KEY TO ABBREVIATIONS

+	continued on later pages of same issue	jr	junior
abp	archbishop	jt auth	joint author
abr	abridged	ltd	limited
Ag	August	m	monthly
Ap	April	Mr	March
arch	architect	My	May
assn	association	N	November
av	avenue	no	number
bart	baronet	O	October
bibliog	bibliography		
bibliog f	bibliographical foot-notes	por	portrait
		pseud	pseudonym
bi-m	bimonthly	pt	part
bi-w	biweekly	pub	published, publisher, publishing
bldg	building		
bp	bishop	q	quarterly
co	company	rev	revised
comp	compiled, compiler		
cond	condensed	S	September
cont	continued	semi-m	semimonthly
corp	corporation	soc	society
		Spr	Spring
D	December	sq	square
dept	department	sr	senior
ed	edited, edition, editor	st	street
		Sum	Summer
F	February	sup	supplement
Hon	Honorable	supt	superintendent
il	illustrated, illustration, illustrator	tr	translated, translation, translator
inc	incorporated		
introd	introduction, introductory	v	volume
		w	weekly
Ja	January	Wint	Winter
Je	June		
Jl	July	yr	year

Readers' Guide to
Periodical Literature

MARCH 1965—FEBRUARY 1966

READERS' GUIDE TO
PERIODICAL LITERATURE

Cumulated Volumes

READERS' GUIDE TO PERIODICAL LITERATURE

An Author and Subject Index

MARCH 1965—FEBRUARY 1966

Edited by
ZADA LIMERICK

Indexers
ANNE W. FURNESS
LINDA LACK HOY
LOVISA J. JENKINS

THE H. W. WILSON COMPANY
NEW YORK   1966

PRINTED IN THE UNITED STATES OF AMERICA

Library of Congress Catalog Card No. (6-8232)

ACKNOWLEDGMENTS

In addition to the staff members whose names appear on the title page we wish to acknowledge the contributions of Valerie F. Oldland, Muriel M. Phillips, Barbara L. Stanley, Josephine Samudio and Virginia Turrell who indexed for this volume.

Z. L.

ABBREVIATIONS OF PERIODICALS INDEXED

March 1965—February 1966

FOR FULL INFORMATION, CONSULT PAGES IX–XI

ALA Bul—ALA Bulletin
Am Artist—American Artist
Am City—American City
Am Ed—American Education
Am For—American Forests
*Am Heritage—American Heritage
Am Hist R—American Historical Review
Am Home—American Home
Am Rec G—American Record Guide
America—America
Américas—Américas
Ann Am Acad—Annals of the American Academy of Political and Social Science
Antiques—Antiques
Arch Forum—Architectural Forum
 (Publication suspended with Ag-S '64; resumed Jl-Ag '65)
Arch Rec—Architectural Record
Art N—Art News
*Atlan—Atlantic
Audubon Mag—Audubon Magazine
Aviation W—Aviation Week & Space Technology

Bet Hom & Gard—Better Homes and Gardens
Bsns W—Business Week
Bul Atomic Sci—Bulletin of the Atomic Scientists

Cath World—Catholic World
*Changing T—Changing Times
Christian Cent—Christian Century
Commentary—Commentary
Commonweal—Commonweal
Cong Digest—Congressional Digest
Consumer Bul—Consumer Bulletin
Consumer Rep—Consumer Reports
Craft Horiz—Craft Horizons
Cur Hist—Current History

Dance Mag—Dance Magazine
Dept State Bul—Department of State Bulletin
Design—Design
Duns R—Dun's Review and Modern Industry

Ebony—Ebony
Electr World—Electronics World
Esquire—Esquire

*Farm J—Farm Journal (Eastern edition)
Field & S—Field & Stream
Flower Grower—Flower Grower, The Home Garden
Flying—Flying
Focus—Focus
*For Affairs—Foreign Affairs
Fortune—Fortune

*Good H—Good Housekeeping

*Harper—Harper's Magazine
Harvard Bsns R—Harvard Business Review
Hi Fi—High Fidelity incorporating Musical America
Hobbies—Hobbies
*Holiday—Holiday
*Horizon—Horizon
Horn Bk—Horn Book Magazine
Horticulture—Horticulture
Hot Rod—Hot Rod
House & Gard—House & Garden incorporating Living for Young Homemakers
House B—House Beautiful

Int Concil—International Conciliation

*Ladies Home J—Ladies' Home Journal
Library J—Library Journal
Life—Life
Liv Wildn—Living Wilderness
Look—Look (Middle Atlantic edition)

McCalls—McCall's
Miss & Roc—Missiles and Rockets
Mlle—Mademoiselle
Mo Labor R—Monthly Labor Review
Mod Phot—Modern Photography
Motor B—Motor Boating
Motor T—Motor Trend

NEA J—NEA Journal
N Y Times Mag—New York Times Magazine
*Nat Geog Mag—National Geographic Magazine
Nat Parks Mag—National Parks Magazine
Nat R—National Review (36p issue only, pub. in alternate weeks)
Nation—Nation
Nations Bsns—Nation's Business
Natur Hist—Natural History incorporating Nature Magazine
Negro Hist Bul—Negro History Bulletin
New Repub—New Republic
New Yorker—New Yorker
*Newsweek—Newsweek

Opera N—Opera News
Outdoor Life—Outdoor Life

PTA Mag—PTA Magazine
Parents Mag—Parents' Magazine and Better Homemaking
Plays—Plays
Poetry—Poetry
Pop Electr—Popular Electronics
Pop Gard—Popular Gardening & Living Outdoors
Pop Mech—Popular Mechanics
Pop Phot—Popular Photography
Pop Sci—Popular Science Monthly
Pub W—Publishers' Weekly

*Read Digest—Reader's Digest (Great Lakes edition)
Recreation—Recreation
Redbook—Redbook
Reporter—The Reporter

Sat Eve Post—Saturday Evening Post
Sat R—Saturday Review
Sch & Soc—School and Society
Sch Arts—School Arts
Sci Am—Scientific American
Sci Digest—Science Digest
Sci N L—Science News Letter
Science—Science
Seventeen—Seventeen
Sky & Tel—Sky and Telescope
*Sports Illus—Sports Illustrated
Sr Schol—Senior Scholastic (Teacher edition)
Suc Farm—Successful Farming (Eastern edition)
Sunset—Sunset (Central edition)

Time—Time
Todays Health—Today's Health
Travel—Travel

UN Mo Chron—UN Monthly Chronicle
UNESCO Courier—UNESCO Courier
U S Camera—U.S. Camera & Travel
U S News—U.S. News & World Report

Vital Speeches—Vital Speeches of the Day
Vogue—Vogue

Wilson Lib Bul—Wilson Library Bulletin
Writer—Writer

Yachting—Yachting
Yale R—Yale Review

* Available for blind readers on talking books, in braille, or on magnetic tape. For information address Division for the Blind, Library of Congress, Washington, D.C. 20540

LIST OF PERIODICALS INDEXED

All data as of latest issue received

ALA Bulletin—available only to members. m (bi-m Jl-Ag) American Library Association, 50 E Huron St, Chicago 60611

America—$8. w (bi-w year-end issue) America Press, 106 W 56th St, New York 10019

The American Academy of Political and Social Science Annals—$10. free to members. bi-m American Academy of Political and Social Science, 3937 Chestnut St, Philadelphia 19104

American Artist—$7. m (S-Je) American Artist, 2160 Patterson St, Cincinnati, Ohio 45214

The American City—$7. m Buttenheim Pub. Corp, 757 3d Av, New York 10017

American Education—$4.50 m (bi-m D, Jl) American Education, Superintendent of Documents, U.S. Government Printing Office, Washington, D.C. 20402

American Forests—$6. m American Forestry Association, 919 17th St, NW, Washington, D.C. 20006

*American Heritage—$15. bi-m American Heritage, 383 W Center St, Marion, Ohio 43302

The American Historical Review—$10. free to members of the American Historical Association, q The Macmillan Co, 60 5th Av, New York 10011

The American Home—$3. m (bi-m Ja, Jl) The American Home, Independence Sq, Philadelphia 19105

The American Record Guide—$4.50. m American Record Guide, P.O. Box 319, Radio City Station, New York 10019

Américas—$4. m Pan American Union, Washington, D.C. 20006

Antiques—$10.50. m Straight Enterprises, Inc, 551 5th Av, New York 10017

The Architectural Forum—$10. m (bi-m Ja, Jl) The Architectural Forum, 111 W 57th St, New York 10019
   (Publication suspended with Ag-S '64; resumed Jl-Ag '65)

Architectural Record—$5.50. m (semi-m My) Architectural Record, P.O. Box 430, Hightstown, N.J. 08520

Art News—$11.50. m (q Je-Ag) The Art Foundation Press, Inc, 4 E 53d St, New York 10022

*The Atlantic—$8.50. m Atlantic Monthly Co, 8 Arlington St, Boston 02116

Audubon Magazine—$7. bi-m National Audubon Society, 1130 5th Av, New York 10028

Aviation Week & Space Technology—$8. w Aviation Week, P.O. Box 430, Hightstown, N.J. 08520

Better Homes and Gardens—$3. m Better Homes and Gardens, 1716 Locust St, Des Moines, Ia. 50303

Bulletin of the Atomic Scientists—$7. m (S-Je) Bulletin of the Atomic Scientists, 935 E 60th St, Chicago 60637

Business Week—$8. w Business Week, P.O. Box 430, Hightstown, N.J. 08520

The Catholic World—$6. m Catholic World, Harristown Road, Glen Rock, N.J. 07452

*Changing Times—$6. m Changing Times, The Kiplinger Magazine, Editors Park, Md. 20782

The Christian Century—$7.50. w Christian Century Foundation, 407 S Dearborn St, Chicago 60605

Commentary—$8. m American Jewish Committee, 165 E 56th St, New York 10022

Commonweal—$9. w (bi-w year-end issue, mid-Jl-mid-S) Commonweal Pub. Co, Inc, 232 Madison Av, New York 10016

Congressional Digest—$10. m (S-Je) Congressional Digest Corp, 3231 P St, NW, Washington, D.C. 20007

Consumer Bulletin—$5. m Consumers' Research, Inc, Washington, N.J. 07882

Consumer Reports—$6. m Consumers Union of U.S, Inc, 256 Washington St, Mount Vernon, N.Y. 10550

Craft Horizons—$8. bi-m American Craftsmen's Council, 44 W 53d St, New York 10019

Current History—$8. m Current History, Inc, 1822 Ludlow St, Philadelphia 19103

Dance Magazine—$7. m Dance Magazine, 268 W 47th St, New York 10036

The Department of State Bulletin—$10. w Department of State Bulletin, Superintendent of Documents, U.S. Government Printing Office, Washington, D.C. 20402

Design—$4.50. bi-m (S-Je) Design Magazine, 1100 Waterway Blvd, Indianapolis, Ind. 46207

Dun's Review and Modern Industry—$5. m Dun & Bradstreet Pub. Corp, 99 Church St, New York 10007

Ebony—$5. m Johnson Pub. Co, Inc, 1820 S Michigan Av, Chicago 60616

Electronics World—$5. m Electronics World, Portland Pl, Boulder, Colo. 80301

Esquire—$6.50. m Esquire, Portland Pl, Boulder, Colo. 80301

*Farm Journal (Eastern edition)—$1. m Farm Journal, Inc, 230 W Washington Sq, Philadelphia 19105

Field & Stream—$4. m Holt, Rinehart and Winston, Inc, 383 Madison Av, New York 10017

Flower Grower, The Home Garden—$3.50. m Flower Grower, 1031 Broadway, Albany, N.Y. 12201

Flying—$6. m Flying, Portland Pl, Boulder, Colo. 80301

Focus—$1.25. m (S-Je) American Geographical Society, Broadway at 156th St, New York 10032

*Foreign Affairs—$6. q Council on Foreign Relations, Inc, 58 E 68th St, New York 10021

Fortune—$12. m Fortune, 540 N Michigan Av, Chicago 60611

*Good Housekeeping—$4. m Good Housekeeping, Box 517, New York 10019

*Harper's Magazine—$8.50. m Harper's Magazine, 381 W Center St, Marion, Ohio 43302

Harvard Business Review—$10. bi-m Harvard Business Review, Soldier's Field Station, Boston 02163

High Fidelity incorporating Musical America—$7. m High Fidelity, 2160 Patterson St, Cincinnati, Ohio 45214

Hobbies—$4. m Lightner Pub. Corp, 1006 S Michigan Av, Chicago 60605

*Holiday—$5.95. m Holiday, Independence Sq, Philadelphia 19105

*Horizon—$16. q Horizon, 379 W Center St, Marion, Ohio 43302

The Horn Book Magazine—$6. bi-m Horn Book, Inc, 585 Boylston St, Boston 02116

Horticulture—$4. m Horticulture, 300 Massachusetts Av, Boston 02115

Hot Rod—$5. m Petersen Pub. Co, 5959 Hollywood Blvd, Los Angeles 90028

House & Garden incorporating Living for Young Homemakers—$6. m House & Garden, Boulder, Colo. 80301

House Beautiful—$6. m House Beautiful, 250 W 55th St, New York 10019

International Conciliation—$2.25. 5 times a yr (S-My) Carnegie Endowment for International Peace, 345 E 46th St, New York 10017

*Ladies' Home Journal—$3. m Ladies' Home Journal, Independence Sq, Philadelphia 19105

Library Journal—$10. semi-m (m Jl-Ag) R. R. Bowker Co, 1180 Avenue of the Americas, New York 10036

Life—$7.75. w (except one issue at year-end) Life, 540 N Michigan Av, Chicago 60611

The Living Wilderness—$5. q The Wilderness Society, 729 15th St, NW, Washington, D.C. 20005

Look (Middle Atlantic edition)—$4. bi-w Look, Look Bldg, Des Moines, Ia. 50304

McCall's—$3. m McCall's, McCall St, Dayton, Ohio 45401

Mademoiselle—$5. m Mademoiselle, Boulder, Colo. 80301

Missiles and Rockets—$5. w (bi-w year-end issue) Missiles and Rockets, 1001 Vermont Av, NW, Washington, D.C. 20005

Modern Photography—$5. m Modern Photography, 2160 Patterson St, Cincinnati, Ohio 45214

Monthly Labor Review—$7.50. m Superintendent of Documents, U.S. Government Printing Office, Washington, D.C. 20402

Motor Boating—$6. m Motor Boating, P.O. Box 544, New York 10019

Motor Trend—$5. m Petersen Pub. Co, 5959 Hollywood Blvd, Los Angeles 90028

NEA Journal—available only to members. m (S-My) National Education Association of the United States, 1201 16th St, NW, Washington, D.C. 20036

The Nation—$10. w (bi-w Jl-Ag) Nation Associates, Inc, 333 6th Av, New York 10014

*National Geographic Magazine—$8. m The Secretary, National Geographic Society, Washington, D.C. 20036

National Parks Magazine—$5. m National Parks Association, 1300 New Hampshire Av, NW, Washington, D.C. 20036

National Review—$9. bi-w (36p issue) National Review, Box 1601, Des Moines, Ia 50306

Nation's Business—$19.75. (3 yrs) m Chamber of Commerce of the U.S, 38 S Dearborn St, Chicago 60603

Natural History incorporating Nature Magazine—$5. m (bi-m Je-S) American Museum of Natural History, Central Park W at 79th St, New York 10024

The Negro History Bulletin—$3. m (O-My) Association for the Study of Negro Life and History, Inc, 1538 9th St, NW, Washington, D.C. 20001

The New Republic—$8. w (bi-w Jl-Ag) New Republic, 381 W Center St, Marion, Ohio 43301

The New York Times Magazine—$28.50. w (complete Sunday ed; not sold separately) New York Times, Times Bldg, 229 W 43d St, New York 10036

The New Yorker—$8. w New Yorker Magazine, Inc, 25 W 43d St, New York 10036

*Newsweek—$8. w Newsweek, 117 E 3d St, Dayton, Ohio 45402

Opera News—$7. w (24 issues S 25-Je 4) The Metropolitan Opera Guild, 1425 Broadway, New York 10018

Outdoor Life—$4. m Outdoor Life, Boulder, Colo. 80313

The PTA Magazine—$1.50. m (S-Je) The PTA Magazine, 700 N Rush St, Chicago 60611

Parents' Magazine and Better Homemaking—$4. m Parents' Magazine, Bergenfield, N.J. 07621

Plays—$6. m (O-My) Plays, Inc, 8 Arlington St, Boston 02116

Poetry—$10. m (bi-m Ap-My) Modern Poetry Association, 1018 N State St, Chicago 60610

Popular Electronics—$4. m Popular Electronics, Portland Pl, Boulder, Colo. 80301

Popular Gardening & Living Outdoors—$3.50. m (bi-m My-D) Holt, Rinehart & Winston, Inc, 383 Madison Av, New York 10017

Popular Mechanics—$4. m Popular Mechanics, Box 646, New York 10019

Popular Photography—$5. m Popular Photography, Portland Pl, Boulder, Colo. 80301

Popular Science Monthly—$4. m Popular Science, P.O. Box 1083, Boulder, Colo. 80313

Publishers' Weekly—$15. w (bi-w year-end issue) R. R. Bowker Co, 1180 Avenue of the Americas, New York 10036

*Reader's Digest (Great Lakes edition)—$2.97. m Reader's Digest Association, Inc, Pleasantville, N.Y. 10570
Enlarged type edition available from Xerox Corp, P.O. Box 3300, Grand Central Station, New York, N.Y. $4.50 a month or $25.65 for six months.

Recreation—$5. m (S-Je) National Recreation Association, 8 W 8th St, New York 10011

Redbook—$3. m Redbook, McCall St, Dayton, Ohio 45401

The Reporter—$7. bi-w (2 summer issues omitted) The Reporter, 660 Madison Av, New York 10021

The Saturday Evening Post—$3.95. 26 issues per year The Saturday Evening Post, Independence Sq, Philadelphia 19105

Saturday Review—$8. w Saturday Review, Inc, 380 Madison Av, New York 10017

School and Society—$8.50. bi-w (O-My, including summer annual) Society for the Advancement of Education, Inc, 1860 Broadway, New York 10023

School Arts—$7. m (S-Je) School Arts, Printers Bldg, Worcester, Mass. 01608

Science—$8.50. w American Association for the Advancement of Science, 1515 Massachusetts Av, NW, Washington, D.C. 20005

Science Digest—$5. m Science Digest, 250 W 55th St, New York 10019

Science News Letter—$5.50. w Science Service, Inc, 1719 N St, NW, Washington, D.C. 20036

Scientific American—$7. m Scientific American, 415 Madison Av, New York 10017

Senior Scholastic—(Teacher edition)—$4.50. w (S-My) Senior Scholastic, 902 Sylvan Av, Englewood Cliffs, N.J. 07632

Seventeen—$6. m Seventeen, Radnor, Pa. 19088

Sky and Telescope—$6. m Sky Pub. Corp, Harvard College Observatory, Cambridge, Mass. 02138

*Sports Illustrated—$7.50. w Sports Illustrated, 540 N Michigan Av, Chicago 60611

Successful Farming (Eastern edition)—$1. m Successful Farming, 1716 Locust St, Des Moines, Ia. 50303

Sunset (Central edition)—$3. in Calif, Ore, Wash, Idaho, Ariz, Nev, Utah, Hawaii. $4 in other states m Sunset Magazine, Menlo Park, Calif. 94025

Time—$10. w Time, 540 N Michigan Av, Chicago 60611

Today's Health—$4. m Today's Health, 535 N Dearborn St, Chicago 60610

Travel—$6. m Travel, Travel Bldg, Floral Park, N.Y. 11001

UN Monthly Chronicle—$6. m (except in Ag) UN Monthly Chronicle, Publishing Service, United Nations, N.Y. 10027

The UNESCO Courier—$5. m (bi-m Jl-Ag) UNESCO Pub. Center, 317 E 34th St, Department WS, New York 10016

U.S. Camera & Travel—$5. m U.S. Camera & Travel, Box 562, Des Moines, Ia. 50302

U.S. News & World Report—$8. w U.S. News & World Report, 435 Parker Av, Dayton, Ohio 45401

Vital Speeches of the Day—$8. semi-m City News Pub. Co, Inc, 1 Wolf's Lane, Pelham, N.Y. 10803

Vogue—$10. semi-m (m My-Jl, D) Vogue, Boulder, Colo. 80301

Wilson Library Bulletin—$4. m (S-Je) The H. W. Wilson Co, 950 University Av, Bronx, N.Y. 10452

The Writer—$5. m The Writer, Inc, 8 Arlington St, Boston 02116

Yachting—$6. m Yachting Pub. Corp, 50 W 44th St, New York 10036

The Yale Review—$5. q Yale Review, 92-A Yale Station, New Haven, Conn. 06520

*Available for blind readers on talking books, in braille, or on magnetic tape. For information address Division for the Blind, Library of Congress, Washington, D.C. 20540

KEY TO ABBREVIATIONS

+	continued on later pages of same issue
abp	archbishop
abr	abridged
Ag	August
Ap	April
arch	architect
assn	association
av	avenue
bart	baronet
bibliog	bibliography
bibliog f	bibliographical foot-notes
bi-m	bimonthly
bi-w	biweekly
bldg	building
bp	bishop
co	company
comp	compiled, compiler
cond	condensed
cont	continued
corp	corporation
D	December
dept	department
ed	edited, edition, editor
F	February
Hon	Honorable
il	illustrated, illustration, illustrator
inc	incorporated
introd	introduction, introductory
Ja	January
Je	June
Jl	July

jr	junior
jt auth	joint author
ltd	limited
m	monthly
Mr	March
My	May
N	November
no	number
O	October
por	portrait
pseud	pseudonym
pt	part
pub	published, publisher, publishing
q	quarterly
rev	revised
S	September
semi-m	semimonthly
soc	society
Spr	Spring
sq	square
sr	senior
st	street
Sum	Summer
sup	supplement
supt	superintendent
tr	translated, translation, translator
v	volume
w	weekly
Wint	Winter
yr	year

Sample entry: IMMIGRATION and emigration law
Americanizing our immigration laws. O.
Handlin. il Holiday 39:8+ Ja '66

Explanation: An illustrated article on the subject IM-MIGRATION and emigration law entitled "Americanizing our immigration laws," by O. Handlin, will be found in volume 39 of Holiday, page 8 (continued on later pages of same issue) the January 1966 number

READERS' GUIDE TO
PERIODICAL LITERATURE

March 1965—February 1966

AA. See Alcoholics anonymous

AACSB. See American association of collegiate schools of business

AALL. See American association of law libraries

AAMC. See American association of medical colleges

AAPC. See American association of pastoral counselors

AASA. See American association of school administrators

AASL. See American association of school librarians

AAU. See Amateur athletic union of the United States

AAUP. See American association of university professors; Association of American university presses

A and A distributors, incorporated
   A & A's new quarters greatly improving service. il Pub W 188:16-19 Ag 16 '65

A and P company. See Great Atlantic and Pacific tea company

ABA. See American bar association; American booksellers association

ABC. See American broadcasting company

ABGR tester (alternator, battery, generator and regulator tester) See Testing instruments

ABPC. See American book publishers council

AC generators. See Electric generators, Alternating current

ACDA. See United States—Arms control and disarmament agency

ACE. See American council on education

ACEI. See Association for childhood education international

ACLU. See American civil liberties union

ACT (American conservatory theater). See Pittsburgh—Theater

ACWA. See Amalgamated clothing workers of America

ADA. See Americans for democratic action

ADC (Aid to dependent children) See Child welfare—United States

ADI. See American documentation institute

AEC. See United States—Atomic energy commission

AES (Apollo earthorbiting station) See Space stations

AFA. See American forestry association

AFBF. See American farm bureau federation

AFCA. See American football coaches association

AFFA. See Air freight forwarders association

AFL. See American football league

AFL-CIO. See American federation of labor and Congress of industrial organizations

AFM. See American federation of musicians

AFSCME. See American federation of state, county and municipal employees

AFT. See American federation of teachers

AHA. See American heart association

AI. See Artificial insemination

AIA. See American institute of architects

AIA-Sunset Western home awards. See Western home awards

AID. See United States—Agency for international development

AIFLD. See American institute for free labor development

AIFT. See American institute for foreign trade

AIGA. See American institute of graphic arts

AILS (advanced integrated landing system) See Airplanes—Landing

AISI. See American iron and steel institute

AKC. See American kennel club

ALA. See American library association

ALPA. See Air line pilots association, International

ALTA. See American library trustee association

AMA. See American medical association

AMA-ERF institute. See American medical association—Institute for biomedical research

AMC. See American motors corporation; American music center (organization)

AMF. See American machine and foundry company

AOCA. See Associated opera companies of America

AP (advanced placement) See College entrance examination board—Advanced placement program

APA. See Association of producing artists

APGA. See American personnel and guidance association

ARA. See United States—Area redevelopment administration

ARPA. See United States—Defense, Department of—Advanced research projects agency

ASCD. See Association for supervision and curriculum development

ASCE. See American society of civil engineers

ASFTA. See American Shakespeare festival theatre and academy, Stratford, Conn.

ASPAU. See African scholarship program of American universities

ASSET (aerothermodynamic/elastic structural systems environmental tests) See Space vehicles—Atmospheric entry

ASW (anti-submarine warfare) See Submarine warfare

AT and T. See American telephone and telegraph company

ATA. See Air transport association of America

ATP. See Adenosine triphosphate

ATPI. See American textbook publishers institute

ATS (advanced technology satellite) See Communications satellites

AUPS. See American university press services, incorporated

AAKVIK, Helmer
   Legendary triumph of Helmer Aakvik. J. G. Hubbell. il Read Digest 86:214-17+ Ap '65

AARDVARKS
   Nature note; ant bear. Sci N L 88:44 Jl 17 '65

AARON, Daniel
   Unbuttoned Titan. Reporter 32:37-9 Je 3 '65

AARON, Henry
   Soak the poor is the new trend in taxation. New Repub 153:12 S 4 '65

AARON, Sam
   Vintage review. House & Gard 128:292+ N '65

ABACO ISLANDS. See Bahama Islands

ABBETT, Robert K.
   Robert Abbett, illustrator. F. Whitaker. il por Am Artist 29:48-53+ Je '65

ABBEY, Fred M.
   Oriental poppy. Horticulture 43:24-5+ My '65

ABBEY, J. R.
   Major Abbey's modern bookbindings. H. Nixon. il Craft Horiz 25:28-31 Jl '65

ABBOTT, R. Tucker
   Wonderful world of shells. Sci Digest 58:66-73 D '65

ABBOTT, Walter M.
Freedom meals. America 112:883 Je 19 '65
ABBOTT laboratories
Drug lab caught in crossfire; FDA's handling of label mixups. Bsns W p30 O 30 '65
10,000,000 bottles; inspection of intravenous solutions manufacturing department. J. Ridgeway. New Repub 153:12-14 N 6 '65
ABDUCTION. See Kidnaping
ABDULLAH, Mohammad
Kashmir, India and Pakistan. For Affairs 43:528-35 Ap '65

about

Lion recaged. il Newsweek 65:56+ My 24 '65
ABDULLAH al-Salim al Subah, Sir
Man for all Arabs; Kuwait's mourning. il Time 86:39 D 3 '65
ABEEL, Erica
Daedalus at the Rollerdrome. Sat R 48:51-3 Ag 28 '65
ABEL, I. W.
Is collective bargaining a myth? statement, October 18, 1965. por U S News 59:108 N 15 '65

about

Abel holds edge in USW tally. Bsns W p31 Mr 6 '65
After steel election, the strike outlook now. il por U S News 58:87-8 F 22 '65
Battle for leadership: a major revolt in steel union. U S News 58:22 F 22 '65
Campaign '65: men of steel. il por Newsweek 65:64+ F 8 '65
Chances of avoiding a steel strike. U S News 58:93-4 Ap 26 '65
Decision time again: is a steel strike coming? il por U S News 59:70-1 Ag 23 '65
Man steel is watching. por Bsns W p48+ Mr 27 '65
New leader for a big union; here's a look at his ideas. por U S News 58:70 My 31 '65
New temper in the steelworkers. Bsns W p43-4 Je 5 '65
Passing the gavel. il por Newsweek 65:90 Je 14 '65
Photo finish in USW? il pors Bsns W p98-100 Ja 30 '65
Pressure on steel union to extend May 1 deadline for strike. por U S News 58:72 Mr 8 '65
Steel negotiators get down to brass tacks. por Bsns W p55-6 Je 19 '65
Steel strike threat loses impact. por Bsns W p79-80 Ag 7 '65
Steelworkers' hard-nosed boss. il pors Life 58: 45-6+ Je 25 '65
Two new leaders tell their aims. U S News 58:80 Je 14 '65
U.S. sweats out the steel vote. il por Newsweek 65:77-8 F 22 '65
ABEL, Lionel
Is there a tragic sense of life? Commentary 38:35-40 D '64; 39:20+ My '65
(tr) See Sartre, J. P. Why I will not go to the United States

about

Wives. Criticism
Commonweal 82:444-5 Je 25 '65
Nation 200:628 Je 7 '65
Reporter 33:42 Jl 1 '65
ABEL, Robert B. and Lindquist, C. B.
Inner space, sea of opportunity. pors Am Ed 1:4-8 Mr '65
ABEL, Theodore
Book reviews. America 113:294 S 18 '65
ABELIAS
Just give abelias a chance. il Sunset 135:194 D '65
ABELL, C. W. and others
Uracil mustard: a potent inducer in lung tumors in mice. bibliog Science 147:1443-5 Mr 19 '65
ABELSON, Philip
Are the tame cats in charge? Sat R 49:100-3 Ja 1 '66
ABERCROMBIE, Thomas J.
Saudi Arabia. il Nat Geog Mag 129:1-53 Ja '66
ABERCROMBIE and Fitch company
Out to launch. J. Skow. il Sat Eve Post 238:20 Ag 28 '65
ABERDEEN-Angus cattle. See Cattle—Breeds
ABERNAT, René d'
Russia has lost its race with U.S.; a French size-up; reprint. U S News 59:84 N 8 '65
ABERNETHY, Roy
Mandatory inspection a sensible requirement; excerpts from testimony, July 1965. por U S News 59:101 Ag 9 '65

ABERNETHY, Theodore, J.
Wood research in a hymn to Hippocrates. F. A. Strenge. il por Am For 71:42-5+ My '65
ABERNETHY, Thomas Gerstle
Excerpt from remarks, July 28, 1965. Cong Digest 44:201 Ag '65
ABILITY
See also
Motor ability
ABILITY grouping in education
Grouping the gifted. B. Bettelheim; K. Mott. il NEA J 54:8-11 Mr '65
ABILITY tests
Hiring tests wait for the score; Myart vs. Motorola. Bsns W p45-6+ F 13 '65
ABLATION shielding. See Shielding (heat)
ABNORMAL psychology. See Psychology, Pathological
ABNORMALITIES (animals)
Growth of mouse mammary glands in vivo after monolayer culture. C. W. Daniel and K. B. DeOme. bibliog il Science 149:634-6 Ag 6 '65
ABNORMALITIES (man) See Deformities
ABOLITIONISTS
First to speak for freedom. H. Hansen. Sat R 48:81-2 My 22 '65
General Benjamin Franklin Butler and the Negro: the evolution of the racial views of a practical politician. N. Weiss. bibliog Negro Hist Bul 29:3-4+ O '65
Grant or Greeley? the abolitionist dilemma in the election of 1872. J. M. McPherson. bibliog f Am Hist R 71:43-61 O '65
Pioneers in protest. L. Bennett, jr. See issues of Ebony
ABOMINABLE snowman. See Animals, Mythical
ABORTION
Abortion. R. A. McCormick. America 112:877-81 Je 19 '65
Abortion and sterilization: the search for answers. W. Goodman. Redbook 125:70-1+ O '65
Abortion and the sick mind. America 113: 37-8 Jl 10 '65
Abortion law reform. America 112:703 My 15 '65
Abortion; questions and answers; excerpt from Encyclopedia of mental health. H. Rosen. Todays Health 43:24-5+ Ap '65
Abortions on the increase. America 113:311 S 25 '65
Abortions sought abroad. Sci N L 88:63 Jl 24 '65
Agony of mothers about their unborn; with editors' note. il Life 58:3, 24-31 Je 4 '65
Catholic abortions; Life's admission of falsehood. America 113:273 S 18 '65
Dear babe that almost was. C. Shade. Redbook 125:48-9+ Jl '65
Gains for birth control; need for new legislation. Newsweek 66:94 D 13 '65
Growing tragedy of illegal abortion. J. Star. Look 29:149-50+ O 19 '65
Miscarriage; skin patch gives hope to victims of a medical enigma. R. P. Goldman. il Sat Eve Post 238:72-3+ Jl 17 '65
Morality and policy. America 112:520-1 Ap 17 '65
More abortions: reasons why. il Time 86:82 S 17 '65
One woman's abortion. Mrs X. Atlan 216:66-8 Ag '65; Discussion. 216:48+ O '65
Psychotherapeutic abortion; bill under consideration in California. R. P. Vaughan. America 113:436-8 O 16 '65
Question of emphasis; CBS special report, Abortion and the law. America 112:513 Ap 17 '65
Scandal of abortion laws. L. Lader. N Y Times Mag p32+ Ap 25 '65
Science vs. morality? America 112:411 Mr 27 '65
Should abortion laws be liberalized? W. Best and F. S. Jaffe. Parents Mag 40:50-1+ Je '65
Tragic pregnancy; case of German measles. il Good H 162:12+ Ja '66
When abortion is justified. L. R. Dice. il Nation 200:189-91 F 22 '65; Discussion. 200: inside cover Mr 8 '65
ABORTION, Vibrionic
New vaccines for vibriosis. Suc Farm 63:28 My '65
You can control vibriosis. J. B. Herrick. il Suc Farm 63:38A Mr '65
ABRAHAM, Willard
Is your child ready for kindergarten? Todays Health 43:40-1+ Mr '65
Misunderstood child; interview. Todays Health 43:26-9 Ap '65
Slow learner, surrounded and alone. Todays Health 43:58-61+ S '65
Solving the dilemma of the underachiever. Todays Health 43:34-7+ D '65

ACOUSTICS, Architectural—*Continued*
What belongs in acoustical specifications. R.
  Farrell. il Arch Rec 138:227-30+ S; 203-6
  N '65
    See also
  Acoustical materials
ACQUISITIONS, College library. See College
  libraries—Acquisitions
ACQUISITIONS, Library. See Libraries—Acqui-
  sitions
ACQUISITIONS, School library. See School li-
  braries—Acquisitions
ACRIDINES
Mutagenicity of a monofunctional alkylating
  agent derivative of acridine in neurospora.
  H. E. Brockman and W. Goben. bibliog il
  Science 147:750-1 F 12 '65
ACROBATICS, Aerial. See Aviation—Stunt
  flying
ACROMEGALY
Treat acromegaly by freezing pituitary. Sci
  N L 88:376 D 11 '65
ACRYLAMIDE
Serum protein electrophoresis in acrylamide
  gel: patterns from normal human subjects.
  A. C. Peacock and others. bibliog il Sci-
  ence 147:1451-3 Mr 19 '65
ACRYLIC paint. See Paint
ACRYLIC sheets. See Plastics, Transparent
ACTING
Anne Bancroft: hey, ma, I can do that! R.
  Lemon. il Sat Eve Post 238:86-8+ N 20 '65
Boys never gave me a tumble. S. Field.
  Seventeen 25:50 Ja '66
I dig that! ed. by E. Miller. Ann-Margret.
  il Seventeen 24:138-9+ F '65
I like people to like me. D. Watson. Seven-
  teen 25:37 Ja '66
I want to be like everyone else; ed. by
  E. Miller. P. Gozzi. il Seventeen 25:82-
  3+ Ja '66
I was a teen-ager for ten years; ed. by
  E. Miller. D. Hickman. il Seventeen 24:94-
  5+ Je '65
Russian evenings; New York visit of the
  Moscow art theatre. R. Brustein. New
  Repub 152:26-8 F 27 '65
Singing or acting? age-old dilemma for opera
  singers. B. Thebom. il Opera N 29:8-11 Ap 3
  '65
    See also
  Amateur theatricals
  Dramatization in education
ACTINOMYCIN
Actinomycin D and hydrocortisone: intracel-
  lular binding in rat liver. C. W. Dingman
  and M. B. Sporn. bibliog il Science 149:
  1251-4 S 10 '65
Actinomycin D and the response to vitamin
  D. A. W. Norman. bibliog il Science 149:
  184-6 Jl 9 '65
Actinomycin D: inhibition of protein syn-
  thesis unrelated to effect on template RNA
  synthesis. G. R. Honig and M. Rabinovitz.
  bibliog il Science 149:1504-6 S 24 '65
Actinomycin D inhibition of vitamin D
  action. J. E. Zull and others. bibliog il
  Science 149:182-4 Jl 9 '65
Vaccinia virus directed RNA: its fate in the
  presence of actinomycin. A. J. Shatkin and
  others. bibliog il Science 148:87-90 Ap 2 '65
ACTION painting. See Art, Abstract
ACTIONS and defenses
ABPC again files amicus brief for John
  Goldfarb. Pub W 187:51 Mr 22 '65
Appellate court reverses John Goldfarb de-
  cision. Pub W 187:133-4 F 22 '65
Champion; court cases of F. L. Shuttles-
  worth. il Time 86:73-4 N 26 '65
Court of appeals OK's John Goldfarb. Pub W
  187:25 Mr 29 '65
    See also
  Libel and slander
ACTIVATION analysis. See Radioactivation
  analysis
ACTIVITIES, Student. See Student activities
ACTON, Charles
Ireland's tribute. Hi Fi 15:168 S '65
ACTORS and actresses
Salute: tribute by Broadway to the fair. New
  Yorker 41:36-8 Ap 24 '65
Spotlight on the nonwoman. J. Simon. Holi-
  day 38:153-4+ N '65
Tomorrow's stars. L. Tornabene. il Good H
  160:20+ Mr '65
    See also
  Acting
  Children as actors
  Moving picture actors and actresses
    also names of actors and actresses, e.g.
  V. Gassman
ACTOR'S workshop. See San Francisco—The-
  ater

ACTRESSES. See Actors and actresses; Moving
  picture actors and actresses
ACTUARIES. See Insurance actuaries
ADA, Okla.
Tennis on top of the tank. P. S. Karr. il
  Am City 80:108-9 O '65
ADAGES. See Maxims
ADAK ISLAND. See Aleutian Islands
ADAM, Karl
Top strokes. il Time 86:48+ Jl 16 '65
ADAM, Yaacov K.
Tighter decks, and how. pors Motor B 115:
  26-8+ Mr '65
ADAMO, S. J.
Anonymousitis. America 114:154+ Ja 22 '66
Dilemma in the Catholic press. America 113:
  154-8 Ag 14 '65
Feeding a myth. America 113:730+ D 4 '65
Truth will out. America 113:610-12 N 13 '65
Two views. America 114:26-7 Ja 1 '66
Whole truth. America 113:480-1 O 23 '65
ADAMS, Abigail (Smith)
Miss Adams in love. L. Mayo. il por Am
  Heritage 16:36-49+ F '65
ADAMS, Adrienne
Color separation. Horn Bk 41:152-7 Ap '65
    about
Adrienne Adams. D. Waugh. il por Am
  Artist 29:54-9+ N '65
ADAMS, Alice
Baker's art. Craft Horiz 25:8-17 N '65
Mary Walker Phillips. Craft Horiz 25:24-7
  Ja '65
ADAMS, Alvin
Little people. Ebony 20:104-6+ O '65
ADAMS, Charles
Face to face with a working diplomat. por
  Seventeen 24:145 O '65
ADAMS, Charles Francis
Sailing with Uncle Charlie. G. C. Homans.
  Atlan 216:39-45 Jl '65
ADAMS, Chuck. See Adams, Charles
ADAMS, Cindy
(ed) See Sukarno. For Sukarno so loves the
  world
ADAMS, Darwin P.
Tunnel diode sweep trigger. Electr World 74:
  94-6 N '65
ADAMS, F. B. Jr
Codex Pithoeanus of Phaedrus; address, Jan-
  uary 13, 1965. Horn Bk 41:260-6 Je '65
ADAMS, Hampton
Obituary
  Christian Cent 82:828 Je 30 '65
ADAMS, Henry
Henry Adams, by E. Samuels. Review
  Nation 200:171-2 F 15 '65. L. Marx
What was the matter with Henry Adams?
  M. Cunliffe. Commentary 39:66-71 Je '65
ADAMS, Henry Babcock
Doctoral studies for pastors. Christian Cent
  82:560+ Ap 28 '65
ADAMS, J. B.
Megaloscience; adaptation of address, No-
  vember 5, 1964. Science 148:1560-4 Je 18
  '65
ADAMS, J. Donald
Dilemma of success. Sat R 48:19+ Ja 30;
  21 Mr 6 '65
Does anyone know what creative writing is?
  Sat R 48:23-5 S 18 '65
ADAMS, John
John Adams at 18. Time 86:57 Jl 9 '65
Miss Adams in love. L. Mayo. il por Am
  Heritage 16:36-49+ F '65
ADAMS, Judith, and Dubrow, Heather
Something to talk about on campus. Mlle 61:
  312-15 Ag '65
ADAMS, Leon D.
Stupid highway signs can kill. Pop Sci 186:
  104-8+ My '65
ADAMS, Mildred
President Frei and the copper goose. New
  Repub 153:10-12 D 18 '65
ADAMS, Phoebe Lou
Canals of Copenhagen. Atlan 215:65-8 Je '65
How to sleep with a dyne. Atlan 215:82-4+
  My '65
Potpourri. See issues of Atlantic
Six viking ships. Atlan 215:88-92 Ap '65
Slow boat on the Göta Canal. Atlan 216:82-6
  N '65
Tower at Fåborg. Atlan 216:51-5 Jl '65
ADAMS, Richard N.
Pattern of development in Latin America;
  with questions and answers. Ann Am Acad
  360:1-10 Jl '65
Sudden development. Américas 17:3-6 Ag '65
ADAMS, Thomas E.
Sled; story. Parents Mag 41:56-8 Ja '66
ADAMS, Velma
Forgotten field sales manager. Duns R 85:
  45-6+ Mr '65
Why the old products last. Duns R 85:46-7+
  Ap '65

ADAMS House, Quincy, Mass. See Quincy,
  Mass.—Historic houses, etc.
ADANSONIA digitata. See Baobab trees
ADAPTATION (biology)
  Evolution of fitness in experimental popula-
    tions of drosophila serrata. F. J. Ayala.
    bibliog il Science 150:903-5 N 12 '65
  Evolution of nest building. N. E. Collias. il
    Natur Hist 74:40-7 bibliog(p74) Ag '65
  Genetic adaptation of caenorhabditis elegans
    (nematoda) to high temperatures. J. Brun.
    il Science 150:1467 D 10 '65
  Hemoglobin and oxygen: affinities in seven
    species of sciuridae. F. G. Hall. bibliog il
    Science 148:1350-1 Je 4 '65
    See also
  Evolution
  Genetics
ADAPTATION (music) See Musical arrange-
  ment
ADAPTATION, Visual. See Eye—Accommoda-
  tion and refraction
ADAPTERS, Radio. See Radio apparatus
ADARKAR, Vivek B.
  Examination; story. Seventeen 24:154-5 Ap '65
ADCOCK, Betty Sharp
  His gift; poem. Nation 202:48 Ja 10 '66
ADCOCK, Cynthia
  When workers unite. Nation 200:228-9 Mr 1
    '65
ADDAMS, Charles Samuel
  Sixteenth man. il por Newsweek 66:81 Jl 5
    '65
ADDICTS, Drug. See Narcotic addicts
ADDING machines
  Keeping mistakes from computers; Addo. il
    Bsns W p 166+ Je 12 '65
  Machines to do the family's figuring. il
    Changing T 20:31-2 Ja '66
ADDISS, Steve
  Senior scholastic interview; ed. by R. Hem-
    ming. por Sr Schol 86:20 Mr 11 '65
ADDITIONS, House. See Houses, Remodeled
ADDITIVES, Food. See Food additives
ADDONIZIO, Hugh J.
  Negroes move toward power. J. O'Shea. il
    Atlan 216:90-2+ N '65
ADEDIRE, Abraham
  Mission of mercy. H. J. Massaquoi. il pors
    Ebony 20:149-52+ My '65
ADELIE penguins. See Penguins
ADELSON, Joel. See Brodie, A. F. jt. auth.
ADEN
  Back to colonialism. Time 86:47 O 8 '65
  Hard to leave. Newsweek 66:63 O 11 '65
  I'm hit; terrorist attacks. Newsweek 66:39-40
    S 13 '65
    See also
  United Nations—Aden
ADENAUER, Konrad
  Adenauer at ninety. K. Kellen. For Affairs
    44:275-90 Ja '66
  Almost the end. Time 86:21 D 31 '65
  Der Alte returns. W. S. Schlamm. por Nat R
    17:811-12 S 21 '65
  Intimations of immortality. por Newsweek
    66:44 S 27 '65
ADENINE
  Hydrogen-bonded dimers of adenine and
    uracil derivatives. R. M. Hamlin, jr. and
    others. bibliog il Science 148:1734-7 Je 25
    '65
ADENOSINE triphosphatase
  Dynein: a protein with adenosine triphos-
    phatase activity from cilia. I. R. Gibbons
    and A. J. Rowe. bibliog il Science 149:424-6
    Jl 23 '65
ADENOSINE triphosphate
  Fireflies to light the way in NASA effort to
    chart earth's biosphere. W. S. Beller. Miss
    & Roc 16:31 Mr 8 '65
  Serotonin and adenosine triphosphate: syner-
    gistic effect of the beat frequency of cilia
    of mussel gills. S. L. Schor. bibliog il Sci-
    ence 148:500-1 Ap 23 '65
  Tracking the spark of life beyond earth.
    J. Lear. il Sat R 48:45-7 Ap 3 '65
ADENOSYLMETHIONINE
  Adenosylmethionine elevation in leukemic
    white blood cells. R. J. Baldessarini and P.
    P. Carbone. bibliog il Science 149:644-5 Ag
    6 '65
ADENOTA vardoin. See Antelopes
ADENOVIRUSES. See Viruses
ADHESIVE tape
  Adhesive self-sticking tapes, how good are
    they? il Consumer Bul 48:28-31 O '65
ADHESIVES
  With today's miracle adhesives, you can mend
    anything. R. C. Whitman. Am Home 68:98-9
    Ap '65
    See also
  Glue

ADINOLFI, Anthony G.
  New kind of client with $1.5 billion to spend.
    W. McQuade. il por Fortune 71:165-6 Mr
    '65
ADIPOSE tissue. See Fat
ADIRONDACK MOUNTAINS
  Adirondack reader; ed. by P. F. Jamieson.
    Review
    Liv Wildn 29:31-3 Spr '65. P. H. Oehser
ADIRONDACK trail. See Roads—New York
  (state)
ADJUSTMENT, Social
  As a psychiatrist sees pressures on middle-
    class teen-agers. S. Berman. il NEA J 54:
    16-17+ F '65
  Dial F for fiction; plea for having life imitate
    art. S. Hixon. Seventeen 24:116 Ag '65
  Is sex morality out of date? with discussion
    group program, by E. G. Neisser. R.
    Thomas. Parents Mag 40:31-2+, 39+ My
    '65
  Jet-age malady; foreign culture difficulties.
    E. Vargas. il Sat R 48:18-19 My 29 '65
  New girl in town; what to do when you move
    to a new school. R. Greer. il Seventeen 24:
    366+ Ag '65
  Parental overprotection and political dis-
    trust. F. A. Pinner. bibliog f il Ann Am
    Acad 361:58-70 S '65
  Person who changed my life; symposium;
    ed. by A. Ebert. il Seventeen 24:156-7+ Ap
    '65
  Scholastic teacher interview: mental health as
    applied to children, teen-agers, teachers,
    and parents; ed. by H. J. Langer. B. Spock.
    Sr Schol 86:sup9-11 Ap 1; sup7-8 Ap 8 '65
  Since Malachi. B. Y. Glassberg. PTA Mag
    60:6-7 S '65
  Social life in the grades; with study-discus-
    sion program, by D. Harris and E. Harris.
    E. J. LeShan. bibliog il PTA Mag 59:
    20-2, 34-6 Mr '65
  Sometime during your teen years someone is
    likely to urge you to drink: what will you
    say? D. Klein. il Seventeen 24:140-1+ S '65
  Summit meeting; introd. to her parents.
    J. Wescott. il Seventeen 24:6 Je '65
  Teenagers need someone to tell their troubles
    to. J. Wakeman. il Parents Mag 40:56-8+
    Ap '65
  Time of juveniles. E. Hoffer. Harper 230:
    16+ Je '65
  V.I.T.'s; programs for teenagers. il Recrea-
    tion 58:242-4, 288-90+, 394-6+ My-Je,
    O '65
    See also
  Aged—Adjustment problems
  College students—Adjustment
  Conformity
  Individual and society
  Maturity
ADLER, Bill
  (ed) What Americans expect from Robert
    Kennedy; excerpts from Dear Senator
    Kennedy. Ladies Home J 82:71+ O '65
  (comp) See Johnson, L. B. LBJ's funny
    stories about his family
ADLER, Irving
  Mathematics for the low achiever. NEA J
    54:28-30+ F '65
  On writing science books for children. Horn
    Bk 41:524-9 O '65
ADLER, Kurt Herbert
  Stanislavsky and Opera. Opera N 29:6-7
    F 6 '65
    about
  Ladies and gentlemen. A. M. Lingg. il por
    Opera N 29:12-16 Mr 20 '65
ADLER, Myles
  Turning the tables. U S Camera 28:50-1 Ag
    '65
    about
  Barrel of fun on ice. il U S Camera 28:16-17
    Mr '65
ADLER, Renata
  Letter from Selma. New Yorker 41:121-2+ Ap
    10 '65
  Life movie review. Life 59:18+ N 26 '65
  Onward and upward with the arts. New
    Yorker 41:63-4+ F 20 '65
  Reporter at large. New Yorker 41:195-202 D 11
    '65
ADMA (automatic drafting machine) See
  Drawing instruments
ADMINISTRATION, Public
  Administrators in the county of tomorrow;
    address, November 24, 1964. B. F. Hillen-
    brand. Vital Speeches 31:243-7 F 1 '65
  Allocation of responsibilities and resources
    among the three levels of government. J.
    C. Charlesworth. il Ann Am Acad 359:71-
    80 My '65
    See also
  Bureaucracy

ADULTHOOD. See Maturity

ADVANCED management program, Harvard
university. See Harvard university—Graduate school of business administration

ADVANCED placement program. See College
entrance examination board—Advanced
placement program

ADVANCED research and technology, Office of.
See United States—National aeronautics
and space administration—Advanced research and technology, Office of

ADVANCED research projects agency. See
United States—Defense, Department of—
Advanced research projects agency

ADVANCED technology satellite. See Communications satellites

ADVENT
We mark the Advent. V. P. McCorry. il
America 113:inside back cover N 27 '65

ADVENTURE and adventurers
Adventure & the American individualist;
Time essay. Time 86:60-1 N 19 '65
Five against the gods. R. Daley. il Esquire
64:96-101+ N '65
On running away. J. Keats. il Holiday 37:8+
Je '65
One step to adventure. E. S. Hill. il Read Di-
gest 87:129-32 S '65

ADVERTISEMENTS. See Advertising

ADVERTISEMENTS, Classified
Advertising's little giants. D. L. Lionel.
Sat R 48:61+ My 8 '65

ADVERTISING
Advertising as a communicating force; ad-
dress, February 9, 1965. J. E. Swearingen.
Vital Speeches 31:304-7 Mr 1 '65
Advertising in the 1970s. E. Roper. Sat R
48:74-5 F 13 '65
As long as you're up, get their attention. il
Time 85:87-8 Ap 23 '65
Best $10 investment; course on persuasive
writing. J. W. Young. Sat R 48:67 Ap 10 '65
Dream world of advertising. il Am Heritage
16:70-5 Ag '65
Great potato-chip war. il Newsweek 66:
71 Jl 26 '65
Madison avenue: the big invisible sell.
M. Mayer. il Sat Eve Post 238:23-31 Mr 13
'65
Naming names. il Time 86:70-1 Ag 20 '65
News behind the ads. See issues of Changing
times
Show window for industry: Madison ave. Sr
Schol 86:19+ Ap 15 '65
See also
Propaganda
Public relations
Publicity
Sales promotion
Slogans
also subhead Advertising under various
subjects, e.g. Childrens literature—Adver-
tising; *also* Television advertising and
similar headings

Bibliography
Books in communications. J. F. Fixx. See
second issue of each month of Saturday
review

Moral aspects
See Advertising ethics

Psychology
Discovering the inner Jones. E. Dichter.
Harvard Bsns R 43:6-8+ My '65
Spoofing and schtik; gimmicks used to at-
tract new generation. P. Kael. Atlan 216:
84-5 D '65

Sex appeal
Anything (almost) goes. il Newsweek 66:98+
D 6 '65
Notes and comment. il New Yorker 41:37
My 22 '65

Study and teaching
Advertising education. C. R. Hill. Sat R 48:70-
1 F 13 '65; Reply. L. D'Armand. 48:66 Ap 10
'65

Asia
Sexy sell. Time 85:102 My 21 '65

Russia
Run it up the flagpole, even reds salute. il
Newsweek 65:74-6 My 3 '65

ADVERTISING, Fraudulent
Calories do count. Nation 200:351-2 Ap 5 '65
Non sequitur, red-on-red; FTC vs advertis-
ing of G.R.I.'s over fifty capsulets. Con-
sumer Rep 30:226-7 My '65
Regimen & responsibility; judgment against
ad agency promoting a fraudulent product.
Time 85:92 My 14 '65

ADVERTISING, Outdoor
Good-by, Burma-Shave. W. K. Zinsser. il
Read Digest 86:103-6 F '65
Unsung bards of Burma-Shave; signs in the
Smithsonian institution. Changing T 19:47
F '65
Verse by the side of the road; excerpts.
F. Rowsome, jr. il Am Heritage 17:102-5
D '65
Why sell for your competitors? dairy farm
advertising. F. A. Cooper. Farm J 89:66D
Mr '65
See also
Billboards

ADVERTISING, Public service
SR's thirteenth annual advertising awards.
W. D. Patterson. il Sat R 48:69-74+ Ap 10
'65
Smokey the Bear and his friends. J. E.
Frazer. il Read Digest 87:134-8 Jl '65

ADVERTISING agencies
Advertising agency services: make or buy?
D. A. Newton. Harvard Bsns R 43:111-18
Jl '65
Getting the brass in; relations between com-
panies and their ad agencies. Bsns W p28-
9 My 15 '65
How's that again? esthetic values before
practical values. J. Kaselow. Sat R 48:56
Jl 10 '65
Knock in advertising; name-calling. G.
Lazarus. Sat R 48:77-8 D 11 '65
Multi-agency marketing. G. Lazarus. Sat R
48:59-60 Ag 14 '65
Wheeling and dealing on the coast; Los
Angeles agencies. G. Lazarus; reply. R. C.
Frojen. Sat R 48:67 F 13 '65
See also
Foote, Cone and Belding
Kastor, Hilton, Chesley, Clifford and Ather-
ton, incorporated

Fees
New way of life for Madison avenue? il
Bsns W p76-8+ My 1 '65

Securities
Rating the agency stocks. il Fortune 73:218+
Ja '66

ADVERTISING and Negroes
Colorful ads; Negroes in advertisements.
Christian Cent 82:262 Mr 3 '65

ADVERTISING campaigns
Tiger goes abroad; Esso's tiger with the
high-octane tail. il Time 85:100-1 My 28 '65

ADVERTISING ethics
Because you have always told half-truths;
excerpt from Bamboozled; or, How busi-
ness is bamboozled by the ad-boys. N. Sam-
stag. Sat R 49:112-15 Ja 8 '66
Civil war on Madison avenue. Nation 201:
235 O 18 '65
Knock in advertising; name-calling. G.
Lazarus. Sat R 48:77-8 D 11 '65
Name-droppers; advertisers call competitors
by name. il Newsweek 66:92 N 15 '65
Who says shoppers are stupid? il Nations
Bsns 53:34-5+ Mr '65
See also
Advertising, Fraudulent

ADVERTISING mediums

Buttons
Advertising buttons. D. F. Brown. il Hobbies
70:50-1 D '65

Motor buses
Sponsorless: New York bus riders digest,
posters by New York bus advertising, inc.
New Yorker 41:49-50 O 23 '65

Newspapers
Appreciation day; editor of four Holmes
County weeklies suggests Negro boycott to
keep papers alive. Newsweek 66:70 D 13 '65

Packaging
Scramble in the marketplace. L. A. Blumenthal. il Duns R 86:pt2 86-7+ D '65

Periodicals
Ottawa restricts U.S. ads. Bsns W p36 S 4
'65
Splits, spots and metros; 1965 revenues. il
Newsweek 67:41 Ja 10 '66

ADVERTISING men
Because you have always told half-truths;
excerpt from Bamboozled; or, How business is bamboozled by the ad-boys.
N. Samstag. Sat R 49:112-15 Ja 8 '66

ADVERTISING research
Must advertising communicate to sell? C. K.
Ramond. bibliog f il Harvard Bsns R 43:
148-56+ S '65

ADVERTISING signs. See Signs and sign-
boards
ADVICE columns. See Newspapers—Advice
columns
ADVISORY committee on monetary arrange-
ments. See United States—Advisory com-
mittee on monetary arrangements
ADVISORY council on the arts. See United
States—National council on the arts
ADVISORY councils, Government. See United
States—Executive departments
ADVISORY service, Readers. See Libraries—
Readers advisory service
AEGEAN ISLANDS
Greek islands. M. Goodman. il Atlan 215:
124+ F '65
Greek islands. il Sat R 48:46 Mr 13 '65
Inkfish and shark kabob; the sun and seafood
of the Aegean; with recipes. F. Du Plessix.
Vogue 146:288-90+ S 1 '65
Two Greek islands. E. Perényi. Vogue 146:
269+ O 1 '65
See also
Cyclades (islands)
AERIAL cameras. See Cameras
AERIAL photography. See Photography, Aerial
AERIAL reconnaissance
L'affaire Voodoo; photos of Pierrelatte bomb
plant taken by U.S. air force officer. Time
86:20 Jl 30 '65
De Gaulle seen viewing RF-101 flight as
future political weapon. L. L. Doty. Avia-
tion W 83:21 Jl 26 '65
Errant camera; air force above Pierrelatte,
France. il Newsweek 66:35 Ag 2 '65
Radar imagery; used for mapping purposes
by reconnaissance aircraft. J. L. Nelson. il
Electr World 74:42-3+ Ag '65
War in Vietnam; O-1F observers perform
major role in aerial recon. C. Brownlow.
il Aviation W 82:52-3+ My 17 '65
AERIAL reconnaissance cameras. See Cameras
AERIAL routes. See Airways
AERO commander, incorporated
Aero commander management shifts set. D.
A. Brown. il Aviation W 83:20-1 Jl 19 '65
Larger Guppy aimed at S-4B transport. H.
D. Watkins. il Aviation W 82:43+ Ap 19 '65
Super Guppy to make first flight Aug. 25.
H. D. Watkins. il Aviation 83:42-3 Ag 23
'65
AEROBATICS. See Aviation—Stunt flying
AEROCLASSIC. See Aviation—Exhibitions
AERODYNAMICS
X-21A tests verify laminar flow gains.
I. Stone. il Aviation W 83:98-9+ S 27 '65
AEROFLOT (airline) See Airlines—Russia
AEROJET-General corporation
Aerometrics division
Aerojet expands into commercial market;
Aerometrics division to capitalize in aero-
space technology. R. G. O'Lone. il Aviation
W 83:81+ N 15 '65
Aerojet pleased with commercial entry. R.
Pay. Miss & Roc 17:36 N 15 '65
AERONAUTIC education. See Aeronautics—
Study and teaching
AERONAUTIC instruments
Cost factors key to future of ILAAS; in-
tegrated light attack avionics system for
VAL aircraft. B. Miller. il Aviation W 82:
62-3+ F 22 '65
IHAS program may establish precedents in
concepts, technology; integrated helicopter
avionics system. B. Miller. il Aviation W 82:
40-1+ Je 21 '65
IHAS uses special incremental computer;
integrated helicopter avionics system. B.
Miller. il Aviation W 82:88-9+ Je 28 '65
Latest avionics equipment planned for C-5A.
Aviation W 82:23 My 3 '65
Navy proposes production start on IHAS,
seeks additional funds. il Aviation W 83:22
N 1 '65
Package will measure flight stress data; VGH
recorders. K. J. Stein. il Aviation W 82:61+
Mr 8 '65
Pilot reaction to Sperry display assessed;
windshield projection display. il Aviation W
83:115+ Ag 9 '65
Rainbow optical projector aids landing. P. J.
Klass. il Aviation W 83:63-5 Ag 23 '65
Re-entry data system assists X-15 pilot.
G. Alexander. il Aviation W 83:79+ S 27
'65
Regency who? miniscule navcom systems. A.
Trammell. Flying 77:45-6 Jl '65
Reliability study cites transistor duty cycle.
Aviation W 82:86-7+ Ap 19 '65
Stationkeeping system effective in tests. B.
Miller. il Aviation W 82:36-7+ Mr 22 '65

VOR/DME, localizer developed for budget-
minded customers. il Aviation W 83:104+
O 25 '65
See also
Altimeters
Automatic pilot (airplanes)
Inertial guidance systems
Space vehicles—Instrument boards
AERONAUTIC meteorology. See Meteorology,
Aeronautic
AERONAUTIC museums
In San Diego, the history of flight; Aerospace
museum, Balboa park. il Sunset 135:62+ N
'65
See also
Smithsonian institution—National air and
space museum
AERONAUTIC research
Monroney asks more civil air research. Avia-
tion W 82:31 Je 21 '65
NASA studies SST operational problems.
Aviation W 83:127+ O 25 '65
AERONAUTICS
History
Airman's almanac. il Flying 77:79 N '65
Aviation and the collector. E. D. Collins.
il Hobbies 70:30-1 Ap '65
Safety devices and measures
See Aviation—Safety devices and meas-
ures
Study and teaching
Making math & science soar; high school
course in flying, Atlanta. il Time 87:44 Ja
14 '66
Terminology
V/STOL terminology. Aviation W 83:90 N 15
'65
AERONAUTICS, Commercial
Aerospace leaders see aviation rebirth. G. C.
Wilson. Aviation W 82:23 F 8 '65
International aspects
See Aviation—International aspects
Alaska
Alaska route shifts set merger climate. R. G.
O'Lone. Aviation W 82:39-40 Ap 5 '65
Arab states
Thirteen Arab nation airlines organize re-
gional unit patterned on IATA; Arab air
carrier organization. Aviation W 83:52 N
15 '65
United States
Jet-age expert gives some blunt answers;
interview, ed. by B. Kocivar. N. Halaby. il
Look 29:50+ D 14 '65
See also
Airlines—United States
Airplane industry and trade—United States
AERONAUTICS, Military
Major joint tactical defense effort seen. C.
Brownlow. Aviation W 84:104-5+ Ja 17 '66
See also
Airplanes, Military
Bombing, Aerial
Helicopters—Military applications
Canada
Canada shifts defense emphasis in tactical
air force buildup. Aviation W 82:287 Mr
15 '65
France
French continue nuclear delivery buildup in
six-year plan. il Aviation W 82:268-9+ Mr
15 '65
Great Britain
See also
Great Britain—Royal air force
Russia
Air defense featured in Soviet film on mis-
siles. il Miss & Roc 17:16-17 S 13 '65
Naked country. W. J. Coughlin. Miss & Roc
17:46 S 20 '65
Sweden
Sweden maintains A37 program funding. W.
C. Wetmore. il Aviation W 82:94-8 Ap 5 '65
Switzerland
See also
Airplanes, Military—Switzerland
United States
AWAC future hinges on feasibility tests.
P. J. Klass. Aviation W 82:80-1+ F 22 '65
B-52 raids seen spurring F-111 bomber.
C. Brownlow. Aviation W 83:22 Ag 30 '65
Big emphasis is on airlift, sealift. il Miss &
Roc 16:117-18+ Mr 29 '65

AERONAUTICS, Military—United States—
Continued
Forward protection called major deficiency. il Miss & Roc 16:101-2+ Mr 29 '65
McNamara seeks improved anti-aircraft. G. C. Wilson. Aviation W 82:25-6 F 22 '65
McNamara stresses air defense system. Miss & Roc 16:18 F 22 '65
Naked country. W. J. Coughlin. Miss & Roc 17:46 S 20 '65
Tactical weaponry pushed by air force. il Aviation W 82:72-5 Mr 15 '65
See also
Airplanes, Military—United States
Space flight—Military applications

Vietnam (Republic)
See also
Vietnamese war, 1957- —Aerial operations
AERONOMY satellites. See Artificial satellites —Use in research
AERONUTRONIC division. See Ford motor company—Aeronutronic division
AEROSOL hair sprays. See Hair preparations
AEROSOLS
New tools for painters. il Consumer Rep 31:40-1 Ja '66
AEROSPACE corporation
Aerospace: congressional study of AF contractor raises questions about proper role of nonprofits. E. Langer. Science 149:1076-9 S 3 '65
Aerospace corp. agrees to open its books. K. Johnsen. Aviation W 82:36 My 17 '65
Aerospace corp. given MOL task. H. Taylor. Miss & Roc 17:15-16 O 18 '65
Aerospace elephant. W. J. Coughlin. Miss & Roc 17:50 S 27 '65
House probe of Aerospace corp. begun; with editorial comment. H. M. David. Miss & Roc 16:16, 46 My 10 '65
House unit hits aerospace corp. spending. K. Johnsen. Aviation W 82:38-9 My 10 '65
How to succeed by being a nonprofit organization. Time 86:114+ S 17 '65
Into the think tank. Newsweek 66:56+ S 6 '65
Is Aerospace corp. necessary? Nation 200:547 My 24 '65
Military's research groups under fire. il Bsns W p34 S 11 '65
Nonprofits again; concerning report of subcommittee of House committee on armed services. Nation 201:262-3 O 25 '65
Report blasts Aerospace violations. Miss & Roc 17:14 Ag 23 '65
Report lashes air force, Aerospace corp. K. Johnsen. Aviation W 83:34-5 Ag 23 '65
AEROSPACE industries
See also
Government investigations—Aerospace industries
Employees
Aerospace employment leveling off. S. Montgomery. Miss & Roc 17:17 S 6 '65
Employment experience of discharged defense workers. R. Brandwein. il Mo Labor R 88:1213-14 O '65
Finance
Aerospace industry financial results, 1964. il Aviation W 83:66-7 S 20 '65
Industry profits rise despite sales drop; with tables. Aviation W 82:96-7 Ap 26 '65
Meaning of backlogs. Fortune 71:80 Ap '65
Securities
Aerospace stocks in strong surge. H. M. David. il Miss & Roc 17:16-17 N 15 '65
Europe, Western
Europe firm on space transporter goals. il Aviation W 82:77+ Je 28 '65
Special report on European aerospace industry; symposium. Aviation W 82:74-91+ Je 14 '65
See also
Eurospace
France
French continue nuclear delivery buildup in six-year plan. il Aviation W 82:268-9+ Mr 15 '65
U.K. France sign aircraft, engine pact. H. J. Coleman. Aviation W 82:18 My 24 '65
Germany (Federal Republic)
German firms prepare satellite designs. W. C. Wetmore. Aviation W 83:95+ Ag 9 '65
German industry hungry for funding. M. Getler. il Miss & Roc 17:29-30+ Jl 19 '65
West German mergers realign industry. Aviation W 82:285+ Mr 15 '65

Great Britain
British need for joint projects stressed. H. J. Coleman. Aviation W 82:22-4 F 15 '65
Buy American policy supported by British aviation consultant. H. J. Coleman. Aviation W 83:89+ Jl 19 '65
U.K. France sign aircraft, engine pact. H. J. Coleman. Aviation W 82:18 My 24 '65
U.K. groups edgy over new U.S. orders. H. J. Coleman. Aviation W 83:26-8 N 22 '65
U.K. industry awaits review findings; with editorial comment. Miss & Roc 17:15, 46 Jl 5 '65
U.K. merger seen step to nationalization; British aircraft corp. and Hawker Siddeley aviation. H. J. Coleman. Aviation W 83:28 D 27 '65
U.K. national plan report depicts top-heavy aerospace industry. H. J. Coleman. Aviation W 83:32 S 27 '65
Japan
Japanese build gradually in aerospace. il Aviation W 82:272-5+ Mr 15 '65
Sweden
Flygmotor develops small hybrid rocket. W. C. Wetmore. il Aviation W 83:55-6+ Jl 19 '65
United States
Aerospace: a new life for a billion-dollar industry? with interview with E. G. Brown. il U S News 58:109-11 My 24 '65
Aerospace companies give California a hand. Bsns W p84 F 20 '65
Aerospace employment leveling off. S. Montgomery. Miss & Roc 17:17 S 6 '65
Aerospace industry; address, February 15, 1965. K. G. Harr. Vital Speeches 31:500-4 Je 1 '65
Aerospace industry financial results, 1964. il Aviation W 83:66-7 S 20 '65
Aerospace interlocks with other firms; table. Aviation W 82:91 Ap 19 '65
Aerospace leaders see aviation rebirth. G. C. Wilson. Aviation W 82:23 F 8 '65
Aerospace raises ante; demands of unions in bargaining. il Bsns W p 124 My 15 '65
Aerospace stocks in strong surge. H. M. David. il Miss & Roc 17:16-17 N 15 '65
California aerospace firms again lead nation in space agency dollars. il Miss & Roc 16:21 Je 21 '65
Changing aerospace market; excerpts from address. D. J. Haughton. Aviation W 83:21 Ag 9 '65
Collaboration viewed as barrier to U.S; Anglo-French collaboration on advanced civil and military aircraft projects. L. L. Doty. Aviation W 82:19 My 24 '65
Defense dept. push for export sales seen backfiring in Europe. C. Brownlow. Aviation W 82:23-4 Je 21 '65
DOD briefing emphasizes tactical needs. H. D. Watkins. Aviation W 82:16-17 Mr 8 '65
Downhill path. W. J. Coughlin. Miss & Roc 18:50 Ja 10 '66
Europeans get eyeful of U.S. space work; delegates to Eurospace conference amazed by U.S. plants. il Bsns W p 134+ My 15 '65
Excess profit claims settled by four firms. Aviation W 83:20 Jl 5 '65
Healthy industry. R. Hotz. Aviation W 83:17 O 4 '65
House group details corporate interlocks. G. C. Wilson. Aviation W 82:92+ Ap 12 '65
How healthy is the aerospace industry? Aviation W 82:11 F 8 '65
How not to sell abroad. W. J. Coughlin. Miss & Roc 16:50 Je 28 '65
Industry may receive $23.7 billion. il Miss & Roc 16:10-11+ F 1 '65
Industry profit performance confounds critics. R. Hotz. Aviation W 82:64-5 Mr 15 '65
Industry profits rise despite sales drop; with tables. Aviation W 82:96-7 Ap 26 '65
Industry within. W. J. Coughlin. Miss & Roc 17:70 S 6 '65
Johnson maps strong aerospace efforts; with editorial comment. G. C. Wilson. il Aviation W 82:11, 16-18 F 1 '65
Laurels for 1965. R. Hotz. Aviation W 83:11 D 27 '65
Myriad R&D problems await solution. il Miss & Roc 16:40-3+ Mr 29 '65
New aerospace products. See issues of Aviation week & space technology
Next step; aerospace programs to apply space-age know-how to the Nation's social and economic problems. W. J. Coughlin. Miss & Roc 17:46 N 15 '65
Onward and upward. W. J. Coughlin. Miss & Roc 16:54 F 8 '65
Problems for the Hill. W. J. Coughlin. Miss & Roc 16:54 F 22 '65

AEROSPACE industries—United States—*Cont.*
Space (cont) il Life 59:35-6 Jl 9 '65
Space and society; excerpts from remarks. R. C. Seamans, jr. Aviation W 83:17 N 22 '65
Space industries expand. Sci N L 88:100 Ag 14 '65
U.S. firms demanding fair play at Paris. L. L. Doty. Aviation W 83:33-4 Ag 2 '65
What aerospace sees on the ground; long-range programs for California. il Bsns W p87-8+ S 25 '65
    See also
Lockheed aircraft corporation
McDonnell aircraft corporation
Strikes—United States—Aerospace industries

AEROSPACE medical division. See United States—Air force—Systems command

AEROSPACE medicine, School of. See United States—Air force—Systems command

AEROSPACE museums. See Aeronautic museums

AEROSPACE telemetry. See Space telemetry

AEROTHERMODYNAMICS. See Thermodynamics

AESCHYLUS
Oresteia. K. Rexroth. Sat R 48:21 Ag 14 '65

AESOP'S fables
Codex Pithoeanus of Phaedrus; address, January 13, 1965. F. B. Adams, jr. Horn Bk 41:260-6 Je '65

AESTHETIC values. See Worth

AESTHETICS
Bad taste factor. W. Sheed. Commonweal 82:256-7 My 14 '65
Fair and change; dividing lines between authentic and phony. C. J. McNaspy. America 112:645 My 1 '65
Object: function, craft, and art. R. Slivka. Craft Horiz 25:10-11 S '65
Object: lost and found. V. D'Amico. il Craft Horiz 25:26-7 S '65
On seeing and believing. A. Heckscher. Sat R 48:125-6 Mr 13 '65
    See also
Nature (aesthetics)

AETNA Trix lenses. See Lenses, Photographic

AFFECTION. See Friendship; Love

AFFILIATION disputes. See Trade unions—Jurisdictional disputes

AFFLERBACH, Lois. See Bry, I, jt. auth.

AFGHANISTAN
    See also
Technical assistance in Afghanistan

Foreign relations
Nonaligned Afghans. E. Hugh-Jones. New Repub 152:10-11 Ap 17 '65
So far, yet it's so near; pro-U.S. turn. R. Rowan. il Life 59:98A-98B D 10 '65

History
Afghanistan. E. Reiner and A. Taylor. bibliog il Focus 15:1-6 Ja '65

Politics and government
Kingly accomplishment; new art: politics. il Time 86:36+ D 3 '65
So far, yet it's so near. R. Rowan. il Life 59:98A-98B D 10 '65

AFLATOXIN. See Fungi

AFRICA
Africa, 1965; symposium. bibliog f il Cur Hist 48:193-231+ Ap '65
Africa's pattern of violence. A. Campbell. New Repub 152:17-18 Je 12 '65
Importance of being black: an Asian looks at Africa, by F. Moraes. Review
    Reporter 32:55+ Mr 25 '65. T. Sterling
Two tough minds. G. M. Carter. Nation 201:198-200 O 4 '65
    See also
Airlines—Africa
Art—Africa
Communism—Africa
Economic assistance in Africa
Hunting—Africa
Marriage—Africa
Mental illness—Africa
Newspapers—Africa
Publishers and publishing—Africa
Water supply—Africa
Women—Africa

Antiquities
Africa's golden past (cont) W. L. Hansberry and E. H. Johnson. il Ebony 20:62-5+ F; 70-2+ Mr; 136-7+ Ap '65

Bibliography
Drama and anguish in Africa. E. R. F. Sheehan. Harper 231:128-33 D '65

Colonization
    See also
Negroes—Colonization

Economic conditions
Africa: from independence to tomorrow, by D. Hapgood. Review
    Nation 201:200-2 O 4 '65. S. Meisler
For black Africa: five years of freedom, and now. A. J. Meyers. il U S News 59:56-9 Jl 5 '65
Widening gap. il Newsweek 66:40-1 Jl 12 '65
    See also
United Nations—Economic commission for Africa

Economic policy
Capitalism and African economic development; excerpts from African nettle. ed. by F. S. Meyer. P. T. Bauer. Nat R 17:542-5 Je 29 '65

Foreign relations
Nonalignment in Africa. T. P. Melady. bibliog f Ann Am Acad 362:52-61 N '65

History
Africa's golden past (cont) W. L. Hansberry and E. H. Johnson. il Ebony 20:62-5+ F; 70-2+ Mr; 136-7+ Ap '65
Can you find Liberia? A. Wilson. il Christian Cent 82:212-13 F 17 '65
Glorious age in Africa, by D. Chu and E. Skinner. Review
    Negro Hist Bul 28:160+ Ap '65
Nations of Africa; date of independence. il Cur Hist 48:224-5 Ap '65

Bibliography
Articles and other books received; comp. by D. E. Gardinier. See issues of American historical review

Maps
Africa, 1965; symposium. bibliog f Cur Hist 48:193-231+ Ap '65
Map of Africa (cont) Sr Schol 87:33 S 30 '65

Nationalism
Africa: a political travelogue, by T. Molnar. Review
    Sat R 48:29-30 S 4 '65. H. Lehrman
Fire this time. D. Wiley. Christian Cent 82:200-3 F 17 '65

Native races
Washing of the spears: a history of the rise of the Zulu nation under Shaka and its fall in the Zulu war of 1879, by D. R. Morris. Review
    Nat R 17:882-3 O 5 '65. J. Hart
    Sat R 48:27-8 S 4 '65. C. Miller
    See also
Negroes in Africa
Somalis

Politics
Africa: a political travelogue, by T. Molnar. Review
    Nat R 17:833-5 S 21 '65. A. Lejeune
    Sat R 48:29-30 S 4 '65. H. Lehrman
Biggest bloc; Organisation commune africaine et Malgache. il Time 85:30 Je 4 '65
Capitalism and African economic development; excerpts from African nettle, ed. by F. S. Meyer. P. T. Bauer. Nat R 17:542-5 Je 29 '65
Frankness from Dr Banda; opinions on Afro-Asian solidarity. America 113:558 N 13 '65
Loneliest men; reprint, March 12, 1960. J. Burnham. Nat R 17:1069 N 30 '65
Lost goals in Africa. A. Rivkin. For Affairs 44:111-26 O '65
New scramble for Africa; Soviets and red Chinese race for influence. il Sr Schol 86:6-9 F 11 '65
Nonalignment in Africa. T. P. Melady. bibliog f Ann Am Acad 362:52-61 N '65
Red China's year in Africa. E. Huxley. il Nat R 17:95-6+ F 9 '65
Revolutionaries adrift. Time 85:28 Mr 26 '65
    See also
Organization of African unity

Race problems
Black skins, white masks, by F. Fanon. Review
    Commentary 40:67-71 Jl '65. H. R. Isaacs
Moving toward chaos in black Africa? il U S News 59:68-70 D 20 '65
We want our country. il Time 86:40-2+ N 5 '65
    See also subhead Race problems under names of African countries, e.g. South Africa—Race problems

AFRICA, CENTRAL
African encounter. T. Sterling. Holiday 38:
52-3+ Ag '65
See also
Chad
Malawi

AFRICA, EAST
Anti-American week. Time 85:32 F 26 '65
Farewell to arms; Uganda's arms scandal.
Time 85:30 Je 4 '65
Leakeys of Africa; family in search of pre-
historic man. M. M. Payne. il Nat Geog
Mag 127:194-231 F '65
See also
Great Rift Valley
Somalia
Zoology—Africa, East

Politics
Letter from Nairobi. V. P. McCorry.
America 114:20-1 Ja 1 '66
Three's a crowd: Kenya, Tanzania and
Uganda disagree. il Time 85:40 My 28 '65

AFRICA, NORTH
Nature of modernization; the Middle East
and north Africa. W. R. Polk. For Affairs
44:100-10 O '65
See also
Sahara Desert

Civilization
Baal, Christ and Mohammed, by J. K. Cooley.
Review
Commonweal 82:672-3 S 17 '65. J. Krit-
zeck

Description and travel
Traveling with Mlle: North Africa and the
Middle East. D. Beal. il Mlle 61:205-6 S '65

Foreign relations
North Africa: active crossroads. D. D. Newsom. il Dept State Bul 53:315-22 Ag 23 '65

History
Baal, Christ and Mohammed, by J. K. Cooley.
Review
Commonweal 82:672-3 S 17 '65. J. Krit-
zeck

Politics
North Africa: active crossroads. D. D. Newsom. il Dept State Bul 53:315-22 Ag 23
'65

AFRICA, SOUTHWEST. See Southwest Africa

AFRICA, WEST
New motifs in West Africa. W. A. E. Shur-
nik. il Cur Hist 48:207-12+ Ap '65
See also
Dahomey
Ivory Coast
Timbuktu
Togo

AFRICA and Asia
Letter from Algiers. R. Shaplen. il New
Yorker 41:38-40+ Jl 17 '65
This brave new world of Afro-Asia; racial
and religious antagonisms. America 113:
312-13 S 25 '65

AFRICAN art. See Art, African

AFRICAN languages

Alphabet
New alphabets for five African languages. R.
Greenough. Sch & Soc 93:375-6 O 16 '65

AFRICAN lilies
Two happy August companions. il Sunset
135:144 Ag '65

AFRICAN magic. See Magic

**AFRICAN scholarship program of American
universities**
How many lions? U.S. orientation course.
Newsweek 66:51 S 6 '65

AFRICAN sculpture. See Sculpture, African

AFRICAN students
Education: U.S. institutions prepare African
students for development tasks at home.
L. J. Carter. Science 149:1213-15 S 10 '65

**AFRICAN students in Great Britain; in Rus-
sia; etc.** See Foreign students in Great
Britain; Foreign students in Russia; etc.

AFRICAN violets
Home garden notebook. J. B. Brimer. il
Flower Grower 52:31-2 O '65
Summer care of African violets. Mrs W. F.
Prescott. il Horticulture 43:36-7 My '65

AFRICAN witch doctors. See Medicine men

AFRICANS
Africans lionize a pride of spacemen. il Life
59:44-5 O 8 '65
On the rounds with a witch doctor. M. Gelfand. il N Y Times Mag p44-5+ Mr 14 '65
Two tough minds. G. M. Carter. Nation 201:
198-200 O 4 '65

AFRICANS in the United States
Africans in darkest New York; United Na-
tions delegates. J. K. Rosen. il N Y Times
Mag p30-1+ F 28 '65

**AFRO-ASIAN people's solidarity conference,
Algiers, 1965**
Afro-Asia: a myth, and a somber reality;
Widening gap; Algiers summit conference
wrecked. il Newsweek 66:39-41 Jl 12 '65
Chou gets socked twice; postponement of Al-
gerian conference. G. De Carvalho. il pors
Life 59:62A-62B+ Jl 9 '65
End of a myth; adjourns for sake of unity.
A. de Borchgrave. il Newsweek 66:58 N 15
'65
Faded dream; failure of conference. Time 86:
40 N 12 '65
Myth dissolves. Nat R 17:1016+ N 16 '65
Seesaw summit; postponement until November
5, 1965. il Time 86:22 Jl 2 '65

**AFRO-ASIAN people's solidarity conference,
Winneba, Ghana, 1965**
Solidarity forever? Time 85:42 My 21 '65

AFRO-ASIAN studies. See Area studies

AFTER all these years; story. See Knowlton,
R. A.

AFTER images
Oh, say can you see? op art. il Time 87:70-1
Ja 14 '66
See also
Phosphenes

AFTERIMAGES. See After images

AGAMMAGLOBULINEMIA
Defective RNA synthesis in lymphocytes from
patients with primary agammaglobulinemia.
M. J. Cline and H. H. Fudenberg. bibliog
il Science 150:1311-12 D 3 '65

AGAPANTHUS africanus. See African lilies

AGAR
Bacteria as an indicator of formation of antibodies by single spleen cells in agar. S. A.
Schwartz and W. Braun. bibliog Science
149:200 Jl 9 '65

AGASSIZ, Louis
Science in the grand tradition. V. Miller.
Nat R 17:243-4 Mr 23 '65

**AGATE FOSSIL BEDS NATIONAL MONU-
MENT**
Monument to miocene mammals. Nat Parks
Mag 39:20 Ag '65
Monument to miocene mammals. P. M.
Tilden. Natur Hist 74:64-6 Ag '65

AGE
See also
Aging
Old age

AGE (plants)
Desert locusts: sexual maturation delayed by
feeding on senescent vegetation. P. E. Ellis
and others. bibliog il Science 149:546-7 Jl
30 '65
Photoperiodic induction of senescence in
xanthium plants. D. T. Krizek and others.
bibliog il Science 151:95-6 Ja 7 '66

AGE and employment
Hiring policies, prejudices, and the older
worker. il Mo Labor R 88:968-70 Ag '65
New plans for older workers. C. A. Betts.
il Sci N L 87:298-9 My 8 '65
Next: job law for older workers? those over
forty-five. U S News 59:84-5 Jl 12 '65
Old before their time; men over fifty-five.
America 113:147 Ag 14 '65
See also
Retirement from business, etc.

AGE determination by radioactivity. See Radioactive dating

AGE for action; story. See Hale, N.

AGE of the earth. See Earth—Age

AGED
America's oldest worker; age: 100. J. Star. il
Look 29:M8+ D 14 '65
Tomorrow started yesterday; symposium. il
Recreation 58:220-3+ My '65
Voluntarism in retirement; address, 1964. G.
Meyer. Recreation 58:219+ My '65
See also
Old age
Retirement from business, etc.
Retirement income
United States—Aging, Administration on

Adjustment problems
Old people's home often benefits senior
citizens. Sci N L 88:362 D 4 '65
Reporter at large; effects of urban renewal
on old people in South End of Boston.
J. Colebrook. New Yorker 41:35-6+ Ja 1
'66

AGED—*Continued*

Care and hygiene

New way to care for the aged & infirm; Hunterdon program. il Changing T 19:22-4 Mr '65

Private geriatrics hospital; Terra Linda Valley hospital, Marin County. Calif. il Arch Rec 137:178-9 F '65
See also
Aged—Housing

Clubs
See Recreation for the aged

Economic conditions

This is the age of the aged. J. Horwitz. il N Y Times Mag p25+ My 16 '65

Employment
See Age and employment

Housing

Eccentricity under the sun. R. Carson. il Holiday 38:106+ O '65

How can you choose the right place to retire? N. Kuehnl and G. Bush. Bet Hom & Gard 43:6+ D '65

New lease on life; high-rise retirement apartment. il Time 87:43 Ja 7 '66

New places to live when you retire. il Changing T 19:24-9 O '65

Reporter at large; effects of urban renewal on old people in South End of Boston. J. Colebrook. New Yorker 41:35-6+ Ja 1 '66

U.S. retirement cities. T. B. Lesure. il Travel 123:36-40 Mr '65

Where life begins at sixty-five; Rossmoor leisure world. P. Friggens. Read Digest 88:15\(\)-8+ Ja '66

Medical care

Medical care for the aged. S. Hollos. il America 112:309-12 Mr 6 '65; Discussion. 112:442-3, 470, 501-2, 622, 850-2+ Ap 3-17, My 1, Je 12 '65

Nutrition

Meals on wheels grows. Sci N L 87:388 Je 19 '65

Recreation
See Recreation for the aged

Statistics

Aged: a new frontier. Christian Cent 82:325 Mr 17 '65

This is the age of the aged. J. Horwitz. il N Y Times Mag p25+ My 16 '65

AGEE, James
Way of seeing; excerpts. Horizon 7:49-50 Sum '65

about

On Chaplin, Verdoux and Agee. D. Macdonald. Esquire 63:18+ Ap '65

AGEE, William C.
Synchromism, the first American movement. Art N 64:28-31+ O '65

AGENCIES, Employment. See Employment agencies

AGENCIES, Regulatory. See Independent regulatory commissions

AGENCY for international development. See United States—Agency for international development

AGENTS. See Literary agents

AGENTS, Purchasing. See Purchasing agents

AGENTS, Talent. See Theatrical agencies

AGERATUMS
Dependable ageratum. C. Christensen. Flower Grower 52:43 D '65

AGGLUTININS
Interferon-like virus-inhibitor induced in human leukocytes by phytohemagglutinin. E. F. Wheelock. bibliog il Science 149:310-11 Jl 16 '65

AGGRESSION (international law)
U.S. calls for deeds, not words, in U.N. committee on defining aggression; statements, April 5 and April 8, 1965. F. T. P. Plimpton. Dept State Bul 52:775-85 My 17 '65
See also
United Nations—Committee on the question of defining aggression

AGGRESSIVENESS
Rats attack when hurt. Sci N L 89:6 Ja 1 '66

AGING
Age, postponement: a doctor speaks; questions and answers. il Vogue 146:62-5+ Ag 15 '65

Aging and everyman. N. J. Berrill. il Atlan 217:86-90 Ja '66

Do you act your age? questions and answers. J. Daugherty and M. Daugherty. il Sci Digest 57:92-4 My '65

Elderly keep brain power. Sci N L 88:22 Jl 10 '65

Search for ways to keep youthful. G. A. W. Boehm. il Fortune 71:138-42+ Mr '65

AGING, Administration on. See United States —Aging, Administration on

AGING of plants. See Age (plants)

AGNES, Sister
Plato: a girl's thought; poem. Commonweal 81:739 Mr 5 '65

Three acts of love; poem. Commonweal 83:236 N 26 '65

AGNES Scott college, Decatur, Ga.
Modern cloister for art studies; Dana fine arts building. il Arch Rec 138:158-60 O '65

AGNEW, C. R. Jr
New vigor in French sports. Recreation 58:66-7+ F '65

AGNEW, H. W. Jr. See Webb, W. B. jt. auth.

AGNOSTICISM
Dialogue with campus agnostics. R. E. Kavanaugh. America 114:126-8 Ja 22 '66
See also
Irreligion

AGOUTI locus. See Color of animals

AGRAWAL, H. O. and others
Rotation technique in electron microscopy of viruses. bibliog Science 148:638-40 Ap 30 '65

AGREEMENTS, International. See Treaties

AGRICULTURAL administration

Asia

Economic development in Asia; address, April 23, 1965. W. W. Rostow. Dept State Bul 52:845-53 My 31 '65

Latin America

Urban concentration, agriculture, and agrarian reform; with questions and answers. G. J. Eder. bibliog f Ann Am Acad 360:27-47 Jl '65

Russia

Butter versus guns. Newsweek 65:43-4 Ap 5 '65

Plowing up. Time 85:31 Ap 2 '65

Russia again tackles farm problem. il U S News 58:82 Ap 12 '65

Underdeveloped areas

Backward nations: aid and resources. W. C. Paddock and P. Paddock. il Nation 200:414-17 Ap 19 '65

Need self-help programs. Sci N L 87:374 Je 12 '65

United States

Across the editor's desk. D. Hanson. Suc Farm 63:6 Ap '65

Bumper crop of cash. il Fortune 72:32+ S '65

Congress cuts new pattern for cotton; omnibus farm bill. Bsns W p56 Ag 14 '65

Dairy report from Washington. Farm J 89:A12 Jl '65

Desegregating agriculture. New Repub 152:7-8 Ap 10 '65

Farewell to farmer Tuttle. J. Bird. il Sat Eve Post 238:34-8+ D 4 '65

Great myths of agricultural policy. D. Paarlberg. Suc Farm 63:29+ Ag; 41+ S '65

Great society, country style. Time 85:19 F 12 '65

How to shoot Santa Claus. il Time 86:22-6 S 3 '65

Johnson trims farm tab; transfer cost of higher grain supports to consumers. Bsns W p38 Ap 10 '65

Last minute report straight from Washington. See issues of Farm journal

Liquidation ahead for 2.4 million farmers? il U S News 58:59-60 Mr 22 '65

Look, the soil bank is back; Cropland adjustment program. C. W. Gifford. Farm J 90:39 Ja '66

Monster government; crop-subsidy program. H. Hazlitt. Newsweek 65:82 Ap 26 '65

Now there's talk of a bread tax. il U S News 59:32 Jl 26 '65

Speaking out; get the government off the farm. A. P. Bean. Sat Eve Post 238:10+ My 8 '65; Same abr. Read Digest 87:83-5 Jl '65

Subsidy crackdown? LBJ decides no. U S News 58:12 F 15 '65

Want to retire your whole farm? C. W. Gifford. Farm J 89:27+ Je '65

What the new farm bill means. C. W. Gifford. Farm J 89:31+ My '65

What's ahead in farm programs? il Suc Farm 63:52-3 F '65
See also
Farm produce—Prices
United States—Agriculture, Department of

AGRICULTURAL airplanes. See Airplanes in agriculture

AGRICULTURAL and technical college at Canton. See New York state university—Agricultural and technical college at Canton

AGRICULTURAL associations. See Agricultural societies

AGRICULTURAL chemicals
   See also
Fungicides
Herbicides

AGRICULTURAL chemistry
   See also
Fertilizers and manures

AGRICULTURAL colleges
   See also
Iowa state university of science and technology, Ames
New York state university—Agricultural and technical college at Canton

AGRICULTURAL credit
Do you borrow enough money? Farm J 89:50H Mr '65
How to stay ahead of your lender; handbook for bankers. B. Brantley. il Suc Farm 63:74 N '65
   See also
Farm finance

AGRICULTURAL economics. See Agriculture—Economic aspects

AGRICULTURAL education
Girls in Vo-ag? we've tried it! denied official FFA membership. H. Haynes. Farm J 90:52P Ja '66

AGRICULTURAL exhibitions
Gold in them thar hills; state-fair circuit, gold mine of show business. il Time 86:53-4 S 10 '65
I went to the country fair; in Monroe County, Mo. M. M. McBride. McCalls 92:40+ S '65
Odd time in Du Quoin, Illinois; Hambletonian trotting race and state fair. M. Kram. il Sports Illus 23:24-31 Ag 30 '65
Why Hickory farms goes to the fair. il Bsns W p70-2 S 4 '65
Yes yes, three in a row for My My, and Sweetie Face, too; Kentucky state fair horse show. A. Higgins. Sports Illus 23:76 O 11 '65
   See also
Livestock shows

AGRICULTURAL extension work
   See also
4-H clubs

AGRICULTURAL forecasts
Farmcast for the eastern states. See issues of Farm journal
What are farming prospects in the next five years? views of four experts; ed. by B. Brantley. il Suc Farm 63:50-1+ Ap '65

AGRICULTURAL labor. See Farm labor

AGRICULTURAL laws and legislation
Big farm fight; with editorial comment. C. W. Gifford. Farm J 89:5, 35+ F '65
Farm journal's poll. Farm J 89:150 Ap '65
How to understand and use this year's wheat-feed grain programs. B. Brantley and F. Bailey, jr. Suc Farm 63:52-3 Mr '65
No time for semantics; 1965 farm bill passed by Senate. Time 86:27 S 24 '65
Speaking out; get the government off the farm. A. P. Bean. Sat Eve Post 238:10+ My 8 '65; Same abr. Read Digest 87:83-5 Jl '65
Swinging a scythe on farm surplus; omnibus bill launches new subsidy program. Bsns W p29-30 O 23 '65
Toward a real solution; ten point basic program. Farm J 89:120 S '65
What farmers will get now: a look at the coming law. il U S News 59:135-7 O 11 '65
What's in that new farm bill. C. W. Gifford. Farm J 89:33+ N '65
Which of these do you want from Congress? with editorial comment. Farm J 89:5, 20-1 F '65

AGRICULTURAL machinery
Agriculture's fantastic new machines. J. N. Miller. il Read Digest 86:117-21 F '65
Machinery management. P. B. Jones. il Suc Farm 64:55 Ja '66
Machinery parade; photographs. See issues of Farm journal
Machinery parade: preview for 1966; photographs. Farm J 90:32-7 Ja '66
Money-saving tax guidelines on machinery. F. Bailey, jr. il Suc Farm 64:60+ Ja '66
Power farming news; photographs. See issues of Farm journal
What you need to know about special steels. Suc Farm 64:88 Ja '66
What's new. See issues of Successful farming
   See also
Corn harvesting machinery
Corn planters
Feed handling
Hay making machinery
Seeding machinery

Leasing
Buy or lease equipment? Suc Farm 63:39-40 My '65
Should you own, lease, or custom hire machinery? D. O. Hull and E. D. Petersen. il Suc Farm 64:56-7+ Ja '66

Prices
How many acres to pay for that machine? Farm J 89:34D Jl '65
How much will it cost to: il Suc Farm 64:64-5 Ja '66
Tips on borrowing to buy machinery. J. Brake. il Suc Farm 64:84 Ja '66

Repairing
Get more hours between valve jobs: farm engine. G. E. Melvin. Suc Farm 64:76D Ja '66
Now is the time to: W. J. Fletcher. il Suc Farm 64:68-9 Ja '66

Storage
Make winter storage pay. Suc Farm 64:92 Ja '66

AGRICULTURAL missions. See Missions

AGRICULTURAL organizations. See Agricultural societies

AGRICULTURAL pests
   See also
Plant quarantine
   also subhead Diseases and pests under names of crops, e.g. Corn—Diseases and pests

AGRICULTURAL research
Backward nations: aid and resources. W. C. Paddock and P. Paddock. il Nation 200:414-17 Ap 19 '65
   See also
Radiation—Agricultural applications

AGRICULTURAL societies
Farmers need a unified voice. D. Paarlberg. Suc Farm 64:33 Ja '66

AGRICULTURAL subsidies. See Agricultural administration—United States

AGRICULTURAL surplus products. See Surplus products, Agricultural

AGRICULTURAL tractors. See Tractors

AGRICULTURAL workers. See Farm labor

AGRICULTURE
   See also
Dairying
Diversified farming
Food supply
Indians of North America—Agriculture
Reclamation of land

Economic aspects
Agricultural export programs; address, February 9, 1965. C. R. Eskildsen. Vital Speeches 31:326-8 Mr 15 '65
Dozen ways to have money when you need it. Farm J 90:52 Ja '66
Farm business. See issues of Farm journal
Farm gains help boost incomes. il Bsns W p84-5 Jl 24 '65
Farm income is changing. D. Hanson. Suc Farm 63:20 Ag '65
Farmcast for the eastern states. See issues of Farm journal
Farmer discusses change. D. Hanson. Suc Farm 63:8 Je '65
For farmers, things are the best in years. il U S News 59:82 Ag 16 '65
I want to make money, not records; ed. by J. Bickers. J. Kirkpatrick. il Farm J 89:34-5+ Je '65
Importance of agricultural issues in Kennedy round: statement, February 3, 1965. C. A. Herter. Dept State Bul 52:251-2 F 22 '65
Jungle law in the farm belt. D. Kramer. il Nation 200:587-9 My 31 '65
1966, another good year. C. W. Gifford. Farm J 89:34-5+ D '65
Ten ways to more spendable income. B. Brantley. Suc Farm 63:25+ Jl '65
U.S. agriculture in 1965; poverty amidst plenty. il Sr Schol 86:13-14 Ap 15 '65
What a surprising year! Farm journal staff report; ed. by G. W. Gifford. il Farm J 89:20-1+ Ag '65
What's ahead for farmers in '66? D. Hanson. Suc Farm 63:25 D '65
What's new in money management. See issues of Successful farming
Why corn-belt farmers are happy; hog prices, spiraling upward. il U S News 59:69 D 27 '65
   See also
Agricultural laws and legislation
Farm produce—Prices
Wheat trade

Exhibitions
See Agricultural exhibitions

AGRICULTURE—*Continued*

Federal aid
See Agricultural administration—United States

History
Ancient life was hard. Sci N L 87:199 Mr 27 '65

Ecology of early food production in Mesopotamia. K. V. Flannery. bibliog il Science 147:1247-56 Mr 12 '65

Human skeletons of Tehuacán. J. E. Anderson. bibliog il Science 148:496-7 Ap 23 '65; Reply. E. A. Sweeney. 149:1118 S 3 '65

International aspects
Agricultural export programs; address, February 9, 1965. C. R. Eskildsen. Vital Speeches 31:326-8 Mr 15 '65

Kennedy round; address, March 8, 1965. W. M. Blumenthal. Dept State Bul 52:628-35 Ap 26 '65

Public relations
Manure odors can land you in court! J. Russell. Farm J 89:19+ Ag '65

Statistics
Another bountiful harvest. America 114:34 Ja 8 '66

New picture of agriculture. Farm J 89:74 Jl '65

That ain't hay; 1965 record crop production. Newsweek 67:42 Ja 3 '66

Study and teaching
See also
Agricultural education

Africa
Agricultural development in Africa; address, January 7, 1965. G. M. Williams. Dept State Bul 52:104-7 Ja 25 '65

Argentina
Revolution on the pampas, by J. S. Scobie. Review
Américas il 17:38 Ag '65. N. Ras

California
Grapes of wrath; Delano district strike. il Newsweek 66:57-8 D 27 '65

Let them eat crow; giant harvest. Newsweek 66:82+ O 25 '65

Union organizing in the fields. V. Salandini. America 113:400-1 O 9 '65

China
Wooden ox: the world's first wheelbarrow; engineering and agriculture in ancient China. L. Petech. il UNESCO Courier 18:28-9 My '65

China (People's Republic)
Agriculture in China today. K. Chao. bibliog f il Cur Hist 49:170-5 S '65

Dominican Republic
Agriculture in the Dominican Republic. F. Dorta-Duque. America 112:348 Mr 13 '65

Europe, Eastern
Reds reap another thin crop, and why. il Newsweek 66:49-50 N 8 '65

Europe, Western
Report from Europe. W. E. Swegle. il Suc Farm 63:38-9+ N; 36-7+ D '65; 64:6+ Ja '66

India
Has India an economic future? C. E. Lindblom. For Affairs 44:239-52 Ja '66

Japan
Farming under wraps; vinyl cultivation. il Newsweek 65:33 Je 28 '65

Missing farmers; abandoning families for city life. Newsweek 66:53-4 D 6 '65

Mexico
Mexico: 1966 and beyond. F. Brandenburg. bibliog f Cur Hist 50:32-7+ Ja '66

Nigeria
Heritage of survival: Kofyar terraces preserve soil and water. R. M. Netting. il Natur Hist 74:14-21 Mr '65

Poland
Poland's perennial problem. C. McWilliams. Nation 201:118-21 S 6 '65

Russia
Dust bowl Khrushchev created; Kazakhstan. U S News 60:9 Ja 3 '66

Management, distribution, planning: new Russian revolution. M. Miller. il Nation 201:437-9+ D 6 '65

Private plot vs. collective farm. A. B. Ballard. il N Y Times Mag p 14-15+ Je 13 '65

Reds reap another thin crop, and why. il Newsweek 66:49-50 N 8 '65

Soviets reap a crop of trouble. Bsns W p31 Ag 21 '65

Tomatoes in February; peasant vendors. il Newsweek 65:44 F 8 '65

Southern states
Unrepresented Negro farmers in the South; Department of agriculture's Agricultural stabilization and conservation service. P. Wieck. New Repub 153:8-9 D 25 '65

Turkey
Threshing sledge. J. Bordaz. il Natur Hist 74:26-9 Ap '65

Underdeveloped areas
Concept of a national market and its economic growth implications; address, September 1, 1965. W. W. Rostow. Dept State Bul 53:520-3 S 27 '65

Cooperation, international development, and the problem of hunger. H. J. Waters. Dept State Bul 53:816-19 N 22 '65

Private investment in world agriculture. S. Williams. Harvard Bsns R 43:95-105 N '65

United States
Answers to hard problems; dwindling farm surpluses. il Newsweek 66:66 Ag 23 '65

Farmcast for the eastern states. See issues of Farm journal

Great myths of agricultural policy; we no longer need farm programs. D. Paarlberg. Suc Farm 63:41+ S '65

Growing up on a farm; Willis Hammer. jr. J. Star. il Look 29:109-14+ Je 15 '65

Jungle law in the farm belt. D. Kramer. il Nation 200:587-9 My 31 '65

Last minute report straight from Washington. See issues of Farm journal

Secretary Wirtz on farming. Farm J 89:86 Ag '65

Seven wonders of American agriculture. L. Palmer. il Farm J 89:38-41+ N '65

What's new in Washington. See issues of Successful farming
See also
Agricultural administration—United States
Agriculture—Economic aspects

History
Farewell to farmer Tuttle. J. Bird. il Sat Eve Post 238:34-8+ D 4 '65

AGRICULTURE, Cooperative
See also
Collective farms

AGRICULTURE and climate. See Plants, Effect of climate on

AGRICULTURE and state. See Agricultural administration

AGRICULTURE as a profession
How to tell if you should be farming. E. H. Logsdon. Farm J 89:14 My '65

AGROBACTERIUM tumefaciens
Agrobacterium tumefaciens: thermal inactivation of tumor-inducing ability. J. A. Lippincott and B. B. Lippincott. bibliog il Science 147:1578-9 Mr 26 '65

AGUNG, MOUNT. See Volcanoes

AHIDJO, Ahmadou
Colored rulers. G. C. Turner. por Negro Hist Bul 29:13-14 O '65

AHLERS, Arvel
Quiet revolution in slide projectors. Pop Phot 56:64-7 Mr '65

AHLERS, Eleanor E.
Book lists for young people. Sr Schol 86:sup23 Mr 4 '65

Selection, quality, balance: a guide to the NDEA guidelines. por Library J 90:1461-3 Mr 15 '65

AHMAD, Eqbal
Revolutionary warfare; how to tell when the rebels have won. Nation 201:95-100 Ag 30 '65

AHMAD, M. S.
Great Asian highway. UNESCO Courier 18:12-17 Je '65

AHMADJIAN, V.
Artificial reestablishment of the lichen cladonia cristatella. bibliog Science 151:199-201 Ja 14 '66

AID to dependent children (program) See Child welfare—United States

AIDA; opera. See Verdi, G.

AIDES, Teachers. See Teachers aides
AIDIT, Dipa Nusantara
Simple man in pursuit of power. N. Sheehan.
il pors N Y Times Mag p9+ Ag 15 '65
AIDS in education. See Teaching—Aids and
devices
AIKEN, Henry David
Action criticism. Commentary 39:104-8 Je '65
AILES, Stephen
Power for peace; address, May 13, 1965. Vital
Speeches 31:534-7 Je 15 '65

about

Advocate for the army. il por Time 85:26
My 28 '65
AIMS in education. See Education—Aims and
objectives
AIMS of recreation. See Recreation—Aims and
objectives
AIN, Gregory
Form follows faction. Arch Rec 137:108-9 My
'65
AINTREE race course. See Race tracks
AIR Afrique. See Airlines—Africa
AIR agreements. See Aviation—International
aspects
AIR bases
French town, an American base, a frontier;
Châteauroux air base. A. Menen. il N Y
Times Mag p 14-15+ Ja 31 '65
Spaceport for the military: close-up of a
mammoth base; Vandenberg air force base
manned orbiting laboratory program. il U S
News 59:42-4+ D 13 '65
Vandenberg begins expanding for MOL. R.
Lindsey. il Miss & Roc 18:35-6 Ja 10 '66
AIR cargo containers. See Containers for ship-
ping
AIR conditioning
Air-conditioning the whole house. H. Wright.
il Arch Rec 137:7+ mid-My '65
How much do you know about air condition-
ing? quiz. il Parents Mag 40:55-7 Jl '65
New ice age. Newsweek 66:85 Jl 26 '65
See also subhead Air conditioning under
various subjects. e.g. Automobiles—Air
conditioning
AIR conditioning equipment
Air conditioning: what to expect and how to
get it. Good H 160:144+ Je '65
Central air conditioning. il Consumer Rep 30:
244-7 My '65
Heating and cooling for housing. F. H.
Kluckhuhn. il Arch Rec 138:211-12 O '65
Mechanical services for a large courthouse;
temperature control. A. Schroeder. il Arch
Rec 138:205-8 O '65
Performance ratings for induction units. B. C.
Smith. il Arch Rec 137:223-4+ Je '65
Small-room air conditioners. il Consumer
Rep 30:276-82 Je '65
Window air conditioners. il Consumer Bul
48:6-10 Jl '65
See also
Heat pumps
Humidifiers
AIR coolers. See Air conditioning equipment
AIR currents. See Winds
AIR cushion vehicles. See Ground effect
machines
AIR defense. See Aeronautics, Military
AIR defense command. See United States—Air
force—Air defense command
AIR engines
Stirling refrigeration cycle. J. W. L. Köhler.
il Sci Am 212:119-25+ bibliog(p 160) Ap '65
AIR ferries. See Airplanes, Freight
AIR filters
How to choose cleaner air for your home.
Bet Hom & Gard 43:146 N '65
AIR filters, Automobile
Dust and smog stoppers. R. E. Jennings. il
Motor T 17:44-6 Je '65
AIR force academy. See United States air
force academy, Colorado Springs
AIR force diet. See Diet
AIR force eastern test range. See Proving
grounds
AIR force flight test center. See Proving
grounds
AIR force officers. See United States—Air force
—Officers
AIR force systems command. See United States
—Air force—Systems command
AIR France. See Airlines—France
AIR freight forwarders association
Air freight forwarder finds ceiling unlimited.
il Bsns W p87-8+ O 16 '65
AIR freight handling. See Freight handling

AIR freight service
Agriculture dept. airlines seek boost for U.S.
-Italy calf traffic. Aviation W 82:47+ Je 28
'65
Air cargo's future flight pattern. J. F. Olesky.
il Duns R 85:pt2 114-17+ Je '65
Airlines draft cargo container program. J. R.
Ashlock. Aviation W 83:30 Jl 19 '65
Auto parts crises dictate air shipments. J.
W. Carter. il Aviation W 83:38-9 S 20 '65
C-130 completes Zambia copper airlift. il
Aviation W 83:29-30 D 20 '65
Cargo shippers cite ground handling lags.
J. W. Carter. Aviation W 83:38-9 S 13 '65
Carriers seek heavier traffic in produce. J.
W. Carter. il Aviation W 83:40-1+ Ag 9 '65
CAB weighs appeal on blocked-space. R. G.
O'Lone. Aviation W 82:41 Ap 26 '65
CAB will weigh new cargo aids if courts rule
out blocked space. J. W. Carter. Aviation W
82:34 Mr 29 '65
Eastern keys cargo resurgence to 727QC. ex-
pansion of staff. J. W. Carter. Aviation W
83:41 N 8 '65
Freight boom brings handling challenge.
J. W. Carter. il Aviation W 83:56-7+ O
25 '65
Honeywell plans all-air export shipment.
J. W. Carter. Aviation W 83:28-9 N 29 '65
IATA carriers report 64.5 per cent cargo gain.
Aviation W 82:43 My 17 '65
North Atlantic cargo advances called sign of
industry maturity. J. W. Carter. Avia-
tion W 83:45-6 Ag 16 '65
Sears relying on DC-8F Honolulu service. J.
W. Carter. il Aviation W 83:33-4 Jl 26 '65
Shipping weights in pounds of total U.S.
exports and imports by air, year 1964;
table. Aviation W 83:198 O 25 '65
Tonnage in the sky; European airlines. il
Time 86:57 D 24 '65
U.S. air cargo showing 26 per cent rise in
1965. J. W. Carter. Aviation W 83:32-3 D 27
'65
World cargo rate structure seen continuing
after IATA session. L. L. Doty. Aviation W
82:27 My 31 '65
See also
Emery air freight corporation

Rates

Japan air lines, Pan American file proposals
to cut freight rates. Aviation W 83:37 Ag
9 '65
AIR freight terminals. See Airport buildings
AIR glow. See Airglow
AIR Jamaica. See Airlines—Jamaica
AIR-jet landing craft. See Landing craft
AIR lanes. See Airways
AIR line pilots association, International
Pilot opinions on FAA Category 2 landing
minimums vary widely. W. Wright. Avia-
tion W 83:37 O 11 '65
AIR lines. See Airlines
AIR mail service
Government tightens reins on revenues. W,
H. Gregory. il Aviation W 83:38-9 Ag 23
'65
Postal, CAB officials seeking expedited letter
mail service. J. W. Carter. Aviation W
83:39 O 11 '65
AIR national guard (United States) See United
States—Air national guard
AIR pilots
Pilots of Danang aren't flyboys. J. Raymond.
il N Y Times Mag p 16-17+ Ag 15 '65
Pilots who saved England. R. L. Inglis. il
Harper 231:52-7 S '65
See also
Airplanes—Piloting
Drinking and airplane accidents
Helicopter pilots
International federation of air line pilots as-
sociations
Negro air pilots
Women as air pilots

Diseases

Medical flying problems. Sci N L 87:150 Mr 6
'65

Hours of labor

Duty hours major issue in Pan Am strike.
Aviation W 82:45 Ap 5 '65

Training

Blank check; FAA requirement for biennial
checks of flight instructors. R. B. Parke. il
Flying 77:32 N '65
Carriers evaluate business jet aircraft. D. A.
Brown. Aviation W 84:25-6 Ja 3 '66

AIR pilots—Training—*Continued*
Follow me through. G. J. Schlaeger. Flying 77:116 O '65
Follow me through. W. K. Kershner. il Flying 77:130+ S; 91 N; 110 D '65
How to become an airline pilot; TWA's international training center, Kansas City, Mo. D. Francis. il Pop Sci 187:70-3 Ag '65
Less than a plumber; flight instructors, ed. by B. E. Burk. H. Johnson. Flying 77:83 S '65
Space training flights in NF-104A near; Aerospace research pilot school, Edwards AFB, Calif. C. M. Plattner. il Aviation W 83:80-1+ Ag 9 '65
VNAF seeks means to train own pilots. C. Brownlow. il Aviation W 82:62-3 Je 7 '65
See also
Aeronautics—Study and teaching
Aviation schools
Flight simulators

AIR plants
See also
Bromeliads

AIR pollution
Air and water; enforcement of legislation. New Repub 152:6-7 Ap 24 '65
Air conservation report reflects national concern. J. P. Dixon and J. P. Lodge. Science 148:1060-6 My 21 '65
Air pollution. P. H. Abelson. Science 147:1527 Mr 26 '65
Air pollution control news. See issues of American city
Air pollution: federal standards likely unless states and localities take early action. L. J. Carter. Science 150:467-8+ O 22 '65
Airborne particulates in Pittsburgh: association with p,p'-DDT. P. Antommaria and others. bibliog il Science 150:1476-7 D 10 '65
America the dirty. C. B. Luce. McCalls 92:28 Jl '65
Beauty spot. New Repub 152:7 F 27 '65
Big sewer in the sky; attempts to cut down on noxious gases from motor vehicles. Life 59:4 Ag 13 '65
Breath of life, by D. E. Carr. Review
New Repub 152:36 Ap 17 '65. J. Ridgeway
Death is in the air in New York city. U S News 59:13 Jl 5 '65
Environmental pollution; report of a President's science advisory committee. Nat Parks Mag 40:19 Ja '66
For air conservation. J. P. Dixon. Bul Atomic Sci 21:17-12 Je '65
Fouling of the American environment; symposium. il Sat R 48:31-48+ My 22 '65; Discussion. 48:21 Je 26 '65
Lead isotopes in gasoline and aerosols of Los Angeles basin, California. T. J. Chow and M. S. Johnstone. bibliog il Science 147:502-3 Ja 29 '65
Man and his habitat: problems of pollution; symposium. Bul Atomic Sci 21:18-30 Mr '65
Metabolism of cities. A. Wolman. il Sci Am 213:178-88+ bibliog(p278) S '65
Meteorology of air pollution. D. H. Pack; reply. E. M. Winkler. Science 147:459 Ja 29 '65
Monoxide rides the freeways. il Time 85:70 F 19 '65
Our deadly atmosphere. C. W. Griffin, jr. Reporter 33:49-50 Jl 15 '65
Poison air around us. D. E. Carr. il Sat R 48:17-19+ F 27 '65; Discussion. 48:21 Mr 27; 29 Ap 10; 29 Ap 17 '65
Poison gas of peace. B. Tufty. il Sci N L 88:262+ O 23 '65
Poison in the air; comment on E. K. Faltermayer's and G. D. Friedlander's articles. Nation 201:347 N 15 '65
Pollution politics; LBJ retreats on opposition to measure curbing pollution from automobile exhaust. E. Langer. Science 148:611-13 Ap 30 '65
Pollution: PSAC panel takes a panoramic view. J. Walsh. Science 150:1006-8 N 19 '65
Presidential findings on air, water pollution. Am City 80:8 D '65
Purifying the effluent society; efforts by industrial plants. il Time 86:106+ N 19 '65
Their master's voice; confusion in pollution control program. New Repub 152:8-9 Ap 17 '65
350,000 tons of smog a day; and the fight against it. il U S News 58:68-9 Mr 1 '65
UCLA meteorologist sees civilization suffocating. Sci N L 88:136 Ag 28 '65
Up in the air; question of air pollution and cancer. il Newsweek 65:60 Ap 19 '65
We can afford clean air. E. K. Faltermayer. il Fortune 72:158-63+ N '65

Where is science taking us? accelerating ratio of carbon dioxide in the air. M. Neiburger. il Sat R 48:40-2 Jl 3 '65
With every breath you take, by H. R. Lewis. Review
Am For 71:44 Je '65. M. Bush
Sci Digest il 57:35-6 Ap '65. H. Pryor
With every breath you take; excerpt. H. R. Lewis. il Read Digest 87:63-8+ S '65
See also
Plants, Effect of air pollution on
Smog
Smoke prevention

Bibliography

Books in review; man's ecological crisis. W. Vogt. Natur Hist 74:4+ D '65

AIR pollution and cancer. See Cancer—Causes
AIR ports. See Airports
AIR pressure support
Building with air and steel. il Bsns W p 184 O 23 '65
AIR purification
Clean air to live in. Good H 161:160+ Ag '65
AIR purifiers
Advance air cleaner protects sweeper engines. il Am City 80:13 S '65
AIR raid shelters
See also
Atomic bomb shelters
AIR raids
See also
London—Air raids

Protective measures

See also
Radar—Military applications

AIR rescue service. See United States—Air force—Air rescue service
AIR rights
No land? then build it on air! erecting structures over railroads, highways and other buildings. C. Peet. il Pop Mech 125:134-8+ Ja '66
AIR routes. See Airways
AIR ships. See Airships
AIR shows. See Aviation—Exhibitions
AIR stewardesses. See Airlines—Hostesses
AIR-supported building. See Air pressure support
AIR taxi service
Air taxi. R. Shippee. il Flying 77:60-1 D '65
CAB proposal seen stimulating expansion of third-level carriers. R. G. O'Lone. Aviation W 82:40 Ap 19 '65
Roof heliport gives copter line a lift; seven minutes from New York's Pan Am building to Kennedy airport. il Bsns W p 18-20 D 25 '65
S-64 sky lounge demonstration sought. H. D. Watkins. Aviation W 83:43 N 8 '65
Taxis in the sky. il Time 86:75 Ag 27 '65
AIR traffic control
Computer aid to traffic control expands. P. J. Klass. Aviation W 83:107-11 N 15 '65
North Atlantic jam nears acute stage. D. A. Brown. Aviation W 83:93+ O 25 '65
Pilot group disputes separation rule. J. R. Ashlock. Aviation W 83:38-9 D 13 '65
Still seeking air safety. il Bsns W p 154+ D 11 '65
To make flying safer in busy airlanes: Alpha numerics. il U S News 59:12 D 20 '65
See also
Airports—Traffic control
AIR transport agreements. See Aviation—International aspects
AIR transport association of America
Air fares flying on collision course. Bsns W p75 Ja 1 '66
Commission rate change proposals stir row among agents, carriers. J. R. Ashlock. Aviation W 82:45 My 17 '65
AIR travel
Air travel from N Y shows sharp increase. Aviation W 83:28-9 Jl 19 '65
Come fly with me. Time 85:90+ Je 25 '65
Flying more than ever. Bsns W p27 Jl 10 '65
Gone flying to St Pierre. R. C. Mock. il Flying 77:52-6 Jl '65
How to get ready for a plane trip. Bet Hom & Gard 43:86 Ag '65
Off on the economic jetstream. il Bsns W p 104-6+ N 20 '65
Record jet sale; what it means to air travel; record order for planes placed by United air lines. il U S News 58:16 Ap 19 '65
Second wave. R. Hotz. Aviation W **83**:37 O 25 '65
Supersonic adventure. B. K. O. Lundberg. il Bul Atomic Sci 21:29-33 F '65

AIR travel—*Continued*

SST: super-sonic transports. W. E. Becker. il Travel 125:29-31+ Ja '66

Supersonic transports, too fast for comfort? T. E. Stimson. il Pop Mech 125:88-92+ Ja '66

Those circadian rhythms; what really happens to jet-age travelers. il Time 86:66 D 17 '65

Tired and listless jet-age blues; FAA study psychological effects. Life 60:4 Ja 14 '66

Travel notes; European flights. R. Joseph. Esquire 63:52+ Je '65

See also

Airlines

India

India-Pakistan struggle disrupts civil air service to both nations. L. L. Doty. Aviation W 83:27-8 S 13 '65

Pakistan

India-Pakistan struggle disrupts civil air service to both nations. L. L. Doty. Aviation W 83:27-8 S 13 '65

United States

Failure snarls air traffic in Northeast. J. W. Carter. Aviation W 83:27-9 N 15 '65

Gone flying to Virginia. K. Magner and J. Magner. il Flying 77:52-6 Ag '65

Gone flying to Washington. K. Magner and J. Magner. il Flying 77:62-7 N '65

U.S. travel push. C. S. Murphy. Aviation W 83:11 N 29 '65

Visit U.S.A. fares gain among trunks. W. Wright. Aviation W 83:26-7 N 1 '65

What can you do when you miss a plane connection? Bet Hom & Gard 43:27-8 N '65

AIR turbines

See also

Rotors

AIR turbulence. See Atmospheric turbulence

AIRBUSES. See Airplanes, Jet propelled

AIRCRAFT carriers

C-Scan goal is 8 x 4 mi. approach window. K. J. Stein. il Aviation W 82:69+ Mr 29 '65

AIRCRAFT computers. See Computers—Aeronautic applications

AIRFRAME industry. See Airplane industry and trade

AIRGLOW

Gemini pictures show glowing layer of air. Sci N L 88:246 O 16 '65

Sounding rocket camera captures nightglow photo. il Miss & Roc 17:15 S 27 '65

AIRLINE hostesses. See Airlines—Hostesses

AIRLINES

Zooming airlines grab for new jets. il Bsns W p 186+ My 22 '65

Consolidations and mergers

Alaska route shifts set merger climate. R. G. O'Lone. Aviation W 82:39-40 Ap 5 '65

Credit cards

See Credit cards

Employees

Training

Mohawk presses jet, turboprop training. J. W. Carter. il Aviation W 82:32-3 Je 7 '65

Fares

Air fares flying on collision course. Bsns W p75 Ja 1 '66

Airline initiative to determine fare action. J. R. Ashlock. il Aviation W 83:35-6 Ag 9 '65

American proposes 50 per cent youth jet fare. Aviation W 83:30 D 20 '65

Atlantic promotional fare cut seen as IATA rejects CAB proposal. Aviation W 83:41 S 27 '65

Big fight over the Atlantic. il Duns R 86:43-4+ S '65

CAB calls meeting with airlines to analyze jet fare policy impact. Aviation W 83:33 O 4 '65

CAB chairman sees no reason for immediate over-all fare cuts. W. Wright. Aviation W 83:37-8 N 8 '65

CAB seeks surcharge dilemma solution. J. R. Ashlock. il Aviation W 84:28-9 Ja 3 '66

Coast-to-coast air fare of $100 proposed by CAB planning officer. R. G. O'Lone. Aviation W 82:27-8 Mr 8 '65

Eastern's shuttle service. J. Ridgeway. New Repub 154:8-9 Ja 15 '66

Fare prodding elicits diverse responses. Aviation W 83:37-8 D 13 '65

Fare slash talks set for IATA meeting. J. R. Ashlock. Aviation W 83:40 Ag 23 '65

Fare sparring leaves objectives undefined. W. H. Gregory. Aviation W 83:26 N 29 '65

Government pushing harder for fare cuts. J. R. Ashlock. Aviation W 83:49-50+ O 25 '65

IATA Atlantic fares to get CAB approval. Aviation W 83:38-9 N 8 '65

IATA slashes group, excursion tariffs. il Aviation W 83:38 O 11 '65

Jet fare policy seen costing $200 million. J. R. Ashlock. Aviation W 83:25 N 29 '65

Lower family fares generate new traffic. W. Wright. Aviation W 83:32-3 O 4 '65

Murphy forecasts revised fare policy. Aviation W 84:37-8 Ja 10 '66

New overseas fare bill in Senate. Aviation W 82:29 F 8 '65

Northeast asks fares geared to seat needs. Aviation W 82:45 Ap 19 '65

Pan Am proposes cut in fares from Europe. Aviation W 82:52 My 10 '65

Refined fare elasticity measure sought. W. H. Gregory. il Aviation W 84:40-3 Ja 17 '66

TWA proposes experimental cut in domestic family coach fares. Aviation W 82:42 Ap 26 '65

$25 fare approved for first-time riders. Aviation W 83:37 N 22 '65

Two basic charter decisions facing CAB. R. G. O'Lone. Aviation W 82:36-7 F 22 '65

United jet fare rejection shakes industry. J. R. Ashlock. Aviation W 83:34-5 S 6 '65

Visit U.S.A. fares gain among trunks. W. Wright. Aviation W 83:26-7 N 1 '65

Finance

Airline income and expenses; tables. See occasional issues of Aviation week & space technology

Airline initiative to determine fare action; with table. J. R. Ashlock. il Aviation W 83:35-6 Ag 9 '65

Airlines gear for massive financing. Bsns W p65 Mr 6 '65

Alitalia profit, growth rate hold steady. E. Walford. il Aviation W 83:49+ Ag 16 '65

CAB baggage decision could cost U.S. airlies $17 million annually. Aviation W 83:29-30 Jl 26 '65

Domestic trunk profits continue surge. J. R. Ashlock. Aviation W 83:36 Ag 2 '65

Economic growth spurs surge in traffic. W. H. Gregory. il Aviation W 83:26-8 Jl 19 '65

Government tightens reins on revenues. W. H. Gregory. il Aviation W 83:38-9 Ag 23 '65

Increases in U.S. airline operating revenues; first six months 1965 over 1964 (table) Aviation W 83:43 S 27 '65

T.W.A: the struggle for the corporate cockpit. J. McDonald. il Fortune 71:106-11+ My '65

Trunk battle intensifies as profits swell. J. R. Ashlock. il Aviation W 82:159-61 Mr 15 '65

Trunkline profits surge to record level. W. Wright. Aviation W 83:30-1 D 27 '65

Turbine-powered aircraft 1964 operating expense, dollars per total aircraft hour; tables. Aviation W 82:36-7 My 31 '65

Turboprop aircraft operating expense; table. Aviation W 83:50 N 8 '65

United order stresses spending requirements. W. H. Gregory. Aviation W 82:39 Ap 12 '65

U.S. airline assets and liabilities. il Aviation W 83:43 O 4 '65

U.S. airline operating revenues and expenses, 1964-1965; table (title varies) Aviation W 82:54-5+ My 10; 83:47 S 13 '65

Wire choice of capital open to trunklines. W. H. Gregory. il Aviation W 82:38-41 My 17 '65

See also

Airlines—Securities

Freight service

See Air freight service; Airplanes, Freight

Hostesses

Girls, girls, girls; shortage of recruits. il Newsweek 65:69 Mr 29 '65

Isle-hoppers, aisle-walkers; The powder-blue yonder. H. Sutton. il Sat R 48:36-8+ My 15 '65

Wanted: girls for the wide blue yonder. G. Jennings. il Read Digest 88:83-6 Ja '66

Why airlines run a bride school. il Bsns W p 164-6+ D 11 '65

Wild hue yonder; Pucci designs uniform suited to jet age. il Life 59:76-7 D 3 '65

Winged women. Holiday 37:162-3 My '65

International aspects

See Aviation—International aspects

AIRLINES—*Continued*

Maintenance and repair
TBO fading as guide to reliability concept. M. L. Yaffee. Aviation W 83:36-7+ D 27 '65

Passenger service
Airline talks fail to end movie deadlock. J. W. Carter. Aviation W 82:29 F 8 '65
Airlines' movie war. New Repub 152:7 My 8 '65
Astrovision; an in-flight entertainment system. L. C. Keene and T. E. Pierson. il Electr World 73:42-3+ Mr '65
Baggage bonanza; no weight limit on domestic routes. il Newsweek 66:76+ Jl 26 '65
Better passenger service. R. Hotz; discussion. Aviation W 82:98 F 8 '65
Board refuses to back inflight movie ban. J. R. Ashlock. Aviation W 82:28 Je 7 '65
Booked for travel; purple planes for plain people; post-journey critique. H. Sutton. il Sat R 48:77-9 D 4 '65
Boyd warns of possible major international dispute on movies. J. W. Carter. Aviation W 82:30 My 3 '65
CAB baggage decision could cost U.S. airlines $17 million annually. Aviation W 83:29-30 Jl 26 '65
CAB seen delaying inflight movie ruling. J. R. Ashlock. Aviation W 82:30 My 24 '65
End of the run? movies on transatlantic routes. Newsweek 65:79 Mr 15 '65
Flicks in flight. H. Sutton. Sat R 48:45-6 My 8 '65
Getting there is half the difficulty. H. Sutton. il Sat R 48:32-4 O 2 '65
Great escape-vision in the sky. A. Levy. il Life 59:57-8+ O 29 '65
Inflight movies rebound from TWA blow. J. W. Carter. Aviation W 82:28 Mr 22 '65
IATA proposes entertainment surcharge. Aviation W 83:25 N 1 '65
Justice dept. may block IATA movie ban. J. W. Carter. Aviation W 82:40-1 My 10 '65
Movies up in the air; agreement to end inflight showings on transatlantic flights. Bsns W p 164 Ap 24 '65
New baggage rule facilitates handling. Aviation W 83:39 Ag 9 '65
Pan American seeking to force inflight entertainment decision. Aviation W 83:34 O 18 '65
TWA move may be death blow for films. J. W. Carter. Aviation W 82:26-7 Mr 8 '65
TWA to renew movie contract; entertainment future uncertain. J. W. Carter. Aviation W 82:39 Ap 19 '65

Passenger traffic
See Airlines—Traffic

Rates
See Airlines—Fares

Routes
See Airways

Safety devices and measures
See Aviation—Safety devices and measures

Securities
Airline stocks begin bucking a head wind. il Bsns W p 172 S 25 '65

Statistics
Airline traffic. See occasional issues of Aviation week & space technology
Increases in U.S. trunkline traffic; table. Aviation W 83:31 D 27 '65
International airlines report major gains. J. W. Carter. il Aviation W 82:172-3+ Mr 15 '65
International flag off-route charter flights between the U.S. and Europe; table. Aviation W 83:50 O 25 '65
Intra-European traffic 1960-64 by carrier; table. Aviation W 83:67 O 25 '65
1964 air passengers between the United States and other countries by flag of carrier; table. Aviation W 83:54-5 O 25 '65
1964 international air passengers at U.S. ports; table. Aviation W 83:186 O 25 '65
1964 U.S. air, sea passengers; table. Aviation W 83:172 O 25 '65
North Atlantic air passengers and load factors; table. Aviation W 83:46-7 O 25 '65
Shipping weights in pounds of total U.S. exports and imports by air, year 1964; table. Aviation W 83:198 O 25 '65
Turbojet load factors in scheduled service; tables. Aviation W 83:32 O 18 '65
U.S. airline scheduled service traffic growth; first six months, 1965 over 1964; table. Aviation W 83:54 S 20 '65

U.S. airlines: flying high or low? il Sr Schol 86:6-9 Mr 25 '65
U.S. scheduled service load factors, Jan.-June, 1965; table. Aviation W 83:53 S 20 '65

Taxation
New aviation user taxes planned to allay federal airways costs. J. R. Ashlock. il Aviation W 82:31-2 F 1 '65

Tickets
Airlines vs. travel agents; proposed new commissions add fuel to smoldering fire. Bsns W p200 My 15 '65
Commission rate change proposals stir row among agents, carriers. J. R. Ashlock. Aviation W 82:45 My 17 '65
10,000 ticket items disappear in Congo. il Aviation W 82:32 Mr 8 '65
U.S. accuses six in ticket credit swindle. F. Cogan. Aviation W 83:36 N 22 '65

Traffic
Air traffic takes a startling zoom. Bsns W p78 F 27 '65
Airline traffic hits record holiday level. W. Wright. Aviation W 83:39 D 6 '65
Atlantic bookings point to new records. J. W. Carter. Aviation W 82:39-40 Ap 26 '65
Carriers boosting Florida seat capacity. J. W. Carter. Aviation W 84:29-30 Ja 3 '66
CAB staff predicts ten-year traffic gains. il Aviation W 83:29-30 N 1 '65
Economic growth spurs surge in traffic. W. H. Gregory. il Aviation W 83:26-8 Jl 19 '65
Failure snarls air traffic in Northeast. J. W. Carter. Aviation W 83:27-9 N 15 '65
Flying more than ever. Bsns W p27 Jl 10 '65
Intra-European frequency expansion lags. L. L. Doty. Aviation W 83:47+ S 20 '65
Surge in world airline traffic is forcing reexamination of predicted growth rate. W. H. Gregory. il Aviation W 83:40-5 O 25 '65; Discussion. 83:126 D 13 '65
Trunk battle intensifies as profits swell. J. R. Ashlock. il Aviation W 82:159-61 Mr 15 '65

Africa
Air Afrique emphasizes measured growth. W. Wright. il Aviation W 83:30-1+ N 29 '65

Arab states
Thirteen Arab nation airlines organize regional unit patterned on IATA; Arab air carrier organization. Aviation W 83:52 N 15 '65

Australia
Qantas gears to meet growing demands. E. Walford. il Aviation W 83:45+ D 13 '65

Belgium
Belgian carrier to show deficit reduction. E. Walford. il Aviation W 82:37+ Je 21 '65

Brazil
Brazil's Varig tackles the world; rival for Pan Am. il Bsns W p 128+ Ap 10 '65
Too many wings; Panair do Brasil airline ordered to cease operations. il Time 85:41-2 F 26 '65

Denmark
Danish carrier to get turbojets; Sterling airways. il Aviation W 82:48 F 22 '65

Europe
Travel notes. R. Joseph. Esquire 63:52+ Je '65

Europe, Western
European carriers push equipment plans. L. L. Doty. il Aviation W 82:88-9 Je 14 '65
Flying high on their own. il Time 86:83 S 3 '65
Intra-European frequency expansion lags. L. L. Doty. Aviation W 83:47+ S 20 '65

France
Air France earnings may end subsidy need. Aviation W 83:41 Ag 23 '65

Germany (Federal Republic)
Lufthansa profit may reach $10 million. E. Walford. il Aviation W 82:34+ F 15 '65
Sales drive, jet expansion cited in $9-million Lufthansa profit. E. Walford. Aviation W 83:55-6 S 13 '65

Great Britain
See also
British European airways corporation
British overseas airways corporation
British united air ferries

AIRLINES—*Continued*

Hungary

Hungarian carrier seeks route expansion. E. Walford. il Aviation W 83:37+ Jl 19 '65

Iceland

Charters are main CL-44J sales target. il Aviation W 83:42-3+ D 20 '65
Icelandair ordering first jet transport. J. W. Carter. il Aviation W 83:32-3 Jl 5 '65

Italy

Alitalia DC-9 order curb denied. Aviation W 84:47 Ja 17 '66
Alitalia profit, growth rate hold steady. E. Walford. il Aviation W 83:49+ Ag 16 '65

Jamaica

Air Jamaica permit could involve new authorities for BOAC, BWIA. Aviation W 83: 36 S 13 '65

Japan

Bilateral sparks JAL global service plan. K. Johnsen. Aviation W 84:26-7 Ja 3 '66

Netherlands

Dutch carrier nearing break-even point. E. Walford. il Aviation W 83:37+ N 29 '65

Nigeria

Nigerian official studies U.S, U.K. jets. Aviation W 83:43+ Ag 2 '65

Russia

Aeroflot traffic falls short of targets. il Aviation W 82:175+ Mr 15 '65

Switzerland

Swissair planning all-jet fleet in 1968. E. Walford. Aviation W 83:53-4+ S 27 '65
Swissair profit rises 77.3 per cent in first half. Aviation W 83:46 O 4 '65

United States

Automation reshapes airline management, operatitons. P. J. Klass. il Aviation W 83: 70-1+ O 25 '65
Booked for travel; purple planes for plain people; post-journey critique. H. Sutton. il Sat R 48:77-9 D 4 '65
Come fly with me. Time 85:90+ Je 25 '65
Competition broadens scope of planning. il Aviation W 83:62+ O 25 '65
Domestic trunk profits continue surge. J. R. Ashlock. Aviation W 83:36 Ag 2 '65
Examiner backs supplemental awards. W. Wright. Aviation W 83:36-7 S 6 '65
Flying cash registers. il Time 85:85-6 Ap 16 '65
High-flying airlines soar higher. il Newsweek 66:50-1 D 27 '65
Jet-age expert gives some blunt answers: interview, ed. by B. Kocivar. N. Halaby. il Look 29:50+ D 14 '65
Refined fare elasticity measure sought. W. H. Gregory. il Aviation W 84:40-3 Ja 17 '66
Stability sought for supplemental carriers. R. G. O'Lone. Aviation W 82:30-1 Mr 29 '65
Trunk battle intensifies as profits swell. J. R. Ashlock. il Aviation W 82:159-61 Mr 15 '65
U.S. airlines; flying high or low? il Sr Schol 86:6-9 Mr 25 '65
Wide choice of capital open to trunklines. W. H. Gregory. il Aviation W 82:28-41 My 17 '65
See also
Government investigations—Airlines
Local service airlines
Strikes—United States—Airlines
also names of airlines e.g. Eastern air lines

Vietnam (Republic)

Flying above the war; Air Viet Nam. il Time 86:84 Jl 23 '65

Virgin Islands

Amphibians reduce transit times on Virgin Island intercity routes. P. J. Klass. il Aviation W 83:41 D 20 '65

AIRLINES, Local service. See Local service airlines

AIRPLANE accidents. See Aviation—Accidents

AIRPLANE accidents, Liability for. See Liability (law)

AIRPLANE collisions. See Aviation—Accidents

AIRPLANE crews

Clothing

Braniff overhauls services, appearance. E. J. Bulban. il Aviation W 83:40-1 N 15 '65

AIRPLANE decoration

Braniff overhauls services, appearance. E. J. Bulban. il Aviation W 83:40-1 N 15 '65

AIRPLANE engines

C-5A engines feature basic differences. Aviation W 82:22 My 3 '65
Engine management. J. Diblin. il Flying 78: 56-9 Ja '66
U.S. reciprocating engines; specifications (cont) Aviation W 82:220-1 Mr 15 '65
U.S, U.K. near joint lift engine decision; V/STOL powerplant development program. C. Brownlow. Aviation W 82:27 F 22 '65
See also
Carburetors
Gas turbines, Aircraft
Jet airplane engines
Jet propulsion

Failures

DC-8 lands after engine fire. il Aviation W 84:27 Ja 3 '66
GE YJ93 operates despite severe damage by ingestion. M. L. Yaffee. il Aviation W 83:64-5+ O 18 '65
Stamp out vmc. R. Blodget. il Flying 77: 106-8 O '65

Fuel

Hydrogen-fueled aircraft study planned. I. Stone. Aviation W 83:69+ Ag 16 '65
See also
Gas turbines, Aircraft—Fuel

Maintenance and repair

See also
Jet airplane engines—Maintenance and repair

Noise

See Airplanes—Noise

AIRPLANE fares. See Airlines—Fares

AIRPLANE hostessess. See Airlines—Hostesses

AIRPLANE industry and trade

Federal aid

Monroney urges federally financed SST. J. R. Ashlock. Aviation W 82:38 Ap 19 '65
SST contracts complicate airline plans. J. R. Ashlock. Aviation W 83:26-7 Jl 12 '65

Finance

Public-private enterprise; excerpts from address. W. M. Allen. Aviation W 83:21 D 6 '65

International aspects

An-22 spurs airbus discussions in West. L. L. Doty. Aviation W 83:24-5 Jl 5 '65
Single chain of command aids Atlantic consortium; building turboprop antisubmarine aircraft. il Aviation W 82:240-1+ Je 14 '65

Statistics

U.S. business & utility aircraft shipments; tables. See occasional issues of Aviation week & space technology

Canada

See also
Canadair, limited

Czechoslovakia

Czechs push for Western market entry. E. Walford. il Aviation W 82:281+ Je 14 '65

Europe, Western

Consortium nearing completion to build West German VFW 614. L. L. Doty. Aviation W 83:38 S 27 '65
European defense efforts mold future of avionics. P. J. Klass. il Aviation W 82:108-9+ Je 14 '65
Europeans push air force modernization. L. L. Doty. Aviation W 83:34 O 11 '65
Europe's jet makers boost sales effort. il Aviation W 82:259-61 Mr 15 '65
Foreign accent. J. Fricker. il Flying 78: 22-3 Ja '66
Large European market seen for COIN. W. C. Wetmore. Aviation W 83:57-8+ S 20 '65
Lift, vectored engine compete in Europe. il Aviation W 82:250-1 Mr 15 '65

France

Dassault plans Mystere 20 production increase, Mercury aimed at feederline sales. H. J. Coleman. il Aviation W 82:260-3+ Je 14 '65

Germany (Federal Republic)

Civil VTOL effort focusing on Germany. il Aviation W 82:95+ Je 14 '65
FAA test program continues on HFB-320. il Aviation W 82:295-9+ Je 14 '65

AIRPLANE industry and trade—Germany
(Federal Republic)—*Continued*
Germany's VFW seeks transport foothold. il
  Aviation W 82:252-4 Je 14 '65
Italians gain full F-104S license rights.
  Aviation W 84:69 Ja 3 '66
Planes or ashtrays? il Newsweek 66:90 N 8 '65
West German mergers realign industry. Avi-
  ation W 82:285+ Mr 15 '65

Great Britain

Britain trims wings of aircraft industry;
  abandons independent British role in air,
  seeks joint projects with U.S. and France.
  il Bsns W p30-1 F 20 '65
Britain wields a modernizing ax. V. K.
  McElheny. Science 147:1429-31 Mr 19 '65
British need for joint projects stressed. H. J.
  Coleman. Aviation W 82:22-4 F 15 '65
British position on F-111 cloudy as Labor
  defeats TSR.2 censure. H. J. Coleman. Avi-
  ation W 82:35 Ap 19 '65
Buy American policy supported by British
  aviation consultant. H. J. Coleman. Avia-
  tion W 83:89+ Jl 19 '65
In the TFX dispute: a McNamara victory;
  British switch to the F-111. U S News 58:19
  Ap 19 '65
Labor policies jolt British industry. H. J.
  Coleman. il Aviation W 82:265-7 Mr 15 '65
Now that Britain decides to buy U.S. planes.
  U S News 58:16 F 15 '65
Plowden report supports nationalization. H.
  J. Coleman. Aviation W 83:25-6 D 20 '65
TSR-2 cancellation brings censure move.
  H. J. Coleman. Aviation W 82:26-7 Ap 12 '65
U.K. groups edgy over new U.S. orders. H.
  J. Coleman. Aviation W 83:26-8 N 22 '65
U.S. extends Britain's option for F-111A.
  Aviation W 83:23 D 20 '65

Italy

Italians gain full F-104S license rights.
  Aviation W 84:69 Ja 3 '66
Italy approves G.91Y, G.222 prototypes; tacti-
  cal reconnaissance/fighter aircraft and
  V/STOL medium-range transport. L. L.
  Doty. il Aviation W 83:62-3+ Jl 19 '65
Italy ponders F-104 program follow-on. L. L.
  Doty. Aviation W 82:75+ F 15 '65
PD-808 certification planned for year-end. il
  Aviation W 82:268-9+ Je 14 '65

Japan

Mooney's air circus. R. Blodget. il Flying 77:
  53-9 D '65

Netherlands

High-density feederline routes expected to
  provide key market for Fokker F-28. il
  Aviation W 82:246-7+ Je 14 '65

Russia

Giant planes: is U.S. really trailing Russia?
  AN-22 and TU-144. il U S News 58:14 Je 28
  '65
Russians fly high at Paris air show; Soviets
  outshine U.S. with An-22. il Bsns W p 146-
  7+ Je 19 '65
Russia's big surprise. il Newsweek 65:72 Je 28
  '65
Soviets make strong sales effort with Paris
  exhibit. il Aviation W 83:84-5 Jl 19 '65
USSR builds super-plane; Antonov 22. Sci
  N L 88:15 Jl 3 '65

Sweden

High-flying Saab. il Time 85:104 Ap 30 '65
Saab sets up a neutral's defense. il Bsns W
  p 124+ Je 19 '65

United States

Arms & the salesman; purchases by foreign
  nations. Time 85:82+ F 12 '65
Aviation industry teamster ranks swell. J.
  W. Carter. Aviation W 83:35 N 22 '65
Commercial jet orders exceed forecasts. Avia-
  tion W 83:39 S 27 '65
Convair striving to maintain COIN competi-
  tion despite Charger crash. Aviation W 83:
  19 N 1 '65
High cost of competition; Lockheed aircraft
  gets contract for C-5A. il Time 86:95-6 O
  8 '65
Jets to stimulate business aircraft sales.
  E. J. Bulban. il Aviation W 82:255-8 Mr 15
  '65
Large European market seen for COIN.
  W. C. Wetmore. Aviation W 83:57-8+ S 20
  '65
Latest on the superjet; why U.S. is lagging,
  SST. il US News 59:108-9 N 1 '65
Monroney urges federally financed SST. J. R.
  Ashlock. Aviation W 82:38 Ap 19 '65
1965 jet orders may reach $1.5 billion. J. R.
  Ashlock. il Aviation W 83:44-5 Ag 16 '65

Nosing into the jumbo jet race; Lockheed,
  Boeing and Douglas. il Bsns W p31-2 D 25
  '65
Slowdown in supersonic timetable; British-
  French may fly off with the market. Bsns
  W p50+ Jl 10 '65
SST firms to receive USAF aircraft data. J.
  R. Ashlock. Aviation W 83:33-4 N 22 '65
USAF to hear C-5A briefings this week.
  C. M. Plattner. il Aviation W 82:35-8 Ap
  26 '65
  See also names of airplane manufactur-
  ing companies, e.g. Piper aircraft corpora-
  tion

AIRPLANE insurance. See Insurance, Aviation
AIRPLANE luggage. See Luggage
AIRPLANE models
Modeling the pivot-wing F-111. R. L.
  Clough, jr. il Pop Mech 124:170-3 O '65
AIRPLANE museums. See Aeronautic museums
AIRPLANE pilots. See Air pilots
AIRPLANE propellers
It all began with a bedstead. J. Gilbert. il
  Flying 77:50-3 S '65
AIRPLANE racing
Once you start down that runway the fear
  goes. J. Underwood. il Sports Illus 23:68-
  70 O 4 '65
AIRPLANE service stations
United uses underground service system;
  renovations at San Francisco international
  airport. il Aviation W 82:49+ My 10 '65
AIRPLANE taxi service. See Air taxi service
AIRPLANE travel. See Air travel
AIRPLANE wings
Delta vs. swing. il Newsweek 66:56-7 Jl 5 '65
Delta-wing X-15 configuration proposed. il
  Aviation W 83:22 O 18 '65
Lockheed SST wing and forward fuselage
  design altered. C. M. Plattner. il Aviation
  W 82:38-9+ Mr 29 '65
Research program extending X-15 life. H.
  Taylor. Miss & Roc 17:14 O 11 '65

Testing

Design for hot-cycle rotor/wing studied. il
  Aviation W 82:74 Je 21 '65
AIRPLANES
Leading international aircraft; specification
  (cont) Aviation W 82:201+ Mr 15 '65
U.S. commercial transports; specifications
  (cont) Aviation W 82:196 Mr 15 '65
  See also
Seaplanes

Accidents

  See Aviation—Accidents

Altitude flying

  See Aviation—Altitude flying

Carburetors

  See Carburetors

Chartering

Two basic charter decisions facing CAB. R.
  G. O'Lone. Aviation W 82:36-7 F 22 '65

Collectors and collecting

Mavericks of sport aviation. R. Bach. il
  Flying 78:32-9 Ja '66

Control

Reliability is key to subsystem progress.
  W. Wright. il Aviation W 83:165+ O 25 '65
  See also
Airplanes, Military—Control

Decoration

  See Airplane decoration

Design

New equipment round widens spectrum.
  R. G. O'Lone. il Aviation W 82:161-2 Mr
  15 '65
  See also
Airplanes, Light—Design
Helicopters—Design

Electric equipment

Constant-frequency a.c. system developed.
  P. J. Klass. il Aviation W 82:84-6 Ap 19 '65

Electronic equipment

European defense efforts mold future of
  avionics. P. J. Klass. il Aviation W 82:108-
  9+ Je 14 '65
New aerospace products. See occasional issues
  of Aviation week & space technology
New avionic products. See issues of Aviation
  week & space technology
  See also
Automatic pilot (airplanes)

AIRPLANES—*Continued*

Emergency landing
See Airplanes—Landing

Equipment
New equipment round widens spectrum. R. G. O'Lone. il Aviation W 82:161-2 Mr 15 '65
Reliability is key to subsystem progress. W. Wright. il Aviation W 83:165+ O 25 '65
See also
Aeronautic instruments
Altimeters
Magnetic recorders and recording
Oxygen apparatus
Radio telephone on aircraft

Escape devices
Ejection modification for F-106 may extend to other fighters. Aviation W 83:67 Ag 2 '65

Fuel tanks
Tank sealing improved in XB-70A no. 2. C. M. Plattner. il Aviation W 82:60-1+ My 24 '65

Fuselage
Lockheed SST wing and forward fuselage design altered. C. M. Plattner. il Aviation W 82:38-9+ Mr 29 '65

Gages
See Gages

Ice protection
Flying weather signposts. H. T. Harrison. il Flying 77:49-51 N '65

Inspection
Lear jet inspections ordered. Aviation W 83:24 N 29 '65

Instruments
See Aeronautic instruments

Insurance
See Insurance, Aviation

Interior decoration
See Airplane decoration

Landing
Clickety-click and no hands; British European airways' automatic landing device. America 113:3 Jl 3 '65
Fantastic descent to a bridge; George Washington bridge landing. il Life 60:34B-34C Ja 7 '66
FAA begins category 2 airport equipment programs; no plans to substitute the new AILS for existing ILS systems. il Aviation W 83:116-17+ O 25 '65
General aviation category 2 rules follow pattern set for airlines. H. D. Watkins. Aviation W 83:20 O 18 '65
On a wing & a prayer; Pan American's flight 843 after takeoff checklist with Captain C. Kimes from San Francisco's International airport. il Time 86:23-4 Jl 9 '65
Pilot opinions on FAA Category 2 landing minimums vary widely. W. Wright. Aviation W 83:37 O 11 '65
Pilot reaction to Sperry display assessed; windshield projection display. il Aviation W 83:115+ Ag 9 '65
Rainbow optical projector aids landing. P. J. Klass. il Aviation W 83:63-5 Ag 23 '65
707 survives lost engine, wing section. H. D. Watkins. il Aviation W 83:27-8 Jl 5 '65
Wing and a prayer. il Newsweek 66:30 Jl 12 '65
See also
Airplanes, Jet propelled—Landing

Landing gear
Douglas tests C-5A landing gear designs. C. M. Plattner. il Aviation W 82:52-3+ Ap 26 '65

Landing on carriers
C-Scan goal is 8 x 4 mi. approach window. K. J. Stein. il Aviation W 82:69+ Mr 29 '65

Leasing
United expands use of leasing. Aviation W 82:39 My 17 '65

Lightning hazards
See Aviation—Lightning hazards

Lubrication
See also
Gas turbines, Aircraft—Lubrication

Maintenance and repair
Al's place. A. Trammell. il Flying 77:45-7 D '65
See also
Airlines—Maintenance and repair
Airplanes, Business—Maintenance and repair
Airplanes, Jet propelled—Maintenance and repair
Airplanes, Supersonic—Maintenance and repair

Noise
Law of noise. Time 86:37-8 S 10 '65
Noise may bar stretched DC-8s at JFK. J. W. Carter. il Aviation W 83:37-8 D 6 '65
Stethoscope for jet engines. il Time 86:52 Ag 13 '65

Operation
See Airplanes—Piloting

Piloting
All save one. L. W. Bartlett, jr. il Flying 77:72+ Jl '65
Engine management. J. Diblin. il Flying 78:56-9 Ja '66
I learned about flying from that. See issues of Flying
My romance with Three One Zulu; training aircraft. R. Starnes. Field & S 70:12-15+ D '65
Pilot error? R. B. Parke. il Flying 77:28 D '65
Safety check. H. Blackburn. Flying 77:118+ O '65
See also
Drinking and airplane accidents
Meteorology, Aeronautic

Power supply
Constant-frequency ac. system developed. P. J. Klass. il Aviation W 82:84-6 Ap 19 '65

Prices
Business airplanes: who needs 'em? with airplane buyer's guide. il Flying 77:59-60+ O '65

Private ownership
Buy your own airliner; and fly away! World samplers club. il Changing T 20:21-3 Ja '66
Flying status. R. B. Parke. Flying 77:38 O '65
See also
Airplanes in business
Private flying

Racing
See Airplane racing

Radio equipment
See Radio apparatus on aircraft

Range
See also
Airplanes, Military—Range

Refueling
See also
Airplane service stations

Safety devices and measures
Boeing, airline moves follow 727 crashes. J. R. Ashlock. Aviation W 83:27-8 D 20 '65
Explosion suppression system planned for TWA's jet aircraft. il Aviation W 83:39 Ag 9 '65
Lessons from the 727; suggested new precautions. Time 86:15A D 31 '65
Majority of lives lost in crashes can be saved. Sci N L 88:265 O 23 '65
See also
Airplanes—Ice protection
Aviation—Safety devices and measures
Oxygen apparatus

Speed
Stamp out vmc. R. Blodget. il Flying 77:106-8 O '65
See also
Airplanes, Supersonic

Stability and stabilizers
See also
Airplanes, Military—Stability and stabilizers

Stalling
BAC III accident laid to illusion of stall; August 20, 1964. Aviation W 82:102-3+ Ap 26 '65
Better C-133 stall performance sought; Douglas turboprop transports. C. M. Plattner. Aviation W 82:87 My 31 '65
Stable stall ruled BAC 111 crash cause; accident, October 22, 1963. il Aviation W 82:94-5+ Ap 19 '65

AIRPLANES—*Continued*

Storm hazards
See Aviation—Storm hazards

Submarine combination
See Submarine boats—Airplane combination

Testing
See also
Airplanes, Experimental—Testing
Airplanes, Jet propelled—Testing
Airplanes, Light—Testing

AIRPLANES, Amphibious
Amphibians reduce transit times on Virgin Island intercity routes. P. J. Klass. il Aviation W 83:41 D 20 '65

AIRPLANES, Business
Aircraft use aids Champion sales effort. D. A. Brown. il Aviation W 83:100-1+ Ag 9 '65
Beech accelerates drive in twin market. E. J. Bulban. il Aviation W 83:95+ Ag 2 '65
Beech moves to provide customer options, increased power in 1966 aircraft line. il Aviation W 83:112-13 N 8 '65
Boeing introducing business 737 at NBAA convention this week. Aviation W 83:50 O 11 '65
Business airplanes: who needs 'em? with airplane buyer's guide. il Flying 77:59-60+ O '65
Cessna moving into big airplane field with 411 twin. D. A. Brown. il Aviation W 82:80-1+ F 15 '65
Europe's jet makers boost sales effort. il Aviation W 82:259-61 Mr 15 '65
Firm's use of HS-125 exceeds estimate; Britain's first corporately-owned turbojet aircraft. D. A. Brown. il Aviation W 83:85+ Jl 26 '65
First delivery of Gulfstream 2 set in 1967; eighteen orders reported; Grumman's twin-turbofan business transport. Aviation W 82:31 My 24 '65
Grumman Gulfstream 2 aimed at ease of maintenance. D. A. Brown. il Aviation W 83:82-3+ N 29 '65
Is Bill Lear taking off again? low-cost executive jet. il Fortune 72:138-40+ Jl '65
Jet class. R. B. Parke. il Flying 77:88-92 O '65
Jet fleet gives Rexall greater flexibility. H. D. Watkins. il Aviation W 83:97-101+ S 13 '65
Jet service utilizes military procedures. D. A. Brown. il Aviation W 83:83+ O 18 '65
Jet to stimulate business aircraft sales. E. J. Bulban. il Aviation W 82:255-8 Mr 15 '65
Leading turbine-powered business aircraft: specifications. Aviation W 82:193 Mr 15 '65
Lear jet designing twin-engine, single-propeller pusher aircraft. Aviation W 83:32 N 22 '65
Limousine trade. R. B. Weeghman. il Flying 77:42-9 O '65
Merlin 2 deliveries may begin this year; turboprop business airplane. il Aviation W 82:107 My 10 '65
Mooney MU-2B offers speed, low price. D. A. Brown. il Aviation W 83:90-1+ N 22 '65
New aircraft, sales drives mark NBAA. il Aviation W 83:19-20 O 18 '65
New business aircraft given Paris debut. H. J. Coleman. il Aviation W 83:76-7+ Jl 5 '65
New business jets considered, designed. Aviation W 82:19 My 31 '65
Piper Cherokee six offers ease of handling, high payload. D. A. Brown. il Aviation W 82:82-6+ My 24 '65
Piper Comanche series capacity increased; photographs. Aviation W 83:97 S 20 '65
Sales of business jets expected to total 1,500-2,000 by 1970. Aviation W 82:85 Je 7 '65
Shell way. J. Gilbert. il Flying 77:54-8 O '65
Shopper's guide to corporate jets. il Fortune 72:141-3 Jl '65
Turbo Commander to sell for $299,950. il Aviation W 82:109-10 F 22 '65
Two new light twins planned by Mooney. E. J. Bulban. il Aviation W 83:101+ D 6 '65
U.S. business, personal and utility aircraft: specifications. Aviation W 82:194 Mr 15 '65
See also
Airplanes in business
Helicopters, Business

Design
Dassault plans Mystere 20 production increase, Mercury aimed at feederline sales. H. J. Coleman. il Aviation W 82:260-3+ Je 14 '65

Maintenance and repair
General motors air transport section, in-house effort stressed in maintenance. D. A. Brown. Aviation W 82:113+ Ap 12 '65

Prices
See Airplanes—Prices

Testing
FAA test program continues on HFB-320; twin-jet executive aircraft. il Aviation W 82:295-9+ Je 14 '65
Stick-pusher set for HFB 320 after accident induced by stall. Aviation W 82:19 Je 7 '65

AIRPLANES, Drone
Germany joins Canada, Britain in drone task; surveillance drone. il Miss & Roc 17:33 D 20 '65
Plane in photos looks like Firebee; pilotless reconnaissance airplane. D. L. Zylstra. il Miss & Roc 16:17 Ap 12 '65
U.S. drones and target missiles; specifications (cont) Aviation W 82:222 Mr 15 '65

AIRPLANES, Experimental
Delta-wing X-15 configuration proposed. il Aviation W 83:22 O 18 '65
USAF seeks funds to speed its scramjet, hypersonic flight program. M. L. Yaffee. il Aviation W 83:52-3+ Jl 12 '65

Testing
I'll fly anything! ed. by W. S. Griswold. M. Thompson. il Pop Sci 186:62-4+ Mr '65
Research program extending X-15 life. H. Taylor. Miss & Roc 17:14 O 11 '65
X-21A tests verify laminar flow gains. I. Stone. il Aviation W 83:98-9+ S 27 '65

AIRPLANES, Freight
Added cargo jets spur Atlantic activity. J. W. Carter. Aviation W 83:40-1 S 27 '65
Air ferry puts wings on travelers' cars. il Bsns W p108-9+ S 11 '65
Auto parts crises dictate air shipments. J. W. Carter. il Aviation W 83:38-9 S 20 '65
Larger Guppy aimed at S-4B transport. H. D. Watkins. il Aviation W 82:43+ Ap 19 '65
Quick-change jet sales portend broadened cargo service. il Aviation W 83:158-60+ O 25 '65
Super Guppy to make first flight Aug. 25. H. D. Watkins. il Aviation W 83:42-3 Ag 23 '65
See also
Airplanes, Military transport

AIRPLANES, Hypersonic. See Airplanes, Supersonic

AIRPLANES, Jet propelled
An-22 spurs airbus discussions in West. L. L. Doty. Aviation W 83:24-5 Jl 5 '65
Boeing planning stretched 320B/C, 727; triturbofan transport. Aviation W 83:38 Ag 9 '65
Boeing 727 service experience. J. R. Ashlock. Aviation W 82:37-9 Ap 5;42-3 Ap 12 '65
Comfortable but costly; BOAC's Super VC 10. il Time 85:92 Ap 2 '65
Commercial jet orders exceed forecasts. Aviation W 83:39 S 27 '65
DC-9B will have greater range, capacity. J. R. Ashlock. Aviation W 82:29 Mr 8 '65
Douglas' new plane; short-range DC-9 jet. il Time 86:85-6 D 17 '65
Explosion suppression system planned for TWA's jet aircraft. il Aviation W 83:39 Ag 9 '65
Few problems noted in BAC 111 phase-in. il Aviation W 83:145-7 O 25 '65
Military versions of 727 proposed by Boeing. il Aviation W 82:40-1 F 15 '65
Mohawk blazes a trail. il Bsns W p74+ Je 26 '65
1965 jet orders may reach $1.5 billion. J. R. Ashlock. il Aviation W 83:44-5 Ag 16 '65
Nosing into the jumbo jet race; Lockheed, Boeing and Douglas. il Bsns W p31-2 D 25 '65
Second wave. R. Hotz. Aviation W 83:37 O 25 '65
Short-medium versions proliferating as traffic swells. C. M. Plattner. il Aviation W 83:148-52 O 25 '65
Stretched Super VC.10 will carry 265. il Aviation W 83:43+ Jl 12 '65
Technology for C-5A studied for commercial version. il Aviation W 83:154-6 O 25 '65
United bets a bundle; contracting for $750-million worth of new jet planes by 1970. Bsns W p36 Ap 10 '65
Zooming airlines grab for new jets. il Bsns W p 186+ My 22 '65
See also
Airplanes, Business

AIRPLANES, Jet propelled—*Continued*

Design

Boeing increases size of 737 transport. C. M. Plattner. il Aviation W 82:26-8 Mr 1 '65

Boeing studies three civil C-5A versions. I. Stone. il Aviation W 83:46-9+ D 27 '65

Lear liner sales to near 500 in decade. D. A. Brown. il Aviation W 83:86-7+ N 1 '65

Quick-change jet sales portend broadened cargo service. il Aviation W 83:158-60+ O 25 '65

Three stretched DC-8 versions planned. H. D. Watkins. il Aviation W 82:54-7+ Ap 12 '65

United begins broad equipment program. J. W. Carter. il Aviation W 82:38+ Ap 12 '65

United 737-222 has extended fuselage. Aviation W 82:41 Ap 12 '65

Landing

All-weather system evolving gradually. il Aviation W 83:111-12+ O 25 '65

Category 3 simulator will test displays. B. Miller. il Aviation W 83:73-5+ N 29 '65

I flew in the airliner that lands itself! D. Francis. il Pop Sci 186:78-80 F '65

Now: pea-soup landings; Boeing-Bendix automatic landing system. il Sci Digest 58: 32-3 Ag '65

Pan Am asks lower DC-8 limits. Aviation W 82:30 Mr 1 '65

Pan Am expected to purchase Boeing-Bendix landing system. Aviation W 82:34 My 31 '65

707/720 landing system approval seen. C. M. Plattner. il Aviation W 82:38-9+ Mr 8 '65

Touchdown by computer; Autoflare system. il Time 85:64 Je 18 '65

Maintenance and repair

Boeing 727 service experience. J. R. Ashlock. Aviation W 82:37-9 Ap 5; 42-3 Ap 12 '65

Eastern sees accelerated training with video-taped maintenance data. Aviation W 83:29 N 29 '65

Stethoscope for jet engines. il Time 86:52 Ag 13 '65

Noise

See Airplanes—Noise

Testing

BAC 111-400 reflects pilot suggestions. H. J. Coleman. il Aviation W 83:55-7 N 1 '65

Douglas plans DC-9 stall tests, may beat certification schedule. il Aviation W 82:30 Mr 8 '65

Simplification, stability featured in DC-9. C. M. Plattner. il Aviation W 83:37+ N 1 '65

AIRPLANES, Light

Cessna accelerates Model 150 production. D. A. Brown. Aviation W 83:83 Jl 5 '65

Cessna 150. R. B. Weeghman. il Flying 77: 83-5 O '65

Cherokee six. R. Weeghman. il Flying 77:98-102 Jl '65

Horse of a different color. A. Trammell. il Flying 77:57-60 Ag '65

Lockheed Vega; a pilot report. F. Tallman. il Flying 77:74-9 S '65

Mr Piper's club. J. Gilbert. il Flying 77:30-5 S '65

Pilot report: the Cessna Super Skymaster. J. Gilbert. il Flying 77:40-4 N '65

Swearingen of San Antone; manufacturer of Merlin II. A. Trammell. il Flying 77:70-3 N '65

U.S. business, personal and utility aircraft; specifications. Aviation W 82:194 Mr 15 '65

Used aircraft pilot report; the Swift 125. R. B. Weeghman. il Flying 78:70-2 Ja '66

Design

BD-1. R. B. Weeghman. il Flying 77:34-9 N '65

Model 18. R. B. Parke. il Flying 77:28-33 Jl '65

Piloting

See Airplanes—Piloting

Testing

Comanche Bs; pilot report. J. Gilbert. il Flying 77:68-71 D '65

Mooney's air circus. R. Blodget. il Flying 77: 53-9 D '65

Pilot report Fairchild Hiller turbo Porter. J. Gilbert. il Flying 77:30-5 D '65

Pilot report: Volaire 10A. A. H. Sanfelici. il Flying 77:47-9 Jl '65

AIRPLANES, Military

Large European market seen for COIN. W. C. Wetmore. Aviation W 83:57-8+ S 20 '65

Military jet teams dominate Paris flying. H. J. Coleman. il Aviation W 82:20-3 Je 28 '65

Soviet air chief blasts theorists forecasting manned aircraft end. Aviation W 84:34 Ja 10 '66

Systems integration boosts ASW effort. P. J. Klass. il Aviation W 82:36-7+ Mr 1 '65

Tailor-made jet for the Vietnam war: A-7A Corsair II. il U S News 59:16 N 15 '65

Armaments

Modified AAFSS studied for Vietnam. Aviation W 83:31 S 27 '65

Control

Control augmentation aids A-7A stability. B. Miller. il Aviation W 83:61-2+ Ag 16 '65

Cost factors key to future of ILAAS; integrated light attack avionics system for VAL aircraft. B. Miller. il Aviation W 82:62-3+ F 22 '65

USAF to test triple-redundancy system. il Aviation W 83:87-8 N 22 '65

Design

F-111A stretch, inlet changes planned. C. M. Plattner. il Aviation W 83:93+ S 27 '65

Single chain of command aids Atlantic consortium; building turboprop antisubmarine aircraft. il Aviation W 82:240-1+ Je 14 '65

USAF to hear C-5A briefings this week. C. M. Plattner. il Aviation W 82:35-8 Ap 26 '65

Vertol tests monocyclic control system. D. A. Brown. il Aviation W 82:46-7+ Mr 8 '65

Electronic equipment

Advanced instrumentation tests planned. il Aviation W 83:87+ S 6 '65

AF awaits F-111A weapons studies. D. L. Zylstra. Miss & Roc 16:18 Je 7 '65

Loran-D designed as limited war navaid. P. J. Klass. il Aviation W 83:71-2 Jl 26 '65

Low-flying navigator. il Time 86:39 Jl 30 '65

Projects face tough technical scrutiny. P. J. Klass. il Aviation W 82:227-30+ Mr 15 '65

Systems approach sought for avionics. B. Miller. il Aviation W 82:235-6+ Mr 15 '65

Tester may simplify carrier maintenance; versatile avionic shop tester. P. J. Klass. il Aviation W 83:87+ Ag 2 '65

USAF to test suitcase Navaid for F-111. B. Miller. il Aviation W 83:52-3+ Ag 23 '65

Engines

See Airplane engines

Equipment

Latest avionics equipment planned for C-5A. Aviation W 82:23 My 3 '65

See also

Airplanes, Military—Electronic equipment

Radio telephone on aircraft

Escape devices

See Airplanes—Escape devices

Landing gear

See Airplanes—Landing gear

Maintenance and repair

Ship to aid Vietnam aircraft maintenance; USS Corpus Christi Bay, former USS Albemarle. R. D. Hibben. il Aviation W 83: 63+ Ag 30 '65

Manufacture

First A-7A Corsair 2 nears August rollout; with pictures. Aviation W 83:76-7 Jl 26 '65

Materials

Honeycomb used extensively in F-111 A/B. E. J. Bulban. il Aviation W 83:73+ O 4 '65

Range

Range seen limiting F-111 in bomber role; British option on aircraft. G. C. Wilson. Aviation W 82:27-8 Ap 12 '65

Records

See Aviation records

Stability and stabilizers

Control augmentation aids A-7A stability. B. Miller. il Aviation W 83:61-2+ Ag 16 '65

Testing

Carrier tests planned in study of X-22A's ASW potential; V/STOL research aircraft. il Aviation W 82:40-1+ My 24 '65

Convair striving to maintain COIN competition despite Charger crash. Aviation W 83: 19 N 1 '65

DOD threat clouds future of navy F-111. G. C. Wilson. Aviation W 83:16 N 1 '65

Douglas Ta-4E in maiden flight; navy will have 35 by late 1966. il Aviation W 83:21 Jl 5 '65

AIRPLANES, Military—Testing—*Continued*
Flight tests of navy F-111 pass 70-hr. mark; photographs. Aviation W 83:102-3 D 13 '65
General dynamics COIN to begin STOL flight testing this week. Aviation W 82:26 Mr 22 '65
Lift fans gain favor for VTOL aircraft. M. L. Yaffee. il Aviation W 83:52-5+ Ag 9 '65
Low-level flight capabilities studied. I. Stone. Aviation W 83:101-2 O 11 '65
Navy F-111 rolled out; fleet use to be determined in flight tests. G. C. Wilson. Aviation W 82:35 My 17 '65
Space training flights in NF-104A near. C. M. Plattner. il Aviation W 83:80-1+ Ag 9 '65
Total A-7A order exceeds $200 million. E. J. Bulban. il Aviation W 83:30-3 N 8 '65
USAF orders production F-111s; TF30 again fails supersonic test. G. C. Wilson. Aviation W 82:27 Ap 19 '65
YAT-37D shows agility in COIN role. D. A. Brown. il Aviation W 83:66-7+ Jl 12 '65

Canada

Canada plans $215-million F-5A, B order. Aviation W 83:29 Jl 12 '65

Europe, Western

Europeans push air force modernization. L. L. Doty. Aviation W 83:34 O 11 '65

Great Britain

Britain continues TSR.2 for evaluation. H. J. Coleman. Aviation W 82:16-17 F 8 '65
Labor policies jolt British industry. H. J. Coleman. il Aviation W 82:265-7 Mr 15 '65
TSR-2 cancellation brings censure move. H. J. Coleman. Aviation W 82:26-7 Ap 12 '65
U.K. aircraft buy totals $650 million. Aviation W 82:23 F 15 '65
U.S. extends Britain's option for F-111A. Aviation W 83:23 D 20 '65

Italy

Italy approves G.91Y, G.222 prototypes; tactical reconnaissance/fighter aircraft and V/STOL medium-range transport. L. L. Doty. il Aviation W 83:62-3+ Jl 19 '65

Russia

An-22. SST model climax Soviet display. R. Hotz. il Aviation W 82:28-31 Je 21 '65
Details of An-22 logistics transport shown; with photographs. Aviation W 83:94-7 Jl 12 '65
USSR military and civil aircraft; specifications (cont) Aviation W 82:223 Mr 15 '65

Sweden

Sweden maintains A37 program funding. W. C. Wetmore. il Aviation W 82:94-8 Ap 5 '65
Swedes adopt PERT for Viggen program. il Aviation W 82:257+ Je 14 '65

Switzerland

New delays threaten Swiss mirage plan. L. L. Doty. Aviation W 82:111+ Mr 22 '65
Revived P.16 planned for low-level roles; counter-insurgency attack fighter. L. L. Doty. il Aviation W 82:111+ My 17 '65

United States

A-6A fills interdiction mission in Vietnam. D. A. Brown. il Aviation W 83:18-20 D 27 '65
AMSA goal limits F-111 bomber design; advanced manned strategic aircraft. G. C. Wilson. il Aviation W 83:21-2 D 20 '65
Advances may extend life of F-4 program. W. H. Gregory. il Aviation W 82:67+ F 15 '65
Air force increasing use of Cessna fleet. Aviation W 82:65+ Mr 8 '65
Air force plans F-111A briefing. il Aviation W 83:29 D 13 '65
B-52 raids seen spurring F-111 bomber. C. Brownlow. Aviation W 83:22 Ag 30 '65
Bad news, good news. il Newsweek 66:25 D 20 '65
Billion-dollar baby, the birth of XB-70. K. Wheeler. il Read Digest 87:128-33 Jl '65
Bomber slash follows B-111 fund rebuff. Aviation W 83:26-7 D 13 '65
Bombers lose again to missiles; cutback of B-52s and B-58s. Bsns W p33 D 11 '65
C-5A award spurs new CX-6A interest. C. Brownlow. il Aviation W 83:91+ N 15 '65
C-5A market potential put at 300 aircraft. C. Brownlow. il Aviation W 83:26-8 O 11 '65
COIN selection anticipated about Jan. 1. C. M. Plattner. Aviation W 83:23 O 4 '65

Cost factors key to future of ILAAS; integrated light attack avionics system for VAL aircraft. B. Miller. il Aviation W 82:62-3+ F 22 '65
DOD threat clouds future of navy F-111. G. C. Wilson. Aviation W 83:16 N 1 '65
Detailed analysis to affect selection of army aircraft. G. Wilson. il Aviation W 82:80-1+ Mr 15 '65
Douglas tests C-5A landing gear designs. C. M. Plattner. il Aviation W 82:52-3+ Ap 26 '65
F-111 breaks another barrier. il Bsns W p34 Mr 13 '65
F-111 flies Mach 1.2; compressor problems persisting with TF30. Aviation W 82:289-90 Mr 15 '65
First operational SR-71 delivered to SAC. R. G. O'Lone. il Aviation W 84:33-4 Ja 17 '66
Flight tests of navy F-111 pass 70-hr. mark; photographs. Aviation W 83:102-3 D 13 '65
Future of V/STOL; excerpts from address. W. A. Davis. Aviation W 83:21 N 15 '65
GE YJ93 operates despite severe damage by ingestion. M. L. Yaffee. il Aviation W 83:64-5+ O 18 '65
How large a future for F-111? Bsns W p29 D 18 '65
In the TFX dispute: a McNamara victory; British switch to the F-111. U S News 58:10 Ap 19 '65
Latest Charger recon configuration shown. il Aviation W 83:95 S 20 '65
Lockheed C-5A builds on C-141 advances. J. R. Ashlock. il Aviation W 82:50-2+ Je 28 '65
Low, slow, well-armed; newest military plane. OV-10A. il Bsns W p34 Jl 10 '65
Military versions of 727 proposed by Boeing. il Aviation W 82:40-1 F 15 '65
Multi-service planes coming in future. Sci N L 88:57 Jl 24 '65
Navy F-111 rolled out; fleet use to be determined in flight tests. G. C. Wilson. Aviation W 82:35 My 17 '65
Navy pushes new VFAX aircraft combining F-4, A-7A capabilities. G. C. Wilson. Aviation W 84:23 Ja 3 '66
North American accelerates COIN work. D. E. Fink. il Aviation W 82:20-2 F 8 '65
Of planes and men; U.S. air force wages cold war and hot. K. F. Weaver. il Nat Geog Mag 128:298-349 S '65
Order for 257 OV-10A aircraft seen; COIN aircraft. D. E. Fink. Aviation W 83:28-9 D 13 '65
Plane in photos looks like Firebee; pilotless reconnaissance airplane. D. L. Zylstra. il Miss & Roc 16:17 Ap 12 '65
Plane that gets you there before you left; SST. J. Atwater. il Sat Eve Post 238:21-5 F 13 '65
Range seen limiting F-111 in bomber role; British option on aircraft. G. C. Wilson. Aviation W 82:27-8 Ap 12 '65
Second life: XB-70. il Newsweek 65:50 My 31 '65
$7 billion goody; F-111 (né the TFX) il Newsweek 65:103-4 My 24 '65
Takes off straight up, lands straight down; army's new XV-5A. il Pop Sci 186:106-7 Ap '65
Tank sealing improved in XB-70A no. 2. C. M. Plattner. il Aviation W 82:60-1+ My 24 '65
Total A-7A order exceeds $200 million. E. J. Bulban. il Aviation W 83:30-3 N 8 '65
USAF, army consider major COIN uses. D. E. Fink. il Aviation W 83:32-4 Jl 12 '65
USAF minimizes F-111 test delay. Aviation W 82:26 F 8 '65
USAF orders production F-111s; TF30 again fails supersonic test. G. C. Wilson. Aviation W 82:27 Ap 19 '65
U.S. air force plane is fastest in world; YF-12A. il(p 149) Sci N L 88:152 S 4 '65
U.S. military aircraft; specifications (cont) Aviation W 82:185-6 Mr 15 '65
Vertol tests monocyclic control system. D. A. Brown. il Aviation W 82:46-7+ Mr 8 '65
YAT-37D shows agility in COIN role. D. A. Brown. il Aviation W 83:66-7+ Jl 12 '65
Zuckert cites technology gains of XB-70. Aviation W 82:93-4 My 10 '65
See also
McDonnell aircraft corporation

AIRPLANES, Military transport
All-jet airlift begins to shape up. il Bsns W p28-9 My 1 '65
Biggest, cheapest lift ever: the C-5. J. Mecklin. il Fortune 72:179-80+ N '65
By '69: biggest jet that has ever flown; C-5A il U S News 59:6 O 11 '65
C-5A award spurs new CX-6A interest. C. Brownlow. il Aviation W 83:91+ N 15 '65

AIRPLANES, Military transport—*Continued*

C-5A: Lockheed's path to the future. il Bsns W p32-3 O 9 '65

C-5A market potential put at 300 aircraft. C. Brownlow. il Aviation W 83:26-8 O 11 '65

Details of An-22 logistics transport shown; with photographs. Aviation W 83:94-7 Jl 12 '65

Dornier military VTOL transport readied for flight test. L. L. Doty. il Aviation W 84: 32-4 Ja 3 '66

Lockheed C-5A builds on C-141 advances. J. R. Ashlock. il Aviation W 82:50-2+ Je 28 '65

Lockheed sees management key to C-5A. C. Brownlow. Aviation W 83:55-7+ O 18 '65

Lockheed's big victory; winning contract for world's largest airplane, C-5A. il Newsweek 66:80 O 11 '65

Nosing into the jumbo jet race; Lockheed, Boeing and Douglas. il Bsns W p31-2 D 25 '65

Ordeal of the plane makers: the C-5. J. Mecklin. il Fortune 72:158-9+ D '65

Pentagon tests one-stop bidding. il Bsns W p99-100+ N 6 '65

Systems analysis by land, air, and sea. il Fortune 72:121+ Jl '65

Technology for C-5A studied for commercial version. il Aviation W 83:154-6 O 25 '65

Tomorrow's air transportation; address, January 27, 1965. W. M. Allen. Vital Speeches 31:297-300 Mr 1 '65

Twenty-hour airlift to Vietnam; portfolio. Fortune 72:135-7 Ag '65

Vietnam war pace strains C-141 program. Aviation W 83:30-1 S 13 '65

Wrapping mobility in a total package: C-5A cargo plane and the fast deployment logistics ship. Bsns W p34 N 27 '65

AIRPLANES, Restored

Mavericks of sport aviation. R. Bach. il Flying 78:32-9 Ja '66

AIRPLANES, Short take-off and landing

Breguet studies large STOL transport. W. C. Wetmore. il Aviation W 82:77-8 F 8 '65

Convair COIN ends STOL tests, data, drawings submitted to navy. Aviation W 82:26 My 24 '65

CX-6A follow-on design studies to use lift-fan engine as basis. Aviation W 83:21 Jl 19 '65

France, Britain agree to collaborate on V/STOL. il Aviation W 82:234-5+ Je 14 '65

Future of V/STOL; excerpts from address. W. A. Davis. Aviation W 83:21 N 15 '65

U.S. and Canadian STOL aircraft; specifications. Aviation W 82:195 Mr 15 '65

V/STOL terminology. Aviation W 83:90 N 15 '65

VAK-191B prototype may fly by 1967. il Aviation W 82:305+ Je 14 '65

AIRPLANES, Supersonic

An-22, SST model climax Soviet display. R. Hotz. il Aviation W 82:28-31 Je 21 '65

Billion-dollar baby, the birth of XB-70. K. Wheeler. il Read Digest 87:128-33 Jl '65

Boeing chief calls for SST prototypes. Aviation W 82:33-4 F 1 '65

Certification of Boeing SST seen sixteen months after maiden flight. Aviation W 83: 103 N 15 '65

Companies balk at SST contract clauses. E. H. Kolcum. Aviation W 83:28 Jl 12 '65

Concorde hews to schedule for first flight in March, 1968. H. J. Coleman. il Aviation W 83:130-1+ O 25 '65

Concorde lead in SST race seen growing. L. L. Doty. Aviation W 83:38-9 Jl 12 '65

Congress to approve SST money request. G. C. Wilson. Aviation W 83:35 Ag 30 '65

Decision on supersonic airliner. C. A. Betts. il Sci N L 87:106-7 F 13 '65

Delay hampers U.S. Mach 2.7 transport. il Aviation W 83:135+ O 25 '65

Delta vs. swing. il Newsweek 66:56-7 Jl 5 '65

Departure of Bain spurs concern over future FAA direction of SST. Aviation W 83:36 Ag 30 '65

Did we goof on the SST? Sci Digest 58:54-5 Jl '65

Facts about supersonic flight. Good H 160: 177 My '65

Flights urged to test SST boom theory. Aviation W 82:28-9 My 3 '65

Flogging with feathers. R. Hotz. Aviation W 83:11 Jl 5 '65

Here comes the flying stovepipe; scramjets. il Time 86:46+ N 26 '65

Hydrogen-fueled aircraft study planned. I. Stone. Aviation W 83:69+ Ag 16 '65

Industry-government SST talks continue. Aviation W 83:30 Jl 26 '65

Johnson advisers split on SST financing. J. R. Ashlock. Aviation W 83:36 O 11 '65

Latest on the superjet; why U.S. is lagging. SST. il U S News 59:108-9 N 1 '65

McKee calls SST next step in transport. Aviation W 83:28-9 O 18 '65

McKee issue may swell SST opposition. J. R. Ashlock. Aviation W 82:31 Je 28 '65

McNamara group analyzing SST studies. Aviation W 82:41 Ap 5 '65

Missing the market. R. Hotz. Aviation W 83:21 Ag 23 '65

Monroney urges federally financed SST. J. R. Ashlock. Aviation W 82:38 Ap 19 '65

NASA studies SST operational problems. Aviation W 83:127+ O 25 '65

No contest seen for SST. J. Eberhart. Sci N L 88:343 N 27 '65

Over a billion for the first plane; American entry into civil aerospeed race. R. Burkhardt. New Repub 153:10-11 Jl 3 '65

Plane that gets you there before you left; SST. J. Atwater. il Sat Eve Post 238:21-5 F 13 '65

Possible market for 500 SSTs forecast. E. J. Bulban. Aviation W 82:27-8 My 24 '65

Present radar systems insufficient for SST. Sci N L 88:100 Ag 14 '65

Public-private enterprise; excerpts from address. W. M. Allen. Aviation W 83:21 D 6 '65

Public-private funding for SST possible if Congress cuts request. J. R. Ashlock. Aviation W 82:30 F 8 '65

Push for the SST. il Time 85:96 Mr 19 '65

Second life; XB-70. il Newsweek 65:50 My 31 '65

Slowdown in supersonic timetable; British-French may fly off with the market. Bsns W p50+ Jl 10 '65

Supersonic adventure. B. K. O. Lundberg. il Bul Atomic Sci 21:29-33 F '65

Supersonic airliner begins to take shape; Anglo-French Concorde ready to fly by 1967. il Bsns W p54-6 Jl 24 '65

Supersonic question mark. W. V. Shannon. Commonweal 82:518-19 Jl 23 '65

SST bidders given two concessions as negotiations approach deadline. Aviation W 83:37 Ag 2 '65

SST contracts complicate airline plans. J. R. Ashlock. Aviation W 83:26-7 Jl 12 '65

SST firms to receive USAF aircraft data. J. R. Ashlock. Aviation W 83:33-4 N 22 '65

SST program seen emphasizing engines. J. R. Ashlock. Aviation W 82:25 My 31 '65

SST; super-sonic transports. W. E. Becker. il Travel 125:29-31+ Ja '66

Supersonic transports, too fast for comfort? T. E. Stimson. il Pop Mech 125:88-92+ Ja '66

That other plane; government development program. il Time 86:68 Ag 20 '65

Tomorrow's air transportation; address, January 27, 1965. W. M. Allen. Vital Speeches 31:297-300 Mr 1 '65

U.K. committee attacks Concorde costs. Aviation W 83:42 Ag 2 '65

USAF seeks funds to speed its scramjet, hypersonic flight program. M. L. Yaffee. il Aviation W 83:52-3+ Jl 12 '65

Vendor, equipment capabilities cited as SST development keys. Aviation W 83:71-2 D 6 '65

What's in a name? XB-70A's record for continuous supersonic flight. Time 85:25 Ap 2 '65

Design

Boeing SST changes seek drag reduction. C. M. Plattner. Aviation W 82:27-8 F 8 '65

Design for flying, 1975 style. il Bsns W p42-4 Je 12 '65

Hypersonic transport concept evolving in Ames studies. R. G. O'Lone. il Aviation W 83:120-1+ O 25 '65

Lockheed begins freezing SST features. J. R. Ashlock. il Aviation W 84:43+ Ja 10 '66

Lockheed SST wing and forward fuselage design altered. C. M. Plattner. il Aviation W 82:38-9+ Mr 29 '65

Sixteen design objectives specified for SST. Aviation W 83:27 Jl 12 '65

Stretched version of Concorde proposed in response to urging of customers. il Aviation W 82:100-3+ Je 14 '65

Maintenance and repair

Improved maintenance seen necessary for SST success. G. Alexander. il Aviation W 83: 104-5+ N 8 '65

Maintenance problems confront Russians. Aviation W 82:93-5+ My 17 '65

AIRPLANES, Supersonic—*Continued*

Testing

SST to challenge non-destructive testing. Aviation W 83:43-4 D 27 '65

AIRPLANES, Toy

It's a Sopwith camel, almost. il Sunset 134: 152+ My '65

AIRPLANES, Used

Used aircraft pilot report; the Swift 125. R. B. Weeghman. il Flying 78:70-2 Ja '66

AIRPLANES, Vertical take-off and landing

Beer barrels aloft. il Time 85:70 Je 4 '65

Bell studies folding-rotor VTOL vehicles. il Aviation W 82:81+ Mr 22 '65

Carrier tests planned in study of X-22A's ASW potential; V/STOL research aircraft. il Aviation W 82:40-1+ My 24 '65

Civil version of XC-142A being studied. E. J. Bulban. il Aviation W 82:27-8 F 15 '65

Civil VTOL effort focusing on Germany. il Aviation W 82:95+ Je 14 '65

Design for hot-cycle rotor/wing studied. il Aviation W 82:74 Je 21 '65

Dornier military VTOL transport readied for flight test. L. L. Doty. il Aviation W 84: 32-4 Ja 3 '66

Final design for U.S.-German joint V/STOL fighter expected in year. C. Brownlow. Aviation W 83:23-4 S 6 '65

Flip-top plane flies two ways. il Life 58: 101+ My 21 '65

France, Britain agree to collaborate on V/STOL. il Aviation W 82:234-5+ Je 14 '65

Future of V/STOL; excerpts from address. W. A. Davis. Aviation W 83:21 N 15 '65

Helicopter that isn't; XC-142A. il Sci Digest 57:41 Ap '65

Lift fans gain favor for VTOL aircraft. M. L. Yaffee. il Aviation W 83:52-5+ Ag 9 '65

Lift, vectored engine compete in Europe. il Aviation W 82:250-1 Mr 15 '65

Nord basing VTOL on flying platform. il Aviation W 82:59+ Je 28 '65

Plane that can fly like a helicopter; XC-142A. il Time 85:51 F 12 '65

Plane that flies on rings; Tri-service X-22A, research airplane. il Sci Digest 58:37 Ag '65

Takes off straight up, lands straight down; army's new XV-5A. il Pop Sci 186:106-7 Ap '65

10-ton-payload USAF V/STOL studied. il Aviation W 82:22-3 Je 21 '65

U.S. VTOL aircraft; specifications (cont) Aviation W 82:198 Mr 15 '65

V/STOL terminology. Aviation W 83:90 N 15 '65

VAK-191B prototype may fly by 1967. il Aviation W 82:305+ Je 14 '65

VTOL competition causing rift in Europe. L. L. Doty. il Aviation W 82:18-21 Je 21 '65

VTOL strides spur civil interest. Aviation W 82:247-9 Mr 15 '65

Vertical-takeoff planes: how soon will you fly in one? W. Cloud. il Pop Sci 187:42-5+ Ag '65

Wide applications seen for X-22 versions; V/STOL research aircraft. Aviation W 82: 21 My 31 '65

X-22A first flight now scheduled for fall. il Aviation W 83:84-5 Ag 2 '65

XC-142 nears Edwards testing. Aviation W 82:115 My 17 '65

AIRPLANES in agriculture

FAA issues first agricultural rules. Aviation W 83:80 Jl 5 '65

Snow agplane bought by Rockwell-Standard. Aviation W 83:31 N 22 '65

U.S. agricultural aircraft; specifications. Aviation W 82:195 Mr 15 '65

Wide-swath method may cut spray time. E. J. Bulban. il Aviation W 82:89+ My 3 '65

Yugoslav UTVA 65 agplane features STOL capability. il Aviation W 83:113 Jl 12 '65

AIRPLANES in business

Centralized control key to Socony Mobil's air operations. D. A. Brown. il Aviation W 82: 60-1+ Je 21 '65

For love and money. T. Baxter. See issues of Flying

Front-door fliers; fly-in industrial parks. il Time 86:102+ D 10 '65

General motors air transport section. D. A. Brown. Aviation W 82:53-4+ Ap 5; 113+ Ap 12 '65

In good company; facts and figures on business flying. W. K. Lawton. Flying 77:50-3 O '65

Jet fleet gives Rexall greater flexibility. H. D. Watkins. il Aviation W 83:97-101+ S 13 '65

Teaming up to roam the airways; Sky roamers of Los Angeles, cooperative flying group. il Bsns W p28-9 Ap 24 '65

Time-savings value of aviation stressed. D. A. Brown. Aviation W 82:105+ My 17 '65

See also
Airplanes, Business

AIRPLANES in fire protection

California brush fire fought by thirty-five aircraft. Aviation W 83:35 S 27 '65

AIRPLANES in insect control
See also
Helicopters in insect control

AIRPLANES in rescue work
See also
Helicopters in rescue work

AIRPLANES in research

Cambridge laboratories KC-135 equipped to study the ionosphere. Aviation W 84:99 Ja 10 '66

AIRPORT buildings

BOAC may expand JFK cargo terminal. il Aviation W 83:39-41 N 22 '65

BOAC plans $19.6-million JFK terminal. il Aviation W 82:43 Ap 5 '65

Recalled to active duty; new version of Quonset hut. il Bsns W p200+ S 11 '65

AIRPORTS

Front-door fliers; fly-in industrial parks. il Time 86:102+ D 10 '65
See also
Airplane service stations
Heliports

Equipment

FAA begins category 2 airport equipment programs. il Aviation W 83:116-17+ O 25 '65

Ground equipment inventory is undergoing steady change. il Aviation W 83:170-3 O 25 '65

Federal aid

FAA allocates $84.5 million for airports. il Aviation W 83:40 S 13 '65

Finance

How to operate a small-city airport. E. Will. il Am City 80:129 Je '65

Fires and fire protection

Navy tests light water airborne fire-fighting system; combating crash fires on and off airfields. il Aviation W 83:90-1 Ag 23 '65

Lighting

Airport pancake lights serve as traffic markers. il Am City 81:129+ Ja '66

Blackout spurs FAA airport design role; possibility of on-site emergency power generators. P. J. Klass. il Aviation W 83:26-7 N 15 '65

Runways

Anti-skid coating aids wet runway stops. R. G. O'Lone. il Aviation W 83:39+ D 20 '65

Mile of runway to everywhere; Manhattan, Kan. D. C. Wesche. il Am City 80:148-9 Jl '65

New directions; circular runway. il Time 86: 61 D 31 '65

New runways built on stilts; LaGuardia airport. il Pop Sci 188:94-5 Ja '66

Runway stress may limit transport size. H. D. Watkins. Aviation W 83:31 O 4 '65

Spray-on landing field aids VTOL planes. Sci N L 87:162 Mr 13 '65

Snow and ice removal

Reverse-bent blades skim over the bumps; John F. Kennedy airport. il Am City 80: 30 Ag '65

Surfaces

Anti-skid coating aids wet runway stops. R. G. O'Lone. il Aviation W 83:39+ D 20 '65

Traffic control

Controlling traffic by numbers. il Time 85:80 Ap 23 '65

Digitrac to aid Sweden's traffic control. P. J. Klass. il Aviation W 83:87+ Jl 5 '65

FAA begins category 2 airport equipment programs. il Aviation W 83:116-17+ O 25 '65

FAA considers standby radars after major traffic jam at O'Hare. Aviation W 83:43 S 20 '65

Ground equipment inventory is undergoing steady change. il Aviation W 83:170-3 O 25 '65

Radar beacon display system cuts costs. P. J. Klass. il Aviation W 82:60-1+ My 3 '65

Transportation problems

Ground access grows as airport problem. il Aviation W 83:185-7 O 25 '65

AIRPORTS—*Continued*

Austria

See also
Vienna—Airports

New York (state)

See also
New York (city)—Airports

Russia

See also
Moscow—Airports

Tennessee

Old airport up-jets; Chattanooga, Tenn. il Am City 80:114-15 S '65

Texas

Texas airport may cover 21,000 acres. il Aviation W 83:35 O 4 '65

United States

Airport city, U.S.A. il Newsweek 65:90 Ap 5 '65
Airport congestion is forcing new wave of expansion. H. D. Watkins. il Aviation W 83:174-5+ O 25 '65
Report criticizes airport planning by FAA. R. G. O'Lone. Aviation W 82:28-9 My 24 '65
Twenty-five airports to get standby power units. Aviation W 83:41 N 22 '65
See also subhead Airports under names of cities, e.g. New York (city)—Airports
AIRS above the ground; story. See Stewart, M.
AIRSHIPS
Dinosaur of air travel. il Sr Schol 86:7 My 6 '65
Last of the sky monsters. J. Gilbert. il Flying 78:48-52 Ja '66
AIRSTRIPS. See Airports—Runways
AIRWAYS
Board delays Hawaii route award. Aviation W 83:41 S 13 '65
CAB awards Florida-Texas route to Eastern, affirming 1961 ruling. R. G. O'Lone. Aviation W 82:29 Je 7 '65
Northeast keys Florida bid to new jets. W. Wright. Aviation W 83:45 Ag 23 '65
Northwest routes suggested for three trunks. Aviation W 83:27 N 29 '65
Northwest-Southwest route case moves to airline testimony phase. Aviation W 83:41 S 20 '65
Panagra disputes CAB bureau on South American route awards. Aviation W 83:39 N 8 '65
Quest for the Holy Grail; American airlines petition for routes to Hawaii and Japan. Newsweek 67:70 Ja 17 '66

Traffic control

See Air traffic control
AIX-EN-PROVENCE festival. See Music festivals—France
AJANTA cave temples. See Cave temples
AJELLO, Libero. See Shields, A. B. jt. auth.
AJEMIAN, Robert
He stirred the hope that he could make things better. Life 59:45 N 12 '65
Tough decision for a flock of Lindsays. Life 58:34-5 My 28 '65
AKADEMEGORODOK, Siberia
New science city in Siberia. H. Koprowski and others. il Science 149:947-9 Ag 27 '65
AKASOFU, Syun-Ichi
Aurora; with biographical sketch. il Sci Am 213:10, 54-62 bibliog(p 126) D '65
AKERS, Milburn Peter
Watchdog in Chicago. il por Time 85:38+ Je 18 '65
AKERS, W. H.
Pliocene-pleistocene boundary, northern Gulf of Mexico. bibliog Science 149:741-2 Ag 13 '65
AKHZIV. See Achziv
AKRON, Ohio

City planning

Goodrich helps Akron get a renewal project. Bsns W p29 Je 26 '65

Education

Seis meses en Akron. A. E. Fitzpatrick. il Am Ed 1:6-7 S '65
Two-lane highway; prekindergarten classes and parent clubs. M. Essex. il PTA Mag 60:30-2 Ja '66

Lighting

Project mercury; relighting project. E. Butler, jr. il Am City 80:114+ N '65

Recreation

Out of a clay pit; Mason Park, recreation development. A. Youngblood. Recreation 58: 429-30 N '65

ALABAMA

Alabama story: newspaper editors tour by invitation of Governor Wallace. W. J. Cook. il Newsweek 65:65 Je 21 '65
Image-polishing in Alabama; out-of-state editors and reporters on tour at invitation of Governor Wallace. il Time 85:38 Je 18 '65
See also
Law—Alabama

Industries

Latest look at Alabama's image. il U S News 58:64-5 Je 28 '65

Politics and government

Alabama unbound; will Flowers bloom in the spring? A. Kopkind. New Repub 153:12-16 N 27 '65; Reply with rejoinder. W. B. Huie. 153:36 D 18 '65
Brave politician in the South; Attorney General R. M. Flowers. Life 59:4 N 5 '65
Filibustered. Newsweek 66:34-5 O 25 '65
Portrait of a southern liberal in trouble; Senator J. Sparkman. R. Sherrill. il N Y Times Mag p46-7+ N 7 '65
Wallace hangs on. H. Wolman. Commonweal 83:313-14 D 10 '65

Race problems

Boycott the boycott? Christian Cent 82:515 Ap 28 '65
Remarks to the New York police department Holy name society, April 4, 1965. W. F. Buckley, jr. Nat R 17:324-6 Ap 20 '65
Reporter at large; attempts of Negroes to register in Tuskegee. B. Taper. New Yorker 41:58+ Jl 24 '65
Summer strategy. Newsweek 65:28-9 Ap 12 '65
White Alabamans worship terror. Christian Cent 82:422 Ap 7 '65
Who's riding whom? concerning editorial in Presbyterian survey. Christian Cent 82: 956-7 Ag 4 '65
Wolf or shepherd? church segregation. Newsweek 65:66-7 Ap 12 '65
See also
Birmingham, Ala.—Negroes
ALABAMA library association
Movement in Mobile. E. Moon. Library J 90: 2509 Je 1 '65
ALABAMA. University, Tuscaloosa
Bear Bryant Hilton. il Sports Illus 23:42-5 O 11 '65
ALADDIN, incorporated; drama. See Hark, M. and McQueen, N.
ALAMOGORDO, N.Mex.
Alamogordo, mon amour. W. L. Laurence. il Esquire 63:118-21+ My '65
ALARM clocks. See Clocks
ALARMS
See also
Burglar alarms
Electric alarms
ALASKA
Russian America, by H. Chevigny. Review Time il 85:110+ Ap 16 '65
See also
Admiralty Island
Aeronautics, Commercial—Alaska
Aleutian Islands
Botany—Alaska
Camping—Alaska
Dams—Alaska
Earthquakes—Alaska
Geology—Alaska
Glacier Bay National Monument
Hunting—Alaska
Pribilof Islands
Radioactive fallout—Alaska
Waterways—Alaska
Yukon River

Description and travel

Alaska: the hard country; with report by M. Leatherbee. il Life 59:64-79+ O 1 '65
Alaska's marine highway; ferry route to the north. W. E. Garrett. il Nat Geog Mag 127: 776-819 Je '65
Be a modern pioneer. A. Heist. il Sr Schol 86:sup22-3 Ap 15 '65
Ferryboat into the sourdough past. R. Dunlop. il Todays Health 43:40-5 Ap '65
Five faces of Alaska. B. Fish. il Read Digest 87:146-52 S '65
Tent trailer to Alaska. E. A. Bauer. il Field & S 70:37-9 Je '65

Economic conditions

New Alaska; ready to take off. il U S News 59:54-6 Ag 16 '65
Plot to strangle Alaska; proposed Rampart Canyon Dam; with reply by P. Brooks. E. Gruening. Atlan 216:56-9 Jl; 52 S '65

ALASKA—*Continued*

History

49th: the United States' big bargain. il Sr Schol 86:5 Mr 25 '65

Poetry

Skylines of Alaska. E. W. Shaw. il Am For 71:40-1 Ap '65

Politics and government

Most powerful governor in the U.S.A. M. Morgan. Harper 231:98+ O '65

Relief work

Medicine at work in a disaster. H. G. Earl. il Todays Health 43:46-7+ Ap '65

Religious institutions and affairs

News of the Christian world (cont) Christian Cent 82:1456 N 24 '65

ALASKA in literature
  See also
  Alaska—Poetry

ALASKANS
Alaska: the hard country; with report by M. Leatherbee. il Life 59:64-79+ O 1 '65

ALATIS, James E.
Our own language barrier. por Am Ed 1:12-13 D '64

ALBA, Italy
Mere truffle; truffle snufflers at Battista Monchiero school. il Newsweek 66:51-2 D 13 '65

ALBA/Reyes Spanish dance company. See Dance companies

ALBANESE, Licia
Albanese anniversary. C. L. Osborne. Hi Fi 15:135 Ap '65

ALBANY, Ga.

Negroes

Two nuns in Georgia: gentle crusaders. il Look 29:M9+ N 2 '65

ALBANY, N.Y.

Institute of history and art

Art galleries: exhibition: Art-in-science. R. M. Coates. New Yorker 41:205-8+ O 16 '65

ALBAR, Syed Jaafar
Expulsion of Singapore. C. P. FitzGerald. il Nation 201:208-12 O 11 '65

ALBEE, Edward
John Gielgud and Edward Albee talk about the theater; ed. by R. S. Stewart. Atlan 215:61-8 Ap '65

  about

Malcolm: dramatization of novel by J. Purdy. Criticism
  Newsweek il 67:82 Ja 24 '66
  Time il 87:50 Ja 21 '66
Tiny Alice. Criticism
  America 112:336-7 Mr 6 '65
  Cath World 200:384 Mr '65
  Esquire 63:58+ Ap '65
  Sat R 48:43 S 4 '65
  Sat R il(p 1) por 48:38-9+ Ja 30 '65;
    Reply. E. Lipton. 48:21 F 20 '65
  Vogue 145:50 F 15 '65
Zoo story. Criticism
  Commonweal 82:501-2 Jl 9 '65

ALBERS, Anni
Conversation with Anni Albers; interview, ed. by N. Welliver. il Craft Horiz 25:17-21+ Jl '65

ALBERT, Heinrich Friedrich
Thrifty spy on the Sixth avenue el. E. Wittenberg. il Am Heritage 17:60-4+ D '65

ALBERT Lasker awards
1965 Lasker awards go to Sabin, Holley. Sci N L 88:323 N 20 '65
Recognition for Sabin; and Dr R. W. Holley. Newsweek 66:93 N 22 '65

ALBERTS, Zita D.
Pittsburgh collection of Höchst. Antiques 89:122-6 Ja '66

ALBINOS and albinism
Men, mink and cattle have same rare ills. Sci N L 87:157 Mr 6 '65

ALBIZZIA julibrissin. See Silk trees

ALBOHN, Ann
Meyer lemon. Horticulture 43:12-13 D '65

ALBRECHT, Margaret
Three, going on four. Parents Mag 41:44-5+ Ja '66
Two-year-olds take their time. Parents Mag 40:48-9+ Ag '65

ALBRIGHT, Frank P.
Crafts of Salem. Antiques 88:94-8 Jl '65

ALBRIGHT, Ivan Le Lorraine
Art galleries: exhibition at the Whitney. R. M. Coates. New Yorker 40:128+ F 13 '65
Ivan Albright: mystic realist. M. W. Dulac. il Am Artist 30:32-7+ Ja '66

ALBRIGHT, Tenley. See Gardiner, T. A.

ALBRIGHT-Knox art gallery, Buffalo, N.Y.
Can this be Buffalo? Festival of the arts today. il Life 58:63-4+ Ap 23 '65
Many sides of cubism: Albright-Knox art gallery recent acquisitions. K. Kuh. il Sat R 48:24-5 Ag 28 '65
Pop and op in Buffalo. F. Getlein. New Repub 153:33-4 D 4 '65

ALBUMINS
Histones and basic polyamino acids stimulate the uptake of albumin by tumor cells in culture. H. J.-P. Ryser and R. Hancock. bibliog il Science 150:501-3 O 22 '65
Serum prealbumin: polymorphism in man. M. K. Fagerhol and M. Braend. bibliog il Science 149:986 Ag 27 '65

ALBUQUERQUE, N.Mex.
Scientific couple finds success in Albuquerque. il Ebony 20:67-70+ Je '65

Education

Albuquerque's climate for in-service education. il NEA J 54:26-7 Mr '65

Parks and playgrounds

Tot area on a shoe-string. V. L. Bedford. il Recreation 58:171-2 Ap '65

Public buildings

Working city hall. il Am City 80:206+ Mr '65

Sanitary affairs

Indian designs on sidewalk ashtrays. il Am City 80:16 Ag '65
Vote for good service. J. Gill. il Am City 80:96-7 My '65

Water supply

Pumps, tanks and automation. C. Gonzales and H. J. Dull. il Am City 80:95-7 Ag '65

ALBURN, Harvey E. See Grant, N. H. jt. auth.

ALCINDOR, Lewis
California, here I come. il por Time 85:81 My 14 '65
College of his choice. Newsweek 65:88+ My 17 '65
Don't call us. il por Newsweek 65:60-1 F 15 '65
Height of temerity. il por Newsweek 66:66 D 13 '65
High Alcindor: basketball's Mt Everest. W. J. McKean. il pors Look 29:86-90 F 9 '65
Oh. baby. il por Time 86:91 D 10 '65

ALCOA. See Aluminum company of America

ALCOHOL
Ultimate prohibition. Sci Am 212:57-8 Je '65

Physiological effects

Excessive drink causes heart muscle disease. Sci N L 87:114 F 20 '65
No hiding place in a bottle; interview, ed. by K. N. Anderson. M. A. Block. il Todays Health 43:32-3+ Mr '65
  See also
Drinking and airplane accidents

ALCOHOL dehydrogenases. See Dehydrogenases

ALCOHOLICS

Rehabilitation

Fallen priests; Via Coeli refuge in N.Mex. S. De Gramont. il Sat Eve Post 238:99-103 N 20 '65
Whisky priests. il Newsweek 67:58 Ja 10 '66

ALCOHOLICS anonymous
William James and alcoholics anonymous. R. J. Roth. America 113:48-50 Jl 10 '65

ALCOHOLISM
My nightmare as an alcoholic; ed. by D. Lester. il Good H 160:75+ F '65
New York drink survey uses religious categories. Sci N L 87:233 Ap 10 '65
Rehabilitated may drink. E. Lederer. Sci N L 87:307 My 15 '65
Rising tide of alcoholism. W. B. Terhune. Read Digest 86:123-6 Je '65
Wine and spaghetti; alcoholism more prevalent in France than in Italy. il Sci Digest 59:36-7 Ja '66
  See also
Delirium tremens
Liquor problem
Temperance

Therapy

Accidental help for alcoholics. Time 86:67 N 12 '65
Hope for alcoholics; Lutheran institute of human ecology. A. P. Klausler. Christian Cent 82:221 F 17 '65
Photos help alcoholics. Sci N L 88:370 D 11 '65
Pill for alcoholism; metronidazole. Newsweek 66:82 N 15 '65

ALCOHOLS
Lignin: its constitution and formation from
p-hydroxycinnamyl alcohols; adaptation of
address, May 25, 1964. K. Freudenberg.
bibliog il Science 148:595-600 Ap 30 '65
ALCOR, incorporated
Al's place. A. Trammell. il Flying 77:45-7 D
'65
ALDA, Alan
Owl and the pussycat. il pors Ebony 20:98-
103 F '65
ALDEBURGH festival. See Music festivals—
England
ALDEN, Robert. See Dukelow, D. A. jt. auth.
ALDEN, Vernon R.
Making of college presidents. Sat R 48:86-7
F 20 '65
Planning for education's forgotten men. Sat
R 48:68-9+ My 15 '65
Why Washington needs more businessmen.
Duns R 86:36-7+ Ag '65
ALDERMAN, Michael
Structure of American medicine. New Repub
153:26-8 S 4 '65
ALDOSTERONE
Diabetes & blood pressure; adrenal-gland
disorder. Time 86:69 D 3 '65
ALDRICH, David V. See Ray, S. M. jt. auth.
ALDRICH, Dorothy. See Hart, M. jt. auth.
ALDRICH, S. R.
Why the 5-star high-yield system works.
por Suc Farm 63:34-5+ N '65
—and Feight, J. J.
Let' take a new look at lime. Suc Farm 63:
42-3+ O '65
ALDRIDGE, Helen
Term papers: the best part of the course.
Sr Schol 87:sup 11 D 2 '65
ALDRIDGE, John W.
What happened to the postwar authors? Sr
Schol 87:sup 16-17+ S 23 '65
ALECHINSKY, Pierre
Gremlinologist. il por Time 85:76 Je 25 '65
ALEMANY, Joseph Sadoc
Archbishop comes home. J. B. McGloin.
America 112:360-1 Mr 13 '65
ALEPA, F. Paul, and Terry, W. D.
Genetic factors and polypeptide chain sub-
classes of human immunoglobulin G de-
tected in chimpanzee serums. bibliog Sci-
ence 150:1293-4 D 3 '65
ALEUTIAN ISLANDS
Adak: a woman behind every tree. E. Asinof.
il Sat Eve Post 238:66+ Jl 17 '65
See also
Amchitka Island
Earthquakes—Aleutian Islands
ALEUTIAN ISLANDS national wildlife refuge.
See Wildlife sanctuaries
ALEWIVES (fishes)
Predation, body size, and composition of
plankton. J. L. Brooks and S. I. Dodson.
bibliog il Science 150:28-35 O 1 '65
ALEXANDER I, emperor of Russia
Czar who wouldn't die. por Time 86:39 N 26
'65
ALEXANDER, Christopher
Theory and invention of form. Arch Rec 137:
177-86 Ap '65
ALEXANDER, D. E. See Poneleit, C. G. jt.
auth.
ALEXANDER, Florence M.
How to choose a nursing school. Todays
Health 44:45-9 Ja '66
ALEXANDER, Herbert E. and Meyers, H. B.
Switch in campaign giving. Fortune 72:170-2+
N '65
ALEXANDER, Joseph K. and Brown, L. W.
Radio telescope for amateurs. bibliog il Sky
& Tel 29:212-14 Ap '65
ALEXANDER, Lloyd
Flat-heeled muse. Horn Bk 41:141-6 Ap '65
ALEXANDER, Myrna
Texas minister's Israeli honeymoon. E. Nadel.
il pors Look 29:M10+ Je 15 '65
ALEXANDER, R. W.
Safe little house; story. Good H 161:80-1 O
'65
So dear to my heart; story. Good H 160:88-9
My '65
Sudden silence; story. Good H 160:90-1 Ap '65
This small stranger; story. Good H 160:94-5
Mr '65
ALEXANDER, Ralph
Texas minister's Israeli honeymoon. E. Nadel.
il pors Look 29:M10+ Je 15 '65
ALEXANDER, Raymond Pace
Church, a symbol of commitment. por Negro
Hist Bul 28:77-8+ Ja '65
Message of greeting and challenge. por Negro
Hist Bul 28:183-4 My '65
Phila. jurist visits trouble spots in Far East;
address, August 20, 1965. por Negro Hist
Bul 29:11-12+ O '65
ALEXANDER, Robert E, and associates
How to stay small and provide big-firm serv-
ices. Arch Rec 137:104-5 My '65

ALEXANDER, Robert J.
Democratic revolution in Venezuela. Ann Am
Acad 358:150-8 Mr '65
Political experiment in Venezuela. Cur Hist
49:336-41+ D '65
ALEXANDER, Shana
Feminine eye. See issues of Life
ALEXANDER, Shirley
Base and noble metals in illumination. Natur
Hist 74:30-9 bibliog(p66) D '65
ALEXANDER, Susanna
Missouri regional librarian resigns after year
of far right pressures. Library J 90:3230-1
Ag '65
ALEXANDER, Tom
It's grow or die at Boise Cascade. Fortune 72:
180-3+ D '65
Millions of people just won't smoke cigars.
Fortune 72:164-7+ S '65
Motionless bird in space. Fortune 72:130-1+
O '65
Synectics: inventing by the madness method.
Fortune 72:165+ Ag '65
What Del Webb is up to in Nevada. Fortune
71:130-2+ My '65
ALEXANDER, W. M. and others
Zodiacal dust: measurements by Mariner IV.
Science 149:1240-1 S 10 '65
**ALEXANDER'S department stores, incorpo-
rated**
Bargain house invades silk-stocking district;
moves into stylish East side. il Bsns W p
112-14 Ag 7 '65
ALFALFA
During year of seeding grow three to five
tons of forage per acre. J. L. Parsons and
L. E. Zeman. il Suc Farm 63:46-7+ F '65
How to feed green-chop. Suc Farm 63:76
O '65
More hay, better pasture; with fertilizer.
Farm J 89:45+ F '65
Pay off: six tons of hay per acre. L. E.
Zeman. il Suc Farm 63:34-5 Ag '65

Hybrids

Hybrid alfalfas: ready next year? B. Fowler.
il Farm J 89:36 Jl '65
ALFALFA weevils
Alfalfa weevil hits sixty-five more counties.
Farm J 89:30 Jl '65
ALFRED the Great, king of England
Alfred the Great, by P. J. Helm. Review
America 112:463 Ap 3 '65. J. F. Bernard
ALFRED, William
One Saturday in Brooklyn. New Yorker 41:42-
6 D 18 '64
about
Hogan's goat. Criticism
Commonweal 83:441 Ja 14 '66
Nation 201:427-8 N 29 '65
New Repub 153:46 N 27 '65
New Yorker 41:150-2 N 20 '65
New Yorker 41:42-6 D 18 '65
Newsweek 66:92 D 6 '65
ALFRED A. Knopf, incorporated. See Knopf,
Alfred A, incorporated
ALFRINK, Bernardus Johannes, cardinal
Dutch cardinal speaks out. America 113:359
O 2 '65
ALFVÉN, Hannes
Origin of the moon. bibliog Science 148:476-7
Ap 23 '65
about
Celestial coexistence. por Time 86:91 N 19 '65
ALGAE
Algal cultures: ability to reduce turbulent
friction in flow. J. W. Hoyt and G. Soli.
bibliog il Science 149:1509-11 S 24 '65
Blue-green algae: fine structure of the gas
vacuoles. C. C. Bowen and T. E. Jensen.
bibliog il Science 147:1460-2 Mr 19 '65
Brucite in carbonate secreted by the red alga
goniolithon sp. R. F. Schmalz. bibliog il
Science 149:993-6 Ag 27 '65
Brucite in the calcareous alga goniolithon.
J. N. Weber and J. W. Kaufman. bibliog
il Science 149:996-7 Ag 27 '65
Chloroplast mutagenesis: effect of N-
methyl-N'-nitro-N-nitrosoguanidine and
some other agents on euglena. D. R.
McCalla. bibliog il Science 148:497-9 Ap
23 '65
Controlling algae in a pool. Sunset 134:122+
Ap '65
Fatty acids in blue-green algal mat com-
munities. P. L. Parker and R. F. Leo.
bibliog il Science 148:373-4 Ap 16 '65
Green algae divide to multiply. W. Patnode.
il Natur Hist 74:28-9 Mr '65
Invisible multitudes in your life. R. Platt.
il Read Digest 86:213-14+ F '65
Mineralogic changes during growth in the
red alga, clathromorphum compactum. K.
E. Chave and B. D. Wheeler, jr. bibliog
il Science 147:621 F 5 '65

ALGAE—*Continued*
Mutation of the blue-green alga, anacystis nidulans. C. Van Baalen. bibliog Science 149:70 Jl 2 '65
Pressure-induced color mutation of euglena gracilis. bibliog Science 147:741-2 F 12 '65
Productivity of microalgae in Antarctic Sea ice. P. R. Burkholder and E. F. Mandelli. bibliog il Science 149:872-4 Ag 20 '65
Scenedesmus obliquus sexuality. F. R. Trainor and C. A. Burg. bibliog il Science 148:1094 My 21 '65
See also
Kelp
Lichens

ALGAE, Fossil
Ancient algae found. Sci N L 88:276 O 30 '65

ALGEBRA
Math for the few; reprint. il Sci Digest 57: 38-41 Mr '65

ALGER, Horatio, 1832-1899
Stairway to the stars. P. W. Schmidtchen. il por Hobbies 70:106-7 Jl '65

ALGERIA
Algeria: zigzag path to socialism. S. Corvell. il Nation 200:277-9 Mr 15 '65
Atlantic report. Atlan 216:14+ S '65
See also
Justice, Administration of—Algeria
Sahara Desert
Socialism—Algeria
Women—Algeria

Economic conditions
Africa's latest Caesar. C. Sterling. il Reporter 32:10-13 Je 3 '65
Letter from Algeria. R. Shaplen. il New Yorker 41:147-8+ O 30 '65

Foreign relations
Africa's latest Caesar. C. Sterling. il Reporter 32:10-13 Je 3 '65
Bridge over the River Kiss. il Time 85:42 My 21 '65

History
Rebellion, 1954-1962
Wretched of the earth, by F. Fanon.
Review
Nation 200:674-6 Je 21 '65. C. C. O'Brien
New Yorker 41:115-17 Ja 15 '66. N. Hentoff

Politics and government
Adventurers, go home! Boumedienne's Algeria-for-Algerians theme. Time 86:26 Jl 9 '65
Aftermath. il Newsweek 66:35-6 Jl 5 '65
Ahmed ben Bella, would-be leader of the third world. R. W. Howe. New Repub 152: 10-11 Je 19 '65
Algeria: a break for the West? il U S News 59:10 Jl 5 '65
Algeria: a rude awakening for the left. E. Taylor. Reporter 33:31-2 Jl 15 '65
Algeria: strong man out. il Newsweek 65:31-2 Je 28 '65
Closing the door. Newsweek 66:38 Jl 12 '65
Concern for reform. il Time 86:32 Ag 20 '65
Crash of glass; overthrow of Ben Bella. il Time 85:36-7 Je 25 '65
French conscience; artists and intellectuals appeal on behalf of A. Ben Bella. Nation 201:179 O 4 '65
Global tremors from Algeria. A. Werth. Nation 201:31-2 Jl 19 '65
Letter from Algeria. R. Shaplen. il New Yorker 41:147-8+ O 30 '65
Letter from Algiers. R. Shaplen. il New Yorker 41:38-40+ Jl 17 '65
New face in Algiers. America 113:2 Jl 3 '65
Reluctant strong man. il Newsweek 66:32 Jl 19 '65
Seesaw summit; postponement of Afro-Asian conference. il Time 86:22 Jl 2 '65
Who and what is the real Boumedienne? R. W. Howe. New Repub 153:11-12 Jl 3 '65
Who's on first? il Time 86:22-3 Jl 2 '65

ALGREN, Nelson
Question of Simone de Beauvoir. Harper 230:134+ My '65
Speaking out. por Sat Eve Post 238:10+ O 23 '65
about
Correspondent to the underworld. S. Yurick. Nation 201:283-4 O 25 '65

ALHAMBRA
Cluster of soap bubbles. M. Cable. il Horizon 7:80-91 Sum '65

ALI, Amjad
United Nations commemoration address, June 25, 1965. UN Mo Chron 2:135-8 Jl '65

ALI, Muhammad. See Clay, C.

ALICE, Sister Mary-. See Mary-Alice, Sister

ALICE, Tex.
Better-water benefits start early. L. E. Weber. il Am City 80:97-8 Ap '65

ALICE in Wonderland. See Carroll, L, pseud.

ALIGNMENT. See Alinement

ALIMONY
Fraternity of crippled men. M. Gunther. il N Y Times Mag p34-5+ S 19 '65

ALINEMENT
Machine a hole-aligner. W. E. Burton. il Pop Sci 188:143 Ja '66

ALINSKY, Saul David
Professional radical; ed. by M. K. Sanders. Harper 230:37-47 Je; 231:52-9 Jl '65
about
Gadfly of the poverty war. R. Young. por Newsweek 66:30+ S 13 '65
Greatest good for all. Christian Cent 82:827-8 Je 30 '65
Poverty Soviets. Nat R 17:907-8 O 19 '65
Poverty-war project under fire: training school of agitators? il por U S News 59: 52 Ag 23 '65
Saul Alinsky in smugtown. J. Ridgeway. New Repub 152:15-17 Je 26 '65
Thank you, no, Mr Alinsky. Christian Cent 82:701 Je 2 '65

ALITALIA (airline) See Airlines—Italy

ALKALI metals
Helium-glow photometer for picomole analysis of alkali metals. G. G. Vurek and R. L. Bowman. bibliog il Science 149:448-50 Jl 23 '65
Rock degradation by alkali metals: a possible lunar erosion mechanism. J. J. Naughton and others. bibliog il Science 149:630-2 Ag 6 '65

ALKALINE batteries. See Storage batteries

ALKALINE phosphatases. See Phosphatases

ALKALOIDS
Biosynthesis of alkaloids. E. Leete. bibliog il Science 147:1000-6 F 26 '65
See also
Ergoline

ALKAN, Charles Henri Valentin
Mystery man; reprint. H. C. Schonberg. por Am Rec G 31:1132-4 Ag '65
Rebirth of an old romantic. R. Eyer. Life 59:22 N 26 '65

ALKYD paint. See Paint

ALL about mothers; drama. See Boiko, C.

ALL-America cities
All America cities. D. R. Maxey and C. S. Wren. il Look 29:90-4+ My 4 '65
All-America cities for 1964. Am City 80:144+ My '65

ALL-America football team. See Football players

ALL America selections. See Plants—All America selections

ALL fools day. See April fools day

ALL in good time; drama. See Naughton, B.

ALL my yesterdays; story. See Nutt, M. E.

ALL the years of her life; story. See Callaghan, M.

ALL trades, their tackle and trim; story. See Williams, T.

ALLAGASH RIVER
Allagash; Maine's counter proposal; with text. il Am For 71:26-9 F '65

ALLAGASH WILDERNESS WATERWAY (proposed) See Wilderness areas

ALLALIN glacier, Switzerland. See Glaciers

ALLAN, Robert M. Jr
Bob Allan on weather strategy. Yachting 117:40+ Je '65

ALLAN, Skip
Crew's-eye view of the Transpac. Yachting 118:97+ S '65

ALLEGHENY MOUNTAINS

Anecdotes, facetiae, satire, etc.
Tragic story of Magic Mountain. M. R. Cutler. il Liv Wildn 29:7-9 Sum '65

ALLEGHENY observatory. See Astronomical observatories

ALLELES. See Allelomorphism

ALLELOMORPHISM
Serum prealbumin: polymorphism in man. M. K. Fagerhol and M. Braend. bibliog il Science 149:986 Ag 27 '65

ALLEN, Arthur T.
Ethos of the teller of tales; address, 1965. bibliog por Wilson Lib Bul 40:356-8 D '65

ALLEN, Betty
Sean Connery takes over Rock Point. Mlle 62:127+ D '65

ALLEN, Casey
Beyond cheesecake. U S Camera 28:42-3+ My '65

ALLEN, Dwight W. and Gross, R. E.
Microteaching. NEA J 54:25-6 D '65
ALLEN, Eddie
Most unforgettable character I've met! T.
Collison. por Read Digest 86:107-12 F '65
ALLEN, Elizabeth
Hidden heart; story. Good H 160:84-5 F '65
Whatever happened to Peggy? Writer 78:11-
13 Je '65
ALLEN, Frances H. and Allen, J. E.
Cavities can be prevented. Parents Mag 40:
52-3+ Jl '65
ALLEN, Fred
Quiet please; Mr Allen is back on the air;
letters, ed. by J. McCarthy; excerpts from
Fred Allen's letters. por Esquire 63:64-6+
Mr '65
about
Art of constructing pyramids of absurdity.
G. Weales. Commonweal 82:599-600 Ag 20
'65
Beware the leaches. por Newsweek 65:98+
Ap 26 '65
Nostalgic stroll up Allen's alley. S. Moore.
Life 59:22 N 12 '65
Vaudeville ritual. J. K. Hutchens. por Sat
R 48:33 N 27 '65
Wayward reader. G. Frazier. Holiday 37:
18+ My '65
ALLEN, Greer
Half a dozen are memorable. Pub W 187:92-
3+ My 3 '65
ALLEN, Ivan, 1911-
Ivan ho! por Time 86:39 S 17 '65
Mayor surrenders Atlanta. J. Minter. il por
Sports Illus 23:14-17 Jl 12 '65
ALLEN, James E. Jr
School personnel and educational policy. PTA
Mag 59:12-14 Je '65
ALLEN, John Alexander
Dinosaurs at the fair; poem. Atlan 216:133
S '65
Heron; poem. Sat R 48:48 Je 19 '65
ALLEN, John E. See Allen, F. H. jt. auth.
ALLEN, John M. and Beard, M. E.
α-Hydroxy acid oxidase: localization in renal
microbodies. bibliog Science 149:1507-9 S 24
'65
ALLEN, Linda
(ed) The look you like; questions and
answers. See issues of Today's health
ALLEN, Louis A.
Where small business goes wrong. Duns R
85:60-1+ My '65
ALLEN, Lucille
Sex at Stanford. Newsweek 65:53-4 Mr 1 '65
ALLEN, M. B.
Marine microorganisms. Science 147:638-9 F
5 '65
ALLEN, Patricia Hunt, and others
(ed) Junior books appraised. Library J 90:
5498+ D 15 '65
—See Davis, E. L. jt. ed.
about
Patricia Allen heads Lj cards, Nancy Paige
joins SLJ. por Library J 90:1492-3 Mr 15 '65
ALLEN, Rita
English ABC of playing-cards. Hobbies 70:
118-19 Jl '65
ALLEN, Robert E.
Follett program. Wilson Lib Bul 40:59-60 S
'65
ALLEN, Robert Thomas
Are sportsmen becoming extinct? Read Digest
87:43+ N '65
ALLEN, Robert V.
(comp) Articles and other books received;
Soviet Union. See issues of American his-
torical review
ALLEN, Sue S.
Save our substitutes. Sr Schol 87:sup20-1 S
23 '65
ALLEN, Tom
Snook hunt along the shores of the Spanish
Main; paintings with account. Sports Illus
24:36-41 Ja 3 '66
Tarpon of the jungle; paintings. Sports Illus
22:44-9 Mr 8 '65
ALLEN, Ward P.
OAS informed of U.S. move to help Cuban
refugees; statement, October 6, 1965. Dept
State Bul 53:663-4 O 25 '65
ALLEN, William M.
Public-private enterprise; address, November
1, 1965. Vital Speeches 32:112-15 D 1 '65;
Excerpts. Aviation W 83:21 D 6 '65
Tomorrow's air transportation; address, Jan-
uary 27, 1965. Vital Speeches 31:297-300 Mr
1 '65
ALLERGY
Allergies: a problem not to be sneezed at.
il Bsns W p66+ Ag 21 '65

Allergies plague 19 million. F. Marley. il(p33)
Sci N L 88:42 Jl 17 '65
Hay fever, allergies: latest on cause and
treatment. il U S News 59:60-3 Jl 12 '65
See also
Hay fever
ALLERS, Franz
Singer's man; interview, ed. by Q. Eaton.
por Opera N 30:16 D 25 '65
ALLEY, Paul
Soup's on. il por Newsweek 66:58 Ag 23 '65
ALLEY theater, Houston. See Houston, Tex.—
Theater
ALLGEIER, Daniel L. See Brewer, J. H. jt.
auth.
ALLIANCE for progress
Aid to libraries in Latin America. M. D.
Shepard. il Wilson Lib Bul 39:778-82 My '65
Alliance comes of age; third annual meeting;
with summary of CIAP report. W. Velloso.
il Américas 17:1-5 F '65
Alliance for progress: a partnership of mu-
tual help; address, June 10, 1965. D. Rusk.
Dept State Bul 53:2-5 Jl 5 '65
Alliance for progress: failures and oppor-
tunities. T. J. Draper. Yale R 55:182-90 D
'65
Alliance for progress; four years of forward
movement; address, August 17, 1965. L. B.
Johnson. Dept State Bul 53:426-30 S 13 '65;
Excerpts. Cur Hist 49:362 D '65
Alliance for progress notes. See issues of
Américas
Alliance for reaction. E. Flores. Nation 200:
659-62 Je 21 '65
Alliance for what? R. Roth. il Nat R 17:189-
90+ Mr 9 '65
Alliance is a partnership; address, April 14,
1965. H. H. Humphrey. il Américas 17:1-5
My '65
At last, a partnership. Time 85:32 Mr 26 '65
Chapter that Keynes never wrote; address,
February 24, 1965. W. W. Rostow. Dept
State Bul 52:454-9 Mr 29 '65
Colombia's dangerous doldrums. R. Eder. il
Reporter 33:36-8 O 7 '65
Common quest for freedom and prosperity in
the American republics; address, November
22, 1965; with texts of resolutions adopted
at Rio de Janeiro conference. D. Rusk. bib-
liog f Dept State Bul 53:985-95, 996-8 D 20
'65
Cooperating for progress in Latin America;
address, February 27, 1965. E. Bunker.
Dept State Bul 52:465-71 Mr 29 '65
Foreign assistance program for 1966; state-
ment, March 9, 1965. D. Rusk. Dept State
Bul 52:482-8 Ap 5 '65
Housing and urban development in Latin
America; address, June 14, 1965. J. H.
Vaughn. Dept State Bul 53:66-70 Jl 12 '65
Marines have landed; intellectual poverty
of administration's policy. W. V. Shannon.
Commonweal 82:278-9 My 21 '65
New man in Rio: J. H. Vaughn. il Newsweek
66:48-9 N 29 '65
Only a beginning; concerning OAS foreign
ministers' meeting in Rio. Time 86:40+
D 3 '65
Peace corps approach. Time 85:41 F 26 '65
Progress for the Alliance? il Sr Schol 86:10-
13 My 20 '65
Reassuring the neighbors; Latin American
countries. il Time 86:25 Ag 27 '65
Review of U.S. policy in Latin America; re-
port, September 10, 1965. J. H. Vaughn.
Dept State Bul 53:548-9 O 4 '65
75th anniversary of the Organization of Amer-
ican states: the record of the inter-Ameri-
can system; address, April 14, 1965. H. H.
Humphrey. bibliog f Dept State Bul 52:
726-31 My 10 '65
Spiritless alliance. R. B. Goldmann. New
Repub 153:13-15 O 30 '65; Reply. D. B.
Atkinson. 153:34-5 N 13 '65
States to people aid; new program called
Partners of the alliance. Time 85:41 F 19
'65
Success of sorts; foreign ministers meeting.
Newsweek 66:54 D 13 '65
Sweet talk. il Newsweek 66:46 Ag 30 '65
Third annual meeting of Inter-American eco-
nomic and social council. F. B. Morse. Dept
State Bul 52:640-3 Ap 26 '65
Three on the go; off the crisis list: Nicaragua,
Honduras, Paraguay. il Time 86:43 N 26 '65
ALLIANCES
Cold war alliances (cont) Sr Schol 87:37 S
30 '65
Nonalignment in foreign affairs; symposium,
ed. by C. V. Crabb, jr. bibliog f Ann Am
Acad 362:1-138 N '65
See also
North Atlantic treaty organization

ALLIED chemical corporation
Bubbling retort at Allied chemical. J. Thackray. il Duns R 85:51-4 Je '65
Tower; building in Times square. New Yorker 41:49-50 D 11 '65
ALLIGATORS
Gater poachers. G. Laycock. il Field & S 70:40-3+ Jl '65
ALLIGATORS; story. See Updike, J.
ALLISON, Horatio
Welded apartment framing cuts costs. Arch Rec 138:223-6 S '65
ALLISON, James L. and others
DNA: reaction with chloroquine. bibliog Science 149:1111-13 S 3 '65
ALLISON, John M.
Establishing freedom by force. Sat R 48:36 N 6 '65
Less than ten feet tall. Sat R 48:38-9+ Ag 14 '65
Looking back, he wasn't so bad. Sat R 48:63 My 22 '65
Two ways to one world. Sat R 48:39-40 S 25 '65
Way to the man is the heart. Sat R 48:37-8 N 20 '65
ALLOTT, Gordon
Republicans do think; address, April 6, 1965. Vital Speeches 31:477-80 My 15 '65
ALLOWANCES, Duty free. See Duty free importation
ALLOWAY, Lawrence
World is a painting: Rauschenberg. Vogue 146:100-3+ O 15 '65
ALLOYS
See also
Aluminum alloys
ALL'S right with the world; story. See Malpass, E.
ALLTUCKER, John
Cross that inflames a city. T. Armbrister. il por Sat Eve Post 238:36-7 Jl 3 '65
ALLYN, Gerould
Guide to the use of acrylic paints. Arch Rec 138:217-18 O; 211-12 N '65
ALLYN and Bacon, incorporated
Allyn & Bacon and CBS call off merger talks. Pub W 188:67 D 27 '65
CBS to acquire Allyn & Bacon. Pub W 188:43-4 O 4 '65
ALMAIN, Jacques
Almain and Major: conciliar theory on the eve of the reformation. F. Oakley. bibliog f Am Hist R 70:673-90 Ap '65
ALMANACS
Soldier's almanac; printed at Newcastle in the early 1800's. D. Powills. il Hobbies 70:118-19 Ja '66
ALMQUIST, Ray
Fragrance that lasts and lasts. il Flower Grower 52:24-5 Je '65
Signs of the times. Design 66:28-9 Ja '65
ALONSO-DEFLORIDA, F. and others
Anaphylactic reaction of denervated skeletal muscle in the guinea pig. bibliog Science 147:1155-6 Mr 5 '65
ALONSO PIÑEIRO, Armando
Two worlds of Jorge Luis Borges. Américas 17:11-15 Mr '65
ALOPECIA. See Baldness
ALOU brothers
Brothers three of baseball. il Ebony 20:73-4+ S '65
ALPERN, Mathew. See Doesschate, J. T. jt. auth.
ALPERT, Herb
Newest sound. il Time 86:83 N 12 '65
ALPERT, Hollis
David Lean recipe: a whack in the guts. N Y Times Mag p32-3+ My 23 '65
Dog days at Cannes. Sat R 48:23-4 Je 26 '65
Happiness is a film-maker in London. Sat R 48:10-13+ D 25 '65
Japanese screen. Sat R 48:35 D 25 '65
Offbeat director in outer space. N Y Times Mag p 14-15+ Ja 16 '66
Saga of Greta Lovisa Gustafsson. N Y Times Mag p26-7+ S 5 '65
ALPHABET
I/t/a: a reading revolution? initial teaching alphabet. il Library J 90:5058 N 15 '65
I/t/a paperback series. W. D. Boutwell. il Sr Schol 86:sup 18 Mr 4 '65
IRA focus: reading instruction in transition; statements. E. Malmquist. il Sr Schol 86:sup 1-2 My 20 '65
Learning to read with i/t/a; Initial teaching alphabet. W. D. Boutwell. il Sr Schol 86:sup8-9 Mr 4 '65
New alphabet eases job of learning to read; ITA. Sci N L 88:139 Ag 28 '65
New phonetic alphabets; Initial teaching alphabet and Unifon. N. Larrick. il Parents Mag 40:49-53+ O '65

Our far-flung correspondents; G. B. Shaw's interest in phonetic and initial teaching alphabets. J. Bainbridge. New Yorker 41:162-4+ N 6 '65
Second international i/t/a conference. A. J. Mazurkiewicz. Sch & Soc 93:482+ D 11 '65
UNIFON system; Foundation for a compatible and consistent alphabet. J. R. Malone. il Wilson Lib Bul 40:63-5 S '65
When a new alphabet was treated for a year; Initial teaching alphabet. il U S News 59:16 Jl 26 '65
World i.t.a. thrust forecast at conference. il Sr Schol 87:sup4 S 23 '65
See also
African languages—Alphabet
ALPHABETS. See Alphabet
ALPHAND, Hervé
Changing the guard. il por Newsweek 66:44+ S 27 '65
ALPHAND, Nicole Merenda (Bunau-Varilla)
Race to succeed Nicole. M. Cheshire. il pors Life 59:93-4+ N 12 '65
ALPINE climbing. See Mountaineering
ALPINE flora
Fall in the mountains. D. E. Rose. Horticulture 43:16 O '65
Floras of the tundra; Colorado. P. D. Kilburn. il Natur Hist 74:52-9 Ag '65
ALPINE tunnels. See Tunnels and tunneling
ALPORT, Peter, and Dufresne, Frank
Neglected cutthroats. Field & S 69:48-9 Ap '65
ALPS
Alps: man's own mountains. R. Gray. il Nat Geog Mag 128:350-95 S '65
Doomsday roar in the Alps. il Life 58:38A My 28 '65
Mountain-top Shangri-las. I. C. Kuhn. il Travel 124:28-35 O '65
Reporter at large; Chamonix, France. J. Bernstein. il New Yorker 41:43-6+ Mr 6; 109-10+ Mr 20 '65
See also
Grépon
Matterhorn
Maps
Europe's snowy crown portrayed on double map. il Nat Geog Mag 128:396-7, Sup (folded map) S '65
ALSACE
Battle line, 1965; industrialized area. il Time 86:107-8 N 12 '65
ALSOP, Joseph
Books. New Yorker 41:114+ Ag 28 '65
Diet that finally did it; air force diet. McCalls 92:138+ My '65; Same abr. with title What about that painless air force diet? Read Digest 87:89-92 Jl '65
ALSOP, Stewart
Affairs of state. See issues of Saturday evening post
America's new big rich. Sat Eve Post 238:23-7+ Jl 17 '65
Intellectuals and Vietnam. Sat Eve Post 238:18 Je 5 '65; Same abr. Read Digest 87:136-8 Ag '65
Meaning of the dead. Sat Eve Post 238:16 Ap 24 '65; Same abr. Read Digest 87:54-6 Jl '65
Two views of Lyndon Johnson; excerpts. U S News 58:34 F 1 '65
We can't let them down. Sat Eve Post 238:18 Mr 27 '65; Same abr. Read Digest 86:116-18 Je '65
What the people really think. Sat Eve Post 238:18, 27-31 O 23 '65
ALSTON, Ralph E. See Melchert, T. E. jt. auth.
ALT, Franz L.
Mechanical translation: U.S.-Japan joint conference. Science 147:1599-600 Mr 26 '65
ALTAI MOUNTAINS
Frozen tombs of the Scythians. M. I. Artamonov. il Sci Am 212:100-9 bibliog(p 151) My '65
ALTBACH, Philip G.
Crisis in south India. Christian Cent 82:403-4 Mr 31 '65
Focus on Berkeley. Christian Cent 82:1356-7 N 3 '65
Indo-Pakistan frustration. Christian Cent 82:1512 D 8 '65
Suicide of the Indian left. Christian Cent 82:1190-2 S 29 '65
ALTER, Robert
Epitaph for a Jewish magazine; notes on the Menorah journal. Commentary 39:51-5 My '65
In the community. Commentary 40:71-5 S; 77-82 D '65
ALTERNATING currents. See Electric currents, Alternating

ALTERNATORS. See Electric generators, Alternating current

ALTIMETERS
Altimeter monitors its own performance; radio altimeter. P. J. Klass. il Aviation W 83:99+ Jl 12 '65
General aviation radar altimeter features low cost, light weight. il Aviation W 83:89-90 N 29 '65
Laser altimeter may aid photo mapping. B. Miller. il Aviation W 82:60-1+ Mr 29 '65
Laser beam successful low-level altimeter. Sci N L 87:248 Ap 17 '65
New York collision investigators study possible error in altimetry. D. A. Brown. Aviation W 83:39-40 D 13 '65
Self-testing navaids correct own errors. radio altimeter and navigation receiver. il Aviation W 83:105+ Jl 12 '65

ALTITUDE, Influence of
Amateur scientist; apparatus for simulating high altitudes. il Sci Am 213:239-40+ S '65
Fatty-tissue changes in rats with acclimatization to altitude. C. M. Blatteis and L. O. Lutherer. il Science 149:1383-5 S 17 '65
Getting high in Mexico city; high altitude's effect on athletes. B. Ottum. il Sports Illus 23:30-1 O 25 '65
In the high, thin air; Mexico city. il Time 86: 70 D 31 '65
See also
Anoxemia

ALTITUDE chambers. See Altitude, Influence of

ALTITUDE flying. See Aviation—Altitude flying

ALTIZER, Thomas J. J.
Creative negation in theology. Christian Cent 82:864-7 Jl 7 '65

ALTMANN, Stuart A.
Primates: communication and social interactions. Science 149:886-7 Ag 20 '65

ALTOMARE, Alvaro A.
Dust-free gun cabinet. Pop Mech 124:176-7 O '65

ALTOONA, Pa.
Anti-poverty program
One city's war on poverty. G. Nikolaieff. il Sr Schol 87:21 D 9 '65

ALTSCHUL, Frank
Arguments for accommodation. Sat R 48:40 Ag 14 '65
More than one way to win a world. Sat R 48:54-5 Ap 17 '65

ALTSHULER, Kenneth Z. See Brebbia, D. R. jt. auth.

ALTUS, William D.
Birth order and its sequelae. bibliog Science 151:44-9 Ja 7 '66

ALUMINUM
See also
Bauxite
Plants, Effect of aluminum on

Prices
Aluminum: battle over prices. il Sr Schol 87: 17-18 D 2 '65
Aluminum: crackdown and rollback. il Newsweek 66:77-8 N 22 '65
Aluminum foiled; industry to bow to government pressure. il Time 86:105-6 N 19 '65
Aluminum price hike kicks up a tempest. Bsns W p29-30 N 6 '65
Aluminum starts retreat on prices; Pentagon compromises on stockpile. il Bsns W p38-9 N 13 '65
Businessmen size up lesson on aluminum; top executive opinion concerning wage-price guideposts. il Bsns W p37-8 N 20 '65
Fighting to hold the line; with editorial comment. Bsns W p37-8, 204 N 13 '65
Great aluminum rattle. Time 86:103-103A N 12 '65
Is the honeymoon really over? LBJ and business face new spats over price policies. il Newsweek 66:78+ N 22 '65
LBJ and the aluminum-price flap. Newsweek 66:91 N 15 '65
Risky way to stabilize prices. Life 59:4 N 26 '65
That wrong war on aluminum. Fortune 72: 133-4 D '65
To hold price line: a new crackdown. il U S News 59:37-9 N 22 '65
Washington desk. J. R. Slevin. Duns R 86: 5-6 D '65
Without benefit of law; excerpts from editorials: New York times and Washington post, November 10, 1965. U S News 59:132 N 22 '65

Protection
Electroplate or anodize your electronic projects. W. B. Ford. il Pop Electr 22:55-9+ Je '65

ALUMINUM, Structural
Beach house made of aluminum sandwiches; polystyrene foam between two sheets of aluminum. il Sports Illus 23:42-5 Ag 9 '65

ALUMINUM alloys
Pyrofuze finds ordnance application; palladium and aluminum in a bimetallic composite. J. F. Judge. il Miss & Roc 16:32-4 My 24 '65

ALUMINUM boats. See Boats—Materials

ALUMINUM cans
See also
Beer containers

ALUMINUM company of America
Aluminum gets a lift. Bsns W p 107-8 Je 5 '65
Aluminum starts retreat on prices; Pentagon compromises on stockpile. il Bsns W p38-9 N 13 '65
First team at Alcoa. il Time 85:100 Ap 30 '65

ALUMINUM finishing. See Metal finishing

ALUMINUM industry and trade

France
On a worldwide hunt for aluminum growth; Pechiney of France. il Bsns W p96+ Mr 20 '65

United States
Aluminum comes next; bargaining spotlight shifts. Bsns W p 136 My 8 '65
Aluminum: crackdown and rollback. il Newsweek 66:77-8 N 22 '65
Aluminum crisis. Commonweal 83:228-9 N 26 '65
Aluminum foiled; industry to bow to government pressure. il Time 86:105-6 N 19 '65
Aluminum price hike kicks up a tempest. Bsns W p29-30 N 6 '65
Booming economy tests self-control. America 113:561-2 N 13 '65
Copper's competitors race for its markets; aluminum, plastics, and clad metals. il Bsns W p86+ D 11 '65
Fighting to hold the line; with editorial comment. Bsns W p37-8, 204 N 13 '65
Great aluminum rattle. Time 86:103-103A N 12 '65
Headlines for aluminum. America 113:615-16 N 20 '65
Productivity in an expanding industry. J. M. Cleaver. il Mo Labor R 88:373-7 Ap '65
Risky way to stabilize prices. Life 59:4 N 26 '65
See also
Aluminum company of America

ALUMNI funds. See Colleges and universities—Gifts, legacies, etc.

ALVAREZ, A.
Polish scene; excerpt from Under pressure. Commentary 39:75-9 Mr '65

ALVAREZ VIDAURRE, Antonio
United Nations commemoration address, June 25, 1965. UN Mo Chron 2:111-13 Jl '65

ALVARY, Lorenzo
Figure of controversy; interview, ed. by F. Stevenson. por Opera N 30:29 Ja 15 '66

ALVES, Margaret
Some trade spoons. Hobbies 70:46 S '65

ALVIN Ailey American dance theater. See Ballet companies

ALWORTH, Lance
They all go bang! at Bambi. E. Shrake. il pors Sports Illus 23:32-4+ D 13 '65

AMABILE, George
Twink drives back, in a bad mood, from a party in Massachusetts; poem. New Yorker 41:36 Mr 6 '65

AMADOR, F. V. Garcia-. See Garcia-Amador, F. V.

AMALGAMATED association of iron, steel, and tin workers
Battle at Homestead; excerpt from Lockout. L. Wolff. il Am Heritage 16:64-79 Ag '65

AMALGAMATED clothing workers of America
Pins and needles, and progress. I. Ross. il Read Digest 86:37-8+ Mr '65

AMALGAMATED lithographers of America
Gospel according to Swayduck. Fortune 73: 118 Ja '66

AMALGAMATION, Racial. See Intermarriage of races

AMARNATH pilgrimages. See Pilgrims and pilgrimages

AMARYLLIS
Just watch them grow. il Sunset 135:246 N '65

AMARYLLIS belladonna. See Belladonna lilies

AMATEUR astronomers. See Astronomers, Amateur

AMATEUR athletic union of the United States
AAU plays by international rules; reprint. D. F. Hull. il Recreation 58:281-2 Je '65
Off to Russia, without love; AAU women's track and field team at Kiev. J. Jares. il Sports Illus 23:20-1+ Jl 12 '65

AMATEUR athletic union of the United States
—*Continued*
What the men can do for an encore; Russia's Brumel and U.S.'s Mills at the National AAU indoor championship. G. S. Brown. il Sports Illus 22:45-7 Mr 1 '65
AMATEUR golf. See Golf
AMATEUR moving pictures. See Moving pictures, Amateur
AMATEUR photography. See Photography
AMATEUR radio operators. See Radio operators, Amateur
AMATEUR radio stations. See Radio stations, Amateur
AMATEUR rocketry. See Rockets—Amateur experiments
AMATEUR scientists. See Scientists, Amateur
AMATEUR theatricals
Drama in the barn; Valley round theatre, Corvallis, Ore. V. Rankin. il Recreation 58: 279+ Je '65
AMATEURISM (sports)
See also
Amateur athletic union of the United States
AMAZON jungle. See Jungle
AMAZON VALLEY
For South America travelers, here is detour to adventure; Amazon basin and Leticia. il Sunset 135:34-6+ N '65
AMBASSADORS
Unhappy draw; West Germany and Israel select ambassadors. il Newsweek 66:35 Jl 19 '65
See also
Negro ambassadors
United States—Diplomatic and consular service
Women as ambassadors
AMBASSADORS for friendship. See Foreign students in the United States
AMBER
Infrared spectra as a means of determining botanical sources of amber. J. H. Langenheim and C. W. Beck. bibliog il Science 149:52-5 Jl 2 '65
AMBLARD, Manuel
Twenty-three years in Franco's jails; tr. by G. Rabassa. Nation 200:305-7 Mr 22 '65
AMBLYOPIA. See Eye—Diseases and defects
AMBULANCE driver; story. See Buechler, J.
AMBULANCES
Ambulance is not a hearse; Louisville's police-operated system. R. H. Berg. il Look 29:40-2+ D 14 '65
Miniature ambulance saves lives at football stadium. il Todays Health 43:70 Ag '65
AMBYSTOMA. See Salamanders
AMCHITKA ISLAND
Atomic blast vs otter? S. McCutcheon. il Audubon Mag 67:376-81 N '65
AMDUR, Irving
Two strategies for peace. Bul Atomic Sci 21:31 O '65
AMEN, Grover
Scholar of Bourbon street; story. New Yorker 40:32-8 F 13 '65
AMEN corner; drama. See Baldwin, J.
AMENDMENTS to the Constitution. See United States—Constitution—Amendments
AMERICA
Founding of new societies, by L. Hartz and others. Review
Nation 200:562-4 My 24 '65. H. Zinn
Antiquities
See also
Mayas
Discovery and exploration
Columbus' doctors. L. H. Roddis. il Américas 17:35-7 Je '65
Enduring Saint Brendan. R. Valente. il Américas 17:22-7 N '65
Westviking; the ancient Norse in Greenland and North America, by F. Mowat. Review
Sat R il 48:33 D 18 '65. S. Thorne
Who discovered America? il Sat Eve Post 238:104 N 20 '65
Windblown Leif. il Time 86:25B O 22 '65
See also
Vikings
Maps
Columbus vs. Ericson, what science says. D. Cohen. il Sci Digest 59:10-15 Ja '66
Map of history; Vinland map. il Time 86: 120+ O 15 '65
New light on discovery of the New World. il U S News 59:8-9 O 25 '65
New World mapped, 1440. Sci N L 88:263 O 23 '65
New World on the map. Am Heritage 16:11 O '65
Seeing America first; Viking map of 1440. il Newsweek 66:103-4 O 18 '65

Vinland map and the Tartar relation, by R. A. Skelton and others. Review
America 114:87 Ja 15 '66. H. Musurillo
Sat R 48:46-8 O 16 '65. S. Thorne
Vinland map and the Tartar relation; excerpts, with introd. by O. Jensen. R. Skelton and G. D. Painter. il Am Heritage 16:4-10+ O '65
What did the Norsemen discover? Sat R 48: 49-52 N 6 '65; Discussion. 48:90-1 D 4 '65
When American was called Vinlanda; Vikings' view of New World; with report by M. Steinmann. Life 59:61+ O 22 '65
Who was first? Sr Schol 87:17 O 28 '65
Yale press publishes map discovery of the century. il Pub W 188:31-4 O 11 '65
AMERICA (periodical)
America; editorial and headquarters changes. T. N. Davis. America 113:inside cover Jl 3 '65
Musings of a poetry editor. J. Moffitt. America 113:262 S 11 '65; Discussion. 113:484-5 O 30 '65
Of many things: America's new home. T. N. Davis. America 113:269 S 18 '65
AMERICA (song)
America sings; recorded by the glassmaker. T. H. Marsh. il Hobbies 70:88-9 Je '65
AMERICA in literature
Operas on American subjects, by H. E. Johnson. Review
Opera N il 29:26-8 My 1 '65. Q. Eaton
AMERICA in opera. See America in literature
AMERICA the beautiful. See Songs, American
AMERICAN academy of arts and letters
Political troubles jar American academy; concerning speech by L. Mumford. Pub W 187: 32 My 31 '65
AMERICAN academy of parish clergy (proposed)
American academy of parish clergy; why not? G. E. Westberg. Christian Cent 82:557-8 Ap 28 '65
AMERICAN academy of political and social science, Philadelphia
Latin America tomorrow; report on annual meeting. F. L. Phelps. il Américas 17:13-15 Je '65
Report of the board of directors to the members of the American academy of political and social science for the year 1964. il Ann Am Acad 359:165-70 My '65
Seventy-five years of the Academy; with articles of incorporation. J. C. Charlesworth. il Ann Am Acad 360:172-7 Jl '65
AMERICAN airlines, incorporated
American proposes 50 per cent youth jet fare. Aviation W 83:30 D 20 '65
Astrovision; an in-flight entertainment system. L. C. Keene and T. E. Pierson. il Electr World 73:42-3+ Mr '65
Great air race; transpacific air-transport market. il Time 87:78-9 Ja 14 '66
Previous commercial sales marks broken by American Boeing order. Aviation W 83:34 O 4 '65
Quest for the Holy Grail; American airlines petition for routes to Hawaii and Japan. Newsweek 67:70 Ja 17 '66
AMERICAN arbitration association
Automation has made strikes senseless. A. H. Raskin. il N Y Times Mag p45+ O 31 '65
AMERICAN art biennial of Córdoba. See Art —Exhibitions
AMERICAN artists. See Artists, American
AMERICAN arts council. See Arts councils of America
AMERICAN association for the advancement of science
Election of AAAS officers. il Science 149: 1522-5 S 24 '65
Integrity of science; concerning report of Committee on science in the promotion of human welfare. Sci Am 212:50 F '65
Science cutbacks opposed. Sci N L 89:36 Ja 15 '66
Use of animals in research and teaching. Science 150:147 O 8 '65
Meetings, 1964
Association affairs. il Science 147:891-932+ F 19 '65
Meetings, 1965
Are we finding a way to study the action of the mind? il Science 150:922-4 N 12 '65
Association affairs. Science 148:257-8+; 150: 1638+ Ap 9, D 17 '65
Evolution; background material for papers to presented at AAAS annual meeting. il Science 150:639-42 O 29 '65
Fourth Berkeley meeting. R. L. Taylor. il Science 148:1116-25; 149:454-8 My 21, Jl 23 '65

AMERICAN association for the advancement
of science—Meetings, 1965—*Continued*
Materials science in dentistry, medicine, and
pharmacy; synthetic materials. il Science
150:784 N 5 '65
Natural environment; plans for sessions of
annual meeting. il Science 150:510-12 O 22
'65
132nd AAAS annual meeting, Berkeley, California, 26-31 December 1965; program. il
Science 150:1323-62+ D 3 '65
Physical science. il Science 150:1058-62 N 19
'65
Science fuels its own chain reaction; AAAS
meeting in Berkeley. il Bsns W p 18-19 Ja 1
'66
Steroid hormones and the pill. il Science
150:1189-91 N 26 '65
AMERICAN association of collegiate schools of
business
Stumping the deans. il Bsns W p 106+ My
8 '65
AMERICAN association of junior colleges
Deprived student in the two-year college;
new breed with a new need; summary of
speeches at Conference on the teaching
of remedial English and math. il Pub W
189:26-31 Ja 3 '66
AMERICAN association of law libraries
Copyright controversy; 58th annual meet-
ing. E. J. Bander. il Library J 90:3221-3
Ag '65
AMERICAN association of medical colleges
Who should govern medicine? J. Lear. il
Sat R 48:39-42 Je 5 '65; Discussion. 48:43-5
Jl 3; 56-8 S 4 '65
AMERICAN association of pastoral counselors
Standards needed! Christian Cent 82:692 My
26 '65
AMERICAN association of physical anthro-
pologists
American association of physical anthropolo-
gists; report on 34th annual meeting, 1965.
F. E. Johnston. Science 149:1526 S 24 '65
AMERICAN association of school administra-
tors
Meeting, 1965. Sr Schol 86:sup4 Mr 4 '65
Washington report; annual convention. J.
Lloyd. Sr Schol 86:sup4 Mr 11 '65
AMERICAN association of school librarians
AASL plans its programs for ALA, NEA con-
ferences. Library J 90:2346-8 My 15 '65
Coming of age; report on the youth divisions,
ALA conference, 1965. E. Geller. Library J
90:3699-700 S 15 '65
See also
Knapp school libraries project
AMERICAN association of university professors
A for affluence. il Newsweek 65:68 Ap 19 '65
Academic revolution at St John's. F. Cana-
van. America 113:136-40 Ag 7 '65
Family planning at St John's. J. Leo. Com-
monweal 82:184-8 Ap 30 '65
T.R.B. from Washington; blacklisting col-
leges. New Repub 152:4 Je 26 '65
AMERICAN astronomical society
American astronomers report; highlights of
some papers (cont) il Sky & Tel 29:141-4,
218-22, 356-8; 30:14-15, 211, 275-8 Mr-Ap,
Je-Jl, O-N '65
AMERICAN athletes. See Athletes
AMERICAN authors. See Authors, American
AMERICAN ballet theatre
American ballet theatre. R. Krokover. il
Hi Fi 15:120+ Je '65
Back on solid ground. il Time 85:73 Ap 9 '65
Ballet American style. il Newsweek 65:100
Ap 12 '65
Ballet theatre at twenty-five. E. Coleman.
il Sat R 48:51-3 F 27 '65
Gallery of American ballet theatre choreog-
raphers. J. Anderson. il Dance Mag 40:38-
45 Ja '66
Human element; triumphant 25th anniver-
sary season at New York state theater.
D. Hering. il Dance Mag 39:42-7+ My '65
Music to my ears; Ballet theatre season. I.
Kolodin. Sat R 48:30 Ap 24 '65
Musical events; opening of spring season at
the New York state theatre. W. Sargeant.
New Yorker 41:173 Mr 27 '65
Musical events; performance of Les noces.
W. Sargeant. New Yorker 41:114-15 Ap 10
'65
AMERICAN bankers association
No-strings federal aid finds backers at
forum; Heller plan, supported at ABA
symposium. il Bsns W p28-9 Ap 3 '65
Stop, look, listen, count three; annual con-
ference. il Newsweek 66:85 O 18 '65
AMERICAN Baptist convention. See Baptists
in the United States
AMERICAN bar association
A.B.A.'s no. one issue. Time 86:46 Ag 20
'65
AMERICAN behavioral scientist (periodical)
Universal reference system. Wilson Lib Bul
39:826+ Je '65

AMERICAN Bible society
Op art show at Bible society promotes its
design aims; contemporary art and photog-
raphy used in Bible society publications.
il Pub W 187:150-2 Je 14 '65
AMERICAN bison. See Buffaloes
AMERICAN book company
American company wins piracy suit in Iran.
Pub W 188:37 D 6 '65
AMERICAN book publishers council
ABPC: annual meeting stresses markets,
world trade, freedom to read; symposium;
with editorial comment. il Pub W 187:18-
31, 41 My 24 '65
ABPC: annual sales trends il Pub W 188:
43-5 S 20 '65
ABPC files amicus brief in Ralph Ginzburg
case. Pub W 188:36 N 29 '65; Reply. H. S.
Manges. 188:21 D 13 '65
ABPC files new statement on copyright revi-
sion. Pub W 188:88 S 27 '65
ABPC management seminar discusses sales
stimulants. Pub W 187:38-9 Mr 15 '65
Author-publisher relation viewed in RPG dis-
cussion; meeting of the Religious publishers
group. Pub W 189:46-7 Ja 3 '66
Highspots of activity in major organizations;
1965 in review. Pub W 189:80-1 Ja 17 '66
Marketing committee starts moving. C. B.
Grannis. Pub W 187:53 Mr 1 '65
Scholarly religious book: editing, pricing,
marketing; Religious publishers group
meeting. Pub W 187:20-4 Mr 29 '65
Stanley Heath named an ABPC director.
Pub W 188:63 S 13 '65
Study under way on copyright and tech-
nology. Pub W 189:41 Ja 3 '66
AMERICAN booksellers association
ABA honors the late John W. Barnes. il
Pub W 187:39 My 3 '65
ABA: lively exhibit and discussions mark
65th annual convention; symposium. Pub W
187:42-56 Je 21 '65
ABA: panels on children's book fairs and
trade communications; symposium. il Pub
W 187:43-51 Je 28 '65
ABA regional: booksellers, publishers meet
for two days at Los Angeles. il Pub W
188:28-39 O 25 '65
ABA regional: censorship, expenses, promo-
tion are topics at San Francisco. Pub W
188:40 O 25 '65
ABA regional, Detroit: trade issues and a
new association; summaries of discussions
at meeting. il Pub W 188:36-40 O 4 '65
ABA regionals and local problems. J. A.
Duffy. Pub W 188:75-7 S 13 '65
ABA section. See every other issue of Pub-
lishers' weekly
Highspots of activity in major organizations;
1965 in review. Pub W 189:82-3 Ja 17 '66
Long range role of the ABA. J. A. Duffy.
Pub W 188:323-6 Ag 30 '65
Registration of 2250 at ABA 65th annual
meeting. Pub W 187:74-5 Je 14 '65
AMERICAN broadcasting company
De Gaulle and ABC enter their bids. R.
Burkhardt. New Repub 153:8-9 O 23 '65
Goldenson touch. il Newsweek 65:92+ Ap 19
'65
New show at ABC; N. Simon largest stock-
holder. Time 86:64 Jl 30 '65
Who, me? Hunt and McCall holdings. News-
week 66:55-6 Ag 2 '65
AMERICAN broadcasting company-Interna-
tional telephone and telegraph company merger. See
Business consolidations and mergers
AMERICAN business men. See Business men
AMERICAN can company
Philosophy, American can, and William May.
J. F. Olesky. Duns R 86:73+ O '65
AMERICAN cancer society
Behind the cancer crusade; American can-
cer society's public relations program. L.
L. L. Golden. Sat R 48:75 Ap 10 '65
Bill Gargan's greatest role; actor speaks out
against cancer. il Life 59:63-4 D 3 '65
AMERICAN Catholicism. See Catholic church
in the United States
AMERICAN Catholics. See Catholics in the
United States
AMERICAN chemical society
Duplicating life, by chemistry; highlights of
Atlantic City meeting. il Bsns W p 119-20
S 25 '65
AMERICAN children. See Children—United
States
AMERICAN citizenship. See Citizenship
AMERICAN city (periodical)
American city awards bring recognition. il
Am City 80:170+ Je '65
Busby wins American city aid-to-education
award. Am City 80:12 O '65
1965 merit award winners. il Am City 81:83-6
Ja '66

AMERICAN civil liberties union
ACLU and civil rights for children. V. C.
Blum. America 113:160-3 Ag 14 '65; Reply.
J. G. Neumann and others. 113:249 S 11 '65
A.C.L.U. attacks capital punishment. Christian Cent 82:1150 S 22 '65
ACLU, Authors league, 111 friends urge Supreme court to hear Ginzburg. Library J 90:836 F 15 '65
Civil liberties union backs dean on novel;
Another country. Pub W 187:76 Je 21 '65
Education vs. culture: strange case of the Burbank public library. T. Schoenman.
ALA Bul 60:27-30 Ja '66
New attacks on postal censorship. R. H.
Smith. Pub W 187:63 F 1 '65

AMERICAN coins. See Coins

AMERICAN college students. See College students

AMERICAN colonial history. See United States
—History—Colonial period

AMERICAN Communist party. See Communist party (United States)

AMERICAN conservative union. See Political clubs and associations

AMERICAN conservatory theater. See Pittsburgh—Theater

AMERICAN cookery. See Cookery, American

AMERICAN council on education
Dysphoric generation? Washington meeting.
Newsweek 66:98 O 18 '65

AMERICAN dance festival. See Dance festivals

AMERICAN dance theater
American dance theater, New York state theater. M. Marks. Dance Mag 39:74-6 Ap '65
Repertory dance theater. E. Stodelle. Nat R 17:205-6 Mr 9 '65
Thorny evangelists. il Newsweek 65:92 Mr 15 '65

AMERICAN dancing. See Dancing

AMERICAN designers. See Costume designers

AMERICAN documentation institute
ADI to publish annual review of information science. Library J 90:5229 D 1 '65

AMERICAN drama
America's lost plays, ed. by B. H. Clark.
Review
Nation 200:647-9 Je 14 '65. H. Popkin
Two revolutions: Negro and sexual (or homosexual). R. Brustein. New Repub 152:26-7 Mr 27 '65

AMERICAN eagles. See Eagles

AMERICAN economic assistance. See Economic assistance, American

AMERICAN education (periodical)
From the editor. Am Ed 1:inside cover D '64

AMERICAN education week
Open house in your school; excerpts. il Sr School 87:sup 12-13 O 21 '65

AMERICAN electric power company
Bright lights of American electric. J. Thackray. il Duns R 86:37-8+ D '65
Utility builds power with a hard sell. il Bsns W p77-8+ O 30 '65

AMERICAN express cards. See Credit cards

AMERICAN express company
Oil, vinegar & sugar. il Time 86:81 S 3 '65

AMERICAN express field warehousing corporation
Salad oil mystery. M. Kempton. New Repub 153:9-11 Jl 24 '65

AMERICAN farm bureau federation
Farm bureau plan: end food surpluses. Farm J 90:62 Ja '66
How to shoot Santa Claus. il Time 86:22-6 S 3 '65

AMERICAN federation of labor and Congress of industrial organizations
AFL-CIO convention; strong arm of the status quo. B. J. Widick. Nation 201:516-18 D 27 '65
AFL-CIO council girds for a shake-up; shift to younger leaders. il Bsns W p 162+ S 25 '65
AFL-CIO fights Klan infiltration. Bsns W p47-8 O 23 '65
AFL-CIO looks for new goals. Bsns W p 128 D 4 '65
AFL-CIO units map their 1966 goals.
Bsns W p 148 D 11 '65
AFL-CIO's inner struggle. il Newsweek 66:81-2+ D 20 '65
American labor abroad; Lovestone diplomacy;
with editorial comment. S. Lens. il Nation 201:2, 10-16+ Jl 5 '65
Awaiting Johnson's word on labor. Bsns W p52 My 1 '65

Business joins a union show: Union industries show. Pittsburgh. il Bsns W p 113-14 My 29 '65
Exeunt kookies; biennial convention. il Time 86:14 D 24 '65
Final curtain; labor's aging leaders. Time 86:33 O 1 '65
Hidden power of labor's professionals. T. O'Hanlon. il Duns R 85:58-9+ Ap '65
How much will Johnson do for the unions? il Bsns W p 128+ Mr 6 '65
How the unions would change the country. U S News 59:62-3 D 27 '65
Labor takes a harder line overseas; AFL-CIO is threatening to boycott two top international labor groups. Bsns W p 139-40 Ap 24 '65
Labor's hardening arteries. T. R. Brooks. Duns R 86:45-7 Ag '65
Looking for issues to excite them; shifted emphasis toward social and political goals. il Bsns W p 104-6 D 18 '65
More union differences with LBJ. U S News 58:84 Mr 15 '65
Mutual aid pact eases inter-union disputes; craft and industrial unions pledge unity. il Bsns W p 132 Mr 6 '65
New alliance shapes up in Dixie; AFL-CIO's interest in strike on cotton plantation. il Bsns W p 124+ Jl 10 '65
Nudging out the old guard; AFL-CIO putting younger leaders on its executive council. il Bsns W p 124+ F 20 '65
Old-age club; question of age of members of AFL-CIO council. il Newsweek 65:77 Mr 8 '65
Organized labor's ten years together. New Repub 153:7-8 D 11 '65
Put your dreams away; biannual convention. Nat R 17:1184 D 28 '65
Reuther pours old zip into new campaigns; interested in becoming AFL-CIO president. il Bsns W p92+ N 20 '65
Senate stalls repeal of 14(b) Bsns W p 163-4+ O 9 '65
Ten years of togetherness. T. R. Brooks. il Duns R 86:55-6+ D '65
Union recruiting: new ideas. U S News 59:102 N 15 '65
Unions act on threats to privacy. il Bsns W p87-8 Mr 13 '65
Unions' big goals for '66. il U S News 59:73-4 D 20 '65
Unions seek second round on 14(b) Bsns W p54 O 23 '65
Walter Reuther looks ahead. U S News 59:88 N 29 '65
What unions asked of LBJ: and what they got, repeal of right to work laws. U S News 58:67-9 My 31 '65
Youth movement in top ranks of AFL-CIO; what it means. il U S News 59:89-90 D 13 '65

Building and construction trades department
Union lobby gets the word to fight; attempt to repeal section of Taft-Hartley act. il Bsns W p 134-6 My 8 '65

Committee on political education
Labor's next decade. il Nations Bsns 53:31-3+ Jl '65

Economic policy committee
Push for full employment. T. R. Brooks. Duns R 85:83+ My '65

Industrial union department
Bolstering the rolls; unions campaign for members. Bsns W p60+ Je 19 '65
Labor drives to close the South's open shop; illegal reprisals by Stevens company for union activities. V. Rony. il Reporter 33:31-4 N 18 '65
Next IUD target: the working poor; low-paid service industries. il Bsns W p62+ N 13 '65
Union bid meets rebuff in South; North Carolina vs AFL-CIO campaign. Bsns W p 116 Mr 20 '65

AMERICAN federation of musicians
Unions, legislation, and the courts. L. E. Lunden. Mo Labor R 88:1177-81 O '65

AMERICAN federation of state, county and municipal employees
New constitution for the AFSCME. Mo Labor R 88:III-IV Ag '65

AMERICAN federation of teachers
49th convention of the Federation of teachers. J. F. Strickland. Mo Labor R 88:1204-5 O '65
Should teachers join a union? H. Rudoff; G. Hillman. Parents Mag 40:60-1+ O '65
Teachers' unions: rift without differences. S. Elam. il Nation 201:247-9 O 18 '65

AMERICAN fiction
Crisis in creativity. E. Capouya. il Sat R 48: 32-4 Ap 17 '65
Greatness as a literary standard. S. Kauffman. il Harper 231:151-6 N '65
Other lost generation; literary scene of the 1890s. L. Ziff. Sat R 48:15-18 Mr 20 '65
Wanted: a Protestant novelist. L. Kriegel. Commonweal 83:273+ D 3 '65
Warsaw book fair. H. R. Lottman. Pub W 188:24-7 Jl 26 '65
Willa Cather and The professor's house; anti-Semitism in American literature of the 1920's. J. Schroeter. Yale R 54:494-512 Je '65
See also
Best sellers
Literature, Comparative—English and American
Western stories

AMERICAN flag. See Flags—United States

AMERICAN folk art. See Folk art

AMERICAN folk songs. See Folk songs, American

AMERICAN football coaches association
High-priced bash in Buffalo; All-America game. D. Jenkins. il Sports Illus 23:16-17 Jl 5 '65

AMERICAN football league
Another good Joe for the AFL; rookie game of Boston Patriots vs New York Jets. J. Underwood. il Sports Illus 23:46-9 Ag 9 '65
Bills come storming in; Buffalo wins by defeating San Diego Chargers. E. Shrake. il Sports Illus 24:16-19 Ja 3 '66
Scouting reports. E. Shrake. il Sports Illus 23:72-9 S 13 '65
Separate but equal. il Time 86:74 D 17 '65
Upstaging the AFL. Newsweek 67:44 Ja 10 '66
Where the crowds are. il Newsweek 66:60 O 4 '65

AMERICAN forestry association
AFA's birthday; ninety years of service; revision of 1956 article. S. T. Dana. il Am For 71:14-17+ S '65
Let's talk parks. Am For 71:26-9 Mr '65
Looking ahead at ninety. il Am For 71:13 S '65
Redwoods and parks. S. T. Dana and K. B. Pomeroy. bibliog f il Am For 71:1-32 My '65
Seeds for agreement; AFA for Humboldt. K. B. Pomeroy. il Am For 71:16-18+ Je '65
See also
Trail riders of the wilderness

Committee on forest land ownership
Minnesota compromise; AFA's Minnesota land ownership study. Am For 71:18-19 F '65

AMERICAN Friends service committee
Clarence E. Pickett. H. E. Snyder. Sat R 48: 25+ Ap 24 '65
To succor the suffering; establishment of fund to aid the family of James J. Reeb. Christian Cent 82:357 Mr 24 '65

AMERICAN furniture. See Furniture, American

AMERICAN goldfinches. See Goldfinches

AMERICAN greetings corporation
How the no. 2 greeter is playing its cards. il Bsns W p 154+ F 13 '65

AMERICAN heart association
Heart prescription: an ounce of prevention. il Bsns W p52+ N 6 '65
Lady's hand guides fight on heart disease; H. Taussig, president of AHA. il Bsns W p 130-2+ N 20 '65

AMERICAN high school students. See High school students

AMERICAN historical association
Washington meeting, 1964. Am Hist R 70:957-74 Ap '65

AMERICAN home products corporation

American home foods division
Hurry-up luncheon dishes. M. B. Keiser. il Parents Mag 40:30+ O '65

AMERICAN hospital association
Elderly crowd. Newsweek 66:80 S 13 '65

AMERICAN hot rod association Winter championship. See Automobile racing

AMERICAN humor. See Humor, American

AMERICAN imperialism. See Imperialism

AMERICAN Indian exposition. See Festivals—Oklahoma

AMERICAN institute for foreign study
See also
Travel study courses

AMERICAN institute for foreign trade
Trade school for traders. il Fortune 71:96+ Je '65

AMERICAN Institute for free labor development
American institute for free labor development. M. F. Riche. bibliog f il Mo Labor R 88:1049-55 S '65
American labor abroad; Lovestone diplomacy; with editorial comment. S. Lens. il Nation 201:2, 10-16+ Jl 5 '65
Latin labor's alarming Christians. G. Delmas. il Reporter 32:27-30 F 25 '65

AMERICAN institute of aeronautics and astronautics
AIAA meeting focuses on thermal degradation. R. Pay. Miss & Roc 17:41+ S 27 '65
AIAA meeting reflects new complexity. W. J. Coughlin and others. il Miss & Roc 17:10-13 Ag 2 '65
AIAA stressing better understanding; with preview of second annual meeting. il Miss & Roc 17:18+ Jl 19 '65

AMERICAN institute of architects
A.I.A. announces honor awards for 1965. il Arch Rec 138:43+ Jl '65
A.I.A. details plans for 97th convention. Arch Rec 137:23 Ap '65
A.I.A. discloses designs of three runners-up in headquarters competition. il Arch Rec 137:14+ Mr '65
A.I.A. elects thirty-seven Fellows. Arch Rec 137:23 My '65
Architects pledge major effort in support of environmental goals of Great society. il Arch Rec 138:35-6+ Jl '65
Blueprint of the future. il Newsweek 65:54 Je 28 '65
Cities and people; Cities of the New World conference, symposium, ed. by M. S. Haverstock. il Américas 17:20-5 Ag '65
Convention. il Arch Forum 123:28-9 Jl '65
Gulf states awards. il Arch Rec 137:26 My '65
Harlem's streetcorner architects; Architects renewal committee in Harlem. A. Lopen. il Arch Forum 123:50-1 D '65
Mitchell/Giurgola win A.I.A. competition; design of headquarters building. il Arch Rec 137:10 F '65

AMERICAN institute of graphic arts
AIGA children's book show; summary. P. A. Bennett. il Pub W 188:76-8+ S 6 '65
AIGA: stimulus for excellence. C. B. Grannis. Pub W 187:44 My 3 '65
Attracting young people is topic of Trade book clinic; production end of publishing. Pub W 188:114-15 D 6 '65
Children's book show of 1965, AIGA. C. B. Grannis. Pub W 188:63 Ag 9 '65
Color in print: AIGA-Safran seminar on color language and reproduction. il Pub W 187: 106-11 Mr 1 '65
Leonard Baskin, graphic artist; AIGA medalist, 1965. J. A. Bennett. il Pub W 187: 70-1+ Ap 5 '65

Trade book clinic
In defense of children's books: price, quality, durability; summary of addresses at meeting. U. Nordstrom; D. Hagen; R. Kraus. Pub W 187:33-4 Mr 15 '65

AMERICAN institute of iron and steel. See American iron and steel institute

AMERICAN institute of nutrition
Metric conversion: petition to Congress. R. W. Engel. Science 148:1670 Je 25 '65

AMERICAN institute of steel construction
Familiar buildings win A.I.S.C. awards. Arch Rec 138:346+ O '65

AMERICAN intellectuals. See Intellectuals

AMERICAN investments abroad. See Investments, Foreign

AMERICAN iron and steel institute
Four winners are announced in steel awards competition. il Arch Rec 137:10 Mr '65
How steel widens its targets; promotes off-beat uses. il Bsns W p 120+ Mr 27 '65
Steel takes stock, stays on cheerful side; AISI meeting. il Bsns W p30-1 Je 5 '65

AMERICAN kennel club
Immaculate doghouse. R. H. Boyle. il Sports Illus 22:64-8+ F 15 '65

AMERICAN LaFrance corporation
Stripped down for action, at fires. il Bsns W p 108 S 18 '65

AMERICAN legion
Mr Ottinger sees it through. Nation 200:518 My 17 '65

AMERICAN legion magazine
Profile of a magazine. R. B. Pitkin. Writer 78:3-4 O '65

AMERICAN liberalism. See Liberalism

AMERICAN libraries abroad
Attacks on U.S. libraries abroad. W. W. Brickman. Sch & Soc 93:204 Ap 3 '65
Crucial battle for the minds of men; USIA libraries. H. W. Axford. bibliog Library J 90:2499-503 Je 1 '65

AMERICAN library association—Membership—
  Continued
New benefits under ALA group insurance.
  R. N. Foulk. ALA Bul 59:110-11 F '65
Opinions in black and white. D. M. Broderick.
  il Library J 90:1994-5 Ap 15 '65
President vs. parliamentarian; midwinter
  conference report. E. Moon. il Library J
  90:1063-6 Mr 1 '65

Notable books council
  See American library association—Adult
  services division

Office for recruitment
  See American library association—Library administration division

Program evaluation and budget
  committee
Program evaluation and budget committee;
  midwinter conference report. ALA Bul 59:
  196-8 Mr '65

Research and development, Office of
ALA library research clearinghouse. J. F.
  Krug. ALA Bul 60:72 Ja '66

Subscription books committee
Subscription books reviewing by ALA.
  H. K. Prince. ALA Bul 59:685 S '65

Young adult services division
Adult books for young people, 1964. Library J
  90:1493-4 Mr 15 '65; Same. Pub W 187:45-6
  Mr 1 '65; Wilson Lib Bul 39:608+ Ap '65
Coming of age; report on the youth divisions.
  ALA conference, 1965. E. Geller. il Library J 90:3700 S 15 '65
AMERICAN library directory
Questionnaires sent for library directory.
  Pub W 188:35 N 1 '65
AMERICAN library trustee association
Planning team. C. E. Reid. Library J 90:
  3214-15 Ag '65
AMERICAN literature
Literary mind. A. Kazin. Nation 201:203-6
  S 20 '65
Men of the '30s. R. Kostelanetz. Commonweal 83:266-9 D 3 '65
Sagas of the underprivileged. G. Hicks. il
  Sat R 48:29-30 Ag 28 '65
  See also
American fiction
American poetry
Authors, American

History
Decolonization of American literature; address, April 1965. K. Shapiro. il Wilson Lib
  Bul 39:842-53 Je '65; Discussion. 40:172-5 O
  '65

Jewish authors
Analyzing the American dream. G. Hicks.
  Sat R 48:33-4 My 1 '65
Jews and Americans, by I. Malin. Review
  Commentary 39:97-100 Je '65. G. P. Elliott
  Nat R 17:556+ Je 29 '65. M. Geltman
Sentimentalizing the Jews. R. Alter. Commentary 40:71-5 S '65; Discussion. 40:27-8+
  D '65

South
Notes in the literary scene: their own language. D. L. Rubin, jr. Harper 230:173-5
  Ap '65
AMERICAN Lutheran church. See Lutheran
  church in the United States
AMERICAN machine and foundry company
Aiming at a high score in bowling; AMF's
  automatic pinspotters. il Bsns W p 124-5+
  N 27 '65
AMERICAN management association
Papers from the AMA winter conference, excerpts. M. E. Stone; H. G. Crook. Mo Labor
  R 88:401-2 Ap '65
Schools make news; Impact of educational
  technology conference issues. Sat R 48:57
  Ag 21 '65
AMERICAN medical association
AMA and the Catholic press. B. L. Masse.
  America 113:583+ N 13 '65
AMA asks hospital aid. Sci N L 88:167 S 11
  '65
AMA budget. New Repub 152:6 Je 5 '65
A.M.A. convention. New Yorker 41:18 Jl 3 '65
AMA: doctors' organization faces growing
  outside criticism, wide range of policy problems. E. Langer. Science 149:282-3+ Jl 16
  '65
AMA in disarray. New Repub 153:7 Jl 10 '65
AMA shifts criticism; attacking proposed
  heart disease, cancer and stroke plan. F.
  Marley. Sci N L 88:85 Ag 7 '65

AMA: the restrictive power. E. Rayack. il
  Nation 200:470-9 My 3 '65
Colds, gout, overweight: what's new; meeting. U S News 59:12 D 13 '65
Doctor prescribes for the AMA; hard look at
  record of organized medicine in United
  States. J. G. Freymann. Harper 231:76-80
  Ag '65
Doctor Ward's last words; AMA opposition
  to medicare bill. Time 85:28-9 My 21 '65
Doctors' debate: what to do when medicare
  comes is main topic of stormy AMA session.
  E. Langer. Science 149:164-7 Jl 9 '65
Doctors' revolt in U.S? the battle over medicare; meeting. il U S News 59:26-8 Jl 5 '65
Eldercare v. medicare. Time 85:22 F 19 '65
Health program attacked. Sci N L 87:284 My
  1 '65
How AMA research into smoking will help
  you. R. M. McKeown. Todays Health 43:
  12-13 Ag '65
Impact of medicare. S. Meisler. il Nation 200:
  481 My 3 '65
In medicine, a year of wide gains; highlights
  of AMA convention. il Bsns W p60-1 Jl
  3 '65
Just a minute, doctor. K. Crawford. Newsweek 65:34 Mr 15 '65
Medicare vs. the AMA's latest substitute.
  Consumer Rep 30:148-9 Mr '65
New health act; AMA criticism reflected in
  adoption of bill on heart, cancer, and
  stroke. E. Langer. Science 150:323-4 O 15
  '65
Texas tornado. il Time 85:54 My 28 '65
Tobacco and health; research report. K. N.
  Anderson. il Todays Health 43:26-34 Jl: 34-
  40+ S '65
Wait & see; annual convention. il Time 86:36
  Jl 2 '65
What the AMA really fears. W. P. Keim.
  New Repub 152:11-12 F 13 '65; Discussion.
  152:35-6 Mr 6; 27-9 Mr 20; 28-9 Ap 10; 44
  Ap 17 '65
What the doctors ordered. il Newsweek 66:
  59-60 Jl 5 '65
Why are doctors out of step? L. Lasagna;
  reply. E. L. Young. New Repub 152:29
  F 6 '65
Your doctor and the A.M.A. J. Bird. il Sat
  Eve Post 239:13-17+ Ja 1 '66

Institute for biomedical research
Research with the brakes off; symposium.
  Todays Health 43:41-59 N '65
AMERICAN merchant marine. See Merchant
  marine—United States
AMERICAN meteorological society
Cloudy and dry; forty-fifth annual meeting.
  New Yorker 41:30-1 F 20 '65
AMERICAN military assistance. See Military
  assistance, American
AMERICAN motors corporation
AMC slowdown. Newsweek 66:85 D 20 '65
AMC's troubles. il Newsweek 65:76+ F 15
  '65
At American motors, length and luxury.
  J. P. Norbye. il Pop Sci 187:83 O '65
Better way: restyled cars. il Time 85:92 My
  14 '65
Holding action for AMC? Newsweek 66:75-6
  S 20 '65
How to bury a job; U.A.W.'s Kenosha strike.
  il Time 86:77-8 S 3 '65
Is auto union asking a veto? il U S News
  59:77-8 S 6 '65
Now, layoffs by one auto maker. U S News
  59:76 D 20 '65
Rambler drives away from old ad agency;
  Geyer, Morey & Ballard. Bsns W p 108+
  Mr 6 '65
Ready for the big race; aiming to fight the
  big three. il Bsns W p36 S 18 '65

Kelvinator division
Making the kitchen a decorator's dream;
  Kelvinator originals. il Bsns W p 116-17+
  N 20 '65
AMERICAN museum of natural history, New
  York
Beachboy caper. J. Roth. Esquire 64:118-19+
  S '65
Nature behind the scenes; photographs. G.
  Berliner. Natur Hist 74:34-9 My '65
Science in action; confessions of a curator.
  S. Anderson. Natur Hist 74:60-4 O '65
Science in action; students in the museum.
  B. M. Hecht. Natur Hist 75:66-7 Ja '66
AMERICAN music center (organization)
American music center. J. Browning. il Opera
  N 29:33 Ap 3 '65
AMERICAN Negroes. See Negroes in the
  United States

AMERICAN newspaper guild
Crack appears in press deadlock; Herald tribune resumes publication. il Bsns W p 116+ O 2 '65
Newsmen v. printers; typographers defiance of automation. Time 86:74 S 3 '65
Papers back in New York. Bsns W p70 O 16 '65
AMERICAN newspapers. See Newspapers— United States
AMERICAN novelists. See Novelists, American
AMERICAN novels. See American fiction
AMERICAN nurses association
Impact of integration on the nursing profession; historical sketch. M. E. Carnegie. bibliog Negro Hist Bul 28:154-5+ Ap '65
AMERICAN occupation of Japan. See Japan— History—Allied occupation, 1945-1952
AMERICAN opera society
Billy Budd returns. J. W. Freeman. il Opera N 30:14-15 Ja 1 '66
Donizetti's Lucrezia Borgia; concert performance in Carnegie Hall. P. J. Smith. il Hi Fi 15:98 Jl '65
Music to my ears; new version of Billy Budd. I. Kolodin. Sat R 49:48 Ja 22 '66
Music to my ears; performance of Donizetti's Roberto Devereux. I. Kolodin. Sat R 49:38 Ja 1 '66
Musical events; concert performance of Donizetti's Lucrezia Borgia. W. Sargeant. New Yorker 41:177-8 My 1 '65
Musical events; performance of Britten's Billy Budd. W. Sargeant. New Yorker 41:103 Ja 15 '66
Musical events; performance of Donizetti's Roberto Devereux. W. Sargeant. New Yorker 41:52 D 25 '65
New York international. R. D. Daniels. Opera N 29:33 My 1 '65
New York; performance of Roberto Devereux at Carnegie Hall. R. D. Daniels. il Opera N 30:33 Ja 15 '66
Trump and no-trump; Turco in Italia. R. D. Daniels. Opera N 29:33 Mr 20 '65
AMERICAN overseas libraries. See American libraries abroad
AMERICAN painting. See Painting, American
AMERICAN personnel and guidance association
Meeting, 1965. Sr Schol 86:sup 1 My 6 '65
AMERICAN philosophical society
APS elects twenty-five members. Sci N L 87:308 My 15 '65
AMERICAN philosophy. See Philosophy, American
AMERICAN playwrights theatre (organization)
Aptitude test; Dallas theater center production. H. Hewes. il Sat R 48:28 Je 19 '65
Fifty stages for one good show. T. Prideaux. Life 59:20 N 19 '65
AMERICAN poetry
Books in the field; poetry. R. Hart. bibliog il Wilson Lib Bul 40:440-59 Ja '66
Weighed and found wanted. W. Stafford. Poetry 106:429-32 S '65
World and self; instances. G. Sorrentino. Poetry 106:306-9 Jl '65
See also
Poetry (periodical)
AMERICAN portraits. See Portraits, American
AMERICAN power boat association
More power to you. M. Crook. See issues of Yachting
AMERICAN propaganda. See Propaganda
AMERICAN public opinion. See Public opinion —United States
AMERICAN public works association
APWA story. Am City 80:8 Ag '65
AMERICAN reporters. See Reporters and reporting
AMERICAN research development corporation
Idealist, with a realistic touch; build up creative men and support their ideas. il Bsns W p 166-8+ Mr 20 '65
AMERICAN revolution. See United States— History—Revolution
AMERICAN rocket society. See American institute of aeronautics and astronautics
AMERICAN SAMOA
Classroom TV comes to Samoa. T. Kaser. il Sat R 48:58-9+ Je 19 '65
Samoa: America's showplace of the South Seas. C. W. Hall. il Read Digest 87:157-64+ N '65
Talofa, Normal N. Anderson. il Ebony 21:54-6+ Ja '66
AMERICAN school in Switzerland
Breather year; precollege travel and European studies program. il Time 85:77-8 My 28 '65
AMERICAN scientists. See Scientists, American
AMERICAN seamen. See Seamen

AMERICAN Shakespeare festival theatre and academy, Stratford, Conn.
Finding Shakespeare. J. Novick. Nation 201:45-7 Jl 19 '65
Gags & good intentions can't tame a shrew. E. Coleman. Life 59:13 Jl 23 '65
Stratford: a theatre in search of itself. R. Hapgood. il Reporter 33:37-9 S 9 '65
Stratford II. J. Novick. Nation 201:65-6 Ag 2 '65
Style in progress; season's productions. H. Hewes. Sat R 48:23 Jl 10 '65
AMERICAN slang. See Slang
AMERICAN society for Christian ethics conference. See Religious conferences
AMERICAN society of civil engineers
Four projects vie for engineering award. Am City 80:177+ Mr '65
AMERICAN society of landscape architects
Landscape architects hold 65th annual meeting. il Arch Rec 138:356+ S '65
AMERICAN society of newspaper editors
Freedom of information. W. J. Coughlin. Miss & Roc 16:46 Ap 26 '65
AMERICAN society of range management
Range management convention. Nat Parks Mag 39:24 My '65
AMERICAN society of tool and manufacturing engineers
Cheaper automatic machining; numerical controls. il Bsns W p58-60 Ap 10 '65
AMERICAN soldiers. See United States—Army
AMERICAN specialist program. See United States—Diplomatic and consular service
AMERICAN standards association
Standards to protect the buying public; proposed creation of a national standards institute. J. Ridgeway. New Repub 152:9-10 My 1 '65
AMERICAN stock exchange
Retreat from Wall Street. il Newsweek 66:68 Ag 16 '65
AMERICAN strategy. See Strategy
AMERICAN students. See College students
AMERICAN students in foreign countries
Students on the move. G. D. Patterson; H. D. F. Kitto. il Sat R 48:67-8+ F 20 '65
Wandering scholars. il Sr Schol 86:12-13 Mr 11 '65
AMERICAN students in Germany; in Israel; etc. See Foreign students in Germany; Foreign students in Israel; etc.
AMERICAN symphony orchestra
Musical events (cont) W. Sargeant. New Yorker 41:170 Ap 17; 169 My 8; 202 O 16 '65
AMERICAN teachers in foreign countries
My fourteen originals; creative writing course at American university in Cairo. J. Stuart. il Sr Schol 86:sup5-6 My 20 '65
AMERICAN technical assistance. See Technical assistance, American
AMERICAN telephone and telegraph company
A.T.&T: a study in federalism. R. Sheehan. il Fortune 71:142-7+ F '65
Competing with AT&T; Los Alamos telephone system. New Repub 152:7 F 6 '65
Specialists try a wider track; management development problem. il Bsns W p56-7 Jl 31 '65
Wage chronology: A.T.&T. long lines department, 1953-64. il Mo Labor R 88:48-60 Ja '65
See also
Government investigations—American telephone and telegraph company
AMERICAN textbook publishers institute
ATPI and the textbook: a coming of age; annual meeting. il Pub W 187:22-35 My 17 '65
Deprived student in the two-year college; new breed with a new need; summary of speeches at Conference on the teaching of remedial English and math. il Pub W 189:26-31 Ja 3 '66
Highspots of activity in major organizations; 1965 in review. Pub W 189:81 Ja 17 '66
Study under way on copyright and technology. Pub W 189:41 Ja 3 '66
Textbook needs in urban education; American textbook publishers institute and the Great cities research council meeting, Los Angeles; summaries of addresses. il Pub W 188:16-27 D 6 '65
AMERICAN tiger club. See Aviation clubs
AMERICAN tobacco company
Passing the sweets; American tobacco company moves to acquire Chicago's Consolidated foods corp. Time 85:84+ F 12 '65
AMERICAN tourists. See Travelers
AMERICAN translators association
English with tears; Ford grant to establish a national translation center. D. Dempsey. Sat R 48:38+ F 13 '65

AMERICAN trucking association, incorporated
Truckers shift gears for a changing load; surge of less-than-truckload freight. il Bsns W p 166+ N 6 '655

AMERICAN university press services, incorporated
AUPS, international projects, reports, debates; report of annual membership business meeting of AAUP. il Pub W 188:55-7+ Jl 19 '65

AMERICAN visitors in England; in India; etc.
See Foreign visitors in England; Foreign visitors in India; etc.

AMERICAN water works association
Spotlight on water supply; annual conference. Am City 80:8 Je '65

AMERICAN West publishing company
George Pfeiffer starts new publishing company. il Pub W 187:97-8 F 8 '65

AMERICAN wines. See Wine

AMERICAN women. See Women—United States

AMERICAN writers. See Authors, American

AMERICANISM
See also
Patriotism

AMERICANS
America the middle-aged. L. Heren. Harper 231:100+ Ag '65
American image will take care of itself. D. Acheson. il N Y Times Mag p24-5+ F 28 '65
Americans: the national experience, by D. J. Boorstin. Review
America 113:412-13 O 9 '65. W. L. Lucey
Time il 86:118+ O 1 '65
America's mood today. L. Gross. il Look 29: 15-21 Je 29 '65
Bold men, bold dreams. C. D. Bowen. Read Digest 87:49-53 Jl '65
Changing mood of America; what a nation-wide survey shows. il U S News 58:36-43 My 31 '65
Goodness is as goodness does; our image abroad; address, May 30, 1965. J. A. McCain. Vital Speeches 31:598-600 Jl 15 '65
How America lives (cont) Ladies Home J 82:56+ Ap; 56-9+ My; 68-9+ Je; 62-3+ Jl; 74-5+ Ag; 74-5+ S; 82-4+ O; 92-3+ N '65
Man in the American mask. J. Barzun. For Affairs 43:426-35 Ap '65
Mea culpa; worries about personal failings. il Newsweek 65:29 Je 21 '65
Parochial American. W. Pfaff. Commonweal 82:581-2 Ag 20 '65
Search for identity, ed. by R. L. Shinn. Review
Christian Cent 82:1131-2 S 15 '65. S. J. Rowland, jr
What motivates American whites? K. B. Clark. il Ebony 20:69-74 Ag '65
See also
Californians
Southerners
Texans
Women—United States

AMERICANS abroad. See Americans in foreign countries

AMERICANS for democratic action
Crrrack! criticism of Johnson administration by ADA. Nat R 17:1061-2 N 30 '65

AMERICANS in Austria
Fellow-American. R. Berczeller. New Yorker 41:50-6 S 25 '65

AMERICANS in Ecuador
Peace corps forestry: there's a forest in your future! F. Friedman. il Am For 71: 20-1+ F '65

AMERICANS in England
Yank in Sherwood Forest. K. Kister. bibliog il Library J 90:4914-20 N 15 '65

AMERICANS in Europe
Notes of a bad American. A. Karlen. il Holiday 38:8+ Jl '65

AMERICANS in foreign countries
Americans around the world; symposium, ed. by G. Nikolaiess. il Sr Schol 86:6-20+ Mr 11 '65
Discrimination against overseas Americans; Arab states and South Africa. Christian Cent 83:4 Ja 5 '66
Globe-trotting t-men follow the taxpayers; help Americans abroad with tax returns. il Bsns W p 112+ Mr 27 '65
In my opinion; living abroad is a drag, unless you truly leave home. D. Buitron. Seventeen 24:194 D '65
Innocents abroad: the expatriates' lot. G. F. Dickover. Mo Labor R 88:143-5 F '65
Jobs overseas: daydreams and data. R. Hoffmann. il Mlle 60:178-81+ Mr '65

What youngsters learn from foreign lands. B. Miles. il Parents Mag 40:52-3+ Ap '65
Yankees who don't go home; American businessman abroad. il Bsns W p48+ Jl 24 '65
See also
American teachers in foreign countries
United States—Armed forces—Forces in foreign countries

AMERICANS in France
Speaking out; I hate Paris in the springtime. R. Daley. Sat Eve Post 238:10+ Je 5 '65
See also
United States—Air force—Forces in France

AMERICANS in Germany
See also
United States—Armed forces—Forces in Europe

AMERICANS in Great Britain
Miss Adams in love; London in 1785. L. Mayo. il Am Heritage 16:36-49+ F '65

AMERICANS in Israel
Settling in Israel? R. Sanders. Commentary 40:37-44 Ag; Discussion. 40:24+ N '65

AMERICANS in Paris. See Americans in France

AMERICANS in Russia
My life as a Soviet prisoner. P. Landerman. il Sat Eve Post 239:32-6+ Ja 15 '66
Tell my parents not to worry; P. Landerman, only American prisoner in Russia. G. Feiffer. il Sat Eve Post 238:33-4+ F 13 '65

AMERICANS in Switzerland
Mack Sennett comedy. N. Stewart. New Yorker 41:46-8 O 2 '65

AMERICANS in Turkey
Banished American: K. Baldwin. il Time 85: 44 Je 25 '65

AMERICANS in Vietnam
Good-by, Saigon; evacuation of U.S. dependents. W. Tuohy. il Newsweek 65: 35-6 F 22 '65
Loaded with morality; murder of J. Grainger by Viet Cong. Newsweek 65:38 Ap 26 '65
President sends Christmas greetings to Americans in Viet-Nam; Presidential message, December 23, 1964. L. B. Johnson. Dept State Bul 52:76 Ja 18 '65

AMERICAS. See America

AMERICA'S future, incorporated
America's future promotes library gift book package. Library J 90:2800+ Je 15 '65

AMERICIUM
Inventor of the month; two new elements, two patents. S. V. Jones. Sci Digest 57: 15 F '65

AMERICUS, Ga.
Americus the beautiful. il Newsweek 66:30 S 20 '65

AMERIKA (periodical)
Sellout in the Soviet; Kennedy issue. il Newsweek 65:83 Ap 5 '65

L'AMÉRIQUE; drama. See Barrault, J. L.

AMERY, Julian
Trouble in Palestine. New Repub 153:30-2 D 4 '65

AMES, Nancy
This is the girl that is. por Newsweek 65:58 Ap 5 '65

AMES, Winslow
Vermont statehouse and its furniture. Antiques 88:200-4 Ag '65

AMES, Ia.
City girds for the Dutch-elm-disease battle. R. E. Speer, jr. il Am City 80:132-3 Je '65

AMEX. See American express company; American stock exchange

AMFT, M. J.
Becky and I; story. Seventeen 24:128-9 N '65
Is it a vice or a talent? story. Seventeen 24: 136-7 My '65
Michael I and Michael II; story. Seventeen 24:228-9 Ag '65
My most unforgettable experience of last summer; story. Seventeen 24:140-1 F '65

AMHERST, Mass.

Courts

Lest the world forget; Justice Charles I. Lincoln's final report to the town. Time 85:63 Mr 26 '65

AMIBEN. See Herbicides

AMIGOS (student welfare project) See Mexico —Relief work

AMIN, Mustafa
Down and out. por Newsweek 67:30-1 Ja 10 '66
Interrupted lunch. il por Time 86:35 Ag 6 '65

AMINO acids
Amino acid changes provoked by streptomycin in a polypeptide synthesized in vitro. D. Old and L. Gorini. bibliog il Science 150: 1290-2 D 3 '65
Amino acids made simply. il Sci N L 87:227 Ap 10 '65

AMINO acids—*Continued*

Amino acids released from the cerebral cortex in relation to its state of activation. H. H. Jasper and others. bibliog il Science 147:1448-9 Mr 19 '65

Control of enzyme activity in growing bacterial cells by concerted feedback inhibition. L. Burlant and others. bibliog il Science 148:1351-3 Je 4 '65

Hemoglobin Ftexas: gamma-chain variant. R. G. Schneider and R. T. Jones. bibliog il Science 148:240-2 Ap 9 '65

Histones and basic polyamino acids stimulate the uptake of albumin by tumor cells in culture. H. J.-P. Ryser and R. Hancock. bibliog il Science 150:501-3 O 22 '65

Immunoglobulin structure: partial amino acid sequence of a Bence Jones protein. K. Titani and others. bibliog il Science 149:1090-2 S 3 '65

New symbols for the amino acid residues of peptides and proteins. D. Wellner and A. Meister. il Science 151:77-8 Ja 7 '66

Optical second-harmonic generation in crystalline amino acids. K. E. Rieckhoff and W. L. Peticolas. bibliog il Science 147:610-11 F 5 '65

Peptide synthesis from amino acids in aqueous solution. C. Ponnamperuma and E. Peterson. bibliog il Science 147:1572-4 Mr 26 '65

Protein synthesis in rat liver: influence of amino acids in diet on microsomes and polysomes. A. Fleck and others. bibliog il Science 150:628-9 O 29 '65

Release of dissolved amino acids by marine zooplankton. R. E. Johannes and K. L. Webb. bibliog Science 150:76-7 O 1 '65

Second mutant gene affecting the amino acid pattern of maize endosperm proteins. O. E. Nelson and others. bibliog il Science 150:1469-70 D 10 '65

What's so important about proteins? D. G. Cooley. il Todays Health 43:46-51+ O '65
    See also
Phenylalanine

AMINODICHLOROBENZOIC acid. See Herbicides

AMINOLEVULINATE dehydratase. See Enzymes

AMIS, Kingsley

Does James Bond really hate women? excerpt from James Bond dossier. Ladies Home J 82:47+ Jl '65

Science fiction: a practical nightmare. Holiday 37:8+ F '65

AMISANO, Joseph

Why did you make the building black? Arch Rec 138:150-1 D '65

AMISH Mennonites. See Mennonites

AMMI visnagi. See Umbelliferae

AMMIDON, Hoyt

Making risk-taking pay at U.S. trust. il por Bsns W p 138-40+ Mr 20 '65

AMMONIA

Ammonia's new world: more plant, less crew; largest synthetic ammonia plant, Lake Charles, La. il Bsns W p 134-6+ N 13 '65

Customers rush for the ammonia. il Bsns W p70-1 Jl 24 '65

AMMONIUM dihydrogen phosphate. See Ammonium phosphates

AMMONIUM phosphates

Growth layers on ammonium dihydrogen phosphate. J. L. Torgesen and R. W. Jackson. bibliog il Science 148:952-4 My 14 '65

AMMONS, A. R.

Halfway; Landscape with figures; Ithaca, N.Y; Composing; poems. Poetry 106:270-3 Jl '65

AMMUNITION
    See also
Bullets
Cartridges

AMNESIA

Anticholinesterase-induced amnesia and its temporal aspects. J. A. Deutsch and others. bibliog il Science 151:221-3 Ja 14 '66

Brief temporal gradient of retrograde amnesia independent of situational change. D. Quartermain and others. bibliog il Science 149:1116-18 S 3 '65

Difficult childhood may cause amnesia. Sci N L 88:259 O 23 '65

AMNESTY International (organization)

They fight to free the world's prisoners of conscience I. Ross. Read Digest 86:131-5 F '65

AMNION

Triploidy in a human cell line. J. D. Regan and J. B. Smith. bibliog il Science 149:1516-17 S 24 '65

AMOR Artis, incorporated. See Choral groups and societies

AMOROSO, Shirley

Face to face: with a girl who couldn't cry. por Seventeen 24:202 My '65

AMORTIZATION deductions

Easing the write-off rules: liberalization of depreciation allowances. Bsns W p31 F 20 '65

Money-saving tax guidelines on machinery. F. Bailey, jr. il Suc Farm 64:60+ Ja '66

AMORY, Cleveland

Calorie crisis in dietland. Sat R 48:40 Ap 10 '65

AMORY, Miss.

Up-to-the-minute middle school for very low cost. il Arch Rec 137:178-9 Mr '65

AMOS, Wayne

Riley's route to the eternal now. Read Digest 86:227-8+ F '65

AMOS, William H.

Living sand. il Nat Geog Mag 127:820-33 Je '65

AMPAL-American Israel corporation

Priming Israel's economy. il Bsns W p45-6+ Mr 6 '65

AMPHETAMINES

Drug puzzle; student use of drugs. M. Herr. Mlle 61:246-7+ Ag '65

Thrill-pill menace. B. Davidson. il Sat Eve Post 238:23-7 D 4 '65

Use of pep pills; a growing problem. U S News 58:8 F 22 '65

AMPHIBIA
    See also
Eye (amphibia)

            Eggs

Protein synthesis in enucleated eggs of rana pipiens. L. D. Smith and R. E. Ecker. bibliog il Science 150:777-9 N 5 '65

AMPHIBIANS (airplanes) See Airplanes, Amphibious

AMPHIBIOUS motor trucks. See Motor trucks, Amphibious

AMPHIPOD

Hotspur and the amphitoe. A. F. Loomis. il Yachting 117:212+ Ap '65

AMPLIFIERS

Amplifier gain nomogram. M. H. Applebaum. il Electr World 74:25 Ag '65

Amplifier module electrifies guitar. M. E. McGrew and N. Fried. il Pop Electr 22:64-6 Je '65

Booster for FM stereo. L. Cantor. il Electr World 73:83-4 My '65

Build a stereo bal. D. Gordon. il Pop Electr 22:48-9+ Je '65

Flame used as amplifier to produce intense sound. Sci N L 89:38 Ja 15 '66

Fluid amplifiers gain wider industrial niche. il Bsns W p 118+ N 13 '65

Interflex; hi-fi and stereo speaker system. E. Stowell. il Pop Mech 124:194-8 S '65

Low-noise TV and FM signal booster. R. B. Cooper. il Electr World 74:30 N '65

Negative feedback, positive result. I. B. Berger. Sat R 48:71 N 27 '65

New challenger to electronics; fluid amplification. H. E. Klein. il Duns R 85:48-50 Je '65

Partaking of power. I. B. Berger. Sat R 48:61 Je 12 '65

Power-output nomogram. M. H. Applebaum. il Electr World 73:29 My '65

Power pitfalls. I. B. Berger. Sat R 48:67+ Ap 24 '65

Selective audio amplifiers. J. Kyle. il Electr World 74:84-8 Jl '65

Silicon transistor i.f. amplifier for FM tuner. D. R. Von Recklinghausen. il Electr World 74:32-3+ O '65

Solid-state designs for hi-fi amplifiers. P. Marcus and L. Zide. il Electr World 73:49-52+ Je '65

Solid-state 6-watt amplifier for ten bucks. C. E. Fenoglio. il Pop Electr 23:73-5+ N '65

Sound advice. R. Flanzraich. Mod Phot 29:101 Ap '65

Two-compactron stereo amplifier. P. E. Hatfield. il Pop Electr 23:43-6 Jl '65

200-watt solid-state stereo amplifier. M. Sharma and R. Berkovitz. il Electr World 73:44-7 Mr '65
    See also
Man amplifiers
Masers
Transistors
Traveling wave tubes
Tunnel diodes

            Noise

Low-noise r.f. amplifiers. J. Kyle. il Electr World 74:71-4 D '65

AMSBERG, Claus von

Love conquers all. il por Newsweek 66:41-2 Jl 12 '65

Prince watsisname. il Time 86:29 Jl 2 '65

AMSTERDAM, Anthony G.
Prodigious professor. por Time 86:68 D 10 '65
AMSTERDAM, Netherlands

Music

Amsterdam. J. Mindszenthy. il Opera N 30:
34 Ja 15 '66
Mozart and Haydn in Holland. B. Jacobson.
il Hi Fi 15:167 S '65
Notes from our correspondents (cont) J. de
Kruijff. Hi Fi 15:22+ O '65
AMULETS
See also
Charms
AMUSEMENT parks
Disneyland East; Florida project. Newsweek
66:82 N 29 '65
Disney's wider world; Florida project. il
Bsns W p21 D 25 '65
Japan's playland puts car makers in driver's
seat; Suzuka circuit amusement park. il
Bsns W p52-4 Ap 3 '65
See also
Coney Island
Disneyland park, Anaheim, Calif.

Concessions

See Concessions (food, etc)
AMUSEMENTS
Where are they going? teen-agers choices. il
Esquire 64:46-7 Jl '65
See also
Childrens amusements
Hobbies
Night clubs
AMVER (automated merchant vessel report
system) See United States—Coast guard
AMY, Robert L. and Storb, R.
Selective mitochondrial damage by a ruby
laser microbeam: an electron microscopic
study. bibliog Science 150:756-8 N 5 '65
AMY Loveman national award
Barns, books, and a bonanza; 1965 Amy Love-
man award. J. F. Fixx. Sat R 48:25 Je 19
'65
AMYGDALA. See Cerebellum
ANAEROBIC bacteria. See Bacteria, Anaerobic
ANAHEIM, Calif.
See also
Disneyland park

Education

Brookhurst plan; an experiment in flexible
scheduling, Brookhurst junior high school.
E. B. Hofmann. il NEA J 54:50-2 S '65
ANALEPTICS
Drug for the comatose; methylphenidate. Sci
Digest 58:36 O '65
New treatment for coma. Time 86:67-8 Jl
16 '65
ANALOG computers. See Computers—Analog
computers
ANARCHISM and anarchists
Aftermath to Harlem riot; Epton anarchy
trial. F. J. Donner. il Nation 201:355-8+
N 15 '65
Anarchists. by J. Joll. Review
Commonweal 82:296-8 My 21 '65. R.
Sanders
Newsweek il 65:90 Mr 29 '65
Sat R 48:34-5 Ap 24 '65
Seeds of liberation, ed. by P. Goodman.
Review
New Repub 152:20-2 Mr 20 '65. A. Kop-
kind
We want bread and roses too. J. L. Feather-
stone. New Repub 152:26+ Ap 17 '65; Re-
ply. P. Cowan. 152:34+ My 1 '65
ANARCHISTS. See Anarchism and anarchists
ANATOMICAL models
Human body; how it works. il Sci Digest
57:69-70 Mr '65
ANATOMY
See also
Anatomical models

Study and teaching

Bodies by bequest. il Time 86:70 Ag 27 '65
ANCESTRY. See Heredity
ANCHOR Bible. See Bible—Versions
ANCHOR corporation
Lonely responsibility of Tom Jones; institu-
tional traders. il Bsns W p 164 O 23 '65
When change hits a billion-dollar fund. il
Bsns W p 158+ O 23 '65
ANCHORAGE, Alaska

Sanitary affairs

Inspecting 11½ miles of sewers from the inside. H. D. Shanks. il Am City 80:118+ S
'65

ANCIENT history. See History, Ancient

AND be my love; story. See Humason, S. W.
M.
AND things that go bump in the night; drama.
See McNally, T.
ANDALUSIA, Spain
Zany Costa del Sol. P. Bowles. Holiday
37:78-9+ Ap '65
ANDELMAN, Morten B.
Let's wipe out measles this year. por Parents
Mag 40:36 My '65
ANDERS, Edward
Diamonds in meteorites; with biographical
sketch. Sci Am 213:10, 26-36 O '65
—and Arnold, J. R.
Age of craters on Mars. bibliog Science 149:
1494-6 S 24 '65
ANDERS paints a picture; drama. See As-
brand, K.
ANDERSEN, Christian A. See Lovering, J. F.
jt. auth.
ANDERSEN, Hans Christian
Duckling into swan. por Newsweek 66:109-
109A+ D 6 '65
Wild swan, by M. Stirling. Review
Sat R 49:81 Ja 8 '66. H. T. Moore
Time il por 86:62 D 24 '65
ANDERSON, Andy D.
Color it green. il Newsweek 65:76 Mr 8 '65
ANDERSON, Benedict R.
Indonesia: united against progress. Cur Hist
48:75-81 F '65
ANDERSON, C. Alan
New developments in New Thought. bibliog f
Christian Cent 83:78-80 Ja 19 '66
ANDERSON, Charles B.
About booksellers and bookselling; adapta-
tion of address. Pub W 188:64-5 Jl 5 '65
ANDERSON, Clifton
Great commoner. Christian Cent 82:1481 D
1 '65
ANDERSON, Clinton Presba
Atoms for peace: the dream, the reality. N Y
Times Mag p 10-11+ Ag 1 '65
Books. Bul Atomic Sci 21:42-4 Mr '65
Excerpt from address, January 6, 1965. Cong
Digest 44:78+ Mr '65
Excerpt from debate, June 24, 1964. Cong
Digest 44:48+ F '65
Wilderness act, a constructive measure. Liv
Wildn 86:3-4 Spr '64
ANDERSON, Donald Jack
Old fur trader. Field & S 70:50-2+ O '65
Old Snakeroot. Field & S 69:40-1+ Mr '65
Rabbits; some with antlers. Field & S 70:
48-50+ N '65
Water wolves. Field & S 70:40-2+ Je '65
ANDERSON, Donny
Lone Star Ranger. H. L. Masin. por Sr Schol
87:20 O 28 '65
ANDERSON, Duwayne M. and Hoekstra, Pieter
Crystallization of clay-adsorbed water. bib-
liog Science 149:318-19 Jl 16 '65
ANDERSON, Erica
Albert Schweitzer: the African years. Sat R
48:19-20+ S 25 '65
Schweitzer and Lambaréné; photographs.
Sat R 48:28-9 S 25 '65
ANDERSON, Forddy
Tradition sprouts in a cornfield. G. Holland.
il pors Sports Illus 24:42-5 Ja 10 '66
ANDERSON, Frank J.
Recruitment release. Library J 90:829 F 15
'65
ANDERSON, Gail V.
What kind of anesthetic for childbirth? ex-
cerpt. Redbook 124:32+ Mr '65
ANDERSON, Gary
He shot the works! H. L. Masin. il Sr Schol
86:34 My 6 '65
ANDERSON, Henry
Note on hedonic price indexes. bibliog Mo
Labor R 88:658-60 Je '65
ANDERSON, Hugh R.
Spacecraft description and encounter se-
quence. Science 149:1226-8 S 10 '65
ANDERSON, Irvin C. See Mitchell, R. L. jt.
auth.
ANDERSON, J. W.
Special hell for children in Washington.
Harper 231:51-6 N '65
ANDERSON, Jack
Anna Galina. Dance Mag 39:25-7 Je '65
Dancer's bookshelf (cont) Dance Mag 39:49+
Je: 47-8+ N '65
Don't say you're a dancer! Dance Mag 39:
47-9 F '65
For looking, for learning, and for fun. Dance
Mag 39:28-30 S '65
Night, window, wind; poem. Nation 200:263
Mr 8 '65
Rembrandt's The anatomy lesson. Dance Mag
39:46-8 Je '65
Spring; poem. Nation 200:286 Mr 15 '65
Towards a dance film library. Dance Mag
39:40-2 S '65
(ed) See Tamiris, H. First and second
thoughts about a dance career

ANESTHESIOLOGISTS. See Anesthetists

ANESTHETICS
Feeling no pain. J. J. Lentz. il Todays Health 43:60-3+ D '65
New anesthetic powerful. Sci N L 88:326 N 20 '65
What kind of anesthetic for childbirth? excerpt. G. V. Anderson. Redbook 124:32+ Mr '65

ANESTHETISTS
Anesthesia: which drugs are used when? G. G. Greer. Bet Hom & Gard 43:38+ Jl '65
Responsibility beyond surgery. il Time 86: 70+ N 5 '65

L' ANGE de feu; opera. See Prokof'ev, S. S.

ANGEL, James Crawford
Bush pilot of Angel Falls. C. Mydans. il por Life 59:80-2+ O 15 '65

ANGEL FALLS, Venezuela
Bush pilot of Angel Falls; son's pilgrimage to the wonder found by his father. C. Mydans. il Life 59:80-2+ O 15 '65
To the highest waterfall in all the world. il Sunset 135:24-6+ S '65

ANGEL of fire; opera. See Prokof'ev, S. S.

ANGELL, Roger
Keeping up with the outs. New Yorker 41:24-7 My 29 '65
NCMSB report. New Yorker 41:47-8+ F 20 '65
Send now for birchbark brochure. New Yorker 41:40-1 Mr 27 '65
Sporting scene (cont) New Yorker 41:192+ O 30 '65

ANGELOFF, Sam
Go to V.D.C. house, say I sent you. por Life 59:110+ D 10 '65

about
Blond beard for a four-week Vietnik. G. P. Hunt. pors Life 59:3 D 10 '65

ANGELS, Christmas. See Christmas decorations

ANGER
Rage in the lab; Feshbach experiment. R. G. G. Price. il Atlan 216:116-18 D '65
Why it's dangerous to get mad. C. Price. il Farm J 89:D6 Mr '65

ANGINA pectoris. See Heart—Diseases

ANGIONEUROTIC edema. See Edema

ANGIOSPERM parasite. See Parasitic plants

ANGIOTENSIN
Arterial hypertension elicited by subpressor amounts of angiotensin. J. W. McCubbin and others. il Science 149:1394-5 S 17 '65

ANGKOR, Cambodia
Angkor before and after. R. Sneyers. il UNESCO Courier 18:28-9 Ja '65

ANGLES (metal work)
Build anything with slotted angle. il Pop Mech 125:158-9 Ja '66

ANGLEWORMS. See Earthworms

ANGLICAN church. See Church of England

ANGLING. See Fishing

ANGLO-AMERICAN relations (non-political) See England and the United States

ANGLO-SAXON poetry
See also
Beowulf

ANGUS, Robert
Sound advice. Mod Phot 29:30+ F; 36+ Mr; 12+ Jl; 80+ O '65
Survey of solid-state stereo receivers. Hi Fi 16:50-5 Ja '66

ANHALT, Edward
Life of a wordsmith. por Time 85:76+ Ap 16 '65

ANHEUSER-Busch, incorporated
Can is lighter if not the brew; all-aluminum cans. il Bsns W p90+ Jl 10 '65

ANHINGA trail. See Everglades National Park

ANIMAL behavior. See Animals—Habits and behavior

ANIMAL calling
Anyone can call predators; tape recordings. R. Tinsley. il Field & S 70:10-12+ N '65
Art of varmint calling. D. Niehuis. il Outdoor Life 136:36-9+ Ag '65

ANIMAL communication
Animal communication. T. A. Sebeok. bibliog il Science 147:1006-14 F 26 '65
Dancing, buzzing show bee language evolution. Sci N L 88:79 Jl 31 '65
Sound: an element common to communication of stingless bees and to dances of the honey bee. H. Esch and others. bibliog il Science 149:320-1 Jl 16 '65
Subtle talk of animals gives clues for humans. Sci N L 87:343 My 29 '65
See also
Sound production by animals

ANIMAL doctors. See Veterinarians

ANIMAL ecology. See Zoology—Ecology

ANIMAL experimentation
Animal-care legislation; letter. E. D. Jacobson. Science 149:375 Jl 23 '65; Discussion. 149:917; 150:1536 Ag 27, D 17 '65
Arthropod preparation for behavioral, electrophysiological, and biochemical studies. W. C. Corning and others. bibliog il Science 148:394-5 Ap 16 '65
Costly cat aids deafness research. il Todays Health 43:75 Je '65
High blood pressure? it may be in your genes; experiments on rats at Brookhaven national laboratory. il Bsns W p90+ Ap 3 '65
Mice swim in drug study. Sci N L 88:355 D 4 '65
Primate colony dedicated; Yerkes regional primate research center, Atlanta, Ga. il Sci N L 88:311 N 13 '65
See also
Laboratory animals
Maze tests
Vivisection

ANIMAL intelligence
See also
Animals—Habits and behavior
Learning, Psychology of
Memory

ANIMAL language. See Animal communication

ANIMAL locomotion
Mechanics of a turnover: bell contractions propel jellyfish. V. N. Argo. il Natur Hist 74:26-9 bibliog(p74) Ag '65
See also
Horses—Paces, gaits, etc.

ANIMAL pets. See Pets

ANIMAL populations
Disaster from overcrowding. B. H. Frisch. il Sci Digest 58:69-73 Jl '65
Out of the park; Kenya's elephant surplus. il Newsweek 66:42 S 20 '65
Self-regulating systems in populations of animals; adaptation of address, December 26, 1964. V. C. Wynne-Edwards. bibliog Science 147:1543-8 Mr 26 '65; Discussion. 148: 892-3, 1669; 149:135+, 814 My 14, Je 25, Jl 9, Ag 20 '65
Territorial needs and limits. E. T. Hall. il Natur Hist 74:12-19 bibliog(p66) D '65
Winter animal show is now under way in snowy Yellowstone. il Sunset 135:31-2 D '65

Control
Birth control planned to halt the coyote; stilbestrol for preventing pregnancy. Sci N L 87:152 Mr 6 '65
Early population checked. Sci N L 87:231 Ap 10 '65
Ill-advised program; tsetse-fly control through elimination of big-game animal populations in Southern Rhodesia. Nat Parks Mag 39:19 Ap '65
Ranches for wild beasts. B. Tufty. il Sci N L 87:234-5 Ap 10 '65
Regional dog-control program; Sussex County, N.J. B. C. Spragg. il Am City 80: 104-5 N '65

ANIMAL repellents
Controlling animals in the garden. W. R. Eadie. il Horticulture 44:26-7 Ja '66

ANIMAL sculpture
Buffalo sculpture for a California high school. R. Reynolds. il Am Artist 30:54-7+ Ja '66

ANIMAL shelters
Mother Cecilia's revolt. il Life 58:45-6 Je 4 '65

ANIMAL sounds. See Sound production of animals; Sound production by fishes

ANIMAL stealing. See Animal thefts

ANIMAL stories. See Newspapers—Animal stories

ANIMAL surgery. See Veterinary surgery

ANIMAL temperature. See Temperature, Animal and human

ANIMAL thefts
Lost pets that stray to the labs; unscrupulous dognappers. C. Phinizy. il Sports Illus 23:36-8+ N 29 '65

ANIMAL toys. See Toys

ANIMAL tracks and trails
Mysterious horseshoe tracks on Wolf Mountain; Jackson County, N.C. M. N. Reed. il Am For 71:32-4 N '65
Wandering enteropneust from the abyssal Pacific, and the distribution of spiral tracks on the sea floor. D. W. Bourne and B. C. Heezen. bibliog il Science 150:60-3 O 1 '65

ANIMALS
Nature note; animal kingdom. Sci N L 88: 155 S 4 '65
See also
Pets
Wildlife
Zoological gardens
Zoology
also names of animals, e.g. Bears

Accidents and hazards
See also
Automobile driving—Animal hazards

Diseases and pests
Wasting disease induced with cortisol acetate; studies in germ-free mice. N. D. Reed and J. W. Jutila. bibliog il Science 150:356-7 O 15 '65

Eyes
See Eye (animals)

Food
Eatometer: a device for continuous recording of free-feeding behavior; experiment with rats. D. Fallon. bibliog il Science 148: 977-8 My 14 '65; Reply with rejoinder. P. B. Porter. 149:764 Ag 13 '65

Habits and behavior
Anatomy of violence. J. P. Scott. il Nation 200:662-6 Je 21 '65
Animal behavior quiz. J. Daugherty and M. Daugherty. il Sci Digest 58:87-9 N '65
Day length and food caches; photoperiods cue the flying squirrel. I. Muul. il Natur Hist 74:22-7 Mr '65
Dream phase necessary; paradoxical sleep of cats. Sci N L 87:342 My 29 '65
Endocrines, behavior, and population. J. J. Christian and D. E. Davis; reply with rejoinder. N. C. Negus and E. Gould. Science 149:376+ Jl 23 '65
Food imprinting in the snapping turtle, chelydra serpentina. G. M. Burghardt and E. H. Hess. bibliog il Science 151:108-9 Ja 7 '66
Genotype and prenatal and premating stress interact to affect adult behavior in rats. J. M. Joffe. bibliog il Science 150:1844-5 D 31 '65
Isle Royale: laboratory of Lake Superior; links between timber wolf, moose and browse. L. D. Mech. il Nat Parks Mag 39: 4-8 D '65
Mus musculus: experimental induction of territory formation. P. K. Anderson and J. L. Hill. bibliog il Science 148:1753-5 Je 25 '65
Paradoxical sleep: deprivation in the cat. J. Siegel and T. P. Gordon. bibliog il Science 148:978-80 My 14 '65
Primates: communication and social interactions; report on international symposium. S. A. Altmann. Science 149:886-7 Ag 20 '65
Rabbit: frequency of suckling in the pup. M. X. Zarrow and others. bibliog il Science 150:1835-6 D 31 '65
Return of the wild beasts. E. Will. il Am For 71:6-7+ Ag '65
Safari! Africa. G. A. Kistler. il Sr Schol 86:sup 13-14 Mr 18 '65
Self-regulating systems in populations of animals; adaptation of address, December 26, 1964. V. C. Wynne-Edwards. bibliog il Science 147:1543-8 Mr 26 '65; Discussion. 148: 892-3, 1669; 149:135+, 814 My 14, Je 25, Jl 9, Ag 20 '65
Territorial needs and limits. E. T. Hall. il Natur Hist 74:12-19 bibliog(p66) D '65
Tooth and a claw; what makes animals fight? J. George. il Read Digest 88:149-50+ Ja '66
Why the lion leaps; territorial instinct. il Newsweek 67:51 Ja 3 '66
Wild heritage, by S. Carrighar. Review
  Life 58:12+ Mr 26 '65. F. Russell
Wildlife; exhibit at Time and Life building. New Yorker 41:43-4 S 11 '65
See also
Courtship of animals
Hibernation
Periodicity
Sex behavior

Language
See Animal communication

Memory
See Memory

Migration
Orientation of ambystoma maculatum: movements to and from breeding ponds. C. R. Shoop. mibliog il Science 149:558-9 Jl 30 '65
See also
Orientation

Orientation
See Orientation

Photographs
Animal pictures make good fillers; excerpts from Baby animals, ed. by H. Reich. il Sat R 48:72-3 D 11 '65

Protection
Of whales and whaling. N. Simon. Science 149:943-6 Ag 27 '65
On endangered species. P. M. Tilden. Natur Hist 75:12A Ja '66
Saved: Australia's delightful wildlife. il Sci Digest 58:58-65 S '65
Surinam animal rescue; new dam traps wildlife in high water. J. R. Smith. il Natur Hist 75:24-9 Ja '66
Threatened animals. P. M. Tilden. Natur Hist 74:66 Ag '65
See also
Animals—Treatment
Wildlife conservation
Wildlife sanctuaries

Protective equipment
See Defense mechanisms (biology)

Sight
See Sight—Animals

Sleep
See Animals—Habits and behavior

Stories
See also
Newspapers—Animal stories

Training
Animal act; A. A. Dobritch, agent for performing animals. il Newsweek 65:95A-95B Mr 15 '65
Domesticated dolphin. il Sci Digest 57:14-15 My '65
In defense of bird brains. R. J. Herrnstein. il Atlan 216:101-4 S '65
Monkeys for the moon; with pictures. Sci Digest 58:66-9 O '65
Trained porpoise released in the open sea. K. S. Norris. bibliog Science 147:1048-50 F 26 '65

Treatment
All heaven in a rage, by E. S. Turner. Review
  Newsweek il 65:91 Mr 29 '65
  Sports Illus 22:10+ Ap 19 '65. D. Barnes
Do animals have rights? Nation 201:404 N 29 '65
On the bestial floor. W. S. Merwin. Nation 200:313-14 Mr 22 '65
What does violence say about man? J. W. Krutch. Sat R 48:18-19 Mr 27 '65; Discussion. 48:29 Ap 24; 25 My 8 '65

ANIMALS, Blessing of. See Blessing
ANIMALS, Cruelty to. See Animals—Treatment
ANIMALS, Domestication of. See Domestication
ANIMALS, Effect of cold on; Effect of radiation on; etc. See Cold—Physiological effects; Radiation—Physiological effects; etc.
ANIMALS, Experiments on. See Animal experimentation
ANIMALS, Extinct
See also
Dinosaurs
ANIMALS, Food habits of. See Animals—Food
ANIMALS, Geographical distribution of. See Geographical distribution of animals and plants
ANIMALS, Laboratory. See Laboratory animals
ANIMALS, Mythical
Sir Tashi and the yeti. N. W. Ross. il Horizon 7:104-11 Spr '65
ANIMALS, Performing. See Animals—Training
ANIMALS, Predatory
Close look at predator control. T. Trueblood. il Field & S 69:28+ Ap '65
New federal predator policy? recommendation of Department of Interior's advisory board on wildlife management. C. W. Buchheister. Audubon Mag 67:221 Jl '65

Bounties
Bounty system; South Dakota's fox-pheasant relationship. Nat Parks Mag 39:20 Ap '65
ANIMALS, Rescue of. See Animals—Protection
ANIMALS, Respiration of. See Respiration
ANIMALS, Sound production by. See Sound production by animals
ANIMALS, Treatment of. See Animals—Treatment

ANIMALS as carriers of infection
Hemorrhagic fever war rages; suspected carriers; rodents and bats. F. Marley. il Sci N L 87:74-5 Ja 30 '65
Visiting pet monkey gives children dysentery. Sci N L 87:265 Ap 24 '65

ANIMALS in art
Portfolio of animals in art, with commentary by the editors. il Am Artist 29:73-9 Je '65
See also
Animal sculpture
Design, Decorative—Animal forms

ANIMALS in fiction. See Animals in literature

ANIMALS in literature
Babar pays us a visit at last. il Life 59:107-9 N 26 '65
See also
Bestiaries
Pets in literature

ANIMALS on television programs
Welcome Lassie; conservation background of new series. E. H. Gregg, jr. and G. A. Kovar. il Am For 71:2-3+ Mr '65

ANIMATED cartoons. See Moving pictures—Animated cartoons

ANISE
Touch of aniseed. C. Claiborne. il N Y Times Mag p41 Jl 25 '65

ANISFIELD-Wolf awards
SR-Anisfield-Wolf awards. R. Brown. il Sat R 48:44+ My 1 '65

ANISOMORPHA buprestoides. See Walking-sticks (insects)

ANKER, Susie
Curl up and read. Seventeen 24:170 O; 144+ D '65

ANN-MARGRET
I dig that! ed. by E. Miller. pors Seventeen 24:138-9+ F '65

ANN ARBOR, Mich.
Ann Arbor's trees; Miss Dean's bequest to city for planting, care, replacement and maintenance of its trees. A. H. Wing. Horticulture 43:16 D '65
Holding basin cuts bypasses. J. C. Seeley. Am City 80:22 D '65

ANNA Lisa's nose; story. See Berriault, G.

ANNAPOLIS naval academy. See United States naval academy, Annapolis

ANNE, princess of Great Britain
England's firebrand princess. R. Lecler. il pors Good H 160:20+ My '65

ANNELIDS
Annelid ciliary photoreceptors. P. A. Lawrence and F. B. Krasne. bibliog il Science 148: 965-6 My 14 '65
Nature note; segmented worms. Sci N L 89: 31 Ja 8 '66

ANNUAL meetings, Stockholders. See Stockholders meetings

ANNUALS (plants)
Annuals for the New Year; 1966. Pop Gard 17:28-9 Ja '66
Modern annuals for modern gardens. J. B. Brimer. il Flower Grower 52:38-9 F '65
Sixteen annuals for spring and how to use them. il Flower Grower 52:38-9 Ap '65
Taking care of your annuals. il Sunset 135: 160+ Jl '65
You'll see red when you see these annuals. E. G. Pierce. il Pop Gard 17:24-5+ Ja '66

ANNUALS, High school. See High school annuals

ANNUITIES
See also
Insurance, Life

ANNULMENT of marriage. See Marriage—Annulment

ANODIZING of aluminum. See Aluminum—Protection

ANOMALOUS dispersion. See Dispersion

ANOMALY'S eyes; story. See MacNeal, M.

ANONYMOUS telephone calls. See Telephone calls

ANOTHER Cinderella; drama. See Fontaine, R.

ANOTHER man's family; drama. See Cable, H.

ANOUILH, Jean
Colombe. Criticism
Newsweek 65:93 Mr 15 '65

ANOXEMIA
Fatty change of the granular pneumocyte. E. Valdivia and others. bibliog il Science 151:213-14 Ja 14 '66
Hepatic glycogen depletion in amphiuma during induced anoxia. F. L. Rose and others. bibliog il Science 147:1467-8 Mr 19 '65
Hypoxia: a medical aid? Sci N L 87:150 Mr 6 '65
Oxygen deficiency may damage offspring. Sci N L 88:312 N 13 '65

ANOXIA. See Anoxemia

ANSAY, Nadine
Champion turns a wrong into right. C. Goren. il Sports Illus 23:60-1 S 27 '65

ANSERMET, Ernest
Only one of its kind, introd. to Pelléas et Mélisande. por Am Rec G 31:692-3 Ap '65

ANSOFF, H. Igor
Firm of the future. Harvard Bsns R 43:162-3+ S '65

ANSON, Ruth
Teen-age TV reporter. S. Gordon. il pors Look 29:44+ O 5 '65

ANT bears, African. See Aardvarks

ANTARCTIC ice fish. See Ice fish, Antarctic

ANTARCTIC REGIONS
Anomalous erosional topography in Victoria Land, Antarctica; Wright Dry Valley. H. T. U. Smith. bibliog il Science 148:941-2 My 14 '65
Antarctica, continent of international science; adaptation of address, December 28, 1965. L. M. Gould. il Science 150:1775-81 D 31 '65
Antarctica: world's most fascinating icebox. J. Wolfert. Read Digest 87:119-23 S '65
Life at Antarctic U. T. O. Jones. il Am Ed 1:29-32 N '65
Rescue in the polar ice pack. E. A. McDonald. il Pop Mech 124:92-6+ D '65
Science probes Antarctica. B. Tufty. il Sci N L 87:358-9+ Je 5 '65
See also
Botany—Antarctic Regions
Geology—Antarctic Regions
Queen Maud Range
Zoology—Antarctic Regions

ANTARCTIC research. See Polar research

ANTARCTIC treaty, 1959
Antarctica, continent of international science; adaptation of address, December 28, 1965. L. M. Gould. il Science 150:1775-81 D 31 '65
President Johnson meets with Antarctic policy group; statement, May 1, 1965 and remarks, May 20, 1965. L. B. Johnson. Dept State Bul 52:1013-15 Je 21 '65

ANTARCTICITE. See Calcium chloride hexahydrate

ANTELOPE ground squirrels. See Squirrels

ANTELOPE hunting
Sables are hard to hit. J. O'Connor. il Outdoor Life 136:44-5+ Jl '65
Up to our necks in nyalas. J. O'Connor. il Outdoor Life 135:50-1+ Je '65
Waterbuck by the yard. W. Page. il Field & S 70:26-7 Ag '65
See also
Pronghorn hunting

ANTELOPE refuges. See Wildlife sanctuaries

ANTELOPES
Right horn implantation in the common duiker. G. Child and A. S. Mossman. Science 149:1265-6 S 10 '65
Territorial behavior among puku in Zambia. A. De Vos. il Science 148:1752-3 Je 25 '65

ANTENNA rotators. See Television antennas

ANTENNAS (electronics)
Antenna will withstand nuclear blast. il Miss & Roc 17:33-5 Jl 5 '65
Antenna with big ideas. Consumer Rep 30: 165-6 Ap '65
ETR antenna gets wide-range ability. R. Pay. il Miss & Roc 16:26-7 My 24 '65
Hardened antennas pose problems. J. F. Judge. il Miss & Roc 17:24+ N 1 '65
RAE to utilize 750-1,000-ft. antennas; radio astronomy explorer satellite. D. E. Fink. il Aviation W 83:106-7+ S 27 '65
S-band shakedown slated at Guam. C. D. LaFond. il Miss & Roc 17:34-5 S 20 '65
Unique low-noise antenna developed; rugged antenna for ground use in satellite communication. C. D. LaFond. il Miss & Roc 16:24-5 Je 21 '65
See also
Radar—Antenna and scanning mechanisms
Radio antennas
Television antennas

ANTES, Horst
Madcap moralist; German expressionist. il Time 86:86-7 O 1 '65

ANTES, John
Birth of chamber music in America. J. W. Barker. il Am Rec G 32:34-6 S '65

ANTHEMS
Music to be patriotic by. Time 86:44+ O 15 '65

ANTHOLOGIES
Fiction writer faces facts. N. Hale. il Sat R 48:23-5+ Je 12 '65
Weighed and found wanted. W. Stafford. Poetry 106:429-32 S '65

ANTHONY, H. M.
From CQ to Mayday. Motor B 115:140+ My '65

ANTHONY, Irvin
Cats with more than nine lives. Yachting 117:210+ Mr '65
ANTHONY, Katharine Susan
Obituary
Pub W 188:43-4 N 29 '65
ANTHONY, Mother Mary. See Mary Anthony, Mother
ANTHONY, Mary
Day is mine, the land is mine. J. Fox. il pors Dance Mag 39:50-3 Mr '65
Mary Anthony; Jack Moore and companies, East 74th street theatre. J. Maskey. Dance Mag 40:18 Ja '66
ANTHONY, Susan B.
Heiresses of Susan B. Anthony. P. Mesta. McCalls 92:86 F '65
ANTHRACENE
Structure of 9,9,10,10-tetrachloroanthracene. N. F. Yannoni and others. bibliog il Science 148:231 Ap 9 '65
ANTHRAX
Annals of medicine; case of skin anthrax, with report by P. S. Brachman. B. Roueché. New Yorker 41:51-2+ Ap 24 '65
ANTHROPOLOGICAL museums
Mexico city has a stunning new museum; Museum of anthropology. il Sunset 135:54+ N '65
ANTHROPOLOGY
Some present aspects of physical anthropology. W. W. Howells. bibliog f Ann Am Acad 357:127-33 Ja '65
See also
American association of physical anthropologists
Man
Man, Prehistoric
ANTIARTHRITIC substances
New drugs aid arthritis; indocin and butazolidin. Sci N L 88:373 D 11 '65
ANTIBIOTICS
Antibiotics, how pediatricians use them. L. W. Sauer. il PTA Mag 60:33-4 Ja '66
Antibiotics: the duplication problem; letter. S. A. Waksman. bibliog Science 147:1396-7 Mr 19 '65
Antimicrobial agents and chemotherapy; report on fourth Interscience conference on antimicrobial agents and chemotherapy. M. H. Lepper and D. Perlman. Science 147:522 Ja 29 '65
Base specificity in the interaction of polynucleotides with antibiotic drugs. D. C. Ward and others. bibliog il Science 149:1259-63 S 10 '65
Cancerous tumor masses shrunk by antibiotic; mithramycin. Sci N L 87:98 F 13 '65
Drug antagonism between lincomycin and erythromycin. L. J. Griffith and others. bibliog il Science 147:746 F 12 '65
Inhibition of protein synthesis by spectinomysin. J. Davies and others. bibliog il Science 149:1096-8 S 3 '65
Osteomyelitis checked by effective new drug; Lincocin. Sci N L 88:313 N 13 '65
See also
Actinomycin
Kasugamycin
Penicillin
Pesticins
Puromycin
Streptomycin
Tetracyclines
ANTIBODIES. See Antigens and antibodies
ANTICHOLINESTERASES
Anticholinesterase-induced amnesia and its temporal aspects. J. A. Deutsch and others. bibliog il Science 151:221-3 Ja 14 '66
ANTICOAGULANTS (medicine)
Cancer, clotting linked. Sci N L 87:114 F 20 '65
ANTI-COLONIALISM. See Colonies
ANTI-COMMUNIST measures. See Communism—Anti-Communist measures
ANTI-COMMUNIST measures in the United States. See Communism—United States—Anti-Communist measures
ANTI-COMMUNIST movements

Cuba
Man for one season; E. G. Menoyo. Newsweek 65:49 F 8 '65

Indonesia
Indonesian army sets back Communists; Indonesian Communist party, PKI. Bsns W p31-2 O 16 '65
Justice in Djakarta; anti-Chinese campaign. il Time 86:39B-40 O 22 '65
One place Communists met a setback. il U S News 59:46+ O 18 '65
ANTI-DEPRESSANTS. See Depressants

ANTI-DEPRESSION measures. See United States—Economic policy
ANTIDEUTERON. See Particles (nuclear physics)
ANTIEVOLUTION legislation. See Evolution—Laws and legislation
ANTI-FREEZE solutions
Anti-freeze. il Consumer Bul 48:2+ N '65
ANTIGENS and antibodies
Abnormal immune mechanism in allogeneic radiation chimeras. N. Gengozian and others. bibliog il Science 149:645-7 Ag 6 '65
Adaptive enzyme synthesis: its inhibition as a possible analogue of immunological tolerance. D. W. van Bekkum and H. T. M. Nieuwerkerk. bibliog il Science 149:548-50 Jl 30 '65
Adult thymectomy: effect on recovery from immunologic depression in mice. A. P. Monaco and others. bibliog il Science 149:432-5 Jl 23 '65
Antibodies against the component polypeptide chains of bovine insulin. Y. Yagi and others. bibliog il Science 147:617-19 F 5 '65
Antibodies in gastric juice. J. M. Fisher and others. bibliog il Science 150:1467-9 D 10 '65
Antibodies to DNA and a synthetic polydeoxyribonucleotide produced by oligodeoxyribonucleotides. O. J. Plesca and others. bibliog Science 148:1102-3 My 21 '65
Antibody-complement complexes. W. F. Willoughby and M. M. Mayer. bibliog il Science 150:907-8 N 12 '65
Antibody induction and tolerance; excerpts from address, February 25, 1965. O. Smithies. bibliog Science 149:151-6 Jl 9 '65
Antigen-antibody reaction: nature of complex initiating delayed hypersensitivity. B. B. Levine. bibliog il Science 149:205-7 Jl 9 '65
Bacteria as an indicator of formation of antibodies by single spleen cells in agar. S. A. Schwartz and W. Braun. bibliog il Science 149:200 Jl 9 '65
Bursa of Fabricius in chickens: possible humoral factor. R. L. St Pierre and G. A. Ackerman. bibliog il Science 147:1307-8 Mr 12 '65
Cellular origin of hyaluronateprotein in the human synovial membrane. S. Blau and others. bibliog il Science 150:353-5 O 15 '65
Complement and hemolytic antibody: changes in their activity induced by mercaptoethanol. M. M. Frank and others. bibliog il Science 147:742-3 F 12 '65
Contact-induced cytotoxicity by lymphoid cells containing foreign isoantigens. E. Möller. bibliog il Science 147:873-4+ F 19 '65
Focal antibody production by transferred spleen cells in irradiated mice. J. H. L. Playfair and others. bibliog il Science 149:998-1000 Ag 27 '65
Hybrid antibody molecules with allotypically different L-polypeptide chains. M. Mannik and H. Metzger. bibliog il Science 148:383-5 Ap 16 '65
Immunoadsorbent for the isolation of purine-specific antibodies. H. H. Weetall and N. Weliky. bibliog il Science 148:1235-7 My 28 '65
Immunodiffusion: detection of a murine leukemia virus, Rauscher. M. A. Fink and C. A. Cowles. bibliog il Science 150:1723-5 D 24 '65
Immunoelectrophoresis reveals collagen solubility in human serum. J. Frey and others. bibliog il Science 150:751-2 N 5 '65
Immunogenicity and role of size: response of guinea pigs to oligotyrosine and tyrosine derivatives. F. Borek and others. bibliog il Science 150:1177-8 N 26 '65
Immunoglobulin structure: amino- and carboxyl-terminal peptides of type I Bence Jones proteins. K. Titani and F. W. Putnam. bibliog Science 147:1304-5 Mr 12 '65
Immunologic tolerance in thymectomized, irradiated rats grafted with thymus from tolerant donors. K. Isaković and others. bibliog il Science 148:1333-5 Je 4 '65
Induction in vitro of antibodies to phage T2: antigens in the RNA extract employed. H. P. Friedman and others. bibliog il Science 149:1106-7 S 3 '65
Involvement of thymus in immune response of rabbits to somatic polysaccharides of gram-negative bacteria. M. Landy and others. bibliog il Science 147:1591-2 Mr 26 '65
Isoantigens of gamma globulin in pigs. B. A. Rasmusen. bibliog il Science 148:1742-3 Je 25 '65
Kidney homografts: uptake of fluorochrome-labeled tissue extracts by lymph node cells. J. L. Tong and others. bibliog il Science 149:753 Ag 13 '65

ANTIGENS and antibodies—*Continued*

Lattice formation in complement fixation: studies with univalent rabbit antibody. H. H. Fudenberg and others. bibliog il Science 148:91-3 Ap 2 '65

Lens fiber differentiation and gamma crystallins: immunofluorescent study of Wolffian regeneration. C. Takata and others. bibliog il Science 147:1299-301 Mr 12 '65

Lymphocytic-choriomeningitis virus in hamster tumor: spread to hamsters and humans. A. M. Lewis, jr. and others. bibliog Science 150:363-4 O 15 '65

Macroglobulin-producing plasma-cell tumor in mice: identification of a new light chain. K. R. McIntire and others. bibliog il Science 150:361-3 O 15 '65

Malignant lymphomas following allogenic disease: transition from an immunological to a neoplastic disorder. R. S. Schwartz and L. Beldotti. bibliog il Science 149:1511-14 S 24 '65

Moloney virus-induced leukemias of mice: measurement in vitro of specific antigen. G. Haughton. bibliog il Science 147:506-7 Ja 29 '65

Passive transfer of the action of Freund's adjuvant by serum of rabbits injected with the adjuvant. D. L. Dawe and others. bibliog il Science 148:1345-7 Je 4 '65

Polypeptide chains of antibody: effective binding sites require specificity in combination. O. A. Roholt and others. bibliog il Science 147:613-15 F 5 '65

Primary immune reactions in organ cultures. A. Globerson and R. Auerbach. bibliog il Science 149:991-3 Ag 27 '65

Rabbit 19S antibodies with allotypic specificities of the a-locus group. G. W. Stemke and R. J. Fischer. bibliog il Science 150:1298+ D 3 '65

Rubella complement fixation test. J. L. Sever and others. bibliog il Science 148:385-7 Ap 16 '65

Serologic codes: interpretation of immunogenetic systems. J. Hirschfeld. bibliog il Science 148:968-71 My 14 '65

Specificity of macroglobulin antibody synthesized by the normal human fetus. W. V. Epstein. bibliog il Science 148:1591-2 Je 18 '65

Surgery in the womb: study of immune reaction in lamb. il Newsweek 66:42-3 Ag 2 '65

Template activity of RNA from antibody-producing tissues. B. Mach and P. Vassalli. bibliog il Science 150:622-6 O 29 '65

Tumor and virus antigens of simian virus 40: differential inhibition of synthesis by cytosine arabinoside. F. Rapp and others. bibliog il Science 147:625-7 F 5 '65

See also
Complement fixation
Complements (immunity)
Haptens
Rh factors

ANTIGO, Wis.

Doctor Strangewater; fluoridation battle. Newsweek 65:34 Ap 26 '65

ANTIGUA, Guatemala

Antigua. G. De Zendegui. il Américas 17:10-19 Ag '65

ANTI-INFLATION measures. See Inflation (finance)

ANTI-KNOCK gasoline. See Gasoline—Anti-knock and anti-knock mixtures

ANTILLES air boats, incorporated. See Airlines—Virgin Islands

ANTIMISSILE defense system. See Guided missiles—Defenses

ANTI-MISSILE missile programs. See Guided missiles—Defenses

ANTIN, David

Passenger's; poem. New Yorker 41:60 N 13 '65

Regarding a door; poem. New Yorker 41:162 N 20 '65

ANTI-NAZI movement

German resistance on American perspective; address, July 20, 1965. K. Brandt. Vital Speeches 31:713-17 S 15 '65

ANTI-NEGRO prejudice. See Race prejudice

ANTI-PARTICLES. See Particles (nuclear physics)

ANTIPASTO. See Appetizers

ANTIPERSPIRANTS. See Cosmetics

ANTI-POVERTY program, 1964-

All power to the Soviets! community councils in war on poverty. Nat R 17:492-4 Je 15 '65

America's other war. H. C. Wallich. Newsweek 66:81 Jl 12 '65

Another job for all faiths; the war on poverty calls for ecumenical action. H. Smith. America 112:542-3 Ap 17 '65

Appalachia, a new greenery of this spring. Bsns W p32+ Ap 24 '65

Appalachia, poverty, beauty and poverty. R. Cleghorn. il N Y Times Mag p 12-13+ Ap 25 '65

As the poverty program gets into gear. il U S News 58:56-8 Mr 8 '65

Atlanta fights poverty. J. Ridgeway. New Repub 152:12-14 My 29 '65

Atlantic report; tactics in the poverty war. Atlan 217:8+ Ja '66

Churches and the war on poverty. B. L. Masse. America 113:208-9+ Ag 28 '65

Do antipoverty funds aid parochial schools? charge made by American Jewish congress; reply. S. Poller. Christian Cent 82:308 Mr 10 '65

Fiesta of politics; criticism of the program by Congressman Powell. il Newsweek 65:29-30 Ap 26 '65

Fighting poverty and city hall; Syracuse university's anti-poverty project. E. Knoll and J. Witcover. il Reporter 32:19-22 Je 3 '65

First skirmish. Commonweal 82:68 Ap 9 '65

Fleecing the consumer; fraud cases in the slums. New Repub 153:7 Ag 21 '65

Hard-fought fiestas. Commonweal 82:180-1 Ap 30 '65

Harvester corps? New Repub 152:6-7 Ap 3 '65

How goes the war on poverty? S. Shriver. il Look 29:30-1+ Jl 27 '65

Larger battleground; J. Farmer as president of Center for Community-action education, inc. Newsweek 67:22-3 Ja 10 '66

LBJ's war at home; the economics of escalation. L. J. Walinsky. il New Repub 154:19-22 Ja 15 '66

Mr Shriver and the savage politics of poverty. W. F. Haddad. il Harper 231:43-50 D '65

Mixed-up war on poverty. C. E. Silberman. il Fortune 72:156-61+ Ag '65

More boon than doggle; predictable pattern of controversy, red tape and scandal. il Time 86:33 O 15 '65

New attacks on the war on poverty; excerpts from statements. U S News 59:9 O 25 '65

New kind of school; prekindergarten school. M. J. E. Senn. il McCalls 92:48+ S '65

Our friends, the poor; Welcome anti-poverty conference. P. Jacobs. Commonweal 81:722-3 Mr 5 '65

Pas de Dirksen. il Time 86:14 Ag 27 '65

Payoff in Chicago. L. Wille. New Repub 153:11 O 23 '65

Politics and the poor: Shriver's second thoughts. J. Witcover and E. Knoll. Reporter 33:23-5 D 30 '65

Politics and the poverty war; a look around the country. il U S News 59:61-3 S 6 '65

Poor in their place; maximum feasible participation. New Repub 153:5-6 N 20 '65

Poor no more; concerning program's problems. il Time 86:20-1 D 17 '65

Poverty and the economy. L. H. Keyserling. il Nation 200:615-17 Je 7 '65

Poverty war: birth pains. il Newsweek 65:23-4 Mr 29 '65

Poverty war has wars of its own; local battles over misuse of funds. il Bsns W p30-1 Ap 3 '65

Poverty war out of hand? il U S News 59:48-52 Ag 23 '65

Poverty's neglected battlefront: legal aid. J. Witcover. Sat R 48:29-30 S 11 '65

Poverty's wars; areas of conflict. Nation 200:434-5 Ap 26 '65

Progress, protest & politics. il Time 86:19-20 Jl 16 '65

Raising anti-poverty's ante. Time 86:12 Jl 30 '65

Real story of the poverty war. il U S News 58:37-40 Je 14 '65

Rockefeller and Shriver clash, why. U S News 59:20 Jl 12 '65

Safe bureaucratic decision; family planning opportunities denied to poor single women. New Repub 153:9 S 18 '65

Shriver and the war on poverty. il Newsweek 66:22-6+ S 13 '65

Sin, morality and poverty; social upheavals afflicting American society. W. Stringfellow. Christian Cent 82:703-6 Je 2 '65

Southern girl's diary of discovery; North Carolina. S. Sterling. il Look 29:107-13 Jl 13 '65

Specter of the poor; psychological defenses. J. P. Sisk. Commonweal 82:437-40 Je 25 '65

Talents of the poor. America 113:741 D 11 '65

Threaten antipoverty program; Economic opportunity act of 1964 in jeopardy. Christian Cent 82:516-17 Ap 28 '65

War on poverty; are the poor left out? R. A. Cloward. il Nation 201:55-60 Ag 2 '65

War on poverty materials assembled in ALA packet. Pub W 188:31 D 13 '65

ANTI-POVERTY program, 1964- —*Continued*
War on poverty needs a battle plan. Life 59:4 D 3 '65
War on poverty needs you. J. Friedberg. il Mlle 61:118-19+ Je '65
War on poverty; realistic battle, or just a political boondoggle? il Sr Schol 87:6-9+ O 21 '65
War on poverty: Washington vs. City hall. il U S News 59:54-6 N 22 '65
War on rural poverty. Christian Cent 82:731 Je 9 '65
War within a war; administrators of schemes challenged. il Newsweek 66:26-7 D 20 '65
What poverty war is about. Life 59:6 Jl 16 '65
When federal aid can backfire. Nations Bsns 53:27-8 Je '65
Where there's objection to a poverty grant. U S News 58:11 Mr 1 '65
Why the poverty war seems a muddle. J. Ridgeway. New Repub 153:7-8 O 9 '65; Discussion. 153:36-8 O 23; 39 N 6 '65
See also
Altoona, Pa.—Anti-poverty program
Laredo, Tex.—Anti-poverty program
Los Angeles—Anti-poverty program
Newark, N.J.—Anti-poverty program
Philadelphia—Anti-poverty program
Project head start
United States—Economic opportunity, Office of
United States—Job corps
Volunteers in service to America
ANTIQUARIAN book fair. See Book fairs
ANTIQUE airplane association
Mavericks of sport aviation. R. Bach. il Flying 78:32-9 Ja '66
ANTIQUE airplanes

Collectors and collecting
See Airplanes—Collectors and collecting
ANTIQUE automobiles

Collectors and collecting
See Automobiles—Collectors and collecting; Automobile museums
ANTIQUE automobiles in art. See Automobiles in art
ANTIQUE dealers
Where the world's past is sold; Portobello road, London's antiques market. il Bsns W p820-2 My 29 '65
ANTIQUE dolls. See Dolls
ANTIQUES
Antiques; questions & answers. T. H. Ormsbee. See issues of House & garden incorporating Living for young homemakers
Best of three centuries. G. O'Brien. il N Y Times Mag p76-7 Mr 14 '65
How to live with antiques and love them. il House & Gard 127:128-39 Je '65
Living with antiques:
Grosse Point home of Mr and Mrs Walter E. Simmons. G. G. Gibson. il Antiques 87:716-19 Je '65
Hudson Valley home of Mrs Henry M. Sage. N. S. Rice. il Antiques 88:806-11 D '65
Mynderse farmhouse in Saugerties, New York. E. Gaines. il Antiques 88:352-5 S '65
New York apartment of Colonel and Mrs Roger Brunschwig. R. Davidson. il Antiques 87:448-53 Ap '65
Providence home of Mrs R. H. Ives Goddard. B. Snow. il Antiques 87:580-5 My '65
Virginia home of Mr and Mrs Walter Major. L. P. McGrath. il Antiques 87: 208-11 F '65
Scotia furnishings. J. M. Graham, 2d. il Antiques 89:99-105 Ja '66
Some eighteenth-century classics from the collection of I. Austin Kelly III. A. Winchester. il Antiques 87:200-3 F '65
Where the world's past is sold; Portobello road, London's antiques market. il Bsns W p80-2 My 29 '65
See also
Collectors and collecting

Bibliography
Books about antiques. R. Davidson. See issues of Antiques

Exhibitions
Armory show; East Side house settlement's winter antiques show. New Yorker 40:23 F 13 '65
Calendar of shows. See issues of Antiques
Current and coming. R. Davidson. See issues of Antiques
ANTIQUES shops
Shops with historical backgrounds. il Hobbies 70:84 Ag '65

ANTIQUITY of man. See Man—Origin and antiquity
ANTI-SEMITISM
Anguish of the Jews, by E. H. Flannery. Review
Sat R 48:34 Je 19 '65. A. L. Sachar
Camden Catholics polled. America 112:384 Mr 20 '65
Cultural genocide in Russia. H. E. Fey. Christian Cent 82:914-16 Jl 21 '65
Little-known chapter in American history; column for Horace Greeley's Tribune, by Marx and Engels. M. Geltman. il Nat R 17:865-7 O 5 '65
Willa Cather and The professor's house; anti-Semitism in American literature of the 1920's. J. Schroeter. Yale R 54:494-512 Je '65
See also
Jews—Persecutions
ANTI-SLAVERY movement. See Slavery—United States
ANTI-SMOG devices. See Automobile engines—Exhaust
ANTI-SMOKING clinics. See Smoking
ANTI-STRIKE legislation. See Labor laws and legislation—United States
ANTI-SUBMARINE airplanes. See Airplanes, Military
ANTI-SUBMARINE warfare. See Submarine warfare
ANTITRUST division. See United States—Justice, Department of—Antitrust division
ANTITRUST legislation. See Trusts, Industrial—Law
ANTI-VIETNAM demonstrations. See Vietnamese war 1957- —Protests, demonstrations, etc. against
ANTIVIRAL drugs. See Drugs
ANTIVIRAL proteins. See Interferon
ANTIVIRUS vaccines. See Vaccines
ANTIVIVISECTION. See Vivisection
ANTOINE, Jim
Safe use of chemicals. Recreation 58:93 F '65
ANTOMMARIA, Phillip, and others
Airborne particulates in Pittsburgh: association with p,p'-DDT. bibliog Science 150: 1476-7 D 10 '65
ANTON, Richard J.
Change or consequences; address, October 27, 1964. Vital Speeches 31:274-9 F 15 '65
ANTONITIS, Joseph
Coral lily. Horticulture 43:16-17+ Je '65
ANTREI, Albert
Oregon's Hart Mountain antelope and sage hen refuge. Nat Parks Mag 39:16-19 Je '65
ANTROPOLOGIA. See Mexico (city)—Galleries and museums
ANTS
Ant venoms, attractants, and repellents. G. W. K. Cavill and P. L. Robertson. bibliog il Science 149:1337-45 S 17 '65
Biochemical polymorphism in ants. J. H. Law and others. bibliog il Science 149:544-6 Jl 30 '65
Circadian rhythms in male ants of five diverse species. E. S. McCluskey. bibliog il Science 150:1037-9 N 19 '65
Dorylines: raiding and in bivouac. T. C. Schneirla. il Natur Hist 74:44-51 O; 40-7 N '65
Great ant hunt. Sci Digest 58:82 S '65
Nature note; farmer ants. Sci N L 87:335 My 22 '65
Stridulation in leaf-cutting ants. H. Markl. bibliog il Science 149:1392-3 S 17 '65
Subversion among the ants; parasite ants subvert fire ant colonies. Time 85:100+ Je 11 '65
Tiny parasitic ant may curb dread fire ant. Sci N L 87:318 My 15 '65
Tree ants build a nest. il Natur Hist 75:64-5 Ja '66
ANXIETY
Firstborns more anxious. Sci N L 88:311 N 13 '65
No simple prescription for treating anxiety. Sci N L 87:226 Ap 10 '65
See also
Worry
ANYA; musical comedy. See Musical comedies, revues, etc.—Criticisms, plots, etc.
ANYONE can buy an Easter lily; story. See Strehlow, L.
ANZUS council
ANZUS ministers exchange views on world problems; text of a communique of meeting, June 28, 1965. Dept State Bul 53:135-7 Jl 19 '65
AORTA

Surgery
See Blood vessels—Surgery

APACHE Indian reservation. See Indians of
North America—Reservations

APARTHEID. See South Africa—Race problems

APARTMENT building research. See Building
research

APARTMENT houses
Apartment house rotates to change the view;
La Jolla, Calif. J. J. Fry. il Pop Sci 187:
118-19 N '65
Apartments? here? never! il Changing T 19:
41-3 Mr '65
Building types study. Arch Rec 137:197-220
Ap '65
Cities higher than mountains. N. Mailer.
il N Y Times Mag p 16-17+ Ja 31 '65
High-rise apartment structures of masonry.
R. M. Gensert. il Arch Rec 137:182-7 F '65
Rooms with a view in San Francisco; Eichler
summit. il Fortune 73:173 Ja '66
Condominium plan ownership
Nob Hill elegance by Warnecke. il Arch Rec
137:198-201 Ap '65
Own your apartment? it can be done. il
Good H 160:184 Ap '65
Cooperative ownership
Co-operators; United Nations plaza. il News-
week 66:74 Ag 23 '65
Foggy Bottom's dolce vita; executives co-
operative overlooking the Potomac. F.
Gutheim. Nation 201:395-7 N 22 '65
Own your apartment? it can be done. il
Good H 160:184 Ap '65
Lobbies
See Lobbies (architecture)

APARTMENT houses, Revolving. See Apartment houses

APARTMENTS
Accenting the arch. L. Hammel. il N Y Times
Mag p 122-3 D 5 '65
At home in four centuries; apartment of
Nereo Fioratti. B. Plumb. il N Y Times
Mag p94-5+ D 12 '65
At home with Carol Channing. il House &
Gard 128:210-13 S '65
Bee Dabney's drawing room. il Vogue 145:
184-9 Ap 1 '65
Checklist for apartment hunters. il Good H
161:167 S '65
Collector's apartment. il House & Gard 128:
96-9 Jl '65
Critic's choice; a newspaperman feathers his
aerie on San Francisco's Telegraph hill. il
House & Gard 128:272-5 N '65
E pluribus unum; Chicago apartment decorat-
ed by B. Gregga. G. O'Brien. il N Y Times
Mag p74-5 F 14 '65
Fool the eye penthouse filled with treasures.
il House & Gard 127:136-41 Ap '65
Improving one's background. G. O'Brien. il
N Y Times Mag p68-9 F 7 '65
Life inside a bouquet. il Vogue 146:146-9 O 15
'65
Living with antiques; New York apartment
of Colonel and Mrs Roger Brunschwig. R.
Davidson. il Antiques 87:448-53 Ap '65
Making it their own. R. Reif. il N Y Times
Mag p54-5 Ag 22 '65
Mixture, Italian style; Nino Carozzi's duplex
apartment. B. Plumb. il N Y Times Mag
p36-7 Ag 1 '65
Pick an apartment to fit your personality.
il Changing T 19:34-6 D '65
Reed team. il Vogue 147:114-17+ Ja 15 '66
Rooftop eyrie gives a modern designer ex-
actly the home he wants. il House & Gard
127:116-21 F '65
Second-cityscape. E. Sverbeyeff. il N Y
Times Mag p98-9 Ap 11 '65

APARTMENTS, Remodeled
Walls came tumbling down. R. Reif. il N Y
Times Mag p 114-15 S 19 '65

APATHY
Self-reliance or self-destruction; address.
April 27, 1965. G. Dudley, jr. Vital Speeches
31:632-4 Ag 1 '65

APEL, Erich
Ally's reward. Newsweek 66:39-40 D 20 '65
Curious case of Dr Apel. il Time 86:20 D 31
'65
How Russia plunders its allies. il U S News
59:47 D 27 '65

APES
Field studies of Old World monkeys and apes.
S. L. Washburn and others. bibliog Science
150:1541-7 D 17 '65
See also
Gibbons
Primates

APGAR, Virginia
What every mother-to-be should know. por
Todays Health 44:35+ Ja '66

APHELANDRAS
Tamed zebra. G. R. Robinson. il Pop Gard
17:53 Ja '66

APHELORIA corrugata. See Millipeds

APHIDS. See Plant lice

APHORISMS and apothegms
Old Ben Franklin and his miserable maxims.
S. L. Clemens. Read Digest 86:137-8 Je '65

APHRODISIAS
Aphrodite's city resuscitated. UNESCO
Courier 18:18-23 Ja '65; Reply. K. T. Erim.
18:33 Je '65

APICAL dominance. See Growth (plants)

APICAL meristems. See Plant cells and tissues

APOLLO (space vehicle) See Space vehicles

APOLLO project. See Space flight to the moon

APOLOGETICS
Contra the new theologies. P. L. Holmer.
Christian Cent 82:329-32 Mr 17 '65; Dis-
cussion. 82:742-3 Je 9 '65

APOPLEXY. See Cerebral hemorrhage

APOSTLE ISLANDS NATIONAL LAKE-
SHORE (proposed) See National parks and
reserves—United States

APOSTLES
See also
Peter, Saint

APOSTROPHE. See Punctuation

APPALACHIAN MOUNTAINS
See also
Shawangunk Mountains

APPALACHIAN REGION
Appalachia, a new greenery this spring.
Bsns W p32+ Ap 24 '65
Appalachia as symbol; Appalachian regional
development program. Nation 200:182 F 22
'65
Appalachia beyond free enterprise; the Ap-
palachian regional development act. S.
Harrington. il Commonweal 82:213-16 My 7
'65; Reply with rejoinder. E. Easterly. 82:
426-7+ Je 25 '65
Appalachia, poverty, beauty and poverty. R.
Cleghorn. il N Y Times Mag p 12-13+ Ap
25 '65
Appalachian aid and libraries. ALA Bul 59:
611 Jl '65
Books for the mountain children; providing
libraries in the schools of Appalachia.
J. Moorhead. il PTA Mag 59:2-3 Mr '65
Christmas without Santa Claus; Currence
family of Mill Creek, W.Va. C. Morrison.
il Look 29:18-21 D 28 '65
Environment traps young American of
promise; Appalachia teener. il Ebony 20:
115-21 Ag '65
How one billion for Appalachia will be spent.
il U S News 58:12 Mr 15 '65
Is there a future for yesterday's people?
excerpt from Yesterday's people; life in
contemporary Appalachia. J. E. Weller. il
Sat R 48:33-6 O 16 '65
Million books for Appalachia; librarians com-
pile most wanted list. Library J 90:1490+
Mr 15 '65
No more pork barrel: the Appalachia ap-
proach. J. Ter Horst. il Reporter 32:27-9
Mr 11 '65; Discussion. 32:6 Ap 8 '65
Proliferating Appalachias. D. Oberdorfer. il
Reporter 33:22-3+ S 9 '65; Discussion. 33:
8+ O 7 '65
Report from Appalachia; experience of a
VISTA volunteer. N. Krell. il Seventeen 25:
92-3+ Ja '66
Such easy charity; Books for Appalachia proj-
ect. E. Geller. Library J 90:1956 Ap 15 '65
Yesterday's people, by J. Weller. Review
Sat R 48:60 O 30 '65. D. M. Potter
See also
Education—Appalachian Region

Anecdotes, facetiae, satire, etc.
Tragic story of Magic Mountain. M. R. Cutler. il Liv Wildn 29:7-9 Sum '65

Recovery program, 1965–
Happy pappies of Handshoe Holler. il Time
86:38-9 N 5 '65
Ministering to Appalachia. J. Weller. Chris-
tian Cent 82:935-6 Jl 28 '65
Misdeal in Appalachia; relief program.
H. M. Caudill. Atlan 215:43-7 Je '65; Reply
with rejoinder. C. E. Hodges. 216:58+
O '65
Mountains of misery; Appalachia. M. Orovan.
il U S Camera 28:58-61+ My '65
New way to beat poverty: the plan for Ap-
palachia. il U S News 59:68-70 S 27 '65

APPALACHIAN regional commission. See
United States—Appalachian regional commission

APPALACHIAN trail
Appalachian trail: most famous footpath in the world. G. Nelson. il Am For 71:24-7 D '65

APPARATUS for the blind. See Blind, Apparatus for the

APPARITIONS. See Ghosts

APPELLATE procedure
See also
Briefs

APPENDICITIS
Vagaries of appendicitis in children. L. W. Sauer. PTA Mag 59:23-4 My '65
Virus, appendicitis linked. Sci N L 88:69 Jl 31 '65

APPETIZERS
And stir like hell: recipe for foie gras de poulet; letter to the editor. T. Caldwell. Nat R 17:902 O 19 '65
First course idea: have a hot appetizer pie. il Sunset 136:100 Ja '66
Help-yourself appetizers. il Sunset 134:239-40 Je '65
Holiday cheese appetizers. il Sunset 135:136 D '65
Italian way to start off; with menu and recipes by E. Graves. il Life 60:86-7+ Ja 21 '66
It's a cheese appetizer tree. il Sunset 135:175 D '65
Sit down to a first-course appetizer. il Sunset 134:222-3 Ap '65
These little Greek pastries are petes. il Sunset 136:106-7 Ja '66
They're bite-sized and in cups; mushroom caps. il Sunset 134:232+ My '65

APPLEBAUM, Max H.
Amplifier gain nomogram. Electr World 74:25 Ag '65
Parallel-resistor nomogram. Electr World 74:27 S '65
Power-output nomogram. Electr World 73:29 My '65
RC time-constant nomogram. Electr World 74:29 Jl '65
Transformer turns ratio nomogram. Electr World 74:29 N '65
U.H.F.-TV half-wave shorting-stub nomogram. Electr World 73:29 Je '65

APPLEBY, L. Thomas. See Miller, W. L. jt. auth.

APPLEBY, Thomas
Real inventor of wireless. Pop Electr 23:64-6+ O '65

APPLEMAN, Morris
Catering affair; Syosset, L.I, synagogue. Newsweek 66:56 Ag 30 '65

APPLES
See also
Cookery—Fruit
Crab apples

APPLES, Baked. See Cookery—Fruit

APPLESAUCE. See Cookery—Fruit

APPLICATIONS for admission to colleges. See Student selection

APPLICATIONS for positions
Tips for first-time job hunters. il Changing T 19:33-4 Jl '65

APPLICATIONS technology satellites. See Communications satellites

APPLIED science. See Technology

APPLIQUÉ work
Curtain cut-ups. J. Holmstrand. il Suc Farm 63:114-15 Ap '65

APPOMATTOX campaign, 1865
Appomattox where Grant and Lee made peace with honor a century ago. U. S. Grant, 3d. il Nat Geog Mag 127:435-69 Ap '65

APPOMATTOX court house
Tale of a table. M. A. Benjamin. il Am Heritage 16:100-1 Ap '65

APPORTIONMENT (election law)
A+B+C+D=NY²; New York state reapportionment case. M. Greenfield. il Reporter 33:32-5 D 2 '65
Are farmers better than city people? one man, one vote principle. Sat Eve Post 238:90 Je 19 '65
Baseball, pure and undefiled: anti-reapportionment amendment. A. Kopkind. New Repub 153:9-10 Ag 7 '65
Big game; choosing sides in the Senate. K. Crawford. Newsweek 65:50 Je 14 '65
Bye-bye Dirksen; amendment defeated. Nat R 17:716 Ag 24 '65
Congress and the Supreme court. il Sr Schol 86:10-11+ F 18 '65
Counting Dirksen out. Newsweek 66:19 Ag 16 '65
Dirksen amendment. G. Miller, jr. New Repub 153:30 Jl 3 '65; Discussion. 153:38 Ag 7, 36 S 4 '65
Dirksen's defeat. Time 86:17 Ag 13 '65

Dirksen's double play. P. R. Wieck. New Repub 152:13-14 Ap 17 '65; Reply. D. Dobson. 152:37 My 15 '65
Dirksen's last chance. K. Crawford. Newsweek 66:40 D 6 '65
Ev's curve ball. il Time 86:17 S 10 '65
In the federal v. state ticket. Time 86:65 Jl 23 '65
Let the people decide! Court decision on reapportionment, with editorial comment. Farm J 89:5, 150 F '65
Lumps in Olympia. il Newsweek 65:29 F 8 '65
Old order against new. K. Crawford. Newsweek 66:30 Ag 2 '65
One man, one vote. D. I. Wells. New Repub 152:11-12 Je 26 '65
One man, one vote? K. Crawford. Newsweek 65:24 Mr 22 '65
One-man, one-vote rule. W. Lippmann. Newsweek 65:33 My 10 '65
One man, one vote; Senate fails endorse Dirksen amendment. America 113:180 Ag 21 '65
One person, one vote; who wins, who loses. il U S News 59:42-3 Ag 23 '65
Reapportionment and redistricting. R. C. Silva. il Sci Am 213:20-7 bibliog(p 142) N '65
Reapportionment comes to Connecticut. E. J. Bell. il Nat R 17:685-7+ Ag 10 '65
Reapportionment goes to town. R. P. Claude. il Am City 80:163-6 My '65
Reapportionment mess. R. Moley. Newsweek 65:104 Je 21 '65
Reapportionment: shall the Court or the people decide? H. Harvey and K. O. Gilmore. Read Digest 86:111-16 Mr '65
Reapportionment thicket. il Time 85:31-2 Je 11 '65
Senator Dirksen vs. the Court; proposed amendment to nullify one man, one vote reapportionment ruling. R. M. Christenson. Nation 201:60-1 Ag 2 '65
Senator Dirksen's unexpected allies; proposed constitutional amendment. J. Duscha. il Reporter 32:26-8 Ap 22 '65; Discussion. 32:6 My 20 '65
Should California be chopped in half? il U S News 58:61-2 F 8 '65
Statehouse shuffle: will business be the loser? il Nations Bsns 53:68-70+ Je '65
Urge to amend; proposed amendment of one-man, one-vote ruling as applied to state legislatures. Time 86:24-5 Ag 6 '65
Vermont House gets remodeled; new House of representatives. V. Maerki. il Reporter 33:38-9 O 7 '65
Warren's monkey wrench: one man, one vote principle. New York state. Nat R 17:628-9 Jl 27 '65
When one person, one vote came up. il U S News 59:20 Ag 16 '65
Will Americans have the last laugh? F. Morley. il Nations Bsns 53:25-6 Ag '65
Will you win the reapportionment fight? C. W. Gifford. Farm J 89:76-7 Ap '65

APPRAISAL of books. See Book reviews

APPRAISER; story. See Wood, M.

APPRECIATION of music. See Music—Appreciation

APPRENTICE; story. See Fisher, D. C.

APPRENTICE teaching. See Student teaching

APPRENTICES
See also
Employees—Training

APPRENTICESHIP; story. See Jacobson, D.

APPROVAL; story. See Gerber, M. J.

APRIL
In April; few of the dates, memorable and not so, coming up next month (title varies) (cont) N Y Times Mag p41 Mr 28 '65

APRIL fools day
April fish; hoaxes in France. Newsweek 65:58 Ap 12 '65
I'd like to speak to Mr Lyon. il Sr Schol 86:7 Ap 1 '65

Quotations, maxims, etc.
Fools day; comp. by E. Murphy. N Y Times Mag p71 Mr 28 '65

APRONS
Party aprons. il Ladies Home J 82:110-11+ O '65

APTHEKER, Bettina
Berkeley, one year later. por Time 86:46+ D 3 '65

APTHEKER, Herbert
Three characters in search of an offer. por Newsweek 67:18 Ja 10 '66

APTITUDE tests
Aptitude tests separate smart from smarter. Sci N L 88:22 Jl 10 '65
Are aptitude tests valid for the highly able? H. Chauncey and T. L. Hilton. bibliog il Science 148:1297-304 Je 4 '65; Discussion. 149:245-6, 583, 708; 150:553-4 Jl 16, Ag 6-13, O 29 '65
Developing tests for the culturally different. W. E. Coffman. bibliog f Sch & Soc 93: 430-3 N 13 '65
Solution to the problem of distributing course grades; using Minnesota scholastic aptitude test. R. F. Berdie. Sch & Soc 93: 373-5 O 16 '65
Test your creativity. il Nations Bsns 53:80-3+ Je '65; Same abr. with title Are you creative? Read Digest 87:181-2 O '65
Test your science aptitude. il Sci N L 87: 118+ F 20 '65

AQUANAUTS
Deep thoughts; aquanauts. il Time 86:67 O 8 '65
Life under pressure; Sealab II. il Newsweek 66:56 S 13 '65
Man tests his limits in the ocean's depths; navy's Sealab II. il Bsns W p66-8+ S 11 '65
Sealab, Gemini similar. Sci N L 88:163 S 11 '65

AQUARIUMS
Aquarama; Philadelphia's marineland. il Travel 124:39-41 N '65
Instant ocean plus care keep fragile fish alive; Aquarium of Niagara Falls. il Sci N L 87: 391 Je 19 '65
Porpoises do an aerial hula at Sea Life park; Oahu oceanarium. il Sunset 135:20-2+ O '65
Right way to start a home aquarium. il Good H 160:145 F '65
Under space programs; show at San Diego's Sea world. H. Sutton. Sat R 48:45-6 F 6 '65

AQUARIUMS, Salt water. See Aquariums

AQUATIC plants
How to over-winter aquatic plants. P. A. Nutt. il Horticulture 43:34-5+ N '65

AQUATIC safety. See Safety education

AQUATIC shows
Mo-maids in the swim; University of Missouri swim club. G. A. Voss. il Recreation 58:499-500 D '65

AQUATIC sports
And the riding is easy; tubing. il Time 86: 34 Jl 30 '65
Fun craft. F. M. Paulson. il Field & S 70:96-8 Jl '65
Sailboarding: exciting new water sport. S. N. Darby. il Pop Sci 187:138-41 Ag '65
Skin and scuba training games; summary of report. F. J. Scalli. il Recreation 58:136-7 Mr '65
    See also
Boats and boating
Surf riding
Swimming
Water skis and skiing

AQUATINT
Aquatint views of our infant cities. A. H. Mayor il Antiques 88:314-18 S '65

AQUATINTS
Aquatint views of our infant cities. A. H. Mayor. il Antiques 88:314-18 S '65

AQUEOUS solutions. See Solutions

AQUINAS, Thomas, Saint. See Thomas Aquinas, Saint

AQUINAS, Thomas, Brother. See Thomas Aquinas, Brother

ARAB-Israel war, 1948-1949. See Israel-Arab war, 1948-1949

ARAB-Jewish relations. See Jewish-Arab relations

ARAB league. See Arab states

ARAB refugees. See Refugees, Arab

ARAB states
Commando decision; meeting of premiers of Arab league in Cairo. Time 85:30 Je 4 '65
Tunisian torpedo: H. Bourguiba absent from Arab league meeting. Time 86:42 S 24 '65
    See also
Aeronautics, Commercial—Arab states
Airlines—Arab states
Kuwait
    Foreign relations
Challenge to Nasser; Bourguiba's castigation. New Repub 152:7 My 15 '65
Nonalignment in the Arab world. D. Peretz. bibliog f Ann Am Acad 362:36-43 N '65

    History
Arab world's heavy legacy. C. Issawi. For Affairs 43:501-12 Ap '65

    Politics
Arab world in ferment. il Sr Schol 86:14-16+ My 6 '65
Bourguiba: portrait of a nonconformist. J. Lacouture. il N Y Times Mag p26-7+ Je 6 '65
Taking the pledge; Casablanca summit conference. il Newsweek 66:54 S 27 '65

    Social conditions
Arab world's heavy legacy. C. Issawi. For Affairs 43:501-12 Ap '65

ARABELLA; opera. See Strauss, R.

ARABIA
    See also
Saudi Arabia

ARABIDOPSIS
Arabidopsis research; report on first international symposium. G. Röbbelen. Science 150:1192 N 26 '65

ARABS
    See also
Arab states
Iraq—Native races
Jewish-Arab relations

ARABS in Israel
Arab refugees; a Zionist view. M. Syrkin. Commentary 41:23-30 Ja '66

ARACHNIDS
Courtship behavior of arachnids. T. Savory. il Natur Hist 74:52-6 My '65

ARAGON, Leopoldo
Cuba, guns and sugar. New Repub 152:13-15 Je 19 '65

ARAGON, Louis
Letter from Paris. Genêt. New Yorker 41: 112+ Je 12 '65

ARALIAS
Christmas aralia, at home, as a gift. il Sunset 135:62-3 D '65

ARANGO Y PARREÑO, Francisco de
Beginnings of industrialism in Latin America. J. L. Martí. il por Américas 17:1-7 O '65

ARANOW, Zedra Jurist
Case for the caboose. McCalls 92:42+ Mr '65

ARBITRATION, Industrial
Compulsory arbitration: a broad view. P. L. Kleinsorge and R. E. Smith. bibliog f Cur Hist 49:97-105+ Ag '65
    See also
Industrial relations

    United States
Business, labor, and the White House. il Duns R 86:44-5+ N '65
Collective coercion? D. Lawrence. U S News 59:120 S 20 '65; Same abr. with title Must collective bargaining be sabotaged? Read Digest 87:113-14 D '65
High cost of automation; strain on nation's professional arbitrators. T. R. Brooks. Duns R 85:61 F '65
Question of resolving major labor disputes by compulsory arbitration; pro and con. P. M. Flipse; R. Mathews. Cong Digest 44:208-10+ Ag '65
Thank you, Mr President; intervention in every labor dispute. Nat R 17:802+ S 21 '65
When LBJ moves to halt strikes. U S News 59:77 Ag 30 '65
    See also
American arbitration association
Trade agreements
United States—Federal mediation and conciliation service

ARBITRATION, International
    See also
International court of arbitration, The Hague
International law
Peace

ARBITRATION association, American. See American arbitration association

ARBONA, Guillermo
Up by the bootstraps. por Time 86:77 O 29 '65

ARBOR day
Liberty tree. V. L. Hebert. il Horticulture 43:38-9+ Ap '65

ARBOR viruses. See Viruses

ARBORETUMS
Seattle, Washington's University of Washington arboretum. J. A. Witt. il Horticulture 43:30-1+ Jl '65
    See also
Botanical gardens

ARBOUSSIER, Gabriel Marie d'
International co-operation; man's new dimension; address. UN Mo Chron 2:74-84 F '65

ARBOVIRUSES. See Viruses

ARC, M.
Prison culture, from the inside. N Y Times Mag p52-3+ F 28 '65
ARC, Electric. See Electric arc
ARC welding. See Electric welding
ARC welding machines. See Electric welding machines
ARCADIAN owls. See Owls
ARCATA redwood company
J. W. Clement company acquired by syndicate. Pub W 188:43-4 S 6 '65
ARCEUTHOBIUM. See Mistletoe
ARCHDIOCESE of Los Angeles. See Catholic church—Dioceses
ARCHEOLOGICAL photography. See Photography in archeology
ARCHEOLOGICAL research
1965 science review. il Sci N L 88:389 D 18 '65
Paleotemperatures and chronology at archeological cave site revealed by thermoluminescence; Jaguar cave, Idaho. W. Dort, jr. and others. bibliog il Science 150:480-1 O 22 '65
Rubidium magnetometer in archeological exploration. S. Breiner. bibliog il Science 150: 185-93 O 8 '65
ARCHEOLOGY
See also
Cave drawings and paintings
Stone age
Study and teaching
Iron age village built; project of Historical archaeological experimental center, Denmark. Sci N L 88:66 Jl 31 '65
ARCHEOLOGY, Submarine
They dive into history. G. Gaskill. il Read Digest 86:131-6 Je '65
Underwater archaeology; Ceylon. il Sci Digest 57:48+ F '65
ARCHER, Glenn L.
Clericalism bypassed. Christian Cent 82:176 F 10 '65
ARCHER, Marguerite P.
(ed) Individualized instruction. bibliog Library J 90:1977-90 Ap 15 '65
ARCHER, Vern B. and others
POINT points the way. NEA J 54:29-30 O '65
ARCHERY
Archery outlook, 1966. G. H. Gillelan. il Outdoor Life 137:114-16 Ja '66
See also
Fishing with bow and arrow
Equipment
Costs of archery. G. H. Gillelan. il Outdoor Life 135:24+ Ap '65
Gadgets for bowmen. G. H. Gillelan. il Outdoor Life 136:24-5 N '65
Why bowhunters miss. G. H. Gillelan. il Outdoor Life 136:16+ O '65
See also
Bow and arrow
ARCHES
Arch that was Grecian for the road that was Roman; Greek arches found in Elea. il Time 86:47 Jl 9 '65
ARCHES of science award. See Seattle—Pacific science center
ARCHILOCHUS
Archilochus not quite revived. J. Redfield. Poetry 105:329-31 F '65
ARCHIMEDES principle. See Specific gravity
ARCHITECTS
Architect as leader in a golden age? E. Goble. Arch Rec 138:9 Ag '65
Architect as mentor to a tortured world. E. Goble. Arch Rec 137:9 Je '65
Architects: a chance for greatness; photographs by H. Namuth. W. McQuade. Fortune 73:151-8+ Ja '66
Architects of the Record houses of 1965. il Arch Rec 137:133 mid-My '65
How architects practice interior design; summary of interviews (cont) W. B. Foxhall. il Arch Rec 137:105+ Ap '65
Who takes the blame when the roof leaks? E. Goble. Arch Rec 138:9 Jl '65; Reply. N. Williams. 138:9 O '65
See also
American institute of architects
Le Corbusier
Pan American congress of architects
Women as architects
ARCHITECTS, Landscape. See Landscape gardening
ARCHITECTS, Women. See Women as architects
ARCHITECTS offices. See Offices
ARCHITECTURAL acoustics. See Acoustics, Architectural

ARCHITECTURAL conferences
Harvard holds ninth urban design conference. M. F. Schmertz. il Arch Rec 137:23+ Je '65
On the calendar. See issues of Architectural record
ARCHITECTURAL designs. See Architecture, Domestic—Designs and plans
ARCHITECTURAL education
Form follows faction. G. Ain. Arch Rec 137: 108-9 My '65
ARCHITECTURAL engineering. See Structural engineering
ARCHITECTURAL firms
Architects for the developing; Rome-based American firms. il Time 85:88 F 12 '65
Architects of the Record houses of 1965. il Arch Rec 137:133 mid-My '65
See also
Alexander, Robert E, and associates
Giffels and Rossetti, incorporated
Mitchell and Giurgola associates
ARCHITECTURAL follies. See Follies (architecture)
ARCHITECTURAL plans. See Architecture, Domestic—Designs and plans
ARCHITECTURAL societies
See also
Pan American congress of architects
ARCHITECTURAL space. See Space (architecture)
ARCHITECTURE
Art in architecture. il Design 66:21-4 Ja '65
Buildings in the news. See issues of Architectural record
Focus: monthly review of notable buildings. il Arch Forum 123:26-9 N; 26-9 D '65
Monthly review of events and ideas. Arch Forum 123:1 Jl; 17-20+ S; 13-16+ O; 11-14+ N; 9-12+ D '65
Redesigning the twentieth century; with editorial comment. il Esquire 64:3, 214-23 D '65
Soaring legacy of a titan; with tribute to Le Corbusier by V. Scully. il Life 59:118-21, 123-4 S 24 '65
Structure & design. W. McQuade. See issues of Fortune
See also
Bank buildings
City planning
Clubhouses
College architecture
Domes
Follies (architecture)
Heating
Laboratories—Architecture
Library architecture
Municipal buildings
Office buildings
Orchestra shells
Recreation buildings
Recreation centers
Swimming pools
Towers
Vaults (architecture)
also subhead Architecture under names of cities, e.g. London—Architecture
Bibliography
Required reading. See issues of Architectural record
Competitions, awards, etc.
Awards. il Arch Forum 123:69 N '65
Competitions. il Arch Forum 123:30+ Jl; 75 S; 65-6 O; 63 D '65
Eighteen structures honored in Canada's Massey awards. il Arch Rec 137:12-15+ Ap '65
Toronto city hall: continuing controversy. il Arch Rec 138:165-72 N '65
Winner announced in Boston competition. il Arch Rec 137:12-13+ Mr '65
Conservation and restoration
Castle under siege; campaign to keep Olana, home of F. Church intact. K. Kuh. il Sat R 48:46-7 N 27 '65
Crowninshield-Bentley House in Salem, a documentary restoration. D. A. Fales, jr. il Antiques 88:486-93 O '65
Destroying the past by development. R. Kirk. Nat R 17:285 Ap 6 '65
Keep your town's historic landmarks. il Changing T 19:11-13 S '65
Living history vs. progress, profit, and apathy. il Sr Schol 86:12-16 Mr 18 '65
Menace of the bulldozers; excerpts from study. J. O. Brew. il UNESCO Courier 18: 33-6 Ja '65
Monuments in peril. UNESCO Courier 18:4-6 Ja '65
Noble past; saving the country's fine architecture. Nation 200:98 F 1 '65

ARCHITECTURE—Conservation and restoration—*Continued*
Preserving America's past. M. Frome. il Holiday 37:151-6 Mr '65
10,000 youngsters to the rescue; restoration of Chateau de Guise, France. il UNESCO Courier 18:21 Jl '65
See also
Houses, Restored

Designs and plans
Theory and invention of form. C. Alexander. il Arch Rec 137:177-86 Ap '65

Details
Architectural details (cont) il Arch Rec 137:133-48 F; 138:143-58 Ag '65
See also
Doors
Roofs

Exhibitions
Architecture; Museum of modern art's exhibition, Sixty-five years of modern architecture in the United States. W. McQuade. il Nation 201:86-7 Ag 16 '65

History
Books; author: S. Giedion. L. Mumford. New Yorker 41:158+ Mr 6 '65
Eternal present: the beginnings of architecture, by S. Giedion. Review
Nat R il 17:160-2 F 23 '65. H. Kenner

Philosophy
Kiesler by Kiesler; manifesto of correalism. F. Kiesler. il Arch Forum 123:64-72 S '65

Social aspects
Case for one total profession. A. Meyer. il Arch Rec 138:189-94 O '65
City and psyche. A. E. Parr. Yale R 55:71-85 O '65
Mark Jaroszewicz says something; excerpts from address; with editorial comment. M. Jaroszewicz. il Arch Forum 123:64 D '65

Australia
See also
Sydney, Australia—Architecture

Belgium
See also
Brussels—Architecture

Canada
Monumental civic architecture, modest in scale; Fathers of confederation memorial; Charlottetown on Prince Edward Island. il Arch Rec 137:161-8 Ap '65
See also
Montreal—Architecture
Toronto—Architecture

England
See also
London—Architecture

Finland
Visit to Pihlajamäki; residential district near Helsinki. J. Barnett. il Arch Rec 138:121-8 D '65

France
See also
Architecture, Domestic—France

Germany (Federal Republic)
Photography contest held in Germany; top winners. il Arch Rec 138:42-3 N '65

Hawaii
Shooting lodge high on a volcano; Mauna Kea, dormant volcano of Hawaii. P. Knight. il Sports Illus 23:64-6 N 8 '65

India
Doshi; architecture for a time of change. P. Blake. il Arch Forum 123:52-9 D '65
India's environment designer. il Fortune 72:174 O '65

Israel
See also
Jerusalem—Architecture

Italy
See also
Venice—Architecture

Japan
See also
Tokyo—Architecture

Malaysia
Mosque for tomorrow. il Time 86:70-3 O 8 '65

Mexico
See also
Architecture, Domestic—Mexico

North Carolina
See also
Winston-Salem, N.C.—Architecture

Spain
See also
Barcelona—Architecture

United States
Architecture; Museum of modern art's exhibition, Sixty-five years of modern architecture in the United States. W. McQuade. il Nation 201:86-7 Ag 16 '65
Astride the open road. P. Blake. Life 59:49 D 24 '65
Buildings in the news. See issues of Architectural record
California design conference called by governor to encourage excellence in state architecture. il Arch Rec 137:20+ F '65
Cities higher than mountains. N. Mailer. il N Y Times Mag p 16-17+ Ja 31 '65
No land? then build it on air! erecting structures over railroads, highways and other buildings. C. Peet. il Pop Mech 125:134-8+ Ja '66
Proud shapes; Towers in the West. il Life 59:84-7 D 24 '65
Small buildings by SOM. il Arch Rec 138:167-76 S '65
See also subhead Architecture under names of cities, e.g. San Francisco—Architecture

ARCHITECTURE, Ancient
Birth of functional architecture: town planning and housing in ancient Rome. M. W. Frederiksen. il UNESCO Courier 18:30-2 My '65

ARCHITECTURE, Domestic
Room at the bottom; underground homes. il Newsweek 65:87 My 3 '65
See also
Apartment houses
Bathrooms
Beach architecture
Building materials
Hillside architecture
Houses, Prefabricated
Houses, Remodeled
Laundries
Pavilions
Summer homes
Vacation houses

Designs and plans
Award-winning mountain house has deck and bridge above the snow. il Sunset 136:64-6 Ja '66
Better homes and gardens editors' choice houses for 1965. Bet Hom & Gard 43:47-55 Je '65
Dutch colonial updated. N. Seney. il Bet Hom & Gard 43:100 D '65
For families who want room to grow. il Parents Mag 40:78 Mr '65
French provincial with a great plan! N. Seney. il Bet Hom & Gard 43:98+ F '65
Here's a compact house with exceptional style and comfort. J. D. Bloodgood. il Bet Hom & Gard 43:48-51+ Mr '65
H&G's Hallmark house for 1965: the return to absolute simplicity. il House & Gard 127:124-35+ Ap '65
H&G's house of color. il House & Gard 128:200-9 S '65
House divided to span the years. R. Martens. il Farm J 89:46-8 Jl '65
House floats inside itself. il Pop Mech 124:126-7 S '65
House of surprises; central patio in year-round house in New England. il House & Gard 128:82-95 Ag '65
House to fit that problem lot. N. Seney. Bet Hom & Gard 43:14+ O '65
House with a natural point of view; built around an atrium. il Good H 161:127-36 O '65
House women want. il McCalls 92:112 Jl '65
How to plan a sound-conditioned house. il House & Gard 127:-154-5 Ap '65
Lot of house on a small lot. il Bet Hom & Gard 43:62-5 Ag '65
1965 editors' choice houses. il Bet Hom & Gard 43:48-55 S '65
On the up and up. E. Sverbeyeff. il N Y Times Mag p70-1 My 23 '65
Record houses of 1965. Arch Rec 137:53-136+ mid-My '65
Roomy two-story was built within astonishingly low budget of $16,000. il Sunset 135:68-9 Jl '65
Three-level living in steep Sausalito. il Sunset 135:84-5 Jl '65
Three new prefabs with a custom-built look. R. Charles. il Parents Mag 40:76-81 Ag '65

ARCHITECTURE, Domestic—Designs and plans
—*Continued*
Two small houses designed to grow. il House & Gard 127:124-33 My '65
Very natural approach to family living. N. Seney. il Bet Hom & Gard 44:36-9+ Ja '66
Very relaxing house. J. D. Bloodgood. il Bet Hom & Gard 43:84-7 Ap '65
What they did was turn everything around. il Sunset 135:70 Ag '65
Why settle for a bad house? il Bet Hom & Gard 43:50-65 N '65
You can expand this home yourself. il Parents Mag 40:62 My '65
Young children in the family? here's a house for you! il Am Home 68:84 Ap '65
Your plans for a second home start here! J. D. Bloodgood. il Bet Hom & Gard 43:102-3 Jl '65

Alabama
Home in classic style; design by P. Rudolph for Mr & Mrs J. W. Wallace of Athens, Ala. il Life 58:94-7+ F 26 '65
Vivid restatement of southern neo-classicism. il Arch Rec 137:58-61 mid-My '65

Arizona
Modular steel frame raises house above seasonal floods. il Arch Rec 137:78-81 mid-My '65

California
Bold splash of a beach home. il Life 58:90-3+ Ap 16 '65
California cliff-hanger. J. Peter. il Look 29:102+ Jl 13 '65
Changes in level adapt house to hillside. il Arch Rec 138:135-8 D '65
Easy extra home; weekend cabin near Carmel, Calif. il Life 58:124-7+ My 7 '65
House divided by a glimmering pool. il House & Gard 128:190-5 S '65
House laced with light. il House & Gard 127:122-9+ Mr '65
House planned for leisure, easy care and retirement. il Arch Rec 137:62-5 mid-My '65
Imaginative split-level planning. il Arch Rec 137:94-7 mid-My '65
Privacy and outdoor living on tiny lot. il Arch Rec 137:193-6 Ap '65
Two exterior treatments of one basic plan. il Arch Rec 137:130-2 mid-My '65

Colorado
Exposed steel straps stabilize hillside house. il Arch Rec 137:183-6 My '65

Connecticut
Contemporary Camelot. R. Reif. il N Y Times Mag p64-5 Ag 29 '65
House of glass today. il House & Gard 128:184-7 O '65
Making the most of inherent riches. il House & Gard 127:104-7 F '65
U shaped wings radiate from central core. il Arch Rec 137:118-21 mid-My '65

Florida
Cantilevered upper floor increases space. il Arch Rec 137:106-9 mid-My '65
Clutter-free house. il House & Gard 128:82-9 Jl '65
House that time cannot wither, nor custom stale; Casa Contenta; with editorial comment. il House & Gard 128:173-81 O '65
Lighthearted pavilion: Nicholas du Pont Palm Beach house. V. Lawford. il Vogue 145:140-5+ Je '65
Outdoor rooms treble space in builder house. il Arch Rec 137:70-3 mid-My '65
Patios around development house add privacy. il Arch Rec 137:86-9 mid-My '65

France
New place in the sun: Castellaras. il Vogue 147:78-80 Ja 15 '66

Georgia
Exploded columns enclose space within space. il Arch Rec 137:126-9 mid-My '65
Powerful roofs dominate design; family house. il Arch Rec 137:171-4 Je '65

Hawaii
Two-house idea keeps gaining favor; Honolulu house of Mr and Mrs David Barry, jr. il Sunset 135:86-7 S '65

Illinois
House that welcomes personal treasures. il House & Gard 128:284-9 N '65
Sliding roof gives house year round use of patio. il Arch Rec 137:157-60 F '65

Libya
Villa Velpi, exotic palace in Tripoli. R. Cameron. il Vogue 145:126-33+ Ap 15 '65

Long Island, N.Y.
Architect's weekend home; G. Bunshaft's East Hampton home. E. Stoller. il Holiday 38:52-7 S '65
Expansion in three directions. il House & Gard 127:90-5 F '65
Fortress by the sea; home of Lawrence Buttenwieser family. il Life 59:82-5+ Ag 13 '65
Saltbox split in two. il Arch Forum 123:58-61 S '65
Strength achieved by horizontal emphasis. il Arch Rec 138:199-202 O '65

Louisiana
Light pyramids add drama to flexible spaces. il Arch Rec 137:98-101 mid-My '65
Patio life behind walls; Curtis house in New Orleans. il Life 58:92-5+ Mr 12 '65

Maryland
Remarkable space and height in small houses. il Arch Rec 137:102-5 mid-My '65

Massachusetts
Bold roof expression for architect's own house. il Arch Rec 137:54-7 mid-My '65
High-up house; T. Rantoul's home at Martha's Vineyard with plans. il Life 59:78-81+ S 3 '65
How a family bought H&G's house of surprises. il House & Gard 128:68+ O '65
McNulty House: a space wrapped in concrete. il Arch Forum 123:30-5 N '65
Music room is dominant feature of house. il Arch Rec 137:74-7 mid-My '65
Sculpture for living; McNulty home, Lincoln. il Life 59:124-7+ D 3 '65
Variety in levels creates interesting spaces. il Arch Rec 137:110-13 mid-My '65

Mexico
One artist's colony. il N Y Times Mag p40-1 S 5 '65

Michigan
Clustered development gets park as bonus. il Arch Rec 137:114-17 mid-My '65
Modular scheme provides disciplined variety. il Arch Rec 137:90-3 mid-My '65
Well-zoned house has bold spaces. il Arch Rec 137:163-6 Mr '65

Minnesota
Brick columns and a broad roof shelter a glass-walled house. il Arch Rec 138:167-70 Ag '65
H&G's Hallmark house for 1965: the return to absolute simplicity. il House & Gard 127:124-35+ Ap '65

Missouri
Stepped-back walls; Cosby home in St Louis. il Life 59:142-6+ O 15 '65

New Jersey
Domestic architecture of New Jersey. J. E. Boucher. il Antiques 88:184-9 Ag '65

New York (state)
Handsome house, practical plan. N. Seney. il Bet Hom & Gard 43:70-1+ N '65
Old house: new plan for city living; home of the Richard Mewman's in New York city. M. White. il Ladies Home J 58-63 Ja '66

North Carolina
Architecture of Salem. W. J. Murtagh. il Antiques 88:69-80 Jl '65
Salem interiors. F. L. Horton. il Antiques 88:81-91 Jl '65

Oregon
House of wood today. il House & Gard 128:188-91 O '65
Two-level house adapts well to slope. il Arch Rec 137:122-5 mid-My '65

Pennsylvania
Country house highlights regional qualities. il Arch Rec 137:82-5 mid-My '65
Modern architect-designed house for under $16,000. il Am Home 68:52-5 Mr '65

Texas
Treetop living pavilion of steel and glass. il Arch Rec 137:66-9 mid-My '65

United States
Architects' own houses; eleven new residences. il Arch Rec 138:177-88 S '65
House divided; separating active living areas from quiet ones. B. Plumb. il N Y Times Mag p94-5 N 7 '65
How long will modern last? il House & Gard 128:182-91 O '65

ARCHITECTURE, Domestic—United States
—*Continued*
Ideas in houses (cont) il Life 58:94-7+ F 26;
90-3 Ap 16; 124-7+ My 7; 88-91+ Je 4 '65
Older homes outsell the new. Bsns W p 144+
Ja 15 '66
Preview of housing for 1966. R. Charles. il
Parents Mag 41:69-71+ Ja '66

Utah
Fun of variety and the cash savings of pre-
fabrication; houses in Salt Lake City. il
Sunset 135:100-3 N '65

Virginia
House that grew and grew; Dower house,
Fairfax County, Va. M. White. il Ladies
Home J 82:84-9 N '65

Washington (state)
This sky-lit house was owner-built. il Sunset 134:88-9 F '65

Western states
See also
Western home awards

Wisconsin
For adults only; home of Mr. G. Nickoll. il
Life 59:90-3+ Jl 16 '65
ARCHITECTURE, Ecclesiastical. See Church
architecture
ARCHITECTURE, Fantastic
Reporter at large; Watts towers, Los An-
geles. C. Trillin. il New Yorker 41:72+ My
29 '65
Watts; the forgotten slum; Towers' place in
history. C. McWilliams. Nation 201:90 Ag
30 '65
Wonderful towers of Sabatino Rodia. il Sun-
set 134:108-9 My '65
ARCHITECTURE, Gothic
A. J. Davis' greatest Gothic; Lyndhurst, N.Y.
J. N. Pearce. il Antiques 87:684-9 Je '65
ARCHITECTURE, Hillside. See Hillside archi-
tecture
ARCHITECTURE, Hotel. See Hotels, taverns,
etc.
ARCHITECTURE, Mexican
The new Mexico. M. Simons. il Look 30:54-7
Ja 25 '66
ARCHITECTURE, Modern
Architects for the developing. il Time 85:88
F 12 '65
Bold structures enclose large spaces at low
cost. il Arch Rec 138:177-88 O '65
In pursuit of diversity; pharmaceutical fac-
tory for the Endo laboratories, Garden City
and IBM building, Cranford, N.J. il Time
86:56-8 Jl 2 '65
McNulty House; a space wrapped in con-
crete. il Arch Forum 123:30-5 N '65
Ten buildings that point the future; portfolio.
Fortune 72:174-9 D '65
ARCHITECTURE, Pueblo. See Pueblo archi-
tecture
ARCHITECTURE, School. See School buildings
ARCHITECTURE and state. See Art and state
ARCHITECTURE in art
Ben Eisenstat finds personality in buildings.
H. C. Pitz. il Am Artist 29:56-61+ D '65
Some Venetian *vedute* painters in the Wads-
worth atheneum. W. G. Constable. il Anti-
ques 88:669-73 N '65
Subject is houses. F. Hanley. il Am Artist 30:
66-9+ Ja '66
Views of Philadelphia 1750-1770. M. P. Snyder.
il Antiques 88:674-80 N '65
ARCHIVES
See also
Vatican—Archives

United States
See also
United States—National archives
ARCTANDER, Erik
Civilized cycles; everybody rides 'em now.
Pop Sci 187:68-72 Jl '65
ARCTIC maneuvers. See Military maneuvers
ARCTIC OCEAN
Scientists ride ice islands on Arctic odysseys.
L. Thomas, jr. il Nat Geog Mag 128:670-91
N '65
ARCTIC REGIONS
North toward the Pole on skis. B. O. Staib.
il Nat Geog Mag 127:254-81 F '65
See also
Aleutian Islands
Botany—Arctic Regions
Disarmament—Arctic Regions
Eskimos
Ice—Polar Regions
Mackenzie River, Canada
Yukon

Description and travel
Scientists ride ice islands on Arctic odysseys.
L. Thomas, jr. il Nat Geog Mag 128:670-91
N '65

Maps
Top of the world map focuses on intercon-
tinental crossroads. il Nat Geog Mag 128:
692-3, sup(folded map) N '65
ARCTIC research. See Polar research
ARCTOSTAPHYLOS. See Bearberries
ARDEN, John
Armstrong's last goodnight. Criticism
New Yorker 41:102-3 Ag 14 '65
Live like pigs. Criticism
Nation 200:681-2 Je 21 '65
Sat R 48:45 Je 26 '65
ARDENNES, Battle of the, 1944-1945
Woman who stayed where she was. F. L.
Keefe. New Yorker 41:208+ N 6 '65
ARDITTI, Joseph
Orchids; with biographical sketch. Sci Am
214:14, 70-8 bibliog(p 135) Ja '66
ARDOIN, John
Culture from Patagonia. Sat R 48:53 Je 26 '65
From the heart. Opera N 29:14-15 My 1 '65
Richter and Christmas. Sat R 48:53 D 18 '65
ARDURA, Ernesto
Ortega y Gasset. Américas 17:15-19 D '65
ARE you decent, mem-sahib? story. See Perel-
man, S. J.
AREA redevelopment administration. See
United States—Area redevelopment admin-
istration
AREA studies
Needed: Afro-Asian studies. T. P. Melady.
America 112:709-10+ My 15 '65
Non-western studies in liberal arts colleges.
D. L. Hamilton. Sch & Soc 93:244+ Ap 17
'65
Secretary to set up procedures for foreign
affairs research; letter to Secretary Rusk,
August 2, 1965. L. B. Johnson. Dept State
Bul 53:323 Ag 23 '65
World we have to know; NDEA language and
area centers programs. M. Flapan. il Am
Ed 1:30-2 O '65
AREA trade schools. See Trade schools
ARECIBO telescope. See Radio telescope
ARELLANO, Osvaldo López. See López Arel-
lano, O.
ARENAS
See also
New York (city)—Madison Square Garden
ARÉVALO MARTÍNEZ, Rafael
Literature of the absurd. G. P. Nemes. il por
Américas 17:6-10 F '65
ARFONS, Art
Enemies in speedland. J. Olsen. il por Sports
Illus 23:80-2+ N 29 '65
Fastest man on wheels. J. Reddy. il Read
Digest 86:94-8 Mr '65
How I'll drive faster than sound; ed. by
D. Francis. il pors Pop Sci 187:46-9+ Jl
'65
ARFONS, Walter
Enemies in speedland. J. Olsen. il por Sports
Illus 23:80-2+ N 29 '65
ARGELANDER, Friedrich Wilhelm August
Argelander and the BD. A. T. Moffet. il por
Sky & Tel 29:276-8 My '65
ARGENTINA
Argentina: reconciliation with the Peronists.
S. L. Baily. Cur Hist 49:356-60+ D '65
See also
Agriculture—Argentina
Córdoba
Education—Argentina
Elections—Argentina
Money—Argentina
Space research—Argentina

Economic conditions
Atlantic report. Atlan 215:34+ F '65
Best year. M. J. Kubic. il Newsweek 66:
33 S 6 '65
Changing the Rx. il Newsweek 65:53-4 Ap 5
'65
Giving in to inflation. Time 85:42 F 26 '65
Going it alone. Time 85:49 Ap 30 '65

Politics and government
Atlantic report. Atlan 215:34+ F '65
Fading image. il Time 86:38 O 29 '65
Grumbling in the barracks; Onganía's resig-
nation. Time 86:40 D 3 '65
Shadow of Peron. New Repub 152:7-8 Mr 27
'65
Third woman; I. Perón's peace mission fails.
Newsweek 66:56 O 25 '65
ARGENTINE cookery. See Cookery, Argentine
ARGENTINE gauchos. See Gauchos
ARGENTINE musicians. See Musicians, Ar-
gentine

ARGERICH, Martha
Dark victor. il por Time 85:64 Mr 26 '65
ARGIRO, Larry
Mosaic art. il Sch Arts 64:10-14 Je '65
ARGO, Virgil N.
Mechanics of a turnover. Natur Hist 74:26-9 bibliog(p74) Ag '65
ARGON
Extraterrestrial dust as a source of atmospheric argon. R. A. Schmidt. bibliog il Science 151:223 Ja 14 '66

Isotopes
Half-lives of argon-37, argon-39, and argon-42. R. W. Stoenner and others. bibliog il Science 148:1325-8 Je 4 '65
ARGOSY (periodical)
When Argosy looks for stories. B. Cassiday. Writer 78:25 Ag '65
ARGOT. See Slang
ARGUMENT
Gentle art of executive persuasion; excerpt from Effective psychology for managers. M. Feinberg. il Duns R 86:41-7 D '65
See also
Logic
ARGUS, M. K.
Last time I saw Petrograd; story. Sat R 48:8 Ap 17 '65
ARIADNE exposed; drama. See Nightingale, E. M.
ARIAS ESPINOSA, Ricardo Manuel
What will be the instruments of Latin-American advancement? address, April 10, 1965. Ann Am Acad 360:78-84 Jl '65
ARID regions
Harvested rain; collecting rainfall in semiarid and desert regions. Sci Am 213:53 N '65
ARIF, Abdul Salam Mohammed
Historical accident. il por Newsweek 66:44 Jl 26 '65
ARISMAN, J. Michael
Gathering of the Klan. Commonweal 82:373-4 Je 11 '65
New Negro casualties. Commonweal 83:372-3 D 24 '65
ARIZONA
See also
Canyon de Chelly National Monument
Fishing—Arizona
Hunting—Arizona
Organ Pipe Cactus National Monument
Petrified Forest National Park
Roads—Arizona
Saguaro National Monument
Salt River
Sonoran Desert
Water supply—Arizona
White Mountains

Antiquities
See Indians of North America—Antiquities—Arizona

Description and travel
Among the books: Standing up country. M. T. Musselman. il Liv Wildn 29:29-31 Sum '65
Baptism by sunset. J. Cowan. Vogue 147: 128+ Ja 15 '66
Desert traditions, decorative riches. M. Roche. il House & Gard 128:254-9+ N '65

Parks and reserves
Along the Arizona-California water border you can explore the desert leisurely by boat. il Sunset 134:34-6+ Mr '65
Rest stop at the Painted Rocks. il Sunset 135:67-8 O '65
ARIZONA meteorite crater. See Meteorite craters
ARIZONA republic (newspaper) See Phoenix, Ariz.—Newspapers
ARK, Noah's. See Noah's ark
ARKANSAS
See also
Buffalo River
Education—Arkansas
School laws and legislation—Arkansas

Race problems
Wilkins calls Little Rock integration top achievement. il Ebony 20:134+ My '65

Recreation
See Recreation—United States
ARKANSAS RIVER
Riches for a new region; harnessing the Arkansas River. il U S News 59:66-8 Jl 12 '65
ARKIN, Joseph, and Glazer, Dorothy
Tuberous begonias. Pop Gard 16:27-9 Jl '65
ARKOFF, Samuel Zachary
Peekaboo sex, or How to fill a drive-in. A. Levy. il por Life 59:81-2+ Jl 16 '65

ARLEN, M. J.
Current cinema. New Yorker 41:59-61 Jl 17; 87-8 Jl 24 '65
ARLINGTON House. See Virginia—Historic houses, etc.
ARMAGNAC, Alden P.
Those new sandwich coins. Read Digest 87: 21-2+ D '65
ARMAMENTS
Arms embargo; industrialized nations race to sell arms to the underdeveloped. Nation 201:318 N 8 '65
Arms race: chicken or egg? America 113: 361 O 2 '65
Cost of the arms race. K. Keane. America 113:372-4 O 2 '65
See also
Disarmament
Munitions
Warships—Armaments
ARMBRISTER, Trevor
Cross that inflames a city. Sat Eve Post 238:36-7 Jl 3 '65
Sammy Davis: don't call him junior anymore. Sat Eve Post 238:89-93 F 13 '65
Watch out, here it comes! Sat Eve Post 238: 74-7 F 27 '65
ARMCO steel corporation
Squeezing costs out of casting. il Bsns W p 163-4 Je 12 '65
ARMED forces medical library. See United States—National library of medicine
ARMED forces of national liberation. See Political parties—Venezuela
ARMED robbery. See Robberies and assaults
ARMELAGOS, George J. See Carlson, R. L. jt. auth.
ARMENIANS in the United States
Ah-ha, the cat saw the mouse. W. Saroyan. il Sat Eve Post 238:70-2 F 27 '65
ARMENTIÈRES, France
Hinky dinky, parley-voo? town's mademoiselle honored. il Time 86:22+ S 10 '65
ARMIES
Soldiers and the nation-state. D. B. Bobrow. bibliog f il Ann Am Acad 358:65-76 Mr '65

Medical service
See also
European war, 1914-1918—Medical and sanitary affairs
ARMISTICE, Korean. See Korean war, 1950-1953—Peace and mediation
ARMITSTEAD, Austin H.
New York: dispirited city. Christian Cent 82: 1319-21 O 27 '65
ARMORED cars. See Motor trucks, Armored
ARMORED vessels
Resurrection of an ironclad: union gunboat Cairo salvaged; with contemporary account of sinking by G. Yost. il Life 58:41-2+ F 12 '65
ARMOUR, Richard
But I'm a good salesman. Pub W 187:33-4 Mr 8 '65
Flick of the wrist; poem. McCall's 92:161 F '65
Floored by floors; poem. McCalls 93:128 Ja '66
Leave me your number, and I'll have her call you; poem. McCalls 92:188 Ap '65
Light verse: questions and answers. Writer 78:26-8 S '65
Perfect renter; poem. McCalls 92:177 Mr '65
They won't let me stop smoking. Read Digest 86:83-5 My '65
ARMOUR and company
Report and appraisal: the Armour fund's Sioux City project. E. H. Conant. Mo Labor R 88:1297-301 N '65
Soap making goes modern. M. B. Keiser. il Parents Mag 40:18+ N '65
ARMS, Isabel
(ed) See Gatti, O. School art festival
ARMS control. See Disarmament
ARMS control and disarmament agency. See United States—Arms control and disarmament agency
ARMSTRONG, April (Oursler)
Speaking out. por Sat Eve Post 238:8+ D 18 '65
ARMSTRONG, Charles M. See Kowitz, G. T. jt. auth.
ARMSTRONG, Clara Franzini-. See Franzini-Armstrong, C.
ARMSTRONG, Louis
Jazz records. W. Balliett. New Yorker 41: 108+ Ja 15 '66
Satchmo goes home. Newsweek 66:98 N 8 '65
Satchmo returns to his home town, briefly. A. Kopkind. New Repub 153:10-11 N 13 '65
ARMSTRONG, Marion
Gift; poem. Christian Cent 82:1575 D 22 '65

ARMSTRONG, O. K.
Damning case against pornography. Read Digest 87:131-4 D '65
Fight against the smut peddlers. Read Digest 87:177-8+ S '65
Must our movies be obscene? Read Digest 87:154-6 N '65
War the reds can't win; excerpt from Religion can conquer communism. Read Digest 86:37-8+ Ap '65

ARMSTRONG, Richard
Bobby Kennedy and the fight for New York. Sat Eve Post 238:29-31+ N 6 '65
Book reviews. America 112:434-5 Mr 27 '65
Explosive revival of the far left. Sat Eve Post 238:27-32+ My 8 '65
Second man at City hall. N Y Times Mag p 12-14+ D 26 '65
Will Snick overcome? Sat Eve Post 238:79-83 Ag 28 '65

ARMSTRONG-JONES, Antony Charles Robert, 1st earl of Snowdon. See Snowdon, A. C. R. A.-J.

ARMSTRONG'S last goodnight; drama. See Arden, J.

ARMY dogs. See Dogs, War use of

ARMY engineers. See United States—Army—Corps of engineers

ARMY materiel command. See United States—Army—Materiel command

ARMY research office. See United States—Army research office

ARMY reserves. See United States—Army—Reserves

ARMY rifles. See Rifles

ARMY slang. See Slang

ARNDT, Adolf
Nazi murders & German politics. D. Schoenbaum. Commentary 39:72-7 Je '65

ARNEY, Thomas
Arney's army. il por Newsweek 66:80 Ag 23 '65

ARNHEIM, Rudolf
What is a critic? Sat R 48:26-7 Ag 28 '65

ARNO, Stephen F.
Great sleeper. il Nat Parks Mag 39:20 O '65

ARNOLD, Dexter Otis
At home with the Arnolds; traditional warmth meets contemporary ease. il pors Good H 160:98-106+ Ja '65

ARNOLD, Elliott
Accident; story. Redbook 124:54-5 F '65

ARNOLD, Gayle
Photography. Sch Arts 65:23-6 S '65

ARNOLD, Helen A.
Wild flower rescue squad. Flower Grower 53:13 Ja '66

ARNOLD, James R. See Anders, E. jt. auth.

ARNOLD, Margaret
At home with the Arnolds; traditional warmth meets contemporary ease. il pors Good H 160:98-106+ Ja '65

ARNOLD, Oren
Should homework be abolished? NEA J 54:22+ F '65

ARNOLD, Stanley
Factory for million-dollar ideas. il pors Bsns W p64+ O 30 '65

ARNOLD, Stanley and associates. See Stanley Arnold and associates

ARNOLD, Sue
Chameleon; poem. America 112:547 Ap 17 '65

ARNOLD, Thurman Wesley
Combative life devoted to ridiculing unreality. E. V. Rostow. Life 59:10 Jl 9 '65
Machiavelli of the New deal. J. Featherstone. New Repub 153:22-6 Ag 7 '65; Reply. J. F. Bowen. 153:36 S 4 '65
On the side of law and a new order. M. Feldman. Sat R 48:19 Jl 31 '65

ARNOLD, W. E.
Sartre as performer and literary illusionist. Commonweal 82:566-7 Ag 6 '65

ARNOLD, Walter M.
All-age, all-job program. por Am Ed 1:8-11 D '64

ARNON, Daniel I.
Ferredoxin and photosynthesis. bibliog Science 149:1460-70 S 24 '65

ARNOSI, Eduardo
Her name was Salome. Opera N 29:31 Mr 13 '65
Season's start at Teatro Colón. Hi Fi 15:166 S '65

ARNSTEIN, F. G.
Lament; poem. Christian Cent 82:1011 Ag 18 '65

AROMATIC hydrocarbons. See Hydrocarbons

ARON, Raymond
Treading between abysses. S. Hoffmann. Nation 200:198-200 F 22 '65

ARONOFF, S.
Catalase: kinetics of photooxidation. bibliog Science 150:72-3 O 1 '65

AROUND the world flights. See Aviation—World flights

ARP, Halton
Faint ring around the spiral galaxy M82. bibliog Science 148:363-4 Ap 16 '65

ARRAES, Miguel
Hard blow for the hard line. por Time 85:46 Ap 30 '65

ARRAN (island)
Home to Arran, Scotland's magic isle. J. H. Howells. il Nat Geog Mag 128:80-99 Jl '65

ARRANGEMENT (music) See Musical arrangement

ARRANGEMENT of flowers. See Flowers, Arrangement of

ARRANGEMENT of fruits, vegetables, etc. See Fruits, vegetables, etc. in decoration

ARRANGEMENT of furniture. See Furniture, Arrangement of

ARREST
Arts of arrest. il Time 85:56 Mr 19 '65
Don't resist, sue; false arrest. il Time 86:61 N 12 '65
No socking, please. Commonweal 82:372 Je 11 '65
Right guy; arrest on murder charge in Janice Wylie and Emily Hoffert case. il Newsweek 65:30-1 F 8 '65
Squared suspect; wrongful arrest in Wylie-Hoffert murders. il Time 85:69 F 5 '65

ARRIVALS and departures; story. See Weiss, M. S.

ARROW de Centro America, ltd. See Guatemala—Industries

ARROW points. See Arrowheads

ARROW worms. See Arrowworms

ARROWHEADS
Arrow-heads. C. Miles. Hobbies 70:114-17+ Je '65

ARROWWORMS
Nature note. Sci N L 88:318 N 13 '65

ARROYO, Martina
Full circle; interview, ed. by R. D. Daniels. por Opera N 30:26 D 11 '65

ARRUPE, Pedro
Father Pedro Arrupe, new Father General of Jesuits. R. C. Dressman. America 112:818-19 Je 5 '65
Jesuit general's speech at the Vatican council. America 113:429-30 O 16 '65
New Black Pope. por Time 85:88 My 28 '65
Shintoist Jesuit. Newsweek 65:74 My 31 '65

ARSON
Fraud fires flare up; arson-for-profit. I. Ross. il Read Digest 86:33-5+ My '65
They help stamp out firebugs. F. Tinker. il Pop Mech 124:98-102+ S '65

ART
Ironies of art. K. Kuh. Sat R 48:49 S 25 '65
See also
Circus in art
Creation (literary, artistic, etc)
Cubism
Drawings
Graffiti
Graphic arts
Illustration of books and periodicals
Impressionism (art)
Mannerism (art)
Nude in art
Performing arts
Realism in art
Surrealism (art)
Water color painting
also subhead Art under names of cities e.g. London—Art

Appreciation

Are we connoisseurs of art or just consumers? report debating value of art, music and literature in the United States. R. Bendiner. il Redbook 125:78-9+ O '65

Bibliography

Art books: 1965. M. Kozloff. Nation 201:503-8 D 20 '65
Book review section. See issues of Design
Book reviews. See issues of American artist
Books. K. Marantz. See issues of School arts
Gift of art: from the Greeks to the vanguard. G. H. Hamilton. Sat R 48:60+ D 4 '65

Collections

See Art—Private collections

Competitions

Competitions and awards. See issues of American artist
1965 Scholastic magazines art awards. il Sr Schol 86:18-19 My 20 '65
See also
Childrens art—Competitions

ART—*Continued*

Copyright
See Copyright—Art

Distortion
Art of distortion. R. Barrio. il Design 67:14-17 N '65

Education
See Art education

Exhibitions
American artist travelogue. il Am Artist 29:61-9+ Ap '65

Art. M. Kozloff. See issues of Nation

Art galleries. R. M. Coates. See issues of New Yorker

Art in the park; Linden, N.J. M. Poston. il Recreation 58:278-9 Je '65

At the Metropolitan; good history, indifferent art; Three centuries of American painting. J. Jacobs. il Reporter 32:36-7 Je 3 '65

Biennial bash in Brazil. il Time 86:79 S 10 '65

Big show Venice; Biennale competition. C. Tomkins. il Harper 230:98-104 Ap '65

Brazilian bouillabaisse; eighth São Paulo bienal. E. C. Baker. il Art N 64:30-1+ D '65

Bulletin board. See issues of American artist

Charlemagne's dream; exhibition at Aachen. P. Schneider. il Art N 64:22-6+ N '65

Coming soon, art exhibits. See issues of Design

Current and coming. R. Davidson. See issues of Antiques

Explosion to the South; major exhibitions of contemporary Latin American art. il Newsweek 65:88 My 3 '65

From pecans to paint; Mead corp.'s Art across America exhibit. il Newsweek 66:104-5 S 27 '65

From Russia with love; French masterpieces from Hermitage and Moscow's Pushkin museums at Bordeaux gallery of fine arts. il Newsweek 65:79 Je 7 '65

Goings on about town. See issues of New Yorker

Met moves in; 300 years of American painting. F. Getlein. New Repub 152:26-8 My 8 '65

Museum calendar. See issues of American artist

New pictorial language; exhibition of selections from second American biennial of art in Córdoba, at Pan American union. D. Suro. il Américas 17:9-13 S '65

New York school question; exhibition at Los Angeles museum; interview, ed. by N. A. Levine. B. Newman. il Art N 64:38-42+ S '65

Now its neon; exhibition at the University of Pennsylvania's Institute of contemporary art. il Life 58:116-19 My 21 '65

Op is up; Responsive eye exhibit at the Museum of modern art. C. J. McNaspy. America 112:403-4 Mr 20 '65

Reviews and previews. See issues of Art news

Seedbed; art of the 1920s, exhibition at Huntington Hartford's Gallery of modern art. il Newsweek 66:84 Jl 26 '65

Sixteenth man; art exhibition, American federation of arts gallery, New York. il Newsweek 66:81 Jl 5 '65

Three centuries of American painting; exhibition to be shown at the Metropolitan museum, New York. R. Davidson. il Antiques 87:252 Mr '65

Twenty-ninth Corcoran biennial; op works. F. Getlein. New Repub 152:23-4 Mr 20 '65

What is mannerism? exhibitions of 16th-century European art in Paris. A. Chastel. il Art N 64:22-5+ D '65

Where and when to exhibit; exhibition calendar. See issues of Art news

Yamato-e time-machine; Trans-Pacific loan show. G. Kuwayama. il Art N 64:40-3+ N '65

See also
American institute of graphic arts
Exhibitions, Traveling

Galleries and museums
Havoc wrought by vandals. il UNESCO Courier 18:16-17 N '65

In re museums; philosophy and practice; U.S. museums. A. Frankfurter. Art N 64:27+ Mr '65

In the museums. R. Davidson. See issues of Antiques

Learning to look, looking to learn; parents and children swarm among the masterpieces. A. Z. Silver. il N Y Times Mag p 132+ N 14 '65

Michelin for museums. G. R. Marek. il Sat R 48:44+ Mr 13 '65

Opening the door; Taiwan museum for Chinese art. il Time 86:94 N 19 '65

Playground of paints; museums of the French Riviera. E. Peer. il Newsweek 66:84-5 S 13 '65

Stones for the spirit; Maeght museum, Saint-Paul-de-Vence, France. il Time 86:70-1 Jl 16 '65

Thief-proofing our art museums. R. LeBlanc. il UNESCO Courier 18:4-7+ N '65

See also names of museums, e.g. Sterling and Francine Clark art institute, Williamstown, Mass.

Architecture
See Museums—Architecture

History
Books; author: S. Giedion. L. Mumford. New Yorker 41:158+ Mr 6 '65

Criticism, interpretative art. E. R. Fagan. il Sch Arts 65:21-5 N '65

What is mannerism? exhibitions of 16th-century European art in Paris. A. Chastel. il Art N 64:22-5+ D '65

See also
Art nouveau (movement)

Periodicals
Letter from Paris; Arts; List of ten greatest artists over last twenty years, poll of one hundred personalities of Paris art world. Genêt. New Yorker 41:84+ Ag 7 '65

Philosophy
Forms of rationality. R. A. Smith. bibliog il Sch Arts 64:19-23 My '65

How's that again? museum directors define attitudes on photography. O. Wittmann; R. E. Fuller; T. S. Buechner. Mod Phot 29:108+ S '65

Visual arts and the sciences; a proposal for collaboration. G. Kepes. il Arch Rec 137:145-56 My '65

When art becomes propaganda; excerpt from Man as an end. A. Moravia. Sat R 48:23-5+ Ap 17 '65

See also
Nature (aesthetics)

Prices
Bull market in art. C. J. McNaspy. America 114:129-31 Ja 22 '66

Doubleheader; auction of modern art works a record for the western hemisphere. il Time 85:66 Ap 23 '65

Pricing the priceless; worth of masterpieces in Florence's Uffizi gallery. Time 86:56 Jl 2 '65

Private collections
Adventurous taste of Sergei Shchukin. il Life 58:45-58 Ap 9 '65

Archetypical China; Singer collection of early Chinese objects on show at Asia House, New York. H. A. La Farge. il Art N 63:32-5+ F '65

Bull market in art. C. J. McNaspy. America 114:129-31 Ja 22 '66

Celebrated choices of Ivan Morosov. il Life 58:45-8 Ap 9 '65

Collecting is its own reward; N. Simon collections; portfolio. Fortune 71:152-9 Je '65

Collectors of the world, unite! proposed registration of all art before 1920, whether in state museums or private hands. Nat R 17:141 F 23 '65

Cuzco school; Pastor collection shown at Pan American union. J. Gómez-Sicre. il Américas 17:4-11 Jl '65

Gambit in Graustark; offer from Simon for Da Vinci's Ginevra. il Time 86:74 D 3 '65

Great family collections; excerpts, ed. by D. Cooper. il Antiques 88:333-5 S '65

Hitler's art and Göring's acquisitions on view at Schleissheim palace. Newsweek 66:106 N 15 '65

In the American grain; W. Benton's art collection. K. Kuh. il Sat R 48:68-70 O 30 '65

Letter from London; Spencer-Churchill collection. M. Panter-Downes. New Yorker 41:88-9 Je 26 '65

Previewing the Spencer-Churchill sale. J. Russell. il Art N 63:40-3+ F '65

Princely price; sale of Prince Franz Josef's Ginevra dei Benci refused. il Newsweek 66:93-4 D 6 '65

Redressing a spiral showcase; Thannhauser collection bequeathed to Manhattan's Guggenheim museum. il Time 85:86 My 7 '65

Treasure from the past; Aubrey House, London. il Newsweek 66:84 S 13 '65

Unknown treasure; Cintas collection; with editorial comment. L. Lastra. il Américas 17:18-26 F '65

ART—Private collections—*Continued*
Without portfolio. C. B. Luce. McCalls 92:
42+ Ag '65
You bought it now live with it; pop art col-
lectors and their collections. il Life 59:
56–61 Jl 16 '65
See also
Frick collection, New York

Scholarships and fellowships

Competitions and awards. See issues of American artist
Competitions, scholarships. See issues of Art
news

Study and teaching

Art gets the tag end of Friday. R. C. Osborn.
il Am Ed 1:5–7 F '65; Same abr. with title
Cheating our children out of beauty. il
McCalls 93:78+ N '65
Artist on the campus. il Time 85:58+ Ap 2
'65
Discovery. S. Jones. il Sch Arts 64:23–4 Ap
'65
Elementary art grades one-six; symposium.
il Sch Arts 65:5–43 D '65
Points in color; work of ninth grade stu-
dents. E. M. Bollo. il Sch Arts 64:15–17
Mr '65
Saturday classes in the creative arts. M. R.
Mancini and J. M. Someroski. il Sch Arts
64:27–34 F '65
Should the artist come to the campus?
adaptation of address. J. A. Perkins. il
Sat R 48:54–6+ Jl 17 '65
Student teaching via closed circuit televi-
sion. J. E. Van Haren. il Sch Arts 65:
29–31 O '65
Whole secret is feeling. J. Lidstone. il Sch
Arts 64:22–8 Mr '65
See also
Art education
Art schools

Materials

Carpet composition. P. Reynolds. il Sch Arts
65:36 O '65
Cloth relief; new dimensions in fabric. M.
Pappas. il Sch Arts 64:38–40 Je '65
Notes on art. P. Greenberg. il Sch Arts 64:
8–11 Mr '65
Sponge painting; elementary grades. J.
Morkos. il Design 66:33 My '65
String painting; fifth grade. W. Karre. il
Sch Arts 65:10–11 O '65
Tempera and starch; project for the upper
elementary and junior high school pupil.
S. A. Batzka. il Sch Arts 64:29 Mr '65
Toothpick structures. M. F. Tressler. il Sch
Arts 64:12–14 Ap '65
Vanishing color. H. Ringgenberg. il Design
66:27–9 My '65
Wax resist. S. Gruenberg. il Sch Arts 64:
28–9 Je '65
See also
Sculpture—Study and teaching—Materials

Projects

Art & the city; Views of our city, eighth
grade projects. H. Topper. il Sch Arts 65:
12–13 N '65
Art on a fence; summer art class, Beverly
Hills, Calif. P. Vandervoort, 3d. il Sch Arts
64:12–14 My '65
Fire bird. T. B. Heidinger and E. Hungar. il
Sch Arts 65:16 D '65
Frames and tempera. H. S. Rush. Sch Arts
64:38 My '65
Help young eyes identify form; kindergarten
animals. D. Perkins. il Sch Arts 65:40–1 D
'65
Lite bulb zoo; different sizes of bulbs to
make papier mache animals. il Design 67:
18–19 S '65
Metal casting for the grades. J. Burgner. il
Design 67:32–7 S '65
Quilting party. H. Ringgenberg. il Design 67:
38–9 N '65
Roman ladies; can covers to beautify bath-
room. H. S. Rush. il Design 67:27 S '65
Shades of Tom Sawyer; painting on a ninety
foot plywood construction barrier. T. Ram-
say. il Sch Arts 65:16–19 S '65
Spot dots, 3-D. M. Guendling. il Sch Arts 65:
38–9 D '65
Theater of the string puppet. H. Bedford. il
Sch Arts 64:25–32 Ap '65
Twenty minute puppets; hand puppets in the
elementary classroom. J. Burgner. il Sch
Arts 65:5–9 N '65
Wood assemblage; a children's art project.
J. Someroski and R. Myers. il Sch Arts
65:14–17 N '65
See also
Christmas projects

Themes

Art in architecture. il Design 66:21–4 Ja '65
John Fulton, artist & matador. I. Murdoch.
il Am Artist 29:22–7+ Ap '65

Man who paints those big eyes. J. Howard.
il Life 59:39–40+ Ag 27 '65
Painting the feeling of autumn. D. Greene. il
Design 67:36–7 N '65
Pictures in search of a subject. H. C. Pitz.
il Am Artist 29:28–33 N '65
Three centuries of the art of Niagara Falls.
N. Lansdale. il Am Artist 29:34–9+ Ap '65
See also
Hell in art
Indians in art
Negroes in art
West in art

Africa

Africa's golden past. W. L. Hansberry and
E. H. Johnson. il Ebony 20:70–2+ Mr '65

California

Assemblage at the frontier; West Coast art.
il Time 86:106–8 O 15 '65

Czechoslovakia

See also
Prague—Art

England

Crusade for the arts in Britain. M. Wechsler.
New Repub 154:23–4 Ja 1 '66

Russia

When art becomes propaganda; excerpt from
Man as an end. A. Moravia. Sat R 48:23–5+
Ap 17 '65; Reply. R. H. Berman. 48:25 My 8
'65

United States

Who wants art? R. Lynes. il Harper 231:
26+ Jl '65
See also
Painting, American

ART, Abstract
Anxious object, by H. Rosenberg. Review
New Repub 152:26–7 F 20 '65
Sat R il 48:48–9 Ja 23 '65; Reply. H. Ros-
enberg. 48:24 Mr 27 '65
Art galleries; exhibition at the Janis. R. M.
Coates. New Yorker 40:130+ F 13 '65
Expressionism with corners; exhibition at
New York university. I. H. Sandler. Art N
64:38–40+ Ap '65
Importance of being casual. N. Edgar. il
Art N 64:44–5 D 6 '65
Motherwell; exhibition at Museum of modern
art. M. Kozloff. Nation 201:256–8 O 18 '65
Object is symbol. M. Friedman. il Art N 64:
32–5+ N '65
Other side of freedom; Carl Holty's new
paintings. il Art N 64:32–4+ Sum '65
Paint a mosaic. R. Barrio. il Design 67:10–13
S '65
Perception is the medium. B. Riley. il Art N
64:32–3+ O '65
Pictures in search of a subject. H. C. Pitz.
il Am Artist 29:28–33 N '65
Sander at the mixolydian edge; exhibition at
Kootz gallery, N.Y. J. Schuyler. il Art N
64:26–7+ D '65
Satisfactions of Robert Motherwell; exhibi-
tion at Museum of modern art, New York.
N. Edgar. il Art N 64:38–41+ O '65
Voulkes; redemption through ceramics. J.
Coplans. il Art N 64:38–9+ Sum '65
Youngerman; liberty in limits. M. Benedikt.
il Art N 64:43–5+ S '65
ART, African
Art under apartheid. il N Y Times Mag p72–4
Mr 28 '65
ART, American
Americans; Metropolitan's Three hundred
years of American art. M. Kozloff. Nation
200:541–3 My 17 '65 (to be cont)
Big show in Venice; Biennale competition.
C. Tomkins. il Harper 230:98–104 Ap '65
See also
Artists, American
Painting, American
Whitney museum of American art, New York
ART, Australian (aboriginal)
Big mob of work mother; Dorothy Bennett
arranging exhibitions of aboriginal art. il
Newsweek 65:83 Je 28 '65
ART, Baroque
Baroque revolution in Italy; loan exhibition
at the Detroit institution. D. Posner. il
Art N 64:32–4+ Ap '65
Flowering, bursting, exuberant; enchanting
conceits of baroque and rococo. il Vogue
146:232–48 D '65
ART, British
Adventure of making Private view. J. Rus-
sell. Vogue 146:97+ N 15 '65
English on the ball; new young artists. il
Newsweek 65:88 F 15 '65
From England's green and pleasant bowers.
S. Simon. il Art N 64:28–31+ Ap '65
Private view, by B. Robertson and others.
Review
Sat R il 48:33–4 D 11 '65. M. R. Weiss;
J. T. Soby

ART, Buddhist
  See also
Sculpture, Buddhist
ART, Byzantine
  Vogue's eye view of Springtime of the spirit;
  Byzantine fresco of Nativity in Mistra,
  Peloponnesus. il Vogue 146:169-73 D '65
ART, Chinese
  Archetypical China; Singer collection of early
  Chinese objects on show at Asia House,
  New York. H. A. La Farge. il Art N 63:
  32-5+ F '65
  Four jade carvings of the Ch'ien Lung period.
  L. F. Reals. il(p 1) Hobbies 70:32 Ja '66
ART, Coptic
  Cross and orb in Egypt. J. D. Cooney. il
  Natur Hist 74:40-9 bibliog(p68) Ap '65
ART, Dutch
  Master rediscovered; Terbrugghen exhibition
  at Art institute. il Newsweek 66:108+ N 8
  '65
ART, Egyptian
  See also
Art, Coptic
ART, English. See Art, British
ART, Eskimo. See Eskimos—Art
ART, European
  Charlemagne's dream; exhibition at Aachen.
  P. Schneider. il Art N 64:22-6+ N '65
ART, Fantastic
  Return of playfulness. A. Bush-Brown. il
  House & Gard 127:116-17+ Je '65
ART, French
  See also
Painting, French
ART, Icelandic
  See also
Painting, Icelandic
ART, Indonesian
  Indonesian decorative design (cont) G. Kaler.
  il Hobbies 69:42-5+ F; 70:42+ Mr; 44+ Ap;
  44+ My '65
ART, Israeli
  How good is Israeli art? exhibition at Jewish
  museum, New York. H. Kramer. Commen-
  tary 39:62-4 F '65
ART, Italian
  Art news from Italy. M. Gendel. il Art N
  64:48-9+ S '65
  Baroque revolution in Italy; loan exhibition
  at the Detroit institute. D. Posner. il
  Art N 64:32-4+ Ap '65
  Hartford glimpses the pre-renaissance; ex-
  hibition at Wadsworth atheneum. S. J.
  Wagstaff, jr. il Art N 64:32-4+ My '65
ART, Japanese
  Avant-garde in Nippon. il Newsweek 65:101
  My 24 '65
  Beauty from poverty; exhibition at Man-
  hattan's Asia House gallery. il Time 85:
  64-5 Je 4 '65
  Eastern art for western eyes. A. Waley. Har-
  per 230:124-7 F '65
  Yamato-e time-machine; Trans-Pacific loan
  show. G. Kuwayama. il Art N 64:40-3+ N
  '65
  See also
Netsukes
ART, Jewish
  Heritage of Judaism; exhibition at Israel
  museum, Jerusalem. J. R. Moskin. il Look
  29:56-65 O 5 '65
  See also
Art, Israeli
ART, Latin American
  Art. See issues of Américas
  Explosion to the South; major exhibitions of
  contemporary Latin American art. il News-
  week 65:88 My 3 '65
  Young art of the Americas; exhibit at the
  Pan American union. F. Getlein. il Améri-
  cas 17:20-5 Je '65
  Young Latin scene; Esso salon of young
  artists, IBM gallery, New York. F. Getlein.
  New Repub 152:23-5 Je 12 '65
  See also
Art, Pre-Columbian
Painting, Latin American
ART, Medieval
  Baby renaissance; Carolingian art works on
  view in Aachen, Germany. il Time 86:62-3
  Ag 27 '65
  See also
Art, Byzantine
ART, Mexican
  See also
Pottery, Mexican
ART, Minoan
  See also
Crete—Antiquities
ART, Modern. See Modernism (art)
ART, Peruvian
  Architecture and the decorative arts on a
  Peruvian tour. R. Davidson. il Antiques
  88:16+ Jl '65

  Cuzco school; Pastor collection shown at Pan
  American union. J. Gómez-Sicre. il Amér-
  icas 17:4-11 Jl '65
ART, Pre-Columbian
  Gold of the Indies; excerpts from introduc-
  tion to Sweat of the sun and tears of the
  moon. A. Emmerich. Américas 17:23-9 My
  '65
ART, Primitive
  Books in review; art in a new context. D.
  Newton. Natur Hist 74:6+ O '65
  Exotic; exhibition of Leff collection of an-
  cient tribal art at the Museum of natural
  history. New Yorker 41:23-4 Je 19 '65
  See also
Art, Australian (aboriginal)
Art, Pre-Columbian
Sculpture, Primitive
ART, Religious. See Christian art and sym-
  bolism
ART, Renaissance
  What is mannerism? exhibitions of 16th-
  century European art in Paris. A. Chastel.
  il Art N 64:22-5+ D '65
ART, Rococo
  Flowering, bursting, exuberant; enchanting
  conceits of baroque and rococo. il Vogue
  146:232-48 D '65
ART and industry
  Company and the arts. il Duns R 86:40-1+
  Jl '65
  Corporation as art collector. C. Willard. il
  Look 29:67-72 Mr 23 '65
  For more than art's sake; New York Marl-
  borough-Gerson gallery exploits modern
  selling methods. il Bsns W p 150-2+ My
  15 '65
  Mural panels for a publisher's office; dec-
  orative scheme for the foyer of the
  Thomas Y. Corwell company offices. A. A.
  Watson. il Am Artist 29:46-51+ O '65
  Notes and comment; exhibition of early
  American paintings and artifacts at the
  I.B.M. gallery sponsored by King Korn
  trading stamp co. New Yorker 41:23-4 F
  27 '65
  See also
Design, Industrial
ART and mathematics
  Mathematical games; relation between mathe-
  matics and ordered patterns of op art.
  M. Gardner. il Sci Am 213:100-3 Jl '65
ART and music
  Art motivation from music; art experience
  for the middle grades. J. Kujawski and L.
  Gutetter. il Design 66:20-3 My '65
ART and nature. See Nature (aesthetics)
ART and photography
  Eleven great photographs; selections from
  Kodak pavilion at the World's fair. N.
  Kent. il Am Artist 29:31-7+ S '65
  How's that again? museum directors define
  attitudes on photography. O. Wittmann; R.
  E. Fuller; T. S. Buechner. Mod Phot 29:
  108+ S '65
  Painting impressions. R. Barrio. il Design
  66:6-10 My '65
  Shadow designs. W. Bock. il Sch Arts 65:
  18-20 N '65
  Visual arts 1955-1965. G. Davenport. Nat R
  17:1111-12 N 30 '65
ART and politics
  Arts in America. H. Taylor. il Dance Mag
  39:35-9+ N '65
  Invitation to a conversation; implication of
  Polish art show in New York. Nation 201:
  515 D 27 '65
  See also
White House festival of the arts, 1965
ART and religion
  Conscience of an art colony; Anatomy of
  prejudice, symposium at Rockport, Mass.
  F. Potter. il Nation 201:410-14 N 29 '65
  How autonomous is art? Christian Cent 82:
  635-6 My 19 '65
  Nature and grace in art, by J. W. Dixon, jr.
  Review
    Christian Cent 82:744 Je 9 '65. H.
    Ehrensperger
  See also
Christian art and symbolism
ART and science
  Art in science; exhibit at 1965 annual meet-
  ing of the AAAS. D. G. Barry. il Science
  150:1486-7 D 10 '65
  Art, science, and reality. G. R. Walker; reply.
  B. Stewart. Bul Atomic Sci 21:34-5 F '65
  Automation and imagination. J. Hawkes.
  Harper 231:92-4+ O '65
  Visual arts and the sciences; a proposal for
  collaboration. G. Kepes. il Arch Rec 137:
  145-56 My '65
ART and society
  Art and work; adaptation of address, 1964.
  H. Rosenberg. Craft Horiz 25:26+ My '65
  Art as a way of life. S. White. il Sch Arts
  64:5-8 F '65

ART and society—*Continued*
Arts in a New World. A. Heckscher. Craft Horiz 25:11 My '65
Arts in America. H. Taylor. il Dance Mag 39:35-9+ N '65
Can culture explode? notes on subsidizing the arts. S. Kauffmann. Commentary 40:19-28 Ag '65
Lincoln Center: tomb of the future. B. Boretz. il Nation 200:299-304+ Mr 22 '65
Time & light. N. Kent. Am Artist 29:3+ S '65

ART and state
Artists in the Great society? T. B. Hess. Art N 64:21 S '65
Arts: crash program. Nation 200:294 Mr 22 '65
Biting the hand; Arts endowment. New Repub 153:8 O 2 '65
California design conference called by governor to encourage excellence in state architecture. il Arch Rec 137:20+ F '65
Can culture explode? notes on subsidizing the arts. S. Kauffmann. Commentary 40:19-28 Ag '65
Congressman looks at the arts. J. V. Lindsay. Sat R 48:23+ Mr 13 '65
Federal aid? concerning recognition of photography. B. Downes. Pop Phot 57:16 Jl '65
Government in the arts; National endowment for the arts. J. L. Collier. Holiday 38:117-18 S '65
Moderns in the White House. F. Getlein. New Repub 153:34-5 O 23 '65
New federal architecture. il Arch Rec 137:135-46 Mr '65
Next on the subsidy list: plays, opera, orchestras. il U S News 58:64-5 Mr 15 '65
Paintings in the President's house. F. Getlein. New Repub 153:34-6 O 16 '65
President outlines housing and arts subsidy programs, names National council on arts. Arch Rec 137:20+ Ap '65
Roger and the rabbits. F. Getlein. New Repub 152:25+ Ap 3 '65
Something for the arts; findings of Rockefeller panel. M. Straight. New Repub 152:11-15 Mr 13 '65; Reply. H. Green. 152:28 Ap 3 '65
Support from the state. A. M. Lingg. il Opera N 30:13-15 Ja 15 '66
See also
Arts councils of America (organization)
State encouragement of science, literature and art
United States—National council on the arts
United States—National foundation on the arts and the humanities

ART as recreation. See Recreation—Activities
ART buildings, College. See College architecture
ART centers
For an art center: free-flowing space; Kalamazoo art center. il Arch Rec 138:168-9 S '65
ART chemistry. See Art objects—Conservation and restoration
ART clubs
Bell rang in one hour; Artists' sketching club of New York. il Am Heritage 16:74-9 Je '65
ART collections. See Art—Private collections
ART colonies. See Artists colonies
ART criticism
Anxious object, by H. Rosenberg. Review Commentary 39:104-8 Je '65. H. D. Aiken
Criticism, interpretative art. E. R. Fagan. il Sch Arts 65:21-5 N '65
ART critics
What is a critic? R. Arnheim. Sat R 48:26-7 Ag 28 '65
ART dealers
Art over the counter; retailers open more art departments. Time 85:94+ My 7 '65
Bull market in art. C. J. McNaspy. America 114:129-31 Ja 22 '66
Cash expressionism; de Kooning and dealer Janis sue each other. Newsweek 65:96 Ap 12 '65
Dealer's choice; S. Kaner's Court gallery, Copenhagen. il Newsweek 66:76 Ag 30 '65
I had the wild guys; E. Halpert's new gallery. Newsweek 66:94+ S 20 '65
Man who invented modern art dealing. J. Russell. il Vogue 146:146-9+ S 15 '65
Synchromism, the first American movement; exhibition at Knoedler, New York. W. C. Agee. il Art N 64:28-31+ O '65

Tirana caper; purchase of Goya painting for Broadway art gallery, Worcestershire. il Newsweek 65:96 Ap 12 '65
See also
Sotheby and company

History
Paris *marchands-merciers* and French eighteenth-century taste; adaptation of address, May 1964. F. J. B. Watson. il Antiques 88:347-51 S '65
ART editors. See Editors and editing
ART education
Art education 1965; prospects and problems. J. J. Hausman. il Sch Arts 64:7-11 Ap '65
Art for the high school students. M. F. Andrews. il Sch Arts 64:33-8 Ap '65
Developmental approach to crafts. N. Krevitsky. il Sch Arts 64:30-5 Je '65
Innovation in art & education. J. W. Cataldo. il Sch Arts 64:2-3 Je '65
Letters. Sch Arts 64:47 Mr; 65:48 O '65
Research in art education. W. J. Kasza. il Sch Arts 64:24-6 My '65
R.I.S.D. hypotheses. D. Manzella. il Sch Arts 65:31-3 S '65
Toward a new art. H. Burgart. il Sch Arts 54:5-9 O '65
ART exhibitions. See Art—Exhibitions
ART exhibitions, Traveling. See Exhibitions, Traveling
ART forgeries. See Forgery of works of art
ART galleries, Commercial. See Art dealers
ART galleries and museums. See Art—Galleries and museums
ART glass. See Glass, Ornamental
ART in industry. See Art and industry
ART in the home
Have your own art gallery. B. Derig. il Suc Farm 64:105+ Ja '66
Life with pop. E. Sverbeyeff. il N Y Times Mag p98-9 My 2 '65
Where to put the things you love to look at. il House & Gard 128:100-5 Jl '65
See also
Antiques
ART institute, Chicago. See Chicago art institute
ART libraries
See also
Metropolitan museum of art, New York
ART literature
Christmas on the coffee table. F. Getlein. New Repub 153:33-5 D 18 '65
ART loans
French paintings from Russia at the Louvre. M. E. Davies. il Antiques 88:584+ N '65
Red faces at the Louvre; cultural exchange from Russia's hermitage and Pushkin collections. il Time 86:74 O 29 '65
Russian delegation to Paris. P. M. Grand. il Art N 64:34-5+ O '65
ART metal work
Arc welding as a means of expression. B. White. il Sch Arts 65:29-31 N '65
Color and metal. J. Brzostoski; J. McDevitt; A. Ventura. il Craft Horiz 25:26-37+ N '65
Malay metal art. G. Kaler. il Hobbies 70:46-7+ O '65
Metal lathe cutting as art form. W .F. Dominick. il Sch Arts 64:36-7 My '65
Mural of copper repoussé for our school. S. L. Dieffenbach. il Sch Arts 64:19-21 Je '65
Village blacksmiths; Japhia interiors. il Ebony 21:96-8+ D '65
See also
Goldsmithing
ART museums. See Art—Galleries and museums
ART nouveau (movement)
Art nouveau. Am Home 68:112 Ap '65
ART objects
Some eighteenth-century classics from the collection of I. Austin Kelly III. A. Winchester. il Antiques 87:200-3 F '65
Where to put the things you love to look at. il House & Gard 128:100-5 Jl '65
See also
Antiques
Art in the home

Collectors and collecting
Collectors' corners. E. Sverbeyeff. il N Y Times Mag p34-5 My 30 '65
Four ways to spend $1000 for real. il Esquire 64:130-3 N '65

Conservation and restoration
New science of art conservation. H. J. Plenderleith. il UNESCO Courier 18:7-10 Ja '65

Copyright
See Copyright—Art

ART objects—*Continued*

Transportation

See Transportation of works of art

ART of living. See Conduct of life

ART patronage
Who pays the piper? J. L. Collier. Holiday 38:168+ D '65
Who wants art? R. Lynes. il Harper 231:26+ Jl '65

ART prices. See Art—Prices

ART sales
Art sale in the supermarkets. il Newsweek 65:75-6+ Je 21 '65
Auction by Early bird; Parke-Bernet & Sotheby's transaction. R. Lynes. il Harper 231:28+ Ag '65
Champagne and Chagall; double auction and il Newsweek 65:86-7 Ap 26 '65
Cold plunge; Cézanne's Bathers, purchased by Britain's National gallery. il Time 85:68-9 F 12 '65
Coming auctions. See issues of Art news
Doubleheader; auction of modern art works a record for the western hemisphere. il Time 85:66 Ap 23 '65
Early bird brightens the fine art scene; first transatlantic art auction. il Bsns W p34-5 My 29 '65
For more than art's sake; New York Marlborough-Gerson gallery exploits modern selling methods. il Bsns W p 150-2+ My 15 '65
London auction prices. R. Davidson. il Antiques 88:430+ O '65
Originals; sale of paintings at Menlo Park branch of Woolworth's. New Yorker 41:36-8 Ap 10 '65
Rembrandt standard; London auctions. Time 85:73 Ap 2 '65
Simon says; sale of Rembrandt's portrait of his son Titus at Christie's, London. il Newsweek 65:80 Mr 29 '65
Son of Rembrandt; painting of the artist's son Titus auctioned at Christie's in London. il Time 85:70 Mr 26 '65
See also
Parke-Bernet galleries, incorporated

ART schools
Art school directory. Am Artist 29:83-98 Mr '65
Travel & study; survey of study opportunities, with directory. il Craft Horiz 25:27-41 My '65
What is an art school for? N. Kent. Am Artist 29:3+ Mr '65

ART societies
See also
Society of illustrators

ART studios. See Artists studios

ART teachers
Artist-teachers in America. G. Byrd, bibliog il Sch Arts 65:21-5 O '65 (to be cont)
Great artists as art teachers. D. L. Smith. il Am Artist 29:58-63 S '65
N.C.C.A.E in Cincinnati; third biennial workshop. il Sch Arts 64:30-1 Mr '65
Printmaker. S. Chafetz. il Sch Arts 64:27-30 My '65
Shoji Hamada. A. R. Park. bibliog il Sch Arts 64:23-7 Je '65

Education

Undergraduate training of an art teacher. F. R. Schwartz. bibliog Sch Arts 64:36-8 F '65

ART thefts
Duke returns. il Newsweek 65:78-9 Je 7 '65
Duke's thief; Kempton Bunton. por Newsweek 66:64-5 Ag 2 '65
Fifty-seven oil paintings lost in a single robbery; Annonciade museum at St Tropez. il UNESCO Courier 18:14-15 N '65
French menus and master thieves. H. Frankel. Sat R 49:79 Ja 8 '66
Interpol; theft warnings alert police in ninety-five countries. il UNESCO Courier 18:8-9 N '65
Thief-proofing our art museums. R. LeBlanc. il UNESCO Courier 18:4-7+ N '65

ART trade
See also
Art dealers
Art sales

ART vandalism. See Vandalism

ARTAMONOV, M. I.
Frozen tombs of the Scythians; with biographical sketch. Sci Am 212:18, 100-9 bibliog(p 151) My '65

ARTANDI, Susan A.
Keeping up with mechanization. por Library J 90:4715-17 N 1 '65

ARTEMISIA. See Wormwood

ARTERIES
Blood-flow relation between hepatic artery and portal vein. J. L. Ternberg and H. R. Butcher, jr. bibliog il Science 150:1030-1 N 19 '65

Surgery

See Blood vessels—Surgery

ARTERIOSCLEROSIS
Cigarettes and atherosclerosis. Sci Am 213:40 D '65
Diet; heart of the matter? il Newsweek 65:53-7 F 8 '65
Fighting fire with fire; gas endarterectomy. il Newsweek 66:93 N 22 '65
Hewing the fat; gas surgery. il Time 86:59 N 26 '65
How well nourished should our children be? relationship of nutrition and exercise to arteriosclerosis. B. Spock. Redbook 125:44+ S '65
Milk-drinking could affect artery clogging. Sci N L 89:25 Ja 8 '66

ARTERIOSCLEROSIS research
Chickens that exercise lack clogged arteries. il Sci N L 88:326 N 20 '65

ARTERY clips. See Surgical instruments

ARTHRITIS
Chemistry and arthritis. Newsweek 65:60 Ap 19 '65
Unusual arthritis type linked to excess iron. Sci N L 88:46 Jl 17 '65
See also
Antiarthritic substances

Therapy

Arthritis. M. Markham. Parents Mag 40:60-1+ D '65

ARTHROPODS
Cousin to mite and spider; tardigrades are arthropods of microscopic dimensions. L. J. Gandek and D. Pramer. il Natur Hist 74:63 N '65
Nature note; joint-legged animals. Sci N L 89:46 Ja 15 '66
Pink creature lives closest to South Pole. Sci N L 87:183 Mr 20 '65
See also
Parasites—Arthropods

ARTHUR, Chester Alan
Chester A. Arthur, twenty-first President. F. Freidel. il pors Nat Geog Mag 127:694-7 My '65

ARTHUR, Gloria
If your plants aren't healthy, check your water supply. Flower Grower 52:35 O '65

ARTHUR, Jay
Pictures in sound; tape recorders. Pop Phot 57:116-17 D '65

ARTHUR, Kay
Moonlight is when; drama. Plays 24:3-16, 42 Mr '65

ARTHUR Guinness, son and company, limited. See Guinness, Arthur, son and company, limited

ARTHUR S. Flemming awards. See Rewards, prizes, etc.

ARTICHOKES
Artichokes are just good looking. il Sunset 134:282 My '65

ARTICHOKES, American. See Jerusalem artichokes

ARTICLES for periodicals. See Periodical literature

ARTIFICIAL bait. See Fishing lures, flies, etc.

ARTIFICIAL body parts. See Prosthesis

ARTIFICIAL bone. See Bone, Artificial

ARTIFICIAL flowers. See Flowers, Artificial

ARTIFICIAL heart. See Heart, Artificial

ARTIFICIAL heart valves. See Heart—Surgery

ARTIFICIAL insemination
Are A.I. rules strangling purebreds? H. H. Stonaker and J. A. Rohlf. il Farm J 89:31+ D '65
Here's the latest on swine AI. J. Harvey. il Suc Farm 63:56-7+ Mr '65
Mass ovulation and foster mother cows make litters of 100s. il Life 59:74-5 S 10 '65

ARTIFICIAL insemination, Human
Pregnancy by artificial insemination fills need. Sci N L 88:135 Ag 28 '65
Secrets of AI. il Newsweek 66:81-2 N 15 '65

ARTIFICIAL organs. See Prosthesis

ARTIFICIAL reefs. See Reefs, Artificial

ARTIFICIAL respiration. See Respiration, Artificial

ARTIFICIAL rubber. See Rubber, Artificial

ARTIFICIAL satellites
Missiles and rockets astrolog; current status of U.S. missile and space programs. See occasional issues of Missiles and rockets

ARTIFICIAL satellites—*Continued*
Missiles and rockets world missile/space encyclopedia 1965. il Miss & Roc 17:37-44+ Jl 26 '65
Roster of current space activity. R. N. Watts, jr. Sky & Tel 31:28-9 Ja '66
Sky elevator proposed to link space to earth; Project Skyhook. Sci N L 88:50 Jl 24 '65
Space vehicle log (cont) Aviation W 82:125 Mr 15 '65
Timers quiet satellites. Sci N L 87:262 Ap 24 '65
US, Soviet space probes; US lead in space race. New Repub 152:7 Je 19 '65
Unmanned scientific satellites; future hinges on manned project plans. il Miss & Roc 17:98-100 N 29 '65
See also
Space vehicles

Astronomical applications
Five telescopes in orbit to study stars in 1967; for one of the orbiting astronomical observatories. Sci N L 87:248 Ap 17 '65
Good look at NGC 4565. N. G. Roman. il Am Ed 1:5-8 O '65
Mars vehicle becomes major scientific program; groundwork for expanded solar and interplanetary program. D. E. Fink. il Aviation W 82:116-18+ Mr 15 '65
NASA orbits solar observatory. Aviation W 82:25 F 8 '65
NASA orders three more OSOs. Aviation W 83:30 S 6 '65
New spacecraft are designed to carry whole observatory units. T. D. Nicholson. il Natur Hist 74:28-30 N '65
OAO-B telescope will scan stars mapped by first OAO; orbiting astronomical observatory. R. D. Hibben. il Aviation W 83:74-6+ Jl 19 '65
OGO 2 satellite in orbit. R. N. Watts, jr. il Sky & Tel 30:353-4 D '65
Plans told for manned observatories. W. S. Beller. il Miss & Roc 16:28-30+ My 17 '65
Prototype telescope for OAO-C tested. R. D. Hibben. il Aviation W 82:71+ Mr 22 '65
RAE to utilize 750-1,000-ft. antennas; radio astronomy explorer satellite. D. E. Fink. il Aviation W 83:106-7+ S 27 '65
Second orbiting solar observatory. R. N. Watts, jr. il Sky & Tel 29:151-2 My '65
Second sun-watching satellite now in orbit; OSO-B2. il Sci N L 87:115 F 20 '65
75-mile space antennas under study. R. Pay. il Miss & Roc 17:32-3 N 1 '65
Space balloon vehicles seen inflating in orbit. il Sci N L 89:37 Ja 15 '66
Space observatory successfully launched; orbiting geophysical observatory. Sci N L 88:264 O 23 '65
Space science stresses optics, antennas. K. Johnson. Aviation W 82:34 Ap 5 '65
300-in.-dia. liquid orbiting eye proposed. R. Pay. il Miss & Roc 16:43 Je 14 '65

Communication applications
See Communications satellites

Equipment
See Space vehicles—Equipment

Launching
AF gets two OV's for dual launch. W. E. Wilks. Miss & Roc 17:18 D 6 '65
And eight makes 300; eight US satellites orbited in one launching. Newsweek 65:51 My 31 '65
Eight satellites at once. R. N. Watts, jr. Sky & Tel 30:87 Ag '65
First industry-built Saturn 1 puts Pegasus-2 in precise orbit. Aviation W 82:21 My 31 '65

Mapping applications
Benchmarks in space can aid mapping; laser beam to photograph Explorer 22. W. S. Beller. il Miss & Roc 16:33+ Ap 12 '65
Geos-A launched, returns data from orbit higher than planned. Aviation W 83:38 N 15 '65
PAGEOS to help find size and shape of earth; Passive geodetic earth orbiting satellite. il(cover) Sci N L 88:133 Ag 28 '65
SECOR V upgrading geodetic effort. il Miss & Roc 17:18 Ag 16 '65

Meteorological applications
Balloons and satellites could track weather. Sci N L 87:105 F 13 '65
Cold line chill; lack of cooperation by Soviet Union. Reporter 32:14+ Mr 11 '65
DOD steps up weather satellite work. D. L. Zylstra. Miss & Roc 16:16 My 31 '65
Early bird speeds chart transmission; data gathered by Tiros IX. il Miss & Roc 17:35+ Jl 5 '65

GAO charge to spur Nimbus investigation. Aviation W 82:99+ F 22 '65
Geophysical observations from Nimbus I. W. Nordberg. bibliog il Science 150:559-72 O 29 '65
Global weather observation system urged; testing Ghost for global horizontal sounding technique, with launch of Nimbus B. D. E. Fink. Aviation W 83:34 D 6 '65
Hurricane Betsy viewed by TIROS satellites; photographs. Miss & Roc 17:18 S 20 '65
John o' Groats to Timbuctoo; photographs taken by the Nimbus weather satellite. Sci Digest 57:inside back cover Mr '65
Latest weather monitor; Tiros 9. R. N. Watts, jr. Sky & Tel 29:151 Mr '65
NASA launches first cartwheel satellite; TIROS (television infrared observation satellite) il(p81) Sci N L 87:88 F 6 '65
NASA weather satellite plans. il Aviation W 84:40-2+ Ja 3 '66
Radiation, inc. equipping Nimbus-B satellite. M. Getler. Miss & Roc 16:35 Mr 8 '65
Satellite could show temperatures, pressures. Sci N L 87:152 Mr 6 '65
Tiros 10 monitors tropical storm belt. Aviation W 83:36 Jl 12 '65
Weather buoy-satellite link is studied. W. H. Gregory. il Aviation W 82:54-5+ F 8 '65

Military applications
Base where MOL will be born; air force's Vandenberg. il Bsns W p70-2+ N 13 '65
Cosmos 57 believed destroyed by Soviets; photographic reconnaissance spacecraft. W. J. Normyle. Aviation W 82:34 Ap 12 '65
Douglas gets a jump with MOL; manned space laboratory. il Bsns W p50-2 D 25 '65
From Washington: the air force in space and peacekeeping assessments. H. Margolis. Bul Atomic Sci 21:34-7 O '65
Satellite photo station ready soon; Electro-optical surveillance station. R. Pay. Miss & Roc 17:42 Jl 19 '65
Schriever reveals MIDAS advances. Miss & Roc 16:12-13 My 24 '65
Soviet article raps DOD space role; summary of report. M. Golyshev. Miss & Roc 17:17 N 22 '65

Navigational applications
Satellites to aid in sea studies; nine oceanographic ships planned. H. Taylor. il Miss & Roc 17:41-2+ S 6 '65
Ships and planes navigated by satellites. W. Von Braun. il Pop Sci 186:76-7+ My '65

Power supply
See Space vehicles—Power supply

Tracking
ALOTS advances airborne tracking. R. Pay. il Miss & Roc 17:26-7 N 22 '65
He keeps score for the space race; B. Lovell and his radiotelescope at Britain's Jodrell bank. il Bsns W p96-8+ O 30 '65
How hams track space shots. R. Gannon. il Pop Sci 186:99-102 My '65
Satellite photo station ready soon; Electro-optical surveillance station. R. Pay. Miss & Roc 17:42 Jl 19 '65
Track man; expert schoolboy. Newsweek 65:69 Mr 15 '65
Western satellite research network. G. A. McCue and others. il Sky & Tel 30:88-90 Ag '65
Where do dead satellites go? I. Asimov. il Sci Digest 58:86-7 D '65
See also
Communications satellites—Tracking

Use in research
Aerojet demonstrates solid pulse motors. Aviation W 82:30 Ap 19 '65
AF drafting own animal satellites; biosatellite program. H. M. David. Miss & Roc 16:32 Mr 22 '65
AF gets two OV's for dual launch. W. E. Wilks. Miss & Roc 17:18 D 6 '65
Application satellite technology; report will decide navigation role. il Miss & Roc 17:91-2+ N 29 '65
AE-B to probe higher in atmosphere. W. S. Beller. il Miss & Roc 17:28+ N 15 '65
Benchmarks in space can aid mapping; laser beam to photograph Explorer 22. W. S. Beller. il Miss & Roc 16:33+ Ap 12 '65
Biosatellite hardware nearly ready. H. M. David. il Miss & Roc 16:34+ F 22 '65
Decision nearing on cislunar MDS; meteoroid detection satellite. Miss & Roc 16:14 Ap 26 '65
ESRO II in early test phase; experiments dealing with solar radiation measurements. il Miss & Roc 17:26-7 Jl 5 '65

ARTIFICIAL satellites—Use in research—*Cont.*
Explorer 26. R. N. Watts, jr. Sky & Tel 29:96 F '65
Explorer 30. R. N. Watts, jr. Sky & Tel 31:30 Ja '66
Hope grows for follow-on Pegasus. M. Getler. il Miss & Roc 16:14-15 F 22 '65
Improved solar cells planned for IMP-D. R. D. Hibben. il Aviation W 83:53+ Jl 26 '65
Measuring meteoroids; orbiting Pegasus launched. il Time 85:58 F 26 '65
Meteoroid program may be expanded. Miss & Roc 16:17 My 31 '65
Michigan satellite design near completion. R. D. Hibben. il Aviation W 83:75+ N 22 '65
Micrometeoroid measurements. J. H. Wujek, jr. il Electr World 74:42-3+ N '65
NASA plans two optical experiment awards. D. E. Fink. Aviation W 83:33 S 13 '65
NASA will pick two contractors for preliminary OTS design work; optical technology satellite. Aviation W 83:22 Jl 5 '65
OAR to use own vehicles for OV shots. R. Pay. il Miss & Roc 18:32-4+ Ja 17 '66
OV2-1 will seek to determine extent of Van Allen belt threat; orbital vehicle. il Aviation W 83:113+ S 27 '65
Pegasus returning meteoroid flux data. il Aviation W 82:28 F 22 '65
Pegasus satellite flies. R. N. Watts, jr. il Sky & Tel 29:210 Ap '65
Pegasus 2 launched; meteoroid-detection satellite. R. N. Watts, jr. il Sky & Tel 30:18-19 Jl '65
Pegasus 3; meteoroid-collecting satellite. R. N. Watts, jr. il Sky & Tel 30:215 O '65
Proposed optical satellite described; optical technology satellite. M. Getler. Miss & Roc 16:30+ Mr 29 '65
Radiation-monitoring satellite awaits Titan 111-C launching. S. Butler. Miss & Roc 17:15 S 20 '65
Satellites while orbiting could aid agriculture. Sci N L 87:216 Ap 3 '65
Study of advanced meteoroid detection satellite is planned. Aviation W 83:34 Ag 9 '65
UK-3 to probe lightning's RF noise. Miss & Roc 16:30+ Je 21 '65

ARTIFICIAL satellites, British
UK-3 to probe lightning's RF noise. Miss & Roc 16:30+ Je 21 '65

ARTIFICIAL satellites, French
Fr-1 bolsters French civil space ambition. W. C. Wetmore. il Aviation W 84:54-5+ Ja 10 '66
France enters the space race, but—. il U S News 59:8 D 6 '65
France in orbit. il Newsweek 66:66 D 6 '65
France injects first satellite into orbit. L. L. Doty. il Aviation W 83:29 D 6 '65
France's first satellite. R. N. Watts, jr. Sky & Tel 31:27 Ja '66
France's silent satellite. Bsns W p54 D 4 '65
French FR-1A satellite orbited. Aviation W 83:36 D 13 '65
Pre-election satellite launching sought by de Gaulle government. Aviation W 83:29 S 20 '65
Satellite balloon-watch; Project EOLE to measure air currents, pressures and temperatures. Sci N L 87:115 F 20 '65

ARTIFICIAL satellites, Japanese
Japan moves toward launch of home-built satellite in '68. il Miss & Roc 17:29-30 D 20 '65

ARTIFICIAL satellites, Russian
Cosmos 57 believed destroyed by Soviets; precursor to manned Soviet flights. W. J. Normyle. Aviation W 82:34 Ap 12 '65
New pictures of Elektron and Cosmos. il Miss & Roc 16:15 My 24 '65
Operational Russian satellites scan U.S. E. H. Kolcum. il Aviation W 82:22 F 22 '65
Russians believed deploying Comsat net. P. J. Klass. Aviation W 83:29 O 11 '65
Russians rap U.S. satellites; Molyna-1 launching. Bsns W p 126 O 23 '65
Soviet satellite tests space transmissions. Aviation W 82:21 My 3 '65
Soviet satellites watching us. R. N. Watts, jr. il Sky & Tel 29:359-60 Je '65
Soviets boost recon satellite launch rate; 1965 Cosmos satellites. il Aviation W 83:32 Ag 16 '65

ARTIFICIAL teeth. See Teeth, Artificial

ARTISTIC ability. See Creation (literary, artistic, etc)

ARTISTIC cookery. See Cookery, Ornamental

ARTISTIC photography. See Photography, Artistic

ARTISTS
Great artists as art teachers. D. L. Smith. il Am Artist 29:58-63 S '65
Letter from Paris; Arts: List of ten greatest artists over last twenty years, poll by one hundred personalities of Paris art world. Genêt. New Yorker 41:84+ Ag 7 '65
Reviews and previews: new names this month. See issues of Art news
    See also
Women as artists

ARTISTS, American
Artist-teachers in America. G. Byrd. bibliog il Sch Arts 65:21-5 O '65 (to be cont)
Artists speak. il Time 87:59 Ja 7 '66
Bell rang in one hour; Artists' sketching club of New York. il Am Heritage 16:74-9 Je '65
Five famous artists in their personal backgrounds. il House & Gard 128:176-83 D '65
What is not in New York; platoons of painters and sculptors. F. Getlein. New Repub 153:32+ O 2 '65
    See also
Cloud, C. C.
Painting, American
Smith, C. W.

ARTISTS, British
English on the ball; new young artists. il Newsweek 65:88 F 15 '65

ARTISTS, Ethiopian
    See also
Tekle, A.

ARTISTS, French
    See also
Degas, E.
Matisse, H.

ARTISTS, Italian
Airlift; Italian artists fly to New York with works to benefit two hospitals. New Yorker 41:38-9 Mr 13 '65

ARTISTS, Uruguayan
    See also
Frasconi, A.

ARTISTS colonies
Artists in paradise. H. Frost. il Opera N 29:6-11 F 27 '65
Greenish village; Nashville, Ind. il Design 66:30-2 My '65

ARTISTS materials
Art mart. See issues of American artist
Buffalo sculpture for a California high school. R. Reynolds. il Am Artist 30:54-7+ Ja '66
Eleventh annual buyer's guide of art materials (cont) il Am Artist 30:BG1-16 Ja '66
New medium for sculpture. D. Mortillito. il Am Artist 29:44-9+ D '65
Painting with tissue paper. R. P. Benson. il Design 67:6-8 S '65
Plastic paints. N. Roukes. il Sch Arts 64:20-4 F '65
Ralph Mayer's technical question & answer page. R. Mayer. See issues of American artist

ARTISTS studios
Atelier crisis. il Time 86:62 Ag 27 '65
City of art; Paris studio complex nears completion. Newsweek 66:93 O 4 '65

ARTS and crafts
Contemporary craftsman. P. P. Hatgil. il Sch Arts 64:36-7 Je '65
Object: act. il Craft Horiz 25:36-7+ S '65
    See also
Glass, Ornamental
Handicraft
Paper work
Weaving
World crafts council

Bibliography

Book review section. See issues of Design
Books (cont) Craft Horiz 25:50-2 Ja; 60 My; 54-6 N '65

Competitions

Creative problem to solve. il Design 66:16 Ja '65

Exhibitions

American Indian student: two educational programs; exhibition at New York's Museum of contemporary crafts. A. Thorpe; M. Libhart. il Craft Horiz 25:12-13+ Jl '65
Calendar; Where to show. See issues of Craft horizons
California design nine; triennial juried exhibition of the Pasadena art museum. P. Soldner. il Craft Horiz 25:18-23 My '65
Collector: object environment; summer show at New York's Museum of contemporary crafts. il Craft Horiz 25:22-7 Jl '65
Exhibitions. See issues of Craft horizons
Fabric collage; exhibition at Museum of contemporary crafts, New York. K. Sawyer. il Craft Horiz 25:16-21+ Mr '65

ARTS and crafts—Exhibitions—*Continued*
Fiber, clay, metal; seventh biennial show of the Saint Paul art center, Saint Paul, Minn. D. Zachai. il Craft Horiz 25:10-17+ Ja '65; Discussion. 25:11+ Mr '65
Northwest craftsmen's exhibition. L. Harrington. il Craft Horiz 25:12-17 My '65
Object: adornment; current show at Museum of contemporary crafts. W. Berkson. il Craft Horiz 25:12-25 S '65

Study and teaching
Alaska's designer-craftsman training project. M. Libhart. il Craft Horiz 25:16+ Jl '65
Crafts classes for children. M. R. Mancini and J. M. Someroski. il Sch Arts 65:32-5 O '65
Crafts in education. W. Mahoney. il Sch Arts 65:7-10 S '65
Developmental approach to crafts. N. Krevitsky. il Sch Arts 64:30-5 Je '65
Peace corps in art: a report. F. Friedman. il Am Artist 29:80+ Je '65
Travel & study; survey of study opportunities, with directory. il Craft Horiz 25:27-41 My '65

Denmark
Going places, finding things in Denmark. N. S. Hazelton. il House & Gard 127:36+ Mr '65

Egypt
Poetic world fashioned on the weaver's loom. R. W. Wassef. il UNESCO Courier 18:32-9 Jl '65

India
Golden one: government-of-India-sponsored handicraft shop in Corning glass building. New Yorker 41:20-1 Je 26 '65

Latin America
In defense of crafts. G. de Zéndegui. Américas 17:inside cover N '65

Malaya
Malay metal art. G. Kaler. il Hobbies 70: 46-7+ O '65

Spain
Spain: impressions and influences. il Ladies Home J 82:48-53+ F '65

United States
Crafts of Salem. F. P. Albright. il Antiques 88:94-8 Jl '65
Doing their home work. il Newsweek 66:66-7+ Ag 30 '65

ARTS and crafts, Indian. See Indians of North America—Industries

ARTS and humanities branch (agency) See United States—Education, Office of—Arts and humanities branch

ARTS council of Great Britain
Subsidies and the British. il Hi Fi 15:43 Ap '65

ARTS councils of America (organization)
Arts in Washington; notes on conference in Washington, D.C. June 16 to 19. Q. Eaton. Opera N 30:6 S 25 '65

ARTSAY, Aida Favia-. See Favia-Artsay, A.

ARTSCHWAGER, Richard
Object: still life; interview. por Craft Horiz 25:28-30+ S '65

ARTURO Ui: drama. See Brecht, B.

ARTZYBASHEFF, Boris
Letter from the publisher. B. M. Auer. il Time 86:17 O 29 '65
Obituary
Time por 86:13 Jl 23 '65

ARUBA (island)
Go Dutch treat! see Aruba and Curaçao, two Dutch islands in the Caribbean. E. Gay. il U S Camera 28:18-19 My '65

ARZHAK, Nikolai, pseud. See Daniel, Y.

ARZT, Karl, family
I took the wrong baby home from the hospital; case in Scheibbs, Austria. F. Spelman. il McCalls 92:62+ Ap '65

ASAHI (newspaper) See Newspapers—Japan

ASAHI Pentax Spotmatic cameras. See Single-lens reflex cameras

ASBELL, Bernard
Best weapon in the fight for better education. Redbook 125:58-9+ My '65
Bright new spirit in Tonyville. Good H 162: 60-1+ Ja '66
Six years old is too late. Redbook 125:53+ S '65
Trial of Patricia Gardelius. Redbook 126:46-8+ D '65
(ed) See Goodman, Mrs R. W. My son didn't die in vain

ASBRAND, Karin
Anders paints a picture; drama. Plays 25:55-60 Ja '66

ASCHER, Marcia. See Ascher, R. jt. auth.

ASCHER, Robert, and Ascher, Marcia
Recognizing the emergence of man. bibliog Science 147:243-50; 148:168 Ja 15, Ap 9 '65

ASCHOFF, Jürgen
Circadian rhythms in man. bibliog Science 148:1427-32 Je 11 '65

ASCOLI, Max
Editorial. See issues of The reporter
On reading Hammarskjöld. Reporter 32:37-40 My 20 '65

ASCOMYCETES
Study in specificity; minute fungi parasitize living arthropods. R. K. Benjamin. il Natur Hist 74:42-9 Mr '65

ASCORBIC acid. See Vitamins—Vitamin C

ASERINSKY, Eugene
Periodic respiratory pattern occurring in conjunction with eye movements during sleep. bibliog Science 150:763-6 N 5 '65

ASH, Lee
Final call for Who's who; letter. Library J 90:3830 O 1 '65
WLB biography (cont) Wilson Lib Bul 39: 694+, 921 Ap, Je '65

ASH (tree)
Often an ash is the answer. il Sunset 135:192-3 D '65

ASHA, Rafik
United Nations commemoration address, June 26, 1965. UN Mo Chron 2:152-6 Jl '65

ASHBAUGH, Byron L.
Guideposts to a nature center. Audubon Mag 67:148-51 My '65

ASHBERY, John
Art news from Paris (cont) Art N 64:52-3+ O; 37+ D '65
Expressionist in Paris. Art N 64:44-5+ Ap '65
Paris: from pre-history to outer space. Art N 64:45-7 Sum '65

ASHBROOK, Joseph
Astronomical scrapbook. See issues of Sky and telescope

ASHBROOK, William
Real hero. Opera N 29:24-5 Mr 27 '65

ASHBURY, Howard H.
Bigger hospitals or bigger people? Sat R 48: 59-60 N 6 '65

ASHBY, Lyle W. and Kramer, I .L.
Building on a legacy of change. NEA J 54: 52-4 O '65

ASHBY, Neal
Easterner's impression of Canyonlands. Am For 71:24-5+ Ag '65
Maple gives New York a first. Am For 71:16-19+ Ap '65

ASHE, Arthur, Jr
Ace. il Time 86:50 Ag 13 '65
American ace. il por Time 86:78 N 19 '65
Arthur was king for a day. J. Jares. il Sports Illus 23:36-7+ S 20 '65
Enter Arthur Ashe. il pors Life 59:61-2+ O 15 '65
Pioneer in white pants. H. Gordon. il pors N Y Times Mag p6-7+ Ja 2 '66
Understudy takes charge. F. Deford. il pors Sports Illus 23:18-19 Ag 9 '65

ASHEIM, Lester E.
University libraries in developing countries; address, July 1965. por ALA Bul 59:795-802 O '65

ASHER, Fronie
Tribute to Miss Fronie. D. Hering. il por Dance Mag 39:54+ F '65

ASHER, Joseph
Rabbi asks: isn't it time we forgave the Germans? pors Look 29:84-6+ Ap 20 '65

ASHER, Robert E.
UN aid to the USA, 1980. New Repub 153: 13-15 Jl 10 '65

ASHEVILLE-Biltmore college, Asheville, N.C.
Asheville-Biltmore in red, white and black. A. A. Whitman. il Library J 90:5204-5 D 1 '65

ASHFORD, Douglas E.
Bureaucrats and citizens. bibliog f Ann Am Acad 358:89-100 Mr '65

ASHLEY, Thomas William Ludlow
Hanky-panky in the House. J. Ridgeway. New Repub 153:8 O 30 '65

ASHMORE, P. G.
On teaching high school chemistry. Science 148:1312-14 Je 4 '65

ASHRAMS. See Retreats, Spiritual

ASHTON, Sir Frederick
New order at the Royal ballet. C. Barnes. il por Dance Mag 39:44-7+ Ap '65

ASHWOOD-SMITH, M. J. and others
Ultraviolet damage to bacteria and bacteriophage at low temperatures. bibliog Science 149:1103-5 S 3 '65

ASHWORTH, L. A. E. and Green, C.
Plasma membranes: phospholipid and sterol content. bibliog Science 151:210-11 Ja 14 '66

ASHWORTH, Lee J. Jr, and others
Aflatoxins: environmental factors governing occurrence in Spanish peanuts. bibliog Science 148:1228-9 My 28 '65

ASIA
Discrimination & discord in Asia; Time essay. Time 85:32-3 Ap 9 '65
See also
Advertising—Asia
Agricultural administration—Asia
Communism—Asia
Development banks—Asia
Economic assistance in Asia
Food supply—Asia
Publishers and publishing—Asia
Roads—Asia
United Nations—Economic commission for Asia and the Far East

Commerce
Economic development in Asia; address, April 23, 1965. W. W. Rostow. Dept State Bul 52:845-53 My 31 '65

Description and travel
Far lands grow nearer; Asia and the Pacific; symposium. il Sat R 48:35-40+ S 18 '65

Economic conditions
Asia out of control? interview. R. P. Martin. il U S News 59:38-42 O 4 '65
Progress and problems in the Far East; address, October 5, 1965. W. P. Bundy. Dept State Bul 53:709-16 N 1 '65
Widening gap. il Newsweek 66:40-1 Jl 12 '65
See also
Colombo plan

Economic policy
Economic development in Asia; address, April 23, 1965. W. W. Rostow. Dept State Bul 52:845-53 My 31 '65

Foreign relations
Asian nonalignment. S. K. Gupta. bibliog f Ann Am Acad 362:44-51 N '65
Notes from Asia and Germany. B. G. Lall. Bul Atomic Sci 21:33-5 N '65
Reflections on Asian anti-Communists. W. H. Judd. Nat R 18:27 Ja 11 '66
Twenty years after: why GI's are still fighting in Asia; with interview with K. S. Chiang. il U S News 59:41-9 Ag 9 '65

History
Bibliography
Articles and other books received; comp. by H. Conroy; C. Hobbs. See issues of American historical review

Maps
Map of Asia (cont) Sr Schol 87:34 S 30 '65

Politics
Editor's easy chair. J. Fischer. Harper 231:21-2+ Ag '65; Discussion. 231:6+ O; 13-14+ N '65
Letter from the publisher; Time's news tour of Asia. B. M. Auer. il Time 85:14-15 F 19 '65
Power politics of Asia. W. Lippmann. Newsweek 66:23 S 27 '65

Population
What exit for Asia? Pyrrho. Nat R 17:638-41 Jl 27 '65

Reconstruction
See also
Colombo plan

Social conditions
Continent of villages. R. G. Wesson. Nation 200:705-7 Je 28 '65

ASIA, CENTRAL
Modern history of Soviet Central Asia, by G. Wheeler. Review
Sat R il 48:31 F 20 '65. H. E. Salisbury

ASIA, SOUTHEASTERN
Dilemma in southeast Asia; symposium. bibliog f il Cur Hist 48:65-108+ F '65
Peking-Djakarta axis. D. Warner. il Reporter 33:25-7 S 23 '65
Toward peace in Asia. W. Lippmann. Newsweek 65:19 F 15 '65
See also
Communism—Asia, Southeastern
Mekong River
Water supply—Asia, Southeastern

Foreign relations
In southeast Asia: no way out for U.S? il U S News 58:30-2 Mr 1 '65
Rays of hope for U.S. in Asia; winning ground at expense of red China. il Bsns W p25-7 N 6 '65

Reasons for the top-level visits to Asia. il U S News 58:20 F 15 '65
Southeast Asia; fallacy of the dominoes. C. P. Fitzgerald. il Nation 200:700-2+ Je 28 '65
Spreading war for U.S. in Asia? il U S News 59:29-32 D 20 '65

Politics
American policy in South Viet-Nam and southeast Asia; address, January 23, 1965. W. P. Bundy. Dept State Bul 52:168-75 F 8 '65
Expulsion of Singapore. C. P. FitzGerald. il Nation 201:208-12 O 11 '65
Japan, the two Reischauers. A. Axelbank. New Repub 153:11-12 N 13 '65
Prospect for southeast Asia; symposium. il Sat R 48:25-37+ O 30 '65
Regional cooperation in southeast Asia. B. K. Gordon. bibliog f il Cur Hist 48:103-8+ F '65
Southeast Asia; fallacy of the dominoes. C. P. Fitzgerald. il Nation 200:700-2+ Je 28 '65
Southeast Asia isn't scared of the Chinese dragon. S. Topping. il N Y Times Mag p 12-13+ Ja 16 '66
Why we are fighting in Asia. F. V. Drake. il Read Digest 87:61-5 O '65

Bibliography
War in Asia: more questions than answers. R. Dudman. Sat R 48:34-5 N 27 '65

ASIA and Africa. See Africa and Asia

ASIA foundation
Asia book project passes 5,000,000 mark. Pub W 188:41 O 4 '65

ASIA MINOR
Antiquities
See also
Aphrodisias

ASIAN development bank. See Development banks—Asia

ASIANS
See also
Chinese

ASIMOV, Isaac
Anatomy of a man from Mars. Esquire 64:113-17+ S '65
Life in 1990; reprint. Sci Digest 58:63-70 Ag '65
Science in search of a subject. N Y Times Mag p52-3+ My 23 '65
Views on science books. See issues of Horn book magazine
Where do dead satellites go? Sci Digest 58:86-7 O '65

ASINOF, Eliot
Adak: a woman behind every tree. Sat Eve Post 238:66+ Jl 17 '65
Big shrimp of pro football. N Y Times Mag p52-3+ D 12 '65
Word for Johnny Keane is: patience. N Y Times Mag p24-8 My 30 '65

ASPARAGUS
See also
Cookery—Vegetables

ASPEN, Colo.
Aspen's awful problem: surfers on skis; with report by R. Bradford. il Life 58:42-4+ Mr 12 '65
Ski life at Aspen. il Mlle 62:106-7+ D '65

ASPEN award. See Aspen institute for humanistic studies

ASPEN institute for humanistic studies
Mr Britten and the loudspeaker. Hi Fi 15:33 Jl '65

ASPEN music festival. See Music festivals—Colorado

ASPERGILLUS
Phosphatase mutants in aspergillus nidulans. G. Dorn. bibliog il Science 150:1183-4 N 26 '65

ASPHYXIA
Three new miracle treatments to keep babies alive. B. Merson. Good H 161:68-9+ Jl '65

ASPIC
Elegance of aspic; with recipes. C. Claiborne. il N Y Times Mag p41 Jl 11 '65

ASPINALL, Wayne N.
Underlying principles of wilderness legislation as I see them; adaptation of statement, July 30, 1964. Liv Wildn 86:6-9 Spr '64

ASPIRIN
Beware of too much aspirin. Sci Digest 58:35-6 O '65

ASQUITH, Herbert Henry, 1st earl of Oxford and Asquith. See Oxford and Asquith, H. H. A.

ASSASSINATION
See also
Kennedy, J. F.—Assassination
Malcolm X—Assassination

ASSATEAGUE ISLAND
Reporter at large. P. Matthiessen. il New Yorker 41:116+ Ap 3 '65
ASSATEAGUE ISLAND NATIONAL SEASHORE
Assateague joins the parks. Nat Parks Mag 38:26 N '65
Assateague Seashore hearings. Nat Parks Mag 39:24 My '65
For a public park, a seashore island. il U S News 59:14 S 27 '65
National seashore or a national loss? Assateague Island. P. Innis. il Audubon Mag 67:86-7 Mr '65
Saved! excerpts from address, September 21, 1965. L. B. Johnson. il Am For 71:4-5 N '65
ASSEMBLY of captive European nations
Converging toward what? J. Burnham. Nat R 17:970 N 2 '65
ASSENHEIMER, Roy C.
Interracial apostolate. America 112:560-1 Ap 17 '65
ASSES and mules
See also
Mule racing
ASSETS, Liquid. See Liquidity (economics)
ASSISTANT; story. See O'Hara, J.
ASSOCIATED colleges at Claremont, Calif.
Ecumenical Claremont: Immaculate heart college to move to site adjacent to Claremont campus. il Newsweek 65:53 Mr 1 '65
See also
Pitzer college, Claremont, Calif.
ASSOCIATED opera companies of America
A.O.C.A. G. Fitzgerald. il Opera N 30:19 N 6 '65
ASSOCIATED publishers, incorporated
Profile: The associated publishers. B. Quarles. Negro Hist Bul 28:81 Ja '65
ASSOCIATION and associations. See Associations
ASSOCIATION for childhood education international
Meeting, 1965. Sr Schol 86:sup 1+ My 13 '65
ASSOCIATION for higher education
What's wrong with our students? characteristics of the ideal administrator. D. Hollowell. New Repub 152:24 F 20 '65
ASSOCIATION for supervision and curriculum development
Meeting, 1965. Sr Schol 86:sup 1-2 Mr 25 '65
ASSOCIATION for the study of Negro life and history
Doctor Wesley receives award at ASNLH annual meeting, Detroit, 1964. il Negro Hist Bul 28:100 F '65
In appreciation: reminiscences, greetings, challenges. il Negro Hist Bul 28:180-6+ My '65
Natchez J. college branch: an active chapter. il Negro Hist Bul 28:83 Ja '65
Our fiftieth year; the golden anniversary, 1965. C. H. Wesley. Negro Hist Bul 28:172-3+ My '65
ASSOCIATION of American colleges
Meeting, 1965. W. W. Anderson. Sch & Soc 93:274 My 1 '65
ASSOCIATION of American medical colleges
AAMC: a broader leadership role in health education prescribed for Association of medical colleges. J. Walsh. Science 148:1700-2 Je 25 '65; Reply. J. T. Flynn. 150:554 O 29 '65
ASSOCIATION of American railroads
Trainmen yank brakes on featherbed label; AAR demands reforms in union work rules. il Bsns W p 102+ N 27 '65
ASSOCIATION of American university presses
AAUP award books: an awareness of quality; with editorial comment. P. A. Bennett. bibliog il Pub W 187:103-5+ Je 14 '65
AAUP meeting, May 23-25 in Lexington, Kentucky. Pub W 187:49-50 Mr 22 '65
AAUP meets in Kentucky for largest annual convention. Pub W 187:143-4 Je 7 '65
Full tax exemption granted to AAUP. Pub W 188:44 Ag 2 '65
Highspots of activity in major organizations; 1965 in review. Pub W 189:81-2 Ja 17 '66
Next steps for the university presses. C. B. Grannis. Pub W 188:70 Jl 19 '65
University presses review domestic and world concerns; AAUP convention. il Pub W 188:36-57+ Jl 19 '65
See also
American university press services, incorporated
ASSOCIATION of college and research libraries
Five individuals, 157 institutions receive ACRL fund or equipment grants. Library J 90:600+ F 1 '65

Rare books section
Rare books and bing bing boys; institute in Detroit. E. Wolf, 2d. Library J 90:3210-11 Ag '65
ASSOCIATION of council secretaries
Primacy of the local. L. Peterson. Christian Cent 82:945-6 Jl 28 '65
ASSOCIATION of lunar and planetary observers
Convention in Milwaukee. W. E. Shawcross. il Sky & Tel 30:132-6 S '65
ASSOCIATION of nations. See United Nations
ASSOCIATION of producing artists
Better than topic A. il Time 85:53-4 Ap 23 '65
Herakles at Ann Arbor. T. Prideaux. Life 59:10 D 3 '65
ASSOCIATION of research libraries
ARL suggests $5 million for cataloging be included in higher education bill; excerpts from testimony, March 19, 1965. W. S. Dix. Library J 90:2109-10 My 1 '65
LC, CRL division of duties suggested by ARL committee. Library J 90:3410 S 1 '65
Meeting, 1965. Library J 90:1272+ Mr 15 '65
ASSOCIATIONS
Contact with the outside world: national organizations at invitational conference at Airlie House, Warrenton, Va, sponsored by ALA. E. Moon. Library J 90:2104-5 My 1 '65
How to prevent organizational dry rot. J. W. Gardner. Harper 231:20+ O '65
See also
Trade associations
ASSOCIATIONS, Trade. See Trade associations
ASSYRO-BABYLONIAN literature
See also
Gilgamesh
ASTAIRE, Fred
Old dog's new tricks at 66; interview, ed. by D. Zeitlin. pors Life 59:89+ O 29 '65
ASTEROIDS
Asteroid belt probe. J. Eberhart. Sci N L 87:115 F 20 '65
Discovery of Icarus. R. S. Richardson. il Sci Am 212:106-15 bibliog(p 158+ Ap '65
Icarus and general relativity. Sky & Tel 30:211 O '65
Interest rises in comets, asteroid belt. H. D. Watkins. il Aviation W 82:89-90+ F 22 '65
ASTHMA
Asthma: its causes and treatment. il Good H 160:178 Mr '65
Asthma seen a syndrome instead of disease. Sci N L 88:95 Ag 7 '65
Drug helps asthmatics. Sci N L 87:260 Ap 24 '65
Treat bronchial asthma with baking soda. Sci N L 87:409 Je 26 '65
ASTRIONICS. See Space vehicles—Electronic equipment
ASTRODOME, Houston. See Stadiums
ASTROLABES
Improved pendulum astrolabe. G. S. Mumford. il Sky & Tel 30:85 Ag '65
ASTROLOGY
Fault is in our stars. R. P. Lister. Mlle 60:146+ Ap '65
ASTRONAUTICAL Instruments. See Space vehicles—Electronic equipment
ASTRONAUTS
Adventure into emptiness; first human satellite. il Time 85:85-6 Mr 26 '65
Astro-scientists. il Time 86:21-2 Jl 9 '65
Hardest rendezvous of all, on the ground. J. Hicks. il Life 59:113-14+ O 1 '65
Here comes Gemini. il Time 85:25 F 19 '65
Moonbound scholars. il Newsweek 66:59 Jl 12 '65
NASA names first scientist-astronauts. E. J. Bulban. il Aviation W 83:18 Jl 5 '65
NASA names Gemini-8 crew. Bsns W p 124 S 25 '65
Now scientists are astronauts. il Sci Digest 58:13-15 S '65
Space-walkers needed. J. Eberhart. Sci N L 87:196 Mr 27 '65
Troubles of astronaut Edward Dwight. C. L. Sanders. il Ebony 20:29-32+ Je '65
Ugly American: proposed interview between American astronauts and Soviet cosmonauts in Athens not held due to poor NASA press relations. W. J. Coughlin. Miss & Roc 17:54 O 4 '65
See also
Barman, F.
Conrad, C. jr.
Cooper, G.
Grissom, V.
Lovell, J.
McDivitt, J. A.
Schirra, W. M.
Stafford, T. P.
White, E. H. 2d

ASTRONAUTS—*Continued*

Clothing

Accelerating Gemini pace clouds future of extra-vehicular plans. W. J. Normyle. Aviation W 83:18 O 18 '65

Adventure into emptiness; first human satellite. il Time 85:85A-85B Mr 26 '65

Apollo suit configuration may be set in early '67. Miss & Roc 17:33 N 22 '65

Apollo suit substantially redesigned. H. M. David. il Miss & Roc 16:26+ Ap 26 '65

Design verification under way on Apollo suit backpack; Block 2 Apollo suit tests. D. E. Fink. il Aviation W 83:52-3+ D 13 '65

GT-4 crew to wear EVA spacesuits; extra-vehicular activity suits. J. Mercer. il Miss & Roc 16:24 Ap 19 '65

GT-7 crew wants shirtsleeve flight. Miss & Roc 17:17 Jl 19 '65

How will man suit up for space? A. Rosenfeld. il Life 58:56+ Ap 16 '65

Longest step: space suits; with painting by N. Rockwell. B. Kocivar. il Look 29:109-12 Ap 20 '65

Lunar suit and backpack design selected. D. E. Fink. Aviation W 83:37 N 15 '65

New space suits considered for Gemini-7. Aviation W 83:22 Jl 26 '65

New suit to be worn aboard Gemini 7. J. Mercer. il Miss & Roc 17:17 O 18 '65

Photos show details of Vostok cabin, suits. il Aviation W 82:58-60 My 31 '65

Protective spacesuit developed for Apollo. il Sci N L 87:355 Je 5 '65

Refined Apollo suit nearing final form. R. D. Hibben. il Aviation W 82:56-7+ F 1 '65

Shirtsleeve garb eases tasks in Gemini 7. E. J. Bulban. il Aviation W 83:30-1 D 13 '65

Thermal manikin to aid MSC. M. Getler. il Miss & Roc 16:49+ My 17 '65

Three entries vie for Apollo lunar suit selection. il Miss & Roc 17:18 O 11 '65

Walk and a leapfrog; McDivitt-White flight. il Newsweek 65:53-4 Je 7 '65

What an astronaut will wear on the moon. W. Von Braun. il Pop Sci 186:87-8+ Ap '65

Training

AF pilots to simulate Apollo flight. H. M. David. Miss & Roc 16:84-5 My 31 '65

Men in space exercise. Sci N L 88:358 D 4 '65

Soviets at Athens detail Voskhod training. W. C. Wetmore. Aviation W 83:35 S 20 '65

ASTRONOMERS, Amateur

Amateur astronomers. See issues of Sky and telescope

Boy who redeemed his father's name; K. Ikeya's discovery. T. Morris. il Redbook 125:86-7+ O 65; Same abr. Read Digest 88: 107-11 Ja '66

Five more amateur observatories. W. E. Shawcross. il Sky & Tel 29:284-6 My '65

Gleanings for ATM's; ed. by R. E. Cox. See issues of Sky and telescope

Here and there with amateurs. Sky & Tel 30:226-32 O '65

See also
Western amateur astronomers

ASTRONOMICAL clocks

Gebhard astronomical and world clock. J. E. Coleman and J. F. Hagans. il Hobbies 70: 44-5+ N; 44 D '65; 44-5 Ja '66

ASTRONOMICAL distances

Moon's distance. G. S. Mumford. Sky & Tel 30:84 Ag '65

See also
Stars—Distance

ASTRONOMICAL instruments

See also
Astrolabes
Interferometers
Sextants
Telescope

ASTRONOMICAL league

Convention in Milwaukee. W. E. Shawcross. il Sky & Tel 30:132-6 S '65

ASTRONOMICAL models

Moon glow will aid in mapping. il Miss & Roc 16:25-6 Mr 1 '65

ASTRONOMICAL names. See Astronomy—Nomenclature

ASTRONOMICAL observations. See Astronomy—Observations

ASTRONOMICAL observatories

Crisis at Allegheny; closing down University of Pittsburgh's Allegheny observatory. Sky & Tel 29:135+ Mr '65

Eighth wonder; ancient observatory at Stonehenge. il Time 86:98 N 12 '65

Harvard observatory's new patrol cameras. H. C. Ingrao. il Sky & Tel 29:200-4 Ap '65

Kitt Peak 150-inch telescope. D. L. Crawford. il Sky & Tel 29:268-73 My '65

Largest mobile antennas to be built next year; Owens Valley radio observatory, Calif. Sci N L 87:131 F 27 '65

Leuschner observatory to move. G. S. Mumford. il Sky & Tel 30:352 D '65

Mount Cuba observatory in Delaware. L. G. Glasser. il Sky & Tel 30:4-7 Jl '65

New observatory at King college in Tennessee. E. W. Burke, jr. and W. W. Rolland. il Sky & Tel 30:172-6 S '65

Notes on some planetary problems; Lowell observatory, Flagstaff, Ariz. B. T. Lynds. il Sky & Tel 30:80-3 Ag '65

Rotatable telescope for polarization studies; Yerkes observatory, University of Chicago. W. A. Hiltner and R. Schild. il Sky & Tel 30:144-7 S '65

See also
National radio astronomy observatory, Green Bank, W.Va.

Chile

Site survey for the inter-American observatory in Chile. J. Stock. il Science 148:1054-9 My 21 '65

Germany (Federal Republic)

Argelander and the BD; Bonn observatory. A. T. Moffet. il Sky & Tel 29:276-8 My '65

India

Stones of Jaipur speak of astronomy. il UNESCO Courier 18:18-21 Je '65

Korea

Seventh century Korean observatory. P. S. Kim. il Sky & Tel 29:229-30 Ap '65

Sweden

Europe's second largest Schmidt telescope; Uppsala observatory, Sweden. A. Wallenquist. il Sky & Tel 29:136-40 Mr '65

ASTRONOMICAL photography

Amateur scientist; deep-sky photographs. R. T. Little. il Sci Am 213:106-9 D '65

Celestial photography at different wavelengths. E. A. Harlan. il Sky & Tel 30: 314-15 N '65

December's well-observed lunar eclipse. il Sky & Tel 29:72-7 F '65

Experiments in cooled-emulsion photography. E. Kreimer. il Sky & Tel 30:384-8 D '65

Faint ring around the spiral galaxy M82. H. Arp. bibliog Science 148:363-4 Ap 16 '65

Finest deep-sky objects. J. Mullaney and W. McCall. il Sky & Tel 30:280-3, 356-8; 31:13-16 N '65-Ja '66

Harvard observatory's new patrol cameras. H. C. Ingrao. il Sky & Tel 29:200-4 Ap '65

How to study the onion. il Sci Digest 57:37-9 Ap '65

Photography of faint stars. G. S. Mumford. Sky & Tel 30:352 D '65

ASTRONOMICAL photometry. See Photometry, Astronomical

ASTRONOMICAL research

Good look at NGC 4565. N. G. Roman. il Am Ed 1:5-8 O '65

Great Swedish astronomer. T. L. Page. il Sky & Tel 30:142-3 S '65

Ground-based astronomy: a ten-year program; summary of report; discussion. Science 147:1087-8 Mr 5 '65

1965 science review. Sci N L 88:389-90 D 18 '65

ASTRONOMICAL societies

See also names of astronomical societies, e.g. Astronomical league

ASTRONOMY

Astronomy. J. Stokley. See issues of Science news letter

Ground-based astronomy: a ten-year program; summary of report; discussion. Science 147:1087-8 Mr 5 '65

Updating a blueprint for American astronomy; with summary of recommendations and costs. Sky & Tel 30:212-13 O '65

See also
Astronomical research
Astrophysics
Comets
Constellations
Eclipses, Solar
Life on other planets
Occultations
Radio astronomy

Bibliography

Books and the sky. See issues of Sky and telescope

Mandate of heaven. P. Morrison. il Nation 200:339-41 Mr 29 '65

Charts, diagrams, etc.

Sky reporter. T. D. Nicholson. See issues of Natural history incorporating Nature magazine

ASTRONOMY—Charts, diagrams, etc.—*Cont.*
Southern stars. See issues of Sky and telescope
Stars for [the month] See issues of Sky and telescope

History

Long night of selenography. J. Ashbrook. il Sky & Tel 29:92-4 F '65
Science in action; steps to new astronomy. G. A. Rothrock. Natur Hist 74:64-8 My '65
Seventh century Korean observatory. P. S. Kim. il Sky & Tel 29:229-30 Ap '65
Some astronomical anniversaries. See issues of Sky and telescope
Supernova in 1006. Sky & Tel 29:218-19 Ap '65

Nomenclature

Notes and comment; names to be given to discoveries in outer space. New Yorker 41:35 Ap 10 '65

Observations

Astronomy on the moon. Sky & Tel 31:3+ Ja '66
Finest deep-sky objects. J. Mullaney and W. McCall. il Sky & Tel 30:280-3, 356-8; 31:13-16 N '65-Ja '66
New objects in sky. A. Ewing. Sci N L 87: 181 Mr 20 '65

Tables, etc.

Events of 1966 in the graphic time table. Sky & Tel 31:33-5 Ja '66
ASTRONOMY, Nautical. See Nautical astronomy
ASTRONOMY, Spherical and practical
Practical astronomy from shipboard. W. S. Von Arx. bibliog il Sky & Tel 29:340-5 Je '65
ASTROPHYSICS
Relativistic astrophysics. L. C. Green. il Sky & Tel 29:145-9, 226-9 Mr-Ap '65
Relativistic astrophysics; report on symposium sponsored by the University of Texas and the Southwest center for advanced studies, Dallas. B. M. Biram. Science 148:112-14 Ap 2 '65
See also
Magnetic field (cosmic physics)
Stars—Atmospheres
ASTROQUARTZ. See Quartz
ASTRO-SCIENTISTS. See Astronauts
ASWAN HIGH DAM
High Dam at Aswan: Egypt's 20th-century colossus. I. Johnson and E. Johnson. il Nat Geog Mag 127:614-15 My '65
Race to save Abu Simbel. G. Gaskill. il Read Digest 88:163-5+ Ja '66
Rescue of a Pharaoh gazing upon a rising Nile. il Life 59:28-33 O 29 '65
ASYLUM, Right of
Diplomatic asylum, by C. N. Ronning. Review
Américas 17:36 N '65. C. G. Fenwick
Zulu limbo; case of dancers at World's fair. Reporter 32:10 Je 17 '65
ATATÜRK, Kamâl
Atatürk, by Lord Kinross. Review
Commonweal 82:166-9 Ap 23 '65. G. Gersh
Time il por 85:108+ Ap 9 '65
Turk who turned West. D. Stewart. Nation 200:512 My 10 '65
ATAXIA
Immunoglobulin A production in ataxia telangiectasia. D. E. McFarlin and others. bibliog il Science 150:1175-7 N 26 '65
ATCHISON, Robert W. and others
Adenovirus-associated defective virus particles. bibliog Science 149:754-6 Ag 13 '65
ATCHISON, Kan.
Miracle on Main Street. A. Thelen. il Am City 80:75-6 N '65
ATCHITY, Kenneth J.
Luci Johnson and history. America 113:334+ S 25 '65
ATHEISM
Atheism: Marxist style. America 112:799 My 29 '65
Can we talk to Marxian atheists? P. Ehlen; D. I. MacLean. America 113:112-17 Jl 31 '65
Christian atheism: God is dead movement. il Time 86:61-2 O 22 '65
Dialogue with atheists; Pope Paul VI's efforts. America 112:186 F 6 '65
God today: Catholic dialogue with unbelievers on the subject of God. America 112:477 Ap 10 '65
Jesuit general's speech at the Vatican council. America 113:429-30 O 16 '65
More dialogue with atheists: challenges Secretariat for nonbelievers. America 113: 456 O 23 '65
See also
Agnosticism

ATHENAGORAS I, patriarch
Bishop in check. Commonweal 82:205 My 7 '65
Imperiled patriarch. D. Peerman. Christian Cent 82:1470-1 D 1 '65
Turks persecute religion. America 113:454 O 23 '65
ATHENS
Athens. P. L. Fermor. il Holiday 37:40-51+ Je '65

Hotels, restaurants, etc.

Greece as the Greeks know it. H. Sutton. Sat R 48:32-3+ Ag 7 '65
ATHEROSCLEROSIS. See Arteriosclerosis
ATHLETES
New fastest human. il Newsweek 65:81 F 8 '65
O.K. everybody: beat America! D. Jenkins. il Sports Illus 23:12-17 Jl 26 '65
Scramble for college athletes; increasing professionalism. P. H. Giddens. il Atlan 216: 49-52 D '65
When the season's over; athletes ground themselves for gainful second careers. il Newsweek 65:70-2 F 8 '65
See also
Baseball players
Basketball players
Football players
Negro athletes

Recruiting

Scramble for college athletes; increasing professionalism. P. H. Giddens. il Atlan 216:49-52 D '65

Training

Man for the next few seasons; F. Broyles of Arkansas Razorbacks. D. Jenkins. il Sports Illus 23:30-2+ N 8 '65
ATHLETE'S foot (disease) See Ringworm
ATHLETIC dormitories. See Dormitories
ATHLETICS
See also
Athletes
Gymnastics
Running
Sportsmanship
Track athletics
ATHLETICS, Intercollegiate. See College athletics
ATITLÁN, LAKE
Giant grebe of Guatemala. A. L. Bowes. il Audubon Mag 67:88-90 Mr '65
ATKINS, Nora
Learning to sail: how and where. bibliog il por Motor B 115:41+ Je '65
ATKINS, Thomas V.
Rebuilding the bridge to Poland. Reporter 32: 39-41 F 25 '65
ATKINSON, Brooks
Rendezvous in our driveway. Audubon Mag 67:312 S '65

about

Brooks Atkinson: a calm, strong, voice for nature. J. C. Devlin. il pors Audubon Mag 67:310-13 S '65
ATKINSON, Daniel E.
Biological feedback control at the molecular level. bibliog Science 150:851-7 N 12 '65
ATKINSON, Paul E.
Sun ship rides new building crest. il Bsns W p58-60+ N 27 '65
ATL, Dr. See Murillo, G.
ATLANTA
Atlanta rose to the occasion; dinner to celebrate winning of Nobel peace prize by M. L. King. Christian Cent 82:164 F 10 '65
Marching to Georgia; attractions for football and baseball leagues. Time 85:69 Je 18 '65
Remarkable dinner: Atlanta celebrates Nobel award to M. L. King; with editorial comment. il Life 58:4, 34-34A F 12 '65

Architecture

Why did you make the building black? Peachtree-Palisades office building. J. Amisano. il Arch Rec 138:150-1 D '65

Banks

Big banks dip into factoring; Atlanta's Citizens & Southern buying Joel Hurt factors, inc. Bsns W p58+ My 22 '65

City planning

Atlanta area revives old residential lure; Ansley Park. il Bsns W p 146 Ja 15 '66

Crime

How Atlanta and Chicago reduced crime. Fortune 72:259 D '65

ATLANTA—*Continued*

Description

Atlanta. P. Deutsch and R. Deutsch. il Redbook 125:72-3+ My '65

Education

Making math & science soar; high school course in flying. il Time 87:44 Ja 14 '66

Negroes

Beyond the voting rights act. P. Good. il Reporter 33:25-9 O 7 '65
Black man, go South. F. Powledge. il Esquire 64:72-4+ Ag '65

Newspapers

Invasion of the Harvards; editors of nation's newest weekly, Southern courier. il Newsweek 66:81-2 Jl 26 '65

Politics and government

Ivan ho! four years as mayor. Time 86:39 S 17 '65

Prisons and reformatories

Captive class; computer programming course at the Atlanta federal penitentiary. Newsweek 66:78 N 8 '65
GE opens a prison door with computer training; teaching programming to inmates of Atlanta penitentiary. il Bsns W p96+ N 20 '65

Sanitary affairs

Crematory for animal disposal. R. D. Speer. il Am City 80:121-2 Ag '65
New strength for an old sewer. R. A. Nixon. il Am City 80:33 Ap '65

Social conditions

Atlanta fights poverty. J. Ridgeway. New Repub 152:12-14 My 29 '65

Water supply

Visualizing the invisible; Atlanta shows how to dedicate water service; ed. by P. D. Eimon. il Am City 80:130+ N '65

ATLANTA university

School of library service

Atlanta library school announces first of three education conferences. Library J 90:1685 Ap 1 '65
ATLANTIC alliance. See Atlantic community
ATLANTIC and Pacific tea company. See Great Atlantic and Pacific tea company
ATLANTIC coast
See also
Geology—Atlantic coast
ATLANTIC Coast line-Seaboard merger. See Railroads—Consolidations and mergers
ATLANTIC community
Alliance and the future of Germany. F. Erler. For Affairs 43:436-46 Ap '65
Alliance immobilized. W. V. Shannon. Commonweal 82:102-3 Ap 16 '65
Atlantic community. by D. Middleton. Review Sat R 48:37 D 18 '65. P. Van Slyck
Atlantic partnership and European unity; address, March 9, 1965. G. C. McGhee. Dept State Bul 52:582-8 Ap 19 '65
Atlantic partnership; emerging new Europe; address, April 12, 1965. Prince Bernhard. Vital Speeches 31:644-6 Ag 15 '65
Diplomacy on collision course. E. J. Hughes. Newsweek 65:29 Je 14 '65
Europe, the United States, and world trade; address, February 4, 1965. C. A. Herter. Dept State Bul 52:294-9 Mr 1 '65
European political cooperation; address, February 11, 1965. M. Stewart. Vital Speeches 31:329-31 Mr 15 '65
European version of neutralism. J. Freymond. bibliog f Ann Am Acad 362:28-35 N '65
Firm foreign policy; unity with Europe; address, May 28, 1965. W. W. Scranton. Vital Speeches 31:652-4 Ag 15 '65
Illusionist: why we misread de Gaulle. H. A. Kissinger. Harper 230:69-70+ Mr '65
Other end of the telescope; address, October 21, 1965. H. Cleveland. Dept State Bul 53:781-7 N 15 '65
Our Atlantic policy; address, March 6, 1965. D. Rusk. Dept State Bul 52:427-31 Mr 22 '65
Persistent friend of Atlantic unity; French economist-philosopher P. Uri. il Bsns W p68+ My 8 '65
Policy of France; independence of Europe; address, June 17, 1965. G. Pompidou. Vital Speeches 31:617-19 Ag 1 '65
Technologically, the Atlantic community exists. V. K. McElheny. Science 149:1080-2 S 3 '65

United States and Germany: common goals; address, February 9, 1965. G. C. McGhee. Dept State Bul 52:375-80 Mr 15 '65
United States policy toward Europe; address, March 19, 1965. W. W. Rostow. Dept State Bul 52:576-82 Ap 19 '65
Washington, Europe, and the Tower of Babel. M. Frankel. Harper 231:108+ D '65
See also
North Atlantic treaty organization
ATLANTIC OCEAN
Brave self far at sea; R. Manry's Atlantic crossing. L. Wainwright. Life 59:18 S 3 '65
Ocean-bottom topography: the divide between the Sohm and Hatteras Abyssal Plains. R. M. Pratt. bibliog il Science 148:1598-9 Je 18 '65
Sands of the Mid-Atlantic Ridge. P. J. Fox and B. C. Heezen. bibliog il Science 149:1367-70 S 17 '65
See also
Gulf Stream
ATLANTIC refining company
Atlantic refining steps out. J. Thackray. il Duns R 86:40-2+ S '65
Loner of many talents enters oil's big league; R. O. Anderson. il Bsns W p36+ My 29 '65
ATLANTIC states
See also
Water supply—Alantic states
ATLANTIC union (proposed)
See also
Atlantic community
ATLANTIS II (ships) See Ships, Research
ATLAS (launching vehicle) See Space vehicles—Propulsion systems
ATLASES
See also
Moon—Atlases
ATMOSPHERE
Atmospheric noble gases: solar-wind bombardment of extraterrestrial dust as a possible source mechanism. D. Tilles. bibliog Science 148:1085-8 My 21 '65
Fireflies to light the way in NASA effort to chart earth's biosphere. W. S. Beller. Miss & Roc 16:31 Mr 8 '65
Stratosphere and troposphere: transport of material between them. J. L. Kroening. il Science 147:862-4 F 19 '65
See also
Winds
ATMOSPHERE, Upper
Anomalous abundance of upper atmosphere sodium, 1964. C. R. Burnett. bibliog Science 147:736-7 F 12 '65
Atmospheric density at extreme heights. G. S. Mumford. Sky & Tel 29:281 My '65
Magnetosphere. L. J. Cahill, jr. il Sci Am 212:58-68 Mr '65
Research within the ionosphere. R. E. Bourdeau. bibliog il Science 148:585-94 Ap 30 '65
Stratosphere and troposphere: transport of material between them. J. L. Kroening. il Science 147:862-4 F 19 '65
ATMOSPHERE Explorer B (satellite) See Artificial satellites—Use in research
ATMOSPHERIC electricity
See also
Auroras
Lightning
ATMOSPHERIC entry problems. See Space vehicles—Atmospheric entry
ATMOSPHERIC pollution. See Air pollution
ATMOSPHERIC pressure
More flying weather signposts; low atmospheric pressure. H. T. Harrison. il Flying 77:79-81 D '65
See also
Wind pressure
ATMOSPHERIC research
Research within the ionosphere. R. E. Bourdeau. bibliog il Science 148:585-94 Ap 30 '65
Where is science taking us? accelerating ratio of carbon dioxide in the air. M. Neiburger. il Sat R 48:40-2 Jl 3 '65
See also
National center for atmospheric research
ATMOSPHERIC turbulence
CAB accident investigation report; Northwest airlines crash in Everglades National Park. February 12, 1963. il Aviation W 83:104-5+ Ag 16; 93+ Ag 23 '65
Mysterious air crashes: why they happen. W. R. Young. il Read Digest 86:106-10 Mr '65
Scientists go higher to study air turbulence; clear air turbulence. Sci N L 88:120 Ag 21 '65
Where is science taking us? accelerating ratio of carbon dioxide in the air. M. Neilburger. il Sat R 48:40-2 Jl 3 '65
See also
Mountain waves
ATOM smashing apparatus. See Accelerators (electrons, etc)

ATOMIC age
Atomic age begins. il Sr Schol 86:9+ My 20 '65

Atomic era twenty years old. C. A. Betts. Sci N L 88:55 Jl 24 '65

Fire of a thousand suns. K. W. Thompson. Sat R 48:112-13 S 18 '65

ATOMIC blasting
Atlantic report; possibility of nuclear excavation for new canal in Latin America. Atlan 215:28+ My '65

Deep nuclear blasts tap lodes of data; AEC's underground test program. il Bsns W p 134+ O 9 '65

Explosions to increase natural gas yield; Gasbuggy, part of Plowshare program. Sci N L 88:27 Jl 10 '65

Plowshare program, developing peaceful uses of nuclear explosives; statement, January 5, 1965. G. T. Seaborg. Dept State Bul 52:116-18 Ja 25 '65

Radioactivity; distribution from cratering in basalt. N. A. Bonner and J. A. Miskel. bibliog il Science 150:489-93 O 22 '65

ATOMIC bomb shelters
Anyone for survival? A. Balk. il Sat Eve Post 238:72+ Mr 27 '65

Atomic defense tunnels. Sci N L 89:3 Ja 1 '66

Expense of civil defense. C. A. Betts. Sci N L 88:282-3 O 30 '65

No holocaust for V.I.P.s; Iron mountain. Nation 201:430-1 D 6 '65

ATOMIC bombs
China and the bomb, by M. H. Halperin. Review
Sat R 48:54 Ap 17 '65. H. C. Hinton

Conversation with President Kennedy; concerning Communist China as a nuclear power, ed. by S. Alsop. J. F. Kennedy. il Sat Eve Post 239:9 Ja 1 '66

5:29 a.m. and the world was changed forever. R. E. Lapp. Life 59:14+ Jl 16 '65

Ground zero at Hiroshima twenty years later. il Life 59:32-3 Ag 20 '65

Johnson-Erhard communiqué; no nuclear status for West Germany. Christian Cent 83:5 Ja 5 '66

Nuclear power of China. R. E. Lapp. il Life 58:86-90+ My 28 '65; Same abr. with title Does red China understand the bomb? Read Digest 87:49-53 S '65

Nuclear proliferation; status & security; Time essay. Time 86:30-1 Jl 23 '65

600 million Chinese + communism = the bomb = ? S. Slessinger. Commonweal 82: 506 Jl 9 '65

So? Communist China's nuclear development; summary of address; December 15, 1965. R. S. McNamara. Nat R 18:12-13 Ja 11 '66

Spread of nuclear weapons; excerpt from Great debate. R. Aron; discussion. Atlan 215:40+ Mr '65

Taste of life in Hiroshima now. A. M. Rosenthal. il N Y Times Mag p4-5+ Ag 1 '65

Ten more countries that can make nuclear bombs. il U S News 59:50-1 D 6 '65
See also
Hydrogen bombs

Ethical aspects
See Atomic warfare—Ethical aspects

History
A-bomb is twenty. H. Pryor. il Sci Digest 58:20-6 Ag '65

Bomb: from Hiroshima to.... il Newsweek 66:52-7 Ag 9 '65

Hiroshima: in a flash it was gone; with editorial comment. R. Steinberg. il Sat Eve Post 238:28-35, 80 Ag 14 '65

Little boy's long, long journey; how the decision to drop the bomb was made. H. W. Baldwin. il N Y Times Mag p6-7+ Ag 1 '65

Manufacture
Chinese bombshell. D. R. Inglis. Bul Atomic Sci 21:19-21 F '65

It was the greatest secret. M. Levitas. il N Y Times Mag p2+ Ag 1 '65

Secret city on the magic mountain. D. Masters. il Sat Eve Post 238:36-40+ Ag 14 '65

Worldwide race for A-bombs, can it be stopped? interview. G. T. Seaborg. U S News 59:60-5 Jl 19 '65

Would you make the bomb again? symposium; ed. by W. L. Laurence. N Y Times Mag p8-9 Ag 1 '65; Discussion. p4+ Ag 15; 6+ Ag 22; 16+ Ag 29 '65

Physiological effects
See Radioactivity—Physiological effects

Testing
Alamogordo, mon amour. W. L. Laurence. il Esquire 63:118-21+ My '65

Atomic era twenty years old. C. A. Betts. Sci N L 88:55 Jl 24 '65

Bomb no. two; second test by Communist China. Newsweek 65:48+ My 24 '65

Bomb the bang; China's second nuclear explosion. Nat R 17:449+ Je 1 '65

China upsets the applecart. D. Cohen. il Sci Digest 58:27-9 Ag '65

China's bomb: exploitation and reactions. R. L. Powell. For Affairs 43:616-25 Jl '65

De Gaulle is set for big blast; preparing to explode H-bomb soon. il Bsns W p 16-17 Jl 31 '65

Explosion of October 16. D. R. Inglis; A. S. Lall; R. Guillain. Bul Atomic Sci 21:19-25 F '65

5:29 a.m. and the world was changed forever. R. E. Lapp. Life 59:14+ Jl 16 '65

Gravest decision; problem of growing menace of Chinese nuclear capability. R. Hotz. Aviation W 82:11 My 24 '65

In the shock wave of red China's second A-bomb—. il U S News 58:6 My 24 '65

Peking statement on nuclear test, October 16, 1964. Cur Hist 48:109-10+ F '65

Red China: firecracker no. 2. il Time 85:34-5 My 21 '65

Red China on its way to H-bomb; second nuclear test. il Bsns W p49-50 My 29 '65

Red China's nuclear threat: the time grows shorter. U S News 58:28-9 My 31 '65

Strontium isotopes; global circulation after the Chinese nuclear explosion of 14 May 1965. P. K. Kuroda and others. bibliog il Science 150:1289-90 D 3 '65

Tahiti learns about the bomb. H. B. Jacobs. il N Y Times Mag p46-7+ D 5 '65

Trinity plus twenty; anniversary of first atomic bomb test. il Newsweek 66:50-2 Jl 19 '65

Testing, Detection of
Breakthrough in test detection? large-aperture seismic array. Sci Am 212:54 Mr '65

Funding for nuclear test detection reaches $250-million annual level. Aviation W 83: 68 Jl 5 '65

H-bomb blast gives U.S. seismic test earful. il Bsns W p56 N 6 '65

Nuclear listening post; Montana system. Large aperture seismic array. il Time 86: 52-3 Ag 13 '65

Progress in seismic recording and analysis; report on meeting of the Royal society. V. K. McElheny. il Science 147:1271-3 Mr 12 '65

Seismic array refines blast detection. W. S. Beller. il Miss & Roc 16:24-5 F 22 '65

Spy game revolutionized. C. A. Betts. Sci N L 88:71 Jl 31 '65

Third NDS pair launched; nuclear detection satellites. Miss & Roc 17:29-31 Jl 26 '65

USAF launches third set of Vela satellites. Aviation W 83:23 Jl 26 '65

United States takes note of Soviet nuclear test; statements by Atomic energy commission and Department of state, January 19 and January 25, 1965. Dept State Bul 52: 187 F 8 '65

Testing, Suspension of
First committee adopts resolution; nuclear tests suspension. UN Mo Chron 2:66-70 D '65

National security and the nuclear-test ban. J. B. Wiesner and H. F. York; discussion. Sci Am 211:8+ D '64; 212:8+ F; 6+ Ap '65

Testing, Underground
Atomic blast vs otter? Operation long shot. S. McCutcheon. il Audubon Mag 67:376-81 N '65

Deep nuclear blasts tap lodes of data; AEC's underground test program. il Bsns W p 134+ O 9 '65

Iron minerals formed by a nuclear explosion in a salt bed. M. W. Nathans and others. bibliog Science 150:1027 N 19 '65

Long shot to LASA; additional means of monitoring secret tests. Newsweek 66:72 N 8 '65

Nuclear blasts yield valuable science data. Sci N L 87:296 My 8 '65

Seismic array refines blast detection. W. S. Beller. il Miss & Roc 16:24-5 F 22 '65

Uproar over otters; Amchitka Island nuclear test dispute. il Life 59:151-2 O 15 '65

ATOMIC clocks
Portable atomic frequency standard. il Electr World 73:45+ Je '65

Saga of the flying clocks. il Sci Digest 57:38-9 Je '65

ATOMIC energy. See Atomic power
ATOMIC energy commission. See United States
—Atomic energy commission
ATOMIC medicine. See Radiology, Medical;
Radiotherapy
ATOMIC nuclei
Doctor Pauling proposes new theory of atomic
nucleus. Sci N L 88:259 O 23 '65
History of the theory of structure of the
atomic nucleus: address, December 12, 1963.
J. H. D. Jensen. bibliog Science 147:1419-
23 Mr 19 '65
Nucleus action probed; SU-6 theory. Sci
N L 87:85 F 6 '65

Fission
See Nuclear fission
ATOMIC piles. See Nuclear reactors
ATOMIC power
Atom and the U.S. twenty years after. il Sr
Schol 87:6-10 N 4 '65
Protection of U.S. naval nuclear propulsion
plant information: Department statement,
February 9, 1965. Dept State Bul 52:300
Mr 1 '65
See also
Atomic bombs
Nuclear reactors

Economic aspects
As cost of A-power falls. G. T. Seaborg. U S
News 59:62-5 Jl 19 '65
Atom in your future. G. T. Seaborg. Seven-
teen 24:162+ Mr '65
Atomic power comes of age. J. F. Blank.
Read Digest 87:109-12 D '65
Atoms for peace and the effort to halt the
spread of nuclear weapons. J. G. Palfrey.
Dept State Bul 53:393-7 S 6 '65
Atoms for peace: the dream, the reality.
C. P. Anderson. il N Y Times Mag p 10-
11+ Ag 1 '65
Electric power remains emphasis of India's
nuclear energy program. V. K. McElheny.
il Science 149:284-7 Jl 16 '65
$.5 billion/year market possible result of
planned high-energy physics effort. W. S.
Beller. il Miss & Roc 17:26-8 O 11 '65
International cooperation on the peaceful uses
of atomic energy; statement, September
22, 1965. G. T. Seaborg. Dept State Bul
53:677-82 O 25 '65
Nuclear energy, public policy and the law,
ed. by E. J. Bloustein. Review
Bul Atomic Sci 21:43-4 Mr '65. C. P.
Anderson
Nuclear power and proliferation; address, No-
vember 17, 1965. H. D. Smyth. Dept State
Bul 54:28-36 Ja 3 '66
Peaceful atom progress. Sci N L 87:101 F 13
'65
Ramifications of nuclear energy. B. I.
Spinrad. Bul Atomic Sci 21:21-4 My '65
Why it's time for atom police. S. Eklund.
il Sat R 48:66-7 O 2 '65
See also
Atomic blasting
Atomic power plants
Nuclear reactors

Industrial aspects
See Atomic power—Economic aspects

International aspects
Atoms for peace: concern growing that pro-
gram is spreading means for more na-
tions to build weapons. D. S. Greenberg.
Science 147:843-4 F 19 '65; Reply. F. J.
Bradley. 148:733 My 7 '65
Atoms for peace, or war. J. A. Hall. For
Affairs 43:602-15 Jl '65
Hard talk about hardware: question of
nuclear sharing. Time 86:20 D 17 '65
Worldwide race for A-bombs, can it be
stopped? interview. G. T. Seaborg. U S
News 59:60-5 Jl 19 '65
See also
European atomic energy community

International control
Atomic water vs. atomic power: difficulties
of nuclear control compounded. Nation 201:
263-4 O 25 '65
Bobby on the bomb. il Newsweek 66:30-1 O
25 '65
Committee considers draft resolutions; non-
proliferation of nuclear weapons; UN. UN
Mo Chron 2:18-23 N '65
Nuclear club: why the outs want in. M.
Viorst. il Nation 201:235-9 O 18 '65
Nuclear power and proliferation; address, No-
vember 17, 1965. H. D. Smyth. Dept State
Bul 54:28-36 Ja 3 '66
Nuclear weapons for Germany; grave dangers
of electronic safeguards. Nation 201:458 D
13 '65

Realism about nuclear spread. D. B. Bobrow.
Bul Atomic Sci 21:20-2 D '65
Ten more countries that can make nuclear
bombs. il U S News 59:50-1 D 6 '65

Laws and regulations
Atoms for peace, or war. J. A. Hall. For
Affairs 43:602-15 Jl '65

Medical applications
See Radiology, Medical

Social aspects
Atomic insurance: the ticklish statistics.
D. E. Pesonen. il Nation 201:242-5 O 18 '65

China (People's Republic)
Nuclear power of China. R. E. Lapp. il Life
58:86-90+ My 28 '65; Same abr. with title
Does red China understand the bomb?
Read Digest 87:49-53 S '65

Europe, Western
Power play. il Time 86:110 N 19 '65

Great Britain
Britain and atomic energy 1939-1945, by M.
Gowing. Review
Bul Atomic Sci 21:26-7 O '65. J. H. Man-
ley

India
What about a nuclear guarantee for India?
R. D. Masters. New Repub 153:9-10 D 25 '65;
Reply. C. Kaysen and J. J. Stone. 154:13-14
Ja 15 '66

United States
See Atomic power
ATOMIC power plants
Atomic insurance: the ticklish statistics.
D. E. Pesonen. il Nation 201:242-5 O 18 '65
Bodega Head, a partisan view. J. W. Hedg-
peth. Bul Atomic Sci 21:2-7 Mr '65; Discus-
sion. 21:27-8 O; 23 D '65
Cheapest atomic power; new station, Dun-
geness, England. Sci Am 213:46 Jl '65
Competitive nuclear power. il Fortune 71:
183-4 Mr '65
Desalination: emphasis is on dual-purpose
nuclear power and desalting plants.
J. Walsh. il Science 147:1117-19 Mr 5 '65
Good and bad subsidies; privately-owned
Public service company of Colorado. New
Repub 153:7 D 25 '65
Power play; more power reactors in western
Europe than in the U.S. il Time 86:110 N 19
'65
Rivers of fresh water from the sea. A. P.
Armagnac. il Pop Sci 187:82-5 N '65
U.S. utilities check nuclear power costs.
Sci N L 88:200 S 25 '65
Where is science taking us? excerpt from
the 1964 report of the director of Oak Ridge
national laboratory. A. M. Weinberg. il
Sat R 48:56-7 F 6 '65

Accidents and injuries
Is atomic industry risking your life? W.
Cloud. il Pop Sci 186:45-9+ Je '65; Discus-
sion. 187:38+ S '65
ATOMIC power plants, Portable. See Space
vehicles—Atomic power plants
ATOMIC powered locomotives. See Locomo-
tives, Atomic powered
ATOMIC research
Atom and the U.S. twenty years after. il
Sr Schol 87:6-10 N 4 '65
Peril and a hope: the scientists' movement
in America, 1945-47, by A. K. Smith. Re-
view
Sci Am 213:257-8+ S '65. P. Morrison
Why pure science? Bul Atomic Sci 21:28-9 S
'65
See also
Accelerators (electrons, etc)
Atomic research laboratories
Hanford works, Richland, Wash.

China (People's Republic)
Ten years of secrecy. R. Guillain. Bul Atomic
Sci 21:24-5 F '65

Europe, Western
See also
European atomic energy community
European organization for nuclear research

India
Electric power remains emphasis of India's
nuclear energy program. V. K. McElheny.
il Science 149:284-7 Jl 16 '65

United States
See Atomic research

ATOMIC research laboratories
New lab will speed radiation studies. H. M.
David. il Miss & Roc 17:34-5 N 15 '65
See also
Oak Ridge national laboratory
United States—Atomic energy commission

ATOMIC test ban treaty. See Nuclear test
ban treaty, 1963

ATOMIC warfare
Bigger wars ahead? interview. H. Kahn. il
U S News 58:42-9 Je 7 '65
Great debate: theories of nuclear strategy,
by R. Aron; tr. by E. Pawel. Review
New Repub 152:21-2 F 13 '65. R. D.
Senter
More than a bad dream. Christian Cent 82:
861 Jl 7 '65
On escalation, by H. Kahn. Review
Commentary 40:101-2+ N '65. G. Kateb
When do we seize the initiative? T. A. Lane.
Nat R 17:384-5 My 4 '65
See also
Atomic weapons
Civil defense

Defenses
Can we take chances on survival? D. Law-
rence. U S News 58:104 F 1 '65
Defense against ballistic missiles. F. J.
Dyson; reply with rejoinder. R. H. Mc-
Mahan, jr. Bul Atomic Sci 21:37-40 Mr '65
Sting of the bee in saturation parity. L.
Szilard. il Bul Atomic Sci 21:8-13 Mr '65
Strategic problems detailed by McNamara;
testimony before the House armed services
committee. R. S. McNamara. Aviation W
82:62-6 Mr 1 '65
U.S. vs. Russia: next round in arms race.
il U S News 59:66-7 N 29 '65

Ethical aspects
Back to the fundamentals. N. Cousins. Sat R
48:26 N 6 '65
Claimants of Hiroshima. R. A. Falk. il Na-
tion 200:157-61 F 15 '65
Controversial European play. H. Popkin.
Vogue 146:296-8+ S 1 '65
Corruption of innocent neutrons. W. H.
Auden. il N Y Times Mag p 18-20+ Ag 1
'65; Same abr. with title Of man and the
atom. Read Digest 87:219-20+ N '65
Men of peace. J. O'Gara. Commonweal 81:779
Mr 19 '65; Discussion. 82:99+, 175, 202 Ap
16-23, My 7 '65

Social aspects
Scientists and civil defense; dialogue at
Berkeley. J. Walsh. Science 151:53-7 Ja 7
'66

ATOMIC warfare, Prevention of. See War,
Prevention of
ATOMIC warfare and children. See War and
children

ATOMIC weapons
Bomb: from Hiroshima to... il Newsweek
66:52-7 Ag 9 '65
Chinese and ballistic missile defense. J. I.
Coffey. Bul Atomic Sci 21:17-19 D '65
Halting the spread of nuclear weapons; new
British proposals. New Repub 152:12-13 F
13 '65
Is Russia slowing down in arms race? inter-
view. R. S. McNamara. il U S News 58:52-
6+ Ap 12 '65
National security and the nuclear-test ban.
J. B. Wiesner and H. F. York; discussion.
Sci Am 211:8+ D '64; 212:8+ F; 6+ Ap '65
Non-dissemination of nuclear weapons; ad-
dress, August 19, 1965. Chalfont. Vital
Speeches 31:679-81 S 1 '65
Nuclear fallout. Newsweek 66:29 D 6 '65
Nuclear proliferation: status & security; Time
essay. Time 86:30-1 Jl 23 '65
On proliferation: where's the danger? J. J.
Stone. Bul Atomic Sci 21:15-18 N '65
Pompeii revisited; our adaptation to the
terrorizing fact of the bomb. Christian Cent
82:955 Ag 4 '65; Discussion. 82:1128-9 S 15
'65
President's opportunity; Gilpatric report on
the spread of nuclear weapons. H. Bran-
don. Sat R 48:16-17 F 13 '65
Realism about nuclear spread. D. B. Bobrow.
Bul Atomic Sci 21:20-2 D '65
Should U.S. reshape its strategic might? il
Bsns W p33-4 Jl 17 '65
Stopping the spread. Commonweal 82:180 Ap
30 '65
Three on nuclear policies. il Bul Atomic Sci
21:27-36 Ap '65
U.S. restates policy on nuclear warheads for
NATO allies; statement, November 22, 1965.
B. D. Moyers. Dept State Bul 53:939 D 13
'65

What about a nuclear guarantee for India?
R. D. Masters. New Repub 153:9-10 D 25 '65;
Reply. C. Kaysen and J. J. Stone. 154:13-14
Ja 15 '66

International control
Kennedy and China; concerning prevention
of nuclear proliferation. New Repub 153:
5-6 Jl 3 '65
New directions in arms control and disarma-
ment. W. C. Foster. For Affairs 43:587-601
Jl '65
Nuclear weapons for Germany; grave dangers
of electronic safeguards. Nation 201:458 D
13 '65
President meets with Committee on nuclear
proliferation; White House announcement;
January 21, 1965, with statement by
President Johnson. Dept State Bul 52:187-8
F '65
Should we give Japan some bombs? Nat R 17:
908+ O 19 '65
Space arms control. A. Frye. Bul Atomic Sci
21:30-3 Ap '65

Safety devices and measures
To reduce the possibility of nuclear catas-
trophe. J. Larus. Bul Atomic Sci 21:33-6
Ap '65

ATOMIC weapons and disarmament
Anti-ballistic-missile ban. Sci Am 214:46-7
Ja '66
Antimissile systems and disarmament. N.
Talensky. Bul Atomic Sci 21:25-9 F '65;
Discussion. 21:25-6 F; 29-30 O '65
Arms control and disarmament; some sober
truths; remarks, May 27, 1965. L. B. John-
son. Dept State Bul 52:973-4 Je 14 '65
Arms control, foundation stone in the ram-
parts we watch; address, March 31, 1965.
W. C. Foster. Dept State Bul 52:659-64 My 3
'65
Atoms for peace and the effort to halt the
spread of nuclear weapons. J. G. Palfrey.
Dept State Bul 53:393-7 S 6 '65
Banning the bomb. J. O'Gara. Commonweal
82:522 Jl 23 '65
Can we take chances on survival? D. Law-
rence. U S News 58:104 F 1 '65
Containing the arms race. J. J. Stone. Bul
Atomic Sci 21:18-21 S '65
Disarmament commission concludes general
debate. UN Mo Chron 2:27-45 Je '65
First committee considers twenty-seven pow-
er draft resolution; denuclearization of
Africa. UN Mo Chron 2:70-2 D '65
Freeze on strategic delivery systems. P.
Doty. Bul Atomic Sci 21:2-6 F '65
From Washington; notes on gas and dis-
armament. H. Margolis. Bul Atomic Sci
21:30-2 N '65
Heading the other way; White House con-
ference on international cooperation. New
Repub 153:5-6 D 11 '65
International cooperation: LBJ gets confer-
ence proposals. L. J. Carter. il Science 150:
1431-2+ D 10 '65
Kennedy and China; concerning prevention
of nuclear proliferation. New Repub 153:5-6
Jl 3 '65
Neat dilemma. il Newsweek 66:36 Jl 26 '65
Neutralist world and disarmament negotia-
tions. J. L. Nogee. bibliog f Ann Am Acad
362:71-80 N '65
New directions in arms control and disarma-
ment. W. C. Foster. For Affairs 43:587-601
Jl '65
Non-proliferation of nuclear weapons; with
text of resolution. UN Mo Chron 2:62-6 D
'65
Nuclear club; why the outs want in. M.
Viorst. il Nation 201:235-9 O 18 '65
Nuclear weapons; nonproliferation and test-
ban talks to be resumed. L. J. Carter.
Science 151:57-60 Ja 7 '66
Perspectives on inspection for arms control.
B. G. Lall. Bul Atomic Sci 21:51-3 Mr '65
Roadblock to arms control and disarmament
negotiations; address, June 4, 1965. W. C.
Foster. Dept State Bul 53:77-84 Jl 12 '65
Scientists speak. Bul Atomic Sci 21:47 F '65
U.N. calls for renewed efforts on non-
proliferation treaty; statements, October
18, 27 and November 8, 1965; with text of
resolution. W. C. Foster. Dept State Bul
53:873-84 N 29 '65
United States summarizes position on dis-
armament and arms control; statement,
April 26, 1965. A. E. Stevenson. bibliog f
Dept State Bul 52:762-73 My 17 '65

ATOMIC weapons and disarmament—*Cont.*
War-peace establishment, by A. Herzog. Review
  Commonweal 82:730-1 O 1 '65. S. Maloff
What Germany has become; rediscovered identity. A. Clément. New Repub 153:12-14 O 23 '65
  See also
Atomic bombs—Testing. Suspension of

Conference of the Eighteen-nation committee on disarmament, Geneva, 1962-

ATOMS
Atoms ionized then sorted. Sci N L 88:37 Jl 17 '65
Field ion microscopy. E. W. Müller. bibliog il Science 149:591-601 Ag 6 '65
New method for studying the atom. S. Bashkin. bibliog il Science 148:1047-53 My 21 '65
  See also
Matter
Neutrinos
Nuclear physics
Quantum theory

ATOMS for peace program. See Atomic power—Economic aspects; Atomic power—International aspects

ATOMTOD; opera. See Manzoni, G.

ATROCITIES
Nazis on trial; pages from a journal. tr. by W. J. Dannhauser. J. Lind. Commentary 39:69-72 Ap '65

ATSATT, P. R.
Angiosperm parasite and host: coordinated dispersal. bibliog Science 149:1389-90 S 17 '65

ATTACHÉ cases
Attaché cases. il Consumer Rep 30:558-61 N '65

ATTACK on Pearl Harbor, 1941. See Pearl Harbor, Attack on, 1941

ATTARDI, D. Gandini, and others
Submaxillary gland of mouse: effects of a fraction on tissues of mesodermal origin in vitro. bibliog Science 150:1307-9 D 3 '65

ATTASSI, Farhan Abdelhadi
Of hate & espionage; Syrian charges against US. il Time 85:31 Mr 5 '65
Spy season. il Newsweek 65:44 Mr 8 '65

ATTENBOROUGH, John
Attenborough and Harwood speak on distribution; summary of address. por Pub W 187:73-4 Je 21 '65

ATTENTION
Art of intelligent listening. J. N. Miller. Read Digest 87:83-6 S '65
Put your mind on the spot. W. M. Marston. Read Digest 86:68-71 My '65

ATTIE, David
David Attie. il Pop Phot 56:92-7+ Je '65
How David Attie creates montages in his darkroom. L. Solmssen. il Mod Phot 29:80-5 Mr '65

ATTITUDES
Derogatory images of the Negro and Negro history. G. E. Cunningham. Negro Hist Bul 28:126-7+ Mr '65
Race and shared belief as factors in social choice. M. Rokeach and L. Mezei. bibliog il Science 151:167-72 Ja 14 '66
Some of my best friends are white. E. B. Thompson. il Ebony 20:154+ Ag '65
What whites can learn from Negroes. il Ebony 20:158-9 Ag '65
  See also
Moral attitudes
Political thought
Public opinion

ATTORNEY, Power of. See Power of attorney

ATTORNEY General (United States) See United States—Justice, Department of

ATTRACTANTS, Insect. See Insect sex attractants

ATTWATER prairie chickens. See Prairie chickens

ATWATER, James
Cosmic room to stagger the mind. Sat Eve Post 238:30-1 Ap 24 '65
Golden hawk of hockey. Sat Eve Post 239:56-9 Ja 1 '66
Is America ready for the Cord? Sat Eve Post 238:58-60 Ag 14 '65
Plane that gets you there before you left. Sat Eve Post 238:21-5 F 13 '65
Tormented life of a pro linebacker. Sat Eve Post 238:26-31 D 18 '65
—See Taylor, T. jt. auth.

ATWATER, Maxine
Mexican trio. Travel 124:44-6 O '65
Resort hopping in the Orient. Travel 124:36-8 N '65

ATZ, James W.
Hermaphroditic fish. Science 150:789-92+ N 5 '65

AUBREY, James Thomas, Jr
CBS: the money machine. il por Newsweek 65:60-2 F 22 '65
Fall of a television czar. M. Kempton. New Repub 152:9-10 Ap 3 '65; Reply. J. G. Dunne. 152:42 Ap 17 '65
Only you, Jim Aubrey. il por Newsweek 65:62-3 Mr 15 '65
Regency firing. il por Time 85:80+ Mr 12 '65
TV's week that was: FCC probe; CBS storm. il por Bsns W p28 Mr 6 '65
Tyrant's fall that rocked the TV world. R. Oulahan and W. Lambert. il pors Life 59:90-2+ S 10 '65
What are friends for? G. Ace. Sat R 48:13 Mr 20 '65

AUBREY, N.Y.
Town where the Mets are champs. J. Izenberg. il Sat Eve Post 238:84+ Ap 24 '65

AUBURN Mets farm club (Minor league baseball) See Baseball

AUBURN university, Alabama
College students change majors. M. O. Cook. il Sch & Soc 93:271-3 My 1 '65

AUCTIONS
Bidding at auction. B. McVay. il Motor T 17:34-5 Je '65
Blissful are they that give; Combined arts of San Diego. il Time 86:104+ N 5 '65
Broadway hijinks at an Angus auction; Black Watch farms, Wappingers Falls, N.Y. il Bsns W p32-3 O 23 '65
For sale: vacation sites from Uncle Sam. E. Kerr. il Pop Sci 186:138-40 Je '65
Sotheby builds up a bid for old-car collectors. il Bsns W p42-4 N 20 '65
  See also
Parke-Bernet galleries, incorporated

AUCTIONS, Art. See Art sales

AUDEN, Wystan Hugh
Books (cont) New Yorker 41:159-60+ Ap 3; 227-8+ O 23 '65
Corruption of innocent neutrons. N Y Times Mag p 18-20+ Ag 1 '65; Same abr. with title Of man and the atom. Read Digest 87:219-20+ N '65
Epithalamium for Peter Mudford & Rita Auden; poem. New Yorker 41:34 Jl 31 '65
  about
Auden: a poet's joy in a new home. R. Phelps. Life 59:17 Ag 13 '65
Auden as critic. W. Meredith. Poetry 107:118-20 N '65
Elvish mode; meeting of the Tolkien society of America. New Yorker 41:24 Ja 15 '66
Poet's voice in the crowd. R. D. Spector. Sat R 48:29 Ag 7 '65
Slender affirmations. F. J. Warnke. New Repub 154:28+ Ja 15 '66

AUDIENCES
Audience: its strengths and weaknesses. W. Weaver. il Opera N 29:8-11 F 6 '65
Let them eat bananas; unruly audience. il Time 87:58+ Ja 21 '66
You're a spectator; excerpt from Seventeen book of etiquette and entertaining. E. A. Haupt. Seventeen 24:318 Ag '65
  See also
Television audiences

AUDIO fairs
Audio '66; 1965 New York high fidelity music show with directory. I. Berger. Sat R 48:58-9+ S 25 '65
Heard at the High fidelity show. I. Berger. Sat R 48:74 O 16 '65
High fidelity newsfronts. N. Eisenberg. il Hi Fi 15:36+ D '65
1965 audio show: notes and impressions. L. Zide. il Am Rec G 32:206-7 N '65
Sound advice; New York high fidelity music show. R. M. Angus. Mod Phot 29:30+ F '65

AUDIO-visual aids
Color slides. R. Miller. U S Camera 28:36 S '65
Constitution: team teaching approach with A-V aids. M. Benefield. Sr Schol 86:sup7-8 Mr 11 '65
Realistic A-V content; excerpts from address, November 1965. L. W. Ingraham. il Sr Schol 87:sup9 D 9 '65
  See also
Educational media index
Libraries and audio-visual materials
Magnetic recorders and recording—Educational applications

AUDIO-visual Instruction
American's impressions: audio visuals in Britain. R. H. Burgert. Sr Schol 87:sup8 O 28 '65
  See also
Libraries and audio-visual materials
Moving pictures in education

AUDITIONS. See Dancing—Auditions

AUDITIONS, Metropolitan. See Singing—Competitions

AUDITORIUMS
Boston bids for big clambakes; War memorial auditorium to lure national conventions. il Bsns W p 150+ F 13 '65
Campus City, Chicago; the hub; design revolves about lecture center. il Arch Forum 123:34-5 S '65
Circular auditorium subdivides into four. il Arch Rec 137:180 Mr '65
Double duty for Dinner Key auditorium, Miami. W. Coburn. il Yachting 118:56+ N '65

AUDRIETH, L. F.
Scientists on tap or on top? we are missing the real issues. Bul Atomic Sci 21:24-5 S '65
—and Chinn, H. I.
State department seminar. Bul Atomic Sci 21: 43-4 My '65

AUDUBON, John James
Audubon: naturalist into artist. E. H. Dwight. il por Art N 64:35-7+ My '65
Eyes in the wilderness; exhibition of watercolors and drawings at Morgan library. F. Getlein. New Repub 153:24+ S 18 '65
Unpublished Audubon originals. E. H. Dwight. il Antiques 87:454-5 Ap '65

AUDUBON medal
Laurance Rockefeller awarded Audubon medal; with note of appreciation. L. S. Rockefeller. il Audubon Mag 67:112-13 Mr '65

AUDUBON nature camps
910 attended Audubon camps. C. W. Buchheister. Audubon Mag 67:357 N '65
Our Wisconsin camp has winning ways. E. Roark. il Audubon Mag 67:103-7 Mr '65

AUDUBON prints. See Birds in art

AUERBACH, Arnold. See Auerbach, Red

AUERBACH, Arnold M.
Brief rebellion of the American male. Harper 230:85-7 F '65

AUERBACH, Jerold S.
Influence of the New deal. bibliog f Cur Hist 48:334-9+ Je '65

AUERBACH, Red
Man. por Time 87:75 Ja 14 '66
They all boo when Red sits down. G. Rogin. pors Sports Illus 22:100-2+ Ap 5 '65

AUERBACH, Robert. See Globerson, A. jt. auth.

AUERT, Edward
Peasant renewal of earth; poem. Nation 200: 344 Mr 29 '65
Sunday to a close at Gritman hospital; poem. Nation 201:232 O 11 '65

AUGELLI, John P.
Dominican Republic. bibliog Focus 15:1-6 My '65

AUGER, Pierre
Limits to science. Bul Atomic Sci 21:21-2 N '65

AUGSTEIN, Rudolf
How Der Spiegel wins profits and enemies. il por Bsns W p 132-4 Ja 30 '65
Man who holds the mirror to Germany. A. J. Olsen. il pors N Y Times Mag p30-1+ F 7 '65

AUGUST, Kendall
New complexities in plant security. Duns R 85:pt2 142-3+ Mr '65

AUGUSTA civic ballet (organization) See Ballet companies

AUGUSTA national golf club course. See Golf courses

AUROCHS. See Bison, European

AURORAS
Auroral phenomena. B. J. O'Brien. bibliog il Science 148:449-60 Ap 23 '65

Spectra
Aurora. S.-I. Akasofu. il Sci Am 213:10, 54-62 bibliog(p 126) D '65

AURTHUR, Robert Alan
Going back to boot camp, Parris Island, S.C. Esquire 64:127-30+ S '65
TV: the 21" bore. Nation 201:227-31 S 20 '65

AUSCHWITZ concentration camp. See Concentration camps—Poland

AUSLAND, John C. and Richardson, H. F.
Crisis management: Berlin, Cyprus, Laos. For Affairs 44:291-303 Ja '66

AUSLANDER, Joseph
I will leave this house; poem. McCalls 92: 202 Ap '65
She made home happy; poem. McCalls 92:152 Mr '65

AUSTEN, Jane
Jane Austen, by A. W. Litz. Review
Reporter 32:45-6+ My 20 '65. A. Ward
Sat R por 48:76 My 22 '65. H. T. Moore

AUSTIN, J. Paul
Modern communication; address, January 16, 1965. Vital Speeches 31:271-4 F 15 '65

AUSTIN, Mary C.
Dropouts or readers? bibliog f Sr Schol 86: sup26-7 Mr 4 '65

AUSTIN, Robert W.
Responsibilty for social change. Harvard Bsns R 43:45-52 Jl '65

AUSTIN, Tex.
Education
New wing at Casis; elementary school library. A. B. McGuire. il Library J 90:5460-2 D 15 '65

AUSTRALIA
See also
Airlines—Australia
Australians
Canberra
Great Barrier Reef
Immigration and emigration—Australia
Iron mines and mining—Australia
Money—Australia
Paleontology—Australia
Private schools—Australia
Publishers and publishing—Australia
Strikes—Australia
Western Australia
Youth—Australia
Zoology—Australia

Defenses
Australia and the defense of southeast Asia. S. Paltridge. For Affairs 44:49-61 O '65
Australia girds for defense. D. Warner. Reporter 32:20-2 Mr 11 '65
Australia modernizes air forces to meet threat from Indonesia. il Aviation W 82:279-80 Mr 15 '65
Sukarno has done us a favor. U S News 58: 32 Mr 1 '65

Description and travel
Australia: out back and in town. P. Durdin. il Sat R 48:64+ S 18 '65
Going places, finding things in Australia. D. Stivens. il House & Gard 128:62-4+ O '65
Let's travel. il Mlle 62:135-8 D '65
Travel's picture portfolio. Travel 124:50-5 N '65

Economic conditions
Rich, easygoing Australia: the challenge ahead. E. J. Drechsel. il U S News 58:80-3 Ap 5 '65
Traveler on the rim of Asia. C. J. V. Murphy. il Fortune 71:264+ Je '65

Foreign relations
Asia, Southeastern
Australia and the defense of southeast Asia. S. Paltridge. For Affairs 44:49-61 O '65

Indonesia
Australia girds for defense. D. Warner. Reporter 32:20--2 Mr 11 '65
Sukarno has done us a favor. U S News 58:32 Mr 1 '65

Industries
See also
Cattle industry and trade
Mines and mineral resources—Australia

Native races
Australia's aborigines step out of the stone age. E. Huxley. il N Y Times Mag p 10-11+ Je 20 '65
Consciences down under. Christian Cent 82: 486 Ap 21 '65

Politics and government
Exit burly Bob; H. Holt replaces Menzies. Newsweek 67:44 Ja 24 '66

Population
Australia's aborigines step out of the stone age. E. Huxley. il N Y Times Mag p 10-11+ Je 20 '65

Religious institutions and affairs
News of the Christian world (cont) Christian Cent 82:1173-4 S 22 '65

Royal air force
Australia modernizes air forces to meet threat from Indonesia. il Aviation W 82:279-80 Mr 15 '65

Social conditions
See also
Australia—Population

Social life and customs
Cocktail party. B. Grant. il Reporter 33:46-8+ O 21 '65

AUSTRALIA, New Zealand and United States treaty council. See ANZUS council

AUSTRALIA, WESTERN. See Western Australia

AUSTRALIA and the United States
Purpose that binds America and Australia; a toast in honor of Sir R. Menzies, June 7, 1965. L. B. Johnson. Dept State Bul 52: 1050-1 Je 28 '65

AUSTRALIAN (newspaper) See Newpapers— Australia

AUSTRALIAN art. See Art, Australian (aboriginal)

AUSTRALIAN national insect collection. See Insects—Collection and preservation

AUSTRALIAN Open golf tournament. See Golf —Tournaments

AUSTRALIAN snails. See Snails

AUSTRALIAN tiger snakes. See Snakes

AUSTRALIANS
Traveling with Mlle: the adventurous young Australians. il Mlle 62:131-4 D '65

AUSTRALOPITHECUS africanus. See Man, Prehistoric

AUSTRIA
Atlantic report. Atlan 215:40+ My '65
See also
Americans in Austria
Elections—Austria
Fishing—Austria
Music festivals—Austria
Political parties—Austria

Defenses
What lock on the door? purchase of antiaircraft guns. il Time 86:47 N 19 '65

Description and travel
Tall tales of the Vienna woods. J. Wechsberg. il Sat R 48:36+ Mr 13 '65

Economic conditions
Disneyland of Europe. il Time 85:38+ My 21 '65
Genius for compromise. Time 85:92 Ap 2 '65

History
Bibliography
Articles and other books received; comp. by A. H. Price. See issues of American historical review

Politics and government
Operetta state. il Newsweek 65:34-5 Je 7 '65
Tenth anniversary of signing of Austrian state treaty; remarks, May 15, 1965. D. Rusk. Dept State Bul 52:898-9 Je 7 '65
See also
Political parties—Austria

Treaties
Tenth anniversary of signing of Austrian state treaty; remarks, May 15, 1965. D. Rusk. Dept State Bul 52:898-9 Je 7 '65

AUSTRIAN cookery. See Cookery, Austrian

AUSTRIAN humor. See Humor, Austrian

AUTHORITARIANISM
Touch of tyranny; views of W. P. Bundy in regard to underdeveloped nations. R. F. Hamilton. Nation 201:75-8 Ag 16 '65

AUTHORITY
Imperatives of authority; excerpt from Managers for tomorrow. Duns R 85:49-50+ F '65

AUTHORITY (religion)
See also
Catholic church—Infallibility

AUTHORS
Frank Dobie ranch sought for writers' retreat. Pub W 188:39 O 11 '65
Is the Nobel prize for literature political? R. J. Clements. il Sat R 48:41-2+ D 4 '65
King of the cats, by F. W. Dupee. Review Sat R 48:27-8 Jl 10 '65. G. Hicks
Literature of the early sixties; reprint. S. Kauffmann. bibliog il Wilson Lib Bul 39:748-56+ My '65
Merry Christmas: here is your gift. L. Conger. Writer 78:9-10 D '65
Off the cuff. L. Conger. Writer 78:9-10 Je; 7-8 Jl; 7-8 O '65
Rebellion and response. S. Babb. Writer 79: 9-11 Ja '66
Retirement bill for authors introduced in Congress. Pub W 187:35 Mr 8 '65
Silences, when writers don't write: adaption of address. T. Olsen. il Harper 231:153-6+ O '65
Those angry authors, why their protests fail. I. Brown. Sat R 48:18-19+ Ag 28 '65
To him who would a writer be. G. Hicks. Sat R 49:23-4 Ja 1 '66

Writers on vacation. R. Barthes. Nation 201:474 D 13 '65
Writer's public image; letter. J. Michener. Esquire 64:150+ D '65
See also
Authorship
Copyright
Literary agents
Literature
Novelists
PEN club
Poets
Prisoners as authors
Publishers and publishing
Royalties
Women as authors

Homes and haunts
See Literary landmarks

AUTHORS, American
Coming revolution in literature. H. Swados. Sat R 48:14-17 Ag 21 '65
Go West, young writer; great Californian novel yet to be written. W. Murray. Holiday 38:20+ O '65
How Alfred Knopf saw his authors; A. A. Knopf's documentary film. Dialogue. M. R. Weiss. il Sat R 48:26-8 Je 12 '65
How to act like a writer in New York and London. A. Pryce-Jones. il Harper 231:146-50 N '65
Literary mind. A. Kazin. Nation 201:203-6 S 20 '65
Literary mine in the gold country; San Francisco scene. J. K. Hutchens. Sat R 48:37-8 S 25 '65
Memoranda of a decade; excerpts from symposium; ed. by M. Cowley and R. Cowley. il Am Heritage 16:33-40 Ag '65
Men of the '30s. R. Kostelanetz. Commonweal 83:266-9 D 3 '65
Reformers in the ghetto. R. Sanders. Commentary 40:78-80+ N '65
They never left Texas; three native writers. F. H. Wardlaw. Sat R 48:25-8 S 18 '65
Willa Cather and The professor's house; anti-Semitism in American literature of the 1920's. J. Schroeter. Yale R 54:494-512 Je '65
Writer can't keep to his attic; concern over grave issues such as Vietnam. I. Howe. il N Y Times Mag p43-5+ D 5 '65
See also
Adams, H.
American literature
Clemens, S. L.
Dupee, F. W.
Elkin, S.
Fitzgerald, F. S. K.
Ford, N. R.
French, A.
Gardner, E. S.
James, H.
Kerouac, J.
Mailer, N.
Mencken, H. L.
Merton, T.
O'Connor, F.
Ossoli, S. M. F. d'
Rand, C.
Thoreau, H. D.
Thurber, J.
Villard, O. G.
Wilder, T. N.
Wilson, E.
Winsor, K.
Zinn, H.

AUTHORS, Argentine
See also
Borges, J. L.

AUTHORS, English
How to act like a writer in New York and London. A. Pryce-Jones. il Harper 231:146-50 N '65
See also
Brogan, D. W.
Conrad, J.
English literature
Golding, W.
Hudson, W. H.
Maugham, W. S.
Snow of Leicester, C. P. S.

AUTHORS, European
And quiet flow the words; smuggling of manuscripts. il Time 86:33 D 17 '65
Letter from Rome; fourth international congress of the European community of writers. E. M. Borgese. Nation 201:313-16 N 1 '65

AUTHORS, Finnish
See also
Salama, H.

AUTHORS, French
  See also
Aragon, L.
Beauvoir, S. de
Camus, A.
French literature
Genet, J.
Jarry, A.
Proust, M.
Sade, D. A. F. de
Saint Exupéry, A. de
Sartre, J. P.
Weil, S.
AUTHORS, German
  See also
Grass, G.
Mann, T.
AUTHORS, Greek
  See also
Kazantzakis, N.
AUTHORS, Irish
  See also
Behan, B.
Joyce, J.
AUTHORS, Italian
  See also
Praz, M.
AUTHORS, Jewish
What's in it for me? I. B. Singer. il Harper
  231:172-3 O '65
  See also
American literature—Jewish authors
Singer, I. B.
Swados, H.
Weil, S.

AUTHORS, Russian
And quiet flow the words; smuggling of
  manuscripts. il Time 86:33 D 17 '65
Arrests in Russia; case of Andrei Sinyavsky
  and Yuli Daniel. New Repub 154:7 Ja 22 '66
Moscow summer, by M. Mihajlov. Review
  Sat R 48:41-2 D 11 '65. P. Viereck
Writers in the Soviet Union. New Repub
  153:9-10 D 11 '65; Discussion. 154:36+ Ja
  1 '66
  See also
Gorky, M.
Pasternak, B. L.
Pushkin, A. S.
Tarsis, V.
Tertz, A.
AUTHORS, South African
Letter from South Africa; writers in dissent.
  S. Uys. New Repub 153:36-7 S 25 '65
AUTHORS, Spanish
Wounded generation: Spanish writers born
  during or since Spanish Civil war. A. M.
  Matute. Nation 201:420-4 N 29 '65
AUTHORS, Venezuelan
  See also
Picón-Salas, M.
AUTHORS agents. See Literary agents
AUTHORS and libraries. See Libraries and au-
thors
AUTHORS and politics
Arrests in Russia; case of Andrei Sinyavsky
  and Yuli Daniel. New Repub 154:7 Ja 22 '66
Writer can't keep to his attic. I. Howe. il
  N Y Times Mag p43-5+ D 5 '65
AUTHORS and publishers
Author-publishers relation viewed in RPG
  discussion; meeting of the Religious pub-
  lishers group. Pub W 189:46-7 Ja 3 '66
Author, the publisher and the fifty-fifty split.
  P. R. Reynolds. Pub W 189:62-4 Ja 10 '66
Authors' alterations: are they really neces-
  sary? comments at American book pub-
  lishers council conference. B. L. Stratton.
  Pub W 187:21-2 Ap 5 '65
But I'm a good salesman. R. Armour. Pub W
  187:33-4 Mr 8 '65
Doctor Spock loses first round in Pocket
  books suit. Pub W 188:67 D 27 '65
Doctor Spock sues pocket books for ruling
  to end inserts. Pub W 188:52 O 25 '65
Notes on authors alterations and the new
  technology. D. Melcher. Pub W 187:35-6
  My 3 '65; Discussion. 188:34-5 Jl 19 '65
Publishing from the cider mill; publishing of
  L. Rue's New Jersey out-of-doors. A. L.
  Crosby. il Pub W 188:41-3 Jl 5 '65; Reply.
  R. M. Huber. 188:11-12 Ag 16 '65
Publishing parties: their do's and don'ts.
  Pub W 188:33-4 D 6 '65
What is the law when author and publisher
  can't agree? H. F. Pilpel. Pub W 188:86
  S 27 '65
  See also
Literary agents
Royalties
AUTHORS and readers
Wanted: a new dialogue between authors &
  readers; excerpt from Revolution in books.
  R. Escarpit. il UNESCO Courier 18:11-14
  S '65

AUTHORS conferences
Letter from Rome; fourth international con-
  gress of the European community of writ-
  ers. E. M. Borgese. Nation 201:313-16 N 1
  '65
Memory of a writers' conference. M. P. War-
  ren. Writer 78:23-4 Ap '65
Workshops for writers; with list of con-
  ferences. G. Munson. il Sat R 48:46-9+
  Ap 24 '65
Writers' conferences 1965. Writer 78:25-30 Ap
  '65
AUTHORS guild of America. See Authors
league of America—Authors guild
AUTHORS league of America
New attacks on postal censorship. R. H.
  Smith. Pub W 187:63 F 1 '65
      Authors guild
Authors guild elects new officers and coun-
  cil. Pub W 187:38 Mr 15 '65
AUTHORS vocabulary. See Vocabulary
AUTHORSHIP
Are writers made, not born? R. Diers. Sat R
  48:52-3 Ag 14 '65
Article queries that sell. M. Gunther. Writer
  78:19-21+ Ag '65
Book-writing venture. Y. I. Kim. Writer 78:
  28-30 O '65
Can you learn to write? L. McLaughlin.
  Writer 78:31-3 D '65
Distilled experience; concerning The 1001
  nights of Jean Macaque. S. Cloete. il Writer
  78:19 Jl '65
Family skeleton with solid gold teeth. V.
  Henry. Writer 78:14-15+ Ap '65
Final approach. M. Lodeesen. Writer 78:12-
  13 Jl '65
Here comes a chopper. S. Lund. Vogue 145:
  68+ Ap 1 '65
Manner of speaking; dear editor: how do I
  become a writer? J. Ciardi. Sat R 48:20 Ag
  21 '65
Taking self-inventory. L. D. Peabody. Writer
  78:26-8 Ag '65
Thinking man's waste land; excerpts from
  address. S. Bellow. Sat R 48:20 Ap 3 '65
Where to sell manuscripts. See issues of
  Writer
Writer & the common world. C. Raines. Li-
  brary J 90:1622 Ap 1 '65
Writer's life; symposium. il Harper 231:141-
  56+ O; 141-71 N '65
  See also
Authors
Biography
Drama—Technique
Fiction—Technique
Literary research
Plagiarism
Plots (drama, novel, etc)
Short stories
Style, Literary

    Anecdotes, facetiae, satire, etc.
Author's anguish. R. E. Wolseley. ALA Bul
  59:1002 D '65
Literary interview: Pussy Adore. R. Bongartz. il Nation 200:598-9 My 31 '65
Why write a book? H. Schwartz. Sat R 48:
  22-3 Ag 14 '65

      Bibliography
Writer's library. See issues of Writer

      Collaboration
Confessions of a speechwriter. D. Lynch. il
  Duns R 86:42-3+ N '65
Who's writing LBJ's speeches. il U S News
  58:57 Je 28 '65
AUTISM
Screams, slaps and love; new treatment for
  withdrawn children at UCLA Neuropsychi-
  atric institute; with report by D. Moser.
  il Life 58:90A-96+ My 7 '65
AUTO-buses. See Automobiles
AUTO-engine analyzers. See Testing instru-
ments
AUTO radios. See Automobiles—Radio equip-
ment
AUTOBAHN. See Roads—Germany (Federal
Republic)
AUTOBIOGRAPHY
Books. M. Muggeridge. Esquire 63:54+ F '65
Distilled experience; concerning The 1001
  nights of Jean Macaque. S. Cloete. il Writer
  78:19 Jl '65
AUTOGRAPHING parties. See Booksellers and
bookselling—Publicity
AUTOGRAPHS
Paper celebrities; auction at Manhattan's
  Gotham hotel. il Time 85:41-2 Ap 2 '65
Trade winds; John F. Kennedy's use of secre-
  taries and Autopen. J. Beatty, jr. il Sat R
  48:10+ N 6 '65

AUTOMATED teaching aids. See Teaching—
  Aids and devices
AUTOMATIC canteen company of America
  Where profits are really food and drink.
    il Bsns W p88-90 Jl 3 '65
AUTOMATIC control
  Electronic timers for automatic control. S. L.
    Silver. il Electr World 73:39-41+ Mr '65
    See also
  Machine tools—Control
  Machinery, Automatic
AUTOMATIC data processing. See Electronic
  data processing
AUTOMATIC drafting macnine. See Drawing
  instruments
AUTOMATIC exposure cameras. See Cameras
AUTOMATIC landing systems. See Airplanes—
  Landing
AUTOMATIC machinery. See Machinery, Auto-
  matic
AUTOMATIC mail handling. See Mail han-
  dling
AUTOMATIC pilot (airplanes)
  I flew in the airliner that lands itself!
    D. Francis. il Pop Sci 186:78-80 F '65
  Pan Am expected to purchase Boeing-Bendix
    landing system. Aviation W 82:34 My 31
    '65
  707/720 landing system approval seen; auto-
    pilot equipment. C. M. Plattner. il Avia-
    tion W 82:38-9+ Mr 8 '65
  737 autopilot exploits avionics advances. B.
    Miller. il Aviation W 83:113+ N 15 '65
  Thinking man's autopilot. A. Trammell. il
    Flying 77:45-8 N '65
AUTOMATIC sprinklers. See Sprinklers
AUTOMATIC teaching. See Teaching machines
AUTOMATIC transmission. See Automobiles—
  Transmission
AUTOMATIC typesetting machines. See Type-
  setting machines
AUTOMATION
  Are we educating our children for the wrong
    future? R. M. Hutchins. il Sat R 48:66-7+
    S 11 '65
  Automation: a job creator not a job de-
    stroyer; excerpts from address. Y. Brozen.
    il U S News 58:94-8 Mr 8 '65
  Automation and jobs. il Sr Schol 87:12-14 N
    11 '65
  Automation and mankind. D. Lyons. il Cath
    World 201:126-31 My '65
  Automation and national policy; address,
    February 10, 1965. R. R. Eppert. Vital
    Speeches 31:316-18 Mr 1 '65
  Automation has made strikes senseless. A. H.
    Raskin. il N Y Times Mag p45+ O 31 '65
  Automation is here to liberate us. E. Hoffer.
    il N Y Times Mag p48-9+ O 24 '65
  Automation not as bad as many people think.
    Sci N L 87:313 My 15 '65
  Automation; past, present and future; ad-
    dress, October 8, 1965. T. J. Watson, jr.
    Vital Speeches 32:48-51 N 1 '65
  Challenge of automation. G. R. Comstock. bib-
    liog f Cur Hist 49:71-6+ Ag '65
  Electronic composing room; how near is it?
    J. Tebbel. il Sat R 48:75-6 Je 12 '65
  Last word in automation; new British daily.
    il Time 86:53-4 S 24 '65
  Learning to live with science. E. G. Mes-
    thene. Sat R 48:14-17 Jl 17 '65
  Logging plant operated by data processing
    il(p 193) Sci N L 88:201 S 25 '65
  Man must halt threat of rule by automation.
    Sci N L 88:216 O 2 '65
  Real news about automation. C. E. Silber-
    man; discussion. Fortune 71:74+ Mr '65
  Sixth sense on the production line. H. E.
    Klein. il Duns R 85:57-9+ My '65
  Taming the specter. Newsweek 67:46 Ja 3
    '66
  Ten corporations and automation; report on
    questions sent to presidents of twenty
    California corporations. A. Juvinall. Chris-
    tian Cent 82:271-3 Mr 3 '65
  Time to kill, automation, leisure and jobs.
    E. Larrabee. Nation 201:198-202 S 20 '65
    See also
  Computers—Industrial applications
  Electronic data processing
  Libraries—Automation
  Machinery, Automatic
  Shipping—Automation
  Unemployment, Technological
AUTOMATONS
  I was an 18-foot robot. J. R. Berry. il Pop
    Mech 124:63-6+ Ag '65
  It walks like a man. R. Bongartz. il Nation
    200:645-6 Je 14 '65
AUTOMOBILE accessories. See Automobiles—
  Equipment
AUTOMOBILE accidents. See Traffic accidents
AUTOMOBILE auctions. See Auctions

AUTOMOBILE boat trailers
  Build this flyweight boat trailer. B. Whittier.
    il Pop Sci 186:116-17 F '65
  Clearance lights for trailer boats. il Sunset
    134:131 Ap '65
  Dunking is not for trailers. F. C. Clark, jr.
    il Yachting 118:60-1+ Jl '65
  Pointers on trailering. F. M. Paulson. il Field
    & S 70:62-3 Ja '66
  Tips on boat trailers. F. M. Paulson. Field &
    S 69:145+ Mr '65
  To Nova Scotia by trailer. H. Modavis. il
    Yachting 117:88-9+ Ap '65
  Tricks with trailers. J. Martenhoff. il Pop
    Sci 187:74-7 Jl '65
  When you go down to the sea with your ship.
    il Pop Sci 186:122-3 F '65
AUTOMOBILE bodies. See Automobiles—Bodies
AUTOMOBILE brakes. See Brakes, Automobile
AUTOMOBILE buying. See Automobiles—Pur-
  chasing
AUTOMOBILE clubs
  Durable A; convention of the Model A re-
    storers club. il Time 86:58-9 Ag 20 '65
  Mustangers, unite! M. Lamm. il Motor T 17:
    76-7 Jl '65
  Parlor game on wheels; rally staged by
    Sports car club of America. D. Francis.
    il Pop Sci 188:64-7+ Ja '66
  They call it a sport now, sarge; four-wheel
    driving vehicles. B. Gilbert. il Sports Illus
    24:50-6+ Ja 10 '66
  Trophy team; Lansing, Mich. R. Huntington.
    il Hot Rod 18:54-5+ Ag '65
AUTOMOBILE dealers
  Detroit adds power to its dealer training. il
    Bsns W p54+ Ag 28 '65
  One-stop center for buying cars; Riverside
    auto center, Calif. il Bsns W p92-4 O 16
    '65
  Why auto dealers don't like cash buyers;
    Supreme court vs General motors franchise
    system. il Consumer Rep 30:258-61 My '65
AUTOMOBILE decoration
  Custom how-to: side scoops; with photo-
    graphs. Hot Rod 18:86-7 S '65
AUTOMOBILE drivers
  From a boy's point of view; love affair with
    his car. J. Wescott. il Seventeen 24:96 N
    '65
  How good a driver are you? J. E. Gibson.
    il Todays Health 43:34-6 My '65
  No sport for gentlemen; Indianapolis race
    driver. B. Ottum. il Sports Illus 22:32-6+
    My 31 '65
  Should a teen own a car? comments from
    parents and teens. Farm J 89:104 D '65
  Some medicines make you a dangerous driv-
    er. il Changing T 20:43-5 Ja '66
  Teen scene. Changing T 19:14-16 Je '65
  Wider moral sense; immorality of reckless
    driving. America 112:414 Mr 27 '65
  Worst drivers. C. W. Morton. il Atlan 216:
    125 Jl '65
  Your eyes, your auto and your life; with
    eye tests. P. W. Kearney. il Read Digest
    87:115-18 D '65
    See also
  Taxicab drivers

Licenses

  Are we licensing drivers to kill? J. R. Berry.
    il Pop Sci 186:64-7 Je '65
  If you're living abroad and you want an
    American car: license and customs regu-
    lations in Munich; letter from an Ameri-
    can citizen. il U S News 58:75 Ap 19 '65
  News on wheels; minimum age for drivers.
    Sr Schol 87:48 N 11 '65

Testing

  Are we licensing drivers to kill? J. R. Berry.
    il Pop Sci 186:64-7 Je '65
  Can driver's license laws really save lives?
    interview. ed. by D. Gregg. W. F. Suep-
    pel. Bet Hom & Gard 43:23-4+ Jl '65
  Driving tests should be tougher. C. Leed-
    ham. il N Y Times Mag p40+ F 14 '65
  Examination time; CBS National driver's
    test sponsored by Shell. Newsweek 66:76
    Ag 23 '65
  Testing what? National drivers' test. R. L.
    Shayon. Sat R 48:48 Je 19 '65
AUTOMOBILE driving
  Are you as good a driver as you think you
    are? reprint of National drivers test. CBS
    news broadcast, with answers. il PTA Mag
    60:23-7 N '65
  Complete guide to vacation driving. Bet
    Hom & Gard 43:20+ Je '65
  Defensive driving. Motor T 17:61-2 Jl '65
  Epileptics drive safely. Sci N L 89:46 Ja 15
    '66
  Help! proposed highway emergency locating
    plan. Time 85:77 F 12 '65

AUTOMOBILE driving—*Continued*
If you drive muddy roads. Sunset 134:52 **F** '65
News on wheels; nighttime driving hazards. D. Chu. Sr Schol 87:40 D 9 '65
Tailgating, invitation to tragedy. P. W. Kearney. Read Digest 87:103-6 O '65
Ten common driving emergencies. il Travel 123:46-9 Mr '65
Ubiquitous auto: man's servant or master? il Sr Schol 86:6-9 F 4 '65
What truckers say about your driving; tips from pros. Read Digest 86:73-5 F '65
See also
Automobile drivers
Automobile touring

Animal hazards
Protect your liabilities when your animals get on the road. N. G. P. Krausz. Suc Farm 63:64 Jl '65

Laws and regulations
See Automobile laws and regulations

Study and teaching
Attack on two fronts; driver-safety campaign in Washington state. Changing T 19:12-14 Je '65
Fast-reflex school for patrolmen. M. Mann. il Pop Mech 124:96-100 Ag '65
Simulators in driver education. R. B. Hayes. NEA J 54:58 Ap '65

AUTOMOBILE driving simulators. See Simulators

AUTOMOBILE engines
Chevy's fabulous new 396. R. Huntington. il Motor T 17:52-5 Je '65
Chevy's new flying wedge. E. Dahlquist. il Hot Rod 18:28-33+ Mr '65
Detroit's hot-heads; combustion-chamber design. R. E. Jennings. il Motor T 17:42-7 Mr '65
Dry-sump your racer. E. Rickman. il Hot Rod 18:46-7 D '65
Famous four-banger Offy is tendered last rites. S. Yunick. Pop Sci 186:67 Ap '65
In and out; Buick Chevy swap. J. McFarland, jr. il Hot Rod 18:78-80 Ag '65
Indy notes. C. Nerpel. il Motor T 17:64 My '65
It's white tie & tails for Chevy Caprice 396. J. Ethridge. il Motor T 17:48-53 Je '65
New cars; what's ahead in 1966? A. Markovich. il Pop Mech 124:96-100+ O '65
One engine has the best chance to win this 500. S. Yunick. Pop Sci 186:85 Mr '65
One hairy sedan! N. Thatcher's mighty Plymouth hemi. D. Francisco. il Hot Rod 18:40-1 F '65
Rotary engine gets on the road; commercial models of NSU's little Spider powered by Wankel engine. il Bsns W p 118-20 Ap 3 '65
Sensational new OHC six from Pontiac. J. P. Norbye. il Pop Sci 187:37-41 Ag '65
65½ cars; hotter engines and tougher suspensions. J. P. Norbye. il Pop Sci 186:70-3 My '65
Tempest's tall six. D. Francisco. il Hot Rod 18:30-5+ S '65
Thirsty Comet. il Hot Rod 18:48 Jl '65
Three hot engines hit the street. J. Dunne. il Pop Mech 125:100-2+ Ja '66
396 wedge, Yunick style. S. Yunick. il Hot Rod 18:34-8+ D '65
Three-ton rod; Summers' quadra-hemi LSR machine. E. Rickman. il Hot Rod 18:66-9 Je '65
Your serviceman looks at the '66 cars. T. Douglas. il Pop Mech 125:106-9+ Ja '66
See also
Anti-freeze solutions
Tachometers

Cooling
Battery, heat riser & radiator check-out. R. E. Jennings. il Motor T 17:84-7+ F '65

Exhaust
Action in the war on auto fumes. U S News 60:12 Ja 17 '66
Air pollution. P. H. Abelson. Science 147:1527 Mr 26 '65
Big sewer in the sky; attempts to cut down on noxious gases from motor vehicles. Life 59:4 Ag 13 '65
Breath of life, by D. E. Carr. Review
New Repub 152:36 Ap 17 '65. J. Ridgeway
Detroit's cars and the big smog problem. R. Huntington. Consumer Bul 48:35-7 Ap '65
Dust and smog stoppers. R. E. Jennings. il Motor T 17:44-6 Je '65
Ideas that work. G. Harkins. il Hot Rod 18:11 N '65

News on wheels; curb on exhaust fumes. Sr Schol 87:49 N 11 '65
Pollution politics; LBJ retreats on opposition to measure curbing pollution from automobile exhaust. E. Langer. Science 148:611-13 Ap 30 '65
Smog today & smog tomorrow; main offender: motor vehicles. M. Neiburger. il Nation 201:432-5 D 6 '65
See also
Carbon monoxide

Filters
See Air filters, Automobile

Fuel consumption
Corvair economy hop-up. E. Rickman. il Hot Rod 18:74-5+ Je '65
How fast can you stop? Pure oil performance trials. D. Francis. il Pop Sci 186:82-6+ Ap '65
Inventor of the month; he earned his own success; designing fuel control valve for cars. S. V. Jones. il Sci Digest 58:28 N '65
Mobil's mileage melee. J. Ethridge. il Motor T 17:64-5 Jl '65
Mobil's mileage misers. D. Wells. il Hot Rod 18:86-7+ Je '65
Pure oil trials. B. Robinson. il Motor T 17:70-3 Ap '65
Teen-age driver sets precedent; M. Payne first Negro in Mobil economy run. il Ebony 20:49-50+ Jl '65
You can get more miles per gallon. M. J. Schultz. il Pop Mech 125:184-8 Ja '66

Fuel feeding
See also
Fuel pumps

History
Where are they now; with photographs. H. M. Hershberger. Hot Rod 19:78-80 Ja '66

Ignition
Additional notes on SCR auto ignition system. W. Sturgeon. il Electr World 73:70-1 My '65
Automotive electronics; transistor ignition and CD systems. B. Ward. il Pop Electr 22:51-3 F '65
Build your own capacitor-discharge ignition system. H. G. McEntee. il Pop Sci 186:94-7+ My '65
Electronic go-go for your car. B. Ward. il Pop Mech 124:196-9 O '65
Magic eye. E. Dahlquist. il Hot Rod 18:42-3+ Ap '65
Now! a universal CD ignition system. M. Gellman. il Pop Electr 23:69-71+ O '65
Transistorized capacitor discharge ignition system. M. Gellman. il Pop Electr 22:43-7+ Je '65
Transistorized ignition; status 1965; with buyer's guide. L. Buckwalter. il Pop Electr 22:35-42+ Je '65

Lubrication
See Automobiles—Lubrication

Repairing
Shop talk. D. Clark. See issues of Hot rod

Starting
See Automobiles—Starting

Superchargers
Chrysler snout on a Chevy shaft. L. Smith. il Hot Rod 18:76-7 O '65
Corvair economy hop-up E. Rickman. il Hot Rod 18:74-5+ Je '65
Don't bury the Offy. E. Rickman. il Hot Rod 19:70-1 Ja '66

Testing
Auto-engine analyzer you build from a kit. R. M. Benrey. il Pop Sci 186:136-7 Ap '65
Knight-kit KG-375 universal auto analyzer. il Pop Electr 22:52-3 F '65
Red line 7000. il Hot Rod 18:112-13 O '65
396 Chevy, loaded & legal. E. Rickman. il Hot Rod 19:64-9+ Ja '66

Valves
Adjust your valves. R. E. Jennings. il Motor T 17:70-2 Mr '65
Wind up with light valves. R. Huntington. il Hot Rod 18:82+ Ag '65

AUTOMOBILE exhibitions. See Automobiles—Exhibitions
AUTOMOBILE factories

Employees
How workers like early retirement. il U S News 59:96-8+ O 18 '65
AUTOMOBILE financing. See Instalment plan

AUTOMOBILE graveyards
Solution for junk car problem suggested. Sci
N L 88:136 Ag 28 '65

AUTOMOBILE industry and trade
Automotive products agreement with Canada
becomes effective; statements, October 22,
1965, with texts of the proclamation and
the order. L. B. Johnson. Dept State Bul
53:793-5 N 15 '65
Department supports bill to carry out auto
agreement with Canada; statement, April
27, 1965. T. C. Mann. Dept State Bul 52:
830-3 My 24 '65

Advertising
Indirect sell. Time 86:90+ O 29 '65
Playing musical cars; importance of rental
market to auto companies. Newsweek 65:79
Ap 19 '65
Rambler drives away from old ad agency;
Geyer, Morey & Ballard. Bsns W p 108+
Mr 6 '65

Employees
See Automobile factories—Employees

History
Mobile status symbol. J. Warner. Sat R 49:
83 Ja 8 '66

International aspects
Big race for world auto markets. il Bsns W
p 106-8+ O 9 '65
Multi-national corporation; address, January
13, 1965. L. A. Townsend. Vital Speeches
31:444-8 My 1 '65

Canada
President asks authority to remove duties
on Canadian auto products; letter, March
31, 1965. L. B. Johnson. Dept State Bul
52:638-9 Ap 26 '65

Europe, Eastern
Unhappy motoring. il Newsweek 67:28-9 Ja 3
'66

Europe, Western
Catching up with Detroit. il Time 86:104 S 24
'65
GM shakes Europe's auto makers; will build
$100-million assembly plant at Antwerp. il
Bsns W p 130 Ja 30 '65
Latest on Europe's car boom. il U S News
59:125-6 O 25 '65
Rabbits and the greyhound. il Fortune 71:49-
50+ Mr '65

France
Peugeot's rearguard action. il Bsns W p 101-
2+ Ap 17 '65

Germany (Federal Republic)
Herr Uhlenhaut: the great lap forward. D.
Bartley. il Esquire 63:96-9+ F '65

Great Britain
Safety with exhilaration: the new Jensen;
four-wheel-drive touring car. J. Lovesey. il
Sports Illus 23:68-70 N 8 '65
Taming the wildcat in British industry; labor
government looks hard at unauthorized
strikes. il Bsns W p 152+ S 18 '65
See also
Rolls-Royce, limited
Rootes motors, incorporated

Greece, Modern
Outdoing Hephaestus; National motor co. of
Athens to build threewheeled utility truck.
il Time 85:81A+ Mr 26 '65

Italy
Fiat toots new horn at its rivals. il Bsns W
p90+ Ag 14 '65

Japan
Japan's playland puts car makers in driver's
seat; Suzuka circuit amusement park. il
Bsns W p52-4 Ap 3 '65

Latin America
Another boom in autos; south of the border.
il U S News 58:84-6 Mr 1 '65

Mexico
Mexico's auto makers switch to home brew.
il Bsns W p68-70 Jl 31 '65

Russia
Fiat in Ivan's future. Time 86:91+ Jl 16 '65
Russia revs up for a car race; Moskvich-
408. il Bsns W p47-8+ Ap 10 '65
Russia's cars. R. Katz. il Motor T 17:36-9
Jl '65
Wheels for the masses; expansion plans.
Newsweek 66:81-2 D 13 '65

Spain
Auto men shout ole! as sales rise in Spain;
British, European, and U.S. companies
fight for market. Bsns W p48 Ap 3 '65
Spain's man with the golden touch; E. Bar-
reiros in partnership with Chrysler. il Bsns
W p 153-4+ N 13 '65

Sweden
Volvo among the giants. il Fortune 73:87-8
Ja '66

United States
America rolling along; '66. il Sr Schol 87:A1-
2+ O 14 '65
Auto industry's road ahead. W. Bowen. il
Fortune 71:137-9+ Je '65
Auto racing: Detroit fights it out. L. Levine.
il Nation 200:559-61 My 24 '65
Auto sales: barometer of prosperity. Sr Schol
87:16+ O 14 '65
Autos: latest on the '66 models. il U S News
59:94-5 S 6 '65
Autos: they're buying everything; sales, pro-
fits and production. il Newsweek 66:77 N 8
'65
Big race for world auto markets. il Bsns W
p 106-8+ O 9 '65
Booming Detroit hits talk of lag. il Bsns W
p28-9 Je 19 '65
Buoyed by '65 record, Detroit gears for '66.
il Bsns W p27 Ag 21 '65
Changeover in Detroit. il Time 86:65 Ag 13
'65
Detroit: a peek at '66. il Newsweek 65:67-8 Ap
5 '65
Detroit listening post. E. Nelson. See issues
of Popular mechanics
Detroit scents 9-million; record car sales.
il Bsns W p31-2 F 27 '65
Detroit sees an all-plus future; optimistic
forecasts for 1966. il Bsns W p62+ O 16
'65
End of cliffhanger; January's sales figures.
il Time 85:84 F 12 '65
Excising the poor. W. V. Shannon. Common-
weal 82:398-9 Je 18 '65
Fast start: sales figures for 1966 models. Time
86:105 O 22 '65
Finding new ways to make autos. il Bsns W
p 190-2+ S 11 '65
For autos, a red-hot start on '66. il Bsns W
p23-4 O 30 '65
Industry leader looks at the auto boom and
its future; interview. A. R. Miller. U S
News 58:78-9 Ap 5 '65
Into 1966 at top speed; fifth good year. il
Bsns W p25-6 D 18 '65
Ladies first in Detroit; influence on selection
and purchase of a car. G. Lazarus. Sat R
48:148 Mr 13 '65
Length, luxury, power; 1966 cars. il Time
86:101-2 O 1 '65
Nine-million year for sure; car sales. il Bsns
W p23-4 Ap 17 '65
1966 cars. A. Rothenberg. il Look 29:120 O 19
'65
Quality control, warranties, and a crisis in
confidence; industry's sloppiness irks buyers. Consumer Rep 30:173-5 Ap '65
'65 car sales; off to a record. il U S News 58:
92-3 F 15 '65
'66 another record year for autos? il U S
News 59:70 D 27 '65
Snakes, butter beans and Mister Cobra;
American sports car. C. Phinizy. il Sports
Illus 22:36-8+ My 17 '65
Sour notes mar auto pact harmony; disputes
over GM's cancellation of strikes' Christmas bonus, and Ford plant's white-collar
organizers. Bsns W p 108 D 18 '65
Stock talk. B. Robinson. See issues of Motor
trend
T.R.B. from Washington; what price cars?
New Repub 153:4 O 2 '65
$12 billion boom: the aftermarket. il News-
week 66:55-6 D 27 '65
UAW mounts campaign against monopsony;
vs Detroit's Big three. Bsns W p43-4 Jl 24
'65
See also
Automobile dealers
Automobiles—Prices
Strikes—United States—Automobile industry
and trade
United automobile, aerospace and agricultural
implement workers of America
also names of automobile manufacturing
companies, e.g. American motors corporation

AUTOMOBILE industry strikes. See Strikes—
United States—Automobile industry and
trade

AUTOMOBILE insurance. See Insurance, Automobile

AUTOMOBILE racing—*Continued*
No sport for gentlemen; Indianapolis race driver. B. Ottum. il Sports Illus 22:32-6+ My 31 '65
Once around the clock swiftly rolling; paintings, with account by B. Ottum. A. Mardon. Sports Illus 22:28-35 Mr 22 '65
One that was missing; German Grand prix victory. Time 86:51 Ag 13 '65
Out of the orchard and up a tantalizing hill; Bugatti automobile on Prescott Hill, Gloucestershire, England. K. W. Purdy. il Sports Illus 22:42-4+ My 3 '65
Parlor game on wheels. D. Francis. il Pop Sci 188:64-7+ Ja '66
Pikes Peak hill climb. R. Brock. il Hot Rod 18:96-101 S '65
Profiles; E. Ferrari. W. Sargeant. New Yorker 41:40-2+ Ja 15 '66
Racing car's horrifying take-off; fatal spill at West Sacramento's capital speedway. il Life 58:92-4 Ap 30 '65
Rear engines out front; Lotus-Fords at Indianapolis qualifying heats. il Newsweek 65:58 My 31 '65
Riverside! big blast. E. Dahlquist. il Hot Rod 18:36-44+ S '65
Road race of champions; first world series to select national class champs. J. Ethridge. il Motor T 17:88-9 F '65
Roaring beasts of the drag strips; with photographs. Pop Sci 186:114-15 Je '65
Show & go. See issues of Hot rod
So there, chaps; Prix de l'endurance. il Time 85:55-6 Ap 2 '65
SCTA opener, El Mirage. L. Smith. il Hot Rod 18:48-51 S '65
Stock to Hot; American hot rod association's world championships, Long Beach, Calif. J. McFarland. il Hot Rod 18:38-44+ N '65
Stocks & bombs; Winternationals. B. McVay. il Motor T 17:61-3 My '65
Sundown of a champion; P. Hill. R. Daley. il Sat Eve Post 238:46+ My 8 '65
Sweet wet win for America at Sebring; Italy's Ferraris challenged by Chaparrals and Fords. H. Whall. il Sports Illus 22:93-6+ Ap 5 '65
Those magnificent men and their speed machines. D. Wells. il Hot Rod 19:50-7+ Ja '66
Today's hero at the 500 is often tomorrow's bum. S. Yunick. Pop Sci 186:81 F '65
Tripping the lights fantastic. E. Dahlquist. il Hot Rod 19:82-6+ Ja '66
Trophy team; Lansing, Mich. R. Huntington. il Hot Rod 18:54-5+ Ag '65
View from the top. Newsweek 66:52 Ag 16 '65
Virginia 500. B. Robinson. il Motor T 17:70-2 Jl '65
Vroom at the top; racing up hills in Europe. il Time 86:63 Ag 6 '65
Who said the Offy was dead? B. Ottum. il Sports Illus 22:60 My 3 '65
Wisconsin warrior; sports car racing at Elkhart Lake, Wis; photographs. J. Cooke. Sports Illus 22:28-33 Je 21 '65
World series; 1965 drag racing, Cordova, Ill. il Hot Rod 18:76-8 N '65
Yankee 300. G. Moore. il Motor T 17:73-5 Jl '65
Yankee 300. R. Brock. il Hot Rod 18:38+ Jl '65
See also
Automobile speed records
Automobiles, Racing

History
Famous transcontinentalists. B. Russo. il Motor T 17:74-9 Mr '65
AUTOMOBILE renting. See Automobiles—Renting
AUTOMOBILE service stations
Changes at the pump; new style gas stations. il Time 86:90 Jl 9 '65
Electronic car doctor; Mobil oil diagnostic center. S. L. Englebardt. il Sci Digest 59:45-7 Ja '66
Electronic clinics for sick cars. P. Bryan. il Pop Mech 125:116-19+ Ja '66
For auto ills, a new trend in treatment: auto clinics. il U S News 60:10-11 Ja 24 '66
Now, the analyst. il Time 86:51-2 D 3 '65
Still the dealers aren't happy. il Bsns W p 144 My 29 '65
AUTOMOBILE shows. See Automobiles—Exhibitions
AUTOMOBILE signals. See Signals and signaling
AUTOMOBILE speed records
How the rest was won; Tulsa, NHRA, and the world championship finals for 1965. D. Wells. il Hot Rod 19:36-40+ Ja '66

Land mark; Breedlove's world-record land speed. il Newsweek 66:75-6 N 15 '65
Mr & Mrs Speedlove; Bonneville Salt Flats of Utah. il Time 86:75-6+ N 12 '65
News on wheels; land speed records. D. Chu. il Sr Schol 87:40 D 9 '65
AUTOMOBILE stickers. See Labels
AUTOMOBILE styling. See Automobiles—Design
AUTOMOBILE thefts. See Automobiles, Theft of
AUTOMOBILE tires. See Tires, Automobile
AUTOMOBILE touring
If you're planning to take an automobile tour abroad; useful news for American tourists. il U S News 58:80-3 Ap 26 '65
Notes for nomads. il Travel 125:58 Ja '66

Accommodations
See Automobile trailer camps

Economic aspects
Ways to cut the cost of family travel. il Changing T 19:29-32 Jl '65

Europe, Western
Holiday handbook; motoring in Europe; general guide and seven tours. D. Dodge. il Holiday 38:89-94 Ag '65
Station wagon abroad. E. Brouwer. il Travel 123:56-8 Mr '65

Mexico
Cuidado! el traffic cop. C. Darlington. il Atlan 216:115-16 D '65
AUTOMOBILE traffic. See Road traffic; Street traffic
AUTOMOBILE trailer camps
Here come the trailers! P. Warren, jr. il Am For 71:36-9+ Je '65
AUTOMOBILE trailers
Global trailer travel. W. Thoms. il Travel 123:26-31+ My '65
Hitch & go. C. Isica. See issues of Motor trend
Imagine yourself in a trailer home. il Changing T 19:15-17 S '65
Tent trailer basics; travel trailer. B. Behme. il Field & S 69:60-3 F '65
Those wheeled industrialized houses. il Fortune 72:174+ Jl '65
Variations for the open road. il Newsweek 66:72-3 Jl 26 '65
Which vacation-on-wheels is best for you? L. Oertle. il Pop Sci 186:112-17 Ap '65

Renting
How to rent a vacation. E. Kiester, jr. il Redbook 124:46+ Mr '65
AUTOMOBILE trips. See Automobile touring
AUTOMOBILE trucks. See Motor trucks
AUTOMOBILE warranty. See Warranty
AUTOMOBILE wheels. See Automobiles—Wheels
AUTOMOBILE wiring. See Automobiles—Electric wiring
AUTOMOBILE workers. See Automobile factories—Employees
AUTOMOBILES
Automobile in American life; symposium. il Atlan 216:73-108+ Jl '65; Discussion. 216:52+ S '65
Automobiles. il Consumer Rep 30:408-42 D '65
Automobiles, 1966 model review. R. Huntington. il Consumer Bul 48:27-32 D '65
Autos: latest on the '66 models. il U S News 59:94-5 S 6 '65
Autos 1965. il Consumer Rep 30:169-75 Ap '65
Buyer's guide to the big three: Plymouth, Chevrolet, Ford. J P. Norbye. il Pop Sci 187:74-8+ N '65
Cars in your family. See issues of Better homes and gardens
Charger. E. Dahlquist. il Hot Rod 19:30-2 Ja '66
Chevrolet's new rival for the Mustang: the Panther. J. P. Norbye. il Pop Sci 187:43-5 D '65
Chevy showcase: Concours. il Motor T 17:68 Jl '65
Chrysler and Jeep; the 1966 models. il U S News 59:9 Ag 30 '65
Custom-build your car on the order form. J. P. Norbye. il Pop Sci 187:65-83 O '65
Detroit's bets are down; 1966 models. il Bsns W p23-4 O 2 '65
Duesenberg back from the romantic past. J. Dunne. il Pop Mech 125:112-15 Ja '66
Five medium-priced V-8s: Chrysler Newport, Mercury Monterey; Pontiac Catalina; Oldsmobile Dynamic 88; Buick Le Sabre. il Consumer Rep 30:250-4 My '65

AUTOMOBILES—*Continued*

Four 1965 automobiles: Chevy II Nova 6 and V-8; Mercury Comet 6; Plymouth Belvedere II V-8; Dodge Dart 6. il Consumer Bul 48: 11-15 Mr '65

Full-size automobiles. il Consumer Bul 48: 18-28 My '65

GM won't even tell it to the judge. Consumer Rep 30:425-7 S '65

Here are more glimpses of the 1966 automobiles. il U S News 59:78-9 S 27 '65

In Detroit they're going like '66. il Newsweek 66:71-4+ O 4 '65

Length, luxury, power; 1966 cars. il Time 86: 101-2 O 1 '65

New-car parade rolls on. il U S News 59:84-7 O 4 '65

New cars for '66: latest entries. il U S News 59:96-7 O 11 '65

New cars; what's ahead in 1966? A. Markovich. il Pop Mech 124:96-100+ O '65

1966 cars; roundup of facts & figures. il Changing T 19:7-11 D '65

1966 models. J. P. Norbye. il Pop Sci 187: 57-64 O '65

Plymouth Fury. il Pop Mech 124:88-91+ Ag '65

Route: '66. E. Dahlquist. il Hot Rod 18:30-7+ O; 30-6+ N '65

Spotlight on that preposterous Mini-Moke. A. Markovich. il Pop Mech 124:30-1 O '65

Tenth annual Look preview; 1976 drivers show off 1966 cars. A. Rothenberg. il Look 29:106-16+ O 19 '65

Three 1966 automobiles: Dart 270 six; Falcon Futura 6; Plymouth Fury II V-8. il Consumer Bul 49:16-20 Ja '66

Toronado. R. Huntington. il Hot Rod 18:82-4+ O '65

Toronado, shakedown by T-bird fans. A. Markovich. il Pop Mech 124:101-3+ O '65

Toronados, Turbos & TV; Detroit's stylish new and future wares. il Time 86:81 Jl 23 '65

Trailer, towing vehicle combine in house car. il Travel 125:58 Ja '66

See also
Automobile graveyards
Sports cars
Station wagons

Accessories
See Automobiles—Equipment

Accidents
See Traffic accidents

Advertising
See Automobile industry and trade—Advertising

Air conditioning
Car air conditioner you install yourself. P. McCafferty. il Pop Sci 186:126-8 Mr '65

Axles
Axle ratios, key to performance + economy. R. Huntington. il Motor T 17:58-9 My '65

Batteries
See Storage batteries

Bearings
Fantastic Fabroid. E. Rickman. il Hot Rod 18:68-9 O '65

Bibliography
Mobile status symbol. J. Warner. Sat R 49: 83 Ja 8 '66

Bodies
Bodies and dimensions. il Consumer Rep 30: 186-7 Ap '65

Design a body for the PM suburba-car and win this chassis! il Pop Mech 124:88-9+ N '65

Pontiac bodies bold & beautiful. il Motor T 17:63-7 F '65

Brakes
See Brakes, Automobile

Burglar alarms
See Burglar alarms

Carburetors
See Carburetors

Care
After tuneup, what? M. J. Schultz. il Pop Mech 124:182-5 N '65

Electronic car doctor. S. L. Englebardt. il Sci Digest 59:45-7 Ja '66

Electronic clinics for sick cars. P. Bryan. il Pop Mech 125:116-19+ Ja '66

How to keep your car looking new. E. D. Fales, jr. il Pop Sci 187:158-61 S '65

How to keep your cars on the go this winter! Bet Hom & Gard 43:30 D '65

How to reduce your car expenses. il Good H 160:179 Ap '65

News on wheels; time to winterize. Sr Schol 87:49 N 11 '65

Notes for a super tune. J. McFarland. il Hot Rod 19:42-4 Ja '66

Secrets of a trouble-free automobile. S. Yunick. il Pop Sci 186:77-88 Je '65

Yes, you can beat the problems of rust and road salt. Bet Hom & Gard 44:13 Ja '66

Your car needs a spring cleaning too. W. J. Toth. Am Home 68:24-5 Ap '65

See also
Automobiles—Repairing

Caricatures and cartoons
Cars & what they are doing to us! Osborn. Atlan 216:98-101 Jl '65

Chassis
Design a body for the PM suburba-car and win this chassis! il Pop Mech 124:88-9+ N '65

Collectors and collecting
Back on the road and purring; restoration of antique cars. il Bsns W p42-4 D 25 '65

Rembrandts of the road. il Newsweek 65: 100+ My 17 '65

Sotheby builds up a bid for old-car collectors. il Bsns W p42-4 N 20 '65

Vintage gems from jalopy graveyards. W. Waltner and E. Waltner. il Pop Mech 124: 106-9+ O '65

Where are they now; with photographs. H. M. Hershberger. Hot Rod 19:78-80 Ja '66

World's greatest automobile collection; W. Harrah of Reno, Nev. K. Purdy. il Atlan 216:84-92 Jl '65

Dashboards
Gauges or idiot lights. il Consumer Bul 48:28 Ag '65

Depreciation
See Depreciation

Design
Chevy with frosting; Caprice custom sedan. il Bsns W p25 F 6 '65

Compact and intermediate cars. il Consumer Bul 48:6-16 Ap '65

Compact sixes. Consumer Rep 30:194-205 Ap '65

Comparing the compacts: Valiant, Falcon, American, Chevy II. J. P. Norbye. il Pop Sci 187:90-4+ N '65

Designing for safety: it can be done. il Consumer Rep 30:182 Ap '65

Designing the Marlin. R. Teague. il Motor T 17:28-9 Mr '65

Detroit: a peek at '66. il Newsweek 65:67-8 Ap 5 '65

Detroit's secrets for 1966. J. P. Norbye. il Pop Sci 187:35-9 Jl '65

Engineering the new Pontiacs. J. Z. De-Lorean. il Motor T 17:68-71 F '65

Formula S; Plymouth Barracuda. E. Dahlquist. il Hot Rod 18:30-5 F '65

Four intermediate sixes; Plymouth Belvedere, Pontiac Tempest, Ford Fairlane, and Chevelle Malibu. il Consumer Rep 30:89-93 F '65

Galaxie 427. E. Dahlquist. il Hot Rod 18:28-31 Ap '65

How good is fwd? il Motor T 17:44-6 My '65

How plush is a luxury car? Cadillac, Imperial, Lincoln Continental, Jaguar 4.2 Mk X, Mercedes-Benz 600 and Rolls-Royce Silver Cloud III. J. Dunne and A. Markovich. il Pop Mech 125:94-9+ Ja '66

How safe are small cars? il Good H 161:171-3 N '65

Is America ready for the Cord? J. Atwater. il Sat Eve Post 238:58-60 Ag 14 '65

It's the curve that counts. R. Caplan. il Consumer Rep 30:183-5 Ap '65

It's white tie & tails for Chevy Caprice 396. J. Ethridge. il Motor T 17:48-53 Je '65

Limousine in your future? il Time 85:45 Ap 16 '65

Missing link in transportation. J. Doblin. il Pop Mech 124:84-7+ N '65

1966 in sight. M. Lamm. il Motor T 17:26-31 Jl '65

Olds 442. E. Dahlquist. il Hot Rod 18:38-43+ Mr '65

Physicians as activists. Nation 200:463 My 3 '65

Pontiac bodies bold & beautiful. il Motor T 17:63-7 F '65

AUTOMOBILES—Design—*Continued*

Profits vs. engineering: the Corvair story; excerpts from Unsafe at any speed. R. Nader. il Nation 201:295-301 N 1 '65

Report on the '66 cars from Chrysler. J. P. Norbye. il Pop Sci 187:76-8+ S '65

Show stoppers. il Motor T 17:56-7 Ap '65

65½ cars. J. P. Norbye. il Pop Sci 186:70-3 My '65

Spotlight on Detroit; forecasts, facts and rumors. See issues of Motor trend

Spotlight on the Dodge Pursuit car. E. Nelson. il Pop Mech 124:32-3 Ag '65

That luxurious feeling. il Time 85:99 My 28 '65

Twenty years from now. R. Loewy. Atlan 216:93-7 Jl '65

Two for the money, one for the show; Bertone Mustang; Duesenberg, and Oldsmobile's Toronado. D. Bartley. il Esquire 64:90-3 O '65

U.S. compacts: with road tests of Falcon and Valiant Sixes. il Consumer Rep 30:151-3 Mr '65

What the '66 cars will be like. il U S News 58:52-5 My 10 '65

What's new in the '66 cars; looking at the road ahead, from '67 and '68 on. il Sr Schol 87: A7+ O 14 '65

Who said mom won't drive a bus! R. Charles. il Parents Mag 40:60-1+ F '65

See also

Automobiles—Bodies

Automobiles—Safety devices and measures

Anecdotes, facetiae, satire, etc.

There's a Freud in your future. M. Bennett. il Atlan 216:126 Jl '65

Driving

See Automobile driving

Electric equipment

Don't let electrical problems stop your car. B. Ward. il Pop Mech 124:198-201 N '65

Protect your car's electrical system. C. E. Cohn. il Pop Electr 23:66 N '65

See also

Automobiles—Electric wiring

Electric wiring

Checking out your circuits. M. J. Schultz. il Pop Mech 124:177-81+ S; 180-4 O '65

Equipment

Big year of luxury options; with report by C. Welles. il Life 59:84-6+ N 12 '65

Car-top carrier for vacation luggage. E. E. Hickman. il Pop Sci 187:138-9 Jl '65

Car-top craft. F. M. Paulson. il Field & S 69:100-1+ F '65

Carnegie Hall on wheels; dashboard stereo-tape player in 1966 models. Time 85:98+ Ap 30 '65

Classic caps: eternal emblems; radiator caps and mascots. il Esquire 64:115-17 Je '65

Complete roundup of 1966 car comfort options. Bet Hom & Gard 43:39-40 O '65

Dashboard tape player for highway hi-fi. il Pop Sci 187:103 S '65

Gun rest for your car. il Pop Sci 187:152 D '65

How to wagon-top a boat. H. G. Tapply. il Field & S 69:66 Mr '65

New products. See issues of Motor trend

Personalize your new used car. J. Ethridge. Motor T 17:42-3 Je '65

Sound advice; tape recorders for cars. H. Manoogian. il Mod Phot 29:24+ My '65

Tape for turnpikes; dashboard tape players. L. Buckwalter. il Hi Fi 15:42-4+ Je '65

Tuff wheels; teen-ager's ideal car. il Esquire 64:76-7 Jl '65

What extras do auto fleet operators buy? Changing T 19:23 O '65

What optional equipment should you order? Consumer Rep 30:510-11 O '65

What to buy for car owners. il Consumer Rep 30:556-7 N '65

What's new. See issues of Hot rod

Will stereo tapes bring music to Detroit ears? il Bsns W p34 N 6 '65

See also

Automobiles—Safety devices and measures

Automobiles for the disabled

Odometers

Exhaust

See Automobile engines—Exhaust

Exhibitions

Foreign cars hope they're here to stay; importers displaying at New York's auto show. il Bsns W p86-8+ Ap 10 '65

Girls, gold and beasts on wheels; Ninth international automobile show in New York city's Coliseum. J. Keats. Life 58:12 Ap 30 '65

Glare: protest against chromium windshield wipers at ninth annual International automobile show at Coliseum. New Yorker 41: 35-7 Ap 17 '65

Oakland roadster show. il Hot Rod 18:36-7 Je '65

Salon era. H. Pfau. il Motor T 17:92-5 F '65

Show & go. See issues of Hot rod

Show schedules. Hot Rod 18:94-5 F; 88-9 Mr; 88-9+ Ap; 90-1 Jl '65

Village car show; Greenfield Village, Mich. il Motor T 17:71-3 My '65

Four wheel drive

Safety with exhilaration: the new Jensen; British car with four-wheel drive and brakes. J. Lovesey. il Sports Illus 23:68-70 N 8 '65

Front drive

See Automobiles—Front wheel drive

Front wheel drive

Coast to coast in a Toronado; Oldsmobile front-wheel drive. J. Dunne and A. Markovich. il Pop Mech 124:76-80+ D '65

How good is fwd? il Motor T 17:44-6 My '65

Is America ready for the Cord? J. Atwater. il Sat Eve Post 238:58-60 Ag 14 '65

Is front-wheel drive for you? H. Luckett. il Pop Sci 188:55-9+ Ja '66

New Olds front-wheel drive! sneak preview of the '66 Holiday. il Pop Sci 186:63-6+ Ap '65

New Peugeot has front drive, crosswise engine. il Pop Sci 187:55 Jl '65

Olds' seven-year secret; a racy front drive; GM's Toronado. B. Grossman and B. Ottum. il Sports Illus 23:55-8 S 27 '65

Frames

Traction-bars: why and how. J. R. Kunkle. Hot Rod 18:110-11 D '65

Fuel tanks

Rubber-lined gas tanks to make '65 racer safer. S. Yunick. Pop Sci 186:81 My '65

Gearing

All about gear drives. R. Huntington. il Hot Rod 18:76-8 Je '65

Tall cogs for GM compacts. L. Smith. il Hot Rod 18:108+ O '65

See also

Automobiles—Transmission

Heating and ventilation

Electric cloth to warm you. il Sci Digest 58: 36-7 D '65

History

Classic comments. R. J. Gottlieb. See issues of Motor trend

Cole, the old king. A. Leich and R. Leich. il Motor T 17:42-5 Jl '65

Dog: Model A Ford to sniff out moonshine stills. C. Cahill. il Motor T 17:68 Ap '65

From the putt-putt to the purr. il Sr Schol 87: A2+ O 14 '65

Roper's steamer; America's first car. T. Robinson. il Pop Mech 124:110-11+ O '65

Sportsmen loved the automobile. il Field & S 70:56-7 Jl '65

What a way to go; excerpts from Gallery of the American automobile, with commentary by J. J. Bradley. C. P. Hornung. il Am Heritage 17:65-79 D '65

Whippet; early American compact. D. E. Earnshaw. il Motor T 17:54-5 Je '65

Ignition

See Automobile engines—Ignition

Insurance

See Insurance, Automobile

Leasing

Lowdown on leasing a car, instead of buying one. il Changing T 19:29-31 Ag '65

Lighting

Dymwatt. D. Lancaster. il Pop Electr 22: 71-3+ My '65

Keep your lights beaming. A. Laidlaw. il Pop Sci 187:136-9 N '65

Simple auto light minder. R. L. Winklepleck. il Pop Electr 22:45 My '65

Lubrication

50,000 miles without an oil change. D. Francis and D. Sneigr. il Pop Sci 186:57-61+ Mr '65

How to cure an oil hog. A. Laidlaw. il Pop Sci 186:168-71 My '65

AUTOMOBILES—Lubrication—*Continued*
Secondhand oil, any good? il Changing T 19: 41-2 F '65
Truth about multigrade oils. W. O. Koehler. il Pop Sci 188:106-8+ Ja '66

Manufacture

Engineering the new Pontiacs. J. Z. De-Lorean. il Motor T 17:68-71 F '65
Giants that back up the assembly lines. il Fortune 71:140-1 Je '65
  See also
Automobile industry and trade

Parking

See Automobile parking

Prices

GM cuts '66 prices in a surprise move. Bsns W p28 S 25 '65
How much a new car can really cost. il U S News 59:78-9 N 1 '65
What the new autos will cost. il U S News 59:82 O 4 '65
What's good for G.M. Commonweal 83:43-4 O 15 '65

Purchasing

How to buy a good used car. B. Taylor. il Pop Sci 186:96-9 Ap '65
Is there a best way to finance a new car? Bet Hom & Gard 43:47+ F '65
Look before you leap! V. L. Oertle. il Motor T 17:30-3 Je '65
Oh Dad, poor dad, junior's doubled our car payments and I'm feelin' so sad. D. Bartley. Esquire 64:75+ Jl '65
. . . Or fix up the old car instead? il Changing T 19:13-15 N '65
Repos & rentals. T. Mills. il Motor T 17:39 Je '65

Radio equipment

Now it's easy to install your own car radio. R. M. Benrey. il Pop Sci 187:130-1 O '65
Special report on a new safety concept: road signs that talk! radio-road alert system. Bet Hom & Gard 43:40+ O '65

Rating

Quality control, warranties, and a crisis in confidence; industry's sloppiness irks buyers. Consumer Rep 30:173-5 Ap '65
Ratings of the 1965 autos. il Consumer Rep 30:192-205 Ap '65

Renting

Playing musical cars; importance of rental market to auto companies. Newsweek 65:79 Ap 19 '65
Repos & rentals. T. Mills. il Motor T 17:39 Je '65
Status on wheels; traveling limousine-style. il Newsweek 66:71 Ag 9 '65
When you rent a car. E. D. Fales, jr. il Pop Sci 187:90-3+ D '65
  See also
Hertz corporation

Repairing

After tuneup, what? M. J. Schultz. il Pop Mech 124:182-5 N '65
Gus Wilson's model garage (title varies) M. Bunn. See issues of Popular science monthly
. . . Or fix up the old car instead? il Changing T 19:13-15 N '65
R for automobiles. J. B. Kemmerer. il Motor T 17:30-5 Mr '65
Say, Smokey; questions and answers. S. Yunick. See issues of Popular science monthly
Shop talk. D. Clark. See issues of Hot rod
$12 billion boom: the aftermarket. il Newsweek 66:55-6 D 27 '65
Weekend mechanic. R. E. Jennings. See issues of Motor trend
  See also
Automobile service stations

Safety devices and measures

Are you in more danger in a small car? pro and con discussion. M. Mann; D. Francis. il Pop Sci 186:71-3+ F '65
At stake: 48,000 lives: problem of highway safety. Bsns W p29 Mr 27 '65
Attack on Detroit. J. Ridgeway. New Repub 152:13-14 Mr 6 '65
Auto safety inquiry. New Repub 153:6 Jl 24 '65
Auto safety: new study criticizes manufacturers and universities. E. Langer. Science 150:1136-9 N 26 '65
Auto safety probers put Detroit on grill; Senate committee hearing on highway safety. il Bsns W p30-1 Jl 17 '65
Auto safety: who will take the lead? il Newsweek 66:67-8 Jl 26 '65

Car safety battle sharpens; auto executives to attend Senate hearings. Bsns W p26-7 Jl 10 '65
Car safety: miracles or mayhem? A. Rothenberg. il Look 29:92-4+ My 18 '65
Cars, roads, drivers and safety. Life 59:4 Jl 23 '65
Crashproof car? il Newsweek 65:69 F 8 '65
Drive for safety; Senate government operations subcommittee investigating auto safety. il Time 86:81 Jl 23 '65
Gauges or idiot lights. il Consumer Bul 48:28 Ag '65
Health & safety. Commonweal 82:134 Ap 23 '65
Henry Ford II talks about car safety. H. Ford, 2d. il Pop Sci 187:62-5+ D '65
How can we stop the slaughter on our nation's highways? forum discussion. il Sr Schol 87:14-15 O 14 '65
How safe are small cars? il Good H 161:171-3 N '65
How to make cars safer: the auto industry ideas; symposium. il U S News 59:100-3 Ag 9 '65
Majority of lives lost in crashes can be saved. Sci N L 88:265 O 23 '65
Making cars safer: what one auto company plans for '66 models. il U S News 59:14-15 Jl 19 '65
Making cars safer: what to expect. U S News 59:10 Jl 12 '65
Many voices of Ford motor co. Consumer Rep 30:473-4 O '65
Mars and motor cars; legislation to establish minimum safety and performance standards for tires. Nation 201:51 Ag 2 '65
More safety for autos; changes in the works. il U S News 58:64-5 Je 7 '65
Numbers game in tires; maximum load standard set. New Repub 153:9 S 18 '65
Passing the buck; manufacturers blame drivers. Nation 201:150-1 S 27 '65
Price of safety. Time 85:87A+ Ap 16 '65
Prospects for safer autos. D. Klein and W. Haddon, jr. il Consumer Rep 30:176-81 Ap '65
Ribicoff's wrench; proposed penalty tax on new cars without safety devices. Newsweek 65:70 Je 21 '65
Road research. Newsweek 66:53-4 Ag 2 '65
Safer car seat for children. il Consumer Bul 48:43 Mr '65
Safety car study uses systems approach. R. D. Hibben. Aviation W 83:53+ D 20 '65
Safety features in the new 1966 cars. G. J. Hect. il Parents Mag 41:51-5+ Ja '66
Safety surge. Newsweek 66:67-8 Jl 19 '65
Safety: the industry has begged off long enough. il Consumer Rep 30:168-9 Ap '65
Special report on a new safety concept: road signs that talk! radio-road alert system. Bet Hom & Gard 43:40+ O '65
Steps toward safety. il Time 86:83 Jl 16 '65
Strict liability suits pile up for auto makers. Bsns W p30+ Ag 28 '65
Those little auto accidents cost plenty: five tips to help avoid them. il Changing T 19: 45-6 O '65
What safety features to look for in a new car. Bet Hom & Gard 43:44+ S '65
Why can't we make cars safer? R. F. Kennedy. il Pop Sci 187:63-7+ N '65
Word to Detroit. Nation 200:182-3 F 22 '65
  See also
Safety belts

Scrapping

See Automobiles—Wrecking

Service stations

See Automobile service stations

Shock absorbers

See Shock absorbers

Social aspects

Can we live with our cars? E. C. Guggenheimer. il Nation 201:164-6 S 27 '65

Specifications

Comfort-livability index to the 1966 cars. Pop Mech 125:104-5 Ja '66
Guide to the specifications table. Consumer Rep 30:188-91 Ap '65
How the 1966 cars compare by length, width. Bet Hom & Gard 43:16 N '65

Speed

Cars coming faster and faster. J. A. Kouwenhoven. Harper 232:97-9 Ja '66
Hot pursuit of turnpike flyers. L. Wainwright. Life 59:28 S 17 '65

AUTOMOBILES—Speed—*Continued*
How fast will we drive? proposed Century expressway to link Boston and Washington, D.C. E. D. Fales, jr. il Pop Sci 187:98-101+ O '65
See also
Automobile speed records
Speedometers

Springs and suspension

Bouncer tamer. D. Wells. il Hot Rod 18:98-101 Je '65
Traction-bars: why and how. J. R. Kunkle. Hot Rod 18:110-11 D '65
What's Watts? I. Poling. il Hot Rod 18:108-9 Je '65

Stability and stabilizers

Bouncer tamer. D. Wells. il Hot Rod 18:98-101 Je '65

Starting

Dipstick oil heaters; easier winter starting for your car. il Consumer Bul 48:17-18 N '65

Steering gear

Case of the much-sued Corvair. il Consumer Rep 30:174 Ap '65
New twist in driving; Mercury's new system. B. McVay. il Motor T 17:62-3 Je '65
Straightening out a steering system. F. Greenwald. il Pop Sci 186:140-3+ Ap '65
Will a twist of the wrist steer your next car? il Pop Sci 186:89 Ap '65

Stopping

How fast can you stop? D. Francis. il Pop Sci 186:82-6+ Ap '65

Testing

Almighty Malibu! J. Ethridge. il Motor T 17:32-4 Jl '65
Chrysler's letter car. E. Dahlquist. il Hot Rod 18:46-7 Jl '65
Coast to coast in a Toronado; Oldsmobile front-wheel drive. J. Dunne and A. Markovich. il Pop Mech 124:76-80+ D '65
Comparing the compacts: American; Chevy II; Valiant; Falcon. J. Whipple. il Pop Sci 186:92-6 F '65
Dodge Monaco road test. J. Ethridge. il Motor T 17:63-7 Ap '65
Ford Fairlane vs. Plymouth Satellite; newest of the intermediates. J. P. Norbye. il Pop Sci 187:54-7+ D '65
GTO. E. Dahlquist. il Hot Rod 18:30-3 Jl '65
How fast can you stop? Pure oil performance trials. D. Francis. il Pop Sci 186:82-6+ Ap '65
How good are American cars? J. R. Bond. Atlan 216:121-4 Jl '65; Same abr. Read Digest 87:174-6 S '65
How hot the hemi? E. Dahlquist. il Hot Rod 18:28-31+ D '65
Imperial's posh LeBaron. B. McVay. il Motor T 17:46-8 Jl '65
Lincoln Continental road test. B. McVay. il Motor T 17:32-5 Ap '65
Mobil's mileage melee. J. Ethridge. il Motor T 17:64-5 Jl '65
Mobil's mileage misers. D. Wells. il Hot Rod 18:86-7+ Je '65
MT road test:
Catalina for the family. B. McVay. il Motor T 17:44-7+ F '65
Chrysler 300-L. J. Ethridge. il Motor T 17:36-41 Mr '65
Comets: hot & cool. J. Ethridge. il Motor T 17:24-31 My '65
Coronet 426. B. McVay. il Motor T 17:56-60 Je '65
Ferocious GTO. J. Ethridge. il Motor T 17:28-31+ F '65
Fiery Grand Prix. J. Ethridge. il Motor T 17:32-5+ F '65
Olds Delta 88. B. McVay. il Motor T 17:50-5 Mr '65
Olds F-85 4-4-2. B. McVay. il Motor T 17:38-43 My '65
Pontiac Bonneville. B. McVay. il Motor T 17:40-3+ F '65
Rambler rag tops. B. McVay. il Motor T 17:78-83 Jl '65
Tamed Tempest Six. B. McVay. il Motor T 17:48-51+ F '65
Plenty hot the hemi. E. Dahlquist. il Hot Rod 19:33+ Ja '66
Road testing the new fastback: Marlin. J. Ethridge. il Motor T 17:22-7 Mr '65
Road tests of low-priced V8 sedans; Ford Galaxie 500, Plymouth Fury III, Pontiac Catalina, Chevrolet Impala. il Consumer Rep 31:17-23 Ja '66
Skylark Gran Sport road test. B. McVay. il Motor T 17:32-7 My '65

Test-driving the intermediates; Chevy Chevelle, Dodge, Coronet, Rambler Classic, and Ford Fairlane. J. Whipple. il Pop Sci 186:72-6+ Mr '65
Three intermediate V-8s: Buick Special deluxe; Dodge Coronet 440; Rambler Ambassador 990; and Mustang V-8. il Consumer Rep 30:360-5 Jl '65
3000 miles in a Marlin. E. Dahlquist. il Hot Rod 18:28-32 Je '65
U.S. compacts: with road tests of Falcon and Valiant Sixes. il Consumer Rep 30:151-3 Mr '65
See also
Automobile engines—Fuel consumption

Tires

See Tires, Automobile

Transmission

Is Chevy stuck in 2nd? R. Huntington. il Motor T 17:56-7 Mr '65
Transmissions: who uses what. il Consumer Rep 30:172 Ap '65
What is a hydrostatic transmission? J. B. Liljedahl. il Suc Farm 63:51 O '65

Wheels

Custom wheels: are they really safe? J. Ethridge. il Motor T 17:24-31 Ap '65

Windshield wipers

Glare: protest against chromium windshield wipers at ninth annual International automobile show at Coliseum. New Yorker 41:35-7 Ap 17 '65

Windshields

Problem of icy windshields; plastic windshield protector. Consumer Bul 48:18 Mr '65

Wrecking

Junk-car plague. Nation 200:630 Je 14 '65
Junk car problem can and must be solved. Sci N L 88:73 Jl 31 '65
Waging war on abandoned autos; Chicago. G. S. Lloyd and R. McCann. il Am City 80:98-100 N '65

AUTOMOBILES, Armored
How Brink's guards its profits, too. il Bsns W p54-6+ F '65

AUTOMOBILES, Care of. See Automobiles—Care

AUTOMOBILES, Electric
Electronic roads for tomorrow's traffic; Cornell lab study for Commerce dept. il Bsns W p160+ Ap 24 '65
Postscript; concerning report by William T. Reid in the Battelle technical review on possible running methods. J. Lear. il Sat R 48:42 Jl 3 '65

AUTOMOBILES, Foreign
Bug forever; Volkswagen. il Time 86:71 Ag 13 '65
Comeback of foreign cars: still bigger years in prospect. il U S News 59:78-9 Ag 2 '65
First of Europe's '66 cars. il Pop Sci 187:60-1 D '65
Foreign cars hope they're here to stay; importers displaying at New York's auto show. il Bsns W p86-8+ Ap 10 '65
Gordini-a-go-go. il Motor T 17:65-7 Je '65
How plush is a luxury car? Cadillac, Imperial, Lincoln Continental, Jaguar 4.2 Mk X, Mercedes-Benz 600 and Rolls-Royce Silver Cloud III. J. Dunne and A. Markovich. il Pop Mech 125:94-9+ Ja '66
New foreign cars come up with some surprises. il Pop Sci 187:64-5 Jl '65
New Peugeot has front drive, crosswise engine. il Pop Sci 187:55 Jl '65
Porsche faces reality. il Time 86:101 N 5 '65
'65 VW. il Consumer Bul 48:31-3 My '65
Two gems for car lovers; BMW 1800 TI and Rover 2000. J. P. Norbye. il Pop Sci 187:60-3+ Jl '65
VW's competition; Datsun PL 410; Saab; and Simca 1000. Consumer Rep 30:406-11 Ag '65

Marketing

Foreign automakers' marketing drive. J. F. Olesky. Duns R 85:73-4 My '65

AUTOMOBILES, Jet propelled
Four in a row gotta go! E. Rickman. il Hot Rod 18:44-7 Mr '65

AUTOMOBILES, Midget. See Karts (midget cars)

AUTOMOBILES, Miniature. See Automobile models

AUTOMOBILES, Old

Collectors and collecting
See Automobiles—Collectors and collecting

AUTOMOBILES, Racing

Baby bottle bomb; photographs. L. Nehamkin and E. Rickman. Hot Rod 18:60-1 D '65
Beetlemania; rebuilt Volkswagen competing at Carlsbad, Calif. E. Dahlquist. il Hot Rod 18:30-3 Ag '65
Bill Burke, Hot rodding's Mr Prolific. D. Wells. il Hot Rod 18:38-42+ Je '65
Brutes, brawls and boosters; Daytona 500. B. Ottum. il Sports Illus 22:14-17 F 22 '65
Building fast cars on a shoestring; C. Shelby, ex-racing driver. il Bsns W p66-8+ Ag 14 '65
Building toward Indy. J Ethridge. il Motor T 17:68-71 Je '65
Cars; photographs. See issues of Hot rod
Elapsed-time bomb. E. Rickman. il Hot Rod 18:76-80 Jl '65
Fastest man on wheels; A. Arfons, the Green Monster's builder and driver. J. Reddy. il Read Digest 86:94-8 Mr '65
Fiery 500 for a cool Scot; English Lotus powered by American Ford engine. B. Ottum. il Sports Illus 22:18-21 Je 7 '65
Ford, new era at Indy. E. Rickman. il Hot Rod 18:36-42+ Ag '65
Goodyear gets back on the race track; Indianapolis 500. il Bsns W p 144-6+ My 22 '65
How I'll drive faster than sound; ed. by D. Francis. A. Arfons. il Pop Sci 187:46-9+ Jl '65
It was murder Italian style; American Ford team loses at Le Mans to Ferrari from Italy. J. Lovesey. il Sports Illus 22:32-3 Je 28 '65
Lesson of Le Mans. il Newsweek 66:53 Jl 5 '65
Looking through the sound barrier. R. Huntington. il Hot Rod 18:42-4+ Jl '65
Match race stockers (cont) E. Dahlquist. il Hot Rod 18:42-7+ F '65
Motor trend 500. il Hot Rod 18:32-3 Ap '65
Mustang GT-350. J Ethridge. il Motor T 17:66-9 My '65
No sport for gentlemen; Indianapolis race driver. B. Ottum. il Sports Illus 22:32-6+ My 31 '65
Once around the clock swiftly rolling; paintings, with account by B. Ottum. A. Mardon. Sports Illus 22:28-35 Mr 22 '65
Out of the orchard and up a tantalizing hill; Bugatti automobile on Prescott Hill, Gloucestershire, England. K. W. Purdy. il Sports Illus 22:42-4+ My 3 '65
Pettys strike the strip. il Motor T 17:58-60 Mr '65
Phoenix 200. P. Biro. il Motor T 17:67-9 Mr '65
Profiles; E. Ferrari. W. Sargeant. New Yorker 41:40-2+ Ja 15 '66
Rear engines out front; Lotus-Fords at Indianapolis qualifying heats. il Newsweek 65:58 My 31 '65
Record route '66; unlimited wheel-driven vehicles. B. McVay. il Motor T 17:75 Ap '65
Return of the Hudson. E. Dahlquist. il Hot Rod 18:82-5 Jl '65
Riverside! big blast. E. Dahlquist. il Hot Rod 18:36-44+ S '65
750 mph, here I come; Spirit of America. C. Breedlove. il Pop Mech 124:88-92+ S '65
Snakebite; Cobra makers at Thames Ditton, England. il Newsweek 66:80 D 6 '65
Spirit of America; Sonic I. E. Rickman. il Hot Rod 18:46-51 O '65
Stock to Hot; American hot rod association's world championships, Long Beach, Calif. J. McFarland. il Hot Rod 18:38-44+ N '65
Streamlining, dragster dilemma? T. Cooke. il Hot Rod 18:94-101+ Ag '65
Summers on standby; with photographs. Hot Rod 18:86-7 N '65
Super-car built like a fine watch; Lotus-Ford, with report by J. Clark. il Life 59:72-6 Jl 16 '65
Sweet wet win for America at Sebring; Italy's Ferraris challenged by Chaparrals and Fords. H. Whall. il Sports Illus 22:93-6+ Ap 5 '65
That blood-red Ferrari mystique. R. Daley. il N Y Times Mag p22-3+ Jl 25 '65
Those magnificent men and their speed machines. D. Wells. il Hot Rod 19:50-7+ Ja '66
Who said the Offy was dead? B. Ottum. il Sports Illus 22:60 My 3 '65

Acceleration

ABG's of acceleration; G-meter for evaluation of changes in car velocity. D. Wells. il Hot Rod 18:82-3+ D '65

Design

Dodge country. E. Dahlquist. il Hot Rod 18:46-8+ Je '65
Dragwinder. il Hot Rod 18:34-7 Mr '65

New approach for dragster design. B. Greene. il Hot Rod 18:70-3+ O '65
Nicholson's super Cyclone. E. Rickman. il Hot Rod 18:48-51 Ap '65
Petty's powder keg; Barracuda. il Hot Rod 18:48-51 F '65
Project: 200 MPH. E. Dahlquist. il Hot Rod 18:78-83+ Mr; 44-7+ Ap '65
Race cars of the world. D. Todd. il Pop Sci 186:130-1 F '6b
T-Q's; Three quarter midgets. A. Bagnall. il Hot Rod 18:36-9 F '65

Exhibitions

National scene. See issues of Hot rod

Specifications

International race-car specs. Pop Sci 186:132-3 F '65

AUTOMOBILES, Remodeled

Back on the road and purring; restoration of antique cars. il Bsns W p42-4 D 25 '65
Beetlemania; rebuilt Volkswagen competing at Carlsbad, Calif. E. Dahlquist. il Hot Rod 18:30-3 Ag '65
Hemi under glass; Plymouth Barracuda. il Hot Rod 18:78-81 Ap '65
Modern A; photographs. Hot Rod 18:91-5 Je '65
Petty's powder keg; Barracuda. il Hot Rod 18:48-51 F '65
Ultimate A/GS. E. Dahlquist. il Hot Rod 19:46-9+ Ja '66
Vintage gems from jalopy graveyards. W. Waltner and E. Waltner. il Pop Mech 124:106-9+ O '65

AUTOMOBILES, Steam

Roper's steamer; America's first car. T. Robinson. il Pop Mech 124:110-11+ O '65

AUTOMOBILES, Theft of

How cops spot stolen cars. W. J. Griswold. il Pop Sci 186:66-8 Mr '65
Key to thefts; master-key mail-order houses make car thievery easy. il Newsweek 66:68 Ag 9 '65
Stop, thief! T. McMullen. il Hot Rod 18:76-7 Mr '65
To keep your car from being stolen. P. W. Kearney. il Read Digest 87:249-50+ N '65

AUTOMOBILES, Toy

Slot car racing fad gets on a faster track; demand for more powerful and complicated toy cars. il Bsns W p 190-2 N 13 '65

AUTOMOBILES, Used

Giving the facts fast; warranty protection system. il Bsns W p 126+ N 20 '65
How important is low mileage when you choose a used car? il Bet Hom & Gard 43:46 My '65
How to buy a good used car. B. Taylor. il Pop Sci 186:96-9 Ap '65
Used cars; symposium. il Motor T 17:23-35+ Je '65
See also
Automobiles—Wrecking

AUTOMOBILES, Winter conditioning. See Automobiles—Care

AUTOMOBILES for the disabled

Limbless youth drives specially engineered car. Sci N L 88:39 Jl 17 '65

AUTOMOBILES in art

What a way to go; excerpts from Gallery of the American automobile, with commentary by J. J. Bradley. C. P. Hornung. il Am Heritage 17:65-79 D '65

AUTOMOTIVE engineers, Society of. See Society of automotive engineers

AUTOMOTIVE safety foundation

Automotive safety. R. Moley. Newsweek 67:92 Ja 24 '66

AUTONOMY

Gamble worth taking; independence for British Guiana. T. M. Petry. America 113:743 D 11 '65

AUTOPILOTS. See Automatic pilot (airplanes)

AUTOPSY

Fewer, better autopsies needed for research. Sci N L 88:201 S 25 '65

AUTORADIOGRAPHY

Autoradiography: technique for drastic reduction of exposure time to alpha particles. J. J. C. Hsieh and others. il Science 150:1821-2 D 31 '65
Bacterial chromsome. J. Cairns. il Sci Am 214:36-44 Ja '66

AUTUMN

Autumn: season of seeds. B. Tufty. il(p 177) Sci N L 88:186-7 S 18 '65
See also
October

AUTUMN crocuses

Colchicums. R. C. Hands. il Horticulture 43:33 Ag '65
Crocus on the window sill. R. C. Baur. il Pop Gard 16:53 S '65

AUTUMN full of apples; story. See Wake-field, D.

AUTUMN leaves. See Leaves

AUTUMN music festival, Naples. See Music festivals—Italy

AUVERGNE, France
Wild mushrooms, whortleberries, and thou. N. Barry. il Sat R 48:60+ Mr 13 '65

AUXINS
Auxin transport, gibberellin, and apical dominance. W. P. Jacobs and D. B. Case. bibliog il Science 148:1729-31 Je 25 '65
Gibberellic acid: action in barley endosperm does not require endogenous auxin. R. Cleland and N. McCombs. bibliog il Science 150:497-8 O 22 '65
See also
Indoleacetic acid

AVALANCHES
All gone; mining camp wiped out in British Columbia. il Newsweek 65:50 Mr 1 '65
Avalanche disaster not likely in U.S. Sci N L 88:169 S 11 '65
Doomsday roar in the Alps. il Life 58:38B My 28 '65
Much too much snow for Portillo, Chile 1966 F.I.S. competition canceled. B. Ottum. il Sports Illus 23:64+ Ag 23 '65
Under the Allalin; Switzerland's worst avalanche in eighty-four years. il Newsweek 66:40+ S 13 '65
Unpredictable ice; Allalin glacier, Switzerland. il Time 86:22 S 10 '65

AVANT-garde literature. See Literature

AVANT-garde moving pictures. See Moving pictures

AVANT-garde music. See Music

AVCO corporation
Avco building boron filament plant. J. F. Judge. il Miss & Roc 17:22-3+ N 15 '65
Rockets from a six-shooter. il Bsns W p84 Ap 10 '65

AVEC la bébé-sitter; story. See Updike, J.

AVEDON, Elliott M.
Enable the disabled. por Recreation 58:70-2 F '65

AVEDON, Richard
Marilyn Monroe. Pop Phot 58:105-9 Ja '66
We talk to. . ; interview. por Mlle 61:229+ Ag '65
about
Avedon show. J. Durniak. il Pop Phot 56:52-5 My '65
On Avedon's controversial book. B. Downes. Pop Phot 56:24 Mr '65

AVENATTI, Bob
Barnyard serenade. Recreation 58:425-6 N '65

AVERILL, Lloyd J.
Dynamics of unfaith. Christian Cent 83:41-4 Ja 12 '66
On a certain faithlessness. Christian Cent 82:1087-90 S 8 '65

AVERY, George S.
Learn to create bonsai. Horticulture 43:26-8 D '65

AVERY, Milton
American masters. il por Newsweek 65:88 Je 21 '65

AVERY ISLAND, Incorporated
Enchantment in the Louisiana marshes; manufacturers of tabasco sauce. K. Hamill. il Fortune 72:158-64 O '65
Sweet and hot; island history and resources. H. Sutton. il Sat R 49:46-7 Ja 15 '66

AVIAN adenoviruses. See Viruses

AVIATION
See also
Air travel
Airlines
Private flying
also headings beginning Aeronautic, Aeronautics, Airplane, Airplanes

Accident investigation
CAB boasts high score in solving crash puzzles. Sci N L 88:137 Ag 28 '65

Accidents
Air safety; lethal lapses. K. M. Ruppenthal. il Nation 201:525-7 D 27 '65
Altimeter setting error cited on Comet; accident at Nairobi, Kenya, February 2, 1964. Aviation W 82:99+ Ap 5 '65
American 727 crash probe starts; Cincinnati airport accident, November 8, 1965. Aviation W 83:39 N 15 '65
BAC III accident laid to illusion of stall; August 20, 1964. Aviation W 82:102-3+ Ap 26 '65

CAB accident investigation report: improper loading cited in D18s crash; Gainesville, Fla, February 3, 1964. Aviation W 82:83-5+ F 8 '65
CAB accident investigation report: lightning ignites 707 fuel/air mixture; accident, December 8, 1963, near Elkton, Md. il Aviation W 82:76-8+ My 3 '65
CAB accident investigation report: Northwest airlines crash in Everglades National Park, February 12, 1963. il Aviation W 83:104-5+ Ag 16; 93+ Ag 23 '65
CAB accident investigation report: premature descent cited in F-27A crash; November 15, 1964. Aviation W 83:105+ D 13 '65
CAB accident investigation report: slick crash laid to ice accretion on tail; March 10, 1964. il Aviation W 82:88-93 F 1 '65
CAB accident investigation report: technique cited in IFR go-around mishap; Los Angeles international airport, December 17, 1963. Aviation W 83:88-91+ O 4 '65
CAB accident investigation report: VFR deviation cited in Tahoe crash; March 1, 1964. Aviation W 83:90-7+ Ag 30 '65
CAB finds Pan Am Elkton crash probably caused by lightning hit. Aviation W 82:28 Mr 8 '65
Collision at 11,000 feet; Boeing 707 and Constellation collision over Danbury, Conn. il Newsweek 66:29 D 13 '65
FAA denies near-miss preceded Eastern DC-7 crash in Atlantic. Aviation W 82:32 F 15 '65
Fiat G-91 jet fighter crashes at Le Bourget. Aviation W 82:30 Je 28 '65
Flight 901A. . , California's Paradise airlines Constellation crash near Lake Tahoe, March 1, 1964. il Time 86:15 Jl 30 '65
Florida 720B crash blamed on turbulence. Aviation W 82:33 Je 7 '65
Good night; Eastern air lines flight 663 plunges into ocean off Jones Beach. il Time 85:24 F 19 '65
In good company; facts and figures on business flying. W. K. Lawton. Flying 77:50-3 O '65
Investigation of third 727 crash begun by Civil aeronautics board. Aviation W 83:37 N 22 '65
Mid-air collision and two steady pilots; Eastern airlines Constellation and TWA jet over North Salem, N.Y. il Life 59:33 D 17 '65
Montserrat crash flight recorder being analyzed by CAB for British. Aviation W 83:39 S 27 '65
New radar cuts hazard of mid-air collisions. P. Geraci. il Pop Sci 186:74-7+ Ap '65
New York collision investigators study possible error in altimetry. D. A. Brown. Aviation W 83:39-40 D 13 '65
On a wing & a prayer; Pan American's flight 843 after takeoff checklist with Captain C. Kimes from San Francisco's International airport. il Time 86:23-4 Jl 9 '65
Propeller windmilling seen cause of crash; accident of General dynamics/Convair model 48, October 9, 1965. Aviation W 83:34 N 8 '65
707 leaves glide path, rolls off runway; at John F. Kennedy international airport, April 7, 1964. il Aviation W 82:68-71+ Mr 8 '65
707 survives lost engine, wing section. H. D. Watkins. il Aviation W 83:27-8 Jl 5 '65
Sight few have seen and lived to tell about; engine fire of Pan American jet after takeoff from San Francisco; with comments by passengers. il Life 59:20-7 Jl 9 '65
Stable stall is cited in BAC 111 crash; test program criticized; accidents October 22, 1963, and August 20, 1964. Aviation W 82:50 Ap 5 '65
Stable stall ruled BAC 111 crash cause; accident, October 22, 1963. il Aviation W 82:94-5+ Ap 19 '65
Still seeking air safety; mid-air collision of Boeing 707 and Constellation shows weakness in traffic control. il Bsns W p 154+ D 11 '65
Third time unlucky; Boeing's 727 Cincinnati and Salt Lake crashes. il Time 86:43B N 19 '65
Triple trouble; three Boeing 727 crashes in three months. il Newsweek 66:33 N 22 '65
Village where people cared; Humlikon, Switzerland. O. Schisgall. il Read Digest 86:55-60 F '65
Viscount crash finding changed; accident at Freeland, Mich. April 6, 1958. Aviation W 82:38 F 22 '65
What happened to 663? Eastern air lines crash off Long Island. Newsweek 65:23-4 F 22 '65

AVIATION—Accidents—*Continued*
Windshield, oxygen bottle failure investigated in Lear jet crashes. H. D. Watkins. Aviation W 83:30 N 22 '65
Wing and a prayer. il Newsweek 66:30 Jl 12 '65
See also
Damages
Drinking and airplane accidents
Helicopters—Accidents

Altitude flying
O_2 fly in the troposphere. A. Trammell. il Flying 77:36-40 S '65

Anecdotes, facetiae, satire, etc.
Report the brewery; reprint. Flying 77:78 Jl '65

Bibliography
Book reviews. See issues of Flying

Bird hazards
Autumn bird migration brings hazards to planes. Sci N L 88:281 O 30 '65

Competitions
Duel at Rockford; aerobatic demonstration at Experimental aircraft association meeting. il Flying 77:49-51 Ag '65

Exhibitions
Aero classic. il Flying 77:58-61 N '65
Aero classic essay winners. il Flying 77:82-5 D '65
Aero classic progress award winners. il Flying 78:78 Ja '66
Aeroclassic; Palm Springs, Calif. R. Blodget. il Flying 77:60-5 Jl '65
Astronauts recoup space prestige; Paris show. M. Getler. il Miss & Roc 16:16-17 Je 28 '65
Astronauts seek to boost U.S. image at show; with editorial comment. il Aviation W 82:11, 24-5 Je 28 '65
Competition in the air; Paris air show. il Time 85:88 Je 18 '65
Costly mistake. R. Hotz. Aviation W 82:13 Je 21 '65
Dulles air show backers seek legislation; proposed International aerospace and science exposition. Aviation W 83:40 Jl 12 '65
European display significant progress in space at Paris air show; with photographs. Miss & Roc 17:16-17 Jl 5 '65
Europeans show new tactical missiles; with editorial comment. M. Getler. il Miss & Roc 16:16-17. 50 Je 21 '65
Jet teams demonstrate precision at Paris show; with photographs. Aviation W 83:58-61 Jl 5 '65
Long hot air show; Paris air show. J. Fricker. il Flying 77:54-6 S '65
NBAA display reflects international flavor. il Aviation W 83:90-1 N 1 '65
Nationalistic sales drives rule Paris show; with editorial comment. il Aviation W 82:69, 74-6 Je 14 '65
Post mortem on Paris. R. Hotz. Aviation W 83:11 Jl 19 '65
Russians fly high at Paris air show; Soviets outshine U.S. with An-22. il Bsns W p 146-7+ Je 19 '65
Russia's big surprise; Paris air show. il Newsweek 65:72 Je 28 '65
U.S. firms demanding fair play at Paris. L. L. Doty. Aviation W 83:33-4 Ag 2 '65
VTOL competition causing rift in Europe. L. L. Doty. il Aviation W 82:18-21 Je 21 '65

Fog problem
Fog chamber aids research on minimums. R. G. O'Lone. il Aviation W 83:40-1 O 11 '65

History
See Aeronautics—History

Ice storm hazards
See Aviation—Storm hazards

International aspects
Airline liability heads for take-off; U.S. moving to raise the maximum passenger coverage on international flights. Bsns W p 105-6 S 11 '65
Airplanes abroad; crashes and consequences. K. M. Ruppenthal. il Nation 201:408-10 N 29 '65
American bids for Tokyo routes in wake of U.S.-Japan bilateral. J. W. Carter. il Aviation W 84:38-9 Ja 10 '66
Big fight over the Atlantic. il Duns R 86:43-4+ S '65
Bilateral sparks JAL global service plan. K. Johnsen. Aviation W 84:26-7 Ja 3 '66
Bitterness in the air; Japan's air rights into U.S. Time 86:83 S 3 '65

Boyd warns of possible major international dispute on movies. J. W. Carter. Aviation W 82:30 My 3 '65
BOAC enters Leningrad dispute. Aviation W 83:29 Jl 19 '65
Canada bilateral to spur 15-20 route bids. K. Johnsen. Aviation W 84:40 Ja 10 '66
CAB strengthens U.S. carriers' South American service structure. Aviation W 82:23 My 31 '65
Cooperation, the cornerstone of international civil aviation. R. P. Boyle. Dept State Bul 53:820-7 N 22 '65
Great air race; transpacific air-transport market. il Time 87:78-9 Ja 14 '66
Hungarian carrier seeks route expansion. E. Walford. il Aviation W 83:37+ Jl 19 '65
International airlines report major gains. J. W. Carter. il Aviation W 82:172-3+ Mr 15 '65
International congress on air technology to be held in U.S. Dept State Bul 53:524 S 27 '65
Joint South American services proposed. Aviation W 82:32 F 8 '65
Mexico and U.S. extend Civil air agreement to 1970. Dept State Bul 53:357-8 Ag 30 '65
More supplementals get Atlantic rights. Aviation W 82:39 Ap 26 '65
Oseibo from the U.S.; Japan air lines to fly from Tokyo to New York and London. il Time 87:87 Ja 7 '66
Overseas carriers press for U.S. rights. J. R. Ashlock. Aviation W 83:38-9 Ag 30 '65
Pending CAB decisions could alter U.S. international route pattern. W. Wright. Aviation W 83:28-9 Jl 26 '65
U.S. and Peru agree to amend Air transport agreement. Dept State Bul 53:961 D 13 '65
U.S., Mexico reach bilateral agreement. W. Wright. Aviation W 83:36-7 Ag 9 '65
What is a life worth? U.S. proposes raise of liability limit. Time 86:98 O 29 '65
See also
International air transport association
International civil aviation organization

Laws and regulations
Airline liability heads for take-off; U.S. moving to raise the maximum passenger coverage on international flights. Bsns W p 105-6 S 11 '65
Scott's corner. D. H. Scott. Flying 77:22 Ag '65
Washington clipboard. R. Burkhardt. il Flying 77:25 Ag '65
See also
United States—Civil aeronautics board
United States—Federal aviation agency

Lightning hazards
CAB accident investigation report; lightning ignites 707 fuel/air mixture; accident, December 8, 1963, near Elkton, Md. il Aviation W 82:76-8+ My 3 '65

Medical aspects
See also
Air pilots—Diseases

Meteorological aspects
See Meteorology, Aeronautic

Mountain flying
Flying the mountain wave; ed. by B. Hicks. I. Leverton. il Flying 77:68-73 Ag '65

Physiological aspects
Command pilots' hearts beat faster. H. M. David. Miss & Roc 17:28 Jl 5 '65
Those circadian rhythms; what really happens to jet-age travelers. il Time 86:66 D 17 '65

Psychological aspects
Solo flyers not lonely. Sci N L 88:370 D 11 '65

Safety devices and measures
Air safety; lethal lapses. K. M. Ruppenthal. il Nation 201:525-7 D 27 '65
Boeing, airline moves follow 727 crashes. J. R. Ashlock. Aviation W 83:27-8 D 20 '65
New radar cuts hazard of mid-air collisions. P. Geraci. il Pop Sci 186:74-7+ Ap '65
Research funds sought to cut accidents. R. G. O'Lone. Aviation W 82:41-2 My 10 '65
Scott's corner; lighting of television towers. D. H. Scott. il Flying 77:70 Jl '65
See also
Airplanes—Ice protection
Airplanes—Safety devices and measures

AVIATION—*Continued*

Snowstorm hazards
See Aviation—Storm hazards

Statistics
In good company; facts and figures on business
flying. W. K. Lawton. Flying 77:50-3 O '65

Storm hazards
Flying weather signposts. H. T. Harrison.
il Flying 77:49-51 N '65
Go or no go. R. Hynes. il Flying 77:88+ Ag
'65
Mysterious air crashes: why they happen.
W. R. Young. il Read Digest 86:106-10
Mr '65
Thunderstorm menace. F. C. Bates. il Flying
77:74-80 O '65

Study and teaching
See Aeronautics—Study and teaching

Stunt flying
Duel at Rockford; aerobatic demonstration
at Experimental aircraft association meeting. il Flying 77:49-51 Ag '65
I'll put on one hell of a show. T. Taylor and
J. Atwater. il Sat Eve Post 238:74-7 O 9
'65
Rumble at Rockford. J. Gilbert. il Flying
78:40-3 Ja '66
Turn over please! American tiger club's
school of aerobatics. J. Gilbert. il Flying
77:40-3 Jl '65

Terminology
See Aeronautics—Terminology

Transatlantic flights
Atlantic bookings point to new records. J.
W. Carter. Aviation W 82:39-40 Ap 26 '65
North Atlantic jam nears acute stage. D. A.
Brown. Aviation W 83:93+ O 25 '65
Pilot group disputes separation rule. J. R.
Ashlock. Aviation W 83:38-9 D 13 '65

World flights
Loser. J. Gilbert. il Flying 77:80-4 Ag '65

United States
See also
Airlines—United States
AVIATION, Commercial. See Aeronautics,
Commercial
AVIATION and health. See Aviation—Phys-
iological aspects
AVIATION associations
Aerospace calendar. See issues of Aviation
week & space technology
Calendar. See issues of Flying
See also names of aviation associations,
e.g. Experimental aircraft association
AVIATION clubs
Buy your own airliner; and fly away! World
samplers club. il Changing T 20:21-3 Ja '66
Turn over please! American tiger club's
school of aerobatics. J. Gilbert. il Flying
77:40-3 Jl '65
AVIATION education
See also
Aeronautics—Study and teaching
AVIATION instructors. See Air pilots—Train-
ing
AVIATION insurance. See Insurance, Aviation
AVIATION museums. See Aeronautic museums
AVIATION records
Seven tentative flight records set by USAF/
Lockheed YF-12As. Aviation W 82:33 My
10 '65
AVIATION research. See Aeronautic research
AVIATION schools
Czech L-29, MiG-21 play role in training at
Soviet Kachinskoye school for pilots; pho-
tographers. Aviation W 83:88-9 Ag 23 '65
AVIATORS. See Air pilots
AVIATORS, Military. See Air pilots
AVILA PIRES, Fernando Dias de. See Pires,
F. D. de A.
AVIONICS industry. See Electronic apparatus
industry and trade
AVOCATIONS. See Hobbies
AVON, Anthony Eden, 1st earl of
Birth of the U.N. por N Y Times Mag p12-
13+ Je 20 '65
Burden of leadership. For Affairs 44:229-38
Ja '66
New evaluation of the big three; excerpts
from Reckoning. por U S News 58:20 Ap
5 '65

about
Anthony Eden and the cacophony of nations.
H. Feis. For Affairs 44:78-89 O '65
Legacy of the wartime big three. T. Molnar.
por Nat R 17:1037-8 N 16 '65
Lord Avon's vantage point. P. O'Donovan.
New Repub 152:24-5 My 15 '65
Minister's report on the past. J. H. Plumb.
por Sat R 48:27-8 Mr 27 '65
AVONDALE shipyards, New Orleans. See Ship-
yards
AWARDS. See Rewards, prizes, etc.
AXE handles. See Handles (machines, tools,
etc)
AXELBANK, Albert
Japan, the two Reischauers. New Repub 153:
11-12 N 13 '65
Japan's non-military buildup. Reporter 34:35-7
Ja 13 '66
AXELROD, George
Virna Lisi: experiment in star making. J.
Hamilton. il pors Look 29:60-6+ My 18
'65
AXELROD, Herbert R.
Strange fish and stranger times of Dr Her-
bert R. Axelrod. R. H. Boyle. il pors
Sports Illus 22:76-8+ My 3 '65
AXELROD, Julius, and Daly, John
Pituitary gland: enzymic formation of meth-
anol from S-adenosylmethionine. bibliog
Science 150:892-3 N 12 '65
—See Snyder, S. H.; Wurtman, R. J. jt.
auths.
AXFORD, H. William
Crucial battle for the minds of men. bibliog
por Library J 90:2499-503 Je 1 '65
AXLES
See also
Automobiles—Axles
AYALA, Francisco J.
Evolution of fitness in experimental popula-
tions of drosophila serrata. bibliog Science
150:903-5 N 12 '65
AYD, Frank J. jr
Book reviews. America 112:866-7 Je 12 '65
AYER, A. J.
Chance; with biographical sketch. Sci Am
213:10, 44-52+ O '65
AYLER, Albert
Albert Ayler for example. M. Williams. il
por Sat R 48:69-70 N 27 '65
AYOT ST LAWRENCE, England
Our far-flung correspondents. J. Bainbridge.
New Yorker 41:137-8+ N 6 '65
AYRES, John N.
Unique 99¢ speaker enclosure. Pop Electr
23:52-3 N '65
AYRES, Stephen M. and others
Carboxyhemoglobin: hemodynamic and re-
spiratory responses to small concentrations.
bibliog Science 149:193-4 Jl 9 '65
AYUB KHAN, Mohammad
Exchange of greetings; exchange of toasts
with President Johnson, December 14, 1965.
Dept State Bul 54:3, 5-7 Ja 3 '66
Kashmir dispute; address, October 2, 1965.
Vital Speeches 32:8-9 O 15 '65
New experiment in democracy in Pakistan.
Ann Am Acad 358:109-13 Mr '65

about
Ayub's basic democracy. R. Knox. il Reporter
32:34-6 F 11 '65
Building on image. il Time 85:28-9 Ap 2 '65
Chillier U.S. for President Ayub. il por U S
News 59:16 D 20 '65
Ending the suspense. il por Time 86:44-8 S
17 '65
Pakistan's Ayub: once an ally; now? il pors
U S News 59:24 S 20 '65
Playing the honest broker. il por Newsweek
67:36+ Ja 17 '66
Plugged in. il por Newsweek 66:20+ D 27
'65
AZAGUANINE. See Triazolo pyrimidin amino
AZALEAS
Royal azalea, spring and fall. il Flower Grow-
er 52:30 Ag '65
AZAURACIL
Morphogenetic effects of 6-azauracil and 6-
azauridine. R. M. Rizki and T. M. Rizki.
bibliog il Science 150:222-3 O 8 '65
AZAURIDINE
Morphogenetic effects of 6-azauracil and 6-
azauridine. R. M. Rizki and T. M. Rizki.
bibliog il Science 150:222-3 O 8 '65
AZIKIWE, Nnamdi
Essentials for Nigerian survival. For Affairs
43:447-61 Ap '65
AZNAVOUR, Charles
Of love & deeper sorrows. por Time 86:102+ O
22 '65
Tiny troubadour. por Newsweek 66:102+ O 25
'65

B

BART (Bay area rapid transit) See San Francisco—Rapid transit
BBB. See Better business bureaus
BBC symphony orchestra
B.B.C. in New York. B. Boretz. Nation 200: 682-3 Je 21 '65
BBC symphony orchestra. E. Laderman. Hi Fi 15:114+ Ag '65
Music to my ears; concert at Carnegie Hall. I. Kolodin. Sat R 48:22 My 29 '65
Musical events; avant-garde concert in Carnegie Hall. W. Sargeant. New Yorker 41: 173-4 My 15 '65
Musical events; concert in Carnegie Hall. W. Sargeant. New Yorker 41:169-70 My 22 '65
BEA. See British European airways corporation
BIA. See United States—Indian affairs, Bureau of
BIC. See United States—International commerce, Bureau of
BIS. See Bank for international settlements
BLM. See United States—Land management, Bureau of
BMI. See Book manufacturers' institute
BOAC. See British overseas airways corporation
BÅÅK, Tryggve
Sulfur: a new high-pressure form. bibliog Science 148:1220-1 My 28 '65
BAAL; drama. See Brecht, B.
BAARS, J. W. M. and Mezger, P. G.
First observations at short wavelengths with the 140-foot radio telescope. Sky & Tel 31:7-10 Ja '66
BABAA, Khalid I.
Third force and the United Nations. bibliog f Ann Am Acad 362:81-91 N '65
—and Crabb, C. V. Jr
Nonalignment as a diplomatic and ideological credo. bibliog f Ann Am Acad 362:6-17 N '65
BABB, Sanora
Rebellion and response. Writer 79:9-11 Ja '66
BABBITT, Milton
This man is composing music. B. H. Frisch. il por Sci Digest 57:72-7 F '65
BABCOCK, Havilah
How old Bill finally wound up. Field & S 69:50-2+ Ap '65
about
Obituary
Field & S 69:52 Ap '65
BABCOCK, M. J.
Common sense about vitamins. Ladies Home J 82:26+ F '65
BABICH, Frank R. and others
Transfer of response to naive rats by injection of ribonucleic acid extracted from trained rats. bibliog Science 149:656-7 Ag 6 '65
BABIES. See Infants
BABY blues; story. See Gerber, M. J.
BABY care. See Infants—Care and hygiene
BABY carriers. See Carriers (infants)
BABY showers. See Entertaining
BABY sitters
What counts most in hiring a baby sitter. Good H 160:131 Ja '65
BABY teeth. See Teeth
BACALL, Lauren
New baby. il por Time 87:68-9 Ja 7 '66
BACCALAUREATE addresses
Beyond civil rights; dealing with President Johnson's address at Howard university. America 112:875 Je 19 '65
Commencement 1965: the generational conflict; Time essay. Time 85:32 Je 18 '65
Dissent on dissent. il Newsweek 65:86 Je 21 '65
Riding the commencement circuit; government officials. H. Hamilton. America 112: 874 Je 19 '65
BACH, Harry
Clear and present danger: the books, or the censors? reprint. bibliog por Library J 90: 3681-5 S 15 '65
BACH, Johann Sebastian
Bach, the baroque and the fugue. R. De Toledano. Nat R 17:695 Ag 10 '65
Bach's Forty-eight, on the piano as a piano should sound. B. Jacobson. Hi Fi 16: 76-7 Ja '66
Brandenburgs, so musical a discourse. N. Broder. il Hi Fi 15:76-7 D '65
From Angelicum, a recording of great musical and pedagogical value. H. Glass. Am Rec G 31:534 F '65

Interpretation like no other. H. Glass. Am Rec G 31:822 My '65
Mighty Forty-eight. R. Kammerer. il Am Rec G 32:214-15 N '65
On records; Easter oratorio; St John passion. Opera N 29:34 Ap 10 '65
On records; St Matthew passion. Opera N 30: 34 D 11 '65
Posthumous career of J. S. Bach. L. Marcus. Hi Fi 16:56-8+ Ja '66
Scherchen's superabundant Musical offering. H. Glass. Am Rec G 31:1147 Ag '65
Year-round bargain from the Musical heritage society; Christmas oratorio. H. Glass. Am Rec G 31:511 F '65
BACH, Richard
Climbing the wind. Holiday 38:102+ Ag '65
Invisible 99s. Flying 77:38-41 Ag '65
Mavericks of sport aviation. Flying 78:32-9 Ja '66
BACHARACH, Burt
Soft touch. il por Newsweek 66:63 Ag 2 '65
BACHELORS
Bachelors more unhappy. E. Lederer. Sci N L 87:342 My 29 '65
Eligible bachelors for 1965. il Ebony 20:131-2+ Je '65

Anecdotes, facetiae, satire, etc.
Sex and the single boy. S. J. Perelman. New Yorker 41:40-3 My 8 '65
BACHMAN, Gregory
Though an arrow destines fall; poem. Christian Cent 82:802 Je 23 '65
BACHMANN, John F.
New look in radar. Electr World 73:32-5+ F '65
BACILLUS anthracis. See Anthrax
BACK packs. See Packs
BACK yards
Could this be your backyard? how to transform it into a garden. il Bet Hom & Gard 43:60-1 Ag '65
We grow a dogproof garden. G. Frerichs. il Pop Gard 16:8-9 Jl '65
BACKACHE
If your back is out, you're in. M. Smith. il Life 58:70-2+ Ap 9 '65; Same abr. Read Digest 87:157-8+ S '65
What is a slipped disc? Good H 161:148-9 Jl '65
When the trouble is gynecological backache. il Good H 162:141 Ja '66
Your aching back, and what to do about it. C. Mitchell. il Read Digest 88:78-82 Ja '66
BACKER, William Slade
Down the Danube by canoe. pors Nat Geog Mag 128:34-79 Jl '65
BACKGROUND in fiction. See Fiction—Technique
BACKGROUND in photography. See Composition (photography)
BACKMAN, Jules
How your competition will change. Nations Bsns 53:38-9+ F '65
Steel company answers the White House on wages; excerpts from report. U S News 59:77 Ag 16 '65
BACKMAN, Susie
Queen of shrimpers. il pors Ebony 21:131-4+ N '65
BACKSTER, Norma V. See Gero, M. J. jt. auth.
BACKWARD areas. See Underdeveloped areas
BACKWARD children. See Slow learning children
BACKYARDS. See Back yards
BACMEISTER, Rhoda W.
Mistakes many mothers make: will your children ever be friends? Parents Mag 40: 54-5+ Ap '65
Play is more than fun and games. Parents Mag 40:62-3+ Jl '65
Preparing preschoolers for the new math. Parents Mag 40:64-5+ S '65
BACON, Francis, viscount St Albans
Search for Francis Bacon. C. D. Bowen. por Atlan 217:68-74 Ja '66
BACON, Robert L. See Connell, R. S. jt. auth.
BACON, W. Stevenson
Science newsfront. Pop Sci 187:25-6+ N; 19-20+ D '65; 188:27-8+ Ja '66
BACON
Different bacon at a different price. Consumer Rep 30:109-10 Mr '65
Where pork bellies bring home the bacon; futures leading at Chicago's Mercantile exchange. il Bsns W p88-90 Ag 7 '65
See also
Cookery—Meat

BACTERIA
Bacteria as an indicator of formation of antibodies by single spleen cells in agar. S. A. Schwartz and W. Braun. bibliog il Science 149:200 Jl 9 '65
Bacterial contamination of some carbonaceous meteorites. J. Oró and T. Tornabene. bibliog il Science 150:1046-8 N 19 '65
Control of enzyme activity in growing bacterial cells by concerted feedback inhibition. L. Burlant and others. bibliog il Science 148:1351-3 Je 4 '65
See also
Agrobacterium tumefaciens
Chromatium
Colostridium botulinum
Electric power production from bacteriological action
Microorganisms
Pseudomonas

Mutation
See Mutation (bacteria)
BACTERIA, Anaerobic
Biological formation of molecular hydrogen. C. T. Gray and H. Gest. bibliog il Science 148:186-92 Ap 9 '65
BACTERIA, Fossil. See Micropaleontology
BACTERIA, Pathogenic
Bacterial stimulation of sporangium production in phytophthora cinnamomi. G. A. Zentmyer. bibliog Science 150:1178-9 N 26 '65
Bipolarity of information transfer from the salmonella typhimurium chromosome. P. Margolin. bibliog il Science 147:1456-8 Mr 19 '65
Food poisoning, and how to avoid it; salmonella. J. H. Winchester. Read Digest 86:161-2+ My '65
Molecular basis of heredity; report on symposium held under the auspices of the United States-Japan cooperative science program. S. E. Luria. Science 150:80-2 O 1 '65
Salmonella germs traced. Sci N L 88:303 N 6 '65
Salmonella in the water; Riverside County, Calif. Newsweek 66:56 Jl 12 '65
Ways to guard against a common food poisoning. Good H 160:172 Je '65
See also
Microorganisms, Pathogenic
Pasteurella pestis
Staphylococci
BACTERIAL oxidation. See Oxidation, Physiological
BACTERIAL viruses. See Bacteriophage
BACTERIOLOGICAL research
Photoplasts and L-forms; report on meeting of the American society for microbiology. T. R. Hamilton. Science 147:635-6+ F 5 '65
BACTERIOLOGICAL warfare. See Biological warfare
BACTERIOLOGY
See also
Staphylococci
BACTERIOLYSIS
Lysis of pleuropneumonia-like organisms by staphylococcal and streptococcal toxins. A. W. Bernheimer and M. Davidson. bibliog il Science 148:1229-31 My 28 '65
BACTERIOPHAGE
Complexes of F-pili and RNA bacteriophage. R. C. Valentine and M. Strand. bibliog il Science 148:511-13 Ap 23 '65
Genetics of a bacterial virus. R. S. Edgar and R. H. Epstein. il Sci Am 212:70-8 F '65
Inactivation by nitrogen mustard of single-and double-stranded DNA and RNA bacteriophages. N. Yamamoto and T. Naito. bibliog il Science 150:1603-4 D 17 '65
Induction in vitro of antibodies to phage T2; antigens in the RNA extract employed. H. P. Friedman and others. bibliog il Science 149:1106-7 S 3 '65
Mutagenic effects of hydroxylamine in vivo. I. Tessman and others. bibliog il Science 148:507-8 Ap 23 '65
Recombination in bacteriophage T4: a mechanism. E. Simon. bibliog il Science 150:760-3 N 5 '65
Suppression in vitro: identification of a serine-sRNA as a nonsense suppressor. M. R. Capecchi and G. N. Gussin. bibliog il Science 149:417-22 Jl 23 '65
BAD breath. See Halitosis
BAD scene at Buffalo Jump; story. See Fiedler, L.
BAD taste. See Vulgarity

BADEN-POWELL, Robert Stephenson Smyth Baden-Powell, 1st baron
Baden-Powell: the two lives of a hero, by W. Hillcourt. Review
New Yorker 41:190+ Ap 24 '65. N. Bliven
My most unforgettable character. W. Hillcourt. por Read Digest 87:203-4+ Jl '65
BADER, John P.
Transformation by Rous sarcoma virus: a requirement for DNA synthesis. bibliog Science 149:757-8 Ag 13 '65
BADER, Lawrence Joseph
Dead or alive? il por Newsweek 65:29 F 22 '65
Man with two wives: amnesia or hoax? C. Welles. il pors Life 58:41-2+ Mr 5 '65
BADHAM, Michael
Transatlantic passage. por Yachting 117:56-7+ Je '65
BADLANDS
Good fun in the Badlands. B. Ballantine. il Holiday 37:20+ Je '65
BADMINTON
Shopwalk; Reinforced shuttlecocks limited of Sandwich, Kent, and Altoona, Pa. J. A. M. Graham. Sports Illus 23:8 S 13 '65
BAECK, Leo
Encounters with God. por Time 85:61 F 19 '65
BAEHLER, Richard
PAC, the friendly octopus. Flying 77:41-3 S '65
BAER, Alban
Books. Commonweal 82:729-30 O 1 '65
BAER, Paul E. See Fuhrer, M. J. jt. auth.
BAGBY, Kenneth W.
Folks, by all rights I should be dead; letter. U S News 59:41 D 13 '65
BAGDIKIAN, Ben H.
Behold the grass-roots press, alas! Harper 229:102-5+ D '64; 230:14 F '65
Five different Washingtons. N Y Times Mag p8-9+ D 26 '65
I'm out of a job, I'm all through. Sat Eve Post 238:32-6+ D 18 '65
In the hearts of the right, Goldwater lives! N Y Times Mag p6-7+ Jl 18 '65
Inner inner circle around Johnson. N Y Times Mag p21+ F 28 '65
Oil can is mightier than the sword. N Y Times Mag p30-1+ Mr 14 '65
BAGLEY, Wayne
Spring on the Columbia River. il Yachting 117:62-3 My '65
BAGNALL, Art
T-Q's. Hot Rod 18:36-9 F '65
BAGS
Sew 'n' tote. il Seventeen 24:204 N '65
Travelers' aids; tote bags. il Seventeen 24:146-7 My '65
BAHADUR, Surendra
Season for kites. New Yorker 41:44-5 S 18 '65
BAHAISM
Bahá'í: a way of life for millions. il Ebony 20:48-50+ Ap '65
BAHAMA ISLANDS
Abaco adventure. B. Robinson. il Yachting 118:45-6+ N '65
East from Florida. J. Hart. il Yachting 118:44-5+ S '65
Science in action; survey of the Bahamas. C. L. Smith. Natur Hist 74:62-5 D '65
See also
Fishing—Bahama Islands
Grand Bahama Islands
Tourist trade—Bahama Islands

Description and travel
Find your family's ideal island. N. Kuehnl. il Bet Hom & Gard 43:93-8 D '65
Gulf Stream's coral spine; the Exumas. L. Smith. il Sports Illus 24:36-41 Ja 17 '66
Treasure cay; Great Abaco Island. M. Delman. il Travel 124:47-9 O '65
BAHAMA sloops. See Sloops
BAHER, Constance Whitman
Enchanted princess; drama. Plays 24:55-64 My '65
BAHREIN
Two down for Nasser. il Time 86:28+ Jl 9 '65
BAHUTU. See Burundi—Native races
BAIL
High price of civil rights protest. R. Goldfarb. New Repub 153:11-12 O 16 '65
Penalizing the poor; modifications of federal bail procedures proposed. Christian Cent 82:197-8 F 17 '65
Ransom, by R. Goldfarb. Review
Sat R 49:30 Ja 1 '66. M. Feldman
Unbounded bondsmen; Tyrone Collins seized by Alabama bondsmen in Philadelphia. il Time 87:74 Ja 7 '66
Who goes to prison; caste and careerism in crime. B. Jackson. il Atlan 217:52-7 Ja '66
BAILEY, Anthony
Our far-flung correspondents. New Yorker 41:129-30+ My 8 '65

BAILEY, Dorothy L.
Teachers' children. NEA J 54:12-14 Mr '65
BAILEY, Fred, Jr
Tax rules you should know before you sell property. Suc Farm 63:34+ F '65
BAILEY, George
Field day for the left in Athens. Reporter 33:25-7 Ag 12 '65
Greece and Turkey: the second round. Reporter 33:14-18 S 9 '65
No change in Germany. Reporter 33:32-3 O 7 '65
Russian at Reims. Reporter 32:34-6 My 20 '65
Tales of the Vienna hoods. Reporter 32:36-40 Mr 25 '65
Under the Berlin wall. Reporter 33:18-23 N 4 '65
West Germany's economic romantics. Reporter 33:37-41 S 23 '65
Where Titoism was tried. Reporter 33:13-18 Jl 1 '65
Windischgraetz caper. Reporter 32:30-4 F 11 '65
BAILEY, Howald T.
Perfect achievement. Opera N 29:24-5 Mr 6 '65
BAILEY, J. Russell
Mr Architect, listen. por Library J 90:5147-51 D 1 '65
BAILEY, J. W.
Six ways to dehorn cattle. Suc Farm 63:54-5 My '65
Veterinary helps. See issues of Successful farming
BAILEY, James
Case history of a failure. Arch Forum 123:22-5 D '65
Making precast concrete do more for less. Arch Forum 123:52-5 N '65
BAILEY, John T.
Determining meter resistance. Electr World 74:49 Ag '65
BAILEY, Richard Eugene
Maitre d' of sports TV. G. S. Brown. il por Sports Illus 23:52-4 N 8 '65
BAILEY, Stephen K.
Education for responsible citizenship; adaptation of address. NEA J 54:16-18 My '65
BAILEY acacias. See Acacias
BAILY, Samuel L.
Argentina: reconciliation with the Peronists. Cur Hist 49:356-60+ D '65
BAIN, Myrna
Everybody's protest play. Nat R 17:249 Mr 23 '65
BAINBRIDGE, John
Letter from Liechtenstein. New Yorker 41:68+ Ag 7 '65
Our far-flung correspondents. New Yorker 40:136+ F 13; 41:62+ Jl 3; 137-8+ N 6 '65
BAINES, Joseph Wilson, family
His mother's story of LBJ; excerpts from manuscript. R. B. Johnson. il U S News 58:48-52 F 15 '65
BAINTON, Roland H.
Books. Commonweal 83:65-7 O 15 '65
BAIRD, Butch
Laugher for the team from Texas. A. Wright. il por Sports Illus 23:84+ D 20 '65
BAIT
How not to strike out. A. J. McClane. il Field & S 69:78-82 Mr '65
Offbeat baits. H. G. Tappiy. il Field & S 70:56 Ag '65
See also
Fishing lures, flies, etc.
BAJA CALIFORNIA. See California, Lower
BAKAL, Carl
Traffic in guns; a forgotten lesson of the assassination. Harper 229:62-8 D '64; 230-12 F '65
BAKED beans. See Cookery—Vegetables
BAKER, Carroll
Baby doll grows up. por Newsweek 65:94-6 Ap 26 '65
Carroll Baker: the lady was a tramp. R. W. Lewis. il pors Sat Eve Post 238:36-8+ F 27 '65
BAKER, Diane
Diane Baker: Peck's good girl. H. Ehrlich. il pors Look 29:56-8+ Mr 23 '65
BAKER, Elizabeth C.
Brazilian bouillabaisse. Art N 64:30-1+ D '65
BAKER, George. See Divine, M. J.
BAKER, Leonard
Compliance. Am Ed 1:24-6 S '65
BAKER, Nancy
Resource in the fight against censorship. ALA Bul 59:529-30 Je '65
BAKER, Robert Gene
Case of Bobby Baker and the courageous senator. J. Barron. Read Digest 87:112-18 S '65
Cave vendor; current financial woes. por Time 86:40 S 17 '65

Change in fortune. il por Newsweek 67:26 Ja 17 '66
Comeuppance for the Pickens kid. il por Time 87:21B Ja 14 '66
See also
Government investigations—Baker case
BAKER, Russell
How Barry Sosostris will save TV. Sat Eve Post 238:24 N 6 '65
It's Middletown-on-the-Potomac. N Y Times Mag p32-3+ F 14 '65
Man who beat the rat race. Sat Eve Post 239:18 Ja 15 '66
We were eyeball to eyeball with victory. Sports Illus 23:40-1 O 11 '65
When the ideal wife marries the absolutely perfect husband. Ladies Home J 82:66-7 S '65
BAKER, Samm Sinclair
How to become a creative writer in twelve not-so-easy steps. Writer 78:9-11 My '65
BAKER, Virgil L.
Role of human values in communication: address, April 2, 1965. bibliog Vital Speeches 31:434-7 My 1 '65
BAKER and Taylor company
Baker & Taylor plans western division in Reno. Pub W 188:32 N 29 '65
BAKER Street irregulars. See New York (city)
—Clubs
BAKER street; musical comedy. See Musical comedies, revues, etc.—Criticisms, plots, etc.
BAKERS and bakeries
Making a cake as fast as you can; portfolio. Fortune 71:134-7 Mr '65
BAKERSFIELD, Calif.
See also
Kern County museum
BAKING
Cupboard full of seasonal sweets; with recipes. il McCalls 93:114-15+ D '65
These farm women cook and bake big! with recipes. N. Nichols. il Farm J 89:86-8+ F '65
See also
Bread
Cake
Cookies
Muffins
Pie
BAKING industry. See Bakers and bakeries
BAKU university. See Colleges and universities—Russia
BAKURIANI, Russia
Russ-skis; Russian ski resort. il Newsweek 65:94+ Mr 15 '65
BALABANOFF, Angelica
Angelica Balabanoff: 1878-1965. T. Pol. Nation 201:482-3 D 13 '65
BALAGUER, Joaquín
Campaign opener; return to Dominican Republic. Newsweek 66:50 Jl 12 '65
Homecoming. por Time 86:34+ Jl 9 '65
Third man. por Newsweek 65:66 Je 14 '65
BALANCE of nature
Massive extinctions in biota at the end of Mesozoic time. M. N. Bramlette. bibliog Science 148:1696-9 Je 25 '65; Discussion. 149:922+; 150:1240 Ag 27, D 3 '65
BALANCE of payments
All aboard, for where? il Fortune 71:104-5 Ap '65
Balance of payments needs a balance of priorities. Fortune 72:125-6 N '65
Balance-of-payments program and the Congress; Cabinet report, May 13, 1965. H. H. Fowler. Dept State Bul 52:963-4 Je 14 '65
Balance-of-payments program to be intensified in 1966; letters, December 2, and December 6, 1965; with report of cabinet committee. L. B. Johnson; J. T. Connor. Dept State Bul 54:22-7 Ja 3 '66
Balancing act. il Time 85:89-90 F 19 '65
Bankers learn to live with foreign loan limits; lending abroad. il Bsns W p40-1 Jl 3 '65
Battle of Britain, 1965. il Newsweek 66:59-61+ S 6 '65
Battle to save the pound; what it does for the dollar. il U S News 59:99 S 27 '65
Best way to help the dollar. Bsns W p206 S 18 '65; Reply. America 113:459 O 23 '65
Bittersweet smell of success. il Newsweek 66:63 Ag 30 '65
Breathing spell for the dollar? dollar controls: a critical view. il U S News 58:84+ Mr 29 '65
Business and the balance of payments; top executives discuss administration's voluntary program. il Duns R 86:37-9+ S '65
Business cool to payments program; with editorial comment. il Bsns W p26-7, 160 F 20 '65
Call for volunteers; measures to cure deficit. il Newsweek 65:78+ F 22 '65

BALANCE of payments—*Continued*
Congeries of uncertainties. il Fortune 71: 25-6 Mr '65
Crash next year? why it's a real danger, and how it can be avoided. P. F. Drucker. Harper 230:59-64 Je '65
Credit joins the payments battle. il Bsns W p34-5 F 27 '65
De Gaulle v. the dollar. il Time 85:81-2 F 12 '65
De Gaulle's nugget. il Fortune 71:92-3 Mr '65
Dollar under stress. Fortune 71:30+ Mr '65
Dollar's future: what companies will do; interview. A. L. Nickerson. Nations Bsns 53:32-3+ My '65
Dollars start coming back home; what Commerce wants. Bsns W p 133-4 Mr 20 '65
Drain on dollars. New Repub 152:8-9 F 13 '65
Edging closer to monetary reform; with editorial comment. il Bsns W p68+, 160 Je 26 '65
Experts take new look at gold drain measure. il Bsns W p 116+ My 1 '65
Foreign aid and the balance of payments; statement, March 9, 1965. D. E. Bell. Dept State Bul 52:498-502 Ap 5 '65
Foreign assistance program for 1966; statement, March 9, 1965. D. Rusk. Dept State Bul 52:482-8 Ap 5 '65
Foreign balance. il Fortune 72:32+ Ag '65
Government-business partnership on balance-of-payments problem; remarks, February 18, 1965. L. B. Johnson. Dept State Bul 52: 335-7 Mr 8 '65
How good is the news about the U.S. balance of payments? Sr Schol 87:12-13+ O 7 65
International economic policies; excerpt from economic report of the President and annual report of the Council of economic advisers. Dept State Bul 52:254-60 F 22 '65
International monetary problems; strong, sound and stable dollar; address, July 10, 1965. H. H. Fowler. Vital Speeches 31:646-9 Ag 15 '65
Into the black: a modest triumph. il Newsweek 66:67 Jl 19 '65
Looking for change. il Time 85:85 Mr 12 '65
LBJ strikes a balance for business. il Newsweek 65:69-70 Mr 1 '65
Making a strong pitch to build U.S. exports; government and businessmen unite. il Bsns W p80+ My 8 '65
New steps to improve international monetary arrangements; address, July 10, 1965. H. H. Fowler. Dept State Bul 53:209-14 Ag 2 '65
Outflow of funds is facing new curb; corporate investments abroad face stiffer program. il Bsns W p53-4+ O 9 '65
Phantom funds; U.S.-owned foreign currency abroad. R. Moley. Newsweek 65:92 Mr 29 '65
Pin-pointing problems in payments reform; highlights of Ossola group study. il Bsns W p87 Ag 14 '65
Plans to plug the dollar drain. Bsns W p 110 Ja 30 '65
Plumbing our leaky payments balance. N. McKitterick. New Repub 152:10-11 F 27 '65
President's partnership; US businessmen briefed on President's plan. il Time 85:85 F 26 '65
Role of the dollar; address, September 21, 1965. J. W. Barr. Vital Speeches 32:18-21 O 15 '65
Self-restraint, or else; Johnson attacks the dollar drain; with editorial comment. il Bsns W p25-6, 166 F 13 '65
Shell game: three sets of statistics for third quarter of year. il Newsweek 66:71-2 N 29 '65
Shrinking deficit. il Newsweek 65:84 My 10 '65
Social responsibility: a subversive doctrine. M. Friedman. Nat R 17:721-3 Ag 24 '65
Stanching the dollar outflow; investing abroad. il Bsns W p38-9 Jl 3 '65
Standby credit braces sterling; Britain's sterling crisis is over. il Bsns W p27-8 S 18 '65
Surprising scapegoat; private foreign investment. H. Hazlitt. Newsweek 65:78 Mr 1 '65
Swallow from the Scilly Isles; import-export figures show narrowing of trade gap. il Newsweek 66:57 Ag 23 '65
Temporary gains. Time 86:73 Ag 27 '65
Thinking ahead in federal tax policy; U.S. balance of payment; address, November 9, 1965. J. F. Oates, jr. Vital Speeches 32: 105-9 D 1 '65
Tightening the screws. Newsweek 66:79 D 13 '65
Trade and the balance of payments; statement, March 16, 1965. G. G. Johnson. Dept State Bul 52:502–7 Ap 5 '65

Trends in international economics. C. P. Kindleberger. bibliog f Ann Am Acad 358: 170-9 Mr '65
Two-way ticket. il Time 85:91-2 My 7 '65
United States and international cooperation; address, March 26, 1965. W. A. Harriman. Dept State Bul 52:621-8 Ap 26 '65
U.S. citizens in India may buy counterpart currency. Dept State Bul 52:907 Je 7 '65
U.S. exports fight to hold '64 level. il Bsns W p 138+ O 16 '65
United States fiscal policy; address, March 19, 1965. D. Dillon. Vital Speeches 31:388-91 Ap 15 '65
U.S. hails easing of dollar drain. Bsns W p33 Ag 21 '65
U.S. tries to sell a new system for world's money. U S News 59:103-4 S 13 '65
Visit from Grim Jim. il Newsweek 66:71-2 Jl 12 '65
Washington desk. J. R. Slevin. Duns R 85: 5-6 F '65
Washington desk; voluntary credit control program. J. R. Slevin. Duns R 85:5-6 My '65
What LBJ's dollar drive means to U.S. business; executives tell their plans and problems. il U S News 58:47-9 Mr 8 '65
Why Martin spoke out; believes dollar must be defended; with editorial comment. il Bsns W p36-7, 188 Je 12 '65
Why the dollar is in danger. J. Daniel and J. B. Shuman. Read Digest 87:130-4 N '65
Will LBJ's plea nip the boom? slow down on investment in Europe. il Newsweek 65:73-4 Mr 8 '65
World markets are still a lure; McGraw-Hill's survey of overseas investment. il Bsns W p26-7 Ag 7 '65
Wrong way to fight the gold outflow? interview, ed. by G. R. Rosen. J. N. Behrman. il Duns R 85:48-9+ Ap '65

BALANCE of power
Asian nonalignment. S. K. Gupta. bibliog f Ann Am Acad 362:44-51 N '65
Red world vs. the West, which is stronger? il U S News 60:34-6 Ja 10 '66
See also
World politics

BALANCE of trade. See Balance of payments

BALANCED diet. See Diet

BALANCHINE, George
Mr B talks about ballet. pors Life 58:94A-98+ Je 11 '65

about

Balanchine dances; role of Don Quixote. il pors N Y Times Mag p39-40 My 16 '65
Balanchine's Don Quixote. R. Krokover. il por Hi Fi 15:123 Ag '65
Ballet in America: one-man show? R. Krokover and H. C. Schonberg; discussion. Harper 229:13 N '64; 230:8+ Mr '65
Lark from Russia. il Newsweek 65:87 F 15 '65
Mr B as Don Q. por Newsweek 65:82 Je 7 '65
Mr B: God creates, I assemble. S. Massie. il pors Sat Eve Post 238:34-7 O 23 '65
Musical events; performance in title role of his Don Quixote with New York city ballet. W. Sargeant. New Yorker 41:144 Je 5 '65
No lousy little stories. Time 86:104 S 17 '65
People are talking about: G. Balanchine. il por Vogue 145:94-5 Je '65

BALANOGLOSSUS
Acorn worm makes tracks. il(p273) Sci N L 88:276 O 30 '65
Iodine: accumulation by balanoglossus gigas. F. B. De Jorge and others. bibliog il Science 150:1182-3 N 26 '65
Wandering enteropneust from the abyssal Pacific, and the distribution of spiral tracks on the sea floor. D. W. Bourne and B. C. Heezen. bibliog il Science 150:60-3 O 1 '65

BALASARASWATHI
Balasarasvati, 92nd street Y. D. Hering. Dance Mag 39:157-8 D '65

BALASURIYA, Tissa
World apartheid. Commonweal 83:363-6 D 24 '65

BALCHIN, Nigel
Speaking out. por Sat Eve Post 238:10+ O 9 '65

BALD eagles. See Eagles

BALDESSARINI, Ross J. and Carbone, P. P.
Adenosylmethionine elevation in leukemic white blood cells. bibliog Science 149:644-5 Ag 6 '65

BALDET, Fernand
Obituary
Sky & Tel 29:283 My '65. G. S. Mumford

BALDINA, Alexandra
Baldina; interview, by D. Leddick. pors Dance Mag 39:21-3 N '65

BALDNESS
Baldness; medicine's first breakthrough. L. R. Chevalier. Ladies Home J 82:34+ Je '65
Hormone cream restores lost hair. il Sci Digest 57:22-3 Mr '65
Male hormone produces hair on bald heads. Sci N L 87:184 Mr 20 '65

BALDWIN, Brooks, and Gorham, B. F.
Just before dawn; story. Good H 161:66-7 Ag '65

BALDWIN, Ed
Wildflowers in Alaska. Horticulture 43:22-3 Ag '65

BALDWIN, H. A. and others
Glass-coated tungsten microelectrodes. bibliog Science 148:1462-4 Je 11 '65

BALDWIN, Hanson Weightman
After fifty years the cry of Ypres still echoes, gas! N Y Times Mag p28-9+ Ap 18 '65
Little boy's long, long journey. N Y Times Mag p6-7+ Ag 1 '65
NATO's uneven steps toward integration. Reporter 32:32-4 Mr 11 '65
Vietnam: new policy in the making. Reporter 33:16-20 Ag 12 '65
We must choose: (1) bug out; (2) negotiate; (3) fight. N Y Times Mag p8-9+ F 21 '65
What we must do to win in Asia. Read Digest 87:111-16 N '65

BALDWIN, James
American dream and the American Negro. por N Y Times Mag p32-3+ Mr 7 '65
White man's guilt. Ebony 20:47-8 Ag '65

about
Amen corner. Criticism
America 112:690 My 8 '65
Cath World il 201:215-16 Je '65
Commonweal 82:221-2 My 7 '65
Life 58:16 My 14 '65
Nation 200:514-15 My 10 '65
New Yorker 41:85 Ap 24 '65
Newsweek 65:90 Ap 26 '65
Sat R 48:49 My 1 '65
Time il 85:59 Ap 23 '65
Vogue 145:68 Je '65
Blues for Mister Baldwin. J. Featherstone. New Repub 153:34-6 N 27 '65
Blues for Mister Charlie. Criticism
Harper 231:34+ S '65
James Baldwin's jeremiad. A. B. Southwick. Christian Cent 82:362-4 Mr 24 '65
Negro and the American dream. W. F. Buckley, jr. Nat R 17:273 Ap 6 '65
On Avedon's controversial book. B. Downes. Pop Phot 56:24 Mr '65

BALDWIN, Kenneth
Back to the army. Time 86:24 Jl 30 '65
Banished American. il por Time 85:44 Je 25 '65
Yankee please stay. H. Bowser. Sat R 48:18 Ag 21 '65

BALDWIN, Louis
Irrelevance of Vatican II. por Cath World 201:260-3 Jl '65

BALDWIN, Ralph B.
Mars: an estimate of the age of its surface. bibliog Science 149:1498-9 S 24 '65

BALDWIN, Roger N.
Defining our legal liberties. Sat R 49:28 Ja 1 '66
Haters among us. Sat R 48:36 Je 19 '65

BALENCIAGA, Cristobal
Balenciaga; tr. by A. White. V. Leduc. por Vogue 145:82-3+ Ap 15 '65

BALEWA, Sir Abubakar Tafawa
Nigerian tragedy. por Newsweek 67:39-40 Ja 24 '66

BALFOUR, L. G, company
Gold in those fingers; class rings. il Newsweek 65:74-5 Je 7 '65

BALFOUR declaration. See Zionism

BALIN, Robert P.
Scope-trace quiz. Pop Electr 22:71+ Mr '65
Voltage function quiz. Pop Electr 22:73+ F '65

BALING machinery
Easy-out bale handling. il Farm J 89:65 F '65

BALK, Alfred
Anyone for survival? Sat Eve Post 238:72+ Mr 27 '65
Builder who makes integration pay. Harper 231:94-9 Jl '65
ICY; report on the White House conference on International cooperation year. Sat R 49:24-8 Ja 22 '64
Should boxing be abolished? Todays Health 43:18-23 Ag '65
Water crisis on the Great Lakes. Read Digest 86:165-6+ Mr '65
Where are tomorrow's journalists? Sat R 49:105-6 Ja 8 '66

BALL, George Wildman
Dangers of nostalgia; address, March 16, 1965. Dept State Bul 52:532-7 Ap 12 '65
Department asks for flexibility on surplus food sales to U.A.R; statement, February 1, 1965. Dept State Bul 52:262-3 F 22 '65
Department opposes bill to amend export control act of 1949; statement, May 24, 1965. Dept State Bul 53:35-7 Jl 5 '65
Department urges enactment of coffee legislation; statement, January 27, 1965. Dept State Bul 52:260-2 F 22 '65
George Ball: talking tough to de Gaulle; excerpts from address. por U S News 58:15 Mr 29 '65
Hard problems of a turbulent world; address, September 16, 1965. Dept State Bul 53:588-92 O 11 '65
Mr Ball discusses U.S. relations with Europe on BBC; interview, ed. by A. Burnet, October 2, 1965. Dept State Bul 53:653-60 O 25 '65
Mr Ball discusses Viet-Nam on Issues and answers; interview, August 1, 1965; ed. by W. R. Downs, jr. and J. Scali. Dept State Bul 53:310-14 Ag 23 '65
New diplomacy; address, June 6, 1965. Dept State Bul 52:1042-8 Je 28 '65
Outer space and the advancement of human understanding; remarks, September 15, 1965. Dept State Bul 53:552 O 4 '65
SEATO council ministers hold 10th meeting at London; statement, May 3, 1965. Dept State Bul 52:920-3 Je 7 '65
United States and Canada: common aims and common responsibilities; address, March 22, 1965. Dept State Bul 52:572-6 Ap 19 '65

about
De Gaulle peace move in Vietnam? por U S News 59:19 S 13 '65

BALL, William
Upon your imaginary forces, ACT! American conservatory theatre. H. Hewes. Sat R 48:43 S 4 '65

BALL, William B.
Court and birth control. Commonweal 82:490-3, 579+ Jl 9, Ag 20 '65
Family planning as law: a lawyer's objections. Cath World 202:144-50 D '65
Johnson education bill. Commonweal 81:638-40 F 12 '65
New era for public and private schools; interview, ed. by C. L. Palms. Cath World 201:227-32 Jl '65
Practice of religious liberty. por Cath World 201:369-74 S '65

BALL point pens. See Fountain pens

BALLADS
See also
Phonograph records—Songs

BALLANTINE, H. Thomas, Jr
Needling the brain. il por Newsweek 66:80 S 13 '65

BALLANTINE, William
Circus! Sat Eve Post 238:30-7 Ap 10 '65
Good fun in the Badlands. Holiday 37:20+ Je '65

BALLARD, Allen B.
Private plot vs. collective farm. N Y Times Mag p 14-15+ Je 13 '65

BALLARD, Ernesta Drinker
Greenhouse in my window. Horticulture 43:26-7 O '65

BALLARD, James
Wild honey; story. Atlan 217:63-7 Ja '66

BALLARD, W. F. R.
Computer produces 120-volume planning reference. Am City 80:110+ Jl '65

BALLERINAS. See Dancers

BALLET
American ballet theatre. R. Krokover. il Hi Fi 15:120+ Je '65
Ballet in America: one-man show? R. Krokover and H. C. Schonberg; discussion. Harper 229:13 N '64; 230:8+ Mr '65
Castor et Pollux. Concert opera association, Philharmonic Hall. M. Marks. Dance Mag 39:32 Mr '65
Dancer's life. A. Markova. Seventeen 24:126+ D '65
Funny Phyllis Diller is serious about ballet. V. H. Swisher. Dance Mag 40:28-30 Ja '66
Man in motion; career of Nureyev in the West. il Time 85:48-52 Ap 16 '65
Metropolitan opera: Faust, Pique dame. D. Hering. Dance Mag 39:18-19 N '65
Mr B talks about ballet. G. Balanchine. il Life 58:94A-98+ Je 11 '65
Presstime news. See issues of Dance magazine
Regional ballet, USA. D. Hering. See issues of Dance magazine
Reviews. See issues of Dance magazine

BALLET—*Continued*
Royal ballet; at Metropolitan opera house. R. Krokover. il Hi Fi 15:99+ Jl '65
Who pays the piper? J. L. Collier. Holiday 38:168+ D '65
See also
Choreography
Moving pictures—Dance film

History
Baldina; interview. ed. by D. Leddick. A. Baldina. il Dance Mag 39:21-3 N '65
Invitation to the dance; ballet in America. F. Russell. il Nat R 17:202+ Mr 9 '65
La Sylphide: epitome of the romantic ballet. L. Moore. il Dance Mag 39:42-7 Mr '65

Study and teaching
Anatomy for the ballet teacher; ed. by W. Como. R. Gelabert. See issues of Dance magazine
Class with Mme Pereyaslavec. L. Joel. il Dance Mag 39:24-7 Jl '65
Connoisseurs in the making. E. L. Raichle. il NEA J 54:29-30 N '65
Mme Anderson-Ivantzova, a little Bolshoi on 56 st. M. Horosko. il Dance Mag 39:54-6 Je '65
Project Buffalo; workshops, seminars, lecture-demonstrations, by members of New York city ballet. J. P. Dwyer. il Dance Mag 40:54-5 Ja '66

Canada
See also
National ballet of Canada
Royal Winnipeg ballet

Denmark
Something new in Denmark; report on recent developments. S. Sorgenfrey. il Dance Mag 39:26-7 Ag '65
See also
Royal Danish ballet

France
Béjart at the Paris festival. M. Seif. Sat R 49:49+ Ja 15 '66

Germany (Federal Republic)
Materials of publicity: the press book. D. Duncan. Dance Mag 39:14-17 Mr '65

Great Britain
See also
Royal academy of dancing
Royal ballet, Great Britain

Japan
Banzai ballet: M. Civecawa and Terror reign. il Newsweek 66:52-3 D 13 '65

Mexico
See also
Ballet folklórico of Mexico

Sweden
Choreographic institute; program of Swedish government. B. Hager. il Dance Mag 39: 14-15 F '65
Time for dance in Stockholm; Royal Swedish ballet festival. S. J. Cohen. il Sat R 48:55+ Je 26 '65

BALLET companies
Annual directory of dance attractions: soloists, companies, choreographers, lecturers. Dance Mag 39:14-16+ D '65
Classicism, romanticism, and color; Ballet classique, new touring group, on the West coast. C. H. Swisher. il Dance Mag 39:118-19+ D '65
Dance and decentralization; regional ballet companies; excerpts from interview; ed. by A. H. Reiss. D. Hering. il Dance Mag 39: 124-6 D '65
Go somewhere! Washington's Capitol ballet. D. Hering. il Dance Mag 39:56-60 My '65
Letter from Augusta: or the launching of a regional ballet company. Mrs I. Beaufort. Dance Mag 40:68-9 Ja '66
Out of pride; Alvin Ailey American dance theater. il Time 85:69 My 28 '65
Paul Taylor dance company, Hunter college playhouse. D. Hering. Dance Mag 39:155-6 D '65
Regional ballet, USA. D. Hering. See issues of Dance magazine
Robert Joffrey ballet, Delacorte theater. M. Marks. Dance Mag 39:60+ O '65
Success story; First chamber dance quartet. J. Anderson. il Dance Mag 39:100-2+ D '65

White House festival of the arts. il Dance Mag 39:36-8 Ag '65
See also
American ballet theatre
Boston ballet company
Harkness ballet (organization)
Metropolitan opera ballet
National ballet of Canada
New York city ballet
Pennsylvania ballet company
Royal ballet, Great Britain
San Francisco ballet (organization)

BALLET dancers. See Dancers
BALLET exercises. See Exercise
BALLET festivals. See Dance festivals
BALLET folklórico of Mexico
Ballet folklórico de Mexico at City center. M. Marks. Dance Mag 39:32+ Mr '65
Mexico's Folklórico. L. Lerman. il Mlle 60: 178-9 Ap '65

BALLET in art. See Dancing in art
BALLET theatre. See American ballet theatre
BALLETS
Music to my ears; the Royal ballet's Romeo. I. Kolodin. Sat R 48:48 My 8 '65
San Francisco's pop art ballet. H. Caen. il Dance Mag 39:48-9 Ap '65
Three Graham restorations: Primitive mysteries, Appalachian spring, Cave of the heart. L. Leatherman. il Dance Mag 39:42-6 N '65
Three Romeos. C. Barnes. il Sat R 48:58-9 Ap 24 '65

Choreographies
See Choreography

Criticisms
Coppelia
  New Yorker 41:234 D 11 '65
Don Quixote
  America 113:450-1 O 16 '65
  Dance Mag il 39:33-7 Jl '65
  Dance Mag 39:30+ Ag '65
  Dance Mag 39:32-3+ N '65
  Harper 231:33 Ag '65
  Hi Fi il 15:123 Ag '65
  New Yorker 41:144 Je 5 '65
  New Yorker 41:184 O 2 '65
  Newsweek 65:82 Je 7 '65
  Sat R 48:34+ Je 12 '65
Dream
  Sat R 48:32 My 15 '65
Harlequinade
  Dance Mag il 39:67-70 Mr '65
  New Yorker 40:154 F 13 '65
  Newsweek il 65:87 F 15 '65
Les noces
  New Yorker 41:114-15 Ap 10 '65
Ode to joy
  UNESCO Courier il 18:60-1 Jl '65
Rites of spring
  New Yorker 41:168-71 My 15 '65
Romeo and Juliet
  New Yorker 41:118+ F 20 '65
  New Yorker 41:178-9 My 1 '65
Le sacre du printemps. See Rites of spring. above
Sleeping beauty
  Dance Mag il 40:20-1 Ja '66
Swan Lake
  Dance Mag 39:36-40+ O '65
La sylphide
  New Yorker 41:158 D 18 '65

BALLIETT, Whitney
Books (cont) New Yorker 41:174-7 My 22; 242+ N 13 '65
Jazz concerts. See issues of New Yorker
Jazz (cont) New Yorker 41:92-3 Mr 6; 174+ Mr 27; 156-8 Ap 3; 132-4 N 6 '65
Jazz records. See occasional issues of New Yorker

BALLINGER, Harry Russell
Cover. il Am Artist 29:4 Je '65

BALLOON racing
Fine but farcical British balloon race. P. Mandel. il Life 58:49-52+ Je 11 '65
Old-time balloon race. M. J. Pedersen. il Pop Mech 124:220N O '65

BALLOONS
Day the balloon came to town; excerpt from William Faulkner of Oxford. ed. by J. W. Webb and A. W. Green. M. Falkner. il Am Heritage 17:46-9 D '65

Use in research
Costly research balloons return to earth safely. Sci N L 88:245 O 16 '65
Fireflies to light the way in NASA effort to chart earth's biosphere. W. S. Beller. Miss & Roc 16:31 Mr 8 '65
Good look at NGC 4565. N. G. Roman. il Am Ed 1:5-8 O '65

BALLOONS—Use in research—*Continued*
Interplanetary balloons could hover over Venus. Sci N L 87:393 Je 19 '65
Pageos balloon satellite. R. N. Watts, jr. Sky & Tel 29:210-11 Ap '65
Shower micrometeorites collected by balloon. il Sky & Tel 30:276-7 N '65
  See also
  Balloons, Meteorological

BALLOONS, Meteorological
Balloons to spot weather. Sci N L 88:7 Jl 3 '65
NASA may aid in French program; Project Eole. W. S. Beller. il Miss & Roc 17:22-3 Jl 5 '65
Satellite balloon-watch; Project EOLE to measure air currents, pressures and temperatures. Sci N L 87:115 F 20 '65

BALLPARKS. See Stadiums

BALLS
Boom with a bounce: Super ball, Wham-O mfg. co's success. il Life 59:69-70+ D 3 '65
It's a bird, it's a plane: Super ball. il Time 86: 69-70 O 22 '65
Way the ball bounces: Super ball, success of Wham-O manufacturing co. il Newsweek 66:80 N 29 '65
  See also
  Golf balls
  Tennis balls

BALLS; drama. See Foster, P.

BALLVÉ, Julieta
Night walk; story. Americas 17:34-6 D '65

BALSLEY, Eugene D.
Count three and stick your foot in it; story. Sat Eve Post 238:64-5 F 13 '65

BALTIMORE
Wildflowers in an asphalt jungle: Cylburn project. il Recreation 58:112-14 Mr '65

Education
Mount Royal elementary; remodeling library. M. B. Wiese and A. Rusk. il Library J 90:5457-9 D 15 '65

Fire department
Mobile air supply cuts casualties. il Am City 80:42 O '65

Housing
Mies in Baltimore: slender frame of concrete. D. Canty. il Arch Forum 123:36-9 D '65

Music
Angels in Baltimore. G. M. Eby. Opera N 29:36 My 1 '65
  See also
  Baltimore civic opera company

Negroes
Child seller; with account by R. Stolley. il Life 59:109-10+ O 8 '65

Newspapers
Stubbornness in Baltimore. Time 85:55 My 21 '65
  See also
  Strikes—United States—Newspapers

Police
Blockbuster; Finan report findings. il Newsweek 67:31 Ja 24 '66

Social life and customs
Baltimore boy. R. Kotlowitz. Harper 231: 62-6+ D '65

Stores
Regional center has open axis mall: Reisterstown road plaza. il Arch Rec 137:204-5 My '65

BALTIMORE and Ohio railroad
Merger that takes a slow track; C&O-B&O. il Bsns W p66-8+ F 13 '65

BALTIMORE Bullets (basketball team) See Basketball teams

BALTIMORE civic opera company
Philadelphia, Hartford, Baltimore. G. Fitzgerald. il Opera N 30:29-30 D 4 '65
Twin capitals. J. Ardoin. Opera N 29:31 Ap 3 '65

BALTIMORE college of dental surgery
Old school, new style. il Time 85:78-9 Mr 19 '65

BALTIMORE Colts (football club) See Football clubs

BALTIMORE COUNTY, Md. public library
Area branches for Baltimore: Catonsville area and North Point area branches. C. W. Robinson. il Library J 90:5183-5 D 1 '65
Book catalog: diving in. C. W. Robinson. il Wilson Lib Bul 40:262-8 N '65

BALTIMORE newspaper strike. See Strikes— United States—Newspapers

BALTIMORE Orioles (baseball) See Baseball clubs

BALTIMORE sun
Eclipse of The Sun. New Repub 152:9 My 15 '65
Other side of the Sun; strike against Sunpapers. il Newsweek 65:82 My 3 '65
Stubbornness in Baltimore. Time 85:55 My 21 '65

BAMBERG, Germany
City's shame. il Newsweek 66:40 Jl 5 '65

BAMBOO
When bamboo goes traveling; how to prevent spreading growth. il Sunset 134:276-7 Ap '65

BANCROFT, Anne
Anne Bancroft: hey, ma, I can do that! R. Lemon. il pors Sat Eve Post 238:86-8+ N 20 '65

BAND instruments
  See also
  Drum

BAND wagons. See Circus equipment

BANDA, Hastings Kamuzu
Colored rulers. G. C. Turner. bibliog Negro Hist Bul 28:107-8 F '65
Frankness from Dr Banda. America 113:558 N 13 '65
Good-by, Mr Chips? il por Newsweek 65:40+ Ap 26 '65

BANDAGES and bandaging
What's new in bandages. il Good H 160:148 F '65

BANDARANAIKE, Sirimavo
Change in direction? Sr Schol 86:25 Ap 15 '65
Madame's exit. Time 85:29-30 Ap 2 '65
More like a thorn. il por Newsweek 65:44 Mr 29 '65

BANDER, Edward J.
Copyright controversy. Library J 90:3221-3 Ag '65

BANDITS. See Brigands and robbers

BANDS (music)
Jazz concerts; B. Tate and band in Museum of modern art series. W. Balliett. New Yorker 41:112-13 Ag 28 '65
Kansas City perspective; position in the jazz story. S. Dance. Sat R 48:36-7 Jl 31 '65
Letter from Port Of Spain; annual Steel band music festival. B. Taper. il New Yorker 41:203-4+ O 23 '65
Past, present and yet to come; G. Lombardo, ghost of New Year's. W. K. Zinsser. il Life 59:82+ D 17 '65
Senior scholastic interview; trail blazer for the modern jazz quartet; ed. by R. Hemming and G. Berg. J. Lewis. Sr Schol 86: 21-2 My 6 '65
Soul of Antigua; R. Sterling and his North star all steel drum band. F. E. Vasta. il Negro Hist Bul 28:131+ Mr '65
Stringing them along; banjo parlors. il Newsweek 66:85 Jl 26 '65
Trumpets fade; Ottumwa, Ia, municipal band. il Newsweek 66:66 S 6 '65

BANDS, Childrens
Grade schoolers strike up the rhythm band. il Todays Health 43:32-3+ S '65

BANDSAWS. See Saws

BANDWAGONS. See Circus equipment

BANERJEE, P. K.
Existence through co-existence; address, May 29, 1965. Vital Speeches 31:562-5 Jl 1 '65

BANFIELD, William G. and others
Mosquito transmission of a reticulum cell sarcoma of hamsters. bibliog Science 148: 1239-40 My 28 '65

BANGKOK
Souvenir from the klongs. M. Connelly. il Sat R 48:47-8 S 18 '65
Well traveled camera. H. Keppler. il Mod Phot 29:56+ F; 52 Mr '65

BANISTER, Judith
Fakes, forgeries, and duty dodgers in English silver; excerpts from Old English silver. Antiques 88:330-2 S '65

BANISTER, Manly
It sure beats raking! Pop Mech 124:170-3 S '65
Your radial saw can sharpen itself. Pop Mech 124:192-4 O '65

BANK architecture. See Bank buildings

BANK buildings
For a motor bank: a crisp elegance. il Arch Rec 138:-170-1 S '65
Modern Medici. il Time 86:44-7 Ag 13 '65
New offices for your friendly banker. il Fortune 72:171-2 Jl '65
Notable low budget building; First national bank of Memphis. il Arch Rec 137:149-56 F '65
Small banks; sampling of current work. il Arch Rec 137:191-200 Je '65

BANK consolidations and mergers
Antitrust chaos; Manufacturers and Hanover merger. H. Hazlitt. Newsweek 65:74 Mr 29 '65
Bank bill stalled; with editorial comment. Bsns W p26, 116 Ag 28 '65
Bank weighs appeal against breakup order; Justice dept. anti-trust suit against Manufacturers Hanover trust co. il Bsns W p35 Mr 20 '65
Congress listens to the bankers. D. Sanford. New Repub 153:16 S 11 '65
Court says no to banks. Bsns W p27 Mr 13 '65
Hanky-panky in the House; House banking and currency committee mutiny. J. Ridgeway. New Repub 153:8 O 30 '65
Money for mañana; updating of Spain's banking structure. Time 86:98 N 26 '65
Settling an account; Manufacturers Hanover union declared illegal. Time 85:95-6 Mr 19 '65
Taking antitrust heat off bank mergers; contest among three compromise bills. il Bsns W p 170+ O 9 '65
Unscrambling an egg? antitrust suit by Justice department against Manufacturers Hanover trust company. Newsweek 65:72 Mr 22 '65
Urge to unmerge. Time 86:74 Ag 27 '65
When Chairman Patman faced a revolt. U S News 59:16 N 1 '65
Who's to control bank mergers? U S News 59:80 Ag 23 '65
Working to untangle the bank merger mess; with editorial comment. il Bsns W p30-1, 150 My 29 '65
BANK employees
Earnings in banks. November-December 1964. J. C. Bush. il Mo Labor R 88:1331-4 N '65
BANK failures
Bank that should never have opened; Brighton national bank, Brighton, Colo. H. B. Meyers. il Fortune 72:126-7+ Jl '65
How two janitors bought white bank in Texas. L. Robinson. il Ebony 20:119-22+ Je '65
Senate investigates how to buy a bank. il Bsns W p24-5 Mr 13 '65
BANK for international settlements
Dollar moves win applause; International settlements bank. Bsns W p50 Je 19 '65
Warning to U.S. on easy credit. U S News 58:95 Je 28 '65
BANK for reconstruction and development, International. See International bank for reconstruction and development
BANK loans. See Loans, Bank
BANK of America national trust and savings association
Charge-it plan that really took off; BankAmericards. il Bsns W p58+ F 27 '65
BANK of China
Two-headed bank. il Time 86:115-16+ O 22 '65
BANK rates. See Interest
BANK robberies. See Robberies and assaults
BANKAMERICARDS. See Credit cards
BANKERS
See also
Negro bankers
BANKING and currency committee (House of representatives). See United States—Congress—House of representatives—Banking and currency committee
BANKING and currency committee (Senate). See United States—Congress—Senate—Banking and currency committee
BANKING law
Chase listing: catalyst for crisis? shares on New York stock exchange. Bsns W p 102+ F 6 '65
Necessary step for sound banking. Bsns W p 152 Jl 17 '65
Taking antitrust heat off bank mergers; contest among three compromise bills. il Bsns W p 170+ O 9 '65
Working to untangle the bank merger mess; with editorial comment. il Bsns W p30-1, 150 My 29 '65
See also
Banks and banking—Regulation
BANKLIGHTS, Photographic. See Electric lamps, Flashlight
BANKRUPTCY
Crackdown on bankruptcies? U S News 58:104 My 17 '65
New York bank blows whistle on Zeckendorf; action against Webb & Knapp in bankruptcy court. il Bsns W p30-1 My 15 '65
Rising tide of bankruptcies. U S News 58:89-90 F 8 '65
BANKS, Louis
Economy under new management. Fortune 71:96-9+ My '65

BANKS, Lynne Reid
Thirtieth birthday of Clara Hawkins; story. McCalls 92:118-19 Mr '65
BANKS, Coin
Old mechanical banks. F. H. Griffith. See issues of Hobbies
BANKS and banking
See also
Development banks
Discount
Government investigations—Banks and banking
Loans, Bank
Postal savings banks
Safe deposit boxes
Savings and loan associations

Bill payment service
Next in banking: pay bills by phone; Bank of Delaware Touch-tone card dial system. il Bsns W p82+ N 13 '65

Checking accounts
What's the best way to balance a checkbook? Bet Hom & Gard 43:114 O '65

Consolidations
See Bank consolidations and mergers

Drive-in and curb services
See Drive-in and curb services

Employees
See Bank employees

Foreign subsidiaries
Glamorous side; foreign branches operated by U.S. banks. il Time 85:99 Je 25 '65
Soviet banks abroad pile up profits; institutions in London and Paris. il Bsns W p72+ O 23 '65

Laws
See Banking law

Regulation
Too many regulators in banking? why thirteen banks failed. il Bsns W p28-9 Mr 27 '65

Safety devices and measures
Heisters increase their haul. C. Remsberg and B. Remsberg. il N Y Times Mag p61+ Ja 16 '66

Savings departments
Perpetual money machine? il Changing T 19:27-8 Jl '65
See also
Savings deposits

Securities
Chase listing: catalyst for crisis? shares on New York stock exchange. Bsns W p 102+ F 6 '65
Some stocks most people overlook. il Changing T 19:16 D '65
Why bank shares are lagging; investors fear profit squeeze. il Bsns W p68-9 D 25 '65

Wages and hours
Earnings in banks. November-December 1964. J. C. Bush. il Mo Labor R 88:1331-4 N '65

California
See also
Bank of America national trust and savings association

China
See also
Bank of China

China (People's Republic)
See also
Bank of China

Europe, Western
Banking American-style. Time 87:86 Ja 7 '66

France
See also
Paris—Banks

Great Britain
Bank methods of 100 years ago; unpublished letter; with introd. by C. Clemens. N. Biddle. Hobbies 70:104+ O 65

Russia
Soviet banks abroad pile up profits; institutions in London and Paris. il Bsns W p72+ O 23 '65

Spain
Money for mañana; updating of Spain's banking structure. Time 86:98 N 26 '65

BANKS and banking—*Continued*

Switzerland

Banking scandal. il Time 85:91-2 Je 11 '65
Europe's bank scandal: the meaning; Muñoz case. il U S News 58:108 Je 21 '65
Gnomes of Zurich; Union bank of Switzerland. il Time 85:91 Mr 12 '65
Secrets of the Swiss banks. T. R. Fehrenbach. Atlan 216:33-8 Jl '65

Thailand

Low interest, high principles: Bangkok bank. il Time 86:81 Ag 6 '65

United States

But 1965 may not be so lush. il Bsns W p98+ F 6 '65
How investment bankers see outlook for 1966. il U S News 59:94-7 D 13 '65
New York banks struggle to expand. il Bsns W p 122+ D 11 '65
Saxon charm draws Chase bank; Chase Manhattan to switch to national charter from state charter. il Bsns W p 121+ Jl 24 '65
Who's on first? disarray among the federal banking agencies. il Newsweek 65:68 F 15 '65
Your bank: how to choose it, how to use it. il Changing T 19:29-32 Ap '65
See also
American bankers association
Bank failures
Bank of America national trust and savings association
Banking law
Federal deposit insurance corporation
Government investigations—Banks and banking
Morgan guaranty trust company
Savings banks
Transamerica corporation
United States—Federal reserve board
also subhead Banks under names of cities, e.g. Denver—Banks

History

Bank methods of 100 years ago; unpublished letter; with introd. by C. Clemens. N. Biddle. Hobbies 70:104+ O '65

BANKS and banking, International
See also
International bank for reconstruction and development
BANKS and banking, State. See Banks and banking—United States
BANNER, William P.
Fps creativity. U S Camera 28:72-3+ Jl '65
BANNERS. See Flags
BANTAM books (firm)
Bantam's Churchill book another production feat. il Pub W 187:121+ Mr 1 '65
Trade winds; lightning publication of book on Sir Winston Churchill. J. G. Fuller. il Sat R 48:10 F 20 '65
BANTUS. See South Africa—Native races
BANUS, Mario D.
Pressure dependence of the alpha-beta transition temperature in silver selenide. bibliog Science 147:732-3 F 12 '65
BAOBAB trees
Nature note. Sci N L 88:62 Jl 24 '65
BAPTISM
After Luci Johnson was baptized; question of rebaptism. il U S News 59:16 Jl 19 '65
Another Catholic in the White House; open letter to Bishop Pike, regarding rebaptism of Luci Johnson. V. Eller. Christian Cent 82:1007-8 Ag 18 '65; Discussion. 82:1194-5, 1388-9 S 29, N 10 '65
Baptism of fire; controversy over L.B. Johnson's rebaptism. il Time 86:73 Jl 16 '65
Catholic priest stubs ecumenical toe; rebaptism of converts. Christian Cent 82: 932 Jl 28 '65
Do they or don't they? rebaptism of Roman Catholic converts. Christian Cent 82:909 Jl 21 '65
Rites and wrongs: L. Johnson rebaptism. il Newsweek 66:79 Jl 19 '65
BAPTIST world alliance
Baptist alliance meets in Miami. Christian Cent 82:885 Jl 14 '65; Correction. 82:1086 S 8 '65
Leader from Liberia; first Negro president. Time 86:50 Jl 9 '65
BAPTISTS
See also
Baptist world alliance
BAPTISTS in Cuba
Castro arrests Baptist churchmen; charges spying for U.S. Christian Cent 82:485 Ap 21 '65
Purging the Baptists. Time 85:40 Ap 16 '65
BAPTISTS in the United States
American Baptists in convention. E. T. Culver. Christian Cent 82:784+ Je 16 '65

Baptist coquetry; discussion of Consultation on church union merger plans. K. Haselden. Christian Cent 82:1437-8 N 24 '65; Discussion. 83:51-2 Ja 12 '66
Baptist image challenged; anti-intellectual stamp. America 113:426 O 16 '65
Baptists conscience; Texas Baptist standard's influence. Newsweek 66:65 O 25 '65
Baptists in a bind; question of accepting federal funds for Baptist-related colleges. Christian Cent 82:1502 D 8 '65
Blunting the cutting edge; resolution adopted by National Baptist convention, U.S.A, inc, Tulsa. Christian Cent 82:883-4 Jl 14 '65
Ferment at Furman; university owned by South Carolina Baptist convention. Newsweek 66:80 Ag 23 '65
In a spirit of repentance; admission of sin regarding racial issues. il Time 85:68 Je 11 '65
Lawsuit in a Richmond church; First Baptist again. S. Nichols. Christian Cent 83: 24 Ja 5 '66
New climate down South? Southern Baptist convention. Christian Cent 82:907 Jl 21 '65
New spirit in the S.B.C; world-consciousness among Southern Baptist leadership. Christian Cent 82:1309-10 O 27 '65; Discussion. 82:1581-2 D 22 '65
Put seminary eggs in fewer baskets; policy regarding Baptist seminaries. Christian Cent 82:1341 N 3 '65
Toward integration; Christian life commission. Time 86:68 N 26 '65
What will we say or do? Southern Baptist convention's annual meeting. il Newsweek 65:94 Je 14 '65
BAR HARBOR, Me.
Bar Harbor. J. McCarthy. il Holiday 38:46-53+ Jl '65
BARBASH, Jack
Architecture of union political action. Mo Labor R 88:653-5 Je '65
BARBE, Walter B.
Personalized reading. Library J 90:1978-80, 5442 Ap 15, D 15 '65
BARBECUE cookery
Argentine barbecue idea: you cook over coals, but slowly; with recipes. il Sunset 135:146-7+ S '65
Barbecued spareribs. il Pop Gard 16:50+ Mr '65
Big barbecue roundup: newest equipment. il McCalls 92:54+ Je '65
Blues on the coals; bluefish barbecue; with menu and recipes by E. Graves. il Life 59:70-1+ Jl 30 '65
Enjoy outdoor eating modern style; barbecued meats; with recipes. G. Maddox. il Todays Health 43:60-5 Je '65
Fall barbecue specials. il Bet Hom & Gard 43:99-100 S '65
It's barbecue time. R. Hanna. il Suc Farm 63:66-7+ Ag '65
Twenty-five barbecues from twenty-five years; our greatest recipes! M. Johnston. il Bet Hom & Gard 43:72-9+ Je '65
You can't barbecue without sauce. il Redbook 125:74-5 Jl '65
BARBECUE grills
Barbecue the safe way. il Good H 161:152 Jl '65
Gas-fired barbecue pit. E. Widdis. il Pop Mech 124:145 Ag '65
Letter from Stan Delaplane. S. Delaplane. il Todays Health 43:78 Ap '65
Now, cook with gas in the back yard. il Pop Sci 186:150-1 My '65
Sure-fire specials for outdoor chefs. il Good H 161:112-13+ Jl '65

Equipment

Care and safekeeping of barbecues. il House & Gard 127:174-5 Je '65
Gas-grill cooking. il House & Gard 127:167-9 Je '65
Hot-off-the-grill barbecue tips. B. G. Wadsworth. Parents Mag 40:130 Je '65
How to make a barbecue asador; Argentine-style. il Sunset 135:114+ S '65
BARBEE, Bobbie
Annual baseball roundup: 1965; the year of the pitchers. Ebony 20:152-8+ Je '65
BARBER, Lawrence
Regulations hassle, the Northwest. Yachting 117:177-9 F '65
BARBER, Samuel
On records; Vanessa. Opera N 29:34 Ap 3 '65
To weep and remember. J. W. Freeman. il por Opera N 29:24-6 Ap 3 '65
Vanessa. Criticism
New Yorker 41:174 Mr 20 '65
Opera N il 29:17-20 Ap 3 '65
Opera N il 29:24-6 Ap 3 '65
Sat R 48:22 Mr 27 '65

BARNETT, Lincoln
Voice heard round the world; excerpt from Conquest of silence. Am Heritage 16:50-9+ Ap '65
BARNETT, Richard
New Knick with a knack. W. Leggett. il pors Sports Illus 24:18-20+ Ja 17 '66
BARNETT, Ross
Integration at Ole Miss, by R. H. Barrett. Review
  Sat R 48:43 Ap 10 '65. E. M. Yoder, jr
BARNETT, Sarah L.
Making hospital rounds with the science lady. J. H. Pollack. il pors Todays Health 43:37-41 My '65
BARNETT, Vincent MacDowell, 1913-
College looks ahead; adaptation of address, October 15, 1964. Sch & Soc 93:219-20 Ap 3 '65
BARNETT Frummer accepts with pleasure; story. See Trillin, C.
BARNETT Frummer and Rosalie Mondle meet Superman: a love story; story. See Trillin, C.
BARNETTE, Aubrey
Black Muslims are a fraud; ed. by E. Linn. pors Sat Eve Post 238:23-9 F 27 '65
BARNS and stables
He built a '65 feed lot around a 1939 barn. P. B. Jones. il Suc Farm 63:48-9 S '65
New life for your old bank barn. I. Bigalow. il Farm J 89:70B Ap '65
New use for old horse barn. R. J. Reiman. il Suc Farm 63:50 O '65
Summer and winter, his feeder cattle eat inside. P. B. Jones. il Suc Farm 63:50-1 My '65

Equipment

Beef confinement, what's happening. W. J. Fletcher and D. Malena. il Suc Farm 63:46-7 Jl '65
New dairy setup with winter comfort. J. R. Borcherding. il Suc Farm 63:58-9 Mr '65
Use free stalls of right size. il Suc Farm 63:70A My '65

Floors

Cows clean these barns; mats, slats new stall designs. il Farm J 89:64D-64E F '65
Cows won't slip on these floors. R. J. Wyndham. Farm J 89:54H Ap '65

Heating and ventilation

Cold weather ideas for livestock. P. B. Jones and J. Harvey. il Suc Farm 63:42-3 N '65
Three ways to cool cows. il Farm J 89:34C Jl '65
BARNSLEY, Alan Gabriel
Splendid old. Harper 230:104-6 F '65
BARNSTONE, Gertrude
Lady stirs her city's conscience. G. Zimmermann. il pors Look 29:66+ S 21 '65
BARNSTONE, Willis
Lapland; poem. New Yorker 41:199 O 2 '65
BARNUM and Bailey circus. See Circus
BARO, Gene
In a northern wood; poem. New Yorker 41:180 N 27 '65
Street; poem. New Yorker 41:130 Je 5 '65
Tide running out; poem. New Yorker 41:83 Ja 15 '66
Waking to sleep; poem. New Yorker 41:191 O 30 '65
BAROLINI, Antonio
Outing at Sant' Erasmo; story. Reporter 33:39-42 Ag 12 '65
BARON, Bea
Tyger, tyger. Mlle 61:200+ Ag '65
BARON, Samuel
Ordeal of a Hoffa victim. B. Davidson. il pors Sat Eve Post 238:23-7 Je 19 '65
BARON, Seymour H. See Schoenfeld, W. N. jt. auth.
BAROODY, William J.
Erosion of rational debate; address, June 10, 1965. Vital Speeches 31:720-4 S 15 '65
BAROQUE art. See Art, Baroque
BARR, Joseph W.
Role of the dollar; address, September 21, 1965. Vital Speeches 32:18-21 O 15 '65
BARR, June
Buried treasure; drama. Plays 24:77-80, 95 Mr '65
BARR, Neal
Augusta: where old masters are on display; photographs. Sports Illus 22:34-9 Ap 5 '65
BARR, S. and Jankus, E. V.
Micrometeorology. Science 148:108+ Ap 2 '65
BARR, Stephen
Letters patent; story. Mlle 60:110-11 F '65
BARRACLOUGH, Solon
No plumbing for Negroes. Atlan 216:105-9 S '65

BARRAGÁN, Luis
The new Mexico. M. Simons. il pors Look 30:54-7 Ja 25 '66
BARRAT, Robert
New priests. Commonweal 82:49-51 Ap 2 '65
Schism in France? Commonweal 82:651-2 S 17 '65
BARRATT, P. E. H. See Beh, H. C. jt. auth.
BARRAULT, Jean Louis
Touch of magic; interview, ed. by P. J. Smith. por Opera N 30:8-9 S 25 '65
L'Amérique; dramatization of Amerika by F. Kafka. Criticism
  New Yorker 41:146+ Ap 3 '65
BARRE publishing company, incorporated
Barre duplicates Mayan prints, dating to 1842. il Pub W 189:94+ Ja 3 '66
BARREIROS RODRIGUEZ, Eduardo
Spain's man with the golden touch. il por Bsns W p 153-4+ N 13 '65
BARRELS
Over the barrel; shortage in Scotland. Time 85:92 Mr 12 '65
BARRENECHEA, Mauro
Training Latin America's leaders. America 112:447 Ap 3 '65
BARRETT, B. L.
Passion of Daisy Hall; story. Sat Eve Post 238:66-8 N 6 '65
BARRETT, George
Detective. J. Mills. il pors Life 59:90D-101+ D 3 '65
Good cop and crime prevention. Life 60:4 Ja 7 '66
BARRETT, Marvin
Akond of swock. Reporter 33:50+ Ag 12 '65
At the movies: Southern way of death. Reporter 33:40-2 N 18 '65
Cart before the horse. Reporter 33:43-4+ D 30 '65
BARRETT, Peter
Family safari. Field & S 70:36-9+ Ag '65
BARRETT, William
Reader's choice. See issues of Atlantic
BARRIENTOS ORTUÑO, René
Bulletproof general. Newsweek 65:53 Ap 5 '65
Flying high. por Time 86:31 Jl 2 '65
On to elections. il por Time 87:36 Ja 14 '66
Steve Canyon of the Andes. il por Time 85:36 Ap 2 '65
BARRIGER, John Walker
Katy puts an old hand in the cab. il pors Bsns W p 192+ O 9 '65
BARRIO, Raymond
Art of distortion. Design 67:14-17 N '65
Paint a mosaic. Design 67:10-13 S '65
Painting impressions. il Design 66:6-10 My '65
BARRON, John
Case of Bobby Baker and the courageous senator. Read Digest 87:112-18 S '65
FBI's secret war against the Ku Klux klan. Read Digest 88:87-92 Ja '66
BARRON, Paul
Tactiles. Design 67:24-6 S '65
BARRS, H. D.
Psychrometric measurement of leaf water potential: lack of error attributable to leaf permeability. bibliog Science 149:63-5 Jl 2 '65
BARRY, D. G.
Art in science. Science 150:1486-7 D 10 '65
BARRY, David
Kids aid Kennedy fund. por Pop Phot 56:22+ F '65
BARRY, Gerald J.
Wine list for patriots. Esquire 64:238-9+ D '65
BARRY, John
Aboard the bandwagon. il por Time 87:62+ Ja 14 '66
BARRY, Lawrence E.
Indian in a cultural trap. America 112:482-4 Ap 10 '65
BARRY, Les
ISFTPOBAWP. Pop Phot 57:57+ Jl '65
On the go. See issues of Popular photography
Travel. Pop Phot 57:44+ S; 28+ O; 10+ D '65; 58:24+ Ja '66
BARRY, Naomi
Holiday handbook: Mediterranean pleasure-spots. Holiday 39:93-8 Ja '66
Wild mushrooms, whortleberries, and thou. Sat R 48:60+ Mr 13 '65
BARRY, Rick
Rick, Rick, hooray! H. L. Masin. il por Sr Schol 86:26 F 4 '65
BARS and barrooms
Moriarty's wonderful saloon: speakeasy operating as gentleman's club. L. Beebe. il Am Heritage 16:65-9+ Ag '65
Night butterflies; Japanese hostesses. B. Krisher. il Newsweek 66:45-6 S 13 '65

BARS and barrooms—*Continued*
P.J.s: bars and other businesses with these initials on Third avenue between Forty-second and Eighty-sixth streets. New Yorker 41:35-6 Mr 13 '65
Portable bars. il House & Gard 128:22+ Ag '65
Potted pounds. Newsweek 66:57 Ag 2 '65
Protocol at the Spotted cow; English pub. J. A. M. Graham. Esquire 63:110-11 My '65

BARSKI, Georges, and Jung, K. Y.
Immunization against Rauscher mouse leukemia with tissue culture material. bibliog Science 149:751-2 Ag 13 '65

BART, Lily, pseud.
Some reflections on the rich. Mlle 62:130+ D '65

BART, Peter
California sound. Atlan 215:140+ My '65
Image polished. Esquire 64:80-1+ Jl '65
Los Angeles: no end in sight. Sat R 48:39-40 My 22 '65
Los Angeles: second-hand water. Sat R 48:41-2 O 23 '65
New look at the Times. Sat R 48:68+ Je 12 '65

BARTELME, Elizabeth
Let it be printed. Commonweal 81:701-3 F 26 '65

BARTENDERS

Anecdotes, facetiae, satire, etc.
Upstaging the British. C. W. Morton. il Atlan 216:128 S '65

BARTER
Big men and disks of shell; exchange of kesa in transactions. H. W. Scheffler. il Natur Hist 74:20-5 D '65
How to buy without money; secret is swapping. F. Maynard. il Good H 160:146+ Mr '65
So who needs money? il Time 86:68 D 31 '65
Trade! trade! who'll hoss trade? swapfest of sports equipment; Jefferson County, Ky. J. McLain. il Recreation 58:187-8 Ap '65
U.S.-Soviet Kula. M. Orans. Bul Atomic Sci 21:44-5 Mr '65

BARTH, Robert H. Jr
Insect mating behavior: endocrine control of a chemical communication system. bibliog Science 149:882-3 Ag 20 '65

BARTHEL, Joan
What a TV producer produces. N Y Times Mag p38-9+ N 21 '65

BARTHÉLÉMY, Nicolau
Reporter at large. J. Bernstein. il New Yorker 41:115-16+ Mr 20 '65

BARTHELME, Donald
Edward and Pia; story. New Yorker 41:46-9 S 25 '65
Game; story. New Yorker 41:29-30 Jl 31 '65
Indian uprising; story. New Yorker 41:34-7 Mr 6 '65
Snap snap. New Yorker 41:108+ Ag 28 '65

BARTHES, Roland
Writers on vacation. Nation 201:474 D 13 '65

BARTHOLOMEW, Paul C.
Warren court by the Warren court. Nat R 17:143-5 F 23 '65

BARTLETT, Laurence W. Jr
All save one. Flying 77:72+ Jl '65

BARTLETT, Lynn M.
New era in Michigan education. por Sr Schol 86:sup 10-11 Mr 25 '65

BARTLETT, Neil R. and White, C. T.
Evoked potentials and correlated judgments of brightness as functions of interflash intervals. bibliog Science 148:980-1 My 14 '65

BARTLETT, P. D. and others
Robert Burns Woodward, Nobel prize in chemistry for 1965. Science 150:585-7 O 29 '65

BARTLEY, Diana
Herr Uhlenhaut: the great lap forward. Esquire 63:96-9+ F '65
Oh dad, poor dad, junior's doubled our car payments and I'm feelin' so sad. Esquire 64:75+ Jl '65
Two for the money, one for the show. Esquire 64:90-3 O '65

BARTLEY, Marge
This old gal went back to college. por Library J 90:5351-3 D 15 '65

BARTLING, Julia
Reference books of 1964. por Library J 90:1809-17 Ap 15 '65

BARTO, Elizabeth. See Shaw, C. R. jt. auth.

BARTÓK, Béla
Bartók and Bloch: isolated in our time. Discus. Harper 230:120 Je '65
Feast of piano music by Bartók. R. Jones. il Am Rec G 32:22-5+ S '65

From Antal Dorati via Mercury, the best Miraculous mandarin yet. J. Diether. Am Rec G 31:978+ Je '65
Juilliard string quartet: Bartók string Quartets nos. 1-6. C. J. Luten. il Am Rec G 31:772-4 My '65
Shadow of genius. R. Ellsworth. il pors Am Rec G 32:26-33 S '65
Touch like a paving stone. F. V. Grunfeld. il Reporter 33:38-41 Jl 15 '65

BARTON, Bruce
Man nobody knows; condensation. Read Digest 86:215-18+ Mr; 247-50+ Je '65

BARTON, Francis L.
Daysailing in Maine. il Motor B 116:101+ Jl '65

BARUCH, Bernard Mannes
Bernard Baruch, 1870-1965. il pors Life 59:56B-56C Jl 2 '65
Bernard M. Baruch, RIP. Nat R 17:582 Jl 13 '65
Empty bench. il por Newsweek 66:27 Jl 5 '65
Man behind the legend por Time 86:18-19 Jl 2 '65
Two great men. America 113:38 Jl 10 '65

BARUCHELLO, Gianfranco
Topography from Lilliput. il por Time 87:74 Ja 21 '66

BARWICH, Heinz
Defector's odyssey; personal look at Soviet-bloc science provided by high-ranking German physicist. D. S. Greenberg. Science 149:40-2 Jl 2 '65

BARY, Shura
Renting boats abroad. Travel 123:44-7 My '65

BARYTON. See Baritone (musical instrument)

BARZEL, Ann
Films for remembrance. por Dance Mag 39:22-6 S '65

BARZINI, Luigi
Great and lonely man. Reporter 32:29-31 Je 3 '65
Growing up Italian. Nation 200:482-3 My 3 '65
Italy's solid bricks make a fragile wall. Life 59:13+ O 1 '65
Mastroianni the man, the actor, the reluctant lover. Vogue 146:96-9+ O 15 '65
Slim, jaunty, with deep, velvety eyes. por Life 59:81-2 O 22 '65

about
Second fame: good food. N. Lyon. por Vogue 146:150-2 O 15 '65

BARZUN, Jacques
Man in the American mask. For Affairs 43:426-35 Ap '65

BASALT
Potassium, rubidium, strontium, thorium, uranium, and ratio of strontium-87 to strontium-86 in oceanic tholeiitic basalt. M. Tatsumoto and others. bibliog il Science 150:886-8 N 12 '65

BASALYGA, Annette
Saint Kevin and the blackbird; poem. Commonweal 83:24 O 8 '65

BASCHET, François
Mephisto's musings. il Hi Fi 15:161 D '65
Sound shaper. il pors Newsweek 66:112-13 O 18 '65

BASCOM, David F.
Wretched mess of type, mostly about fishing. R. Cantwell. il por Sports Illus 23:71-4 D 20 '65

BASEBALL
Baseball 1965: immutable but changing. W. Leggett. il Sports Illus 22:42-4 Ap 19 '65
Business of baseball. il Newsweek 65:66-70 Ap 26 '65
Hustler's handbook; excerpts. W. L. Veeck and E. Linn. il Sports Illus 22:87-9+ My 17; 40-2+ My 24; 50-2+ My 31; 32-4+ Je 7; 48-50+ Je 14 '65
In-Sain view of the Twins: Minnesota pitching starr; interviews, ed. by H. L. Masin. J. Sain. il Sr Schol 87:50 S 30 '65
Last angry old man; C. Stengel of New York Mets. E. Linn. il Sat Eve Post 238:75-8 Jl 31 '65
Perfect loser. Newsweek 65:52 Je 28 '65
Redbirds on the grapefruit. il Time 85:58 Mr 19 '65
Red-hot baseball in the Valley of the Sun; Sun Devils of Arizona state. J. Mann. Sports Illus 22:66-8+ My 24 '65
Sandy makes a pitch for posterity; compares with Feller and Diz. J. Jares. il Sports Illus 23:10-13 Ag 2 '65
Silly season. il Newsweek 66:64-5 Jl 12 '65
Sort of postscript: apology on forgetting name. B. L. Standish of Frank Merriwell fame. J. K. Hutchens. Sat R 48:23 Ag 21 '65
Steal producer; M. Wills. il Newsweek 66:48-9 Jl 19 '65

BASEBALL—*Continued*

Strikes and strokes. il Newsweek 66:68-9 Ag 23 '65

Town where the Mets are champs; Auburn Mets farm club for National league. J. Izenberg. il Sat Eve Post 238:34+ Ap 24 '65

Very minor leagues. il Newsweek 66:53-4 Ag 30 '65

Wait till next year. Time 85:83 Ap 23 '65

Willie the virtuoso hurtles on to the finish; W. May's success. il Life 59:26-33 O 1 '65

See also

Radio broadcasting—Sports

World series (baseball)

Accidents and injuries

Ben Casey at the ball park; R. Kerlan of Los Angeles Dodgers. J. Murphy. il N Y Times Mag p 18-19+ Ag 22 '65

Black cats are stalking the Redbirds. J. Mann. il Sports Illus 23:54-6 Jl 5 '65

Deadly slide for the Dodgers; T. Davis broke his ankle. Dodgers pennant dream shattered. J. Mann. il Sports Illus 22:30-1 My 10 '65

Wounded but winning; Minnesota Twins. il Time 86:50 Ag 13 '65

Bibliography

Books on first base. J. K. Hutchens. Sat R 48:38 Ap 17 '65

Organization and administration

General who? Lt. Gen. W. D. Eckert appointed commissioner. Newsweek 66:62 N 29 '65

Slow search for another Frick; baseball's owners search for new commissioner. J. Mann. il Sports Illus 23:18-19 Ag 2 '65

Uninvited guest spills baseball's beans; major league owners search for new commissioner. W. Furlong. il Sports Illus 23: 62-4 N 1 '65

Unknown soldier; new baseball commissioner. Time 86:86 N 26 '65

Quotations, maxims, etc.

Game time; comp. by E. F. Murphy. il N Y Times Mag p 101 My 16 '65

Statistics

Quick look back at a most peculiar season. M. Mulvoy. il Sports Illus 23:72-3 O 11 '65

Some significant baseball statistics. Sports Illus 22:70+ Ap 19 '65

Tickets

Customer problem: the world series; fans of Minnesota Twins demand for tickets. Bsns W p70 O 2 65

Japan

Take me out to the old *yakyu*. L. Shecter. il Sat Eve Post 237:82+ F 13 '65

BASEBALL, Commissioner of. See Baseball— Organization and administration

BASEBALL accidents. See Baseball—Accidents and injuries

BASEBALL clubs

Angel who doesn't fear to tread. M. Cope. il Sat Eve Post 238:95-9 Ap 10 '65

Annual baseball roundup; 1965; the year of the pitchers. B. Barbee. il Ebony 20:152-8+ Je '65

Another gone with the wind; Milwaukee franchise to Atlanta in 1966; excerpt from Hustler's handbook. B. Veeck and E. Linn. il Sports Illus 22:32-4+ Je 7 '65

Atlanta you can have the rest, leave us Eddie Mattress, our hero. W. Leggett. il Sports Illus 22:24-5+ Ap 26 '65

Baltimore Orioles: birds on the road. G. Astor. il Look 29:85-8+ My 18 '65

Baseball's week. See issues of Sports illustrated

Beachy and Wesley and LBJ; unsung Dodgers in National league pennant race. W. Leggett. il Sports Illus 23:30-1 O 11 '65

Better mouse beats a path; base stealer M. Wills of Los Angeles Dodgers. J. Murphy. il Sat Eve Post 238:72-3 O 9 '65

Black cats are stalking the Redbirds. J. Mann. il Sports Illus 23:54-6 Jl 5 '65

Bo and Dr Strangeglove; Phillies. il Newsweek 65:56 Ap 5 '65

Boom go the big Red bats; Cincinnati Redlegs. J. Brosnan. il Sports Illus 23:12-13+ Ag 16 '65

Boss of the Yankees; new manager J. Keane. il Newsweek 65:60 Mr 29 '65

Brand-new trend in Twins; Minnesota Twins fighting White Sox for league lead. W. Leggett. il Sports Illus 22:30-2+ My 17 '65

Busch, beer and baseball; St Louis Cardinals. A. A. Busch, jr. il N Y Times Mag p32-3+ Ap 11 '65

Business of baseball. il Newsweek 65:66-70 Ap 26 '65

CBS, Yankees score in capital. Bsns W p42 F 27 '65

Champions on the loose; Minnesota Twins and Dodgers. il Time 86:56 O 8 '65

Conversation with Gussie Busch, ed. by W. Leggett. A. A. Busch, jr. il Sports Illus 22:50-1 Ap 19 '65

Decline and fall of a dynasty; New York Yankees; with editorial comment. J. Mann. il Sports Illus 22:4, 20-5 Je 21 '65

Deron who? Cincinnati Reds. il Newsweek 66:58+ S 13 '65

Desperate hours; National league pennant race. il Sports Illus 23:24-5 O 4 '65

Destiny's whipping boys; Washington Senators. J. Mann. il Sports Illus 22:68-70+ Ap 5 '65

Different kind of season; White Sox vs Yankees. W. Leggett. il Sports Illus 22:26-8+ Je 7 '65

Don't call me coach; L. Durocher to run Chicago Cubs. il Newsweek 66:65 N 8 '65

Down to the wire and than Sandy Koufax settled it all; Meanwhile, a Twin killing. J. Lake. il Newsweek 66:68-70 O 11 65

Everybody pick up a drum; Minnesota Twins lead in American league. W. Leggett. il Sports Illus 23:16-19+ Ag 23 '65

Five way fight for a pennant; American league pennant race. J. Mann. il Sports Illus 23:12-15 Jl 19 '65

Garter on the Sox. il Time 85:56 My 28 '65

Genius & the kid; San Francisco Giants. il Time 86:83 S 24 '65

Gentlemen, the Dodgers. Time 86:53 Jl 2 '65

Great wall of Boston; Fenway park's left-field fence. J. Mann. il Sports Illus 22:42-8+ Je 28 '65

In-Sain view of the Twins; Minnesota pitching staff; interviews, ed. by H. L. Masin. J. Sain. il Sr Schol 87:50 S 30 '65

Long Island's own; the Met set. W. J. McKean. il Look 29:M5-M7 S 7 '65

McCarver of the Cardinals; masked menace. T. Cohane. il Look 29:99-100+ Je 15 '65

Man and a mule in Missouri; baseball needs showmanship. E. Shrake. il Sports Illus 23: 36-8+ Jl 19 '65

Mayor surrenders Atlanta; Braves and NFL franchise in Atlanta. J. Minter. il Sports Illus 23:14-17 Jl 12 '65

Meanwhile, consider poor Milwaukee. J. Mann. Sports Illus 23:18-19 S 6 '65

Mecca lunch kid; White Sox third-baseman. M. Cope. il Sat Eve Post 238:70+ Ag 14 '65

Metamorphosis in Minnesota; St Paul-Minneapolis Twins. il Time 86:74 Jl 23 '65

Mickey Mantle: Oklahoma to Olympus; New York Yankees. G. Astor. il Look 29:70-5 F 23 '65

Mouse who builds the mountains; Dodger's M. Wills, holder of stolen-base record. W. Leggett. il Sports Illus 23:38-42 Jl 12 '65

New comic act in New York; austere Yankees now dedicated to fun. J. Mann. il Sports Illus 22:30-2+ My 3 '65

Nice to have Met you. Time 85:68 Je 25 '65

Octopus under the big eye; CBS purchase of New Yankees; excerpt from Hustler's handbook. W. L. Veeck and E. Linn. il Sports Illus 22:40-2+ My 24 '65

Old-fashioned National league tangle; close pennant race. W. Leggett. Sports Illus 23:15 Ag 30 '65

Pitcher a forty-four; Mets' Spahn. Newsweek 65:72 My 10 '65

Pitcher goes to bat against the catcher; Marichal-Roseboro fight. il Life 59:34-5 S 3 '65

Players pick the Reds. il Sports Illus 23:37 S 13 '65

Please, please, Ed Spiezio, won't you please pop up? St Louis Cardinals rookie third baseman. T. C. Brody. il Sports Illus 22:80-1 Ap 12 '65

Quick look back at a most peculiar season. M. Mulvoy. il Sports Illus 23:72-3 O 11 '65

Rampaging Twins want the series, too. W. Leggett. il Sports Illus 23:26-8 O 4 '65

Regroup! retrench! dig in! Giants slim lead in pennant race. il Time 86:92 O 1 '65

Rise and fall of the fabulous Phillies; photographs by W. Iooss, jr; with account by W. Leggett. il Sports Illus 22:52-63 Mr 1 '65

Scouting reports (cont) il Sports Illus 22: 52-60+ Ap 19 '65

September song: strain; National league's six contenders in pennant race. il Sports Illus 23:14-17 S 6 '65

Sporting scene; world series. Dodgers vs. Twins. R. Angell. il New Yorker 41:192+ O 30 '65

BASEBALL clubs—*Continued*

Sultan of swat from Sparrows Point; R. Swoboda hero of New York Met fans. W. Leggett. il Sports Illus 22:70+ Je 14 '65

Team that made leaving Milwaukee famous. Time 86:69 Ag 27 '65

They can't even give it away; National league pennant race. Time 86:91 S 10 '65

They love Herman and Willie; Giants in National league race. J. Mann. il Sports Illus 23:24-6+ S 27 '65

They'd rather pitch than hit; Los Angeles Dodgers. W. Leggett. il Sports Illus 22: 30-2+ Mr 29 '65

Tony Oliva: Twins' lonely star. T. Cohane. il Look 29:83+ Je 1 '65

Valiant Yankee-chaser; A. Lopez, manager of Chicago White Sox. G. Rogin. il Sports Illus 22:36-8+ Mr 22 '65

We were eyeball to eyeball with victory; why Washington Senators were removed to Minnesota and renamed Minnesota Twins. R. Baker. Sports Illus 23:40-1 O 11 '65

Week to remember; Cardinals National league champions; photographs. M. E. Newman. Sports Illus 22:44-9 Ap 19 '65

Weirdest race rolls on; National league pennant race. W. Leggett. Sports Illus 23:36-7 S 13 '65

Word for Johnny Keane is: patience. E. Asinof. il N Y Times Mag p24-8 My 30 '65

Wounded but winning; Minnesota Twins. il Time 86:50 Ag 13 '65

Yankees that look like mud hens. il Time 85:81 My 14 '65

Year the Yankees; behind league-leading White Sox. il Newsweek 65:57-8 My 31 '65

Anecdotes, facetiae, satire, etc.

Making of a pastime; 1971. F. P. Tullius. New Yorker 41:212-14 O 16 '65

BASEBALL coaches. *See* Physical directors

BASEBALL fans

Atlanta you can have the rest, leave us Eddie Mattress, our hero. W. Leggett. il Sports Illus 22:24-5+ Ap 26 '65

BASEBALL managers

Wait till this year; Mauch of the calamity Phils. J. R. McDermott. il Life 58:75-6+ Mr 26 '65

See also
Franks, H.
Keane, J.
Mele, S.
Stengel, C.

BASEBALL players

Annual baseball roundup; 1965; the year of the pitchers. B. Barbee. il Ebony 20:152-8+ Je '65

Bat day; fight during Giant-Dodger game at Candlestick park, San Francisco. il Newsweek 66:44 S 6 '65

Battle of San Francisco; bloodiest brawl in baseball history between Dodgers and Giants. J. Mann. il Sports Illus 23:12-15 Ag 30 '65

Beachy and Wesley and LBJ; unsung Dodgers in National league pennant race. W. Leggett. il Sports Illus 23:30-1 O 11 '65

Ben Casey at the ball park; R. Kerlan of Los Angeles Dodgers. J. Murphy. il N Y Times Mag p 18-19+ Ag 22 '65

Boom go the big Red bats; Cincinnati Redlegs. J. Brosnan. il Sports Illus 23:12-13+ Ag 16 '65

Brothers three of baseball. il Ebony 20:73-4+ S '65

Decline and fall of a dynasty; New York Yankees; with editorial comment. J. Mann. il Sports Illus 22:4, 20-5 Je 21 '65

Destiny's whipping boys: Washington Senators. J. Mann. il Sports Illus 22:68-70+ Ap 5 '65

Different kind of season; White Sox vs Yankees. W. Leggett. il Sports Illus 22: 26-8+ Je 7 '65

Five way fight for a pennant; American league pennant race. J. Mann. il Sports Illus 23:12-15 Jl 19 '65

Genius & the kid; San Francisco Giants. il Time 86:83 S 24 '65

Hustler's handbook; excerpts. W. L. Veeck and E. Linn. il Sports Illus 22:87-9+ My 17; 40-2+ My 24; 50-2+ My 31; 32-4+ Je 7; 48-50+ Je 14 '65

Latins storm *las grandes ligas.* R. H. Boyle. il Sports Illus 23:24-6+ Ag 9 '65

Look! it's the monster; D. Radatz relief pitcher for Boston Red Sox. J. Jares. Sports Illus 22:101-5 Ap 19 '65

Mean man named Mauch sounds off; Philadelphia Phillie manager G. Mauch. J. Mann. Sports Illus 23:45-7 Jl 26 '65

New comic act in New York; austere Yankees now dedicated to fun. J. Mann. il Sports Illus 22:30-2+ My 3 '65

Pitcher goes to bat against the catcher; Marichal-Roseboro fight. il Life 59:34-5 S 3 '65

Rookie cookies, 1965. H. L. Masin. il Sr Schol 86:24 Mr 25 '65

Scouting reports (cont) il Sports Illus 22: 52-60+ Ap 19 '65

Sporting scene; world series. R. Angell. il New Yorker 41:192+ O 30 '65

They'd rather pitch than hit; Los Angeles Dodgers. W. Leggett. il Sports Illus 22:30-2+ Mr 29 '65

Time for tension; brawl during Giant-Dodger game. il Time 86:64 S 3 '65

Time of the third basemen. H. L. Masin. Sr Schol 86:30 Ap 29 '65

When your eye is off the pitcher; photographs. Sports Illus 22:48-53 My 10 '65

Year of the rookie. pors Time 85:68 Je 4 '65

You can take the boy out of the country; D. Chance. M. Kram. il Sports Illus 22:36-8+ Mr 8 '65

See also names of baseball players, e.g. S. Koufax

Recruiting

Cold draft; first free agent draft. Time 85:68-9 Je 18 '65

BASEBALL players, High school

Fight, teen, fight! H. L. Masin. il Sr Schol 86:30 Ap 8 '65

BASEBALL scoreboards. *See* Scoreboards

BASEBALL stadiums. *See* Stadiums

BASEBALL teams. *See* Baseball clubs

BASEBALL umpires. *See* Umpires (sports)

BASEBALLS

Something on the ball; charges of frozen baseballs leveled against the White Sox. Newsweek 66:53 Ag 16 '65

BASEMENT insulation. *See* Insulation (heat)

BASEMENTS and cellars

Basements can be family rooms. J. LemMon. il Suc Farm 63:52-5 Jl '65

Is your basement dreary or cheery? il Farm J 90:92-3 Ja '66

Step by step to a finished basement. R. H. Kruse. il Bet Hom & Gard 43:68-9+ N '65

Your own big show in the basement. il Bet Hom & Gard 43:72-3 Ap '65

See also
Dampness in buildings

BASES (chemistry)

Acids and bases. R. G. Pearson. bibliog il Science 151:172-7 Ja 14 '66

Soft and hard acids and bases. Sci Am 213: 46 Ag '65

BASES, Guided missile. *See* Guided missile bases

BASES, Military. *See* Military bases

BASHKIN, Stanley

New method for studying the atom. bibliog Science 148:1047-53 My 21 '65

BASIC research. *See* Research

BASIDIOMYCETES

Spore discharge in basidiomycetes; a unified theory. D. B. O. Savile; reply with rejoinder. L. S. Olive. Science 148:533 Ap 23 '65

BASIE, Count

Kansas City perspective. S. Dance. por Sat R 48:36-7 Jl 31 '65

BASIE, William. *See* Basie, C.

BASIN HARBOR, Vt. *See* Ferrisburg, Vt.

BASKET making

Indian & Eskimo basketry exhibit in Chicago. C. Miles. Hobbies 70:114 N '65

BASKETBALL

Aces are high in Evansville; Purple Aces, best small-college basketball team. F. Deford. il Sports Illus 22:24-7 F 15 '65

Agony of Lefty Driesell. J. Jares. il Sports Illus 22:32-5 Mr 8 '65

Basketball's week. M. Hyman. See issues of Sports illustrated published during basketball season

Big little five; Evansville college. il Newsweek 65:54+ Mr 8 '65

Can anyone beat the Bruins? UCLA. H. L. Masin. il Sr Schol 87:26-7 D 2 '65

College basketball 1966; top twenty teams in order of rank. il Sports Illus 23:48+ D 6 '65

Dispirit of '76. il Time 85:82 Ap 23 '65

Doctor of ferocity; St Joseph's college of Philadelphia. il Time 86:37 D 24 '65

Five immovable objects stood fast; New Mexico's Lobos vs Brigham Young and Utah. F. Deford. il Sports Illus 22:52+ F 22 '65

Harder they fall; college basketball il Time 87:76 Ja 7 '66

Hawk is a mighty hunter; St Joseph's vs Temple. F. Deford. il Sports Illus 24:20-3 Ja 10 '66

BASKETBALL—*Continued*
Hex wrecks 'em in Peoria; Bradley university's basketball team champion of Missouri Valley conference. J. Jares. il Sports Illus 24:14-15 Ja 17 '66
Hot Brubabes; UCLA freshman team defeats UCLA varsity. J. Jares. il Sports Illus 23:46-7 D 6 '65
How the West won; battle for the N.C.A.A. championship. il Time 85:44 Mr 26 '65
Lost weekend in Carolina; UCLA loses to Duke. F. Deford. il Sports Illus 23:30-2 D 20 '65
My life in a bush league; ed. by B. Ottum. W. Chamberlain. il Sports Illus 22:32-4+ Ap 12; 38-41+ Ap 19 '65
Oh baby; U.C.L.A. team. il Time 86:91 D 10 '65
Power of the press; UCLA zone press and the Bruins victories. F. Deford. il Sports Illus 22:20-5 Mr 29 '65
Press that panics them all; UCLA's swarming defensive style. M. Hyman. il Sports Illus 23:77-80+ D 6 '65
Providence provides. il Time 85:80 F 19 '65
Real Miami stands up; Miami of Ohio. F. Deford. il Sports Illus 22:50+ F 1 '65
Shooting is the least important part of basketball; UCLA team. J. Wooden. il Look 30:66+ Ja 25 '66
Twelve flew out of the pressure cooker; college basketball coaches. J. Underwood. il Sports Illus 22:70-1 Mr 22 '65

Intermissions
Show for center court; half-time colorful performances by talented coeds. il Sports Illus 22:44-9 F 22 '65

Refereeing
See Sports officiating

Rules
Amendment for the fifth; player banished from game for fifth personal foul. Sports Illus 22:11 F 15 '65
Flaw in basketball. Sports Illus 22:11 Mr 29 '65

BASKETBALL coaches. See Physical directors
BASKETBALL fans
They all boo When Red sits down; A. Auerbach, coach of Boston Celtics. G. Rogin. il Sports Illus 22:100-2+ Ap 5 '65
BASKETBALL players
Basketball all America. il Look 29:87-91 Mr 23 '65
Celtics isn't dead yet. J. Jares. il Sports Illus 23:32-5 N 15 '65
Elgin Baylor comes back. il Ebony 20:35-6+ F '65
Hawk is a mighty hunter; St Joseph's vs Temple. F. Deford. il Sports Illus 24:20-3 Ja 10 '66
Hoop ace of Evansville. il Ebony 20:84-6+ Ap '65
Kids are mighty useful; pro basketball scouting report. il Sports Illus 23:40-2+ O 25 '65
Little slice of heaven; Hot Rod Hundley, All-America basketball player. F. Deford. il Sports Illus 23:62-4+ N 29 '65
1965 All-American H.S. basketball squad. H. L. Masin. il Sr Schol 86:32 My 13 '65
Psych, and my other tricks; stars of world champion Boston Celtics; ed. by B. Ottum. B. Russell. il Sports Illus 23:32-4+ O 25 '65
See also names of basketball players, e.g. G. Rodgers

Recruiting
Negro athlete is invited home; A. Beard to matriculate at University of Louisville. F. Deford. il Sports Illus 22:26-7 Je 14 '65
BASKETBALL scouting
Kids are mighty useful; pro basketball scouting report. il Sports Illus 23:40-2+ O 25 '65
BASKETBALL teams
Celtics isn't dead yet. J. Jares. il Sports Illus 23:32-5 N 15 '65
Height of temerity; UCLA's varsity vs UCLA freshmen. i Newsweek 66:66 D 13 '65
Kids are mighty useful; pro basketball scouting report. il Sports Illus 23:40-2+ O 25 '65
Lost Bullets in disasterville; no prospects for NBA title. M. Kram. il Sports Illus 23:26-7 N 8 '65
New Knick with a knack; New York Knickerbockers' D. Barnett. W. Leggett. il Sports Illus 24:18-20+ Ja 17 '66

Play that won the title: Boston Celtics win from Philadelphia 76ers. il Sports Illus 22:30-1 Ap 26 '65
Playoff child's play; Los Angeles Lakes lose; Boston Celtics win their seventh world title. F. Deford. il Sports Illus 22:28-9 My 3 '65
Psych, and my other tricks; stars of world champion Boston Celtics; ed. by B. Ottum. B. Russell. il Sports Illus 23:32-4+ O 25 '65
Race in the West, a shoo-in the East. F. Deford. il Sports Illus 24:46-7 Ja 3 '66
Smashing hurrah for the Lakers. J. Underwood. il Sports Illus 22:12-17 F 8 '65
They all boo when Red sits down, A. Auerbach, coach of Boston Celtics. G. Rogin. il Sports Illus 22:100-2+ Ap 5 '65
BASKETBALL tournaments
Open season on the Wolverine; NCAA championship pairings. F. Deford. il Sports Illus 22:24-7 Mr 15 '65
Playoff was child's play; Los Angeles Lakes lose; Boston Celtics win their seventh world title. F. Deford. il Sports Illus 22:28-9 My 3 '65
Whole team touched by stardust; Princeton winner of Eastern title, NCAA tournament. F. Deford. il Sports Illus 22:20-3 Mr 22 '65
BASKETRY. See Basket making
BASKETS
These basket gifts are Papago. il Sunset 135:64-5 D '65
BASKETTE, Kirtley
Gift of Debbie. Good H 160:92-3+ Mr '65
Needless tragedy of Linda Darnell. Good H 161:42+ S '65
Never look back in sorrow. Good H 160:66-7+ Ja '65
BASKIN, Leonard
Leonard Baskin, graphic artist. P. A. Bennett. il por Pub W 187:70-1+ Ap 5 '65
BASKIN, R. J. and Paolini, P. J.
Muscle volume changes: relation to the active state. bibliog Science 148:971-2 My 14 '65
BASLER, Roy
Old photographs; poem. Poetry 106:345-6 Ag '65
BASOV, Nikolai Gennadevich
Semiconductor lasers; address, December 11, 1964. bibliog Science 149:821-7 Ag 20 '65
BASS, Abraham Z.
Platform for citizen-students. Sat R 48:84 O 16 '65
BASS
Striped bass breakthrough. A. J. McClane. il Field & S 70:88-90+ Jl '65
BASS fishing
Bass-bugging with trout tackle. H. G. Tapply. il Field & S 70:74 S '65
Brackish water black bass. J. Brooks. il Outdoor Life 135:40-1+ My '65
Brown bass of the Buffalo. H. Bradshaw. il Outdoor Life 135:56-9+ Ap '65
Check these hot lakes. G. Gresham. il Outdoor Life 136:48-9+ D '65
Fish in your own backyard. C. Elliott. il Outdoor Life 136:52-3+ O '65
Fooling late-fall smallmouths. W. Davis. il Outdoor Life 136:126-8 N '65
Hartwell is hot. C. Elliott. il Outdoor Life 136:50-1+ N '65
Horseshoe bass. T. Janes. il outdoor Life 136:56-7+ Jl '65
Hot-weather bass. T. Trueblood. il Field & S 70:22+ Jl '65
125 years of bass savvy. C. Chatfield. il Outdoor Life 136:28-31+ Ag '65
Ozark big uns bite best in winter. H. Bradshaw. il Field & S 70:104-7+ Ja '66
Pop for bass. J. Brooks. il Outdoor Life 136:64-5+ N '65
Stealthy approach for stripers. P. McLain. il Field & S 70:18-20+ Je '65
Stripers are my downfall! C. R. Meyer il Yachting 117:120-1+ Je '65
Ten sure tips to catch bass. G. Laycock. Farm J 89:68-9 My '65
They're after trophy-sized bass; Santa Margarita Lake, Calif. il Sunset 134:33 Mr '65
Where the fish are. J. Chiappetta. il Field & S 70:16-18 My '65
Workingman's fish. M. Ellis. il Field & S 70:58-9+ N '65
World's biggest bass lakes. B. East. il Outdoor Life 135:33-5+ Je '65
BASSANI, Giorgio
Dear, dead days. T. G. Bergin. por Sat R 48:46 Jl 24 '65
BASSETT, C. Andrew L.
Electrical effects in bone; with biographical sketch. Sci Am 213:10, 18-25 O '65
BASSETT, Patricia
It's easy to travel with a baby. Parents Mag 40:56-7+ Ag '65
BASSETT, William A. See Takahashi, T. jt. auth.

BASTIAT, Frédéric
Bastiat for '65. H. Hazlitt. Nat R 17:154-5 F 23 '65
BASTOGNE, Battle of. See Ardennes, Battle of the, 1944-1945
BASUTOLAND
See also
Elections—Basutoland
BAT rabies. See Rabies
BATAVIA, N.Y.
Tire failure no longer a problem. G. A. Kandra. il Am City 80:104-5 Mr '65
BATCHELDER, Alan B.
Economic forces serving the ends of the Negro protest. bibliog f Ann Am Acad 357: 80-8 Ja '65
BATCHELDER, Mildred L.
International scene. por Library J 90:5039-40 N 15 '65
Learning about children's books in translation; address, July 1965. por ALA Bul 60: 33-42 Ja '66
BATCHELDER, Richard D.
Today's militant teachers. NEA J 54:18-19 S '65
about
Batch. il pors NEA J 54:42-3 O '65
BATCHELOR, E. A. jr
Century of progress; reprint. Library J 90:2757-60 Je 15 '65
BATEMAN, Hester (Needham)
Hester Bateman. G. Kaler. Hobbies 70:46 S '65
BATES, Carl H. and others
High-pressure transitions of germanium and a new high-pressure form of germanium. bibliog Science 147:860-2 F 19 '65
BATES, Darrell
Short stories: how to begin and how to end. Writer 79:19-20+ Ja '66
BATES, Fred C.
Thunderstorm menace. Flying 77:74-80 O '65
BATES, Gilbert H.
Sergeant Bates' march. M. Lomask. il pors Am Heritage 16:12-17 O '65
BATESON, Frank M.
Eclipse expeditions on Manuae atoll. Sky & Tel 30:78-9 Ag '65
BATH preparations
Bubble bath: another warning. il Consumer Rep 30:376-7 Ag '65
BATH rooms. See Bathrooms
BATHING. See Baths
BATHING beaches. See Beaches
BATHING suits
Beach brevity. il Time 86:50 Ag 6 '65
Less for sea than seeing. il Time 86:56-61 D 31 '65
New skimpy, backless bikinis. il Look 30: 64-5 Ja 11 '66
So now I own a net bikini. S. Alexander. Life 58:33 My 7 '65
Topless triumph; topless-bathing-suit wearer acquitted in French court. Time 85:73 Mr 12 '65
BATHROOM scales. See Scales (weighing instruments)
BATHROOMS
Architect's notes on kitchen and bathroom planning. P. M. Bolton. il Arch Rec 137: 15-16+ mid-My '65
Bathroom pretty-ups. il Seventeen 24:156+ F '65
Bathroomology; Cornell's survey report. Newsweek 66:69 D 13 '65
Bright ideas for 5x7 bathrooms. il Bet Hom & Gard 43:114-15 S '65
Here's help for old bathrooms. J. Holmstrand. il Suc Farm 63:90-3 My '65
Low-cost ways to improve any bathroom. il Good H 161:171 O '65
More space to hang towels. il Farm J 89:77 S '65
New color accents for your bathroom. il House & Gard 128:198-9 S '65
Splash your bath with color. il Good H 160: 116-21 F '65
Take the age out of any bathroom. il Bet Hom & Gard 43:66-7 Ap '65
That little old porch is now a roomy new bath. il Sunset 134:151 My '65
Why settle for a bad house? il Bet Hom & Gard 43:60-1 N '65
BATHS
Bath: a study in time and motion. il Mlle 61:136-7 O '65
Have as much fun as your youngsters do at bathtime. L. D. Kirk. il Parents Mag 40: 108 Mr '65
History
Art of cleanliness. J. G. Harmount. il Todays Health 43:49-51+ D '65

BATHS, Vapor
Homemade sauna. L. Burgess. il Flower Grower 52:50-1 F '65
Importance of being poached. J. Skow. il Sat Eve Post 238:88-91 My 8 '65
BATHYSCAPHE
Searchers beneath the seas. il Newsweek 66: 84-5 S 27 '65
BATIK
Batiks; Columbia high school. T. W. Kundsen. il Sch Arts 64:3-8 My '65
Put your designs on cotton. il Design 67:18-19 N '65
BATS
Hearing sensitivity in bats. J. I. Dalland. bibliog il Science 150:1185-6 N 26 '65
Histoplasma capsulatum from the liver of a bat in Colombia. C. J. Marinkelle and E. Grose. bibliog Science 147:1039-40 F 26 '65
Moths and ultrasound. K. D. Roeder. il Sci Am 212:94-102 Ap '65
Trinidad and bat research. A. M. Greenhall. il Natur Hist 74:14-21 Je '65
BATTELLE memorial institute of Columbus, Ohio
Fast-growing lab regroups on the run. il Bsns W p67-70 F 6 '65
Postscript; concerning report by William T. Reid in the Battelle technical review. J. Lear. il Sat R 48:42 Jl 3 '65
BATTERIES, Electric. See Electric batteries
BATTERIES, Solar. See Solar batteries
BATTERY chargers. See Storage battery chargers
BATTIN, Dalton
Pixies in Eden park; reprint. Recreation 58: 475-6 D '65
BATTLE of Britain. See World war, 1939-1945—Great Britain
BATTLE of Dunkirk, 1940. See Dunkirk, Battle of, 1940
BATTLE of Squashy Hollow; story. See Wodehouse, P. G.
BATTLE of the sexes. See Women and men
BATTLE of Waterloo. See Waterloo, Battle of, 1815
BATTLESHIPS. See Warships
BATZKA, Stephen A.
Tempera and starch. Sch Arts 64:29 Mr '65
BAUER, Erwin A.
All outdoors for rent. pors Outdoor Life 136: 20-3+ Ag '65
Buck the hard way. pors Outdoor Life 136: 60-3+ Jl '65
Christmas adventure. por Outdoor Life 136: 36-9+ D '65
Fishing Baja California. il Yachting 117:110-12+ Je '65
Muskie explosion. Outdoor Life 135:18-23+ Mr '65
My secret of summertime escape. por Outdoor Life 135:40-3+ Je '65
Rocky road to paradise. Field & S 69:43-7 F '65
Stalking winter wildlife. por Outdoor Life 137:48-51+ Ja '66
Tent trailer to Alaska. Field & S 70:37-9 Je '65
BAUER, Florence Marvyne. See Bauer, W. W. jt. auth.
BAUER, Peter T.
Capitalism and African economic development; excerpts from African nettle, ed. by F. S. Meyer. Nat R 17:542-5 Je 29 '65
BAUER, W. W. and Bauer, F. M.
All girls have problems; excerpts from Way to womanhood. Todays Health 43:24-7+ F '65
Man to marry; excerpt from Way to womanhood. Todays Health 43:38-9+ Ap '65
Those difficult years of change; excerpts from Way to womanhood. Todays Health 43: 46-9+ Mr '65
BAUERMEISTER, Mary
Powerhouse. New Yorker 41:24-7 Jl 31 '65
BAULER, Mathias J.
Paddy's last hurrah. por Newsweek 65:31-2 F 8 '65
BAUM, Gregory
Birth control, what happened? Commonweal 83:369-71 D 24 '65
Books. Commonweal 82:542-3 Jl 23 '65
Council ends. Commonweal 83:402-5 Ja 7 '66
Final session; off to a good start. Commonweal 83:52-5 O 15 '65
Five decrees. Commonweal 83:237-40 N 26 '65
Indulgences at the council. Commonweal 83: 307+ D 10 '65
On the modern world. Commonweal 83:117-20 O 29 '65
Peace, priests and the missions. Commonweal 83:175-8 N 12 '65
BAUM, Lyman Frank
Child's garden of bewilderment. M. Gardner. il Sat R 48:18-19 Jl 17 '65

BAUM, Morton
He calls the tunes at the City Center. R. Kotlowitz. il por N Y Times Mag p44-5+ My 2 '65
BAUMAN, Carol
Political grocery store. Nat R 17:884-5 O 5 '65
BAUMAN, John Nevin
White molds the parts. il por Bsns W p 159-60+ O 16 '65
BAUMAN, Robert E.
Home is where the heart is. Nat R 17:286-7 Ap 6 '65
BAUMGARTNER, Warren
Warren Baumgartner, 1894-1963. N. Kent. il por Am Artist 29:46-7+ Ap '65
BAUMGOLD, Julie
Come up and see her sometime: poem. Mlle 61:324 Ag '65
BAUS, Paul J.
Men, beeswax, and molten metal. Natur Hist 74:18-25 bibliog(p74) Ag '65
BAUTISTA, Jose. See Hamlin, G. H. jt. auth.
BAUXITE
Australia stumbles onto new Golconda. il Bsns W p68-72 Ag 7 '65
BAVARIA
    See also
    Bayreuth
        Politics and government
What was Lola? Newsweek 66:40 D 20 '65
BAVARIAN ALPS. See Alps
BAVETTA, Lucien A. See Nimni, M. E. jt. auth.
BAVIER, Robert N. Jr
Changes in the racing rules. Yachting 117:51+ Mr '65
Race that broke the Bird. Sports Illus 23:34-40 Ag 16 '65
BAWGUS, Emma
Environment traps young American of promise. il pors Ebony 20:115-21 Ag '65
BAXENDALE, J. H. and Gilbert, G. P.
Electron yield in the γ-radiolysis of water vapor. bibliog Science 147:1571 Mr 26 '65
—and others
Pulse radiolysis of dioxane solutions. bibliog Science 148:637 Ap 30 '65
BAXTER, Dow V.
Our land speaks. Liv Wildn 87:16-21 Wint '64
BAXTER, Percival Proctor
Mister Maine and the mountain. E. W. Smith. il por Field & S 70:10-11+ D '65
BAXTER, Tom
For love and money. See issues of Flying
BAXTER STATE PARK. See Maine—Parks and reserves
BAY area rapid transit. See San Francisco—Rapid transit
BAY CITY, Mich.
No monopoly on snow-fighting. R. K. Mc-Gillivray. il Am City 80:102-3 D '65
BAY OF PIGS invasion. See Cuba—History—Invasion, 1961
BAYER, Ann
Secret infidelity of Arthur Nydes; story. Sat Eve Post 238:70-1 S 25 '65
BAYH, Birch
Filling a void. Sr Schol 86:30-1 F 18 '65
BAYLOR, Elgin
Elgin Baylor comes back. il pors Ebony 20:35-6+ F '65
BAYLOR, J. E. and others
How to tell if hay is top quality. por Suc Farm 62:32-3+ Jl '65
BAYREUTH festival
Bayreuths 14-karat ring. E. Davidson. il Opera N 30:25-6 N 6 '65
Cult and myth on the green hill; Wieland Wagner's staging of the Ring des Nibelungen. G. Loney. il Hi Fi 15:160-1 O '65
Freudian ring. il Time 86:66 Ag 6 '65
Wagner's Bayreuth. il Opera N 29:14-16 Mr 6 '65
BAZAARS, Charitable
Memories of another fair. J. Canady. il N Y Times Mag p71-2 Ap 18 '65
BAZELON, David Lionel
U.S. judge would restrict police; excerpts from letter. U S News 59:66 Ag 16 '65
    about
Police find lawyer friends. Life 59:4 Ag 20 '65
BAZELON, David T.
Big business & the Democrats: excerpts from What is power? Commentary 39:39-46 My '65
Prescription and prices. Commentary 39:75-7 F '65

BAZIOTES, William
Baziotes: modern mythologist; retrospective at the Guggenheim. I. H. Sandler. il por Art N 63:28-31+ F '65
Silent mirrors. il por Newsweek 65:69-70 F 22 '65
BEA, Augustin, cardinal
Bea denies revisions in Catholic-Jewish draft. Christian Cent 82:637 My 19 '65
Crisis of growth. America 112:516 Ap 17 '65
Ecumenical journey. America 112:746 My 22 '65
BEACH, Frank A.
Books. Sci Am 212:147-50+ Ap '65
BEACH, Norton L.
(ed) International education. por Sr Schol 86:sup 1, 9-14 My 20 '65
What we can learn from schools abroad. Sr Schol 86:sup9 My 20 '65
BEACH architecture
Beach house made of aluminum sandwiches, polystyrene foam between two sheets of aluminum. il Sports Illus 23:42-5 Ag 9 '65
Bold splash of a beach home. il Life 58:90-3+ Ap 16 '65
Pavilion in the dunes; Fire Island beach house. E. Sverbeyeff. il N Y Times Mag p38-9 Je 20 '65
They live at the beach both summer and winter. il Sunset 135:56-7 Ag '65
Transplanted beach house. il House & Gard 127:122-5 F '65
BEACH buggies. See Motor vehicles
BEACH erosion
Case of the vanishing beaches; California. W. Marx. il Am For 71:10-13+ N '65
    See also
Shore protection
BEACH party; story. See Grau, S. A.
BEACHES
California loses another beach; Dilton Beach. K. S. Roe. il Audubon Mag 67:110-11 Mr '65
Case of the vanishing beaches; California. W. Marx. il Am For 71:10-13+ N '65
Turkish delights; Turkish Riviera. il Time 86:58 Ag 20 '65
BEACONS
    See also
Lighthouses
BEACONS, Radar. See Radar in aviation
BEAD curtains. See Curtains and draperies
BEADLE, George W.
How to transmit culture; summary of address. Sci N L 89:5 Ja 1 '66
BEADLE, Muriel
But, please George, write it in English! excerpt from Pomona today. Sat R 48:53-4 Ap 3 '65
Talent grows in small towns, too. Sat R 48:64-5 Jl 17 '65
BEADS
Bead making. P. Greenberg. il Sch Arts 65:20-2 S '65
BEAGLE, Charles
WAM builds a street in one day. pors Am City 80:86-8 D '65
BEAGLE, Peter S.
Long way to go. Holiday 37:62-7+ F; 78-81+ Mr '65
My last heroes. Holiday 38:8+ Ag '65
Wayward reader. Holiday 37:35-8 Je '65
BEAHM, Sherman E.
Epiphyllums. Horticulture 43:22-3 Jl '65
BEAL, Doone
Going places, finding things in Crete. House & Gard 129:18-20+ Ja '66
Traveling with Mlle. Mlle 61:206-6 S '65
BEALE, James H.
Dogwoods star in all seasons. Flower Grower 52:27-9 Mr '65
BEALS, Carleton
In quest of Sandino, imperialism still rides. Nation 201:83-7 S 20 '65
BEAM, Jacob D.
Strengthening peace through arms control and disarmament. Dept State Bul 53:398-400 S 6 '65
BEAME, Abraham
Beame: campaign in Manhattan. New Yorker 41:50-2 O 23 '65
Statement sent to the press, November 3, 1965. W. F. Buckley, jr. Nat R 17:1014 N 16 '65
Switcheroo. il por Newsweek 66:29-30 S 27 '65
This Tuesday's winner, and loser. W. Weaver, jr. il por N Y Times Mag p 46-7+ O 31 '65
Victory. New Yorker 41:41-2 S 25 '65
BEAN, Alice Pearse
Speaking out. por Sat Eve Post 238:10+ My 8 '65; Same abr. Read Digest 87:83-5 Jl '65
BEAN, Louis H. and Drummond, Roscoe
How many votes does Goldwater own? Look 29:75-6 Mr 23 '65

BEANS
See also
Cookery—Vegetables
BEAR, Firman E.
Danger signs in plants. Horticulture 43:26-7 Je '65
Read the label on the fertilizer sack. Horticulture 44:22-3+ Ja '66
BEAR, Fred
Bag it with a bow. Pop Mech 124:106-9+ S '65
BEAR hunting
Bear stroganoff; Intourist safari. Newsweek 65:40 Mr 8 '65
Bonus: 500-pound bear. L. H. Johns. il Outdoor Life 137:38-9+ Ja '66
Boy into a man; Chip's first bear hunt. R. Starnes. Field & S 70:22-4+ O '65
No time to climb. G. McKechnie. il Outdoor Life 136:48-9+ O '65
Wake up, Willie! D. DeHart. il Outdoor Life 135:48-9+ My '65
Wind River bear run. L. Miracle. il Outdoor Life 135:54-5+ Ap '65
World's rarest trophy? H. Shelley. il Outdoor Life 136:36-9+ Jl '65
You can't figure bears. A. Laha. il Outdoor Life 136:58-9+ N '65
BEARBERRIES
God's little apples. R. Coudy. il Am For 71:36-7 Mr '65
They do nicely on steep banks. il Sunset 134:257 My '65
BEARD, Alfred
Negro athlete is invited home. F. Deford. il por Sports Illus 22:26-7 Je 14 '65
BEARD, Charles A.
Scholar in an age of conflicts; reprint of a 1936 article. Sch & Soc 93:43-4+ Ja 23 '65
BEARD, James A.
Happy marriages of wine and meat. House & Gard 128:226+ O '65
Roast meat cook book. House & Gard 128:229+ O '65
Wine; the farsighted wedding gift. il House & Gard 127:172+ My '65
BEARD, Margaret E. See Allen, J. M. jt. auth.
BEARD, Peter
Misty haven for sportsmen; photographs. Sports Illus 22:50-4 My 17 '65
BEARDSLEY, Aubrey
Tyger, tyger... F. Stevenson. il por Opera N 29:28-31 Mr 6 '65
BEARDSLEY, Helen
Who gets the drumstick? excerpt. pors Good H 161:86-9+ O '65
BEARING walls. See Walls
BEARINGS (machinery)
See also
Automobiles—Bearings
BEARN, Alexander G. See Danes, B. S. jt. auth.
BEARS
Are the days of the Arctic's king running out? R. Murphy. il N Y Times Mag p38-40 Mr 28 '65
Bare bear facts. Sports Illus 23:12 S 27 '65
Bear nightmare. D. DeCleene. il Outdoor Life 135:17-19+ Mr '65
Grizzly outlook: cloudy to fair; excerpt from report. V. H. Cahalane. il Audubon Mag 67:170-1 My '65
Grizzly; story of five hikers. A. Ruffin. il Life 59:73-4+ Ag 27 '65
Ins & outs of bears. il Changing T 19:44-5 Ag '65
Nature note; American black bear. Sci N L 87:93 F 6 '65
Nature note; polar bear. Sci N L 87:407 Je 26 '65
Warden's view of bears. F. G. Smith. il Outdoor Life 135:56-7+ Je '65
White Russian bear. Nation 200:463 My 3 '65
Year of the bear; in New Hampshire. Sports Illus 23:25 O 11 '65
BEASLEY, Thomas M. See Palmer, H. E. jt. auth.
BEAT generation. See Beatniks
BEATLES
B is for Beatles and baroque; concerning Baroque Beatles book. R. Freed. il Sat R 48:57+ D 25 '65
Beatlemania and the fast buck: Beatle-touched items sold at fancy prices. Christian Cent 82:230 F 24 '65
Beatlemania: the most or the worst? pro and con discussion. il Sr Schol 86:10-11 F 4 '65
Beauty and the Beatles. il McCalls 92:78-83+ Jl '65
Best of the Beatles. il Time 86:36 D 31 '65
Beware, the red Beatles. pors Newsweek 65:89A F 15 '65
Blue-chip Beatles. il Newsweek 66:82 O 4 '65
Buying the Beatles. Time 85:94 F 19 '65

Day the King of swing met the Beatles. R. Goodman. il Esquire 64:52-3+ Jl '65
Hear that big sound; with report by T. Thompson. il Life 58:90-4+ My 21 '65
High-brows vs no-brows. A. Chasins. il McCalls 92:42+ S '65
I wanna hold your stock. Newsweek 65:70-1 Mr 1 '65
Letter from Liverpool, almost. B. Comden. Vogue 146:120+ D '65
Mopheads, M.B.E. il Newsweek 65:38 Je 28 '65
On the scene with the Beatles; ed. by E. Miller. il Seventeen 24:230-1+ Ag '65
Ringo, Ringo, let down your hair! S. Alexander. Life 59:28 S 10 '65
Ringo Starr: domesticated Beatle. R. Deardorff. il Redbook 125:60-1+ S '65
Trade winds; phenomenal success. J. G. Fuller. il Sat R 48:14+ S 18 '65
What every woman should know about the Beatles. A. Levy. il Good H 161:12+ Jl '65
BEATNIKS
Beatniks' friend; proprietor of Chez Popoff. il Newsweek 66:36+ Ag 23 '65
Beauty and the Beatniks; Spanish Steps, Rome. W. S. Schlamm. Nat R 18:23-4 Ja 11 '66
Colder children. S. Kempton. il Esquire 64:58:61 Jl '65
Death of hip; the changing hipster. M. Magid. il Esquire 63:89-103+ Je '65
BEATON, Cecil
Cecil Beaton, photographer, designer. Harper 230:62-3 Ap '65
Golden Picasso. il Vogue 146:142-5+ S 15 '65
BEATRICE and Benedict; opera. See Berlioz, H.
BEATRICE foods company
FTC spells out a merger. Bsns W p32 My 22 '65
BEATRIX, princess of the Netherlands
In Margaret's steps; plans for wedding in Amsterdam. Newsweek 66:61 N 15 '65
Love conquers all. il por Newsweek 66:41-2 Jl 12 '65
Prince watsisname. il por Time 86:29 Jl 2 '65
Vote for love; Parliament approval of marriage. il por Time 86:47 N 19 '65
BEATTY, Clyde Raymond
King of the beasts. il por Time 86:54-5 Jl 30 '65
BEATTY, Jerome, jr
Me and my terrible talent. Read Digest 87:93-5 Ag '65
No uncertain terms. Atlan 215:118+ Je '65
Trade winds. See issues of Saturday review
BEATTY, John, and Beatty, Patricia
Watch your language, you're writing for young people! Horn Bk 41:34-40 F '65
BEATTY, Patricia. See Beatty, J. jt. auth.
BEATTY, Robert O.
Teenage gunners only. Field & S 70:110-11 N '65
BEATTY, W. Donald
Chilean dilemma. bibliog f Cur Hist 49:342-8+ D '65
BEATY, Katie
I wait; poem. Horn Bk 41:674 D '65
BEAUCHAMP, Emerson
Stop the greasepaint, I want to smell the crowd! New Yorker 41:68+ Jl 17 '65
BEAUCHAMP, James. See Hiller, L. jt. auth.
BEAUCHEMIN, David J.
Nineteen-year-old marine in Vietnam. C. S. Wren. il pors Look 29:19-23 Ag 24 '65
BEAUDOIN, Isabel
Group mosaics by elementary students. Design 66:16-18 Mr '65
That bulletin board in the hall. Design 67:41 N '65
BEAUFORT, Mrs Ira
Letter from Augusta. Dance Mag 40:68-9 Ja '66
BEAUFORT COUNTY, N.C.
Phosphate bonanza ready to be tapped. il Bsns W p88+ Mr 27 '65
BEAUTIFICATION of landscape. See Landscape improvement
BEAUTIFICATION of roadsides. See Roadside improvement
BEAUTIFUL to behold; story. See Plagemann, B.
BEAUTIFYING of cities. See Municipal improvement
BEAUTY, Personal
All girls have problems; excerpts from Way to womanhood. W. W. Bauer and F. M. Bauer. il Todays Health 43:24-7+ F '65
Beach beauty guide. il Seventeen 24:64-9 Je '65
Beauty and the Beatles. il McCalls 92:78-83+ Jl '65
Beauty bulletin. See issues of Vogue
Beauty checkout. See issues of Vogue

BEAUTY, Personal—*Continued*
Beauty clinic. See issues of Good housekeeping
Beauty: in a wild new spin. S. Harney. il Ladies Home J 82:72-3 S '65
Beauty life, beauty homework, new lessons to learn. il Mlle 61:98-9+ Je '65
Beauty life: Mlle guest editors make the beauty scene. il Mlle 61:272-80+ Ag '65
Beauty of being yourself; beauty secrets of several young women. S. Harney. il Ladies Home J 82:68-9 Ag '65
Beauty register; detective work on the beauty behavior of five moving women. il Vogue 147:102-9 Ja 15 '66
Beauty register; six case histories from Vogue's private files. il Vogue 146:96-101 Jl '65
Beautywise words. il Good H 160:132-3 My '65
Business of being merely beautiful G. B. Leonard. il Look 30:18-21 Ja 11 '66
Cookie cutter beauty. il Seventeen 24:128-9 F '65
Dear beauty editor. See issues of Seventeen
Does he or doesn't he? W. K. Zinsser. il Sat Eve Post 238:16 O 9 '65
Dressing table talk. See issues of Seventeen
Good looks. L. D. Kirk. See issues of Parents' magazine and better homemaking
Have you met Miss May? il Mlle 61:154-5 My '65
Hey, beautiful. il Seventeen 24:100-1 D '65
How to make your figure fit the fashion. il Vogue 145:120-5+ F 15 '65
I wish, I wish, I wish. il Seventeen 25:70-5 Ja '66
The look you like; questions and answers, ed. by L. Allen. See issues of Today's health
Memo to the hurried homemaker. Am Home 68:28 Mr '65
Man talk; plain and fancy. D. Newman and R. Benton. il Mlle 61:90 O '65
My problem was me. il Good H 160:63+ My '65
New kind of flash. il Seventeen 24:110-11 S '65
Now you can have your hair restored ($1 a hair) your eyelids tightened ($500) D. D. Harris. il Esquire 64:134-6+ N '65
120 ways to please a man. il Good H 161:104-26+ O '65
Open letter on beauty. Good H 160:225 My '65
Private beauty life of a model. il Seventeen 24:94-9 O '65
Quick change and long-range ways to a prettier you. Am Home 68:38 Ap '65
Seventeen ways to look and feel great! il Good H 160:74-7 Ja '65
She wants to grow up pretty! il Good H 160:132-5 Mr '65
Time to be beautiful; post natal exercise and beauty routine. il Redbook 125:70-1+ My '65
Twelve sparkling ways to summer beauty. il Good H 161:110-11+ Jl '65
Weekend beauty camp. il Seventeen 24:100+ Jl '65
Young London look. il Seventeen 24:128-9 Mr '65
Young mothers talk about their hair, skin and other beauty problems; ed. by R. Drake. il Redbook 125:38+ Jl '65
See also
Cosmetics
Exercise
Hairdressing
Lips
Make-up
Manicuring

BEAUTY bush
June rivals. E. S. Henderson. il Pop Gard 16:31+ My '65

BEAUTY contests
Discovery of Miss America; D. Bryant as Miss Kansas. D. L. Goodrich. il Sat Eve Post 238:36-41 N 6 '65
Negro girl in Miss America race; wins Miss Rochester title. il Ebony 20:70-2+ Jl '65
Switched on: L. Bass, winner of Miss American teen-ager at Young naturals, ltd. New Yorker 41:42-5 S 25 '65
What Miss America is made of. J. Canaday. il N Y Times Mag p 124+ S 19 '65

BEAUTY culture
Face race: Institute of cosmetology, Russia. il Time 86:20 D 31 '65

BEAUTY of scenery. See Landscape

BEAUTY preparations. See Cosmetics

BEAUTY shops
Salon-sleuthing; Chicago, Los Angeles. Mlle 61:76 S '65

BEAUVOIR, Françoise (Brasseur) de
Very easy death. S. de Bauvoir. il por McCalls 93:74-5+ Ja '66

BEAUVOIR, Simone de
Very easy death. por McCalls 93:74-5+ Ja '66
What love is and isn't. McCalls 92:71+ Ag '65

about
Beauvoir's reflections on her middle years. A. Mayhew. Commonweal 82:728-9 O 1 '65
Bonjour, tristesse. por Time 85:111 My 14 '65
Books; The shadow and the substance. N. Bliven. New Yorker 41:104+ Ja 8 '66
Dutiful Simone de Beauvoir. M. Ellmann. Commentary 40:59-62 Ag '65
Intellectual passion, logical love. A. Darack. Sat R 48:29-30 My 8 '65
Question of Simone de Beauvoir. N. Algren. Harper 230:134+ My '65
Sartre talks of Beauvoir; interview, ed. by M. Gobeil, tr. by B. Frechtman. J. P. Sartre. por Vogue 146:72-3 Jl '65
Second sex and second thoughts. W. S. Schlamm. Nat R 17:692-4 Ag 10 '65
Wayward reader. T. Wolfe. Holiday 38:14+ Ag '65
Woman first. il por Newsweek 65:124-5 My 10 '65

BEAVAN, John
Way it was in the blitz. N Y Times Mag p 12-13+ S 5 '65

BEAVER, R. Pierce
Christian ashrams in India. Christian Cent 82:887-9, 1357-8 Jl 14, N 3 '65

BEAVERS
Beaver returns to Maine. B. Geagan. il Nat Parks Mag 40:12-14 Ja '66

BECENTI, Ernest
We are legion. por PTA Mag 59:19-20 F '65

BÉCHET, Sidney
Jazz records. W. Balliett. New Yorker 41:175-9 My 15 '65

BECHTEL corporation
Bringing the campus to the office; University of California sends classroom instruction to Bechtel corp. il Bsns W p72-3 D 25 '65

BECHUANALAND
Walking the tightrope: Bechuanaland's first prime minister. il Time 85:29 Mr 12 '65

BECK, Beth L.
Ranchwoman's treasury of sounds and smells. por Farm J 89:76-7 O '65

BECK, Curt W. See Langenheim, J. H. jt. auth.

BECK, Hans Johannes Christian
Bournonville preserved. T. G. Veale. il pors Dance Mag 39:52-3+ Ag '65

BECK, James H.
All the paintings of. Art N 64:45+ My '65

BECK, Joan
(ed) Big question for teens; morality. por Todays Health 43:24+ My '65
Financing your college education. Todays Health 43:32-5+ F '65
How well do you know teen-agers? Todays Health 43:47-8+ F '65
Mono: the medical mimic. Todays Health 43:36-7+ F '65
Other face of the problem: the unmarried teen father. Todays Health 43:28-31+ F '65

BECK, Ray
Great hellbender. Field & S 69:64-6+ Ap '65

BECKER, Dan
Photography's new breed. U S Camera 28:64-7+ F '65

BECKER, Howard S.
Deviance and deviates. Nation 201:115-19 S 20 '65
Stamping out addiction. Commentary 40:76-8 Ag '65

BECKER, Joseph
Data processing equipment in libraries (cont) ALA Bul 59:293-6, 823-6 Ap, O '65

BECKER, Joseph M.
Unemployment insurance. America 113:73-6 Jl 17 '65

BECKER, William E.
SST. Travel 125:29-31+ Ja '66

BECKETT, Samuel
Happy days. Criticism Nation 201:258-9 O 18 '65

BECKY and I; story. See Amft, M. J.

BED linens. See Linens, Household

BED-sitting rooms. See Bedrooms

BED; story. See Robinson, B.

BED wetting. See Urine—Incontinence

BEDAU, Hugo Adam
When is law natural? Nation 200:398-401 Ap 12 '65

BEDDING
Late report on big beds and big bed linens. il House & Gard 128:26+ S '65

BEDE, James
BD-1. R. B. Weeghman. il por Flying 77:34-9 N '65

BEDE Sullivan, Sister. See Sullivan, B.
BEDE aviation corporation
  BD-1. R. B. Weeghman. il Flying 77:34-9 N
    '65
BEDELL, Eugenia
  Booked for travel. Sat R 48:40+ Mr 20 '65
BEDFORD, Harry
  Rare evergreen defies extinction. il Audubon
    Mag 67:182-3 My '65
  Theater of the string puppet. Sch Arts 64:
    25-32 Ap '65
BEDFORD, Nicole (Schneider) Milinaire Rus-
    sell, duchess of
  Christmas at Woburn Abbey; interview.
    House & Gard 128:136-8+ D '65
BEDFORD, Sybille
  Her Majesty's incorruptible, imperturbable,
    incomparable judges. Esquire 64:78-82+
    O '65
  House of lords. Horizon 7:4-13+ Autumn '65
  This blessed plot, this earth, this realm, this
    Denmark. Esquire 64:212+ D '65
BEDFORD, Virginia L.
  Tot area on a shoe-string. Recreation 58:
    171-2 Ap '65
BEDICHEK, Roy
  They never left Texas. F. H. Wardlaw.
    Sat R 48:25-8 S 18 '65
BEDROOM furnishings. See Household fur-
    nishings
BEDROOMS
  Bedrooms: emphasis on. M. White. il Ladies
    Home J 82:68-73 Ap '65
  Bedtime stories. il Seventeen 24:142-3 S '65
  Dream room is... il Seventeen 25:122-5 O
    '65
  First step to a new room is a new idea. il
    Seventeen 24:140-1 My '65
  Four ways to make a big change in a small
    room. il Seventeen 24:138-41 Mr '65
  Living with the London look. il Seventeen
    24:180+ Mr '65
  Lucky Seventeen room. il Seventeen 24:240-
    1+ Ag '65
  Planning a new room? il Seventeen 24:176+
    My '65
  Space-makers for small rooms. il Seventeen
    24:152+ F '65
  Teeners' haven. il House & Gard 127:150-1
    Je '65
  You be the decorator. il Seventeen 24:84-5+
    Je '65
    See also
  Childrens rooms
BEDS
  Late report on big beds and big bed linens.
    il House & Gard 128:26+ S '65
  Seven ways to find space for a guest bed.
    C. T. Sigman. il Pop Sci 186:140-4 Mr '65
  Somebody gets to sleep upstairs; bunk beds.
    il Sunset 134:98-9 Ap '65
    See also
  Hospital beds
  Yachts—Berths

    Anecdotes, facetiae, satire, etc.
  Early to bed and late to rise. D. Herold. il
    Read Digest 87:29-30+ Ag '65
BEDTIME story telling. See Story telling
BEE hunts. See Bees
BEE stings. See Insect bites and stings
BEE-tree hunting. See Bees
BEEBE, Lucius
  Moriarty's wonderful saloon. Am Heritage
    16:65-9+ Ag '65
BEECH aircraft corporation
  Beech expands data center capabilities. il
    Aviation W 84:97-8 Ja 10 '66
BEECHAM, Sir Thomas
  Sir Thomas and the gramophone, 1910-1960;
    with discography. W. Botsford. por Hi Fi
    15:45-8+ Je '65
BEEF
    See also
  Cookery—Meat
    Prices
    See Meat—Prices
BEEF grading. See Meat—Grading and stand-
    ardization
BEEF industry. See Meat industry and trade
BEEHIVE House. See Salt Lake City—His-
    toric houses, etc.
BEELER, Joe
  School of old paint. il Newsweek 66:107-8 N
    8 '65
BEER
  Suntory brews a drive for its beer in Japan.
    il Bsns W p 118-20 S 4 '65
    Advertising
  At the fair, beer garden is heady surprise;
    Lowenbrau beer gets back $750,000 sunk
    in promotion at World's fair. il Bsns W
    p56-7+ Ag 21 '65

BEER containers
  Can is lighter if not the brew; all-aluminum
    cans. il Bsns W p90+ Jl 10 '65
  Steel rolls new weapon into can market
    fight; tin-free stock. il Bsns W p62+ N 6
    '65
BEERBOHM, Sir Max
  Alone with his wit. S. Weintraub. il Sat R
    48:46-7 Ap 17 '65
  Max, by D. Cecil. Review
    Commonweal 82:452-3 Je 25 '65. B. Ber-
      gonzi
    Life 58:8+ Ap 16 '65. S. N. Behrman
    New Yorker 41:227-8+ O 23 '65. W. H.
      Auden
    Newsweek pors 65:104+ Ap 19 '65
    Time por 85:109-10+ Ap 16 '65
  Maximum Max. S. Kauffmann. New Repub
    152:19-22 Ap 10 '65
BEES
  Danger from the African queens; Brazil. il
    Time 86:75 S 24 '65
  Great wild bee safari. B. Gilbert. il Sat
    Eve Post 238:28-9 Jl 17 '65
  Sound: an element common to communica-
    tion of stingless bees and to dances of the
    honey bee. H. Esch and others. bibliog il
    Science 149:320-1 Jl 16 '65
BEESON, Jack
  Lizzie Borden. Criticism
    New Yorker 41:154-5 Ap 3 '65
    Sat R 48:87 Ap 10 '65
    Time 85:67 Ap 2 '65
BEETHOVEN, Ludwig van
  Amazing man, Rubinstein. C. J. Luten. Am
    Rec G 31:1149 Ag '65
  Beethoven sonatas, by divers hands. H.
    Goldsmith. il Hi Fi 15:58-60 My '65
  Books. W. Sargeant. New Yorker 41:192-4
    Ap 17 '65
  Disc for history, knowledge enhanced, esteem
    confirmed. A. Rich. il Hi Fi 15:60 Je '65
  Fidelio. Criticism
    Hi Fi 16:148-9 Ja '66
    Opera N il 30:17-20 Ja 22 '66
    Opera N il 30:24-5 Ja 22 '66
    Sat R 49:48 Ja 22 '66
  Glenn Gould, some of today's finest Beet-
    hoven playing. R. Kammerer. Am Rec G
    31:980 Je '65
  Lateiner's Beethoven. J. M. Conly. il Re-
    porter 32:46+ F 11 '65
  Musical gold from Washington, D.C. A.
    Cohn. il Am Rec G 31:1136-7 Ag '65
  New York concerts. H. Goldsmith. Hi Fi
    15:137-8+ Ap '65
  On records: Egmont. Opera N 29:34 Mr 6 '65
  On records: Fidelio. Opera N 30:34 Ja 22 '66
  Serkin: Beethoven, Fourth piano concerto.
    E. Belov. il Am Rec G 32:120-1 O '65
  Serkin's Beethoven, once with Toscanini, to-
    day with Ormandy. H. Goldsmith. il Hi Fi
    15:80-1 O '65
  Szell and Beethoven on Epic. J. Lyons. il Am
    Rec G 32:48 S '65
  They shall have music. H. Kupferberg. il
    Atlan 217:112-13 Ja '66
BEETLES
  Chilocorus similis Rossi: disinterment and
    case history. S. G. Smith. bibliog il Science
    148:1614-16 Je 18 '65
  Dendroctonus pseudotsugae; a hypothesis re-
    garding its primary attractant. H. J. Heik-
    kenen and B. F. Hrutfiord. bibliog il Sci-
    ence 150:1457-9 D 10 '65
  Report on cereal leaf beetle. M. C. Wilson.
    Il Suc Farm 63:80 Mr '65
    See also
  Bark beetles
  Fireflies
  Japanese beetles

    Wings
    See Insects—Wings
BEETS
    See also
  Sugar beets
BEGEMANN, Egbert Haverkamp-. See Haver-
    kamp-Begemann, E.
BEGGING and beggars
  Trade winds; New York's gentlemen pan-
    handlers. J. Beatty, jr. il Sat R 48:16+
    N 20 '65
BEGONIAS
  Behold the beautiful begonia. il Am Home
    68:50-1 Mr '65
  Color perfection with tuberous begonias. C.
    Lewis. il Horticulture 43:18-19+ Mr '65
  Grow and enjoy tantalizing begonias. C. J.
    Davis. il Pop Gard 16:38-40 Mr '65
  Tuberous begonias. J. Arkin and D. Glazer. il
    Pop Gard 16:27-9 Jl '65
BEH, Helen C. and Barratt, P. E. H.
  Discrimination and conditioning during sleep
    as indicated by the electroencephalogram.
    bibliog Science 147:1470-1 Mr 19 '65

BEHAIM, Martin
Was Christopher Columbus really Martin Behaim? P. W. Schmidtchen. il Hobbies 70:106-7+ D '65
BEHAN, Brendan
Last playboy of the western world. K. Sullivan. Nation 200:283-7 Mr 15 '65
BEHAVIOR. See Etiquette
BEHAVIOR (psychology)
Calipers on the human mind. J. W. Krutch. Sat R 48:22-5 Je 19 '65
Games people play, by E. Berne. Review Life 58:15+ Je 11 '65. K. Vonnegut, jr
Good advice from the social scientists. R. L. Dean. Cath World 202:80-3 N '65
How good is your mental health? H. Levinson. Read Digest 87:54-8 S '65
How your body can shape your personality. R. Mines. il Sci Digest 57:79-83 Je '65
Man's nature and his communities, by R. Niebuhr. Review
Nation 202:19-22 Ja 3 '66. M. Wreszin
Uncommitted, by K. Keniston. Review
Reporter 33:46-8 D 30 '65. E. T. Chase
Sat R 49:84 Ja 8 '66. R. J. Levin
Up from peeping tom. Newsweek 66:100 O 11 '65
See also
Human nature
Motivation (psychology)
BEHAVIOR, Criminal. See Criminal psychology
BEHAVIOR, Group. See Groups (sociology)
BEHAVIOR of animals. See Animals—Habits and behavior
BEHAVIORAL sciences
Ethological study of behavior; report on ninth International ethological conference. J. C. Fentress. Science 151:110-11 Ja 7 '66
1965 science review. Sci N L 88:390 D 18 '65
Pattern for success. W. Wingo. il Nations Bsns 53:48-52+ O '65
BEHIND-the-lens meters. See Exposure meters
BEHME, Bob
Instant trailering. Field & S 70:154-7+ My '65
Last chance at San Carlos. Field & S 70:73-5 O '65
Nothing like it on the Oregon coast. Field & S 70:10-11+ S '65
Piñatas and pescados. Field & S 70:33-5 D '65
Tent trailer basics. Field & S 69:60-3 F '65
BEHNKE, Ruth
Sugar-cured ham from a country kitchen. Farm J 89:87 N '65
BEHR, Edward
Find another de Gaulle. Sat Eve Post 238: 28-9 D 4 '65
BEHRENDT, Thomas. See Duane, T. D. jt. auth.
BEHRENS, John C.
Cranberry Glades. Am For 71:12-13+ D '65
BEHRMAN, Daniel
Conversations on an Indian campus. UNESCO Courier 18:34-6 My '65
BEHRMAN, Jack N.
Wrong way to fight the gold outflow? interview, ed. by G. R. Rosen. por Duns R 85:48-9+ Ap '65
BEHRMAN, S. N.
Riddle of Max and its masterly solution. Life 58:8+ Ap 16 '65
BEHRSTOCK, Julian
UNESCO and the world of books. UNESCO Courier 18:21-2 S '65
BEICHMAN, Arnold
Study in academic freedom. N Y Times Mag p 14-15+ D 19 '65
BEILENSON, Betsy
Children's book week and the bookseller. Pub W 188:54-6 N 8 '65
BEIRUT
Description
Sport on the far shores of Eden; photographs by P. Turner; with account by F. R. Smith. Sports Illus 22:38-9 Mr 29 '65
BEISE, S. Clark
San Francisco: getting together. Sat R 49: 50+. Ja 8 '66
BEISWANGER, George
Swan Lake in Atlanta. Dance Mag 39:36-40+ O '65
BEITING, Ralph W.
CAP is born. E. M. Raabe. America 112: 608-10 Ap 24 '65
BEITZ, Berthold
Idea. Newsweek 65:68+ F 15 '65
Krupp forges a new German trade weapon. il pors Bsns W p92-4 F 6 '65
BEJAR, Feliciano
One artist's colony. il por N Y Times Mag p40-1 S 5 '65

BÉJART, Maurice
Béjart at the Paris festival. M. Seif. por Sat R 49:49+ Ja 15 '66
Letter from Paris; choreography Opéra's Stravinsky ballet gala. Genêt. New Yorker 41:168-71 My 15 '65
BEKKUM, D. W. van, and Nieuwerkerk, H. T. M.
Adaptive enzyme synthesis: its inhibition as a possible analogue of immunological tolerance. bibliog Science 149:548-50 Jl '65
BELAÚNDE TERRY, Fernando
Architect of progress. il por Time 85:45-6 F 5 '65
New conquest. il pors Time 85:32-42 Mr 12 '65
Peru: encouraging new spirit. J. C. Carey. bibliog f Cur Hist 49:321-7 D '65
Shock of recognition. Newsweek 66:39+ Jl 19 '65
BELDOTTI, Lorraine. See Schwartz, R. S. jt. auth.
BELÉM-Brazilia highway. See Roads—Brazil
BELFORD, John A.
Case for a consistent company labor policy. Mo Labor R 88:148 F '65
BEL GEDDES, Joan
Bringing up baby. Redbook 125:65+ Ag '65
BELGIAN CONGO. See Congo (capital Leopoldville)
BELGIAN cookery. See Cookery, Belgian
BELGIANS in the United States
Vacation notes: letter from a Belgian settled in Georgia. A. T. Renson. Nat R 17: 803 S 21 '65
BELGIUM
See also
Elections—Belgium
Foreign relations
America and Belgium; a community of interests; address, June 16, 1965. D. MacArthur, 2d. Dept State Bul 53:118-22 Jl 19 '65
History
Bibliography
Articles and other books received; comp. by H. H. Rowen. See issues of American historical review
Industries
Big get bigger; Société générale de Belgique. Time 86:108 O 8 '65
Languages
Belgium divided. America 112:817 Je 5 '65
Confusion of tongues. il Newsweek 65:35-6 Je 7 '65
Politics and government
Belgium divided. America 112:817 Je 5 '65
Congo of Europe; Flemings vs. Walloons. Time 86:34 Ag 6 '65
Royal family
Regal mourners of Belgium's Queen without frontiers. il Life 59:49 D 10 '65
BELGRADE
Those friendly Beogradjani. D. Binder. il N Y Times Mag p92+ N 21 '65
BELIÁEV, Pavel Ivanovich
See also
Space flight—Manned flights—Beliáev-Leonov flight, 1965
—and Leonov, A. A.
How bright it is, how incredibly beautiful! pors Life 58:44+ My 14 '65
about
Adventure into emptiness. il pors Time 85: 85-86 Mr 26 '65
Hardest rendezvous of all, on the ground J. Hicks. il pors Life 59:113-14+ O 1 '65
BELIEF and doubt
Belief and unbelief, by M. Novak. Review Christian Cent 83:49 Ja 12 '66. P. M. Van Buren
Commonweal 83:221-2 N 19 '65
Campaign on many fronts. R. M. Brown. Christian Cent 82:577-9 My 5 '65; Discussion. 82:717 Je 2 '65
Dynamics of unfaith. L. J. Averill. Christian Cent 83:41-4 Ja 12 '66
See also
Creeds
BELIEF in God. See Faith
BELITT, Ben
Late dandelions; poem. New Yorker 41:197 O 23 '65
View from the gorge; poem. New Yorker 41: 26 Jl 3 '65
about
Poetry of Ben Belitt. W. Fowlie. Poetry 105: 324-5 F '65

BELK, W. H, family
Holdout in a world of chains. il Bsns W
p 113-14+ O 23 '65
BELK department stores. See Department
stores—Management
BELL, Alexander Graham
Voice heard round the world; excerpt from
Conquest of silence. L. Barnett. il pors Am
Heritage 16:50-9+ Ap '65
BELL, Charles
Building this sailing dink is a breeze.
Motor B 116:43-5 D '65
Care and repair of fiberglass boats. il Motor
B 115:42-4 Mr '65
FRP; fiberglass forum. Motor B 116:86+ Jl '65
Inner space program for your boat. Motor B
116:74-5+ N '65
BELL, Charles W.
Put your leaves to work. Am City 80:112-13
Ag '65
BELL, Daniel
Worker's search for security; reprint from
June 1963 issue. Mo Labor R 88:789-92
Jl '65
BELL, David Elliott
Challenge of the developing countries; ad-
dress, May 23, 1965. Dept State Bul 53:
173-7 Jl 26 '65
Foreign aid and the balance of payments;
statement, March 9, 1965. Dept State Bul
52:498-502 Ap 5 '65
Foreign aid program for 1966; statement,
February 4, 1965. Dept State Bul 52:343-8
Mr 8 '65; Excerpt. Cong Digest 44:183+
Je '65
BELL, E. and others
Configuration of inactive and active poly-
somes of the developing down feather. bib-
liog Science 148:1739-41 Je 25 '65
—See Reeder, R. jt. auth.
BELL, Edward J.
Along the peace front. Nat R 17:506-7, 575
Je 15, Jl 13 '65
National review: 1883-1960. Nat R 17:1117+
N 30 '65
Reapportionment comes to Connecticut. Nat
R 17:685-7+ Ag 10 '65
Sit down, you're rocking the boat. Nat R
17:983+ N 2 '65
BELL, Elsie
Nonconformist; story. NEA J 55:10-11 Ja '66
BELL, Enid
My wood sculpture. il por Am Artist 29:34-
9+ Mr '65
BELL, Joseph N.
Three giant steps to the moon. Pop Mech
124:104-8+ D '65
(ed) See Hollenbeck, A. I fought against
hatred among my neighbors
BELL, Marvin
Four young poets. Poetry 106:370-2 Ag '65
Hole in the sea; poem. New Yorker 41:149
Mr 6 '65
What songs the soldiers sang; Three corners
of reality; Coat of arms; Poor Jew; Things
we dreamt we died for; Her dream house;
poems. Poetry 105:381-6 Mr '65
BELL, Mrs Marvin R.
Dried plants offer design bonus. Design 66:
22-5 Mr '65
BELL, S. Alexander
Cruise of the Alsanal. por Motor B 116:22-5+
Ag; 44-6+ S; 74+ O '65
BELL, Vic
Color-TV set-up problems & adjustments.
Electr World 74:24-5+ D '65
BELL and Howell company
Evolution of the Bluejays. L. Lipton. il Pop
Phot 56:68-70+ Je '65
BELL helicopter company
Bell studies folding-rotor VTOL vehicles. il
Aviation W 82:81+ Mr 22 '65
BELL telephone hour (television program)
See Television broadcasting—Music
BELL telephone laboratories
Switchboard that will run forever. il Bsns W
p66-7 My 1 '65
BELL telephone system
AT&T; folksy octopus; Western union-
AT&T-Bell battle. D. Smith. il Nation
202:16-18 Ja 3 '66
BELLA, Ahmed Ben. See Ben Bella, A.
BELLA, Sita
Iran's education corps and illiteracy. Sch &
Soc 93:156-7 Mr 7 '65
BELLADONNA lilies
Two happy August companions. il Sunset 135:
144 Ag '65
BELLAGIO Road school, Bel Air. See Los
Angeles—Education
BELLANCA, Joe
Collages by Bellanca. il U S Camera 28:26-7
Ag '65
BELLER, Henry K. See Morant, R. B. jt.
auth.
BELLERIVE country club course, St Louis.
See Golf courses

BELLEVILLE, Ill, public library
Audiatur et altera pars: charge of censor-
ship by POAU against librarian. Wilson Lib
Bul 40:9+ S '65
Church, state, and freedom to read, charge
of censorship by POAU against librarian.
E. J. Gaines. ALA Bul 59:785-6 O '65
BELLI, Melvin Mouron
Trial of Jack Ruby, by J. Kaplan and J. R.
Waltz. Review
New Repub 153:25-8 N 27 '65. M. Kemp-
ton
BELLINI, Vincenzo
Joan Sutherland as Norma. P. L. Miller. Am
Rec G 31:604-5 Mr '65
On records; Norma. Opera N 29:39 My 1 '65
BELLINO, Joe
Another good Joe for the AFL. J. Under-
wood. il por Sports Illus 23:46-9 Ag 9 '65
BELLMAN, Richard
Is science big enough to cope with society?
with biographical sketch. por Sat R 48:
43-4 Je 5 '65
BELLMON, Henry
Oklahoma's education war. S. Kalkstein. il
Look 30:82+ Ja 25 '66
Teachers give Oklahoma a lesson. B. Carter.
Reporter 33:34-7 S 9 '65
BELLOW, Saul
Orange soufflé; text. Esquire 64:130-1+ O
'65
Thinking man's waste land; excerpt from
address. por Sat R 48:20 Ap 3 '65
about
Herzog and the passion. R. F. Capon. America
112:425-7 Mr 27 '65
Writer & the common world. C. Raines. Li-
brary J 90:1622 Ap 1 '65
BELLOWS, George Wesley
Gallery for young people. C. B. Johnson. il
Sch Arts 65:44 S '65
BELLS
Bells; Good humor bells. L. Springer. Hobbies
70:54 Ag '65
More about altar bells. L. E. Springer. il
Hobbies 70:123+ Jl '65
Parties that ring bells. E. J. L. Porter. il
Recreation 58:477-8 D '65
See also
Doorbells. Electric

Collectors and collecting
Farm and school bells. J. Mebane. il Bet
Hom & Gard 43:10+ O '65
Some inanimate bells. L. Springer. il Hob-
bies 7:44 S '65
BELLS of Ireland. See Shell flowers
BELLUSCHI, Pietro
Concerned with old-fashioned qualities. Arch
Rec 138:144-5 D '65
BELMONDO, Jean Paul
Son of Bogie. R. Grenier. por Esquire 65:
66-9+ Ja '66
BELMONT stakes. See Horse racing
BELOIT college, Beloit, Wis.
College with a plan. Newsweek 66:59 Ag
16 '65
BELOV, Evelyn
Serkin: Beethoven, Fourth piano concerto.
Am Rec G 32:120-1 O '65
BELSER, Karl
Santa Clara: the bulldozer crop. J. P.
Degnan. il Nation 200:242-5 Mr 8 '65
BELSER, William L. See Vacquier, V. D. jt.
auth.
BELTING
How to keep V-belts running longer. Suc
Farm 64:76 Ja '66
BELTON, Michael J. S.
Dynamics of interplanetary dust. bibliog
Science 151:35-44 Ja 7 '66
BELTON, Winstel R.
After a soldier fasted to avoid Vietnam duty.
U S News 59:8 O 18 '65
BELTRAMINI, Alessandro
Downfall of the man with the dog. M. Acoca.
il pors Life 58:72C-72D Ap 30 '65
BELTS, Machine. See Belting
BELTS, Safety. See Safety belts
BEMELMANS, Ludwig
Last of Bemelmans. H. Sutton. il Sat R
48:49+ F 20 '65
BEMIS, Samuel Flagg
America's first peace mission. Sat R 48:56-7
O 2 '65
BEN, Philip
Dead end of nonalignment. Reporter 32:19-22
My 20 '65
Limits of the U.N. Reporter 34:32-3 Ja 13
'66
Opinion in Paris: China won't fight. New
Repub 153:18 S 25 '65

BEN, Philip—*Continued*
  Poland takes a French lesson. Reporter 33:
    38-9 N 18 '65
  Romania's new national communism. Re-
    porter 33:32-3 S 9 '65
  Russia and Vietnam. New Repub 153:15-16
    Jl 10 '65
BEN BARKA, Mehdi
  Missing exile. por Time 86:43 N 12 '65
  St-Germain caper; Mehdi Ben Barka kidnaped
    in Paris. Newsweek 66:61-2 N 15 '65
  Shaking the throne. Newsweek 66:39 N 29 '65
BEN BELLA, Ahmed
  Africa's latest Caesar. C. Sterling. il Re-
    porter 32:10-13 Je 3 '65
  Aftermath. il Newsweek 66:35-6 Jl 5 '65
  Ahmed ben Bella, would-be leader of the
    third world. R. W. Howe. New Repub 152:
    10-11 Je 19 '65
  Algeria: a break for the West? il por U S
    News 59:10 Jl 5 '65
  Algeria; strong man out. il por Newsweek
    65:31-2 Je 28 '65
  Atlantic report. Atlan 216:14+ S '65
  Crash of glass. il por Time 85:36-7 Je 25 '65
  French conscience. Nation 201:179 O 4 '65
  Letter from Algeria. R. Shaplen. il New
    Yorker 41:147-8+ O 30 '65
  Letter from Algiers. R. Shaplen. il New York-
    er 41:38-40+ Jl 17 '65
  New face in Algiers. America 113:2 Jl 3 '65
BEN GURION, David
  Facts of Jewish exile; excerpt from Ben
    Gurion looks back. Harper 231:47-51 S '65

  about

  Back into battle. il por Time 86:45 O 22 '65
  Ben-Gurion woos the Diaspora. Christian
    Cent 82:765 Je 16 '65
  Ben-Gurion's failure. New Repub 153:16-17
    N 20 '65
  Old man and the young Sabras. C. Sterling.
    il Reporter 33:35-8 N 4 '65
  Salute to Israel's grand old man. H. Lehr-
    man. il por Sat R 48:39-40 Ap 10 '65
  Warrior's return. por Newsweek 66:37-8 Jl
    12 '65
BEN Franklin in Paris; musical comedy. See
    Musical comedies, revues, etc.—Criticisms,
    plots, etc.
BENACERRAF, Baruj. See Levine, B. B. jt.
    auth.
BENARES, India
  Well traveled camera. H. Keppler. il Mod
    Phot 29:36+ D '65; 30:26+ Ja '66
BENATTAR, Cecilia
  Toughest woman in real estate; with ex-
    cerpts from interview with D. Lurie. il
    pors Life 59:49-50+ O 1 '65
BENCE Jones proteins. See Proteins
BENCHES
  Build these benches for patio or deck. il
    Bet Hom & Gard 43:124+ Je '65
  Simple-to-make redwood bench. R. A. Henry.
    il Pop Gard 16:20+ My '65
  They're playing chess-on-a-bench. il Sunset
    136:74 Ja '66
BENCHLEY, Nathaniel
  First snow; story. New Yorker 41:194+ N 20
    '65
  Funny thing happened. New Yorker 41:78+
    Ja 15 '66
  World & Nantucket. il Am Heritage 16:28-
    31+ Je '65
BENCHLEY, Robert
  Most unforgettable character I've met. M.
    Connelly. por Read Digest 86:72-8 My '65
BENDA, Ernst
  Nazi murders & German politics. D. Schoen-
    baum. Commentary 39:72-7 Je '65
BENDA, Harry J.
  Decolonization in Indonesia: the problem of
    continuity and change. bibliog f Am Hist
    R 70:1058-73 Jl '65
BENDAÑA, F. E. and Galston, A. W.
  Hormone-induced stabilization of soluble
    RNA in pea-stem tissue. bibliog Science
    150:69-70 O 1 '65
BENDICH, Aaron, and others
  Circulating DNA as a possible factor in on-
    cogenesis. bibliog Science 148:374-6 Ap 16
    '65
BENDINER, Robert
  Are we connoisseurs of art or just con-
    sumers? Redbook 125:78-9+ O '65
  In that dawn to be alive. Reporter 33:57-8
    D 2 '65
  Personal note. por Nation 201:39-41 S 20 '65
  What has happened to America the beauti-
    ful? Redbook 125:50-1+ Je '65
  Who started the war on poverty? Redbook
    124:48-9+ F '65
BENDING
  NAA system would avoid booster bending.
    R. Pay. Miss & Roc 16:38-9 Ap 5 '65

BENDIX corporation
  Room for one more. il Time 86:82 S 10 '65
BENEDETTO, William R.
  How to help your wife cope with a hurricane.
    Harper 230:106 Mr '65
BENEDICT, H. Courtney. See Bonner, W. A.
    jt. auth.
BENEDICT, Lynne
  Why doesn't he write? Seventeen 24:326+
    Ag '65
BENEDICT, Nelson
  Big one! Bimini, 1965. il Yachting 118:32-3+
    Ag '65
  Sportfishing. See issues of Yachting
  Where the diesel makes sense. Yachting 117:
    108-9+ Je '65
BENEDICT Mar Gregorios, abp
  Kerala; agricultural slum. America 112:701
    My 15 '65
BENEDIKT, Michael
  Bonnard's own Bonnards. Art N 64:42-3+
    D '65
  Choices and risks. Poetry 105:332-6 F '65
  Some old men; Landscape; Enormous dang-
    ling sack-like net; Eye; poems. Poetry
    106:274-7 Jl '65
  Youngerman: liberty in limits. Art N 64:43-
    5+ S '65
BENEFIELD, Marilyn
  Constitution: team teaching approach with
    A-V aids. Sr Schol 86:sup7-8 Mr 11 '65
BENEVELLI, Frank N.
  Lowest responsible bidder, who is he? Am
    City 80:146+ Mr '65
BENGALI literature
    See also
  Bengali poetry
BENGALI poetry
  Note on the Vaishnava lyrics. E. C. Dimock,
    jr. Poetry 107:182-3 D '65
BENGSTON, Carl R.
  Plastic sewers serve a wharf. Am City 80:
    94-5 S '65
BENIGN myalgic encephalomyelitis. See Epi-
    demic neuromyasthenia
BENIN sculpture. See Sculpture, Bini
BENIRSCHKE, K. and others
  Chromosome complement: differences between
    equus caballus and equus przewalskii, Polia-
    koff. bibliog Science 148:382-3 Ap 16 '65
BENITEZ, Jaime
  Leadership crisis. Sat R 48:20 Jl 17 '65
BENITEZ, Manuel. See Cordobes
BENJAMIN, Curtis G.
  Relating to ETV. por Pub W 187:15-17 Ap
    5 '65
BENJAMIN, Lois
  Have you heard? See issues of Ladies' home
    journal
  Pet news. Ladies Home J 82:28+ My; 12+
    Je; 18 Jl '65
  Sight & sound. See issues of McCall's to
    August 1965
BENJAMIN, Mary A.
  Tale of a table. Am Heritage 16:100-1 Ap
    '65
BENJAMIN, Richard K.
  Study in specificity. Natur Hist 74:42-9 Mr
    '65
BENNETT, Charles G.
  New York: engineers vs politicians. Sat R
    48:43-4 O 23 '65
  New York: too little, too late? Sat R 48:45-6
    My 22 '65
BENNETT, Edna
  Boom in picture books. U S Camera 28:68-71+
    Mr '65
  Mister Japan in the U.S.A. U S Camera 28:
    18+ Je '65
  Photography is his business. U S Camera
    28:78+ N '65
  —and Saito, Fred
  History of Japanese photography. U S
    Camera 28:64-5+ Je '65
BENNETT, Hank
  Short-wave listening (cont of) Monthly short-
    wave report. See issues of Popular elec-
    tronics
BENNETT, Harmon
  Education vs. culture. T. Schoenman. ALA
    Bul 60:28-30 Ja '66
BENNETT, Joan Eastman, and Freedman,
    Elaine
  How practical is your front walk? Flower
    Grower 53:38-40 Ja '66
BENNETT, John C.
  Protestant views religious liberty. por Cath
    World 201:362-8 S '65
BENNETT, Lerone, jr
  Black power. Ebony 21:28-9+ N; 51-2+ D
    '65; 116-22 Ja '66 (to be cont)
  Pioneers in protest. See issues of Ebony
  SNCC: rebels with a cause. Ebony 20:146-53
    Jl '65
  White problem in America. Ebony 20:29-30+
    Ag '65

BENNETT, Lynn W.
  Outboard cruising is in. Motor B 115:35-7+
    Ap '65
BENNETT, Margaret, pseud.
  Don't give us your tired, your poor. Atlan
    215:93-5 My '65
  There's a Freud in your future. Atlan 216:126
    Jl '65
BENNETT, Paul A.
  AAUP award books; an awareness of qual-
    ity. bibliog Pub W 187:104-5+ Je 14 '65
  AIGA children's book show; summary. Pub
    W 188:76-8+ S 6 '65
  Keepsake for Alfred A. Knopf. Pub W 188:
    72-4+ Ag 9 '65
  Leonard Baskin, graphic artist. Pub W 187:
    70-1+ Ap 5 '65
  Recollections of F. W. Goudy: his types,
    books and press. Pub W 187:88+ Mr 1
    '65
  Remarkable exhibit in Baltimore: 2000 years
    of calligraphy. Pub W 188:106-8+ Jl 19 '65
  William Nicoll and Edit, inc. Pub W 188:
    88-92 D 6 '65
BENNETT, Raymond D. and Heftmann, Erich
  Progesterone: biosynthesis from pregnenolone
    in holarrhena floribunda. bibliog Science
    149:652-3 Ag 6 '65
BENNETT, Richard M.
  Teamwork. Christian Cent 82:941-2 Jl 28 '65
BENNETT, Tony
  Mature Mr Bennett. N. Hentoff. Holiday 38:
    158+ N '65
BENNETT, Vernon
  Stroke: second greatest crippler. G. Astor.
    il pors Look 29:120+ Je 15 '65
BENNETT, Ward
  Rooftop eyrie gives a modern designer ex-
    actly the home he wants. il House & Gard
    127:116-21 F '65
BENNETT, William Tapley, 1917-
  Diplomat who called for the marines. por
    U S News 58:24 My 17 '65
  How did it happen? B. van Voorst. il por
    Newsweek 65:49-50+ My 17 '65
BENNETT college, Greensboro, N.C.
  Bennett's proper pickets. M. A. Guitar. il
    Mlle 61:112-15+ Je '65
BENNINGTON college, Bennington, Vt.
  Bennington college dance department; 92nd
    street Y. J. Maskey. Dance Mag 40:59 Ja
    '66
  Bennington man. Newsweek 66:58-9 Jl 5 '65
  Pie in the face, poetry in a tree. il Time 86:
    56-7 Jl 9 '65
BENSON, Charles S.
  Two exercises in educational policy making;
    excerpt from Cheerful prospect: a state-
    ment on the future of American education.
    Sch & Soc 93:305-8 Sum '65
BENSON, George C. S.
  Trends in intergovernmental relations. bib-
    liog f Ann Am Acad 359:1-9 My '65
BENSON, Reed
  Birchers settle in. R. Stolley. Life 58:43 Je 18
    '65
  We Birchers are trained to look for patterns.
    J. Witcover. New Repub 152:8-9 My 8 '65
BENSON, Rosamond P.
  Painting with tissue paper. il Design 67:6-8
    S '65
BENSON, Sidney W. and King, J. W. Jr
  Electrostatic aspects of physical adsorption:
    implications for molecular sieves and gase-
    ous anesthesia. bibliog Science 150:1710-13
    D 24 '65
BENSUSAN, Howard B. and Klein, L.
  Catabolism of collagen. Science 148:1758-9
    Je 25 '65
BENTHAM, Josephine
  With love and cold water soap; story. Mc-
    Calls 92:90-1 Ag '65
BENTLEY, Beth
  Nuns at the Dali exhibit art in jewels; poem.
    Nation 200:207 F 22 '65
BENTLEY, Eric
  Peter Weiss and Wolf Biermann. Nation
    202:31 Ja 10 '66
  Treason of the experts. Nation 201:466-70
    D 13 '65
  (tr) See Brecht, B. Mother Courage and her
    children
BENTON, Robert. See Newman, D. jt. auth.
BENTON, Ruth
  Meadowlark's bill of rights. Am For 71:56
    N '65
  Security's price; poem. Am For 71:47 Je '65
BENTON, Thomas Hart
  Down the wide Missouri with an old S.O.B.
    R. Wernick. il pors Sat Eve Post 238:92-7
    O 23 '65
BENTON, William
  What worries the men in the Kremlin. Look
    29:67-8+ Ap 20 '65

about
  Cuckoo's egg in the Britannica. R. A. Free-
    man. il Nat R 17:514-18 Je 15 '65
  In the American grain. K. Kuh. il por Sat
    R 48:68-70 O 30 '65
BENTON HARBOR malleable industries
  Union tactics stall justice thirteen years. il
    Nations Bsns 53:31-3 N '65
BENZEDRINE. See Amphetamines
BENZOPYRANO
  Visnagin: biosynthesis and isolation from
    ammi visnagi suspension cultures. B. Kaul
    and E. J. Staba. bibliog il Science 150:
    1731-2 D 24 '65
BEOGRAD. See Belgrade
BEOWULF
  Beowulf. K. Rexroth. Sat R 48:27 Ap 10 '65
  On translating Beowulf. B. Raffel. Yale R
    54:532-46 Je '65
BEQUESTS. See Colleges and universities—
    Gifts, legacies, etc; Wills
BERAN, Josef, cardinal
  Two interventions on behalf of religious lib-
    erty. Cath World 202:177 D '65

about
  Four men: four stories. America 112:449-50
    Ap 3 '65
BERCZELLER, Richard
  Fellow-American. New Yorker 41:50-6 S 25
    '65
  M. Zuckerberg's heart. New Yorker 41:98+
    S 4 '65
BERDIE, Ralph F.
  Solution to the problem of distributing
    course grades. Sch & Soc 93:373-5 O 16 '65
BERENDT, John
  Esquire the younger. Esquire 63:158-61 Ap '65
BERENSON, Bernard
  BB as collector. L. Steinberg. Harper 230:
    154-6 Mr '65
  Game of the spirit. il por Time 86:122 O 22
    '65
  In love with the renaissance. A. Darack. por
    Sat R 48:53 O 9 '65
  Two centenarians. A. Frankfurter. Art N 63:
    23 F '65
BERENSON, Sara
  City summer; poem. Christian Cent 82:1011
    Ag 18 '65
BERENSTAIN, Janice. See Berenstain, S. jt.
    auth.
BERENSTAIN, Stanley, and Berenstain, Janice
  It's all in the family. See issues of McCall's
BERG, Alban
  Berg's Wozzeck, all made lucid and urgent.
    C. L. Osborne. il Hi Fi 15:75-7 D '65
  Lulu. Criticism
    Hi Fi 15:176-7 D '65
  On records: Wozzeck (excerpts) Opera N 29:
    34 F 6 '65
  On records; Wozzeck. Opera N 30:34 Ja 8 '66
  Wozzeck. Criticism
    Opera N 29:30 Mr 20 '65
    Opera N il 30:6-7 N 20 '65
    Opera N il 30:32 Ja 1 '66
    Sat R 48:26 Mr 13 '65
  Wozzeck. A. Sperber. il Am Rec G 32:338-41
    D '65
  Wozzeck strikes back. Discus. Harper 232:
    102-3 Ja '66
BERG, Eugene Paulsen
  Digging out from under. il por Bsns W p 106-
    7+ Ag 28 '65
BERG, Howard C. and others
  Erythrocyte membrane: chemical modifica-
    tion. bibliog Science 150:64-7 O 1 '65
BERG, Louis
  Peddlers in Eldorado. Commentary 40:63-7
    Jl '65
BERG, Norman
  Strategic planning in conglomerate com-
    panies. bibliog f Harvard Bsns R 43:79-92
    My '65
BERG, Roland H.
  New hope for drug addicts. Look 29:23-4
    N 30 '65
BERG, Stephen
  And so on; poem. Poetry 106:394 S '65
  Wife talks to herself; poem. New Yorker
    40:111 Ja 30 '65
BERGÉ, Carol
  Winter song. Poetry 105:365 Mr '65
BERGE, Glenn L. and Seielstad, G. A.
  Magnetic field of the galaxy; with biographi-
    cal sketches. Sci Am 212:20, 46-54 bib-
    liog(p 146) Je '65
BERGEN, Candy
  What I did last summer. por Esquire 64:
    234-7+ D '65

about
  Candy Bergen: what will she do when she
    grows up? il pors Look 29:39-41 S 7 '65

BERGEN, Polly
Polly Bergen sets the holiday scene. il Good H 161:38+ D '65
BERGER, Bennett M.
Teen-agers are an American invention. N Y Times Mag p 12-13+ Je 13 '65
BERGER, Elmer
United States and the Middle East; address, November 4, 1965. Vital Speeches 32:184-90 Ja 1 '66
BERGER, Ivan
Audio '66. Sat R 48:58-9 S 25 '65
Heard at the High fidelity show. Sat R 48: 74 O 16 '65
How loud is loud? Sat R 48:61+ F 27 '65
How to hook up hi-fi. Sat R 48:62 Je 26 '65
Loudness under control. Sat R 48:59+ Mr 27 '65
Negative feedback, positive result. Sat R 48:71 N 27 '65
Partaking of power. Sat R 48:61 Je 12 '65
Power pitfalls. Sat R 48:67+ Ap 24 '65
Riding gain. Sat R 48:59 Ag 28 '65
Sweetest sounds. Esquire 64:112-13+ N '65
BERGER, Jason
How to tip just enough: interview. Changing T 19:33-6 S '65
BERGER, K. C. and others
Polonium-210 analyses of vegetables. cured and uncured tobacco, and associated soils. bibliog Science 150:1738-9 D 24 '65
BERGER, Rainer. See Orr, P. C. jt. auth.
BERGER, Robert B.
Shopping for tools. See issues of Popular mechanics
BERGER, Roland
North Korea: nation at school. Nation 200: 530-1 My 17 '65
BERGER, Senta
She's Paulette, Hedy and Ava, all in one. il pors Life 59:80-1 S 10 '65
BERGER, Suzanne
Edouard Leclerc: grocer of France. Yale R 55:90-106 O '65
BERGER, Thomas
Jonathan Winters: always on. Holiday 38: 101-3+ N '65
Monkey of his own; story. Sat Eve Post 238:66-70 My 22 '65
BERGIN, Thomas G.
Dante; poem. Yale R 55:86 O '65
Dear, dead days. Sat R 48:46 Jl 24 '65
BERGNER, Per-Erik E.
Exchangeable mass: determination without assumption of isotopic equilibrium. bibliog Science 150:1048-50 N 19 '65
BERGONZI, Bernard
Books. Commonweal 82:452-3 Je 25 '65
BERGSAGEL, Daniel E. and others
Myeloma proteins and the clinical response to melphalan therapy. bibliog Science 148: 376-7; 149:564-5 Ap 16, Jl 30 '65
BERGSTROM purifier. See Oil filters
BERGTHOLD, Linda
Why I'm staying in teaching. por NEA J 54:20 O '65
BERING STRAIT
Bering Strait studied as land and sea. Sci N L 87:244 Ap 17 '65
First Americans: the evidence of mud. P. Colinvaux. Yale R 54:397-410 Mr '65
Quaternary correlations across Bering Strait. D. M. Hopkins and others. bibliog il Science 147:1107-14 Mr 5 '65
BERKELEY, Busby
Current cinema. B. Gill. New Yorker 41:110+ D 4 '65
100 lighted violins. il por Newsweek 66:104+ D 13 '65
BERKEY, Ben
Photography is his business. E. Bennett. il por U S Camera 28:78+ N '65
BERKMAN, Dave
Robert McNamara, crime syndicate head. Nat R 17:282+ Ap 6 '65
BERKOVITZ, Robert. See Sharma, M. jt. auth.
BERKOWITZ, Jesse M. See Gregor, H. P. jt auth.
BERKSHIRE Eagle (newspaper) See Pittsfield, Mass.—Newspapers
BERKSHIRE symphonic festival
Lohengrin complete; Tanglewood report. W. B. Syer. il Hi Fi 15:203+ N '65
BERKSON, William
Object: adornment. Craft Horiz 25:12-25 S '65
BERKWITT, George
Escalating war in metalworking. Duns R 86: 44-6+ Jl '65
Glitter in glass. Duns R 86:32-4+ S '65
Inevitable science of human engineering. Duns R 86:45-7+ O '65
Rise in industrial gases. Duns R 86:39-40+ D '65

BERLAND, Theodore
Headache: our most common malady. Todays Health 43:20-1+ F '65
Your doctor as a disease detective. Todays Health 43:62-5 S '65
BERLE, Adolf A.
Interference in the White House. Sat R 48: 29-30 Ag 21 '65
Stitch in time. Reporter 32:22-3 My 20 '65
BERLENGA ISLAND
Island asylum for mad fishermen. J. Olsen. il Sports Illus 23:74-6+ N 8 '65
BERLIN
One-way traffic. Time 86:20 D 31 '65

History
Allied occupation, 1945-
See also
Berlin wall, 1961-

Libraries
Prize awarded for design of Berlin national library. Library J 90:607 F 1 '65

Music
Berlin. J. H. Sutcliffe. Opera N 30:33 Ja 1 '66
Notes from our correspondents (cont) Hi Fi 16:28+ Ja '66

Theater
Etc; Berliner ensemble. R. J. Schroeder. Commonweal 83:62-3 O 15 '65
Live blossoms in dead soil; Berliner ensemble. R. Brustein. New Repub 153:33-6 Ag 7 '65

BERLIN (East Berlin)
East Berlin on July 4! letter to Dick Hanson. W. E. Swegle. Suc Farm 63:6+ S '65

Music
Berlin bouquet. J. H. Sutcliffe. il Opera N 29:32 F 20 '65
Opera East and West. P. Moor. il Hi Fi 15: 86X-86Y Mr '65

BERLIN (West Berlin)
Autobahn stop-go; Communist harassment to protest West German parliament meeting West Berlin. Sr Schol 86:27 Ap 29 '65
Berlin: the cultural capital. Holiday 38:102 S '65
Island and the sea; Soviet harassment during Bundestag meeting. il Newsweek 65:38+ Ap 19 '65
Simple signpost; Bundestag session in West Berlin in defiance of Soviet wishes. il Time 85:32 Ap 16 '65
Smiles change to snarls in Berlin; the meaning; Communist harassment around Berlin to protest the meeting of the West German Parliament in West Berlin. il U S News 58:52 Ap 19 '65

Music
Berlin bouquet. J. H. Sutcliffe. il Opera N 29:32 F 20 '65
Great opera houses: Berlin. H. Koegler. il Opera N 29:26-30 Mr 13 '65
Notes from our correspondents. P. Moor. Hi Fi 15:16+ Jl '65
Opera East and West. P. Moor. il Hi Fi 15: 86X-86Y Mr '65

BERLIN conference, 1945
Our war aims were wrong. L. J. Halle. il N Y Times Mag p 12-13+ Ag 22 '65; Discussion. p 14+ S 12 '65
BERLIN festival. See Music festivals—Germany (Federal Republic)
BERLIN film festival. See Moving picture festivals
BERLIN philharmonic orchestra
Musical events; performances of Beethoven cycle in Carnegie Hall, conducted by H. von Karajan. W. Sargeant. New Yorker 40:64-5 Ja 30; 98 F 6 '65
BERLIN question, 1945-
U.S. protests harassment on access routes to Berlin; note, April 7, 1965. Dept. State Bul 52:658 My 3 '65
See also
Berlin wall, 1961-
BERLIN wall, 1961-
Berlin wall, four years of failure. R. Drummond. il Read Digest 88:155-6 Ja '66
Catacomb instinct; rescuing people from East Berlin. B. van Voorst. il Newsweek 66:36 Ag 23 '65
Distractions at the wall. Time 85:25A Mr 12 '65
Since August 13, everything's different; end of hope for 17 millions. A. J. Olsen. il N Y Times Mag p36-7+ S 19 '65
Under the Berlin wall. G. Bailey. il Reporter 33:18-23 N 4 '65

BERLIN wall, 1961—*Continued*
Wall and the Pope. L. Wainwright. Life 58:28
Mr 19 '65
Wall: three years later. E. von Kuegelgen.
Nat R 17:764-5 S 7 '65
BERLIND, Bruce
Heidelberg 1963; poem. Poetry 105:240-3 Ja
'65
BERLINER, Gert
Nature behind the scenes; photographs.
Natur Hist 74:34-9 My '65
BERLINER ensemble. See Berlin—Theater
BERLINERS
Wall: three years later. E. von Kuegelgen.
Nat R 17:764-5 S 7 '65
BERLIOZ, Hector
Beatrice and Benedict. Criticism
New Yorker 41:122+ My 29 '65
Berlioz by Ormandy, and others. R. Law-
rence. Sat R 48:82 O 30 '65
Berlioz by Toscanini. P. L. Miller. il Am
Rec G 31:962-3 Je '65
Dread day of wrath, and the whisper of
compassion. R. D. Darrell. il Hi Fi 15:86-7
N '65
Music to my ears; concert performance of
Benvenuto Cellini in Philarmonic Hall. I.
Kolodin. Sat R 48:87+ Ap 10 '65
New York international. Benvenuto Cellini.
F. Merkling. Opera N 29:33 My 1 '65
On records; Roméo et Juliette. Opera N 30:
35 D 25 '65
BERLITZ schools of languages
Crowell Collier to buy Berlitz language
schools. Pub W 188:68 D 27 '65
BERMAN, Claire
TV's female brain trust. Good H 161:42 Jl
'65
BERMAN, Leonid. See Leonid
BERMAN, Sidney
As a psychiatrist sees pressures on middle-
class teen-agers. NEA J 54:16-17+ F '65
BERMEL, Albert
Getting out from under an image. Harper
230:38+ Ap '65
Split personality of USIA. Harper 231:116-
18+ S '65
BERMUDA
See also
Tourist trade—Bermuda

Description and travel
Bermuda moods. M. M. Davis. il Travel 124:
45-7 Ag '65
Gone flying to Bermuda. W. Strohmeier. il
Flying 77:44-9+ S '65
BERNA, James J.
Election in Kerala. America 112:316-17 Mr 6
'65
BERNADOTTE, Kerstin, countess
Sweden. Look 29:60-2 F 9 '65
BERNAM, Mel
Enna auto-magic interchangeable-lens sys-
tem. il Pop Phot 56:82-3 Ap '65
How to get the most out of polarizers they're
especially valuable with today's SLR's. Pop
Phot 56:84-7+ Je '65
New: Bilora Bellina 127 camera. Pop Phot
56:132-3 Ap '65
BERNARD, John V.
Science in the small school: Green River,
Wyoming. Atlan 215:95-8 Ap '65
BERNAYS, Edward L.
Men at the top: a Bernays'-eye view; ex-
cerpts from Biography of an idea. por For-
tune 72:138-9+ O '65

about
Cart before the horse. M. Barrett. Reporter
33:43-4+ D 30 '65
BERNBROCK, William F.
Furniture selection and specification. Arch
Rec 138:93+ S '65
BERNER, Robert A.
Dolomitization of the mid-Pacific atolls. bib-
liog Science 147:1297-9 Mr 12 '65
BERNFIELD, Merton R. and Nirenberg, M. W.
RNA codewords and protein synthesis. bib-
liog Science 147:479-84 Ja 29 '65
BERNHARD, consort of Juliana, queen of the
Netherlands
Atlantic partnership; address, April 12, 1965.
Vital Speeches 31:644-6 Ag 15 '65
Rediscovery of the UN. Nation 200:433 Ap
26 '65
BERNHARDT, Sarah
All that glitters. il por Time 86:68-71 Jl 23
'65
BERNHEIMER, Alan W. and Davidson, Mor-
ton
Lysis of pleuropneumonia-like organisms by
staphylococcal and streptococcal toxins.
bibliog Science 148:1229-31 My 28 '65

BERNHEIMER, Martin
BSO Schönberg. Sat R 48:30 Ap 17 '65
Imported baroque. Sat R 48:63-4 F 27 '65
Klemperer and the flute. Sat R 48:50 Mr 27 '65
Late Strauss from Vienna. Sat R 48:57-8 Ap
24 '65
Messiahs via Munich and Berlin. Sat R 48:
51 My 29 '65
Music to my ears. Sat R 48:48-9 My 8 '65
BERNI, Antonio
Antonio Berni: reprint. R. Squirru. il
Américas 17:20-9 O '65
BERNICCHI, Robert V.
Sampling by helicopter. Am City 80:80-2 N
'65
BERNSON, Marcella
In my opinion. por Seventeen 24:246 N '65
BERNSTEIN, Burton
Any book in this store twenty-nine cents.
New Yorker 41:122+ Je 12 '65
BERNSTEIN, Cal
Eight Japanese women. il Look 29:53-9 Ag
24 '65
BERNSTEIN, Edward Morris
Experts take new look at gold drain meas-
ure. il Bsns W p 116+ My 1 '65
BERNSTEIN, Jeremy
Books (cont) New Yorker 41:180-2+ My 1;
231-8+ N 6 '65
Reporter at large. New Yorker 41:43-6+ Mr
6; 130+ Mr 13; 109-10+ Mr 20 '65
BERNSTEIN, Leonard
In this age of dodecaphonics; premiere of
Chichester psalms. Time 86:52 Jl 23 '65
Musical events; Ives' Third and Mahler's
Ninth symphonies, performed by New York
philharmonic. W. Sargeant. New Yorker 41:
200-1 D 4 '65
Musical events; performance of Mahler's
Eighth symphony in Philharmonic Hall. W.
Sargeant. New Yorker 41:156+ D 18 '65
Musical events; performance of Mahler's
Seventh symphony and A. von Webern's
Symphony with New York philharmonic.
W. Sargeant. New Yorker 41:236 D 11 '65
Musical show minus the show. C. Harman.
Life 59:12 Jl 30 '65
Professor Bernstein's required readings. R.
Lawrence. Hi Fi 15:164 F '65
Summer nights at the Philharmonic. I. Kolo-
din. Sat R 48:41 Jl 31 '65
BERNSTEIN, Lou
What's there? il Mod Phot 29:91+ O '65
BERNSTEIN, Marion
Making the moment. il U S Camera 29:52-3
Ja '66
BERNSTEIN, Richard J.
Charles Sanders Peirce & The nation. Nation
200:308-10 Mr 22 '65

about
How to rate a teacher. il Time 85:48 Mr 12
'65
Protest at Yale. Nation 200:266-7 Mr 15 '65
Uprising at Yale. il Newsweek 65:89 Mr 15
'65
Yale's tenure trouble. N. S. Care. New Repub
152:13-14 Mr 27 '65
BERNSTEIN, Robert L.
Robert Bernstein named president of Ran-
dom House. por Pub W 188:29 D 13 '65
BERNSTEIN, Theodore M.
Cool that low talk and that high talk. N Y
Times Mag p 12-13 Jl 4 '65
BEROZA, Morton. See Jacobson, M. jt. auth.
BERRIAULT, Gina
Anna Lisa's nose; story. Esquire 63:74-5 Je
'65
BERRIES
Miraculous fruit makes sour foods taste
sweet. Sci N L 88:329 N 20 '65
See also
Spraying and dusting
also names of berries, e.g. Raspberries
BERRIGAN, Daniel
Question; poem. Christian Cent 82:1157 S 22
'65
Selma and Sharpeville. Commonweal 82:71-5
Ap 9 '65
Who is deprived? address. Commonweal 82:
53-5 Ap 2 '65
about
Father Berrigan, round two. Commonweal
83:328-9 D 17 '65
From glory to shame. Commonweal 83:261
D 3 '65
Lucky you! letter from pen-ultimate. Chris-
tian Cent 83:31 Ja 5 '66
Question of freedom. por Time 86:43 D 24 '65
Storm over Fr. Berrigan and again in New
Jersey. America 113:736 D 11 '65
BERRIGAN, Philip
Newburgh again. Commonweal 82:239 My 14
'65
Why and what. Commonweal 82:483-4 Jl 9 '65

BERRIGAN, Ted
Painter to the New York poets. Art N 64:
44-7+ N '65
BERRILL, N. J.
Aging and everyman. Atlan 217:86-90 Ja '66
BERRY, Charles
Doctor who worried about mumps in space.
M. Durham. il pors Life 58:76-7 Je 18 '65
BERRY, George Packer
No. 1 at no. 1. por Time 86:55 Jl 9 '65
BERRY, James R.
Are we licensing drivers to kill? Pop Sci 186:
64-7 Je '65
How they rescued me 200 feet underground.
Pop Sci 187:89-91+ O '65
Miniature world of microcircuits. Pop Mech
124:120-3 S '65
Voiceprints: poison for the telephone rat.
Pop Sci 187:80-3 S '65
Way-out world of antimatter. Pop Mech 124:
98-102+ D '65
BERRY, John
Banker in the news. Duns R 86:53-4 S '65
BERRY, Paul L.
Space race at LC. por Library J 90:3179-83
Ag '65
BERRY, Wendell
From The handing down. Poetry 106:1-9 Ap
'65
My great-grandfather's slaves; poem. Nation
200:199 F 22 '65
Two elegiac poems. Nation 201:220 S 20 '65
Tyranny of charity. Nation 201:161-4 S 27 '65

about

Three poets. H. Carruth. Poetry 106:310 Jl
'65
BERRYMAN, John
Berryman's dream songs. F. Seidel. Poetry
105:257-9 Ja '65
Couch and poetic insight. M. L. Rosenthal.
Reporter 32:53-4 Mr 25 '65
BERRYMAN, Phillip E.
Punishment of a priest. G. S. Mitrovich.
Christian Cent 82:782+ Je 16 '65
BERTHOLD, Robert V. See Herrett, R. A. jt.
auth.
BERTHS on yachts. See Yachts—Berths
BERTLES, John F. See Borgese, T. A. jt.
auth.
BERTOLUCCI, Bernardo
Starburst by a gifted twenty-two year-old.
P. Kael. Life 59:12 Ag 13 '65
BERTON, Pierre
Relics from the 20th century; excerpt from
My war with the 20th century. Read Digest
88:105-6 Ja '66
BERTRAM, Richard H.
Offshore powerboat racing, and a great man.
Yachting 117:58-9+ Mr '65
BERTRAND, Héloïse
Incident at Versailles. M. Cousins. il Mc-
Calls 92:114-15+ My '65
BERTRAND, Raymond
New life for priest workers. America 113:
669-70 N 27 '65
Wave of French conservatism. America 112:
248-9 F 20 '65
BERWICK, W. Phillips
Aid to parochial schools. Christian Cent 82:
374+ Mr 24 '65
BERWYN, Ill.
New street signs spell out good community
relations. il Am City 80:129 My '65
BERYLLIUM
Beryllium material offers more ductility. il
Aviation W 82:97+ F 22 '65
BESSE, Ralph M.
Metropolitan education; address, January 27,
1965. Vital Speeches 31:307-10 Mr 1 '65
1965: age of the shrug; address, November 9,
1965. Vital Speeches 32:154-8 D 15 '65
BESSER, Marianne
Children can learn to be quiet. Parents Mag
40:50-1+ F '65
BEST, Peter
Best of the Beatles. il por Time 86:36 D 31
'65
BEST, Winfield
Now! something better than the pill? McCalls
92:42+ F '65; Same with title Something
new in birth control. Read Digest 86:79-82
Ap '65
—and Jaffe, F. S.
Should abortion laws be liberalized? Parents
Mag 40:50-1+ Je '65
BEST of times; story. See Bradbury, R.
BEST sellers
Best sellers. See issues of Publishers' weekly
Best sellers and the public taste; letter to
the editor. B. C. Black Writer 78:5 S '65
Hardcover best sellers of 1965 in the U.S.
book trade. A. P. Hackett. il Pub W 189:
60-4 Ja 17 '66
1965 paperback best sellers in the bookstores.
il Pub W 189:64-7, 90-3 Ja 17 '66

BESTER, Alfred
Compleat hobbyist. Holiday 38:140-2+ D '65
BESTER, John F. See Moser, C. M. jt. auth.
BESTIARIES
Book as an artist's medium: Theobald's
bestiary. il Pub W 187:114+ F 1 '65
BÉTEILLE, André. See Srinivas, M. N. jt.
auth.
BETHE, H. A.
H. A. Bethe discusses high energy physics.
por Science 147:1551-2 Mr 26 '65
BETHGE, Eberhard
Profiles: D. Bonhoeffer. V. Mehta. New
Yorker 41:70+ N 27 '65
BETHLEHEM steel company
Wage chronology: Bethlehem Atlantic ship-
yards; supplement no. 4, 1962-65. W. Fridie.
il Mo Labor R 88:421-4 Ap '65
BETJEMANN, Christopher
Inventor of the month; box that won a U.S.
patent. S. V. Jones. il por Sci Digest 58:36
Ag '65
BETTELHEIM, Bruno
Dialogue with mothers. Ladies Home J 82:
55-6 N '65; 83:20 Ja '66
Grouping the gifted. NEA J 54:8-10 Mr '65
(ed) How mothers-in-law disrupt marriages;
an old problem in new forms. Redbook 124:
54-5+ Mr '65
Teaching the disadvantaged. NEA J 54:8-12
S '65
(ed) What our daughters-in-law didn't tell
you: an unexpected response from a group
of mothers-in-law. Redbook 124:66-7+ Ap
'65
When children lie or steal. Redbook 125:
74-5+ O '65
BETTER business bureaus
What is a better business bureau anyhow?
il Changing T 19:17-19 O '65
BETTI, Ugo
Queen and the rebels. Criticism
New Yorker 41:80 Mr 6 '65
Troubled waters. Criticism
Nation 200:681 Je 21 '65
BETTINA. See Bodin, S.
BETTING. See Gambling
BETTINI, Giovanni
Bettini: Sembrich cylinder and three cata-
logs. A. Favia-Artsay. il Hobbies 70:33-4 O
'65
Signor Bettini's cylinders. P. G. Davis. il
Hi Fi 15:24+ Ag '65
BETTIS, Valerie
Dance theatre workshop, inc, works by
Valerie Bettis, Anna Sokolow, Deborah
Jowitt; East 74th street theatre. J. Maskey.
Dance Mag 39:160-1 D '65
BETTS, Charles A.
Expense of civil defense. Sci N L 88:282-3
O 30 '65
BETTS, Lee F.
Make a charming entrance. Am City 81:94-5
Ja '66
BETWEEN the dark and the daylight; story.
See Hale, N.
BEUM, Robert
Lux urbanitatis; poem. Commonweal 83:151
N 5 '65
BEUTLER, Ernest, and Collins, Zeola
Hybridization of glucose-6-phosphate dehy-
drogenase from rat and human erythro-
cytes. bibliog Science 150:1306-7 D 3 '65
—See Krill, A. E. jt. auth.
BEV accelerators. See Accelerators (electrons,
etc)
BEVERAGES
Drinks that delight. il Ebony 21:110+ Ja '66
Greece bottles a drink with a familiar shape;
Tam Tam, grape-based soft drink. il
Bsns W p 146+ O 16 '65
Here's looking at you. il Sunset 135:144 S
'65
HoJo challenges the giants. J. F. Olesky.
Duns R 86:59+ S '65
Lighter side of Christmas drinking. J. A.
Beard. House & Gard 128:186+ D '65
Mellowed kickapoo. il Newsweek 65:80 F 22
'65
Milk punch; with recipes. M. Kaytor. il
Look 29:52-3 F 23 '65
Summer sipping; with recipes. D. Durham.
il Ladies Home J 82:72-3+ Jl '65
Super coolers for sizzling days. il Ebony 20:
138+ Jl '65

BEVERAGES—*Continued*
Through deepest summer with zest and cube.
Vogue 143:152 Ag 1 '65
Your conch runneth over; eight new ways
to hold your liquor. il Esquire 63:92-3 My
'65
See also
Coca-Cola company
Lemonade
Liquors
Punch (beverage)
Tea
Wine

BEVERLY HILLS, Calif.

Crime
Snatch that failed; L. K. Firestone. il Newsweek 67:31+ Ja 24 '66

Street traffic
Putting traffic-control practices to work. E.
E. Tufte. il Am City 80:125-6 Ag '65

BEXELIUS, Alfred
Our far-flung correspondents. J. Bainbridge.
New Yorker 40:136+ F 13 '65

BEYER, Malcolm K.
Caliph of caviar. A. J. McClane. il por Field
& S 70:36-8+ D '65

BEYLE, Marie Henri
History, stuff of dreams. P. G. Valderrama.
il por Americas 17:29-33 D '65

BHATTACHARYA, Deben
Forbidden and ecstatic circle. il Dance Mag
39:44-5+ F '65
Mile in the sky. il Dance Mag 39:46-9 Jl '65

BHATTACHARYA, P. K. and others
Nucleic acid and protein changes in wheat
leaf nuclei during rust infection. bibliog
Science 150:1605-7 D 17 '65

BIALER, Severyn
Men who run Russia's armed forces. N Y
Times Mag p 14-15+ F 21 '65

BIALOWIESKA FOREST. See Bialowieza
Forest

BIALOWIEZA FOREST
Return of the mighty bison; herd of Euro-
pean bison in the Bialowieska Forest. D.
Stivens. il Sci Digest 58:59-61 N '65

BIANCHI, Eugene C.
Los Angeles: tragedy and opportunity. Amer-
ica 113:260-1 S 11 '65
Pope of renewal. Cath World 202:178-9 D '65
Workshop on Christian unity. America 113:
95-6 Jl 24 '65
(ed) See Rahner, K. Karl Rahner in New
York

BIBB, Leon Douglas
They preach black to be the ideal. Negro
Hist Bul 28:132-3 Mr '65

BIBBY, Geoffrey
Celts. Horizon 7:20-31 Spr '65

BIBLE
Presenting the Bible: Anchor Bible. D.
Daiches. Commentary 40:47-55 S '65
Scripture and tradition; Vatican council ap-
proves constitution on Divine revelation.
America 113:456 O 23 '65

Antiquities
See also
Jerusalem—Antiquities
Jordan—Antiquities

Bibliography
Gift Bibles for the holiday season. il Pub W
188:77-83 S 27 '65
New Bibles and related books for the spring
season. il Pub W 187:84-8 F 8 '65

Biography
Meet Herodias; Richard Strauss' Salome. A.
M. Lingg. il Opera N 29:16 Mr 13 '65

Criticism, interpretation, etc.
Conversation with the Bible, by M. Barth.
Review
Christian Cent 82:1130 S 15 '65. F. V.
Filson
Jerusalem and Albion, by H. Fisch. Review
Commentary 39:73-5 F '65. D. Daiches

Bibliography
Book reviews. W. M. Abbott. il America 113:
720-4 D 4 '65
Books about the Bible. il Pub W 187:89-93
F 8 '65
Gift Bibles for the holiday season. il Pub W
188:83-5 S 27 '65

Editions
See Bible—Versions

Illustrations
See Bible—Pictorial illustrations

Interpretation
See Bible—Criticism, interpretation, etc.

Pictorial illustrations
Dali's astonishing new drawings to appear in
Rizzoli Bible. il Pub W 188:130+ Jl 19 '65

Publication and distribution
See also
Gideons international (organization)

Stories
See Bible stories

Study
See Bible study

Translations
See Bible—Versions

Versions
Common Bible nearer. America 112:872 Je 19
'65
Our new translation of the Bible. R. E.
Brown; discussion. America 112:168-9, 272-3
Ja 30, F 27 '65
Parables for cool squares. il Time 85:44
Mr 5 '65
Presenting the Bible: Anchor Bible. D.
Daiches. Commentary 40:47-55 S '65
See also
Bible—New Testament—Versions

Old Testament
Manuscripts
See also
Dead Sea scrolls

New Testament
See also
Jesus Christ

Versions
Catholic R.S.V. Commonweal 82:549 Ag 6 '65
Miracle of R.S.V; Catholic edition. C. North-
cott. Christian Cent 82:862 Jl 7 '65
New New Testament; new Confraternity ver-
sion. B. Vawter. Cath World 201:290-5 Ag
'65
New Testament; revised standard version:
Catholic edition. Review
Cath World 202:52-3 O '65. E. H. Peters
One for all; Catholic revised standard ver-
sion. Time 86:72 Jl 23 '65
Translation on trial; unfinished Confraternity
Bible. Time 85:90 My 28 '65

Gospels
Study of the synoptic gospels, by A. Bea; ed.
by J. A. Fizmyer. Review
Sat R 49:27 Ja 1 '66. Q. Quesnell

Matthew
On reading Matthew; question of a Judeo-
Christian tradition. M. Himmelfarb. Com-
mentary 40:56-65 O '65

BIBLE characters. See Bible—Biography

BIBLE in the schools. See Public schools and
religion

BIBLE society, American. See American Bible
society

BIBLE stories
Book your children will treasure; Children's
bible. L. M. Palmer. Farm J 89:64 Jl '65

BIBLE study
Ecumenism and the Ephesians; discussion
groups in Princeton. M. Wade. America
112:753 My 22 '65
Mustard-seed Bible schools; organization and
operation of a summer Bible school. M. A.
Carey. America 112:361-4 Mr 13 '65

BIBLICAL drama. See Religious drama

BIBLIOGRAPHIES
Networks of scientific papers; adaptation of
address, March 17, 1964. D. J. de S. Price.
bibliog il Science 149:510-15 Jl 30 '65

BIBLIOGRAPHY
Bibliographical challenges in the age of the
computer; excerpts from editorial in Mental
health book review index. I. Bry and L.
Afflerbach. il Library J 90:813-18 F 15 '65
Integrated bibliography; address. R. R. Shaw.
Library J 90:819-22 F 15 '65
Needless pains caused by heedless editors;
letter. I. H. Page. Science 147:1241 Mr 12
'65; Discussion. 148:443-4, 1174; 149:8, 815
Ap 23, My 28, Jl 2, Ag 20 '65
See also
Cataloging, Cooperative

Bibliography
Childrens literature
Book lists for young people. E. E. Ahlers.
Sr Schol 86:sup23 Mr 4 '65

BILLINGTON, Grace. See Norton, E. jt. auth.
BILLINGTON, Ray Allen
History is a dangerous subject. Sat R 49:
59-61+ Ja 15 '66
BILLUPS, J. W.
Telemetry: our eyes and ears in space. Pop
Electr 23:53-7+ O '65
BILLY Budd; opera. See Britten, B.
BILLY Liar; drama. See Waterhouse, K. and
Hall. W.
BILORA Bellina cameras. See Cameras
BIMAT film. See Photography—Films
BIMS, Hamilton J.
CORE: wild child of civil rights. Ebony 20:
35-8+ O '65
Deacons for defense. Ebony 20:25-8+ S '65
Housing, the hottest issue in the North.
Ebony 20:93-4+ Ag '65
New life for Ron Sturrup. Ebony 21:115-20+
D '65
Rocket age comes to tiny Triana. Ebony 20:
106-8+ Mr '65
BIMSON, Walter R.
My hunt of a lifetime. Sports Illus 23:82-
6+ O 25 '65
BINARY stars. See Stars, Double
BINDER, David
Rumania declares a sort of independence.
N Y Times Mag p43-9+ Je 6 '65
Those friendly Beogradjani. N Y Times Mag
p92+ N 21 '65
BINDING (books) See Bookbinding
BINDING dies. See Dies (metal work)
BINDRA, Dalbir, and others
Judgments of sameness and difference: ex-
periments on decision time. bibliog Science
150:1625-7 D 17 '65
BINDZI, Benoit
United Nations commemoration address, June
25, 1965. UN Mo Chron 2:99-102 Jl '65
BING, Rudolf
Importance of Bing. F. Merkling. il por Opera
N 29:8-11 Ap 17 '65
BING Crosby national pro-amateur champion-
ship. See Golf—Tournaments
BINGHAM, Jonathan B.
Excerpt from debate, September 20, 1965.
Cong Digest 44:285+ N '65
BINGHAM, Sallie
Bare bones; story. Redbook 124:52-3 Mr '65
BINGHAM, Wheelock H. and Yunich, D. L.
Retail reorganization. Harvard Bsns R 43:
129-32+ Jl '65
BINGHAMTON, N.Y.

Street traffic

Controller that meters traffic electronically. il Am City 80:120+ Jl '65

Water supply

Fluoridate the automatic way. C. V. Costello.
il Am City 80:183-4+ Je '65
BINI sculpture. See Sculpture, Bini
BINOCULARS. See Field glasses
BINSFELD, Edmund L.
Can any lover; poem. Christian Cent 83:14
Ja 5 '66
Nightingale on a jet; poem. Christian Cent
82:767 Je 16 '65
BINZEN, Peter
How to pick a school board. Sat R 48:72-3+
Ap 17 '65
Philadelphia's Negroes challenge a will. Re-
porter 33:43-5 O 21 '65
BIOASTRONAUTICS. See Space flight—Physio-
logical aspects
BIOCHEMISTRY
Are we finding a way to study the action
of the mind? il Science 150:922-4 N 12 '65
Biological formation of molecular hydrogen.
C. T. Gray and H. Gest. bibliog il Science
148:186-92 Ap 9 '65
Chemicals control body. Sci N L 89:4 Ja 1
'66
Control of biochemical reactions. J. P.
Changeux. il Sci Am 212:36-45 bibliog(p
158) Ap '65
Duplicating life, by chemistry; highlights of
ACS meeting, Atlantic City. il Bsns W
p 119-20 S 25 '65
Insect biochemistry; report on pioneering
insect biochemistry seminar, Chiba, Japan.
L. Levenbook. Science 150:643-4 O 29 '65
Significance of the gunflint, Precambrian
microflora. P. E. Cloud, jr. bibliog Sci-
ence 148:27-35 Ap 2 '65
Stereospecificity; report on symposium. A.
Sehon. Science 148:401-4+ Ap 16 '65
See also
Biosynthesis
Oxidation, Physiological

BIOCLIMATOLOGY
Bioclimatology; report on meeting at Sap-
poro, Japan. F. Sargent, 2d and S. Itoh.
Science 147:761-2+ F 12 '65
BIOELECTRIC control. See Electrophysiology
BIOELECTRONICS. See Medical electronics
BIOENGINEERING. See Human engineering
BIOGRAPHICAL dictionaries
Project to publish science biography dic-
tionary. Pub W 187:40 Mr 8 '65
See also
Biographical encyclopaedia and who's who
of the American theatre
Who's who in library service
BIOGRAPHICAL encyclopaedia and who's who
of the American theatre
In research of theater. H. Hewes. Sat R 48:
33 S 18 '65
BIOGRAPHY
Art of biography, by P. M. Kendall. Review
New Repub 152:25-7 Mr 6 '65. L. Edel
Lives and letters: a history of literary
biography in England and America, by
R. D. Altick. Review
Sat R 48:37 N 27 '65. L. Untermeyer
Perils and paradoxes of writing biography.
P. M. Kendall. Sat R 48:14-16+ Mr 27 '65
Reality of real people. A. Pryce-Jones. Com-
monweal 83:88-9+ O 22 '65

Bibliography

Biography (cont) F. J. Gallagher. America
112:672-4; 113:690-2 My 8, N 27 '65
Eight lives. P. Schlueter. Christian Cent
82:1158-9 S 22 '65
BIOLOGICAL apparatus and supplies
Automated synthesis of peptides. R. B.
Merrifield. bibliog il Science 150:178-85 O
8 '65
Constant volume, self-filling nanoliter pipette
construction and calibration. D. J. Prager
and others. il Science 147:606-8 F 5 '65
Disposable hydrogen generator: producing
hydrogen gas for anaerobe jars. J. H.
Brewer and D. L. Allgeier. bibliog il Sci-
ence 147:1033-4 F 26 '65
Protein solutions: concentration by a rapid
method. W. F. Blatt and others. bibliog
il Science 150:224-6 O 8 '65
See also
Homogenizers
BIOLOGICAL batteries. See Electric power
production from bacteriological action
BIOLOGICAL chemistry. See Biochemistry
BIOLOGICAL cycles. See Periodicity
BIOLOGICAL luminescence
Tracking the spark of life beyond earth.
J. Lear. il Sat R 48:45-7 Ap 3 '65
BIOLOGICAL physics
See also
Cells
BIOLOGICAL power. See Electric power pro-
duction from bacteriological action
BIOLOGICAL research
Are we finding a way to study the action
of the mind? il Science 150:922-4 N 12 '65
Biomedical science in Europe. R. P. Grant
and others; reply. R. K. Appleyard. Science
147:556-7 F 5 '65
Brain research; report on second seminar of
International brain research organization.
E. Costa. Science 148:865-6+ My 7 '65
Fundamental biology at the Weizmann insti-
tute. V. K. McElheny. il Science 148:641-18
Ap 30 '65
1965 science review. Sci N L 88:390-1 D 18
'65
Toxicology and the biomedical sciences. B. B.
Brodie and others. bibliog Science 148:
1547-54 Je 18 '65
See also
Cold—Physiological effects
Federation of American societies for ex-
perimental biology
Fishery research
Salk institute for biological studies, San
Diego. Calif.
BIOLOGICAL sciences curriculum study. See
Biology—Study and teaching
BIOLOGICAL warfare
Forthright CBR policy urged. W. S. Beller.
il Miss & Roc 16:27-8+ Ap 19 '65
Peril of non-nuclear weapons. B. H. Frisch.
il Sci Digest 57:8-13 Mr '65
BIOLOGY
See also
Cells
Death (biology)
Evolution
Life (biology)
Mendelism
Mutation (biology)
Polymorphism (biology)
Regeneration (biology)
Sex (biology)

BIOLOGY—*Continued*

International aspects

See Science—International aspects

Study and teaching

Brains, newts, legs, eggs, and sea shells; Science center of the Los Angeles school system. D. Turpin. il Am Ed 1:1-4 Ap '65

Curriculum reform: success hasn't spoiled NSF program, but biology study's status reflects problems; Biological sciences curriculum study. J. Walsh. Science 149:280-2 Jl 16 '65

Will evolution come to Arkansas? T. Dearmore. Reporter 34:34 Ja 13 '66

BIOLUMINESCENCE. See Luminescence, Biological

BIOMEDICAL engineering

TV camera to monitor biodynamics. M. Getler. il Miss & Roc 16:32-3 My 3 '65

BIOMEDICAL research. See Medical research

BIONICS

Brains without bodies. B. H. Frisch. il Sci Digest 58:10-14 N '65

BIONUCLEONICS laboratories. See Atomic research laboratories

BIOSATELLITE. See Artificial satellites—Use in research

BIOSYNTHESIS

Biological synthesis of cholesterol; address, December 11, 1964. K. Bloch. bibliog il Science 150:19-28 O 1 '65

Biosynthesis of alkaloids. E. Leete. bibliog il Science 147:1000-6 F 26 '65

Biosynthesis of histones and acidic nuclear proteins under different conditions of growth. L. S. Hnilica and others. bibliog il Science 150:1470-2 D 10 '65

Biosynthesis of vitamin A with rat intestinal enzymes. D. S. Goodman and H. S. Huang. bibliog il Science 149:879-80 Ag 20 '65

Cholesterol biosynthesis: mevalonate synthesis inhibited by bile salts. G. M. Fimognari and V. W. Rodwell. bibliog il Science 147:1038 F 26 '65

Control of glutamine synthetase in the embryonic retina in vitro. A. A. Moscona and D. L. Kirk. bibliog il Science 148:519-21 Ap 23 '65

Cyclopentanoid terpene biosynthesis in a phasmid insect and in catmint. J. Meinwald and others. bibliog il Science 151:79-80 Ja 7 '66

Dicyandiamide possible role in peptide synthesis during chemical evolution. G. Steinman and others. bibliog Science 147:1574 Mr 26 '65

Glycoprotein biosynthesis in human reticulocytes: a lesion in thalassemia. E. H. Eylar and G. T. Matioli. bibliog il Science 147:869-70 F 19 '65

Inheritance of linoleic and oleic acids in maize. C. G. Poneleit and D. E. Alexander. bibliog il Science 147:1585-6 Mr 26 '65

Nucleotide synthesis under possible primitive earth conditions. C. Ponnamperuma and R. Mack. bibliog il Science 148:1221-3 My 28 '65

Peptide synthesis from amino acids in aqueous solution. C. Ponnamperuma and E. Peterson. bibliog il Science 147:1572-4 Mr 26 '65

Protein synthesis and the mitotic apparatus. J. Mangan and others. bibliog il Science 147:1575-8 Mr 26 '65

BIOTECHNOLOGY. See Bionics

BIOTITE

Kink-bands: shock deformation of biotite resulting from a nuclear explosion. D. Cummings. bibliog il Science 148:950-2 My 14 '65

BIRAM, Brenda M.

Relativistic astrophysics. Science 148:112-14 Ap 2 '65

BIRCH, John, society. See John Birch society

BIRCH

Birches; the West's most popular. il Sunset 135:98-101 O '65

Make room for birch trees. D. Wyman. il Pop Gard 16:32-3+ My '65

BIRCH bark

Science in action; winter bark, slow fire; excerpt from The woods and the sea. D. C. Lunt. Natur Hist 74:57-8 Ap '65

BIRCH bark canoes. See Canoes and canoeing; Indians of North America—Boats

BIRD, John

Farewell to farmer Tuttle. Sat Eve Post 238:34-8+ D 4 '65

Fischer quints: summer on the farm. Sat Eve Post 238:28-35 Jl 31 '65

Lyndon Johnson's religion. Sat Eve Post 238:80-1+ Mr 27 '65

Merry Christmas for the quints. Sat Eve Post 238:21-5 D 18 '65

Your doctor and the A.M.A. Sat Eve Post 239:13-17+ Ja 1 '66

BIRD, Thomas E.

Collegiality and the cardinalate. Christian Cent 82:490-1 Ap 21 '65

Red hats as red flags. Commonweal 82:9-13, 301+ Mr 26, My 21 '65

Sidelight on Cyprus; fate of a patriarch. Commonweal 82:374-5 Je 11 '65

BIRD calling

Gift of gabbling. T. Janes. il Outdoor Life 137:44-5+ Ja '66

BIRD calls. See Birds—Song

BIRD census

Making the Yuletide count. L. B. Taylor, jr. il Audubon Mag 67:350-5 N '65; Same abr. with title Great day for bird lovers. Read Digest 87:83-7 D '65

BIRD dogs

Brag dog. C. Ford. il Field & S 69:6+ Mr '65

See also

Field trials (dogs)

Pointers (dogs)

BIRD feeders. See Feeders (birds)

BIRD houses

Birds aren't fussy. C. P. Fox. il Flower Grower 52:47 Ap '65

BIRD populations

Control

Anesthetize pest birds; with tribromethanol for humane removal. C. M. Moser and J. F. Bester. Am City 80:30+ My '65

BIRD sanctuaries

Pintail ducks and friends gather here; Richardson Bay wildlife sanctuary, Calif. il Sunset 135:36+ O '65

See also

Wildlife sanctuaries

BIRD shooting. See Shooting

BIRD songs. See Birds—Song

BIRD study

Air battles close to home. M. Michaud. il Audubon Mag 67:116-20 Mr '65

Bird finding. O. S. Pettingill, jr. See issues of Audubon magazine

Birdwatching, an all-year, all-time hobby. J. Cole. il Parents Mag 40:87 Je '65

Know the birds by name. J. K. Terres. il Flower Grower 52:23+ Ag '65

Making the Yuletide count. L. B. Taylor, jr. il Audubon Mag 67:350-5 N '65; Same abr. with title Great day for bird lovers. Read Digest 87:83-7 D '65

Sense of wonder; excerpts. R. Carson. il McCalls 92:76-83+ Je '65

Walk with the Birdman; R. T. Peterson. J. Roddy. il Look 29:106+ My 18 '65

Wondrous birds and a wondrous lady. E. W. Teale. il Audubon Mag 67:222-8 Jl '65

See also

Audubon magazine

Birds—Identification

BIRD watching. See Bird study

BIRDFOOT violets. See Violets

BIRDOFF, Harry

Erminie, a Victorian extravaganza. Hobbies 70:35 D '65

BIRDS

Bird finding. O. S. Pettingill, jr. See issues of Audubon magazine

Bird quiz. J. Daugherty and M. Daugherty. il Sci Digest 58:83-5 Ag '65

Birds in your garden. See issues of Popular gardening & living outdoors

Bring a song to your garden. J. K. Terres. il Pop Gard 16:24-5 S '65

See also names of birds, e.g. Crows

Accidents and hazards

Bird mortality after spraying for Dutch elm disease with DDT. C. F. Wurster, jr. and others. bibliog Science 148:90-1 Ap 2 '65; Reply with rejoinder. I. N. McDaniel. 149:326 Jl 16 '65

Bibliography

Birds and things. M. Bush. Am For 71:69+ My '65

Of interest to birders. E. Eisenmann. Natur Hist 74:6+ Je '65

Diseases and pests

See also

Botulism

Extermination

Bird mortality after spraying for Dutch elm disease with DDT. C. F. Wurster, jr. and others. bibliog Science 148:90-1 Ap 2 '65

BIRDS—*Continued*

Eyes
See Eye (birds)

Food and feeding
Attract birds to your garden. E. A. Mason. il Horticulture 43:20-1+ D '65
Choice feeders and foods for eastern birds; excerpts. V. E. Davison. Audubon Mag 67:393-4+ N '65
Energy intake of the mourning dove zenaidura macroura marginella. W. D. Schmid. bibliog il Science 150:1171-2 N 26 '65
Food choices of some choice species; excerpts. V. E. Davison. il Audubon Mag 67:322+ S '65 (to be cont)
Low cost bird feeding. C. Niewoehner. Audubon Mag 67:257 Jl '65
Margie's porridge, make it for the birds. M. D. Hodgins. il Flower Grower 53:66 Ja '66
New menu suets catbirds. R. B. Fischer. il Audubon Mag 67:121 Mr '65
Who needs a grouse dog? N. Smith. il Outdoor Life 136:44-7+ O '65
See also
Feeders (birds)

Habits and behavior
Birds that see in the dark with their ears. E. S. Ross. il Nat Geog Mag 127:282-90 F '65
Friendly ones. J. K. Terres. il Flower Grower 52:36+ My '65
Lonely tunesmiths of nature, men and the birds. W. H. Thorpe and M. E. W. North. il Sat R 48:85-7 D 4 '65
See also
Birds—Food and feeding

Identification
Identification test for bird enthusiasts. L. J. Kopp. il Nat Parks Mag 39:22-3+ My '65

Language
See Birds—Habits and behavior

Migration
Night flight with a thrush. R. R. Graber. il Audubon Mag 67:368-74 N '65
Painting swans for science. P. Innis. il Audubon Mag 67:292-5 S '65
Rendezvous in our driveway. B. Atkinson. Audubon Mag 67:312 S '65
Wondrous birds and a wondrous lady. E. W. Teale. il Audubon Mag 67:222-8 Jl '65
See also
Orientation

Nests
See Nests

Orientation
See Orientation

Physiology
Bursa of Fabricius in chickens: possible humoral factor. R. L. St Pierre and G. A. Ackerman. bibliog il Science 147:1307-8 Mr 12 '65
Changes in the tail feathers of the adolescent lyrebird. L. H. Smith. il Science 147:510-13 Ja 29 '65; Correction 149:565 Jl 30 '65
Countercurrent multipliers in avian kidneys. T. L. Poulson. bibliog il Science 148:389-91 Ap 16 '65

Protection
Your garden can attract birds and people too. M. Costigan. il Flower Grower 52:38+ Mr '65

Sanctuaries
See Bird sanctuaries

Song
Bird song: the anatomy of a miracle. D. J. Borror. il Audubon Mag 67:159-63 My '65
Lonely tunesmiths of nature, men and the birds. W. H. Thorpe and M. E. W. North. il Sat R 48:85-7 D 4 '65
Science in action; the sounds of singing; East Africa. G. S. Keith. Natur Hist 74:61-4 Je '65
White-throated sparrow knows neighbor's pitch. Sci N L 88:137 Ag 28 '65

Study
See Bird study

Alaska
Pribilofs; excerpt from The Bird watcher's America, ed. by O. S. Pettingill. il Audubon Mag 67:72-7 Mr '65

California
From Monterey to the Sierras; excerpt from Bird watcher's America, ed. by O. S. Pettingill, jr. il Audubon Mag 67:208-11 Jl '65

Florida
Inside the Everglades; excerpt from Bird watcher's America, ed. by O. S. Pettingill, jr. W. B. Robertson, jr. Audubon Mag 67:274+ S '65
See also
Nenes

Hawaii
See also
Nenes

Missouri
Show birds of the show-me state. G. Campbell. Audubon Mag 67:122-3 Mr '65

New Zealand
Bird that stood 10 feet tall. R. A. Caras. il Sci Digest 59:57-60 Ja '66

North America
Water, prey, and game birds: a new singing book. Review
  Nat Geog Mag il 128:528-35 O '65. M. B. Grosvenor
See also
Bird census

North Carolina
Visit to Hatteras. O. S. Pettingill, jr. il Audubon Mag 67:343-4+ N '65

South Dakota
Black Hills of South Dakota; excerpt from The bird watcher's America, ed. by O. Pettingill. H. Krause. il Audubon Mag 67:140+ My '65

Texas
Wonderous birds and a wondrous lady. E. W. Teale. il Audubon Mag 67:222-8 Jl '65

United States
See also
Bird census

BIRDS, Extinct
See also
Moas

BIRDS as pets. See Pets

BIRDS' Christmas carol; drama. See Miller, H. L.

BIRDS in art
Audubon: naturalist into artist. E. H. Dwight. il Art N 64:35-7+ My '65

BIRDS nests. See Nests

BIRMINGHAM, Stephen
American youth: a generation under the gun. Holiday 37:42-61+ Mr '65
Palm Springs, gold-plated mirage. Holiday 37:32-45 F '65
Restive youth of Spain. Holiday 37:88-93+ Ap '65

BIRMINGHAM, William
Books. Commonweal 82:222-3, 538-40 My 7, Jl 23 '65
What the theologians are saying. Commonweal 81:705-8 F 26 '65

BIRMINGHAM, Ala.

Negroes
Birmingham two years later. P. Good. il Reporter 33:21-7 D 2 '65
Where good men don't count. H. Brandon. Sat R 48:12 Ap 24 '65

Politics and government
Birmingham two years later. P. Good. il Reporter 33:21-7 D 2 '65

BIRMINGHAM, Ala. civic opera company
Birmingham's tenth. A. M. Lingg. il Opera N 29:31 Ap 10 '65

BIRMINGHAM, Mich.
Structural form defines bank areas. il Arch Rec 137:195 Je '65

BIRMINGHAM news
Riot act in Alabama. Newsweek 65:75 Ap 12 '65

BIRNBAUM, Hubert C.
Signed with a grin. il U S Camera 28:48-9 O '65

BIRNKRANT, Milton
Inventor of the month. por S. V. Jones. por Sci Digest 57:30 Ap '65

BIRNN, Roland
U.S. Coast guard auxiliary. See issues of Yachting

BIRO, Pete
Phoenix 200. Motor T 17:67-9 Mr '65

BIRRELL, Lowell McAfee
Birrell break. Newsweek 65:72 Je 28 '65

BIRTH. See Childbirth

BIRTH, Multiple
Fantastic drug that creates quintuplets. il Life 59:24-31 Ag 13 '65
See also
Quintuplets
Triplets

BIRTH control

Back in business; Connecticut law ruled unconstitutional. il Newsweek 65:60 Je 21 '65
B—th c-nt—l. New Repub 153:5-6 S 25 '65; Reply. R. T. Bushell. 153:36-7 O 9 '65
Birth control: academy report stresses burdens of high birth rate among the impoverished here. E. Langer. Science 148: 1205-6+ My 28 '65
Birth control hearings. Commonweal 82:484-5 Jl 9 '65
Birth control pills: an up-to-date report. il Good H 161:159-61 S '65
Birth control: private initiative and public debate. E. Langer. Science 150:1433 D 10 '65
Birth rate. W. F. Buckley, jr. Nat R 17:231 Mr 23 '65
Breakthrough in birth control: answer to population explosion? il U S News 59:56-8 O 4 '65; Same abr. with title Breakthrough in birth control. Read Digest 88:61-4 Ja '66
Businessmen back it. Bsns W p34 My 15 '65
By the clock; cycle dial to show a woman's period of probable fertility. il Time 86:61 Jl 9 '65
Climate changes for federal birth control aid. Christian Cent 82:229 F 24 '65
Coming: more federal help on birth control. U S News 59:11 N 15 '65
Connecticut decision. Commonweal 82:427-8 Je 25 '65
Consensus grows on birth control: federal agencies support programs for family planning. Bsns W p36 O 9 '65
Contraception and morals; concerning address given by Donald B. Straus. America 112:741 My 22 '65
Court and birth control. W. B. Ball. Commonweal 82:490-3 Jl 9 '65; Reply with rejoinder. M. L. Wulf. 82:578-9+ Ag 20 '65
Discuss birth control; Hamilton County Cincinnati welfare workers. F. Stauffer. Christian Cent 82:693-4 My 26 '65
Drift toward disaster; Belgrade conference sponsored by UN, a failure. Christian Cent 82:1309 O 27 '65
End of term decisions; Connecticut's anti-birth control statute unconstitutional. New Repub 152:7-8 Je 19 '65
Family planning as law: a lawyer's objections. W. B. Ball. Cath World 202:144-50 D '65
Family planning clock; Lady 13021. il Consumer Rep 30:522-3 N '65
Famine is here. New Repub 153:6 S 18 '65
Federal birth control: progress without policy. W. Greene. il Reporter 33:35-7 N 18 '65
Forgotten amendment; Griswold v. Connecticut, right to marital privacy and rediscovery of Ninth amendment. J. D. Carroll. Nation 201:121-2 S 6 '65
Gains for birth control; Ford foundation grants to Columbia-Presbyterian medical center and Population council; foreign aid recommendations. Newsweek 66:94 D 13 '65
Health and population. C. E. Taylor. For Affairs 43:475-86 Ap '65
Hidden crisis. J. D. Rockefeller, 3rd. il Look 29:75-6+ F 9 '65
How births can be controlled. A. F. Guttmacher. Nat R 17:641-2 Jl 27 '65
If we ignore the plight. . ; bill to establish assistant secretaryships for population control. Time 86:16 Jl 2 '65
Indian birth control plant holds clues to glands. Sci N L 87:281 My 1 '65
Kentucky doctor: one man's war against southern poverty. L. Bergquist. il Look 29:76-80 N 16 '65
Lemmings: federal policy and programs. Nation 201:402-3 N 29 '65
Life, liberty and privacy; Connecticut law forbidding the use of contraceptives declared unconstitutional. Life 59:4 Jl 2 '65
Mister birth control; Ernest Gruening, interest and proposals. R. Stolley. Life 59: 40D Jl 2 '65
More U.S. aid soon for birth control? U S News 59:10 Jl 5 '65
Myth-busters. il Newsweek 66:19 Jl 5 '65
National population policy. W. E. Moran, jr. il Cath World 202:138-43 D '65
New books. E. H. Peters. Cath World 201: 403-6 S '65
Now it's official: U.S. backs birth control aid. il U S News 58:64-6 Mr 22 '65
Now, legal family planning; Connecticut birth control law unconstitutional. H. G. Lewis. Christian Cent 82:970+ Ag 4 '65
Of many things; Chicago program aimed at poor Negroes. T. N. Davis. America 113: 511 N 6 '65
Population committee formed; Population crisis committee. Nat Parks Mag 39:20 Je '65

Population explosion and anti-babyism. Life 58:6 Ap 23 '65
Population politics: new bill introduced by Gruening brings birth control issues to Congress. E. Langer. Science 148:1702-3 Je 25 '65
Population problems are still critical. Sci N L 87:374 Je 12 '65
Promoting birth control. America 112:238 F 20 '65
Promoting family planning; CWS planned parenthood. Christian Cent 82:980 Ag 11 '65
Public birth control; programs conducted by state and local governments. America 112: 513 Ap 17 '65
Purely biological: nature and meaning of human sexuality; letter. M. Ortiz. America 112:195-6 F 6 '65
Regulation at last? America 112:275 F 27 '65
Reproduction and the whole man. F. W. Carney. il America 112:245-7 F 20 '65
Safe bureaucratic decision; family planning opportunities denied to poor single women. New Repub 153:9 S 18 '65
Science vs. morality? America 112:411 Mr 27 '65
Silence is broken; protests against government's involvement in birth control programs. America 113:256 S 11 '65
Supreme court reverses birth control law; Connecticut birth control laws banned. Christian Cent 82:796 Je 23 '65
U. S. population problem; family planning. Sci Am 213:46 Jl '65
Why did birth control fail for me? B. Seaman. Ladies Home J 82:166-7 N '65
Why U.S. birth rate is heading downward. il Bsns W p 108+ F 13 '65
Words and deeds are not identical: absence of information in a library's collections. E. J. Gaines. ALA Bul 59:605-6 Jl '65
See also
Abortion
Contraceptives

Religious aspects

Beyond contraception. America 112:478 Ap 10 '65; Reply. J. J. McEleney. 112:696 My 15 '65
Birth control: a new Catholic policy soon? U S News 58:16 Ap 12 '65
Birth control decision. America 112:875-6 Je 19 '65
Birth control decision. Commonweal 83:296 D 10 '65
Birth control revolution. S. M. Spencer. il Sat Eve Post 239:21-5+ Ja 15 '66
Birth control, what happened? G. Baum. Commonweal 83:369-71 D 24 '65
Catholic agency opposes birth control ban; Catholic council on civil liberties. Christian Cent 82:262 Mr 3 '65
Catholic church reconsiders birth control. J. Cogley. il N Y Times Mag p7+ Je 20 '65
Catholic revolution. J. Roddy. il Look 29:26-7 F 9 '65
Catholics and population. G. Wills. Nat R 17:643-8 Jl 27 '65; Discussion. 17:706+ Ag 24 '65
Church & birth control: from Genesis to genetics. Time 86:73-4 Jl 16 '65
Contraception, by J. T. Noonan. Review Commonweal 82:538-40 Jl 23 '65. W. Birmingham
Council on contraception. R. A. McCormick. America 114:47-8 Ja 8 '66; Reply with rejoinder. J. C. Ford. 114:103+ Ja 22 '66
Critical juncture; licit means of family limitation. Commonweal 82:99-100 Ap 16 '65
Division on birth control; Pope Paul's advisory commission. Time 85:80 Ap 2 '65
Ecclesiology of birth control. M. Novak. Christian Cent 82:454-5 Ap 14 '65
Irony out of Liverpool; Catholic laymen seek revision of church teaching. America 112: 598 Ap 24 '65
Lady doctor defies her church. J. Roddy. il Look 27:73+ Ag 10 '65
Mater si, magistra, si! L. B. Bozell. Nat R 17:772+ S 7 '65; Reply. G. Wills. 17:933 O 19 '65
Morals in Massachusetts: amending the birth control laws. J. L. Dorsey. Commonweal 82:188-90 Ap 30 '65
New approach in sex morals. America 113: 176 Ag 21 '65
New books. E. H. Peters. Cath World 201: 206-7 Je '65
Papal statement on birth control. America 113:558 N 13 '65
Pope and the pill; Pope Paul's special commission on birth and population control. il Newsweek 65:66 Ap 12 '65
Rediscovering the obvious; Catholic discussion over the morality of birth control. V. R. Ruggiero. America 112:613-15 Ap 24 '65

BIRTH control—Religious aspects—*Continued*
Subtle shift. Newsweek 66:43 S 6 '65
This baby will be my last; explanation by a Catholic mother. B. J. Taylor. Redbook 125:6+ Jl '65
Vatican II and responsible parenthood. R. Fagley. Christian Cent 82:332-3 Mr 17 '65
Will Rome take the pill? C. Northcott. Christian Cent 82:518 Ap 28 '65

Colombia
Family planning; experiment in Cali. R. Guerrero. America 112:665-6 My 8 '65

France
Letter from Paris. Genêt. New Yorker 41: 169-70+ N 13 '65

India
Billion Indians by 2000 A.D? S. Chandrasekhar. il N Y Times Mag p32-3+ Ap 4 '65
Loop way. Time 86:24 Jl 23 '65

Latin America
Opinions of Latin-American intellectuals on population problems and birth control; with questions and answers. J. M. Stycos. bibliog f il Ann Am Acad 360:11-26 Jl '65
Problem of our time. Time 86:34 Ag 20 '65

United States
See Birth control

BIRTH defects. See Deformities
BIRTH marks. See Birthmarks
BIRTH order
Birth order and its sequelae. W. D. Altus. bibliog Science 151:44-9 Ja 7 '66

BIRTH rate
See also
Birth control
Population, Increase of

India
We help build the population bomb. W. Vogt. il N Y Times Mag p32+ Ap 4 '65

United States
End of the baby boom in America. il U S News 58:67 Je 14 '65
Why U.S. birth rate is heading downward. il Bsns W p108+ F 13 '65

BIRTHDAY of the infanta; drama. See Nolan, P. T.
BIRTHDAY parties. See Childrens parties
BIRTHDAY picnics. See Picnics
BIRTHMARKS
Birthmark treatment. Sci Digest 58:38-9 O '65
Hemangiomas: Mother Nature's vanishing act. V. H. Witten. il Todays Health 43: 48-9+ S '65

BISCUITS
Perfect biscuits. Am Home 68:75 Ap '65
BISHKO, C. J.
(comp) Articles and other books received; Spain and Portugal. See issues of American historical review
BISHOP, Charles W.
Pilot was a pioneer. por Outdoor Life 136: 52-5+ D '65
BISHOP, Claire Huchet
Reading and singing. Commonweal 83:153-4 N 5 '65
What Chinese children read. Commonweal 82:323-5 My 28 '65
BISHOP, Elizabeth
On the railroad named delight. N Y Times Mag p30-1+ Mr 7 '65
(tr) See Andrade, C. D. de. Travelling in the family
BISHOP, Jim
Bishop & the dictator; columns on Haiti. Time 86:62 S 10 '65
BISHOP, Jordan
Tremors in Bolivia. Commonweal 83:339-42 D 17 '65
Yankees in Roman collars. Commonweal 82: 469-71 Jl 2 '65
BISHOP, Lews G. and Stark, Lawrence
Pupillary response of the screech owl, otus asio. Science 148:1751-2 Je 25 '65
BISHOP, Morris
Dante's pilgrimage. Horizon 7:4-15 Sum '65
BISHOPS
Applied collegiality. Commonweal 83:171-2 N 12 '65
Bishops and criticism. Commonweal 82:260-1 Jl 2; 83:173 N 12 '65
Catholic revolution; authority of bishops and supremacy of the pope. J. Roddy. il Look 29:21-7 F 9 '65; Reply. America 112:213 F 13 '65

Collegiality: its meaning. L. M. Örsy. America 112:705-9 My 15 '65; Reply. J. Finnegan. 112:842-3 Je 12 '65
Negro heads bishops' council; Methodist church's Council of bishops. Christian Cent 82:606 My 12 '65
New currents swirling around Peter's rock. J. K. Jessup. il Life 59:27-9+ D 17 '65
Papacy, the episcopacy, and collegiality, by W. Bertrams. Review
Commonweal 82:360-1 Je 4 '65. P. E. Sigmund
Time is now: bishops must lead. J. G. Lawler. Commonweal 82:691-4 S 24 '65
See also
Episcopacy
BISMARCK, Otto, fürst von
Bismarck, by W. Richter, tr. by B. Battershaw. Review
Sat R il por 48:25+ Ap 3 '65. L. L. Snyder
Time por 85:100 Mr 26 '65
BISMARCK, N.D.
Planning parking and plowing. E. J. Booth. il Am City 80:87-9 S '65
BISON, European
Return of the mighty bison; herd of European bison in the Bialowieska Forest. D. Stivens. il Sci Digest 58:59-61 N '65
BISQUE figurines. See Figurines
BISSELL, Richard
Lighthearted tour of America. Holiday 38:30-43+ Jl '65
BISSELL, Trim
Archaic song. Poetry 105:249 Ja '65
BITS, Boring. See Drilling and boring machinery
BITTER, Francis
Ultrastrong magnetic fields; with biographical sketch. Sci Am 213:16, 64-73 Jl '65
BITTERMAN, M. E. See Kirk, K. L. jt. auth.
BITTERS
Bitters, the tangy mixers. H. Johnson. House & Gard 127:152+ Je '65
BITTNER, William
Poet's day of grace. Sat R 48:44 O 30 '65
BIZET, Georges
Carmen. Criticism
Opera N 30:28 O 23 '65
Sat R 48:64 N 20 '65
On records: Carmen. Opera N 29:34 F 27 '65
On records; Carmen. Opera N 30:44 O 23 '65
BJORKMAN, Donald
Workshop: vacuum forming of plywood. Craft Horiz 25:38-40 S '65
BLACK, Barbara
Battle against insects and diseases of plants. Horticulture 43:26-7+ Jl '65
For easy maintenance, a self-controlled landscape. Pop Gard 17:32-3 Ja '66
Green mansions. Pop Gard 16:38-41 My '65
If you are moving plants interstate. Horticulture 43:32-3+ O '65
Mail order catalogs. Horticulture 43:42-4 D '65
Saga of a garden center. Flower Grower 52: 37-9 Je '65
Tree is forever. Pop Gard 16:18-20 Mr '65
BLACK, Charles
Git or git got. il por Newsweek 66:88 D 6 '65
BLACK, Clanton C.
Reduction of trimethylene dipyridyl with illuminated chloroplasts. bibliog Science 149: 62-3 Jl 2 '65
BLACK, Eugene Robert
LBJ's choice for aid-to-Asia job. il por U S News 58:22 Ap 19 '65
Mr Black reports on southeast Asia economic development. Dept State Bul 53:215 Ag 2 '65
Why LBJ wants men ten feet tall. P. Lisagor. por Nations Bsns 53:23-4 O '65
BLACK, Hillel
School where children teach themselves. Sat Eve Post 238:80-1+ Je 19 '65
BLACK, Martin L. and Gay, I. D.
Some kinetic properties of a deterministic epidemic confirmed by computer simulation. bibliog Science 148:981-5 My 14 '65
BLACK, Shirley (Temple) See Temple, S.
BLACK, Sue
Shirley's big daughter. il pors Life 59:65-6+ Jl 30 '65
BLACK Angus cattle. See Cattle—Breeds
BLACK bass fishing. See Bass fishing
BLACK bear hunting. See Bear hunting
BLACK death
See also
Plague
BLACK Hawks (hockey team) See Hockey teams

BLACK HILLS, S. D.
Black Hills of South Dakota; excerpt from
The bird watcher's America, ed. by O.
Pettingill. H. Krause. il Audubon Mag 67:
140+ My '65
On your way to the Black Hills. . . E. Walt-
ner. il Travel 124:35-7 S '65
    See also
Mount Rushmore National Memorial
BLACK Muslim movement
After Malcolm X. J. O'Gara. Commonweal
82:8 Mr 26 '65
Black Muslims are a fraud; ed. by E. Linn.
A. Barnette. il Sat Eve Post 238:23-9 F 27
'65
Brief return from Mecca. E. Capouya. il Sat
R 48:42+ N 20 '65
Cassius Clay must be beaten; with editorial
comment. F. Patterson. Sports Illus 23:19,
78-80+ O 11 '65
Death of a desperado; assassination of Mal-
colm X. il Newsweek 65:24-5 Mr 8 '65
James Baldwin's jeremiad. A. B. Southwick.
Christian Cent 82:362-4 Mr 24 '65
Malcolm X. Nation 200:239 Mr 8 '65
Meaning of Malcolm X. C. E. Lincoln.
Christian Cent 82:431-3 Ap 7 '65
Muslim influence great. Sci N L 88:165 S 11
'65
Now it's Negroes vs. Negroes in America's
racial violence. il U S News 58:6 Mr 8 '65
They preach black to be the ideal. L. D.
Bibb. Negro Hist Bul 28:132-3 Mr '65
Vendetta by rivals feared. il Sr Schol 86:21
Mr 11 '65
BLACKBURN, Clark W.
Substitute mothers. PTA Mag 59:28-30 Je '65
BLACKBURN, Hal
Safety check. Flying 77:118+ O '65
BLACKBURN, Paul
Lower case poem. Nation 200:654 Je 14 '65
Stone; poem. New Yorker 41:59 N 20 '65
BLACKETT, Patrick Maynard Stuart
Blackett chosen president of Royal society.
V. K. McElheny. por Science 150:1437-9 D
10 '65
BLACKFISH fishing. See Tautog fishing
BLACKHAM, E. Donnell
Physics of the piano; with biographical
sketch. Sci Am 213:10, 88-96+ bibliog(p 128)
D '65
BLACKIE, William
President Johnson receives report on in-
creasing trade with U.S.S.R; remarks,
January 7, 1965. Dept State Bul 52:101-2
Ja 25 '65
BLACKLISTING
Blooped out; J. Muir out of Girl talk. Nation
202:30 Ja 10 '66
    See also
Boycott
BLACKOUTS (electric power) See Electric
power
BLACKS; drama. See Genet, J.
BLACKSMITHS
Whatever became of the village blacksmith?
C. B. Randall. il Pop Mech 124:106-7+ N '65
BLACKWATER fever
Rare disease hits troops. C. A. Betts. Sci
N L 88:35 Jl 17 '65
BLACKWELL, R. Quentin, and others
Hemoglobin J$_{Korat}$ in Thais. bibliog Science
150:1614-15 D 17 '65
BLACKWELL, Vera
Avant-garde in Prague. Nation 200:650-2 Je
14 '65
BLADDER
        Diseases
Medical problem every woman should under-
stand. Good H 160:181 My '65
BLAINE, Graham B. Jr
Teenagers in search of themselves. Parents
Mag 40:46-8+ D '65
BLAIR, Eric. See Orwell, G. pseud.
BLAIR, James P.
Fair reopens; photographs. Nat Geog Mag
127:504-29 Ap '65
BLAIR, Robert Dike
Imaginative selling in small town shop. P.
Johnson. jr. il Pub W 188:51-2 Ag 9 '65
BLAIR, William L. See Wright, J. C. jt. auth.
BLAISDELL, Harold F.
Home of the fish. por Field & S 70:37-9+
Jl '65
Landlock break-out. por Outdoor Life 135:
58-60+ My '65
BLAISDELL, Neal S.
GOP mayor in his eleventh year. il pors
Look 29:62-3 F 23 '65
BLAKE, Catherine (Boucher)
Pronounced golgonooza? L. Zukofsky. Poetry
107:65-8 O '65

BLAKE, Eugene Carson
We nominate Blake. Christian Cent 83:68-
9 Ja 19 '66
BLAKE, Hector
Hard Toe right to the jaw. M. Kram. il por
Sports Illus 22:32-3 My 10 '65
Worrying is the way to win. M. Kram. il
pors Sports Illus 23:48-50+ N 22 '65
BLAKE, John Lauris
Parson Blake and the farmer's wife; summary
of Farmer's everyday book, ed. by M. W.
Steer. Am Heritage 16:42-5 Je '65
BLAKE, L. C.
Busy life came to a close. K. Fleming. il por
Newsweek 66:18-19 D 27 '65
BLAKE, Peter
Astride the open road. Life 59:49 D 24 '65
BLAKE, Toe. See Blake, H.
BLAKE, William
On Yeats and others. H. Carruth. Poetry 107:
194-5 D '65
Pronounced golgonooza? L. Zukofsky. Poetry
107:65-8 O '65
BLAKEMORE, W. B.
Catholic and Protestant renewal. Cath World
201:183-8 Je '65
BLAKESLEE, Alton L.
Today's health news. See issues of Today's
health
BLAKEY, G. Robert
Crisis in crime control. America 113:238-40
S 4 '65
BLANCH, Lesley
And so perfumed that the winds were love-
sick with them. Vogue 146:127-8+ N 15 '65
Exotic and the erotic. Vogue 145:106-11+ Ap
15 '65
Iran. Vogue 146:130-9+ Ag 15 '65
Match me such marvel! Vogue 146:180-201+
D '65
BLANCHARD, Eric D.
Delta ministry. Christian Cent 82:337-8 Mr
17 '65
BLANCO BOUZA, Julio David
Self-portrait of a Cuban teenager; excerpts
from interview; ed. by W. Johnson. por
Sr Schol 87:18 N 18 '65
BLANK, B. D.
Crump's craft. Nation 200:402 Ap 12 '65
BLANK, Joseph P.
Atomic power comes of age. Read Digest 87:
109-12 D '65
John F. Kennedy school no. 1. Read Digest
86:54-8 Mr '65
Twenty minutes of horror. Read Digest 86:
141-4 Ap '65
BLANKETS
Blankets; questions and answers. il Good H
160:164+ F '65
Loosely blanketed; thermal blanket. Time
85:67 Mr 26 '65
Thermal weave blankets. il Consumer Bul
48:2+ D '65
Winter warmers. B. G. Wadsworth. il Par-
ents Mag 40:112 Mr '65
BLANSHARD, Brand
Eliot in memory. Yale R 54:635-40 Je '65
BLANTON, Smiley
Magic of being in touch. Read Digest 87:76-8
Ag '65
BLASER, Robin
Medium; poem. Nation 201:126 S 6 '65
BLASINGAME, Ralph, Jr
Equalization of opportunity; address, Octo-
ber 1964. por Library J 90:2071-5 My 1 '65
—See Ricking, M. jt. auth.
BLASPHEMY
Finnish author, publisher prosecuted for
blasphemy. Pub W 187:100 F 8 '65
BLASS, Bill
Bare-ish. il Newsweek 65:57 Je 7 '65
BLASSINGAME, John W.
Freedom fighters. bibliog Negro Hist Bul 28:
105-6 F '65
BLASTING
    See also
Atomic blasting
BLASZKA, Felix
Brief biography. S. Goodman. pors Dance
Mag 39:50-1 F '65
BLATNIK, John A.
Water pollution: federal role is strengthened
by law authorizing new agency and quality
standards. E. Langer. por Science 150:198-
9+ O 8 '65
BLATT, Genevieve
New books. Cath World 202:187-8 D '65
Wanted: more men for all seasons, and
women too. por Cath World 201:56-61 Ap '65
BLATT, William F. and others
Protein solutions: concentration by a rapid
method. bibliog Science 150:224-6 O 8 '65
BLATTEIS, Clark M. and Lutherer, L. O.
Fatty-tissue changes in rats with accli-
matization to altitude. Science 149:1383-5
S 17 '65

BLAU, Amram
Lost leader. il por Time 86:73 S 10 '65
Rabbi's shiksa. il por Newsweek 66:77 Ag 9 '65

BLAU, Herbert
Blau & Irving come out of the West. M. Harris. il por N Y Times Mag p 16-17+ F 21 '65
Enter the gadflies. por Newsweek 65:82-3 F 8 '65
People are talking about... por Vogue 146:204-5 O 1 '65

BLAU, Sheldon, and others
Cellular origin of hyaluronateprotein in the human synovial membrane. bibliog Science 150:353-5 O 15 '65

BLAUKOPF, Kurt
Notes from our correspondents. See issues of High fidelity incorporating Musical America

BLAUSHILD, David
Fight to save Lake Erie. H. Titus. il por Field & S 69:10-12+ Mr '65

BLEACHES. See Bleaching materials

BLEACHING (photography) See Photography —Retouching

BLEACHING materials
Fine-fabric bleaches. E. Taylor. il Good H 160:154 Ja '65
Vanishing color. H. Ringgenberg. il Design 66:27-9 My '65

BLEDSOE, Stewart
I spent a winter in politics. pors Farm J 90:38+ Ja '66

BLEEDERS disease. See Hemophilia

BLENDERS, Electric. See Electric apparatus and appliances, Domestic

BLENDING. See Mixing

BLEPHARISMA intermedium. See Ciliata

BLESSED Sacrament. See Catholic church—Eucharist

BLESSING
Day before Easter on Olvera street: blessing of animals in Los Angeles. il Sunset 134:40+ Ap '65

BLEWETT, John
They asked me why I came. America 113:469-70 O 23 '65

BLIMPS. See Airships

BLIND
Sonar system of the blind: size discrimination. C. E. Rice and S. H. Feinstein. bibliog il Science 148:1107-8 Mr 21 '65
See also
Libraries—Work with blind
School libraries—Work with blind

Education
Long steep hill to victory; blind scientist graduate. L. T. Henderson. il Read Digest 86:103-7 Je '65

BLIND, Apparatus for the
Blind test themselves; sensory aids for evaluation. Sci N L 87:119 F 20 '65
How the blind use sonar. il Sci Digest 58:33 S '65
Sensory research discussion: sonar and electronic reading for the blind; report on proceedings. H. Freiberger. Science 147:1163 Mr 5 '65

BLIND, Books for the
See also
Talking books

BLIND, Checks for the
Checks in braille. Time 85:87 F 12 '65

BLIND, Periodicals for the
See also
Talking books

BLINDNESS
Condemned before birth. Sci Digest 57:20 Je '65
Glories I've seen! M. Jackson. Read Digest 87:95-8 S '65

BLINDNESS, Color. See Color blindness

BLINDNESS, Snow. See Snow blindness

BLINDS
Timeless traditions for windows; venetian blind. il House & Gard 128:256-7 O '65

BLISS, Marion
Curl up and read. Seventeen 24:28 Jl '65

BLISS, Ray Charles
Election aftermath: how Republicans see the future; interview. por U S News 59:34-6 N 15 '65

about

Bliss rides the elephant. D. S. Broder. il pors N Y Times Mag p49-50+ Mr 21 '65
Mr Bliss' dilemma. W. F. Buckley, jr. Nat R 17:630 Jl 27 '65
More and more problems for Bliss. por U S News 59:16 Jl 5 '65
New era of Bliss. W. R. Buckley, jr. Nat R 17:318 Ap 20 '65

New GOP chairman. G. F. Jenks. New Repub 152.8-9 F 6 '65
Ordeal of Ray Bliss. R. Evans and R. Novak. il pors Sat Eve Post 238:32-5 N 6 '65
Republicans' comeback trail, where it begins. il U S News 58:70-1 F 8 '65

BLISTERS
Can anything be done about cold sores? Good H 161:175 O '65
Those pesky mouth sores. E. J. Driscoll and E. A. Graykowski. il Todays Health 44:32-4 Ja '66

BLITZSTEIN, Marc
Marc Blitzstein's The cradle will rock. T. Brown. il por Am Rec G 31:800-5 My '65

BLIVEN, Bruce
Tempest over Teapot. Am Heritage 16:20-3+ Ag '65

BLIVEN, Naomi
Books (cont) New Yorker 41:190+ Ap 24; 126-8 My 29; 153-5 Je 12; 80-4 Jl 10; 124-7 Ag 21 '65; 104+ Ja 8 '66

BLIXEN, Karen (Dinesen) baronesse
Challenge of the myth and mask. V. Lange. por Sat R 48:43 Mr 6 '65
Isak Dinesen conquers Rome. E. Walter. por Harper 230:46-54 F '65

BLOATING
Tips on bloat. L. A. Baker. Farm J 89:A10 Jl '65

BLOCH, Ernest
Bartók and Bloch: isolated in our time. Discus. Harper 230:120+ Je '65
From Columbia, a Bloch, Stern, Zakin triumph. E. Belov. il Am Rec G 31:1067 Jl '65

BLOCH, Konrad
Biological synthesis of cholesterol; address, December 11, 1964. bibliog Science 150:19-28 O 1 '65

BLOCK, Jean Libman
Many lives of Maureen O'Sullivan. Good H 161:28+ N '65
Many talents of Mrs Hubert Humphrey. por Good H 160:42+ Je '65

BLOCK, Libbie
Where did all the flowers go? story. McCalls 92:90-1 Mr '65

BLOCK, Marvin A.
No hiding place in a bottle; interview, ed. by K. N. Anderson. Todays Health 43:32-3+ Mr '65

BLOCK, Nancy
In my opinion. por Seventeen 24:204 O '65

BLOCK, Ruth
(comp) Machiavelli speaks. N Y Times Mag p57-8 Mr 14 '65
(comp) Of want. N Y Times Mag p25+ Jl 25 '65

BLOCK, S. and others
High-pressure single-crystal studies of ice VI. bibliog Science 148:947-8 My 14 '65

BLOCK ISLAND race week. See Regattas

BLOCKADE
Blockade saves lives. R. Moley. Newsweek 67:60 Ja 3 '66
Freedom of the seas; goods of war to North Vietnam. R. Moley. Newsweek 66:74 D 27 '65

BLOCKER, Chris
O.K. let's start again; pro debut of a rookie. il por Sports Illus 24:10-11 Ja 17 '66

BLOCKER, Dan
Bonanza. R. W. Lewis. il pors Sat Eve Post 238:84-9 D 4 '65

BLODGET, Robert
Aeroclassic. Flying 77:60-5 Jl '65
Once around the parking lot. Flying 77:62-6 S '65

BLOESCH, Donald G.
Spiritual ecumenism. Christian Cent 82:1450-1 N 24 '65

BLOMDAHL, Karl Birger
Herr von Hancken. Criticism
Opera N il 30:23 N 6 '65

BLOOD
Blood of a cockroach: unusual cellular behavior. H. Ritter, jr. bibliog il Science 147:518-19 Ja 29 '65
Can you answer these questions about blood? L. Galton. il Pop Sci 186:122-5+ Mr '65
See also
Erthropoiesis
Leucocytes

Circulation
Blood-flow relation between hepatic artery and portal vein. J. L. Ternberg and H. R. Butcher, jr. bibliog il Science 150:1030-1 N 19 '65

Coagulation
Hageman factor: alterations in physical properties during activation. V. H. Donaldson and O. D. Ratnoff. bibliog il Science 150:754-6 N 5 '65

BLOOD—Coagulation—*Continued*
Visual excitation and blood clotting. G. Wald. bibliog il Science 150:1028-30 N 19 '65
See also
Anticoagulants (medicine)

Corpus and platelets

See also
Lymphocytes

Diseases

Granulocytosis; promoting extract of mouse tumor tissue; partial purification. L. Delmonte and R. A. Liebelt. bibliog il Science 148:521-3 Ap 23 '65
See also
Anemia
Hemophilia
Leukemia

Freezing

Sugar best preservative in quick freezing blood. Sci N L 87:313 My 15 '65

Pigments

See also
Hemoglobin

Plasma

Hageman factor: alterations in physical properties during activation. V. H. Donaldson and O. D. Ratnoff. bibliog il Science 150:754-6 N 5 '65
Inheritance of two alkaline phosphatase variants in fowl plasma. G. R. J. Law and S. S. Munro. bibliog il Science 149:1518 S 24 '65
Protein conformations in the plasma membrane. A. H. Maddy and B. R. Malcolm. bibliog il Science 150:1616-18 D 17 '65

Proteins

See also
Serum globulins

Testing

PKU test kit price hit. F. Marley. Sci N L 87:357 Je 5 '65
What blood can tell. Sci Digest 57:34-5 F '65

Transfusion

Transfusions we don't need. Sci Digest 58:17 Ag '65

BLOOD donors
Blood in your future. J. B. Hartney. Todays Health 43:5+ D '65

BLOOD groups
Automatic blood sorter. il Sci Digest 57:21-2 Ap '65
Hemoglobin J$_{Korat}$ in Thais. R. Q. Blackwell and others. bibliog Science 150:1614-15 D 17 '65
See also
Rh factors

BLOOD pressure
Carotid sinus and aortic reflexes in the regulation of circulation during sleep. M. Guazzi and others. bibliog il Science 148:397-9 Ap 16 '65
See also
Hypertension

BLOOD spots in eggs. See Eggs—Grading and standardization

BLOOD substitutes
See also
Dextran

BLOOD sugar
New culprit in heart disease? Time 86:59 Jl 23 '65

BLOOD vessels
See also
Capillaries

Surgery

Gas clears arteries. Sci N L 88:341 N 27 '65
Hewing the fat; gas surgery. il Time 86:59 N 26 '65
Man who should have died; complete shutdown in aorta. il Time 86:92 O 8 '65
Stroke victims treated by neck artery surgery. Sci N L 88:297 N 6 '65

BLOOM, Claire
Beauty and the beast; ed. by A. Guerin. il pors Life 59:45-6+ O 29 '65

BLOOM, Murray Teigh
How to protect those valuable papers. Read Digest 87:127-30 D '65
Justice for the poor. Read Digest 86:126-30 Ap '65
Why many criminals go free. Read Digest 87:19-20+ Ag '65

BLOOMINGDALES (store) See New York (city)
—Stores

BLOOMSBURY group
Cast of characters: a Bloomsbury memoir; excerpts from Taken care of. E. Sitwell. Reporter 32:43-5 Ap 8 '65

BLOUSES
Shirts and blouses permanent press? well, yes if you have an electric or gas dryer. il Consumer Bul 49:37-40 Ja '66

BLOUSTEIN, Edward J.
Bennington man. por Newsweek 66:58-9 Jl 5 '65

BLOWER, David
David Blower: watercolorist. il por Am Artist 29:28-9+ My '65

BLOWERS, Snow. See Snow blowers, throwers, etc.

BLUE, Elizabeth M.
Please, Mr Superintendent. NEA J 54:49-50 My '65

BLUE baby. See Tetralogy of Fallot

BLUE collar workers. See Labor and laboring classes

BLUE cross hospital services. See Insurance, Hospitalization

BLUE green algae. See Algae

BLUE kite; story. See Marqués, R.

BLUE laws. See Sunday legislation

BLUE lily of the Nile. See African lilies

BLUE RIDGE MOUNTAINS
We took the high road. W. Hartley. il Redbook 124:70-1 Mr '65
See also
Shenandoah National Park

BLUEBIRDS
Birds in your garden. J. K. Terres. il Pop Gard 16:10-11 Mr '65
Tanager and a bluebird jousting. J. Vosbergh. il Audubon Mag 67:374-5 N '65

BLUEFIELD, W. Va.
Bluefield: example for Appalachia? il U S News 59:102-3 Jl 12 '65

BLUEFISH fishing
Blue blitzes; Montauk trolling spree. G. Heinold. il Outdoor Life 136:42-3+ Ag '65
June blues. K. Osborne. il Field & S 70:124-7 Je '65

BLUEGRASS. See Grasses

BLUES (music) See Negro music

BLUES for Mister Charlie; drama. See Baldwin, J.

BLUHDORN, Charles
Man of many parts. il por Time 86:89 D 3 '65

BLUM, Albert A.
Labor and the federal government: 1850-1933. bibliog f Cur Hist 48:328-33+ Je '65

BLUM, Daniel
Obituary
Pub W 187:41 Mr 15 '65

BLUM, Etta
Words for Eli; poem. Poetry 106:194-8 Je '65

BLUM, Isabelle
Habit. New Yorker 41:31-3 Je 5 '65

BLUM, John M.
Schlesinger's Kennedy. New Repub 153:21-4 D 4 '65

BLUM, Ralph
Book bag of thrillers. Vogue 146:54+ D '65
Books (cont) Vogue 145:51 F 15; 60 Mr '65; 67 Je; 146:50 Ag 1 '65
Carp; story. New Yorker 40:30-6 F 6 '65
Movies. Vogue 146:64 O 15 '65; 147:70 Ja 1 '66
Reporter at large (cont) New Yorker 41:40-2+ Ag 28; 32-6+ S 4; 168+ S 11 '65

BLUM, Sam
And now, a message about commercial. N Y Times Mag p26-7+ Ap 11 '65
Do doctors still care about their patients? Redbook 126:51+ N '65
Pill. Redbook 126:33-5+ Ja '66
Why couples quarrel. Redbook 125:46-7+ Je '65
—and Welles, Sara
What young husbands really think about marriage. Redbook 125:60-1+ Ag '65

BLUM, Sigmund F.
Triangular plot shapes triple tower. Arch Rec 138:140-3 D '65

BLUM, Virgil C.
ACLU and civil rights for children. America 113:160-3 Ag 14 '65
New plan for tuition grants. America 113:499 O 30 '65

BLUMBERG, Ralph
If ever a devil... il por Time 86:109 N 5 '65

BLUMENFELD, Hans
Modern metropolis. Sci Am 213:64-74 bibliog(p276) S '65

BLUMENTHAL, George
Wandering patio. New Yorker 40:23-4 F 6 '65

BLUMENTHAL, Lassor
Are sales incentives a waste? Duns R 86:66-8+ O '65
Machinery revolution. Duns R 86:pt2 95-7+ D '65
Scramble in the marketplace. Duns R 86:pt2 86-7+ D '65
Soft sell in sales meetings. Duns R 86:48-9+ N '65
Utilities and appointments come of age. Duns R 85:pt2 138-41+ Mr '65

BLUMENTHAL, W. Michael
Commercial policy at the crossroads; address, September 16, 1965. Dept State Bul 53:665-71 O 25 '65
Kennedy round; address, March 8, 1965. Dept State Bul 52:628-35 Ap 26 '65
World trade and the Kennedy round; address, July 15, 1965. Dept State Bul 53:249-55 Ag 9 '65

BLUMER, Max
Organic pigments: their long-term fate. bibliog Science 149:722-6 Ag 13 '65
—and Snyder, W. D.
Isoprenoid hydrocarbons in recent sediments, presence of pristane and probable absence of phytane. bibliog Science 150:1588-9 D 17 '65
—and Thomas, D. W.
Phytadienes in zooplankton. Science 147:1148-9 Mr 5 '65
Zamene, isomeric C₁₉ monoolefins from marine zooplankton, fishes, and mammals. bibliog Science 148:370-1 Ap 16 '65

BLUNDERS
Don't upset the apricot. B. Conklin. Sat Eve Post 238:18 S 25 '65
Small world; comments by elementary school children on scenic wonders of America; ed. by H. Dunn. Travel 124:47-9+ D '65

BLYND, Alan
Critic's choice. N. Rothschild. il Pop Phot 57:72-3+ Ag '65

BLYTH, Myrna
Perils of a Ph.T. Read Digest 87:143-6 O '65

BOAK, Robert I.
Putting new life in old volumes; interview. Pub W 188:115-18 Jl 19 '65

BOAR testing. See Swine—Performance records and registration

BOARD of governors of the Federal reserve system. See United States—Federal reserve board

BOARD of trade, Chicago. See Chicago board of trade

BOARDING homes for children. See Foster home care

BOARDMAN, Thomas Leslie
Something missing here. Newsweek 67:83-4 Ja 17 '66

BOARDMAN, Walter S.
Attwater prairie chicken. Nat Parks Mag 39:16-17 Mr '65

BOARDS of education. See School boards

BOAT berths. See Yachts—Berths

BOAT building. See Boatbuilding

BOAT camping. See Camping

BOAT cockpits
Easy to make cockpit panels. G. P. Manning. il Motor B 116:42 N '65

BOAT harbors. See Marinas

BOAT landings. See Docks

BOAT ownership. See Boats—Purchasing

BOAT propellers. See Propellers

BOAT racing
See also
Motor boat racing
Rowing
Sailboat racing

BOAT selling. See Boats—Purchasing

BOAT shows. See Boats—Exhibitions

BOAT trailers. See Automobile boat trailers

BOATBUILDING
Boating business. W. Robberson. See issues of Yachting beginning March 1965
Build bigger engine hatches. H. Clark. il Motor B 116:120-1 N '65
Build this three-way boat for less than $50. G. Daniels. il Pop Sci 186:126-33+ Ap '65
Building this sailing dink is a breeze. C. Bell. il Motor B 116:43-5 D '65
Building your own. J. A. Emmett. il Outdoor Life 136:144-7 O '65
Built on the Lakes. il Yachting 117:53 My '65
Donsy, baby, this is your Sam; second annual Sam Griffith memorial powerboat race. L. Evans. Sports Illus 22:60-2 F 15 '65
Florida boatbuilding. J. A. Sutor. il Yachting 117:172 F '65
From backyard boats to yachts; Pearson yachts. il Bsns W p28-9 Ag 28 '65
Packaged fun. F. M. Paulson. il Field & S 70:94-9 N '65
Penguins in glass. B. Cobb, jr. il Yachting 118:61-3+ O '65
Plyfoam boat building. il Pop Mech 124:154:5+ N '65
Proving ground for fast boats and tough men; Sam Griffith memorial ocean race, Miami to Bahamas race. il Bsns W p28-30 F 20 '65

Rich rush of a Rybo; Florida's John Rybovich and sons. H. Whall. il Sports Illus 23:22-4 Ag 2 '65
Sandwich into boat: plyfoam. il Motor B 116:40-2 D '65
Sloops of Friendship. R. F. Duncan. il Yachting 117:184-6 F '65
Teacup; a basic-basic sailboat. M. M. Matthews. il Pop Mech 125:146-51+ Ja '66
Tiki Nui of Tahiti. N. J. Lays. il Motor B 116:80-1 D '65
Yachting asks about wooden-kit boatbuilding; interviews, ed. by E. Robberson. L. Humes; D. McNair; R. Cess. il Yachting 117:61-4+ Mr '65
See also
Chrysler corporation
Yacht building

BOATHOUSES
How to build piers, floats, boathouses. G. Daniels. il Pop Sci 186:104-7 F '65
Kitchen of surprises for families with a passion for cruising and fishing. il House & Gard 129:122-9 Ja '66

BOATS
Burglar alarms
See Burglar alarms

Care
Care and repair of aluminum boats. G. Carr. il Motor B 115:56-7+ Ap '65
Care and repair of fiberglass boats. C. Bell. il Motor B 115:42-4 Mr '65
Case against ventilation; fiberglass boat. J. A. English. Motor B 116:98-9 D '65
Fiberglassing with cellophane; the cellofinish process. B. Cobb, jr. il Yachting 117:60-1+ My '65
Fine art of fitting-out. il Motor B 115:22-3 Mr '65
Going overboard for maintenance and fun. W. S. Kals. il Yachting 118:52-3+ N '65
Spring work. J. A. Emmett. il Outdoor Life 135:28+ Ap '65
Yachting special report, maintenance; symposium. il Yachting 117:62-76+ Ap '65

Cockpits
See Boat cockpits

Design
Boats for the sport fisherman. il Yachting 117:126-7 Je '65
Designs. W. H. deFontaine. See issues of Yachting
Designs of note. il Motor B 116:36-9 N; 46-9 D '65
How hulls are made. G. Daniels. il Pop Sci 186:108-11 F '65

Electric equipment
A.C. afloat. E. Robberson. il Yachting 117:64-6+ Je '65
Electrical and electronic maintenance. E. Robberson. il Yachting 117:74-5+ Ap '65

Electronic equipment
Electrical and electronic maintenance. E. Robberson. il Yachting 117:74-5+ Ap '65
Electronic boating in your future. G. Rounds. il Motor B 116:22-5 N '65
Electronics for the sport fisherman. il Yachting 117:125 Je '65
VHF-FM: transmit and be heard. R. Humphrey. il Motor B 116:26-7+ N '65

Equipment
Cabin talk. M. Wiley. See issues of Yachting
Easily built dish rack. G. P. Manning. il Motor B 116:43 N '65
Fitting out for fun. P. M. Paulson. il Field & S 69:104-9 Mr '65
Gadgets and gilhickies. H. deFontaine. See issues of Yachting
How to equip your boat. W. E. Swegle. il Suc Farm 63:52 Je '65
Inner space program for your boat. C. Bell. il Motor B 116:74-5+ N '65
New for '66, as seen at the Chicago trade show. Yachting 118:164-6 O '65
1966 motor buyer's guide. F. M. Paulson. il Field & S 70:54-7 Ja '66
Peggy Slater on boat preparation. P. Slater. il Yachting 117:39-40 Je '65
Sailaway, sailaway, sailaway home. G. P. Manning. il Motor B 116:30-4+ S '65
Stainless steel surprises. E. Kopecki. il Motor B 115:56-9 My '65
Sure-to-please Christmas gifts; for all the boating people. il Motor B 116:28-35 N '65
This winter make a handsome transom swim platform. R. Dean. il Motor B 116:84-5+ N '65

BOATS—Equipment—*Continued*
Waterfront news. M. Wiley. See issues of Yachting
What's new? See issues of Motor boating
Yachting special report, maintenance; symposium. il Yachting 117:62-76+ Ap '65
See also
Burglar alarms
Sailboats—Equipment

Exhibitions

Boat-show calendar (cont) Outdoor Life 137:76 Ja '66
New for '66, as seen at the Chicago trade show. Yachting 118:164-6 O '65
Off-season soundings; Manhattan's National boat show. il Time 87:56-7 Ja 21 '66
Rig for sea and showtime; paintings. N. Solovioff. Sports Illus 24:20-5 Ja 3 '66
See also
Motor boats—Exhibitions

Lighting

Removable stern light. N. Meiners. il Motor B 116:37 D '65

Materials

Boom in portables. J. A. Emmett. il Outdoor Life 137:62-5+ Ja '66
Building a stock fiberglass cruiser (cont) B. Cobb, jr. il Yachting 117:49-51+ F '65
Care and repair of aluminum boats. G. Carr. il Motor B 115:56-7+ Ap '65
Care and repair of fiberglass boats. C. Bell. il Motor B 115:42-4 Mr '65
Fiberglass maintenance. B. Cobb, jr. il Yachting 117:76+ Ap '65
FRP; fiberglass forum. C. Bell. Motor B 116:86+ Jl '65
Hatteras fifty. il Motor B 116:40-1 N '65
Penguins in glass. B. Cobb, jr. il Yachting 118:61-3+ O '65
Plyfoam boat building. il Pop Mech 124:154-5+ N '65
Sandwich into boat: plyfoam. il Motor B 116:40-2 D '65

Mooring

Anchoring and mooring. F. M. Paulson. il Field & S 69:132-4+ Ap '65
Build a floating drydock. F. M. Paulson. il Field & S 70:84-7 Jl '65
How to dock and depart with dignity. W. Swegle. il Pop Sci 186:118-21 F '65
Put down a mooring. J. A. Emmett. il Outdoor Life 136:116-18 S '65

Names

Boat name contest. il Motor B 115:56 F '65

Painting

Advice for amateur painters. B. G. Hatch. Motor B 115:166-8 Je '65
Boat finishes. J. Hand. il Pop Sci 186:100-3 Mr '65
Is your brightwork getting dull? il Motor B 116:52 Ag '65
Painter's checklist. W. H. deFontaine. il Yachting 117:72-3 Ap '65
Top ideas for boat bottoms. Motor B 115:25 Mr '65

Propellers

See Propellers

Purchasing

Anecdotes, facetiae, satire, etc.
Boat for sale, reasonable. J. D. Williamson. il Motor B 116:28-9+ S '65

Radio equipment

See Radio apparatus on ships, boats, etc.

Renting

Renting boats abroad. S. Bary. il Travel 123:44-7 My '65

Repairing

Care and repair of aluminum boats. G. Carr. il Motor B 115:56-7+ Ap '65
Care and repair of fiberglass boats. C. Bell. il Motor B 115:42-4 Mr '65
Covering your boat; canvas and fiberglass covering. J. A. Emmett. il Outdoor Life 136:16+ D '65
For weeping seams a silicone sealant. W. A. Evanko. il Motor B 115:29 Mr '65
Rubber hull coating seals old leakers. il Motor B 116:96 O '65
Tighter decks, and how. Y. K. Adam. il Motor B 115:26-8+ Mr '65

Speed

See also
Speedometers

Storage

Hang it all! G. Byrnes. il Motor B 116:76-8 D '65
Kitchen of surprises for families with a passion for cruising and fishing. il House & Gard 129:122-9 Ja '66
Two de-icing systems for wet storage in winter. C. Kucyn; M. Jancsics, jr. il Motor B 116:100-2 O '65

Transportation

Car-top craft. F. M. Paulson. il Field & S 69:100-1+ F '65
How to wagon-top a boat. H. G. Tapply. il Field & S 69:66 Mr '65
See also
Automobile boat trailers

BOATS, Ice. See Ice boats and ice boating

BOATS, Rubber
Boats that blow up; inflatable rubber craft. F. M. Paulson. il Field & S 70:102-6 Je '65

BOATS, Solar powered
Army shows interest in solar-powered boat. Sci N L 87:281 My 1 '65
Solar boat: army evaluators record a plus for novel craft. J. Walsh. il Science 147:1559-60 Mr 26 '65

BOATS and boating
Art of trading up for a song. H. Leavitt. il Motor B 116:48+ N '65
Boating. J. A. Emmett. See issues of Outdoor life
Boating; ed. by F. M. Paulson. See issues of Field & stream
Boats and boating; symposium. il Pop Sci 186:99-123 F '65
Boats for hunting. J. A. Emmett. il Outdoor Life 136:136-8 N '65
Boom in portables. J. A. Emmett. il Outdoor Life 137:62-5+ Ja '66
Calendar of coming events; comp. by R. B. Smith. See issues of Motor boating
Children aboard. N. A. Kline. il Yachting 118:148-9 S '65
Cows on the quay; cruise on the Grand Canal, Ireland. P. Redford. il Atlan 215:178+ Mr '65
Field & stream boatman's handbook. F. M. Paulson. il Field & S 70:51-66 Ja '66
How to be a good guest on a cruise. L. O'Brien. il Motor B 116:56+ Jl '65
Hunt with your boat. F. M. Paulson. il Field & S 69:129 F '65
Incredible saga of Twinkle-Twinkle. H. G. Smith. il Yachting 117:217-18 My '65
Landlubbers ahoy! Changing T 19:6 Ap '65
Let's go gunkholing. A. Woodle. il Motor B 115:30+ Je '65
Man and his boat; twenty-eight feet of good living. B. Crabtree. il Yachting 118:55-7+ O '65
Marblehead gunning dory. L. Dietz. il Field & S 70:54-7+ N '65
Mile high in Teton country. R. C. Lillie. il Motor B 116:22-5+ My '65
News from yachting centers. See issues of Yachting
Outdoor life boating 1966. J. A. Emmett. il Outdoor Life 137:52-66+ Ja '66
Outrigger stabilizer for small craft. V. L. Oertle. il Pop Mech 124:146-7 Ag '65
Pontoon craft. J. A. Emmett. il Outdoor Life 135:130-2 Je '65
Power or pedal water bike. H. Clark. il Pop Mech 124:148-53 Ag '65
Recreation. Consumer Rep 30:287-91 D '65
Renting boats abroad. S. Bary. il Travel 123:44-7 My '65
Rescue at tin can grounds; Long Island Sound. J. Ridgeway. New Repub 153:14-16 Jl 24 '65
Rugged johnboat. J. A. Emmett. il Outdoor Life 135:134-6 My '65
Seasoned skipper. See issues of Motor boating
Summer thoughts for winter thinking. D. DeBartolo. il Motor B 116:22-3+ D '65
Today's Arkansas traveler is a boatman. J. Heuston. il Motor B 116:28-31 Jl '65
Ultimate motorboat tour. W. T. McKeown. il Esquire 63:110-11+ Je '65
Under the lee of the longboat. See issues of Yachting
What is this thing called seamanship? R. M. Clancy. il Motor B 116:24-6+ D '65
What's new? See issues of Motor boating
Yachting special report, southern California; symposium. il Yachting 117:38-52+ Je '65
See also
Canoes and canoeing
Cat boats
Cookery, Marine
Decks
Indians of North America—Boats

BOATS and boating—See also—*Continued*
Motor boats
Navigation
River trips
Sailboats
Sailing
Women in boating
Yachts and yachting

Accidents
Disaster at Cat Cay. R. Marston. Yachting 117:196+ Je '65
Eight boating crises. R. Petrow. il Pop Sci 186:114-18 My '65
Hard way south; voyage to St Thomas. D. C. Stone. il Yachting 118:60-1+ N '65
Hell on an island; interview, ed. by J Rearden. F. C. Johnson. il Outdoor Life 136:50-3+ S '65
How to cope with water emergencies. il Good H 160:168 Je '65
How to make a boating rescue. G. Daniels. il Pop Sci 187:80-1+ Jl '65
Man overboard. A. F. Loomis; R. Choy. Yachting 118:60+ O '65
See also
Fishing—Accidents and injuries
Yachts and yachting—Accidents

Anecdotes, facetiae, satire, etc.
Compleat boat. T. J. King. il Yachting 118: 152 S '65

Bibliography
Book reviews. See issues of Yachting

Laws and regulations
Boat handling. F. M. Paulson. il Field & S 70:58-61 Ja '66
Live and let live. L. E. Penso. il Yachting 118:60-2+ Ag '65
Marine law enforcement. J. Miner. il Yachting 118:63-5+ Ag '65
New boating laws and regulations. W. T. Stone. il Yachting 117:68-71+ Ap '65
New international rules of the road. W. H. DeFontaine. il Yachting 118:60 S '65
Regulations hassle, the Northwest. L. Barber. Yachting 117:177-9 F '65
Rules of the road; Regulations for preventing collisions at sea. il Sports Illus 23:28-9 Ag 2 '65
Seven common controversies; questions and answers. F. M. Paulson. il Field & S 70: 108-14 O '65
Washington report. W. T. Stone. See issues of Yachting
We're being swamped with boating laws. J. Speirs. il Pop Mech 124:106-9+ Ag '65

Safety devices and measures
Goal of the week: the year's safety. N. C. Barnard. Motor B 115:126-7 Je '65
Man overboard. A. F. Loomis; R. Choy. Yachting 118:60+ O '65
Seven common controversies; questions and answers. F. M. Paulson. il Field & S 70: 108-14 O '65
Summer insanity. il Travel 123:40-3 Je '65
See also
Life preservers

Study and teaching
Coast guard auxiliary offers free boating courses. il Motor B 116:123-4 Ag '65
Fleet thinking; how to launch a community small-craft program. C. W. Russell. il Recreation 58:132-3 Mr '65
U.S. power squadrons free instruction in boat operation starts next month. J. Wilde. il Motor B 116:120-2 Ag '65

BOAZ, Martha
ALA's intellectual freedom committee. por Wilson Lib Bul 39:651 Ap '65
Situation we face; address, January 1965. por ALA Bul 59:470+ Je '65

BOAZ, Ruth
My thirty years with Father Devine. pors Ebony 20:88-90+ My '65

BOB Jones university, Greenville, S.C.
Bob Jones university; new curricula for bigotry. R. G. Sherrill. il Nation 200:326-33 Mr 29 '65

BOBBIE Brooks, incorporated
Girls and machine team up to spot style trends, or I was a teen-age computer; Bobbie Brooks company award scheme. il Life 59:81-3+ Ag 6 '65

BOBCAT hunting
Cat that liked cabrito. B. W. Dalrymple. il Field & S 70:37-9+ Ja '66
Little cat is big stuff. J. Philbrick. il Outdoor Life 136:56-7+ D '65

BOBER, Harry
Books in review. Natur Hist 74:6+ Mr '65

BOBROW, Davis B.
Realism about nuclear spread. Bul Atomic Sci 21:20-2 D '65
Soldiers and the nation-state. bibliog f Ann Am Acad 358:65-76 Mr '65

BOBSLEDDING. See Coasting
BOBSLEDS. See Sleds
BOBWHITE shooting. See Quail shooting

BOCA RATON, Fla.
We vacuum-filter lime softening sludge. G. Hager. il Am City 80:105-7 Je '65

BOCHER, Main Rousseau. See Mainbocher

BOCK, Frederick
And a variable compass. Poetry 106:229-31 Je '65
Big, fat summer, and the lean and hard; poem. New Yorker 41:38 Ag 21 '65
Far; Catch a man forty; That strait-jacket case; Crowd and performer; poems. Poetry 105:295-9 F '65

BOCK, Walter
Shadow designs. Sch Arts 65:18-20 N '65

BOCKMAN, Charles
Choreographer in the second city. L. L. Bram. il pors Dance Mag 39:52-3+ F '65

BODANSKY, Oscar. See Nisselbaum, J. S. jt. auth.

BODE, Elroy
Visit home; story. Redbook 125:48-9 Ag '65

BODEGA BAY, Calif.
Bodega Head, a partisan view. J. W. Hedgpeth. Bul Atomic Sci 21:2-7 Mr '65; Discussion. 21:27-8 O: 23 D '65

BODENWEIN, Gordon
Saint James parish. Cath World 202:238-41 Ja '66

BODIN, Simone
Bettina: the adventures of a passionate traveller; excerpts from journal; tr. by F. Frenaye. pors Vogue 147:138-43+ Ja 1 '66

BODONI, Giovanni Battista
Bodoni's Manuale Tipografico is reproduced in Parma, Italy. il Pub W 188:129-30 Jl 19 '65

BODY, Human. See Physiology
BODY chemistry. See Biochemistry
BODY fat. See Fat
BODY fluids
See also
Urine
BODY odors. See Odors
BODY temperature. See Temperature, Animal and human
BODY water. See Water in the body
BODY weight. See Weight (physiology)

BOEHM, George A. W.
Amazing alchemy of ultrahigh pressure. Read Digest 86:144E-144F+ Mr '65
Countdown for Nike-X. Fortune 72:132-7+ N '65
Search for ways to keep youthful. Fortune 71:138-42+ Mr '65

BOEING-Boeing; drama. See Cross, B.

BOEING company
Boeing, airline moves follow 727 crashes. J. R. Ashlock. Aviation W 83:27-8 D 20 '65
Boeing chief calls for SST prototypes. Aviation W 82:33-4 F 1 '65
Boeing increases size of 737 transport. C. M. Plattner. il Aviation W 82:26-8 Mr 1 '65
Boeing introducing business 737 at NBAA convention this week. Aviation W 83:50 O 11 '65
Boeing studies extended fuselage growth versions of 707 series. Aviation W 82:291 Mr 15 '65
Boeing studies three civil C-5A versions. I. Stone. il Aviation W 83:46-9+ D 27 '65
Previous commercial sales marks broken by American Boeing order. Aviation W 83:34 O 4 '65
United for Boeing; choice of a short-range jet. il Newsweek 65:80 Ap 19 '65

Aerospace division
U.S. keeps wary eye on strike at Boeing. il Bsns W p 166+ S 25 '65

Vertol division
How Vertol vies for skilled labor. Bsns W p46+ O 30 '65
Revivalist zeal in the drive for perfect parts; Zero defects gaining converts in aerospace and defense industries. il Bsns W p 158+ My 8 '65
Vertol tests monocyclic control system. D. A. Brown. il Aviation W 82:46-7+ Mr 8 '65
Vertol to increase helicopter production. D. E. Fink. il Aviation W 83:61-5 N 29 '65

BOETH, Richard
Behind the magnolia curtain. Atlan 216:46-52 Ag '65

BOGALUSA, La.
Armed justice? administration of justice in the South. Commonweal 82:517 Jl 23 '65
Bleeding Bogalusa. Time 85:32 Je 11 '65
Blot on Bogalusa; murder of Negro sheriff. Newsweek 65:38 Je 14 '65
Bullets in Bogalusa. il Newsweek 66:25 Jl 19 '65
Caught in the civil rights crossfire; Crown Zellerbach target of CORE demonstrations. il Bsns W p 102-4+ Ag 7 '65
Deacons; for defense and justice, Negro vigilantes. il Newsweek 66:28-9 Ag 2 '65
Help wanted. Newsweek 66:32 Jl 26 '65
In murky waters. Newsweek 65:21 Je 7 '65
Klantown, USA. P. Good. il Nation 200:110-13 F 1 '65
Man in the middle. il Time 86:19 Jl 23 '65

Police
Where is the flag? Time 86:25 Ag 6 '65

BOGAN, Louise
Verse (cont) New Yorker 41:193-4+ Ap 10 '65

BOGART, Humphrey
Bogey boom. il pors Newsweek 66:94-94A+ N 1 '65
Last days of Humphrey Bogart; excerpt from Bogie, the biography of Humphrey Bogart. J. Hyams. il pors Good H 162:54-7+ Ja '66

BOGART, Max
Paperbacks on the march. Sr Schol 87:sup21-2 O 28 '65

BOGDANOVICH, Peter
Go-go, and hurry; it's later than you think. Esquire 63:86-91 F '65

BOGERT, Jane R.
Barns, books, and a bonanza. J. F. Fixx. por Sat R 48:25 Je 19 '65

BOGOTÁ, Colombia

Historic houses, etc.
Bolívar's villa. L. Zalamea. il Américas 17:20-7 D '65

Social conditions
Latin-American shantytown. S. Schulman. il N Y Times Mag p30-1+ Ja 16 '66

BOHAN, Peter J.
Early American gold. Antiques 88:812-19 D '65
La BOHÈME; opera. See Puccini, G.

BOHEMIAN glass. See Glassware

BOHEMIANISM
Girls of Greenwich Village. A. Geracimos and J. Ferris. Mlle 61:82-3+ Je '65
See also
Beatniks

BOIARDI, Hector
Hurry-up luncheon dishes. M. B. Keiser. il Parents Mag 40:30+ O '65

BOIGNY, Christiane (Hervé-Dupenher) Houphouet-. See Houphouet-Boigny, C. H.-D.

BOIGNY, Guillaume Houphouet-. See Houphouet-Boigny, G.

BOIKO, Claire
All about mothers; drama. Plays 24:71-4. 86 My '65
Clean sweep; drama. Plays 25:73-7 Ja '66
Lion to lamb; drama. Plays 24:81-4, 96 Mr '65
Meet the Pilgrims! drama. Plays 25:74-8 N '65
Mother Goose's Christmas surprise; drama. Plays 25:77-82 D '65
Runaway bookmobile; drama. Plays 25:60-6 N '65
Small crimson parasol; drama. Plays 25:67-72. 78 Ja '66
Spaceship Santa Maria; drama. Plays 25:61-7 O '65
Star bright; drama. Plays 25:63-7 D '65

BOILERS
Foster Wheeler mends its house from within; maker of boilers remodels its operations. il Bsns W p 116-18+ D 18 '65

Electric heating
Hot new ideas in home heaters! thermo-temp electric boilers. J. Ingersoll. il Pop Mech 124:110-14+ N '65

BOILING water reactors. See Nuclear reactors

BOISE Cascade corporation
Idaho Ivy league. Newsweek 66:79-80 O 11 '65
It's grow or die at Boise Cascade. T. Alexander. il Fortune 72:180-3+ D '65

BOLER, John F.
Behind the protests at Berkeley. Commonweal 81:602-5 F 5 '65

BOLES, Paul Darcy
Big beast; story. Sat Eve Post 238:48-51 Ag 14 '65
Night watch; story. Seventeen 24:160-1 Ap '65
Running of the deer; story. Seventeen 24: 86-7 Jl '65

BOLÍVAR, Simón
It was Bolívar's last home. il Sunset 135:8 Ag '65

BOLIVIA
See also
Railroads—Bolivia
Tin mines and mining—Bolivia

Economic conditions
Atlantic report. Atlan 216:14+ D '65

Politics and government
Atlantic report. Atlan 216:14+ D '65
Flying high. Time 86:31 Jl 2 '65
Gamble in the Andes. il U S News 59:22 O 4 '65
In until when. il Time 85:49 My 21 '65
More trouble from the mines. Time 86:46 O 1 '65
No room for compromise. Time 85:29 My 28 '65
On to elections. Time 87:36 Ja 14 '66
Plea for a miracle; miners riots. il Newsweek 66:58 O 4 '65
Revolution and stability in Bolivia. D. B. Heath. bibliog f Cur Hist 49:328-35+ D '65
Steve Canyon of the Andes. il Time 85:36 Ap 2 '65
Transition and uncertainty. M. Arias. Christian Cent 82:757-8 Je 9 '65
Tremors in Bolivia. J. Bishop. Commonweal 83:339-42 D 17 '65
Two heads, one mind. il Time 85:35+ Je 4 '65

Social conditions
Revolution and stability in Bolivia. D. B. Heath. bibliog f Cur Hist 49:328-35+ D '65

BOLIVIAN hemorrhagic fever. See Hemorrhagic fever

BÖLL, Heinrich
Like a bad dream; story; tr. by L. Vennewitz. Harper 231:61-4 O '65
Peace; story. Sat Eve Post 238:50-7 Ag 28 '65
Recollections of 1945. Esquire 64:111-12 S '65
Secret of the box; story. Sat Eve Post 238: 60-3 Jl 17 '65
about
Outgrowing Germany. S. Koch. Nation 200: 484-6 My 3 '65
Worlds of desolation. V. Lange. New Repub 153:36-8 N 27 '65

BOLLO, Eda M.
Points in color. Sch Arts 64:15-17 Mr '65

BOLOGNA, Sando
Museum village. Travel 124:60-2 Ag '65

BOLT, Richard H. and others
Doctoral feedback into higher education. bibliog Science 148:918-28 My 14 '65

BOLTON, Guy
Experience. New Yorker 41:49-50 N 27 '65

BOLTON, Preston M.
Architect's notes on kitchen and bathroom planning. Arch Rec 137:15-16+ mid-My '65

BOLTON, William
(ed) That's a good question. See issues of Today's health

BOMB shelters. See Atomic bomb shelters

BOMBING, Aerial
Cubic proposes sharpening targeting; high accuracy targeting sub-system. R. Pay. Miss & Roc 16:36+ My 17 '65
Ordeal by fire; interview, ed. by R. Tunley. A. Wahle. il Ladies Home J 82:63-5+ Mr '65

BON voyage; story. See Coward, N.

BONAIRE (island)
Reader's choice. D. E. W. Tisdale. Travel 123:13 Mr '65

BONAPARTE, Napoleon. See Napoleon I, emperor of the French

BONARDI, Peter Martin
Here I am, back at Alcatraz East. A. Buchwald. il pors Life 59:70-4+ Ag 13 '65

BONATTI, Walter
Five against the gods. R. Daley. il por Esquire 64:96-7+ N '65
Master of the mountain peaks. G. Kent and J. Reddy. il por Read Digest 87:102-7 S '65
Three days on a rope. il por Time 85:82 F 26 '65

BONAVENA, Oscar Natalio
Making of a heavyweight. H. Tuckner. il pors N Y Times Mag p32+ F 7 '65

BONAVENTURA, Mario di
Dartmouth's congregation. O. Daniel. por Sat R 48:35+ Jl 31 '65

BOND, A. C.
Space simulation: man-rated testing and vacuum generation. Science 147:523-7 Ja 29 '65

BOND, Edward
Saved. Criticism
New Yorker 41:228+ D 11 '65

BOND, James (literary character) See Spies
   in literature
BOND, John R.
   How good are American cars? Atlan 216:121-4
   Jl '65; Same abr. Read Digest 87:174-6 S
   '65
BOND, Julian
   One word too many. por Time 87:20 Ja 21 '66
   Two-time loser. Newsweek 67:26+ Ja 24 '66
BOND, Mary Wickham
   Did a Barbados hunter shoot the last Eskimo
   curlew? Audubon Mag 67:314-16 S '65
BOND campaigns. See Municipal bonds
BONDERI, Elmi
   Epic love of Elmi Bonderi. M. Laurence.
   Holiday 38:35+ N '65
BONDONE, Giotto di. See Giotto di Bondone
BONDOR, George S.
   Keep tab on your speedometer. Pop Sci 187:
   28 Jl '65
BONDS
   As stocks pass 900; advice experts are giving
   to investors. il U S News 58:40-2 F 15 '65
   Bonds across the sea; overseas-bond-financing
   technique. Time 87:81-2 Ja 14 '66
   Bonds feel squeeze of downward pressure.
   il Bsns W p 170 S 25 '65
   Return you can get on your money now. U S
   News 59:115-16+ N 22 '65
   What the new year holds for investors and
   savers. il U S News 60:78-80 Ja 10 '66
   What's ahead in stock market now; as ex-
   perts see it; symposium. il U S News 58:
   44-50 Je 28 '65
   Where the yields are; new look of the bond
   market. Fortune 73:217-18 Ja '66
      See also
   State bonds
BONDS, Chemical. See Chemical bonds
BONDS, Government
   Competition for savings bonds? U S News
   58:102-3 My 17 '65
   Little-known facts about savings bonds. B.
   Brantley. il Suc Farm 63:112 Mr '65
   Record savings in U.S. bonds. U S News 59:
   90 Ag 16 '65
   Soon: higher yields on savings bonds? il
   U S News 60:64 Ja 3 '66
      See also
   State bonds
BONDS, Institutional
   Church bonds ride the population wave. il
   Bsns W p 138+ Mr 13 '65
BONDS, Municipal. See Municipal bonds
BONDS, Revenue
   Chicago's toll skyway hits a fiscal pothole.
   il Bsns W p68+ D 4 '65
BONDS, State. See State bonds
BONDY, Sebastián Salazar. See Salazar
   Bondy, S.
BONE
   Biology of hard tissues; report from con-
   ference, Princeton, N.J. 20-23 June 1965.
   A. M. Budy. Science 151:225-6 Ja 14 '66
   Bone density measurements in vivo; im-
   provement of X-ray densitometry. R. L.
   Mason and C. Ruthven. bibliog il Science
   150:221-2 O 8 '65
   Electrical effects in bone. C. A. L. Bassett.
   il Sci Am 213:18-25 O '65
   Thyrocalcitonin: inhibitor of bone resorption
   in tissue culture. J. Friedman and L. G.
   Raisz. bibliog il Science 150:1465-7 D 10 '65
BONE, Artificial
   Man-made human bones; cerosium. il Sci
   Digest 57:28 Mr '65
BONE, Transplantation of. See Transplantation
   of organs, tissues, etc.
BONE densitometers. See Densitometers
BONE marrow. See Marrow
BONE surgery. See Orthopedia
BONEAU, C. Alan, and others
   Color-discrimination performance of pigeons:
   effects of reward. Science 149:1113-14 S 3 '65
BONEFISH fishing
   Is it true what they say about bonefish?
   H. Modavis. il Field & S 70:72-4+ Je '65
BONES
   Fluoride protection of bones and teeth.
   R. F. Sognnaes. bibliog il Science 150:989-
   93 N 19 '65
   Tetracycline: effect of osteogenesis in vitro.
   L. Saxén. bibliog il Science 149:870-2 Ag
   20 '65
      Diseases
   Detect fragile bones; osteoporosis. Sci N L
   88:275 O 30 '65
      See also
   Osteomyelitis
BONES, Fossil. See Paleontology
BONEY, Knowles
   Study of a group of English salt-glaze ware.
   Antiques 88:834-7 D '65

BONGARTZ, Roy
   It walks like a man. Nation 200:645-6 Je
   14 '65
   Literary interview: Pussy Adore. Nation 200:
   598-9 My 31 '65
   To each his own buffalo. Sat Eve Post 238:
   22 O 23 '65
   Wanted: one lovely monster. Sat Eve Post
   238:22 Jl 3 '65
      about
   Books. R. M. Elman. Commonweal 82:573-5
   Ag 6 '65
   View from the West side. E. Merriam. Nation
   200:620-2 Je 7 '65
BONHAM CARTER, Lady Violet (Asquith)
   Courtship: all the fun of an obstacle race. il
   por Vogue 146:126-7 Ag 1 '65
BONHOEFFER, Dietrich
   Beyond Bonhoeffer? H. Cox. Commonweal
   82:653-7 S 17 '65; Reply. S. S. Schwarz-
   child. 83:227+ N 26 '65
   Bonhoeffer: representative Christian. Chris-
   tian Cent 82:420-1 Ap 7 '65
   Faith and the facts of life. W. Hamilton.
   Nation 200:424-6 Ap 19 '65
   Man for others. J. T. Elson. il pors Life
   58:108-9+ My 7 '65
   Profiles. V. Mehta. New Yorker 41:65-8+
   N 27 '65
BONIN ISLANDS
   A look inside a secret U.S. base; Chichi-Jima.
   il U S News 59:62-3 Ag 23 '65
BONING of fishes. See Fish as food
BONIS, L. J.
   Surface phenomena. Science 150:1630-1 D 17
   '65
BONK, Wallace J.
   Reference encounter. por Library J 90:1818-
   24 Ap 15 '65
BONN, George S.
   (comp) Technical books of 1964. por Library J
   90:1041-7 Mr 1 '65
BONN observatory. See Astronomical observ-
   atories—Germany (Federal Republic)
BONNARD, Pierre
   Bonnard's own Bonnards; exhibition at
   Acquavella, N.Y. M. Benedikt. il Art N
   64:42-3+ D '65
   Pierre Bonnard exhibit. B. Kaufman. Com-
   monweal 81:676-7 F 19 '65
BONNER, Charles
   What's in it for me. Harper 231:170-1 N '65
BONNER, Norman A. and Miskel, J. A.
   Radioactivity: distribution from cratering
   in basalt. bibliog Science 150:489-93 O
   22 '65
BONNER, William A. and Benedict, H. C.
   Spin away your black & white blues. U S
   Camera 28:54-5+ D '65
BONSAI. See Trees, Dwarf
BONSMA, J. C.
   New way to pick the best breeders; by eye.
   C. E. Ball. il Farm J 89:38-9+ F '65
BONTEMPS, Arna
   Why I returned. Harper 230:176-82 Ap '65
BONUS system
   Bonus formula for division heads; based on
   relative profitability of profit centers. J.
   Dearden and W. S. Edgerly. Harvard Bsns
   R 43:83-90 S '65
BOOK, William H.
   William H. Book, RIP. M. S. Evans. Nat R
   17:454 Je 1 '65
BOOK advertising. See Books—Advertising
BOOK and periodical giving campaigns
   Such easy charity; Books for Appalachia
   project. E. Geller. Library J 90:1956 Ap 15
   '65
BOOK awards, National. See National book
   awards
BOOK binding. See Bookbinding
BOOK buying, Personal. See Libraries,
   Private
BOOK buying for libraries. See Libraries—
   Acquisitions
BOOK buying for school libraries. See School
   libraries—Acquisitions
BOOK catalogs. See Catalogs, Library
BOOK censorship. See Censorship
BOOK cloth. See Bookbinding—Materials
BOOK club guild, inc. See Book clubs
BOOK clubs
   Meredith publishing buys Book club guild,
   inc. Pub W 187:25 Mr 29 '65

BOOK collecting
Barns, books, and a bonanza; 1965 Amy Loveman award. J. F. Fixx. Sat R 48:25 Je 19 '65
Great book collectors. P. W. Schmidtchen. il Hobbies 70:106-7+ Ap '65
Infallible calling. P. W. Schmidtchen. il Hobbies 70:106-7 My '65
See also
Libraries, Private
Manuscripts

BOOK covers
Book jackets: the new wave; design and designers. D. Dempsey. il Sat R 48:46-7 D 4 '65
Feds nix postage stamps on postmaster's jacket. Pub W 188:181 Jl 12 '65
Jacket of Little, Brown novel uses animated tip-on. il Pub W 188:100 D 6 '65; Reply. M. Powers. 189:61 Ja 10 '66
Non-woven cover materials approved for textbook use; joint committee on textbook specifications. Pub W 188:96-8 S 6 '65
Paperback cover designs are tasteful and effective. bibliog il Pub W 187:94-6+ F 1 '65
Pocket books' art direction committee of consultants to the art director. Pub W 189: 90 Ja 3 '66
San Francisco censors Bantam books cover. Pub W 187:54 Je 28 '65
Seventy-one outstanding book jackets in T&R contest. il Pub W 187:112-16 Mr 1 '65
Sheep in wolves' clothing: or Never judge a children's book by its cover. L. Russ. Pub W 187:57-8 My 10 '65
Swift advances cited in printing of covers; summary of discussion at panel held by Women's national book association. il Pub W 187:90 My 3 '65

BOOK design
AIGA children's book show; summary. P. A. Bennett. il Pub W 188:76-8+ S 6 '65
AAUP: two aspects of production: computers and fine design; summaries of discussions at annual convention. Pub W 188:120-5 Jl 19 '65
Does design affect reviewing? three reviewers say yes! summary of discussion at meeting of the Trade book clinic of the American institute of graphic arts. R. Kluger; H. A. Kenny; V. A. Bradley. Pub W 187:32-3 Ap 12 '65
Fifty books of 1964: too little innovation seen in AIGA show. M. Colman. il Pub W 187: 72-4 My 3 '65
Golden press' new juveniles in shapes and blocks. il Pub W 188:95-6 D 6 '65
Half a dozen are memorable; Chicago book clinic's 16th annual exhibit. G. Allen. il Pub W 187:92-3+ My 3 '65
New England book show of 1964 design. bibliog il Pub W 187:104-5+ F 1 '65
Shorewood's New York uses fourteen antique faces for heads. il Pub W 188:96-8+ D 6 '65
William Nicoll and Edit, inc. P. A. Bennett. il Pub W 188:88-92 D 6 '65

Competitions
Thirty-four books chosen for Ninth annual midwestern show; one display at AAUP convention, Lexington. L. S. Thompson. Pub W 188:125+ Jl 19 '65

BOOK detector. See Library protection systems
BOOK development council
British form international Book development council. Pub W 187:37 My 17 '65
BOOK digest. See Books, Condensed
BOOK donations. See Libraries—Gifts, legacies, etc.
BOOK drives. See Book and periodical giving campaigns
BOOK exhibits
AIGA children's book show; summary. P. A. Bennett. il Pub W 188:76-8+ S 6 '65
AAUP award books: an awareness of quality; with editorial comment. P. A. Bennett. bibliog il Pub W 187:103-5+ Je 14 '65
AAUP: two aspects of production: computers and fine design; summaries of discussions at annual convention. Pub W 188:120-5 Jl 19 '65
Children's book show of 1965, AIGA. C. B. Grannis. Pub W 188:63 Ag 9 '65
Currents; new books preview, 1965. Pub W 188:41-2 S 13 '65
Fifty books of 1964: too little innovation seen in AIGA show. M. Colman. il Pub W 187: 72-4+ My 3 '65
Half a dozen are memorable; Chicago book clinic's 16th annual exhibit. G. Allen. il Pub W 187:92-3+ My 3 '65

Materials for the underprivileged, theme of New books preview dinner. Library J 90: 4536 O 15 '65
New England book show of 1964 design. bibliog il Pub W 187:104-5+ F 1 '65
1965 new books preview. il Pub W 188:40-2 S 20 '65
Skira art books on exhibit in Moscow. il Pub W 187:78 Je 21 '65
Thirty-four books chosen for Ninth annual midwestern show; one display at AAUP convention, Lexington. L. S. Thompson. Pub W 188:125+ Jl 19 '65
Western books exhibition to open at AIGA. il Pub W 188:98-100+ S 6 '65
See also
Book fairs

BOOK fairs
Bridgeport book fair highlights jobber's activities; sponsored by King Cole supermarket. il Pub W 180:28-31 N 1 '65
CBC plans for book week and large fairs. il Pub W 188:178-80 Jl 12 '65
Children's libraries; public library and the school book fair, Kansas City public library. J. A. Merrill. Wilson Lib Bul 39: 913 Je '65
Eleven miles of books; Frankfurt book fair. C. Northcott. Christian Cent 82:1382 N 10 '65
Fair at Nashville Baptist bookstore attracts over 10,000 children. il Pub W 188:56-7 D 13 '65
Frankfurt fair, 1965: rich and famous. il Pub W 188:20-31 N 22 '65
Organizing and managing children's book fairs; summary of informal discussion. M. Childs and D. Thompson. Pub W 187:43-4 Je 28 '65
Second annual book fair at Nashville Baptist store. Pub W 188:52-3 N 1 '65
Sixth Antiquarian fair a success, dealers report. Pub W 187:106 Ap 26 '65
Special issue on book fairs; symposium. il Sr Schol 86:sup 13-18 Ap 29 '65
Warsaw book fair. H. R. Lottman. Pub W 188:24-7 Jl 26 '65

BOOK illustration. See Illustration of books and periodicals
BOOK imports. See Books—Importation
BOOK indexes. See Indexes
BOOK industries and trade
Attracting young people is topic of Trade book clinic; production end of publishing. Pub W 188:114-15 D 6 '65
BMI; government concern, industry outlook, 1966; summaries of addresses at 33rd annual convention. il Pub W 188:68-70+ D 6 '65
BMI: scheduling, personnel problems; areas of mutual interest; summaries of addresses at 33rd annual convention. il Pub W 188: 72-4+ N 8 '65
Bookmaking. See first issue of each month of Publishers' weekly
International publishers congress in Washington, D.C; symposium. il Pub W 187:30-42 Je 28 '65
Revolution in books; symposium. bibliog il UNESCO Courier 18:4-32 S '65
See also
Book manufacturers' institute
Bookazine company, incorporated
Booksellers and bookselling
Copyright
Printing
Printing industry
Publishers and publishing
Royalties

Advertising
See Books—Advertising

Bibliography
Books about bookmaking. il Pub W 188:92-4 Ag 9 '65

International aspects
Feffer and Simons wins E award for export. il Pub W 188:89 S 27 '65
Franklin book programs: global publishing aid is varied and expanded. il Pub W 187: 28-32 Mr 15 '65
In Washington, they say, culture is now in; free flow of books. R. H. Smith. Pub W 188:48 O 4 '65
International book trade developments; 1965 in review. Pub W 189:79-80 Ja 17 '66
United States book import and export figures, 1963-1964. il Pub W 188:34-5 O 4 '65

Law
But can you do that? H. F. Pilpel. See last issue of each month of Publishers' weekly

BOOK industries and trade—*Continued*

Statistics

United States book import and export figures, 1963-1964. il Pub W 188:34-5 O 4 '65

Denmark

See also
Publishers and publishing—Denmark

England

See also
National book league

France

See also
Publishers and publishing—France

Great Britain

See also
Book development council

India

India's first high-speed bindery; Four oceans bindery. R. B. Ellis. il Pub W 187:103-5 My 3 '65

Latin America

See also
Publishers and publishing—Latin America

Spain

See also
Publishers and publishing—Spain

Sweden

Sweden's net book agreement ended by government board. T. R. Buckman. il Pub W 187:26-31 My 3 '65

United States

ABPC seminar held on mail order. Pub W 187:65-6 F 15 '65

Goals for 1966: book trade association leaders look at the year ahead; symposium. il Pub W 188:55-60 D 27 '65

Growth, prosperity and a measure of chaos. C. B. Grannis. Pub W 189:109 Ja 17 '66

Highspots of activity in major organizations; 1965 in review. Pub W 189:80-3 Ja 17 '66

1965 in review; statistics, news and trends in the industry. il Pub W 189:68-73 Ja 17 '66

Portents of doom in time of plenty; march of new technology can turn industry upside down. D. Rustin. Pub W 188:71 N 8 '65

See also
Booksellers and bookselling—United States
Publishers and publishing—United States

BOOK jackets. See Book covers

BOOK jobbers

Book wholesaling and supply in California. F. H. Potter. Pub W 188:57-9 N 22 '65

Bookseller and a jobber look at U.P. books; summary of panel discussion at AAUP. il Pub W 188:50-2 Jl 19 '65

See also
Academic book service, incorporated
Baker and Taylor company

BOOK lists. See Childrens literature—Bibliography; Reading lists

BOOK making (betting)

See also
Horse race betting

BOOK manufacturers' institute

BMI: convention stresses relations with publishers and government; plans. Pub W 188:96 O 4 '65

BMI endorses proposals of Register of copyrights. Pub W 187:57 F 1 '65

BMI, government concern, industry outlook, 1966; summaries of addresses at 33rd annual convention. il Pub W 188:68-70+ D 6 '65

BMI; scheduling, personnel problems; areas of interest; summaries of addresses at 33rd annual convention. il Pub W 188:72-4+ N 8 '65

Book manufacturing, 1966, theme of BMI conference. Pub W 188:118-19 S 6 '65

Policy statement drafted at BMI convention. Pub W 188:116 D 6 '65

BOOK marks. See Bookmarks

BOOK mending. See Books—Conservation and restoration

BOOK of common prayer. See Church of England—Book of common prayer

BOOK-of-the-month club

See also
Dorothy Canfield Fisher library awards

BOOK orders, School library. See School libraries—Acquisitions

BOOK plates. See Bookplates

BOOK press

Friedman, Johns announce purchase of the Book press. il Pub W 189:100 Ja 3 '66

BOOK prices. See Books—Prices

BOOK processing in libraries. See Libraries—Technical processes

BOOK publication. See Publishers and publishing

BOOK rarities

Books. P. W. Schmidtchen. See issues of Hobbies

See also
Association of college and research libraries—Rare books section
Manuscripts

Facsimiles

Alice ms. facsimile starts Xerox subsidiary's program. il Pub W 188:41-2 Ag 2 '65

BOOK repairing. See Books—Conservation and restoration

BOOK reports

How to succeed in book reports without really reading; Reading avoidance service. J. Biermann and B. Toohey. il Library J 90:5348-50 D 15 '65

BOOK restoration. See Books—Conservation and restoration

BOOK review digest

Depleted Book review digest; coverage of children's books. D. Broderick. Library J 90:945 F 15 '65

BOOK reviewers. See Critics

BOOK reviews

Authors league panel: book reviews and reviewers. il Pub W 187:38-41 Mr 22 '65

Bias in book reviewing and book selection. H. Regnery. ALA Bul 60:57-62 Ja '66

Boston book review editors express views; summary of addresses. H. Kenny and A. Duhamel. Pub W 187:39 My 17 '65

Caveats and contradictions: fiction reviews in Lj; letter, with editorial comment. J. C. Pine. Library J 90:3828+ O 1 '65; Reply. C. D. Pipes. 90:5124 D 1 '65

Depleted Book review digest; coverage of children's books. D. Broderick. Library J 90:945 F 15 '65

Does design affect reviewing? three reviewers say yes! summary of discussion at meeting of the Trade book clinic of the American institute of graphic arts. R. Kluger; H. A. Kenny; V. A. Bradley. Pub W 187:32-3 Ap 12 '65

On reviewing children's books. R. H. Vigures. Horn Bk 41:23 F '65

Reviewer on review. J. K. Hutchens. Sat R 48:25-6 F 20 '65

Reviewing of university press books; report of panel discussion at AAUP convention. il Pub W 188:45-7+ Jl 19 '65

WLB review of books. J. C. Haden; N. W. Polsby; R. Hart. bibliog il Wilson Lib Bul 40:420-59 Ja '66

See also
American library association—Subscription books committee
Literary criticism
Radio broadcasting—Book programs
Television broadcasting—Book programs

BOOK selection

Administrative policy and book stock provision; views of a British public library administrator. S. C. Holliday. il Library J 90:4907-11 N 15 '65

Benefit of the doubt; address, May 2, 1963. E. Moon. il Wilson Lib Bul 39:663-7+ Ap '65

Bias in book reviewing and book selection. H. Regnery. ALA Bul 60:57-62 Ja '66

Book purchasing by university and college libraries; report of group meeting at AAUP convention. il Pub W 188:44-5 Jl 19 '65

Children's libraries: Jack-of-all-trades: book selection coordinator and critic. A. Izard. Wilson Lib Bul 39:689 Ap '65

Crucial battle for the minds of men; USIA libraries. H. W. Axford. bibliog Library J 90:2499-503 Je 1 '65

Hidden persuaders in book selection. J. Cushman. il Library J 90:3553-8 S 15 '65

In, out, or neglected? books chosen in response to an Lj book selection survey; with editorial comment. il Library J 91:57-64, 68 Ja 1 '66

More than lip service. E. Geller. Library J 90:3640 S 15 '65

Pursuing a policy; excerpts from Library reaches out, ed. by K. Coplan and E. Castagna. A. C. Lake. Library J 90:2491-4 Je 1 '65

Selection, quality, balance: a guide to the NDEA guidelines; school library holdings. E. Ahlers. il Library J 90:1461-3 Mr 15 '65

BOOK selection—*Continued*
They play it safe; North Carolina public libraries, report of survey. E. W. Tamblyn. il Library J 90:2495-8 Je 1 '65; Reply. E. Moon. 90:2980-1 Jl '65
Unsavory answer; discarding twice as costly as acquiring. W. Brahm. Library J 90: 5222-3 D 1 '65

BOOK stands. See Bookcases

BOOK thefts
Librarian and bookdealer convicted in Scranton (Pa) book theft trial. Library J 90: 2774 Je 15 '65
Mirrors and TV for security. T. W. McConkey. il Library J 90:1692-3 Ap 1 '65
See also
Library protection systems

BOOK titles. See Titles of books, stories, etc.

BOOK trade. See Book industries and trade

BOOK week
Catholic book week, 1965. D. L. Flaherty. America 112:254-6 F 20 '65
CBC plans for book week and large fairs. il Pub W 188:178-80 Jl 12 '65
Children's book week and the bookseller. B. Beilenson. il Pub W 180:54-6 N 8 '65

BOOKAZINE company, incorporated
How two leading book jobbers prepare for Christmas. Pub W 188:37-9 Ag 23 '65

BOOKBINDER, Hyman
Poverty's armchair generals. New Repub 153:36-8 O 23 '65

BOOKBINDING
Barrow report discusses adhesives used for perfect or unsewn binding. Library J 91:74 Ja 1 '66
Binding with vat-made papers; C. Delpierre and K. Vinding revive centuries-old art. A. Karlikow. il Craft Horiz 25:12-15+ Mr '65
Handbinding Churchill's biography; Royal binder of the book Mansell. il Pub W 188: 98-9 O 4 '65
India's first high-speed bindery; Four oceans bindery. R. B. Ellish. il Pub W 187:103-5 My 3 '65
Major Abbey's modern bookbindings. H. Nixon. il Craft Horiz 25:28-31 Jl '65
See also
Book covers

Cost
Libraries estimate processing costs in library binding institute survey. Library J 90:2991 Jl '65

Materials
Columbia mills completes new plant in Ontario. il Pub W 188:110 O 4 '65

BOOKBINDING machinery
Tools of the trade. Pub W 188:98-9 Ag 9 '65

BOOKCASES
Lectern bookcase. il Pop Mech 124:168 O '65
Reading matter. R. Reif. il N Y Times Mag p 134-5+ O 24 '65

BOOKING agencies. See Theatrical agencies

BOOKLETS. See Pamphlets

BOOKMARKS
Bejeweled bookmarks. il McCalls 93:128-9 D '65

BOOKMOBILES
Bookmobile; bookstore on wheels visits high schools. il Sr Schol 86:sup8-9 Ap 29 '65
Books on the mountain; North Carolina. B. Davenport. il Am Ed 1:12-15 Mr '65
Colorful trailers serve as mobile libraries; Lakeland, Fla. W. H. Murphy. il Am City 80:106-7 Jl '65
Community action; Henderson County public library, Hendersonville, N.C. M. Seagle. Wilson Lib Bul 40:256 N '65
Evaluating bookmobile services; changes in bookmobile clientele. G. K. Schenk. Wilson Lib Bul 39:687 Ap '65

BOOKPLATES
Art of the bookplate. F. Johnson. il Am Artist 29:48-53+ My '65

BOOKS
Revolution in books; symposium. bibliog il UNESCO Courier 18:4-32 S '65
See also
Best sellers
Royalties

Advertising
Adclub examines handling of religious books. Pub W 188:70-2 D 27 '65
ABPC management seminar discusses sales stimulants. Pub W 187:38-9 Mr 15 '65
FTC hearing forecasts federal book banning; opinions in advertising. S. Wagner. Pub W 188:30-1 O 11 '65
FTC offers a plan for voluntary compliance; determination to eliminate anticompetitive discriminatory promotional programs. C. B. Grannis. Pub W 188:33 O 18 '65

January books; major campaigns. il Pub W 188:26-34 N 8 '65
Large ad campaign budgeted for Atlanta bookstores; Elson's book stores. Pub W 188:43 O 18 '65
Literary agents find much ignorance in advertising; summary of Publishers' ad club meeting. Pub W 187:34-6 My 24 '65
Tips; C. Brown's Manchild in the promised land. il Pub W 188:38-9 Jl 26 '65
See also
Childrens literature—Advertising

Anecdotes, facetiae, satire, etc.
Any book in this store twenty-nine cents. B. Bernstein. New Yorker 41:122+ Je 12 '65

Care
Care and safekeeping of books. House & Gard 127:34-5+ My '65
Ways to care for your books. Sunset 134: 118-19 Ap '65

Collectors and collecting
See Book collecting

Conservation and restoration
Continuing quest; care of LC's collections. P. E. Edlund. il Library J 90:3397-402 S 1 '65
Preservation of deteriorating books; excerpts from report. G. R. Williams. bibliog Library J 91:51-6 Ja 1 '66
Putting new life in old volumes; interview. R. I. Boak. il Pub W 188:115-18 Jl 19 '65
US support for book preservation proposed in ARL committee report; summary; with editorial comment. G. Williams Library J 90:1271, 1272+ Mr 15 '65
Vitamins restore old books at Vatican City laboratory. il Pub W 188:79+ Ag 9 '65

Exhibitions
See Book exhibits

Importation
Importing books for the college store. Pub W 187:65-6 Je 14 '65

Mutilation, defacement, etc.
Mirrors and TV for security. T. W. McConkey. il Library J 90:1692-3 Ap 1 '65

Paper covered books
See Paperback books

Pirated editions
See Copyright—Unauthorized reprints

Prices
Cost indexes for library materials. M. Chicorel. il Wilson Lib Bul 39:896-900+ Je '65
Pre-Christmas price book; is it a bane or a blessing? Pub W 187:18-20 Ap 5 '65
Sticky problem of price stickers. H. J. Houlihan. Pub W 187:60-1 My 24 '65
Sweden's net book agreement ended by government board. T. R. Buckman. il Pub W 187:26-31 My 3 '65
See also
Libraries—Finance

Repairing
See Books—Conservation and restoration

Reprints
OP publishing; the new look in reprints; with selected list of OP publishers. D. Dempsey. Sat R 48:37-8+ Je 12 '65
See also
Paperback books

Reprints, Unauthorized
See Copyright—Unauthorized reprints

Storage
See also
Warehouses

Translations
See Translations and translating

BOOKS, Censorship of. See Censorship

BOOKS, Chinese. See Chinese literature

BOOKS, Condensed
How to succeed in book reports without really reading; Reading avoidance service. J. Biermann and B. Toohey. il Library J 90:5348-50 D 15 '65

BOOKS, Filmed. See Film adaptations

BOOKS, Illustrated. See Illustrated books

BOOKS, Illustration of. See Illustration of books and periodicals

BOOKS, incorporated
Publishers company, inc. merges book divisions. Pub W 188:44 Jl 5 '65

BOOKS, Paper covered. See Paperback books
BOOKS, Titles of. See Titles of books, stories, etc.
BOOKS and reading
  Books. M. Muggeridge. See issues of Esquire
  Can reading affect delinquency? address, January 1965. W. C. Kvaraceus. bibliog f ALA Bul 59:516-22 Je '65
  Catch up with L. Lerman. Mlle 61:104 S; 62:80 N '65
  Confidential question. W. S. Maugham. NEA J 54:19 Ap '65
  Curl up and read. See issues of Seventeen
  Great misconceptions? every new scientific invention death knell of reading and libraries. W. Brahm. Library J 90:594+ F 1 '65
  In, out, or neglected? books chosen in response to an Lj book selection survey; with editorial comment. il Library J 91:57-64, 68 Ja 1 '66
  Let's don't be too solemn about books; address, October 30, 1964. J. K. Galbraith. ALA Bul 59:112-14 F '65
  Letter to parents. N. Larrick. Sr Schol 86:sup 15 Mr 4 '65
  Life book review. See issues of Life
  Outlook tower; books of interest to high school students; comp. by M. C. Scoggin. See issues of Horn book magazine
  Preview of new books. P. K. Cuneo. America 113:409+ O 9 '65
  Reading matter; quotations; comp by E. F. Murphy. il N Y Times Mag p 102 Ap 25 '65
  Should we censor what adolescents read? with study-discussion program, by C. Smallenburg and H. Smallenburg. H. Norris; J. R. Squire; R. F. Hogan. bibliog il PTA Mag 59:10-12, 36 Mr '65
  Summer reading: risks, rules & rewards; Time essay. Time 86:34-5 Ag 13 '65
  This is reading, by F. G. Jennings. Review Pub W 187:58-60 F 15 '65
    Sat R 48:88-9 F 20 '65. C. J. Calitri
  Twelve-year-old adult reader. D. M. Broderick. il Library J 90:2321-7 My 15 '65
  Under cover (cont) C. Stinnett. Ladies Home J 82:20+ F '65
  WLB review of books. J. C. Haden; N. W. Polsby; R. Hart. bibliog il Wilson Lib Bul 40:420-59 Ja '66
  Writing for the in-betweenster. F. Kohner. Writer 78:22-4 Ag '65
  See also
  Authors and readers
  Best sellers
  Biography
  Book selection
  Childrens literature
  Childrens reading
  College students—Reading
  Immoral literature and pictures
  Libraries, Private
  Libraries and readers
  National book committee
  Reading lists
  Reference books

    Anecdotes, facetiae, satire, etc.
  Why mommy can't read. J. Kerr. McCalls 93:51+ Ja '66

    Best books
  Adult books for young people, 1964. Library J 90:1493-4 Mr 15 '65; Same. Pub W 187:45-6 Mr 1 '65; Wilson Lib Bul 39:608+ Ap '65
  America's survey of notable fall books. America 113:676-7+ N 27 '65
  Books; critics' choices for Christmas. Commonweal 83:281-91 D 3 '65
  Books to be noted, 1965. America 112:672-87+ My 8 '65
  Nais chooses ten best adult books of 1964. Pub W 187:30 Mr 29 '65
  New books appraised; ed. by M. Cooley and others. See issues of Library journal
  Notable books of 1964; a selected list. ALA Bul 59:221-2 Mr '65; Same. Library J 90:1279 Mr 15 '65; Pub W 187:44-5 Mr 1 '65; NEA J 54:60+ Ap '65; Sr Schol 86:sup 1-2 Ap 1 '65; Wilson Lib Bul 39:607-8 Ap '65
  Reader looks at the notable books; address, 1964. J. Cushman. ALA Bul 59:105-10 F '65
  Titles to thaw out by. P. Bunker. Sat R 48:35-6 Ap 17 '65
  See also
  Best sellers

    Bibliography
  Basic library of trash. D. Newman and R. Benton. Esquire 63:78-9+ F '65
  Books for adults beginning to read. il Wilson Lib Bul 40:66-70 S '65
  Books for Christmas giving. il Sat R 48:52-4+ D 4 '65

Books to come; ed. by I. E. Stokvis and J. Putnam (cont) Library J 90:686-772+ F 1 '65
  Books to come; ed. by J. Putnam and R. Grossman. Library J 90:2598-600+ Je 1 '65
  Books to come; ed. by J. Putnam and others. Library J 90:4126-247 O 1 '65
  Bookworm's boutique. House & Gard 128:207-8 D '65
  Current titles of interest to Nation readers. Nation 201:66 Ag 2 '65
  Fall highlights. M. E. Marty. Christian Cent 82:1223-5 O 6 '65
  From the university presses. il Library J 90:2766-71 Je 15 '65
  Just off the press! new books of special interest to teachers. il Sr Schol 86:sup28 Mr 4 '65
  Materials for the illiterate; symposium. bibliog il Wilson Lib Bul 40:51-64 S '65
  Money isn't everything; subject range available with price list. H. Frankel. Sat R 48:47-8 D 4 '65
  New books for young adults. J. Rowell. Sr Schol 86:sup32-3 Ap 15 '65
  New reading for junior and senior high school students. H. R. Finch. il Sr Schol 87:sup8-9 S 30 '65
  New textbooks for high school students. Sr Schol 87:sup 14-16 N 18 '65
  Nobel prize-winners: a selected gift list. Sat R 48:41 D 4 '65
  Paperbacks for teenage readers. H. R. Finch. Sr Schol 87:sup30-1 O 28 '65
  Potpourri. P. Adams. See issues of Atlantic
  SR's check list of the week's new books; comp. R. Brown. See issues of Saturday review
  School library or bookatheque? education of youth and war on poverty. C. K. Brooks. Library J 90:1989-90 Ap 15 '65
  September books; some top early fall campaigns. il Pub W 187:88-106 Je 7 '65
  This week. See issues of Christian century
  Time listings. See issues of Time

    International aspects
  Challenge of the sixties; Congress of the International publishers association. D. Dempsey. il Sat R 48:27-8+ Je 26 '65
  U.S. publishers survey textbook needs in U.A.R. Pub W 187:37 Mr 8 '65

    Reading aloud
  Books my father read to me. R. Kilmer. Horn Bk 41:319-20 Je '65

    Religious aspects
  Freedom to read and religious problems: address, January 1965. T. Gill. ALA Bul 59:59:477-83 Je '65

    United States
  See Books and reading
BOOKS as gifts
  Books to make friends happy. G. Davenport. Nat R 17:1163-4 D 14 '65
  Children's books: worth reading before wrapping. C. H. Simonds. Nat R 17:1165 D 14 '65
  For creatures great and small; some children's books for adults. L. Russ. il Pub W 188:28-9 O 11 '65
  Horizontal-enrichment: information-wise; books not to give. A. B. Heath. Nat R 17:1189-90 D 28 '65
BOOKS for children. See Childrens literature
BOOKS for girls. See Childrens literature
BOOKS USA, incorporated
  Books U.S.A. poster invites donations. il Pub W 187:80-1 Ap 26 '65
BOOKSELLERS and bookselling
  Active agenda for booksellers. C. B. Grannis. Pub W 187:81 Je 21 '65
  Bookseller and a jobber look at U.P. books; summary of panel discussion at AAUP. il Pub W 188:49-52 Jl 19 '65
  Check-out cashiers can give efficient service. M. L. Levin. Pub W 187:96-7 F 15 '65
  Children's books and the trade sales representative; summary of discussion of Children's book council. Pub W 189:66-7 Ja 10 '66
  Hiring and training personnel for the bookstore. B. R. Mark. Pub W 187:68-71 Mr 1 '65
  Management tools for bookstores and general college stores: summary of workshops during annual meeting of National association of college stores. il Pub W 188:66-71 S 20 '65
  Publishers should put more effort on their staple stock. B. Schweid. il Pub W 187:45 My 31 '65

BOOKSELLERS and bookselling—*Continued*
Wednesday is biddy day; excerpt from Customer is always. L. Meyer. Pub W 187: 56-7 Mr 8 '65
Working one's way through the ABA trade show. M. Kain. Pub W 187:58-60 My 24 '65
See also
Books—Prices
College bookstores

Catholic literature
See Booksellers and bookselling—Religious literature

Childrens literature
Children's book shop sponsors storybook art show; House of the magic rabbit, New York city. Pub W 187:54-5 Mr 15 '65
Children's book week and the bookseller. B. Beilenson. il Pub W 188:54-6 N 8 '65
Selling children's books from a rabbit warren; House of the magic rabbit, N.Y. il Pub W 188:46-8 O 18 '65
Selling children's books; summary of panel discussion at ABA Los Angeles meeting. il Pub W 188:35-9 O 25 '65
Sheep in wolves' clothing; or Never judge a children's book by its cover. L. Russ. Pub W 187:57-8 My 10 '65

Paperback books
A&A's new quarters greatly improving service. il Pub W 188:16-19 Ag 16 '65
ABA regional, Detroit; trade issues and a new association; summaries of discussions at meeting. il Pub W 188:36-8 O 4 '65
Bookmobile; bookstore on wheels visits high schools. il Sr Schol 86:sup8-9 Ap 29 '65
1965 paperback best sellers in the bookstores. il Pub W 189:64-7, 90-3 Ja 17 '66
Paperbacks in the bookstore; report of discussion at ABA Los Angeles meeting. il Pub W 188:29-31 O 25 '65
Paperbacks, problems, profits and! ! ! PW survey. il Pub W 188:58-60 Ag 2 '65
Summer reading lists for secondary schools; with Yale co-op's list of paperbacks. G. R. Smith. Pub W 188:108-14 S 27 '65

Publicity
Autographing parties around the country. il Pub W 188:43-5 O 18 '65
Autographing parties in seven cities. il Pub W 189:60-1+ Ja 3 '66
Successful autographing tours by three personalities. il Pub W 188:53-6 D 13 '65
Unusual ad campaign of small New England store; Vermont book shop ad in Saturday evening post. Pub W 188:57 N 8 '65
See also
Show windows

Reference books
Colorado booksellers association plan; combat doorbell-pushing encyclopedia salesman; with plan lists. il Pub W 188:15-16, 25 N 29 '65

Religious literature
Ecumenical council; effect on sales of books in three Catholic stores. F. Henderson; G. Jeannot; J. C. Drahos. Pub W 187:118-19 F 8 '65
Promotion plays vital role in Minneapolis Catholic shop; St Francis shop. il Pub W 188:115-16 S 27 '65

Returns policy
Review of returns. J. A. Duffy. Pub W 188: 56-7 Ag 2 '65

Scientific literature
New efforts in retailing of scientific-technical books. C. B. Grannis. Pub W 188:78 N 15 '65

Statistics
ABPC: annual sales trends. il Pub W 188: 43-5 S 20 '65

Stock
Management tools for bookstores and general college stores; summary of workshops during annual meeting of National association of college stores. il Pub W 188:67-9 S 20 '65
Store directories simplify stock control. M. G. Hurtig. il Pub W 188:48-52 D 27 '65

Technical literature
New efforts in retailing of scientific-technical books. C. B. Grannis. Pub W 188:78 N 15 '65
See also
Professional and scientific sales group

California
ABA regional. Pub W 188:28-51 O 25 '65
Antiquarian bookshop honors author of new book; Alta California bookstore in Berkeley. Pub W 189:82 Ja 10 '66
Book wholesaling and supply in California. F. H. Potter. Pub W 188:57-9 N 22 '65
California booksellers join forces to combat censorship. W. S. Chleboun. Pub W 188: 30-1 Ag 16 '65
Children's books well received in I. Magnin toy depts. Pub W 188:52 N 1 '65
Cody's books in Berkeley moves into 6500-foot store. il Pub W 189:126-8 Ja 17 '66
S.F. bookshops cooperate with airline to promote books. il Pub W 188:50 D 6 '65
Shorebird bookstore caters to cultivated well-to-do residents; Palos Verdes Peninsula. il Pub W 187:46-8 My 31 '65

Canada
Canadian bookshop's sale at 50 per cent off grosses $13,000; M. G. Hurtig booksellers ltd. il Pub W 187:94-5 Ap 19 '65
Store directories simplify stock control. M. G. Hurtig. il Pub W 188:48-52 D 27 '65
See also
Canadian booksellers association

Colorado
Area meeting of booksellers held in Denver; second biennial Mountain-Plains booksellers convention; summaries of discussions. il Pub W 188:14-25 N 29 '65
Currents from the Chinook: putting a bookstore on the map; Chinook bookshop, Colorado Springs. J. Noyes. il Pub W 187:58-60 Ap 12 '65
May-D&F, Denver, combines sale of original art and art books. Pub W 180:61 N 22 '65
Mismanagement blamed for Boulder shop closing; Village bookstall. Pub W 187:56 My 31 '65

Connecticut
Book fair in Westport store benefits private school; Klein's. Pub W 189:59 Ja 3 '66
Brentano's in Hartford is city's largest bookstore. il Pub W 188:46-7 D 27 '65
Brentano's opens new store; enlarges two others. Pub W 188:78-9 S 13 '65
Klein's, Westport, Conn. expands. W. Pitkin, jr. il Pub W 188:58-9 N 29 '65

England
See also
National book league

Florida
Betsy caused limited damage but business has suffered. Pub W 188:58 O 4 '65
Lutheran church supply store opens in Orlando, Florida. il Pub W 189:84 Ja 10 '66

France
Christmas in France: selling books in English. H. R. Lottman. il Pub W 188:22-4 D 13 '65
Visiting bookmen in France. A. T. Hamlin. ALA Bul 59:815-18 O '65

Georgia
Century-old Macon, Ga. shop prospers in new location; Brown's book store. il Pub W 187:52-4 Mr 15 '65
Unorthodox bookstore methods pay off for Atlanta store; Lenox Square bookstore. il Pub W 188:62-4 O 11 '65

Hungary
Book buying in Budapest; letter to the editor. D. Gratz. Library J 90:4652 N 1 '65

Illinois
Book shop in Aurora, Ill; personality plus. P. Kohn. il Pub W 187:60-3 My 10 '65
Paul Romaine defense fund; Chicago bookseller guilty under Illinois anti-obscenity statute. R. H. Smith. Pub W 187:63 Je 28 '65

Indiana
Ayres' new store completes first Christmas season. Pub W 189:82-4 Ja 10 '66

Italy
Remainders book italiano: Italian, English-language titles. il Pub W 188:58-60 D 13 '65

Latin America
Savior and nemesis; concerning publication *Libros en venta.* letter to the editor. J. G. Veenstra. Library J 90:4650+ N 1 '65

BOOKSELLERS and bookselling—*Continued*

Louisiana

Betsy caused limited damage but business has suffered. Pub W 188:58 O 4 '65

Twenty-fifth anniversary party for Harnett Kane in Louisiana; Marion Harris' book store in Metairie. il Pub W 188:60 N 22 '65

Massachusetts

A&A's new quarters greatly improving service. il Pub W 188:16-19 Ag 16 '65

Bookshop with a belfry; Baucom's textbook co, Amherst. P. Johnson, jr. il Pub W 187: 98-100 F 15 '65

Religious store's recent annual sale was biggest in thirty years; Whittemore associates, Boston. il Pub W 187:58-9 My 17 '65

Minnesota

Book Case marks its third year in downtown Minneapolis. il Pub W 188:54-5 N 1 '65

Promotion plays vital role in Minneapolis Catholic shop; St Francis shop. il Pub W 188:115-16 S 27 '65

New Jersey

Brentano's opens new store; enlarges two others. Pub W 188:78-9 S 13 '65

New Mexico

Santa Fe book & stationary co: an old shop in modern dress. il Pub W 187:180-1 Je 7 '65

New York (state)

Books for four-to-ten-year olds major concern of upper East Side N.Y. store; Drewdale books and cards on Madison ave. il Pub W 187:163-4 F 22 '65

Booksellers, a summer of uncertainty; New York state censorship legislation. R. H. Smith. Pub W 188:45 Ag 2 '65

Brentano's Fifth avenue suggests Old World shopping arcade. il Pub W 188:42-5 D 27 '65

Brentano's N.Y. store enlarged; now third largest bookshop in U.S; Fifth avenue, NYC. il Pub W 187:72-4 Mr 1 '65

Brentano's will open shop in Greenwich Village. Pub W 189:59 Ja 3 '66

Children's book shop sponsors storybook art show; House of the magic rabbit, New York city. Pub W 187:54-5 Mr 15 '65

Eighth Street bookshop has avant-garde flavor. il Pub W 189:36-8 Ja 3 '66

Expansion brings business in Buffalo; Ulbrich's bookstore. il Pub W 188:44-5 Jl 26 '65

Health food store sells 1100 copies of book at party; Carlton Fredericks Facts and fallacies. Pub W 188:50 D 6 '65

Laurel book center in New York makes some changes. Pub W 188:61 N 22 '65

Lost in the bookshop of New York. A. Levy. il Harper 231:148-52 O '65

N.Y. anti-obscenity laws passed to protect minors. Pub W 188:181 Jl 12 '65

Outlook bullish for new shop; Book center paperback store in Kingston, N.Y. J. A. Ellithorpe, jr. il Pub W 188:327-8 Ag 30 '65

Trade winds; bookstore boom on Fifth avenue; Rizzoli international bookstore and Brentano's. J. Beatty, jr. Sat R 48:14+ O 9 '65

Wise men fish here: the story of Frances Steloff and the Gotham book mart, by W. G. Rogers. Review
Sat R 48:31 F 6 '65. W. Bower

Ohio

Store's first year sales meet owner's projections; Fields' Book store of severance, inc, Cleveland Heights. Pub W 187:82 F 1 '65

Pennsylvania

Facelifting increases sales in Pittsburgh Cokesbury store. il Pub W 187:58-9 My 3 '65

South America

See Booksellers and bookselling—Latin America

Spain

Savior and nemesis; concerning publication *Libros en venta*, letter to the editor. J. G. Veenstra. Library J 90:4650+ N 1 '65

Sweden

Sweden's net book agreement ended by government board. T. R. Buckman. il Pub W 187:26-31 My 3 '65

Tennessee

Fair at Nashville Baptist bookstore attracts over 10,000 children. il Pub W 188:56-7 D 13 '65

Second annual book fair at Nashville Baptist store. Pub W 188:52-3 N 1 '65

United States

About booksellers and bookselling; adaptation of address at N.Y. women's national book association, April 13, 1965. C. B. Anderson. Pub W 188:64-5 Jl 5 '65

ABA; panels on children's book fairs and trade communications; symposium. il Pub W 187:43-51 Je 28 '65

Bookseller year 1965. L. Epstein. Pub W 187:80 F 1 '65

Bookselling. See issues of Publishers' weekly

Call for meaningful cooperation for bookstores; excerpts from article in American scholar, with comments by R. H. Smith. W. Jovanovich. Pub W 188:42 O 11 '65

Christmas 1965; record sales were achieved by retail bookstores. il Pub W 189:121-4 Ja 17 '66

Christmas pot pourri; ideas and suggestions for holiday season. Pub W 188:46-8 Ag 23 '65

Hooked on books; sales jump. il Time 86:96 O 15 '65

Lasser report; distribution of books by publishers. J. A. Duffy. Pub W 188:51-2 D 13 '65

New bookshops opened in 1965; the West was most popular region. Pub W 189:125-6 Ja 17 '66

1964 failure rate drops for book-stationery stores. Pub W 188:46 Jl 26 '65

Planning and making the move to a new store. E. Young. Pub W 188:56-60 O 11 '65

Publishers' executives review order-time survey; Lasser survey report; summary of discussion at ABPC luncheon. Pub W 188: 29-30 D 13 '65

Sidelines and the American bookstore; nonbook merchandise. J. A. Duffy. Pub W 188:68-70 O 25 '65

Snob sidelines: chess sets, jigsaw puzzles, literary dolls. E. C. Lowry. il Pub W 187: 100-3 Ap 26 '65

What some booksellers have been promoting. il Pub W 187:178-9 Je 7 '65

Who shall silence all the airs and madrigals? address, November 1964. J. Zeitlin. il Library J 90:2479-83 Je 1 '65

Will bookstore machinery be adequate for 1975-1985? C. B. Grannis. Pub W 187:152 Je 7 '65

See also

American booksellers association

Christian booksellers association

Department stores—Book departments

Vermont

Imaginative selling in small town shop; Vermont book shop, Middlebury. P. Johnson, jr. il Pub W 188:51-2 Ag 9 '65

Personal touch in Vermont; Yankee bookshop in Woodstock. P. Johnson, jr. il Pub W 188:58-60 S 6 '65

Unusual ad campaign of small New England store; Vermont book shop ad in Saturday evening post. Pub W 188:57 N 8 '65

Virginia

Advertising and promotion helped build up Rule book shop in Lynchburg. il Pub W 187:40-2 Ap 5 '65

Washington (state)

Bellevue, Wash. shop is five years old; Bell, Book & Candle. il Pub W 188:88-90 D 27 '65

BOOKSELLERS' league of New York

Booksellers' league of New York celebrates 70th birthday. il Pub W 187:56-7 F 15 '65

BOOKSHELVES. See Bookcases

BOOKSTORE windows. See Show windows

BOOKSTORES. See Booksellers and bookselling; College bookstores

BOOKSTORES, Traveling. See Bookmobiles

BOOMS, Real estate. See Real estate business

BOORMAN, Howard

Report from Peking. Sat R 49:35 Ja 15 '66

BOORMAN, John

Dave Clark five make a movie! ed. by E. Miller. por Seventeen 24:90 Jl '65

BOOSTER heart. See Heart, Artificial

BOOSTERS for space vehicles. See Space vehicles—Propulsion systems

BOOT and shoe industry. See Shoes—Trade and manufacture

BOOT jacks. See Bootjacks

BOOTH, Arch N.
America will be different because of you;
address, May 6, 1965. Vital Speeches 31:
537-9 Je 15 '65
BOOTH, Edward J.
Planning parking and plowing. Am City 80:
87-9 S '65
BOOTH, Franklin
Drawings of Franklin Booth. J. Jellico. il
por Am Artist 30:42-6+ Ja '66
BOOTH, John E.
Veteran against veteran. Atlan 216:88-91 O
'65
BOOTH, John Wilkes
Assassination! excerpt from Twenty days.
D. M. Kunhardt and P. B. Kunhardt, jr.
il por Am Heritage 16:12-35 Ag '65; Dis-
cussion. 16:7 Ap; 93 O '65
BOOTH, Philip
Tenants' harbor: poem. New Yorker 41:48 S
11 '65
BOOTH, Roland L.
Linseed oil cuts spalling damage. Am City
80:96-7 S '65
BOOTH, Wayne C.
College education for what? NEA J 54:14-16
D '65
BOOTH, William
Booth led boldly with his big bass drum;
Salvation army's 100th anniversary. Chris-
tian Cent 82:885-6 Jl 14 '65
General next to God; condensation. R. Collier.
il Read Digest 86:265-8+ F '65
BOOTJACKS
Treasure hunt; flatirons and bootjacks. J.
Mebane. il Bet Hom & Gard 43:25+ My '65
BOOTS, Mary Jo
We never say we can't afford it. por Farm
J 90:75 Ja '66
BOOTS and shoes. See Shoes
BORAGES
Borage. J. Lindeman. Horticulture 43:55 My
'65
BORAGO officinalis. See Borages
BORCH, Gerard ter, 1617-1681
Terborch's Lady at her toilet. E. Haver-
kamp-Begemann. il Art N 64:38-41+ D '65
BORCHARDT, Georges
Report on French publishing. Pub W 187:
27-9 My 31 '65
BORDAZ, Jacques
Threshing sledge. Natur Hist 74:26-9 Ap '65
BORDEAUX wines. See Wines
BORDEN company
America's favorite food. M. B. Keiser. il
Parents Mag 40:28+ Ag '65
BORDERS, Garden. See Garden borders
BOREK, Felix, and others
Immunogenicity and role of size: response
of guinea pigs to oligotyrosine and tyrosine
derivatives. bibliog Science 150:1177-8 N
26 '65
BORETZ, Benjamin
Lincoln Center: tomb of the future. Nation
200:299-304+ Mr 22 '65
Records (cont) Nation 200:458-60; 201:286-7
Ap 26, O 25 '65
BORGES, Jorge Luis
Books. J. Updike. New Yorker 41:223-4+ O
30 '65
Two worlds of Jorge Luis Borges. A. A.
Piñeiro. por Américas 17:11-15 Mr '65
BORGESE, Elisabeth Mann
Letter from Rome. Nation 201:313-16 N 1 '65
BORGESE, Thomas A. and Bertles, J. F.
Hemoglobin heterogeneity: embryonic hemo-
globin in the duckling and its disappear-
ance in the adult. bibliog Science 148:50° ·11
Ap 23 '65
BORIDES
See also
Tungsten borides
BORING (woodwork) See Drilling and boring
(woodwork)
BORING bits. See Drilling and boring machin-
ery
BORING machinery. See Drilling and boring
machinery
BORIS Godunov; opera. See Musorgskiĭ, M. P.
BORLAND, Hal
October splendor; excerpt from Sundial of
the seasons. Read Digest 87:25-6 O '65
Spacious days of summer; excerpt from Sun-
dial of the seasons. Read Digest 87:187-8+
Ag '65
BORMAN, Frank
We felt content, cozy and safe and never
got bored. il pors Life 60:68-72 Ja 14 '66
See also
Space flight—Manned flights—Borman-Lovell
flight, 1965
BORMANN, Martin
End of the Hitler gang; excerpts from Last
100 days. J. Toland. il Look 29:72+ Je 1 '65

Wanted: 1,000 Nazis still at large. G.
Samuels. il por N Y Times Mag p26-7+
F 28 '65
World's most wanted criminal. B. Clark.
por Read Digest 86:74-7 Mr '65
BORN, Max
Recollections of Max Born. por Bul Atomic
Sci 21:3-6 S: 9-13 O; 3-6 N '65
BORNEO
See also
North Borneo
BORNEO, North. See North Borneo
BORNS, Harold W. jr
Late glacial ice-wedge casts in northern
Nova Scotia, Canada. bibliog Science 148:
1223-6 My 28 '65
BORNSTEIN, Murray B. and Crain, S. M.
Functional studies of cultured brain tissues
as related to demyelinative disorders. bib-
liog Science 148:1242-4 My 28 '65
BORNSTEIN, Paul, and Piez, K. A.
Collagen: structural studies based on the
cleavage of methionyl bonds. bibliog Sci-
ence 148:1353-5 Je 4 '65
BOROFF, David
Don't call it the borscht belt. N Y Times Mag
p48+ My 9 '65
Kind of proletarian Harvard. N Y Times
Mag p28-9+ Mr 28 '65
NYU: mecca for transfers. Sat R 48:68-9+
Ap 17 '65
New Yorker's report on New Mexico. Harper
230:72-8 F '65
What ails the journalism schools. Harper
231:77-8+ O '65
about
Obituary
Nation por 201:14 S 20 '65. J. J. Star-
row, jr
BORON, Calif.
Boron. H. D. Brown. il Hobbies 70:124-5
Mr '65
BORON
Avco building boron filament plant. J. F.
Judge. il Miss & Roc 17:22-3+ N 15 '65
Boron research focusing on components. I.
Stone. il Aviation W 83:49+ D 20 '65
Miles and miles of boron. Miss & Roc 16:55
Mr 29 '65
BORON nitride
Inorganic fiber production readied. J. F.
Judge. il Miss & Roc 17:32+ D 13 '65
BORROR, Donald J.
Bird song: the anatomy of a miracle. pors
Audubon Mag 67:159-63 My '65
BORROW pits. See Sand and gravel pits
BORROWERS, Registration of. See Libraries
—Registration
BORROWING of money. See Credit; Debt;
Loans
BORROWMAN, Merle
Conant's fight for better teaching. Atlan 215:
113-17 Ap '65
BORSOS, Tibor, and Rapp, H. J.
Complement fixation on cell surfaces by 19S
and 7S antibodies. bibliog Science 150:505-
6 O 22 '65
BORZOI books. See Knopf, Alfred A. in-
corporated
BOSC, Robert
European looks at the New York world's
fair. America 113:77 Jl 17 '65
What de Gaulle's re-election means. Amer-
ica 114:72-4 Ja 15 '66
BOSCH, Juan
Communism and democracy in the Domini-
can Republic. por Sat R 48:13-15+ Ag 7 '65
Dominican revolution. New Repub 153:19-21
Jl 24 '65
about
Angry Bosch back from exile. M. Acoca. il
por Life 59:46B O 8 '65
Back to Bosch? New Repub 153:9 S 18 '65
Dominican crisis. T. Draper. Commentary
40:33-68 D '65
In the shadow of Trujillo. Reporter 32:14 My
20 '65
Juan Bo's return. Newsweek 66:59 O 4 '65
Juan Bosch, bitter as he calls it quits. por
Life 58:38B-38C My 14 '65
Tragedy of Juan Bosch. F. Dorta-Duque. il
America 112:824-5+ Je 5 '65
Trouble for Bosch. Time 86:46+ D 10 '65
Two key men in the Dominican flare-up. U S
News 58:20 My 10 '65
Unheroic return. il por Time 86:46 O 1 '65
BOSE, Nirmal Kumar
Calcutta: a premature metropolis; with bio-
graphical sketch. Sci Am 213:28, 90-102 S
'65

BOSOM. See Breast

BOSOMTWE, LAKE. See Meteorite craters

BOSS rule
House that Tweed built; New York County courthouse. A. B. Callow, jr. il Am Heritage 16:64-9 O '65

BOSTON, Ralph
With a quarter inch between. il por Time 85:80 F 26 '65

BOSTON
Big overhaul. il Life 59:80-1 D 24 '65

Architecture
Boston bids for big clambakes; War memorial auditorium to lure national conventions. il Bsns W p 150+ F 13 '65
Boston upbeat. M. M. Davis. il Travel 123:11 Je '65
Winner announced in Boston competition. il Arch Rec 137:12-13+ Mr '65

Art
Reviews: Boston. J. H. Kay. Art N 63:17+ S '64; 21 F; 64:23 Sum '65

City planning
Bold Boston gladiator, Ed Logue. il Life 59:126-34 D 24 '65
My renewed city. F. Russell. il Nat R 17: 1108-11 N 30 '65
Structure & design. P. Herrera. il Fortune 72:179-80+ S '65
What's happening to proper old Boston? il Newsweek 65:77-9 Ap 26 '65

Crime
Boston's South End; center of the city's colored vice. J. Colebrook. il New Repub 152:8-12 Mr 6 '65; Discussion. 152:35-7 Mr 27 '65
Chicago on the Charles; Chicago-style murders. Time 86:27 N 26 '65
Then there were none; thugs against each other. il Newsweek 66:33 N 29 '65

Description
Invitation to Boston: NCTE convention. H. L. Walen. il Sr Schol 87:sup 10 N 11 '65
My Boston. E. M. Kennedy. il Esquire 64: 174-9 D '65

Education
Boston's busing battle; Louise Day Hicks fight to keep Negroes from busing their children out of black districts into white neighborhood schools. il Time 86:70 S 24 '65
Bussing in Boston. R. Coles. New Repub 153:12-15 O 2 '65
How to learn a secret name; South End school. B. Spacks. il Am Ed 1:7-12 Je '65
Rebalancing Boston; report on de facto segregation. il Newsweek 65:60-1 Ap 26 '65
Scholars and athletes; classics at Boston college high school. America 112:654 My 8 '65

Galleries and museums
See also
Boston museum of fine arts

History
Early cards of Boston. B. Finnegan. il Hobbies 70:124-5+ D '65

Hospitals
Code 99; signal for teamwork on the double; Pratt clinic-New England center hospital. il Todays Health 43:90-1 My '65
Restarting the heart; Samuel A. Levine cardiac center at Peter Bent Brigham hospital. il Newsweek 65:68 F 22 '65

Hotels, restaurants, etc.
Home at last; the Sheraton-Boston. Time 85:92 Ap 23 '65

Industries
Great Boston power play. W. Hines. Read Digest 88:99-104 Ja '66

Libraries
See also
Boston public library

Music
Special repertoire in a special way. M. Steinberg. Hi Fi 15:125 Ag '65
Subduing the passions; 150th birthday of Handel and Haydn society. Newsweek 66: 89-90 N 1 '65

Negroes
Boston's race dilemma: threat to cut off U.S. school funds. U S News 59:37 Ag 23 '65
Bussing in Boston. R. Coles. New Repub 153: 12-15 O 2 '65

Newspapers
See also
Globe (Boston)

Politics and government
Vote of confidence: L. D. Hicks. Newsweek 66:36 O 4 '65

Rapid transit
To keep Boston's wheels turning; new regional transit authority for seventy-seven neighboring towns. il Bsns W p 144+ F 20 '65

Social conditions
Boston's South End; center of the city's colored vice. J. Colebrook. il New Repub 152:8-12 Mr 6 '65; Discussion. 152:35-7 Mr 27 '65
My renewed city. F. Russell. il Nat R 17: 1108-7 N 30 '65
Reporter at large; effects of urban renewal on old people in South End. J. Colebrook. New Yorker 41:35-6+ Ja 1 '66

Stores
Scramble at Filene's; sale of furs salvaged from Neiman-Marcus fire in Dallas. il Newsweek 65:87 F 22 '65

Street traffic
Big drop in public-transportation use. il Am City 80:137+ O '65

Water supply
Outboard motor speeds treatment of algae. C. H. Reed. il Am City 80:38 N '65

BOSTON ballet company
Boston ballet company. John Hancock hall, Boston. I. Ferguson. Dance Mag 39:61-2 Mr '65

BOSTON Celtics (basketball team) See Basketball teams

BOSTON children's medical center. See Children—Hospitals

BOSTON college high school. See Boston—Education

BOSTON herald
Boston book review editors express views; summary of addresses. H. Kenny and A. Duhamel. Pub W 187:39 My 17 '65

BOSTON marathon. See Running

BOSTON museum of fine arts
Enrichment of a famous textile collection. R. Davidson. il Antiques 88:534+ O '65
Trove of Doughtys. T. N. Maytham. il Antiques 88:681-5 N '65

BOSTON opera company
Boston opera company, by Q. Eaton. Review Am Rec G 32:132+ O '65. J. Maclain Opera N 29:29 Ap 17 '65. D. Warren
Boston opera company, 1909-1914. D. Warren. Am Rec G 32:130-2 O '65; Reply with rejoinder. P. L. Miller and A. F. R. Lawrence. 32:382 D '65

BOSTON opera group, incorporated
Nono? yes and no; first American performance of Intolerance, 1960. il Newsweek 65: 84 Mr 8 '65
She puts the oomph in the opera. D. J. Hamblin. il Life 58:77-8+ Mr 5 '65
Swatches & splashes; production of Intolleranza. il Time 85:66 Mr 5 '65

BOSTON pops orchestra
Master of the pops. H. Kupferberg. il Atlan 215:130+ F '65

BOSTON public library
ABCD in Boston. J. M. Carroll and E. J. Montana, jr Wilson Lib Bul 40:248-50 N '65
Age of the acronym; address, February 1965. J. Manthorne. Wilson Lib Bul 40:84-6 S '65

BOSTON Red Sox (baseball) See Baseball clubs

BOSTON symphony orchestra
BSO plays Lohengrin. H. Kupferberg. il Atlan 216:174+ N '65
BSO Schönberg; violin concerto. M. Bernheimer. Sat R 48:30 Ap 17 '65
See also
Boston pops orchestra

BOSWELL, James
Withering wit of Samuel Johnson. W. H. Chamberlin. Sat R 48:14-15+ S 4 '65

BOTANICAL chemistry
See also
Alkaloids
Photosynthesis

BOTANICAL gardens
Huntington botanical gardens, San Marino, Calif. M. Kimnach. il Horticulture 43:34-6+ S '65
School botanic garden; Sacramento. il Sunset 135:272+ O '65
See also
Brooklyn botanic garden
New York botanical garden
Santa Barbara botanic garden

BOTANICAL research
Arabidopsis research: report on first international symposium. G. Röbbelen. Science 150:1192 N 26 '65
BOTANICAL specimens. See Plants—Collection and preservation
BOTANY
See also
Chromosomes (botany)
Desert vegetation
Flowers
Plants
Seeds
Trees
Physiology
Differential enzymatic activity in ecological races of typha latifolia L. S. J. McNaughton. bibliog il Science 150:1829-30 D 31 '65
See also
Chloroplasts
Germination
Photosynthesis
Alaska
Wildflowers in Alaska. E. Baldwin. il Horticulture 43:22-3 Ag '65
Antarctic Regions
Antarcticana: mosses. New Yorker 41:33-4 Je 5 '65
Arctic Regions
Polyploidy and environment in Arctic Alaska. A. W. Johnson and J. G. Packer. bibliog il Science 148:237-9 Ap 9 '65
California
Redding to Red Bluff in flowers; spring wildflowers in the Cascade foothills. il Sunset 134:44-5 Mr '65
Sierra Nevada has varied climate, plants. Sci N L 87:290 My 8 '65
Colorado
Floras of the tundra. P. D. Kilburn. il Natur Hist 74:52-9 Ag '65
England
Concise British flora in colour, by W. K. Martin. Review
New Yorker 41:65 Jl 31 '65. M. Panter-Downes
Mexico
Sabino grove ecology study. E. Leshan and others. il Natur Hist 74:14-23 My '65
Southwestern states
Plant formations in the natural history interpretation of southwestern desert regions. F. R. Gehlbach. il Nat Parks Mag 40:16-18 Ja '66
BOTANY, Medical
Cancer folk medicine effective in test tube; study on milkweed and dogbane. Sci N L 87:393 Je 19 '65
Plants that cure. quiz. J. Daugherty and M. Daugherty. il Sci Digest 58:92-4 O '65
See also
Umbelliferae
BOTELHO, Stella Y.
Medicine in the year 2000. Science 147:1164+ Mr 5 '65
BOTHMER, Bernard V.
Split chief minister. il Time 85:66-7 Ap 23 '65
BOTRAN. See Fungicides
BOTSFORD, Keith
Farewell to Muñoz Marin. Commentary 39:86-9 Je; 40:10+ O '65
My friend Fuentes. Commentary 39:64-7 F '65
Other candidate in France. N Y Times Mag p8-9+ D 19 '65
BOTSFORD, Ward
Sir Thomas and the gramophone, 1910-1960. Hi Fi 15:45-8+ Je '65
BOTTEL, Helen
Down to the sea on skis. Motor B 116:38-9 Jl '65
BOTTLE caps and seals
Lathe fun from Alpine novelties; smoking caliph and bottle stoppers. H. Sibley. il Pop Mech 125:164-7 Ja '66
BOTTLE charts
Soda pop bottles chart sea currents. Sci N L 87:136 F 27 '65
BOTTLE messages
Messages in bottles. New Yorker 41:50-2 D 4 '65
BOTTLE-nosed dolphins. See Dolphins (mammals)
BOTTLES; story. See Stewart, N.
BOTULINUM toxin. See Toxins and antitoxins

BOTULISM
Dangers of canned food should not be ignored. Sci N L 88:164 S 11 '65
Dead loon mystery. J. Van Coevering. il Audubon Mag 67:229-30 Jl '65
See also
Clostridium botulinum
BOUCHER, Anthony
Of fortune and faro. Opera N 30:8-12 Ja 15 '66
BOUCHER, Jack E.
Domestic architecture of New Jersey. il Antiques 88:184-9 Ag '65
BOUGHTON, Audrey A.
Visitor: story. Sat Eve Post 238:66-7 Jl 3 '65
BOUGHTON, H. G.
Train for Topolobampo. por Outdoor Life 136:40-3+ N '65
BOUGUEREAU, William Adolphe
From salon to saloon. il Time 87:70 Ja 14 '66
BOULDER, Colo.
Description
Springtime in the Rockies; Table Mesa. L. P. Hudson. il Reporter 32:42-5 F 11 '65
BOULDING, Kenneth E.
Books. Sci Am 212:139-40+ My '65
Postscript: a moderately Great society. New Repub 153:15-16 D 18 '65
Reflections on protest. Bul Atomic Sci 21:18-20 O '65
BOUMEDIENNE, Houari
Aftermath. il por Newsweek 66:35-6 Jl 5 '65
Algeria; strong man out. il por Newsweek 65:31-2 Je 28 '65
Atlantic report. Atlan 216:14+ S '65
Closing the door. por Newsweek 66:38 Jl 12 '65
Concern for reform. il por Time 86:32 Ag 20 '65
Crash of glass. il por Time 85:36-7 Je 25 '65
Letter from Algeria. R. Shaplen. il New Yorker 41:147-8+ O 30 '65
Letter from Algiers. R. Shaplen. il New Yorker 41:38-40+ Jl 17 '65
New face in Algiers. America 113:2 Jl 3 '65
Reluctant strong man. il por Newsweek 66:32 Jl 19 '65
Who and what is the real Boumedienne? R. W. Howe. New Repub 153:11-12 Jl 3 '65
Who's on first? il Time 86:22-3 Jl 2 '65
BOUNDARIES
See also subhead Boundaries under names of countries, e.g. Russia—Boundaries
BOUNDARIES (gardens) See Garden boundaries
BOUNDARY WATERS CANOE AREA. See Wilderness areas
BOUNTY; story. See McCarthy, C.
BOUQUETS
How to make a corsage. il Sunset 134:252+ Je '65
BOUQUETS, Dried. See Flowers, Dried
BOURDEAU, Robert E.
Research within the ionosphere. bibliog Science 148:585-94 Ap 30 '65
BOURGUIBA, Habib ben Ali
Shock waves; interview, ed. by E. Behr. Newsweek 65:50+ My 10 '65
about
Arab voice for peace. Life 58:4 My 7 '65
Atlantic report. Atlan 216:24+ N '65
Bourguiba: portrait of a nonconformist. J. Lacouture. il pors N Y Times Mag p26-7+ Je 6 '65
Challenge to Nasser. New Repub 152:7 My 15 '65
Man to anger Nasser. por Time 85:42+ My 7 '65
Maverick kicks up. por Newsweek 65:46+ My 3 '65
Tunisian torpedo. Time 86:42 S 24 '65
BOURGUIGNON, Serge
Good drizzle after a big sizzle. D. Zeitlin. il pors Life 58:45-6+ F 26 '65
BOURJAILY, Vance
Outdoors (cont) Esquire 63:48+ F '65
BOURKE, George
From tip to top in Florida. See issues of Travel
BOURLIÈRE, François
Sanctuaries astride frontiers. UNESCO Courier 18:15-21 F '65
BOURNE, Donald W. and Heezen, B. C.
Wandering enteropneust from the abyssal Pacific, and the distribution of spiral tracks on the sea floor. bibliog Science 150:60-3 O 1 '65
BOURNE, Randolph Silliman
World of Randolph Bourne, ed. by L. Schlissel. Review
New Repub 152:28+ My 15 '65. L. Grauman

BOURNE, St Clair
Young publisher with problems; Brooklyn
Peace corps volunteer puts out Spanish
newspaper in slum of Lima, Peru. il pors
Ebony 21:101-2+ N '65
BOUTWELL, Albert Burton
Birmingham two years later. P. Good. il Re-
porter 33:21-7 D 2 '65
BOUTWELL, William D.
Motivating the slow learner; excerpt from an
address, April 1965. por Wilson Lib Bul
40:75-7+ S '65
What's happening in education? See issues of
PTA magazine
BOUZA, Julio David Blanco. See Blanco Bouza,
J. D.
BOVINE insulin. See Insulin
BOW, Clara
Girl who had It. por Time 86:60+ O 8 '65
Last act for the "It Girl". il pors Life 59:
106B-107 O 8 '65
BOW and arrow
Case for two bows. G. H. Gillelan. il Out-
door Life 135:110-11+ Mr '65
    See also
Hunting with bow and arrow
BOW hunting. See Hunting with bow and
arrow
BOWDEN, James H.
On seeing a lunatic in church on Whitsun;
poem. Christian Cent 82:710 Je 2 '65
BOWDOIN college, Brunswick, Me.
Blended simplicity for Bowdoin; Hawthorne-
Longfellow library. R. Harwell. il Li-
brary J 90:5192-3 D 1 '65
Ivory tower for Bowdoin college; Senior
center. il Arch Rec 137:146-9 Je '65
BOWEN, C. C. and Jensen, T. E.
Blue-green algae: fine structure of the gas
vacuoles. bibliog Science 147:1460-2 Mr 19
'65
BOWEN, Catherine Drinker
Bold men, bold dreams. Read Digest 87:49-53
Jl '65
Search for Francis Bacon. Atlan 217:68-74
Ja '66
BOWEN, Ezra
New ski boom in France. Mlle 62:202-3+
N '65
BOWEN, Susan
Royal fantasies. Design 66:32-5 Mr '65
BOWEN, William
Auto industry's road ahead. Fortune 71:137-
9+ Je '65
Crime in the cities: an unnecessary crisis.
Fortune 72:140-5+ D '65
Water shortage is a frame of mind. Fortune
71:144-6+ Ap '65
What's new about the new Hubert Hum-
phrey. Fortune 72:142-5+ Ag '65
BOWER, Beverly
Fresh valkyries; interview, ed. by E. R.
Rizzo. por Opera N 29:13 Mr 6 '65
BOWER, T. G. R.
Stimulus variables determining space per-
ception in infants. bibliog Science 149:88-9
Jl 2 '65
BOWER, Warren
Open door to innovation. Sat R 48:31 F 6 '65
BOWER plants
On the ground or in the air. il Sunset 134:
250 Mr '65
BOWERING, George
Seven poets. M. McCloskey. Poetry 105:270-3
Ja '65
BOWERS, Edgar
From autumn shade; Field marshal; poems.
Poetry 105:290-4 F '65
BOWERS, Faubion
Looking and listening. House & Gard 127:
40+ Je; 128:10+ Ag; 246-7+ O; 34+ N;
183-4+ D '65
Opening the door to music for the musically
shy adult. House & Gard 128:196-7 S '65
No theater. Opera N 30:8-13 Ja 1 '66
(ed) See Richter, S.   Richter on Scriabin
BOWERS, Jack
Bowers details Convair market aims. W. E.
Wilks. il Miss & Roc 17:35-6+ O 25 '65
BOWES, Anne Labastille
Giant grebe of Guatemala. il por Audubon
Mag 67:88-90 Mr '65
BOWES, Betty M.
Uses a mixed aqueous technique. il por Am
Artist 29:34-5+ N '65
BOWFISHING. See Fishing with bow and
arrow
BOWIE, Harold E.
Recent developments in mathematics educa-
tion. Sch & Soc 93:252-4 Ap 17 '65
BOWIE knives
Hunting knife. A. Russell. il Field & S 70:54-
7+ Je '65

BOWKER, Richard Rogers
Student lounge named for Mr Bowker. il
Pub W 188:43 N 22 '65
BOWKER, R. R. company
Bowker plans new edition of Publishers'
world. Pub W 188:32 D 13 '65
Dramatic book trade expansion shown in
Bowker publications. Library J 90:5357 D
15 '65
Forthcoming books, new Bowker bi-monthly.
Pub W 188:35 D 6 '65
    See also
Carey-Thomas award
Library journal cards, incorporated
BOWL football games. See Football
BOWLES, Carl
One family's strange journey. H. Champion.
il por Life 59:80-1 Jl 23 '65
BOWLES, Chester
India dedicates Sharavathy hydroelectric
project; address, January 24, 1965. Dept
State Bul 52:305-7 Mr 1 '65
Oldest new nation. Yale R 54:321-30 Mr '65
    about
How the State department baffled him; ex-
cerpts from A thousand days. A. M.
Schlesinger, jr. il Life 59:18-27 Jl 30 '65
Secret conquest. il por Newsweek 66:19-20
Ag 23 '65
BOWLES, Paul
Zany Costa del Sol. Holiday 37:78-9+ Ap '65
BOWLING, Lawrence
Thoreau's social criticism as poetry. Yale R
55:255-64 D '65
BOWLING
Commercial recreation: an ally. J. L. Wilson.
il Recreation 58:76+ F '65
Pétanque comes West. J. W. Metcalfe. il
Recreation 58:292-4 Je '65
Poor man's tour begins to strike it rich;
Firestone tournament of champions. J.
Jares. il Sports Illus 22:112-14 Ap 19 '65
What they're playing is pétanque; lawn
bowling. il Sunset 135:8 O '65
BOWLING alleys

Equipment and supplies
Aiming at a high score in bowling; AMF's
automatic pinspotters. il Bsns W p 124-5+
N 27 '65
BOWLING on the green
Department of correction and amplification;
pétanque, a version of jeux de boules. J. W.
Metcalfe. New Yorker 41:113-14 Ap 3 '65
BOWLS
June Schwarcz: electroforming and enamel.
A. Ventura. il Craft Horiz 25:36-7+ N '65

Anecdotes, facetiae, satire, etc.
How to turn Bartók into a fruit bowl. H. B.
Jacobs. New Yorker 41:199-200+ My 15 '65
BOWLS (game) See Bowling on the green
BOWMAN, Byrne A.
Nothing beats money. Time 86:77 N 19 '65
BOWMAN, Clarice M.
Teaching in the spirit. Christian Cent 82:
1229-30 O 6 '65
BOWMAN, Garda W. and others
Are women executives people Harvard
Bsns R 43:14-16+ Jl '65
BOWMAN, Robert L. See Chen, R. F.; Vurek,
G. G. jt. auths.
BOWSER, Hallowell
International cooperation year. Sat R 48:20
Mr 6 '65
Rattling good history. Sat R 48:26 Ap 3 '65
Yankee please stay. Sat R 48:18 Ag 21 '65
BOWYER, C. Stuart
Galactic X-ray astronomy. Sky & Tel 30:
264-6 N '65
BOX lunches. See Lunches
BOXERS
Making of a heavyweight; O. Bonavena, un-
defeated Argentinian. H. Tuckner. il N Y
Times Mag p32+ F 7 '65
BOXES, cases, etc.
It's the busy box. il Sunset 135:68-9 D '65
Royal fantasies. S. Bowen. il Design 66:32-5
Mr '65
    See also
Sewing boxes
BOXES, Display. See Exhibition cases
BOXING
Alas, poor Cassius! il Ebony 20:144-5 Jl '65
American dream; Torres v. Pastrano. News-
week 65:102 Ap 12 '65
AMA proposes methods for safe boxing
matches. Sci N L 88:98 Ag 14 '65
Angry Tiger jumps on Joey; D. Tiger vs
J. Giardello in Madison Square Garden.
W. Leggett. il Sports Illus 23:20-1 N 1 '65

BOXING—*Continued*

Baddest of all looks over the universe; observations of Patterson, Chuvalo fight. T. Maule. il Sports Illus 22:20-3 F 15 '65

Big fight moves to small town; Liston-Clay fight from Boston to Lewiston, Me. J. Underwood. il Sports Illus 22:22-3 My 17 '65

Big muddle among the big ones; boxing's heavyweight division. il Ebony 20:106-8+ My '65

Big week for boxing; House of representatives passed bill to create federal boxing commission. Sports Illus 23:7 Ag 30 '65

Bitter end for Sugar Ray. M. Kane. il Sports Illus 23:89-90 N 22 '65

Carlos and the king of con. M. Kram. il Sports Illus 24:28-31 Ja 10 '66

Cassius Clay must be beaten; with editorial comment. F. Patterson. Sports Illus 23:19, 78-80+ O 11 '65

Cassius to win a thriller; Liston-Clay fight to be in Lewiston, Me. T. Maule. il Sports Illus 22:22-5 My 24 '65

Champion as long as he wants; Clay-Patterson fight. G. Rogin. il Sports Illus 23:20-5 N 29 '65

Champion of nonviolence; W. Pastrano. M. Cope. il Sat Eve Post 238:84-7 Mr 27 '65

Champ's first time down, and out; Pastrano-Torres fight. il Life 58:62-3 Ap 9 '65

Croatian candidate; Chuvalo fights Patterson. G. Rogin. il Sports Illus 22:54-60 F 1 '65

Dumb broad at a dumb fight. S. Alexander. Life 58:23 Je 4 '65

Family man; welterweight E. Griffith. il Time 85:52-3 Ap 9 '65

Floyd is beginning to see the light, finally; Patterson-Herring fight in Stockholm. J. Lovesey. Sports Illus 22:72-3 My 24 '65

For all the cheese; World boxing association's world championship fight. Time 85:83A Mr 12 '65

400 blows; Clay-Patterson fight. il Newsweek 66:64 D 6 '65

Giant they love to hate; Clay-Patterson fight in Las Vegas; with account by G. Rogin. il Sports Illus 23:40-5+ D 6 '65

Greatest meets the grimmest; Clay vs. Patterson in Las Vegas. M. Kane. il Sports Illus 23:36-8+ N 15 '65

Hare was no rabbit; impressions of Patterson-Chuvalo fight. Muhammad Ali. il Life 58:97-8 F 12 '65

Head for figures; Main bout inc. to handle Clay title defense. Newsweek 67:79 Ja 24 '66

He's just got that look; S. Liston. B. La Fontaine. il Sports Illus 22:32-4+ Ap 26 '65

I was wrong! Cassius Clay and the Chuvalo-Patterson fight. il Time 85:40 F 12 '65

Liver trouble and high living; J. Torres-W. Pastrano fight. E. Shrake. il Sports Illus 22-28-9+ Ap 12 '65

Lunch for a lion; Clay-Patterson fight. il il Time 86:73 D 3 '65

Maine bout; Clay-Liston bout from Boston to Lewiston, Me. Sports Illus 22:16 My 17 '65

Maine event; Clay v. Liston in Lewiston Me. il Newsweek 65:58-9 Je 7 '65

No phantom punch; Clay-Liston fight, Lewiston, Me; with account by J. Murray. il Sports Illus 22:48-53 Je 7 '65

No place to wear his crown; Terrell-Machen fight. T. Maule. il Sports Illus 22:28-9 Mr 15 '65

Okay, but don't bring on Clay; F. Patterson-G. Chuvalo fight. T. Maule. il Sports Illus 22:18-19 F 8 '65

Quick, hard right and a needless storm of protest; Clay-Liston fight, Lewiston, Me. T. Maule. il Sports Illus 22:22-5 Je 7 '65

Rabbit hunt in Vegas; Clay-Patterson championship fight. G. Rogin. il Sports Illus 23:34-9 N 22 '65

Sad case of a neglected Tiger; Dick Tiger vs Rubin Carter. M. Kram. il Sports Illus 22:28-9 My 31 '65

Shark ran into a tiger; C. Ortiz-I. Laguna lightweight title fight. M. Kram. il Sports Illus 22:32-4+ Ap 19 '65

Sickening spectacle in a ring; Clay-Patterson fight. il Life 59:42-42A D 3 '65

Sugar: down but not quite out. L. L. King. il Sports Illus 23:58-66 S 6 '65

Svengali returns! C. D'Amato, manager of J. Torres. R. H. Boyle. il Sports Illus 22:24-7 Ap 12 '65

Tempest in a beanpot; rematch between Cassius Clay and Sonny Liston. Sports Illus 22:17 Ap 19 '65

Theater of the absurd; Clay-Liston fight in Lewiston. il Time 85:68-9 Je 4 '65

True picture; Clay-Liston fight, Lewiston, Me. Sports Illus 22:12 Je 7 '65

Two-for-one revival meeting at the Garden; Torres-Pastrano and Stable-Griffith fights. E. Shrake. il Sports Illus 22:59-60+ Mr 22 '65

While Ali babbled; Patterson against Chuvalo. il Newsweek 65:60 F 15 '65

Willie Pep's art of self-defense. S. Gelman. il Esquire 64:194-5+ D '65

Accidents and injuries

Patterson's glass jaw; no one fully recovers from a K.O; with report by D. Brown. il Life 59:115-16+ N 19 '65

History

That was New York. A. Logan. il New Yorker 41:41-2+ F 27 '65

Laws and regulations

Job opening; Hart-Kefauver bill for boxing. Sports Illus 22:14 Je 21 '65

Moral and religious aspects

Should boxing be abolished? A. Balk. il Todays Health 43:18-23 Ag '65

BOXING for shipment. See Packing for shipment

BOY from Chillicothe; story. See Flynn, R. L.

BOY in a box; story. See Crosman, P. R.

BOY scouts

Baden-Powell: the two lives of a hero, by W. Hillcourt. Review
    New Yorker 41:190+ Ap 24 '65. N. Bliven

Boy scouts. C. Davis. il Esquire 64:69-71+ Jl '65

Boy scouts visit White House on 55th anniversary of scouting; remarks, February 8, 1965. L. B. Johnson. Dept State Bul 52:289-90 Mr 1 '65

Five notions I won't buy; address, December 15, 1964. W. MacPeek. Vital Speeches 31:247-9 F 1 '65

My most unforgettable character; Lord Baden-Powell. W. Hillcourt. Read Digest 87:203-4+ Jl '65

Explorer scouts

Explorers in the surf; Coronado, Calif. G. D. Hunsacker. il Recreation 58:286-7+ Je '65

BOYAR, Burt
(ed) See Davis, S. jr. Yes I can

BOYAR, Jane
(ed) See Davis, S. jr. Yes I can

BOYARSKY, Saul. See Catacutan-Labay, P. jt. auth.

BOYCE, Peter B. and Sinton, W. M.
Infrared spectroscopy with an interferometer. pors Sky & Tel 29:78-80 F '65

BOYCE Thompson southwestern arboretum, Superior, Ariz.
Boyce Thompson southwestern arboretum. J. E. Thompson, jr. il Horticulture 43:44-5+ F '65

BOYCOTT, Brian B.
Learning in the octopus; with biographical sketch. Sci Am 212:16, 42-50 bibliog(p 138) Mr '65

BOYCOTT
Boycotting Alabama. A. Kopkind. New Repub 152:11-13 Ap 17 '65

Department opposes bill to amend export control act of 1949; statement, May 24, 1965. G. W. Ball. Dept State Bul 53:35-7 Jl 5 '65

Latin dockers join Castro boycott. Bsns W p50+ My 1 '65

Money & the flag. Time 86:97 N 26 '65

BOYD, Alan S.
Planes, trains, ships, roads: an official look ahead; interview. por U S News 60:48-51 Ja 24 '66

about

Boyd role to bolster Commerce office. R. G. O'Lone. Aviation W 82:27 My 3 '65

Boyd views new Commerce post as focus of transportation policy. Aviation W 82:26 My 31 '65

Can he set an industry course? por Bsns W p49-50+ S 18 '65

BOYD, Ann S.
James Bond: modern-day dragonslayer. Christian Cent 82:644-7 My 19 '65

BOYD, Catharine
Endless chain; story. Redbook 124:68-9 Mr '65

In the face of life; story. McCalls 92:96-7 My '65

More the merrier; story. Redbook 126:44-5 D '65

BOYD, Howard T.
Boyd of El Paso. por Fortune 71:37 Mr '65
BOYD, Malcolm
Movies (cont) Christian Cent 82:216-18, 336-7, 713, 839-40, 942-3, 1262, 1547-8; 83:17 F 17, Mr 17, Je 2, 30, Jl 28, O 13, D 15 '65, Ja 5 '66
Violence in Los Angeles. Christian Cent 82:1093-5 S 8 '65
Violence or nonviolence in the Deep South? Christian Cent 82:1126-8 S 15 '65
Who speaks for the church? Christian Cent 82:493-5 Ap 21 '65

about

Where the people are. il por Newsweek 65:91 My 3 '65
BOYD, Robin
Cruciform window onto heaven. Arch Forum 123:50-5 S '65
BOYD, Susan Kuehn
Encounter with a stranger; story. Redbook 124:70-1 Ap '65
BOYKIN, Frank William
All for love. Time 86:15A D 31 '65
BOYKIN, John E.
(ed) See Potter, E. J. I hit the ground at 150 mph
BOYLAN, Brian Richard. See De Costa, E. J. jt. auth.
BOYLE, Andrew
Churchill as prophet. Commonweal 81:658-9 F 19 '65
BOYLE, Kay
One sunny morning; story. Sat Eve Post 238:61-2 Jl 3 '65
BOYLE, Robert H.
America down the drain? Read Digest 86:235-6+ Ap '65
Conservation. Sports Illus 22:81-2+ Ap 26 '65
Fishing (cont) Sports Illus 23:94-6+ S 13 '65
Sam's pigeons don't leave nuthin' for nobody. Sports Illus 23:102-4+ N 22 '65
Show-biz Sonny and his quest for stars. Sports Illus 23:66-72 Jl 19 '65
Strange fish and stranger times of Dr Herbert R. Axelrod. Sports Illus 22:76-8+ My 3 '65
BOYLE, Robert P.
Cooperation, the cornerstone of international civil aviation. Dept State Bul 53:820-7 N 22 '65
BOYS
Boy into a man; Chip's first bear hunt. R. Starnes. Field & S 70:22-4+ O '65
Can a girl change a boy? questions and answers. A. Wood. il Seventeen 24:98-9+ Je '65
From a boy's point of view. J. Wescott. See issues of Seventeen
Good grooming for boys? L. D. Kirk. il Parents Mag 41:82 Ja '66
Little things mean a lot. J. Gibbs. il Seventeen 25:104+ Ja '66
Possessive male; questions and answers. A. Wood. il Seventeen 24:128-9+ O '65
Why am I unlucky in love? questions and answers. A. Wood. il Seventeen 24:152-3+ Ap '65
Why doesn't he write? L. Benedict. il Seventeen 24:326+ Ag '65
See also
Runaway boys and girls
School children
BOYS as actors. See Children as actors
BOYS brotherhood republic of New York, incorporated
Where kids are kings. J. Olsen. il Sr Schol 86:sup 10-11 Mr 4 '65
BOYS clubs
See also
Boys brotherhood republic of New York, incorporated
BOYS rooms. See Childrens rooms
BOYS schools. See Private schools
BOZELL, L. Brent
Dialogue in Vermont. Nat R 17:1153-6 D 14 '65
Open question. por Nat R 17:772+ S 7 '65
Who is accommodating to what? Nat R 17:374+ My 4 '65
BRACELAND, Francis J.
Book reviews. America 113:289-90 S 18 '65
BRACELETS, Medic alert. See Identification tags, bracelets, etc.
BRACEROS. See Migrant labor
BRACHIOPODS, Fossil
Shell structure of recent articulate brachiopoda. D. B. Sass and others. il Science 149:181-2 Jl 9 '65
BRACHMAN, Philip S.
Annals of medicine; Hoffman case, report. New Yorker 41:67-8+ Ap 24 '65

BRACHNEY, Robert
Race; poem. Negro Hist Bul 28:200 My '65
BRACKEN, Peg
First aid for the fish wife. Ladies Home J 82:52 Ag '65
Husbands vs. wives vs. Christmas. Ladies Home J 82:46 D '65
Seven things one should never do. . . Ladies Home J 82:60 O '65
BRADBURY, Ray
Best of times; story. McCalls 93:60-3+ Ja '66
Machine-tooled happyland. Holiday 38:100-2+ O '65
Secret mind; excerpt from Afterword to Anthem sprinters and other antics. Writer 78:13-16 N '65

about

World of Ray Bradbury. Criticism New Yorker 41:197-8 O 16 '65
BRADEMAS, John
Excerpt from remarks addressed, September 20, 1965. Cong Digest 44:281+ N '65
Foundation of our educational system; teachers of high quality. NEA J 54:17 D '65
BRADEN, Spruille
Immorality and communism; address, January 15, 1965. Vital Speeches 31:365-8 Ap 1 '65
BRADFORD, Franklin
BLM's tenor in the timber. Am For 71:32-3+ Je '65
BRADFORD, Lawrence, Jr
Couple of whizzes go to Washington. il pors Ebony 20:75-8 Je '65
BRADFORD, Robert
Players call him Shadow. Life 59:64+ O 15 '65
What day is it? who cares? Life 58:44+ Mr 12 '65
BRADLEY, Bill
Bradley: good man and true. P. O'Neil. il pors Life 58:93-4+ Ap 2 '65
God and man at Nassau. il por Newsweek 65:86 Mr 15 '65
Tiger in Princeton's tank! H. L. Masin. por Sr Schol 86:40 F 18 '65
Whole team touched by stardust. F. Deford. il pors Sports Illus 22:20-3 Mr 22 '65
BRADLEY, C. Paul
Malaysia's first year. bibliog f Cur Hist 48:82-8+ F '65
BRADLEY, Harold
Young man with worlds to conquer. il pors Ebony 20:119-20+ S '65
BRADLEY, Harry L.
Obituary
Nat R 17:718 Ag 24 '65
BRADLEY, James J.
Wheelsville, USA. por Library J 90:2752-6 Je 15 '65
BRADLEY, Richard C.
Attack on Grand Canyon. Liv Wildn 87:3-7 Wint '64
BRADLEY, Sam
African in this different land; Impossible situation; poems. Poetry 105:247-8 Ja '65
O Christmas come, against vast Babel; poem. Christian Cent 82:1545 D 15 '65
Testament of the ringed snake; poem. Nation 201:123 S 6 '65
Token; poem. Christian Cent 82:1408 N 17 '65
BRADLEY, W. H.
Vertical density currents. bibliog Science 150:1423-8 D 10 '65
BRADLEY, William Warren. See Bradley, B.
BRADNER, Harry
Slurry waterproofs 'em all. Am City 80:86-8 Jl '65
BRADSHAW, George
Adventurers: skulduggery aboard the Madame V. Vogue 146:202-3+ D '65
Rhodes, Julius Caesar cut classes. Vogue 146:73 Ag 15 '65
Travel. Vogue 145:138-40 My; 146:74 S 15; 151 D '65
View from a tall glass oasis: subliminal pleasures of Hilton hotels. Vogue 146:82+ Jl '65
Who buys all the watches? travel notes found on a matchbook. Vogue 145:98-9+ Je '65
BRADSHAW, Hank
Brown bass of the Buffalo. Outdoor Life 135:56-9+ Ap '65
How to hunt pheasants. Field & S 70:41-3+ S '65
Now, a bullet without a case. Pop Sci 187:173 O '65
Now is the time for sauger fishing. il Suc Farm 63:88 Ap '65
Ozark big uns bite best in winter. por Field & S 70:104-7+ Ja '66
Twelve foolproof ways to rig a fishline. Pop Sci 187:146-9+ Jl '65

BRADSHAW, Hank—*Continued*
Underground animals, good targets. il Suc Farm 63:54-5 O '65
—and Bradshaw, Vera
Following the trail of the cottontail. il Todays Health 44:22-4+ Ja '66
Six easy-on-the-budget cruises. Todays Health 43:18-22 Je '65
—See Bradshaw, H. jt. auth.
BRADY, D. Norman
Greatest little boat. Yachting 118:48-50+ Jl '65
BRADY, Mildred Edie
Let the reader beware; reprint. Consumer Rep 30:496 O '65

about
Mildred Edie Brady 1906-1965. il pors Consumer Rep 30:494-5 O '65
Obituary
Consumer Rep por 30:426 S '65
BRADY, Terry T.
Rampart Dam: white elephant of the Yukon Flats. il Nat Parks Mag 39:4-7 O '65
BRADY, Tex.
First we built the reservoir; triple benefits from dam. J. C. Feazelle. il Am City 80:135-6 N '65
BRADY, Thomas Pickens
Education of Tom Brady. por Time 86:94+ O 22 '65
BRADYKININ. See Kallikrein
BRAEND, Mikael. See Fagerhol, M. K. jt. auth.
BRAENDEL, Helmuth G.
Amphibious cruise in a day sailer. Yachting 117:38-40+ F '65
BRAESTRUP, Peter
Cruel desert is Algeria's wealth. N Y Times Mag p76-7+ N 7 '65
BRAGG, Lawrence
Schools lectures at the Royal institution. Science 150:1420-3 D 10 '65
BRAHE, Tycho. See Brahe, Tyge
BRAHE, Tyge
Tycho Brahe's nose. J. Ashbrook. por Sky & Tel 29:353+ Je '65
BRAHM, Walter
On the grindstone (cont) Library J 90:594+, 1080, 1623, 2106, 2510-11, 2982, 3226+, 3409, 4022, 4726, 5222-3 F 1, Mr 1, Ap 1, My 1, Je 1, Jl-S 1, O 1, N 1, D 1 '65
BRAHMS, Johannes
Karajan: after the Beethovens, the Brahmses. C. J. Luten. Am Rec G 31:720 Ap '65
Karajan's Brahms requiem, visionary eloquence. R. Sabin. Am Rec G 31:983 Je '65
Now on Vox: Brahms, Loewe, and Wolf lieder by Prey, magnificent. H. Glass. Am Rec G 31:526-7 F '65
On records; Four serious songs. Opera N 30:38 Ja 15; 34 Ja 22 '66
On records; German requiem. Opera N 30:30 N 20 '65
Szell's Brahms, an outstanding release. C. J. Luten. Am Rec G 31:632 Mr '65
Vox boxful of Brahms and Schumann quartets. A. Cohn. Am Rec G 32:233-4 N '65
BRAID
Making gifts with braid. il Sunset 134:109-10 F '65
BRAIN, George
Evaluating teacher effectiveness. NEA J 54:35-6 F '65
BRAIN, Walter Russell Brain, 1st baron
Science and antiscience; address, December 27, 1964. bibliog Science 148:192-8 Ap 9 '65
BRAIN
Altered effect of potassium ions on cerebral respiration in vitro following subcortical lesions. B. F. Roth and J. A Harvey. bibliog il Science 148:1356-7 Je 4 '65
Are we finding a way to study the action of the mind? il Science 150:922-4 N 12 '65
Attenuation of aversive properties of peripheral shock by hypothalamic stimulation. V. C. Cox and E. S. Valenstein. bibliog il Science 149:323-5 Jl 16 '65
Background and evoked activity in the auditory pathway: effects of noise-shock pairing. D. Galin. bibliog il Science 149:761-3 Ag 13 '65
Brain and how it changes; adaptation of address, April 1964. E. R. John. Bul Atomic Sci 21:12-14 N '65
Brain control by radio; electrical stimulation of the brain. J. A. Osmundsen. il Pop Mech 124:130-3+ N '65
Brain research; report on second seminar of International brain research organization. E. Costa. Science 148:865-6+ My 7 '65
Brain revolution. J. B. Sheerin. Cath World 201:223-6 Jl '65

Cerebral temperature changes accompanying sexual activity in the male rat. C. D. Hull and others. bibliog il Science 149:89-90 Jl 2 '65
Dark may impair brain. Sci N L 89:4 Ja 1 '66
Dogs' brains isolated. Sci N L 87:242 Ap 17 '65
Elevation in brain temperature during paradoxical sleep. H. Kawamura and C. H. Sawyer. bibliog il Science 150:912 N 12 '65
Evoked brain potential correlates of psychophysical responses: heterochromatic flicker photometry. J. B. Siegfried and others. bibliog il Science 149:321-3 Jl 16 '65
Functional studies of cultured brain tissues as related to demyelinative disorders. M. B. Bornstein and S. M. Crain. bibliog il Science 148:1242-4 My 28 '65
Human body; master control, the brain; reprint. D. E. Wooldridge. il Sci Digest 57:77-81 Mr '65
Intracranial reinforcement compared with sugar-water reinforcement. W. E. Gibson and others. bibliog il Science 148:1357-9 Je 4 '65
Matter over mind; symposium at meeting of the American association for the advancement of science. Newsweek 67:45 Ja 10 '66
Mirror display in the squirrel monkey, saimiri sciureus. P. D. MacLean; reply with rejoinder. P. Hershkovitz. Science 147:1156-7 Mr 5 '65
Model of the brain, by J. Z. Young. Review Sci Am 212:147-50+ Ap '65. F. A. Beach
See also
Cerebral cortex
Memory
Sleep

Diseases
Cerebellar disease in cats induced by inoculation of rat virus. L. Kilham and G. Margolis. bibliog il Science 148:244-6 Ap 9 '65
Molecular abnormality seen in brain disease; metachromatic leukodystrophy. Sci N L 89:6 Ja 1 '66
Myelin membrane: a molecular abnormality. J. S. O'Brien and E. L. Sampson. bibliog il Science 150:1613-14 D 17 '65
Particles resembling papova viruses in human cerebral demyelinating disease. G. M. Zu Rhein and S. M. Chou. bibliog il Science 148:1477-9 Je 11 '65
See also
Cerebral hemorrhage
Encephalitis
Mental illness
Sleeping sickness

Localization of functions
Chemical coding of behavior in the brain. N. E. Miller. bibliog il Science 148:328-38 Ap 16 '65
Role of orbital cortex in regulation of thalamocortical electrical activity. M. Velasco and D. B. Lindsley. bibliog il Science 149:1375-7 S 17 '65
Site of short-term memory. Sci Am 212:52-3 F '65
Vocalization evoked from the optic lobe of a songbird. J. L. Brown. bibliog il Science 149:1002-3 Ag 27 '65

Surgery
False senility cured; drainage of cerebrospinal fluid from brain ventricles. Sci N L 88:53 Jl 24 '65
Needling the brain; giving psychosurgery a second chance. il Newsweek 66:80 S 13 '65
Road back; surgery following stroke. il Time 85:37 Mr 26 '65
Through the neck & into the brain; tumor excised at base of skull. il Time 85:58 Ap 16 '65
See also
Cryogenic surgery

Wounds and injuries
First aid. C. J. Potthoff. Todays Health 43:86 F '65
Lesions in the medial forebrain bundle; delayed effects on sensitivity to electric shock. J. A. Harvey and C. E. Lints. bibliog il Science 148:250-2 Ap 9 '65
BRAIN, Transplantation of. See Transplantation of organs, tissues, etc.
BRAIN hemorrhage. See Cerebral hemorrhage
BRAIN surgery. See Brain—Surgery
BRAIN telestimulator. See Physiological apparatus
BRAIN tumors. See Tumors
BRAINARD, Franklin
Lost lands; poem. Horn Bk 41:487 O '65

BRAINWASHING
On parole; cases of G. E. Smith and C. McClure. il Newsweek 66:37-8 D 13 '65

BRAKE, John
Tips on borrowing to buy machinery. Suc Farm 64:84 Ja '66

BRAKES, Automobile
Disc brakes for early Fords. L. T. Smith. il Hot Rod 18:56-8+ D '65
Disk brakes, do you need them? Consumer Rep 31:24 Ja '66
Give your brakes a break. M. J. Schultz. il Pop Mech 124:154-7 Ag '65
How brakes will be better than ever in '66; disk and drum brakes. J. P. Norbye. il Pop Sci 186:56-9+ Je '65

Testing
How fast can you stop? D. Francis. il Pop Sci 186:82-6+ Ap '65

BRAKKE, Myron K. and Daly, J. M.
Density-gradient centrifugation: non-ideal sedimentation and the interaction of major and minor components. bibliog Science 148: 387-9 Ag 16 '65

BRAM, Leon L.
Choreographer in the second city. Dance Mag 39:52-3+ F '65

BRAMBILLA, Luisa
Bigamy Italian style. D. J. Hamblin. il Life 59:52A-52B Jl 23 '65

BRAMLETTE, M. N.
Massive extinctions in biota at the end of Mesozoic time. bibliog Science 148:1696-9 Je 25 '65

BRANCH libraries. See Libraries—Branches and stations

BRANCO, Humberto Castello. See Castello Branco, H.

BRAND, Mario
Doctor Atl, 1875-1964. Américas 17:35-7 Ag '65

BRAND names. See Trade names

BRANDBORG, Stewart M.
Guidelines to wilderness action; excerpt from address, May 15, 1965. Liv Wildn 29: 36-7 Spr '65
Job ahead under the Wilderness act; Interpretation of the Wilderness act. Liv Wildn 86:13-18 Spr '64

BRANDEIS, Louis Dembitz
Friendship of Holmes and Brandeis. F. Biddle. por Atlan 216:86-91 D '65

BRANDEIS university, Waltham, Mass.
Broadway postscript; Nate B. and Frances Springold theater arts center opens with Volpone. H. Hewes. Sat R 48:63 D 25 '65
Coeducational dormitories. il Arch Rec 138: 120-1 Ag '65

BRANDENBURG, Frank
Mexico: 1966 and beyond. bibliog f Cur Hist 50:32-7+ Ja '66

BRANDES, David, and others
Nuclear mitochondria? Science 149:1373-4 S 17 '65

BRANDING, Cattle. See Cattle—Branding

BRANDON, Henry
J.F.K. remembered. Sat R 48:58-9 D 11 '65
State of affairs. See issues of Saturday review

BRANDON, O. K.
Do-it-yourself pays in many ways. Am City 80:97 O '65

BRANDS, Advertised. See Advertising

BRANDS, Private. See Private brands

BRANDT, Karl
German resistance in American perspective; address, July 20, 1965. Vital Speeches 31: 713-17 S 15 '65

BRANDT, Thomas O.
Foreign language summer camps for children. Sch & Soc 93:372-3 O 16 '65

BRANDT, Willy
As Germans vote: what's at stake. por U S News 59:26 S 20 '65
Heavy winner. Newsweek 66:46+ O 4 '65
Making of the chancellor 1965. il por Newsweek 66:26 S 6 '65

BRANDYWINE CREEK
House by the Brandywine. S. S. Ralston. il Read Digest 87:126-7 Jl '65

BRANIFF international airways
Braniff overhauls services, appearance. E. J. Bulban. il Aviation W 83:40-1 N 15 '65
Braniff plans extensive changes; seeks all-jet equipment by 1967. Aviation W 82:32 Je 21 '65
Braniff refuels on razzle-dazzle; fancy paint on planes and new costumes for hostesses. il Bsns W p 110+ N 20 '65
Color it Braniff. il Newsweek 67:76 Ja 24 '66
First Braniff BAC 111 delivered; twinturbofan aircraft. il Aviation W 82:31 Mr 22 '65
New course for Braniff. Time 85:92 F 19 '65

Wild hue yonder; Pucci designs uniform suited to jet age. il Life 59:76-7 D 3 '65

BRANNEY, Joseph J.
Colorado's first goat hunt. pors Outdoor Life 136:33-5+ O '65

BRANSTEN, Thomas R.
Reed: the Mavericks and the Mandarinate. Mlle 60:188-90+ Ap '65

BRANT. See Geese, Wild

BRANTLY helicopter corporation
Brantly aiming 305 at executive market. D. A. Brown. il Aviation W 82:88-9+ My 31 '65
Four new Brantly helicopters planned; three turbine-powered. Aviation W 83:21 N 29 '65

BRASÍLIA, Brazil
Brasília neurosis. il Newsweek 65:56 My 3 '65
Capital becoming a capital. il Time 86:36 Jl 9 '65

BRASS coins. See Coins

BRASS dies. See Dies (metal work)

BRASSENS, Georges
My last heroes. P. S. Beagle. il Holiday 38: 8+ Ag '65

BRASSIERES
Women's brassieres. il Consumer Bul 48: 24-7 Mr '65

Advertising
Vogue and vague; nudes in Exquisite form bra ads. il Newsweek 65:90 Mr 22 '65

BRATGE, Willi
Day Hitler lost the war; excerpts from Last 100 days. J. Toland. il pors Look 29:38-40+ My 4 '65

BRATTON, Clyde B. and others
Nuclear magnetic resonance studies of living muscle. bibliog Science 147:738-9 F 12 '65

BRATTON, Fred Gladstone
Oasis in a desert of time. Sat R 48:21-2 S 4 '65

BRAUCHER, Howard
Playgrounds build for the new era. Recreation 58:154 Ap '65

BRAUN, Armin C.
Reversal of tumor growth; with biographical sketch. Sci Am 213:14, 75-81+ bibliog (p 143) N '65

BRAUN, Eva
End of the Hitler gang; excerpts from Last 100 days. J. Toland. il Look 29:70-2+ Je 1 '65

BRAUN, Peggy. See Braun, S. jt. auth.

BRAUN, Saul, and Braun, Peggy
I Playboy, take thee, Reader's digest... Esquire 64:83 Ag '65

BRAUN, Werner. See Schwartz, S. A. jt. auth.

BRAUNSTEIN, Joseph
Make a continuity tester for your appliance test bench. Pop Mech 125:189 Ja '66

BRAUWEILER, J .W. See Hirschmann, W. B. jt. auth.

BRAVERMAN, Miriam
Mississippi summer. Library J 90:5045-7 N 15 '65

BRAVERY. See Courage

BRAVES (baseball) See Baseball clubs

BRAY, Donald W.
Chilean crazy quilt. Nation 201:450 D 6 '65

BRAYMAN, Harold
Du Pont team. L. L. L. Golden. Sat R 48:78 Je 12 '65

BRAZIERS
Clay pot hibachi. il Pop Gard 16:53 My '65

BRAZIL
Brazil: land of massive problems. R. H. Bolton; reply. A. R. Kratz. Christian Cent 82:748 Je 9 '65
See also
Brasília
Finance—Brazil
Fishing—Brazil
Hunting—Brazil
Investments, Foreign (in Brazil)
Iron mines and mining—Brazil
Manaus
Money—Brazil
Moving picture industry—Brazil
Opera—Brazil
Portuguese language in Brazil
Railroads—Brazil
Rio de Janeiro—Description
Rites and ceremonies—Brazil
Roads—Brazil
Taxation—Brazil

Colonization
New West. M. J. Kubic. il Newsweek 66:48 Ag 16 '65

BRAZIL—*Continued*

Economic conditions

Close-up of South America's worst trouble spot; northeast Brazil. J. N. Wallace. il U S News 59:66-8 S 6 '65

Hope in the Northeast. il Time 85:46+ Ap 30 '65

If Brazil fails to make it this time. J. N. Wallace. il U S News 59:84-6 O 11 '65

On the road to dreams; effects of Belém to Brasília highway. il Time 87:34 Ja 7 '66

Toward stability. il Time 86:29 D 31 '65

Economic policy

Perils of stabilization. il Fortune 72:97-8+ D '65

Economic relations

What is so rare? il Newsweek 66:45-6 Ag 23 '65

Industries

See also

Iron industry and trade—Brazil

Native races

See also

Indians of South America—Brazil

Politics and government

Act two; Branco assumes near-dictatorial powers. Newsweek 66:60 N 8 '65

Answer for a critic; Lacerda arguing for new military coup. Time 86:53 O 22 '65

Brazil: second act; intensification of dictatorship. Nation 201:345 N 15 '65

Brazil swings again toward dictatorship. il Bsns W p31 O 30 '65

Brazil's revolution. New Repub 152:8 Ap 24 '65

Chapter II of a revolution; army tightens up in Brazil. U S News 59:60 N 8 '65

Clamp-down in Brazil. New Repub 153:8 N 13 '65

Detribalizing politics. Time 86:32 Jl 23 '65

Eying a new system; Branco's government. Time 86:41 S 3 '65

Facade crumbles. Newsweek 66:48 Ag 16 '65

Hard blow for the hard line; release of M. Arraes. Time 85:46 Ap 30 '65

Hard line of Castello Branco. Time 86:56+ N 5 '65

If Brazil fails to make this time. J. N. Wallace. il U S News 59:84-6 O 11 65

Interim regime in Brazil. R. M. Schneider. bibliog f Cur Hist 49:349-55+ D '65

Man from Ipanema; Kubitschek returns name. il Newsweek 66:71 O 18 '65

Military clamps down. Sr Schol 87:7-8 N 18 '65

Other barrel. Time 86:46 N 12 '65

Out of the past. il Time 86:52 O 15 '65

Riding the tiger; new governor of Guanabara. il Newsweek 66:50 D 20 '65

Running things his way. Time 86:51 D 10 '65

South American impasse. E. M. von Kuehnelt-Leddihn. Nat R 17:191 Mr 9 '65

South America's moment of truth. L. Gross. il Look 29:30-40+ Mr 23 '65

Suppressing the future. R. H. Chilcote; reply with rejoinder. J. Magalhaes. Nation 200: inside cover+ F 15 '65

Year after. Time 85:36 Ap 2 '65

Year-end report. Newsweek 65:63 Ap 12 '65

Race problems

Does amalgamation work in Brazil? E. B. Thompson. il Ebony 20:27-30+ Jl; 33-42 S '65 (to be cont)

Religious institutions and affairs

Afro-Brazilian rites. J. Elbein. il Américas 17:16-19 Je '65

News of the Christian world (cont) Christian Cent 82:312, 1205-6 Mr 10, S 29 '65

BRAZILIAN cookery. See Cookery, Brazilian

BRAZILLER, George, incorporated

Braziller wins art award in anniversary year; 1965 Art in America award. Pub W 189:71-2 Ja 10 '66

BRAZING

NASA increasing use of brazed fittings. il Aviation W 83:63+ Jl 26 '65

Secrets of good brazing. T. Moore. il Pop Sci 186:150-3+ Ap '65

BRAZZAVILLE teen-ager; story. See Friedman, B. J.

BREAD

Baked in U.S.A. C. Claiborne. il N Y Times Mag p 129-30 N 14 '65

Baker's art; holiday show at New York's Museum of contemporary crafts. A. Adams. il Craft Horiz 25:8-17 N '65

Bread and rolls baked at home add flavor to your family meal. G. Maddox. il Todays Health 43:52-7 F '65

Bread of the Pueblos is easy to make at home. il Sunset 135:84-5 S '65

Christmas gathering. il Good H 161:126-7+ D '65

Easiest breads in the world; need no kneading. il Ladies Home J 82:82-3+ S '65

Easter breads, a delicious tradition. il Bet Hom & Gard 43:100+ Ap '65

Four fragrant breads of Christmas; with recipes. il Sunset 135:72-5 D '65

Full-flavored international breads. B. S. Brown. il Good H 161:156 N '65

Home-baked breads the quick and easy way. il McCalls 92:114-16+ Je '65

Homemade breads in half the time. il Bet Hom & Gard 43:82 S '65

Hot breads cook book. E. Ross. il House & Gard 127:163+ Mr '65

Hot cross buns and other tasty Easter treats. il Sunset 134:204+ Ap '65

It is peasant bread and it is very good. il Sunset 134:180+ Mr '65

It's a dessert bun; Swedish semlor. il Sunset 134:221 Ap '65

Quick breads; with recipes. il Redbook 125: 84-5+ S '65

Refrigerator rolls; with recipes. B. L. Henry. Farm J 89:91 F '65

Special cereal breads. il Bet Hom & Gard 43:95-6 Mr '65

Successful recipes; Christmas breads. il Suc Farm 63:85-6 N '65

Successful recipes; quick breads. il Suc Farm 63:127-8 F '65

Susan makes crisscross corn bread. M. F. Williams. il Good H 160:126 Ja '65

Susan makes giant popovers. M. F. Williams. il Good H 160:220 Mr '65

They're made with refrigerator dough; cinnamon rolls. il Sunset 134:204+ Je '65

To bagelville and beyond. H. Sutton; discussion. Sat R 47:33 D 12; 21 D 26 '64; 48:43 Ja 9; 21 Ja 16; 37 Ja 23; 21 Ja 30; 23 F 6; 21 F 20; 22 Mr 20 '65

Variety of homemade breads. il Ebony 20: 156+ O '65

See also

Coffee cake

Muffins

BREAD plates, Glass. See Glassware

BREAKABLE cup; story. See Lewis, J.

BREAKERS. See Newport, R.I.—Historic houses

BREAKFASTS

Breakfast around the world; with recipes. il McCalls 92:106-7+ Ag '65

Breakfasts that serve themselves; with recipes and menus. il Redbook 125:32+ S '65

Good morning breakfasts; menus with recipes. B. M. Stover. il Parents Mag 40:74-7+ S '65

Hunt breakfast; with recipes. M. Kaytor. il Look 29:98-101+ O 19 '65

Memorable breakfasts; menus with recipes. M. R. Hamm. il Parents Mag 40:71+ S '65

Out of the groove breakfasts. B. Pierson. il Farm J 89:92-3 S '65

See also

Brunches

Outdoor meals

Wedding

BREAKING it off; story. See Mallet-Joris, F.

BREAST

Escalation; injections of liquid silicone for bust development. il Newsweek 66:110+ O 25 '65

Surgery

News about breast surgery. Sci Digest 58: 15 Ag '65

Over-surgery questioned; mastectomy for breast cancers. Sci N L 88:2 Jl 3 '65

BREAST cancer. See Cancer

BREAST feeding. See Infants—Nutrition

BREAST tumors. See Tumors

BREATH, Shortness of. See Emphysema

BREATH odor. See Halitosis

BREATHING. See Respiration

BREATHING apparatus. See Respiratory apparatus

BREBBIA, D. Robert, and Altshuler, K. Z. Oxygen consumption rate and electroencephalographic stage of sleep. bibliog Science 150:1621-3 D 17 '65

BRECHER, Edward. See Brecher, R. jt. auth.

BRECHER, Ruth, and Brecher, Edward
Can you still get bargains in discount stores?
Redbook 124:62-3+ Ap '65; Same abr. with
title How big are bargains in discount
stores? Read Digest 87:79-82 Jl '65
Getting to work and back. Consumer Rep
30:56-65, 128-33, 206-9 F-Ap '65
BRECHT, Bertolt
Arturo Ui. Criticism
New Repub 153:34 Ag 7 '65
Baal. Criticism
Commonweal 82:413-14 Je 18 '65
Nation 200:625-8 Je 7 '65
New Yorker 41:158+ My 15 '65
Newsweek 65:81 Je 7 '65
Time il 85:64 My 14 '65
Etc. R. J. Schroeder. Commonweal 83:62-3
O 15 '65
Exception and the rule. Criticism
America 113:62 Jl 10 '65
Commonweal 82:414 Je 18 '65
Newsweek 65:81 Je 7 '65
In London: Berliner ensemble, better with
low Brecht. H. Popkin. Vogue 146:65 O 15
'65
Mother Courage and her children; tr. by E.
Bentley. Criticism
New Repub 152:29 Je 26 '65
Squire Puntila and his servant Matti. Crit-
icism
Christian Cent 82:1097 S 8 '65
BRECKENRIDGE, Bruce
Object: still life. Craft Horiz 25:33-5 S '65
BRECKENRIDGE, Nicholas
What a man looks for when he hires a girl.
Mlle 60:146+ F '65
BREE, Germaine
Stranger in this world. Sat R 48:26-7 F 20 '65
BREEDER reactors. See Nuclear reactors
BREEDING
See also
Cattle breeding
Eugenics
Genetics
BREEDLOVE, Craig
750 mph, here I come. Pop Mech 124:88-92+
S '65
about
Land mark. il por Newsweek 66:75-6 N 15 '65
Mr & Mrs Speedlove. por Time 86:75-6+ N
12 '65
News on wheels; land speed records. D. Chu.
il pors Sr Schol 87:40 D 9 '65
BREEDLOVE, Lee
Mr & Mrs Speedlove. por Time 86:75-6+ N
12 '65
News on wheels; land speed records. D. Chu.
il por Sr Schol 87:40 D 9 '65
BREELING, Jim
Nuclear medicine's two explosive decades.
Todays Health 43:54-9+ Jl '65
BREESE, S. S. Jr, and others
Rotational symmetry in foot-and-mouth
disease virus and models. bibliog Science
150:1303-5 D 3 '65
BREIDENSTEIN, B. C.
New changes in beef grading, here's what
they'll mean. Suc Farm 63:31 Je '65
BREINER, Sheldon
Rubidium magnetometer in archeological ex-
ploration. bibliog Science 150:185-93 O 8 '65
BREIT, Harvey
(ed) See Frost, R. Robert Frost speaks
prose
BREMBECK, Cole S. See Hanson, J. W. jt.
auth.
BREMNER, Donald
Maryland college case: a clear test for school
aid? Reporter 32:36-8 F 25 '65
BRENDAN, Saint
Enduring Saint Brendan. R. Valente. il
Américas 17:22-7 N '65
BRENHOLT, Richard A.
Beyond question. Flying 77:86 N '65
BRENNAN, D. G.
Books. Bul Atomic Sci 21:25-30 D '65
BRENNAN, Maeve
Shadow of kindness; story. New Yorker 41:
30-6 Ag 14 '65
BRENNECKE, Harry E.
Nobel prize; poem. Negro Hist Bul 28:146
Ap '65
BRENNER, Paul David
I believe; ed. by C. Lydon. por Seventeen
24:220-1 Mr '65
BRENNER, William
Inventor of the month. S. V. Jones. por Sci
Digest 57:32 Mr '65
BRENT, Ralf
Education by electronics; address, December
3, 1965. Vital Speeches 32:175-8 Ja 1 '66
BRESLER, Harvey
Radio's rabid priest. Nation 200:401-2 Ap 12
'65

BRESLIN, James E. See Breslin, J.
BRESLIN, Jimmy
I am a fugitive from the Diners' club. Sat
Eve Post 238:20 Ag 14 '65
about
Pundit and the prole; J. B. Reston and J. E.
Breslin in Saigon. il por Newsweek 66:49-
50 S 6 '65
BRESSI, Betty
Spontaneity in children's painting. Sch Arts
65:26-8 N '65
BRESSON, Henri Cartier-. See Cartier-Bres-
son, H.
BRETHREN, Church of the. See Church of the
Brethren
BRETT, J. R.
Swimming energetics of salmon; with bio-
graphical sketch. Sci Am 213:11, 80-5 Ag
'65
BREUNING, Oswald von Nell-. See Nell-
Breuning, O. von
BREW, John O.
Menace of the bulldozers; excerpts from
study. UNESCO Courier 18:33-6 Ja '65
BREWER, Gay, Jr
Laugher for the team from Texas. A. Wright.
il por Sports Illus 23:84+ D 20 '65
BREWER, John H. and Allgeier, D. L.
Disposable hydrogen generator. bibliog Sci-
ence 147:1033-4 F 26 '65
BREWERIES
Across a sea of Löwenbräu; Oktoberfest in
Munich. il Time 86:110 O 1 65
BREWING industries
Brewing up new business. il Time 86:77 Jl
2 '65
See also
Anheuser-Busch, incorporated
BREWSTER, Willie
Uncolored justice. Newsweek 66:34 D 13 '65
BREZHNEV, Leonid Il'ich
Brezhnev's new farm nightmare. America
113:232 S 4 '65
Kremlin mood: strain and anxiety. il por
Newsweek 65:31 Mr 29 '65
One year, two views. R. J. Korengold; L.
Volkov. il Newsweek 66:56-7 O 18 '65
Soviet Union today. il por Sr Schol 86:12-16
F 4 '65
BRIAN HEAD
Brian Head. N. N. Dodge. il Nat Parks Mag
39:18-19 Mr '65
BRIBERY
No inferences, please; bribery charges by
Mayor R. Wagner against State Chairman
W. McKeon. il Time 85:25 F 5 '65
See also
Politics, Corruption in
Anecdotes, facetiae, satire, etc.
Fifty-dollar bill. D. Hall il Esquire 63:106 F
'65
BRICK. See Bricks
BRICK construction
Brick columns and a broad roof shelter a
glass-walled house. il Arch Rec 138:167-70
Ag '65
BRICK floors. See Floors, Brick
BRICK industry
See also
Clay industries
BRICK walls. See Walls, Brick
BRICKMAN, William W.
Foreign books for educators. Sch & Soc
93:125-34, 406-12 F 20, O 30 '65
Half-century of School and society. Sch &
Soc 93:34+ Ja 23 '65
U.S. books for educators. Sch & Soc 93:320-
6+, 505-8+ Sum, D 25 '65
BRICKS
Beauty of brick. il House & Gard 128:218-21
O '65
Brick. J. H. Ingersoll. il Pop Gard 16:18-21 N
'65
How to take care of brick. House & Gard
128:240 O '65
BRIDAL showers. See Entertaining
BRIDE, Joseph, Jr
Smudge on the cadet code. Life 58:82+ F
5 '65
BRIDGE (game)
Add a fifth to the Bermuda bowl. C. Goren.
il Sports Illus 23:50-1 Ag 9 '65
Case of the double squeeze. C. Goren. il
Sports Illus 23:103 S 13 '65
Cooke with a recipe for victory; Goren bridge
cruises. C. Goren. il Sports Illus 22:60 F
22 '65
Dizzy makes a different kind of pitch; play-
ing duplicate bridge. C. Goren. il Sports
Illus 23:74 O 11 '65

BRIDGE (game)—*Continued*

Experts' substitute for X-ray eyes. C. Goren. il Sports Illus 23:50-1 Ag 16 '65

Magic of hands that fit. C. H. Goren. il McCalls 93:94+ N '65

Maugham never forgot the day I trumped his ace. C. Goren. il Sports Illus 24:50-1 Ja 17 '66

Message from agent O-32.92. C. Goren. il Sports Illus 22:65-6 Je 28 '65

Mysteries of the short club. C. H. Goren. il McCalls 92:40 Ap '65

New kind of double makes a hit; unpenalty double. C. Goren. il Sports Illus 22:85 My 17 '65

Perfect partner makes a perfect play. C. Goren. il Sports Illus 23:72 N 8 '65

Pros and cons of a capital hand. C. Goren. il Sports Illus 23:50 Ag 30 '65

Quiz to see if you like to fight. C. Goren. il Sports Illus 23:88-90 D 20 '65

Rogues, rascals and reprobates. C. H. Goren. il McCalls 92:28 Je '65

Safety play that led to ruin; shipboard contract bridge. C. Goren. il Sports Illus 22:74 Je 14 '65

Somewhat artificial victory. C. Goren. il Sports Illus 22:48-9 F 1 '65

Tattletale from the living room. C. Goren. il Sports Illus 22:66 Mr 22 '65

Way to signal success. C. H. Goren. il McCalls 92:26+ Jl '65

Why do people cheat? Reese, Shapiro scandal at World's championship tournament. C. H. Goren. il McCalls 92:30+ S '65

Wise time to fool your partner; bidding systems must be public record. C. Goren. il Sports Illus 22:52 F 15 '65

Zero doubled is no worse than zero. C. Goren. il Sports Illus 22:90 Ap 5 '65

BRIDGE CANYON DAM (proposed) See Dams

BRIDGE design. See Bridges—Design

BRIDGE parties. See Entertaining

BRIDGE players

Backdoor entry to center stage; Great Britain or France in world championship representing Europe. C. Goren. il Sports Illus 23:66-7 N 1 '65

Baron abdicates his throne; Italians win European championship. C. Goren. il Sports Illus 23:90+ O 18 '65

Basic fallacy of the trials; selection of American team to represent us in the World bridge championship. C. Goren. il Sports Illus 22:71 My 3 '65

Beware of anonymous opponents. C. Goren. il Sports Illus 23:59 Jl 19 '65

Cheating scandal rocks the bridge world. M. Smith. il Life 58:32-3 Je 4 '65

Cocky kid makes a grand slam bid; J. Rubens. C. Goren. il Sports Illus 22:107 Ap 19 '65

Farewell to an understanding lady: Ruth Sherman. C. Goren. il Sports Illus 22:72 My 31 '65

Finding the trials guilty; selecting contenders for U.S. team. C. Goren. il Sports Illus 23:98+ N 22 '65

Nip-and-tuck finish to a long trial; competition for North American team. C. Goren. il Sports Illus 23:70+ N 29 '65

Perfect partner makes a perfect play. C. Goren. il Sports Illus 23:72 N 8 '65

Tall man takes a long chance. C. Goren. il Sports Illus 23:116 S 20 '65

Tribute to a longtime friend; O. Peterson. C. Goren. il Sports Illus 22:50 Mr 1 '65

Young master with the old touch; twenty-one-year-old Ohio state university sophomore J. Wisemiller became Life master of American contract bridge league. C. Goren. il Sports Illus 22:72 My 10 '65

BRIDGE tournaments

Add a fifth to the Bermuda bowl. C. Goren. il Sports Illus 23:50-1 Ag 9 '65

Backdoor entry to center stage; Great Britain or France in world championship representing Europe. C. Goren. il Sports Illus 23:66-7 N 1 '65

Baron abdicates his throne; Italians win European championship. C. Goren. il Sports Illus 23:90+ O 18 '65

By the way, Italy won again; seventh straight victory. C. Goren. il Sports Illus 22:57 Je 21 '65

Champion turns a wrong into right; Tournament of champions, in Deauville, France. C. Goren. il Sports Illus 23:60-1 S 27 '65

Cheating scandal rocks the bridge world. M. Smith. il Life 58:32-3 Je 4 '65

Eleventh-hour victory at 3 a.m. C. Goren. il Sports Illus 22:79 Ap 12 '65

Finding the trials guilty; selecting contenders for U.S. team. C. Goren. il Sports Illus 23:98+ N 22 '65

Fingered; British pair accused of cheating in World contract bridge tournament. il Newsweek 65:59-60 Je 7 '65

Five-finger exercise; cheating by British players at World bridge championship, Buenos Aires. il Time 85:42 Je 4 '65

Four-finger exercise; Great Britain's leading players accused of cheating. J. Gerber; T. Reese. il Sports Illus 22:56+ Je 7 '65

Four masters from Canada; Masters knockout team championship. C. Goren. il Sports Illus 23:55 S 6 '65

Letter from the publisher; Men's team championship in the Fall nationals. G. Valk. Sports Illus 23:4 D 13 '65

Luck always helps in a game of skill. C. Goren. il Sports Illus 22:66 Mr 8 '65

Up-and-down in San Francisco; Team trials and the Fall nationals. C. Goren. il Sports Illus 23:100+ D 6 '65

BRIDGEMAN, Donald

Planning play areas. il Recreation 58:169-70 Ap '65

BRIDGEPORT, Conn.

Bridgeport book fair highlights jobber's activities; sponsored by King Cole supermarket. il Pub W 188:28-31 N 1 '65

BRIDGES, Julia W.

Helping children to speak effectively. NEA J 54:20-1 Mr '65

BRIDGES

Bridges that span three continents; portfolio. Fortune 72:154-7 N '65

Rejected beams span water hazards; Orangebrook golf course, Hollywood, Fla. W. A. Peterson. il Am City 80:98-9 My '65

Steelwork starts on new bridge; Delaware memorial bridge. il Am City 81:39 Ja '66

See also subhead Bridges under names of cities, e.g. New York (city)—Bridges

Design

Design a bridge and win a prize. il Am City 80:30 D '65

Steel gains a trump with new bridge deck; orthotropic bridges. il Bsns W p100-2+ S 18 '65

Foundations and piers

Pouring concrete into a river, with a purpose; Delaware River bridge. il Bsns W p40-1 Mr 20 '65

BRIDGES, Foot

How to bridge a gap. il Pop Gard 16:54 Mr '65

Rejected beams span water hazards; Orangebrook golf course, Hollywood, Fla. W. A. Peterson. il Am City 80:98-9 My '65

BRIDGES, Iron and steel

Bridge erected in one day; Humphreys Creek, Sparrow Point, Md. il Am City 80:18 F '65

Steel gains a trump with new bridge deck; orthotropic bridges. il Bsns W p 100-2+ S 18 '65

BRIDGES, Steel. See Bridges, Iron and steel

BRIDGES, Suspension

Fall of Galloping Gertie. R. Kraske. il Sci Digest 58:61-5 D '65

BRIDSTON, Keith R.

Ecumenical criticism. Christian Cent 82:1608 D 29 '65

BRIDWELL, Lowell K.

International cooperation year, a challenge to transportation. Dept State Bul 53:835-9 N 22 '65

BRIDWELL, Margaret M.

Tea caddy spoons. Antiques 88:528-31 O '65

BRIEFS

Some of your best friends will go to court for you; amicus curiae brief, attacking law that bans sale of contraceptives in Connecticut. il Time 85:50 F 26 '65

BRIEN, Alan

Theatre. Vogue 146:49 Ag 1; 75 S 15 '65

BRIER, Herb S.

Across the ham bands. See issues of Popular electronics

Amateur radio (cont of) Across the ham bands. See issues of Popular electronics

BRIGANDS and robbers

Return of sure shot; Tiro Fijo responsible for murders in Columbia. Time 85:37 Ap 9 '65

BRIGGS, Austin

Fast changing South; paintings. Look 29:33-8 N 16 '65

BRIGHTON, Colo.

Bank that should never have opened; Brighton national bank. H. B. Meyers. il Fortune 72:126-7+ Jl '65

BRIMBLE, Lionel John Farnham

Obituary

Science 150:1138 N 26 '65. V. K. McElheny

BRIMER, John Burton
Cooling water or fountain. Pop Sci 186:142-4+ My '65
Flower grower's home garden notebook. See issues of Flower grower, the home garden magazine
Modern annuals for modern gardens. il Flower Grower 52:38-9 F '65
Warm weather hardiness and roses. Horticulture 43:22-3 N '65

BRIMMER, Andrew F.
Five more boom years ahead; interview. pors Nations Bsns 53:60-2+ Je '65

BRIN, Judith
Don't splinter the dance! Dance Mag 39:34-5 Ag '65

BRINHART, Betty
First aid for winter-scarred lawns. Pop Gard 16:44-5+ Ap '65
Hollyhocks, the flower with old-fashioned charm. Pop Gard 16:6-7+ Jl '65
Zinnias, rainbow colors all season bloom. Flower Grower 52:36-7+ Mr '65

BRINK, David
Fipple in the mouth. Recreation 58:399 O '65
Ready, set, ski! Recreation 58:443 N '65

BRINKLEY, David
Leading from strength: LBJ in action. Atlan 215:49-54 F '65

BRINK'S incorporated
How Brink's guards its profits, too. il Bsns W p54-6+ F 6 '65

BRION, Marcel
City of the dead. UNESCO Courier 18:27-31 Je '65

BRISKIN, Jacqueline
Tsunami; story. Seventeen 24:108-9 Jl '65

BRISTER, Bob
Mystery geese. Field & S 70:44-6+ S '65

BRISTOL, Horace
Accent on the exotic. Sat R 48:38-9 My 29 '65
Asahi Pentax Spotmatic. U S Camera 28:57-9+ Mr '65

BRISTOL-Myers company
Is it true Bristol has more fun? il Time 85:86 F 12 '65

BRISTOL Siddeley engines, limited
Bristol Siddeley presses rocket studies. H. J. Coleman. il Aviation W 83:83+ Ag 23 '65

BRITCHES thief; story. See Ford, J. H.

BRITISH aircraft corporation
BAC 111-400 reflects pilot suggestions. H. J. Coleman. il Aviation W 83:55-7 N 1 '65
BAC studying new VC.10 configurations. R. G. O'Lone. il Aviation W 82:30 Mr 22 '65
Letter from London. M. Panter-Downes. New Yorker 40:106+ Ja 30 '65

BRITISH art. See Art, British

BRITISH artificial satellites. See Artificial satellites, British

BRITISH artists. See Artists, British

BRITISH broadcasting corporation
Auntie adjusts her skirts. Time 85:30-1 Ap 9 '65
Auntie's indiscretions. il Newsweek 65:70 12 '65
TVs' battle of Britain. S. Hynes. Commonweal 82:564-6 Ag 6 '65

BRITISH COLUMBIA
See also
Gardens—British Columbia

Description and travel
Be a modern pioneer. A. Heist. il Sr Schol 86:sup22-3 Ap 15 '65

BRITISH COMMONWEALTH. See Commonwealth of nations

BRITISH cookery. See Cookery, English

BRITISH council of churches
Evangelicals see red. C. Northcott. Christian Cent 82:799 Je 23 '65

BRITISH European airways corporation
BEA reservation system keyed to two Univac 490 computers. Aviation W 83:47 S 27 '65
Trident introductory costs cited as factor in lower BEA profits. H. J. Coleman. il Aviation W 83:39 S 6 '65

BRITISH Ford. See Ford motor company, limited, Dagenham, England

BRITISH GUIANA
See also
Medical relief work—British Guiana

Politics and government
Birth of Guyana. Newsweek 66:49 N 29 '65
British Guiana's future. T. M. Petry. America 113:51 Jl 10 '65
End of a mission; continuing racial conflict. Newsweek 65:50 Mr 1 '65
Gamble worth taking. T. M. Petry. America 113:743 D 11 '65

Independence ahead. Time 86:43 N 26 '65
Repairing the damage; Forbes Burnham's administration. Time 85:36+ F 19 '65

Race problems
British Guiana's future. T. M. Petry. America 113:51 Jl 10 '65

Religious institutions and affairs
News of the Christian world. Christian Cent 82:818 Je 23 '65

BRITISH HONDURAS
Atlantic report. Atlan 217:24+ Ja '66
Let George do it. Newsweek 65:60 Mr 15 '65

BRITISH imperialism. See Imperialism

BRITISH Labor party. See Labor party (Great Britain)

BRITISH library association. See Library association

BRITISH military bases. See Military bases, British

BRITISH national trust. See National trust for places of historic interest on natural beauty

BRITISH NORTH BORNEO. See North Borneo

BRITISH Open. See Golf—Tournaments

BRITISH overseas airways corporation
BAC studying new VC.10 configurations. R. G. O'Lone. il Aviation W 82:30 Mr 22 '65
BOAC enters Leningrad dispute. Aviation W 83:29 Jl 19 '65
BOAC may expand JFK cargo terminal. il Aviation W 83:39-41 N 22 '65
BOAC plans $19.6-million JFK terminal. il Aviation W 82:43 Ap 5 '65
BOAC reports $19.6-million net profit. H. J. Coleman. Aviation W 83:50 Ag 2 '65
Stretched Super VC.10 will carry 265. il Aviation W 83:43+ Jl 12 '65

BRITISH petroleum company
Sinking of the Sea Gem; quest for gas under the North Sea. il Time 87:87 Ja 7 '66

BRITISH press. See Newspapers—Great Britain

BRITISH royal ballet. See Royal ballet, Great Britain

BRITISH sailors See Seamen

BRITISH sculpture. See Sculpture, British

BRITISH singers. See Singers

BRITISH SOMALILAND. See Somalia

BRITISH student Christian movement. See Student Christian movement

BRITISH united air ferries
Air ferry puts wings on travelers' cars. il Bsns W p 108-9+ S 11 '65

BRITISH united airways
Jets intensify U.K. domestic competition. Aviation W 84:52 Ja 17 '66

BRITISH WEST INDIES federation. See West Indies (federation)

BRITTANY
France meets the sea in Brittany. H. Walker. il Nat Geog Mag 127:470-503 Ap '65

BRITTEN, Benjamin
Billy Budd returns. J. W. Freeman. il Opera N 30:14-15 Ja 1 '66
Britten's new cello symphony. J. Diether. il Am Rec G 31:1056-8 Jl '65
Double star; Gemini variations, quartet for two players. I. Goodwin. il por Newsweek 66:80-1 Jl 5 '65
From Peter Pears, his third and best Britten Serenade. J. Diether. Am Rec G 31:1150-2 Ag '65
London's Albert Herring. Am Rec G 31:1060-3 Jl '65
Midsummer night's dream. Criticism
New Yorker 41:173 Mr 20 '65
Mr Britten and the loudspeaker. Hi Fi 15:33 Jl '65
Music to my ears; new version of Billy Budd. I. Kolodin. Sat R 49:48 Ja 22. '66
On records; Albert Herring. Opera N 29:34 Ap 3 '65

BRITTENUM, Jon
Arkansas on top of the world. D. Jenkins. il Sports Illus 23:24-7+ O 25 '65

BRITTER, Marguerite S.
(ed) Book notes and reviews. Yachting 117:100-1 My; 191-2+ Je; 118:86-7 Jl; 155 Ag; 78 S '65

BRITTON, Wright
Roller wings. Yachting 118:54-6+ Ag '65
Tune up! Motor B 115:42+ My '65

BRIZEE, Alan A.
Computer that puts the budget in order every day. Am City 80:116-17 Mr '65

BRNO, Czechoslovakia
Brno; opera house. C. N. Welsh. il Opera N 30:31 D 4 '65

BRO, Margueritte Harmon
Feminine voice. Christian Cent 82:918 Jl 21 '65

BROADBENT, D. E.
Information processing in the nervous system. bibliog Science 150:457-62 O 22 '65

BROADBENT, Robert V.
Grand climax. pors Outdoor Life 135:36-9+ My '65

BROADBILL swordfish fishing. See Swordfish fishing

BROADFIELD, George W.
Different drum. Nation 201:161-5 S 20 '65

BROADHURST, Allan R.
Education: worth of the individual; address, February 24, 1965. Vital Speeches 31:360-2 Ap 1 '65

BROADWAY, New York (theater district) See New York (city)—Theater

BROADWAY actors and actresses. See Actors and actresses

BROCK, Clifton
Implementing the depository law. bibliog por Library J 90:1825-33 Ap 15 '65

BROCK, Paul
Ingredients of happiness. Sci Digest 58:83-5 S '65
It's an old English custom. Travel 124:56-61 D '65
Odd tricks of the human eye. Sci Digest 58: 74-7 D '65

BROCK, Stanley E.
Tight turn with a tigre. por Outdoor Life 135:36-9+ Mr '65

BROCK, Van K.
Landscapes for voyagers; poem. Yale R 55: 251 D '65
Sea birds. New Yorker 41:62 O 23 '65

BROCK, William R.
As it was, as it is. Nation 201:197-8 O 4 '65

BROCKETT, Ernest Delwin, 1913–
Businessmen in the news. por Fortune 73:77 Ja '66

BROCKMAN, H. E. and Goben, Wini
Mutagenicity of a monofunctional alkylating agent derivative of acridine in neurospora. bibliog Science 147:750-1 F 12 '65

BRODER, David S.
Bliss rides the elephant. N Y Times Mag p49-50+ Mr 21 '65
California's political free-for-all. Look 29: 61-2+ Jl 13 '65
Dale Miller: the President's favorite lobbyist. Look 29:66-8 Ap 6 '65
Forty-eight freshmen build their fences. N Y Times Mag p51+ D 12 '65

BRODER, Nathan
Brandenburgs, so musical a discourse. Hi Fi 15:76-7 D '65
Haydn's oratorios, a simple faith, sublimest craft. Hi Fi 15:82 O 65
Mozart's last six from the indefatigable Klemperer. Hi Fi 15:59 Jl '65

BRODERICK, Carlfred B.
Family communication. PTA Mag 60:4-6 bibliog(p36) D '65

BRODERICK, Dorothy M.
Carping critics, instant experts. Library J 90:3690-2 S 15 '65
Catalog. Library J 90:5492-4 D 15 '65
Depleted Book review digest. Library J 90: 945 F 15 '65
Opinions in black and white. Library J 90: 1994-5 Ap 15 '65
Spy who got locked in the ice box. Library J 90:1478-9 Mr 15 '65
Twelve-year-old adult reader. por Library J 90:2321-7 My 15 '65

BRODEUR, Paul
Hydrography; story. New Yorker 40:28-31 F 13 '65
Secret; story. Seventeen 24:104-5 D '65
Spoiler; story. New Yorker 41:28-34 Ja 8 '66
Turtle; story. Sat Eve Post 238:42-4 Mr 27 '65

BRODIE, Arnold F. and Adelson, Joel
Respiratory chains and sites of coupled phosphorylation. bibliog Science 149:265-9 Jl 16 '65

BRODIE, Bernard
Politics of strategy. Reporter 33:57-9 S 23 '65

BRODIE, Bernard B. and others.
Toxicology and the biomedical sciences. bibliog Science 148:1547-54 Je 18 '65

BRODIE, Fawn M.
Parks and politics in Los Angeles. Reporter 32:39-42 F 11 '65

BRODIE, Henry
Commodity agreements, a partial answer to the trade problems of developing countries. Dept State Bul 53:111-17 Jl 19 '65

BRODKEY, Harold
On the waves; story. New Yorker 41:24-7 S 4 '65

BRODSKII, Iosif
Reporter at large. R. Blum. New Yorker 41:192+ S 11 '65

BRODY, Jacob A. and others
Soviet search for viruses that cause chronic neurologic diseases in the U.S.S.R. bibliog Science 147:1114-16 Mr 5 '65

BRODY, Thomas C.
Baseball (cont) Sports Illus 22:80-1 Ap 12 '65
Hockey. Sports Illus 23:68+ D 13 '65

BROECKER, Wallace S. and Thurber, D. L.
Uranium-series dating of corals and oolites from Bahaman and Florida Key limestones. bibliog Science 149:58-60 Jl 2 '65

BROEG, Bob
What makes Stan Musial The Man? por Pop Sci 187:126-8+ O '65

BROFSKY, Miriam
Nijinsky. M. Marks. il por Dance Mag 39: 28-9 Je '65

BROGAN, Colm
Churchill: a profile in greatness. Nat R 17: 99-100+ F 9 '65
Letter from London (cont) Nat R 17:195-6, 1026-7 Mr 9. N 16 '65

BROGAN, Sir Denis William
Harrington on the human condition. New Repub 153:25-6 Jl 24 '65
Impending crisis of the deep South. Harper 230:147-51 Ap '65
Speaking out; hypocrisy is no sin. por Sat Eve Post 238:10+ Ag 14 '65

about
Doctor Brogan in the cabbage patch. G. Dangerfield. Nation 200:176-8 F 15 '65

BROHI, A. K.
Problem of international co-operation in the contemporary world; address. UN Mo Chron 2:71-88 Mr '65

BROILER-house litter feed. See Feeding and feeding stuffs—Poultry house litter

BROILERS, Electric. See Electric apparatus and appliances, Domestic

BROILING
All-in-one broiler meals; with recipes. il Redbook 126:58-61+ Ja '66

BROKERS
Brokers open doors to economy; economists as security analysts. il Bsns W p76+ N 6 '65
Fed holds the key on action; brokers look for trouble if Fed should tighten money. il Bsns W p 141-2 D 11 '65
Gone for broke; Yamaichi securities co, Japan. Newsweek 65:72 Je 7 '65
New setback in Tokyo; Yamaichi securities co, $214-million in debt. Bsns W p 122 My 29 '65
Pacesetter of change for Europe's investors; Netherlands' Robeco. il Bsns W p 156+ Ap 17 '65
SEC draws a bead on top men. Bsns W p 151 N 20 '65
What are the customer's rights? Fortune 72:246 N '65
See also
Harris, Upham and company
Merrill Lynch, Pierce, Fenner and Smith, incorporated
Women as brokers

Advertising
Where Wall Street meets Madison avenue; advertising by brokerage houses. il Bsns W p 130-2+ F 13 '65

Commissions
Haze over brokers' fees. il Fortune 72:89-90 S '65
Life among the no-loads. C. J. Loomis. il Fortune 72:86+ O '65

BROKERS, Marriage. See Marriage brokers

BROMELIADS
Bromeliads. M. B. Foster. il Horticulture 43: 24-5+ Je '65
Can you kill a bromeliad? H. Mason and R. O'Harra. il Bet Hom & Gard 44:40-3+ Ja '66

BROMLEY, D. A. See Zucker, A. jt. auth.

BRONCHIAL asthma. See Asthma

BRONCO busting. See Rodeos

BRONCOS (football club) See Football clubs

BRONK, Detlev W.
Rockefeller university: science in a different key. J. Walsh. il por Science 150:1692-5 D 24 '65

BRONK, H.
(tr) See Kung, H. What has the council done?

BRONOWSKI, Jacob
Panic in modern man; excerpt from Identity of man. por Sci Digest 58:82-5 D '65

about
Lecturer. New Yorker 41:35-8 Ap 3 '65

BRONSON, F. H. and Eleftheriou, B. E.
Adrenal response to fighting in mice: separation of physical and psychological causes. bibliog Science 147:627-8 F 5 '65
BRONX high school of science. See New York (city)—Education
BRONX zoo. See New York zoological park
BRONZES
Patination of bronzes. J. Brzostoski. il Craft Horiz 25:26-31 N '65
BROOK, Peter
Peter Brook: a natural saboteur of order. P. Gilliatt. por Vogue 147:102-5 Ja 1 '66
BROOK street bureau of Mayfair, limited. See Employment agencies
BROOKE, Edward W.
Negro leader's advice to Republicans; interview. pors U S News 58:66-70 F 1 '65

about

Free for all. il por Newsweek 67:20-1 Ja 10 '66
Running Brooke. Reporter 34:12+ Ja 13 '66
Saltonstall's successor. M. F. Nolan. New Repub 154:8 Ja 22 '66
BROOKFIELD, Ill.
First computer center billing. F. E. McGuire. il Am City 80:102-3 My '65
BROOKINGS institution
Best of both worlds. il Newsweek 66:82-3 Jl 12 '65
Bureaucrats meet company brass. il Bsns W p 176-8 My 22 '65
Changing the rules on growth. il Bsns W p 142+ Mr 6 '65
Gaining a clearer view of the top; Brookings' dialogue for bureaucrats and corporate brass. il Bsns W p84-6 Ag 7 '65
Powerhouse of economic thought; K. Gordon joins its staff. il Bsns W p 124-6+ Je 5 '65
BROOKLYN
See also
Coney Island

Description

One Saturday in Brooklyn. W. Alfred. New Yorker 41:42-6 D 18 '65

Education

Wrap-up senior lesson; Erasmus Hall high school. J. Sverdlik. il Library J 90:4516-19+ O 15 '65

Hospitals

Law on human guinea pigs; experiments at the Jewish chronic disease hospital. J. Lear. Sat R 48:56 Ap 3 '65
Patient's right to know; experiments at Jewish chronic disease hospital. J. Lear. Sat R 48:20 Je 26 '65
Specialist finds many tropical diseases on Brooklyn waterfront. il Todays Health 43:71 Ag '65

Music

See also
Brooklyn academy of music

Newspapers

See also
Brooklyn eagle

BROOKLYN academy of music
Brooklyn; Mozart festival. F. Stevenson. Opera N 30:29 D 4 '65
BROOKLYN botanic garden
Brooklyn botanic garden; many gardens within a garden. R. C. Hands. il Horticulture 43:36-9 O '65
BROOKLYN bridge
Brooklyn bridge, by A. Trachtenberg. Review
Reporter 33:36-7 Jl 1 '65. H. Cohen
BROOKLYN eagle
Brooklyn daily eagle and its post cards. B. McCague. il Hobbies 70:118-19 Mr '65
BROOKLYN polytechnic institute. See Polytechnic institute, Brooklyn
BROOKLYNITES. See New Yorkers
BROOKNER, Anita
Prud'hon's The union of love and friendship. Art N 64:36-8+ N '65
BROOKNER, Jack
Ruminations on social security. Nat R 17:868-9 O 5 '65
BROOKS, Charlotte K.
School library or bookatheque? por Library J 90:1989-90 Ap 15 '65
BROOKS, Cleanth
On the grave. Yale R 55:275-9 D '65
BROOKS, Colleen
Invitation to the harvest. New Yorker 41:86+ Ap 10 '65
BROOKS, Edward M.
Two Peruvian solar eclipses. Sky & Tel 29:86-7 F '65
BROOKS, Elaine C.
Book reviews. Negro Hist Bul 28:138-9 Mr '65

BROOKS, Harvey
Brooks succeeds Kistiakowsky as head of NAS committee on public policy. por Science 149:953 Ag 27 '65
BROOKS, Joe
Brackish water black bass. Outdoor Life 135:40-1+ My '65
Flies worth their salt. Outdoor Life 135:60-3+ Je '65
Great tailwalker. Outdoor Life 136:58-60+ D '65
Pop for bass. por Outdoor Life 136:64-5+ N '65
School for anglers. Field & S 70:32-3 Jl '65
BROOKS, John
Profiles (cont) New Yorker 41:52-4+ Ap 3; 51-2+ Ap 10 '65
Reporter at large. New Yorker 40:72+ Ja 30 '65
BROOKS, John Langdon, and Dodson, S. I.
Predation, body size, and composition of plankton. bibliog Science 150:28-35 O 1 '65
BROOKS, Patricia K.
How to be outlandish. Sat R 48:40-1+ Mr 13 '65
BROOKS, Paul
Plot to drown Alaska. Atlan 215:53-9 My; 216:59 Jl '65; Same abr. Read Digest 87:79-83 Ag '65
BROOKS, Phyllis
Bouquet; poem. Nation 201:26 Jl 5 '65
To a good friend at a rest home; poem. Nation 201:202 O 4 '65
BROOKS, Robert A.
Harvard square; poem. New Yorker 41:54 N 13 '65
BROOKS, T. E.
Nothing box; story. Seventeen 24:132-3 N '65
BROOKS, Thomas R.
Books. Commonweal 82:361-2 Je 4 '65
Death of a craft? Commonweal 82:46-9 Ap 2 '65
Dock strike. Commonweal 81:728-30 Mr 5 '65
Labor front. See issues of Dun's review and modern industry
Necessary force or police brutality? N Y Times Mag p60-1+ D 5 '65
New York's finest. Commentary 40:29-36 Ag '65
To the East of the Communist party. N Y Times Mag p9+ Ap 25 '65
Voice of the new campus underclass. N Y Times Mag p25-7+ N 7 '65
BROOKS, Van Wyck
Critic and imperial consciousness. Q. Anderson. New Repub 152:15-17 Ap 17 '65
BROOKS, creeks, etc.
How to build a brook. J. Hyypia. il Pop Gard 16:26-7+ Mr '65
BROOME, Harvey
Among the books. Liv Wildn 29::29-31 Spr '65
Great Smoky Mountains National Park. Nat Parks Mag 39:4-7 Mr '65
Importance of wilderness; excerpt from remarks. Liv Wildn 86:44-6 Spr '64
BROOMS (shrubs)
Broom; yellow-flowered shrub. M. J. Dietz. il Flower Grower 52:35 Mr '65
BROPHY, George Patrick
Thirteenth mission; ed. by D. MacDonald. Read Digest 87:78-82 D '65
BROPHY, John
Obituary
Pub W 188:37 D 13 '65
BROPHY, Marjorie
Every day is mother's day. See issues of Good housekeeping
BROSIO, Manlio
Function of the Atlantic alliance; address, October 4, 1965. Vital Speeches 32:41-6 N 1 '65
BROSNAN, Dennis William
One way to run a railroad: go to it! il por Newsweek 66:89-90+ O 18 '65
BROSNAN, Jim
Boom go the big Red bats. Sports Illus 23:12-13+ Ag 16 '65
BROTHELS. See Prostitution
BROTHER industries. See Japan—Industries
BROTHER international corporation. See Japan—Industries
BROTHERHOOD of man
Man belongs to man; excerpt from Teaching of reverence for life. A. Schweitzer. Read Digest 87:77-8 Jl '65
Night watch. R. Popkin. il Read Digest 87:81-2 S '65

Bibliography

Books for brotherhood. il Commonweal 81:698-700 F 26 '65

BROTHERHOOD of teamsters. See Internation-
al brotherhood of teamsters, chauffeurs,
warehousemen and helpers of America
BROTHERHOODS
   See also
Brothers (Catholic)
BROTHERS, Joyce
On being a woman. See issues of Good house-
keeping
BROTHERS (Catholic)
Brother. K. B. O'Leary. il Commonweal 82:
142-6 Ap 23 '65; Reply. D. Darst. 82:366-7
Je 4 '65
BROTHERS and sisters. See Siblings
BROTHERS and sisters have I none; story. See
Loeser, K.
BROUGHTON, Jacqueline
Santa Barbara botanic garden. Horticulture
43:28-32 N '65
BROUGHTON, James
Gift of the stag; In the wind's eye; poems.
Poetry 106:192-3 Je '65
BROUGHTON, T. Robert S.
(comp) Articles and other books received;
ancient. See issues of American historical
review
BROUWER, Edith
Station wagon abroad. Travel 123:56-8 Mr '65
BROUWER, Luitzen Egbertus Jan
Fixed-point theorems. M. Shinbrot. il Sci Am
214:106-10 Ja '66
BROWARD COUNTY, Fla.
Complete combustion with minimum excess
air. J. D. Easterlin. il Am City 80:99-101 F
'65
BROWER, Brock
Always the challenger. Life 59:94-6+ S 24
'65
Freeing the children. Holiday 38:60-7+ S '65
Worthy try at covering a big story. Life 60:
15 Ja 21 '66
BROWER, David
Wilderness and the constant advocate; re-
print. Liv Wildn 86:42-3 Spr '64
BROWN, Albert Bush-. See Bush-Brown, A.
BROWN, Allen
Scouting around Nova Scotia. Hobbies 70:
114 O '65
BROWN, Bianca S.
Fascinating foods of the U.S.A. Good H 162:
118 Ja '66
Foods with a foreign flavor. See issues of
Good housekeeping
BROWN, Bruce L. and Nagle, S. C. Jr
Preservation of mammalian cells in a chem-
ically defined medium and dimethylsulfox-
ide. bibliog Science 149:1266-7 S 10 '65
BROWN, Carlton
What's new in records. Redbook 124:46 Ap;
125:64 O '65
BROWN, Charles
Epic of Ashton Jones. Ebony 20:45-8+ O '65
BROWN, Claude
Nobody wants to hear that nonsense in Har-
lem; excerpts from television discussion.
New Repub 153:20 O 16 '65
Saturday night in Harlem; a memoir; excerpt
from Manchild in the promised land. Com-
mentary 40:47-53 Jl '65
   about
Books. W. Balliett. New Yorker 41:242+
N 13 '65
Claude Brown's world. G. Daniels. New
Repub 153:26-8 S 25 '65
Cry from Harlem. C. Brossard. il pors Look
29:125-6+ D 14 '65
In defense of Uncle Toms. G. Wills. Com-
monweal 83:178-80 N 12 '65
In the promised land. R. A. Schroth. America
113:213 Ag 28 '65
Survivor. por Newsweek 66:81 Ag 16 '65
Tips. il Pub W 188:38-9 Jl 26 '65
BROWN, Clayton M.
TV or the herded tour. por Library J 90:
2214-18 My 15 '65
BROWN, Courtney C.
Academic fund raising: yesterday and today.
Sch & Soc 93:240-2 Ap 17 '65
BROWN, D. S.
In-shop or on-site figuring of large telescope
mirrors? Sky & Tel 29:350-2 Je '65
BROWN, Delmer M.
Eastern route to the western way. Sat R 48:
35 N 6 '65
BROWN, Deming
Muffled voice of Russian liberalism. N Y
Times Mag p 10-11+ D 19 '65
BROWN, Doil C.
Four myths that hurt farm boys. por Farm J
89:68 Ap '65
BROWN, Dolores
Terror of the pack train. Outdoor Life 135:
48-51+ Ap '65

BROWN, Dorothy Foster
Button collecting. See issues of Hobbies
BROWN, Drew
Floyd, fight like he slapped your mother.
Life 59:120+ N 19 '65
BROWN, Eastman
Obituary
Pub W 188:23 Ag 16 '65
BROWN, Edmund Gerald Pat
College by plan. por Am Ed 1:9-11 Mr '65
Down-to-earth use for space brains; inter-
view. por U S News 58:111 My 24 '65
   about
Big Daddy vs. Pat. por Newsweek 65:30+
Ap 5 '65
Great row in California. S. Alsop. por Sat
Eve Post 238:18 My 8 '65
BROWN, Edward T.
Community college's learning laboratory. por
Wilson Lib Bul 40:80-3 S '65
BROWN, Frank Arthur 1908-
Orbiting potato. J. Lear. il Sat R 48:47-50
S 4 '65
BROWN, G. W. Jr
Ornithine carbamoyltransferase in liver of
the dipnoan protopterus aethiopicus. bib-
liog Science 149:1515 S 24 '65
BROWN, George M. and Levy, H. A.
α-D-glucose: precise determination of crystal
and molecular structure by neutron-diffrac-
tion analysis. bibliog Science 147:1038-9
F 26 '65
BROWN, George MacKay
Black furrow, gray furrow; poem. Atlan 216:
74 O '65
Country girl; poem. Atlan 215:98 My '65
Seven houses; poem. Atlan 215:48 Je '65
BROWN, Gifford
Game of chess; story. New Yorker 41:37-46
Je 12 '65
BROWN, Guillermo
Spell of the rainbow; story. Américas 17:32-4
Ag '65
BROWN, Gwilym S.
Golf (cont) Sports Illus 22:64-7 Mr 15 '65
Track & field (title varies) (cont) Sports
Illus 22:48-9 F 8; 45-7 Mr 1; 66-7 My 31;
79-81 Je 14 '65; 24:44-5 Ja 3 '66
BROWN, H. Douglas
Gems and minerals. See issues of Hobbies
BROWN, Harold
New air force secretary has a scientific back-
ground. por Science 149:404 Jl 23 '65
Personality of the month; scientist takes
over the air force. por Sci Digest 57:17 O
'65
BROWN, Harold O. J.
Intellectual climate and Christian belief. Nat
R 17:1022-5 N 16 '65
Protestant deformation. Nat R 17:464-6 Je 1
'65
BROWN, Helen Evans
Shrimp cook book. House & Gard 127:175+
Ap '65
BROWN, Helen Gurley
New direction for Cosmopolitan. Writer 78:
20 Jl '65
   about
Helen Gurley Brown turns editor. C. Welles.
il pors Life 59:65-6+ N 19 '65
Sex & the editor. por Time 85:40 Mr 26 '65
BROWN, Irving
American labor abroad; Lovestone diplomacy;
with editorial comment. S. Lens. il Nation
201:2, 10-16+ Jl 5 '65
BROWN, Ivor
Those angry authors, why their protests
fail. Sat R 48:18-19+ Ag 28 '65
BROWN, Jack Kenneth
Magnificent obsession of Colonel Brown. J.
Phelan. il Sat Eve Post 238:98-101 My 8 '65
BROWN, James
Explosive Mr Brown. il pors Ebony 20:57-8+
Mr '65
BROWN, James Nathaniel
Look at me, man! pors Time 86:80+ N 26 '65
BROWN, Jeff
Tahoe notebook. Holiday 38:76-86+ D '65
BROWN, Jerram L.
Vocalization evoked from the optic lobe of a
songbird. bibliog Science 149:1002-3 Ag 27
'65
BROWN, John Mason
Worlds of Robert E. Sherwood; preview with
brief excerpts. por(p 1) Sat R 48:16-20+
Ag 14 '65
BROWN, Kenneth Irving
Vision that rescues; address, May 31, 1965.
Vital Speeches 31:567-70 Jl 1 '65
BROWN, Kenneth T. and Watanabe, Kosuke
Neural stage of adaptation between the recep-
tors and inner nuclear layer of monkey
retina. bibliog Science 148:1113-15 My 21 '65

BROWN, Larry W. See Alexander, J. K. jt. auth.

BROWN, Lewis
Lewis Brown, artist in the theater. J. H. Michel. il Am Artist 30:47-53+ Ja '66

BROWN, Norman S. and Huff, W. H.
Cost indexes for 1965: serial services. Library J 90:2966-7 Jl '65

BROWN, P. E. and others
Thymine addition to ethanol: induction by gamma irradiation. Science 151:68-70 Ja 7 '66

BROWN, Pat. See Brown, E. G. P.

BROWN, Philip S.
House & garden's outdoor menu cook book. House & Gard 128:117+ Jl '65
Mexican drinks. House & Gard 128:218+ S '65

BROWN, Richard
Zambia and Rhodesia: a study in contrast. Cur Hist 48:201-6+ Ap '65

BROWN, Richard F.
Art wagon. Nation 201:459-60 D 13 '65
Broken harness. il por Time 86:76+ N 26 '65
Drawing the line in L.A. il por Newsweek 66:98 N 22 '65
Happy New Year, Dr Brown. S. Alexander. Life 60:20 Ja 7 '66

BROWN, Robert McAfee
Agenda for men of good will. Sat R 48:21-3 F 13 '65
Campaign on many fronts. Christian Cent 82: 577-9, 717 My 5, Je 2 '65
Paul Tillich. Commonweal 83:471-3 Ja 21 '66
Protestant viewpoint (cont) Commonweal 82: 380-2, 697-9; 83:58-60, 211-14 Je 11, S 24, O 15, N 19 '65

about
Brown's word: when a structure is in the way, it must be axed. il por Newsweek 67:34-5 Ja 3 '66

BROWN, Ruth
SR-Anisfield-Wolf awards. Sat R 48:44+ My 1 '65
(comp) SR's check list of the week's new books. See issues of Saturday review
(comp) SR's check list of University press books. Sat R 48:91-2 My 22 '65

BROWN, Sandra
Whale and I. Seventeen 24:93+ Jl '65

BROWN, Stanley H.
Detroit: slow healing of a fractured city. Fortune 71:142-5+ Je '65
Univac isn't a business to jump in and out of. Fortune 71:120-3+ Ap '65
What guides the steelworkers? Fortune 72: 156-8+ S '65

BROWN, Tally
Marc Blitzstein's The cradle will rock. Am Rec G 31:800-5 My '65

BROWN, Warren
September hurricane. Yachting 118:38-40+ S '65

BROWN, Wenzell
Defense of the bedside pad. Writer 78:15-17 S '65

BROWN, Willis E.
Expectant mother. Redbook 126:31+ D '65

BROWN fat. See Fat

BROWN pelican. See Pelicans

BROWNE, Harry L.
Is the Supreme court increasing power of unions? por U S News 58:104-6 Je 7 '65

BROWNE, Malcolm W.
Letters. Sat Eve Post 238:6 N 6 '65
This is guerrilla warfare. Read Digest 87: 87-93 S '65

BROWNE, Roland A.
Never such roses. Flower Grower 52:40+ F '65

BROWNE, William R. See Coffman, J. A. jt. auth.

BROWNELL, Beverly. See Brownell, W. jt. auth.

BROWNELL, Samuel Miller
Keeping the schools human. PTA Mag 59:6-8 F '65
Schools in the cities; address, January 27, 1965. Vital Speeches 31:380-4 Ap 1 '65

BROWNELL, William, and Brownell, Beverly
Spanish fiestas. Travel 125:24-8 Ja '66

BROWNFELD, Allan C.
Intermarriage and the Court. Commonweal 81:609-10 F 5 '65

BROWNIES. See Cake

BROWNING, James
Wagner for young and old. Opera N 29:32 F 13 '65

BROWNING, John
Busiest fingers on the keys; interview, ed. by S. Schmidt. il pors Life 59:89-90+ N 26 '65

BROWNLEE, J. L.
Fewer fire stations serve better. Am City 80:107-9 D '65

BROWNLEE, John
Miracle in Manhattan. Q. Eaton. il por Opera N 30:14-15 D 18 '65

BROWNS (football club) See Football clubs

BROWNSON, Orestes Augustus
Orestes Brownson. F. E. McMahon. Commonweal 83:260 D 3 '65

BROYLES, Frank
Man for the next few seasons. D. Jenkins. il pors Sports Illus 23:30-2+ N 8 '65

BROŽEK, Josef. See Simonson, E. jt. auth.

BROZEN, Yale
Automation: a job creator not a job destroyer; excerpts from address. por U S News 58:94-8+ Mr 8 '65

BRUBACHER, John S.
Deeper bases of policy in higher education; excerpt from Bases for policy in higher education. bibliog f Sch & Soc 93:308-19 Sum '65

BRUBAKER, Claude A.
Church in the Wildwood. C. West. il por Am For 71:8-9 Je '65

BRUBAKER, R. R. and others
Pasteurella pestis: role of pesticin I and iron in experimental plague. bibliog Science 149:422-4 Jl 23 '65

BRUBAKER, Robert L.
Manuscripts make history. Hobbies 70:110-11+ Ja '66

BRUCE, Betty
I dreamed I went on a photo safari with Betty Bruce & my Nikon F; interview, ed. by K. Burroughs. il por Mod Phot 29: 36+ O '65

BRUCE, Charles M.
Fruits and nuts of the South. Horticulture 43:38-9+ F '65

BRUCE, Helen Finn
Command performance: newest one-act cameras. House & Gard 128:72+ N '65

BRUCE, Lenny
Books. M. Muggeridge. Esquire 64:65-6 N '65

BRUCE, Robert. See Robert I, king of Scotland

BRUCITE
Brucite in carbonate secreted by the red alga goniolithon sp. R. F. Schmalz. bibliog il Science 149:993-6 Ag 27 '65
Brucite in the calcareous alga goniolithon. J. N. Weber and J. W. Kaufman. bibliog il Science 149:996-7 Ag 27 '65

BRUCKER, Herbert
Crack in Canon 35. Sat R 48:48-9 Jl 10 '65
Mass man and mass media; adaptation of address. Sat R 48:14-16+ My 29 '65

BRUCKNER, Anton
Bruckner; from Lyrichord, the E minor Mass. J. Diether. il Am Rec G 31:788-90 My '65
From Furtwängler; the true Brucknerian affinity. A. Rich. il Hi Fi 15:78-9 S '65
Furtwängler Bruckner. C. J. Luten. Am Rec G 31:1052-3 Jl '65
Musical events; performance of Bruckner's Fifth symphony by N.Y. philharmonic. W. Sargeant. New Yorker 41:121-2 My 29 '65
Musical events; performance of Bruckner's Ninth symphony by N.Y. philharmonic. W. Sargeant. New Yorker 41:150 F 20 '65

BRUDER, W. H.
This parking garage. Am City 80:98-100 D '65

BRUGGHEN, Hendrick ter. See Terbrugghen, H.

BRUHN, Erik
Interview with Erik Bruhn; ed. by O. Maynard. por Dance Mag 40:22-3 Ja '66

about
High & the mighty. il Time 86:62 D 10 '65
Melancholy Dane. il por Newsweek 66:92-3 D 13 '65
Toronto: excitement. il pors Dance Mag 39: 22-3 F '65

BRUMBERG, Abraham
Cold wind from Moscow: detente illusions die hard. Reporter 33:40-2 O 21; 10 D 2 '65
End to Soviet censorship? New Repub 153: 19-21 O 2 '65

BRUMEL, Valerii
Warm visit with a Russian rival; with account by J. Thomas. il pors Life 58:69-70+ Je 18 '65
What the men can do for an encore. G. S. Brown. il por Sports Illus 22:45-7 Mr 1 '65

BRUMMELL, O. B.
Folk music (cont) Hi Fi 15:121-2 Mr; 95 My; 81 Jl; 123-4 S; 54 N '65; 16:42 Ja '66

BRUN, Helen L.
New York's Finger Lakes point to pleasure. Motor B 116:22-5 Jl '65

BRUN, J.
Genetic adaptation of caenorhabditis elegans (nematoda) to high temperatures. Science 150:1467 D 10 '65

BRUNCHES
Open house A.M; P.M; Christmas entertaining; with recipes. il McCalls 93:118-21+ D '65
Party; Sunday morning brunch. il Ladies Home J 82:114-15+ O '65
Saucepans and the single girl; excerpts. J. Kragen and J. Perry. il Ladies Home J 82:94+ Ag '65
Spring weekend brunches. D. Durham. il Ladies Home J 82:86-9+ Ap '65
Weekend brunch. il Bet Hom & Gard 53: 76-7+ N '65
BRUNER, Louise
Landscape paintings of Richard Kozlow. Am Artist 29:54-9+ My '65
BRUNHOFF, Jean de
Babar pays us a visit at last. il Life 59:107-9 N 26 '65
BRUNHOFF, Laurent de
Babar pays us a visit at last. il por Life 59: 107-9 N 26 '65
BRUNING, Walter F.
Multipurpose equipment for all seasons; excerpts from address, 1964. Recreation 58:493 D '65
BRUNO, Chris
Discovery. P. Caulfield. il Mod Phot 29:62-3+ O '65
BRUNSWICK, Ohio
Industry wasn't interested. K. Hotz. il Am City 80:32 O '65
BRUNTON, Frank M.
Pyrannosaurus Rex; F. M. Brunton charging Bishop Pike with heresy. il Newsweek 66: 56 Ag 30 '65
BRUSH, Charles F.
Pox pottery; earliest identified Mexican ceramic. bibliog Science 149:194-5 Jl 9 '65
BRUSH fires
Brush fire warning system. Sunset 135:115 O '65
BRUSHES
Brush with beauty. S. Harney. il Ladies Home J 82:48 Je '65
See also
Paint brushes
BRUSSELS
Architecture
Modern Medici. il Time 86:44-7 Ag 13 '65
Galleries and museums
Century of Rubens; exhibition at Brussels' Royal museums of fine arts. il Newsweek 66:93 D 6 '65
Music
Brussels. L. Mueller. Opera N 30:34 D 25 '65
Brussels ups and downs. L. Mueller. Opera N 29:31 Ap 3 '65
BRUST, Paul
Furniture selection and specification. Arch Rec 138:93+ S '65
BRUSTEIN, Robert
Russian evenings. New Repub 152:26-8 F 27 '65
Theater. See issues of New republic
Who's killing the novel? New Repub 153:22-4 O 23; 36-7 N 13 '65
BRUTON, Paul W.
Law of church and state; address, October 13, 1965. Vital Speeches 32:149-54 D 15 '65
BRY, Ilse, and Afflerbach Lois
Bibliographical challenges in the age of the computer; excerpts from editorial. Library J 90:813-18 F 15 '65
BRYAN, C. D. B.
Sade: chronicles of a misanthrope. New Repub 153:20-3 O 30 '65
BRYAN, Diana
Notes for the hostess. See issues of House & garden incorporating Living for young homemakers
BRYAN, Pack
Electronic clinics for sick cars. Pop Mech 125:116-19+ Ja '66
Gary Player tests fiberglass clubs. Pop Mech 124:86-7 Ag '65
BRYAN, William Jennings
Defender of the faith, by L. W. Levine. Review
Christian Cent 82:1481 D 1 '65. C. Anderson
BRYANT, Anita
Person who changed my life. por Seventeen 24:157+ Ap '65
BRYANT, Deborah
Discovery of Miss America. D. L. Goodrich. il pors Sat Eve Post 238:36-41 N 6 '65
What Miss America is made of. J. Canaday. il por N Y Times Mag p 124+ S 19 '65
BRYANT, Nelson
Bog-trot for trout. por Outdoor Life 135: 46-7+ Ap '65

BRYANT, Paul
'Bama plows them under. J. Underwood. il por Sports Illus 23:36-9 D 6 '65
Southern football: the Bear of Alabama. G. Astor. il por Look 29:101+ N 16 '65
BRYCE, Dorothy
Calories do count. Nation 200:351-2 Ap 5 '65
BRYN MAWR, Pa.
Try a multi-bed filter. K. E. Shull. il Am City 80:77-9 N '65
BRYN MAWR college, Bryn Mawr, Pa.
Another kind of castle; dormitory. J. M. Dixon. il Arch Forum 123:58-65 N '65
BRYSON, John
Marilyn Monroe. Pop Phot 58:144+ Ja '66
BRZESKA, Henri Gaudier-. See Gaudier-Brzeska, H.
BRZOSTOSKI, John
Patination of bronzes. Craft Horiz 25:26-31 N '65
BUBAS, Vic
Mr Bubas' business. il por Time 86:71 D 31 '65
BUBBLE bath. See Bath preparations
BUBBLE chambers
Please explain; what is a bubble chamber? I. Asimov. il Sci Digest 58:86-7 Ag '65
BUBER, Martin
All life is a meeting. por Time 85:82 Je 25 '65
He made the universal transparent. Christian Cent 82:796 Je 23 '65
Martin Buber. Commonweal 82:461 Jl 2 '65
Martin Buber: in memoriam. R. Niebuhr. Sat R 48:37 Jl 24 '65
Martin Buber. RIP. W. Herberg. Nat R 17: 539 Je 29 '65
Presence of greatness. por Newsweek 65: 76 Je 28 '65
Two great men. America 113:38 Jl 10 '65
Wise old teacher of I-thou. F. Kappler. pors Life 58:97-8 Je 25 '65
BUBONIC plague. See Plague
BUCHAN, Alastair
Arms nobody wants to control. New Repub 153:17-18 N 6 '65
Changed setting of the Atlantic debate. For Affairs 43:574-86 Jl '65
Onward and upward with Herman Kahn. New Repub 152:19-21 Je 5 '65
BUCHAN, John, 1st baron Tweedsmuir
Founding father. il por Newsweek 67:87A-87B Ja 17 '66
BUCHANAN, Ian. See Buchanan, K. jt. auth.
BUCHANAN, James M.
Economists and economists. Nat R 17:777-8+ S 7 '65
BUCHANAN, Kirsten, and Buchanan, Ian
Family quiz game. Parents Mag 40:24+ S; 42+ O; 36+ N; 24+ D '65
BUCHANAN, Wiley T. Jr
It's the most fascinating job in Washington. por Life 58:74-5 Mr 12 '65
BUCHANAN, William
Politics and federalism: party or anti-party? bibliog f Ann Am Acad 359:107-15 My '65
BUCHER, Charles A.
Health, physical education, and academic achievement. NEA J 54:38-40 My '65
BUCHHEISTER, Carl W.
President reports to you. See issues of Audubon magazine
BUCHINGER, Maria
To save our natural resources. Américas 17: 26-31 Ag '65
BUCHMAN, Frank Nathan Daniel
M.R.A: the new Druseanism. M. E. Marty. Christian Cent 82:399-401 Mr 31 '65
BÜCHNER, Georg
Danton's death. Criticism
America 113:647-8 N 20 '65
Christian Cent 82:1578 D 22 '65
Commentary 41:55-6+ Ja '66
Commonweal 83:191-2 N 12 '65
Nation 201:370-1 N 15 '65
New Repub 153:37-8 N 6 '65
New Yorker 41:108+ O 30 '65
Newsweek il 66:86-7 N 1 '65
Reporter 34:43 Ja 13 '66
Sat R 48:41 N 6 '65
Time 86:84 O 29 '65
Vogue 146:146 D '65
Leonce and Lena. Criticism
Nation 202:26-7 Ja 3 '66
BUCHSBAUM, Walter H.
Color-TV ghosts. Electr World 74:33-5 D '65
Electronic intrusion alarms. Electr World 73:25-8 Je '65
Line-operated transistor TV sets: RCA. Electr World 74:32-3 N '65
New soldering tools and techniques. Electr World 73:46-8+ F '65

BUCHWALD, Art
Anatomy of a revolt; reprint. Sch & Soc 93: 371-2 O 16 '65
Art Buchwald. por Ladies Home J 82:26 Ap; 55 Je; 12 N '65
Art Buchwald on taxes, LBJ, automation, the stock market and a whole bunch of other things; interview. pors Nations Bsns 53: 38-40+ Ag '65
Here I am, back at Alcatraz East. pors Life 59:70-4+ Ag 13 '65
Liz and I. por Ladies Home J 83:26 Ja '66
Visit that didn't come off. Read Digest 86: 235-6 F '65

about

Capital wit of Art Buchwald. il pors Newsweek 65:47-51 Je 7 '65
If Goldwater had won; A. Buchwald on President Johnson's policy in Vietnam. Time 85:72 Mr 19 '65

BUCK, Dorothy
So you want to work in Europe next year. Dance Mag 39:32+ O '65

BUCK, Griffith J.
What causes plant hardiness? Horticulture 43:22-3 O '65

BUCK, Jim
Coach. New Yorker 40:24-6 F 6 '65

BUCK, Pearl (Sydenstricker)
At home with Pearl Buck. por Ladies Home J 82:36 Jl '65
Come in Mary. Read Digest 87:229-30+ N '65
Joy of children; excerpts. Read Digest 87: 145-53 Jl '65
My world (cont) Ladies Home J 82:36+ Mr '65

BUCK, Robert N.
Man who makes me think young. Read Digest 86:259-60+ Ap '65

BUCK, Warren L. See Schmidt, K. H. jt. auth.

BUCKINGHAM, Frank, and Fletcher, W. J.
Get ready for fall plowing. Suc Farm 63:40-1 O '65

BUCKLER, Helen
Surgeon who dared; excerpt from Doctor Dan. Todays Health 43:46-7+ S '65

BUCKLEY, Kevin P. and Cotton, Richard
Chicago: the marchers and the machine. Reporter 33:30-1 N 4 '65

BUCKLEY, Priscilla L.
How Margaret took Sherman. Nat R 18:33-4 Ja 11 '66
Notes on a tenth anniversary. por Nat R 17: 1113-15 N 30 '65
Theater (cont) Nat R 17:561-2 Je 29 '65

BUCKLEY, William Frank, 1925–
American dream and the American Negro. por N Y Times Mag p88-9 Mr 7 '65
Approaching end of Edgar H. Smith, jr. Esquire 64:116-20+ N '65
On the right. See issues of National review
Remarks at the anniversary dinner; November 11, 1965. por Nat R 17:1127-9 N 30 '65
Remarks to the New York police department Holy name society, April 4, 1965. Nat R 17:324-6 Ap 20 '65
Statement by Wm. F. Buckley jr. announcing his candidacy for mayor of New York, June 24, 1965; with questions and answers. por Nat R 17:586-9 Jl 13 '65
Statement sent to the press, November 3, 1965. Nat R 17:1014 N 16 '65
Statement to the friends of National review. Nat R 17:448 Je 1 '65

about

Bill Buckley, how to have a certain amount of fun. por Newsweek 66:28-9 S 20 '65
Bouquet for Buckley. Christian Cent 82:1028 Ag 25 '65
British press postscript. J. Fletcher. il Nat R 18:25-6 Ja 11 '66
Buckley; campaign in Manhattan. New Yorker 41:50-1 O 30 '65
Buckleyism forever? K. Crawford. Newsweek 66:49 N 15 '65
Defending the police. Commonweal 82:100 Ap 16 '65
Different kind of candidate. por Time 86:18 Jl 2 '65
Religion in the N.Y. mayoral campaign. J. Leo. Commonweal 83:170 N 12 '65
Special election supplement; symposium. il Nat R 17:973-82 N 2 '65
Tongue-in-cheek candidate; with excerpts from conversations, ed. by S. Angeloff. il pors Life 59:49-50+ S 17 '65
Very dark horse in New York. J. Leo. il pors N Y Times Mag p8-9+ S 5 '65
William F. Buckley, jr. M. Kempton. New Repub 153:9 Jl 10 '65

BUCKMAN, Gertrude
All in all, a most enlightening happening. Mlle 61:162-3+ O '65
House can be a home. Mlle 61:148-9 S '65

BUCKMAN, Thomas R.
Sweden's net book agreement ended by government board. Pub W 187:26-31 My 3 '65

BUCKOW, Ed
To catch a king. Field & S 70:96-8+ D '65

BUCKWALTER, Len
Extension speakers. Hi Fi 15:70-3 Mr '65
New citizens band circuits (cont) Electr World 73:48-9 Mr; 48-50 My; 74:65-7 S; 60-1 N '65
Tape for turnpikes. Hi Fi 15:42-4+ Je '65
Transistorized ignition; status 1965. Pop Electr 22:35-42+ Je '65

BUCYRUS-Erie company
Digging out from under. il Bsns W p 106-7+ Ag 28 '65

BUDAPEST

Music

Mad for music. E. Helm. Hi Fi 15:134-5 My '65

BUDDHA and Buddhism
Buddhism: a serene religion, and political dynamite? il Sr Schol 86:10-13+ Mr 25 '65
Year and a half too late; New York times' reporting of political turmoil in South Vietnam. America 112:412 Mr 27 '65

BUDDHIST sculpture. See Sculpture, Buddhist

BUDDHISTS
Last days for South Vietnam? close look at latest crisis. R. P. Martin. il U S News 58:36-7 F 8 '65
Manipulators; Buddhism as a political force in Vietnam. il Newsweek 65:37 F 8 '65
Our friends, the Buddhists; impending purge of Catholic generals from the South Vietnamese armed forces. America 112:597 Ap 24 '65

BUDELL, Elizabeth E.
What does the local representative do? address, July 1964. ALA Bul 59:303-5 Ap '65

BUDGET

Great Britain

Britain's budget: a blow to pride and purse. il Newsweek 65:77-9 Ap 19 '65
Letter from London (cont) M. Panter-Downes. New Yorker 41:174-6 Ap 17; 98+ Ag 14 '65
Next-to-last defense. Time 86:80-1 Ag 6 '65
Penny stupid, pound foolish. Nat R 17:313 Ap 20 '65
Toward deflation? Time 85:33-4 Ap 16 '65

Russia

Bad omens. Newsweek 66:39 D 20 '65

United States

Art of unbalancing the budget; potential GNP. N. W. Chamberlain. il Atlan 217: 58-62 Ja '66
As bankers look at the new economics; symposium. il U S News 58:86-90 Je 21 '65
Atlantic report; President, working on new budget. Atlan 216:6 D '65
Budget escalates; $12-billion added for Vietnamese war, with editorial comment. Bsns W p27-8, 114 Ja 8 '66
Budget lifts the old lid. il Bsns W p27-8 S 4 '65
Budget of the United States government for the fiscal year ending June 30, 1966; excerpts from message to Congress, January 25, 1965. L. B. Johnson. il Dept State Bul 52:207-11 F 15 '65
Budget: portrait of a growing nation; Johnson calls for $99.7-billion. il Bsns W p78-80+ Ja 30 '65
Budget swing from give to take will be less than expected for '66. U S News 59:104 D 6 '65
Budgetry; concerning President Johnson's State of the Union message. H. C. Wallich. Newsweek 67:77 Ja 24 '66
Burdens on the budget. il Fortune 71:32+ Je '65
Catching the rabbit. Time 86:11 D 24 '65
Changed morality of a boom budget. Life 58: 4 F 5 '65
Cracks in the ceiling. Time 86:16 S 10 '65
Cult of deficits. H. Hazlitt. Newsweek 65:81 F 15 '65
Cutting the melon. H. C. Wallich. Newsweek 65:74 F 8 '65
Decisions under the gun; with editorial comment. il Bsns W p 11-13, 84 D 25 '65
Dilemma of the budget. America 114:36 Ja 8 '66
Directional signals. Nation 200:125 F 8 '65
Great fiscal debate. H. J. Samuels; W. F. Carey. Duns R 85:52-3+ F '65

BUDGET—United States—Continued

How Congress may bust the budget. C. B. Seib. il Nations Bsns 53:38-9+ Mr '65

How federal spending will soar in '66, war or no war. il U S News 60:75-7 Ja 10 '66

How last year's budget came out. U S News 59:66 Ag 2 '65

How LBJ wins at the budget game; with editorial comment. il Bsns W p30-1, 160 Je 26 '65

It's still a one-way budget: up. il U S News 58:75-8 F 1 '65

Johnson administration budget science oriented. Sci N L 87:105 F 13 '65

LBJ's budget: a closer look. il U S News 60:90-1 Ja 24 '66

LBJ's budget dilemma. H. Hazlitt. Newsweek 67:79 Ja 17 '66

LBJ's budget dilemma: cut or tax. il Newsweek 67:12-13 Ja 3 '66

LBJ's budget: set for bigger war. U S News 60:31 Ja 17 '66

LBJ's new budget. Nat R 17:91-2 F 9 '65

Now it's the surplus problem. Time 86:83 Jl 16 '65

Our unbalanced federal budget. D. Lawrence. Read Digest 86:103-4 Ap '65

Phoney baloney in welfare spending. R. A. Freeman. il Nat R 17:823-6 S 21 '65

President proposes two amendments to 1966 Department budget. Dept State Bul 52:388 Mr 15 '65

Real budget: it's up six billions. il U S News 58:88-9 F 8 '65

'66 budget; war takes precedence over the Great society. G. L. Perry. New Repub 153:12-15 D 25 '65

State of the Union. R. Hotz. Aviation W 84:21 Ja 17 '66

State of the Union, and the war: President prepares message. il Newsweek 67:15-16 Ja 17 '66

State of the Union; concerning President's message. America 114:113 Ja 22 '66

Story of 127 billion dollars; where some of the billions go. il U S News 58:29-32 F 8 '65

Union & the war; concerning State of the Union address. il Time 87:19-19B Ja 21 '66

Vietnam puts squeeze on the Great society; with editorial comment. il Bsns W p31, 132 D 18 '65

Vietnam war threatens the Great society budget. R. H. Smith. Pub W 189:74 Ja 10 '66

War costs set pace for jump in spending. il Bsns W p28-30 D 4 '65

Where does all the money go? J. D. Weaver. il McCalls 93:26+ Ja '66

Where your money goes. il Nations Bsns 53:38-9 S '65

Whittled, hacked & squeezed. il Time 87:21A-21B Ja 14 '66

Will business tempo start to slow '66? impact of Johnson's programs. il Bsns W p60+ F 13 '65

See also

Taxation—United States

United States—Appropriations and expenditures

United States—Budget, Bureau of the

BUDGET, Household

Budgeting back home; a lesson for Mr Gordon. M. Gordon. Read Digest 87:49 O '65

Eating low on the hog. A. B. Spalding. il Harper 230:139-40+ Mr '65

Family money management; questions and answers. N. Kuehnl and G. Bush. See issues of Better homes and gardens

Home furnishings; how much people spend; guide for budgeting. il Changing T 19:13-15 Ag '65

How to match your money to your dreams; with group discussion program, by C. W. Mattuck. P. McLean. il Parents Mag 40:58-9+, 130-1 F '65

Live better, spend less; cost-cutting formula. il Changing T 19:21-3 Je '65

Monthly survey of family budgets in the U.S.S.R. J. W. DePauw. bibliog f il Mo Labor R 88:681-7 Je '65

Poker problems. il Good H 161:12+ S '65

So you think you don't need a budget. il Changing T 19:33-5 O '65

BUDGET, Library. See College libraries—Finance

BUDGET, Personal

Be sure your budget is this year's model. Changing T 20:47 Ja '66

Kids and money; with case history of the Martin family of Barrington, Ill. G. Zimmermann. il Look 29:49-53+ N 2 '65

Mother, I'd rather buy it myself! excerpts. G. Frank. il Seventeen 24:132-3+ S '65

We never say we can't afford it. B. J. Boots. il Farm J 90:75 Ja '66

See also

Estate planning

Finance, Personal

Saving and savings

BUDGET bureau (United States) See United States—Budget, Bureau of the

BUDGETS, Library. See Libraries—Finance

BUDKA, Metchie J. E.

(tr) See Niemcewicz, J. U. Visit to Mount Vernon

BUDY, Ann M.

Biology of hard tissues. Science 151:225-6 Ja 14 '66

BUECHLER, James

Ambulance driver; story. Sat Eve Post 238:64-6 Ap 24 '65

Second-best girl; story. Redbook 126:36-7 Ja '66

BUECHNER, Georg. See Büchner, G.

BUECHNER, Thomas S.

How's that again. Mod Phot 29:112+ S '65

BUEGELEISEN, Sally

Abbott's rib. pors Flying 77:34-7+ Ag; 68-72 S '65

Skirts flying. por Flying 77:22 N; 20 D '65; 78:28 Ja '66

BUENOS AIRES

Music

Buenos Aires. G. Knepler. il Opera N 30:32-3 D 11 '65

Season's start at Teatro Colón. E. Arnosi. Hi Fi 15:166 S '65

Tucker at the Colon; opera program for 1965. M. T. Meyer. Sat R 48:63 Ag 28 '65

BUETTNER-JANUSCH, John, and Hill, R. L.

Molecules and monkeys. bibliog Science 147:836-42 F 19 '65

BUFALINI, J. J. and Purcell, J. C.

Nitrogen: formation by photooxidation of ethylene in the presence of its oxides. bibliog Science 150:1161 N 26 '65

BUFFALO, N.Y.

Can this be Buffalo? Festival of the arts today, at the Albright-Knox gallery. il Life 58:63-4+ Ap 23 '65

Project Buffalo; workshops, seminars, lecture-demonstrations by members of New York city ballet. J. P. Dwyer. il Dance Mag 40:54-5 Ja '66

Galleries and museums

See also

Albright-Knox art gallery

Libraries

See also

Buffalo and Erie County, N.Y. public library

Music

Foss. New Yorker 40:22-4 Ja 30 '65

Theater

Broadway postscript; rebirth of Studio arena theatre. H. Hewes. Sat R 48:74 O 23 '65

BUFFALO AND ERIE COUNTY, N.Y. public library

Buffalo bridges its site. J. B. Rounds and P. M. Rooney. il Library J 90:5173-5 D 1 '65

BUFFALO Bills (football club) See Football clubs

BUFFALO meat

If you hunger for buffalo. il Sunset 135:213-14+ O '65

BUFFALO philharmonic orchestra

New frontier: the word is out; Buffalo report. J. Dwyer. Hi Fi 16:146+ Ja '66

BUFFALO RIVER, Ark.

Buffalo River. J. Heuston. il Travel 124:56-9 Ag '65

BUFFALO university. See New York state university—University at Buffalo

BUFFALOES

Artist as buffalo hunter. H. Dinnerstein. il Esquire 64:184-9 D '65

To each his own buffalo. R. Bongartz. il Sat Eve Post 238:22 O 23 '65

BUFFET meals

Five great D.I.Y. parties, do it yourself; with recipes. il Seventeen 24:146-9+ O '65

Give a cool party; with menu. H. Worth. il Parents Mag 40:69-72+ Ag '65

Outdoors if the weather's good, indoors if it isn't. il Sunset 134:172-3 Ap '65

BUGS; drama. See White, J.

BUILDING

Building a new house: no trauma; excerpts from House in the country. N. Fairbrother. Vogue 145:210+ My '65

Giant venture in Viet Nam; large and swift construction programs. il Time 86:86 D 17 '65

BUILDING—*Continued*
Monthly review of events and ideas. Arch Forum 123:1 Jl; 17-20+ S; 13-16+ O; 11-14+ N; 9-12+ D '65
Some radical proposals. il Esquire 64:222-3 D '65
Structure & design. W. McQuade. See issues of Fortune
See also
Concrete construction
Foundations
Framing (building)
Heating
Masonry

Contracts and specifications
How one office handles problems in specifying new materials. il Arch Rec 138:104-5 S 65

Cost
Building construction costs. W. H. Edgerton. See issues of Architectural record
Is great architecture worth what it costs? E. Goble. Arch Rec 138:9 S '65
Record houses 1965 comparative building costs for selected cities. il Arch Rec 137:134-5 mid-My '65
See also
Housing—Costs

Employees
See Building workers

Finance
No increase seen in long-term interest rates. G. A. Christie. il Arch Rec 137:18 My '65

Statistics
Current construction trends. G. A. Christie. See issues of Architectural record
F. W. Dodge construction outlook for 1966. il Arch Rec 138:121+ N '65
BUILDING, Ice and snow
Processed snow may be used for polar houses. Sci N L 87:293 My 8 '65
See also
Snow houses
BUILDING, Stormproof
Buildings that stood up to Betsy; prefab resort abuilding. il Bsns W p56+ S 25 '65
BUILDING and construction trades department. See American federation of labor and Congress of industrial organizations—Building and construction trades department
BUSINESS and droughts. See Weather and business
BUILDING and earthquakes. See Earthquakes and building
BUILDING fittings
Never-before building materials that will change the way you live. il House & Gard 129:112-15 Ja '66
Product reports. See issues of Architectural record

Bibliography
New literature for home-planning. Arch Rec 137:182+ mid-My '65
BUILDING industry
Builders fight to stay even; residential construction. Bsns W p25-7 Ag 21 '65
Building pace is stalled; with charts. Bsns W p 190+ O 23 '65
Canada takes chill off winter unemployment; building of public works and houses. il Bsns W p 118+ Ja 15 '66
Employment effects of construction expenditures. C. M. Ball. il Mo Labor R 88:154-8 F '65
Fuse is lit for another office building boom. il Bsns W p28+ Jl 24 '65
German programs to curb winter construction layoffs. E. M. Bussey. Mo Labor R 88:434-7 Ap '65
His bets are lit on real estate; T. Crow. il Bsns W p 140+ S 18 '65
Homebuilders try to sell a city; Philadelphia-area builders woo families to be transferred by Defense dept. il Bsns W p60+ Ap 3 '65
Houses, anyone? slump in southern California. Newsweek 66:92 N 15 '65
Housing takes a long view. il Bsns W p23-4 Ap 24 '65
How to make a quick million in real estate. D. M. Friedenberg. il Esquire 63:122-3+ Je '65
Investors move into the dorms. il Bsns W p47-8+ N 6 '65
Italy's new empire; projects in Africa. il Fortune 72:74+ O '65
Menace of the bulldozers; excerpts from study. J. O. Brew. il UNESCO Courier 18:33-6 Ja '65

Preview of housing for 1966. R. Charles. il Parents Mag 41:69-71+ Ja '66
Rolling readjustment. Time 85:84+ Je 11 '65
What's happened to the building boom? interview. G. C. Smith. il U S News 59:90-5 N 29 '65
See also
Fuller, George A, company
BUILDING machinery industry and trade
See also
Koehring company
BUILDING materials
Giant wave of wood; redwood structure. Hydraulic laboratory. E. J. Long. il Am For 71:31+ Ag '65
How one office handles problems in specifying new materials. il Arch Rec 138:104-5 S '65
Never-before building materials that will change the way you live. il House & Gard 129:112-15 Ja '66
New growth rings for U.S. plywood. il Bsns W p72-5 Jl 24 '65
New materials for quick remodeling. A. J. Maher. il Pop Mech 124:133-7 S '65
New products for improving walls and ceilings. il Pop Sci 187:124-5 S '65
Product reports. See issues of Architectural record
Products you can use to improve your home. il Pop Sci 186:162-3 Mr '65
Why buy brand names? Bet Hom & Gard 43:34 F '65
See also
Bricks
Flooring
Roofing
Siding (building)
Tiles

Bibliography
New literature for home-planning. Arch Rec 137:182+ mid-My '65
BUILDING research
Progress in building a research project puts new techniques to the test of use. E. T. Shiffer. il Arch Forum 123:80-3 Jl '65
BUILDING sites
Integrated site planning and design for a small college; Concordia Lutheran junior college, Ann Arbor, Mich. il Arch Rec 138:189-96 S '65
Modular steel frame raises house above seasonal floods. il Arch Rec 137:78-81 mid-My '65
See also
Hillside architecture
Housing projects—Site planning
BUILDING workers
Grass-roots social justice; employment in building St Mary's cathedral. America 113:392 O 9 '65
Ironworker on high. il Ebony 20:64-6+ Mr '65
BUILDINGS
Focus: monthly review of notable buildings. il Arch Forum 123:26-9 N; 26-9 D '65
See also
Medical buildings
BUILDINGS, Prefabricated
See also
Houses, Prefabricated
BUILDINGS, Remodeled
Old mill streamlined; 237-year old grain mill, Solingen, Germany. B. Plumb. il N Y Times Mag p 136-7 N 14 '65
See also
Houses, Remodeled
Remodeling (architecture)
BUILDINGS, Restoration of. See Architecture —Conservation and restoration
BUILDINGS, Temporary. See Air pressure support
BUILDINGS, Underwater. See Underwater structures
BUILDINGS, Wrecking of. See Wrecking
BUILDINGS in art. See Architecture in art
BUITRAGO, Fanny
Dirty heron; story. Américas 17:30-2 Mr '65
BUITRON, Diana
In my opinion. por Seventeen 24:194 D '65
BUKSTEIN, Ed
Alpha-com. Pop Electr 23:81-2 N '65
Computer control of industrial processes. Electr World 74:42-3+ D '65
Computers in business. Electr World 73:41-3 F '65
Readout indicators for solid-state computers. Pop Electr 22:49-52+ Mr '65
Scientific computers. Electr World 73:34-5+ Mr '65

BULB planters. See Garden tools, equipment and supplies

BULBS
Big spring color from small bulbs. H. Mason. il Bet Hom & Gard 43:66-7+ N '65
Bulbs. J. A. Eaton. il Horticulture 43:20-1+ S '65
Bulbs for winter bloom. il Flower Grower 52:20 N '65
For bulb color from January onward. il Sunset 135:256-7 O '65
It's bulb planting time. R. M. Peters. il Pop Gard 16:40-7 S '65
News about bulbs. Flower Grower 52:16 O '65
One way we manage our bulbs at Sunset. il Sunset 135:263 O '65
Out of the ordinary small bulbs. J. Thibodeau. il Horticulture 43:28-9 Mr '65
Pot spring bulbs now for color and fragrance this winter. J. Shiels. il Horticulture 43:24-5+ O '65
Sample summer's riches. E. S. Henderson. il Pop Gard 16:36-7 Ap '65
Small gems for your rock garden. B. Miles. il Pop Gard 16:22-3+ N '65
Spring bulbs for the terrace. il Flower Grower 52:22 O '65
These strangers all are happy here. il Sunset 135:182-3 S '65
See also
Amaryllis
Crocuses
Forcing (plants)
Narcissus
BULBS, Light. See Electric lamps
BULGAKOV, Mikhail
Dead souls; dramatization of novel by N. V. Gogol'. Criticism
New Repub 152:26-8 F 27 '65
New Yorker 40:76+ F 13 '65
Sat R 48:43 F 20 '65
Time il 85:78 F 12 '65
BULGARIA
Balkan welcome. P. L. Fermor. Holiday 37:82-3+ My '65
Experiments with reforms stir Bulgarian interest. il Bsns W p 194 N 20 '65
Most faithful. il Newsweek 66:40+ Jl 5 '65

Politics and government
Black sheep; anti-government plotters. il Time 85:39B Ap 30 '65
Coup that failed. Newsweek 65:46 My 3 '65
BULGARIA and the United States
I remember Dobry. R. H. Wagner. il Horn Bk 41:342-8 Ag '65
BULGARIAN literature
See also
Childrens literature—Bulgaria
BULGARIAN poetess; story. See Updike, J.
BULGE, Battle of the. See Ardennes, Battle of the, 1944-1945
BULGER, Ruth Ellen, and others
Endoplasmic reticulum in rat renal interstitial cells; molecular rearrangement after water deprivation. bibliog Science 151:83-6 Ja 7 '66
BULKELEY, Houghton. See Chase, A. R. jt. auth.
BULL fights. See Bullfights
BULL RUN, First battle of, 1861
So eager were we all; condensation, with an introd. by B. Catton. L. H. Metcalf. il Am Heritage 16:32-41 Je '65
BULLARD, Robert W. See Van Beaumont, W. jt. auth.
BULLETIN boards
Bulletin boards as teaching aids; Alexander Hamilton high school, Los Angeles. S. Cochell. Sr Schol 87:sup6 N 4 '65
That bulletin board in the hall. I. Beaudoin. il Design 67:41 N '65
BULLETS
Blast away indoors with wax bullets. il Pop Mech 124:132-4 O '65
Bullet's the thing. J. O'Connor. il Outdoor Life 135:116+ Je '65
Controlled expanding bullets. W. Page. il Field & S 69:112-17 Mr '65
Now, a bullet without a case. H. Bradshaw. il Pop Sci 187:173 O '65
Point of the bullet. W. Page. il Field & S 69:108-10+ F '65
Selection of hunting bullets. J. B. Miller. Consumer Bul 48:16-18 O '65
See also
Cartridges
BULLFIGHTERS
Death of the afternoon. il Time 86:41 S 24 '65
Five against the gods. R. Daley. il Esquire 64:98+ N '65
BULLFIGHTS
Afternoon in Spain; excerpts. M. Simont. il Horizon 7:118-20 Autumn '65

Beatnik of the bull ring; El Cordobés; with account by L. Hall. il Life 59:62D-68 Ag 6 '65
Brain control by radio; electrical stimulation of the brain. J. A. Osmundsen. il Pop Mech 124:130-3+ N '65
Crazy month; controversial El Cordobés, aiming at title of número uno. E. Gress. il Newsweek 66:68 Ag 23 '65
John Fulton, artist & matador. I. Murdoch. il Am Artist 29:22-7+ Ap '65
¡Olé! for the brave Club Taurino! paintings. M. Simont. Sports Illus 23:32-9 Ag 23 '65
Radio-controlled bullfight; experiment controlling the brain externally. il Sci Digest 58:38-9 Ag '65
Spaniards discover bullfighting. R. Daley. il N Y Times Mag p32-3+ Ag 29 '65
Speaking of shooting the bull; bullfight pictures. L. Barry. il Pop Phot 56:16+ Ap '65
BULLFROGS. See Frogs
BULLOUGH, Vern L.
Streetwalking, theory and practice. por Sat R 48:52-4 S 4 '65
BULLS
Beef bull costs dairyman $400 per calf. Farm J 89:D10 Ap '65
Sex and the single bull; operation performed on prize bull, Lindertis Evulse. il Newsweek 66:53 Ag 2 '65
This helps you select better A1 bulls. Farm J 89:46 My '65
BULTMANN, Rudolf Karl
Profiles; concerning Honest to God, by J. Robinson. V. Mehta. New Yorker 41:64+ N 13 '65
Schweitzer letter presented by librarian; excerpts from letter to R. Bultmann. A. Schweitzer. Wilson Lib Bul 40:217+ N '65
BUMBA, V. and Howard, Robert
Solar magnetic fields. bibliog Science 149:1331-7 S 17 '65
BUMPERS, Door. See Door stops
BUNDRA, Mike
But why me, coach? G. Plimpton. il pors Sports Illus 23:18-21 D 13 '65
BUNDY, Carter F.
New Floridian; the scarlet ibis. Audubon Mag 67:84-5 Mr '65
BUNDY, McGeorge
International cooperation; a realistic appraisal; address, March 23, 1965. Dept State Bul 52:562-5 Ap 19 '65
Low marks for the professors. por Time 85:24 My 7 '65
Uses of responsibility; reply to A. MacLeish. por Sat R 48:13-14+ Jl 3 '65
Viet-Nam: winning the peace; television interview, August 23, 1965. Dept State Bul 53:431-44 S 13 '65
White House conference on international cooperation; address, November 29, 1965. Dept State Bul 53:970-3 D 20 '65

about
Attacks in retaliation. il por Time 85:13 F 12 '65
Bundy and beyond. H. Brandon. Sat R 49:18 Ja 22 '66
Dear McGeorge; LBJ accepts resignation. il por Newsweek 66:24-5 D 20 '65
Everybody's catalyst. por Time 86:19 D 17 '65
Importance of being Bundy. M. Frankel. il pors N Y Times Mag p32-3+ Mr 28 '65
Second traveler. il por Newsweek 65:38 F 15 '65
Top trouble shooter; why LBJ relies on Bundy. U S News 58:15 My 31 '65
Two powerful men who stayed. R. Dudman. por Esquire 64:94+ N '65
Two worlds of McGeorge Bundy. J. Kraft. Harper 231:106+ N '65; Discussion. 232:8 Ja '66
Use of power with a passion for peace. il pors Time 85:26-9 Je 25 '65
BUNDY, Mary Lee, and Thornton, M. V.
Who runs ALA? excerpts from Social and political aspects of librarianship. Library J 91:67 Ja 1 '66
BUNDY, William Putnam
American policy in South Viet-Nam and southeast Asia; address, January 23, 1965. Dept State Bul 52:168-75 F 8 '65
Department officers discuss Viet-Nam situation. Dept State Bul 52:291-4 Mr 1 '65
Japan and the United States; the essentials of partnership; address, October 25, 1965. Dept State Bul 53:777-80 N 15 '65
Korea, a free-world partner in the Far East; address, September 20, 1965. Dept State Bul 53:593-6 O 11 '65

BUNDY, William Putnam—*Continued*
Perspective on U.S. policy in Viet-Nam; address, May 27, 1965. Dept State Bul 52: 1001-5 Je 21 '65
Perspective on U.S. policy in Viet-Nam; address, November 5, 1965. Dept State Bul 53:890-4 D 6 '65
Progress and problems in the Far East; address, October 5, 1965. Dept State Bul 53:709-16 N 1 '65
Reality of myth concerning South Viet-Nam; address, May 13, 1965. Dept State Bul 52:890-6 Je 7 '65
United States expresses views on Laurel-Langley agreement; statement, March 8, 1965. Dept State Bul 52:664 My 3 '65
U.S.-Japanese trends and prospects; address, October 30, 1965. Dept State Bul 53:770-7 N 15 '65

about
Touch of tyranny. R. F. Hamilton. Nation 201:75-8 Ag 16 '65
BUNGE, Charles A.
(comp) Statewide public library surveys and plans, 1944-64. ALA Bul 59:364+ My '65
BUNK beds. See Beds
BUNKE, Harvey C.
Priests without cassocks. Harvard Bsns R 43:103-9 My '65
BUNKER, Ellsworth
Cooperating for progress in Latin America; address, February 27, 1965. Dept State Bul 52:465-71 Mr 29 '65
OAS foreign ministers provide for establishment of inter-American force in Dominican Republic; statements, May 1-14, 1965. Dept State Bul 52:854-69 My 31 '65
OAS Secretary General to represent meeting of consultation of Dominican Republic; Brazilian to command inter-American force; statements and notes, May 15-22, 1965. Dept State Bul 52:908-12 Je 7 '65
U.S. acts to meet threat in Dominican Republic; statement, April 30, 1965. Dept State Bul 52:739-42 My 17 '65
United States and Latin America; special ties of interest and affection; address, January 30, 1965. Dept State Bul 52:301-4 Mr 1 '65

about
Bunker and Bung. Reporter 32:8 My 6 '65
BUNKER, Patricia
Titles to thaw out by. Sat R 48:35-6 Ap 17 '65
BUNKS, Boat. See Yachts—Berths
BUNN, Martin
Gus Wilson's model garage (title varies) See issues of Popular science monthly
BUNNY Berigan: wasn't he a musician or something? story. See Cormier, R.
BUNTING, J. Whitney
(ed) See Dirksen, E. M. Congress and business; Senators Mansfield and Dirksen debate outlook
(ed) See Mansfield, M. Congress and business; Senators Mansfield and Dirksen debate outlook
BUNTING, Mary Ingraham
Experiment in womanhood. A. P. Cooper. por Sat R 48:52-3 Mr 6 '65
BUÑUEL, Luis
Luis Buñuel: an eye in the wilderness. R. Carson. por Holiday 37:123-4+ Ap '65
BUONINSEGNA, Duccio di. See Duccio di Buoninsegna
BUOYANT vests. See Life saving suits
BUOYISH fishing. See Tripletail fishing
BUOYS
Weather buoy-satellite link is studied; meteorological buoys. W. H. Gregory. il Aviation W 82:54-5+ F 8 '65
BURAU, R. and Stout, P. R.
Trans-aconitic acid in range grasses in early spring. bibliog Science 150:766-7 N 5 '65
BURBANK, Calif.
Growing voluntary hospital complex; St Joseph's hospital. il Arch Rec 137:170-2 F '65
BURBANK, Calif. public library
Education vs. culture. T. Schoenman. ALA Bul 60:27-30 Ja '66
BURCH, Claire
We leave our house. Good H 161:44+ Ag '65
BURCH, Dean
Dean Burch's view: most Americans are conservative; excerpts from address. February 15, 1965. por U S News 58:16 Mr 1 '65
Speaking out. por Sat Eve Post 238:12+ Mr 27 '65

about
Final refrain. Newsweek 65:27 Mr 15 '65

BURCK, Charles
Valley's lopsided boom. Fortune 73:131 Ja '66
BURCK, Gilbert H.
Boiling world of oil. Fortune 71:126-31+ F '65
Guns, butter, and then-some economy. Fortune 72:118-21+ O '65
Union carbide's patient schemers. Fortune 72:146-53+ D '65
U.S. oil: a giant caught in its own web. Fortune 71:113-19+ Ap '65
World's biggest merger. Fortune 71:176-9+ Je; 72:128-31+ Jl '65
BURDEN, Amanda Mortimer
Goodbye Jackie, hello Amanda! pecking order among the world's best-dressed women. il por Time 87:56 Ja 21 '66
BURDEN, Jean
Charwoman at St Patrick's; poem. Sat R 48:84 My 15 '65
For Hildegarde who received for Christmas a moon-window in a wall; poem. Sat R 48:40 F 13 '65
BURDICK, Eugene
Three Californias. Holiday 38:60-75 O '65

about
Obituary
Pub W 188:34-5 Ag 9 '65
BUREAU of intelligence and research. See United States—State, Department of—Intelligence and research, Bureau of
BUREAU of ships. See United States—Navy department—Ships, Bureau of
BUREAUCRACY
Bitter refrain: orders from Washington; Vietnam fighting front. il U S News 59:40 D 27 '65
Bureaucrats and citizens. D. E. Ashford. bibliog f Ann Am Acad 358:89-100 Mr '65
Crisis management: Berlin, Cyprus, Laos. J. C. Ausland and H. F. Richardson. For Affairs 44:291-303 Ja '66
HEW: running the Great society. E. Langer. il Science 150:1272-4 D 3 '65
Men may come, and men may go; attempt to save a man from the electric chair in Pennsylvania. W. F. Buckley, jr. Nat R 17:683 Ag 10 '65
New Soviet oligarchy. C. W. Thayer. Harper 230:64-8+ Ap '65
Politics of bureaucracy, by G. Tullock. Review
Nat R 18:75-6 Ja 25 '66. J. Chamberlain
BUREAUS of the United States government. See name of bureau, inverted under United States, e.g. United States—Indian affairs, Bureau of
BURFORD, William
Barcelona; Space; Future? it was the beginning; poems. Poetry 106:338-40 Ag '65
High office; poem. Nation 201:287 O 25 '65
Local God; poem. Sat R 48:61 O 9 '65
BURG, Carol Ann. See Trainor, F. R. jt. auth.
BURG, Ellen A. See Burg, S. P. jt. auth.
BURG, Stanley P. and Burg, E. A.
Ethylene action and the ripening of fruits. bibliog Science 148:1190-6 My 28 '65
BURGART, Herbert
Toward a new art. il Sch Arts 65:5-9 O '65
BURGDERFER, Donald E.
It's an icicle world up close. U S Camera 28:16+ F '65
BURGE, Boyce W. and Pfefferkorn, E. R.
Conditional-lethal mutants of an animal virus: identification of two cistrons. bibliog Science 149:959-60 My 14 '65
BURGER, Chester
Meanwhile, back on earth, where's 3-D today? Pop Phot 57:56-9+ S '65
World's fair picture-taking & exposure guide. il Pop Phot 56:62-7+ Ap '65
BURGESS, Anthony
Docter Rowse meets Dr Faustus. Nation 200:115+ F 1 '65
BURGESS, Bob
Quiet boom in the Bahamas. Field & S 70:48-50+ Ja '66
BURGESS, Howard
Watchdog mobile monitor. Pop Electr 23:67-8+ O '65
BURGESS, Jackson
Affluent poor. Esquire 63:82-7+ Ap '65
BURGESS, Lorraine
Busy hands make happy holidays. Flower Grower 52:28-9 D '65
Gardener's kitchen. il Flower Grower 53:46-7 Ja '66
Homemade sauna. il Flower Grower 52:50-1 F '65
Practical & pretty: crocks to cover up pots. il Flower Grower 52:48 Ag '65
Shopping center with take-home ideas. il Flower Grower 53:34-5 Ja '66
Weathered treasures. il Flower Grower 52:26 Ag '65

BURGESS, Quentin
Tribute to Dr Wesley. por Negro Hist Bul 28:103 F '65
BURGESS, Robert F.
New bream bonanza. Field & S 69:130-2+ F '65
Spooky grays of Tate's hell. pors Outdoor Life 136:48-51+ Jl '65
BURGESS, Roger
Whatever happened to the temperance movement? Christian Cent 82:984-7 Ag 11 '65
BURGESS, Thornton Waldo
Obituary
Pub W 187:80 Je 14 '65
BURGHARDT, Gordon M. and Hess, E. H.
Food imprinting in the snapping turtle, chelydra serpentina. bibliog Science 151: 108-9 Ja 7 '66
BURGLAR alarms
Burglar alarm for boats. J. F. Jayne. il Motor B 115:175+ Je '65
Magic box that thiefproofs your car. R. M. Benrey. il Pop Sci 188:164-7+ Ja '66
Simple self-resetting tamper-alarm; automotive burglar alarm system. R. Seese. il Pop Electr 23:61-2 Jl '65
BURGLARY and burglars
Beachboy caper. J. Roth. Esquire 64:118-19+ S '65
New target of thieves: fashionable D.C. area. il U S News 58:12 F 8 '65
BURGNER, Jack
Metal casting for the grades. Design 67:32-7 S '65
Twenty minute puppets. Sch Arts 65:5-9 N '65
BURIAL, Cost of. See Funerals, Cost of
BURIANEK, Elizabeth T.
Confidentiality of student records. NEA J 55:28+ Ja '66
BURIED treasure; drama. See Barr, J.
BURK, Bill E.
(ed) See Johnson, H. Less than a plumber
BURKE, Betsy
What stress can do to you and for you. Parents Mag 40:45+ Ap '65
BURKE, Carl F.
Parables for cool squares. il por Time 85:44 Mr 5 '65
BURKE, Dennis J.
Teaching religion in Catholic high schools. por Cath World 201:113-18 My '65
BURKE, Edmund
Relevance of Edmund Burke, ed. by P. J. Stanlis. Review
Nat R 17:112-13 '65. S. J. Tonsor
BURKE, Edward W. Jr, and Rolland, W. W.
New observatory at King college in Tennessee. pors Sky & Tel 30:172-6 S '65
BURKE, Frank
Thrifty spy on the Sixth avenue el. E. Wittenberg. il Am Heritage 17:62-4+ D '65
BURKE, Helena
Going places, finding things in Corfu. House & Gard 127:42-4+ My '65
BURKE, Herbert C.
Sight is the eye of the mind; poem. Commonweal 81:672 F 19 '65
BURKE, Jack, Jr
Jack and Jimmy hold a bash in the Big Thicket. A. Wright. il por Sports Illus 22: 62-3 Mr 29 '65
BURKE, James
Himalayas; photographs. Life 58:56-68 My 28 '65
BURKE, Kenneth
Technology and insight. G. S. Fraser. Poetry 106:366-8 Ag '65
BURKE, Marvin E.
Long-distance jumper on the ski wear trail. il pors Bsns W p 140-1 F 27 '65
BURKE, Thomas A.
Book reviews. America 113:347-8 S 25 '65
BURKETT, Lowell A.
Conversation on industrial arts and vocational education; interview. por NEA J 54:25-8 N '65
BURKHALTER, Lois
My real friend, Joe. Am Heritage 16:44-5 Ap '65
BURKHARDT, Robert
De Gaulle and ABC enter their bids. New Repub 153:8-9 O 23 '65
Flying porkbarrels. New Repub 153:11 Ag 7 '65
Over a billion for the first plane. New Repub 153:10-11 Jl 3 '65
Washington clipboard. See issues of Flying
BURKHOLDER, Paul R. and Mandelli, E. F.
Productivity of microalgae in Antarctic Sea ice. bibliog Science 149:872-4 Ag 20 '65
BURKS, David D.
Cuba seven years after. Cur Hist 50:38-44 Ja '66

BURLANT, Louise, and others
Control of enzyme activity in growing bacterial cells by concerted feedback inhibition. bibliog Science 148:1351-3 Je 4 '65
BURLESQUE. See Vaudeville
BURLINGTON industries, incorporated
Weaving a profit pattern. il Bsns W p72-4+ Mr 6 '65
BURLS
If you are sure they are burls, you can ignore them. il Sunset 135:158 Jl '65
BURMA
Behind closed doors. R. K. McCabe. il Newsweek 67:20+ Ja 3 '66

Politics and government
Strength through weakness. il Time 85:28-9 Mr 5 '65
See also
Socialism—Burma
BURMA-Shave signs. See Advertising, Outdoor
BURMAN, Ben Lucien
Computer critic's Christmas. Sat R 48:44-5 D 4 '65
Opal miners of Lightning Ridge. Read Digest 86:171-6 Je '65
BURMEISTER, Walther
Potassium-40 content as a basis for the calculation of body cell mass in man. bibliog Science 148:1336-7 Je 4 '65
BURNERS, Oil. See Oil burners
BURNET, Alastair
(ed) See Ball, G. W. Mr Ball discusses U.S. relations with Europe on BBC
about
Top people's paper. il por Newsweek 65:84 Ap 26 '65
BURNETT, C. R.
Anomalous abundance of upper atmosphere sodium, 1964. bibliog Science 147:736-7 F 12 '65
BURNETT, Constance Buel
Frances Hodgson Burnett: episodes in her life; excerpt from Happily ever after. Horn Bk 41:86-94 F '65
BURNETT, Frances Hodgson
Racketty-Packetty house; dramatization. See Kimball, R. P.
about
Frances Hodgson Burnett: episodes in her life; excerpt from Happily ever after. C. B. Burnett. il Horn Bk 41:86-94 F '65
BURNETT, Ivy Compton-. See Compton-Burnett, I.
BURNETT, Wayne
Wisconsin warrior; photographs. J. Cooke. Sports Illus 22:28-33 Je 21 '65
BURNHAM, Daniel Hudson
Americans not everybody knows. C. W. Ferguson. il por PTA Mag 60:18-20 D '65
BURNHAM, Donald Clemens
Remarks on talent search. Sci N L 87:164 Mr 13 '65
BURNHAM, James
Open question. Nat R 17:720 Ag 24 '65
Third world war. See issues of National review
about
Burnham on medicare; letters to the editor. Nat R 17:750 S 7 '65
BURNHAM, Philip
Unreasonable. New Yorker 41:35-6 Mr 27 '65
BURNHAM, Walter Dean
Back to the drawing board. Commonweal 81: 780-2 Mr 19 '65
Elections. Commonweal 83:233-6 N 26 '65
Goldwater rallies the troops. Commonweal 82: 552-5 Ag 6 '65
BURNING mill; story. See Dethier, V. G.
BURNING of land
See also
Weeds—Control by fire
BURNING of weeds. See Weeds—Control by fire
BURNING; story. See Cady, J.
BURNS, Arthur Edward
Rising cost of overkill. Sat R 48:26 Ag 7 '65
BURNS, Arthur F.
Danger signs in the boom? warning from a top economist; excerpts from address, October 26, 1965. por U S News 59:104-5 N 8 '65
Top economist's formula for keeping the boom alive; excerpts from address, November 9, 1965. por U S News 59:94+ N 22 '65
Wages and prices by formula? address. Harvard Bsns R 43:55-64 Mr '65

BURNS, Eveline M.
　Poor need money. Nation 200:613-15 Je 7 '65
　Welfare programs in evolution. Mo Labor R
　88:294-5 Mr '65
BURNS, Haywood
　Rule of law in the South. Commentary 40:
　80+ S; 24 D '65
BURNS, James MacGregor
　Psychology of the radical right. Sat R 48:
　37-8 D 25 '65
　Shadow presidency. Nation 201:115-18 S 6 '65
　Sting of responsibility. Harper 230:118+ F
　'65
BURNS, John Lawrence
　Businessmen in the news. por Fortune 72:
　41 Ag '65
　On top again. Time 86:74+ Jl 2 '65
BURNS, John T. and Riker, A. P.
　Today's hospital techniques save ailing new-
　borns. Parents Mag 40:46-7+ Ap '65
BURNS, Leroy
　Shoeshine. New Yorker 41:40-1 My 22 '65
BURNS and scalds
　Black magic; healing qualities of silver
　nitrate. il Time 85:73 Mr 5 '65
　Burn treatment improved. Sci N L 88:295
　N 6 '65
　End to X-ray agony? Time 86:101 O 22 '65
　Filigree of skin: new grafting technique for
　severe burns. il Life 59:51+ O 29 '65
　Germ-free bubble; airtight plastic keeps out
　infection. il Life 58:39-40+ Je 4 '65
　New burn treatment: silver nitrate. Sci Di-
　gest 57:21 Je '65
　New burn treatments. Sci Digest 58:37 Jl
　'65
　New help for the burn-injured child; Shrin-
　ers burns institutes. G. E. Maxwell. il To-
　days Health 43:43-5+ Jl '65
　Synthetic skin aids burns. Sci N L 88:243 O
　16 '65
　Synthetic skin tests lift hopes in burn cases.
　il Bsns W p52 D 4 '65
BURNSIDE, Orvin C.
　How to avoid a herbicide residue problem. Suc
　Farm 63:70F Ap '65
BURRESS, Lee A. jr
　Censorship and the public schools: address,
　January 1965. bibliog por ALA Bul 59:491-9
　Je '65
BURRIER, Tom
　Electrifying race. Motor B 115:60 F '65
　Round Whidbey outboard marathon. Motor B.
　116:26+ Jl '65
BURROS, Daniel
　Jewish Nazi. il por Newsweek 66:110-12 N
　15 '65
　Klansman's secret. por Time 86:54 N 12 '65
BURROUGHS, John
　Control the contrast. Pop Sci 186:120-4 My
　'65
　Fourth rule for soft soldering. Pop Sci 186:
　130-3+ Mr '65
　How to cut metal with woodworking power
　tools. Pop Sci 186:128-30 Je '65
　Improving your home wiring. Pop Sci 187:
　159-63+ N '65
　In appliances, it's the contacts that count.
　Pop Sci 186:156-9 F '65
　Make your own arc welder. Pop Sci 187:142-
　5+ N '65
BURROUGHS, Ken
　(ed) See Bruce, B. I dreamed I went on a
　photo safari with Betty Bruce & my
　Nikon F
BURROUGHS, R. D.
　Lewis and Clark expedition's botanical dis-
　coveries. Natur Hist 75:56-62 Ja '66
BURROUGHS, William
　New immoralists. W. Phillips. Commentary
　39:66-9 Ap '65; Discussion. 40:10+ Ag '65
BURROWING owls. See Owls
BURROWS, Abe
　Abe Burrows: what he does to earn $2,000
　a day. E. J. Kahn, jr. pors McCalls 92:
　116-17+ F '65
　Cactus flower; adaptation of play by P. Bar-
　illet and J. P. Grédy. Criticism
　　America 114:54 Ja 8 '66
　　Commonweal 83:410 Ja 7 '66
　　New Yorker 41:152+ D 18 '65
　　Newsweek il 66:92 D 20 '65
　　Sat R 48:41 D 25 '65
　　Time il 86:40 D 17 '65
BURROWS, Larry
　One ride with Yankee Papa 13; photographs.
　Life 58:24-34C Ap 16 '65
BURSA of Fabricius. See Birds—Physiology
BURSK, Edward C.
　Businessman's bookshelf. Sat R 49:87-8 Ja
　8 '66
BURSON, Phyllis S.
　Project opportunity in Corpus Christi. por
　Wilson Lib Bul 40:257-61 N '65

BURT, Nathaniel
　Presidents in the family. Sat R 48:37 Jl 10
　'65
BURTON, Richard
　Burton writes of Taylor. Vogue 145:128-33 Mr
　1 '65
　Joy. McCalls 93:25 D '65

about

　King and queen. J. Hamilton. il por Look 29:
　26-8+ Mr 9 '65
　Mind and heart of Richard Burton. il pors
　Good H 160:84-7+ Je '65
BURTON, Sybil
　I've never done anything with more clarity
　in my life; interview, ed. by D. Lurie. por
　Life 58:78 Je 25 '65

about

　Can a simple Welsh lass of thirty-six find
　happiness with a Macedonian rock-and-roll
　star of twenty-four? E. Dundy. il pors
　Esquire 64:164-5+ D '65
　Rise and surprise of Sybil Burton. il pors
　Life 58:72-7 Je 25 '65
　Wild scene at Arthur. L. Bergquist. il pors
　Look 29:40-2+ N 30 '65
BURTON, Thomas E.
　Translator and publisher: the popular tech-
　nical book. Pub W 187:62-4 Ap 19 '65
BURTON, Walter E.
　Cutting glass. Pop Mech 124:148-55+ O '65
　Machine a hole-aligner. Pop Sci 188:143 Ja
　'66
　Make a model Tesla turbine. Pop Mech 124:
　188-93 S '65
　Three trays you can make. il Pop Sci 187:
　148-51 N '65
　You can make your own deep-hole drill. Pop
　Mech 124:166-8 Ag '65
BURTT, E. T. and Catton, W. T.
　Perception by locusts of rotated patterns.
　Science 151:224 Ja 14 '66
BURUNDI
　Bahutu are restless; abortive coup. Newsweek
　66:48+ N 1 '65
　Dark days for the rule of law. Time 87:40 Ja
　14 '66
　Josy and the king. il Newsweek 67:41 Ja 24
　'66
　Lesson of sorts; Chinese Ambassador expelled.
　il Time 85:29-30 F 12 '65
　Lucky Mwami; revolt caused by tribal rival-
　ry. Time 86:37 O 29 '65

Native races

　Bahutu are restless; animosities between
　Watusi and Bahutu. Newsweek 66:48+ N 1
　'65
BURZELL, Linden R.
　Water service beyond the meter. Am City
　80:122-3+ O '65
BUS; story. See Jackson, S.
BUSBY, Edward O.
　Busby wins American city aid-to-education
　award. Am City 80:12 O '65
BUSCH, August A. jr
　Conversation with Gussie Busch, ed. by W.
　Leggett. por Sports Illus 22:50-1 Ap 19 '65

about

　Busch, beer and baseball. L. Koppett. il pors
　N Y Times Mag p32-3+ Ap 11 '65
BUSCH, Noel F.
　John Marshall Harlan: today's great dis-
　senter. Read Digest 86:201-4+ Je '65
　Red Skelton: television's clown prince. Read
　Digest 86:145-8 Mr '65
BUSH, George. See Kuehnl, N. jt. auth.
BUSH, Janet
　Let's travel: on the high seas. Mlle 61:183-6
　O '65
　University of the Seven Seas. Mlle 60:147-9
　F '65
BUSH, John William
　Old ways at the ICC nearing end of line.
　por Bsns W p74 Ja 1 '66
BUSH, Monroe
　Reading about resources. See issues of
　American forests
BUSH, Vannevar
　Churchill and the scientists. Atlan 215:94-
　101 Mr '65
　Limitations of science. por Time 85:81 My 7
　'65
　Science pauses. por Fortune 71:116-19+ My
　'65
BUSH-BROWN, Albert
　Return of playfulness. House & Gard 127:
　116-17+ Je '65

BUSH babies. See Lemurs

BUSHNELL, Horace
Nature and the supernatural in the theology of Horace Bushnell, by W. A. Johnson. Review
    Christian Cent 82:176 F 10 '65. F. Kirschenmann

BUSINESS
Needs of business; talent and knowledge; address, June 5, 1965. J. T. Connor. Vital Speeches 31:583-6 Jl 15 '65
Tiny flame; competition and profit; address, October 26, 1965. R. G. Wingerter. Vital Speeches 32:158-60 D 15 '65
    See also
Airplanes in business
Christmas business
Free enterprise
Industrial mobilization
Location in business and industry
Marketing
Monopolies
Retail trade
Success

Bibliography
Business books of 1964; comp. by J. B. Woy. il Library J 90:1048-52 Mr 1 '65
Business books to come; ed. by J. Putnam and J. Lindheim. Library J 90:4810-19 N 1 '65
Business books to come; ed. by J. Putnam and R. Grossman. Library J 90:1150-8, 3078-82 Mr 1, Jl '65
Businessman's bookshelf. E. C. Bursk. Sat R 49:87-8 Ja 8 '66
Executive bookshelf. See issues of Dun's review and modern industry
How to start a business library; in one easy lesson. C. Georgi. il Library J 90:1058-62 Mr 1 '65

Directories
Global yellow pages; International yellow pages. il Time 86:102+ S 24 '65

Exhibitions
    See Exhibitions

Foreign expansion
Bonds across the sea; overseas-bond-financing technique. Time 87:81-2 Ja 14 '66
Executives abroad: the American way overseas. il Nations Bsns 53:58-60+ Mr '65
Passport for world markets; government and foreign investment; address, June 21, 1965. R. R. Eppert. Vital Speeches 31:663-8 Ag 15 '65
Science, technology and the gold drain. P. H. Abelson. Science 147:989 F 26 '65; Discussion. 148:894; 149:583 My 14, Ag 6 '65
Technologically, the Atlantic community exists. V. K. McElheny. Science 149:1080-2 S 3 '65
U.S. business stake in Europe. il Newsweek 65:67-8+ Mr 8 '65
Yankees who don't go home; American businessman abroad. il Bsns W p48+ Jl 24 '65
    See also
Corporations—Foreign subsidiaries

Forms, blanks, etc.
Business forms and controls. il Duns R 86: pt2 146-8+ S '65
    See also
Business records

History
Traditional role of management. W. G. Caples. bibliog f Cur Hist 49:9-16+ Jl '65

International aspects
Breaking the red's sound barrier; support of Radio free Europe by American businessmen. il Bsns W p 108-10 Je 12 '65
Business and industry in International cooperation year. A. B. Trowbridge. Dept State Bul 53:406-11 S 6 '65
Hunters behind the Curtain; west European businessmen. il Time 86:107 D 10 '65
International management; address, October 5, 1965. D. A. Shepard. Vital Speeches 32: 178-81 Ja 1 '66
Labor relations abroad; American business overseas. T. R. Brooks. Duns R 86:75-6 N '65
LBJ strikes a balance for business. il Newsweek 65:69-70 Mr 1 '65
U.S. factoring leaps Atlantic; First national of Boston led parade, followed by Heller of Chicago. Bsns W p86+ Ja 30 '65
World business: what to expect. See issues of Nation's business

Bibliography
Guides to international operations; descriptive writings, practical guides, analyses, and case studies. W. S. Barnes. Harvard Bsns R 43:26-8+ N '65

Periodicals
There's no business like business. N. L. Cahners; reply. M. M. Badler. Sat R 48:141+ Mr 13 '65

Political aspects
After fifteen months, what businessmen think of LBJ. il U S News 58:98-102 F 22 '65
Anti-communism & the corporations. A. F. Westin; discussion. Commentary 37:19-24 Ap; 14 Je; 38:6 N '64; 39:14+ F '65
Big business & the Democrats; excerpts from What is power? D. T. Bazelon. Commentary 39:39-46 My '65
Business and the G.O.P. J. Berry. il Duns R 86:34-6+ D '65
Business as usual; Toward an age of greatness, souvenir book of U.S. industry. Newsweek 66:26 D 20 '65
Business, Washington, and conflict of interest; interview, ed. by J. Berry. L. L. Strauss. Duns R 86:48-50+ O '65
First thirty-five years of Fortune; with editorial comment. H. R. Luce. il Fortune 71:115-16, 136-7+ F '65
How businessmen size up LBJ, outlook, spending, hiring. il U S News 58:94-5 My 10 '65
Johnson and the businessmen. G. R. Rosen. il Duns R 85:40-3+ My '65
LBJ and business now; not quite so friendly. U S News 58:82 Je 14 '65
LBJ and businessmen; climate gets cooler. il U S News 59:39-41 N 29 '65
Our growing responsibilities in a changing world; address, December 8, 1964. G. Champion. Vital Speeches 31:282-5 F 15 '65
Power of big business. R. L. Heilbroner. Atlan 216:89-93 S '65
What business wants from Lyndon Johnson. E. K. Faltermayer. il Fortune 71:122-5+ F '65
Why politics is for you. G. Champion. il Nations Bsns 53:40-1+ Mr '65
Why Washington needs more businessmen. V. R. Alden. il Duns R 86:36-7+ Ag '65

Public relations
Ford's citizenship program. L. L. L. Golden. Sat 48:77 F 13 '65
Not by divine right; corporate manager's role. L. L. L. Golden. Sat R 48:129 S 18 '65
Turnaround boys; Lippincott & Marguiles, inc. il Time 86:84 Jl 16 '65
Where do they come from? L. L. L. Golden. Sat R 48:60-1 Ag 14 '65

Small business
    See Small business

Social aspects
Auto safety: new study criticizes manufacturers and universities. E. Langer. Science 150:1136-9 N 26 '65
Business can save America's cities. L. Smith. il Nations Bsns 53:38-9+ N '65
Capitalism today. B. B. Seligman. Commentary 39:88-90 Ap '65
Is the corporation above the law? J. F. A. Taylor. bibliog f Harvard Bsns R 43:119-30 Mr '65
Let there be light. Duns R 85:39 My '65
Responsibility for social change; business or government? R. W. Austin. Harvard Bsns R 43:45-52 Jl '65

Anecdotes facetiae, satire, etc.
Silvertoe; financial adventure of James Debenture. W. L. Safire. il Harvard Bsns R 43:110-18 My '65

BUSINESS, Retirement from. See Retirement from business, etc.

BUSINESS airplanes. See Airplanes, Business

BUSINESS and art. See Art and industry

BUSINESS and droughts. See Weather and business

BUSINESS and education
Academic fund raising: yesterday and today. C. C. Brown. Sch & Soc 93:240-2 Ap 17 '65
Bright key, by M. E. Spaght. Review
    Sat R 48:60 Ag 21 '65. A. T. Hill
Business lectures professors; Monsanto woos chemistry graduates to marketing by teaching their teachers. il Bsns W p65-6 Jl 10 '65
Colleges soft sell fund pleas; use of executive seminar to win over potential donors. il Bsns W p81-2+ D 11 '65

BUSINESS and education—Continued
Corporations and education. L. L. L. Golden. Sat R 48:100-1 N 13 '65
Letter from the publisher; Time, inc. in partnership with GE to serve education. B. M. Auer. Time 86:19 N 26 '65
New firm will finance educational technology. Pub W 188:30-1 Jl 26 '65
See also
Business education

BUSINESS and professional women
Behind every successful woman: outstanding Thai businesswomen. il Time 86:91-2 D 17 '65
Girl in Georgetown; Jo Ann Christiansen. C. S. Wren. il Look 29:93-6 Ap 6 '65
Is someone kidding the college girl? creativity in college, then typing in a NY office. J. Shepherd. il Look 30:36-8 Ja 11 '66
Ivy league girls on the road. M. Decter. il Esquire 64:103+ S '65
See also
Women as executives

BUSINESS and state. See Industry and state

BUSINESS and the community. See Business —Social aspects

BUSINESS and war. See War—Economic aspects

BUSINESS and weather. See Weather and business

BUSINESS charts
Corporate charts go global. Bsns W p52+ S 11 '65

BUSINESS communication. See Communication in management

BUSINESS conditions
Bill Martin's red flag; similarities between our present prosperity and the fabulous '20s. il Time 85:83 Je 11 '65
Business and finance. See issues of Newsweek
Business outlook. See issues of Business week
Business roundup. See issues of Fortune
Business tides. H. Hazlitt. See issues of Newsweek
Caution signal. Duns R 86:31 Jl '65
Cities in U.S. where business is best; with charts (cont) U S News 58:82-5 Je 7; 59: 74-8+ N 29 '65
Confidence high, pace brisk. il Bsns W p25-6 Je 26 '65
Excise tax cut; any effects on business? il U S News 59:86 Jl 12 '65
How Europe sees outlook for U.S. boom. il U S News 59:32-5 Jl 5 '65
Just a hint of chill; no recession in sight; with editorial comment. il Bsns W p23-6, 140 Je 5 '65
Keeping up a hot pace; gains in GNP and corporate profits. il Bsns W p 19-20 Jl 24 '65
Key to continued growth. Bsns W p 160 Jl 10 '65
Myth of the inevitable cycle. Bsns W p96 Jl 3 '65
No dog days in business. il Bsns W p25-6 Jl 17 '65
Now 1966: problems of prosperity. il Newsweek 67:49-52 Ja 10 '66
Plus & minus; business activity of the week. See issues of U.S. news & World report
Spotlight on business. See issues of Newsweek
Then and now. H. C. Wallich. Newsweek 65:92 Je 14 '65
Trend of American business. See issues of U.S. news & World report
Trend of business. J. Phillips. See issues of Dun's review and modern industry
What the boom did for people and business in 1965. il U S News 60:76-7 Ja 3 '66
See also
Business depression
Business forecasting
Economic conditions
Inflation (finance)
also subhead Economic conditions under names of countries, states, e.g. Canada—Economic conditions

BUSINESS conferences
Letter from the publisher; gathering of Time-Life international advertising directors and Russian advertising officials in Moscow. B. M. Auer. il Time 86:25 N 12 '65
Martinis for breakfast. Newsweek 65:79 Mr 1 '65
Stauffer board meeting moves south of border; to Mexico City. il Bsns W p 112-14 F 6 '65
See also
Business meetings
International industrial conference

BUSINESS consolidations and mergers
ABC's for ITT. Newsweek 66:82-3 D 13 '65
Anatomy of a big deal; Continental oil co. to acquire Consolidation coal co. il Time 86:106+ O 22 '65
Antitrust gets a new gospel. Bsns W p27 Ag 14 '65
Big skid at Yale express. R. J. Whalen. il Fortune 72:144-9+ N '65
Can you merge? now even government isn't sure. il U S News 58:102-3 My 24 '65
Clore's next coup? offer to take over Selfridges. il Newsweek 66:78+ N 1 '65
Curious pursuit of Pure oil. T. A. Wise. il Fortune 72:112-15+ Jl '65
Easing the pangs of growth. il Bsns W p 108-10 Jl 24 '65
Fizz & chips; Pepsi-Cola to merge with Frito-Lay, inc. Time 85:88+ Mr 5 '65
Goulash in the making; Restaurant associates to merge with Waldorf system, inc. il Time 85:94+ My 21 '65
Into the $1 billion club. Time 86:69 Ag 20 '65
McGraw-Hill delays merger with Standard & Poor's. Pub W 188:67 D 27 '65
McGraw-Hill set to acquire Standard & Poor's. Pub W 188:55 O 25 '65
Marriage brokers; merger brokers. Time 86: 109 N 19 '65
Mating call; electronics firms marrying technology to academe. Newsweek 67:74+ Ja 24 '66
Merger: bad word in U.S. lifesaver to Europe. il U S News 58:120-1 My 17 '65
Mergers and acquisitions. B. R. Wakefield. bibliog Harvard Bsns R 43:6-8+ S '65
Natural; merger of Società Montecatini and Società Edison, Italy. Newsweek 66:51 D 27 '65
New colossus; proposed I.T.&T.-ABC merger. Time 86:53 D 17 '65
New look in mergers frowned on by FTC. Bsns W p 136 Mr 13 '65
Passing the sweets; American tobacco company moves to acquire Chicago's Consolidated foods corp. Time 85:84+ F 12 '65
Perilous quest for acquisitions. J. B. Weiner. il Duns R 86:32-5+ Jl '65
Prize union; merger negotiations with California's Union oil co. Time 85:86+ F 26 '65
Putting facts together; Standard & Poors to merge with McGraw-Hill. Time 86:92 O 29 '65
Rash of mergers: new crackdown? il U S News 58:72 Mr 29 '65
Report on Washington; debate on how to bring antitrust laws up to date. Atlan 216: 8+ Ag '65
Some questions about mergers; attitude of government; address, September 27, 1965. G. H. Love. Vital Speeches 32:9-12 O 15 '65
Supercolossus; merger between Montecatini and the Edison group. il Time 86:56 D 24 '65
T.R.B. from Washington; evidence about mergers gathered by the Judiciary subcommittee on antitrust and monopoly. New Repub 152:4 Ap 24 '65
Trying to spin out of trouble; consolidation and streamlining of two of Japan's leading cotton-spinning companies. il Time 86: 97 N 26 '65
What ITT is seeking from ABC. Bsns W p 144 D 11 '65
See also
Bank consolidations and mergers
Petroleum industry and trade—Consolidations and mergers
Railroads—Consolidations and mergers

BUSINESS consultants
Consultants: the men who came to dinner. W. Guzzardi, jr. il Fortune 71:138-41+ F '65
Seagram's recipe: a dash of advice; operates own management consulting service. il Bsns W p 126+ Ja 30 '65
Striking it big in oil without drilling a well; DeGolyer & MacNaughton, petroleum consulting concern. il Bsns W p60+ N 20 '65
See also
Stanley Arnold and associates

BUSINESS council
Briefing the brass. il Bsns W p30-1 My 8 '65

BUSINESS cycles
Business cycle rides a smoother wave length. Bsns W p 116 F 20 '65
See also
Business conditions

BUSINESS depression
Another 1929? why there's little chance. il U S News 58:94-5 Je 21 '65
Can we avoid a recession D. Lawrence. U S News 59:104 D 20 '65

BUSINESS depression—*Continued*
Could we ever have another depression? il
Changing T 20:7-12 Ja '66
Does monetary history repeat itself? present
& the past; address, June 1, 1965. W. M.
Martin, jr. Vital Speeches 31:580-3 Jl 15
'65; Excerpts. U S News 58:84-6 Je 14 '65;
Summary. Newsweek 65:79 Je 14 '65
No more recessions? what the planners say.
il U S News 58:36-9 F 15 '65
Washington desk; Mr Johnson intends to pre-
vent a downturn. J. R. Slevin. Duns R 86:
5-6 Ag '65
We are depression (but not recession) proof.
E. L. Dale, jr. il N Y Times Mag p36-7+ Ap
4 '65
Why recessions are obsolete. R. Newcomb.
Nations Bsns 53:62-4 My '65
See also
Business conditions
BUSINESS districts
Comeback of downtown: big plans in big
cities. il U S News 59:64-9 Jl 26 '65
Fresno mall. D. Haimbach. il Am City 80:91-
3 Ap '65
Upgrading downtown; downtown renewal. il
Arch Rec 137:175-90 Je '65
See also
Shopping centers
BUSINESS education
America's most wanted students; Seattle's
public schools' program of business edu-
cation. G. B. Leonard. il Look 29:46-51 Jl
27 '65
Changes at the source. il Time 85:92+ My 7
'65
Mating call; electronics firms marrying tech-
nology to academe. Newsweek 67:74+ Ja 24
'66
Purdue gives and gets a lesson. il Bsns W
p 186-8+ Ap 17 '65
Stately homes are B-schools for the British;
manor houses now schools for managers.
il Bsns W p52-3+ Jl 17 '65
Stumping the deans. il Bsns W p 106+ My 8
'65
They teach business how to make decisions;
incident process method. il Bsns W p72+
S 18 '65
What kind of managers for tomorrow's
world? address, January 19, 1965. M. J.
Rathbone. Vital Speeches 31:372-5 Ap 1
'65
What's new in business education? John
Marshall high school, Richmond, Va. il
NEA J 54:12-13 Ap '65
See also
American institute for foreign trade
Chicago. University—Graduate school of busi-
ness
Executives—Training
BUSINESS enterprises, New. See New business
enterprises
BUSINESS entertaining
Maybe it's deductible; entertainment expen-
diture. B. Mills. Motor B 115:50+ Mr '65
Party's over; office Christmas party. News-
week 66:70 D 27 '65
Publishing parties: their do's and don'ts.
Pub W 188:33-4 D 6 '65
Tax dodgers, British style. U S News 59:86
Jl 26 '65
BUSINESS equipment exposition. See Office
appliances—Exhibitions
BUSINESS ethics
Business administration: three recent legal
violations. New Repub 152:8 My 15 '65
Business ethics, your trade association, and
the invisible hand; address, May 10, 1965.
D. Fromson. Vital Speeches 32:28-32 O 15
'65
Down with brand X. Consumer Rep 31:6-7
Ja '66
Ethics in business. T. A. Kelly. America 113:
716 D 4 '65
When private news is public. Time 86:86
Jl 16 '65
See also
Advertising ethics
Better business bureaus
Trade practices
Trade secrets
BUSINESS expenses. See Expense accounts
(business)
BUSINESS failures
Business failures. R. Wyant. See issues of
Dun's review and modern industry
1964 failure rate drops for book-stationery
stores. Pub W 188:46 Jl 26 '65
See also
Bank failures
Bankruptcy
BUSINESS films. See Moving pictures in in-
dustry
BUSINESS flying. See Airplanes in business

BUSINESS forecasting
After steel dispute: the outlook for business.
il U S News 59:93-4 S 13 '65
Another year of good times? as LBJ sees
the future. il U S News 58:102-3 F 8 '65
Businessmen's expectations (cont) K. Dieter.
il Duns R 85:11 Mr '65
Businessmen's expectations (cont) il Duns R
85:11 Mr; 15 Je; 86:11 S; 13 D '65
Businessmen's forecast: more boom in '66.
il Nations Bsns 53:31-3+ O '65
Butter plus guns: new boom ahead? il U S
News 59:70-2 Ag 16 '65
Call it the cheerful science. Bsns W p 116
Ag 28 '65
Danger signs in the boom? warning from a
top economist; excerpts from address, Octo-
ber 26, 1965. A. F. Burns. U S News 59:
104-5 N 8 '65
Fallible forecasting. H. Hazlitt. Newsweek
66:76 Jl 19 '65
Firm of the future. H. I. Ansoff. il Harvard
Bsns R 43:162-3+ S '65
Halfway through the soaring '60s. il U S
News 58:35-6 F 15 '65
How investment bankers see outlook for 1966.
il U S News 59:94-7 D 13 '65
How thirteen leading economists see the
'66 business outlook; symposium. il U S
News 60:52-9 Ja 10 '66
Look ahead. See issues of Nation's business
Look at the odds. il Fortune 72:27-8 Ag '65
Management's forgotten sales forecast. J. D.
Louth. il Duns R 86:69+ O '65
New look at the business future; how the
forecasters see it. il U S News 59:36-41 Ag
30 '65
1966: everybody's optimistic. il Newsweek 66:
81 O 25 '65
On the long view. il Fortune 71:25-6 Ap '65
On the plateau. il Fortune 71:27-8 Je '65
Outlook now for business. il U S News 59:42-
5 Jl 19 '65
Outlook now for business: interview. J. T.
Connor. il U S News 58:72-7 My 24 '65
Presidential prophecies. H. C. Wallich.
Newsweek 66:74 Jl 26 '65
Problem: to keep a lid on; with editorial
comment. il Bsns W p 11-13, 84 Ja 1 '66
Prop for business in '66; increase in the
number of newlyweds. il U S News 58:82
Ap 19 '65
Signs still point up, with a few go-slows. il
Bsns W p92+ S 4 '65
Times are good, but ... U S News 59:106
O 25 '65
Trend of American business. See issues of
U.S. news & World report
What 1966 holds for business; excerpts from
report. W. W. Heller. U S News 59:110-11
S 27 '65
What top businessmen see ahead. il U S News
58:65 My 17 '65
Where business will grow fastest. il Nations
Bsns 53:56-8+ Ag '65
Will '60s go on soaring? business advisers
say this; with forecast by industry econo-
mists. il U S News 59:102-4 O 11 '65
See also
Forecasts (economics)
BUSINESS forms. See Business—Forms,
blanks, etc.
BUSINESS gifts. See Gifts in business
BUSINESS letters. See Commercial correspon-
dence
BUSINESS libraries. See Libraries, Business
BUSINESS literature
See also
Publishers and publishing—Business litera-
ture
BUSINESS location. See Location in business
and industry
BUSINESS management and organization
ASPC: planning for profits in publishing; re-
port on conference at Princeton inn. D.
Melcher and G. McCorkle. Pub W 187:32-5
My 10 '65
A.T.& T: a study in federalism. R. Sheehan.
il Fortune 71:142-7+ F '65
Boss will always be human; Diebold research
program. il Bsns W p 100-1 Ag 7 '65
Bureaucrats meet company brass; Brookings
institution seminars. il Bsns W p 176-8 My
22 '65
Case of the punctilious president. J. J. Han-
sen. il Harvard Bsns R 43:160-3+ N '65
Diagnosing the marketing takeover; excerpt
from Marketing management: analysis,
planning, and control. P. Kotler. il Harvard
Bsns R 43:70-2 N '65
Engineer the job to fit the manager. F. E.
Fiedler. il Harvard Bsns R 43:115-22 S '65
Executive trends. See issues of Nation's
business
Famous firsts: composer of management classics. Bsns W p84+ N 27 '65

BUSINESS management and organization—
Continued

Fine art of high-yield management. J. B. Weiner. il Duns R 86:38-41+ O '65

Firm of the future. H. I. Ansoff. il Harvard Bsns R 43:162-3+ S '65

Gaining a clearer view of the top; Brookings' dialogue for bureaucrats and corporate brass. il Bsns W p84-6 Ag 7 '65

Grass roots market research. L. W. Stern and J. L. Heskett. bibliog f il Harvard Bsns R 43:83-96 Mr '65

How business keeps prices down. R. Dreyfack. il Nations Bsns 53:34-5+ S '65

How to prevent organizational dry rot. J. W. Gardner. Harper 231:20+ O '65

How to succeed in business in Japan. Il Newsweek 65:80-2 My 17 '65

International management; address, October 5, 1965. D. A. Shepard. Vital Speeches 32: 178-81 Ja 1 '66

ITT: can profits be programmed? J. B. Weiner. il Duns R 86:38-41+ N '65

It's grow or die at Boise Cascade. T. Alexander. il Fortune 72:180-3+ D '65

Man on the moon; profit motive and change; address, March 11, 1965. R. E. Williams. Vital Speeches 31:624-9 Ag 1 '65

Management assistance for small business. L. T. White. Harvard Bsns R 43:67-74 Jl '65

Management in the coming decade; address, October 23, 1964. W. F. May. Vital Speeches 31:285-8 F 15 '65

Management of government programs S. Ramo. Harvard Bsns R 43:6-8+ Jl '65

Management's men in the middle. J. B. Weiner. il Duns R 85:38-9+ Ap '65

Managing a worldwide business. W. J. Butler and J. Dearden. Harvard Bsns R 43:93-102 My '65

Mergers and acquisitions. B. R. Wakefield. bibliog Harvard Bsns R 43:6-8+ S '65

Norton Simon says thumbs down. R. J. Whalen. il Fortune 71:146-51+ Je '65

Pendulum of management control; adaptation of address, February 10, 1965. G. E. Morse. bibliog Harvard Bsns R 43:158-60+ My '65

Personal values and corporate strategy. W. D. Guth and R. Tagiuri. bibliog f il Harvard Bsns R 43:123-32 S '65

Preparation, perspiration, participation; address, May 12, 1965. C. Daugherty. Vital Speeches 31:539-42 Je 15 '65

Product management, vision unfulfilled. D. J. Luck and T. Nowak. il Harvard Bsns R 43: 143-50+ My '65

Purposeful pursuit of profits and growth in business; address, April 7, 1965. C. G. Mortimer. Vital Speeches 31:636-40 Ag 1 '65

R&D entrepreneur: profile of success. H. Schrage. bibliog f il Harvard Bsns R 43:56-69 N '65

Team at the top. D. R. Daniel. Harvard Bsns R 43:74-82 Mr '65

Teamwork and corporate goals; amplifying the individual; address, November 11, 1964. B. E. Phillips. Vital Speeches 31:509-11 Je 1 '65

Think small. A. Uris. il Nations Bsns 53:94-6+ My '65

Traditional role of management. W. G. Caples. bibliog f Cur Hist 49:9-16+ Jl '65

Union carbide's patient schemers; with portfolio. G. Burck. Fortune 72:146-53+ D '65

What kind of managers for tomorrow's world? address, January 19, 1965. M. J. Rathbone. Vital Speeches 31:372-5 Ap 1 '65

Where small business goes wrong. L. A. Allen. il Duns R 85:60-1+ My '65

See also
Computers—Business applications
Conflict of interests (business)
Decision making
Department stores—Management
Diversification in industry
Executives
Industrial management and organization
Industrial relations

BUSINESS meetings
Business meetings add a dash of the past; Williamsburg, Va. Conference center. il Bsns W p 178-80+ N 6 '65
Business meetings: more message, less meringue. il Nations Bsns 53:40-1+ Ap '65
See also
Sales conventions
Stockholders meetings

BUSINESS men
Businessmen in the news. See issues of Fortune
Egg man; leader among West German entrepreneurs. Time 86:76+ Ag 27 '65
How the sons rise. il Time 85:96+ My 28 '65
How to do business with a Frenchman. E. R. Eggers. Harper 231:41-4 Ag '65

Moderates speak; voice of southern businessmen. Newsweek 65:79 Ap 26 '65

SR's businessman of the year: J. C. Wilson. W. D. Patterson. Sat R 49:72+ Ja 8 '66

When the season's over; athletes ground themselves for gainful second careers. il Newsweek 65:70-2 F 8 '65
See also
Executives

Health and hygiene
See Men—Health and hygiene

Political activities
See Business—Political aspects

BUSINESS names
We've got to call it something; picking a name for new gadget, or company. M. Gunther. il Sat Eve Post 238:60-1 S 11 '65
See also
Trade names

BUSINESS organization. See Business management and organization

BUSINESS recession. See Business depression

BUSINESS records
Paperwork explosion: can we control it? excerpts from Modern records management; a basic guide to records control, filing, and information retrieval. E. J. Leahy and C. A. Cameron. il Nations Bsns 53:102-4+ S '65
Watch your minutes. R. S. Holzman. bibliog f Harvard Bsns R 43:162-4+ Mr '65
See also
Business—Forms, blanks, etc.
Card system in business, etc.

BUSINESS schools. See Business education

BUSINESS secrets. See Trade secrets

BUSINESS statistics
Figures of the week. See issues of Business week
Kroger co. adds data to its wares; Product movement index. Bsns W p38 S 4 '65
See also
Business forecasting

BUSINESS success. See Success

BUSINESS travel
Battle for industry's travel dollar. il Duns R 85:nt2 136-7+ Je '65

BUSINESS women. See Business and professional women

BUSINESSES, Moving of. See Moving

BUSONI, Ferruccio Benvenuto
Brilliant Busonian tour de force. R. Kammerer. por Am Rec G 31:722 Ap '65

BUSSE, James G.
Silent sea engine for nuclear subs. Pop Sci 188:112-14+ Ja '66

BUTCHART gardens. See Gardens—Canada

BUTCHER, Harvey R, Jr. See Ternberg, J. L. jt. auth.

BUTCHER, Russell D.
Redwood National Park. Nat Parks Mag 39: 4-9 F '65
Redwood National Park, but where, and how much? Liv Wildn 29:11-15 Spr '65
Redwoods face a race against time. il Audubon Mag 67:234-9 Jl '65

BUTKUS, Dick
Year of the rookie, especially this one; with report by J. R. McDermott. il pors Life 59:72D-75+ N 5 '65

BUTLER, Benjamin Franklin
General Benjamin Franklin Butler and the Negro: the evolution of the racial views of a practical politician. N. Weiss. bibliog Negro Hist Bul 29:3-4+ O '65
Lincoln's scapegoat general, by R. S. West, jr. Review
Sat R 48:29 My 15 '65. W. B. Catton
Time por 85:115+ Mr 19 '65

BUTLER, Edward, Jr
Project mercury. Am City 80:114+ N '65

BUTLER, Edward W.
Fixed resistor industry. por Electr World 73: 37 Ap '65

BUTLER, John
Dance magazine's 1964 awards. por Dance Mag 39:36+ Mr '65

BUTLER, Joseph T.
Innovative furniture of the nineteenth century. Antiques 87:332-5 Mr '65

BUTLER, Richard
End of the Newman club. Commonweal 82: 627-30 S 3 '65

BUTLER, Sue
Leveling trouble plagues crawler. Miss & Roc 16:17 My 10 '65
Radiation-monitoring satellite awaits Titan 111-C launching. Miss & Roc 17:15 S 20 '65
Vacuum chambers to check Apollo 011. Miss & Roc 17:27 D 6 '65

BUTLER, W. Jack, and Dearden, John
Managing a worldwide business. Harvard Bsns R 43:93-102 My '65

BUTTER
Butter fights back against colored margarine. D. Hagen. Farm J 89:50 Je '65
BUTTERCUPS
Ranunculus make a gay display. il Sunset 135:242-3 N '65
BUTTERFAT. See Milk—Fat content
BUTTERFLIES
Churchill's interest in animal life. L. H. Newman. il Audubon Mag 67:240-3 Jl '65
Defensive secretion of a caterpillar, Papilio. E. Eisner and Y. C. Mainwald. bibliog il Science 150:1733-5 D 24 '65
When Churchill brought butterflies to Chartwell. L. H. Newman. il Audubon Mag 67: 154-8 My '65

Collection and preservation
Our kids collect butterflies. J. D. Rossio. il Parents Mag 40:62-3+ Ag '65
BUTTERFLIES, Photography of. See Photography of insects
BUTTLAR, Haro von, and Wiik, B.
Enrichment of tritium by thermal diffusion and measurement of dated Antarctic snow samples. bibliog Science 149:1371-3 S 17 '65
BUTTNER, Marguerite
Iceland poppies. Pop Gard 16:27-9 Jl '65
BUTTONS
Button collecting. D. F. Brown. See issues of Hobbies
Buttons. il Design 66:40-1 Ja '65
BUTTS, Dorothy
Deed of friendship. Newsweek 65:30 Ap 26 '65
BUTZ, Earl L.
Let's help farmers retire early. por Farm J 89:20+ Mr '65
BUTZER, Karl W.
Acheulian occupation sites at Torralba and Ambrona, Spain: their geology. bibliog Science 150:1718-22 D 24 '65
BUWEPS. See United States—Navy department —Weapons, Bureau of
BUXTON, Charles Lee
Back in business. il por Newsweek 65:60 Je 21 '65
BUYING. See Purchasing, Household; Shopping and shoppers
BUZBEE, Ellen W.
Parent and child. N Y Times Mag p87+ D 12 '65
BUZZATI-TRAVERSO, Adriano A.
Scientific research: the case for international support. bibliog Science 148:1440-4 Je 11 '65
BY-elections. See Elections—Great Britain
BYERS, Sanford O. See Friedman, M. jt. auth.
BYG, D. M. and Gill, W. E.
Here's how to lick corn harvesting losses. Suc Farm 63:47 S '65
BYLIN, James E.
Day we run out of water; reprint. Sci Digest 58:74-9 Jl '65
BYLINSKY, Gene
Acrobats in space. New Repub 152:14-15 Ap 3 '65
Two spacemaps to the moon. N Y Times Mag p6-7+ My 30 '65
When the countdown is one. his pulse is 135. N Y Times Mag p 14-15+ Ag 15 '65
BYNNER, Witter
Four poems: I had an appointment with myself; Blue heron all by himself; He will walk here always; Life and death might be the stakes. Poetry 106:212 Je '65
BYRD, Gibson
Artist-teachers in America. bibliog Sch Arts 65:21-5 O '65 (to be cont)
BYRD, Harry Flood, 1887-
Other side of the voting-rights bill; excerpts from statement. por U S News 58:86-8 Ap 12 '65

about
End of an era. por Sr Schol 87:20 D 9 '65
Extinct Byrd. K. Crawford. Newsweek 66: 34 N 29 '65
Look alike, think alike: Harry F. Byrd, sr. and jr. il por U S News 59:20 N 29 '65
New dominion. Reporter 33:20+ O 21 '65
Primogeniture. New Repub 153:9 N 27 '65
Senator Harry Byrd: a symbol steps down. por U S News 59:21 N 22 '65
Sic transit Byrd. V. F. Callahan, jr. Commonweal 83:312-13 D 10 '65
Swan song? il por Time 86:43A N 19 '65
Time has come. il por Newsweek 66:40 N 22 '65
Virginia catches up with history. J. N. Eller. America 113:664 N 27 '65
BYRD, Harry Flood, 1914-
End of an era. por Sr Schol 87:20 D 9 '65
Look alike, think alike: Harry F. Byrd, sr. and jr. il por U S News 59:20 N 29 '65

BYRD, Robert C.
Can subsidies solve America's problems? por Nations Bsns 53:30-1+ Ag '65
Should equal rights mean equal responsibility? excerpts from address, August 23, 1965. por U S News 59:14-15 S 6 '65
BYRNE, James J.
Anyone for survival? A. Balk. il pors Sat Eve Post 238:72+ Mr 27 '65
BYRNES, George
Hang it all! Motor B 116:76-8 D '65
BYRNES, James B.
Edgar Degas' New Orleans paintings. Antiques 88:664-8 N '65
BYRON, Gilbert
Harvard's Algonquin. Liv Wildn 29:17-19 Sum '65
BYZANTINE art. See Art, Byzantine
BYZANTINE empire
Fall of Constantinople 1453, by S. Runciman. Review
Reporter il 33:54-7 O 7 '65. G. Vidal

C

CAB. See United States—Civil aeronautics board
CAIP. See Catholic association for international peace
CAP. See Christian Appalachian project, incorporated; United States—Civil air patrol
CAPEI. See Central American program of economic integration
CAR. See Central African Republic
CARE. See Cooperative for American relief everywhere, incorporated
CAT (clear air turbulence) See Atmospheric turbulence
CATV (community antenna television systems) See Television antennas
CB radio. See Citizens radio service
CBA. See Christian booksellers association
CBC. See Childrens book council
CBS. See Columbia broadcasting system
CCNY. See New York (city) City university of New York—City college
CDL. See Citizens for decent literature and motion pictures, incorporated
CEA. See United States—Council of economic advisers
CED. See Committee for economic development
CERN (Conseil européen pour la recherche nucléaire) See European organization for nuclear research
CIA. See United States—Central intelligence agency
CIAP (Inter-American committee on the Alliance for progress) See Alliance for progress
CLR. See Council on library resources, incorporated
CND. See Campaign for nuclear disarmament (organization)
COC (combat operations center) See North American air defense command
COFO. See Council of federated organizations
CORE. See Congress of racial equality
COSATI (committee on scientific and technical information) See United States—Federal council for science and technology
COSPAR. See International council of scientific unions—Committee on space research
CPSU (Congress of the Communist party of the Soviet Union) See Communist party (Russia)
CRI. See Composers recordings, incorporated
CSD. See American library association—Childrens services division
CU. See Consumers union of United States
CUNY. See New York (city) City university of New York
CURV (cable-controlled underwater research vehicle) See Oceanographic research— Equipment
CAAMAÑO DEÑO, Francisco
Broken record. il Time 85:35 Je 18 '65
Death and jasmine. il por Newsweek 65:46+ My 17 '65
Fighting resumes. il Time 85:49 Je 25 '65
CAB drivers. See Taxicab drivers
CABALLÉ, Montserrat
Spanish treasure; interview, ed. by P. J. Smith. pors Opera N 30:13 S 25 '65

CABALLÉ, Montserrat—*Continued*

about

Big find. por Time 86:47 D 24 '65
From Odeon, the first recording by Montserrat Caballé. P. L. Miller. por Am Rec G 32:125 O '65
Lady from Spain. por Newsweek 66:67 D 27 '65
Music to my ears; Caballé's Lucrezia. H. Weinstock. Sat R 48:49 My 8 '65
Music to my ears; role of Elizabeth Tudor in Donizetti's Roberto Devereux. I. Kolodin. Sat R 49:38 Ja 1 '66
Music to my ears; role of Marguerite. I. Kolodin. Sat R 49:76 Ja 8 '66
Musical events; concert performance of Donizetti's Lucrezia Borgia, with American opera society. W. Sargeant. New Yorker 41:177-8 My 1 '65
New soprano from Spain. C. L. Osborne. por Hi Fi 15:106 O '65
Notes from our correspondents. E. Greenfield. Hi Fi 15:28 N '65

CABIN cruisers. See Yachts and yachting

CABINET

United States

See United States—Cabinet

CABINET (Great Britain) See Great Britain—Cabinet

CABINET officers
Close-up of the team now running the U.S. il U S News 58:36-8 My 3 '65
Weaver's long wait. il Time 87:19C Ja 21 '66
Will we have a Negro in the Cabinet? Christian Cent 82:1533 D 15 '65
See also
United States—Cabinet

CABINET work. See Cabinetmakers

CABINETMAKERS
Cabinetmakers of the Norwich area; with Connecticut historical society list. H. Comstock. il Antiques 87:696-9 Je '65
Notes on Rhode Island cabinetmakers. J. F. Ott. Antiques 87:572 My '65
Providence cabinetmakers of the eighteenth and early nineteenth centuries. E. B. Monahon. il Antiques 87:573-9 My '65
Tyranny of charity; furniture makers plight in east Kentucky. W. Berry. il Nation 201: 161-4 S 27 '65
See also
Cogswell family
Howard, T. jr
Krause, J.

CABINETS (furniture)
ABCs of building chests and cabinets (cont) R. J. De Cristoforo. il Pop Sci 186:160-4 F '65
How to judge good cabinet work. il Bet Hom & Gard 43:142 Je '65
It's neat if you don't peek; sewing cabinets. il Sunset 134:140 Je '65
Lateral compartment file. T. W. McConkey. il Library J 90:1101 Mr 1 '65
Shallow cabinet for a hallway. T. B. Shearer. il Pop Sci 186:172-3 F '65
Storage doors are window shades. il Sunset 135:158+ O '65
See also
Kitchen cabinets
Medicine cabinets
Phonograph record cabinets

CABINS
Cabin in the snow. J. Peter. il Look 29:76-9 F 23 '65
Cabin on stilts; cash cost, $2,500; prefabricated cabin. il Sunset 134:110-11 My '65
Camp-out with comforts. A. C. Borg. il Am Home 68:46-7 Ap '65
Easy living in mountain home; weekend cabin near Carmel, Calif. il Life 58:124-7+ My 7 '65
Why not build a roof house? A. C. Borg. il Am Home 68:44 Ap '65
Wilderness retreat, the "wickiup". il Sunset 134:124-5 My '65

CABLE, Harold
Another man's family; drama. Plays 25:1-14 D '65
Last stop; drama. Plays 24:15-29 My '65

CABLE, Mary
Cluster of soap bubbles. Horizon 7:80-91 Sum '65
Marble cottages. Horizon 7:18-27 Autumn '65
Palace in the sun. Horizon 7:65-75 Spr '65
She who shall be nameless. Am Heritage 16:50-5 F '65
Silk of Thailand. Atlan 217:107-11 Ja '66

CABLES
See also
Electric cables

CABLEWAYS
They came by the highest tramway; to the summits of Pico Bolívar and Pico Espejo. il Sunset 135:22+ N '65

CABOT, John
Did Columbus or Cabot see the map? excerpt from Vinland map and the Tartar relation. R. A. Skelton. il Am Heritage 16:103-6 O '65

CABOT, Paul Codman
Harvard's Midas. por Time 85:57 Ap 16 '65

CABRAL, Donald Reid
Dominican crisis. T. Draper. Commentary 40: 33-68 D '65
Nobody's yes man. il por Time 85:31-2 Mr 26 '65

CACOYANNIS, Michael
Second fame: good food. N. Lyon. por Vogue 145:230-2 My '65

CACTUS
Cacti and succulents in the garden. L. Cutak. il Horticulture 43:18-21+ O '65
Cactus for Christmas. M. M. Leister. il Flower Grower 52:26-7+ D '65
Christmas cactus. A. MacDougall. il Horticulture 43:29+ D '65
Concerning the Saguaro. Nat Parks Mag 39: 21 S '65
Grow cactus from seeds. L. L. Stroud. Flower Grower 52:42 D '65
Nature note; saguaro. Sci N L 87:399 Je 19 '65
Saguaro problem and grazing in southwestern national monuments. W. A. Niering and R. H. Whittaker. bibliog il Nat Parks Mag 39:4-9 Je '65
See also
Epiphyllums

CACTUS flower; drama. See Burrows, A.

CADAVERS
On giving oneself away. E. T. Harris; discussion. Harper 230:8+ F '65

CADDEN, Vivian
How women see themselves. Redbook 125: 46-7+ My '65
Women who bought Main Street. Redbook 124: 60-1+ Mr '65

CADDIES (golf)
Even iron man couldn't win for Arnie; Nat Avery, Palmer's caddie. D. Jenkins. il Sports Illus 22:28-9 Ap 19 '65

CADOO, Emil
Images etched in time. J. Morris. il U S Camera 28:46-9+ Jl '65

CADY, Jack
Burning; story. Atlan 216:53-7 Ag '65

CADY, Steve
Race horses are a cash crop. N Y Times Mag p26-7+ Je 13 '65

CAEN, Herb
San Francisco's pop art ballet. Dance Mag 39:48-9 Ap '65

CAENORHABDITIS elegans. See Nematodes

CAESAR, Caius Julius
Julius Caesar, by J. F. C. Fuller. Review Nat R por 18:73+ Ja 25 '66. G. F. Eliot
They made our world. L. Rosten. pors Look 29:78-9 D 28 '65

CAESAR, Gene
Michigan's Upper Peninsula. Holiday 37:68-9+ Je '65

CAETANI, Marguerite (Chapin) principessa
Marguerite Caetani. I. Origo. il por Atlan 215:81-8 F '65

CAFÉS. See Restaurants

CAFÉS, Parisian. See Paris—Hotels, restaurants, etc.

CAGE, John
Second fame: good food. N. Lyon. il por Vogue 146:256-8 O 1 '65

CAHALANE, Victor H.
Cougars in the U.S. are barely holding their own; excerpt from Preliminary study of distribution and numbers of cougar, grizzly and wolf in North America. Audubon Mag 67:108-9 Mr '65
Grizzly outlook; cloudy to fair; excerpt from report. Audubon Mag 67:170-1 My '65

CAHILL, Carl
Dog. Motor T 17:68 Ap '65

CAHILL, Laurence J. jr
Magnetic fields in interplanetary space. bibliog Science 147:991-1000 F 26 '65
Magnetosphere; with biographical sketch. Sci Am 212:17. 58-68 Mr '65

CAHILL, P. Joseph
It's a strange one. Christian Cent 82:1039 Ag 25 '65

CAHILL, Thomas J.
Special unit revives police-community relations. por Am City 80:166+ Je '65

CAIN, James Mallahan
Hard-boiled school. G. Hicks. Sat R 48:27-8 Ag 14 '65

CAIN, Stanley A.
Interior appointment. Nat Parks Mag 39: 19 Ap '65

CAINE, Michael
People are talking about. . . por Vogue 146: 154 N 1 '65

CAIRNS, John
Bacterial chromosome; with biographical sketch. Sci Am 214:14, 36-44 Ja '66
CAJETAN, cardinal
Almain and Major: conciliar theory on the eve of the reformation. F. Oakley. bibliog f Am Hist R 70:673-90 Ap '65
CAKE
Brownie of another hue. C. Claiborne. il N Y Times Mag p89-90 N 7 '65
Christmas party chimney cake; with recipes. il Seventeen 24:114-15+ D '65
Guy Fawkes bread; ginger parkin recipe. il Sunset 135:169 N '65
Happy marriage holiday white fruitcake: with recipe. il McCalls 93:60 N '65
How you can make the Black Forest cherry cake. il Sunset 134:134 F '65
I-love-you cake; with recipes. il Seventeen 24:144-5+ F '65
Jam-bar cake. il Farm J 89:91 S '65
Let the season decide what goes inside il Sunset 135:112 Jl '65
New tricks with cake mix. il Bet Hom & Gard 43:86 S '65
1,000 (almost) layer cake. il Sunset 134:233 Ap '65
On a lazy summer afternoon, you just happen to have a frozen torte all ready to serve. il Sunset 135:66-7 Jl '65
Orange-pecan loaf. M. F. Williams. il Good H 161:144 S '65
Original recipe is a closely guarded secret; sachertorte. il Sunset 135:183 O '65
Party-best recipe: apple pie cake. il Seventeen 24:174 N '65
Slice of history; English fruit cake, Simnel cake. J. Hewitt. il N Y Times Mag p87 Mr 28 '65
Springtime cakes. il Bet Hom & Gard 43:113-14 Ap '65
Stop by for homemade ice cream and cake. il Farm J 89:66-7+ Ag '65
Successful recipes; cakes for spring. il Suc Farm 63:119-20 Ap '65
Viennese cream torte; with recipes. il Seventeen 24:178 S '65
Was there a cake in Catherine's dowry? C. Claiborne. il N Y Times Mag p 112 S 19 '65
See also
Cheesecake
Icings
CAKE decorations. See Icings
CALADIUMS
Caladiums for color. M. D. Logan. il Pop Gard 16:21+ Mr '65
CALAMITIES. See Disasters
CALCIFICATION
See also
Bone
CALCITE
Mineralogic changes during growth in the red alga, clathromorphum compactum. K. E. Chave and B. D. Wheeler, jr. bibliog il Science 147:621 F 5 '65
CALCIUM chloride hexahydrate
Antarcticite: a new mineral, calcium chloride hexahydrate, discovered in Antarctica. T. Torii and J. Ossaka. bibliog il Science 149:975-7 Ag 27 '65
CALCIUM cyclamate. See Sugar substitutes
CALCIUM in the body
Clycerinated skeletal and smooth muscle; calcium and magnesium dependence. R. S. Filo and others. bibliog il Science 147:1581-3 Mr 26 '65
See also
Hypercalcemia
CALCULATING charts. See Charts, Calculating
CALCULATING devices
Know the price per ounce! Consumer Bul 48:19 N '65
CALCULATING machines. See Computers
CALCULATIONS, Numerical. See Numerical calculations
CALCULI, Biliary
Gallstones produced experimentally by litho-cholic acid in rats. R. H. Palmer. bibliog il Science 148:1339-40 Je 4 '65
Stones people get: causes, treatment; interview. L. Laster. il U S News 59:37-8 O 25 '65
CALCULI, Urinary
Stones people get: causes, treatment; interview. L. Laster. il U S News 59:37-8 O 25 '65
CALCUTTA
Calcutta: a premature metropolis. N. K. Bose. il Sci Am 213:90-102 S '65
CALDECOTT medal
Beni Montresor. J. Karl. il Library J 90:1465-7 Mr 15 '65
Children's Pulitzers; 1965 winners. il Newsweek 65:102+ Mr 15 '65

Newbery and Caldecott award winners. il ALA Bul 59:238 Ap '65
Newbery and Caldecott winners: Wojcie-chowska, Montresor. il Pub W 187:26-8 Mr 8 '65
Newbery-Caldecott awards. Wilson Lib Bul 39:627 Ap '65
Spring brings the winners. A. Dalgliesh. il Sat R 48:32-3 Mr 27 '65
CALDER, Alexander
Calder the pioneer. F. Getlein. New Repub 152:31-2 Mr 27 '65
Mobile maker's giddy whirl. il pors Life 58:47-8+ Mr 5 '65
Mobiles: the soaring art of Alexander Calder. R. Lemon. il por Sat Eve Post 238:30-5 F 27 '65
CALDER, Ritchie
Science and the common man. UNESCO Courier 18:4-8+ F: 17+ Mr '65
Speed of change. Bul Atomic Sci 21:2-5 D '65
CALDERA, Rafael
Democratic revolutions. Commonweal 83:120-4 O 29 '65
CALDERONE, Mary Steichen
How young men influence the girls who love them; adaptation of address. Redbook 125:45+ Jl '65
Teenagers and sex. PTA Mag 60:4-7 bibliog(p37) O '65
CALDURA, Maria Perego
Inventor of the month. S. V. Jones. il por Sci Digest 59:32 Ja '66
CALDWELL, Erskine
Deep South's other venerable tradition. N Y Times Mag p 10-11+ Jl 11 '65
In search of Bisco. Esquire 63:120-1+ Ap '65
about
Books. W. Balliett. New Yorker 41:174-7 My 22 '65
CALDWELL, Sam
Gloriosa-lilies. il Flower Grower 52:8 Je '65
Plastic sheeting, a useful aid. il Flower Grower 52:6+ Ap '65
CALDWELL, Sarah
She puts the oomph in the opera. D. J. Hamblin. il pors Life 58:77-8+ Mr 5 '65
CALDWELL, Taylor
And stir like hell: recipe for foie gras de poulet; letter. Nat R 17:902 O 19 '65
CALDWELL, N.J.
New idea in sludge dewatering. G. A. Valente. il Am City 80:95-7 Jl '65
CALENDAR
Manner of speaking; year's end when leaves fall: primitive and present day systems. J. Ciardi. Sat R 48:21-2 O 30 '65
CALENDARS
Betsy McCall calendar for 1966; making instructions. il McCalls 93:134 Ja '66
Calendars to welcome 1966. il House & Gard 128:206 D '65
Doomsday calendar; with the girls. il Esquire 64:224-9 D '65
CALENDULAS
Calendulas. R. C. Hands. il Horticulture 43:36-7 Jl '65
CALF contracts. See Contracts, Agricultural
CALF roping. See Rope tricks
CALGARY, Alberta
Downtown traffic responds to the computer. il Am City 80:134 O '65
CALHOUN, Mary
Writing the picture book story. Writer 78:16-19 Ap '65
CALIAN, Carnegie Samuel
Social consciousness in Eastern orthodoxy. Christian Cent 82:1284-6 O 20 '65
CALIBRATORS
Simple Simon voltage calibrators. F. Chapman. il Pop Electr 22:48+ Mr '65
Tachometer & engine idle speed calibrator. J. S. Shreve. il Pop Electr 22:54-5+ F '65
CALIFANO, Joseph A. Jr
Crisis solver for LBJ. por Bsns W p34+ Ja 15 '66
CALIFORNIA
Biggest and richest? Newsweek 66:71 Jl 19 '65
California loses another beach; Dilton Beach. K. S. Roe. il Audubon Mag 67:110-11 Mr '65
California without clichés; symposium. il Holiday 38:8+ O '65
What aerospace sees on the ground. il Bsns W p87-8+ S 25 '65
See also
Agriculture—California
Architecture—California
Architecture, Domestic—California
Art—California
Birds—California
Booksellers and bookselling—California

CALIFORNIA—*Continued*
Botany—California
Camping—California
Colleges and universities—California
Courts—California
Crime and criminals—California
Education—California
Feather River
Fishing—California
Gardens—California
Housing—California
Hunting—California
Land—California
Lava Beds National Monument
Law—California
Libraries—California
Music festivals—California
Petroleum—California
Prisons—California
Public welfare—California
Radioactive fallout—California
Reclamation of land—California
Salton Sea
San Francisco Bay Region
Squaw Valley
Stanislaus River
Tehachapi Mountains
Water supply—California

Description and travel

Cable cars, a Russian fort and San Simeon. il Holiday 38:148-9 O '65
California coast. C. Kentfield. il Holiday 38:80-91+ O '65
Gone flying to Shelter Cove. R. Blodget. il Flying 78:60-2 Ja '66
If you're going to Watsonville. il Sunset 134:62+ Mr '65
Refugio road, pleasantly lonesome: southern California. il Sunset 135:36+ D '65
Three Californias: North, South, the City. E. Burdick. il Holiday 38:60-75 O '65

Economic conditions

Industry studies California problems; special report. W. E. Wilks. il Miss & Roc 16:24-5+ F 15 '65
Researching social needs. New Repub 152:7 My 15 '65

Economic policy

Defense: California planners try novel approach to problems of economic reconversion. E. Langer. Science 148:482 Ap 23 '65

Industries

Aerospace: a new life for a billion-dollar industry? with interview with E. G. Brown. il U S News 58:109-11 My 24 '65
California's science monopoly. H. Pryor. il Sci Digest 57:22-5 F '65
Down to earth: aerospace industry working on social problems. W. J. Coughlin. Miss & Roc 17:46 Ag 2 '65
Industry studies California problems; special report. W. E. Wilks. il Miss & Roc 16:24-5+ F 15 '65
Next step; aerospace programs to apply space-age know-how to the Nation's social and economic problems. W. J. Coughlin. Miss & Roc 17:46 N 15 '65
State systems study lauded: four aerospace companies attacking social problems with systems engineering know-how. Miss & Roc 17:32 Jl 26 '65

Legislature

Should California be chopped in half? il U S News 58:61-2 F 8 '65

Missions

El Camino Real. B. Finnegan. il Hobbies 70:124-5+ Jl '65
Lost mission west of Yuma. il Sunset 134:83 Mr '65

Moral conditions

Going together: teen-agers. J. Poppy. il Look 29:80-5 Jl 13 '65

Parks and reserves

Autumn walk through the Smith River redwoods. il Sunset 135:20 N '65
California playground. F. Dufresne. il Field & S 69:42-5 Mr '65
Damaged parks back in shape; flood-damaged region along north coast. il Sunset 134:47 My '65
Fern canyon and Gold Bluffs beach acquired for California state park system. il Nat Parks Mag 39:21 Ag '65
Four-lane menace to California's redwoods. L. P. Hudson. il Reporter 33:34-8 Ag 12 '65
Holiday handbook: California's state parks. V. McHugh. il Holiday 38:141-6 O '65

Power-line playground; Southern California Edison company right-of-ways. R. Laudenslayer. Recreation 58:168 Ap '65
Rare evergreen defies extinction. H. Bedford. il Audubon Mag 67:182-3 My '65
Recollections of a trip with Mr John D. Rockefeller, jr, in California's Humboldt Redwoods State Park, July 1926. N. B. Drury. il Nat Parks Mag 39:8-9 My '65
Redwood National Park; Jedediah Smith Redwoods State Park, Del Norte Coast Redwoods State Park and Prairie Creek Redwoods State Park. R. D. Butcher. il Nat Parks Mag 39:4-9 F '65
See also
Death Valley National Monument

Politics and government

Antic politics of California. P. Seabury. Harper 230:82-4+ Je '65
Big Daddy vs. Pat; Democratic gubernatorial nomination. il Newsweek 65:30+ Ap 5 '65
Brown vs Reagan. New Repub 154:7-8 Ja 22 '66
California's political free-for-all: race for the governorship. D. S. Broder. il Look 29:61-2+ Jl 13 '65
Democratic dissidence. il Newsweek 66:33-4 N 29 '65
Democrats' minuet. il Time 86:17B Ag 13 '65
Enter Ronald Reagan. il Newsweek 67:31-2 Ja 17 '66
Good guy; R. Reagan. S. Alsop. Sat Eve Post 238:18 N 20 '65
How is Ronald Reagan doing? W. F. Buckley, jr. Nat R 18:17 Ja 11 '66
Milkman cometh; Republican gubernatorial nomination. Time 86:38 N 5 '65
Polls apart; gubernatorial race contenders. Time 86:27 S 24 '65
Reagan rides East. il Newsweek 66:42 O 11 '65
Real Ronald Reagan stands up. R. Oulahan and W. Lambert. il Life 60:70-2+ Ja 21 '66
Ronald Reagan for governor? S. Alexander. Life 59:22 Ag 13 '65
Ronald Reagan story; or. Tom Sawyer enters politics. L. E. Litwak. il N Y Times Mag p46-7+ N 14 '65
Running wild. A. Kopkind. New Repub 153:15-19 O 30 '65
Stage to Sacramento? il Time 86:13-14 Jl 30 '65
Where are the new Republicans? Reporter 33:16+ O 7 '65
Will he size up? R. Reagan. il Newsweek 65:18-19 Je 7 '65

Population

California, the Nation's first. America 113:275 S 18 '65
Destruction of California, by R. F. Dasmann. Review
Newsweek il 66:67 S 6 '65

Race problems

Round one to Proposition fourteen. il Time 85:74 F 12 '65
See also
Los Angeles—Riots

Religious institutions and affairs

News of the Christian world (cont) Christian Cent 82:348-50, 898-900, 1044 Mr 17, Jl 14, Ag 25 '65

Sanitary affairs

Scientists' report: choice for California: act fast, or be like a sewer by 1990. U S News 59:46 O 4 '65

Social life and customs

Affluent poor. J. Burgess. il Esquire 63:82-7+ Ap '65
Eccentricity under the sun. R. Carson. il Holiday 38:92-9+ O '65
Three Californias; North, South, the City. E. Burdick. il Holiday 38:60-75 O '65

CALIFORNIA, LOWER
Baja, the other California. W. W. Johnson. il Holiday 38:112-15 Ag '65
New boat, a new venture. E. Newmark. il Yachting 118:61-4+ D '65 (to be cont)
Yachting special report, southern California; symposium. il Yachting 117:38-52+ Je '65
See also
Fishing—California, Lower
Hunting—California, Lower
Tourist trade—California, Lower

Description and travel

Where the westerlies blow. il Yachting 117:38-9+ Je '65

CALIFORNIA authors. See Authors, American

CALIFORNIA caves. See Caves
CALIFORNIA condors. See Condors
CALIFORNIA highway patrol academy. See Police, State—Training
CALIFORNIA institute of technology, Pasadena
Apotheosis of the practical joke. il Esquire 64:99 S '65
Caltech, campus for genius. il Sci Digest 58: 48-55 O '65
  See also
Jet propulsion laboratory
CALIFORNIA marine parks and harbors association, incorporated
California's marine watchdogs. D. Selby. Yachting 117:195-6 Ap '65
CALIFORNIA pipeline. See Gas, Natural—Pipe lines
CALIFORNIA state college, Los Angeles
TV or the herded tour: large numbers of entering freshmen. C. M. Brown. il Library J 90:2214-18 My 15 '65
CALIFORNIA. University
After Berkeley: California looks ahead; new campuses. il Newsweek 66:99-100+ O 4 '65
Breaking up the big systems; plans to decentralize authority. P. Woodring. Sat R 48:51-2 Jl 17 '65
Fresh look at the University of California. W. Trombley. New Repub 153:14-15 Jl 3 '65
On the campus: a troubled reflection of the U.S. M. Ways. il Fortune 72:140-7+ O '65
State as a campus. N. Morgan. il Holiday 38:78-9+ O '65
What's ahead for the university? academic freedom; address, September 10, 1965. E. W. Strong. Vital Speeches 32:24-8 O 15 '65

Berkeley campus
Antiwar marches and how they happen; with report by S. Angeloff. il Life 59:108-10+ D 10 '65
Behind the campus revolt: California uprising. J. Poppy; L. Gross. il Look 29:30-8+ F 23 '65
Behind the protests at Berkeley. J. F. Boler. Commonweal 81:602-5 F 5 '65
Berkeley affair: Mr Kerr vs. Mr Savio & co. A. H. Raskin. il N Y Times Mag p24-5+ F 14 '65
Berkeley: free speech and free verse; poetry conference. D. Wesling. Nation 201:338-40 N 8 '65
Berkeley, one year later. il Time 86:46+ D 3 '65
Berkeley student revolt, ed. by S. M. Lipset and S. S. Wolin. Review
  Newsweek 66:51 S 6 '65
  Sat R 48:77 S 11 '65. P. Woodring
Berkeley's civil war. New Repub 152:6-7 Mr 27 '65
Bonaparte's retreat; Savio quits as leader of the Free speech movement. Time 85:54 My 7 '65
Choices at Berkeley; convicted students sentenced. il Newsweek 66:74-5 Ag 9 '65
Coeds in rebellion. B. H. Hoffman. il Ladies Home J 82:32-4+ O '65
Crisis at Berkeley. E. Langer. bibliog il Science 148:198-202, 346-9 Ap 9-16 '65; Discussion. 148:1273-8 Je 4 '65
Cure for campus riots; interview. M. Rafferty. il U S News 58:70-2 My 17 '65
Dysphoric generation; ACE assesses student demonstrations. Newsweek 66:98 O 18 '65
Escalation in California. N. Cousins; reply. C. Kerr. Sat R 48:21+ Mr 6 '65
Extremism in the defense of ... R. E. Fitch; discussion. Christian Cent 82:147-50 F 3 '65
Focus on Berkeley. P. G. Altbach. Christian Cent 82:1356-7 N 3 '65
Gallery spaces defined by many changes of level. il Arch Rec 138:132-4 D '65
Horrors at Berkeley, or did architecture make students riot? F. MacShane. il Art N 64: 30-3+ S '65
How campus discord forced a university president to resign. il U S News 58:22 Mr 22 '65
Lesson of Berkeley; question of student political activities. S. M. Lipset and P. Seabury; discussion. Reporter 32:6+ F 25 '65
Lesson of Clark Kerr; withdraws resignation. il Newsweek 65:53 Mr 22 '65
Letter from Berkeley. C. Trillin. New Yorker 41:52-4+ Mr 13 '65
Letter from the Berkeley underground. M. Miller. Esquire 64:85-7+ S '65
Man for tomorrow; Yesterday's rebels. il Time 86:49 Ag 6 '65
Nonstudent left; significance of the Mulford law. H. S. Thompson. il Nation 201:154-8 S 27 '65

On the campus: a troubled reflection of the U.S. M. Ways. il Fortune 72:130-5+ S '65
Self-criticism at Cal; reports on student disorders. Time 85:58 My 21 '65
Sowing future trouble; Berkeley judge passes sentence on students involved in the demonstrations. Nation 201:70 Ag 16 '65
Spider strikes; collection of festering excerpts from semimonthly malcontent manifesto of Berkeley. il Esquire 64:90-1 S '65
Stiffening the spine; question of university discipline. il Time 85:48 Mr 19 '65
They march, doubting they will overcome; Vietnam day committee marchers. New Repub 153:9 O 30 '65
To the big game and to the barricades. A. Wright. il Sports Illus 24:48-54 Ja 3 '66
Trouble again at Cal and Kerr calls it quits. il Life 58:43 Mr 19 '65
University has become a factory; interview, ed. by J. Fincher. M. Savio. Life 58:100-1 F 26 '65
Verdict on Berkeley; committee report on student revolt. Newsweek 65:64 My 24 '65
What happened at Berkeley. J. Cass; discussion. Sat R 48:62+ F 20; 56 Mr 20 '65
What happened at Berkeley. N. Glazer. Commentary 39:39-47 F '65; Reply with rejoinder. P. Selznick. 39:80-5 Mr '65
Why campus crisis flares again. il Bsns W p38-9 Mr 20 '65

Libraries
New campuses program: San Diego (UCSD) Irvine (UCI) and Santa Cruz (UCSC). M. J. Voigt and J. H. Treyz. il Library J 90: 2204-8 My 15 '65
  See also
California. University—Los Angeles campus—Libraries

Los Angeles campus
Can anyone beat the Bruins? UCLA. H. L. Masin. il Sr Schol 87:26-7 D 2 '65
College or career for dancers? UCLA's answer. E. Stodelle. il Dance Mag 39:48-53 My; 40-1+ Je '65
Fire from the maddened crowd; librarianship a profession? E. Moon. Library J 90:578-81 F 1 '65
Good time at UCLA; an English view. R. Gilbert. Harper 230:75-80+ Ap '65
L.A. ambitions. A. Goldberg. Opera N 29: 31 Mr 20 '65
Shooting is the least important part of basketball; UCLA team. J. Wooden. il Look 30:66+ Ja 25 '66
Student filmmakers; UCLA's festival. il Newsweek 66:114+ O 25 '65
UCLA gets contract for pilot study on decentralization of MEDLARS. Library J 90:603 F 1 '65

Libraries
Lending research library. J. R. Cox. il Library J 90:2219-25 My 15 '65

Santa Cruz campus
Academic order and the humane scale. R. Kirk. Nat R 17:241 Mr 23 '65

Scripps institution of oceanography
Biggest classroom in the world. il Sci Digest 57:57-61 Je '65
Giant wave of wood; redwood structure, Hydraulic laboratory. E. J. Long. il Am For 71:31+ Ag '65

CALIFORNIA wines. See Wine
CALIFORNIANS
California without clichés; symposium. il Holiday 38:8+ O '65
CALISHER, Hortense
Will we get there by candlelight? Reporter 33:38-40+ N 4 '65
CALITRI, Charles J.
Love affair with words. Sat R 48:88-9 F 20 '65
CALKINS, Robert De Blois
Best of both worlds. por Newsweek 66:82-3 Jl 12 '65
CALL, Hughie
Always listen for the bells. Redbook 126:42-3+ D '65
CALL Washington 1776; drama. See Miller, H. L.
CALLAGHAN, James
Britain props the pound. il por Bsns W p27-8 Ap 10 '65
Letter from London. M. Panter-Downes. New Yorker 41:174-6 Ap 17 '65
Visit from Grim Jim. il por Newsweek 66: 71-2 Jl 12 '65
CALLAGHAN, Morley
All the years of her life; story. Parents Mag 40:50-2 Ag '65
Legends of the old man. Sat R 48:43 Ag 28 '65

CALLAHAN, Daniel
Comment. Commonweal 83:149-51, 260-1. 346-8, 474-6 N 5. D 3, 17 '65, Ja 21 '66
Constitution on the church and the laity. Cath World 202:21-5 O '65
New freedom. Commonweal 82:401-5 Je 18 '65
Preparing for diversity; value of creative confusion. Commonweal 82:694-6 S 24 '65
Relevance of honesty in the church; excerpt from Honesty in the church. por Cath World 200:333-8 Mr '65
Risk of faith; excerpt from Honesty in the church. Commonweal 81:755-8 Mr 12 '65
Schools. Commonweal 81:473-6, 622-3 Ja 8, F 5 '65
Secular city. Commonweal 83:189-90 N 12 '65
Toward a theology of secularity. Commonweal 82:658-62; 83:5+, 165-6 S 17, O 8, N 5 '65
Unworldly wisdom. Commentary 39:90+ Ap '65

CALLAHAN, Sidney Cornelia
Mature married woman. por Cath World 201:102-6 My '65

CALLANISH. See Callernish, Scotland

CALLAS, Maria
Callas. M. Duras. il por Vogue 146:192-3 O 1 '65
Callas fan brightens opera night. il por Life 58:105-6 Ap 2 '65
Encore, Callas. il por Newsweek 65:78 Mr 29 '65
Four Americans. M. Mayer. Esquire 63:36+ Ap '65
Letter from Paris; performance of Puccini's Tosca. Genêt. New Yorker 41:162+ Mr 20 '65
Maria Callas returns to Tosca. J. Maclain. il por Am Rec G 31:688-90+ Ap '65
Music to my ears; the Callas-Corelli-Gobbi Tosca. I. Kolodin. Sat R 48:28 Ap 3 '65
Musical events; performance of Puccini's Tosca. W. Sargeant. New Yorker 41:171-2 Mr 27 '65
Notes from our correspondents. R. McMullen. il por Hi Fi 15:20+ Mr '65
Return of the prodigal daughter; Callas, in Tosca, returns to the Met. por Time 85:64 Mr 26 '65
Woman of the week. H. Weinstock. por Opera N 29:26-7 Mr 20 '65

CALLERNISH, Scotland
Callanish, a Scottish Stonehenge. G. S. Hawkins; reply with rejoinder. Y. Schwartz. Science 148:444 Ap 23 '65

CALLIGRAPHY
Exhibitions
Remarkable exhibit in Baltimore: 2000 years of calligraphy. P. A. Bennett. il Pub W 188:106-8+ Jl 19 '65
2,000 years of calligraphy; exhibition in Baltimore. F. Johnson. il Am Artist 29:40-5+ O '65

CALLING, Animal. See Animal calling

CALLISON, Charles H.
National capital report. por Audubon Mag 67:114-15 Mr '65

CALLOSE. See Polysaccharides

CALLOW, Alexander B. jr
House that Tweed built. Am Heritage 16:64-9 O '65

CALLS for animals. See Animal calling

CALLS of birds. See Birds—Song

CALLWOOD, June
Infidelity: a growing problem in American marriages. Ladies Home J 82:76-7+ Ap '65
What is courage? excerpt from Love, hate, fear, anger and the other lively emotions. Read Digest 86:117-19 Mr '65

CALOCEPHALUS
Cushion bush is happy on the coast. il Sunset 134:266 My '65

CALOIA, Leo
Hold your audience! U S Camera 28:70-1+ S '65

CALOMEE, Gloria
Vacation in Las Vegas. il Ebony 20:180-2 Je '65

CALORIES, Food. See Food values

CALORIMETRY conference
Calorimetry; report of 20th calorimetry conference. R. Hultgren. Science 150:928-9 N 12 '65

CALTECH. See California institute of technology, Pasadena

CALVES
Care
Hasn't lost a calf in twelve years. O. Bay and G. Lorang. il Farm J 89:C1 S '65

Diseases and pests
Why are there calving deaths? Suc Farm 63:64 Je '65

CALVO, Juan A.
Terror in the embassy. Read Digest 87:104-8 D '65

CAM RANH BAY. See Camranh Bay

CAMARGO, Alberto Lleras. See Lleras Camargo, A.

CAMBODIA
Snookie's snub. il Time 85:36 My 7 '65
We don't live in the clouds. B. Krisher. il Newsweek 65:46-7 Ap 5 '65
See also
Economic assistance in Cambodia
United Nations—Cambodia
United States—Foreign relations—Cambodia

Antiquities
See also
Angkor

Foreign relations
Big puffs & old paper; riding with the Chinese tiger. Time 86:35 O 29 '65
Close-up of a red sanctuary; Cambodia and its leaky border. S. W. Sanders. il U S News 60:48-9 Ja 3 '66
Real reason why Prince Sihanouk broke with America. U S News 58:24 My 17 '65
Scuttled hopes; Sihanouk cuts diplomatic relations with U.S. il Newsweek 65:56+ My 17 '65
Sihanouk, stay home! Soviet snub. Newsweek 66:53 N 1 '65
When a prince got a kick in the pants. il U S News 59:26 N 8 '65

Politics and government
Atlantic report. Atlan 216:20+ Jl '65
Embattled prince. Time 87:25B Ja 21 '66

CAMBRIDGE research laboratories. See United States—Air force—Cambridge research laboratories

CAMBRIDGE. University
City that is not Oxford. C. Northcott. Christian Cent 82:1535-6 D 15 '65

CAMDEN, Ala.
Camden, Alabama: last summers of a dreamlike world; with excerpts from Ordways, by W. Humphrey. J. Poppy. il Look 29:64-8+ N 16 '65

CAMELLIAS
Crazy for camellias. P. Deutsch and R. Deutsch. il Read Digest 88:133-7 Ja '66
Yellow camellia. M. Peer-Morris. Horticulture 43:33+ Jl '65

CAMELOT project. See Project Camelot

CAMELS
Desert nomads' economy depends on camel; photographs. N. Ekstrom. Natur Hist 74:36-9 Ag '65

CAMERA cases
Keppler on the SLR. H. Keppler. il Mod Phot 29:38+ F '65

CAMERA clubs
Fountain of youth; senior citizens. Sun City, Ariz. Z. L. Roshovsky. il U S Camera 28:22-3+ F '65
Should you join a camera club? M. Morrison. U S Camera 29:24+ Ja '66

CAMERA guaranty. See Warranty

CAMERA shutters
Electronic shutters are on the way. B. Sherman. il Mod Phot 30:74-5+ Ja '66

CAMERA stores. See Photographic apparatus industry and trade

CAMERA tripods
Tripods. Pop Phot 58:69-70 Ja '66

CAMERAS
Aerial camera with rotary lens designed to give improved resolution. D. A. Brown. il Aviation W 82:72-3+ Ap 26 '65
All that's new in 35! il Pop Phot 57:78-80+ Ag '65
Are lower priced cameras equal to high priced cameras in quality? interview, ed. by M. A. Matzkin. M. B. Forscher. il Mod Phot 29:72-5+ My '65
Back to yesterday's hardware? N. Rothschild. il Pop Phot 58:157-8 Ja '66
Behind the scenes. See issues of Modern photography
Big comeback of the big camera. J. Forney. il Pop Phot 57:62+ S '65
Big world of little cameras; subminiature cameras. G. Gilbert. il U S Camera 28:62-3+ O '65
Camera on the comeback trail. B. Pierce. Pop Phot 56:83-4 F '65
Cameras, lenses, meters, accessories. il U S Camera 28:58-61 Ag '65
Cameras: which one? for what? how much? C. W. Kennedy. il Pop Phot 57:64-7 N '65

CAMERAS—*Continued*
Christmas shopping guide. il Mod Phot 29:
147-51 D '65
Closeups with RF & TLR. G. Gilbert. il U S
Camera 28:54-5+ F '65
Command performance: newest one-act cam-
eras. H. F. Bruce. House & Gard 128:72+
N '65
Don't get hooked buying a camera. T. Karp.
Mod Phot 29:67+ D '65
Electric-eye 35mm cameras. il Consumer Bul
48:6-10 Mr '65
Evolution of the Bluejays. L. Lipton. il Pop
Phot 56:68-70+ Je '65
Fun with a nearsighted camera. R. Zentner.
il Pop Mech 125:160-1 Ja '66
Half-frame cameras are catching on. P.
Wahl. il Pop Sci 187:114-17 D '65
Harvard observatory's new patrol cameras:
Damon cameras. H. C. Ingrao. il Sky &
Tel 29:200-4 Ap '65
How far have we gone? Purma Special 127
camera. il Mod Phot 29:90+ Jl '65
Instamatic vs Rapid. il Mod Phot 29:68-9
Ag '65
Instant-loading cameras make it big. il Bsns
W p50-2+ My 8 '65
IPEX '65. il U S Camera 28:74-7 Je '65
IPEX '65 guide. il Mod Phot 29:87-102 Je '65
Is the rangefinder more precise? B. Sher-
man. il Mod Phot 29:66-7+ My '65
Large camera. A. Feininger. See issues of
Modern photography
Large camera: Graflex xl and the Koni-
Omega. A. Feininger. il Mod Phot 29:
32+ Ag; 58-9 S '65
Magic eye. il Seventeen 24:174 My '65
Meanwhile, back on earth, where's 3-D today?
C. Burger. il Pop Phot 57:56-9+ S '65
Memories of the memo. P. Stackpole. U S
Camera 28:24+ Jl '65
Modern tests. See issues of Modern photog-
raphy
New. B. C. Brown and C. W. Kennedy. il
Pop Phot 56:108-11+ Je '65
New: Bilora Bellina 127 camera. M. Bernam.
il Pop Phot 56:132-3 Ap '65
New cameras, lenses, meters, accessories. il
U S Camera 28:26 D '65
New: capsule comments from our correspond-
ents. il Pop Phot 57:80-4+ S '65
New for camera fans. il Consumer Rep 30:
340-1 Jl '65
Nikon crowds into Leica's picture. il Bsns W
p49-50+ D 11 '65
Olympus Pen-EM: big step in half-35 automa-
tion. C. W. Kennedy. il Pop Phot 57:100-1 S
'65
Omega is back! il Pop Phot 56:142 Je '65
Photography. il Consumer Rep 30:308-26 D '65
Photography for inept sophisticates. H. Wolf.
il Esquire 65:62-4 Ja '66
Pictures in a moment. J. Wolbarst. il Mod
Phot 29:26+ Ag '65
Presto picture. il Time 85:53 My 14 '65
RFDR: when, why; symposium. il Mod Phot
29:68-9 My '65
Rapid arrives. M. Edelson. il U S Camera
28:54-5+ Ag '65
Show windup; 1965 IPEX. M. A. Matzkin
and others. il Mod Phot 29:66-7+ Ag '65
Single-frame 35mm cameras. il Consumer
Rep 30:291-5 Je '65
Six new rapids: German and Japanese 35-mm
cameras. il Pop Phot 56:54-5 Ap '65
Some thoughts on buying another camera. P.
Stackpole. U S Camera 29:36+ Ja '66
Super 8; equipment designed to take Kodak's
Super 8 film. il U S Camera 28:70-1 Je '65
Techniques tomorrow; cameras being used
in space. B. Sherman. il Mod Phot 29:40+
D '65
Test reports. See issues of Popular photogra-
phy
That amphibious camera: the Nikonos. P.
Gowland. il Pop Phot 56:17-18 Mr '65
35mm: lens-to-film distance. J. Wolbarst. il
Mod Phot 29:14+ S '65
35mm; non-nostalgic comparison. J. Wol-
barst. Mod Phot 29:18+ D '65
35mm; Rapid cameras. J. Wolbarst. Mod
Phot 29:40 Ag '65
Thirty years of American progress. E. Han-
nigan. il U S Camera 28:52-3+ N '65
2¼x2¼ camera roundup. D. L. Miller. il Mod
Phot 29:74-7 N '65
251 new cameras detailed; comp. by D. L.
Miller. il Mod Phot 29:105-28 D '65
USC test report. See issues of U.S. camera
Vagabond camera. W. Lane. il Travel 124:62-3
N '65
War of the photo systems. E. H. Ortner. il
Pop Sci 187:88-92+ Jl '65
What's new at Honeywell? N. Rothschild.
Pop Phot 56:34+ My '65

Where are we headed? automatic devices.
W. Clark. il U S Camera 28:52-3 Ag '65
Where is all this automation leading us? P.
Stackpole. U S Camera 28:16+ N '65
See also
Eastman Kodak company
Graflex cameras
Mirrors for cameras
Moving picture cameras
Polaroid Land cameras
Single-lens reflex cameras
Television cameras
Twin-lens cameras
View finders

Care

As I see it. E. Hannigan. U S Camera 29:38
Ja '66
Rothschild on repairs; National camera repair school, Englewood, Colo. N. Rothschild.
il Pop Phot 56:74-7+ My '65

Loading

Inside super 8; how it was developed at
Eastman Kodak. J. S. Forney. il Pop Phot
57:40-1+ D '65
New fast-load cameras focus on U.S. mar-
ket; Rapid cameras vs Kodak's Instamatic.
il Bsns W p 122+ F 13 '65
Rapid arrives. M. Edelson. il U S Camera
28:54-5+ Ag '65
Rapid vs. standard cartridge. N. Rothschild.
il Pop Phot 56:80-1+ F '65
Straight facts; super 8. L. Lipton. il Pop
Phot 57:42+ D '65
35mm: Instamatic/Rapid competition. J.
Wolbarst. il Mod Phot 29:50 Jl '65
Vagabond camera. W. Lane. il Travel 123:
62-3 F; 124:64-5 D '65

Repairing

Keppler on the SLR. H. Keppler. Mod Phot
29:124+ N '65

Testing

Ansco memo camera. P. Farber. il U S
Camera 28:34-5+ Ap '65
Home tests. T. Karp. il Mod Phot 29:70-1+
D '65
Store checks. T. Karp. il Mod Phot 29:68-9+
D '65
Sub-minis; those mighty midget cameras. B.
Berger. il Pop Mech 124:122-5 N '65
CAMERAS, Stomach. See Medical instruments
and apparatus
CAMERAS, Used
Can flash synchronization be added to a
used camera? comp. by A. C. Muller. Mod
Phot 29:104 D '65
Don't get hooked buying a camera. T. Karp.
Mod Phot 29:67+ D '65
Good buys in used SLR's. il Mod Phot 29:
70-1+ S '65
276 used cameras compared; comp. by N. M.
Grossman. il Mod Phot 29:73-104 D '65
CAMERON, Christopher A. See Leahy, E. J.
jt. auth.
CAMERON, J. M.
Churchill as whig. Commonweal 81:659-60 F
19 '65
Farewell to America. Commonweal 82:617-18 S
3 '65
Post-Waugh insight. Commonweal 83:114-15
O 29 '65
CAMERON, James
Conduit in North Viet Nam. il por Time
86:78 D 17 '65
Inside Hanoi. por Newsweek 66:69 D 20 '65
CAMERON, Roderick
Villa Volpi. Vogue 145:126-33+ Ap 15 '65
CAMEROON REPUBLIC
Atlantic report. Atlan 215:44+ Ap '65
Colored rulers. G. C. Turner. Negro Hist
Bul 29:13-14 O '65
See also
Technical assistance in the Cameroon Re-
public

Religious institutions and affairs

News of the Christian world. Christian Cent
82:1611+ D 29 '65
CAMMACK, Floyd M.
Library/USA's first season. por ALA Bul 59:
115-19 F '65
Radio active library. por Library J 90:4300-2
O 15 '65
CAMOLETTI, Marc
Boeing-Boeing; adaptation. See Cross, B.
CAMP (term)
Call it camp. G. Frazier. il Holiday 38:12+
N '65
Not good taste, not bad taste, it's camp. T.
Meehan. il N Y Times Mag p30-1+ Mr
21 '65

CAMP cookery
Cabin guests just help themselves. il Sunset 135:62-3 Ag '65
Food for a camping vacation; with menus. B. M. Stover. il Parents Mag 40:71-4+ Ap '65
Here are eight delicious one-pan meals for backpackers. Sunset 135:122-3 Ag '65
See also
Barbecue cookery
CAMP equipment. See Camping outfits
CAMP fires
Campfires. T. Trueblood. il Field & S 70:24+ Je '65
CAMP lighting
Electricity in camp. C. B. Colby. il Outdoor Life 136:100-1+ Ag '65
CAMP sites. See Camps
CAMP stoves
Cooking on the front page; newspaper-burning grill. C. Conley. il Field & S 70:145 My '65
Take along your own campfire. M. Lindberg. il Pop Sci 186:152-5 Je '65
Testing the Gaz S-200. il Field & S 69:117 F '65
CAMPAIGN for nuclear disarmament (organization)
British peace movement: looking for the marchers. T. Roszak. il Nation 201:273-7 O 25 '65
Where have all the young men gone? N. Moss. il Sat R 48:26-7+ Ap 17 '65
CAMPAIGN funds
Dollars (15,000) for Democrats. A. Kopkind. New Repub 154:15-16 Ja 8 '66
Staggering cost of running for office. U S News 59:8 D 6 '65
Switch in campaign giving. H. E. Alexander and H. B. Meyers. il Fortune 72:170-2+ N '65
Who's responsible now? National council for civic responsibility and Democratic party. Nat R 17:224-6 Mr 23 '65
CAMPAIGNS, Advertising. See Advertising campaigns
CAMPAIGNS, Money raising. See Fund raising
CAMPAIGNS, Political. See Political campaigns
CAMPAIGNS, Presidential. See Presidential campaigns
CAMPBELL, Alan K.
National-state-local systems of government and intergovernmental aid. bibliog f Ann Am Acad 359:94-106 My '65
CAMPBELL, Alex
Mann to watch. New Repub 152:13-15 Je 5 '65
Nehru: sixty years to power. New Repub 152:20+ My 1 '65
Not for attribution. New Repub 152:7-8 Mr 13 '65
Since Hiroshima. New Repub 153:27-8 Ag 7 '65
CAMPBELL, Angus. See Eckerman, W. C. jt. auth.
CAMPBELL, Bryn
Right way to zoom. U S Camera 28:66-7+ Ap '65
CAMPBELL, Clarence
Private game: no admittance! J. Olsen. il Sports Illus 22:64-6+ Ap 12 '65
CAMPBELL, Gladys
Show birds of the show-me state. Audubon Mag 67:122-3 Mr '65
CAMPBELL, Gladys (professor)
Some recollections of the Poetry club at the University of Chicago. Poetry 107:110-17 N '65
CAMPBELL, Henry C.
New ways with old books. por Library J 90:5043-4 N 15 '65
CAMPBELL, John C.
Decision at Sinai. Sat R 48:55-6 Ap 17 '65
CAMPBELL, Joseph
Watchdog agency tugs on leash. por Bsns W p76+ Je 12 '65
CAMPBELL, Jule
Way out West in the Bois de Boulogne. Sports Illus 23:56-8 Ag 23 '65
CAMPBELL, Lawrence
Other side of freedom. Art N 64:32-4+ Sum '65
CAMPBELL, Patton
Costume in the theatre. Opera N 30:36 Ja 15 '66
CAMPBELL, Richard D.
Cell proliferation in hydra: an autoradiographic approach. bibliog Science 148:1231-2 My 28 '65
CAMPBELL, T. L.
Long-lived solid-state circuits. Science 147:1472-7 Mr 19 '65
CAMPBELLITES. See Disciples of Christ

CAMPERS and coaches, Truck
Camping on wheels. C. B. Colby. il Outdoor Life 136:26+ N '65
Expandable camper spreads its sides. il Pop Sci 186:82-3 F '65
Gains for truck sales zip past rise in autos. il Bsns W p25 Mr 6 '65
Hitch & go. C. Isica. See issues of Motor trend
Indoor comfort for outdoorsmen; Dreamer pickup camper rally in Hershey, Pa. il Bsns W p30-1 Ag 7 '65
New look in pickups. R. Barlow. il Field & S 69:24+ Mr '65
Newest campers and camp trailers. il Bet Hom & Gard 43:138+ Ap '65
She bought a camper van, then she remodeled it; Mrs M. Ehrman's ideas. il Sunset 135:92+ S '65
Swing low, sweet status symbol. R. Starnes. Field & S 69:22+ F '65
Tent trailer to Alaska. E. A. Bauer. il Field & S 70:37-9 Je '65
Testing a travel wagon; Clark Cortez. R. Barlow. il Field & S 70:36+ My '65
Variations for the open road. il Newsweek 66:72-3 Jl 26 '65
We rented a roving cabin. G. S. Wells. il McCalls 93:60+ O '65
Which vacation-on-wheels is best for you? L. Oertle. il Pop Sci 186:112-17 Ap '65

Renting
Instant trailering. B. Behme. il Field & S 70:154-7+ My '65
CAMPING
Be my guest! Apache Indian reservation open to campers. B. Hackett. il Recreation 58:115+ Mr '65
Camping. C. B. Colby. See issues of Outdoor life
Family approach to regional planning; Rocky Mountain National Park. D. S. Moore. Nat Parks Mag 39:19 S '65
Indoor comfort for outdoorsmen; Dreamer pickup camper rally in Hershey, Pa. il Bsns W p30-1 Ag 7 '65
Let's take a family camping vacation! R. Charles. Parents Mag 40:68+ Ap '65
New horizons in camping. il Recreation 58:124-5 Mr '65
Personal business. Bsns W p 173-4 My 22 '65
Road to camp right. P. L. Levin. il N Y Times Mag p68+ Mr 7 '65
Secrets of camping pleasure; excerpt from Anyone can camp in comfort. J. R. Johnson. il Field & S 69:48-51 F '65
You meet such wonderful people. D. Lambert. il Field & S 70:46-7+ Je '65
See also
Camping outfits
Camps
Outdoor life

Activities
Something new every day; Chicago Park District day camps. G. Thomas. il Recreation 58:129 Mr '65

Caricatures and cartoons
There's a good place! J. A. Chapleau. Field & S 69:68-9 F '65

Health aspects
How to be happy though outdoors. J. Martenhoff. il Outdoor Life 136:58-9+ Jl '65

Safety devices and measures
What to do about wild animals. C. B. Colby. Outdoor Life 135:124-7 Mr '65

Alaska
Jet age camping; cabin camping in Alaska's Tongass national forest. H. E. McLean. il Am For 71:16-17+ Jl '65

California
They are trespass-camping. il Sunset 135:34 O '65

Canada
We explore Saskatchewan. C. B. Colby. il Outdoor Life 136:22-4+ D '65; 137:112-13+ Ja '66

Europe, Western
Traveling with Mlle; camping in Europe. R. Leaper. Mlle 61:121-2 Je '65

Mexico
What's it like to camp in Mexico? Sunset 135:50+ S '65

Michigan
Campurbia; crowded tent and trailer cities. H. M. Gregerson. il Am For 71:18-20 Jl '65

CAMPING—*Continued*

Minnesota

Try Paul Bunyan country for vacation size; northern Minnesota. J. Engh. il Todays Health 43:18-23 Jl '65

Russia

We camped in Soviet Russia. C. B. Colby. il Outdoor Life 136:48-9+ S '65

Southern states

Go South for camping. J. R. Gregg. il Field & S 69:70-3 F '65

Utah

My secret of summertime escape. E. A. Bauer. il Outdoor Life 135:40-3+ Je '65

CAMPING outfits

Family camping was never like this! R. Charles. il Parents Mag 40:82-6 Ap '65

First overnight camp. C. B. Colby. il Outdoor Life 135:16+ Ap '65

Recreation. il Consumer Rep 30:262-72 D '65

Some best buys in camping gear. il Changing T 19:21-3 My '65

That small emergency. C. B. Colby. il Outdoor Life 136:100-2 Jl '65

What's new in camping. C. B. Colby. il Outdoor Life 135:20+ My '65

What's new in camping equipment. il Good H 160:170-1 Je '65

Which vacation-on-wheels is best for you? L. Oertle. il Pop Sci 186:112-17 Ap '65

See also
Camp cookery
Clothing and dress—Sports clothes
Sleeping bags
Tents

CAMPION, Donald R.

Book of the month. Cath World 201:269-70 Jl '65

Book reviews. America 113:166-8 Ag 14 '65

Books. Commonweal 83:318 D 10 '65

Books to be noted; home scene. America 112:684-7+ My 8 '65

New trend in encyclicals? Commonweal 82:714-15 O 1 '65

Phenomenon of Teilhard. America 112:480-1, 697 Ap 10, My 15 '65

War on addiction. America 112:356-9 Mr 13 '65

CAMPO DEL CIELO crater. See Meteorite craters

CAMPOS, Roberto de Oliveira

That man in Rio; target of C. Lacerda's criticism. por Time 85:45 Je 11 '65

CAMPS

Acculturation at camp; summer camp under Christian auspices. J. C. Evans. Christian Cent 82:1182 S 29 '65

Choosing your day camp site. M. Melamed. il Recreation 58:122-3 Mr '65

How to choose a good camp. H. G. Gibbs. il Parents Mag 40:72-4+ Mr '65

National youth science camp has convened. Sci N L 88:40 Jl 17 '65

Road to camp right. P. L. Levin. il N Y Times Mag p68+ Mr 7 '65

Summer camp education for underprivileged children; Edgewater creche, 1884-1964. F. M. Cordasco and J. G. Redd. bibliog f Sch & Soc 93:299 Sum '65

What camp for your child? excerpt from Today's health guide. il Todays Health 43:35-7 Jl '65

See also
Audubon nature camps
Labor camps
Music camps

Anecdotes, facetiae, satire, etc.

Send now for birchbark brochure. R. Angell. New Yorker 41:40-1 Mr 27 '65

CAMPS for the handicapped

Giant stride; VA hospital, Bedford, Mass. P. Poulicakos. Recreation 58:131+ Mr '65

Trial at Tippecanoe; Logansport state hospital, Ind. C. A. Lubbert. Recreation 58:130-1 Mr '65

CAMPUS CITY, Chicago. See Illinois. University, Urbana—Chicago campus

CAMPUS life. See Student life

CAMPUS planning

Building types study. il Arch Rec 137:143-66 Je '65

CAMRANH BAY

Mecca on the bay; supply base at Cam Ranh Bay. F. Sully. Newsweek 66:34+ S 13 '65

Port of entry for U.S. power; Cam Ranh Bay. K. M. Chrysler. il U S News 59:50-2 O 11 '65

CAMUS, Albert

Casebook of conscience. por Newsweek 66:122 O 25 '65

His doubt was not without hope. A. Darack. por Sat R 48:59-60 O 23 '65

Letter from Paris. Genêt. New Yorker 40:115-16 F 6 '65

Portrait of a secular moralist. T. S. Szasz. New Repub 153:32-3 N 27 '65

Substance of spirit. H. Clurman. Nation 201:310-11 N 1 '65

CAN (periodical) See College and school journalism

CANADA

Canada: carving out a new future? il Sr Schol 86:12-15 My 13 '65

Canada's great debate. il Bsns W p84-6+ My 22 '65

Why fear the future? complacency in a land of plenty; address, June 28, 1965. W. C. Mainwaring. Vital Speeches 31:691-6 S 1 '65

See also
Aeronautics, Military—Canada
Airplanes, Military—Canada
Architecture—Canada
Booksellers and bookselling—Canada
Camping—Canada
Church unity—Canada
Crime and criminals—Canada
Dams—Canada
Elections—Canada
Fishing—Canada
Frontier and pioneer life—Canada
Gardens—Canada
Georgian Bay
Hunting—Canada
Income tax—Canada
Insurance, Health—Canada
Investments, Foreign (in Canada)
Libraries—Canada
Mackenzie River
Opera—Canada
Paleontology—Canada
Periodicals—Canada
Public welfare—Canada
Quebec (province)
Strikes—Canada
Tariff—Canada
Tourist trade—Canada
Trails—Canada
Yukon

Commerce

Common market for U.S. and Canada? interview. H. G. Johnson. il U S News 58:98-101 F 8 '65

Domino effect; collapse of Atlantic acceptance corp. Newsweek 66:80-1 O 4 '65

Moving wheat to Russia. il Time 86:34 Ag 20 '65

U.S. and Canada trade relations; address, December 15, 1964. S. J. Randall. Vital Speeches 31:251-4 F 1 '65

Commercial treaties and agreements

Automotive products agreement with Canada becomes effective; statements, October 22, 1965, with texts of the proclamation and the order. L. B. Johnson. Dept State Bul 53:793-5 N 15 '65

President asks authority to remove duties on Canadian auto products; letter, March 31, 1965. L. B. Johnson. Dept State Bul 52:638-9 Ap 26 '65

U.S. and Canada sign agreement on trade in automotive products; exchange of remarks; with text of agreement, January 16, 1965. L. B. Johnson; L. B. Pearson. Dept State Bul 52:191-4 F 8 '65

Defenses

Canada shifts defense emphasis in tactical air force buildup. Aviation W 82:287 Mr 15 '65

See also
North American air defense command

Description and travel

Canada: islands galore. N. D. Ford. il Travel 124:26-31 Ag '65

Canada: land of contrast and diversity. V. S. Pritchett. il Read Digest 86:200-2+ Ap '65

Cruising the Rideau. F. M. Paulson. il Field & S 70:40-3 Ja '66

Just across the border. P. P. Coleman. il Sr Schol 86:sup8-9 Ap 15 '65

North of the border; Bob Kane's Canada. R. S. Kane. il Pop Phot 56:88-91+ Je '65

Vacation high spots in Canada. il Bet Hom & Gard 43:151-6 My '65

Economic conditions

Boom to the North; Canada cashes in. il U S News 58:72-4 Je 28 '65

Canada rides a crest, Japan fights recession; inflation worries Latin America. il Bsns W p48-9 Ja 1 '66

CANADA—Economic conditions—*Continued*
Edging close to full capacity. il Bsns W p98-9 Ja 8 '66
When good times hit Canadian prairies. il U S News 59:138-9 O 18 '65

Economic policy
Canada takes chill off winter unemployment; building of public works and houses. il Bsns W p 118+ Ja 15 '66
Wheat deal adds yeast to Canadian politics. il Bsns W p36+ S 4 '65

Economic relations
United States
Canada and the United States, principles for partnership; report, June 28, 1965. L. T. Merchant and A. D. P. Heeney. Dept State Bul 53:193-208 Ag 2 '65

Foreign relations
Canada; with editorial comment. H. Mac-Lennan. il Am Heritage 17:4, 6-45+ D '65
Shastri-Pearson talks. Nation 200:686 Je 28 '65
United States
Between friends. Newsweek 66:51 Jl 26 '65
Canada and the United States, principles for partnership; report, June 28, 1965. L. T. Merchant and A. D. P. Heeney. Dept State Bul 53:193-208 Ag 2 '65
Canadian complaints. America 113:277-8 S 18 '65
Canadian national elections; campaign issues. B. Fraser. New Repub 153:10-11 N 6 '65
What Canada's election means to the U.S. il U S News 59:78 N 22 '65

Historic houses, etc.
To Canada in '67? reconstruction of Ste Marie Among-the-Hurons mission center. America 112:795 My 29 '65

History
Canada; with editorial comment. H. Mac-Lennan. il Am Heritage 17:4, 6-45+, D '65
See also
Frontier and pioneer life—Canada

Nationalism
Guy Trimble vs. Guy Tremblay; clash of English and French could destroy Canada. J. Walz. il N Y Times Mag p38-9+ S 19 '65

Politics and government
All those rusty wires. Time 85:45 F 5 '65
Atlantic report (cont) Atlan 215:14+ Ap '65
Back in harness; Pearson's 1965 legislative program. Newsweek 65:52 Ap 19 '65
Canada, by G. Clark. Review
    Sat R 48:49+ N 13 '65. R. T. Elson
Canada's quiet revolution; a degree of autonomy for Quebec. A. Deming. il Newsweek 65:58-60 Mr 15 '65
Changing the line-up. il Time 86:28 D 24 '65
Halfway housecleaning. Time 86:39 Jl 16 '65
Last hurrah as the power failed. N. McKenty. America 113:665 N 27 '65
Lining up for Canada's next round. il Bsns W p38 O 9 '65
O Canada, by E. Wilson. Review
    Sat R 48:37 My 29 '65. R. T. Elson
Survival issue. Newsweek 66:50 S 20 '65
Teasing game. il Time 86:31 S 10 '65
We're nothing, but we want to be something; attitudes of students at University of Montreal, and McGill. R. Hoffmann. il Mlle 62:155-7+ N '65
See also
Elections—Canada
Federal and provincial relations (Canada)
French Canadians
Political parties—Canada
Socialism—Canada

Religious institutions and affairs
News of the Christian world (cont) Christian Cent 82:1587-8 D 22 '65
See also
Church unity—Canada
Presbyterian church in Canada

Royal Canadian mounted police
Royal Canadian mounted police. D. F. Brown. il Hobbies 70:46-7+ Mr '65

Secession
See Canada—Politics and government

Social life and customs
See also
Christmas—Canada

CANADA and China (People's Republic)
No-enterprise system; full-time correspondent in China of Toronto's Globe and mail. Nation 201:178 O 4 '65

CANADA and the United States
Canadian complaints. America 113:277-8 S 18 '65
United States and Canada: common aims and common responsibilities; address, March 22, 1965. G. W. Ball. Dept State Bul 52:572-6 Ap 19 '65

Anecdotes, facetiae, satire, etc.
American's view of Canada dimly seen through the mists of Niagara Falls; pictorial map. Am Heritage 17:2-3 D '65

CANADA geese. See Geese, Wild

CANADA-United States permanent joint board on defense. See Permanent joint board on defense, United States and Canada

CANADAIR, limited
Charters are main CL-44J sales target. il Aviation W 83:42-3+ D 20 '65

CANADAY, John
Art that pulses, quivers and fascinates. N Y Times Mag p 12-13+ F 21 '65
Giotto and Duccio. Horizon 7:92-107 Sum '65
Memories of another fair. N Y Times Mag p71-2 Ap 18 '65
What Miss America is made of. N Y Times Mag p 124+ S 19 '65

CANADIAN booksellers association
CBA: speeding up distribution is theme of Toronto meeting; 14th annual convention. Pub W 187:57-62+ Je 21 '65

CANADIAN Eskimos. See Eskimos

CANADIAN library association
Canadian library association to meet in Toronto; June 25-July 1, 1965. E. H. Morton. ALA Bul 59:394 My '65
New directions; 20th annual conference. S. Havens. il Library J 90:3217-21 Ag '65

CANADIAN MARITIME PROVINCES. See Maritime Provinces, Canada

CANADIAN mounted police. See Canada—Royal Canadian mounted police

CANADIAN opera company
Canadian east. R. Ubriaco. il Opera N 30:25-6 N 20 '65

CANADIAN ROCKIES, Trail riders of the. See Trail riders of the Canadian Rockies

CANADIANS
We're nothing, but we want to be something; attitudes of students at University of Montreal, and McGill. R. Hoffmann. il Mlle 62:155-7+ N '65

CANADIENS (hockey team) See Hockey teams

CANAIMA, Venezuela
To the highest waterfall in all the world. il Sunset 135:24-6+ S '65

CANAL ZONE. See Panama Canal Zone

CANALS
Where shall we build the new canal? C. W. Hall. il Read Digest 87:213-14+ S '65
See also
Panama Canal

Canada
See also
Rideau Canal

Central America
Atlantic report; possibility of nuclear excavation for new canal. Atlan 215:28+ My '65
Canal hitch; proposed new sea-level canal connecting the Atlantic and Pacific. il Time 85:32 F 12 '65
Marine biology and a new canal; letter. J. D. Davis. Science 148:579-80 Ap 30 '65
Mr Ailes and Mr Mann hold opening talks on sea-level canal; Department announcement, January 21, 1965. Dept State Bul 52:164 F 8 '65
Science in action: mixing oceans and species. I. Rubinoff. Natur Hist 74:69-72 Ag '65
Sea-level canal: how and where. J. H. Stratton. For Affairs 43:513-18 Ap '65
Where shall we build the new canal? C. W. Hall. il Read Digest 87:213-14+ S '65
See also
United States—Interoceanic canal commission

Florida
Cross-Florida Barge Canal. Liv Wildn 29:39 Sum '65

Ireland
Cows on the quay; cruise on the Grand Canal. P. Redford. il Atlan 215:178+ Mr '65

Middle western states
Midwest canal plan barges toward decision; to link Ohio River with Lake Erie. il Bsns W p 194+ My 15 '65

CANALS—*Continued*

Sweden

See also
Gota Canal

United States

Ditched again; Washington's pork-barrel engineers. Nation 201:290 N 1 '65
See also
Erie Canal

Le CANARD enchaîné (newspaper) See Newspapers—France

CANAVAN, Francis P.
Academic revoluion at St John's. America 113:136-40 Ag 7 '65
Book review. America 113:417+ O 9 '65
Books to be noted; world scene. America 112:681-3 My 8 '65
Changing Jewish attitudes. America 112:214 F 13 '65
Reflections on the revolution in sex. America 112:312-15, 458 Mr 6, Ap 3 '65
St John's university: the issues. America 114:122-4 Ja 22 '66

about

New education bill. America 112:108-9+ Ja 23 '65; Correction. 112:275 F 27 '65

CANAVERAL, CAPE. See Kennedy, Cape

CANBERRA, Australia
After the long wait, Canberra's ready. il Sunset 135:30 O '65

CANCER
Bill Gargan's greatest role; actor speaks out against cancer. il Life 59:63-4 D 3 '65
Breast cancer reported in girls fourteen and seventeen. Sci N L 88:194 S 25 '65
Cancer: what medicine can do about it now. G. G. Greer. Bet Hom & Gard 43:32+ Ag '65
Chromosomal breakage in a rare and probably genetically determined syndrome of man. J. German and others. bibliog il Science 148:506 Ap 23 '65
Eye cancer can be cured. F. Marley. Sci N L 88:327 N 20 '65
Feather of a dove; a husband's tribute to his wife; excerpt from More than booty. B. Crile. il Redbook 126:42-3+ Ja '66
Indicting a virus; affinity between Burkitt's tumor and leukemia. il Time 87:68 Ja 14 '66
Let's stop these needless cancer deaths! excerpt from Climate is hope. W. S. Ross. il McCalls 92:82+ Ap '65
Over-surgery questioned; mastectomy for breast cancers. Sci N L 88:2 Jl 3 '65
Pigmented nevi and malignant melanomas as studied with a specific fluorescence method. B. Falck and others. bibliog Science 149:439 Jl 23 '65
Tumor village; Buggiano's cancer mortality. il Newsweek 66:86 S 20 '65
Zeroing in on three killer diseases. Bsns W p 170+ O 23 '65
See also
Cancer research
Sarcoma

Causes

Bracken, cancer link seen. Sci N L 88:402 D 25 '65
Can we really cure cancer? F. Marley. il Sci N L 87:250-1 Ap 17 '65
Cancer linked to trauma. Sci N L 88:22 Jl 10 '65
Cancer, personality link; feelings of despair typical of patients. Sci N L 87:245 Ap 17 '65
Circulating DNA as a possible factor in oncogenesis. A. Bendich and others. bibliog il Science 148:374-6 Ap 16 '65
New clues to the mystery of cancer. M. Clark. Read Digest 87:157-8+ Jl '65
Pinning down the suspects; industrial smog and cigarette smoke. Newsweek 66:96 N 8 '65
Putting the clues to work. R. M. Deutsch. Read Digest 87:160+ Jl '65
Why cancer may be psychosomatic; reprint. il Sci Digest 58:75-8 S '65

Diagnosis

Cancer detection risky. Sci N L 87:229 Ap 10 '65
Diagnose uterine cancer; fluorometric test. Sci N L 87:341 My 29 '65
Level of urine enzymes gives clue to cancer. Sci N L 88:168 S 11 '65
Way to control the cancer no one talks about; colon-rectum cancer. Good H 160:173-4 Mr '65

Hospitals

Doctors too immature; question of cancer centers. Sci N L 89:2 Ja 1 '66

Prevention and control

Cancer, clotting linked. Sci N L 87:114 F 20 '65
Do-it-yourself test that could cut the toll; Davis test for uterine cancer. il Bsns W p74+ Mr 13 '65
Formula for beating cancer. S. S. Steinberg. il Todays Health 43:36-7+ Ap '65
New war against cancer brings control closer. Sci N L 87:229 Ap 10 '65
Rising hope in war on cancer. il U S News 58:55-6 Ap 19 '65
See also
American cancer society
Strang clinic, New York

Statistics

More than two million cancer patients alive. Sci N L 88:312 N 13 '65

Therapy

Adenosylmethionine elevation in leukemic white blood cells. R. J. Baldessarini and P. P. Carbone. bibliog il Science 149:644-5 Ag 6 '65
Approve treating cancer in pregnancy. Sci N L 88:398 D 18 '65
Can we really cure cancer? F. Marley. il Sci N L 87:250-1 Ap 17 '65
Cancerous tumor masses shrunk by antibiotic; mithramycin. Sci N L 87:98 F 13 '65
Injections could help breast cancer patients. Sci N L 88:360 D 4 '65
Laser on the cancer frontier; with account by M. Steinmann. il Life 59:70-1+ Jl 9 '65
Myeloma proteins and the clinical response to melphalan therapy. D. E. Bergsagel and others. bibliog il Science 148:376-7 Ap 16 '65; Discussion. 149:564-5 Jl 30 '65
Now, A-blasts for cancer. A. J. Snider. il Sci Digest 58:16-17 D '65
Peggy was dying; first cancer cure by methotrexate. W. S. Ross. il Ladies Home J 82:50-1+ Jl '65
Rising hope in war on cancer. il U S News 58:55-6 Ap 19 '65

CANCER centers. See Cancer—Hospitals

CANCER producing substances
Carcinogenic aromatic hydrocarbons: special vulnerability of rats. C. B. Huggins and others. bibliog il Science 147:1153-4 Mr 5 '65
Fluoride and cancer. A. Taylor. Sat R 48:73 O 2 '65
See also
Cycasin
Uracil

CANCER research
Beta-solamarine: tumor inhibitor isolated from solanum dulcamara. S. M. Kupchan and others. bibliog il Science 150:1827-8 D 31 '65
Cancer folk medicine effective in test tube; study on milkweed and dogbane. Sci N L 87:393 Je 19 '65
Cancer research; report on nineteenth annual symposium. D. N. Ward. Science 150:1063-4+ N 19 '65
Cancer research: why a top authority is optimistic; interview. F. L. Horsfall, jr. il U S News 58:57+ Ap 19 '65
Cancer: the long war. M. Clark. il Newsweek 65:68-9 Ap 12 '65
Cell division and cancer; address, My 13, 1965. A. Szent-Györoyi. bibliog Science 149:34-7 Jl 2 '65
Coming: a cancer breakthrough; reprint. H. M. Schmeck, jr. il Sci Digest 58:57-62 Ag '65
Curb cancer development. Sci N L 88:36 Ag 7 '65
Irradiated cells repaired. F. Marley. Sci N L 87:259 Ap 24 '65
Mosquito gives cancer. F. Marley. Sci N L 87:371 Je 12 '65
New clues to the mystery of cancer. M. Clark. Read Digest 87:157-8+ Jl '65
Patient's right to know; experiments at Jewish chronic disease hospital. J. Lear. Sat R 48:20 Je 26 '65
Putting the clues to work. R. M. Deutsch. Read Digest 87:160+ Jl '65
Radiation carcinogenesis: the sequence of events. L. J. Cole and P. C. Nowell. bibliog il Science 150:1782-6 D 31 '65
Separation and partial purification of plasma-membrane fragments from Ehrlich ascites carcinoma microsomes. V. B. Kamat and D. F. H. Wallach. bibliog il Science 148:1343-5 Je 4 '65

CANCER research—*Continued*
Up in the air; question of air pollution and cancer. il Newsweek 65:60 Ap 19 '65
War on cancer, 1965. il Sci Digest 58:33-4 Jl '65
See also
Sloan-Kettering institute for cancer research
CANCER tests. See Cancer—Diagnosis
CANCER viruses
Big cancer riddle. Sci Digest 59:38 Ja '66
Brain tumors, gliomas induced in hamsters by Bryan's strain of Rous sarcoma virus. G. F. Rabotti and others. bibliog il Science 147:504-6 Ja 29 '65
Successive transformations of an established cell line by polyoma virus and SV40. G. J. Todaro and H. Green. bibliog il Science 147:513-14 Ja 29 '65
Tumor and virus antigens of simian virus 40: differential inhibition of synthesis by cytosine arabinoside. F. Rapp and others. bibliog il Science 147:625-7 F 5 '65
CANDAU, Marcolino G.
United Nations commemoration address, June 25, 1965. UN Mo Chron 2:138-40 Jl '65
CANDIDATES, Political
California's political free-for-all: race for the governorship. D. S. Broder. il Look 29: 61-2+ Jl 13 '65
Taking a stand; endorsement by radio stations. Newsweek 66:71 N 8 '65
See also
Political campaigns
CANDIED fruit. See Confectionery
CANDIED grapefruit peel. See Confectionery
CANDLE holders. See Candlesticks
CANDLES
Christmas by candlelight. M. White. il Ladies Home J 82:78-9 D '65
Handcrafted candles using chip carving or sgraffito. il Sunset 135:106 D '65
CANDLESTICKS
Two candle holders of unique design. il Pop Sci 187:150-1 N '65
CANDY
Candies without cooking, or almost. il Ladies Home J 82:66-7+ D '65
Holiday candies, sweets, and comfits. il House & Gard 128:202-3 D '65
Night before Christmas; poem; with holiday suggestions. il Redbook 126:49-61+ D '65
Recipes from a good cook's notebook; holiday season cookery. R. Hanna. il Suc Farm 63: 60-1+ D '65
Sweet conceits. il House & Gard 128:140-3 D '65
See also
Confectionery
CANFIELD, Jane
Findings in a valley. Read Digest 86:86-90 My '65
CANHAM, Erwin D.
Why the Monitor changed. Sat R 48:78-9 Ap 10 '65
CANKERS
Those pesky mouth sores. E. J. Driscoll and E. A. Graykowski. il Todays Health 44:32-4 Ja '66
CANNED food
Take a can of seafood. V. T. Habeeb. il Am Home 68:62+ Mr '65
CANNED hams. See Meat, Canned
CANNES international film festival
Annual rites at Cannes. A. Schlesinger, jr. Harper 230:79-84 F '65
Cannes caper. W. Wiser. Reporter 33:43-4+ N 18 '65
Cannes sans brio. il Newsweek 65:80 Je 7 '65
Dog days at Cannes; 1965 entries. H. Alpert. il Sat R 48:23-4 Je 26 '65
CANNIBALISM
Indian ate Indian thirty centuries ago. Sci N L 87:217 Ap 3 '65
CANNING and preserving
Dangers of canned food should not be ignored. Sci N L 88:164 S 11 '65
See also
Jelly, jam, etc.
CANNING and preserving industry and trade
Reporter at large; Eskimo canneries for Eskimo foods, results of sampling in district of Keewatin. E. Iglauer. New Yorker 41:121-2+ Ap 24 '65
CANNON, Poppy
Line a day. Ladies Home J 82:96 D '65; 83:87 Ja '66
CANOE racing
1965 Little Miami River canoe races. il Motor B 116:52 S '65
CANOE trips
Arctic adventure. C. E. Gillham. il Field & S 70:40-2+ Ag '65

Bird, the vow and the child; search through the marshlands of southern New Jersey. B. Gilbert. il Sports Illus 23:58-62+ Ag 30 '65
Down the Danube by canoe; Dartmouth canoe club. W. S. Becker. il Nat Geog Mag 128:34-79 Jl '65
See also
Canoes and canoeing
CANOES and canoeing
Bark canoes and skin boats of North America, by E. T. Adney and H. I. Chapelle. Review
Am Heritage 16:72-4 F '65. B. Catton
Canoeing made easy; Shenandoah River. F. M. Paulson. il Field & S 70:110-13 S '65
Family canoe trip; Minnesota-Ontario boundary waters canoe area. J. R. Gregg. il Field & S 70:58-60+ Je '65
See also
Indians of North America—Boats
Accidents
See Boats and boating—Accidents
CANON law. See Ecclesiastical law
CANON law society of America
Letter and spirit. America 112:183 F 6 '65; Discussion. 112:301, 507+ Mr 6, Ap 17 '65
CANON Pellix reflex cameras. See Single lens reflex cameras
CANONSBURG, Pa.
Renegotiated contract brings better service. Am City 80:128 S '65
CANT, Gilbert
Intelligent woman's guide to the population explosion. McCalls 92:32+ F '65; Same abr. with title What the population explosion really means. Read Digest 86:103-6 My '65
Joint for next season. Sports Illus 22:38-41 F 8 '65
CANTAGIRO. See Singing—Competitions
CANTALOUPES. See Muskmelons
CANTATAS
See also
Phonograph records—Cantatas
CANTATE (record company) See Phonograph record industry—Germany (Federal Republic)
CANTELON, John E.
Whatever happened to Religious emphasis week? Christian Cent 82:396-8 Mr 31 '65
CANTERBURY, Arthur Michael Ramsey, abp of. See Ramsey, A. M.
CANTILEVERED girders. See Girders
CANTON, China
China, birth control and Bibles. R. Terrill. New Repub 152:13-14 F 6 '65
CANTOR, Arnold
Election and negotiation in Rochester. por NEA J 54:22-3 S '65
CANTOR, Lon
Booster for FM stereo. Electr World 73:83-4 My '65
Coax vs twinlead. Electr World 74:34-6 Jl '65
How to improve color TV antenna installations. Pop Electr 22:52-3+ My '65
How to stack TV antennas to increase signal strength and to reduce ghosts. Pop Electr 23:63-5+ N '65
Indispensable antenna. Hi Fi 15:64-7+ O '65
CANTOR, Milton
Inheritors of the faith. Nation 200:366-8 Ap 5 '65
Tooth, fang and trust. Sat R 48:41 Ap 10 '65
CANTOR, Sol M.
Obituary
Pub W 187:41 Mr 15 '65
CANTWELL, Robert
Field hockey. Sports Illus 22:68-70 My 31 '65
Lacrosse. Sports Illus 22:70+ My 17 '65
CANVAS
Canvas. P. Corey. il Pop Gard 16:28-31 Mr '65
CANVAS boats. See Boats—Materials
CANVASSING, Political. See Political campaigns
CANYON DE CHELLY NATIONAL MONUMENT
Nature and man in Canyon de Chelly. M. M. Guillet. il Nat Parks Mag 39:9-11 Jl '65
CANYON DIABLO crater. See Meteorite craters
CANYONLANDS NATIONAL PARK
Canyonland: newest national park. E. A. Floor. il Travel 124:56-7 Jl '65
Easterner's impression of Canyonlands. N. Ashby. il Am For 71:24-5+ Ag '65
In Utah, an early look at our newest national park. il Sunset 134:32+ Ap '65
Jouncy journey in a new parkland; Utah's Canyonlands. A. Higgins. il Sports Illus 23:50-6+ Jl 26 '65
Upheaval Dome. R. H. Rose. il Nat Parks Mag 39:11-15 S '65

CANYONS
Standing up country, by C. G. Crampton. Review
Liv Wildn il 29:29-31 Sum '65. M. T. Musselman
CANZONE festival, San Remo. See Music festivals—Italy
CAPA, Cornell
Like an iguana sitting on a log. G. P. Hunt. por Life 59:3 O 29 '65
CAPACITANCE, Electric. See Electric capacitance
CAPACITORS. See Electric capacitors
CAPE COD
Cape Cod. C. S. Dotts. il U S Camera 28:78-9+ Jl '65
Series of villages built around recreation; New Seabury, Waquoit. il Arch Rec 138:148-51 N '65
CAPE COD NATIONAL SEASHORE
Cape Cod's Marconi station site. C. R. Koehler. il Nat Parks Mag 39:18 S '65
CAPE HENLOPEN. See Henlopen, Cape
CAPECCHI, Mario R. and Gussin, G. N.
Suppression in vitro: identification of a serine-sRNA as a nonsense suppressor. bibliog Science 149:417-22 Jl 23 '65
CAPILLARIES
60,000 miles of tunnels form capillary network. Sci N L 88:56 Jl 24 '65
CAPITAL
See also
Liquidity (economics)
CAPITAL gains tax. See Income tax—Capital gains tax
CAPITAL investments
Biggest year ever coming up; McGraw-Hill survey of capital spending plans; with editorial comment. il Bsns W p70-2+, 192 N 6 '65
Boom: sign of a slack ahead? il Newsweek 65:75 Mr 15 '65
Breaking through $50-billion. il Bsns W p23-4 Mr 13 '65
Business pumps millions into depressed areas: job-creating investments. il Nations Bsns 53:36-7+ Mr '65
Changing the rules on growth; Brookings study report. il Bsns W p 142+ Mr 6 '65
Expansion gets larger share of spending; survey; with editorial comment. il Bsns W p24-6, 138 My 1 '65
Forecast for capital outlays: sunny. il Bsns W p 112+ S 25 '65
Investment analysis: coping with change. W. B. Hirschmann and J. R. Brauweiler. il Harvard Bsns R 43:62-72 My '65
On your marks, get set, spend. il Newsweek 66:55 S 6 '65
Respite for investment. il Fortune 71:28+ Je '65
Running to excess. il Fortune 72:48+ D '65
Slight pinch for cash. il Bsns W p45-6 Je 19 '65
Strength ahead. il Newsweek 65:72 Je 7 '65
Taking the rise in stride. il Bsns W p25-7 D 11 '65
CAPITAL market. See Money market
CAPITAL punishment
A.C.L.U. attacks capital punishment. Christian Cent 82:1150 S 22 '65
Capital punishment, W. Lester. il America 112:484-6 Ap 10 '65; Discussion. 112:831-3 Je 5 '65
Death for the death penalty? il Time 85:62-3 Ap 2 '65
Death penalty abolished; action in Iowa. P. B. Mather. Christian Cent 82:382 Mr 24 '65
End to the chair. Nation 200:575 My 31 '65
Exit the death penalty. Nation 200:266 Mr 15 '65
Last mile? death sentence dying out in the U.S. il Newsweek 65:26+ Mr 8 '65
Loophole for vengeance. Nation 200:435 Ap 26 '65
New attempts under way to abolish death penalty; What a poll shows. U S News 58:13 Ap 5 '65
New York abolishes death. Time 85:61 Je 11 '65
New York Senate would curtail capital punishment. Christian Cent 82:669 My 26 '65
On the death penalty. Nat R 17:406 My 18 '65
Power of life and death, by M. V. DiSalle. Review
Sat R 49:29-30 Ja 1 '66. J. F. Fixx
Question of value; death penalty in case of assassination of president or vice president. Time 86:16-17 Jl 2 '65
Russia shoots its business crooks; executions for economic crimes. G. Feifer. il N Y Times Mag p32-3+ My 2 '65
Toward a more humane society; abolishing the death penalty. Christian Cent 82:261 Mr 3 '65

Without portfolio. C. B. Luce. McCalls 92:12+ My '65
See also
Hanging
CAPITAL spending. See Capital investments
CAPITALISM
Accidental century, by M. Harrington. Review
Commonweal 82:667-8 S 17 '65. E. Capouya
Capitalism today. B. B. Seligman. Commentary 39:88-90 Ap '65
Inheritors of the faith. M. Cantor. Nation 200:366-8 Ap 5 '65
Socialism and capitalism: an international misunderstanding. R. K. White. il For Affairs 44:216-28 Ja '66
CAPITALISM and communism. See Communism and democracy
CAPITALISTS and financiers
See also
Millionaires
CAPITOL (United States) See United States—Capitol
CAPITOL ballet of Washington, D.C. See Ballet companies
CAPITOL records, incorporated
Broadway on records; Capitol at twenty-three; with discography. M. Kreuger. il Am Rec G 32:112-17+ O '65
CAPITOLS
See also subhead Capitol under names of countries, states, etc. e.g. North Carolina—Capitol
CAPITULATIONS, Military
Heart of deterrence. R. K. Coffey. il Bul Atomic Sci 21:27-9 Ap '65
CAPLAN, Gerald M.
Downgraded rights. Nat R 17:694 Ag 10 '65
CAPLAN, Ralph
It's the curve that counts. Consumer Rep 30:183-5 Ap '65
CAPLES, William G.
Traditional role of management. bibliog f Cur Hist 49:9-16+ Jl '65
CAPLIN, Mortimer Maxwell
What's wrong with our tax system? interview; ed. by G. R. Rosen. por Duns R 85:36-7+ F '65
about
Caplin takes over. Newsweek 65:70+ My 31 '65
New payroll plan: more taxes from weekly checks. por U S News 59:74-5 D 27 '65
Profiles; federal income-tax. J. Brooks. New Yorker 41:66+ Ap 3 '65
CAPOFERRI, Joseph
Wild windswept strand; Down to the sea; poems. Liv Wildn 29:16 Spr '65
CAPON, Robert F.
Herzog and the passion. America 112:425-7 Mr 27 '65
Priest with a breezy way. il pors Life 59:79-80 D 3 '65
CAPOTE, Truman
Annals of crime; In cold blood. New Yorker 41:57-60+ S 25; 57-60+ O 2; 58-62+ O 9; 62-4+ O 16 '65
Curious gift. Redbook 125:52-3+ Je '65
Sylvia Odyssey. il Vogue 147:68-75 Ja 15 '66
about
Author. H. Frankel. por Sat R 49:36-7 Ja 22 '66
Book reviews. T. Greene. America 114:142+ Ja 22 '66
Capote in Kansas. S. Kauffmann. New Repub 154:19-21+ Ja 22 '66
Country below the surface; crime reporter. il por Time 87:83 Ja 21 '66
Horror spawns a masterpiece. il pors Life 60:58-62 Ja 7 '66
In a novel way. por Time 86:74+ O 8 '65
In cold blood, an American tragedy. il pors Newsweek 67:59-63 Ja 24 '66
People are talking about... pors Vogue 146:94-5 O 15 '65
Six-year literary vigil. J. Howard. il por Life 60:70-2+ Ja 7 '66
Story of an American tragedy. G. Hicks. Sat R 49:35-6 Ja 22 '66
Truman Capote and the country studio he designed for work. il pors Vogue 146:208-11 N 1 '65
CAPOUYA, Emile
Books. Commonweal 82:224-5, 568, 667-8 My 7, Ag 6, S 17 '65
Brief return from Mecca. Sat R 48:42+ N 20 '65
Crisis in creativity. Sat R 48:32-4 Ap 17 '65
Descendants of Eve. Sat R 48:34-5 Jl 17 '65
Existence behind the evidence. Sat R 48:28-9 Mr 28 '65

CAPOUYA, Emile—*Continued*
Free self in a captive society. Sat R 48:40-1
Je 12 '65
From rebellion to responsibility. Sat R 48:45
O 30 '65
Imperialism and the native. Sat R 48:38+
D 11 '65
Language of democracy. Sat R 48:31-2 My 8
'65
Mind on the heart of the matter. Sat R 48:55
O 2 '65
Protest march on purgatory. Sat R 48:41-2
S 25 '65
Time to turn a tide of violence? Sat R 48:
33-4 Ap 24 '65
To America, with some regret. Sat R 48:101
S 18 '65
Triumph of wit. Sat R 48:19 F 20 '65
Writer as subject. Sat R 48:35 Ag 14 '65

CAPP, Al
My life as an immortal myth. il Life 58:97-
100+ Ap 30 '65
Person who changed my life. por Seventeen
24:157 Ap '65
about
Getting their kicks; kigmies. Newsweek 66:
62 Jl 19 '65
Mellowed kickapoo. il Newsweek 65:80 F 22
'65

CAPPAERT, Lael
We keep a kitchen library. Parents Mag 40:
90 Je '65

CAPPEL, Heinz H.
Look to your lifelines. Motor B 116:102-3+
N '65

CAPPS, Benjamin
Up the river and over the Rockies. Sat R
48:27 F 20 '65

CAPRICCIO; opera. See Strauss, R.

CAPS, Bottle. See Bottle caps and seals

CAPSULES
Capsules that act on command; National
cash register co.'s encapsulation process.
il Bsns W p96 Jl 10 '65

CAPTIVE nations week
Captive nations week, 1965; proclamation. L.
B. Johnson. Dept State Bul 53:171 Jl 26 '65

CAPUCHINS
Capuchin cache of embarrassment; cigarette
smuggling monks. R. Espinosa. il Life 58:
38A My 28 '65
Capuchins' caper; smuggled American cigarettes found in monastery at Albano. il
Newsweek 65:47-8 My 31 '65

CAPUCINE
Hottest icicle. por Time 86:89 D 10 '65

CAR ferries. See Train ferries

CAR shelters. See Shelters

CAR-sitter; story. See Jordan, E. H.

CARACAS, Venezuela
Letter from Caracas. B. Taper. il New
Yorker 41:101-2+ Mr 6 '65

CARADON, Hugh Foot, baron
United Nations commemoration address, June
26, 1965. UN Mo Chron 2:165-8 Jl '65

CARAJÁ Indians. See Indians of South America—Brazil

CARAMOOR festivals. See Music festivals—
New York (state)

CARAS, Roger A.
Bird that stood 10 feet tall. Sci Digest 59:57-
60 Ja '66

CARAVAGGIO, Michelangelo Merisi da
Caravaggio: rehabilitation of a long-disdained
genius. il por UNESCO Courier 18:18-23
My '65

CARAVANS
I joined a Sahara salt caravan. V. Englebert.
il Nat Geog Mag 128:694-711 N '65
She bought a camper van, then she remodeled
it; Mrs M. Ehrman's ideas. il Sunset 135:
92+ S '65

CARAVANS, Motor. See Motor caravans

CARAWAN, Guy
Moment of history. New Yorker 41:37-8 Mr
27 '65

CARBANILIC acid
Enzyme from soil bacterium hydrolyzes
phenylcarbamate herbicides. P. C. Kearney
and D. D. Kaufman. Science 147:740 F 12
'65

CARBINES. See Rifles

CARBOHYDRATES
Reduction-like effect of carbohydrates on
cytochrome c. P. T. Mora and others. bibliog il Science 149:642-4 Ag 6 '65

CARBON
Carbon abundances in chondritic meteorites.
C. B. Moore and C. Lewis. bibliog il Sci-
ence 149:317 Jl 16 '65

Isotopes
Carbon-14 content of 18th- and 19th-century
wood: variations correlated with sunspot
activity. M. Stuiver. bibliog il Science 149:
533-5 Jl 30 '65
Carbon traces changes. Sci N L 87:116 F 20
'65
Free carbon atom chemistry. C. MacKay
and R. Wolfgang. bibliog il Science 148:
899-907 My 14 '65
Temperature dependence of carbon isotope
composition in marine plankton and sediments. W. M. Sackett and others. bibliog
il Science 148:235-7 Ap 9 '65
See also
Radiocarbon dating

CARBON compounds
See also
Hydrocarbons

CARBON dioxide
Carbon dioxide changed to breathable oxygen.
Sci N L 88:105 Ag 14 '65
Productivity of microalgae in Antarctic Sea
ice. P. R. Burkholder and E. F. Mandelli.
bibliog il Science 149:872-4 Ag 20 '65
Transhydrogenation in root tissue: mediation
by carbon dioxide. I. P. Ting and W. M.
Dugger, jr. bibliog il Science 150:1727-8 D
24 '65
See also
Plants, Effect of carbon dioxide on

CARBON 14. See Carbon—Isotopes

CARBON monoxide
Carboxyhemoglobin: hemodynamic and res-
piratory responses to small concentrations.
S. M. Ayres and others. bibliog il Science
149:193-4 Jl 9 '65
CO on the highway. Sci Am 212:52+ My '65
Exhaust fumes threaten driver in heavy
traffic. Sci N L 87:201 Mr 27 '65

CARBON tetrachloride
Avoid the risks of these toxic fumes. Good H
160:181 Mr '65

CARBON zinc batteries. See Storage batteries

CARBONACEOUS rocks. See Rocks, Sedimentary

CARBONATE-apatite
Carbonate in hydroxylapatite. D. R. Simpson.
bibliog il Science 147:501-2 Ja 29 '65

CARBONATE rocks. See Rocks

CARBONATES
Carbonates: association with organic matter
in surface seawater. K. E. Chave. bibliog
il Science 148:1723 Je 25 '65

Isotopes
Systematic relationships between carbon and
oxygen isotopes in carbonates deposited by
modern corals and algae. M. L. Keith and
J. N. Weber. bibliog il Science 150:498-501
O 22 '65

CARBONE, Paul P. See Baldessarini, R. J. jt.
auth.

CARBONYLHEMOGLOBIN
Carboxyhemoglobin: hemodynamic and respiratory responses to small concentrations.
S. M. Ayres and others. bibliog il Science
149:193-4 Jl 9 '65

CARBORUNDUM company
Distributors fight for their take; manufac-
turers of grinding wheels. Bsns W p33
Ja 8 '66
Inorganic fiber production readied. J. F.
Judge. il Miss & Roc 17:32+ D 13 '65
Spiderweb for a plant. il Bsns W p82 Ja 1
'66

CARBOXYHEMOGLOBIN. See Carbonylhemoglobin

CARBOXYLIC acids
Tricarboxylic acid cycle mutants in saccharomyces: comparison of independently
derived mutants. M. Ogur and others. bibliog Science 147:1590 Mr 26 '65

CARBURETORS
About that carburetor. C. F. Oldershaw. il
Flying 77:104+ S '65
Carburetor overhaul: with photographs. T.
Smith. Motor T 17:57-9 Jl '65
Know your carburetor. F. L. Greenwald. il
Pop Sci 187:94-8 Jl '65

CARCASS disposal
Crematory for animal disposal; Atlanta. R. D.
Speer. il Am City 80:121-2 Ag '65
How to dispose of dead birds. il Suc Farm
63:38B My '65

CARCASSES

Decomposition
Insect morticians; decomposition of dead
bodies. il Time 87:77 Ja 21 '66
Nature's morticians. J. A. Payne. Sci Am
214:51 Ja '66

CARCINOGENIC substances. See Cancer producing substances

CARCINOGENS. See Cancer producing substances
CARCINOMA. See Cancer
CARD games. See Cards
CARD sharping. See Cardsharping
CARD system in business, etc.
　Famous firsts: it was all in the cards. il
　　Bsns W p74-5 D 25 '65
CARDBOARD cutouts. See Paper work
CARDIAC resuscitation
　　See also
　Heart-lung machines
CARDIJN, Joseph, cardinal
　Belgium's apostle of working youth. America
　　113:455 O 23 '65
CARDINALS
　American princes of the church. G. Zimmer-
　　mann. il Look 29:24-8+ Ag 24 '65
　Another U.S. cardinal. U S News 58:16 F 8
　　'65
　Baltimore cardinal; and the others. America
　　112:181 F 6 '65
　Collegiality and the cardinalate; recent de-
　　velopments concerning the College of
　　cardinals. T. E. Bird. Christian Cent 82:
　　490-1 Ap 21 '65
　New red hats; twenty-seven new cardinals.
　　il Newsweek 65:80 F 8 '65
　Papal fraternity; twenty-six new members
　　of the Sacred college. il Newsweek 65:61
　　Mr 8 '65
　Red hats as red flags. T. E. Bird. Common-
　　weal 82:9-13 Mr 26 '65; Discussion. 82:274-
　　5+ My 21 '65
　Toned-down consistory. il Time 85:42 Mr 5 '65
　Twenty-seven more cardinals. il Time 85:56+
　　F 5 '65
CARDINALS (baseball) See Baseball clubs
CARDINALS (football club) See Football clubs
CARDINALS, College of. See Cardinals
CARDIOVASCULAR diseases. See Heart—Dis-
eases
CARDIOVASCULAR strokes. See Heart—Dis-
eases
CARDONA, Hernando
　Window for the blind. Sci Digest 58:18 D '65
CARDONA-HINE, Alvaro
　Listen Galaxea; poem. Nation 201:46 Jl 19
　　'65
CARDS
　Of fortune and faro; gambling in opera. A.
　　Boucher. il Opera N 30:8-12 Ja 15 '66
　Playing cards. D. Powills. See issues of Hob-
　　bies
　　See also
　Bridge (game)
　Cardsharping
　Rummy (game)
　　　　　　　　History
　And West is West: suit signs of the western
　　world. D. Powills. il Hobbies 70:118-19+
　　My '65
　East is East: suit signs of the eastern world.
　　D. Powills. il Hobbies 70:120-1+ Ap '65
CARDS, Catalog. See Catalog cards
CARDS, Greeting. See Greeting cards
CARDSHARPING
　Cheating scandal rocks the bridge world.
　　M. Smith. il Life 58:32-3 Je 4 '65
　Fingered; British pair accused of cheating
　　in World contract bridge tournament. il
　　Newsweek 65:59-60 Je 7 '65
　Five-finger exercise; cheating by British
　　players at World bridge championship,
　　Buenos Aires. il Time 85:42 Je 4 '65
　Four-finger exercise; Great Britain's leading
　　players accused of cheating at bridge tour-
　　nament. J. Gerber; T. Reese. il Sports Illus
　　22:56+ Je 7 '65
　Rogues, rascals and reprobates. C. H. Goren.
　　il McCalls 92:28 Je '65
　Why do people cheat? Reese, Shapiro scandal
　　at World's championship tournament. C. H.
　　Goren. il McCalls 92:30+ S 65
CARDUS, Neville
　Decades of Klemperer. Sat R 48:45-7+ My 29
　　'65
CARE, Norman S.
　Inner activity of Friedrich Nietzsche. New
　　Repub 152:24-6 Je 26 '65
　Russians as philosophers. New Repub 153:
　　30-1 S 25 '65
　Theory and practice of socialism. New
　　Repub 153:25-7 D 25 '65
　Yale's tenure trouble. New Repub 152:13-14
　　Mr 27 '65
CARE of firearms. See Firearms—Care
CARE of paintings. See Paintings—Conserva-
tion and restoration
CAREER counseling. See Vocational guidance

CAREER girls. See Business and professional
　women
CAREER literature. See Vocational literature
CAREERS. See Occupations
CAREERS for women. See Woman—Employ-
　ment; Woman—Occupations
CAREFREE years; story. See McGiffin, L.
CAREY, Mother Marie Aimée
　Mustard-seed Bible schools. America 112:361-
　　4 Mr 13 '65
CAREY, J. B. Jr, and Williams, G.
　Lithocholic acid in human-blood serum. bib-
　　liog Science 150:620-2 O 29 '65
CAREY, James B.
　Carey's comeuppance. Time 85:26 Ap 16 '65
　Carey's fall causes union quake. il por Bsns
　　W p 140+ Ap 10 '65
　Counted out. M. Kempton. New Repub 152:
　　16-18 Ap 24 '65
　Great vote steal. por Newsweek 65:82-3 Ap
　　19 '65
　Reuther's offer to IUE: one stronger union.
　　por Bsns W p28 F 13 '65
　Why the electrical workers union turned
　　against its president. U S News 58:94 Ap
　　19 '65
CAREY, James C.
　Peru: encouraging new spirit. bibliog f Cur
　　Hist 49:321-7 D '65
CAREY, Walter F.
　Let's try balance the budget. por Duns R
　　85:53+ F '65
CAREY, William D.
　Proposal for a yearly presidential report on
　　science. Sat R 48:57-8 N 6 '65
CAREY-Thomas award
　Carey-Thomas award given for Sierra club
　　exhibit series. Pub W 187:75 Ap 26 '65
　Carey-Thomas awards are presented. il Pub
　　W 187:32-4 My 3 '65
CARGILL, incorporated
　Two-billion-dollar company that lives by the
　　cent. H. Kay. il Fortune 72:166-9+ D '65
CARGO airlines. See Air freight service
CARGO handling. See Freight handling
CARGO passenger ships. See Freight vessels
CARGO planes. See Airplanes, Freight; Air-
　planes, Military transport
CARGO ships. See Freight vessels
CARGO vessels. See Freight vessels
CARIBBEAN cookery. See Cookery, West
　Indian
CARIBBEAN REGION
　Retire to the Caribbean? how practical, real-
　　ly? il Changing T 20:35-8 Ja '66
　Tight little islands; boom in winter vacation.
　　Time 85:49-50 Mr 5 '65
　　See also
　Communism—Caribbean Region
　Paleontology—Caribbean Region
　Real property—Caribbean Region
　Tourist trade—Caribbean Region
　West Indies (Federation)
　　　Description and travel
　Find your family's ideal island. N. Kuehnl.
　　il Bet Hom & Gard 43:93-8 D '65
　Let's travel to sea, sand, sun. il Mlle 60:223+
　　Ap '65
　Mlle's inside report on summer 1965. T. Van
　　Doren. Mlle 60:211+ Ap '65
　　　Economic conditions
　Time bomb in U.S. front yard. il U S News
　　58:35-9 Je 7 '65
　　　　Politics
　Caribbean: intervention, when and how. J. N.
　　Plank. For Affairs 44:37-48 O '65
CARIBOU
　Daffy deer. F. Dufresne. il Field & S 70:
　　34-6+ Ja '66
CARIBOU hunting
　Eleventh hour caribou. J. R. Johnson. il
　　Field & S 70:32-5+ Ag '65
CARICATURES and cartoons
　Drawing blood; political cartoonists. J. D.
　　Weaver. Holiday 38:72-3+ Ag '65
　Feiffer. J. Feiffer. See issues of New republic
　Indignation in the North; irate cartooning
　　provoked by reports from Selma. Time 85:71
　　Mr 19 '65
　Love is walking hand in hand; excerpt. C.
　　M. Schulz. Ladies Home J 82:70-1 Jl '65
　Muddled, mirthful world of Burr Shafer.
　　J. F. Fixx. Sat R 48:54-5 Jl 10 '65
　Nation gallery. Nation 201:88-91 S 20 '65
　1965 as it looked to Mauldin. W. H. Mauldin.
　　New Repub 154:17-19 Ja 8 '66
　Opening night; Metropolitan opera house,
　　New York. J. Stevenson. Opera N 30:16-18
　　N 6 '65

CARICATURES and cartoons—*Continued*
Wordless workshop. R. Doyt. See issues of
Popular science monthly
See also
Comics (books, strips, etc)
Humor, Pictorial
CARIES, Dental. See Teeth—Diseases
CARILLI, Anthony, and others
Backward bird. Good H 161:156-7 D '65
CARINGELLA, Charles
Super selectivity for your receiver. Pop Electr
25:53-6 Ag '65
CARISSA grandiflora. See Natal plums
CARL, Herbert A. See Price, P. P. jt. auth.
CARLETON, R. Milton
What causes brown patches? Flower Grower
52:41-2 F '65
CARLETON college, Northfield, Minn.
Natural, appropriate use of concrete shells:
men's gymnasium. il Arch Rec 137:129-32
F '65
CARLI, Giovanni Rinaldo, conte
Coinage, commodities, and Count Carli. A.
Sackley. il Mo Labor R 88:817-21 Jl '65
CARLINE, Donald E.
Paperbacks for curriculum enrichment. Sr
Schol 86:sup 12 Mr 4 '65
CARLINGTON, Alicia
Triumph of a stubborn lady. J. Poppy. il
pors Look 29:64-6+ F 9 '65
CARLISLE, Norman, and Kessler, K. O.
Here's your guide to successful inventing;
questions and answers; excerpts from The
successful inventor's guide. Pop Sci 186:89-
93 Mr '65
CARLISLE, Olga
Russian woman. Sat Eve Post 238:28-38+ Je
19 '65
CARLISLE, Thomas John
Juvenile highjinksery; poem. Horn Bk 41:76
F '65
Word is; poem. Horn Bk 41:529 O '65
CARLOS, Dorcas Brennan
How to stretch Christmas. House & Gard
128:234+ N '65
CARLQUIST, Sherwin
Rare cypress clings to coast habitat. Natur
Hist 74:38-43 O '65
CARLSBERG, Arthur
Land speculator. il por Time 86:89 D 3 '65
CARLSON, Burton L.
Falconer; poem. Christian Cent 82:936 Jl 28
'65
CARLSON, Chester
Man who started it all. il por Newsweek 66:
86 N 8 '65
Xerox: the invention that hit the jackpot. D.
Wharton. il por Read Digest 86:121-4 Mr '65
CARLSON, Jerry A.
Programmed farming finds your best chance
to make money. Farm J 89:31+ Mr '65
CARLSON, Leland H.
(comp) Articles and other books received:
British Commonwealth and Ireland. See
issues of American historical review
CARLSON, O. D.
Transistor FM multiplexer. Pop Electr 22:
45-9+ F '65
CARLSON, Paul Earle
Stanleyville massacre; excerpt from 111 days
in Stanleyville. D. Reed. il Read Digest 87:
233-8+ S '65
Tragedy in the Congo. Read Digest 86:88-92
F '65
CARLSON, Roy L. and Armelagos, G. J.
Cradleboard hoods, not corsets. bibliog
Science 149:204-5 Jl 9 '65
CARLSON, Ruth Kearney
Curious whether and how. por Library J 90:
1981-3 Ap 15 '65
CARLUCCI, Frank
Wawa moves East. Time 85:40 F 5 '65
CARMELITA cultural center. See Pasadena,
Calif.—Galleries and museums
CARMEN; opera. See Bizet, G.
CARMICHAEL, Joel
Opinion on religion. por Mlle 61:124+ S '65
CARMICHAEL, Leonard
Remarks on talent search. Sci N L 87:164+
Mr 13 '65
CARMICHAEL, Stokely
Two for SNCC; interviews, excerpts from
Who speaks for the Negro? ed. by R. P.
Warren. Commentary 39:42-8 Ap '65
Who is qualified? New Repub 154:20-2 Ja 8
'66
about
Worker hits the freedom road. J. Shepherd.
il pors Look 29:M16+ N 16 '65
CARMICHAEL, Thomas N.
Waterloo: 1815. Life 58:68-87 Je 11 '65
about
Since toy soldier days, a Waterloo buff. G.
P. Hunt. por Life 58:3 Je 11 '65

CARNATIONS
Carnations and the pinks. il Sunset 135:258
O '65
CARNEGIE, Mary Elizabeth
Impact of integration on the nursing profes-
sion. bibliog por Negro Hist Bul 28:154-5+
Ap '65
CARNEGIE corporation of New York
Carnegie corp. plans education TV study.
Sr Schol 87:sup3-4 D 2 '65
CARNEGIE steel company
Battle at Homestead; excerpt from Lockout.
L. Wolff. il Am Heritage 16:64-79 Ap '65
See also
Homestead strike, 1892
CARNEY, Francis W.
Reproduction and the whole man. America
112:245-7 F 20 '65
CARNIVAL
Carnival beat; carnival in Rio. il Vogue 145:
76-93 Je '65
Mardi gras; mid-winter cruise to Ensenada,
Mexico. C. West. il Motor B 115:38-9+ My
'65
Mardi gras: the golden age. L. V. Huber.
il Am Heritage 16:16-23 F '65
State of Comus; Mardi gras in New Orleans.
il Newsweek 65:94 Mr 15 '65
CARNOVSKY, Leon
Toward world literacy; address, April 1965.
bibliog por Wilson Lib Bul 39:887-95 Je '65
CARO, Lucien G. and Schnös, Maria
Tritium and phosphorus-32 in high-resolution
autoradiography. bibliog Science 149:60-2
Jl 2 '65
—See Gross, J. D. jt. auth.
CAROL, Raymond L.
Book reviews. America 113:141-2 Ag 7 '65
CAROTENOIDS
Absence or singular specificity of carotenoids
in some lower fishes. D. L. Fox and G. F.
Crozier. bibliog il Science 150:771-3 N 5 '65
CAROUSEL; musical comedy. See Musical
comedies, revues, etc.—Criticisms, plots, etc.
CAROZZA, Michael J.
Prudent equipment purchasing. Am City 80:
107+ O '65
—and Theroux, R. J.
Vacuum flotation replaces primary settling.
Am City 80:79-81 F '65
CARP fishing
Tough fish with the big punch. W. Davis. il
Outdoor Life 136:54+ Ag '65
CARP; story. See Blum, R.
CARPENTER, Elizabeth
First lady's Lady Boswell. N. Robertson.
il pors N Y Times Mag p 130-1+ Ap 11 '65
CARPENTER, Scott
Thirty days in Sealab. por Life 59:100A-100B+
O 15 '65
about
Deep thoughts. il por Time 86:67 O 8 '65
Exploring depths of sea and men. L. Wain-
wright. Life 59:21 Ag 20 '65
CARPENTERS

Wages and hours
For carpenters, $5.80 an hour. U S News 58:
78 Je 7 '65
CARPENTRY
How to start fair and square. il Bet Hom
& Gard 43:26 Je '65
See also
Joints (carpentry)
CARPETS. See Rugs and carpets
CARPETS for libraries. See Rugs and carpets
CARPINTERIA, Calif.
Pot-picking time; boys arrested for growing
marijuana. Newsweek 65:42 My 17 '65
CARPORTS. See Garages
CARR, Archie
Navigation of the green turtle; with bio-
graphical sketch. Sci Am 212:18, 78-86 bib-
liog(p 151) My '65
CARR, Donald E.
Poison air around us. Sat R 48:17-19+ F 27
'65
CARR, Grant
Care and repair of aluminum boats. Motor B
115:56-7+ Ap '65
CARR, Joe
You're all right, Pete. A. Wright. il Sports
Illus 23:32-5 S 13 '65
CARR, John Dickson
Murder-fancier recommends . . . Harper 231:
104 Jl '65
CARR, Rachel E.
Containers for today; and how to get the
most from them. Flower Grower 52:30-2 N
'65
CARR, William G.
Fit to teach, fit to vote. NEA J 54:11 Ap '65
Los Angeles riots; handling the topic in class.
Sr Schol 87:sup9 O 7 '65; Same, 87:12+
O 28 '65

CARR-HARRIS, Peter
Star-crossed voyage. Newsweek 66:50 D 20
'65
CARRAGEEN
Department of amplification; Irish-moss
blancmange. K. S. White. New Yorker 41:
70 Jl 10 '65
CARRAGEENIN
Induced hypersensitivity to cold. H. Selye.
il Science 149:201 Jl 9 '65
CARRE, John le, pseud. See Cornwell, D. J. M.
CARRICK, Lynn
Obituary
Pub W por 188:51 S 20 '65
CARRICK, Robert W.
Case for roller reefing. Yachting 118:44-5+
Jl '65
Get the pitch. Yachting 117:63+ Je '65
Outboard wells for the small auxiliary (cont)
Yachting 117:53-5+ F '65
Winches have taken a turn for the better.
Yachting 118:58-60+ D '65
CARRIER corporation
Warm news at Carrier. il Time 85:88 Mr 5
'65
CARRIERS
See also
Transportation
United States—Interstate commerce commis-
sion
CARRIERS (infants)
You just pick up baby and basket and go. il
Sunset 134:100 F '65
CARRIERS, Automobile. See Automobiles—
Equipment
CARRIERS, Car-top. See Automobiles—Equip-
ment
CARRIERS of infection
See also
Animals as carriers of infection
CARRIGHAR, Sally
Culture of animals, a lesson in evolution;
excerpt from Wild heritage. Sat R 48:56-7
My 1 '65
Sex: the silent bell; excerpt from Wild herit-
age. Atlan 215:102-9 Mr '65

about
Tips. por Pub W 187:47-8 Mr 8 '65
CARRILLO DE ALBORNOZ, A. F.
Religious freedom: intrinsic or fortuitous?
bibliog f Christian Cent 82:1122-6 S 15 '65
CARROLL, Hanson
Chair-lift rabbits. Field & S 70:27-9+ D '65
CARROLL, James D.
Forgotten amendment. Nation 201:121-2 S 6 '65
CARROLL, Jock
From red China: with love. Esquire 64:127+
Ag '65
Up in Ivan's room. Holiday 38:62-3+ D '65
CARROLL, John M.
Book selection for the Job corps trainees;
excerpts from guidelines. por Library J 90:
934 F 15 '65
—and Montana, E. J. Jr
ABCD in Boston. Wilson Lib Bul 40:248-50
N '65
CARROLL, Lewis, pseud.
Century of Alice. il por Newsweek 66:86 Jl
12 '65
Child's garden of bewilderment. M. Gardner.
il Sat R 48:18-19 Jl 17 '65; Discussion. 48:26
Ag 14 '65
Life: what is it but a dream? P. W.
Schmidtchen. il Hobbies 70:106-7 O '65
Millions in wonderland. G. L. Potter. il Horn
Bk 41:593-7 D '65
CARROLL, Lucille
Carpet composition. P. Reynolds. il Sch Arts
65:36 O '65
CARROLL, Paul
My mouth quick with many bees; poem. Na-
tion 200:346 Mr 29 '65
CARROLL, Robert L.
Lungfish burrows from the Michigan coal
basin. bibliog Science 148:963-4 My 14 '65
CARROTHERS, George E.
Teaching through stagesetting. Sch & Soc
93:220-2 Ap 3 '65
CARROTS
Ontogeny of adventive embryos of wild car-
rot. W. Halperin and D. F. Wetherell. bib-
liog il Science 147:756-8 F 12 '65
CARRUTH, Hayden
Contra mortem; poem. Poetry 106:10-25 Ap '65
Freedom and style. Poetry 106:358-60 Ag '65
Informal epic. Poetry 105:259-61 Ja '65
On Yeats and others. Poetry 107:192-5 D '65
Reverting still again; poem. Nation 201:200
O 4 '65
Spruce of Marshall washer's; poem. Nation
201:104 Ag 30 '65
Three poets. Poetry 106:309-11 Jl '65

Upon which to rejoice. Poetry 106:239-41 Je
'65
Voix-de-la-rose; poem. Nation 200:178 F 15
'65
about
Northness of North. J. Harrison. Nation 200:
180 F 15 '65
CARSON, Doris M.
Cataloging nonbook materials. bibliog por
Wilson Lib Bul 39:562-4 Mr '65
CARSON, Gerald
Acknowledgments from an author; address,
July 3, 1965. Wilson Lib Bul 40:271-4+ N
'65
Piano in the parlor; excerpts from Polite
Americans. Am Heritage 17:54-9+ D '65
CARSON, Johnny
Great Carsoni. il pors Time 85:84+ My 28 '65
Insomniacs-ville. il por Newsweek 66:78 Jl
19 '65
Johnny Carson, the prince of chitchat, is a
loner. B. Rollin. il pors Look 30:98-102
Ja 25 '66
Twenty-four hours in the life of Johnny Car-
son. E. Havemann. por McCalls 92:58+ Mr
'65
CARSON, Rachel
Sense of wonder; excerpts. McCalls 92:76-83+
Je '65
CARSON, Robert
Eccentricity under the sun. Holiday 38:92-9+
O '65
Luis Buñuel: an eye in the wilderness. Holi-
day 37:123-4+ Ap '65
CARSON, Ruth
What does a school counselor do? Parents
Mag 40:66-8+ S '65
CARTER, Albert Howard
In the wilderness; poem. Christian Cent 82:
457 Ap 14 '65
CARTER, Barbara
Can the Job corps do the job? Reporter 32:
21-6 Mr 25 '65
Great society: a man with a problem. Reporter
32:32-3 My 20 '65
Integrating the Negro teacher out of a job.
Reporter 33:31-3 Ag 12 '65
Teachers give Oklahoma a lesson. Reporter
33:34-7 S 9 '65
CARTER, Edward William
West's biggest chain. il por Time 86:96+
S 24 '65
CARTER, G. Emmett, bp
Conciliar Rome. America 112:423-5 Mr 26 '65
CARTER, Genevieve W.
Social trends and recreation planning: ad-
dress, 1964. Recreation 58:378-80 O '65
CARTER, Giles F.
Analysis of copper and brass coins of the
early Roman empire. bibliog Science 151:
196-7 Ja 14 '66
CARTER, Gwendolen M.
Two tough minds. Nation 201:198-200 O 4 '65
CARTER, Hodding
Furl that banner? N Y Times Mag p8-9+ Jl
25 '65
Unvarnished Faulkner. Américas 17:30-3 O
'65
CARTER, Jane
Largo; poem. Christian Cent 83:6 Ja 5 '66
CARTER, Luther J.
Education: U.S. institutions prepare African
students for development tasks at home.
Science 149:1213-15 S 10 '65
International cooperation: LBJ gets confer-
ence proposals. Science 150:1431-2+ D 10
'65
CARTER, Manfred A.
Dark skeleton; poem. Christian Cent 83:38
Ja 12 '66
Words on the wind; poem. Christian Cent
82:389 Mr 31 '65
CARTER, Margaret
Darling, said Amanda; story. Ladies Home J
82:56-7 S '65
CARTER, Mary
Face of the moon; story. McCalls 93:108-9
N '65
CARTER, Norman W. See Dietschy, J. M. jt.
auth.
CARTER, Sally
Mix fun with glamor. P. Gowland. por Pop
Phot 56:24+ My '65
CARTER, Shirley Verrett-. See Verrett-Carter.
S.
CARTER, Thomas M.
Preparation of teachers in a liberal arts col-
lege. Sch & Soc 93:242-4 Ap 17 '65
CARTER, Lady Violet (Asquith) Bonham. See
Bonham Carter, V. A.
CARTHEW, Anthony
As a British observer reports the war. New
Repub 152:7 Ap 17 '65

CASTAGNA, Edwin
ALA at Pacem in terris. ALA Bul 59:273
Ap '65
Something drastic must be done about school
libraries, you can help! por Parents Mag
40:42+ Ap '65
CASTAGNA, Mary
Fort Ross. il Nat Parks Mag 40:15 Ja '66
CASTAGNO, A. A.
Breaking a common bond of poverty. Sat R
48:42-3 Jl 24 '65
CASTE
Creatures of prejudice; the burakumin of
Japan. Newsweek 65:45 Ap 19 '65
See also
Untouchables
CASTEL, Albert
Sam Houston's last fight. Am Heritage 17:
80-7 D '65
CASTELLARAS, France
New place in the sun: Castellaras. il Vogue
147:78-80 Ja 15 '66
CASTELLI, Leo
Antic arts; Leo Castelli: the artful entre-
preneur. M. Elkoff. il por Holiday 37:95-7+
Je '65
CASTELLO BRANCO, Humberto
Act two. por Newsweek 66:60 N 8 '65
Brazil swings again toward dictatorship. il
por Bsns W p31 O 30 '65
Chapter II of a revolution: army tightens
up in Brazil. por U S News 59:60 N 8 '65
Clamp-down in Brazil. New Repub 153:8 N 13
'65
Laying the ground rules. por Time 86:31 Jl
2 '65
Military clamps down. Sr Schol 87:7-8 N 18 '65
Running things his way. Time 86:51 D 10 '65
Soldier as reformer. il por Newsweek 66:45
Ag 23 '65
Year after. por Time 85:36 Ap 2 '65
CASTER dolly. See Casters, glides, etc (hard-
ware)
CASTERS, glides, etc (hardware)
More wheels for washers, etc; Caster dolly.
il Consumer Rep 30:322 Jl '65
Smart new look in casters. G. Daniels. il
Pop Sci 186:174-9 F '65
CASTING (fishing) See Fishing
CASTING (sculpture)
Sand cast sculpture: fine art in fine sand. C.
H. Larson. il Design 66:6-9 Mr '65
CASTING, Continuous. See Continuous casting
CASTING, Precision. See Lost wax process
CASTINGS, Steel. See Steel castings
CASTLES
Fashions for castle hopping. S. Kirtland. il
Holiday 38:78-83 N '65
10,000 youngsters to the rescue; restoration
of Chateau de Guise, France. il UNESCO
Courier 18:21 Jl '65
CASTRO, Fidel
Beyond harassment. J. Finn. Commonweal
82:720-3 O 1 '65
Castroism, by T. Draper. Review
America 113:99 Jl 24 '65. G. MacEoin
Commonweal 83:126-8 O 29 '65. W. C.
McWilliams
Nat R por 17:656-8 Jl 27 '65. M. Lazo
Nation 201:62-4 Ag 2 '65. S. Shapiro
Castro's turn next? il U S News 58:44-7 My
17 '65
Cuba is in Fidel's shirt pocket. P. Hofmann.
il pors N Y Times Mag p7+ Je 13 '65
Cuba si, Castro no: Fidel's sister speaks up:
excerpt from statement. June 11, 1965. J.
Castro. U S News 58:22 Je 21 '65
How Castro spreads the revolution. R. S.
Strother. Read Digest 87:205-6+ N '65
On the spot in Cuba,. our distant neigh-
bor: Castro's Cuba today; symposium. ed.
by W. Johnson. il pors Sr Schol 87:9-23+
N 18 '65
Petrified forest. il por Time 86:36-40 O 8
'65
Terror in the embassy. J. A. Calvo. il Read
Digest 87:104-8 D '65
Turning the tables: Cubans offered free
flights to join relatives in U.S. Newsweek
66:65 O 11 '65
What Castro is doing to Cuba; an eyewitness
report. C. Migdail. il por U S News 58:70-2
Mr 1 '65
Where Castro brews new trouble for U.S.
il por U S News 59:38-40 O 18 '65
Why Castro allows Cubans to flee; the
dictator's worries. il por U S News 59:49-
51 N 8 '65
CASTRO, Francisco Lyon de
Censorship harasses Portuguese publisher.
Pub W 188:20 Ag 16 '65
CASTRO, Juanita
Cuba si, Castro no: Fidel's sister speaks up:
excerpt from statement, June 11, 1965. por
U S News 58:22 Je 21 '65

CASUALTY insurance companies. See Insur-
ance companies
CAT boats
Cats with more than nine lives. I. Anthony.
il Yachting 117:210+ Mr '65
CATACUTAN-LABAY, Peregrina, and Boyar-
sky, Saul
Bradykinin: effect on ureteral peristalsis. bib-
liog Science 151:78-9 Ja 7 '66
CATALAND, George. See Plumb, H. H. jt.
auth.
CATALASE
Catalase: kinetics of photooxidation. S.
Aronoff. bibliog il Science 150:72-3 O 1 '65
Catalase photoinactivation. R. L. Mitchell
and I. C. Anderson. bibliog il Science 150:
74 O 1 '65
CATALOG cards
Classification schedules and subject headings
to be distributed by card division; Library
of Congress. E. Hamer and A. McCor-
mick. ALA Bul 59:991-2 D '65
In praise of error. D. Gore. il Library J 90:
582-5 F 1 '65
LJ cards, book processing service starts
April 15. Pub W 187:38 Mr 8 '65
LC card division to distribute classification
schedules. Library J 90:4312 O 15 '65; Same.
Wilson Lib Bul 40:227+ N '65
Program to expand LC cataloging proposed
at 65th ARL conference. Library J 90:1274+
Mr 15 '65
Reducing the cataloging backlog: Library
of Congress cards; letter to the editor.
W. E. Jorgensen. Library J 90:4880+ N 15
'65
CATALOG houses. See Mail order business
CATALOGERS
Centralized cataloging: its implications to
personnel; address, November 1963. R. M.
Pierson. il Library J 90:826-8 F 15 '65
CATALOGING
Cataloging nonbook materials. D. M. Carson.
bibliog Wilson Lib Bul 39:562-4 Mr '65
Centralized cataloging: its implications to
personnel; address, November 1963. R. M.
Pierson. il Library J 90:826-8 F 15 '65
Commercial cataloging services. B. Westby.
Wilson Lib Bul 39:560-1+ Mr '65
LC, CRL division of duties suggested by ARL
committee: Centralized cataloging program.
Library J 90:3410 S 1 '65
Saga of the cataloger; letters to the editor.
Library J 90:2050+ My 1 '65; Discussion.
90:2694+ Je 15 '65
Why catalog books? W. Brahm. Library J
90:2510-11 Je 1 '65

Cost
ARL suggests $5 million for cataloging be
included in higher education bill; excerpts
from testimony, March 10, 1965. W. S. Dix.
Library J 90:2109-10 My 1 '65
In praise of error. D. Gore. il Library J 90:
582-5 F 1 '65
Rugged stupidity: rugged individualism in
cataloging practices in Canadian academic
libraries. E. Moon. Library J 90:3406 S 1 '65
CATALOGING, Cooperative
Bibliographic information exchange; address,
November 1963. J. T. Popecki. il Library J
90:823-6 F 15 '65
CATALOGS
See also
Phonograph records—Catalogs
CATALOGS, Library
Book catalog. C. W. Robinson; B. Vavrek.
il Wilson Lib Bul 40:262-70 N '65
Machine-readable catalog copy discussed;
summary of conference. ALA Bul 59:188 Mr
'65
CATALOGS, Mail order
Where it's always spring: catalogue mer-
chandising. il Time 87:69B Ja 21 '66
CATALOGS, Publishers
Catalogs: meeting librarians' demands.
Pub W 188:53 Jl 19 '65
CATALOGS, Seed and plant
Garden catalogues. D. Biddle. il Pop Gard
16:37+ N '65
Mail order catalogs. B. Black. Horticulture
43:42-4 D '65
CATALONIA
Curious Catalonians. R. J. Misch. il Sat R 48:
48+ Mr 13 '65
CATALPA
Catalpa, the pros and cons. il Sunset 134:254
My '65
CATAMARANS
Bottoms up down under; photographs. Pop
Mech 124:128-9 N '65
Cat bites whale. J. Schultz and C. Pyle. il
Yachting 118:48-50+ D '65
Handling the multihull; excerpt from Basic
sailing; ed. by A. Piver. M. B. George.
il Motor B 116:38-9 S '65

CATAMARANS—*Continued*

Design

Fat cat is three boats in one; Stranger, the cruising catamaran. H. Whall. il Sports Illus 22:22-5 F 1 '65

CATARACT

Cataracts due to drugs. Sci N L 87:109 F 13 '65

X-ray exposure causes hereditary rat cataracts. Sci N L 87:121 F 20 '65

CATASTROPHE coverage. See Insurance—Catastrophe coverage

CATASTROPHES. See Disasters

CATAWBA language. See Indians of North America—Languages

CATCH me if you can; drama. See Weinstock, J.

CATCHERS, Baseball. See Baseball players

CATE, Curtis

Chabert of Tain l'hermitage. Atlan 216:168+ N '65

Footloose in Prague; a Marxist Bohemia. Atlan 215:100-4+ F '65

Zermatt. Atlan 215:138+ Ap '65

CATE, William B.

Traditional approach. Christian Cent 82:1324 O 27 '65

CATECHETICS

Challenge to modern catechetics. M. J. Link. America 113:42-4 Jl 10 '65

CATECHOLAMINES

Brain catecholamines; relation to the defense reaction evoked by amygdaloid stimulation in cat. D. J. Reis and L.-M. Gunne. bibliog il Science 149:450-1 Jl 23 '65

Chemicals control body. Sci N L 89:4 Ja 1 '66

CATER, Douglas G.

Church and the reliefers. Christian Cent 82:232-5 F 24 '65

CATERPILLARS

See also

Butterflies

Moths

CATHEDRAL church of St Peter and St Paul. See Washington, D.C.—Churches

CATHEDRAL of St John the Divine. See New York (city)—St John the Divine, Cathedral of

CATHEDRALS

England

Affection for cathedrals; Winchester and Salisbury. W. Golding. Holiday 38:35-9+ D '65

See also

London—Westminster abbey

France

Day we saved Chartres cathedral. G. Gaskill. il Read Digest 87:102-7 Ag '65

See also

Notre Dame cathedral, Paris

Italy

Mother church, Orvieto. R. M. Coates. il Horizon 7:76-95 Spr '65

Japan

Cruciform window onto heaven; Kenzo Tange creates cathedral in Tokyo. R. Boyd. il Arch Forum 123:50-5 S '65

United States

See also

Washington, D.C.—Washington cathedral

CATHER, Willa Sibert

Willa Cather and The professor's house. J. Schroeter. Yale R 54:494-512 Je '65

Willa Cather: her masquerade. Q. Anderson. New Repub 153:28-31 N 27 '65

CATHERINE II, empress of Russia

Catherine the great, by Z. Oldenbourg. Review

Nation 200:290 Mr 15 '65. H. Chevigny

Catherine's campaign for culture. Life 58:82+ Ap 2 '65

CATHODE ray tubes

Direct-view storage tubes. J. B. Pegram. il Electr World 73:25-8 F '65

CATHODIC protection. See Corrosion and anticorrosives

CATHOLIC action

Financing the lay apostolate. America 113:233 S 4 '65

CATHOLIC art. See Christian art and symbolism

CATHOLIC association for international peace

CAIP evaluates Vietnam policy. America 113:126 Ag 7 '65

CATHOLIC authors

Introducing Thomas Gallagher. B. Cook. Cath World 202:96-101 N '65

See also names of Catholic authors e.g. F. O'Connor

CATHOLIC book awards, National. See National Catholic book awards

CATHOLIC book week. See Book week

CATHOLIC church

Aggiornamento. See issues of Catholic world

Aggiornamento si, NR no; May 4 issue; letters to the editor. Nat R 17:565 Je 29 '65

Case for Catholic humility. M. Novak. Christian Cent 82:1406-8 N 17 '65

Catholic and Protestant renewal. W. B. Blakemore. Cath World 201:183-8 Je '65

Changes for Catholics? Pope has some new plans. U S News 58:21 Je 21 '65

Christian in the world; drafting of a final conciliar text on the church in the modern world. America 112:350 Mr 13 '65

Church and the world; interview, ed. by C. L. Palms. B. Haring. Cath World 202:17-20 O '65

Council, the church and the human person; end of session observations. J. B. Sheerin. Cath World 202:199-203 Ja '66

Crisis of growth; Cardinal Bea's remarks concerning conflict between authority and freedom in the church. America 112:516 Ap 17 '65

Dialogue with atheists; Pope Paul VI's efforts. America 112:186 F 6 '65

Dilemmas of change. D. Callahan. Commonweal 83:474-6 Ja 21 '66

Ecumenical backlash. il Newsweek 65:67 Ap 19 '65

Erosion of rational debate; authority of church and state; address, June 10, 1965. W. J. Baroody. Vital Speeches 31:720-4 S 15 '65

Generation of the third eye; young Catholic leaders view their church, ed. by D. Callahan. Review

Nat R 17:380+ My 4 '65. F. D. Wilhelmsen

Glorious freedom of God's sons. C. Davis. America 113:97 Jl 24 '65

Growing up Catholic; excerpt from Generation of the third eye. W. Sheed. il Commonweal 81:692-5 F 26 '65; Discussion. 82:2-3+, 132-3+ Mr 26, Ap 23 '65

Guide to Protestant ploys; concerning Catholicism. M. Novak. Christian Cent 83:39-40 Ja 12 '66

Honesty in the church, by D. Callahan. Review

Commonweal 82:222-3 My 7 '65. W. Birmingham

Is Roman Catholicism reformable? R. Rueher. Christian Cent 82:1152-4 S 22 '65

Mixed marriages; Church's laws. Commonweal 81:719-20 Mr 5 '65; Discussion. 82:66, 202 Ap 9, My 7 '65

New Catholicism. J. R. Nelson. Christian Cent 82:1068-9 S 1 '65

New constitution on the church; a new approach. F. X. Murphy. Cath World 200:346-53 Mr '65

New freedom; revolution in the church. D. Callahan. Commonweal 82:401-5 Je 18 '65; Discussion. 82:514-15, 546 Jl 23-Ag 6 '65

On the present positions of Catholics. G. Wills. il Nat R 71:375-7 My 4 '65

Open season on the church? aggiornamento. W. Herberg. Nat R 17:363-4 My 4 '65

Our 100th anniversary and the new era of the Holy Spirit; analysis of the vatican council's Constitution on the church. J. B. Sheerin. Cath World 201:11-14 Ap '65

Overburdened pilgrims. C. Davis. America 113:626 N 20 '65

Protestant surveys schema thirteen; The church in the modern world. C. Nelson. Cath World 201:394-9 S '65

Relevance of honesty in the church; excerpt from Honesty in the church. D. A. Callahan. Cath World 200:333-8 Mr '65

Schema thirteen and private property. America 113:394 O 9 '65

Theology for renewal, by K. Rahner. Review

Christian Cent 82:1383 N 10 '65. R. Goetz

To the catacombs; concerning article in National review. Newsweek 65:74 My 10 '65

Unreformed church, by R. E. McNally. Review

America 113:724-5 D 4 '65. J. J. Healy

Commonweal 83:232 N 26 '65. J. O'Gara

Warning? Traditionalist movement points up the need for discussion in the church. J. Gallagher. America 112:611 Ap 24 '65

Who is accommodating to what? L. B. Bozell. il Nat R 17:374+ My 4 '65

Widening the fold by fiat. Christian Cent 82:515-16 Ap 28 '65

Word. V. P. McCorry. America 112:811-12 My 29 '65

CATHOLIC church—*Continued*
World is already Christic; Christian secularity.
T. E. Clarke. America 112:800-3 My 29 '65
See also
Concordats
Confession
Councils and synods
Indulgences
Jesuits
Mass
Modernism
Novenas
Papacy
Parish missions
Priests
Reformation
Vatican
Vatican council, 2d
Women and the church
Worker priests

Anecdotes, facetiae, satire, etc.

Gnostics on a train. M. R. O'Connell. il
Nat R 17:151-3 F 23 '65

Art

See Christian art and symbolism

Authority

See Church—Authority

Bibliography

Roundup of some new liturgical works. C. J.
McNaspy. America 113:216 Ag 28 '65
Summer reading in the age of Christian renewal; comp. by V. Kendall. Cath World
201:312-13 Ag '65

Ceremonies and practices

Pope and pomp. Commonweal 82:713 O 1 '65
Pope is clearly worried; warns of danger
threatening Catholic orthodoxy. America
113:177 Ag 21 '65
Post-tribal worship; benefits of liturgical reform in English language. J. J. Ryan.
Commonweal 82:586-9 Ag 20 '65; Discussion. 82:648-9+; 83:4 S 17, O 8 '65
Specter of modernism. J. Ratte. Commonweal
82:530-3 Jl 23 '65; Discussion. 82:610 S 3 '65
What is to be done. L. T. Mahon. Commonweal 82:590-2+ Ag 20 '65

Clergy

Another nun in the paddy wagon. America
113:151-2 Ag 14 '65
Diocesan priest and the intellectual life; ex-
cerpt from Seminary in crisis. S. Poole.
Commonweal 82:78-81 Ap 9 '65; Reply. T.
Merriam. 82:229 My 7 '65
Where are the shepherds? America 113:35 Jl
10 '65
See also
Negro clergy
Vatican council, 2d

Converts

See Converts, Catholic

Dioceses

Punishment of a priest; for preaching on
race. G. S. Mitrovich. Christian Cent 82:
782+ Je 16 '65

Discipline

Another priest, another ban. T. Lickona.
Commonweal 83:298-9 D 10 '65
Father Berrigan, round two. Commonweal 83:
328-9 D 17 '65
From glory to shame; case of Father Daniel
Berrigan. Commonweal 83:261 D 3 '65
Let it be printed; imprimatur today. E.
Bertelme. il Commonweal 81:701-3 F 26 '65
News & views; rigid interpretation of canon
law. J. Leo. Commonweal 83:294 D 10 '65
Storm over Fr. Berrigan and again in New
Jersey. America 113:736 D 11 '65; Discus-
sion. 114:30-1 Ja 8 '66
Why and what. Commonweal 82:483-4 Jl 9 '65
See also
Index librorum prohibitorum
Indulgences

Education

America's 1965 directory of Catholic colleges.
America 113:578-9 N 13 '65
Are colleges slipping? symposium. America
112:451-3 Ap 3 '65
Back to the schools. J. O'Gara. Commonweal
82:183 Ap 30 '65
Blueprint for seminaries. H. Ottensmeyer.
America 113:780-1 D 18 '65
Catholic college forecast; summary of ad-
dress, March 16, 1965. K. J. Alter. America
112:446 Ap 3 '65
Catholic colleges; a modest proposal. L.
Swidler; discussion. Commonweal 81:683+,
719+; 82:174 F 26-Mr 5, Ap 23 '65

Catholic education in America, by N. G.
McCluskey. Review
America 112:562 Ap 17 '65. F. Canavan
Catholic education; next ten years. A. M.
Greeley. America 112:522-4+ Ap 17 '65;
Reply. A. Paule. 112:696 My 15 '65
Catholic education once more. G. N. Shuster.
Cath World 201:50-4 Ap '65
Catholic school enrollment up. America 113:
359 O 2 '65
Catholic universities as a cultural force.
J. Hitchcock. Cath World 201:233-6 Jl '65
Christian commitment and catholic schools.
V. M. Novak. America 113:40-2 Jl 10 '65
Colleges vs. high schools. America 113:106
Jl 31 '65
Criticizing the schools. J. O'Gara. Common-
weal 82:138 Ap 23 '65
Ecumenism and the Catholic seminary. K.
Conley. Christian Cent 82:523-5 Ap 28 '65
Editorial dissent: articles on the NORC re-
port. J. O'Gara. Commonweal 81:657 F 19
'65; Reply. P. A. Lockrey. 82:95 Ap 9 '65
Education of Catholic girls, by J. E. Stuart.
Review
Commonweal 82:673-5 S 17 '65. D. Hunt.
Encyclical on education? America 113:454 O
23 '65
God, man, and holy cross; report of Na-
tional Catholic educational association con-
vention. E. J. Hughes. Newsweek 65:21
My 3 '65
Laymen of the future. America 112:277 F
27 '65
Letter from the council. R. E. Tracy. America
113:432-3 O 16 '65
Louisville story; Bellarmine and Ursuline
colleges to coordinate academic and ad-
ministrative operation. America 112:345 Mr
13 '65
Newman apostolate is not enough. J. J.
Kirvan. Cath World 201:308-11+ Ag '65
On thinking Latin America. K. J. Pollinger.
America 113:214-15 Ag 28 '65
One year later; further thoughts on Are
parochial schools the answer? M. P. Ryan.
Commonweal 82:139-41 Ap 23 '65; Reply. L.
L. Routhier. 82:306-7+ My 28 '65
Scholars and athletes; classics at Boston col-
lege high school. America 112:654 My 8 '65
School boards of the future. O. C. D'Amour.
America 113:316-17 S 25 '65
Teacher today; amateurs not tolerated in
Catholic education; adaptation of address
at National Catholic educational associa-
tion convention, April 21, 1965. A. Thomas.
Cath World 202:40 O '65
Theology and the university, ed. by J. Coul-
son. Review
Commonweal 82:702 S 24 '65. L. Swidler
Three ways out for small Catholic colleges.
L. C. Vaccaro. America 113:580-2 N 13 '65
See also
Georgetown university, Washington, D.C.
National Catholic educational association
Notre Dame, Ind. University
Parochial schools, Catholic
St Johns university, Collegeville, Minn.
St John's university, Jamaica, N.Y.
St Michael's college, Winooski Vt.
Webster college, Webster Groves, Mo.

Eucharist

Encyclical on the eucharist; mystery of faith.
America 113:308 S 25 '65
Mysterium fidei. Commonweal 82:681 S 24 '65;
Discussion. 83:42, 44-5 O 15 '65
New trend in encyclicals? D. R. Campion.
Commonweal 82:714-15 O 1 '65
Pope strikes conservative note for fourth ses-
sion. Christian Cent 82:1181 S 29 '65
What is transignification all about? concern-
ing Pope Paul's encyclical, Mysterium fidei.
C. O'Neill. il Cath World 202:204-10 Ja '66

Finance

Dispute in Buffalo; bishop's right to tax
parishes. Commonweal 81:720-1 Mr 5 '65
How rich? Newsweek 66:74+ Jl 26 '65

Government

American princes of the church. G. Zimmer-
mann. il Look 29:24-8+ Ag 24 '65
Catholic aggiornamento. O. Hastings. il Re-
porter 33:19-22 D 30 '65
Elections in the church. J. O'Donoghue. Com-
monweal 82:281-4 My 21 '65
New currents swirling around Peter's rock.
J. K. Jessup. il Life 59:27-9+ D 17 '65
Vatican council ends: reform on borrowed
time? F. E. Cartus. Harper 231:100-3+
S '65
What the council did. il Newsweek 66:60+
D 20 '65
See also
Vatican council, 2d

CATHOLIC church—*Continued*

History

Almain and Major: conciliar theory on the eve of the reformation. F. Oakley. bibliog f Am Hist R 70:673-90 Ap '65

Infallibility

Is Roman Catholicism reformable? R. Ruether. Christian Cent 82:1152-4 S 22 '65

Liturgy and ritual

Birdcages in Dutch churches. E. Schoenmaeckers. America 113:408 O 9 '65

Early report from Rome and the council. R. E. Tracy. America 113:330+ S 25 '65

Liturgy, Asian style. R. J. Ledogar. Commonweal 82:43-5 Ap 2 '65

Liturgy; contemporary liturgical renewal. G. F. Simons. Commonweal 82:678 S 24 '65

Plea for uniformity in the liturgy. D. M. Murphy. il Cath World 201:296-300 Ag '65

Pope Paul on the liturgy; excerpts from addresses, January 13 and March 17, 1965. Cath World 201:198-201 Je '65

Post-tribal worship; benefits of liturgical reform in English language. J. J. Ryan. Commonweal 82:586-9 Ag 20 '65; Discussion. 82:648-9+; 83:4 S 17, O 8 '65

Putting the new liturgy to work; understanding the meaning of the changes. O. V. Foxhoven. America 113:204-6 Ag 28 '65

Traditionalist manifesto; movement to resist liturgical changes. Time 85:60 Ap 9 '65

Traditionalist manifesto; objections to the church's current reforms in the liturgy. America 112:477-8 Ap 10 '65; Discussion. 112:697 My 15 '65

What is to be done. L. T. Mahon. Commonweal 82:590-2+ Ag 20 '65

See also
Liturgical language
Liturgical movement—Catholic church
Mass
Missals

Missions

Cross and crucifix in mission, by N. A. Horner. Review
America 113:604 N 13 '65. W. J. Richardson
Cath World 202:246 Ja '66. H. D. Noyes

Government of the missions. America 113:660-1 N 27 '65

Latin America in the church's global mission: what priority? with reply by T. E. McCarrick. R. Hoffman. America 114:68-71 Ja 15 '66

Money for missions. America 112:892 Je 26 '65

Peace, priests and the missions. G. Baum. Commonweal 83:175-8 N 12 '65

See also
Jesuits—Missions

Relations

Jews

Absolution of the Jews. America 113:660 N 27 '65

An end to shame? Christian and anti-Semitism. Commonweal 82:237-8 My 14 '65

Anguish of the Jews, by E. H. Flannery. Review
Commonweal 82:542-3 Jl 23 '65. G. Baum

Catholic view on anti-Semitism. U S News 59:15 N 1 '65

Christian insolence reaches new height; Catholic church absolves Jews of crucifixion of Christ. Christian Cent 82:1181 S 29 '65

Declaration on the Jews. America 113:5-6 Jl 3 '65

Declaration on the Jews. Commonweal 83: 112 O 29 '65

Declaration on the Jews. J. B. Sheerin. Cath World 202:134-7 D '65

How the Jews changed Catholic thinking. J. Roddy. il Look 30:18-23 Ja 25 '66

Jewish declaration. J. O'Gara. Commonweal 83:332 D 17 '65

Jewish declaration; dissenting voice. H. J. Morgenthau. Commonweal 83:142-4 N 5 '65; Discussion. 83:295+ D 10 '65

Last minute skulduggery; future dialogue with Jews. America 113:516 N 6 '65

New revisions in the Declaration on the Jews. America 113:430 O 16 '65

Patriarch enflames Arab prejudices; defamation of Jews. Christian Cent 82:132 F 3 '65

Pope and the Jews. M. D. Zeik. Commonweal 82:181-2 Ap 30 '65; Reply. M. McCrimmon. 82:482 Jl 9 '65

Statement on the Jews: an inadequate document. D. Polish. Christian Cent 82:1475-7 D 1 '65; Reply. A. B. Williams. 83:84-5 Ja 19 '66

Three-fourths of a loaf; Vatican council II's declaration on Jews. Christian Cent 82:1373-4 N 10 '65

Vatican II & the Jews. F. E. Cartus; discussion. Commentary 39:31-2+ Je '65

Vatican's dilemma. Christian Cent 82:859-60 Jl 7 '65

Vote against prejudice; declaration accepted by Vatican council. il Time 86:61 O 22 '65

Who kills Christ now? Christian Cent 82: 571-2 My 5 '65

Orthodox Eastern church

Ecumenical journey; Cardinal Bea's view of the role of American Orthodox and Catholic ecumenists. America 112:746 My 22 '65

Ecumenism and argument; establishment of a joint W.C.C.-Catholic committee. Commonweal 81:751-2 Mr 12 '65

Protestant churches

Baptists and Catholicism. America 112:627 My 1 '65

Dialogue on marriage; Protestant-Catholic. E. Gibson. Christian Cent 82:297-300 Mr 10 '65

Ecumenism and argument; establishment of a joint W.C.C.-Catholic committee. Commonweal 81:751-2 Mr 12 '65

Ecumenism and teetotalism. J. C. Evans. Christian Cent 82:798-9 Je 23 '65; Discussion. 82:1040-1 Ag 25 '65

Evangelicals see red. C. Northcott. Christian Cent 82:799 Je 23 '65

Learning the language of mutual respect. Christian Cent 82:702 Je 2 '65

Lutherans and Catholics seek areas of common action. Christian Cent 82:910 Jl 21 '65

Protestant hopes for the fourth session. J. B. Sheerin. Cath World 202:5-9 O '65

Vatican special delivery; question of interfaith services. Newsweek 65:64 Mr 15 '65

Wonderful communion of the faithful; divided Christian family; excerpt from commentary on the Decree on ecumenism. T. F. Stransky. Cath World 202:48-51 O '65

Relations (diplomatic)

Listening post? Commonweal 82:179-80 Ap 30 '65

See also
Nuncios, Papal

Communist countries

Cardinals & commissars; negotiations with east European regimes. il Time 85:61-2 F 19 '65

United States

Another point of view. R. A. Graham. America 113:710-11 D 4 '65

Listening post? Commonweal 82:179-80 Ap 30 '65

U.S. representative at the Vatican? J. J. Hennesey. America 113:707-11 D 4 '65; Reply. J. E. Russell. 114:61 Ja 15 '66

Roman curia

Catholic aggiornamento. O. Hastings. il Reporter 33:19-22 D 30 '65

Collision course in Rome; goal of the progressive bishops at Vatican II. Newsweek 66:60 N 1 '65

Council, the church and the human person; end of session observations. J. B. Sheerin. Cath World 202:199-203 Ja '66

Italian prelates still control curia. Christian Cent 82:165 F 10 '65

New currents swirling around Peter's rock. J. K. Jessup. il Life 59:27-9+ D 17 '65

Retirement in the church; probable retirement age for officials of the Roman curia. America 112:277 F 27 '65

St John and St Pius? Pope Paul's concern for consensus for reform. Newsweek 66:86 N 29 '65

Study of the synoptic gospels, by A. Bea; ed. by J. A. Fizmyer. Review
Sat R 49:27 Ja 1 '66. Q. Quesnell

What the council did. il Newsweek 66:60+ D 20 '65

Societies

See also
Catholic association for international peace
Knights of Columbus
Newman clubs
Pax Romana
Secular institutes
Serra international

Theology

See Theology

CATHOLIC church and communism

Church of caution in Czechoslovakia. Cath World 201:254-9 Jl '65

CATHOLIC church and communism—*Cont.*
Communist priests in South America. R.
Peter. Nat R 17:876 O 5 '65
Council condemnation of communism? America 113:561 N 13 '65
Dialogue in Vermont; conference sponsored by St Michael's college, Winooski, Vt. L. B. Bozell. Nat R 17:1153-6 D 14 '65
Dialogue with Marxists. Time 85:76+ My 14 '65
Four men: four stories. America 112:449-50 Ap 3 '65
Ideology of *aggiornamento*. T. Molnar. Nat R 17:365-6 My 4 '65
Marxist's Christ. G. D. Kumlien. Commonweal 82:471-2 Jl 2 '65
Pacem in terris, Ecclesiam Suam and communism. C. Wallace; reply with rejoinder. J. P. Conneally. Cath World 201:219-220 Jl '65
Political or pastoral? Secretariat for non-believers. America 112:890 Je 26 '65
CATHOLIC church and international relations. See Church and international relations
CATHOLIC church and politics. See Church and politics
CATHOLIC church and psychiatry. See Psychiatry and religion
CATHOLIC church and race problems. See Church and race problems
CATHOLIC church and the press. See Church and the press
CATHOLIC church and war. See War and religion
CATHOLIC church in Asia
Liturgy, Asian style. R. J. Ledogar. Commonweal 82:43-5 Ap 2 '65
CATHOLIC church in Communist countries. See Catholic church and communism
CATHOLIC church in Czechoslovakia
Beran and the Czech reds. America 112:302 Mr 6 '65
Church of caution in Czechoslovakia. Cath World 201:254-9 Jl '65
CATHOLIC church in France
Eldest daughter in turmoil; anxieties over church's current reforms. Time 85:68 Je 11 '65
New life for priest workers. R. Bertrand. America 113:669-70 N 27 '65
New priests, a controversial French novel. R. Barrat. Commonweal 82:49-51 Ap 2 '65
Schism in France? R. Barrat. Commonweal 82:651-2 S 17 '65
Schism in French Catholicism? R. Rouquette. Cath World 202:34-9 O '65
They are priests and workers, both. J. Cogley. il N Y Times Mag p6-7+ D 26 '65
Wave of French conservatism. R. Bertrand. America 112:248-9 F 20 '65; Discussion. 112:378, 500-1 Mr 20, Ap 17 '65
CATHOLIC church in Germany
Hands across the Oder-Neisse; Polish bishops seeking reconciliation between Poland and Germany. Christian Cent 83:69 Ja 19 '66
CATHOLIC church in Hungary
Hollow tolerance; priests convicted of conspiring against the Communist system. il Time 86:24 Jl 23 '65
Lapse of the U.S. press: 1964 negotiations between the Vatican and the Hungarian regime. America 113:390 O 9 '65
CATHOLIC church in India
India after the Pope. B. Griffiths. Commonweal 81:641-2 F 12 '65
CATHOLIC church in Ireland
New Ireland: needs an alert and resourceful Irish Catholicism. America 112:626 My 1 '65
CATHOLIC church in Italy
See also
Papacy
CATHOLIC church in Latin America
I failed in Puno; Papal volunteer. R. F. Clark; discussion. America 112:152, 470 Ja 30, Ap 10 '65
Latin America and revolution; new mood in the churches. J. A. Mackay. Christian Cent 82:1439-43 N 24 '65
Latin America in the church's global mission; what priority? with reply by T. E. McCarrick. R. Hoffman. America 114:68-71 Ja 15 '66
Priest corps; help for the church in Latin America. Commonweal 81:652 F 19 '65
Yankees in Roman collars. J. Bishop. Commonweal 82:469-71 Jl 2 '65
CATHOLIC church in Poland
Hands across the Oder-Neisse; Polish bishops seeking reconciliation between Poland and Germany. Christian Cent 83:69 Ja 19 '66
CATHOLIC church in Spain
All-pervasive church. H. Thomas. Holiday 37:86-7+ Ap '65

Spain and freedom; reply. F. de Villalonga. America 112:341 Mr 13 '65
Voice of the church in Spain. America 113:424 O 16 '65
CATHOLIC church in the Congo
Church in the Congo; tr. by E. O'Gorman. J. Jadot. Cath World 201:247-53 Jl '65
CATHOLIC church in the Netherlands
Birdcages in Dutch churches. E. Schoenmaeckers. America 113:408 O 9 '65
Dutch cardinal speaks out. America 113:359 O 2 '65
CATHOLIC church in the United States
American Catholicism after the council. M. Novak. Commentary 40:50-8 Ag '65
Bourgeois church. America 114:119 Ja 22 '66
Catholic church in modern America. B. Haring. Cath World 201:27-31 Ap '65
Charter for laymen, 1822. G. Traynor; discussion. Commonweal 81:555+, 750 Ja 29, Mr 12 '65
End to isolationism? J. O'Gara. Commonweal 83:116 O 29 '65
Father DePauw returns. J. Leo. Commonweal 83:458-9 Ja 21 '66
Knights, Masons and ecumenism. America 113:426 O 16 '65
Laity today and tomorrow. J. Cogley. Cath World 201:32-40 Ap '65
Less ecumenism, please. Time 85:74 Mr 12 '65
Nonecclesiastical Catholicism. K. L. Woodward. Christian Cent 82:779-80 Je 16 '65
Open parish in the open society. J. H. Fichter. Cath World 201:16-21 Ap '65
Priest corps; help for the church in Latin America. Commonweal 81:652 F 19 '65; Reply. R. Hoffman. 82:94-5 Ap 9 '65
Real problems of the American church. A. M. Greeley. America 113:571-2+ N 13 '65; Discussion. 113:766 D 18 '65
Thread of renewal. J. P. Marschall. America 113:622-5 N 20 '65
See also
Catholics in the United States
Knights of Columbus

History
Through other eyes, ed. by D. Herr and J. Wells. Review
Commonweal 82:509-10 Jl 9 '65. A. Fremantle
CATHOLIC church in Venezuela
Vocationless Venezuela; shortage of native born priests. P. J. Cunningham. Cath World 201:189-93 Je '65
CATHOLIC colleges. See Catholic church—Education
CATHOLIC converts. See Converts, Catholic
CATHOLIC council on civil liberties
Some of your best friends will go to court for you; amicus curiae brief, attacking law that bans sale of contraceptives in Connecticut. il Time 85:50 F 26 '65
CATHOLIC education. See Catholic church—Education
CATHOLIC encyclopedia
See also
New Catholic encyclopedia
CATHOLIC encyclopedia for school and home
Book of the month. J. M. Fitzgerald. Cath World 202:244-5 Ja '66
McGraw-Hill launches new Catholic reference set. il Pub W 188:62 S 13 '65
CATHOLIC high schools. See Catholic church—Education
CATHOLIC Indian missions. See Missions—Indians of North America
CATHOLIC intellectuals. See Intellectuals
CATHOLIC laymen. See Laity
CATHOLIC learning and scholarship
See also
Catholics—Intellectual life
CATHOLIC library association
See also
Regina award
CATHOLIC literature
Morality of Catholic censorship. B. A. Curtis. Christian Cent 82:772-5 Je 16 '65
See also
Publishers and publishing—Catholic literature

Bibliography
Catholic world of books for Christmas. V. Kendall. Cath World 202:160-1 D '65
Religion (cont) E. S. Stanton. America 112:679-81; 113:684-6 My 8, N 27 '65
That favorable time; Lenten reading. D. L. Flaherty and others. America 112:321-2+ Mr 6 '65
CATHOLIC missionary society
Ecumenism and converts; concerning speech by Cardinal Heenan. America 112:798 My 29 '65

CATHOLIC newspapers. See Catholic press
CATHOLIC periodicals. See Catholic press
CATHOLIC press
AMA and the Catholic press. B. L. Masse. America 113:583+ N 13 '65
Anonymousitis. S. J. Adamo. il America 114:154+ Ja 22 '66
Catholic press. J. G. Deedy. jr. Commonweal 81:666-7 F 19 '65; Reply with rejoinder. J. A. Breig. 82:34 Ap 2 '65
Catholic press, beware. Commonweal 81:753 Mr 12 '65
Cheeky reporter; Kansas City's National Catholic reporter. Time 86:118+ N 19 '65
Dilemma in the Catholic press. S. J. Adamo. America 113:154-8 Ag 14 '65
Feeding a myth; reactions to Rolf Hochhuth's play, The deputy. S. J. Adamo. America 113:730+ D 4 '65
Truth will out. S. J. Adamo. il America 113: 610-12 N 13 '65; Reply M. Clayton. 114:1-2 Ja 1 '66
See also
Critic (periodical)
Ramparts (periodical)
CATHOLIC-Protestant marriages. See Marriages, Mixed
CATHOLIC relief services. See National Catholic welfare conference
CATHOLIC scholars. See Scholars Catholic
CATHOLIC schools. See Parochial schools, Catholic
CATHOLIC students
Crash program for the Newman apostolate. J. L. Quinn. Cath World 202:166-70 D '65
Newman Apostolate jubilee. America 112:345 Mr 13 '65
CATHOLIC teachers. See Teachers
CATHOLIC universities. See Catholic church —Education
CATHOLIC worker movement
Catholic worker; R. A. LaPorte burns self to death. il Newsweek 66:71 N 22 '65
CATHOLIC world (periodical)
Centennial salute. America 112:521 Ap 17 '65
Human rights: divine, fundamental, practical; reprint of June 1887. I. T. Hecker. Cath World 202:47 O '65
Our 100th anniversary and the new era of the Holy Spirit. J. B. Sheerin. Cath World 201:11-14 Ap '65
Why we publish what we publish; reprint of February 1868. I. T. Hecker. Cath World 201:307 Ag '65
CATHOLICISM. See Catholic church
CATHOLICS
Catholics and Lent. M. Novak. Christian Cent 82:323 Mr 17 '65
Generation of the third eye: young Catholic leaders view their church, ed. by D. Callahan. Review
Nat R 17:380+ My 4 '65. F. D. Wilhelmsen
Growing up Catholic; excerpt from Generation of the third eye. W. Sheed. il Commonweal 81:692-5 F 26 '65; Discussion. 82:2-3+, 132-3+ Mr 26, Ap 23 '65
Honesty in the church, by D. Callahan. Review
Commonweal 82:222-3 My 7 '65. W. Birmingham
How life will be different for Catholics. il U S News 59:52-3 D 20 '65
On the present positions of Catholics. G. Wills. il Nat R 17:375-7 My 4 '65
Principles for the dialogue: more friendliness to non-Catholics urged. America 113:311 S 25 '65
Relevance of honesty in the church; excerpt from Honesty in the church. D. A. Callahan. Cath World 200:333-8 Mr '65
Risk of faith; excerpt from Honesty in the church. D. Callahan. Commonweal 81:755-8 Mr 12 '65; Reply. J. Barrera. 82:458-9+ Jl 2 '65
Self-conscious Catholicism. E. C. Kennedy. America 113:434-6 O 16 '65; Discussion. 113: 551-2+ N 13 '65

Intellectual life
Catholic intellectualism again. P. Gleason; discussion. America 112:236 F 20 '65
Diocesan priest and the intellectual life; excerpt from Seminary in crisis. S. Poole. Commonweal 82:78-81 Ap 9 '65; Reply. T. Merriam. 82:229 My 7 '65
CATHOLICS in Italy
Catholics left and right. G. D. Kumlien. Commonweal 82:16-17 Mr 26 '65
Florentines: hope of Italy? G. Natoli. il Cath World 200:339-45 Mr '65
CATHOLICS in literature
Guide to Protestant ploys; concerning Catholicism. M. Novak. Christian Cent 83:39-40 Ja 12 '66

CATHOLICS in the United States
American Catholic is changing. J. Leo. il N Y Times Mag p45+ N 14 '65
Catholic imprint. M. Novak. Christian Cent 82:990 Ag 11 '65
Catholics in colonial America, by J. T. Ellis. Review
America 113:100 Jl 24 '65. C. E. O'Neill
Chicago's Archdiocesan office of urban affairs. J. H. Fichter. America 113:462-5 O 23 '65
Dialogue with Evangelicals like Billy Graham. J. B. Sheerin. Cath World 201:158-61 Je '65; Discussion. 201:346-7 S 15 '65
Fifteen most important. Christian Cent 82: 1591 D 22 '65
New challenges to American Catholics, by G. MacEoin. Review
America 113:219-20 Ag 28 '65. J. Martin Cath World 201:331-3 Ag '65. T. Greene Commonweal 82:602-4 Ag 20 '65. J. G. Deedy, jr
Wanted: more men for all seasons, and women too. G. Blatt. Cath World 201:56-61 Ap '65
CATLIN, George
Americans not everybody knows. C. W. Ferguson. il por PTA Mag 60:20-3 O '65
Eyes in the wilderness; Smithsonian's collection on exhibition. F. Getlein. New Repub 153:24+ S 18 '65
My real friend, Joe; with portrait of J. Chadwick. L. Burkhalter. Am Heritage 16:44-5 Ap '65
CATNIP
One man's meat. Sci Am 212:54 F '65
CATO, pseud.
Focus on Washington. See issues of National review
CATS
Campaign for top cat. D. R. Maxey. il Look 29:M8-10 Jl 27 '65
How to make your kitten purr. il Todays Health 43:80 N '65
Tyger, tyger. B. Baron. Mlle 61:200+ Ag '65
Tylotrich (hair) follicle: association with a slowly adapting tactile receptor in the cat. S. J. Mann and W. E. Straile. bibliog il Science 147:1043-5 F 26 '65
What every young cat ought to know; excerpt from Silent miaow. P. W. Gallico and S. Szasz. il Read Digest 86:178-82 F '65
See also
Lynxes

Stories
Little. M. Rukeyser. il Ladies Home J 82: 82-5 F '65

Training
How to housebreak dogs and cats. il Good H 160:134-5 Ja '65
CATSKILL MOUNTAINS
Catskills: land of milk and money. M. Richler. il Holiday 38:56-63+ Jl '65
Don't call it the borscht belt. D. Boroff. il N Y Times Mag p48+ My 9 '65
CATSKILL photo center. See Photography— Galleries and museums
CATTELL, David T.
Soviet foreign policy: a broad view. bibliog f Cur Hist 49:208-13 O '65
CATTLE

Branding
Branding makes cattle record keeping easy. M. Vance. il Suc Farm 63:108 Ap '65

Breeding
See Cattle breeding

Breeds
Are Charolais really that good? J. A. Rohlf. il Farm J 89:40-1+ Mr '65
Broadway hijinks at an Angus auction; Black Watch farms, Wappingers Falls, N.Y. il Bsns W p32-3 O 23 '65

Dehorning
See Dehorning

Diseases and pests
Here's how to identify and control beef cattle insects. R. E. Roselle. il Suc Farm 63:48-9+ My '65
Veterinarian tells: how to treat fresh feedlot cattle. W. Schaulis. il Suc Farm 63: 46+ S '65
See also
Bloating
Cows—Diseases and pests
Foot-and-mouth disease

Feeding
Chopped bales feed easier. il Farm J 89:50F Mr '65

CAVANAGH, Jerome Patrick—*Continued*
Why cities are turning to Washington for cash; interview. por U S News 59:44-5 Ag 23 '65

about

Cavanagh is willin'. S. Friedman. New Repub 153:10 N 27 '65
Detroit: slow healing of a fractured city. S. H. Brown. il por Fortune 71:142-5+ Je '65
Mayor who woke up a city. E. Dunbar. il pors Look 29:34-8+ S 21 '65
Restoring the heart. il por Time 86:24 S 24 '65

CAVANAUGH, Arthur
Offering; story. McCalls 93:90-1 D '65
Wonderful prize; story. Redbook 126:64-5 D '65

CAVE, Hugh
Change of heart; story. Good H 161:84-5 S '65
Double wedding; story. Good H 161:88-9 Jl '65
End of the road; story. Good H 160:100-1 Mr '65
He loves me! story. Good H 161:102-3 O '65
To trust in Andy; story. Good H 160:102-3 Ap '65

CAVE drawings and paintings
On the way to Nirvana; Buddhist monastery-caves at Ajanta. A. Menen. Holiday 37: 144+ Mr '65
20,000-year-old cave painting found. Sci N L 87:184 Mr 20 '65

CAVE rescues. See Rescue work

CAVE temples
On the way to Nirvana; Buddhist monastery-caves at Ajanta. A. Menen. Holiday 37: 144+ Mr '65

CAVELL, Edith
She was more than a patriot. P. G. Fredericks. il por N Y Times Mag p 110+ D 5 '65

CAVENDISH, Spencer Compton, 8th duke of Devonshire. See Devonshire, S. C. C.

CAVERLY, Joseph M.
Recreation supervision crisis. Recreation 58: 342-3 S '65

CAVES
Conservation and American caves; Wyandotte cave. W. R. Halliday. il Nat Parks Mag 39:17-19 D '65
Paleotemperatures and chronology at archeological cave site revealed by thermoluminescence; Jaguar cave, Idaho. W. Dort, jr. and others. bibliog il Science 150:480-1 O 22 '65
Subway cave is a lava tube. il Sunset 135: 44 S '65

CAVIAR
Caliph of caviar; retired Marine general. M. Beyer. A. J. McClane. il Field & S 70:36-8+ D '65
Caveat caviar; synthetic caviar. Newsweek 65:36-7 Je 7 '65
Vanishing taste; possible reduction of Caspian sturgeon breeding grounds. Time 85: 45 Ap 16 '65

CAVILL, G. W. K. and Robertson, P. L.
Ant venoms, attractants, and repellents. bibliog Science 149:1337-45 S 17 '65

CAVIN, Patty
L.B.J.'s grass widows. Ladies Home J 82:64+ N '65

CAVIN, Valerie
Curl up and read. Seventeen 24:106 Mr '65

CAXTON, William, Jr
Alfred Knopf keepsake. Am Artist 29:38-43+ S '65

CAXTON printers. See Printing—Private presses

CAZES, Marcellin
Lemonader extraordinary. il Newsweek 66: 54+ O 25 '65

CEAUSESCU, Nicolae
Docile guests. il por Time 86:23 Jl 30 '65

CEBIK, Ronald James
Freedom beyond polity. Christian Cent 82: 1379-82 N 10 '65

CECIL, Andrew R.
World peace through the law never tried; address, May 1965. Vital Speeches 31:557-62 Jl 1 '65

CECIL, Henry
Nothing but the truth? Holiday 37:12+ Mr '65

CECIL, Robert Arthur Talbot Gascoyne-, 3d marquis of Salisbury. See Salisbury, R. A. T. G.-C.

CECILE, Mother Mary. See Mary Cecile, Mother

CECILIA Mary, Mother
Mother Cecilia's revolt. il pors Life 58:45-6 Je 4 '65
Show-down in a nunnery. Commonweal 83:79 O 22 '65

CEDAR
New cedars of Lebanon. il UNESCO Courier 18:18-19 O '65

CEDAR BREAKS NATIONAL MONUMENT
Brian Head. N. N. Dodge. il Nat Parks Mag 39:18-19 Mr '65

CEDAR POINT, Ohio. See Summer resorts

CEDAR RAPIDS, Ia.

Architecture
United they built; Senior citizen center. N. G. Zook. Recreation 58:427-8 N '65

CEILINGS
See also
Plaster and plastering

CELA, Camilo José
European literary scene. R. J. Clements. por Sat R 48:57 O 23 '65

CELEBRATIONS
See also
Festivals

CELEBRITIES
Brief essay on the subject of celebrity with numerous digressions and particular attention to the actress, Rita Hayworth. E. S. Connell, jr. il Esquire 63:114-16 Mr '65
Me? a movie about me? Manny, it's a natural. il Esquire 65:48-9 Ja '66
My V.I.P. trip. D. Considine. il Seventeen 28:114-15+ F '65
Repressed desires; well-known personalities tell what they want for Christmas. House & Gard 128:239 N '65
Six English self-portraits; symposium. il Harper 230:56-63 Ap '65
Squires at large (cont) Esquire 63:78 My; 64:70 Ag '65; 65:107 Ja '66
See also
Great men
Women, Famous

CELENT, Christopher M.
Art of xerography. Electr World 74:25-8+ Jl '65

CELERY ripeness is all; story. See Freedman, M.

CELESTIAL navigation. See Navigation (space flight)

CELESTIAL photography. See Astronomical photography

CELESTIAL simulators. See Simulators

CELIBACY
Credit where credit is due. V. P. McCorry. il America 114:54+ Ja 8 '66
Discussing celibacy in the press. America 113:109 Jl 31 '65
Papal letter on celibacy. F. Canavan. America 113:500 O 30 '65
Pope vetoes celibacy debate; fourth session of Vatican council II. Christian Cent 82: 1311 O 27 '65
Protestant celibacy; Baptist view. H. Winter. America 113:470-1 O 23 '65
Sister considers chastity. M. R. Jones. America 112:488-90 Ap 0 '65; Reply. M. Chabanel. 112:651 My 8 '65

CELIBIDACHE, Sergiu
Man without. il por Time 85:44 Je 4 '65

CELL division (biology)
Abrogation of allogeneic inhibition by cortisone. K. E. Hellström and others. bibliog il Science 149:82-4 Jl 2 '65
Cell division and cancer; address, May 13, 1965. A. Szent-Györgyi. bibliog Science 149: 34-7 Jl 2 '65
Mitosis; induction by cultures of human peripheral lymphocytes. N. Hashem. bibliog il Science 150:1460-2 D 10 '65
Protein synthesis and the mitotic apparatus. J. Mangan and others. bibliog il Science 147:1575-8 Mr 26 '65
Radiation resistance in lipovirus-altered human cells. J. B. Little and R. S. Chang. bibliog il Science 148:1746-7 Je 25 '65

CELL growth. See Cells

CELL separator. See Physiological apparatus

CELLARS. See Basements and cellars

CELLER, Emanuel
Excerpt from address, May 12, 1964. Cong Digest 44:154+ My '65
Induction, or jail? two sides of a growing fight over use of the draft; letter. U S News 60: 39 Ja 10 '66

about

Mr Celler's statement on copyright revision. R. H. Smith. Pub W 188:53 S 20 '65

CELLINI, William F.
Stump removal wins public favor. Am City 80:82-3 F '65

CELLISTS. See Violoncellists

CELLS
Aging and everyman. N. J. Berrill. il Atlan 217:86-90 Ja '66

CELLS—*Continued*
Bacteria as an indicator of formation of antibodies by single spleen cells in agar. S. A. Schwartz and W. Braun. bibliog il Science 149:200 Jl 9 '65
Bone: formation by autoinduction. M. R. Urist. bibliog il Science 150:893-9 N 12 '65
Cell proliferation in hydra: an autoradiographic approach. R. D. Campbell. bibliog il Science 148:1231-2 My 28 '65
Cell research gets NIH grant of $1.2 million. Sci N L 88:361 D 4 '65
Cellular dynamics: the cell cycle; report on third conference on cellular dynamics. E. W. Taylor. Science 148:1364 Je 4 '65
Cellular segregation and heterocytic dominance in hydra. H. M. Lenhoff. bibliog il Science 148:1105-7 My 21 '65
Constitution, viability, and lactate dehydrogenase in stationary-phase L-cell suspension cultures. A. D. Glinos and others. bibliog il Science 150:350-3 O 15 '65
Galactose metabolism and cell sociology. H. M. Kalckar. bibliog il Science 150:305-13 O 15 '65
HeLa cells: effects of temperature on the life cycle. P. N. Rao and J. Engelberg. bibliog Science 148:1092-4 My 21 '65
Human body; from cell to man. il Sci Digest 57:71-6 Mr '65
Hybrid cells of mouse and man. Sci Am 212:62 Ap '65
Intercellular communication: renal, urinary bladder, sensory, and salivary gland cells. W. R. Loewenstein and others. bibliog il Science 149:295-8 Jl 16 '65
Irradiated cells repaired. F. Marley. Sci N L 87:259 Ap 24 '65
Lactate dehydrogenase isozyme patterns of human platelets and bovine lens fibers. E. S. Vesell. bibliog il Science 150:1735-7 D 24 '65
Lymphoma growth in vivo: electronic discrimination between tumor and stroma cells. G. Haughton and others. il Science 150:769-71 N 5 '65
Mouse and human cells fused by scientists. Sci N L 87:182 Mr 20 '65
Physical basis of life and learning; adaptation of address, April 23, 1965. F. O. Schmitt. bibliog Science 149:931-6 Ag 27 '65
Potassium-40 content as a basis for the calculation of body cell mass in man. W. Burmeister. bibliog Science 148:1336-7 Je 4 '65
Proteins and disulfide groups in the aggregation of dissociated cells of sea sponges. G. J. Gasic and N. L. Galanti. bibliog il Science 151:203-5 Ja 14 '65
Revolution in the cell; Lwoff and others discover. Newsweek 66:77 O 25 '65
Spectrophotometer: new instrument for ultrarapid cell analysis. L. A. Kamentsky and others. bibliog il Science 150:630-1 O 29 '65
Successive transformations of an established cell line by polyoma virus and SV40. G. J. Todaro and H. Green. bibliog il Science 147:513-14 Ja 29 '65
Turnover of ribosomal RNA in rat liver. J. N. Loeb and others. bibliog il Science 149:1093-5 S 3 '65
Uncoupling of an epithelial cell membrane junction by calcium-ion removal. M. Nakas and others. bibliog il Science 151:89-91 Ja 7 '66
See also
Chromosomes
Cilia and ciliary motion
Macrophages
Membranes (biology)
Nerve cells
Plasma membranes

CELLULAR glass. See Glass, Cellular
CELLULAR metabolism. See Tissue metabolism
CELLULAR plastics. See Plastics, Cellular
CELLULAR therapy
I took the Niehans treatment. H. Worden. Vogue 147:76-7+ Ja 15 '66
CELLULOSE
See also
Lignin
CELOSIA. See Cockscombs
CELTIC literature
Celtic heritage in Ireland. A. Moray. il Horizon 7:32-9 Spr '65
CELTICS (basketball team) See Basketball teams
CELTS
Celts. G. Bibby. il Horizon 7:20-31 Spr '65
CEMENT
See also
Concrete

CEMENT industry and trade
Cement strives to pour the proper profit mix; River cement company's giant rotary kiln. il Bsns W p 144-6+ Jl 17 '65
CEMENT kilns
Cement strives to pour the proper profit mix; River cement company's giant rotary kiln. il Bsns W p 144-6+ Jl 17 '65
CEMENT, lime and gypsum workers international union. See United cement, lime and gypsum workers international union
CEMETERIES
Tomb with a view: Nanda Vigo's design for windowless concrete towers in northern Italy. il Time 85:76-7 F 12 '65
See also
Service mens graves
CEMETERY vandalism. See Vandalism
CENOZOIC period. See Geology, Stratigraphic—Cenozoic
CENSORSHIP
Against pornography. G. P. Elliott. Harper 230:51-60 Mr '65
ABPC files amicus brief in Ralph Ginzburg case. Pub W 188:36 N 29 '65; Reply. H. S. Manges. 188:21 D 13 '65
ACLU, Authors league, 111 friends urge Supreme court to hear Ginsburg. Library J 90:836 F 15 '65
California booksellers join forces to combat censorship. W. S. Chieboun. Pub W 188: 30-1 Ag 16 '65
Censoring sex: Los Angeles times screening board. il Time 85:71 F 12 '65
Censorship and cultural rebellion; excerpts from address, October 1964. H. E. Fey. il Library J 90:2473-8 Je 1 '65
Censorship and the freedom to read; 1965 in review. Pub W 189:77-9 Ja 17 '66
Censorship situation in California; report of session at ABA San Francisco meeting. il Pub W 188:41-5 O 25 '65
Civil liberties union backs dean on novel; Another country. Pub W 187:76 Je 21 '65
High court review asked on Mass. Fanny Hill ruling. Pub W 188:31-2 Ag 9 '65
How can we protect our children from obscenity? B. Spock. Redbook 124:18+ Ap '65
James Baldwin novel attacked in Chicago. Pub W 187:58-9 F 1 '65
Let it be printed; imprimatur today. E. Bartelme. il Commonweal 81:701-3 F 26 '65
Literature and obscenity. R. Tracy. Christian Cent 82:769-72 Je 16 '65
Literature and obscenity. R. Tracy. Christian Cent 82:769-72 Je 16 '65; Discussion. 82:993 Ag 11 '65
Manner of speaking; right to read: New Jersey committee activities. J. Ciardi. Sat R 48:12 N 6 '65
Massachusetts finds Fanny Hill obscene. Pub W 187:37-8 My 3 '65
Nation of peeping toms; discussion. America 112:34. 179 Ja 9, F 6 '65
Passionate pursuit of pornography. E. J. Gaines. ALA Bul 59:99-100 F '65
Paul Romaine defense fund; Chicago bookseller guilty under Illinois anti-obscenity statute. R. H. Smith. Pub W 187:63 Je 23 '65
San Francisco censors Bantam books cover. Pub W 187:54 Je 28 '65
Should we censor what adolescents read? with study-discussion program, by C. Smallenburg and H. Smallenburg. H. Norris; J. R. Squire; R. F. Hogan. bibliog il PTA Mag 59:10-12, 36 Mr '65
Supporting the Library bill of rights; proceedings of midwinter conference sponsored by ALA Intellectual freedom committee. bibliog ALA Bul 59:469-533 Je '65
Supreme court and obscenity; censorship a defensive weapon; address, May 2, 1965. J. T. Regan. Vital Speeches 31:592-5 Jl 15 '65
Two faces of the Chicago tribune; controversy over James Baldwin's Another country as college required reading. Christian Cent 82:132-3 F 3 '65
See also
Government and the press
Immoral literature and pictures
Index librorum prohibitorum
Libraries—Censorship
Moving picture censorship
Postal censorship
School libraries—Censorship
Television broadcasting—Censorship

France
Maurice Girodias: in trouble for his d.b.'s. Pub W 188:34-5 O 11 '65

Great Britain
Be unbuggable, Harold Wilson; Britain's biggest bookseller bans Bunkside book from shelves. Life 59:4 D 10 '65

CENSORSHIP—*Continued*

Ireland

Irish censors deny entry to John McGahern novel; ban against The dark. Pub W 188:40, 48 O 11 '65

Italy

Banning The deputy. Commonweal 81:721 Mr 5 '65

Portugal

Censorship harasses Portuguese publisher. Pub W 188:20 Ag 16 '65

Russia

And quiet flow the words; smuggling of manuscripts. il Time 86:33 D 17 '65

Arrests in Russia; case of Andrei Sinyavsky and Yuli Daniel. New Repub 154:7 Ja 22 '66

End to Soviet censorship? A. Brumberg. New Repub 153:19-21 O 2 '65

Writers in the Soviet Union. New Repub 153: 9-10 D 11 '65; Discussion. 154:36+ Ja 1 '66

Spain

Little battle; cancellation of a scheduled concert by Raimón. Nation 201:422 N 29 '65

United States

See Censorship

Yugoslavia

Ungentle ways of Marshal Tito; concerning M. Mihajlov's Summer in Moscow. T. Molnar. Nat R 17:595+ Jl 13 '65

CENSORSHIP, Library. See Libraries—Censorship

CENSORSHIP of mail. See Postal censorship

CENSURE of Joseph R. McCarthy. See Government investigations—McCarthy censure

CENTAUR booster. See Space vehicles—Propulsion systems

CENTER for research libraries, Chicago
Center for research libraries: its new organization and programs. G. Williams. il Library J 90:2947-51 Jl '65

CENTER for the study of democratic institutions, Santa Barbara, Calif.
Convocation; four days at New York Hilton. New Yorker 41:30-2 Mr 6 '65

Convocation on Pacem in terris; world leaders study Pope John's words. P. J. Henriot. America 112:223-4 F 13 '65

Pacem in terris; convocation of world leaders to examine the requirements for peace in the context of the encyclical. il Sat R 48:19 F 13 '65

Peace and pathos; study of Pope John's encyclical Pacem in terris. N. O'Gorman. Commonweal 81:783-5 Mr 19 '65

Peace at the Hilton; convocation on Pacem in terris. G. Wills. il Nat R 17:233-6 Mr 23 '65

Peace on earth? New York convocation discusses Pope John XXIII's encyclical Pacem in terris; with report by J. K. Jessup. il Life 58:32-36A+ Mr 5 '65

Pope John speaks again; International convocation on Peace on earth. America 112: 307-8 Mr 6 '65

Requirements of peace; conference on Pope John XXIII's encyclical Pacem in terris (Peace on earth) il Time 85:36-8 F 26 '65

Rim of hell; How the United States got involved. Nation 201:110 S 6 '65

When the world's peoples talked peace; excerpts from speeches at the Pacem in terris convocation, with list of participants. il Sat R 48:22-6+ My 1 '65

CENTERPIECES. See Table decoration

CENTO. See Central treaty organization

CENTRAL AFRICAN REPUBLIC
African encounter. T. Sterling. Holiday 38: 52-3+ Ag '65

Another blow to red China; expelling all nationals of Communist China. America 114: 63 Ja 15 '66

Fast shuffle; government coup. il Newsweek 67:40 Ja 17 '66

Soldiers on the march. Time 87:39 Ja 14 '66

CENTRAL airlines
Central plans twin-jet aircraft, seeks expanded route structure. Aviation W 83:47 D 6 '65

CENTRAL AMERICA
Central America today; symposium. bibliog f il Cur Hist 50:1-44 Ja '66
See also
Canals—Central America
Economic assistance in Central America

Economic conditions

Why Central America moves to a faster beat. il Bsns W p 114+ S 11 '65

Economic policy

See also
Central American program of economic integration

History

Republic of Central America; an old dream, a new hope. H. Martínez Montero. il Américas 17:18-23 Mr '65

Industries

Go South, young man! D. S. Stroetzel. Read Digest 88:189-94 Ja '66

Politics

Republic of Central America; an old dream, a new hope. H. Martínez Montero. il Américas 17:18-23 Mr '65

CENTRAL AMERICAN common market. See Central American program of economic integration

CENTRAL AMERICAN program of economic integration
New Common market. H. C. Wallich. Newsweek 65:80 Mr 8 '65

New octopus; Mexico's trade with CACM. il Newsweek 67:38 Ja 10 '66

Why Central America moves to a faster beat. il Bsns W p 114+ S 11 '65

CENTRAL ARIZONA project (proposed)
Grand Canyon cash registers. Life 58:4 My 7 '65

CENTRAL ASIA. See Asia, Central

CENTRAL CITY, Colo.

Music

Opera in a bonanza town. R. C. Marsh. Hi Fi 15:153+ O '65

CENTRAL CITY festival. See Music festivals—Colorado

CENTRAL CITY opera association, Colo.
Central City triple play; Lakmé, Manon and Barber of Seville. A. Young. Opera N 30: 26 S 25 '65

CENTRAL EUROPE
See also
Danubian countries

CENTRAL intelligence agency. See United States—Central intelligence agency

CENTRAL MICHIGAN university, Mount Pleasant
They lead two lives in Central Michigan university's five-year teacher intern program. C. E. Nash and others. NEA J 54:12-14 My '65

CENTRAL nervous system. See Nervous system

CENTRAL opera service
Man on the move; interview, ed. by A. M. Lingg. R. L. B. Tobin. Opera N 30:13 N 6 '65

CENTRAL park. See New York (city)—Parks and playgrounds

CENTRAL treaty organization
Central treaty organization marks 10th anniversary; exchange of messages; with announcement of U.S. celebration, and remarks. L. B. Johnson; A. A. Khalatbary; D. Rusk. Dept State Bul 52:389-90 Mr 15 '65

Central treaty organization meets at Tehran; statement, April 7, 1965, with final communique. D. Rusk. Dept State Bul 52: 685-8 My 3 '65

CENTRALIZATION in government. See Decentralization in government

CENTRALIZED authority in business. See Business management and organization

CENTRALIZED cataloging. See Cataloging

CENTRIFUGAL homogenizers. See Homogenizers

CENTRIFUGES
Simple microcentrifuge for use in the field. B. Holmstedt. bibliog il Science 149:977-8 Ag 27 '65

CENTURY expressway (proposed) See Expressways highways

CERAMI, Charles A.
For success; work twenty-five hours a day. Nations Bsns 53:78-80 Ag '65

Test your leadership skill. Nations Bsns 53:74-5 Ap '65

CERAMIC materials
Ceramic i.f. filters. D. L. Pippen. il Electr World 74:34-5+ N '65

Man-made human bones; cerosium. il Sci Digest 57:28 Mr '65

CERAMIC sculpture
Voulkos: redemption through ceramics. J. Coplans. il Art N 64:38-9+ Sum '65

CERAMICS. See Pottery; Tiles

CERASTIUM. See Snow-in-summer

CERATOCYSTIS ulmi. See Elm—Diseases and pests

CERDA, Luis Escobar
Social science and development; excerpt from Social sciences in Latin America, ed. by M. Diégues, jr. and B. Wood. por Américas 17:1-7 N '65
CEREAL breads. See Bread
CEREAL foods
See also
Cookery—Cereals
CEREAL leaf beetles. See Beetles
CEREBELLAR cortex
Cerebellar disease in cats induced by inoculation rat virus. L. Kilham and G. Margolis. bibliog il Science 148:244-6 Ap 9 '65
CEREBELLUM
Brain catecholamines: relation to the defense reaction evoked by amygdaloid stimulation in cat. D. J. Reis and L.-M. Gunne. bibliog il Science 149:450-1 Jl 23 '65
CEREBRAL cortex
Amino acids released from the cerebral cortex in relation to its state of activation. H. H. Jasper and others. bibliog il Science 147: 1448-9 Mr 19 '65
Duplication of evoked potential waveform by curve of probability of firing of a single cell. S. S. Fox and J. H. O'Brien. bibliog il Science 147:888-90 F 19 '65
Facilitation: electrical response enhanced by conditional excitation of cerebral cortex. L. T. Rutledge. bibliog il Science 148:1246-8 My 28 '65
Prolonged excitation in the visual cortex of the cat. C. R. Evans and A. D. J. Robertson. bibliog il Science 150:913-15 N 12 '65
CEREBRAL hemorrhage
Can strokes be prevented? Good H 161:135-7 Ag '65
Her best performance; case of P. Neal. il Newsweek 65:55 My 31 '65
New insight gained into origin of stroke. Sci N L 87:137 F 27 '65
Patricia Neal: a woman's fight to live. S. Frank. il Good H 161:64-5+ Ag '65
Personal business; strokes. Bsns W p 161 Mr 27 '65
Stroke: second greatest crippler. G. Astor. il Look 29:120+ Je 15 '65
Stroke victims treated by neck artery surgery. Sci N L 88:297 N 6 '65
Zeroing in on three killer diseases. Bsns W p 170+ O 23 '65
CEREBRAL palsy. See Paralysis
CERF, Jay H.
We should do more business with Communists. N Y Times Mag p70-1+ D 5 '65
CERN (Conseil européen pour la recherche nucléaire) See European organization for nuclear research
CEROSIUM. See Ceramic materials
CERRUTI, James
Hunting the wild mushroom. Holiday 38:96-100 Ag '65
CESIUM
Ribosomes: analysis by cesium sulfate gradient centrifugation. F. M. DeFilippes. bibliog il Science 150:610-12 O 29 '65
CESIUM in the body
Radioactive meat eaten; cesium 137 found among Eskimos at Anaktuvuk Pass. Sci N L 87:142 F 27 '65
CESS, Robert
Yachting asks about wooden-kit boatbuilding; interview, ed. by E. Robberson. por Yachting 117:61-4+ Mr '65
CESTODA
Cestode echinococcus multilocularis in foxes in North Dakota. P. D. Leiby and O. W. Olsen; reply. T. B. Magath. il Science 147: 632 F 5 '65
Cestode in North Dakota: echinococcus in field mice. P. D. Leiby. bibliog Science 150:763 N 5 '65
CEYLON
See also
Elections—Ceylon
Political campaigns—Ceylon

History
Pearl on the toe of India. S. Rama Rau. il Horizon 7:50-63 Autumn '65

Politics and government
Change in direction? Sr Schol 86:25 Ap 15 '65
New deal in Ceylon. America 113:618 N 20 '65
Pledge to battle. Time 85:28 Ap 9 '65
CÉZANNE, Paul
Cold plunge. il por Time 85:68-9 F 12 '65
Letter from London: exhibition of painting: Les grandes baigneuses at the National gallery. M. Panter-Downes. New Yorker 40: 108+ Ja 30 '65

CHABAS, Yves
Christians and Marxists. Christian Cent 82: 1286-8 O 20 '65
CHACO CANYON NATIONAL MONUMENT
Confusing rock; prehistoric masonry work, Pueblo Bonito, N.Mex. L. Kinnear and W. Kinnear. il Nat Parks Mag 39:17-19 N '65
CHAD
Guelta of the bleak Sahara; source of water is mystery in the Tchad. W. G. Dyer. il Natur Hist 74:36-9 N '65
CHADWICK, Florence
Last one in is a zero figure! Mlle 61:148-9 My '65
CHADWICK, Joe
My real friend. Joe; with portrait by G. Catlin. L. Burkhalter. Am Heritage 16: 44-5 Ap '65
CHAENICHTHYIDAE. See Ice fish, Antarctic
CHAETOGNATHA. See Arrowworms
CHAFETZ, Sidney
Printmaker. Sch Arts 64:27-30 My '65
CHAFFARD, Georges
Is the Vietcong such a sure winner after all? excerpt. Life 58:87+ Ap 30 '65
CHAGALL, Marc
Chagallicisms. Time 85:94 Ap 16 '65
Midsummer night's dreamer. il pors Time 86:42-50 Jl 30 '65
Poor little Chagall from Vitebsk. E. Roditi. il pors N Y Times Mag p50-1+ D 5 '65
CHAGRIN VALLEY
Hijinks at the hee-haw derby; Chagrin Valley Mule point-to-point. L. Smith. il Sports Illus 22:34-6+ Je 21 '65
CHAI, S. Y. and Vogelhut, P. O.
Activation energy of direct-current electrical conductivity of ice with HF and NH3 added. bibliog Science 148:1595-8 Je 18 '65
CHAIKIN, Miriam
Gwendolyn Julie Rebecca McBroom; poem. Good H 160:30 Mr '65
CHAIN, Ernst Boris
We tamed penicillin; ed. by J. D. Ratcliff. Read Digest 86:89-93 Mr '65
about
E. B. Chain accused of contempt of Italian judiciary. V. K. McElheny. Science 150: 1573-5 D 17 '65
CHAIN stores
Art sale in the supermarkets. il Newsweek 65:75-6+ Je 21 '65
Mexico's drug store changes prescription; Sanborns restaurants, chain, and retail stores under Walgreen co. il Bsns W p72-4+ My 15 '65
West's biggest chain; Broadway-Hale. il Time 86:96+ S 24 '65
Why Hickory farms goes to the fair. il Bsns W p70-2 S 4 '65
See also
National association of convenience stores
Penney, J. C. company
Woolworth, F. W. company
CHAIRMEN
Pointers on conducting a meeting. Recreation 58:333+ S '65
CHAIRS
Chairs in pairs. il House & Gard 127:178 Mr '65
Nineteenth-century contour chairs. C. J. Otto. il Antiques 87:193-5 F '65
CHALET, Pierre
In an eastern woodlot; poem. Am For 71:53 Ap '65
Miracle of the Blue Ridge; poem. Am For 71: 43 Jl '65
CHALFONT, Alun Gwynne-Jones, baron
Non-dissemination of nuclear weapons; address, August 19, 1965. Vital Speeches 31: 679-81 S 1 '65
CHALMERS, Bruce, and Williamson, R. B.
Crystal multiplication without nucleation. bibliog Science 148:1717-18 Je 25 '65
CHAMBER music
For the joy of it; Amateur chamber music players. Time 86:47 D 24 '65
See also
Phonograph records—Chamber music
CHAMBER of commerce of the United States
New blow at Connally; U.S. chamber of commerce calls for repeal of the Connally reservation. Time 85:24 My 7 '65
Partisan reporting; views of the Education department of the U.S. chamber of commerce on federal aid to private schools. America 112:413 Mr 27 '65
CHAMBER orchestras
Princeton chamber orchestra; Decca records. J. W Barker. il Am Rec G 32:51 S '65
CHAMBERLAIN, John
Rival to Cosa nostra? Harper 231:118+ D '65
Strange case against fourteen-B. Nat R 17: 500-2+ Je 15 '65

CHAMBERLAIN, John Maxwell
Extended effort; excerpts from Climate is hope, ed. by W. Ross. Todays Health 44:62-6+ Ja '66

CHAMBERLAIN, Neil W.
Art of unbalancing the budget. Atlan 217:58-62 Ja '66
Corporation as a college. Atlan 215:102-4 Je '65

CHAMBERLAIN, Neville
Dreamer wide awake; letter. J. F. Kennedy. Am Heritage 16:80-1 O '65

CHAMBERLAIN, Wilt
My life in a bush league; ed. by B. Ottum. pors Sports Illus 22:32-4+ Ap 12; 38-41+ Ap 19 '65

CHAMBERLIN, Anne
Great Swampoodle gazette. Sat Eve Post 238:90+ Ap 10 '65
See America first. Sat Eve Post 238:25-31+ Ag 28 '65
Soviet fashions: a hesitant hint of glamour. Sat Eve Post 238:82-3 My 22 '65

CHAMBERLIN, Thomas Chrowder
Method of multiple working hypotheses; reprint from Science, 1890. por Science 148:754-9 My 7 '65

CHAMBERLIN, William Henry
Magnificent middlebrow. Sat R 48:28-9+ O 9 '65
Thucydides: the historian as prophet. Sat R 48:22-3+ My 8 '65
Withering wit of Samuel Johnson. Sat R 48:14-15+ S 4 '65

CHAMBERS, Whittaker
Wallace vs. Chambers; letter to the editor. F. C. Waldrop. Nat R 18:6+ Ja 11 '66
Whittaker Chambers. J. Finn. Commonweal 81:696-7 F 26 '65
Witness from the past. J. O'Gara. Commonweal 81:687 F 26 '65

CHAMONIX, France
Reporter at large. J. Bernstein. il New Yorker 41:43-6+ Mr 6; 130+ Mr 13; 109-10+ Mr 20 '65

CHAMORROS
Letter from Guam. E. J. Kahn, jr. il New Yorker 40:39-40+ F 13 '65

CHAMPAGNAT, Alfred
Protein from petroleum. Sci Am 213:13-17 O '65

CHAMPAGNE
Fizz, bubbly, pop; historical background. E. Waugh. Vogue 146:156+ S 1 '65
Wine, women and so on. P. Cannon. Ladies Home J 83:103 Ja '66

CHAMPAIGN, Ill.
Two master controllers, one smooth-flowing traffic network. F. B. Noonan. il Am City 80:150 Je '65

CHAMPION, George
Government-by-guideline; address. por Duns R 86:17-18+ Jl '65
New threat to economic freedom; address, May 25, 1965. Vital Speeches 31:521-4 Je 15 '65
Our growing responsibilites in a changing world; address, December 8, 1964. Vital Speeches 31:282-5 F 15 '65
Why politics is for you. pors Nations Bsns 53:40-1+ Mr '65

about
Banker in the news. J. Berry. por Duns R 86:53-4 S '65
New phase? por Newsweek 65:70-1 Je 7 '65

CHAMPION, Gower
Broadway's Champion. G. P. Gates. por Holiday 37:87-8+ F '65

CHAMPION, Hale
One family's strange journey. por Life 59:80-1 Jl 23 '65

CHAMPION Red Archer; story. See Sinclair, T.

CHAMPION spark plug company
Aircraft use aids Champion sales effort. D. A. Brown. il Aviation W 83:100-1+ Ag 9 '65

CHAMPLIN, Beulah
Tomorrow I'll see the sun; ed. by M. Longwell. por Farm J 90:73+ Ja '66

CHAN, Y. C. See Rudnick, A. jt. auth.

CHANCE, Dean
Angel who doesn't fear to tread. M. Cope. il pors Sat Eve Post 238:95-9 Ap 10 '65
Take a chance. H. L. Masin. por Sr Schol 86:36 Ap 15 '65
You can take the boy out of the country. M. Kram. il pors Sports Illus 22:36-8+ Mr 8 '65

CHANCE
Chance. A. J. Ayer. il Sci Am 213:44-52+ O '65
See also
Probabilities

CHANCE of a lifetime; story. See Culver, M.

CHANCELLOR, John William
Change for the Voice: TV newsman named chief. U S News 59:14 Ag 9 '65
New voice at VOA. por Time 86:52 Ag 6 '65
Voice of the Voice. Newsweek 66:27+ Ag 9 '65

CHANDLER, Patti
Success overtakes Patti Chandler. H. Ehrlich. il pors Look 29:33-7 Je 29 '65

CHANDLER, Raymond
Lost fortnight. J. Houseman. Harper 231:55-61 Ag '65

CHANDRASEKHAR, S.
Billion Indians by 2000 A.D? N Y Times Mag p32-3+ Ap 4 '65

CHANEL, Gabrielle
Interview with Chanel; ed. by J. Barry. pors McCalls 93:120-1+ N '65

CHANG, R. Shihman. See Little, J. B. jt. auth.

CHANGE, Social. See Social change

CHANGE, Technological. See Technological change

CHANGE of heart; story. See Cave, H.

CHANGE of life. See Menopause

CHANGE of plan; story. See Friedman, B. J.

CHANGEUX, Jean-Pierre
Control of biochemical reactions. Sci Am 212:36-45 bibliog(p 158) Ap '65

CHANNEL ISLANDS (English Channel)
See also
Sark

CHANNEL ISLANDS, Calif. See Santa Barbara Islands

CHANNEL tunnel. See English Channel tunnel (proposed)

CHANNING, Carol
At home with Carol Channing. il pors House & Gard 128:210-13 S '65
Jonathan Winters of our discontent. G. Ace. Sat R 48:14 Ap 24 '65
New doll in town. il por Newsweek 66:74-5 Ag 16 '65

CHANOCK, Robert M.
Cure for the common cold? interview. por U S News 58:46-8 My 3 '65

CHAO, Kang
Agriculture in China today. bibliog f Cur Hist 49:170-5 S '65

CHAPARRAL
Plants resistant to fire; replacing highly inflammable chaparral with fireresistant plants. Sci N L 88:124 Ag 21 '65

CHAPEL HILL, N.C.
Free men. by J. Ehle. Review
Sat R 48:38 My 1 '65. W. Spearman

CHAPEL HILL, N.C. rehabilitation center. See Rehabilitation centers

CHAPELLE, Dickey
Dickey Chapelle killed. por Sr Schol 87:7 N 18 '65
Dickey Chapelle, RIP. C. Wiley. Nat R 17:1066 N 30 '65
Reporter's death. Newsweek 66:52 N 15 '65
Woman at war. il por Time 86:54 N 12 '65

CHAPELS
Chapel for the University Presbyterian church, Rochester, Mich. il Arch Rec 137:160-2 Mr '65
Processional elements in Houston; chapel for St Thomas university. il Arch Rec 137:159 Je '65

CHAPELS, Miniature
Two miniature chapels. S. A. Parvin. il Hobbies 70:122-3 Ap '65

CHAPIN, Francis
Francis Chapin: an exuberant painter. F. Messersmith. il por Am Artist 29:28-33+ Mr '65

CHAPIN, Katherine Garrison
Courage of irony: poetry of Allen Tate. New Repub 153:22-4 Jl 24 '65

CHAPLAINS, College. See Colleges and universities—Religious life

CHAPLAINS, Military
Linking arms in a common cause: four chaplains. il Sr Schol 86:5 F 4 '65

CHAPLAINS, Prison
Books. A. Nebolsine. Commonweal 82:476 Jl 2 '65
Ministers behind bars. il Time 85:55 Je 18 '65

CHAPLEAU, J. A.
There's a good place! il Field & S 69:68-9 F '65

CHAPLIN, Charles
Books. M. Muggeridge. Esquire 63:54+ F '65
On Chaplin. Verdoux and Agee. D. Macdonald. Esquire 63:18+ Ap '65

CHAPLIN, Charles, family
Charlie Chaplin and his children. G. Frank. il Ladies Home J 82:70-1+ My '65
Entrancing new actress; ed. by E. Miller. G. Chaplin. il Seventeen 24:92-3+ D '65

CHAPLIN, George
Opening up the underneath. Sat R 48:74+
S 18 '65
CHAPLIN, Geraldine
Charlie Chaplin's daughter; interview. ed. by
R. Deardorff. pors Redbook 124:58-9+ Mr
'65
Entrancing new actress; ed. by E. Miller.
pors Seventeen 24:92-3+ D '65
about
Female Chaplin makes the movies. G. Zimmermann. il pors Look 29:57-60+ Ap 20
'65
CHAPMAN, Carleton B. and Mitchell, J. H.
Physiology of exercise; with biographical
sketches. Sci Am 212:18, 88-94+ My '65
CHAPMAN, Fred
Simple Simon voltage calibrators. Pop Electr
22:48+ Mr '65
CHAPMAN, John
My most unforgettable character. Read Digest
86:111-15 Je '65
CHAPMAN, Maxine L. See Fisher, R. jt. auth.
CHAPMAN, Robert D.
TPG-65, Paris exposition: a production man's
view. Pub W 188:64-8+ Ag 9 '65
CHAPMAN-Reinhold, incorporated
Medical economics, Reinhold merge as Chapman-Reinhold. Pub W 189:43 Ja 3 '66
CHAR fishing
Home of the fish. H. F. Blaisdell. il Field & S
70:37-9+ Jl '65
Magnificent Arctic char. W. Davis. il Outdoor
Life 137:98-100 Ja '66
We found the hidden char. G. Laycock. il
Field & S 70:49-51+ My '65
CHARACTER
Ethology and experimental psychology; report
on an international conference in Rome.
W. N. Schoenfeld and S. H. Baron. Science
147:634-5 F 5 '65
Words and the tensile strength of character. B. W. Overstreet. il PTA Mag 59:16-18
Je '65
See also
Responsibility
Self reliance
CHARACTER sketches
My most unforgettable character (title
varies) See issues of Reader's digest
CHARACTER tests
See also
Personality tests
CHARACTERIZATION
Off the cuff. L. Conger. Writer 78:5-6 N '65
Stories are about people. L. Wibberley. Writer
78:9-11+ Ag '65
Whatever happened to Peggy? E. Allen.
Writer 78:11-13 Je '65
You can change puppets to people. H. Hinckley. Writer 78:12-16 My '65
CHARACTERS in literature
Author Rex Stout vs. the FBI; Nero Wolfe
takes on a surprising villain; observations;
ed. by S. Schmidt. il Life 59:127-8+ D 10
'65
Birth of a story. L. Egri. Writer 78:20-2 Je
'65
Can anyone invent adventures for famous
character? H. F. Pilpel. Pub W 188:56 S
13 '65
Case of the durable detective: Sherlock
Holmes. J. Stewart-Gordon. il Read Digest
86:207-10 F '65
Century of Alice. il Newsweek 66:86 Jl 12 '65
Don Quixote. K. Rexroth. Sat R 48:19 My 15
'65
Hardy as a modern novelist; excerpt from
introd. to new edition of Jude the obscure.
I. Howe. New Repub 152:19-22 Je 26 '65
Herzog and the passion. R. F. Capon. America 112:425-7 Mr 27 '65
Lazarus as hero: the novels of Lagerkvist.
W. Weathers. Commonweal 81:688-91 F 26
'65
On the grave. C. Brooks. Yale R 55:275-9 D
'65
Roosevelt Grady and the children of Asia.
L. B. Shotwell. il Horn Bk 41:252-4 Je '65
Sentimental journey to Dracula's home town;
Borgo Pass. G. Smith. il Sat Eve Post 238:
76-9 Mr 27 '65
Speed dash. E. S. Gardner. Atlan 215:55-7
Je '65
Spy who got locked in the ice box: childrens
fiction and the real world. D. M. Broderick.
il Library J 90:1478-9 Mr 15 '65
To Valhalla with twin exhausts: J. Bond.
A. Lejeune. il Nat R 17:776-7 S 7 '65
With a little wand. A. Iverson. Writer 78:
16-19 Je '65
See also
Characterization
Jews in literature
Spies in literature
Uncle Tom

CHARACTERS in opera
Fiddling devil; E. T. A. Hoffmann's mad
violinist. N. Paganini. J. W. Stedman. il
Opera N 29:14-16 F 27 '65
Meet Herodias; Richard Strauss' Salome.
A. M. Lingg. il Opera N 29:16 Mr 13 '65
Ramerrez rides again; Dick Johnson alias
Ramerrez, in Girl of the golden West. J.
W. Stedman. il Opera N 30:6-7 Ja 8 '66
Real hero: Sharpless, not Pinkerton. W. Ashbrook. il Opera N 29:24-5 Mr 27 '65
Three under stress: Forza's tormented principals. K. McDonald. il Opera N 29:24-5
F 6 '65
CHARCOAL braziers. See Braziers
CHARDIN, Pierre Teilhard de. See Teilhard de
Chardin, P.
CHARGE accounts (retail trade)
Next in banking: pay bills by phone; Bank
of Delaware Touch-tone card dial system.
il Bsns W p82+ N 13 '65
What it costs to say charge it; new kinds
of accounts, revolving account. il Changing T 19:17-19 Je '65
CHARGERS (football club) See Football clubs
CHARGERS, Battery. See Storage battery
chargers
CHARISMATA. See Gifts, Spiritual
CHARITIES
Tithe that binds; Jewish fund-raising techniques. il Newsweek 66:86-7 D 13 '65
See also
Charity organization society of the city of
New York
Corporations—Charitable contributions
Foundations, Charitable and educational
Fund raising
Giving
Salvation army
CHARITY
Thing beyond compare. C. Davis. America
112:667 My 8 '65
CHARITY organization society of the city of
New York
Summer camp education for underprivileged
children; Edgewater creche, 1884-1964. F. M.
Cordasco and J. G. Redd. bibliog f Sch &
Soc 93:299 Sum '65
CHARLATANRY. See Quacks and quackery
CHARLEMAGNE, king of the Franks
Baby renaissance. il Time 86:62-3 Ag 27 '65
Charlemagne's dream; exhibition at Aachen.
P. Schneider. il Art N 64:22-6+ N '65
CHARLES, prince of Wales
Toughening Charles at Timbertop. il Time
86:64 O 29 '65
CHARLES, Alan
Everyone plays the company game. il por
Bsns W p34 F 6 '65
CHARLES, Robert Horne
Carrots and sticks: the Pentagon's new incentive pricing formula. por Fortune 72:280
D '65
CHARLES Hamilton autographs, incorporated.
See Hamilton, Charles, autographs, incorporated
CHARLES Pfizer and company. See Pfizer,
Charles, and company
CHARLESWORTH, James C.
Allocation of responsibilities and resources
among the three levels of government. Ann
Am Acad 359:71-80 My '65
(ed) Latin America tomorrow. bibliog f
Ann Am Acad 360:1-138 Jl '65
Seventy-five years of the Academy. Ann
Am Acad 360:172-7 Jl '65
CHARLOTTETOWN, Prince Edward Island
Public buildings
Monumental civic architecture, modest in
scale; Fathers of confederation memorial.
il Arch Rec 137:161-8 Ap '65
CHARM schools. See Personality training and
development
CHARMS
Charms and amulets. Mrs. J. D. Whiting. il
Hobbies 70:45+ O '65
CHAROLAIS cattle. See Cattle—Breeds
CHARPIE, Robert Alan
Power of the mind; address, June 14, 1965.
Vital Speeches 31:668-70 Ag 15 '65
CHARROS. See Rodeos
CHARTER of the United Nations. See United
Nations—Charter
CHARTERING of yachts. See Yachts—Chartering
CHARTRES cathedral. See Cathedrals—France
CHARTS, Calculating
Amplifier gain nomogram. M. H. Applebaum.
il Electr World 74:25 Ag '65
Handy lumber calculator. Pop Sci 187:147 N
'65
Instant color correction! color filter nomography. il Mod Phot 29:60-1 O '65

CHARTS, Calculating—*Continued*
Line-of-sight nomogram; required antenna heights for various reception ranges. D. L. Pippen. il Electr World 73:27 Mr '65
Parallel-resistor nomogram. M. H. Applebaum. il Electr World 74:27 S '65
Power-output nomogram. M. H. Applebaum. il Electr World 73:29 My '65
RC time-constant nomogram. M. H. Applebaum. Electr World 74:29 Jl '65
Resistor noise graphs. R. Jones. il Electr World 73:42-3 Ap '65
Transformer turns ratio nomogram. M. H. Applebaum. il Electr World 74:29 N '65
U.H.F.-TV half wave shorting-stub nomogram M. H. Applebaum. il Electr World 73:29 Je '65

CHARTS, Scientific. See Science—Charts, graphs, etc.

CHARTS, Stock. See Stocks—Price indexes and averages

CHASE, Ada R. and Bulkeley, Houghton
Thomas Harland's clock, whose case? Antiques 87:700-1 Je '65

CHASE, Edward T.
Native aliens. Reporter 33:46-8 D 30 '65
Shape of things to come. New Repub 153:28-9 Jl 10 '65
Tracking the American intellectual. Nation 200:564-6 My 24 '65

CHASE, Stuart
Historical necessity of peace. Sat R 48:129 Mr 13 '65
More power, less security. Sat R 48:32-3 Jl 17 '65

CHASE, William W.
Schoolhouses for big cities. por Am Ed 1:12-19 F '65

CHASE Manhattan bank. See New York (city)—Banks

CHASEMAN, Joel
Sound of news. New Yorker 41:18-19 Je 26 '65

CHASINS, Abram
High-brows vs no-brows. McCalls 92:42+ S '65
Moscow philharmonic. Hi Fi 16:131+ Ja '66
Rubinstein, adventurer and elder statesman. Hi Fi 15:113+ My '65
Sviatoslav Richter returns. Hi Fi 15:100-1 Jl '65
Vladimir Horowitz. Hi Fi 15:122+ Ag '65
You call that music? McCalls 92:76+ Ap '65; Same abr. Read Digest 87:141-4 Ag '65
(ed) See Horowitz, V. Horowitz.

CHASSIER, Suzanne M.
My daughter Laure. por Redbook 124:8+ Mr '65

CHASSIS, Automobile. See Automobiles—Chassis

CHASTEL, André
What is mannerism? Art N 64:22-5+ D '65

CHASTITY. See Sexual ethics

CHASTITY of Magda Wickwire; story. See Konecky, E.

CHATEAUROUX, France
French town, an American base, a frontier. A. Menen. il N Y Times Mag p 14-15+ Ja 31 '65

CHATEAUROUX air base. See Air bases

CHATFIELD, Chester
Big trout! Outdoor Life 135:48-9+ Mr '65
Flight to never-never land. por Outdoor Life 135:52-3+ Ap '65
Lost like a goose. por Outdoor Life 136:60-3+ N '65
125 years of bass savvy. Outdoor Life 136:28-31+ Ag '65

CHATHAM marine shell museum, Mass.
Cape Cod's Chatham shell museum. A. G. Melvin. il Hobbies 70:130+ My '65

CHATTAHOOCHEE RIVER
Atlanta: the waiting game; pollution problems. R. McGill. Sat R 48:42-3 My 22 '65

CHATTANOOGA, Tenn.
Old airport up-jets. il Am City 80:114-15 S '65

CHATTERS, R. M. See Olson, E. A. jt. auth.

CHAUCER, Geoffrey
Chaucer. K. Rexroth. Sat R 48:23 D 25 '65

CHAUNCEY, Henry, and Hilton, T. L.
Are aptitude tests valid for the highly able? bibliog Science 148:1297-304 Je 4 '65

CHAVE, Keith E.
Carbonates: association with organic matter in surface seawater. bibliog Science 148:1723 Je 25 '65
—and Wheeler, B. D. Jr
Mineralogic changes during growth in the red alga, clathromorphum compactum. bibliog Science 147:621 F 5 '65

CHEAT; story. See O'Connor, F.

CHEATHAM, Owen Robertson
Second growth of Georgia-Pacific. J. B. Weiner. il por Duns R 85:47-9+ My '65

CHEATING at cards. See Cardsharping

CHEATING in schoolwork
Amount of cheating on U.S. campuses; who are the cheaters in college? il U S News 58:10 F 8 '65
Cadet involved sizes up the scandal; honor code violation at U S air force academy. il Life 58:68-73 F 12 '65
Cadets in cheating scandal. Sr Schol 86:17 F 11 '65
Cheating and symbols; report of a special committee called by the secretary of the air force to consider cases of cheating. Commonweal 82:277 My 21 '65
Cheating by air cadets; the brass is blamed. U S News 58:16 My 17 '65
Classroom incident; examination stolen. NEA J 55:52-3 Ja '66
Fields of friendly strife. Nation 200:126 F 8 '65
Honor bound to what? Air force academy code of honor. New Repub 152:9-10 F 13 '65; Discussion. 152:26-7 Mr 13; 28-9 Ap 3 '65
Lengthening list; buying and selling of stolen exams at Air force academy. Newsweek 65:83-4 F 8 '65
Letter from Paris; thefts of examination papers for the baccalaureate. Genêt. New Yorker 41:96-7 Je 26 '65
Rules of the game; revision of administration of honor code. Newsweek 66:65 N 29 '65
Scandal at Colorado Springs; sale of exam papers. il Time 85:62 F 5 '65
Smudge on the cadet code; cheating ring at Air force academy. J. Bride, jr. il Life 58:82+ F 5 '65
Startling survey on college cribbing; study by the Bureau of applied research, Columbia university. Life 58:84 F 5 '65
Tarnished buttons; cheating scandal at Air force academy. S. Alexander. Life 58:25 F 12 '65
Topkapi in Colorado; cheating scandal at the Air force academy. il Newsweek 65:82 F 15 '65
What to do when children cheat. O. Palmer. il Parents Mag 41:38-9+ Ja '66

CHEBOYGAN, Mich.
Shared time in action. case history. il U S News 58:54 My 3 '65

CHECKING accounts. See Banks and banking—Checking accounts

CHECKS for the blind. See Blind, Checks for the

CHECKUP, Medical. See Physical examinations

CHEER leaders
Paratrooper runs tough school for cheerleaders. il Life 59:71-2+ S 17 '65

CHEESE
Art of serving fruit and cheese. il McCalls 92:94-6+ Jl '65
Cheese chart. il McCalls 92:52-3 Mr '65
Thirty-six different ways to say cheese. il Bet Hom & Gard 43:78-9 Mr '65
See also
Cookery—Cheese

CHEESECAKE
Let's make dessert together; creamcake recipe. il Seventeen 24:170-1 Ap '65
Pleasant ending; creamy cheesecake with fruit. il Sunset 135:230+ O '65

CHEETAHS
Champion sprinters of the animal world. il UNESCO Courier 18:18-19 F '65

CHEEVER, John
Geometry of love; story. Sat Eve Post 239:34-9 Ja 1 '66
about
Oracle of subocracy. J. Scully. Nation 200:144-5 F 8 '65

CHEFS. See Cooks

CHEKHOV, Anton Pavlovich
Cherry orchard. Criticism
Nation 201:87-8 Ag 16 '65
New Repub 152:26-8 F 27 '65
New Yorker 41:54+ F 20 '65
Newsweek 65:93-4 F 22 '65
Three sisters. Criticism
Harper 231:32+ S '65
New Repub 152:26-8 F 27 '65
New Yorker 41:96+ F 27 '65
Newsweek il 65:94 F 22 '65

CHELMINSKI, Rudolph
Goodby at Lambarene. Life 59:90-2+ S 17 '65
(ed) See Nguyen-cao-Ky. General Nguyen Ky: we've got to go fast

CHELMSFORD, Mass.
Two churches that respect tradition: Trinity Lutheran church. il Arch Rec 137:155-9 Mr '65

CHELSEA flower show. See Flower exhibits

CHEMICAL additives in food. See Food additives

CHEMICAL apparatus and supplies
   See also
Centrifuges
CHEMICAL bonds
  Hydrogen-bonded dimers of adenine and uracil derivatives. R. M. Mamlin, jr. and others. bibliog il Science 148:1734-7 Je 25 '65
CHEMICAL elements
   See also names of chemical elements, e.g. Plutonium
CHEMICAL engineers
  Business lectures professors; Monsanto woos chemistry graduates to marketing by teaching their teachers. il Bsns W p65-6 Jl 10 '65
CHEMICAL equilibrium
   See also
Donnan equilibrium
CHEMICAL evolution. See Biosynthesis
CHEMICAL industries
   See also
Allied chemical corporation
Du Pont de Nemours, E. I, and company
General aniline and film corporation
Grace, W. R. and company
Mallinckrodt chemical works
Monsanto company
Olin Mathieson chemical corporation
Stauffer chemical company
Union carbide corporation

      Exhibitions
Applied chemistry; Exposition of chemical industries at the Coliseum. New Yorker 41:41-2 D 18 '65
Russia hunts chemical knowhow; European participation in Moscow exhibition. il Bsns W p70+ S 25 '65

      Italy
Italy gets a chemical giant; merger of Montecatini, Edison company. Bsns W p20 D 25 '65

      Russia
Russia hunts chemical knowhow; European participation in Moscow exhibition. il Bsns W p70+ S 25 '65
CHEMICAL nomenclature. See Chemistry—Nomenclature
CHEMICAL reactions
  Chemistry at high velocities. R. Wolfgang. il Sci Am 214:82-90 Ja '66
  Kinetics and analysis of very fast chemical reactions; address, January 14, 1965. R. G. W. Norrish. bibliog il Science 149:1470-82 S 24 '65
  Molecular transitions and chemical reaction rates. B. Widom. bibliog Science 148:1555-60 Je 18 '65
  Reactions occur in ice. Sci N L 89:38 Ja 15 '66
   See also
Precipitation (chemistry)

      Velocity
  See Chemical reactions
CHEMICAL research
  Chemistry: a little science would like a little more money; with editorial comment. D. S. Greenberg. il Science 150:1247, 1267-70 D 3 '65
  1965 science review. Sci N L 88:391-2 D 18 '65
  Order from chaos; address, March 19, 1965. J. H. Hildebrand. bibliog il Science 150:441-50 O 22 '65
   See also
Gordon research conferences
CHEMICAL warfare
  Chemical agents may decrease war savagery. Sci N L 88:137 Ag 28 '65
  Forthright CBR policy urged. W. S. Beller. il Miss & Roc 16:27-8+ Ap 19 '65
  Peril of non-nuclear weapons. B. H. Frisch. il Sci Digest 57:8-13 Mr '65
   See also
Gases in warfare
CHEMISTRY
   See also
Acids
Atoms
Biochemistry
Solution (chemistry)

      Nomenclature
Zamene, isomeric C₁₉ monoolefins from marine zooplankton, fishes, and mammals. M. Blumer and D. W. Thomas. bibliog il Science 148:370-1 Ap 16 '65

      Study and teaching
Education in chemistry: United States and Japan; report on United States-Japan conference on chemistry education. B. Tamamushi. Science 147:1163 Mr 5 '65
NAS urges increase in chemistry program. Sci N L 89:24 Ja 8 '66

      Textbooks
On teaching high school chemistry. P. G. Ashmore. Science 148:1312-14 Je 4 '65
CHEMISTRY, Analytic
  Analytical chemistry in nuclear technology; report on eighth Conference on analytical chemistry in nuclear technology. C. D. Susano and others. Science 147:523 Ja 29 '65
   See also
Precipitation (chemistry)
Radioactivation analysis
Thermal analysis
CHEMISTRY, Biological. See Biochemistry
CHEMISTRY, Organic
  Organic fluorine chemistry. C. G. Krespan. bibliog il Science 150:13-18 O 1 '65
   See also
Proteins
CHEMISTRY, Physical and theoretical
   See also
Adsorption
Critical point
Precipitation (chemistry)
Solution (chemistry)
CHEMISTRY sets. See Toys
CHEMISTS
  Scientific couple finds success in Albuquerque. il Ebony 20:67-70+ Je '65
CHEMOTHERAPY
  Antimicrobial agents and chemotherapy; report on fourth Interscience conference on antimicrobial agents and chemotherapy. M. H. Lepper and D. Perlman. Science 147:522 Ja 29 '65
   See also
Antibiotics
CHEN, King
  Peking's strategy in Indochina. Yale R 54:550-66 Je '65
CHEN, Raymond F.
  Fluorescence quantum yield measurements: vitamin B₆ compounds. bibliog Science 150:1593-5 D 17 '65
—and Bowman, R. L.
  Fluorescence polarization: measurement with ultraviolet-polarizing filters in a spectrophotofluorometer. bibliog Science 147:729-32 F 12 '65
CHEN, Theodore H. E.
  New citizens for a new society. bibliog f Cur Hist 49:155-63 S '65
CHEN, Yi
  Sukarno struts as Chen Yi snoozes. il Life 59:36-36A S 3 '65
CHENEY, Frances Neel
  Current reference books. See issues of Wilson library bulletin
CHEONG, W. H. and others
  Anopheles balabacensis balabacensis identified as vector of simian malaria in Malaysia. bibliog Science 150:1314-15 D 3 '65
CHERNE, Leo
  Twenty-five year look back; address, January 5, 1965. Vital Speeches 31:349-52 Mr 15 '65
  Why we can't withdraw. Sat R 48:17-21 D 18 '65
CHEROKEE, Ia.
  Culture comes to Cherokee. D. J. Henahan. Holiday 38:21-6 Jl '65
CHERRY, Elaine
  Garden indoors. Horticulture 43:30-1 Mr '65
  Grow a complete garden indoors under lights. Flower Grower 52:20-1+ O '65
CHERRY, Joe H. and Van Huystee, R. B.
  Comparison of messenger RNA in photoperiodically induced and noninduced xanthium buds. bibliog Science 150:1450-3 D 10 '65
CHERRY orchard; drama. See Chekhov, A. P.
CHERRY VALLEY, N.Y.
  Green leaves of summer; excerpts from Happy valley. P. D. Taft. il Am Heritage 16:56-63 O '65
CHERT
  Chert: modern inorganic deposition in a carbonate-precipitating locality. M. N. A. Peterson and C. C. Von Der Borch. bibliog il Science 149:1501-3 S 24 '65
CHESAPEAKE and Ohio Canal national historical park. See Potomac River
CHESAPEAKE and Ohio railway
  Merger that takes a slow track; C&O-B&O. il Bsns W p66-8+ F 13 '65
CHESAPEAKE and Ohio railway-Norfolk and Western merger. See Railroads—Consolidations and mergers
CHESEBROUGH, H. E.
  There is not and never will be a completely safe auto; excerpts from testimony, July 1965. por U S News 59:100 Ag 9 '65
CHESEBROUGH-Pond's, incorporated
  Capsules that act on command; National cash register co.'s encapsulation process. il Bsns W p96 Jl 10 '65

CHESHIRE, Maxine
Race to succeed Nicole. Life 59:93-4+ N 12 '65
CHESS, Stella, and Thomas, Alexander
Toilet training need not be a battle. Parents Mag 40:54-5+ F '65
Why some babies are difficult. Parents Mag 40:35+ Jl '65
—and others
How babies differ; excerpt from Your child as a person. McCalls 92:72-3+ Jl '65
CHESS
Hot-line chess. il Newsweek 66:44-5 S 6 '65
CHESSBOARDS
They're playing chess-on-a-bench. il Sunset 136:74 Ja '66
CHESSMEN
Easy-to-make chess set. il House & Gard 128:174-5 D '65
CHESSON, Frederick W.
Tonal darkroom timer or metronome. Pop Electr 23:95-6 N '65
CHEST. See Lungs
CHESTER Dale collection. See National gallery of art, Washington, D.C.
CHESTS
ABCs of building chests and cabinets (cont) R. J. De Christoforo. il Pop Sci 186:160-4 F '65
Chest for toys. R. Gilmore. il Pop Sci 187: 152-3 N '65
Nomadic chest. il House & Gard 128:60 Jl '65
CHEVALIER, Lois R.
Baldness. Ladies Home J 82:34+ Je '65
High IQ and the small bosom: do they really go together? McCalls 92:87+ Mr '65
Now doctors can end monthly problems. Ladies Home J 82:44+ Ag '65
CHEVALIER, Maurice
Love affair. por Newsweek 65:100-1 Ap 12 '65

about

Chevalier at 77. W. Sheed. Commonweal 82: 155-7 Ap 23 '65
Maurice Chevalier at 77. H. Hewes. Sat R 48:44 Ap 17 '65
Maurice Chevalier at 77. T. Lewis. America 112:590 Ap 17 '65
CHEVIGNY, Hector
Gift of survival. Nation 200:290 Mr 15 '65
CHEVROLET motor company. See General motors corporation—Chevrolet division
CHEYENNE MOUNTAIN
Come visit the village inside a mountain. D. Francis. il Pop Sci 187:96-9+ N '65
Finally: an attack-proof center for U.S. defense; NORAD's Combat operations center. il U S News 60:54-7 Ja 24 '66
Norad operations center. P. J. Klass. il Aviation W 82:66+ F 1; 65-8 F 8 '65
CHEZ Lipp, Paris. See Paris—Hotels, restaurants, etc.
CHIANG, Ching-kuo
Visitors from China. il por Time 86:20 O 1 '65
CHIANG, Kai-shek
Task of U.S: to regain victory from a lost peace; interview, ed. by R. P. Martin. por U S News 59:46-9 Ag 9 '65
CHIANG, Kai-shek, Mme. See Chiang, M. L. S.
CHIANG, Mei-ling (Sung)
Return of Missimo. il por Newsweek 66:20+ S 6 '65
CHIAPPETTA, Jerry
Where the deer are. Field & S 70:126-9 O '65
Where the fish are. Field & S 70:16-18 My '65
CHICAGO
Chicago: yachting at the office door. J. Roe. il Yachting 117:44-5+ My '65

Air pollution
Chicago: doing something about it. G. Lazarus. il Sat R 48:41-2 My 22 '65

Architecture
Above the hurly-burly; plans of John Hancock insurance co. for a 100-story building. il Time 85:42 Ap 2 '65
Campus City, Chicago; University of Illinois' new urban campus. il Arch Forum 123:21-45 S '65
Chicago builds a new skyline for business. il Bsns W p 126-8+ My 1 '65
Marina City adds a strong horizontal line. il Arch Rec 138:152-5 D '65
Mies designs Federal center. il Arch Rec 137: 125-34 Mr '65
Tower in a new kind of urban space; Equitable's new headquarters. il Arch Rec 138: 161-8 O '65

Art
Art news from Chicago (cont) J. Kind. Art N 64:52 Ap; 52-4 Sum; 52+ D '65

Crime
Bad bounce; Robert Lee Lassiter held on charges of murder by arson. Newsweek 66: 28 D 27 '65
Brotherly boom in burglaries; Panczko brothers criminal career. K. Wheeler. il Life 59:71-2+ Ag 6 '65
Chicago squeeze; Illinois crime investigating commission hearings. il Newsweek 67:34-5 Ja 24 '66
How Atlanta and Chicago reduced crime. Fortune 72:259 D '65
Rest is silence; Chicago mobster. il Time 86:15 D 24 '65

Description
New time for Old Town. il Time 86:68+ S 10 '65

Education
Brookses and the Gowsters. S. Alsop. il Sat Eve Post 238:16 D 4 '65
Chicago postpones federal testing. Sr Schol 87:sup2-3 O 21 '65
Confrontation in Chicago; Mayor Daley meets the movement. L. Wille. il Nation 201: 92-5 Ag 30 '65
Federal crackdown starts on local schools. il U S News 59:57-8 O 18 '65
King comes to Chicago; demonstrations against public school superintendent Benjamin C. Willis. Christian Cent 82:979 Ag 11 '65
Leaning on HEW; Office of education federal aid decision overruled. il Newsweek 66:98 O 18 '65
Priest in jail; Chicago demonstration. J. J. Hill. Commonweal 82:615-17 S 3 '65; Discussion. 92:710 O 1 '65
Segregation crisis: Chicago's troubled schools. J. Star. Look 29:59+ My 4 '65
That they might learn; Chicago college students' SWAP program offer tutoring help to children of ghetto schools. il Ebony 20:93-4+ Mr '65
What one big city learned about federal aid to schools; interview. B. C. Willis. U S News 59:58-9 N 8 '65
See also
Illinois. University. Urbana—Chicago campus

Education, Board of
Chicago: the marchers and the machine. K. P. Buckley and R. Cotton. Reporter 33:30-1 N 4 '65; Discussion. 33:10 D 2 '65

Finance
Maintenance contracts. il Am City 80:101+ D '65
Research programs can solve purchasing problems, reduce costs. R. H. Vlerick. Am City 80:150+ Ap '65

Forestry and parkways, Bureau of
Chicago's community Christmas tree; composed of seventy-five smaller trees. D. J. Coman. il Am City 80:81-2 D '65

Housing
Buyers prefer four-bedroom town houses. il Arch Rec 137:206-7 Ap '65
Marina city: Chicago's pies in the sky. R. Atcheson. Holiday 38:24+ D '65
Modern design for a city ghetto; Robert R. Taylor homes. S. Castan. il Look 29:M8-12 S 21 '65

Libraries
See also
Chicago public library

Metropolitan district
Platform towns; Chicago west project. il Life 59:162-3 D 24 '65

Music
See also
Chicago symphony orchestra
Lyric opera of Chicago

Negroes
Chicago a racial battleground: what the fight is about. il U S News 59:54-5 Ag 2 '65
Confrontation in Chicago; Mayor Daley meets the movement. L. Wille. il Nation 201: 92-5 Ag 30 '65
King comes to Chicago; demonstrations against public school superintendent Benjamin C. Willis. Christian Cent 82:979 Ag 11 '65

CH.LD-adult relationship
Art of talking with children. H. G. Ginott. il Parents Mag 40:58-9+ O '65
Fathers-at-large; New York group gives fatherless children male affection. il Good H 161:32-3 Jl '65
Gift of understanding. P. Villiard. il Read Digest 86:58-61 Je '65
Good-by, my son. R. W. Wells. il Read Digest 86:130-2 Mr '65
I am a lone boy; excerpts from papers written by fifth-graders. ed. by E. F. Murphy. N Y Times Mag p89+ D 5 '65
Person who changed my life; symposium; ed. by A. Ebert. il Seventeen 24:156-7+ Ap '65
Pied Piper of suburbia. M. C. Martin. il Parents Mag 40:60-1+ Mr '65

CHILD beating. See Cruelty to children

CHILD care center, Chicago. See Day nurseries

CHILD delinquency. See Juvenile delinquency

CHILD development group of Mississippi. See Project head start

CHILD health. See Children—Care and hygiene

CHILD labor
United States
Canal-boat children; reprint from February 1923 issue. E. M. Springer. Mo Labor R 88:798 Jl '65

CHILD murder. See Murder

CHILD of the Sacred Heart; story. See Dalton, E.

CHILD prodigies. See Children, Gifted

CHILD psychiatry
Dangerous ones; help for children with twisted minds. A. Ribicoff. Harper 230:88-90 F '65
Saving the trouble-prone. N. E. Hall, jr. il NEA J 54:26-8 Ap '65
Treating the mentally ill; study of southern children. R. Coles. New Repub 152:17-20 F 20 '65

CHILD psychology. See Child study

CHILD study
Art of talking with children. H. G. Ginott. il Parents Mag 40:58-9+ O '65
Betsy's wonderful blanket. S. Szasz. il Parents Mag 40:64-5 Ap '65
Children in the line of march; question of involving children in social and political issues. K. D. Fishman. il N Y Times Mag p92+ N 7 '65
Don't rob them of their childhood. F. R. Horwich. NEA J 54:14-15 F '65
Good mothers, impossible children. E. J. Leshan. il Redbook 124:59+ Ap '65
How babies differ; excerpt from Your child as a person. S. Chess and others il McCalls 92:72-3+ Jl '65
Little excitement goes a long way. B. Spock. Redbook 125:24+ Je '65
Mistakes many mothers make: dawdling is a necessary nuisance. R. Thomas. il Parents Mag 40:70-1+ Mr '65
Time of juveniles. E. Hoffer. Harper 230:16+ Je '65
What parents ask about how children learn and grow. M. J. E. Senn. McCalls 92:34+ Ag '65
See also
Children—Language
Children, First-born
Children and death
Gesell institute of child development
Parent-child relationship
Playmates
Psychology, Educational

CHILD welfare
See also
Adoption
Cruelty to children
Detention homes
Foster home care
United Nations children's fund
United States
Church and the reliefers; urban Negro slum-dwellers. D. G. Cater. Christian Cent 82:232-5 F 24 '65
Mystery of rising relief costs; aid to dependent children. il U S News 58:39-43 Mr 8 '65
Triumph of a stubborn lady; Aid to dependent children, Olympia, Wash. J. Poppy. il Look 29:64-6+ F 9 '65

CHILDBIRTH
Diary of my baby's birth. H. Freedman. il Parents Mag 40:44-5+ Ag '65
Every year, 3.5 million miracles. il Newsweek 66:67-70+ O 25 '65
Expectant mother; what happens to you in the hospital. W. E. Brown. Redbook 126:31+ D '65
Expectant mother; what is an episiotomy? ed. by D. Meilach. H. A. Kaminetzky. Redbook 125:30 S '65
Father watches the birth of his son; natural childbirth. R. Spero. il Redbook 125:54-5+ My '65
How much does it cost to have a baby? il Good H 160:175 Je '65
Natural or unnatural? il Newsweek 65:96-7 Mr 15 '65
Only a woman can own this moment. G. B. Leonard. il Look 30:22-3 Ja 11 '66
Pushed out into a hostile world. A. Rosenfeld. Life 58:70+ Ap 30 '65
What kind of anesthetic for childbirth? excerpt. G. V. Anderson. Redbook 124:32+ Mr '65
Why forceps may be used in delivering a baby. Good H 161:145 Ag '65
See also
Pregnancy

CHILDHOOD memories. See Reminiscence
CHILDHOOD poisoning. See Poisons
CHILDHOOD schizophrenia. See Schizophrenia
CHILDLESSNESS. See Sterility

CHILDREN
Guardian angel of the air well. R. Hamilton. il Read Digest 88:95-8 Ja '66
Middle-aged child. R. Kramer. il N Y Times Mag p65-6+ My 23 '65
What two generations can do about children and their grandparents. K. B. Garner and I. V. Sperry. Farm J 89:97 My '65
Why I bought my children a woods. R. W. Wells. Ladies Home J 82:39-40 F '65
See also
Adoption
Birth order
Boys
Cookery by children
Family, Size of
Family life
Fathers
Girls
Infants
Mothers
Negro children
Parents
School children
Siblings
Stepparents
Television broadcasting and children
Travel with children
Twins

Adjustment
See Adjustment, Social

Amusements
See Childrens amusements

Anecdotes, facetiae, satire, etc.
Red mittens! children's playground at Fifth avenue and eighty-fifth. New Yorker 41:32-3 Mr 6 '65

Care and hygiene
Good health for every school child. S. S. Rosenberg. il Parents Mag 40:50-1+ S '65
Growing pains. See issues of Today's health
Health, physical education, and academic achievement. C. A. Bucher. il NEA J 54:38-40 My '65
How to have clean children. il Redbook 125:78-9+ Ag '65
How well nourished should our children be? relationship of nutrition and exercise to arteriosclerosis. B. Spock. Redbook 125:44+ S '65
Sick children; Boston survey shock. Nation 201:347 N 15 '65
Your child is a person, by S. Chess and others. Review
Life 59:10 N 19 '65. J. Mitford
Your child's health. L. W. Sauer. See issues of PTA magazine
See also
Baby sitters
Poisons

Caricatures and cartoons
Small wonders. R. Marcus. See issues of Good housekeeping

Clothing and dress
See Clothing and dress—Children

Day care
See Day nurseries

Development
See Children—Growth and devolpment

CHILDREN—*Continued*

Photographs
Boy and balloon; Jeff Wheaton in Central park. Look 29:76-7 Jl 27 '65

Preparation for medical and dental care
Jordy has his tonsils out. L. Jacobs, jr. il Parents Mag 40:77-9 N '65

Psychology
See Child study

Punishment
See Children—Management and training

Religion
See also
Sunday schools

Sayings
Before the age of discretion. G. Hechinger and F. M. Hechinger. il N Y Times Mag p39 Ja 31 '65
Out of the mouths of babes. See issues of Parents' magazine and better homemaking

Sex behavior
See Sex behavior

Singing
See Singing

Social and economic status
Headstart for children in slums. G. Lewis and H. Mackintosh. il Am Ed 1:30, inside back cover D '64
See also
Socially handicapped children
Students—Social and economic status

Suicide
See Suicide

Surgery
Major advances being scored in surgery for tiny infants. Todays Health 43:92 N '65
See also
Children—Preparation for medical and dental care

Training
See Children—Management and training

United States
American kids? H. Fairlie. il N Y Times Mag p 116+ N 14 '65
Children in the line of march; question of involving children in social and political issues. K. D. Fishman. il N Y Times Mag p92+ N 7 '65
See also
Child labor—United States
Child welfare—United States

CHILDREN, Adoption of. See Adoption

CHILDREN, Backward. See Slow learning children

CHILDREN, Cost of raising. See Domestic finance

CHILDREN, Cruelty to. See Cruelty to children

CHILDREN, Delinquent. See Juvenile delinquency

CHILDREN, Education of. See Education of children

CHILDREN, Exceptional
Misunderstood child; interview. W. Abraham. il Todays Health 43:26-9 Ap '65
See also
Problem children

Bibliography
Books. D. DuBose. Sr Schol 86:sup 12-13 My 6 '65

CHILDREN, First born
Birth order and its sequelae. W. D. Altus. bibliog Science 151:44-9 Ja 7 '66
Differences between first-born and other children. B. Spock. il Redbook 125:12+ My '65
Two's a crowd; what the first-born feels when new baby arrives. V. Valaitis. il Parents Mag 40:42-3 Jl '65

CHILDREN, Gifted
Gifted child (handle with care) ed. by S. Frank. R. Ricci. il McCalls 92:88+ F '65
How to tell if a child is gifted. il Good H 160:180-1 Ap '65
Nicest young genius in the U.S; M. Grost. J. Howard. il Life 58:104-6+ My 21 '65

CHILDREN, Handicapped
Brighter future for disabled children. H. A. Rusk. il Parents Mag 40:66-7+ N '65
No time for tears. il Ebony 20:75-8+ Ap '65
Redbook's guide to the major diseases and handicaps of children. A. Lake. Redbook 125:33-40 Je '65

Education
Education of handicapped children in residential schools. P. P. Hunter. bibliog f il Sch Life 47:9-12 D '65
Montessori expands; teaching of brain-damaged children. P. McBroom. Sci N L 88:375 D 11 '65
See also
Special classes and special schools

CHILDREN, Illegitimate. See Illegitimacy

CHILDREN, Mentally ill. See Mentally ill

CHILDREN, Preschool. See Preschool children

CHILDREN, Problem. See Problem children

CHILDREN, Runaway. See Runaway boys and girls

CHILDREN, Sick. See Sick, The

CHILDREN and adults. See Child-adult relationship

CHILDREN and death
Anne and the sand dobbies. B. J. Lifton. Horn Bk 41:80 F '65
Breaking the news of death. P. L. Levin. N Y Times Mag p47 F 21 '65
How to tell your child about death. W. Duckat. il Ebony 20:48-50+ Mr '65
Mysterious disappearances. L. R. Young. il McCalls 92:60+ My '65
What death means to children; with discussion group program, by M. Smart. H. H. Gibney. il Parents Mag 40:15-16, 64-5+ Mr '65

CHILDREN and music. See Music and children

CHILDREN and parents. See Parent-child relationship

CHILDREN and television. See Television broadcasting and children

CHILDREN as actors
Audition: boys for principal role in musical version of The yearling. New Yorker 41:20-3 S 4 '65
Big push for Danny's charmer. il Life 58:57-8+ Mr 19 '65
Child stars, by N. J. Zierold. Review Reporter 33:42-3 N 18 '65. J. Crist
See also
Childrens plays
Dramatization in education

CHILDREN as photographers
Let kids take their own pictures! C. B. Nieberding. il Pop Phot 57:144-5 N '65
Turning the tables. M. Adler. il U S Camera 28:50-1 Ag '65

CHILDREN in art
See also
Art—Themes

CHILDREN in their masks; story. See Thomson, M.

CHILDREN of migrant laborers
Our brother the migrant. J. L. Corker. Christian Cent 82:1192-3 S 29 '65

Education
From their hands, a feast. H. Morales. il Am Ed 1:1-5 N '65
What migrant farm children learn. R. Coles. il Sat R 48:73-4+ My 15 '65

CHILDREN of teachers
Teachers' children. D. L. Bailey. il NEA J 54:12-14 Mr '65

CHILDRENS allowances
Kids and money; with case history of the Martin family of Barrington, Ill. G. Zimmermann. il Look 29:49-53+ N 2 '65

CHILDRENS amusements
At the Gibson Ranch park, your children are welcome to meet the animals. il Sunset 135:64-5 Jl '65
Children like simple pleasures best. E. G. Neisser. il Parents Mag 40:58-9+ Je '65
How to perform waiting room magic. R. Worthington. Parents Mag 40:22 N '65
Mud is more than just dirt to kids. A. Schwartz. il Parents Mag 40:48-9+ Ap '65
Take them back to the farm; California's Gibson ranch county park. S. Parenteau. il Nat Parks Mag 39:12-13 N '65
These games keep children occupied on trips. il Good H 161:152 Jl '65
What'll I do today? simple play projects. il Todays Health 43:23-4+ Je '65
Your child deserves more than packaged creativity. K. Gay. Am Home 68:15+ Ap '65
See also
Childrens parties
Games
Paper work
Piñatas
Playgrounds
Playhouses
Skateboarding
Story telling

CHILDRENS art

All children are artists. R. U. Hildebrand. il Parents Mag 40:58-9+ D '65

All the children sculpture with wire. E. Sitts and M. Sitts. il Sch Arts 64:9-13 F '65

Art motivation from music; art experience for the middle grades. J. Kujawski and L. Gutetter. il Design 66:20-3 My '65

Backward bird; graphic lesson for disabled kindergarten children. A. Carilli and others. il Good H 161:156-7 D '65

Child's world opens wide. H. W. Rivers. il Horn Bk 41:81-5 F '65

Elementary art grades one-six; symposium. il Sch Arts 65:5-43 D '65

Instant sculpture. E. Welch. il Design 66:12-14 Mr '65

Spontaneity in children's painting. B. Bressi. il Sch Arts 65:26-8 N '65

Wax resist. S. Gruenberg. il Sch Arts 64:28-9 Je '65

We want to make something. J. Lidstone. il Sch Arts 65:11-15 S '65

See also
Paper work

Competitions

Special issue of children's art in 1965. il Sch Arts 64:20-8 Mr '65

Exhibitions

Displaying art work. P. Greenberg. il Sch Arts 64:9-11 My '65

School art festival; interview, ed. by I. Arms. O. Gatti. il Sch Arts 64:31-3 My '65

Wav-out art exhibition; work of teenage schoolboys at the Terry Clune galleries, Sydney, Australia. il Design 67:30 N '65

CHILDRENS bands. See Bands, Childrens

CHILDRENS book council

CBC plans for book week and large fairs. il Pub W 188:178-80 Jl 12 '65

Children's book week and the bookseller. B. Beilenson. il Pub W 188:54-6 N 8 '65

CHILDRENS book editors. See Editors and editing

CHILDRENS book exhibits. See Book exhibits

CHILDRENS book fairs. See Book fairs

CHILDRENS book week. See Book week

CHILDRENS books. See Childrens literature

CHILDRENS bookshops. See Booksellers and bookselling—Childrens literature

CHILDRENS camps. See Camps

CHILDRENS clothing. See Clothing and dress —Children

CHILDRENS competitions. See Competitions

CHILDRENS concerts. See Music for children

CHILDRENS costume. See Costume

CHILDRENS dictionaries. See Dictionaries, Childrens

CHILDRENS diseases. See Children—Diseases

CHILDRENS encyclopedias. See Encyclopedias

CHILDRENS fears. See Fear

CHILDRENS football. See Football, Childrens

CHILDRENS friends. See Playmates

CHILDRENS furniture. See Furniture, Childrens

CHILDRENS games. See Games

CHILDRENS gardens

For children a new adventure. Pop Gard 16:6-7 N '65

Gardening is child's play. B. Brilmayer. il Flower Grower 52:54-5 Mr '65

Paul's garden. P. Mawicke. il Flower Grower 52:34-5 Je '65

See also
School gardens

CHILDRENS haircuts. See Haircutting

CHILDRENS historical literature. See Historical literature

CHILDRENS homes. See Homes, Institutional

CHILDRENS hospital, Boston. See Children— Hospitals

CHILDRENS hospital, Detroit. See Children— Hospitals

CHILDRENS libraries. See Libraries, Childrens

CHILDRENS literature

All-white world of children's books. N. Larrick. il Sat R 46:63-5+ S 11 '65; Discussion. 48:78-9 O 16 '65

And so they lived happily ever after. E. Enright. il McCalls 93:116-17+ D '65

Anne and the sand dobbies. B. J. Lifton. Horn Bk 41:80 F '65

Babar pays us a visit at last. il Life 59:107-9 N 26 '65

Books children want to read. T. V. Comstock. Writer 78:26-7 Je '65; Discussion. 78:2-4 S '65

Carping critics, instant experts. D. M. Broderick. il Library J 90:3690-2 S 15 '65

Children's books and the trade sales representative; summary of discussion of Children's book council. Pub W 189:66-7 Ja 10 '66

Child's garden of bewilderment; Alice's adventures in Wonderland and Wonderful Wizard of Oz compared. M. Gardner. il Sat R 48:18-19 Jl 17 '65; Discussion. 48:26 Ag 14 '65

Comedy in wax, or Lucy and their majesties; with correspondence between M. M. Dodge and B. L. Farjeon. E. Farjeon. il Horn Bk 41:358-63 Ag '65

Common ground; adaptation of address, November 16, 1964. A. Petry. Horn Bk 41:147-51 Ap '65

Doctor Seuss: what am I doing here? C. R. Jennings. il Sat Eve Post 238:105-9 O 23 '65

Doll book as old as Victoria; importance of children's literature in study of dolls. C. H. Fawcett. il Hobbies 70:38+ O '65

Education of the doll. C. H. Fawcett. Hobbies 70:38 N '65

Flowers of delight; excerpts. L. De Vries. il McCalls 92:110-13 F '65

For creatures great and small; some children's books for adults. L. Russ. il Pub W 188:28-9 O 11 '65

Imagination and the child; symposium bibliog il Wilson Lib Bul 40:332-58 D '65

In defense of children's books: price, quality, durability; summary of addresses at meeting of AIGA trade book clinic. U. Nordstrom; D. Hagen; R. Kraus. Pub W 187:33-4 Mr 15 '65

Let there be light! R. Caudill. Horn Bk 41:585 D '65

Let's build a skyscraper, but let's find a good book first; reprint. R. Dahl. Writer 78:27-8+ F '65

Lose not the nightingale; excerpts. F. C. Sayers. Horn Bk 41:299-301 Je '65

Mountain of books for mountain children; PTA project, Books for Appalachia. E. May. il PTA Mag 60:8-10 S '65

Once upon a time. E. E. Philpott. ALA Bul 59:810-14 O '65

Responsibility of writing for children; excerpts from address, November 26, 1965. R. Godden. Sr Schol 87:sup 14 D 9 '65

Roosevelt Grady and the children of Asia. L. R. Shotwell. il Horn Bk 41:252-4 Je '65

Shadow of a kid; Newbery award acceptance; address, July 6, 1965. M. Wojciechowska. il Horn Bk 41:349-52 Ag '65

Spy who got locked in the ice box; childrens fiction and the real world. D. M. Broderick. il Library J 90:1478-9 Mr 15 '65

Teaching by delight. M. Nash. Horn Bk 41:158-60 Ap '65

Teaching Johnny to cop out. S. Maloff. Commonweal 82:321-3 My 28 '65

Transatlantic editing. G. A. Hogarth. Horn Bk 41:520-3 O '65

Writing for the in-betweenster. F. Kohner. Writer 78:22-4 Ag '65

See also
Book selection
Book week
Booksellers and bookselling—Childrens literature
Childrens book council
Childrens reading
Frontier and pioneer life—United States— Childrens literature
Libraries, Childrens
Newbery medal
Paperback books
Picture books for children
Publishers and publishing—Childrens literature
Scientific literature for children—Bibliography

Advertising

Promotions that help sell children's books in the stores. il Pub W 187:160-2 F 22 '65

Bibliography

Best books of the season for children. E. Sheehan. America 113:637-40+ N 20 '65

Booklist (title varies) R. H. Viguers and others. See issues of Horn book magazine

Books (cont) E. Maxwell. New Yorker 41:217-20+ D 4 '65

Books for boys & girls. D. E. Leland. See issues of Parents' magazine and better homemaking

Books for children; Christmas list. C. Jackson. Atlan 216:152-60 D '65

Books for young people. A. Dalgliesh. See issues of Saturday review

Children's books of 1964-65. NEA J 54:65-8 N '65

CHILDRENS literature—Bibliography—*Cont.*
Children's books; some leading titles to be published this spring. il Pub W 187:92-131 F 22 '65
Children's books: worth reading before wrapping. C. H. Simonds. Nat R 17:1165 D 14 '65
Children's paperbacks; comp. by J. Thomson. Library J 90:2355-70+, 3725-6+ My 15, S 15 '65
Choice for children at Christmas. Christian Cent 82:1546-7 D 15 '65
Christmas books, 1965. N. Paige. il Library J 90:4529-31+ O 15 '65
Elementary school library collection, ed. by M. V. Gaver. Review
  Library J 90:5492-4 D 15 '65. D. M. Broderick
For the lower shelves. Christian Cent 82: 838-9 Je 30 '65
Junior books appraised See second issue of each month of Library journal
Million books for Appalachia; librarians compile most wanted list. Library J 90:1490+ Mr 15 '65
New children's books. G. Shalit. il McCalls 92:64+ Je '65
New fall children's books; comp. by J. C. Thomson. Library J 90:4560-600 O 15 '65
New spring children's books; comp. by J. C. Thomson. Library J 90:1508-40 Mr 15 '65
Notable children's books of 1964. Wilson Lib Bul 39:611+ Ap '65; Same. Pub W 187:40-1 Ap 12 '65; ALA Bul 59:285-8 Ap '65; Library J 90:1998 Ap 15 '65
Read! open your future and theirs. L. Nix. bibliog il PTA Mag 59:32-4 Ap '65
Selected list of children's books. A. T. Eaton. il Commonweal 83:154-65 N 5 '65
Selected list of children's books. E. M. Graves. il Commonweal 82:327-34 My 28 '65
Some leading children's books for fall, 1965. il Pub W 188:128-75 Jl 12 '65
Vacation reading for children. E. Sheehan. America 112:899-902 Je 26 '65

Book reviews
See Book reviews

Collectors and collecting
New ways with old books: results of the Toronto colloquium. H. C. Campbell. il Library J 90:5043-4 N 15 '65

Exhibitions
See Book exhibits

Illustrations
See Illustration of books and periodicals

Study and teaching
Summoned by books. R. H. Viguers. Horn Bk 41:244-5 Je '65

Technique
Cry of the curlew, call to freshness. J. Karl. Pub W 188:176-8 Jl 12 '65
Flat-heeled muse. L. Alexander. Horn Bk 41: 141-6 Ap '65
On spies and applesauce and such. R. H. Viguers. Horn Bk 41:74-6 F '65
Our dreams are tales. R. Manning. il Horn Bk 41:24-7 F '65

Translating
Learning about children's books in translation; address, July 1965. M. L. Batchelder. il ALA Bul 60:33-42 Ja '66

Bulgaria
I remember Dobry. R. H. Wagner. il Horn Bk 41:342-8 Ag '65

China (People's Republic)
What Chinese children read. C. H. Bishop. il Commonweal 82:323-5 My 28 '65
CHILDRENS manners. See Etiquette for children and youth
CHILDREN'S monument. See Hiroshima—Monuments, statues, etc.
CHILDRENS national book week. See Book week
CHILDRENS opinions
Man is daddy: childrens definitions. M. Cohen. il Redbook 125:60-1+ Je '65
CHILDRENS parties
Delights of a small guest list; small sons at a full-dress dinner party. E. S. Oshin. House & Gard 128:56+ O '65
Making it a happy birthday. R. Kramer. il N Y Times Mag p 128+ D 5 '65

Parties for children. il Farm J 89:83 F '65
Party; birthday party nursery-size. il Ladies Home J 82:116-19+ O '65
Party of the month! B. Clark. See issues of Parents' magazine and better homemaking
Pink is for parties; recipes. il McCalls 93: 142-3+ O '65
CHILDRENS periodicals
Prescription for progress. J. Krishnayya. il Horn Bk 41:202-5 Ap '65
CHILDRENS phonograph records. See Phonograph records—Childrens records
CHILDRENS plays
Creative dramatics in Philadelphia; program in the children's room of free library. C. W. Field. il Wilson Lib Bul 40:344+ D '65
Curtain going up! L. James. il Parents Mag 40:46-7+ Ag '65
  See also
Amateur theatricals

Texts
Middle grades; lower grades. See issues of Plays
CHILDRENS poems (by children)
First grade poems. Sister Mary Claude. il Sch Arts 65:38 N '65
Horn book league. See issues of Horn book magazine
I never saw another butterfly. Review
  Commentary 39:86-7 F '65. M. Ellmann
CHILDRENS poetry
Fox in socks. Dr Seuss. il Ladies Home J 82:66-9+ Mr '65
Speaking to the imagination. S. F. Morse. Horn Bk 41:255-9 Je '65
CHILDRENS questions
Making friends with facts. B. W. Overstreet. il PTA Mag 59:28-9 My '65
CHILDRENS reading
Books help boys and girls discover their feelings. W. C. Fitzgibbon. il Parents Mag 40:50-1+ Ap '65
Imagination and the child; symposium. bibliog il Wilson Lib Bul 40:332-58 D '65
Read! open your future and theirs. L. Nix. bibliog il PTA Mag 59:32-4 Ap '65
Reading with John. F. Foster. il Sat R 48: 40-2 My 15 '65
Root-room for delight. V. Kumblé. Horn Bk 41:247-51 Je '65
Their improbable treasure; excerpts from address, 1965. M. Wojcienchowska. il Library J 90:4511-13 O 15 '65
What's happening in education? summer reading. W. D. Boutwell. PTA Mag 59:17 My '65
  See also
Childrens literature
Libraries, Childrens
CHILDRENS rooms
Children just live differently. il Sunset 136: 60-1 Ja '66
Children's rooms for two to share. il Parents Mag 40:75+ F '65
Children's rooms that act their age. il Good H 161:114-21 Jl '65
Gordon gets a new room. il Sunset 135:120+ N '65
New wing for a new baby. il House & Gard 127:96-9 F '65
Study corner that grows. R. Hoppough. il Pop Sci 187:112-13 S '65
These children's rooms are colorful and carefree! il Bet Hom & Gard 43:96+ O '65
Two World's fair rooms your children will love. N. Pierce. il Parents Mag 40:78-9+ S '65
What one built-in can do for a small room. il Bet Hom & Gard 43:134 Ap '65
  See also
Playhouses
CHILDRENS safety seat. See Automobiles—Safety devices and measures
CHILDRENS services division, American library association. See American library association—Childrens services division
CHILDRENS shopping. See Shopping and shoppers
CHILDRENS speech defects. See Speech defects
CHILDREN'S spring book festival awards. See Rewards, prizes, etc.
CHILDRENS stories
Alligator case; excerpt. W. P. Du Bois. il Ladies Home J 82:62-3+ Ag '65
CHILDRENS theater. See Theater, Childrens
CHILDRENS zoos. See Zoological gardens
CHILDRESS, William
Addict: poem. Poetry 106:207 Je '65
Korea bound, 1952; poem. Harper 231:64 O '65
CHILDS, Gailand
Call alert for two-way radio. Electr World 74:83 Jl '65

CHILE
Chilean dilemma. W. D. Beatty. bibliog f
Cur Hist 49:342-8+ D '65
Project Camelot. Newsweek 66:18-19 Jl 5 '65
See also
Astronomical observatories—Chile
Copper mines and mining—Chile
Earthquakes—Chile
Elections—Chile
Political parties—Chile
Portillo
Technical assistance in Chile

Economic policy
Change in Chile: what it means to U.S. business; interview, ed. by J. N. Wallace. E.
Frei. U S News 58:84-5 Ap 26 '65
Green light for reformer; in Chile, changes
ahead. U S News 58:22 Mr 22 '65

Foreign relations
Profitable trip; President Frei's journey of
international understanding. il Time 86:36
Ag 6 '65
See also
Project Camelot

Politics and government
Adios siesta? end to three-hour lunch hour.
Time 87:36+ Ja 14 '66
Alternative to Castro. Newsweek 66:39 Ag 2
'65
Atlantic report. Atlan 215:22+ Je '65
Copper-bill crisis. M. J. Kubic. il Newsweek
66:52 S 13 '65
Nationalism and communism in Chile, by E.
Halperin. Review
Nation 201:450 D 6 '65. D. W. Bray
Over the hump; copper bill approved. Newsweek 66:50 S 20 '65
Prudence by fiat; presidential decrees. Newsweek 67:38 Ja 10 '66
Stuck on dead center. Time 85:46 F 5 '65
See also
Elections—Chile
Political parties—Chile

Relief work
Again, natural disaster. P. Zottele. Christian Cent 82:1136+ S 15 '65
CHILEAN squids. See Squids
CHILI con carne. See Cookery—Meat
CHILOCORUS similis. See Beetles
CHIMPANZEES
New discoveries among Africa's chimpanzees.
J. Van Lawick-Goodall. il Nat Geog Mag
128:802-31 D '65
CHIN, William, and others
Naturally acquired quotidian-type malaria in
man transferable to monkeys. bibliog Science 149:865 Ag 20 '65
CHINA
See also
Agriculture—China
Taiwan

Antiquities
Sensing of time in China; J. Needham's conclusions on Chinese priority in clockmaking.
J. Lear. il Sat R 49:95-100 Ja 1 '66

History
Role of the horse in Chinese history. H. G.
Creel. bibliog f Am Hist R 70:647-72 Ap '65

1900-
Giant's awakening. Sr Schol 87:5 O 7 '65

Social life and customs
Report from a Chinese village, by J. Myrdal.
Review
New Repub 152:22-3 Je 26 '65. E. Snow
CHINA (People's Republic)
Anniversary thoughts. il Newsweek 66:55-6
O 11 '65
Blueprint for conquest. Newsweek 66:37 S
20 '65
Communist China, 1965; symposium. bibliog f il Cur Hist 49:129-75 S '65
Conversation with President Kennedy; concerning Communist China as a nuclear
power, ed. by S. Alsop. J. F. Kennedy. il
Sat Eve Post 239:9 Ja 1 '66
Red China: an insistent presence. il Newsweek 65:36-8+ Mr 15 '65
Red China on its way to H-bomb; second
nuclear test. il Bsns W p49-50 My 29 '65
600 million Chinese + communism + the
bomb = ? S. Slessinger. Commonweal 82:
506 Jl 9 '65
Trip to China. R. Terrill; reply. R. M.
Pfeffer. New Repub 152:28 F 13 '65
We must stop red China now! interview.
W. E. Griffith. Read Digest 86:67-72 F '65

Where is China? Peiping's plans; address,
July 28 ,1965. S. K. Chow. Vital Speeches
31:699-702 S 1 '65
See also
Agriculture—China (People's Republic)
Atomic research—China (People's Republic)
Canton
Communism—China (People's Republic)
Education—China (People's Republic)
Foreign visitors in China
Forests and forestry—China (People's Republic)
Hainan
Newspapers—China (People's Republic)
Science—China (People's Republic)
Secret service—China (People's Republic)
United Nations—China (People's Republic)

Armed forces
Communist China as a military power. R. L.
Powell. bibliog f Cur Hist 49:136-41+ S '65
How sharp are the dragon's claws? People's
liberation army. C. Johnson. il N Y Times
Mag p22-3+ F 28 '65
How strong is China's army? J. A. Rose. il
Reporter 32:23-5 Mr 11 '65
If red China does jump into Vietnam war—.
il U S News 58:68-9 Mr 29 '65
Test for tigers. il Time 85:25-9 F 26 '65
Their weapon; infantrymen. il Time 85:26-7
F 19 '65

Commerce
Political price of Japan's China trade. J.
Schechter. il Reporter 33:28-30 S 23 '65
Reds reach for cash in Hong Kong; Communist China opens department store. il
Bsns W p 140-2+ N 6 '65

Defenses
China and the bomb, by M. H. Halperin. Review
Sat R 48:54 Ap 17 '65. H. C. Hinton
Gravest decision; problem of growing menace
of Chinese nuclear capability. R. Hotz.
Aviation W 82:11 My 24 '65
How strong is China's army? J. A. Rose. il
Reporter 32:23-5 Mr 11 '65

Economic conditions
Communist China's economy: critical questions. Y. L. Wu. bibliog f Cur Hist 49:164-
9 S '65
Just how much of a threat is red China? il
U S News 58:40-2 F 22 '65
Red China: paper tiger? il U S News 59:40-
2+ O 25 '65; Same abr. with title How
strong is red China? Read Digest 88:124-7
Ja '66
Slow creep forward. il Time 86:19 D 31 '65
Village life in Communist China; excerpts
from Report from a Chinese village; ed. by
J. Myrdal. il Sat R 48:24-6+ Ap 10 '65
What to expect next from red China. il Nations Bsns 53:42-4+ O '65

Economic policy
Communist China's economy: critical questions. Y. L. Wu. bibliog f Cur Hist 49:164-9
S '65
Image and reality: China from within. C.
Taylor. il Nation 201:180-4 O 4 '65

Economic relations
Busy bees of Peiping. America 112:894 Je 26
'65
Paris-Peking trade; Marianne & the dragon.
J. S. Prybyla. Nation 200:99-102 F 1 '65
Unrequited friendship; economic-warfare. E.
Taylor. Reporter 32:12 Ap 8 '65
What to expect next from red China. il Nations Bsns 53:42-4+ O '65

Foreign opinion
China and the peace of Asia, ed. by A.
Buchan. Review
New Repub 153:25-6 N 20 '65. C. P. Fitzgerald

Foreign relations
Atlantic report. Atlan 216:6+ N '65
Bull in China's shop. K. Crawford. Newsweek 66:38 N 8 '65
Busy travelers. il Time 85:27-8 Ap 9 '65
Challenges to freedom and peace; address,
October 31, 1965. W. A. Harriman. Dept
State Bul 53:863-7 N 29 '65
Chance for Soviet-American diplomacy. H.
Brandon Sat R 48:18+ O 23 '65
China goes it alone. R. MacFarquhar. Atlan
215:69-75 Ap '65
China's strategy: a critique. D. S. Zagoria.
Commentary 40:61-6 N '65
Chinese riddle. Commonweal 82:711-12 O 1 '65
Chou gets socked twice; postponement of Algerian conference. G. De Carvalho. il Life
59:62A-62B+ Jl 9 '65

CHINA (People's Republic)—Foreign relations
—*Continued*
Communist China and the uncommitted zone.
H. M. Vinacke. bibliog f Ann Am Acad
362:113-20 N '65
Dead end of nonalignment. P. Ben. il
Reporter 32:19-22 My 20 '65
Image and reality: China from within. C.
Taylor. il Nation 201:180-4 O 4 '65
Interview with Mao; ed. by E. Snow. New
Repub 152:17-23 F 27 '65; Reply. M. Lind-
say. 152:27 Mr 13 '65; Summary. Newsweek
65:36+ F 22 '65
Just how much of a threat is red China? il
U S News 58:40-2 F 22 '65
Light at the end of the tunnel: red China's
expansion failures. W. Lippmann. News-
week 66:29 N 8 '65
Mao's blueprint for chaos. Life 59:4 S 17 '65
Peking and the third world; nonaligned and
left-of-center countries. S. Y. Dai. bibliog f
Cur Hist 49:142-9 S '65
People's wars. New Repub 153:7-8 S 18 '65
Political effects of the Chinese bomb. A.
S. Lall. Bul Atomic Sci 21:21-4 F '65
Putting on the dog. il Time 86:36 O 15 '65
Rays of hope for U.S. in Asia. il Bsns W
p25-7 N 6 '65
Red China: paper tiger? il U S News 59:40-
2+ O 25 '65; Same abr. with title How
strong is red China? Read Digest 88:124-7
Ja '66
Red China's nuclear threat: the time grows
shorter. U S News 58:28-9 My 31 '65
So? Communist China's nuclear development;
summary of address; December 15, 1965.
R. S. McNamara. Nat R 18:12-13 Ja 11 '66
Some payoffs for patience. Life 59:4 N 12
'65
U.N. General assembly again rejects move to
change representation of China; statements,
November 8, 16 and 17, 1965; with texts of
resolutions. A. J. Goldberg; C. W. Yost.
Dept State Bul 53:940-52 D 13 '65
Vietnam and China. G. Lichtheim. Commen-
tary 39:56-9 My '65
When red China is a nuclear tiger. U S
News 59:6 D 27 '65
Why China leaves Hong Kong alone. D.
Kirk. Reporter 33:31-2 S 23 '65
Why hold the line in Vietnam? Adlai Steven-
son's answer. A. E. Stevenson. il News-
week 66:20 D 27 '65
Why we are fighting in Asia. F. V. Drake. il
Read Digest 87:61-5 O '65

Africa

Busy bees of Peiping. America 112:894 Je 26
'65
French Africa; Communist subversion. E.
Taylor. Reporter 32:29-31 Mr 25 '65
Hell-raisers. P. R. Webb and A. de Borch-
grave. il Newsweek 65:42+ F 22 '65
Red China's year in Africa. E. Huxley. il
Nat R 17:95-6+ F 9 '65

Asia

Reflections on Asian anti-Communists. W. H.
Judd. Nat R 18:27 Ja 11 '66

Asia, Southeastern

Peking's strategy in Indochina. K. Chen.
Yale R 54:550-66 Je '65
Southeast Asia isn't scared of the Chinese
dragon. S. Topping. il N Y Times Mag
p 12-13+ Ja 16 '66

Cuba

Rice bomb; Castro charges against China.
Newsweek 67:49-50 Ja 24 '66

Indonesia

Indonesia's Communists: down but not out.
D. Warner. il Reporter 33:23-6 N 18 '65
Just a pinprick? Sukarno orders halt to
anti-Communist and anti-Chinese demonstrations. il Newsweek 66:53 N 1 '65
Peking-Djakarta axis. D. Warner. il Reporter
33:25-7 S 23 '65
Sukarno struts as Chen Yi snoozes; during
anniversary parade. il Life 59:36-36A S
3 '65

Japan

Political price of Japan's China trade. J.
Schecter. il Reporter 33:28-30 S 23 '65

Kenya

Casual correspondent; Wang Te-ming expelled from Nairobi. Newsweek 66:45 Ag 9
'65

Middle East

If a million die. Reporter 32:10-11 Ap 22 '65

Pakistan

Peking and the third world; nonaligned and
left-of-center countries. S. Y. Dai. bibliog f
Cur Hist 49:142-9 S '65

Rumania

Come to the funeral! Newsweek 65:43 Ap 5
'65

Russia

Communist division. Commonweal 81:684 F
26 '65
Deepening split. Newsweek 65:30+ Mr 22 '65
Dialectic of the split. J. Burnham. Nat R 17:
274 Ap 6 '65
Enemies fall out; Russian-Chinese split. J.
O'Gara. Commonweal 82:70 Ap 9 '65
High price of horse meat. Time 85:31 Ap 2
'65
In venom veritas? concerning accusations
made in official journal of Chinese Com-
munist party. K. Crawford. Newsweek 65:
42 My 17 '65
Mao vs. Moscow. S. Slessinger. Commonweal
81:759-61 Mr 12 '65
Military aspects of the Sino-Soviet dispute.
M. Mackintosh. Bul Atomic Sci 21:14-17
O '65
Rickety revisionists v. leftist adventurers.
Time 86:19 D 31 '65
Strictly temporary. Time 85:34 Mr 19 '65
Vilification as before. Newsweek 65:43 Je 28
'65
Where danger grows on a 4,500-mile border.
R. P. Martin. il U S News 59:44-7 D 6 '65
With a tight smile; red Chinese inhospitality
to Kosygin. il Time 85:20 F 12 '65

Tibet

Where guerrillas are giving reds a lot of
trouble. il U S News 59:54 O 11 '65

United States

Atlantic report. Atlan 216:6+ N '65
China's new leap forward. M. Ascoli. Re-
porter 33:24 S 23 '65
Not so dark. Nation 202:57-8 Ja 17 '66
Target U.S.A, a warning from Peking; com-
ment on article by Lin Piao. S. Topping.
Read Digest 87:208-9 N '65
Test for tigers. il Time 85:25-9 F 26 '65
United States and red China; address, April
29, 1965. R. L. Walker. Vital Speeches 31:
527-34 Je 15 '65
Vietnam crisis and China. H. J. Morgenthau.
Bul Atomic Sci 21:27 Je '65
War with China? H. J. Morgenthau. New
Repub 152:11-14 Ap 3 '65

Vietnam (Democratic Republic)

Peking statement on North Vietnam; excerpts from resolution of National people's
congress, April 20, 1965. Cur Hist 49:177-8
S '65

Vietnam (Republic)

On the other side. il Newsweek 65:20 Mr 1
'65

History

Communist China: the early years, 1949-1955,
by A. D. Barnett. Review
　Cath World 201:141-3 My '65. P. K. T.
　Sih
Speaking out; we must woo red China. A. J.
Toynbee. Sat Eve Post 238:10+ Jl 17 '65

Industries

Of geese & ballyhoo; trade fair at Canton.
il Time 86:98 N 26 '65

Politics and government

It doesn't matter who succeeds Mao. J. Mar-
cuse. il N Y Times Mag p8-9+ Jl 11 '65
Leadership and succession in Communist
China. W. F. Dorrill. bibliog f Cur Hist 49:
129-35+ S '65
Mao and the Chinese revolution, by J. Ch'en.
Review
　Nation 200:703-4 Je 28 '65. C. P. Fitzger-
　ald
To Mao we are the prime enemy. M. Gayn.
il N Y Times Mag p46-7+ O 24 '65
See also
Communism—China (People's Republic)

Religious institutions and affairs

China, birth control and Bibles. R. Terrill.
New Repub 152:13-14 F 6 '65

CHINA (People's Republic)—*Continued*

Social conditions

Report from a Chinese village, by J. Myrdal.
Review
Reporter il 33:33-4+ Jl 1 '65. H. R. Lie-
berman
Sat R 48:39-40 Je 12 '65. M. H. Fried
Year of the Swedes in China. J. A. Cohen.
Harper 231:130-2 O '65
See also
Communism—China (People's Republic)

**CHINA (People's Republic) and the United
States**
Ahab and the China whale. Nation 200:519
My 17 '65
Communist China as a problem in U.S.
policymaking; address, February 26, 1965.
M. Green. Dept State Bul 52:449-53 Mr 29
'65
Finding out about red China; need for ex-
change of information. L. H. Evans. il Sat
R 48:17-18 Je 26 '55
Good sense on China. Nation 200:294 Mr 22
'65
No-enterprise system; full-time correspond-
ent in China of Toronto's Globe and mail.
Nation 201:178 O 4 '65

CHINA trade porcelain. See Pottery, Chinese

CHINAMEN. See Chinese

CHINATOWN, San Francisco. See San Francisco—Chinatown

CHINAWARE. See Pottery

CHINCOTEAGUE ISLAND
Wild horses couldn't hold us back. Z. Taylor.
il Motor B 115:30-3+ Ap '65

CHINESE
China: the grand tour; photographs. K. Ku-
makiri. Newsweek 67:36-8 Ja 17 '66
Expulsion of Singapore. C. P. FitzGerald. il
Nation 201:208-12 O 11 '65
Where is China? Peiping's plans; address.
July 28, 1965. S. K. Chow. Vital Speeches
31:699-702 S 1 '65

CHINESE art. See Art, Chinese

CHINESE atomic bomb test. See Atomic
bombs—Testing

CHINESE books. See Chinese literature

CHINESE cookery. See Cookery, Chinese

CHINESE economic assistance. See Economic
assistance, Chinese

CHINESE fiction. See Chinese literature

CHINESE folk songs. See Folk songs, Chinese

CHINESE hibiscus. See Hibiscus

CHINESE in Singapore
Singapore's restless Chinese. S. S. King. il
Reporter 33:20-2 Ag 12 '65

CHINESE-Indian border dispute, 1957-. See
Sino-Indian border dispute, 1957-

CHINESE literature
Dream of the red chamber; characteristics of
the Chinese novel. K. Rexroth. Sat R 49:
19 Ja 1 '66
See also
Chinese poetry

CHINESE opera. See Opera, Chinese

CHINESE poetry
On translating Mao's poetry. D. Davie. Nation 200:704-5 Je 28 '65
Out of China. A. Fang. Poetry 107:196-9 D
'65

CHINESE scientists. See Scientists, Chinese

CHINITZ, Benjamin
New York: a metropolitan region; with biographical sketch. Sci Am 213:30, 134-8+
bibliog(p277) S '65

CHINN, H. I. See Audrieth, L. F. jt. auth.

CHIONANTHUS. See Fringe trees

CHIOS
Two Greek islands. E. Perényi. Vogue 146:
269+ O 1 '65

CHIP circuit. See Electronic circuits

CHIPEMBERE, Henry Masauko
Good-by, Mr Chips? il por Newsweek 65:40+
Ap 26 '65

CHIPMAN, Robert A.
De Forest and the triode detector; with
biographical sketch. Sci Am 212:18, 92-100
bibliog(p 140) Mr: 10 My '65

CHIPMUNKS
Charming cheater, the chipmunk. J. George.
il Read Digest 86:215-16+ My '65

CHIPPING: story. See Gerber. M. J.

CHIRICO, Giorgio de
Gallery for young people. C. B. Johnson. il
Sch Arts 65:42 O '65

CHIROPRACTORS
Chiropractic: science or swindle? excerpt
from Health hucksters. R. L. Smith. il
Todays Health 43:56-61 My '65

CHITONS
Cyclic variations in the digestive gland and
glandular oviduct of chitons (mollusca)
A. L. Lawrence and others. bibliog il Science 147:508-10 Ja 29 '65

CHLEBOUN, William S.
California booksellers join forces to combat
censorship. Pub W 188:30-1 Ag 16 '65

CHLORINATION of water. See Water purification

CHLORINE gases in warfare. See Gases in warfare

CHLOROPHYL
Role of chlorophyll in photosynthesis. E. I.
Rabinowitch and Govindjee. il Sci Am 213:
74-83 Jl '65
See also
Chloroplasts

CHLOROPLASTS
Chloroplast mutagenesis: effect of N-methyl-
N'-nitro-N-nitrosoguanidine and some other agents on euglena. D. R. McCalla. bibliog il Science 148:497-9 Ap 23 '65
Differential enzymatic activity in ecological
races of typha latifolia L. S. J. Mc-
Naughton. bibliog il Science 150:1829-30 D
31 '65
Kinetin-induced chloroplast maturation in
cultures of tobacco tissue. D. A. Stetler
and W. M. Laetsch. bibliog il Science
149:1387-8 S 17 '65
Reduction of trimethylene dipyridyl with illuminated chloroplasts. C. C. Black. bibliog il Science 149:62-3 Jl 2 '65
See also
Ferredoxin

CHLOROQUINE
DNA: reaction with chloroquine. J. L. Alli-
son and others. bibliog il Science 149:1111-13
S 3 '65

CHLORPROMAZINE
Tranquilizers can reduce psychotic symtoms;
effectiveness of thorazine and related drugs.
Sci N L 89:29 Ja 8 '66

CHOATE, Elizabeth R.
Honkin' good time. Atlan 215:122-4 Ap '65
Soft touch. Atlan 216:81-3 D '65

CHOCO Indians. See Indians of South America
—Colombia

CHOCOLATE
How to tell one chocolate from another. il
Good H 161:174 N '65

CHOCOLATE desserts. See Desserts

CHOICE of college. See College, Choice of

CHOICE of occupations. See Occupations

CHOISEUL ISLAND. See Solomon Islands

CHOISYA ternata. See Mexican oranges

CHOLERA
Cholera resurgent. il Time 86:59-60 D 3 '65

CHOLESTEROL
Biological synthesis of cholesterol; address,
December 11, 1964. K. Bloch. bibliog il Sci-
ence 150:19-28 O 1 '65
Cholesterol biosynthesis: mevalonate synthe-
sis inhibited by bile salts. G. M. Fimog-
nari and V. W. Rodwell. bibliog il Science
147:1038 F 26 '65
Cholesterol implicated. Sci Digest 58:39 S '65
Cholesterol reduced by pancreatic extract.
Sci N L 87:150 Mr 6 '65
Diet: heart of the matter? il Newsweek
65:53-7 F 8 '65
Forget about cholesterol. Sci N L 88:2 Jl 3
'65
More blood, less fat. Time 86:72 N 5 '65

CHOLINESTERASE
Ciguatera fish poison: a cholinesterase inhibitor. K. M. Li. bibliog il Science 147:
1580-1 Mr 26 '65

CHOLTITZ, Dietrich von
General who defied Hitler. H. Ehrlich. il pors
Look 30:46+ Ja 25 '66

CHONDRITES. See Meteorites

CHONDROITIN sulfate
Chondroitin sulfate: inhibition of synthesis
by puromycin. G. De La Haba and H.
Holtzer. bibliog il Science 149:1263-5 S 10
'65

CHONDRULES
Chondrule in the Chainpur meteorite. K.
Fredriksson and A. M. Reid. bibliog il
Science 149:856-60 Ag 20 '65

CHOPIN, Frédéric François
Gilt-edged Chopin by Gilels and Ormandy.
C. J. Luten. il Am Rec G 31:797 My '65
Rubinstein's potent art vs. the critical
faculties. C. J. Luten. Am Rec G 32:143 O
'65

CHOPIN international piano competition. See
Music—Competitions

CHOPS. See Cookery—Meat

CHORAL groups and societies
Choral festival in New York city; International uni7ersity choral festival, at Lincoln Center for the performing arts. Américas 17:45 Ag '65
Music to my ears; the other Richter. M. Bernheimer. Sat R 48:48 My 8 '65
New York; Amor artis chorale and orchestra present Semele. E. R. Rizzo. Opera N 30:31 Ja 1 '66
No rock, no mop, but a big hit; M. Anderson's group. il Life 59:67-8 Ag 13 '66
CHORAL music
See also
Handel and Haydn society
Phonograph records—Choral music
CHORAL singing
See also
Choral groups and societies
CHOREOGRAPHIC institute. See Dance schools—Sweden
CHOREOGRAPHY
Americans abroad; American choreographers influencing Europe. C. Barnes. il Dance Mag 39:40-3+ Jl '65
Don't say you're a dancer! J. Anderson. il Dance Mag 39:47-9 F '65
Gallery of American ballet theatre choreographers. J. Anderson. il Dance Mag 40:38-45 Ja '66
Human element; American ballet theatre's 25th anniversary season; new productions and others. D. Hering. il Dance Mag 39:42-7+ My '65
Lincoln square YMCA theatre, West side YMCA. J. Maskey. Dance Mag 39:30+ Mr '65
Peril and delight; interview, ed. by W. Como. il Dance Mag 39:25-7+ My '65
Rembrandt's The anatomy lesson inspires new ballet. J. Anderson. il Dance Mag 39:46-8 Je '65
Robert Joffrey ballet. Delacorte theater. M. Marks. Dance Mag 39:60+ O '65
Start with the body. il Newsweek 66:77 Ag 30 '65
Tatjana Gsovsky: a prayer to the deity. W. Sorell. il Dance Mag 39:14-15 Ag '65
Unexpected assemblage! unique collaboration of four artists with dancers. D McDonagh. il Dance Mag 39:42-5+ Je '65
Viewpoint: Agnes De Mille; interview, ed. by H. Loxton. A. De Mille. il Dance Mag 39:42-3+ Ap '65
Young choreographer's concert. Clark center for the performing arts. J. Maskey. Dance Mag 40:19+ Ja '66
CHORIONIC gonadotrophin. See Hormones
CHORLEY, Jean Travers
English earthenware in the Chorley collection. Antiques 87:182-7 F '65
CHOROVER, Stephan L. See Mendelson, J. jt. auth.
CHORUS in opera. See Opera—Chorus
CHOU, En-lai
Chou gets socked twice. G. De Carvalho. il pors Life 59:62A-62B+ Jl 9 '65
From one, many; visit to Tanzania. il por Newsweek 65:44 Je 21 '65
Life magazine? of America? very sorry, goodby; G. De Carvalho's attempt to interview Chou En-lai. G. P. Hunt. Life 59:3 Jl 9 '65
Safari that failed; Chou has troubles in Africa. U S News 58:21-2 Je 21 '65
Why we guard against subversion; visit to Tanzania. il por Time 85:40 Je 11 '65
You can go home again; early return from African visit. Time 85:31B Je 18 '65

Anecdotes, facetiae, satire, etc.

On the bongo beat of history; or, Black mischief revisited. Nat R 17:538-9 Je 29 '65
CHOU, Shi-ming. See Zu Rhein, G. M. jt. auth.
CHOW, Shu-kai
Where is China? address, July 28, 1965. Vital Speeches 31:699-702 S 1 '65
CHOW, Tsaihwa J. and Johnstone, M. S.
Lead isotopes in gasoline and aerosols of Los Angeles basin. California. bibliog Science 147:502-3 Ja 29 '65
CHOWDER
Chowder at the beach; with fish and shellfish; recipes. il Sunset 135:90-1 N '65
CHOY, Rudy
Man overboard; in the Pacific. Yachting 118:60+ O '65
CHRISLIN Insta-cameras. See Cameras
CHRIST. See Jesus Christ
CHRISTENBERRY, Herbert William
Where is the flag? por Time 86:25 Ag 6 '65
CHRISTENSEN, Ernst T.
Betsy in the Everglades: report. Nat Parks Mag 39:22 N '65

CHRISTENSEN, Lew
Dash & control. il por •Time 85:67 Mr 5 '65
East meets West! Newsweek 65:88 Ap 26 '65
CHRISTENSON, Reo M.
Senator Dirksen vs. the Court. Nation 201:60-1 Ag 2 '65
CHRISTGAU, Robert
New but muddy wave. Pop Phot 56:118-19+ My '65
VanDerBeek: master of animation. Pop Phot 57:106-11 S '65
CHRISTIAN, J. See Taylor, J. L. jt. auth.
CHRISTIAN, John J. and Davis, D. E.
Endocrines, behavior, and population. bibliog Science 146:1550-60; 149:376+ D 18 '64, Jl 23 '65
CHRISTIAN anti-Communist crusade
Tell it to the navy. New Repub 152:8 F 6 '65
CHRISTIAN Appalachian project, incorporated
CAP is born; plight of the people of Appalachia. E. M. Raabe. America 112:608-10 Ap 24 '65
CHRISTIAN art and symbolism
Ecclesiastical art in Russia. G. Murray. Christian Cent 83:54 Ja 12 '66
See also
Art, Coptic
Art and religion
Mary, Virgin—Art

Exhibitions

Battle against vulgarity. C. J. McNaspy. America 113:693 N 27 '65
Letter from Paris; treasures of French churches at Musée des arts décoratifs. Genêt. New Yorker 41:150+ Mr 6 '65
CHRISTIAN booksellers association
Christian booksellers association tops convention records. A. Hustwitt. il Pub W 188:38-41 S 6 '65
CHRISTIAN century (periodical)
Editorial policies, questions and answers. Christian Cent 82:517 Ap 28 '65
No offense intended; Zondervan publishing house advertisement in May 12 issue. Christian Cent 82:797-8 Je 23 '65
What's new? concerning editorials in 1915 copies. Christian Cent 82:956 Ag 4 '65
CHRISTIAN character. See Christian life
CHRISTIAN crusade (organization)
Oh, to be in Manitou! Christian Cent 82:599 My 5 '65
CHRISTIAN democrats (Chile) See Political parties—Chile
CHRISTIAN democrats (Germany) See Political parties—Germany (Federal Republic)
CHRISTIAN democrats (Italy). See Political parties—Italy
CHRISTIAN democrats (Latin America) See Political parties—Latin America
CHRISTIAN doctrine. See Theology
CHRISTIAN education. See Religious education
CHRISTIAN ethics
Christian faith and moral action. J. M. Gustafson. Christian Cent 82:1345-7 N 3 '65
Man as nature's man. P. Hefner; reply. T. Dobzhansky. Christian Cent 82:242 F 24 '65
Revolution for Christmas. E. J. Hughes. Newsweek 66:11 D 27 '65
Sin, liberty and law, by L. Monden. Review Cath World 201:401 S '65. J. D. Conway
Situation ethics: between law & love. il Time 87:55 Ja 21 '66
Validity of absolutes; with reply by J. Fletcher and rejoinder. H. McCabe. Commonweal 83:432-7, 439-40 Ja 14 '66
See also
Conscience
Humility
War and religion
CHRISTIAN herald
End to nostalgia; editor retires. Time 86:48 D 24 '65
CHRISTIAN institute of southern Africa. See Theological schools
CHRISTIAN life
Can we talk to Marxian atheists? P. Ehlen; D. I. MacLean. America 113:112-17 Jl 31 '65
Christian faith and moral action. J. M. Gustafson. Christian Cent 82:1345-7 N 3 '65
Christian in the world; drafting of a final conciliar text on the church in the modern world. America 112:350 Mr 13 '65
Christian renewal in a changing world, by B. Haring. Review Cath World 201:64+ Ap '65. K. A. Lynch
Decree on religious life. L. M. Orsy. America 114:12-13+ Ja 1 '66
Glorious freedom of God's sons. C. Davis. America 113:97 Jl 24 '65
Herzog and the passion. R. F. Capon. America 112:425-7 Mr 27 '65

CHRISTIAN life—*Continued*
Needed: a new status for the single woman. V. Lindbeck. Cath World 202:151-7 D '65
On a certain faithlessness. L. J. Averill. Christian Cent 82:1087-90 S 8 '65; Discussion. 82:1358 N 3 '65
Parish of the future; San Miguelito, Panama City. J. P. Fitzpatrick. America 113:521-3 N 6 '65
Spiritual guidance; reprint from Catholic world, February 1888. I. T. Hecker. Cath World 202:165 D '65
Who is deprived? address. D. Berrigan. Commonweal 82:53-5 Ap 2 '65
World as sacrament. A. Schmemann. Cath World 201:132-7 My '65
   See also
Faith

CHRISTIAN medical society
Where the needy get free medical care; Christian medical clinics. H. G. Earl. il Todays Health 43:26-9+ Mr '65

CHRISTIAN missions. See Missions

CHRISTIAN names. See Names, Personal

CHRISTIAN pacifism. See Pacifism

CHRISTIAN peace conference, Budapest. See Peace conferences

CHRISTIAN peace conference, Sofia, Bulgaria. See Peace conferences

CHRISTIAN peace conference movement. See Peace conferences

CHRISTIAN Science
New developments in New Thought. C. A. Anderson. bibliog f Christian Cent 83:78-80 Ja 19 '66

CHRISTIAN Science monitor (newspaper)
Change at the Monitor. il Newsweek 65:70 Mr 15 '65
Monitor's new look. Time 85:63 Mr 12 '65
Why the Monitor changed. E. D. Canham. il Sat R 48:78-9 Ap 10 '65; Discussion. 48:57+ My 8 '65

CHRISTIAN sociology. See Sociology, Christian

CHRISTIAN tribune (periodical)
Formosan Christians launch weekly. Christian Cent 82:1119 S 15 '65

CHRISTIAN year
   See also
Lent

CHRISTIAN youth corps (organization)
New rightist group lures youth; qualifications for membership include rifle, six-inch hunting knife and 1,000 rounds of ammunition. Christian Cent 82:486 Ap 21 '65

CHRISTIANITY
Battle of the Bible; new Reformation. T. G. Harris. il Look 29:17-20 Jl 27 '65
Beyond Bonhoeffer; future of religionless Christianity. H. Cox. Commonweal 82:653-7 S 17 '65
Campaign on many fronts. R. M. Brown. Christian Cent 82:577-9 My 5 '65; Discussion. 82:717 Je 2 '65
Canadian collegians and The comfortable pew; concerning P. Berton's book. W. A. Sadler, jr. Christian Cent 82:1353-6 N 3 '65
Creative negation in theology. T. J. J. Altizer. Christian Cent 82:864-7 Jl 7 '65; Discussion. 82:1015-16, 1195, 1351-2 Ag 18, S 29, N 3 '65
Dividing of Christendom, by C. Dawson. Review
   America 112:432 Mr 27 '65. C. J. McNaspy
Intellectual climate and Christian belief. H. O. J. Brown. il Nat R 17:1022-5 N 16 '65
No access to God's diaries. C. G. Rutenber. bibliog f Christian Cent 82:1570-3 D 22 '65
Power and a goodness. R. R. Niebuhr. Christian Cent 82:1472-5 D 1 '65
Profiles; concerning Honest to God, by J. Robinson. V. Mehta. il New Yorker 41:63-4+ N 13; 60-2+ N 20 '65
Rebirth of Christ; essay on C. S. Lewis. J. Hart. il Nat R 17:1192-6 D 28 '65
Self-conscious Catholicism. E. C. Kennedy. America 113:434-6 O 16 '65; Discussion. 113:551-2+ N 13 '65
Shaw and Christianity, by A. S. Abbott. Review
   Christian Cent 82:1579 D 22 '65. J. A. Davidson
Swallowed up by godlessness. G. Vahanian. Christian Cent 82:1505-7 D 8 '65
Theology in the context of culture. P. M. Van Buren. Christian Cent 82:428-30 Ap 7 '65
We stand or fall together. H. E. Fey. Christian Cent 82:612-14 My 12 '65; Discussion. 82:841 Je 30 '65
Why this non-God-talk? death-of-God theologians. Christian Cent 82:1467-8 D 1 '65

Word; Christian faith. V. P. McCorry. America 112:868-9 Je 12 '65
World is already Christic; Christian secularity. T. E. Clarke. America 112:800-3 My 29 '65
   See also
Catholic church
Christian ethics
Christian life
Church
Fundamentalism
Jesus Christ
Missions
Protestantism
Religion and science
Theism
Theology
War and religion

History
Dividing of Christendom, by C. Dawson. Review
   Commonweal 82:570-1 Ag 6 '65. J. Ratte

CHRISTIANITY and communism. See Catholic church and communism; Communism and religion

CHRISTIANITY and international affairs. See Church and international relations

CHRISTIANITY and other religions
Jew and Christmas; to observe or not? from a new generation, a new answer. L. Gross. il Look 29:22-4 D 28 '65
On reading Matthew; question of a Judeo-Christian tradition. M. Himmelfarb. Commentary 40:56-65 O '65
Relations with non-Christians. America 113:490-1 O 30 '65
Setting of the Sermon on the mount, by W. D. Davies. Review
   Commentary 40:73-5 Ag '65. S. Siegel
Social consciousness in Eastern orthodoxy; long hampered by subservience to Islamic rule. C. S. Calian. Christian Cent 82:1284-6 O 20 '65
We Jews and Jesus, by S. Sandmel. Review
   Commentary 40:107-8+ S '65. P. Winter

CHRISTIANITY and psychiatry. See Psychiatry and religion

CHRISTIANITY and science. See Religion and science

CHRISTIANITY and social problems. See Church and social problems

CHRISTIANITY and war. See War and religion

CHRISTIANS
Freedom in action; Christian's situation in world today. J. H. Smylie. Christian Cent 82:1067-8 S 1 '65

CHRISTIANS in Communist countries
Church in the storm of our time. R. Terrill. Christian Cent 82:1280-3 O 20 '65

CHRISTIANS in Germany
Christians and Marxists. Y. Chabas. Christian Cent 82:1286-8 O 20 '65

CHRISTIANS in India
Christian ashrams in India; disciplined rule of worship, meditation. R. P. Beaver. Christian Cent 82:887-9 Jl 14 '65; Reply. E. S. Jones. 82:1160-2+ S 22 '65; Rejoinder. 82:1357-8 N 3 '65

CHRISTIANS in Indonesia
Indonesia today. H. P. Van Dusen. Christian Cent 82:616-17 My 12 '65

CHRISTIANS in Japan
   See also
United church of Christ in Japan

CHRISTIE, George A.
Current construction trends. See issues of Architectural record

CHRISTIE, Julie
Voom! voom! it's Julie Christie. il pors Newsweek 66:88-91 D 20 '65

CHRISTIE, Trevor L.
Booked for travel (cont) Sat R 48:41-2+ S 4 '65
Easy adventure: Ethiopia. Travel 124:56-9 N '65

CHRISTINA, Sister M. See M. Christina, Sister

CHRISTINE, Emma Ruth
Why not listen to the librarian? ALA Bul 59:1010-11 D '65

CHRIST-JANER, Albert
Visions from the greenhouse. il Time 86:74-5 D 31 '65

CHRISTMAS
Bah and humbug to Dr Spock. Life 59:4 D 10 '65
Christmas after Christmas; religiously ridiculous. R. H. Hamill. Christian Cent 82:1486-7 D 1 '65
Christmas in other lands. M. Mead. Redbook 126:24+ D '65
Christmas in the first person. Christian Cent 82:1563 D 22 '65
Christmas is for joy. L. H. Valbracht. il Suc Farm 63:55+ D '65

CHRISTMAS—*Continued*

Christmas symbols around the world. Good H 161:166 D '65

Great festival. il Time 86:70-5 D 10 '65

Great myrth and melody; traditions. il House & Gard 128:135 D '65

Magic of Christmas. R. J. McCracken. Parents Mag 40:40 D '65

Making the holidays pleasant for children and their parents. B. Spock. Redbook 126:20+ D '65

Restore Christmas to Christ! discussion. Christian Cent 82:243 F 24 '65

Someday, a real Christmas; excerpts from editorial, December 23, 1955. D. Lawrence. U S News 59:84 D 27 '65

Vogue's eye view of Springtime of the spirit; Byzantine fresco of Nativity in Mistra, Peloponnesus. il Vogue 146:169-73 D '65

What are we celebrating, and why? H. Cox. il Redbook 126:40-1+ D '65

See also

Jesus Christ—Nativity

Anecdotes, facetiae, satire, etc.

Passed present. G. Ace. Sat R 49:12 Ja 22 '66

Caricatures and cartoons

And a Merry Christmas from Little Nemo! W. McCay. Redbook 126:70-1 D '65

Canada

Prairie winter. M. Creal. il Ladies Home J 82:60-1+ D '65

England

Christmas at Woburn Abbey; interview. Duchess of Bedford. il House & Gard 128: 136-8+ D '65

Christmas in England. G. Zimmermann. il Look 29:31-5 D 28 '65

Tradition in England: the food of Christmas day; Thomas Rivers family of Hertfordshire. M. Kaytor. il Look 29:36-8 D 28 '65

Greece, Modern

Night the war stopped for a moment; Christmas eve in 1943. J. Hawk. il Redbook 126: 6+ D '65

India

Christmas in the midday sun. S. Rama. Rau. House & Gard 128:162-3 D '65

Japan

Oh, little town of Tokyo. A. Gonzalez and G. Gonzalez. il Sat R 48:81-2 S 18 '65

United States

Always listen for the bells; personal reminiscence of Christmas in Montana. H. Call. il Redbook 126:42-3+ D '65

Boy borrowed for Christmas; reprint. H. J. Taylor. il Good H 161:107+ D '65

Christmas at Pine Mountain. M. Rogers. il Horn Bk 41:587-92 D '65

Christmas at the White House. Sr Schol 87:29 D 9 '65

Christmas in the country. il Farm J 89:81 D '65

Christmas is people; poet recalls family holidays. P. Engle. il McCalls 93:79-81+ D '65

Christmas, the Messiah and the small town. J. Sittler. Christian Cent 82:1576-7 D 22 '65

Christmas tree for the children; excerpts from diary during West Coast flood, December 1964. Am For 71:17 Mr '65

Christmas without Santa Claus; Currence family of Mill Creek, W.Va. C. Morrison. il Look 29:18-21 D 28 '65

Early starter: Christmas in America. E. M. Marshall. il Travel 124:42-4 N '65

How to stretch Christmas. D. B. Carlos. House & Gard 128:234+ N '65

How we put ourselves into Christmas. il Farm J 89:88-9 D '65

If I were king, Todays Health 43:21+ D '65

Jew and Christmas; to observe or not? from a new generation, a new answer. L. Gross. il Look 29:22-4 D 28 '65

Littlest traditions. E. S. Oshin. House & Gard 128:45+ D '65

Merry Christmas for the quints: Fischers holiday. J. Bird. il Sat Eve Post 238:21-5 D 18 '65

Nativity in the Smokies; Marshall, N.C. R. C. Davids. il Farm J 89:38-9 D '65

Polly Bergen sets the holiday scene. il Good H 161:38+ D '65

Seventy-five ways to save time during the holidays. Good H 161:163-4 D '65

Speaking out: let's keep Christmas commercial. A. O. Armstrong. il Sat Eve Post 238: 8+ D 18 '65

What do our hearts treasure? northerners in Florida for Christmas. E. B. White. New Yorker 41:29-30 Ja 15 '66

CHRISTMAS angels. See Christmas decorations

CHRISTMAS breads. See Bread

CHRISTMAS business

Christmas employment picture. Pub W 188: 56-7 S 6 '65

Christmas in France; selling books in English. H. R. Lottman. il Pub W 188:22-4 D 13 '65

Christmas 1965: record sales were achieved by retail bookstores. il Pub W 189:121-4 Ja 17 '66

Christmas pot pourri; ideas and suggestions for holiday season. Pub W 188:46-8 Ag 23 '65

Christmas trade: record boom? il U S News 59:37-9 N 8 '65

Christmas window displays; interview. J. Schwartz. il Pub W 188:36-8 Ag 23 '65

How two leading book jobbers prepare for Christmas. Pub W 188:37-9 Ag 23 '65

I'm dreaming of a white tornado; hints for a bookseller at Christmas time. L. Russ. Pub W 188:28 D 6 '65

More for more; Christmas shopping record. il Time 87:81-2 Ja 7 '66

Project headstart: Christmas 1965. il Newsweek 66:75-6+ D 6 '65

Retailers ringing up merriest season ever. il Bsns W p28-9 D 18 '65

Some hardy perennials and important annuals for the coming holiday season; list by Oklahoma bookseller. L. Meyer. Pub W 188: 58-9 N 8 '65

Stores load shelves, brace for record Yule. il Bsns W p30-1 N 6 '65

Stores say holiday buying lags in many parts of the country; sampling of bookstores. il Pub W 188:56-7 N 29 '65

When buyers swamped stores; the biggest Christmas boom. il U S News 59:65-6 D 27 '65

CHRISTMAS cactus. See Cactus

CHRISTMAS cake. See Cake

CHRISTMAS candy. See Candy

CHRISTMAS cards

Case for Christmas cards. C. B. Luce. il McCalls 93:28+ D '65

Christmas & other card ideas; photographic Christmas cards. D. B. Eisendrath, jr. Pop Phot 57:6+ D '65

Christmas cards; listing of nonprofit suppliers. il Consumer Rep 30:484-5 O '65

Famous cards from famous people. il Good H 161:50+ D '65

Winter scene: the Johnsons' Christmas card. il U S News 59:11 D 20 '65

Young people can print their own. il Sunset 135:76-7 D '65

CHRISTMAS carols

Stories behind famous carols. il Good H 161: 165 D '65

See also

Phonograph records—Christmas music

CHRISTMAS clubs

Christmas clubs; silly way to save? il Changing T 19:33 D '65

CHRISTMAS cookery. See Christmas dinners; Christmas meals; Cookery; Cookery, Ornamental

CHRISTMAS cookies. See Cookies

CHRISTMAS decorations

Anyplace; ideas to make Christmas merrier. il Pop Gard 16:29 N '65

Band of angels. W. Waltner and E. Waltner. il Pop Mech 124:136-7 D '65

Busy hands make happy holidays. L. Burgess. il Flower Grower 52:28-9 D '65

Christmas claybake, 1965. il Ladies Home J 82:26 D '65

Christmas comes. B. Plumb. il N Y Times Mag p47-9 D 19 '65

Christmas Eve in pine cone land. M. Perry. il Flower Grower 52:30-2+ D '65

Christmas ornaments from fruit dividers. H. S. Rush. il Design 67:12-13 N '65

Designed for Christmas. il Flower Grower 52: 22-5 D '65

Fifty easy ideas for the holiday house. il Good H 161:110-18 D '65

Glorious Christmas ornaments for 1965. il House & Gard 128:138-47 D '65

Glorious wreath; new designs you can make yourself. il House & Gard 128:148-51 D '65

Great festival: department store decorations. il Time 86:70-5 D 10 '65

High and dry for Christmas; dried arrangements. il Sunset 135:184-5 D '65

Home grown Christmas shop. M. Perry. il Flower Grower 52:40-1 N '65

It's not too early for Christmas crafts! M. Garrity. il Bet Hom & Gard 43:84+ N '65

Making your own medallions. il Sunset 135: 111-12 D '65

Mexican fantasies. il House & Gard 128:144-7 D '65

CHRISTMAS decorations—*Continued*
One pattern makes all three. il Sunset 135:80 D '65
Rainbow star. W. Waltner and E. Waltner. il Pop Mech 124:140-1 D '65
Reflections of the past; decorated mirrors. il McCalls 93:104-7 D '65
Trim your treasures for the hoidays. il McCalls 93:102-3 D '65
Wire core in our conifer balls. il Sunset 135: 92+ D '65
See also
Christmas greens
Christmas projects
Christmas trees

CHRISTMAS decorations, Outdoor
Add action to your Christmas displays. D. M. Swartwout. il Pop Mech 124:128-33 D '65
Build a hat-tipping snowman. il Pop Sci 187:153 D '65
Great festival. il Time 86:70-5 D 10 '65

CHRISTMAS dinners
Dinner straight out of Dickens; with recipes. il McCalls 93:86-7+ D '65
Dinners. il Good H 161:122-5+ D '65
Golden goose of Christmases past; with recipes and menu. E. Graves. il Life 59: 90-1+ D 17 '65
Magnificent Christmas bird. il Bet Hom & Gard 43:64-5+ D '65
Tradition in England: the food of Christmas day; with recipes. M. Kaytor. il Look 29: 36-8 D 28 '65
Yuletide feasting in Pennsylvania; with menu and recipes. M. B. Wilson. il Parents Mag 40:71-4+ D '65

CHRISTMAS employment. See Part time employment

CHRISTMAS eve
Night the war stopped for a moment; Christmas eve in 1943. J. Hawk. il Redbook 126: 6+ D '65

CHRISTMAS eve; story. See Fremantle, A.

CHRISTMAS fables. See Fables

CHRISTMAS festivals. See Festivals

CHRISTMAS gifts
Advice to relatives, or Hand this to your wife. T. Trueblood. Field & S 70:16+ D '65
Bejeweled bookmarks. il McCalls 93:128-9 D '65
Best buy gifts. il Consumer Rep 30:524-6 N '65
Better Christmas giving, better year round living. Consumer Bul 48:18-19 D '65
Bull market Christmas. il Esquire 64:196-203 D '65
Christmas art books. H. Rosenberg. Vogue 146:148-50 D '65
Christmas avalanche; guide to the best illustrated books. il Time 86:116+ D 10 '65
Christmas classified; Mlle's annual charibotée. L. Lerman. il Mlle 62:162-5 N '65
Christmas on the coffee table; the art book. F. Getlein. New Repub 153:33-5 D 18 '65
Christmas science selection. F. L. Snakenberg. il Sci N L 88:314-15 N 13 '65
Gamy days ahead; photographs by L. St John; with account by P. Knight. Sports Illus 23:72-7 N 22 '65
Gift-making time is here again! ideas from the Needlework & sewing center. il Good H 161:112-15+ N '65
Gift of photography. D. S. Gelatt. il Pop Phot 57:148-9+ D '65
Gifts for a child to sew. C. Houck. il Parents Mag 40:76 D '65
Gifts for the travel-minded. S. Robinson. il McCalls 93:40+ D '65
Gifts from museums (cont) il Consumer Rep 30:540-1 N '65
Give homemade gifts this Christmas. J. LemMon. il Suc Farm 63:78-81 N '65
Glittering novelties, easy to do. C. T. Richardson. il Design 67:35 N '65
In gifts keyed to current crazes. il House & Gard 128:264-5 N '65
Night before Christmas; poem; with holiday suggestions. il Redbook 126:49-61+ D '65
Project headstart: Christmas 1965. il Newsweek 66:75-6+ D 6 '65
Sewing is a mother's art for gifts galore. il Bet Hom & Gard 43:40-1+ D '65
Sixty-six treasures under $6. il House & Gard 128:260-3 N '65
Speaking out; let's keep Christmas commercial. A. O. Armstrong. il Sat Eve Post 238: 8+ D 18 '65
Stocking stuffers. il House & Gard 128:205 D '65
Sure-to-please Christmas gifts; for all the boating people. il Motor B 116:28-35 N '65
Try Christmas shopping at the museum. il Changing T 19:46-7 N '65

We give promises for presents. L. Campbell. il Farm J 89:82 D '65
What's new in gifts for Christmas. Outdoor Life 136:94+ O '65
See also
Books as gifts
Christmas projects
Food as gifts
Gifts in business
Toys
Wrapping of packages

Anecdotes, facetiae, satire, etc.
Annual crisis of love. L. Wainwright. Life 59:18 D 17 '65
Repressed desires; well-known personalities tell what they want for Christmas. House & Gard 128:239 N '65

CHRISTMAS gifts for children
Children Santa forgot; cases of seventeen children. il Ladies Home J 82:48+ D '65
Children's gifts with dividends. il House & Gard 128:308-9 N '65
Christmas gifting. il Parents Mag 40:111-13 D '65
Christmas toys with a purpose. L. Steckler. il Pop Mech 124:124-7 D '65
Here are some projects dad might not think he can do (but he can) il Bet Hom & Gard 43:48-9+ D '65
On and off the avenue (cont) New Yorker 41:151-2+ D 11 '65
Personal business; shopping for toys. Bsns W p 145-6 D 4 '65
Personal business; some ideas on picking presents. Bsns W p 161-2 D 11 '65
Shoppers gallery. il Good H 161:101 D '65
These are mostly games and very quick to make. il Bet Hom & Gard 43:52-3+ D '65
Treats to tickle a child's fancy. il House & Gard 128:268-9 N '65

CHRISTMAS gifts for men
For the men in your life, play Santa. il Seventeen 24:122-5 D '65
How to please the men. il Farm J 89:84 D '65
Man talk; what not to buy for men at Christmas. D. Newman and R. Benton. Mlle 62: 40 D '65
Shoppers gallery. il Good H 161:100 D '65

Anecdotes, facetiae, satire, etc.
Husband vs. wives vs. Christmas. P. Bracken. il Ladies Home J 82:46 D '65

CHRISTMAS gifts for the home
Checklist of small electric appliances, equally delightful to give or to receive. il McCalls 93:50 D '65
Christmas is a family day. R. Charles. il Parents Mag 40:81+ D '65
Christmas shopper. il Craft Horiz 25:24-5 N '65
Coveted pleasures; clues to the happiest gifts of all. il House & Gard 128:270-1 N '65
Fabulous finds for the house. il House & Gard 128:266-7 N '65
From our kitchen to yours; token gift. il McCalls 93:52 D '65
Good gifts for the family. il Bet Hom & Gard 43:12+ D '65
GH's famous gift list. il Good H 161:8+ D '65
On and off the avenue (cont) New Yorker 41:166+ D 4 '65
Personalized gifts. il Farm J 89:86-7 D '65
Shoppers gallery. il Good H 161:102-6+ D '65

CHRISTMAS gifts for women
Girl pleasers; surefire ways to play Santa. il Seventeen 24:118-21 D '65
How to please farm women. il Farm J 89:85 D '65
On and off the avenue (cont) New Yorker 41:164+ N 20; 182+ N 27 '65
Shopper's gallery. il Good H 161:98-9 D '65

CHRISTMAS greens
Busy hands make happy holidays. L. Burgess. il Flower Grower 52:28-9 D '65
Christmas ball. il Sunset 135:56-9 D '65
Glorious wreath; new designs you can make yourself. il House & Gard 128:148-51 D '65
Here are some idea wreaths. il Sunset 135: 208 D '65
What's in a wreath? H. W. Dengler. il Am For 71:10-11 D '65
Wreaths are wonderful; let's make one! H. W. Dengler. il Am For 71:6-9 D '65
Yuletide geography; symposium. il Pop Gard 16:26-9 N '65
See also
Christmas trees
Holly

CHRISTMAS house; drama. See Waite, H. E. and Hoppenstedt, E. M.

CHRISTMAS meals
  Bright beginning for Christmas morning. il
    Bet Hom & Gard 43:62-3+ D '65
  Casserole ideas for busy Christmas eve. il
    Sunset 135:122+ D '65
  From eighty years of good housekeeping:
    a Christmas gathering of favorite dishes.
    il Good H 161:120-38+ D '65
  Holiday insides for brioche. il Sunset 135:
    116 D '65
  Holiday party cook book. il House & Gard
    128:187+ D '65
  Tureen supper for Christmas eve. il Bet Hom
    & Gard 43:60-1+ D '65
      See also
  Christmas dinners
CHRISTMAS music
  Heigh, Sir Ass, oh heigh; Play of Daniel and
    the Play of Herod. F. Bowers. il House &
    Gard 128:183-4+ D '65
      See also
  Phonograph records—Christmas music
CHRISTMAS pageants. See Pageants
CHRISTMAS parties. See Entertaining
CHRISTMAS plays
      See also
  Pageants

                    Texts
  Birds' Christmas carol; dramatization of
    story by K. D. Wiggin. H. L. Miller. Plays
    25:87-96 D '65
  Christmas house. H. E. Waite and E. M.
    Hoppenstedt. Plays 25:15-22 D '65
  Christmas snowman. M. Hark and N.
    McQueen. Plays 25:41-50, 96 D '65
  Empty room at the inn. G. Du Bois. Plays
    25:23-31 D '65
  Queen's Christmas cake. F. B. Watts. Plays
    25:69-75 D '65
  Star bright. C. Boiko. Plays 25:63-7 D '65
CHRISTMAS poetry
  And there were shepherds. S. K. Freiberg.
    Christian Cent 82:1545 D 15 '65
  Annunciation. R. Spargur. Christian Cent
    82:1545 D 15 '65
  Christmas in the Southwest. J. C. Mergard.
    Farm J 89:107 D '65
  Christmas poems. il America 113:776-7 D 18
    '65
  Christmas presents. G. Dickerson. Mlle 62:48
    D '65
  Christmas story. J. R. Quinn. Christian
    Cent 82:1569 D 22 '65
  Christmas tree in Rockefeller center. M. N.
    Hoyer. il Am For 71:37 D '65
  Christmas trees after the event. D. Gottlieb.
    Mlle 62:48 D '65
  Early American carol. F. Frieseke. il Horn
    Bk 41:612 D '65
  Gift. W. C. Williams. il Good H 161:70-1 D
    '65
  Hand of God. M. Plowman. Christian Cent
    82:1569 D 22 '65
  In the Black Forest. O. Lilly. Christian
    Cent 82:1569 D 22 '65
  Nativity. A. N. Wilder. Christian Cent 82:
    1568 D 22 '65
  O Christmas come, against vast Babel. S.
    Bradley. Christian Cent 82:1545 D 15 '65
  Poems for Christmas. Commonweal 83:374
    D 24 '65
  Two haiku for Christmas. G. Gilsdorf.
    Cath World 202:143 D '65
  Who's afraid of Franz Gruber? M. J. Irion.
    Christian Cent 82:1569 D 22 '65
      See also
  Santa Claus—Poetry
CHRISTMAS presents. See Christmas gifts
CHRISTMAS projects
  Christmas crafts. il Bet Hom & Gard 43:35-
    66+ D '65
  Christmas gifts children can make. B. Pierce.
    il Todays Health 43:40-5 D '65
  Christmas in the castle; fourth grade Christ-
    mas project. A. Gustafson and others. il
    Sch Arts 65:29-30 D '65
  Christmas memory book you can make. il
    McCalls 93:124-5 D '65
  Decorate-it-yourself Christmas ideas. il Suc
    Farm 63:58-9 D '65
  Silvery sculptures fashioned from foil. il Mc-
    Calls 93:110-11+ D '65
  Think Christmas! J. Wolcott. il Recreation
    58:455 N '65
  Wreaths are wonderful: let's make one! E.
    W. Dengler. il Am For 71:6-9 D '65
CHRISTMAS roses
  Rose of Christmas, not a rose. R. C. Hands.
    il Horticulture 43:36-7 D '65
CHRISTMAS savings plans. See Christmas
    clubs
CHRISTMAS snowman; drama. See Hark. M.
    and McQueen. N.

CHRISTMAS stars. See Christmas decorations
CHRISTMAS stories
  Christmas books, 1965. N. Paige. il Library J
    90:4529-31+ O 15 '65
  Christmas that was nearly lost. R. Sawyer.
    il Parents Mag 40:49-51 D '65
  Foxer. B. Cleeve. il Sat Eve Post 238:48-9
    D 18 '65
  Journey for love. R. A. Knowlton. il Good H
    161:82-3 D '65
  Joy to the whole wide world. C. Scovel. il
    McCalls 93:108-9 D '65
  King Merrily's Merry Christmas. T. Tiche-
    nor. il Good H 161:72-81 D '65
  Merry Little Christmas; excerpt from Little
    Christmas. A. S. Turnbull. il Read Digest
    88:65-70 Ja '66
  Milk is good for skinny kids. G. Stein. il
    Redbook 126:62-3 D '65
  More the merrier. C. Boyd. il Redbook 126:
    44-5 D '65
  Offering. A. Cavanaugh. il McCalls 93:90-1
    D '65
  Sea Christmas. E. Enright. Horn Bk 41:662-
    72 D '65
  Surprise package. B. Robinson. il McCalls
    93:112-13 D '65
  Well, a little more time. Todays Health 43:
    20-1 D '65
  When the heart remembers. L. Dowty. il
    Good H 161:84-5 D '65
  Wonderful prize. A. Cavanaugh. il Redbook
    126:64-5 D '65

              Bibliography
  Christmas stories the young will enjoy.
    Good H 161:179 N '65
CHRISTMAS that was nearly lost; story. See
    Sawyer. R.
CHRISTMAS trees
  Be safe with your Christmas tree. Consumer
    Bul 48:43 D '65
  Bend in the trend; harvesting of trees not
    detrimental to forests. Am For 71:15 D '65
  Chicago's community Christmas tree; com-
    posed of seventy-five smaller trees. D. J.
    Coman. il Am City 80:81-2 D '65
  Come gather round the Christmas tree! il
    Changing T 19:24-5 D '65
  How to make our fairy-tale cover tree. il
    Good H 161:36-7 D '65
  How to transplant a live Christmas tree. il
    Good H 161:166 D '65
  Pixies in Eden park; reprint. D. Battin. il
    Recreation 58:475-6 D '65
  Presidents and their Christmas trees. W. K.
    Williams. il Am For 71:16-19+ D '65
  Ribbon trees, so nice and easy. il Bet Hom
    & Gard 43:50-1+ D '65
  Trees of Christmas. Todays Health 43:15 D
    '65
  Trees the family can do its own very special
    way. il Bet Hom & Gard 43:44-5+ D '65
CHRISTMAS wrappings. See Wrapping of pack-
    ages
CHRISTMAS wreaths. See Christmas greens
CHRISTOLOGY. See Jesus Christ
CHRISTOPHE, Louis A.
  Dismantling Abu Simbel. UNESCO Courier
    18:24-9 N '65
CHRISTOPHER, George
  Milkman cometh. por Time 86:38 N 5 '65
CHRISTOPHER, Jordan
  Wild scene at Arthur. L. Bergquist. il pors
    Look 29:40-2+ N 30 '65
CHRISTOPHER, Russell
  Emperors two; interview, ed. by A. M. Lingg.
    por Opera N 29:31 F 27 '65
CHRISTOPHER, Sybil Burton. See Burton. S.
CHROMATIN
  Sex chromatin of cone cells of human retina.
    R. L. Teplitz. bibliog il Science 150:1828-9
    D 31 '65
CHROMATIUM
  Alternative forms of triosephosphate dehy-
    drogenase in chromatium. G. A. Hudock
    and others. bibliog il Science 150:776-7 N 5
    '65
CHROMATOGRAPHIC analysis
  Thin-layer chromatography of plant pig-
    ments on mannitol or sucrose. L. W.
    Smith and others. il Science 148:508-9 Ap
    23 '65
CHROMIUM
  Volume measurements on chromium to pres-
    sure of 30 kilobars. W. E. Evenson and
    H. T. Hall. bibliog il Science 150:1164-5
    N 26 '65
CHROMOSOMES
  Bacterial chromosome. J. Cairns. il Sci Am
    214:36-44 Ja '66
  Chromosomal breakage in a rare and prob-
    ably genetically determined syndrome of
    man. J. German and others. bibliog il Sci-
    ence 148:506 Ap 23 '65

CHROMOSOMES—Continued

Chromosome complement: a fertile hybrid between equus prjewalskii and equus caballus. L. Koulischer and S. Frechkop. bibliog il Science 151:93-5 Ja 7 '66

Chromosome complement: differences between equus caballus and equus przewalskii. Poliakoff. K. Benirschke and others. bibliog il Science 148:382-3 Ap 16 '65

Chromosomes of American marsupials. J. D. Biggers and others. bibliog il Science 148: 1602-3 Je 18 '65

Cytological basis of sex ratio in drosophila pseudoobscura. E. Novitski and others. bibliog il Science 148:516-17 Ap 23 '65

Sex chromatin in newborns: presumptive evidence for external factors in human nondisjunction. A. Robinson and T. T. Puck. bibliog il Science 148:83-5 Ap 2 '65

Sex-linkage of glucose-6-phosphote dehydrogenase in the horse and donkey. J. M. Trujillo and others. bibliog il Science 148: 1603-4 Je 18 '65

Significance of a dark spot; possible correlation between Barr spots and the effects of testosterone. Time 85:78 Mr 19 '65

Triploidy in a human cell line. J. D. Regan and J. B. Smith. bibliog il Science 149: 1516-17 S 24 '65

Triploidy in parthenogenetic species of the teiid lizard, genus cnemidophorus. L. A. Pennock. bibliog il Science 149:539-40 Jl 30 '65

X chromosome DNA replication: developmental shift from synchrony to asynchrony. R. B. Nicklas and R. A. Jaqua. bibliog il Science 147:1041-3 F 26 '65

See also
Chromatin

CHROMOSOMES (botany)

Bipolarity of information transfer from the salmonella typhimurium chromosome. P. Margolin. bibliog il Science 147:1456-8 Mr 19 '65

DNA content of a chromosome of trillium erectum: effect of cold treatment. J. Woodard and others. bibliog il Science 151: 215-16 Ja 14 '66

Polyploidy and environment in Arctic Alaska. A. W. Johnson and J. G. Packer. bibliog il Science 148:237-9 Ap 9 '65

Relative radiosensitivities of woody and herbaceous spermatophytes. R. C. Sparrow and A. H. Sparrow. bibliog il Science 147:1449-51 Mr 19 '65

CHRONOMETRY, Mental. See Time perception

CHRYSANTHEMUMS

Chrysanthemum show winners. il Sunset 135: 254 O '65

Here is how to cascade chrysanthemums. il Sunset 134:265 My '65

Increase chrysanthemums the quick way. B. Brinhart. il Flower Grower 52:32 My '65

It's practical & easy to tailor-make chrysanthemums. C. Ackerson. il Flower Grower 52:56-7 My '65

Manner of speaking. J. Ciardi. Sat R 48: 20+ N 20 '65

CHRYSLER corporation

At Chrysler corporation, middle cars are the stars. J. P. Norbye. il Pop Sci 187:71-4 O '65

Chrysler launches a new flotilla ;pleasure boats and equipment. il Bsns W p60-2 Jl 17 '65

Chrysler's rescue mission; partnership with Rootes motors of Britain. il Fortune 72:63-4 Jl '65

Doing business abroad: a top businessman's view; new plant in Turkey; excerpts from address, January 13, 1965. L. A. Townsend. U S News 58:94-5 F 1 '65

Giving the facts fast; warranty protection system. il Bsns W p 126+ N 20 '65

Industry's Saturn I scores hit. il Bsns W p52+ My 29 '65

Making mileage at Chrysler. il Time 85:75 Mr 26 '65

Price of success at Chrysler. R. Sheehan. il Fortune 72:138-43+ N '65

CHU, Dan

News on wheels. Sr Schol 87:40 D 9 '65

CHU, Janet Pattee

Blueprint for a school forest. por Am For 71:34-9+ F '65

CHUB. See Trout

CHUKAR shooting. See Partridge shooting

CHULA VISTA, Calif.

Revised report speeds police work. V. H. Seiveno. il Am City 80:42 F '65

CHUMASH Indians

Ruth collection. C. Miles. il Hobbies 70:114-16 Jl '65

CHUN KING corporation

Chow mein king spices up market drive; packaged Chinese-American foods. il Bsns W p 100-2+ Mr 6 '65

CHURCH, Frank

Excerpt from address, February 17, 1965. Cong Digest 44:115+ Ap '65

How many Dominican Republics and Vietnams can we take on? N Y Times Mag p44-5+ N 28 '65

Speaking out. por Sat Eve Post 238:10+ Ap 24 '65

We are in too deep in Asia and Africa. por N Y Times Mag p30-1+ F 14 '65

CHURCH, Frederick Edwin

Castle under siege. K. Kuh. il por Sat R 48:46-7 N 27 '65

Olana, the center of the world. D. C. Huntington. il Antiques 88:656-63 N '65

CHURCH, R. J. Harrison

Niger Republic. bibliog Focus 16:1-6 S '65

CHURCH

Canadian collegians and The comfortable pew; concerning P. Berton's book. W. A. Sadler, jr. Christian Cent 82:1353-6 N 3 '65

Church as it appears today: a disquieting denunciation; address, November 16, 1965. G. O. Hand. Vital Speeches 32:143-5 D 15 '65

Ecumenics: the science of the church universal, by J. A. Mackay. Review
Christian Cent 82:1132+ S 15 '65. C. N. Kraus

See also
Catholic church
Christianity
Women and the church

Authority

Authority under fire. Time 85:74+ Mr 19 '65

Church of De Pauw; relation between freedom of priests and loyalty to their bishop. Commonweal 82:181 Ap 30 '65; Reply. J. Gallagher. 82:306 My 28 '65

Collegiality: it's meaning. L. M. Örsy. America 112:705-9 My 15 '65; Reply. J. Finnegan. 112:842-3 Je 12 '65

Crisis of obedience. America 112:520 Ap 17 '65

Father Hecker, a bridge between Catholic and Protestant thought. R. T. Handy. Cath World 202:158-9+ D '65

Murray and liberty. R. M. Healey. Christian Cent 82:1130-1 S 15 '65

Papacy, the episcopacy, and collegiality, by W. Bertrams. Review
Commonweal 82:360-1 Je 4 '65. P. E. Sigmund

Religious freedom: intrinsic or fortuitous? A. F. Carrillo de Albornoz. bibliog f Christian Cent 82:1122-6 S 15 '65

Word. V. P. McCorry. America 112:441 Mr 27 '65

CHURCH, Negro. See Negroes in the United States—Religion

CHURCH and art. See Art and religion

CHURCH and education

College aid bill. America 112:892 Je 26 '65

Johnson education bill. W. B. Ball. Commonweal 81:638-40 F 12 '65

School aid: a threat to the parish; President's proposal for supplementary education centers. R. S. Shaper. Christian Cent 82:394-6 Mr 31 '65

See also
Catholic church—Education

CHURCH and international relations

Arranged by the Defense department; clergymen's mission to southeast Asia. Christian Cent 82:1150 S 22 '65

Letter from the council. R. E. Tracy. America 113:432-3 O 16 '65

Pope and President at the UN? America 113: 179-80 Ag 21 '65

Protest trends in foreign policy. Christian Cent 82:861 Jl 7 '65

Red China at St Louis: World order study conference. K. Haselden. Christian Cent 82:1243-4 N 3 '65

Religion and the UN. America 113:37 Jl 10 '65

Speaking out on foreign policy. Time 86:53 Jl 30 '65

Vatican City: council debate on The church in the modern world. R. E. Tracy. America 113:461 O 23 '65

See also
National council of the churches of Christ in the United States of America—Commission on international affairs

CHURCH and labor

Lessons of the Detroit experience; early injustices. R. Niebuhr. Christian Cent 82:487-90 Ap 21 '65

CHURCH and peace. See War and religion

CHURCH and politics

Another nun in the paddy wagon. America 113:151-2 Ag 14 '65

Are we serious about social action? E. R. Wilson. Christian Cent 82:169-71 F 10 '65

California churches in the aftermath of defeat; Proposition fourteen, repeal of Rumford fair housing act. P. Wogaman. Christian Cent 82:139-41 F 3 '65; Discussion. 82:435-6 Ap 7 '65

Demythologizing neoevangelicalism. Christian Cent 82:1115-16 S 15 '65

Healthy backlash in New York election. Christian Cent 82:1436 N 24 '65

Peace priests muzzled. Christian Cent 82: 1500-1 D 8 '65

Politics, Italian style. Commonweal 81:653-4 F 19 '65

Priests and politics; Kerala elections. America 112:473 Ap 10 '65

Sacred politics. C. Davis. America 112:898 Je 26 '65

Unwarranted search; Christian institute of southern Africa and police. D. M. Norman. Christian Cent 82:820-1 Je 23 '65

Vigil at the Pentagon; Interreligious committee on Vietnam pickets Pentagon. il Newsweek 65:66 My 24 '65

Why and what. Commonweal 82:483-4 Jl 9 '65

See also

Church and international relations

Church and state

CHURCH and race problems

Beauty for ashes; Committee of concern organized to rebuild Negro churches bombed and burned in Mississippi. il Time 85:61 F 5 '65

Bells in the Delta; Episcopal civil rights activists. Time 85:71 F 26 '65

Blunting the cutting edge; resolution adopted by National Baptist convention, U.S.A. inc, Tulsa. Christian Cent 82:883-4 Jl 14 '65

Catholic involvement in civil rights. J. B. Sheerin. Cath World 201:93-6 My '65

Church, a symbol of commitment. R. P. Alexander. Negro Hist Bul 28:77-8+ Ja '65

Church in Mississippi. S. Sicotte. Commonweal 82:487-8 Jl 9 '65

Clergy and nuns march; No outsiders. America 112:411 Mr 27 '65

Clergy heeds a new call. J. Cogley. il N Y Times Mag p42-3+ My 2 '65

Conflict of concerns; tensions affecting southern Presbyterians. J. H. Smylie. Christian Cent 82:1602-6 D 29 '65

Council rescinds restrictions; clergymen's participation in racial justice projects. Christian Cent 82:293 Mr 10 '65

Darkness of life; reprint. U S News 59:84 Ag 2 '65

Delta ministry. E. D. Blanchard. Christian Cent 82:337-8 Mr 17 '65

Does anyone really care? Negroes who rioted in Los Angeles. Christian Cent 82: 1148 S 22 '65

Doing is the difference; Student interracial ministry; reply. R. C. Assenheimer. America 112:560-1 Ap 17 '65

Ferment in the churches; the new Christian soldiers. H. Cox. il Nation 201:216-20 O 11 '65

Financing fair employment. Time 85:88+ My 28 '65

Flocking of good shepherds; participation in civil rights demonstrations. L. Wainwright. Life 58:23 Ap 16 '65

Freedom revolution and the churches, by R. W. Spike. Review
    Christian Cent 82:1013-14 Ag 18 '65. G. Fackre

Harlem priest reports on Selma; interview, ed. by C. L. Palms. E. T. Dugan. Cath World 201:171-6 Je '65

Hollow gestures or omens of unity? election of Negroes to highest honorary posts in white-dominated Protestant churches. Christian Cent 82:884 Jl 14 '65

How it is in Mississippi. W. Rowland. Christian Cent 82:340+ Mr 17 '65

How the civil rights struggle challenges our churches. A. Whitman. il Redbook 125:55-7+ Ag '65

In a spirit of repentance; admission of sin regarding racial issues by Southern Baptist convention. il Time 85:68 Je 11 '65

Integrating Methodism; elimination of central jurisdiction. Christian Cent 83:3-4 Ja 5 '66

Is the clergyman changing his role? D. Lawrence. U S News 58:116 Ap 19 '65

Justice, southern style; Ashton Jones vs Atlanta's First Baptist church. J. Gillies; discussion. Christian Cent 81:270-2; 82:732 F 26 '64, Je 9 '65

Lawsuit in a Richmond church; First Baptist again. S. Nichols. Christian Cent 83:24 Ja 5 '66

Mockery of tokenism; meeting of Catholic Negroes and whites in Memphis. America 112:444 Ap 3 '65

Mormon missionaries and the race question; condemned by NAACP. G. W. Davidson. Christian Cent 82:1183-6 S 29 '65; Discussion. 82:1452 N 24 '65

Nuns at Selma. Sister Thomas Marguerite. America 112:454-6 Ap 3 '65

Old wounds reopened; southern churchmen attack integration activities of the NCC. America 112:239 F 20 '65

Our churches answer the challenge of civil rights. A. Whitman. il Redbook 125:64-5+ S '65

Our churches' sin against the Negro; excerpts from Freedom revolution and the churches. R. W. Spike. il Look 29:29-31 My 18 '65

Plight of the colored clerisy; incidents at Selma, Ala. R. Kirk. Nat R 17:551 Je 29 '65

Racism and the Christian understanding of man, by G. D. Kelsey. Review
    Christian Cent 83:50 Ja 12 '66. D. Kitagawa

Reconciliation through anger; Delta ministry. il Time 86:70-1 Jl 2 '65

Selma, civil rights, and the church militant. il Newsweek 65:75-6+ Mr 29 '65

Selma spirit. il Time 85:59-60 Ap 9 '65

So much Christian unity in Selma; congregation at the memorial service for the Rev. James Reeb. M. McGrory. America 112:448 Ap 3 '65

Theology of demonstration; interrelation between freedom movement and Christianity. G. Winter. Christian Cent 82:1249-52 O 13 '65

Toward integration; Christian life commission. Time 86:68 N 26 '65

Turning point for the church; march from Selma, Ala. to Montgomery. C. S. Wren. il Look 29:32-7 My 18 '65

Wolf or shepherd? church segregation in Alabama. Newsweek 65:66-7 Ap 12 '65

See also

National Catholic conference on interracial justice

Un-Christian Christian. M. L. King, jr. il Ebony 20:76-80 Ag '65

WASP and ACE. America 113:620 N 20 '65

CHURCH and social problems

Another job for all faiths; the war on poverty calls for ecumenical action. H. Smith. America 112:542-3 Ap 17 '65

Another priest, another ban. T. Lickona. Commonweal 83:298-9 D 10 '65

Are we serious about social action? E. R. Wilson. Christian Cent 82:169-71 F 10 '65

Breakthroughs: Covenant House in Philadelphia. J. Hemenway. Christian Cent 82: 1316-19 O 27 '65

Christ the church and the poor, by P. Gauthier. Review
    America 112:434-5 Mr 27 '65. R. Armstrong

Church and marriage in Africa. K. Hughes. Christian Cent 82:204-8 F 17 '65; Reply. L. Andrews. 82:497 Ap 21 '65

Church and the reliefers; urban Negro slum-dwellers. D. G. Cater. Christian Cent 82: 232-5 F 24 '65

Church and urban renewal, by G. D. Younger. Review
    Commonweal 82:540 Jl 23 '65. R. Robbins

Church in the world. America 112:629 My 1 '65

Church, unity and community. L. M. Madigan. Cath World 202:91-5 N '65

Churches and the war on poverty. B. L. Masse. America 113:208-9+ Ag 28 '65

Citizens vs. crime. W. W. Richardson. Christian Cent 82:1456+ N 24 '65

Clergy-laity schism. L. Davis; discussion. Christian Cent 82:58-61, 372+ Ja 13, Mr 24 '65

Crisis to the south; condition of the poor in Latin America. J. O'Gara. Commonweal 81:754 Mr 12 '65

Demythologizing neoevangelicalism. Christian Cent 82:1115-16 S 15 '65

Discuss birth control; Hamilton County Cincinnati welfare workers. F. Stauffer. Christian Cent 82:693-4 My 26 '65

Essence of the ministry; teaching the Christian doctrine; address, June 6, 1965. R. W. Croskery. Vital Speeches 31:570-2 Jl 1 '65

Ferment in the churches; the new Christian soldiers. H. Cox. il Nation 201:216-20 O 11 '65

Grapes of wrath; church involvement in union recognition for grape pickers. il Time 86:96 D 10 '65

CHURCH and social problems—*Continued*
Is God changing our society? E. A. Smith. Cath World 202:74-9 N '65
Justice and beyond justice; United church's Council for Christian social action. Christian Cent 82:227-8 F 24 '65; Reply with rejoinder. R. M. Davidson. 82:436 Ap 7 '65
Ministering to Appalachia. J. Weller. Christian Cent 82:935-6 Jl 28 '65
Ministers vs. Miljay, inc. Knox County, Ill. L. M. Martin. Christian Cent 82:679-80 My 26 '65
N.C.C. agenda. K. Haselden. Christian Cent 82:766-7 Je 16 '65
News of the Christian world. See issues of Christian century
Odds for religion in Las Vegas. Christian Cent 82:422-3 Ap 7 '65
Other dialogue, by J. Gremillion. Review Cath World 201:68+ Ap '65. C. L. Palms
Plunge; Urban training center for Christian mission, Chicago. il Newsweek 65:83 F 15 '65
Poor: French vs. American viewpoint. D. O'Grady. Cath World 201:177-82 Je '65
School for a new creation; Urban training center for Christian mission. il Time 86: 124+ N 19 '65
Why so much secrecy? consultation on the role of the churches in urban organization and development. Christian Cent 82:163 F 10 '65; Discussion. 82:376-7 Mr 24 '65
World around us (cont of) News of the Christian world. Christian Cent 83:23-30. 53-4 Ja 5-12 '66
World poverty; responsibility of the church. America 112:630 My 1 '65
World poverty secretariat; proposal of Bishop Swanstrom. America 113:455 O 23 '65
See also
Birth control—Religious aspects
Christian ethics
Church and labor
Church and race problems
Church work with migrants
CHURCH and state
Another nun in the paddy wagon. America 113:151-2 Ag 14 '65
Christian motivation for political concern; address, February 23, 1965. G. W. Forell. Vital Speeches 31:368-72 Ap 1 '65
Church and state: is the wall of separation rising or falling? J. P. Williams. Sch & Soc 93:112-13 F 20 '65
Coalition of conscience & power. il Time 86: 68+ S 3 '65
Conflict without calumny; interpretation of First amendment. Christian Cent 82:933 Jl 28 '65
Federal aid and judicial review. Christian Cent 82:451-2 Ap 14 '65
H.R. 2362. Christian Cent 82:196-7 F 17 '65
Law of church and state; freedom of the mind; address, October 13, 1965. P. W. Bruton. Vital Speeches 32:149-54 D 15 '65
Murray and liberty. R. M. Healey. Christian Cent 82:1130-1 S 15 '65
Ramparts and the gate. America 113:616 N 20 '65
Religion and American constitutions, by W. G. Katz. Review Christian Cent 82:144 F 3 '65. T. G. Sanders
Religion and the Constitution, by P. G. Kauper. Review Christian Cent 82:176 F 10 '65. G. L. Archer
School aid: a threat to the parish; President's proposal for supplementary education centers. R. S. Shaper. Christian Cent 82:394-6 Mr 31 '65
See also
Concordats
Parochial schools, Catholic
Protestants and other Americans united for separation of church and state
Religious liberty
Secularization
CHURCH and state in Israel
Israel has still to find its way. M. Lazega. Cath World 202:84-90 N '65
Israeli notebook, updated. G. Kennedy. Christian Cent 82:237-8 F 24 '65
CHURCH and state in Latin America
Church and the Latin American revolution, by F. Houtart and E. Pin. Review Commonweal 82:540-2 Jl 23 '65. A. Mayhew
CHURCH and state in Switzerland
Swiss reconsider anticlerical articles; articles of exception in constitution of Switzerland. Christian Cent 83:70 Ja 19 '66
CHURCH and the press
Bishops and criticism. Commonweal 82:460-1 Jl 2 '65

Conciliar cloak and dagger; counterfeit news stories at Vatican council. America 112:627 My 1 '65
Role of the press. Commonweal 82:372-3 Je 11 '65
Separation of church and press. A. E. P. Wall. America 113:285-6 S 18 '65
Two views. S. J. Adamo. il America 114: 26-7 Ja 1 '66
CHURCH architecture
Baptist church by Weese; Columbus, Ind. il Arch Rec 138:113-17 D '65
Christ and architecture, by D. J. Bruggink and C. H. Droppers. Review Christian Cent 82:941-2 Jl 28 '65. R. M. Bennett
Cruciform window onto heaven; Kenzo Tange creates cathedral in Tokyo. R. Boyd. il Arch Forum 123:50-5 S '65
Down with the cathedral! 26th National conference on church architecture. il Newsweek 65:74 My 10 '65
Eight churches receive design awards. il Arch Rec 137:12-13 Je '65
How to build a church; outcome of Cleveland meeting. C. J. McNaspy. America 113:168-9 Ag 14 '65
Liturgy and tradition shape designs for three faiths. M. F. Schmertz. il Arch Rec 138: 133-42 N '65
Two churches that respect tradition. il Arch Rec 137:155-62 Mr '65
Unitarian church by Belluschi; May memorial Unitarian church, Syracuse, N.Y. il Arch Rec 138:118-20 D '65
Welded pipe trussed frame roofs open air tabernacle. il Arch Rec 137:224-5 Ap '65
What's a church for? C. J. McNaspy. America 112:495-6 Ap 10 '65
See also
Mosques
National conference on church architecture
Bibliography
Architecture in print. C. J. McNaspy. America 112:204-5 F 6 '65
CHURCH bells. See Bells
CHURCH colleges. See Denominational colleges
CHURCH conferences. See Religious conferences
CHURCH cooperation. See Religious cooperation
CHURCH councils. See Councils and synods
CHURCH decoration and ornament
What we can learn from English church arrangements. Mrs A. H. Smith. il Horticulture 43:20-3 Mr '65
See also
Glass painting and staining
CHURCH fairs. See Bazaars, Charitable
CHURCH finance
Price of conviction; churches' commitment to civil rights. Time 86:118 N 19 '65
CHURCH government
See also
Church unity
Episcopacy
CHURCH history
Dividing of Christendom, by C. Dawson. Review America 112:432 Mr 27 '65. C. J. McNaspy
From the apostolic community to Constantine, by K. Baus. Review America 113:296 S 18 '65. C. P. Loughran
See also
Creeds
Reformation
CHURCH in the world (conference) See Religious conferences
CHURCH law. See Ecclesiastical law
CHURCH libraries. See Libraries, Church
CHURCH membership
Looking for a church. Christian Cent 82: 886 Jl 14 '65
Membership up, attendance down. Time 87: 51 Ja 14 '66
CHURCH music
Cool creeds; liturgical jazz. il Time 86:48 Jl 9 '65
Ecumenical Ellington; concert in San Francisco's Grace cathedral. S. Dance. il Sat R 48:70-1 O 16 '65
New songs unto the Lord. N. O'Connor. Sat R 48:88-9+ Ap 10 '65
Sing unto the Lord; concerts. J. Roddy. il Hi Fi 15:117 My '65
See also
Phonograph records—Choral music
CHURCH of England
Methodism, 1784-1970; plans to heal Anglican-Methodist breach. il Newsweek 65:74 My 31 '65

CHURCH of England—*Continued*
Spirit of Anglicanism, by H. R. McAdoo. Review
  Christian Cent 82:1265 O 13 '65. C. Northcott

Book of common prayer
Changing a way of worship. il Time 86:50 D 31 '65

CHURCH of Jesus Christ of Latter-day saints. See Mormons and Mormonism

CHURCH of Scotland
Church of Scotland assembly. I. Logan. Christian Cent 82:811-12 Je 23 '65
Church of the soil? C. Northcott. Christian Cent 82:607 My 12 '65

CHURCH of the Brethren
Church of the Brethren: new involvement. I. Long. Christian Cent 82:924-6 Jl 21 '65

CHURCH of the Holy Sepulcher. See Jerusalem—Church of the Holy Sepulcher

CHURCH property

Taxation
End to tax exemption? proposed amendment to Oregon's constitution. M. A. Talney. Christian Cent 82:1297-8+ O 20 '65

CHURCH related colleges. See Denominational colleges

CHURCH-related schools. See Church schools

CHURCH schools
ACLU and civil rights for children. V. C. Blum. America 113:160-3 Ag 14 '65; Reply. J. G. Neumann and others. 113:249 S 11 '65
Take back your aid; Southern Baptist preachers' view of federal funds for Baptist schools. Newsweek 66:86 N 29 '65
Why church-related Negro colleges? Christian Cent 82:1179-80 S 29 '65
  See also
Parochial schools

CHURCH services
Agony and the wild cry; worship service, Chicago's First congregational church. Christian Cent 82:910 Jl 21 '65; Discussion. 82:1070-2, 1211-12, 1516 S 1, O 6, D 8 '65
Arney's army; Sunday services on Lake Texoma. il Newsweek 66:80 Ag 23 '65
  See also
Liturgies

CHURCH-sponsored camps. See Camps

CHURCH suppers, breakfasts, etc.
Let's talk about food: assuring safety of foods prepared for groups. P. L. White. Todays Health 43:5+ F '65

CHURCH unity
Baptist coquetry; discussion of Consultation on church union merger plans. K. Haselden. Christian Cent 82:1437-8 N 24 '65; Discussion. 83:51-2 Ja 12 '66
Breaking the habit of division; same prayers for the Week of prayer. Christian Cent 83:35 Ja 12 '66
Concord at Lexington. R. M. Brown. Commonweal 82:330-2 Je 11 '65
Concord at Lexington; Consultation on church union. J. R. Nelson. Christian Cent 82:575-6 My 5 '65
Ecumenicity of Vatican II. America 114:8 Ja 1 '66
Ecumenism and the Ephesians; discussion groups in Princeton. M. Wade. America 112:753 My 22 '65
Ecumenism down the Street. America 113:563 N 13 '65
Freedom beyond polity; is episcopacy the answer? R. J. Cebik. Christian Cent 82:1379-82 N 10 '65
Holy Cross, holy dream; question of merging Holy Cross Lutheran church and St Margaret's Episcopal church in Newport, Wash. il Time 86:50 D 31 '65
Join, consolidate, or drift? Time 86:42 Ag 13 '65
Less ecumenism, please. Time 85:74 Mr 12 '65
Neighborhood ecumenism; Interchurch council of Holbrook, Mass. America 112:796 My 29 '65
On primacy: thinking the unthinkable. M. E. Marty. Cath World 202:26-31 O '65
Presbyterians on unity. America 112:846 Je 12 '65
Public aye, private fear; fourth annual Consultation on church union. Time 85:76 Ap 23 '65
Things that make for unity; reprint. I. T. Hecker. Cath World 201:53-9 Ap '65
Town with too many churches; Schellsburg, Pa. votes for United church. N. M. Lobsenz. il Redbook 126:70-1+ N '65
Turning in the never buttons. Time 86:68 Jl 2 '65

Union without renewal? critique of the Methodist-E.U.B. negotiations. J. E. Will. Christian Cent 82:588+ My 5 '65; Discussion. 82:809-11, 815 Je 23 '65
Unity in freedom: reflections on the human family, by A. C. Bea. Review
  Sat R 48:40 F 6 '65
Walking the road together; excerpt from address, April 21, 1965. J. J. Krol. Cath World 201:329-30 Ag '65
Workshop on Christian unity; report of 2d annual meeting. E. C. Bianchi. America 113:95-6 Jl 24 '65
  See also
Ecumenical movement

Canada
Canadian churches engaged to be engaged; Anglican church of Canada and the United church of Canada. Christian Cent 82:860 Jl 7 '65
Church union in Canada. America 113:254 S 11 '65
More church union in Canada? J. R. Mutchmor. Christian Cent 82:1090-3 S 8 '65

Great Britain
Anglicans and Methodists move toward union. Christian Cent 82:765 Je 16 '65
Gambling on God; Anglican-Methodist merger. C. Northcott. Christian Cent 82:765-6 Je 16 '65

Nigeria
Hands down in Nigeria. C. Northcott. Christian Cent 82:1438 N 24 '65

CHURCH vestments
Pope and pomp. Commonweal 82:713 O 1 '65

CHURCH work with migrants
Poverty spurs ecumenism; Michigan council of churches and the Michigan Catholic conference cooperate. America 112:475 Ap 10 '65

CHURCH world service
New division meets. W. A. Geier. Christian Cent 82:1360 N 3 '65
Promoting family planning; CWS planned parenthood. Christian Cent 82:980 Ag 11 '65

CHURCHES

Acoustics
See Acoustics, Architectural

Membership
See Church membership

England
Faith that moved a church; Church of St Mark, Biggin Hill, Kent. G. Kent. Read Digest 86:61-5 Ap '65

United States
Church in the Wildwood; Mt Zion Baptist church, Montgomery County, Md. C. West. il Am For 71:8-9 Je '65
New Mexico's missions; Spanish mission churches. W. F. Heald. il Travel 123:36-41 F '65

CHURCHES, Remodeled. See Remodeling (architecture)

CHURCHILL, Clementine Ogilvy (Hozier) Spencer, lady
Lion's heart. D. Cooper. il pors Atlan 215:59-62 Mr '65

CHURCHILL, Edward George Spencer-. See Spencer-Churchill, E. G.

CHURCHILL, Sir Winston Leonard Spencer
Churchill on America: a legacy in words; quotations. por U S News 58:38-9 F 8 '65; Same abr. with title Churchill legacy in words. Read Digest 86:214B-214C My '65
Churchill on America; quotations. il U S News 58:38-9 F 8 '65

about
All in one life's span. il pors U S News 58:46-8 F 1 '65
As he lay dying; defeat of Labor party in Leyton by-election. Nat R 17:89 F 9 '65
Be ye men of valour. H. La Fay. il pors Nat Geog Mag 128:158-95 Ag '65
Churchill: a profile in greatness. C. Brogan. il por Nat R 17:99-100+ F 9 '65
Churchill as historian. H. L. Hurwitz. il por Sr Schol 86:1T F 11 '65
Churchill as prophet. A. Boyle. Commonweal 81:658-9 F 19 '65
Churchill as Whig. J. M. Cameron. Commonweal 81:659-60 F 19 '65
Churchill by Churchill, and Murrow. por Am Rec G 31:671 Mr '65
Churchill: his greatest utterances. H. Kupferberg. il por Atlan 215:184-6 Mr '65
Churchill I knew. D. D. Eisenhower. il pors Nat Geog Mag 128:153-7 Ag '65

CHURCHILL, Sir Winston Leonard Spencer—
about—Continued
Churchill in the balance. W. F. Buckley, jr. Nat R 17:147 F 23 '65
Churchill: newly discovered set of camera close-ups. il pors Look 29:94-6+ F 23 '65
Churchill records. P. J. Smith. por Hi Fi 15:71-2 Ap '65
Churchill: unrivaled statesman. Christian Cent 82:133 F 3 '65
Churchill's interest in animal life. L. H. Newman. il Audubon Mag 67:240-3 Jl '65
Death and the hero. M. Ascoli. Reporter 32:20 F 11 '65
Grist to the historian's mill. S. Leslie. il por Nat R 17:603-5 Jl 13 '65
Letter from London. M. Panter-Downes. New Yorker 40:106+ Ja 30; 41:116 F 20 '65
Letter from Paris. Genêt. New Yorker 40:112 F 6 '65
Literary Churchill. J. H. Plumb. por Sat R 48:17-20+ F 6 '65
Man for all times; with excerpts from tributes from leaders around the globe. por Sr Schol 86:17-18 F 4 '65
Notes and comment. New Yorker 40:21 Ja 30 '65
Obituary
    Pub W 187:61-2 F 1 '65
Personal memoir of Churchill. S. Leslie. por Nat R 17:288+ Ap 6 '65
Sir Winston Churchill, 1874-1965; symposium. il pors Atlan 215:49-101 Mr '65
Sir Winston Churchill; excerpts from a tribute. A. L. Rowse. il por Vogue 145:120-1 Mr 1 '65
Sir Winston Churchill: tributes in the United Nations. il por UN Mo Chron 2:16-21 F '65
U.S. leaders express sorrow at death of Winston Churchill; executive order with statements. L. B. Johnson. Dept State Bul 52:206 F 15 '65
Vision of invincibility. Nation 200:125 F 8 '65
Wavell: scholar and soldier, by J. Connell. Review
    Reporter 33:43-5 S 9 '65. G. A. Craig
When Churchill brought butterflies to Chartwell. L. H. Newman. il pors Audubon Mag 67:154-8 My '65
Winston Churchill: a footnote. S. Alsop. por Sat Eve Post 238:20 F 27 '65
Winston Churchill and the human potential. N. Cousins. Sat R 48:18 F 6 '65
Winston Churchill, by V. B. Carter. Review
    Commonweal 82:639-40 S 3 '65. A. Fremantle
    Sat R il por 48:33 My 29 '65. J. H. Plumb
Winston Churchill; letter. R. Sencourt. Commonweal 81:750-1 Mr 12 '65
Winston Churchill; reply. C. Oglesby. New Repub 152:29 F 13 '65
Winston Churchill: the sound of a man's voice. E. J. Hughes. Newsweek 65:14-15 F 8 '65
W. S. C. S. Potter. il pors Am Rec G 31:600-3+ Mr '65

Caricatures and cartoons
Cartoons by Low. D. Low. Atlan 215:85 Mr '65

Funeral rites and ceremonies
Final tribute. C. B. Patterson. il por Nat Geog Mag 128:199-225 Ag '65
Last honors; with reports by A. Moorehead and L. Hall. il pors Life 58:26-36B+ F 5 '65
Last post for an old warrior. il Newsweek 65:17-22 F 8 '65
Letter from London. M. Panter-Downes. New Yorker 40:122-6 F 6 '65
Requiem for greatness. il por Time 85:26-33B F 5 '65
World pays its last respects to Churchill. il Sr Schol 86:19 F 11 '65

Statues, portraits, etc.
Sir Winston Churchill, 1874-1965. Atlan 215:65-8 Mr '65

CHURCHILL-Stalin-Truman conference. See Berlin conference, 1945

CHURRUCA, Francisco
Jai alai: fury at the fronton. J. Olsen. il pors Sports Illus 22:68-70+ Mr 29 '65

CHUTNEYS. See Pickles and relishes

CHUVALO, George
Croatian candidate. G. Rogin. il pors Sports Illus 22:54-60 F 1 '65
Okay, but don't bring on Clay. T. Maule. il por Sports Illus 22:18-19 F 8 '65

CIARDI, John
Alphabestiary. Sat R 48:15 Jl 3; 26 Jl 10; 26 Jl 17; 16 Jl 24; 11 Jl 31 '65
Damnation of pigeons; poem. Sat R 48:30 O 16 '65

[Dante's Paradiso: canto five; translation] Poetry 107:75-84 N '65

Magus; poem. Sat R 48:26 D 25 '65
Manner of speaking. See issues of Saturday review
Natural propositions; poem. Sat R 48:31 F 13 '65
Relevance of Dante. Sat R 48:16-18+ My 15; 51-3 My 22 '65
    about
More comic spirit. E. Sandeen. Poetry 106:231-3 Je '65

CICIONI, Mirna
Year of seven new words. pors Seventeen 24:126-7+ O '65

CIGAR humidors. See Humidors

CIGAR industry

Wages and hours
Cigar manufacturing earnings in April-May 1964. J. C. Bush. il Mo Labor R 88:312-14 Mr '65

CIGARETTE labels. See Labels

CIGARETTES
Beauty checkout: giving up smoking. Vogue 145:58+ Mr 1 '65
Caution: cigarette smoking may be hazardous to your health; warning to be on every cigarette pack and carton. Consumer Rep 30:488-91 O '65
Cigarette warning: too late and too little. Christian Cent 82:1118 S 15 '65
Cigarettes and atherosclerosis. Sci Am 213:40 D '65
Has the smoking scare ended? il U S News 59:132 O 18 '65
How to stop smoking without really quitting. il Sci Digest 57:32-3 F '65
Man who couldn't stop; case of Dr Louis F. Fieser. Newsweek 66:94 N 22 '65
Polonium-210 content of mainstream cigarette smoke. T. F. Kelley. bibliog il Science 149:537-8 Jl 30 '65
Quiet victory of the cigarette lobby. E. B. Drew. Atlan 216:76-80 S '65
Six quitters, six smokers; symposium. Esquire 63:68-9 My '65
Smouldering issue. il Sr Schol 86:20 F 11 '65
Tobacco: Congress moves closer to requiring warning of danger included on cigarette packages. D. S. Greenberg. Science 148:478-9 Ap 23 '65
What government plans on cigarette warnings; Smoking on the rise again. U S News 58:14 Ap 12 '65
Where there's smoke; TV commercial hooks actor. R. L. Shayon. Sat R 48:51 S 25 '65
Will new tobacco blends make cigarettes safer? Pop Sci 187:20+ Jl '65
    See also
Smoking

Advertising
Bad joke. Nation 200:267 Mr 15 '65
Britain's TV ban; blackout on TV commercials for cigarettes. Newsweek 65:88 F 22 '65
British ban TV cigarette ads. Bsns W p 100 F 13 '65
Cigarette ads. New Repub 152:7 My 22 '65
Cigarette label battle. C. A. Betts. Sci N L 87:223 Ap 3 '65
Deadlock looms ahead on tobacco control; health warning labels on cigarette packages. Sci N L 88:25 Jl 19 '65
Smokeless screen; British government bans cigarette advertising. Time 85:94+ F 19 '65
Toadying to tobacco. New Repub 152:7 Ap 10 '65

Anecdotes, facetiae, satire, etc.
They won't let me stop smoking. R. Armour. il Read Digest 86:83-5 My '65

Statistics
New brands, tastes spur cigarette sales; with tables. il Bsns W p64-6+ D 11 '65

CIGARS
Millions of people just won't smoke cigars. T. Alexander. il Fortune 72:164-7+ S '65

CIGUATERA fish poison. See Fish poisons

CILIA and ciliary motion
Annelid ciliary photoreceptors. P. A. Lawrence and F. B. Krasne. bibliog il Science 148:965-6 My 14 '65
Dynein: a protein with adenosine triphosphatase activity from cilia. I. R. Gibbons and A. J. Rowe. bibliog il Science 149:424-6 Jl 23 '65
Respiratory cilia; report on symposium. K. H. Kilburn and J. V. Salvano. Science 148:1618-19 Je 18 '65; Reply with rejoinder. L. C. Cole. 149:1176 S 10 '65

CILIATA
Blepharisma intermedium: ultraviolet resistance of pigmented and albino clones. A. C. Giese. bibliog il Science 149:540-1 Jl 30 '65

CINCINNATI

Music

Sense of tradition; May festival. R. C. Marsh. Hi Fi 15:128+ Ag '65

Newspapers

See also
Cincinnati enquirer

Parks and playgrounds

Pixies in Eden park; reprint. D. Battin. il Recreation 58:475-6 D '65
Shopping for recreation; suburban shopping plaza transforms ravine into usable playspace. il Recreation 58:402 O '65

Streets

Galvanizing guards a people barrier. F. V. Cornelius. il Am City 80:22 N '65

CINCINNATI enquirer
March of the proudfoot; efficiency study. il Newsweek 65:54+ F 22 '65

CINCINNATI Reds (baseball) See Baseball clubs

CINCINNATI summer opera association
Destiny in Cincinnati. H. S. Humphreys. il Opera N 30:25 S 25 '65

CINCINNATI. University

Libraries

Visiting bookmen in France. A. T. Hamlin. ALA Bul 59:815-18 O '65

CINDERELLA; opera. See Rossini, G.

CINNAMON rolls. See Bread

CINTAS, Oscar B.
Unknown treasure: Cintas collection; with editorial comment. L. Lastra. il por Américas 17:18-26 F '65

CIOPPINO. See Stew

CIPHER and telegraph codes
From CQ to Mayday. H. M. Anthony. Motor B 115:140+ My '65

CIRCADIAN rhythm. See Periodicity

CIRCUIT breakers. See Electric circuit breakers

CIRCULAR saws. See Saws

CIRCUS
Circus! B. Ballantine. il Sat Eve Post 238:30-7 Ap 10 '65
Florida's three-ring city; Ringling memorabilia remains in Sarasota. H. Sutton. il Sat R 48:64+ O 16 '65
It's Wenatchee's sprightly Youth circus. il Sunset 134:112-13 Je '65
Resurgence: Ringling brothers, Barnum and Bailey circus in New York. New Yorker 41:38-9 Ap 10 '65
Unhappiest circus; Hubert de Malafosse's circus stranded in Lebanon. L. Griggs. il Life 58:83 Ap 23 '65

CIRCUS equipment
Historic bandwagons. il Design 66:28-31 Mr '65

CIRCUS in art
Circus comes to town. F. M. Kelly. il Sch Arts 65:34 S '65

CIRCUS magic; drama. See Vahl, R.

CIRCUS performers
See also
Clowns

CISMARU, Alfred
We beat the educationists. Nat R 17:413-14 My 18 '65

CISNEROS, Alberto López. See López Cisneros, A.

CISSELL, Helen. See Cissell, R. jt. auth.

CISSELL, Robert, and Cissell, Helen
Automation and jobs. America 112:459-61 Ap 3 '65

CISTERNS
Need water? build a cistern. C. F. Marley. il Suc Farm 63:73 N '65

CITADEL record club. See Phonograph record clubs

CITATIONS, Bibliographic. See Bibliographies

CITGO. See Cities service oil company

CITHERONIINAE. See Imperial moths

CITIES, Imaginary. See Geographical myths

CITIES and towns
See also
City and country
Education, Urban
New towns
Playgrounds
Slums
Sociology, Urban
Street lighting
Urbanization
also headings beginning City, Community, Municipal, Street

Decoration
See Christmas decorations, Outdoor

Federal aid
See Federal and municipal relations

Growth

City as environment. K. Lynch. il Sci Am 213:209-14+ bibliog(p280) S '65
Everybody's going to town. J. Peter. il Look 29:31-3 S 21 '65
Fastest-growing metropolitan area. Am City 80:172+ Mr '65
What's to come. W. R. Young. il Life 59:143+ D 24 '65
See also
Metropolitan areas

History

Origin and evolution of cities. G. Sjoberg. il Sci Am 213:54-63 S '65

Industries

Industry wasn't interested; Brunswick, Ohio. K. Hotz. il Am City 80:32 O '65

Names
See Names, Geographical

Religious life
See City churches

Transportation
See Rapid transit

Water supply
See Water supply

Zone system
See Zoning

Canada
See also
Windsor, Ontario

Far East
Cities of the Orient. Am City 80:44+ Je '65

Latin America
See also
Urbanization—Latin America

United States

American city: crisis or renaissance? il Sr Schol 86:6-9 Ap 29 '65
Cities in U.S. where business is best; with charts (cont) U S News 58:82-5 Je 7; 59:74-8+ N 29 '65
Crisis of the cities. W. V. Shannon. Commonweal 83:264-5 D 3 '65
Danger facing big cities; equal rights not complete answer to Negro problems. il U S News 59:29-33 S 6 '65
Future of the American city. J. V. Lindsay. Sat R 49:70 Ja 8 '66
Making American cities more livable; symposium, with introd. by F. B. Wilde. il Sat R 49:37-41+ Ja 8 '66
Notes for a gazetteer. P. Hamburger. See occasional issues of New Yorker to September 18, 1965
Our sick cities; symposium. il Look 29:27-38+ S 21 '65
Pleasant places to live in the U.S; where they are. il U S News 58:50-5+ Mr 29 '65
Problems are not all solved; new tools to refashion our cities. Am City 80:6 N '65
Problems the cities face: what U.S. mayors say. il U S News 58:88 Je 14 '65
Spending and saving in urban and rural areas. K. R. Murphy. il Mo Labor R 88:1169-76 O '65
Spot check on police brutality in the cities. il U S News 59:40 S 6 '65
U.S. city. il Life 59:5-7+ D 24 '65
Urban 1966?!! Am City 81:6 Ja '66
What cities are doing to people. il U S News 59:54-7 S 20 '65
See also
All-America cities
Metropolitan areas
United States—Housing and urban development, Department of

History

Great days of build and rebuild. il Life 59:50-62 D 24 '65

CITIES and towns. Ancient
See also
Mohenjo-Daro

CITIES and towns, Movement to. See Cities and towns—Growth

CITIES and towns, Ruined, extinct, etc.
See also
Pella, Greece (ancient city)

CITIES service company
Cities service hangs new shingle; new brand name Citgo. il Bsns W p72+ My 8 '65
On top again. Time 86:74+ Jl 2 '65
What's in a name? brand name changed to Citgo. Newswook 65:89 My 10 '65

CITIZENS and Southern national of Atlanta. See Atlanta—Banks

CITIZENS band radio. See Citizens radio service

CITIZENS for decent literature and motion pictures, incorporated
Anti-pornographers plan court appearances. Pub W 188:35-6 N 8 '65
Censorship: fanatics and fallacies. N. Mark. il Nation 201:5-7 Jl 5 '65
Smut hunters; new jurisprudery. H. Junker. il Nation 201:358-60 N 15 '65

CITIZENS radio service
Annual report on CB equipment. J. D. Gillespie. il Pop Electr 23:67-75+ Ag '65
Getting the most out of CB radio. R. M. Benrey. il Pop Sci 186:162-5+ Je '65
H.E.L.P. CB radio to rescue stranded motorists. il Pop Electr 22:64 Mr '65
New citizens band circuits (cont) L. Buckwalter. il Electr World 73:48-9 Mr; 48-50 My; 74:65-7 S; 60-1 N '65
New CB rules effective April 26, 1965. Pop Electr 22:86 My '65
New CB rules; HELP. W. A. Stocklin. Electr World 73:8 My '65
On the citizens band. M. P. Spinello. See issues of Popular electronics

CITIZENSHIP
Bureaucrats and citizens. D. E. Ashford. bibliog f Ann Am Acad 358:89-100 Mr '65
Lady in the dark; investigation of citizenship of R. Eitani. Time 85:65 F 12 '65
National citizenship test; excerpt from CBS TV presentation. il PTA Mag 60:17-21 Ja '66
Parties and the masses. K. H. Silvert. bibliog f Ann Am Acad 358:101-8 Mr '65
Who's giving up citizenship; and why, American citizenship. il U S News 59:12 Jl 5 '65
See also
Patriotism
Social ethics

CITIZENSHIP, Education for
Are we preparing our children for world citizenship? J. M. Spiegelman. il Parents Mag 40:42 S '65
Education and political enlightenment in America. E. Litt. bibliog f Ann Am Acad 361:32-9 S '65
Education for responsible citizenship; adaptation of address. S. K. Bailey. NEA J 54:16-18 My '65
Good citizenship must begin in childhood. H. I. Willett. Parents Mag 40:40 Je '65
National citizenship test. P. Dilts. il Sr Schol 87:29 N 4 '65
See also
Boys brotherhood republic of New York, incorporated
Education and democracy
Patriotism—Study and teaching

CITRUS fruit industry
Orange men get caught in squeeze; Florida's citrus problem. il Bsns W p 156+ D 4 '65

CITRUS fruits
When should you harvest citrus? Sunset 135:186 D '65

CITY and country
Choice forced upon us. il Life 58:54-63 F 5 '65
Urban concentration, agriculture, and agrarian reform; with questions and answers. G. J. Eder. bibliog f Ann Am Acad 360:27-47 Jl '65
We like the suburbs but. E. Simonds. il Parents Mag 40:54-5+ D '65

CITY and town life
Our right to privacy. M. Mead. Redbook 124:15-16 Ap '65
Small towns; a new role for old communities? M. Mead. Redbook 125:20+ S '65
U.S. city. il Life 59:5-7+ D 24 '65
Waiting for reality, birth of the megalopolis. S. Greer. Nation 201:98-102 S 20 '65
We like the suburbs but. E. Simonds. il Parents Mag 40:54-5+ D '65
What cities are doing to people. il U S News 59:54-7 S 20 '65
See also
City and country

CITY center of music and drama. See New York city center of music and drama

CITY churches
Life together in the city; address, February 1965. J. J. Harmon. il Cath World 201:322-8 Ag '65
Planning for Protestantism in urban America, by L. E. Schaller. Review
Christian Cent 82:711 Je 2 '65. W. Kloetzli

CITY college of New York. See New York (city) City university of New York—City college

CITY colleges. See Colleges and universities, Municipal

CITY councils. See Municipal government

CITY gardens
City gardens. P. Truex. il Horticulture 43:26-7+ My '65

CITY government. See Municipal government

CITY growth. See Cities and towns—Growth

CITY halls
City hall built from winning design; Eugene, Ore. il Arch Rec 137:170-1 My '65
City hall should be a show place; Paducah, Ky. T. Wilson. il Am City 80:106-7 My '65
Civic center leads downtown renewal; Redondo Beach, Calif. il Arch Rec 137:172-3 My '65
Singular symbol for Toronto. il Arch Forum 123:15-21 N '65
Spanish modern city hall; Fullerton, Calif. T. W. Oglesby. il Am City 80:84-5 F '65
Symbol for a city; new city hall, Toronto. il Time 86:98 S 17 '65
Toronto city hall: continuing controversy. il Arch Rec 138:165-72 N '65
Working city hall; Albuquerque, N.M. il Am City 80:206+ Mr '65

CITY improvement. See Municipal improvement

CITY life. See City and town life

CITY manager plan
Who likes council-manager government? Am City 80:7 Mr '65

CITY managers
Recent city manager appointments. See issues of American city

CITY noise. See Noise

CITY planning
America down the drain? with statement by Secretary Udall. R. H. Boyle. il Read Digest 86:235-6+ Ap '65
Case for building 350 new towns. W. Von Eckardt. il Harper 231:85-8+ D '65
Cities and people; Cities of the New World conference, symposium, ed. by M. S. Haverstock. il Américas 17:20-5 Ag '65
Future of the American city. J. V. Lindsay. Sat R 49:70 Ja 8 '66
Harvard holds ninth urban design conference. M. F. Schmertz. il Arch Rec 137:23+ Je '65
Housing progress: four steps forward; how many back? il Arch Forum 123:70-89 Jl '65
Long look at city planning. D. F. Parker. il Am City 80:90-2+ Jl '65
Making American cities more livable; symposium, with introd. by F. B. Wilde. il Sat R 49:37-41+ Ja 8 '64
Need for suburban planning. M. Polner. America 112:188-90 F 6 '65
Nine tough pros sound off. il Life 59:137-41 D 24 '65
Open-space planning process; excerpt from address, 1964. A. A. Davis. il Recreation 58:400-2 O '65
Opinion, please from New York. R. Marker. il Mlle 61:38+ Je '65
People like cul-de-sacs; Naperville, Ill. D. Wiegand. il Am City 80:108 Mr '65
Redesigning the twentieth century; with editorial comment. il Esquire 64:8, 214-15 D '65
Ubiquitous auto: man's servant or master? il Sr Schol 86:6-9 F 4 '65
Uses of land in cities. C. Abrams. il Sci Am 213:150-6+ bibliog(p277) S '65
See also
Business districts
Cities and towns
Regional planning
Urban renewal
also subhead City planning under names of cities, e.g. London—City planning

Zone system
See Zoning

CITY products corporation
Taking a front seat in furniture. il Bsns W p50+ Ag 14 '65

CITY school systems. See Public schools

CITY traffic. See Street traffic

CITY transit. See Rapid transit

CITY trees. See Trees in cities

CITY university of New York. See New York (city) City university of New York

CIUDAD GUAYANA
Ciudad Guayana: a new city. L. Rodwin. il Sci Am 213:122-30+ S '65

CIVIC buildings. See Municipal buildings

CIVIL aeronautics board. See United States—Civil aeronautics board

CIVIL air patrol. See United States—Civil air patrol

CIVIL air patrol cadets. See United States—Civil air patrol

CIVIL aviation. See Aeronautics, Commercial

CIVIL defense
No time for civilians. W. J. Coughlin. Miss & Roc 17:46 Ag 9 '65
Scientists and civil defense: dialogue at Berkeley. J. Walsh. Science 151:53-7 Ja 7 '66
What happened to civil defense? E. B. Drew. il Reporter 32:37-40 Ap 8 '65
See also
Atomic bomb shelters

Economic aspects
Expense of civil defense. C. A. Betts. Sci N L 88:282-3 O 30 '65

CIVIL disobedience. See Passive resistance to government

CIVIL liberties union, American. See American civil liberties union

CIVIL liberty. See Liberty

CIVIL procedure
See also
Jury

CIVIL rights
Fluoride and civil liberty. J. Lear; discussion. Sat R 48:55-6 Ap 3 '65
International concern for social justice and human rights; statement, July 26, 1965. F. H. Williams. Dept State Bul 53:532-6 S 27 '65
Let habeas corpus be worldwide: World peace through law conference agenda. Life 59:4 S 3 '65
Songs of freedom; with photographs by A. Kane. C. S. Wren. Look 29:83-9 N 16 '65
See also
American civil liberties union
Catholic council on civil liberties
Inter-American commission on human rights
Negroes in the United States—Civil rights
Privacy
United Nations—Commission on human rights
United States—Commission on civil rights
Woman—Equal rights

Israel
Israel has still to find its way. M. Lazega. Cath World 202:84-90 N '65

United States
After Hayneville; exclusion of Negroes from jury box. Reporter 33:16+ O 21 '65
Civil equity; wrongs to be righted; address, November 17, 1965. W. W. Wirtz. Vital Speeches 32:135-8 D 15 '65
Enforcing civil-rights laws: a prohibition-size job? il U S News 59:55-7 D 6 '65
Greatest good for all; not the greater good for the greater number. Christian Cent 82:827-8 Je 30 '65
Human-rights committee in action; Modesto, Calif. J. C. Keefe. il Am City 80:116-18 O '65
I want my rights. R. O. Johann. America 112:805 My 29 '65
Is this the land of the free? D. Lawrence. U S News 59:108 Jl 12 '65
NEA's civil rights school project. Sch & Soc 93:239 Ap 17 '65
Professional radical moves in on Rochester; conversations with S. Alinsky, ed. by M. K. Sanders. il Harper 231:52-9 Jl '65; Discussion. 231:6 S '65
See also
United States—Constitution—Bill of rights

Civil rights bill, 1963-1964
See also
Civil rights act of 1964

CIVIL rights act of 1964
After freedom; conditions a year after passage of law. New Repub 153:5-6 Jl 10 '65
Highlights of Title VII. B. L. Masse. America 113:23 Jl 3 '65
Integrate or get nothing; how big is the crackdown? il U S News 58:41-4 My 3 '65
Learning on HEW; power politics force reversal of governments attempt to use Title VI. il Newsweek 66:98 O 18 '65
Now: new rights for workers, new rules for employers; questions and answers. il U S News 58:69-70 Je 28 '65

Prospects for equal employment: conflicting portents. R. Marshall. il Mo Labor R 88:650-3 Je '65
Red-tape gambit; problem of how to enforce Title VI. R. Stolley. Life 59:40D Jl 2 '65
Sex & VII; Equal employment opportunity section. Time 86:62 Jl 9 '65
South weighs the cost of defiance on schools; if racial discrimination is permitted, federal aid withheld. Bsns W p29-30 My 8 '65
Spirit of civil rights. America 113:110 Jl 31 '65
Strong arm of the law. Nat R 17:230 Mr 23 '65
Title VI: southern education faces the facts; guidelines to school authorities. G. W. Foster, jr. il Sat R 48:60-1+ Mr 20 '65
Title VI: universities, others affected by federal moves to end discrimination by aid recipients. E. Langer. Science 147:488-9 Ja 29 '65; Reply. M. D. Garrick. 148:22 Ap 2 '65
Title VII stumbles over sex. America 113:231 S 4 '65
Unexpected dividend for the South. P. M. Stern. Harper 230:66-72 My '65
Unfinished business of Negro jobs; Title VII of Civil rights act. il Bsns W p82-4+ Je 12 '65
U.S. government policies on desegregation of elementary and secondary schools. Sch & Soc 93:377-80+ O 16 '65
Where civil rights law is going wrong. Nations Bsns 53:60-2+ N '65

CIVIL rights demonstrations
American tragedy; state troopers charge marching Negroes at Selma, Ala. il Newsweek 65:18-21 Mr 22 '65
Another march to the monuments; March on Washington slated for November 27, 1965. L. Lorrinson. America 113:493 O 30 '65
Behind the Selma march. M. L. King, jr. il Sat R 48:16-17+ Ap 3 '65
Beyond the bridge; race relations in Selma, Ala. P. Good. il Reporter 32:23-6 Ap 8 '65
Boomerang in Neverland; Selma, Ala. il Sr Schol 86:17-19 Mr 25 '65
By the book; police role in racial conflicts. Newsweek 65:34+ Mr 1 '65
Caught in the civil rights crossfire; Crown Zellerbach target of CORE demonstrations. il Bsns W p 102-4+ Ag 7 '65
Central point; Negro struggle to achieve the right to vote. il Time 85:23-8 Mr 19 '65
Changing character of Negro protest. J. H. Laue. bibliog f Ann Am Acad 357:119-26 Ja '65
Children in the line of march. K. D. Fishman. il N Y Times Mag p92+ N 7 '65
Clergy and nuns march; No outsiders. America 112:411 Mr 27 '65
Clergy heeds a new call. J. Cogley. il N Y Times Mag p42-3+ My 2 '65
Dangers of mass disobedience. C. E. Whittaker. Read Digest 87:121-4 D '65
Doctor King's policy: invitation to racial violence? excerpts from address, September 21, 1965. J. S. Kemper. U S News 59:22 O 4 '65
Electric charges; march from Selma, Ala. to Montgomery. il Time 85:19-20 Mr 26 '65
Ethics of Selma. M. L. Stackhouse. Commonweal 82:75-7 Ap 9 '65
Fallacy of civil disobedience. D. Lawrence. Read Digest 87:111-12 O '65
50,000 march on Montgomery. S. Booker. il Ebony 20:46-8+ My '65
Free men, by J. Ehle. Review
  Sat R 48:38 My 1 '65. W. Spearman
Freedom march ends in a murder; Selma to Montgomery march. il Life 58:45 Ap 2 '65
High price of civil rights protest. R. Goldfarb. New Repub 153:11-12 O 16 '65
Home to roost; violence between white and black in America. Commonweal 81:752 Mr 12 '65
Hot & dry; protests in Chicago. il Time 85:26 Je 18 '65
How the army got set to move into Selma; What really happened on Alabama march? excerpts from statement to Congress, April 27, 1965. W. L. Dickinson. il U S News 58:16-17 My 10 '65
Impact and anger; events in Selma lead to nation-wide protests. il Newsweek 65:21-2 Mr 22 '65
Instruments of freedom; discussion of methods of civil rights movement. G. Winter; A. I. Waskow; A. T. Davies. Christian Cent 82:1249-58 O 13 '65
It looks like a hot summer; with Selma the beginning. il U S News 58:32-3 Mr 22 '65
Journey of conscience: midnight plane to Alabama. G. B. Leonard. il Nation 200:502-5 My 10 '65

CIVIL service pensions
Early civil service retirement. Mo Labor R 88:III-IV Ja '65
Exodus of federal employees. America 114: 62 Ja 15 '66
Eye on the states; public pension funds move into stocks. il Fortune 71:87+ F '65
People's spoilsport. Fortune 72:114 O '65
CIVIL war (United States) See United States—History—Civil war
CIVIL war centennial. See United States—History—Civil war—Centennial, 1961-1965
CIVILIAN defense. See Civil defense
CIVILIAN-military relations. See United States—Armed forces—Relations with civilians
CIVILIAN morale. See Morale, National
CIVILIZATION
Civilization in 2100 A.D. P. McBroom. il(p289) Sci N L 88:298-9 N 6 '65
Problem of international co-operation in the contemporary world; address. A. K. Brohi. UN Mo Chron 2:71-88 Mr '65
Subversive West. T. H. Von Laue. Bul Atomic Sci 21:25-8 My '65
Toward an intellectual community; tr. by J. Dekker. D. Ćosić. Bul Atomic Sci 21:2-6 Je '65
    See also
Art
Culture
Inventions
Progress
Religions
Renaissance
Social change
Technology and civilization
United States—Civilization

    Philosophy
Idea of progress: a critical reassessment; adaptation of paper, September 1964. G. G. Iggers. bibliog f Am Hist R 71:1-17 O '65

    Preservation of records
American city magazine article in 5,000-year time capsule; New York world's fair. il Am City 80:123 F '65
Notes and comment: burial of second Westinghouse time capsule. il New Yorker 41:47 O 30 '65
Time capsule II deposited for 5,000 years at fair. il Sci N L 88:260 O 23 '65

CIVILIZATION, Ancient

    Bibliography
Books in review; a gallery of antiquity. H. Bober. Natur Hist 74:6+ Mr '65
CIVILIZATION, Greek
Greeks and the Hebrews. C. H. Gordon. il Sci Am 212:102-6+ bibliog(p 136) F '65
CIVILIZATION, Minoan
    See also
Crete—Antiquities
CIVILIZATION, Modern. See Civilization
CIVILIZATION, Semitic
Greeks and the Hebrews. C. H. Gordon. il Sci Am 212:102-6+ bibliog(p 136) F '65
CIVILIZATION and science. See Science and civilization
CIVILIZATION and technology. See Technology and civilization
CLAD metals. See Metals, Clad
CLADOCERAN
Diapause induction in daphnia requires two stimuli. R. G. Stross and J. C. Hill. bibliog il Science 150:1462-4 D 10 '65
CLAGGETT, Mary Frances
Janus in the classroom. Sat R 48:70+ D 18 '65
CLAGHORN, James L. and others
Spontaneous opiate addiction in rhesus monkeys. bibliog Science 149:440-1 Jl 23 '65
CLAIBORNE, Craig
Food. See issues of New York times magazine
    about
Dishing it up in the Times. il por Time 86:57 O 29 '65
CLAIMS
U.S. and Canada sign agreement on claims relating to Gut Dam; Department statement, March 25, 1965, with text of agreement. Dept State Bul 52:643-6 Ap 26 '65
    See also
Restitution claims
CLAIROL, Incorporated
Clairol puts on a new face; expanding into full cosmetic line. il Bsns W p 124-6+ Je 12 '65
CLAIRVOYANCE
    See also
Extrasensory perception
CLAMPITT, Amy
Books. See issues of Audubon magazine

CLAMPS
Make your own hand-screws. E. P. Kushner, sr. il Pop Mech 124:194-5 N '65
CLAMPS, Camera. See Photography—Apparatus and supplies
CLAMS
Dirty-clam caper: Great Narragansett Bay quahog war. J. Skow. il Sat Eve Post 238: 44+ F 27 '65
Growth rate of giant clam tridacna gigas at Bikini atoll as revealed by radioautography. K. Bonham. bibliog il Science 149:300-2 Jl 16 '65
    See also
Cookery—Fish
CLANCY, Roger M.
What is a cutter? Motor B 115:182-3+ My '65
What is this thing called seamanship? Motor B 116:24-6+ D '65
CLAPP, Edwin R.
Why the devil don't you teach freshmen to write? Sat R 48:63-5+ F 20 '65
CLAPP, Margaret
Point in time at Wellesley. por Time 86:55-6 Ag 20 '65
Stopping in midstream. por Newsweek 66: 72-3 Ag 23 '65
CLAPP, Verner W.
Interview with Verner Clapp; ed. by K. Molz. pors Wilson Lib Bul 40:150-6 O '65
Profile: Luther H. Evans; reprint. Library J 90:3384-91 S 1 '65
CLAPPERTON, Jane
Capsule history of hospitality. Holiday 37: 46-7 F '65
CLAREMONT colleges. See Associated colleges at Claremont, Calif.
CLARION music society
Musical events; performance of Dittersdorf's Arcifanfano, king of fools. W. Sargeant. New Yorker 41:103-4+ Ja 15 '66
CLARK, Alice M.
De facto integration in Bel Air. Sat R 49: 72-3 Ja 15 '66
CLARK, Blake
America's unconventional master builder. Read Digest 86:192-6 F '65
They help the blind to see. Read Digest 86: 197-200 Mr '65
World's most wanted criminal. Read Digest 86:74-7 Mr '65
Young lives, brave actions. Read Digest 87: 187-8+ N '65
CLARK, Bobbie
Party of the month! See issues of Parents' magazine and better homemaking
CLARK, Dave
Dave Clark five make a movie! ed. by E. Miller. pors Seventeen 24:91+ Jl '65
    about
Kathy's wild weekend. K. Sheron. il pors Seventeen 24:136-7 N '65
CLARK, Dennis
Police under pressure. Cath World 202:228-32 Ja '66
CLARK, Don
Shop talk. See issues of Hot rod
CLARK, Edward
Tie me kangaroo down. por Newsweek 65: 20-1 Je 28 '65
CLARK, Eleanor
Portrait in blue. Vogue 146:122+ S 1 '65
CLARK, Eugenie
Mating of groupers. Natur Hist 74:22-5 Je '65
    about
Lovely lady with a very fishy reputation. C. Phinizy. il pors Sports Illus 23:46-50 O 4 '65
CLARK, F. C. Jr
Dunking is not for trailers. il Yachting 118: 60-1+ Jl '65
Northwest's islands of discovery. Yachting 117:66-8 Mr '65
CLARK, Gordon
Jaunty Ireland. Travel 123:24-8 Mr '65
CLARK, Grenville
Second Dublin declaration. Sat R 48:28-9 D 11 '65
CLARK, Hank
Build bigger engine hatches. Motor B 116: 120-1 N '65
Power or pedal water bike. Pop Mech 124: 148-53 Ag '65
CLARK, Howard Longstreth
Oil, vinegar & sugar. il por Time 86:81 S 3 '65
CLARK, J. Desmond
Later pleistocene cultures of Africa. bibliog Science 150:833-47 N 12 '65
CLARK, Jim
Forced march. il Newsweek 65:24+ F 22 '65

CLARK, Jim, 1937?-
Airplane without wings. il por Life 59:78 Jl 16 '65

about

Close call at Silverstone. Time 86:53 Jl 16 '65
Easy does it. il por Time 85:80 Je 11 '65
Fiery 500 for a cool Scot. B. Ottum. il por Sports Illus 22:18-21 Je 7 '65
Gentleman Jim. il por Newsweek 65:96+ Je 14 '65
Hero with a hot shoe. il pors Time 86:78-82 Jl 9 '65; Same abr. Read Digest 87:200-2+ O '65
One that was missing. Time 86:51 Ag 13 '65
View from the top. Newsweek 66:52 Ag 16 '65

CLARK, John Abbot
John Abbot Clark. RIP. R. Kirk. Nat R 17:1018 N 16 '65

CLARK, Joseph S.
Excerpt from address, May 14, 1965. Cong Digest 44:277+ N '65
Key to peace. Sat R 49:28 Ja 15 '66

CLARK, Ken
Brother coon never had it so good! Field & S 69:49-51 Mr '65

CLARK, Kenneth Bancroft
Civil rights mystique. Sat R 48:60-1 O 16 '65
Delusions of the white liberal; excerpt from Dark ghetto. N Y Times Mag p27+ Ap 4 '65
Role for librarians in the relevant war against poverty; address, May 15, 1965. por Wilson Lib Bul 40:42-7 S '65
What motivates American whites? por Ebony 20:69-74 Ag '65
Wonder is there have been so few riots. N Y Times Mag p 10-11+ S 5 '65

about

Light on the ghetto. il por Newsweek 65:78+ My 31 '65
Precious irrelevance. J. Berry. Library J 90: 2772 Je 15 '65

CLARK, Marguerite
New clues to the mystery of cancer. Read Digest 87:157-8+ Jl '65

CLARK, Michael
Model boy. il Newsweek 65:46 My 10 '65

CLARK, Petula
Everyone's Pet. por Time 85:52 Ap 23 '65
Pappy, listen to Petula. C. Harman. Life 59:23 D 10 '65
Pretty Pet. por Newsweek 65:82 F 8 '65

CLARK, Phil
New York botanical garden. Horticulture 43:38-41 Je '65

CLARK, Ramsey
Excerpts from testimony, April 27 and July 15, 1965. Cong Digest 44:239+ O '65

CLARK, Thomas
Advent; poem. Nation 200:116 F 1 '65
Gestures of deliberation. Poetry 107:121-4 N '65
Instruction; poem. Nation 200:654 Je 14 '65
Zukofsky's all. Poetry 107:55-9 O '65

CLARK, Walter Houston
Do seminaries teach religion? Christian Cent 82:520-2+ Ap 28 '65

CLARK, Walter Van Tilburg
Are writers made, not born? R. Diers. por Sat R 48:52-3 Ag 14 '65

CLARK, Willard
Black & white. U S Camera 29:40-1 Ja '66
Now: automatic speedlight. U S Camera 28: 46-7+ O '65
Where are we headed? U S Camera 28:52-3 Ag '65

CLARK, Sterling and Francine art institute. See Sterling and Francine Clark art institute, Williamstown, Mass.

CLARK institute. See Sterling and Francine Clark art institute, Williamstown, Mass.

CLARK university, Worcester, Mass.
Architecture that transforms a campus. il Arch Rec 137:157-68 My '65
Focal point at Clark university; Goddard library. il Arch Rec 137:150-3 Je '65

CLARKE, Arthur Charles
Beyond the stars. New Yorker 41:38-9 Ap 24 '65

CLARKE, Dick
Outfox the foxes! Motor T 17:40-1 Je '65

CLARKE, J. Harold
Hand-me-down garden ideas. Horticulture 43:28-9 Ag '65

CLARKE, John
Whippoorwill; poem. Atlan 216:166 N '65

CLARKE, Richard
Job consultant for big business. il pors Ebony 20:115-16+ Ap '65

CLARKE, Ron
Big three are miles apart. J. Underwood. por Sports Illus 22:26-7+ Je 21 '65
Ron runs the world ragged. G. M. Brown. il por Sports Illus 23:24-5 Jl 26 '65
Running philosopher. Time 86:75 Jl 23 '65
Two stirring triumphs over men and the clock. G. S. Brown. il Sports Illus 22:79-81 Je 14 '65

CLARKE, Thomas E.
World is already Christic. America 112:800-3 My 29 '65

CLARKE and Way. See October house, incorporated

CLASS distinction
Protestant establishment, by E. D. Baltzell. Review
Commentary 39:83-6 Je '65. D. H. Wrong
See also
Caste
Equality
Middle classes

CLASS reunions. See College graduates

CLASS rings. See Rings

CLASS size
NEA research division looks at secondary school class size. R. C. Maul. il NEA J 54:44-5 Mr '65

CLASSES, Special. See Special classes and special schools

CLASSICAL education
See also
Humanities

CLASSICAL literature
Classics revisited. K. Rexroth. Sat R 48:19 Mr 20; 17 Mr 27; 18 Ap 3; 27 Ap 10; 27 My 1; 19 My 15; 17 My 29; 15 Je 5; 29 Je 12; 19 Je 26; 19 Jl 10; 21 Ag 14; 20 Ag 28; 31+ S 11; 29 S 18; 25 O 2; 40 N 13; 27 N 27; 27 D 11; 23 D 25 '65; 49:19 Ja 1 '66

CLASSICAL music. See Music

CLASSICS, The. See Classical literature

CLASSIFICATION, Decimal
Dewey abroad. S. K. Vann. bibliog il Wilson Lib Bul 39:550-4 Mr '65
Dewey 17: a preview and report. B. A. Custer. Wilson Lib Bul 39:555-9 Mr '65

CLASSIFIED advertisements. See Advertisements, Classified

CLASSIFIED defense information. See Defense information, Classified

CLASSIFIED documents. See Security classification (government documents)

CLASSROOM furniture. See School furniture, equipment, etc.

CLASSROOM libraries. See School libraries

CLASSROOM management
Big-city school: problems and prospects. J. I. Goodlad and M. C. Hunter. il PTA Mag 59:8-10 Ap '65
Classroom incident. NEA J 54:52-3 S '65
Discipline is. . . . Sister Marian Frances. il NEA J 54:26-8 S '65
Editor's notebook. M. S. Fenner. NEA J 54:72 Ap '65
I was an innocent in the classroom. R. St Germain. NEA J 54:21 O '65
Way it spozed to be. J. Herndon. il Harper 231:79-87 S '65
What can the schools do? D. M. Lee. il NEA J 54:25-7 F '65

CLASSROOM teachers. See Teachers

CLASSROOMS
See also
Home economics departments

CLATHRATES. See Crystallography

CLATHROMORPHUM. See Algae

CLAUDE, Sister Mary. See Mary Claude, Sister

CLAUDE, R. P.
Reapportionment goes to town. Am City 80: 163-6 My '65

CLAUSEN, Mads
Danish industry grows amidst the farm-lands. il por Bsns W p60-2 Je 26 '65

CLAWSON, Marion
Public land review. Am For 71:10-13+ Mr; 34-9+ Ap; 50-3+ My; 20-3+ Je; 26-9+ Jl; 12-15+ Ag '65

CLAY, Cassius
Hare was no rabbit. pors Life 58:97-8 F 12 '65

about

Alas, poor Cassius! il por Ebony 20:144-5 Jl '65
Cassius Clay must be beaten; with editorial comment. F. Patterson. Sports Illus 23: 19, 78-80+ O 11 '65
Cassius to win a thriller. T. Maule. il pors Sports Illus 22:22-5 My 24 '65
Champion as long as he wants. G. Rogin. il pors Sports Illus 23:20-5 N 29 '65

CLAY, Cassius—about—*Continued*
Floyd, fight like he slapped your mother. D. Brown. il por Life 59:120+ N 19 '65
400 blows. il por Newsweek 66:64 D 6 '65
Giant they love to hate; with account by G. Rogin. il pors Sports Illus 23:40-5+ D 6 '65
Greatest meets the grimmest. M. Kane. il por Sports Illus 23:36-8+ N 15 '65
Head for figures. Newsweek 67:79 Ja 24 '66
Lunch for a lion. il por Time 86:73 D 3 '65
Man in the champ's corner. G. Rogin. Sports Illus 22:32-6+ My 24 '65
No phantom punch; with account by J. Murray. il pors Sports Illus 22:48-53 Je 7 '65
Poetic knockout. Sports Illus 23:10 N 1 '65
Quick, hard right and a needless storm of protest. T. Maule. il por Sports Illus 22:22-5 Je 7 '65
Rabbit hunt in Vegas. G. Rogin. il pors Sports Illus 23:34-9 N 22 '65
Sickening spectacle in a ring. il por Life 59:42-42A D 3 '65
Theater of the absurd. il por Time 85:68-9 Je 4 '65
While Ali babbled. il por Newsweek 65:60 F 15 '65
World champion is refused a meal. G. Plimpton. il pors Sports Illus 22:24-7 My 17 '65

CLAY
Anchorage's feet of clay. il Time 86:62 D 17 '65
Make your own tiles and trivets. il Design 66:26-7 Mr '65
See also
Illite

CLAY industries

Wages and hours
Wages in structural clay products, July-August 1964. C. M. O'Connor. il Mo Labor R 88:1089-92 S '65

CLAY pigeons. See Trap shooting

CLAYTON, Roderick K.
Biophysical problems of photosynthesis. bibliog Science 149:1346-54 S 17 '65

CLEAN rooms. See Factories—Cleanliness

CLEAN sweep; drama. See Boiko, C.

CLEANER wrasses. See Wrasses

CLEANERS, Electric. See Vacuum cleaners

CLEANING
Ways you can help your dry cleaner. il Good H 162:133 Ja '66
See also
House cleaning

CLEANING compositions
Cleaning agents harmful. Sci N L 87:375 Je 12 '65
Detergents: effects on the chemical senses of the fish ictalurus natalis, (le sueur) J. E. Bardach and others. bibliog il Science 148:1605-7 Je 18 '65
Hard look at soft detergents. C. H. Wayman. il Bul Atomic Sci 21:22-6 Ap '65
Laundry detergent steps up. M. B. Keiser. il Parents Mag 40:16+ Ap '65
Less suds for the Nation's rivers; new-type detergent. il U S News 59:16 Jl 12 '65
Oven cleaners. il Consumer Bul 49:43 Ja '66
Oven cleaners. Consumer Rep 30:70-1 F '65
Soft detergents pass practical field tests. Am City 80:16 Mr '65

CLEANING machinery and appliances
See also
Vacuum cleaners

CLEANING of fishes. See Fish as food

CLEANLINESS
See also
Factories—Cleanliness

CLEAR air turbulence. See Atmospheric turbulence

CLEARING of lakes. See Lakes—Clearing

CLEARY, Robert E.
Southern political culture and school desegregation. bibliog f Sch & Soc 93:392-4 O 30 '65

CLEATH, Robert L.
Balaam's ass in the seminary. R. Kirk. Nat R 17:934 O 19 '65

CLEEVE, Brian
Foxer; story. Sat Eve Post 238:48-9 D 18 '65

CLEGHORN, Reese
Appalachia, poverty, beauty and poverty. N Y Times Mag p 12-13+ Ap 25 '65
Two faces of Sheriff Rainey. N Y Times Mag p 10-11+ F 21 '65

CLELAND, Robert, and McCombs, Nancy
Gibberellic acid: action in barley endosperm does not require endogenous auxin. bibliog Science 150:497-8 O 22 '65

CLEMATIS
This is a clematis tree. il Sunset 134:292 Ap '65

CLEMENS, Cyril
Chat with Joseph Conrad. Hobbies 70:85+ Ja '66

CLEMENS, Samuel Langhorne
Old Ben Franklin and his miserable maxims. Read Digest 86:137-8 Je '65
about
Expergation of Huckleberry Finn; excerpt from Susy and Mark Twain. E. C. Salsbury. Am Heritage 16:112 O '65
Innocents at home. J. Swan. il por Am Heritage 16:58-61+ F '65

CLEMENS, Susy
Expergation of Huckleberry Finn; excerpt from Susy and Mark Twain. E. C. Salsbury. Am Heritage 16:112 O '65

CLÉMENT, Alain
What Germany has become. New Repub 153:12-14 O 23 '65

CLEMENT, David
Big Joe no 1. il por Time 86:25 Ag 20 '65

CLÉMENT, René
Letter from Paris. Genêt. New Yorker 41: 142-3 S 18 '65

CLEMENTE, Roberto Walker
Pirate booty. H. L. Masin. por Sr Schol 87: 34 S 16 '65

CLEMENTS, Robert D.
Letters. Sch Arts 65:48 O '65

CLEMENTS, Robert J.
Critic alone with his text. Sat R 48:36 D 25 '65
European literary scene (cont) Sat R 48:36-7 F 13; 25-6 Mr 20; 39+ Ap 17; 26-7+ My 15; 30-1 Je 19; 30-1 Jl 17; 21-2 Ag 7 '65
He questioned all the answers. Sat R 48: 50-1 O 16 '65
Is the Nobel prize for literature political? Sat R 48:41-2+ D 4 '65
Latin America's neglected literature. Sat R 48:60-1 My 22 '65
Talent for evil. Sat R 48:45-6 S 11 '65

CLEPPER, Henry
Well governed angler. Am For 71:4-5+ F '65

CLERGY
American minister. H. H. Martin. il Sat Eve Post 238:19-23+ Ap 24 '65
Brave Englishman in a Midwest pulpit. P. Watkins. Harper 231:96-8+ D '65
Darkness of life; reprint. U S News 59:84 Ag 2 '65
Day in the life of a man who tries; E. Cole of Indianapolis. il Sat Eve Post 238:24+ Ap 24 '65
Ferment in the churches; the new Christian soldiers. H. Cox. il Nation 201:216-20 O 11 '65
Flocking of good shepherds; participation in civil rights demonstrations. L. Wainwright. Life 58:23 Ap 16 '65
How to become a bishop without being religious, by C. M. Smith. Review Time 85:65-6 F 12 '65
Is the clergyman changing his role? D. Lawrence. U S News 58:116 Ap 19 '65
Ministry to millionaires. Time 86:42 Ag 13 '65
New models for ministers; concerning E. Werner's article in the American scholar; reply. A. G. Taylor. Christian Cent 82:374 Mr 24 '65
No solicitors allowed; parish minister in urban center. Christian Cent 82:165-6 F 10 '65; Discussion. 82:475-6 Ap 14 '65
Parochial syndrome. L. Davis. Christian Cent 82:1543-5 D 15 '65
Pastor and the world, by G. J. Fackre. Review
Christian Cent 82:582-3 My 5 '65. R. E. Wentz
Selma, civil rights, and the church militant. il Newsweek 65:75-6+ Mr 29 '65
See also
Catholic church—Clergy
Laity
Missionaries
Preaching
Priests
Theologians
Theological students
Women as ministers
Women as priests

Costume
Dressing down. il Newsweek 66:61 Ag 2 '65
See also
Church vestments

Education
Beyond seminary; movement for continuing education of ministers. M. Rich. Christian Cent 82:877-8 Jl 7 '65

CLERGY—*Continued*

Salaries

Disappearing discount: clergyman's discount. Time 86:48+ Jl 9 '65
Salaries and ministry. America 112:347 Mr 13 '65

CLERGY, Negro. See Negro clergy

CLERGY conferences
43rd annual event: Pastoral conference. E. T. Culver. Christian Cent 82:380-2 Mr 24 '65

CLERGY in literature
How to become a bishop without being religious, by C. M. Smith. Review
Life 58:20 Je 18 '65 F. B. Sayre, jr

CLERICAL dress. See Clergy—Costume

CLERICAL workers. See Office workers

CLEVA, Fausto
Poem of the West. Opera N 30:24-5 Ja 8 '66
about
Notary public. J. W. Freeman. por Opera N 29:12-13 Ap 17 '65

CLEVELAND, Grover
Grover Cleveland, twenty-second, 1885-1889 and twenty-fourth President, 1893-1897. F. Freidel. il pors Nat Geog Mag 127:698-703 My '65

CLEVELAND, Harlan
Broadcasting of world politics; address, November 3, 1965. Dept State Bul 53:896-901 D 6 '65
Building blocks of world order; address, March 23, 1965. Dept State Bul 52:566-9 Ap 19 '65
Disarmament and international cooperation; statement, May 12, 1965. Dept State Bul 52:967-71 Je 14 '65
How to live together. por Am Ed 1:1-5 My '65
Other end of the telescope; address, October 21, 1965. Dept State Bul 53:781-7 N 15 '65
Peace comes in parcels; address, March 31, 1965. Dept State Bul 52:613-18 Ap 26 '65
Politics of outer space; address, May 27, 1965. Dept State Bul 52:1007-13 Je 21 '65
Special issue of the Bulletin. Dept State Bul 53:383 S 6 '65
U.N: hope for the future; remarks, February 19, 1965. Dept State Bul 52:380-1 Mr 15 '65
View from up there; address, July 2, 1965. Dept State Bul 53:151-6 Jl 26 '65

CLEVELAND, Ohio

City planning

How one big city is planning a comeback. il U S News 58:58-61 My 31 '65

Lighting

No eerie view of Erieview. A. Nichols. il Am City 81:121 Ja '66
Private lighting program rids city of darkness. A. Nichols. il Am City 80:134 Ap '65

Music

See also
Cleveland orchestra

Negroes

Bitter and insistent plague: misery of the house on Hough; with report by P. Welch. il Life 59:106-17+ D 24 '65

Newspapers

Scoop at sea; rivalry between Cleveland plain dealer and Cleveland press in reporting R. Manry's voyage. il Time 86:48 Ag 20 '65
Tigerish; Cleveland plain dealer. il Newsweek 66:78-9 Jl 5 '65
See also
Cleveland press

Politics and government

Black and white issue. il Newsweek 66:36+ N 15 '65

Social conditions

How one big city is planning a comeback. il U S News 58:58-61 My 31 '65

Transportation

Rapid transit pays own fare: Cleveland's little Shaker Heights line. il Bsns W p80+ S 11 '65

Water supply

Cleveland: saving Lake Erie. L. B. Seltzer. il Sat R 48:36+ O 23 '65
Multiple jets prevent filter upset. T. E. Stanton. il Am City 80:28 F '65

CLEVELAND Browns (football club) See Football clubs

CLEVELAND museum of art
In the museums; French porcelain and pottery from the Norweb collection. R. Davidson. il Antiques 89:134-6+ Ja '66

CLEVELAND orchestra
Profiles: G. Szell. J. Wechsberg. New Yorker 41:59-62+ N 6 '65
Triumph abroad. il Time 85:69 My 28 '65

CLEVELAND press
Mr Cleveland bows out. il Time 87:58 Ja 14 '66
Something missing here; T. L. Boardman replaces L. B. Seltzer. Newsweek 67:83-4 Ja 17 '66

CLEVELAND symphony orchestra. See Cleveland orchestra

CLEVER, Ulrich. See Schin. K. S. jt. auth.

CLICQUOT, Barbe Nicole (Ponsardin)
Fizz, bubbly, pop. E. Waugh. Vogue 146:156+ S 1 '65

CLIFFE, Lionel
Tanzania: myth and reality. Cur Hist 48:219-23+ Ap '65

CLIFFORD, Donald K. Jr
Leverage in the product life cycle. Duns R 85:62-4+ My '65

CLIFT, David H.
After the ALA reorganization; address, July 1965. ALA Bul 59:727-32 S '65
Memo to members. por ALA Bul 59:170-1, 335-7 Mr, My '65
Memo to members; letter to G. T. Stevenson. por ALA Bul 59:248-9 Ap '65

CLIFTON, Chester Victor, 1913-
Aid who aided. il por Time 86:17A Ag 13 '65

CLIMATE
See also
Plants, Effect of climate on
Weather
also subhead Climate under names of continents, countries, states, etc. e.g. Europe—Climate

CLIMATE and business. See Weather and business

CLIMATOLOGY, Agricultural. See Plants, Effect of climate on

CLIMBING plants
Placing and spacing trees, shrubs, and vines. il Bet Hom & Gard 43:126 Ap '65
Trees and vines. il Bet Hom & Gard 43:22 Mr '65
Trees and vines for every setting. H. Mason and others. il Bet Hom & Gard 43:56-61 Mr '65
Vines. C. B. Lees. il Horticulture 44:36-40 Ja '66
When your vines invade trees. il Sunset 135:148+ Ag '65
See also
Bower plants
Gourds
Morning glories
Wisteria

CLIMBING roses. See Roses

CLIMBING strawberries. See Strawberries

CLINE, M. J. and Fudenberg, H. H.
Defective RNA synthesis in lymphocytes from patients with primary agammaglobulinemia. bibliog Science 150:1311-12 D 3 '65

CLINE, Ralph
Patriot talks about his portrait. Life 58:122 My 14 '65

CLINICAL laboratories. See Medical laboratories

CLINICAL research. See Medical research

CLINICS. See Health clinics

CLINOENSTATITE
Clinoenstatite: high-low inversion. A. J. Perrotta and D. A. Stephenson. bibliog il Science 148:1090-1 My 21 '65

CLIPS, Surgical. See Surgical instruments

CLIQUES. See Groups (sociology)

CLITENNESTRA: opera. See Pizzetti, I.

CLOCK and watch makers
New England country clocks and movements; Shelburne museum, Vermont exhibition. il Antiques 88:34+ Jl '65
Thomas Harland's clock, whose case? A. R. Chase and H. Bulkeley. il Antiques 87:700-1 Je '65

CLOCK and watch making
Watch movement, to West Indies; loophole in tariff permits duty-free entry into U.S. il Bsns W p 132+ Je 5 '65
Willing hands on Japanese watches; K. Hattori & co. il Fortune 72:144-8 Jl '65

CLOCK cases
Thomas Harland's clock, whose case? A. R. Chase and H. Bulkeley. il Antiques 87:700-1 Je '65

CLOCKS
Alarm clocks. L. W. Slaughter. il Hobbies 70:50-1 Ap '65
Capsule history of timepieces. R. Condon. Holiday 38:42-3 Ag '65
Clocks by Riley Whiting. E. T. Goodnow. Hobbies 70:44 O '65

CLOTHING and dress—Sports clothes—*Cont.*
Fancy pants maker stretches into new lines; Jack Winter, inc. Milwaukee. il Bsns W p60-2 Mr 20 '65
High-mountain down; insulation against chill of deep-powder country. M. E. Newman. il Sports Illus 23:68-72 N 15 '65
Hunting clothes. T. Trueblood. il Field & S 70:34+ S '65
Jaunty look for boatmen. F. M. Paulson. il Field & S 70:94-8 Ag '65
Long-distance jumper on the ski wear trail; ski jackets. il Bsns W p 140-1 F 27 '65
Many-layered golf; golfers prefer turtleneck sweaters. il Sports Illus 22:72-6 Ap 12 '65
Snow job; ski togs. il Time 86:46 D 17 '65
Sporting look. See issues of Sports illustrated
This summer everybody will be on the team. il Sports Illus 22:64-5 My 24 '65
Tips for your winter outdoor vacation. Todays Health 44:85-6 Ja '66
Tournament play; fishin' fashions for all hands. F. Rohr. il Motor B 115:35-40 Je '65
What to wear when sport fishing. il Yachting 117:128 Je '65

Study and teaching

Threads of fashion. P. A. Janssen. il Am Ed 1:9-11 N '65
CLOTHING industry

Wages and hours

Earnings in men's shirt and nightwear plants, 1964. F. L. Bauer. il Mo Labor R 88:957-9 Ag '65
Earnings in work clothing industry, May-June 1964. C. M. O'Connor. il Mo Labor R 88:555-7 My '65

France

Paris puts its magic into ready-to-wear. il Bsns W p78-80+ D 18 '65

Russia

Soviets set style for profit; Moscow clothing plant aims to please consumer taste. il Bsns W p 104+ Mr 20 '65

United States

Garment makers bolt to bonded materials. il Bsns W p40-1 D 25 '65
Wooing the cautious male. il Time 86:96+ O 8 '65
See also
New York (city)—Industries
CLOUD, C. Carey
Full cycle. il pors Design 66:38-41 My '65
CLOUD, Preston E. Jr
Significance of the gunflint. Precambrian microflora. bibliog Science 148:27-35 Ap 2 '65
—and others
Carbonaceous rocks of the Soudan iron formation early Precambrian. bibliog Science 148: 1713-16 Je 25 '65
CLOUD, Wallace
Science newsfront. See issues of Popular science monthly to October 1965
CLOUD seeding. See Rain making
CLOUDS
Lidar observation of cloud. R. T. H. Collis. il Science 149:978-81 Ag 27 '65
Luminous spiderwebs of heaven; noctilucent clouds. J. Lear. il Sat R 48:54-6 N 6 '65; Reply with rejoinder. T. E. Uehling, jr. 48:90 D 4 '65
Some observations of noctilucent clouds. D. A. Rodger. il Sky & Tel 29:250-1 Ap '65
CLOUGH, Roy L. Jr
Jet-fighter kite. Pop Sci 186:134-5 Mr '65
Modeling the pivot-wing F-111. Pop Mech 24:170-3 O '65
Singing steel guitar. Pop Mech 124:129-31+ Ag '65
CLOWARD, Richard A.
War on poverty; are the poor left out? Nation 201:55-60 Ag 2 '65
CLOWNS
Day his funny friends frolicked in grief. M. Mok. il Life 58:40B-40C Ap 30 '65
CLUB houses. See Clubhouses
CLUBHOUSES
Ingenious use of a narrow site. il Arch Rec 138:161-4 N '65
Mile-high clubhouse; John F. Kennedy municipal golf course, Denver, Colo. il Recreation 58:430 N '65
Special lighting for an atrium; Waterbury club. Waterbury, Conn. S. R. Shemitz. il Arch Rec 138:171-2 D '65
They own their own homes. il NEA J 54: 36-7 My '65

CLUBS
Clubs for commoners; Wythenshawe and other workingmen's clubs. il Newsweek 67:20 Ja 3 '66
Now; social clubs face new taxes. U S News 58:99-101 Mr 22 '65
See also
Aviation clubs
Fishing clubs
Science clubs
Yacht clubs
also subhead Clubs under names of cities, e.g. Paris—Clubs
CLUBS, Merchandising. See Merchandising clubs
CLUETT, Peabody and company
Expanding today for business manana; Arrow de Centro America, ltda. il Bsns W p 120 S 11 '65
CLUM, Neda S.
Get together for a clam steam. Parents Mag 40:61+ Jl '65
CLURMAN, Harold Edgar
Notes from afar. Nation 201:84-6,105-6 Ag 16, 30 '65
Substance of spirit. Nation 201:310-11 N 1 '65
Theatre. See issues of Nation
Theatre; the laggard art. Nation 201:221-6 S 20 '65
about
How to succeed in the theatre without really being successful. E. Dundy. il Esquire 63: 88-9+ My '65
CLUSTER housing. See Housing projects—Site planning
CLUTTER, Herbert William, family
Annals of crime; In cold blood. T. Capote. New Yorker 41:57-60+ S 25; 57-60+ O 2; 58-62+ O 9; 62-4+ O 16 '65
Horror spawns a masterpiece; T. Capote's In cold blood inspired by murders; excerpt; with report by J. Howard. il Life 60:58-72+ Ja 7 '66
In cold blood, an American tragedy; concerning T. Capote's book. il Newsweek 67:59-63 Ja 24 '66
In cold blood, by T. Capote. Review America 114:142+ Ja 22 '66; T. Greene Sat R 49:35-6 Ja 22 '66. G. Hicks
CLYMER, Adam
How the government won the third Liuzzo trial. Reporter 33:25-6 D 30 '65
COACH dogs. See Dalmatian dogs
COACH museum, Lisbon. See Museums
COACHES (athletics) See Physical directors
COACHES and coaching
Our far-flung correspondents; driving route of Edinburgh royal mail up Old North road to Grantham. H. W. Wind. il New Yorker 41:138-46+ My 22 '65
COACHING (athletics) See Athletes—Training
COAGULATION, Water. See Water purification
COAL and steel community. See European coal and steel community
COAL dusting. See Ice on rivers, lakes, etc. —Control
COAL industry

Great Britain

Lord Coal's troubles; Britain's national coal board. Time 86:92 D 17 '65

United States

See also
Consolidation coal company
COAL miners
See also
Strikes—United States—Coal mines and mining
COAL mines and mining

Contract system

Investment nobody knows about. T. J. Murray. il Duns R 85:40-3+ Ap '65

Stripping operations

Louisville; law or license? contamination of land and water. N. E. Isaacs. il Sat R 48: 44-5 My 22 '65
Strip mining heals its own scars. il Bsns W p 140+ N 13 '65
Strip mining; Kentucky begins to close the reclamation gap. J. Walsh. il Science 150: 36-9 O 1 '65
Strip mining; TVA in middle in reclamation controversy. J. Walsh. il Science 150:194-8 O 8 '65

Wages and hours

Wage chronology; bituminous coal mines; supplement no. 6, 1960-66. P. B. Smith. il Mo Labor R 88:425-8 Ap '65

COAL mines and mining—*Continued*

Europe, Western

See also
European coal and steel community

Germany (Federal Republic)
West Germany's Ruhr: coal, steel, and trouble. il U S News 58:80-1 Mr 8 '65

Russia
Dash forward; increasing production under Libermanism. Time 85:26 Je 4 '65

COALINGA, Calif, district library
Library and librarian attacked in California censorship case. Library J 90:1683 Ap 1 '65

COAN, Max
Mastery in billfishing. il Motor B 115:43-4+ Ap '65

COAST and geodetic survey (United States)
See United States—Coast and geodetic survey

COAST guard academy, United States. See United States coast guard academy, New London, Conn.

COAST guard auxiliary. See United States—Coast guard auxiliary

COASTAL marshes. See Salt marshes

COASTING
Rule Britannia for now. il Time 85:88 F 5 '65

COASTS
United States
See also
Pacific coast

COAT hangers. See Clothes hangers

COATES, Paul
Underdogs' favorite. il por Time 85:72 Mr 19 '65

COATES, Robert M.
Art galleries. See issues of New Yorker
Mother church, Orvieto. Horizon 7:76-95 Spr '65
Polyphemus unbound. Reporter 33:49-51 D 16 '65

COATIS
Curious coati. L. L. Hothem. il Field & S 70:47+ Ja '66

COATS, Alfred C.
Temperature effects on the peripheral auditory apparatus. bibliog Science 150:1481-3 D 10 '65

COATS, Betty, and Wood, Kay
Paper doll people. Parents Mag 40:93 Jl '65

COATS and Clark, incorporated
Industry enrolls in 4-H clubs. il Bsns W p36 D 4 '65

COATS
See also
Fur coats, wraps, etc.

COATS of arms. See Heraldry

COAXIAL cables
See also
Television cables

COBB, Boughton, Jr
Building a stock fiberglass cruiser (cont) Yachting 117:49-51+ F '65
Fiberglass maintenance. Yachting 117:76+ Ap '65
Fiberglassing with cellophane. Yachting 117:60-1+ My '65
Penguins in glass. Yachting 118:61-3+ O '65

COBB, Charlie
Whose society is this? New Repub 153:13-15 D 18 '65

COBB, John B. Jr
Christian natural theology and Christian existence. Christian Cent 82:265-7 Mr 3 '65

COBBLERS (desserts) See Desserts

COBERG, Almeda
Old trunks; how to turn them into treasures. House & Gard 128:78+ S '65

COBIA fishing. See Sergeant fish fishing

COBLENTZ, Stanton A.
Out of the wilderness; poem. Liv Wildn 86:12 Spr '64

COBURN, Walt
Double duty for Dinner Key. Yachting 118:56+ N '65

COCA-COLA company
Coke makes switch to a new staff setup; brand manager system. Bsns W p 128 N 20 '65
Thaw that refreshes; Coca-Cola in Bulgaria. Time 86:98 D 3 '65

COCCINELLIDAE. See Beetles

COCCIOLI, Carlo
Carlo Coccioli. T. F. Staley. Commonweal 83:95-8 O 22 '65

COCHELL, Shirley
Bulletin boards as teaching aids. Sr Schol 87:sup6 N 4 '65
How to help students plan reading lists. Sr Schol 87:sup 10 D 2 '65
Writing unit on statistics. Sr Schol 86:8T F 11 '65

COCHRAN, Bert
Personalities around the President. Sat R 48:51 D 4 '65

COCHRAN, Dwight M.
Gleaning new ventures from farming profits. il por Bsns W p89-90+ O 23 '65

COCKPITS. See Boat cockpits

COCKROACHES
American cockroach sex attractant. M. Jacobson and M. Beroza. bibliog Science 147:748-9 F 12 '65
Blood of a cockroach: unusual cellular behavior. H. Ritter, jr. bibliog il Science 147:518-19 Ja 29 '65
Photoreception and entrainment of cockroach activity rhythms. S. K. Roberts. bibliog il Science 148:958-9 My 14 '65
Regulation of cockroach fat-body metabolism by the corpus cardiacum in vitro. A. W. Wiens and L. I. Gilbert. bibliog il Science 150:614-16 O 29 '65

COCKSCOMBS
Diverse celosias. R. C. Hands. il Horticulture 43:28-31 O '65

COCKTAIL tables. See Tables

COCKTAILS
Cocktail lore and legend. C. G. Martinez. House & Gard 127:174+ Ap '65
Drinks that delight. il Ebony 21:110+ Ja '66
Mexican drinks. P. S. Brown. House & Gard 128:218+ S '65
Wine, women and so on; premixed cocktails. P. Cannon. Ladies Home J 82:32 O '65

COCLÉ Indians. See Indians of Central America

COCOA, Fla.
Making the Yuletide count. L. B. Taylor, jr. il Audubon Mag 67:350-5 N '65; Same abr. with title Great day for bird lovers. Read Digest 87:83-7 D '65

COCOA
Prices
Cocoa working party; United Nations cocoa conference. UN Mo Chron 2:47-8 N '65

COCONUT
See also
Cookery—Coconut

COD fishing
Cold dawn run from Witless Bay to Erewhon. F. Russell. il Sports Illus 22:64-6+ Ap 26 '65
Wintertime codfishing. M. Rosko. il Travel 124:42-4 D '65

CODES (signals) See Signals and signaling

CODES of behavior. See Children—Management and training

CODY, John Patrick, abp
Cody for Chicago. il por Newsweek 65:77 Je 28 '65
New man in town. Christian Cent 82:1085 S 8 '65
Next cardinal. por Time 85:82 Je 25 '65
People of the week. por U S News 58:16 Je 28 '65

COE, Burr D.
Best place for vocational education. NEA J 54:50-1 D '65

COE, William R.
Tikal, Guatemala, and emergent Maya civilization. bibliog Science 147:1401-19 Mr 19 '65

COEDS. See College students, Women

COEDUCATION
In my opinion: girls have their place, but it's not on my college campus. J. Gibbs. Seventeen 24:266 Ap '65
Where girls are inconvenient; universities. Time 85:69 F 19 '65

COELACANTHS
Coelacanth displayed for first time in U.S. il Sci N L 87:199 Mr 27 '65

COELENTERATES
See also
Hydra (zoology)

COESITE
Coesite discovered in tektites; Muong Nong type tektites from Thailand. L. S. Walter. bibliog il Science 147:1029-32 F 26 '65; Reply. S. R. Taylor. 149:658-9 Ag 6 '65

COEXISTENCE. See World politics, 1945-

COFFEE
Come for coffee and . . . il Sunset 135:168 D '65

COFFEE cake
Coffee break breads. R. Hanna. il Suc Farm 63:116-17+ Ap '65
This sweet bread ring is cheese-filled. il Sunset 134:227-8 My '65
COFFEE houses
Coffee house ministry; new style of evangelism. J. D. Perry, jr. Christian Cent 82:180-1+ F 10 '65
Intersection: point of meeting; enterprise in San Francisco. R. J. Hawthorne. Christian Cent 82:1599-602 D 29 '65
Splendors and miseries of the literary cafe. H. R. Lottman. il Sat R 48:34-5+ Mr 13 '65
COFFEE parties. See Entertaining
COFFEE pots, percolators, etc.
Dollar gift for a bachelor, maybe; one-cup coffee-maker. il Consumer Rep 30:520 N '65
Electric coffee urns. il Consumer Rep 30:82-5 F '65
COFFEE trade
Big stir in coffee. J. M. Salazar. Read Digest 87:31-2+ D '65
Department urges enactment of coffee legislation; statement, January 27, 1965. G. W. Ball. Dept State Bul 52:260-2 F 22 '65
President signs bill on coffee agreement; statement, May 24, 1965. Dept State Bul 52:975 Je 14 '65
COFFEY, J. I.
Chinese and ballistic missile defense. Bul Atomic Sci 21:17-19 D '65
COFFEY, Raymond R.
HUAC in Chicago: this is not a court. Nation 200:633-6 Je 14 '65
People beneath the war. Nation 202:61-3 Ja 17 '66
To the right of reason: the patrioteers convene. Nation 200:520-1 My 17 '65
COFFEY, Rosemary Klineberg
Heart of deterrence. Bul Atomic Sci 21:27-9 Ap '65
COFFEY, Warren
Ashes and irony. Commentary 39:82+ Ap '65
Flannery O'Connor. Commentary 40:93-9 N '65
COFFIN, Frank M.
Economic development in south and southeast Asia; statement, November 19, 1964. Dept State Bul 52:77-81 Ja 18 '65
COFFIN, Tristram
Maryland's Montgomery County: the changing suburban dream. Holiday 38:54-5+ Jl '65
COFFIN, William Sloane, jr
Don't tell them to play it safe. por Life 58:31 Ap 30 '65
On the roots of prejudice. Mlle 60:176-7 Ap '65
about
Contemporary revival. J. C. Evans. Christian Cent 82:392-3 Mr 31 '65
COFFMAN, John A. and Browne, W. R.
Corona chemistry; with biographical sketches. Sci Am 212:20+, 91-6+ bibliog(p 147) Je '65
COFFMAN, William E.
Developing tests for the culturally different. bibliog f Sch & Soc 93:430-3 N 13 '65
COFIELD, Tom
For whom do storm signals fly? Motor B 116:46-7+ O '65
COGEN, Charles
AFT head asks national standards; statements. Sr Schol 87:sup2 D 9 '65
Los Angeles riots: handling the topic in class. Sr Schol 87:sup9-10 O 7 '65
COGLEY, John
Catholic church reconsiders birth control. N Y Times Mag p7+ Je 20 '65
Clergy heeds a new call. N Y Times Mag p42-3+ My 2 '65
Conciliar Rome. America 112:420-2 Mr 27 '65
Laity today and tomorrow. por Cath World 201:32-40 Ap '65
Pope is not pontifical. N Y Times Mag p44-7+ S 12 '65
They are priests and workers, both. N Y Times Mag p6-7+ D 26 '65
COGSWELL family
Five secretaries and the Cogswells. M. A. Young. il Antiques 88:478-85 O '65
COHEN, Abraham B.
Designing the hi-fi loudspeaker. Electr World 73:61-4+ Ap '65
COHEN, Alexander H.
Cohen's coddled public. T. Prideaux. il pors Life 58:137-8 Ap 2 '65
Pitching for Holmes. New Yorker 41:31-3 F 20 '65
COHEN, Arthur Allen
Of many things; what has happened to Catholicism and editorial censorship. T. N. Davis. America 113:173 Ag 21 '65

COHEN, Benjamin V.
Using the United Nations; adaptation of address. New Repub 152:13-16 My 8 '65
COHEN, Carl
Punishment by conscription. Nation 201:520-2 D 27 '65
COHEN, Daniel
Jeane Dixon: psychic star of the year. Nation 201:470-3 D 13 '65
Return of flying saucers. Nation 201:131-4 S 13 '65
COHEN, David
At the wake; poem. Christian Cent 82:203 F 17 '65
On seeking employment in America; poem. Christian Cent 82:869 Jl 7 '65
COHEN, E. D. and Trumbore, C. N.
Alkyl iodide-iodine exchange and the szilard-chalmers effect. bibliog Science 148:1460-1 Je 11 '65
COHEN, Harry B. and Dement, W. C.
Sleep: changes in threshold to electroconvulsive shock in rats after deprivation of paradoxical phase. bibliog Science 150:1318-19 D 3 '65
COHEN, Hennig
Instinct for misanthropy. Reporter 33:51-2 D 16 '65
Roebling's wonderful span. Reporter 33:36-7 Jl 1 '65
COHEN, Jerome A.
Year of the Swedes in China. Harper 231:130-2 O '65
COHEN, Julia. See Grobstein, C. jt. auth.
COHEN, Martin
Grand tour, family style: a Redbook guide to travel vacations. Redbook 124:49-56 Ap '65
Man is daddy. Redbook 125:60-1+ Je '65
COHEN, Melvin, and Jacklet, J. W.
Neurons of insects: RNA changes during injury and regeneration. bibliog Science 148:1237-9 My 28 '65
COHEN, Nathan
Theater (cont) Nat R 17:660; 18:37-9 Jl 27 '65, Ja 11 '66
COHEN, Robert David
Barber and I; poem. New Yorker 41:71 My 29 '65
Day on kind continent; poem. New Yorker 41:52 S 25 '65
Face to face with a successful poet. por Seventeen 24:107 Jl '65
Man-song, river-song. New Yorker 41:48 Mr 27 '65
Monody; poem. New Yorker 41:66 N 27 '65
Poem for Daniel; I am not wholly asleep; poems. Seventeen 24:132 Jl '65
COHEN, Selma Jeanne
Meeting with Rallou Manou. Dance Mag 39:57 Je '65
Time for dance in Stockholm. Sat R 48:55+ Je 26 '65
COHEN, Sheldon S.
New tax collector. por Nations Bsns 53:31+ Ap '65
about
New payroll plan: more taxes from weekly checks. por U S News 59:74-5 D 27 '65
COHEN, Sidney
LSD and the anguish of dying. Harper 231:69-72+ S '65
—and others
Temperature-sensitive repression of staphylococcal penicillinase. bibliog Science 149:877-9 Ag 20 '65
COHEN, Wilbur J.
Excerpt from statement, January 5, 1965. Cong Digest 44:88-9 Mr '65
COHN, Arthur
Divine document, the Ives Fourth. Am Rec G 32:220-2 N '65
Music of Arnold Schoenberg. Am Rec G 32:12-13 S '65
On five labels simultaneously, more music by Chas. E. Ives. Am Rec G 31:958-61 Je '65
Two views of the avant-garde repertoire at Philharmonic Hall. Am Rec G 32:355-6 D '65
COHN, Charles Erwin
Protect your car's electrical system. Pop Electr 23:66 N '65
COHN, Elie
Of hate & espionage; Syria accuses E. Cohn of spying for Israel. il Time 85:31 Mr 5 '65
Spy season. il Newsweek 65:44 Mr 8 '65
COHN, Lawrence
Folk bookshelf. Sat R 48:59+ My 15 '65
Recording reports (cont) Sat R 48:134 Mr 13; 62 Ag 28 '65
COHN, Roy Marcus
Days of shame, by C. E. Potter. Review Sat R 48:49 O 16 '65. N. S. Finney

COHN, Victor
Are we really telling the people about science? adaptation of address, December 28, 1964. Science 148:750-3 My 7 '65
Medicine today. Ladies Home J 82:44 Ap; 24 My '65
(ed) See Wright, P. M. Medicine today

COIFFURE. See Hairdressing

COIMBRA, Portugal
Conimbriga the Roman city in Portugal. P. James. il U S Camera 28:62 Ap '65

COIN aircraft. See Airplanes, Military—United States

COIN banks. See Banks, Coin

COINAGE. See Coins; Silver as money

COINS
About those new coins you're beginning to see. il U S News 59:51-3 N 15 '65
Ambassadors of art and history. O. P. Wenger. il UNESCO Courier 18:27-31 F '65
Analysis of copper and brass coins of the early Roman empire. G. F. Carter. bibliog il Science 151:196-7 Ja 14 '66
Coin quiz. C. French. See issues of Hobbies
Coin shortage: crisis with a silver lining. Sr Schol 86:25 Mr 4 '65
Coins without silver, but what kind? il U S News 58:92 Ap 12 '65
In answer to your questions about silver. il U S News 58:118-19 Je 21 '65
New coins begin to roll. il Bsns W p29 Ag 7 '65
New dimes, quarters, halves; here's the plan. il U S News 58:91-3 Je 14 '65
Numismatics. C. French. See issues of Hobbies
Run on silver coins? worry over hoarders. il U S News 58:56-7 My 3 '65
Silverless coins lighter. W. McCann. Sci N L 88:23 Jl 10 '65
See also
Silver as money

Analysis
See Metals—Analysis

Collectors and collecting
Coin collecting police clerk. il Ebony 21:126-8+ D '65
Europe's coin collecting has skyrocketed. C. French. Hobbies 70:102 D '65
Protect your collection. C. French. Hobbies 70:102 Je '65
Watch the coin bills in Congress. C. French. Hobbies 70:102 S '65

COIT, Margaret L.
Election year to remember. Sat R 48:29-31 Jl 10 '65
Free man with a free mind. Sat R 48:51-2 O 9 '65
Legislation with representation. Sat R 48:62-3 Ap 10 '65
Money talked and the people paid. Sat R 48:24-5 Jl 31 '65

COLA beverages. See Beverages

COLBY, Carroll B.
Camping. See issues of Outdoor life

COLBY, S. R.
Herbicide metabolism: N-glycoside of amiben isolated from soybean plants. bibliog Science 150:619-20 O 29 '65

COLCHICUMS. See Autumn crocuses

COLD
See also
Low temperature research

Physiological effects
Activity in mammalian peripheral nerves during supercooling. L. K. Miller. bibliog il Science 149:74-5 Jl 2 '65
Adaptations to cold. L. Irving. il Sci Am 214:94-101 bibliog(p 135-6) Ja '66
First aid. C. J. Potthoff. Todays Health 43:74 Mr '65
How to cope with cold weather. A. Hamilton. il Sci Digest 58:56-60 D '65
Induced hypersensitivity to cold. H. Selye. il Science 149:201 Jl 9 '65

Therapeutic applications
Freeze on death? Newsweek 65:55 My 31 '65
Ice aids snakebite cure. Sci N L 88:99 Ag 14 '65
See also
Cryogenic surgery

COLD (disease)
Personal business; self-medication can be dangerous. Bsns W p 147 F 13 '65
Still common cold. il Time 85:44 F 12 '65
Warming up for attack on the common cold; Purdue university research report. Bsns W p55 N 6 '65
When your baby catches cold. C. A. Holmes. il Parents Mag 41:36-7+ Ja '66

Vaccines
Common cold: a hopeful, new look. S. L. Englebardt. il Sci Digest 58:56-9 O '65
Cure for the common cold? capsule vaccine? interview. R. M. Chanock and R. J. Huebner. U S News 58:46-8 My 3 '65
New light on an old mystery: the common cold; interferon. M. J. E. Senn. il McCalls 93:136-7+ N '65
Type of common cold prevented by vaccine. Sci N L 87:377 Je 12 '65

COLD frames
Portable frame you can build. R. E. Wester and W. E. Edgerley. il Horticulture 43:24-5 Mr '65

COLD remedies. See Medicines, Patent, proprietary, etc.

COLD sores. See Blisters

COLD soups. See Soups

COLD SPRING HARBOR, N.Y.
Cold Spring Harbor high school; decentralized libraries. Z. R. George. il Library J 90:5475-7 D 15 '65

COLD typography. See Printing

COLD war. See Communism and democracy; World politics, 1945-

COLD war (United States and Russia) See United States—Foreign relations—Russia

COLD weather, Physiological effect of. See Temperature—Physiological effects

COLD welding. See Welding

COLDFRAMES. See Cold frames

COLDS. See Cold (disease)

COLE, Dandridge M.
Dandridge Cole: G.E.'s way-out man. B. H. Frisch. il pors Sci Digest 58:9-15 Jl '65

COLE, Elbert
Day in the life of a man who tries. il pors Sat Eve Post 238:24+ Ap 24 '65

COLE, Eva
Welcome, parents; drama. Plays 25:56-9 N '65

COLE, Gladys A.
Furnishing doll houses became a business. S. A. Parvin. il Hobbies 70:122 Ja '66

COLE, Janet
Birdwatching. Parents Mag 40:87 Je '65

COLE, Joseph J.
Cole, the old king. A. Leich and R. Leich. il por Motor T 17:42-5 Jl '65

COLE, Leonard J. and Nowell, P. C.
Radiation carcinogenesis: the sequence of events. bibliog Science 150:1782-6 D 31 '65
—See Nowell, P. C. jt. auth.

COLE, Marget Cochrane
Not for eating. Flower Grower 52:29 O '65

COLE, Maria (Hawkins)
Why I am returning to show business. pors Ebony 21:45-50+ Ja '66

COLE, Nat King
King. il por Time 85:60 F 26 '65
King of song dies, and a friend remembers him. T. Thompson. por Life 58:36 F 26 '65
Life and death of Nat King Cole. L. Robinson. il pors Ebony 20:123-34 Ap '65
Soft answers. por Newsweek 65:81 Mr 1 '65

COLE, Tom
On the edge of Arcadia; story; excerpt from End to chivalry. Atlan 216:81-8 S '65

COLE national corporation
Key maker Cole sharpens its vision; largest vendor of replacement keys. il Bsns W p84+ Ja 15 '66

COLEBROOK, Joan
Boston's South End. New Repub 152:8-12 Mr 6; 37 Mr 27 '65
Reporter at large. New Yorker 41:47-8+ Je 12 '65; 35-6+ Ja 1 '66

COLEMAN, Dorothy
Doll convention in nation's capitol. Hobbies 70:38+ D '65

COLEMAN, Elliott
Solo; poem. Poetry 106:278 Jl '65

COLEMAN, Emily
Ballet theatre at twenty-five. Sat R 48:51-3 F 27 '65
Fine new Mimi sings everywhere at once. Life 59:23 O 29 '65
Gags & good intentions can't tame a shrew. Life 59:13 Jl 23 '65
Hi-fi hit for Wagner's masterwork. Life 59:22 Jl 2 '65

COLEMAN, J. E. and Hagans, J. F.
Gebhard astronomical and world clock. Hobbies 70:44-5+ N: 44 D '65; 44-5 Ja '66

COLEMAN, James Plemon
Armed justice? Commonweal 82:517 Jl 23 '65
Haunting litany. Newsweek 66:17-18 Jl 12 '65
Judge Coleman? New Repub 152:7 My 29 '65
Judgment on a judge. Newsweek 66:30-1 Jl 26 '65
Mississippi's best. por Time 86:17-18 Jl 23 '65
Stirring controversy, two LBJ nominations. U S News 59:10 Jl 26 '65

COLEMAN, Ornette
Jazz concerts; composer of the new thing. W. Balliett. New Yorker 41:122-4 F 27 '65
Ornette Coleman: innovator or incompetent? B. Whitworth. il Holiday 38:81-2+ S '65

COLEMAN, Patricia P.
Travel tips (cont) Sr Schol 86:10T F 25; sup 10 My 13 '65

COLEMAN, Thomas L.
Hayneville justice. il Newsweek 66:36+ O 11 '65
License to kill. por Time 86:34-5 O 8 '65
Trial in Hayneville. Sr Schol 87:17 O 14 '65

COLEOPTERA. See Beetles

COLES, Robert
Anatomy of perversion. New Repub 153:25-7 O 16 '65
Bussing in Boston. New Repub 153:12-15 O 2 '65
Compelling summons. Reporter 33:59-62 O 21 '65
Mind of the poor. New Repub 152:21-3 F 6 '65
Pills they push. New Repub 154:25-7 Ja 1 '66
Poor don't want to be middle-class. N Y Times Mag p7+ D 19 '65
Public evil and private problems: segregation and psychiatry. Yale R 54:513-31 Je '65
Treating the mentally ill. New Repub 152:17-20 F 20 '65
Voices from the South. Harper 230:165 Ap '65
What colonialism does. New Repub 153:20+ S 18 '65
What migrant farm children learn. Sat R 48:73-4+ My 15 '65

COLETTI, Anthony
How we feed college cows. por Suc Farm 63:106+ F '65

COLETTI, Antonio Magini-. See Magini-Coletti, A.

COLEUS
If you are a fancy leaf fancier. il Sunset 134:241 Mr '65

COLGATE Palmolive company
Laundry detergent steps up. M. B. Keiser. il Parents Mag 40:16+ Ap '65

COLGATE university, Hamilton, N.Y.
College looks ahead; adaptation of address, October 15, 1964. V. M. Barnett, jr. Sch & Soc 93:219-20 Ap 3 '65

COLIC
What to do for the colicky baby. M. I. Levine. il Parents Mag 40:54-5+ O '65

COLIJN, Helen
Do's and don'ts in Europe. Seventeen 24:93 My '65

COLINVAUX, Paul A.
First Americans: the evidence of mud. Yale R 54:397-410 Mr '65
Origin of ice ages: pollen evidence from Arctic Alaska. bibliog Science 145:707-8; 147:633 Ag 14 '64, F 5 '65

COLLAGE
Black clouds & pink rain; cloth collage. L. Webber. il Sch Arts 65:13 D '65
Collages by Bellanca. il U S Camera 28:26-7 Ag '65
Fabric collage; exhibition at Museum of contemporary crafts, New York. K. Sawyer. il Craft Horiz 25:16-21+ Mr '65
Revolution from refuse; work of K. Schwitters. il Time 85:64 Je 4 '65

COLLAGEN
Cable of collagen. Sci Am 212:61 Je '65
Catabolism of collagen; report on workshop. H. B. Bensusan and L. Klein. Science 148:1758-9 Je 25 '65
Collagen defect induced by penicillamine. M. E. Nimni and L. A. Bavetta. bibliog il Science 150:905-7 N 12 '65
Collagen: structural studies based on the cleavage of methionyl bonds. P. Bornstein and K. A. Piez. bibliog il Science 148:1353-5 Je 4 '65
Collagenase: effect on the morphogenesis of embryonic salivary epithelium in vitro. C. Grobstein and J. Cohen. bibliog il Science 150:626-8 O 29 '65
Immunoelectrophoresis reveals collagen solubility in human serum. J. Frey and others. bibliog il Science 150:751-2 N 5 '65
Protein chain unraveled. Sci N L 87:227 Ap 10 '65
Synthetic skin tests lift hopes in burn cases. il Bsns W p52 D 4 '65

COLLECTING. See Collectors and collecting

COLLECTIVE bargaining
Antitrust law moves into bargaining room; unions forfeit exemption. Bsns W p 139-40 Je 12 '65
Bargaining weather: fair and mild; few contracts open; with chart. Bsns W p37-9 Ja 1 '66

Business, labor, and the White House. il Duns R 86:44-5+ N '65
Collective bargaining; address, April 14, 1965. V. B. Day. Vital Speeches 31:437-41 My 1 '65
Collective bargaining solutions to technological change; excerpt from address, December 1964. A. Weber. Mo Labor R 88:17-18 Ja '65
Contract talks enter a long, tough alley; administration trouble-shooters believe. Bsns W p43-4 Mr 27 '65
Factory workers under bargaining agreements. A. Strasser. il Mo Labor R 88:164-7 F '65
Joint consultation devices in collective bargaining. Mo Labor R 88:173 F '65
Labor-management since World war II. J. P. Goldberg. Cur Hist 48:346-52+ Je '65
Labor relations in the Common market. C. W. Summers. il Harvard Bsns R 43:148-50+ Mr '65
Labor: the rank-and-file revolt. T. R. Brooks. il Duns R 85:34-5+ Mr '65
Let's stop Labor board's unfair practices. S. Rothman. il Nations Bsns 53:34-5+ My '65
Multiemployer bargaining and the balancing of power. Mo Labor R 88:III-IV Ap '65
Multiemployer bargaining; extent rationale and future. C. M. Rehmus. Cur Hist 49:91-6+ Ag '65
Shifting winds of collective bargaining. M. E. Stone. Mo Labor R 88:401 Ap '65
Trade union alliances for collective bargaining. Mo Labor R 88:III-IV My '65
See also
Industrial relations
Trade agreements

Electric industries
Six unions team up for electrical talks. Bsns W p 166 O 9 '65

Petroleum industry
Prospects rise for pact in oil; money gap narrow, strike may be averted. il Bsns W p 120-1 O 2 '65

Steel industry
After steel dispute: the outlook for business. il U S News 59:93-4 S 13 '65
Eye to eye; negotiations between the United steelworkers union and the steel industry. il Newsweek 66:56 S 6 '65
How the terms fit the guidelines. il Bsns W p 167-8 S 11 '65
In steel, a deal close to guidelines; with editorial comment. il Bsns W p28-30, 122 S 4 '65
Is collective bargaining a myth? excerpts from address, October 14, 1965. with reply by I. W. Abel. R. C. Cooper. il U S News 59:104-6+ N 15 '65
New steel pact: its meaning. il U S News 59:96+ S 13 '65
Pacesetter's pace. il Time 86:113-14 S 17 '65
Steel answers and real questions. il Newsweek 66:19-20 S 13 '65
Steel negotiators get down to brass tacks. Bsns W p55-6 Je 19 '65
Steel settlement with a difference. Fortune 72:111-12 O '65
Steel sights ray of hope; negotiations in critical stage. Bsns W p86 Ap 3 '65
Steel talks come into the homestretch. il Bsns W p25 Ag 28 '65
Steelworkers vote: prelude to the strike. B. J. Widick. il Nation 200:214-16 Mr 1 '65
To the brink in steel; Pittsburgh. il Time 86:19-20 S 3 '65
USW hears rumble on local issues: dissatisfaction over bargaining techniques. Bsns W p69 O 16 '65
Wage barrier looms in steel bargaining. il Bsns W p 144+ Ap 10 '65
What happens to bargaining now? il Newsweek 66:71-2+ S 20 '65
When the President cracked his whip; with editorial comment. il Bsns W p24-5, 204 S 11 '65
Where do unions go after steel? Bsns W p 150 S 18 '65
Whole stack; determination to avert nationwide steel strike. il Time 86:15-16 S 10 '65

COLLECTIVE bargaining, Industry wide
New tool for union bargainers; privilege granted by National labor relations board. U S News 59:114 O 11 '65

COLLECTIVE farms

Russia
Private plot vs. collective farm. A. B. Ballard. il N Y Times Mag p 14-15+ Je 13 '65

COLLECTIVE security. See International security

COLLECTIVE settlements
Communistic societies of the United States. by C. Nordhoff. Review
Newsweek il 67:59 Ja 3 '66

Israel
Kibbutzing in Israel. J. Lieber. il Travel 123: 48-51+ F '65

COLLECTORS and collecting
And everything in its place; some collectors and their displays. B. Plumb. il N Y Times Mag p 136-7 S 12 '65
Antiques' travel guide. See issues of Antiques
Collectors' notes. E. Gaines. See issues of Antiques
I have a dream house. il Seventeen 25:86-7+ Ja '66
Out in the open. E. Sverbeyeff. il N Y Times Mag p90-1 Ap 18 '65
Show off in your own gallery; ways to display collections and decorate your room. il Seventeen 25:39-40 Ja '66
Treasure hunt. J. Mebane. il Bet Hom & Gard 43:25+ My; 82-3 Je; 96 Ag; 41-2 S; 10+ O; 47-8 N '65; 44:54-5+ Ja '66
Treasure hunt; flatirons and bootjacks. J. Mebane. il Bet Hom & Gard 43:25+ My; 82-3 Je '65
See also
Antiques
Art—Private collections
Book collecting
also subhead Collectors and collecting under various subjects, e.g. Rocks—Collectors and collecting

COLLEGE, Choice of
College & careers. D. Klein. il Seventeen 24:104-5 Ap; 216-17 My; 166-7 Je; 20+ Jl; 30+ Ag; 246-8 S; 56+ O; 20+ N; 32+ D '65
Looking ahead to college and careers. J. Hawkes. See issues of Seventeen through March 1965
Which college is best? J. A. Perkins. il Sat R 48:71-2+ S 11 '65

COLLEGE administration. See Colleges and universities—Administration

COLLEGE administrators. See College officials

COLLEGE admission. See Colleges and universities—Entrance requirements

COLLEGE and school drama
University theater. R. A. Duprey. il Cath World 201:240-6 Jl '65
Yes, we are collegiate! J. Anderson. il Dance Mag 39:46 F '65

Texts
Junior and senior high. See issues of Plays

COLLEGE and school journalism
Can the comedy; MIT freshman magazine. il Newsweek 65:105-6 Je 14 '65
Diamond in the college press; University of Michigan's Daily celebrates its seventy-fifth anniversary. R. L. Tobin. Sat R 48: 115-16 S 18 '65
Invasion of the Harvards; editors of nation's newest weekly, Southern courier. il Newsweek 66:81-2 Jl 26 '65
Putting out the school newspaper. H. Morganti. NEA J 54:41-2 Mr '65
School literary magazines; what's out, what's in. il Seventeen 24:152-3+ S '65
Spider strikes; collection of festering excerpts from semimonthly malcontent manifesto of Berkeley. il Esquire 64:90-1 S '65
Student publications and the Tufts plan (or alma mater, yours in pride) J. Ciardi. Sat R 48:20-2 S 11 '65
Where have all the young writers gone? report on the 1965 student magazine contest. S. B. Chickering. il Sat R 48:26-7 O 9 '65

COLLEGE architecture
Architecture and art building will introduce Netsch's new geometries. il Arch Forum 123:42-3 S '65
Architecture that transforms a campus; Clark university. il Arch Rec 137:157-68 My '65
Building types study. il Arch Rec 137:143-66 Je; 138:137-60 O '65
Campus City, Chicago; University of Illinois' new urban campus. il Arch Forum 123:21-45 S '65
Container to fit the contained; new building for Harvard graduate school of education. il Time 87:64-6 Ja 21 '66
Harvard tweed; Roy E. Larsen Hall. il Newsweek 66:94 O 11 '65
Horrors at Berkeley, or did architecture make students riot? F. MacShane. il Art N 64:30-3+ S '65
In Canada, the continent's first single-structure campus. D. Lyndon. il Arch Forum 123:13-21 D '65

Integrated site planning and design for a small college; Concordia Lutheran junior college, Ann Arbor, Mich. il Arch Rec 138: 189-96 S '65
Ivyless halls of Yale. il Holiday 37:76-81 My '65
Labor and material required for college housing. S. F. Miller. il Mo Labor R 88:1100-4 S '65
Late Frank Lloyd Wright is completed in Kansas; Corbin education center, Wichita state U. il Fortune 71:186 Je '65
New kind of client with $1.5 billion to spend; New York state university construction fund. W. McQuade. il Fortune 71:165-6 Mr '65
New look of campus living. R. C. Weaver. il Am Ed 1:14-21 D '64
University building by a master hand; Alvar Aalto's new classroom complex for the Finnish technical institute, Helsinki; with commentary by F. Gutheim. il Arch Rec 137:169-76 Ap '65
See also
Dormitories
Gymnasiums

COLLEGE athlete recruiting. See Athletes—Recruiting

COLLEGE athletes. See Athletes

COLLEGE athletics
Scramble for college athletes; increasing professionalism. P. H. Giddens. il Atlan 216: 49-52 D '65
See also
Basketball
Cheer leaders
Football
Rowing
Track athletics
Wrestling

COLLEGE auditoriums. See Auditoriums

COLLEGE bookstores
Chicago's newest showcase; U. of Illinois bookstore. E. B. Vest. il Pub W 189:32-5 Ja 3 '66
Fifty college stores using mail call promotion. il Pub W 188:38 O 11 '65
Management tools for bookstores and general college stores; summary of workshops during annual meeting of National association of college stores. il Pub W 188:66-71 S 20 '65
MIT tech coop honors Wiley authors on campus. il Pub W 188:90 N 15 '65
NACS annual meeting; books, education and the college store. il Pub W 187:52-4 Je 14 '65
NACS merchandising awards presented at NACS convention. Pub W 187:89-90 Je 14 '65
Tech coop; service to faculty, students, industry; MIT. il Pub W 188:52-4 D 6 '65
When planning a college store, call in an expert; sessions at annual meeting of National association of college stores. il Pub W 188:36-40 Jl 5 '65

COLLEGE degrees. See Degrees, Academic

COLLEGE dining halls. See Colleges and universities—Dining halls

COLLEGE discipline
Crisis on our campuses; excerpts from address. J. A. Logan. Read Digest 86:124-6 F '65
Cure for campus riots; interview. M. Rafferty. il U S News 58:70-2 My 17 '65
Escalation in California. N. Cousins; reply. C. Kerr. Sat R 48:21+ Mr 6 '65
Stiffening the spine; question of university discipline. il Time 85:48 Mr 19 '65
What parents think about campus morals. Read Digest 86:141-4 My '65

COLLEGE dormitories. See Dormitories

COLLEGE dropouts. See Dropouts

COLLEGE education
American higher education in 1980. R. Gross. Sch & Soc 93:484-5 D 11 '65
College education for what? W. C. Booth. il NEA J 54:14-16 D '65
College grad has been short-changed. A. Hacker. il N Y Times Mag p25+ Je 6 '65
Colleges of tomorrow. A. T. Hill. Sat R 48: 78-9 S 11 '65
Commencement '65; implications of protests during 1964-1965 academic year. Commonweal 82:397 Je 18 '65
Deeper bases of policy in higher education; excerpt from Bases for policy in higher education. J. S. Brubacher. bibliog f Sch & Soc 93:308-19 Sum '65
Higher education and 1984; adaptation of address. November 2, 1964. L. Wilson Sch & Soc 93:343-6 O 2 '65

COLLEGE education—*Continued*
Is the college student becoming a forgotten man? adaptation of address, October 22, 1964. L. Wilson. Sch & Soc 93:78-81 F 6 '65
Job that buys a dream; work-study programs. J. T. Farrell. il Am Ed 1:1-4 O '65
Toward academic emphasis in American higher education; excerpts from address, November 12, 1965. W. W. Brickman. Sch & Soc 94:4 Ja 8 '66
What's going on in schools & colleges. See issues of Changing times
See also
Coeducation
Colleges and universities—Curriculum
Junior colleges
Liberal education
Technical education

COLLEGE education, Cost of
Graduate speed-up. J. Neugeboren. Commonweal 83:8 O 8 '65
How to beat the high cost of college; excerpts. C. Cox. il Seventeen 24:134-5+ F '65
How your child can afford to go to college. F. Bailey, jr. il Suc Farm 63:64+ My '65
Loans that really pay off; borrowing for education. D. Hanson. Suc Farm 63:6 O '65

COLLEGE education, Experimental
See also
Union for research and experimentation in higher education

COLLEGE education, Value of
Loans that really pay off; borrowing for education. D. Hanson. Suc Farm 63:6 O '65
No, you don't have to go to college. il Changing T 19:7-10 Ap '65
Speaking out; colleges are obsolete. R. M. Hutchins. Sat Eve Post 238:10+ S 25 '65
What next for your teen-ager? symposium. Farm J 89:57-9 Je '65
What people think about college. W. C. Eckerman and A. Campbell. il Am Ed 1:30-2 F '65

COLLEGE enrollment. See Colleges and universities—Attendance

COLLEGE entrance examination board
College boards fail the test. B. Hoffmann. il N Y Times Mag p52-3+ O 24 '65; Discussion. p40 N 7 '65
How to write without thinking. N. Cousins. Sat R 48:30 My 1; 20 My 29 '65; Discussion. 48:17-18 Je 5 '65
Those college boards! O. Palmer. Seventeen 24:136-7+ S '65
Unreasonable: English teachers reading of examination essays at Nassau inn, Princeton. New Yorker 41:35-6 Mr 27 '65
See also
Colleges and universities—Entrance requirements

Advanced placement program
AP; bright new tone in education. S. Schuler. il PTA Mag 59:4-7 Je '65; Same abr. with title Bright new horizons for the gifted student. Read Digest 87:33-4+ S '65
Way to do college work in high school. il Good H 161:143 Ag '65

Scholastic aptitude test
Educational testing: the SAT. R. Hoffmann. il Mlle 62:112-13+ D '65

COLLEGE entrance requirements. See Colleges and universities—Entrance requirements

COLLEGE ethics. See Student ethics

COLLEGE faculties. See College professors and instructors

COLLEGE fees. See Colleges and universities—Finance

COLLEGE football. See Football

COLLEGE football players. See Football players

COLLEGE fraternities
Fraternities at the University of Rochester. Sch & Soc 93:77+ F 6 '65
See also
Hazing

Desegregation
Federal aid and segregated fraternities. Sch & Soc 93:336+ O 2 '65
Fraternities get the grip. il Time ;85:53 Je 25 '65
Troubled heart of Sigma chi; attempt to pledge a Negro at University of Michigan. H. Higdon. il N Y Times Mag p48-9+ N 14 '65
What happens when Sigma chi pledges a Negro. il Look 29:36-40 Jl 27 '65

COLLEGE freshmen. See College students

COLLEGE girls. See College students, Women

COLLEGE glee clubs. See Choral groups and societies

COLLEGE graduates
Commencement '65; implications of protests during 1964-1965 academic year. Commonweal 82:397 Je 18 '65
Ethics of executive selection. L. B. Ward. bibliog f il Harvard Bsns R 43:6-8+ Mr '65
For college grads: no job problem. U S News 58:88 My 24 '65
How different we were! 25th reunion at Yale. W. Gibson. il N Y Times Mag p8-9+ Je 13 '65
How does religion influence job choice? Harvard study. il Bsns W p 178+ Ap 17 '65
Industry plugs positive Negro job message; Opportunity center. il Bsns W p34 Je 26 '65
Is business letting young people down? P. F. Drucker. Harvard Bsns R 43:49-55 N '65
They're not trying to succeed in business; college seniors. L. Stessin. il N Y Times Mag p76+ Mr 28 '65
See also
College education, Value of
Colleges and universities—Graduate work

COLLEGE graduates, Women
Is someone kidding the college girl? creation in college, then typing in a NY office. J. Shepherd. il Look 30:36-8 Ja 11 '66

COLLEGE interviews. See Interviewing

COLLEGE journalism. See College and school journalism

COLLEGE laboratories

Architecture
See Laboratories—Architecture

COLLEGE libraries
Campus library. J. G. Lorenz and P. P. Muirhead. il Am Ed 1:12-19 My '65
How to succeed in book reports without really reading; Reading avoidance service. J. Biermann and B. Toohey. il Library J 90:5348-50 D 15 '65
Librarians' Pugwash, or INTREX on the Cape; conference on MIT's program, Wood Hole, Mass. J. H. Shera. bibliog Wilson Lib Bul 40:359-62 D '65
University libraries in developing countries; address, July 1965. L. E. Asheim. ALA Bul 59:795-802 O '65
Vision of university library of 1975 emerges from Woods Hole conference; MIT's project INTREX (Information transfer experiments) Library J 90:4024 O 1 '65

Acquisitions
Haphazard acquisitioning. P. Smith. Library J 90:2916+ Jl '65
Library at a crossroad; excerpt from the University of Colorado libraries annual report, 1964-65. R. E. Ellsworth. Library J 90:5344 D 15 '65
Scholarship on a budget. B. Thomas. bibliog il Library J 90:2209-14 My 15 '65

Architecture
See Library architecture

Book selection
See Book selection

Circulation, loans, etc.
See also
Research libraries—Circulation, loans, etc.

Cooperation
Univ. of North Dakota library ends statewide loan service. Library J 90:2520 Je 1 '65

Departmental and divisional libraries
Divisional reading room; college and university libraries. G. Fitzgerald. Wilson Lib Bul 39:565-6+ Mr '65

Finance
Costs of academic library services forecast in Canadian library brief. Library J 90:1090 Mr 1 '65
Legislature is not convinced; state-suppported academic library budget. R. E. Ellsworth. il Library J 90:2199-203 My 15 '65; Discussion. 90:3156+ Ag '65
Library at a crossroad; excerpt from the University of Colorado libraries annual report, 1964-65. R. E. Ellsworth. Library J 90:5344 D 15 '65
Usual: visit to the United States university average library. J. Weatherford. il Library J 90:5345-7 D 15 '65

Instruction in use
See Libraries—Instruction in use

COLLEGE libraries—*Continued*

Reserve systems
Unreserved book. J. Berry. Library J 90:2228 My 15 '65

Science collections
See Libraries—Science collections

COLLEGE libraries and audio-visual materials. See Libraries and audio-visual materials

COLLEGE library architecture. See Library architecture

COLLEGE life. See Student life

COLLEGE newspapers. See College and school journalism

COLLEGE of agriculture at Cornell university, Ithaca. See New York state university—College of agriculture at Cornell university, Ithaca

COLLEGE of cardinals. See Cardinals

COLLEGE of the desert, Palm Desert, Calif. Colonnades in a desert landscape. il Arch Rec 137:160-1 Je '65

COLLEGE officials
Training college administrators. Sch & Soc 93:135 F 20 '65
See also
College presidents

COLLEGE operas, revues, etc.
Bloomington; I. U. music school. Q. Eaton. il Opera N 30:26-30 Ja 8 '66
Denver's Falstaff. A. Young. Opera N 29:33 Ap 10 '65
L.A. ambitions. A. Goldberg. Opera N 29:31 Mr 20 '65
Midwest medley; University of Chicago and Northwestern. J. W. Stedman. il Opera N 29:33 Ap 10 '65

COLLEGE PARK, Md.
One-man refuse collection. J. P. McDonald. il Am City 80:93 S '65

COLLEGE periodicals. See College and school journalism

COLLEGE presidents
Making of college presidents. V. R. Alden. Sat R 48:86-7 F 20 '65
Presidential perils. il Time 85:58 Je 18 '65
What's wrong with our students? characteristics of the ideal administrator. D. Hollowell. New Repub 152:24 F 20 '65

COLLEGE professors and instructors
Beleaguered professors. I. Howe. il Atlan 216:115-18 N '65
But is the teacher also a citizen? adaptation of address, April 14, 1965. A. M. Weinberg. bibliog Science 149:601-6 Ag 6 '65; Discussion. 150:141-2+, 965 O 8, N 19 '65
Crescendo on the campus: our new music centers; Indiana university's school of music. H. Pleasants. il Reporter 33:52-6 S 23 '65
Doctoral feedback into higher education. R. H. Bolt and others. bibliog il Science 148:918-28 My 14 '65
Education's faceless factories shortchange our students. F. Morley. il Nations Bsns 53:27-8 F '65
Grass roots of campus freedom. F. Heimberger. il Sat R 48:60-1+ Jl 17 '65
Human dimension in college teaching. E. R. Hilgard. il NEA J 54:43-5 S '65
New reality; God is dead; proclamation by T. J. J. Altizer. Newsweek 66:71-2 N 22 '65
Opening the classroom door; experts observe techniques and assess abilities of lecturers at Earlham college. il Time 85:74 Je 11 '65
Oxford's magnificent oddballs. J. Morris. Harper 231:69-74 N '65
Path to promotion; hiring and firing. A. Mizener. il Atlan 216:135-8 N '65
Professional teacher or dedicated amateur? address, March 3, 1965. R. H. Garrison. Sch & Soc 93:390-2 O 30 '65
Should the artist come to the campus? adaptation of address. J. A. Perkins. il Sat R 48:54-6+ Jl 17 '65
Suggestions for the college supervisor. G. Margosian. NEA J 54:39 Ap '65
Ubiquitous TA. il Time 85:49-50 Je 4 '65
What are professors for? P. H. Abelson. Science 148:1545 Je 18 '65; Discussion. 149:910+, 1047 Ag 27-S 3 '65
Why Harvard still ranks first; oldest graduate economics department. il Bsns W p 118-20+ Ap 24 '65
See also
Academic freedom
Colleges and universities—Administration
Colleges and universities—Teaching
Teachers and students

Education
Faculty education and income in Negro and white colleges. il Mo Labor R 88:537-40 My '65

Political activities
Morally suffocating? dismissal of teachers. Newsweek 66:65 D 27 '65
What is a Socialist? first annual Socialist scholars conference. J. O'Connor. Nation 201:195-6 O 4 '65
See also
Teach-ins

Publications
Publish or perish; publishing vs. quality of teaching. H. M. Wriston. Sat R 48:59 Jl 17 '65; Discussion. 48:47 Ag 21 '65
Publish or perish. Commonweal 81:776-7 Mr 19 '65
Publish or perish, why Prof. Edelweiss has little time for junior. R. Langbaum. il N Y Times Mag p74-5+ N 14 '65

Qualifications
Educational equipment of the professor of education. W. W. Brickman. Sch & Soc 93:111 F 20 '65
Teachers as scholars. F. T. Worrell; reply. R. S. Alexander. Science 147:1087 Mr 5 '65
Teaching is better than ever. J. R. Killian, jr. il Atlan 216:53-6 D '65

Rating
Grading the graders; Yale committee proposes official status for student evaluations of teachers. Newsweek 66:98 O 25 '65
How to rate a teacher; case of R. J. Bernstein at Yale. il Time 85:48 Mr 12 '65
Yale's tenure trouble; case of R. J. Bernstein. N. S. Care. New Repub 152:13-14 Mr 27 '65; Reply. C. Mitchell. 152:29 Ap 10 '65

Rating by students
How do they rate you, professor? H. G. Shane. il NEA J 54:18-20 N '65

Salaries
A for affluence. il Newsweek 65:68 Ap 19 '65
Faculty education and income in Negro and white colleges. il Mo Labor R 88:537-40 My '65
Professors' salaries still near bottom of scale. Sci N L 87:281 My 1 '65

Supply and demand
Scientists drift from teaching. il Bsns W p52-3 Ja 8 '66

Tenure
Kearns case. J. Leo; discussion. Commonweal 81:718-19, 774-5+; 82:31, 34-5+, 178-9+ Mr 5, 19-Ap 2, 30 '65
Protest at Yale. Nation 200:266-7 Mr 15 '65
Publish or perish; publishing vs. quality of teaching. H. M. Wriston. Sat R 48:59 Jl 17 '65; Discussion. 48:47 Ag 21 '65
Students & tenure at Yale. Time 86:64 O 22 '65
Yale's tenure trouble; case of R. J. Bernstein. N. S. Care. New Repub 152:13-14 Mr 27 '65; Reply. C. Mitchell. 152:29 Ap 10 '65

COLLEGE professors and instructors, Women. See Women as teachers

COLLEGE recruiting. See Employment systems

COLLEGE reunions. See College graduates

COLLEGE sports. See College athletics

COLLEGE stores association. See National association of college stores

COLLEGE students
Adults view: kids under pressure. il Newsweek 65:60+ Mr 22 '65
Campus '65. il Newsweek 65:43-8+ Mr 22 '65
Causes of the student revolution. J. Katz and N. Sanford. il Sat R 48:64-6+ D 18 '65
College presidents look at the students; subject at American council on education meeting. H. H. Miller. New Repub 153:9-10 O 23 '65
College students change majors. M. O. Cook. il Sch & Soc 93:271-3 My 1 '65
College students: the new breed. J. L. Jarrett. il Sat R 48:64-5+ Mr 20 '65; Reply. G. F. Lewis. 48:75-6 S 11 '65
Cool hours; TV viewing. il Newsweek 67:80 Ja 17 '66
Do junior college transfers make the grade? survey findings. J. H. Nelson. il NEA J 54:55-7 O '65
Drug puzzle; student use of drugs. M. Herr. Mlle 61:246-7+ Ag '65
Letter from the Berkeley underground. M. Miller. Esquire 64-85-7+ S '65
Little sex without love. Time 85:46 Ap 9 '65
Minority view: tradition of free student expression upheld by Tufts university. Commonweal 82:276 My 21 '65

COLLEGE students—*Continued*

Morals on the campus; a professor and a minister disagree on the present state of student morality. N. Sanford; A. Kinsolving. NEA J 54:20-4 Ap '65

New voices on campus; interview, ed. by W. McWhirter. F. D. Murphy. Mlle 61:302+ Ag '65

New voices on campus; symposium of student-activists. il Mlle 61:303-5+ Ag '65

Non-academic profile of college freshmen. Sch & Soc 93:292-3 Sum '65

Phila. jurist visits trouble spots in Far East; address, August 20, 1965. R. P. Alexander. Negro Hist Bul 29:11-12+ O '65

Pill and morality. A. Hacker. il N Y Times Mag p32-3+ N 21 '65

Politically ignorant college students; recrudescent Communist movement on the campus. R. Kirk. Nat R 17:423 My 18 '65

Robert McNamara, crime syndicate head; test shows ignorance of current events. D. Berkman. Nat R 17:282+ Ap 6 '65

Salvation on the campus; why existentialism is capturing the students. J. G. Gray. Harper 230:53-9 My '65; Discussion. 231:12+ Jl '65

Second time around; transfer students. il Newsweek 65:86 My 3 '65

Stealing their way through college. R. Hodesh. Esquire 64:96+ S '65

Student protest and commitment; address, June 15, 1965. N. M. Pusey. Sch & Soc 93:471-4 D 11 '65

Student tastes: a sandy culture. il Newsweek 65:58-60 Mr 22 '65

Surf, snow, sex & protest; spring-vacationing students. il Time 85:61 Ap 2 '65

This year's freshmen: more and better! A. D. Holt. il NEA J 54:29-30 Ap '65

Troubled campus; symposium. il Atlan 216:107-12+ N '65

Twenty-eight people who count; heroes of the California rebels. il Esquire 64:97 S '65

Who speaks for today's youth? R. E. Fitch. Christian Cent 82:1348-50 N 3 '65

Why the students revolt. B. Ward; reply. K. Auletta. Nation 200:inside cover F 22 '65

See also
American students in foreign countries
Coeducation
Cuban students
Foreign students in the United States
National student Christian federation
Student activities
Student demonstrations
Student life
Student volunteer movement
Study
Teachers and students
United States national student association
Young Americans for freedom (organization)

Adjustment

Help for freshmen. W. H. Cornog. Sat R 48:79 S 11 '65

Post-industrial generation: roots of student discontent. M. B. Freedman. il Nation 200:639-43 Je 14 '65

What the college catalogues don't tell you. il Seventeen 24:238-9+ Ag '65

Age

Students, or grown-ups posing as students? J. W. Ramsey. NEA J 55:16-18 Ja '66

Aid

Battling for student loan market. il Bsns W p47-50 Jl 17 '65

Cash for college careers. il Ebony 20:40-2+ Ap '65

Good news for students short on cash. R. C. Davids. Farm J 89:59 Je '65

Need money for graduate study? how & where to find it. il Changing T 19:43-4 O '65

New plan for tuition grants. V. C. Blum. America 113:499 O 30 '65

What's the current picture on college financial aid? Bet Hom & Gard 43:148 O '65

See also
Scholarships and fellowships
Student loans

Anecdotes, facetiae, satire, etc.

Get those people out of my cellar! J. E. Varney. il Read Digest 86:244-6+ F '65

Caricatures and cartoons

John Held, jr. and his world. J. Shuttleworth. Am Heritage 16:28-32 Ag '65

Cheating

See Cheating in schoolwork

Communist activities

Are campus radicals more red than the reds? excerpts from testimony. S. T. Possony. U S News 59:10 S 6 '65

Behind the campus protests over draft and Vietnam. U S News 59:6 O 25 '65

Campus Communists: America's time bomb? interview. S. T. Possony. il U S News 59:42-5 N 1 '65

Explosive revival of the far left. R. Armstrong. il Sat Eve Post 238:27-32+ My 8 '65

March, countermarch. Nat R 17:964+ N 2 '65

New American revolution. P. A. McCombs. il Nat R 17:766-8+ S 7 '65

New wave of unrest on college campuses? U S News 59:15 O 18 '65

Where reds are busy on the campuses. il U S News 58:53-4 Je 7 '65

Dating

See Dating

Discipline

See College discipline

Employment

Butler goes to college. S. Gordon. il Look 29:106-8 My 4 '65

Financing your college education. J. Beck. il Todays Health 43:32-5+ F '65

Expenditures

See also
College education, Cost of

Failures

See Dropouts

Grading

See Grading and marking (students)

Housing

Married students housing; University of Georgia. il Arch Rec 138:119 Ag '65

New look of campus living. R. C. Weaver. il Am Ed 1:14-21 D '64

See also
Dormitories

Political activities

Activists, protesting too much? il Newsweek 65:48+ Mr 22 '65

Behind the protests at Berkeley. J. F. Boler. Commonweal 81:602-5 F 5 '65

Berkeley student revolt, ed. by S. M. Lipset and S. S. Wolin. Review Newsweek 66:51 S 6 '65

Crisis at Berkeley. E. Langer. bibliog il Science 148:198-202, 346-9 Ap 9-16 '65; Discussion. 148:1273-8 Je 4 '65

Exit arguing; Columbia pickets. il Newsweek 65:102 Je 14 '65

Here we go again. W. F. Buckley, jr. Nat R 17:411 My 18 '65

Letter from Berkeley. C. Trillin. New Yorker 41:52-4+ Mr 13 '65

Nature of dissent in a democracy; student action; address, August 23, 1965. H. H. Humphrey. Vital Speeches 31:741-3 O 1 '65

New fraternity; student and crypto-student organizations. F. Powledge. il Esquire 64:88-9+ S '65

Nonstudent left; significance of the Mulford law. H. S. Thompson. il Nation 201:154-8 S 27 '65

Now the Vietnik; demonstrations against U.S. policy in Viet Nam. il Time 86:25A O 22 '65

Platform for citizen-students; campus governments. A. Z. Bass. Sat R 48:84 O 16 '65

Public universities and student freedom. Sch & Soc 93:342 O 2 '65

Some ways toward campus peace. V. A. Rapport. Sch & Soc 93:296-7 Sum '65

Sowing future trouble; Berkeley judge passes sentence on students involved in the demonstrations. Nation 201:70 Ag 16 '65

Spanish students rebel. G. Jackson. Commonweal 83:469-71 Ja 21 '66

State dept. on campus: sit down and shut up. D. Janson. il Nation 200:547-50 My 24 '65

Student unrest in U.S. and Latin-American universities. R. R. Renner. Sch & Soc 93:294-5 Sum '65

Students: mostly on target. Life 58:4 Ap 2 '65

Sublimating student aggression. Sch & Soc 93:208+ Ap 3 '65

Vote for student protest. M. N. Gonzales. Atlan 216:112 N '65

What happened at Berkeley. J. Cass; discussion. Sat R 48:62+ F 20; 56 Mr 20 '65

What happened at Berkeley. N. Glazer. Commentary 39:39-47 F '65; Reply with rejoinder. P. Selznick. 39:80-5 Mr '65

COLLEGE students—Political activities—
—*Continued*

What the students want. J. L. Walsh. Commonweal 83:206-9 N 19 '65

What's bugging the students. I. Kristol. il Atlan 216:108-11 N '65

Young America's newest vocation; awakening the disadvantaged and the disinterested to their political opportunities and responsibilities. A. I. Waskow. il Sat R 48:12-14+ Je 5 '65

See also

Students for a democratic society (organization)

Teach-ins

Vietnamese war, 1957- —Protests, demonstrations, etc. against

Reading

Janus in the classroom. M. F. Claggett. il Sat R 48:70+ D 18 '65

Pony boom: the object is to pass, isn't it? il Newsweek 66:101-2+ N 22 '65

Recreation

See Student life

Religion

Belief in God, highly qualified. il Newsweek 65:57-8 Mr 22 '65

Catholics on campus. J. O'Gara. Commonweal 82:376 Je 11 '65; Reply. D. Hood. 82:458 Jl 2 '65

Dialogue with campus agnostics. R. E. Kavanaugh. America 114:126-8 Ja 22 '66

Students talk of their faith; Joint consultation of Pax Romana and the World student Christian federation at Taizé. J. J. Megivern. America 112:636-8 My 1 '65

See also

Colleges and universities—Religious life

Selection

See Student selection

Volunteer service

See Volunteer service

COLLEGE students, Catholic. See Catholic students

COLLEGE students, Married

Divorce, college style. il Newsweek 65:105 Je 14 '65

Perils of a Ph.T. M. Blyth. il Read Digest 87:143-6 O '65

Housing

See College students—Housing

COLLEGE students, Men

Dress

See Clothing and dress—Men

COLLEGE students, Mentally superior

Caltech, campus for genius. il Sci Digest 58:48-55 O '65

COLLEGE students, Negro. See Negro students

COLLEGE students, Women

Coeds in rebellion. B. H. Hoffman. il Ladies Home J 82:82-4+ O '65

How the girls really are; Princeton's publication Where the girls are, refuted by Life's explorations of eastern women's colleges. il Life 59:66A-71 D 17 '65

If your daughter wants to go to college. . . il U S News 58:54-5 My 24 '65

Ivy league girls on the road. M. Decter. il Esquire 64:103+ S '65

Sexual behavior of college girls. il Sch & Soc 93:208 Ap 3 '65

Tigers on the prowl; Princeton booklet. il Newsweek 66:58 N 1 '65

See also

Coeducation

COLLEGE students fads. See Fads

COLLEGE teachers. See College professors and instructors

COLLEGE teaching. See Colleges and universities—Teaching

COLLEGE verse

Ten undergraduate poems. America 112:546-7 Ap 17 '65

COLLEGE women (graduates) See College graduates, Women

COLLEGES and universities

Questions and answers about college bookings of dancers; interview, ed. by I. Fisher. F. Taylor. Dance Mag 40:52-3+ Ja '66

See also

Academic freedom

College education

College students

International association of universities

Summer schools

Vocational education

Administration

Academic organization in physical science. H. G. Booker; reply. H. J. Gray. Science 147:557-8 F 5 '65

Crisis at Berkeley. E. Langer. bibliog il Science 148:198-202, 346-9 Ap 9-16 '65; Discussion. 148:1273-8 Je 4 '65

Future administrators. D. Wolfle. Science 150:1411 D 10 '65

Good time at UCLA; an English view. R. Gilbert. Harper 230:75-80+ Ap '65

Governance of higher education; adaptation of annual report. W. K. Selden. Science 149:711 Ag 13 '65

Inefficient colleges. R. Moley. Newsweek 66: 124 O 25 '65

New voices on campus; interview, ed. by W. McWhirter. F. D. Murphy. Mlle 61:302+ Ag '65

Nonstudent left; significance of the Mulford law. H. S. Thompson. il Nation 201:154-8 S 27 '65

On the campus: a troubled reflection of the U.S. M. Ways. il Fortune 72:140-7+ O '65

Post-industrial generation: roots of student discontent. M. B. Freedman. il Nation 200: 639-43 Je 14 '65

University bosses. R. Presthus. New Repub 152:20-4 F 20 '65; Discussion. 152:28-9 Mr 13 '65

Who makes university policy? P. Woodring. Sat R 48:65-6 Ap 17 '65

Faculty participation

Dictatorship of the majority. W. L. Hickman. Sch & Soc 93:346-9 O 2 '65

Admission standards

See Colleges and universities—Entrance requirements

Attendance

Enrollment in colleges and universities, fall 1964. W. V. Grant. il Am Ed 1:back cover D '64

I am very sorry that . . . pressure of enrollment primarily in the East. il Newsweek 65:86 My 3 '65

Some reflections on graduate school enrollments. M. Kinnane. Sch & Soc 93:114 F 20 '65

Statistics of attendance in American universities and colleges, 1965-66. G. G. Parker. il Sch & Soc 94:7-22 Ja 8 '66

Where the students are. Newsweek 66:100 D 20 '65

See also

Student selection

Business schools

See Business education

Choice

See College, Choice of

Cooperation

Academic cooperation: Big ten style. S. F. Salwak. Sch & Soc 93:397-8+ O 30 '65

And Los Angeles; Immaculate Heart college to build on a site adjacent to the Associated colleges of Claremont. America 112:345 Mr 13 '65

Dream college; estimated opening date of September 1968. Hampshire college. Newsweek 66:58 Ag 16 '65

Louisville story; Bellarmine and Ursuline colleges to coordinate academic and administrative operation. America 112:345 Mr 13 '65

More colleges co-operate. America 112:414 Mr 27 '65

Regional pacts: cooperation flourishes in higher educatoin. M. Zeiger. Science 150: 728-30 N 5 '65

School with four parents; Hampshire college scheduled to open in 1969. il Time 86:49 Ag 13 '65

Curriculum

New breed of BA's; some alternatives to boredom and unrest. C. Jencks. New Repub 153:17-21 O 23 '65; Discussion. 153: 40 N 6; 36 D 4 '65

New curriculum in English, speech, and communications. S. Simonson. Sch & Soc 93: 394-5 O 30 '65

Of time and the doctorate. D. Wolfle. Science 148:1045 My 21 '65

Should the artist come to the campus? adaptation of address. J. A. Perkins. il Sat R 48:54-6+ Jl 17 '65

COLLEGES and universities—Curriculum—
—*Continued*
To eccentricity and beyond: fragmentation is
part of college life; address, September 10,
1964. G. Reddick. bibliog Vital Speeches 31:
310-16 Mr 1 '65
Which college gives the courses you want?
il Changing T 19:17-18 D '65
See also
Colleges and universities—Music departments
Liberal education

Desegregation

Perils of integration. il Newsweek 65:61 Ap
5 '65
She came through; V. Malone. il Newsweek
65:37-8 Je 14 '65
Southern political culture and school desegregation. R. E. Cleary. bibliog f Sch &
Soc 93:392-4 O 30 '65
Why church-related Negro colleges? Christian Cent 82:1179-80 S 29 '65

Dining halls

Dormitories and dining commons at Clark
university. il Arch Rec 137:158-68 My '65
Revising the gothic revival; dining hall at
Swarthmore. il Arch Rec 137:154-5 Je '65

Discipline

See College discipline

Education departments

Preparation of teachers in a liberal arts
college. T. M. Carter. Sch & Soc 93:242-4
Ap 17 '65

Enrollment

See Colleges and universities—Attendance

Entrance requirements

Can you win an argument with your high
school? lack of courses required for college
entrance. D. Klein. Seventeen 24:20+ N '65
College admissions: a cure for chaos? J. B.
Conant's proposals. J. Cass. Sat R 48:69-70
N 20 '65
Getting into college: will it be easier? il
U S News 59:47-8 Ag 30 '65
If your daughter wants to go to college. . .
il U S News 58:54-5 My 24 '65
Latest on getting into college; with inter-
view with R. E. Mahn. il U S News 60:
50-5 Ja 3 '66
Now: crisis for state universities? with inter-
view with D. D. Henry. il U S News 58:55-
60 F 1 '65
100,000 to be crowded out of colleges? with
interview with J. K. Hitt. U S News 58:
58-61 My 10 '65
Race to college. R. P. Wolff. il Atlan 216:
145-8 N '65
Your college interview. D. Klein. Seventeen
24:56+ O '65
See also
College entrance examination board
College entrance examination board—Scholastic aptitude test
Student selection

Anecdotes, facetiae, satire, etc.

How to make the college of daddy's choice
without really knowing anything. O. Palmer. il Nation 200:251-3 Mr 8 '65

Extension

See University extension

Faculties

See College professors and instructors

Federal aid

See Federal aid to education

Finance

Academic fund raising: yesterday and today.
C. C. Brown. Sch & Soc 93:240-2 Ap 17 '65
Cost of quality: ten-year drive to raise $360
million at University of Chicago. Newsweek 66:58 N 1 '65
Education and the bond market. E. C. Deering and J. Du Von. il Am Ed 1:28 S; 23 O;
28 N '65
Education and the bond market. E. C. Deering and P. K. Nance. il Am Ed 1:22 D '64;
20 F; 28 Mr '65
Education and the bond market. E. C. Deering
and J. Trevor Thomas. il Am Ed 1:28 Ap;
22 My; 30 Je; 29 Jl '65
Fiscal dilemma of academic science. W. V.
Consolazio. il Bul Atomic Sci 21:15-18 F '65
From the bottom to the top; roles of public
and private universities in the U.S; address, February 4, 1965. G. Romney. Vital
Speeches 31:290-2 Mr 1 '65

Manner of speaking; who writes the con-
tract? J. Ciardi. Sat R 48:45+ O 23 '65
Money from heaven? question of spending so
much for science. Commonweal 81:595-6 F
5 '65
See also
Council for financial aid to education
Federal aid to education

Gifts, legacies, etc.

Academic fund raising: yesterday and today.
C. C. Brown. Sch & Soc 93:240-2 Ap 17 '65
Colleges soft sell fund pleas; use of executive
seminar to win over potential donors. il
Bsns W p81-2+ D 11 '65
Giving is growing; private support of higher
education. il Time 85:67 F 26 '65

Graduate work

Editor's bookshelf; admission and degree requirements. P. Woodring. Sat R 48:86-7
N 20 '65
Graduate schools: grants awarded to encourage stronger programs. L. J. Carter.
il Science 150:1139-41 N 26 '65
Great grad school gold rush. J. Keats. il
Life 58:107-8+ Je 11 '65
NDEA fellowships; expansion doubles and
redoubles number. J. Walsh. Science 150:
1270-2 D 3 '65
Race to college. R. P. Wolff. il Atlan 216:
145-8 N '65
Some reflections on graduate school enrollments. M. Kinnane. Sch & Soc 93:114 F
20 '65

Music departments

New generation. B. Boretz. Nation 200:345-8
Mr 29 '65

Overseas extension

Palo Alto in Europe; Stanford's permanent
campuses in Europe. il Time 87:43 Ja 14
'66

Publishing

See also
University presses

Religious life

Campus ministry, ed. by G. L. Earnshaw.
Review
Christian Cent 82:780+ Je 16 '65. B. Gibson
Contemporary revival: Religious emphasis
week's Willson lectures. J. C. Evans. Chris-
tian Cent 82:392-3 Mr 31 '65
Crash program for the Newman apostolate.
J. L. Quinn. Cath World 202:166-70 D '65
Helping students make the spiritual passage.
il Time 86:85 O 1 '65
Whatever happened to Religious emphasis
week? J. E. Cantelon. Christian Cent 82:
396-8 Mr 31 '65
See also
College students—Religion

Research

Big money and high politics of science. D. R.
Fleming. Atlan 216:41-5 Ag '65; Reply. M.
W. Keith. 216:56+ N '65
But is the teacher also a citizen? adaptation
of address, April 14, 1965. A. M. Weinberg.
bibliog Science 149:601-6 Ag 6 '65; Discus-
sion. 150:141-2+, 965 O 8, N 19 '65
Congress: subcommittee surveys effects of
federally supported research on higher edu-
cation. J. Walsh. Science 149:42-4 Jl 2 '65;
Reply. D. T. Denhardt. 149:918+ Ag 27 '65
Federal research aid harms higher educa-
tion. Sci N L 88:328 N 20 '65
Fiscal dilemma of academic science. W. V.
Consolazio. il Bul Atomic Sci 21:15-18 F '65
Indirect costs: House legislation embodies
new cost-sharing formula for federal re-
search grants. J. Walsh. Science 149:525-6
Jl 30 '65
Institutional grants of the National science
foundation. E. J. Merton. il Science 148:
1693-6 Je 25 '65
One-sided criticism of university research.
P. H. Abelson. Science 148:1177 My 28 '65;
Discussion. 149:243 Jl 16 '65
One small college and research. J. Grennan.
Am Ed 1:14-15 Je '65
Partnership in research. D. F. Shaughnessy.
il Am Ed 1:1-4 F '65
Public domain. W. E. Mylecraine. Am Ed 1:
7-8 N '65
R&D boom: House report sees harm to higher
education. D. S. Greenberg. Science 150:
464-6 O 22 '65; Discussion. 150:1766-8+ D
31 '65
Universities and federal science policies; ad-
dress, October 11, 1965. D. F. Hornig. Sci-
ence 150:847-51 N 12 '65
University and the exploration of space; address, October 11, 1965. H. L. Dryden.
Science 150:1129-33 N 26 '65

COLLEGES and universities—*Continued*

Social life
See Student life

Standards
Are colleges slipping? symposium. **America** 112:451-3 Ap 3 '65
Berkeley and beyond; excerpt from Semester of crisis. I. Howe. New Repub 152:14-17 My 1 '65; Discussion, 152:36-8 My 29; 28 Je 19 '65
Three ways out for small Catholic colleges. L. C. Vaccaro. America 113:580-2 N 13 '65

Teaching
How do they rate you, professor? H. G. Shane. il NEA J 54:18-20 N '65
Is there a teacher on the faculty? J. Fischer. il Harper 230:18+ F '65; Same abr. Read Digest 86:76-80 Je '65; Discussion. Harper 230:6+ Ap '65
New breed of BA's some alternatives to boredom and unrest. C. Jencks. New Repub 153:17-21 O 23 '65; Discussion. 153: 40 N 6; 36 D 4 '65
One sided criticism of university research. P. H. Abelson. Science 148:1177 My 28 '65; Discussion. 149:243 Jl 16 '65
Path to promotion; hiring and firing. A. Mizener. il Atlan 216:135-8 N '65
Professional teacher or dedicated amateur? address, March 3, 1965. R. H. Garrison. Sch & Soc 93:390-2 O 30 '65
See also
College professors and instructors

Alabama
See also
Auburn university

Arkansas
See also
Arkansas. Southern state college, Magnolia

California
College by plan. E. G. Brown. il Am Ed 1:9-11 Mr '65
See also
Associated colleges at Claremont
California institute of technology
California state college, Los Angeles
California. University
College of the desert, Palm Desert
Pitzer college, Claremont
San Francisco. University
Southern California university, Los Angeles
Stanford university, Stanford

Canada
Flowering up North; new universities. il Time 85:48+ Ap 23 '65
See also
McGill university, Montreal
Waterloo, Ont. University

China (People's Republic)
Science in mainland China: a tourist's impressions. C. H. G. Oldham. bibliog il Science 147:706-14 F 12 '65; Reply. P. A. Chenoweth. 148:1172 My 28 '65

Colorado
See also
Colorado college, Colorado Springs
Colorado. University, Boulder

Congo (capital Leopoldville)
Free university of the Congo. J. Egerton. Christian Cent 83:60-2 Ja 12 '66
Investment in the Congo; National school of law and administration. America 112:817 Je 5 '65

Egypt
My fourteen originals; creative writing course at American university in Cairo. J. Stuart. il Sr Schol 86:sup5-6 My 20 '65

England
See also
Cambridge. University

Europe, Western
European students strike for academic reforms. D. C. Watt. il Reporter 33:42-4 D 16 '65

Florida
Bustle down South. il Time 85:63 F 5 '65
See also
Florida Atlantic university, Boca Raton
Florida state university, Tallahassee
New college, Sarasota

France
Jacques Monod: further comments on French universities. V. K. McElheny. Science 150: 1701 D 24 '65

Anecdotes, facetiae, satire, etc.
Baudelaire in three injections. L. Simpson. Harper 230:48-50 Je '65

Georgia
See also
Agnes Scott college, Decatur

Germany
Edith and Alice Hamilton: students in Germany. A. Hamilton. il Atlan 215:129-32 Mr '65

Great Britain
Oh, to be in England! D. Klein. Seventeen 24:42+ N '65
Politics and higher education; address, June 10, 1964. E. Hutchinson; reply. F. S. Barnes. Science 147:823 F 19 '65
Revolution in British higher education? T. R. McConnell. NEA J 54:55-6+ My '65

Hawaii
See also
Hawaii. University, Honolulu

Illinois
See also
Chicago. University
Illinois. University. Urbana
Shimer college, Mount Carroll

India
Bombay institute of technology. V. A. Javoronkoy; D. Behrman. il UNESCO Courier 18:14-17+, 33-6 My '65

Indiana
See also
Earlham college, Richmond
Evansville college
Indiana. University. Bloomington
Notre Dame, Ind. University
Purdue university, Lafayette

Iowa
See also
Cornell college, Mount Vernon
Drake university, Des Moines

Israel
Forty years in Jerusalem. il Newsweek 66:58 Jl 5 '65

Maine
See also
Bowdoin college, Brunswick

Maryland
Maryland college case: a clear test for school aid? D. Bremner. il Reporter 32:36-8 F 25 '65
See also
Maryland. University, College Park
St John's college, Annapolis, Md.—Santa Fe campus

Massachusetts
See also
Brandeis university, Waltham
Clark university, Worcester
Hampshire college
Harvard university
Massachusetts institute of technology, Cambridge
Tufts university, Medford

Michigan
See also
Central Michigan university, Mount Pleasant
Henry Ford community college, Dearborn
Michigan state university of agriculture and applied science, East Lansing
Michigan technological university, Houghton
Oakland university, Rochester
Wayne state university, Detroit

Middle western states
Academic cooperation: Big ten style. S. F. Salwak. Sch & Soc 93:397-8+ O 30 '65

Minnesota
See also
Carleton college, Northfield

Mississippi
See also
Mississippi. University

Missouri
See also
St Louis university, St Louis
Washington university, St Louis
Webster college, Webster Groves

COLLEGES and universities—*Continued*

Nebraska

See also
Hiram Scott college, Scottsbluff
Nebraska. University, Lincoln

Nevada

See also
Nevada. University, Reno

New Hampshire

See also
Dartmouth college, Hanover

New Jersey

Harvesting neglect in New Jersey. il Time 87:43-4 Ja 14 '66
See also
Princeton university

New Mexico

See also
New Mexico. University, Albuquerque

New York (state)

See also
Colgate university, Hamilton
Columbia university
Eisenhower college, Seneca Falls, N.Y.
Ithaca college
New York state university
New York state university—Agricultural and technical college at Canton
Rensselaer polytechnic institute, Troy
Rochester institute of technology, Rochester

North Carolina

See also
Asheville-Biltmore college
Davidson college
North Carolina. University, Chapel Hill

Ohio

See also
Cincinnati. University
Miami university, Oxford
Oberlin college, Oberlin
Ohio state university, Columbus

Oklahoma

See also
Panhandle agricultural and mechanical college, Goodwell

Oregon

See also
Portland state college
Reed college, Portland

Pennsylvania

Pennsylvania accent; state help for private universities. Time 86:59 D 10 '65
Political control in the state colleges of Pennsylvania. M. Anello. bibliog f Sch & Soc 93:83-5 F 6 '65; Reply with rejoinder. R. E. Heiges. 93:235-6 Ap 17 '65
See also
Bryn Mawr college, Bryn Mawr
La Salle college, Philadelphia
Pittsburgh. University
Swarthmore college, Swarthmore
Villanova university

Peru

Operation community service; volunteers in Peru's university community cooperation movement. E. Barclay. il UNESCO Courier 18:17-20 Jl '65

Russia

Africans don't go to Russia to be brainwashed. N. Nyangira. il N Y Times Mag p52+ My 16 '65
Old college try; Lumumba university. Newsweek 65:33-4 Je 28 '65

South Carolina

See also
Bob Jones university, Greenville
Furman university, Greenville

Southern states

Good southern universities. V. Dabney. il Harper 230:86-8+ Mr '65
In the new South: the way the colleges are changing. il U S News 58:62-4 My 31 '65
On the move in the South. il Time 86:94 D 17 '65

Spain

Cry for liberty; students' defiance of government. Newsweek 66:33-4 D 27 '65
Restive youth of Spain. S. Birmingham. il Holiday 37:88-93+ Ap '65
Spanish students rebel. G. Jackson. Commonweal 83:469-71 Ja 21 '66

Tennessee

See also
University of the South, Sewanee

Texas

Big business influences education in Texas. J. C. Evans. Christian Cent 82:425 Ap 7 '65
See also
University of St Thomas, Houston

Underdeveloped areas

University libraries in developing countries; address, July 1965. L. E. Asheim. ALA Bul 59:795-802 O '65

United States

Academic order and the humane scale. R. Kirk. Nat R 17:241 Mr 23 '65
Academy; excerpts from American dissent; decade of modern conservatism. J. Hart. Nat R 17:A32-4 N 30 '65
Artist on the campus. il Time 85:58+ Ap 2 '65
Berkeley and beyond; excerpt from Semester of crisis. I. Howe. New Repub 152:14-17 My 1 '65; Discussion. 152:36-8 My 29; 28 Je 19 '65
Campus '65. il Newsweek 65:43-8+ Mr 22 '65
College grad has been short-changed. A. Hacker. il N Y Times Mag p25+ Je 6 '65
Colleges that still have room. il Changing T 19:17-20 My '65
Diversity of institutional goals. D. Wolfle. Science 150:969 N 19 '65
Does the small private college have a future? P. Woodring; discussion. Sat R 48:96 F 20 '65
Education in a pressure cooker. P. Woodring. Sat R 48:55 Mr 20 '65; Discussion. 48:76 My 15 '65
Ivyless league: profiles of four new campuses. V. Kelley; M. Franklin; V. Voss. il Mlle 61:148-9+ O '65
Large university. D. Klein. il Seventeen 24:246-8 S '65
Meaning of a university. H. M. Jones. Atlan 216:157-60 N '65
Misuses of the university: anxiety in academe; address, June 17, 1965. F. A. Johnson. Vital Speeches 31:586-18 Jl 15 '65
Nature of the American college. W. W. Brickman. Sch & Soc 93:139 Mr 6 '65
New design for the college of liberal arts and sciences. G. D. Stoddard. il Sch & Soc 93:265-7 My 1 '65
Old college try gets harder. il Bsns W p 144+ Je 26 '65
On the campus: a troubled reflection of the U.S. M. Ways. il Fortune 72:130-5+ S '65
Our colleges aren't ready for today's students. H. Howe, 2d. il Sat R 48:77-9+ My 15 '65
Picking order; most desirable colleges. Time 85:59 F 12 '65
Politics and higher education; address, June 10, 1964. E. Hutchinson; reply. F. S. Barnes. Science 147:823 F 19 '65
Public universities face civil rights challenge. Sch & Soc 94:22+ Ja 8 '66
T.R.B. from Washington; blacklisting colleges. New Repub 152:4 Je 26 '65
Troubled campus; symposium. il Atlan 216:107-12+ N '65
Vital role of a modern college; address, April 3, 1965. L. C. Dowdy. Vital Speeches 31:475-7 My 15 '65
What's ahead for the university? academic freedom; address, September 10, 1965. E. W. Strong. Vital Speeches 32:24-8 O 15 '65
What's going on in schools & colleges. See issues of Changing times
Womb-clingers; non-students on college campuses. il Time 85:53-4 Je 25 '65
See also
Coeducation
Colleges and universities, State
Denominational colleges
Junior colleges
Medical colleges
Union for research and experimentation in higher education

Bibliography

Guide to college guides. Consumer Rep 30:310-11 Je '65

Vermont

Progress at Vermont state colleges. T. N. Stern. bibliog f Sch & Soc 93:267-9 My 1 '65
See also
Bennington college
Middlebury college, Middlebury
St Michael's college, Winooski

Virginia

Two-a-day circuit in Virginia colleges. R. Lynes. il Harper 230:26+ Je '65

COLLEGES and universities—*Continued*
Washington, D.C.
See also
Howard university

Washington (state)
See also
Washington (state) University, Seattle

Wisconsin
New plan for tuition grants. V. C. Blum.
America 113:499 O 30 '65
See also
Beloit college, Beloit
Wisconsin. University, Madison

COLLEGES and universities, Municipal
Asphalt-league colleges. D. Klein. il Seventeen
24:30+ Ag '65
See also
New York (city) City university of New
York—City college

COLLEGES and universities, State
Legislature is not convinced; state-supported
academic library budget. R. E. Ellsworth.
il Library J 90:2199-203 My 15 '65; Discus-
sion. 90:3156+ Ag '65
Now: crisis for state universities? with inter-
view with D. D. Henry. il U S News 58:55-
60 F 1 '65
Political control in the state colleges of
Pennsylvania. M. Anello. bibliog f Sch &
Soc 93:83-5 F 6 '65; Reply with rejoinder.
R. E. Heiges. 93:235-6 Ap 17 '65
Progress at Vermont state colleges. T. N.
Stern. bibliog f Sch & Soc 93:267-9 My 1
'65
See also names of state colleges and
universities, e.g. Michigan state university
of agriculture and applied science, East
Lansing

COLLEGES and universities, Traveling
Learning on the Seven Seas. il Time 85:69
F 19 '65
University of the Seven Seas. J. Bush. il
Mlle 60:147-9 F '65

COLLEGES for Negroes. See Negroes in the
United States—Education

COLLEGES for women
How the girls really are; Princeton's publication Where the girls are, refuted by Life's
explorations of eastern women's colleges.
il Life 59:66A-71 D 17 '65
See also names of womens colleges, e.g.
Wellesley college, Wellesley, Mass.

COLLEGES of liberal arts. See Liberal education

COLLETT family
Collett coat-of-arms. H. K. Eilers. il Hobbies
70:126-7+ My '65

COLLIAS, Nicholas E.
Evolution of nest building. Natur Hist 74:
40-7 bibliog(p74) Ag '65

COLLIER, James Lincoln
Government in the arts. Holiday 38:117-18 S
'65
Who pays the piper? Holiday 38:168+ D '65
Who's in charge here? Read Digest 87:117-
19 N '65
You take progress, I'll take tooth powder.
Read Digest 88:197-200 Ja '66

COLLIER, Marie
Texas Tosca; interview, ed. by R. D. Daniels.
por Opera N 30:14 D 4 '65

COLLIER, Richard
General next to God; condensation. Read
Digest 86:265-8+ F '65

COLLIER trophy
Collier trophy, B. Kocivar. il Look 29:77+ N
2 '65

COLLIE'S magpie jay. See Jays

COLLIGNON, Joseph
Phenomenon of Teilhard. Christian Cent 82:
426-8 Ap 7 '65

COLLINS, Bessie F.
Color of laughter; poem. Horn Bk 41:160 Ap
'65

COLLINS, Blanche
Ordeal at Long Beach. por Library J 90:
2486-90+ Je 1 '65

COLLINS, Charlene
Free spirits; poem. Negro Hist Bul 29:23
O '65

COLLINS, Doreen
Verdict for Corvair. il Time 86:46+ Ag 20
'65

COLLINS, E. D.
Aviation and the collector. Hobbies 70:30-1
Ap '65

COLLINS, George
Very special redwoods. il Liv Wildn 87:22-6
Wint '64

COLLINS, Jean
Battle of the species: he vs. she. Mlle 62:
93+ D '65

COLLINS, John Frederick
Saltonstall's successor. M. F. Nolan. New
Repub 154:8 Ja 22 '66

COLLINS, John R.
Glass for electronics. Electr World 74:44-6+
N '65
Liquid flow measurement. Electr World 73:38-
40+ Je '65

COLLINS, Larry, and Lapierre, Dominique
Is Paris burning? condensation. Read Digest
86:269-73+ Ap '65
Is Paris burning? excerpts. Ladies Home J
82:89-90+ O '65
Name is Moreau (not Bardot) N Y Times
Mag p46-7+ Mr 21 '65

COLLINS, Lorence G.
Finding rare beauty in common rocks. il por
Nat Geog Mag 129:120-9 Ja '66

COLLINS, Trudy
Compensating the victim. por Newsweek 67:
16 Ja 3 '66

COLLINS, Zeola. See Beutler, E. jt. auth.

COLLIS, Ronald T. H.
Lidar observation of cloud. Science 149:978-81
Ag 27 '65

COLLISIONS at sea
Where oil and ships don't mix; offshore oil
and shipping in Gulf of Mexico. il Bsns W
p 178+ Je 19 '65

COLLISON, Thomas
Most unforgettable character I've met! Read
Digest 86:107-12 F '65

COLM, Gerhard
Dismal science and the good life. Reporter
33:46-8 Jl 15 '65

COLMAN, Morris
Fifty books of 1964. por Pub W 187:72-4+
My 3 '65
about
Children's book illustrators honor an art di-
rector. il por Pub W 187:90-1 F 22 '65

COLMAN, William G.
Role of the federal government in the design
and administration of intergovernmental
programs. Ann Am Acad 359:23-34 My '65

COLOMBE; drama. See Anouilh, J.

COLOMBIA
See also
Birth control—Colombia
Bogota
Cauca Valley
Communism—Colombia
Crime and criminals—Colombia
Economic assistance in Colombia
Food relief—Colombia
Hunting—Colombia
Indians of South America—Colombia
Leticia
Technical assistance in Colombia
Zipaquirá

Commercial treaties and agreements
U.S. and Colombia conclude cotton textile
agreement; Department announcement,
June 9, 1965, with agreement and related
letters. il Dept State Bul 53:89-92 Jl 12 '65

Economic conditions
Another Latin-American country that can
blow up. J. N. Wallace. il U S News 58:
70-2 Je 21 '65
Colombia's dangerous doldrums. R. Eder. il
Reporter 33:36-8 O 7 '65
Permanently on the defense; economic re-
forms. Time 86:54+ S 17 '65
South America's shattered showcase. P. Siek-
man. il Fortune 72:164-9+ N '65

Native races
See Indians of South America—Colombia

Politics and government
Colombia's dangerous doldrums. R. Eder. il
Reporter 33:36-8 O 7 '65
General unrest. Time 85:32 F 12 '65
New force in Colombia; Unión de traba-
jadores de Colombia. V. Andrade. America
112:828-9 Je 5 '65
Next victim? D. Weber. Newsweek 65:58 My
24 '65
Rebel priest in Colombia. V. Andrade. Amer-
ica 113:287 S 18 '65; Reply with rejoinder.
A. Vanistendael. 113:512-13 N 6 '65
South America's shattered showcase. P. Siek-
man. il Fortune 72:164-9+ N '65
Splinters in the front. Time 85:29 My 28 '65
Students strike in Colombia. M. M. Loftus.
America 113:98 Jl 24 '65
Turn to the front; two Llerases. il Time 86:
28 D 24 '65

Religious institutions and affairs
Rebel priest in Colombia. V. Andrade. Amer-
ica 113:287 S 18 '65; Reply with rejoinder.
A. Vanistendael. 113:512-13 N 6 '65

COLOMBIA—*Continued*

Social conditions
Urban concentration, agriculture, and agrarian reform; with questions and answers. G. J. Eder. bibliog f Ann Am Acad 360:27-47 Jl '65

COLOMBIAN Indians. See Indians of South America—Colombia

COLOMBO, Umberto, and others
Magnetite oxidation: a proposed mechanism. bibliog Science 147:1033 F 26 '65

COLOMBO plan
Economic development in south and southeast Asia; annual meeting of Consultative committee, November 19, 1964, with communique and chapter of report. F. M. Coffin. Dept State Bul 52:77-86 Ja 18 '65

COLON, Cancer of the. See Cancer

COLONIAL dependencies. See Colonies

COLONIAL history

United States
See United States—History—Colonial period

COLONIAL life and customs
See also
Williamsburg, Va.

COLONIALISM. See Colonies

COLONIES
Black skin, white masks, by F. Fanon. Review
  Commentary 40:67-71 Jl '65. H. R. Isaacs
Colonizer and the colonized, by A. Memmi. Review
  Nation 201:535-7 D 27 '65. P. F. Semonin
  Sat R 48:38+ D 11 '65. E. Capouya
Hidden politics of language. M. Pei. Sat R 49:22-4 Ja 15 '66
New colonialism: who's oppressing whom in the 20th century? il Sr Schol 86:14-17 Mr 4 '65
Wretched of the earth, by F. Fanon. Review
  Nation 200:674-6 Je 21 '65. C. C. O'Brien
  New Yorker 41:115-17 Ja 15 '66. N. Hentoff
  Sat R 48:33-4 Ap 24 '65. E. Capouya
See also
Imperialism
Underdeveloped areas
United Nations—Special committee on the situation with regard to implementation of declaration on granting of independence to colonial countries and peoples

COLONIZATION
Some legal aspects of the colonial problem in Latin America; address, April 10, 1965; with questions and answers. C. M. Velazquez. bibliog f Ann Am Acad 360:110-19 Jl '65
See also
Brazil—Colonization

COLONIZATION of Negroes. See Negroes—Colonization

COLONY development company
New ways to squeeze oil out of a stone; pilot plant in Colorado extracting oil from shale. il Bsns W p78-9+ Jl 10 '65

COLOR
Color, a world of wonders. D. S. Gelatt. il Pop Phot 57:80-3 Jl '65
Great ideas on color; ed. by D. S. Gelatt. il Pop Phot 57:64-9+ Jl '65
Patination of bronzes. J. Brzostoski; J. McDevitt; A. Ventura. il Craft Horiz 25:26-37+ N '65
3-D through tints; work of eighth graders. A. Heidt. il Design 67:24-5 N '65
Vanishing color. H. Ringgenberg. il Design 66:27-9 My '65
See also
Colorimeters and colorimetry

Psychology
Are color choices clues to personality? Good H 162:134 Ja '66
Who are you? and who are all those others? color and psychic makeup. R. Warfield. il Vogue 146:84-5+ S 15 '65

COLOR blindness
If identifying colors is a problem. il Good H 160:146 F '65
More men color-blind. Sci N L 87:291 My 8 '65
Red-light thresholds in heterozygote carriers of protanopia: genetic implications. A. E. Krill and E. Beutler. bibliog il Science 149:186-8 Jl 9 '65

COLOR films. See Photography—Films
COLOR filters. See Light filters
COLOR in gardens. See Gardens—Color

COLOR in house decoration
Craze for color; J. R. Laury, designer. J. Peter. il Look 29:53 O 5 '65
Deeper colors move into the kitchen. il House & Gard 127:154-7 Mr '65
Great expectations; 1966 viewpoints. il House & Gard 129:100-5 Ja '66
H&G's current color hit: jade. il House & Gard 127:134-5 My '65
Introducing H&G colors for 1966; symposium. House & Gard 128:173-87, 198-209 S '65
Most imaginative color schemes we've ever published! il Bet Hom & Gard 43:48-59 F '65
Put a one-two punch in your color scheme. P. Rumely and E. T. Lawyer. il Bet Hom & Gard 43:58-67 S '65

COLOR in hunting clothing. See Hunting—Safety devices and measures

COLOR measurement
See also
Colorimeters and colorimetry

COLOR of animals
Agouti locus: homology of its method of operation in rats and mice. W. K. Silvers. bibliog il Science 149:651-2 Ag 6 '65
Body composition and coat color correlation in different phenotypes of viable yellow mice. G. L. Wolff. bibliog il Science 147:1145-7 Mr 5 '65

COLOR of flowers
Green flowers and herb trees. B. Mellon. il Vogue 146:208-11 D '65
You'll see red when you see these annuals. E. G. Pierce. il Pop Gard 17:24-5+ Ja '66

COLOR of insects
Insect survival and selection for pattern. H. B. D. Kettlewell. bibliog il Science 148:1290-6 Je 4 '65

COLOR of leaves
Autumn color you can count on; bigleaf maple. il Sunset 135:72 O '65

COLOR of man
Four-letter word that hurts: race. M. H. Fried. Sat R 48:21-3+ O 2 '65

COLOR of plants
See also
Color of flowers

COLOR organ
Low-cost hi-fi color organ. D. Lancaster. il Pop Electr 22:43-7 Mr '65

COLOR photography
Age of color? not yet. B. Downes. Pop Phot 57:191 D '65
Are color photographers born or made? R. Miller. il U S Camera 28:26 O '65
Caulfield on color. P. Caulfield. See issues of Modern photography
Color clinic. D. B. Eisendrath, jr. See issues of Popular photography
Color critique. H. Flatow. U S Camera 29:59-61 Ja '66
Color's infinite variety; selection of color pictures. il Pop Phot 57:70-7 Jl '65
Creative color. A. Rothstein. See issues of U.S. camera & travel
Feininger on color; excerpts from Complete photographer. A. Feininger. Mod Phot 29:73-9 O '65
How to get the most out of Polacolor. H. M. Kinzer. il Pop Phot 57:78-9+ Jl '65
Keep it warm. il U S Camera 28:42-5 Jl '65
Kodak Ektachrome infrared aero; two-part test report. M. Iger and N. Rothschild. il Pop Phot 57:158-61+ D '65
Mexico. N. Rothschild; J. M. Zanutto. il Pop Phot 57:90-7+ O '65
Negative color: this mystery world. il Pop Phot 56:66-7 My '65
New colors in your prints. il U S Camera 28:42-5 Ap '65
Norman Rothschild's color refresher; questions and answers. N. Rothschild. il Pop Phot 57:84-91+ Jl '65
Psycolorgy. D. Gilbert. il Pop Phot 56:56-7+ Mr '65
Quiet war on bad processing; color quality. J. Durniak. il Pop Phot 56:64 Je '65
Secrets of shooting color at night. H. T. Gurley. il Pop Sci 187:92-5 S '65
Walk softly and carry a long lens. L. Barry. il Pop Phot 57:68-71+ Ag '65
Who knows more about color than the National geographic? D. B. Eisendrath, jr. il Pop Phot 57:58-63 Jl '65

Bibliography
Caulfield on color. P. Caulfield. Mod Phot 29:28+ Je '65

COLOR preference tests. See Personality tests
COLOR prejudice. See Race prejudice
COLOR print meters. See Exposure meters

COLOR printing
As one craftsman to another. G. P. Hunt.
il Life 58:3 My 14 '65
Color in print: AIGA-Safran seminar on color
language and reproduction. il Pub W 187:
106-11 Mr 1 '65
Hornung's luxurious prints of the American
automobile. il Pub W 187:90-1 Ap 5 '65
How the Sierra club does it; remarkable
color reproduction. il Pub W 187:94-5+ Mr
1 '65

COLOR prints (reproductions) See Reproduction of works of art

COLOR sense
Color vision in the antelope ground squirrel.
F. Crescitelli and J. D. Pollack. bibliog il
Science 150:1316-18 D 3 '65
Evoked visual potentials and human color
vision. T. Shipley and others. bibliog il
Science 150:1162-4 N 26 '65
Spectral sensitivity of color mechanisms:
derivation from fluctuations of color appearance near threshold. J. Krauskopf and
R. Srebro. bibliog il Science 150:1477-9 D 10
'65

COLOR-slide projectors. See Projection apparatus

COLOR standards. See Colorimeters and colorimetry

COLOR television. See Television, Color

COLOR television receiving apparatus. See
Television receiving apparatus—Color receivers

COLORADO
See also
Architecture, Domestic—Colorado
Booksellers and bookselling—Colorado
Botany—Colorado
Cheyenne Mountain
Fishing—Colorado
Hunting—Colorado
Paleontology—Colorado
Prisons—Colorado

Industries
Oil rush; shale extraction experiment at Rifle,
Colo. R. Fleming. New Repub 153:11 S 18
'65

Religious institutions and affairs
News of the Christian world (cont) Christian
Cent 82:1076-7 S 1 '65

COLORADO college, Colorado Springs
Fearless tot from Possum Trot: S. D. Sabol.
T. C. Brody. il Sports Illus 23:64+ N 22 '65

COLORADO RIVER
Attack on Grand Canyon; building dams as
part of Southwest water plan. R. C. Bradley. il Liv Wildn 87:3-7 Wint '64
Colorado, America's Nile. il Fortune 71:147-9
Ap '65
Funds requested for salinity control on lower
Colorado River. Dept State Bul 52:637 Ap
26 '65
Increase water supply, don't allocate shortages. S. B. Nelson. il Am City 80:96-8 Mr
'65
Sweetening the salt: US-Mexican agreement.
Time 85:34+ Ap 9 '65
Think big: open letter to the Secretary of the
Interior to build two dams on Colorado
River. B. Stewart. il Harper 231:62-3 Ag
'65; Discussion. 231:8+ N '65
Triumph of goodwill; problem of salt water
solved. il Newsweek 65:54 Ap 5 '65
See also
Central Arizona project (proposed)
Grand Canyon
Salton Sea

COLORADO SPRINGS

Streets
Arrows mark the way. D. L. Smith. il Am
City 80:124+ D '65

COLORADO state prison. See Prisons—Colorado

COLORADO. University, Boulder
Colorado football's galloping disaster; memoirs of a big-time coach. B. Davis. il Harper 231:50-3 O '65
Poor are getting richer. F. S. Barnes. Science 147:823 F 19 '65

COLORED glass. See Glass, Colored

COLORIMETERS and colorimetry
Amateur scientist; on constructing and using
a photoelectric colorimeter. S. Epstein. il
Sci Am 212:118-23 F '65
Colorimetry in color television. J. F. Holahan. il Electr World 74:21-3+ D '65

COLORING books
Are coloring books good for children? il
Good H 161:178-9 N '65

COLORING of metals. See Metal coloring

COLQUITT, Betsy Feagan
Metaphor; poem. Christian Cent 82:1374 N 10
'65

COLT revolvers. See Revolvers

COLTMAN, Derek
(tr) See Leduc, V. La bâtarde

COLTS (football club) See Football clubs

COLUMBIA
See also
Tourist trade—Columbia

COLUMBIA, Md.
New town of Columbia proposes ten villages
to accommodate 110,000. il Arch Rec 137:14
F '65
Peopleless town surveyed for library needs.
Pub W 188:92 S 27 '65

COLUMBIA, Mo.
Now you can read the signs. T. I. Maupin. il
Am City 80:114-15 Ag '65

COLUMBIA, Mo, public library
Missouri regional librarian resigns after year
of far right pressures; Daniel Boone regional library. Library J 90:3230-1 Ag '65

COLUMBIA, S.C.
Weep no more, Columbia. il Newsweek 65:27-
8+ My 3 '65

COLUMBIA broadcasting system
Allyn & Bacon and CBS call off merger talks.
Pub W 188:67 D 27 '65
Bigger than all of us; agreement between
CBS and the N.F.L. il Time 87:68 Ja 7 '66
CBS: the money machine. il Newsweek 65:
60-2 F 22 '65
CBS to acquire Allyn & Bacon. Pub W 188:
43-4 O 4 '65
CBS, Yankees score in capital. Bsns W p42
F 27 '65
Invitation to return to Cam Ne; Saturday
review project to rebuild destroyed houses.
N. Cousins. Sat R 48:16+ S 4 '65; Discussion. 48:33-4+ S 25 '65
Killing the mad monk; charge against CBS
dramatization. il Newsweek 66:38 N 1 '65
NFL-CBS pact nails prime time, top cash. il
Bsns W p 17 Ja 1 '66
Octopus under the big eye; CBS purchase
of New York Yankees; excerpt from Hustler's handbook. W. L. Veeck and E. Linn. il
Sports Illus 22:40-2+ My 24 '65
Only you, Jim Aubrey; TV president J. T.
Aubrey replaced by J. A. Schneider. il
Newsweek 65:62-3 Mr 15 '65
Pad 19: TV coverage of Grissom-Young flight.
New Yorker 41:38-40 Ap 3 '65
Prince & the monk; suit against CBS for
invasion of privacy. il Time 86:49-50 O 29
'65
Regency firing; J. Aubrey toughly sacked. il
Time 85:80+ Mr 12 '65
SR's readers and Cam Ne. N. Cousins. Sat R
48:30 O 9 '65
Slattery's saga; Slattery's people. il Newsweek 65:82+ My 31 '65
TV looks at TV ratings. Bsns W p62 Jl 17 '65
TV's week that was: FCC probe; CBS storm.
il Bsns W p28 Mr 6 '65
Those CBS reports; distorted report of
marine assault on Camne. America 113:175
Ag 21 '65
Tyrant's fall that rocked the TV world. R.
Oulahan and W. Lambert. il Life 59:90-2+
S 10 '65
What are friends for? G. Ace. Sat R 48:13
Mr 20 '65

COLUMBIA Jays. See Jays

COLUMBIA mills, incorporated
Columbia mills completes new plant in Ontario. il Pub W 188:110 O 4 '65

COLUMBIA records, incorporated
Broadway on records; Columbia, six decades
of innovation; with discography. M.
Kreuger. il Am Rec G 32:322-3+ D '65

COLUMBIA RIVER
Chromium-51 as a radioactive tracer of Columbia River water at sea. C. Osterberg
and others. bibliog il Science 150:1585-7
D 17 '65

Power utilization
Arrogant river's golden promise; Canadian-American treaty for joint development of
the river and its tributaries. W. S. Ellis.
il N Y Times Mag p42-6+ Mr 28 '65

COLUMBIA RIVER basin
Arrogant river's golden promise; Canadian-American treaty for joint development of
the river and its tributaries. W. S. Ellis.
il N Y Times Mag p42-6+ Mr 28 '65

COLUMBIA savings and loan association
How to win star billing for an S&L. il Bsns
W p90-2 My 1 '65

COLUMBIA university

Columbia buckles under; demonstration against and postponement of Naval reserve officer training corps awards ceremony. E. J. Bell. il Nat R 17:506-7 Je 15 '65; Reply with rejoinder. J. S. Reed, jr. 17:575 Jl 13 '65

Exit arguing; concerning propriety of student political activities. il Newsweek 65: 102 Je 14 '65

Graduate speed-up. J. Neugeboren. Commonweal 83:8 O 8 '65

COLUMBUS, Christopher

Columbus' doctors. L. H. Roddis. il Américas 17:35-7 Je '65

Did Columbus or Cabot see the map? excerpt from Vinland map and the Tartar relation. R. A. Skelton. il Am Heritage 16:103-6 O '65

Was Christopher Columbus really Martin Behaim? P. W. Schmidtchen. il pors Hobbies 70:106-7+ D '65

Windblown Leif. il Time 86:25B O 22 '65

Drama

Admiral leads on. F. Shriner. Plays 25:79-82, 86 O '65

Poetry

Columbus' voyage. C. K. Leverett. Horn Bk 41:530 O '65

COLUMBUS, Ind.

Baptist church by Weese. il Arch Rec 138: 113-17 D '65

Architecture

Columbus, Indiana. J. M. Dixon. il Arch Forum 123:40-9 D '65

City planning

Columbus, Indiana. J. M. Dixon. il Arch Forum 123:40-9 D '65

COLUMNISTS. See Newspapers—Sections, columns, etc.

COLUMNS (architecture)

Exploded columns enclose space within space. il Arch Rec 137:126-9 mid-My '65

COLUMNS (newspapers) See Newspapers—Sections, columns, etc.

COLVILLE, Derek

Shoddy revolution in British education. Yale R 54:464-77 Mr '65

COLVILLE, W. L. and Zeman, L. E.

Corn soybeans sorghum; how thick should you plant? Suc Farm 64:36-7+ Ja '66

COLVIN, Frances

Glass blower; poem. Commonweal 83:60 O 15 '65

Wildcat; poem. Commonweal 83:345 D 17 '65

COLY. See Mousebirds

COMA

New treatment for coma. Time 86:67-8 Jl 16 '65

COMAN, Daniel J.

Chicago's community Christmas tree. Am City 80:81-2 D '65

COMBAT fatigue. See Neuroses

COMBINATION record player-filmstrip projector. See Projection apparatus—Phonograph combination

COMBINES. See Harvesting machinery

COMBUSTION chambers. See Automobile engines

COMDEN, Betty

Big girl's notes on little girls' legs. Esquire 63:41 Je '65

Letter from Liverpool, almost. Vogue 146: 120+ D '65

To those of you who remember Eric Linden in Are these our children? I say: are these our parents? Esquire 65:12+ Ja '66

COME back, Peter. . . come back, Paul; story. See Prasniewski, M.

COMEDIANS

See also
Hayes, P. L.
Mills, S.
Negro comedians
Rivers, J.
Vernon, J.
Winters, J.

COMEDY

See also
Humor
Moving pictures—Comedy
Television broadcasting—Humor

COMEN, Priscilla, and Jacobson, Rovena

New way to clean water and reuse it. Sci Digest 57:89-91 My '65

COMET probes. See Space probes

COMETS

Boy who redeemed his father's name; K. Ikeya's discovery. T. Morris. il Redbook 125:86-7+ O '65; Same abr. Read Digest 88:107-11 Ja '66

Bright comet nears sun; Ikeya-Seki. Sci N L 88:246 O 16 '65

Bright new comet: how to spot it; Ikeya-Seki. il U S News 59:10 O 25 '65

Comet breaks in three; nucleus of Ikeya-Seki. Sci N L 88:325 N 20 '65

Comet holds records; Ikeya-Seki. A. Ewing. Sci N L 88:286 O 30 '65

Evidence from a distant comet; Ikeya-Seki comet. il Time 86:95 N 5 '65

Great comet of 1965; with editorial comment. B. G. Marsden. il Sky & Tel 30:331-7 D '65

Ikeya-Seki calls. il Newsweek 66:56-7 N 1 '65

Interest rises in comets, asteroid belt. H. D. Watkins. il Aviation W 82:89-90+ F 22 '65

Midafternoon view of the elusive comet Ikeya-Seki. il Life 59:40-40A N 5 '65

New comets cross sky. Sci N L 88:230 O 9 '65

Origin of comets; new theory. D. Robey. il Sat R 48:37-41 Ag 7 '65

Photographs of comet Ikeya-Seki. il Sky & Tel 30:342-6; 31:20-3 D '65-Ja '66

Reports of comet Ikeya-Seki (1965f) L. J. Robinson. il Sky & Tel 31:52-6 Ja '66

Rich harvest of comets; Ikeya-Seki; Two periodic comets recovered. il Sky & Tel 30:284-5 N '65

Splendor in the night; Ikeya-Seki comet. il Time 86:72+ O 22 '65

Strange story of comet de Vico-Swift. B. G. Marsden. il Sky & Tel 30:139-40 S '65

Twin Chinese comets; Purple Mountain comets. G. S. Mumford. il Sky & Tel 29: 223-4 Ap '65

Whisk broom in the sky; Ikeya-Seki. J Reinert. il Sci Digest 59:39-41 Ja '66

Orbits

Effect of the planetary system on comet orbits. G. S. Mumford. Sky & Tel 31:25 Ja '66

Spectra

Sodium D lines in comet Ikeya-Seki. W. Livingston and others. il Sky & Tel 31:24-5 Ja '66

COMFORTERS. See Quilts

COMIC literature. See Humor

COMIC strips. See Comics (books, strips, etc)

COMICS (books, strips, etc)

Censoring Orphan Annie. Time 85:52 F 26 '65

Champ for all time!!! Joe Palooka. R. H. Boyle. il Sports Illus 22:120-4+ Ap 19 '65

Comics, etc. D. Cort. Commonweal 82:503-5 Jl 9 '65

Good grief: Peanuts. il Time 85:80-4 Ap 9 '65

Great comic book heroes, by J. Feiffer. Review
Life 59:12+ D 17 '65. R. Schickel
Newsweek 66:104+ N 22 '65

Modern Mona Lisa; international exhibition of comic strips. il Time 85:41 Mr 5 '65

My life as an immortal myth; experiences at the first International exhibition of the comics. A. Capp. il Life 58:97-100+ Ap 30 '65

No laughing matter; first International convention on the comics. il Newsweek 65:62 Mr 8 '65

Pop! goes the poster; pop art portraits of comic-book favorites. il Newsweek 65:72 Mr 29 '65

Superfans and batmaniacs. il Newsweek 65: 89-90 F 15 '65

Superman revisited. R. Nordell. il Atlan 217:104-5 Ja '66

Syndicate producing books from color comic strips; Spadea spectaculars. Pub W 187: 52 Mr 22 '65

Collectors and collecting

ComiCon; second annual convention of Academy of comic-book fans and collectors. New Yorker 41:23-4 Ag 21 '65

Moral aspects

Gospel according to Peanuts, by R. L. Short. Review
Christian Cent 82:276 Mr 3 '65. R. P. Nelson

COMMAGER, Henry Steele

Historian looks at our political morality. Sat R 48:16-18 Jl 10 '65

Problem of dissent. Sat R 48:21-3+ D 18 '65

Search for a usable past. Am Heritage 16: 4-9+ F '65

Why history. por Am Ed 1:26-9 Je '65

COMMANDAY, Robert

Lulu; West Coast premiere. Hi Fi 15:176-7 D '65

Mozart era. Hi Fi 15:156+ O '65

COMMENCEMENT addresses. See Baccalaureate addresses

COMMENCEMENTS
Joyous farewell to the best years. L. Wainwright. Life 58:20 Je 25 '65
COMMENTATORS, Radio. See Radio broadcasting—News

COMMERCE
Business around the globe. See issues of Fortune
Challenges facing United States trade policy; address, October 21, 1965. A. M. Solomon. Dept State Bul 53:787-93 N 15 '65
Commercial policy at the crossroads; address, September 16, 1965. W. M. Blumenthal. Dept State Bul 53:665-71 O 25 '65
Commodity agreements, a partial answer to the trade problems of developing countries. H. Brodie. Dept State Bul 53:111-17 Jl 19 '65
Competing for tomorrow's world markets; address, November 18, 1964. F. G. Donner. Vital Speeches 31:279-82 F 15 '65
Disparities in progress between nations; address, April 9, 1965. T. C. Mann. Dept State Bul 52:720-4 My 10 '65
Europe, the United States, and world trade; address, February 4, 1965. C. A. Herter. Dept State Bul 52:294-9 Mr 1 '65
International trade; address, March 31, 1965. T. C. Mann. Dept State Bul 52:665-7 My 3 '65
Trade windows to the world. W. M. Roth. Dept State Bul 53:401-5 S 6 '65
Trends in international economics. C. P. Kindleberger. bibliog f Ann Am Acad 358:170-9 Mr '65
World trade and the Kennedy round; address, July 15, 1965. W. M. Blumenthal. Dept State Bul 53:249-55 Ag 9 '65
See also
Balance of payments
Barter
Free trade and protection
Investments, Foreign
Reciprocity
also subhead Commerce under names of countries, e.g. France—Commerce

Statistics
Facts and figures of the Americas; income from exports. il Américas 17:47 F '65

COMMERCE, Interstate. See Interstate commerce
COMMERCIAL contests. See Competitions
COMMERCIAL correspondence
Take a letter, cheap; World wide dictation service. Newsweek 66:71+ Jl 19 '65
COMMERCIAL ethics. See Business ethics
COMMERCIAL geography. See Geography, Commercial
COMMERCIAL law
See also
Trusts, Industrial—Law
COMMERCIAL medical laboratories. See Medical laboratories
COMMERCIAL photography. See Photography, Commercial
COMMERCIAL products
Months ahead; guide for your work and personal living. See issues of Changing times
See also
Quality of products
COMMERCIAL treaties and agreements
Commodity agreements, a partial answer to the trade problems of developing countries. H. Brodie. Dept State Bul 53:111-17 Jl 19 '65
COMMERCIALISM
Monumental shame. J. H. Winchester. il Travel 123:58-60 My '65
COMMERCIALS. See Television advertising
COMMISSION merchants
See also
Factors
COMMISSION of the churches on international affairs. See World council of churches
COMMISSION on international affairs. National council of the churches of Christ in the United States of America—Commission on international affairs
COMMISSION on law enforcement and administration of justice. See United States—President's commission on law enforcement and administration of justice
COMMISSION on national goals. See United States—President's commission on national goals
COMMISSION on the humanities
Humanity's previous attempts... to transcend the world it inhabits; recommendation for establishment of a National humanities foundation. Sat R 48:60 F 6 '65
COMMISSION on the status of women. See United Nations—Commission on the status of women

COMMISSIONER of baseball. See Baseball—Organization and administration
COMMISSIONER of education. See United States—Education, Office of
COMMISSIONS, independent regulatory. See Independent regulatory commissions
COMMISSIONS of the United States government. See name of the commission as subhead under United States, e.g. United States—Commission on civil rights
COMMITTEE for a sane nuclear policy. See National committee for a sane nuclear policy
COMMITTEE for an effective and durable peace in Asia
Presidential front; formation of committee. Nation 201:207 O 11 '65
COMMITTEE for economic development
Keeping watch on the economy; meaning of 1946 employment act. K. Schriftgiesser. Sat R 49:65-6+ Ja 8 '66
COMMITTEE for industrial development. See United Nations—Committee for industrial development
COMMITTEE of twenty-four. See United Nations—Special committee on the situation with regard to implementation of declaration on granting of independence to colonial countries and peoples
COMMITTEE on forest land ownership. See American forestry association—Committee on forest land ownership
COMMITTEE on space research. See International council of scientific unions—Committee on space research
COMMITTEES, Congressional. See United States—Congress—Committees
COMMODITIES price index. See Index numbers
COMMODITY control
Commodity agreements, a partial answer to the trade problems of developing countries. H. Brodie. Dept State Bul 53:111-17 Jl 19 '65
COMMODITY prices. See Prices
COMMON market in Central America. See Central American program of economic integration
COMMON market in Latin America. See Latin American free trade association
COMMON market in western Europe. See European economic community
COMMON stocks. See Stocks
COMMONS, House of. See Great Britain—Parliament—House of commons
COMMONWEALTH educational conference
Meeting, 1964. Sch & Soc 93:105-6 F 6 '65
COMMONWEALTH of nations
Atlantic report; Gibraltar. Atlan 216:30+ D '65
Britain gropes for ways to dissolve an empire; Rhodesian crisis. il Bsns W p27-8 O 30 '65
Britain is right on Rhodesia. Life 59:4 N 26 '65
Colonial office; a final inventory. N. Mostert. il Reporter 33:24-6 Jl 1 '65
Eleventh hour in Rhodesia. N. M. Shamuyarira. Nation 201:319-22 N 8 '65
Independence day? Prime Minister H. Wilson's efforts to deter Rhodesia. il Newsweek 66:50+ N 22 '65
Proposed solution to the Rhodesian crisis. W. B. George. Christian Cent 83:13-14 Ja 5 '66
Rebellion brews in Rhodesia. R. W. Howe. il Reporter 32:26+ Je 3 '65; Reply with rejoinder. D. T. M. Williams. 33:6+ S 9 '65
Rhodesian rebellion. G. I. Smith; R. W. Howe. il Reporter 33:27-32 D 2 '65
Unblessed are the peacemakers; Commonwealth peace-making mission. Time 86:29 Jl 2 '65
See also
Prime ministers conferences
COMMONWEALTH prime ministers conferences. See Prime ministers conferences
COMMUNICABLE diseases
See also
Immunity
Venereal diseases
also names of communicable diseases, e.g. Smallpox
COMMUNICATION (speech, writing, etc)
Communications; ed. by R. L. Tobin. See issues of Saturday review
Hobo signs; designs by students at the Herron school of art. il Design 66:36-9 Mr '65
Making free speech audible. C. A. Reich. il Nation 200:138-41 F 8 '65
Marshall McLuhan: Canada's intellectual comet. R. Schickel. Harper 231:62-8 N '65
Modern communication; address, January 16, 1965. J. P. Austin. Vital Speeches 31:271-4 F 15 '65

COMMUNICATION (speech, writing, etc)
—*Continued*
Please send two free tickets. il Sci Digest 57:26-7 F '65
Role of human values in communication; address, April 2, 1965. V. L. Baker. bibliog Vital Speeches 31:434-7 My 1 '65
Watch your language; everyone else does! E. Pearson. Farm J 89:55 S '65
See also
Computers—Communication applications
Language and languages
Language arts
Mass media

International aspects
Cooperation in international communications. L. Loevinger. Dept State Bul 53:828-34 N 22 '65
One world; views of D. Sarnoff. Nation 201: 207 O 11 '65
Picture of the future; changes in world communications. N. P. Hurley. America 112: 218-19 F 13 '65

Religious aspects
Intersection: point of meeting; enterprise in San Francisco. R. J. Hawthorne. Christian Cent 82:1599-602 D 29 '65

Social aspects
Family communication; with study-discussion program, by C. Smallenburg and H. Smallenburg. C. B. Broderick. bibliog il PTA Mag 60:4-6, 35-6 D '65

COMMUNICATION, Animal. See Animal communication

COMMUNICATION and traffic

History
Spanning time and space; picture section. UN Mo Chron 2:67-74 My '65

International aspects
Comsat compromise starts a revolution. J. McDonald. il Fortune 72:128-9 O '65
International cooperation year, a challenge to transportation. L. K. Bridwell. Dept State Bul 53:835-9 N 22 '65

COMMUNICATION arts. See Language arts

COMMUNICATION in management
Are you getting across to employees? il Nations Bsns 53:74-7 Jl '65
Clear communications for chief executives. R. N. McMurry. il Harvard Bsns R 43: 131-2+ Mr '65
Communication aids; telephone aids, intercoms, telescribers, pneumatic tubes and document conveyors. il Duns R 86:pt2 164-5+ S '65
Communicator; employer, employee relations; address, June 24, 1965. L. A. Townsend. Vital Speeches 31:670-2 Ag 15 '65
Data transmission and the real-time systems. il Duns R 86:pt2 159-61+ S '65
Escape from the grapevine. L. L. L. Golden. Sat R 48:79 D 11 '65
How do you keep informed? symposium. il Duns R 85:50-1+ My '65
Pendulum of management control; adaptation of address, February 10, 1965. G. E. Morse. bibliog Harvard Bsns R 43:158-60+ My '65
Ten ways to sell them. R. J. Tiernan. il Nations Bsns 53:84-6+ Je '65

COMMUNICATION in science
Conference literature. E. H. Ahrens, jr. Science 148:313 Ap 16 '65
Free source materials. Sci N L 87:340 My 29 '65
Group interaction among scientists. P. H. Abelson. Science 148:447 Ap 23 '65; Reply. F. Fremont-Smith. 148:1669-70 Je 25 '65
Information exchange group no. 1; letter. D. E. Green. Science 148:1543 Je 18 '65
Information race; letters. W. Loveland; A. Mather. Science 148:314 Ap 16 '65
Networks of scientific papers; adaptation of address, March 17, 1964. D. J. de S. Price. bibliog il Science 149:510-15 Jl 30 '65
Science of science. D. J. de S. Price. Bul Atomic Sci 21:2-8 O '65
Scientific information exchange in psychology. W. D. Garvey and B. C. Griffith; reply. F. A. Coyle, jr. and R. Eisenman. Science 149:375 Jl 23 '65
See also
Science—Information services

COMMUNICATIONS, Military
See also
Communications satellites—Military applications
United States — Air force — Communication systems

COMMUNICATIONS research
Tickle talk, now you can hear with your fingers; cutaneous communication. C. P. Gilmore. il Pop Sci 188:104-5 Ja '66

COMMUNICATIONS satellite corporation
As Comsat gets down to business. il U S News 58:112 Ap 12 '65
Bird on one wing. Newsweek 66:72 Ag 16 '65
Comsat bid on defense system faces fight. Aviation W 82:71+ F 8 '65
Comsat: center of controversy. il U S News 59:54 Jl 5 '65
Comsat compromise starts a revolution. J. McDonald. il Fortune 72:128-9 O '65
Comsat corp. briefing for NASA system draws thirty-five avionics bidders. Aviation W 83: 31 Ag 9 '65
Comsat launches no. 1; Early bird satellite. il Bsns W p33 Ap 10 '65
Comsat lease rights to determine growth of space communications. K. Johnsen. Aviation W 83:27-8 N 8 '65
Comsat seeking bids for military system. Aviation W 82:35 F 22 '65
Comsat seeks joint NASA-public system. K. Johnsen. Aviation W 83:35 S 13 '65
Comsat seeks studies of multi-role vehicle. Aviation W 84:21 Ja 3 '66
Comsat squares off at Pentagon. Bsns W p29 Mr 6 '65
Comsat's first try; launch of first communications satellite. Early bird. il Time 85:92 Ap 9 '65
New boss for Comsat. Time 86:108+ O 22 '65
Opposition hits direct Comsat use. Aviation W 84:34 Ja 17 '66
President Johnson transmits report on communications satellite system; letter of transmittal, Febraury 15, 1965, with excerpts from report. L. B. Johnson. Dept State Bul 52:340-2 Mr 8 '65
Quarrels over Comsat; question of rates for use of Early bird. il Time 85:88 Je 25 '65
Reporter at large. J. Brooks. New Yorker 40: 72+ Ja 30 '65
Setting sights higher; satellite to service all of U.S. il Bsns W p32+ Je 5 '65
Song of the Early bird. il Newsweek 65:74 Ap 19 '65
Stations for Early bird. il Fortune 72:197 Jl '65
TRW systems wins Comsat nod. il Miss & Roc 17:19 D 20 '65
Transistors pace Early bird launch date. B. Miller. Aviation W 82:20-1 Mr 22 '65
U.S. share in Comsat consortium decreases. Aviation W 82:67 Mr 8 '65

COMMUNICATIONS satellites
Apollo Comsats built for multiple access. B. Miller. il Aviation W 84:78-80 Ja 17 '66
ATS expanding to study large antennas. D. E. Fink. Aviation W 83:91-2 N 8 '65
ATS to aid airline communications tests; Advanced technology satellite. P. J. Klass. Aviation W 83:117+ Ag 9 '65
Auction by Early bird; Parke-Bernet & Sotheby's transaction. R. Lynes. il Harper 231-28+ Ag '65
Bird on one wing. Newsweek 66:72 Ag 16 '65
Bird: two-way transatlantic television program. New Yorker 41:46-8 My 15 '65
Birds on the wing; cost of using Early bird for transatlantic broadcasts. Newsweek 65: 70 My 24 '65
Broadcast satellite studies sought. Aviation W 84:23 Ja 3 '66
Commercial communications satellites; global network operation seen by '68. il Miss & Roc 17:155-6+ N 29 '65
Communications revolution. il Sci Digest 58: 30-1 Ag '65
Comsat delay may spur penalties; late delivery of the Early bird communication satellite. Aviation W 82:23 Mr 8 '65
Comsat lease rights to determine growth of space communications. K. Johnsen. Aviation W 83:27-8 N 8 '65
Comsat rings the bell. il Bsns W p32 My 1 '65
De Gaulle and ABC enter their bids. R. Burkhardt. New Repub 153:8-9 O 23 '65
Early bird aloft. il Time 85:64 Ap 16 '65
Early bird and Molniya 1. R. N. Watts, jr. Sky & Tel 29:360 Je '65
Early bird brightens the fine art scene; first transatlantic art auction. il Bsns W p34-5 My 29 '65
Early bird gets the word. il Life 58:63-4 My 7 '65
Early bird going into business. S. Montgomery. Miss & Roc 16:24 Je 28 '65
Early bird on way to equatorial station. Aviation W 82:31 Ap 12 '65
Early bird operation may be speeded. S. Montgomery. il Miss & Roc 16:12 Ap 12 '65

COMMUNICATIONS satellites—*Continued*
Early bird outdoes itself. Bsns W p 140 My 15 '65
Early bird speeds chart transmission. il Miss & Roc 17:35+ Jl 5 '65
End run; American broadcasting company's proposed domestic version of the Early bird. Time 85:84 My 28 '65
Feeding the Bird; first telecasts via Early bird. il Newsweek 65:86 My 17 '65
First ATS payload experiments selected; Applications technology satellite program. Aviation W 83:25 N 22 '65
Golden egg; Early bird sports coverage from abroad. Sports Illus 22:10 Je 28 '65
Hughes proposes TV broadcast satellite. B. Miller. il Aviation W 82:75+ F 1 '65
More nations sign communications satellite agreements; Department announcement, February 12, 1965. Dept State Bul 52:356-7 Mr 8 '65
Motionless bird in space. T. Alexander. il Fortune 72:130-1+ O '65
Optical technology satellite data sought. R. D. Hibben. il Aviation W 82:31-2 Ap 5 '65
Oscar III: A OK. il Pop Electr 22:50 Je '65
Oscar III: ham radio's new 2-meter space station. R. N. Tellefsen and H. C. Gabrielson. il Pop Electr 22:39-42+ Mr '65
President inaugurates commercial telephone service by satellite; remarks, June 28, 1965. L. B. Johnson. Dept State Bul 53:117 Jl 19 '65
President issues executive order on Communications satellite act; text, January 4, 1965. L. B. Johnson. Dept State Bul 52:112 Ja 25 '65
President Johnson transmits report on communications satellite system; letter of transmittal, February 15, 1965, with excerpts from report. L. B. Johnson. Dept State Bul 52:340-2 Mr 8 '65
Putting space to work to educate the world; Johnson plan. il Bsns W p 17 D 25 '65
Quarrels over Comsat; question of rates for use of Early bird. il Time 85:88 Je 25 '65
RCA, GE study TV broadcast satellites. P. J. Klass. il Aviation W 84:115+ Ja 10 '66
Room-size world; significance and potential of Early bird. il Time 85:84-6+ My 14 '65
Russians believed deploying Comsat net. P. J. Klass. Aviation W 83:29 O 11 '65
Satellite for you; Early Bird. il Sci Digest 57:inside back cover Je '65
Satellite TV predicted. Sci N L 88:246 O 16 '65
Satellites offer wide uses to airlines. B. Miller. il Aviation W 83:86+ O 25 '65
Setting sights higher; satellite to service all of U.S. il Bsns W p32+ Je 5 '65
Song of the Early bird. il Newsweek 65:74 Ap 19 '65
Spectrum of satellite Echo I. A. Przybylski. il Sky & Tel 30:217 O '65
Support grows for airline VHF Comsat. P. J. Klass. il Aviation W 83:83-6 N 22 '65
Switchboards in space: a look into the future; interview. D. Sarnoff. il U S News 59:50-4 Jl 5 '65
Transistors pace Early bird launch date. B. Miller. Aviation W 82:20-1 Mr 22 '65
Weather buoy-satellite link is studied. W. H. Gregory. il Aviation W 82:54-5+ F 8 '65
Where Soviets may challenge U.S. next; excerpts from address May 26, 1965. D. Sarnoff. U S News 58:20 Je 7 '65
See also
Communications satellite corporation

Electronic equipment
LES-4 satellite transponder succeeds in communications test; Lincoln experimental satellite. Aviation W 84:80 Ja 10 '66

Launching
Comsat launches no. 1; Early bird satellite. il Bsns W p33 Ap 10 '65
Comsat's first try; launch of first communications satellite. Early bird. il Time 85:92 Ap 9 '65
Russians rap U.S. satellites; Molyna-1 launching. Bsns W p 126 O 23 '65
Titan III-A hits near-perfect orbit; boosting LES-I. D. L. Zylstra. il Miss & Roc 16:21 F 22 '65

Military applications
Compact Comsat ground station designed for tactical applications. il Aviation W 83:125 N 15 '65
Comsat bid on defense system faces fight. Aviation W 82:71+ F 8 '65
Comsat squares off at Pentagon. Bsns W p29 Mr 6 '65

Comsat terminal design resists jamming. P. J. Klass. il Aviation W 82:56-7+ Je 21 '65
USAF plans attempt to transmit radio signals between satellites. M. L. Yaffee. il Aviation W 83:80-1+ Ag 16 '65

Tracking
Compact Comsat ground station designed for tactical applications. il Aviation W 83:125 N 15 '65
Comsat terminal design resists jamming; Lincoln experimental terminal. P. J. Klass. il Aviation W 82:56-7+ Je 21 '65
More ground stations planned by Comsat. Sci N L 89:40 Ja 15 '66
Unique low-noise antenna developed; rugged antenna for ground use in satellite communication. C. D. LaFond. il Miss & Roc 16:24-5 Je 21 '65

COMMUNICATIONS satellites ground stations. See Radio stations

COMMUNICATIONS workers

Wages and hours
Wage rates of communications workers. J. C. Bush. il Mo Labor R 88:40-4 Ja '65

COMMUNISM
Burdens of power. C. Marcy. Sat R 48:11-13 S 4 '65
Communism, facing a clouded future. il U S News 60:34-7 Ja 3 '66
Communism today: a refresher course; Time essay. Time 86:26-7 Ag 6 '65
Communists never give up; condensation of address, December 1, 1964. T. J. Dodd. Read Digest 86:61-6 Mr '65
Free self in a captive society. E. Capouya. Sat R 48:40-1 Je 12 '65
Immorality and communism; address, January 15, 1965. S. Braden. Vital Speeches 31:365-8 Ap 1 '65
Is communism folding up? J. Burnham. Nat R 17:631 Jl 27 '65
Karl Marx's theories need reevaluation. Sci N L 88:165 S 11 '65
Kremlin's difficult choice: ideology vs. national interests. R. Lowenthal. Atlan 215:76-83 Ap '65
Marxism: 100 years in the life of a doctrine, by R. D. Wolfe. Review
  Sat R 48:38-9 Je 12 '65. R. Strausz-Hupe
Principles and heresies: a crystallization of ten years. F. S. Meyer. il Nat R 17:1076-8 N 30 '65
World communism: the disintegration of a secular faith, by R. Lowenthal. Review
  Commentary 39:94-6 Ap '65. L. A. Coser
See also
Socialism

Anti-Communist measures
  See also
United States—Foreign relations—Anti-Communist measures

Anecdotes, facetiae, satire, etc.
Closing the game gap; anti-Communist games. C. M. Curtis. il Atlan 216:150-1 O '65

Study and teaching
Looking ahead in teaching about communism; excerpt from Teaching about communism. R. I. Miller. bibliog f Sch & Soc 93:502-5 D 25 '65

Africa
Busy bees of Peiping. America 112:894 Je 26 '65
New scramble for Africa; Soviets and red Chinese race for influence. il Sr Schol 86:6-9 F 11 '65

Asia
Asia out of control? interview. R. P. Martin. il U S News 59:38-42 O 4 '65
Communism in Asia. D. S. Zagoria. Commentary 39:53-8 F '65; Reply with rejoinder. S. Bialer. 39:8+ Ap '65

Asia, Southeastern
Australia and the defense of southeast Asia. S. Paltridge. For Affairs 44:49-61 O '65
Point of no return. W. V. Shannon. Commonweal 82:580-1 Ag 20 '65
Present objectives and future possibilities in southeast Asia; address, April 19, 1965. L. Unger. Dept State Bul 52:712-19 My 10 '65
Southeast Asia; fallacy of the dominoes. C. P. Fitzgerald. il Nation 200:700-2+ Je 28 '65
Southeast Asia isn't scared of the Chinese dragon. S. Topping. il N Y Times Mag p 12-13+ Ja 16 '66

COMMUNISM—Asia, Southeastern—*Continued*
What we must do to win in Asia. H. W.
Baldwin. il Read Digest 87:111-16 N '65
Why U.S. risks big war in Asia; with in-
terview with Thanat Khoman; ed. by R. P.
Martin. il U S News 58:31-4+ Mr 15 '65

Cambodia
Close-up of a red sanctuary; Cambodia and
its leaky border. S. W. Sanders. il U S
News 60:48-9 Ja 3 '66

Caribbean Region
Caribbean: intervention, when and how. J.
N. Plank. For Affairs 44:37-48 O '65
Time bomb in U.S. front yard. il U S News
58:35-9 Je 7 '65

Chile
See also
Communist party (Chile)

China (People's Republic)
China, by H. Schwartz. Review
Sat R 49:35 Ja 15 '66. H. L. Boorman
China goes it alone. R. MacFarquar. Atlan
215:69-75 Ap '65
China, Russia & the experts. G. Lichtheim.
Commentary 39:62-6 Mr '65
Delusions of power. New Repub 153:5-6 O 16
'65
How to talk to the Chinese in Peking.
J. Marcuse. il N Y Times Mag p24-5+ My
23 '65
Image and reality: China from within. C.
Taylor. il Nation 201:180-4 O 4 '65
Mao and the Chinese revolution, by J. Ch'en.
Review
Nation   200:703-4 Je 28 '65. C. P.
Fitzgerald
Mao's blueprint for chaos. Life 59:4 S 17 '65
Red China. G. Zimmermann. il Look 29:29-46
N 2 '65
Through the bamboo curtain. Nat R 17:537
Je 29 '65
See also
Communist party (China [People's Republic])

Colombia
Another Latin-American country that can
blow up. J. N. Wallace. il U S News 58:70-2
Je 21 '65

Cuba
Beyond harassment. J. Finn. Commonweal
82:720-3 O 1 '65
Castroism, by T. Draper. Review
America 113:99 Jl 24 '65. G. MacEoin
Nat R 17:656-8 Jl 27 '65. M. Lazo
Nation 201:62-4 Ag 2 '65. S. Shapiro
Sat R 48:28-9 Ag 21 '65. H. Lavine
Cuba seven years after. D. D. Burks. il Cur
Hist 50:38-44 Ja '66
Cuba si, Castro no; Fidel's sister speaks up;
excerpt from statement, June 11, 1965.
J. Castro. U S News 58:22 Je 21 '65
Cuba's brazen blueprint for subversion. K. O.
Gilmore. Read Digest 87:67-75 Ag '65
Exporter of communism. il Time 86:36 Ag 6
'65
How Castro spreads the revolution; FALN
goals. R. S. Strother. Read Digest 87:205-
6+ N '65
Imprisoned by Castro. G. de los Reyes. Read
Digest 86:114-18 My '65
What Castro is doing to Cuba; an eye witness
report. C. Migdail. il U S News 58:70-2
Mr 1 '65

Dominican Republic
After the battle in the Caribbean. H. Handle-
man. il U S News 58:33-7 My 17 '65
As Communists surface in Dominican Re-
public. il U S News 59:48 S 6 '65
Bitter salt of a stranger's bread; letter. E.
Wessin y Wessin. Nat R 17:911 O 19 '65
By which people? J. Burnham. Nat R 17:
864 O 5 '65
Caribbean riddle: how to let go. il U S News
58:25-7 My 31 '65
Close view of Santo Domingo. S. Rodman.
il Reporter 33:20-7 Jl 15 '65
Communism and democracy in the Dominican
Republic. J. Bosch. Sat R 48:13-15+ Ag 7
'65
Coup that became a war. il Time 85:28-32
My 7 '65
Dominican intervention: forward or backward
for Uncle Sam? with press comments. il Sr
Schol 87:6-8, 10-11 S 16 '65
Dominican prospect. J. Burnham. Nat R 17:
1019 N 16 '65
Dominican reds: taking over? il U S News
59:45 O 18 '65

Full story of Caribbean war; how reds plotted
a take-over. H. Handleman. il U S News
58:32-5 My 10 '65
Has U.S. turned over a nation to the reds?
two sides. H. Handleman. U S News 59:
50-2+ S 27 '65
New terror planned by Dominican reds? excerpts from testimony. E. Wessin y Wessin.
U S News 59:16 N 29 '65
Official record: how reds captured the Dominican revolt. il U S News 58:78-9 My 17 '65
Revolt rocks hemisphere. il Sr Schol 86:19-
20 My 13 '65
Security council authorizes U.N. representative in Dominican Republic; statements,
May 3-5, 1965, with text of resolution
adopted May 14, 1965. A. E. Stevenson.
bibliog f Dept State Bul 52:869-85 My 31 '65

Europe, Eastern
East Europe in flux; symposium. bibliog f
il Cur Hist 48:129-74+ Mr '65
Impact of change in eastern Europe on the
Atlantic partnership; address, April 3, 1965.
J. R. Schaetzel. Dept State Bul 53:161-71
Jl 26 '65

Europe, Western
Communism in western Europe. J. R. Staro-
bin. bibliog f For Affairs 44:62-77 O '65

France
See also
Communist party (France)

Germany (Democratic Republic)
Stirrings behind the wall: East Germany's
muted revolution. W. Hangen. il Harper
230:77-83 My '65

Guatemala
New red offensive; kidnaping. Time 87:34
Ja 7 '66

India
Soviet bid for India; hate America campaign.
E. Taylor. il Reporter 33:18-23 N 18 '65
Suicide of the Indian left. P. G. Altbach.
Christian Cent 82:1190-2 S 29 '65

Indonesia
Another big country about to go to the reds.
S. W. Sanders. il U S News 58:80-2 My 17
'65
Blowup in Indonesia: what it means to U.S.
and reds. il U S News 59:43-4 O 11 '65
Bung stands alone; housecleaning of all reds.
Time 86:39 D 10 '65
Following the mob. il Newsweek 65:36+ Mr
29 '65
Indonesia today. H. P. Van Dusen. Christian
Cent 82:584-8 My 5 '65
Sukarno makes trouble in the Philippines.
O. S. Villadolid. Reporter 33:22-4 Ag 12 '65
Sukarno, the would-be emperor. D. Warner.
Reporter 32:24-7 My 20 '65
U.S. survivors await Sukarno's ax. il Bsns W
p52+ Je 26 '65
See also
Communist party (Indonesia)

Italy
See also
Communist party (Italy)

Latin America
Communist priests in South America. R.
Peter. Nat R 17:876 O 5 '65
Communist strategy for Latin America. il
U S News 58:35 My 10 '65
Communist strategy in Latin America. J.
Kalvoda. Yale R 55:191-208 D '65
Cuba's brazen blueprint for subversion. K. O.
Gilmore. Read Digest 87:67-75 Ag '65
Decline of communism in Latin America. E.
Halperin. il Atlan 215:65-70 My '65
Hispaniola. M. Ascoli. Reporter 33:14 Jl 15
'65
Hopes rise south of the border; Communists
losing ground. il Bsns W p97-8 My 29 '65
How Castro spreads the revolution; FALN
goals. R. S. Strother. Read Digest 87:205-
6+ N '65
New communism in South America: address,
January 6, 1965. J. B. Powers. Vital
Speeches 31:318-20 Mr 1 '65
New strategy. il Time 85:40 Ap 23 '65
Now, a new round of red subversion. il U S
News 58:8 F 8 '65
OAS moves in, slowly; Dominican turmoil. il
Bsns W p36 My 15 '65
Roots of revolt. il Newsweek 65:30-1 Je 7
'65
This month's feature: the U.S. and western
hemisphere security. Cong Digest 44:257-88
N '65

COMMUNISM—Latin America—*Continued*
Vietnam and Latin America; danger of a hemispheric Vietnam; address, August 25, 1965. T. J. Dodd. Vital Speeches 31:706-9 S 15 '65
When a few Communists start to seize power. U S News 58:12 Je 28 '65
Where Castro brews new trouble for U.S. il U S News 59:38-40 O 18 '65

Malaysia
Another red threat to southeast Asia? U S News 60:11 Ja 10 '66

Peru
Battling the Castroites; terrorists in Peru. il Time 86:39 Jl 16 '65

Philippines
Now: an old friend turning away from U.S? with interview with D. Macapagal. il U S News 58:68-71 Je 14 '65
See also
Hukbalahaps

Poland
Who may come to Czestochowa? Time 87:34 Ja 14 '66

Rumania
Atlantic report. Atlan 215:32+ Je '65
See also
Communist party (Rumania)

Russia
American worker's daughter reports on workers' paradise. B. Humenny. il U S News 59:82-3 N 8 '65
China, Russia & the experts. G. Lichtheim. Commentary 39:62-6 Mr '65
No short cut to Soviet paradise. M. Nomad. il Sat R 48:39+ N 20 '65
Permanent crisis within Soviet Union; address, March 7, 1965. M. S. Pap. Vital Speeches 31:405-10 Ap 15 '65
Problems of dictatorship; the Russian experience. J. R. Strayer. For Affairs 44:264-74 Ja '66
Speaking out; Communism is not what we think. G. Feifer. Sat Eve Post 238:10+ F 27 '65
Underground view of the U.S.S.R; concerning articles by A. Tertz. il N Y Times Mag p52-3+ O 31 '65
See also
Communist party (Russia)

Thailand
And now Thailand. Nation 202:29 Ja 10 '66
How secure is Thailand? A. J. Dommen. New Repub 152:8-9 My 1 '65
Next target; Communist infiltration in northeast region. Newsweek 65:23 Mr 1 '65
Report from Thailand: reds' next target in Asia. il U S News 58:69-70+ Mr 22 '65
Thai countermeasures to Communist threat; excerpt from address, March 14, 1965. M. Green. Dept State Bul 52:489-91 Ap 5 '65
Thailand: next Vietnam? an on-the-scene report. S. W. Sanders. il U S News 59:30-3 Ag 2 '65
Thailand: Peking's new front. D. Warner. il Reporter 32:32-4 Je 17 '65

United States
American friends of the Vietcong; radical peace movements. H. Romerstein. il Nat R 17:278-9 Ap 6 '65
Communists and civil rights: how closely linked? Chicago and Montgomery, Ala. il U S News 59:12 Jl 12 '65
Faith of freedom; crime problem; address, October 19, 1965. J. E. Hoover. Vital Speeches 32:71-4 N 15 '65
From J. Edgar Hoover: a report on campus reds; excerpts from testimony, March 4, 1965. J. E. Hoover. il U S News 58:84 My 31 '65
Here we go again; Communist front type organization: Artists protest. Nat R 17:578-9 Jl 13 '65
Little old pink man who called Ike red; concerning address at Howard university by R. Welch. D. Sanford. New Repub 153:8 N 20 '65
Nobody but us agrarians: A. L. Strong. I. Epstein. F. Coe. J. Burnham. Nat R 17:684 Ag 10 '65
Politically ignorant college students; recrudescent Communist movement on the campus. R. Kirk. Nat R 17:423 My 18 '65
Reds and civil rights: a senator's warning; excerpts from address, March 18, 1965. J. O. Eastland. U S News 58:8 Mr 29 '65
To the East of the Communist party. T. R. Brooks. il N Y Times Mag p9+ Ap 25 '65

What's left of the left? H. Swados. Nation 201:108-14 S 20 '65
Why I quit the extreme left. P. A. Luce. Sat Eve Post 238:32-3 My 8 '65
See also
College students—Communist activities
Communist party (United States)
Trade unions—Communist activities

Anti-Communist measures
Anti-communism & the corporations. A. F. Westin; discussion. Commentary 37:19-24 Ap; 14 Je; 38:6 N '64; 39:14+ F '65
Days of shame, by C. E. Potter. Review Sat R 48:49 O 16 '65. N. S. Finney
How much freedom now for U.S. reds? Supreme court decision; McCarran and Smith acts; with editorial comment. il U S News 59:56, 116 N 29 '65
Last act; McCarran act of 1950. New Repub 153:9 N 27 '65
McCarran act; new lease on malignancy. A. A. Morris. il Nation 200:295-9 Mr 22 '65
New McCarthyism. Commonweal 83:138 N 5 '65
Plot to take over the PTA. E. Dunbar. il Look 29:27-31 S 7 '65
Ring loud the tocsin. Nation 201:29-30 Jl 19 '65
Up from the underground; court prohibits government from compelling individual party members to register. il Time 86:26 N 26 '65
See also
Conservatism
John Birch society
Loyalty, Oaths of

Venezuela
Cuba's brazen blueprint for subversion. K. O. Gilmore. Read Digest 87:67-75 Ag '65

Vietnam (Democratic Republic)
Other side of the Vietnam war; peasants under Communist control and red guerrillas. il U S News 59:48 Jl 12 '65
Why war in Vietnam goes on and on. il U S News 59:24-5 Ag 23 '65

Vietnam (Republic)
Communism has many faces in the Vietnam war. il U S News 58:35 My 3 '65
Untold story of Vietnam war. il U S News 60:29-32 Ja 24 '66
See also
Guerrillas—Vietnam (Republic)

West Indies
Those troubled islands in America's front yard. il U S News 59:77-80 Jl 12 '65

Yugoslavia
Constitutional socialism in Yugoslavia. I. Maksimović. bibliog f Ann Am Acad 358:159-69 Mr '65
Paunchy revolution; Tito's twilight. M. Mestrovic. Commonweal 83:336-9 D 17 '65

COMMUNISM and democracy
Advancing the goals of the U.N. charter; address, October 26, 1965. A. J. Goldberg. Dept State Bul 53:868-71 N 29 '65
Cold war alliances in a changing world. il Sr Schol 87:36 S 30 '65
Communist view. il Sat Eve Post 239:80 Ja 15 '66
Contagion of hope. E. J. Hughes. Newsweek 66:23 O 4 '65
East Berlin on July 4! letter to Dick Hanson. W. E. Swegle. Suc Farm 63:6+ S '65
False analogy. Nation 200:436 Ap 26 '65
From commissars to capitalists; comparing economic systems. Sr Schol 86:22+ Ap 15 '65
Future of nonalignment. M. S. Rajan. Ann Am Acad 362:121-8 N '65
Ideology of foreign policy; equal opportunities for all people; address, December 1, 1965. P. Dean. Vital Speeches 32:173-5 Ja 1 '66
Negotiated settlement; toward ending the Cuban stalemate. L. Dewart. Commonweal 82:717-20 O 1 '65; Reply. F. Pirez. 83:203+ N 19 '65
President's constituency; relation of cold war operations to the working of democracy. C. C. O'Brien. New Repub 153:28-31 Ag 21 '65
United States policy toward Europe; address, March 19, 1965. W. W. Rostow. Dept State Bul 52:576-82 Ap 19 '65
U.S. program of economic assistance to Africa; statement, February 10, 1965. G. M. Williams. Dept State Bul 52:349-54 Mr 8 '65

COMMUNIST party (United States)—*Continued*
Communists again on trial. America 113:616-17 N 20 '65
Going public; convicted for failure to register. Newsweek 66:25 N 29 '65
How much freedom now for U.S. reds? Supreme court decision: McCarran and Smith acts; with editorial comment. il U S News 59:56, 116 N 29 '65
Popular front party coming? neo-Progressive party. J. Burnham. Nat R 18:18 Ja 11 '66
Reds' registration overruled; Supreme court decision. Sr Schol 87:14 D 2 '65
Up from the underground; court prohibits government from compelling individual party members to register. il Time 86:26 N 26 '65

COMMUNIST periodicals
Explosive revival of the far left. R. Armstrong. il Sat Eve Post 238:27-32+ My 8 '65
To the East of the Communist party. T. R. Brooks. il N Y Times Mag p9+ Ap 25 '65

COMMUNIST propaganda. See Propaganda, Communist

COMMUNIST spies. See Spies

COMMUNIST strategy
Bull in China's shop. K. Crawford. Newsweek 66:38 N 8 '65
Challenges to freedom and peace; address, October 31, 1965. W. A. Harriman. Dept State Bul 53:863-7 N 29 '65
China's new leap forward. M. Ascoli. Reporter 33:24 S 23 '65
China's strategy; a critique. D. S. Zagoria. Commentary 40:61-6 N '65
Chinese riddle. Commonweal 82:711-12 O 1 '65
Communist strategy in Latin America. J. Kalvoda. Yale R 55:191-208 D '65
Impact of change in eastern Europe on the Atlantic partnership; address, April 3 1965. J. R. Schaetzel. Dept State Bul 53:161-71 Jl 26 '65
Light at the end of the tunnel; red China's expansion failures. W. Lippmann. Newsweek 66:29 N 8 '65
Soviet bid for India; hate America campaign. E. Taylor. il Reporter 33:18-23 N 18 '65
Target U.S.A., a warning from Peking; comment on article by Lin Piao. S. Topping. Read Digest 87:208-9 N '65
Vietnam: a debate; why we can't withdraw. L. Cherne. Sat R 48:17-21 D 18 '65; Discussion. 49:29 Ja 15 '66

COMMUNISTIC settlements. See Collective settlements

COMMUNITY and the school. See School and the community

COMMUNITY antenna television systems. See Television antennas

COMMUNITY arts councils, incorporated. See Arts councils of America

COMMUNITY centers
Something for everybody; new community center, Greensboro, N.C. O. T. Hester. il Am City 80:88-9 N '65
See also
Recreation centers

COMMUNITY college. See Junior colleges

COMMUNITY development
Would you fight poverty this way? Willow Run association for neighborhood development. il Nations Bsns 53:104+ Ap '65

COMMUNITY House. See Middlebury, Vt.—Historic houses, etc.

COMMUNITY life
Dawn of a community-defining federalism. H. C. Hart. bibliog f Ann Am Acad 359:147-56 My '65

COMMUNITY organization. See Community life

COMMUNITY planning. See Regional planning

COMMUNITY property
Who owns what when it's community property. il Good H 160:178 Je '65

COMMUNITY relations service. See United States—Community relations service

COMMUNITY service
College serves the community; cooperation in recreation programs, Cerritos college district, Calif. J. Larez. Recreation 58:485 D '65
They wouldn't let their small town die! il Suc Farm 63:74+ F '65
War on poverty; are the poor left out? R. A. Cloward. il Nation 201:55-60 Ag 2 '65
See also
Volunteer service

COMMUNITY welfare work. See Community service

COMMUTER service. See Railroads—Passenger traffic

COMMUTERS
Electronic roads for tomorrow's traffic; Cornell lab study for Commerce dept. il Bsns W p 160+ Ap 24 '65
For New York riders, the rail crisis deepens. il Bsns W p74-6+ Mr 20 '65
Getting to work and back. R. Brecher and E. Brecher. il Consumer Rep 30:56-65, 128-33, 206-9 F-Ap '65; Discussion. 30:299-301 Je '65
Hardest look yet at rail commuters; in Philadelphia. il Bsns W p 164+ My 8 '65
Man from L.I.R.R. tells a few. C. B. Palmer. il N Y Times Mag p 154+ N 28 '65

Anecdotes, facetiae, satire, etc.
To heck in a handcar. M. Kitman. il Sat Eve Post 238:16 D 18 '65

COMO, William
(ed) See Gelabert, R. Anatomy for the ballet teacher

COMPACT cars. See Automobiles—Design

La COMPAGNIE de Saint-Gobain. See France—Industries

COMPANION; story. See Gabbard, A.

COMPANY magazines. See House organs

COMPANY of Jesus. See Jesuits

COMPANY presidents. See Executives

COMPARATIVE education. See Education, Comparative

COMPARATIVE literature. See Literature, Comparative

COMPASS
Outboard in fog. B. Whittier. il Yachting 117:66-7+ My '65
Pocket compasses. il Consumer Rep 30:399-401 Ag '65

COMPENSATION (law)
Are new laws needed for good samaritans? U S News 58:18 Ap 26 '65
Proposed solution to the Rhodesian crisis. W. B. George. Christian Cent 83:13-14 Ja 5 '66
See also
Damages

COMPENSATION claims. See Claims

COMPENSATION for victims of crime. See Reparation

COMPETITION
How your competition will change. J. Backman. il Nations Bsns 53:38-9+ F '65
Tiny flame; competition and profit; address, October 26, 1965. R. G. Wingerter. Vital Speeches 32:158-60 D 15 '65
See also
Free enterprise
Monopolies
Price cutting

COMPETITION, Unfair
See also
Industrial property

COMPETITIONS
Boat name contest. il Motor B 115:56 F '65
My own favorite contest; favorite book contest for children. M. F. Howard. Pub W 188:88-9 Jl 19 '65
Prize contests, the secrets of winning. il Changing T 19:13-15 D '65
Soup's on; winner of Campbell's soup contest. il Newsweek 66:58 Ag 23 '65
Success story; the all-American girl enters Mademoiselle's college competitions. il Mlle 62:130-1 N '65
See also subhead Competitions under various subjects, e.g. Art—Competitions

COMPETITIVE bidding. See Contracts; Contracts, Government

COMPETITIVE sports. See Sports

COMPLAINTS
Put your complaint in writing! Consumer Bul 48:26-7 O '65

COMPLEMENT fixation
Complement fixation on cell surfaces by 19S and 7S antibodies. T. Borsos and H. J. Rapp. bibliog il Science 150:505-6 O 22 '65
Complement; inactivation of second component by p-hydroxymercuribenzoate. M. A. Leon. bibliog il Science 147:1034-5 F 26 '65
Lattice formation in complement fixation; studies with univalent rabbit antibody. H. H. Fudenberg and others. bibliog il Science 148:91-3 Ap 2 '65
Nonspecific binding of complement by digestion fragments from antiviral gamma globulin. N. E. Cremer and others. bibliog il Science 149:84-5 Jl 2 '65
Rubella complement fixation test. J. L. Sever and others. bibliog il Science 148:385-7 Ap 16 '65

COMPLEMENTS (immunity)
Complement; increased efficiency of the second component after treatment with iodoacetamide. M. J. Polley and H. J. Müller-Eberhard. bibliog il Science 148:1728-9 Je 25 '65

COMPLEXION. See Skin

COMPOSERS
Unfashionable generation; twentieth-century music. P. J. Pirie. il Hi Fi 16:59-62 Ja '66
See also
International rostrum of composers

COMPOSERS, American
New generation. B. Boretz. Nation 200:345-8 Mr 29 '65
See also
Bloch, E.
Copland, A.
Gottschalk, L. M.
Ives, C. E.

COMPOSERS, Austrian
Composers of Vienna; photographs. Opera N 30:14-16 Ja 22 '66
See also
Bruckner, A.
Mozart, J. C. W. A.
Schoenberg, A.
Webern, A.

COMPOSERS, Brazilian
See also
Villa-Lobos, H.

COMPOSERS, Czech
See also
Janáček, L.
Smetana, B.

COMPOSERS, Danish
See also
Nielsen, C.

COMPOSERS, Finnish
See also
Sibelius, J. J. C.

COMPOSERS, French
See also
Debussy, C.
Dukas, P.
Varèse, E.

COMPOSERS, German
See also
Beethoven, L. van
Loewe, C.
Schütz, H.

COMPOSERS, Hungarian
See also
Bartók, B.
Kálmán, E.
Kodály, Z.

COMPOSERS, Italian
See also
Donizetti, G.
Nono, L.
Zandonai, R.

COMPOSERS, Russian
See also
Tchaikovsky, P. I.

COMPOSERS recordings, incorporated
CRI explores the universe of Harry Patch. R. Ellsworth. il Am Rec G 31:606-8 Mr '65

COMPOSITAE
See also
Tithonia

COMPOSITE materials. See Materials

COMPOSITE photographs. See Montage

COMPOSITION (art)
Landscape painting composition and its relation to abstract design. D. Frantz. il Design 67:31-3 N '65
Paint a mosaic. R. Barrio. il Design 67:10-13 S '65

COMPOSITION (music)
At white heat; Il Trovatore written in a month. H. Klein. il Opera N 30:24-5 D 4 '65
See also
International rostrum of composers

COMPOSITION (photography)
Add the background later. Gowland. il Pop Phot 56:34+ Je '65
Backgrounds help make pictures. S. H. Gottscho. il Horticulture 43:18-19+ Jl '65
Decomposition. D. Vestal. Pop Phot 56:82-3+ Je '65
Images etched in time; double exposure and blending of texture with person. J. Morris. il U S Camera 28:46-9+ Jl '65
On the beach. il U S Camera 28:38-41 My '65
Photographic abstracts. R. B. Walker. il Design 67:14-16 S '65
Precise moment. P. Caulfield and H. Keppler. il Mod Phot 29:67-73 Ap '65
What center of interest? with photographs by Louis Stettner. U S Camera 28:54-5 S '65
See also
Photography—Still life

COMPOSITION (printing) See Typesetting

COMPOSITION, English. See English language—Composition

COMPOSTS. See Fertilizers and manures

COMPOUNDS, Organic. See Organic compounds

COMPOUNDS, Periodic. See Periodic compounds

COMPTON, Neil
American dreams. Commentary 39:73-4+ My '65
Camping in the wasteland. Commentary 41:58-60+ Ja '66
Consensus television. Commentary 40:67-8+ O '65

COMPTON-BURNETT, Ivy
Alarming qualities of Ivy Compton-Burnett. P. Devlin. por Vogue 146:252-3+ S 1 '65

COMPTON, Calif.
250 feet of sewer obstruction. D. W. Robins. il Am City 80:136+ F '65

COMPTROLLER general, Office of. See United States—General accounting office

COMPULSORY arbitration. See Arbitration, Industrial

COMPULSORY military service. See Military service, Compulsory

COMPUTER industry
Dutch computers hit the European market; Holland's Electrologica. il Bsns W p 110+ Jl 10 '65
New computer prodigy? Scientific data systems. J. F. Olesky. Duns R 86:71-2 N '65
Vast expansion in computer use seen; advances in batch-fabrication processes. R. Pay. Miss & Roc 16:32-3 Ap 26 '65
Wanted: compatible computers. Bsns W p34 Mr 6 '65
See also
International business machines corporation
Scientific data systems, incorporated

Europe, Western
Europe's counterattack. Newsweek 66:70 Ag 16 '65

COMPUTER process control. See Computers—Industrial applications

COMPUTER processing. See Electronic data processing

COMPUTER workers
Lots of new jobs in computers; careers in electronic data processing. il Changing T 19:21-3 Ag '65
New look at how machines make jobs. il Nations Bsns 53:58-60+ S '65

COMPUTERS
Big eight computer spectrum. D. E. Weisberg. il Duns R 86:pt2 152 S '65
Criminal identification in three seconds; new system at St Louis metropolitan police department. H. S. Priest. il Am City 80:46 Mr '65
Cybernated generation. il Time 85:84-8+ Ap 2 '65
Games, logic and computers. H. Wang. il Sci Am 213:98-104+ N '65
Good-by to Gutenberg; concepts incubating in laboratories. il Newsweek 67:85-8 Ja 24 '66
Hologram and the computer; new proposal for mechanical character recognition. Sci Am 214:48 Ja '66
Honeywell calls a computer bet; Series 200 line challenges IBM and RCA. il Bsns W p 102+ F 13 '65
How computers are used. F. K. Fukuchi. il Sci Digest 57:58-62 Mr '65
How computers will change your life. J. Pfeiffer. McCalls 92:34 My '65
How to pick a computer. H. Pryor. il Sci Digest 57:75-9 Ap '65
Hybrid computers; combination of analog and digital techniques. L. E. Frenzel, jr. il Electr World 74:64-6 O '65
IBM pulls switch on computers. Bsns W p68 My 1 '65
Inventor of the month; coming, computers without one-track minds. S. V. Jones. il Sci Digest 58:22 S '65
Learn, vote by computer. Sci N L 87:395 Je 19 '65
My IBM baby; blindness out of blind dates. il Time 86:84+ N 19 '65
New job for computers with atom smashers. Sci N L 87:233 Ap 10 '65
New look in selling; intensive training requirements. L. Velie. Read Digest 86:251-2+ My '65
Next big jump is near in printing. il Bsns W p92+ Ap 24 '65
Notes and comment; failure to demonstrate Pauline letters were by six authors. New Yorker 40:23 F 6 '65
Some problems still stymie the computers. Sci N L 88:263 O 23 '65
Track, fast; bets, too; automated system handling bets. il Bsns W p66-7 N 27 '65
Univac isn't a business to jump in and out of. S. H. Brown. Fortune 71:120-3+ Ap '65
Vast expansion in computer use seen; advances in batch-fabrication processes. R. Pay. Miss & Roc 16:32-3 Ap 26 '65

COMPUTERS—*Continued*

What computers can do. S. L. Englebardt. il Sci Digest 57:61-5 F '65

What computers can't do. L. Eisenberg. il Harper 231:96-9 Ag '65

When a computer needs a friend; thinking machines vs. human judgment. il Bsns W p 146+ Mr 6 '65

See also
Control data corporation
Data processing service centers
Electronic data processing
International business machines corporation
Programming (computers)
Publishers and publishing—Computer installations

Aeronautic applications

Automation reshapes airline management, operations. P. J. Klass. il Aviation W 83: 70-1+ O 25 '65

BEA reservation system keyed to two Univac 490 computers. Aviation W 83:47 S 27 '65

Computer aid to traffic control expands. P. J. Klass. Aviation W 83:107-11 N 15 '65

Computer offers multiple program level. B. Miller. il Aviation W 83:72-3+ S 6 '65

Computer use in flight planning to spread. J. W. Carter. Aviation W 82:29-30 F 15 '65

Digitrac to aid Sweden's traffic control. P. J. Klass. il Aviation W 83:87+ Jl 5 '65

Inflight engine-data recording evaluated. il Aviation W 83:71+ N 1 '65

Phoenix data unit decision near. Aviation W 82:23 Je 7 '65

Re-entry data system assists X-15 pilot. G. Alexander. il Aviation W 83:79+ S 27 '65

Sale, exchange of engineering data becoming common among airlines. Aviation W 82:35 Mr 8 '65

Systems integration boosts ASW effort. P. J. Klass. il Aviation W 82:36-7+ Mr 1 '65

Touchdown by computer; Autoflare system. il Time 85:64 Je 18 '65

Univac flies with United. Bsns W p33 D 25 '65

Agricultural applications

Now you can hire computer bookkeeping. Farm J 89:54B Ap '65

Programmed farming finds your best chance to make money. J. A. Carlson. il Farm J 89: 31+ Mr '65

What computers are ready to do for you; with editorial comment. J. Carlson. il Farm J 89:5, 21-3 Jl '65

Analog computers

Beech expands data center capabilities; using analog computers in missile and aircraft design work. il Aviation W 84: 97-8 Ja 10 '66

Anecdotes, facetiae, satire, etc.

Is there a God? Newsweek 67:55-6 Ja 10 '66

R U there? ed. by M. Levin. C. L. Melaro. Sat R 48:6+ Ag 14 '65; Same. Read Digest 87:199-200+ N '65

Rating week; Swell 7, our leader. P. H. Kendall. Sat R 48:8+ Jl 17 '65

Architectural applications

Computer-aided design and automated working drawings. J. Barnett. bibliog il Arch Rec 138:85+ O '65

Computers can simplify architect's work. Sci N L 87:139 F 27 '65

Bibliographic applications

Computer reference system speeds bibliographies; Universal reference system. Pub W 187:42 My 3 '65

Business applications

Automating chores in the office; Business equipment exposition at New York's Coliseum. il Bsns W p 104+ O 30 '65

Computers and the college store. Pub W 187: 62-4 Je 14 '65

Computers in business. E. Bukstein. il Electr World 73:41-3 F '65

Data transmission and the real-time systems. il Duns R 86:pt2 159-61+ S '65

Giving the facts fast; warranty protection system. il Bsns W p 126+ N 20 '65

How to organize information systems. J. Dearden. bibliog f il Harvard Bsns R 43: 65-73 Mr '65

Communication applications

Computer-based terminal system to handle Department cable flow. Dept State Bul 53: 645 O 18 '65

Western union hums with data; computer data transmission. il Bsns W p 150-2+ F 20 '65

Control applications

Process-control computers. il Fortune 71:223-4 Ap '65

Cooperative use

Computer time sharing goes on the market; service of Keydata corp, Boston. Bsns W p 116 D 4 '65

Lot of little users share a big computer. il Bsns W p61-3 Ag 7 '65

Sharing the computer's time. Time 86:104 N 12 '65

Digital computers

Is science big enough to cope with society? R. Bellman. il Sat R 48:43-4 Je 5 '65

Rx for hospitals; computers; information system at Massachusetts general hospital and Missouri medical center. il Bsns W p 142+ My 15 '65

Reinforcement schedule generated by an on-line digital computer. B. Weiss and V. G. Laties. bibliog il Science 148:658-61 Ap 30 '65

Educational applications

Computer-aided instruction. J. A. Swets and W. Feurzeig. bibliog Science 150:572-6 O 29 '65

In so far as. . . attempt to see if computers can evaluate essay style. Newsweek 65:61 Ap 5 '65

School scheduling by computer; Generalized academic simulation programs. Sch & Soc 93:143+ Mr 6 '65

Engineering applications

Beech expands data center capabilities; using analog computers in missile and aircraft design work. il Aviation W 84: 97-8 Ja 10 '66

Computer designs circuit board layouts. P. J. Klass. il Aviation W 84:72-3 Ja 3 '66

Electronic draftsman. W. R. Wise. il Electr World 74:70-1 Jl '65

Ford lifts lid on secret; numerical control in auto production. il Bsns W p 140+ Ja 15 '66

New machine speeds diagram production. P. J. Klass. il Aviation W 83:77+ O 18 '65

Errors

Keeping mistakes from computers; Addo. il Bsns W p 166+ Je 12 '65

Government applications

Uncle Sam's wonderful tax machine. D. Oberdorfer. il Sat Eve Post 238:28-9 Ap 10 '65

Wanted: compatible computers. Bsns W p34 Mr 6 '65

What computers are doing to your tax return. il Changing T 19:31-2 N '65

When machines check on taxes. U S News 58:103-4 Ap 19 '65

When the machines get your tax return. il U S News 58:110-11 Ap 26 '65

Industrial applications

AAUP: two aspects of production; computers and fine design; summaries of discussions at annual convention. il Pub W 188:120-5 Jl 19 '65

Black-box plant is coming. E. Landes. il Duns R 85:pt2 114-17+ Mr '65

Computer control of industrial processes. E. Bukstein. il Electr World 74:42-3+ D '65

Executive denies computer costs force small firms into mergers. G. C. Wilson. Aviation W 83:124+ S 13 '65

How steel jobs are dwindling; computer-controlled mills. il Bsns W p75-6+ Ag 14 '65

IBM's answer to time-sharing. Bsns W p50 Mr 13 '65

Keeping ahead on real time. il Bsns W p 166-8+ Mr 27 '65

New edge in glass; Owens-Corning computer runs glass furnace by itself. Bsns W p60+ Ap 10 '65

Process-control computers. il Fortune 71:223-4 Ap '65

Input-output equipment

Information acquisition and display. il Duns R 86:pt2 153-5+ S '65

What's ahead in information technology. J. Diebold. il Harvard Bsns R 43:76-82 S 65

Medical applications

Adverse drug effects data available to all. Sci N L 88:326 N 20 '65

Computer spots disease. Sci N L 88:294 N 6 '65

Computer that psychoanalyzes you. M. Maruyama. il Sci Digest 59:70-5 Ja '66

Diagnosis by computer speeds heart check-up. il Bsns W p34 O 2 '65

COMPUTERS—Medical applications—*Continued*
New medical uses for computers. il Good H 160:183 Ap '65
Some kinetic properties of a deterministic epidemic confirmed by computer simulation. M. L. Black and I. D. Gay. bibliog il Science 148:981-5 My 14 '65

Military applications

New computer aimed at tactical role. M. Getler. il Miss & Roc 16:28+ F 1 '65
On-line computing dominance foreseen. R. Pay. Miss & Roc 16:32-4 Mr 1 '65
Phoenix data unit decision near. Aviation W 82:23 Je 7 '65
Univac delivers A-NEW computer; unit for air, surface or underwater manned military tactical systems. C. D. LaFond. il Miss & Roc 16:60+ My 17 '65

Municipal applications

Automatic purchase orders; Phoenix, Ariz. B. A. Gragg. Am City 80:140+ F '65
Computer produces 120-volume planning reference; City planning commission, New York, N.Y. W. F. R. Ballard. il Am City 80:110+ Jl '65
Computer that puts the budget in order every day; Oakland, Calif. A. A. Brizee. il Am City 80:116-17 Mr '65
Computerize your purchases and save; use of computers by Department of purchase, New York city. G. A. Wechsler. il Am City 80:86-7 N '65
Cycle-basis billing; Nutley, N.J. W. J. Jernick. il Am City 80:104+ O '65
First computer center billing; Brookfield, Ill. F. E. McGuire. il Am City 80:102-3 My '65
Solving land-use determinations electronically; Norristown, Pa. D. B. Witwer. il Am City 80:90-1 F '65

Musical applications

Computer makes music of trumpet sounds. il Sci N L 88:375 D 11 '65

Navigational applications

Seagoing computer; aboard research vessel, Atlantis II. il Sci Digest 57:24-5 My '65

Photographic applications

Computer-produced movies. K. C. Knowlton. il Science 150:1116-20 N 26 '65

Police applications

Computers play cops and robbers. il Bsns W p 132-4+ Ja 15 '66
Electronic pinch; computer oriented retrieval of auto larcenists. il Sci Digest 58:23 N '65
Instant arrest by Univac; Operation corral. il Pop Sci 188:76 Ja '66

Printing applications

Behind the glamor of computer composition. A. E. Gardner. Pub W 188:90+ O 4 '65
Exit the computer. Newsweek 66:50 S 6 '65
PIA convention, publisher as printer; electronics house to become typesetting house; summaries of speeches. il Pub W 188:97-8+ N 8 '65
R&E reviews computers and electronics in the graphic arts; annual meeting. Pub W 187:123-4 Je 14 '65
Setting type by computer; McGraw-Hill's Electronics buyers' guide. il Bsns W p 140+ Ag 21 '65
Survey shows computer use more than doubles in year. Pub W 188:125 N 8 '65

Psychiatric applications

See Computers—Medical applications

Readout systems

Readout indicators for solid-state computers. E. Bukstein. il Pop Electr 22:49-52+ Mr '65

Scientific applications

Can we improve on nature too much? A. Smith. il Sci Digest 58:88-91 O '65
Computer aids chemistry. Sci N L 87:372 Je 12 '65
Computer experiments in fluid dynamics. F. H. Harlow and J. E. Fromm. il Sci Am 212:104-10 bibliog(p 140) Mr '65
Computer studies atoms. A. Ewing. Sci N L 87:247 Ap 17 '65
Computing methods applied to reactor problems; report on international conference at Argonne national laboratory. W. Sangren. Science 149:1268+ S 10 '65
Is science big enough to cope with society? R. Bellman. il Sat R 48:43-4 Je 5 '65
Liquid waves by computer. F. H. Harlow and others. il Science 149:1092-3 S 3 '65
Nervous system research with computers. G. D. McCann. bibliog il Science 148:1565-71 Je 18 '65

New computer simulates man's behavior in crisis. Sci N L 87:264 Ap 24 '65
Recording Lissajous figures. I. L. Finkle. il Science 148:1541-2 Je 18 '65; Reply. J. Potzick. 149:1446 S 24 '65
Scientific computers. E. Bukstein. il Electr World 73:34-5+ Mr '65
Theoretical morphology of the coiled shell. D. M. Raup and A. Michelson. bibliog il Science 147:1294-5 Mr 12 '65

Simulation programs

Make believe for real; forecasting war maneuver or business move. S. L. Englebardt. il Sci Digest 58:73-7 N '65

Social aspects

Cybernated generation. il Time 85:84-8+ Ap 2 '65

Space flight applications

Abort backup for LEM near production. B. Miller. il Aviation W 84:106-7+ Ja 10 '66
Analog digital computer combination will aid in MOL mission simulation. Miss & Roc 16:34-5 Mr 15 '65
Athena impact accuracies point to possibility of longer unguided flights. R. Pay. il Miss & Roc 17:26-7 Jl 12 '65
Biggest brain built at spacecraft center. Sci N L 87:344 My 29 '65
Computer has speed, compactness. C. D. LaFond. il Miss & Roc 16:28+ Mr 22 '65
Computer lab to serve entire center; section of ERC's Instrumentation and data processing division. Miss & Roc 16:61 My 31 '65
Firms detail computer systems at fall show. R. Pay. Miss & Roc 17:28+ D 13 '65
Instrumentation and data processing; Instrumentation and data processing division of ERC. il Miss & Roc 16:45-6 My 31 '65
Tiny computers steer mightiest rockets. W. Von Braun. il Pop Sci 187:94-5+ O '65

Standards

Wanted: compatible computers. Bsns W p34 Mr 6 '65

Terminology

What those words mean. Sci Digest 57:78-9 Ap '65

Testing

Firm matches computers with jobs; systems and computers evaluation and review technique. J. F. Judge. il Miss & Roc 16:24-5 Je 7 '65

Traffic control applications

Can computers call the signals? il Bsns W p80-1+ N 20 '65

Transportation applications

Downtown traffic responds to the computer; Calgary, Alberta. il Am City 80:134 O '65
Let the computer plan your traffic program. E. Nussbaum. il Am City 80:102-4 Jl '65
Toting commuters by computers; San Francisco Bay area rapid transit district. il Bsns W p 122-4+ Ap 10 '65

COMSAT. See Communications satellite corporation

COMSTOCK, Helen
Cabinetmakers of the Norwich area. Antiques 87:696-9 Je '65
—See Strachan, R. jt. auth.

COMSTOCK, Randolph G.
Challenge of automation. bibliog f Cur Hist 49:71-6+ Ag '65

COMSTOCK, Thelma Vest
Books children want to read. Writer 78:26-7 Je '65

COMTE, Gilbert
Letter from Africa. Nat R 17:509-10 Je 15 '65
Letter from Cairo. Nat R 17:728 Ag 24 '65

CON men. See Fraud

CONANT, Howell
Expert at pushing girls around. G. P. Hunt. por Life 58:3 Mr 19 '65

CONANT, James Bryant
Doctor James B. Conant answers questions you ask about schools. por Changing T 20:24-9 Ja '66
Role of the states in education; address, July 27, 1965. Vital Speeches 31:686-8 S 1 '65
University and the high school; reprint of a 1939 article. Sch & Soc 93:52-6 Ja 23 '65

about

College admissions: a cure for chaos? J. Cass. Sat R 48:69-70 N 20 '65
Conant's fight for better teaching. M. Borrowman. por Atlan 215:113-17 Ap '65

CONANT, Margaret M.
How well should children mind? PTA Mag 59:10-12 bibliog(p43) F '65
CONARD-Pyle company
One red rose, symbol of a bond. E. M. Shisler. il Pop Gard 16:58 S '65
CONCENTRATION. See Attention
CONCENTRATION camps
Holocaust kingdom, by A. Donat. Review
Commonweal 81:644 F 12 '65. E. T. Gargan

Germany

Germany today. G. Astor. il Look 29:44-5+ My 4 '65
Nazis on trial; pages from a journal, tr. by W. J. Dannhauser. J. Lind. Commentary 39:69-72 Ap '65

Philippines

Santo Tomas story, by A. V. Hartendorp. Review
America 112:641-2 My 1 '65: J. F. Hurley

Poland

Return to Auschwitz. A. Schalk. Commonweal 82:498-501 Jl 9 '65; Reply. L. X. Tarpey, sr. 82:546 Ag 6 '65

Russia

Et tu, Tito? Yugoslav report on Stalin's concentration camps. Time 85:27 F 19 '65
Now it can be told, by the Russians. M. Mihajlov. il N Y Times Mag p25+ Mr 14 '65
CONCERT audiences. See Audiences
CONCERT halls
Festival hall reopened. T. Heinitz. Sat R 48:62 F 27 '65
CONCERT managers
Questions and answers about college bookings; interview, ed. by I. Fisher. F. Taylor. Dance Mag 40:52-3+ Ja '66
CONCERT opera association
Music to my ears; production of Tchaikovsky's Pique dame. I. Kolodin. Sat R 48:30 Mr 6 '65
Musical events; concert performance of Berlioz's Benvenuto Cellini in Philharmonic Hall. W. Sargeant. New Yorker 41:155-6 Ap 3 '65
Musical events; performance of Tchaikovsky's Pique dame. W. Sargeant. New Yorker 41:119-21 F 27 '65
New York international; Benvenuto Cellini at Philharmonic Hall. F. Merkling. Opera N 29:33 My 1 '65
Trump and no-trump; Queen of spades. F. Merkling. Opera N 29:33 Mr 20 '65
CONCERTOS
See also
Phonograph records—Concertos
CONCERTS
Musical events; Spanish promenade concert at Philharmonic Hall. W. Sargeant. New Yorker 41:128+ Je 12 '65
CONCERTS for children. See Music for children
CONCESSIONS (food, etc)
Their business is peanuts; feeding spectators at sports events. J. Jares. il Sports Illus 24:52-8 Ja 17 '66
Where profits are really food and drink; Automatic canteen co. of America. il Bsns W p88-90 Jl 3 '65
CONCHOLOGY. See Shells (conchology)
CONCILIATION, Industrial. See Arbitration, Industrial
CONCILIUM (periodical)
Concilium appears; reply. J. T. Ellis. America 112:301 Mr 6 '65
CONCORDATS
What about the concordats? Vatican council II's Declaration on religious liberty. Christian Cent 82:1244 O 13 '65
CONCORDIA Lutheran Junior college, Ann Arbor, Mich.
Integrated site planning and design for a small college. il Arch Rec 38:189-96 S 65
CONCRETE
Ready-mix in small batches; new service for do-it-yourself home workmen. il Sunset 134:105-6 F '65

Prestressing

Tall buildings in prestressed concrete. T. Y. Lin. il Arch Rec 138:165-70 D '65
CONCRETE, Precast
Detailing a precast panel facade. M. Wolff. il Arch Rec 137:191-3 Mr '65
Making precast concrete do more for less; new IBM headquarters in Milwaukee. J. Bailey. il Arch Forum 123:52-5 N '65
Three precast bearing walls. il Arch Rec 137:218-20 My '65

CONCRETE, Reinforced
Saarinen's skyscraper: Columbia broadcasting system's office tower, New York city. il Arch Rec 138:111-18 Jl '65
CONCRETE block walls. See Walls, Concrete
CONCRETE construction
Concrete for shade and pattern; design for Child care center, Chicago. il Arch Rec 138:159-60 N '65
Girder wall is all precast. il Arch Rec 137:217-18 Je '65
Mies in Baltimore: slender frame of concrete. D. Canty. il Arch Forum 123:36-9 D '65
See also
Bridges—Foundations and piers

Forms

Appearance of board-formed concrete. J. G. Wilson. bibliog il Arch Rec 138:173-6 Ag '65
McNulty House: a space wrapped in concrete. il Arch Forum 123:30-5 N '65
CONCRETE girders. See Girders
CONCRETE pavements. See Pavements, Concrete
CONCRETE slabs
Easy way to raise sunken concrete slabs. R. Day. il Pop Sci 186:146-9 Je '65
CONCRETE walls. See Walls, Concrete
CONDENSED books. See Books, Condensed
CONDITIONED response
Brightness discrimination in the collared lizard. V. J. Vance and others. bibliog il Science 147:758-9 F 12 '65
Classical conditioning of electric organ discharge rate in mormyrids. F. J. Mandriota and others. bibliog il Science 150:1740-2 D 24 '65
Color-discrimination performance of pigeons; effects of reward. C. A. Boneau and others. il Science 149:1113-14 S 3 '65; Reply. J. A. Nevin. 150:1057 N 19 '65
Color vision in the antelope ground squirrel. F. Crescitelli and J. D. Pollack. bibliog il Science 150:1316-18 D 3 '65
Differential-approach tendencies produced by injection of RNA from trained rats. A. L. Jacobson and others. il Science 150:636-7 O 29 '65
Differential classical conditioning: verbalization of stimulus contingencies. M. J. Fuhrer and P. E. Baer. bibliog il Science 150:1479-81 D 10 '65
Efficiency of the conditioned eyelid response. I. Martin and A. B. Levey. bibliog il Science 150:781-3 N 5 '65
Facilitation: electrical response enhanced by conditional excitation of cerebral cortex. L. T. Rutledge. bibliog il Science 148:1246-8 My 28 '65
Humoral mediation of radiation-induced motivation in parabiont rats. E. L. Hunt and others. bibliog il Science 150:1747-8 D 24 '65
Hypothalamic motivational processes as reflected by their hippocampal electrical correlates. E. Grastyán and others. bibliog il Science 149:91-3 Jl 2 '65
Interocular transfer in goldfish: color easier than pattern. D. J. Ingle. bibliog il Science 149:1000-2 Ag 27 '65
Lateral hypothalamus: learning of food-seeking response motivated by electrical stimulation. E. E. Coons and others. bibliog il Science 150:1320-1 D 3 '65
Observable changes of hypotheses under positive reinforcement. P. Suppes and M. Schlag-Rey. bibliog il Science 148:661-2 Ap 30 '65
Probability-learning by the turtle. K. L. Kirk and M. E. Bitterman. bibliog il Science 148:1484-5 Je 11 '65
Reinforcement schedule generated by an on-line digital computer. B. Weiss and V. G. Laties. bibliog il Science 148:658-61 Ap 30 '65
Retrograde amnesia from electroconvulsive shock in a one-trial appetitive learning task. S. S. Tenen. bibliog il Science 148:1248-50 My 28 '65; Reply with rejoinder. S. L. Chorover and P. H. Schiller. 149:1521 S 24 '65
Signal detection in fixed-ratio schedules. M. Rilling and C. McDiarmid. bibliog il Science 148:526-7 Ap 23 '65
Temperature independence of an arbitrary temporal discrimination in the goldfish. P. Rozin. bibliog il Science 149:561-3 Jl 30 '65
Two-stage paired-associate learning and eye movements. P. D. McCormack and E. J. Haltrecht. bibliog il Science 148:1749-50 Je 25 '65

CONDOMINIUM plan ownership. See Apartment houses—Condominium plan ownership
CONDON, Richard
Capsule history of timepieces. Holiday 38:42-3 Ag '65

CONDON-Wadlin act.   See Labor laws and legislation—New York (state)

CONDORS
Annual condor count planned. C. W. Buchheister. Audubon Mag 67:357 N '65
Crucial meeting on the condor. C. W. Buchheister. Audubon Mag 67:285 S '65
Grave threat to the condor. C. W. Buchheister. il Audubon Mag 67:82-3 Mr '65
Our campaign to save the condor. C. W. Buchheister. Audubon Mag 67:180 My '65
Remaining California condors menaced by dams. il Nat Parks Mag 39:22 Mr '65
There soars the condor. G. A. Morse. il Am For 71:22-4+ F '65
Wilderness and the condor. Nat Parks Mag 40:19-20 Ja '66

CONDUCT of life
Centering: toward a new humanism. E. Navaretta. Craft Horiz 25:37+ Mr '65
Choose one of five; it's your life; address, May 30, 1965. E. S. Sampson. Vital Speeches 31:661-3 Ag 15 '65
Don Marquis to the young; letter, ed. by C. O'Neill. D. Marquis. Esquire 63:77+ My '65
Findings in a valley; letter to my oldest grandchild. J. Canfield. il Read Digest 86: 86-90 My '65
Ideals can be disquieting; with study-discussion program, by C. Smallenburg and H. Smallenburg. W. J. Anderson; H. Long. bibliog il PTA Mag 59:14-16, 36-7 My '65
In solitary witness: the life and death of Franz Jägerstätter, by G. C. Zahn. Review Nation 200:426-8 Ap 19 '65. T. Roszak
Interview with Erich Fromm; ed. by R. Heffner. E. Fromm. McCalls 93:132-3+ O '65
Myths by which we live; address, March 7, 1965. L. Rosten. Vital Speeches 31:410-14 Ap 15 '65
Once more, a beginning. J. Moorhead. il PTA Mag 59:2-3 Ap '65
Opinion on religion. J. Carmichael. Mlle 61: 124+ S '65
Plato, the penthouse, and the girl who hesitates. G. Roy. Mlle 60:199+ Mr '65
Power of the mind; dedication to a contributing life; address, June 14, 1965. R. A. Charpie. Vital Speeches 31:668-70 Ag 15 '65
Secret of the right word. E. A. Autry. Farm J 89:62B O '65
Some quotes from John Gardner on excellence, self-renewal and other matters. J. Gardner. Science 149:614-15 Ag 6 '65
Time on our hands. R. Lazarus. NEA J 54: 15 My '65
Try everything once. W. M. Marston. Read Digest 86:93-6 F '65
Vision that rescues; self-awareness, creativeness and strength; address, May 31, 1965. K. I. Brown. Vital Speeches 31:567-70 Jl 1 '65
See also
Character
Charity
Christian life
Conscience
Ethics
Friendship
Honesty
Human relations
Hypocrisy
Love
Resolutions
Self-denial
Service
Worth

CONDUCTED tours. See Travel

CONDUCTING (music)
Afternoon with an autocrat; interview, ed. by F. Stevenson. Z. Mehta. Opera N 30:27 Ja 1 '66
High-voltage conductor; interview, ed. by Q. Eaton. W. Steinberg. il Opera N 29:11 Mr 20 '65
Maestro remembers; excerpt from It's all in the music, by D. G. Monteux. P. Monteux. Opera N 30:26-7 D 25 '65
Preparing a performance; ed. by A. M. Lingg. G. Schick. il Opera N 29:8-12 Mr 27 '65

CONDUCTING, Choral
Song leading simplified. S. H. Frieswyk. il Recreation 58:480-1 D '65

CONDUCTORS (music)
Maestros on the road, Metropolitan opera national company conductors; interviews, ed. by Q. Eaton. R. La Marchina and S. Krachmalnick. il Opera N 30:20 O 23 '65
Notary public. J. W. Freeman. Opera N 29:12-13 Ap 17 '65
Tomorrow's grand old men. L. Marcus. Hi Fi 15:119 Je '65

Top face; Negro conductor triumphs at La Scala. il Time 86:49 D 31 '65
Wandmanship; Piatigorsky's analysis of the conductor's role. il Time 85:72+ F 5 '65
See also
Bernstein, L.
Carvalho, E. de
Celibidache, S.
De Carvalho, E.
Irving, R.
Karajan, H. v
Leinsdorf, E.
Maazel, L.
Martinon, J.
Mehta, Z.
Schippers, T.
Simon, S.
Szell, G.

Anecdotes, facetiae, satire, etc.
Of time and time beaters. H. Von Hochmeister. Hi Fi 15:136-7 Ag '65

CONE, Bonnie
School Miss Bonnie built. il por Time 86:56 Jl 16 '65

CONE, Fairfax M.
What's bad for TV is worse for advertising. por Fortune 72:102+ Jl '65
about
Fairfax Cone, the FCC, and TV advertising. R. L. Tobin. Sat R 48:49-50 Ag 14 '65
It's Cone two to one. por Newsweek 66:68-70 Ag 16 '65

CONERICO was here to stay; drama. See Gagliano, F.

CONEY ISLAND
I remember Coney. B. Finnegan. il Hobbies 70:124-5+ N '65

CONFECTIONERY
How to make and use candied grapefruit peel. F. Imlay. il Farm J 89:97 D '65
Sweets blend old and new; Mexican recipes. S. M. Fertitta. il Look 30:63 Ja 25 '66
See also
Candy

CONFEDERATE memorial of Stone Mountain. See Stone Mountain memorial

CONFEDERATE STATES of America
See also
Flags—Confederate States of America
United States—History—Civil war
Army
War within a war, by C. Beals. Review Sat R 48:61-2 O 16 '65. W. B. Catton

CONFERENCE of the Eighteen-nation committee on disarmament, Geneva, 1962-
Back to Geneva. Time 86:23 Jl 30 '65
Building a shrine for disarmament. N. Moss. il Reporter 33:33-5 O 7 '65
Conference of 18-nation disarmament committee reconvenes at Geneva; statement, July 27, 1965; with message from President Johnson. W. C. Foster. Dept State Bul 53:333-7 Ag 23 '65
Disarmament at the U.N. H. A. Jack. Christian Cent 82:991-2 Ag 11 '65
Disarmament committee reconvenes; summary of message. Thant. UN Mo Chron 2:26-7 Ag '65
Disarmament conference: United States position; address. A. E. Stevenson. Vital Speeches 31:482-8 Je 1 '65
Disarmament impasse may alter alliances. Aviation W 83:32 Ag 30 '65
Eighteen-nation disarmament committee considers U.S. draft treaty to prevent spread of nuclear weapons; statements, August 17 and August 31, 1965; with text of draft treaty. L. B. Johnson; W. C. Foster. Dept State Bul 53:466-75 S 20 '65
Growing U.S.-Soviet rift palls renewed disarmament discussion. Aviation W 83:30 Ag 9 '65
Just an exercise? Newsweek 66:46 Ag 30 '65
Neutralist world and disarmament negotiations. J. L. Nogee. bibliog f Ann Am Acad 362:71-80 N '65
Nuclear weapons: nonproliferation and testban talks to be resumed. L. J. Carter. Science 151:57-60 Ja 7 '66
Report of Conference of Eighteen-nation committee. UN Mo Chron 2:29-31 O '65
Till next time. Time 86:36 S 24 '65
United States arms control and disarmament agency; excerpts from report to Congress, January 1, 1964-December 31, 1964. bibliog f Dept State Bul 52:308-17 Mr 1 '65
U.S. expresses views on convening of U.N. disarmament committee; statement. A. E. Stevenson. Dept State Bul 52:601 Ap 19 '65

CONFERENCE of the Seventeen-nation committee on disarmament. See Conference of the Eighteen-nation committee on disarmament, Geneva, 1962-

CONFERENCE on military electronics. See Military electronics conference

CONFERENCE on the church and the new morality. See Religious conferences

CONFERENCES
See also
Diebold conferences
Inter-American conferences
Library conferences
Religious conferences

CONFERENCES on science and world affairs. See Pugwash conferences on science and world affairs

CONFESSION
Confession: public or private? il Time 86:70 Ag 6 '65
More meaning in confession. America 113: 661 N 27 '65

CONFESSION (law)
Confession controversy. il Time 86:62+ D 3 '65
Confession of confusion: Escobedo vs. Illinois mass confusion cases. il Newsweek 66:29 D 20 '65
Confessions any good in court any more? U.S. Supreme court decision. U S News 58: 12 Je 14 '65
Confusion on confessions; ruling of U.S. Court of appeals in Philadelphia. Time 85:52 Je 4 '65
Courts vs the police. Life 58:4 My 21 '65
Fighting crime; Senate bill on new interpretation of Mallory rule. A. M. Bickel. New Repub 153:11-12 S 18 '65; Reply with rejoinder. M. H. Freedman. 153:36-8 O 16 '65
Should confessions be outlawed? A. Poinsett. il Ebony 20:173-4+ My '65
Still waiting on confessions. il Time 85:61 Je 11 '65
Suspect confesses, but who believes him? G. Whitmore affair. S. E. Zion. il N Y Times Mag p30-1+ My 16 '65
Under review by Supreme court: just what rights do suspects have? il U S News 59: 10 D 6 '65
Unspoken confession; Graves decision. Time 86:58 Jl 30 '65

CONFESSION stories. See Short stories
CONFESSIONS of faith. See Creeds
CONFIDENCE men. See Fraud
CONFLICT, Social. See Social conflict
CONFLICT of interests (business)
Aerospace interlocks with other firms; table. Aviation W 82:91 Ap 19 '65
House group details corporate interlocks. G. C. Wilson. Aviation W 82:92+ Ap 12 '65
Outside directors under attack; proposed legislation against interlocks in corporate management. A. R. Towl. il Harvard Bsns R 43:135-47 S '65

CONFLICT of interests (public office)
Business, Washington, and conflict of interest; interview, ed. by J. Berry. L. L. Strauss. Duns R 86:48-50+ O '65
Financial bosom-baring: a test of ethics? J. N. Eller. America 112:745 My 22 '65
University microfilm head requests inquiry; charges of conflict of interests between roles as officer of the publishing house and regent of University of Michigan. Pub W 188:34-5 N 29 '65
What Connor loses by joining Cabinet. il U S News 58:20 F 1 '65

CONFORMITY
Conformity as a tactic of ingratiation. E. E. Jones. bibliog il Science 149:144-50 Jl 9 '65
Hair styles and harebrains. J. Ciardi. Sat R 48:18 My 1 '65
Kind word for conformity; American life in the 1960s. M. W. Fishwick. il Sat R 48:22-4 D 11 '65
Topic: The unreasonable man; excerpts from College entrance examination papers. P. L. Levin. il N Y Times Mag p92+ Mr 28 '65
Two cheers for conformity. P. L. Levin. il N Y Times Mag p79+ Ap 25 '65

CONGENITAL malformations. See Deformities

CONGER, Lesley
Off the cuff. Writer 78:9-10 F; 6-8 Mr; 7-8 Ap; 7-8 My; 9-10 Je; 7-8 Jl; 7-8 Ag; 8-10 S; 7-8 O; 5-6 N; 9-10 D '65; 79:7-8 Ja '66

CONGO (capital Brazzaville)
See also
United States—Foreign relations—Congo (capital Brazzaville)

Foreign relations
Little neighborliness; two Congos. Time 86: 43-4 N 12 '65

Politics and government
Abbé in exile. Time 85:34+ Ap 16 '65
To burn, to bury or to hang? Time 86:35 Ag 6 '65

CONGO (capital Leopoldville)
Certain gain; clean up of Congolese rebels. il Time 85:32 Ap 23 '65
Congo; is what is happening another Boxer rebellion? M. Pfaff. Commonweal 81:599-601 F 5 '65
Congo vortex. Christian Cent 82:195-6 F 17 '65
Double intrusion; charges made that Congolese planes bombed two Ugandan villages. P. Webb. Newsweek 65:44 Mr 8 '65
Eastern Congo's chaotic rebellion. R. W. Howe. il Reporter 32:35-6 Mr 11 '65; Discussion. 32:6+ Ap 8 '65
Moise's black magic. il Time 85:34 F 19 '65
Red arsenals arm the Simbas; with eye-witness reports from Life correspondents. il Life 58:26-33 F 12 '65
Resolutions on the Congo; excerpts from the O.A.U. resolution, September 10 and text of the Security council resolution, December 30, 1964. Cur Hist 48:237-8 Ap '65
Victory and despair. il Newsweek 65:44-5 Ap 26 '65
See also
Colleges and universities—Congo (capital Leopoldville)
Elections—Congo (capital Leopoldville)
Katanga
Rites and ceremonies—Congo (capital Leopoldville)
Stanleyville
United Nations—Congo (capital Leopoldville)

Army
Changing guard. Time 86:30 D 17 '65
Road to Fizi; attack on Simbas by mercenaries. il Time 86:43-4 O 15 '65

Economic conditions
Visit with Tshombe; is peace possible in the Congo? E. Dunbar. il Look 29:83-6+ Mr 9 '65
See also
Congo (capital Leopoldville)—Industries

Foreign relations
Congo and its neighbors. New Repub 152:9 Ap 24 '65
Little neighborliness; two Congos. Time 86: 43-4 N 12 '65

History
Fire this time. D. Wiley. Christian Cent 82:200-3 F 17 '65

Industries
Big companies still thrive in the Congo. il Bsns W p70+ F 20 '65

Massacre, 1964
See Congo massacre, 1964

Politics and government
Bad news for Communists. il U S News 59: 20 D 6 '65
But he has survived. J. Lelyveld. il N Y Times Mag p52-3+ N 28 '65
Congo realities and United States policy; address, April 25, 1965. G. M. Williams. Dept State Bul 52:793-805 My 24 '65
Fight for a leopard-skin chair; test of strength between Kasavubu and Tshombe. Time 86:37 N 26 '65
How to win wars & elections. il Time 85: 30-1 Ap 2 '65
I am president; self proclamation by J. Mobutu. Newsweek 66:47-8 D 6 '65
Kind of progress; Kimba replaces Tshombe. Newsweek 66:48 O 25 '65
Looking for votes; meeting of the Organization of African unity. Time 85:26+ Mr 12 '65
Military takes over. Sr Schol 87:19 D 9 '65
New, five-year (?) government. il Time 86: 34-5 D 3 '65
New Tshombe. P. E. Sigmund. Commonweal 82:559-63 Ag 6 '65
Political awakening in the Congo: the politics of fragmentation, by R. Lemarchand. Review
Commentary 40:112-14+ N '65. C. Legum
Rebellion in the Congo. M. D. Markowitz and H. F. Weiss. il Cur Hist 48:213-18+ Ap '65
Short-sleeved society. il Time 86:27 D 24 '65
Stanleyville massacre; excerpt from 111 days in Stanleyville. D. Reed. il Read Digest 87:233-8+ S '65
Strongman Tshombe: ousted, but ... il U S News 59:20 O 25 '65

CONGO (capital **Leopoldville**)—Politics and government—*Continued*
Tshombe may seek anti-white role; election preview. R. W. Howe. New Repub 153:14-15 S 18 '65
Uniform of the day. Newsweek 66:41 D 27 '65
View from the terrace; Tshombe's ouster. il Time 86:40+ O 22 '65
Visit with Tshombe; is peace possible in the Congo? E. Dunbar. il Look 29:83-6+ Mr 9 '65

Religious institutions and affairs
See also
Catholic church in the Congo

CONGO massacre, 1964
Carnage in the Congo; discussion. Christian Cent 82:146 F 3 '65
Fire this time. D. Wiley. Christian Cent 82:200-3 F 17 '65; Discussion. 82:474 Ap 14 '65
Grim siesta of Stanleyville. J. Lelyveld. il N Y Times Mag p28-9+ My 16 '65
111 days in Stanleyville, by D. Reed. Review Sat R il 48:37-8 D 11 '65. C. Miller
Stanleyville massacre; excerpt from 111 days in Stanleyville. D. Reed. il Read Digest 87:233-8+ S '65
Tragedy in the Congo. Read Digest 86:88-92 f '65

CONGO massacres, 1965-
Arrows to heaven. Time 85:40 Je 11 '65
Flare-up. Newsweek 65:58 Je 14 '65

CONGO villages. See Villages

CONGOLESE
Congo is Kibweta, not Leopoldville. J. A. Lukas. il N Y Times Mag p24-5+ Mr 7 '65
See also
Simbas

CONGREGATIONAL Christian churches. See United church of Christ

CONGREGATIONAL churches
Renewing England's free churches. C. Northcott. Christian Cent 82:829-30 Je 30 '65

CONGRESS of racial equality
Congress of racial equality and its strategy. M. Rich. Ann Am Acad 357:113-18 Ja '65
CORE: wild child of civil rights. H. Bims. il Ebony 20:35-8+ O '65
Happy anniversary; convention, Durham, N.C. Newsweek 66:31 Jl 12 '65
One war at a time; CORE's annual convention in Durham, N.C. Newsweek 66:22+ Jl 19 '65

CONGRESS party (India) See Political parties—India

CONGRESSIONAL committees. See United States—Congress—Committees

CONGRESSIONAL hearings. See United States—Congress—Committees

CONGRESSIONAL medal of honor. See Medal of honor (United States)

CONGRESSIONAL quarterly
Instant encyclopedia. il Newsweek 66:78-9 S 13 '65

CONGRESSIONAL record
Great Swampoodle gazette. A. Chamberlin. il Sat Eve Post 238:90+ Ap 10 '65

CONGRESSMEN
Congress: a crop of bright young men. il Newsweek 66:35 N 8 '65
Congress: one new member brings an engineering PH.D. background in research, business to the job. J. Walsh. il Science 147:1016-18 F 26 '65
CODELS are coming; lawmakers survey foreign lands. il Newsweek 66:32 D 13 '65
Duty of Congress; representatives organize public discussions in own districts. Nation 201:457-8 D 13 '65
Freshman class that votes like a bloc; non-southern-bloc freshman Democrats. il Time 86:12 Jl 30 '65
It's world-travel season for Congress; with a record in sight. il U S News 59:72-3 D 6 '65
Key men in the 89th. Sr Schol 86:15 F 18 '65
New faces in Washington. P. Mesta. il McCalls 92:24+ Ap '65
Occupation: member of Congress. D. Reische. il Sr Schol 86:16-19 F 18 '65
Quiet junketeers. Time 86:14-15 D 31 '65
Seductive odor of pork; congressmen's pet projects. Life 59:4 S 17 '65
When to ask your congressmen for help. il Changing T 20:13-14 Ja '66
See also
Negro congressmen
Senators
United States—Congress

CONGREVE, William
Way of the world. Criticism
Life 58:8+ Je 4 '65

CONIDIA. See Spores (botany)

CONIFERS
H&G's gardener's month: San Francisco's Strybing arboretum. il House & Gard 127:182-4 Mr '65

CONIGLIARO, Tony
Tony Conigliaro: Red Sox high note. T. Cohane. il pors Look 29:102-4 My 4 '65

CONIMBRIGA. See Coimbra, Portugal

CONINE, Ernest
Communism's new economics. Harvard Bsns R 43:53-61 My '65

CONKLIN, Bill
Don't upset the apricot. Sat Eve Post 238:18 S 25 '65

CONKLING, Laurette Kristine
Queen of the little Kings. H. Ehrlich. il pors Look 29:80-4 Je 29 '65

CONLEY, Clare
Anything can happen hunt. Field & S 70:47-9+ S '65
Cooking on the front page. Field & S 70:145 My '65
Great steelhead hang-up. Field & S 69:44-7+ Ap '65
Hurrah for the real elk hunter. Field & S 70:50-1+ Ag '65
It's in the bag. Field & S 69:64-7+ F '65
Lightning: nature's deadly fireworks. Field & S 70:52-3+ My '65

CONLEY, Kieran
Ecumenism and the Catholic seminary. Christian Cent 82:523-5 Ap 28 '65

CONLY, John M.
Aaron Copland looks ahead. Reporter 33:54+ Ag 12 '65
Lateiner's Beethoven. Reporter 32:46+ F 11 '65
Record clubmen. Reporter 32:46+ Ap 8 '65
Welcome back, maestri. Reporter 33:41-2 Jl 1 '65

CONNABLE, Roma
Case for girls in law. Mlle 61:188-90+ My '65

CONNALLY, John B.
Connally's Texas. A. Kopkind. New Repub 153:9-12 N 20 '65
People of the week. por U S News 58:20 Ap 12 '65

CONNALLY amendment. See International court of justice, The Hague

CONNECTICUT
See also
Architecture, Domestic—Connecticut
Booksellers and bookselling—Connecticut
Education—Connecticut
Fishing—Connecticut
Gardens—Connecticut
Housing—Connecticut
Hunting—Connecticut
Law—Connecticut
Roads—Connecticut

Politics and government
Reapportionment comes to Connecticut. E. J. Bell. il Nat R 17:685-7+ Ag 10 '65

Religious institutions and affairs
News of the Christian world (cont) Christian Cent 82:1584+ D 22 '65

CONNECTICUT opera association
Gallic Hartford. W. Miranda. Opera N 29:33 F 20 '65
Opera in Connecticut. W. B. Syer. il Hi Fi 15:126-7 Je '65
Philadelphia, Hartford, Baltimore. G. Fitzgerald. il Opera N 30:29-30 D 4 '65

CONNELL, Evan S. Jr
Brief essay on the subject of celebrity with numerous digressions and particular attention to the actress, Rita Hayworth. Esquire 63:114-16 Mr '65
St Augustine's pigeon; story. Sat Eve Post 238:52-3 Mr 13 '65
about
WLB biography. N. Morgan. por Wilson Lib Bul 39:695 Ap '65

CONNELL, Reid S. and Bacon, R. L.
Nucleoside phosphatases of fetal and maternal blood cells: electron microscope study. bibliog Science 150:503-4 O 22 '65

CONNELLY, Dolly
How did I get myself into this? Sports Illus 22:56-8+ Ap 5 '65
Yoo-hoo to Namu the whale. Sports Illus 23:18-23+ Jl 26 '65

CONNELLY, Marc
Most unforgettable character I've met. Read Digest 86:72-8 My '65
On the fringe; ed. by H. Frankel. por Sat R 48:40 Jl 24 '65
Souvenir from the klongs. Sat R 48:47-8 S 18 '65
about
Dewdrop man. por Newsweek 65:88+ Je 28 '65

CONNERY, Sean
Big Bond bonanza. W. K. Zinsser. il pors Sat Eve Post 238:76-81 Jl 17 '65
Bondomania. il por Time 85:59 Je 11 '65

CONNERY, Sean—*Continued*
007-the spy with the golden touch. F. Stewart-Gordon. Read Digest 87:113-17 O '65
James Bond conquers all in Thunderball. G. Zimmermann. il pors Look 29:45-50+ Jl 13 '65
Sean Connery takes over Rock Point. B. Allen. il Mlle 62:127+ D '65

CONNESS, John
Yosemite's hundredth birthday. W. R. Jones. il por Nat Park Mag 39:14-17 Ap '65

CONNIFF, James C. G.
Those chemicals in our food. McCalls 92:83+ F '65
(ed) See Giordano, H. L. Dope-smuggling diplomats

CONNOLLY, Francis X.
Obituary
Pub W 188:43 N 29 '65

CONNOLLY, Thomas E.
Who's in the trap? America 113:716 D 4 '65

CONNOR, John Thomas
Letter to businessmen, December 6, 1965. Dept State Bul 54:24-7 Ja 3 '66
Needs of business; address, June 5, 1965. Vital Speeches 31:583-6 Jl 15 '65
Outlook now for business; interview. pors U S News 58:72-7 My 24 '65

about

Connor: how he works for business; seeking bigger voice for business in government. il pors Nations Bsns 53:36-7+ N '65
New Secretary of commerce. por Fortune 71:47 F '65
Voice for business in U.S. policy. il pors Bsns W p96-8+ Mr 13 '65
What Connor loses by joining Cabinet. il por U S News 58:20 F 1 '65

CONOLLY, John R. and Ewing, Maurice
Ice-rafted detritus as a climatic indicator in Antarctic deep-sea cores. bibliog Science 150:1822-4 D 31 '65

CONQUEST, Robert
Nabokov's Eugene Onegin. Poetry 106:236-8 Je '65

CONRAD, Charles, Jr
We had our orbit: it was the cat's bandana. pors Life 59:84C-84D S 24 '65

about

Africans lionize a pride of spacemen. il por Life 59:44-5 O 8 '65
Fuel-cell flight. il Time 86:46-8 Ag 27 '65
Hardest rendezvous of all, on the ground. J. Hicks. il pors Life 59:113-14+ O 1 '65
Keeping house in orbit. il por Newsweek 66:64 S 20 '65
See also
Space flight—Manned flights—Cooper-Conrad flight, 1965

CONRAD, Charles, Jr, family
Long wait at home for a star that's brighter than heck. M. Acoca. il pors Life 59:38-9 S 10 '65

CONRAD, Joseph
Chat with Joseph Conrad. C. Clemens. Hobbies 70:85+ Ja '66

CONRAD, Pete. See Conrad, C. jr

CONROY, Hilary
(comp) Articles and other books received; east Asia. See issues of American historical review

CONSCIENCE
Announcing mortal sins. C. Davis. America 112:193 F 6 '65; Discussion. 112:340-1 Mr 13 '65
Fiery pangs of conscience; why N. Morrison committed suicide. L. Wainwright. Life 59:34 N 12 '65
High cost of conscience. L. R. Young. il McCalls 93:81-2+ O '65
Worst censorship; personal reprisal for acts of conscience. Nation 201:459 D 13 '65
See also
Truth

CONSCIENTIOUS objectors
Any God will do; Selective service act's test of supreme-being belief. il Time 85:74 Mr 19 '65
Conscientious objectors: how many, what they do. U S News 59:12 N 15 '65
Conscientious objectors: U.S. Supreme court upholds right to military draft. America 112:381 Mr 20 '65
Do pacifists embarrass the churches? Christian Cent 82:1404-5 N 17 '65
Right to say no? Commonweal 83:7 O 8 '65
Supreme court broadens scope of conscientious objection. Christian Cent 82:356-7 Mr 24 '65
Test for believers; Supreme court decision. il Newsweek 65:64 Mr 22 '65
See also
Military service, Compulsory—United States

CONSCIOUSNESS
Research in America; Ranger 8 findings. J. Lear. il Sat R 48:47-8 Ap 3 '65
See also
Self

CONSCRIPTION. See Military service, Compulsory

CONSEIL européen pour la recherche nucléaire. See European organization for nuclear research

CONSERVATION associations
See also
American forestry association

CONSERVATION education. See Conservation of resources—Study and teaching

CONSERVATION of parity. See Wave functions

CONSERVATION of resources
America down the drain? with statement by Secretary Udall. R. H. Boyle. il Read Digest 86:235-6+ Ap '65
America, the beautiful; President Johnson's message to Congress on natural beauty. il Time 85:54-5 F 19 '65
Beware: the spoilers are on the march! waste, destruction, pollution. J. Shivers. il Recreation 58:448-50 N '65
Big new issue. Nation 200:237 Mr 8 '65
Conservation and natural beauty. P. H. Abelson. Science 150:1539 D 17 '65
Conservation critique; summary of address, February 8, 1965. M. Goddard. Am For 71:8-9+ Ap '65
Conservation; ed. by H. Titus. See issues of Field & stream
Conservation revolt; excerpt from address, March 8, 1965. H. H. Humphrey. Audubon Mag 67:252-4 Jl '65
Destruction of California, by R. F. Dasmann. Review
Holiday 38:171-4 O '65. W. O. Douglas
Nation 201:252-4 O 18 '65. K. Lamott
Duty to the future. S. L. Udall. Sat R 48:48+ My 22 '65
Ecology of man and the land ethic. S. L. Udall. il Natur Hist 74:32-41 Je '65
Flight from folly. il Time 86:62-72 S 17 '65
For a more beautiful America; excerpts from remarks, February 8, 1965. L. B. Johnson. Recreation 58:107-8+ Mr '65
For a more beautiful U.S; the President asks this; with interview with C. A. T. Johnson. il U S News 58:71-6 F 22 '65
Fouling of the American environment; symposium. il Sat R 48:31-48+ My 22 '65; Discussion. 48:21 Je 26 '65
Guidelines to wilderness action; excerpt from address, May 15, 1965. S. M. Brandborg. Liv Wildn 29:36-7 Spr '65
How to do something about it. T. Trueblood. il Field & S 69:18+ Mr '65
Is shale-oil boom on the way at last? il U S News 58:100 My 31 '65
Looking forward. A. W. Smith. Nat Parks Mag 40:2 Ja '66
Matching funds; program for conserving soil and water resources. New Repub 154:6 Ja 22 '66
Matching growth with beauty. Life 58:4 Mr 5 '65
Message from the President of the United States, February 8, 1965; excerpt. L. B. Johnson. Liv Wildn 87:2 Wint '64; Recreation 58:107 Mr '65
National capital report. C. H. Callison. Audubon Mag 67:114-15 Mr '65
Natural beauty and conservation. P. H. Abelson. Science 147:1245 Mr 12 '65
News and commentary. See issues of National parks magazine
1965 science review. Sci N L 88:392 D 18 '65
People's money and the national welfare. A. W. Smith. Nat Parks Mag 39:2 Je '65
Peripatetic reviewer. E. Weeks. Atlan 215:188-9 Mr '65
Preserving vegetation in parks and wilderness. E. C. Stone. bibliog il Science 150:1261-7 D 3 '65
President Johnson outlines programs for realization of the Great society. il Arch Rec 137:23+ Mr '65
President's message on natural beauty. P. M. Tilden. Nat Parks Mag 39:2 Mr '65
Report of president and general counsel to the general membership of National park association; May 20, 1965. Nat Parks Mag 39:I-IV My '65
Shale oil: the cartel's ace in the hole. R. Fleming. il Nation 200:274-6 Mr 15 '65
Speaking out; let's spoil the wilderness. R. Wernick. il Sat Eve Post 238:12+ N 6 '65
Still talkin' about the Tetons; Johnsons hailed on conservation. D. Fleeson. il Am For 71:22-5 N '65
University research program. Nat Parks Mag 39:21 Jl '65

CONSERVATION of resources—*Continued*
Wasters. J. P. Degnan; J. Hillaby. il **Nation** 200:242-7 Mr 8 '65
Wilderness and the Land and water conservation fund act; outdoor enjoyment. F. Gregg. il Liv Wild 29:25-8 Sum '65
See also
Forest conservation
Inter-American specialized conference to deal with problems relating to the conservation of renewable natural resources in the western hemisphere
International union for the conservation of nature and natural resources
Natural resources
United States—Conservation, Department of (proposed)
United States—Interior, Department of
Water conservation
Wilderness areas
Wildlife conservation

History
George Perkins Marsh; conservation's forgotten man. C. E. Randall. Am For 71:20-3 Ap '65

Study and teaching
Blueprint for a school forest; Yellow Springs school forest, Ohio. J. P. Chu. il Am For 71:34-9+ F '65
New York checks up. J. J. Shomon. Audubon Mag 67:388-90 N '65
Why outdoor conservation education? excerpt from Manual of outdoor conservation. J. J. Shomon. Recreation 58:101 Mr '65

CONSERVATION of wildlife. See Wildlife conservation
CONSERVATION of works of art. See Art objects—Conservation and restoration
CONSERVATISM
Conservatism after Goldwater. D. Danzig. Commentary 39:38-42 Mr '65
Conservatism, liberalism, and religion. W. Herberg. il Nat R 17:1087-8 N 30 '65
Conservative mindlessness. R. H. Rovere. Commentary 39:31-7 Mr '65
Dean Burch's view: most Americans are conservative; excerpts from address, February 15, 1965. D. Burch. U S News 58:16 Mr 1 '65
Horizons of conservatism. F. S. Meyer. Nat R 17:197 Mr 9 '65
John Birch society and the conservative movement; editors of National review; symposium. Nat R 17:914-20+ O 19 '65; Discussion. 17:1141 D 14 '65
Myth of American conservatism. R. Lechtreck. America 114:44-6 Ja 8 '66
Need to maintain a civilization; first national meeting of the Philadelphia society. G. Davenport. Nat R 17:283-4 Ap 6 '65
Principles and heresies: a crystallization of ten years. F. S. Meyer. il Nat R 17:1076-8 N 30 '65
Richard Cornuelle and the third sector. F. S. Meyer. Nat R 17:103 F 9 '65
Sit down, you're rocking the boat; rightwing in New Jersey and Virginia. E. J. Bell. Nat R 17:983+ N 2 '65
Some reason for cheerfulness: rumination on Conservative thoughts and action. R. Kirk. Nat R 17:1079-81 N 30 '65
Stridence on the right. Christian Cent 82:323-4 Mr 17 '65
Uncertain trumpet; Chicago congress of conservatives. Newsweek 65:45 My 10 '65
See also
Liberalism
Minutemen (organization)
Right and left (political science)

Bibliography
Growth of conservative thought. F. S. Meyer. Nat R 17:1097-8 N 30 '65
CONSERVATIVE library association
Why a conservative L.A? letter to the editor. B. Harrison. Library J 90:2446+ Je 1 '65; Reply. H. V. Deale. 90:3156 Ag '65
CONSERVATIVE party (Great Britain)
Britain's next prime minister? E. Heath. new type of Conservative leader. I. Ross. Read Digest 87:97-101 N '65
Could Maudling win for the Tories? P. Worsthorne. il N Y Times Mag p28-9+ F 14 '65
Exit Sir Alec. S. Hagerty. il Newsweek 66: 34-5 Ag 2 '65
Gentlemanly affair; new leader chosen. Time 86:30+ Ag 6 '65
Heath's middle road to Downing street. L. Malkin. il Reporter 33:39+ D 16 '65
Last of the amateurs. Time 86:19-20 Jl 30 '65
Meeting the folks; E. Heath at party conference. Newsweek 66:53 O 25 '65
Not by tongue alone; new leader. Newsweek 66:36+ Ag 16 '65

Shadows reshuffled; Tory shadow cabinet. il Time 85:32 F 26 '65
Tories arm for tough new assault on Labor; new Conservative leader. Bsns W p26 Jl 31 '65
Tory change at the top. P. Crane. America 113:159 Ag 14 '65
Tough man for the Tories. il Newsweek 66: 37-8 Ag 9 '65
What hope for Conservatives? A. Lejeune. Nat R 17:1071-2 N 30 '65
CONSIDINE, Bob
Greatest news story; excerpt from Christmas stocking. Todays Health 43:18-19 D '65
CONSIDINE, Debbie
My V.I.P. trip. Seventeen 24:114-15+ F '65
CONSOLAZIO, William V.
Fiscal dilemma of academic science. Bul Atomic Sci 21:15-18 F '65
CONSOLE. See Phonograph
CONSOLIDATED Edison company of New York
Battle of the Hudson. T. Lawrence. il Am For 71:12-15+ Ap '65
Con Edison: the Hudson River caper. D. Cort. il Nation 201:387-9 N 22 '65; Reply. R. L. Ottinger. 201:inside cover D 6 '65
Debacle; northeastern failure. Nation 201: 373 N 22 '65
Hydropower and the Hudson Highlands. P. M. Tilden. Nat Parks Mag 39:2 Ap '65
Smoke watch. New Yorker 41:23-5 Jl 17 '65
Stink of dead stripers; Con Ed under attack over killing of fish at Hudson's bass spawing grounds. R. H. Boyle. il Sports Illus 22:81-2+ Ap 26 '65
Storm over stripers; Commission to hold hearings on power project's threat to Hudson's striped bass fishery. G. Heinold. il Outdoor Life 135:10-12+ My '65
What went wrong? something called 345 KV. T. H. White. il Life 59:46B+ N 19 '65
World's biggest wet storage battery; Storm King Mountain. H. Walton. il Pop Sci 187: 52-3 Ag '65
CONSOLIDATED foods corporation
Consolidated foods plans its diet; Con foods-American tobacco combination called off. il Bsns W p65-6 My 22 '65
Passing the sweets; American tobacco company moves to acquire Chicago's Consolidated foods corp. Time 85:84+ F 12 '65
CONSOLIDATED gas company of New York. See Consolidated Edison company of New York
CONSOLIDATED schools
Big ideas for small schools; Western states small schools project. O. F. Parody. il Am Ed 1:1-3 Jl '65
CONSOLIDATION, Railroad. See Railroads—Consolidations and mergers
CONSOLIDATION coal company
Anatomy of a big deal; Continental oil co. to acquire Consolidation coal co. il Time 86:106+ O 22 '65
Consol. Hanna sell-offs stun Street. il Bsns W p 166+ O 16 '65
CONSOLIDATIONS, Business. See Business consolidations and mergers
CONSPIRACY
Charged: a plot to blow up U.S. shrines. il U S News 58:8 Mr 1 '65
Dynamiters; Black liberation front plot to dynamite Statue of Liberty. il Newsweek 65:33-4 Mr 1 '65
Landmarks target: plot to dynamite Statue of Liberty, the Liberty bell, and the Washington monument. il Sr Schol 86:23-4 Mr 4 '65
Monumental plot; Black liberation front plans to blow up the Statue of Liberty. il Time 85:22 F 26 '65
Plot to behead the Statue of Liberty. M. Mok. il Life 58:38-9 F 26 '65
CONSTABLE, John
Total immersion in landscape. G. Reynolds. il Art N 64:42-5+ O '65
CONSTABLE, Rosalind
Avant-garde fun for the family. Life 58:71 Ap 23 '65
Styles too are pushed further out by pop. Life 58:59-60+ F 26 '65
CONSTABLE, W. G.
Some Venetian *vedute* painters in the Wadsworth atheneum. Antiques 88:669-73 N '65
CONSTANT of gravitation. See Gravitation
CONSTANTINE II, king of the Hellenes
End in sight? il por Sr Schol 87:17-18 O 14 '65
Greek crisis. E. M. von Kuehnelt-Leddihn. Nat R 17:763 S 7 '65
King is on trial in Greece. C. L. Sulzberger. il pors N Y Times Mag p 12-13+ Ag 15 '65
Looking for a solution. il por Newsweek 66: 34 Ag 16 '65
New crisis in Greece: and the king in the middle. por U S News 59:13 Ag 2 '65

CONSTANTINE II, king of the Hellenes—*Cont.*
Violent days: Greek against Greek. il por Newsweek 66:33 Ag 2 '65
What the palace fears. C. Poulos. il por Nation 201:158-61 S 27 '65

CONSTANTINE, Eddie
Constantine the Great. L. Peer. il por Newsweek 66:70B-71 S 6 '65

CONSTELLATION (frigate)
New life for an old warrior: the frigate Constellation. il Motor B 116:35+ S '65

CONSTELLATIONS
Thoughts about constellation figures. O. R. Norton. il Sky & Tel 30:203-5 O '65
See also
Pleiades

CONSTRUCTION (United States) See United States—Constitution

CONSTRUCTION. See Building

CONSTRUCTION industry. See Building industry

CONSTRUCTION workers. See Building workers

CONSULTATION on church union. See Church unity

CONSULTATIVE committee for economic development in south and southeast Asia. See Colombo plan

CONSUMER complaints. See Complaints

CONSUMER credit. See Credit

CONSUMER education
Big secret: federal government's consumer reports service. New Repub 152:7 My 22 '65; Discussion. 152:30 Je 5; 37 Je 26 '65
Buying guide issue (cont) Consumer Rep 30:1-448 D '65
Education for consumers. E. Peterson. NEA J 55:15 Ja '66
That young consumers be good consumers. Consumer Rep 30:424 S '65
USDA's role as the consumer's adviser. Consumer Bul 48:39-40 N '65
See also
Consumer protection

CONSUMER goods. See Commercial products

CONSUMER price index. See Price indexes

CONSUMER protection
Docket: notes on government actions taken to enforce consumer protection laws. See issues of Consumer reports
Let the reader beware; reprint. M. E. Brady. Consumer Rep 30:496 O '65
Put your complaint in writing! Consumer Bul 48:26-7 O '65
Truly a consumer council: President's consumer advisory council. Consumer Rep 30:456 S '65
Truth about two truth bills; lending and packaging. Consumer Rep 30:166-7 Ap '65
What Congress plans for you. Changing T 19:6 My '65
What's new at the Institute? lots of things. il Good H 161:124-7 S '65

CONSUMER surveys
Consumers on upbeat; University of Michigan survey. il Bsns W p31 O 9 '65

CONSUMER union of United States
Staff openings at CU. Consumer Rep 30:523 N '65

CONSUMERS
Confidence at a peak; Survey research center report. il Bsns W p76 Jl 24 '65
Fleecing the consumer; fraud cases in the slums. New Repub 153:7 Ag 21 '65
Happiness is a satisfied consumer. Consumer Rep 31:4-5 Ja '66
It never looked better; consumer confidence. il Bsns W p23-5 Mr 27 '65
No sag in buying plans: University of Michigan survey, with table. Bsns W p38 Ja 8 '66
Riding a new crest. il Bsns W p24-5 Ap 17 '65
Speaker for the house. C. Montgomery. See issues of Good housekeeping
See also
Consumer education
Consumer protection

CONSUMERS preferences
Discovering the inner Jones. E. Dichter. Harvard Bsns R 43:6-8+ My '65
Marketers tell women the shopper is boss; conference sponsored by advertising women of New York. il Bsns W p74-5+ Ap 17 '65
Modular production, a new concept. M. K. Starr. il Harvard Bsns R 43:131-2+ N '65
More sense about market segmentation. W. H. Reynolds. bibliog f il Harvard Bsns R 43:107-14 S '65
Why they buy. Newsweek 66:104 O 11 '65
Willing to buy, maybe to splurge. il Bsns W p22-3 Ag 28 '65

CONSUMERS' research, incorporated
Consumers' research is not consumer research! Consumer Bul 48:34-5 My '65
Sad tale of a consumer pioneer. Consumer Rep 30:80-1 F '65

CONSUMERS union of United States
New executive director for CU; W. Sandbach. il Consumer Rep 30:323 Jl '65
These calls were not from CU. Consumer Rep 30:224 My '65
To serve you better; acquired major test facilities. il Consumer Rep 30:72-3 F '65

CONSUMPTION (economics)
Consumer equation. Fortune 72:30+ O '65
Food expenditures of urban families, 1950 to 1960-61. L. M. Webb. il Mo Labor R 88:150-3 F '65
More money for spending. il Bsns W p21-2 Ag 28 '65
Spending and saving in urban and rural areas. K. R. Murphy. il Mo Labor R 88:1169-76 O '65
Strings on the purse. il Fortune 71:26+ Mr '65
U.S. paychecks: bigger share for luxuries. il U S News 58:100-1 F 1 '65
See also
Supply and demand

CONTACT printing. See Photography—Printing processes

CONTAINERS
Special report on packaging; symposium. il Duns R 86:pt2 86-92+ D '65
See also
Beer containers
Capsules
Milk containers

CONTAINERS for flowers. See Vases

CONTAINERS for shipping
Airlines draft cargo container program. J. R. Ashlock. Aviation W 83:30 Jl 19 '65
Containerization: the unhappy marriage. J. L. Eyre. il Duns R 85:pt2 134-5+ Je '65
Inventor of the month; box that won a U.S. patent; combined shipping container and showcase. S. V. Jones. il Sci Digest 58:36 Ag '65

CONTAMINATION of Mars (planet) See Mars (planet)—Contamination

CONTE, Silvio O.
Excerpt from remarks, January 14, 1965. Cong Digest 44:187+ Je '65

CONTEMPORARY dance, incorporated
Young choreographers' concert, 41st street theatre. J. Maskey. Dance Mag 39:63 My '65

CONTEMPT of court
Slight case of contempt; New vs. Neal. il Time 86:58 Jl 30 '65

CONTENTMENT
See also
Happiness

Les CONTES d'Hoffmann; opera. See Offenbach, J.

CONTESTS. See Competitions

CONTINENTAL airlines
Continental air lines diversifies with southeast Asia operations. C. M. Plattner. Aviation W 83:37 Ag 30 '65
Continental orders twelve convertible DC-9s. il Aviation W 82:32 Mr 22 '65
Continental seeks new U.S. Pacific routes. il Aviation W 83:26 N 1 '65
Out of the nest: executive changes. Newsweek 65:88 F 22 '65
Two basic charter decisions facing CAB. R. G. O'Lone. Aviation W 82:36-7 F 22 '65

CONTINENTAL drift
Ancient rocks hold key to supercontinent theory. Sci N L 88:297 N 6 '65
See also
Continents

CONTINENTAL oil company
Anatomy of a big deal; Continental oil co. to acquire Consolidation coal co. il Time 86:106+ O 22 '65

CONTINENTAL shelf
Continental shelf. D. Wolfle. Science 148:25 Ap 2 '65; Reply. A. L. Shalowitz. 148:1412 Je 11 '65
Ocean drilling on the continental margin; Joint oceanographic institutions' deep earth sampling program. bibliog il Science 150:709-16 N 5 '65

CONTINENTAL slope. See Continental shelf

CONTINENTAL telephone corporation
Continental dials M for merger. il Bsns W p86+ N 6 '65

CONTINENTS
Huge meteors may have created continents. Sci N L 87:297 My 8 '65
Microcontinents sought. il Sci N L 88:229 O 9 '65

CONTINI, Jeanne
Somalia walks the tightrope. N Y Times Mag p 14-15+ Ag 8 '65

CONTINUITY testers. See Testing instruments

CONTINUOUS casting
Squeezing costs out of casting. il Bsns W p 163-4 Je 12 '65
CONTINUOUS-progress plan in education. See Ungraded classes
CONTOUR chairs. See Chairs
CONTRA COSTA COUNTY, Calif.
Rumble strips jar dreamy drivers. M. Kermit. il Am City 80:94-5 N '65
CONTRABAND trade. See Smuggling
CONTRACEPTION. See Birth control
CONTRACEPTIVES
Birth control by IUCD; intra-uterine contraceptive device. il Newsweek 66:80 Jl 26 '65
Birth control pill found safe for 11,711 women. Sci N L 87:242 Ap 17 '65
Birth control revolution. S. M. Spencer. il Sat Eve Post 239:21-5+ Ja 15 '66
Contraceptive loop safe; Birth control pill probe like that of all drugs. Sci N L 88: 374 D 11 '65
Does nature know best? natural versus artificial products. Time 85:76 My 7 '65
Gains for birth control; Ford foundation grants to Columbia-Presbyterian medical center and Population council; foreign aid recommendations. Newsweek 66:94 D 13 '65
Is the pill the answer? K. N. Anderson. il Todays Health 43:28-34+ Je '65
Longer-lasting contraception; experimental Deladroxate injections. Time 85:83 My 21 '65
Master of the pill; Syntex corp. il Time 87:85 Ja 7 '66
Now! something better than the pill? intra-uterine devices. W. Best. il McCalls 92:42+ F '65; Same with title Something new in birth control; intrauterine devices. Read Digest 86:79-82 Ap '65
Pill. S. Blum. il Redbook 126:33-5+ Ja '66
Pill and morality. A. Hacker. il N Y Times Mag p32-3+ N 21 '65
Pill on the campus. Newsweek 66:92-3 O 11 '65
Pills in white & pink. il Time 85:86 Ap 30 '65
Population control takes a forward step; ruling against Connecticut's anti-birth control statutes. Bsns W p 108+ Je 19 '65
Precaution on the pill. il Newsweek 66:82 N 29 '65
Pregnancy vaccination? P. McBroom. Sci N L 89:22 Ja 8 '66
Pronuclear ovum from a patient using an intrauterine contraceptive device. R. W. Noyes and others. bibliog il Science 147:744 F 12 '65
Quest for more effective means of birth control. il Life 59:70-1 S 10 '65
Steroid hormones and the pill. il Science 150:1189-91 N 26 '65
What's new in family planning. A. L. Southam. il Parents Mag 40:82-4+ N '65
Will Rome take the pill? C. Northcott. Christian Cent 82:518 Ap 28 '65
CONTRACT bridge. See Bridge (game)
CONTRACT labor, Farm. See Farm labor
CONTRACTION, Muscular. See Muscles
CONTRACTORS
Italy's new empire; projects in Africa. il Fortune 72:74+ O '65
See also
Fuller, George A, company
CONTRACTS
Art and science of competitive bidding; executive judgment and computer analysis combined. F. Edelman. il Harvard Bsns R 43:53-66 Jl '65
Mephisto's musings; movement toward year-round contracts, higher salaries, and increased benefits for players. il Hi Fi 15: 188+ N '65
See also
Exclusive agencies
Leases
CONTRACTS, Agricultural
Heifer contracts that work. J. Russell and O. Bay. il Farm J 89:52J My '65
CONTRACTS, Government
Bid asked on Apollo experiment bed. Miss & Roc 17:19 S 27 '65
C-5A: Lockheed's path to the future; giant military cargo plane contract to Lockheed-Georgia co. il Bsns W p32-3 O 9 '65
California aerospace firms again lead nation in space agency dollars. il Miss & Roc 16:21 Je 21 '65
Carrots and sticks: the Pentagon's new incentive pricing formula. Fortune 72:280 D '65
Committee seeks DOD, GAO conformity; on contract policies. Aviation W 82:20 My 31 '65

Companies balk at SST contract clauses. E. H. Kolcum. Aviation W 83:28 Jl 12 '65
Contracts and procurements (title varies) See issues of Missiles and rockets
Defense dept. lists 100 top contractors. Aviation W 83:75+ D 20 '65
DOD, GAO reach truce on pricing policy. K. Johnsen. Aviation W 83:68-70 D 27 '65
Department of defense lists top 100 prime contractors for fiscal 1964. il Aviation W 82:88-91 Ap 12 '65
Downhill path. W. J. Coughlin. Miss & Roc 18:50 Ja 10 '66
GAO contracts policy is criticized. Miss & Roc 16:18 My 31 '65
GAO willing to help protect contractors. K. Johnsen. Aviation W 83:87 Jl 19 '65
House group will recommend changes in GAO defense contract audit practices. H. M. David. Miss & Roc 17:23 Jl 19 '65
Industry voices concern over GAO power. K. Johnsen. Aviation W 82:20 Je 7 '65
Lab focus changing as funds shift; plans for federal R&D spending. il Bsns W p47-8+ D 4 '65
Lockheed holds a steady lead; heads defense contractor list. il Bsns W p35 N 27 '65
Lockheed retains top contract rank. il Aviation W 83:24 N 29 '65
Lockheed scrambles for the battle of the primes. C. J. V. Murphy. il Fortune 71:148-52+ F '65
Lockheed tops DOD contractor list. il Miss & Roc 16:21 Mr 22; 17:14 N 29 '65
Loosening the red tape; Contract administration service. Bsns W p 130 Ap 3 '65
Low fees may undermine incentive goal; cost plus incentive fee. B. Backe; reply. G. C. Bannerman. Aviation W 82:67-8 Mr 1 '65
Management of government programs. S. Ramo. Harvard Bsns R 43:6-8+ Jl '65
Midwest electronics, a changing pattern of growth. J. A. Kennedy. il Electr World 74:25-8 O '65
Move up in space, win points; Martin co. steering Titan II program toward a profit. il Bsns W p92-4+ S 25 '65
NASA list of FY 1964 top 100 prime contractors. il Miss & Roc 16:21 F 15 '65
NASA list of FY 1965 top 100 prime contractors. il Miss & Roc 17:20 D 20 '65
NASA procurement up 51 per cent in first half of fiscal 1965; North American top contractor; with tables. Aviation W 83:82-3 Jl 12 '65
NASA's top 100 contractors. Aviation W 82: 70-1 Mr 1 '65
New profits for the primes. C. J. Loomis. il Fortune 71:75-6+ Ap '65
Pentagon tests one-stop bidding. il Bsns W p99-100+ N 6 '65
Rising cost of overkill; money devoted to defense program. A. E. Burns. Sat R 48: 26 Ag 7 '65
Selection of contractors nearing for Apollo technology adaptation. W. J. Normyle. Aviation W 83:25 S 6 '65
Selling R&D to the government. S. F. Divita. il Harvard Bsns R 43:62-75 S '65
Services dominate $14-million market; promotion of fluidics. il Miss & Roc 16:30-2+ F 8 '65
Services draft source selection guides. G. C. Wilson. Aviation W 82:88-9 My 17 '65
Support service fight has $8 billion stake. C. Brownlow. Aviation W 82:16-18 Mr 22 '65
Three top contractors planned for AES; Apollo extension system. Miss & Roc 16: 13 My 10 '65
Top 100 fiscal 1965 NASA contractors listed. il Aviation W 83:66-8 D 27 '65
Watchdog agency tugs on leash; GAO checks U.S. expenditures. Bsns W p76+ Je 12 '65
Who gets lion's share of arms-research funds. U S News 59:14-15 Jl 19 '65
Who gets the big contracts; fifty top defense contractors. il Bsns W p45 Mr 13 '65
Wrapping mobility in a total package; C-5A cargo plane and the fast deployment logistics ship. Bsns W p34 N 27 '65
See also
Government investigations—Government contracts
United States—National aeronautics and space administration—Procurement

Labor problems

How Vertol vies for skilled labor. Bsns W p46+ O 30 '65

Renegotiation

See also
United States—Renegotiation board

CONTRACTS, Government—*Continued*

Subcontracting

Douglas reopens MOL subcontracting. Miss &
Roc 17:18 S 27 '65
MOL subcontract bidding re-opened. Avia-
tion W 83:26 S 27 '65
Navy/LTV A-7A vendors listed; subcon-
tractors and suppliers on A-7A Corsair 2
light attack aircraft. Aviation W 83:87 N
15 '65
CONTRACTS, Municipal. See Municipal con-
tracts
CONTRACTS, Teachers. See Teachers—Con-
tracts
CONTRERAS, Gloria
Gloria Contreras and company. 92nd street
Y. J. Maskey. Dance Mag 39:60 Je '65
CONTROL data corporation
Control data widens line; smaller, cheaper
computer is its bid. il Bsns W p88 O 2 '65
Draftsman with speed to spare; mechani-
cal plotter directed by computer. il Bsns W
p64+ My 29 '65
CONTROL of insects. See Insects, Injurious
and beneficial—Control
CONTROL of production. See Production con-
trol
CONTROL panels (space vehicles) See Space
vehicles—Instrument boards
CONVAIR division. See General dynamics cor-
poration—Convair division
CONVALESCENT homes. See Nursing homes
CONVECTIVE storms. See Storms
CONVENIENCE foods. See Food—Ready-to-
cook food
CONVENIENCE stores. See National associa-
tion of convenience stores
CONVENTIONS
Boston bids for big clambakes; War memori-
al auditorium to lure national conventions.
il Bsns W p 150+ F 13 '65
Business meetings: more message, less mer-
ingue. il Nations Bsns 53:40-1+ Ap '65
CONVERSATION
Art of intelligent listening. J. N. Miller. Read
Digest 87:83-6 S '65

Anecdotes, facetiae, satire, etc.

You have to say something; excerpt from
Hohenzollerns in America. S. Leacock. Read
Digest 86:226B-226C F '65
CONVERSATION corners. See Living rooms
CONVERSATION radio programs. See Radio
broadcasting—Conversation programs
CONVERSATION television programs. See Tele-
vision broadcasting—Conversation programs
CONVERSION
See also
Converts
CONVERTER lenses. See Lenses, Photographic
CONVERTERS. See Electric current con-
verters
CONVERTERS, Radio. See Radio converters
CONVERTERS, Television. See Television ap-
paratus
CONVERTIBLE furniture. See Furniture, Con-
vertible
CONVERTS
From conversion to concern. il Time 85:76
My 14 '65
CONVERTS, Catholic
After Luci Johnson was baptized; question of
rebaptism. il U S News 59:16 Jl 19 '65
Ecumenism and converts; concerning speech
by Cardinal Heenan. America 112:798 My
29 '65
Why the President's daughter turned to the
Catholic church. N. Robertson. Ladies
Home J 82:76+ Ag '65
CONVERTS, Protestant
Catholic leakage; Chicago survey findings.
America 112:846 Je 12 '65
CONVEYING machinery
See also
Ore handling
CONVICTS. See Prisoners
CONWAY, J. D.
Book of the month. Cath World 201:401 S '65
CONWAY, Jack T.
AFL-CIO's inner struggle. il por Newsweek
66:82+ D 20 '65
Next IUD target: the working poor. por
Bsns W p62+ N 13 '65
CONYNGHAM, William
Books. Commonweal 82:733-4 O 1 '65
CONYNGTON, Mary
Government's wage policy; reprint from June
1920 issue. Mo Labor R 88:795 Jl '65
COOK, Bruce
Ayn Rand: a voice in the wilderness. Cath
World 201:119-24 My '65
Cold war fiction. Commonweal 83:342-5 D 17
'65
Introducing Thomas Gallagher. por Cath
World 202:96-101 N '65

COOK, Chauncey William Wallace
Chief Cook. il por Time 85:85 Mr 12 '65
Ready for instant growth. il por Bsns W p68-
9+ Ap 24 '65
COOK, Clair M.
Battle over 14(b) Christian Cent 82:937-9 Jl
28 '65
Evaluating A.R.A. Christian Cent 82:1097-8
S 8 '65
COOK, Donald C.
LBJ's outside man. por Bsns W p27 F 13 '65
Turndown. Time 85:29 Mr 19 '65
Utility builds power with a hard sell. il
por Bsns W p77-8+ O 30 '65
COOK, Fred J.
Billion-dollar mystery. Nation 200:380-97 Ap
12 '65
Draft boards escalate. N Y Times Mag p54-
5+ S 12 '65
I come from Julius. Nation 201:361-3+ N
15 '65
Iranian aid story: new twists to the mys-
tery. Nation 200:550-6 My 24 '65
Rich, respectable racketeers. Sat R 48:31 F
27 '65
River dies, and is born again. N Y Times Mag
p22-3+ Ap 18 '65
Snoopers & tappers. Nation 201:496-501 D 20
'65
COOK, Leslie G. and Hazzard, G. W.
Mature research institutions and the older
scientist. bibliog Science 150:716-19 N 5 '65
COOK, M. Olin
College students change majors. Sch & Soc
93:271-3 My 1 '65
COOK, Roderick
Books in brief. Harper 230:127-9 F; 117-20
Ap; 231:138-41 S; 128-33 N '65; 232:99-101 Ja
'66
COOK ISLANDS
See also
Elections—Cook Islands
United Nations—Cook Islands
COOKBOOKS
Fighting Fannie Farmer. il Newsweek 65:
112+ Je 14 '65
Holiday handbook; exotic recipes from the
United Nations cookbook. comp. by B.
Kraus. il Holiday 38:95-100 S '65
Michael Field's cooking school. Review
Life 59:21 Jl 16 '65. E. O'Connor
Michael Field's cooking school; excerpts. il
Ladies Home J 82:86-7+ S '65
Redbook's timesaver cookbook; with recipes.
il Redbook 125:96-102+ O '65

Bibliography

Books. M. F. K. Fisher. New Yorker 41:145-
50+ Je 5 '65
Cookbooks for Christmas giving. Parents Mag
40:117 D '65
Cookbooks for fall selling. il Pub W 188:
44-54 S 13 '65
New foreign cookbooks. Parents Mag 40:50
N '65
COOKE, Barclay
Cooke with a recipe for victory. C. Goren. il
Sports Illus 22:60 F 22 '65
COOKE, Blaize
Monterey to San Francisco: what we wanted
was wind. Motor B 115:138-9+ My '65
COOKE, Eileen D. See Krettek, G. jt. auth.
COOKE, Hope. See Hope Namgyal, maharani of
Sikkim
COOKE, Jerry
Wisconsin warrior; photographs. Sports Il-
lus 22:28-33 Je 21 '65
COOKE, Sam
Tragic death of Sam Cooke. L. Robinson. il
pors Ebony 20:92-6 F '65
COOKE, Terry
Streamlining, dragster dilemma? Hot Rod
18:94-101+ Ag '65
COOKERY
Afternoon tea; recipes. il Redbook 126:80-1+
N '65
Basic guide to planning, preparing and serv-
ing good meals. il Redbook 124:74-82 F '65
Christmas specialties from good farm cooks.
il Farm J 89:98-100+ D '65
Come for potluck; with recipes. J. Figg. il
Suc Farm 63:140-1+ Mr '65
Cooking club (cont) il House & Gard 127:
186-8 Ap; 186-9 My; 167-9 Je '65
Cupboard full of seasonal sweets; with
recipes. il McCalls 93:114-15+ D '65
Delicious make-ahead meal will ease task of
hostess. il Ebony 20:192+ My '65
Fifteen-minute meals with a flair. il Redbook
124:78-9+ Ap '65
Flaming finales. P. Cannon. il Ladies Home
J 82:76-7+ D '65
Flash in the pan cooking. M. Johnston. il
Bet Hom & Gard 43:90-3+ Ap '65
Flowers that bloom in the spring signal
added freshness for recipes. G. Maddox. il
Todays Health 43:49-55 Ap '65

COOKERY—Fish—*Continued*

New fish recipes, southern specialties. L. Heinold. il Outdoor Life 135:8+ Ap '65
Outdoor fish feast. il Pop Gard 16:52 Ap '65
Savannah oyster roast. M. Kaytor. il Look 29:92-3 N 16 '65
Scallops; with recipes. il McCalls 92:108-9+ S '65
Sea food for Lent. il Ebony 20:138+ Mr '65
Sea's own season: great seafood casseroles. il McCalls 92:128-9+ Mr '65
Shellfish on ice. il Sunset 135:72-3 S '65
Shrimp cook book. H. E. Brown. il House & Gard 127:175+ Ap '65
Successful recipes; tuna and salmon. il Suc Farm 63:143-4 Mr '65
Take a can of seafood. V. T. Habeeb. il Am Home 68:62+ Mr '65
See also
Chowder
Fish as food

Flowers
See Flowers as food

Frogs
Frogs legs in a white-wine sea; with menu. E. Graves. il Life 59:90-1+ Ag 20 '65

Fruit
Accent on apples. J. Hewitt. il N Y Times Mag p 109-10 N 21 '65
Apples are basic; with recipes. M. Kaytor. il Look 29:71-2 N 2 '65
Courtesy of C. Columbus; oranges to the New World. C. Claiborne. il N Y Times Mag p82 Ap 25 '65
Cranberry salads, relish. il Bet Hom & Gard 43:101-2 N '65
Fresh fruit: summer's own dessert. il Redbook 125:72-3+ Jl '65
Fresh ripe fruit; with recipes. M. Kaytor. il Look 29:70-1 Ag 10 '65
Fruit of the season: strawberries; with recipes. il Ladies Home J 82:88-9+ Je '65
Fruits of the season. Parents Mag 40:24 Ag '65
Happy marriage; fresh-peach torte. il McCalls 92:68 Ag '65
Have you faced a persimmon? with recipes. Sunset 135:171 N '65
If you bring home fresh figs; with recipes. Sunset 135:137 S '65
It's the berry. J. Hewitt. il N Y Times Mag p68 My 23 '65
Midsummer's fabulous fruits! glamorized in different ways; with recipes. il Bet Hom & Gard 43:66-73+ Ag '65
Peaches and cream; with recipes. M. Kaytor. il Look 29:74-5 Jl 13 '65
Pineapple desserts. il Bet Hom & Gard 43:95-6 Mr '65
Serve a goblet of summer. il McCalls 92:110-11+ Ag '65
Spring strawberries. il Sunset 134:188-9 Ap '65
These call for last-minute action at the table; fresh strawberry desserts. il Sunset 134:208+ Je '65

Game
Cooking your own goose. N. Riley. il Outdoor Life 136:42-3+ D '65
For dinner tonight we're having tasty rabbit stew. il Sunset 135:170 O '65
Hunter's bag. C. Claiborne. il N Y Times Mag p 125-6 D 5 '65

Leftovers
Build up leftovers for hearty cold plates. B. L. Henry. il Farm J 89:68 Ag '65
Successful recipes; second day turkey. il Suc Farm 64:113-14 Ja '66

Meat
Bacon, a bargain in flavor. il Farm J 89:100 Ap '65
Barbecued spareribs. il Pop Gard 16:50+ Mr '65
Battle plan for the feast; lamb chop shis kebab. E. Graves. il Life 59:87 Jl 2 '65
Beefsteak pie and steak and kidney pie. il Sunset 134:188 Mr '65
Braising and stewing. il House & Gard 127:186-8 Ap '65
Burgers and hot dogs. R. Hanna. il Suc Farm 63:56-7+ Jl '65
Chicken boats, salmon boats, lamb boats, and ham boats. il Sunset 134:172 Je '65
Country cooking; with recipes. il McCalls 92:110-11+ S '65
Creamy white French veal stew. Sunset 136:112 Ja '66
Deep in the heart of Texans; chili con carne. C. Claiborne. il N Y Times Mag p72 My 16 '65

Eating 'in'. J. Hewitt. il N Y Times Mag p27 D 26 '65
Exotic hamburger; with recipes. il McCalls 93:86-7+ Ja '66
Exotic new ways with lamb. il Bet Hom & Gard 43:82 Mr '65
French provincial classic: it's beef a la mode; with recipe. il Sunset 135:154+ N '65
Fresh ham as a Christmas roast. il Sunset 135:167 D '65
Gastronomy; goulash. J. Wechsberg. Esquire 64:126-8+ D '65
Guests tomorrow? you start these today: beef and veal roasts, with recipes. il Sunset 135:134-5 S '65
Ham loaf that's sweet and sour. il Sunset 134:198 Ap '65
Happiness is a hamburger; with recipes. C. Claiborne. il N Y Times Mag p 127 O 24 '65
Happy marriage: roast beef with Yorkshire pudding. il McCalls 93:43 D '65
Happy marriage; sauerbraten with red cabbage. il McCalls 92:84 F '65
Holiday hams. il Ladies Home J 82:70-1+ D '65
How to win new converts to sweetbreads. Sunset 135:186+ O '65
If a roast is on your holiday menu. Good H 161:169 D '65
In the pot; hearty beef dishes. il Ladies Home J 82:84-5+ Ap '65
It's delicious hot or cool; meat and mushroom pie. il Sunset 134:245 Ap '65
Juicy entrees; adding fruit juice to meats. il Bet Hom & Gard 43:90 My '65
Knife and fork sandwiches. il Sunset 134:223-4+ Mr '65
Like to do kabobs just like those on our cover? Bet Hom & Gard 43:115 Je '65
Made in a matter of minutes. il McCalls 92:138-9+ F '65
Meat for hearty midday meals. il Parents Mag 40:40 F '65
Meatballs from a press; frikadeller. il Sunset 134:196+ My '65
Modern meat primer. R. Staggs. il Parents Mag 40:77+ O '65
Moneywise main dishes with menus to match! il Good H 162:82-98 Ja '66
Oriental favorites. il Bet Hom & Gard 43:113-14 Ap '65
Peerless roast of lamb. C. Claiborne. il N Y Times Mag p47 S 5 '65
Pork with red cabbage. il Sunset 136:97 Ja '66
Quick roast on top of the range. Sunset 135:147 Jl '65
Roast meat cook book. J. A. Beard. il House & Gard 128:229+ O '65
Round steak specials. il Bet Hom & Gard 43:95-6 F '65
Skewer ideas: lamb rolls or steak with lobster; with recipes. il Sunset 134:168 Je '65
Stuffed meats. il Bet Hom & Gard 43:101-2 N '65
Successful recipes; pork chops. il Suc Farm 63:89-90 O '65
Such elegance, chopped meat; with recipes. il Ladies Home J 82:84-5+ S '65
Sugar-cured ham from a country kitchen. R. Behnke. il Farm J 89:87 N '65
Susan's stuffed pork chops. M. F. Williams. il Good H 160:168 My '65
There are other ways with liver. Sunset 135:119 Jl '65
Those other cuts of beef. il Am Home 68:58-9+ Mr '65
Three skillet dinners; with recipes. Seventeen 24:181 Ap '65
Turnover treats; deep-fried meat pastry. C. Claiborne. il N Y Times Mag p32 Jl 18 '65
Using the juices from a veal roast. il Sunset 134:162 Mr '65
What goes on a hamburger? everything! with recipes. il Seventeen 24:164-5+ My '65
What it needs is stuffing; breast of veal. il Sunset 134:170-1 Mr '65
When the cooking is easy: hamburgers; with recipes. D. Durham. il Ladies Home J 82:84-5+ Je '65
When you slice the first slice, watch their faces; pâté en croûte. il Sunset 135:156 D '65
Wiener schnitzel: the Viennese veal cutlet. il Sunset 134:182-3+ My '65
See also
Barbecue cookery
Broiling
Stew

Milk
Dairy foods are tops. il Parents Mag 40:116 Je '65

Mushrooms
Make room for mushrooms. C. Claiborne. il N Y Times Mag p 102 Ap 4 '65

COOKERY—*Continued*

Nuts

Making desserts with western nuts. il Sunset 135:196-8 O '65
Using chopped macadamias. il Sunset 134:224+ Ap '65

Poultry

Battle plan for the feast: a winery chicken stew. E. Graves. Life 58:109-10 Ap 30 '65
Best chicken dishes. il Redbook 125:76-7+ My '65
Chicken à la stroganoff. M. F. Williams. il Good H 161:148 N '65
Chicken has a right to crow! il Good H 160:114-31 My '65
Chicken: the native dish. D. Durham. il Ladies Home J 82:78-9+ My '65
Chicken Tuscany takes time. Sunset 134:164 F '65
Chicken with a foreign accent il McCalls 92:110-11+ Je '65
Divers ways with livers. J. Hewitt. il N Y Times Mag p 129-30 S 12 '65
Dove à la mamma and other great scoff. R. Starnes. Field & S 69:16+ Ap '65
Exciting chicken recipes to delight the taste. G. Maddox. il Todays Health 44:52-7 Ja '66
Five ways they do chicken in Hawaii. il Sunset 134:188+ My '65
Four ways to feed a crowd with turkey. il Sunset 134:230+ Je '65
Fried chicken; with recipes. M. Kaytor. il Look 29:50-1 Je 1 '65
Gourmet artist cooks duck; with recipes. M. Kaytor. il Look 29:58-9 S 7 '65
House & garden's turkey cook book. J. A. Beard. il House & Gard 128:293+ N '65
More ways to use turkey. il Sunset 136:105 Ja '66
Poultry fills the bill. il Parents Mag 40:112 My '65
Things to do with packaged stuffings. il Ladies Home J 82:116+ N '65
Turkey: main dish and more. il McCalls 93:71-2+ D '65
Turkey postscripts. il Bet Hom & Gard 43:83-4 D '65
Turkey roasting tips. il Good H 161:236 N '65
Two quick chicken dinners. il Sunset 135:170 D '65
What's new about turkey? il Bet Hom & Gard 43:88 N '65
When fowl is fare. C. Claiborne. il N Y Times Mag p82+ Mr 21 '65
You can do so much with chicken! B. Pierson. il Farm J 89:50-1+ Jl '65

Rhubarb

If you are a rhubarb fan. Sunset 134:208 My '65
Strawberries and rhubarb. R. Hanna. il Suc Farm 63:94-5+ My '65
Three foolproof rhubarb desserts. il Bet Hom & Gard 43:98 My '65

Rice

Rice is nice. C. Claiborne. il N Y Times Mag p34 Je 20 '65
Rice: the long and short of it. il Redbook 124:70-3+ F '65

Vegetables

Anyone for sp-n-ch? C. Claiborne. il N Y Times Mag p 102 My 2 '65
Cabbages for kings. J. Hewitt. il N Y Times Mag p56 Ja 15 '66
Concoctions with corn. C. Claiborne. il N Y Times Mag p92 Ap 18 '65
Cooking the miniatures; peas and carrots. il Sunset 134:230 My '65
Cook's discovery: fresh fennel; with recipes. il Sunset 135:172-4 N '65
Corn. il McCalls 92:92-3 Jl '65
Gallic way with beans; with menu and recipes by E. Graves. il Life 59:134-5+ O 8 '65
Green-up time; early spring vegetables. il Ladies Home J 82:52+ Ap '65
Here are asparagus casseroles. il Sunset 134:202 Ap '65
How to pare, dice, cut, cube and mince. M. F. Williams. il Good H 160:158-9 F '65
It's both bitter and elegant; with recipes. il Sunset 135:189+ N '65
Let's give a party together; baked bean pies; with recipe. il Seventeen 24:168-9 Ap '65
Look what you can do with squash. R. Hanna. il Suc Farm 63:86-7+ O '65
Plant now; Cook later; with recipes. M. Kaytor and J. Peter. il Look 29:51-3 My 4 '65
Prettiest potatoes come in packages. il McCalls 92:140-1+ F '65
Rah-tah-too yeh; French vegetable classic. il Sunset 135:52-3 Ag '65

Season's fare. H. S. Witty. Flower Grower 52:8+ S '65
Stuffed to perfection; stuffed vegetables for luncheon or supper entrees. C. Claiborne. il N Y Times Mag p50 Ag 15 '65
Successful recipes: spring vegetables. il Suc Farm 63:77-8 Je '65
Susan makes festive fresh corn sauté. M. F. Williams. il Good H 161:130 Ag '65
They aren't afraid of turnips; less popular vegetables. Sunset 135:227+ O '65
Time to bring out the bean pot. M. Bierman. il Farm J 89:86 O '65
Twelve great vegetable recipes. M. Johnston and others. il Bet Hom & Gard 43:76-9+ My '65
Using the juices from a veal roast; mushroom pie. il Sunset 134:162 Mr '65
Vegetable kingdom. il McCalls 92:112-14+ Ag '65
Vegetable season offers tasty dishes. G. Maddox. il Todays Health 43:56-61 Ag '65
What she's serving is a vegetable soufflé; with recipes. il Sunset 135:172+ S '65
Wild new ways with roasting ears. il Ladies Home J 82:90-1 Ag '65
With fresh corn cut off the cob. il Sunset 135:134 Jl '65
    See also
Stew

Wine

Classic wine cookery. il McCalls 92:132-3 My '65
Cooking with berry wines. il Sunset 134:216+ Ap '65
Holiday handbook; cooking with wines and spirits. M. Field. il Holiday 37:115-20 Je '65

Yogurt

Summer snacks from the Balkans: yogurt and cheese pie. M. Kaytor. il Look 29:44-5 Jl 27 '65

COOKERY, American
All-America recipes and All American roses. M. Johnston and H. Mason. il Bet Hom & Gard 43:68-77+ F '65
All-American menu. il Ebony 20:160+ Ag '65
Colonial recipes for the jet age. G. Maddox. il Todays Health 43:52-7 D '65
Fascinating foods of the U.S.A. B. S. Brown. il Good H 162:118 Ja '66
Introduce your family to New Orleans cookery. il Am Home 68:62-3+ Ap '65
Savannah oyster roast. M. Kaytor. il Look 29:32-3 N 16 '65
Score of recipes in the Shaker tradition. il Bet Hom & Gard 43:78-81+ O '65
Senators' choice: soup of the inner sanctum, also other specialties; with recipes. M. Kaytor. il Look 29:38-9 Ap 6 '65
COOKERY, Argentine
Argentine barbecue idea: you cook over coals, but slowly; with recipes. il Sunset 135:146-7+ S '65
COOKERY, Austrian
He likes to cook. il Bet Hom & Gard 43:88 Ag '65
Wiener schnitzel: the Viennese veal cutlet. il Sunset 134:182-3+ My '65
COOKERY, Belgian
Foods with a foreign flavor; great treats from little Belgium. Good H 161:143 Jl '65
COOKERY, Brazilian
Brazilian steak dinner with rice. il Sunset 134:174+ Ap '65
Exotic dishes from tropical Brazil. il Ebony 20:140+ S '65
COOKERY, Chinese
Chinese, home style. il Ladies Home J 82:82-3 My '65
Cooking with antique tangerine peel. Sunset 134:194+ Mr '65
Feasting, Chinese style. C. Claiborne. il N Y Times Mag p90+ D 12 '65
Making your own Chinese pastries; with recipes. il Sunset 134:192+ Je '65
Shopping for *fun, go, ha gow, jin dui*, and other Chinese pastry treats. il Sunset 134:98-9 Je '65
Think Chinese! good to eat, great for next party. il Am Home 68:60-1+ Mr '65
COOKERY, Danish
Danes call it burning love. il Sunset 136:102 Ja '66
From Denmark, a six-salad buffet. il Sunset 135:152+ S '65
COOKERY, English
Of bangers, blighters, and bloaters. H. Sutton. il Sat R 48:24-5 Jl 10; 43-5 Jl 17 '65
COOKERY, Foreign. See Cookery, International
COOKERY, French
French menus and master thieves. H. Frankel. Sat R 49:79-80 Ja 8 '66
French provincial classic: it's beef a la mode; with recipe. il Sunset 135:154+ N '65

COOKERY, French—_Continued_
It's a pie to start arguments; Quiche Lorraine. il Sunset 134:80-1 F '65
Louise de Vilmorin; second fame: good food. N. Lyon. Vogue 146:122-4 Jl '65
Napoleon and friends; millefeuilles; with recipes. il McCall 93:88-90+ Ja '66
Poem of a dish; cassoulet. C. Claiborne. il N Y Times Mag p66 F 7 '65

COOKERY, German
From Germany with great gusto. B. S. Brown. Good H 160:156 Ap '65
German cook book. N. S. Hazelton. il House & Gard 127:137+ F '65
How you can make the Black Forest cherry cake. il Sunset 134:134 F '65

COOKERY, Greek
Freighter fare; meals on the SS Eurymachus; with recipes. M. Kaytor. il Look 29:50-2+ My 18 '65
Inkfish and shark kabob; the sun and seafood of the Aegean; with recipes. F. Du Plessix. Vogue 146:288-90+ S 1 '65
These little Greek pastries are petes. il Sunset 136:106-7 Ja '66
Wrapped in grape leaves. il Sunset 135:210 O '65

COOKERY, Hawaiian
Five ways they do chicken in Hawaii. il Sunset 134:188+ My '65
When the luau idea crosses the Pacific; with menus. il Sunset 134:182-4+ Je '65

COOKERY, Hungarian
But never for breakfast; Hungarian pancakes. il Sunset 135:100-3 Ag '65
Gastronomy; goulash. J. Wechsberg. Esquire 64:126-8+ D '65

COOKERY, Indian
Art of American Indian cooking; recipes. il Ladies Home J 82:108-9+ N '65

COOKERY, Indian (East Indian)
Indian party; with recipes. il Ladies Home J 82:74-7+ Jl '65
This curry actually is easier here than in India; with recipes. il Sunset 135:204+ N '65

COOKERY, International
Chicken with a foreign accent. il McCalls 92:110-11+ Je '65
Foods with a foreign flavor. B. S. Brown. See issues of Good housekeeping
From one basic batter; three great pancakes. M. Kaytor. il Look 29:110-11 Mr 23 '65
Holiday handbook; exotic recipes from the United Nations cookbook, comp. by B. Kraus. il Holiday 38:95-100 S '65
How to celebrate Thanksgiving in ten languages; recipes. G. Maddox. il Todays Health 43:70-5 N '65
How to diet in five languages. il McCalls 92:136-7+ Ap '65
Line a day. P. Cannon. il Ladies Home J 82:85 Ag '65
Line a day; daily foods from home and abroad. P. Cannon. il Ladies Home J 83:87 Ja '66
Reader's tastes, exotic. C. Claiborne. il N Y Times Mag p34-5 Ja 2 '66
World's fare to enjoy at the World's fair or to savor at home. B. M. Stover. il Parents Mag 40:81+ Mr '65

COOKERY, Irish
Table for two. Ladies Home J 82:25 Mr '65

COOKERY, Israeli
Young Israel; old in tradition. B. S. Brown. il Good H 161:152 S '65

COOKERY, Italian
Glory that is Rome. B. S. Brown. il Good H 161:146 O '65
Happy marriage; old-world lasagna. il McCalls 93:32 O '65
Italian way to start off; with menu and recipes by E. Graves. il Life 60:86-7+ Ja 21 '66
Italians have a way with salads in summer; with recipes. M. Kaytor. il Look 29:50-1 Je 29 '65
Pasta repast. C. Claiborne. il N Y Times Mag p66 Ja 9 '66
Table for two. Ladies Home J 82:24 F '65
See also
Macaroni

COOKERY, Japanese
Ten minute gourmet cookbook; excerpts. Y. Tarr. il Ladies Home J 83:82-3 Ja '66

COOKERY, Jewish
For Passover. C. Claiborne. il N Y Times Mag p96+ Ap 11 '65
Happy time of Passover. Am Home 68:78-9 Ap '65
Knishes by the dozen. il Sunset 134:219-20 Mr '65

COOKERY, Lenten. See Lenten menus

COOKERY, Marine
Cook in any storm. M. Knowlton. il Motor B 115:44-5+ My '65
Cooking without a galley. il Sunset 135:141-2 Jl '65

COOKERY, Mediterranean
Season's fare. H. S. Witty. Flower Grower 52:15 Ag '65

COOKERY, Mexican
Mexican cook book. E. L. de Ortiz. House & Gard 128:219+ S '65
Sweets blend old and new; with recipes. S. M. Fertitta. il Look 30:62-3 Ja 25 '66
Twelfth night party, north of the Rio Grande; with menu. il House & Gard 128:158-9+ D '65

COOKERY, Middle Eastern
Great classic of the Near East; moussaka. il Sunset 135:102-4 O '65

COOKERY, Oriental
Oriental favorites. il Bet Hom & Gard 43:113-14 Ap '65
Outdoor dining oriental style. K. Smith. il Pop Gard 16:48-9 Mr '65

COOKERY, Ornamental
Baked; exhibition of traditional breads and modern dough sculpture at Museum of contemporary crafts, New York. New Yorker 41:19-20 Ja 8 '66
Baker's art; holiday show at New York's Museum of contemporary crafts. A. Adams. il Craft Horiz 25:8-17 N '65
Christmas is the special ingredient. C. Claiborne. il N Y Times Mag p52-3 D 19 '65
Decorating ideas for February holidays. il McCalls 92:163 F '65
Easter breads, a delicious tradition. il Bet Hom & Gard 43:100+ Ap '65
Gingerbread pony, gingerbread sleigh; filled with the world's most loved cookies; with recipes. il McCalls 93:88-9+ D '65
Great staples to help you turn out masterpieces. V. T. Habeeb. il Am Home 68:60-1+ Ap '65
See also
Cake
Icings

COOKERY, Outdoor
Fiesta for fall; menu with recipes. il Pop Gard 16:39+ S '65
House & garden's outdoor menu cook book. P. S. Brown. il House & Gard 128:117+ Jl '65
Most magnifique pique-nique. il Life 59:84-6 Ag 27 '65
See also
Barbecue cookery
Camp cookery
Camp stoves
Outdoor meals

COOKERY, Portuguese
How the Portuguese like their ribs. il Sunset 134:178+ Ap '65
Pleasures of Portugal. B. S. Brown. il Good H 161:120 Ag '65

COOKERY, Quantity
Fit for a bride. C. Claiborne. il N Y Times Mag p30 My 30 '65
New toppings for angel food; with recipes. B. Pierson. il Farm J 89:92-3 F '65
Refrigerator rolls; with recipes. B. L. Henry. Farm J 89:91 F '65
These farm women cook and bake big! with recipes. N. Nichols. il Farm J 89:86-8+ F '65

COOKERY, Shaker. See Cookery, American

COOKERY, Southern. See Cookery, American

COOKERY, Spanish
Spain: great taste, versatility in food. D. Durham. il Ladies Home J 82:70-1+ F '65
Spanish food; a new excitement. S. Spitzer. il Holiday 37:94-6+ Ap '65
Spanish treasure: paella. C. Claiborne. il N Y Times Mag p72 F 14 '65

COOKERY, Swedish
Deft Swedish touch. B. S. Brown. Good H 160:142 Ja '65
How the Swedes use mushrooms. il Sunset 134:150 F '65
Two Swedish national favorites; with recipes. il Look 29:58-9 F 9 '65

COOKERY, Turkish
Turkish meze. il Sunset 135:190-2+ O '65

COOKERY, Viennese. See Cookery, Austrian

COOKERY, West Indian
Have yourself an island fling! B. S. Brown. il Good H 160:152 My '65

COOKERY, Yugoslav
Foods of Yugoslavia; with recipes. M. Kaytor. il Look 29:88-91+ Je 15 '65

COOKERY books. See Cookbooks

COOKERY by children
Kids in the kitchen. il Ladies Home J 82:114 F '65
Our teenage cook. M. F. Williams. See issues of Good housekeeping

COOKERY by children—*Continued*
Our teenage cook Susan makes meringue shells à la mode. il Good H 161:134 Jl '65
She's making tasty meringue sculptures. il Sunset 135:98 Ag '65

COOKERY by men
Chefs of the West. See issues of Sunset
He likes to cook (cont) il Bet Hom & Gard 43:30+ Ap; 80 Jl; 88 Ag '65
Meals for mother's day off. il Redbook 125: 82-3+ Ag '65
Well-kept refrigerator for the man-about-town; with recipes. M. Kaytor. il Look 29: 86+ S 21 '65

COOKERY in literature
Our hungry authors; quotations from world of literature. C. Claiborne. il N Y Times Mag p 134-5 O 31 '65

COOKERY on yachts. See Cookery, Marine

COOKIE cutters
See also
Cookie press

COOKIE press
New cooky press. il Consumer Bul 48:19 D '65

COOKIES
Baker's art; holiday show at New York's Museum of contemporary crafts. A. Adams. il Craft Horiz 25:8-17 N '65
Christmas gathering. il Good H 161:134-5 D '65
Christmas is a cookie. il Ladies Home J 82:68-9+ D '65
Cookie art; a joyous Christmas tradition. il House & Gard 128:152-3 D '65
Cookie jigsaw. il Good H 161:96-7 D '65
Cookies: fun-to-eat nourishment; with recipes. G. Maddox. il Todays Health 43:52-7 S '65
Gingerbread pony, gingerbread sleigh; filled with the world's most loved cookies; with recipes. il McCalls 93:88-9+ D '65
Make-ahead cookies to freeze and keep. il Sunset 134:236-7 Ap '65
Night before Christmas; poem; with holiday suggestions. il Redbook 126:49-61+ D '65
Put them all together, they spell Santa: a jigsaw-puzzle cookie. il McCalls 93:136-7+ D '65
Recipes from a good cook's notebook; holiday season cookery. R. Hanna. il Suc Farm 63:60-1+ D '65
Successful recipes. il Suc Farm 63:69-70 Ag '65
Sugar cooky May baskets and hand painted cookies to go with them. il Sunset 134:184+ My '65
These are crisp vanilla horns. il Sunset 134: 220 My '65
These candy cookies are cooky candies; Florentines, with recipe. il Sunset 135: 180-1 N '65
Twice-baked Italian cookies. il Sunset 134: 196 Ap '65
Your gingerbread boys can carol, cavort, kick high, or just yawn. il Sunset 135:60-1 D '65

COOKING. See Cookery

COOKING thermometers. See Thermometers, Cooking

COOKING utensils. See Kitchen utensils

COOKING utensils, Electric. See Electric apparatus and appliances, Domestic

COOKS, Wilmer
When he sacrifices, watch out! por Sports Illus 23:51 S 20 '65

COOKS
Most magnifique pique-nique. il Life 59:84-6 Ag 27 '65

COOKY press. See Cookie press

COOLEY, Donald G.
What's so important about proteins? Todays Health 43:46-51+ O '65

COOLEY, Harold Dunbar
Sweet talk. Reporter 33:10 S 9 '65

COOLEY, Margaret, and others
(ed) New books appraised. See issues of Library journal

COOLEY's anemia. See Anemia

COOLIDGE, Calvin
Thirtieth President 1923-1929. F. Freidel. il pors Nat Geog Mag 128:566-71 O '65

COOLING
Cooling tips for homes in summer. Good H 161:149 Jl '65
See also
Air conditioning
Gas and oil engines—Cooling

COOLING of food. See Food, Cooling of

COOLING of livestock. See Livestock, Cooling of

COON hunting. See Raccoon hunting

COONEY, John D.
Cross and orb in Egypt. Natur Hist 74:40-9 bibliog(p68) Ap '65

COONS, Edgar E. and others
Lateral hypothalamus: learning of food-seeking response motivated by electrical stimulation. bibliog Science 150:1320-1 D 3 '65

COOPER, Alice P.
Experiment in womanhood. Sat R 48:52-3 Mr 6 '65

COOPER, Annie Lee
Selma. contd. Time 85:24 F 5 '65

COOPER, Diana (Manners) viscountess Norwich
Lion's heart. Atlan 215:59-62 Mr '65
about
Private line from London. V. Cowles. Vogue 146:148 S 1 '65

COOPER, Douglas
(ed) Great family collections; excerpts. Antiques 88:333-5 S '65

COOPER, Everett
My daughter, the policeman. il pors Ebony 20:82-4+ O '65

COOPER, Gordon
For a time we looked like history's shortest eight-day mission. pors Life 59:87-8 S 24 '65
about
Africans lionize a pride of spacemen. il pors Life 59:44-5 O 8 '65
At the controls. il por Newsweek 65:54 F 22 '65
Fuel-cell flight. il Time 86:46-8 Ag 27 '65
Hardest rendezvous of all, on the ground. J. Hicks. il pors Life 59:113-14+ O 1 '65
Keeping house in orbit. il por Newsweek 66:64 S 20 '65
See also
Space flight—Manned flights—Conrad-Cooper flight, 1965

COOPER, Gordon, family
Long wait at home for a star that's brighter than heck. M. Acoca. il pors Life 59:38-9 S 10 '65

COOPER, Joseph D.
Onward the management of science: The Wooldridge report. Science 148:1433-9; 149: 705-6 Je 11, Ag 13 '65

COOPER, Kent
AP's K.C. Newsweek 65:63 F 15 '65

COOPER, Lawson P.
Letters. Sch Arts 64:47 Mr '65

COOPER, Leroy Gordon. See Cooper, G.

COOPER, R. Conrad
Is collective bargaining a myth? excerpts from address, October 14, 1965. por U S News 59:104-6+ N 15 '65
Steel's warning on union power; excerpts from address, October 14, 1965. U S News 59:98 O 25 '65

COOPER, Richard
Chicago, the low rent district. New Repub 153:15-16 Jl 3 '65

COOPER, Robert B.
Low-noise TV and FM signal booster. Electr World 74:30 N '65

COOPERATION
See also
Educational cooperation
Industrial cooperation
International cooperation
Interracial cooperation
Library cooperation

Latin America
Toward a Latin American parliament. J. Ignacio Rasco. il Américas 17:12-17 Jl '65

COOPERATION, Inter-American. See Inter-American relations

COOPERATION in education. See Colleges and universities—Cooperation; Educational cooperation

COOPERATIVE apartment houses. See Apartment houses—Cooperative ownership

COOPERATIVE associations
Everyone else is organized; farmers should be, too. D. Paarlberg. Suc Farm 63:31+ O '65

United States
See also
National rural electric cooperative association

COOPERATIVE cataloging. See Cataloging, Cooperative

COOPERATIVE commonwealth federation. See Political parties—Canada

COOPERATIVE education. See Education, Cooperative

COOPERATIVE for American relief everywhere, incorporated
Need self-help programs. il Sci N L 87:374 Je 12 '65
New Tom Dooleys; with pictures. Sci Digest 57:60-3 My '65

COOPERATIVE marketing. See Marketing. Cooperative

COOT shooting
You've got to be crazy to hunt coot; Long Island Sound. N. Karas. il Field & S 70:66-9+ S '65

COPE, Don E.
It's what's happening, baby. Nat R 17:930-2 O 19 '65

COPE, Jack
Name of Patrick Henry; story. New Yorker 41:55-61 O 16 '65
Power; story. Mlle 62:144-7 D '65

COPE, Myron
Angel who doesn't fear to tread. Sat Eve Post 238:95-9 Ap 10 '65
Champion of nonviolence. Sat Eve Post 238:84-7 Mr 27 '65
Mecca lunch kid. Sat Eve Post 238:70+ Ag 14 '65
Prince of Pittsburgh. Sports Illus 23:84+ S 13 '65
Speaking out. por Sat Eve Post 238:10+ D 4 '65

COPELAND, George
George Copeland; at 82, incredibly, still the peerless interpreter of Debussy. R. Kammerer. Am Rec G 31:538 F '65

COPELAND, John
Sander stand swallows its own dust. Pop Sci 186:158-61 My '65

COPELAND, Lammot du Pont
Du Pont's great search for surprises. il Read Digest 86:155-6 F '65

COPENHAGEN
Description
Canals of Copenhagen. P. L. Adams. Atlan 215:65-8 Je '65
Copenhagen. W. Marchant. il Holiday 38:30-43+ S '65
Copenhagen, like a canaletto freshly restored. D. Messinesi. Vogue 145:149 Ap 15 '65
Some pleasures of Copenhagen. il Sunset 134:56+ Ap '65
Music
Nielsen centennial. F. Stevenson. il Hi Fi 15:138 Ag '65

COPEPODS
Sex conversion induced by hydrostatic pressure in the marine copepod tigriopus californicus. V. D. Vacquier and W. L. Belser. bibliog il Science 150:1619-21 D 17 '65

COPLAND, Aaron
Aaron Copland looks ahead. J. M. Conly. Reporter 33:54+ Ag 12 '65
Thank you, Aaron Copland; messages from his colleagues, former students and friends on his 65th birthday. por Am Rec G 32:196-205+ N '65

COPLANS, John
Art news from Los Angeles. Art N 63:51-4 F; 64:52+ D '65
Los Angeles: the scene. Art N 64:28-9+ Mr '65
Voulkos: redemption through ceramics. Art N 64:38-9+ Sum '65

COPLEY, John Singleton
American milestone comes to Washington; Watson and the shark, 1778. il Art N 64:35+ Mr '65
Copley: eye & idea. B. N. O'Doherty. il por Art N 64:22-7+ S '65
A Copley returns to Boston. Am Artist 29:4+ Mr '65
First American-born master. R. Davidson. il Antiques 88:270 S '65
Hand across the sea. F. Getlein. New Repub 153:32-3+ O 9 '65
John Singleton Copley; Washington's National gallery exhibition. il por Newsweek 66:92-3 O 4 '65
Man who left home. pors Time 86:74-5 O 29 '65

COPPELIA; ballet. See Ballets—Criticisms

COPPER
Prices
After aluminum: U.S. action on copper. il U S News 59:40-1 N 29 '65
Fitful at 42. il Time 87:81 Ja 14 '66
Holding copper in line. Bsns W p36 Ja 15 '66
Rollback: copper's turn. il Newsweek 66:71 N 29 '65

COPPER coins. See Coins

COPPER dies. See Dies (metal work)

COPPER industry and trade
Chile
Chile gives copper a lift; government woos U.S. companies. Bsns W p 172+ S 18 '65
Copper-bill crisis. M. J. Kubic. il Newsweek 66:52 S 13 '65
United States
Copper fights to block upward price pressure. Bsns W p44 N 20 '65
Copper's competitors race for its markets; aluminum, plastics, and clad metals. il Bsns W p86+ D 11 '65
Holding copper in line. Bsns W p36 Ja 15 '66
Rollback: copper's turn. il Newsweek 66:71 N 29 '65

COPPER mines and mining
Chile
President Frei and the copper goose. M. Adams. New Repub 153:10-12 D 18 '65

COPPER pipes. See Pipes, Copper

COPPOCK, John O.
Books. Bul Atomic Sci 21:40 F '65

COPPOLA, Frank
Underworld links. por Newsweek 66:26+ Ag 16 '65

COPTIC art. See Art, Coptic

COPTIC manuscripts. See Manuscripts, Coptic (papyri)

COPYING processes
Boon to business; or piracy for everyman. C. B. Grannis. Pub W 188:75 O 4 '65
British system will enlarge diazo copies; method of focusing ultra-violet light permits use of microfilm. Bsns W p 148 F 27 '65
Copying, duplicating and printing. il Duns R 86:pt2 143+ S '65
Reprography and the law; adaptation of address, December 16, 1964. P. F. Willig. Recreation 58:353-5 S '65
Techniques tomorrow; Diazo process and Kalvar technique. B. Sherman. Mod Phot 29:56+ N '65
Techniques tomorrow; report on United States navy and the Society of photographic scientists and engineers symposium. B. Sherman. Mod Phot 29:34 O '65
Turnaround; new copier unveiled. Newsweek 66:76+ S 27 '65
What's new, copycat? Time 86:98 N 5 '65
See also
Photography—Copying
Photostat
Xerography

COPYRIGHT
Frances Hodgson Burnett: episodes in her life; excerpt from Happily ever after. C. B. Burnett. il Horn Bk 41:86-94 F '65
Art
Case leaves a lot of questions unanswered; copied design. H. F. Pilpel. Pub W 188:29 Jl 26 '65
You may have lost rights if you don't insist on them; question of copyright on Mad magazine's Alfred E. Neumann. H. F. Pilpel. Pub W 188:29-30 N 29 '65
Law reports, digests, etc.
Who does own the copyright? H. F. Pilpel. Pub W 87:19 Mr 29 '65
Music
Copyright law revision and music librarians. A. A. Goldman. il Library J 90:1268.70 Mr 15 '65
Unauthorized reprints
American company wins piracy suit in Iran. Pub W 188:37 D 6 '65
Candy covered copyright. D. Dempsey. Sat R 48:40+ O 2 '65
Grove gets injunction vs. bootleg Thief's journal; edition issued by Greenleaf publishing company. Pub W 188:64 Jl 19 '65
Thief's journal copying ruled infringement. Pub W 188:26-7 O 18 '65
You can't just claim statutory damages; copyright infringement case. H. F. Pilpel. Pub W 188:55 S 13 '65
Canada
Copyright: Canadian, U.S. and international; summary of address. Pub W 187: 71-3 Je 21 '65
Great Britain
British cope with photocopying and fair use. R. H. Smith. Pub W 188:39 D 13 '65

COPYRIGHT—*Continued*

United States

ABPC files new statement on copyright revision. Pub W 188:88 S 27 '65

Anatomy of copyright revision; subcommittee of the House committee on the judiciary. R. H. Smith. Pub W 187: 81 Je 14 '65

BMI endorses proposals of Register of copyrights. Pub W 187:57 F 1 '65

Books, not copying machines, are the longterm answer; address, March 1964. L. C. Deighton. il Library J 90:2087-92 My 1 '65

Boon to business; or piracy for everyman. C. B. Grannis. Pub W 188:75 O 4 '65

British cope with photocopying and fair use. R. H. Smith. Pub W 188:39 D 13 '65

Candy copyrights applied for. Pub W 187:48-9 Mr 22 '65

Care and feeding of intellectual property. J. H. Munster, jr. and J. C. Smith. bibliog Science 148:739-43 My 7 '65

Copying grab-bag: observations on the new copyright legislation. C. F. Gosnell. bibliog f ALA bul 60:46-55 Ja '66

Copyright controversy; 58th annual meeting of American association of law libraries. E. J. Bander. il Library J 90:3221-3 Ag '65

Copyright crisis. America 113:236 S 4 '65

Copyright debate clarified on computer uses. Pub W 188:36-7 O 11 '65

Copyright office refuses to register Candy. Pub W 187:36 Ap 12 '65

Copyright revision and the writer; reprint. D. Lacy. Writer 78:19-21 My '65

Copyright revision bill introduced in Congress. Library J 90:1086+ Mr 1 '65

Everybody knows everybody in room 2226; hearings on copyright revision bill. R. H. Smith. Pub W 188:71 Ag 23 '65

General revision of the copyright law; 1965 in review. Pub W 189:74-7 Ja 17 '66

H.R. 4347 and you; bill for the general revision of the copyright law. D. Linton. Pop Phot 57:51+ S '65

Hearings reveal deadlock on manufacturing clause; subcommittee of House judiciary committee; August 11 and August 12. Pub W 188:49-55 Ag 23 '65

Hearings reveal main issues in copyright revision. il Pub W 188:18-23 Jl 26 '65

House copyright hearings: education and fair use. Pub W 188:291 Ag 30 '65

IPA congress hits U.S. on copyright and foreign policies. Pub W 187:141-3 Je 7 '65

Issue of access considered a crucial factual one; copyright infringement. H. Pilpel. Pub W 189:40 Ja 3 '66

Library position on copyright law revision; excerpts from statement, June 3, 1965. R. D. Rogers. Library J 90:3403-5 S 1 '65

Long amendment and the book industry; inclusion of copyright for public domain treatment. R. H. Smith. Pub W 187:37 My 31; 188:52 Jl 5 '65

Mr Celler's statement on copyright revision. R. H. Smith. Pub W 188:53 S 20 '65

Neither the word nor the music. Pub W 187: 53 Je 28 '65

New copyright bill introduced. A. Hamer and A. McCormick. ALA Bul 59:262-3 Ap '65

New copyright revision bill submitted to Congress; with editorial comment. Pub W 187:61-2, 77 F 15 '65

No place for poetic license; the copyright office at LC. B. A. Ringer. il Library J 90: 2958-63 Jl '65

Patents and copyrights: Congress moves toward comprehensive policy on federally financed research. J. Walsh. Science 148:54-6 Ap 2 '65

Publisher wins map copyright suit; pentron corporation to pay Rand McNally and destroy the plates used. Pub W 189:69 Ja 10 '66

Reprography and the law; adaptation of address, December 16, 1964. P. F. Willig. Recreation 58:353-5 S '65

Revising the copyright law. Atlan 216:10+ Ag '65

Rights and permissions. P. Nathan. See issues of Publishers' weekly

Senate opens hearings on copyright revision. Pub W 188:289-90 Ag 30 '65

Similarities compel the inference of copying; concerning story of Grania O'Malley; common law copyright. H. F. Pilpel. Pub W 188:30-1 N 29 '65

Study under way on copyright and technology. Pub W 189:41 Ja 3 '66

Tax relief denied creator of an idea. H. F. Pilpel. Pub W 187:73 Ap 26 '65

Teaching, publishing, and copyright. W. W. Brickman. Sch & Soc 93:419 N 13 '65

Test is not whether he could have created it. H. F. Pilpel. Pub W 188:30 N 29 '65

Up for grabs; Putnam's suit against Lancer books over publishing of Candy. il Newsweek 65:88+ F 8 '65

What is a proper copyright notice? H. F. Pilpel. Pub W 188:87 S 27 '65

Why the copyright law needs revision. W. Steif. Sat R 48:126-8 S 18 '65; Reply. R. Corbin. 48:64+ O 9 '65

COPYRIGHT office. See United States—Copyright office

CORAL

Neoplasia in a coral? D. F. Squires. bibliog il Science 148:503-5 Ap 23 '65

CORAL lilies. See Lilies

CORAL reefs and islands
See also
Eniwetok
Great Barrier Reef

CORAL REEFS ISLANDIA NATIONAL MONUMENT (proposed) See National monuments

CORALS

Myriad colors in coral. B. Hunter. il Natur Hist 75:30-3 Ja '66

Nature note; red coral. Sci N L 88:252 O 16 '65

CORBETT, Elizabeth

Who'd rather be deaf? Atlan 216:116+ O '65

CORBUSIER, Le. See Le Corbusier

CORDASCO, Frank M. and Redd, J. G.

Summer camp education for underprivileged children. bibliog f Sch & Soc 93:299 Sum '65

CORDIER, Andrew W.

Weaponry of quiet diplomacy. Sat R 48:28-9+ Jl 24 '65

CORDIGLIA, Achille Judica-. See Judica-Cordiglia, A.

CORDIGLIA, Gian Battista Judica-. See Judica-Cordiglia, G. B.

CORDLESS electric appliances. See Electric apparatus and appliances, Cordless

CÓRDOBA, Argentina

Bullets for a consul. il Newsweek 65:55 Je 21 '65

CÓRDOBA biennial. See Art—Exhibitions

el CORDOBÉS

Beatnik of the bull ring; with account by L. Hall. il pors Life 59:62D-68 Ag 6 '65

Crazy month. E. Gress. il por Newsweek 66:68 Ag 23 '65

Death of the afternoon. il por Time 86:41 S 24 '65

Five against the gods. R. Daley. por Esquire 64:98+ N '65

CORDOTOMY. See Spinal cord—Surgery

CORDS, Electric. See Electric cords

CORDYLINE terminalis. See Ti plant

COREN, Alan

Power and the glory. Atlan 216:130-2 S '65

COREY, Paul

Canvas. Pop Gard 16:28-31 Mr '65

CORFMAN, Philip A. and others

Response of the rabbit oviduct to a tissue adhesive. bibliog Science 148:1348-50 Je 4 '65

CORFU (island)

Going places, finding things in Corfu. H. Burke. il House & Gard 127:42-4 My '65

CORIOLANUS; drama. See Shakespeare, W.—Plays

CORKE, Hilary

Freya observed; poem. New Yorker 41:52 S 11 '65

CORKER, Jeanne L.

Our brother the migrant. Christian Cent 82: 1192-3 S 29 '65

CORKSCREW swamp sanctuary. See Wildlife sanctuaries

CORLETT, T. B. Jr, and Hoffer, J. R.

Pilot plant points the way to a rate decrease. Am City 80:113-15 O '65

CORMIER, Robert

Bunny Berigan; wasn't he a musician or something? story. Redbook 126:40-1 Ja '66

President Cleveland, where are you? story. Redbook 125:48-9 My '65

about

Books. M. Murray. Commonweal 82:477 Jl 2 '65

CORN, Nelson S.

Cash-and-carry justice. Newsweek 65:37-8 My 24 '65

CORN

Animal protein from plants; opaque-2 maize. Sci Am 213:44 Ag '65

Growth of rats fed on opaque-2 maize. E. T. Mertz and others. bibliog il Science 148:1741 -2 Je 25 '65

Inheritance of linoleic and oleic acids in maize. C. G. Poneleit and D. E. Alexander. bibliog il Science 147:1585-6 Mr 26 '65

CORN—*Continued*
Molybdenum content of corn plants exhibiting varying degrees of potassium deficiency. J. B. Jones, jr. il Science 148:94 Ap 2 '65
Renter who bought a farm with corn. R. D. Wennblom. il Farm J 89:26-7+ Jl '65
Second mutant gene affecting the amino acid pattern of maize endosperm proteins. O. E. Nelson and others. bibliog il Science 150:1469-70 D 10 '65
Versatile kernel. R. Yoshioka. il Sci N L 88:250-1+ O 16 '65

Cultivation

Biggest year yet for minimum tillage. il Farm J 89:36-7 My '65
Fifty bu. more corn for $24. D. Seim. il Farm J 89:42+ Mr '65
557 acres of corn in twenty-inch rows. L. E. Zeman. il Suc Farm 63:27-8+ D '65
Five-star high-yield system. L. E. Zeman. il Suc Farm 63:43-5+ F '65
From pop-up fertilizer, a 21-bu. kick. D. Hagen. il Farm J 89:70 Ap '65
How to make more money growing corn. Suc Farm 63:45 Mr '65
100-bu. corn on hillside pasture. J. Bickers. il Farm J 89:70G Ap '65
These farmers shoot the works on corn. R. J. Reiman and L. E. Zeman. il Suc Farm 63:54-5+ Mr '65
Why the 5-star high-yield system works; with editorial comment. S. R. Aldrich. il Suc Farm 63:34-5+ N '65

Diseases and pests

Corn insects, here's how to control them. Suc Farm 63:84-5 Mr '65
How to identify and control corn diseases. M. Shurtleff and J. J. Feight. il Suc Farm 63:44-5+ Ap '65
Latest report on maize dwarf mosaic. M. C. Shurtleff and J. J. Feight. il Suc Farm 63:56-7+ F '65
Report on postemergence weed killers for corn. E. Knake. Suc Farm 63:79 Mr '65
Report on preemergence weed killers for corn and soybeans. Suc Farm 63:88-9 Mr '65
See also
Corn rootworms

Drying

Dryeration, faster, cheaper corn drying for you? P. B. Jones. il Suc Farm 63:40-1 Ag '65
How to dry corn as fast as you pick. G. W. Wormley. il Farm J 89:30-1+ S '65

Harvesting

Five ways to speed up corn harvest. il Farm J 89:38-9 O '65
Here's how to lick corn harvesting losses. D. M. Byg and W. E. Gill. il Suc Farm 63:47 S '65

History

Corn pollen in swamp hints early agriculture: Dismal Swamp, Va. Sci N L 88:359 D 4 '65
Prehistoric maize in southeastern Virginia. D. R. Whitehead. bibliog il Science 150:881-3 N 12 '65

Hybrids

Five-star high-yield system. L. E. Zeman. il Suc Farm 63:43-5+ F '65

Seeding

Corn without plowing; subsoil as you plant. B. Hardy. il Farm J 89:B8 My '65
Here come those thirty-inch corn rows. D. Seim. il Farm J 89:32-3+ My '65
Just how early can you plant corn? il Suc Farm 63:14 Ap '65
100-bu. corn on hillside pasture. J. Bickers. il Farm J 89:70G Ap '65
Too cold, too early? plant corn anyway! J. Russell. il Farm J 89:34-5+ Ap '65

Storage

Protect corn with plastic. P. W. Rexroat. il Suc Farm 63:74 O '65

CORN, Sweet
How to enjoy a longer season of sweet corn E. M. Schroeder. il Flower Grower 52:61 Ap '65
If you grow sweet corn, try super-sweet. W. D. Pardee. Suc Farm 63:58B My '65
See also
Cookery—Vegetables

CORN borers. See European corn borers

CORN bread. See Bread

CORN dwarf mosaic. See Viruses, Plant

CORN harvesting machinery
Machinery for narrow rows. W. J. Fletcher. il Suc Farm 63:48-9 Ap '65

CORN picking. See Corn—Harvesting

CORN planters
Machinery for narrow rows. W. J. Fletcher. il Suc Farm 63:48-9 Ap '65
CORN products
Versatile kernel. R. Yoshioka. il Sci N L 88:250-1+ O 16 '65
CORN products company
When cruzeiros spiral, think dollars. il Bsns W p 107-8+ Mr 13 '65
CORN rootworms
Late word on corn rootworm controls. Farm J 89:47 Ap '65
One treatment controls rootworm and corn borer. W. G. Lovely. il Suc Farm 63:92 Mr '65
CORN silage. See Silage
CORNEAL transplants. See Transplantation of organs, tissues, etc.
CORNELL, Joseph
Cornell: the compass of boxing. D. Waldman. il Art N 64:42-5+ Mr '65
CORNELL, Robert
How to get more life out of your TV picture tube. Pop Electr 23:39-41+ O '65
CORNELL, Thomas C.
Why I am burning my draft card. Commonweal 83:205 N 19 '65
CORNELL aeronautical laboratory
Electronic roads for tomorrow's traffic. il Bsns W p 160+ Ap 24 '65
CORNELL college, Mount Vernon, la.
After the money came; Ford foundation grant. K. P. Buckley. Newsweek 66:66+ N 8 '65
CORNELSEN, Leroy A.
Investment yield on manpower development. Mo Labor R 88:672 Je '65
CORNER, F. H.
United Nations commemoration address, June 25, 1965. UN Mo Chron 2:129-32 Jl '65
CORNFELD, Bernard
Foreign beachhead on U.S. funds. por Bsns W p 146+ Je 12 '65
CORNING, W. C. and others
Arthropod preparation for behavioral, electrophysiological, and biochemical studies. bibliog Science 148:394-5 Ap 16 '65
CORNING glass center, Corning, N.Y.
Corning museum accessions in glass. R. Davidson. il Antiques 88:846+ D '65
CORNOG, William H.
Help for freshmen. Sat R 48:79 S 11 '65
CORNUELLE, Richard C.
Richard Cornuelle and the third sector. F. S. Meyer. Nat R 17:103 F 9 '65
CORNUS florida. See Dogwood
CORNWALL, England
Curious Cornwall. P. Friggens. il Travel 123:37-40 My '65; Same abr. with title In the land of King Arthur. Read Digest 86:171-6 My '65
CORNWELL, David John Moore
Looking glass war: novel. Ladies Home J 82:63-7 Ap; 54-5 My '65
What every writer wants. Harper 231:142-5 N '65
Wrong man on Crete. Holiday 38:74-5 D '65
about
John le Carré: will his success spoil David Cornwell? J. Wechsberg. il pors Ladies Home J 82:122+ Ap '65
Men who throw cold water on hot spies. por Vogue 146:94-5 Jl '65
CORONA (electricity)
Corona chemistry. J. A. Coffman and W. R. Browne. il Sci Am 212:91-6+ bibliog(p 147) Je '65
CORONADO, Calif.
Explorers in the surf. G. D. Hunsaker. il Recreation 58:286-7+ Je '65
CORONADO national forest. See National forests
CORONARY artery disease. See Arteriosclerosis
CORONARY heart disease. See Heart—Diseases
CORONARY thrombosis. See Thrombosis
CORPORAL punishment
Discipline in the dark: on beating school children. R. M. Gummere, jr. il Nation 201:442-5 D 6 '65; Reply with rejoinder. R. F. McKeen, jr. 202:inside cover Ja 10 '66
CORPORATE acquisitions. See Business management and organization
CORPORATE giving. See Corporations—Charitable contributions
CORPORATION farming. See Farms, Incorporated
CORPORATION law
Break for stockholders; reforms. Time 85:82 Je 4 '65
CORPORATIONS
Federal court considers where is a corporation: Louisiana case against Time, inc. H. F. Pilpel. Pub W 187:74 Ap 26 '65

CORPORATIONS—*Continued*

Is the corporation above the law? J. F. A. Taylor. bibliog f Harvard Bsns R 43:119-30 Mr '65

Power of big business. R. L. Heilbroner. Atlan 216:89-93 S '65

See also

Bonds

Business consolidations and mergers

Executives

Farms, Incorporated

Monopolies

Accounting

Accounting stalemate: management's move now? il Duns R 85:55-6+ My '65

Big skid at Yale express. R. J. Whalen. il Fortune 72:144-9+ N '65

Pensions and profits. Fortune 71:69-70 My '65

Advertising

Getting the brass in; relations between companies and their ad agencies. Bsns W p28-9 My 15 '65

Charitable contributions

Involuntary charity; private utilities' donations to good works at consumers' expense. New Repub 153:8 N 20 '65

Performing arts find an angel in business. il Bsns W p52+ Mr 13 '65

See also

Foundations, Charitable and educational

Directories

Fortune directory; 500 largest U.S. industrial corporations (cont) il Fortune 72:149-68 Jl '65

Fortune directory; 200 largest industrials outside the U.S., and the 50 largest U.S. commercial banks, life-insurance, merchandising, transportation, and utility companies. il Fortune 72:169-80 Ag '65

Directors

See also

Interlocking directorates

Finance

Case for retiring stock. il Fortune 72:245-6 N '65

Corporate giants: an American success story. il U S News 59:84+ N 15 '65

Higher profits across the board. il Newsweek 66:63 Ag 9 '65

How much recovery for stocks? il Bsns W p 114+ Jl 17 '65

How officials are sizing up their companies' stocks. il U S News 58:102-3 Ap 5 '65

Investment analysis: coping with change. W. R. Hirschmann and J. R. Brauweiler. il Harvard Bsns R 43:62-72 My '65

It's another big quarter for profits; with chart. U S News 59:74 Ag 2 '65

It's still an uptrend in profits; with chart. U S News 58:94 F 15 '65

Keeping up a hot pace; gains in GNP and corporate profits. il Bsns W p 19-20 Jl 24 '65

More companies are buying back their stock. L. A. Guthart. il Harvard Bsns R 43:40-2+ Mr '65; Discussion. 43:31+ Jl '65

New look at cash. il Fortune 72:96 Ag '65

New offerings perk up. il Bsns W p 134 Ap 3 '65

New peaks; corporate profits. il Time 86:89 O 29 '65

New way to prosper; with editorial comment. il Bsns W p23-4, 156 Mr 6 '65

Profits ride still higher; third-quarter gain; with charts. Bsns W p25-6 O 23 '65

Profits roll on: another quarter at record level; with chart. U S News 59:106 N 1 '65

Repurchase stock to revitalize equity. C. D. Ellis. il Harvard Bsns R 43:119-28 Jl '65

Rise in earnings may slow in 66. il Bsns W p30-2 Ja 1 '66

Security analyst and the corporation. il Duns R 85:41-2+ Mr '65

Setting records already; with charts. Bsns W p23-5 F 6 '65

Slight pinch for cash. il Bsns W p45-6 Je 19 '65

Story on profits; again, it's a record; with chart. U S News 58:66 My 3 '65

Telling their secrets; unlisted companies comply with SEC disclosure requirements. Bsns W p 170+ O 16 '65

Topping all expectations; corporate earnings. il Bsns W p21-2 My 1 '65

Variety of secondary stocks. il Duns R 85:137-8 Ap '65

What's unknown to stockholders; true picture of company earnings. U S News 58:77 Mr 8 '65

When cruzeiros spiral, think dollars; strategy of Corn products co. il Bsns W p 107:8+ Mr 13 '65

Where does the money come from? address, April 6, 1965. G. K. Funston. Vital Speeches 31:467-72 My 15 '65

Who pays the profit? G. R. Vila. il Duns R 86:50-2+ S '65

Why growth companies go wrong. J. B. Weiner. il Duns R 85:42-4+ Je '65

See also

Capital investments

Dividends

Profit

Foreign expansion

See Business—Foreign expansion

Foreign subsidiaries

Challenge and change abroad. il Duns R 85: pt2 144-5+ Mr '65

Corporate charts go global. Bsns W p52+ S 11 '65

Executive gap; problem of American subsidiaries in Mexico. il Fortune 71:63-4 Ap '65

Flow chart of U.S. funds. Bsns W p75 N 27 '65

Goodby, Geneva; hello, Brussels. il Fortune 71:58 My '65

Growing overseas without dollars; U.S. companies raise money abroad. il Bsns W p 107-8+ O 2 '65

Guidelines tighten on foreign investment; to reduce balance-of-payments deficit. il Bsns W p29-31 D 11 '65

How to do business with a Frenchman. E. R. Eggers. Harper 231:41-4 Ag '65

Innocents abroad; animosity toward American subsidiaries. H. C. Wallich. Newsweek 66:84 N 29 '65

Innocents abroad: the expatriates' lot. G. F. Dickover. Mo Labor R 88:143-5 F '65

Labor relations abroad: American business overseas. T. R. Brooks. Duns R 86:75-6 N '65

Local man makes good. il Time 85:94 Je 25 '65

Managing a worldwide business. W. J. Butler and J. Dearden. Harvard Bsns R 43:93-102 My '65

Multi-national corporation; address, January 13, 1965, L. A. Townsend. Vital Speeches 31:444-8 My 1 '65

Oil and power mix; Esso Standard eastern. Fortune 71:70+ F '65

Outflow of funds is facing new curb; corporate investments abroad face stiffer program. il Bsns W p53-4+ O 9 '65

Piggyback sales gain momentum; piggyback exporting. Bsns W p70+ D 18 '65

To build abroad, borrow abroad. Newsweek 67:41 Ja 3 '66

Top salary mix abroad changes; U.S. expatriates and foreign nationals working for American controlled companies. il Bsns W p98 O 2 '65

U.S. checks up on dollar drain; Commerce dept. calls for data on foreign investments. Bsns W p31-2 N 6 '65

U.S. companies recross the Alps; ban on hiring Swiss personnel. il Bsns W p90-2+ My 8 '65

What U.S. companies are doing abroad. See issues of U.S. news & World report

When cruzeiros spiral, think dollars; strategy of Corn products co. il Bsns W p 107-8+ Mr 13 '65

Laws and legislation

See Corporation law

Public relations

See Business—Public relations

Real estate operations

Towering empire; purchase of Schine holdings by Wien and Helmsley. il Time 86:63B Jl 30 '65

Reports

See Reports

Social aspects

See Business—Social aspects

Taxation

From business: $43 billion for welfare. il Nations Bsns 53:120-1 O '65

Monumental muddle in state taxes. J. F. Olesky. il Duns R 86:61+ N '65

New U.S. agency urged to run some state taxes; sales and use levies on out-of-state companies. Bsns W p58-9 Jl 3 '65

Pinch on margins. il Fortune 72:52+ N '65

Watch your minutes. R. S. Holzman. bibliog f Harvard Bsns R 43:162-4+ Mr '65

CORPORATIONS—*Continued*

Valuation

Fine art of high-yield management. J. B. Weiner. il Duns R 86:38-41+ O '65

Reliable consumer; eight producers of consumer nondurables. il Duns R 86:143-5 O '65

CORPORATIONS, Foreign

See also
Corporations, International

CORPORATIONS, International

Multi-national corporation; address, January 13, 1965. L. A. Townsend. Vital Speeches 31:444-8 My 1 '65

CORPORATIONS, Nonprofit

Military's research groups under fire. il Bsns W p34 S 11 '65

Nonprofits again; concerning report of subcommittee of House committee on armed services. Nation 201:262-3 O 25 '65

CORPORATIONS and education. See Business and education

CORPS of engineers. See United States—Army —Corps of engineers

CORPULENCE

Best diet is exercise. J. Mayer. il N Y Times Mag p34-5+ Ap 25 '65

Bypassing the small bowel; super-surgery for the super-obese. il Time 86:77 O 29 '65

Diet that finally did it; air force diet. J. Alsop. il McCalls 92:138+ My '65; Same abr. with title What about that painless air force diet? Read Digest 87:89-92 Jl '65

Hormone helps reduce weight; chorionic gonadotrophin. Sci Digest 58:36-7 Jl '65

I wrote The drinking man's diet. R. Wernick. il Sat Eve Post 238:84+ My 22 '65

Reduction of Happy Humphrey; case of William J. Cobb. il Time 86:31 Jl 30 '65

Social weight control. Sci Digest 58:39 O '65

Stout-hearted men; well-rounded opera singers. A. M. Lingg. il Opera N 29:12-13 F 6 '65

Thin book by a formerly fat psychiatrist. T. I. Rubin. il McCalls 93:54-5+ Ja '66

See also
Weight reducing preparations

CORPUS CHRISTI, Tex.

Libraries

See also
La Retama public library

CORPUS CHRISTI BAY (repair ship) See Ships—Repairing

CORREAS, Edmundo

Liberators of the South. Américas 17:14-21 S '65

CORRECTIONAL institutions. See Reformatories

CORRESPONDENCE schools and courses

Home study courses: how well can you learn by mail? il Good H 161:170-1 O '65

See also
International correspondence schools

CORRESPONDENTS, Foreign. See Reporters and reporting

CORRESPONDENTS, Newspaper. See Reporters and reporting

CORRESPONDENTS, War. See War correspondents

CORRETTE, Michel

Real sleeper, this one! J. W. Barker. Am Rec G 31:1154-5 Ag '65

CORRIGAN, Dean

Student teacher. NEA J 54:40 Ap '65

CORRIGAN, John E. See Lehman, D. J. jt. auth.

CORRIGAN, Robert W.

Books. Vogue 146:77 S 15 '65

Theatre. Vogue 146:68 N 15; 146 D '65; 147: 34 Ja '66

CORRINGTON, John William

Seven poets. M. McCloskey. Poetry 105:270-3 Ja '65

CORRINGTON, Julian D.

Nature and the microscope (cont) Natur Hist 74:61-6 Ap '65

CORROSION and anticorrosives

Checklist on galvanic corrosion. Yachting 117:171 F '65

Corrosion hampers AF development; comprehensive materials symposium. J. F. Judge. il Miss & Roc 16:26-7+ Je 14 '65

Corrosion of metals under water. E. Crimin. il Motor B 115:33-4+ Mr '65

New corrosion inhibitor checks salt damage to cars; Davenport, Ia. il Am City 80:66 O '65

Oakland, N.J. proving ground for cathodic protection. N. D. Fagerlund. il Am City 80:106-8 S '65

Reverse current keeps ferry afloat. W. P. Brothers. il Pop Electr 23:78 D '65

$7 billion rust spot. M. J. Walker. il Sci N L 89:26-7 Ja 8 '66

Softening rock salt's bite. il Bsns W p160 Mr 13 '65

CORRUPTION in politics. See Politics, Corruption in

CORSAGES (flowers) See Bouquets

CORSETS. See Foundation garments

CORSICA

Corsica. R. S. Kane. il Travel 124:47-9 N '65

Corsican curse. il Time 86:36 O 29 '65

CORSO, Gregory

(ed) Life, death and dancing: a Buffalo shindig; excerpts from interviews with teenagers. Esquire 64:34-5 Jl '65

CORSON, Martha

Girl to marry; story. Good H 162:52-3 Ja '66

CORT, David

Another visit to the undertaker. Nation 200: 420-1 Ap 19 '65

Comics, etc. Commonweal 82:503-5 Jl 9 '65

Con Edison: the Hudson River caper. Nation 201:387-9 N 22 '65

On how to be a revolutionary in your spare time. Commonweal 81:615-16 F 5 '65

Soccer; the rabble game. Nation 201:100-1 Ag 30 '65

Statesman on Madison avenue. Nation 200: 118-19 F 1 '65

Vulgar press. Commonweal 81:761-3; 82:173 Mr 12, Ap 23 '65

Well-informed spy. Nation 200:136-8 F 8 '65

Westchester gorillas. Nation 201:249-50+ O 18 '65

CORT, John C.

Adlai Stevenson. Commonweal 82:556-8 Ag 6 '65

CORTE, Arturo E.

Particle sorting by repeated freezing and thawing. bibliog Science 142:499-501, 148: 1617 O 25 '63, Je 18 '65

CORTEX, Cerebral. See Cerebral cortex

CORTICOSTEROIDS

Steroid stimulation of beating of cultured rat-heart cells. R. L. McCarl and others. bibliog il Science 150:1611-13 D 17 '65

CORTISOL. See Hydrocortisone

CORTISONE

Abrogation of allogeneic inhibition by cortisone. K. E. Hellström and others. bibliog il Science 149:82-4 Jl 2 '65

CORTRIGHT, Edgar M.

Space: a White House endorsement and a NASA view on the attitudes of scientists toward the program. D. S. Greenberg. Science 147:1270 Mr 12 '65

CORTRIGHT, Richard W.

Laubach method. bibliog Wilson Lib Bul 40: 50-4 S '65

CORVALLIS, Ore.

Drama in the barn; Valley round theatre. V. Rankin. il Recreation 58:279+ Je '65

CORYELL, Schofield

Algeria: zigzag path to socialism. Nation 200:277-9 Mr 15 '65

COSA nostra. See Mafia

COSBY, Bill

Senior scholastic interview; ed. by R. Hemming. por Sr Schol 86:17 Mr 18 '65

about

Bill Cosby: variety is the life of spies. S. Karnow. il por Sat Eve Post 238:86+ S 25 '65

I spy. il pors Ebony 20:65-6+ S '65

That's the truth, and other Cosby stories. C. L. Mee, jr. pors N Y Times Mag p96-7 Mr 14 '65

COSER, Lewis A.

Fear of positive thinking. Nation 201:166-70 S 20 '65

Monolithic myth. Commentary 39:94-6 Ap '65

COSGROVE, Frank D.

Community recreation tries hosteling programs. Recreation 58:337 S '65

COSI fan tutte; opera. See Mozart, J. C. W. A.

ĆOSIĆ, Dobrica

Toward an intellectual community; tr. by J. Dekker. Bul Atomic Sci 21:2-6 Je '65

COSINDAS, Marie

How to get the most out of Polacolor. H. M. Kinzer. il por Pop Phot 57:78-9+ Jl '65

COSMETIC industry and trade

Big boom in men's beauty aids; not by soap alone. C. Welles. il Life 59:39-40 Ag 13 '65

See also
Chesebrough-Pond's, incorporated
Revlon, incorporated

Securities

Cosmetic stocks on sale. il Fortune 72:93-4+ Ag '65

COSMETIC surgery. See Surgery, Plastic

COSMETICS

Beauty memo; weather-vain; lash-proud. Mlle 62:128 N '65

Beauty with all the answers; Revlon research center. il Vogue 146:110-13 Ag 1 '65

COSMETICS—*Continued*
Clairol puts on a new face; expanding into full cosmetic line. il Bsns W p 124-6+ Je 12 '65
For a perfect tan. Seventeen 24:146 Je '65
Hormone cream restores lost hair. il Sci Digest 57:22-3 Mr '65
How a precocious 18-year-old plays with paints. il Mlle 62:166-9 N '65
Jar of hope; concerning Mrs Neuberger's drive for labeling cosmetics. Newsweek 65:64 My 31 '65
New aerosol deodorants and anti-perspirants. il Consumer Bul 48:2+ S '65
New beauty university; Revlon research center opened. Vogue 146:36 Ag 1 '65
Quick change and long-range ways to a prettier you. Am Home 68:38 Ap '65
Tender is the skin. Mlle 61:142+ My '65
See also
Lipstick
Make-up

COSMETICS for men
Big boom in men's beauty aids; not by soap alone. C. Welles. il Life 59:39-40 Ag 13 '65
Does he or doesn't he? W. K. Zinsser. il Sat Eve Post 238:16 O 9 '65

COSMETOLOGY. See Beauty culture

COSMIC dust. See Matter, Interstellar

COSMIC physics
See also
Astrophysics
Magnetic field (cosmic physics)

COSMIC radio noise. See Radio astronomy

COSMIC rays
Fossil particle tracks and uranium distributions in minerals of the Vaca Muerta meteorite. R. L. Fleischer and others. bibliog il Science 148:629-32 Ap 30 '65
Major energy cosmic? Sci N L 88:339 N 27 '65
Thermal neutron activation: measurement of cross section for manganese-53. H. T. Millard, jr. bibliog il Science 147:503-4 Ja 29 '65

COSMOGONY
In the beginning... bang! Newsweek 65:50 My 31 '65
Notes and comment; explosion theory of creation. New Yorker 41:31 Je 5 '65
Notes and comment; universe has a heartbeat. New Yorker 41:23 Jl 17 '65
Whisper from a bang; new evidence to support Big Bang theory of the universe. il Time 85:98+ Je 11 '65

COSMOLOGY
Continual creation. G. S. Mumford. Sky & Tel 29:88 F '65
Discovery of time, by S. Toulmin and J. Goodfield. Review
New Yorker 41:231-8+ N 6 '65. J. Bernstein
Not according to Hoyle; F. Hoyle denies his theory of a steady-state universe. Newsweek 66:77 O 25 '65

COSMONAUTS. See Astronauts

COSMOPOLITAN (periodical)
Helen Gurley Brown turns editor. C. Welles. il Life 59:65-6+ N 19 '65
New direction for Cosmopolitan. H. G. Brown. Writer 78:20 Jl '65
Sex & the editor. Time 85:40 Mr 26 '65

COSMOS
Count on cosmos. M. C. Ohlander. il Flower Grower 52:43 Mr '65

COSMOS (artificial satellites) See Artificial satellites, Russian

COSPAR. See International council of scientific unions—Committee on space research

COST accounting
Budget wins a new role. il Bsns W p 128-30+ Ap 21 '65
How to measure marketing performance. R. A. Feder. il Harvard Bsns R 43:132-42 My '65
Next place for paring costs. il Bsns W p 132+ My 1 '65
See also
Value analysis

COST of college education. See College education, Cost of

COST of food. See Food—Prices

COST of living
See also
Domestic finance
Standard of living

United States
Consumer and wholesale prices; tables. See issues of Monthly labor review
Lid coming off living costs? U S News 58:87 Je 14 '65

Poverty: the word and the reality. H. H. Lamale. bibliog f il Mo Labor R 88:822-7 Jl '65
See also
Food—Prices
Price indexes
Prices—United States

COST of medical service. See Medical service, Cost of

COST of sickness. See Medical service, Cost of

COSTA, E.
Brain research. Science 148:865-6+ My 7 '65

COSTA, Mary
Costa diva; interview, ed. by E. R. Rizzo. por Opera N 29:30 Ap 3 '65

COSTA E SILVA, Artur da. See Silva, A. da Costa e

COSTA RICA
Costa Rica, free of the volcano's veil. R. De Roos. il Nat Geog Mag 128:122-52 Jl '65
Costa Rica: mighty midget. C. H. Gardiner. bibliog f Cur Hist 50:8-13+ Ja '66

Description and travel
Costa Rica. C. Cress. il Travel 124:56-8+ S '65

Religious institutions and affairs
News of the Christian world (cont) Christian Cent 82:1045-6 Ag 25 '65

COSTA RICAN national science fair. See Science fairs

COSTA RICAN poetry
Eight Costa Rican poets; with poems. il Américas 17:29-34 S '65

COSTAIN, Thomas Bertram
Obituary
Pub W 188:32 O 18 '65

COSTANTINI, Egidio
Melodies for the eye. il por Time 86:98-101 S 17 '65

COSTANZO, G. A.
Latin America; address, May 13, 1965. Vital Speeches 31:551-4 Jl 1 '65

COSTE, Brutus
Yalta twenty years after. Nat R 17:142+ F 23 '65

about
Converging toward what? J. Burnham. Nat R 17:970 N 2 '65

COSTELLO, Charles V.
Fluoridate the automatic way. Am City 80:183-4+ Je '65

COSTIGAN, Daniel M.
Microfilm and electronics. Electr World 74:37-9 Ag '65

COSTIGAN, Madeleine
Your garden can attract birds and people too. il Flower Grower 52:38+ Mr '65

COSTUME
Children's party costumes. C. Houck. il Parents Mag 40:118 O '65
See also
Fashion

Europe, Eastern
New class. il Time 86:28-9 Ag 13 '65

Japan
Do you like kimono? excerpt from The kimono mind. B. Rudofsky. il Horizon 7:48-53 Spr '65
See also
Netsukes

COSTUME, Indian. See Indians of North America—Costume and adornment

COSTUME, Theatrical
Costume in the theatre. P. Campbell. Opera N 30:36 Ja 15 '66
Lewis Brown, artist in the theater. J. H. Michel. il Am Artist 30:47-53+ Ja '66

COSTUME design
Bare-ish. il Newsweek 65:57 Je 7 '65
Beautiful daughters of Israel. il Holiday 37:68-73 F '65
Bravura year for Italian beauty. il Life 59:70-9 O 22 '65
Bugles, bangles & all woman; Sarmi creations. il Time 85:62 Je 25 '65
But, M. Courrèges, what about Mrs Bottomley? M. Mannes. il N Y Times Mag p34-5+ Mr 28 '65
Fall '65: season of contrasts; seven individualists in their showrooms. T. Owett. il Ladies Home J 82:68-71 S '65
Feather merchants; fall clothes. il Time 86:50 Ag 6 '65
Gernreich's progress: or, Eve unbound. G. Steinem. il N Y Times Mag p 18-22+ Ja 31 '65
Girl with a golden bra; metallic dresses and pants. il Newsweek 66:69 D 13 '65
Great idea boy; R. Gernreich. L. H. Lapham. il Sat Eve Post 238:74-81 F 13 '65

COSTUME design—*Continued*
High style; space-age designs by Courrèges. il Newsweek 65:86 Mr 22 '65
It's op from toe to top; dresses displayed at the Museum of modern art's op show. il Life 58:52-4 Ap 16 '65
Lord of the space ladies. il Life 58:47-50+ My 21 '65
Low couture; inexpensive copies of European couture. il Newsweek 66:64 O 4 '65
Made in America; Coty American critics' awards. il Newsweek 66:110 O 25 '65
Pajama game. il Newsweek 67:58-9 Ja 17 '66
Return of the leg; fall collections in New York. il Newsweek 65:90 Je 21 '65
Return of the woman; Paris fashion showings. il Newsweek 65:78-9 F 8 '65
Soviet fashions: a hesitant hint of glamour. A. Chamberlin. il Sat Eve Post 238:82-3 My 22 '65
Styles too are pushed further out by pop. R. Constable. il Life 58:59-60+ F 26 '65
Where did all the women go? T. Meehan. il Sat Eve Post 238:26-31 S 11 '65
Young actress tries them all on; new styles from Paris. il Life 58:54-6+ Mr 5 '65
COSTUME designers
After Courrèges, what future for the haute couture? F. Giraud. il N Y Times Mag p50-1+ S 12 '65
Battle of Pitti Palace; fashion shows open in Florence and Rome. il Newsweek 66:44 Ag 2 '65
Betsey's world; a tale about what a lot of talent can do. il Mlle 62:178+ N '65
Courage of Courrèges. il Time 85:48+ Ap 9 '65
Fashionable savages, by J. Fairchild. Review Sat R il 48:69 N 13 '65
Only the young. il Time 86:63 Ag 13 '65
Paris puts its magic into ready-to-wear. il Bsns W p78-80+ D 18 '65
Threads of fashion. P. A. Janssen. il Am Ed 1:9-11 N '65
Two American girls show Paris; M. Fonssagrives and V. Tiel. il Life 58:94-6+ F 5 '65
See also
Balenciaga, C.
Blass, B.
Courrèges, A.
Gernreich, R.
Mori, H.
St Laurent, Y. M.
Stephen, J.

Anecdotes, facetiae, satire, etc.
Tyranny of hairdressers and fashion designers. M. Mannes. McCalls 93:34+ Ja '66
COSTUME in art
Study of dress in the works of the old masters. S. M. Newton. il Antiques 88:650-5 N '65
COSTY, Alan
Somebody out there hates the Mayor. New Repub 153:8-9 S 4 '65
CÔTE D'AZUR. See Riviera
COTHRAN, Tilman C.
Negro protest against segregation in the South. bibliog f Ann Am Acad 357:65-72 Ja '65
COTLER, Gordon
Selected shorts. New Yorker 41:188-90 D 18 '65
COTONEASTERS
Rock cotoneaster. J. E. Dwyer. il Pop Gard 16:8 My '65
COTTAGES
Remarkable space and height in small houses. il Arch Rec 137:102-5 mid-My '65
Three family vacation houses, all within reach. J. D. Bloodgood. il Bet Hom & Gard 43:62-7 F '65
Yes, you can own a vacation home. A. C. Borg. il Am Home 68:41-7 Ap '65
COTTAGES, Summer. See Summer homes
COTTON, Dorothy Whyte
Introducing our new editor. il pors Parents Mag 40:55 Mr '65
COTTON, Norris
Excerpt from address, August 26, 1965. Cong Digest 44:301+ D '65
COTTON, Richard. See Buckley, K. P. jt. auth.
COTTON
Prices
Cotton candy from Congress. A. Hamilton. New Repub 153:9-10 O 9 '65; Reply with rejoinder. J. A. Schnittker. 153:35+ N 20 '65
COTTON fabrics
Creasing
Inventor of the month; he gave cotton a reprieve. S. V. Jones. il Sci Digest 57:27 My '65

COTTON growing
What is she growing? cotton. il Sunset 134:270-2 Ap '65
COTTON industry and trade
British textiles spin revival with synthetics. il Bsns W p50-2+ Ja 15 '65
Congress cuts new pattern for cotton; omnibus farm bill. Bsns W p56 Ag 14 '65
Cotton candy from Congress. A. Hamilton. New Repub 153:9-10 O 9 '65; Reply with rejoinder. J. A. Schnittker. 153:35+ N 20 '65
King cotton; completely subsidized. Time 85:21-2 Mr 5 '65
Trying to spin out of trouble; consolidation and streamlining of two of Japan's leading cotton-spinning companies. il Time 86:97 N 26 '65
U.S. and Colombia conclude cotton textile agreement; Department announcement, June 9, 1965, with agreement and related letters. il Dept State Bul 53:89-92 Jl 12 '65
U.S. and Japan amend bilateral cotton textile arrangement; joint announcement, May 19, 1965, with U.S. note. Dept State Bul 52:980-1 Je 14 '65
U.S. and Korea conclude cotton textile agreement; Department announcement, January 26, 1965, with agreement and related letters. il Dept State Bul 52:274-8 F 22 '65
U.S. and Pakistan conclude cotton textile agreement; Department announcement, with text of U.S. note, February 26, 1965. G. G. Johnson. il Dept State Bul 52:391-4 Mr 15 '65
COTTON seed. See Cottonseed
COTTON workers
See also
Strikes—United States—Cotton workers
COTTONSEED
Ribosomal-RNA synthesis in the absence of ribosome synthesis in germinating cotton seeds. L. Waters and L. Dure, 3d. bibliog il Science 149:188-91 Jl 9 '65
COTTONTAIL hunting. See Rabbit hunting
COUDY, Robert
God's little apples. il Am For 71:36-7 Mr '65
COUFFER, Jack
Nature and photography. Natur Hist 74:66-9 Je '65
COUGAR hunting. See Puma hunting
COUGARS. See Pumas
COUGHLIN, Charles Edward
Father Coughlin & the New deal, by C. J. Tull. Review
Commonweal 82:121-2 Ap 16 '65. J. R. Mellow; Reply. G. N. Shuster. 82:231 My 7 '65; Rejoinder. 82:335 My 28 '65
Nation 200:401-2 Ap 12 '65. H. Bresler
COUGHLIN, George G.
King can do wrong. Read Digest 87:31+ O '65
COUGHLIN, William J.
Editorial. See issues of Missiles and rockets
COULOMBE, Harry N. and others
Respiratory water exchange in two species of porpoise. bibliog Science 149:86-8 Jl 2 '65
COUNCIL for Christian social action. See United church of Christ
COUNCIL for financial aid to education
Bright key, by M. E. Spaght. Review Sat R 48:60 Ag 21 '65. A. T. Hill
COUNCIL for the encouragement of music and the arts. See Arts council of Great Britain
COUNCIL-manager plan. See City manager plan
COUNCIL of community churches. See International council of community churches
COUNCIL of economic advisers. See United States—Council of economic advisers
COUNCIL of Europe
See also
Court of human rights
COUNCIL of federated organizations
Freedom libraries; program in Mississippi. F. W. Heinze. il Library J 90:1991-3 Ap 15 '65; Reply. R. B. Layton. 90:2308+ My 15 '65
Meanwhile, in Mississippi. B. L. Smith. Commonweal 82:39-42 Ap 2 '65
COUNCIL of foreign ministers, Geneva, 1954
That Geneva agreement; how the French got out of Vietnam. B. B. Fall. il N Y Times Mag p28-9+ My 2 '65
COUNCIL of Trent. See Trent, Council of, 1545-1563
COUNCIL on books in wartime
Wartime council's assets transferred to Franklin. Pub W 189:68 Ja 10 '66
COUNCIL on library resources, incorporated
Council awards six grants for improving library service. Pub W 188:58 Ag 23 '65
CLR announces new reports and a $24,000 grant. Pub W 187:42 My 3 '65

COUNCIL on library resources, incorporated
—*Continued*
CLR grants for statistics meeting and manual on book care and repair. Library J 90: 4312+ O 15 '65
Council on library resources; grants to further research and technological advances in services and equipment. Wilson Lib Bul 40:15+ S '65
Microfiche camera, archives congress among latest CLR-supported projects. Library J 90:3414-15 S 1 '65
New center at LC to coordinate copying of foreign manuscripts. Library J 90:3413 S 1 '65

COUNCILS and synods
New synod. J. O'Gara. Commonweal 83:46 O 15 '65
Next council; need for a new council in ten years. W. J. Nagle. Commonweal 82:688-91 S 24 '65
Synod of bishops. America 113:358 O 2 '65
See also
Vatican council, 2d

COUNSELING
Guidance in the elementary school; teacher vs. specialist. R. R. Ferris; S. L. Leiter. NEA J 54:48-9+ S '65
Pastoral counseling. F. D. Shafer. Christian Cent 82:1420+ N 17 '65
Special issue on guidance. J. A. Keith; H. L. Hurwitz; N. E. Hearn. bibliog Sr Schol 87:sup4-sup6+ N 11 '65
Young living; questions and answers. A. Wood. See issues of Seventeen

Anecdotes, facetiae, satire, etc.
Answers to poets' questions. N. Perrin. New Yorker 41:23 Je 26 '65

COUNSELING, Educational. See Educational guidance
COUNSELING service, School. See Personnel service (education)
COUNSELORS
See also
School counselors
COUNT, Ellen
Mr Clean; poem. Sat R 48:30 Ag 14 '65
COUNT three and stick your foot in it; story. See Balsley, E. D.
COUNTERFEIT money. See Counterfeits and counterfeiting
COUNTERFEITS and counterfeiting
Windischgraetz caper; Hungarian counterfeiting scandal of 1925-1926. G. Bailey. il Reporter 32:30-4 F 11 '65
COUNTERGLOW
Gemini V experiments on zodiacal light and gegenschein. E. P. Ney and W. F. Huch. bibliog il Science 150:53-6, 1629 O 1, D 17 '65
COUNTER-insurgency aircraft. See Airplanes, Military—United States
COUNTER-Reformation
See also
Trent, Council of, 1545-1563
COUNTERTENORS. See Singers
COUNTRIES, Imaginary. See Geographical myths
COUNTRY and city. See City and country
COUNTRY clubs
Teen city; first teen-age country club, Denver. Newsweek 66:120+ N 15 '65
COUNTRY doctors. See Physicians
COUNTRY estates
English dream: Mrs Nancy Lancaster's Haseley court; with account by V. Lawford. il Vogue 146:112-21+ Jl '65

Ireland
Lure of Tollymore. E. V. Malone. il Am For 71:30-1 F '65
COUNTRY houses
Lady Hesketh and her small, perfect palace; Easton Neston. D. McEwen. il Vogue 147: 144-51+ Ja 1 '66
COUNTRY life
Country feast. R. W. Wells. Ladies Home J 82:23 Mr '65
Country living in the West (cont) Sunset 134:116 Ap; 135:124 O '65
See also
Farm life
Recreation, Rural
COUNTRY towns. See Cities and towns
COUNTRY wife; drama. See Wycherley, W.
COUNTRY women. See Farm women
COUNTY buildings
Gold in the hills of California; Marin County, Calif, county center. il Fortune 82:162-4 Ag '65
COUNTY centers. See County buildings
COUNTY fairs. See Agricultural exhibitions

COUNTY recreation. See Recreation, Rural
COUPLINGS, Electric
Multiset couplers: operation and problems. il Electr World 73:36+ F '65
COUPONS
Meet Sugar Bear. J. Ciardi. Sat R 48:26 My 22 '65
See also
Trading stamps
COUPS d'etat. See Revolutions
COURAGE
Bold men, bold dreams. C. D. Bowen. Read Digest 87:49-53 Jl '65
In solitary witness: the life and death of Franz Jägerstätter, by G. C. Zahn. Review Nation 200:426-8 Ap 19 '65. T. Roszak
Other side of apathy. F. Sondern, jr. il Read Digest 86:113-16 F '65
She only cried once. L. David. il Good H 161:74-5+ S '65
What is courage? excerpt from Love, hate, fear, anger and the other lively emotions. J. Callwood. Read Digest 86:117-19 Mr '65
Young lives, brave actions. B. Clark. il Read Digest 87:187-8+ N '65
COURIER-journal
Noble experiment in Louisville; six-column newspaper. R. L. Tobin. il Sat R 48:139-40 Mr 13 '65
COURRÈGES, André
I warned my house, no Duchess; interview, ed. by N. Liber. por Life 58:54+ My 21 '65

about
After Courrèges, what future for the haute couture? F. Giraud. il por N Y Times Mag p50-1+ S 12 '65
Courage of Courrèges. il Time 85:48+ Ap 9 '65
Courrèges. V. Leduc. il Vogue 145:208-9+ My '65
Courrèges controversy. A. Zill. il por Look 29:98-100 Jl 13 '65
High style. il Newsweek 65:86 Mr 22 '65
Lord of the space ladies. il pors Life 58:47-50+ My 21 '61
Where did all the women go? T. Meehan. il por Sat Eve Post 238:26-31 S 11 '65
COURSES of study
Curriculum revolution in the 'sixties: address, July 1964. J. Goodlad. il Library J 90:927-31 F 15 '65
Pressures on students and teachers; questions and answers. G. Hechinger and F. M. Hechinger. McCalls 92:180-1 Ap '65
Reform movement or panacea? curriculum development. T. R. Sizer. il Sat R 48:52-4+ Je 19 '65
Scholastic teacher interview: ed. by H. Langer. A. W. Foshay. Sr Schol 86:6T-9T F 18 '65
Toward a B.A. in alcohol? proposal to provide students with group experiences in drinking. il Time 87:64+ Ja 21 '66
See also
Association for supervision and curriculum development
Colleges and universities—Curriculum
English language—Courses of study
High schools—Curriculum
Vocational education
COURT, Contempt of. See Contempt of court
COURT martial. See Courts martial
COURT of customs and patent appeals. See United States—Court of customs and patent appeals
COURT of human rights. See European court of human rights
COURT reporting (by newspapers) See Newspaper court reporting
COURTESY
Children's manners. A. Vanderbilt. Ladies Home J 82:52 Je '65
Interracial etiquette. America 112:796 My 29 '65
What do you get for what you pay? courteous service. M. Mannes. McCalls 92:14+ Jl '65
What manner of men? ill-mannered Americans. il Newsweek 66:92+ N 1 '65
See also
Sportsmanship
COURTHOUSES
Mechanical services for a large courthouse; temperature control. A. Schroeder. il Arch Rec 138:205-8 O '65
COURTNEY, Marguerite
Keeping company with a parakeet. Harper 230:30+ My '65; Same abr. with title Petie, the perplexing parakeet. Read Digest 87: 123-6 Ag '65
COURTROOMS
No longer decrepit and dull; County court house in Mankato, Minn. il Am City 80: 124 O '65

COURTRY, Sylvaine Thybon de, baroness. See
Thybon de Courtry, S.
COURTS
See also
Criminal procedure
Domestic relations courts
Jury
Justice, Administration of
Oaths

California
Pioneering California; California Supreme
court. il Time 87:48-9 Ja 21 '66

Great Britain
Call her mister. Time 86:40 Ag 27 '65

Oklahoma
Oklahoma's shocking scandal; bribery
charges against justices. il Time 85:47 Ap
16 '65

Pennsylvania
Price-tag problem; putting a specific price
tag on the injury at issue. Time 86:59 O 1
'65

Russia
See also
Law—Russia

United States
Mississippi's best; J. P. Coleman, new
member of Fifth circuit Court of appeals.
Time 86:17-18 Jl 23 '65
U.S. judge would restrict police; excerpts
from letter with reply by N. B. Katzen-
bach. D. L. Bazelon. U S News 59:66-7 Ag
16 '65
Why many criminals go free; indictment
delay tactics. M. T. Bloom. Read Digest
87:19-20+ Ag '65
See also
Justice, Administration of—United States
United States—Supreme court
COURTS, Military. See Courts martial
COURTS martial
Service courts of friendly foreign forces
within the United States; proclamation,
October 10, 1965. L. B. Johnson. Dept State
Bul 53:758 N 8 '65
Serviceman's rights; Uniform code of military
justice. il Time 86:36+ Ag 13 '65
COURTSHIP
Legitimate pickup. A. Ellis and R. Nathan.
il Mlle 61:198+ My '65
See also
Dating
COURTSHIP of animals
Froggie went a-courtin; excerpt from Sex
life of the animals. H. Wendt. il Sat R 48:
50 S 4 '65
Territorial behavior among puku in Zambia.
A. De Vos. il Science 148:1752-3 Je 25 '65
COURTSHIP of insects
Courtship behavior of arachnids. T. Savory.
il Natur Hist 74:52-6 My '65
Insect mating behavior: endocrine control
of a chemical communication system.
R. H. Barth, jr. bibliog il Science 149:
882-3 Ag 20 '65
COURTYARDS
Small courtyard with a spacious look. il Pop
Gard 16:41 Mr '65
COUSINS, Frank
Setback for socialism; British vote a blow
to Wilson. il U S News 58:20 F 1 '65
COUSINS, Margaret
Incident at Versailles. McCalls 92:114-15+ My
'65
San Antonio, I love you! McCalls 93:72+ N
'65
COUSINS, Norman
Life begins at twenty-five. Sat R 48:26-8
Ap 24 '65; Correction. 48:49 My 22 '65
Outstretched hand. Sat R 48:20-1 F 13 '65
What matters about Schweitzer. Sat R 48:
30-2 S 25 '65
COUSTEAU, Jacques Yves
Talk with Cousteau; ed. by E. Miller. por
Seventeen 24:56 F '65
about
Up from success. il por Time 86:72 O 22 '65
COUSY, Bob
Playing it nice and Cousy. H. L. Masin. il
por Sr Schol 86:32 Mr 18 '65
COUTURIERS. See Costume designers
COVARRUBIAS, John
Kamikaze in Nevada. il Newsweek 65:30
Ap 26 '65
COUVE DE MURVILLE, Maurice
International situation; address, October 20,
1965. Vital Speeches 32:35-9 N 15 '65
about
De Gaulle carries on. il por Newsweek 66:
55-6 N 15 '65

COVELL, Roger
Sutherland comes home. Hi Fi 15:162-3 O '65
COVENANT House, Philadelphia. See Philadel-
phia—Social work
COVENANT; story. See Cassill, R. V.
COVENT Garden. See London—Covent Gar-
den
COVENT Garden opera company
Other side; thwarted attempt to present
Schönberg's Moses and Aaron at the Royal
opera house. T. Heinitz. Sat R 48:43 Jl 31
'65
COVER design. See Book covers
COVER plants
Bulbs & groundcovers, good bedfellows. R. M.
Peters. il Pop Gard 16:46-7 S '65
Groundcovers for the Northwest. E. A. Wood
and C. H. Potter. il Horticulture 43:36-7+
N '65
Groundcovers for the South. F. Heutte. il
Horticulture 43:22-3+ Je '65
Using roses as ground covers. il Sunset 134:
178+ F '65
See also
Pachysandra
COVERED bridges
Bridges with a past. G. Gould and T. Gould.
il Hobbies 70:124-5+ Ag '65
COVERLETS
Quilts and coverlets; homespuns of the North-
west Territory. il Antiques 87:327-9 Mr '65
COVERS, Book. See Book covers
COVINA, Calif.
Smartness in police uniform. il Am City 80:
22 Jl '65
COWAN, John
Baptism by sunset. Vogue 147:128+ Ja 15
'66
COWARD, Noel
Bon voyage; story. McCalls 92:86-7 Je '65
COWBIRDS
Nature note. Sci N L 87:139 F 27 '65
COWBOY hall of fame. See National cowboy
hall of fame and western heritage center
COWBOYS
Negro cowboys, by P. Durham and E. L.
Jones. Review
Time il 85:103+ F 26 '65
See also
Gauchos
McCauley, J. E.
National cowboy hall of fame and western
heritage center
COWDRAY, Weetman John Churchill Pearson,
3d viscount
Country lord and the city lord. por Fortune
72:104 D '65
COWES regatta. See Regattas
COWES-Torquay offshore powerboat race. See
Motor boat racing
COWES week. See Regattas
COWLES, Carolyn A. See Fink, M. A. jt. auth.
COWLES, John, Jr
New hand at Harper's. il por Newsweek 65:
98 My 10 '65
COWLES, Virginia
In East Africa and London, two writing
women. Vogue 145:98 Ap 1 '65
Private line from London (cont) Vogue 145:
205-6 Mr 1; 156 Mr 15; 159-60 Je; 146:34
Ag 15 '65
COWLEY, Malcolm, and Cowley, Robert
(eds) Memoranda of a decade; excerpts. Am
Heritage 16:33-40 Ag '65
COWLEY, Robert. See Cowley, M. jt. ed.
COWRIES
Golden cowry. A. G. Melvin. il Hobbies 70:130
Je '65
COWS
See also
Dairying
Heifers
Milking

Breeding
See Cattle breeding

Care
See also
Calves—Care

Diseases and pests
Now dairymen squirt away ketosis. il Farm
J 89:48 Ap '65
See also
Mastitis

Feeding
Do cows need fancy feed? symposium. il
Farm J 89:A7 Jl '65
He full-feeds grain, with $3.50 milk! D.
Hagen. il Farm J 89:34-5+ N '65
How to mix groughage. Farm J 89:50 Ap '65
How we feed college cows. A. Coletti. il Suc
Farm 63:106+ F '65

COWS—Feeding—*Continued*
Latest on corn in silos for dairy cows. D.
Hillman. il Suc Farm 63:36-8+ Ag '65
Lesson from a champ. O. Bay. il Farm J
89:57 N '65
New silage-feeding ideas. J. R. Borcherding
and J. Albino. il Suc Farm 63:36-7 N '65
Summer dairy feeding ideas. il Suc Farm
63:54+ Je '65
Why we switched to soft corn. D. K. O'Brien.
il Farm J 89:36-7+ D '65

Grading and standardization
They're here: graded heifers. N. Reeder. il
Farm J 89:62E O '65

Milk production
See Milk—Production

Testing
Those new-fangled dairy records. J. R.
Borcherding. il Suc Farm 63:56-7+ My '65

COWS, Cooling of. See Livestock, Cooling of

COWS, Sacred. See Cows in religion, folklore, etc.

COWS in religion, folklore, etc.
Why Go Matha is loved. R. K. Narayan. il
N Y Times Mag p 12-13+ My 30 '65

COX, Arthur N. and others
Thirty-six miles in the shadow. Sky & Tel
30:72-5 Ag '65

COX, Claire
How to beat the high cost of college; excerpts. Seventeen 24:134-5+ F '65

COX, Harvey
Beyond Bonhoeffer? Commonweal 82:653-7 S
17 '65
Ferment in the churches; the new Christian
soldiers. Nation 201:216-20 O 11 '65
Marx, the many, and the mentors. Sat R 48:
107-8 S 18 '65
Place and purpose of theology. Christian
Cent 83:7-9 Ja 5 '66
Secular city. Commonweal 83:186-9 N 12 '65
What are we celebrating, and why? Red-
book 126:40-1+ D '65
about
Today's city: threat or promise? M. L. Stack-
house. Christian Cent 82:1537-41 D 15 '65

COX, James R.
Lending research library. por Library J 90:
2219-25 My 15 '65

COX, Joan Etchingham
Capsule history of perfume. Holiday 38:44-5
S '65

COX, Robert E.
(ed) Gleanings for ATM's. See issues of Sky
and telescope

COX, Verne C. and Valenstein, E. S.
Attenuation of aversive properties of peripheral shock by hypothalamic stimulation.
bibliog Science 149:323-5 Jl 16 '65

COX, William Harold
Impeach Judge Cox. A. M. Bickel. New
Repub 153:13 S 4 '65
No federal case? por Newsweek 65:25 Mr 8
'65
True to form. Time 85:25 Mr 5 '65

COXE, Louis
Fire in winter; poem. Atlan 215:83 Ap '65

COXSACKIE viruses
Coxsackie A9 virus: mutation from drug dependence to drug independence. H. J.
Eggers and I. Tamm. bibliog il Science 148:
97-8 Ap 2 '65

COY, John
John Coy dance company. 92nd street Y.
J. Maskey. Dance Mag 39:29 F '65

COYOTE hunting
Song of the coyote. B. W. Dalrymple. il Outdoor Life 135:64-5+ Je '65

COYOTES
Howl over coyotes; Pasadena, Calif. Nat
Parks Mag 39:25 N '65

COZUMEL ISLAND
Cozumel: a Mexican isle for the idle; with
report by M. Leatherbee. il Life 58:120-3+
Mr 5 '65
Mexico: *ayer, hoy y mañana*. R. Joseph. il
Esquire 64:104-6 N '65

CRAB apples
Selecting the right crabapple. R. C. Hands.
Horticulture 43:16 Ap '65

CRAB CREEK
Ghosts along Crab Creek. il Sunset 134:72+
My '65

CRABAPPLES. See Crab apples

CRABB, A. L.
Hint of the future in the last day program;
story. PTA Mag 60:15-17 D '65

CRABB, Cecil V. Jr
(ed) Nonalignment in foreign affairs. bibliog f Ann Am Acad 362:1-138 N '65
United States and the neutralists: a decade
in perspective. bibliog f Ann Am Acad
362:92-101 N '65
—See Babaa, K. I. jt. auth.

CRABS
United States and U.S.S.R. sign king crab
fishing agreement; Department announcement, February 6, 1965, with text of agreement. Dept State Bul 52:320-1 Mr 1 '65
See also
Cookery—Fish

CRABS eye. See Eye (crustacea)

CRABTREE, Bruce
Man and his boat. Yachting 118:55-7+ O '65

CRADDOCK, Campbell, and others
Glossopteris discovered in west Antarctica.
bibliog Science 148:634-7 Ap 30 '65

CRAFT, Robert
Sacre de Diaghilev. Vogue 145:124-5+ Ap 15
'65

CRAFTS. See Arts and crafts; Handicraft

CRAFTSMANSHIP
See also
Fisher body craftsman's guild

CRAFTSMEN. See Labor and laboring classes

CRAIG, Gordon A.
Pillars of ice. Reporter 32:39-40 Je 17 '65
Waging war with Winston. Reporter 33:43-5
S 9 '65

CRAIG, James
1840 North Carolina capitol and its furniture.
Antiques 88:205-7 Ag '65

CRAIG, James B.
B. Frank Heintzleman: history's child. Am
For 71:39 Ag '65
How private are private lands? Am For 71:
22-3+ D '65
—and Moore, I. M.
White House conference on natural beauty.
Am For 71:12-15 Je '65

CRAIG, Ralph C.
Pleasures of photography. il por Pop Phot
56:110-12 My '65

CRAIN, Stanley M. See Bornstein, M. B. jt.
auth.

CRAMER, Jean
Painting on burlap. Design 67:34-5 N '65

CRAMER, William C.
Excerpt from remarks, September 20, 1965.
Cong Digest 44:282+ N '65

CRAMPTON, Bruce
Double, double toil and trouble. A. Wright.
il por Sports Illus 22:12-17 F 1 '65

CRAMPTON, M. R.
Faraday society discussion: proton transfer
processes. Science 149:208-9 Jl 9 '65

CRANBERRIES
Juicing up cranberry sales. J. Olesky. Duns
R 85:84-5 Ap '65
Spreading sassamanesh; broader base for in-
dustry. il Time 86:104 N 12 '65
See also
Cookery—Fruit

CRANBERRY GLADES. See Richwood, W.Va.

CRANE, Frances
Research for the mystery writer. Writer 78:
15-17 F '65

CRANE, Julian C. and Van Overbeek, J.
Kinin-induced parthenocarpy in the fig, ficus
carica L. bibliog Science 147:1468-9 Mr 19
'65

CRANE, Les
Lowering the Crane. Newsweek 65:83 Mr 8
'65

CRANE, Paul
Tory change at the top. America 113:159 Ag
14 '65

CRANE, Ralph
Alaska: the hard country; photographs. Life
59:64-79 O 1 '65
about
He gets up earlier and goes more places.
G. P. Hunt. por Life 59:7 O 1 '65

CRANES (birds)
Bird named Lady, or Lyndon; whooping
crane. J. O'Reilly. il Sports Illus 22:46-7 F
1 '65
Day we rescued a whooping crane. N. S.
Novakowski. il Audubon Mag 67:230-3 Jl
'65
Endangered species report; whooping crane
and trumpeter swan. Nat Parks Mag 40:21
Ja '66
Whooper nest sits for a rare portrait. L. H.
Walkinshaw. il Audubon Mag 67:299-301
S '65
Whooping crane. Sci N L 87:366 Je 5 '65

CRANHAM, Gerry
Big week at Cowes; photographs. Sports
Illus 23:30-4 Jl 12 '65

CRANIN, A. Norman, and Lobsenz, N. M.
Your children's teeth. Redbook 125:55-62 O
'65
CRANK calls. See Telephone calls
CRANKSHAW, Edward
Russia discovers the customer is always
right. N Y Times Mag p26-7+ Mr 28 '65
CRAPE myrtle
Great flowering plant for hot summers. il
Sunset 134:266-7 Je '65
CRASH diets. See Diet
CRASSOSTREA. See Oysters
CRATER LAKE NATIONAL PARK
Life as a fire lookout in Crater Lake National
Park. L. Neuberger and R. Neuberger. il
Nat Parks Mag 39:16-19 Ag '65
Mazama and Glacier Peak pumice glass: uni-
formity of refractive index after weather-
ing. V. C. Steen and R. Fryxell. bibliog il
Science 150:878-80 N 12 '65
Mazama and Glacier Peak volcanic ash lay-
ers: relative ages. R. Fryxell. bibliog il Sci-
ence 147:1288-90 Mr 12 '65
Titanium dioxide in pyroclastic layers from
volcanoes in the Cascade Range. G. K.
Czamanske and S. C. Porter. bibliog il Sci-
ence 150:1022-5 N 19 '65
CRATERS
Better cratering extrapolation seen. il Miss
& Roc 16:23-4 Mr 1 '65
Largest volcanic crater? Valle Grande. il
Sunset 135:66+ N '65
See also
Haleakala
Meteorite craters
CRATERS, Moon. See Moon—Surface
CRAWFORD, Cheryl
How to succeed in the theatre without really
being successful. E. Dundy. il Esquire 63:
88-9+ My '65
CRAWFORD, David L.
Kitt Peak 150-inch telescope. por Sky & Tel
29:268-73 My '65
Problems of constructing large telescopes.
Sky & Tel 29:354-5 Je '65
CRAWFORD, Jack, Jr
Ship; Camels pass in smoke; Behind the
brow; Bright flesh; I stand as on a battle-
ground; poems. Poetry 105:304-7 F '65
Suddenly falling earth. Poetry 105:410-14 Mr
'65
CRAWFORD, Joan
Second fame: good food. N. Lyon. il por
Vogue 146:212-14 N 1 '65
CRAWFORD, Kenneth
Kidding the kids. por Newsweek 65:47 My
10 '65; Same abr. with title Let's not kid
the kids about Vietnam. Read Digest 87:
56-7 Jl '65
Washington. See issues of Newsweek
CRAWFORD, Marc
In a roaring inferno burn, baby, burn. Life
59:27 Ag 27 '65
CRAWFORDVILLE, Ga.
Even Stephens. il Time 86:31 O 15 '65
Georgia: a haymaker and a flying tackle. il
Life 59:47 O 22 '65
Twilight zone. il Newsweek 66:48 O 18 '65
CRAWHALL, J. C. and Thompson, C. J.
Cystinuria: effect of D-penicillamine on plas-
ma and urinary cystine concentrations.
bibliog Science 147:1459-60 Mr 19 '65
CRAWLER tractors
Apollo crawler bearing design changed. il
Aviation W 83:100 N 8 '65
How about a crawler? il Suc Farm 63:62 F
'65
Leveling trouble plagues crawler. S. Butler.
il Miss & Roc 16:17 My 10 '65
CRAYFISH
Crusty crustacean. E. P. Creaser, sr. il
Audubon Mag 67:364-5 N '65
CREAL, Margaret
Prairie winter. Ladies Home J 82:60-1+
D '65
CREAM, Sour
See also
Cookery—Cream, Sour
CREASER, Edwin P.
Crusty crustacean. Audubon Mag 67:364-5 N
'65
CREASEY, John
Prolific Mr Creasey stumps television panel. il
por Pub W 187:99 F 8 '65
CREASING of textiles
Clothes that never need ironing: wash-and-
wears with permanent press. Changing T
19:11-12 N '65
Crease & increase: Koratron co. il Time 86:88
D 17 '65
Farewell to wrinkles; permanent press fabrics.
il Bsns W p34+ S 18 '65
Permanent press clothing. il Consumer Bul
48:6-10 N '65

Permanent-press shirts. il Consumer Rep 30:
534-5 N '65
Shirts and blouses permanent press? well,
yes if you have an electric or gas dryer. il
Consumer Bul 49:37-40 Ja '66
See also
Cotton fabrics—Creasing
CREATION
See also
Cosmogony
CREATION (literary, artistic, etc)
Art of distortion. R. Barrio. il Design 67:14-17
N '65
Arthur Seller: pictures by design, not acci-
dent. A. Seller. il Pop Phot 57:150-1+ N
'65
Calendar of creation. H. Rosenberg. Vogue
146:228-9 S 1 '65
Call for originality. America 112:244 F 20
'65
Can the public school foster creativity? R. J.
Mueller; reply. J. O. Goodsell. Sat R 48:
96 F 20 '65
Does anyone know what creative writing is?
J. D. Adams. Sat R 48:23-5 S 18 '65
Have faith in your subconscious. C. Mercer.
Writer 78:12-14 Mr '65
How a writer finds his material. E. W.
Stone. il Harper 231:157-61 N '65
I like to present a problematical situation,
and let the viewer come to grips with it;
interview, ed. by H. M. Kinzer. J. Uels-
mann. il Pop Phot 57:140-3+ N '65
Keppler on the SLR; creativity vs the me-
chanics. H. Keppler. il Mod Phot 29:112+
O '65
Painting with film. J. Foldes. il U S Cam-
era 28:50-1+ O '65
Parthenon and the bull. I. Pirovano. il Amér-
icas 17:33-5 Jl '65
Saturday classes in the creative arts. M. R.
Mancini and J. M. Someroski. il Sch Arts
64:27-34 F '65
Silences, when writers don't write; adapta-
tion of address. T. Olsen. il Harper 231:
153-6+ O '65
Sing and tell; with study-discussion program,
by R. Strang. K. Osborn and P. P. W.
Knapp. bibliog il PTA Mag 59:7-9, 34 Mr
'65
Think with me about creativity, by E. W.
Eisner. Review
Sch Arts 65:50 O '65. R. J. Saunders
Thinking man's waste land; excerpts from
address. S. Bellow. Sat R 48:20 Ap 3 '65
Translating reality into fiction; excerpt
from Modern fiction techniques. F. A.
Rockwell. Writer 78:16-18+ Jl '65
We want to make something. J. Lidstone. il
Sch Arts 65:11-15 S '65
What every writer wants. J. le Carré. il Har-
per 231:142-5 N '65
Where have all the young writers gone? re-
port on the 1965 student magazine contest.
S. B. Chickering. il Sat R 48:26-7 O 9 '65
Your child deserves more than packaged cre-
ativity. K. Gay. Am Home 68:15+ Ap '65
CREATIVE ability. See Creation (literary,
artistic, etc)
CREATIVE dramatics. See Childrens plays
CREATIVE imagination. See Imagination
CREATIVE playthings, incorporated
Toymaker for schools moves into the home.
il Bsns W p90-2+ O 9 '65
CREATIVE teaching. See Teaching
CREATIVE thinking. See Thought and think-
ing
CREATIVE writing. See English language—
Composition—Creative activities
CREDIT
Bait the hook with merchandise. il Con-
sumer Rep 30:457-61 S '65
Borrowers want more than ever. il Bsns W
p64-5 Ja 1 '66
Borrowing money? here's what's new. R. E.
Geyer. Suc Farm 63:45+ My '65
Credit at the crossroads. il Fortune 71:32+
My '65
Credit men begin to look wary; consumer
borrowing heading up. il Bsns W p54 My
22 '65
Installment credit soars to a record; with
table. Bsns W p46+ Ja 8 '66
Is credit quality getting too low? private
debt outpaced economic growth. il Bsns W
p75-6+ O 2 '65
Living high on the old homestead; refinancing
mortgages. il Bsns W p47-8 Ap 24 '65
Money debate. il Fortune 72:52+ D '65
Pleasures & pitfalls of being in debt; Time
essay. Time 86:20-1 Jl 2 '65; Same abr.
Read Digest 87:87-90 O '65

CREDIT—*Continued*
Tips on borrowing to buy machinery.. J. Brake. il Suc Farm 64:84 Ja '66
Use these eight rules for credit buying. Suc Farm 63:98 My '65
See also
Agricultural credit
Debt
Discount
Farm finance
Instalment plan
Loans
Loans, Bank
Loans, Personal
CREDIT, Municipal. See Municipal finance
CREDIT cards
Charge-it plan that really took off; Bank-Americards. il Bsns W p58+ F 27 '65
Credit card companies come into the chips. Bsns W p54+ S 4 '65
First nation's full house. il Time 86:102+ O 1 '65
Flying on air. Time 85:101-101A F 5 '65
Hole card; credit cards for medical and funeral expenses. Newsweek 65:86 Mr 22 '65
Toward a cashless society. il Time 86:97A N 5 '65
See also
Diners' club, incorporated
CREDIT unions
Credit union reverie. R. Q. Strain. NEA J 54:29-30 Mr '65
Progress of credit unions. America 113:274 S 18 '65
CREEDS
Creeds and confessions. R. M. Brown. Commonweal 83:211-14 N 19 '65
Script-writers take over; Presbyterians confession of faith. M. E. Marty. Christian Cent 82:733-5 Je 9 '65
CREEGAN, Robert F.
Albany symposium on the renaissance. Sch & Soc 93:302-3 Sum '65
CREEKMORE, C. J.
Decision east of Suez. Nat R 17:457-9 Je 1 '65
CREEL, Austin B.
Unscrewing the inscrutable? Christian Cent 82:894+ Jl 14 '65
CREEL. H. G.
Role of the horse in Chinese history. bibliog f Am Hist R 70:647-72 Ap '65
CREELEY, Robert
Answer; Dimensions; Night, sky; World; poems. Poetry 106:26-31 Ap '65
. . . Paradise/our/speech. . . Poetry 107:52-5 O '65
CREEPER; drama. See Macaulay, P.
CRÈME brûlée. See Custards
CREMER, Jan
Trade winds. J. Beatty, jr. Sat R 48:14 O 23 '65
CREMER, Natalie E. and others
Nonspecific binding of complement by digestion fragments from antiviral gamma globulin. bibliog Science 149:84-5 Jl 2 '65
CREMIN, Lawrence A.
Making history. por Newsweek 65:58 Mr 8 '65
CRENNA, Richard
Slattery's saga. il por Newsweek 65:82+ My 31 '65
CRENSHAW, John W.
Radiation-induced increases in fitness in the flour beetle tribolium confusum. bibliog Science 149:426-7 Jl 23 '65
CRENSON, Gus A.
How to move 15,400,000 children. por Am Ed 1:10-12 Jl '65
CRESCITELLI, Frederick, and Pollack, J. D.
Color vision in the antelope ground squirrel. bibliog Science 150:1316-18 D 3 '65
CRESPIN. Régine
Stars at home. il pors Opera N 29:26-8 Ap 17 '65
Tosca at last. R. Lawrence. il Hi Fi 15:113-14 Je '65
CRESS, Cy
Costa Rica. Travel 124:56-8+ S '65
CRESSMAN, George P.
Numerical weather prediction in daily use. bibliog Science 148:319-27 Ap 16 '65
CRESSY, Philip J. jr, and Shedlovsky, J. P.
Cosmogenic radionuclides in the bondoc meteorite. bibliog Science 148:1716-17 Je 25 '65
CRESTED flycatchers. See Flycatchers (birds)
CRESTS. See Heraldry
CRETACEOUS period. See Paleontology—Cretaceous
CRETE
Anecdotes, facetiae, satire, etc.
Wrong man on Crete. D. J. M. Cornwell. Holiday 38:74-5 D '65

Antiquities
Kato Zakro: rediscovered palace. N. Platon. il Horizon 7:76-9 Sum '65
Rediscovery of Crete. M. I. Finley. il Horizon 7:64-75 Sum '65

Description and travel
Going places, finding things in Crete. D. Beal. il House & Gard 129:18-20+ Ja '66
Those golden Greek isles. H. Sutton. il Holiday 39:62-71 Ja '66
CREVALLÉ fishing
Tough jack crevallé. G. Heinold. il Outdoor Life 135:12+ Mr '65
CREWEL work
Quick crewel for all ages. il Ladies Home J 82:76-81 S '65
CREWS, Judson
Poet facing up to life; Perfection; poems. Poetry 105:308-9 F '65
CRICKET (game)

Anecdotes, facetiae, satire, etc.
It isn't the game that's impossible, it's the people. T. S. Matthews. Vogue 146:154 D '65
CRILE. Barney
Feather of a dove; excerpt from More than booty. por Redbook 126:42-3+ Ja '66
CRIME and criminals
Aiding the victims. Commonweal 83:139-40 N 5 '65
See also
Capital punishment
Conspiracy
Crime in literature
Criminal investigation
Embezzlement
Fraud
Juvenile delinquency
Kidnaping
Murder
Parole
Police—United States
Prostitution
Robberies and assaults
Sex crimes

International aspects
See also
International criminal police organization
United Nations congress on the prevention of crime and the treatment of offenders

Law
See Criminal law

Statistics
See Criminal statistics

California
Motorcycle gangs: losers and outsiders. H. S. Thompson. il Nation 200:522-6 My 17 '65
Taxonomy to the rescue; Space-General corp.'s report. Time 86:20 S 10 '65
Wild ones; Hell's Angels, motorcycleriding hoodlums. il Newsweek 65:25 Mr 29 '65

Canada
Another nation where crime rise is a worry. U S News 58:13 Ap 26 '65

Colombia
See also
Kidnaping

Florida
Angels of the East; murder by South Florida motorcycle club outlaws. il Newsweek 66:28 D 27 '65

France
Embattled Nice; headquarters of the Riviera underworld. Newsweek 66:46 Jl 26 '65
See also
Prisons—France

Great Britain
Crime does pay because we do not back up the police. Shawcross. il N Y Times Mag p44-5+ Je 13 '65
Criminal is living in a golden age; excerpts from address, October 11, 1965. Shawcross. il U S News 59:80-2 N 1 '65
Ghosts on the moors; children's murders in Great Britain. il Time 86:54 N 5 '65
Haunted moor; charges against Ian Brady and Myra Hindley. il Newsweek 66:32 D 27 '65
Letter from London. M. Panter-Downes. New Yorker 41:57 Ja 1 '66
Limehouse gang; quicksilver robberies. Newsweek 65:89 My 24 '65
On England's misty moors, a grisly search; case of multiple murder. il Life 59:46-7 N 12 '65

CRIME and criminals—Great Britain—*Cont.*
Speedier justice in Britain: we reformed our laws in the 19th century and U.S. didn't; interview. J. Foster. U S News 58:42-3 Mr 22 '65
See also
Liverpool—Crime

Italy

Capuchin cache of embarrassment; cigaret smuggling monks. R. Espinosa. il Life 58: 38A My 28 '65
Matter of style. Newsweek 65:52+ Mr 15 '65

Kansas

Annals of crime; In cold blood, murder of H. W. Clutter family. T. Capote. New Yorker 41:57-60+ S 25; 57-60+ O 2; 58-62+ O 9; 62-4+ O 16 '65
Horror spawns a masterpiece; T. Capote's In cold blood inspired by Clutter family murders; excerpt; with report by J. Howard. il Life 60:58-72+ Ja 7 '66
In cold blood, an American tragedy; concerning T. Capote's book. il Newsweek 67:59-63 Ja 24 '66
In cold blood, by T. Capote. Review Sat R 49:35-6 Ja 22 '66. G. Hicks

Massachusetts

Reporter at large; Massachusetts correctional institution, Framingham. J. Colebrook. il New Yorker 41:47-8+ Je 12 '65

Mexico

Horse-show whodunits; series of unrelated tragedies. A. Higgins. il Sports Illus 23: 40 S 20 '65

Philippines

Dirty campaign on the corruption issue. G. De Carvalho. il Life 59:78B-80+ N 26 '65

Poland

Butchers on the block. Newsweek 66:56+ N 15 '65

Russia

Watch and ward, U.S.S.R. druzhinniki. Newsweek 65:50 Je 21 '65

Sicily

See also
Mafia

Switzerland

Exile; H. L. F. Van Vlissingen expelled for building violation. il Newsweek 66:56 O 25 '65

Turkey

Topkapi revisited; biggest armed robbery in Turkish history. il Newsweek 66:52 S 27 '65

United States

Attack on crime; And the Haters. America 112:412 Mr 27 '65
Behind the crime scare. G. Shadoan. il Nation 200:495-7 My 10 '65
Climate of crime. S. Grafton. il McCalls 92: 92-3+ Mr '65
Crime in the cities: an unnecessary crisis. W. Bowen. il Fortune 72:140-5+ D '65
Crime in the suburbs. P. Pierce. il Ebony 20:167-72 Ag '65
Crime rise: what the record shows. U S News 58:6 Ap 19 '65
Crime; rising tide. il Newsweek 66:20-2+ Ag 16 '65
Crime runs wild; will it be halted? with statements by J. E. Hoover and interview with W. H. Parker. il U S News 59:64-9 Ag 9 '65
Crime that threatens every woman. S. Grafton. McCalls 92:122-3+ F '65
Crisis in crime control. G. R. Blakey. America 113:238-40 S 4 '65
Declaration of war. Newsweek 66:30 Ag 9 '65
Faith of freedom; crime problem; address, October 19, 1965. J. E. Hoover. Vital Speeches 32:71-4 N 15 '65
Greatest need: a safe society. D. Lawrence. U S News 58:108 F 8 '65
Horse-show whodunits: series of unrelated tragedies. A. Higgins. il Sports Illus 23: 38-40 S 20 '65
Is crime in U.S. out of hand? why LBJ worries; with interview with F. E. Inbau. il U S News 58:38-43 Mr 22 '65
It's really rising. Time 86:15 D 24 '65
Lawlessness galore; address, August 26, 1965. F. E. Inbau. Vital Speeches 32:95-6 N 15 '65; Excerpt. U S News 59:82 S 13 '65
Lawlessness in U.S. warning from a top jurist; address, June 17, 1965. C. E. Whittaker. il U S News 59:60-3 Jl 5 '65

Malignant enemy. il Time 85:29 Mr 19 '65
Of crime and punishment. S. Grafton. McCalls 92:73+ Je '65
Police find lawyer friends; right of law-abiding citizens to freedom from criminal molestation. Life 59:4 Ag 20 '65
Rise in crime, as new FBI report shows it; with chart. U S News 59:10-11 Ag 2 '65
Slippery worm; G. Lemay caught. il Newsweek 66:35 O 4 '65
Terror in the streets? W. Sparks. Commonweal 82:345-8 Je 4 '65
This month's feature: moves to strengthen law enforcement. Cong Digest 44:225-56 O '65
Two good cops in bad trouble; M. Hannon and T. O'Neal. S. Alexander. Life 59:16 Jl 30 '65
U.S. judge would restrict police; excerpts from letter with reply by N. B. Katzenbach. D. L. Bazelon. U S News 59:66-7 Ag 16 '65
Up, up, up. Newsweek 66:29-30 Ag 2 '65
We ask the wrong questions about crime. W. M. McCord. il N Y Times Mag p27+ N 21 '65
West side story; death of Manny Skar. il Newsweek 66:31 S 27 '65
What do we want from our policemen? S. Grafton. il McCalls 92:110-11+ My '65
When the cops were not handcuffed. Y. Kamisar. il N Y Times Mag p34-5+ N 7 '65
Who goes to prison; caste and careerism in crime. B. Jackson. il Atlan 217:52-7 Ja '66
See also
Criminal statistics
Gambling
Gangs
Mafia
Prisons—United States
Racketeering
United States—Federal bureau of investigation
    also subhead Crime under names of cities, e.g. Chicago—Crime

CRIME and the press
British verdict on trial-by-press. A. Lewis. il N Y Times Mag p 14-15+ Je 20 '65
Code for justice? new restrictions on press releases in a federal criminal case. Newsweek 65:85 Ap 26 '65
Free press and fair trial; address, April 15, 1965. N. deB. Katzenbach. Vital Speeches 31:518-21 Je 15 '65
Trial by headline? Tucson judge issues injunction restraining local law-enforcement officials from discussing details of murder case in Arizona city. il Newsweek 66:70 D 13 '65

CRIME commission. See United States—National crime commission

CRIME detection. See Criminal investigation

CRIME in literature
Seat of power, by J. D. Horan. Review Newsweek 66:50+ Ag 16 '65
See also
Detective and mystery stories

CRIME news. See Newspapers—Crime reporting

CRIME novels. See Detective and mystery stories

CRIME prevention
Watch and ward, U.S.S.R. druzhinniki. Newsweek 65:50 Je 21 '65
See also
Juvenile delinquency—Prevention
Police
United Nations congress on the prevention of crime and the treatment of offenders

CRIME syndicates. See Crime and criminals—United States

CRIME wave. See Crime and criminals—United States

CRIMEA conference, Yalta, Russia, 1945
New evaluation of the big three; excerpts from Reckoning. Avon. il U S News 58:20 Ap 5 '65
Yalta twenty years after. B. Coste. il Nat R 17:142+ F 23 '65

CRIMINAL behavior. See Criminal psychology

CRIMINAL investigation
Century of the detective, by J. Thorwald. Review Time il 86:118+ N 12 '65
How cops spot stolen cars. W. J. Griswold. il Pop Sci 186:66-8 Mr '65
Revolution in criminal justice; Time essay. Time 86:22-3 Jl 16 '65
Snoopers & tappers; Edward V. Long's investigation into the invasion of privacy. F. J. Cook. il Nation 201:496-501 D 20 '65

CRIMINAL investigation—*Continued*
To catch a thief; new crime-detection devices. il Time 86:59 Jl 30 '65
  See also
Electronics in criminal investigation, espionage, etc.
Lie detectors
Photography in criminal investigation
Radioactivity analysis
Television in criminal investigation
United States—Federal bureau of investigation

CRIMINAL Justice, Office of. See United States—Justice, Department of—Office of criminal justice

CRIMINAL Justice bill. See Criminal law

CRIMINAL law
After Escobedo; constitutional rights of state criminal defendants. il Time 85:74-5 F 12 '65
Britain pays the victim of the crime; state compensation for victims of criminal violence. C. Hussey. il N Y Times Mag p 19-20+ F 21 '65
Criminal law and the Bill of rights. J. S. Wright. il Reporter 32:23-5 Je 3 '65
Equality v. deterrence; concerning exchange of letters between Attorney General N. Katzenbach and Chief Judge D. Bazelon of the U.S. Court of appeals. Time 86:41 Ag 13 '65
Have you ever been convicted of a felony? Midwestern district judge's remarks to boys who borrowed cars for joy-rides. Read Digest 87:99-100 S '65
Improbable cause; concerning M. Smith's and guests' arrests for possession of marijuana. il Time 87:55 Ja 14 '66
Reasonable rape; statutory rape. Time 87:49 Ja 21 '66
Running afoul of the law; Innocent offender. L. Strong. il N Y Times Mag p53-4 Ja 16 '66
Should the government compensate crime victims? pro and con discussion. Sr Schol 86:10-11 Ap 8 '65
  See also
Criminal procedure
Entrapment (law)
Obscenity (law)

CRIMINAL procedure
Another confession problem: unjoining the joint trial. il Time 86:31 D 24 '65
As Congress takes a hand in war against rising crime. il U S News 59:10 S 13 '65
Confession controversy. il Time 86:62+ D 3 '65
Court & the cop; panel at conference of federal judges and lawyers. Time 86:74 S 17 '65
Court vs the police. Life 58:4 My '65
Crime in the streets and the new McCarthyism; accusing people in high places of being soft on criminals. J. S. Wright. New Repub 153:10-11 O 9 '65; Discussion. 153:38 O 23; 28 O 30; 37-8 N 13 '65
Criminal is living in a golden age; excerpts from address, October 11, 1965. Shawcross. il U S News 59:80-2 N 1 '65
Doughty dean's defense; Supreme court's reversal of state criminal decisions. il Time 85:63 My 21 '65
Fighting crime; Senate bill on new interpretation of Mallory rule. A. M. Bickel. New Repub 153:11-12 S 18 '65; Discussion. 153:38 O 2; 36-8 O 16 '65
Freeing people & police. Time 86:47 Ag 20 '65
Gideon's impact; lawyers for indigents in trials of serious crimes. Time 86:39 D 17 '65
Orderly public procedures; public trial for demonstrators in Russia. Time 86:27 D 24 '65
Policing the police; undesirable restrictions by Supreme court. H. L. Packer. New Repub 153:17-21 S 4 '65; Reply. J. R. Piland. 153:38 O 16 '65
Revolution in criminal justice; Time essay. Time 86:22-3 Jl 16 '65
This month's feature: moves to strengthen law enforcement. Cong Digest 44:225-56 O '65
Why many criminals go free; indictment delay tactics. M. T. Bloom. Read Digest 87:19-20+ Ag '65
Winner take nothing. il Time 85:46 Ap 23 '65
  See also
Arrest
Bail
Jury

CRIMINAL psychology
Anatomy of violence. J. P. Scott. il Nation 200:662-6 Je 21 '65
  See also
Forensic psychiatry
Psychology, Pathological

CRIMINAL statistics
Safest large city. il Am City 80:160+ Ag '65

CRIMMIN, Eileen
Corrosion of metals under water. Motor B 115:33-4+ Mr '65
Gold cup. Motor B 116:116-17 S '65
Love lyrics to a lake. Motor B 116:40-1+ S '65
One year later, what happened in Alaska. Sci Digest 57:42-6 Mr '65
Pain clinic. Sci Digest 57:66-70 F '65
Portrait of a racing lady; S. M. McDonald. Motor B 116:115-16 Ag '65
Whatta way to go! See issues of Motor boating

CRINOIDS
Nature note; sea lilies. Sci N L 88:363 D 4 '65

CRIPPLES
Rehabilitation
  See Rehabilitation

CRIST, Judith (Klein)
Opinion, please from New York. Mlle 61:12+ Jl '65
Slaughter of the innocents. Reporter 33:42-3 N 18 '65
  about
Super pan. il por Time 85:48 My 14 '65

CRIST, Mary
In my opinion. por Seventeen 24:179 Je '65

CRISTOFANO, Sam
Slurry seal drops costs, boosts quality. Am City 80:96-8 F '65

CRISWELL, Marianne
My mother and Joey; story. Seventeen 24:96-7 Je '65

CRITCHFIELD, Richard
Background to conflict. Reporter 33:28-30 N 4 '65

CRITES, Stephen
Beloved of cats; poem. Christian Cent 82:710 Je 2 '65

CRITIC (periodical)
Fifteen most important; Catholics in U.S.A. Christian Cent 82:1591 D 22 '65

CRITICAL path analysis
Swedes adopt PERT for Viggen program. il Aviation W 82:257+ Je 14 '65

CRITICAL point
Critical-point phenomena; report on conference. M. S. Green. Science 150:229-32+ O 8 '65

CRITICISM
Bishops and criticisms. Commonweal 83:173 N 12 '65
  See also
Dramatic criticism
Literary criticism
Moving picture plays—Criticisms, plots, etc.
Music—History and criticism
Television criticism

CRITICISM, Personal. See Self evaluation

CRITICS
Big four; music critics of the golden age: H. E. Krehbiel, H. T. Finck, W. J. Henderson and J. G. Huneker. E. H. Huneker. il Opera N 30:8-13 D 18 '65
Common reader and the uncommon critic. C. Fadiman. Holiday 39:109-11 Ja '66
Critical thoughts; quotations; comp. by G. Flatley. il N Y Times Mag p 117+ S 19 '65
Doctor in the house; drama critic. E. Norton. il Newsweek 65:76 Ap 12 '65
England's stingingest gadfly; K. Tynan. G. Smith. il N Y Times Mag p26-7+ Ja 9 '66
New man on the aisle; S. Kauffmann comes to the Times. Newsweek 66:92 D 20 '65
New reviewers address PPA luncheon. Pub W 188:36-7 N 1 '65
Useful critic. A. Kazin. Atlan 216:73-4+ D '65
View from Women's wear; drama critic. il Time 86:109-10 N 5 '65
  See also
Art critics
Dramatic criticism

Anecdotes, facetiae, satire, etc.
My wife, the critic; the human comedy. M. Kitman. il Sat Eve Post 238:18 My 22 '65

CRITTENDEN, Brian S.
Religious liberty; study in doctrinal development. Cath World 200:354-5+ Mr '65

CRITTENDEN, Rupert
Sowing future trouble. Nation 201:70 Ag 16 '65

CROAGH PATRICK
Up Ireland's holy mountain. il Look 29:78-9+ Mr 23 '65

CROCE, Arlene
Ballet. Nat R 17:607-9 Jl 13 '65
Movies (cont) Nat R 17:1104-5+ N 30 '65

CROCKER, John
Change at Groton. il por Newsweek 65:79
Je 28 '65
CROCKER, Thomas D.
In Polk & Hillsborough Counties, Florida.
Bul Atomic Sci 21:17-19 Je '65
CROCODILE fish. See Ice fish, Antarctic
CROCUSES
Crocus by the dozens. il Flower Grower 52:
26-7 S '65
CROCUSES, Autumn. See Autumn crocuses
CROFUT, Bill
Senior scholastic interview; ed. by R. Hem-
ming. por Sr Schol 86:20 Mr 11 '65
La CROIX. See Paris—Newspapers
CROLY, Herbert David
Croly and The promise of American life.
A. Schlesinger, jr. New Repub 152:17-22
My 8 '65
CROMER, George Rowland Stanley Baring,
3d earl of
Protector of the pound. por Time 85:90 F 26
'65
CRONE additive C. See Photography—Develop-
ing and developers
CRONKITE, Walter
Aboard the 35' ketch Wyntie with Walter
Cronkite. G. Sloane. il pors Motor B 116:
42-3 Ag '65
Pad 19. New Yorker 41:38-40 Ap 3 '65
CROOK, Harry G.
Union pressures for pension changes. Mo
Labor R 88:402 Ap '65
CROOK, Mel
More power to you. See issues of Yachting
CROONERS. See Singers
CROPS
Crops news. See issues of Farm Journal
What's new. See issues of Successful farm-
ing
Statistics
See Agriculture—Statistics
CROPS and climate. See Plants, Effect of
climate on
CROPS reports. See Agriculture—Statistics
CROSBY, Alexander
Library school at Liberty bell. Library J
90:2334-5 My 15 '65
Publishing from the cider mill. Pub W 188:
41-3 Jl 5 '65
CROSBY, Bing
Bing's bash. il por Newsweek 67:78 Ja 24
'66
CROSBY, H. Ashton
Nato tomorrow. Bul Atomic Sci 21:18-21
My '65
CROSBY, John
To serve the cause of opera. P. J. Smith. il
Hi Fi 15:198+ N '65
CROSBY, Muriel
Everybody gets into the act. NEA J 54:22-4
N '65
about
Wilmington finds an answer; city salvages
underprivileged pupils. il pors Ebony 20:
57-60+ Jl '65
CROSKERY, Robert William
Essence of the ministry; address, June 6,
1965. Vital Speeches 31:570-2 Jl 1 '65
CROSS, Beverley
Boeing-Boeing; adaptation of play by M.
Camoletti. Criticism
New Yorker 40:76 F 13 '65
Newsweek 65:84 F 15 '65
CROSS, Gilbert
Marvel of maps. Holiday 38:106+ Jl '65
CROSS, Jennifer
Recompense for violence. Nation 201:304-5 N
1 '65
CROSS and crosses
Cross that inflames a city; controversy over
cross erected in Eugene, Ore. T. Arm-
brister. il Sat Eve Post 238:36-7 Jl 3 '65
CROSS breeding. See Hybridization
CROSS country skiing. See Skis and skiing
CROSSCUT saws. See Saws
CROSSING over (genetics)
Hybrid resistance to parental marrow grafts:
association with the K region of H-2.
G. Cudkowicz and J. H. Stimpfling. bibliog
il Science 144:1339-40 Je 12 '64; Correction.
147:1056 F 26 '65
CROSSMAN, E. R. F. W.
Model for the prediction of manpower require-
ments; excerpt from address, April 15, 1965.
bibliog f Mo Labor R 88:669-71 Je '65
CROSSMAN, Patricia
Boy in a box; story. Redbook 126:74-5 N '65
Time out of yesterday; story. Good H 160:
78-9 Je '65

CROSSWORD puzzles
World's hardest crossword puzzle. il Esquire
63:77 F '65
CROSTHWAIT, Charles
Censorship and the school library. bibliog
por Wilson Lib Bul 39:670-2 Ap '65
CROTHERS, Bill
One Canadian takes charge of three meets.
G. S. Brown. por Sports Illus 22:48-9 F 8
'65
CROUCH, Winston W.
Conflict and co-operation among local gov-
ernments in the metropolis. bibliog f Ann
Am Acad 359:60-70 My '65
CROW, John
Schools for the first Americans. por Am Ed
1:15-22 O '65
CROW, Trammell
His bets are still on real estate. pors Bsns W
p 140+ S 18 '65
CROWE, Cecily T.
Kilraven castle; story. Redbook 126:147 D '65
CROWELL, David H. and others
Galvanic skin reflex in newborn humans.
bibliog Science 148:1108-11 My 21 '65
CROWELL, Robert L.
Little bit of censoring. por Wilson Lib Bul
39:652-7 Ap '65
CROWELL Collier and Macmillan, incorporated
Collier's affair; a rueful memoir; excerpt
from personal file. P. C. Smith; reply. W.
Wirsig. Esquire 63:150+ Je '65
Crowell-Collier renamed; new directors
elected. il Pub W 187:40 My 17 '65
Crowell Collier to buy Berlitz language
schools. Pub W 188:68 D 27 '65
New Crowell Collier. Newsweek 66:86 N 22
'65
CROWELL-Collier publishing company. See
Crowell Collier and Macmillan, incorporated
CROWLEY, Elmer S.
Breakthrough for professional autonomy.
NEA J 54:46-7 N '65
CROWN, James Tracy
Symbol of a moment. Nation 200:707-8 Je
28 '65
CROWN gall
Agrobacterium tumefaciens; thermal inacti-
vation of tumor-inducing ability. J. A. Lip-
pincott and B. B. Lippincott. bibliog il Sci-
ence 147:1578-9 Mr 26 '65
Crown-gall tumorigenesis; effect of temper-
ature on wound healing and conditioning.
J. Lipetz. bibliog il Science 149:865-7 Ag
20 '65
CROWN imperials
Crown imperial. il Horticulture 43:32-3 My
'65
CROWN Zellerbach corporation
Caught in the civil rights crossfire. il Bsns W
p 102-4+ Ag 7 '65
CROWS
Beach bird. il Look 29:132+ Je 15 '65
Bird, the vow and the child; search through
the marshlands of southern New Jersey.
B. Gilbert. il Sports Illus 23:58-62+ Ag 30
'65
I love those ornery rascals. R. Starnes. Field
& S 70:16+ S '65
CROWTHER, Bosley
Birth of The birth of a nation. N Y Times
Mag p24-5+ F 7 '65
CROWTHER, C. Edward, bp
Angry young bishop. il por Time 87:52 Ja
14 '66
CROZIER, George
Medicine. Sports Illus 23:48-50 Jl 12 '65
CROZIER, George F. See Fox, D. L. jt. auth.
CRUCIBLE steel company of America
New St George. il Time 87:69A Ja 21 '66
Raider to the rescue. Newsweek 67:68 Ja 24
'66
CRUCIFIXION of Christ. See Jesus Christ—
Crucifixion
CRUELTY to animals. See Animals—Treat-
ment
CRUELTY to children
Helping physicians protect children; Illinois
law to exempt physicians from libel suits
by parents. Christian Cent 82:516 Ap 28
'65
10,000 children battered and starved. il To-
days Health 43:24+ S '65
CRUICKSHANK, Donald R.
Don't use schoolwork as punishment. NEA J
55:53 Ja '66
CRUISES. See Cruising
CRUISING
Adventurers; skulduggery aboard the Madame
V. G. Bradshaw. Vogue 146:202-3+ D '65
Amphibious cruise in a day sailer. H. G.
Braendel. il Yachting 117:38-40+ F '65
Barnyard boating; Okeechobee Waterway,
Fla. I. Deibert. il Yachting 118:57+ N '65

CRUISING—*Continued*
Brotherly cruise on the Black Sea. G. Feifer. il Harper 230:78-84 Mr '65
Cruise of the Alsanal. S. A. Bell. il Motor B 116:22-5+ Ag; 44-6+ S; 74+ O '65
Cruising down east. A. W. Moffat. il Yachting 118:38-40+ Jl; 57-9+ Ag '65
Cruising the West coast of Mexico. S. Murray and R. Poole. il Yachting 117:50-2+ Je; 118:54-6+ Jl '65
Cruising through history on Long Island Sound; fifth Heritage cruise. L. A. Solomon. il Motor B 115:22-9+ Ap '65
Day on the Runeberg; from Helsinki to Porvoo. N. Lindgren. il Travel 124:28-30 Jl '65
East from Florida. J. Hart. il Yachting 118:44-5+ S '65
Finisterre sails the Windward Islands. G. Mitchell. il Nat Geog Mag 128:755-801 D '65
Gentle adventure: from Lake Erie to the sea. N. Nadel. il Yachting 118:44-6+ Ag; 48-9+ S '65
Greatest little boat. D. N. Brady. il Yachting 118:48-50+ Jl '65
Handy Pied-à-Terre for a sailorman. C. Mitchell. il Sports Illus 22:79-80+ My 24 '65
High speed in the Caribbean; with comment by D. Newick. D. Teague. il Yachting 117:58-9+ Je '65
Let's travel: on the high seas. J. Bush. il Mlle 61:183-6 O '65
Motor boating's guide to winter cruising. il Motor B 116:22-3 O '65
Motorboating in the Mediterranean. M. W. keeler. il Yachting 117:42-4+ Mr; 82-4+ Ap '65
New boat, a new venture; Baja California. E. Newmark. il Yachting 118:61-4+ D '65 (to be cont)
New York's Finger Lakes point to pleasure. H. L. Brun. il Motor B 116:22-5 Jl '65
North Channel cruise. C. H. Vilas. il Yachting 117:46-8+ My; 60-2+ Je '65
Notes to Mrs Charterer; when Bahamas or Caribbean bound. B. Weinman. Yachting 117:173-4 F '65
Rich delights of Tidewater, Virginia. E. S. Maloney. bibliog il Motor B 116:22-7+ S '65
Sailaway, sailaway, sailaway home. G. P. Manning. il Motor B 116:30-4+ S '65
Six easy-on-the-budget cruises. H. Bradshaw and V. Bradshaw. il Todays Health 43:18-22 Je '65
South American cruise; Moore-McCormack luxury cruise. T. B. Lesure. il Travel 124:28-32+ N '65
Sylvia Odyssey; month sliding among the Greek islands and along the stark coast of southern Turkey. T. Capote. il Vogue 147:68-75 Ja 15 '66
Teen travel talk; windjammer Caribbean cruises. il Seventeen 24:182 My '65
Triangle of cruising contrasts; Ontario's Golden triangle. B. Koelbel. il Motor B 115:22-5+ Je '65
See also
River trips
Voyages

Anecdotes, facetiae, satire, etc.
Some call it Slocumania. G. K. Gould. il Motor B 116:42-3+ S '65
CRUISING with children. See Travel with children
CRUMP, Edward Hull
Mr Crump of Memphis, by W. D. Miller. Review
Nation 200:402 Ap 12 '65. B. D. Blank
CRUST of the earth. See Earth—Surface
CRUSTACEA
See also
Amphipod
Crayfish
Isopoda
CRUZ, J. See Gallego, A. jt. auth.
CRYING
What kind of men cry? symposium. il Ebony 20:47+ Je '65
See also
Infants—Crying
CRYOGENIC research. See Low temperature research
CRYOGENIC surgery
Cold that cures. il Time 85:85-6 Ap 30 '65
Healing with an icy lance. il Life 58:98B-100+ Ap 2 '65
Near-freezing of brain permits lengthy surgery. Sci N L 88:213 O 2 '65
New world of surgery; hottest heat and coldest cold perform operating-room miracles. R. Berg. il Look 29:78-82+ My 4 '65
CRYOGENICS. See Low temperatures
CRYOSURGERY. See Cryogenic surgery

CRYOTHERAPY. See Cold—Therapeutic applications
CRYPTOCOCCUS neoformans. See Fungi, Pathogenic
CRYSTAL, Minn. See Minneapolis
CRYSTAL. See Quartz
CRYSTAL CITY, Tex.
CASA, not PASO; Mexican American city councilmen. Time 85:27 Ap 16 '65
CRYSTAL diodes. See Tunnel diodes
CRYSTALLIZATION
Device rids impurities. Sci N L 88:228 O 9 '65
Gel aids crystal growth. Sci N L 88:379 D 11 '65
CRYSTALLOGRAPHY
Ceramic whisker output boost seen. J. F. Judge. il Miss & Roc 17:28+ Ag 23 '65; Reply. L. R. Standifer. 17:6 O 4 '65
Clathrate crystalline form of silica. B. Kamb. bibliog il Science 148:232-4 Ap 9 '65
Crystal multiplication without nucleation. B. Chalmers and R. B. Williamson. bibliog il Science 148:1717-18 Je 25 '65
Crystallization and molecular folding. P. H. Lindenmeyer. bibliog il Science 147:1256-62 Mr 12 '65
Glide mechanisms in experimentally deformed minerals. C. B. Raleigh. bibliog il Science 150:739-41 N 5 '65
Growth layers on ammonium dihydrogen phosphate. J. L. Torgesen and R. W. Jackson. bibliog il Science 148:952-4 My 14 '65
Hexamethylenetetramine hexahydrate: a new type of clathrate hydrate. G. A. Jeffrey and T. C. W. Mak. bibliog il Science 149:178 Jl 9 '65
Intercrystalline links in bulk polyethylene. H. D. Keith and others. Science 150:1026-7 N 19 '65
Nucleation of crystals from solution. A. G. Walton. bibliog il Science 148:601-7 Ap 30 '65
Point defects in insulators. C. C. Klick. bibliog il Science 150:451-6 O 22 '65
Process promises ultra-high purity. Miss & Roc 17:25 O 4 '65
Room temperature slip in titanium diboride produced by high pressure. F. W. Vahldiek and others. bibliog il Science 149:747-8 Ag 13 '65
Structure of crystal surfaces. L. H. Germer. il Sci Am 212:32-41 Mr '65
Whiskers in quantity; silicon carbide. Sci Am 212:56 Mr '65
See also
Crystallization
Dislocations in crystals

X ray studies
α-D-glucose: precise determination of crystal and molecular structure by neutron-diffraction analysis. G. M. Brown and H. A. Levy. bibliog il Science 147:1038-9 F 26 '65
Anomalous dispersion method: its power for protein structure analysis. G. N. Ramachandran and S. Parthasarathy. bibliog il Science 150:212-14 O 8 '65
Clathrate structure of silicon Na₈Si₄₆ and Na×Si₁₃₆. J. S. Kasper and others. bibliog il Science 150:1713-14 D 24 '65
Crystal packing of molecules. D. E. Williams. bibliog Science 147:605-6 F 5 '65
Crystallization of clay-adsorbed water. D. M. Anderson and P. Hoekstra. bibliog il Science 149:318-19 Jl 16 '65
Germanium and silicon disulfides: structure and synthesis. C. T. Prewitt and H. S. Young. bibliog il Science 149:535-7 Jl 30 '65
High-pressure single-crystal studies of ice VI. S. Block and others. bibliog il Science 148:947-8 My 14 '65
Phase relations in the system Na₂Si₂O₅SiO₂. J. Williamson and F. P. Glasser. bibliog il Science 148:1589-91 Je 18 '65
Structure of ice VI. B. Kamb. bibliog il Science 150:205-9 O 8 '65
Structure of 9,9,10,10-tetrachloroanthracene. N. F. Yannoni and others. bibliog il Science 148:231 Ap 9 '65
Sulfur: a new high-pressure from. T. Bååk. bibliog il Science 148:1220-1 My 28 '65
X-ray analysis of complicated molecules: address. December 11, 1964. D. C. Hodgkin. bibliog il Science 150:979-88 N 19 '65
CRYSTALS. See Crystallography
CRYSTALS, Ice. See Ice
CRYSTALS, Snow. See Snow
CUBA
Cuba seven years after. D. D. Burks. il Cur Hist 50:38-44 Ja '66
Letter from Havana. P. Schmid. Commentary 40:56-63 S '65

CULTURE
Culture on a local level; international conference examines culture. Recreation 58:407 O '65
How to transmit culture; summary of address. G. W. Beadle. Sci N L 89:5 Ja 1 '66
See also
Civilization
Popular culture
    also subheads Civilization; Intellectual life; Popular culture, under names of countries, e.g. United States—Civilization

CULTURE, Primitive. See Eskimos—Culture; Indians of North America—Culture

CULTURE of tissues. See Tissues—Culture

CULVER, Elsie Thomas
American Baptists in convention. Christian Cent 82:784+ Je 16 '65

CULVER, Monty
Chance of a lifetime; story. Sat Eve Post 239:58-63 Ja 15 '66

CUMMINGS, Abbott Lowell
History in houses. Antiques 88:506-10 O '65

CUMMINGS, David
Kink-bands: shock deformation of biotite resulting from a nuclear explosion. bibliog Science 148:950-2 My 14 '65

CUMMINGS, Nathan
Consolidated foods plans its diet. il por Bsns W p65-6 My 22 '65

CUNARD, Nancy
Letter from Paris. Genêt. New Yorker 41:148+ Ap 3 '65

CUNARD steamship company
Queen's shipbuilder. il Time 85:92+ Mr 12 '65

CUNEO, Paul K.
Of many things. America 114:101 Ja 22 '66
Preview of new books. America 113:409+ O 9 '65

CUNHA, Vasco Tristão Leitão da. See Leitão da Cunha, V. T.

CUNLIFFE, Marcus
What was the matter with Henry Adams? Commentary 39:66-71 Je '65

CUNLIFFE-LISTER, Philip, 1st earl of Swinton. See Swinton, P. C.-L.

CUNNINGHAM, Billy
Kangaroo Kid. H. L. Masin. il por Sr Schol 86:28 Mr 11 '65

CUNNINGHAM, George E.
Derogatory images of the Negro and Negro history. Negro Hist Bul 28:126-7+ Mr '65

CUNNINGHAM, J. V.
Indirections of reason. W. Stafford. Poetry 105:262-4 Ja '65
Poet of plainness. R. M. Elman. Commonweal 82:250-1+ My 14 '65

CUNNINGHAM, Merce
Merce Cunningham and dance company, Hunter college playhouse. M. Marks. Dance Mag 39:32-3 Ap '65

CUNNINGHAM, Phillip J.
Vocationless Venezuela. Cath World 201:189-93 Je '65

CUNNINGHAM, Robert
Sinkbox shoot; paintings. Sports Illus 23:40-5 O 4 '65

CUNNINGHAM, Ross L.
Seattle: nature was a good provider. Sat R 48:76-7 O 23 '65

CUPBOARDS
She even has a cupboard inside another cupboard. il Sunset 135:112 O '65
See also
Kitchen cabinets

CUPERTINO, Calif.
Vote yes for parks. J. G. Parham. Recreation 58:405+ O '65

CUPS
Cups and beakers. G. Kaler. il Hobbies 70:46+ N '65

CURAÇAO
Go Dutch treat! See Aruba and Curaçao, two Dutch islands in the Caribbean. E. Gay. il U S Camera 28:18-19 My '65

CURATORS, Museum. See Museum workers

CURIA romana. See Catholic church—Roman curia

CURIOSITIES
Here is the odd paradise of the record maniac. Guinness book of records. J. A. M. Graham. il Sports Illus 22:54-8+ F 8 '65; Same abr. with title Book to end arguments. Read Digest 86:152-4+ My '65

CURIUM
Inventor of the month; two new elements, two patents. S. V. Jones. Sci Digest 57:15 F '65

CURLEWS
Did a Barbados hunter shoot the last Eskimo curlew? M. W. Bond. il Audubon Mag 67:314-16 S '65

CURLEY, Daniel
Animal witnesses; poem. America 113:671 N 27 '65

CURLEY, Thomas F.
High-Irish. Commentary 39:84-8 My '65
Vulgarity of O'Neill. Commonweal 83:443-6 Ja 14 '66

CURLING
Jam can curling. C. A. Barbour. il Recreation 58:64 F '65
Oooh, what a drawing game! Wisconsin's national champion curlers. J. Lovesey. il Sports Illus 22:28-9 Mr 29 '65
Stone's throw to a playdown; U.S. curling championships. B. La Fontaine. il Sports Illus 22:20-3+ Mr 15 '65

CURRAN, Donald J.
Problem of metropolis. America 114:38-40 Ja 8 '66

CURRELL, B. R.
Thermal analysis. Science 149:765-6 Ag 13 '65

CURRENCY convertibility
U.S. citizens in India may buy counterpart currency. Dept State Bul 52:907 Je 7 '65

CURRENCY question
Business hedges on British pound. Bsns W p 117-18 F 13 '65
More heat on the pound; sterling crisis. il Bsns W p23-4 Ap 3 '65

CURRENT events
Affairs of state. S. Alsop. See issues of Saturday evening post
Atlantic report on the world today. See issues of Atlantic
Constancy in all affairs. B. L. Masse. America 112:744 My 22 '65
Contemporary affairs test (cont) il Sr Schol 87:26 S 16 '65
Flop, flap, flip, is nothing sacred? il Newsweek 65:15-16 Je 7 '65
Life on the newsfronts of the world. See issues of Life
March of events. See issues of Senior scholastic
March of the news; front page of the week. See issues of U.S. news & World report
Month in review. See issues of Current history
Press section; excerpts from newspapers and periodicals. See issues of Reader's digest
U.S. and world affairs annual, 1965-66; ed. by E. R. Floyd and others. il Sr Schol 87:12-41+ S 30 '65
Washington report; ed. by R. Stolley. See issues of Life
World around. America 112:343, 410, 472, 596, 659, 749, 823; 113:72 Mr 13, 27, Ap 10, 24, My 8, 22, Je 5, Jl 17 '65

Study and teaching
Editors, teachers discuss contemporary affairs. Sr Schol 87:sup9+ D 9 '65
News in the classroom. J. H. Haefner. il Sat R 49:71 Ja 15 '66

CURRENTS, Ocean. See Ocean currents

CURRICULUM. See Colleges and universities—Curriculum; Courses of study; High schools—Curriculum

CURRICULUM development, Association for. See Association for supervision and curriculum development

CURRIE, Lauchlin
Sleep softly, myth. Nat R 17:494+ Je 15 '65

CURRIER, Herbert H. See Webster, D. B. jt. auth.

CURRIER, Ruth
Ruth Currier, Jeff Duncan & companies, East 74th street theatre. J. Maskey. Dance Mag 40:58 Ja '66

CURRY, David
Creche in the madhouse; poem. Commonweal 83:374 D 24 '65

CURRY, Peggy Simson
Plot, a pattern created by people. Writer 78:20-6+ F '65

CURRY, Tom
Wild western rides again. Sat R 48:70+ D 11 '65

CURRY
Curries and condiments. M. Field. il McCalls 93:68+ O '65
How to curry flavor; with recipes. il McCalls 93:136-7+ O '65
This curry actually is easier here than in India; with recipes. il Sunset 135:204+ N '65

CURTAINS and draperies
Curtain cut-ups. J. Holmstrand. il Suc Farm 63:114-15 Ap '65
Curtain excitement ready-made! il Good H 160:136-43 Ap '65
Give windows a fresh outlook. il Bet Hom & Gard 43:63 Ap '65
How to make beads for airy screens and curtains. il House & Gard 127:148-9+ Je '65
Monticello swag. il House & Gard 127:38-9 Je '65

CURTAINS and draperies—*Continued*
  Shopping ideas for windows. B. G. Wadsworth. Parents Mag 40:94 N '65
  Strap headings for curtains. il House & Gard 128:66-7 N '65
  Windows: the romantic view. M. White. il Ladies Home J 82:70-7 Je '65
  Wonderful ways with windows. il Parents Mag 40:97+ N '65

Care

  Curtain care. E. Taylor. il Good H 160:241 Ap '65
CURTAYNE, Alice
  Dante's vision. America 113:751-3 D 11 '65
CURTIN, Thomas J.
  Education for patriotism in our schools. Sr Schol 86:10T+ F 4 '65
CURTIS, Bernard A.
  Morality of Catholic censorship. Christian Cent 82:772-5 Je 16 '65
CURTIS, C. J.
  Söderblom: ecumenical churchman and theologian. Christian Cent 83:47-8 Ja 12 '66
CURTIS, C. Michael
  Closing the game gap. Atlan 216:150-1 O '65
  New folklorist. Atlan 215:139-40 My '65
CURTIS, Carl Thomas
  Excerpt from debate, September 1, 1964. Cong Digest 44:81+ Mr '65
CURTIS, Charlotte
  Don't run up hills or run down people. N Y Times Mag p38-9+ Ap 4 '65
  Sociologist on the society beat. il por Time 85:51 F 19 '65
CURTIS, Christine
  Allure. pors Vogue 146:186, 188-9 O 1 '65
CURTIS, Gordon
  Gordon Curtis on race organization. Yachting 117:210+ Je '65
CURTIS, Joseph E.
  Reduce your money needs. Am City 80:32 My '65
  What's in a budget? por Recreation 58:82-3 F '65
CURTIS, K. D.
  Charnley's fabulous guns. Hobbies 70:116-17+ Ap '65
CURTIS, Thomas B.
  Wage-price guidelines; address, August 31, 1965. Vital Speeches 31:727-9 S 15 '65
CURTIS circulation company
  Large magazine distributors charged by Justice dept. Pub W 187:76 Je 21 '65
CURTIS publishing company
  Curtis caper. Newsweek 66:68 N 22 '65
  Curtis' green acres; faith in future. il Time 86:52 N 26 '65
  Hitting the iceberg. Time 85:63 Mr 12 '65
CURTISS, Thomas Quinn
  Paris: the Cisco kid speaks French. Sat R 49:46-7+ Ja 1 '66
CUSHING, Charles Phelps
  Cushing; main streets are his specialty. J. Deschin. il por Pop Phot 56:104-5+ F '65
CUSHING, Minnie
  Lineage of beauty. il pors Vogue 145:56-63 F 15 '65
CUSHION bush. See Calocephalus
CUSHIONS
  See also
  Pillows
CUSHMAN, Cliff
  We rejoice in our sufferings: letter. por Sr Schol 86:30 Mr 4 '65
CUSHMAN, Jerome
  Hidden persuaders in book selection. por Library J 90:3553-8 S 15 '65
  Reader looks at the notable books; address, 1964. por ALA Bul 59:105-10 F '65
CUSTARDS
  Back on the scene: old-fashioned custard; with recipes. il McCalls 92:114-16+ S '65
  Baked caramel custard, and French vanilla custard pie. il Bet Hom & Gard 43:116 Ap '65
  Cut calories but not dessert. Farm J 89:82 O '65
  Susan makes caramel-topped custard. M. F. Williams. il Good H 160:188 Ap '65
  This dessert is burnt cream, it's delicious and elegant; crème brûlée. il Sunset 134:202+ My '65
CUSTER, Benjamin A.
  Dewey 17: a preview and report. por Wilson Lib Bul 39:555-9 Mr '65
CUSTIS, Nelly Parke
  Visit to Mount Vernon; excerpts from Travels through America; tr. and ed. by M. J. E. Budka. J. U. Niemcewicz. il por Am Heritage 16:64-71 F '65
CUSTODIANS, School. See Janitors

CUSTOMER relations
  Customer is SO right. il Time 86:100+ D 10 '65
  Wanted: concern for the customer; address, September 29, 1965. J. I. Straus. Vital Speeches 32:109-12 D 1 '65
CUSTOMS. See Manners and customs
CUSTOMS (tariff) See Tariff
CUSTOMS service

United States

  Customs clears way to progress; Negro personnel moves up in U.S. agency. il Ebony 21:104-6+ D '65
CUT glass. See Glassware
CUTAK, Ladislaus
  Cacti and succulents in the garden. il Horticulture 43:18-21+ O '65
CUTANEOUS communication. See Communications research
CUTCH, Rann of
  At it again; border war in Rann of Kutch. Newsweek 66:34-5 Ag 23 '65
  Judgment of Rann. il Time 86:25 Jl 9 '65
  Kutch and Kashmir, how the war started. G. Woodcock. Commonweal 82:724-6 O 1 '65
  Milestone in the rain. Newsweek 66:38 Jl 12 '65
  Run-in on the Rann. il Time 85:39 My 7 '65
  Tiny war; fighting over Great Rann of Kutch. il Newsweek 65:52 My 10 '65
  War in a windblown waste called the Rann of Kutch. il Life 58:30-6 Je 11 '65
  War where U.S. is caught in the middle; skirmishing in Rann of Cutch. il U S News 58:12 My 10 '65
CUTLER, Ann
  Persistent Russian. Esquire 63:66-7+ My '65
CUTLER, Bruce
  Poetry chronicle. R. Howard. Poetry 106:299-301 Jl '65
CUTLER, M. Rupert
  Tragic story of Magic Mountain. Liv Wildn 29:7-9 Sum '65
CUTRER, Jesse H. Jr
  In murky waters. por Newsweek 65:21 Je 7 '65
CUTTERS (boats) See Sailboats
CUTTING tools
  See also
  Paper cutters (tools)
  Saws
CUTTS, Warren G.
  Reading research and improvement: a time for change. por Sr Schol 86:sup 6+ Ap 29 '65
CUYAHOGA FALLS, Ohio
  Flexible guard posts. il Am City 80:117 My '65
CUZCO, Peru
  Cuzco school; Pastor collection shown at Pan American union. J. Gómez-Sicre. il Américas 17:4-11 Jl '65
CYANOGUANIDINE
  Dicyandiamide possible role in peptide synthesis during chemical evolution. G. Steinman and others. bibliog Science 147:1574 Mr 26 '65
CYBERNETICS
  Space movement studied. il Sci N L 87:262 Ap 24 '65
  See also
  Bionics
CYCASIN
  Cycasin: radiomimetic effect. H. J. Teas and others. bibliog il Science 149:541-2 Jl 30 '65
CYCLADES (islands)
  Those golden Greek isles. H. Sutton. il Holiday 39:62-71 Ja '66
CYCLAMATE. See Sugar substitutes
CYCLES, Biological. See Periodicity
CYCLING
  Bicycle popularity sweeping country. il Todays Health 43:80-1 My '65
  Bike's comeback; bikes, ways to transport them, and bicycle touring in the West. il Sunset 135:50-7 Jl '65
  Can they pass the test? rights and wrongs of way. il Recreation 58:224 My '65
  Get a bike! reprint. il Am For 71:26-7 Ag '65
  Return of the cycle. il Newsweek 66:102+ N 8 '65
  See also
  Bicycle racing

Safety devices and measures

  Taking the hazards out of bicycling; excerpt from Today's health guide. il Todays Health 43:40-2 Jl '65
CYCLING clubs
  Bike clubs invite you along; northern California. il Sunset 135:36 Jl '65

CYCLING trips
Where the biking's good; California. il Sunset 135:40+ Jl '65
CYCLOBUTADIENE
Cyclobutadiene made. Sci N L 88:75 Jl 31 '65
CYCLONES
See also
Tornadoes
CYMBIDIUMS. See Orchids
CYPRESS
Rare cypress clings to coast habitat. S. Carlquist. il Natur Hist 74:38-43 O '65
CYPRIPEDIUM. See Ladys slippers
CYPROLIDOL. See Depressants
CYPRUS
Anger from all; United Nations study of the Cyprus problem. Time 85:29-30 Ap 9 '65
Cyprus dispute. H. J. Psomiades. bibliog f il Cur Hist 48:269-76+ My '65
Greece and Turkey: the second round. G. Bailey: C. Sterling. il Reporter 33:14-22 S 9 '65
Jitters again. il Newsweek 65:45 Ap 5 '65
New bloodletting? Newsweek 65:36 Mr 29 '65
Ready to explode again. il Time 85:27 Mr 26 '65
Shots in the orchard; Makarios' men in control. Time 86:43 N 12 '65
Toward peace in Cyprus. New Repub 152:10 Ap 17 '65
Who cares about Cyprus? C. Poulos. Nation 201:493-6 D 20 '65
See also
United Nations—Cyprus
CYR, Don
Peter Voulkas. il Sch Arts 65:27-30 S '65
CYSTATHIONINE
Cystathioninuria: nature of the defect. G. W. Frimpter. bibliog il Science 149:1095-6 S 3 '65
Genetic disorder found; homocystinuria. F. Marley. Sci N L 88:131 Ag 28 '65
CYSTIC fibrosis
Fingernails aid diagnosis. Sci N L 87:182 Mr 20 '65
Living with cystic fibrosis. il Time 86:43 Ag 20 '65
CYSTINURIA. See Intestines—Diseases
CYSTITIS. See Bladder—Diseases
CYTISUS. See Brooms (shrubs)
CYTOCHROMES
Reduction-like effect of carbohydrates on cytochrome c. P. T. Mora and others bibliog il Science 149:642-4 Ag 6 '65
CYTOKININS. See Peptides
CYTOLOGY. See Cells
CYTOSINE
Tumor and virus antigens of simian virus 40: differential inhibition of synthesis by cytosine arabinoside. F. Rapp and others. bibliog il Science 147:625-7 F 5 '65
CZAMANSKE, Gerald K. and Porter, S. C.
Titanium dioxide in pyroclastic layers from volcanoes in the Cascade Range. bibliog Science 150:1022-5 N 19 '65
CZECH philharmonic orchestra
Music to my ears: concerts in Carnegie Hall. I. Kolodin. Sat R 48:69 D 4 '65
Musical events; concert in Carnegie Hall. W. Sargeant. New Yorker 41:174-5 N 27 '65
CZECHOSLOVAKIA
Change in Czechoslovakia. E. Taborsky. bibliog f Cur Hist 48:168-74+ Mr '65
Western ideas come back in Czechoslovakia. il Bsns W p 180 N 20 '65
See also
Airplane industry and trade—Czechoslovakia
Brno
Merchant marine—Czechoslovakia
Music festivals—Czechoslovakia
Opera—Czechoslovakia
Piestany
Prague
Economic conditions
Crowning failure. Time 86:21 D 31 '65
Something new in east Europe: the customer is right. A. Kucherov. il U S News 58:80-3 Je 28 '65
Economic policy
Change in Czechoslovakia. E. Taborsky. bibliog f Cur Hist 48:168-74+ Mr '65
Industries
Gambling on the Czechs; exclusive sales agent in the western hemisphere for the heavy machine tools of the Skoda works. il Fortune 72:103-4 D '65
Religious institutions and affairs
Deepening the Christian-Marxist dialogue. D. Peerman. Christian Cent 82:1566-8 D 22 '65
See also
Catholic church in Czechoslovakia

CZEGLEDY, Alexander
Hungarian theologian speaks out on the God is dead vogue. Christian Cent 82:1351-2 N 3 '65
CZURA, Pete
Female wins retriever Nationals. Field & S 69:146-9 F '65
Flavor-testing Fido. Field & S 70:144-6+ Je '65
Land of smiling waters. Field & S 70:66-8+ Je '65
Rattle up a deer this year! Pop Mech 124:108-9+ N '65

D

DAR. See Daughters of the American revolution
D. C. Heath and company. See Heath, D. C, and company
DDC. See Classification, Decimal
DDT (insecticide)
DDT in Antarctica. Sci Am 213:80+ S '65
High DDT levels found in Midwest fish and birds. Sci N L 88:169 S 11 '65
Pesticides spread, even to Antarctica. Sci N L 88:56 Jl 24 '65
This malaria spray caused a chain reaction; in British Guiana, reprint. Audubon Mag 67:215 Jl '65
Injurious effects
Airborne particulates in Pittsburgh: association with p,p'-DDT. P. Antommaria and others. bibliog il Science 150:1476-7 D 10 '65
Bird mortality after spraying for Dutch elm disease with DDT. C. F. Wurster, jr. and others. bibliog Science 148-90-1 Ap 2 '65; Reply with rejoinder. I. N. McDaniel. 149:326 Jl 16 '65
Insecticide kills cats. Sci N L 88:21 Jl 10 '65
Quails stop learning when fed excessive DDT. Sci N L 88:155 S 4 '65
DESP. See National education association—Department of elementary school principals
DMO. See Dimethyl oxazolidinedione
DMSO. See Methyl sulfoxide
DNA. See Deoxyribonucleic acid
D'ABERNAT, René. See Abernat, R. d'
DABNEY, Beatrice Whistler
Bee Dabney's drawing room. il por Vogue 145:184-9 Ap 1 '66
DABNEY, Joseph
Georgia jinx. Travel 123:47-51 Je '65
DABNEY, Virginius
Good southern universities. Harper 230:86-8+ Mr '65
Is a mixed race inevitable? excerpt from The pace is important. U S News 58:67 My 10 '65
DA CUNHA, Vasco Tristão Leitão. See Leitão da Cunha, V. T.
DADDARIO, Emilio Q.
Daddario study says NSF should be in forefront of policymaking. D. S. Greenberg. Science 151:177-9 Ja 14 '66
DADE COUNTY, Fla.
Education
Library cooperation in Dade County. J. P. McIntyre. ALA Bul 59:540-2 Je '65
DAFFODILS. See Narcissus
DAHL, Lewis K.
High blood pressure? it may be in your genes. il Bsns W p90+ Ap 3 '65
DAHL, Roald
Let's build a skyscraper, but let's find a good book first; reprint. Writer 78:27-8+ F '65
My wife, Patricia Neal. pors Ladies Home J 82:53-5+ S '65
DAHLBERG, Edward
Majorca: an island haven. Holiday 37:48-51 F '65
about
Some poets in their prose. R. Howard. Poetry 105:398-400 Mr '65
DAHLBERG, James E. and Haselkorn, Robert
Ribosomes from escherichia coli: lack of specificity for viral RNA. bibliog Science 149:78-80 Jl 2 '65
DAHLIAS
Dwarf dahlias. A. M. Murphy. Horticulture 43:53 F '65
Dwarf dahlias, grow them with other garden flowers. M. M. Leister. il Flower Grower 52:37+ Ap '65

DAHLIAS—*Continued*
More dahlias for your money. B. C. Kilvert. jr. il Pop Gard 16:37 Mr '65
Ways with dahlias. il Flower Grower 52:30-1 My '65

DAHLSTRÖM, Annica B. and Zetterström, B. E. M.
Noradrenaline stores in nerve terminals of the spleen: changes during hemorrhagic shock. bibliog Science 147:1583-4 Mr 26 '65

DAHOMEY
Fast shuffle: government coup. il Newsweek 67:40 Ja 17 '66
Royal monuments from Africa's past. UNESCO Courier 18:31 Ja '65
Soldiers on the march. Time 87:39 Ja 14 '66

DAHOOD, Thomas S.
Line thickness can produce depth. Design 66:18-19 My '65

DAI, Shen-yu
Peking and the third world. bibliog f Cur Hist 49:142-9 S '65

DAICHES, David
Hebraism reconsidered. Commentary 39:73-5 F '65
Presenting the Bible. Commentary 40:47-55 S '65

DAILY news, Chicago. See Chicago daily news

DAILY worker (London)
Daily something; name change recommended. Newsweek 67:56 Ja 24 '66

DAIMLER-Benz, ag. See Automobile industry and trade—Germany (Federal Republic)

DAIN, Martin J.
Faulkner's county. A. Goldsmith. il Pop Phot 56:62-3+ F '65

D'AIRO, Leonard J.
Tabletop radio goes portable. Pop Mech 124:176-80+ D '65

DAIRY farm management
Ideas from the East's biggest dairyman. B. Hardy. il Farm J 89:30-1+ Je '65
Seventy cows; but no plows! D. Hagen. Farm J 89:56 Ag '65

DAIRY farm records
Easier ways to keep records on dairy cows. N. Reeder and O. Bay. il Farm J 89:25 Je '65
Those new-fangled dairy records. J. R. Borcherding. il Suc Farm 63:56-7+ My '65

DAIRY farming. See Dairying

DAIRY farms
Thinking of expanding? W. B. Ward and J. R. Borcherding. il Suc Farm 63:46-7+ Ap '65
See also
Dairy farm management

DAIRY inspection
Those milk inspectors! L. Lambert. Farm J 89:44 Ag '65

DAIRY products
See also
Butter

Prices
Business report. C. W. Gifford. Farm J 89:All Jl '65
See also
Milk—Prices

DAIRYING
Dairy extra; symposium. il Farm J 89:A1-2+ Jl '65
Dairy news. See issues of Farm journal
Dairying and a town job; industrial arts teacher, Carl Balsam. J. Russell. Farm J 89:64 N '65
How to stay in the dairy business: ed. by J. R. Borcherding. R. Hoglund. il Suc Farm 64:40-1+ Ja '66
Milk 'em one lactation and sell 'em? B. Hardy. il Farm J 89:48-9 Mr '65
Thinking of expanding? W. B. Ward and J. R. Borcherding. il Suc Farm 63:46-7+ Ap '65
What's new. See issues of Successful farming
See also
Dairy farm management

DAISIES, Shasta. See Shasta daisies

DAKIN, Leonard
Green leaves of summer; excerpts from Happy valley. P. D. Taft. il Am Heritage 16:56-63 O '65

DAKOTA, SOUTH. See South Dakota

DAKOTA Indians
More lost Indians; Pine Ridge reservation. J. Ridgeway. New Repub 153:19-22 D 11 '65

DALAI Lama XIV
I visit Tibet's Dalai Lama. P. S. Buck. Ladies Home J 82:36+ Mr '65

DALCROZE, Émile Jaques-. See Jaques-Dalcroze, E.

DALCROZE method. See Eurythmics

DALE, Chester
For the people. il por Newsweek 65:103-7 My 10 '65

DALE, Chester, collection. See National gallery of art, Washington, D.C.

DALE, Edwin L. jr
Big gun on poverty. New Repub 153:13-15 Ag 7 '65
Uncle Sam's $50,000,000,000 surplus. N Y Times Mag p32-3+ N 7 '65
We are depression (but not recession) proof. N Y Times Mag p36-7+ Ap 4 '65

DALEY, Richard J.
Confrontation in Chicago; Mayor Daley meets the movement. L. Wille. il Nation 201:92-5 Ag 30 '65

DALEY, Robert
Five against the gods. Esquire 64:96-101+ N '65
Spaniards discover bullfighting. il N Y Times Mag p32-3+ Ag 29 '65
Speaking out. por Sat Eve Post 238:10+ Je 5 '65
Sundown of a champion. Sat Eve Post 238:46+ My 8 '65
That blood-red Ferrari mystique. N Y Times Mag p22-3+ Jl 25 '65

DALGLIESH, Alice
Books for young people. See issues of Saturday review

DALI, Salvador
Avida dollars. A. Werner. il Reporter 34:45-7 Ja 13 '66
Comedian & the straight man. il por Time 86:74 D 31 '65
Dali, gala and moolah; exhibition at Huntington Hartford's Gallery of modern art, New York. il por Newsweek 66:68-9 D 27 '65
Dali's astonishing new drawings to appear in Rizzoli Bible. il Pub W 188:130+ Jl 19 '65
Is Dali disgusting? two Dali shows. G. R. Swenson. il pors Art N 64:50-1+ D '65
Melina Mercouri and Salvador Dali match wits in a discussion of love, wealth, fidelity and death. por Redbook 124:52-3+ F '65
Spain: Casa Dali. il pors Ladies Home J 82:121-5 F '65

DALL sheep hunting. See Mountain sheep hunting

DALLAND, John I.
Hearing sensitivity in bats. bibliog Science 150:1185-6 N 26 '65

DALLAS, Philip
Italian land bargains. Atlan 215:124+ Je '65
Wines of Italy. House & Gard 127:136+ F '65

DALLAS

City planning
Self-help: an answer to urban renewal; Dallas project for slum rehabilitation. R. S. Strother. Read Digest 86:223-6 F '65

Music
See also
Dallas civic opera, company

Religious institutions and affairs
Breakthroughs: renewal in the local church; three Methodist congregations lead the way. J. C. Evans. Christian Cent 82:1443-7 N 24 '65

Stores
Texas-size fire sale at Neiman-Marcus. il Bsns W p44 Mr 20 '65

DALLAS civic opera company
Dallas. J. Rosenfield. Opera N 30:31 Ja 1 '66
Texas. A. Holmes. il Opera N 30:30 D 11 '65

DALLAS symphony orchestra
Dallas symphony at North Texas state. P. Yates. Hi Fi 15:127+ Ag '65

DALMATIAN dogs
Dog at cross-porpoises. il Look 30:90+ Ja 25 '66

D'ALPUGET, Lou
Challenge. il Yachting 118:42-4+ D '65

DALRYMPLE, Byron W.
Bird that thinks it's a rabbit. Field & S 70:53+ Je '65
Cat that liked cabrito. Field & S 70:37-9+ Ja '66
Living end for bluegills. Outdoor Life 136:64-5+ Jl '65
New techniques for old toms. Field & S 70:51-3+ N '65
Number one combo. Field & S 70:48-9+ O '65
Song of the coyote. Outdoor Life 135:64-5+ Je '65

DALRYMPLE, Jean
U.S. showtime abroad. Travel 123:44-6 Je '65

DALTON, Elizabeth
Child of the Sacred Heart; story. New Yorker 41:59-66 O 23 '65

DALTRY, Patience M.
Back to beginnings; reprint. Writer 78:14-15 Jl '65

DALY, Bill
Carlos and the king of con. M. Kram. il por Sports Illus 24:28-31 Ja 10 '66
DALY, J. M. See Brakke, M. K. jt. auth.
DALY, John. See Axelrod, J. jt. auth.
DALY, Maureen
Connecticut Yankee finds her destiny in Spain. Ladies Home J 82:60-1+ F '65
DALY, Maxine Lindley
Journey to Gitchee Gumee. Travel 124:40-2 S '65
DALY, Ronald O.
Professional negotiation. NEA J 54:30-1 My '65
DAMAGES
Attorney & his client; A. Garrett awarded $1,500,000 for punitive damages. Time 86:35 Jl 2 '65
Biggest settlement; first million-dollar award for a single death in air crash. Newsweek 65:66 My 31 '65
Companionship & compensation; damage suits. Time 85:63 My 28 '65
Price-tag problem; putting a specific price tag on the injury at issue. Time 86:59 O 1 '65
See also
Liability (law)
D'AMATO, Cus
Svengali returns. R. H. Boyle. il pors Sports Illus 22:24-7 Ap 12 '65
DAMBORIENA, Prudencio
Pentecostal fury. Cath World 202:217-23 Ja '66
D'AMICO, Victor
Object: lost and found. Craft Horiz 25:26-7 S '65
DAMMAN, A. W. H. See Peterson, E. B. jt. auth.
DAMON, Virgil G. and Taves, Isabella
War between mother and daughter. por Look 30:30+ Ja 11 '66
DAMON cameras. See Cameras
D'AMOUR, O'Neil C.
School boards of the future. America 113:316-17 S 25 '65
DAMPING (mechanics)
See also
Vibration absorbers
DAMPNESS in buildings
Dangerous basement waterproofer; X-33 water repellent. Consumer Bul 48:18 Je '65
Fix basement leaks now. W. J. Fletcher. il Suc Farm 63:47 O '65
DAMS
Attack on Grand Canyon. R. C. Bradley. il Liv Wildn 87:3-7 Wint '64
Battle of the Grand Canyon; dam builders vs. conservationists. A. Hano. il N Y Times Mag p56-7+ D 12 '65
Grand Canyon dams? C. W. Buchheister. Audubon Mag 67:181 My '65
Little Tennessee River jeopardized; Tellico Dam near Vonore, Loudon County, Tenn. Liv Wildn 29:38 Spr '65
Low-cost relief for droughts? dam of rubberized fabric, answer to water shortage. il Bsns W p54+ Ag 7 '65
Myths of the western dam. W. Stegner. il Sat R 48:29-31 O 23 '65
Senecas lose again. Nat Parks Mag 39:21 F '65
Shall our wild rivers be eternally dammed? dam builders vs conservationists. R. Starnes. Field & S 69:14+ Mr '65
Tellico Dam. Nat Parks Mag 39:23-4 D '65
Think big: open letter to the Secretary of Interior to build two dams on Colorado River. B. Stewart. il Harper 231:62-3 Ag '65; Discussion. 231:8+ N '65
U.S. and Canada sign agreement on claims relating to Gut Dam; Department statement. March 25, 1965, with text of agreement. Dept State Bul 52:643-6 Ap 26 '65
Versatile new dam that comes and goes away; Fabridam, inflatable dam for Sunbury, Pa. il Pop Sci 187:52-3 D '65
Water and power for the Southwest; Bridge Canyon and Marble Canyon dams. A. W. Smith. Nat Parks Mag 39:2 S '65
Water for Arizona and Bridge and Marble Canyon Dams; statements, August 1965. A. W. Smith. Nat Parks Mag 39:I-IV D '65
Water Valley Dam unlikely. Nat Parks Mag 39:21 Jl '65
See also
Fish ladders

Alaska
Plot to drown Alaska; Rampart Dam project. P. Brooks. il Atlan 215:53-9 My '65; Same abr. Read Digest 87:79-83 Ag '65; Discussion. Atlan 216:26+ Jl '65

Plot to strangle Alaska; proposed Rampart Canyon Dam; with reply by P. Brooks. E. Gruening. Atlan 216:56-9 Jl; 52 S '65
Rampart Canyon Dam proposal; plans for sessions of AAAS meeting to be held in Berkeley. il Science 150:510-11 O 22 '65
Rampart Dam: white elephant of the Yukon Flats. T. T. Brady. il Nat Parks Mag 39:4-7 O '65
Rampart, foolish dam. G. H. Wood. il Liv Wildn 29:3-7 Spr '65
Rampart project. P. M. Tilden. Natur Hist 75:12A Ja '66

Canada
Caging a river to build a skyscraper dam; Manic 5. J. C. Rehfield. il Pop Sci 186:126-9 F '65

Egypt
See also
Aswan High Dam

Italy
Geologic disaster; failure of Vaiont Dam. Sci Am 213:48 Jl '65
Night the mountain fell; Vaiont Dam disaster. G. Gaskill. il Read Digest 86:59-67 My '65

Netherlands
War without end; projects progress. S. Hagerty. il Newsweek 66:58+ N 15 '65
DANA, Nathalie
Avant-garde. pors Opera N 29:8-13 F 13 '65
DANA, Robert
Riddles; poem. Nation 201:67 Ag 2 '65
DANA, Samuel T.
AFA's birthday; ninety years of service. por Am For 71:14-17+ S '65
—and Pomeroy, K. B.
Redwoods and parks. bibliog f Am For 71:1-32 My '65
DANAHER, Dan
Packtrain hunt in New York. Outdoor Life 136:36-9+ O '65
DANCE, Stanley
Recordings reports: jazz LPs. See issues of Saturday review
DANCE bands. See Bands (music)
DANCE caravan U.S.A. See Dance institutes and workshops
DANCE companies
Alba/Reyes Spanish dance company. Brooklyn academy of music. M. Marks. Dance Mag 40:18 Ja '66
Alba-Reyes Spanish dance company, 92nd st. Y. D. Hering. Dance Mag 39:61 F '65
John Coy dance company, 92nd street Y. M. Marks. Dance Mag 39:157 D '65
Nederlands Dans theater at Jacob's Pillow. D. Hering. il Dance Mag 39:31-2+ S '65
See also names of dance companies. e.g. Moiseyev dance company
DANCE conferences
In our discontent; dance teachers devote a week to urgent self-appraisal. D. Hering. il Dance Mag 39:54-8 O '65 (to be cont)
Summer '65 teacher meetings. il Dance Mag 39:18-23 O '65
DANCE festivals
Calendar of summer international dance events. il Dance Mag 39:34-7 My '65
Eighteenth American dance festival, Connecticut college. D. Hering. Dance Mag 39:68-72 O '65
Regional ballet USA: sixth Northeast regional ballet festival. D. Hering. il Dance Mag 39:56-9+ Jl '65
Regional ballet USA: tenth annual Southeastern regional ballet festival. D. Hering. il Dance Mag 39:50-3+ Je '65
Regional ballet USA: third annual Southwestern regional ballet festival. D. Hering. il Dance Mag 39:54-7 Ag '65
Reviews: Rebekah Harkness foundation festival. M. Marks; J. Maskey. Dance Mag 39:35 O '65
DANCE films. See Moving pictures—Dance films
DANCE institutes and workshops
All aboard for Dance caravan; tour through Europe. E. LeMone. il Dance Mag 39:59-60 N '65
Excitement on 20th street; Dance theatre workshop. L. Moser. il Dance Mag 39:30-1 N '65
DANCE magazine
Dance magazine awards presentation party; symposium. il Dance Mag 39:38-41+ My '65
Dance magazine's 1964 awards. Dance Mag 39:34-7+ Mr '65

DANCE music
Next dance will be what is Meyer Davis doing while Oedipus and the mothers drop trousers? G. Frazier. Esquire 65:60-1+ Ja '66
   See also
Bands (music)
Jazz music
DANCE notation
Copyright by Hanya Holm. il Dance Mag 39:44 Jl '65
DANCE production
Backstage views; audition; rehearsal. il Dance Mag 39:22-3 Ag '65
On the gypsy circuit. See issues of Dance magazine
DANCE recitals
All aboard for Dance caravan; tour through Europe. E. LeMone. il Dance Mag 39:59-60 N '65
Dancer's theatre company, 92nd street Y. M. Marks. Dance Mag 39:34 Ap '65
Excitement on 20th street; Dance theatre workshop. L. Moser. il Dance Mag 39:30-1 N '65
DANCE schools
Beaupre; letters from a camper at summer arts school in the Berkshires. E. Parker. il Dance Mag 39:22-4 Mr '65
Give them a chance to dance. J. Kass. il Parents Mag 40:55-7+ S '65

Sweden

Choreographic institute; program of Swedish government. B. Hager. il Dance Mag 39:14-15 F '65
DANCE studios
Ballet in the barn: Carlisle, Pa. il Dance Mag 39:64-5 F '65
Day is mine, the land is mine. J. Fox. il Dance Mag 39:50-3 Mr '65
DANCE teachers
Feeling in your bones; ed. by J. Dougherty. R. Rossellat. il Dance Mag 39:54-7 Ap '65
In our discontent; dance teachers devote a week to urgent self-appraisal. D. Hering. il Dance Mag 39:54-8 O; 54-5+ N '65
New Year's message from the publisher. R. Orthwine. il Dance Mag 40:31 Ja '66
Summer '65 teacher meetings. il Dance Mag 39:18-23 O '65
   See also
Asher, F.
Holm, H.
DANCE theatre workshop. See Dance institutes and workshops
DANCE therapy
Learning is fun when you dance it; program in Washington, D.C. to prepare slum children for reading. C. Schmais. il Dance Mag 40:33-5 Ja '66
Sliver of hope; concerning film about dance and the mentally disturbed. D. Hering. il Dance Mag 39:46-8 S '65
Social dance: an aid to rehabilitation. E. J. Jacobs. Recreation 58:494-6 D '65
DANCE workshops. See Dance institutes and workshops
DANCER, Stanley
Hambo in the gloaming. P. Ryan. il Sports Illus 23:38-9 S 13 '65
Mud in Stanley's eye. il Time 86:92 S 10 '65
DANCERS
Annual directory of dance attractions: soloists, companies, choreographers, lecturers. Dance Mag 39:14-16+ D '65
Brief biographies. S. Goodman. See issues of Dance magazine
Dance magazine's 1964 awards. Dance Mag 39:34-7+ Mr '65
Fourteen stars-in-ascendant of the greatest ballet company in the world. Britain's Royal. L. Lerman. il Mlle 60:218-19 Mr '65
In the news; photographs. See issues of Dance magazine
Interview with Erik Bruhn; ed. by O. Maynard. E. Bruhn. Dance Mag 40:22-3 Ja '66
On the gypsy circuit. See issues of Dance magazine
Presstime news. See issues of Dance magazine
SEG or SAG; what union for Hollywood dancers? V. H. Swisher. Dance Mag 39:108-9 D '65
So you want to work in Europe next year. D. Buck. il Dance Mag 39:32+ O '65
DANCING
About dancing. J. Waring. il Dance Mag 39:35 F '65
Contemporary dance: three points of view. Carnegie recital hall. J. Maskey. Dance Mag 39:155 D '65
Daedalus at the Rollerdrome; dances by Robert Rauschenberg. E. Abeel. il Sat R 48:51-3 Ag 28 '65

Dance. A. Todd. bibliog il NEA J 54:16-19 Mr '65
Dance: phoenix of the arts. il Dance Mag 39:34-9 Je '65
Dancers, buildings, and people in the streets, by E. Denby. Review Sat R 49:52-3 Ja 15 '66. I Kolodin
Discothèque. N. Poirier. il Sat Eve Post 238:21-7 Mr 27 '65
Discothèque man. C. L. Mee, jr. il N Y Times Mag p92+ Ja 9 '66
Don't splinter the dance! dance in Minneapolis. J. Brin. Dance Mag 39:34-5 Ag '65
Hal Grego jazz ballets. 92nd street Y. M. Marks. Dance Mag 39:62+ N '65
Hanya Holm asks and answers. J. Anderson. il Dance Mag 39:32-3 Ag '65
How I became a dancer. M. Graham. il Sat R 48:54 Ag 28 '65
How not to cut a rug; portable dance floor. J. Peter. il Look 29:52 Jl 27 '65
In my opinion; critics of teen dances see moral danger where none exists. N. Block. Seventeen 24:204 O '65
Martha Graham's retrospective season. J. Martin. il Sat R 48:60+ D 11 '65
Minneapolis muse; modern dance. N. Hauser. il Dance Mag 39:48-50 Ag '65
Mlle; new dance. il Mlle 60:208-9 Mr '65
Opera sampler; Metropolitan opera and New York city opera productions. D. Hering. il Dance Mag 39:25-6 Ap '65
Outdoors in North Carolina; history re-created in summer pageants. D. Nesbitt. il Dance Mag 39:31 Ag '65
Parades and changes, scandal and delight; A. Halprin's dancers workshop on a European tour. R. Hartley. il Dance Mag 39:50-1+ O '65
Presstime news. See issues of Dance magazine
Questions and answers about college bookings; interview, ed. by I. Fisher. F. Taylor. Dance Mag 40:52-3+ Ja '66
Reviews. See issues of Dance magazine
Untamed surge of modern dance; with report by C. Barnes. il Life 59:96B-108 N 12 '65
Visitor from Yugoslavia; observing dance life in the United States. J. Anderson. Dance Mag 39:18-20 Jl '65
You start to smile. New Yorker 41:18-19 Jl 10 '65
   See also
Ballet
Choreography
Dance therapy
Eurythmics
Jazz music
Moving pictures—Dance films
Moving pictures—Dancing
Royal academy of dancing
Square dancing
Television broadcasting—Dancing

Auditions

Backstage views; audition; rehearsal. il Dance Mag 39:22-3 Ag '65

Bibliography

Dancer's bookshelf (cont) J. Anderson. il Dance Mag 39:49+ Je; 47-8+ N '65

Economic aspects

Contemporary look; changing times call for new knowledge about support for dance. A. Reiss. il Dance Mag 39:95-8+ D '65

Production and direction
See Dance production

Publicity

Materials of publicity: the press book (cont) D. Duncan. Dance Mag 39:14-17 Mr '65

Study and teaching

After graduation, what? D. Hering. il Dance Mag 39:50-1+ Ap '65
All aboard for Dance caravan; tour through Europe. E. LeMone. il Dance Mag 39:59-60 N '65
College or career for dancers? UCLA's answer. E. Stodelle. il Dance Mag 39:48-53 My; 40-1+ Je '65
Feeling in your bones; ed. by J. Dougherty. R. Rossellat. il Dance Mag 39:54-7 Ap '65
Filming in the studio; amateur dance films. F. De Lagrange. il Dance Mag 39:52-3+ S '65
Films for notation; study of choreography. H. P. Rogers. il Dance Mag 39:55-7 S '65
First and second thoughts about a dance career; interview, ed. by J. Anderson. H. Tamiris. il Dance Mag 39:30+ My '65
For looking, for learning, and for fun; use of films in regional ballet companies and their schools. J. Anderson. il Dance Mag 39:28-30 S '65

DANCING—Study and teaching—*Continued*
Give them a chance to dance. J. Kass. il
Parents Mag 40:55-7+ S '65
I hate academies; modern dance is an indi-
vidual quest; excerpt from Choreographers
on choreography, ed. by S. J. Cohen. A.
Sokolow. il Dance Mag 39:38-9 Jl '65
In our discontent; dance teachers devote a
week to urgent self-appraisal. D. Hering.
il Dance Mag 39:54-8 O: 54-5+ N '65
Old and new, new and old; P. Koner in Japan.
il Dance Mag 39:51 Ag '65
See-do films. W. Como. il Dance Mag 39:54
S '65
Small town teacher; D. R. Sellars of Florala,
Ala. J. Anderson. il Dance Mag 39:52-5
Jl '65
Whole secret is feeling. J. Lidstone. il Sch
Arts 64:.24-8 Mr '65
See also
Dance studios

Europe, Western
Live & let live, kiss & letkiss. Time 85:31
Mr 5 '65
DANCING (in religion, folklore, etc)
Still point. W. Glenesk. il Dance Mag 39:
39-41 Ap '65
DANCING, Greek
Meeting with Rallou Manou. S. J. Cohen. il
Dance Mag 39:57 Je '65
DANCING, Indian (East Indian)
Mile in the sky; folk dancing of Himalayan
Mountain people. D. Bhattacharya. il Dance
Mag 39:46-9 Jl '65
Story dancers of India. Philharmonic Hall.
M. Marks. Dance Mag 39:67 Je '65
DANCING, Japanese
Japanese classical dance, Fashion institute of
technology. M. Marks. Dance Mag 39:66 Je
'65
DANCING, Mexican
Dances of Anahuac, by G. P. Kurath and
S. Marti. Review
Dance Mag il 39:49+ Je '65. J. Anderson
DANCING, Russian
See also
Moiseyev dance company
DANCING, Spanish
See also
Flamenco
DANCING, Turkish
Forbidden and ecstatic circle. D. Bhat-
tacharya. il Dance Mag 39:44-5+ F '65
DANCING in art
Edgar Degas: the sentimental cynic. W.
Sorell. il Dance Mag 39:62-5 Je '65
DANCING in moving pictures. See Moving
pictures—Dancing
DANCING in television. See Television broad-
casting—Dancing
DANE, Genevieve O.
Grant programs for fiscal 1966. por Am Ed
1:5-9 Jl '65
DANELSKI, David J.
Supreme court justice steps down. Yale R
54:411-25 Mr '65
DANERS, B. Shannon, and Bearn, A. G.
Hurler's syndrome: demonstration of an in-
herited disorder of connective tissue in cell
culture. bibliog Science 149:987-9 Ag 27 '65
D'ANGELO, Armand
Blimp trip. New Yorker 41:23-4 Jl 31 '65
DANGER meters. See Automobiles—Safety de-
vices and measures
DANGERFIELD, George
Doctor Brogan in the cabbage patch. Na-
tion 200:176-8 F 15 '65
DANIEL, Charles W. and DeOme, K. B.
Growth of mouse mammary glands in vivo
after monolayer culture. bibliog Science
149:634-6 Ag 6 '65
DANIEL, D. Ronald
Team at the top. Harvard Bsns R 43:74-82
Mr '65
DANIEL, James
Hands across many seas. Read Digest 86:
155-8+ Mr '65
VITA has the answer. Read Digest 87:123-6
O '65
—and Shuman, J. B.
Why the dollar is in danger. Read Digest
87:130-4 N '65
DANIEL, Jean
Leader of Europe and arbiter between blocs.
New Repub 152:10-11 F 20 '65
DANIEL, Oliver
Americans from Vienna. Sat R 48:51-3 Je 26
'65
Dartmouth's congregation. Sat R 48:35+ Jl
31 '65
Music from the cantons. Sat R 48:49-50 D
25 '65
Take me to your lieder. Sat R 48:84-5 O 30
'65

DANIEL, Wayne
Hymn for the consecration of a church.
Christian Cent 82:1408 N 17 '65
DANIEL, Yuli
Forever amber? Newsweek 66:48 N 1 '65
DANIEL Boone regional library. See Columbia,
Mo, public library
DANIELI, Fidel A.
Reviews: Los Angeles. Art N 64:65 My '65
DANIELS, Danny
Danny Daniels says, grumble. J. Anderson. il
por Dance Mag 39:122-3+ D '65
DANIELS, Elizabeth A.
Jessie White Mario: Victorian in Italy. Na-
tion 202:13-16 Ja 3 '66
DANIELS, George
Build this three-way boat for less than $50.
il Pop Sci 186:126-33+ Ap '65
How hulls are made. Pop Sci 186:108-11 F '65
How to build piers, floats, boathouses. Pop
Sci 186:104-7 F '65
How to make a boating rescue. Pop Sci 187:
80-1+ Jl '65
Improving your home wiring. Pop Sci 187:
140-5+ Jl; 122-7+ Ag; 138-42 S; 154-9+
O '65; 188:158-63+ Ja '66
Smart new look in casters. Pop Sci 186:174-9
F '65
You can rent almost anything! Pop Sci 186:
132-4+ Je '65
DANIELS, Guy
Claude Brown's world. New Repub 153:26-8
S 25 '65
Does English usage exist? New Repub 153:
32-4 Ag 21 '65
Project Mayakovsky. New Repub 153:24+ D
4 '65
Pushkin and the lepidopterist. New Repub
152:19-21 Ap 3 '65
DANIELS, Jonathan
Ever-ever land. Harper 230:183-4+ Ap '65
In the crusading tradition. Sat R 48:142-4
Mr 13 '65
Raleigh: a long look ahead. Sat R 48:40 My
22 '65
DANIELS, Jonathan Myrick
Catalyst for reconciliation. Christian Cent
82:1084-5 S 8 '65
Death in the Black Belt. il por Time 86:12
Ag 27 '65
In the heart of life. Newsweek 66:20 Ag 30 '65
DANISH cookery. See Cookery, Danish
DANISH royal ballet. See Royal Danish ballet
DANNHAUSER, Werner J.
Decline of reason. Commentary 39:100-4 Je '65
(tr) See Lind, J. Nazis on trial; pages from
a journal
DANOVITZ, Saul
Area technical high school. NEA J 54:41-3
My '65
DANTE Alighieri
Paradiso; canto five; tr. by J. Ciardi. Poetry
107:75-84 N '65

about

Dante; The Inferno and its illustrators with
report by K. Kappler. Life 59:38-43+ D
17 '65
Dante vivo. America 112:746-7 My 22 '65
Dantean music: celebration of Dante centen-
nial at Fairfield university. C. J. McNaspy.
America 112:839-40 Je 5 '65
Dante's novel of the self: Divine comedy.
J. Freccero. por Christian Cent 82:1216-18
O 6 '65
Dante's pilgrimage. M. Bishop. il por Hori-
zon 7:4-15 Sum '65
Dante's vision. A. Curtayne. America 113:751-
3 D 11 '65
European literary scene; celebration of
Dante's 700th anniversary. R. J. Clements.
il Sat R 48:26-7+ My 15 '65
Man for the ages. il pors Time 86:100+
Jl 9 '65
Relevance of Dante. J. Ciardi. il por Sat R
48:16-18+ My 15; 51-3 My 22 '65
700 years after: the relevance of Dante. J.
Ciardi. il por Sat R 48:16-18+ My 15 '65
(to be cont)
Two great Florentines. R. Moley. Newsweek
65:120 My 24; 88 My 31 '65
Vehement soul. por Newsweek 65:121 My 10
'65
DANTE prize
Unforeseen development on Mount Parnassus.
D. Dempsey. Sat R 48:29 Mr 13 '65
DANTON'S death; drama. See Büchner, G.
DANUBE RIVER
Down the Danube by canoe; Dartmouth canoe
club. W. S. Backer. il Nat Geog Mag 128:
34-79 Jl '65
DANUBIAN countries
Down the Danube by canoe; Dartmouth canoe
club. W. S. Backer. il Nat Geog Mag 128:
34-79 Jl '65

DANZIG, David
Conservatism after Goldwater. Commentary 39:31-7 Mr '65
Republican parties. Christian Cent 82:326 Mr 17 '65

DAPHNES
Daphne, fussy but irresistible. il Sunset 134: 192+ F '65

DAPHNIA. See Cladoceran

DA PONTE, Lorenzo
That true phoenix: Lorenzo da Ponte. G. Rogoff. il Hi Fi 15:58-61+ N '65

DARACK, Arthur
Art for the ages or temper of the times? Sat R 48:37-8 S 11 '65
Great ones loved him. Sat R 48:100-1 S 18 '65
His doubt was not without hope. Sat R 48: 59-60 O 23 '65
In love with the renaissance. Sat R 48:53 O 9 '65
Intellectual passion, logical love. Sat R 48: 29-30 My 8 '65
When life was but a dream. Sat R 48:59 O 30 '65

DARBY, George
Most unforgettable character I've met. H. W. McKervill. il por Read Digest 87:223-4+ O '65

DARBY, S. Newman
Sailboarding: exciting new water sport. Pop Sci 187:138-41 Ag '65

DARDANELLES
Great Britain and the 1914-1915 Straits agreement with Russia; the British promise of November 1914. C. J. Smith, jr. bibliog f Am Hist R 70:1015-34 Jl '65

DARGOMYZHSKII, Aleksandr Sergeevich
On records: Rusalka; The stone guest. Opera N 29:40 My 1 '65

DARIAUX, Genevieve Antoine
Sensible woman's guide to entertaining; excerpts from Entertaining with elegance. Redbook 125:56-7+ Jl '65

DARIEN, Conn.
Education
Integrating a white ghetto; Darien, Conn. program of exchanges. J. V. Davis. il Sat R 48:84-5+ N 20 '65

DARK, Harris Edward
His first trip to school? make it a safe one. Todays Health 43:50-1+ S '65

DARK glasses. See Sun glasses

DARKE, Kenneth H.
SEC vs. Texas Gulf raises sticky questions; bonanza trouble. C. Welles. il por Life 59:29-30+ Ag 6 '65

DARKROOM exposure meters. See Exposure meters

DARKROOM meters. See Photography—Apparatus and supplies

DARKROOMS. See Photography—Studios and darkrooms

DARLEY, Ward
Where is science taking us? Sat R 48:55-6 S 4 '65

DARLING, David W.
Team teaching; Wisconsin improvement program. NEA J 54:24-5 My '65

DARLING, said Amanda; story. See Carter, M.

DARLINGTON, Celia
Cuidado! el traffic cop. Atlan 216:115-16 D '65

DARLINGTON manufacturing company. See Deering, Milliken and company

DARNELL, Linda
Needless tragedy of Linda Darnell. K. Baskette. il pors Good H 161:42+ S '65

DARRELL, Robert Donaldson
Dread day of wrath, and the whisper of compassion. Hi Fi 15:86-7 N '65
Sonic showcase. See issues of High fidelity incorporating Musical America
Stokowski's Scheherazade. Hi Fi 15:87-8 Mr '65
Tape deck. See issues of High fidelity incorporating Musical America

DARRING, Walter
Surprised by me; poem. New Yorker 41:32 Jl 24 '65

DART, Justin Whitlock
Rexall Darts ahead. por Newsweek 66:75 Jl 19 '65

DARTMOUTH college, Hanover, N.H.
Hopkins center
Dartmouth's congregation: summer music program. O. Daniel. Sat R 48:35+ Jl 31 '65
Krenek on campus: Congregation of the arts. C. L. Osborne. il Hi Fi 15:148-9 O '65

DASBURG, Andrew
Out there in the universe; exhibition at Knoedler gallery. il por Newsweek 66:88 N 1 '65

DAS GUPTA, N. N. and Moore, D. H.
Electron microscopy in the Far East. Science 148:1126-7 My 21 '65

DASH, Joan
Sephardim. Américas 17:8-14 O '65

DA SILVA, Howard, and Leon, Felix
Zulu and the zayda. Criticism
America 113:762 D 11 '65
Commonweal 83:316 D 10 '65
New Yorker 41:149 N 20 '65
Newsweek il 66:97 N 22 '65
Time il 86:97 N 19 '65
Vogue 147:72 Ja 1 '66

DASSAULT, Marcel
Mystère man. E. Behr. il por Newsweek 66: 68+ S 13 '65

DASSAULT, Marcel, company. See Airplane industry and trade—France

DATA processing service centers
Data link. W. O. Reed. il Am Ed 1:31-2 Je '65

DATA processing workers. See Computer workers

DATA storage and retrieval systems. See Information storage and retrieval systems

DATA transmission systems. See Computers—Communication applications

DATING
Blind dates; excerpt from Seventeen book of etiquette and entertaining. E. A. Haupt. Seventeen 24:43 Je '65
Boys never gave me a tumble. S. Field. Seventeen 25:50 Ja '66
Can a girl change a boy? questions and answers. A. Wood. il Seventeen 24:98-9+ Je '65
Going steady, who needs it? A. Landers. Read Digest 87:88-90 D '65
Going together; teen-agers in southern California. J. Poppy. il Look 29:80-5 Jl 13 '65
Handicapped girl; questions and answers. A. Wood. il Seventeen 24:102-3 D '65
How do bachelors get away with it? five young men tell all to a tape recorder. Mlle 60:105-6+ F '65; Discussion. 61:183-5+ S '65
Little things mean a lot. J. Gibbs. il Seventeen 25:104+ Ja '66
Love and sex. D. Sugarman and R. Hochstein. Seventeen 24:94-5+ Jl '65
My IBM baby; blindness out of blind dates. il Time 86:84+ N 19 '65
No date for the dance; questions and answers. A. Wood. il Seventeen 24:152-3+ N '65
Opinion, please from Philadelphia; young man's first dance. J. A. Snyder. Mlle 61: 144+ Ag '65
Possessive male; questions and answers. A. Wood. il Seventeen 24:128-9+ O '65
Talking it over with Gay Head; questions and answers. Gay Head. See issues of Senior scholastic
That weekend date. J. Wescott. il Seventeen 24:196 O '65
Townies; quartet of off-campus cuties. il Esquire 64:92-5 S '65
When is a steady un-steady? J. Wescott. il Seventeen 24:13 Mr '65
When is old enough? questions and answers. A. Wood. il Seventeen 24:160-1 F '65
When the sap begins to flow. G. Naismith. il Todays Health 43:44-6+ F '65
Why am I unlucky in love? questions and answers. A. Wood. il Seventeen 24:152-3+ Ap '65

DATING, Radiocarbon. See Radiocarbon dating

DATURA
See also
Jimson weed

DAUBER, Samuel
Obituary
Pub W 187:40 My 24 '65

DAUGHERTY, A. C.
Let's have more research on research; address, September 23, 1965. Vital Speeches 32:89-93 N 15 '65

DAUGHERTY, Clark
Preparation, perspiration, participation; address, May 12, 1965. Vital Speeches 31:539-42 Je 15 '65

DAUGHERTY, Hugh Duffy
Don't get Duffy mad. il por Time 86:75 N 12 '65
Duffy's Hawaiian punch. G. Astor. il por Look 29:85-8 D 28 '65

DAUGHERTY, James Henry
Out there in the universe; exhibition at Knoedler gallery. il por Newsweek 66:88 N 1 '65

DAUGHERTY, John, and Daugherty, Molly
Animal behavior quiz. Sci Digest 58:87-9 N '65
Bird quiz. Sci Digest 58:83-5 Ag '65
Do you act your age? questions and answers. Sci Digest 57:92-4 My '65
Do you know your metals? questions and answers. Sci Digest 57:88-90 Je '65
Do you smell something? questions and answers. Sci Digest 58:89-91 Jl '65

DAUGHERTY, John, and Daugherty, Molly—
  Continued
  Electricity and magnetism quiz. Sci Digest
    58:91-4 D '65
  How do you figure? questions and answers.
    Sci Digest 57:95-7 F '65
  Inventors quiz. Sci Digest 57:93-4 Mr '65
  Plants that cure, quiz. Sci Digest 58:92-4 O
    '65
  Quiz; how we use rocks and minerals. Sci
    Digest 57:89-91 Ap '65
  Spider quiz. Sci Digest 58:90-2 S '65
  Which is older, the earth or the sun? quiz.
    Sci Digest 59:92-4 Ja '66
DAUGHERTY, Molly. See Daugherty, J. jt.
  auth.
DAUGHTERS
  Joy. R. Burton. McCalls 93:25 D '65
    See also
  Fathers
  Girls
DAUGHTERS and mothers. See Parent-child
  relationship
DAUGHTERS and parents. See Parent-child
  relationship
DAUGHTERS of the American revolution
  Argumentum ad ridiculum; concerning Sen-
    ate publishing of DAR annual report. New
    Repub 153:7 Jl 24 '65
  Hobbies salutes diamond jubilee of the
    D.A.R. and its president general. il
    Hobbies 70:72-3 Ap '65
DAUTERMAN, Carl C.
  Chinese imagery on restoration silver. An-
    tiques 88:511-15 O '65
DAVENPORT, Arthur
  100-a-day at Enfield. Field & S 70:43-5+ Je
    '65
DAVENPORT, Barbara
  Books on the mountain. Am Ed 1:12-15 Mr
    '65
DAVENPORT, Guy
  Books to make friends happy. Nat R 17:1163-
    4 D 14 '65
  Cretan glance. Nat R 17:937-8 O 19 '65
  Need to maintain a civilization. Nat R 17:
    283-4 Ap 6 '65
  Visual arts 1955-1965. Nat R 17:1111-12 N 30
    '65
DAVENPORT, Gwen
  Practical joker; story. Sat Eve Post 239:40-5
    Ja 1 '66
DAVENPORT, John
  Book review. Life 59:12+ D 10 '65
DAVENPORT, John, 1904-
  Troubled world of international money. For-
    tune 73:136-40+ Ja '66
DAVENPORT, Ia.
  New corrosion inhibitor checks salt damage
    to cars. il Am City 80:66 O '65
DAVID, Lester
  Are you really in love? questions and answers.
    Read Digest 86:33-4+ Je '65
  (ed) My nightmare as an alcoholic. Good H
    160:75+ F '65
  My son was a drug addict. Good H 160:53+
    Ja '65
  Our daughter was a victim of the world's
    cruelest hoax. Good H 161:81+ N '65
  Our son was different. Good H 162:51+
    Ja '66
  Promise and perils of the miraculous DMSO.
    Good H 161:68-9+ Ag '65
  Questions for young people, and for parents.
    Read Digest 86:213-14 Mr '65
  She only cried once. Good H 161:74-5+ S '65
  (ed) See McNeil, V. A. I'm glad I tried to
    help
DAVIDS, Richard C.
  Welcome to Happy Hollow. Farm J 89:82-3
    My '65
DAVIDSON, Bill
  Jeane Dixon predicts the future. Ladies
    Home J 82:74+ N '65
  Mafia can't crack Los Angeles. Sat Eve Post
    238:23-7 Jl 31 '65
  Ordeal of a Hoffa victim. Sat Eve Post 238:
    23-7 Je 19 '65
  Teen-age drinking. Sat Eve Post 238:23-7
    Ap 10 '65
  Who killed your favorite TV show? Sat Eve
    Post 238:84-7 F 27 '65
  Your eye can't lie. Sat Eve Post 239:76-9
    Ja 15 '66
DAVIDSON, Eric H.
  Hormones and genes; with biographical
    sketch. Sci Am 212:20, 36-45 bibliog (p 146)
    Je '65
DAVIDSON, Erika
  (ed) See King, J. Homecoming
DAVIDSON, Frank P.
  Chunnel. For Affairs 44:314-19 Ja '66
DAVIDSON, Glen W.
  Mormon missionaries and the race question.
    Christian Cent 82:1183-6 S 29 '65
DAVIDSON, Homer L.
  Let the sun power your portable. Pop Electr
    23:85-6 D '65

DAVIDSON, J. A.
  Not just a bad joke. Christian Cent 82:1579
    D 22 '65
DAVIDSON, Morton. See Bernheimer, A. W.
  jt. auth.
DAVIDSON, Muriel
  What prayer means to me. Good H 160:90-1
    Je '65
  What Princess Grace likes and doesn't like
    about the life she leads. Good H 160:58-63+
    Ja '65
  (ed) See Farr, F. My husband, Jack Lem-
    mon
DAVIDSON, Patricia
  Gold of Alexander. Art N 64:32-5+ D '65
DAVIDSON, Peter
  Gifts; poem. Atlan 216:98 O '65
DAVIDSON, Ruth
  Books about antiques. See issues of Antiques
  Current and coming. See issues of Antiques
  In the museums. See issues of Antiques
DAVIDSON, Treat
  Moths that behave like hummingbirds. il
    Nat Geog Mag 127:770-5 Je '65
  Tree snails, gems of the Everglades. il Nat
    Geog Mag 127:372-87 Mr '65
DAVIDSON college, Davidson, N.C.
  Agony of Lefty Driesell. J. Jares. il Sports
    Illus 22:32-5 Mr 8 '65
DAVIE, Donald
  After Sedley, after Pound. Nation 201:311-13
    N 1 '65
  On translating Mao's poetry. Nation 200:
    704-5 Je 28 '65
DAVIES, Alfred T.
  Law and morality in race relations. Chris-
    tian Cent 82:1256-8 O 13 '65
DAVIES, James C.
  Family's role in political socialization. bib-
    liog f Ann Am Acad 361:10-19 S '65
DAVIES, John Paton, Jr
  How Russia has changed and what it means
    to us. il Look 29:81-3 My 18 '65
  Yankee go home? stay home? intervene?
    N Y Times Mag p28-9+ My 23 '65
DAVIES, Julian, and others
  Inhibition of protein synthesis by spectinom-
    ycin. bibliog Science 149:1096-8 S 3 '65
DAVIES, Margaret E.
  French paintings from Russia at the Louvre.
    Antiques 88:584+ N '65
DAVIES, William Henry
  Vagabond muse. L. Untermeyer. Sat R 48:
    51+ O 16 '65
DAVIS, Al
  Thunder out of Oakland. il por Sports Illus
    23:86-8+ N 15 '65
DAVIS, Arthur A.
  Open-space planning process; excerpt from
    address, 1964. Recreation 58:400-2 O '65
DAVIS, Benjamin Oliver, 1912-
  Cadet who refused to quit. R. S. Strother.
    por Read Digest 87:71-5 S '65
DAVIS, Bette
  Pro. I. Mothner. il pors Look 29:20-5 Mr 9 '65
DAVIS, Bob
  Wee bit of Irish yachting. por Motor B 116:
    26-7+ Ag '65
DAVIS, Bud
  Colorado football's galloping disaster. Harper
    231:50-3 O '65
DAVIS, Burke
  WLB biography. L. Ash. por Wilson Lib
    Bul 39:694+ Ap '65
DAVIS, Catherine
  Cold comfort; poem. Poetry 106:204 Je '65
DAVIS, Charles
  Theological asides (cont) America 112:193,
    394, 667; 113:97, 284, 626 F 6, Mr 20, My 8,
    Jl 24, S 18, N 20 '65
DAVIS, Chester
  Moravians of Salem. Antiques 88:60-4 Jl '65
DAVIS, Christopher
  Boy scouts. Esquire 64:69-71+ Jl '65
  Go, Massillon, go! Esquire 64:206-7+ D '65
  Man of affairs; story. Esquire 63:70 My '65
DAVIS, Clara J.
  Grow and enjoy tantalizing begonias. Pop
    Gard 16:38-40 Mr '65
DAVIS, Claude W.
  Louisiana iris in South. Horticulture 43:27+
    Mr '65
DAVIS, David E. See Christian, J. J. jt. auth.
DAVIS, E. Louise, and Allen, P. H.
  (eds) Junior books appraised. See second
    issue of each month of Library journal to
    February 15, 1965
  —and Thomson, J.C.
  (eds) Junior books appraised. Library J 90:
    5070+ N 15 '65
  —and others
  (ed) Junior books appraised. Library J 90:
    1541-2+, 2009-10+, 2393-4+, 2880-92+,
    3120-37, 3776+, 4602+ Mr 15, Ap 15, My
    15, Je 15, Jl, S 15, O 15 '65
DAVIS, Eileen
  Paint a movie on film! Pop Phot 56:120 My
    '65

DAVIS, Florence Follwell
Herbs; on your windowsill. Horticulture 43
47-8 F '65
DAVIS, Glover
Monuments; poem. Poetry 106:282 Jl '65
DAVIS, Hazel
What teachers say about evaluation of teach-
ers. NEA J 54:37-9 F '65
DAVIS, James
Pope John set to music. Am Rec G 32:60 S
'65
DAVIS, Jefferson
Jefferson Davis. R. Moley. Newsweek 66:72
S 6 '65
La. state univ. to do Jefferson Davis papers.
Pub W 187:51 Mr 1 '65
DAVIS, Joan V.
Integrating a white ghetto. Sat R 48:84-5+
N 20 '65
DAVIS, John W.
Open window of history. por Negro Hist Bul
28:183 My '65
DAVIS, Keith
Big red. Esquire 65:28-30 Ja '66
DAVIS, Kingsley
Urbanization of the human population; with
biographical sketch. Sci Am 213:28, 40-53
S '65
DAVIS, Leroy
Parochial syndrome. Christian Cent 82:1543-5
D 15 '65
DAVIS, M. Edward
Expectant mother. Redbook 125:33+ Ag '65
DAVIS, Marguerite Norris
Pots of pleasure. Flower Grower 52:18+ F '65
DAVIS, Melton S.
First the pasta, then the play. N Y Times
Mag p 10-11+ Ja 2 '66
Hamlet who wants to play clowns. N Y Times
Mag p46-7+ S 19 '65
DAVIS, Meyer
Next dance will be what is Meyer Davis
doing while Oedipus and the mothers drop
trousers? G. Frazier. Esquire 65:60-1+ Ja
'66
DAVIS, Miles Dewey
Rollins and Davis renewed. M. Williams. por
Sat R 48:91 O 30 '65
DAVIS, Norman M.
For Pearl Harbor day; poem. Cath World 202:
140-3 D '65
DAVIS, Peter G.
Fine sound in the Fine arts center. Hi Fi
15:202 N '65
Harvest of hosannas. Hi Fi 15:28+ D '65
Notes from our correspondents. Hi Fi 15:36
Ap; 16+ My; 24+ Je; 22+ Jl; 26+ N; 14+
D '65; 16:16+ Ja '66
Signor Bettini's cylinders. Hi Fi 15:24+ Ag
'65
DAVIS, Robert K. and Knetsch, J. L.
Conflct in outdoor recreation. Am For 71:26-
9+ N '65
DAVIS, Sammy
How I got into show business; excerpt from
Yes I can. Harper 231:87-90 Ag '65
Military ordeal of Sammy Davis jr; excerpt
from Yes I can. pors Ebony 21:151-4+ D '65
Yes I can; excerpt. ed. by J. Boyar and
B. Boyar. pors Ladies Home J 82:77-84 Ag
'65
about
I gotta get bigger. por Newsweek 66:80+
Ag 9 '65
Man of many selves. il pors Time 86:92 N
5 '65
Sammy could and did. T. Thompson. Life
59:21 N 5 '65
Sammy Davis: don't call him junior any-
more. T. Armbrister. il pors Sat Eve Pos
238:89-93 F 13 '65
DAVIS, Shawn
New breed of bronc buster. J. R. McDermott.
por Life 59:60+ Ag 20 '65
DAVIS, Sol
Audio power wattmeter. Electr World 74:77
D '65
DAVIS, Stuart
American masters. il por Newsweek 65:88 Je
21 '65
Art galleries; memorial exhibition at Whit-
ney museum. R. M. Coates. New Yorker
41:193-4+ O 2 '65
Davis retrospective; exhibition at the Whit-
ney museum. New York. B. Kaufman. Com-
monweal 83:69-70 O 15 '65
Stuart Davis in memoriam. F. Getlein. New
Repub 153:36-7 Jl 24 '65
DAVIS, Tommy
Deadly slide for the Dodgers. J. Mann. il
Sports Illus 22:30-1 My 10 '65
DAVIS, W. A.
Future of V/STOL; excerpts from address.
Aviation W 83:21 N 15 '65

DAVIS, Watson
Free source of materials. Sci N L 87:340 My 29
DAVIS, Wynn
Angling. See issues of Outdoor life
Five tips for opening day. Outdoor Life 135:
33-5+ Ap '65
Squaretail country. Outdoor Life 135:48-9+
Je '65
DAVIS cup. See Tennis
DAVISON, Peter
Bright being; poem. Atlan 216:65 N '65
Eurydice in darkness; poem. Atlan 216:65 Ag
'65
Gilt edge of reputation; twelve months of
new poetry. Atlan 217:82-5 Ja '66
Lunch at the Coq d'or; poem. Reporter 34:
47 Ja 13 '66
Unwilling to wake; poem. Atlan 216:83 D '65
DAVISON, Verne E.
Choice feeders and foods for eastern birds;
excerpts. Audubon Mag 67:393-4+ N '65
Food choices of some choice species; excerpts.
Audubon Mag 67:322+ S '65 (to be cont)
Nest sites of 400 eastern species. Audubon
Mag 67:258-9 Jl '65
DAWBER, Thomas R.
Heart attack, what's the risk? Todays Health
43:46-7+ Ag '65
DAWDLING. See Procrastination
DAWE, D. L. and others
Passive transfer of the action of Freund's
adjuvant by serum of rabbits injected with
the adjuvant. bibliog Science 148:1345-7 Je
4 '65
DAWIDOWICZ, Lucy S.
Pastor and the Jews. Commentary 40:110-12
N '65
DAWKINS, Michael J. R. and Hull, David
Production of heat by fat; with biographical
sketches. Sci Am 213:11, 62-7 bibliog(p 119)
Ag '65
DAWN, Marpessa
Girl on the go in Paris. il pors Ebony 20:
100+ My '65
DAWN redwood. See Metasequoia
DAWSON, Christopher
Dawson's new contribution to dialogue.
C. J. McNaspy. America 112:432 Mr 27 '65
DAWSON, Daniel
Haunted man's perilous search; with report
by D. Moser. il pors Life 58:26-35+ Mr 12
'65
I finally met the Vietcong and became their
prisoner. D. Dawson. il por Life 59:121-2+
O 8 '65
DAWSON, Donald
I am black and blue and every bone hurts.
por Life 58:64-8 Mr 12 '65
I finally met the Vietcong and became their
prisoner; with introduction. pors Life 59:
121-2+ O 8 '65

about

Haunted man's perilous search; with report
by D. Moser. il pors Life 58:26-35+ Mr 12
'65
DAWSON, Kenneth E.
Conversation on industrial arts and voca-
tional education; interview. por NEA J 54:
25-8 N '65
DAWSON, Robert
Rafters; poem. Atlan 216:95-6 S '65
DAY, Beth
Jot it down. Read Digest 87:31-2+ Jl '65
—See Liley, M. jt. auth.
DAY, Doris
Doris Day cuts up; photographs. Good H
161:72-3 O '65
DAY, J. Edward
When in Washington: hang up while you're
talking; excerpt from My appointed round.
por Nations Bsns 53:38-9+ Jl '65
DAY, Richard
Easy way to raise sunken concrete slabs.
Pop Sci 186:146-9 Je '65
Is your plumbing double-crossing you? Pop
Mech 124:160-3+ Ag '65
Three trays you can make. il Pop Sci 187:
148-51 N '65
DAY, Richard L.
Captain of his ship. Yachting 117:59+ My
'65
DAY, Virgil B.
Collective bargaining; address, April 14, 1965.
Vital Speeches 31:437-41 My 1 '65
DAY, William L.
Where urban renewal brings history to life.
il por Bsns W p78-9+ O 23 '65
DAY-LEWIS, C.
Poems, 1964: St Anthony's shirt; Days before
a journey. Harper 230:85 Mr '65
Stephanotis; poem. Atlan 215:62 Je '65
DAY camps. See Camps

DAY care for children. See Day nurseries

DAY lilies
Discover new colors in daylilies. il Pop Gard 16:11-12 Ap '65
It's day-lily time. il Flower Grower 52:24 Jl '65
Modern daylilies. W. B. Flory. il Horticulture 43:16-17+ Jl '65
No sooner said than done. il Flower Grower 52:37 Ag '65
Outstanding day-lily; Midwest star. Flower Grower 52:41 D '65

DAY nurseries
Concrete for shade and pattern; design for Child care center, Chicago. il Arch Rec 138:159-60 N '65
Day care centers for children with no place to go. K. B. Oettinger. Parents Mag 40: 42 F '65

DAY of absence; drama. See Ward, D. T.

DAY of the tortoise; musical comedy. See Musical comedies, revues, etc.—Criticisms, plots, etc.

DAY schools, Jewish. See Jews—Education

DAY the time changed; story. See Mandel, G.

DAY the whores came out to play tennis; drama. See Kopit, A.

DAYE, J. R. and Heron, A. deF.
Stationary snow melter overcomes dumping dilemma. Am City 80:86-9 F '65

DAYLIGHT saving
As clocks change: crazy-quilt confusion. U S News 58:14 My 3 '65
Letter from Stan Delaplane. S. Delaplane. il Todays Health 43:8 Jl '65
Time after time; confusion over DST in U.S. Newsweek 65:39-40 My 10 '65
What time have you got? Nation 200:491 My 10 '65

DAYLIGHTING. See Lighting

DAYLILIES. See Day lilies

DAYS between; drama. See Anderson, R.

DAYTON, Ohio

Galleries and museums
Master rediscovered; Terbrugghen exhibition at Art institute. il Newsweek 66:108+ N 8 '65

Water supply
Designed for split treatment. R. C. Stout and B. S. Shuey. il Am City 80:108-11 My '65

DAYTON trial. See Tennessee evolution controversy

DAYTONA international speedway. See Speedways

DAYTON'S department store. See Minneapolis —Stores

DEACONESSES
Communion from a woman. Time 85:91-2 Ap 30 '65
See also
Edwards, P.

DEACONS for defense of justice (organization) See Civil rights organizations

DEAD, Resuscitation of. See Resuscitation

DEAD, The. See Death

DEAD SEA scrolls
Dead Sea scrolls: a new historical approach. by C. Roth. Review
Sat R 48:22-3 S 4 '65. T. H. Gaster
Endless cave in Jerusalem; shrine for Israel's collection of Dead Sea scrolls. il Time 85: 82-4 Ap 30 '65
Scroll search controlled by Jordan government. Sci N L 87:178 Mr 20 '65
Shrine of the book: the great new museum in Jerusalem. il Vogue 145:186-7 My '65

DEAD souls; drama. See Bulgakov, M.

DEAF
Telephones for the deaf; reprint. G. M. Smith. il Sci Digest 57:55-9 My '65

Education
Help for the child with impaired hearing. W. Formaad. NEA J 54:45-6 D '65
School for the deaf adds facilities for pre-primary training; New York school for the deaf, White Plains, N.Y. il Arch Rec 137:181-3 Mr '65
Talk. talk. talk to deaf children; John Tracy clinic. Mrs S. Tracy. il Am Ed 1:4-7 D '64

DEAF, Apparatus for the
See also
Hearing aids

DEAF, Moving pictures for the
Films with meaning for the deaf. il Am Ed 1:23 Mr '65

DEAF, Sports for the. See International games for the deaf

DEAF Olympics. See International games for the deaf

DEAFNESS
Black cat gains fame as hearing loss patient. il Sci N L 88:131 Ag 28 '65
Costly cat aids deafness research. il Todays Health 43:75 Je '65
Hearing, lost and found. A. N. Lemon. il Todays Health 43:49-50 Jl '65
Who'd rather be deaf? E. Corbett. Atlan 216:116+ O '65

DEAFNESS research foundation
Costly cat aids deafness research. il Todays Health 43:75 Je '65

DEAGAN, J. P.
Cool on a hot curl. N Y Times Mag p72-3 Ag 22 '65

DEAKIN, James
How to out-fox the majority. New Repub 152:13-14 F 27 '65
Humphrey. New Repub 152:10-12 My 29 '65

DEAL, Babs H.
To ride an elephant; story. Redbook 125: 50-1 Ag '65

DEAL, Borden
Long way to go; story. Good H 161:65-7 Jl '65

DEALER relations
All the world's a stage for business meetings. il Bsns W p74-5 F 6 '65
Seagram's recipe: a dash of advice; operates own management consulting service. il Bsns W p 126+ Ja 30 '65

DEALERS, Art. See Art dealers

DEALERS, Automobile. See Automobile dealers

DEALERS, Farm equipment. See Farm equipment dealers

DEALERS in antiques. See Antique dealers

DEAN, Dizzy
Dizzy makes a different kind of pitch; playing duplicate bridge. C. Goren. il Sports Illus 23:74 O 11 '65

DEAN, Jay Hanna. See Dean, D.

DEAN, Sir Patrick Henry
Ideology of foreign policy; address, December 1, 1965. Vital Speeches 32:173-5 Ja 1 '66
President Johnson receives book on the Magna carta; remarks, July 22, 1965. Dept State Bul 53:235 Ag 9 '65

DEAN, Robert
This winter make a handsome transom swim platform. Motor B 116:84-5+ N '65

DEAN, Robert L.
Case for a narrow education. America 112: 553 Ap 17 '65
Good advice from the social scientists. por Cath World 202:80-3 N '65
Sneaky summer word-makers. America 113: 135 Ag 7 '65

DEAN, Stuart E.
Nongraded school. bibliog f Sch Life 47:19-23 D '64

DEAN, Vera Micheles
He left his country a future. Sat R 48:26-7 Mr 27 '65

DEANE, Philip, pseud.
Old man from Crete. New Repub 153:26-7 O 2 '65

DEANGELIS, Anthony
Great salad oil swindle. by N. C. Miller. Review
Harper 231:118+ D '65. J. Chamberlain
Reporter 33:54-7 D 2 '65. H. Robinson
Judgment day for Tino. Newsweek 65:75-6 Je 7 '65
Man who fooled everybody. il por Time 85: 20-1 Je 4 '65
Salad oil mystery. M. Kempton. New Repub 153:9-11 Jl 24 '65
Twenty years for Tino. il por Newsweek 66: 70+ Ag 30 '65

DEARBORN, Mich.
Fresh-air heater stops negative pressure problems. il Am City 80:94 Jl '65

Politics and government
One million per cent; segregation. Newsweek 66:27-8 Jl 5 '65

DEARDEN, John
How to organize information systems. bibliog f Harvard Bsns R 43:65-73 Mr '65
—and Edgerly, W. S.
Bonus formula for division heads. Harvard Bsns R 43:83-90 S '65
—See Butler, W. J. jt. auth.

DEARDORFF, Robert
Ringo Starr; domesticated Beatle. Redbook 125:60-1+ S '65
Valais variety. Travel 123:58-61 Je '65
(ed) See Chaplin, G. Charlie Chaplin's daughter

DEARMENT, W. E.
We solved a filter-media problem. Am City 80:83-5 D '65

DEARMORE, Tom
Will evolution come to Arkansas? Reporter 34:34 Ja 13 '66

DEATH
Death isn't necessary; condensed from address. A. W. Galston. Sci Digest 58:80-5 Jl '65
Death of death? concerning L. Boros' Mystery of death. il Newsweek 67:53 Ja 24 '66
Feather of a dove; a husband's tribute to his wife; excerpt from More than booty. B. Crile. il Redbook 126:42-3+ Ja '66
On death as a constant companion; Time essay. Time 86:52-3 N 12 '65
See also
Children and death
Euthanasia
Immortality
Suicide

Causes
Cause of death: fright. Newsweek 66:62 D 27 '65
Enigma of sudden infant death. M. R. Dische. Ladies Home J 82:48+ Mr '65
Today's health guide; safety in the home; excerpts. il Todays Health 43:35-42 Je '65
See also
Heat—Physiological effects

DEATH (biology)
Can deep freeze conquer death? cryogenic interment. R. C. W. Ettinger. il Ebony 21:60-1+ Ja '66
Frozen Christian; cryogenic interment. R. C. W. Ettinger. Christian Cent 82:1313-15 O 27 '65; Reply. L. J. Putnam. 82:1550+ D 15 '65
How to delay death. V. Negovsky and V. Soboleva. il Sci Digest 57:60-5 Ap '65
Lasting indefinitely. R. C. W. Ettinger. il Esquire 63:63-5+ My '65

DEATH and children. See Children and death
DEATH penalty. See Capital punishment
DEATH tax. See Inheritance tax

DEATH VALLEY NATIONAL MONUMENT
Sunny winter holiday at Furnace Creek. il Sunset 134:42+ F '65

DEATHLESS lovers; story. See Woiwode, L.

DEBAKEY, Michael Ellis
Tell me, doctor. Ladies Home J 82:30 Ap '65

about
Texas tornado. il pors Time 85:46-8+ My 28 '65

DEBARTOLO, Dick
Summer thoughts for winter thinking. Motor B 116:22-3+ D '65

DEBAT, Alphonse Massamba-. See Massamba-Debat, A.

DEBATES and debating
See also
Oxford University—Oxford union society

DEBATING societies
Forensic furore can be resolved; representation of Catholic high schools in the National forensic league. America 112:212 F 13 '65; Reply. G. René. 112:340 Mr 13 '65
See also
Oxford University—Oxford union society

DEBETZ, Georghi F.
Biology looks at race. UNESCO Courier 18:4-7 Ap '65

DE BEUS, J. G.
United Nations commemoration address, June 25, 1965. UN Mo Chron 2:121-2+ Jl '65

DE BOLT, William Walter
Lucky Pilate; poem. Christian Cent 82:430 Ap 7 '65

DE BREMAECKER, J. Cl.
Microseisms from hurricane Hilda. bibliog Science 148:1725-7 Je 25 '65

DEBT
American way of debt. Time 85:82 Je 18 '65
Pay-later economy. Nation 201:178-9 O 4 '65
Young mother revisited; how Hubbell family extricated themselves. J. Robbins and J. Robbins. il Redbook 125:8+ S '65
Your debts: too big? how much people owe. il U S News 58:45-8 Je 14 '65
See also
Bankruptcy
Credit
Debtor and creditor
Farm finance

DEBT counseling. See Debtor and creditor

DEBTOR and creditor
Those damned Joneses; Counseling services aid debtors. il Newsweek 67:78 Ja 17 '66

DEBTS, Public
If nations only paid U.S. what they owe: World war I, II and postwar debt. il U S News 58:78 Mr 15 '65
No hope of collecting what others owe U.S? U S News 58:13 Mr 29 '65
World war I debts. R. Moley. Newsweek 65:90 Mr 1 '65

United States
As bankers look at the new economics; symposium. il U S News 58:86-90 Je 21 '65
Federal debt management. R. V. Roosa. Duns R 85:33+ Je '65
High-cost borrowing; meaning to taxpayers; carrying public debt. il U S News 60:95-7 Ja 17 '66
Only $30 billion in the red! D. Lawrence. U S News 58:112 My 10 '65

DEBUS, Allen
Florrie Forde. Hobbies 70:36 Jl '65
Sheet music; I. Franklin and B. Green. Hobbies 70:36+ S '65

DEBUSSCHERE, David Albert
Young man with three heads. T. C. Brody. por Sports Illus 22:20-1+ Mr 1 '65

DEBUSSY, Claude
As never before, London's Pelléas et Mélisande. H. Glass. il Am Rec G 31:694-6 Ap '65
George Copeland; at 82, incredibly, still the peerless interpreter of Debussy. R. Kammerer. Am Rec G 31:538 F '65
Pelléas et Mélisande. Criticism
Am Rec G 31:692-3 Ap '65
Pelléas in stereo, with Ansermet in brilliant form. C. L. Osborne. Hi Fi 15:72-3 Ap '65

DEBUTANTES
Teens make debut for grown-up cause; Link's Oakland cotillion. il Ebony 20:70-2+ F '65
Triplets take a bow. B. Leavitt. il Look 29:M9-13 O 19 '65

DE CARVALHO, Eleazar
City to emulate. P. Yates. por Hi Fi 15:112-13 Jl '65

DE CARVALHO, George
Ancient hatred builds toward war. Life 58:44+ Je 18 '65
Chou gets socked twice. Life 59:62A-62B+ Jl 9 '65
Dirty campaign on the corruption issue. Life 59:78B-80+ N 26 '65
Everything's up to date in Kuwait. Life 59:96-8+ S 17 '65
In New Delhi an uneasy mood; in a village the smoking ruins from attack by stealth. Life 59:44-44A S 17 '65
Yemen's desert fox. Life 58:97-8+ F 19 '65

about
Life magazine? of America? very sorry, goodby. G. P. Hunt. Life 59:3 Jl 9 '65

DECCA navigation
Decca IFR use approved for NY airways. J. W. Carter. il Aviation W 82:39 F 22 '65

DECCA records, incorporated
Broadway on records; Decca, where it all started; with discography. M. Kreuger. il Am Rec G 32:6-11, 76-7 S '65

DECEDENTS estates. See Estates, Decedents

DECEMBER
In December, few of the dates, memorable and not so, coming up next month (title varies) (cont) il N Y Times Mag p56+ N 28 '65

DECENTRALIZATION in government
Eisenhower on the choice Americans must make; interview. D. D. Eisenhower. il Nations Bsns 53:34-7+ O '65
People or personnel, by P. Goodman. Review Atlan 216:88-91 Ag '65. M. Harrington
New Yorker 41:124-7 Ag 21 '65. N. Bliven

DECENTRALIZING authority in business. See Business management and organization

DECIBELS
Decibel wheel; technique for reading decibel values of voltage, current, and power directly. J. Kyle. il Electr World 73:29 F '65

DECIMAL classification. See Classification, Decimal

DECIMAL system
Aussies ring up currency change; switch from pound to decimal currency. il Bsns W p58+ Ja 15 '66

DECIO, Arthur Julius
Mobile manufacturer. il por Time 86:88 D 3 '65

DECISION by firelight; story. See Shyer, M. F.

DECISION making
Deciding the tough ones; interview. M. J. Rathbone. Nations Bsns 53:34-5+ Je '65
How do you keep informed? symposium. il Duns R 85:50-1+ My '65
Personal values and corporate strategy. W. D. Guth and R. Tagiuri. bibliog f il Harvard Bsns R 43:123-32 S '65
Sensing who can command; interview. C. H. Greenewalt. il Nations Bsns 53:40-1+ O '65
Strategic planning in conglomerate companies. N. Berg. bibliog f il Harvard Bsns R 43:79-92 My '65

DECISION making—*Continued*
Team at the top. D. R. Daniel. Harvard Bsns R 43:74-82 Mr '65
They teach business how to make decisions; incident process method. il Bsns W p72+ S 18 '65
DECISIONS (psychology) See Judgment (psychology)
DECKS
Tighter decks, and how. Y. K. Adam. il Motor B 115:26-8+ Mr '65
DECKS (outdoor rooms) See Outdoor rooms
DECLARATION of war. See War, Declaration of
DECLEENE, Doris
Bear nightmare.   Outdoor Life 135:17-19+ Mr '65
DECLINE and fall of the entire world as seen through the eyes of Cole Porter revisited; revue. See Musical comedies, revues, etc. —Criticisms, plots, etc.
DECOMPOSITION
See also
Carcasses—Decomposition
DECONTAMINATION (from gases, chemicals, etc)
See also
Space vehicles—Sterilization
DECORATION and ornament
Ring in the new; decorations for New Year's eve. B. Plumb. il N Y Times Mag p30-1 D 26 '65
Royal fantasies. S. Bowen. il Design 66:32-5 Mr '65
Yuan trellis. J. Burroughs. il Pop Mech 124: 161 O '65
See also
Appliqué work
Christmas decorations
Cookery, Ornamental
House decoration
Jewelry
Mural painting and decoration
Needlework
Paper work
Table decoration
Wall hangings
DECORATION and ornament, Architectural
Arts and architecture: functionalism versus decoration; condensation of debate. E. L. Barnes; J. L. Larsen. il Craft Horiz 25:24-5+ My '65
Explosive forms of Piotr Kowalski; interview, ed. by B. P. Spring. P. Kowalski. il Arch Forum 123:30-5 D '65
Gargoyle snatchers. il Time 85:74 Mr 5 '65
Man from AARS; Anonymous arts recovery society. il Newsweek 65:75 My 31 '65
See also
Gargoyles
Tiles
DECORATIONS, Christmas. See Christmas decorations
DECORATIONS of honor
All for reciprocity; awards of the Legion of honor in Latin America. il Newsweek 65: 49 F 8 '65
Hot radishes; Legion of honor presentations in Ecuador. Time 85:46 F 5 '65
DECORATIVE design. See Design, Decorative
DECORATIVE panels. See Panels, Decorative
DECORATIVE tiles. See Tiles
DE COSTA, Edwin J. and Boylan, B. R.
Expectant mother. Redbook 126:26-7 Ja '66
DECOYS (hunting)
Decoys for diving ducks. B. Popowski. il Outdoor Life 136:50-1+ D '65
DECRAENE, Philippe
France's changing policy in Africa. Reporter 34:37-9 Ja 13 '66
DE CRISTOFORO, R. J.
ABCs of building chests and cabinets (cont) Pop Sci 186:160-4 F '65
Desks you can size to suit your home. Pop Sci 187:132-4 D '65
Notched jigs for your table saw. Pop Sci 187:112-14 Ag '65
Offbeat tricks with your radial-arm saw. Pop Mech 124:188-92 N '65
Secret of successful stairs. Pop Mech 124:158-62 D '65
Secrets of drill-press mortising. Pop Sci 187: 146-50 D '65
Thingamajig for cutting tapers. Pop Sci 188:128-31 Ja '66
Tool that cuts lumber costs. Pop Sci 188: 140-1+ Ja '66
Your table saw will cut circles. Pop Sci 188:136-9 Ja '66
DECTER, Midge
Ivy league girls on the road. Esquire 64:103+ S '65
Movies & messages. Commentary 40:77-8 N '65

DEDERICH, Charles E.
Where junkies learn to hang tough. G. Samuels. il por N Y Times Mag p30-1+ My 9 '65
DEDERICH, Chuck. See Dederich, C. E.
DEDIJER, Stevan
Soviets take a new look at science.   Bul Atomic Sci 21:40-1 Mr '65
DEDOLPH, R. R. and others
Geoelectric effect and geotropic curvature. bibliog Science 148:1100-1 My 21 '65
DEE, Ruby
Gags & good intentions can't tame a shrew. E. Coleman. Life 59:13 Jl 23 '65
DEEDS of men; story. See Meade, W.
DEEDY, John G. Jr
Books. Commonweal 82:602-4 Ag 20 '65
Catholic press. Commonweal 81:666-7; 83:34 F 19, Ap 2 '65
DEEMER, Bill
Diana; Poem: The room is damp & rain scented, smelling of berry vines; Poem: Asleep, electric heaters whir; windows moisten & cloud. Poetry 107:98-9 N '65
about
Four young poets. M. Bell. Poetry 106:370-1 Ag '65
DEEP RIVER, Conn.
Inexpensive alerting system brings fire safety to private buildings. J. F. Olson. il Am City 80:119+ O '65
DEEP sea anglers club swordfish tournament. See Fishing—Competitions
DEEP sea deposits
Clostridium botulinum type F from marine sediments. M. W. Eklund and F. Poysky. bibliog il Science 149:306 Jl 16 '65
Deep-sea stratigraphy; report on conference supported by the National science foundation. R. F. Flint. Science 149:660-1 Ag 6 '65
Dolomitization of the mid-Pacific atolls. R. A. Berner. bibliog il Science 147:1297-9 Mr 12 '65
Ice-rafted detritus as a climatic indicator in Antarctic deep-sea cores. J. R. Conolly and M. Ewing. bibliog il Science 150:1822-4 D 31 '65
Morphology and sediments of a portion of the Mid-Atlantic ridge. T. H. van Andel and others. bibliog il Science 148:1214-16 My 28 '65
Pleistocene epoch in deep-sea sediments. D. B. Ericson and others; discussion. bibliog il Science 148:1037+, 1488 My 21, Je 11 '65
Pliocene-pleistocene boundary, northern Gulf of Mexico. W. H. Akers. bibliog il Science 149:741-2 Ag 13 '65
Subbottom profile of abyssal sediments in the central equatorial Pacific. G. R. Heath and T. C. Moore, jr. bibliog il Science 149: 744-6 Ag 13 '65
Suspended matter in deep ocean water. M. Ewing and E. M. Thorndike. bibliog il Science 147:1291-4 Mr 12 '65
Temperature dependence of carbon isotope composition in marine plankton and sediments. W. M. Sackett and others. bibliog il Science 148:235-7 Ap 9 '65
DEEP sea diving. See Diving, Submarine
DEEP sea drilling. See Underwater drilling
DEEP sea fishes. See Fishes, Deep sea
DEEPSTAR.   See Oceanographic research— Equipment
DEER
What scares a deer? D. M. Newell. il Field & S 69:46-8+ Mr '65
See also
Caribou
DEER hunting
Best deer hunting this season; symposium. il Outdoor Life 36:65-80 O '65
Big buck on the Snake. J. O'Connor. il Outdoor Life 135:42-3+My '65
Big bucks of the Badlands. G. Gresham. il Outdoor Life 136:52-5+ N '65
Bring a buck to horn; antler rattling. D. Klepper. il Field & S 70:68-9+ O '65
Buck at the secret crossing. A. Rutledge. il Outdoor Life 135:46-7+ Mr '65
Bucks above the smog zone. L. Oertle. il Field & S 70:124-6+ S '65
Family affair. J. Vadon. il Outdoor Life 136: 54-5+ O '65
Fundamentals of deer hunting. T. Trueblood. il Field & S 70:20+ N '65
Guessing the giants. W. Page. il Field & S 70:79-81+ O '65
I made my death bed; ed. by B. East. R. Fisher. il Outdoor Life 135:60-1+ Ap '65
I read my own stuff. T. Janes. il Outdoor Life 136:40-1+ D '65
Packtrain hunt in New York. D. Danaher. il Outdoor Life 136:36-9+ O '65

DEER hunting—*Continued*
Prepare now for deer hunting. G. H. Gillelan. il Outdoor Life 136:30+ Jl '65
Rattle up a deer this year! P. Czura. il Pop Mech 124:108-9+ N '65
Redcoats return to Bucks County. J. O'Reilly. il Sports Illus 23:78-80+ N 22 '65
10,000 miles from Thuringia. E. Schwiebert. il Field & S 70:67-9+ Ja '66
Trophy takes more doing; mule deer head. E. Park. il Outdoor Life 136:44-7+ Ag '65
Trophy to remember; the shooting. C. Elliott. il Outdoor Life 136:25-7+ S '65
Utah, still the promised land. V. L. Oertle. il Field & S 70:10-12+ Ag '65
Way to get deer. K. Gilsvik. il Outdoor Life 136:36-9+ N '65
Where do you hunt deer? W. Page. il Field & S 70:92-7 O '65
Where the deer are. J. Chiappetta. il Field & S 70:126-9 O '65
Where's the best bowhunting? G. H. Gillelan. il Outdoor Life 136:104-6 S '65
Whether you walk or sit or stand; secrets of success are silence and knowledge of terrain. W. Page. il Field & S 70:60-3 N '65
Whitetails can make mistakes. L. A. Anderson. il Field & S 70:70-2+ O '65
Whitetails don't hesitate. E. Park. il Outdoor Life 135:44-7+ Je '65
DEERING, Elmer C. and Du Von, Jay
Education and the bond market. Am Ed 1:28 S; 23 O; 28 N '65
—and Nance, P. K.
Education and the bond market. Am Ed 1:22 D '64; 20 F; 28 Mr '65
—and Trevor, T. J.
Education and the bond market. Am Ed 1:28 Ap; 22 My; 30 Je; 29 Jl '65
DEERING, Milliken and company
Meshing managers and computers: Deering. Milliken's new total information center. il Bsns W p82-3 Jl 3 '65
New rules for employers from the Supreme court; Darlington manufacturing company case. il U S News 58:101-3 Ap 12 '65
DEFAMATION. See Libel and slander
DEFECTIVE speech. See Speech defects
DEFECTORS, Political
Chinese lawyer. il Time 86:14-15 Ag 27 '65
Flight of the Gypsy Baron; Wladyslaw Tykocinski, chief of the Polish military mission to West Berlin, defects to the West. Time 85:34 My 28 '65
Prize defector: Li Tsung-jen. Time 86:18 Jl 30 '65
Propaganda coup. Newsweek 66:36+ Ag 2 '65
Return of a native. S. Liu. il Newsweek 66:45 Ag 30 '65
Threepenny tragedy; C. Weisbrod's return to East Berlin. il Time 86:54 N 5 '65
DEFENDERS, Public. See Public defenders
DEFENSE, Civilian. See Civil defense
DEFENSE, Department of. See United States—Defense, Department of
DEFENSE appropriations. See United States—Armed forces—Appropriations and expenditures
DEFENSE buying. See United States—Armed forces—Procurement
DEFENSE contracts. See Contracts, Government
DEFENSE industries. See Munitions industries
DEFENSE information, Classified
Freedom of information. W. J. Coughlin. Miss & Roc 16:46 Ap 26 '65
Truth and the MOL. W. J. Coughlin. Miss & Roc 17:46 N 22 '65
DEFENSE laboratories. See Military research
DEFENSE language institute. See United States—Army—Defense language institute
DEFENSE mechanisms (biology)
Ant venoms, attractants, and repellents. G. W. K. Cavill and P. L. Robertson. bibliog il Science 149:1337-45 S 17 '65
Asian insects in disguise. E. S. Ross. il Nat Geog Mag 128:432-9 S '65
Defensive spray of a phasmid insect. T. Eisner. bibliog il Science 148:966-8 My 14 '65
Insect survival and selection for pattern. H. B. D. Kettlewell. bibliog il Science 148:1290-6 Je 4 '65
Insect's scales are asset in defense. T. Eisner. il Natur Hist 74:26-31 Je '65
Mystery of a millipede; hydrogen cyanide produced by apheloria corrugata. T. Eisner and H. E. Eisner. il Natur Hist 74:30-7 Mr '65
DEFENSE research and engineering, Director of. See United States—Defense research and engineering, Director of
DEFENSE work. See Contracts, Government

DEFFERRE, Gaston
Can de Gaulle be upset? Socialist mayor will try. por U S News 58:20 Ap 5 '65
Hanging together. Newsweek 65:46 Je 21 '65
In quest of unity. il por Time 85:31 Je 18 '65
Letter from Paris (cont) Genêt. New Yorker 41:77-8 Jl 10; 82-3 Ag 7 '65
Man who. il por Newsweek 65:39 F 22 '65
Out of the ring. Newsweek 66:38+ Jl 5 '65
DEFICIT spending. See Government spending policy
DEFILIPPES, Frank M.
Ribosomes: analysis by cesium sulfate gradient centrifugation. bibliog Science 150:610-12 O 29 '65
DEFLORIDA, F. Alonso-. See Alonso-DeFlorida, F.
DEFONTAINE, Ham
Gadgets and gilhickies. See issues of Yachting
DEFONTAINE, W. H.
Designs. See issues of Yachting
DEFORD, Frank
Basketball (cont) Sports Illus 22:50+ F 1; 52+ F 22 '65
Pro basketball (cont) Sports Illus 24:46-7 Ja 3 '66
DEFORD, Sara
We are all spirits; poem. Cath World 200:353 Mr '65
DE FOREST, Lee
De Forest and the triode detector. R. A. Chipman. il por Sci Am 212:92-100 bibliog(p 140) Mr '65; Reply with rejoinder. il Espenschied. 212:8+ My '65
DeForest's early audions. P. G. Watson. il Electr World 74:82-3 S '65
DEFORMITIES
Birth defects studied. il Sci N L 88:243 O 16 '65
Deformity of forelimb in rats: association with high doses of acetazolamide. W. M. Layton, jr. and D. W. Hallesy. bibliog il Science 149:306-8 Jl 16 '65; Reply with rejoinder. T. H. Maren. 150:79 O 1 '65
Feeling dizzy? drug labels. J. Ridgeway. New Repub 153:15-16 S 25 '65
Right to be well born. R. E. Hall. il PTA Mag 60:13 Ja '66
DEFRANCE, Edward
Group of poems; Birdnotes; Choruses for the redwoods; Moon; crutch of midnight; I marry earth; Sonnet; March shivers under snowy afterbirth. Liv Wildn 29:23-4 Sum '65
DEGAS, Edgar
Degas' American cousins. il por Life 59:52-5+ Jl 2 '65
Edgar Degas' New Orleans paintings. J. B. Byrnes. il Antiques 88:664-8 N '65
Edgar Degas: the sentimental cynic. W. Sorell. il por Dance Mag 39:62-5 Je '65
DE GAULLE, Charles. See Gaulle, C. de
DEGAUSSING. See Demagnetization
DEGLER, Carl N.
Aid for parochial schools, a question of education, not religion. N Y Times Mag p 11+ Ja 31 '65
Divided South. Reporter 32:46+ Mr 11 '65
DEGNAN, James P.
Books. Commonweal 82:510-11 Jl 9 '65
Santa Clara: the bulldozer crop. Nation 200:242-5 Mr 8 '65
DEGOLYER and MacNaughton consultants. See Business consultants
DE GRAAFF, Jan
Hybrid lilies indoors. Horticulture 44:24-5+ Ja '66
about
"Consider the (new-style) lilies. . ." F. J. Taylor. il por Read Digest 87:154-9 Ag '65
DEGRADATION (chemistry)
Rock degradation by alkali metals: a possible lunar erosion mechanism. J. J. Naughton and others. bibliog il Science 149:630-2 Ag 6 '65
DE GRAMONT, Sanche
Fallen priests. Sat Eve Post 238:99-103 N 20 '65
Pope Paul VI. Atlan 216:99-103 O '65
Who murdered General Delgado? Sat Eve Post 239:49-51 Ja 1 '66
DE GRAZIA, Edward
Defending the freedom to read in the courts. por ALA Bul 59:507-15 Je '65
Sex and the stuffy librarian. por Library J 90:2483-5 Je 1 '65
DEGREE mills. See Diplomas, Fraudulent
DEGREES, Academic
Academic degrees: universities ask strict control on federal agencies' power to grant them. J. Walsh. Science 147:844-6 F 19 '65; Reply. N. B. Reynolds. 148:168 Ap 9 '65

DEGREES, Academic—*Continued*
Degree value questioned. Sci N L 88:36 Jl 17 '65
Doctoral feedback into higher education. R. H. Bolt and others. bibliog il Science 148:918-28 My 14 '65
Great grad school gold rush. J. Keats. il Life 58:107-8+ Je 11 '65
Of time and the doctorate. D. Wolfle. Science 148:1045 My 21 '65
Ph.D: new demands, same old response. E. Walters; F. W. Ness. il Sat R 49:62-5+ Ja 15 '66
See also
Diplomas, Fraudulent

Anecdotes, facetiae, satire, etc.
Universal education. Commonweal 82:517-18 Jl 23 '65

DEGREES, Honorary
Kudos (cont) Time 85:77-8 Je 11; 61-2 Je 18 54 Je 25 '65
DEHART, Don
Day on the Slana. Outdoor Life 135:36-9+ Je '65
Wake up, Willie! Outdoor Life 135:48-9+ My '65
DEHARTOG, Jan
Author shakes up a city. B. Paisner. il pors Life 58:47-9 Mr 26 '65
DE HEEREN, Cristina
Allure. por Vogue 146:191 O 1 '65
DEHLER, Thomas
Nazi murders & German politics. D. Schoenbaum. Commentary 39:72-7 Je '65
DEHORNING
Six ways to dehorn cattle. J. W. Bailey. il Suc Farm 63:54-5 My '65
DEHYDRATION (physiology)
Endoplasmic reticulum in rat renal interstitial cells; molecular rearrangement after water deprivation. R. E. Bulger and others. bibliog il Science 151:83-6 Ja 7 '66
DEHYDROGENASES
Alcohol dehydrogenase in drosophila melanogaster: isozymes and genetic variants. E. H. Grell and others. bibliog il Science 149:80-2 Jl 2 '65
Alternative forms of triosephosphate dehydrogenase in chromatium. G. A. Hudock and others. bibliog il Science 150:776-7 N 5 '65
Autosomally determined polymorphism of glucose-6-phosphate dehydrogenase in peromyscus. C. R. Shaw and E. Barto. bibliog il Science 148:1099-100 My 21 '65
Constitution, viability, and lactate dehydrogenase in stationary-phase L-cell suspension cultures. A. D. Glinos and others. bibliog il Science 150:350-3 O 15 '65
Glucose-6-phosphate dehydrogenase mosaicism: utilization as a cell marker in the study of leiomyomas. D. Linder and S. M. Gartler. bibliog il Science 150:67-9 O 1 '65
Histone regulation of lactic dehydrogenase in embryonic chick brain tissue. B. C. Goodwin and I. W. Sizer. bibliog il Science 148:242-4 Ap 9 '65
Hybridization of glucose-6-phosphate dehydrogenase from rat and human erythrocytes. E. Beutler and Z. Collins. bibliog il Science 150:1306-7 D 3 '65
Lactate dehydrogenase isozyme patterns of human platelets and bovine lens fibers. E. S. Vesell. bibliog il Science 150:1735-7 D 24 '65
Lactate dehydrogenase isozymes: substrate inhibition in various tissues. E. S. Vesell. bibliog il Science 150:1590-3 D 17 '65
Lactate dehydrogenases in trout: evidence for a third subunit. E. Goldberg. bibliog il Science 148:391-2 Ap 16 '65
Polymorphism of human lactate dehydrogenase isozymes. E. S. Vesell. bibliog il Science 148:1103-5 My 21 '65
Rabbit muscle lactate dehydrogenase 5; a regulatory enzyme. P. J. Fritz. bibliog il Science 150:364-6 O 15 '65
Sex-linkage of erythrocyte glucose-6-phosphate dehydrogenase in two species of wild hares. S. Ohno and others. bibliog il Science 150:1737-8 D 24 '65
Sex-linkage of glucose-6-phosphate dehydrogenase in the horse and donkey. J. M. Trujillo and others. bibliog il Science 148:1603-4 Je 18 '65
X-linked 6-phosphogluconate dehydrogenase in drosphila: subunit associations. H. H. Kazazian, jr. and others. bibliog il Science 150:1601-2 D 17 '65
DEIBERT, Irv
Barnyard boating. il Yachting 118:57+ N '65
DE-ICERS. See Ice on rivers, lakes, etc.—Control

DEIGHTON, Lee C.
Books, not copying machines, are the long-term answer; address March 1964. por Library J 90:2087-92 My 1 '65
DEIGHTON, Len
Men who throw cold water on hot spies por Vogue 146:94-5 Jl '65
DEINDORFER, Robert G.
(ed) See Loscuito, N. N. jr. Letters from a soldier
DEJ, Gheorghe Gheorghiu-. See Gheorghiu-Dej, G.
DEJONG, David Cornel
Humors of summer; poem. Sat R 48:76 D 18 '65
Ritual; Survivor; poems. Poetry 106:286-8 Jl '65
Spectator sport; poem. Reporter 33:52 N 4 '65
Spring comes to New England; poem. Horn Bk 41:201 Ap '65
DE JORGE, F. B. and others
Iodine: accumulation by balanoglossus gigas. bibliog Science 150:1182-3 N 26 '65
DEKKER, Jan
(tr) See Ćosić, D. Toward an intellectual community
DEKKER, Marcel, incorporated
Dekker firm publishes its first science list. il Pub W 187:69-70 Ap 19 '65
DE KOONING, Willem
Cash expressionism. por Newsweek 65:96 Ap 12 '65
De Kooning's new Women. T. B. Hess. il por Art N 64:36-8+ Mr '65
Prisoner of the seraglio. il Time 85:74-5 F 26 '65
DELACATO, Carl. See Doman, G. jt. auth.
DELADROXATE. See Contraceptives
DE LA FUENTE, Marianne Petrillo. See Haimoff, S. H. jt. auth.
DE LAGRANGE, Frances
Filming in the studio. Dance Mag 39:52-3+ S '65
DE LA HABA, G. and Holtzer, H.
Chondroitin sulfate: inhibition of synthesis by puromycin. bibliog Science 149:1263-5 S 10 '65
DE LANUX, Eyre
Adlai. Adlai, what was the fifth word? New Yorker 41:176+ S 25 '65
DELANY, Elvira
State and local developments. See issues of Recreation to December 1965
DELAPLANE, Stan
Letter from Stan Delaplane. See issues of Today's health
DE LAUTER, Alice
Self-direction for teachers. NEA J 55:49-51 Ja '66
DELAWARE
See also
Henlopen, Cape

Education
See also
Wilmington, Del.—Education

Politics and government
Statehouse shuffle: will business be the loser? il Nations Bsns 53:68-70+ Je '65

Religious institutions and affairs
News of the Christian world. Christian Cent 82:442-3, 900 Ap 7, Jl 14 '65
DELAWARE memorial bridge. See Bridges
DELAWARE RIVER
Rebirth of the shad. J. S. Martin. il Atlan 215:90-3 Je '65
DELAWARE RIVER bridge. See Bridges
DELEON, Archer
More than 1,000 million under-25's; interview. UNESCO Courier 18:50-2 Jl '65
DELGADO, Enrique
U.S. loan to support economic integration of Central America; remarks, July 29, 1965. Dept State Bul 53:332 Ag 23 '65
DELGADO, Humberto
Under the eucalyptus trees. por Time 85:39 My 14 '65
Who murdered General Delgado? S. De Gramont. pors Sat Eve Post 239:49-51 Ja 1 '66
DELGADO, José M. R.
Sequential behavior induced repeatedly by stimulation of the red nucleus in free monkeys. bibliog Science 148:1361-3 Je 4 '65
DELGADO trades and technical institute, New Orleans
Moss amid the oaks; Moss library. C. Stross. il Library J 90:5206-7 D 1 '65

DELHI, India
  Description
  Well traveled camera. H. Keppler. il Mod
    Phot 29:29+ O; 50+ N '65
DELHOM, M. Mellanay. See Gregg, R. N. jt.
    auth.
DE LIMA, Francisco Negrão. See Negrão de
    Lima, F.
DELINQUENT children. See Juvenile delin-
    quency
DELINQUENTS. See Juvenile delinquency
DELIRIUM tremens
  Treat delirium tremens. Sci N L 88:244 O 16
    '65
DELIUS, Anthony
  Verwoerd tightens the screws. Reporter 33:
    29-31 Jl 1 '65
DELL, E. T. Jr
  Bishops of Rome. Christian Cent 82:244 F 24
    '65
DELL publishing company
  All-rush service the goal at new Dell ware-
    house; Montvill warehouse, New Jersey. il
    Pub W 188:19-22 O 18 '65
  Dell plans child care line with Boston hospital.
    Pub W 188:29-30 D 6 '65
  Dell publishing acquires Noble & Noble. Pub
    W 187:34 My 24 '65
DELLER, Alfred
  Lonely as a lark. por Time 86:54 N 26 '65
DELMAN, Maury
  Treasure cay. Travel 124:47-9 O '65
DELMAR, Viña
  Enchanted; novel. McCalls 92:102-5 F: 88-9
    Mr: 132-3 Ap '65
DELMAS, Gladys
  Latin labor's alarming Christians. Reporter
    32:27-30 F 25 '65
DEL MONICO, Charles
  Needlepoint justice. Newsweek 65:29-30 F
    22 '65
DELMONTE, L. and Liebelt, R. A.
  Granulocytosis-promoting extract of mouse
    tumor tissue; partial purification. bibliog
    Science 148:521-3 Ap 23 '65
DEL NORTE COAST REDWOODS STATE
    PARK. See California—Parks and reserves
DELOACH, Cartha D.
  His master's voice. Newsweek 66:25 D 27 '65
DELOREAN, John Z.
  Engineering the new Pontiacs. Motor T 17:
    68-71 F '65
DELPHINIUMS
  Delphinium. P. Shedesky. il Pop Gard 16:
    26-9 Jl '65
DELPIERRE, Claude
  Binding with vat-made papers. A. Karlikow.
    il Craft Horiz 25:12-15+ Mr '65
DELTA air lines
  Delta begins scheduled service with DC-9.
    il Aviation W 83:41 D 13 '65
DELTA wings. See Airplane wings
DE LUCIA, Sam
  Sam's pigeons don't leave nuthin' for nobody.
    R. H. Boyle. il por Sports Illus 23:102-4+
    N 22 '65
DELUSIONS. See Errors, Popular
DEMAGNETIZATION
  Automatic degausser. il Electr World 73:77
    Mr '65
DEMARE, Jean Legault-. See Legault-Demare,
    J.
DEMARET, Jimmy
  Jack and Jimmy hold a bash in the Big
    Thicket. A. Wright. il por Sports Illus 22:
    62-3 Mr 29 '65
DEMARIS, Ovid
  Toughest customers. Esquire 64:77+ O '65
DEMARTINI, F. E. and others
  Lactic acid metabolism in hypertensive pa-
    tients bibliog Science 148:1482-4 Je 11 '65
DEMENT, William
  Reporter at large. C. Trillin. il New Yorker
    41:58-60+ S 18 '65
DEMENT, William C. See Cohen, H. B. jt.
    auth.
DE MILLE, Agnes
  Viewpoint: Agnes De Mille; interview, ed.
    by H. Loxton. por Dance Mag 39:42-3+
    Ap '65
DEMING, Frederick L.
  Problem of international liquidity; address,
    April 29, 1965. Dept State Bul 52:955-63 Je
    14 '65
DEMING, Lucille A.
  Color lasts all summer when you grow
    geraniums. Flower Grower 52:22-3+ Jl '65
DEMIREL, Suleyman
  Ride to victory. Time 86:46 O 22 '65
DEMOCRACY
  1865: the great transition. A. S. Eisenstadt.
    il Nation 201:54-61 S 20 '65
  New experiment in democracy in Pakistan.
    M. Ayub Khan. Ann Am Acad 358:109-13
    Mr '65

Politicians, bureaucrats, and development in
    India. W. Wilcox. bibliog f Ann Am Acad
    358:114-22 Mr '65
  Worldwide status of democracy; Time essay.
    Time 85:30-1 Ap 23 '65
    See also
  Communism and democracy
  Education and democracy
  Liberty
DEMOCRACY and communism. See Commun-
    ism and democracy
DEMOCRACY and education. See Education
    and democracy
DEMOCRATIC party
  Big business & the Democrats; excerpts
    from What is power? D. T. Bazelon. Com-
    mentary 39:39-46 My '65
  Bobby Kennedy and the fight for New York.
    R. Armstrong. il Sat Eve Post 238:29-31+
    N 6 '65
  Conviction or convenience; the trap of the
    Great society. R. F. Hamilton. il Nation
    201:384-7 N 22 '65
  Dollars (15,000) for Democrats. A. Kop-
    kind. New Repub 154:15-16 Ja 8 '66
  Government by freshmen: Maine's year of
    the donkey. D. L. Graham. il Nation 202:
    43-5 Ja 10 '66
  Party of one; National committee shakeup.
    Reporter 34:17-18 Ja 13 '66
  This may be LBJ's Achilles' heel. P. Lis-
    agor. il Nations Bsns 53:23-4 N '65
DEMOGRAPHY. See Population
DEMOLITION of buildings. See Wrecking
DEMONOLOGY
  School of one; S. Jackson's interest in the
    black arts. Newsweek 66:83B Ag 23 '65
DEMONSTRATIONS against Vietnamese war.
    See Vietnamese war, 1957- —Protests,
    demonstrations, etc, against
DEMOTT, Benjamin
  How to win at cocktails; story. Sat Eve Post
    238:52-5 Ag 14 '65
  With-it boys in England. Reporter 33:55-7 O
    21 '65
DEMPSEY, David
  Challenge of the sixties. Sat R 48:27-8+ Je
    26 '65
  Foundations: a welfare state for writers?
    Harper 231:165-71 O '65
  Great manuscript rush. Sat R 48:28-9 My
    1 '65
  Package deal. Sat R 48:45 Ap 17 '65
  Publishing scene. See occasional issues of
    Saturday review
  Teaching librarians to fight back. Sat R 48:
    20-1+ F 27 '65
  What to read till the doctor comes. Sat R
    48:29 Jl 17 '65
DEMPSEY, William H. Jr
  Books. Commonweal 82:227-8 My 7 '65
DEMYELINATIVE disorders. See Nervous sys-
    tem—Diseases
DE NAVE, Connie
  Image in the marketplace. E. Dundy. il por
    Esquire 64:82-3+ Jl '65
DENBO, Bruce F.
  Gathering on the bluegrass; comp. by R.
    Brown. il Sat R 48:58-9+ My 22 '65
DENBY, Edwin
  About Don Quixote. Dance Mag 39:33-7 Jl '65
DENCKLAU, Sharon
  Blue ribbon girl. pors Seventeen 24:136-7+
    Mr '65
DENDROCTONUS. See Beetles
DENDROCTONUS monticolae. See Pine—Dis-
    eases and pests
DENEUVE, Catherine
  Sister stars of France. T. G. Harris. il pors
    Look 29:90-3 Je 1 '65
DE NEVERS, Noel
  Secondary recovery of petroleum; with bi-
    ographical sketch. Sci Am 213:16, 34-42 bib-
    liog(p 124) Jl '65
DENGLER, Harry William
  What's in a wreath? Am For 71:10-11 D '65
  Wreaths are wonderful: let's make one! Am
    For 71:6-9 D '65
DENGUE
  Dengue type 2 virus in naturally infected
    aedes albopictus mosquitoes in Singapore.
    A. Rudnick and Y. C. Chan. bibliog il
    Science 149:638-9 Ag 6 '65
DENISON, Russell E.
  Rate and upgrade your street cleaning. Am
    City 80:120-2 Ap '65
DENMARK
    See also
  Airlines—Denmark
  Arts and crafts—Denmark
  Ballet—Denmark
  Copenhagen
  Libraries—Denmark
  Publishers and publishing—Denmark
  Schools—Denmark

DENMARK—*Continued*

Antiquities

Six viking ships; found in Roskildefjord. P. L. Adams. Atlan 215:88-92 Ap '65

Description and travel

Going places, finding things in Denmark. N. S. Hazelton. il House & Gard 127:36+ Mr '65

How to sleep with a dyne. P.-L. Adams. Atlan 215:82-4+ My '65

This blessed plot, this earth, this realm, this Denmark. S. Bedford. Esquire 64:212+ D '65

Tower at Fåborg. P. L. Adams. il Atlan 216: 51-5 Jl '65

Industries

Danish industry grows amidst tne farmlands; Danfoss. il Bsns W p60-2 Je 26 '65

DENNETT, John Richard
1865: the South as it is. Nation 201:153-6 S 20 '65

DENNIS, Jack. See Easton, D. jt. auth.

DENNIS, Sandy
New ingénue. R. Hoban. por Holiday 37:131+ Mr '65

DENNISON, George
Cooling it. Commentary 41:82-4 Ja '66
Demagogy of Le Roi Jones. Commentary 39: 67-70 F '65

DEÑÓ, Francisco Caamaño. See Caamaño Deñó, F.

DENOMINATIONAL colleges
Aid to church colleges; Maryland state grants. America 112:414 Mr 27 '65
Baptists in a bind; question of accepting federal funds for Baptist-related colleges. Christian Cent 82:1502 D 8 '65
Public aid to church-related colleges and universities. Sch & Soc 93:404-5 O 30 '65

Desegregation

Desegregates despite church's opposition. Christian Cent 82:260 Mr 3 '65

DENSITOMETERS
Bone density measurements in vivo: improvement of X-ray densitometry. R. L. Mason and C. Ruthven. bibliog il Science 150:221-2 O 8 '65

DENSITY. See Specific gravity

DENT, Paul
Book reviews. America 113:725-6 D 4 '65

DENT, W. A.
Quasi-stellar sources: variation in the radio emission of 3C 273. bibliog Science 148: 1458-60 Je 11 '65

DENTAL caries. See Teeth—Diseases

DENTAL fillings. See Teeth

DENTAL hygiene. See Teeth—Care and hygiene

DENTAL insurance. See Insurance, Dental

DENTISTRY

History

Dentistry 100 years ago: crude, quaint & painful; excerpts from Dentists to the world. J. Jackson and E. Jackson. il Todays Health 43:20-1+ Mr '65

DENTISTS
Pedodontics: children's own dentistry. M. J. E. Senn. il McCalls 93:38+ Ja '66

Supply and demand

If you find it hard now to get to see a dentist—. il U S News 59:80-1 D 6 '65

DENTON, Tex.

Music

Dallas symphony at North Texas state. P. Yates. Hi Fi 15:127+ Ag '65

DENTURES, Artificial. See Teeth, Artificial

DENVER
Denver peaks into a mile-high seller's dream. il Bsns W p 182-4+ S 25 '65
Ranchmen have their big fling in Denver; nine-day National western stock show. il Bsns W p 120-2 Ja 30 '65

Architecture

Mile-high clubhouse; John F. Kennedy municipal golf course. il Recreation 58:430 N '65

Banks

Banking in the garage; Denver U.S. national bank, world's largest motor bank. M. J. Pedersen. il Pop Mech 124:91 D '65

Education

Importance of the individual: East high school, Denver. W. J. Ehrenkrook. Atlan 215:89-92 F '65

Operation brainstorm; projects of Denver classroom teachers association. J. E. Larson. NEA J 54:41 N '65

Music

Golschmann's quiet conquest. A. Young. Hi Fi 15:86L-86M Mr '65

Negroes

Where Negroes keep out other Negroes; reprint. L. Larsen. il U S News 59:62-3 O 18 '65

Streets

Fighting the flurries. J. A. Wikgren. il Am City 80:98-9 O '65

DENVER Broncos (football club) See Football clubs

DENVER Chicago trucking company
Across the ocean by truck; business in Europe. il Time 86:91 D 17 '65

DENVER United States national bank. See Denver—Banks

DEODORANTS
New aerosol deodorants and anti-perspirants. il Consumer Bul 48:2+ S '65

DEOME, K. B. See Daniel, C. W. jt. auth.

DEOXYRIBONUCLEIC acid
Antibodies to DNA and a synthetic polydeoxyribonucleotide produced by oligodeoxyribonucleotides. O. J. Plesca and others. bibliog Science 148:1102-3 My 21 '65
Bacterial chromosome. J. Cairns. il Sci Am 214:36-44 Ja '66
Circulating DNA as a possible factor in oncogenesis. A. Bendich and others. bibliog il Science 148:374-6 Ap 16 '65
Complex DNA isolated. Sci N L 87:391 Je 19 '65
Cyclic structure of adenovirus DNA. K. O. Smith. bibliog il Science 148:100-2 Ap 2 '65
Death isn't necessary; condensed from address. A. W. Galston. Sci Digest 58:80-5 Jl '65
DNA-dependent synthesis of RNA is not implicated in growth response of chick comb to androgens. G. P. Talwar and others. bibliog il Science 150:1315-16 D 3 '65
DNA: reaction with chloroquine. J. L. Allison and others. bibliog il Science 149: 1111-13 S 3 '65
DNA, RNA synthesized in lab the easy way. Sci N L 88:53 Jl 24 '65
DNA synthesis in aluminum-treated roots of barley. M. Sampson and others. bibliog il Science 148:1476-7 Je 11 '65
Electron spin resonance of irradiated DNA. P. S. Pershan and others. bibliog il Science 148:378-80 Ap 16 '65
Genetic transfer in bacterial mating. J. D. Gross and L. Caro. bibliog il Science 150: 1679-84 D 24 '65
Inactivation by nitrogen mustard of single- and double-stranded DNA and RNA bacteriophages. N. Yamamoto and T. Naito. bibliog il Science 150:1603-4 D 17 '65
Inhibition of L1210 tumor growth by thymus DNA. J. L. Glick and A. R. Goldberg. bibliog il Science 149:997-8 Ag 27 '65
Isolation and characterization of DNA from kinetoplasts of leishmania enriettii. H. G. Du Buy and others. bibliog il Science 147: 754-6 F 12 '65
Lability of host-cell DNA in growing cell cultures due to mycoplasma. C. C. Randall and others. bibliog il Science 149:1098-9 S 3 '65
Nearer the secret of life. il Sci Digest 57: 15-16 Je '65
Nitrous acid mutation of transforming DNA: consideration of mode of action. S. H. Goodgal and E. H. Postel. bibliog Science 148: 1095-7 My 21 '65
Quenching of DNA phosphorescence. I. Isenberg and others. bibliog il Science 150:1179-81 N 26 '65
Recombination in bacteriophage T4: a mechanism. E. Simon. bibliog il Science 150:760-3 N 5 '65
Secret of life; today's most fascinating mystery story. M. Gunther. il Sat Eve Post 238:25-9 Jl 3 '65
Three-base code confirmed. Sci Am 212:56-7 Je '65
Thymine photoproducts but not thymine dimers found in ultraviolet-irradiated bacterial spores. J. E. Donnellan, jr. and R. B. Setlow. bibliog il Science 149:308-10 Jl 16 '65
Transformation by Rous sarcoma virus: a requirement for DNA synthesis. J. P. Bader. bibliog il Science 149:757-8 Ag 13 '65
What happens when life begins. W. Goodman. Redbook 125:54-5+ Jl '65

DEOXYRIBONUCLEIC acid—*Continued*
X chromosome DNA replication: developmental shift from synchrony to asynchrony. R. B. Nicklas and R. A. Jaqua. bibliog il Science 147:1041-3 F 26 '65
DEPARTMENT of elementary school principals. See National education association—Department of elementary school principals
DEPARTMENT of housing and urban development. See United States—Housing and urban development, Department of
DEPARTMENT store decorations. See Christmas decorations
DEPARTMENT store mergers. See Department stores—Consolidations and mergers
DEPARTMENT stores
Check list for department store programing. D. Schwartzman. Arch Rec 137:188-90 My '65
Children's books well received in I. Magnin toy depts. Pub W 188:52 N 1 '65
Customer is SO right. il Time 86:100+ D 10 '65
See also
Alexander's department stores, incorporated
Chain stores
Macy, R. H. and company
May department stores company
Saleswomen
also subhead Stores under names of cities, e.g. Dallas—Stores

Book departments
Ayres' new store completes first Christmas season. Pub W 189:82-4 Ja 10 '66
Bloomingdale's intermingles paperbacks, modern library with hardbound books. il Pub W 188:53-4 D 27 '65
Donaldson's, Minneapolis, takes over its book department. Pub W 187:63 Mr 22 '65
88 per cent of discount stores have book departments. Pub W 187:57 My 17 '65
Moderate sales rise for first half of 1965. Pub W 188:59 S 13 '65
Stock turnover rate increased in dept. store book sections; 1963 to 1964. Pub W 188:61 O 11 '65

Consolidations and mergers
Halting department store mergers; FTC warns major retailers no more acquisitions of local companies. Bsns W p36 Ag 21 '65

Employees
How top retailers build executives; modern methods used to recruit and train. il Bsns W p88+ Je 5 '65
Organizing with an adman's touch; southern California locals of RCIA applying Madison avenue techniques to recruit department store employees. il Bsns W p72+ O 16 '65

Management
Holdout in a world of chains; Belk's stores run family-style. il Bsns W p 113-14+ O 23 '65
Retail reorganization; example of R. H. Macy and company. W. H. Bingham and D. L. Yunich il Harvard Bsns R 43:129-32+ Jl '65
DEPARTMENTAL libraries. See College libraries—Departmental and divisional libraries
DEPAS, Spencer
Spencer Depas and knotting. N. Znamierowski. il Craft Horiz 25:32-3+ Mr '65
DEPATTA, Margaret
Jewelry by Margaret DePatta. Y. Uchida. il Craft Horiz 25:22-5 Mr '65
DE PAUL, Stephen
Washington front. America 114:37 Ja 8 '66
DEPAUR, Starletta
Cat lady of Philadelphia. A. Peters. il pors Ebony 21:76-8+ D '65
DE PAUW, Gommar A.
Church of De Pauw. Commonweal 82:181 Ap 30 '65; Reply. J. Gallagher. 82:306 My 28 '65
Ecumenical backlash. il por Newsweek 65:67 Ap 19 '65
Father DePauw returns. J. Leo. Commonweal 83:458-9 Ja 21 '66
Traditionalist manifesto: movement to resist liturgical changes. Time 85:60 Ap 9 '65
Warning? Traditionalist movement points up the need for discussion in the church. J. Gallagher. America 112:611 Ap 24 '65
DEPENDENT children. See Homes, Institutional
DEPENDENT classes. See Poor
DE PIETRO, Albert
Summer sundown; poem. Cath World 201:168 Je '65
DEPILATORIES. See Hair, Removal of
DE PINNA. See New York (city)—Stores

DEPLETION allowances
Deductible water; case of farmer Shurbet in Texas. il Time 86:62+ Jl 9 '65
DEPORTATION
Oh, to be in England; efforts to deport P. Ricca. Newsweek 66:38 N 8 '65
DEPOSIT stations, Library. See Libraries—Branches and stations
DEPOSITION (geology) See Sedimentation and deposition
DEPOSITORY libraries. See Libraries, Depository
DEPRECIATION
How old a car should you buy? with depreciation charts. M. Lamm. il Motor T 17:24-6 Je '65
Tax rules you should know before you sell property. F. Bailey, jr. Suc Farm 63:34+ F '65
See also
Amortization deductions
DEPRESSANTS
Drug affects neurotic animals specifically; cyprolidol. Sci N L 88:194 S 25 '65
See also
Imipramine
DEPRESSED areas aid. See Economic assistance, Domestic
DEPRESSION, Business. See Business depression
DEPRESSION, Mental
Depression treated with drug, desipramine. Sci N L 88:311 N 13 '65
Injections for depression. Time 85:75 My 7 '65
Pills for depression more effective on men. Sci N L 87:242 Ap 17 '65
DEPTH indicators
New sounds underwater. E. Robberson. il Yachting 118:50-3+ Ag '65
DEPTH of field. See Photography—Focusing
DEPTH sounders. See Sounding and soundings
DEPUE, George, Jr
Adman in the pulpit. J. Shepherd. il pors Look 29:M14+ D 14 '65
DEPUE, Palmer
Multiple choice and the either-or fallacy. Sch & Soc 93:154-6 Mr 6 '65
DERBER, Milton
Labor-management in World war II. Cur Hist 48:340-5 Je '65
DERDON, Ed
You need long lens, high flying camera to film an eagle. L. Jacobs, jr. il Mod Phot 29:89+ Mr '65
DER HOVANESSIAN, Diana
For midnight; poem. Ladies Home J 83:112 Ja '66
DERIG, Betty
Have your own art gallery. Suc Farm 64:105+ Ja '66
DERKERT, Siri
Grandma Siri. por Newsweek 66:107-8 O 25 '65
DERMATITIS. See Skin—Diseases
DERMOOPTICAL perception. See Sight
DE ROOS, Robert
Costa Rica, free of the volcano's veil. Nat Geog Mag 128:122-52 Jl '65
Jumping frogs of Angels camp. Read Digest 87:21-2+ S '65
DEROUNIAN, Steven Boghos
How to beat a good congressman. N. Freeman. por Nat R 17:547-50 Je 29 '65; Discussion. 17:672-3 Ag 10 '65
DERVISHES
Forbidden and ecstatic circle. D. Bhattacharya. il Dance Mag 39:44-5+ F '65
DERWINSKI, Edward J.
Excerpt from address, August 9, 1965. Cong Digest 44:307+ D '65
DESALINIZATION. See Water purification—Desalting
DESALTING of sea water. Sea water—Desalting
DESAUTELS, Paul E.
Interaction between light and minerals. Natur Hist 74:52-7 O '65
DE SCHAUENSEE, Max
Lubin revisited. Opera N 30:26-8 Ja 22 '66
DESCHIN, Jacob
Cushing; main streets are his specialty. Pop Phot 56:104-5+ F '65
Ducrot, fashion reporter with a camera. Pop Phot 56:29+ Je '65
Gottscho, always in love with his medium. Pop Phot 56:28+ Ap '65
Market newspaper for photographers. Pop Phot 56:100-1 F '65
Mikoda, peacocks, astronauts, and Vikings. Pop Phot 56:26+ Mr '65
[Monthly column] See issues of Popular photography
DESEGREGATION. See Colleges and universities—Desegregation; Public schools—Desegregation

DESERT flora. See Desert vegetation

DESERT gardens. See Gardens, Desert
DESERT locusts. See Grasshoppers
DESERT vegetation
Plant formations in the natural history interpretation of southwestern desert regions. F. R. Gehlbach. il Nat Parks Mag 40:16-18 Ja '66
    See also
Succulent plants
DESERT vehicles. See Motor vehicles
DESERTS
    See also
Arid regions
Sahara Desert
Sonoran Desert
DE SEYNES, Philippe
International perspective on the world economy; statement, October 5, 1965. UN Mo Chron 2:146-58 N '65
DESIGN
Good design makes good giving; Ben Thompson's selections. J. Peter. il Look 29:M10+ D 28 '65

Exhibitions
Best of the West; California design IX in Pasadena museum of art. G. O'Brien. il N Y Times Mag p90-1 Mr 28 '65
California design show: here's a look at the shape of things to come. il Sunset 134:92-3 Ap '65

Study and teaching
Decorated mink boards. Sister Mary Mercy. il Sch Arts 65:10-11 N '65
Line design with pen and ink; junior high school. K. Lakewold. il Sch Arts 64:32 Mr '65
On decoration. G. Joe. il Design 67:38-9 S '65
Secret of creative mask design; fifth grade. L. S. Roe. il Design 67:28-30 S '65
Shape, color, space, a la Mondrian. E. Welch. il Design 67:20-1 S '65
DESIGN, Book. See Book design
DESIGN, Decorative
Indonesian decorative design. G. Kaler. il Hobbies 70:44+ Ap '65
Realistic hallucinations: kaleidoscopic patterns. P. Max. il Horizon 7:116-20 Spr '65

Animal forms
Indonesian decorative design. G. Kaler. il Hobbies 69:42-4 Ja; 70:42+ Mr '65

Plant forms
Indonesian decorative design. G. Kaler. il Hobbies 70:44+ My '65
Nature thought of them first; English gardener exposes the origins of classic decorative motifs. B. Nichols. il House & Gard 128:96-7 Ag '65
Not for eating. M. C. Cole. il Flower Grower 52:29 O '65
Spatter prints. M. M. Ridenour. il Flower Grower 52:20-2 Ag '65

Study and teaching
See Design—Study and teaching
DESIGN, Industrial
Technology races ahead; research, way of life for packaging men. il Duns R 86:pt2 90-2+ D '65
Where the designer rules the roost; success of Braun appliances in West Germany. il Bsns W p40-2 Jl 31 '65
DESIGN of automobiles. See Automobiles—Design
DESIST, Samuel
Stupefying Sam. il Time 86:15B D 31 '65
DESK fan See Electric fans
DESK furnishings
Pipe-rack desk clock. il Pop Sci 187:156 N '65
DESKS
Desks you can size to suit your home. R. J. De Cristoforo. il Pop Sci 187:132-4 D '65
Five secretaries and the Cogswells. M. A. Young. il Antiques 88:478-85 O '65
Renewed study of Salem secretaries. R. Strachan and H. Comstock. il Antiques 88:502-5 O '65
DESMOND, James
Albany hippodrome: Wagner, Rocky and the Kennedy act. Nation 200:184-5 F 22 '65
Mischievous Robert Wagner. Nation 200:688-90 Je 28 '65
DESPRADEL ROGUES, Fidelio
June 14th; the young rebels. M. Acoca. il Life 59:56A Ag 13 '65
DESSAUER, Herbert C. See Gorman, G. C. jt. auth.

DESSERTS
And she cooks! M. Smith. il Seventeen 25:102-3+ Ja '66
Bake a giant cookie shell; heap it high, like this. il McCalls 92:142-3+ F '65
Big pan desserts that carry well. B. L. Henry. il Farm J 90:80-3 Ja '66
Blender and the sweet tooth. Sunset 135:138-9 Jl '65
Candy-size desserts; with recipes. il Seventeen 24:154-5+ N '65
Chocolate desserts. il Bet Hom & Gard 43:99-100 S '65
Christmas gathering. il Good H 161:128-31+ D '65
Coffee-flavored treats. il Bet Hom & Gard 43:95-6 F '65
Crème brûlée. M. F. Williams. il Good H 161:232 O '65
Department of amplification; Irish-moss blancmange. K. S. White. New Yorker 41:70 Jl 10 '65
Dessert of the month. V. V. Voboril. See issues of Good housekeeping
Festive desserts. il Bet Hom & Gard 43:83-4 D '65
Fire when ready; flambé desserts; with recipes. il McCalls 93:144-5+ N '65
Flaming desserts. il Ebony 21:166 D '65
Frosted gelatin-fruit molds for salad or dessert. B. Pierson. il Farm J 89:76-7 N '65
Grand finales; recipes. il McCalls 93:144-6+ O '65
Happiness is a yummy dessert. B. B. Smith. il Parents Mag 40:69-72+ Je '65
Happy marriage; chocolate mousse. il McCalls 92:38 S '65
How to be nice to chocolate fanciers; chocolate mousse. Sunset 134:187 Mr '65
Ice cream pizza; with recipes. il Seventeen 24:162-3+ S '65
It's a fresh fruit whip; with recipe. il Sunset 134:175 Je '65
Lemon desserts. il Bet Hom & Gard 43:99-100 Je '65
Look what you can make with pudding mix! il Bet Hom & Gard 43:110-11 S '65
Luscious fruit cobblers. B. L. Henry. il Farm J 89:58-9 Jl '65
Making desserts with western nuts. il Sunset 135:196-8 O '65
New fall desserts made with mincemeat. Farm J 89:84-5 N '65
Old-time sweets. il McCalls 92:130-2+ Mr '65
Pineapple desserts. il Bet Hom & Gard 43:95-6 Mr '65
Puddings and cobblers. il Bet Hom & Gard 43:99-100 Jl '65
Successful recipes; summertime desserts. il Suc Farm 63:61-2 Jl '65
Talk about dazzling desserts! il Good H 160:98-114 F '65
Tangerine boom. il Sunset 134:76-9 F '65
Trifles are not trivial. C. Claiborne. il N Y Times Mag p68+ My 9 '65
    See also
Cake
Cheesecake
Cookery—Fruit
Custards
Fruit
Ice cream, ices, etc.
Meringue
Pie
Shortcake
D'ESTAING, Valéry Giscard. See Giscard d'Estaing, V.
DETECTION of crime. See Criminal investigation
DETECTION threshold. See Sight
DETECTIVE and mystery stories
Book bag of thrillers. R. Blum. Vogue 146:54+ D '65
Murder-fancier recommends... J. D. Carr. il Harper 231:104 Jl '65
Paper bag mystery. H. L. Miller. Plays 25:47-55 N '65
Thrillers for eggheads. A. Campbell. New Repub 153:25-6 Jl 3 '65
    See also
Television broadcasting—Crime programs

Bibliography
Criminal record. J. T. Winterich. See last issue of each month of Saturday review
Mystery, detective, suspense. M. K. Grant. See first issue of each month of Library journal

Technique
Defense of the bedside pad. W. Brown. Writer 78:15-17 S '65
Research for the mystery writer. F. Crane. Writer 78:15-17 F '65
There's a dividend in mysteries. P. McGerr. Writer 78:9-11 Ap '65

DETECTORS
Leak detector wins M/R competition. Miss & Roc 16:32 Ap 19 '65
Light that measures fog. il Sci Digest 57: 32-3 Je '65
See also
Smoke detectors

DETENTION homes
Improbable successes of Ettie Lee; Ettie Lee homes, inc. S. W. Taylor. Read Digest 87:187-8+ D '65

DETERGENTS. See Cleaning compositions

DETERRENCE (strategy) See Strategy

DETERRENT; story. See Williams, G.

DETHIER, Vincent G.
Burning mill; story. Cath World 202:171-5 D '65

DE TOLEDANO, Ralph
Records (cont) Nat R 17:385-7, 695, 940-2 My 4, Ag 10, O 19 '65

DETROIT
Detroit: slow healing of a fractured city. S. H. Brown. il Fortune 71:142-5+ Je '65
Restoring the heart. il Time 86:24 S 24 '65

Architecture
Round and tall; Cobo Hall and Michigan gas building. il Life 59:82-3 D 24 '65
Triangular plot shapes triple tower. S. F. Blum. il Arch Rec 138:140-3 D '65

Banks
Four Michigan branch banks by one architectural firm. il Arch Rec 137:198-200 Je '65

Description
Four fascinating worlds. M. Jerome. il Sr Schol 86:sup26-7 Ap 15 '65
Nation's new leader among convention cities. C. M. Mohrhardt. il ALA Bul 59:547-51 Je '65
New Detroit: setting of ALA's 1965 annual conference. J. P. Cavanagh. il ALA Bul 59:289-92 Ap '65

Education
High school clusters little schools in an expandable plan. il Arch Rec 137:174-5 Mr '65

Galleries and museums
Wheelsville, USA. J. J. Bradley. il Library J 90:2752-6 Je 15 '65

Hotels, restaurants, etc.
Detroit restaurants; comp. by M. Robideau. ALA Bul 59:397-401 My '65

Industries
Four fascinating worlds. M. Jerome. il Sr Schol 86:sup26-7 Ap 15 '65

Libraries
Inquiring librarian's guide. W. H. Kaiser. il Library J 90:2761-5 Je 15 '65
Library tours announced for Detroit ALA conference. Library J 90:2519 Je 1 '65; Same. ALA Bul 59:561-2 Je '65; Correction. Library J 90:2700 Je 15 '65
See also
Detroit public library

Lighting
Modern lighting helps to fight blight. H. Pearson. il Am City 80:140+ Je '65

Music
See also
Detroit symphony orchestra

Newspapers
Investing in the future; Detroit press club cash appeal for journalist scholarships. Newsweek 66:91 N 1 '65

Parades
Faw down & go boom; walk for peace in Vietnam disrupted by young conservatives. Nat R 17:314 Ap 20 '65

Politics and government
Cavanagh is willin'; Detroit's mayor could be called to higher duties. S. Friedman. New Repub 153:10 N 27 '65; Reply. M. M. Ramsey. 153:38 D 11 '65
Mayor who woke up a city. E. Dunbar. il Look 29:34-8+ S 21 '65

Riots
Detroit race riot: a study in violence, by R. Shogan and T. Craig. Review
Negro Hist Bul 29:17 O '65. C. E. Stewart

DETROIT childrens hospital. See Children— Hospitals

DETROIT public library
Automation in the Detroit public library. C. M. Mohrhardt. il ALA Bul 59:829-33 O '65
Century of progress; reprint. E. A. Batchelor, jr. il Library J 90:2757-60 Je 15 '65
Detroit public library: century of progress. il ALA Bul 59:556-8 Je '65

DETROIT Red Wings (hockey team) See Hockey teams

DETROIT RIVER
Detroit: Cadillac liked it. G. E. Van. il Yachting 117:42-3+ My '65

DETROIT symphony orchestra
Fifty years old, and full steam ahead. F. Gill. Hi Fi 15:121 My '65
Go-go symphony; new season; success assured· il Newsweek 66:110 O 18 '65
Musical events; concert at Carnegie Hall. W. Sargeant. New Yorker 41:130+ N 6 '65

DETZER, Karl
They work wonders with wood. Read Digest 86:233-4+ My '65

DEUS dixit; story. See Updike, J.

DEUTERIUM
Anti-world may exist; discovery of antiparticle called antideuteron, largest known particle of antimatter. Sci N L 87:402 Je 26 '65

Isotopes
Low deuterium content of Lake Vanda, Antarctica R. A. Ragotzkie and I. Friedman. bibliog il Science 148:1226-7 My 28 '65

DEUTSCH, J. A. and others
Anticholinesterase-induced amnesia and its temporal aspects. bibliog Science 151:221-3 Ja 14 '66

DEUTSCH, Karl W. and Rieselbach, L. N.
Recent trends in political theory and political philosophy. bibliog f Ann Am Acad 360: 139-62 Jl '65

DEUTSCH, Martin
Great society; a man with a problem; antipoverty project, Head start. B. Carter. il Reporter 32:32-3 My 20 '65

DEUTSCH, Patricia, and Deutsch, R. M.
Atlanta. Redbook 125:72-3+ My '65
Crazy about camellias. Read Digest 88:133-7 Ja '66
Hidden threat to children's eyes. Todays Health 43:29-32+ Ag '65; Same abr. Read Digest 87:63-6 Ag '65
Plantation country. Holiday 37:30+ My '65

DEUTSCH, Ronald M.
Putting the clues to work. Read Digest 87: 160+ Jl '65
—See Deutsch, P. jt. auth.

DEUTSCHER, Isaac
Constellations of lobbies. Nation 200:352-4 Ap 5 '65
Kremlin diplomacy; first year for the new team. Nation 202:32-3 Ja 10 '66
Moscow restoration; dragon of bureaucracy. Nation 201:264-6 O 25 '65
Russia vs. China; clash over Vietnam. Nation 201:3-4 Jl 5 '65
Vietnam, another Dienbienphu? Nation 200: 212-14 Mr 1 '65

DEVALUATION of currency. See Currency question

DEVANE, William Clyde
Obituary
Yale R 55:159-60 O '65

DEVANEY, Bob
Organization man. Newsweek 66:60 O 4 '65
Rhymes with uncanny. il por Time 86:78+ N 19 '65

DE VAUCOULEURS, Gerard
Charting the Martian surface. bibliog Sky & Tel 30:196-201 O '65

DEVELOPING (photography) See Photography —Developing and developers

DEVELOPING nations. See Underdeveloped areas

DEVELOPMENT. See Evolution

DEVELOPMENT, Economic. See Economic development

DEVELOPMENT banks

Asia
Asian development bank; special preparatory meeting in Bangkok. UN Mo Chron 2:48 N '65
Lift out of the morass; Asian development bank. Time 86:97 O 29 '65
New temple; headquarters to be in Manila. Time 86:107 D 10 '65
Sharing the wealth. Newsweek 66:57-8 N 8 '65
U.S. participates in founding of Asian development bank; White House announcement, November 26; with statements by President Johnson, November 26, and December 4, 1965. Dept State Bul 53:1015-16 D 27 '65

DEVELOPMENT of children. See Children— Growth and development

DEVELOPMENT programme of the United Na-tions. See United Nations—Development programme

DEVEUSTER, Damien
Father Damien in Washington: proposed statue in the U.S. Capitol's Statuary hall. America 112:699 My 15 '65

DEVIANT behavior. See Behavior (psychology)

DEVILFISH. See Octopus

DEVILLE superjet siphon. See Photography— Apparatus and supplies

DEVILS; drama. See Whiting, J.

DEVLIN, John
I hadda shoot. M. Kempton. New Repub 152:13-15 Mr 20 '65

DEVLIN, John C.
Brooks Atkinson: a calm, strong, voice for nature. Audubon Mag 67:310-13 S '65

DEVLIN, Patrick Arthur Devlin, baron
Death of a president: the established facts. Atlan 215:112-18 Mr '65

DEVLIN, Polly
Alarming qualities of Ivy Compton-Burnett. Vogue 146:252-3+ S 1 '65
Encounter with Jean Shrimpton. Vogue 146: 28+ O 15 '65

DEVLIN, Wende
Beat poems of a beat mother. Good H 160: 60-1 My; 161:54 O '65

DEVON horse show. See Horse shows

DEVONIAN period. See Paleontology—Devo-nian

DEVONSHIRE, Spencer Compton Cavendish, 8th duke of
Patricians; excerpts from Proud tower. B. W. Tuchman. por Vogue 146:158-9+ N 1 '65

DE VOS, A.
Territorial behavior among puku in Zambia. Science 148:1752-3 Je 25 '65

DEVOTION to the Sacred Heart. See Sacred Heart, Devotion to

DEVOTIONS. See Prayer

DE VRIES, Leonard
Flowers of delight; excerpts. McCalls 92: 110-13 F '65

DEWAR, John A.
Phasing speaker systems. Pop Electr 23:66+ S '65

DEWART, Leslie
Negotiated settlement. Commonweal 82:717-20 O 1 '65

DEWEY, John
Education and our present social problems; reprint of a 1933 article. Sch & Soc 93:39-43 Ja 23 '65

DEWEY, Thomas E.
Vietnam or California; address, December 11, 1965. Vital Speeches 32:170-3 Ja 1 '66

DEWEY classification. See Classification, Decimal

DEXTER, Gerry L.
How to get those hard-to-get QSL's. Pop Electr 22:60-1+ Je '65

DEXTRAN
More blood, less fat. Time 86:72 N 5 '65

DEY, Joseph Charles
Man who makes the grass grow. A. Wright. il por Sports Illus 22:40-4+ Je 14 '65

DEY mansion, Wayne. See New Jersey— Historic houses, etc.

DEZETTEL, L. M.
Photoflood dimmer. Pop Electr 23:68-9 D '65

DIABETES
Diabetes & blood pressure; adrenal-gland disorder. Time 86:59 D 3 '65
New look at diabetes. Time 85:79 Je 25 '65
Sorbitol pathway: presence in nerve and cord with substrate accumulation in dia-betes. K. H. Gabbay and others. bibliog il Science 151:209-10 Ja 14 '66
Taking the danger out of diabetes; excerpts from Today's health guide. il Todays Health 43:56-7+ Ap '65
You and your diet; sweet recipes for di-abetics. il Good H 161:155-7 Ag '65

Diagnosis
Early diabetes signs. Sci Digest 58:17 D '65

DIAGHILEV, Sergei Pavlovich
Sacre de Diaghilev. I. Stravinsky; R. Craft. il pors Vogue 145:124-5+ Ap 15 '65

DIAGNOSIS
Condition critical: cause unknown. D. Murray. il Read Digest 86:145-8+ F '65
Medical lab tests: dangerous mistakes. A. Lake. McCalls 92:116-17+ My '65; Same abr. with title Laboratory test: medicine's Achilles' heel. Read Digest 87:70-4 O '65
Trouble with doctors is me. J. West. Ladies Home J 82:42+ Mr '65
Your doctor as a disease detective. T. Ber-land. Todays Health 43:62-5 S '65
See also
Photography, Medical
Ultrasonic waves—Medical applications

DIAGNOSIS, Radioscopic
Radiation danger reduced; new technique with scintillation camera. Sci N L 88:226 O 9 '65

DIAGRAMS
New machine speeds diagram production. P. J. Klass. il Aviation W 83:77+ O 18 '65

DIAL (periodical)
Aristocrat of the twenties. R. Sklar. il Re-porter 32:51-2 F 11 '65

DIAMOND mines and mining
Price of prosperity. P. Webb. il Newsweek 66:45 Ag 16 '65

DIAMONDS
Diamond history. H. D. Brown. Hobbies 70: 116-17 S '65
Diamonds in meteorites. E. Anders. il Sci Am 213:26-36 O '65
Hope diamond glows red in ultraviolet light. Sci N L 88:216 O 2 '65
If you want to sell a diamond. il Good H 160:179 Mr '65

Anecdotes, facetiae, satire, etc.
Capsule history of diamonds. G. Endore. Holiday 37:52-23 Je '65

DIAPAUSE. See Insects—Development

DIAPERS, Infants
Diapers. il Consumer Rep 30:402-5 Ag '65

DIARIES
John Adams at 18; discovery of John Adams' lost diary. Time 86:57 Jl 9 '65

DIAS, Earl J.
Knights of the square table; drama. Plays 25:51-62 D '65
Mountain madness; drama. Plays 24:17-28 F '65
Sophia the seamstress; drama. Plays 24:1-14 Ap '65
Thar she blows; drama. Plays 25:37-46, 84 N '65

DIAS DE AVILA PIRES, Fernando. See Pires, F. D. de A.

DIASPORA. See Refugees, Religious

DIAZO process. See Copying processes

DIAZ ORDAZ, Gustavo
Consensus. il por Time 86:28+ S 10 '65
Mexico: 1966 and beyond. F. Brandenburg. bibliog f Cur Hist 50:32-7+ Ja '66
Soothing words from a new colossus. il por Time 87:39 Ja 21 '66

DIBELER, Vernon H.
Photon and electron impact. Science 150:786-7 N 5 '65

DIBLIN, Joe
Engine management. Flying 78:56-9 Ja '66

DICE, Lee R.
When abortion is justified. Nation 200:189-91 F 22 '65

DICHLOROBENZYL methylcarbamate. See Herbicides

DICHTER, Ernest
Discovering the inner Jones. Harvard Bsns R 43:6-8+ My '65

DICKEL, J. R. and others
Andromeda galaxy: extension of the 610.5-megacycle-per-second map. bibliog Science 150:883-4 N 12 '65

DICKENS, Charles
Oliver Twist; dramatization. See Side, R. K.

about
Taking Dickens seriously. B. McCabe. Com-monweal 82:244-7 My 14 '65
What the Dickens; Pickwick papers adapted to musical. Newsweek 66:114 O 18 '65

DICKERSON, George
Christmas presents; poem. Mlle 62:48 D '65
Opinion, please from New York. Mlle 61:62+ My '65

DICKEY, James
Aura; poem. New Yorker 41:38 Je 5 '65
Birthday dream; poem. Nation 201:170 S 27 '65
Buckdancer's choice; poem. New Yorker 41: 36 Je 19 '65
Celebration; poem. Harper 230:50 Je '65
Coming back to America; poem. New Yorker 41:57 S 18 '65
False youth: summer; poem. Harper 231:115 S '65
Hedge life; poem. New Yorker 41:34 S 4 '65
Shark's parlor; poem. New Yorker 40:32-3 Ja 30 '65
Slave quarters; poem. New Yorker 41:28-9 Ag 14 '65
Sustainment; poem. Yale R 54:547-8 Je '65

DICKIE, Margaret M. See Schlager, G. jt. auth.

DICKINSON, David B.
Germination of lily pollen: respiration and tube growth. bibliog Science 150:1818-19 D 31 '65

DICKINSON, Dwight
Trust Territory of the Pacific Islands; statement, May 28, 1965. Dept State Bul 53:280-1 Ag 16 '65
DICKINSON, Edwin
Dickinson: reality of reflection. D. Waldman. il por Art N 64:28-31+ N '65
DICKINSON, William L.
How the army got set to move into Selma; What really happened on Alabama march? excerpts from statement to Congress, April 27, 1965. por U S News 58:16-17 My 10 '65

about

Kiss and tell? il por Newsweek 65:40 My 10 '65
Mud in the House. por Time 85:27 My 7 '65
DICTATORSHIP
Problems of dictatorship; the Russian experience. J. R. Strayer. For Affairs 44:264-74 Ja '66
Reign in Spain stays mainly the same. Christian Cent 82:763-4 Je 16 '65
    See also
Totalitarianism
DICTION
    See also
Singing—Diction
DICTIONARIES
    See also
English language—Dictionaries
DICTIONARIES, Childrens
French dictionary; excerpt from Cat in the hat beginner book dictionary in French. P. D. Eastman. il McCalls 93:66+ N '65
DICYANDIAMIDE. See Cyanoguanidine
DID I say it was funny? story. See Lee, M.
DIDION, Joan
Books. Vogue 146:66 O 15 '65
John Wayne: a love song. Sat Eve Post 238:76-9 Ag 14 '65
Movies. See issues of Vogue
New museum in Mexico. Vogue 146:48 Ag 1 '65
Notes from a native daughter. Holiday 38:76-7+ O '65
Questions about the new fiction. Nat R 17:1100-2 N 30 '65
DIDYMIUM nigripes. See Myxomycetes
DIEBENKORN, Richard
Diebenkorn. B. Kaufman. Commonweal 81:744-5 Mr 5 '65
DIEBOLD, John
What's ahead in information technology. Harvard Bsns R 43:76-82 S '65

about

Advice seller. por Time 86:90 D 3 '65
DIEBOLD conferences
Boss will always be human; Diebold research program. il Bsns W p 100-1 Ag 7 '65
DIEFENBAKER, John George
Canada's election: clash of personalities. por U S News 59:21 S 20 '65
Pearson's tempest. Newsweek 66:39 Jl 19 '65
Till the pub closes. por Time 85:36 F 19 '65
DIEFFENBACH, Shirley L.
Mural of copper repoussé for our school. Sch Arts 64:19-21 Je '65
DIEFFENBACHIAS
Fancy-leafed dieffenbachias. il Sunset 135:191 D '65
DIEGO GARCIA (atoll)
New beginning? Britain gaining atoll of Diego Garcia. il Time 86:45-6 N 19 '65
DIÉGUES, Manuel, Jr
(ed) See Cerda, L. E. Social science and development
DIELECTRICS
Point defects in insulators. C. C. Klick. bibliog il Science 150:451-6 O 22 '65
DIEM, Ngo-dinh-. See Ngo-dinh- Diem
DIENBIENPHU, Battle of. See Indochina, French—History—Civil war, 1946-1954
DIENSTAG, Eleanor
Feminine touch. New Repub 153:21-2 D 18 '65
DIENSTFREY, Harris
Books. Commonweal 83:64-5 O 15 '65
DIERS, Richard
Are writers made, not born? Sat R 48:52-3 Ag 14 '65
DIES (metal work)
Copper binding dies: faster, better, cheaper. il Pub W 187:86+ My 3 '65
DIESEL engines
Help engines beat the heat. Suc Farm 63:58 My '65

Fuel

Avoid fuel storage problems. Suc Farm 64:78 Ja '66
Know your diesel fuels. Suc Farm 64:83 Ja '66

DIESEL engines, Automotive
    See also
Motor truck engines
DIESEL engines, Marine
Where the diesel makes sense. N. Benedict. il Yachting 117:108-9+ Je '65
DIESKAU, Dietrich Fischer-. See Fischer-Dieskau, D.
DIET
Beware the drinkers' diet; crash diets. Sci Digest 58:13-14 Ag '65
Calories still count; Mayo clinic disclaims any association with diets. il Time 86:102 N 19 '65
Challenge to the American diet; interview. P. L. White. il Todays Health 44:12-13+ Ja '66
Diet: heart of the matter? il Newsweek 65:53-7 F 8 '65
Diet on whipped cream. Sci N L 87:259 Ap 25 '65
Diet that finally did it; air force diet. J. Alsop. il McCalls 92:138+ My '65; Same abr. with title What about that painless air force diet? Read Digest 87:89-92 Jl '65
Dieters' clipboard. See issues of Seventeen
Dollars in figures; effect on industries. T. R. Brooks. il Duns R 85:62-4+ Ap '65
Drinking man's danger. Time 85:72-3 Mr 5 '65
Feeding by machine helps reduce weight. Sci N L 87:89 F 6 '65
Fourteen day diet & pep-up plan. il Good H 162:144-6+ Ja '66
Good food habits for better health. D. G. Van Bortel. il Parents Mag 40:87-90 N '65
Good nutrition can be spiced by variety; with recipes. G. Maddox. il Todays Health 43:54-9 O '65
Gourmet diet cook book. J. A. Beard. il House & Gard 127:153+ Je '65
How to diet in five languages. il McCalls 92:136-7+ Ap '65
How to keep your weight down; advice from specialists. il U S News 58:66-70 Je 7 '65
I wrote The drinking man's diet. R. Wernick. il Sat Eve Post 238:84+ My 22 '65
Let 'em eat hay; Hay diet. il Todays Health 43:91 O '65
Mismanaged diets: some don'ts and dos for college girls. il Mlle 61:293 Ag '65
Overweight society, by P. Wyden. Review Sat R 48:40 Ap 10 '65. C. Amory
Personal business; dangers in fad diets. Bsns W p 157 Ap 24 '65
Proper diet decreases repeat heart attacks. Sci N L 88:328 N 20 '65
Reduction of Happy Humphrey; case of William J. Cobb. il Time 86:31 Jl 30 '65
Risks of that new eat-all-you-want diet. il Good H 160:171-3 My '65; Same abr. with title Risks in the low-carbohydrate diet. Read Digest 87:92-3 Jl '65
You and your diet. See issues of Good housekeeping
    See also
Children—Nutrition
Corpulence
Food
Food fads
Food preferences
Nutrition
Nutrition education
Nutrition research
Proteins
Weight reducing preparations
DIET, Deficient
Vitamin E harmful? Sci N L 88:402 D 25 '65
DIET in disease
How to eat well on a gluten-free diet. il Todays Health 43:38-40+ O '65
Trade winds; concerning Adelle Davis' Let's get well. J. Beatty, jr. il Sat R 49:12+ Ja 15 '66
You and your diet; recipes that limit fats. il Good H 161:203-5 O '65
    See also
Ketogenic diet
DIETARY studies. See Diet
DIETER, Kathleen
Businessmen's expectations (cont) Duns R 85:11 Mr; 15 Je '65
DIETHER, Jack
At last in stereo. Schoenberg's Gurre lieder. Am Rec G 32:208-12 N '65
Britten's new cello symphony. Am Rec G 31:1056-8 Jl '65
Bruckner. Am Rec G 31:788-90 My '65
Deutsche grammophon presents the first stereo recordings of the two ultra-Moravian vocal works by Janáček. Am Rec G 31:710-14 Ap '65
From Philips, the best complete recording of L'histoire du soldat. Am Rec G 31:610-11+ Mr '65
Messiah, two new versions. Am Rec G 32:306-8 D '65
Something new for Joan Baez, Villa-Lobos. Am Rec G 31:502-4 F '65

DIETS. See Diet

DIETSCHY, John M. and Carter, N. W.
Active transport of 5,5-dimethyl-2,4-oxazolidinedione. bibliog Science 150:1294-6 D 3 '65

DIETZ, Albert G. H.
Where is science taking us? por Sat R 49:104-5 Ja 1 '66

DIETZ, George. See Forsberg, R. jt. auth.

DIETZ, Lew
Long hard winter. Field & S 69:56-7+ Mr '65
Marblehead gunning dory. Field & S 70:54-7+ N '65
Odd fellow of the alder runs. Field & S 70:56-7+ S '65
Trembling prairie. Field & S 69:56-9+ F '65

DIETZ, Robert S.
Colston symposium: marine geology and geophysics. Science 149:94-5 Jl 2 '65

DIFFERENCES, Racial. See Racial differences

DIFFERENTIAL thermal analysis. See Thermal analysis

DIFFERENTIALS, Wage. See Wage differentials

DIFFERENTIATION (biology)
Hemoglobin and transferrin electrophoresis and relationships of island populations of anolis lizards. G. C. Gorman and H. C. Dessauer. bibliog il Science 150:1454-5 D 10 '65

DIFFICULT children. See Problem children

DIFFUSION
Neon isotope fractionation during transient permeation. S. N. I. Rama and S. R. Hart. bibliog Science 147:737-8 F 12 '65
Oxygen-hemoglobin system: a model for facilitated membranous transport. D. B. Zilversmit. bibliog il Science 149:874-6 Ag 20 '65
Tension gradients accompanying accelerated oxygen transport in a membrane. P. F. Scholander. bibliog il Science 149:876-7 Ag 20 '65

DIGEPOL. See Secret service—Venezuela

DIGESTIVE glands. See Glands

DIGESTIVE system

Diseases
See also
Diabetes
Stomach—Diseases

DI GIOVANNI, Norman Thomas
In the Apuan Alps. Atlan 216:134+ S '65

DIGITAL computers. See Computers—Digital computers

DIGITAL simulators. See Flight simulators

DIGITALIS (drug)
William Withering and the purple foxglove. J. W. Estes and P. D. White. il Sci Am 212:110-16+ Je '65

DIGITALIS purpurea. See Foxgloves

DIHYDROXYMETHYL valeric acid
α-D-glucose: precise determination of crystal and molecular structure by neutron-diffraction analysis. G. M. Brown and H. A. Levy. bibliog il Science 147:1038-9 F 26 '65

DILATION, Pupillary. See Pupil (eye)

DILKE, Sir Charles Wentworth, 2d bart
Victorian scandal, by R. Jenkins. Review
Nat R 18:80-1 Ja 25 '66. S. Leslie

DILL, William R. and others
Strategies for self-education. bibliog f Harvard Bsns R 43:119-30 N '65

DILLE, John
Good copters, but bum tactics. Life 58:34D Ap 16 '65

DILLER, Phyllis
Funny Phyllis Diller is serious about ballet. V. H. Swisher. pors Dance Mag 40:28-30 Ja '66

DILLIARD, Irving
Origins of the Bill of rights. New Repub 153: 38-40 N 27 '65
St Louis: one city's contribution. Sat R 48:77-8 O 23 '65

DILLON, Clarence Douglas
Assessment of the international monetary system; address, March 19, 1965. Dept State Bul 52:593-8 Ap 19 '65
United States fiscal policy; address, March 19, 1965. Vital Speeches 31:388-91 Ap 15 '65

about
Mr Dillon's valedictory. America 112:602-3 Ap 24 '65

DILLON, Richard H.
Confessions of fellow traveler. Library J 90:5484-5 D 15 '65
Profile: Lawrence Clark Powell. Library J 90:5341-3 D 15 '65

DILORENZO, Alexander
Quiet giants. Time 85:86 Mr 12 '65

DILTS, Peggy
Look and listen. See issues of Senior scholastic
Looking and listening. See issues of Senior scholastic

DIM light. See Electric lighting—Control

DIMAGGIO, Charlie
East side Earp. Time 86:21 Ag 20 '65

DIMARE, Dominic
Dominic DiMare. H. Giambruni. il por Craft Horiz 25:18-21+ N '65

DIMETHYL oxazolidinedione
Active transport of 5,5-dimethyl-2,4-oxazolidinedione. J. M. Dietschy and N. W. Carter. bibliog il Science 150:1294-6 D 3 '65

DIMETHYL sulfoxide. See Methyl sulfoxide

DIMITRI Mitropoulos international music competition. See Music— Competitions

DIMMED room light. See Electric lighting—Control

DIMMERS. See Electric lighting—Control

DIMMERS, Automobile. See Automobiles—Lighting

DIMOCK, Edward C. Jr
Note on the Vaishnava lyrics. Poetry 107:182-3 D '65
—and Levertov, Denise
Six Vaishnava lyrics. Poetry 107:176-81 D '65

DIMONDSTEIN book company, incorporated
How two leading book jobbers prepare for Christmas. Pub W 188:37-9 Ag 23 '65

DINERS' club, incorporated

Anecdotes, facetiae, satire, etc.
I am a fugitive from the Diners' club. J. Breslin. il Sat Eve Post 238:20 Ag 14 '65

DINERS' club magazine
I am a fugitive from the Diners' club. J. Breslin. il Sat Eve Post 238:20 Ag 14 '65

DINESEN, Isak, pseud. See Blixen, K. D.

DINGHIES. See Boats and boating

DINGLE, A. Nelson
Stratospheric tapping by intense convective storms: implication for public health in the United States. bibliog Science 148:227-9 Ap 9 '65

DINGMAN, C. W. and Sporn, M. B.
Actinomycin D and hydrocortisone: intracellular binding in rat liver. bibliog Science 149:1251-4 S 10 '65

DINING halls
See also
Colleges and universities—Dining halls

DINING room furniture
New ways to seat your guests. il House & Gard 129:108-11 Ja '66

DINING rooms
Great dining room comeback. G. O'Brien. il N Y Times Mag p70-1 Mr 7 '65
How to add zest to your dining room. il House & Gard 128:240-7 N '65

DINKINS, Lloyd, and Bickers, Jack
Partway partnership. Farm J 89:D2 F '65

DINKLER, Cornelia Vandegaer
Connie's club for homeless glitterbugs. A. Wright. il pors Sports Illus 23:40-2+ D 13 '65

DINNERS and dining
Dinner for the boss. il Ebony 20:110+ F '65
Dinner-in-a-jiffy; with recipes. il Good H 160:112-29+ Mr '65
Dinners that wait for you; recipes. il Redbook 126:82-4+ N '65
Do-ahead meals. B. B. Smith. il Parents Mag 41:61+ Ja '66
Duck dinner. il Bet Hom & Gard 43:73+ N '65
Gourmet feast for Americans; with menu. il Esquire 64:243-5 D '65
Great dinners. See occasional issues of Life
Happy marriage; a little French dinner. il McCalls 92:38 Ap '65
How to give a perfect party every time. il Bet Hom & Gard 43:72+ N '65
How to give dashing parties; Philadelphia association of gourmets. il House & Gard 128:248-53 N '65
Table for two (cont) Ladies Home J 82:24 F; 50 Ap; 88 My; 94 Je; 100 Ag; 102 S; 118 N '65
Taste of spring. il McCalls 92:140-1+ Ap '65
Teeny-tiny dinners for six; with recipes. il Mlle 62:186-7+ N '65
See also
Christmas dinners
Food, Frozen
Outdoor meals
Thanksgiving dinners

DINNERSTEIN, Harvey
Artist as buffalo hunter. il Esquire 64:184-9 D '65

DINOFLAGELLATES
Bioelectric control of bioluminescence in the dinoflagellate noctiluca. R. Eckert. bibliog il Science 147:1140-5 Mr 5 '65

DINOSAURS
Dinosaur footprints on the ceiling; Queensland, Australia. il Sci Digest 57:inside cover Ap '65
New species of dinosaur claimed by Chinese. Sci N L 88:101 Ag 14 '65
-Were dinosaurs a failure? A. Smith. il Sci Digest 58:86-9 S '65

DINSMORE, William H.
Dear stockholders: everything looks rosy. . . Harper 230:133-6+ Mr '65

DIODES
DeForest's early audions. P. G. Watson. il Electr World 74:82-3 S '65
Using diodes to protect circuits. T. Kaarto. il Electr World 73:82 F '65
Using silicon diodes. C. L. Fair. il Pop Electr 23:58-60 Jl '65

Testing
Simple go no-go diode testers. il Pop Electr 23:88 Ag '65

DIODES, Tunnel. See Tunnel diodes

DIORAMAS
Art of the diorama. R. Strong. il Am Artist 29:34-9+ O '65

DIOSPYROS. See Persimmons

DIOXANE
Pulse radiolysis of dioxane solutions. J. H. Baxendale and others. bibliog il Science 148:637 Ap 30 '65

DIPAGLIA, Floren
Case of the too hot golfer. G. S. Brown. il pors Sports Illus 23:42-4+ N 22 '65

DIPLOMACY
Computerized diplomacy. W. Pfaff. Commonweal 82:520-1 Jl 23 '65
Limits to secrecy. Commonweal 81:627-8 F 12 '65
New diplomacy; address, June 6, 1965. J. W. Ball. Dept State Bul 52:1042-8 Je 28 '65
See also
International relations
World war, 1939-1945—Diplomatic history
also subhead Foreign relations under names of countries, e.g. Russia—Foreign relations

DIPLOMAS, Fraudulent
Mail-order college; action to prevent Central Christian college, Huntington, W.Va. from selling worthless degrees and diplomas. Newsweek 66:86 Jl 26 '65

DIPLOMATIC and consular service
Race to succeed Nicole; the entries. M. Cheshire. il Life 59:93-4+ N 12 '65
Western village in Moscow. J. Wolfenden. il N Y Times Mag p21+ F 7 '65
See also
Diplomats
Nuncios, Papal
also subhead Diplomatic and consular service under names of countries, e.g. France—Diplomatic and consular service

DIPLOMATIC etiquette
How ya gonna keep 'em down in Upper Volta after they've met Lloyd Hand? E. Wittenberg. Esquire 64:24+ D '65
It's the most fascinating job in Washington. W. T. Buchanan, jr. il Life 58:74-5 Mr 12 '65

DIPLOMATIC privileges and immunities
Cracking the nest eggs; private sale of imported duty-free automobiles prohibited. Time 85:32 Mr 26 '65

DIPLOMATS
Affairs at state, by H. S. Villard. Review Time il 86:121+ O 1 '65
Dope-smuggling diplomats; ed. by J. C. G. Conniff. H. L. Giordano. il Pop Sci 186:100-3+ Je '65
See also
United States—Foreign service

DIPOLE antennas. See Radio antennas

DIRECT energy conversion
Army presses for better field systems. il Miss & Roc 16:77-8+ Mr 29 '65
See also
Solar batteries

DIRECT-view storage tubes. See Storage tubes

DIRECTION, Sense of. See Orientation

DIRECTION finding
Swede compass; long pole. G. J. Tucker. il Outdoor Life 137:108-9 Ja '66

DIRECTION finding apparatus
See also
Hydrophones
Range finding

DIRECTIONAL antennas. See Radio antennas

DIRECTORATES, Interlocking. See Interlocking directorates

DIRECTORIES
See also subhead Directories under various subjects, e.g. Theological schools—Directories

DIRECTORS. See Interlocking directorates; Moving picture directors

DIRIGIBLES. See Airships

DIRKSEN, Everett McKinley
Congress and business: Senators Mansfield and Dirksen debate outlook; ed. by J. W. Bunting. pors Nations Bsns 53:76-80+ Mr '65
Excerpt from address, February 18, 1965. Cong Digest 44:112+ Ap '65
If a man die, shall he live again? U S News 59:124+ N 8 '65
Look ahead by the Republicans; interview. por U S News 60:70-4 Ja 17 '66
Republican future; interview. pors U S News 58:60-4 My 3 '65

about
Are farmers better than city people? por Sat Eve Post 238:90 Je 19 '65
Baseball, pure and undefiled. A. Kopkind. New Repub 153:9-10 Ag 7 '65
Blackmail and blackjack. Newsweek 66:24 S 20 '65
Bobby and Teddy. K. Crawford. Newsweek 65:38 My 24 '65
Bye-bye Dirksen. Nat R 17:716 Ag 24 '65
Counting Dirksen out. por Newsweek 66:19 Ag 16 '65
Dirksen's defeat. il por Time 86:17 Ag 13 '65
Dirksen's double play. P. R. Wieck. New Repub 152:13-14 Ap 17 '65
Ev's curve ball. il por Time 86:17 S 10 '65
Ev's extendalong. por Time 86:30 O 15 '65
Grand old king of the Senate. P. O'Neil. il pors Life 58:88-90+ Mr 26 '65; Same abr. Read Digest 87:84-8 Ag '65
Inscrutable Pekinese. K. Crawford. Newsweek 65:34 Ap 26 '65
Oil can is mightier than the sword. B. H. Bagdikian. il pors N Y Times Mag p30-1+ Mr 14 '65
Pas de Dirksen. il Time 86:14 Ag 27 '65
Senate stalls repeal of 14(b) por Bsns W p 163-4+ O 9 '65
Senator Dirksen vs. the Court. R. M. Christenson. Nation 201:60-1 Ag 2 '65
Senator Dirksen's unexpected allies. J. Duscha. il Reporter 32:26-8 Ap 22 '65
Visit with the Dirksens. P. R. Smith, jr. il pors Flower Grower 52:36-7 N '65
When one person, one vote came up. por U S News 59:20 Ag 16 '65

DIRTY heron; story. See Buitrago, F.

DISABILITY insurance. See Insurance, Disability

DISABLED. See Handicapped

DISADVANTAGED children. See Socially handicapped children

DISARMAMENT
Arms nobody wants to control; proliferation of non-nuclear weapons. A. Buchan. New Repub 153:17-18 N 6 '65
Assembly adopts resolution; World disarmament conference; with text of resolution. UN Mo Chron 2:46-52 D '65
Disarmament and international cooperation; statements, May 12, 1965. H. Cleveland; A. S. Fisher. Dept State Bul 52:967-73 Je 14 '65
Disarmament inches ahead; new lease of life for ACDA. N. K. Herzfeld. Commonweal 82:631-5 S 3 '65
Disarmament proposal. D. K. Sen. Bul Atomic Sci 21:35-6 F '65
Key to peace. J. S. Clark. Sat R 49:28 Ja 15 '66
Problems of peace-making; address, September 9, 1965. Thant. UN Mo Chron 2:118-22 O '65
Strategy and conscience. by A. Rapoport. Review
Bul Atomic Sci 21:25-30 D '65; D. G. Brennan; with reply by A. Rapoport. 21:31-6 D '65
Strengthening peace through arms control and disarmament. J. D. Beam. Dept State Bul 53:398-400 S 6 '65
U.S.-red Chinese bilateral urged. Aviation W 83:36 D 6 '65
United States summarizes position on disarmament and arms control; statement, April 26, 1965. A. E. Stevenson. bibliog f Dept State Bul 52:762-74 My 17 '65
See also
Armaments
Atomic weapons and disarmament
Conference of the Eighteen-nation committee on disarmament. Geneva, 1962-
International security
United Nations—Disarmament commission

DISARMAMENT—*Continued*

Economic aspects

Defense is no longer a big growth business. Bsns W p29 S 11 '65

Report released on economic impact of defense and disarmament; letter, September 4, 1965; with White House announcement. L. B. Johnson. Dept State Bul 53:515-18 S 27 '65

Inspection

Perspectives on inspection for arms control. B. G. Lall. Bul Atomic Sci 21:51-3 Mr '65

Arctic Regions

Arctic proposed to be nuclear-free zone. Sci N L 87:392 Je 19 '65

Europe, Western

Prospects for arms control in Europe. W. Young. Bul Atomic Sci 21:22-4 S '65

Recent arms control research in Europe. J. B. Teeple. Bul Atomic Sci 21:37-9 O '65

Great Britain

See also
Campaign for nuclear disarmament (organization)

DISARMAMENT agency. See United States—Arms control and disarmament agency

DISASTERS

Beauty and chivalry of the United States assembled; explosion of Peacemaker, cannon on U.S. steam sloop Princeton, 1844. D. B. Webster, jr. il Am Heritage 17:50-3+ D '65

Winter's toll; catastrophes in Chile. il Time 86:26 Ag 27 '65

See also
Explosions
Floods
Hurricanes
Insurance—Catastrophe coverage
Relief work

DISCHARGE, Military

Alive again; precedent-setting decision concerning dishonorable discharge. il Time 87:74 Ja 7 '66

DISCHARGED prisoners. See Prisoners, Discharged

DISCHE, M. Renate

Enigma of sudden infant death. Ladies Home J 82:48+ Mr '65

DISCIPLES of Christ

Concord at Lexington; Consultation on church union. J. R. Nelson. Christian Cent 82:575-6 My 5 '65

Lyndon Johnson's religion. J. Bird. il Sat Eve Post 238:80-1+ Mr 27 '65

DISCIPLINE

How much is too much discipline? H. Van Stockum. il Parents Mag 40:56-7+ Je '65

How well should children mind? with study-discussion program, by R. Strang. M. M. Conant. bibliog il PTA Mag 59:10-12, 43 F '65

Six on a honeymoon. A. Lee. il Parents Mag 41:42-3+ Ja '66

See also
Children—Management and training
College discipline
School discipline

DISCIPLINE, Library. See Library administration

DISCOTHEQUE. See Night clubs

DISCOUNT

Abroad: warm on rate, cool on dollar curbs. Bsns W p31-2 D 11 '65

Bankers applaud, businessmen accept; Feds decision to raise bank rate; with editorial comment. il Bsns W p27-9 D 11 '65

Fait accompli. Time 86:18-19 D 17 '65

Fed's surprise: tighter money: raise in discount rate. il Newsweek 66:75-6+ D 13 '65

Fixing interest rates. H. Hazlitt. Newsweek 66:86 D 20 '65

Haves vs. have-nots; disagreement between Johnson and Martin over discount rate. K. Crawford. Newsweek 66:30 D 20 '65

Manipulating money. H. Hazlitt. Newsweek 67:47 Ja 3 '66

Patman on the warpath. il Newsweek 66:51 D 27 '65

Pressures & passions; hearings about the Federal reserve's discount-rate rise. il Time 86:53-4 D 24 '65

Raising the cost of money. New Repub 153:8-9 D 18 '65

Rate & its ripples; effects of the Federal reserve's move. il Time 86:85 D 17 '65

Taking the rise in stride; stepped-up spending plans by corporations and government. il Bsns W p25-7 D 11 '65

Up go the rates and the roof; protests. il Newsweek 66:75-6 D 20 '65

Up with the discount rate. il Time 86:99 D 10 '65

DISCOUNT, Trade

Disappearing discount; clergyman's discount. Time 86:48+ Jl 9 '65

DISCOUNT houses (retail trade)

America's discount houses: bargain bonanzas or retail junkyards? pro and con discussion. il Sr Schol 87:12-13 S 16 '65

Can you still get bargains in discount stores? R. Brecher and E. Brecher. il Redbook 124:62-3+ Ap '65; Same abr. with title How big are bargains in discount stores? Read Digest 87:79-82 Jl '65

88 per cent of discount stores have book departments. Pub W 187:57 My 17 '65

Great discount delusion, by W. H. Nelson. Review
Nation 201:255-6 O 18 '65. V. Lebow
Sat R 48:22 Jl 31 '65. V. Packard

Is success spoiling discount stores? il Bsns W p97-8+ Je 26 '65

Mix discounts and art and make sales jump; Honest Ed's in Toronto. il Bsns W p50-2 F 20 '65

Mixed bag of gimmicks. W. H. Nelson. Pub W 188:34-7 Ag 2 '65

Show card, get discount; Ratio markts, West Germany. il Bsns W p48-50+ My 22 '65

See also
Masters, incorporated

DISCOURTESY. See Courtesy

DISCOVERIES in science. See Inventions; Patents; Research; Science

DISCRIMINATION

See also
Anti-Semitism
Race discrimination
United Nations—Sub-commission on prevention of discrimination and protection of minorities

DISCRIMINATION in education

Chicago: the marchers and the machine. K. P. Buckley and R. Cotton. Reporter 33:30-1 N 4 '65; Discussion. 33:10 D 2 '65

Leaning on HEW; Office of education federal aid decision overruled. il Newsweek 66:98 O 18 '65

Philadelphia dilemma; trouble resulting from segregation clause in will providing for Girard college. il Time 86:65 Jl 23 '65

Philadelphia's Negroes challenge a will. P. H. Binzen. il Reporter 33:43-5 O 21 '65

DISCRIMINATION in employment

Committee for professional opportunity; letter. T. Hayashi. Science 148:1411 Je 11 '65

Conference on equal employment opportunity. G. Potts. Mo Labor R 88:1320-1 N '65

Different drum. G. W. Broadfield. Nation 201:161-5 S 20 '65

Hiring tests wait for the score; Myart vs. Motorola. Bsns W p45-6+ F 13 '65

Meritocracy of labor. M. Kempton. New Repub 152:14-17 F 6 '65

Milwaukee: a fair deal; Voluntary equal employment opportunity council activities. E. L. Winter. il Sat R 49:54+ Ja 8 '66

Mississippi business plans for integration. Bsns W p32 Ap 17 '65

Prospects for equal employment: conflicting portents. R. Marshall. Mo Labor R 88:650-3 Je '65

Racial inequality in employment: the patterns of discrimination. H. Hill. bibliog f Ann Am Acad 357:30-47 Ja '65

Sex and nonsense. New Repub 153:10 S 4 '65; Reply. 153:26+ S 18 '65

Sex & VII; Equal employment opportunity section. Time 86:62 Jl 9 '65

When is the difference unequal? question of sex bias. Time 86:36 D 10 '65

Where civil rights law is going wrong. Nations Bsns 53:60-2+ N '65

See also
Negroes in the United States—Employment

DISCRIMINATION in housing

California churches in the aftermath of defeat; Proposition fourteen, repeal of Rumford fair housing act. P. Wogaman. Christian Cent 82:139-41 F 3 '64; Discussion. 82:435-6 Ap 7 '65

Dilemmas of urban America, by R. C. Weaver. Review
Sat R 49:85 Ja 8 '66. C. W. Griffin, jr.

From the polls to the Court; problems in California resulting from passage of Prop. 14. America 113:87 Jl 24 '65

Housing, the hottest issue in the North. H. J. Bims. il Ebony 20:93-4+ Ag '65

DISCRIMINATION in housing—*Continued*
Protest against housing segregation. L. Miller. bibliog f Ann Am Acad 357:73-9 Ja '65
Round one to Proposition fourteen. il Time 85:74 F 12 '65
See also
Housing—Desegregation
Negroes in the United States—Housing
DISCRIMINATION learning. See Learning, Psychology of
DISCUS, pseud.
Music in the round. See issues of Harper's magazine
DISCUSSION
Coffee house ministry; new style of evangelism. J. D. Perry, jr. Christian Cent 82:180-1+ F 10 '65
See also
Conversation
Forums (discussion and debate)
DISEASE, Diet in. See Diet in disease
DISEASE resistance. See Immunity
DISEASES
Analyze laughing sickness; kuru. Sci N L 88:374 D 11 '65
Cripplers; excerpts from Today's health guide. il Todays Health 43:33-7 Ag '65
Let's end these unnecessary deaths. J. D. Ratcliff. il Read Digest 87:124-8 S '65
Medical news of the month. M. Fishbein. See issues of McCall's
See also
Diagnosis
Venereal diseases
also names of diseases, e.g. Histoplasmosis

Causes and theories of causation

Sex chromatin in newborns: presumptive evidence for external factors in human nondisjunction. A. Robinson and T. T. Puck. bibliog il Science 148:83-5 Ap 2 '65
What you don't see can hurt you! R. Martin. il Todays Health 43:42-7 N '65
DISEASES, Hereditary. See Heredity of disease
DISEASES, Industrial
Human side of industry. F. R. Schreiber and M. Herman. il Sci Digest 57:41-3 F '65
See also
Anthrax
DISEASES, Mental. See Mental illness
DISEASES, Prehistoric. See Paleopathology
DISEASES, Psychosomatic. See Medicine, Psychosomatic
DISEASES of plants. See Plants—Diseases and pests
DISGUISES
False faces for the real me. L. Wainwright. Life 58:21 Ap 30 '65
DISHES. See Pottery
DISHONESTY. See Honesty
DISHWASHING
How to get out of the kitchen after dinner. il Redbook 126:76-7+ N '65
If you wash dishes by hand. il Good H 160: 201 Mr '65
DISHWASHING and drying machines
Automatic dishwashers. il Consumer Bul 48: 20-6 D '65
Dishes and dishwashers. Consumer Rep 30: 32-8 D '65
Dishwashers. il Consumer Rep 30:527-33 N '65
Dishwashing facts for old-fashioned girls. V. T. Habeeb. Am Home 68:76 Mr '65
Drudgery is for dishwashers! il Good H 160: 134-5 My '65
Five ways to find space for a dishwasher. H. R. Pfister. il Pop Sci 187:108-10 S '65
Of machines and marriage. M. Davidson. il Ladies Home J 82:34 Ag '65
You can't afford to wash dishes by hand. N. Pierce and B. G. Wadsworth. il Parents Mag 40:59-61 My '65
DISK brakes. See Brakes, Automobile
DISLOCATIONS in crystals
Dislocation networks in folded-chain polyethylene crystals. V. F. Holland and P. H. Lindenmeyer. bibliog il Science 147: 1296-7 Mr 12 '65
Screw dislocations in graphite. G. R. Hennig. bibliog il Science 147:733-4 F 12 '65
DISMISSAL of employees. See Employees—Dismissal
DISMISSAL wage. See Wages—Dismissal wage
DISNEY, Dorothy Cameron
(ed) Can this marriage be saved? case histories. See issues of Ladies home journal
DISNEY, Roy
Disney's live-action profits. il pors Bsns W p78-82 Jl 24 '65

DISNEY, Walt
Day with Disney. F. Whitaker. il por Am Artist 29:44-8+ S '65
Disneyland East. Newsweek 66:82 N 29 '65
Disney's live-action profits. il pors Bsns W p78-82 Jl 24 '65
Fantasy that paid off. L. E. Litwak. il N Y Times Mag p22-3+ Je 27 '65
Tinker Bell, Mary Poppins, cold cash. il por Newsweek 66:74-6 Jl 12 '65
DISNEY, Walt, productions
Day with Disney. F. Whitaker. il Am Artist 29:44-8+ S '65
Too long at the sugar bowls: Frances C. Sayers raps Disney; statements. F. C. Sayers. Library J 90:4538 O 15 '65
Walt Disney accused; interview. F. C. Sayers. Horn Bk 41:602-11 D '65
DISNEYLAND East. See Amusement parks
DISNEYLAND park, Anaheim, Calif.
Fantasy that paid off. L. E. Litwak. il N Y Times Mag p22-3+ Je 27 '65
Foamrubbersville. J. Ciardi. Sat R 48:20 Je 19 '65
Machine-tooled happyland. R. Bradbury. il Holiday 38:100-2+ O '65
Tinker Bell, Mary Poppins, cold cash. il Newsweek 66:74-6 Jl 12 '65
DISPERSION
Anomalous dispersion method: its power for protein structure analysis. G. N. Ramachandran and S. Parthasarathy. bibliog il Science 150:212-14 O 8 '65
DISPLAY boxes. See Exhibition cases
DISPLAY cases. See Exhibition cases
DISPLAYS, Window. See Show windows
DISPOSAL of refuse. See Refuse and refuse disposal
DISTANCES
Measurement
See also
Range finding
DISTANCES, Astronomical. See Astronomical distances
DISTILLATION
See also
Water, Distilled
DISTILLATION apparatus
See also
Solar stills
DISTILLERS corporation-Seagrams, limited. See Seagram, Joseph E, and sons
DISTILLING, Illicit. See Moonshining
DISTILLING industries
See also
Seagram, Joseph E, and sons
DISTORTION, Art. See Art—Distortion
DISTRESS signals. See Signals and signaling
DISTRIBUTION, Physical. See Distribution of goods
DISTRIBUTION cost analysis. See Cost accounting
DISTRIBUTION of animals and plants. See Geographical distribution of animals and plants
DISTRIBUTION of goods
Art of physical distribution. H. C. Meal. il Duns R 85:pt2 118-19+ Je '65
Concept of a national market; address, September 1, 1965. W. W. Rostow. Vital Speeches 31:717-20 S 15 '65
DISTRIBUTION stations. See Warehouses
DISTRICT Judges. See Judges
DISTRICT of Columbia. See Washington, D.C.
DISTRICT schools. See Rural schools
DISULFIDES. See Sulfides
DITCHLEY foundation
Quiet place fosters U.S.-British harmony; meeting of U.S. senators and representatives and British officials to discuss world's most disturbing problems. il Bsns W p32-3 F 13 '65
DIVERS. See Diving, Submarine
DIVERSIFICATION in industry
Case of the diversification dilemma: symposium, ed. by C. H. Kline. il Harvard Bsns R 43:12-14+ My '65
Finding the right combination; Philadelphia & Reading corp. Bsns W p49-50+ Ag 21 '65
Gates rubber: plenty of bounce. il Bsns W p 112-14+ O 16 '65
Gleaning new ventures from farming profits; Kern County land co diversifies. il Bsns W p89-90+ O 23 '65
How to feed profits as well as babies; Gerber products. il Bsns W p64-6+ Ja 8 '66
Industry studies California problems; special report. W. E. Wilks. il Miss & Roc 16: 24-5+ F 15 '65
Joy digs from under its burden of coal. il Bsns W p 100-2+ Ja 8 '66

DIVERSIFICATION in industry—*Continued*
New look at Pet milk. J. B. Weiner. il Duns R 85:36-8+ Mr '65
Oil is no longer enough; Jersey Standard moves into chemical, power, realty. il Bsns W p48-50+ Jl 3 '65
Pet milk spills over into other pastures. il Bsns W p58-60+ Jl 31 '65
Railroads switch to other tracks. Bsns W p45-6 Ag 7 '65
Second growth of Georgia-Pacific. J. B. Weiner. il Duns R 85:47-9+ My '65
Smucker spreads out beyond jam and jelly. il Bsns W p 194+ N 13 '65
Strategic planning in conglomerate companies. N. Berg. bibliog f il Harvard Bsns R 43:79-92 My '65
Univac isn't a business to jump in and out of. S. H. Brown. Fortune 71:120-3+ Ap '65
Wilson, lean, fit, ready for action. il Bsns W p80-3 N 27 '65

DIVERSIFIED farming
Here's proof that diversified farming isn't dead! W. Messerly. il Suc Farm 63:72 N '65

DIVIDENDS
Catch to soaring dividends. il Bsns W p59 N 20 '65
Raises for the stockholders. Time 85:87 F 12 '65

DIVINA commedia. See Dante Alighieri

DIVINE, Father. See Divine, M. J.

DIVINE, Major J.
Deity derepersonifitized; Father Divine's death. il por Time 86:41 S 17 '65
Father Divine's righteous government. G. Harkness. Christian Cent 82:1259-61 O 13 '65
Life with Father. il por Newsweek 66:28 S 20 '65
My thirty years with Father Divine. R. Boaz. il pors Ebony 20:88-90+ My '65

DIVINE comedy. See Dante Alighieri

DIVING
Which way is up? dangers of dizziness. Time 86:48 S 10 '65

Safety devices and measures
Diving injuries. C. J. Potthoff. Todays Health 43:64 Ag '65

DIVING, Submarine
Divers' agenda; Underwater society of America convention. il Life 59:41-2 S 3 '65
Five men swim down to giant mountain peak. il(p 1) Sci N L 88:8 Jl 3 '65
Frogmen on pickup duty. il Life 58:80 Je 18 '65
Ghost in the blue hole; Banner Reef, southwest of Jamaica in the open Caribbean. C. Phinizy. il Sports Illus 22:68-70+ Mr 8 '65
Going overboard for maintenance and fun. W. S. Kals. il Yachting 118:52-3+ N '65
How Jon Lindbergh works on the ocean floor. G. Soule. il Pop Sci 187:50-3 S '65
I could dive all day. J. Duffy; S. Brown; M. Krasovetz. Seventeen 24:92-3+ Jl '65
Old men of the sea; San Diego's G. Orr. C. Phinizy. il Sports Illus 23:72-4+ Ag 23 '65
Skin and scuba training games; summary of report. F. J. Scalli. il Recreation 58:136-7 Mr '65
Talk with Cousteau; ed. by E. Miller. J. Y. Cousteau. Seventeen 24:56 F '65
Their business is going under; Underwater tours, ltd, Nassau, Bahama Islands. G. Rogin. il Sports Illus 22:80-4+ Je 7 '65
What's going on down there? J. Dugan. il Holiday 37:70-9+ Je '65
Why they invade the sea. J. Jones. il N Y Times Mag p47+ Mr 14 '65
See also
Archeology, Submarine

Safety devices and measures
AMA warns divers of gas, pressure dangers. Sci N L 87:281 My 1 '65

DIVING apparatus
Depth problems yielding to research. H. M. David. il Miss & Roc 17:56-9 S 6 '65
Going overboard for maintenance and fun. W. S. Kals. il Yachting 118:52-3+ N '65
Why they invade the sea. J. Jones. il N Y Times Mag p47+ Mr 14 '65
See also
Bathyscaphe

DIVINITY of Christ. See Jesus Christ—Divinity
DIVINITY schools. See Theological schools
DIVINITY students. See Theological students
DIVISION of overseas ministries. See National council of the churches of Christ in the United States of America
DIVITA, Sal F.
Selling R&D to the government. Harvard Bsns R 43:62-75 S '65

DIVORCE
Problems of a broken home; questions and answers. A. Wood. il Seventeen 24:162-3+ My '65
Trouble in paradise; some complaints voiced by spouses seeking divorces; comp. by H. Helfer. il N Y Times Mag p56 Ap 25 '65
See also
Alimony
Domestic relations courts
Marriage

Great Britain
Divorce in Britain; Sir Jocelyn Simon's proposed reforms. America 112:849 Je 12 '65

Italy
Concubinage, Italian style. il Time 85:56 F 19 '65

Mexico
Divorce across the border. il Time 86:62 Jl 23 '65
Divorce Mexican style. il Newsweek 66:31-2 Jl 26 '65
To Juárez on the divorce run. G. Samuels. il N Y Times Mag p78+ S 12 '65

United States
Bankrupt marriages; rights of the children. America 112:344 Mr 13 '65
Divorce across the border; validity of Mexican divorces. il Time 86:62 Jl 23 '65
Divorce Mexican style. il Newsweek 66:31-2 Jl 26 '65
Fathers without children. E. T. Eberhart. il Parents Mag 40:66-7+ Ap '65
How movies break up marriages. il Ebony 20:98-100+ S '65
Last of the divorce ranches; Donner Trail ranch, Nev. R. Wernick. il Sat Eve Post 238:30-2+ Jl 17 '65
Legal facts about divorce, separation and annulment. il Good H 160:180 Mr '65
Long, lonely wait of a young divorcée. B. Leavitt. il Look 30:78-81 Ja 11 '66
Rites of Reno. il Holiday 37:62-7 Je '65
When parents divorce. R. Kramer. il N Y Times Mag p77-8 F 14 '65

DIX, William S.
ARL suggests $5 million for cataloging be included in higher education bill; excerpts from testimony, March 10, 1965. Library J 90:2109-10 My 1 '65

DIXON, Dorothy
Lure of the wilderness. Am For 71:42-4+ Mr '65

DIXON, James P.
For air conservation. Bul Atomic Sci 21:7-12 Je '65
—and Lodge, J. P.
Air conservation report reflects national concern. Science 148:1060-6 My 21 '65

DIXON, Jeane
Crystal ball; condensation from Gift of prophecy. R. Montgomery. il Read Digest 87:235-42+ Jl '65
Gift of prophecy, by R. Montgomery. Review Life il pors 59:69+ O 8 '65. J. Howard
Jeane Dixon predicts the future. B. Davidson. por Ladies Home J 82:74+ N '65
Jeane Dixon: pyschic star of the year. D. Cohen. il Nation 201:470-3 D 13 '65
Seer in Washington. il por Time 86:59-60 Ag 13 '65
Successful autographing tours by three personalities. il por Pub W 188:53-6 D 13 '65
Time and telepathy. J. T. Winterich; H. Frankel. il por Sat R 48:44-5 S 11 '65

DO I hear a waltz? musical comedy. See Musical comedies, revues, etc.—Criticisms, plots, etc.

DO-it-yourself-work
Let Hans do it; shortage of workers in West Germany. il Newsweek 66:80+ O 4 '65
See also
Kit building

DO not pass go; drama. See Nolte, C.

DOANE, D. Howard
Will it earn the extra cost? Farm J 89:48I Je '65

DOAR, John Michael
Honest broker. il por Newsweek 65:27-8 Ap 5 '65

DOBBIN, John E.
Still testing, testing, testing. PTA Mag 60:4-6 bibliog(p37) Ja '66

DOBIE, J. Frank
They never left Texas. F. H. Wardlaw. Sat R 48:25-8 S 18 '65

DOBLIN, Jay
Missing link in transportation. Pop Mech 124:84-7+ N '65

DOBRITCH, Alexander Alexandroff
Animal act. il por Newsweek 65:95A-95B Mr 15 '65

DOBROF, Alfred, and Jablin, J. N.
Developing an amateur radio project; summary of article in Jewish community center program aids. Recreation 58:453-4 N '65

DOBYNS, Henry F. See Holmberg, A. R. jt. auth.

DOCCIA pottery. See Pottery, Italian

DOCK workers. See Longshoremen

DOCKS
Dandiest dock in Darien. S. F. Manning. il Yachting 118:146 S '65
How to build piers, floats, boathouses. G. Daniels. il Pop Sci 186:104-7 F '65
See also
Ports

DOCTOR Love strikes again; story. See Leasor, J.

DOCTOR Putney's darkest hour; story. See Heinemann, A.

DR Seuss, pseud. See Geisel, T. S.

DOCTORATES. See Degrees, Academic

DOCTORS. See Physicians

DOCTORS of philosophy. See Degrees, Academic

DOCTORS strike (Canada) See Strikes—Canada

DOCTRINE, Religious. See Theology

DOCUMENTARY films. See Moving pictures—Documentary films—Criticisms, plots, etc.

DOCUMENTARY television programs. See Television broadcasting—Documentary programs

DOCUMENTATION
See also
American documentation institute

DOCUMENTATION institute, American. See American documentation institute

DOCUMENTS
See also
United States—National archives

DODD, Allen R. Jr
Home for orphan shots. Pop Phot 56:124 Ap '65

DODD, Robert T. Jr, and others
Merrihueite, a new alkali-ferromagnesian silicate from the Mezö-Madaras chondrite. bibliog Science 149:972-4 Ag 27 '65

DODD, Thomas Joseph
Communists never give up; condensation of address, December 1, 1964. Read Digest 86:61-6 Mr '65
Excerpt from address. Cong Digest 44:305+ D '65
Excerpt from address, February 23, 1965. Cong Digest 44:116+ Ap '65
Excerpt from address, September 16, 1965. Cong Digest 44:270+ N '65
Key senator warns: appeasers are hurting U.S. excerpts from statement, June 10, 1965. por U S News 58:21 Je 21 '65
Let's limit the sale of guns. McCalls 93:166+ N '65
Mail-order guns. Ladies Home J 82:74-5+ Mr '65; Same abr. with title Guns by mail. Read Digest 86:183-6 Je '65
Vietnam and Latin America; address, August 25, 1965. Vital Speeches 31:706-9 S 15 '65
Was U.S. wrong in Dominican crisis? statements. por U S News 59:20 S 27 '65; Same. Nat R 17:859 O 5 '65; Sr Schol 87:15 O 7 '65

about
How two officials size up Vietnam. por U S News 58:26 My 17 '65
King acts for peace; condemnation of M. L. King's statement on Vietnamese war. Christian Cent 82:1180 S 29 '65

DODGE, David
Chinese side of the story. Sat R 48:60 O 23 '65
Holiday handbook. Holiday 38:89-94 Ag '65
Quick look at Nice's carnival. Holiday 39:60-1 Ja '66
Travel in Spain. Holiday 37:153-60 Ap '65

DODGE, F. W, corporation
F. W. Dodge construction outlook for 1966. il Arch Rec 138:121+ N '65

DODGE, Mary (Mapes)
Comedy in wax, or Lucy and their majesties; with correspondence between M. M. Dodge and B. L. Farjeon. E. Farjeon. il Horn Bk 41:360-3 Ag '65

DODGE, Natt N.
Brian Head. Nat Parks Mag 39:18-19 Mr '65

DODGERS (baseball) See Baseball clubs

DODGSON, Charles Lutwidge. See Carroll, L. pseud.

DODOTH (native race) See Uganda—Native races

DODSON, Dan W.
Urgent concern. Sat R 48:82-3 My 15 '65

DODSON, Helen W. and others
Solar activity during the first fourteen months of the International years of the quiet sun. bibliog Science 148:1328-31 Je 4 '65

DODSON, Stanley I. See Brooks, J. L. jt. auth.

DOERMANN, Humphrey
Financing higher education. Sat R 48:80-2+ N 20 '65

DOERSCHUK, Ernest Edwin, 1914-
Day at State library. J. N. Berry, 3d. il por Library J 90:4013-18 O 1 '65

DOESSCHATE, Jurriaan ten, and Alpern, Mathew
Response of the pupil to steady-state retinal illumination; contribution by cones. bibliog Science 149:989-91 Ag 27 '65

DOG breeds. See Dogs

DOG food
Diet discovery. J. Stetson. il Field & S 70:138-40 O '65
Dogs need special diets, too. Consumer Bul 48:37-8 O '65
Flavor-testing Fido. P. Czura. il Field & S 70:144-6+ Je '65

DOG houses. See Kennels

DOG racing
Brother coon never had it so good! World championship coonhound water races. K. Clark. il Field & S 69:49-51 Mr '65
Racing beneath the peaks; tracks surrounding Phoenix and Santa Anita. M. R. Werner. il Sports Illus 22:50-2+ Mr 8 '65

DOG schools. See Dogs—Training

DOG shows
Dogs, it's a man's life; 89th Westminster kennel club show. T. Flaherty. Life 58:16 Mr 12 '65
Going to the dogs; Westminster kennel club 89th annual show. il Newsweek 65:56+ Mr 1 '65
Immaculate doghouse. R. H. Boyle. il Sports Illus 22:64-8+ F 15 '65
Raggedy go at the Garden; Westminster dog show. L. Smith. il Sports Illus 22:22-5 Mr 1 '65

DOG sleds and sledding
On March 6, Californians can go to the dogs; sled-dog races. il Sunset 134:31+ F '65

DOG training. See Dogs—Training

DOG trials. See Field trials (dogs)

DOGNAPPING. See Animal thefts

DOGS
Buttercup meets the baby. J. R. Moskin. il Look 29:114-16+ Mr 23 '65
Dog response like man's. Sci N L 87:242 Ap 17 '65
Dogs. D. M. Duffey. See issues of Outdoor life
Every boy should have a dog. C. Ford. il Field & S 69:6+ F '65
Genetics and the social behavior of the dog, by J. P. Scott and J. L. Fuller. Review Sci Digest il 58:23-5 Jl '65. D. Cohen
Gun dogs; ed. by J. Stetson. See issues of Field & stream
Is that so? T. Trueblood. il Field & S 70:14+ Ag '65
Picking a puppy to love; common sense guide to choosing a pet. M. Gross. il Parents Mag 40:62-3+ Je '65
Regional dog-control program; Sussex County, N.J. B. C. Spragg. il Am City 80:104-5 N '65
Soft touch; experiences with stray dogs. E. R. Choate. il Atlan 216:81-3 D '65
What dogs tell us about man's future; SR preview of Genetics and the social behavior of the dog, J. P. Scott and J. L. Fuller. il Sat R 48:47-51 Mr 6 '65; Reply with rejoinder. L. Perrine. 48:64 My 1 '65
Who's who in American dogs. P. O'Keefe. McCalls 92:202 F '65
See also
Dalmatian dogs
Dog shows
Field trials (dogs)
Hunting dogs
Pointers (dogs)
Watchdogs

Care
Beat the heat. J. Stetson. il Field & S 70:138-9 S '65
Dog care. D. M. Duffey. il Outdoor Life 136:106-9 Ag '65
Dog-walking dolls. M. Mok. il Life 58:65-6 Je 11 '65

DOGS—*Continued*

Diseases and pests

Diet discovery. J. Stetson. il Field & S 70: 138-40 O '65

Threat of hip dysplasia. D. M. Duffey. il Outdoor Life 136:128-30+ S '65

See also

Fleas

Feeding

See also

Dog food

Stories

How old Bill finally wound up. H. Babcock. il Field & S 69:50-2+ Ap '65

Training

Basic training for spaniels. D. M. Duffey. il Outdoor Life 136:160-4 O '65

Coach: J. Buck's dog school. New Yorker 40: 24-6 F 6 '65

How to housebreak dogs and cats. il Good H 160:134 Ja '65

Making sense of scents. J. Stetson. il Field & S 70:104+ D '65

Mere truffle; truffle snufflers at Battista Monchiero school, Alba, Italy. il Newsweek 66:51-2 D 13 '65

New tools for training. R. A. Wolters. il Field & S 70:178-9+ My '65

Putting a dog on the spot. J. Stetson. il Field & S 70:120-2 N '65

Scent pointing without birds. G. B. Evans. il Field & S 69:180-2+ Ap '65

Second-season madness. D. M. Duffey. il Outdoor Life 137:128-30+ Ja '66

Snow training. J. Stetson. il Field & S 69: 156-7+ Mr '65

Training and terms. J. Stetson. il Field & S 70:132-3+ Jl '65

We grow a dogproof garden. G. Frerichs. il Pop Gard 16:8-9 Jl '65

See also

American kennel club

DOGS, War use of

Parapooches; Finnish army dogs. il Life 59: 105-6 N 19 '65

Sentry dogs: big help in Vietnam war. il U S News 59:14 N 8 '65

DOGS, Wild. See Wild dogs

DOGS in war. See Dogs, War use of

DOGS on television programs. See Animals on television programs

DOGWOOD

Dogwoods star in all seasons. J. H. Beale. il Flower Grower 52:27-9 Mr '65

DOHERTY, John Stephen

Rare route south. Yachting 118:45-7+ D '65

DOHERTY, Kathryn B.

Jordan waters conflict. bibliog f Int Concil 553:3-66 My '65

DOLE, Vincent Paul

Now, a drug that cures drug addicts. J. Reinert. por Sci Digest 58:38-41 N '65

DOLES. See Unemployment—Relief measures

DOLL, Richard

Licorice & ulcers. Time 85:77 F 26 '65

DOLL houses

Doll houses: points to check. Good H 161:168 D '65

Furnishing doll houses became a business. S. A. Parvin. il Hobbies 70:122 Ja '66

Miniaturia (cont) S. A. Parvin. il Hobbies 70: 120 Ag; 120 N; 120-1+ D '65

Our *puppenhaus.* H. A. Mitchell. il Hobbies 70:40-1 Je '65

This year our doll house is four stories tall; with building plans. il Sunset 135:78-9 N '65

Three Christmas dollhouses. il Pop Mech 124: 142-7 D '65

DOLLAR. See Money—United States

DOLLAR bills. See Paper money—United States

DOLLAR gap. See Balance of payments

DOLLS

Doll convention in nation's capitol. D. Coleman. il Hobbies 70:38+ D '65

Dollology. C. H. Fawcett. See issues of Hobbies

Family story told by dolls. R. E. Meyer. il Hobbies 70:40+ S '65

Famous wooden statues or effigies and dolls. C. H. Fawcett. il Hobbies 70:40-2+ Ja '66

Hello, dolly? dolls with human faces. il Newsweek 65:92 F 22 '65

Oriental dolls. C. H. Fawcett. il Hobbies 70: 37-40 Ap '65

Sown, seed for a doll museum; Ruth's doll museum, Kokomo, Ind. S. A. Parvin. il Hobbies 70:120-1+ N; 120-1+ D '65

Wax dolls. C. H. Fawcett. il Hobbies 70: 38-9+ Ag '65

Poetry

To an old doll in an antique shop. L. Myers. Hobbies 70:40 My '65

Repairing

Doll museum in Santa Monica; Hawkins' modern doll hospital and museum. il Sunset 135:58 S '65

DOLMATCH, Theodore B.

Color me brown, I'm integrated. por Sat R 48:73 S 11 '65

DOLMATHES. See Cookery, Greek

DOLOMITE (mineral)

Dolomitization of the mid-Pacific atolls. R. A. Berner. bibliog il Science 147:1297-9 Mr 12 '65

DOLPHIN fishing

Rainbows of the sea. G. Heinold. il Outdoor Life 137:16+ Ja '66

DOLPHINS (mammals)

Communication between dolphins in separate tanks by way of an electronic acoustic link. T. G. Lang and H. A. P. Smith. bibliog il Science 150:1839-44 D '31 '65

Dog at cross-porpoises. il Look 30:90+ Ja 25 '66

Dolphins can mimic human voice duration. Sci N L 87:73 Ja 30 '65

Domesticated dolphin. il Sci Digest 57:14-15 My '65

Intelligent life on this world; bottle-nosed dolphins. H. Downs. il Sci Digest 57:88-91 Mr '65

New light shed on dolphins. il Life 59:122-3+ O 22 '65

Porpoises do an aerial hula at Sea Life park; Oahu oceanarium. il Sunset 135:20-2+ O '65

Respiratory water exchange in two species of porpoise. H. N. Coulombe and others. bibliog il Science 149:86-8 Jl 2 '65

Trained porpoise released in the open sea. K. S. Norris. bibliog Science 147:1048-50 F 26 '65

What science knows about dolphin talk. A. Hamilton. il Sci Digest 57:9-13 My '65

DOMAN, Glenn, and Delacato, Carl

Train your baby to be a genius. McCalls 92: 65+ Mr '65

DOME stadium, Houston. See Stadiums

DOMENACH, Jean Marie

De Gaulle's bomb. Commonweal 81:668-9 F 19 '65

DOMES

Aluminum and plastic dome for a plant room. il Arch Rec 137:194 Mr '65

Designed by youth for modern living; geodesic domes with plastic covers. il UNESCO Courier 18:48-9 Jl '65

Profiles; R. B. Fuller, inventor of geodesic dome. C. Tomkins. New Yorker 41:35-6+ Ja 8 '66

Spiderweb for a plant; Carborundum co.'s new geodesic dome. il Bsns W p82 Ja 1 '66

DOMESTIC animals

See also

Domestication

Pets

Veterinary medicine

Vaccination

Inoculation schedule for pets. Good H 160:174 My '65

DOMESTIC appliances. See Electric apparatus and appliances, Domestic; Household appliances

DOMESTIC architecture. See Architecture, Domestic

DOMESTIC economic assistance. See Economic assistance, Domestic

DOMESTIC employees. See Household employees

DOMESTIC finance

Family money management; questions and answers. N. Kuehnl and G. Bush. See issues of Better homes and gardens

How much to raise a child? il Changing T 19:31-2 F '65

Net worth: a guide to family financial health. il Good H 160:140 Ja '65

Spending your money; questions and answers. S. Porter. Ladies Home J 82:52 O; 62 N; 42+ D '65; 83:24 Ja '66

See also

Budget, Household

Debt

DOMESTIC peace corps. See Volunteers in service to America

DOMESTIC relations

Legal facts about divorce, separation and annulment. il Good H 160:180 Mr '65

See also

Divorce

Family life

Marriage

Quarrels

DOMESTIC relations courts
Family courts at work; New York state's family court; ed. by M. R. Sherwin. J. Jiudice. il Parents Mag 40:64-6+ Ag '65
Time of many fevers; family court; address, June 10, 1965. R. W. Hansen. Vital Speeches 31:603-5 Jl 15 '65
DOMESTIC service. See Household employees

DOMESTICATION
Ecology of early food production in Mesopotamia. K. V. Flannery. bibliog il Science 147:1247-56 Mr 12 '65

DOMINGUIN, Miguel
Redbook dialogue: Deborah Kerr, Peter Viertel and Miguel Dominguin. por Redbook 125:50-1+ My '65

DOMINICA (island)
Island; photographs. J. Dominis. Life 59:46-59 Ag 6 '65

DOMINICAN REPUBLIC
Bloodiest day. Newsweek 65:44+ Je 28 '65
Coup that became a war. il Time 85:28-32 My 7 '65
OAS moves in, slowly; Dominican turmoil. il Bsns W p36 My 15 '65
Routine assignment. F. Schulke. il Mod Phot 29:18+ S '65
Stitch in time. A. A. Berle. il Reporter 32: 22-3 My 20 '65
Yankee go home? stay home? intervene? J. P. Davies, jr. il N Y Times Mag p28-9+ My 23 '65
See also
Agriculture—Dominican Republic
Communism—Dominican Republic
Economic assistance in the Dominican Republic
Forests and forestry—Dominican Republic
Natural resources—Dominican Republic
Newspapers—Dominican Republic
Santo Domingo
United Nations—Dominican Republic
United States—Armed forces—Forces in Dominican Republic
United States—Foreign relations—Dominican Republic

Economic conditions
Dominican eyewitness: in the capital, stalemate; outside, a dying country. H. Handleman. il U S News 59:34-8 Ag 2 '65
It could be a great little country, if... il U S News 58:39 My 24 '65
Troubled days. il Time 86:30 Ag 13 '65

Economic policy
And now: what next in Santo Domingo? H. Handleman. il U S News 58:41 Je 7 '65
U.S. aid while the bullets fly; the real Dominican story. A. Firfer. il U S News 59:48-50 Jl 19 '65

Foreign relations
Bitter salt of a stranger's bread; letter. E. Wessin y Wessin. Nat R 17:911 O 19 '65

United States
International law, morality and American interventions. W. V. O'Brien. Cath World 201:388-93 S '65

History
Dominican Republic. J. P. Augelli. bibliog il Focus 15:1-6 My '65

Politics and government
All the king's men; attempt to settle the civil war. il Time 85:27-8 My 28 '65
And now: what next in Santo Domingo? H. Handleman. il U S News 58:41 Je 7 '65
Angry Bosch back from exile. M. Acoca. il Life 59:46B O 8 '65
As new crisis came to a troubled isle. U S News 60:12 Ja 17 '66
Assessment of the situation in the Dominican Republic; statement, June 17, 1965. L. B. Johnson. Dept State Bul 53:19-21 Jl 5 '65
Back to Bosch? New Repub 153:9 S 18 '65
Between rebels and rightists. H. Lavine. Sat R 48:36 N 27 '65
Bingo night. Time 87:39 Ja 14 '66
Broken record. il Time 85:35 Je 18 '65
Calling a halt: a dialogue; imaginary conversation. A. Francois-Poncet. Reporter 32: 6 Je 3 '65
Caribbean blind alley. Nat R 17:495 Je 15 '65
Cease-fire that never was. il Time 85:44+ My 21 '65
Chaos and a search for peace. il Newsweek 65:32+ My 31 '65
Close view of Santo Domingo. S. Rodman. il Reporter 33:20-7 Jl 15 '65
Comedy & public violence; García-Godoy's government under pressure from all sides. il Time 86:40 D 3 '65
Communism and democracy in the Dominican Republic. J. Bosch. Sat R 48:13-15+ Ag 7 '65

Crisis on U.S. doorstep that won't go away. il U S News 60:21 Ja 3 '66
Disaster in Santiago. il Newsweek 67:31 Ja 3 '66
Dominican crisis; case study in American policy. T. Draper. Commentary 40:33-68 D '65
Dominican crisis ended; with text of Act of Dominican reconciliation. il Américas 17:41-2 S '65
Dominican crisis: help from the OAS. il Newsweek 65:44+ My 17 '65
Dominican eyewitness: in the capital, stalemate; outside, a dying country. H. Handleman. il U S News 59:34-8 Ag 2 '65
Dominican imbroglio. N. Gall. New Repub 153:12-13 Jl 3 '65
Dominican military. J. Thackray. New Repub 153:12 Ag 7 '65
Dominican puzzle: reds halted, but how to win the peace? il U S News 58:37-9 My 24 '65
Dominican Republic; address, May 2, 1965. L. B. Johnson. Vital Speeches 31:450-2 My 15 '65
Dominican revolution. J. Bosch. New Repub 153:19-21 Jl 24 '65
Dominican situation in the perspective of international law; address, June 9, 1965. L. C. Meeker. Dept State Bul 53:60-5 Jl 12 '65
Erratic attack. Time 86:44 S 24 '65
Exile of the general. Time 86:54 S 17 '65
Farewell to arms. Newsweek 66:50 S 20 '65
Fighting resumes. il Time 85:49 Je 25 '65
Formulas by airplane. il Time 85:32+ Je 4 '65
Government, at last. il Time 86:28 S 10 '65
Hate in the streets. il Newsweek 67:49 Ja 17 '66
Homecoming; return of J. Balaguer. Time 86:34+ Jl 9 '65
How did it happen? reasons for US intervention in revolt. B. van Voorst. il Newsweek 65:49-50+ My 17 '65
Human rights: investigations of execution of political prisoners. il Américas 17:40-1 Ag '65
In the nick of time; OAS prevents replay of civil war. il Time 86:61 N 5 '65
Inside the drama and chaos of the Dominican upheaval; with report by J. B. Martin. il Life 58:26-31+ My 28 '65; Same abr. with title Assignment Santo Domingo. Read Digest 87:94-102 Jl '65
Juan Bo's return. Newsweek 66:59 O 4 '65
June 14th: the young rebels; men behind the movement. M. Acoca. il Life 59:56A Ag 13 '65
Leadership crisis. J. Benitez. Sat R 48:20 Jl 17 '65
Letter from Washington. R. H. Rovere. New Yorker 41:204+ My 15 '65
Moving in was easy, but... U S News 58:75 Je 21 '65
My life as Trujillo's prisoner; ed. by L. Berg-quist. F de O. Trujillo. il Look 29:52-3+ Je 29 '65
My tormented life as Trujillo's daughter; ed. by L. Bergquist. F. de O. Trujillo il Look 29:44-6+ Je 15 '65
No consensus. Newsweek 66:33 S 6 '65
Nobody's yes man. il Time 85:31-2 Mr 26 '65
Non-trusteeship. Newsweek 66:47 Jl 5 '65
Odd reconciliation. Time 86:51 O 15 '65
Officers' mess. Newsweek 66:46 Ag 23 '65
On the tightrope. Newsweek 66:54 S 27 '65
One step forward. il Newsweek 66:51 S 13 '65
OAS achieves reconciliation in Dominican Republic; statements, September 1, 1965; with declaration to the Dominican people. L. B. Johnson. Dept State Bul 53:477-80 S 20 '65
OAS foreign ministers provide for establishment of inter-American force in Dominican Republic; statements, May 1-14, 1965, with texts of resolutions and Act of Santo Domingo. E. Bunker. Dept State Bul 52: 854-69 My 31 '65
OAS in action; OAS continues efforts in Dominican Republic. il Américas 17:42-4 Je '65
OAS in action; peace force authorized for Dominican Republic. il Américas 17:41-3 My '65
OAS Secretary General to represent meeting of consultation in Dominican Republic; Brazilian to command inter-American force; statements and notes, May 15-22, 1965, with resolutions adopted by the meeting. E. Bunker. Dept State Bul 52:908-13 Je 7 '65
OAS to help restore democratic order in Dominican Republic; statement, June 2, 1965, with text of resolution. D. Rusk. Dept State Bul 52:1017-18 Je 21 '65

DOMINICAN REPUBLIC—Politics and government—*Continued*
O.A.S. turns a corner; peace-keeping in Santo Domingo. Life 58:4 Je 11 '65
Peace that failed. il Newsweek 65:26-7 My 24 '65
Power and the ticking of the clock; attempted Communist take-over; with report by J. Barnes. il Newsweek 65:35-8 My 10 '65
Report from Santo Domingo. J. F. Fixx. il Sat R 48:30-2+ Je 12 '65
Report from Santo Domingo; Ad hoc committee. Américas 17:43 N '65
Revolution is over, but—. H. Handleman. U S News 59:53 S 20 '65
Round for the pessimists; resurgence of violence. il Time 86:24 D 31 '65
Routine kill. D. Weber. il Newsweek 66:64 O 11 '65
Santo Domingo. Commonweal 82:459-60 Jl 2 '65
Santo Domingo: can we withdraw? S. Shapiro. Nation 200:556-9 My 24 '65
Santo Domingo revisited. Commonweal 83:455-6 Ja 21 '66
Santo Domingo's activist adventurers. M. Clos. il Reporter 32:29-31 Je 17 '65
Secretary discusses Dominican situation on NBC-TV; interview, ed. by J. Chancellor. D. Rusk. Dept State Bul 52:947-9 Je 14 '65
Secretary Rusk's news conference of May 26, 1965; with questions and answers. D. Rusk. Dept State Bul 52:938-47 Je 14 '65
Situation in Santo Domingo; Ad hoc committee. Américas 17:41-2 D '65
Solution nears in Dominican Republic; Ad hoc committee proposal, text. il Américas 17:39-40 Jl '65
Squabbling continues. Newsweek 66:39 Ag 2 '65
Stalemate of hate; role of OAS team in the Dominican Republic. il Time 86:30-1 Jl 2 '65
Sticky stalemate in Santo Domingo; with report by W. Just. il Newsweek 65:27-8 Je 7 '65
Still elusive Dominican peace. M. Acoca. Life 59:32B Jl 23 '65
Terror in the night. Newsweek 65:55 Je 21 '65
Third man; choice for next president. Newsweek 65:66 Je 14 '65
Tragedy of Juan Bosch. F. Dorta-Duque. il America 112:824-5+ Je 5 '65
Trouble for Bosch. Time 86:46+ D 10 '65
Turmoil in the Dominican Republic. H. Wells. il Cur Hist 50:14-21 Ja '66
Two governments, face to face. il Time 85:31-3 My 14 '65
Uncertain solution. Time 86:34-5 Ag 20 '65
Unfinished experiment, by J. Bosch. Review Atlan 217:119-20 Ja '66. E. Weeks
U.N. Security council considers situation in Dominican Republic; statements, May 19-21, 1965. A. E. Stevenson. Dept State Bul 52:913-19 Je 7 '65
U.S. acts to meet threat in Dominican Republic; statements and letter, April 28-May 2, 1965; with texts of three resolutions. L. B. Johnson; A. E. Stevenson; E. Bunker. bibliog f Dept State Bul 52:738-48 My 17 '65
U.S. steps into another hornet's nest; sending troops to Santo Domingo. il Bsns W 28-9 My 8 '65
U.S. submits to U.N. security council OAS documents on Dominican Republic; statement, June 18, 1965; with texts of documents. A. E. Stevenson. Dept State Bul 53:132-5 Jl 19 '65
Waiting for Godoy. Time 86:39 Jl 16 '65
When the marines stormed ashore in Santo Domingo; excerpt from thirty days in May. T. Szulc. il Sat Eve Post 238:36-8+ Jl 31 '65
Whiff of buckshot. il Newsweek 67:49 Ja 24 '66
Who will rule now in Dominican Republic? il U S News 58:38 My 17 '65

Anecdotes, facetiae, satire, etc.
Medicare for the Dominican Republic. S. Huck. Nat R 18:66+ Ja 25 '66

Relief work
President comments on situation in Dominican Republic; statements, June 1, 1965. L. B. Johnson. Dept State Bul 52:992-3 Je 21 '65
Relief operation. OAS. Américas 17:41 O '65

Social conditions
Search for a durable peace in the Dominican Republic; address, May 28, 1965. L. B. Johnson. Dept State Bul 52:989-92 Je 21 '65

DOMINICAN REPUBLIC and the United States
Dominican revolution. J. Bosch. New Repub 153:19-21 Jl 24 '65
DOMINICK, Willard F.
Metal lathe cutting as art form. Sch Arts 64:36-7 My '65
DOMINIONS, British. See Commonwealth of nations
DOMINIS, John
Island; photographs. Life 59:46-59 Ag 6 '65
DOMINO, Edward F. and Yamamoto, Ken-ichi
Nicotine; effect on the sleep cycle of the cat. bibliog Science 150:637-8 O 29 '65
DOMINOES (game)
More fun than the watusi. R. Cantwell. il Sports Illus 22:50-2+ Mr 29 '65
DOMMEN, Arthur J.
How secure is Thailand? New Repub 152:8-9 My 1 '65
Neutralization experiment in Laos. Cur Hist 48:89-94+ F '65
DON Carlo; opera. See Verdi, G.
DON Giovanni; opera. See Mozart, J. C. W. A.
DON Juan in Dublin; story. See O'Faolain, S.
DON Quichotte; opera. See Massenet, J.
DON Quixote (literary character) See Characters in literature
DON Quixote; ballet. See Ballets—Criticisms
DONAHUE, Ralph J.
Life cycle of seclusion. Natur Hist 74:50-1 My '65
DONALDSON, Lauren R.
College-bred fish for man's delight. M. Morgan. il por Harper 231:47-51 Jl '65; Same abr. Read Digest 87:193-5 O '65
DONALDSON, Virginia H. and Ratnoff, O. D.
Hageman factor; alterations in physical properties during activation. bibliog Science 150:754-6 N 5 '65
DONAT, Alexander
Ashes and irony. W. Coffey. Commentary 39:82+ Ap '65
DONATIEN, Frank
Snow cruising. Travel 125:40-1 Ja '66
DONELSON, Loren E.
Obituary
Farm J por 89:5 Ap '65
DONEN, Stanley
Senior scholastic interview; ed. by M. Ronan. por Sr Schol 87:20 D 2 '65
DONGEN, Kees van
Wild beast of high life. K. Levin. il por Art N 64:28-9+ D '65
DONINI, Piero
Two medical pioneers that all would-be mothers now desperately want to see. il por Life 59:28-9 Ag 13 '65
DONIZETTI, Gaetano
Believable and ingratiating Don Pasquale. H. Glass. il Am Rec G 31:968-9 Je '65
Elixir of love (L'elisir d'amore) Criticism
New Yorker 41:154 N 20 '65
Sat R 48:40 N 27 '65
New York. R. D. Daniels. il Opera N 30:33 Ja 15 '66
On records; Don Pasquale. Opera N 30:34 D 11 '65
DONLEY, Marshall O. and Murray, D. J.
More we grow, the more we do. NEA J 54:26-7 My '65
DONLON, Roger H. C.
Battle for Nam Dong; excerpt from Outpost of freedom; ed. by W. Rogers. pors Sat Eve Post 238:38-42+ O 23 '65
DONNAN equilibrium
Osmotic flow in a rigid porous membrane. A. Mauro. bibliog il Science 149:867-9 Ag 20 '65
DONNELLAN, J. E. Jr, and Setlow, R. B.
Thymine photoproducts but not thymine dimers found in ultraviolet-irradiated bacterial spores. bibliog Science 149:308-10 Jl 16 '65
DONNELLY, Dorothy
Roses of ashes; poem. Commonweal 82:146 Ap 23 '65
DONNELLY, Russell J.
Nonequilibrium thermodynamics, variational techniques, and stability. Science 149:1119-20 S 3 '65
DONNER, Frank J.
Aftermath to Harlem riot; Epton anarchy trial. Nation 201:355-8+ N 15 '65
DONNER, Frederic G.
Competing for tomorrow's world markets; address, November 18, 1964. Vital Speeches 31:279-82 F 15 '65
DONNER Trail ranch, Nev. See Ranches
DONOHUE, Jack
High Alcindor; basketball's Mt Everest. W. J. McKean. il por Look 29:86-90 F 9 '65
DONOVAN, Bernard Eugene
New York's take-charge man. por Time 85:57 Ap 16 '65

DONOVAN, James B.
Educational politics. Reporter 32:12+ Mr 25 '65

DONOVAN, Robert J.
Over-nominated under-elected, still a promising candidate. N Y Times Mag p 14-15+ Ap 25 '65

DONOVAN, Winkie
How a precocious 18-year-old plays with paints. il pors Mlle 62:166-9 N '65

DONS. See College professors and instructors

DON'T bother to call; story. See Flannery, J.

DON'T give my body to science, the dying mother said; story. See Loeser, K.

DON'T send for Hector; drama. See Slattery, M. E.

DON'T stop the carnival; story. See Wouk, H.

DONZI marine. See Boatbuilding

DOOLEY, Roger B.
Poor little self-pitying rich boy. Sat R 49:31 Ja 1 '66

DOOLEY, Thomas Anthony
New Tom Dooleys. il por Sci Digest 57:60-3 My '65

DOOLEY, William
Met's new star is named Dooley. il pors Life 58:43-4+ Ap 16 '65

DOOLITTLE, Jerome H.
After finishing his morning coffee, this man hopped a freight. il por Esquire 63:80-3+ My '65

DOOR stops
Many ways to stop a door. il Sunset 134:129-31 Je '65

DOORBELLS, Electric
Tiny electric eye to guard your home. S. Hoberman. il Pop Sci 187:100-2 S '65

DOORS
Case for the pre-hung door. il Sunset 135:139-40 O '65
Controlling the effects of sun's heat on steel doors. J. I. Yellott. il Arch Rec 138:177-8 D '65
Curbing a clear and present danger; injuries to people who barge through glass doors and panels. il Bsns W p84+ Jl 10 '65
First thing they did was remodel their front door. il Sunset 134:149-50 Mr '65
Glass doors, use of safety glass reduces accidents. il Consumer Rep 30:121-3 Mr '65
New doors and how to buy them. il House & Gard 128:214-15 S '65
Old door into new door. D. Swartwout. il Pop Mech 124:136-7 Ag '65
See also
Doorways

DOORSTOPS. See Door stops

DOORWAYS
English decorative arts at the Art institute of Chicago; architectural treatments of the eighteenth century. A. Wardwell. il Antiques 89:79-82 Ja '66
New entry is less abrupt, better looking. il Sunset 136:68 Ja '66

DOPE smuggling. See Smuggling

DORATI, Antal
Non-traveling opera por Opera N 29:6-7 Ap 17 '65

DORCHESTER equine preparatory school, Ocala, Fla. See Horse training

DORFMAN, Earl
Break's over, Mac. Mac! Mac! il por Life 60:39-40+ Ja 21 '66

DORIES. See Boats and boating

DORIOT, Georges F.
Idealist, with a realistic touch. il pors Bsns W p 166-8+ Mr 20 '65

DORLÉAC, Françoise
Sister stars of France. T. G. Harris. il pors Look 29:90-3 Je 1 '65
Young actress tries them all on. il pors Life 58:54-6+ Mr 5 '65

DORMAN, Sonya
Some of the time, all of the time; story. Sat Eve Post 238:50-2 F 27 '65
Zero on the compass; story. Sat Eve Post 238:58-66 My 8 '65

DORMITORIES
Another kind of castle; dormitory at Bryn Mawr college. J. M. Dixon. il Arch Forum 123:58-65 N '65
Bear Bryant Hilton; athletic dormitory at University of Alabama. il Sports Illus 23:42-5 O 11 '65
Building types study; college dormitories. il Arch Rec 138:113-36 Ag '65
Dormitories and dining commons at Clark university. il Arch Rec 137:158-68 My '65
For a dormitory: reflection of a system; Lake Forest academy, Ill. il Arch Rec 138:172-3 S '65
Furniture selection and specification; designs for college dormitories. P. Brust and W. F. Bernbrock. il Arch Rec 138:93+ S '65

Investors move into the dorms. il Bsns W p47-8+ N 6 '65
University housing in residential scale; University of Michigan. il Arch Rec 137:208-9 Ap '65
See also
College students—Housing

DORN, Alva L.
Doscher exposure system. U S Camera 28:44-7+ Mr '65

DORN, Edward
Gestures of deliberation. T. Clark. Poetry 107:124 N '65

DORN, G.
Phosphatase mutants in aspergillus nidulans. bibliog Science 150:1183-4 N 26 '65

DOROTHY Canfield Fisher library awards
Annual book-of-the-month library awards announced. Pub W 187:96 F 8 '64

DOROZYNSKI, Alexander
Two miracles, Russian style. G. Feifer. Harper 230:106+ Je '65

DORRILL, William F.
Leadership and succession in Communist China. bibliog f Cur Hist 49:129-35+ S '65

DORROS, Sidney
Case for independent professional teachers' associations. Mo Labor R 87:543; 88:536 My '64, My '65

DORSEY, Joseph L.
Morals in Massachusetts. Commonweal 82:188-90 Ap 30 '65

DORT, Wakefield, jr, and others
Paleotemperatures and chronology at archeological cave site revealed by thermoluminescence. bibliog Science 150:480-1 O 22 '65

DORTA-DUQUE, Francisco
Agriculture in the Dominican Republic. America 112:348 Mr 13 '65
Tragedy of Juan Bosch. America 112:824-5+ Je 5 '65

DORYLINE ants. See Ants

DOSCHER, John W.
Doscher exposure system. A. L. Dorn. il U S Camera 28:44-7+ Mr '65

DOSHI, Balkrishna Vithaldas
Doshi. P. Blake. il por Arch Forum 123:52-9 D '65

DOSIMETERS. See Radiometers

DOTSON, Janie
Eye and I. Seventeen 24:140-1+ N '65
In my opinion. por Seventeen 25:48 Ja '66

DOTTS, Charles S.
Cape Cod. U S Camera 28:78-9+ Jl '65

DOTY, Paul
Freeze on strategic delivery systems. Bul Atomic Sci 21:2-6 F '65
—See Thach, R. E. jt. auth.

DOTY, Roy
Wordless workshop. See issues of Popular science monthly

DOUBLE fusee skeleton clocks. See Clocks

DOUBLE snapper; story. See Faust, I.

DOUBLE standard in sexual ethics. See Sexual ethics

DOUBLE time. See Overtime

DOUBLE wedding; story. See Cave, H.

DOUBLEDAY and company
Doubleday acquires J. G. Ferguson companies. Pub W 187:138 F 22 '65

DOUGH
Some new ways to use sourdough; with recipes. il Sunset 135:201-3 N '65

DOUGHERTY, John
(ed) See Rossellat, R. Feeling in your bones

DOUGHTY, Frances W.
Selection criteria: science books for children. Horn Bk 41:195-200 Ap '65

DOUGHTY, Thomas
Trove of Doughtys. T. N. Maytham. il Antiques 88:681-5 N '65

DOUGLAS, Archibald G. and Mair, B. J.
Sulfur: role in genesis of petroleum. bibliog Science 147:499-501 Ja 29 '65

DOUGLAS, Lewis W.
Qualities of leadership: Churchill as diplomat. Atlan 215:86-9 Mr '65

DOUGLAS, Paul Howard
Excerpt from testimony, March 1, 1965. Cong Digest 44:150+ My '65
Senator's indictment of de Gaulle; excerpts from address, June 3, 1965. U S News 58:8 Je 14 '65
What shall we do about de Gaulle? New Repub 152:7-10 Je 12 '65
When big business gets too big. Sat R 48:29-30 F 27 '65
about
When one person, one vote came up. por U S News 59:20 Ag 16 '65

DOUGLAS, Todd
Your serviceman looks at the '66 cars. Pop Mech 125:106-9+ Ja '66

DOUGLAS, William Orville
Animal man needs to hike. pors N Y Times Mag p34-5 Mr 21 '65
Excerpts from the opinion of the Court, June 7, 1965. Cong Digest 44:222-3 Ag '65
Land despoiled. Holiday 38:171-4 O '65
Law and survival; address, March 24, 1965. Vital Speeches 31:400-3 Ap 15 '65
North River, town of Norwell, Plymouth County, Mass. Bul Atomic Sci 21:11 My '65

about

Dangerous climb: storm traps Justice Douglas. il por U S News 58:16 Mr 1 '65
Emanations from a penumbra. il por Time 85:47-8 Je 18 '65
For Justice Douglas, a third divorce suit. il por U S News 59:11 D 27 '65
Walkin' and hollerin'. C. Ritter. il pors Am For 71:6-7+ Je '65

DOUGLAS-HOME, Sir Alexander Frederick
Exit Home, enter Heath. A. Lejeune. Nat R 17:723-4 Ag 24 '65
Exit Sir Alec. S. Hagerty. il por Newsweek 66:34-5 Ag 2 '65
Labor delight. por Newsweek 65:39 Ap 5 '65
Last of the amateurs. por Time 86:19-20 Jl 30 '65
Sir Alec loses, and wins. P. Worsthorne. il pors N Y Times Mag p33+ Mr 21 '65
Still at Home. Newsweek 65:48+ F 15 '65
Tory change at the top. P. Crane. America 113:159 Ag 14 '65

DOUGLAS aircraft company
Douglas gets a jump with MOL: manned space laboratory. il Bsns W p50-2 D 25 '65
Douglas upgrades the apprentice: on-the-job training program for skilled workers. Bsns W p80 Ja 8 '66
Simplification, stability featured in DC-9. C. M. Plattner. il Aviation W 83:37+ N 1 '65

DOUGLAS fir

Diseases and pests

Dendroctonus pseudotsugae: a hypothesis regarding its primary attractant. H. J. Heikkenen and B. F. Hrutfiord. bibliog il Science 150:1457-9 D 10 '65

DOUGLAS fir beetles. See Beetles
DOUGLASS, James W.
Council and the bomb. Commonweal 81:725-8 Mr 5 '65
DOVE shooting. See Mourning dove shooting
DOVER, N.H.
Two Dovers relight. il Am City 80:135 Mr '65
DOVER, Ohio
Two Dovers relight. il Am City 80:135 Mr '65
DOVISCH among the savages; story. See Wilner, H.
DOW chemical company
Small town, big company. L. L. L. Golden. Sat R 48:57 Jl 10 '65
DOW-Jones averages. See Stocks—Price indexes and averages
DOWDY, Lewis Carnegie
Vital role of a modern college; address, April 3, 1965. Vital Speeches 31:475-7 My 15 '65
DOWNES, Bruce
[Monthly column] See issues of Popular photography
DOWNES, Edward
Bigger than life. Opera N 30:24-5 Ja 22 '66
Kindling word. Opera N 29:24-5 Mr 20 '65
Wings of the storm. Opera N 29:24-6 F 13 '65
DOWNES, Mollie Panter-. See Panter-Downes, M.
DOWNEY, Hugh F.
Yankee please stay. H. Bowser. Sat R 48:18 Ag 21 '65
DOWNING, Alfred
Mosquitoes, mules, and men: Pacific Northwest; with sketches. B. Le Roy. Am Heritage 16:102-7 Ap '65
DOWNING, Antoinette F.
John Brown House. Antiques 87:556-63 My '65
DOWNS, Hugh
All the fun is getting there. por Sci Digest 58:92-4 Jl '65
Hugh Downs column. See issues of Science digest
Let's invest in buggy whips. por Sci Digest 59:80-3 Ja '66

about

Hugh Downs: Today's star is South Seas bound. G. Sloane. il por Motor B 116:76-8 Jl '65
DOWNTOWN areas. See Business districts
DOWRY
Bride price; Kenya dowry reformation movement. Time 86:25 Jl 30 '65

DOWST, Loring
Country dining around Philadelphia. Holiday 37:80-1+ Je '65
DOWTY, Leonhard
Cook's tour; poem. Good H 161:24-5 Jl '65
Fanfare for fathers; poem. Good H 160:186 Je '65
When the heart remembers; story. Good H 161:84-5 D '65
DOXIADIS, Constantinos Apostolos
What I have learned; learning how to learn. por Sat R 49:16-18+ Ja 1 '66
DOYLE, Sir Arthur Conan
Case of the durable detective. J. Stewart-Gordon. il Read Digest 86:207-10 F '65
Singular set of people, Watson. W. S. Baring-Gould. il Esquire 65:92-5+ Ja '66
DRACULA (literary character) See Characters in literature
DRAFT law. See Military service, Compulsory
DRAFTEES. See Soldiers
DRAFTING instruments. See Drawing instruments
DRAFTING room practice. See Drawing room practice
DRAG racing. See Automobile racing
DRAGADZE, Peter
Happiness is a bad liver. Life 59:95+ N 26 '65
DRAGONFLIES
What dragonflies see, and how. Sci Digest 58:36 S '65
DRAIN, James Andrew
Joy digs from under its burden of coal. il pors Bsns W p 100-2+ Ja 8 '66
DRAINAGE
Drainage: first step to high profits. H. Galloway and D. Sisson. il Suc Farm 63:42-3+ S '65
DRAINAGE, House
Is your run-off system doing its job? il Pop Mech 124:158-64+ N '65
DRAKE, Francis Vivian
Why we are fighting in Asia. Read Digest 87: 61-5 O '65
—and Drake, Katharine
Paupers in uniform. Read Digest 86:49-53 Mr '65
DRAKE, Katharine. See Drake, F. V. jt. auth.
DRAKE, William P.
Where Pennsalt got its new pep. il pors Bsns W p 170-2+ Je 19 '65
DRAKE university, Des Moines, Ia.
Mies provides for journalism at Drake. il Arch Rec 138:144-6 O '65
DRAMA
See also
College and school drama
Dramatic criticism
Television broadcasting—Drama
Theater

Study and teaching

Bruner on drama: excerpts from address, July 1965. Sr Schol 87:sup 12 D 2 '65
See also
Dramatization in education

Technique

Author! author! writing and production of On trial. E. Rice. il Am Heritage 16:46-9+ Ap '65

Themes

Father's day on Broadway. T. Frideaux. il Life 59:72A-72B N 5 '65
DRAMA, Medieval
Heigh, Sir Ass, oh heigh; Play of Daniel and the Play of Herod. F. Bowers. il House & Gard 128:183-4+ D '65
DRAMA, Religious. See Religious drama
DRAMA critics. See Critics
DRAMA festivals
Actors studio in London, or, the Broadway boiler-house abroad. P. Gilliatt. Harper 231:32+ S '65
Big little theater; Chichester festival theatre. il Newsweek 66:78 Ag 30 '65
Guthrie's getaway season; new productions of Minnesota theatre company at Tyrone Guthrie theatre. H. Hewes. Sat R 48:34 Ag 7 '65
Happening: second Festival of free expression, at Montparnasse. il Time 85:26 Je 4 '65
Letter from London; Chichester festival (cont) M. Panter-Downes. New Yorker 41: 102-4 Ag 14 '65
Repertory's rising requirements. H. Hewes. Sat R 48:22 Jl 3 '65
DRAMA in education. See Dramatization in education

DRAMAS

Gnädiges fräulein. T. Williams. il Esquire
64:102+ Ag '65
Mutilated. T. Williams. il Esquire 64:96-101
Ag '65
Orange soufflé. S. Bellow. il Esquire 64:130-1+
O '65
There's some milk in the icebox. B. J. Hen-
derson. il Mlle 62:176-7+ N '65
See also
Childrens plays
College and school drama—Texts
Detective and mystery plays
Fairy plays
Valentines day—Drama
also subhead Theater under names of
cities, e.g. London—Theater

Criticisms, plots, etc.

Bald primaqueera. S. O'Casey. Atlan 216:
69-74 S '65
Best of the 1964-65 theater season. H. Hewes.
il Sat R 48:49-51 Je 12 '65
Broadway postscript. H. Hewes. See issues
of Saturday review
Goings on about town. See issues of New
Yorker
Off Broadway. E. Oliver. See issues of New
Yorker
Stage. W. Sheed. See issues of Commonweal
Theatre. H. Clurman. See issues of Nation
Theatre. J. McCarten. See issues of New
Yorker
Theater. R. Brustein. See issues of New re-
public
Theatre. T. Lewis. See issues of America
Theater (cont) Nat R 17:561-2, 660; 18:37-9
Je 29, Jl 27 '65, Ja 11 '66
Time listings. See issues of Time

Single works

See name of author for full entry
All in good time. B. Naughton
Amen corner. J. Baldwin
L'Amérique. J. L. Barrault
And things that go bump in the night. T.
McNally
Armstrong's last goodnight. J. Arden
Arturo Ui. B. Brecht
Baal. B. Brecht
Balls. P. Foster
Billy Liar. K. Waterhouse and W. Hall
Blacks. J. Genet
Blues for Mister Charlie. J. Baldwin
Boeing-Boeing. B. Cross
Bugs. J. White
Cactus flower. A. Burrows
Catch me if you can. J. Weinstock
Cherry orchard. A. P. Chekhov
Colombe. J. Anouilh
Conerico was here to stay. F. Gagliano
Country wife. W. Wycherley
Creeper. P. Macaulay
Danton's death. G. Büchner
Day of absence. D. T. Ward
Day the whores came out to play tennis.
A. Kopit
Days between. R. Anderson
Dead souls. M. Bulgakov
Devils. J. Whiting
Do not pass go. C. Nolte
Enemies. A. Leokum
Entertainer. J. Osborne
Entertaining Mr Sloane. J. Orton
Exception and the rule. B. Brecht
Exhaustion of our son's love. J. Max
Friends. A. Leokum
Generals' tea party. See Le goûter des
généraux, below
Generation. W. Goodhart
Glass menagerie. T. Williams
Le goûter des généraux. B. Vian
Happy days. S. Beckett
Happy ending. D. T. Ward
Herakles. A. MacLeish
Hogan's goat. W. Alfred
Home free! L. Wilson
Homecoming. H. Pinter
Impossible years. B. Fisher and A. Marx
In the case of J. Robert Oppenheimer. H.
Kipphardt
Inadmissible evidence. J. Osborne
Les joies de la famille. See Very rich woman,
below
Judith. J. Giraudoux
Kremlin chimes. N. Pogodin
Leonce and Lena. G. Buechner
Life of Joseph. M. Rej
Live like pigs. J. Arden
Lovey. J. Morgenstern
Luv. M. Schisgal
Malcolm. E. Albee
Marat/Sade. P. Weiss
Matty and the moron and madonna. H.
Lieberman
Mrs Dally. W. Hanley

Mother Courage and her children. B. Brecht
Odd couple. N. Simon
On trial. E. Rice
Owl and the pussycat. B. Manhoff
Patrick—the first. B. Larnen
Patriot for me. J. Osborne
Persecution and assassination of Marat as
performed by the inmates of the asylum of
Charenton under the direction of the Mar-
quis de Sade. See Marat/Sade. above
Piege pour un homme seul. See Catch me
if you can, above
Pigeons. L. Osgood
Playroom. M. Drayton
Poor Richard. J. Kerr
Prodigal son. L. Hughes
Queen and the rebels. U. Betti
Race of hairy men! E. Hunter
Rhinoceros. E. Ionesco
Ride a cock horse. D. Mercer
Right honourable gentleman. M. Dyne
Room. H. Pinter
Royal hunt of the sun. P. Shaffer
Saved. E. Bond
Say nothing. J. Hanley
Les séquestrés d'Altona. J. P. Sartre
Sign in Sidney Brustein's window. L. Hans-
berry
Sing to me through open windows. A. Kopit
Slave. L. Jones
Slight ache. H. Pinter
Slow dance on the killing ground. W. Hanley
Sound of silence. H. Willis
Square in the eye. J. Gelber
Squire Puntila and his servant Matti. B.
Brecht
Subject was marigolds. P. Zindel
Sweet enemy. J. C. Oates
Tango. S. Mrozek
Tartuffe. J. B. P. Molière
Three sisters. A. P. Chekhov
Tiny Alice. E. Albee
Toilet. L. Jones
Trigon. J. B. Lynne
Trojan women. Euripides
Troubled waters. U. Betti
Veronica. J. White
Very rich woman. R. Gordon
View from the bridge. A. Miller
War and peace. A. Neumann and others
Way of the world. W. Congreve
White devil. J. Webster
Wives. L. Abel
Women. C. B. Luce
World of Ray Bradbury. R. Bradbury
Xmas in Las Vegas. J. Richardson
You can't take it with you. M. Hart and
G. S. Kaufman
Zoo story. E. Albee
Zulu and the zayda. H. Da Silva and F. Leon

DRAMATIC art. See Acting

DRAMATIC criticism
Bad moment on Broadway; cast reading re-
views of J. Kerr's Poor Richard. C. Bros-
sard. il Look 29:67-70 Mr 9 '65
Divided men on the aisle; review system
under reform? Newsweek 67:84 Ja 17 '66
See also
Critics

DRAMATIC critics. See Critics

DRAMATIC production. See Theatrical production

DRAMATIC production (in education) See
Dramatization in education

DRAMATIC readings
Broadway postscript; Evening's Frost. H.
Hewes. Sat R 48:74 O 30 '65
Frost as drama; An evening's Frost. W.
Sheed. Commonweal 83:147-8 N 5 '65
Off Broadway; Evening's Frost. E. Oliver.
New Yorker 41:96+ O 23 '65

DRAMATICS for children. See Childrens plays

DRAMATICS in schools. See Dramatization in
education

DRAMATISTS
Theatre of revolt, by R. Brustein. Review
Commentary 39:77-80 F '65. J. Gross

DRAMATISTS, American
See also
Jones, L.
O'Neill, E. G.
Simon, N.

DRAMATISTS, French
See also
Genet, J.

DRAMATIZATION by children. See Childrens
plays

DRAMATIZATION in education
Building tomorrow's audience. J. S. Morrison.
il Am Ed 1:24-7 O '65

DRANE, James F.
Kashmir: a religious war. por Cath World
202:212-16 Ja '66

DRAPER, Theodore
Dominican crisis. Commentary 40:33-68 D '65

DRAPER, Thomas J.
Alliance for progress: failures and opportunities. Yale R 55:182-90 D '65
DRAPERIES. See Curtains and draperies
DRAT! the cat! musical comedy. See Musical comedies. revues. etc.—Criticisms, plots. etc.
DRAVNIEKS, Andrew
You and your olfactronics. il por Life 59:103-4 D 10 '65
DRAWERS
ABCs of building chests and cabinets: fine art of drawer making. R. J. De Cristoforo. il Pop Sci 186:160-4 F '65
DRAWING
Drawing with pen and pencil for senior high school students. F. Snider. il Sch Arts 64:18 My '65
Line drawings of Thoreau MacDonald. N. Kent. il Am Artist 29:36-41+ D '65
See also
Perspective
Silhouettes
Study and teaching
I asked them to draw. J. Kick. il Sch Arts 65:21-4 D '65
DRAWING, Childrens. See Childrens art
DRAWING instruments
Draftsman with speed to spare; mechanical plotter directed by computer. il Bsns W p64+ My 29 '65
Electronic draftsman; automatic drafting machine. W. R. Wise. il Electr World 74:70-1 Jl '65
DRAWING room practice
Draftsmen with speed to spare; mechanical plotter directed by computer. il Bsns W p64+ My 29 '65
DRAWINGS
Sketches of the banned. il Time 86:50 Ag 20 '65
Straight from the hand and mouth of Steinberg; excerpts from New world; with interview. ed. by J. Vanden Heuvel. il Life 59:59-60+ D 10 '65
See also
Graffiti
Exhibitions
Artist's record; sketches of great men. N Y Times Mag p 146-7 Ap 4 '65
DRAYTON, Mary
Playroom. Criticism
New Yorker 41:152+ D 18 '65
Newsweek 66:92 D 20 '65
Sat R 48:41 D 25 '65
Time 86:42 D 17 '65
DREADNOUGHTS. See Warships
DREAM; ballet. See Ballets—Criticisms
DREAMS
Dreamers are examining the day's novel events. Sci N L 87:342 My 29 '65
ESP and the dreamer. il Newsweek 65:68 My 24 '65
Please don't call me Fireball. T. Meehan. il Sat Eve Post 238:18 Jl 31 '65
Reality of dreams. E. Lederer. il Sci N L 87:282-3 My 1 '65
Reporter at large; Rapid eye movement sleep. C. Trillin. il New Yorker 41:58-60+ S 18 '65
Scientists use new techniques to study the complex activity called sleep. M. Markham. Parents Mag 40:60-1+ Ag '65
Tell it like it is. baby. R. Ellison. Nation 201:129-36 S 20 '65
DREAMS of Rosemary; story. See Holland. B.
DRED Scott case
Without fear or favor. by W. Lewis. Review Time 86:122+ D 10 '65
DREDGING
See also
Lakes—Cleaning
Die **DREIGROSCHENOPER;** opera. See Weill, K.
DREISER, Theodore
Dreiser among the slicks; excerpt from Dreiser. W. A. Swanberg. il por Horizon 7:54-61 Spr '65
Dreiser. by W. A. Swanberg. Review
Commonweal 82:640-1 S 3 '65. J. T. Farrell
Life 58:10+ My 14 '65. S. Kauffmann
Nation 201:102-5 Ag 30 '65. L. Marx
Reporter 32:37-9 Je 3 '65. D. Aaron
Time il por 85:108+ My 7 '65
Liar in search of the truth. G. Hicks. Sat R 48:31-2 Ap 24 '65
DRENNEN, D. A.
Book review. America 113:754 D 11 '65
DRESDEN, Marc, and Hoagland, M. B.
Polyribosomes from escherichia coli: enzymatic method for isolation. bibliog Science 149:647-9 Ag 6 '65

DRESS. See Clothing and dress
DRESS design. See Costume design
DRESS designers. See Costume designers
DRESS shops. See Stores
DRESSING, Poultry. See Cookery—Poultry
DRESSMAKING
Spring, summer fashion news. C. D. Legg. il Farm J 89:92-4 Ap '65
See also
Clothing and dress—Study and teaching
Sewing
DRESSMAN, Robert C.
Father Pedro Arrupe, new Father General of Jesuits. America 112:818-19 Je 5 '65
DREW, Elizabeth Brenner
Lady Bird's beauty bill. Atlan 216:68-72 D '65
Long trial of public housing. Reporter 32:15-18 Je 17; 33:8 Jl 15 '65
New housing at rents families can afford. New Repub 153:9-10 Ag 21 '65
Quiet victory of the cigarette lobby. Atlan 216:76-80 S '65
What happened to civil defense? Reporter 32:37-40 Ap 8 '65
DREYFACK, Raymond
How business keeps prices down. Nations Bsns 53:34-5+ S '65
Where do you stand with the boss? Nations Bsns 53:74-5+ N '65
DRIED flowers. See Flowers, Dried
DRIESELL, Lefty
Agony of Lefty Driesell. J. Jares. il pors Sports Illus 22:32-5 Mr 8 '65
DRIEU LA ROCHELLE, Pierre
Books. J. Updike. New Yorker 41:216+ O 2 '65
DRIFT bottles. See Bottle charts
DRIFTERS. See Unemployables
DRILL press. See Drilling and boring machinery
DRILLING, Underwater. See Underwater drilling
DRILLING and boring (earth and rocks)
USSR plans to drill through earth's crust. Sci N L 88:216 O 2 '65
See also
Mohole project
Underwater drilling
DRILLING and boring (woodwork)
It pays to know the best bits for boring wood. H. Walton. il Pop Sci 186:146-9+ Ap '65
Secrets of drill-press mortising. R. J. De Cristoforo. il Pop Sci 187:146-50 D '65
DRILLING and boring machinery
Five accessories for your drill press. W. G. Waggoner. il Pop Sci 186:168-70 Ap '65
Getting there the hot way; molybdenum drill bit. Time 85:52 F 12 '65
How to get the best from twist drills. H. Walton. il Pop Sci 186:148-50+ F '65
It pays to know the best bits for boring wood. H. Walton. il Pop Sci 186:146-9+ Ap '65
New high-speed drill melts. penetrates rocks. Sci N L 88:41 Jl 17 '65
Shockproof drill with high power, too. il Consumer Rep 30:55 F '65
Trigger varies its speed: portable electric drill. il Consumer Rep 30:108 Mr '65
Undoutedly the handiest power tool of them all; electric drill. il Sunset 134:135-8+ Ap '65
You can make your own deep-hole drill. W. E. Burton. il Pop Mech 124:166-8 Ag '65
DRILLS and marches
So forget the Beatles; Royal Marines tattoo touring North America. il Time 86:60 O 8 '65
DRINAN, Robert F.
Independence of the bar; address, November 13, 1965. Vital Speeches 32:102-5 D 1 '65
Reflections on the first decade of the freedom movement (1955-1965) address, July 20, 1965. Vital Speeches 31:619-22 Ag 1 '65
DRINK question. See Alcoholism; Temperance
DRINKING, Social. See Liquor problem
DRINKING and airplane accidents
Sober truth. R. B. Parke. il Flying 77:28 S '65
DRINKING customs
I dreamt I drank in marble halls. J. Hay. il Holiday 37:92-3+ My '65
Vertical drinking in the Soviet Union. H. Lees. il Atlan 216:164-6 N '65
DRINKING in the opera. See Drinking songs
DRINKING songs
Bravo Bacchus! drinking in opera; reprint. G. Jellinek. il Opera N 30:8-9 O 23 '65
DRINKING water. See Water
DRINKS. See Beverages; Liquors

DRINKWATER, Terrell C.
Western's jets fly over profit ceiling. il por Bsns W p54-5+ Mr 6 '65
DRISCOLL, Edward J. and Graykowski, E. A.
Those pesky mouth sores. Todays Health 44:32-4 Ja '66
DRIVE-in and curb services
Banking in the garage; Denver U.S. national bank, world's largest motor bank. M. J. Pedersen. il Pop Mech 124:91 D '65
Hamburger king; McDonald's hamburger chain of drive-ins. il Newsweek 66:74-5 S 13 '65
DRIVER, Cecil
All for one, one for all. NEA J 54:45 N '65
DRIVER, Geoffrey, and Fritz, Gary
Another view from Latin America. Christian Cent 82:1292+ O 20 '65
DRIVER, Josephine P.
Young John Marquand. Atlan 216:69-72 Ag '65
DRIVER, Tom F.
Christ's sexuality. il por Time 85:59 Ap 9 '65
DRIVES (money raising) See Fund raising
DRIVEWAYS
How to plan for the cars at your house; with account by N. Seney. il Bet Hom & Gard 43:20, 50-3 Ag '65
DRIVEWAYS, Concrete. See Pavements, Concrete
DRIVING, Automobile. See Automobile driving
DRIVING tests, Automobile. See Automobile drivers—Testing
DROGIN, Marc
Battle-tested hints for the housebound husband. Read Digest 88:19+ Ja '66
What happened to the moment of truth? Read Digest 87:39-40 O '65
DRONE airplanes. See Airplanes, Drone
DROP leaf tables. See Tables
DROPOUTS
Changing liabilities to assets; Job corps program to train school dropouts. il Bsns W p 156+ Mr 20 '65
College dropout and talent utilization; Princeton university conference. Sch & Soc 93:163+ Mr 6 '65
Dad's letter to a dropout: did we love you too little, or too much? Good H 160:77+ Je '65; Discussion. 161:24+ O '65
Does drop-out have to be a dirty word? D. Klein. Seventeen 24:166-7 Je '65
Drop in dropouts. America 112:512 Ap 17 '65
Dropout, by L. F. Cervantes. Review
America 113:342-3 S 25 '65. R. Hassenger
Dropouts or readers? need for summer reading programs. M. C. Austin. bibliog f il Sr Schol 86:sup26-7 Mr 4 '65
Employment of high school graduates and dropouts in 1964. F. A. Bogan. il Mo Labor R 88:637-43 Je '65
Five bold ways to attack the dropout problem. W. Van Til. il Parents Mag 40:58-9+ Mr '65
It's a dead-end road for the dropout. J. N. Miller. il Read Digest 86:125-30 My '65
Mothers, homemakers, and wage earners. B. M. Moore. il NEA J 54:22-3 My '65
Senior scholastic interview; ed. by R. Hemming. B. Cosby, Sr Schol 86:17 Mr 18 '65
Seven who came back. il Sch Life 47:16-18 D '64
Sheepskin psychosis, by J. Keats. Review
Nat R 17:689 Ag 10 '65. R. Kirk
So you want to be a dropout. T. Mayer. il Atlan 216:151-3 N '65
Womb-clingers; non-students on college campuses. il Time 85:53-4 Je 25 '65
DROPSY
Wringing out the water. Time 85:78 F 19 '65
DROSERA. See Sundew
DROSOPHILA
Alcohol dehydrogenase in drosophila melanogaster; isozymes and genetic variants. E. H. Grell and others. bibliog il Science 149:80-2 Jl 2 '65
Amateur scientist: studying genetics of fruit flies with chromatograms. R. LaFond. il Sci Am 212:126-7+ Je '65
Analysis of a gene in drosophila. W. J. Welshons. bibliog il Science 150:1122-9 N 26 '65
Culture of dissociated drosophila embryos: aggregated cells differentiate and sort out. R. J. Lesseps. bibliog il Science 148:502-3 Ap 23 '65
Cytological basis of sex ratio in drosophila pseudoobscura. E. Novitski and others. bibliog il Science 148:516-17 Ap 23 '65
Drosophila phenol oxidases. H. K. Mitchell and U. M. Weber. bibliog il Science 148: 964-5 My 14 '65
Evolution of fitness in experimental populations of drosophila serrata. F. J. Ayala. bibliog il Science 150:903-5 N 12 '65

Interspecific transfer of the sex-ratio agent of drosophila willistoni in drosophila bifasciata and drosophila melanogaster. H. Ikeda. bibliog il Science 147:1147-8 Mr 5 '65
Unique sterol in the ecology and nutrition of drosophila pachea. W. B. Heed and H. W. Kircher. bibliog il Science 149:758-61 Ag 13 '65
X-linked 6-phosphogluconate dehydrogenase in drosophila: subunit associations. H. H. Kazazian, jr. and others. bibliog il Science 150:1601-2 D 17 '65
DROTNING, John E.
Union representation election. bibliog f Mo Labor R 88:938-43 Ag '65
DROUGHT, James
Young man with his own horn. H. Frankel. por Sat R 48:26-8 F 27 '65; Discussion. 48:26 Mr 20; 24+ Mr 27 '65
DROUGHT resistance of plants. See Plants—Drought resistance
DROUGHTS
Downhill winds; drought plaguing northeast U.S. and parts of Canada. il Time 86:21 Jl 16 '65
Drip, drip, drip; emergency program for four drought-plagued northeastern states. Newsweek 66:22 Ag 30 '65
Drought in west Texas; dust bowl in the making? il U S News 58:100-1 Mr 29 '65
Drought! insidious enemy; northeastern United States. B. Tufty. il Sci N L 88:90-1 Ag 7 '65
Drought plight global; Madrid's water cut. Sci N L 88:73 Jl 31 '65
Dry silence in the Northeast; five-year drought. R. Cantwell. il Sports Illus 23:20-3 Ag 9 '65
Fourth dry year for the Northeast? il U S News 58:10 Je 7 '65
Northeast farmers fight fourth year of drouth. B. Hardy. Farm J 89:54B S '65
People-water crisis. il Newsweek 66:48-50+ Ag 23 '65
Reality of drought is always with us. H. E. Thomas. il Natur Hist 74:50-7 N '65
Water crisis: emergency in four eastern states. U S News 59:12 Jl 19 '65
Ways to make dry weather hurt less. R. E. Geyer. Suc Farm 63:28+ Jl '65
DROUGHTS and business. See Weather and business
DROUTHS. See Droughts
DROWNING
See also
Respiration, Artificial
DRUCKER, Peter F.
American directions: a forecast. Harper 230: 39-45 F '65
Crash next year? Harper 230:59-64 Je '65
Is business letting young people down? Harvard Bsns R 43:49-55 N '65
DRUDING, Susan
Coeds in rebellion. B. H. Hoffman. il por Ladies Home J 82:82-4+ O '65
DRUG addicts. See Narcotic addicts
DRUG habit. See Narcotic habit
DRUG labels. See Labels
DRUG laws and legislation
Blame pep pills for murder; murder of F. A. Christiansen by three teenage Chicago boys. Christian Cent 82:199 F 17 '65
Drug abuse: tighter controls placed on amphetamines and barbiturates; law to cover other drugs later. J. Walsh. Science 149: 951-3 Ag 27 '65
Drug lab caught in crossfire; FDA's handling of label mixups. Bsns W p30 O 30 '65
See also
Narcotic laws
United States—Food and drug administration
DRUG plants. See Botany, Medical
DRUG research. See Pharmaceutical research
DRUG trade
Change, challenge and the drug industry; address, October 12, 1965. J. J. Powers, jr. Vital Speeches 32:57-60 N 1 '65
In a few hands: monopoly power in America, by E. Kefauver and I. Till. Review
Sat R 48:29-30 F 27 '65. P. H. Douglas
See also
Bristol-Myers company
Government investigations—Drug trade
Miles laboratories, incorporated
Pfizer, Charles, and company

Securities
Medicare: bonanza or burden for drugs? il Bsns W p 174+ S 11 '65
DRUGGISTS. See Pharmacists

DRUGS

Congress and drugs: political interest in drug problems is at lowest point in five years. E. Langer. Science 147:846-8 F 19 '65

Drugs you use; excerpts from Today's health guide. il Todays Health 43:38-9+ Mr '65

Get rid of those worn-out medicines. J. Lentz. il Todays Health 43:88 F '65

Health and grooming. Consumer Rep 30:348-92 D '65

New hope for drugs to fight viruses. Good H 160:143-5 F '65

Pill board identifies 450 drugs; at Brackenridge hospital, Austin, Tex. il Todays Health 43:68 Je '65

Promise and perils of the miraculous DMSO. L. David. il Good H 161:68-9+ Ag '65

Therapeutic nightmare, by M. Mintz. Review New Repub 154:25-7 Ja 1 '66. R. Coles

U.S. to propose International adverse drug reaction center. Dept State Bul 52:814 My 24 '65

Wanted, drugs to fight the new viruses. B. Slaton and N. Slaton. il Sci Digest 57:81-4 F '65

See also
Antiarthritic substances
Antibiotics
Fertility drugs
Hallucinogenic drugs
Medicines, Patent, proprietary, etc.
United States—Food and drug administration
also names of drugs, e.g. Methadone

Contamination

Infected drugs recalled; FDA controlling penicillin contamination. Sci N L 87:350 My 29 '65

Physiological effects

Addiction by overuse; withdrawal symptoms from non-narcotic, non-barbiturate drugs. Sci N L 87:69 Ja 30 '65

Adverse drug effects data available to all. Sci N L 88:326 N 20 '65

Cataracts due to drugs. Sci N L 87:109 F 13 '65

Cause of bone marrow destruction seen in drug; antibiotic chloramphenicol causing aplastic anemia. Sci N L 88:386 D 18 '65

Cleft palate produced in mice by human-equivalent dosage with triamcinolone. B. E. Walker. bibliog il Science 149:862-3 Ag 20 '65

Drug dangers attacked; by National institutes of health. Sci N L 88:6 Jl 3 '65

Drug ignorance hit. F. Marley. Sci N L 88:3 Jl 3 '65

Drug mixing danger seen; analexin may increase effects of anticoagulants. Sci N L 88:130 Ag 28 '65

Drugs deforming rats safe for human use; diamox. Sci N L 88:88 Ag 7 '65

Drugs that work around the clock. Bsns W p58+ S 4 '65

Drugs your doctor prescribes. L. Lasagna. il Ladies Home J 83:35+ Ja '66

For pregnant women: a warning on three drugs. U S News 59:20 N 8 '65

Hormone hazard; use of steroids by athletes. il Newsweek 66:68 S 27 '65

Mescaline, 3,4-dimethoxyphenylethylamine, and adrenaline: sites of electroencephalographic arousal. Y. Takeo and H. E. Himwich. bibliog il Science 150:1309-10 D 3 '65

New registry to reveal harmful drug reactions. Sci N L 87:285 My 1 '65

Non-narcotic addicts. Time 86:36 Jl 2 '65

Pill addicts; amendments to the U.S. food and drug laws. il Newsweek 66:64 D 20 '65

Some medicines make you a dangerous driver. il Changing T 20:43-5 Ja '66

Tetracycline; effect on osteogenesis in vitro. L. Saxén. bibliog il Science 149:870-2 Ag 20 '65

Those adverse effects; plea for reportage to manufacturers. Time 86:66 D 17 '65

Toxicology and the biomedical sciences. B. B. Brodie and others. bibliog Science 148:1547-54 Je 18 '65

Warning labels ordered; drugs harmful to an unborn child. Sci N L 88:293 N 6 '65

Psychological effects

Drug abuse; tighter controls placed on amphetamines and barbiturates; law to cover other drugs later. J. Walsh. Science 149:951-3 Ag 27 '65

Drug improves memory; Cylert. Sci N L 89:6 Ja 1 '66

Drug to improve memory. Sci N L 88:386 D 18 '65

LSD and the anguish of dying. S. Cohen. Harper 231:69-72+ S '65
See also
Mental illness—Therapy

Testing

Drugs that work around the clock. Bsns W p58+ S 4 '65

Infected drugs recalled; FDA controlling penicillin contamination. Sci N L 87:350 My 29 '65

Toxicity, the therapeutic index, and the ranking of drugs. M. A. Schneiderman and others; discussion. il Science 149:1396-8 S 17 '65

Toxicology and the biomedical sciences. B. B. Brodie and others. bibliog Science 148:1547-54 Je 18 '65

Two new experimental TB drugs effective; capreomycin and ethambutol. Sci N L 88:221 O 2 '65

DRUGS, Resistance to

Coxsackie A9 virus: mutation from drug dependence to drug independence. H. J. Eggers and I. Tamm. bibliog il Science 148:97-8 Ap 2 '65

Quinine-resistant plasmodium berghei in mice. P. E. Thompson and others. bibliog il Science 148:1240-1 My 28 '65

DRUGSTORES

Mexico's drug store changes prescription; Sanborns restaurants, chain, and retail stores under Walgreen co. il Bsns W p72-3+ My 15 '65

DRUM

Drum collecting dental surgeon. il Ebony 20:44-6 S '65

Jazz; Z. Singleton's music. W. Balliett. New Yorker 41:132-4 N 6 '65

Rage for rhythm. F. Bowers. House & Gard 128:10+ Ag '65

DRUM brakes. See Brakes, Automobile

DRUMMER: story. See Frater, A.

DRUMMOND, Ainslie H. Jr
Science news in the classroom. Sat R 48:57 Jl 17 '65

DRUMMOND, Richard H.
Missionary exodus from Japan? Christian Cent 82:672-4 My 26 '65

DRUMMOND, Roscoe
Berlin wall, four years of failure. Read Digest 88:155-6 Ja '66

New forward thrust of freedom. Read Digest 87:133-5 Ag '65

Unofficial volunteers for the great debate. Harper 231:122+ N '65
—See Bean, L. H. jt. auth.

DRUMS. See Drum

DRUNKENNESS. See Alcoholism

DRURY, John
(tr) See Nabuco, J. Dead end in Portugal

DRURY, Michael
Courage to grow and the right to fail; address to 4-H clubs of America. McCalls 93:101+ O '65

Fourth dimension; poem. McCalls 92:199 F '65

Long, hard look at love and marriage. McCalls 92:93+ Ap '65

DRURY, Newton B.
Recollections of a trip with Mr John D. Rockefeller, jr, in California's Humboldt Redwoods State Park, July 1926. Nat Parks Mag 39:8-9 My '65

DRURY, Theodore
Where socialism failed close to home. Nations Bsns 53:66-8+ O '65

DRY cell batteries. See Electric batteries

DRY cleaning. See Cleaning

DRY docks
Build a floating drydock. F. M. Paulson. il Field & S 70:84-7 Jl '65

DRY flies. See Fishing lures, flies, etc.

DRY printing. See Xerography

DRYDEN, Hugh Latimer
International space surge; excerpts from congressional testimony. Aviation W 82:17 F 22 '65

University and the exploration of space; address, October 11, 1965. Science 150:1129-33 N 26 '65

about
Man from Pocomoke City. W. J. Coughlin. Miss & Roc 17:46 D 13 '65

NASA leader dies. M. K. Zeiger. por Science 150:1436 D 10 '65

DRYER, Ivan
Grand Falls of the Little Colorado. il Nat Parks Mag 39:10-12 My '65

DRYERS, Print. See Photography—Apparatus and supplies

DRYING (crops)
See also
Corn—Drying

DRYING apparatus
See also
Clothes dryers

DUANE, Morris
Philadelphia: behind the renaissance. Sat R
49:48+ Ja 8 '66
DUANE, T. D. and Behrendt, Thomas
Extrasensory electroencephalographic induction between identical twins. Science 150:
367; 151:28+ O 15 '65, Ja 7 '66
DUBIN, Robert
Coalitions versus consumers in the analysis
of power. Mo Labor R 88:655-7 Je '65

DUBLIN
Music
Dublin's children. M. E. Davies. Opera N 29:
33 Ap 10 '65
Ireland's tribute. C. Acton. Hi Fi 15:168 S '65
DU BOIS, Donald
What do you know about gun laws? questions
and answers. Outdoor Life 135:12-14 Ap '65
DU BOIS, Graham
Empty room at the inn; drama. Plays 25:
23-31 D '65
DUBOIS, Paul Z.
Myth of the historical society library. por
Library J 90:4279-81 O 15 '65
DU BOIS, William Edward Burghardt
W. E. B. DuBois. R. McGill. por Atlan 216:
78-81 N '65
W. E. B. Du Bois: prophet of protest and
Pan-Africa. L. Bennett, jr. il pors Ebony
20:146-8+ Mr '65
DU BOIS, William Pène
Alligator case; excerpt. il Ladies Home J
82:62-3+ Ag '65
DUBROW, Heather. See Adams, J. jt. auth.
DUBUQUE, Iowa
Religious institutions and affairs
Breakthroughs: Dubuque's experiment in
ecumenism; cooperative graduate programs
and open classes for undergraduates. W. E.
Hulme. Christian Cent 82:1187-90 S 29 '65
DU BUY, Herman G. and others
Isolation and characterization of KNA from
kinetoplasts of leishmania enriettii. bibliog
Science 147:754-6 F 12 '65
DUCCIO di Buoninsegna
Giotto and Duccio. J. Canaday. il Horizon
7:92-107 Sum '65
DUCHAMP, Marcel
Art galleries; exhibition at the Cordier &
Ekstrom gallery. R. M. Coates. New Yorker
40:92+ Ja 30 '65
Duchamp. M. Kozloff. Nation 200:123-4 F 1
'65
J'accuse Marcel Duchamp; show at Cordier-
Ekstrom, New York. T. B. Hess. il por
Art N 63:44-5+ F '65
Pop's dada. il por Time 85:78+ F 5 '65
Profiles. C. Tomkins. por New Yorker 40:37-
40+ F 6 '65
DUCHIN, Peter
Striking the right notes. por Time 86:46+ D
17 '65
DUCK blinds
Sinkbox shoot; paintings by R. Cunningham;
with account by D. Barnes. Sports Illus
23:40-5 O 4 '65
DUCK decoys. See Decoys (hunting)
DUCK shooting
Campout for prairie ducks. J. O. Cartier.
il Outdoor Life 136:60-1+ O '65
Guns for waterfowl. J. O'Connor. il Outdoor
Life 137:82-3+ Ja '66
Marblehead gunning dory. L. Dietz. il Field
& S 70:54-7+ N '65
Sportiest duck hunting of all! J. Madson. il
Farm J 89:50+ O '65
See also
Game laws
DUCKAT, Walter
How to tell your child about death. Ebony
20:48-50+ Mr '65
DUCKETT, Kenneth W.
Harding papers: how some were burned. Am
Heritage 16:24-31+ F '65
about
Harding letters: this case and library censor-
ship. E. J. Gaines. ALA Bul 59:343-4 My '65
DUCKS, Wild
Duck drain. il Time 86:94 O 1 '65
Elusive musk ducks. P. A. Johnsgard. il
Natur Hist 74:26 O '65
Lost like a goose. C. Chatfield. il Outdoor
Life 136:60-3+ N '65
Wood ducks are special. J. O. Cartier. il
Outdoor Life 136:32-3+ Ag '65
Wood ducks for your pond! E. F. Hester. il
Farm J 89:D3 F '65
See also
Duck shooting
DUCROT, Jerome
Ducrot, fashion reporter with a camera.
J. Deschin. il Pop Phot 56:29+ Je '65

DUCTED fan observation platform. See Ground
effect machines
DUDINTSEV, Vladimir
Capitalist exploitation; excerpt from Moscow
summer. M. Mihajlov. por Sat R 48:41 D 11
'65
DUDLEY, Guilford, Jr
Self-reliance or self-destruction; address, April
27, 1965. Vital Speeches 31:632-4 Ag 1 '65
DUDLEY, Pendleton
Give your mind a chance. Read Digest 87:
94-6 N '65
DUDLEY, Sherwood Harris
Playboy of the western night world. il pors
Ebony 20:103-4+ Jl '65
DUDMAN, Richard
Report from the Dominican Republic. New
Repub 152:15-16 Je 5 '65
Rules they use in Vietnam. New Repub 152:
20-1 Je 12 '65
Two powerful men who stayed. Esquire 64:
94-5+ N '65
War in Asia: more questions than answers.
Sat R 48:34-5 N 27 '65
about
Misinformed source. por Newsweek 67:53 Ja
3 '66
Right not to know. K. Crawford. Newsweek
67:18 Ja 3 '66
DUESENBERG automobile. See Automobiles
DUESENBERG, James Stembel
To & from Harvard in the middle of the road.
por Time 87:82 Ja 7 '66
DUFAULT, Peter Kane
Fisherman; poem. New Yorker 41:203 My 15
'65
DUFFEY, David Michael
Dogs. See issues of Outdoor life
DUFFY, Joanne
Discovering the deep. Seventeen 24:93 Jl '65
DUFFY, John
Player piano is back in a popular key. il
por Bsns W p 148+ O 23 '65
DUFFY, Joseph A.
ABA regionals and local problems. Pub W
188:75-7 S 13 '65
Lasser report. Pub W 188:51-2 D 13 '65
Long range role of the ABA. Pub W 188:323-6
Ag 30 '65
Review of returns. Pub W 188:56-7 Ag 2 '65
Sidelines and the American bookstore. Pub W
188:68-70 O 25 '65
DUFRESNE, Frank
California playground. por Field & S 69:42-5
Mr '65
Daffy deer. Field & S 70:34-6+ Ja '66
Snowblind. Field & S 70:30-2+ D '65
That was the storm. Field & S 70:20+ My
'65
—See Alport, P. jt. auth.
DUFY, Raoul
Role for Raoul Dufy. G. R. Swenson. il Art N
64:39+ N '65
DUGAN, Edward T.
Harlem priest reports on Selma; interview,
ed. by C. L. Palms. Cath World 201:171-6
Je '65
DUGAN, James
What's going on down there? Holiday 37:70-
9+ Je '65
DUGGAN, Francis X.
Paul Elmer More: the Nation's conservative
editor. Nation 200:248-51 Mr 8 '65
DUGGAN, R. E. and others
Pesticide residues in total-diet samples. bib-
liog Science 151:101-4 Ja 7 '66
DUGGER, Ronnie
Two men from Moscow pay a call. N Y Times
Mag p34-5+ F 14 '65
DUGGER, W. M. Jr. See Ting, I. P. jt. auth.
DUHÊME, Jacqueline
Full happy life of John F. Kennedy; paint-
ings. Ladies Home J 82:100-5 N '65
DUIKERS. See Antelopes
DUKAS, Paul
Cascade of jewels. R. Lawrence. por Opera N
30:6-7 N 6 '65
DUKE, Angier Biddle
People are talking about... por Vogue 145:
100-1 Mr 15 '65
DUKE, Patty
Aaaaaaahh-wow! il por Newsweek 66:106+
O 18 '65
DUKE, Paul, and Meisler, Stanley
Republicans after the debacle. Reporter 32:
26-8 F 11 '65
—and Sawsilak, A. B.
Group that runs the House; Democratic study
group. Reporter 32:29-31 My 20 '65
DUKE, Robin Chandler
People are talking about... por Vogue 145:
100-1 Mr 15 '65

DUKELOW, Donald A.
Tagged for life. Todays Health 43:58-9+ D '65
—and Alden, Robert
Yellow fever, a new airborne threat. Todays Health 43:30-1+ Mr '65
DULAC, Margarita Walker
Ivan Albright: mystic-realist. Am Artist 30: 32-7+ Ja '66
DULBERG, Eric M.
Amateur scientist. Sci Am 212:136-8+ Ap '65
DULCIN
Dulcin and saccharin taste in squirrel monkeys, rats, and men. G. L. Fisher and others. bibliog il Science 150:506-7 O 22 '65
DULK, George A.
Io-related radio emission from Jupiter. bibliog Science 148:1585-9 Je 18 '65
DULL, H. J. See Gonzales, C. jt. auth.
DULLEA, Keir
Romantic at large; ed. by E. Miller. por Seventeen 24:144-5+ N '65
DULLES international airport. See Washington, D.C.—Airports
DU MAURIER, Daphne
Flight of the Falcon; novel. Good H 160: 66-74 F; 85-7 Mr; 94-5 Ap; 100-1 My '65
DUMBARTON OAKS garden. See Gardens— Washington, D.C.
DUMMLING and the golden goose; drama. See Thane, A.
DUMOND, Dwight L.
Journey in misery. Sat R 48:30 Mr 13 '65
DUMONT, Wayne, Jr.
Chance for a change in the Garden state. J. J. Farmer. Reporter 33:27-9 Ag 12 '65
DUN and Bradstreet
Longtime credit-rater figures its own future; expanding services to management, in U.S. and overseas. il Bsns W p70+ Ap 10 '65
DUNAGIN, Percy E. Jr, and others
Retinoyl beta-glucuronic acid: a major metabolite of vitamin A in rat bile. bibliog Science 148:86-7 Ap 2 '65
DUNAWAY, Jim
Some fanatics whose fun is playing old records. G. Holland. il por Sports Illus 23: 46-7 Ag 2 '65
DUNAWAY, Vic
Campout on Cape Sable. Outdoor Life 135:62-4+ Ap '65
DUNBAR, Leslie W.
Southern regional council. Ann Am Acad 357:108-12 Ja '65
DUNBAR, Paul Laurence
Paul Laurence Dunbar: a new perspective. W. Phillips. bibliog por Negro Hist Bul 29: 7-8 O '65
DUNCAN, Donald
Donald Duncan (June 9, 1914—May 10, 1965) por Dance Mag 39:5 Je '65
DUNCAN, Jeff
Ruth Currier, Jeff Duncan & companies, East 74th street theatre. J. Maskey. Dance Mag 40:58 Ja '66
DUNCAN, Lois
True believer; story. Redbook 125:52 Ag '65
DUNCAN, Marion Moncure
Hobbies salutes diamond jubilee of the D.A.R. il por Hobbies 70:72-3 Ap '65
DUNCAN, Peter
Two Canadians raid Aspen. B. Ottum. Sports Illus 22:50-1 F 8 '65
DUNCAN, Robert
Fire; poem. Poetry 106:32-6 Ap '65
Taking away from God his sound. Nation 200:595-8 My 31 '65
Up rising; poem. Nation 201:146-7 S 13 '65

about

Notes on Robert Duncan. F. Will. Poetry 106: 427-8 S '65
DUNCAN, Robert Blackford
Excerpt from debate, July 28, 1965. Cong Digest 44:206 Ag '65
DUNCAN, Mrs Robert V. H.
Excerpt from testimony, August 10, 1964. Cong Digest 44:153+ My '65
DUNCAN, Roger F.
Sloops of Friendship. Yachting 117:184-6 F '65
DUNCANNON, Pa.
Private lighting goes public. M. Cooper. il Am City 80:113 F '65
DUNCE-cap limpets. See Limpets
DUNDEE, Angelo
Man in the champ's corner. G. Rogin. por Sports Illus 22:32-6+ My 24 '65
DUNDY, Elaine
Can a simple Welsh lass of thirty-six find happiness with a Macedonian rock-and-roll star of twenty-four? Esquire 64:164-5+ D '65
How to succeed in the theatre without really being successful. Esquire 63:88-9+ My '65
Image in the marketplace. Esquire 64:82-3+ Jl '65

DUNE buggies. See Motor vehicles
DUNE vegetation. See Sand dunes
DUNES, Sand. See Sand dunes
DUNETZ, Lora
Riven rock; poem. Christian Cent 82:802 Je 23 '65
DUNHAM, David W.
Occultation highlights, September-November, 1965. Sky & Tel 30:186 S '65
DUNKIRK, Battle of, 1940
Twenty-five years after Dunkirk. E. F. Haylock. il Motor B 115:45-7+ Je '65
DUNLOP, Richard
Doctors on the American frontier; excerpts (cont) Todays Health 43:50-1+ Mr '65
Ferryboat into the sourdough past. Todays Health 43:40-5 Ap '65
Let's throw a star-spangled party! Todays Health 44:36-9+ Ja '66
Matter of taste. Todays Health 43:32-4 O '65
Stroll through Ben Franklin's Philadelphia. Todays Health 43:32-7 N '65
Take charge of your career. Pop Mech 124: 20+ Ag; 30+ S '65
Three days afoot in New York. Todays Health 43:42-9 My '65
Trifle about truffles. Todays Health 43:84-6 O '65
DUNN, Harold
(ed) Small world. Travel 124:47-9+ D '65
DUNN, Michael
Elf's progress. por Time 86:54 Jl 30 '65
DUNNE, George H.
This was Montgomery. America 112:660-1+ My 8 '65
DUNNE, James
Detroit listening post. Pop Mech 124:24 O; 58+ N; 26+ D '65; 125:32+ Ja '66

about

Editor's page. por Pop Mech 124:83 N '65
DUNNE, John Gregory
Embattled nurse of Jackrabbit Flats. Sat Eve Post 238:42-4+ N 20 '65
Hollywood's heedless horseman. Holiday 38: 111-12+ D '65
Take back your Kafka. New Repub 153:32-4 S 4 '65
Television. See issues of New republic
DUNNE, Mary Neil
How I took the menace out of menopause. Farm J 89:101+ Mr '65
DUNNIGAN, Alice E.
Early history of Negro women in journalism. por Negro Hist Bul 28:178-9+ My '65
DUNOVAN, Cass
Voyage of the lollipop; story. Redbook 125: 160-9 Ag '65
DUNSON, William A. and Weymouth, R. D.
Active uptake of sodium by softshell turtles, trionyx spinifer. bibliog Science 149:67-9 Jl 2 '65
DUNTON, Sam
Nature and photography (cont) Natur Hist 74:58-60 D '65
DUPEE, Frederick Wilcox
Discernments. V. S. Pritchett. Commentary 40:104+ N '65
DU PLESSIX, Francine
House that pop art built. House & Gard 127: 158-63 My '65
Inkfish and shark kabob. Vogue 146:288-90+ S 1 '65
True meaning of comfort. House & Gard 128:192-3 O '65
DUPLICATING processes. See Copying processes
DUPLICATORS. See Copying processes
DU PONT DE NEMOURS, E. I. and company
Deal for du Pont; tax problem over holdings of GM stock. Newsweek 65:75-6 F 15 '65
Du Pont team. L. L. L. Golden. Sat R 48:78 Je 12 '65
DuPonts get off easy. Nation 200:183-4 F 22 '65
Du Pont's great search for surprises. il Read Digest 86:151-2+ F '65
In Du Pont-GM divorce: how everybody fared. il U S News 58:98 Mr 1 '65
Kind of charity. Nation 201:30 Jl 19 '65
DUPREY, Richard A.
Movie of the month (cont) Cath World 202: 63-4 O '65
Play of the month (cont) Cath World 201: 151-2 My '65
University theater. por Cath World 201:240-6 Jl '65
DUQUE, Francisco Dorta-. See Dorta-Duque, F.
DUQUESNE, Pa.
Duquesne, Pa, breaks precedent. W. T. McPhee. il Am City 80:93-6 O '65

DU QUOIN, III.
Odd time in Du Quoin, Illinois; Hambleton-
ian trotting race and state fair. M. Kram.
il Sports Illus 23:24-31 Ag 30 '65
Tradition battles expediency; question
whether the Hambletonian will move. P.
Ryan. il Sports Illus 23:22-3 N 1 '65
DURAND, Ruth (Sawyer) See Sawyer, R.
DURANT, Ariel
Essence of the centuries. il por Time 86:48
Ag 13 '65
DURANT, Will
Essence of the centuries. il por Time 86:48
Ag 13 '65
DURANT, William Crapo
Rise & fall of Wm. C. Durant. J. B. Sibbi-
son. il pors Motor T 17:58-61 Ap '65
DURANTE, Jimmy
And another who never went away; show at
the Copacabana in New York. S. Moore. Life
58:12 Ap 9 '65
DURAS, Marguerite
Bardot, Bardot. Vogue 145:170-1+ Ap 1 '65
Callas. Vogue 146:192-3 O 1 '65
Jeanne Moreau. Vogue 146:100-1+ N 15 '65
DURATION of life. See Longevity
DURDIN, Peggy
Australia: out back and in town. Sat R 48:
64+ S 18 '65
DURE, Leon, 3d. See Waters, L. jt. auth.
DÜRER, Albrecht
Pointing to God. il Time 86:86-7 N 12 '65
Taking man's measure; traveling exhibit of
150 drawings. il Newsweek 67:60-1 Ja 10
'66
DURHAM, Diane
Sunday night supper. Ladies Home J 82:
94-5+ Mr '65
DURHAM, Eldon
Modest proposal. Time 86:77 D 3 '65
DURHAM, Helen
Take a deep breath. Read Digest 86:24J Mr
'65
DURHAM, Michael
Man at the switch with no time to argue.
Life 58:74-7 Je 18 '65
DURHAM, N.C.
Gathering of the Klan. J. M. Arisman. Com-
monweal 82:373-4 Je 11 '65
DURIG, Ernest
Great Rodin, his flagrant faker; with report
by D. Seiberling. il por Life 58:64-71 Je 4
'65
DURISCH, Lawrence L.
South: socioeconomic and cultural aspects;
address, April 1965. por Wilson Lib Bul 39:
854-9 Je '65
DURNIAK, John
Focus on Wilson Hicks. Pop Phot 56:58-61+
Ap '65
Three photographers try the Swinger. il Pop
Phot 57:69 S '65
DUROCHER, Leo
Don't call me coach. il por Newsweek 66:65
N 8 '65
DUROSELLE, Jean Baptiste
Historian looks at de Gaulle: why he acts
that way; interview, ed. by F. C. Painton.
por U S News 58:44+ My 10 '65
DURRELL, Gerald
Monkeys' marriage & other improbable tales;
excerpt from Menagerie manor. McCalls
92:80+ Mr '65
DURRELL, Lawrence
Delphi; poem. New Yorker 41:219 N 6 '65
Other T. S. Eliot. Atlan 215:60-4 My '65
Salamis; poem. New Yorker 41:50 N 20 '65
DURRER, Dirk
Heart lived on por Newsweek 66:59 N 1 '65
DURSIN, Margaret
Off-campus love story; story. Harper 232:60-
4 Ja '66
DUSCHA, Julius
Same young fogies. New Repub 153:8 Jl 3
'65
Senator Dirksen's unexpected allies. Reporter
32:26-8 Ap 22 '65
DUST, Radioactive. See Radioactive fallout
DUST free area. See Factories—Cleanliness
DUST jackets. See Book covers
DUST storms
Nature note. Sci N L 88:110 Ag 14 '65
DUSTY miller. See Wormwood
DUTCH, Pennsylvania. See Pennsylvania Ger-
mans
DUTCH art. See Art, Dutch
DUTCH elm disease. See Elm—Diseases and
pests
DUTCH irises. See Irises
DUTIES (tariff) See Tariff
DUTTON, E. P. and company
Dispute over publication of Yevtushenko
poems. Pub W 187:36-7 Mr 15 '65

DUTY
See also
Conscience
DUTY free importation
LBJ again backs bill for Florence agreement.
Pub W 188:32 N 29 '65
LBJ asks implementation of Florence agree-
ment in '65. Pub W 187:77-8 Je 14 '65
President urges implementation of Florence
agreement; statement, with letter, June 1,
1965. L. B. Johnson. Dept State Bul 52:
1015 Je 21 '65
President urges legislation to implement Flo-
rence agreement; statement. November 8,
1965. L. B. Johnson. Dept State Bul 53:
907 D 6 '65
This season $100 duty-free allowance still
applies. il U S News 58:76 Ap 12 '65
DUVALIER, François
Crushing a country. il por Time 86:25 Ag 27
'65
Emperor Duvalier? Newsweek 65:49 Mr 29 '65
Haiti: hatred without hope. H. Gold. il por
Sat Eve Post 238:74-6+ Ap 24 '65
Nightmare. il por Newsweek 65:34+ My 31
'65
DUVEL, William A.
Bad debts: threat to small business. Duns R
85:60-1 Ap '65
DUVENECK, Frank
I studied with Duveneck. H. C. Loughmiller.
il por Am Artist 29:40-5+ Mr '65
DU VON, Jay. See Deering, E. C. jt. auth.
DVOŘÁK, Antonín
First, and beautiful, recording of Rusalka. R.
Zarbock. il Am Rec G 32:348-9 D '65
Too popular to be good? Discus. Harper 231:
139-40 D '65
Whole of Rusalka; lovable, touching, unique-
ly atmospheric. C. L. Osborne. il Hi Fi
15:77-8 S '65
DVORIN, Eugene P.
Chile-California experiment. Bul Atomic Sci
21:35-8 N '65
DWARF dahlias. See Dahlias
DWARF fruit trees. See Fruit trees, Dwarf
DWARF geraniums. See Geraniums
DWARF mistletoe. See Mistletoe
DWARF periwinkles. See Periwinkles
DWARF stars. See Stars, Dwarf
DWARF trees. See Trees, Dwarf
DWARFS
Little people; tiny minority with big prob-
lems. A. Adams. il Ebony 20:104-6+ O '65
DWIGGINS, Clare Victor
Dwigs comics. R. C. Finnegan. il Hobbies
70:124-5+ O '65
DWIGHT, Edward H.
Audubon: naturalist into artist. Art N 64:35-
7+ My '65
Unpublished Audubon originals. Antiques 87:
454-5 Ap '65
DWIGHT, Edward Joseph, 1934?-
Troubles of astronaut Edward Dwight. C. L.
Sanders. il pors Ebony 20:29-32+ Je '65
DWYER, J.
(tr) See Kung, H. What has the council
done?
DWYER, James E.
Accent your patio with a lily pool. Pop Gard
16:33 Ap '65
Rock cotoneaster. Pop Gard 16:8 My '65
—See Purcell, E. J. jt. auth.
DWYER, John P.
New frontier: the word is out. Hi Fi 16:146+
Ja '66
Project Buffalo. Dance Mag 40:54-5 Ja '66
DYAL, James A.
Images in the lonely crowd; address, April 3,
1965. Vital Speeches 31:729-35 S 15 '65
DYCKMAN, John W.
Transportation in cities; with biographical
sketch. Sci Am 213:30, 162-74 bibliog (p278)
S '65
DYE, Charlie
School of old paint. il Newsweek 66:107-8 N 8
'65
DYER, W. Gurnee
Guelta of the bleak Sahara. Natur Hist 74:
36-9 N '65
DYES and dyeing
Do-it-yourself fabric dyeing. E. Taylor. il
Good H 161:186 Ag '65
See also
Hair—Dyeing and bleaching
DYKSTRA, William G. Jr. and Herbst, E. J.
Spermidine in regenerating liver: relation to
rapid synthesis of ribonucleic acid. bibliog
Science 149:428 Jl 23 '65

DYLAN, Bob
Folk and the rock. il por Newsweek 66:88+
S 20 '65
Public writer no. 1? T. Meehan. il pors N Y
Times Mag p44-5+ D 12 '65; Discussion.
p4+ D 26 '65
DYNACHROME films. See Photography—Films
DYNAMICS
Galileo's discoveries in dynamics; adaptation
of address, September 10, 1964. N. R.
Hanson. bibliog il Science 147:471-8 Ja 29
'65
DYNE, Michael
Right honourable gentleman. Criticism
America 113:762 D 11 '65
Commonweal 83:215-16 N 19 '65
Nation 201:398 N 22 '65
New Yorker 41:108 O 30 '65
Newsweek il 66:86 N 1 '65
Reporter 33:50 N 18 '65
Time 86:84 O 29 '65
DYNEIN. See Proteins
DYSAUTONOMIA. See Nervous system—
Diseases
DYSON, Freeman J.
Death of a project. Science 149:141-4 Jl 9
'65
Defense against ballistic missiles. Bul Atomic
Sci 20:12-18 Je '64; 21:40 Mr '65
Tomonaga, Schwinger, and Feynman awarded
Nobel prize for physics. Science 150:588-9
O 29 '65
DYSPEPSIA
How upset stomach is best treated. Good H
160:129-30 Ja '65
DYSTROPHY, Muscular
Enzyme high in dystrophy. Sci N L 88:355
D 4 '65
Neuromuscular diseases. il Todays Health 43:
33-4 Ag '65

E

ECAFE. See United Nations—Economic com-
mission for Asia and the Far East
ECLA. See United Nations—Economic commis-
sion for Latin America
ECM (electrochemical machining) See Electro-
chemical cutting
ECSC. See European coal and steel community
EDM (electrical discharge machining) See
Electric cutting
EDP. See Electronic data processing
EEC. See European economic community
EEOC. See United States—President's equal
employment opportunity commission
EFTA. See European free trade association
EHE. See Executive health examiners (orga-
nization)
E. I. Du Pont de Nemours and company. See
Du Pont de Nemours, E. I, and company
ELDO. See European launcher development
organization
ENI (Ente nazionale idrocarburi) See Petrole-
um industry and trade—Italy
EOS. See Electro-optical systems, incorporated
EPC. See Educational policies commision
E. P. Dutton and company, incorporated. See
Dutton, E. P. and company
EPTA (expanded program of technical assist-
ance) See United Nations—Technical as-
sistance program
ERC. See United States—National areonautics
and space administration—Electronics re-
search center
ESAR (electronically steerable away radars)
See Radar—Antenna and scanning mech-
anisms
ESP. See Extrasensory perception
ESRO. See European space research organiza-
tion
ESSA. See United States—Environmental sci-
ence services agency
ETV. See Television in education
ETV stations. See Television stations, Educa-
tional
EUB. See Evangelical United Brethren church
EVA (extravehicular activity) suit. See
Astronauts—Clothing
EACLES imperialis. See Imperial moths
EADIE, W. Robert
Controlling animals in the garden. Horticul-
ture 44:26-7 Ja '66

EAGAN, W. B.
Tall fences for privacy. Pop Sci 186:139-41
My '65
EAGLE, George
Correspondent in Saigon. New Repub 152:25-7
My 15 '65
EAGLE, Harry
Metabolic controls in cultured mammalian
cells; adaptation of address, June 2, 1964.
bibliog Science 148:42-51 Ap 2 '65
EAGLE, Joanna
Teruo Hara. Craft Horiz 25:32-4 Jl '65
EAGLE (newspaper) See Pittsfield, Mass.—
Newspapers
EAGLE CAP wilderness area. See Wilderness
areas
EAGLES
Case for the golden eagle. Nat Parks Mag
39:10-11 Je '65
Counting our eagles; excerpt from Raccoons
and eagles. P. Redford. il Atlan 216:64-8 Jl
'65
Eagle on the loose; Goldie escapes from
London zoo, with report by J. Hicks. il
Life 58:86A+ Mr 19 '65
First flight: a golden eagle evades capture;
excerpt from Golden eagle. il Audubon Mag
67:244-8 Jl '65
Flying symbol; Goldie, the London zoo's
eagle, escapes. il Time 85:36 Mr 19 '65
Golden eagle, by R. Murphy. Review
Life 59:23 S 10 '65. F. Russell
Underbird; golden eagle escapes from London
zoo. il Newsweek 65:32 Mr 22 '65
EAKIN, Mary M.
Sermon seminar in a parish church. Christian
Cent 83:75-7 Ja 19 '66
EAKINS, Thomas
Artist-teachers in America. G. Byrd. bib-
liog il Sch Arts 65:21-5 O '65
EAR
See also
Deafness
Labyrinth (ear)
Diseases
See also
Tinnitus
Foreign bodies
Beetles in ear included among camping haz-
ards. Sci N L 88:200 S 25 '65
EAR (insects)
Moths and ultrasound. K. D. Roeder. il Sci
Am 212:94-102 Ap '65
EAR, Artificial
New ear for Susan. il Todays Health 43:43
Je '65
EARL, Howard G.
Helping your teen-agers to better nutrition.
Todays Health 43:49-51+ F '65
How jobless are retrained to work in mental
hospitals. Todays Health 43:8-9+ Ap '65
Magna charta: forerunner of the U.S. Con-
stitution. Todays Health 43:54-7 Je '65
Medicine at work in a disaster. Todays
Health 43:46-7+ Ap '65
EARLHAM college, Richmond, Ind.
Opening the classroom door. il Time 85:74
Je 11 '65
EARLY bird (artificial satellite) See Communi-
cations satellites
EARNINGS, Corporate. See Corporations—
Finance
EARNSHAW, Donald E.
Whippet; early American compact. Motor T
17:54-5 Je '65
EARPHONES
Earphone: sound's viewfinder. T. Schwartz.
il Pop Phot 56:24+ F '65
Private ear for silent TV viewing. S. Hahn.
il Pop Mech 125:196-7 Ja '66
To hear a symphony in your skull, try head-
phones. J. Wesson. U S Camera 28:28+ My
'65
EARRINGS
Airy lobes; pierced ears craze. Time 86:70
O 15 '65
Remarkable return of pierced ears. il Chang-
ing T 20:30 Ja '66
EARTH
See also
Cosmology
Geography
Magnetism, Terrestrial
Age
Lead isotopes and the age of the earth. G.
R. Tilton and R. H. Steiger. bibliog il
Science 150:1805-8 D 31 '65
Life 2.7 billion years old. Sci N L 87:339
My 29 '65
Still-earlier life. Sci Am 212:58 Je '65
Which is older, the earth or the sun? quiz.
J. Daugherty and M. Daugherty. il Sci
Digest 59:92-4 Ja '66

EARTH—*Continued*

Crust

See Earth—Surface

Figure

Earth has four corners. il Sci N L 87:390 Je 19 '65

Earth's shape. J. Ashbrook. il Sky & Tel 30: 83+ Ag '65

Internal structure

Composition of the earth's interior. T. Takahashi and W. A. Bassett. il Sci Am 212:100-6+ Je '65

New emphasis on studies of core of earth urged; Upper Mantle project. Sci N L 87:88 F 6 '65

USSR plans to drill through earth's crust. Sci N L 88:216 O 2 '65

See also
Mohole project

Shape

See Earth—Figure

Surface

Crust's origin indicated; mixture of rare-earth metals. Sci N L 88:195 S 25 '65

Terrestrial ratio of potassium to rubidium and the composition of earth's mantle. P. W. Gast. bibliog il Science 147:858-60 F 19 '65

See also
Earth tides
Faults (geology)

Temperature

See Earth temperature

EARTH, Photography of. See Space photography

EARTH magnetism. See Magnetism, Terrestrial

EARTH movements

See also
Earth tides
Seismology

EARTH moving machinery. See Excavating machinery

EARTH pollution. See Soil pollution

EARTH temperature

Terrestrial heat flow: measurement in lake bottoms. S. R. Hart and J. S. Steinhart. bibliog il Science 149:1499-501 S 24 '65

Terrestrial heat flow through salt-marsh peat. A. C. Redfield. bibliog il Science 148:1219-20 My 28 '65

EARTH tides

What we're learning about tides in the earth. A. Hamilton. il Sci Digest 58:55-8 N '65

EARTH waves. See Earthquakes

EARTHQUAKE detectors. See Seismographs

EARTHQUAKES

How to interpret earthquake recordings. il Pop Sci 187:139 D '65

Reduce earthquake deaths. Sci N L 88:283 O 30 '65

Resonant vibrations of the earth. F. Press. il Sci Am 213:28-37 bibliog(p 142) N '65

Seattle earthquake hits earth's weak belt. Sci N L 87:312 My 15 '65

Soliqueous matter may cause earthquakes. Sci N L 88:169 S 11 '65

When the earth rang like a bell. E. Ubell. Read Digest 87:179-80+ Ag '65

See also
Seismographs
Seismology

Research

Aftershocks of the 4 February 1965 Rat Island earthquake. J. N. Jordan and others. bibliog il Science 148:1323-5 Je 4 '65

Alaskan quake taught lesson in preparedness. Sci N L 87:230 Ap 10 '65

Earthquake areas mapped; prediction for southern California. Sci N L 88:215 O 2 '65

Earthquake forecasting. Sci Am 213:52-3 N '65

Earthquake prediction: ESSA and USGS vie for leadership. L. J. Carter. il Science 151: 181-3 Ja 14 '66

Earthquake prediction: OST panel recommends ten-year program. J. Walsh. Science 150:321-3 O 15 '65

One year later, what happened in Alaska. E. Crimmin. il Sci Digest 57:42-6 Mr '65

Predicting the shock: seismograph network to predict earth tremors. Bsns W p 135 O 16 '65

Science and space; U.S. to build seismic clusters. Newsweek 67:82 Ja 17 '66

Solving the riddle of the shuddering earth. L. Lessing. il Fortune 71:164-8+ F '65

Tectonic deformation associated with the 1964 Alaska earthquake. G. Plafker. bibliog il Science 148:1675-87 Je 25 '65

Alaska

Alaskan earthquake, 27 March 1964: vertical extent of faulting and elastic strain energy release. F. Press and D. Jackson. bibliog il Science 147:867-8 F 19 '65

Alaskan glaciers: recent observations in respect to the earthquake-advance theory. A. S. Post. bibliog il Science 148:366-8 Ap 16 '65

Anchorage's feet of clay. il Time 86:62 D 17 '65

Dangerous dirt; some damage in Anchorage earthquake caused by landslides. Sci Am 213:42 D '65

Medicine at work in a disaster. H. G. Earl. il Todays Health 43:46-7+ Ap '65

One year later, what happened in Alaska. E. Crimmin. il Sci Digest 57:42-6 Mr '65

Tectonic deformation associated with the 1964 Alaska earthquake. G. Plafker. bibliog il Science 148:1675-87 Je 25 '65

Aleutian Islands

Aftershocks of the 4 February 1965 Rat Island earthquake. J. N. Jordan and others. bibliog il Science 148:1323-5 Je 4 '65

Chile

August 16, 1906; excerpt from Alvaro and I. S. Guevara. Américas 17:29-32 Jl '65

Chile: the earthquake that one white rabbit survived. M. Acoca. il Life 58:32-32A Ap 9 '65

God and man. il Newsweek 65:63 Ap 12 '65

Quakes hit Chile, Greece. B. Tufty. il Sci N L 87:230 Ap 10 '65

Shakes again. il Time 85:34 Ap 9 '65

Greece, Modern

Quakes hit Chile, Greece. B. Tufty. il Sci N L 87:230 Ap 10 '65

Japan

Living on the brink; Matsushiro prediction. il Newsweek 67:82 Ja 17 '66

United States

California could get it too. Nation 200:210-11 Mr 1 '65

Place is coming apart; quake in Washington. Time 85:27 My 7 '65

Vicious month; Seattle quake and Mississippi floods. il Newsweek 65:45 My 10 '65

EARTHQUAKES and building

Some quake-resistant building designs poor: Alaskan study. Sci N L 87:345 My 29 '65

EARTHWORMS

What good are earthworms? Sunset 135:205 S '65

Worming tricks. H. G. Tapply. il Field & S 69:68 Ap '65

EAST, Ben

New facts on deadly snakes. Outdoor Life 136: 17-19+ Ag '65

World's biggest bass lakes. Outdoor Life 135: 33-5+ Je '65

(ed) See Fisher, R. I made my death bed

(ed) See Loebrich, G. Michigan's first elk hunt

EAST AFRICA. See Africa, East

EAST AFRICAN safari. See Automobile racing

EAST and West

Exotic and the erotic. L. Blanch. il Vogue 145:106-11+ Ap 15 '65

EAST BERLIN. See Berlin (East Berlin)

EAST BERLINERS. See Berliners

EAST GERMAN refugees. See Refugees, German

EAST GERMANS. See Germans

EAST GERMANY. See Germany (Democratic Republic)

EAST HAMPTON, N.Y.

Great schools from little schoolrooms grow. il Look 29:74 S 7 '65

EAST INDIANS in the West Indies

East Indian, West Indian. V. S. Naipaul. Reporter 32:35-7 Je 17 '65

EAST MEADOW, N.Y.

Trailers help to solve park refuse problem. il Am City 80:158 Ag '65

Trials of an interracial couple. il Ebony 20: 66-8+ O '65

EAST ORANGE, N.J.

Education

New community idea; East Orange plans an education plaza. G. L. Lynch; G. M. Skea. Recreation 58:236-7 My '65

EAST Side house settlement winter antiques show. See Antiques—Exhibitions

EAST-West relations. See International relations

EAST-West trade. See Communist countries—Commerce

EASTER
Word. V. P. McCorry. America 112:591-2 Ap
    17 '65
    See also
Holy week

Drama

Case of the forgetful Easter rabbit. H. L.
    Miller. Plays 24:63-9 Ap '65

Poetry

Every man's I A.D; Poem to be read back-
    wards and forward; Easter 1965. W. I.
    Elliott. Christian Cent 82:458 Ap 14 '65
Friday's work. T. Kretz. Christian Cent 82:
    458 Ap 14 '65
Third day. A. N. Wilder. Christian Cent 82:
    458 Ap 14 '65
EASTER bonnets. See Hats
EASTER business. See Retail trade
EASTER eggs
How to make an egghead, or an egg
    menagerie. il Sunset 134:97 Ap '65
EASTER ISLAND
Mystery of Easter Island. D. Cohen. il Sci
    Digest 58:84-6 O '65
EASTERLIN, John D.
Complete combustion with minimum excess
    air. Am City 80:99-101 F '65
EASTERN air lines
CAB awards Florida-Texas route to Eastern,
    affirming 1961 ruling. R. G. O'Lone. Avia-
    tion W 82:29 Je 7 '65
DC-9B will have greater range, capacity.
    J. R. Ashlock. Aviation W 82:29 Mr 8 '65
Eastern confident its jet shuttles will fly into
    Washington national. Aviation W 83:43 N
    15 '65
Eastern initiates cost savings program. Avi-
    ation W 82:37 F 1 '65
Eastern keys cargo resurgence to 727QC,
    expansion of staff. J. W. Carter. Aviation W
    83:41 N 8 '65
Eastern seeks major transpacific routes. W.
    Wright. il Aviation W 83:38-9 Ag 2 '65
Eastern shows reduced deficit. Aviation W
    82:30 F 15 '65
Eastern's aloft again. Bsns W p56-8+ Mr 13
    '65
Eastern's shuttle service. J. Ridgeway. New
    Repub 154:8-9 Ja 15 '66
Fare prodding elicits diverse responses. Avia-
    tion W 83:37-8 D 13 '65
Senate group may probe Eastern shuttle.
    J. R. Ashlock. Aviation W 83:27-8 Jl 26
    '65
Stress on planning key in EAL comeback.
    W. H. Gregory. il Aviation W 83:40-2 Ag
    2 '65
Sunrise at Eastern; increased profits. il
    Newsweek 65:76+ Mr 15 '65
EASTERN EUROPE. See Europe, Eastern
EASTERN GERMANY. See Germany (Demo-
    cratic Republic)
EASTERN Orthodox church. See Orthodox
    Eastern church
EASTERN Orthodox church in the United
    States. See Orthodox Eastern church in the
    United States
EASTERN test range. See Proving grounds
EASTLAKE, William
Kidding our Puritan conscience. Nation 202:
    22-3 Ja 3 '66
EASTLAND, James O.
Reds and civil rights: a senator's warning;
    excerpts from address, March 18, 1965. U S
    News 58:8 Mr 29 '65

about

James Eastland: child of scorn. R. G. Sher-
    rill. il por Nation 201:184-95 O 4 '65
EASTLAND shipwreck. See Shipwrecks
EASTMAN, Max
Man who wrote Moby Dick. Read Digest 86:
    182-4+ Mr '65

about

On coming home to poetry. J. Slater. por
    Sat R 48:30 F 6 '65
On how to be a revolutionary in your spare
    time. D. Cort. Commonweal 81:615-16 F 5
    '65
EASTMAN, P. D.
French dictionary; excerpt from Cat in the
    hat beginner book dictionary in French.
    McCalls 93:66+ N '65
EASTMAN Kodak company
Inside super 8: how it was developed at
    Eastman Kodak. J. S. Forney. il Pop Phot
    57:40-1+ D '65
Kodak picture, sunshine and shadow. R. Shee-
    han. il Fortune 71:126-9+ My '65
Kodak's other activities. N. Rothschild. Pop
    Phot 56:46+ Je '65

EASTMAN museum of photography. See Pho-
    tography—Galleries and museums
EASTON, D. Allan
Church on trial. Christian Cent 82:582 My 5
    '65
EASTON, David, and Dennis, Jack
Child's image of government. bibliog f Ann
    Am Acad 361:40-57 S '65
EATING
    See also
Diet
Food
EATING, Psychology of
Night eating; excerpts from Overweight so-
    ciety. P. Wyden. Ladies Home J 82:39-40+
    Ap '65
Opinion: on gluttony. K. Kellen. Mlle 61:25+
    O '65
EATOMETERS. See Physiological apparatus
EATON, Anne T.
Selected list of children's books. Common-
    weal 83:154-65 N 5 '65
EATON, Burnham
Look deep; poem. Horn Bk 41:259 Je '65
EATON, Charles Edward
Clown; poem. Reporter 32:33 Je 3 '65
Parure; poem. Reporter 33:42 Jl 15 '65
Tree-frog; poem. Sat R 48:130 Mr 13 '65
Turkey; poem. Reporter 33:46 D 2 '65
EATON, Jerome A.
Bulbs. Horticulture 43:20-1+ S '65
Home greenhouse. See issues of Flower
    grower, the home garden magazine
Living with orchids. House & Gard 128:
    290-1+ N '65
EATON, Quaintance
Bloomington. Opera N 30:26-30 Ja 8 '66
Great opera houses; the ghosts. Opera N 29:
    26-9 Mr 27 '65
Ladies on the loose. Opera N 30:32-4 O 23 '65
New World. Opera N 29:26-8 My 1 '65
Roots for Washington. Opera N 29:28-31 F
    13 '65
Steel city stage. Opera N 30:29-32 Ja 22 '66
EAVESDROPPING devices. See Electronics in
    criminal investigation, espionage, etc.
EBAN, Abba
Do we really need the UN? por Look 29:75-6
    Je 29 '65
Modern Israel. America 112:896-7 Je 26 '65
Reality and vision in the Middle East. For
    Affairs 43:626-38 Jl '65
EBEL, Fred E.
Night Ben Franklin called it a day. Pop Electr
    22:62-3+ Je '65
EBERHARD, Hans J. Müller-. See Müller-
    Eberhard, H. J.
EBERHART, E. T.
Fathers without children. Parents Mag 40:
    66-7+ Ap '65
EBERHART, Richard
Hill dream of youth, thirty years later; poem.
    Atlan 216:63 Jl '65
Matin pandemoniums; poem. New Yorker 41:
    42 Ap 10 '65

about

Choices and risks. M. Benedikt. Poetry 105:
    334-6 F '65
EBERT, Alan
(ed) Person who changed my life. Seventeen
    24:156-7+ Ap '65
EBLE, Kenneth
Ordinary anguish. Sat R 48:17 Jl 31 '65
EBONY (periodical)
Ebony's nativity; an evaluation from birth;
    with editorial comment. L. Hughes. il
    Ebony 21:27, 40-2+ N '65
Twenty years of Ebony. il Ebony 21:58-60+
    N '65
White problem; special issue on civil rights.
    il Newsweek 66:76 Ag 9 '65
ECCENTRIC dancing. See Dancing
ECCENTRICS and eccentricities
Charmers and cranks, by I. Ross. Review
    Newsweek il 65:106-7 Ap 19 '65
To eccentricity and beyond: fragmentation
    is part of college life; address, September
    10, 1964. G. Reddick. bibliog Vital Speeches
    31:310-16 Mr 1 '65
ECCLESIASTICAL architecture. See Church
    architecture
ECCLESIASTICAL law
Canon lawyer stereotype; remarks of Fr.
    P. Boyle. America 113:426 O 16 '65
ECHÁNOVE, Carlos A.
José Guadalupe Posada: engraver of Mexican
    life. Américas 17:28-35 N '65
ECHINODERMS
    See also
Crinoids
Starfishes
ECKER, R. E. See Smith, L. D. jt. auth.

ECONOMIC assistance, Domestic
Achievement motivation can be developed; recent experiments. D. C. McClelland. il Harvard Bsns R 43:6-8+ N '65
Appalachia as symbol; Appalachian regional development program. Nation 200:182 F 22 '65
Appalachia beyond free enterprise; the Appalachian regional development act. S. Harrington. il Commonweal 82:213-16 My 7 '65; Reply with rejoinder. E. Easterly. 82:426-7+ Je 25 '65
Bigger slice goes to poorer areas; geographic breakdown of federal spending made by M. L. Weidenbaum. il Bsns W p54+ N 27 '65
Billion for poor areas: just a beginning? U S News 58:14-15 F 15 '65
Coalition of conscience & power. il Time 86: 68+ S 3 '65
Depressed areas built to order. B. B. Van Dusen. Read Digest 86:79-82 My '65
Federal financing for library personnel; provided by Economic opportunity act. 1964; symposium. il Wilson Lib Bul 40:242-61 N '65
Great risk of the Great society. F. Morley. Nations Bsns 53:27-8 Mr '65
Great society: an old New deal. S. W. Rousseas. Nation 200:499-501 My 10 '65
How one billion for Appalachia will be spent. il U S News 58:12 Mr 15 '65
No more pork barrel: the Appalachia approach. J. Ter Horst. il Reporter 32:27-9 Mr 11 '65
Now the war on poverty is called political grab bag. il U S News 58:67-8 Ap 26 '65
Poor need money. E. M. Burns. il Nation 200:613-15 Je 7 '65
Proliferating Appalachias. D. Oberdorfer. il Reporter 33:22-3+ S 9 '65; Discussion. 33: 8+ O 7 '65
Speaking out; do we want to win the war on poverty? C. Jencks. Sat Eve Post 238:10+ Mr 13 '65
What big daddy, alias Uncle Sam, will do for you; Time essay. il Time 86:62-3 N 5 '65
See also
Anti-poverty program. 1964–
Appalachian Region—Recovery program. 1965–
United States—Job corps
Volunteers in service to America

ECONOMIC assistance, French
France's changing policy in Africa. P. Decraene. il Reporter 34:37-9 Ja 13 '66

ECONOMIC assistance, Japanese
Japan's role in south Asia. T. McNelly. il Cur Hist 49:284-93 N '65

ECONOMIC assistance, Russian
Exporting communism. R. Moley. Newsweek 66:72 Ag 2 '65
Soviet trade and aid. M. Kovner. bibliog f il Cur Hist 49:227-34 O '65
Soviet Union and the neutralist world. J. S. Reshetar, jr. bibliog f Ann Am Acad 362: 102-12 N '65
Ugly Russian, by V. Lasky. Review
Nat R il 17:731-2 Ag 24 '65. M. S. Evans

ECONOMIC assistance in Africa
Agricultural development in Africa; address, January 7, 1965. G. M. Williams. Dept State Bul 52:104-7 Ja 25 '65
U.S. program of economic assistance to Africa; statement, February 10, 1965. G. M. Williams. Dept State Bul 52:349-54 Mr 8 '65

ECONOMIC assistance in Asia
Behind the scenes in Vietnam: Asian development bank. H. Brandon. Sat R 48:10+ Ag 14 '65
Chance for Soviet-American diplomacy. H. Brandon. Sat R 48:18+ O 23 '65
Hopes for harnessing the Mekong. il Bsns W p 113 Ap 17 '65
LBJ's choice for aid-to-Asia job; southeast Asia. il U S News 58:22 Ap 19 '65
Mr Black reports on southeast Asia economic development; White House announcement, July 10, 1965. Dept State Bul 53:215 Ag 2 '65
On the Mekong; Mr Johnson's billion dollar offer. J. Ridgeway. New Repub 152:13-14 Ap 24 '65
President and Mr Black discuss Asian economic progress; statement, April 20, 1965. L. B. Johnson. Dept State Bul 52:719 My 10 '65
Progress and problems in the Far East; address, October 5, 1965. W. P. Bundy. Dept State Bul 53:709-16 N 1 '65
Southeast Asia aid program; statements, June 1 and June 3, 1965, and message to Congress. L. B. Johnson: D. Rusk. Dept State Bul 52:1054-60 Je 28 '65
Tragedy, disappointment, and progress in southeast Asia; statement, April 17, 1965. L. B. Johnson. Dept State Bul 52:650-2 My 3 '65

United States aid in Asia; symposium. bibliog f il Cur Hist 49:257-99+ N '65
U.S. peace plan for Asia: will it work? il U S News 58:35-7 Ap 19 '65
Why Johnson is ready to talk on Vietnam; offer of unconditional discussions and $1.billion aid program. il Bsns W p30-1 Ap 10 '65
See also
Colombo plan

ECONOMIC assistance in Cambodia
Thailand, Laos and Cambodia: a decade of aid. A. Roseman. Cur Hist 49:271-7+ N '65

ECONOMIC assistance in Central America
U.S. loan to support economic integration of Central America; remarks, July 29, 1965. L. B. Johnson; E. Delgado. Dept State Bul 53:330-2 Ag 23 '65

ECONOMIC assistance in Colombia
South America's shattered showcase. P. Siekman. il Fortune 72:164-9+ N '65

ECONOMIC assistance in Egypt
Reprieve for Nasser. G. Comte. Nat R 17:728 Ag 24 '65

ECONOMIC assistance in Ghana
When Nkrumah bit the hand that fed him; summary of Neocolonialism: the last stage of imperialism. K. Nkrumah. U S News 59:19 D 6 '65

ECONOMIC assistance in Honduras
Honduras: problems and prospects. W. S. Stokes. Cur Hist 50:22-6+ Ja '66

ECONOMIC assistance in India
India and Pakistan: the major recipients. N. D. Palmer. bibliog f il Cur Hist 49:262-70+ N '65
India dedicates Sharavathy hydroelectric project; address, January 24, 1965. C. Bowles. Dept State Bul 52:305-7 Mr 1 '65
Strong medicine for India. L. Hazard. Atlan 216:43-8 D '65

ECONOMIC assistance in Iran
Billion-dollar mystery; with editorial comment. F. J. Cook. il Nation 200:377-8, 380-97 Ap 12 '65
Iranian aid story: new twists to the mystery. F. J. Cook. Nation 200:550-6 My 24 '65

ECONOMIC assistance in Korea (Republic)
Korea after twelve years: saved from reds, but still in trouble. il U S News 58:46-8 My 31 '65

ECONOMIC assistance in Laos
Thailand, Laos and Cambodia: a decade of aid. A. Roseman. Cur Hist 49:271-7+ N '65

ECONOMIC assistance in Latin America
Housing and urban development in Latin America; address, June 14, 1965. J. H. Vaughn. Dept State Bul 53:66-70 Jl 12 '65
Review of U.S. policy in Latin America; report, September 10, 1965. J. H. Vaughn. Dept State Bul 53:548-9 O 4 '65
Revolution in Latin America. G. C. Lodge. For Affairs 44:173-97 Ja '66
See also
Alliance for progress
Inter-American development bank

ECONOMIC assistance in Nigeria
Should foreign aid include secondary education in Nigeria? L. C. Monroe. il Negro Hist Bul 28:128-9+ Mr '65

ECONOMIC assistance in Pakistan
India and Pakistan: the major recipients. N. D. Palmer. bibliog f il Cur Hist 49: 262-70+ N '65
Should a friend in need be a friend in deed? Time 86:23 Jl 23 '65

ECONOMIC assistance in Peru
Squeeze play. New Repub 154:6 Ja 22 '66
Transformation of peasant societies; report on symposium on Vicos, Peru, project. A. R. Holmberg and H. F. Dobyns. Science 147:1062+ F 26 '65

ECONOMIC assistance in Poland
Rebuilding the bridge to Poland. T. Atkins. il Reporter 32:39-41 F 25 '65

ECONOMIC assistance in southeast Asia. See Economic assistance in Asia

ECONOMIC assistance in Thailand
Thailand, Laos and Cambodia: a decade of aid. A. Roseman. Cur Hist 49:271-7+ N '65

ECONOMIC assistance in the Dominican Republic
Sugar, tourists, dollar aid and unrest on U.S. doorstep. il U S News 58:49-50 My 17 '65
U.S. aid while the bullets fly; the real Dominican story. A. Firfer. il U S News 59:48-50 Jl 19 '65

ECONOMIC assistance in the Philippines
Philippines: a unique effort. J. F. Melby. Cur Hist 49:278-83+ N '65

ECONOMIC assistance in the United Arab Republic
Congress upholds aid. Sr Schol 86:15 F 25 '65
Dealing with Nasser. Commonweal 81:628 F 12 '65
How many cheeks? House ban on surplusfood shipments. Reporter 32:10 F 11 '65

ECONOMIC assistance in Vietnam (Republic)
American aid to Vietnam. W. R. Fishel. il
Cur Hist 49:294-9 N '65
Other side of the Vietnam war; excerpts from
address, May 31, 1965. L. B. Johnson. il
U S News 58:22 My 24 '65
Report to the stockholders; war in Vietnam.
Nation 200:545 My 24 '65
Squaring the circle. il Newsweek 65:54+
Je 14 '65
Viet-Nam: the third face of the war; address,
May 13, 1965. L. B. Johnson. Dept State
Bul 52:838-41 My 31 '65
Vietnamese refugee problem. P. Geyelin. il
Reporter 33:43-5 S 23 '65
ECONOMIC change
Automation and change. Duns R 85:31 F '65
Staying on top of change; interview. J. W.
Tapp. Nations Bsns 53:46-8+ Ag '65
ECONOMIC commissions of the United Na-
tions. See name of commission under
United Nations, e.g. United Nations—Eco-
nomic commission for Africa
ECONOMIC conditions
Business abroad: another good year, for some.
il U S News 60:65-6 Ja 10 '66
Business around the world. See issues of U.S.
news & World report
International perspective on the world econ-
omy; statement, October 5, 1965. P.
De Seynes. UN Mo Chron 2:146-58 N '65
World economic problems; discussion in Sec-
ond committee; UN. UN Mo Chron 2:37-40
N '65
World economic trends surveyed in UN re-
port; summary. UN Mo Chron 2:41 Ag '65
See also
Business depression
Poverty
Social conditions
Standard of living
Underdeveloped areas
also subhead Economic conditions under
names of countries, states, etc. e.g.
France—Economic conditions
ECONOMIC conferences
Money theory comes back in style; high-
lights of University professors conference,
at Purdue. il Bsns W p 110+ S 18 '65
ECONOMIC cooperation. See Industrial coop-
eration; International cooperation
ECONOMIC development
America's commitment to social justice and
progress for all; excerpt from address, June
1, 1965. L. B. Johnson. Dept State Bul
52:1005-6 Je 21 '65
America's great success story. H. H. Hum-
phrey. Read Digest 87:71-4 D '65
Backward nations: aid and resources. W. C.
Paddock and P. Paddock. il Nation 200:414-
17 Ap 19 '65
Behind the mask of success; excerpt from
Our depleted society. S. Melman. Sat R
48:8-10+ Jl 31 '65
Concept of a national market and its eco-
nomic growth implications; address, Sep-
tember 1, 1965. W. W. Rostow. Dept State
Bul 53:518-24 S 27 '65
Development decade in the balance. G. D.
Woods. For Affairs 44:206-15 Ja '66
Disparities in progress among nations. T. C.
Mann. Ann Am Acad 360:63-7 Jl '65
Disparities in progress between nations; ad-
dress, April 9, 1965. T. C. Mann. Dept State
Bul 52:720-4 My 10 '65
Eastern Europe breaks out of its bonds;
special report. il Bsns W p 176-8+ N 20
'65
Economic development in Asia; address, April
23, 1965. W. W. Rostow. Dept State Bul
52:845-53 My 31 '65
Economic factors and political development.
W. Malenbaum. bibliog f Ann Am Acad
358:41-51 Mr '65
Economic growth brings industrial diseases.
Sci N L 88:280 O 30 '65
Efficiency and equity in welfare economics.
C. A. Zebot. bibliog f Mo Labor R 88:528-34
My '65
Effort of every man. H. Hazlitt. Newsweek
66:86 S 27 '65
From now to 1980: amazing growth; predic-
tion by McGraw-Hill economics dept. il
Bsns W p56-8+ O 16 '65
Interdependence of mankind; address, June 9,
1965. H. H. Humphrey. Dept State Bul 53:
56-9 Jl 12 '65
International action and the strategy of
development; half-way mark of the De-
velopment decade. P. de Seynes. UN Mo
Chron 2:55-8 F '65
Kariba case: manmade lakes and resource
development in Africa. T. Scudder. il Bul
Atomic Sci 21:6-11 D '65
Last revolution, by L. J. Lebrat. Review
Commonweal 83:250-2 N 26 '65. V. C.
Ferkiss

Let's outgrow the growth mania. D. Lam-
bert. il Nat Parks Mag 39:4-8 Ap '65
New books. W. J. Gibbons. Cath World 201:
334-5+ Ag '65
New era in world development. C. H. Malik.
America 113:496-8 O 30 '65
Pattern of development in Latin America;
with questions and answers. R. N. Adams.
il Ann Am Acad 360:1-26 Jl '65
Patterns, structures, of modernization and
political development. M. J. Levy, jr. Ann
Am Acad 358:29-40 Mr '65
Rate and costs of political development. M.
Halpern. bibliog f Ann Am Acad 358:20-8
Mr '65
Strengthening the international development
institutions; statement, July 9, 1965. A. E.
Stevenson. Dept State Bul 53:142-51 Jl 26
'65; Same with title International develop-
ment. Vital Speeches 31:610-16 Ag 1 '65
Toward a better life in larger freedom; state-
ment, October 15, 1965. J. Roosevelt. Dept
State Bul 53:798-805 N 15 '65
UN at twenty: Vision of a world economy.
A. Gabriel. il Nation 200:694-6 Je 28 '65
U.S. aid program in Asia. D. E. Lockwood.
bibliog f il Cur Hist 49:257-61+ N '65
What will be the instruments of Latin-
American advancement? address, April 10,
1965. R. M. Arias Espinosa. Ann Am Acad
360:78-84 Jl '65
See also
Development banks
United Nations—Economic commission for
Africa
ECONOMIC education. See Economics—Study
and teaching
ECONOMIC equality. See Equality
ECONOMIC forecasting. See Forecasts (eco-
nomics)
ECONOMIC geography. See Geography, Com-
mercial
ECONOMIC growth. See Economic development
ECONOMIC mobilization. See Industrial mobili-
zation
ECONOMIC opportunity, Office of. See United
States—Economic opportunity, Office of
ECONOMIC opportunity act, 1964. See Eco-
nomic assistance, Domestic
ECONOMIC organizations, International. See
International cooperation
ECONOMIC planning
Accidental century, by M. Harrington. Review
Life 59:11 Ag 20 '65. B. D. Nossiter
New world in the making, by D. Dolci. Re-
view
Sat R 48:61 O 30 '65. G. Gersh
See also
Committee for economic development
ECONOMIC planning, International
Crash next year? why it's a real danger, and
how it can be avoided. P. F. Drucker.
Harper 230:59-64 Je '65
Europe, the United States, and world trade;
address, February 4, 1965. C. A. Herter.
Dept State Bul 52:294-9 Mr 1 '65
Lesson the world hasn't learned: world a
unit in economic sense. D. Lawrence. U S
News 58:108 Mr 1 '65
UN at twenty: Vision of a world economy.
A. Gabriel. il Nation 200:694-6 Je 28 '65
What will be the instruments of Latin-
American advancement? address, April 10,
1965. R. M. Arias Espinosa. Ann Am Acad
360:78-84 Jl '65
See also
European economic community
United Nations—Technical assistance program
ECONOMIC policy
Money theory comes back in style; high-
lights of University professors conference.
at Purdue. il Bsns W p 110+ S 18 '65
ECONOMIC research
Studies of long-term economic growth; focus
on development of alternative projections
of the United States economy to 1970. J.
Alterman. Mo Labor R 88:983-7 Ag '65
See also
Brookings institution
ECONOMIC security. See Social and economic
security
ECONOMIC statistics
Economy at a glance; table. Sr Schol 86:9
Ap 15 '65
ECONOMIC status
See also
Students—Social and economic status
ECONOMIC theory. See Economics
ECONOMICS
Essays in the history of economics, by G.
Stigler. Review
Nat R 17:777-8+ S 7 '65. J. M. Buchanan;
Correction. 17:808 S 21 '65
New orthodoxy: Keynesian policies. H. Haz-
litt. Newsweek 65:82 Je 21 '65

ECONOMICS—*Continued*
On economic knowledge: toward a science of political economics, by A. Lowe. Review
  Reporter 33:46-8 Jl 15 '65. G. Colm
  Sci Am 212:139-40+ My '65 K. E. Boulding
Slippery path of prosperity; how to combine growth with full employment and stable prices. il Bsns W p70-3 Ja 1 '66
We are all Keynesians now. il Time 86:64-67B D 31 '65
  See also
Employment
Liquidity (economics)
Marketing

Bibliography
Development of economic thought. H. Hazlitt. Nat R 17:1102+ N 30 '65

Social and ethical aspects
Efficiency and equity in welfare economics. C. A. Zebot. bibliog f Mo Labor R 88:528-34 My '65

Study and teaching
Teaching the school teachers; Wharton focuses on secondary schools; with editorial comment. il Bsns W p63-4, 144 Ag 14 '65
Why Harvard still ranks first; oldest graduate economics department. il Bsns W p 118-20+ Ap 24 '65
Why there's more heat than light on economics; analysis by Professors G. L. Bach and P. Saunders of Carnegie institute of technology. il Bsns W p 147-8 My 29 '65

Terminology
Economics in the news (cont) il Sr Schol 86:22 F 4; 16 F 25; 25 Mr 4; 21 Mr 18; 22 Ap 8; 87:14-15 S 16; 12-13+ O 7; 16+ O 14; 12-13 O 21; 13-14 O 28; 21-2 N 4; 17-18 D 2; 21 D 9 '65

ECONOMICS, Agricultural. See Agriculture—Economic aspects
ECONOMICS and politics
Bastiat for '65. H. Hazlitt. Nat R 17:154-5 F 23 '65
ECONOMIST (London)
Top people's paper. il Newsweek 65:84 Ap 26 '65
ECONOMISTS
Brokers open doors to economy; economists as security analysts. il Bsns W p76+ N 6 '65
Value of practical eggheads. il Bsns W p52+ F 13 '65
Why there's more heat than light on economics; analysis by Professors G. L. Bach and P. Saunders of Carnegie institute of technology. il Bsns W p 147-8 My 29 '65
  See also
Keynes, J. M.
ECONOMY runs. See Automobile engines—Fuel consumption
ECTOHORMONES. See Pheromones
ECUADOR
  See also
Americans in Ecuador
Schools—Ecuador

Antiquities
See Indians of South America—Antiquities—Ecuador

Politics and government
Atlantic report. Atlan 216:12+ N '65
Impatience with the brass. Time 86:32 Jl 23 '65
Then there were three. Newsweek 66:54 D 13 '65

ECUADORIAN pottery. See Pottery, Ecuadorian
ECUADORIAN visitors in the United States. See Foreign visitors in the United States
ECUMENICAL council, 2d. See Vatican council, 2d
ECUMENICAL councils. See Councils and synods
ECUMENICAL movement
Beyond pronunciamentos. America 112:308 Mr 6 '65
Brisk unity advance. America 112:413 Mr 27 '65
Catholic and Protestant renewal. W. B. Blakemore. Cath World 201:183-8 Je '65
Church tomorrow, by G. H. Tavard. Review
  Commonweal 82:508 Jl 9 '65. E. E. Ryan
Common worship; reaction to the Vatican council's decree on ecumenism. America 112:626-7 My 1 '65
Dialogue with atheists; Pope Paul VI's efforts. America 112:186 F 6 '65

Ecumenical ennui? Cath World 201:22-6 Ap '65
Ecumenical escalation; concerning the schema De oecumenismo. R. M. Brown. Commonweal 81:787-90 Mr 19 '65
Ecumenical movement and the unity of the church, by T. A. Sartory. Review
  Christian Cent 82:304-5 Mr 10 '65. D. Ritschl
Ecumenical qualms; Protestant viewpoint. R. M. Brown. Commonweal 82:697-9 S 24 '65
Ecumenical risk-taking. L. A. Hoch. America 112:446 Ap 3 '65
Ecumenical scandal on Main Street, by W. B. Cate. Review
  Cath World 201:140 My '65. J. B. Sheerin.
Ecumenical suppers. America 112:700 My 15 '65
Ecumenism and converts; concerning speech by Cardinal Heenan. America 112:798 My 29 '65
Educational ecumenism. America 112:512 Ap 17 '65
Eyes to the past? B. Thompson. Christian Cent 82:947-8+ Jl 28 '65
Father Hecker, a bridge between Catholic and Protestant thought. R. T. Handy. Cath World 202:158-9+ D '65
Hold unprecedented ecumenical service; Protestant Episcopal and Roman Catholic joint worship service; discussion. Christian Cent 82:184 F 10 '65
Imperious ecumenism. Christian Cent 82: 1499-500 D 8 '65
It can't happen, but it does; disagreements within Protestantism, separating Christian groups. Christian Cent 82:1436 N 24 '65
Orthodox churches vis-a-vis the ecumenical movement; address, April 28, 1965. Iakovos Cath World 201:237-9 Jl '65
Pioneering for Christian unity. P. M. Minus, jr. America 114:117 Ja 22 '66
Primacy of the local. L. Peterson. Christian Cent 82:945-6 Jl 28 '65
Protestantism in an ecumenical age, by O. A. Piper. Review
  Christian Cent 82:1450-1 N 24 '65. D. G. Bloesch
Students talk of their faith; Joint consultation of Pax Romana and the World student Christian federation at Taizé. J. J. Megivern. America 112:636-8 My 1 '65
Switch or fight? representatives of three dissenting religions at Unitarian universalist fellowship meeting. Newsweek 65:84 My 3 '65
Those who don't want it. Time 86:59-60 Ag 27 '65
We stand or fall together. H. E. Fey. Christian Cent 82:612-14 My 12 '65; Discussion. 82:841 Je 30 '65
  See also
Church unity
Religious conferences
Religious cooperation
ECUMENICAL youth study conference. See Youth conferences
EDDE, Howard
How biological oxidation works in theory and practice. bibliog Am City 80:92-5 F '65
EDDY, Robert M.
Sermon on sex. Newsweek 66:77 Ag 9 '65
EDEL, Leon
Biography and the narrator. New Repub 152:25-7 Mr 6 '65
Good soldier himself. Sat R 48:23-4 S 4 '65
Henry James and the Nation. Nation 201: 237-40 S 20 '65
Literature and life style. Sat R 48:37-8 N 6 '65
Rage against the night. Sat R 48:34 My 29 '65
EDELMAN, Franz
Art and science of competitive bidding. Harvard Bsns R 43:53-66 Jl '65
EDELSON, Michael
How far have we come? il U S Camera 28: 32-3+ Ap '65
How pros edit contact sheets. U S Camera 28:62-5+ Ag '65
How to make a quality print. U S Camera 28:52-3+ S '65
Shoot for quality. U S Camera 28:52-3+ My '65
35mm color films. il U S Camera 28:60-3+ S '65
—and Keppler, Herbert
Close-up which lenses? Mod Phot 29:76-9 Mr '65
EDEMA
Hereditary angioneurotic edema: two genetic variants. F. S. Rosen and others. bibliog il Science 148:957-8 My 14 '65
EDEN, Anthony, 1st earl of Avon. See Avon, A. E.

EDER, George Jackson
Urban concentration, agriculture, and agrarian reform; with questions and answers. bibliog f Ann Am Acad 360:27-47 Jl '65

EDER, Richard
Colombia's dangerous doldrums. Reporter 33:36-8 O 7 '65

EDGAR, Barry
How to take your pet to Europe. House & Gard 128:88+ S '65

EDGAR, Natalie
Importance of being casual. Art N 64:44-5 D '65
Satisfactions of Robert Motherwell. Art N 64:38-41+ O '65

EDGAR, R. S. and Epstein, R. H.
Genetics of a bacterial virus; with biographical sketches. Sci Am 212:16, 70-8 F '65

EDGAR Allan Poe awards. See Mystery writers of America

EDGERLEY, W. E. See Wester, R. E. jt. auth.

EDGERLY, William S. See Dearden, J. jt. auth.

EDGERTON, Henry W.
Vietnam policy; letter. New Repub 152:28-30 My 22 '65

EDGERTON, William H.
Building construction costs. See issues of Architectural record

EDGINGS, Garden. See Garden borders

EDIBLE plants. See Plants, Food

EDINBURGH

Description

Edinburgh boyhood. J. I. M. Stewart. il Holiday 38:60-71+ Ag '65

EDINGER, Lois V.
Big meeting in the big town. NEA J 54:20-1 My '65
Our New York city convention. NEA J 54:42 F '65

EDISON, Thomas Alva
Man who was tired of glory; excerpt from Biography of an idea. E. L. Bernays. por Fortune 72:138-9 O '65
Some mysterious Edison diamond discs. J. Walsh. il Hobbies 70:34-6 Ag '65

EDISON institute. See Henry Ford museum and Greenfield Village, Dearborn, Mich.

EDIT, Incorporated
William Nicoll and Edit, inc. P. A. Bennett. il Pub W 188:88-92 D 6 '65

EDITING. See Editors and editing

EDITING moving pictures. See Moving pictures —Editing

EDITORIAL referees. See Editors and editing

EDITORS and editing
Article queries that sell. M. Gunther. Writer 78:19-21+ Ag '65
Editors are helpful ogres. R. C. Payes. Writer 78:27-8 Mr '65
Editor's trade. J. Fischer. Harper 231:16+ Jl '65; Discussion. 231:10+ S '65
Final approach. M. Lodeesen. Writer 78:12-13 Jl '65
Helen Gurley Brown turns editor. C. Welles. il Life 59:65-6+ N 19 '65
In defense of editing. N. Podhoretz. il Harper 231:143-7 O '65
In the crusading tradition. J. Daniels. Sat R 48:142-4 Mr 13 '65
Mailbag (a letter to would-be summer editors) J. Ciardi. Sat R 48:22 F 20 '65
Needless pains caused by heedless editors; letter. I. H. Page. Science 147:1241 Mr 12 '65; Discussion. 148:443-4, 1174; 149:8, 815 Ap 23, My 28, Jl 2, Ag 20 '65
New direction for Cosmopolitan. H. G. Brown. Writer 78:20 Jl '65
Off the cuff. L. Conger. Writer 78:7-8 My '65
Ones that got away. A. E. Jones. Writer 78:17-18+ My '65
Personal note. F. Kirchwey. Nation 201:27-35 S 20 '65
Reaching toward a higher sophistication. E. Goble. Arch Rec 137:9 My '65
Roy Lindstrom, artist & art director. F. Johnson. il Am Artist 29:50-5+ D '65
Rules for referees: scientific literature. B. K. Forscher. Science 150:319-21 O 15 '65; Discussion. 150:1407-8 D 10 '65
Ten pointers for new article writers. E. H. Matthew. Writer 79:29-30 Ja '66
Transatlantic editing. G. A. Hogarth. Horn Bk 41:520-3 O '65
See also
Villard, O. G.
Women as editors

EDLUND, Paul E.
Continuing quest: care of LC's collections. por Library J 90:3397-402 S 1 '65

EDMAN, David A.
Prayermongering at the public library. Christian Cent 82:462-6 Ap 14 '65

EDMINSTER, Frank C.
Landscaping rural America. Travel 124:30-5 D '65

EDSON, Russell
World dances between our eyes. K. Irby. Poetry 105:418 Mr '65

EDUCATION
Corporation as a college; continuing education in the business world. N. W. Chamberlain. Atlan 215:102-4 Je '65
Do school boards take education seriously? J. Wallace and P. Schneider. il Sat R 48:89-90+ O 16 '65
New strategy for development; excerpts from address, July 9, 1965. R. Maheu. UNESCO Courier 18:10 O '65
Role of paperback books in education examined in depth; summary of conference at Teachers college, Columbia university; with editorial comment. il Pub W 188:13-27, 40 N 1 '65
Teaching and the expanding knowledge. A. Szent-Györgyi; reply. W. F. Battig. Science 147:558 F 5 '65
See also
Catholic church—Education
Correspondence schools and courses
Courses of study
Culture
Home study
Illiteracy
Knowledge, Theory of
Learning, Psychology of
Learning and scholarship
Motivation (education)
Schools
Teaching
also Business education; Religious education; and similar headings

Aims and objectives

Are we educating our children for the wrong future? R. M. Hutchins. il Sat R 48:66-7+ S 11 '65
Case for a narrow education. R. L. Dean. America 112:553 Ap 17 '65
College education for what? W. C. Booth. il NEA J 54:14-16 D '65
Dichotomies in American education. J. J. Van Patten. Sch & Soc 93:474-5 D 11 '65
Education is for thinking. R. D. Patton. Sch & Soc 93:429-30 N 13 '65
Education: what kind, for whom, how much? with study-discussion program, by C. Smallenburg and H. Smallenburg. G. L. Mangum. bibliog il PTA Mag 60:4-7, 34-5 N '65
Excellence in education: foundation of the Great society; excerpt from address, November 24, 1964. H. H. Humphrey. Sch & Soc 93:175-7 Mr 20 '65
Genius of American education, by L. A. Cremin. Review
   Sat R 48:94-5 O 16 '65. F. G. Jennings
How children fail, by J. Holt. Review
   Commonweal 82:386-7 Je 11 '65. N. Hentoff
Intelligence, information, and education; address, September 28, 1964. R. W. Gerard. bibliog Science 148:762-5 My 7 '65
Relation of the school to the social order; excerpt from Formative ideas in American education. V. T. Thayer. bibliog f Sch & Soc 93:183-96 Mr 20 '65
School enrichment; what it is and is not. il Good H 162:138 Ja '66
Toward a theory of education for development; excerpt from Education and the development of nations. J. W. Hanson and C. S. Brembeck. Sch & Soc 93:499-502 D 25 '65
What I have learned: first glimpses of a new world; retrospective and personal summing-up. R. M. Hutchins. Sat R 48:33-5+ D 4 '65

Anecdotes, facetiae, satire, etc.

Grassy. J. Stuart. il NEA J 54:53-4 D '65

Bibliography

Editor's bookshelf. P. Woodring. See issues of Saturday review
Foreign books for educators. W. W. Brickman. Sch & Soc 93:125-34, 406-12 F 20, O 30 '65
New books (cont) Sat R 48:87-8 F 20; 81 Ap 17; 83 My 15 '65
New books for your professional shelf. H. L. Hurwitz. il Sr Schol 86:sup 16-17+ Mr 4 '65
New paperbacks for high school teachers; new professional books. H. L. Hurwitz. il Sr Schol 87:sup24-5+ O 28 '65
Outstanding education books of 1964. NEA J 54:66-9 My '65

EDUCATION—Bibliography—*Continued*
Paperbacks and professional growth; excerpts from address, 1965. W. E. Hoth. Sr Schol 87:sup36 O 28 '65
U.S. books for educators. W. W. Brickman. Sch & Soc 93:320-6+, 505-8+ Sum, D 25 '65

Curricula
See Courses of study

Economic aspects
Education and our present social problems; reprint of a 1933 article. J. Dewey. Sch & Soc 93:39-43 Ja 23 '65
Rib cage of a mighty giant; economy's non-economic supports. il Sr Schol 86:10-11 Ap 15 '65
Tax credits for education. New Repub 152:8 F 13 '65
See also
Colleges and universities—Finance

Exhibitions
NCSS exhibit notes. Sr Schol 87:sup20 D 9 '65
NCTE: exhibit highlights. Sr Schol 87:sup 15 D 9 '65

Federal aid
See Federal aid to education

Finance
See School finance

History
Ancestors of the ball-point pen. L. Pareti. il UNESCO Courier 18:25-7 My '65
Educational history of the western world, by A. E. Meyer. Review
    Sat R 48:66 Jl 17 '65. J. L. Gorin
1965 as a centennial year in the history of education. F. Parker. Sch & Soc 93:85-6 F 6 '65
See also
Education—United States—History

International aspects
Come in, world. See issues of PTA magazine
Education and international understanding. F. Keppel. Dept State Bul 53:812-15 N 22 '65
See also
International education
United Nations educational, scientific and cultural organization

International cooperation
International program in educational administration. Sch & Soc 93:517 D 25 '65
Next, the Great global society; worldwide educational endeavor. Time 86:26 S 24 '65

Objectives
See Education—Aims and objectives

Periodicals
See also
American education (periodical)
School and society (periodical)

Philosophy
Danger of complacency; reprint of a 1952 article. I. L. Kandel. Sch & Soc 93:58-63 Ja 23 '65
Deeper bases of policy in higher education; excerpt from Bases for policy in higher education. J. S. Brubacher. bibliog f Sch & Soc 93:308-19 Sum '65
Philosophy of the New education; reprint of a 1941 article. W. H. Kilpatrick. Sch & Soc 93:56-8 Ja 23 '65
Why teachers fail; address. B. F. Skinner. il Sat R 48:80-1+ O 16 '65

Standards
AFT head asks national standards; statements. Sr Schol 87:sup2 D 9 '65
Big-city schools in trouble resegregation in North. il U S News 59:44-7 S 27 '65
Standards in teacher education and the new image makers. B. Mehl. Sch & Soc 93:81-2 F 6 '65
What's bugging teachers. A. M. West. Sat R 48:88 O 16 '65

State control
See Education and state

Statistics
In school this autumn; more than a fourth of U.S. population. il U S News 59:6 S 6 '65
Magnitude of the American educational establishment, fall 1965. il Sat R 48:68-70 S 11 '65

Statistic of the month. See issues of American education
Washington report. J. Lloyd. Sr Schol 87:sup3 O 21 '65
See also
School attendance

Terminology
Accounting for every pupil; Terms and definitions. J. F. Putnam. Sch Life 47:31-3 D '64

Africa
When foreign-student scholarships are misused. C. Haussamen. il Sat R 48:48-50+ Ag 21 '65
See also
Negro schools—Alabama

Alabama
See also
Negro schools—Alabama

Appalachian Region
Mountain of books for mountain children; PTA project, Books for Appalachia. E. May. il PTA Mag 60:8-10 S '65
Schools of Appalachia. P. Schrag. il Sat R 48:70-1+ My 15 '65
See also
Hazard, Ky.—Education

Argentina
From the editor. Am Ed 1:inside cover Ap '65

Arkansas
Will evolution come to Arkansas? T. Dearmore. Reporter 34:34 Ja 13 '66
See also
School laws and legislation—Arkansas

Asia
When foreign-student scholarships are misused. C. Haussamen. il Sat R 48:48-50+ Ag 21 '65
See also
Private schools—Australia

Australia
See also
Private schools—Australia

California
Theory of maximum use: flexible scheduling; Hueneme school district, Port Hueneme, Calif. libraries. P. M. Sturm. Library J 90:2341 My 15 '65

China (People's Republic)
New citizens for a new society. T. H. E. Chen. bibliog f il Cur Hist 49:155-63 S '65

Colombia
Students strike in Colombia. M. M. Loftus. America 113:98 Jl 24 '65

Congo (capital Leopoldville)
See also
Colleges and universities—Congo (capital Leopoldville)

Connecticut
Do-it-yourself in Granby; experiment to improve educational opportunities. E. D. Stevens. il Sat R 48:62-3 Jl 17 '65
See also
Darien, Conn.—Education
Greenwich, Conn.—Education

Cuba
Exclusive! Cuban education: on-the-spot interviews; ed. by W. Johnson. il Sr Schol 87:sup 1-2, 17-18 N 18 '65

Denmark
See also
Schools—Denmark

District of Columbia
See Washington, D.C.—Education

Egypt
See also
Colleges and universities—Egypt

England
See Education—Great Britain

Europe, Western
European students strike for academic reforms. D. C. Watt. il Reporter 33:42-4 D 16 '65
What we can learn from schools abroad. N. L. Beach. il Sr Schol 86:sup9 My 20 '65

Florida
Where a school of the future is holding classes today; complete education on one campus, South Florida education center, Broward County. il U S News 59:36-9 Jl 5 '65

France
Stab in the bac? il Newsweek 65:40 Je 28 '65

EDUCATION—*Continued*

Germany (Federal Republic)

Political conscience for West German youth. S. M. Shafer. il Sr Schol 86:sup 13 My 20 '65

Third debacle? il Time 86:54 Jl 16 '65

What German boys say about Hitler. D. Schoenbaum. il N Y Times Mag p30-1+ Ja 9 '66

Great Britain

American's impressions: audio visuals in Britain. R. H. Burgert. Sr Schol 87:sup8 O 28 '65

British Commonwealth cooperation in education. Sch & Soc 93:105-6 F 6 '65

Catholic schools in Britain. M. P. Fogarty. Commonweal 83:13-14+ O 8 '65

Leicestershire plan: breakthrough in British education. S. C. Mason. il Sr Schol 86:sup 11 My 20 '65

New directions for British education? M. N. Hennessy. il Sat R 48:58-9+ Ag 21 '65

Privileged education in Britain; future of separate, but not equal schools. B. Wenham. New Repub 153:10-12 D 11 '65

Quality: U.S. v. British; first factual evidence. il Time 86:48 D 3 '65

Shoddy revolution in British education. D. Colville. Yale R 54:464-77 Mr '65

Social service projects in English schools. R. Kirk. Sch & Soc 93:476-7 D 11 '65

Social studies in British schools. R. E. Gross. il Sr Schol 87:sup36-8 S 23 '65

Swot shop; Manchester grammer school considered best secondary school. il Newsweek 66:70 D 6 '65

See also
Schools—England

Greece, Modern

Recent educational tendencies in Greece; excerpt from Tradition and change in education: a comparative study. A. M. Kazamias and B. G. Massialas. bibliog f Sch & Soc 93:275-80 My 1 '65

Guatemala

Petronillo learns to write his name; Guatemala's literacy campaign. A. Howard. il N Y Times Mag p26-7+ F 7 '65

Illinois

See also
Chicago—Education

India

India trains teachers for a new age. E. S. Obourn. il Am Ed 1:16-22 Mr '65

Indiana

See also
Indianapolis—Education

Iowa

Old Order; Amish families defy Iowa education authorities. il Newsweek 66:38 D 6 '65

Iran

Iran's education corps and illiteracy. S. Bella. Sch & Soc 93:156-7 Mr 6 '65

Israel

Integrating the two Israels; Jews from Europe and from north Africa or Asia. H. L. Hurwitz. il Sr Schol 87:sup 18+ S 23 '65

Prejudice in Israel; Jews from north Africa and Asia, Oriental Jews. J. R. Moskin. il Look 29:67+ O 5 '65

Italy

Training for adult education and rural development in southern Italy; National union for the struggle against illiteracy. M. Tabellini. Sch & Soc 93:395-6 O 30 '65

Kentucky

Case of the shocking-purple school. J. Fetterman. Good H 161:276 N '65

See also
Hazard, Ky.—Education
Lexington, Ky.—Education
Louisville—Education

Korea (People's Democratic Republic)

North Korea: nation at school. R. Berger. Nation 200:530-1 My 17 '65

Latin America

Facts and figures of the Americas. il Américas 17:46-7 My '65

Planning for education. G. Meek. il Américas 17:16-17 Mr '65

Three pillars of progress; education, science, culture. J. Posada. il Américas 17:24-9 Ap '65

Maryland

Best weapon in the fight for better education; question of school boards and quality of schools. B. Asbell. il Redbook 125:58-9+ My '65

School libraries: reflections; Harker preparatory school, Potomac, Md. M. H. Lord. Wilson Lib Bul 39:587 Mr '65

See also
Baltimore—Education

Massachusetts

Another first for Massachusetts; ban de facto school segregation. il Time 86:56 Ag 27 '65

See also
Boston—Education

Michigan

New era in Michigan education. L. M. Bartlett. Sr Schol 86:sup 10-11 Mr 25 '65

Shared time in action, case history; Cheboygan. il U S News 58:54 My 3 '65

Sharing good teaching practices. R. O. Lippitt and M. P. Flanders. il NEA J 54:30-2 D '65

Missouri

See also
St Louis—Education

Nevada

See also
Las Vegas—Education

New Jersey

Paperbacks on the march; concerning paperbound books in New Jersey public schools. M. Bogart. il Sr Schol 87:sup21-2 O 28 '65

Profile of a high school; New Jersey paperback study. Sr Schol 87:sup22-3 O 28 '65

New York (state)

Aid for all; state to pay the full cost of textbooks in public schools. America 112:796 My 29 '65

Head start in suburbia; Yorktown, Westchester County. J. Nagy. il Sat R 48:62+ D 18 '65

Humanities in the ninth grade introduced in project Cue. Library J 90:1999-2000 Ap 15 '65

New York textbook bill. America 112:512 Ap 17 '65

Nigeria

Should foreign aid include secondary education in Nigeria? L. C. Monroe. il Negro Hist Bul 28:128-9+ Mr '65

North Carolina

Catching failures in time; costly public boarding school in Winston-Salem for underachievers. il Time 85:49-50 Mr 19 '65

Innovations in foreign language instruction. T. T. Ladu. il Sr Schol 87:sup 16-17 O 14 '65

Oklahoma

Behind a controversy over pay for teachers. U S News 58:16 My 24 '65

Oklahoma's education war; NEA sanctions. S. Kalkstein. il Look 30:80+ Ja 25 '66

Showdown in Oklahoma; battle for more state aid. Time 85:49 Je 4 '65

Subminimal Oklahoma; NEA imposes sanctions because of bad academic conditions. Newsweek 65:64 My 24 '65

Teachers give Oklahoma a lesson; NEA sanctions against state. B. Carter. Reporter 33:34-7 S 9 '65

Oregon

Breakthrough for professional autonomy; status of teaching profession in Oregon. E. S. Crowley. NEA J 54:46-7 N '65

See also
Portland, Ore.—Education

Pennsylvania

See also
Pittsburgh—Education

Peru

See also
Colleges and universities—Peru

Philippines

Philippine science school. Sci N L 87:132 F 27 '65

Russia

Campaign against religion in Soviet schools. W. W. Brickman. Sch & Soc 93:73 F 6 '65

Cuckoo's egg in the Britannica; misleading derogatory comparisons between the Soviet Union and the United States in Britannica book of the year, 1965. R. A. Freeman. il Nat R 17:514-18 Je 15 '65

EDUCATION—Russia—*Continued*
Soviet education in 1964. I. Schlesinger. bibliog f Sch & Soc 93:270-1 My 1 '65
Soviet education's unsolved problems. H. J. Noah. il Sat R 48:54-6+ Ag 21 '65
See also
Colleges and universities—Russia

Saskatchewan
Public-private school upheaval. G. Lane. Christian Cent 82:378-80 Mr 24 '65

Scotland
See also
Schools—Scotland

South Africa
Higher learning for the Bantu; separate institutions under the policy of apartheid. R. Kirk. Nat R 17:150 F 23 '65

South America
See Education—Latin America

Southern states
Black and white schools; separate and unequal schools in South. New Repub 153:5-6 O 9 '65
Integration takes hold in southern schools. il U S News 59:40 S 13 '65
Segregation by integration; problem of Negro teachers. Time 85:58+ Je 18 '65
South; educational resources; address, April 1965. R. Sarratt. il Wilson Lib Bul 39:860-6 Je '65
Title VI; southern education faces the facts; guidelines to school authorities. G. W. Foster, jr. il Sat R 48:60-1+ Mr 20 '65
Toward the new South; Southern region conference. Newsweek 66:65 D 13 '65
Year of compliance. Newsweek 66:19-20 S 6 '65

Southwestern states
Educating Spanish-speaking children. Sch & Soc 93:388 O 30 '65

Spain
Cry for liberty; students' defiance of government. Newsweek 66:33-4 D 27 '65
See also
Colleges and universities—Spain

Switzerland
See also
Schools—Switzerland

Texas
Integrating the Negro teacher out of a job; dilemma in Munday. B. Carter. il Reporter 33:31-3 Ag 12 '65; Discussion. 33:10+ S 23 '65
See also
Austin, Tex.—Education
Colleges and universities—Texas

Thailand
Thailand diary. L. R. Shotwell. NEA J 54:44 O '65

Underdeveloped areas
Can the U.S. teach whole world to read? school aid for backward lands. Bsns W p34 O 23 '65
Putting space to work to educate the world; Johnson plan. il Bsns W p 17 D 25 '65
Toward a theory of education for development; excerpt from Education and the development of nations. J. W. Hanson and C. S. Brembeck. Sch & Soc 93:499-502 D 25 '65

United States
Capital gains. J. Moorhead. PTA Mag 60:2-3 N '65
Cuckoo's egg in the Britannica; misleading derogatory comparisons between the Soviet Union and the United States in Britannica book of the year, 1965. R. A. Freeman. il Nat R 17:514-18 Je 15 '65
Danger of complacency; reprint of a 1952 article. I. L. Kandel. Sch & Soc 93:58-63 Ja 23 '65
Doctor James B. Conant answers questions you ask about schools. J. B. Conant. Changing T 20:24-9 Ja '66
Education in America; ed. by P. Woodring and J. Cass. See issues of Saturday review
Education in 1965; major educational events. W. W. Brickman. Sch & Soc 93:491-2 D 25 '65
Education is for thinking. R. D. Patton. Sch & Soc 93:429-30 N 13 '65
Educational values in disorder. J. Justman. Sch & Soc 93:147-50 Mr 6 '65
Education's faceless factories shortchange our students. F. Morley. il Nations Bsns 53:27-8 F '65

Excellence in education: foundation of the Great society; excerpt from address, November 24, 1964. H. H. Humphrey. Sch & Soc 93:175-7 Mr 20 '65
Faddishness in education. M. Smith. Sat R 48:53 Ag 21 '65
Full educational opportunity; key points of President's message. L. B. Johnson. Sat R 48:84-5 F 20 '65
Genius of American education, by L. A. Cremin. Review
Sat R 48:94-5 O 16 '65. F. G. Jennings
How children fail, by J. Holt. Review
Commonweal 82:386-7 Je 11 '65. N. Hentoff
How much have our schools improved since Sputnik? questions and answers. G. Hechinger and F. M. Hechinger. il McCalls 92:94 F '65
How sinister is the education establishment? D. W. Robinson; reply. M. E. Doyle. Sat R 48:96 F 20 '65
Johnson education bill. W. B. Ball. Commonweal 81:638-40 F 12 '65
LBJ's school program; a revolution in American education? C. Jencks. New Repub 152:17-20 F 6 '65
Magnitude of the American educational establishment, fall 1965. il Sat R 48:68-70 S 11 '65
Message from the President to all who work with youth. L. B. Johnson. Am Ed 1:27 S '65
Metropolitan education; address, January 27, 1965. R. M. Besse. Vital Speeches 31:307-10 Mr 1 '65
Morality and the public school; address, March 18,1965. J. P. Leary. Vital Speeches 31:427-30 My 1 '65
More education needed. Sci N L 87:70 Ja 30 '65
New careers in America's classrooms. L. Velie. Read Digest 86:78-82 F '65
News and trends. See issues of NEA journal
Organizing for continuing change. F. A. J. Ianni and B. D. McNeill. il Sat R 48:55-6+ Je 19 '65
Our children deserve the best in education. H. H. Humphrey. Parents Mag 40:40+ S '65
President Johnson on education; text of remarks, July 2, 1965. L. B. Johnson. Sch & Soc 93:351-4 O 2 '65
President Kennedy and education; excerpt from John F. Kennedy on education. W. T. O'Hara. bibliog f Sch & Soc 93:444-50+ N 27 '65
Quality: U.S. v. British; first factual evidence. il Time 86:48 D 3 '65
Redbook dialogue. C. Heston; R. Hutchins. Redbook 126:68-9+ D '65
Relation of the school to the social order; excerpt from Formative ideas in American education. V. T. Thayer. bibliog f Sch & Soc 93:183-96 Mr 20 '65
Revolution in the schools, by R. Gross and J. Murphy. Review
Commonweal 82:731-2 O 1 '65. J. J. McDermott
Rising levels of education among young workers. J. D. Cowhig and C. L. Beale. il Mo Labor R 88:625-8 Je '65
Role of the states in education; address, July 27, 1965. J. B. Conant. Vital Speeches 31:686-8 S 1 '65
Schools make news (cont) Sat R 48:80-1 Ap 17; 58 Jl 17; 74 S 11; 91 O 16 '65
Transatlantic view of American education. M. Whitney. il Sat R 48:66-7 Mr 20 '65
Two exercises in educational policy making; excerpt from Cheerful prospect; a statement on the future of American education. C. S. Benson. il Sch & Soc 93:305-8 Sum '65
Washington report. J .Lloyd. Sr Schol 86:14T F 4: sup3 My 20; 87:sup3 O 14 '65
What's happening in education? W. D. Boutwell. See issues of PTA magazine
What's happening in education? middle schools. W. D. Boutwell. PTA Mag 60:14 D '65
While school keeps. J. Cass. See issues of Saturday review
See also
American education week
Education and democracy
Education and state
Education of women—United States
High schools
Indians of North America—Education
Jews—Education
National academy of education
National education association
Negroes in the United States—Education
Public schools—United States
School laws and legislation—United States
Service men, Discharged—Education
United States—Education, Office of
Vocational education
White House conference on education, 1965

EDUCATION—United States—*Continued*

Bibliography

Review of books. H. Sondericker. il Sr Schol 87:sup 10 S 30 '65

History

Education for Democracy; address, November 14, 1964. F. Mayer. Vital Speeches 31:254-6 F 1 '65

Evaluations of American education by foreigners; excerpt from Schools in an age of mass culture. W. Rudy. bibliog f Sch & Soc 93:93-104 F 6 '65

Making history; proposed three-volume comprehensive history of American education. Newsweek 65:58 Mr 8 '65

Vietnam (Republic)

With Senior's editor in Viet Nam; questions and answers. R. Hemming. il Sr Schol 86:12-13 Mr 4 '65

Virginia

Green Hedges. F. F. Kilmer. Horn Bk 41: 598-601 D '65

They closed their schools, by B. Smith. Review

Sat R 48:67-8 Jl 17 '65. P. Johnson

When school stopped; case of Prince Edward County. Newsweek 66:81 N 15 '65

Washington (state)

POINT points the way; Project for the orientation and induction of new teachers. V. B. Archer and others. NEA J 54:29-30 O '65

Triumph of a stubborn lady. J. Poppy. il Look 29:64-6+ F 9 '65

See also

Seattle—Education

West Virginia

Head start in West Virginia. B. François. il Sat R 48:61 D 18 '65

See also

Milwaukee—Education

EDUCATION, Adult. See Adult education

EDUCATION, Boards of. See School boards

EDUCATION, Commissioner of. See United States—Education, Office of

EDUCATION, Comparative

Education in modern and primitive societies; excerpt from Educational anthropology. G. F. Kneller. bibliog f Sch & Soc 93:158-63 Mr 6 '65

School that smiles. E. Ferber. il Am Ed 1: 8-10 S '65

EDUCATION, Cooperative

Job that buys a dream; work-study programs. J. T. Farrell. il Am Ed 1:1-4 O '65

EDUCATION, Elementary

Compact K-1 addition features carpets and flexible plan. il Arch Rec 137:172-3 Mr '65

Meeting children where they are; non-graded classes at University elementary school, University of California, Los Angeles. J. I. Goodlad. il Sat R 48:57-9+ Mr 20 '65

Response in elementary education; excerpt from Change and challenge in American education. J. E. Russell. Sch & Soc 93:120-4 F 20 '65

There's a fire truck in the hall; a child's-eye view of modern education. W. Stanton. il Redbook 126:44-5+ Ja '66

Why I don't believe in speeding up primary education. B. Spock. Redbook 125:26+ O '65

See also

Education of children

Montessori method of education

National education association—Department of elementary school principals

EDUCATION, Experimental

See also

Progressive education

EDUCATION, Higher. See College education; Colleges and universities

EDUCATION, Individual. See Individual instruction

EDUCATION, International. See International education

EDUCATION, Liberal. See Liberal education

EDUCATION, Medical. See Medical education

EDUCATION, Musical. See Music—Instruction and study; Musical education

EDUCATION, Nutrition. See Nutrition education

EDUCATION, Office of. See United States—Education, Office of

EDUCATION, Parent. See Parent education

EDUCATION, Physical. See Physical education and training

EDUCATION, Primary. See Education, Elementary

EDUCATION, Primitive

Education in modern and primitive societies; excerpt from Educational anthropology. G. F. Kneller. bibliog f Sch & Soc 93:158-63 Mr 6 '65

EDUCATION, Progressive. See Progressive education

EDUCATION, Religious. See Religious education

EDUCATION, Rural. See Rural schools

EDUCATION, Scientific. See Scientific education

EDUCATION, Secondary

Quality secondary schools of the future (cont) O. F. Parody. Sch Life 47:24-8 D '64

University and the high school; reprint of a 1939 article. J. B. Conant. Sch & Soc 93:52-6 Ja 23 '65

See also

High schools

EDUCATION, Social. See Social education

EDUCATION, State departments of

Data link. W. O. Reed. il Am Ed 1:31-2 Je '65

EDUCATION, Technical. See Technical education

EDUCATION, Urban

Commercial textbooks and urban education. R. H. Smith. Pub W 188:39 D 6 '65

Textbook needs in urban education; American cities research council meeting, Los Angeles; summaries of addresses. il Pub W 188:16-27 D 6 '65

EDUCATION, Value of

Educational values in disorder. J. Justman. Sch & Soc 93:147-50 Mr 6 '65

Stimulus to dialogue; impact of mass culture. M. L. Goldberg. Sat R 48:87-9 N 20 '65

See also

College education, Value of

EDUCATION, Vocational. See Vocational education

EDUCATION and business. See Business and education

EDUCATION and church. See Church and education

EDUCATION and democracy

Danger of extremism. J. Moorhead. NEA J 54:17 S '65

Dictatorship of the majority. W. L. Hickman. Sch & Soc 93:346-9 O 2 '65

Education, democracy, and the human condition. B. O. Wireman. Sch & Soc 93:366-8 O 16 '65

Education for responsible citizenship; adaptation of address. S. K. Bailey. NEA J 54: 16-18 My '65

Effective cooperative decision-making in education. M. Y. Nunnery. Sch & Soc 93:151-2 Mr 6 '65

EDUCATION and economic problems. See School and social and economic problems

EDUCATION and industry. See Business and education

EDUCATION and politics. See Politics and education

EDUCATION and social problems. See School and social and economic problems

EDUCATION and state

Compact for education. P. A. Fitzgerald. America 114:140-1 Ja 22 '66

Compact for education; state action with support from Carnegie corporation and Danforth foundation. Sch & Soc 94:4+ Ja 8 '65

Money from heaven? question of spending so much for science. Commonweal 81:595-6 F 5 '65

Political control in the state colleges of Pennsylvania. M. Anello. bibliog f Sch & Soc 93:83-5 F 6 '65; Reply with rejoinder. R. E. Heiges. 93:235-6 Ap 17 '65

Politics and higher education; address, June 10, 1964. E. Hutchinson; reply. F. S. Barnes. Science 147:823 F 19 '65

Role of the states in education; address, July 27, 1965. J. B. Conant. Vital Speeches 31: 686-8 S 1 '65

Washington report; consideration of new department of education. Sr Schol 87:sup3 N 11 '65

Washington report; new educational programs authorized by Congress. L. Lloyd. Sr Schol 87:sup3 O 7 '65

EDUCATIONAL research
Do-it-yourself in Granby; experiment to improve educational opportunities. E. D. Stevens. il Sat R 48:62-3 Jl 17 '65
Mythology of educational research; the descriptive approach. F. N. Kerlinger. bibliog f Sch & Soc 93:222-5 Ap 3 '65
National testing: the first step? assessing U.S. education. Sr Schol 87:sup2 O 28 '65
Partnership in research. D. F. Shaughnessy. il Am Ed 1:1-4 F '65
Research and development center for learning and re-education. H. J. Klausmeier. Sch & Soc 93:182-3 Mr 20 '65
Research clues; questions and answers. See issues of NEA journal
Research in art education. W. J. Kasza. il Sch Arts 64:24-6 My '65
See also
Colleges and universities—Research

Bibliography
Educational research shelf for teachers. M. D. Engelhart. NEA J 54:63-4 D '65
EDUCATIONAL research council of Greater Cleveland
Reforming social studies in schools. R. Kirk. Nat R 17:775 S 7 '65
EDUCATIONAL segregation. See Segregation in education
EDUCATIONAL sociology
See also
School and social and economic problems
Socially handicapped children—Education
EDUCATIONAL standards. See Education—Standards
EDUCATIONAL statistics. See Education—Statistics
EDUCATIONAL study tours. See Travel study courses
EDUCATIONAL surveys
$1.3 billion requested for school aid; Advance local school study. G. Krettek and E. D. Cooke. Wilson Lib Bul 39:915-16 Je '65
EDUCATIONAL television. See Television in education
EDUCATIONAL television stations. See Television stations, Educational
EDUCATIONAL testing service
Sub-environments and the individual; Invitational conference on testing problems. E. Spremulli. Sch & Soc 93:104-5 F 6 '65
Unreasonable: English teachers reading of examination essays at Nassau inn, Princeton. New Yorker 41:35-6 Mr 27 '65
See also
College entrance examination board
EDUCATIONAL tests and measurements
In my opinion; ineffectiveness of objective tests. J. Dotson. Seventeen 25:48 Ja '66
Multiple choice and the either-or fallacy. P. DePue. Sch & Soc 93:154-6 Mr 6 '65
Still testing, testing, testing; with study-discussion program by C. Smallenburg and H. Smallenburg. J. E. Dobbin. bibliog il PTA Mag 60:4-6, 36-7 Ja '66
See also
Aptitude tests
College entrance examination board—Scholastic aptitude test
Examinations
Grading and marking (students)
Intelligence tests
EDUCATIONAL toys. See Toys
EDUCATIONAL workshops
Library school at Liberty bell; teachers' workshop on using children's literature in the elementary school, Coopersburg, Pa. A. Crosby. il Library J 90:2334-5 My 15 '65
EDUCATORS
See also
College professors and instructors
Teachers
EDWARD VIII, king of Great Britain (abdicated 1936)
Once upon a time. il por Time 85:36+ Mr 19 '65
EDWARD and Pia; story. See Barthelme, D.
EDWARDS, Altivia. See Powell, B.
EDWARDS, Blake
Greatest pie fight ever creates a horrendous splaat! D. Zeitlin. il pors Life 59:34-5+ Jl 9 '65
EDWARDS, Corwin D.
Reweaving the web; Monopoly power in America. Nation 200:680 Je 21 '65
EDWARDS, Frank
Surfing. il pors Ebony 20:109-13 Ap '65
EDWARDS, H. Lynn
Youth crime; some suggested treatments; statement. por U S News 59:46 N 15 '65
EDWARDS, Harlan
Solving leakage problems of parapets. Arch Rec 137:222-3 Ap '65

EDWARDS, Hugh
Hugh Edwards. J. Deschin. por Pop Phot 57:28+ Jl '65
EDWARDS, James
$107 misunderstanding. por Newsweek 65:27 Ap 19 '65
EDWARDS, L. K.
High-speed tube transportation; with biographical sketch. Sci Am 213:11, 30-40 bibliog(p 118) Ag; 6 O '65
EDWARDS, Margaret A.
Fair garden and the swarm of beasts; address, December 1964. Library J 90:3379-83 S 1 '65
EDWARDS, Phyllis
Bishop Lickfield attacks Bishop Pike; condemns recognition of Mrs Edwards as deaconess. Christian Cent 82:1214 O 6 '65
Communion from a woman. por Time 85:91-2 Ap 30 '65
Lady in waiting. il por Newsweek 65:62 Ap 26 '65
EDWARDS, V. C. Wynne-. See Wynne-Edwards, V. C.
EDWARDS, Walter M.
Inventor of the month. S. V. Jones. il por Sci Digest 58:22 Jl '65
EDWARDS air force base flight test center. See Proving grounds
EDWARDS brothers, incorporated, lithographers
Edwards brothers rounds out a remarkable decade. il Pub W 189:84-9 Ja 3 '66
EFF, Johannes
Happiness is a warm pupae that became a hot ten year old St Bernard; poem. Nat R 17:1067 N 30 '65
EFFICIENCY

Anecdotes, facetiae, satire, etc.
Efficiency in its country of origin. A. Page. il Atlan 217:105-6 Ja '66
EFFICIENCY, Agricultural. See Farm management
EFFICIENCY, Industrial
Russia's new economy. S. Lens. Christian Cent 82:236 F 24 '65
EFFICIENCY experts. See Business consultants
EGAN, James
Le high-life in Guadeloupe. Atlan 216:120+ D '65
Private seacoast in Italy. Sat R 48:42-3+ Mr 13 '65
Wheels around the world. Atlan 216:117-20 Jl '65
EGAN, John
Chicago's Archdiocesan office of urban affairs. J. H. Fichter. America 113:462-5 O 23 '65
EGAN, William Allen
Most powerful governor in the U.S.A. M. Morgan. Harper 231:98+ O '65
EGER, Joseph
Mephisto's musings. por Hi Fi 15:142+ O '65
EGERTON, John W.
New missionary. Christian Cent 82:1507-9 D 8 '65
EGG decoration. See Decoration and ornament
EGG industry and trade
Egg producers try quotas. S. Eberly. Farm J 90:52E Ja '66
Six ways to boost egg profits. Suc Farm 63:70A Ap '65
EGG production. See Poultry—Egg production
EGG shell cases. See Boxes, cases, etc.
EGGER, Eugene. See Whitfield, R. P. jt. auth.
EGGER, Hermann
Sundial monument. Sky & Tel 30:220 O '65
EGGERS, E. Russell
How to do business with a Frenchman. Harper 231:41-4 Ag '65
EGGERS, Hans J. and Tamm, Igor
Coxsackie A9 virus: mutation from drug dependence to drug independence. bibliog Science 148:97-8 Ap 2 '65
EGGINTON, Joyce
(ed) See Evers, M. Mississippi widow
EGGS
How to blow an egg. il Sunset 134:96 Ap '65
Iron accumulation in cockerel plasma after estrogen: relation to induced phosphoprotein synthesis. O. Greengard and others. bibliog il Science 147:1571-2 Mr 26 '65
See also
Cookery—Eggs
Easter eggs

Blood spots
See Eggs—Grading and standardization
Care and handling
See also
Eggs—Washing

EGGS—*Continued*

Grading and standardization

New light on losses from blood spots. Farm J 89:50G Mr '65

Prices

Low egg prices jolt Midwest. Farm J 89:54E Ap '65

Washing

Clean eggs with less handling. il Farm J 89:70F Ap '65

EGGS (ova) See Ovum

EGO. See Self

EGRETS

Where and why to watch for the egrets. il Sunset 134:49 F '65

EGRI, Lajos

Birth of a story. Writer 78:20-2 Je '65

EGYPT

Unquiet genius of Egypt. J. Morris. Atlan 216:126-30+ O '65

See also

Arts and crafts—Egypt

Colleges and universities—Egypt

Economic assistance in Egypt

Antiquities

Yankee cruises the storied Nile. I. Johnson and E. Johnson. il Nat Geog Mag 127:583-633 My '65

See also

Abu Simbel, Temples of

Pyramids

Anecdotes, facetiae, satire, etc.

Look what I brought back from ancient Egypt. H. Lees. il Atlan 215:174-5 Mr '65

Economic conditions

Fewer curses, more sense. il Time 86:23 D 31 '65

Keeping Nasser afloat. A. Hottinger. New Repub 153:15-16 N 20 '65

On the verge. il Newsweek 65:40 F 8 '65

Tale of two autocrats. il Time 85:25-6 Mr 26 '65

Economic policy

Sudden freeze. A. Higbee. il Newsweek 66:36 Ag 2 '65

Foreign relations

Nasser's Egypt. G. H. Torrey. il Cur Hist 48:290-5+ My '65

Nonalignment in the Arab world. D. Peretz. bibliog f Ann Am Acad 362:36-43 N '65

One more notch. Newsweek 65:46 Ap 19 '65

Watch on the Nile. il Time 85:30 Mr 5 '65

Arab states

Arab world in ferment. il Sr Schol 86:14-16+ My 6 '65

Death of a dream; Nasser and Faisal sign Yemeni peace pact. il Newsweek 66:29 S 6 '65

Germany (Federal Republic)

Bonn, Cairo, Jerusalem: the triple crisis. W. Z. Laqueur. Commentary 39:29-38 My '65

Caving in. il Time 85:28 F 19 '65

Mideast mix-up: everybody loses. Newsweek 65:29 Mr 22 '65

West Germany trapped in Mideast squeeze. il Bsns W p26-7 Mr 6 '65

What to do about Germany. Time 85:35 Mr 19 '65

Willie Sutton and Abdel Nasser. W. S. Schlamm. Nat R 17:238 Mr 23 '65

Iran

Darius Canal; clash of interests. Newsweek 65:45 F 22 '65

Iraq

Serpentine politics in latter-day Eden; September coup. C. Sterling. Reporter 33:30-2 D 30 '65

Saudi Arabia

Journey to Jedda. il Time 86:20-1 Ag 27 '65

No time for fanfare. il Time 86:29-30 S 3 '65

Yemen

Forgotten war in the desert: a first-hand report. J. Law. il U S News 58:67-9 My 24 '65

History

Invasion, 1956

New look in war. D. Smith. Nation 200:200-2 F 22 '65

Politics and government

Down and out; M. Amin: spy or scapegoat? Newsweek 67:30-1 Ja 10 '66

Keeping Nasser afloat. A. Hottinger. New Repub 153:15-16 N 20 '65

They call him El Rayis, the boss. H. Smith. il N Y Times Mag p32-3+ My 16 '65

Religious institutions and affairs

Cross and crescent; Nasser addressing Coptic orthodox Christians. Newsweek 66:56 Ag 16 '65

Riots

Sense of frustration. Newsweek 66:42 S 20 '65

EGYPTIAN sculpture. See Sculpture, Egyptian

EHLEN, Peter

Can we talk to Marxian atheists? prospects for a dialogue. America 113:112-14 Jl 31 '65

EHLERS, Ernest G. and others

Fossil bacteria in pyrite. Science 148:1719-21 Je 25 '65

EHRENBURG, Il'ia Grigor'evich

His pen was a welcome weapon. A. Werth. il por Sat R 48:32-3 Je 19 '65

Reporter at large. R. Blum. New Yorker 41:82+ Ag 28 '65

EHRENKROOK, Wymond J.

Importance of the individual; East high school, Denver. Atlan 215:89-92 F '65

EHRENREICH, Joe

Mister Japan in the U.S.A. E. Bennett. por U S Camera 28:18+ Je '65

EHRENSBERGER, Ray

Maryland U.'s global classrooms. F. V. Rummell. por Read Digest 86:245-8+ Ap '65

EHRENSPERGER, Harold

Exciting intersection. Christian Cent 82:744 Je 9 '65

EHRLICH, David Alan

Teen-agers; new world problem. Sci Digest 57:16-19 F '65

EHRLICH, P. R.

I learned about flying from that. Flying 77:86 D '65

EHRLING, Sixten

Go-go symphony. por Newsweek 66:110 O 18 '65

EICHELBERGER, Clark M.

Alternative to anarchy. Sat R 48:35+ Jl 24 '65

James Thomson Shotwell; a tribute. Sat R 48:16 Ag 7 '65

EIGHT, The (group) See Painting, American

8mm films. See Photography—Films

EIGHT-pen Dataplotter. See Drawing instruments

EIGHTEEN hundred and sixty-five

1865: the great transition. A. S. Eisenstadt. il Nation 201:54-61 S 20 '65

1865: the South as it is. J. R. Dennett. Nation 201:153-6 S 20 '65

EIGHTEEN-nation disarmament conference. See Conference of the Eighteen-nation committee on disarmament, Geneva, 1962-

EIGHTEENTH century

Age of Voltaire, by W. Durant and A. Durant. Review

Sat R 48:65-6 O 23 '65. L. Gershoy

EIGNER, Larry

Five poems: Baby cries he invokes warmth; To make myself a world; Water dripping; Green garage door; Empty the apartment. Poetry 105:313-17 F '65

EILEEN O'Gorman, Mother. See O'Gorman, E.

EILERS, Hazel Kraft

At the sign of the crest. See issues of Hobbies

EIMERIA tenella. See Protozoa, Pathogenic

EIMON, Pan Dodd

(ed) City tells its story. See issues of American city

EINSTEIN, Albert

Einstein, specific heats, and the early quantum theory; address, December 29, 1964. M. J. Klein. bibliog Science 148:173-80 Ap 9 '65

EINSTEIN theory. See Relativity (physics)

EIRE. See Ireland

EISELEY, Loren C.

Eloquent valedictory from a far valley. Life 59:10 Ag 13 '65

Elvish art of enchantment; reprint. Horn Bk 41:364-7 Ag '65

EISENBERG, Arlene, and Eisenberg, Howard

Choosing your luggage. Holiday 38:131-6 D '65

Trees that need no stars. McCalls 93:30+ D '65

EISENBERG, Dennis

Margaret: the British princess with American tastes. Look 29:68-70+ N 30 '65

EISENBERG, Howard. See Eisenberg, A. jt. auth.

EISENBERG, Lawrence, and others
Radio frequency stimulation: a research and clinical tool. bibliog Science 147:578-82 F 5 '65

EISENBERG, Lucy
What computers can't do. Harper 231:96-9 Ag '65

EISENBERG, Norman
British audio establishment. Hi Fi 15:56-60+ Ap '65
High fidelity newsfronts (cont) Hi Fi 15:29 Jl '65
Magnificent monsters. Hi Fi 15:55-9+ S '65
Stereo question box. Hi Fi 15:61-5+ D '65
Turntables and changers. Hi Fi 15:34-7 Je '65

EISENDRATH, David B. Jr
Color clinic. See issues of Popular photography
Who knows more about color than the National geographic? Pop Phot 57:58+ Jl '65

EISENHOWER, Dwight David
America's place in the world. Read Digest 87:75-81 O '65
Churchill I knew. por Nat Geog Mag 128:153-7 Ag '65
Eisenhower on the choice Americans must make; interview. por Nations Bsns 53:34-7+ O '65
Eisenhower's views on the breakdown in law and order; excerpts from address, September 1, 1965. U S News 59:20 S 13 '65
Faith in the individual; address, December 9, 1964. Vital Speeches 31:228-31 F 1 '65
From Ike, some strong backing for Johnson; excerpts from news conference. U S News 58:8 My 24 '65
Ike on the missile gap: there wasn't any; excerpts from White House years: waging peace, 1956-61. por U S News 59:20 O 4 '65
What is leadership? Read Digest 86:49-54 Je '65
What worries Ike: the breakdown in American morals; statements. por U S News 59:19 O 25 '65
Who pledged what in Vietnam? excerpts from news conference, August 17, 1965. por U S News 59:15 Ag 30 '65

about

Books. R. H. Rovere. New Yorker 41:238+ D 11 '65
Break in the weather; heart attack. por Newsweek 66:42 N 22 '65
Coming up seventy-five, all roses for Ike. J. Steele. il pors Life 59:49-50+ S 24 '65
Eisenhower speaks out at press conference. il por Pub W 188:53-5 O 25 '65
Eisenhower's second term. C. B. Marshall. New Repub 153:25-7 N 6 '65
Eisenhower's 75th birthday. il pors Sr Schol 87:8-9+ O 14 '65
History unleashed. K. Crawford. Newsweek 66:27 Ag 30 '65
How Eisenhower would change Washington. il por U S News 59:64-5 O 18 '65
Ike on Ike. Newsweek 66:69-70 S 27 '65
Man behind the grin. E. R. May. por Sat R 48:48-9 O 16 '65
Military move: trip to Walter Reed hospital. Time 86:26 D 3 '65
Patient in T-4. por Time 86:43 N 19 '65
Present occupation: writer. E. T. Folliard. America 113:460 O 23 '65
Reader's choice; presidential memoirs. O. Handlin. Atlan 216:166+ O '65
That man, those years. P. Jacobs. Nation 201:368 N 15 '65
Thirty-fourth President 1953-1961. F. Freidel. il pors Nat Geog Mag 129:90-9 Ja '66
Years of decision. por Newsweek 66:118F+ O 25 '65

EISENHOWER college, Seneca Falls, N.Y.
Growing importance of Ike U; college to open fall of 1967. il Time 86:52-3 O 1 '65

EISENMANN, Eugene
Books in review. Natur Hist 74:6+ Je '65

EISENSTADT, Abraham S.
1865: the great transition. Nation 201:54-61 S 20 '65

EISENSTAT, Benjamin
Ben Eisenstat finds personality in buildings. H .C. Pitz. il por Am Artist 29:56-61+ D '65

EISENSTEIN, Elizabeth L.
Who intervened in 1788? bibliog f Am Hist R 71:77-103 O '65

EISLER, Colin T.
Sittow Assumption. Art N 64:34-7+ S '65

EISLEY, Richard S.
Japan. U S Camera 28:42-5+ Je '65

EISNER, H. E. See Eisner, T. jt. auth.

EISNER, Thomas
Defensive spray of a phasmid insect. bibliog Science 148:966-8 My 14 '65
Insect's scales are asset in defense. Natur Hist 74:26-31 Je '65
—and Eisner, H. E.
Mystery of a millipede. Natur Hist 74:30-7 Mr '65
—and Meinwald, Y. C.
Defensive secretion of a caterpillar. Papilio. bibliog Science 150:1733-5 D 24 '65
—and Shepherd, Julian
Caterpillar feeding on a sundew plant. bibliog Science 150:1608-9 D 17 '65

EISS, Albert F. and Mulford, Carolyn
How far is space? NEA J 54:14-16 N '65

EISTEDDFODS. See Festivals—Wales

EITANI, Rina
Lady in the dark; investigation of citizenship. por Time 85:65 F 12 '65

EJECTION devices (airplanes) See Airplanes—Escape devices

EKLUND, Henning
Stability of lakes near the temperature of maximum density. Science 149:632-3 Ag 6 '65

EKLUND, Melvin W. and Poysky, Frank
Clostridium botulinum type F from marine sediments. bibliog Science 149:306 Jl 16 '65

EKLUND, Sigvard
Why it's time for atom police. Sat R 48:66-7 O 2 '65

about

Bargainer in plowshares. J. Lear. por Sat R 48:64-5 O 2 '65

EKSTROM, Niki
Desert nomads' economy depends on camel; photographs. Natur Hist 74:36-9 Ag '65

EKTACHROME-X films. See Photography—Films

ELAEAGNUS
Use them to make a screen. il Sunset 135:277 O '65

ELAM, Stanley
Teachers' unions: rift without differences. Nation 201:247-9 O 18 '65

ELASTICITY
See also
Bending
Strains and stresses

ELAZAR, Daniel J.
Shaping of intergovernmental relations in the twentieth century. bibliog f Ann Am Acad 359:10-22 My '65

ELBEIN, Juana
Afro-Brazilian rites. il por Américas 17:16-19 Je '65

ELBRICK, C. Burke
United States and eastern Europe; address, January 5, 1965. Dept State Bul 52:137-42 F 1 '65

EL CORDOBÉS. See Cordobés

ELDERCARE. See Insurance, Health—United States

EL DORADO, Kan.
Records protection system with a plus. R. D. Thomas. il Am City 80:109 S '65

ELDRIDGE, Roy
Jazz. W. Balliett. New Yorker 41:156-8 Ap 3 '65

ELEA. See Velia, Italy

ELECTION day
First Tuesday after the first Monday. il Sr Schol 87:5 N 4 '65

ELECTION districts
See also
Apportionment (election law)
Gerrymander

ELECTION expenses. See Campaign funds

ELECTION forecasts. See Political forecasts

ELECTION laws
See also
Literacy tests (election law)

United States

Achieving voting reform: every teacher's concern. R. Fisher and M. L. Chapman. il NEA J 55:12-14 Ja '66
Amending the voting rights bill. A. M. Bickel. New Repub 152:10-11 My 1 '65
Barrier falls: the U.S. Negro moves to vote; Voting rights act of 1965. il Newsweek 66:15-16 Ag 16 '65
Birth of a bill; the labored progress of voting rights. A. Kopkind. New Repub 152:11-13 My 15 '65
But how many will vote? voting-rights bill. il Newsweek 65:20-1 Je 7 '65
Dirkzenbach bill; question of poll-tax ban in voting-rights bill. il Newsweek 65:39 My 10 '65
Fount; voting-rights bill passed by Senate after cloture. Time 85:18-19 Je 4 '65

ELECTION laws—United States—*Continued*
House and Senate voting bills. A. M. Bickel.
New Repub 153:8 Jl 24 '65
Inscrutable Pekinese; Dirksen amendment to
voting-rights bill. K. Crawford. Newsweek
65:34 Ap 26 '65
Into the ditch; legal fight against voting law
in Mississippi. Time 86:39 S 17 '65
Kiss of death; voting rights bill. Time 86:
17-18 Jl 16 '65
Must we repeal the Constitution to give the
Negro the vote? with editorial comment.
J. J. Kilpatrick. il Nat R 17:312, 319-22,
350+ Ap 20-My 4 '65
Nine eager men; Senate judiciary committee amendments to voting-rights bill. Reporter 32:10+ My 6 '65
Other side of the voting-rights bill; excerpts
from statement. H. F. Byrd. U S News 58:
86-8 Ap 12 '65
Second Appomattox; southern congressmen
and senators divided on the voting-rights
bill. K. Crawford. Newsweek 65:35 My 3
'65
Test: a vote for everyone anywhere. J. N.
Eller. America 112:476 Ap 10 '65
U.S. fever chart; Supreme court to decide
constitutionality of the 1965 Voting rights
act. Time 86:50 O 29 '65
Voting rights act of 1965; address, March 18,
1965. N. deB. Katzenbach. Vital Speeches
31:391-8 Ap 15 '65
Voting rights; Administration's bill. Com-
monweal 82:69 Ap 9 '65
Voting rights bill is tough. A. M. Bickel.
New Repub 152:16-18 Ap 3 '65
Who should vote? il Sr Schol 86:6-9+ Ap 8
'65
Who speaks for Alabama? question of con-
stitutionality of the Voting rights act of
1965. Newsweek 67:17 Ja 3 '66
Your future depends on it; signing of voting
rights bill and its effect. il Time 86:15 Ag
13 '65
    See also
Voters, Registration of
ELECTION tests
    See also
Voters, Registration of
ELECTIONEERING. See Political campaigns
ELECTIONS
To the polls. Commonweal 83:113 O 29 '65
    See also
Political campaigns
Voting

Argentina

Gauging the dose; Peronista vote. il Newsweek 65:49 Mr 29 '65
Voting for a ghost. il Time 85:31 Mr 26 '65

Austria

Holzbein v. Holzkopf. Time 85:26 Je 4 '65

Basutoland

Friend for Verwoerd. il Time 85:40 My 14
'65

Belgium

Confusion of tongues. il Newsweek 65:35-6
Je 7 '65

Brazil

Laying the ground rules; who can and who
cannot run. Time 86:31 Jl 2 '65

Canada

Another election. Time 86:61 N 5 '65
Bad advice. Newsweek 66:56+ N 22 '65
Canada's quiet crisis. Reporter 33:16 N 4 '65
Canadian national elections; campaign issues.
B. Fraser. New Repub 153:10-11 N 6 '65
Galloping apathy. il Newsweek 66:60 N 8 '65
Lining up for Canada's next round. il Bsns
W p38 O 9 '65
Mr Pearson draws a blank. America 113:617
N 20 '65
Non-victory. Time 86:59 N 19 '65
Nothing changed. Sr Schol 87:16 D 2 '65
Pearson squeaks back. Bsns W p48 N 13 '65
Third man; Jean Lesage. Newsweek 66:58
O 4 '65
To the polls, glumly. Time 86:59 S 17 '65
What Canada's election means to the U.S.
il U S News 59:78 N 22 '65

Ceylon

Madame's exit. Time 85:29-30 Ap 2 '65
Shift to the center. Newsweek 65:44 Ap 5 '65

Chile

Appeal to the arbiter. Time 85:35 Mr 5 '65
Big sweep; congressional majority for Frei.
Newsweek 65:38 Mr 22 '65
Mandate to serve; victory for Christian
democrats. il Time 85:42 Mr 19 '65

Congo (capital Leopoldville)

Bumpy road to democracy. il Time 85:30 Ap 9
'65
Improbable elections. il Newsweek 65:44 Ap
5 '65
Nervous at the top. Time 85:40+ My 14 '65
Some other time; fiasco in Leopoldville.
Newsweek 65:51 Ap 12 '65
Tshombe's election campaign. Time 85:41 Mr
19 '65

Cook Islands

Elections under United Nations supervision.
UN Mo Chron 2:26-7 Mr '65
Supervision of elections. UN Mo Chron 2:33-4
Ap '65

France

After victory, a guessing game. il Newsweek
67:19 Ja 3 '66
Also running; J. Lecanuet. Newsweek 66:
50+ N 8 '65
De Gaulle: America's elder statesman. A.
Werth. Nation 201:404-8 N 29 '65
De Gaulle between two elections. Newsweek
66:37 D 20 '65
De Gaulle carries on. il Newsweek 66:55-6
N 15 '65
De Gaulle has an opposition. Life 59:4 D 17
'65
De Gaulle moves to recoup; attempts to
mend domestic and Common market fen-
ces. Bsns W p 15-16 D 25 '65
Down from Olympus. il Time 86:26-7 D 17 '65
Election day in France; I have spoken. il
Newsweek 66:41-2 D 13 '65
France loosens grip of de Gaulle. Bsns W
p32-3 D 11 '65
Frapping de Gaulle. Commonweal 83:329 D 17
'65
French politics at the municipal level. E.
Taylor. il Reporter 32:31-2 Ap 8 '65
Letter from Paris; campaign for and results
of second election. Genêt. New Yorker 41:
61-2+ Ja 1 '66
Letter from Paris; five candidates against
de Gaulle. Genêt. New Yorker 41:186+ D 11
'65
Letter from Paris; metropolitan France and
its overseas départments municipal elec-
tions. Genêt. New Yorker 41:167-8+ Mr 20
'65
Letter from Paris; results of first ballot.
Genêt. New Yorker 41:160-1 D 18 '65
Man who... Newsweek 66:51 O 4 '65
Non, mon général! local elections. il Time
85:32 Ap 2 '65
Le pill; presidential contenders. il Newsweek
66:39-40 N 29 '65
Seven more years for de Gaulle. il Time 86:
18 D 24 '65
So, vive de Gaulle but with reservations. Life
59:4 N 19 '65
Suddenly, politics! il Time 86:38 N 26 '65
This electoral season. M. Ascoli. Reporter
33:10 N 18 '65
What de Gaulle's re-election means. R. Bosc.
America 114:72-4 Ja 15 '66
Will de Gaulle be easier to live with now?
il U S News 59:34-5 D 20 '65

Germany (Democratic Republic)

Day at the races; provincial and local elections. Time 86:46 O 22 '65

Germany (Federal Republic)

Besser ist der Ludwig. il Time 86:40+ O
1 '65
Bonn, the morning after. R. Steel. Common-
weal 83:55-7 O 15 '65
Election slogans in Germany. R. Goldman.
New Repub 153:8 Ag 21 '65
Elections in wonderland. W. S. Schlamm.
Nat R 17:651-2 Jl 27 '65
German vote; meaning for U.S. il U S
News 59:70 O 4 '65
Getting away from it all; US TV coverage.
R. L. Shayon. Sat R 48:53 O 23 '65
Heavy winner; Erhard's victory. Newsweek
66:46+ O 4 '65
No change in Germany. G. Bailey. il Re-
porter 33:32-3 O 7 '65
Pack den tiger in dem tank. H. Moffett.
il Life 59:43-4 O 1 '65
Photo finish? il Time 86:51-2 S 17 '65
Playing it safe; Erhard, most likely to suc-
ceed. Time 86:29 Ag 13 '65
Safety first: the West German election. G.
K. Romoser and C. R. Foster. Bul Atomic
Sci 21:37-9 D '65

Great Britain

Great fight coming. H. Brandon. Sat R 48:
14+ O 30 '65
Labor party jolted; by-election for representative in House of commons. il Sr Schol 86:
19 F 4 '65

ELECTIONS—Great Britain—*Continued*
Labor's delight; Tory defeat in Scottish by-election. Newsweek 65:39 Ap 5 '65
Road to Number 10, by A. Howard and R. West. Review
Commentary 40:114+ D '65. J. Mander

Honduras

His master's voice; Colonel López elected as president. Newsweek 65:50 Mr 1 '65
Unfortunate throwback. il Time 85:41 F 26 '65

India

Election in Kerala. J. J. Berna. America 112:316-17 Mr 6 '65
Priests and politics; Kerala elections. America 112:473 Ap 10 '65
Red upset; Kerala elections. Time 85:25A Mr 12 '65

Ireland

Mixture at before. Time 85:34 Ap 16 '65

Israel

Back into battle; Ben-Gurion's new party. il Time 86:45 O 22 '65
David come to judgment; Eshkol victory. il Time 86:43 N 12 '65
Rivals; Eshkol-Ben-Gurion campaign. Newsweek 66:54 N 8 '65

Mexico

Into the daylight; forthcoming municipal elections. Time 85:40 Ap 23 '65

Nigeria

Flickering light; election rigging causes riots. Newsweek 66:52+ N 22 '65
Way the West was won; post-election violence. Time 86:54 N 19 '65

Northern Ireland

New sense of moderation; pro-British Unionist party back in power. Time 86:32 D 3 '65

Philippines

Dirty campaign on the corruption issue. G. De Carvalho. il Life 59:78B-80+ N 26 '65
Go Marcos. il Newsweek 66:54 N 22 '65
Marcos elected. Sr Schol 87:20 D 9 '65
Struggle in the barrios; presidential race. il Time 86:39 O 1 '65
Surprise in Manila. il Time 86:52 N 19 '65

Rhodesia

Victory for fear. Newsweek 65:54-5 My 17 '65

Tanzania

Campaign of the magic eye. Time 86:48 O 8 '65

Turkey

Battling a ghost. il Time 86:46-7 O 8 '65
Beyond the grave; Justice party back in power. Newsweek 66:48+ O 25 '65
Discovery of politics. C. Poulos. il Nation 201:378-80 N 22 '65
Ride to victory. Time 86:46 O 22 '65
Wavering ally. Newsweek 66:64 O 18 '65

United States

Atlantic report; SOS to Humphrey. Atlan 217:6 Ja '66
Bigger club; state and city levels. il Time 86:27-8 N 12 '65
Election day, 1965. Sr Schol 87:20 N 4 '65
Elections. Nat R 17:1012-13 N 16 '65
Elections; democratic tide is still running strong. W. D. Burnham. Commonweal 83:233-6 N 26 '65
For both parties: some plums. il Sr Schol 87:6 N 18 '65
Major contests on the election calendar. U S News 59:17 N 1 '65
Negro's new force. Time 86:33-4 N 12 '65
Testing, testing; recovery from Goldwater debacle; test areas. Newsweek 66:37 N 1 '65
Victory for confusion. D. Lawrence. U S News 59:128 N 15 '65
What elections showed. il U S News 59:29-31 N 15 '65
See also
Presidents—United States—Election
Voting
also subhead Elections under names of cities, e.g. New York (city)—Elections

History

Grant or Greeley? the abolitionist dilemma in the election of 1872. J. M. McPherson. bibliog f Am Hist R 71:43-61 O '65

Vietnam (Republic)

How democracy returned to Vietnam. B. B. Fall. Nation 200:362-4 Ap 5 '65
Vietnam: free elections? S. Alsop. il Sat Eve Post 238:18 Jl 3 '65

ELECTORAL college
LBJ asks reforms. Sr Schol 86:31 F 18 '65

ELECTRIC alarms
Electronic intrusion alarms. W. H. Buchsbaum. il Electr World 73:25-8 Je '65
Electronics answers a cry for help. il Bsns W p56+ S 11 '65
See also
Burglar alarms

ELECTRIC apparatus and appliances
See also
Electric apparatus industry
Electric batteries
Electric circuit breakers

Control

Solid-state dimmers & power controls. D. Lancaster. il Electr World 73:34-6+ My; 41-4+ Je '65

Protection

See also
Electric fuses

Safety devices and measures

Electrical hazards in appliances as detected and measured in CR's laboratories. il Consumer Bul 48:37-40 Mr '65
How to play it safe with electricity. W. J. Fletcher. il Suc Farm 63:18D Ag '65

Testing

Instruments for determining shock hazard of electrical appliances. il Consumer Bul 48:37-40 Ag '65

ELECTRIC apparatus and appliances, Cordless
Appliances run by batteries. il Consumer Bul 49:13-15 Ja '66
Batteries: which kind runs what? il Changing T 20:46-7 Ja '66
Battery-operated small appliances. Bet Hom & Gard 43:90+ S '65
Cordless electrical appliances. il House & Gard 127:158-9+ Mr '65

ELECTRIC apparatus and appliances, Domestic
Big help from small appliances. J. LemMon. il Suc Farm 63:70-1 Je '65
Big problem with portables; storage. il Sunset 135:86-9 N '65
Blend it; electric blenders. il McCalls 93:88+ N '65
Blenders. il Consumer Bul 49:26-9 Ja '66
Electric juicers, great! il Bet Hom & Gard 43:102 Je '65
Electric skillets, non-stick coatings now prevalent. il Consumer Bul 48:19-22 Je '65
Hazardous electric broiler; Cory Broilitizer model C5. il Consumer Rep 30:166 Ap '65
Kitchen blenders. il Consumer Rep 30:542-7 N '65
Making the kitchen a decorator's dream; Kelvinator originals. il Bsns W p 116-17+ N 20 '65
Newest in kitchen automation. il House & Gard 128:68+ N '65
Other household aids and appliances. il Consumer Rep 30:87-166 D '65
Presenting the newest in small appliance cooking. il Bet Hom & Gard 44:56-64+, 74, 76 Ja '66
Private brands: the inside story. il Changing T 19:25-9 N '65
Serve it hot. M. Davidson. il Ladies Home J 82:30 D '65
Small appliances for broiling; some can be used for baking too. il Consumer Bul 48:6-9 S '65
Where the designer rules the roost; success of Braun appliances in West Germany. il Bsns W p40-2 Jl 31 '65
See also
Laundry equipment
Washing machines

Repairing

In appliances, it's the contacts that count. J. Burroughs. il Pop Sci 186:156-9 F '65

Safety devices and measures

Unplug your appliances after use! il Consumer Bul 48:43 O '65

Storage

Small appliance centers make your kitchen work for you. R. Charles. il Parents Mag 40:75-80 Je '65

Testing

Appliance tester for home use. il Consumer Bul 48:33-4 O '65

ELECTRIC apparatus industry
New necessities. il Time 86:69-70 Ag 20 '65
Where the designer rules the roost; success of Braun appliances in West Germany. il Bsns W p40-2 Jl 31 '65
X marks success; Moulinex. il Time 85:80-1 Mr 26 '65

Securities
Has GE stock hit peak? il Bsns W p 158 N 6 '65

ELECTRIC arc
NOL tunnel advances arc heater art. W. S. Beller. il Miss & Roc 17:27 O 4 '65

ELECTRIC automobiles. See Automobiles, Electric

ELECTRIC batteries
Appliances run by batteries. il Consumer Bul 49:13-15 Ja '66
Army presses for better field systems. il Miss & Roc 16:77-8+ Mr 29 '65
Batteries: the inside story. B. G. Wels. il U S Camera 28:62-3+ F '65
Batteries: which kind runs what? il Changing T 20:46-7 Ja '66
Battery renaissance. W. A. Stocklin. Electr World 74:6 S '65
Cordless electrical appliances. il House & Gard 127:158-9+ Mr '65
Switching the charge on batteries. il Bsns W p 132+ Mr 13 '65
See also
Fuel cells
Storage batteries

ELECTRIC blenders. See Electric apparatus and appliances, Domestic
ELECTRIC broilers. See Electric apparatus and appliances, Domestic
ELECTRIC cables
LTV rejoins civilian ranks; plans to buy Okonite co. Bsns W p96 O 23 '65
See also
Television cables
ELECTRIC capacitance
RC time-constant nomogram. M. H. Applebaum. il Electr World 74:29 Jl '65
ELECTRIC capacitors
Fixed-capacitor industry; symposium. il Electr World 74:37-60 Jl '65
ELECTRIC cars. See Electric railroads
ELECTRIC circuit breakers
This shock preventer could save your life. il Pop Sci 186:155 F '65
This switch caused the big blackout; power plant in Queenston, Ontario. il Life 59:36-7 N 26 '65
ELECTRIC circuits
See also
Electronic circuits
Printed circuits
ELECTRIC clothes dryers. See Clothes dryers
ELECTRIC conductivity
Activation energy of direct-current electrical conductivity of ice with HF and NH_3 added. S. Y. Chai and P. O. Vogelhut. bibliog il Science 148:1595-8 Je 18 '65
Ionizing waves of potential gradient. L. B. Loeb. bibliog il Science 148:1417-26 Je 11 '65
See also
Superconductivity
ELECTRIC conductors
See also
Semiconductors
ELECTRIC control
Clap of light; Sonuswitch trained to respond to sound. Time 86:52 O 29 '65
Remote control system. D. H. Rogers. il Electr World 74:92-3 O '65
Solid-state dimmers & power controls. D. Lancaster. il Eliectr World 73:34-6+ My; 41-4+ Je '65
See also
Photoelectric cells—Control applications
ELECTRIC converters. See Electric current converters
ELECTRIC cordotomy. See Spinal cord—Surgery
ELECTRIC cords
Handyman how-to; cord keeper. il Bet Hom & Gard 43:129 S '65
ELECTRIC couplings. See Couplings, Electric
ELECTRIC cup race. See Motor boat racing
ELECTRIC current converters
A.C. afloat. E. Robberson. il Yachting 117:64-6+ Je '65
Sound advice; putting sound on wheels with an inverter. R. Angus. Mod Phot 29:80+ O '65
ELECTRIC current rectifiers
Build the master control SCR switching center. H. Reed. il Pop Electr 22:53-5 Mr '65
ELECTRIC currents
See also
Hall effect

Grounding
Cheviot Hills goes underground; Los Angeles residential area. Sunset 134:157-8 Mr '65
ELECTRIC currents, Alternating
A.C. afloat. E. Robberson. il Yachting 117:64-6+ Je '65
ELECTRIC currents, Direct
DC power's big comeback. L. Lessing. il Fortune 72:174-6+ S '65
ELECTRIC cutting
This is zero force; electrochemical machining and electrical discharge machining. C. J. Vlahos. il Sci Digest 58:77-9 O '65
ELECTRIC dishwashers. See Dishwashing and drying machines
ELECTRIC distribution
See also
Electric plants—Interconnection
ELECTRIC doorbells. See Doorbells, Electric
ELECTRIC drills. See Drilling and boring machinery
ELECTRIC drills, Portable. See Drilling and boring machinery
ELECTRIC ear. See Electric control
ELECTRIC engineering

Study and teaching
Big blackout: whooping cranes & power failures; need for preserving technology of power engineering. L. J. Hollander. il Nation 202:33-6 Ja 10 '66
ELECTRIC engineers
Electronics industry: products, people, and prospects; special report. il Electr World 73:25-8+ Ap '65
ELECTRIC equipment
See also subhead Electric equipment under various subjects, e.g. Airplanes—Electric equipment
ELECTRIC equipment industry
Tax row revives price-fixing case. Bsns W p76 F 27 '65
ELECTRIC eye. See Photoelectric cells
ELECTRIC-eye door. See Photoelectric cells—Control applications
ELECTRIC fans
Unique tischlüfter. il Consumer Bul 48:2 Ag '65
ELECTRIC field
Electricity in volcanic clouds. R. Anderson and others. bibliog il Science 148:1179-89 My 28 '65
Thunderstorm electrification and raindrop collisions and disjection in an electric field. R. Gunn. Science 150:888-9 N 12 '65
ELECTRIC filters
See also
Radio filters
ELECTRIC fishing. See Harpooning
ELECTRIC frying pans. See Electric apparatus and appliances, Domestic
ELECTRIC fuses
Selecting the proper fuse. A. J. Steele. il Electr World 74:28-30+ Ag '65
Timid girl's guide to the fuse box. il Changing T 19:41-2 N '65
ELECTRIC generators
Amazing new power sources. M. Mann. il Pop Sci 186:100-3+ Ap '65
Build a fail-safe transistor power supply. E. Nawracaj and F. Forman. il Pop Electr 23:74-6 O '65
Build steam powered ham rig. H. B. Smith. il Pop Electr 23:55-7+ Jl '65
Providing blackout lights; auxiliary power generators. il Time 86:102 D 10 '65
Rockets studied as laser power sources; magnetohydrodynamic generators. M. L. Yaffee. il Aviation W 82:85+ Je 28 '65
ELECTRIC generators, Alternating current
Constant-frequency ac. system developed. P. J. Klass. il Aviation W 82:84-6 Ap 19 '65
ELECTRIC grinders. See Grinding machines
ELECTRIC guitar. See Guitar
ELECTRIC harpoons. See Harpooning
ELECTRIC heaters
Portable electric heaters. il Consumer Bul 48:12-16 S '65
Portable electric heaters. il Consumer Rep 30:497-503 O '65
ELECTRIC heating
Electric industry glows over heating prospects. il Bsns W p 162+ Mr 13 '65
ELECTRIC industries
Brighter picture for lights; vapor bulbs. il Bsns W p36 O 23 '65
See also
Collective bargaining—Electric industries
Electric power

ELECTRIC industries—*Continued*

Wages and hours

Output per man-hour, gas and electric utilities. J. E. Dragonette and P. W. Jaynes. il Mo Labor R 88:34-9 Ja '65
  See also
Collective bargaining—Electric industries

ELECTRIC inverters
Wall plug in the wilderness; DC-to-AC inverter. R. M. Benrey. il Pop Sci 187:112-14 Jl '65

ELECTRIC irons
Iron glider; Teflon attachment for electric irons. il Consumer Bul 48:40 S '65

ELECTRIC knives. See Knives

ELECTRIC lamps
Don't buy this dangerous high-intensity lamp! ! Consumer Bul 48:35 My '65
How those high intensity lights work. il Good H 161:164 S '65
How to choose the right lamps. C. Murphy. il Redbook 124:32+ Ap '65
Lamps to light the music. il House & Gard 127:104-5 Mr '65
Light bulbs. il Consumer Rep 30:394-7 Ag '65
Long-lived bulb in a short-lived lamp; high-intensity miniature lamps. il Consumer Rep 30:224 My '65
More on the Perky-D hi-tensity lamp. il Consumer Bul 48:39 Je '65
News about electric light bulbs. H. Manchester. Read Digest 87:102-4 N '65
TV lamp. H. Jackson. il Pop Mech 125:175 Ja '66
Those little high-intensity lamps. il Changing T 19:35-6 Je '65
Tiny lights for closeups. J. Wesson. il U S Camera 28:52-3 F '65

Repairing

Maintenance, the key to a good lighting systems. il Am City 80:114-16 Ap '65

ELECTRIC lamps, Arc
  See also
Electric lamps, Sodium vapor

ELECTRIC lamps, Flashing
Emergency flasher; auto warning signals. D. Yeh. il Pop Electr 23:60 Jl '65

ELECTRIC lamps, Flashlight
Amazing flashcube. E. H. Ortner. il Pop Sci 187:157 S '65
Are you getting the most out of flash? R. Miller. U S Camera 28:32 N '65
Blue flash: universal bulb? N. Rothschild. il Pop Phot 57:22+ Jl '65
Changing habits with the times. D. B. Eisendrath, jr. Pop Phot 57:8+ S '65
Electronic flash: the light that pays for itself. J. Forney. il Pop Phot 57:116-18 N '65
Electronic flash! what's new, what's good, what's coming. T. Karp. il Mod Phot 30:56-61+ Ja '66
Flashcubes. il U S Camera 28:40 O '65
Four-sided flashbulb: how good is it? D. S. Gelatt. il Pop Phot 57:148-9+ N '65
Honeywell's auto/strobonar electronic flash. J. Forney. il Pop Phot 57:63-7+ O '65
Light you can bank on. A. Goldsmith. il Pop Phot 56:70-3+ Mr '65
More power in AG blue bulbs. C. Wright. il Pop Phot 58:30+ Ja '66
Photoflood dimmer. L. M. Dezettel. il Pop Electr 23:68-9 D '65
Strobelight slave. W. F. Gephart. il Pop Electr 22:61-3+ Mr '65
Tony Karp on 35mm. T. Karp. il Mod Phot 30:38+ Ja '66
200 flashes: new ultrablitz circuitry plus revolutionary nickel-cadmium batteries. G. Gilbert. il U S Camera 28:66-7 Mr '65

ELECTRIC lamps, Fluorescent
Battery-operated fluorescent lamp. N. W. Mapham. il Electr World 74:68 O '65
Battery-powered fluorescent light. H. G. McEntee. il Pop Sci 186:116-18 Je '65
D.C.-operated fluorescent light. B. Richards. il Pop Electr 23:40-2 Jl '65

ELECTRIC lamps, Mercury vapor
Mercury vapors brighten underpass, lower costs; Ohio state highway department. il Am City 80:120+ D '65

ELECTRIC lamps, Neon
Call alert for two-way radio; neon lamp memory. G. Childs. il Electr World 74:83 Jl '65
Neon lamp wonder. C. A. Pirolo. il Pop Electr 22:61-4+ Ap '65
Writing with light. J. G. Rabinowitz. il Electr World 74:31 N '65

ELECTRIC lamps, Sodium vapor
Brighter picture for lights; GE's Lucalox. il Bsns W p36 O 23 '65
Sodium vapor used for efficient light source; Lucalox. Sci N L 88:280 O 30 '65

ELECTRIC light bulbs. See Electric lamps

ELECTRIC light fixtures. See Lighting fixtures

ELECTRIC lighting
Improving your home wiring. G. Daniels. il Pop Sci 187:138-42 S; 154-9+ O '65
Lighting, 1966. B. Plumb. il N Y Times Mag p68-9 Ja 9 '66
New light on living. il Good H 161:108-14 Ag '65
Special lighting for an atrium. S. R. Shemitz. il Arch Rec 138:171-2 D '65
Techniques to improve lighting effects. D. A. Mintz. il Arch Rec 138:199-202 N '65
  See also
Electric lamps

Control

Burglar repellents; automatic switches. il Consumer Bul 48:39-40 O '65
Photoflood dimmer. L. M. Dezettel. il Pop Electr 23:68-9 D '65
Solid-state dimmers & power controls. D. Lancaster. il Electr World 73:34-6+ My; 41-4+ Je '65

Rates
  See Electric utilities—Rates

ELECTRIC lines

Grounding
  See Electric distribution—Grounding

Poles

Fiberglas repairs cut pole replacement. il Am City 80:120-1 O '65
Street lights and traffic signals share one pole; Tampa, Fla. S. Heller. il Am City 80:124 N '65

ELECTRIC meters
On-site meter testing; Kissimmee, Fla. C. B. Tyson. il Am City 80:113 S '65

ELECTRIC mixers. See Electric apparatus and appliances, Domestic

ELECTRIC motors
One motor, four tools. il Pop Sci 187:74-5 S '65
Unique rolling-rotor motor can't burn out. D. Scott. il Pop Sci 187:84-5+ S '65

Care

Follow these four cardinal rules; ways to get maximum performance from electrical equipment in water and sewage plants. W. Schneider. il Am City 80:104-6 D '65

Control

Dymwatt. D. Lancaster. il Pop Electr 22:71-3+ My '65
Speed reducer for metal cutting. H. P. Strand. il Pop Mech 124:152-4 D '65

Mounting

Motor mounts that solve shop problems. H. Walton. il Pop Sci 186:152-6 My '65

ELECTRIC outlets. See Electric wire and wiring

ELECTRIC plants
  See also
Atomic power plants

Interconnection

After the blackout, the questions; why the intricate intertie plan failed. il Bsns W p41-3 N 13 '65
Big blackout: whooping cranes & power failures; need for preserving technology of power engineering. L. J. Hollander. il Nation 202:33-6 Ja 10 '66
Blackout study points to new FPC powers. Bsns W p34 D 11 '65
Blackout's cause, cure: some answers, but—. il U S News 59:12 N 29 '65
Lessons from blackouts: a look at power grids. il U S News 59:98-100 D 13 '65
Night they unplugged society; power failure, November 9, 1965. J. Lear. il Sat R 48:81-4 D 4 '65
System couldn't fail, but it did. il Newsweek 66:29 N 22 '65
Working to bar another blackout. il Bsns W p38-40 N 20 '65

ELECTRIC plants, Municipal
Extra electric-plant benefits; Greenfield, Iowa. D. Moore. il Am City 80:187.8 Mr '65
Pressure switches monitor electrical distribution system; Los Angeles. il Am City 80:117 Je '65

ELECTRIC power
After the blackout, the questions; why the intricate intertie plan failed. il Bsns W p41-3 N 13 '65
Amazing new power sources. M. Mann. il Pop Sci 186:100-3+ Ap '65
Backlash from Q-29BW; cause of power failure. il Time 86:28 N 26 '65

ELECTRIC power—*Continued*
Big city lived by the light of the moon; with report by T. H. White. il Life 59:36-46B+ N 19 '65
Blackout spurs FAA airport design role; possibility of on-site emergency power generators. P. J. Klass. Aviation W 83:26-7 N 15 '65
Compactron regulated power supply. P. E. Hatfield. il Pop Electr 22:57-9 F '65
Current-limiting power supply. H. L. Moore. il Electr World 74:85 O '65
Day of the transistor; function during Northeast power blackout. R. L. Tobin. Sat R 48:65-6 D 11 '65
Debacle; northeastern failure. Nation 201:373 N 22 '65
Designing a transistor power supply. T. J. Barmore. il Electr World 73:46-7 My '65
Disaster that wasn't; Northeast blackout. il Time 86:36-43 N 19 '65
Great blackout; its meaning for the future; with questions and answers. il U S News 59:40-2 N 22 '65
Lighting up the blackout. il Newsweek 66:92 N 22 '65
Lights that failed. il Sr Schol 87:14-15 D 2 '65
Longest night. il Newsweek 66:27-8+ N 22 '65
New England's power politics; Dickey-Lincoln school project. P. Barnes. il Reporter 33:36-8 D 16 '65
New power supplies show high reliability; miniature regulated dc. power supplies for solid-state avionics equipment. il Aviation W 83:119+ N 15 '65
Night the lights went out. il Bsns W p44-5 N 13 '65
Night they unplugged society; power failure, November 9, 1965. J. Lear. il Sat R 48:81-4 D 4 '65; Discussion. 49:106 Ja 1 '66
Power from the atom: where U.S. stands, what it plans for the future. il U S News 59:100 D 13 '65
Re the blackout; reprint from National review, July 1, 1961. Nat R 17:1066 N 30 '65
Super engine puts a plus in power distribution; Freeport, N.Y. C. E. Metz. il Am City 80:106-7 N '65
T.R.B. from Washington; rescuing New England; TVA-type power yardstick. New Repub 153:4 O 30 '65
This switch caused the big blackout; power plant in Queenston, Ontario. il Life 59:36-7 N 26 '65
Trapped in a skyscraper; Life magazine carries on. G. P. Hunt. il Life 59:3 N 19 '65
Truth or consequences; blackout of El Paso electric co. Time 86:36 D 10 '65
Ways to make blackout a little less painful; Federal power commission report; excerpts. U S News 59:13-14 D 20 '65
What went wrong? blackout. Newsweek 66:25 N 29 '65
What went wrong? something called 345 KV. T. H. White. il Life 59:46B+ N 19 '65
Whodunit; blackout in Northeast; FPC findings. Newsweek 66:84 D 20 '65
Working to bar another blackout. il Bsns W p38-40 N 20 '65
See also
Hydroelectric power

Rates
See Electric utilities—Rates

Great Britain
Letter from London; power cuts. M. Panter-Downes. New Yorker 41:225-6 D 11 '65
Never to Eskimos; blackout. Newsweek 66:72 N 29 '65
Other blackout. Time 86:38 N 26 '65
Why Britain, too, has power blackouts. il U S News 59:16 D 6 '65

Hong Kong
Oil and power mix; Esso and China light reach agreement. Fortune 71:70+ F '65

United States
See Electric power
ELECTRIC power production
See also
Direct energy conversion
ELECTRIC power production from bacteriological action
In future, electricity may come from sewage. Sci N L 88:37 Jl 17 '65
Milk from coconuts used to produce electricity. Sci N L 88:264 O 23 '65
ELECTRIC power production from chemical action
See also
Fuel cells

ELECTRIC propulsion. See Rocket propulsion
ELECTRIC protective apparatus
See also
Electric circuit breakers
ELECTRIC railroads
Due this year; trains that can go 150 m.p.h; electric cars between New York and Washington. A. P. Armagnac. il Pop Sci 188:88-93 Ja '66
Skokie Swift celebrates first anniversary. il Am City 80:52 Jl '65
Skokie Swift, the answer to a commuter's prayer. B. L. Marsh. il Am City 80:122-3 Je '65
ELECTRIC ranges. See Electric stoves
ELECTRIC rates. See Electric utilities—Rates
ELECTRIC refrigerators. See Refrigerators, Electric
ELECTRIC relays
Magnetic reed switches and relays. G. A. Lehman. il Electr World 74:23-6+ S '65
See also
Electronic relays
ELECTRIC resistance
Determining meter resistance. J. T. Bailey. il Electr World 74:49 Ag '65
RC time-constant nomogram. M. H. Applebaum. il Electr World 74:29 Jl '65
See also
Electric resistors
ELECTRIC resistors
Fixed resistors; symposium. il Electr World 73:37-59 Ap '65
Parallel-resistor nomogram. M. H. Applebaum. il Electr World 74:27 S '65
See also
Thermistors

Noise
Resistor noise graphs. R. Jones. il Electr World 73:42-3 Ap '65
ELECTRIC saws. See Saws
ELECTRIC scoreboards. See Scoreboards
ELECTRIC service, Rural. See United States—Rural electrification administration
ELECTRIC shock
Can electric tools now be shockproof? il Consumer Bul 48:33-4 Jl '65
Electrical hazards in appliances as detected and measured in CR's laboratories. il Consumer Bul 48:37-40 Mr '65
Instruments for determining shock hazard of electrical appliances. il Consumer Bul 48:37-40 Ag '65
Lesions in the medial forebrain bundle: delayed effects on sensitivity to electric shock. J. A. Harvey and C. E. Lints. bibliog il Science 148:250-2 Ap 9 '65
This shock preventer could save your life. il Pop Sci 186:155 F '65
ELECTRIC signs
Writing with light. J. G. Rabinowitz. il Electr World 74:31 N '65
ELECTRIC slicing knives. See Knives
ELECTRIC stoves
Electric ranges. il Consumer Rep 30:436-45 S '65
Everything's under control; new range controls. il McCalls 92:86+ Ap '65
Experts answer your questions about modern ranges. il Redbook 124:72-3+ Mr '65
Kitchen ranges. il Consumer Rep 30:14-31 D '65
Ranges: the news is inside. M. Davidson. il Ladies Home J 82:32 My '65

Testing
Defects, lethal and otherwise; Tappan and RCA Whirlpool. il Consumer Rep 30:445 S '65
ELECTRIC switches
Build the master control SCR switching center. H. Reed. il Pop Electr 22:53-5 Mr '65
Burglar repellents; automatic switches. il Consumer Bul 48:39-40 O '65
Capacitance touch-plate lighting switch. R. W. Simister. il Electr World 74:44+ Ag '65
High-speed switch; use in automated telephone systems. il Electr World 74:85 N '65
Improved switching of inductive loads. J. P. Reed. il Electr World 74:35+ S '65
Improving your home wiring; how to install new switches. H. Walton. il Pop Sci 187:156-61 D '65
Magnetic reed switches and relays. G. A. Lehmann. il Electr World 74:23-6+ S '65
Pressure switches monitor electrical distribution system; Los Angeles. il Am City 80:117 Je '65
Switchboard that will run forever. il Bsns W p66-7 My 1 '65
Testing faster hookup; electronic automatic exchange. il Bsns W p91 N 20 '65

ELECTRIC tools, Portable
Can electric tools now be shockproof? il
Consumer Bul 48:33-4 Jl '65
Fast-set glue gun for the home. J. Hand.
il Pop Sci 187:154-5 D '65
How good are GE's new power tools? H.
Walton. il Pop Sci 187:170-2 N '65
Let electricity ease your hard work. J. Hand.
il Pop Sci 187:60-3 Jl '65
New line of portable power tools. S. M. Gal-
lager. il Pop Sci 186:164-5+ My '65
One motor, four tools. il Pop Sci 187:74-5
S '65
Two shop tools with a low price tag; disk-
belt sander and wood-turning lathe. C. E.
Rhine. il Pop Sci 187:162-3 O '65
Workshop and garden equipment. il Con-
sumer Rep 30:166-202 D '65

Control
Build your own dual-throttle power-tool
speed control. D. Lancaster. il Pop Sci
187:128-30 N '65
Those amazing speed controls. D. Huff. il
Pop Sci 186:137-9+ Mr '65
Variable speed: the big news in tools. il
Pop Sci 187:164-6 O '65

Testing
Four-in-one portable tool. A. W. Lees. il
Pop Mech 124:50+ S '65

ELECTRIC transformers
Ground-level transformers improve city sky-
line; Ukiah, Calif. M. K. Roper. il Am
City 80:100 N '65
Transformer turns ratio nomogram. M. H.
Applebaum. il Electr World 74:29 N '65

ELECTRIC transmission
See also
Corona (electricity)

ELECTRIC utilities
Statist mentality; case of Duke power co.
R. Moley. Newsweek 65:108 Ap 19 '65
Upbeat; plans for new plant and equipment.
Newsweek 65:90+ Ap 12 '65
Utility war heats up. il Newsweek 65:80-2 Mr
15 '65
See also
American electric power company
Consolidated Edison company of New York

Employees
Manpower planning at an electric and gas
utility; displaced employees due to extensive
technological changes. R. W. Riche. Mo
Labor R 88:965-7 Ag '65

Finance
Why utility stocks are lagging. il Bsns W
p86 Ja 8 '66

Investments
Utilities steady growth. il Duns R 85:149-50
My '65

Management
Utility builds power with a hard sell; Amer-
ican electric power co. il Bsns W p77-8+
O 30 '65

Rates
Cost of running all those electric things.
il Changing T 19:24 Mr '65
Electric power: runaway rates. R. J. Straw.
Nation 200:364-5 Ap 5 '65
How to cut your city's electric bill. A.
Lurkis. Am City 80:53+ Je '65
See how your electric bill compares; other
states. Changing T 19:20 O '65
T.R.B. from Washington; rescuing New
England; TVA-type power yardstick. New
Repub 153:4 O 30 '65

ELECTRIC vehicles
Westinghouse aims high with a bus; skybus
for urban rapid transit. il Bsns W p57-8
S 18 '65

ELECTRIC vote counters. See Voting machines

ELECTRIC washing machines. See Washing
machines

ELECTRIC water heaters. See Water heaters

ELECTRIC waves
See also
Microwaves

ELECTRIC welding
Arc welding as a means of expression. B.
White. il Sch Arts 65:29-31 N '65
Steel hybrids take new shapes; high-
frequency. Fortune 73:176 Ja '66

ELECTRIC welding machines
Make your own arc welder. J. Burroughs.
il Pop Sci 187:142-5+ N '65

ELECTRIC wire and wiring
Extension speakers. L. Buckwalter. il Hi Fi
15:70-3 Mr '65

Improving your home wiring. G. Daniels. il
Pop Sci 187:140-5+ Jl; 122-7+ Ag; 138-42
S; 154-9+ O '65; 188:158-63+ Ja '66
Improving your home wiring. J. Burroughs.
il Pop Sci 187:159-63+ N '65
Improving your home wiring; how to install
new switches. H. Walton. il Pop Sci 187:
156-61 D '65
Rewards of electrical power. il House & Gard
127:166-9 My '65
Underground movement. Time 86:62 Ag 13 '65

Safety devices and measures
It's no substitute for adequate wiring; Surge
Limiter. Consumer Rep 30:231-2 Jl '65

ELECTRIC workers
Electronics industry: products, people, and
prospects; special report. il Electr World
73:25-8+ Ap '65
Project choose:
Resident schools. K. Gilmore. il Pop Electr
23:41-8 S '65
Six unions team up for electrical talks.
Bsns W p 166 O 9 '65
See also
Electric utilities—Employees

ELECTRICITY
See also
Corona (electricity)
Electric generators
Fuel cells
Hall effect

Prices
See Electric utilities—Rates

Study and teaching
See also
Electric engineering—Study and teaching

ELECTRICITY in the home
Rewards of electrical power. il House &
Gard 127:166-9 My '65
See also
Electric lighting
Electric wire and wiring

ELECTROBIOLOGY. See Electrophysiology

ELECTROCARDIOGRAPHY
What an EKG does, and doesn't tell your
doctor. G. G. Greer. Bet Hom & Gard 43:20
Ap '65

ELECTROCHEMICAL cutting
This is zero force; electrochemical machin-
ing and electrical discharge machining.
C. J. Vlahos. il Sci Digest 58:77-9 O '65

ELECTROCORTICOGRAMS
Amino acids released from the cerebral cortex
in relation to its state of activation. H. H.
Jasper and others. bibliog il Science 147:
1448-9 Mr 19 '65
Visually evoked electrocortical responses in
kittens: development of specific and nonspecific systems. G. H. Rose and D. B.
Lindsley. bibliog il Science 148:1244-6 My
28 '65

ELECTRODEPOSITION of metals. See Electroforming

ELECTRODES, Glass
Cationic glass electrode response in aqueous
solutions of sodium chloride and potassium chloride. E. W. Moore and J. W. Ross.
bibliog il Science 148:71-2 Ap 2 '65

ELECTROENCEPHALOGRAPHY
Cross-correlation analysis of electroencephalographic potentials and slow membrane transients. M. R. Klee and others.
bibliog il Science 147:519-21 Ja 29 '65
Discrimination and conditioning during sleep
as indicated by the electroencephalogram.
H. C. Beh and P. E. H. Barratt. bibliog
il Science 147:1470-1 Mr 19 '65
Electroencephalographic studies of homing
salmon. T. J. Hara and others. bibliog il
Science 149:884-5 Ag 20 '65
Extrasensory electroencephalographic induction between identical twins. T. D. Duane
and T. Behrendt. il Science 150:367 O 15 '65;
Discussion. 150:1240+; 151:28+ D 3 '65, Ja
7 '66
Mescaline, 3,4-dimethoxyphenylethylamine,
and adrenaline: sites of electroencephalog-
raphic arousal. Y. Takeo and H. E. Him-
wich. bibliog il Science 150:1309-10 D 3 '65
Selective attentiveness and cortical evoked
responses to visual and auditory stimuli.
P. Spong and others. bibliog il Science
148:395-7 Ap 16 '65
Sequential behavior induced repeatedly by
stimulation of the red nucleus in free
monkeys. J. M. R. Delgado. bibliog il
Science 148:1361-3 Je 4 '65
Sleep: effects of a restricted regime. W. B.
Webb and H. W. Agnew, jr. bibliog il
Science 150:1745-7 D 24 '65
Somnambulism: all-night electroencephalo-
graphic studies. A. Jacobson and others.
bibliog il Science 148:975-7 My 14 '65

ELECTRONIC circuits—*Continued*
Microelectronics. W. C. Hittinger and M. Sparks. il Sci Am 213:56-64+ N '65
Miniature frequency synthesizer among goals of expanding microwave firm. Miss & Roc 16:35-6 My 3 '65
Miniature world of microcircuits. J. R. Berry. il Pop Mech 124:120-3 S '65
Oceanography promising market for micro-circuit manufacturers. Miss & Roc 16:37 Ap 5 '65
PreFab electronic building blocks. R. M. Benrey. il Pop Sci 187:118-20 Jl '65
Single silicon slice foreseen yielding up to 1,000 circuits. R. Pay. Miss & Roc 17: 24+ S 20 '65
Sylvania steps up IC market drive. Miss & Roc 17:35 Ag 23 '65
Technical, business trends show semiconductor microcircuit shift. P. J. Klass. il Aviation W 82:107+ Ap 12 '65
Tiny circuits take a fall. il Fortune 72:192+ Jl '65
    See also
Guided missiles—Electronic equipment
Printed circuits
ELECTRONIC components. See Electronic apparatus and appliances
ELECTRONIC computers. See Computers
ELECTRONIC data processing
Computers begin to solve the marketing puzzle. il Bsns W p 114-15+ Ap 17 '65
Computers move up in personnel ranks; IBM's recruitment information system. Bsns W p 118 O 23 '65
Data-processing system you can bank on; system used in Alexandria, Va. F. L. Ventura. il Am City 81:114+ Ja '66
Electronic data processing. il Duns R 86:150-1+ S '65
Electronic information handling; report on conference. A. Kent. Science 148:540-3 Ap 23 '65
Flexible display system gaining users. C. D. LaFond. il Miss & Roc 17:36-7 S 27 '65
New tax collector tells his goals. S. S. Cohen. Nations Bsns 53:31+ Ap '65
Office automation in the insurance industry. A. Freedman. il Mo Labor R 88:1313-19 N '65
On-line computing dominance forseen. R. Pay. Miss & Roc 16:32-4 Mr 1 '65
Picking top men by electronics. il Bsns W p97-8 Mr 6 '65
Small community gets big-time data processing; Windsor, Conn. R. B. Weiss. il Am City 80:103-4 Ap '65
You must use brains; evaluating a city's total data-processing system. D. K. Martin. il Am City 80:95+ D '65
    See also
Data processing service centers
ELECTRONIC data processing workers. See Computer workers
ELECTRONIC digital computers. See Computers—Digital computers
ELECTRONIC drafting machine. See Drafting instruments
ELECTRONIC engineers. See Electric engineers
ELECTRONIC equipment. See Electronic apparatus and appliances
ELECTRONIC flash units. See Electric lamps, Flashlight
ELECTRONIC lens testing. See Lenses, Photographic—Testing
ELECTRONIC listening devices. See Electronics in criminal investigation, espionage, etc.
ELECTRONIC medical apparatus. See Medical instruments and apparatus
ELECTRONIC music. See Music, Electronic
ELECTRONIC organ. See Organ
ELECTRONIC ovens
Industry warms up to microwaves. il Bsns W p 152+ Mr 13 '65
ELECTRONIC parts. See Electronic apparatus and appliances
ELECTRONIC reading aids. See Blind, Apparatus for
ELECTRONIC reading machines. See Reading machines
ELECTRONIC relays
Super-sens. L. E. Garner, jr. il Pop Electr 23:57-62+ N '65
ELECTRONIC service shops
Radio & TV news. See issues of Electronics world
ELECTRONIC specialty company
Easing the pangs of growth. il Bsns W p 108-10 Jl 24 '65
ELECTRONIC surveying. See Electronics in surveying
ELECTRONIC switches. See Electric switches

ELECTRONIC systems division. See United States—Air force—Systems command
ELECTRONIC technicians. See Electric workers
ELECTRONIC test instruments. See Testing instruments
ELECTRONIC thermometers. See Thermometers and thermometry
ELECTRONIC timers. See Timing devices
ELECTRONIC vote counters. See Voting machines
ELECTRONIC vote indicators. See Voting machines
ELECTRONICALLY steerable away radars. See Radar—Antenna and scanning mechanisms
ELECTRONICS
Basic principles of reliability. J. H. Wujek. jr. il Electr World 73:44-5 F '65
Electronic coin tosser. W. Pope. il Pop Electr 22:50-3 Ap '65
Electronic magic at the World's fair. A. Zuckerman. il Pop Electr 23:63-5+ Jl '65
Instant electronics for the home; IRectronics, building blocks. il Sci Digest 57:22 My '65
Microfilm and electronics. D. M. Costigan. il Electr World 74:37-9 Ag '65
Recent developments in electronics. See issues of Electronics world
    See also
Medical electronics
Quantum electronics

Bibliography

Electronics library (cont of) Pop'tronics bookshelf. See issues of Popular electronics
New literature. See occasional issues of Missiles and rockets

Exhibitions

I.E.E.E. and N.E.W. shows. W. A. Stocklin. Electr World 73:6 Je '65
New functional devices dominate meeting; International electron devices meeting. Aviation W 83:69 N 8 '65
Picture brightens; WESCON electronics show. W. J. Coughlin. Miss & Roc 17:46 Ag 23 '65

Military applications

DOD paper urges microcircuitry in all types of military systems. P. J. Klass. Aviation W 83:24 D 20 '65
Systems approach sought for avionics. B. Miller. il Aviation W 82:235-6+ Mr 15 '65
Tactical needs dictate better equipment. il Miss & Roc 16:63-4+ Mr 29 '65

Study and teaching

Project choose:
Resident schools. K. Gilmore. il Pop Electr 23:41-8 S '65
ELECTRONICS, Medical. See Medical electronics
ELECTRONICS in criminal investigation, espionage, etc.
Computers play cops and robbers. il Bsns W p 132-4+ Ja 15 '66
Outwit the electronic eavesdroppers. L. Steckler. il Pop Mech 124:70-4+ D '65
Question time; listening devices at Pension Clausewitz, West Berlin. il Newsweek 65: 49 Mr 1 '65
Too much snooping by federal agencies? il US News 58:10 Mr 1 '65
    See also
Wire tapping

Anecdotes, facetiae, satire, etc.

Notes and comment; protection against electronic snooping. New Yorker 41:35 Mr 13 '65
ELECTRONICS in space flight. See Space vehicles—Electronic equipment
ELECTRONICS in sports
Transistorball; electronic football. il Newsweek 66:64 N 8 '65
ELECTRONICS in surveying
Electronic equipment speeds survey work; San Diego, Calif. F. G. Peters. il Am City 80:122-4 Mr '65
ELECTRONICS in traffic control
City gets the green light; Orlando, Fla. W. L. Thomas. il Am City 80:123-4 S '65
Standardize traffic-control equipment; San Antonio, Tex. S. Fischer. il Am City 80: 117 F '65
ELECTRONICS industry and trade. See Electronic apparatus industry and trade
ELECTRONICS research center. See United States—National aeronautics and space administration—Electronics research center
ELECTRONS
Electron density and electronic properties in noble-metal transition elements. M. A. Jensen and others. bibliog il Science 150:1448-50 D 10 '65

ELECTRONS—*Continued*
Electron yield in the γ-radiolysis of water vapor. J. H. Baxendale and G. P. Gilbert. bibliog il Science 147:1571 Mr 26 '65
Photon and electron impact; report on symposium. V. H. Dibeler. Science 150:786-7 N 5 '65
See also
Plasma (ionized gases)

ELECTRO-OPTICAL surveillance station. See Artificial satellites—Military applications

ELECTRO-OPTICAL systems, incorporated
EOS unveils unique passive reflector. il Miss & Roc 17:38+ O 18 '65

ELECTROPHORESIS
Electrophoretic variation in enzymes. C. R. Shaw. bibliog Science 149:936-43 Ag 27 '65
Leukocyte alkaline phosphatase: electrophoretic variants associated with chronic myelogenous leukemia. J. C. Robinson and others. bibliog il Science 150:58-60 O 1 '65
Microelectrophoresis with alternating electric fields. L. D. Sher and others. bibliog il Science 148:229-31 Ap 9 '65
Serum protein electrophoresis in acrylamide gel: patterns from normal human subjects. A. C. Peacock and others. bibliog il Science 147:1451-3 Mr 19 '65

ELECTROPHYSIOLOGY
Active transport of 5,5-dimethyl-2,4-oxazolidinedione. J. M. Dietschy and N. W. Carter. bibliog il Science 150:1294-6 D 3 '65
Bioelectric control of bioluminescence in the dinoflagellate noctiluca. R. Eckert. bibliog il Science 147:1140-5 Mr 5 '65
Classical conditioning of electric organ discharge rate in mormyrids. F. J. Mandriota and others. bibliog il Science 150:1740-2 D 24 '65
Cross-correlation analysis of electroencephalographic potentials and slow membrane transients. M. R. Klee and others. bibliog il Science 147:519-21 Ja 29 '65
Duplication of evoked potential waveform by curve of probability of firing of a single cell. S. S. Fox and J. H. O'Brien. bibliog il Science 147:888-90 F 19 '65
Electrical effects in bone. C. A. L. Bassett. il Sci Am 213:18-25 O '65
Electrophysiological studies of Chilean squid axons under internal perfusion with sodium-rich media. I. Tasaki and others. bibliog il Science 150:899-901 N 12 '65
Electrostatic aspects of physical adsorption: implications for molecular sieves and gaseous anesthesia. S. W. Benson and J. W. King. jr. bibliog il Science 150:1710-13 D 24 '65
Myo-electricity; the transistorized man. D. S. Halacy. jr. il Pop Electr 22:41-4+ F '65
Nature of the excitatory sarcoplasmic reticular junction. G. Hoyle. bibliog il Science 149:70-2 Jl 2 '65
Sodium pump: its electrical effects in skeletal muscle. A. S. Frumento. bibliog il Science 147:1442-3 Mr 19 '65
Visual excitation and blood clotting. G. Wald. bibliog il Science 150:1028-30 N 19 '65

Apparatus
Arthropod preparation for behavioral, electrophysiological, and biochemical studies. W. C. Corning and others. bibliog il Science 148:394-5 Ap 16 '65
Auditory nerve: electrical stimulation in man. F. B. Simmons and others. bibliog il Science 148:104-6 Ap 2 '65

ELECTROPHYSIOLOGY of plants
Geoelectric effect and geotropic curvature. R. R. Dedolph and others. bibliog Science 148:1100-1 My 21 '65

ELECTROPLATING
Electroplate or anodize your electronic projects. W. B. Ford. il Pop Electr 22:55-9+ Je '65
See also
Electroforming

ELECTRORETINOGRAPHY
Electroretinography in newborn human infants. A. B. Barnet and others. bibliog il Science 148:651-4 Ap 30 '65
Respiratory and electrical responses to light stimulation in the retina of the frog. W. Sickel. bibliog il Science 148:648-51 Ap 30 '65

ELEFTHERIOU, B. E. See Bronson, F. H. jt. auth.

ELEMENTARY and secondary education act of 1965. See Federal aid to education

ELEMENTARY particles. See Particles (nuclear physics)

ELEMENTARY school buildings. See School buildings

ELEPHANT hunting
Tale of two cats. W. Page. il Field & S 70:62-5+ My '65

ELEPHANTS
Out of the park; Kenya's elephant surplus. il Newsweek 66:42 S 20 '65

ELEVATED sidewalks. See Sidewalks, Elevated

ELEVATORS
Basic factors in planning elevator systems. C. W. Lerch. Arch Rec 138:181-2 Jl '65

ELGIN marbles
Greece as the Greeks know it; Great Britain keeps marbles. H. Sutton. Sat R 48:47 Ag 7 '65

ELIASBERG, Ann Pringle
Parent and child (cont) N Y Times Mag p 129+ O 31; 112+ N 21 '65

ELIOT, George Fielding
1914: tragedy of the West. Nat R 17:555-6 Je 29 '65
Onset of empire. Nat R 18:73+ Ja 25 '66
Our one-package landing force. Pop Sci 187:40-3+ Jl '65

ELIOT, John
Three apostles to the Indians. P. W. Schmidtchen. il Hobbies 70:106+ Ag '65

ELIOT, Thomas Stearns
Interview with Eliot; ed. by T. S. Matthews. Mlle 61:68 My '65

about

Eliot in memory. B. Blanshard. Yale R 54:635-40 Je '65
Elusive genius of T. S. Eliot. L. Paul. pors Reporter 32:33-5 Ap 22 '65
Joyce and Eliot: a tale of Shem & Shaun. N. Halper. por Nation 200:590-5 My 31 '65
Letter from London; homage to him at Globe theatre. M. Panter-Downes. New Yorker 41:84+ Je 26 '65
Magical journey of T. S. Eliot. P. Elmen. Christian Cent 82:649-50+ My 19 '65
Memories of T. S. Eliot; excerpt from Table talk. I. Stravinsky. Esquire 64:92-3 Ag '65
Other T. S. Eliot. L. Durrell. por Atlan 215:60-4 My '65
Some non-encounters with Mr Eliot. F. Russell. por Horizon 7:36-41 Autumn '65
T. S. Eliot: a memoir and a tribute. H. Rago. Poetry 105:392-5 Mr '65
Upon which to rejoice. H. Carruth. Poetry 106:239-41 Je '65

ÉLISABETH, consort of Albert I, king of the Belgians
Regal mourners of Belgium's Queen without frontiers. il Life 59:49 D 10 '65

L'ELISIR d'amore; opera. See Donizetti, G.

ELISOFON, Eliot
Vagabond camera. W. Lane. il Travel 123:56-7 My '65

ELIXIR of love; opera. See Donizetti, G.

ELIZABETH II, queen of Great Britain
Queen finally meets her aunt. il por Life 58:41 Mr 26 '65

Visit to Ethiopia, 1965
Old-fashioned hospitality. il por Newsweek 65:46+ F 15 '65
Queen calls on Judah's Lion. il por Life 58:36-7 F 19 '65
Wing on the palace; eight-day visit. il por Time 85:30 F 12 '65

Visit to Germany (Federal Republic) 1965
Auld acquaintance. il por Newsweek 65:36 Je 7 '65
Better late than never. il pors Time 85:32 My 28 '65
Hands across the Rhine. il por Newsweek 65:42+ My 31 '65
Queen's trip; an end to old enmities? il por U S News 58:16 My 31 '65
Royal promise; visit to West Berlin. il por Time 85:25 Je 4 '65

ELIZABETH, princess of Yugoslavia. See Oxenberg, Mrs H.

ELIZALDE, Manuel
Who's who in foreign business. il por Fortune 72:70 O '65

ELK
They're still shooting the tule elk. M. Owings. il Audubon Mag 67:296-8 S '65

ELK hunting
Bull elk in the brush. J. O'Connor. il Outdoor Life 136:50-1+ O '65
Hurrah for the real elk hunter. C. Conley. il Field & S 70:50-1+ Ag '65
Mad bull of Bristol Head. G. A. Wintz. il Outdoor Life 135:56-7+ My '65
Michigan's first elk hunt; ed. by B. East. G. Loebrich. il Outdoor Life 135:36-9+ Ap '65
We learned about elk. N. Smith. il Outdoor Life 136:44-7+ D '65

ELKIN, Lillian
Paul Y. Anderson: Nation's angry man. Nation 200:584-7 My 31 '65

ELM

Diseases and pests

City girds for the Dutch-elm-disease battle; Ames, Ia. R. E. Speer, jr. il Am City 80: 132-3 Je '65

Dutch elm disease: there is no cure. Am For 71:2-3 Ag '65

Phytotoxin isolated from liquid cultures of ceratocystis ulmi. C. A. Salemink and others. bibliog Science 149:202 Jl 9 '65

Way to save the elms. il Fortune 72:192 Jl '65

EL MALLAKH, Ragaei. See Mallakh, R.

ELMAN, Richard M.
Antic arts. Holiday 38:83-7 Ag '65
Books. Commonweal 82:573-5 Ag 6 '65
Educational TV. Nation 200:217-21 Mr 1; inside cover, 421 Ap 19 '65
Poet of plainness. Commonweal 82:250-1+ My 14 '65
Puerto Ricans. Commonweal 83:405-8 Ja 7 '66

ELMEN, Paul
Magical journey of T. S. Eliot. Christian Cent 82:649-50+ My 19 '65

ELMIRA, N.Y.
Elmira to try composting; use in refuse disposal. C. F. Sanford. il Am City 80:93-4 Jl '65

EL PASO natural gas company
They play rough in the gas business; T.G.T. vs. El Paso fight for southern California market. R. A. Smith. il Fortune 73:132-5+ Ja '66

ELPHICK, Ruth L.
Ethel Parton. Horn Bk 41:307-14 Je '65

ELSON, John T.
Man for others. Life 58:108-9+ My 7 '65

ELSON, Robert T.
Country in search of identity. Sat R 48:49+ N 13 '65
In man for the Cabinet. Fortune 72:154-7+ O '65
What the leaders believed. Sat R 49:36 Ja 1 '66
What's going on way up North? Sat R 48:37 My 29 '65

ELTON, Godfrey Elton, 1st baron
Day with Jude the obscure. Horizon 7:62-4 Spr '65

ELVES and the shoemaker; drama. See Thane, A.

ELVINS, Peter
Zandonai: Giulietta e Romeo. Opera N 30:31 N 6 '65

ELWART, Joan P.
Much ado about school readiness. Parents Mag 40:43+ Ag '65

ELY, Gladys
On receiving as a memento a stone from Alaska; poem. Nation 201:506 D 20 '65

EMANCIPATION of women. See Woman—Equal rights

EMANCIPATION proclamation
Great man theory of emancipation. C. H. Wesley. Negro Hist Bul 28:101-2+ F '65

EMANS, Elaine V.
Discovery; poem. Farm J 89:107 D '65
Late perception; poem. Farm J 89:88 Je '65

EMBARGO
Battle act report, 1964; seventeenth report to Congress, January 13, 1965. Dept State Bul 52:148-54 F 1 '65

EMBASSIES (buildings)
Bill authorizing new embassy at Saigon signed by President; statement, May 25, 1965. L. B. Johnson. Dept State Bul 52:974 Je 14 '65
Embassies undergo attacks. il Sr Schol 86: 18-19 Mr 18 '65
Embassy bombed; Saigon. il Sr Schol 86:25-6 Ap 15 '65
Eyewitness report: a single, heavy blast, bodies everywhere; U.S. embassy, Saigon. R. P. Martin. il U S News 58:36-7 Ap 12 '65
Outrages like this; attack on U.S. embassy in Saigon. il Time 85:21-2 Ap 9 '65
Saigon savagery; bombing of U.S. embassy. il Newsweek 65:39-40 Ap 12 '65
U.S. embassy at Saigon damaged; funds for new building requested; statement, March 30, and letter, April 1, 1965, with bill. L. B. Johnson. Dept State Bul 52:571-2 Ap 19 '65
Will Viet war step up? bombing of U.S. embassy in Saigon. il Bsns W p29 Ap 3 '65

EMBEZZLEMENT
Funds disappear, rights leader accused. U S News 59:12 Jl 19 '65
Law and the faithful; Rev Reese, charged with embezzlement. Reporter 33:18+ S 23 '65
Mistakes of the head? Newsweek 66:26 Jl 19 '65
Various forms of embezzlement; case of F. D. Reese. il Time 86:20 Jl 16 '65

EMBLEN, D. L.
Fitchburg railroad; poem. Cath World 201:131 My '65

EMBOSSED stationery. See Stationery

EMBROIDERY
Stitchery for wall hanging; junior high school. B. Springer. il Sch Arts 64:22 Je '65
See also
Crewel work

EMBRYOLOGY
Drama of life before birth; photographs; with report by A. Rosenfeld. L. Nilsson. Life 58:54-70+ Ap 30 '65
See also
Amnion
Cells
Fetus

Birds

Control of glutamine synthetase in the embryonic retina in vitro. A. A. Moscona and D. L. Kirk. bibliog il Science 148: 519-21 Ap 23 '65

Erythropoiesis in the chick embryo: the role of endoderm. F. H. Wilt. bibliog il Science 147:1588-90 Mr 26 '65

Hemoglobin heterogeneity: embryonic hemoglobin in the duckling and its disappearance in the adult. T. A. Borgese and J. F. Bertles. bibliog il Science 148:509-11 Ap 23 '65

Histone regulation of lactic dehydrogenase in embryonic chick brain tissue. B. C. Goodwin and I. W. Sizer. bibliog il Science 148:242-4 Ap 9 '65

Prenatal auditory sensitivity in chickens and ducks. G. Gottlieb. bibliog il Science 147: 1597-8 Mr 26 '65

Short- and long-lived messenger RNA in embryonic chick lens. R. Reeder and E. Bell. bibliog il Science 150:71-2 O 1 '65

Echinoderms

Messenger RNA in early sea-urchin embryos: cytoplasmic particles. A. S. Spirin and M. Nemer. bibliog il Science 150:214-17 O 8 '65

Messenger RNA in early sea-urchin embryos: size classes. M. Nemer and A. A. Infante. bibliog il Science 150:217-21 O 8 '65

Insects

Culture of dissociated drosophila embryos: aggregated cells differentiate and sort out. R. J. Lesseps. bibliog il Science 148:502-3 Ap 23 '65

Mammals

Cleft palate produced in mice by human-equivalent dosage with triamcinolone. B. E. Walker. il Science 149:862-3 Ag 20 '65

Collagenase: effect on the morphogenesis of embryonic salivary epithelium in vitro. C. Grobstein and J. Cohen. bibliog il Science 150:626-8 O 29 '65

EMELYANOV, Vasily S.
For more pure water. Bul Atomic Sci 21: 46-8 S '65

EMENS, John R.
Education begets education. por Am Ed 1: 11-13 S '65

EMERGENCIES. See First aid in illness and injury

EMERGENCY communication systems
See also
Radio communication—Emergency applications

EMERGENCY landing, Airplanes. See Airplanes—Landing

EMERGENCY medical tags. See Identification tags, bracelets, etc.

EMERGENCY planning, Office of. See United States—Emergency planning, Office of

EMERGENCY services, Hospital. See Hospitals—Emergency services

EMERSON, Ralph Waldo
But can they crack a nut? Emerson's views on commodity values vs. beauty. J. B. Craig. Am For 71:7 Jl '65

EMERSON, Roy
Best and best-paid amateur. H. Gordon. il pors N Y Times Mag p36-7+ My 16 '65
¡Ole! Manolo, a little bit too late. E. Shirley. il Sports Illus 24:48-9 Ja 10 '66

EMERSON family
Emerson coat-of-arms. H. K. Eilers. il Hobbies 70:126 N '65

EMERY, Donald G.
What every library needs. Sat R 48:74-5 Ap 17 '65

EMERY, John C.
Air freight forwarder finds ceiling unlimited. il por Bsns W p87-8+ O 16 '65

EMERY air freight corporation
Air freight forwarder finds ceiling unlimited.
il Bsns W p87-8+ O 16 '65
Intervention by Hildred forestalls Emery's
IATA status cancellation. Aviation W 83:
38 D 6 '65
EMIGRATION and immigration law. See Immigration and emigration law
EMINENT men. See Great men
EMMANUEL, Sister Mary. See Mary Emmanuel. Sister
EMMERICH, André
Gold of the Indies; excerpts from introduction
to Sweat of the sun and tears of the moon.
Américas 17:23-9 My '65
Master goldsmiths of Sitio Conte; excerpt
from Sweat of the sun and tears of the
moon. Natur Hist 74:18-25 O '65
EMMETT, J. A.
Boating. See issues of Outdoor life
New boats for 1966. Outdoor Life 137:60-2+
Ja '66
Outdoor life boating 1966. Outdoor Life 137:
56-66+ Ja '66
EMMETT, Jim
Boats we meet: Captain Handy. Camulin
IV. Yachting 118:51-3+ D '65
Boats we meet: Distant Star. Yachting 118:
57-9+ Jl '65
Boats we meet: Out Islander. Yachting 117:
85-7+ Ap '65
Boats we meet: Rocking Chair. Yachting 117:
41-3 F '65
Going south. Yachting 118:154-6 D '65
The Keys. Yachting 118:38-40+ N '65
EMMYS. See Academy of television arts and
sciences
EMOTIONAL maturity. See Maturity
EMOTIONS
Interview with Erich Fromm; ed. by R. Heffner. E. Fromm. McCalls 93:132-3+ O '65
Your emotions are in your voice. F. R.
Schreiber and M. Herman. Sci Digest 57:
31-2 Ap '65
See also
Anger
Anxiety
Facial expression
Jealousy
Love
EMOTIONS and food. See Eating. Psychology
of
EMOTIONS in literature
Satisfying element. P. A. Whitney. Writer
78:11-14+ F '65
EMPHYSEMA
Battle for breath; rise in number of cases.
il Life 58:41-2+ My 28 '65
Is it really emphysema? il Sci Digest 58:35
O '65
Losing life's breath. il Newsweek 65:100+ Je
14 '65
Shortness of breath. Time 85:53-4 F 5 '65
EMPIRE
See also
Imperialism
EMPLOYEE relocation. See Employment systems
EMPLOYEE vacations. See Vacations, Employee
EMPLOYEES
See also
Job transfers
Personnel management

Dismissal
European limitations on employee dismissal.
K. Braun. Mo Labor R 88:67-8 Ja '65
How to know when you're being F.I.R.E.D.
D. Winks. il Esquire 64:104-5+ Ag '65

Qualifications
What do employers want? il Am For 71:35-
7+ S '65

Selection
See Employment systems

Training
Can subsidies solve America's problems? a
city's answer, Oakland, Calif. il Nations
Bsns 53:32-3+ Ag '65
Douglas upgrades the apprentice: on-the-job
training program for skilled workers.
Bsns W p80 Ja 8 '66
How jobless are retrained to work in mental
hospitals. H. G. Earl. il Todays Health 43:
8-9+ Ap '65
New look at how machines make jobs. il
Nations Bsns 53:58-60+ S '65
Nine jobs in your future. Life 58:4 Mr 19 '65
Report and appraisal: the Armour fund's
Sioux City project. E. H. Conant. Mo Labor
R 88:1297-301 N '65
Retraining programs in western Europe. M.
S. Gordon. Mo Labor R 88:292-3 Mr '65

Take charge of your career. R. Dunlop. Pop
Mech 124:20+ Ag '65
Ten corporations and automation; report on
questions sent to presidents of twenty California corporations. A. Juvinall. Christian
Cent 82:271-3 Mr 3 '65
EMPLOYEES, Transfer of
Homebuilders try to sell a city; Philadelphia-
area builders woo families to be transferred by Defense dept. il Bsns W p60+
Ap 3 '65
Report and appraisal: the Armour fund's
Sioux City project. E. H. Conant. Mo Labor
R 88:1297-301 N '65
EMPLOYEES lunches. See Lunches, Employees
EMPLOYEES representation in management
Can employees manage themselves? radical
new theory of management. T. R. Brooks.
il Duns R 86:59-60+ N '65
EMPLOYER-employees relations. See Industrial
relations; Personnel management
EMPLOYERS associations
Fate of 14(b); aid for the unions. S. Lens.
Commonweal 82:662-5 S 17 '65
EMPLOYMENT
Are they asking too much? Peace corps
veterans. F. G. Jennings. Sat R 48:65-6
My 15 '65
Are we turning away from talent? excerpt
from address. F. Keppel. Sat R 48:66 My
15 '65
Can U.S. find jobs for 89 million? il U S
News 58:75 My 8 '65
Choosy class of '65. il Time 85:86 Mr 12 '65
For college grads: no job problem. U S
News 58:88 My 24 '65
Gracious society; ways of putting the unskilled unemployed to work. America 112:
416 Mr 27 '65
How to choose your job, and land it; questions and answers. L. Velie. Read Digest
87:140-3 N '65
National goals; review of Employment act
proposed. H. C. Wallich. Newsweek 66:104
N 15 '65
President Johnson on employment; excerpt
from news conference, April 1, 1965. L. B.
Johnson. Cur Hist 49:45+ Jl '65
Private war on poverty; where industry
creates jobs. U S News 59:75-6 Ag 30 '65
Shortage of skills. Time 86:88 D 17 '65
What life is like when everybody has a job.
il U S News 58:86-8 Ap 5 '65
Where chances for jobs are best. U S News
58:91 My 10 '65
Work that play built. L. Velie. Read Digest
86:151-2+ Je '65
See also
Applications for positions
Seasonal labor
Self employed
Student employment
Unemployment—United States
Woman—Employment
Youth—Employment

Statistics
Employment; tables. See issues of Monthly
labor review
Marital and family characteristics of workers in March 1964. V. C. Perrella. Mo
Labor R 88:260-4 Mr '65
Sixty-one million jobs. Time 86:28 S 24 '65
Work experience of the population in 1963. S.
Saben. il Mo Labor R 88:8-16 Ja '65
See also
Unemployment—Statistics
EMPLOYMENT act of 1946. See Employment
EMPLOYMENT agencies
Executive job hunters get a guide; with
editorial comment. il Bsns W p45-6+, 129-
30 Ja 15 '66
Job consultant for big business. il Ebony
20:115-16+ Ap '65
Management: headhunters by any other
name; executive recruiters. il Newsweek
67:44-6 Ja 3 '66
One-woman show: Britain's largest secretarial employment agency, The Brook street
bureau. il Time 85:106 Mr 19 '65
EMPLOYMENT counseling. See Vocational
guidance
EMPLOYMENT discrimination. See Discrimination in employment
EMPLOYMENT stabilization
German programs to curb winter construction layoffs. E. M. Bussey. Mo Labor R 88:
434-7 Ap '65
EMPLOYMENT systems
Christmas employment picture. Pub W 188:
56-7 S 6 '65
Computers move up in personnel ranks.
IBM's recruitment information system.
Bsns W p 118 O 23 '65

EMPLOYMENT systems—*Continued*
Ethnics of executive selection. L. B. Ward. bibliog f il Harvard Bsns R 43:6-8+ Mr '65; Reply. B. L. Masse. America 112:612 Ap 24 '65
Hiring practices for longshoremen; Labor department study of ten East and Gulf Coast ports. P. Groom. Mo Labor R 88:1289-96 N '65
How does religion influence job choice? Harvard study. il Bsns W p 178+ Ap 17 '65
Sharper tools for the talent hunt; psychological tests for potential executives. il Bsns W p70+ Mr 27 '65
They're not trying to succeed in business; college seniors. L. Stessin. il N Y Times Mag p76+ Mr 28 '65
See also
Applications for positions

Guaranty of employment
Heat is back on for pay raises; job security and job expansion, labor's primary demands. il Bsns W p33-4 Jl 3 '65
New plans for older workers. C. A. Betts. il Sci N L 87:298-9 My 8 '65
UAW expected to stress job security. W. H. Gregory. Aviation W 82:55+ Mr 29 '65
Worker's search for security; reprint from June 1963 issue. D. Bell. Mo Labor R 88: 789-92 Jl '65

EMPTY place; story. See Panter-Downes, M.

EMPTY room at the inn; drama. See Du Bois, G.

ENAMEL and enameling
Enameling; enameling on copper in the ninth grade. J. Madill. il Sch Arts 64:14-16 F '65
Hungarian enamels; application of champlevé. G. Kaler. il Hobbies 70:46-7 Ja '66
June Schwarcz; electroforming and enamel. A. Ventura. il Craft Horiz 25:36-7+ N '65

ENAMELLED glass. See Glassware

ENCAPSULATION. See Capsules

ENCAUSTIC painting
Wax painting. W. Radcliffe. il Sch Arts 64: 25-6 F '65

ENCEPHALITIS
Virus-like particles seen in photographs of brain; patient suffering from sclerosing encephalitis. il Sci N L 89:35 Ja 15 '66

ENCEPHALITIS, Epidemic. See Sleeping sickness

ENCHANTED; novel. See Delmar, V.

ENCHANTED princess; drama. See Baher, C. W.

ENCOUNTER with a stranger; story. See Boyd, S. K.

ENCYCLICALS
Convocation on Pacem in terris; world leaders study Pope John's words. P. J. Henriot. America 112:223-4 F 13 '65
Guidelines to peace; Pacem in terris. M. Frakes. Christian Cent 82:294-6 Mr 10 '65
Lasting vision of Pope John; Pacem in terris. Time 85:37 F 26 '65
New trend in encyclicals? D. R. Campion. Commonweal 82:714-15 O 1 '65
Pacem in terris; symposium. il Sat R 48: 19-30 F 13 '65
Paul's second encyclical: Mense Maio. Nat R 17:408 My 18 '65
Paul's urgent cry: Mense Maio, second encyclical. America 112:698 My 15 '65
Peace and pathos; study of Pope John's encyclical Pacem in terris. N. O'Gorman. Commonweal 81:783-5 Mr 19 '65
Peace and reality; convocation on Pacem in terris. P. Steinfels. Commonweal 81:785-6 Mr 19 '65
Peace on earth? New York convocation discusses Pope John XXIII's encyclical Pacem in terris; with report by J. K. Jessup. il Life 58:32-36A+ Mr 5 '65
Pope John speaks again; International convocation on Peace on earth. America 112: 307-8 Mr 6 '65
Question of tone. J. O'Gara. Commonweal 82: 716 O 1 '65
Requirements of peace; conference on Pope John XXIII's encyclical Pacem in terris (Peace on earth) il Time 85:36-8 F 26 '65
When the world's peoples talked peace; excerpts from speeches at the Pacem in terris convocation, with list of participants. il Sat R 48:22-6+ My 1 '65

ENCYCLOPAEDIA Britannica
Encyclopaedia Britannica; the new edition. H. Finch. Sr Schol 86:sup 12-13 My 13 '65
Friendly Britannica. A. M. Louis. il Nation 200:224-5 Mr 1 '65
Intimacy Q.E.D. Newsweek 65:58+ Mr 8 '65

ENCYCLOPAEDIA Britannica, Incorporated
Britannica joins N.Y. times in social studies program. Pub W 188:69 D 27 '65
EB gives $100,000 to JFK memorial library. il Pub W 187:50 Mr 22 '65
Words in color. H. Goodman. Wilson Lib Bul 40:62 S '65

ENCYCLOPAEDIA Britannica press. See Encyclopaedia Britannica. incorporated

ENCYCLOPAEDIA Britannica school library awards
EB awards to four school library systems. Pub W 187:137 F 22 '65
Ten finalists named for school library awards. Pub W 187:97 F 8 '65

ENCYCLOPEDIAS
Keeping up with knowledge. J. Tebbel. Sat R 48:52-3 Jl 10 '65
Negro biography neglected in children's encyclopedias. Library J 90:2002 Ap 15 '65
Psychosemantics: vagaries of Great Soviet encyclopedia. Reporter 33:16 D 2 '65; Reply. D. H. Norton. 33:6 D 30 '65
What's new in encyclopedias? for children. H. R. Finch. il Sr Schol 86:18T F 18 '65
Your encyclopedia: tool for teaching research skills. W. D. Halsey. Sr Schol 86:sup9 My 6 '65
See also names of encyclopedias, e.g. New Catholic encyclopedia

END of the road; story. See Cave, H.

ENDEMISM. See Geographical distribution of animals and plants

ENDIVE
See also
Cookery—Vegetables

ENDIVE, French. See Chicory

ENDLESS chain; story. See Boyd, C.

ENDOCRINOLOGY
Endocrines, behavior, and population. J. J. Christian and D. E. Davis; reply with rejoinder. N. S. Negus and E. Gould. Science 149:376+ Jl 23 '65
Insect mating behavior: endocrine control of a chemical communication system. R. H. Barth, jr. bibliog il Science 149:882-3 Ag 20 '65

ENDORE, Guy
Capsule history of diamonds. Holiday 37:52-3 Je '65

ENDOTOSCOPE. See Medical instruments

ENDRIN
Food safety program: endrin monitoring in the Mississippi River. A. F. Novak and M. R. R. Rao. bibliog il Science 150:1732-3 D 24 '65

ENDURANCE
You're tougher than you think. R. Gannon. il Pop Sci 186:78-81 Ap '65

ENEMIES; drama. See Leokum, A.

ENEMY: love; story. See Monk, E. G.

ENERGY conversion, Direct. See Direct energy conversion

ENERSEN, Lawrence A. See Lundy, F. A. jt. auth.

Les ENFANTS du Thalia; story. See Williams, G.

ENFORCEMENT of law. See Law enforcement

ENGBERG, Edward
From Du Pont, with love. Commonweal 82: 465-8 Jl 2 '65

ENGEL, Celeste G. and others
Igneous rocks of the Indian Ocean floor. Science 150:605-10 O 29 '65

ENGEL, Leonard
Science crosses specialty lines. Harper 230: 117-18 F '65

ENGELBERG, Joseph. See Rao. P. N. jt. auth.

ENGELHARDT, Manfred, and others
Odorous secretion of normal and mutant tribolium confusum. bibliog Science 150: 632-3 O 29 '65

ENGELHARDT, Nickolaus Louis, 1907-
Unknown shaper. por Time 86:90+ N 12 '65

ENGELHART, Max D.
Educational research shelf for teachers. NEA J 54:63-4 D '65

ENGELS, Friedrich
Little-known chapter in American history; column for Horace Greeley's Tribune. M. Geltman. il Nat R 17:865-7 O 5 '65

ENGELS, John
Cellar springs in winter; poem. Reporter 32:50 F 25 '64
Seasonal poem. Commonweal 83:374 D 24 '65

ENGH, Jeri
Summer in the USA: bumming with a purpose. Mlle 60:132-3+ F '65
Try Paul Bunyan country for vacation size. Todays Health 43:18-23 Jl '65

ENGH, Keith
Praise the Lord and pass the lug wrench. Pop Mech 124:82-5+ D '65

ENGINEER corps. See United States—Army—
Corps of engineers

ENGINEERING
Future of engineering education; address,
June 24, 1965. J. H. Hollomon. Vital
Speeches 31:634-6 Ag 1 '65
Lift the human spirit! a new kind of engi-
neering; excerpts from address. J. R.
Killian, jr. il Sat R 48:58-60 My 1 '65
Social engineering. Nation 201:486-7 D 20 '65
What are we doing to engineering? J. R.
Pierce. il Science 149:397-9 Jl 23 '65
See also
Building
also Electric engineering; Structural en-
gineering; etc.

History
Wooden ox: the world's first wheelbarrow;
engineering and agriculture in ancient
China. L. Petech. il UNESCO Courier 18:
28-9 My '65

Study and teaching
Hayward issues the call; open house for high
school students and teachers. Hayward,
Calif; ed. by P. D. Eimon. il Am City 80:
130+ Jl '65
See also
Engineering education

ENGINEERING, Biomedical. See Biomedical
engineering

ENGINEERING, Medical. See Biomedical engineering

ENGINEERING colleges
Bombay institute of technology. V. A.
Javoronkov; D. Behrman. il UNESCO
Courier 18:14-17+, 33-6 My '65
See also names of engineering colleges,
e.g. Polytechnic institute, Brooklyn

ENGINEERING education
Engineering misdirected; misuse of national
resources by cold war. Nation 201:111 S 6
'65
Future of engineering education; address,
June 24, 1965. J. H. Hollomon. Vital
Speeches 31:634-6 Ag 1 '65
Inventing an education for engineers. T. K.
Glennan. il Sat R 48:72-4+ N 20 '65
Research grants hurt engineering education.
Sci N L 88:88 Ag 7 '65
What are we doing to engineering? J. R.
Pierce. il Science 149:397-9 Jl 23 '65

ENGINEERING materials. See Materials

ENGINEERING research
1965 science review. il(p385) Sci N L 88:394
D 18 '65
Technology races ahead; research, way of
life for packaging men. il Duns R 86:pt2
90-2+ D '65

ENGINEERING societies
See also
Society of automotive engineers

ENGINEERING students
Inventing an education for engineers. T. K.
Glennan. il Sat R 48:72-4+ N 20 '65

ENGINEERS
Average engineer described in survey. Sci
N L 88:56 Jl 24 '65
Lift the human spirit! a new kind of engi-
neering; excerpts from address. J. R.
Killian, jr. il Sat R 48:58-60 My 1 '65
See also
Chemical engineers
Electric engineers
Engineering education

Supply and demand
GM in their future; MTU draws engineering
head-hunters. il Newsweek 67:80 Ja 24
'66
Your career barometer (title varies) C. Peet.
il Pop Mech 124:32+ O; 44+ N '65

ENGINES
See also
Air engines
Diesel engines
Pistons
Solar engines

ENGINES, Toy
Solenoid toy engine will fascinate the PM
boy. W. D. Siprelle. il Pop Mech 124:197+
N '65

ENGLAND, J. Merton
Institutional grants of the National science
foundation. Science 148:1693-6 Je 25 '65

ENGLAND
See also
Art—England
Ayot St Lawrence
Botany—England
Cathedrals—England
Churches—England
Cornwall
Foreign visitors in England

Liverpool
Music festivals—England
Roads—England
Theater—Great Britain
Tourist trade—England
Yorkshire

Antiquities
See also
Stonehenge

Description and travel
Back roads of England. M. Furlong. il Atlan 216:114+ Ag '65
From Guzzle Down to the Tah. L. Martin. il
Sat R 48:52+ Mr 13 '65
1066-1966: history oriented visitor. W. Houlton. il NEA J 55:57-9 Ja '66

Divorce
See Divorce—Great Britain

Education
See Education—Great Britain
National trust
See National trust for places of historic
interest on natural beauty

Religious institutions and affairs
News of the Christian world (cont) Christian
Cent 82:250, 378, 595-6, 753-4, 874, 946 F
24, Mr 24, My 5, Je 9, Jl 7, 28 '65
Renewing England's free churches. C. North-
cott. Christian Cent 82:829-30 Je 30 '65
World around us (cont of) News of the
Christian world. Christian Cent 83:27-8 Ja
5 '66
See also
Reformation

Social life and customs
It's an old English custom. P. Brock. il
Travel 124:56-61 D '65
Last aristocrat. N. Gulbenkian. Esquire 63:
104-7+ Ap '65
See also
Christmas—England

ENGLAND, Church of. See Church of England

ENGLAND and the United States
Opinion, please from London. K. Miller. il
Mlle 60:84+ Mr '65
Sergeant Bates' march. M. Lomask. Am
Heritage 16:16-17 O '65
See also
Americans in England
United States—Foreign opinion—British

ENGLE, George
1320 feet of speed. Motor B 116:40-1+ Ag
'65

ENGLE, Paul
Christmas is people. McCalls 93:79-81+ D '65
Liveliest Republican of them all. N Y Times
Mag p 141-3 Ap 4 '65

about
Paul Engle: poet-grower to the world. T. G.
Harris. il pors Look 29:95-7 Je 1 '65

ENGLEBARDT, Stanley L.
Coming: two-inch TV. Sci Digest 57:55-9 Ap
'65
Common cold: a hopeful, new look. Sci Digest
58:56-9 O '65
Electronic car doctor. Sci Digest 59:45-7
Ja '66
How the armed forces create careers for
specialists. Pop Sci 186:136-8+ F '65
Make believe for real. Sci Digest 58:73-7
N '65
What computers can do. Sci Digest 57:61-5
F '65

ENGLEBERT, Victor
I joined a Sahara salt caravan. il Nat Geog
Mag 128:694-711 N '65

ENGLEWOOD, N.J.
It's easy to plant trees downtown. C. C. Guerrina. il Am City 80:108-9 Ap '65

ENGLISH, John A.
Case against ventilation. Motor B 116:98-9
D '65

ENGLISH, Patricia D. and others
Myoinositol kinase: partial purification and
identification of product. bibliog Science
151:198-9 Ja 14 '66

ENGLISH
Six English self-portraits; symposium. il
Harper 230:56-63 Ap '65

ENGLISH art. See Art, British

ENGLISH CHANNEL tunnel (proposed)
Channel tunnel bores toward contract stage.
il Bsns W p29 Jl 10 '65
Chunnel. F. P. Davidson. For Affairs 44:
314-19 Ja '66

ENGLISH composition. See English language—
Composition

ENGLISH cookery. See Cookery, English
ENGLISH drama
    See also
    London—Theater
ENGLISH fiction
    Angus Wilson's England. W. J. Smith. Commonweal 82:18-21 Mr 26 '65
    See also
    Literature, Comparative—English and American
ENGLISH grammar. See English language—Grammar
ENGLISH holly. See Holly
ENGLISH in the United States
    Brave Englishman in a Midwest pulpit. P. Watkins. Harper 231:96-8+ D '65
    Good time at UCLA; an English view. R. Gilbert. Harper 230:75-80+ Ap '65
ENGLISH language
    Dictionary of modern English usage, by H. W. Fowler. Review
      Life 59:6+ Ag 20 '65. G. Frazier
    Mother tongue, by L. Hogben. Review
      Time 85:98 Ap 2 '65
    Our man in Trotton; revised edition of Fowler's dictionary of modern English usage. New Yorker 41:21-3 Ag 14 '65
    Spitting permitted; revised edition of Fowler's dictionary of modern English usage. Newsweek 65:64+ My 17 '65
    See also
    Slang
    Words

Bibliography

Using the mother tongue. P. Pickrel. Harper 231:118+ N '65

Composition

How to write without thinking; essay requirements for College entrance examination board papers. N. Cousins. Sat R 48:30 My 1; 20 My 29 '65; Discussion. 48:17-18 Je 5 '65
Reeling and writhing; high school English courses. D. Klein. Seventeen 24:32+ D '65
Term papers; the best part of the course. H. Aldridge. il Sr Schol 87:sup 11 D 2 '65
Why the devil don't you teach freshmen to write? E. R. Clapp. il Sat R 48:63-5+ F 20 '65
Writing unit on statistics. S. Cochell. Sr Schol 86:8T F 11 '65
    See also
    Style, Literary

Creative activities

Inviting the muses. M. Young. Mlle 61:194+ S '65
My fourteen originals; creative writing course at American university in Cairo. J. Stuart. il Sr Schol 86:sup5-6 My 20 '65
Research papers in high school English; pro and con discussion. T. E. Taylor; Sister M. Christina. NEA J 54:42-4 N '65
What shall I write about? F. Pryor. il NEA J 54:54-5 N '65
    See also
    College and school journalism

Courses of study

Curriculum revision projects: English and the social studies. W. K. Richards. il Sr Schol 86:13T-14T+ F 18 '65
What's happening in education? instruction in English in high schools. W. D. Boutwell. PTA Mag 60:25 Ja '66

Dictionaries

Dictionaries. W. T. Johnston. il Consumer Bul 48:13-18 Je '65

Grammar

Between you and I; crusading for correct grammar is a hopeless business. G. Ace. Sat R 48:14 D 11 '65
Careful writer, by T. Bernstein. Review
    New Repub 153:32-4 Ag 21 '65. G. Daniels; Reply. L. T. Milic 153:37 S 4 '65
    Reporter il 33:60+ S 23 '65. R. C. Wald
    Sat R 48:27-8 Jl 17 '65. G. Hicks
How to improve sentence structure. R. I. Golden. Sr Schol 86:sup25 Ap 15 '65
New grammar; with transformer's guide. il Newsweek 66:64 D 13 '65
Save the English language! excerpt from Time lurches on. R. Schoenstein. Read Digest 87:45-6 Jl '65
Troublesome S and verb difficulties. R. I. Golden. Sr Schol 86:sup9 Mr 25 '65

Anecdotes facetiae, satire, etc.

Correct usage for he and I. L. J. Leibik. Sr Schol 86:sup4 Mr 25 '65

Word made Flesch; summary of his ABC of style, by D. Hucklesmudge, transcribed and paragraphed by H. Kenner. Nat R 17:558-60 Je 29 '65

Study and teaching

Content specialist in English. J. S. Simmons. Sch & Soc 93:153-4 Mr 6 '65
Curriculum revision projects: English and the social studies. W. K. Richards. il Sr Schol 86:13T-14T+ F 18 '65
Custodians of the language convene. W. Thompson. Nation 200:145-8 F 8 '65
Freedom and discipline in English; report of the College entrance examination board Commission on English. Review
    Sr Schol 87:sup6+ S 30 '65. J. Mersand
Our own language barrier. J. E. Alatis. Am Ed 1:12-13 D '64
Senior-made primers. E. Silverman. il NEA J 54:32-3 O '65
What every high school English teacher should know about using films in the classroom. B. Sullivan. il Sr Schol 87:sup43-4 S 23 '65
What's happening in education? instruction in English in high schools. W. D. Boutwell. PTA Mag 60:25 Ja '66
What's happening in English. H. R. Finch. Sr Schol 87:sup26-7 O 28 '65
Why the devil don't you teach freshmen to write? E. R. Clapp. il Sat R 48:63-5+ F 20 '65
    See also
    English language—Composition
    English language—Grammar
    English literature—Study and teaching
    National council of teachers of English

Terms and phrases

Hail to the cliché; Associated press computer assesses use of clichés. R. L. Tobin; discussion. Sat R 48:66 F 13; 66 Ap 10; 68 My 8 '65
How not to write, what not to say. L. Kronenberger. Atlan 216:97-100 S '65
Notes and comment; telephonic baby farewell: bye-bye. New Yorker 41:29 F 20 '65
Trials of a word-watcher. C. Ogburn, jr. Harper 230:88-90+ Ap '65
Words that are ours (cont) B. W. Overstreet. il PTA Mag 59:15-16 F; 26-8 Mr; 28-30 Ap; 28-9 My; 16-18 Je '65

Anecdotes, facetiae, satire, etc.

On the outness of inness. Sat Eve Post 238:98 S 25 '65

Words

History

Words and the sense of history. B. W. Overstreet. il PTA Mag 59:15-16 F '65
ENGLISH language arts. See Language arts
ENGLISH language in India
    Notes and comment. New Yorker 41:23 Jl 31 '65
ENGLISH literature
    Le morte d'Arthur. K. Rexroth. il Sat R 48:19 Jl 10 '65
    See also
    Literature, Comparative—English and Russian

History

Jerusalem and Albion, by H. Fisch. Review
    Commentary 39:73-5 F '65. D. Daiches

Study and teaching

Motion picture and the teaching of English, by M. C. Sheridan and others. Review
    Sr Schol 87:sup6 D 2 '65. J. Mersand
New records for English and social studies; with discography. J. Muri. il Sr Schol 87:sup 13-14 O 7 '65
    See also
    English language—Study and teaching
ENGLISH sculpture. See Sculpture, British
ENGLISH sheep dogs. See Sheep dogs
ENGLISH silver. See Silverware
ENGLISH songs. See Songs, English
ENGLISH sparrows. See Sparrows
ENGLISH springer spaniel national championship. See Field trials (dogs)
ENGLISH visitors in the United States. See Foreign visitors in the United States
ENGRAVING
    Chinese imagery on restoration silver. C. C. Dauterman. il Antiques 88:511-15 O '65
    See also
    Aquatint
    Lithography
    Postage stamp printing

ENGRAVING tools
Engraver for everything; Dremel model. C.
Conley. il Field & S 70:97 Ja '66
ENGRAVINGS
Engraved sources for American overmantel
panels. N. F. Little. il Antiques 88:494-501
O '65
See also
Prints
ENGRAVINGS, Mexican
José Guadalupe Posada: engraver of Mexican
life. C. A. Echánove. il Américas 17:28-35 N
'65
ENGSTROM, Elmer William
Businessmen in the news. por Fortune 72:
47 O '65
ENIWETOK
Uranium-series ages of Pacific atoll coral.
D. L. Thurber and others. bibliog Science
149:55-8 Jl 2 '65
ENLARGING (photography) See Photography
—Enlarging
ENLARGING meter. See Photography—Appara-
tus and supplies
ENQUIRER, Cincinnati. See Cincinnati en-
quirer
ENRIGHT, D. J.
Updike's ups and downs. Holiday 38:162+
N '65
ENRIGHT, Elizabeth
And so they lived happily ever after. McCalls
93:116-17+ D '65
Sea Christmas: story. Horn Bk 41:662-72 D '65
ENRIGHT, J. T.
Entrainment of a tidal rhythm. bibliog Sci-
ence 147:864-7 F 19 '65
ENROLLMENT, College. See Colleges and uni-
versities—Attendance
ENSENADA, Mexico
Mardi gras. C. West. il Motor B 115:38-9+
My '65
ENSLIN, Theodore
Tangere; poem. Nation 200:208 F 22 '65
about
Gestures of deliberation. T. Clark. Poetry
107:121 N '65
ENTEROPNEUST. See Balanoglossus
ENTERPRISE, Free. See Free enterprise
ENTERTAINER; drama. See Osborne, J.
ENTERTAINERS
Entertainment unions: a progress report. Mo
Labor R 88:III-IV N '65
See also
Beatles
Dancers
ENTERTAINING
Afternoon tea; recipes. il Redbook 126:80-1+
N '65
Books, not booties for a baby shower. Pub
W 188:71 O 25 '65
Coffee pot's on! M. L. Bagley. il Farm J
89:87 Mr '65
Diploma-night party. il Farm J 89:78-9 My
'65
Engagement party; Bridal shower; menus
with recipes. il Redbook 125:68-71+ Je '65
Entertaining made easy; with menus. il Bet
Hom & Gard 43:72-83+ N '65
Etiquette of entertaining. A. Vanderbilt.
Ladies Home J 82:28 Ap '65
For the young and hungry; with recipes.
J. Hewitt. il N Y Times Mag p62 Ag 29
'65
Four holiday parties to give tradition a new
sparkle. il House & Gard 128:156-61+ D '65
Give a party! with recipes. il Seventeen 24:
63-79+ Jl '65
GH's lazy days cookbook; spontaneous snacks
with recipes. il Good H 161:90-107 Jl '65
Good time ideas for all ages. K. Davis. il
Farm J 89:81-3+ F '65
Holiday open house. il Bet Hom & Gard
43:58-9+ D '65
How to give dashing parties; Philadelphia
association of gourmets. il House & Gard
128:248-53 N '65
In twelve hours there will be a party in this
room. il Esquire 65:99-106 Ja '66
Ladies' home journal party portfolio. il
Ladies Home J 82:95-124+ O '65
Let's throw a star-spangled party! R. Dun-
lop. il Todays Health 44:36-9+ Ja '66
Mlle's next word on the real right way
to go to/give a party. il Mlle 62:71-3+ D
'65
Man talk; let me entertain you. D. Newman
and R. Benton. Mlle 62:84 N '65
Mixture as never before. A. Pryce-Jones.
House & Gard 127:146-7 Mr '65
Music for parties. F. Bowers. House & Gard
128:34+ N '65
Notes for the hostess. D. Bryan. See issues
of House & garden incorporating Living for
young homemakers

Open house A.M; P.M; Christmas entertain-
ing; with recipes. il McCalls 93:118-21+ D
'65
Parties that ring bells. E. J. L. Porter. il
Recreation 58:477-8 D '65
Party file. il Ladies Home J 82:100-1 Ap; 90-1
My; 98-9 Je '65
People at parties. W. Stanton. il McCalls
92:55 My '65
Perle Mesta's party notebook. P. Mesta.
McCalls 92:17 My '65
Quick and zesty dips! il Bet Hom & Gard
43:108 O '65
Saucepans and the single girl; excerpts.
J. Kragen and J. Perry. il Ladies Home J
82:36+ My; 90+ Je; 86+ Jl; 94+ Ag; 90+
S '65
Sensible woman's guide to entertaining; ex-
cerpts from Entertaining with elegance.
G. A. Dariaux. il Redbook 125:56-7+ Jl '65
Seven things one should never do . . . P.
Bracken. il Ladies Home J 82:60 O '65
Six ways to make your party fun. il Seven-
teen 24:122-5 F '65
Summer living in Southampton. il House &
Gard 128:100-15 Ag '65
Teen-agers all love slumber parties. Bet Hom
& Gard 43:124 O '65
Two great parties with a new idea; movie
party, bridge party. il House & Gard 127:
136-41 Mr '65
Watching Fords go by; party at New York's
Delmonico hotel before wedding of A.
Ford. il Newsweek 67:46 Ja 10 '66
When you entertain outside your home;
excerpt from Today's etiquette. il Good H
160:183 Ja '65
See also
Buffet meals
Business entertaining
Childrens parties
Games
Government entertaining
Hospitality
Menus
Table setting
    Anecdotes, facetiae, satire, etc.
Pity the poor hostess. R. Hochstein. il
Good H 161:56+ N '65
ENTERTAINING, Government. See Govern-
ment entertaining
ENTERTAINING in sales promotion
Broadway hijinks at an Angus auction;
Black Watch farms, Wappingers Falls,
N.Y. il Bsns W p32-3 O 23 '65
To succeed in Europe, Philco goes European;
introduces multinational line with music
and dancing. il Bsns W p 132-3+ O 2 '65
ENTERTAINING Mr Sloane; drama. See Or-
ton, J.
ENTERTAINMENTS. See Amusements
ENTFÜHRUNG aus dem serail; opera. See
Mozart, J. C. W. A.
ENTRANCE drives. See Driveways
ENTRANCE halls. See Halls
ENTRANCE requirements, College. See Col-
leges and universities—Entrance require-
ments
ENTRANCES (doorways) See Doorways
ENTRAPMENT (law)
To trap a thief. Time 85:56 Je 25 '65
ENVIRONMENT
City as environment. K. Lynch. il Sci Am
213:209-14+ bibliog(p280) S '65
Fouling of the American environment; sym-
posium. il Sat R 48:31-48+ My 22 '65; Dis-
cussion. 48:21 Je 26 '65
Man and his habitat; problems of pollution;
symposium. Bul Atomic Sci 21:18-30 Mr '65
Man and his habitat; problems of water
pollution. il Bul Atomic Sci 21:16-26 Ap
'65
Man and his habitat; symposium. il Bul
Atomic Sci 21:18-30 Mr; 16-26 Ap; 2-11
My; 6-25 Je '65
New boundaries of home. House & Gard
127:87 F '65
Save the world. D. Wolfle. Science 149:819
Ag 20 '65; Reply. A. F. Hofmann. 150:145
O 8 '65
See also
Adjustment, Social
ENVIRONMENTAL laboratories. See Testing
laboratories
ENVIRONMENTAL science services admin-
istration. See United States—Environmental
science services administration
ENZYMES
Adaptive enzyme synthesis: its inhibition as
a possible analogue of immunological
tolerance. D. W. van Bekkum and H. T. M.
Nieuwerkerk. bibliog il Science 149:548-50
Jl 30 '65

ENZYMES—*Continued*

Alcohol dehydrogenase in drosophila melanogaster: isozymes and genetic variants. E. H. Grell and others. bibliog il Science 149:80-2 Jl 2 '65

Biological feedback control at the molecular level. D. E. Atkinson. bibliog il Science 150:851-7 N 12 '65

Biosynthesis of vitamin A with rat intestinal enzymes. D. S. Goodman and H. S. Huang. bibliog il Science 149:879-80 Ag 20 '65

Control of biochemical reactions. J.-P. Changeux. il Sci Am 212:36-45 bibliog(p 158) Ap '65

Control of enzyme activity in growing bacterial cells by concerted feedback inhibition. L. Burlant and others. bibliog il Science 148:1351-3 Je 4 '65

Crystalline human urokinase: some properties. A. Lesuk and others. bibliog il Science 147:880-2 F 19 '65

Delta-aminolevulinate dehydratase activity in mice with hereditary anemia. F. L. Margolis and E. S. Russell. bibliog il Science 150:496-7 O 22 '65

Effect of gamma radiation on dietary and hormonal induction of enzymes in rat liver. H. C. Pitot and others. bibliog il Science 150:901-3 N 12 '65

Electrophoretic variation in enzymes. C. R. Shaw. bibliog Science 149:936-43 Ag 27 '65

Enzymatic synthesis of tri- and tetranucleotides of defined sequence. R. E. Thach and P. Doty. bibliog il Science 148:632-4 Ap 30 '65

5-Hydroxytryptophan decarboxylase in rat brain: effect of hypothalamic lesions. A. Heller and others. bibliog il Science 147:887-8 F 19 '65

Increased activities of glycogenolytic enzymes in liver after splanchnic-nerve stimulation. T. Shimazu and A. Fukuda. bibliog il Science 150:1607-8 D 17 '65

Inhibitory oxidation products of indole-3-acetic acid: enzymic formation and detoxification by pea seedlings. C. C. Still and others. bibliog il Science 149:1249-51 S 10 '65

Isoenzymic specificity of impaired clearance in mice infected with Riley virus. B. W. J. Mahy and K. E. K. Rowson. bibliog il Science 149:756-7 Ag 13 '65

Lactate dehydrogenase isozymes: substrate inhibition in various human tissues. E. S. Vesell. bibliog il Science 150:1590-3 D 17 '65

Level of urine enzymes gives clue to cancer. Sci N L 88:168 S 11 '65

New enzyme discovered by Vermont scientist; esteroproteolytic enzyme. Sci N L 88:6 Jl 3 '65

Nucleoside phosphatases of fetal and maternal blood cells: electron microscope study. R. S. Connell and L. E. Bacon. bibliog il Science 150:503-4 O 22 '65

Ornithine carbamoyltransferase in liver of the dipnoan protopterus aethiopicus. G. W. Brown, jr. bibliog Science 149:1515 S 24 '65

Papain membrane on a collodion matrix: preparation and enzymic behavior. R. Goldman and others. bibliog il Science 150:758-60 N '65

Pituitary gland: enzymic formation of methanol from S-adenosylmethionine. J. Axelrod and J. Daly. bibliog il Science 150:892-3 N 12 '65

Proteins and disulfide groups in the aggregation of dissociated cells of sea sponges. G. J. Gasic and N. L. Galanti. bibliog il Science 151:203-5 Ja 14 '66

Rhythmic enzyme changes in neurons and glia during sleep. H. Hydén and P. W. Lange. bibliog il Science 149:654-6 Ag 6 '65

Square root variations of reciprocal graphing of enzyme kinetic data. P. Stutts and I. Fridovich. il Science 149:447 Jl 23 '65; Reply. J. R. Totter and M. J. Cormier. bibliog 150:1627-9 D 17 '65
See also
Catalase
Cholinesterase
Dehydrogenases
Galactosidases
Glutamic oxaloacetic transaminase
Hyaluronidase
Lipase
Lysozyme
Oxidases
Penicillinase
Phosphatases

Hybrids

Hybridization of glucose-6-phosphate dehydrogenase from rat and human erythrocytes. E. Beutler and Z. Collins. bibliog il Science 150:1306-7 D 3 '65

Nomenclature

Enzyme nomenclature; report on the 1964 recommendations of the International union of biochemistry on nomenclature and classification of enzymes. Science 150:719-21 N 5 '65

EOCENE period. See Paleontology—Eocene

EPERGNES

Powell? Potts? Pitts! the T P epergnes. E. Gaines. il Antiques 87:462-5 Ap '65

EPHRATA, Pa.

For travelers east, here's an interesting Pennsylvania detour; Ephrata Cloister. il Sunset 135:27-8 Jl '65

EPIC poetry

Epic of the gaucho: Martín Fierro, by J. Hernández, with excerpts. C. E. Ward. il Américas 17:8-15 N '65

EPIDEMIC neuromyasthenia

Annals of medicine. B. Roueché. New Yorker 41:205-10+ N 27 '65

EPIDEMICS

Anatomy of an epidemic. Sci Digest 57:35 My '65

Some kinetic properties of a deterministic epidemic confirmed by computer simulation. M. L. Black and I. D. Gay. bibliog il Science 148:981-5 My 14 '65
See also
Cholera
Plague

EPIDENDRUM atropurpureum. See Orchids

EPIDERMIS. See Skin

EPILEPSY

I'm tired of living a lie. Read Digest 86:133-6 Ap '65

New paths opened for epilepsy studies. Sci N L 88:167 S 11 '65

That stardust malady; musicogenic epilepsy. il Time 86:67 Jl 16 '65

What are we doing about epilepsy? H. G. Earl. il Todays Health 44:28-31+ Ja '66

EPILEPTICS

Epileptics drive safely. Sci N L 89:46 Ja 15 '66

I'm tired of living a lie. Read Digest 86:133-6 Ap '65

Living with epilepsy; interview, ed. by E. Keiffer. C. T. Lombroso. Parents Mag 40:72-3+ N '65

EPIPHYLLUMS

Epiphyllums. S. E. Beahm. il Horticulture 43:22-3 Jl '65

EPISCOPACY

Freedom beyond polity; is episcopacy the answer? R. J. Cebik. Christian Cent 82:1379-82 N 10 '65

EPISCOPAL church. See Protestant Episcopal church

EPOXY adhesives

Versatile adhesive putty. Consumer Rep 30:472 O '65

EPPEL, Lou

Are you getting the outboard performance you paid for? Motor B 116:32-3+ Jl '65

Autumn look at your outboard. Motor B 116:51-3+ O '65

EPPERT, Ray R.

Automation and national policy; address, February 10, 1965. Vital Speeches 31:316-18 Mr 1 '65

Passport for world markets; address, June 21, 1965. Vital Speeches 31:663-8 Ag 15 '65

EPPRIDGE, Bill

How Bill Eppridge photographed the world of junkies. Mod Phot 29:22+ Je '65

about

Junkie's life. Newsweek 65:63 Mr 8 '65

EPSTEIN, Emanuel. See Rains, D. W. jt. auth.

EPSTEIN, Eugene V.

American books for American children in Switzerland. Pub W 189:64-5 Ja 10 '66

EPSTEIN, Jason

Stranded in the future. Commentary 39:80-2+ My '65

EPSTEIN, Joseph

Albert's girl. New Repub 152:19-20 Mr 13 '65

Down the line. Commentary 40:101-5 O '65

Intellectualism in American life. New Repub 152:21-4 Je 5 '65

Joe Gould's masterpiece. New Repub 153:26-7+ O 23 '65

New possibilities. New Repub 153:40+ N 27 '65

Rococo and roll. New Repub 153:27-9 Jl 24 '65

Row over urban renewal. Harper 230:55-61 F: 18+ Ap '65

EPSTEIN, Louis

Bookseller year 1965. Pub W 187:80 F 1 '65

EPSTEIN, R. H. See Edgar, R. S. jt. auth.

EPSTEIN, Sam

Amateur scientist. Sci Am 212:118-23 F '65

EPSTEIN, Seymour
In the deep sea; story. Redbook 125:62-3 S
'65
In the place of angels; story. Redbook 124:137
F '65
EPSTEIN, Wallace V.
Specificity of macroglobulin antibody syn-
thesized by the normal human fetus. bibliog
Science 148:1591-2 Je 18 '65
EPTON, William
Aftermath to Harlem riot; Epton anarchy
trial. F. J. Donner. il Nation 201:355-8+
N 15 '65
Mao's man in Harlem. il por Time 86:15
D 31 '65
EQUAL employment opportunity commission.
See United States—President's equal em-
ployment opportunity commission
EQUAL rights for women. See Woman—Equal
rights
EQUALITY
Civil equity; wrongs to be righted; address,
November 17, 1965. W. W. Wirtz. Vital
Speeches 32:135-8 D 15 '65
Equality and liberty, by H. V. Jaffa. Review
Nat R il 17:606-7 Jl 13 '65. S. Parry
Equality, by L. Miller and others. Review
America 113:446-8 O 16 '65. A. A. North
Interdependence of mankind; address, June 9,
1965. H. H. Humphrey. Dept State Bul 53:
56-9 Jl 12 '65
Negroes sharpen call for real equality;
southern justice as main target. il Bsns W
p46 N 20 '65
Project equality is growing; San Antonio
joins. America 113:233 S 4 '65
EQUILIBRIUM, Donnan. See Donnan equilib-
rium
EQUIPMENT renting. See Rental services
EQUISETUM
Nature note; horsetails. Sci N L 87:189 Mr
20 '65
ERASMUS, Desiderius
His wit against the wicked. J. A. Hardon.
Sat R 48:88-9 My 22 '65
They made our world. L. Rosten. il por Look
29:80-1 Je 1 '65
ERASMUS Hall, Brooklyn. See Brooklyn—
Education
ERDMAN, Jean
Jean Erdman and company. Martinique the-
atre. J. Maskey. Dance Mag 39:66-7 Je '65
ERFURTH, Hugo
Psychological document in sadness; portrait
of O. Kokoschka. G. M. Mayer. Pop Phot
56:50-1+ F '65
ERGOLINE
Ergoline alkaloids in tropical wood roses.
J. W. Hylin and D. P. Watson. bibliog il
Science 148:499-500 Ap 23 '65
ERHARD, Ludwig
West Germany's aim; closer ties with the
U.S; interview. por U S News 59:36-7 D 20
'65
—See Johnson. L. B. jt. auth.

about

As Germans vote; what's at stake. por U S
News 59:26 S 20 '65
Back in stride; U.S. visit. il por Newsweek
67:13 Ja 3 '66
Besser ist der Ludwig. il por Time 86:40+
O 1 '65
Bonn, the morning after. R. Steel. Common-
weal 83:55-7 O 15 '65
Chancellor Erhard's visit. America 113:703-4
D 4 '65
Erhard and Wilson: why they plan trips to
U.S. U S News 59:19 N 29 '65
Erhard's free-market concepts go on trial.
por Bsns W p62 D 18 '65
Erhard's goal: to ease U.S.-French strain.
por U S News 58:19 Je 7 '65
Erhard's new mandate. il por Sr Schol 87:9
S 30 '65
German problem heats up. il por U S News
58:45 F 1 '65
German vote: meaning for U.S. il por U S
New 59:70 O 4 '65
Heavy winner. por Newsweek 66:46+ O 4 '65
Knocking eggheads together. il por Time
86:26 Jl 23 '65
Making of the chancellor 1965. il Newsweek
66:26 S 6 '65
Mideast mix-up: everybody loses. Newsweek
65:29 Mr 22 '65
Neglected fences; five-day visit in the U.S.
il por Time 85:29-30 Je 11 '65
Piglet for *onkel*. il por Time 86:33 Ag 20 '65
Rubber lion strikes again. il por Time 86:35
O 29 '65
Sincere Chancellor. Time 85:30-1 F 26 '65
ERICKSON, R. C.
Sex as the writer's new myth. Christian Cent
82:641-3 My 19 '65

ERICSON, Raymond
New life for Gurre-lieder. Sat R 48:85 O
30 '65
ERICSSON, John
Beauty and chivalry of the United States
assembled. D. B. Webster, jr. il por Am
Heritage 17:50-3+ D '65
ERICSSON, Leif. See Leif Ericsson
ERIE, Pa.
Stabilization solves dirt-street problems.
H. P. Wozniak. il Am City 80:60 O '65
We solved a filter-media problem. W. E.
DeArment. il Am City 80:83-5 D '65
ERIE, LAKE
Cleveland: saving Lake Erie. L. B. Seltzer.
il Sat R 48:36+ O 23 '65
Dead sea; problem of pollution. il Newsweek
65:33-4 Ap 12 '65
Fight to save Lake Erie. H. Titus. il Field
& S 69:10-12+ Mr '65
Hideous Hudson River: Lake Erie is dirty,
too. America 113:148 Ag 14 '65
Test case on pollution: big clean-up begins.
il Bsns W p25-6 Ag 14 '65
Time for transfusion. il Time 86:62 Ag 20 '65
ERIE CANAL
Gentle adventure: from Lake Erie to the sea.
N. Nadel. il Yachting 118:44-6+ Ag; 48-9+
S '65
ERIKSEN, Stein
Top-money skier. il pors Look 29:87-8 D 14
'65
ERIOGONUM
They're great for sunny slopes; Santa Cruz
Island buckwheat and St Catherine's lace.
il Sunset 134:274-5 Je '65
ERLER, Fritz
Alliance and the future of Germany. For
Affairs 43:436-46 Ap '65
ERLICHMAN, Joe
Quiet war on bad processing. J. Durniak. il
Pop Phot 56:64 Je '65
ERNANI: opera. See Verdi. G.
ERNEST Orlando Lawrence memorial awards
Five scientists named for Lawrence award.
Sci N L 87:153 Mr 6 '65
ERNST, Max
Second fame. N. Lyon. il por Vogue 145:
150-2 Je '65
ERNST, Morris L.
Some aspects of censorship; excerpts from
address, October 13, 1964. por Wilson Lib
Bul 39:668-9 Ap '65
ERNST, Paul
Once upon a midnight; story. Good H 162:58-
9 Ja '66
EROSION
Anomalous erosional topography in Victoria
Land, Antarctica; Wright Dry Valley. H.
T. U. Smith. bibliog il Science 148:941-2 My
14 '65
ERRORS, Popular
Bunk about health foods. R. L. Smith. il
Todays Health 43:24+ O '65
Profits and risks of simplification. H. Eyring.
Science 150:439 O 22 '65
Science and antiscience; address, December
27, 1964. W. R. Brain. bibliog Science
148:192-8 Ap 9 '65; Reply. D. J. Pletsch.
149:926 Ag 27 '65
You and your diet; false notions about foods.
plus recipes. il Good H 161:205-8 S '65
ERRORS, Typographic
Riot sale; New York post error sells TV sets
at $8.98. il Newsweek 66:81 D 13 '65
ERVIN, Samuel James, 1896-
Excerpt from address, March 4, 1965. Cong
Digest 44:145+ My '65

about

Doubters with points. Time 85:22-3 Ap 2 '65
ERWIN, Henry
Sergeant Erwin and the blazing bomb. C.
Ford. il Read Digest 87:86-8 Jl '65
ERWITT, Elliott
Marilyn Monroe. il Pop Phot 58:140-1 Ja '66
ERYTHROCYTES
Electrophoresis of hemoglobin in single
erythrocytes. G. T. Matioli and H. B.
Niewisch. bibliog il Science 150:1824-6 D
31 '65
Erythrocyte membrane: chemical modifica-
tion. H. C. Berg and others. bibliog il Sci-
ence 150:64-7 O 1 '65
Glutamic-oxaloacetic transaminases in
reticulocytes and erythrocytes. J. S
Nisselbaum and O. Bodansky. bibliog il
Science 149:195-7 Jl 9 '65
Glycoprotein biosynthesis in human reticulo-
cytes: a lesion in thalassemia. E. H. Eylar
and G. T. Matioli. bibliog il Science 147:
869-70 F 19 '65
Hybridization of glucose-6-phosphate dehydrogenase from rat and human erythrocytes.
E. Beutler and Z. Collins. bibliog il Science
150:1306-7 D 3 '65

ERYTHROCYTES—*Continued*
Skin grafts: delayed rejection between pairs of cattle twins showing erythrocyte chimerism. W. H. Stone and others. bibliog il Science 148:1335-6 Je 4 '65

ERYTHROMYCIN
Drug antagonism between lincomycin and erythromycin. L. J. Griffith and others. bibliog il Science 147:746 F 12 '65

ERYTHROPOIESIS
Erthropoiesis in the chick embryo: the role of endoderm. F. H. Wilt. bibliog il Science 147:1588-90 Mr 26 '65
Spleen as a production site for erythropoietin. P. de Franciscis and others. bibliog il Science 150:1831-3 D 31 '65

ESCALATION. See Military art and science

ESCAPE artist; story. See Wagoner, D.

ESCARPIT, Robert
Revolution in books. UNESCO Courier 18: 4-10 S '65
Wanted: a new dialogue between authors & readers; excerpt from Revolution in books. UNESCO Courier 18:11-14 S '65

ESCH, Harald, and others
Sound: an element common to communication of stingless bees and to dances of the honey bee. bibliog Science 149:320-1 Jl 16 '65

ESCHEAT
Espousing easier escheat: Supreme court decision in case of Sun oil company. Time 85:74 F 12 '65

ESCHERICHIA coli
Complexes of F-pili and RNA bacteriophage. R. C. Valentine and M. Strand. bibliog il Science 148:511-13 Ap 23 '65
Genetic transfer in bacterial mating. J. D. Gross and L. Caro. bibliog il Science 150: 1679-84 D 24 '65
Ionizing radiation: effect of irradiated medium on synthetic processes. E. C. Pollard. bibliog il Science 147:1045-7 F 26 '65
Polyribosomes from escherichia coli: enzymatic method for isolation. M. Dresden and M. B. Hoagland. bibliog il Science 149:647-9 Ag 6 '65
Pseudouridine formation: evidence for RNA as an intermediate. S. B. Weiss and J. Legault-Demare. bibliog il Science 149:429-31 Jl 23 '65
Puromycin: effect on messenger RNA synthesis and β-galactosidase formation in escherichia coli 15T-. B. H. Sells. bibliog il Science 148:371-3 Ap 16 '65
Recombination in bacteriophage T4: a mechanism. E. Simon. bibliog il Science 150:760-3 N 5 '65
Ribosomes from escherichia coli: lack of specificity for viral RNA. J. E. Dahlberg and R. Haselkorn. bibliog il Science 149: 78-80 Jl 2 '65
Ultraviolet damage to bacteria and bacteriophage at temperatures. M. J. Ashwood-Smith and others. bibliog il Science 149: 1103-5 S 3 '65

ESCORTED tours. See Travel

ESFANDIARY, F. M.
Iran without veils Nation 200:178-80 F 15 '65

ESHKOL, Levi
Raiding the coop. il Newsweek 67:42+ Ja 24 '66
Search for identity. il por Newsweek 66:64+ N 15 '65

ESHLEMAN, Clayton
Book of Yorunomado; poem. Poetry 106:257-69 Jl '65

ESKILDSEN, C. R.
Agricultural export programs; address, February 9, 1965. Vital Speeches 31:326-8 Mr 15 '65

ESKIMO curlews. See Curlews

ESKIMO snow houses. See Snow houses

ESKIMOS
Alaska: the hard country; with report by M. Leatherbee. il Life 59:76-7+ O 1 '65
Europo-American block; the truly native Americans. C. Miles. Hobbies 70:114+ Ag '65
Reporter at large; return to George River. E. Iglauer. il New Yorker 41:174+ N 6 '65

Art
Eskimo ivory carving. il Design 66:34-6 Ja '65

Culture
Culture areas among the Eskimos and Indians of North America. C. Miles. il Hobbies 70: 112-14 S '65
Eskimo culture area. C. Miles. il Hobbies 70:112-13 O; 112-13 N; 112-13 D '65; 112-14 Ja '66

Food
Reporter at large; Eskimo canneries for Eskimo foods, results of sampling in district of Keewatin. E. Iglauer. New Yorker 41: 121-2+ Ap 24 '65

ESPALIERS. See Trees, Training of

ESPARZA, Elfego
American buffo; interview, ed. by Stevenson. por Opera N 29:32 F 6 '65

ESPINOSA, Ricardo Manuel Arias. See Arias Espinosa, R. M.

ESPINOSA, Robin
Capuchin cache of embarrassment. Life 58: 38A My 25 '65
Making the *bella figura;* a letter from Rome. Mlle 61:181-2 O '65

ESPIONAGE
Invisible government, by D. Wise and T. B. Ross. Review
  Commentary 39:87-9 Mr '65. R. Steel
Spy, by G. Lonsdale. Review
  Newsweek il 66:104+ D 20 '65
Spy in the Kremlin; O. V. Penkovsky. il Newsweek 66:48 N 8 '65
  See also
Electronics in criminal investigation, espionage, etc.
Spies
Wire tapping

ESPIONAGE, Industrial. See Spies, Industrial

ESQUIRE (periodical)
Adversaria. Esquire 64:98-9 O '65
Dedicated to the proposition that thinking can be fun. A. Gingrich. Esquire 64:6 N '65
Esquire is a dress rehearsal for the real world outside. A. Gingrich. Esquire 64:6 S '65
Esquire is a paid-up member in the fellowship of American sport. A. Gingrich. Esquire 64:6 O '65
Esquire's fifth annual dubious achievement awards 1965. il Esquire 65:74-9 Ja '66
Half the fun of travel is reading Richard Joseph. A. Gingrich. Esquire 64:6 Ag '65
Tight pants and full wallets; comment on Esquire's coverage of the American teenager. R. A. Schroth. America 113:80 Jl 17 '65

ESQUIRE literary symposium
Seventh esquire symposium this month at Chapel Hill. A. Gingrich. Esquire 63:6 Ap '65
Seventh literary symposium at Chapel Hill. A. Gingrich. Esquire 64:6 Jl '65

ESSAYS
Competitions
1965 Scholastic magazines writing awards. il Sr Schol 86:20-2+ My 20 '65

ESSEX institute, Salem, Mass.
Essex County furniture. R. Davidson. il Antiques 88:146 Ag '65

ESSO research and engineering company
Electricity from alcohol; Esso's new cell. il Time 85:55 Mr 12 '65

ESSO Standard eastern, incorporated. See Standard oil company (New Jersey)

ESTAING, Valéry Giscard d'. See Giscard d'Estaing, V.

ESTATE planning
Can your wife afford to be a widow? F. J. Taylor. il Read Digest 86:149-52 Ap '65
What death taxes do to you. il Changing T 19:37-9 S '65

ESTATE tax. See Inheritance tax

ESTATES, Decedents
Can your wife afford to be a widow? F. J. Taylor. il Read Digest 86:149-52 Ap '65

ESTEP, Irene
Dwarf fruit trees. Pop Gard 16:22-3 Mr '65

ESTERASES
  See also
Cholinesterase

ESTERQUEST, Ralph T.
High style at Harvard. Library J 90:5186-8 D 1 '65

ESTES, Billie Sol
Crack in Canon 35. H. Brucker. Sat R 48:48-9 Jl 10 '65; Discussion. 48:50-1 Ag 14 '65
Washington's money birds; guide to lobbyist Americanus and his predatory pursuits. L. L. King. il Harper 231:51-4 Ag '65

ESTES, Elliott M.
Like a pretty girl. il Newsweek 65:71+ Mr 1 '65
Pontiac's chiefs. por Motor T 17:76-9 F '65

ESTES, J. Worth, and White, P. D.
William Withering and the purple foxglove; with biographical sketches. Sci Am 212:22, 110-16+ Je '65

ESTES industries, incorporated
Making a bang with mini-missiles; rockets by mail to teen-agers. il Bsns W p79-80 Ap 24 '65

ESTIMATED income tax. See Income tax—Estimates

ESTIVALS, Gabrielle
Algerian woman. Holiday 37:60-1+ Je '65

ESTRADIOL
Radiolysis of estrone and estradiol. O. H. Wheeler and R. Montalvo. bibliog Science 150:493-4 O 22 '65

ESTROGENS
Age, postponement: a doctor speaks; questions and answers. il Vogue 146:62-5+ Ag 15 '65
Iron accumulation in cockerel plasma after estrogen: relation to induced phosphoprotein synthesis. O. Greengard and others. bibliog il Science 147:1571-2 Mr 26 '65
Menopause: is it necessary? A. Lake. Good H 160:85+ Ap '65
Pills to keep women young; excerpt from ERT: the pills to keep women young. A. Walsh. il McCalls 93:104-5+ O '65
Springs of youth. Time 85:59 Ap 16 '65

ESTRONE
Radiolysis of estrone and estradiol. O. H. Wheeler and R. Montalvo. bibliog Science 150:493-4 O 22 '65

ESTRUATION
It's here: timed breeding for livestock; drugs to control heat in beef cattle. J. A. Rohlf. il Farm J 89:24-5+ Jl '65

ETCHING, American
See also
Kowalke, R.

ETERNAL life. See Immortality

ETHACRYNIC acid
Wringing out the water. Time 85:78 F 19 '65

ETHANOL
Glycerol metabolism in the human liver: inhibition by ethanol. F. Lundquist and others. bibliog il Science 150:616-17 O 29 '65
Thymine addition to ethanol: induction by gamma irradiation. P. E. Brown and others. il Science 151:68-70 Ja 7 '66

ETHER
See also
Myristicin

ETHICAL relativism
Cult of relativism; harder right or the easier wrong; address, September 25, 1965. S. Thurmond. Vital Speeches 32:46-8 N 1 '65

ETHICS
Authentic morality, by I. Lepp. Review
Cath World 202:56-8 O '65. E. H. Peters
How does a conscience grow? M. Smart. il Parents Mag 40:58-9+ Ag '65
Man belongs to man; excerpt from Teaching of reverence for life. A. Schweitzer. Read Digest 87:77-8 Jl '65
New morality. J. Fletcher; H. McCabe. Commonweal 83:427-40 Ja 14 '66
Of note: Protestant-Catholic ethics. A. R. Jonsen. Commonweal 81:613-15 F 5 '65
Poets among the demagogues. L. Smith. Sat R 48:24+ O 2 '65
Psychoanalysis and morality. L. H. Farber. Commentary 40:69-74 N '65
See also
Advertising ethics
Business ethics
Cheating in schoolwork
Christian ethics
Honesty
Integrity
Love
Medical ethics
Moral attitudes
Moral conditions
Moral education
Political ethics
Sexual ethics
Social ethics
Truth
War, Ethics of

ETHICS and law. See Law and ethics

ETHIOPIA
See also
Elizabeth II, queen of Great Britain—Visit to Ethiopia. 1965
Natural resources—Ethiopia
Sports—Ethiopia
State encouragement of science, literature and art—Ethiopia

Description and travel
Easy adventure: Ethiopia. T. L. Christie. il Travel 124:56-9 N '65
Ethiopian adventure. N. T. Kenney. il Nat Geog Mag 127:548-82 Ap '65

History
Ethiopia. J. W. Sommer. bibliog il Focus 15:1-6 Ap '65

Politics and government
Lamb in lionskin. S. Meisler. Nation 200:510-12 My 10 '65

Social conditions
Yankee please stay; overseas exploits of ex-G.I.'s K. Baldwin and H. F. Downey. H. Bowser. Sat R 48:18 Ag 21 '65

ETHNIC attitudes. See Attitudes

ETHNIC types
See also
Race

ETHNOLOGY
See also
Racial differences

ETHOLOGY. See Character

ETHRIDGE, Samuel
Integrating the Negro teacher out of a job. B. Carter. il Reporter 33:31-3 Ag 12 '65

ETHYL alcohol. See Alcohol

ETHYLENE
Ethylene action and the ripening of fruits. S. P. Burg and E. A. Burg. bibliog il Science 148:1190-6 My 28 '65
Nitrogen: formation by photooxidation of ethylene in the presence of its oxides. J. J. Bufalini and J. C. Purcell. bibliog il Science 150:1161 N 26 '65

ETIQUETTE
Can't the pendulum swing this way? M. A. Guitar. Am Home 68:8 Mr '65
Etiquette; questions and answers. A. Vanderbilt. See issues of Ladies' home journal
Happy ways of doing things. P. Jones. Am Home 68:33+ Mr '65
What you can eat with your fingers. il Good H 161:163 S '65
When you entertain outside your home; excerpt from Today's etiquette. il Good H 160:183 Ja '65
You're a spectator; excerpt from Seventeen book of etiquette and entertaining. E. A. Haupt. Seventeen 24:318 Ag '65
See also
Courtesy
Diplomatic etiquette

ETIQUETTE for children and youth
Advice to children on behaviour at table; poem; first published about 1830. Redbook 125:64 Ag '65
Children's manners. A. Vanderbilt. Ladies Home J 82:52 Je '65
Let's be little ladies; M. Young's Washington school of social graces for moppets; with excerpts from her book. il Life 59:83-4+ D 3 '65
Talking it over with Gay Head; travel manners. Gay Head. Sr Schol 86:42 My 13 '65

ETNA, MOUNT
Polyphemus unbound. R. M. Coates. il Reporter 33:49-51 D 16 '65

ETTEN, John F.
What's wrong with high school science. por Sci Digest 57:64-8 Mv '65

ETTENBERG, Eugene M.
Philip Kappel, etcher & engraver. Am Artist 29:36-41+ N '65

ETTER, N. Wayne
Guest editorial. por Electr World 74:37 Jl '65

ETTINGER, Robert C. W.
Can deep freeze conquer death? Ebony 21:60-1+ Ja '66
Frozen Christian. Christian Cent 82:1313-15 O 27 '65
Lasting indefinitely. Esquire 63:63-5+ My '65

ETZIONI, Amitai
Chaos in science. Commonweal 82:494-7 Jl 9 '65

EUBANKS, Ralph Travis
Denatured man; address, November 24, 1964. bibliog Vital Speeches 31:241-3 F 1 '65

EUCHARIST. See Lords Supper

EUGENE, Ore.
Cross that inflames a city. T. Armbrister. il Sat Eve Post 238:36-7 Jl 3 '65

Architecture
City hall built from winning design. il Arch Rec 137:170-1 My '65

EUGENICS
Fruit from the tree of knowledge. P. H. Abelson. Science 149:251 Jl 16 '65; Discussion. 149:1171+ S 10 '65

EUGLENA
Nature note; protists. Sci N L 88:162 S 11 '65

EUGLENA gracilis. See Algae

EULER, Robert C. and Olson, A. P.
Split-twig figurines from northern Arizona: new radiocarbon dates. bibliog Science 148:368-9 Ap 16 '65

EULLER, John
Low water on the Lakes. Yachting 117:49+ My '65

EUPHORBIACEAE. See Spurges
EUPLECTELLA. See Sponges
EURATOM. See European atomic energy
community
EURHYTHMICS. See Eurythmics
EURIPIDES
Euripides; critical comparison to other Greek
literati. K. Rexroth. Sat R 48:29 S 18 '65
Trojan women; tr. by J. P. Sartre. Criticism
New Yorker 41:183-4 Ap 17 '65
EUROPE
Europe: hands across the Continent; with
report by A. de Borchgrave. il Newsweek
65:37-8+ My 3 '65
See also
Airlines—Europe
Americans in Europe
Tourist trade—Europe

Climate
Green winter; cold, wet, dreary summer. il
Time 86:28 Ag 13 '65

Commerce
What to watch for in Europe. F. Morley. il
Nations Bsns 53:27-8 Ap '65

Description and travel
Go fever: Europe's biggest season. il News-
week 66:57-61 Jl 19 '65
How to take your pet to Europe. B. Edgar.
il House & Gard 128:88+ S '65
I remember. M. B. Tucker. il NEA J 54:46-8+
F '65
Spanning Europe. T. B. Lesure. il Travel
124:47-9 Jl '65
Trip abroad: plan it to enjoy it. il Changing
T 19:33-4 F '65

Economic integration
West's mission is now in east Europe. Life
58:4 My 28 '65

History
See also
European war, 1914-1918

Bibliography
Articles and other books received; comp. by
O. J. Falnes. See issues of American his-
torical review

1789-1815
See also
Waterloo, Battle of, 1815

Maps
Map of Europe (cont) Sr Schol 87:26 S 30
'65

Politics
See also
European federation
Munich four power agreement, 1938

Social history
Proud tower, by B. W. Tuchman. Review
Newsweek il 67:86+ Ja 17 '66
Sat R il 49:33 Ja 15 '66
EUROPE, EASTERN
East Europe in flux; symposium. bibliog f
il Cur Hist 48:129-74+ Mr '65
Eastern Europe breaks out of its bonds;
special report. il Bsns W p 176-8+ N 20 '65
Hunters behind the Curtain; west European
businessmen. il Time 86:107 D 10 '65
Red world vs. the West, which is stronger?
il U S News 60:34-6 Ja 10 '66
Russia and Vietnam; Soviet prestige in
eastern Europe. P. Ben. New Repub 153:
15-16 Jl 10 '65
See also
Agriculture—Europe, Eastern
Theater—Europe, Eastern
Tourist trade—Europe, Eastern
United States—Foreign relations—Europe,
Eastern

Commerce
West Germany's economic romantics. G.
Bailey. il Reporter 33:37-41 S 23 '65

Description and travel
Iron curtain going up. R. Joseph. il Esquire
63:118-19+ Je '65
Personal business; businessman's guide to
eastern Europe. Bsns W p 171-2 N 20 '65

History
Bibliography
Articles and other books received; comp. by
C. Morley. See issues of American histori-
cal review

Politics
Germany looks at eastern Europe. G.
Schröder. For Affairs 44:15-25 O '65
United States and eastern Europe; address,
January 5, 1965. C. B. Elbrick. Dept State
Bul 52:137-42 F 1 '65
EUROPE, WESTERN
See also
Agriculture—Europe, Western
Airlines—Europe, Western
Airplane industry and trade—Europe,
Western
Automobile industry and trade—Europe.
Western
Automobile touring—Europe, Western
Banks and banking—Europe, Western
Camping—Europe, Western
Communism—Europe, Western
Dancing—Europe, Western
Disarmament—Europe, Western
Education—Europe, Western
Electronic apparatus industry and trade—
Europe, Western
Finance—Europe, Western
Gambling—Europe, Western
Investments, Foreign (in Europe)
Labor and laboring classes—Europe, Western
Music—Europe, Western
Newspapers—Europe, Western
Parks—Europe, Western
Public opinion—Europe, Western
Public welfare—Europe, Western
Restaurants—Europe, Western
Space research—Europe, Western
Steel industry and trade—Europe, Western
Strikes—Europe, Western
Telephone—Europe, Western
Textile industry—Europe, Western
Tourist trade—Europe, Western

Commerce
See also
European free trade association

Defenses
Chancellor Erhard's visit. America 113:703-4
D 4 '65
De Gaulle's bomb. J. M. Domenach. Common-
weal 81:668-9 F 19 '65
European scientists speak. J. Orear and L.
Wolfenstein. il Bul Atomic Sci 21:44-5 Ap
'65
Major joint tactical defense effort seen.
C. Brownlow. Aviation W 84:104-5+ Ja 17
'66
Which way Europe? J. H. Huizinga. For
Affairs 43:487-500 Ap '65
See also
North Atlantic treaty organization

Description and travel
Do U.S. sights surpass those of Europe? il
U S News 58:12 Mr 8 '65
Europe: how to relax and enjoy it! five trips.
G. Bush. il Bet Hom & Gard 44:89-94 Ja
'66
Europe with some reservations; excerpts from
Europe without George. I. Kampen. il
McCalls 92:124-5+ My '65
Gone flying to Europe. R. B. Parke. il Fly-
ing 77:36-9 D '65
How to live like a European in Europe; spend
the summer in a rented home. R. Joseph.
Esquire 64:121+ S '65
Let's travel: student specials. il Mlle 61:335-
8 Ag '65
My V.I.P. trip. D. Considine. il Seventeen
24:114-15+ F '65
Photocade chronicle. L. Barry. il Pop Phot
57:10+ D '65
Station wagon abroad. E. Brouwer. il
Travel 123:56-8 Mr '65
Tips for tourists. M. E. Peltz. Opera N 29:
13 My 1 '65
Travel notes. R. Joseph. Esquire 63:20+ F;
64:50+ S '65
Traveler in spring: thoughts of Europe; sym-
posium. il Sat R 48:33-6+ Mr 13 '65
Wonderful one-day side trips through Europe.
il Bet Hom & Gard 43:159-64 Ap '65

Economic conditions
Downturn becomes an upturn. il Bsns W
p41-2+ Ag 28 '65
Europe: boom slows, but next year. il U S
News 59:78-80 Jl 26 '65
Europe's boom in trouble? how real the
signs are. il U S News 58:74-6 Mr 22 '65
How Europe's boom looks from U.S. il U S
News 59:35 Jl 5 '65
Integration vs. nationalism in the European
economy. C. P. Kindleberger. il Reporter
33:38-40 D 2 '65

EUROPE, Western—*Continued*

Economic integration

One more step; agreement to merge executive bodies of Euratom, European coal and steel community, and the Common market. Newsweek 65:50+ Mr 15 '65

True problems of European integration: address, February 19, 1965. W. Hallstein. Vital Speeches 31:459-67 My 15 '65

Economic policy

See also
European economic community
Taxation—Europe, Western

Economic relations

Impact of change in eastern Europe on the Atlantic partnership; address, April 3, 1965. J. R. Schaetzel. Dept State Bul 53:161-71 Jl 26 '65

Nationalism threatens U.S. investment. R. A. Smith. il Fortune 72:126-31+ Ag '65

Where U.S. patience is wearing thin: Europe gets rich, finds fault, but still wants help. il U S News 58:50-3 Ap 5 '65

Economic union

See European economic community

Foreign opinion
American

How Europe's boom looks from U.S. il U S News 59:35 Jl 5 '65

Foreign relations

Changed setting of the Atlantic debate. A. Buchan. For Affairs 43:574-86 Jl '65

European version of neutralism. J. Freymond. bibliog f Ann Am Acad 362:28-35 N '65

United States

From a French friend: letter. E. Senn. Bul Atomic Sci 49-51 Je '65

Squabble over Europe's future: what the new moves mean; with report by F. B. Stevens. il U S News 59:52-4 D 13 '65

Toward a new European alliance? H. Brandon. Sat R 48:21-2 N 13 '65

Troubled partnership, by H. A. Kissinger. Review
New Repub 152:22-3 My 15 '65. N. McKitterick

History

Decline and rise of Europe, by J. Lukacs. Review
Sat R 48:39 F 13 '65. J. S. Schapiro

Historiography

Writing of west European history: a bird's-eye view of trends between 1960 and 1964. S. L. Thrupp. bibliog f Ann Am Acad 359:157-64 My '65

Maps

Europe's snowy crown portrayed on double map. il Nat Geog Mag 128:396-7. sup(folded map) S '65

Nationalism

Integration vs. nationalism in the European economy. C. P. Kindleberger. il Reporter 33:38-40 D 2 '65

Politics

Anniversary: V-E day. il Time 85:34 My 14 '65

Atlantic report. Atlan 216:6+ Ag '65

1815 & all that. Time 85:38+ Je 25 '65

Europe: decision or drift. D. Acheson. For Affairs 44:198-205 Ja '66

European void. E. M. von Kuehnelt-Leddihn. Nat R 17:1074-5 N 30 '65

Europe's middle way: me-too. il Newsweek 66:48-50 O 4 '65

Toward a new European alliance? H. Brandon. Sat R 48:21-2 N 13 '65

What to watch for in Europe. F. Morley. il Nations Bsns 53:27-8 Ap '65
See also
Atlantic community
European federation
European parliament

Union (proposed)
See European federation

EUROPE and France
So, vive de Gaulle but with reservations. Life 59:4 N 19 '65

EUROPE and the United States
Open letter to the American people. B. Hutchison. Read Digest 87:96-100 Ag '65

View from the other side; address, November 23, 1965. P. R. Harris. Dept State Bul 54:16-19 Ja 3 '66
See also
United States—Foreign opinion—European

EUROPEAN atomic energy community
Biology in Euratom. V. Rabinowitch. Bul Atomic Sci 21:46-7 Mr '65

EUROPEAN authors. See Authors, European

EUROPEAN bison. See Bison, European

EUROPEAN coal and steel community
Steel feels weight of global surplus. il Bsns W p31-2 N 27 '65

EUROPEAN common market. See European economic community

EUROPEAN corn borers
One treatment controls rootworm and corn borer. W. G. Lovely. il Suc Farm 63:92 Mr '65

EUROPEAN council for nuclear research. See European organization for nuclear research

EUROPEAN court of human rights
Palace of perplexity: permanent home, Strasbourg, France. il Time 86:88 O 8 '65

EUROPEAN economic community
And a touch of garlic; import duties to be eliminated in western Europe. Time 85:88 F 12 '65

At sixes and sevens. il Newsweek 66:35-6 Jl 26 '65

Common market edging up a bit; slight rise in EEC's growth rate. il Bsns W p45-6 Ja 1 '66

Common market turns to new mode of living. il Bsns W p30-1 Ja 30 '65

Cost of stubbornness; Eurocrats, de Gaulle and problems over common market in farm produce. Time 85:41-2 Je 25 '65

De Gaulle's Europe; Common market in trouble. America 113:308 S 25 '65

De Gaulle's responsibility; another Common market crisis. America 113:91 Jl 24 '65

End of Europe's big dream? what de Gaulle's revolt means. il U S News 59:46-7 Jl 19 '65

European economic community; address, December 4, 1964. W. Hallstein. Vital Speeches 31:331-7 Mr 15 '65

EEC buckles down to matters of money. il Bsns W p49-50+ Je 26 '65

EEC faces grim test; de Gaulle pulls French representatives out. Bsns W p32+ Jl 10 '65

European economy and European policy; plans for the future; address, July 8, 1965. W. Hallstein. Vital Speeches 31:654-8 Ag 15 '65

General's boycott. Newsweek 66:29 Jl 19 '65

Ghastly problem; Common market and tariffs. Newsweek 66:78+ S 20 '65

International situation; what happened to EEC; address, October 20, 1965. M. Couve de Murville. Vital Speeches 32:85-9 N 15 '65

Is de Gaulle killing the Common market? il U S News 59:84-5 Ag 23 '65

Is General de Gaulle that alarming? B. D. Nossiter. New Repub 153:13-15 O 9 '65

Must anything be done about Europe? willfulness of Charles de Gaulle; Time essay. Time 86:28-9 D 3 '65

One more step; agreement to merge executive bodies of Euratom, European coal and steel community, and the Common market. Newsweek 65:50+ Mr 15 '65

Power of negative thinking; France's desire to extend its community-wide farm-price agreements. Time 86:27 Jl 9 '65

President of EEC commission meets with President Johnson; joint communique, March 18, 1965. L. B. Johnson and W. Hallstein. Dept State Bul 52:491-2 Ap 5 '65

Spain and the E.E.C. L. López Rodó. For Affairs 44:127-33 O '65

Standing up to de Gaulle. Time 86:100 N 5 '65

Supranational stall; France boycotts the Common market. Time 86:31 Jl 16 '65

Tale of two citadels; Vienna meeting of Common market and Outer seven ministers. il Time 85:24 Je 4 '65

Time of paralysis. Time 86:121 S 17 '65

To the brink; Common market crisis. Newsweek 66:41 Jl 12 '65

True problems of European integration: address, February 19, 1965. W. Hallstein. Vital Speeches 31:459-67 My 15 '65

What to watch for in Europe. F. Morley. il Nations Bsns 53:27-8 Ap '65

Who is the real realist? constructive role of de Gaulle. A. de Borchgrave. il Newsweek 66:47-8+ D 13 '65

Why Europe wants more U.S. investment. il Bsns W p74-6 N 27 '65
See also
European parliament

EUROPEAN federation
Atlantic partnership and European unity: address, March 9, 1965. G. C. McGhee. Dept State Bul 52:582-8 Ap 19 '65

Atlantic partnership; emerging new Europe; address, April 12, 1965. Prince Bernhard. Vital Speeches 31:644-6 Ag 15 '65

EUROPEAN federation—*Continued*
End of Europe's big dream? what de Gaulle's revolt means. il U S News 59:46-7 Jl 19 '65
European economic community; address, December 4, 1964. W. Hallstein. Vital Speeches 31:331-7 Mr 15 '65
True problems of European integration: address, February 19, 1965. W. Hallstein. Vital Speeches 31:459-67 My 15 '65
West's mission is now in east Europe. Life 58:4 My 28 '65
Which way Europe? J. H. Huizinga. For Affairs 43:487-500 Ap '65

EUROPEAN free trade association
Moving on tiptoe toward ties; closer trade ties with the EEC. Time 86:100 N 5 '65
Seven keep on the brakes; growth at slower rate. il Bsns W p46-7 Ja 1 '66
Tale of two citadels; Vienna meeting of Common market and Outer seven ministers. il Time 85:24 Je 4 '65
Time of paralysis. Time 86:121 S 17 '65

EUROPEAN launcher development organization
Design efforts for ELDO B accelerated. Aviation W 82:227 Je 14 '65
ELDO, ESRO programs meet slippages. W. Wetmore. il Aviation W 82:127+ Mr 15 '65
European launcher development organization; its changing role. V. K. McElheny. il Science 148:1705-6 Je 25 '65
Increasing costs spark ELDO program review. Aviation W 82:57 F 15 '65
Schedule, performance problems threaten ELDO A booster program. D. E. Fink. il Aviation W 82:188-90+ Je 14 '65
Scientist criticizes European space group. Sci N L 88:71 Jl 31 '65

EUROPEAN literature
Artist's journey into the interior and other essays, by E. Heller. Review
Sat R 49:25-6 Ja 1 '66. E. M. Potoker
European literary scene (cont) R. J. Clements. il Sat R 48:36-7 F 13; 25-6 Mr 20; 39+ Ap 17; 26-7+ My 15; 30-1 Je 19; 30-1 Jl 17 '65
Spirit of the letter, by R. Poggioli. Review
Sat R 48:36 D 25 '65. R. J. Clements

EUROPEAN organization for nuclear research
Why pure science? CERN, the European organization for nuclear research. V. E. Weisskopf. Bul Atomic Sci 21:4-8 Ap '65; Discussion. 21:28-9 S '65

EUROPEAN parliament
Ambitious men of Europe house. E. T. O'Toole. il Reporter 32:24-6 F 25 '65

EUROPEAN rabbit flea. See Fleas

EUROPEAN shopping. See Shopping and shoppers

EUROPEAN space research organization
ELDO, ESRO programs meet slippages. W. Wetmore. il Aviation W 82:127+ Mr 15 '65
European space research organization. R. Lüst. Science 149:394-7 Jl 23 '65
ESRO hopes keyed to impending shots. Aviation W 82:204 Je 14 '65
ESRO II in early test phase. il Miss & Roc 17:26-7 Jl 5 '65
ESRO TD-2 experiments set. Aviation W 84:74 Ja 17 '66
Europeans reviewing space goals through early 1970s. Aviation W 82:198-201 Je 14 '65
French firm wins ESRO 1 award. il Aviation W 82:30 Ap 19 '65
International programs; ESRO to buy U.S. launch vehicle. il Miss & Roc 17:111-12+ N 29 '65

EUROPEAN union. See European federation

EUROPEAN visitors in the United States. See Foreign visitors in the United States

EUROPEAN war, 1914-1918
Proud tower, by B. W. Tuchman. Review
Time il 87:90 Ja 14 '66

Ambulance service
See European war, 1914-1918—Medical and sanitary affairs

Bibliography
Blood of change. R. L. Tobin. il Sat R 48: 36-7 S 4 '65

Campaigns and battles
Men of Vimy. F. Russell. il Nat R 17:474-6 Je 1 '65
Swordbearers: supreme command in the first World war, by C. Barnett. Review
Am Heritage 16:108-10 Ap '65. B. Catton
Yank in the B.E.F, second Battle of the Somme, memoir, with editorial comment. J. Gallagher. il Am Heritage 16:18-27+ Je '65

Balkan front
Gardeners of Salonika, by A. Palmer. Review
Time il 86:86 S 3 '65

Turkey and the Near East
Gallipoli: the history of a noble blunder, by R. R. James. Review
Atlan 216:166 O '65. E. Weeks

Western
After fifty years the cry of Ypres still echoes, gas! H. W. Baldwin. il N Y Times Mag p28-9+ Ap 18 '65
Still quiet on the western front. G. Smith. il Am Heritage 16:20-5+ O '65; Excerpt. Sat Eve Post 238:78-85 N 6 '65

Medical and sanitary affairs
Yank in the B.E.F, memoir, with editorial comment. B. J. Gallagher. il Am Heritage 16:18-27+ Je '65

Peace and mediation
Japanese-German peace negotiations during World war I. F. W. Iklé. bibliog f Am Hist R 71:62-76 O '65

Personal narratives
Yank in the B.E.F, second Battle of the Somme, memoir, with editorial comment. J. Gallagher. il Am Heritage 16:18-27+ Je '65

Pictorial works
Picture post card. B. Finnegan. il Hobbies 70:124-5+ Ja '66

Results
Meaning of the first World war, by R. Albrecht-Carrié. Review
Nat R 17:555-6 Je 29 '65. G. F. Fielding

Secret service
Thrifty spy on the Sixth avenue el; German spies in New York in 1915. E. Wittenberg. il Am Heritage 17:60-4+ D '65

France
See also
European war, 1914-1918—Campaigns and battles

Great Britain
Great Britain and the 1914-1915 Straits agreement with Russia: the British promise of November 1914. C. J. Smith, jr. bibliog f Am Hist R 70:1015-34 Jl '65

Japan
Japanese-German peace negotiations during World war I. F. W. Iklé. bibliog f Am Hist R 71:62-76 O '65

Russia
Great Britain and the 1914-1915 Straits agreement with Russia: the British promise of November 1914. C. J. Smith, jr. bibliog f Am Hist R 70:1015-34 Jl '65

Western
Europe of the great war. R. L. Tobin. il Sat R 48:28 Jl 3 '65

EUROPEAN youth hostels. See Youth hostels

EUROPEANS
Vietnam, LBJ, good times: what Europeans are saying. il U S News 59:70-4 Ag 9 '65

EUROPEANS in Rhodesia
Shadowed world of the white Rhodesians. L. Fellows. il N Y Times Mag p43+ D 12 '65

EUROPEANS in the United States. See Immigrants in the United States

EUROSPACE
Eurospace clings to transporter idea. Miss & Roc 16:18 My 17 '65
Eurospace debates its future; with editorial comment. il Miss & Roc 16:12-13, 46 My 3 '65
Eurospace proposes expanded program; with editorial comment. E. H. Kolcum. Aviation W 82:11, 16-17 My 3 '65
Eurospace views program needs. E. Loewe; E. P. Wheaton. il Aviation W 82:74-5+ My 10 '65

EURYTHMICS
Lessons with Monsieur Jaques. E. Findlay. il Dance Mag 39:40-5 Ag '65

EUTHANASIA
Deed of friendship; M. Happer shot by friend. Newsweek 65:30 Ap 26 '65
Keeping the dying alive; moral problem of mercy killing. America 114:6 Ja 1 '66
Today I killed my best friend; Dorothy Butts shoots Mary Happer. il Time 85:74+ Ap 23 '65

EVACUATION, Military
Twenty-five years after Dunkirk. E. F. Haylock. il Motor B 115:45-7+ Je '65
EVANGELICAL and Reformed church.   See
United church of Christ
EVANGELICAL United Brethren church
Methodist merger maneuvers; Methodist-E.U.B. merger. J. C. Evans. Christian Cent 82:1246-7 O 13 '65; Reply. J. S. Thomas. 82:1518 D 8 '65
Union without renewal? critique of the Methodist-E.U.B. negotiations. J. E. Will. Christian Cent 82:588+ My 5 '65
EVANGELICALISM
Defenders of the faith; Evangelical theological society. Time 87:70 Ja 7 '66
Demythologizing neoevangelicalism. Christian Cent 82:1115-16 S 15 '65
Dialogue with Evangelicals like Billy Graham. J. B. Sheerin. Cath World 201:158-61 Je '65; Discussion. 201:346-7 S '65
Go Evangelical; National assembly of Evangelicals in London. C. Northcott. Christian Cent 82:1311 O 27 '65
See also
Fundamentalism
EVANKO, Walter A.
For weeping seams a silicone sealant. Motor B 115:29 Mr '65
EVANOFF, Vlad
Fish 'n ships. por Motor B 116:54-5+ O; 58+ N; 52+ D '65
EVANS, Allan
Research in action: the Department of state's Bureau of intelligence and research. Dept State Bul 53:359-67 Ag 30 '65
EVANS, Sir Arthur John
Rediscovery of Crete. M. I. Finley. il por Horizon 7:64-75 Sum '65
EVANS, C. R. and Robertson, A. D. J.
Prolonged excitation in the visual cortex of the cat. bibliog Science 150:913-15 N 12 '65
EVANS, Clifford. See Meggers, B. J. jt. auth.
EVANS, Daniel Jackson
E in Olympia. Time por 86:37 N 5 '65
Lumps in Olympia. il por Newsweek 65:29 F 8 '65
EVANS, Dennis C.
Ultraviolet reflectivity of Mars. bibliog il Science 149:969-72 Ag 27 '65
EVANS, E. Ben
Pointers in planning. Library J 90:5455-6 D 15 '65
EVANS, Earnestyne
Report from Mississippi. pors Seventeen 25: 90+ Ja '66
EVANS, Gil
Jazz records. W. Balliett. New Yorker 41: 172-4 My 8 '65
EVANS, Howard E.
Books. Sci Am 214:123-4+ Ja '66
EVANS, J. Claude
Big business influences education in Texas. Christian Cent 82:425 Ap 7 '65
Breakthroughs: renewal in the local church. Christian Cent 82:1443-7 N 24 '65
Contemporary revival. Christian Cent 82:392-3 Mr 31 '65
Do you mean it, Mr Goldwater? Christian Cent 82:1312 O 27 '65
Ecumenism and teetotalism. Christian Cent 82:798-9 Je 23 '65
How to produce a demonstration. Christian Cent 82:134 F 3 '65
Meaningful death. Christian Cent 82:1598 D 29 '65
Methodism's way. Christian Cent 82:1005 Ag 18 '65
Methodist merger maneuvers. Christian Cent 82:1246-7 O 13 '65
Palmetto Republicans. Christian Cent 82:1030 Ag 25 '65
EVANS, Jane M.
Miners and Eskimos; story. Mlle 60:199-200 Ap '65
EVANS, Joseph E.
Saboteurs at work; reprint from Wall street journal. September 20, 1965. U S News 59:120 O 4 '65
EVANS, L. T.
Abscisin II: inhibitory effect on flower induction in a long-day plant. bibliog Science 151:107 Ja 7 '66
EVANS, Luther
Boating. Sports Illus 22:60-2 F 15 '65
Experimental air-jet landing craft. Yachting 118:160 D '65
EVANS, Luther H.
Finding out about red China. Sat R 48:17-18 Je 26 '65
about
Profile: Luther H. Evans; reprint, with editorial comment. V. W. Clapp. il pors Library J 90:3384-91 S 1 '65

EVANS, M. Stanton
Education of a Socialist. Nat R 17:878+ O 5 '65
Is there an enemy? Nat R 17:512-13 Je 15 '65
Kennedy without incense. Nat R 17:242-3 Mr 23 '65
Liberals strike back at Goldwater win. Nat R 17:584+ Jl 13 '65
Sober assessment. Nat R 18:34-7 Ja 11 '66
Ugly is as ugly does. Nat R 17:731-2 Ag 24 '65
William H. Book. RIP. Nat R 17:454 Je 1 '65
EVANS, Mary
Letter from Tokyo. Nation 201:203-4 O 4 '65
EVANS, Rowland, and Novak, Robert
Ordeal of Ray Bliss. Sat Eve Post 238:32-5 N 6 '65
Yarmolinsky affair. Esquire 63:80-2+ F '65
EVANS, W. Leonard, Jr
Full of grace. New Yorker 41:42 S 18 '65
EVANSTON, Ill.

Education
How Evanston passed its bond issue. J. F. Hall. il NEA J 54:42-4 D '65
EVANSVILLE, Ind.

Negroes
Long, hot summer in Indiana; 1924. W. E. Wilson. il Am Heritage 16:56-64 Ag '65
EVANSVILLE college, Evansville, Ind.
Aces are high in Evansville; Purple Ades, best small-college basketball team. F. Deford. il Sports Illus 22:24-7 F 15 '65
EVAPORATION
See also
Reservoirs—Evaporation control
EVELYN, Maude
Idol remembered. por Esquire 64:84-5 Jl '65
EVENING clothes. See Clothing and dress
EVENING of the holiday; story. See Hazzard, S.
EVENING'S Frost (dramatic reading)   See
Dramatic readings
EVENSON, William E. and Hall, H. T.
Volume measurements on chromium to pressure of 30 kilobars. bibliog Science 150: 1164-5 N 26 '65
EVERARD family
Everard coat-of-arms. H. K. Eilers. il Hobbies 69:124 F '65
EVERGLADE kites. See Kites (birds)
EVERGLADES NATIONAL PARK
Betsy in the Everglades; report. E. T. Christensen. il Nat Parks Mag 39:22 N '65
Disaster threatens the Everglades. P. Farb. il Audubon Mag 67:302-9 S '65; Same abr. with title Save the Everglades. Read Digest 87:241-3+ N '65
Everglades water hearings. Nat Parks Mag 39:20 Mr '65
Primeval wilderness, the Everglades. H. Sutton. il McCalls 93:18+ Ja '66
Shrimp need fresh water, too; address, June 1965. C. P. Idyll. Nat Parks Mag 39:14-15 O '65
Water picture in Everglades National Park; report on study by S. Raushenbush for National parks assn, with editorial comment. M. Straight. il Nat Parks Mag 39:2+, 4-9 Ag '65
Water wanted for a parched park; Florida's Everglades. J. O'Reilly. il Sports Illus 22: 70+ Je 7 '65
EVERGREENS
Evergreens. C. W. Price. il Horticulture 43: 36-7+ Je '65
Evergreens for the Plains. G. Viehmeyer. il Horticulture 43:18+ Ag '65
Evergreens keep their good looks. C. Lisle. il Flower Grower 52:30-1+ Ap '65
Right way to prune evergreens. E. F. Steffek. il Horticulture 43:50-1 Ap '65
See also
Christmas trees
Conifers
Holly
Silk tassel bushes

Diseases and pests
Spraying evergreens; schedule for narrow-leaved evergreens. P. P. Pirone. il Horticulture 43:34-7 F '65
EVERHART, William C.
So long, St Louis, we're heading West. Nat Geog Mag 128:642-69 N '65
EVERLY, Jack
Whip Johnsongrass. il Suc Farm 63:102 Ap '65
EVERNGAM, Howard
Movie cameras: super 8 to 16. Pop Phot 57: 70-1 D '65
EVERS, Medgar W.
Mississippi widow; ed. by J. Egginton. M. Evers. il por Look 29:62+ Je 1 '65

EVERS, Medgar W, family
Why I left Mississippi. M. Evers. il Ebony 20:25-8+ Mr '65
EVERS, Myrlie
Mississippi widow; ed. by J. Egginton. pors Look 29:62+ Je 1 '65
Why I left Mississippi. pors Ebony 20:25-8+ Mr '65
EVERSON, R. G.
Outside Joe Beef's; poem. Atlan 215:127 Ap '65
EVERY day is yesterday; story. See McCord, J.
EVERYTHING must go! story. See Elkin, S.
EVIDENCE (law)
Needlepoint justice: question of lie detector tests as evidence. Newsweek 65:29-30 F 22 '65
See also
Confession (law)
EVIL eye
Evil eye; Mexican magic repellents. G. G. Parratt. il Atlan 216:152 O '65
EVIL eye; story. See Gillespie, A.
EVINRUDE award. See Rewards, prizes, etc.
EVOLUTION
Animal proteins provide a study of evolution. Sci N L 87:185 Mr 20 '65
Can we improve on nature too much? A. Smith. il Sci Digest 58:88-91 O '65
Evolution; background material for papers to be presented at AAAS annual meeting. il Science 150:639-42 O 29 '65
Future of Homo sapiens; biologist's view. J. Hiernaux. il UNESCO Courier 18:12-15 Ap '65; Same abr. with title How man will evolve. Sci Digest 58:90-4 Ag '65
Man as nature's man. P. Hefner; reply. T. Dobzhansky. Christian Cent 82:242 F 24 '65
Man evolved like animals; Third species questioned. C. A. Betts. il(p241) Sci N L 87: 243 Ap 17 '65
Molecules and monkeys. J. Buettner-Janusch and R. L. Hill. bibliog il Science 147:836-42 F 19 '65
New man; what will he be like? A. Rosenfeld. Life 59:94-6+ O 1 '65; Same abr. with title Will man direct his own evolution? Read Digest 88:37-42 Ja '66
Vision of Father Pierre. H. Downs. Sci Digest 57:85-91 F '65
When man first stood up. J. Pfeiffer. il N Y Times Mag p70-1+ Ap 11 '65
See also
Life (biology)
Man—Origin and antiquity
Mendelism
Religion and science

Laws and legislation
Anti-evolution law tested. J. Tompkins. Sci N L 89:7+ Ja 1 '66
Will evolution come to Arkansas? T. Dearmore. Reporter 34:34 Ja 13 '66
EVOLUTION, Social. See Social change; Social progress
EVTUSHENKO, Evgenii Aleksandrovich
Chicken-god; story, tr. by D. Mann. Harper 231:64-8 Ag '65
Meeting; poem, tr. by S. J. Parker. Sat R 48: 22 Ag 7 '65
about
Dispute over publication of Yevtushenko poems. Pub W 187:36-7 Mr 15 '65
Reporter at large. R. Blum. New Yorker 41: 32-6+ S 4; 168+ S 11 '65
EWERS, John C.
Deadlier than the male. il Am Heritage 16: 10-13 Je '65
EWERS, Wm. H. and Rose, C. R.
Trematode parasitism and polymorphism in a marine snail. Science 148:1747-8 Je 25 '65
EWES
Culling
See Sheep—Culling
EWING, Ann
Current U.S. patents. Sci N L 88:93, 190 Ag 7, S 18 '65
EWING, Grace D.
Putting TV in its place. PTA Mag 60:8-9 Ja '66
EWING, Maurice
Grappler for life's clues in the world's oceans. il pors Bsns W p68-70+ My 22 '65
—and Thorndike, E. M.
Suspended matter in deep ocean water. bibliog Science 147:1291-4 Mr 12 '65
—See Conolly, J. R; Jacobs, M. B. jt. auths.
EWING TOWNSHIP, N.J.
Less than $3,000 per ton. A. Gruenwald and J. A. Reynolds. il Am City 80:100-1 O '65
EXAMINATION; story. See Adarkar, V. B.

EXAMINATIONS
Examinations, valuable yardstick or useless burden? pro and con discussion. il Sr Schol 86:12-13 My 6 '65
Final exams: ordeal of a borderline co-ed; B. Blake. B. Leavitt. il Look 29:138-44+ Je 15 '65
Letter from Paris: thefts of examination papers for the baccalaureate. Genêt. New Yorker 41:96-7 Je 26 '65
New directions for British education? M. N. Hennessy. il Sat R 48:58-9+ Ag 21 '65
See also
College entrance examination board
Educational tests and measurements
Physical examinations
EXCAVATING machinery
Digging out from under: Bucyrus-Erie company. il Bsns W p 106-7+ Ag 28 '65
Shakers of the earth. il Fortune 71:186+ Je '65
EXCAVATIONS (archeology)
See also
Crete—Antiquities
EXCEPTION and the rule; drama. See Brecht, B.
EXCEPTIONAL children. See Children, Exceptional
EXCHANGE (barter). See Barter
EXCHANGE of persons programs
East-West exchanges: Viet strife has had no immediate effects, but Soviets unresponsive to expansion. D. S. Greenberg. Science 149:950-1 Ag 27 '65
Envoy; Citizen exchange corps. New Yorker 40:24-5 F 13 '65
International visitors and the American society; address, March 19, 1965. D. Rusk. Dept State Bul 52:588-92 Ap 19 '65
President sends Congress reports on cultural and exhibits programs; letters, October 6, 1965. L. B. Johnson. Dept State Bul 53: 673-4 O 25 '65
President sends Congress report on cultural exchange program; letter, February 1, 1965. L. B. Johnson. Dept State Bul 52:263-4 F 22 '65
Scribblers and international relations. C. Frankel. For Affairs 44:1-14 O '65
Six weeks in Russia. E. Koontz. NEA J 54: 51 My '65
U.S. and Rumania sign cultural exchange agreement for 1965-66; Department announcement; with text of U.S. note, December 23, 1964. Dept State Bul 52:87-90 Ja 18 '65
U.S. and U.S.S.R. complete plans for 1965 exchanges program; Department statement, January 30, 1965. Dept State Bul 52:252 F 22 '65
See also
Educational exchanges
EXCHANGE of political prisoners. See Political prisoners, Exchange of
EXCHANGE scholarships. See Scholarships and fellowships
EXCHANGES
Where pork bellies bring home the bacon; futures leading at Chicago's Mercantile exchange. il Bsns W p88-90 Ag 7 '65
See also
Chicago board of trade
Stock exchange
EXCHANGES, Educational. See Educational exchanges
EXCIROLANA chiltoni. See Isopoda
EXCISE tax
Another tax cut: what it will mean. il U S News 58:30-2 My 31 '65
Big excise tax cut makes it; with editorial comment. Bsns W p30-1, 184 Je 19 '65
Biggest markdown. il Newsweek 66:67 Jl 5 '65
Congress gets going on excises. il Bsns W p24-5 My 22 '65
Due soon; more excise cuts. il U S News 59: 102-3 N 29 '65
Excise cut begins to trickle down. il Bsns W p36 Je 26 '65
Excise cut brings no sales spurt. Bsns W p20 Jl 3 '65
Excise cuts: how much, for whom? U S News 59:82-3 Ag 30 '65
Excise tax cut; any effects on business? il U S News 59:86 Jl 12 '65
Excise tax-cutting spree. Life 58:4 Je 4 '65
Excise taxes. il Sr Schol 87:14-15 S 16 '65
Excising the poor. W. V. Shannon. Commonweal 82:398-9 Je 18 '65
Getting ready to widen excise tax reductions. il Bsns W p26-7 My 15 '65
Great discount day. il Time 85:87-8 Je 25 '65
Has tax cut aided photographers? J. Neubauer. Pop Phot 57:59+ N '65
Here's a preview of the next cut in taxes, il U S News 58:99-100 My 3 '65

EXCISE tax—*Continued*
How Congress can save photographers $28,000,000. J. Neubauer. Pop Phot 56:51+ My '65
How excise cuts affected prices. U S News 59:108-9 O 4 '65
In one pocket, out the other: excises cut, state taxes up. il U S News 59:72-4 Jl 5 '65
Jockeying for position; race for excise tax cuts. Bsns W p34 F 20 '65
Lightening the tax load. America 113:6 Jl 3 '65
Logical step; biggest excise-tax cut in U.S. history. Time 85:95 My 28 '65
Personal business; federal excise cuts. Bsns W p 131 My 29 '65
Retailers jump gun on tax cut; pledge refunds. il Bsns W p28-30 My 29 '65
Taxes: honing the knife; proposed cutback. il Newsweek 65:73-4 My 17 '65
We got ours, then they got theirs; tax-cut bill. il Newsweek 65:63-4 My 31 '65
What cuts in excises will mean. il U S News 58:92-5 Je 28 '65
What to do till the excise tax cut comes. il Consumer Rep 30:242-3 My '65
When luxuries become necessities. Time 85:30 Je 11 '65

EXCLUSIVE agencies
Boss yourself; the $15 billion boom. il Newsweek 65:83-4 F 22 '65
Franchising finds it's an industry; franchisers conference at Boston. il Bsns W p72+ Je 19 '65
Is the franchise system legal? General motors vs Supreme court. Bsns W p66+ Ap 3 '65
Mom & pop business of your own; franchise system. il Changing T 19:35-8 Mr '65; Same abr. with title Surest shortcut to being your own boss. Read Digest 86:209-10+ Je '65
Why auto dealers don't like cash buyers; Supreme court vs General motors franchise system. il Consumer Rep 30:258-61 My '65

EX-CONVICTS. See Prisoners, Discharged

EXCRETION
See also
Urinary organs

EXECUTIONS and executioners
See also
Hanging

EXECUTIVE ability
Exploring the paths that lead to the top; W. P. Dommermuth analysis of company presidents. il Bsns W p69-70 S 18 '65
Gentle art of executive persuasion; excerpt from Effective psychology for managers. M. Feinberg. il Duns R 86:41-7 D '65

EXECUTIVE health examiners (organization)
Sugarcoating the executive's health checkup. il Bsns W p68-9 Je 19 '65

EXECUTIVE jet aviation, incorporated
Jet service utilizes military procedures. D. A. Brown. il Aviation W 83:83+ O 18 '65

EXECUTIVE jets. See Airplanes, Business

EXECUTIVE office of the president. See United States—Executive office of the president

EXECUTIVE planes. See Airplanes, Business

EXECUTIVE power
It isn't right just because it's happening. F. Morley. Nations Bsns 53:27-8 O '65

EXECUTIVE recruiting consultants. See Employment agencies

EXECUTIVE responsibility. See Responsibility

EXECUTIVE service corps. See International executive service corps

EXECUTIVES
Executive strains come from within the man. Sci N L 87:102 F 13 '65
Executive suites go on the road; company presidents spend over third of their working year traveling. il Bsns W p92+ O 2 '65
Executives abroad: the American way overseas. il Nations Bsns 53:58-60+ Mr '65
Exploring the paths that lead to the top; W. P. Dommermuth analysis of company presidents. il Bsns W p69-70 S 18 '65
How the sons rise. il Time 85:96+ My 28 '65
How to keep from going out of style; executive's problems of job obsolescence. S. Schuler. il Nations Bsns 53:66+ F '65
It's the men up front that count. il Bsns W p73-5 My 1 '65
Lessons of leadership; symposium. il Nations Bsns 53:34-5+ Je; 40-1+ Jl; 46-8+ Ag; 40-2+ S; 40-1+ O; 40-2+ N '65
Man on the move. Duns R 86:53-4 S; 73+ O; 67-8 N; 49-52 D '65
Management in the coming decade; address, October 23, 1964. W. F. May. Vital Speeches 31:285-8 F 15 '65
Management's men in the middle. J. B. Weiner. il Duns R 85:38-9+ Ap '65

Men at the top: a Bernays'-eye view; excerpts from Biography of an idea. E. L. Bernays. il Fortune 72:138-9+ O '65
Million dollar men of insurance. il Ebony 20:207-10 My '65
Organizational paradox; quiz on control and creativity. L. K. Randall. Harvard Bsns R 43:86-7+ Jl '65
Peace: common stock for business; San Francisco meeting of top executives from sixty-six nations. il Bsns W p80-2 S 25 '65
Private leadership: on way out in U.S? U S News 59:11 D 27 '65
Successful men, then and now; photographs. Nations Bsns 53:86-7 S '65
Team at the top. D. R. Daniel. Harvard Bsns R 43:74-82 Mr '65
Those fund-raising businessmen; moonlighting for charity. R. Sheehan. Fortune 73:148-50+ Ja '66
Tracking conformity to its business lair; Porter survey. Bsns W p74 F 27 '65
When a top rung breaks on the success ladder; two books for the executive. il Bsns W p 106+ N 6 '65
Where do you stand with the boss? R. Dreyfack. il Nations Bsns 53:74-5+ N '65
Who gets to the top in business. il U S News 59:88 Jl 12 '65
See also
Business management and organization
Leadership
Women as executives

Dismissal
See Employees—Dismissal

Health and hygiene
See Men—Health and hygiene

Qualifications
Engineer the job to fit the manager. F. E. Fiedler. il Harvard Bsns R 43:115-22 S '65
Imperatives of authority; excerpt from Managers for tomorrow. Duns R 85:49-50+ F '65
Put new life in your career. A. Uris. il Nations Bsns 53:78+ S '65
R&D entrepreneur; profile of success. H. Schrage. bibliog f il Harvard Bsns R 43:56-69 N '65
Search for the proven man; executive recruiters. Time 86:78+ Ag 6 '65
Sensing who can command; interview. C. H. Greenewalt. il Nations Bsns 53:40-1+ O '65
Technicians moving in at the top. il Bsns W p 118+ Je 12 '65
Tomorrow's executive: new dimensions you'll need; excerpt from Managers for tomorrow. Nations Bsns 53:100-2+ F '65

Retirement
See Retirement from business, etc.

Salaries, allowances, etc.
Bonus formula for division heads; based on relative profitability of profit centers. J. Dearden and W. S. Edgerly. Harvard Bsns R 43:83-90 S '65
Deterioration in top executive pay. A. Patton. il Harvard Bsns R 43:106-18 N '65
Executive pay rides profit tide. il Bsns W p88+ My 15 '65
How Japan's top brass makes the job pay off; through liberal system of expense accounts and fringe benefits. il Bsns W p 100-2+ My 8 '65
More pay to top men in 1964. il Bsns W p 127-8 Ap 3 '65
Top salary mix abroad changes; U.S. expatriates and foreign nationals working for American controlled companies. il Bsns W p98 O 2 '65
Who gets what. il Time 86:68 Ag 13 '65

Selection and appointment
Chances that they take; case histories. Fortune 72:155 S '65
Ethics of executive selection. L. B. Ward. bibliog f il Harvard Bsns R 43:6-8+ Mr '65; Reply. B. L. Masse. America 112:612 Ap 24 '65
How do you find an executive job? with list of agencies. il Changing T 19:35-40 N '65
Management: headhunters by any other name; executive recruiters. il Newsweek 67:44-6 Ja 3 '66
Picking top men by electronics. il Bsns W p97-8 Mr 6 '65
Take labels off your men. J. D. Weinland. Nations Bsns 53:56+ N '65

EXECUTIVES—*Continued*

Supply and demand

Churning market for executives. S. Freedgood. il Fortune 72:152-4+ S '65

Ethnics of executive selection. L. B. Ward. bibliog f il Harvard Bsns R 43:6-8+ Mr '65; Reply. B. L. Masse. America 112:612 Ap 24 '65

Executive gap; problem of American subsidiaries in Mexico. il Fortune 71:63-4 Ap '65

Management: headhunters by any other name; executive recruiters. il Newsweek 67:44-6 Ja 3 '66

Search for the proven man; executive recruiters. Time 86:78+ Ag 6 '65

Wanted: $50,000-a-year men. P. Korenvaes. il Duns R 85:41-6+ F '65

Training

Bringing the campus to the office; University of California sends classroom instruction to Bechtel corp. il Bsns W p72-3 D 25 '65

Charting pitfalls of decision; Kepner-Tregoe & associates, inc, Princeton, N.J. il Bsns W p64-6 Je 5 '65

How GM keeps its top ranks strong. Bsns W p78+ Jl 3 '65

How top retailers build executives; modern methods used to recruit and train. il Bsns W p88+ Je 5 '65

Mexicans get a boost up corporate ladder; training programs by U.S. companies in Mexico. il Bsns W p76+ O 9 '65

New course for canned teaching; teaching machines used in industrial training. il Bsns W p67-9 Jl 24 '65

Specialists try a wider track; management development problem. il Bsns W p56-7 Jl 31 '65

Stately homes are B-schools for the British; manor houses now schools for managers. il Bsns W p52-3+ Jl 17 '65

See also
Harvard university—Graduate school of business administration
Industrial management and organization—Study and teaching

EXECUTIVES as stockholders

On stock dealing by insiders; excerpts from address, October 26, 1965. K. Funston. U S News 59:107 N 8 '65

Way officials size up stocks of their companies. il U S News 59:107-8 O 18 '65

EXECUTORS and administrators

Personal business; appointing your wife as executor. Bsns W p95 Ja 8 '66

EXEMPTION of taxation. See Taxation, Exemption from

EXERCISE

Beach beauty guide. il Seventeen 24:64-9 Je '65

Best diet is exercise. J. Mayer. il N Y Times Mag p34-5+ Ap 25 '65

Disco shape-up; how to dance away 750 calories in four hours. il Mlle 62:174-5 N '65

Dollars in figures; effect on industries. T. R. Brooks. il Duns R 85:62-4+ Ap '65

Exercise. S. Harney. il Ladies Home J 82: 94-5 N '65

Four exercises to trim, tone or relax you. il Good H 161:100 N '65

Fourteen day diet & pep-up plan. il Good H 162:144-6+ Ja '66

Growth hormone: important role in muscular exercise in adults. W. M. Hunter and others. bibliog il Science 150:1051-3 N 19 '65

Interviews with two experts about trimming, toning. J. Roosevelt; J. Limon. il Mlle 60:136-9 F '65

Key to physical fitness. S. E. Smith. il Parents Mag 40:46-7+ Jl '65

Let's tell the truth about isometrics. H. Higdon. il Todays Health 43:58-9+ Je '65

Lie down and gain; with chart showing energy equivalents of food calories expressed in minutes of activity. Sci N L 87:183 Mr 20 '65

Physical fitness and dynamic health, by T. K. Cureton, jr. Review
Time il 86:64-5 Ag 6 '65

Physiology of exercise. C. B. Chapman and J. H. Mitchell. il Sci Am 212:88-94+ My '65

Spring training. il Redbook 124:82-90 Mr '65

Sprinters burn oxygen. Sci N L 87:311 My 15 '65

Time to be beautiful; post natal exercise and beauty routine. il Redbook 125:70-1+ My '65

Warm-up ballet exercises. il McCalls 93:98+ O '65

You can have a far slimmer figure if you stand up straight! il Seventeen 24:132-3 Mr '65

Your aching back, and what to do about it. C. Mitchell. il Read Digest 88:78-82 Ja '66

See also
Physical education and training
Walking

EXERCISES, Spiritual. See Spiritual exercises

EXHAUST gases. See Automobile engines—Exhaust

EXHAUST systems

It's a kitchen smokestack. il Sunset 134:128 Ap '65

See also
Automobile engines—Exhaust

EXHAUSTION of our son's love; drama. See Max, J.

EXHIBITION cases

Displaying books at your fair. il Sr Schol 86:sup 17 Ap 29 '65

Inventor of the month; box that won a U.S. patent; combined shipping container and showcase. S. V. Jones. il Sci Digest 58:36 Ag '65

EXHIBITIONISM

See also
Indecent exposure

EXHIBITIONS

Business joins a union show; Union industries show, Pittsburgh. il Bsns W p 113-14 My 29 '65

Come ski with me; International winter sports and ski show in Coliseum. New Yorker 41:49-50 O 30 '65

Equipment; Business equipment exposition at Coliseum. New Yorker 41:47 N 6 '65

How U.S. makes markets abroad; exports displayed in trade shows. il U S News 59:70 Ag 30 '65

Inventors peddle their wares; International inventors and new products exhibition. M. J. Pederson. il Pop Mech 124:54-7 N '65

Miami boosts Interama; Inter-American trade center project. Bsns W p46 Je 12 '65

New style; Kosygin visits Leipzig trade fair. il Newsweek 65:46 Mr 15 '65

Of geese & ballyhoo; trade fair at Canton. il Time 86:98 N 26 '65

Plastics show takes the train; U.S. exhibitor operates from four railroad cars International plastics exhibition in London. il Bsns W p92-4 Jl 3 '65

President sends Congress reports on cultural and exhibits programs; letters, October 6, 1965. L. B. Johnson. Dept State Bul 53:673-4 O 25 '65

Road show, U.S.A; U.S. Commerce department trade-show program. Newsweek 65: 78 Je 21 '65

SR/1966 world travel calendar. R. Meyer, jr. Sat R 49:55-6+ Ja 1 '66

Some strength & little joy. il Time 85:91-2 Mr 12 '65

They lead small business to bigger markets. R. S. Knowles. Read Digest 87:107-10 O '65

Tightening trade ties with Japan; Pacific Northwest products at industrial fair in Tokyo. il Bsns W p 104-6+ Ap 24 '65

Tower of freedom; Florida's hemi-world's fair. New Repub 153:8 N 6 '65

U.S. concerns go back to Leipzig, but at own risk; Washington ends ban on Leipzig fair in East Germany. il Bsns W p 182-4 S 18 '65

See also
Agricultural exhibitions
International exhibition of paper, printing and graphic arts industries, Paris, 1965
New York (city)—Worlds fair, 1964-1965
also subhead Exhibitions under various subjects, e.g. Education—Exhibitions

EXHIBITIONS, Traveling

Art shows on tour. il Changing T 19:32 Jl '65

Europe's What is man? exhibit; tr. by A. Rosin. R. E. Martinez. Pop Phot 56:8+ Je '65

Flying showcase speeds sales. il Bsns W p84+ My 1 '65

From England's green and pleasant bowers. S. Simon. il Art N 64:28-31+ Ap '65

Gold of Alexander. P. Davidson. il Art N 64:32-5+ D '65

Letter from London: exhibition of sculpture; Virgin and child of Michelangelo. M. Panter-Downes. New Yorker 41:125-6 My 22 '65

They lead small business to bigger markets. R. S. Knowles. Read Digest 87:107-10 O '65

EXHIBITS

Collapsible gaff; Sports, vacation, and travel show at N.Y. coliseum. New Yorker 41: 29-30 Mr 6 '65

EXTRATERRESTRIAL dust. See Matter, Interstellar

EXTRAVEHICULAR activity suits. See Astronauts—Clothing

EXTREMISM. See Right and left (political science)

EXUMA CAYS. See Bahama Islands

EYAL, Zwi, and others
Homograft rabbit skin protection by phenothiazine derivatives. bibliog Science 148:1468-9 Je 11 '65

EYE
Common fallacies about your child's eyes. J. H. Jacobson. il Parents Mag 40:62-3+ N '65
Response of the pupil to steady-state retinal illumination: contribution by cones. J. ten Doesschate and M. Alpern. bibliog il Science 149:989-91 Ag 27 '65
    See also
Pupil (eye)
Retina

Accommodation and refraction
Neural stage of adaptation between the receptors and inner nuclear layer of monkey retina. K. T. Brown and K. Watanabe. bibliog il Science 148:1111-13 My 21 '65

Cancer
See Cancer

Care and hygiene
How smog hurts your eyes. il Sci Digest 58:18 S '65
Patricia couldn't see the board. J. Hunter. il Parents Mag 40:68-9+ Mr '65
    See also
Sight testing

Diseases and defects
Hidden threat to children's eyes; amblyopia. P. Deutsch and R. M. Deutsch. il Todays Health 43:29-32+ Ag '65; Same abr. Read Digest 87:63-6 Ag '65
Personal business; tips on health. Bsns W p 129-30 O 30 '65
Red eyes may mask dangerous glaucoma. Sci N L 88:327 N 20 '65
Sclera graft aids sight; correcting failing sight due to retinal detachment. F. Marley. Sci N L 88:275 O 30 '65
    See also
Blindness
Myopia
Ophthalmology

Movements
Microsaccades and the velocity-amplitude relationship for saccadic eye movements. B. L. Zuber and L. Stark. bibliog il Science 150:1459-60 D 10 '65
Odd tricks of the human eye. P. Brock. il Sci Digest 58:74-7 D '65
Reporter at large; Rapid eye movement sleep. C. Trillin. il New Yorker 41:58-60+ S 18 '65
Visual perception of direction for stimuli flashed during voluntary saccadic eye movements. L. Matin and D. G. Pearce. bibliog il Science 148:1485-8 Je 11 '65

Surgery
New eye transplants. il Sci Digest 59:35 Ja '66
Proton beam saves sight of poor surgical risks. Sci N L 88:152 S 4 '65
Window for the blind. Sci Digest 58:18 D '65

EYE (amphibia)
Frog retina: detection of movement. D. Finkelstein and O. J. Grüsser. bibliog il Science 150:1050-1 N 19 '65
Lens fiber differentiation and gamma crystallins: immunofluorescent study of Wolffian regeneration. C. Takata and others. bibliog il Science 147:1299-301 Mr 12 '65
Respiratory and electrical responses to light stimulation in the retina of the frog. W. Sickel. bibliog il Science 148:648-51 Ap 30 '65

EYE (animals)
Seen through other eyes. J. George. Read Digest 86:141-4 F '65

EYE (birds)
Degeneration of the eyes of tyrosine-deficient chick embryos. C. R. Grau and others. bibliog il Science 148:1743-5 Je 25 '65
Interhemispheric reversal of mirror-image oblique lines after monocular training in pigeons. N. K. Mello. bibliog il Science 148:252-4 Ap 9 '65; Discussion. 149:1518-20 S 24 '65
Short- and long-lived messenger RNA in embryonic chick lens. R. Reeder and E. Bell. bibliog il Science 150:71-2 O 1 '65

EYE (crustacea)
Electrical connections between visual cells in the ommatidium of limulus. T. G. Smith and others. bibliog il Science 147:1446-8 Mr 19 '65

EYE (fishes)
Interocular transfer in goldfish: color easier than pattern. D. J. Ingle. bibliog il Science 149:1000-2 Ag 27 '65
Reversible, light-screening pigment of elasmobranch eyes: chemical identity with melanin. D. L. Fox and K. P. Kuchnow. bibliog il Science 150:612-14 O 29 '65

EYE (insects)
What dragonflies see, and how. Sci Digest 58:36 S '65

EYE, Evil. See Evil eye

EYE make-up. See Cosmetics: Make-up

EYE movements. See Eye—Movements

EYEGLASSES
Dear beauty editor; advice to girls who wear glasses: frame and hairdo. il Seventeen 24:341 Ag '65
Easy on the eyes; what fashion-minded women say on subject; ed. by S. Harney. il Ladies Home J 83:72-3 Ag '66
How not to miss a thing; techniques for doing it dashingly. il Vogue 146:108-11+ Jl '65
Making spectacles. New Repub 153:6 D 25 '65
    See also
Sun glasses

EYELASHES, Artificial
Guide to false eyelashes. il Seventeen 24:28 D '65

    Anecdotes, facetiae, satire, etc.
Eyelash: fur or hair? J. Sargent. Atlan 215:120-2 Je '65

EYELETS, Metal
Here are ways to use grommets. il Sunset 135:162+ O '65

EYELIDS
Efficiency of the conditioned eyelid response. I. Martin and A. B. Levey. bibliog il Science 150:781-3 N 5 '65

EYER, Ron
Life music review. Life 59:16 O 22; 22 N 26 '65

EYESIGHT. See Sight

EYLAR, Edwin H. and Matioli, G. T.
Glycoprotein biosynthesis in human reticulocytes: a lesion in thalassemia. bibliog Science 147:869-70 F 19 '65

EYRE, John L.
Containerization: the unhappy marriage. Duns R 85:pt2 134-5+ Je '65

EYRING, Henry
Profits and risks of simplification. Science 150:439 O 22 '65

EZELL, Judy
I am a farm girl! pors Farm J 89:70-1 S '65

EZELL, Madelon K.
When is a captain; story. Mlle 61:270-1 Ag '65

F

F. JOSEPH, Brother
This is right; that must be wrong. America 112:430 Mr 27 '65

FALN (Armed forces of national liberation)
See Political parties—Venezuela

FASEB. See Federation of American societies for experimental biology

FBI. See United States—Federal bureau of investigation

FCC. See United States—Federal communications commission

FDA. See United States—Food and drug administration

FDIC. See Federal deposit insurance corporation

FDL (fast deployment logistics ships) See Warships—United States

FHA. See United States—Federal housing administration

FHA loans. See United States—Federal housing administration

FHLBB. See United States—Federal home loan bank board

FID. See International federation for documentation

FM. See Radio frequency modulation

FM radio stations. See Radio stations, Frequency modulation

FM receivers. See Radio receiving apparatus—Frequency modulation receivers

FM-stereo antennas. See Radio antennas

FMC corporation
Perilous quest for acquisitions. J. B. Weiner. il Duns R 86:32-5+ Jl '65
Seat pallet van is developed for 727QC. R. G. O'Lone. il Aviation W 83:66-7 N 1 '65
FPC. See United States—Federal power commission
FRB. See United States—Federal reserve board
FTC. See United States—Federal trade commission
FUNY. See Free university of New York
F. W. Woolworth company. See Woolworth, F. W, company
FAAS, Horst
Trick is to get close and stay alive. G. P. Hunt. por Life 59:3 Jl 2 '65
Where the action is. il por Time 85:66-7 Je 25 '65
FABER, John
Your wife may be right. il U S Camera 28: 52-3+ O '65
FABER, Trudie
Your wife may be right. J. Faber. il por U S Camera 28:52-3+ O '65
FABIAN, Bela
Truth about Hungary. America 113:749-51 D 11 '65
FABIANI, Aurelio
A.O.C.A. G. Fitzgerald. il por Opera N 30: 19 N 6 '65
FABLES
Fable of the phoebe bird. M. M. Holloway. il Cath World 202:224-7 Ja '66
Santa and the crown jewels; Christmas fable. J. Glashan. il Holiday 38:44-9 D '65
See also
Aesop's fables
FABRIC wall coverings. See Wall coverings
FABRICS. See Textile fabrics
FABRIDAMS. See Dams
FACE
See also
Facial expression
FACE helmets. See Helmets
FACE of the moon; story. See Carter, M.
FACIAL expression
Origins of facial expressions. R. J. Andrew. il Sci Am 213:88-92+ O '65
FACIALS. See Skin—Care and hygiene
FACKENHEIM, Emil L.
Judaism & the meaning of life; excerpt from Meaning of life in five world religions. Commentary 39:49-55 Ap; 40:13-14 Ag '65
FACKRE, Gabriel
Behind the ism. Christian Cent 82:1236-8 O 6 '65
Kindled fire. Christian Cent 82:1013-14 Ag 18 '65
FACSIMILES of rare books. See Book rarities —Facsimiles
FACTORIES
Special report on industrial facilities; symposium. il Duns R 85:pt2 112-21+ Mr '65

Cleanliness
How clean is clean? reprint. T. J. Foster. il Sci Digest 57:56-60 F '65

Design
Construction: blending function and esthetics. J. Thackray. il Duns R 85:pt2 128-33+ Mr '65

Electric utilities
Utilities and appointments come of age. L. Blumenthal. il Duns R 85:pt2 138-41+ Mr '65

Equipment
Forecast for capital outlays: sunny. il Bsns W p 112+ S 25 '65

Heating and ventilation
Utilities and appointments come of age. L. Blumenthal. il Duns R 85:pt2 138-41+ Mr '65

Location
See Location in business and industry

Protection
New complexities in plant security. K. August. il Duns R 85:pt2 142-3+ Mr '65

Reconversion
Defense: California planners try novel approach to problems of economic reconversion. E. Langer. Science 148:482 Ap 23 '65

Safety devices and measures
New complexities in plant security. K. August. il Duns R 85:pt2 142-3+ Mr '65

FACTORIES, Automatic. See Machinery, Automatic
FACTORING (finance) See Accounts receivable
FACTORS
U.S. factoring leaps Atlantic: First national of Boston led parade, followed by Heller of Chicago. Bsns W p86+ Ja 30 '65
FACTORY management
See also
Foremen
Industrial management and organization
FACTORY produced houses. See Houses, Prefabricated
FACTORY wages. See Wages—United States
FACULTIES, College. See College professors and instructors
FADER, Daniel
Boast of Englishmen. bibliog por Library J 90:1841-3 Ap 15 '65
FADIMAN, Clifton
Anatomizing Oscar: a friend looks at Levant. Holiday 38:27+ N '65
Common reader and the uncommon critic. Holiday 39:109-11 Ja '66
Party of one (cont) Holiday 38:8+ O '65
Wayward reader (cont) Holiday 37:34 Mr '65
FADS
Airy lobes; pierced ears craze. Time 86:70 O 15 '65
Can you invent a million-dollar fad? W. S. Griswold. il Pop Sci 188:78-81+ Ja '66
Ins and outs of pop culture; how to play the game. G. Steinem. il Life 59:72-3+ Ag 20 '65
Ironing hair fad. J. Shepherd. il Look 29: 104+ Ap 20 '65
It's a bird, it's a plane: Super ball. il Time 86:69-70 O 22 '65
Not good taste, not bad taste, it's camp. T. Meehan. il N Y Times Mag p30-1+ Mr 21 '65
Teen scene. See issues of Seventeen
See also
Food fads
FAGAN, Edward R.
Criticism, interpretative art. Sch Arts 65: 21-5 N '65
FAGERHOL, Magne K. and Braend, Mikael
Serum prealbumin: polymorphism in man. bibliog Science 149:986 Ag 27 '65
FAGERLUND, N. D.
Oakland, N.J. proving ground for cathodic protection. por Am City 80:106-8 S '65
FAGLEY, Richard
Vatican II and responsible parenthood. Christian Cent 82:332-3 Mr 17 '65
FAHRENBACH, Wolf H.
Sarcoplasmic reticulum: ultrastructure of the triadic junction. bibliog Science 147:1308-10 Mr 12 '65
FAÏENCE, French. See Pottery, French
FAILURES in business. See Business failures
FAIR, Charles L.
Using silicon diodes. Pop Electr 23:58-60 Jl '65
FAIR, Ronald L.
Many thousand gone; excerpts from novel. por Ebony 20:57-8+ Ap '65
FAIR employment practices. See Discrimination in employment
FAIR play. See Sportsmanship
FAIR today, followed by tomorrow; drama. See Fontaine, R.
FAIRBANKS, Horace
Victoriana in Vermont. il Time 86:50-1 Ag 20 '65
FAIRBROTHER, Nan
Building a new house: no trauma; excerpts from House in the country. Vogue 145:210+ My '65
FAIRCHILD, John Burr
Locomotives; excerpt from Fashionable savages. Ladies Home J 82:47+ S '65
about
Man from WWD. il por Newsweek 66:50 Ag 16 '65
FAIRCHILD camera and instrument corporation
What made a high flier take off at top speed. il Bsns W p 118+ O 30 '65
FAIRCHILD Hiller corporation
Fairchild adds to F-27, FH-227 output, starts turbo-porter line. Aviation W 83:41 Jl 12 '65
FAIRFAX COUNTY, Va.
Battle at Mason Neck. il Nat Parks Mag 39:20-1 D '65
Housing
Deft handling of concrete and brick. il Arch Rec 137:214-15 Ap '65

FAIRLIE, Henry
America, 1965. New Repub 154:15-20 Ja 1
'66
American kids? N Y Times Mag p 116+ N
14 '65
Cheer for American imperialism. N Y Times
Mag p7+ Jl 11 '65
Englishman goes to a Klan meeting. N Y
Times Mag p26-7+ My 23 '65
He was a man of only one season. N Y Times
Mag p28-9+ N 21 '65
Johnson & the intellectuals. Commentary
40:49-55 O '65

FAIRS
See also
Agricultural exhibitions
Bazaars, Charitable
Book fairs
Exhibitions
Festivals

FAIRWEATHER, Arthur. See Faught, M. C. jt.
auth.

FAIRY plays
Another Cinderella. R. Fontaine. Plays
25:91-5 Ja '66
Dummling and the golden goose; dramatiza-
tion of Grimms' fairy tale. A. Thane.
Plays 25:35-44 Ja '66
Elves and the shoemaker; dramatization of
Grimms' fairy tale. A. Thane. Plays 25:33-
40, 62 D '65
Enchanted princess. C. W. Baher. Plays 24:
55-64 My '65
Genie of the bottle. H. Whittaker. Plays
25:79-84 N '65
Hansel and Gretel. A. Thane. Plays 24:41-50
F '65
Knights of the square table. E. J. Dias.
Plays 25:51-62 D '65
Let sleeping beauties lie. R. Fontaine. Plays
24:91-5 F '65
Mother Goose's Christmas surprise. C. Boiko.
Plays 25:77-82 D '65
Storybook revolt. F. B. Watts. Plays 25:
67-73 N '65

FAIRY queen; opera. See Purcell, H.

FAIRY tales
And so they lived happily ever after. E. Enright. il McCalls 93:116-17+ D '65

FAISAL, king of Saudi Arabia. See Feisal

FAITH, Sister Mary. See Mary Faith, Sister

FAITH
Christian faith and moral action. J. M.
Gustafson. Christian Cent 82:1345-7 N 3
'65
Christian natural theology and Christian
existence. J. B. Cobb. jr. Christian Cent
82:265-7 Mr 3 '65; Discussion. 82:496 Ap 21
'65
Contra the new theologies. P. L. Holmer.
Christian Cent 82:329-32 Mr 17 '65; Dis-
cussion. 82:742-3 Je 9 '65
Creativity without guilt; man's relation to
God. R. O. Johann. America 113:165 Ag 14
'65
Dissolution and reconstruction in theology.
L. Gilkey. Christian Cent 82:135-9 F 3 '65;
Discussion. 82:433-5 Ap 7 '65
Dynamics of unfaith. L. J. Averill. Chris-
tian Cent 83:41-4 Ja 12 '66
Existence of God, by W. I. Matson. Review
Sat R 48:39-40 F 6 '65; Discussion. 48:28
Mr 13 '65
Faith and truth. S. M. Ogden. Christian
Cent 82:1057-60 S 1 '65; Reply. H. E. Jen-
sen. 82:1321 O 27 '65
Nature and function of faith. V. A. Harvey.
Christian Cent 82:962-6 Ag 4 '65
Other twenty-nine; prize winning story. R.
T. Schmitt. NEA J 54:12-14 O '65
Power and a goodness. R. R. Niebuhr. Chris-
tian Cent 82:1472-5 D 1 '65
Relevance of religion. R. O. Johann. America
112:287 F 27 '65
Religion of Abraham Lincoln. R. Niebuhr.
Christian Cent 82:172-5 F 10 '65
Theology as risk. C. Welch. Christian Cent
82:707-10 Je 2 '65
Word. V. P. McCorry. America 112:811-12
My 29 '65
See also
Agnosticism
Belief and doubt
Creeds
Hope
Justification

FAITH and order conferences. See Religious
conferences

FAITH cure
Faith and a friar. Newsweek 65:40+ Je 28 '65

FAKERS. See Quacks and quackery

FALCIPARUM malaria. See Malaria

FALCK, B. and others
Pigmented nevi and malignant melanomas as
studied with a specific fluorescence method.
bibliog Science 149:439 Jl 23 '65

FALCONER, G. and others
Late-Wisconsin end moraines in northern
Canada. bibliog Science 147:608-10 F 5 '65

FALCONER, Vera
Films and filmstrips (cont) Sr Schol 86:22T
F 18; sup22 Mr 18; sup34 Ap 15; sup 14
My 13 '65
New films and filmstrips (cont of) Films
and filmstrips. Sr Schol 87:sup24 S 23; sup4
O 21; sup 10-11 O 28; sup 16 N 4 '65

FALCONRY
Hunters of the sky; paintings by F. Golden;
with account by D. Barnes. Sports Illus
23:46-51 N 8 '65

FALES, Dean A. Jr
Crowninshield-Bentley House in Salem, a
documentary restoration. Antiques 88:486-
93 O '65

FALES, E. D. Jr
How fast will we drive? Pop Sci 187:98-101+
O '65
How to keep your car looking new. Pop
Sci 187:158-61 S '65
When you rent a car. Pop Sci 187:90-3+
D '65

FALK, Richard A.
Claimants of Hiroshima. Nation 200:157-61 F
15 '65

FALKNER, Murry
Day the balloon came to town; excerpt from
William Faulkner of Oxford. ed. by J. W.
Webb and A. W. Green. por Am Heritage
17:46-9 D '65

FALL, Albert Bacon
Tempest over Teapot. B. Bliven. il por Am
Heritage 16:22-3+ Ag '65

FALL, Bernard B.
Feuding with the French. New Repub 152:
17-18 Mr 13 '65
How democracy returned to Vietnam. Nation
200:362-4 Ap 5 '65
If Ho Chi Minh's army moves south in
force—. N Y Times Mag p7+ S 5 '65
Mess: three views. Nation 200:534-6 My 17
'65
That Geneva agreement: how the French got
out of Vietnam. N Y Times Mag p28-9+
My 2 '65
Vietnam blitz; report on the impersonal war.
New Repub 153:17-21 O 9; 33-4 N 13 '65
Vietnam: European viewpoints. New Repub
153:13-15 Ag 21 '65
Vietnam: remembrance of things past. New
Repub 153:23-4 Jl 10 '65
Vietnam: the agonizing reappraisal. bibliog f
Cur Hist 48:95-102+ F '65
Year of the hawks. N Y Times Mag p46-9+
D 12 '65

FALL. See Autumn

FALL planting. See Gardening

FALLACI, Oriana
(ed) See Kennedy, R. F. Robert Kennedy
answers some blunt questions

FALLACIES. See Logic

FALLACIES, Food. See Errors, Popular

FALLERS, Lloyd A. and others
Policy proposals: a negotiated stalemate. Bul
Atomic Sci 21:42-5 Je '65

FALLING leaves; story. See Slote, A.

FALLON, Daniel
Eatometer: a device for continuous recording
of free-feeding behavior. bibliog Science
148:977-8; 149:764 My 14, Ag 13 '65

FALLOT'S tetralogy. See Tetralogy of Fallot

FALLOUT shelters. See Atomic bomb shelters

FALLSBURGH, N.Y.
Telemetering ties cut operating costs; centralizing the operation of five small water
districts with a large distribution area.
S. Friedman. il Am City 80:96-7 N '65

FALNES, Oscar J.
(comp) Articles and other books received:
northern Europe. See issues of American
historical review

FALSE lashes. See Eyelashes

FALSE teeth. See Teeth, Artificial

FALTER, Mary Elizabeth
Notes of a happy housekeeper. See issues of
House & garden incorporating Living for
young homemakers

FALTERMAYER, Edmund K.
Coming battle for the color-TV market.
Fortune 73:144-7+ Ja '66
Drift to early retirement. Fortune 71:112-15+
My '65
Half-finished society. Fortune 71:96-7+ Mr
'65

FALTERMAYER, Edmund K.—*Continued*
We can afford clean air. Fortune 72:158-63+ N '65
We're bullish on Mexico. Fortune 72:149-51+ S '65
What business wants from Lyndon Johnson. Fortune 71:122-5+ F '65
about
Poison in the air. Nation 201:347 N 15 '65

FAME
Quotations, maxims, etc.
Famous; comp. by E. F. Murphy. N Y Times Mag p62 O 31 '65

FAMILY
Family's role in political socialization. J. C. Davies. bibliog f Ann Am Acad 361:10-19 S '65
See also
Birth order
Family life
Fathers
Mothers
Widows

FAMILY, Size of
Case for the caboose. Z. J. Aranow. il McCalls 92:42+ Mr '65
Poverty and the size of families. Am City 80:34+ Ap '65
Who gets the drumstick? excerpt. H. Beardsley. il Good H 161:86-9+ O '65

FAMILY affair; drama. See Ward, M.

FAMILY allowances
United States
Family policy for the Nation; with editorial comment. D. P. Moynihan. il America 113:277, 280-3 S 18 '65

FAMILY budget. See Budget, Household

FAMILY circle (periodical)
Past the middle range; booklist for college bound. E. Geller. Library J 90:5016 N 15 '65

FAMILY corporations
Enchantment in the Louisiana marshes; manufacturers of tabasco sauce. K. Hamill. il Fortune 72:158-64 O '65
Two-billion-dollar company that lives by the cent; Cargill, inc. H. Kay. il Fortune 72:166-9+ D '65

FAMILY courts. See Domestic relations courts
FAMILY doctors. See Physicians
FAMILY finance. See Domestic finance
FAMILY life
Don't be a martyr-mother. V. Hyde. il Parents Mag 40:38-9+ Jl '65
Hey, mom, it's party time! S. Mullins. il Farm J 89:61+ Ag '65
How America lives (cont) Ladies Home J 82:56+ Ap; 56-9+ My; 68-9+ Je; 62-3+ Jl; 74-5+ Ag; 74-5+ S; 82-4+ O; 92-3+ N '65
I couldn't have stood marriage; a humorist-artist's account. D. Herold. il Read Digest 87:25-6 S '65
Negro family, by D. P Moynihan. Review New Yorker 41:116+ S 11 '65. R. H. Rovere
Our daughter Ivan the Terrible. E. Thompson. il Redbook 125:8+ O '65
Tiredest night of the week. J. K. Lubold. il Read Digest 87:108-11 S '65
Who gets the drumstick? excerpt. H. Beardsley. il Good H 161:86-9+ O '65
Who won, mom? L. M. Stalvey. Parents Mag 40:87 O '65
See also
Love
Parent-child relationship
Stepparents

Anecdotes, facetiae, satire etc.
Man next door. B. Hillis. See issues of Better homes and gardens

Caricatures and cartoons
It's all in the family. S. Berenstain and J. Berenstain. See issues of McCall's

FAMILY limitation. See Birth control
FAMILY man; story. See Heinemann, A.
FAMILY matter; story. See Phillips, J. R.
FAMILY meadow; story. See Updike, J.
FAMILY planning. See Birth control
FAMILY records
How to protect those valuable papers. M. T. Bloom. Read Digest 87:127-30 D '65
Machines to do the family's figuring. il Changing T 20:31-2 Ja '66

FAMILY recreation. See Recreation
FAMILY rooms. See Living rooms

FAMILY service association of America
Substitute mothers. C. W. Blackburn. il PTA Mag 59:28-30 Je '65
FAMILY vacations. See Vacations
FAMINES
India
Another calamity: famine in India. il U S News 59:58-9 D 27 '65
Famine in India. Christian Cent 82:1596 D 29 '65
See also
Food supply—India

FAMOUS men. See Great men
FAMOUS Rutland pearls; story. See Wilson, R.
FAMOUS women. See Women, Famous
FANALE, F. P. and Schaeffer, O. A.
Helium-uranium ratios for pleistocene and tertiary fossil aragonites. bibliog Science 149:312-17 Jl 16 '65
La FANCIULLA del West; opera. See Puccini, G.
FANCY-leafed geraniums. See Geraniums
FANDANGO; story. See Madocs, R.
FANDEL, John
Economy; poem. Cath World 201:188 Je '65
Oneliners; poems. Commonweal 81:758 Mr 12 '65

FANFANI, Amintore
Human rights day 1965; message. UN Mo Chron 2:i-iii D '65
Letter to President Johnson, November 20, and to Secretary Rusk, December 13, 1965. Dept State Bul 54:11-12 Ja 3 '66
about
Fanfani's helpmeet. Reporter 34:14+ Ja 13 '66
Motor quits. por Newsweek 67:28 Ja 10 '66
Motor's return. por Newsweek 65:57 Mr 15 '65
Peacemaker in a jam; tough lesson for Fanfani. il por U S News 60:17 Ja 10 '66
Touch that failed. il por Time 87:28 Ja 7 '66

FANFANI, Biancarosa
Fanfani's helpmeet. Reporter 34:14+ Ja 13 '66
FANG, Achilles
Out of China. Poetry 107:196-9 D '65
FANGER, Donald
Posthumously rehabilitated. Nation 202:46-7 Ja 10 '66
FANNIN, William Jones
Battle over 14(b) Christian Cent 82:939-40 Jl 28 '65
FANNING, Eleanor Ivanye
Birds in your garden. Pop Gard 17:22+ Ja '66
FANNING, James
Good cutting garden. House & Gard 127:206-9+ My '65
FANON, Frantz
Portrait of a revolutionary. H. R. Isaacs. Commentary 40:67-71 Jl '65
What colonialism does. R. Coles. New Repub 153:20+ S 18 '65
FANS
Fans through the summer; Metropolitan museum exhibition. R. Davidson. il Antiques 87:654+ Je '65
FANS, Electric. See Electric fans
FANS, Ventilating. See Ventilators
FANTAIL willow. See Willow
FANTASIES, Literary
Elvish mode; meeting of the Tolkien society of America. New Yorker 41:24 Ja 15 '66
Flat-heeled muse. L. Alexander. Horn Bk 41:141-6 Ap '65
James Thurber and the art of fantasy. C. S. Holmes. Yale R 55:17-33 O '65
Wells of fancy, 1865-1965; childrens literature; with bibliography. D. MacCann. il Wilson Lib Bul 40:334-43 D '65
See also
Fairy tales
FANTASTIC architecture. See Architecture, Fantastic
FANTASTIC art. See Art, Fantastic
FANTASY finishes. See Decoration and ornament, Architectural
FANTEL, Hans H.
Audio. See issues of Opera news
Bantam hi-fi speaker systems ride on air cushion. Pop Electr 22:40-3+ My '65
Hi-fi stereo for '66, in solid. Pop Electr 23:47-51+ N '65
No stick on a swivel. Pop Electr 23:35-9+ Jl '65
Placing the speakers. Opera N 29:35 F 6 '65
Record hygiene. Opera N 29:35 F 20; 32 Mr 6 '65
Sound waves that see through people. por Pop Mech 124:124-8+ O '65

FANTEL, Hans H.—*Continued*
Tape types. Opera N 29:36 Ap 17 '65
Taping off the air. Opera N 29:35 Mr 20; 35 Ap 3 '65
They're still inventing the telephone. Pop Sci 187:94-6+ D '65
Three giant steps to the moon. Pop Mech 124:90-4+ O '65
Updating your stereo system. Pop Electr 22: 57-60+ Mr '65

FAR EAST
See also
Asia, Southeastern
Cities and towns—Far East
United Nations—Economic commission for Asia and the Far East

Description and travel
Far lands grow nearer; Asia and the Pacific; symposium. il Sat R 48:35-40+ S 18 '65
Resort hopping in the Orient. M. Atwater. il Travel 124:36-8 N '65

FAR right (politics) See Right and life (political science)

FARADAY, Michael
Michael Faraday, by L. P. Williams. Review Time il 86:90 Jl 23 '65

FARADAY society
Faraday society discussion; proton transfer processes; report on meeting. M. R. Crampton. Science 149:208 Jl 9 '65

FARAH, Abdulrahim Abby
United Nations commemoration address, June 26, 1965. UN Mo Chron 2:149-52 Jl '65

FARB, Peter
Disaster threatens the Everglades. Audubon Mag 67:302-9 S '65; Same abr. with title Save the Everglades. Read Digest 87:241-3+ N '65

FARBEN, I.G. See Interessengemeinschaft farbenindustrie aktiengesellschaft

FARBENINDUSTRIE, I.G. See Interessengemeinschaft farbenindustrie aktiengesellschaft

FARBER, Leslie H.
Psychoanalysis and morality. Commentary 40:69-74 N '65

FARBER, Norma
Cymbal; poem. Horn Bk 41:615 D '65
Don't leave off dreaming; poem. Horn Bk 41:267 Je '65
In a cold country; poem. America 113:777 D 18 '65
My son in the ooze; poem. America 112:772 My 22 '65

FARBER, Paul R.
Ansco memo camera. il U S Camera 28:34-5+ Ap '65
Foto facts. See issues of U.S. camera & travel
Try tone lines. il U S Camera 28:72-3+ Ag '65
Twisted easel. il U S Camera 28:60-1+ Mr '65
What is best for closeups il U S Camera 28:57-9+ F '65

FARBERMAN, Harold
From a virtuoso, music for virtuosi. P. L. Miller. por Am Rec G 32:239 N '65

FARES, Airline. See Airlines—Fares

FARGO, Frank
Put new life in old streets. Am City 80: 93-5 Mr '65

FARIÑA, Richard
For the crashing and burning of a Lockheed Electra whose engines had been clogged by passing birds; poem. Mlle 61:110 O '65

FARJEON, Benjamin Leopold
Comedy in wax, or Lucy and their majesties; with correspondence between M. M. Dodge and B. L. Farjeon. E. Farjeon. il Horn Bk 41:358-63 Ag '65

FARJEON, Eleanor
Comedy in wax, or Lucy and their majesties. Horn Bk 41:358-60 Ag '65

about
Continuing radiance. R. H. Viguers. Horn Bk 41:341 Ag '65
Obituary
Horn Bk 41:419-20 Ag '65

FARKAS, George
Bargain house invades silk-stocking district. il por Bsns W p 112-14 Ag 7 '65

FARLEY, James C.
One ride with Yankee Papa 13. L. Burrows. il pors Life 58:24-34C Ap 16 '65

FARM animals

Collisions with automobiles
See Automobile driving—Animal hazards

FARM boys
Four myths that hurt farm boys. D. C. Brown. Farm J 89:68 Ap '65
Opportunities for farm boys. Farm J 89:146 Mr '65

FARM buildings
See also
Swine farrowing crates and pens
Swine houses

FARM bureau federation. See American farm bureau federation

FARM bureaus. See American farm bureau federation

FARM corporations. See Farms, Incorporated

FARM drainage. See Drainage

FARM equipment
Home-made and handy; photographs. See issues of Farm journal
See also
Agricultural machinery

FARM equipment dealers
How dealers can help you. Suc Farm 64:95 Ja '66

FARM fences. See Fences

FARM finance
How farmers finance land purchases. Suc Farm 63:86C F '65
How farmers get money to start farming. Suc Farm 63:36 Ap '65
How these farmers handle debt. J. A. Carlson. Farm J 89:52 Ap '65
How to evaluate your own credit rating. Suc Farm 63:71 Ap '65

FARM girls
What do you want out of life? il Farm J 89: 88-9 Ap '65

FARM income. See Agriculture—Economic aspects

FARM labor
Education of Willard Wirtz. Nation 200:379 Ap 12 '65
Harvester corps? New Repub 152:6-7 Ap 3 '65
On the bench; domestic farm workers. New Repub 153:8 Ag 7 '65
Report from the National farm labor conference. P. Groom. Mo Labor R 88:275-8 Mr '65
These hired hands want to stay; California dairies. Farm J 89:40 S '65
They're out to take your hired man. N. Reeder. Farm J 89:48D Je '65
Train cow milkers in college? N. Reeder. Farm J 89:50H O '65
Wirtz helps growers a little; yields slightly on ban on foreign farm labor. il Bsns W p45-6+ Ap 17 '65
See also
Migrant labor
Strikes—United States—Farm labor

FARM land values. See Land values

FARM leases. See Leases

FARM legislation. See Agricultural laws and legislation

FARM life
Can we keep on being neighborly? H. Stieve. Farm J 89:C2 S '65
Farmer's daughter, 1965. il Farm J 89:69+ S '65
I am a farm girl! J. Ezell. il Farm J 89: 70-1 S '65
I like this side of the fence. M. W. Harper. il Farm J 89:43 Jl '65
Letters from farm women. See issues of Farm journal
See also
Farm women
Ranch life

FARM machinery. See Agricultural machinery

FARM management
How to tell if it'll pay; decision-maker formula. il Farm J 89:56 S '65
No plumbing for Negroes; Ames plantation. S. Barraclough. il Atlan 216:105-9 S '65
Partway partnership. L. Dinkins and J. Bickers. il Farm J 89:D2 F '65
Will it earn the extra cost? D. H. Doane. Farm J 89:48I Je '65
You can't afford to own a farm. C. E. Ball. il Farm J 89:42-3+ Ap '65
See also
Dairy farm management
Dairy farm records
Farm records

FARM odors. See Odors

FARM offices. See Offices

FARM ownership
Buy land on contract to start farming? Suc Farm 63:67 Je '65
Renter who bought a farm with corn. R. D. Wennblom. il Farm J 89:26-7+ Jl '65
You can't afford to own a farm. C. E. Ball. il Farm J 89:42-3+ Ap '65

FARM parity. See Farm produce—Prices
FARM policy. See Agricultural administration
    —United States
FARM ponds. See Ponds
FARM prices. See Farm produce—Prices
FARM produce
    See also
    Surplus products, Agricultural
                Marketing
    Cost of stubbornness: Eurocrats, de Gaulle
        and problems over common market in farm
        produce. Time 85:41-2 Je 25 '65
        See also
    Turkeys—Marketing
                Prices
    Everyone else can set his price, farmers
        should, too. D. Paarlberg. Suc Farm 63:
        31+ N '65
    Great myths of agricultural policy: farm
        prices are made in Washington. D. Paarl-
        berg. Suc Farm 63:29+ Ag '65
    Parity: tackling the farm problem. Sr Schol
        86:16 F 25 '65
    Shortage of Florida crops? U S News 58:82-3
        Mr 1 '65
    Swinging a scythe on farm surplus; omnibus
        bill launches new subsidy program. Bsns W
        p29-30 O 23 '65
    Under LBJ's farm plan: a rise in food
        costs. U S News 58:12 Ap 19 '65
    Why farmer's share is shrinking; study by
        National commission on food marketing.
        il Bsns W p174-6+ My 15 '65
        See also
    Agricultural administration—United States
        also subhead Prices under names of farm
        produce, e.g. Hogs—Prices
FARM records
    How careless farm records hurt you. Suc
        Farm 63:106A Mr '65
    I want to make money, not records; ed. by
        J. Bickers. J. Kirkpatrick. il Farm J 89:
        34-5+ Je '65
FARM shops. See Workshops
FARM subsidies. See Agricultural administra-
    tion—United States
FARM tenancy
    Nothin' to lose: sharecropper strike in Miss-
        issippi. Newsweek 65:33+ Je 21 '65
        See also
    Leases
FARM tours
    City friends for farmers; fourth graders of
        Spokane, Wash. visit a farm. il Farm J
        89:51 N '65
FARM women
    But I'm glad I'm my farmer's wife; ed. by
        M. Longwell. M. Stanley. Farm J 89:107 Ap
        '65
    How to preserve a husband. J. A. Nimrod.
        il Farm J 89:81+ Mr '65
    How young wives help their husbands. R.
        Hanna. il Suc Farm 63:113+ S '65
    Letters from farm women. See issues of Farm
        journal
    No cold war here, nor hot, nor even luke-
        warm; Dublin, Ireland. L. Lane. il Farm J
        89:74-5 N '65
    Parson Blake and the farmer's wife; summary
        of Farmer's everyday book, ed. by M. W.
        Steer. J. L. Blake. il Am Heritage 16:42-5
        Je '65
    Tomorrow I'll see the sun; ed. by M. Long-
        well. B. Champlin. Farm J 90:73+ Ja '66
    Want to stretch your mind? L. Lane. il
        Farm J 89:82-3 Mr '65
    When a woman has a whim. . . J. F. Swan.
        il Farm J 89:77+ My '65
FARM workshops. See Workshops
FARMER, James
    Confusing the cause; civil rights groups U.S.
        foreign policy. Time 86:20 Jl 16 '65
    CORE: wild child of civil rights. H. Bims.
        il pors Ebony 20:35-8+ O '65
    Farmer's war; to head Center for community
        action education. Time 87:23 Ja 7 '65
    Larger battleground. por Newsweek 67:22-3
        Ja 10 '66
    Will success spoil civil rightists Christian
        Cent 83:35-6 Ja 12 '66
FARMER, John J.
    Chance for a change in the Garden state.
        Reporter 33:27-9 Ag 12 '65
FARMER ants. See Ants
FARMER-hunter relations
    Give the farmers a break. R. Uhl. Field &
        S 69:163-4 Mr '65
    Hunters welcome! il Farm J 89:50B D '65

            Anecdotes, facetiae, satire, etc.
    Redcoats return to Bucks County. J.
        O'Reilly. il Sports Illus 23:78-80+ N 22 '65

FARMERS
    Department of agriculture. Farm J 89:126
        D '65
    Four myths that hurt farm boys. D. C. Brown.
        Farm J 89:68 Ap '65
    Growing up on a farm; Willis Hammer, jr.
        J. Star. il Look 29:109-14+ Je 15 '65
    How you voted. il Farm J 89:34-5 Mr '65
    Liquidation ahead for 2.4 million farmers?
        il U S News 58:59-60 Mr 22 '65
    Ultimate weapon in war on poverty. il Na-
        tions Bsns 53:90+ F '65
        See also
    Agriculture
    Farmer-hunter relations
    Negro farmers

            Anecdotes, facetiae, satire, etc.
    When doctors take over farming. E. H. Logs-
        don. Farm J 89:53 F '65

            Health and hygiene
        See Men—Health and hygiene

            Political activities
    Big farm fight; with editorial comment.
        C. W. Gifford. Farm J 89:5, 35+ F '65
    Which of these do you want from Congress?
        with editorial comment. Farm J 89:5, 20-1
        F '65

            Public relations
        See Agriculture—Public relations
FARMERS associations. See Agricultural so-
    cieties
FARMERS retirement. See Retirement from
    business, etc.
FARMERS unions
    Union organizing in the fields. V. Salandini.
        America 113:400-1 O 9 '65
FARMERS wives. See Farm women
FARMHOUSES, Remodeled. See Houses, Re-
    modeled
FARMILOE, Dorothy
    We are all in the dark; poem. America 112:
        547 Ap 17 '65
FARMING. See Agriculture
FARMING, Diversified. See Diversified farm-
    ing
FARMING, Part time. See Part time farming
FARMS
    Barnyard serenade; park and recreation dis-
        trict operates popular small animal farm,
        Norwalk, Calif. B. Avenatti. il Recreation
        58:425-6 N '65
    Eighty miles of faith: Farm journal follows
        the trail of a tornado. J. Carlson. il Farm J
        89:40-1+ O '65
        See also
    Farm management
    Farm ownership
    Horse farms
FARMS, Incorporated
    How 135 farmers buy it wholesale. C. E.
        Ball. Farm J 89:28 F '65
    Will incorporation reduce taxes? il Suc Farm
        63:90 Ap '65
FARMVILLE, Va.
    Encounters in Virginia; freedom teacher &
        gentle ladies. E. Newmark. il Nation 200:
        193-7 F 22 '65
FARNSWORTH, Clyde A.
    Quiet triumph of a gentle man. Ebony 20:
        124-6+ Jl '65
    (comp) Vienna laughs. N Y Times Mag p38
        Mr 7 '65
FARNY, Dave
    Ski-mad family. il pors Look 29:80-3 D 14
        '65
FARO (game) See Cards
FAROUK I, king of Egypt (abdicated 1952)
    Last of Farouk's 1,000 and one nights. il
        pors Life 58:38B Mr 26 '65
    One of the discards. il pors Newsweek 65:
        32+ Mr 29 '65
    Tale of two autocrats. il pors Time 85:25
        Mr 26 '65
FARR, Felicia
    My husband, Jack Lemmon; ed. by M.
        Davidson. por Good H 160:58+ Ap '65
FARR, Finis
    Woman who wrote Gone with the wind; ex-
        cerpt from Margaret Mitchell of Atlanta,
        author of Gone with the wind, by F. Farr
        and S. Mitchell. McCalls 92:84-7+ Jl '65
FARRAN, F. T.
    Old purchasing system takes on a new look.
        por Am City 80:126+ Jl '65
FARRELL, Allan P.
    Power of effective thinking. America 112:517
        Ap 17 '65

FARRELL, Barry
Gallant fight of Pat Neal. Life 59:92-103+
O 22 '65
When facing crowds he felt a twinge of
stage fright. Life 60:26-9 Ja 21 '66

about

Occupation: journalist passport: poet. G. P.
Hunt. por Life 59:3 O 22 '65
FARRELL, Edward
Reporter at large: Watts towers, Los Angeles.
C. Trillin. il New Yorker 41:72+ My 29
'65
FARRELL, Eileen
On records: E. Farrell,. Opera N 29:34 F 20
'65
FARRELL, James T.
Books. Commonweal 82:640-1 S 3 '65
Job that buys a dream. por Am Ed 1:1-4
O '65
FARRELL, Ranger
What belongs in acoustical specifications.
Arch Rec 138:227-30+ S; 203-6 N '65
FARRINGTON, Bob
Trotting to the bank. il por Newsweek 67:
56 Ja 17 '66
FARROW, Mia
Extraordinary girl; ed. by E. Miller. pors
Seventeen 24:136-7+ O '65

about

Seagoing soap opera of captain Sinatra.
T. Thompson. il pors Life 59:34B Ag 20 '65
Voyage of the Southern Breeze. il por Time
86:64 Ag 20 '65
FARROWING crates and pens. See Swine far-
rowing crates and pens
FARROWING of swine. See Swine
FARWELL, Ellen L.
Riverside in yellow brick. Library J 90:5161-3
D 1 '65
FASCELL, Dante B.
Excerpt from debate, September 20, 1965.
Cong Digest 44:284+ N '65
FASCISM

Germany

Account rendered, by M. Maschmann. Review
New Repub 153:23-8 Ag 21 '65. L. Segal
Journal of the Warsaw ghetto; excerpts.
C. A. Kaplan. Commentary 40:42-58 N '65
Preview of a German controversy; W.
Graetz's play. The conspirators. G. K.
Romoser. Nation 201:172-4 S 27 '65
Secret war against Hitler, by F. von Schla-
brendorff. Review
America 113:294 S 18 '65. T. Abel
Spy of God. L. Poliakov. Commentary 40:
67-70 Ag '65
What German boys say about Hitler D.
Schoenbaum. il N Y Times Mag p30-1+
Ja 9 '66

Italy

Visit. A. Vivante. New Yorker 41:29-31 Jl
3 '65

United States

Jewish Nazi. il Newsweek 66:110-12 N 15 '65
FASHION
Best dressed women. il Ebony 20:161-4+ My
'65
Fashionable savages, by J. Fairchild. Re-
view
Sat R il 48:69 N 13 '65
Going to great lengths; grannies. il Time
86:81 O 8 '65
Only the young. il Time 86:63 Ag 13 '65
Paris in the fall. il Newsweek 66:49 Ag 16 '65
Paris: the news as we see it; fall fashion
lines. D. Vreeland. il Vogue 146:254-69 S 1
'65
What is fashion? D. Vreeland. il Look 30:58-9
Ja 11 '66
See also
Clothing and dress
Costume design
Fads
Hairdressing

Anecdotes, facetiae, satire, etc.

Flatten your wallet; high style ahead. S. J.
Perelman. New Yorker 41:34-6 F 20 '65
Man who beat the rat race. R. Baker. il Sat
Eve Post 239:18 Ja 15 '66

History

Dressing through two decades. il Ebony 21:
213-18 N '65

Quotations, maxims, etc.

Fashion footnotes; comp. by G. Flatley. N Y
Times Mag p64 Je 13 '65
FASHION designers. See Costume designers
FASHION magazines. See Periodicals for wom-
en

FASHION photography. See Photography,
Fashion
FASHION shows
Bouleversant! spring showings in Paris. il
Time 85:87 F 5 '65
Fashion fair 1965: fashions in orbit. il Ebony
20:157-60 S '65
Fireworks and feathers; new Paris styles.
il Life 59:46-8+ S 3 '65
New beat; rock 'n' roll fashion show. il
Time 86:70 S 10 '65
FASHIONABLE society. See Upper classes
FAST day menus. See Lenten menus
FAST deployment logistics ships. See War-
ships—United States
FASTENINGS
Fasteners. D. F. Brown. il Hobbies 70:50-1+
S '65
See also
Zippers
FASTS and feasts
See also
Holy week
FAT
Lipase: localization in adipose tissue. M. S.
Moskowitz and A. A. Moskowitz. bibliog il
Science 149:72-3 Jl 2 '65
Production of heat by fat. M. J. R. Dawkins
and D. Hull. il Sci Am 213:62-7 bibliog
(p 119) Ag '65
Protein synthesis inhibition: mechanism for
the production of impaired fat absorption.
S. M. Sabesin and K. J. Isselbacher. bib-
liog il Science 147:1149-51 Mr 5 '65
See also
Corpulence
FAT metabolism
Production of heat by fat. M. J. R. Dawkins
and D. Hull. il Sci Am 213:62-7 bibliog
(p 119) Ag '65
FATHER-child relationship. See Parent-child
relationship
FATHER-daughter relationship. See Parent-
child relationship
FATHER-son relationship. See Parent-child
relationship
FATHERS
Double duty for dad. L. Marett. il Parents
Mag 40:52-5 Je '65
Fathers-at-large; New York group gives
fatherless children male affection. il Good H
161:32-3 Jl '65
Fathers, daughters and holiday fashion; ten
famous fathers. il McCalls 93:92-101 D '65
Man in her life. J. Lawrence. il N Y Times
Mag p52+ Ag 15 '65
Man is daddy; childrens definitions.
M. Cohen. il Redbook 125:60-1+ Je '65
Putting down father. P. L. Levin. il N Y
Times Mag p79 Mr 21 '65
Vanishing American father. M. Lerner. Mc-
Calls 92:95+ My '65; Same abr. Read Di-
gest 87:116-18 Jl '65
See also
Stepparents

Anecdotes, facetiae, satire, etc.

Who's in charge here? J. L. Collier. il Read
Digest 87:117-19 N '65

Poetry

Fanfare for father; poem. L. Dowty. Good H
160:186 Je '65
FATHERS, Unmarried. See Illegitimacy
FATHERS day
For Father's day; gifts. il Seventeen 24:139
My '65
Fragrances for father. il Seventeen 24:119
Je '65
FATIGUE
Fatigue: its causes and how it is relieved.
il Good H 160:153 F '65
Personal business; middle years. Bsns W
p 125-6 Ag 14 '65
See also
Endurance
Noise—Physiological effects
FATIGUE, Combat. See Neuroses
FATS, Minnesota. See Wanderone, R.
FATTY acids. See Acids, Fatty
FAUCHER, Joseph A. and Koleske, J. V.
Sedimentation velocity experiments: position
and motion of schlieren peaks. Science 147:
1152-3 Mr 5 '65
FAUGHT, Millard C. and Fairweather, Arthur
Where free enterprise is building a new fron-
tier. Nations Bsns 53:40-1+ Je '65
FAULKNER, Douglas
Finned doctors of the deep. il Nat Geog Mag
128:866-73 D '65
FAULKNER, John
Day the balloon came to town; excerpt from
William Faulkner of Oxford, ed. by J. W.
Webb and A. W. Green. M. Falkner. il por
Am Heritage 17:46-9 D '65

FAULKNER, William
Mr Acarius; story. Sat Eve Post 238:26-31 O
9 '65

about

Day the balloon came to town; excerpt from
William Faulkner of Oxford, ed. by J. W.
Webb and A. W. Green. M. Falkner il
por Am Heritage 17:46-9 D '65
Faulkner on Faulkner. G. Hicks. Sat R 49:
77-8 Ja 8 '66
Sat R 49:77-8 Ja 8 '66. G. Hicks
How a writer finds his material. E. W.
Stone. il Harper 231:157-61 N '65
Memory of William Faulkner. por Sat Eve
Post 238:88 O 9 '65
Unvarnished Faulkner. H. Carter. il por
Américas 17:30-3 O '65
William Faulkner of Oxford, ed. by J. W.
Webb and A. W. Green. Review
Sat R 48:37-8 O 2 '65. G. Hicks

FAULTS (geology)
Alaskan earthquake, 27 March 1964: vertical
extent of faulting and elastic strain energy
release. F. Press and D. Jackson. bibliog
il Science 147:867-8 F 19 '65
Earthquake areas mapped; prediction for
southern California. Sci N L 88:215 O 2 '65
Transform faults, oceanic ridges, and magnetic anomalies southwest of Vancouver
Island. J. T. Wilson. bibliog il Science 150:
482-5 O 22 '65

FAUNTLEROY family
Fauntleroy coat-of-arms. H. K. Eilers. il
Hobbies 70:126-7 Jl '65

FAURE, Edgar
International co-operation: the three periods
of co-operation; address. UN Mo Chron
2:47-58 Mr '65

FAUST, Irvin
Double snapper; story. Esquire 64:180 D '65

FAUST; opera. See Gounod, C. F.

FAVIA-ARTSAY, Aida
Historical records. See issues of Hobbies

FAVORITE child problem. See Children—Management and training

FAVORITE; story. See Shyer, M. F.

FAVREAU, Guy
Halfway housecleaning. Time 86:39 Jl 16
'65
Scandal in Ottawa. il por Time 86:34 Jl 9 '65

FAWCETT, Clara H.
Dollology. See issues of Hobbies

FAWNS
You know how it is with a mother. F. Morgan. il Good H 160:160 F '65

FAY, Gordon S.
How chance affects your life; with questions
and answers. Sci Digest 58:71-7 Ag; 95-6 N
'65

FAYET-LEROY, Jacqueline
High, dry & disastrous. il por Time 86:67 Ag
13 '65

FAYETTE, Eli
Choosing and using salt water tackle. il
Yachting 117:122-4+ Je '65

FEAR
Why children are afraid of the dark. A.
Schwartz. il Parents Mag 40:44-5+ Je '65
Word. V. P. McCorry. America 112:647-8
My 1 '65
See also
Phobias
Worry

FEATHER, Leonard
(ed) Hierarchy of the jazz anarchy. Esquire
64:123-5+ S '65

FEATHER FALLS scenic area. See Wilderness
areas

FEATHER RIVER
On Feather River, old Cherokee. il Sunset
135:19 Ag '65

FEATHERS
Configuration of inactive and active polysomes of the developing down feather. E.
Bell and others. bibliog il Science 148:1739-
41 Je 25 '65

FEATHERSTONE, Joseph L.
Katherine Anne Porter's harvest. New
Repub 153:23-6 S 4 '65
Machiavelli of the New deal. New Repub
153:22-6 Ag 7 '65
Mrs Wharton and Mr James. New Repub
152:21-4 My 29 '65
Poetry of commonplaces. New Repub 152:27-
9 Mr 6 '65
Red flag of mutiny. New Repub 153:23-5 N
6 '65
We want bread and roses too. New Repub
152:26+ Ap 17 '65

FEATHERSTONE, Ralph
From Selma: the stench of freedom. por
Negro Hist Bul 28:130 Mr '65

FEAZELLE, James C.
First we built the reservoir. Am City 80:135-
6 N '65

FEBRUARY
February; few of the dates, memorable and
not so, coming up next month (title varies)
(cont) il N Y Times Mag p4+ Ja 31 '65

FEDER, Richard A.
How to measure marketing performance.
Harvard Bsns R 43:132-42 My '65

FEDERAL aid. See Art and state; Federal and
municipal relations; Federal and state relations; Grants-in-aid; Subsidies; *also* subhead Federal aid under various subjects,
e.g. Transportation—Federal aid

FEDERAL aid to education
Action and more action. C. B. Grannis.
Pub W 188:46 S 6 '65
Aid for parochial schools, a question of edu-
cation, not religion. C. N. Degler. il N Y
Times Mag p 11+ Ja 31 '65
Aid to education: Administration's bill. New
Repub 152:9 Ap 17 '65
Aid to parochial schools. W. P. Berwick.
Christian Cent 82:374+ Mr 24 '65
AASA favors education bill; annual conven-
tion. Sr Schol 86:sup4 Mr 4 '65
ACLU and civil rights for children. V. C.
Blum. America 113:160-3 Ag 14 '65
AFT head asks national standards; state-
ments. Sr Schol 87:sup2 D 9 '65
Arts & humanities in the U.S. Office of edu-
cation. H. E. Hoffa. Sch Arts 64:52 My '65
Batch of winners; USOE approve 216 of the
first PACE applications. il Newsweek 67:79
Ja 24 '66
Big federal move into education; Time essay.
Time 85:44-5 Ap 30 '65
Biggest push yet for school integration;
threat to cut off aid. il U S News 58:50-1
Mr 1 '65
Bill to aid elhi education runs into trouble.
R. H. Smith. Pub W 187:140 F 22 '65
Break in the ranks; Union of Orthodox Jew-
ish congregations of America disassociate
itself from National community relations
advisory council. America 113:392 O 9 '65
Changing Jewish attitudes; question of in-
cluding parochial schools in federal aid-to-
education programs. F. Canavan. America
112:214 F 13 '65
College aid bill. America 112:892 Je 26 '65
Colleges' turn. Time 86:20 S 3 '65
Compliance. L. Baker. il Am Ed 1:24-6 S '65
Congress: a higher education bill is considered a likely prospect, but hard bargaining lies ahead. J. Walsh. Science 149:162-4
Jl 9 '65
Congress clears higher education bill. Sr
Schol 87:sup2 N 11 '65
Congress: higher education act including
scholarship for needy passed in final days
of session. J. Walsh. Science 150:591-2+
O 29 '65
Congress: subcommittee surveys effects of
federally supported research on higher edu-
cation. J. Walsh. Science 149:42-4 Jl 2 '65
Congress subcommittee surveys effects of
federally supported research on higher
education. J. Walsh. Science 149:42-4 Jl 2
'65; Reply. D. T. Denhardt. 149:918+ Ag
27 '65
Development of federal responsibility in
higher education. Sat R 48:82 N 20 '65
Discrimination in Chicago. Newsweek 66:94
O 11 '65
Dixie disunity; government threat to non-
compliant states. Reporter 32:8-9 Je 3 '65
Education act of 1965 introduced and de-
bated. Library J 90:1486+ Mr 15 '65
Education bill amendments. America 112:275
F 27 '65
Education scoreboard; school aid bill cleared
for House vote. G. Krettek and E. D.
Cooke. ALA Bul 59:349 My '65
Education: what next? C. Jencks. New
Repub 153:21-3 O 16 '65; Correction. 153:40
N 6 '65
Education's muddled bureaucracy. J. Spivak.
il Reporter 32:33-6 Ap 8 '65; Reply. R. L.
Thackrey. 32:6 My 6 '65
Elementary and secondary education act of
1965. ALA Bul 59:184-5 Mr '65
Elementary and secondary education act of
1965; Higher education act of 1965. G.
Krettek and E. D. Cooke. Wilson Lib Bul
39:583-5+ Mr '65
Elementary teachers say: books come first;
results of survey made for Grade teacher.
C. B. Grannis. Pub W 187:82 Ap 26 '65
Federal aid and judicial review. Christian
Cent 82:451-2 Ap 14 '65
Federal aid at last. America 112:602 Ap
24 '65
Federal aid for shared time. America 113:
147 Ag 14 '65
Federal aid to education prospects improve.
Christian Cent 82:231 F 24 '65
Federal aid to education; symposium. Sr
Schol 87:sup4+ O 14 '65

FEDERAL aid to education—*Continued*
Washington report; Republican alternative to education bill in House of representatives. J. Lloyd. Sr Schol 86:sup3 Mr 25 '65
We've got it started; Elementary and secondary education act of 1965. il NEA J 54:33-9 S '65
What price partnership? Johnson administration's bold measure. Newsweek 65:59 F 22 '65
What's happening in education? W. D. Boutwell. PTA Mag 60:11-12 S '65
What's happening in education? concerning President Johnson's education message to Congress. W. D. Boutwell. PTA Mag 59:17-18 Mr '65
What's happening in education? effect of act for federal aid to elementary and secondary education on local communities. W. D. Boutwell. PTA Mag 59:19-20 Je '65
What's happening in education? ten principal events in education in the year 1964. W. D. Boutwell. PTA Mag 59:31-2 F '65
Where federal school spending overlaps. il Nations Bsns 53:82-3 F '65
Who will be aided by federal school aid? R. Kirk. Nat R 17:378 My 4 '65
Who'll get the school-aid money. il U S News 58:40-2+ Ap 19 '65
Who's to get the 1.3 billions in school aid. U S News 58:6 Ap 5 '65
World we have to know; NDEA language and area centers programs. M. Flapan. il Am Ed 1:30-2 O '65
  See also
Libraries and state

Bibliography
Current materials on recent federal programs for education; adaptation. PTA Mag 60:12 O '65

FEDERAL aid to libraries. See Libraries and state

FEDERAL and municipal relations
At the end of the yo-yo, the federal city. W. Marx. Bul Atomic Sci 21:48-50 Mr '65
Cities seek more federal funds. U S News 58:110 Ap 12 '65
Intergovernmental relations in the United States; symposium, ed. by H. W. Reynolds, jr. bibliog f il Ann Am Acad 359:1-156 My '65
Latest plan for perpetual prosperity; city building; LBJ's proposals to Congress. il U S News 58:42-4 Mr 15 '65
More federal aid for cities? U S News 59:88 Ag 9 '65
Schemes for the cities; President's proposals. Bsns W p32+ Mr 6 '65
War on poverty; Washington vs. City hall. il U S News 59:54-6 N 22 '65
Washington report; local schools to remain independent in their management of federal money. J. Lloyd. Sr Schol 87:sup4+ N 18 '65
We'd rather do it ourselves; communities rebuilding without federal doles. il Nations Bsns 53:36-7+ S '65
Why cities are turning to Washington for cash; interview. J. P. Cavanagh. U S News 59:44-5 Ag 23 '65

FEDERAL and provincial relations (Canada)
Breakup warning. Sr Schol 86:19-20 Mr 18 '65
Guy Trimble vs. Guy Tremblay; clash of English and French could destroy Canada. J. Walz. il N Y Times Mag p38-9+ S 19 '65

FEDERAL and state relations
Administrators in the county of tomorrow; address, November 24, 1964. B. F. Hillenbrand. Vital Speeches 31:243-7 F 1 '65
Big change. D. Lawrence. U S News 58:116 Mr 15 '65
Creative federalism and the Great society; more to L.B.J.'s domestic policies than meets the eye. M. Ways. il Fortune 73:120-3+ Ja '66
Eisenhower on the choice Americans must make; interview. D. D. Eisenhower. il Nations Bsns 53:34-7+ O '65
End of road in sight for the states? how states lean on Washington. il U S News 58:41-5 Mr 29 '65
Establishment. R. Moley. Newsweek 66:104 S 20 '65
Industry studies California problems; special report. W. E. Wilks. il Miss & Roc 16:24-5+ F 15 '65
Intergovernmental relations in the United States; symposium, ed. by H. W. Reynolds, jr. bibliog f il Ann Am Acad 359:1-156 My '65
Lincoln without rhetoric; his destruction of the autonomy of the states. F. S. Meyer. Nat R 17:725 Ag 24 '65; Discussion. 17:827-8+, 850+, 898+; 18:71+ S 21-O 19 '65, Ja 25 '66

Lynching the states; proposed Voting rights act of 1965. D. Lawrence. U S News 58:124 Ap 12 '65
Matching funds; program for conserving soil and water resources. New Repub 154:6 Ja 22 '66
New era ahead for your state. T. Sanford. il Nations Bsns 53:56-8+ Jl '65
No strings federal money for the states; pro and con discussion. Sr Schol 86:16-17 Ap 1 '65
Other side of the voting-rights bill; excerpts from statement. H. F. Byrd. U S News 58:86-8 Ap 12 '65
Power to protect; use of federal forces. New Repub 152:5-6 Mr 20 '65
Retarded dialogue; R. Kennedy, N. Rockefeller dispute over aid for the mentally retarded. Newsweek 67:16 Ja 3 '66
South weighs the cost of defiance on schools; if racial discrimination is permitted, federal aid withheld. Bsns W p29-30 My 8 '65

FEDERAL boards, bureaus, commissions, etc. of United States government. See name of board, bureau, commission, etc. under United States, e.g. United States—Federal communications commission

FEDERAL buildings. See Public buildings

FEDERAL correctional institutions. See Reformatories

FEDERAL courts. See Courts—United States

FEDERAL debt (United States) See Debts, Public—United States

FEDERAL deposit insurance corporation
New limit on bank interest? U S News 59:89 Ag 16 '65
Who's on first? disarray among the federal banking agencies. il Newsweek 65:68 F 15 '65

FEDERAL electric corporation
Experiment at Camp Kilmer. W. Welch. il Reporter 33:30-2 O 21 '65

FEDERAL employees. See Government employees

FEDERAL expenditures. See United States—Appropriations and expenditures

FEDERAL government
Engineering of change in the U.S. Constitution; excerpt from Technology, social change, and the Constitution. A. S. Miller. il Sat R 48:52-5 F 6 '65
Government: biggest growth industry? il U S News 59:62-5 N 22 '65
Intergovernmental relations in the United States; symposium, ed. by H. W. Reynolds, jr. bibliog f il Ann Am Acad 359:1-156 My '65
  See also
Federal and state relations

FEDERAL grants. See Grants-in-aid

FEDERAL housing projects. See Housing projects, Government

FEDERAL judges. See Judges

FEDERAL prisons. See Prisons—United States

FEDERAL reserve banks
  See also
United States—Federal reserve board

FEDERAL statistics. See United States—Statistics

FEDERAL urban renewal program. See Urban renewal

FEDERALISM. See Federal government

FÉDÉRATION internationale de documentation. See International federation for documentation

FEDERATION of American societies for experimental biology
Instruments at the FASEB show. D. J. Prager. Science 148:1366+ Je 4 '65

FEDERATION of Europe. See European federation

FEDERATION of Malaysia. See Malaysia

FEDERMANN, Yekutiel Xavier
Who's who in foreign business. il por Fortune 71:66 F '65

FEDORENKO, Nikolai Trofimovich
United Nations commenmoration address, June 26, 1965. UN Mo Chron 2:159-63 Jl '65

FEDOROV, Konstantin
Gulf Stream of the Pacific. UNESCO Courier 18:36-8 D '65

FEEBLE minded. See Mentally handicapped

FEED handling
Easy way to move feed, blow it! C. F. Marley. il Suc Farm 63:64A N '65
Seven ways to handle livestock feed, which one for you? P. B. Jones and R. J. Mutti. il Suc Farm 63:37-9 O '65
Some of my best customers are rats; confessions of feed salesman. R. Gogerty. il Farm J 90:52N Ja '66
What you should know about feed meters. P. B. Jones. il Suc Farm 63:40-1 N '65

FEED meters. See Meters

FEEDERS (birds)
Bird automat. P. T. Hennig. il Pop Mech 124:156-7 N '65
FEEDING and feeding stuffs
See also
Cattle—Feeding
Cows—Feeding
Dog food
Feed handling
Milo
Silage
Swine—Feeding
Urea

Contamination by drugs and pesticides
New drive to head off meat residues. Farm J 89:44 Ap '65

Litter
See Feeding and feeding stuffs—Poultry house litter

Pelleted feed
Successful farming report on field wafering for hay. il Suc Farm 63:50 Je '65

Poultry house litter
Use feed twice, for chickens then cattle! B. Hardy. il Farm J 89:32-3+ Mr '65
FEEDING stations for birds. See Feeders (birds)
FEEDLOTS, Cattle. See Cattle self feeders
FEELEY, Constance
On the edge: story. New Yorker 41:52-6 O 2 '65
FEELINGS. See Emotions
FEENEY, Mary E.
History will creep in. Library J 90:2978-9 Jl '65
FEES, School. See School finance
FEET. See Foot
FEFFER and Simons, incorporated
Feffer and Simons launches overseas textbook program; reprints of American college texts. Pub W 188:42-3 O 4 '65
Feffer and Simons wins E award for export. il Pub W 188:89 S 27 '65
FEHRENBACH, T. R.
Secrets of the Swiss banks. Atlan 216:33-8 Jl '65
FEIBELMAN, Walter A.
Gravitational lens effect: an observational test. bibliog Science 151:73-4 Ja 7 '66
FEIFER, George
Brotherly cruise on the Black Sea. Harper 230:78-84 Mr '65
900 days. Sat R 48:42 D 11 '65
Russia shoots its business crooks. N Y Times Mag p32-3+ My 2 '65
Speaking out. por Sat Eve Post 238:10+ F 27 '65
Tell my parents not to worry. Sat Eve Post 238:33-4+ F 13 '65
Terror sat in judgment. Sat R 48:31 Je 26 '65
Two miracles. Russian style. Harper 230:106+ Je '65
Underlaw. Nation 201:366-8 N 15 '65
FEIFFER, Jules
Feiffer. See issues of New republic
Men really don't like women. Look 30:60 Ja 11 '66

about
Comic valentine. por Newsweek 66:104+ N 22 '65
Prolific pen of Jules Feiffer; with excerpts from conversation, ed. by S. Schmidt. il pors Life 59:111-12+ S 17 '65
FEIGHAN, Michael A.
Obscure congressman to keep an eye on. R. Stolley. Life 58:34 Je 4 '65
FEIGHT, J. J. See Aldrich, S. R.; Shurtleff, M. jt. auths.
FEIN, Mark
Case of the dead bookie. R. Kahn. il por Sat Eve Post 238:34-8+ Mr 13 '65
FEINBERG, Mortimer R.
Confidential memo to busy husbands. Ladies Home J 82:66+ O '65
Gentle art of executive persuasion; excerpt from Effective psychology for managers. Duns R 86:41-7 D '65
What you can learn about yourself. Nations Bsns 53:40-1+ F '65
FEINBERG, Wilhelmina
Chelsea flower show. Horticulture 43:38-9+ My '65
FEININGER, Andreas
Feininger on color; excerpts from Complete photographer. Mod Phot 29:73-9 O '65
Large camera. See issues of Modern photography

FEINSTEIN, Stephen H. See Rice, C. E.; Schusterman, R. J. jt. auths.
FEIS, Herbert
Anthony Eden and the cacophony of nations. For Affairs 44:78-89 O '65
FEISAL, king of Saudi Arabia
Five kinds of time. J. A. Morris, jr. il por Newsweek 65:42-4 My 8 '65
King Faisal's first year. V. Sheean. For Affairs 44:304-13 Ja '66
FELD, Stuart P.
Recently acquired American paintings at the Metropolitan. Antiques 87:439-43 Ap '65
FELDKAMP, Phyllis
World's most exclusive club. Horizon 7:92-6+ Autumn '65
FELDMAN, Fred
Public service. New Yorker 41:44-5 S 11 '65
FELDMAN, Leonard
Inquiry into spatial stereo. Hi Fi 15:38-40+ My '65
FELDMAN, Myer
Best is yet to be told. Sat R 48:65-6 O 30 '65
Laying down the law. Sat R 48:70-2 My 22 '65
On the side of law and a new order. Sat R 48:19 Jl 31 '65
Pay now, justice later. Sat R 49:30 Ja 1 '66
FELDON, Barbara
Sic 'em tigers. il por Newsweek 65:92+ My 3 '65
FELDSPAR
Feldspar in chondrites. B. Mason. bibliog Science 148:943 My 14 '65
FELLINI, Federico
Fantasy, flesh and Fellini. T. Meehan. il pors Sat Eve Post 239:24-8+ Ja 1 '66
Federico Fellini; wizard of film. E. Walter. il pors Atlan 216:62-7 D '65
First the pasta, then the play. M. S. Davis. il por N Y Times Mag p 10-11+ Ja 2 '66
New fantasy by the 8½ man; with report by N. Liber. il por Life 59:50-4 Ag 27 '65
Private jokes of Federico Fellini. E. Walter. il por Vogue 146:274-5+ S 1 '65
Profiles. L. Ross. por New Yorker 41:63-6+ O 30 '65
Second fame: good food. N. Lyon. il por Vogue 147:152-4 Ja 1 '66
FELLOWS, Lawrence
Harambee, says Kenyatta; let's all pull together. N Y Times Mag p36-7+ N 7 '65
Other, and first, Rhodesians. N Y Times Mag p36-7+ N 21 '65
Shadowed world of the white Rhodesians. N Y Times Mag p43+ D 12 '65
FELLOWSHIPS. See Scholarships and fellowships
FELONY. See Criminal law
FELT rugs. See Rugs and carpets
FENCE posts
How to set and align fence posts. il Sunset 134:171-2+ My '65
FENCES
Canvas. P. Corey. il Pop Gard 16:28-31 Mr '65
Create your own private world. J. H. Ingersoll. il Pop Gard 16:30-2 Ap '65
Design your own fence with modular sections. il Pop Sci 187:143 S '65
How to get quick privacy. il Sunset 135:232 '65
Inexpensive fence panels. il Bet Hom & Gard 43:69 Ap '65
New for your yard, an apple fence. H. A. Rollins, jr. il Farm J 89:47 Mr '65
New ideas in fencing. W. J. Fletcher. il Suc Farm 63:104 Mr '65
Role of the garden screen. il Sunset 136:80+ Ja '66
Six good fencing ideas. il Suc Farm 63:46-7 Je '65
Tall fences for privacy. W. B. Eagan. il Pop Sci 186:139-41 My '65
FENCING
Illinois' unheralded champions. il Ebony 20:125-8 Mr '65
FENELL, Stella
Gardenia success story. il Flower Grower 52:28-9+ N '65
FENICHEL, I. Robert, and Horowitz, S. B.
Nonelectrolyte transport in muscle during induced protein loss. bibliog Science 148:80-3 Ap 2 '65
FENN, Jean
Opera is for her: interview, ed. by R. D. Daniels. por Opera N 30:28 Ja 15 '66
FENNEL
See also
Cookery—Vegetables
FENNER, Mildred S.
Editor's notebook. See issues of NEA journal
FENOGLIO, Charles E.
Solid-state 6-watt amplifier for ten bucks. Pop Electr 23:73-5+ N '65

FENTRESS, John C.
Ethological study of behavior. Science 151:110-11 Ja 7 '66
FENWAY park, Boston. See Stadiums
FENWICK, C. G.
Books. Américas 17:36 N '65
FERABOLI, Mario
Artist of note. por Newsweek 65:75 My 31 '65
FERBER, Ellen
School that smiles. Am Ed 1:8-10 S '65
FERGUSON, Charles W.
Americans not everybody knows (title varies)
See issues of PTA magazine
FERGUSON, J. G, associates
Doubleday acquires J. G. Ferguson companies. Pub W 187:138 F 22 '65
FERGUSON, James Henry
Expectant mother. Redbook 125:32+ Jl '65
FERGUSON, Ken
Magnificent Manitoba. Motor B 116:34-7 Jl '65
FERKISS, Victor C.
Books. Commonweal 83:250-2 N 26 '65
FERLINGHETTI, Lawrence
Pound at Spoleto. Sat R 48:20 S 4 '65

about
San Francisco beat. H. Frankel. Sat R 48:20-1 S 4 '65
FERMOR, Patrick Leigh
Athens. Holiday 37:40-51+ Je '65
Balkan welcome. Holiday 37:82-3+ My '65
FERMOR-HESKETH, Christian Mary (Mc-Ewen) baroness Hesketh. See Hesketh, C. M. M. F.-H.
FERN pine. See Podocarpus
FERNANDEZ, Marina
Exclusive! Cuban education: on-the-spot interview; ed. by W. Johnson. por Sr Schol 87:sup 1 N 18 '65
FERNS
Biology of reproduction in ferns. K. A. Wilson. il Natur Hist 74:52-9 Je '65
Ferns set the rich tone you see here. il Sunset 134:254-5 Mr '65
H&G plans two fern windows. il House & Gard 128:164-7 D '65
We in California live in a treasure-house of ferns. il Sunset 134:102-7 Mr '65
FERNS, Fossil
See also
Glossopteris
FERON, James
German ambassador to Israel. N Y Times Mag p 102+ O 31 '65
FERRANTE, Arthur
Theme team. por Time 85:72 F 5 '65
FERRARI, Enzo
Profiles. W. Sargeant. por New Yorker 41:40-2+ Ja 15 '66
That blood-red Ferrari mystique. R. Daley. il por N Y Times Mag p22-3+ Jl 25 '65
FERRÉ, Frederick
Metaphysics makes a comeback. Christian Cent 82:712-13 Je 2 '65
FERREDOXIN
Ferredoxin and photosynthesis. D. I. Arnon. bibliog il Science 149:1460-70 S 24 '65
Key to photosynthesis found in ferredoxin. Sci N L 88:248 O 16 '65
FERRIES
Alaska's marine highway; ferry route to the north. W. E. Garrett. il Nat Geog Mag 127:776-819 Je '65
Salt-water highways of Puget Sound; how to use them on any visit to western Washington. il Sunset 135:42-51 Ag '65
Water highway to the top of the world; British Columbia to Skagway. S. McCutcheon. il Pop Mech 124:102-5 Ag '65
FERRIES, Train. See Train ferries
FERRIS, John. See Geracimos, A. jt. auth.
FERRIS, Robert R.
Guidance in the elementary school. NEA J 54:48+ S '65
FERRISBURG, Vt.
Gone flying with the NPA to Basin Harbor, Vermont. E. D. Muhlfeld. il Flying 77:96-101 O '65
FERROMAGNESIUM mica. See Biotite
FERRY to Vermont; story. See Stewart, D.
FERRYBOATS. See Ferries
FERSH, Seymour
Words under a mask. bibliog f UNESCO Courier 18:9-12+ F '65
FERTIG, Howard
Howard Fertig founds own publishing house. Pub W 189:102 Ja 17 '66
FERTILITY, Human
Fantastic drug that creates quintuplets. il Life 59:24-31 Ag 13 '65
FERTILITY control. See Birth control

FERTILITY drugs
Fantastic drug that creates quintuplets. il Life 59:24-31 Ag 13 '65
Those new fertility drugs. J. Robbins and J. Robbins. il Good H 160:88-9+ Mr '65
FERTILITY testing of cattle. See Cattle—Testing
FERTILIZATION (biology)
Sperm capacitation by uterine fluid or beta-amylase in vitro. K. T. Kirton and H. D. Hafs. bibliog il Science 150:618-19 O 29 '65
FERTILIZATION, Artificial. See Artificial insemination, Human
FERTILIZATION of plants
Late fall best time to feed trees & shrubs. Flower Grower 52:45 O '65
Tender trap; mechanisms of trap flowers. il Time 85:52+ F 12 '65
See also
Pollen
FERTILIZER industry and trade
Monsanto moves into farmers' backyard. il Bsns W p60-2 F 6 '65
See also
International minerals and chemical corporation
FERTILIZER spreaders
Fertilizer spreaders that float. il Farm J 89:40-1 F '65
It's easy to prolong the life of a lawn spreader. B. C. Kilvert, jr. il Flower Grower 52:48-9 Ap '65
FERTILIZERS and manures
Beware of fertilizer quacks; don't settle for substitute! L. E. Zeman. Suc Farm 63:44 O '65
Chemical fertilizers. C. J. Pratt. il Sci Am 212:62-72 Je '65
Chicken manure makes good fertilizer. J. Bickers. Farm J 89:48J Je '65
Fertilizers and soybeans. J. Russell. Farm J 89:60J My '65
Five factors to consider when buying fertilizer. L. Robertson and L. E. Zeman. il Suc Farm 63:30-1 D '65
From pop-up fertilizer, a 21-bu. kick. D. Hagen. il Farm J 89:70 Ap '65
How my Saturday's bargain became a truckload of trouble. W. H. Hull. il Flower Grower 52:42-3 Je '65
How to fertilize for six tons of hay per acre. W. L. Griffeth and L. E. Zeman. il Suc Farm 63:50-1+ Mr '65
Is row fertilizer old-fashioned? L. E. Zeman. il Suc Farm 64:44 Ja '66
More hay, better pasture; with fertilizer. Farm J 89:45+ F '65
Put your leaves to work; popular compost results, Neosho, Mo. C. W. Bell. il Am City 80:112-13 Ag '65
Read the label on the fertilizer sack. F. E. Bear. Horticulture 44:22-3+ Ja '66
Reading labels on fertilizers. Sunset 134:262 My '65
Sulfur may increase yield of winter wheat. Sci N L 88:121 Ag 21 '65
See also
Lime

Handling
New manure handling ideas. J. Harvey and others. il Suc Farm 63:50-3+ S '65
Three nifty ideas on manure handling. il Farm J 89:50F O '65
FESTIVAL of contemporary arts. See Music festivals—Illinois
FESTIVAL of contemporary music. See Music festivals—Ohio
FESTIVAL of two worlds, Spoleto. See Music festivals—Italy
FESTIVALS
SR/1966 world travel calendar. R. Meyer, jr. Sat R 49:55-6+ Ja 1 '66
See also
Moving picture festivals

California
On December 19, two Las Posadas; reenactment of Mary and Joseph's search for lodging. il Sunset 135:44+ D '65

France
Letter from Paris; Marais festival. Genêt. New Yorker 41:94-5 Je 26 '65

Germany (Federal Republic)
Across a sea of Löwenbräu; Oktoberfest in Munich. il Time 86:110 O 1 '65
Oktoberfest in Munich. il Holiday 38:70-5 N '65

Ireland
Orgy, by M. Rukeyser. Review
Nation 200:282-3 Mr 15 '65. D. Johnston

FESTIVALS—*Continued*

New York (state)

Did you ever, ever, ever; Buffalo festival of the arts today. Time 85:55 Mr 19 '65

Whale of a time; Sag Harbor's Old whaler's festival. il Motor B 116:54+ Ag '65

Oklahoma

Oklahoma powwows. J. H. Winchester. il Travel 123:32-6+ Je '65

Spain

Spanish fiestas. W. Brownell and B. Brownell. il Travel 125:24-8 Ja '66

Switzerland

Basel's licensed license; Fasnacht. il Holiday 37:72-7 Mr '65

Wales

Wales, land of bards. A. Villiers. il Nat Geog Mag 127:727-69 Je '65

FETTERMAN, John
Are you accident prone? reprint. Sci Digest 58:53-6 Ag '65
Case of the shocking-purple school. Good H 161:276 N '65

FETUS
Control of life. il Life 59:59-69 S 10 '65
Delta-aminolevulinate dehydratase activity in mice with hereditary anemia. F. L. Margolis and E. S. Russell. bibliog il Science 150:496-7 O 22 '65
Drama of life before birth; photographs; with report by A. Rosenfeld. L. Nilsson. Life 58:62-9 Ap 30 '65
Every year, 3.5 million miracles. il Newsweek 66:67-70+ O 25 '65
Herpes-like virus isolated from neonatal and fetal dogs. S. E. Stewart and others. bibliog il Science 148:1341-3 Je 4 '65
New discoveries about an old miracle. M. Liley and B. Day. McCalls 92:92-3+ Ag '65; Same abr. with title Secret world of the unborn. Read Digest 87:74-7 N '65
Specificity of macroglobulin antibody synthesized by the normal human fetus. W. V. Epstein. bibliog il Science 148:1591-2 Je 18 '65
Treating a baby before birth; reprint. R. Hermann. il Sci Digest 57:70-4 Ap '65
See also
Unborn children (law)

Photographs

Drama of life before birth; photographs; with report by A. Rosenfeld. L. Nilsson. Life 58:62-9 Ap 30 '65

FEUDAL system. See Feudalism

FEUDALISM
Other Eden; Island of Sark. il Time 86:33 Ag 20 '65

FEUER, Lewis S.
Two cheers for hedonism. M. Himmelfarb. Commentary 39:61-5 Ap '65

FEURZEIG, Wallace. See Swets, J. A. jt. auth.

FEVER blisters. See Blisters

FEW words of advice; story. See Stanton, W.

FEY, Harold E.
Censorship and cultural rebellion; excerpts from address, October 1964. por Library J 90:2473-8 Je 1 '65
Cultural genocide in Russia. Christian Cent 82:914-16 Jl 21 '65
Is the U.N. dying? Christian Cent 82:263-4 Mr 3 '65
Japanese peace mission. Christian Cent 82:982-3 Ag 11 '65
On the angels' side. Christian Cent 82:968 Ag 4 '65
Wars of liberation. Christian Cent 82:1054 S 1 '65
We stand or fall together. Christian Cent 82:612-14 My 12 '65

FEYNMAN, Richard Phillips
Nobel prize winners. por Sci N L 88:279 O 30 '65
Tomonaga, Schwinger, and Feynman awarded Nobel prize for physics. F. J. Dyson. por por Science 150:588-9 O 29 '65

FIAT company. See Automobile industry and trade—Italy

FIBBING. See Lying

FIBEL, Lewis R.
Getting ahead; questions and answers. See issues of Popular science monthly to August 1965

FIBER glass. See Glass fibers

FIBER glass boats. See Boats—Materials

FIBER optics
Fiber optics in electronics. F. O. Kahl. il Electr World 73:25-8+ My '65

FIBERGLASS. See Glass fibers

FIBERGLASS boatbuilding. See Boatbuilding

FIBERS
Inorganic fiber production readied. J. F. Judge. il Miss & Roc 17:32+ D 13 '65
Where is science taking us? composite materials for the future. A. G. H. Dietz. il Sat R 49:104-5 Ja 1 '66

FIBROSIS, Cystic. See Cystic fibrosis

FICHTER, Joseph H.
Chicago's Archdiocesan office of urban affairs. America 113:462-5 O 23 '65
Open parish in the open society. por Cath World 201:16-21 Ap '65

FICHTER, Robert
George Eastman house. U S Camera 28:74-5+ N '65

FICTION
All about books. J. Foster. Sr Schol 87:sup22 N 18 '65
Hot property; what happens to a novel kissed by Hollywood. H. Mitgang. il Sat R 48:39-40 O 2 '65
Questions about the new fiction. J. Didion. il Nat R 17:1100-2 N 30 '65
Who's killing the novel? concerning article by N. Podhoretz in Book week. R. Brustein. New Repub 153:22-4 O 23 '65; Reply with rejoinder. R. Kluger. 153:35-7 N 13 '65
See also
Detective and mystery stories
Historical fiction
Jews in literature
Negroes in literature
Novelists
Priests in literature
Realism in literature
Science fiction
Short stories
Spies in literature
also American fiction; Spanish fiction; etc: *also* subhead Fiction under various subjects, e.g. Sports—Fiction

Bibliography

Fiction (cont) W. B. Hill. America 112:676-9; 113:686+ My 8, N 27 '65
Invisible man and Bellow voted best in Book week survey of postwar fiction. Library J 90:4030 O 1 '65; Discussion. 90:4311, 5318+ O 15, D 15 '65
Year's fiction in review. G. Hicks. Sat R 48:27-8 D 25 '65

Technique

Back to beginnings; reprint. P. M. Daltry. Writer 78:14-15 Jl '65
Birth of a story. L. Egri. Writer 78:20-2 Je '65
Confessions of a storyteller; address, July 1965. F. G. Slaughter. ALA Bul 59:1003-5 D '65
Conflict and how to build it. D. V. Swain. Writer 78:22-6 D '65; 79:21-28+ Ja '66
Cornerstone of fiction. A. Myrer. Writer 78:9-11+ O '65
Eye of the story. E. Welty. Yale R 55:265-74 D '65
How to become a creative writer in twelve not-so-easy steps. S. S. Baker. Writer 78:9-11 My '65
Kind of magic. C. Gaffron. Writer 79:12-14 Ja '66
Map is not a journey. P. A. Whitney. Writer 78:7-12 N '65
Mood of your story. M. J. Waldo. Writer 78:12-13+ Ap '65
Off the cuff. L. Conger. Writer 78:7-8 Ag '65
Ones that got away. A. E. Jones. Writer 78:17-18+ My '65
Plan ahead. A. Heinemann. Writer 78:14-16 D '65
Plot, a pattern created by people. P. S. Curry. Writer 78:20-6+ F '65
Plots and plans. P. Ketchum. Writer 78:23-5 Je '65
Rules of the game. M. A. Rodgers. Writer 78:11-14+ S '65
Satisfying element. P. A. Whitney. Writer 78:11-14+ F '65
Secret mind; excerpt from Afterword to Anthem sprinters and other antics. R. Bradbury. Writer 78:13-16 N '65
Setting a scene. E. Taylor. Writer 78:9-11 Jl '65
Slick pattern. M. F. Shyer. Writer 78:12-14 Ag '65
Taking self-inventory. L. D. Peabody. Writer 78:26-8 Ag '65
That lively corpse: the novel. R. Powell. Writer 78:12-14+ O '65
Throw your heart over. N. Lofts. Writer 78:11-13+ D '65
Time was, a long time coming. J. F. West. Writer 78:15-18 Ag '65

FICTION—Technique—*Continued*
Tips for busy beginners. T. McCormick. Writer 78:29-31 F '65
What is a scene? E. S. Fox. Writer 78:17-20 O '65
With a little wand. A. Iverson. Writer 78:16-19 Je '65
Words you write; excerpt from Tricks and techniques of the selling writer. D. V. Swain. Writer 78:18-23 S '65
See also
Characterization
Detective and mystery stories—Technique
Fiction in periodicals and newspapers
Short stories

Themes
See Literature—Themes
FICTION, Comparative

English and American
See Literature, Comparative—English and American

FICTION for children. See Childrens literature
FICTION in periodicals and newspapers
Fiction for Redbook. N. G. Stuart. Writer 78:24-5 N '65
Notes on creative editing; excerpt from address. H. R. Mayes. Writer 78:18-19+ F '65
When Argosy looks for stories. B. Cassiday. Writer 78:25 Ag '65

FICTION manuscripts. See Manuscripts
FICTIONAL characters. See Characterization
FIDELIO; opera. See Beethoven, L. van
FIDGETS. See Nervous habits
FIEDLER, Arthur
Master of the pops. H. Kupferberg. il por Atlan 215:130+ F '65
FIEDLER, Fred E.
Engineer the job to fit the manager. Harvard Bsns R 43:115-22 S '65
FIEDLER, Leslie A.
Bad scene at Buffalo Jump; story. Esquire 63:100-1 Mr '65
about
Books. M. Tucker. Commonweal 82:387-8 Je 11 '65

FIELD, Andrew
Stalin and Stalinism. New Repub 154:27-9 Ja 1 '66
Was Tolstoy a gentleman? Nation 202:47-8 Ja 10 '66

FIELD, Carolyn W.
Creative dramatics in Philadelphia. por Wilson Lib Bul 40:344+ D '65

FIELD, Cyrus West
Americans nobody knows. C. W. Ferguson. por PTA Mag 59:14-16 Mr '65

FIELD, Edward
Unwanted: a villanelle; poem. Harper 232:28 Ja '66

FIELD, Franklyn. See Greenberg, L. jt. auth.

FIELD, Marshall, 1916-1965
Behind the image. K. McArdle. por Sat R 48:72 O 9 '65
Chicago inheritance. il Time 86:69 O 1 '65
Father to son. il Newsweek 66:62-3 O 4 '65

FIELD, Marshall, 1941?-
Father to son. il por Newsweek 66:62-3 O 4 '65

FIELD, Michael
Curries and condiments. McCalls 93:68+ O '65
Holiday handbook; cooking with wines and spirits. Holiday 37:115-20 Je '65
about
Fighting Fannie Farmer. il por Newsweek 65:112+ Je 14 '65

FIELD, Paul
When; poem. McCalls 92:185 Mr '65

FIELD, Rosamond
Walden changes; poem. Nation 200:260 Mr 8 '65

FIELD, Sally
Boys never gave me a tumble. por Seventeen 25:50 Ja '66

FIELD, Magnetic. See Magnetic field

FIELD and stream (periodical)
When we were growing up. il Field & S 70:58-60 Jl '65

FIELD enterprises, incorporated
Battle of hard news; Larry Fanning replaced by Roy Fisher. il Newsweek 67:53 Ja 3 '66
Father to son. il Newsweek 66:62-3 O 4 '65

FIELD glasses
Binoculars as gifts; here are choices. il Sunset 135:24-6+ D '65
Compact and capable. C. Conley. il Field & S 69:119 Mr '65
Look at it this way. C. Fletcher. il Read Digest 86:25-6+ F '65

FIELD hockey
Unobserved invasion from the North; U.S.-Canadian rivalry. R. Cantwell. Sports Illus 22:68-70 My 31 '65

FIELD ion microscope
Field ion microscopy. E. W. Müller. bibliog il Science 149:591-601 Ag 6 '65

FIELD trials (dogs)
Female wins retriever Nationals. P. Czura. il Field & S 69:146-9 F '65
Grounds for trialing. D. M. Duffey. il Outdoor Life 136:150-2+ N '65
Gun dogs; ed. by J. Stetson. See issues of Field & stream
Lot of work for a $25 hatpin; National retriever stake. il Bsns W p36-8 N 27 '65
National springer stake. D. M. Duffey. il Outdoor Life 135:138-40+ Mr '65
Point about a champion is how he does it; bird dogs compete in National field trial championship, Grand Junction, Tenn. D. Barnes. il Sports Illus 22:22-7 F 8 '65
Shooting dog championship. D. M. Duffey. il Outdoor Life 135:144-8 Je '65
Some grousing about no grouse; Grand national grouse championship, Allegheny national forest, Pa. D. Barnes. Sports Illus 23:79-80 D 13 '65
Some western amateurs fight back against the top pros. V. Kraft. il Sports Illus 22:71+ Ap 26 '65
Springer spaniel national; English springer spaniel national stake. il Field & S 69:159+ Mr '65

FIELDING, Gabriel, pseud. See Barnsley, A. G.

FIELDS, Wilease
VISTA brings aid to Indians. il pors Ebony 20:88-90+ S '65

FIESTAS. See Festivals

FIFTY books of the year exhibit. See Book exhibits

FIGHTING. See Boxing

FIGHTING (psychology)
Pilots who saved England. R. L. Inglis. il Harper 231:52-7 S '65
See also
Aggressiveness

FIGS
Kinin-induced parthenocarpy in the fig, ficus carica. L. J. C. Crane and J. Van Overbeek. bibliog il Science 147:1468-9 Mr 19 '65
See also
Cookery—Fruit

FIGUEIREDO, Antonio de
Portugal, imperialism on credit. Nation 201:134-7 S 17 '65

FIGURAL aftereffects
Adaptation to prismatically rotated visual fields. R. B. Morant and H. K. Beller. bibliog il Science 148:530-1 Ap 23 '65
Color adaptation of edge-detectors in the human visual system. C. McCollough. bibliog il Science 149:1115-16 S 3 '65

FIGURE drawing
It's in the bag! M. Hirschl. il Sch Arts 65:36-7 N '65
Lewis Brown, artist in the theater. J. H. Michel. il Am Artist 30:47-53+ Ja '66

FIGURE of the earth. See Earth—Figure

FIGURES of speech
Sound as a dollar. G. Ace. Sat R 49:20 Ja 8 '66

FIGURINES
Large groups and figures in the soft-paste biscuit of Vincennes-Sèvres. W. J. Sainsbury. il Antiques 87:430-3 Ap '65
Small figures and groups in the soft-paste biscuit of Vincennes-Sèvres. W. J. Sainsbury. il Antiques 88:824-8 D '65

FILAMENTS
Avco building boron filament plant. J. F. Judge. il Miss & Roc 17:22-3+ N 15 '65
Miles and miles of boron. Miss & Roc 16:55 Mr 29 '65
Wound Tungsten offers new shapes. J. F. Judge. il Miss & Roc 16:27 Ap 12 '65

FILENE, Edward Albert
Millionaire failure; excerpt from Biography of an idea. E. L. Bernays. por(p 139) Fortune 72:236 O '65

FILENE, Peter
Alienation vs. involvement. Reporter 32:40+ Je 17 '65

FILENE'S sons company. See Boston—Stores

FILES and filing (documents, etc)
See also
Card system in business, etc.

FILING cabinets. See Cabinets (furniture)

FILLING (earthwork)
How to use your completed landfills. bibliog Am City 80:91-4 Ag '65
Solid-waste disposal; sanitary landfills. R. R. Fleming. il Am City 81:101-4 Ja '66

FILM adaptations
Hot property; what happens to a novel kissed by Hollywood. H. Mitgang. il Sat R 48:39-40 O 2 '65
Rights and permissions. P. Nathan. See issues of Publishers' weekly
Transatlantic view. L. Kramer. Pub W 188:26-9 N 29 '65

Anecdotes, facetiae, satire, etc.
Heart of darkness; reading of Lord Jim fifty-two times by R. Brooks before filming. F. P. Tullius. New Yorker 41:125-6 F 27 '65

FILM censorship. See Moving picture censorship

FILM festival, Cannes. See Cannes international film festival

FILM festivals. See Moving picture festivals

FILM speeds. See Photography—Exposure

FILM strips
Films about patriotism. V. M. Falconer. Sr Schol 86:13T F 4 '65
Films and filmstrips (cont) V. Falconer. Sr Schol 86:22T F 18; sup22 Mr 18; sup34 Ap 15; sup 14 My 13 '65
Films and filmstrips for literature units. V. M. Falconer. Sr Schol 86:sup34 Mr 4 '65
Films and filmstrips for teachers and parents. V. M. Falconer. Sr Schol 86:sup 11 My 13 '65
New films and filmstrips (cont of) Films and filmstrips. V. M. Falconer. Sr Schol 87:sup24 S 23; sup4 O 21; sup 10-11 O 28; sup 16 N 4 '65

Projection
See also
Projection apparatus

FILMS, Photographic. See Photography—Films

FILMS from books. See Film adaptations

FILMSTRIPS. See Film strips

FILO, Ronald S. and others
Glycerinated skeletal and smooth muscle: calcium and magnesium dependence. bibliog Science 147:1581-3 Mr 26 '65

FILSON, Floyd V.
Dialogue of lovers. Christian Cent 82:1130 S 15 '65

FILTER plants
Capacity doubled, manpower unchanged; Kenosha, Wis. O. F. Nelson. il Am City 80:118-19+ Ap '65
Salt water in the sewers; North Miami Fla. F. J. Miller. il Am City 80:112+ D '65
We solved a filter-media problem; Erie, Pa. W. E. DeArment. il Am City 80:83-5 D '65
See also
Filters and filtration

FILTERS, Automobile. See Air filters, Automobile

FILTERS and filtration
Multiple jets prevent filter upset; Baldwin plant. Cleveland, Ohio. T. E. Stanton. il Am City 80:28 F '65
We vacuum-filter lime softening sludge; Boca Raton, Fla. G. Hager. il Am City 80:105-7 Je '65
See also
Water purification

FIMOGNARI, Grace M. and Rodwell, V. W.
Cholesterol biosynthesis: mevalonate synthesis inhibited by bile salts. bibliog Science 147:1038 F 26 '65

FINANCE
See also
Bonds
Church finance
Corporations—Finance
Domestic finance
Farm finance
Interest
Investment trusts
Stock exchange
Stocks
United Nations—Finance

Brazil
Harsh curbs generate growing discontent. il Bsns W p56+ Mr 27 '65
Out of chaos, order. Time 86:72 Ag 20 '65

Congo (capital Leopoldville)
See also
Investments, Foreign (in Congo [capital Leopoldville])

Europe, Western
Sharing the dollar's burden; Europe to share world's capital burden. il Bsns W p54+ Je 5 '65

France
Golden fleece. Time 85:94 F 19 '65

Great Britain
Battle to save the pound; what it does for the dollar. il U S News 59:99 S 27 '65
Britain props the pound; tightens domestic spending and overseas investment. il Bsns W p27-8 Ap 10 '65
Defending the pound; British Chancellor of the Exchequer confers with Treasury Secretary in Washington. il Time 86:96 Jl 9 '65
Standby credit braces sterling; Britain's sterling crisis is over. il Bsns W p27-8 S 18 '65
See also
Budget—Great Britain
Money—Great Britain

Japan
See also
Japan—Economic conditions
Stock exchange—Tokyo

Russia
See also
Budget—Russia
Money—Russia

Switzerland
Secrets of the Swiss banks. T. R. Fehrenbach. Atlan 216:33-8 Jl '65

United States
All aboard, for where? il Fortune 71:104-5 Ap '65
Congeries of uncertainties. il Fortune 71:25-6 Mr '65
Great fiscal debate. H. J. Samuels; W. F. Carey. Duns R 85:52-3+ F '65
Manipulating interest. H. Hazlitt. Newsweek 65:84 Mr 15 '65
National-state-local systems of government and intergovernmental aid. A. K. Campbell. bibliog f il Ann Am Acad 359:94-106 My '65
'66 budget; war takes precedence over the Great society. G. L. Perry. New Repub 153:12-15 D 25 '65
Uncle Sam's $50,000,000,000 surplus. E. L. Dale, jr. il N Y Times Mag p32-3+ N 7 '65; Reply. H. Hazlitt. Nat R 17:1151-2 D 14 '65
United States fiscal policy; address, March 19, 1965. D. Dillon. Vital Speeches 31:388-91 Ap 15 '65
Warrior from Patman's switch. H. Kay. il Fortune 71:154-6+ Ap '65
See also
Bonds, Government
Budget—United States
Debts, Public—United States
Inflation (finance)
Money—United States
State finance
Stock exchange—New York (city)
Taxation—United States
United States—Appropriations and expenditures
United States—Economic conditions
United States—Federal reserve board

FINANCE, International
Anglos v. Continentals. il Time 86:82 Jl 23 '65
As good as gold? plan to hike international liquidity with new reserve asset. Bsns W p 178+ S 11 '65
Assessment of the international monetary system; address, March 19, 1965. D. Dillon. Dept State Bul 52:593-8 Ap 19 '65
Battle for the pound. Fortune 72:123-4 S '65
Beyond the dollar. Time 85:94+ Je 25 '65
Closed shop for monetary reform. N. McKitterick. New Repub 153:9-10 S 25 '65
Crash next year? why it's a real danger, and how it can be avoided. P. F. Drucker. Harper 230:59-64 Je '65
Cry for change. il Time 85:90+ Ap 16 '65
De Gaulle v. the dollar. il Time 85:81-2 F 12 '65
Development of international cooperation in financial and monetary affairs. M. Trued. Dept State Bul 53:843-7 N 22 '65
Do we need more money? H. Hazlitt. Newsweek 65:94 Ap 12 '65
Does the world need a new kind of money? interview. P. P. Schweitzer. U S News 59:78-81 O 4 '65
Dollar drought. Time 85:80 Mr 26 '65
Five clubs for moneymen. Time 85:99 My 14 '65
Fowler's odyssey. Newsweek 66:68 S 13 '65
France still serving. il Newsweek 66:77-9 O 11 '65
Global finance men: who they are, how they work. il Time 85:99-100 My 14 '65
Heading for a new monetary unit? dollar and pound under fire. il Bsns W p 132+ F 20 '65

FINANCE, International—*Continued*
Hearing the Europeans; monetary reform. il Time 86:82 S 3 '65
How to lose $8-million on sterling; New York's First national city bank tells how. Bsns W p96+ Jl 24 '65
Improving the world's monetary system; remarks and statements. L. B. Johnson; T. C. Mann; H. H. Fowler. Dept State Bul 53: 614-24 O 18 '65
International economic policies; excerpt from economic report of the President and annual report of the Council of economic advisers. Dept State Bul 52:254-60 F 22 '65
International exchange: a standard better than gold. D. Smith. il Nation 200:437-9 Ap 26 '65
International monetary reform urged; meeting at UN. UN Mo Chron 2:104-5 Jl '65
Missionary for gold wins few U.S. fans; French economist J. Rueff apostle of gold standard; with editorial comment. Bsns W p31-2, 176 Ap 24 '65
Mr Dollar goes abroad. il Time 86:84-84B+ S 10 '65
Monetary conference. H. C. Wallich. Newsweek 66:69 Ag 9 '65
Monetary reform: blood will be spilled. il Newsweek 66:70-3 Jl 5 '65
Monetary reform for the world economy, by R. V. Roosa. Review
Fortune 72:112+ O '65
Nat R 18:78-9 Ja 25 '66. W. F. Rickenbacker
Newsweek 66:78 S 20 '65
Monetary reform gets a timetable. Bsns W p25-6 S 18 '65
Monetary talks get go-ahead. Bsns W p26-7 Jl 17 '65
New steps to improve international monetary arrangements; address, July 10, 1965. H. H. Fowler. Dept State Bul 53:209-14 Ag 2 '65
Perils of the pound. il Sr Schol 87:12-13 O 21 '65
Pound and dollar. Nat R 17:758 S 7 '65
Problem of international liquidity; address, April 29, 1965. F. L. Deming. Dept State Bul 52:955-63 Je 14 '65
Realistic reform. H. C. Wallich. Newsweek 66:82 S 20 '65
Return to Bretton Woods? il Newsweek 66: 68+ Jl 26 '65
Role of the dollar; address, September 21, 1965. J. W. Barr. Vital Speeches 32:18-21 O 15 '65
Scent of change; world monetary reform. Time 87:70 Ja 21 '66
Search for steps to improve international monetary system; statement, August 25, 1965. L. B. Johnson. Dept State Bul 53: 452 S 13 '65
Secretary Fowler reports on monetary talks in Europe; report, September 13, 1965. H. H. Fowler. Dept State Bul 53:553-4 O 4 '65
Spreading perils of the pound. Life 59:4 S 10 '65
Trends in international economics. C. P. Kindleberger. bibliog f Ann Am Acad 358: 170-9 Mr '65
Troubled world of international money. J. Davenport. il Fortune 73:136-40+ Ja '66
United States fiscal policy; address, March 19, 1965. D. Dillon. Vital Speeches 31:388-91 Ap 15 '65
Verdict in Europe: LBJ has six months to rescue the dollar. il U S News 58:43-4 Mr 1 '65
Visit from Grim Jim. il Newsweek 66:71-2 Jl 12 '65
What it costs to borrow money abroad. il U S News 59:115-17 N 1 '65
Will dollars always be as good as gold? il Newsweek 65:70-1 Mr 1 '65
Will 1965 repeat 1931? R. Triffin. il Reporter 32:27-30 Ap 8 '65
See also
Balance of payments
Bank for international settlements
Banks and banking, International
Inter-American development bank
International development association
International monetary fund
Investments, Foreign
Liquidity, International
FINANCE, Local. See Local finance
FINANCE, Municipal. See Municipal finance
FINANCE, Personal
Got to be away for a while? things to attend to before departure. il Changing T 19:31-2 O '65
Spending your money; questions and answers. S. Porter. Ladies Home J 82:52 O; 62 N; 42+ D '65; 83:24 Ja '66
FINANCE, School. See School finance

FINANCE, State. See State finance
FINANCE companies
See also
Ampal-American Israel corporation
Factors
General motors acceptance corporation
FINCH, Elfreda
Conservation: New Jersey style. Pop Gard 16:34-5+ Ap '65
Enjoy summer's flowers. Pop Gard 16:28-9 S '65
FINCH, Hardy
Encyclopaedia Britannica: the new edition. Sr Schol 86:sup 12-13 My 13 '65
New reading for junior and senior high school students. Sr Schol 87:sup8-9 S 30 '65
Paperbacks for teenage readers. Sr Schol 87: sup30-1 O 28 '65
What's happening in English. Sr Schol 87: sup26-7 O 28 '65
What's new in encyclopedias? Sr Schol 86: 18T F 18 '65
FINCHER, Jack
(ed) See Savio, M. University has become a factory
FINCHUM, R. N.
Let's make the most of our school custodians. Sch Life 47:29-31 D '64
FINCK, Henry T.
Big four. E. H. Huneker. por Opera N 30:10-11 D 18 '65
FINDERS, View. See View finders
FINDLAY, Elsa
Lessons with Monsieur Jaques. por Dance Mag 39:40-5 Ag '65
FINDLEY, Paul
Lobbyists; cloud of doubt. Newsweek 66:34 O 25 '65
FINE, Sidney
General motors sit-down strike, 1937: a reexamination. bibliog f Am Hist R 70:691-713 Ap '65
FINES, Trade union. See Trade unions—Dues, fees, etc.
FINGER, Harold B.
Finger cites thermionic power gains. W. S. Beller. Miss & Roc 17:12 N 22 '65
FINGER, Seymour M.
U.S. states views on procedures to amend U.N. charter; statement, September 16, 1965. Dept State Bul 53:642-3 O 18 '65
FINGER LAKES, N.Y.
New York's Finger Lakes point to pleasure. H. L. Brun. il Motor B 116:22-5 Jl '65
FINISHING, Textile. See Textile finishing
FINISHING, Wood. See Wood finishing
FINISHING materials
Interior and exterior masonry finishes. il Consumer Rep 30:138-41 Mr '65
See also
Paint
FINK, Mary Alexander, and Cowles, C. A.
Immunodiffusion: detection of a murine leukemia virus, Rauscher. bibliog Science 150: 1723-5 D 24 '65
FINKBINE, Robert
Historic myopia: a suggested cure. NEA J 55:63-4 Ja '66
FINKEL, Donald
Planh; Metaphysics of snow; Vogelfanger; poems. Poetry 105:358-60 Mr '65
Spring song. New Yorker 41:127 My 22 '65
about
Three poets. H. Carruth. Poetry 106:311 Jl '65
FINKELSTEIN, Daniel, and Grüsser, O. J.
Frog retina: detection of movement. bibliog il Science 150:1050-1 N 19 '65
FINKELSTEIN, Lawrence S.
Books; from Suez to the Congo. Bul Atomic Sci 21:36-7 My '65
FINKELSTEIN, Louis
Earl Kerkam, 1890-1965. Art N 64:28-31+ My '65
FINKLE, Ivan L.
Recording Lissajous figures. Science 148: 1541-2 Je 18 '65; Reply. J. Potzick. 149: 1446 S 24 '65
FINLAND
See also
Architecture—Finland
Opera—Finland
Publishers and publishing—Finland

Army
Parapooches. il Life 59:105-6 N 19 '65

Description and travel
Day on the Runeberg; from Helsinki to Porvoo. N. Lindgren. il Travel 124:28-30 Jl '65

FINLAND and the United States
Finland and the United States, an enduring friendship; address, September 5, 1965; with message from President Johnson. W. A. Harriman. Dept State Bul 53:555-8 O 4 '65

FINLAYSON, J. S. and others
Major urinary protein complex of normal mice; origin. bibliog Science 149:981-2 Ag 27 '65

FINLEY, Charles O.
Man and a mule in Missouri. E. Shrake. il por Sports Illus 23:36-8+ Jl 19 '65

FINLEY, M. I.
Rediscovery of Crete. Horizon 7:64-75 Sum '65

FINN, Hugh
Under the eaves; poem. Atlan 215:93 F '65

FINN, James
Beyond harassment. Commonweal 82:720-3 O 1 '65
Pritchett's New York. Commonweal 82:247-50 My 14 '65
Whittaker Chambers. Commonweal 81:696-7 F 26 '65

FINNEGAN, Bob
Picture post card. See issues of Hobbies

FINNEY, Albert
Albert Finney, actor. Harper 230:61-2 Ap '65

FINNEY, Nat S.
Case against corruption. Sat R 48:45 N 20 '65
McCarthy craze. Sat R 48:49 O 16 '65
National security, global safety. Sat R 48:102+ S 18 '65

FINNISH baths. See Baths, Vapor

FINUCAN, J. Thomas
Let's give shared time a try. America 113:568-70 N 13 '65

FIRE
Fire; in the lives of Indians and Eskimos. C. Miles. il Hobbies 69:112+ F '65
See also
Camp fires

FIRE alarms
Inexpensive alerting system brings fire safety to private buildings; Deep River, Conn. il Am City 80:119+ O '65
Police and fire reporting on a single circuit; Tarrytown, N.Y. il Am City 80:103 Mr '65
Underground alarm center; St Louis, Mo. il Arch Rec 137:176 My '65

FIRE and casualty insurance companies. See Insurance companies

FIRE ants. See Ants

FIRE apparatus, Motor
Fire boat on wheels. il Am City 80:48 N '65
Fire truck that swims. il Pop Sci 187:89 S '65
Stretching the reach of men who fight fires; water cannons, developed by Mack trucks, inc. il Bsns W p34-5 S 4 '65
Stripped down for action, at fires; American LaFrance's assembly-line Pioneer fire pumper. il Bsns W p 108 S 18 '65

FIRE arms. See Firearms

FIRE control (aerial gunnery)
See also
Range finding

FIRE drills
Home fire drills may save your family. A. Mecredy. il Parents Mag 40:87+ Ap '65

FIRE extinguishers
How to shoot out a fire; fire extinguishing powder pneumatically fired at flames. il Sci Digest 57:26 Ap '65
Look at new fire extinguishers. W. Andrews. il Yachting 118:62+ Jl '65
One extinguisher controls all fires. il Pop Sci 187:130-1 D '65

FIRE houses
Fewer fire stations serve better; Fort Worth, Tex. J. L. Brownlee. il Am City 80:107-9 D '65
Fire station for a hillside neighborhood; Sausalito, Calif. il Arch Rec 137:175 My '65
Fire station in a glass pavilion; San Diego, Calif. il Arch Rec 137:174 My '65

FIRE in a paper; drama. See Hagy, L.

FIRE logs. See Fireplaces—Fuel

FIRE making
Fire; in the lives of Indians and Eskimos. C. Miles. il Hobbies 69:112+ F '65
Handful of fire. C. Conley. il Field & S 70:117 O '65
See also
Camp fires

FIRE pits. See Fireplaces, Outdoor

FIRE protection
Brush fire warning system. Sunset 135:115 O '65
Fire-protection charges. il Am City 80:116+ My '65
Fire safety around your country place; California law. Sunset 135:120+ S '65
In case of fire, know what to do. il Good H 161:172-3 O '65

Keep your home safe from fire. Consumer Bul 49:11 Ja '66
Light water smothers fuel-tank fires. il Am City 80:59 Je '65
See also
Airplanes in fire protection
Fire apparatus, Motor
Fire extinguishers
Forest fire protection
Underwriters' laboratories, incorporated

Laws and regulations
New electric-code highlights. Am City 80:16 S '65

FIRE resistant plants. See Plants—Fire resistance

FIRE stations. See Fire houses

FIRE trucks. See Fire apparatus, Motor

FIREARMS
Big change in guns; special report. J. O'Connor. il Outdoor Life 136:61-76 D '65
Cursed gun, the track of C2766; gun fancier J. J. King sues N. deB. Katzenbach for the physical possession of rifle Oswald bought by mail. K. Wheeler. il Life 59:62-5 Ag 27 '65
Deadly souvenirs of the insurrection; Watts riots, Los Angeles. il Life 59:34 Ag 27 '65
Firearms. See issues of Hobbies
Getting the range. J. O'Connor. See issues of Outdoor life
More punch than a .45; rocket-firing small arms. il Pop Sci 187:113 D '65
Recreation. Consumer Rep 30:272-82 D '65
Run on guns; a lethal national problem. il Life 59:59-61 Ag 27 '65
Shooting. J. O'Connor. See issues of Outdoor life
Shooting; ed. by W. Page. See issues of Field & stream
Shooting questions. W. Page. Field & S 69:116 F '65
$13,925.75 worth of guns. O. Godbout. il Esquire 63:109-11 F '65
See also
Ordnance
Pistols
Revolvers
Rifles
Shooting
Shotguns

Care
Get your guns ready now. J. Madson. il Suc Farm 63:52+ O '65

History
Onward and upward with technology; varying interest in guns from mid-sixteenth century on, Japan. N. Perrin. New Yorker 41:211-16+ N 20 '65

Laws and regulations
Battle of the guns; bill to cut mail-order business. il Time 85:24-5 Ap 16 '65
Boom in the suburbs; Philadelphia law. Sports Illus 23:8 N 1 '65
Cops, guns and homicides. S. Rubin. il Nation 201:527-9 D 27 '65
Gun battle; Senator Dodd's firearms control bill. Commonweal 82:309 My 28 '65
Have gun, will kill; mail order guns. Christian Cent 82:701-2 Je 2 '65
High noon in the gun battle. R. Starnes. Field & S 70:12+ Je '65
It could happen here. C. Ford. il Field & S 69:6+ Ap '65
Let's limit the sale of guns. T. J. Dodd. McCalls 93:166+ N '65
Mail-order guns; a senator battles to stem the deadly tide. T. J. Dodd. il Ladies Home J 82:74-5+ Mr '65; Same abr. with title Guns by mail; a national scandal. Read Digest 86:183-6 Je '65
Run on guns; a lethal national problem. il Life 59:59-61 Ag 27 '65
Spy among the Minutemen. R. Stolley. Life 59:40D Jl 2 '65
Traffic in guns; a forgotten lesson of the assassination. C. Bakal; discussion. Harper 230:12 F '65
What do you know about gun laws? questions and answers. D. Du Bois. Outdoor Life 135:12-14 Ap '64

Safety devices and measures
Basic rules of gun safety. Good H 162:139 Ja '66
Safety gun holder. G. O. Mitty. il Field & S 70:101 N '65

Sights
Is your shotgun sighted in? J. Madson. il Suc Farm 63:46 O '65
No sights at all. W. Page. il Field & S 70:84-9 S '65
See also
Telescopic sights

FIREARMS, Miniature. See Miniature objects

FIREFLIES
Aggressive mimicry in photuris; firefly femmes fatales. J. E. Lloyd. bibliog Science 149:653-4 Ag 6 '65
NASA's firefly project. il Life 59:35-6 Jl 9 '65

FIREMEN
Salaries
Trends in salaries of firemen and policemen. A. Sackley. il Mo Labor R 88:159-63 F '65
FIREMEN, Railroad. See Railroads—Employees

FIREPITS. See Fireplaces, Outdoor

FIREPLACE accessories
Fireplace curios; the cauldron. G. Kaler. il Hobbies 70:44+ Jl '65
Fireplace curios; the curfew. G. Kaler. il Hobbies 70:44 Je '65

FIREPLACES
Fuel
Newspaper logs keep the home fires burning. H. Walton. il Pop Sci 187:140-1 D '65
FIREPLACES, Outdoor
Easy-to-make back yard fire pit. D. B. Johnson. il Pop Gard 16:45 Jl '65

FIREPROOF construction
Time-rated acoustical ceiling assemblies. il Arch Rec 137:197-8 F '65

FIRES
Race with fire on the French Riviera. il Life 59:36-36A Ag 13 '65
Texas-size fire sale at Neiman-Marcus. il Bsns W p44 Mr 20 '65
See also
Arson
Brush fires
Fire protection
Ships—Fires and fire protection

Statistics
Fire deaths up; property loss down. Am City 81:28+ Ja '66

FIRESTONE, Leonard Kimball
Missing the cue; attempt to kidnap. il por Time 87:21 Ja 21 '66
Snatch that failed. il por Newsweek 67:31+ Ja 24 '66

FIRESTONE tire and rubber company
Firestone case; cancellation of contract to build plant in Rumania. Newsweek 66:64 Ag 9 '65

FIRETHORN
Firethorn, spring and fall. il Flower Grower 52:31 Ag '65

FIREWOOD. See Wood as fuel

FIRFER, Alexander
U.S. aid while the bullets fly; the real Dominican story. por U S News 59:48-50 Jl 19 '65

FIRING of employees. See Employees—Dismissal

FIRM names. See Business names

FIRST, Ruth
Prisons of apartheid. H. Kuper. Nation 202: 76-8 Ja 17 '66

FIRST aid for animals. See Veterinary first aid

FIRST aid in illness and injury
First aid. C. J. Potthoff. See issues of Today's health
First aid training vital to sailors on remote mission. il Todays Health 43:87 Ap '65
How to cope with water emergencies. il Good H 160:168 Je '65
See also
Ambulances
Burns and scalds
Veterinary first aid

FIRST amendment to the Constitution. See United States—Constitution—Bill of rights

FIRST-born children. See Children, First-born

FIRST chamber dance quartet. See Ballet companies

FIRST committee of the General assembly. See United Nations—Political and security committee

FIRST farewell; story. See Mackey, E.

FIRST frost; story. See Weston, C.

FIRST national city bank of New York. See New York (city)—Banks

FIRST snow; story. See Benchley, N.

FISCALINI, Janet
Night-driving in the Midwest; poem. Commonweal 81:790 Mr 19 '65

FISCHER, Andrew J, family
Fischer quints at two. P. Wright. il pors Ladies Home J 83:53-7+ Ja '66
Fischer quints; summer on the farm. J. Bird. il Sat Eve Post 238:28-35 Jl 31 '65
Merry Christmas for the quints; Fischers holiday. J Bird. il Sat Eve Post 238:21-5 D 18 '65

FISCHER, Antoinette Nicholas
Butterfly's cocoon. Opera N 29:13 Mr 27 '65

FISCHER, Carl
Miniature gladiolus. il Horticulture 43:34-5+ Ap '65

FISCHER, John
Editor's easy chair. See issues of Harper's magazine
Is there a teacher on the faculty? Harper 230:18+ F '65; Same abr. Read Digest 86:76-80 Je '65

FISCHER, Josef E. and Snyder, S. H.
Histamine synthesis and gastric secretion after portacaval shunt. bibliog Science 150: 1034-5 N 19 '65

FISCHER, Louis
Passion that poisons our daily bread. Sat R 48:27 Je 5 '65

FISCHER, R. J. See Stemke, G. W. jt. auth.

FISCHER, Richard B.
New menu suets catbirds. il Audubon Mag 67:121 Mr '65

FISCHER, Robert James
Hot-line chess. por Newsweek 66:44-5 S 6 '65

FISCHER-DIESKAU, Dietrich
Thinking man's baritone. por Time 86:38 Ag 20 '65

FISCHER-WILLIAMS, Barbara
(ed) See Forzano, G. Don't call me maestro

FISCHER quintuplets. See Quintuplets

FISCHMAN, Walter Ian
Great relaxing bonanza. Pop Mech 125:122-5+ Ja '66

FISH, Byron
Five faces of Alaska. Read Digest 87:146-52 S '65

FISH, Chet
Where to go fishing, vacationing, hunting. See issues of Outdoor Life

FISH, Frozen
Frozen breaded fish portions. Consumer Rep 30:235-7 My '65

FISH, Smoked. See Food—Smoking

FISH as food
Basic guide to buying fish. il Good H 161:169 O '65
Seafood freezer; care of the catch. A. J. McClane. il Field & S 69:52-5+ Mr '65
See also
Cookery—Fish

FISH chowder. See Chowder

FISH crows. See Crows

FISH culture
College-bred fish for man's delight. M. Morgan. il Harper 231:47-51 Jl '65; Same abr. Read Digest 87:193-5+ O '65
Exotics U.S.A. A. J. McClane. il Field & S 69:88-94 Ap '65
Striped bass breakthrough. A. J. McClane. il Field & S 70:88-90+ Jl '65

FISH flies. See Fishing lures, flies, etc.

FISH hawks. See Ospreys

FISH industry and trade
Peru nets a boom in fishmeal. il Bsns W p64-5 F 20 '65
See also
Fisheries

FISH ladders
New; a big lift for salmon. J. Rearden. il Outdoor Life 136:26-8+ Jl '65

FISH law. See Fishery laws and legislation

FISH meal
Fishing for meal. D. S. Stroetzel. il Américas 17:18-22 My '65
Peru nets a boom in fishmeal. il Bsns W p64-5+ F 20 '65

FISH mousse. See Cookery—Fish

FISH noises. See Sound production by fishes

FISH poisons
Ciguatera fish poison; a cholinesterase inhibitor. K. M. Li. bibliog il Science 147: 1580-1 Mr 26 '65

FISH stew. See Stew

FISHBECK, James
Solid-state slot car speed control. Pop Electr 23:59-61 D '65

FISHBEIN, Morris
Medical news of the month. See issues of McCall's

FISHEL, Wesley R.
American aid to Vietnam. Cur Hist 49:294-9 N '65

FISHER, Adrian S.
Disarmament and international cooperation; statement, May 12, 1965. Dept State Bul 52:971-3 Je 14 '65

FISHER, Aileen
Hidden meanings; drama. Plays 24:79-80 F '65
Yankee Doodle dandy; drama. Plays 25:61-2 Ja '66
—and Rabe, Olive
Cavalcade of human rights; drama. Plays 24:99-122 My '65
Star for Old Glory; drama. Plays 24:57-61 Ap '65
Wheels within wheels; drama. Plays 24:61-4 F '65

FISHER, Bob, and Marx, Arthur
Impossible years. Criticism
Commonweal 83:243 N 26 '65
Life 59:72B N 5 '65
Newsweek 66:102 O 25 '65
Time 86:103A O 22 '65

FISHER, Dorothy Canfield
Apprentice; story. Parents Mag 40:46-7 My '65

FISHER, G. L. and others
Dulcin and saccharin taste in squirrel monkeys, rats, and men. bibliog Science 150:506-7 O 22 '65

FISHER, Isabelle
(ed) See Taylor, F. Questions and answers about college bookings

FISHER, June Marion, and others
Antibodies in gastric juice. bibliog Science 150:1467-9 D 10 '65

FISHER, M. F. K.
Books. New Yorker 41:145-50+ Je 5 '65
Lost, strayed, stolen; story. New Yorker 41:47-52 Mr 20 '65

FISHER, Robert
I made my death bed; ed. by B. East. por Outdoor Life 135:60-1+ Ap '65

FISHER, Rosaline, and Chapman, M. L.
Achieving voting reform; every teacher's concern. NEA J 55:12-14 Ja '66

FISHER, William H.
Academic freedom for the believer. Sch & Soc 93:475-6 D 11 '65

FISHER body craftsman's guild
Model dream cars build dream careers. H. Shuldiner. il Pop Sci 187:170-2+ O '65
Prize-winning model cars. il Sr Schol 87:30 O 7 '65

FISHER-Price toys, incorporated
Child's play, a serious business. il Bsns W p 124-6 Mr 27 '65

FISHERIES
International aspects
Fishing treaties and salmon of the North Pacific; address, October 21, 1965. W. F. Thompson. il Science 150:1786-9 D 31 '65
Sockeye that swims too far. il Time 85:86 Je 11 '65
U.S. and Canada discuss salmon fisheries. Dept State Bul 53:759 N 8 '65
United States and U.S.S.R. sign king crab fishing agreement; Department announcement, February 6, 1965, with text of agreement. Dept State Bul 52:320-1 Mr 1 '65
U.S., Japan quarrel over salmon fishing; Bristol Bay, Alaska. Bsns W p 102 Je 19 '65

Law
See Fishery laws and legislation

FISHERMEN
World in miniature; Barra do Rio Grande do Sul, Brazil. E. C. Uriburu. il Américas 17:34-6 O '65

FISHERS ISLAND
Island of the discreet shudder. R. H. Boyle. il Sports Illus 23:40-4 S 6 '65

FISHERY laws and legislation
Fewer fish to fry. J. Rutherfoord. il Field & S 69:10-12+ Ap '65
Fishing laws; United States and Canada (cont) Field & S 69:34+ Ap; 70:30-2+ My '65
Fishing seasons (cont) Outdoor Life 135:72-3 Ap; 18+ My; 10+ Je '65
Fishing treaties and salmon of the North Pacific; address, October 21, 1965. W. F. Thompson. il Science 150:1786-9 D 31 '65
Jersey's scofflaws of the sea. R. H. Boyle. Sports Illus 23:94-6+ S 13 '65

FISHERY research
Fish immunogenetics research; report on planning meeting for hematological, immunogenetic, and serological studies of fish. L. M. Sprague. Science 148:1252+ My 28 '65

FISHES
Detergents: effects on the chemical senses of the fish ictalurus natalis, le Sueur. J. E. Bardach and others. bibliog il Science 148:1605-7 Je 18 '65
Doorway to watery wonderlands; National geographic's latest book. M. B. Grosvenor. il Nat Geog Mag 127:388-93 Mr '65

From aawa to zooplankton; concerning the compilation of the Fishing encyclopedia. A. J. McClane. il Field & S 70:46-7 N '65
Lovely lady with a very fishy reputation; E. Clark of Cape Haze marine laboratory, Sarasota, Fla. C. Phinizy. il Sports Illus 23:46-50 O 4 '65
Strange fish and stranger times of Dr Herbert R. Axelrod. R. H. Boyle. il Sports Illus 22:76-8+ My 3 '65
Strange new fish found off coast of Florida; kasidoron edom. il(p289) Sci N L 87:294 My 8 '65
See also
Ice fish; Antarctic
Sound production by fishes
also names of fishes, e.g. Salmon

Extermination
Pollution kills 7,800,000 fish. Am City 80:133 Mr '65

Eye
See Eye (fishes)

Food
Predation, body size, and composition of plankton. J. L. Brooks and S. I. Dodson. bibliog il Science 150:28-35 O 1 '65

Habits and behavior
Art of fish watching; adaptation from paper. W. M. Stephens. Yachting 117:156+ Je '65
Taking temperatures. J. E. Pugh, jr. il Field & S 70:92-6 Je '65
Why does a fish? D. M. Newell. il Field & S 70:66-8+ My '65

Hybrids
Codominance of visual pigments in hybrid fishes. W. N. McFarland and F. W. Munz. bibliog il Science 150:1055-7 N 19 '65

Migration
Electroencephalographic studies of homing salmon. T. J. Hara and others. bibliog il Science 149:884-5 Ag 20 '65
Swimming energetics of salmon. J. R. Brett. il Sci Am 213:80-5 Ag '65

Physiology
Absence or singular specificity of carotenoids in some lower fishes. D. L. Fox and G. F. Crozier. bibliog il Science 150:771-3 N 5 '65
Built-in thermometer gives fish sixth sense. Sci N L 88:361 D 4 '65
Classical conditioning of electric organ discharge rate in mormyrids. F. J. Mandriota and others. bibliog il Science 150:1740-2 D 24 '65
Hermaphroditic fish; report on conference. J. W. Atz. Science 150:789-92+ N 5 '65

Reproduction
Tassels on male fish help produce offspring. Sci N L 88:344 N 27 '65

Stories
Exit, laughing. E. Zern. See issues of Field & stream

FISHES, Breathing of. See Respiration

FISHES, Deep sea
Four-eyed fish captured alive in ocean depths. Sci N L 88:232 O 9 '65

FISHES, Extinct
See also
Coelacanths

FISHES, Fossil
Fossil search aided by U.S. public roads; Cuyahoga County, Ohio. Sci N L 87:231 Ap 10 '65
Lungfish burrows from the Michigan coal basin. R. L. Carroll. bibliog il Science 148:963-4 My 14 '65

FISHES, Photography of. See Photography of fishes

FISHING
Angling. W. Davis. See issues of Outdoor life
Art of plugging. A. J. McClane. il Field & S 70:90-3 Ag '65
Bookmaker to a river. B. Smith. il Field & S 70:52-5 Ag '65
Books for the fisherman. E. Gilligan. Yachting 117:157 Je '65
Fish is a fish. T. Trueblood. il Field & S 70:24+ My '65
Fish 'n ships. V. Evanoff. il Motor B 116:54-5+ O; 58+ N; 52+ D '65
Fishing; ed. by A. J. McClane. See issues of Field & stream
Gist of it; digest of the outdoor news. ed. by H. Moore. See issues of Outdoor life
Luck! T. Trueblood. il Field & S 69:30+ F '65

FISHING—*Continued*

My fishpond; excerpt from Here are my lectures. S. Leacock. Read Digest 86:244B-244E Ap '65

New way to fly cast; with charts. L. Kreh. Outdoor Life 135:28-31+ Mr '65

Put on a boat and go fishing; floater tube fishing. J. Madson. il Farm J 89:46+ Je '65

Regulating the reefs. T. N. Sandifer. il Motor B 115:118+ Mr '65

Ritz has a cast system. J. Olsen. il Sports Illus 23:122-4+ S 20 '65

Sportsman's notebook. H. G. Tapply. See issues of Field & stream

Taking temperatures. J. E. Pugh, jr. il Field & S 70:92-6 Je '65

Where to go fishing, vacationing, hunting. See issues of Outdoor life
  See also
Fisheries
Fishing clubs
Salt water fishing
Trawls and trawling
  also Bass fishing; Grayling fishing; etc.

Accidents and injuries

Death rode the surf. O. C. Johnson. il Outdoor Life 136:52-5+ Jl '65

Anecdotes, facetiae, satire, etc.

First aid for the fish wife. P. Bracken. il Ladies Home J 82:52 Ag '65

How to outsmart a fish. il Todays Health 43:66 S '65

Pop angler's guide to fishing with coffeepots and other original lures. B. Gilbert. il Sports Illus 23:68-70+ N 1 '65

Competitions

Billfish East; People to people international fishing championships. B. Wisner. il Motor B 116:37+ S '65

Fishing for peace; People to people international sportfishing championships. B. Wisner. il Motor B 115:50-1+ My '65

Mastery in billfishing; third Invitational masters angling tournament. M. Coan. il Motor B 115:43-4+ Ap '65

1964 winners; Field & stream fishing contest. Field & S 69:26+ Mr; 60+ Ap '65

Piñas Bay; jungle, Indians and the fightingest fish. Motor B 116:51-3 Jl '65

Search for the big swords; paintings, with account by D. Barnes. D. Passalacqua. Sports Illus 23:30-5 Jl 19 '65

Implements and appliances

Go fly a fishing kite. W. Yolen. il Todays Health 43:58-61+ Mr '65

Third hand for fly fishermen; C. Decker's gadget for changing flies. H. G. Tapply. il Field & S 69:76 F '65

Law
  See Fishery laws and legislation

Study and teaching

School for anglers; Miami Beach rod and reel club. J. Brooks. il Field & S 70:32-3 Jl '65

Alaska

Four men alone. L. Hayes. il Outdoor Life 137:21-3+ Ja '66

Argentina

Homage to Patagonia: a fisherman's tale. E. Schwiebert. il Esquire 63:90-2+ Mr '65

Arizona

New hope for the Gila. R. B. Whitaker. il Field & S 70:48-9+ Ag '65

Arkansas

Brown bass of the Buffalo. H. Bradshaw. il Outdoor Life 135:56-9+ Ap '65

Austria

Angling in Austria. A. J. McClane. il Field & S 69:39-41+ Ap '65

Bahama Islands

Gulf Stream's coral spine; the Exumas. L. Smith. il Sports Illus 24:36-41 Ja 17 '66

Is it true what they say about bonefish? H. Modavis. il Field & S 70:72-4+ Jl '65

Quiet boom in the Bahamas. B. Burgess. il Field & S 70:48-50+ Ja '66

South to Caicos. B. S. Wright. il Field & S 70:49-51+ D '65

Summer fishing in the Bahamas. F. T. Moss. il Yachting 117:102-4+ Je '65

Brazil

Jangada; a seaworthy Brazilian raft. E. C. Uriburu. il Américas 17:34-6 My '65

Rainbows in a strange land. D. C. Proper. il Outdoor Life 136:40-3+ O '65

World in miniature; Barra do Rio Grande do Sul. E. C. Uriburu. il Américas 17:34-6 O '65

California

For solitude and fishing; Budd Lake. il Sunset 135:27 Ag '65

Game grab bag for sportsmen. T. Stimson. il Pop Mech 124:136-8+ O '65

If weather holds, the fishing's fine; June Lakes loop. il Sunset 135:63 O '65

It's an easy walk to Widow; Lassen Volcanic National Park. il Sunset 135:30 Ag '65

They're after trophy-sized bass; Santa Margarita Lake. il Sunset 134:33 Mr '65

Trophy of gold. M. Hayden. il Outdoor Life 135:44-7+ My '65

We gambled on Poison. M. Hayden. il Outdoor Life 136:36-9+ S '65

California, Gulf of

Rocky road to paradise. E. A. Bauer. il Field & S 69:43-7 F '65

California, Lower

Fishing Baja California. E. A. Bauer. il Yachting 117:110-12+ Je '65

Man's man. W. Page. il Field & S 70:31-3 Ja '66

Canada

Bulls of St Mary's; river in Nova Scotia. R. Tuttle. il Outdoor Life 136:46-7+ Jl '65

Flight to never-never land. C. Chatfield. il Outdoor Life 135:52-3+ Ap '65

Land of record breakers. B. Warner. il Field & S 69:152-4+ Ap '65

Magic month for fishing. D. W. Larson. il Outdoor Life 136:30-1+ S '65

Magnificent Arctic char. W. Davis. il Outdoor Life 137:98-100 Ja '66

Return to the Winnipeg. J. Parry. il Outdoor Life 135:66-8+ Je '65

Salmon spree. C. Elliott. il Outdoor Life 135:52-5+ Je '65

Tenacious tiger. M. Ellis. il Field & S 70:80-4+ My '65

To Nova Scotia by trailer. H. Modavis. il Yachting 117:88-9+ Ap '65

Waters of the big fish. C. Elliott. il Outdoor Life 135:40-3+ Mr '65

We found the hidden char. G. Laycock. il Field & S 70:49-51+ My '65

We had a wild time. A. W. Prince. il Outdoor Life 136:33-5+ Jl '65

Where grayling gang; Hatchet Lake. M. Ellis. il Field & S 70:59-61+ S '65

Colorado

Big browns in the Crystal; dry-fly fishing in the Southwest. J. S. Holden. il Atlan 216:84-7 Ag '65

Connecticut

100-a-day at Enfield. A. Davenport. il Field & S 70:43-5+ Je '65

Tricks of trolling. G. Heinold. Outdoor Life 136:8+ Ag '65

Florida

All outdoors for rent. E. A. Bauer. il Outdoor Life 136:20-3+ Ag '65

Campout on Cape Sable. V. Dunaway. il Outdoor Life 135:62-4+ Ap '65

Fisherman's horn of plenty. G. X. Sand. il Outdoor Life 135:52-5+ My '65

Florida offbeat. A. J. McClane. il Field & S 70:90-3 Ja '66

Guide to violence. A. J. McClane. il Field & S 70:74-8+ My '65

Old fish eater. G. Laycock. il Field & S 70:54+ D '65

Spring tide plugging. A. J. McClane. il Field & S 69:100 Ap '65

Tips for tripletails. G. Heinold. il Outdoor Life 136:24+ O '65

Tough jack crevallé. G. Heinold. il Outdoor Life 135:12+ Mr '65

Tricky tilapia. G. X. Sand. il Field & S 70:70-1+ Ja '66

Georgia

Fish in your own backyard. C. Elliott. il Outdoor Life 136:52-3+ O '65

New bream bonanza; Walter F. George reservoir. R. F. Burgess. il Field & S 69:130-2+ F '65

Great Lakes Region

Big fishing hole; Lake Superior. H. Titus. il Field & S 70:64-6 N '65

New things in ice fishing. K. Mason. il Outdoor Life 137:24-7+ Ja '66

World's biggest bass lakes. B. East. il Outdoor Life 135:33-5+ Je '65

Gulf states

Gulf coast fishing fiesta. G. Heinold. il Outdoor Life 136:8+ D '65

FISHING—*Continued*

Indiana

Land of smiling waters. P. Czura. il Field & S 70:66-8+ Je '65

Labrador

Home of the fish. H. F. Blaisdell. il Field & S 70:37-9+ Jl '65

We blazed wild new trails. M. G. Terzlev. il Outdoor Life 135:32-5+ My '65

Louisiana

Chinks are bedded! G. Gresham. il Outdoor Life 135:34-5+ Mr '65

Maine

Fly choice by the Omen method. E. W. Smith. il Field & S 69:62-4+ Mr '65

Fly of last resort. B. Elliot. il Outdoor Life 136:62-4+ O '65

H.C.L. makes the lobsterman happy; high cost of lobster. E. Hill. il N Y Times Mag p 18-19+ Ap 25 '65

Landlock break-out. H. F. Blaisdell. il Outdoor Life 135:58-60+ My '65

Long hard winter. L. Dietz. il Field & S 69:56-7+ Mr '65

Sebago starts back. Sports Illus 23:8+ N 1 '65

Son of the salmon. B. Geagan. il Field & S 69:42-3+ Ap '65

Squaretail country. W. Davis. il Outdoor Life 135:48-9+ Je '65

Mexico

Pinatas and pescados; Christmas in Mexico. B. Behme. il Field & S 70:33-5 D '65

Train for Topolobampo. H. G. Boughton. il Outdoor Life 136:40-3+ N '65

Michigan

Living end for bluegills. B. W. Dalrymple. il Outdoor Life 136:64-5+ Jl '65

Water wolves. D. J. Anderson. il Field & S 70:40-2+ Je '65

Where the fish are. J. Chiappetta. il Field & S 70:16-18 My '65

Wired for walleyes; trolling sinkers. W. Jarvis. il Outdoor Life 136:34-5+ Ag '65

Minnesota

Newest thing on wheels. B. Cary. il Outdoor Life 135:25-7+ My '65

Missouri

Ozark big uns bite best in winter. H. Bradshaw. il Field & S 70:104-7+ Ja '66

New England

Pirate of the pads. A. W. Prince. il Outdoor Life 136:48-9+ Ag '65

New Hampshire

Bog-trot for trout. N. Bryant. il Outdoor Life 135:46-7+ Ap '65

Pint-size speedster. G. Heinold. il Outdoor Life 136:14-15 N '65

New Jersey

Jersey's scofflaws of the sea. R. H. Boyle. Sports Illus 23:94-6+ S 13 '65

Stealthy approach for stripers. P. McLain. il Field & S 70:18-20+ Je '65

New Mexico

Browns and rainbows in a deep, steep box; forbidding canyon on the Rio Grande. E. White. il Sports Illus 22:49-50+ Je 21 '65

New York (state)

Best trout stream in the East; West Branch of the Ausable River. A. Glowka. il Field & S 70:54-7+ My '65

Cold-sport hotspot. N. Karas. il Field & S 70:52-3+ D '65

Expressways to the north; interstate 81. N. Karas. il Field & S 69:61-3+ Ap '65

Newfoundland

Cold dawn run from Witless Bay to Erewhon. F. Russell. il Sports Illus 22:64-6+ Ap 26 '65

Nicaragua

Snook hunt along the shores of the Spanish Main; paintings with account. T. Allen. Sports Illus 24:36-41 Ja 3 '66

Tarpon of the jungle; paintings. T. Allen. Sports Illus 22:44-9 Mr 8 '65

North Carolina

Brackish water black bass. J. Brooks. il Outdoor Life 135:40-1+ My '65

Ohio

Muskie explosion. E. A. Bauer. il Outdoor Life 135:18-23+ Mr '65

Oregon

After your nine-mile hike, a choice of thirty fishing lakes; Oregon's Lake Basin. il Sunset 135:47-8 S '65

Nothing like it on the Oregon coast; Cape Kiwanda. B. Behme. il Field & S 70:10-11+ S '65

Spring salmon ring the bell. R. E. Landsburg. il Outdoor Life 135:40-3+ Ap '65

Steelheads on a rough river. V. Kraft. Sports Illus 23:92+ N 15 '65

Pacific coast

Klamath slot. C. R. Hull. il Outdoor Life 136:40-3+ Jl '65

Portugal

Island asylum for mad fishermen; Berlenga Island. J. Olsen. il Sports Illus 23:74-6+ N 8 '65

Rhode Island

How to work the surf. G. Heinold. il Outdoor Life 136:20+ Jl '65

Southern states

Hartwell is hot. C. Elliott. il Outdoor Life 136:50-1+ N '65

Tennessee

Backwoods browns. H. L. Lawrence. il Field & S 69:12-14+ F '65

Shellcracker fever. C. Vinson. il Outdoor Life 135:58-9+ Je '65

Workingman's fish. M. Ellis. il Field & S 70:58-9+ N '65

Texas

Number one combo; bass-dove combination. B. W. Dalrymple. il Field & S 70:48-9+ O '65

United States

Best fishing this season; symposium. il Outdoor Life 135:65-80 Ap '65

Check these hot lakes. G. Gresham. il Outdoor Life 136:48-9+ D '65

Five tips for opening day. W. Davis. il Outdoor Life 135:33-5+ Ap '65

Float trips U.S.A. A. J. McClane. il Field & S 70:102-7+ O; 86-93 N '65

How to do something about it. T. Trueblood. il Field & S 69:18+ Mr '65

Special section on sportfishing; symposium. il Yachting 117:77+ Je '65

Strangest trout stream on earth; Firehole River in Yellowstone National Park. E. Schwiebert. il Field & S 70:44-7+ Jl '65

Turnabout for trout. J. T. Fowler. il Outdoor Life 136:58-9+ S '65

Vermont

I got the message. G. B. Gordon. il Outdoor Life 136:66-8+ Jl '65

Virginia

How to fish those fished-out lakes. W. Davis. Outdoor Life 136:70-2 Jl '65

June blues. K. Osborne. il Field & S 70:124-7 Je '65

Washington (state)

Big trout! C. Chatfield. il Outdoor Life 135:48-9+ Mr '65

Cruising Puget Sound. F. M. Paulson. il Field & S 70:65-9+ Jl '65

125 years of bass savvy. C. Chatfield. il Outdoor Life 136:28-31+ Ag '65

Runny-nose brigade; winter fly fishermen. R. R. Gerlach. il Outdoor Life 137:54-5+ Ja '66

Winter fishing the Skagit. il Sunset 136:28+ Ja '66

West Virginia

Drums along Otter Creek; limestone neutralizes acid trout waters. J. Hayes. il Outdoor Life 137:4-3+ Ja '66

Horseshoe bass. T. Janes. il Outdoor Life 136:56-7+ Jl '65

Western states

Best trout in the West. F. Dufresne. Field & S 69:84-5 Mr '65

Great steelhead hang-up. C. Conley. il Field & S 69:44-7+ Ap '65

Wisconsin

Edge of heaven; mouth of the Bois Brule River. M. Ellis. il Field & S 70:45-7 O '65

FISHING—*Continued*

Wyoming
Neglected cutthroats. P. Alport and F. Dufresne, jr. il Field & S 69:48-9 Ap '65
Wyoming roundup. A. J. McClane. il Field & S 70:48-52+ Je '65

FISHING, Deep sea. See Salt water fishing

FISHING, Winter
Christmas adventure. E. A. Bauer. il Outdoor Life 136:36-9+ D '65
Cold-sport hotspot. N. Karas. il Field & S 70:52-3+ D '65
Long hard winter. L. Dietz. il Field & S 69:56-7+ Mr '65
New things in ice fishing. K. Mason. il Outdoor Life 137:24-7+ Ja '66
Runny-nose brigade; winter fly fishermen. R. R. Gerlach. il Outdoor Life 137:54-5+ Ja '66

FISHING accidents. See Fishing—Accidents and injuries

FISHING boats
Beach boats. J. A. Emmett. il Outdoor Life 136:90-2 Ag '65
Fish 'n ships. V. Evanoff. il Motor B 116:54-5+ O '65
Jangada; a seaworthy Brazilian raft. E. C. Uriburu. il Américas 17:34-6 My '65
Newest thing on wheels. B. Cary. il Outdoor Life 135:25-7+ My '65

Design
New boats for 1966. J. A. Emmett. il Outdoor Life 137:60-2+ Ja '66
New world each morning; floating fishing palace, El Pador. M. Ellis. il Field & S 69:92-5 F '65

Equipment
Fish 'n ships. V. Evanoff. il Motor B 116:54-5+ O; 58+ N; 52+ D '65
Those silly outriggers; status symbol or secret weapon? M. Payne. il Yachting 117:106-7+ Je '65

FISHING clubs
Where sportfishermen meet. D. W. Thornton. il Motor B 115:144-7 F '65

FISHING flies. See Fishing lures, flies, etc.

FISHING kites. See Fishing—Implements and appliances

FISHING lures, flies, etc.
Big browns in the Crystal; dry-fly fishing in the Southwest. J. S. Holden. il Atlan 216:84-7 Ag '65
Deadliest dries. W. Davis. il Outdoor Life 135:70+ Je '65
Flies worth their salt. J. Brooks. il Outdoor Life 135:60-3+ Je '65
Fly choice by the Omen method. E. W. Smith. il Field & S 69:62-4+ Mr '65
Fly of last resort. B. Elliot. il Outdoor Life 136:62-4+ O '65
Fooling late-fall smallmouths. W. Davis. il Outdoor Life 136:126-8 N '65
How to fish those fished-out lakes. W. Davis. Outdoor Life 136:70-2 Jl '65
How to make an easy-cast bug. H. G. Tapply. il Field & S 70:72 Ja '66
How to tell a fishing story. C. W. Morton. Read Digest 87:201-2 Jl '65
I got the message. G. B. Gordon. il Outdoor Life 136:66-8+ Jl '65
Pop for bass. J. Brooks. il Outdoor Life 136:64-5+ N '65
Seasoned with salt; fly fishing. A. J. McClane. il Field & S 70:102-7 S '65
Tenacious tiger. M. Ellis. il Field & S 70:80-4+ My '65
Tricks fit to be tied. T. Trueblood. il Field & S 70:16+ Ja '66
Try being different. W. Davis. il Outdoor Life 136:134+ O '65
Twelve foolproof ways to rig a fishline. H. Bradshaw. il Pop Sci 187:146-9+ Jl '65
Walking the dry fly. A. J. McClane. il Field & S 70:76-8 D '65
Well governed angler; inventor of artificial trout fly. H. Clepper. il Am For 71:4-5+ F '65

FISHING reels. See Fishing tackle

FISHING research
Yachtsmen and marine science. F. T. Moss. il Yachting 117:44-5+ F '65

FISHING rods. See Fishing tackle

FISHING tackle
Case for the flea rod. A. J. McClane. il Field & S 69:86-90 F '65
Choosing and using salt water tackle. E. Fayette. il Yachting 117:122-4+ Je '65
Exploring with ultralight; ed. by A. J. McClane. il Field & S 70:96-8+ My '65
Fly-fishing rods. il Consumer Rep 30:143-5 Mr '65

Fly leaders for wary trout. W. Davis. il Outdoor Life 135:56+ Mr '65
Making a wider cast to lure the customers; Garcia corp; Teaneck, N.J. il Bsns W p94-6+ Ap 10 '65
Recreation. Consumer Rep 30:282-7 D '65
Shortcuts to better fishing. W. Davis. il Outdoor Life 136:26-7+ D '65
Strength of the light rod; excerpt from Well-tempered angler. A. Gingrich. il Atlan 216:114-16 S '65
Twelve foolproof ways to rig a fishline. H. Bradshaw. il Pop Sci 187:146-9+ Jl '65
Wired for walleyes; trolling sinkers. W. Jarvis. il Outdoor Life 136:34-5+ Ag '65
See also
Shakespeare company

FISHING tournaments. See Fishing—Competitions

FISHING treaties. See Fishery laws and legislation

FISHING with bow and arrow
Bowfishing for sport. G. H. Gillelan. il Outdoor Life 135:28+ Je '65

FISHMAN, George M.
Centennial notes: report on a New Jersey observance. por Negro Hist Bul 28:82-3 Ja '65

FISHMAN, Katharine Davis
Parent and child. N Y Times Mag p92+ N 7 '65

FISHMEAL. See Fish meal

FISHWAYS. See Fish ladders

FISHWICK, Marshall W.
Kind word for conformity. Sat R 48:22-4 D 11 '65

FISK, Cynthia
Cynthia and Mara, Carnegie recital hall. J. Maskey. Dance Mag 39:161-2 D '65

FISSION, Nuclear. See Nuclear fission

FISSION-track dating. See Radioactive dating

FISTLER, Doris
Start at Grundy Center. Library J 90:5465-7 D 15 '65

FITCH, Charles Marden
Lilies need other plants. Flower Grower 52:32-3+ Ag '65

FITCH, Robert E.
Is America ready for a Great society? interview. por U S News 58:50-4 Mr 8 '65; Same abr. with title America's potential for greatness. Read Digest 86:62-6 Je '65
Who speaks for today's youth? Christian Cent 82:1348-50 N 3 '65

FITCH, Val Logsdon
New headache for physicists. B. H. Frisch. il por Sci Digest 58:28-32 Jl '65

FITE, W. L. and Gerjuoy, E.
Electronic and atomic collisions. Science 150:516-18+ O 22 '65

FITHIAN, Janet H.
Should it be off to work for you? Suc Farm 63:69+ Je '65
Something should be done about meetings. Suc Farm 63:77+ N '65

FITNESS, Physical. See Health

FITTING out boats. See Boats—Care

FITZ, Brigitte
Curl up and read. Seventeen 24:70 My '65

FITZGERALD, C. P.
Expulsion of Singapore. Nation 201:208-12 O 11 '65
Mao: patriot and Communist. Nation 200:703-4 Je 28 '65
Southeast Asia: fallacy of the dominoes. Nation 200:700-2+ Je 28 '65
What do we do with China? New Repub 153:25-6 N 20 '65

FITZGERALD, E.
You need long lens, high flying camera to film an eagle. L. Jacobs, jr. il Mod Phot 29:89+ Mr '65

FITZGERALD, Frances
Inside New York state. Mlle 61:199+ My '65

FITZGERALD, Francis Scott Key
My father's letters: advice without consent; with introd. by Frances Scott Fitzgerald Lanahan. Esquire 64:95-7 O '65

about
Books. D. Littlejohn. Commonweal 82:358-60 Je 4 '65
F. Scott Fitzgerald, by H. D. Piper. Review Sat R il 48:17 Jl 31 '65. K. Eble
That big word: integrity. C. E. Shain. Seventeen 24:94-5+ D '65

FITZGERALD, Gerald M. C.
Fallen priests. S. De Gramont. il por Sat Eve Post 238:101-3 N 20 '65

FITZGERALD, Gregory
Divisional reading room. por Wilson Lib Bul 39:565-6+ Mr '65

FITZGERALD, Julia Morris
Book of the month. Cath World 202:244-5
Ja '66
FITZGERALD, Paul A.
Compact for education. America 114:140-1 Ja
22 '66
FITZGERALD, Robert Stuart
Free verse; new appointment to Boylston
chair in rhetoric and oratory at Harvard.
por Time 85:51 Ap 23 '65
FITZGIBBON, Constantine
Young Dylan Thomas; excerpts from The
life of Dylan Thomas. Atlan 216:63-70 O;
66-72 N '65
FITZGIBBON, William C.
Books help boys and girls discover their
feelings. Parents Mag 40:50-1+ Ap '65
FITZPATRICK, Albert E.
Seis meses en Akron. por Am Ed 1:6-7 S '65
FITZPATRICK, Joseph P.
Parish of the future. America 113:521-3 N 6
'65
FITZSIMMONS, R. O.
Confidentiality of student records. NEA J 55:
29-30 Ja '66
FIVE and ten-cent stores
See also
Woolworth, F. W, company
FIVE year plan, Russian. See Russia—Eco-
nomic policy
FIX, Carolos
Greece bottles a drink with a familiar shape.
il Bsns W p 146+ O 16 '65
FIXED capacitors. See Electric capacitors
FIXED-point theorems. See Topology
FIXX, James F.
(ed) As others see us. See issues of Saturday
review
Books in communications. See second issue
of each month of Saturday review
Crime and the ultimate punishment. Sat R
49:29-30 Ja 1 '66
Frustrations of a satisfied viewer. Sat R
48:73 O 9 '65
Great Gallic welcome. Sat R 48:14-17 D 25
'65
Muddled, mirthful world of Burr Shafer.
Sat R 48:54-5 Jl 10 '65
Report from Santo Domingo. Sat R 48:30-2+
Je 12 '65
Startled look at British television. Sat R
48:98+ N 13 '65
Through the iron curtain. Sat R 48:76-7+
Ap 10 '65
When extremists attack the press. Sat R
48:72-3 F 13 '65
FIZER, Charles Patrick
Charles Fizer, 1940-1965. T. G. Harris. Look
29:26-7 O 5 '65
FLACKS, Richard
Some social implications of the teach-ins. Bul
Atomic Sci 21:21 O '65
FLAG poles. See Flagstaffs
FLAGELLATES
Heterothallism in biflagellate aquatic fungi:
preliminary genetic analysis. J. T. Mullins
and J. R. Raper. bibliog Science 150:1174-5
N 26 '65
See also
Euglena
FLAGELLO, Nicolas
Music of Nicolas Flagello. A. Cohn. por Am
Rec G 31:1054-5 Jl '65
FLAGPOLES. See Flagstaffs
FLAGS
New glories; flags and banners by living
artists. il Time 85:76-7 Ap 9 '65
We're flying the flag! J. Robbins. il Read
Digest 86:128-30 Je '65

Confederate States of America
Furl that banner? H. Carter. il N Y Times
Mag p8-9+ Jl 25 '65
FLAGSTAD, Kirsten
Flagstad, a personal memoir. G. Fitzgerald.
Opera N 30:31 D 25 '65
Flagstad's winner. il por Opera N 29:33 Mr
13 '65
Kirsten Flagstad I knew; excerpt from
Flagstad: a personal memoir. E. McArthur.
il pors Sat R 48:55-6+ S 25 '65
FLAGSTAFFS
Pole for Old Glory. il Pop Gard 16:57 Jl '65
FLAHERTY, Daniel L.
Catholic book week, 1965. America 112:254-6
F 20 '65
War safety control. America 112:656 My 8 '65
(ed) See West, M. L. Tragedy of Diem and
the paradox of Asia
—and others
That favorable time. America 112:321-2+
Mr 6 '65

FLAHERTY, Tom
Dogs, it's a man's life. Life 58:16 Mr 12 '65
Virtuoso of three clubs. Life 58:115-18 Ap 23
'65
FLAME cultivation. See Weeds—Control by fire
FLAMENCO
Back to the singing cafés; the real thing
at New York world's fair. il Time 85:73
Je 18 '65
FLAMING (cookery) See Cookery
FLAMING angel; opera. See Prokof'ev, S. S.
FLANAGAN, Val J.
Give the Gulf Coast a try. Motor B 115:50-
1+ Ap '65
Golfing along the Gulf. Travel 123:42-4 F '65
FLANDERS, Harold F.
Public organizes for the fight on censorship.
ALA Bul 59:528-9 Je '65
FLANDERS, Mary Powell. See Lippitt, R. O.
jt. auth.
FLANDORF, Vera S.
(Comp) Medical books for the public library.
Library J 90:4718-23 N 1 '65
FLANEGAN, Eugene B.
Glacier Bay National Monument. Nat Parks
Mag 39:12-15 Je '65
FLANGES
Floor flanges make the job easier. il Pop Sci
188:132 Ja '66
FLANNER, Janet
Letter from Paris. See issues of New Yorker
FLANNERY, Jack
Don't bother to call; story. Redbook 125:
68-9 Jl '65
Limited lone ranger; story. Redbook 125:58-9
Je '65
FLANNERY, Kent V.
Ecology of early food production in Meso-
potamia. bibliog Science 147:1247-56 Mr 12
'65
FLANZRAICH, Robert
Sound advice. Mod Phot 29:101 Ap; 21+ S
'65
FLAPAN, Maxwell
World we have to know. por Am Ed 1:30-
2 O '65
FLARES, Solar. See Solar flares
FLASHBULBS. See Electric lamps, Flashlight
FLASHCUBE adapters. See Photography—Ap-
paratus and supplies
FLASHING
Is your run-off system doing its job? il Pop
Mech 124:158-64+ N '65
FLAT irons. See Flatirons
FLATHEAD RIVER
Wrong consultants; conservation organizations
concern over plans for a pulp mill. Nat
Parks Mag 39:20 F '65
FLATIRONS
Treasure hunt. J. Mebane. il Bet Hom &
Gard 43:25+ My '65
FLATLEY, Guy
(comp) Critical thoughts. N Y Times Mag
p 117+ S 19 '65
(comp) Fashion footnotes. N Y Times Mag
p64 Je 13 '65
(comp) Subject: Ireland. N Y Times Mag
p42 Mr 14 '65
FLATOW, Herbert
Color critique. U S Camera 29:59-61 Ja '66
FLATWORMS. See Planarians
FLAVONOIDS
Flavonoids from the moss mnium affine bland.
T. E. Melchert and R. E. Alston. bibliog
il Science 150:1170-1 N 26 '65
FLAVOR. See Taste
FLEA market, New York. See New York (city)
—Markets
FLEAS
End of fleadom; Sentry collar. C. Conley.
il Field & S 70:111 Jl '65
Fleas: breeding cycle of European rabbit
flea. M. Rothschild. il Sci Am 213:44-53
D '65
FLECK, A. and others
Protein synthesis in rat liver: influence of
amino acids in diet on microsomes and
polysomes. bibliog Science 150:628-9 O 29
'65
FLECK, Richard
Too tame for the Chippeway. Liv Wildn 29:
20-1 Sum '65
FLEESON, Doris
Still talkin' about the Tetons. por Am For
71:22-5 N '65
FLEISCHER, R. L. and others
Fission-track dating of bed I, Olduvai
Gorge. bibliog Science 148:72-4 Ap 2 '65
Fossil particle tracks and uranium distri-
butions in minerals of the Vaca Muerta
meteorite. bibliog Science 148:629-32 Ap 30
'65
Tracks of charged particles in solids. bib-
liog Science 149:383-93 Jl 23 '65

FLEISHMAN, Stanley
Witchcraft and obscenity: twin superstitions; excerpts from address, November 2, 1964. por Wilson Lib Bul 39:640-6 Ap '65

FLEMER, William, 3d
Choose the right tree for your terrace. Pop Gard 16:26-7+ S '65

FLEMING, D. F.
Can Pax Americana succeed? Ann Am Acad 360:127-38 Jl '65
Is containment moral? bibliog f Ann Am Acad 362:18-27 N '65

FLEMING, Donald R.
Big money and high politics of science. Atlan 216:41-5 Ag '65

FLEMING, Ian
European literary scene; European popularity. R. J. Clements. Sat R 48:22 Ag 7 '65
Incredible James Bond. J. F. Olesky. il Duns R 86:75-6 O '65
James Bond: modern-day dragonslayer. A. S. Boyd. Christian Cent 82:644-7 My 19 '65
My Japanese days with Ought-ought seven. R. Hughes. il Sat R 48:38-40+ S 18 '65
Smell of Bond. Nation 200:378 Ap 12 '65
To Valhalla with twin exhausts. A. Lejeune. il Nat R 17:776-7 S 7 '65

FLEMING, Mary Crist
Breather year. il por Time 85:77-8 My 28 '65

FLEMING, Peter
Landfalls in Polynesia. Holiday 37:62-3+ Mr '65

FLEMING, Rodney R.
European parks too formal. Am City 80:100-3+ S '65
Snow-fighting's new techniques; adaptation of address bibliog Am City 80:83-5+ N '65
Solid-waste disposal. Am City 81:101-4 Ja '66 (to be cont)

FLEMING, Roscoe
Oil rush. New Repub 153:11 S 18 '65
Shale oil: the cartel's ace in the hole. Nation 200:274-6 Mr 15 '65

FLEMING, Thomas J.
Good-bye to everything! Am Heritage 16:88-95+ Ag '65
In pursuit of Honest Abe. Good H 160:138+ F '65
Truth and illusion: meaning of the American revolution today; address, February 22, 1965. Vital Speeches 31:345-9 Mr 15 '65
(ed) See James, B. We was amazingly fortunate

FLEMMING, Arthur S, awards. See Rewards, prizes, etc.

FLEMMING, E. W.
Build a Hansel and Gretel playhouse. Parents Mag 40:146 N '65

FLESCH, Rudolf
Word made Flesch. H. Kenner. Nat R 17:558:60 Je 29 '65

FLETCHER, Allen
Finding Shakespeare. J. Novick. Nation 201:45-7 Jl 19 '65

FLETCHER, Colin
Look at it this way. Read Digest 86:25-6+ F '65
Rattlesnake, fact and fancy. Read Digest 86:196-8+ Je '65

FLETCHER, James
British press postscript. Nat R 18:25-6 Ja 11 '66

FLETCHER, Joseph
Agreement and disagreement. Commonweal 83:437-9 Ja 14 '66
Love is the only measure. Commonweal 83:427-32 Ja 14 '66

FLETCHER, William J.
New ideas in fencing. Suc Farm 63:104 Mr '65
New ways to make roof trusses. Suc Farm 63:108 Mr '65
—and Malena, Dave
Beef confinement, what's happening? Suc Farm 63:46-7 Jl '65

FLEXNER, James Thomas
George Washington, businessman; excerpt from George Washington: the forge of experience. Am Heritage 16:94-8 O '65

FLEXNER, Simon
Rockefeller university: science in a different key. J. Walsh. il Science 150:1692-5 D 24 '65

FLICKER phenomena
Evoked brain potential correlates of psychophysical responses: heterochromatic flicker photometry. J. B. Siegfried and others. bibliog il Science 149:321-3 Jl 16 '65
Evoked potentials and correlated judgments of brightness as functions of interflash intervals. N. R. Bartlett and C. T. White. bibliog il Science 148:980-1 My 14 '65
Visual perception of direction for stimuli flashed during voluntary saccadic eye movements. L. Matin and D. G. Pearce. bibliog il Science 148:1485-8 Je 11 '65

Der FLIEGENDE Holländer; opera. See Wagner, R.

FLIES
Books. H. E. Evans. il Sci Am 214:123-4+ Ja '66
See also
Drosophila
Fruit flies

Extermination
1965 dairy fly control guide. H. Stockdale and H. Gunderson. Suc Farm 63:46-7 Je '65
Paper sacks cut fly larval production. il Am City 80:44 N '65

FLIES, Artificial. See Fishing lures, flies, etc.

FLIES as carriers of infection
Flies and disease. B. Greenberg. il Sci Am 213:92-9 Jl '65

FLIGHT
Physiological aspects
See Aviation—Physiological aspects

FLIGHT instructors. See Air pilots—Training

FLIGHT of the Falcon; novel. See Du Maurier, D.

FLIGHT simulators
BAC building simulator system for use as Concorde design tool. il Aviation W 83:43+ O 11 '65
Category 3 simulator will test displays. B. Miller. il Aviation W 83:73-5+ N 29 '65
Fog chamber aids research on minimums. R. G. O'Lone. il Aviation W 83:40-1 O 11 '65
Microcircuits add to simulator flexibility. K. J. Stein. il Aviation W 83:76-7+ N 1 '65
See also
Space flight simulators

FLINDT, Flemming
Introducing Flemming Flindt. J. Anderson. il por Dance Mag 39:26-9 N '65

FLINT, Evelyn Conger
Say it with flowers. Flower Grower 52:22 Mr '65

FLINT, R. F.
Deep-sea stratigraphy. Science 149:660-1 Ag 6 '65

FLINT, Roland
August from my desk; poem. Atlan 215:95 F '65

FLINT
See also
Chert

FLIPSE, Peter M.
Excerpt from testimony, April 9, 1963. Cong Digest 44:208+ Ag '65

FLOATING accelerators. See Accelerators (electrons, etc)

FLOATING docks. See Docks

FLOATING dry docks. See Dry docks

FLOATING electronic bases. See Oceanographic buoys

FLOATING instrument platforms. See Oceanographic buoys

FLOATING platforms. See Oceanographic buoys

FLOATS. See Docks

FLOGGING. See Corporal punishment

FLOOD prevention and control
Floods with us always. Sci N L 87:270 Ap 24 '65

United States
See also
Mississippi River
Missouri River—Flood control projects

FLOODLIGHTING. See Light projection

FLOODLIGHTING, Photographic. See Electric lamps, Flashlight

FLOODS
Floods with us always. Sci N L 87:270 Ap 24 '65

Brazil
Heavens weep; Rio de Janeiro. il Newsweek 67:49 Ja 24 '66

United States
Big flood; Pacific Coast flood. L. Parker. il Am For 71:14-17+ Mr '65
Cruel beauty of the ravages of flood: Mississippi bursts its banks. il Life 58:34-5 Ap 30 '65
Elements: still untamed and deadly; Betsy in Louisiana. il U S News 59:48-9 S 27 '65
First the wind, then the waters; six Midwest states suffer disaster. il Newsweek 65:25-6 Ap 26 '65
Man vs. nature: still a losing fight. il U S News 58:50-2 Ap 26 '65
On the rampage. il Sr Schol 86:28 Ap 29 '65
Teenagers who saved a town; Rock Island, Ill. C. Remsberg and B. Remsberg. il Good H 161:82-3+ S '65
That was the storm. F. Dufresne. il Field & S 70:20+ My '65

FLOODS—United States—*Continued*
Up from the deluge; aftermath of hurricane Betsy. il Time 86:24-5 S 24 '65
Vicious month; Seattle quake and Mississippi floods. il Newsweek 65:45 My 10 '65
Wasters: logging for floods; California, 1964. L. P. Hudson. il Nation 200:531-3 My 17 '65
West coast clears the road back. il Bsns W p90-2 Ja 30 '65
   See also
Mississippi River

FLOOR, Emanuel A.
Canyonland: newest national park. Travel 124:56-7 Jl '65

FLOOR coverings
How to buy smooth-surface flooring. Am Home 68:21 Ap '65
Two new products for covering floors. il Pop Sci 187:119 S '65
   See also
Rugs and carpets
Tiles, Floor

FLOORING
How to choose wood paneling and flooring. Bet Hom & Gard 43:33+ My '65
Wood squares give you a luxury floor fast. D. Huff. il Pop Sci 187:116-18 S '65
Wood: what the new flooring, paneling and furniture can do for a room! D. Popplestone and D. Jordan. il Bet Hom & Gard 43:50-63 My '65

FLOORS
How not to cut a rug; portable dance floor. J. Peter. il Look 29:52 Jl 27 '65
   See also
Swine houses—Floors

Care
Care and safekeeping of masonry floors. House & Gard 128:75-6+ O '65
Help for clean-up time; Armstrong products. M. B. Keiser. il Parents Mag 40:38+ Mr '65
Resilient floors. House & Gard 127:4+ F '65

FLOORS, Brick
Handsome paving patterns. il House & Gard 128:241 O '65

FLOORS, Cement
Oxychloride floors: use and application. C. W. Redeker. il Arch Rec 137:235-6 Ap '65

FLOORS, Wood
Wood squares give you a luxury floor fast. D. Huff. il Pop Sci 187:116-18 S '65

FLORA. See Botany

FLORA, Arctic. See Botany—Arctic Regions

FLORA pacifica, Honolulu. See Flower exhibits

FLORA, the red menace; musical comedy. See Musical comedies, revues, etc.—Criticisms, plots, etc.

FLORAL decoration. See Flowers, Arrangement of

FLORAL design. See Design, Decorative—Plant forms

FLORAL tribute; story. See Tuohy, F.

FLORENCE agreement. See Duty free importation

FLORENCE May festival. See Music festivals—Italy

FLORENTINES
Florentines: hope of Italy? G. Natoli. il Cath World 200:339-45 Mr '65

FLORES, Edmundo
Alliance for reaction. Nation 200:659-62 Je 21 '65

FLORES, Lola
People are talking about... por Vogue 145:184-5 My '65

FLORICULTURE
Flowers say welcome to the farm. L. Donelson. il Farm J 89:83 Je '65
H&G's gardener's month. See issues of House & garden incorporating Living for young homemakers
   See also
Bulbs
Flowers
Gardening
Greenhouses
   also names of flowers, e.g. Tulips

FLORIDA
West coast of Florida wakes up. W. H. Kendall. il Motor B 115:45-9+ Ap '65
   See also
Architecture, Domestic—Florida
Birds—Florida
Booksellers and bookselling—Florida
Canals—Florida
Everglades National Park
Fishing—Florida
Gardens—Florida
Hunting—Florida

Labor and laboring classes—Florida
Land—Florida
Petroleum—Florida
Tourist trade—Florida
Water supply—Florida

Description and travel
Florida nobody knows. B. Thielen. il Holiday 37:21-3+ F '65
Florida's Gulf coast. W. B. Hartley. il Redbook 126:48-9+ Ja '65
From tip to top in Florida. G. Bourke. See issues of Travel
Traveler's choice; Vilano Beach near St Augustine, Fla. E. Melvin. Travel 124:13 N '65

Legislature
Florida's legislature; the pork chop state of mind. R. Sherrill. Harper 231:82+ N '65

Politics and government
Detour to Tallahassee? gubernatorial race. il Time 86:26-7 D 3 '65
   See also
Florida—Legislature

FLORIDA Atlantic university, Boca Raton
Using computers in a new university library. J. Becker. il ALA Bul 59:823-6 O '65

FLORIDA East Coast railway
Carrying people again. il Bsns W p81 Ag 7 '65
Rider's risk. il Newsweek 66:70 Ag 16 '65

FLORIDA Indians. See Seminole Indians

FLORIDA KEYS
The Keys. J. Emmett. il Yachting 118:38-40+ N '65

FLORIDA land boom. See Real estate business

FLORIDA state university, Tallahassee
Renaissance in library history? new publication. J. Shera. Wilson Lib Bul 40:281 N '65

FLORINSKY, Michael T.
Economic policies after Khrushchev. Cur Hist 49:221-6+ O '65

FLORISSANT FOSSIL BEDS NATIONAL MONUMENT (proposed) See National monuments

FLORISTS
Say it with profits. Time 86:68-9 Ag 20 '65

FLORY, Wilmer B.
Modern daylilies. Horticulture 43:16-17+ Jl '65

FLOTOW, Friedrich von
On records; Martha. Opera N 30:34 Ja 8 '66

FLOW meters
Liquid flow measurement. J. R. Collins. il Electr World 73:38-40+ Je '65

FLOWER arrangements. See Flowers, Arrangement of

FLOWER boxes, planters, etc.
Almost every garden can use a big container. il Sunset 135:78-81 S '65
Containers. J. B. Brimer. il Flower Grower 52:41-2 My '65
Easy-to-make redwood baskets. E. Javorsky. il Flower Grower 52:36-7 F '65
How to select pots for your plants. il Good H 160:151 F '65
Make a place for house plants. il Bet Hom & Gard 43:78 Jl '65
Old-fashioned strawberry jar. J. J. Hill, sr. il Flower Grower 52:39 Jl '65
Plants grow everywhere. G. Taloumis. il Horticulture 43:44-7 Mr '65
Pots of pleasure. M. N. Davis. il Flower Grower 52:18+ F '65
You get to know them if you grow them in containers. il Sunset 134:108-11 Je '65

FLOWER exhibits
Chelsea flower show. W. Feinberg. il Horticulture 43:38-9+ My '65
Flora pacifica; exhibit at East-West center, University of Hawaii, Honolulu. C. B. Lees. il Horticulture 43:14-17 N '65
Flower shows. il Horticulture 43:6+ Mr '65
Flower shows and garden tours (cont) il House & Gard 127:16+ Mr '65
Garden events. See issues of Flower grower, the home garden magazine
Garden events [in month] (title varies) See issues of Sunset
If you are proud of your plants, enter a flower show. M. Orans. il Flower Grower 52:25 Ap '65

FLOWER grower (periodical)
Weathervane. R. G. Miner. Flower Grower 52:8 Mr '65

FLOWER pots
Practical & pretty: crocks to cover up pots. L. Burgess. il Flower Grower 52:48 Ag '65

FLOWER-seed industry. See Seed trade

FLOWER shops. See Florists

FLOWER shows. See Flower exhibits

FLOWER trade. See Florists

FLOWERING dogwood. See Dogwood

FLOWERING trees
Early apricot to late cherry. il Sunset 134:82-7 F '65

FLOWERS, Edwin C. and Viebrock, H. J.
Solar radiation: an anomalous decrease of direct solar radiation. bibliog Science 148: 493-4 Ap 23 '65

FLOWERS, Richmond M.
Alabama unbound. A. Kopkind. New Repub 153:13-16 N 27 '65
Brave politician in the South. Life 59:4 N 5 '65
New politician from the old South. C. S. Wren. il pors Look 29:46+ N 16 '65

FLOWERS
More new plants for 1965. il Horticulture 43: 40-2+ F '65
New flowers say spring's coming. G. Logsdon. il Farm J 90:86-7 Ja '66
Spectacular color this summer! H. Mason. il Bet Hom & Gard 43:68-71 My '65
Spotlight these flowers this year; symposium. il Pop Gard 16:26-9+ Jl '65
This is my favorite. See issues of Popular gardening & living outdoors
    See also
Annuals (plants)
Bulbs
Color of flowers
Floriculture
Flowers as gifts
Perennials
Wild flowers
    also names of flowers, e.g. Roses

All America selections
See Plants—All America selections

Bibliography
Onward and upward in the garden. K. S. White. New Yorker 41:164+ D 18 '65

Cut flowers
Fresh flowers. Mrs W. E. Wilkenloh. il Horticulture 43:43 F '65
    See also
Flowers, Arrangement of

Seed
Seeds of success; T. Sakata and company, Japan. M. Noble. il Flower Grower 53:27 Ja '66

FLOWERS, Arrangement of
Accent on foliage. D. Biddle. il Pop Gard 16:14+ Ap '65
Containers for today; and how to get the most from them. R. E. Carr. il Flower Grower 52:30-2 N '65
Enjoy summer's flowers. E. Finch. il Pop Gard 16:28-9 S '65
Flower arrangements. il Horticulture 43:28-9 Je '65
Mixed bouquets. M. White. il Ladies Home J 82:32 Ag '65
Props from my farm. C. McGeoch. il Flower Grower 52:35 S '65
Say it with flowers. E. C. Flint. il Flower Grower 52:22 Mr '65
These are today's Dutch masterpieces! Dick Schuyt's arrangements. E. D. Craster. il Bet Hom & Gard 43:74-5+ My '65
    See also
Church decoration and ornament

FLOWERS, Artificial
Make your own flowers. K. Seibel. il Farm J 89:76 S '65

FLOWERS, Dried
Dried plants offer design bonus. Mrs M. R. Bell. il Design 66:22-5 Mr '65
Extend the abundance of summer. R. C. Hands. il Horticulture 43:24-5 N '65
Flowering Spain. il Ladies Home J 82:113 F '65
High and dry for Christmas. il Sunset 135: 184-5 D '65
    See also
Potpourri

FLOWERS, Forcing of. See Forcing (plants)

FLOWERS, Fragrant. See Gardens, Fragrant

FLOWERS, Wild. See Wild flowers

FLOWERS as food
How to eat a rose. E. Gibbons. House & Gard 128:48+ S '65
To cook a rose. C. Claiborne. il N Y Times Mag p32 Je 27 '65

FLOWERS as gifts
Etiquette of giving flowers. Good H 161:154 Jl '65

FLOWERS in church decoration. See Church decoration and ornament

FLOWERS in house decoration. See Plants in house decoration

FLOYD, Carlisle
Susannah. Criticism
    Opera N 30:21 O 23 '65
    Sat R 48:40 N 27 '65

FLUID amplifiers. See Amplifiers

FLUID dynamics
Coherent matter waves. Sci Am 212:61 Je '65
Computer experiments in fluid dynamics. F. H. Harlow and J. E. Fromm. il Sci Am 212:104-10 bibliog(p 140) Mr '65
Liquid waves by computer. F. H. Harlow and others. il Science 149:1092-3 S 3 '65

FLUIDICS. See Fluids

FLUIDS
Five firms top field in achievement; applications of fluidics. il Miss & Roc 16:36+ F 8 '65
Hard-sphere fluid. H. L. Frisch. bibliog il Science 150:1249-54 D 3 '65
Special report: fluidics; ed. by C. D. LaFond. il Miss & Roc 16:18+ F 8 '65

FLUIDS engineering laboratories. See Hydraulic laboratories

FLUMES
Ride to remember; down lumber flume at Pacific wood, lumber and flume company, Virginia City, Nev. J. C. Hunt. il Am Heritage 16:80-3 Ap '65

FLUORESCENCE
Fluorescence quantum yield measurements: vitamin B$_6$ compounds. R. F. Chen. bibliog il Science 150:1593-5 D 17 '65
Fluorescent contaminants from plastic and rubber laboratory equipment. H. A. Kordan. bibliog Science 149:1382-3 S 17 '65
Pigmented nevi and malignant melanomas as studied with a specific fluorescence method. B. Falck and others. bibliog Science 149:439 Jl 23 '65

FLUORESCENT lamps. See Electric lamps, Fluorescent

FLUORESCENT lighting. See Electric lamps, Fluorescent

FLUORESCENT street lighting. See Street lighting

FLUORIDATION. See Water supply—Fluoridation

FLUORIDES
Fluoride protection of bones and teeth. R. F. Sognnaes. bibliog il Science 150:989-93 N 19 '65
Fluorides help prevent some bone diseases. Sci N L 88:373 D 11 '65

FLUORINE compounds
Organic fluorine chemistry. C. G. Krespan. bibliog il Science 150:13-18 O 1 '65

FLUOROCHEMICALS. See Fluorine compounds

FLUOROMETRIC test. See Cancer—Diagnosis

FLUOROSPECTROPHOTOMETERS. See Medical instruments and apparatus

FLUSHERS, Street. See Street cleaning apparatus

FLUSHING, Mich.
Hometown USA; excerpt from The situation in Flushing. E. G. Love. il Sat Eve Post 238:32-6+ S 11 '65

FLUTE players
    See also
Rampal, J. P.

FLXIBLE company
Bus competitor GM helped build. il Bsns W p 172+ D 11 '65

FLY, Camillas S.
Help wanted in Tombstone. L. Barry. il Pop Phot 56:28+ My '65

FLY casting. See Fishing

FLY leaders. See Fishing tackle

FLY tying. See Fishing lures, flies, etc.

FLYCATCHERS (birds)
Flycatchers in the rose garden. M. D. Hodgins. il Flower Grower 52:14+ Je '65

FLYING boats. See Seaplanes

FLYING clubs. See Aviation clubs

FLYING Dutchman; opera. See Wagner, R.

FLYING saucers
Return of flying saucers. D. Cohen. il Nation 201:131-4 S 13 '65
Should we be serious about UFO's? unidentified flying object. D. Cohen. il Sci Digest 57: 41-4 Je '65
Trade winds: Exeter people give accounts of observations. J. G. Fuller. Sat R 49:14 Ja 22 '66
Tradewinds; report of an unidentified flying object in Exeter, N.H. J. G. Fuller. il Sat R 48:10+ O 2 '65
Why I believe in flying saucers. M. Kantor. il Pop Sci 188:72-4+ Ja '66

FLYING squirrels. See Squirrels

FLYING submarine. See Submarine boats—Airplane combination

FLYING Tiger line, incorporated
Can't hold that Tiger. il Newsweek 66:74
Jl 5 '65

FLYNN, John
Marines get flowers for a tough mission. Life
58:44-5 Mr 19 '65

FLYNN, Robert L.
Boy from Chillicothe; story. Yale R 54:567-77
Je '65

FLYNN, William James
Thrifty spy on the Sixth avenue el. E. Wittenberg. il Am Heritage 17:60-4+ D '65

FLYWHEELS
That old spinning wheel. J. McFarland. il
Hot Rod 19:58-61 Ja '66

FOAMED plastics. See Plastics, Cellular

FOCUSING. See Photography—Focusing

FODOR travel guides. See Guidebooks

FOETUS. See Fetus

FOG
Outboard in fog. B. Whittier. il Yachting 117:
66-7+ My '65
See also
Aviation—Fog problem

FOG detectors. See Detectors

FOGARTY, John E.
Laws, law-makers, and libraries. por ALA
Bul 59:269-73 Ap '65

FOGARTY, Michael P.
Catholic schools in Britain. Commonweal 83:
13-14+ O 8 '65

FOGG, John M. Jr
Magnolias. Horticulture 43:22-5 F '65

FOLDES, Joseph
Close-ups, down-stage center. Pop Phot
56:74-5+ Mr '65
Painting with film. U S Camera 28:50-1+
O '65

FOLDING boats. See Boats and boating

FOLDING screens. See Screens (furniture)

FOLEY, Connie
Living museums. Am For 71:14-17+ N '65

FOLEY, John J.
Paradox of university publishing. America
114:84+ Ja 15 '66

FOLIAGE. See Leaves

FOLK, Mary Lou
That accident did me good! Farm J 89:104
F '65

FOLK art
By the people, for the people. L. Hammel.
il N Y Times Mag p30-1 Jl 18 '65
In defense of crafts; Latin America. G. de
Zéndegui. Américas 17:inside cover N '65
Van Alstyne American folk art collection.
P. C. Welsh. il Antiques 88:208-11 Ag '65
See also
Museum of early American folk arts, New
York

FOLK dancers. See Dancers

FOLK dancing
Many songs, many dances: folk music of the
United States: cultural imprint of foreign
countries. S. G. Knott. il Américas 17:27-33
F '65
Mile in the sky; folk dancing of Himalayan
Mountain people. D. Bhattacharya. il Dance
Mag 39:46-9 Jl '65

FOLK festivals. See Festivals

FOLK music
See also
Folk songs
Bibliography
Recent and worth-while books devoted to
folk music. Am Rec G 31:575 F '65

FOLK schools, Danish. See Schools—Denmark

FOLK singers. See Singers

FOLK song festivals. See Music festivals

FOLK songs
Behind the folk-song frenzy. A. Shaw. il Read
Digest 86:191+ Ap '65
Sing a song of folk. J. Wescott. il Seventeen
24:16 Ap '65
Sound of music? P. L. Levin. il N Y Times
Mag p72+ Mr 14 '65
Young sing the old. Am Home 68:20 Mr '65
Bibliography
Curl up and read. C. A. Lovin. Seventeen
24:30 Ap '65
Folk bookshelf. L. Cohn. Sat R 48:59+ My
15 '65

FOLK songs, American
Dear wayfarers. B. Ives. Seventeen 24:264+
Ag '65
Many songs, many dances: folk music of
the United States: cultural imprint of
foreign countries. S. G. Knott. il Américas
17:27-33 F '65

FOLK songs, Chinese
Songs of the red flag. Review
Esquire 64:127+ Ag '65. J. Carroll

FOLKLORE
See also
Superstition

FOLLETT publishing company
Follett program. R. E. Allen. Wilson Lib Bul
40:59-60 S '65

FOLLIAGE plants. See Plants, Ornamental

FOLLIARD, Edward T.
Washington front. See occasional issues of
America

FOLLICLES
Tylotrich (hair) follicle: association with
a slowly adapting tactile receptor in the
cat. S. J. Mann and W. E. Straile. bibliog
il Science 147:1043-5 F 26 '65

FOLLIES (architecture)
In praise of a folly; Portmeirion, a gay
architectural caprice on the Welsh coast. J.
Morris. il Horizon 7:16-19 Sum '65
Return of playfulness. A. Bush-Brown. il
House & Gard 127:116-17+ Je '65

FOLON, Jean Michel
New York, site unseen; drawings. Horizon
7:116-20 Sum '65

FONDUE. See Cookery—Cheese

FONSSAGRIVES, Mia
Two American girls show Paris. il pors Life
58:94-6+ F 5 '65

FONTAINE, Robert
Androcles and his pal; drama. Plays 24:83-6
My '65
Another Cinderella; drama. Plays 25:91-5 Ja
'66
Fair today, followed by tomorrow; drama.
Plays 24:81-4 Ap '65
Is there a monster in the house? drama.
Plays 25:83-6 D '65
Let sleeping beauties lie; dramatization of
Grimms' fairy tale. Plays 24:91-5 F '65
No quarter asked; story. Parents Mag 40:
48-9 Je '65
Ride your hobby; drama. Plays 25:83-6 O '65
Sex without popcorn. Atlan 215:128+ My '65

FONTANA, Lucio
Second fame: good food. N. Lyon. por Vogue
147:118-20 Ja 15 '66

FONTEYN, Dame Margot
Man in motion; Prince & Swan. il pors Time
85:48-52 Ap 16 '65
Royal academy. New Yorker 41:34-5 Je 5 '65
Royal ballet's eighth New York season.
Metropolitan opera house. D. Hering. Dance
Mag 39:29-30+ Jl '65
Secret of the Nureyev spell. C. Barnes. il
por N Y Times Mag p 30-1+ Ap 18 '65

FOOD
Food and nutrition; special issue; sympo-
sium. il Todays Health 43:18-24+ O '65
Food forum (cont) E. Weston. il McCalls 92:
38 Mr; 34 Ap; 44 My; 36 Je '65
Foods. Consumer Rep 30:73-86 D '65
See also
Cookery
Gelatin
Nutrition
Proteins
Salads
Sandwiches
Space flight—Food problems
Analysis
See also
Food adulteration and inspection
Irradiation
See Food, Effect of radiation on
New sources
See Food supply—New sources
Prices
Calculation of average retail food prices. D.
P. Rothwell. il Mo Labor R 88:61-6 Ja '65
Eating low on the hog. A. B. Spalding. il
Harper 230:139-40+ Mr '65
Food prices: where they're headed. il U S
News 58:54 Je 21 '65
High cost of eating. il Newsweek 65:70+
Je 21 '65
Know the price per ounce! Consumer Bul 48:
19 N '65
Rising cost of living: where higher prices
hit hardest. il U S News 59:64-5 Ag 16 '65
Tips to save you money in buying food.
Suc Farm 63:109 My '65
Why housewives are paying more for food.
il U S News 58:93-4 Je 7 '65
Why you spend so much on groceries. il
Changing T 19:25-8 S '65
Psychology
See Eating, Psychology of

FOOD—*Continued*

Ready-to-cook food

Better days for housewives as food industry changes; convenience foods. il U S News 58:118-20 Mr 22 '65

Instant gourmet; with recipes. il McCalls 92:76+ My '65

Potato favorites instantly! il Bet Hom & Gard 43:105 Ap '65

Saving graces of convenience foods. E. Weston. McCalls 92:44 My '65

Smoking

How to cook a bony fish. K. Wood. il Field & S 69:56-9 Ap '65

How to smoke your own. il Sunset 135:124+ Ag '65

Standards

Firmer food standards proposed for world. Sci N L 87:248 Ap 17 '65

What's in food standards for you? Consumer Bul 48:31-3 Mr '65

Storage

Good housekeeping guide to food storage. il Good H 160:147 F '65

Well-kept refrigerator for the man-about-town; with recipes. M. Kaytor. il Look 29: 86+ S 21 '65

FOOD, Cooling of
Serve it cold. il Ladies Home J 82:32 D '65

FOOD, Cost of
See also
Food—Prices

FOOD, Dried
New food for sportsmen. M. C. Gethman. il Field & S 69:52-5 F '65

FOOD, Effect of radiation on
Radiation: food's new keeper. B. Tufty. il(p33) Sci N L 89:42-3 Ja 15 '66

Radiation preservation of foods; report on international conference. F. P. Mehrlich. Science 147:1600+ Mr 26 '65

Some thoughts for food; preservation of food by radiation. Time 86:55 D 31 '65

FOOD, Frozen
Dinner's almost ready (in the freezer!) with recipes. il Good H 160:116-31 Ap '65

Fabulous feasts, straight from the freezer; with recipes and menus. il McCalls 93:82-3+ Ja '66

Foods. Consumer Rep 30:63-73 D '65

Frozen entrees; stingy portions, mediocre quality make them hardly worthwhile. Consumer Rep 30:492-3 O '65

Frozen fruit pies. il Consumer Rep 30:434-5 S '65

Heat 'n' eat, packaging treat. G. Lazarus. Sat R 48:77 Je 12 '65

How do you mold a main dish? salads with recipes. il Bet Hom & Gard 43:74 Ag '65

Keep a picnic in your freezer. il Bet Hom & Gard 43:82 Jl '65

Saving graces of convenience foods. E. Weston. McCalls 92:44 My '65

What's new, besides ho-ho-ho; Green giant co. il Bsns W p 136+ O 23 '65

FOOD, Irradiated. See Food, Effect of radiation on

FOOD, Smoked
See also
Food—Smoking

FOOD, Synthetic. See Food substitutes

FOOD additives
Let's talk about food. P. L. White. Todays Health 43:5+ Mr '65

Those chemicals in our food. J. C. G. Conniff. il McCalls 92:83+ F '65

FOOD adulteration and inspection
Pesticide residues in total-diet samples. R. E. Duggan and others. bibliog il Science 151:101-4 Ja 7 '66
See also
Meat inspection

FOOD and drug administration. See United States—Food and drug administration

FOOD as carrier of infection. See Food poisoning

FOOD as gifts
From our orchard and woods; for Christmas. L. Helsel. il Farm J 89:83 D '65

Gifts from the freezer; for Christmas. R. Hanna. il Suc Farm 63:82-3+ N '65

Lavish labels for your gourmet gifts. il McCalls 93:126-7 D '65

Merry gifts from the kitchen. il Bet Hom & Gard 43:56-7+ D '65

Treats that add flavor to Christmas. B. L. Henry. il Farm J 89:94-6 D '65

FOOD chain stores. See Chain stores

FOOD columns. See Newspapers—Sections, columns, etc.

FOOD concessions. See Concessions (food, etc)

FOOD fads
Bunk about health foods. R. L. Smith. il Todays Health 43:24+ O '65

Yin, yang, and MB; macrobiotic food. Newsweek 65:90+ Ap 5 '65

FOOD fallacies. See Errors, Popular

FOOD for peace program. See Food relief

FOOD freezers. See Freezers

FOOD grinders, Electric. See Electric apparatus and appliances, Domestic

FOOD habits of animals. See Animals—Food

FOOD industry and trade
Better days for housewives as food industry changes. il U S News 58:118-20 Mr 22 '65

Calculation of average retail food prices. D. P. Rothwell. il Mo Labor R 88:61-6 Ja '65

Fast food and footloose Americans; conference on the problems of the Food service industries held in Fontana, Wis. R. Lynes. Harper 232:26+ Ja '66

Government and the food industry; domestic food marketing; address, September 17, 1965. G. L. Mehren. Vital Speeches 31:755-8 O 1 '65

Why farmer's share is shrinking; study by National commission on food marketing. il Bsns W p 174-6+ My 15 '65
See also
Canning and preserving industry and trade
Consolidated foods corporation
Food, Frozen
General foods corporation
Government investigations—Food industry and trade
Pet milk company

FOOD labels. See Labels

FOOD mixers, Electric. See Electric apparatus and appliances, Domestic

FOOD packaging. See Packaging

FOOD plants. See Plants, Food

FOOD poisoning
Don't invite the bugs to your next picnic. il Todays Health 43:6 Jl '65

Food poisoning, and how to avoid it. J. H. Winchester. Read Digest 86:161-2+ My '65

Food poisoning studied. Sci N L 88:244 O 16 '65

Food poisoning: the sneaky attacker. H. G. Earl. Todays Health 43:64-6+ O '65

Let's talk about food: assuring safety of foods prepared for groups. P. L. White. Todays Health 43:5+ F '65

Ways to guard against a common food poisoning. Good H 160:172 Je '65

FOOD preferences
Paired comparison method for measurement of sugar preference in squirrel monkeys. M. W. Wagner and others. bibliog il Science 148:1473-4 Je 11 '65

Purely personal régimes; choices of celebrities. Vogue 145:108-9+ Je '65

What they eat; teen-agers food preferences. il Esquire 64:48-9 Jl '65

FOOD preservation and preservatives
New processes that make cooking easier. Good H 161:173 N '65
See also
Food, Effect of radiation on
Meat—Preservation

FOOD processing. See Food preservation and preservatives

FOOD production. See Food supply

FOOD relief
Administration of Food for peace transferred to Department of state; memorandum, October 20, 1965, with executive order. L. B. Johnson. Dept State Bul 53:925-6 D 6 '65

Another calamity; famine in India. il U S News 59:58-9 D 27 '65

Breadbasket diplomacy; farm surpluses as lever to make underdeveloped nations grow more food. il Time 86:25 D 3 '65

Cooperation, international development, and the problem of hunger. H. J. Waters. Dept State Bul 53:816-19 N 22 '65

Dwindling farm surplus. S. De Paul. America 114:37 Ja 8 '66

Emotional exports; expanded Food for peace program. Reporter 34:12 Ja 13 '66

Fighting world famine. New Repub 153:7-8 Ag 7 '65

Food for freedom; Shuman's plan. il Time 86:11 D 24 '65

Food for peace? New Repub 154:5-6 Ja 1 '66

Food for peace program and the challenge of the future; message, March 31, 1965. L. B. Johnson. Dept State Bul 52:682-4 My 3 '65

More food for peace. America 112:187 F 6 '65

U.S. industry speeds aid to hungry il Bsns W p62-3 D 25 '65

U.S. shapes fight on world hunger. il Bsns W p34+ D 18 '65

FOOD relief—*Continued*
War against want, by G. S. McGovern.
Review
    Commonweal 82:477-8 Jl 2 '65. A. Mc-
        Cormack
World famine ahead? Gunnar Myrdal's warn-
ing; excerpts from address, March 15, 1965.
G. Myrdal. U S News 58:16 Mr 29 '65

Colombia

Pilot school lunch program begins at Bogota.
Dept State Bul 53:65-6 Jl 12 '65

Latin America

More children; more hunger. G. M. Schultz.
il Todays Health 43:18-23+ O '65

Mexico

Hasty act? U.S. food for peace program cutoff. il Newsweek 66:39 Jl 19 '65

Somalia

U.S. provides emergency food supplies to
Somalia; Department statement, December
29, 1964. Dept State Bul 52:76 Ja 18 '65

United Arab Republic

Clash on the hill; cutoff of surplus-food ship-
ments. Time 85:14 F 12 '65
Department asks for flexibility on surplus
food sales to U.A.R; statement. February
1, 1965. G. W. Ball. Dept State Bul 52:
262-3 F 22 '65
FOOD slicers, Electric. See Electric apparatus
and appliances, Domestic
FOOD standards. See Food—Standards
FOOD stores
    See also
Chain stores
National association of convenience stores
Supermarkets
FOOD substitutes
Solution to hunger; synthetic food. Sci N L
87:68 Ja 30 '65
Synthetic food for tomorrow's billions. A. T.
McPherson. il Bul Atomic Sci 21:6-11 S '65
FOOD supply
Crisis ahead! C. P. Streeter. Farm J 89:33+
O '65
Food for peace? New Repub 154:5-6 Ja 1 '66
Next: the war on hunger. Farm J 89:126 O
'65
Population and food. Nat Parks Mag 39:22
F '65
Too little food and too much fertility; UN
demographers report in Population bulle-
tin. Christian Cent 82:1405 N 17 '65
Will we prevent mass starvation? G. Myrdal.
New Repub 152:14-15 Ap 24 '65
World choice: limit population or face famine.
il U S News 58:64-6 Je 14 '65
World's biggest problem: how experts see it.
il U S News 59:52-5 O 4 '65
    See also
Surplus products, Agricultural

New sources

Protein from petroleum. A. Champagnat. il
Sci Am 213:13-17 O '65

Asia

What exit for Asia? Pyrrho. Nat R 17:638-41
Jl 27 '65

India

Folly of others. il Time 86:22 D 31 '65
Threat of famine. il Time 86:36 D 3 '65
Too little too late? speed up of wheat ship-
ments to India. Newsweek 66:40 D 20 '65
    See also
Famines—India

Latin America

Less & less for more & more. Time 86:43 O
29 '65

Philippines

Are agricultural missions out of date? C. R.
McBride. Christian Cent 82:1606-7 D 29 '65

Underdeveloped areas

Atlantic report: plight of the underfed.
Atlan 216:8+ N '65

Vietnam (Republic)

Squaring the circle; rice shortage. il News-
week 65:54+ Je 14 '65
FOOD values
Calorie count of favorite holiday foods.
Good H 161:181 N '65
Let's talk about food; ed. by P. L. White.
See issues of Today's health

Lie down and gain; with chart showing ener-
gy equivalents of food calories expressed in
minutes of activity. Sci N L 87:183 Mr 20
'65
What is a calorie, anyhow? il Changing T 19:
18 Mr '65
    See also
Diet
Nutrition
FOOD waste disposers. See Refuse grinders
FOOD wrapping materials. See Wrapping ma-
terials
FOODSTUFFS. See Food
FOOT, Hugh, baron Caradon. See Caradon,
H. F.
FOOT, Michael
Harold Wilson: Labour's Lloyd George? Nation
201:518-20 D 27 '65
FOOT
Female foot. il Sci Digest 57:32-3 My '65

Care and hygiene

Foot care for the vacationer. il Good H 161:
144 Ag '65
Protect you; your feet: a perfect pedicure. il
Ladies Home J 82:51 Je '65

Diseases

    See also
Ringworm
FOOT-and-mouth disease
Charolais from France head your way. J. A.
Rohlf. Farm J 89:27 S '65
In Russia, new trouble down on the farm. il
U S News 60:14 Ja 17 '66
Rotational symmetry in foot-and-mouth dis-
ease virus and models. S. S. Breese, jr.
and others. bibliog il Science 150:1303-5
D 3 '65
FOOT racing. See Running
FOOTBALL
American war game; pro football. T. B.
Morgan. il Esquire 64:71-2+ O '65
Arkansas on top of the world; Razorbacks
beat Texas. D. Jenkins. il Sports Illus 23:
24-7+ O 25 '65
'Bama plows them under; Alabama vs. Au-
burn. J. Underwood. il Sports Illus 23:
36-9 D 6 '65
Best, east of Ashtabula; Dartmouth-
Princeton game will decide championship. il
Newsweek 66:66 N 22 '65
Boiled by the Boilermakers; Purdue victory
over Notre Dame. il Time 86:92+ O 1 '65
Bowls: fun with a purpose; photographs; with
account by D. Jenkins. Sports Illus 24:
26-35 Ja 3 '66
College football forecast. T. Cohane. il Look
29:84-6+ S 7 '65
College football 1965. D. Jenkins. il Sports
Illus 23:33-5 S 20 '65
College game is best. J. Underwood. il Sports
Illus 23:94-6+ S 20 '65
Colorado football's galloping disaster; mem-
oirs of a big-time coach. B. Davis. il Har-
per 231:50-3 O '65
Cutting it thin; Texas-Arkansas game. il
Newsweek 66:60 O 25 '65
Day of the underdog; New Year's day bowl
games. il Time 87:74-5 Ja 14 '66
Fearless tot from Possum Trot: S. D. Sabol
of Colorado college. T. C. Brody. il Sports
Illus 23:64+ N 22 '65
Football. See issues of New Yorker published
during football season
Football's Bowl week. il Sports Illus 24:32-41
Ja 10 '66
Football's week. M. Hyman. See issues of
Sports illustrated published during foot-
ball season
For the defense; Michigan state vs. Notre
Dame. il Newsweek 66:61 N 29 '65
Game nobody saw; Buffalo and San Diego.
Time 87:76-7 Ja 7 '66
Go, Massillon, go! cradle of football. C.
Davis. il Esquire 64:206-7+ D '65
Irish revenge; Notre Dame vs Southern Cali-
fornia. il Newsweek 66:63 N 1 '65
Leap for the roses; Purdue loses to Michigan
state. J. Underwood. il Sports Illus 23:16-19
N 1 '65
Little Bruins in a big, big bowl; UCLA team
in the Rose bowl. J. Underwood. il Sports
Illus 23:26-9 N 29 '65
Man for the next few seasons; F. Broyles
of Arkansas Razorbacks. D. Jenkins. il
Sports Illus 23:30-2+ N 8 '65
Nevertheless.., Arkansas and Texas game.
Time 86:93B O 22 '65
Nolo contendere; Pittsburgh, West Virginia
game. il Time 86:77-8 O 15 '65
Not just an old sweet song; Georgia's Bull-
dogs. J. Underwood. il Sports Illus 23:26-9
O 11 '65

FOOTBALL—*Continued*

Oh, that Griese kid stuff! Purdue defeats Notre Dame. D. Jenkins. il Sports Illus 23:30-1+ O 4 '65

One team, one vote; Associated press votes for Alabama. Newsweek 67:56 Ja 17 '66

Operation head start; Jefferson City high, football club. il Newsweek 66:84 S 20 '65

Out of their league; Princeton's success. il Time 86:83 N 5 '65

Punt? what's that? Notre Dame clobbers California. il Time 86:83 S 24 '65

Rhymes with uncanny; University of Nebraska. il Time 86:78+ N 19 '65

Semipro game; football in the rough. W. J. McKean. il Look 29:90-6 N 30 '65

Star is born, about forty minutes too late; Cleveland Browns victorious over College All-Stars in Chicago. D. Jenkins. il Sports Illus 23:47-9 Ag 16 '65

Texas teeners strike back; toughest high school football game, Texas over Pennsylvania. J. Underwood. il Sports Illus 23:20-3 Ag 23 '65

This Tiger is not in the tank; R. Landeck, of Princeton. J. Underwood. il Sports Illus 23:28-31 N 15 '65

To the big game and to the barricades; University of California at Berkeley a symbol of campus unrest. A. Wright. il Sports Illus 24:48-54 Ja 3 '66

Transistorball; electronic football. il Newsweek 66:64 N 8 '65

Two guys named Joe; Joe Bellino of the Patriots and Joe Namath of the Jets. il Newsweek 66:72 Ag 9 '65

See also
American football league
Football players
National football league
Rugby football
Soccer

Accidents and injuries

This stuff is to keep him from getting hurt, it doesn't always work. il Esquire 64:74-5 O '65

Year of agony and decline; ed. by T. Maule. Y. A. Tittle. il Sports Illus 23:42-4+ Ag 30 '65

Economic aspects

New road to riches; story of the boom in pro football. il U S News 60:66+ Ja 17 '66

Pro football kicks off to a profit. il Bsns W p32 Ag 28 '65

Rules

Fifteen dirtiest plays. il Esquire 64:72-3 O '65

FOOTBALL, Childrens

World of Pop Warner. il Newsweek 66:100+ D 6 '65

FOOTBALL accidents. See Football—Accidents and injuries

FOOTBALL clubs

Another good Joe for the AFL; rookie game of Boston Patriots vs New York Jets. J. Underwood. il Sports Illus 23:46-9 Ag 9 '65

Bears unpack 'em; Chicago Bears beat Green Bay Packers. E. Shrake. il Sports Illus 23:22-5 N 8 '65

Big man in Baltimore; Colts' J. Unitas. il Look 29:90+ S 21 '65

Big shrimp of pro football; head coach of New York football Giants. E. Asinof. il N Y Times Mag p52-3+ D 12 '65

Bills come storming in; Buffalo wins by defeating San Diego Chargers. E. Shrake. il Sports Illus 24:16-19 Ja 3 '66

Breaks of the game; Baltimore Colts. il Newsweek 67:49 Ja 3 '66

Burl Toler blows a whistle. il Ebony 21:142-7 D '65

Cards unscramble the East; Eastern division championship race of NFL. T. Maule. il Sports Illus 23:36-9 O 18 '65

Cool masterpiece; Green Bay Packers, National football league champions. T. Maule. il Sports Illus 24:14-19 Ja 10 '66

Doctor Ryan of the Browns; how smart is too smart? J. Olsen. il Sports Illus 23:64-70+ S 27 '65

Extravagant outing for a rare rookie; defeat of Giants by Chicago Bears. T. Maule. il Sports Illus 23:97-9 D 6 '65

49ers lose their cool and get hot; won their second straight at Kezar stadium. T. Maule. il Sports Illus 23:34-6+ O 11 '65

Furious fun below decks; Baltimore and Cleveland lead in the NFL. E. Shrake. il Sports Illus 23:40-1 N 22 '65

Ghostly massacre; Green Bay Packers solid form of 1961-62 take NFL Western division lead from Baltimore Colts. T. Maule. il Sports Illus 23:22-7 D 20 '65

Guessing game; merger negotiations stop, expansion talk follows. Sports Illus 22:17 Je 14 '65

Heroes without any headlines; Baltimore Colts to clinch Western division championship of NFL. T. Maule. il Sports Illus 23:30-2+ N 29 '65

In the AFL; another flag for San Diego; Chargers vs Buffalo Bills. E. Shrake. Sports Illus 23:26-7 D 20 '65

Jet start; New York Jets. il Newsweek 66:62 Jl 26 '65

King of crash, haul and hit; Tom Sestak of Buffalo Bills. E. Shrake. il Sports Illus 23:71-4 O 25 '65

Lining it out; Green Bay Packers vs Cleveland Browns. Newsweek 67:56-7 Ja 17 '66

Love affair with a loser; Denver Broncos. E. Shrake. il Sports Illus 22:26-7+ Nr 29 '65

Matt Snell; Jets' guided missile. G. Astor. il Look 29:87-90 O 5 '65

Mayor surrenders Atlanta; Braves and NFL franchise in Atlanta. J. Minter. il Sports Illus 23:14-17 Jl 12 '65

My life in pro football; ed. by T. Maule. Y. A. Tittle. il Sports Illus 23:27-32 Ag 16; 40-2+ Ag 23; 42-4+ Ag 30 '65

New National football league (?) D. Jenkins. il Sports Illus 22:24-7 My 31 '65

One for the cripples; National football league championship for Green Bay. il Time 87:74 Ja 14 '66

Outlaw and the want-to Cards. E. Shrake. il Sports Illus 23:30-2+ N 1 '65

Packers in a thriller; Green Bay edged Colts. E. Shrake. Sports Illus 23:76+ O 4 '65

Point of some return; Packers, winners of NFL playoff game from Baltimore Colts. T. Maule. il Sports Illus 24:10-13 Ja 3 '66

Pro football forecast. G. Astor. il Look 29:90-1 S 7 '65

Pro football 1965; young pros have taken over. il Sports Illus 23:40-2+ S 13 '65

Scouting reports; National football league; American football league. T. Maule; M. H. Sharnik; E. Shrake. il Sports Illus 23:45-79 S 13 '65

Scrambler; quarterback of the Minnesota Vikings. il Newsweek 66:61 S 13 '65

Show-biz Sonny and his quest for stars; New York Jets of the A.F.L. R. H. Boyle. il Sports Illus 23:66-72 Jl 19 '65

These are the champs? Michigan state. il Newsweek 66:58 D 20 '65

Those fearsome new Packers. T. Maule. il Sports Illus 23:16-21 S 27 '65

Thunder out at Oakland; Raiders could become AFL champions. E. Shrake. il Sports Illus 23:86-8+ N 15 '65

To be seen seeing the Redskins; Washington Redskins. E. Shrake. il Sports Illus 23:52-4+ O 4 '65

Tommy's terrible surprise; Baltimore Colts' quarterback. T. Matte. T. Maule. il Sports Illus 24:16-17 Ja 17 '66

Two for the seesaw in the inscrutable East; Cleveland Browns and St Louis Cardinals. T. Maule. il Sports Illus 23:60-2 N 8 '65

What every man wants. Newsweek 66:65 Jl 12 '65

FOOTBALL clubs, Professional. See Football clubs

FOOTBALL coaches. See Physical directors

FOOTBALL fans. See Sports fans

FOOTBALL gambling. See Gambling

FOOTBALL players

Arkansas on top of the world; Razorbacks beat Texas. D. Jenkins. il Sports Illus 23:24-7+ O 25 '65

Baby bulls; three rookies of National football league teams. il Newsweek 66:75 N 15 '65

Bad boy of the pros; J. D. Looney. M. Smith. il Life 59:85-6+ O 22 '65

Battle of the QBs. il Time 86:96 S 17 '65

Bears unpack 'em; Chicago Bears beat Green Bay Packers. E. Shrake. il Sports Illus 23:22-5 N 8 '65

But why me, coach? cutdown time. G. Plimpton. il Sports Illus 23:18-21 D 13 '65

C=(Frank Ryan)÷2; quarterback of Cleveland Browns, and mathematician. R. Kahn. il Sat Eve Post 238:92+ N 20 '65

College football 1965 scouting reports. D. Jenkins and others. il Sports Illus 23:43-6+ S 20 '65

Confrontations and contrasts at the summit; Browns vs Packers. Sports Illus 24:14-15 Ja 3 '66

Cool masterpiece; Green Bay Packers, National football league champions. T. Maule. il Sports Illus 24:14-19 Ja 10 '66

Detroit Lions' remarkable screwball; Alex Karras; excerpt from Paper lion. G. Plimpton. Harper 232:76-82 Ja '66

FORD, Henry, 1917-
Henry Ford II talks about car safety. por
Pop Sci 187:62-5+ D '65

about

Booming Detroit hits talk of lag. il por
Bsns W p28-9 Je 19 '65
Watching Fords go by; party at New York's
Delmonico hotel before wedding of A. Ford.
il por Newsweek 67:46 Ja 10 '66

FORD, Jesse Hill
Britches thief; story. Atlan 216:87-9 N '65
Messenger; story. Atlan 216:60-3 Jl '65

FORD, Maria Cristina Vettore
Cristina is the new Mrs Ford. il pors Life 58:
87-8 Mr 5 '65

FORD, Norman D.
Canada: islands galore. Travel 124:26-31 Ag
'65

FORD, Norman Robert
Tales of Norman Ford. F. Deford. il pors
Sports Illus 23:80-2+ O 4 '65

FORD, Tirey L.
Very model of model amateur. P. Stackpole.
U S Camera 28:22-3+ Ag '65

FORD, Walter B.
Electroplate or anodize your electronic projects. Pop Electr 22:55-9+ Je '65

FORD foundation
After the money came; Ford foundation
grant to Cornell college, Mount Vernon, Ia.
K. P. Buckley. Newsweek 66:66+ N 8 '65
Again, the Ford millennium; foundation
grant to American orchestras. B. Boretz.
Nation 201:368-70 N 15 '65
English with tears; grant to establish a na-
tional translation center at the University
of Texas. D. Dempsey. Sat R 48:38+ F 13
'65
Ford foundation aids Pittsburgh schools. Sr
Schol 86:1T-2T F 11 '65
Ford foundation grants $750,000 to establish
translation center; University of Texas,
Austin. Library J 90:600 F 1 '65
Ford foundation looks for new top command.
il Bsns W p30-1 O 23 '65
Ford in the future; McGeorge Bundy suc-
ceeds Heald. Newsweek 67:60 Ja 17 '66
Ford in their future; grants to U.S. or-
chestras. Time 86:71 O 29 '65
Gains for birth control; Ford foundation
grants to Columbia-Presbyterian medical
center and Population council; foreign aid
recommendations. Newsweek 66:94 D 13 '65
Giving an upbeat to orchestra finances. Bsns
W p31 O 23 '65
Good-by Mr Chips. Newsweek 66:86 Jl 26
'65
Investment in the Congo; National school of
law and administration. America 112:817
Je 5 '65
Open letter to the Ford foundation. P. M
Stern. Harper 232:83-7 Ja '66

FORD motor company
At Ford motor, brakes and power get a boost.
J. P. Norbye. il Pop Sci 187:66-70 O '65
Carnegie Hall on wheels; dashboard stereo-
tape player in 1966 models. Time 85:98+ Ap
30 '65
Ford lifts lid on secret; numerical control in
auto production. il Bsns W p 140+ Ja 15 '66
Ford's autobahn to success; Taunus cars
capture 19.6 per cent of the German mar-
ket. il Time 85:97 My 7 '65
Ford's citizenship program. L. L. L. Golden.
Sat R 48:77 F 13 '65
Ford's road ahead. J. B. Weiner. il Duns R
86:28-31+ Ag '65
Henry Ford II talks about car safety; re-
search at Automotive safety center. H.
Ford, 2d. il Pop Sci 187:62-5+ D '65
It's time we took on Mr Big; D. Frey of
Ford div. hopes to break Chevrolet's hold
on first place. il Bsns W p 108-11 Ag 7 '65
Many voices of Ford motor co. Consumer
Rep 30:473-4 O '65

Aeronutronic division

Aeronutronic headed for new high. W. E.
Wilks. Miss & Roc 17:33+ O 4 '65

**FORD motor company, limited, Dagenham,
England**
Americanization of Dagenham; wildcatting
started up again. Time 86:98+ D 3 '65

FORD museum. See Henry Ford museum and
Greenfield Village, Dearborn, Mich.

FORDE, Florrie
Florrie Forde. A. Debus. por Hobbies 70:36
Jl '65

FORECASTS
American higher education in 1980. R. Gross.
Sch & Soc 93:484-5 D 11 '65
Civilization in 2100 A.D. P. McBroom. il (p289)
Sci N L 88:298-9 N 6 '65

Future as a way of life. A. Toffler. il Horizon
7:108-15 Sum '65
Higher education and 1984; adaptation of
address, November 2, 1964. L. Wilson.
Sch & Soc 93:343-6 O 2 '65
Jeane Dixon: psychic star of the year. il
D. Cohen. Nation 201:470-3 D 13 '65
Life in 1990; reprint. I. Asimov. Sci Digest
58:63-70 Ag '65
Look ahead ten years. Changing T 19:6 S '65
Newsgram. See issues of U.S. news & World
report
1966: the year of the big if. il Newsweek 67:
26+ Ja 10 '66
Science forecast for 1966. W. Davis. Sci N L
88:403 D 25 '65
Step to man; excerpt. J. R. Platt. Science
149:607-13 Ag 6 '65
World in 1984, ed. by N. Calder. Review
New Repub 153:28-9 Jl 10 '65. E. T. Chase
See also
Business forecasting
Political forecasts
Prophecies
Weather forecasts

FORECASTS (economics)
Ahead of schedule. Fortune 71:29-30 F '65
As top economists see the outlook for money.
il U S News 59:45-6 D 20 '65
Common market turns to new mode of living.
il Bsns W p30-1 Ja 30 '65
Five more boom years ahead; interview. A.
F. Brimmer. il Nations Bsns 53:60-2+ Je '65
Forecaster for the forecasters; D. W. Lusher.
il Bsns W p 158+ Ap 3 '65
Forecasters look again, upward; opinion of
business economists. il Bsns W p58+ O 9
'65
From now to 1980; amazing growth; prediction
by McGraw-Hill economics dept. il Bsns W
p56-8+ O 16 '65
Get ready for the merely good. Fortune 72:
99-100 Jl '65
Hitting a faster beat. il Bsns W p29-30 N
27 '65
How business will be a year from now. Na-
tions Bsns 53:66-9 Jl '65
It can't be that good; forecasts for 1966.
Bsns W p 164 D 4 '65
New era, Fortune's forecast through 1966. il
Fortune 72:27-8+ Jl '65
New times. il Fortune 71:27-8 My '65
New way to prosper; with editorial comment.
il Bsns W p23-4, 156 My 6 '65
1965: better than hoped; with editorial com-
ment. il Bsns W p33-4, 180 Mr 20 '65
Outlook for 1966; address, September 23, 1965.
P. W. McCracken. Vital Speeches 32:15-18
O 15 '65
Part-war economy; Fortune's forecast for
next eighteen months. il Fortune 73:31-2+
Ja '66
Rolling into $700-billion economy. il Bsns W
p23-4 Ag 14 '65
Steadier course ahead. il Bsns W p23-4
My 22 '65
Steaming ahead with no letdown. il Bsns W
p23-4 S 11 '65
Twenty-five year look back: twenty-five year
forward projection; address, January 5, 1965.
L. Cherne. Vital Speeches 31:349-52 Mr 15
'65
Washington business outlook. See issues of
Nation's business
See also
Business forecasting

FOREIGN aid. See Economic assistance
FOREIGN automobiles. See Automobiles, For-
eign
FOREIGN bodies (surgery)
People who swallow things. il Sci Digest 58:
31-2 N '65
See also
Ear—Foreign bodies
FOREIGN born. See Immigrants in the United
States
FOREIGN cookery. See Cookery, International
FOREIGN expansion of business. See Business
—Foreign expansion
FOREIGN investments. See Investments, For-
eign
FOREIGN languages. See Languages, Modern
FOREIGN loans. See Loans, Foreign
FOREIGN news
See also
Newspapers—Foreign news
FOREIGN opinion of the United States. See
United States—Foreign opinion
FOREIGN relations. See International rela-
tions; *also* subhead Foreign relations under
names of countries, e.g. United States—
Foreign relations
FOREIGN scholarships, Board of. See United
States—State, Department of—Foreign
scholarships; Board of

FOREIGN service (United States) See United States—Foreign service

FOREIGN students in Germany
Dropouts and kickouts: expulsion from Harvard, followed by undergraduate years in Germany from 1931 through 1932. F. Russell. Nat R 17:1166-7 D 14 '65

FOREIGN students in Great Britain
Clean, well-lighted place; West African students in London libraries; reprint. J. Wakeman. Library J 90:4912-12 N 15 '65

FOREIGN students in India
India is centuries away; Wisconsin undergraduate year in India; a student recalls. M. C. Vander Wal. il Sat R 48:51-2+ Ag 21 '65

FOREIGN students in Israel
Texas minister's Israeli honeymoon. E. Nadel. il Look 29:M10+ Je 15 '65

FOREIGN students in Russia
Africans don't go to Russia to be brainwashed. N. Nyangira. il N Y Times Mag p52+ My 16 '65
Old college try; Lumumba university. Newsweek 65:33-4 Je 28 '65

FOREIGN students in the United States
College diplomats at work; People-to-people university program. J. Poling. Read Digest 86:197-8+ My '65
Education: U.S. institutions prepare African students for development tasks at home. L. J. Carter. Science 149:1213-15 S 10 '65
Face of the enemy: Japanese student, five years old in World war II. M. Newman. New Yorker 41:132-7 My 22 '65
Showing foreigners the way; postgraduate year of practical experience in U.S. industry for visiting business and engineering students. Bsns W p 116 F 6 '65
Successful foreign aid in education; case of Anees Ahmed from Pakistan. W. R. Shunk. Sch & Soc 93:437-8 N 13 '65
Summer in the USA: bumming with a purpose; Ambassadors for friendship. J. Engh. il Mlle 60:132-3+ F '65
When foreign-student scholarships are misused. C. Haussamen. il Sat R 48:48-50+ Ag 21 '65
Year of seven new words; Rimini, Italy to Nebraska, via American field service scholarship. M. Cicioni. il Seventeen 24:126-7+ O '65

Orientation

How many lions? U.S. orientation course. Newsweek 66:51 S 6 '65

FOREIGN subsidiaries. See Corporations—Foreign subsidiaries

FOREIGN trade. See United States—Commerce

FOREIGN visitors in Africa
Words to wise tourists: Americans abroad. R. Kirk. Nat R 17:632 Jl 27 '65

FOREIGN visitors in China
Jilted lover; J. Roy. il Newsweek 66:58+ O 18 '65

FOREIGN visitors in Ecuador
Intercontinental handshake; Johnson City, Tenn. and Guaranda, Ecuador. il Am City 80:156+ Je '65

FOREIGN visitors in England
Kathy's wild weekend; I won a contest. and a date with the Dave Clark five! K. Sheron. il Seventeen 24:136-7 N '65

Anecdotes, facetiae, satire, etc.

No autographs, please, I'm invisible; American TV personality's last day in London. S. L. Perelman. New Yorker 41:46-9 S 18 '65

FOREIGN visitors in Europe
Do's and don'ts in Europe. H. Colijn. Seventeen 24:93 My '65
Gibson girl romance. A. W. Hinckley. il Am Heritage 17:106-11 D '65
Go! go! go! what makes hosteling fun in Europe. K. Goff. il Seventeen 24:80-1+ Je '65
My V.I.P. trip. D. Considine. il Seventeen 24:114-15+ F '65
Teen travel talk; class project: European holiday for Wolcott high school, Conn. il Seventeen 24:70 O '65
Words to wise tourists: Americans abroad. R. Kirk. Nat R 17:632 Jl 27 '65

FOREIGN visitors in France
French smile. at Americans! campaign of welcome and amiability. T. Foote. il N Y Times Mag p24-6+ Je 20 '65

FOREIGN visitors in Greece
Adlai, Adlai, what was the fifth word? E. De Lanux. New Yorker 41:176+ S 25 '65

FOREIGN visitors in India
Up front in Kashmir. E. Taylor. il Reporter 33:36-9 O 21 '65

FOREIGN visitors in Italy
Guided tour of tourists in Rome. I. Shenker. il N Y Times Mag p24-5+ Jl 11 '65

FOREIGN visitors in Japan
Letter from Tokyo. M. Evans. Nation 201:203-4 O 4 '65

FOREIGN visitors in Russia
Instant ambassador; a chance to explain America to some Russians. L. Wainwright. Life 58:25 Mr 5 '65
Weekend in Moscow; Le tout-Paris; with report by E. Peer. il Newsweek 65:55-6 My 10 '65

FOREIGN visitors in the United States
Airlift; Italian artists fly to New York with works to benefit two hospitals. New Yorker 41:38-9 Mr 3 '65
Europeans get eyeful of U.S. space work; delegates to Eurospace conference amazed by U.S. plants. il Bsns W p 134+ My 15 '65
Farewell to America. J. M. Cameron. Commonweal 82:617-18 S 3 '65
How ya gonna keep 'em down in Upper Volta after they've met Lloyd Hand? E. Wittenberg. Esquire 64:24+ D '65
Innocents at home; visit by Gorky and Mme Andreyeva. J. Swan. il Am Heritage 16:58-61+ F '65
Intercontinental handshake; Johnson City, Tenn. and Guaranda, Ecuador. il Am City 80:156+ Je '65
Letter from Paris; French tourists to America. Genêt. New Yorker 41:116-17 Ag 21 '65
Travels among the Americans; experiences of a visiting English student. D. Widgery. Sat R 49:55-6 Ja 15 '66
Two men from Moscow pay a call; Russian journalists A. N. Druzhinin and S. Kondrashov. R. Gugger. il N Y Times Mag p34-5+ F 14 '65
Use of Mexican border-crossing cards extended; White House statement, August 10, 1965. Dept State Bul 53:368-9 Ag 30 '65
Visit to Mount Vernon; excerpts from Travels through America; tr. and ed. by M. J. E. Budka. J. U. Niemcewicz. il Am Heritage 16:64-71 F '65
Visitor from Yugoslavia: Dr H. Neubauer. J. Anderson. Dance Mag 39:18-20 Jl '65
When children discover America; French family's reactions to U.S. visit. H. Lee. il McCalls 92:76-9 Ag '65

FOREIGN visitors in Vietnam (Democratic Republic)
In Hanoi a show of fists by Ho & co; C. Koch's tour. il Life 59:34-5 O 1 '65
Three characters in search of an offer; U.S. leftists in Hanoi. Newsweek 67:18 Ja 10 '66

FOREIGN visitors in Vietnam (Republic)
Senior scholastic interview: folk singing ambassadors; ed. by R. Hemming. S. Addiss; B. Crofut. il Sr Schol 86:20 Mr 11 '65

FORELL, George W.
Christian motivation for political concern; address, February 23, 1965. Vital Speeches 31:368-72 Ap 1 '65

FOREMEN
Foreman: master and victim of double talk; reprint from an issue of 1945. F. J. Roethlisberger. bibliog f il Harvard Bsns R 43:22-6+ S '65

FORENSIC psychiatry
Crime needs psychiatry; community mental health centers as an alternative to prison isolation. E. Lederer. Sci N L 87:147 Mr 6 '65

FORER, Bernard
War on words. Sat R 48:27 Ap 3 '65

FOREST conservation
Night comes to Admiralty! Tongass national forest, Admiralty Island, Alaska. R. Starnes. il Field & S 70:18-22+ Ag '65
Preserving vegetation in parks and wilderness. E. C. Stone. bibliog il Science 150:1261-7 D 3 '65
See also
Forest fire protection

FOREST fire prevention signs. See Road signs

FOREST fire protection
Greenkeepers; Keep America green program. J. Stevens. il Am For 71:20-1+ D '65
See also
United States—Forest service

FOREST fires
See also
Arson

FOREST HILLS, N.Y. See Queens, N.Y.

FOREST management
Manipulating forests for water; watershed research. K. G. Reinhart and H. W. Lull. il Am For 71:35-7+ N '65

FOREST products laboratory. See United States—Forest products laboratory

FOREST rangers. See United States—Forest service

FOREST reserves. See National forests

FOREST service (United States) See United States—Forest service

FORESTERS
So you want to be a forester? C. E. Randall. il Am For 71:18-34 S '65
What do employers want? il Am For 71:35-7+ S '65

FORESTRY research
See also
United States—Forest products laboratory
Wood research

FORESTRY schools and education
So you want to be a forester? with list of schools. C. E. Randall. il Am For 71:26-9 S '65

FORESTS, National. See National forests

FORESTS, State
Shape of a forest; Savage River State forest, Maryland. P. M. Tilden. Nat Parks Mag 39:2 Ap '65

FORESTS and forestry

Study and teaching
Ann Webb, girl forester. W. B. Morse. il Am For 71:28-9+ Ap '65
Blueprint for a school forest; Yellow Springs school forest, Ohio. J. P. Chu. il Am For 71:34-9+ F '65

China (People's Republic)
Forestry in red China: modern-day Marco Polo visits China. S. D. Richardson. il Am For 71:6-15+ F '65

Dominican Republic
From firefighting to revolution in three days. M. S. Lowden. il Am For 71:16-19+ Ag '65

Ecuador
Peace corps forestry: there's a forest in your future! F. Friedman. il Am For 71:20-1+ F '65

France
France halts forest insects; using biological controls. R. Maury. il Audubon Mag 67:384-5 N '65

Missouri
Visit to a primeval woods. J. P. Jackson. il Am For 71:36-7+ Ag '65

Nebraska
Forest that men made; Nebraska national forest. J. C. Hunt. il Am For 71:18-21+ N: 32-5+ D '65

Spain
Spain plants the plain. C. E. Randall. il Am For 71:24-7+ Je '65

Underdeveloped areas
Forests have vital role in developing countries. Sci N L 88:280 O 30 '65

United States
Forestry in the federal budget, fiscal year ending June 30, 1966. il Am For 71:8 Mr '65
Forests resources report (cont) Am For 71:47 Mr '65
Sounding board. Am For 71:30-1 Ap; 70 My; 34-5 Je; 36-7+ Jl; 2-3 Ag '65
Washington lookout. A. G. Hall. See issues of American forests
See also
Forest conservation
National forests
United States—Forest service

FORGASH, Morris
One big package for the shippers. por Bsns W p74+ S 4 '65

FORGERIES, Art. See Forgery of works of art

FORGERY
See also
Counterfeits and counterfeiting

FORGERY of works of art
Artists speak; how to protect the public. Time 87:59 Ja 7 '66
Chemical standards may authenticate art works. Sci N L 88:296 N 6 '65
Fakes, forgeries, and duty dodgers in English silver; excerpts from Old English silver. J. Banister. Antiques 88:330-2 S '65
Fake's progress. Newsweek 66:90 N 29 '65
Great Rodin, his flagrant faker; with report by D. Seiberling. il Life 58:64-71 Je 4 '65
Lively art of fakery. K. Kuh. Sat R 48:46 Je 26 '65
Still life with pasta; forging of modern Italian masters. il Newsweek 65:42 Je 28 '65

FORGET-me-nots
Your state flower: forget-me-not, Alaska. L. Krelove. Flower Grower 52:45 Ag '65

FORGETTING. See Memory

FORGING
See also
Blacksmiths

FORKER, Barbara
How much leisure can you stand? Suc Farm 63:89+ My '65

FORM in architecture. See Architecture—Philosophy

FORMAAD, William
Help for the child with impaired hearing. NEA J 54:45-6 D '65

FORMAN, Ella Q. See Stevenson, M. jt. auth.

FORMAN, Fred. See Nawracaj, E. jt. auth.

FORMOSA. See Taiwan

FORMS and blanks, Business. See Business—Forms, blanks, etc.

FORNEY, James
Big comeback of the big camera. il Pop Phot 57:62-5+ S '65
Craflex XL: camera with 1,000 faces. il Pop Phot 56:102-3+ Je '65
220: twice as many shots per roll. Pop Phot 56:87-8+ F '65

FORRESTER, Maureen
On records: M. Forrester. Opera N 29:34 F 20 '65

FORSBERG, Ray, and Dietz, George
Cold figures promote warm water. por Am City 80:120-1 Je '65

FORSCHER, Bernard K.
Rules for referees. Science 150:319-21 O 15 '65

FORSCHER, Martin B.
Are lower priced cameras equal to high priced cameras in quality? interview, ed. by M. A. Matzkin. Mod Phot 29:72-5+ My '65

about
Having a problem focusing on your SLR ground glass? M. A. Matzkin. il Mod Phot 29:20+ Mr '65

FORSDALE, Joan Rosengren, and Litten, L.
They start young with film; reprint. Pop Phot 58:103+ Ja '66

FORSYTH, Bryan
Song of the mountains. Liv Wildn 29:27 Spr '65

FORSYTH, John F.
And then there was one. Flying 78:82 Ja '66

FORSYTH, Peter Taylor
Theology of P. T. Forsyth, by J. H. Rodgers. Review
Christian Cent 82:1230+ O 6 '65. D. O. Woodyard

FORT LAUDERDALE, Fla.
Microfilm your records and save. F. H. Marks. Am City 80:152+ Je '65

FORT RILEY, Kan. See Military training camps

FORT ROSS, Calif.
Fort Ross; remnant of czarist Russia's dream of American empire. M. Castagna. il Nat Parks Mag 40:15 Ja '66

FORT WORTH, Tex.
Fewer fire stations serve better. J. L. Brownlee. il Am City 80:107-9 D '65

City planning
Upgrading downtown. il Arch Rec 137:176-8 Je '65

FORT WORTH opera association
Fort Worth, Houston. J. Rosenfield; A. Holmes. Opera N 30:32 Ja 15 '66
State of Texas. J. Rosenfield. il Opera N 30:24 S 25 '65

FORTAS, Abe
Abe, help! LBJ. C. B. Seib and A. L. Otten. il pors Esquire 63:86-8+ Je '65
Fortas appointment. R. Moley. Newsweek 66:84 Ag 16 '65
Fortas to the Court. New Repub 153:7-8 Ag 21 '65
Lawyer & friend. il por Time 86:24 Ag 6 '65
Let not the right hand. Nat R 17:676+ Ag 10 '65
Liberal replaces a liberal. por Bsns W p 19 Jl 31 '65
Mr Justice Fortas; President's choice for Supreme court. por Newsweek 66:25+ Ag 9 '65
New face on Supreme court. por Sr Schol 87:17 O 7 '65
New liberal on the High court, what Abe Fortas believes. por U S News 59:14 Ag 9 '65
Questions & answers; two-hour hearing before Senate judiciary committee. por Time 86:17B Ag 13 '65
Tough lawyer goes to the Court. A. Lewis. por N Y Times Mag p 11+ Ag 8 '65

FORTSON, Warren
Americus the beautiful. il por Newsweek 66:30 S 20 '65

FORTUNE (periodical)
First thirty-five years of Fortune; with editorial comment. H. R. Luce. il Fortune 71:115-16, 136-7+ F '65

FORTY eight (periodical)
Magazine of the year. C. W. Morton. il Atlan 215:62-3 F '65

FORTY-hour week. See Hours of labor

49ERS (football club) See Football clubs

FORTY seven (periodical) See Forty eight (periodical)

FORUMS (discussion and debate)
Are student moral values slipping? round-table discussion from 1965 student burgesses at Williamsburg. il Sr Schol 86:14-16 Ap 29 '65
See also
Center for the study of democratic institutions, Santa Barbara, Calif.
Teach-ins

La FORZA del destino; opera. See Verdi, G.

FORZANO, Giovacchino
Don't call me maestro; interview, ed. by B. Fischer-Williams. por Opera N 30:6-7 Ja 1 '66

FOSBURGH, James Whitney
No business suit and lots of color; concerning portrait of J. F. Kennedy. G. P. Hunt. por Life 59:3 N 5 '65

FOSCA, François
Liotard: the painter who drew the truth from the mythic East. Vogue 145:112-15+ Ap 15 '65

FOSDICK, Raymond B.
White Island. Atlan 216:110-12+ O '65

FOSHAY, Arthur W.
Scholastic teacher interview: ed. by H. Langer. por Sr Schol 86:6T-9T F 18 '65

FOSS, Lukas
Foss. New Yorker 40:22-4 Ja 30 '65

FOSSIL algae. See Algae, Fossil

FOSSIL bones. See Paleontology

FOSSIL brachiopods. See Brachiopods, Fossil

FOSSIL invertebrates. See Invertebrates, Fossil

FOSSIL microorganisms. See Micropaleontology

FOSSIL trees. See Trees, Fossil

FOSTER, Charles R. See Romoser, G. K. jt. auth.

FOSTER, Clyde
Rocket age comes to tiny Triana. H. Bims. il pors Ebony 20:106-8+ Mr '65

FOSTER, Constance
How marriage counseling helps children. Parents Mag 40:42-3+ My '65

FOSTER, Donald L.
Unique gospel in Utah. Christian Cent 82: 890-2 Jl 14 '65

FOSTER, Eugene A.
Hemolysin production in the development of staphylococcal lesions. bibliog Science 149: 1395-6 S 17 '65

FOSTER, Frances
Reading with John. Sat R 48:40-2 My 15 '65

FOSTER, G. W. Jr
Title VI: southern education faces the facts. Sat R 48:60-1+ Mr 20 '65

FOSTER, Gertrude B.
Herbs: in your garden. Horticulture 43:46+ F '65

FOSTER, Irene
Heart of the family; story. Good H 162:62-8 Ja '66

FOSTER, John
England's Peak Park. Am For 71:40-3 Ag '65

FOSTER, Sir John
Speedier justice in Britain: we reformed our laws in the 19th century and U.S. didn't; interview. por U S News 58:42-3 Mr 22 '65

FOSTER, John Stuart, 1922-
DOD: Johnson appoints Foster, chief of weapons laboratory, to head Pentagon research unit. E. Langer. por Science 150: 39-40 O 1 '65
Reorganized DDR&E to put more emphasis on systems engineering. Aviation W 83:33 S 20 '65

FOSTER, Martha Standing
Hosanna! I said; story. Redbook 125:44-5 Je '65

FOSTER, Mulford B.
Bromeliads. Horticulture 43:24-5+ Je '65

FOSTER, Paul
Balls. Criticism
Newsweek il por 65:93 F 22 '65

FOSTER, Stephen Collins
Old Kentucky home. R. H. Woodward. il Hobbies 70:120 My '65

FOSTER, T. J.
How clean is clean? reprint. Sci Digest 57: 56-60 F '65

FOSTER, William C.
Arms control, foundation stone in the ramparts we watch; address, March 31, 1965. Dept State Bul 52:659-64 My 3 '65
Conference of eighteen-nation disarmament committee reconvenes at Geneva; statement, July 27, 1965. Dept State Bul 53:333-7 Ag 23 '65
Eighteen-nation disarmament committee considers U.S. draft treaty to prevent spread of nuclear weapons; statements, August 17 and August 31, 1965. Dept State Bul 53:467-73 S 20 '65
New directions in arms control and disarmament. For Affairs 43:587-601 Jl '65
President Johnson asks four-year extension for ACDA authorization; letter to the President, January 13, 1965. Dept State Bul 52: 145-6 F 1 '65
Roadblock to arms control and disarmament negotiations; address, June 4, 1965. Dept State Bul 53:77-84 Jl 12 '65
U.N. calls for renewed efforts on nonproliferation treaty; statements, October 18, 27 and November 8, 1965. Dept State Bul 53: 873-84 N 29 '65
U.S. agrees to discuss holding of world disarmament conference; statement, November 18, 1965. Dept State Bul 53:1029-32 D 27 '65
United States arms control and disarmament agency; introduction to report. Dept State Bul 52:308-10 Mr 1 '65

FOSTER, William Eaton
Providence pioneer: William E. Foster. J. L. Wheeler. il por Wilson Lib Bul 40:275-8 N '65

FOSTER CITY, Calif.
Wrested from the bay. L. Ham. il Am City 80:102-3 Ag '65

FOSTER home care
Foster care. M. J. E. Senn. McCalls 92:66+ Mr '65
Happy homes for foster children; Women's Christian alliance. il Ebony 20:29-32+ Ap '65

FOSTER Wheeler corporation
Foster Wheeler mends its house from within. il Bsns W p 116-18+ D 18 '65

FOSTORIA, Ohio
Slurry waterproofs 'em all; streets. H. Bradner. il Am City 80:86-8 Jl '65

FOTOVAL enlarging computer. See Photography—Apparatus and supplies

FOULK, Richard N.
New benefits under ALA group insurance. ALA Bul 59:110-11 F '65

FOUND art. See Found objects

FOUND objects
Object: lost and found. V. D'Amico. il Craft Horiz 25:26-7 S '65
Weathered treasures. L. Burgess. il Flower Grower 52:26 Ag '65

FOUNDATION garments
Boom in bustenhalter; Munich's Triumph international, largest manufacturer of foundation garments in Europe. il Time 86:84 Jl 23 '65
Facts of the matter; new lightweight underwear. il Time 85:64 Mr 19 '65
Panty-girdle problem; effect on circulation. il Time 85:46 F 12 '65
See also
Brassieres

FOUNDATION of America (organization)
Want to start something? Am For 71:56 N '65

FOUNDATIONS
Why a complete soil analysis is important; foundation design. E. C. Nordquist. Arch Rec 137:215-16 Je '65
See also
Bridges—Foundations and piers

FOUNDATIONS, Charitable and educational
Foundations: a welfare state for writers? D. Dempsey. Harper 231:165-71 O '65
Foundations for progress. il Newsweek 65: 105-6 Ap 12 '65
Foundations, the new pioneers. J. G. Harrar. Read Digest 87:100-1 O '65
New music, big money; destructive potential. B. Boretz. Nation 201:47-8 Jl 19 '65
Private initiative for the public good. J. W. Gardner. Read Digest 87:98-102 O '65
Repairing cracks in foundations; Treasury report on private tax-exempt groups. Bsns W p34 F 13 '65
See also names of foundations. e.g. Rockefeller foundation

Taxation
New rules urged for foundations. U S News 58:96-7 F 22 '65

FOUNDRY furnaces. See Furnaces, Foundry

FOUNDRY practice
  See also
Continuous casting
Lost wax process
Steel castings
FOUNTAIN, Lawrence H.
  FDA: scientific, medical groups support
  agency in dispute with Fountain over ac-
  cess to drug data. E. Langer. Science 149:
  731-4 Ag 13 '65
FOUNTAIN pens
  Ball-point pens. il Consumer Bul 48:30-4 S
  '65
FOUNTAINS
  Cooling waterfall or fountain. J. Brimer. il
  Pop Sci 186:142-4+ My '65
  Making a big splash. il Newsweek 66:49 Ag
  16 '65
  Rehabilitating a century-old fountain; Pough-
  keepsie, N.Y. R. E. Lapar. il Am City 80:
  20 Ag '65
FOUR academic fantasies; story. See Perrin,
  N.
FOUR-day week. See Hours of labor
4-H clubs
  Industry enrolls in 4-H clubs. il Bsns W p36
  D 4 '65
  Six 4-H club members win National health
  awards. il Todays Health 43:90 Mr '65
  To farm homemakers with love; Cloverleaf
  citation. il Farm J 89:100 O '65
FOUR saints in three acts; opera. See Thom-
  son, V.
FOUR sides of one story; story. See Updike, J.
FOUR wheel drive automobiles. See Automo-
  biles—Four wheel drive
FOURTH committee of the General assembly.
  See United Nations—Trusteeship committee
FOWLER, Henry Hamill
  Balance-of-payments program and the Con-
  gress; Cabinet report, May 13, 1965. Dept
  State Bul 52:963-4 Je 14 '65
  Improving the world's monetary system;
  statement, September 24, 1965. Dept State
  Bul 53:619-24 O 18 '65
  International monetary problems; address,
  July 10, 1965. Vital Speeches 31:646-9 Ag 15
  '65
  More federal controls? what Fowler sees
  ahead; excerpts from address, November
  19, 1965. por U S News 59:20 D 6 '65
  New steps to improve international monetary
  arrangements; address, July 10, 1965. Dept
  State Bul 53:209-14 Ag 2 '65
  Secretary Fowler reports on monetary talks
  in Europe; report, September 13, 1965. Dept
  State Bul 53:553-4 O 4 '65

            about
  Fowler's odyssey. Newsweek 66:68 S 13 '65
  Hearing the Europeans. il por Time 86:82 S 3
  '65
  Markets feel the pressure. por Bsns W p27-8
  O 9 '65
  Mr Dollar goes abroad. il por Time 86:84-
  84B+ S 10 '65
  Old hand for treasury. il por Time 85:23 Mr
  26 '65
  People of the week. por U S News 58:16 Mr
  29 '65
  Right-hand man. por Newsweek 65:25-6 Mr 29
  '65
  Treasury gets its man; Secretary of the
  Treasury. por Bsns W p 152-4 Mr 27 '65
  U.S. tries to sell a new system for world's
  money. por U S News 59:103-4 S 13 '65
FOWLER, John T.
  Turnabout for trout. Outdoor Life 136:58-9+
  S '65
FOWLER'S dictionary of modern English usage.
  See English language
FOWLIE, Wallace
  Poetry of Ben Belitt. Poetry 105:324-5 F '65
FOX, Charles K.
  Trouting with heart and mind. Esquire 63:
  112-14 Je '65
FOX, Charles P.
  Birds aren't fussy. il Flower Grower 52:47
  Ap '65
FOX, Denis L. and Crozier, G. F.
  Absence or singular specificity of carotenoids
  in some lower fishes. bibliog Science 150:
  771-3 N 5 '65
  —and Kuchnow, K. P.
  Reversible, light-screening pigment of elas-
  mobranch eyes: chemical identity with
  melanin. bibliog Science 150:612-14 O 29 '65
FOX, Edward S.
  What is a scene? Writer 78:17-29 O '65
FOX, John Michael
  Fox of United fruit. por Fortune 71:39 My '65
FOX, Josephine
  Day is mine, the land is mine. Dance Mag
  39:50-3 Mr '65

FOX, Marvin
  Kedushah and kavod. Commentary 40:84+
  Jl '65
FOX, Paul Jeffrey, and Heezen, B. C.
  Sands of the Mid-Atlantic Ridge. bibliog Sci-
  ence 149:1367-70 S 17 '65
FOX, Rodney
  Attacked by a killer shark! Read Digest 87:
  49-54 Ag '65
FOX, Stephen S. and O'Brien, J. H.
  Duplication of evoked potential waveform by
  curve of probability of firing of a single
  cell. bibliog Science 147:888-90 F 19 '65
FOX, William Price, Jr
  Conversation with Satchel Paige. Holiday
  38:18+ Ag '65
  Just a friendly little game; story. Sat Eve
  Post 238:54-6 O 23 '65
FOX hunting
  Foxes aren't killed by accident. J. O. Cartier.
  il Outdoor Life 137:52-3+ Ja '66
  Operation foil-a-fox-hunt; Britain's Hunt
  saboteurs association. J. Hicks. il Life
  58:87-8+ Ap 2 '65
FOXER; story. See Cleeve, B.
FOXES
  Airport guest. J. Stuart. Am For 71:4+ Jl '65
FOXGLOVES
  For elegance, foxgloves. D. E. Rose. il Flower
  Grower 52:26-7 My '65
  Foxgloves offer color in the shade. il Sunset
  135:280 O '65
  William Withering and the purple foxglove.
  J. W. Estes and P. D. White. il Sci Am
  212:110-16+ Je '65
FOXHALL, William B.
  How architects practice interior design (cont)
  Arch Rec 137:105+ Ap '65
FOXHOVEN, Omer V.
  Putting the new liturgy to work. America
  113:204-6 Ag 28 '65
FOYERS. See Halls
FOYT, Anthony Joseph, 1935?-
  Champion: hard driver in business, too. il por
  Bsns W p 148 My 22 '65
  Masked marvel of the speedway. B. Ottum.
  il por Sports Illus 22:26-9 My 24 '65
FRACTIONATION. See Isotope separation
FRACTURES
  They're learning new things about broken
  bones. Changing T 19:12 F '65
FRAENKEL, G. and others
  Properties of bursicon: an insect protein
  hormone that controls cuticular tanning.
  bibliog Science 151:91-3 Ja 7 '66
FRAGILE heaven; story. See McKinley, G.
FRAGRANT gardens. See Gardens, Fragrant
FRAIBERG, Selma H.
  American reading problem. bibliog f Com-
  mentary 39:56-65 Je '65
  Friendships are for growing. Parents Mag 40:
  66-8+ D '65
  Thirteen's not a menace. Parents Mag 40:
  52-3+ F '65
FRAKES, Margaret
  Guidelines to peace. Christian Cent 82:294-6
  Mr 10 '65
  United church of Christ general synod:
  ministries approved. Christian Cent 82:
  919-20+ Jl 21 '65
FRALEIGH, Arnold
  How to fail in negotiations without really
  trying. New Repub 154:9 Ja 1 '66
FRAMES for collectors (firm)
  Carving more profits out of antique frames;
  Mario Broeders. il Bsns W p 190-1 O 9 '65
FRAMING (buildings)
  Detailing a precast panel facade. M. Wolff. il
  Arch Rec 137:191-3 Mr '65
  Three solutions in steel framing for light-
  weight, economical construction. il Arch
  Rec 137:188-90 Mr '65
FRANCE
  France transformed: seven years of de
  Gaulle. H. Peyre. il N Y Times Mag p50-1+
  N 14 '65
  Grand subject. H. de Turenne. N Y Times
  Mag p 114 S 12 '65
    See also
  Aerospace industries—France
  Airlines—France
  Airplane industry and trade—France
  Alsace
  Aluminum industry and trade—France
  Americans in France
  Architecture, Domestic—France
  Automobile industry and trade—France
  Auvergne
  Birth control—France
  Booksellers and bookselling—France
  Brittany
  Catholic church in France
  Censorship—France
  Châteauroux
  Clothing industry—France

Armed forces

France without NATO. il U S News 59:75 O 18 '65

Army

Battle of Dienbienphu, by J. Roy. Review Commonweal 82:119-20 Ap 16 '65. W. C. McWilliams

Cabinet

Fertile games. il Time 87:34 Ja 14 '66

Colonies

France's changing policy in Africa. P. Decraene. il Reporter 34:37-9 Ja 13 '66
See also
Saint Pierre and Miquelon (islands)

Commerce

Ghastly problem; Common market and tariffs. Newsweek 66:78+ S 20 '65
Is de Gaulle killing the Common market? il U S News 59:84-5 Ag 23 '65

Defenses

France without NATO. il U S News 59:75 O 18 '65
Gallic version. Newsweek 65:42+ F 8 '65
Sting of the bee in saturation parity. L. Szilard. il Bul Atomic Sci 21:8-13 Mr '65

Description and travel

Barges on the Seine. C. Frankel. il Harper 230:60-5 My '65
Stop & go. H. Sutton. McCalls 92:49-50+ My '65
Travel's picture portfolio. Travel 123:52-7 F '65

Diplomatic and consular service

Changing the guard. il Newsweek 66:44+ S 27 '65

Economic conditions

De Gaulle's glass house. il Time 85:95 Mr 5 '65
End of the French miracle. il U S News 58:81 Je 7 '65
France casts a vote on Gaullist affluence. il Bsns W p76-8+ D 4 '65
Growing rift in French economy. Bsns W p52 Mr 6 '65
Letter from Paris (cont) Genêt. New Yorker 40:112+ F 6 '65
See also
Money—France

Economic policy

De Gaulle & business. Time 86:108+ O 1 '65
Economic hassle for de Gaulle; OECD advice to scrap economic stabilization plan. Bsns W p98+ Ag 14 '65
Life with de Gaulle. H. C. Wallich. Newsweek 66:67 Ag 23 '65
Permissive planning and the French economy. E. Taylor. il Reporter 32:25-8 My 6 '65

Economic relations

De Gaulle launches an economic war on the dollar; with excerpt from interview with J. Rueff. il U S News 58:44-6 F 15 '65

De Gaulle's new triad. Nat R 17:138-40 F 23 '65
Nationalism threatens U.S. investment. R. A. Smith. il Fortune 72:126-31 Ag '65
Oiling on alliance; France's stake in Algerian oil. Time 86:82+ Jl 23 '65
Paris-Peking trade; Marianne & the dragon. J. S. Prybyla. Nation 200:99-102 F 1 '65
Why French pay off to the Viet Cong. il U S News 59:39 Jl 19 '65

Foreign relations

Atlantic report (cont) Atlan 215:38+ Ap '65
Convocation; de Gaulle's eleventh semiannual convocation of the press. il Time 85:21-2 F 12 '65
De Gaulle: America's elder statesman. A. Werth. Nation 201:404-8 N 29 '65
De Gaulle between two elections. Newsweek 66:37 D 20 '65
De Gaulle, Europe, and the dollar. E. Taylor. il Reporter 32:20-3 F 25 '65
De Gaulle on Vietnam; way out of the jungle; with editorial comment. A. Werth. Nation 200:237, 239-42 Mr 8 '65
De Gaulle: pose and policy. H. Lüthy. For Affairs 43:561-73 Jl '65
De Gaulle's Europe; Common market in trouble. America 113:308 S 25 '65
De Gaulle's grand design for U.S. get out. il U S News 59:50-2 Jl 26 '65
De Gaulle's new triad. Nat R 17:138-40 F 23 '65
De Gaulle's responsibility; another Common market crisis. America 113:91 Jl 24 '65
Don't expect de Gaulle to change. M. Gordey. New Repub 153:16-19 D 18 '65
Europe of Charles de Gaulle. T. Molnar. Nat R 17:108-9 F 9 '65
European version of neutralism. J. Freymond. bibliog f Ann Am Acad 362:28-35 N '65
Firecrackers. Time 85:40 Ap 30 '65
If de Gaulle could have his way in Europe. U S News 59:55-6 D 13 '65
If France pulls out, the future of NATO. M. S. Johnson. il U S News 59:40-2 S 27 '65
Illusionist: why we misread de Gaulle. H. A. Kissinger. Harper 230:69-70+ Mr '65
Independence of France; address, April 27, 1965. C. de Gaulle. Vital Speeches 31:514-15 Je 15 '65
Leader of Europe and arbiter between blocs. J. Daniel. New Repub 152:10-11 F 20 '65
Letter from Paris (cont) Genêt. New Yorker 41:106+ F 20 '65
Plain talk by de Gaulle. E. Weintal. Newsweek 66:44 N 1 '65
Policy of France; independence of Europe; address, June 17, 1965. G. Pompidou. Vital Speeches 31:617-19 Ag 1 '65
Seven more years of de Gaulle: what to expect. U S News 60:38 Ja 3 '66
Siren call in Paris. Newsweek 65:52+ My 10 '65
Smiling again. Time 85:37 My 21 '65
Twilight of NATO. M. Frankel. il N Y Times Mag p54-5+ D 5 '65
United States, France, and NATO: a comparison of two approaches; address, January 21, 1965. D. H. Popper. Dept State Bul 52:180-7 F 8 '65
Whatever for? il Newsweek 65:53 F 15 '65
Who is the real realist? constructive role of de Gaulle. A. de Borchgrave. il Newsweek 66:47-8+ D 13 '65
Will de Gaulle be easier to live with now? il U S News 59:34-5 D 20 '65

Africa

France's changing policy in Africa. P. Decraene. il Reporter 34:37-9 Ja 13 '66
French Africa; Communist subversion. E. Taylor. Reporter 32:29-31 Mr 25 '65

Algeria

Algeria: a rude awakening for the left. E. Taylor. Reporter 33:31-2 Jl 15 '65

China (People's Republic)

Mysterious visitor. il Time 86:26B-27 Ag 13 '65

Germany (Federal Republic)

Cooling Franco-German relations. E. M. von Kuehnelt-Leddihn. Nat R 17:650-1 Jl 27 '65
France and Germany: divergent outlooks. A. Grosser. For Affairs 44:26-36 O '65
Necessary guest: President de Gaulle in Bonn. Time 85:30 Je 18 '65
New storm over Germany; de Gaulle's latest maneuver. il U S News 59:65-6 N 8 '65
NATO without France? Time 86:50+ N 5 '65
Once burned; talks between de Gaulle and Erhard. Newsweek 65:47-8 Je 21 '65

FRANCE—Foreign relations—*Continued*

Great Britain

Duck with de Gaulle; meeting with Harold Wilson. il Time 85:31 Ap 9 '65
Slightly warmer. Newsweek 65:54+ Ap 12 '65

Morocco

Shaking the throne; French press points to Gen. M. Oufkir, as instigator of Ben Barka plot. Newsweek 66:39 N 29 '65

Russia

De Gaulle carries on. il Newsweek 66:55-6 N 15 '65
De Gaulle rings Kremlin bells. Bsns W p45 Ap 3 '65
Making Gromyko smile. E. Taylor. Reporter 32:28-9 My 20 '65
Paris-Moscow axis. J. Burnham. Nat R 17: 362 My 4 '65
Paris-Moscow flirtation. M. Gordey. New Repub 152:10-11 My 15 '65

United States

De Gaulle seen viewing RF-101 flight as future political weapon. L. L. Doty. Aviation W 83:21 Jl 26 '65
Historian looks at de Gaulle: why he acts that way; interview, ed. by F. C. Painton. J. B. Duroselle. il U S News 58:44+ My 10 '65
How de Gaulle's anti-U.S. drive is doing. il por U S News 58:19 Je 7 '65
On dealing with de Gaulle. J. M. Gavin. Atlan 215:49-54 Je '65
Senator's indictment of de Gaulle; excerpts from address, June 3, 1965. P. Douglas. U S News 58:8 Je 14 '65

History

Bibliography

Articles and other books received; comp. by B. F. Hyslop. See issues of American historical review

Medieval period to 1515

Miracle of Saint Joan. L. R. Peattie. Read Digest 86:239-40+ My '65

Bourbons, 1589-1789

For the glory of France. C. V. Wedgwood. il Horizon 7:20-9 Sum '65

Revolution

Coming of the French revolution, by G. Lefebvre. Review
Am Hist R 71:77-103 O '65. E. L. Eisenstein
French revolution has been lost. J. F. Revel. il N Y Times Mag p28-9+ N 7 '65

Industries

At Saint-Gobain, the first 300 years were the easiest. R. A. Smith. il Fortune 72:148-50+ O '65
Business á la U.S. now the mode in Paris. il Bsns W p58-60+ O 23 '65
France bets millions on nickel; Societe le nickel. Bsns W p 110+ Ap 24 '65
From a monarch's whim, a great corporation: la Compagnie de Saint-Gobian. il Fortune 72:151-3 O '65
How to do business with a Frenchman. E. R. Eggers. Harper 231:41-4 Ag '65
Michelin stretches its rubber empire; first in tire sales in France. il Bsns W p 136-8+ Jl 17 '65
X marks success; Moulinex. il Time 85:80-1 Mr 26 '65

Moral conditions

See also
Prostitution

Nationalism

De Gaulle's grand design for U.S. get out. il U S News 59:50-2 Jl 26 '65
Historian looks at de Gaulle: why he acts that way; interview, ed. by F. C. Painton. J. B. Duroselle. il U S News 58:44+ My 10 '65

Politics and government

After de Gaulle? two crown princes now: Pompidou and Debré. U S News 60:14 Ja 24 '66
Atlantic report (cont) Atlan 215:30+; 216:14+ Ap, O '65
Bourgeois candidate. il Newsweek 66:28-9 S 6 '65
By word and deed, the once and future king; de Gaulle's invisible government. Newsweek 66:43 D 13 '65
Death of Gaullism. W. S. Schlamm. Nat R 18: 63-5 Ja 25 '66

De Gaulle looks left. E. Taylor. il Reporter 32:13-14 Je 3 '65
De Gaulle's dauphin. Newsweek 66:38 Ag 9 '65
Divided they stand: question of presidential candidates. il Time 86:35-6 S 24 '65
Election day in France: I have spoken; de Gaulle on TV. il Newsweek 66:41-2 D 13 '65
Find another de Gaulle. E. Behr. il Sat Eve Post 238:28-9 D 4 '65
First foray; this year's presidential election campaign. il Time 85:33-4 My 28 '65
Four views on seven years; symposium. il Newsweek 66:44+ D 13 '65
France casts a vote on Gaullist affluence. il Bsns W p76-8+ D 4 '65
Gaullist succession. New Repub 154:8 Ja 1 '66
General's surprises; cabinet reshuffle. Newsweek 67:47-8 Ja 17 '66
In quest of unity. il Time 85:31 Je 18 '65
Letter from Paris (cont) Genêt. New Yorker 41:166+ My 15 '65
Man who; Defferre's dilemma. il Newsweek 65:39 F 22 '65
Next French president. America 113:659-60 N 27 '65
Other candidate in France: F. Mitterrand. K. Botsford. il N Y Times Mag p8-9+ D 19 '65
Out of the ring. Newsweek 66:38+ Jl 5 '65
Permanent opposition. Time 86:21-2 D 31 '65
Seven more years of de Gaulle: what to expect. U S News 60:38 Ja 3 '66
So dies a dream; anti-Gaullist unity. Newsweek 65:40 Je 28 '65
What de Gaulle's re-election means. R. Bosc. America 114:72-4 Ja 15 '66
See also
Communist party (France)
Elections—France
France—Cabinet
Political parties—France
Presidents—France

Religious institutions and affairs

News of the Christian world (cont) Christian Cent 82:316-17 Mr 10 '65
See also
Catholic church in France

Social conditions

See also
Women—France

Social life and customs

See also
Paris—Social life and customs
FRANCE and Europe. See Europe and France
FRANCE and the United States
How to do business with a Frenchman. E. R. Eggers. Harper 231:41-4 Ag '65
See also
Americans in France
United States—Foreign opinion—French
FRANCE-soir (newspaper) See Newspapers—France
FRANCEKEVICH, Al
In the darkroom. See issues of Popular photography
FRANCES, Sister Marian. See Marian Frances, Sister
FRANCESCA, Piero della. See Piero della Francesca
FRANCESCHINI, Romulus
Postscript on Ives's Fourth. Am Rec G 32: 223 N '65
FRANCHISE system (business) See Exclusive agencies
FRANCILLON, Jacques Jacquet-. See Jacquet-Francillon, J.
FRANCIS, Charles E.
Don't junk your old FM tuner. Pop Electr 23: 83-4 N '65
FRANCIS, Devon
Are you in more danger in a small car? no. Pop Sci 186:73+ F '65
—and Sneigr, Denis
50,000 miles without an oil change. Pop Sci 186:57-61+ Mr '65
FRANCIS, Robert
Castro's Cuba today. Newsweek 66:49-50 Jl 12 '65
FRANCIS, Robert (poet)
Come; Emergence; poems. Commonweal 81: 605 F 5 '65
Old men; poem. Commonweal 82:468 Jl 2 '65
FRANCIS: the city; the saint, the statue, the boy; story. See Trott, S.
FRANCISCANS
See also
Capuchins
FRANCISCIS, Pietro de, and others
Spleen as a production site for erythropoietin. bibliog Science 150:1831-3 D 31 '65

FRANCISCO, Don
One hairy sedan! Hot Rod 18:40-1 F '65
Tempest's tall six. Hot Rod 18:30-5+ S '65
FRANCO, Carmen Polo de
Doña Franco comes to town. J. Yglesias.
Holiday 37:44+ Ap '65
FRANCO, Francisco
Awakening land. il por Time 87:26-34D Ja 21 '66
Franco's foes' stop hoping. C. Sterling. il
Reporter 32:33-6 F 25 '65
Hint from the Caudillo. il por Time 87:30 Ja 7 '66
Leader and some notable Spanish faces. il
Holiday 37:70-7 Ap '65
Reign in Spain stays mainly the same. Christian Cent 82:763-4 Je 16 '65
FRANÇOIS, Bill
Enjoy summer all winter long. Pop Gard 16:36+ N '65
Head start in West Virginia. Sat R 48:61 D 18 '65
FRANÇOIS, Pierre
Explosion of vitality. UNESCO Courier 18:8-16 Jl '65
FRANCOIS-PONCET, Andre
Calling a halt: a dialogue. Reporter 32:6 Je 3 '65
FRANK, Adassa
Hungry auntie; poem. Sat R 48:37 Je 19 '65
FRANK, Bernard
Obituary
Liv Wildn il por 87:8-9 Wint '64
FRANK, Bill
Bill Frank and company, Henry street playhouse. J. Maskey. Dance Mag 39:29+ F '65
FRANK, Gerold
Charlie Chaplin and his children. Ladies Home J 82:70-1+ My '65
FRANK, Goldalie
Mother, I'd rather buy it myself! excerpts.
Seventeen 24:132-3+ S '65
FRANK, Jerome D.
Statement on South Vietnam. Bul Atomic Sci 21:32-3 My '65
FRANK, Leo M.
Little girl is dead, by H. Golden. Review
Life 59:15 D 3 '65. W. M. Kunstler
Sat R por 48:32 D 25 '65. E. M. Yoder, jr
FRANK, Michael M. and others
Complement and hemolytic antibody: changes in their activity induced by mercaptoethanol. bibliog Science 147:742-3 F 12 '65
FRANK, Stanley
Patricia Neal: a woman's fight to live.
Good H 161:64-5+ Ag '65
(ed) See Ricci, R. Gifted child (handle with care)
FRANKEL, Charles
Barges on the Seine. Harper 230:60-5 My '65
Scribblers and international relations. For Affairs 44:1-14 O '65
FRANKEL, Haskel
Author: A. Sharp Sat R 48:28 My 8 '65
Author: T. Capote. Sat R 49:36-7 Ja 22 '66
Authors. Sat R 48:41-2 Mr 6 '65
On the fringe. See issues of Saturday review
Time and telepathy. Sat R 48:44-5 S 11 '65
FRANKEL, Max
Importance of being Bundy. N Y Times Mag p32-3+ Mr 28 '65
President's just-a-minute man. N Y Times Mag p48-9+ S 12 '65
Twilight of NATO. N Y Times Mag p54-5+ D 5 '65
Washington, Europe, and the Tower of Babel.
Harper 231:108+ D '65
FRANKENFIELD, Mrs Herbert
Avenues of cooperation. ALA Bul 59:744-5 S '65
FRANKENSTEIN, Alfred
Ives's Fourth symphony, an unplayable work gets played. Hi Fi 15:83-4 N '65
FRANKENTHALER, Helen
Frankenthaler & Olitski. M. Kozloff. Nation 200:374-6 Ap 5 '65
FRANKFORT ON THE MAIN
Music
Guests on the Main. W. B. Rios. il Opera N 29:31 Mr 20 '65
FRANKFURT book fair. See Book fairs
FRANKFURTER, Alfred
Los Angeles: the new museum. Art N 64:30-4+ Mr '65
about
A.F, 1906-1965. il por Newsweek 65:100 My 24 '65
Alfred Frankfurter, 1906-1965. T. B. Hess.
Art N 64:25+ Sum '65
Editor's letters; tributes. Art N 64:6 S '65
FRANKFURTER, Felix
Brush of a comet: letter to President Franklin D. Roosevelt. Atlan 215:90-1 My '65

about
All the trumpets sounded. por Newsweek 65:30-1 Mr 8 '65
Books. W. H. Dempsey, jr. Commonweal 82:227-8 My 7 '65
Felix Frankfurter. Nation 200:238 Mr 8 '65
Felix Frankfurter dies at eighty-two. Christian Cent 82:294 Mr 10 '65
Felix Frankfurter 1882-1965. A. M. Bickel.
New Repub 152:7 Mr 6 '65
Felix Frankfurter, RIP. Nat R 17:182 Mr 9 '65
Former justice dies. por Sr Schol 86:22-3 Mr 11 '65
Judge but not a lawmaker. Life 58:4 Mr 5 '65
Passionate restrainer. il pors Time 85:68+ Mr 5 '65
Talent for joy. A. MacLeish. por Sat R 48:25-6 N 27 '65
FRANKFURTERS
See also
Cookery—Meat
FRANKL, Peter
Frankl in American debut. E. Lewis. Hi Fi 15:139 Ap '65
FRANKLIN, Benjamin
Enlightenment's evangel. J. W. Ward. Reporter 33:52+ D 2 '65
Old Ben Franklin and his miserable maxims.
S. L. Clemens. Read Digest 86:137-8 Je '65
Paradoxical pragmatist. R. B. Morris. Sat R 48:63 N 13 '65
Senior scholastic interviews; ed. by R. Hemming. R. Preston. il por Sr Schol 86:21 Mr 4 '65
FRANKLIN, Glen
King of the rope. il Time 86:76 D 17 '65
FRANKLIN, Irene
Sheet music. A. Debus. il Hobbies 70:36+ S '65
FRANKLIN, Mimi
Pitzer; St John's. Mlle 61:148-9+ O '65
FRANKLIN, Robert D.
Book acquisition costs. por Library J 90:1612-13 Ap 1 '65
Personnel primer: a topical index to library teamwork. por Library J 90:3542-9 S 15 '65
FRANKLIN book programs, incorporated
Books for developing countries. R. Stein. il
Sr Schol 86:sup 14 My 20 '65
Franklin book programs: global publishing aid is varied and expanded. il Pub W 187:28-32 Mr 15 '65
Franklin names directors, reviews year's operations. Pub W 188:42 N 22 '65
Strong and steady light. J. Tebbel. il Sat R 48:145+ Mr 13 '65
Wartime council's assets transferred to
Franklin. Pub W 189:68 Ja 10 '66
FRANKLIN Delano Roosevelt memorial. See
Washington, D.C.—Monuments, statues, etc.
FRANKLIN publications, incorporated. See
Franklin book programs, incorporated
FRANKS, Herman
They love Herman and Willie. J. Mann. il
por Sports Illus 23:24-6+ S 27 '65
FRANTZ, Dorothy
Landscape painting composition and its relation to abstract design. Design 67:31-3 N '65
FRANZINI-ARMSTRONG, Clara. See Porter, K. R. jt. auth.
FRASCONI, Antonio
Antonio Frasconi: inventive bookmaking and graphics. il Pub W 188:80-1 D 6 '65
FRASE, Robert W.
Legislative process; address, January 1965.
bibliog por ALA Bul 59:276-81 Ap '65
FRASER, Lady Antonia (Pakenham)
In East Africa and London, two writing women. V. Cowles. Vogue 145:98 Ap 1 '65
FRASER, Blair
Canadian national elections. New Repub 153:10-11 N 6 '65
FRASER, Dawn
Aussie row over Dawn's night out. il pors
Life 58:36-36A Mr 12 '65
Fun at the games; swimmer suspended for writing a book. por Time 85:82+ Mr 12 '65
Strike at Dawn. il por Newsweek 65:86+ Mr 15 '65
Thunder down under. Sports Illus 22:13 Mr 15 '65
FRASER, Donald M.
American policy toward South Africa; address, March 22, 1965. Vital Speeches 31:398-400 Ap 15 '65
FRASER, G. S.
Technology and insight. Poetry 106:366-8 Ag '65
FRASER, Kathleen
Giants with capes of gold; poem. Poetry 106:205-6 Je '65

FRATELLI Fabbri editori. See Publishers and publishing—Italy

FRATER, Alexander
Drummer; story. New Yorker 41:54-5 N 27 '65

FRATERNITIES. See College fraternities

FRAUD
Bank that should never have opened; Brighton national bank, Brighton, Colo. H. B. Meyers. il Fortune 72:126-7+ Jl '65
1883 gilt nickel. C. French. Hobbies 70:102 Ag '65
Gendlin's effect. Newsweek 65:55-6 My 24 '65
Gyps & swindles & schemes. il Changing T 19:29-32 Je '65
Losers on the road; indictment of top officials for running traffic-fine racket in Greenwood Village, Col. Time 85:46 Ap 23 '65
Man who fooled everybody; case of Tino De Angelis. il Time 85:20-1 Je 4 '65
Mr Smitherman goes to Washington. Time 85:26 Ap 16 '65
$107 misunderstanding: mayor of Selma in Washington. il Newsweek 65:27 Ap 19 '65
Robbing the aged; findings of subcommittee of Senate special committee on aging. America 112:244 F 20 '65
Salad oil mystery. M. Kempton. New Repub 153:9-11 Jl 24 '65
Sleuthing the scammers; quick-buck business fraud. Newsweek 66:70 N 1 '65
10,000 ticket items disappear in Congo. il Aviation W 82:32 Mr 8 '65
Tino's day of reckoning. H. Robinson. Reporter 33:54-7 D 2 '65
Twenty years for Tino; salad-oil master swindler. il Newsweek 66:70+ Ag 30 '65
U.S. accuses six in ticket credit swindle. F. Cogan. Aviation W 83:36 N 22 '65
See also
Advertising, Fraudulent
Diplomas, Fraudulent
Forgery of works of art
Imposters and imposture
Quacks and quackery

FRAUDULENT diplomas. See Diplomas, Fraudulent

FRAZER, John E.
It was on Good Friday. Read Digest 86:76-8 Ap '65
Kashmir: tinderbox of Asia. Read Digest 87:91-6 D '65
Smokey the Bear and his friends. Read Digest 87:134-8 Jl '65

FRAZIER, George
Call it camp. Holiday 38:12+ N '65
Fowler's love affair with the language. Life 59:6+ Ag 20 '65
Next dance will be what is Meyer Davis doing while Oedipus and the mothers drop trousers? Esquire 65:60-1+ Ja '66
Wayward reader. Holiday 37:18+ My '65

FRAZIL ice. See Ice

FREAS, Ralph
Antennas: which, why, when, and how much? Am Home 68:27-8 Ap '65
Faithful sound (cont) Esquire 64:16-17 Jl '65

FRECCERO, John
Dante's novel of the self. Christian Cent 82:1216-18 O 6 '65

FRECHKOP, Serge. See Koulischer, L. jt. auth.

FRECHTMAN, Bernard
(tr) See Sartre, J. P. Sartre talks of Beauvoir

FREDERICK A. Praeger, incorporated. See Praeger, Frederick A, incorporated

FREDERICK, Carl
How I breed and feed for no. 1 hogs. por Suc Farm 63:26-7 Jl '65

FREDERICK, Pauline
View from the world bridge. address, December 3, 1964. Vital Speeches 31:265-7 F 15 '65

FREDERICK, William H. Jr
Let's be honest about hollies. il Horticulture 43:22-3+ D '65
—and Simon, R. A.
Grass. il Horticulture 43:14-15+ Ag '65

FREDERICKS, Carlton
Carlton Fredericks charged in FTC complaint; false advertising. Pub W 188:40 N 22 '65
Vitamin healers. R. L. Smith. il Reporter 33:18-25 D 16 '65; Discussion. 34:6+ Ja 13 '66

FREDERICKS, Pierce G.
She was more than a patriot. N Y Times Mag p 110+ D 5 '65

FREDERIKSEN, M. W.
Birth of functional architecture: town planning and housing in ancient Rome. UNESCO Courier 18:30-3 My '65

FREDLAND, John R.
Getting the Nation on the go. Sat R 48:49-50 D 4 '65

FREDRIKSSON, Kurt, and Reid, A. M.
Chondrule in the Chainpur meteorite. bibllog Science 149:856-60 Ag 20 '65

FREE, John R.
How electricity in the air affects you. Sci Digest 58:50-4 N '65

FREE, Montague
Obituary
Flower Grower il por 52:29 Ap '65
Pub W 187:102 F 8 '65

FREE coupons. See Coupons

FREE enterprise
Changing balance power; with views of leading business executives. il Bsns W p84-5+ Jl 17 '65
Freedom and enterprise; address, April 26, 1965. R. C. Tyson. Vital Speeches 31:497-500 Je 1 '65
Letter from the Vice President; Humphrey on free enterprise. H. H. Humphrey. U S News 59:53 O 25 '65
Public-private enterprise; effects of technology; address. November 1, 1965. W. M. Allen. Vital Speeches 32:112-15 D 1 '65
Where free enterprise is building a new frontier. M. C. Faught and A. Fairweather. il Nations Bsns 53:40-1+ Je '65
See also
Competition
Profit

FREE-lance writing. See Authorship

FREE library of Philadelphia. See Philadelphia —Free library

FREE man; story. See Siegel, B.

FREE masons. See Freemasons

FREE society association
Do you mean it, Mr Goldwater? first newsletter. J. C. Evans. Christian Cent 82:1312 O 27 '65
Goldwater rallies the troops. W. D. Burnham. Commonweal 82:552-5 Ag 6 '65
What a party can't do. R. Moley. Newsweek 66:96 Jl 26 '65

FREE Southern theater. See Theater, Negro

FREE speech
Berkeley affair: Mr Kerr vs. Mr Savio & co. A. H. Raskin. il N Y Times Mag p24-5+ F 14 '65
Berkeley: free speech and free verse; poetry conference. D. Wesling. Nation 201:338-40 N 8 '65
Dissent, consensus, and McCarthyism. J. P. Roche. Reporter 33:10 D 16 '65
Making free speech audible. C. A. Reich. il Nation 200:138-41 F 8 '65
Newburgh again; Father P. Berrigan removed from the faculty of Epiphany Apostolic college. Commonweal 82:239 My 14 '65
Speaker ban: North Carolina law. L. J. Carter. il Science 150:589-91, 725-8 O 29-N 5 '65
Speaker ban: State assembly kills law denying forum to Communists: U.N.C.'s status is believed safe. L. J. Carter. Science 150:1141+ N 26 '65
What happened at Berkeley. N. Glazer. Commentary 39:39-47 F '65; Reply with rejoinder. P. Selznick. 39:80-5 Mr '65
See also
Academic freedom

FREE trade and protection
Competing for tomorrow's world markets; address, November 18, 1964. F. G. Donner. Vital Speeches 31:279-82 F 15 '65
U.S. interest in free trade and peaceful commerce; remarks, June 9, 1965. L. B. Johnson. Dept State Bul 53:30-1 Jl 5 '65
See also
Import quotas

FREE trade area, European. See European free trade association

FREE trade area, Latin American. See Latin American free trade association

FREE universities
Universities, free style. il Newsweek 67:59-60 Ja 10 '66

FREE university of New York
Free university; academy for mavericks. H. Junker. il Nation 201:78-80 Ag 16 '65
Universities, free style. il Newsweek 67:59-60 Ja 10 '66

FREE university of the Congo. See Colleges and universities—Congo (capital Leopoldville)

FREED, Albert
Doctor Albert Freed. J. Deschin. il por Pop Phot 57:33-4+ Ag '65

FREED, Richard
B is for Beatles and baroque. Sat R 48:57+ D 25 '65
J. Strauss: all in the family. Sat R 48:54+ Je 26 '65
Mexico in sight and sound. Sat R 48:92 Ap 10 '65
Recorded literature of Telemann. Sat R 48:81+ O 30 '65

FREED, Simon
Chemical-biochemical signal and noise; adaptation of address, September 23, 1964. bibliog Science 150:576-84 O 29 '65

FREEDGOOD, Seymour
Churning market for executives. Fortune 72: 152-4+ S '65
Uncle to 1,700 grocers. Fortune 71:130-3 Mr '65

FREEDMAN, Elaine. See Bennett, J. E. jt. auth.

FREEDMAN, Helen
Diary of my baby's birth. Parents Mag 40:44-5+ Ag '65

FREEDMAN, Max
I'm devoted to him; Freedman and LBJ. por Newsweek 66:54 Jl 12 '65

FREEDMAN, Mervin B.
Post-industrial generation: roots of student discontent. Nation 200:639-43 Je 14 '65

FREEDMAN, Morris
Celery ripeness is all; story. New Yorker 41: 179-80 N 27 '65

FREEDOM. See Liberty

FREEDOM, Intellectual. See Intellectual liberty

FREEDOM house (organization)
Freedom house speaks out; statement of national purpose in Vietnam. America 113: 126 Ag 7 '65

FREEDOM marches. See Civil rights demonstrations

FREEDOM of information. See Information, Freedom of

FREEDOM of information committee. See American society of newspaper editors

FREEDOM of religion. See Religious liberty

FREEDOM of speech. See Free speech

FREEDOM of teaching. See Academic freedom

FREEDOM of the press
Desperate hours and the right of privacy; concerning the limiting of freedom of speech and the press to protect privacy of private individuals. H. F. Pilpel. Pub W 188:32 N 1 '65
Rigid restriction in Britain; conflict between a free press's right to report criminal proceedings and a defendant's right to an unprejudiced trial. Time 85:71 F 12 '65
When extremists attack the press. J. F. Fixx. Sat R 48:72-3 F 13 '65
See also
Censorship
Libel and slander

FREEDOM schools
Encounters in Virginia; freedom teacher & gentle ladies. E. Newmark. il Nation 200: 193-7 F 22 '65
Freedom libraries: program in Mississippi of Council of federated organizations. F. W. Heinze. il Library J 90:1991-3 Ap 15 '65; Reply. R. B. Layton. 90:2308+ My 15 '65
Friends of freedom libraries to meet during ALA conference. Library J 90:2778 Je 15 '65
Mississippi summer. M. Braverman. il Library J 90:5045-7 N 15 '65
My friends in Mississippi. L. Kabat. New Repub 152:18-20 My 29 '65

FREEDOM to read. See Intellectual liberty

FREEDOM to travel. See Travel regulations

FREEHAFER, Edward G.
Edward G. Freehafer named chairman of N.Y. library agency. por Library J 90:838 F 15 '65

FREEMAN, A. D.
We have; poem. Sat R 48:23 Ap 10 '65

FREEMAN, Arthur
Naples again; poem. New Yorker 41:36 F 27 '65
Occupation; poem. Poetry 106:413-19 S '65

FREEMAN, Arthur J. See Kolm, H. H. jt. auth.

FREEMAN, Don
Man from U.N.C.L.E. Sat Eve Post 238:76+ Je 19 '65

FREEMAN, James Dillet
Wish from us sane people; poem. Sat R 48:16 N 27 '65

FREEMAN, Jean Todd
Pony ring; Sunday drive; poems. McCalls 92:150, 179 Ap '65

FREEMAN, John W.
Billy Budd returns. Opera N 30:14-15 Ja 1 '66
In Dante's wake. Opera N 30:6-7 D 11 '65
To weep and remember. Opera N 29:24-6 Ap 3 '65

FREEMAN, Neal
How to beat a good congressman. Nat R 17:547-50, 673 Je 29, Ag 10 '65

FREEMAN, Norman D.
Gear and gadgets for the one-design. Yachting 117:58-60+ F '65

FREEMAN, Orville Lothrop
Boundary waters canoe area decision. il Liv Wildn 29:20-6 Spr '65

FREEMAN, Roger A.
Cuckoo's egg in the Britannica. Nat R 17:514-18 Je 15 '65
How to railroad a school bill. Nat R 17:419-22 My 18 '65
Phoney baloney in welfare spending. Nat R 17:823-6 S 21 '65

FREEMASONS
Knights, Masons and ecumenism. America 113:426 O 16 '65
Secrets of the Masons. Newsweek 65:66 My 24 '65

FREEPORT, N.Y.
Down go accidents and robberies; changeover in street lighting. il Am City 80:116 N '65
Super engine puts a plus in power distribution. C. E. Metz. il Am City 80:106-7 N '65

FREEWAYS. See Express highways

FREEZER food plans. See Food, Frozen

FREEZERS
Good use tips for refrigerators and freezers. Good H 160:135 Ja '65
Searching for freezer space? stop right here! il Good H 160:132-3 Ap '65

FREEZING
See also
Frostbite

FREEZING (therapy) See Cold—Therapeutic applications

FREEZING of food
Freeze your own tray dinners. B. Pierson. il Farm J 89:74+ Je '65
New way to freeze a garden's goodness. R. Gannon. il Flower Grower 52:10+ Jl '65
One big recipe, enough to freeze for several meals. il Farm J 89:90-1 My '65

FREI, Eduardo
Change in Chile: what it means to U.S. business; interview, ed. by J. N. Wallace. por U S News 58:84-5 Ap 26 '65

about
Alternative to Castro. por Newsweek 66:39 Ag 2 '65
Big sweep. por Newsweek 65:38 Mr 22 '65
Green light for reformer; in Chile, changes ahead. U S News 58:22 Mr 22 '65
Profitable trip. por Time 86:36 Ag 6 '65
Stuck on dead center. por Time 85:46 F 5 '65
Where does Chile go from here? Christian democratic party. il Nat R 17:275-7 Ap 6 '65

FREIBERG, Stanley K.
And there were shepherds; poem. Christian Cent 82:1545 D 15 '65
Flight into Egypt; poem. Christian Cent 82: 1575 D 22 '65

FREIBERGER, Howard
Sensory research discussion: sonar and electronic reading for the blind. Science 147: 1163 Mr 5 '65

FREIDEL, Frank
Political power in trust. Sat R 48:124 Mr 13 '65
Profiles of the Presidents (cont) Nat Geog Mag 127:660-711; 128:536-77; 129:66-119 My, O '65, Ja '66

FREIGHT and freightage
See also
Air freight service
Trucking

FREIGHT car ferries. See Train ferries

FREIGHT cars. See Railroads—Freight cars

FREIGHT handling
Big skid at Yale express. R. J. Whalen. il Fortune 72:144-9+ N '65
Container ships race for a route; U.S. and foreign operators competing. il Bsns W p 198+ N 13 '65
Freight boom brings handling challenge. J. W. Carter. il Aviation W 83:56-7+ O 25 '65
One big package for the shippers. Bsns W p74+ S 4 '65
Seat pallet van is developed for 727QC. R. G. O'Lone. il Aviation W 83:66-7 N 1 '65
See also
Containers for shipping
Trucking

FREIGHT vessels
Container ships race for a route; U.S. and foreign operators competing. il Bsns W p 198+ N 13 '65
Please squeeze the caviar: trip on the Norwegian ship. Ferncliff, from Vancouver to Los Angeles. B. Scott. Seventeen 25:26 Ja '66
Trip abroad: go by freighter, fun, different, a bargain. il Changing T 19:35-6 F '65

FREIGHT vessels—*Continued*

Food service
Freighter fare; meals on the SS Eurymachus: with recipes. M. Kaytor. il Look 29:50-2+ My 18 '65

Trailer transportation
See Trailers—Transportation
FREIGHTER cruises. See Ocean travel
FREILICHER, Jane
Painter to the New York poets. T. Berrigan. il por Art N 64:44-7+ N '65
FREIMER, Earl H. and McCarty, Maclyn
Rheumatic fever; with biographical sketches. Sci Am 213:10, 66-70+ bibliog(p 126+) D '65
FREISER, Leonard H.
Toronto's Education centre library. Sat R 48:76+ Ap 17 '65
FREITAG, George H.
Hurry with your snowball. Writer 78:28-9 My '65
FRELINGHUYSEN, Peter H. B.
U.N, an effective arm of U.S. foreign policy; address, November 3, 1965. Dept State Bul 53:1021-8 D 27 '65
FREMANTLE, Anne
Books. Commonweal 82:509-10, 639-40 Jl 9, S 3 '65
Christmas eve; story. New Yorker 40:110 F 13 '65
FREMONT-SMITH, R.
Emergency radio calls. Yachting 117:190+ Ap '65
FRENAYE, Frances
(tr) See Bodin, S. Bettina: the adventures of a passionate traveller
FRENCH, Alice
Journey to obscurity, by G. McMichael. Review
  Sat R 49:82 Ja 8 '66. I. Haverstick
FRENCH, Bevan M. and Rosenberg, P. E.
Siderite (FeCO₃): thermal decomposition in equilibrium with graphite. bibliog Science 147:1283-4 Mr 12 '65
FRENCH, Charles
Coin quiz. See issues of Hobbies
Numismatics. See issues of Hobbies
FRENCH
French revolution has been lost. J. F. Revel. il N Y Times Mag p28-9+ N 7 '65
French smile; at Americans! campaign of welcome and amiability. T. Foote. il N Y Times Mag p24-6+ Je 20 '65
Grand subject. H. de Turenne. N Y Times Mag p 114 S 12 '65
  See also
Parisians
FRENCH ALPS. See Alps
FRENCH and Indian war, 1755-1763. See United States—History—French and Indian war, 1755-1763
FRENCH artificial satellites. See Artificial satellites, French
FRENCH atomic bomb test. See Atomic bombs —Testing
FRENCH CANADA. See Quebec (province)
FRENCH CANADIANS
French-Canadian dilemma. C. Ryan. For Affairs 43:462-74 Ap '65
Guy Trimble vs. Guy Tremblay; clash of English and French could destroy Canada. J. Walz. il N Y Times Mag p38-9+ S 19 '65
FRENCH cookery. See Cookery, French
FRENCH economic assistance. See Economic assistance, French
FRENCH faience. See Pottery, French
FRENCH fiction
  See also
Goncourt prize
FRENCH language
De Gaulle: president of France calls for a harder line in behalf of French in international science. J. Walsh. Science 148:350-1 Ap 16 '65; Reply. W. S. Wooster. 148:1670 Je 25 '65
Parlons, enfants de la patrie! reverence Frenchmen feel toward language. Time 86:35-6 O 29 '65
FRENCH literature
French authors and Roman indexers. H. M. Watson. America 114:79-83 Ja 15 '66
Gargantua and Pantagruel. K. Rexroth. Sat R 48:20 Ag 28 '65
FRENCH opera. See Opera, French
FRENCH painting. See Painting, French
FRENCH pastry. See Pastry
FRENCH posters. See Posters
FRENCH RIVIERA. See Riviera
FRENCH RIVIERA fire. See Fires

FRENCH singers. See Singers
FRENCH spies. See Spies
FRENCH TOGOLAND. See Togo
FRENCH visitors in the United States. See Foreign vistors in the United States
FRENCH wine. See Wine
FRENI, Mirella
Fine new Mimi sings everywhere at once. E. Coleman. Life 59:23 O 29 '65
Mirella Freni operatic arias. R. Jones. Am Rec G 32:37 S '65
Music to my ears; Freni's Elisir. I. Kolodin. Sat R 48:40 N 27 '65
FRENK, S. See Maturana, H. R. jt. auth.
FRENZEL, Louis E. jr
Design of transistor multivibrators. Electr World 73:52-4 F '65
Hybrid computers. Electr World 74:64-6 O '65
Oscilloscope calibrator. Electr World 74:58-9 Ag '65
Printed-circuit repair. Electr World 74:57 O '65
FREQUENCY, Radio. See Radio frequency
FREQUENCY allocation, Radio. See Radio frequency allocation
FREQUENCY modulation. See Radio frequency modulation
FREQUENCY modulation receivers. See Radio receiving apparatus—Frequency modulation receivers
FRERICHS, Gisela
We grow a dogproof garden. Pop Gard 16:8-9 Jl '65
FRESCOES
Mother church, Orvieto. R. M. Coates. il Horizon 7:85-9 Spr '65
FRESE, Paul F.
Let's keep our natural beauty. Flower Grower 52:15 S '65
FRESHMEN. See College students
FRESNEDO SIRI, Román
Sculpture in light and concrete. J. Villaverde. il por Américas 17:22-8 S '65
FRESNO, Calif.
Vacuum flotation replaces primary settling. M. J. Carozza and R. J. Theroux. il Am City 80:79-81 F '65

City planning
Fresno mall. D. Haimbach. il Am City 80:91-3 Ap '65
Upgrading downtown. il Arch Rec 137:180-3 Je '65

Finance
Prudent equipment purchasing. M. J. Carozza. il Am City 80:107+ O '65
FREUD, Anna
Anna Freud receives White House award. Sci N L 88:265 O 23 '65
FREUD, Sigmund
Freudian slip. J. Wechsberg. il pors N Y Times Mag p 105-8 Je 6 '65
Reality of dreams. E. Lederer. il Sci N L 87:282-3 My 1 '65
FREUDENBERG, Karl
Lignin: its constitution and formation from p-hydroxycinnamyl alcohols; adaptation of address, May 25, 1964. bibliog Science 148:595-600 Ap 30 '65
FREUDISM. See Psychoanalysis
FREUND'S adjuvant. See Antigens and antibodies
FREY, Donald Nelson
It's time we took on Mr Big. il pors Bsns W p 108-11 Ag 7 '65
FREY, J. and others
Immunoelectrophoresis reveals collagen solubility in human serum. bibliog Science 150 751-2 N 5 '65
FREYMANN, John Gordon
Doctor prescribes for the AMA. Harper 231:76-80 Ag '65
FREYMOND, Jacques
European version of neutralism. bibliog f Ann Am Acad 362:28-35 N '65
FRIAR, Kimon
In the footsteps of a world spirit. Sat R 48:37-8 My 29 '65
Kazantzakis report. Sat R 48:34 Ag 14 '65
FRICK, Ford Christopher
Slow search for another Frick. il Sports Illus 23:18-19 Ag 2 '65
FRICK, Henry Clay
Instant and judicial history. Life 59:4 Ag 13 '65
FRICK collection, New York
Uncommon touch. K. Kuh. il Sat R 48:18 S 4 '65
FRICKER, John
Foreign accent. Flying 78:22-3 Ja '66
Long hot air show. Flying 77:54-6 S '65
NBAA, old chap. Flying 78:63-6 Ja '66

FRIDLINGTON, Robert
Fredrick Law Olmsted: launching the Nation.
Nation 202:10-12 Ja 3 '66
FRIDOVICH, Irwin. See Stutts, P. jt. auth.
FRIEBERT, Stuart
Young hunter; poem. Cath World 202:14 O
'65
FRIED, Morton H.
Four-letter word that hurts. Sat R 48:21-3+
O 2 '65
New tidings from Cathay. Sat R 48:39-40 Je
12 '65
FRIED, Norm. See McGrew, M. E. jt. auth.
FRIEDBERG, Judith
War on poverty needs you. Mlle 61:118-19+
Je '65
FRIEDBERG, M. Paul
Super-block play areas. por Recreation 58:
164-6+ Ap '65
FRIEDE, Donald
Obituary
Pub W por 187:151 Je 7 '65
FRIEDENBERG, Daniel M.
How to make a quick million in real estate.
Esquire 63:122-3+ Je '65
Speaking out. por Sat Eve Post 238:12+ Ag
28 '65
FRIEDENBERG, Edgar Z.
Polite encounter between the generations.
N Y Times Mag p 10-11+ Ja 16 '66
Public schools for private enterprise. Nation
201:171-5 S 20 '65
Synanon solution. Nation 200:256-61 Mr 8 '65
FRIEDL, George, Jr
New NASA contract policies; excerpts from
statement. Aviation W 82:11 Mr 1 '65
FRIEDLANDER, Gordon D.
Poison in the air. Nation 201:347 N 15 '65
FRIEDMAN, Arnold P.
What to do about headaches; interview.
Read Digest 86:127-30 F '65
FRIEDMAN, Bruce Jay
Brazzaville teen-ager; story. Esquire 64:78
Jl '65
Change of plan; story. Esquire 65:96-7 Ja
'66
Imposing proportions of Jean Shrimpton. por
Esquire 63:70-5+ Ap '65
New sounds. Holiday 38:44-5+ Jl '65
Punch; story. Esquire 63:116 F '65
Raquel Welch: the definitive chickie. Esquire
64:84-7+ O '65
Speaking out. por Sat Eve Post 239:6+ Ja 15
'66
What's in it for me. Harper 231:168-9 N '65
FRIEDMAN, Fredrica
Peace corps forestry: there's a forest in your
future! Am For 71:20-1+ F '65
Peace corps in art: a report. Am Artist 29:
80+ Je '65
FRIEDMAN, H. P. and others
Induction in vitro of antibodies to phage T2:
antigens in the RNA extract employed.
antigens in the RNA extract employed.
FRIEDMAN, Herbert
Our life-giving star, the sun. por Nat Geog
Mag 128:712-43 N '65
FRIEDMAN, Irving. See Ragotzkie, R. A. jt.
auth.
FRIEDMAN, Judith, and Raisz, L. G.
Thyrocalcitonin: inhibitor of bone resorption
in tissue culture. bibliog Science 150:1465-7
D 10 '65
FRIEDMAN, Martin
Object is symbol. Art N 64:32-5+ N '65
FRIEDMAN, Meyer, and Byers, S. O.
Epinephrine-induced normalization of lipid
metabolism in adrenalectomized rats. bibliog
Science 148:644-6 Ap 30 '65
FRIEDMAN, Milton
Social responsibility: a subversive doctrine.
Nat R 17:721-3 Ag 24 '65
FRIEDMAN, Saul
Cavanagh is willin'. New Repub 153:10 N 27
'65
FRIEDMAN, Sigmund
Record clubmen. J. M. Conly. Reporter 32:
46+ Ap 8 '65
FRIEDMAN, Sol
Telemetering ties cut operating costs. por Am
City 80:96-7 N '65
FRIEL, Brian
Gold in the sea; story. New Yorker 41:32-7 Jl
31 '65
FRIEND, Douglas J. C.
Where is science taking us? por Sat R 48:61-2
My 1 '65
FRIENDLINESS. See Kindness
FRIENDS; drama. See Leokum, A.
FRIENDS, Society of
See also
American friends service committee
FRIENDS of Mary Fowler; story. See Weid-
man, J.

FRIENDS service committee, American. See
American friends service committee
FRIENDSHIP
Pleasures and problems of friendship. R.
Hochstein and D. Sugarman. il Seventeen
24:86-7+ Je '65
That much-abused word, friendship. S. Rama
Rau. McCalls 93:54+ N '65
See also
Playmates
FRIENDSHIP sloop. See Sloops
FRIERMOOD, Elisabeth Hamilton
Where did you get that idea? Horn Bk 41:
655-61 D '65
FRIESEKE, Frances
Early American carol. Horn Bk 41:612 D '65
FRIESWYK, Siebolt H.
Modern theater concepts and community
drama. por Recreation 58:229-33 My '65
Song leading simplified. Recreation 58:480-1
D '65
FRIGGENS, Paul
Curious Cornwall. Travel 123:37-40 My '65;
Same abr. with title In the land of King
Arthur. Read Digest 86:171-6 My '65
Want to sell your house in a hurry? Read
Digest 87:147-50 O '65
We help ourselves. Read Digest 87:134-8 O '65
Where life begins at sixty-five. Read Digest
88:157-8+ Ja '66
FRIGHT of Mrs Yeager; story. See Herlihy,
J. L.
FRIIS, Harald T.
Karl Jansky: his career at Bell telephone
laboratories. Science 149:841-2 Ag 20 '65
FRIMBO, Ernest M.
Current cinema. B. Gill. New Yorker 41:
152-3 Mr 20 '65
FRIMPTER, George W.
Cystathioninuria: nature of the defect. bib-
liog Science 149:1095-6 S 3 '65
FRINGE benefits. See Non-wage payments
FRINGE trees
Fragrant fringe tree. M. J. Dietz. il Flower
Grower 52:40 My '65
FRISBIE, Johnny
Mama Tala. Atlan 215:69-74 F '65
FRISCH, H. L.
Hard-sphere fluid. bibliog Science 150:1249-54
D 3 '65
FRISCH, O. R.
Molecular beams; with biographical sketch.
Sci Am 212:18, 58-72+ My '65
FRITILLARIES
See also
Crown imperials
FRITO-LAY, incorporated
Fizz & chips; Pepsi-Cola to merge with
Frito-Lay, inc. Time 85:88+ Mr 5 '65
FRITZ, Gary. See Driver, G. jt. auth.
FRITZ, Jean
Kelly's girl; story. Seventeen 24:96-7 D '65
FRITZ, Paul J.
Rabbit muscle lactate dehydrogenase 5;
a regulatory enzyme. bibliog Science 150:
364-6 O 15 '65
FRIZELL, Bernard
Drama of Paris set free. Life 58:15 Je 4 '65
FROBE, Gert
Man you hate to love. il por Time 86:94 N 12
'65
FROBISHER, Mary. See Strang, R. jt auth.
FROG called Mystery; story. See Rohde, B.
FROG men. See Diving, Submarine
FROGS
Bullfrogs sing along with jets. S. W. Kress.
il Audubon Mag 67:93-6 Mr '65
Jumping frogs of Angels camp. R. De Roos.
il Read Digest 87:21-2+ S '65
FROGS eye. See Eye (amphibia)
FROM the French quarter; story. See Steele,
M.
FROME, Michael
Adventure without a passport. NEA J 55:54-6
Ja '66
American public gardens. Holiday 38:91-6 Jl
'65
Holiday handbook of summer escape. Holiday
37:105-10 F '65
Preserving America's past. Holiday 37:151-6
Mr '65
FROMM, Erich
Interview with Erich Fromm; ed. by R.
Heffner. por McCalls 93:132-3+ O '65
Psychology of a guaranteed income; excerpt
from Guaranteed income: next step in
economic evolution? Nation 201:439-42 D
6 '65
FROMM, Jacob E. See Harlow, F. H. jt. auth.
FROMSON, David
Business ethics, your trade association;
address, May 10, 1965. Vital Speeches 32:
28-32 O 15 '65

FRONDEL, Clifford, and Klein, Cornelis, Jr
Ureyite, NaCrSi₂O₆: a new meteoritic pyroxene. bibliog Science 149:742-4 Ag 13 '65

FRONT doors. See Doorways

FRONT drive automobiles. See Automobiles—Front wheel drive

FRONT man in line; story. See Packer, N. H.

FRONTIER and pioneer life

Canada

Sketches from northwestern America and Canada. F. Hölzlhuber. Am Heritage 16:49-64 Je '65

United States

Sketches from northwestern America and Canada. F. Hölzlhuber. Am Heritage 16:49-64 Je '65
So long, St Louis, we're heading West. W. C. Everhart. il Nat Geog Mag 128:642-69 N '65
War of the Never Sweats. T. St George. il Nat Parks Mag 39:16-17 S '65
See also
Pioneers

Childrens literature

Frontier faith revisited. W. J. Jacobs. il Horn Bk 41:464-73 O '65

FRONTIERS of the sea; story. See Ustinov, P.

FROOK, John
Then the old sarge says, you're all mine now. Life 59:26-7 Ag 20 '65
Two believed Murhpy and voted innocent. Life 58:38-9 My 21 '65

about

Good man with words and dynamite. G. P. Hunt. por Life 59:3 Ag 20 '65

FROST, Helena
Artists in paradise. Opera N 29:6-11 F 27 '65

FROST, Robert
Robert Frost speaks prose; ed. by H. Breit. por Esquire 64:230+ D '65

about

Broadway postscript. H. Hewes. Sat R 48:74 O 30 '65
Frost as drama. W. Sheed. Commonweal 83:147-8 N 5 '65
Off Broadway. E. Oliver. New Yorker 41:96+ O '65
On Yeats and others. H. Carruth. Poetry 107:194 D '65
Robert Frost: some divisions in a whole man. I. Traschen. Yale R 55:57-70 O '65
Selected letters of Robert Frost, ed. by L. Thompson. Review
  Holiday 37:34 Mr '65. C. Fadiman

FROST protection
How to foil Jack Frost. R. E. Jennings. Flower Grower 52:13 O '65

FROSTBITE
Travel well. E. N. Dye. Travel 125:59-60 Ja '66

FROZEN desserts. See Ice cream, ices, etc.

FROZEN dinners. See Food, Frozen

FROZEN food. See Food, Frozen

FROZEN ground
Particle sorting by repeated freezing and thawing. A. E. Corte; discussion. il Science 148:1616-17; 149:1520 Je 18, S 24 '65

FROZEN vegetables. See Vegetables, Frozen

FRUCHTER, Norman
Style of the thirties. Nation 200:370-1 Ap 5 '65

FRUEHAUF trailer company
Fruehauf hooked up for the long haul. il Bsns W p74-6 D 18 '65

FRUIT
Art of creating fruit fantasies. House & Gard 127:126-7 Je '65
New fruits and vegetables for '66. G. Logsdon. il Farm J 90:60 Ja '66
See also
Cookery—Fruit
Spraying and dusting

Picking

Grapes of wrath; church involvement in union recognition for grape pickers. il Time 86:96 D 10 '65

Ripening

Ethylene action and the ripening of fruits. S. P. Burg and E. A. Burg. bibliog il Science 148:1190-6 My 28 '65

FRUIT bowls. See Bowls

FRUIT cake. See Cake

FRUIT culture
Fruit-truck news. See issues of Farm Journal
Fruits and nuts of the South. C. M. Bruce. il Horticulture 43:38-9+ F '65

FRUIT desserts. See Desserts

FRUIT drinks. See Beverages

FRUIT flies
U.S. ready for fruit fly. Sci N L 87:294 My 8 '65
See also
Drosophila

FRUIT harvesting machinery. See Harvesting machinery

FRUIT industry
See also
Citrus fruit industry

FRUIT juices
Juicy entrees; adding fruit juice to meats. il Bet Hom & Gard 43:90 My '65

FRUIT picking. See Fruit—Picking

FRUIT trees
New money with a sideline orchard. J. Bickers. il Farm J 89:18 Jl '65
See also
Lime trees
Persimmons

Care

Maintenance is easy with the right tools. G. L. Slate. il Pop Gard 16:24-5 Mr '65

Diseases and pests

Virus hiding in your orchard? Farm J 89:50B O '65

FRUIT trees, Dwarf
Dwarf fruit trees. I. Estep. il Pop Gard 16:22-3 Mr '65
Dwarf fruit trees will thrill every home owner; questions and answers. il Flower Grower 52:34-5+ F '65
Maintenance is easy with the right tools. G. L. Slate. il Pop Gard 16:24-5 Mr '65

FRUITS, vegetables, etc. in decoration
Bountiful bouquets; from the vegetable garden. il McCalls 93:114-19 N '65

FRUMENTO, Antonio S.
Sodium pump: its electrical effects in skeletal muscle. bibliog Science 147:1442-3 Mr 19 '65

FRUTKIN, Arnold W.
Space and the International cooperation year: a national challenge. Dept State Bul 53:384-92 S 6 '65

FRYE, Alton
Space arms control. Bul Atomic Sci 21:30-3 Ap '65

FRYE, John C. See Munson, P. J. jt. auth.

FRYE, John T.
Modern broadband CATV system. Electr World 73:37-40+ F '65

FRYING
Favorites from the french fryer. il Bet Hom & Gard 43:86 Mr '65
See also
Cookery—Poultry

FRYING pans. See Skillets

FRYXELL, Roald
Mazama and Glacier Peak volcanic ash layers: relative ages. bibliog Science 147:1288-90 Mr 12 '65
—See Steen, V. C. jt. auth.

FUBINI, Eugene G.
Is the U.S. armed for the wrong war? interview. por U S News 59:60-3 Ag 16 '65

FUCHS, Wolfgang
Under the Berlin wall. G. Bailey. il Reporter 33:18-23 N 4 '65

FUDENBERG, H. Hugh, and others
Lattice formation in complement fixation: studies with univalent rabbit antibody. bibliog Science 148:91-3 Ap 2 '65
—See Cline, M. J. jt. auth.

FUEL
See also
Gas, Natural
Heating
  also subhead Fuel under various subjects, e.g. Diesel engines—Fuel

FUEL cells
Apollo fuel cell part approved for space use. Sci N L 88:34 Jl 17 '65
Army presses for better field systems. il Miss & Roc 16:77-8+ Mr 29 '65
Electricity from alcohol; Esso's new cell. il Time 85:55 Mr 12 '65
Fuel cell may provide practical applications. Sci N L 88:25 Jl 10 '65
Gemini fuel cell studied. Sci N L 88:151 S 4 '65
Those amazing fuel cells. T. Weissmann. il Sci Digest 58:79-82 S '65

FUEL economy
How to save up to 25 per cent on your fuel-oil bill; using firebox liner. J. Ingersoll and C. E. Rhine. il Pop Sci 187:148-51 S '65

FUEL pumps
Fuel pump remedies. R. E. Jennings. il
Motor T 17:75-7 My '65
FUEL tanks
See also
Airplanes—Fuel tanks
Automobiles—Fuel tanks
FUENTES, Carlos
Five secret clues to Mexico. Vogue 147:
108-9+ Ja 1 '66

about
My friend Fuentes. K. Botsford. Commen-
tary 39:64-7 F '65
FUHRER, Marcus J. and Baer, P. E.
Differential classical conditioning: verbaliza-
tion of stimulus contingencies. bibliog Sci-
ence 150:1479-81 D 10 '65
FUJI, MOUNT
Magic mountain. il U S Camera 28:50-1 Je
'65
FUJI photo film company, limited. See Photo-
graphic apparatus industry and trade
FUJIYAMA. See Fuji, Mount
FUKUCHI, Fred K.
How computers are used. Sci Digest 57:58-62
Mr '65
FUKUDA, Aoi. See Shimazu, T. jt. auth.
FUKUYAMA, Betty Adkins
To the modern moderns; poem.   Christian
Cent 82:238 F 24 '65
FULBRIGHT, James William
Excerpt from address, September 15, 1965.
Cong Digest 44:269+ N '65
Excerpt from debate, June 24, 1964. Cong
Digest 44:47+ F '65
Foreign aid? yes, but with a new approach.
N Y Times Mag p27+ Mr 21 '65
Research backlash; excerpts of remarks.
Aviation W 83:17 Ag 30 '65
Should Fulbright be muzzled? summary of
address. Nat R 17:718 Ag 24 '65
Situation in the Dominican Republic; address,
September 15, 1965. Vital Speeches 31:
747-55 O 1 '65
Uses of flexibility; adaptation of address. Sat
R 48:19-21+ My 8 '65
Vietnam: holding action; address, June 15,
1965. Vital Speeches 31:546-8 Jl 1 '65
Was U.S. wrong in Dominican crisis? state-
ments. por U S News 59:20 S 27 '65; Same.
Nat R 17:859 O 5 '65; Sr Schol 87:15 O 7 '65

about
Absentee; widening rift between the Pres-
ident and Senator Fulbright. por Newsweek
67:15 Ja 3 '66
Bill's Baedeker; suggestion for vacation
travel within the United States. por Time
85:23 Mr 12 '65
Charity begins abroad. M. Ascoli. Reporter
33:24 O 7 '65
Common noun spelled f-u-l-b-r-i-g-h-t. D.
Oberdorfer. il N Y Times Mag p79-80+ Ap
4 '65
Crackdown; US policy dissenter. Nation 201:
205-6 O 11 '65
Disinvited guest. Time 86:14 D 31 '65
Erratic attack. por Time 86:44 S 24 '65
Money for tourists. R. Moley. Newsweek 65:
100 Mr 22 '65
Myth and reality II. por Newsweek 66:27 S
27 '65
Senator Fulbright dissents. Nation 201:177-8
O 4 '65
Speechmaker. A. Kopkind. New Repub 153:15-
19 O 2 '65
Two key senators who question LBJ's policy
on Vietnam. por U S News 58:17 My 3 '65
FULBRIGHT international exchange program.
See Scholarships and fellowships
FULBRIGHT students. See Scholarships and
fellowships
FULL employment. See Employment
FULL employment act of 1946. See Employ-
ment
FULLER, Buckminster. See Fuller, R. B.
FULLER, George A, company
Going private. Newsweek 65:72 Je 21 '65
FULLER, John G.
Trade winds. See Issues of Saturday review
FULLER, John Langworthy. See Scott, J. P.
jt. auth.
FULLER, Margaret. See Ossoli, S.M.F. d'
FULLER, Richard Buckminster
Instant slum clearance. J. Meyer. il Esquire
63:108-11 Ap '65
Profiles. C. Tomkins. New Yorker 41:35-6+
Ja 8 '66
FULLER, Richard E.
How's that again. Mod Phot 29:108+ S '65

FULLER, Sam
Low-budget movies with pow! E. Goodman.
il por N Y Times Mag p42-3+ F 28 '65
FULLERTON, Calif.
Spanish modern city hall. T. W. Oglesby.
il Am City 80:84-5 F '65
FULTON, Robert
Fulton steams ahead. il Sr Schol 86:9 My 20
'65
FULTON COUNTY, Ga.
Old purchasing system takes on a new look.
F. T. Farran. il Am City 80:126+ Jl '65
Punched-card votes meet with instant suc-
cess; use of the Votomatic in Atlanta, Ga.
A. F. Klepper and others. il Am City 80:
110-12 S '65
FULWYLER, M. J.
Electronic separation of biological cells by
volume. bibliog Science 150:910-11 N 12 '65
FUMES
Six dangerous fumes from things you may
use often. Bet Hom & Gard 43:33 D '65
FUMIGATION
See also
Soil disinfection
FUND raising
Abuses of sweet charity. Life 58:28 My 21 '65
Christmas fund-raising ideas for clubs. il
Good H 161:176 N '65
Kids aid Kennedy fund; picture taking with
Polaroid Land camera and initiative. D.
Barry. il Pop Phot 56:22+ F '65
Those fund-raising businessmen; moonlight-
ing for charity. R. Sheehan. Fortune 73:
148-50+ Ja '66
See also
Campaign funds
Thrift shops and rummage sales
FUNDAMENTALISM
Bob Jones university: new curricula for
bigotry. F. G. Sherrill. il Nation 200:326-33
Mr 29 '65
Giving the rib a ribbing. Time 85:66 F 12 '65
Modernity of fundamentalism. J. Opie. jr.
Christian Cent 82:608-11 My 12 65; Reply.
J. Goodwin. 82:872-3 Jl 7 '65
See also
Evangelicalism
FUNERAL directors. See Undertakers and un-
dertaking
FUNERAL rites and ceremonies
See also
Mourning customs

Anecdotes, facetiae, satire, etc.
Magyar wedding, Irish funeral. J. Lukacs.
Esquire 64:34+ Ag '65
FUNERAL services. See Funeral rites and cere-
monies
FUNERALS, Cost of
Funeral industry, some harbingers of change?
Consumer Rep 30:283-4 Je '65
See also
Undertakers and undertaking
FUNGI
Aflatoxins: environmental factors governing
occurrence in Spanish peanuts. L. J.
Ashworth, jr. and others. bibliog il Sci-
ence 148:1228-9 My 28 '65
Bizarre world of the fungi. P. A. Zahl. il
Nat Geog Mag 128:502-27 O '65
Broken pods dangerous; peanuts analyzed for
presence of aflatoxin. Sci N L 87:375 Je 12
'65
Moldy peanut poison breaks chromosomes;
aflatoxin. Sci N L 88:87 Ag 7 '65
Mushrooms, molds, and miracles, by L.
Kavaler. Review
Time il 85:106 Je 25 '65
See also
Ascomycetes
Lichens
Neurospora
Sporangium
Spores (botany)
Truffles

Culture media
Sterols and temperature tolerance in the fun-
gus pythium. R. H. Haskins. bibliog Science
150:1615-16 D 17 '65
FUNGI, Pathogenic
Medium for selective isolation of cryptococ-
cus neoformans. A. B. Shields and L.
Ajello. bibliog Science 151:208 Ja 14 '66
FUNGICIDES
Controlling animals in the garden. W. R.
Eadie. il Horticulture 44:26-7 Ja '66
Fungicide stops fruit spoilage. Farm J 89:42B
Ag '65
FUNK, Wilfred J.
It pays to increase your word power. See
issues of Reader's digest

about
Words that sizzled. por Time 85:52+ Je 11
'65

FUNK and Wagnalls company, Incorporated
Reader's digest buys Funk & Wagnalls. Pub W 188:68 D 27 '65
Reader's digest talking merger with Funk & Wagnalls. Pub W 188:33 N 29 '65

FUNK ISLAND, Newfoundland
Life and death on the Funks. F. Russell. il Horizon 7:32-8 Sum '65

FUNKE, Lewis
—See Hayes, H. jt. auth.
(ed) See Hayes, H. Charlie; My faith in prayer

FUNNIES. See Comics (books, strips, etc)

FUNSTON, G. Keith
On stock dealing by insiders; excerpts from address, October 26, 1965. U S News 59:107 N 8 '65
Where does the money come from? address, April 16, 1965. Vital Speeches 31:467-72 My 15 '65

FUR coats, wraps, etc.
Care a fur deserves. Good H 162:140 Ja '66
Fun furs. il Time 86:69 O 22 '65

FUR trade
Old fur trader. D. J. Anderson. il Field & S 70:50-2+ O '65

FURLONG, Monica
Back roads of England. Atlan 216:114+ Ag '65
Fun of being a woman. Read Digest 86:59-60 Mr '65

FURLONG, William Barry
Baseball. Sports Illus 23:62-4 N 1 '65
How doctors use patients as guinea pigs. Good H 161:79+ O '65
Training for the front-all-around-you war. N Y Times Mag p 184+ O 24 '65

FURMAN university, Greenville, S.C.
Desegregates despite church's opposition. Christian Cent 82:260 Mr 3 '65
Ferment at Furman; university owned by South Carolina Baptist convention. Newsweek 66:80 Ag 23 '65

FURNACE CREEK, Calif. See Death Valley National Monument

FURNACES
See also
Heating
Oil burners

FURNACES, Foundry
Workshop: the primitive foundry. E. Tefft. il Craft Horiz 25:26-31 Mr '65

FURNISHINGS, Household. See Household furnishings

FURNITURE
Courtly country homes. il McCalls 92:88-95 S '65
Fine furniture ready to paint. il House & Gard 127:106+ Mr '65
Furniture glossary (cont) il Am Home 68:92 Mr '65
Furniture with a future. See issues of House & garden incorporating Living for young homemakers
Good furniture buys under $100. il Bet Hom & Gard 43:29-30+ O '65
Great expectations; 1966 viewpoints. il House & Gard 129:100-5 Ja '66
Innovative furniture of the nineteenth century; Antiques book preview. J. T. Butler. il Antiques 87:332-5 Mr '65
New products for the house. il Arch Rec 137:137+ mid-My '65
Newest! in living, in furniture. V. D. Hahn. il Am Home 68:39-45 Mr '65
Party furniture. il House & Gard 127:148-9 Mr '65
Redbook's guide to contemporary furniture. il Redbook 125:86-94 S '65
What's new in furnishings and housewares (cont) R. Martens and J. Gillies. il Farm J 89:84-5 Mr '65
Wood: what the new flooring, paneling and furniture can do for a room! D. Popplestone and D. Jordan. il Bet Hom & Gard 43:50-63 My '65

Anecdotes, facetiae, satire, etc.
Desk is a desk is a desk. E. G. Smith. il Redbook 124:97 Ap '65

Care
Keep furniture finish looking like new. B. G. Wadsworth. il Parents Mag 40:14 F '65

Decorating and painting
See Furniture, Painted

Design
Danish has had it in California. W. McQuail. il Arch Forum 123:92 Jl '65
Furniture selection and specification; designs for college dormitories. P Brust; W. F. Bernbrock. il Arch Rec 138:93+ S '65

Object: still life; interview. R. Artschwager. il Craft Horiz 25:28-30+ S '65
Style makes news in furniture. il Good H 160:136-43 My '65

Exhibitions
Essex County furniture. R. Davidson. il Antiques 88:146 Ag '65

Finishing
Antiquing your furniture. B. G. Wadsworth. il Parents Mag 41:112 Ja '66
Masterpieces in the making! new finish-it-yourself furniture. il Good H 160:122-4+ F '65
Refinishing: the new way is the easy way! D. Jordan and D. Popplestone. il Bet Hom & Gard 44:48-53 Ja '66

Refinishing
See Furniture—Finishing

Repairing
Finishing touches: give your room a go-together look. il Seventeen 24:178-9 Mr '65

FURNITURE, American
Cabinetmakers of the Norwich area; with Connecticut historical society list. H. Comstock. il Antiques 87:696-9 Je '65
Essex County furniture. R. Davidson. il Antiques 88:146 Ag '65
Furniture and interiors; old Northwest Territory. il Antiques 87:310-18 Mr '65
John Brown House loan exhibition of Rhode Island furniture. J. K. Ott. il Antiques 87:564-71 My '65
Providence cabinetmakers of the eighteenth and early nineteenth centuries. E. B. Monahan. il Antiques 87:573-9 My '65
Restorations in American furniture, what is acceptable? H. Sack. il Antiques 89:116-21 Ja '66
Rococo style in nineteenth-century American furniture; excerpts from American furniture of the nineteenth century. C. J. Otto. il Antiques 88:325-9 S '65
Scotia furnishings. J. M. Graham, 2d. il Antiques 89:99-102 Ja '66
Shop talk. R. Davidson. il Antiques 87:138+ F '65
Sources of some American regional furniture. J. T. Kirk. il Antiques 88:790-8 D '65 (to be cont)
Thomas Howard jr, Providence cabinetmaker. E. B. Monahon. il Antiques 87:702-4 Je '65

FURNITURE, Arrangement of
Decorating wrongs made right; good traffic pattern. il Bet Hom & Gard 43:28 S '65
These rooms cause talk! il Bet Hom & Gard 43:30+ N '65
Two fast furniture arrangements! P. Rumely. il Bet Hom & Gard 43:52-5 Mr '65

FURNITURE, Childrens
They'll grow as Hilary grows; play table and chairs. il Sunset 134:165-6 My '65
See also
Chests

FURNITURE, Convertible
How to make room for a guest when you don't have a guest room. D. Popplestone. il Bet Hom & Gard 43:54-9 Ag '65
New surprise furniture! Bet Hom & Gard 43:68-71+ Je '65
This furniture makes room for more! P. Rumely and E. T. Lawyer. il Bet Hom & Gard 44:32-5 Ja '66

FURNITURE, English
English decorative arts at the Art institute of Chicago. A. Wardwell. il Antiques 89:78-9, 83-7 Ja '66

FURNITURE, Inflatable
Inventor of the month; furniture you inflate; scientific space utilization. S. V. Jones. Sci Digest 57:30 Ap '65

FURNITURE, Italian
Redbook's guide to Italian furniture. J. Macurdy. il Redbook 125:82-90 My '65

FURNITURE, Metal
New age of metals. R. Reif. il N Y Times Mag p54-5 Ag 8 '65
You can make wrought-iron furniture. P. McCafferty. il Pop Sci 186:122-5 Je '65

FURNITURE, Modern. See Furniture

FURNITURE, Outdoor
Furnishing the great outdoors. B. Plumb. il N Y Times Mag p72-3 My 9 '65
It's an up-jumping umbrella table. il Sunset 135:113 S '65
King-size lawn lounger. S. Ellingson. il Pop Mech 124:140-1 Ag '65
Plastics; the outdoor type. il Good H 161:158 Jl '65
Smart, new look in outdoor furniture. il Bet Hom & Gard 43:36+ My '65

FURNITURE, Painted
Finishing touches: give your room a go-together look. il Seventeen 24:178-9 Mr '65

FURNITURE, Rococo
Rococo style in nineteenth-century American furniture; excerpts from American furniture of the nineteenth century. C. J. Otto. il Antiques 88:325-9 S '65
FURNITURE, Victorian
Galleries of nineteenth-century art in the Victoria and Albert museum. J. F. Hayward. il Antiques 87:690-5 Je '65
FURNITURE dealers. See Furniture industry and trade
FURNITURE finishing. See Furniture—Finishing
FURNITURE industry and trade
Home furnishings head toward a new design; All-industry home furnishings conference. il Bsns W p45-6+ Ag 14 '65
Taking a front seat in furniture. il Bsns W p50+ Ag 14 '65
FURNITURE makers. See Cabinetmakers
FURST, P. T.
Radiocarbon dates from a tomb in Mexico. bibliog Science 147:612-13 F 5 '65
FURTHER tales about men and women. See Maxwell, W.
FURTWÄNGLER, Wilhelm
Who's afraid of the Furtwängler Ring? M. Mayer. Hi Fi 15:32+ O '65
FUSELAGE of airplanes. See Airplanes—Fuselage
FUSES, Electric. See Electric fuses
FUSSELL, Paul
How to sing of a diminished thing. Sat R 48:30-2 Jl 3 '65
FUTURE
Accidental century, by M. Harrington. Review
Life 59:11 Ag 20 '65. B. D. Nossiter
Can we cope with tomorrow? A. Toffler. il Redbook 126:38-9+ Ja '66
Future as a way of life. A. Toffler. il Horizon 7:108-15 Sum '65
Help wanted for the brave new world; address, May 28, 1965. P. G. Peterson. Vital Speeches 31:724-7 S 15 '65
Publisher's foreword. J. J. Starrow, jr. Nation 201:15-17 S 20 '65
Step to man; excerpt. J. R. Platt. Science 149:607-13 Ag 6 '65; Same. il UNESCO Courier 18:4-9+ D '65
What's to come. W. R. Young. il Life 59:143+ D 24 '65
Why fear the future? complacency in a land of plenty; address, June 28, 1965. W. C. Mainwaring. Vital Speeches 31:691-6 S 1 '65
Your child and the world of tomorrow; questions and answers. D. N. Michael. il NEA J 55:33-48 Ja '66
See also
Forecasts
Nineteen hundred and eighty-four
Prophecies
FUTURE life
See also
Death
FUTURES. See Exchanges
FYLE, Clifford M.
Continent in quest of a publishing industry. UNESCO Courier 18:28-31 S '65

G

GAF. See General aniline and film corporation
GAO. See United States—General accounting office
GATT. See General agreement on tariffs and trade
GEM. See Ground effect machines
GI bill of rights. See Service men, Discharged—Education
GM. See General motors corporation
GMAC. See General motors acceptance corporation
G-men. See United States—Federal bureau of investigation
GNP. See Gross national product
GOP. See Republican party
GPO. See United States—Government printing office
GRI. corporation. See Geriatric research, incorporated
GSA. See United States—General services administration
GABBARD, Andrea
Companion; story. Seventeen 25:84-5 Ja '66

GABBAY, Kenneth H. and others
Sorbitol pathway: presence in nerve and cord with substrate accumulation in diabetes. bibliog Science 151:209-10 Ja 14 '66
GABLE, Christopher
Brief biography. S. Goodman. pors Dance Mag 39:50-1 Jl '65
GABLIK, Suzi
Crossing the bar. Art N 64:22-5 O '65
Meta-trompe-l'oeil. Art N 64:46-9 Mr '65
GABON
French in Gabon. R. D. Perry. New Repub 152:29 Je 5 '65; Reply. S. C. Easton. 152:29 Je 19 '65
See also
Lambaréné
GABRIEL, Alexander
Vision of a world economy. Nation 200:694-6 Je 28 '65
GABRIEL, Jack P.
China for Americans. Travel 123:58-61 Ap '65
GABRIELSON, Harley C. See Tellefsen, R. N. jt. auth.
GADFIELD, Mary Jane
In each of us. Sch Arts 65:35-7 S '65
GADGETS
Beauty workshop; getting the goods on the new gadgets. il Mlle 61:150-1 My '65
$40 stand-in for a note pad; Westinghouse H3ORl message center. il Consumer Rep 30:377-8 Ag '65
GADSBY, Margaret
Strike of the railroad shopmen; reprint from December 1922 issue. Mo Labor R 88:796 Jl '65
GAERTNER, Kenneth C.
Unemployed; poem. Christian Cent 82:235 F 24 '65
GAFFNEY, Mason
Applying economic controls. Bul Atomic Sci 21:20-5 Je '65
GAFFRON, Carole
Girl in the camel's-hair coat; story. Redbook 125:76-7 O '65
Kind of magic. Writer 79:12-14 Ja '66
GAGE, Kenneth D.
How to buy tires. Motor T 17:48-50+ My '65
GAGES
Varied uses developing for radioisotopes. B. Miller. il Aviation W 83:42-3+ Jl 19 '65
GAGLIANO, Frank
Conerico was here to stay. Criticism
New Yorker 41:108 Mr 13 '65
Time il 85:58 Mr 12 '65
GAGNÉ, Robert M.
Elementary science: a new scheme of instruction. bibliog Science 151:49-53 Ja 7 '66
GAHUKUS. See New Guinea—Native races
GAIN, Dick
Triad dance company, 92nd street Y. M. Marks. Dance Mag 39:68 Je '65
GAINES, Diana
No game for children; story. Redbook 125:163-85 My '65
GAINES, Edith
Collectors' notes. See issues of Antiques
GAINES, Ervin J.
Intellectual freedom. See issues of ALA bulletin
GAINES, Jack
Fathers-at-large. il por Good H 161:32-3 Jl '65
GAINS tax. See Income tax—Capital gains tax
GALACTIC systems
Andromeda galaxy dominates our view of distant universe. T. D. Nicholson. il Natur Hist 74:38-40 Mr '65
Andromeda galaxy: extension of the 610.5-megacycle-per-second map. J. R. Dickel and others. bibliog il Science 150:883-4 N 12 '65
Atoms span galactic space. Sci N L 87:295 My 8 '65
Cepheids of the Andromeda galaxy. G. S. Mumford. Sky & Tel 31:26 Ja '66
Deep-sky wonders. W. S. Houston. il Sky & Tel 29:186 Mr '65
Evolution of galaxies (cont) T. L. Page. il Sky & Tel 29:81-4 F '65
Exploding universe of quasars. L. Lessing. il Fortune 72:160-5+ D '65
Faint ring around the spiral galaxy M82. H. Arp. bibliog Science 148:363-4 Ap 16 '65
Galactic X-ray astronomy. C. S. Bowyer. il Sky & Tel 30:264-6 N '65
Galaxy's spiral shape. G. S. Mumford. Sky & Tel 29:281 My '65
Helium and the galaxy's age. Sky & Tel 29:219 Ap '65
Hydrogen emission line $n_{110} \rightarrow n_{109}$: detection at 5009 megahertz in galactic H II regions. B. Höglund and P. G. Mezger. bibliog il Science 150:339-40+ O 15 '65

GALACTIC systems—*Continued*
Intergalactic dark cloud? G. S. Mumford.
3d. il Sky & Tel 29:158 Mr '65
Magnetic field of the galaxy. G. L. Berge
and G. A. Seielstad. il Sci Am 212:46-54
bibliog(p 146) Je '65
Quasi-stellar galaxies. il Sky & Tel 30:67+
Ag '65
Ring around the stars. il Sci Digest 58:26-7
Jl '65
Search for cosmic light. Sky & Tel 30:211 O
'65
Search for intergalactic hydrogen in the
Virgo cluster. S. J. Goldstein, jr. bibliog il
Science 151:71-3 Ja 7 '66
Unusual feature near spiral galaxy M81.
G. S. Mumford. il Sky & Tel 29:346; 30:
141 Je, S '65
GALACTOSE metabolism
Galactose metabolism and cell sociology. H.
M. Kalckar. bibliog il Science 150:305-13
O 15 '65
GALACTOSIDASES
Puromycin: effect on messenger RNA syn-
thesis and β-galactosidase formation in
escherichia coli 15T-. B. H. Sells. bibliog
il Science 148:371-3 Ap 16 '65
GALANTI, Norbel L. See Gasic, G. J. jt. auth.
GALBRAITH, Catherine
Nehru: a view from the embassy. Harper
231:76-80 Jl '65
GALBRAITH, Georgie Starbuck
Hubbards revisited; poem. McCalls 92:180 F
'65
Interior decoration; poem. McCalls 93:198 N
'65
Meditation of the mother of the bride; poem.
McCalls 92:133 Jl '65
GALBRAITH, John Kenneth
Foreign policy: the stuck whistle. por Atlan
215:64-8 F '65
Let's don't be too solemn about books; ad-
dress, October 30, 1964. por ALA Bul 59:
112-14 F '65
Sex in college; letter. por Esquire 64:150+
D '65

about
Keynes revolution. por Newsweek 65:66 My
31 '65
New orthodoxy. H. Hazlitt. Newsweek 65:82
Je 21 '65
GALILEE
Land of Galilee. K. MacLeish. il Nat Geog
Mag 128:823-65 D '65
GALILEI, Galileo
Galileo: a great spirit; formally praised by
Pope Paul VI. il Time 85:55 Je 18 '65
Galileo: the man, his work, his misfortunes,
by J. Broderick. Review
Commonweal 82:729-30 O 1 '65. A. Baer
Galileo's discoveries in dynamics; adaptation
of address, September 19, 1964. N. R. Han-
son. bibliog il Science 147:471-8 Ja 29 '65;
Reply with rejoinder. M. M. Mueller. 149:
1048-9 S 3 '65
GALIN, David
Background and evoked activity in the audi-
tory pathway: effects of noise-shock pair-
ing. bibliog Science 149:761-3 Ag 13 '65
GALINA, Anna
Anna Galina. J. Anderson. il pors Dance
Mag 39:25-7 Je '65
GALL, Norman
Domnican imbroglio. New Repub 153:12-13
Jl 3 '65
GALL bladder. See Gallbladder
GALLAGER, Sheldon M.
Shop talk. See issues of Popular science
monthly to May 1965
GALLAGHER, Bernard J.
Yank in the B.E.F. memoir. por Am Herit-
age 16:18-27+ Je '65
GALLAGHER, Buell G.
Campus revolts: why students act that way;
interview. por U S News 58:66-7 Mr 29 '65
Thorns in the groves of academe; adaptation
of address. NEA J 54:52-4 My '65
GALLAGHER, Cornelius Edward
Wanted: more political gadflies. Christian
Cent 82:668 My 26 '65
GALLAGHER, Francis J.
Biography. America 113:690-2 N 27 '65
Book review. America 113:605-6 N 13 '65
Books to be noted; biography (cont) Amer-
ica 112:672-4 My 8 '65
GALLAGHER, J. Roswell
Emerging specialty: adolescent medicine.
D. W. Lewis. il Todays Health 43:38-41 F
'65
GALLAGHER, Joseph
Warning? America 112:611 Ap 24 '65
GALLAGHER, Joseph V.
New books. Cath World 201:143-4 My '65

GALLAGHER, Thomas
Day in the life of a family doctor. Good H
160:78-81+ F '65

about
Introducing Thomas Gallagher. B. Cook. Cath
World 202:96-101 N '65
GALLANT, Kathryn
Are you a good mother? Parents Mag 40:
154-5 N '65
GALLANT, Mavis
In transit; story. New Yorker 41:24-5 Ag
14 '65
Orphans' progress; story. New Yorker 41:49-
51 Ap 3 '65
Statues taken down; story. New Yorker 41:
53-6 O 9 '65
Virus X; story. New Yorker 40:29-40 Ja 30
'65
GALLANTRY; story. See Maloney, R.
GALLATIN, Tenn.
Water worries disappear with the old plant.
D. L. Kuhlman. il Am City 81:110-11 Ja '66
GALLBLADDER
Surgery
Operation in 8 pavilion; President Johnson's
surgery. il Newsweek 66:33 O 18 '65
Presidential cholecystectomy. il Time 86:59
O 15 '65
What doctors say about gall-bladder surgery.
il U S News 59:35 O 18 '65
GALLE, Johann Gottfried
Long career of J. G. Galle. J. Ashbrook. por
Sky & Tel 30:355 D '65
GALLEGO, A. and Cruz, J.
Mammalian retina: associational nerve cells
in ganglion cell layer. bibliog Science 150:
1313-14 D 3 '65
GALLER, David
Jersey marsh; poem. New Yorker 41:166 Mr
13 '65
Makers; poem. New Yorker 41:32 Ja 15 '66
Trust; Habit; Hall; poems. Poetry 105:361-4
Mr '65
GALLERIES and museums. See Art—Galleries
and museums
GALLERIES and museums, Underground. See
Underground structures
GALLICO, Paul William
Mrs 'Arris goes to Parliament; story. Ladies
Home J 82:80-1 Mr '65
Small miracle; story; condensation. Read
Digest 87:203-8 Jl '65
Snow goose; story; condensation. Read Digest
87:226-8 D '65
Writers should be heard but not obscene.
Writer 78:15-16 O '65
—and Szasz, Suzanne
What every young cat ought to know; ex-
cerpt from Silent miaow. il Read Digest
86:178-82 F '65
GALLIPOLI campaign, 1915. See European war,
1914-1918—Campaigns and battles—Turkey
and the Near East
GALLIUM antimonide
Superconducting gallium antimonide. D. B.
McWhan and others. bibliog il Science
147:1441-2 Mr 19 '65
GALLO, Frank
New medium for sculpture, reinforced plas-
tics. il Design 66:15 Mr '65
Plastic people. il por Newsweek 66:90 N 29
'65
GALLO, Marilyn
Pellegrino and the professor; story. Mlle 61:
262-3 Ag '65
GALLOIS, Pierre M.
How U.S. is doing in Europe and Asia, a
French size-up; interview. por U S News
59:58-60 D 20 '65
GALLOWAY, Eilene
International regulation of outer space acti-
vities. Bul Atomic Sci 21:36-9 F '65
GALLOWAY, Harry, and Sisson, Don
Drainage: first step to high profits. Suc Farm
63:42-3+ S '65
GALLSTONES. See Calculi, Biliary
GALLUP, George
You may be smarter than you think; excerpt
from Miracle ahead. Read Digest 86:145+
My '65
GALPHIN, Bruce
Inward and the outward ear. Sat R 48:22 Je
5 '65
GALSTER, George M.
Transistor ignitions, good? bad? and how
can you tell? Motor B 115:82-3+ Mr '65
GALSTON, Arthur W.
Death isn't necessary; condensed from ad-
dress. por Sci Digest 58:80-5 Jl '65
—See Bendaña, F. E. jt. auth.
GALT, John
Inventing to discover. L. Turco. Poetry 106:
370 Ag '65

GALTON, Lawrence
Can you answer these questions about blood?
Pop Sci 186:122-5+ Mr '65
Commuting at 1,000 m.p.h. N Y Times Mag
p76-7+ O 24 '65
Personality of the month. Sci Digest 57:38-40
My '65

GALVIN, Brendan
Dollae Americanae; poem. Atlan 215:93 F '65
New critic; poem. Atlan 216:113 Ag '65

GALVIN, Thomas J.
Reference encounter. por Library J 90:1818-
24 Ap 15 '65

GAMBIA
Blessed are the poor. il Newsweek 65:44+
Mr 1 '65
Newest, smallest: Gambia gains indepen-
dence. il Time 85:32+ F 26 '65
See also
United Nations—Gambia

GAMBLE, Theodore Robert
New look at Pet milk. J. B. Weiner. il por
Duns R 85:36-8+ Mr '65
Pet milk spills over into other pastures. il
por Bsns W p58-60+ Jl 31 '65

GAMBLER; story. See O'Hara, J.

GAMBLING
Case of the dead bookie; R. Markowitz. R.
Kahn. il Sat Eve Post 238:34-8+ Mr 13 '65
Case of the too hot golfer; F. DiPaglia. G. S.
Brown. il Sports Illus 23:42-4+ N 22 '65
Faded youth; teen-agers' casino, Haworth,
N.J. il Newsweek 65:29 Mr 8 '65
Five-figure exercise; Calcuttas. Time 86:59
Ag 20 '65
Gamblers' money, by W. Turner. Review
Life 58:17-18 F 26 '65. W. Lambert
Sat R 48:31 F 27 '65. F. J. Cook
More fun than the watusi; playing of
dominoes by San Francisco society. R.
Cantwell. il Sports Illus 22:50-2+ Mr 29
'65
Poker problems. il Good H 161:12+ S '65
Sin of betting. C. W. Morton. il Atlan 215:
124+ My '65
Tahoe notebook. J. Brown. il Holiday 38:76-
86+ D '65
Third man; Pushkin's Queen of spades. B.
Goldovsky. Opera N 30:26-7 Ja 15 '66
Toughest customers; football gamblers. O.
Demaris. Esquire 64:77+ O '65
Two bit bet; financing a crime empire. B.
Carey. Look 29:131-2+ D 14 '65
Tragedy of a compulsive gambler. A. Poin-
sett. il Ebony 21:133-4+ Jl '65
VIH; Las Vegas gamblers threaten ex-law-
yer. Newsweek 65:32+ Ap 19 '65
What Del Webb is up to in Nevada. T. Alex-
ander. il Fortune 71:130-2+ My '65
When police raided a casino for teen-agers;
Haworth, N.J. il U S News 58-11 Mr 8 '65
Why I gambled and what it cost me; foot-
ball gambling; excerpt from Football and
the single man. P. Hornung. il Look 29:
61-2+ Ag 10 '65
World's biggest gambler; W. F. Harrah,
Tahoe casino owner. R. Wernick. il Sat
Eve Post 238:27-32 F 13 '65
See also
Cardsharping
Horse race betting
Lotteries

Europe, Western
Little bit illicit. il Time 85:31-2 Je 18 '65

Great Britain
God save the ace; London biggest gambling
center. Time 86:70 S 10 '65

United States
See Gambling

GAMBLING machines
Wheels and bells of wills and mills; portfolio. Fortune 71:133-5 My '65

GAME
Big game hunting forecast. il Field & S 70:
106-7 Ag '65

GAME birds
See also
Pheasant shooting
Shooting
also names of game birds, e.g. Ducks,
Wild

GAME calls. See Animal calling

GAME laws
Canadian hunting seasons. Outdoor Life 136:
176 O '65
Field & stream 1965 hunting forecast, small
& big game. il Field & S 70:53-64 O '65
Hunting seasons (cont) Outdoor Life 136:16+
S: 71-4 O '65
Sinkbox shoot; paintings by R. Cunningham;
with account by D. Barnes. Sports Illus 23:
40-5 O 4 '65

GAME of chess; story. See Brown, G.

GAME preserves
Ranches for wild beasts. B. Tufty. il Sci
N L 87:234-5 Ap 10 '65

GAME protection
See also
Game laws
Game preserves
Wildlife conservation

GAME; story. See Barthelme, D.

GAME wardens
Gamest warden of them all. R. Starnes. Field
& S 70:10+ My '65

GAMER, Eleanor E.
Fossil beds of Florissant. Nat Parks Mag
39:16-19 Jl '65

GAMES
Adult games, no easy kid stuff. H. Shuldiner.
il Pop Sci 187:173-5 N '65
Child's play; Merit; Catholic monopoly. il
Newsweek 66:56 Ag 16 '65
Everyone plays the company game; Citibank.
il Bsns W p34 F 6 '65
Gamy days ahead; photographs by L. St
John; with account by P. Knight. Sports
Illus 23:72-7 N 22 '65
Good old games with brand-new twists. Bet
Hom & Gard 43:169 O '65
Irresistible games that prompt a lively party.
il House & Gard 128:216-17 S '65
It's how you play the game; parlor games.
E. Craster. il Bet Hom & Gard 44:44-7
Ja '66
One hobby set and a brain game; Colorada
home screen printing set and Wff'n proof.
il Consumer Bul 49:25 Ja '66
These are mostly games and very quick to
make. il Bet Hom & Gard 43:52-3+ D '65
WFF 'n proof, a game that makes learning
math fun. Pub W 187:92 Ap 19 '65
See also
Bowling on the green
Cards
Childrens amusements
Dominoes (game)
Piñatas
School athletics
Treasure hunts

Anecdotes, facetiae, satire, etc.
Closing the game gap; anti-Communist
games. C. M. Curtis. il Atlan 216:150-1 O '65
In the far-off land of ennui, etc; original
brainteasers. T. Meehan. New Yorker 41:
49-50 N 6 '65

**GAMES, Mathematical. See Mathematical rec-
reations**

GAMES, Theory of
Games, logic and computers. H. Wang il Sci
Am 213:98-104+ N '65

GAMMA globulin
Functional ribosomal unit of gamma-globulin
synthesis. M. D. Scharff and J. W. Uhr.
bibliog il Science 148:646-8 Ap 30 '65
Gamma-globulin factors (Gm and Inv) in
New Guinea: anthropological significance.
E. Giles and others. bibliog il Science 150:
1158-60 N 26 '65
Isoantigens of gamma globulin in pigs. B. A.
Rasmusen. bibliog il Science 148:1742-3 Je
25 '65
Nonspecific binding of complement by digestion fragments from antiviral gamma
globulin. N. E. Cremer and others. bibliog
il Science 149:84-5 Jl 2 '65

GAMMA rays
Gamma rays can spot invisible air movement.
Sci N L 88:291 N 6 '65

GANDAR, Laurence
How to lose friends. Time 86:36 S 3 '65

GANDEK, Linda J. and Pramer, David
Cousin to mite and spider. Natur Hist 74:63
N '65

GANDHI, Indira (Nehru)
Process of change. il por Time 87:22-5 Ja 21
'66

GANDHI, Mohandas Karamchand
Spirit of holiness in men of power. Life 58:
4 Ap 16 '65

GANGES RIVER
Well traveled camera. H. Keppler. il Mod
Phot 30:26+ Ja '66

GANGS
Hell's Angels; outlaw motorcycle club in
Calif. W. Murray. il Sat Eve Post 238:32-9
N 20 '65
Motorcycle gangs; losers and outsiders. H.
S. Thompson. il Nation 200:522-6 My 17
'65
Requiem for an Angel; funeral of J. T. Miles
of the Hell's Angels. il Time 87:57 Ja 21
'66
They no longer bop, they jap. G. Samuels.
il N Y Times Mag p40+ Mr 7 '65

GANGS—*Continued*
Watch out, whitey; Negro youth gangs and violence. L. Yablonsky. New Repub 154:10-12 Ja 1 '66; Reply. T. J. Cummins. 154:29-30 Ja 22 '66
Wilder ones; Hell's Angels of California. il Time 85:23B Mr 26 '65
See also
Juvenile delinquency
GANGSTERS. See Crime and criminals—United States
GANNETT, Lewis
Ripening of the dream. Sat R 48:99-100 S 18 '65
GANNON, Frank
London scene. Nat R 17:838-40 S 21 '65
GANNON, Robert
Balls o' fire! Pop Mech 124:116-19+ S '65
Day I swallowed a camera. por Pop Sci 187:56-7+ Jl '65
How hams track space shots. Pop Sci 186:99-102 My '65
You're tougher than you think. Pop Sci 186:78-81 Ap '65
GANNON, Ruth
New way to freeze a garden's goodness. Flower Grower 52:10+ Jl '65
Three unusual vegetables. Flower Grower 52:54-5 My '65
GANS, Herbert J.
Failure of urban renewal. Commentary 39:29-37 Ap; 40:77-80 Jl; 19-20 N '65
Negro family. Commonweal 83:47-51 O 15 '65
Who's o-o-oh in America. Vogue 145:108+ Mr 15 '65
GANTNER, Edna
How to grow mouthwatering strawberries. Pop Gard 16:32 Mr '65
GARAGES
Clutter-free garage. il House & Gard 128:112-13 Jl '65
Good-looking but inexpensive carport. il Bet Hom & Gard 43:78 Ap '65
Why settle for a bad house? il Bet Hom & Gard 43:58-9 N '65
GARAGES (service stations) See Automobile service stations
GARAGES, Municipal
Planning a downtown parking deck. R. C. Rich. il Arch Rec 137:177-82 My '65
This parking garage; White Plains, N.Y. W. H. Bruder. il Am City 80:98-100 D '65

Heating and ventilation
Fresh-air heater stops negative pressure problems; solution in Dearborn, Mich. il Am City 80:94 Jl '65
GARAGES, Toy
Two-story parking garage. il Sunset 135:96+ D '65
GARAGIOLA, Joe
Sweet sound of success. H. Horn. il pors Sports Illus 22:30-2+ Mr 15 '65
GARBAGE. See Refuse, Utilization of
GARBAGE collection and disposal. See Refuse and refuse disposal
GARBAGE grinders. See Refuse grinders
GARBELL, Maurice A.
Jordan Valley plan; with biographical sketch. Sci Am 212:16, 23-31 Mr '65
GARBER, Benjamin F.
Out there in the universe; exhibition at Knoedler gallery. il Newsweek 66:88 N 1 '65
GARBO, Greta
Saga of Greta Lovisa Gustafson. H. Alpert. il pors N Y Times Mag p26-7+ S 5 '65
GARCIA, Joaquin Torres-. See Torres-García, J.
GARCIA, Pauline Viardot-. See Viardot-García, P.
GARCIA-AMADOR, F. V.
Dominican situation. Américas 17:1-3 Jl '65
Latin American integration. Américas 17:50-3 Ap '65
GARCIA DEL SOLAR, Lucio
United Nations commemoration address, June 25, 1965. UN Mo Chron 2:92-6 Jl '65
GARCIA GODOY, Héctor
Back to Bosch? New Repub 153:9 S 18 '65
Hate in the streets. por Newsweek 67:49 Ja 17 '66
One step forward. il por Newsweek 66:51 S 13 '65
Still elusive Dominican peace. S. Acoca. por Life 59:32B Jl 23 '65
Waiting for Godoy. Time 86:39 Jl 16 '65
GARCIA LORCA, Federico
Sketches of the banned. il Time 86:50 Ag 20 '65
GARCIA corporation
Making a wider cast to lure the customers. il Bsns W p94-6+ Ap 10 '65

GARCILASO DE LA VEGA, el Inca
Inca Garcilaso. A. Salgado. il Américas 17:22-8 Jl '65
GARDELIUS, Patricia
Embattled nurse of Jackrabbit Flats. J. G. Dunne. il pors Sat Eve Post 238:42-4+ N 20 '65
GARDEN barrows. See Wheelbarrows
GARDEN borders
Wood edging for garden beds. il Sunset 135:264-5 O '65
GARDEN boundaries
Ideas to profit by; planting for a boundary. J. B. Brimer. il Flower Grower 52:33 My '65
GARDEN carts. See Carts
GARDEN catalogs. See Catalogs, Seed and plant
GARDEN centers
Saga of a garden center: Greenwich garden center, Greenwich, Conn. B. Black. il Flower Grower 52:37-9 Je '65
GARDEN CITY, N.Y.
Many roads to reading: Homestead school. A. Eisenberg and H. Eisenberg. il Look 29:M7-11 My 4 '65
GARDEN clubs
How to organize a garden club. il Good H 161:163 S '65
See also
Garden centers
National council of state gardens clubs, incorporated
GARDEN design
Here you see a garden gamble paying off; garden of H. L. Dietrich of Sierra Madre. il Sunset 135:230-1 N '65
Lots of garden in a small space. E. McClure. il Pop Gard 16:30 My '65
New look with stone. il Flower Grower 52:28-30 S '65
Planning makes perfect. R. S. Maxwell. il Pop Gard 16:24-7 My '65
Portfolio of plans for little gardens. il Flower Grower 52:20-3 S '65
Take flower show ideas home with you. N. Gillespie. il Horticulture 43:40-1+ Mr '65
Texture is essential in the garden. J. Hudak. il Horticulture 43:28-9+ My '65
See also
Gardening—Planting plans and tables
GARDEN equipment. See Garden tools, equipment and supplies
GARDEN fences. See Fences
GARDEN furniture. See Furniture, Outdoor
GARDEN gates. See Gates
GARDEN hose
Three tips for happy hosing. K. Murray. il Flower Grower 52:5 Ag '65
GARDEN houses, shelters, etc.
Add a place to park your power equipment and garden tools. R. L. Hering. il Pop Gard 16:32-4 S '65
Garden teahouse. J. H. Ingersoll. il Pop Gard 17:30-1+ Ja '66
Our second home is a chicken coop. G. Logsdon. il Farm J 89:19 S '65
Place to pot and putter. S. Stewart. il Pop Gard 17:12-13 Ja '66
These portable pavilions have all sorts of garden uses. il Sunset 135:82-3 S '65
Tool shed houses the dog, too. H. Pfister. il Pop Sci 187:128-30 Ag '65
Total tool shed revisited. il House & Gard 128:132-3 Jl '65
See also
Pergolas
GARDEN lighting. See Gardens—Lighting
GARDEN ornaments
It's a sculptor's retreat. il Sunset 135:171 Jl '65
Little touches that count. W. Radcliffe. il Flower Grower 52:30-1 My '65
New look with stone. il Flower Grower 52:28-30 S '65
One good idea can transform your whole garden. il House & Gard 128:214-17 O '65
See also
Fountains
GARDEN paths. See Walks (paths)
GARDEN pools
Accent your patio with a lily pool. J. E. Dwyer. il Pop Gard 16:33 Ap '65
Controlling algae in a pool. Sunset 134:122+ Ap '65
Flower grower's home garden notebook. J. B. Brimer. il Flower Grower 52:43-4 F '65
Our small terrace pool; excerpt from Rockwells' complete guide to successful gardening. F. F. Rockwell and E. C. Grayson. il Flower Grower 52:39 Mr '65
Pause to reflect. M. Perry. il Flower Grower 52:56-7 Mr '65

GARDEN pools—*Continued*
Pocket-sized pool. il Flower Grower 52:19 N '65
Pools. C. B. Lees. il Horticulture 43:42-5 My '65
Sometimes it's a pool, sometimes a plant stage. il Sunset 134:132 Je '65
This fountain pool cares for itself. il Sunset 135:54-5 Ag '65
Water for your terrace. il Flower Grower 52:24-5 Ag '65
Water: visual, aural and salutary delight. il House & Gard 127:150-3+ Mr '65
See also
Fountains

GARDEN soils. See Gardening—Soil preparation

GARDEN tools, equipment and supplies
Build a gas-powered mulcher. E. F. Lindsley. il Pop Sci 187:136-40 O '65
Care packages for a gardener's Christmas. il House & Gard 128:330-1 N '65
Eleven gifts for plant buyers. il Sunset 135:188 D '65
For every homeowner: basic hand tools. il Pop Gard 16:16 My '65
Have you heard? See issues of Flower grower, the home garden magazine
Let electricity ease your hard work. J. Hand. il Pop Sci 187:60-3 Jl '65
Little engine that does. . . il Flower Grower 52:26-7+ Je '65
New products for better lawns. il Flower Grower 52:54-5 Ap '65
New tool helps you plant anything from bulbs to bedding plants. il Sunset 135:266 O '65
Some slightly unusual garden tool gifts il Sunset 135:180+ D '65
Workshop and garden equipment. Consumer Rep 30:193-202 D '65
See also
Hedge clippers
Hoes
Lawn sweepers
Tractors

Storage
See also
Garden houses, shelters, etc.

GARDEN tours
Flower shows and garden tours. il House & Gard 127:16+ Mr '65
Gardens to visit. D. McFadden. il Pop Gard 16:40-4 Jl '65
Green mansions. B. Black. il Pop Gard 16:38-41 My '65
Victoria, city of charm; 1966 garden tours. M. Perry. il Flower Grower 52:44 D '65
Virginia in the spring. J. E. Dwyer. il Pop Gard 16:16 Mr '65
When private gardens are open to the public. B. Nichols. il Pop Gard 16:37+ Jl '65

GARDEN tractors. See Tractors

GARDEN walks
Brick. J. H. Ingersoll. il Pop Gard 16:18-21 N '65
Paving walks & terraces. J. B. Brimer. il Flower Grower 52:49 Mr '65
Quick & easy paths & patios. il Flower Grower 52:24-5 Mr '65
Try pebble-faced paving for new beauty underfoot. B. Gilmore. il Pop Sci 187:152-4 S '65

GARDEN walls
Build an open brick wall. J. B. Brimer. il Flower Grower 52:40-1 Je '65

GARDENIAS
Gardenia success story. S. Fenell. il Flower Grower 52:28-9+ N '65
Gardenias deserve special care. il Sunset 134:250-1 Je '65

GARDENING
All around the place. J. Milton. Pop Gard 16:51 Mr '65
Fall garden notes; some things to do before winter. B. Brinhart. il Pop Gard 16:8+ S '65
Fruit-truck news. See issues of Farm journal
Hand-me-down garden ideas. J. H. Clarke. il Horticulture 43:28-9 Ag '65
H&G's gardener's month. See issues of House & garden incorporating Living for young homemakers
How to become a better gardener in winter. il Good H 162:135 Ja '66
[Month] gardening where you live! See issues of Better homes and gardens
[Month] in your garden. See issues of Sunset
Offbeat ideas for the garden. il Changing T 19:26 Ap '65
Pop Gardener says. H. R. O'Brien. See issues of Popular gardening & living outdoors
Quick and easy tips. See issues of Popular gardening & living outdoors
Regional gardening; symposium. See issues of Popular gardening & living outdoors

Spring checkup every garden needs. il Good H 160:176 Ap '65
Time to start thinking of spring. Changing T 19:6 Mr '65
What to do in the garden now! autumn work. il Changing T 19:46-7 S '65
See also
Bulbs
Catalogs, Seed and plant
Flowers
Garden centers
Garden tools, equipment and supplies
Gardens
Herbs
Transplanting
Watering of gardens, lawns, etc.

Anecdotes, facetiae, satire, etc.
No-sweat garden guide for spring. W. F. Miksch. il Atlan 215:126+ My '65

Bibliography
Books for holiday giving. E. C. Hall. il Pop Gard 16:10-11+ N '65

Planting plans and tables
Doorway garden. il Flower Grower 52:38-9 My '65
Spring mix-mates to plant this fall. R. M. Peters. il Pop Gard 16:40-1 S '65

Soil preparation
Get your soil in shape. B. C. Kilvert, jr. il Flower Grower 52:44-7 Mr '65
How my Saturday's bargain became a truckload of trouble. W. H. Hull. il Flower Grower 52:42-3 Je '65
How to make a soil sifter. il Sunset 134:264 Mr '65

GARDENING, Landscape. See Landscape gardening

GARDENING, Vegetable. See Vegetable gardening

GARDENS
Good cutting garden. J. Fanning. il House & Gard 127:206-9+ My '65
This garden without a lawn offers variety instead. il Sunset 135:64-5+ Ag '65
What is a garden? C. B. Lees. il Horticulture 43:32-3 Mr '65
See also
Back yards
City gardens
Floriculture
Flowers
Garden design
Gardening
Gardens, Desert

Bibliography
Onward and upward in the garden. K. S. White. New Yorker 41:164+ D 18 '65

Color
For color come winter, plant these annuals now. il Sunset 135:250-1 O '65
For color saturation you can't beat spring bulbs. il House & Gard 128:188-9 S '65
Green garden. J. R. Rebhan. il Flower Grower 52:28-31+ Jl '65
How to be color ahead next summer! H. Mason. il Bet Hom & Gard 43:68-9 S '65
Paints & plants. J. D. Parslow. il Flower Grower 52:26 Mr '65
Plant a golden spring. M. J. Dietz. il Flower Grower 52:23-7 O '65
Spectacular color this summer! H. Mason. il Bet Hom & Gard 43:68-71 My '65
White garden. il Sunset 135:60-1 Ag '65
See also
Color of flowers

Fragrant
See Gardens, Fragrant

Lighting
After dark garden. S. Schuler. il Flower Grower 52:37+ My '65
Garden lights in clay, weathered metal, wood. il Sunset 134:116+ F '65

California
From open lot to quiet, enclosed garden; front garden in La Habra. il Sunset 134:242+ Mr '65
Here you see a garden gamble paying off; garden of H. L. Dietrich of Sierra Madre. il Sunset 135:230-1 N '65
Image of true luxuriance. il House & Gard 127:154-7 My '65
In a great gardener's great garden every plant is king; Hortense Miller's garden at Laguna Beach. il House & Gard 127:166-9+ Ap '65

GARDENS—California—*Continued*
New idea-gardens you can visit in San Francisco's Golden Gate park. il Sunset 135:74-7 S '65
This garden is just four months old. il Sunset 134:270-1 My '65
See also
Santa Barbara botanic garden

Canada

All around the place; Butchart gardens. J. Milton. Pop Gard 16:43 N '65
Victoria's Butchart gardens. M. Perry. il Flower Grower 53:58 9 Ja '66

Connecticut

Poet's garden. M. E. O'Brien. il Pop Gard 16:20-3 S '65

England

When private gardens are open to the public. B. Nichols. il Pop Gard 16:37+ Jl '65
See also
London—Gardens

Florida

Gardener's guide to Florida. E. A. Menninger. il Horticulture 43:30-3+ D '65

Greece, Modern

Good ideas from home gardens in Greece. G. Taloumis. il Flower Grower 52:28-9 F '65

Hawaii

There are many ideas for mainlanders in this Hawaiian garden. il Sunset 134:116-18 My '65

Ireland

Ireland grows more than shamrocks. M. L. Garra. il Horticulture 44:30-1 Ja '66

Louisiana

Great New Orleans garden where elegance looks easy. il House & Gard 127:126-9 F '65

Massachusetts

Gardens at the Adams national historic site; Quincy, Mass. R. C. Hands. il Horticulture 43:40-1+ My '65

Monaco

Above Monte Carlo, the Exotic garden. il Sunset 134:80+ Je '65

New Jersey

Conservation; New Jersey style. E. Finch. il Pop Gard 16:34-5+ Ap '65

New York (state)

Reader's digest gardens, Pleasantville, New York. C. Pintchman. il Horticulture 43:34-6 Ag '65
See also
New York (city)—Gardens

Northeastern states

Gardens to visit. D. McFadden. il Pop Gard 16:40-4 Jl '65

Ohio

Kingwood center, Mansfield, Ohio. J. M. Martin. il Horticulture 43:44-7 Ap '65

United States

American public gardens. M. Frome. il Holiday 38:91-6 Jl '65
English nurseryman comments on American gardens. H. G. Hillier. il Horticulture 43:36-7+ Mr '65
See also subhead Gardens under names of cities, e.g. Washington, D.C.—Gardens

GARDENS, Childrens. See Childrens gardens
GARDENS, City. See City gardens
GARDENS, Desert
Ideas for arid country gardens. L. Burgess. il Flower Grower 52:36 Ag '65
GARDENS, Fragrant
Put fragrance in your summertime living. M. M. Leister. il Flower Grower 52:32-3+ Je '65
GARDENS, Indoor
Garden indoors. E. Cherry. il Horticulture 43:30-1 Mr '65
Grow a complete garden indoors under lights. E. C. Cherry. il Flower Grower 52:20-1+ O '65
Try an indoor garden for an early spring. Suc Farm 63:130 Mr '65
GARDENS, Rock
Good ways to hold up a bank. il Bet Hom & Gard 43:74-5 Ap '65
Small gems for your rock garden. B. Miles. il Pop Gard 16:22-3+ N '65
GARDENS, School. See School gardens

GARDENS, Seaside
Seashore gardens. M. M. Taylor; E. S. Henderson. Pop Gard 16:22-3+ Jl '65
Weatherproof plants for the seashore. G. Taloumis. il House & Gard 128:128-30+ Ag '65
GARDENS, Sunken
Sunken garden; Mormon temple at the New York world's fair. M. Orans. il Pop Gard 16:54 My '65
GARDENS, Vegetable. See Vegetable gardening
GARDER, Michel
Soviet revolution will come around 1970; interview, ed. by F. C. Painton. por U S News 58:46-8 Je 21 '65
GARDINER, C. Harvey
Costa Rica; mighty midget. bibliog f Cur Hist 50:8-13+ Ja '66
GARDINER, Harold C.
Making of an encyclopedia. America 112:668-9 My 8 '65
Scholars, Catholic, who's got the? America 113:442-3 O 16 '65
GARDINER, Tenley Albright
There is a doctor on the ice. B. La Fontaine. il pors Sports Illus 22:28-30+ F 8 '65
GARDINER, Tudor
There is a doctor on the ice. B. La Fontaine. il pors Sports Illus 22:28-30+ F 8 '65
GARDINIER, David E.
(comp) Articles and other books received; Africa. See issues of American historical review
GARDNER, Albert Ten Eyck
American art at the Metropolitan. Antiques 87:434-8 Ap '65
GARDNER, Arthur E.
Behind the glamor of computer composition. Pub W 188:90+ O 4 '65
GARDNER, Dwayne E.
Land-rich or land-poor schools. por Am Ed 1:12-14 N '65
GARDNER, Erle Stanley
My love affair with sand and wheels. pors Pop Sci 187:112-17+ N '65
Speed dash. Atlan 215:55-7 Je '65
about
Case of the busy bookwright. R. Kirsch. il por N Y Times Mag p89+ Mr 21 '65
GARDNER, Frank M.
Library explosion. por Library J 90:4897-901 N 15 '65
GARDNER, Gerald
Kennedys in New York; excerpts. McCalls 92:100-3+ Ag '65
GARDNER, Helen Lieban
Life with music. Opera N 30:6 Ja 22 '66
GARDNER, Isabella
Word from the Piazza del Limbo; poem. Poetry 105:225-6 Ja '65
GARDNER, Isabella (Stewart)
Improper Bostonian. il Time 86:96 S 10 '65
Mrs Jack, by L. H. Tharp. Review Atlan 217:117 Ja '66. E. Weeks
GARDNER, John W.
Education as a way of life. Science 148:759-61 My 7 '65
Health, education, and welfare; excerpts from address, November 18, 1965. Science 150:1684-6 D 24 '65
How to prevent organizational dry rot. Harper 231:20+ O '65
Private initiative for the public good. Read Digest 87:98-102 O '65
Some quotes from John Gardner on excellence, self-renewal and other matters. Science 149:614-15 Ag 6 '65
about
Educator takes on problem pupil, HEW. por Bsns W p32+ Ag 14 '65
Excellence for HEW. por Newsweek 66:27 Ag 9 '65
Explorer for excellence. por Time 86:23 Ag 6 '65
Foundations for progress. il por Newsweek 65:105-6 Ap 12 '65
Gardner appointment. J. Lear. Sat R 48:46 Ag 21 '65
Gardner named new HEW chief. il por Sr Schol 86:sup3 S 16 '65
HEW; as Secretary of Department of health, education and welfare Gardner faces formidable task. J. Walsh. por Science 149:613-16 Ag 6 '65
In man for the Cabinet. R. T. Elson. por Fortune 72:154-7+ O '65
John Gardner becomes HEW head. por Library J 90:3708 S 15 '65
Leadership for education. J. Cass. Sat R 49:57-8 Ja 15 '66

GARDNER John W.—about—*Continued*
Real power in education today. il por U S
News 59:16 Ag 9 '65
White House conference on education and
the emergence of the new guard. F. Parker.
Sch & Soc 93:425-8 N 13 '65
GARDNER, Martin
Child's garden of bewilderment. Sat R 48:
18-19 Jl 17 '65
Mathematical games. See issues of Scientific
American
GARDNER, Paul V.
Eighteenth-century porcelain at the Smith-
sonian. Antiques 88:336-40 S '65
GARDNER, Richard N.
United Nations procedures and power reali-
ties: the international apportionment prob-
lem: address, April 23, 1965. Dept State
Bul 52:701-11 My 10 '65
GARFIELD, James Abram
James A. Garfield, twentieth President. F.
Freidel. il pors Nat Geog Mag 127:690-3
My '65
GARGAN, Edward T.
Reflections on tunneling out of an antheap.
Commonweal 81:644 F 12 '65
GARGAN, William
Bill Gargan's greatest role. il pors Life 59:
63-4 D 3 '65
GARGOYLES
Gargoyles for Washington; National cathe-
dral. E. L. Horwitz. il Horizon 7:46-8 Sum
'65
GARIBALDI, Carole
Movie report. Good H 161:35 D '65
GARLAND, Judy
Triumph of Judy's Liza. il por Life 58:82-4
My 28 '65
GARLAND, Tex.
Garland's PR is showing. Am City 80:154+
My '65
GARLAND of friendship; story. See Manning,
R.
GARLIC
And a touch of garlic; import duties to be
eliminated in western Europe. Time 85:
88 F 12 '65
GARLITS, Don
Champion of champions. D. Wells. il Hot Rod
18:82-3+ F '65
GARMENT workers
See also
Amalgamated clothing workers of America
Clothing industry—Wages and hours
GARN, Stanley M.
Interracial marriage isn't the solution; inter-
view. por U S News 58:59-61 Je 28 '65
GARNER, Erroll
My pleasure. il por Newsweek 65:94+ Je 21
'65
GARNER, Lou
Solid state (cont of) Transistor topics. See
issues of Popular electronics
GARRA, Martha Ludes
Ireland grows more than shamrocks. il Horti-
culture 44:30-1 Ja '66
GARRARD, Mimi
Mimi Garrard and company, Henry street
playhouse. J. Maskey. Dance Mag 39:64
Jl '65
GARRELS, Robert M.
Silica: role in the buffering of natural waters.
bibliog Science 148:69 Ap 2 '65
—See Mackenzie, F. T. jt. auth.
GARRETT, Arthur
Attorney & his client. por Time 86:35 Jl 2
'65
GARRETT, Bernard S.
How two janitors bought white bank in
Texas. L. Robinson. il por Ebony 20:119-22+
Je '65
GARRETT, Mike
Trojan horse. H. L. Masin. por Sr Schol 87:
26 N 4 '65
GARRETT, Robert, and Harris, Michael
Opportunity in foreign bonds. Harvard Bsns
R 43:73-80 N '65
GARRETT, W. E.
Alaska's marine highway. il Nat Geog Mag
127:776-819 Je '65
GARRETT COUNTY, Md.
Snowtime surprise: Maryland. M. C. Roberts.
il Travel 124:33-5 N '65
GARRIGUE, Jean
And a variable compass. F. Bock. Poetry
106:229-31 Je '65
GARRISON, Paul
Flying photographer. Flying 77:110-11 Ag; 108-
9 D '65
GARRISON, Roger H.
Professional teacher or dedicated amateur?
address, March 3, 1965. Sch & Soc 93:390-2
O 30 '65
GARRISON, Winfred E.
Search for truth. Christian Cent 82:1513-14
D 8 '65

GARRITY, Margo
Your own touch on sheets, pillowcases, and
towels. Bet Hom & Gard 43:124+ My '65
GARRYA. See Silk tassel bushes
GARTLAND, Henry J.
Three-dimensional program: Veterans ad-
ministration library service. Library J 90:
4296-9 O 15 '65
GARTLER, Stanley M. See Linder, D. jt. auth.
GARY, Romain
Twilight of the goddess? por Ladies Home
J 82:90-1 Mr '65
GAS, Interstellar. See Matter, Interstellar
GAS, Natural
Down to the sea in rigs; North Sea. Time
86:110+ N 19 '65
Gas fever & coal chills; Europe's newly
discovered riches of natural gas. il Time
86:68+ Ag 13 '65
Regulating natural gas in Texas. J. Ridge-
way. New Repub 152:11-12 F 20 '65
Sinking of the Sea Gem; quest for gas under
the North Sea. il Time 87:87 Ja 7 '66
See also
Liquefied petroleum gas

Pipe lines

Burning issue for gas pipelines; southern
California natural gas market. il Bsns W
p 138+ Ag 14 '65
Dutch gas discovery sets off a boom; natural
gas in Groningen. il Bsns W p97-8+ F 13
'65
They play rough in the gas business; T.G.T.
vs. El Paso fight for southern California
market. R. A. Smith. il Fortune 73:132-5+
Ja '66

Rates

FPC tightens the cap on natural gas prices.
il Bsns W p31-2 Ag 14 '65
Gas pricing: wellhead warriors. M. Wax. il
Nation 200:417-19 Ap 19 '65
Permian landmark. Newsweek 66:67 Ag 16
'65
GAS and oil engines
Controlling twins, twin-screw boat. M. Crook.
il Yachting 118:64-6+ N '65
See also
Diesel engines

Care

Basic care of the four-cycle engine. B. C.
Kilvert, jr. il Flower Grower 52:42 Jl '65
Engine knock. Suc Farm 64:82 Ja '66

Cooling

Corvair takes to water; air-cooled engine. E.
Rickman. il Hot Rod 18:62-4 O '65
Spotlight on the Wayne 100; air-cooled in-
board. P. Parrett. il Pop Mech 124:38-40
S '65
GAS and oil engines, Inboard
Corvair takes to water; air-cooled engine E.
Rickman. il Hot Rod 18:62-4 O '65
Spotlight on the Wayne 100; air-cooled in-
board. P. Parrett. il Pop Mech 124:38-40
S '65
GAS and oil engines, Outboard
Are two outboards better than one? J. Roe.
il Pop Sci 186:110-12 My '65
Are you getting the outboard performance
you paid for? L. Eppel. il Motor B 116:
32-3+ Jl '65
Beware the outboard thief! B. Whittier. il
Yachting 118:53 S '65
Chrysler introduces outboard line. J. A.
Emmett. il Outdoor Life 136:135 N '65
Genesis of an outboard motor. M. Crook. il
Yachting 118:56-7+ D '65
Long happy life of the phenomenal outboard
motor; postwar years, and what next? C. D.
Strang. il Motor B 116:44-7+ Ag '65
More powerful outboard motors. Outdoor
Life 136:10 O '65
New engines for 1966. il Yachting 118:64-5+
O '65
1966 motor buyer's guide. F. M. Paulson. il
Field & S 70:54-7 Ja '66
Outboard wells for the small auxiliary (cont)
R. W. Carrick. il Yachting 117:53-5+ F '65
Outboards à go-go. F. M. Paulson. il Field
& S 70:80-5 D '65
Outdoor life boating 1966. J. A. Emmett. il
Outdoor Life 137:56-9+ Ja '66
Portable power in '66. il Motor B 116:48-50+
O '65
'66 outboards are hotter, handier, and quieter.
J. Roe. il Pop Sci 187:112-17 O '65

Care

Autumn look at your outboard. L. Eppel. il
Motor B 116:51-3+ O '65
Outboard know-how. J. Martenhoff. il Motor
B 115:38-9+ Ap '65
Winterize your outboard. H. B. Notrom. il
Pop Mech 124:186-9 O '65

GAS and oil engines, Outboard—*Continued*

History

Long happy life of the phenomenal outboard motor. C. D. Strang. il Motor B 115:31-4+ Je; 116:43-5+ Jl; 44-7+ Ag '65

Testing

World's best-selling outboard. J. Roe. il Pop Sci 187:70-3+ S '65

GAS as fuel
See also
Gas, Natural

GAS companies
Upbeat; plans for new plant and equipment. Newsweek 65:90+ Ap 12 '65
Utility war heats up. il Newsweek 65:80-2 Mr 15 '65
See also
El Paso natural gas company
Tennessee gas transmission company

GAS endarterectomy. See Blood vessels—Surgery

GAS industry
Rise in industrial gases. G. Berkwitt. il Duns R 86:39-40+ D '65

Employees

Manpower planning at an electric and gas utility; displaced employees due to extensive technological changes. R. W. Riche. Mo Labor R 88:965-7 Ag '65

Regulation

Gas pricing: wellhead warriors. M. Wax. il Nation 200:417-19 Ap 19 '65
See also
United States—Federal power commission

Wages and hours

Output per man-hour, gas and electric utilities. J. E. Dragonette and P. W. Jaynes. il Mo Labor R 88:34-9 Ja '65

GAS rates. See Gas, Natural—Rates

GAS stations. See Automobile service stations

GAS stoves
Built-in gas cooking appliances. il Consumer Bul 48:22-9 N '65
Everything's under control; new range controls. il McCalls 92:86+ Ap '65
Experts answer your questions about modern ranges. il Redbook 124:72-3+ Mr '65
Gas ranges. il Consumer Rep 30:476-83 O '65
Gas vs. electric ranges. Consumer Rep 30:444 S '65
Kitchen ranges. il Consumer Rep 30:21-35 D '65
Ranges: the news is inside. M. Davidson. il Ladies Home J 82:32 My '65

GAS surgery. See Blood vessels—Surgery

GAS tractors. See Tractors

GAS turbines
Sales heat up for gas turbines. il Bsns W p 120-2+ F 6 '65

GAS turbines, Aircraft
Auxiliary turbojet installed in C-47 tail. il Aviation W 82:79 F 8 '65
Better C-133 stall performance sought; Douglas turboprop transports. C. M. Plattner. Aviation W 82:87 My 31 '65
Firm's use of HS-125 exceeds estimate; Britain's first corporately-owned turbojet aircraft. D. A. Brown. il Aviation W 83:85+ Jl 26 '65
First Braniff BAC 111 delivered; twin-turbofan aircraft. il Aviation W 82:31 Mr 22 '65
First delivery of Gulfstream 2 set in 1967; eighteen orders reported; Grumman's twin-turbofan business transport. Aviation W 82:31 My 24 '65
GE completing T64-12 engine assembly. M. L. Yaffee. il Aviation W 88:52-3+ N 8 '65
Grumman Gulfstream 2 aimed at case of maintenance. D. A. Brown. il Aviation W 83:82-3+ N 29 '65
High-bypass engines may be next step. M. Yaffee. il Aviation W 83:140-1+ O 25 '65
Hiller will build FH-1100 utility version: light turbine-powered helicopter. C. M. Plattner. il Aviation W 83:80+ Ag 2 '65
Horse of a different color. A. Trammell. il Flying 77:57-60 Ag '65
ICAO unit adopts rule requiring recorders on all turbine aircraft. Aviation W 83:47 D 13 '65
Leading international gas turbines; specifications (cont) Aviation W 82:218-19 Mr 15 '65
Leading turbine-powered business aircraft; specifications. Aviation W 82:193 Mr 15 '65
Military Spey version reflects new policy at Rolls-Royce. H. J. Coleman. il Aviation W 83:64-5+ O 4 '65

Nord 262 battles competition from auto. D. A. Brown. il Aviation W 83:57+ N 8 '65
Plenum chamber burning feature studied for Hawker P.1127 fighter. H. J. Coleman. il Aviation W 83:90-2+ S 20 '65
Rolls-Royce, Turbomeca basing series on Br.121 engine: turbofan engine. W. C. Wetmore. il Aviation W 83:70-1+ Ag 2 '65
Turbine aircraft 1964 operating costs; table. Aviation W 82:57+ My 10 '65
Turbine aircraft 1964 operating statistics; tables. Aviation W 82:168 Mr 15 '64
Turbine aircraft 1964 traffic statistics; tables. Aviation W 82:169 Mr 15 '65
Turbine-powered aircraft 1964 operating expense; tables. Aviation W 82:36-7 My 31 '65
Turbojet load factors in scheduled service; tables. Aviation W 83:32 O 18 '65
Turbomeca provides technology to Anglo-French Br. 121 trainer. Aviation W 82:232 Je 14 '65
U.S. gas turbine engines; specifications (cont) Aviation W 82:216-17 Mr 15 '65
See also
Helicopter engines
Jet propulsion

Design

GE aims J79/J1B at future F-4 series. M. L. Yaffee. il Aviation W 82:52-3+ Ap 19 '65

Fuel

Turbine fuels, oils keep pace with needs. il Aviation W 83:189-91+ O 25 '65

Lubrication

Improve consumption, stability recorded in use of type 2 oils. Aviation W 83:30 O 18 '65
Turbine fuels, oils keep pace with needs. il Aviation W 83:189-91+ O 25 '65

Statistics

Turboprop aircraft operating expense; table. Aviation W 83:50 N 8 '65
Turboprop load factors in scheduled service; table. Aviation W 83:45 N 8 '65

GAS turbines, Automotive
Car with tomorrow's engine. il Changing T 19:39-42 Ap '65
Turbine drives Chevy truck. il Pop Sci 187:88 O '65

GAS warfare. See Gases in warfare

GASCOYNE-CECIL, Robert Arthur Talbot, 3d marquis of Salisbury. See Salisbury, R. A. T. G.-C.

GASES
See also names of gases, e.g. Carbon dioxide

Industrial applications

Rise in industrial gases. G. Berkwitt. il Duns R 86:39-40+ D '65

GASES, Asphyxiating and poisonous
See also
Chemical warfare
Gases in warfare

GASES, Interstellar. See Matter, Interstellar

GASES, Ionization of. See Ionization of gases

GASES, Rare
Atmospheric noble gases: solar-wind bombardment of extraterrestrial dust as a possible source mechanism. D. Tilles. bibliog Science 148:1085-8 My 21 '65
Primordial rare gases in meteorites. R. O. Pepin and P. Signer. bibliog il Science 149:253-65 Jl 16 '65
See also
Argon
Xenon

GASES in warfare
Chemical warfare: how inhuman, how humane? il Sr Schol 86:10-13 Ap 29 '65
Door best kept closed. New Repub 152:5-6 Ap 3 '65; Reply. J. H. Rothschild. 152:37 My 1 '65
Experiment that failed; use of nonlethal gas in Vietnam. il Newsweek 65:37-8 Ap 5 '65
From Washington: notes on gas and disarmament. H. Margolis. Bul Atomic Sci 21:30-2 N '65
Gas in Vietnam. Commonweal 82:67-8 Ap 9 '65
Gas: nobody's mistake but L.B.J.'s; use of nonlethal gas in Vietnam. Life 58:4 Ap 2 '65
Gas warfare challenged. Sci N L 89:34 Ja 15 '66
Gas warfare: is it justifiable as minimum force? J. Pleasants. Commonweal 82:209-12 My 7 '65; Reply with rejoinder. C. August and others. 82:454-5 Je 25 '65
Great gas flap; use of nonlethal gas by South Vietnamese troops. Time 85:19-21 Ap 2 '65

GASES in warfare—*Continued*
New backing for the use of nausea gas; South Vietnam. U S News 58:6 Ap 12 '65
Non-destructive warfare. Miss & Roc 16:58-9 Mr 29 '65
On the use of gas. W. J. Coughlin. Miss & Roc 16:46 Ap 19 '65
Peril of non-nuclear weapons. B. H. Frisch. il Sci Digest 57:8-13 Mr '65
Secretary Rusk discusses use of tear gas in Viet-Nam; statement, March 24, 1965. D. Rusk. Dept State Bul 52:528-32 Ap 12 '65
Tear gas in Vietnam; freer use ahead? non-lethal, riot-control-type gas. U S News 59:8 O 4 '65
Tempest over gas. Sr Schol 86:18 Ap 8 '65
Truth about gas warfare in Vietnam. U S News 58:48-9 Ap 5 '65
U Thant's credibility; use of gas in South Vietnam. Nation 200:349 Ap 5 '65
U.S. denounces Soviet circulation of note on use of gas in Viet-Nam; letter, April 2, 1965. A. E. Stevenson. Dept State Bul 52: 688 My 3 '65
Use of gas in Vietnam draws a rising protest; non-lethal type used. Bsns W p34 Mr 27 '65
Use of gas in Vietnam sparking violent reaction, strong defense. Aviation W 82:29 Mr 29 '65
Wide range of chemicals available for gas war. Sci N L 87:315 My 15 '65
  See also
Chemical warfare

GASIC, Gabriel J. and Galanti, N. L.
Proteins and disulfide groups in the aggregation of dissociated cells of sea sponges. bibliog Science 151:203-5 Ja 14 '66

GASKILL, Gordon
Day we saved Chartres cathedral. Read Digest 87:102-7 Ag '65
Night the mountain fell. Read Digest 86: 59-67 My '65
Race to save Abu Simbel. Read Digest 88: 163-5+ Ja '66
They dive into history. Read Digest 86:131-6 Je '65

GASOLINE
Best beast in your tank. W. S. Ross. il Esquire 63:86-9+ Mr '65; Same abr. Read Digest 86:139-41 Je '65

  Anti-knock and anti-knock mixtures
Lead in gasoline kept at safe levels by PHS. Sci N L 88:201 S 25 '65

  Prices
Are gas price wars at an end? marketing technology seems to be maturing. il Bsns W p 134-6+ My 29 '65

  Storage
Avoid fuel storage problems. Suc Farm 64: 78 Ja '66

  Taxation
How to get your full gas tax refund. Suc Farm 63:98 S '65

GASOLINE industry
Gas war casualty; Britain. il Time 86:98 O 29 '65

GASOLINE stations. See Automobile service stations

GASOLINE storage. See Gasoline—Storage

GASPERI, Alcide de
Great and lonely man. L. Barzini. il Reporter 32:29-31 Je 3 '65

GASS, Oscar
German unification; prospects and merits. bibliog Commentary 40:25-38 Jl '65
Political economy of the Great society. bibliog f Commentary 40:31-6 O '65
World politics of responsibility. Commentary 40:85-90 D '65

GASSER, Henry
Sunday painting for beginners. por Recreation 58:68-9 F '65

GASSET, José Ortega y. See Ortega y Gasset, J.

GASSETT, William H.
Look for good stocks, buy on market weakness; interview. por U S News 58:46 Je 28 '65

GASSMANN, Vittorio
Hamlet who wants to play clowns. M. S. Davis. il pors N Y Times Mag p46-7+ S 19 '65

GAST, Paul W.
Terrestrial ratio of potassium to rubidium and the composition of earth's mantle. bibliog Science 147:858-60 F 19 '65

GASTER, Theodor H.
Qumran quandary. Sat R 48:22-3 S 4 '65

GASTON, A. G.
Birmingham two years later. P. Good. il Reporter 33:24-7 D 2 '65

GASTONIA, N.C.
Watch dog accounts for every gallon of gas. H. L. Parker. il Am City 80:48 Mr '65

GASTRIC juice
Antibodies in gastric juice. J. M. Fisher and others. bibliog il Science 150:1467-9 D 10 '65
Gastric secretion: mechanism for production of hydrogen ions. H. P. Gregor and J. M. Berkowitz. bibliog il Science 150:773-6 N 5 '65
Pancreatic secretion induced by stimulation of the pyloric gland area of the stomach. R. M. Preshaw and others. bibliog il Science 148:1347-8 Je 4 '65

GASTRIC ulcers. See Peptic ulcers

GASTRO camera. See Medical instruments and apparatus

GASTROPOD shells. See Shells (conchology)

GASTROPODS
Calcite deposition during shell repair by the aragonitic gastropod murex fulvescens. E. O. Muzii and H. C. W. Skinner. bibliog il Science 151:201-3 Ja 14 '66

GASZTOLD, Carmen Bernos de
Creatures' choir; poems excerpts from Choral de bêtes, tr. by R. Godden. McCalls 93:82-5 D '65

GATES, Allen H. and Karasek, Marvin
Hereditary absence of sebaceous glands in the mouse. bibliog Science 148:1471-3 Je 11 '65

GATES, Charles C. Jr
Gates rubber: plenty of bounce. il pors Bsns W p 112-14+ O 16 '65

GATES, David M.
Heat transfer in plants; with biographical sketch. Sci Am 213:10, 76-84 bibliog(p 128) D '65

GATES, Gary Paul
Bad days on Broadway. Holiday 39:118+ Ja '66
Broadway's Champion. Holiday 37:87-8+ F '65

GATES, Thomas Sovereign, 1906–
New master at Morgan. por Newsweek 65:74+ My 17 '65

GATES
Gateway to the Oriental garden. il Pop Gard 16:19 My '65

GATES rubber company
Gates rubber: plenty of bounce. il Bsns W p 112-14+ O 16 '65

GATEWAY arch. See St Louis—Monuments, statues, etc.

GATLIN, Rochelle
Radical frame of mind. Sat R 48:83+ O 16 '65

GATTI, Ora
School art festival; interview. ed. by I. Arms. Sch Arts 64:31-3 My '65

GAUCHOS
Epic of the gaucho: Martín Fierro, by J. Hernández, with excerpts. C. E. Ward. il Américas 17:8-15 N '65
Gaucho Jesus; concerning Creole gospel of Amado Anzi. G. F. Hall. Christian Cent 82:1419 N 17 '65

GAUDIER-BRZESKA, Henri
Illustrious unknown. il por Time 86:68 Jl 23 '65

GAUDIEST thing on wheels; story. See Humphrey, W.

GAUGLER, William M.
Importance of method in art. il por Am Artist 29:42-7+ Je '65

GAUGUIN, Émile
Welcome new world for a son of Gauguin. D. Chapman. il pors Look 29:66-70 Jl 13 '65

GAUGUIN, Paul
Gauguin woodblocks rediscovered. H. Lass. il Am Artist 29:36-41+ My '65
Welcome new world for a son of Gauguin. D. Chapman. il Look 29:66-70 Jl 13 '65

GAULLE, Charles de
Independence of France; address, April 27, 1965. Vital Speeches 31:514-15 Je 15 '65

  about
After victory, a guessing game. por Newsweek 67:19 Ja 3 '66
And seventy-six trombones. por Newsweek 66:40-1 S 20 '65
Après moi, la confusion; decision to run again for the presidency. por Time 86:38 N 12 '65
Atlantic report. Atlan 216:6+ Ag; 14+ O '65
Best-kept secret; rumors of declining health. Newsweek 65:37 Mr 22 '65
By word and deed, the once and future king. Newsweek 66:43 D 13 '65
Can de Gaulle be upset? Socialist mayor will try. U S News 58:20 Ap 5 '65

GAULLE, Charles de—about—*Continued*

Compleat candidate. il por Time 85:41 Je 25 '65

Convocation. il por Time 85:21-2 F 12 '65

Death of Gaullism. W. S. Schlamm. por Nat R 18:63-5 Ja 25 '66

De Gaulle: America's elder statesman. A. Werth. Nation 201:404-8 N 29 '65

De Gaulle between two elections. Newsweek 66:37 D 20 '65

De Gaulle carries on. il por Newsweek 66:55-6 N 15 '65

De Gaulle, Europe, and the dollar. E. Taylor. il Reporter 32:20-3 F 25 '65

De Gaulle has an opposition. Life 59:4 D 17 '65

De Gaulle launches an economic war on the dollar; with excerpt from interview with J. Rueff. il por U S News 58:44-6 F 15 '65

De Gaulle looks left. E. Taylor. il Reporter 32:13-14 Je 3 '65

De Gaulle moves to recoup; attempts to mend domestic and Common market fences. por Bsns W p 15-16 D 25 '65

De Gaulle on Vietnam; way out of the jungle; with editorial comment. A. Werth. Nation 200:237, 239-42 Mr 8 '65

De Gaulle peace move in Vietnam? por U S News 59:19 S 13 '65

De Gaulle: pose and policy. H. Lüthy. For Affairs 43:561-73 Jl '65

De Gaulle: president of France calls for a harder line in behalf of French in international science. J. Walsh. Science 148: 350-1 Ap 16 '65; Discussion. 148:1670; 150: 435-6 Je 25, O 22 '65

De Gaulle proposes U.N. revision. Christian Cent 82:198 F 17 '65

De Gaulle's Europe. America 113:308 S 25 '65

De Gaulle's grand design for U.S. get out. il pors U S News 59:50-2 Jl 26 '65

De Gaulle's new triad. Nat R 17:138-40 F 23 '65

De Gaulle's nugget. il Fortune 71:92-3 Mr '65

De Gaulle's plan for U.N. il U S News 58:46 F 15 '65

De Gaulle's responsibility. America 113:91 Jl 24 '65

Don't expect de Gaulle to change. M. Gordey. New Repub 153:16-19 D 18 '65

Election day in France: I have spoken. il por Newsweek 66:41-2 D 13 '65

End of Europe's big dream? what de Gaulle's revolt means. il por U S News 59:46-7 Jl 19 '65

End of the French miracle. il U S News 58:81 Je 7 '65

Europe of Charles de Gaulle. T. Molnar. Nat R 17:108-9 F 9 '65

Europe's schizophrenia. H. Brandon. Sat R 48:16 S 25 '65

Four views on seven years; symposium. il Newsweek 66:44+ D 13 '65

France loosens grip of de Gaulle. por Bsns W p32-3 D 11 '65

France transformed: seven years of de Gaulle. H. Peyre. il pors N Y Times Mag p50-1+ N 14 '65

Frapping de Gaulle. Commonweal 83:329 D 17 '65

French elections: Gaullism after de Gaulle. C. Sterling. il Reporter 33:33-6 D 16 '65

General ignorance; reception for newsmen. Time 87:29 Ja 7 '66

General's boycott. por Newsweek 66:29 Jl 19 '65

General's gorillas: bodyguards. il por Newsweek 65:41-2 My 31 '65

Grand subject. H. de Turenne. N Y Times Mag p 114 S 12 '65

Historian looks at de Gaulle: why he acts that way; interview, ed. by F. C. Painton. J. B. Duroselle. il por U S News 58:44+ My 10 '65

How de Gaulle's anti-U.S. drive is doing. il por U S News 58:19 Je 7 '65

If de Gaulle could have his way in Europe. por U S News 59:55-6 D 13 '65

Illusionist: why we misread de Gaulle. H. A. Kissinger. Harper 230:69-70+ Mr '65

Is de Gaulle killing the Common market? il por U S News 59:84-5 Ag 23 '65

Is General de Gaulle that alarming? B. D. Nossiter. New Repub 153:13-15 O 9 '65

Leader of Europe and arbiter between blocs. J. Daniel. New Repub 152:10-11 F 20 '65

Letter from Paris (cont) Genêt. New Yorker 41:106+ F 20; 166+ My 15; 77-8 Jl 10; 82-4 Ag 7; 137 S 18; 169-70+ N 13; 186+ D 11; 160-1 D 18 '65; 61-2+ Ja 1 '66

Life with de Gaulle. H. C. Wallich. Newsweek 66:67 Ag 23 '65

Man who upset the world again. U S News 58:19 F 15 '65

New storm over Germany; de Gaulle's latest maneuver. il por U S News 59:65-6 N 8 '65

Next French president. America 113:659-60 N 27 '65

Non, mon général! local elections. por Time 85:32 Ap 2 '65

On dealing with de Gaulle. J. M. Gavin. Atlan 215:49-54 Je '65

Once more, sans feeling; press conference. Time 86:52 S 17 '65

One candidate against de Gaulle. H. de Turenne. il por N Y Times Mag p40-1+ Ag 29 '65

Oracles on the Seine. il por Newsweek 66: 63 O 18 '65

Le penseur. K. Crawford. Newsweek 65:30 F 22 '65

Plain talk by de Gaulle. E. Weintal. Newsweek 66:44 N 1 '65

La question? Nat R 17:759 S 7 '65

Senator's indictment of de Gaulle; excerpts from address, June 3, 1965. P. Douglas. U S News 58:8 Je 14 '65

Sense in that golden nonsense; concerning recent press conference. Life 58:4 F 19 '65

Seven more years for de Gaulle. il por Time 86:18 D 24 '65

Seven more years of de Gaulle: what to expect. U S News 60:38 Ja 3 '66

Siren call in Paris. Newsweek 65:52+ My 10 '65

So, vive de Gaulle but with reservations. Life 59:4 N 19 '65

Supranational stall. Time 86:31 Jl 16 '65

This electoral season. M. Ascoli. Reporter 33:10 N 18 '65

Twilight of NATO. M. Frankel. il por N Y Times Mag p54-5+ D 5 '65

Veto by France? Newsweek 66:44+ N 1 '65

What de Gaulle's re-election means. R. Bosc. por America 114:72-4 Ja 15 '66

What shall we do about de Gaulle? P. H. Douglas. New Repub 152:7-10 Je 12 '65; Discussion. 152:35-7 Je 26 '65

Whatever for? il por Newsweek 65:53 F 15 '65

Which way Europe? J. H. Huizinga. For Affairs 43:487-500 Ap '65

Why de Gaulle thinks U.S. is through as world leader. il por U S News 58:47-8 Mr 1 '65

Will de Gaulle be easier to live with now? il por U S News 59:34-5 D 20 '65

GAUTIER, Felisa Rincón de

New man in La Fortaleza. A. W. Maldonado. il por Reporter 33:32-3 N 4 '65

GAVER, Mary Virginia

Knapp school libraries project: address, July 1965. ALA Bul 59:806-9 O '65

Teacher education and school libraries. bibliog f ALA Bul 60:63-72 Ja '66

about

New ALA officer. E. Hodges. por ALA Bul 59:654+ Jl '65

GAVIN, James M.

Grandiose plan of conquest. Harper 230:148+ Mr '65

On dealing with de Gaulle. Atlan 215:49-54 Je '65

Two fighting generals; Patton and MacArthur. Atlan 215:55-61 F; 40 Je '65

GAXTON, William

William Gaxton, master printer. P. W. Schmidtchen. il Hobbies 70:106-7+ N '65

GAY, Ernest

Go Dutch treat! il U S Camera 28:18-19 My '65

GAY, Ian D. See Black, M. L. jt. auth.

GAY, Jim

Trophy to remember; the shooting. C. Elliott. il por Outdoor Life 136:25-7+ S '65

GAY, Kathlyn

Your child deserves more than packaged creativity. Am Home 68:15+ Ap '65

GAY, Peter

Chains and couches. Commentary 40:93-4+ O '65

GAY Head, pseud.

Talking it over with Gay Head; questions and answers. See issues of Senior scholastic

GAYER family

Gayer coat-of-arms. H. K. Eilers. il Hobbies 70:126-7 Ag '65

GAYN, Mark

To Mao we are the prime enemy. il N Y Times Mag p46-7+ O 24 '65

GAZENKO, Oleg G.

Gazenko discusses Soviet space medicine. Aviation W 82:40-1+ Je 7 '65

GAZZOLA, Pietro

Venice, a sinking city. UNESCO Courier 18: 11-13 Ja '65

GEAGAN, Bill
Beaver returns to Maine. Nat Parks Mag
40:12-14 Ja '66
Son of the salmon. Field & S 69:42-3+ Ap
'65
GEAR and flaps man; story. See Medelman, J.
GEARING. See Automobiles—Gearing
GEBHARD, Christian
Gebhard astronomical and world clock. J. E.
Coleman and J. F. Hagans. il Hobbies 70:
44-5+ N '65
GEBHARD, Paul
1965 Kinsey report. Ladies Home J 82:66-7+
My; 42+ Je '65
GEDDES, Robert L.
Geddes is named dean of architecture at
Princeton. por Arch Rec 137:26 Mr '65
GEERLINGS, Gerald K.
Choosing the right windows. Pop Sci 186:156-9
Ap; 146-9 My '65
GEESE
Gander who likes girls. il Look 29:M16+
Ap 20 '65
Honkin' good time. E. R. Choate. Atlan
215:122-4 Ap '65
GEESE, Wild
Dig those crazy brant; New Jersey's Barnegat
Bay. P. McLain. il Field & S 70:39-41 D
'65
Gift of gabbling. T. Janes. il Outdoor Life
137:44-5+ Ja '66
Goose pays the way. H. Titus. il Field & S
70:100-1 Je '65
Guns for waterfowl. J. O'Connor. il Outdoor
Life 137:82-3+ Ja '66
Life in a goose pit. W. Page. il Field & S
70:80-4 N '65
Mystery geese. B. Brister. il Field & S 70:
44-6+ S '65
There arose such a clatter. J. McFarland. il
Field & S 70:65-7+ O '65
See also
Cookery—Game
Nenes
GEGENSCHEIN. See Counterglow
GEHENNA press. See Printing—Private
presses
GEHLBACH, Albert
Now, cast slats in place. Suc Farm 63:76
S '65
GEHLBACH, Frederick R.
Plant formations in the natural history in-
terpretation of southwestern desert regions.
Nat Parks Mag 40:16-18 Ja '66
GEHMAN, Richard
Amish folk. Nat Geog Mag 128:226-53 Ag '65
GEIB, M. Eugenia
Cold steel, hot blood. Opera N 29:6-7 Mr 27
'65
GEISEL, Theodor Seuss
Fox in socks. Ladies Home J 82:66-9 Mr '65
about
Doctor Seuss: what am I doing here? C. R.
Jennings. il pors Sat Eve Post 238:105-9
O 23 '65
GEISERT, Arthur
Six days of creation. Sch Arts 65:5-8 D '65
GEISHAS
Night butterflies. B. Krisher. il Newsweek
66:45-6 S 13 '65
GELABERT, Raoul
Anatomy for the ballet teacher; ed. by
W. Como. See issues of Dance magazine
GELATIN
Gourmet gelatin. C. Claiborne. il N Y Times
Mag p21 Jl 4 '65
GELATIN salads. See Salads
GELATT, Dorothy S.
Color, a world of wonders. Pop Phot 57:80-3
Jl '65
Focus on Henry M. Lester: photography's
Ben Franklin. Pop Phot 56:60-3+ My '65
(ed) Great ideas on color. Pop Phot 57:64-
9+ Jl '65
GELATT, Roland
Golden twilight. Reporter 33:48 S 9 '65
Off the beaten track. Reporter 33:41-2 D 30
'65
To awake in paradise. Reporter 33:45-6+ D
2 '65
When records reached the supermarket; ex-
cerpt from The fabulous phonograph. Hi
Fi 15:56-60+ D '65
GELB, Lawrence M.
Clairol puts on a new face. il por Bsns W
p 124-6+ Je 12 '65
GELBER, Jack
Square in the eye. Criticism
Commonweal 82:474 Jl 2 '65
New Repub 152:30 Je 26 '65
New Yorker 41:56+ My 29 '65
Newsweek il 65:76 My 31 '65
Reporter 33:42 Jl 1 '65
Time 85:83 My 28 '65
Vogue 146:38 Jl '65

GELFAND, Michael
On the rounds with a witch doctor. N Y
Times Mag p44-5+ Mr 14 '65
GELLER, William S.
Gauging progress; excerpts from address,
June 1964. por Library J 90:3559-62 S 15 '65
GELLHORN, Martha
In East Africa and London, two writing
women. V. Cowles. Vogue 145:98 Ap 1 '65
GELLMAN, Murray
Now! a universal CD ignition system. Pop
Electr 23:69-71+ O '65
Transistorized capacitor discharge ignition
system. Pop Electr 22:43-7+ Je '65
GELMAN, Steve
Willie Pep's art of self-defense. Esquire 64:
194-5+ D '65
GELTMAN, Max
Little-known chapter in American history.
Nat R 17:865-7 O 5 '65
Who's alienated now? Nat R 17:556+ Je 29
'65
Whose ism was it? Nat R 17:990+ N 2 '65
GEM carving. See Carving (art industries)
GEMINI project. See Space flight—Manned
flights
GEMS
Gems and minerals. H. D. Brown. See issues
of Hobbies
See also
Jewelry
GEMZELL, Carl Axel
Two medical pioneers that all would-be
mothers now desperately want to see. il
por Life 59:28-9 Ag 13 '65
GENDEL, Milton
Art news from Italy. Art N 64:48-9+ S '65
Rome: new and old, lost and found. Art
N 64:36-7+ Sum '65
GENDLER, Everett E.
Revolutionary truism. Sat R 48:26-7 F 13
'65
GENEEN, Harold Sydney
ITT: can profits be programmed? J. B.
Weiner. il por Duns R 86:38-41+ N '65
GENERAL accounting office. See United States
—General accounting office
GENERAL agreement on tariffs and trade
Challenges facing United States trade poli-
cy; address, October 21, 1965. A. M. Solo-
mon. Dept State Bul 53:787-93 N 15 '65
GATT contracting parties sign articles on
trade and development. Dept State Bul 52:
355-6 Mr 8 '65
Kennedy round: a progress report; address,
May 20, 1965. C. A. Herter. Dept State Bul
53:31-5 Jl 5 '65
United States delegations to international
conferences; twenty-second session of
GATT contracting parties. Dept State Bul
52:436 Mr 22 '65
World trade and the Kennedy round; address,
July 15, 1965. W. M. Blumenthal. Dept
State Bul 53:249-55 Ag 9 '65
GENERAL aniline and film corporation
Aniline, my Aniline; stock finally marketed.
Time 85:96+ Mr 19 '65
GAF stock sells like hotcakes. Bsns W
p 142+ Mr 13 '65
Inside GAF, formerly Ansco. N. Rothschild.
il Pop Phot 57:18+ N '65
Seized Nazi company sold by U.S. Sr Schol
86:18 Mr 25 '65
Wall Street: we won! terrific Blyth-First
Boston syndicate wins bid to sell US gov-
vernment shares. il Newsweek 65:71 Mr 22
'65
GENERAL assembly of the Presbyterian church
in the United States (southern) See Presby-
terian church in the United States (South)
GENERAL assembly of the United Nations.
See United Nations—General assembly
GENERAL board of the National council. See
National council of the churches of Christ
in the United States of America
GENERAL dynamics corporation
Convair division
Bowers details Convair market aims. W. E.
Wilks. il Miss & Roc 17:35-6+ O 25 '65
GENERAL electric company
GE aims J79/J1B at future F-4 series. M. L.
Yaffee. il Aviation W 82:52-3+ Ap 19 '65
GE completing T64-12 engine assembly. M. L.
Yaffee. il Aviation W 83:52-3+ N 8 '65
GE finds a way to sell to itself; equipment
in housing projects. Bsns W p75 Jl 24 '65
GE opens a prison door with computer train-
ing; teaching programming to inmates of
Atlanta penitentiary. il Bsns W p96+ N
20 '65
GE president sees continuing gains in jet
engine business. Aviation W 83:29 D 27 '65
GE reshapes divisions. Bsns W p20 D 25 '65
Has GE stock hit peak? il Bsns W p 158 N
6 '65

GENERAL electric company—*Continued*
IBM's answer to time-sharing. Bsns W p50 Mr 13 '65
Letter from the publisher; joint enterprise to create and market educational materials, systems and services. B. M. Auer. Time 86:19 N 26 '65
1980; Technical military planning operation. il New Yorker 41:37-8 My 22 '65
Time, inc. and G.E. plan educational materials unit. Pub W 188:32-3 N 29 '65
Where GE peers far into future. il Bsns W p45-6+ S 11 '65

GENERAL foods corporation
Chief Cook. il Time 85:85 Mr 12 '65
Moving day. L. L. L. Golden. Sat R 49:107 Ja 8 '66
Ready for instant growth. il Bsns W p68-9+ Ap 24 '65

GENERAL information tests. See Information tests

GENERAL motors acceptance corporation
Auto buying headaches; lesson in the high-cost of borrowing. J. Osborne. New Repub 152:15-18 Mr 27 '65; Reply. A. J. Manzano. 152:42+ Ap 17 '65

GENERAL motors corporation
At General motors, more variety everywhere. J. P. Norbye. il Pop Sci 187:75-82 O '65
Auto safety: who will take the lead? il Newsweek 66:67-8 Jl 26 '65
Corvair's second case. il Time 86:37 S 10 '65
General motors air transport section. D. A. Brown. Aviation W 82:53-4+ Ap 5; 113+ Ap 12 '65
GM bus suit settled. Bsns W p34 D 4 '65
GM cuts '66 prices in a surprise move. Bsns W p 28 S 25 '65
GM in their future; MTU draws engineering head-hunters. il Newsweek 67:80 Ja 24 '66
GM shakes Europe's auto makers; will build $100-million assembly plant at Antwerp. il Bsns W p 130 Ja 30 '65
GM won't even tell it to the judge. Consumer Rep 30:425-7 S '65
GM's new driver; J. M. Roche. il Newsweek 65:88 Je 14 '65
GM's new president; man with a world view; J. M. Roche. il Bsns W p 114+ Je 5 '65
General motors sit-down strike, 1937: a re-examination. S. Fine. bibliog f Am Hist R 70:691-713 Ap '65
How GM keeps its top ranks strong. Bsns W p78+ Jl 3 '65
In DuPont-GM divorce: how everybody fared. il U S News 58:98 Mr 1 '65
In high gear; fourth straight record year. Newsweek 66:80+ D 6 '65
Is the franchise system legal? General motors vs Supreme court. Bsns W p66+ Ap 3 '65
Managing to succeed; G.M.'s new president. il Time 85:84 Je 11 '65
Profits vs. engineering: the Corvair story; excerpts from Unsafe at any speed. R. Nader. il Nation 201:295-301 N 1 '65
Rise & fall of Wm. C. Durant. J. B. Sibbison. il Motor T 17:58-61 Ap '65
Up from the ranks: GM's new president. U S News 58:14 Je 14 '65
Verdict for Corvair; G.M. vs. D. Collins. il Time 86:46+ Ag 20 '65
What's good for G.M. Commonweal 83:43-4 O 15 '65
What's the key to GM's success? Il Bsns W p25-6 My 8 '65
Why auto dealers don't like cash buyers; Supreme court vs General motors franchise system. il Consumer Rep 30:258-61 My '65

Chevrolet division
Chevy with frosting; Caprice custom sedan. il Bsns W p25 F 6 '65
How Chevrolet sets the pace for Detroit. il Bsns W p58-9+ D 4 '65
It's time we took on Mr Big; D. Frey of Ford div. hopes to break Chevrolet's hold on first place. il Bsns W p 108-11 Ag 7 '65

Electro-motive division
Switching a workhorse; introducing new line of diesel electric freight engines. Bsns W p 186 Je 12 '65

Oldsmobile division
Olds' seven-year secret: a racy front drive; GM's Tornado. B. Grossman and B. Ottum. il Sport Illus 23:55-8 S 27 '65
Toronado; most dynamic car Olds ever built! R. Huntington. il Hot Rod 18:82-4+ O '65

Pontiac motor division
Like a pretty girl; hottest-selling medium-priced car. il Newsweek 65:71+ Mr 1 '65
Pontiac on the market. il Motor T 17:72-5 F '65
Pontiac's chiefs il Motor T 17:76-9 F '65

GENERAL practitioners. See Physicians

GENERAL precision equipment corporation

Lirascope division
Electroluminescent display has controlled image storage. B. Miller. il Aviation W 82:104-5+ Ap 12 '65

GENERAL services administration. See United States—General services administration

GENERAL telephone and electronics corporation
Testing faster hookup; electronic automatic exchange. il Bsns W p91 N 20 '65

GENERAL tire and rubber company
General tire's widening tread. il Time 85:88 Mr 12 '65

GENERAL warrants. See Warrants (law)

GENERALS' tea party; drama. See Vian, B.

GENERATION; drama. See Goodhart, W.

GENERATORS, Electric. See Electric generators

GENES
Agouti locus: homology of its method of operation in rats and mice. W. K. Silvers. bibliog il Science 149:651-2 Ag 6 '65
Analysis of a gene in drosophila. W. J. Welshons. bibliog il Science 150:1122-9 N 26 '65
Genetics of a bacterial virus. R. S. Edgar and R. H. Epstein. il Sci Am 212:70-8 F '65
Hormones and genes. E. H. Davidson. il Sci Am 212:36-45 bibliog(p 146) Je '65
See also
Heredity of disease

GENESCO, incorporated
Should companies promote their own stocks? SEC investigates Genesco. C. J. Loomis. il Fortune 72:184-6+ D '65

GENÊT, pseud. See Flanner, J.

GENÊT, Jean
Blacks. Criticism
Yale R 55:209-26 D '65
New immoralists. W. Phillips. Commentary 39:66-9 Ap '65; Discussion. 40:10+ Ag '65

GENETIC mosaics. See Variegation

GENETIC research
Amateur scientist; studying genetics of fruit flies with chromatograms. R. LaFond. il Sci Am 212:126-7+ Je '65
Biochemical genetics and man: accomplishments and problems. H. E. Sutton. bibliog il Science 150:858-62 N 12 '65
Biological engineering. W. L. Thorkelson. Christian Cent 82:188 F 10 '65
Genes, psychosis linked. Sci N L 88:131 Ag 28 '65
Genetic control of differentiation; Brookhaven symposium in biology. H. H. Smith. Science 150:1847-9 D 31 '65
Genetic punctuation. Sci Am 213:43-4 Ag '65
Genetic transfer in bacterial mating. J. D. Gross and L. Caro. bibliog il Science 150:1679-84 D 24 '65
Three men & a messenger; prize in physiology and medicine. il Time 86:101 O 22 '65

GENETICS
Alcohol dehydrogenase in drosophila melanogaster: isozymes and genetic variants. E. H. Grell and others. bibliog il Science 149:80-2 Jl 2 '65
Biochemical genetics and man: accomplishments and problems. H. E. Sutton. bibliog il Science 150:858-62 N 12 '65
Essays of a humanist, by J. Huxley. Review Sci Am 211:135-8 O '64. A. E. Mirsky; Discussion. 212:6-9 Ja; 8-11 Mr '65
Final defeat for Comrade Lysenko. Time 85:51 F 12 '65
Genetic factors and polypeptide chain subclasses of human immunoglobulin G detected in chimpanzee serums. F. P. Alepa and W. D. Terry. bibliog il Science 150:1293-4 D 3 '65
Johann Gregor Mendel. J. Rostand. il UNESCO Courier 18:16-19 Ap '65
Linkage in control of allotypic specificities on two different γG-immunoglobulins. R. Lieberman and others. bibliog il Science 148:640-2 Ap 30 '65
Radiation-induced increases in fitness in the flour beetle tribolium confusum. J. W. Crenshaw. bibliog Science 149:426-7 Jl 23 '65

What dogs tell us about man's future; SR preview of Genetics and the social behavior of the dog. J. P. Scott and J. L. Fuller. il Sat R 48:47-51 Mr 6 '65; Reply with rejoinder. L. Perrine. 48:64 My 1 '65

GENETICS—*Continued*
What happens when life begins. W. Goodman. Redbook 125:54-5+ Jl '65
See also
Heredity
Heterozygosis
Variegation

Research
See Genetic research

GENETICS (botany)
Inheritance of linoleic and oleic acids in maize. C. G. Poneleit and D. E. Alexander. bibliog il Science 147:1585-6 Mr 26 '65

GENETICS, Medical. See Heredity of disease

GENEVA, Switzerland

Music
Kokoschka. Flute and a new regime; Geneva report. W. Legge. Hi Fi 16:147+ Ja '66

Religious institutions and affairs
News of the Christian world (cont) Christian Cent 82:816 Je 23 '65

GENEVA, LAKE
Thinking man's lake. N. Kotker. il Horizon 7:64-79 Autumn '65

GENEVA conference of foreign ministers. See Council of foreign ministers, Geneva, 1954

GENEVA conventions
U.S. continues to abide by Geneva conventions of 1949 in Viet-Nam; letter, August 10, 1965. D. Rusk. Dept State Bul 53:447 S 13 '65

GENEVA disarmament conference. See Conference of the Eighteen-nation committee on disarmament, Geneva, 1962-

GENGOZIAN, Nazareth, and others
Abnormal immune mechanism in allogeneic radiation chimeras. bibliog Science 149:645-7 Ag 6 '65

GENGRAS, Edmund Clayton
Iconoclast of insurance. il por Duns R 86:62-4 O '65

GENIE of the bottle; drama. See Whittaker, H.

GENNARO, Peter
Dance magazine's 1964 awards. por Dance Mag 39:37 Mr '65

GENOVESE, Eugene D.
Study in academic freedom. A. Beichman. il por N Y Times Mag p 14-15+ D 19 '65

GENRICH, Carl B. jr
Better maps. Am City 80:166+ Jl '65

GENSERT, Richard M.
High-rise apartment structures of masonry. Arch Rec 137:182-7 F '65

GEOCHEMISTRY
Organic pigments; their long-term fate. M. Blumer. bibliog il Science 149:722-6 Ag 13 '65
See also
Earth—Surface

GEOCHRONOLOGY. See Geological time

GOEDESIC domes. See Domes

GEODESY
See also
Earth—Figure

GEODETIC satellites. See Artificial satellites—Mapping applications

GEOELECTRIC effect. See Electrophysiology of plants

GEOGRAPHICAL distribution of animals and plants
Endemism in middle Miocene Caribbean molluscan faunas. W. P. Woodring. bibliog il Science 148:961-3 My 14 '65
Predation, body size, and composition of plankton. J. L. Brooks and S. I. Dodson. bibliog il Science 150:28-35 O 1 '65
Science in action: mixing oceans and species. I. Rubinoff. Natur Hist 74:69-72 Ag '65
Scrap woodlands, transported grassland soils, and concept of grassland climate in the Great Plains Region. P. V. Wells. bibliog il Science 148:246-9 Ap '65
See also
Plants—Migration

GEOGRAPHICAL myths
Inside Xenobia. W. K. Zinsser. il Horizon 7:112-13 Autumn '65

GEOGRAPHICAL names. See Names, Geographical

GEOGRAPHICAL positions
Our young people. S. Miller. il Audubon Mag 67:130 Mr '65

GEOGRAPHY

Study and teaching
Rediscovering the earth. G. F. White. il Am Ed 1:8-11 F '65
See also
National council for geographic education

GEOGRAPHY, Commercial
Geography and foreign affairs. G. E. Pearcy. Dept State Bul 52:1035-41 Je 28 '65

GEOLOGICAL survey (United States) See United States—Geological survey

GEOLOGICAL time
Pleistocene epoch in deep-sea sediments. D. B. Ericson and others; discussion. bibliog il Science 148:1037+, 1488 My 21, Je 11 '65
Rock ages measured. Sci N L 87:180 Mr 20 '65
See also
Radioactive dating
Radiocarbon dating

GEOLOGY
See also
Earth—Age
Faults (geology)
Glacial geology
Petroleum—Geology
Submarine geology

Classification
Taxonomic treatment of genera and species from the lower algal chert, Gunflint formation, animikie series, Ontario, Canada. bibliog Science 147:576-7 F 5 '65

Alaska
Sea-level changes during the last 2000 years at Point Barrow, Alaska. J. D. Hume. bibliog il Science 150:1165-6 N 26 '65

Antarctic Regions
Geology of the central portion of the Queen Maud Range, Transantarctic Mountains. F. A. Wade and others. bibliog Science 150:1808-9 D 31 '65
Glossopteris discovered in west Antarctica. C. Craddock and others. bibliog il Science 148:634-7 Ap 30 '65
Low deuterium content of Lake Vanda, Antarctica. R. A. Ragotzkie and I. Friedman. bibliog il Science 148:1226-7 My 28 '65
Potassium-argon age from a granite at Mount Wilbur, Queen Maud Range, Antarctica. V. H. Minshew. bibliog il Science 150:471-3 N 5 '65

Arctic Regions
Genesis of the Arctic Ocean Basin. E. R. King and others; reply with rejoinder. N. A. Ostenso. bibliog il Science 147:1052-6 F 26 '65

Atlantic coast
Holocene submergence of the eastern shore of Virginia. W. S. Newman and G. A. Rusnak. bibliog il Science 148:1464-6 Je 11 '65

Minnesota
Carbonaceous rocks of the Soudan iron formation early Precambrian. E. P. Cloud, jr. and others. bibliog il Science 148:1713-16 Je 25 '65

North Dakota
Pseudo superglacial till. A. D. Howard. bibliog il Science 148:1461-2 Je 11 '65

Nova Scotia
Late glacial ice-wedge casts in northern Nova Scotia, Canada. H. W. Borns, jr. bibliog il Science 148:1223-6 My 28 '65

Ontario
Precambrian glaciated surface beneath the Gowganda formation, Lake Timagami, Ontario. P. E. Schenk. bibliog il Science 149:176-7 Jl 9 '65

Pennsylvania
Wisconsinan age of the Titusville till, formerly called inner Illinoian, northwestern Pennsylvania. G. W. White and S. M. Totten. bibliog il Science 148:234-5 Ap 9 '65

Quebec (province)
Radiocarbon date from the Lake St John area, Quebec. P. Lasalle. bibliog il Science 149:860-2 Ag 20 '65

Spain
Acheulian occupation sites at Torralba and Ambrona, Spain; their geology. K. W. Butzer. bibliog il Science 150:1718-22 D 24 '65

Tanganyika
Fission-track dating of bed I, Olduvai Gorge. R. L. Fleischer and others. bibliog il Science 148:72-4 Ap 2 '65

United States
Undersea history of America; reprint. M. C. McKenna. il Sci Digest 57:80-3 Ap '65

GEOLOGY, Stratigraphic
Holocene submergence of the eastern shore of Virginia. W. S. Newman and G. A. Rusnak. bibliog il Science 148:1464-6 Je 11 '65

GEOLOGY, Stratigraphic—*Continued*
Low deuterium content of Lake Vanda, Antarctica. R. A. Ragotzkie and I. Friedman. bibliog il Science 148:1226-7 My 28 '65
Radiocarbon date from the Lake St John area, Quebec. P. Lasalle. bibliog il Science 149:860-2 Ag 20 '65
Wisconsinan age of the Titusville till, formerly called inner Illinoian, northwestern Pennsylvania. G. W. White and S. M. Totten. bibliog il Science 148:234-5 Ap 9 '65

Cenozoic
Quaternary correlations across Bering Strait. D. M. Hopkins and others. bibliog il Science 147:1107-14 Mr 5 '65

Pleistocene
Acheulian occupation sites at Torralba and Ambrona, Spain: their geology. K. W. Butzer. bibliog il Science 150:1718-22 D 24 '65
Fossil coral from sand indicates ice age thaw; Wisconsin stage. Sci N L 89:12 Ja 1 '66
Pleistocene epoch in deep-sea sediments. D. B. Ericson and others; discussion. bibliog il Science 148:1037+, 1488 My 21, Je 11 '65
Pleistocene glaciation: a criterion for recognition of its onset. D. H. Krinsley and W. S. Newman. bibliog il Science 149:442-3 Jl 23 '65
Pliocene-pleistocene boundary, northern Gulf of Mexico. W. H. Akers. bibliog il Science 149:741-2 Ag 13 '65
Titanium dioxide in pyroclastic layers from volcanoes in the Cascade Range. G. K. Czamanske and S. C. Porter. bibliog il Science 150:1022-5 N 19 '65

Precambrian
Carbonaceous rocks of the Soudan iron formation early Precambrian. E. P. Cloud, jr. and others. bibliog il Science 148:1713-16 Je 25 '65
Hydrocarbons of biological origin in sediments about two billion years old. J. Oró and others. bibliog il Science 148:77-9 Ap 2 '65
Microorganisms from the Gunflint chert; Precambrian fossils from Ontario. E. S. Barghoorn and S. A. Tyler. bibliog il Science 147:563-77 F 5 '65; Reply. Time 85:56 Mr 12 '65
Paleobiology of a Precambrian shale. E. S. Barghoorn and others. bibliog il Science 148:461-72 Ap 23 '65
Precambrian glaciated surface beneath the Gowganda formation, Lake Timagami, Ontario. P. E. Schenk. bibliog il Science 149:176-7 Jl 9 '65

GEOLOGY, Structural
Tectonic deformation associated with the 1964 Alaska earthquake. G. Plafker. bibliog il Science 148:1675-87 Je 25 '65

GEOMAGNETIC storms. See Magnetic storms
GEOMAGNETISM. See Magnetism, Terrestrial
GEOMETRY
See also
Topology
GEOMETRY of love; story. See Cheever, J.
GEOPHYSICAL research
Data analysis and the frontiers of geophysics; adaptation of address, February 26, 1964. J. W. Tukey. bibliog Science 148:1283-9 Je 4 '65
1965 science review. Sci N L 88:393-4 D 18 '65

GEOPHYSICS
Colston symposium: marine geology and geophysics; report on 17th conference sponsored by the Colston research society. R. S. Dietz. Science 149:94-5 Jl 2 '65
See also
Auroras
Earth—Internal structure
Earth tides
International geophysical year

GEOPOLITICS
Geographic aspects of the struggle in Viet-Nam. G. E. Pearcy. il Dept State Bul 53:487-96 S 20 '65

GEORGE III, king of Great Britain
What ailed George; Hunter-MacAlpine diagnosis. Newsweek 67:81 Ja 17 '66
GEORGE of Poděbrad, king of Bohemia
George of Bohemia: king of heretics, by F. G. Heymann. Review
America 112:463-4 Ap 3 '65. C. L. Hohl, jr.
GEORGE, F. Morrison
F. Morrison George, 1944-1965. S. Gordon. Look 29:25-6 O 5 '65

GEORGE, Jean
Charming cheater, the chipmunk. Read Digest 86:215-16+ My '65
Seen through other eyes. Read Digest 86:141-4 F '65
Tooth and a claw. Read Digest 88:149-50+ Ja '66
Wizardry of webs. Read Digest 87:115-19 Ag '65
GEORGE, M. B.
Handling the multihull; excerpts from Basic sailing; ed. by A. Piver. Motor B 116:38-9 S '65
GEORGE, William B.
Proposed solution to the Rhodesian crisis. Christian Cent 83:13-14 Ja 5 '66
GEORGE, Zale R.
Cold Spring Harbor high school. Library J 90:5475-7 D 15 '65
GEORGE Braziller, incorporated. See Braziller, George, incorporated
GEORGE Eastman house of photography. See Photography—Galleries and museums
GEORGE RIVER
Reporter at large. E. Iglauer. il New Yorker 41:174+ N 6 '65
GEORGETOWN university, Washington, D.C.
Luci Johnson and history; ties between University and White House. K. J. Atchity. America 113:334+ S 25 '65
GEORGI, Charlotte
How to start a business library; in one easy lesson. por Library J 90:1058-62 Mr 1 '65
GEORGIA
Atlanta: the waiting game; pollution problems. R. McGill. Sat R 48:42-3 My 22 '65
See also
Architecture, Domestic—Georgia
Booksellers and bookselling—Georgia
Fishing—Georgia
Stone Mountain

Legislature
Beyond the voting rights act. P. Good. il Reporter 33:25-9 O 7 '65
Georgia legislature's new look for 1966. il Ebony 20:48-50+ S '65
One word too many; seatless legislator Bond. Time 87:20 Ja 21 '66
Two-time loser; J. Bond claims seat as representative. Newsweek 67:26+ Ja 24 '66

Politics and government
Pulling a huhmun. Newsweek 66:26-8 S 20 '65
That changing climate. il Time 85:17-18 F 12 '65
Times have changed; Negro members in Georgia's House. il Newsweek 65:24+ Je 28 '65

Race problems
Things to come; Negroes in the Georgia House of representatives. New Repub 152:7 My 22 '65

GEORGIA library association
Giant step in Georgia; letter to the editor. E. J. Josey. Library J 90:5320 D 15 '65
GEORGIA-Pacific corporation
Second growth of Georgia-Pacific. J. B. Weiner. il Duns R 85:47-9+ My '65
GEORGIA, University, Athens
Married students housing. il Arch Rec 138:119 Ag '65
GEORGIAN BAY
Amphibious cruise in a day sailer. H. G. Braendel. il Yachting 117:38-40+ F '65
GEOS (satellite) See Artificial satellites—Mapping applications
GEOTHERMAL energy. See Steam, Natural
GEOTHERMAL wells. See Water, Underground
GEOTROPISM (botany)
Geoelectric effect and geotropic curvature. R. R. Dedolph and others. bibliog Science 148:1100-1 My 21 '65
GEPHART, W. F.
Strobelight slave. Pop Electr 22:61-3+ Mr '65
GERACI, Phil
Big year for small recorders. Pop Electr 23:47-9 D '65
New radar cuts hazard of mid-air collisions. Pop Sci 186:74-7+ Ap '65
GERACIMOS, Ann, and Ferris, John
Girls of Greenwich Village. Mlle 61:82-3+ Je '65
GERALD, John Bart
Color in England. Commonweal 83:304-6 D 10 '65
GERALD J. McDonnell, incorporated. See McDonnell, Gerald J, incorporated
GERANIUMS
Color lasts all summer when you grow geraniums. L. A. Deming. il Flower Grower 52:22-3+ Jl '65
Geraniums bring a new look to your summer garden picture. M. Orons. il Pop Gard 16:18-20 Jl '65

GERANIUMS—*Continued*
Geraniums new for 1965. M. Orans. il Flower Grower 52:19 Mr '65
How to care for geraniums. il Sunset 135:155 Ag '65
If you fancy them fancy. il Sunset 135:188 S '65
Miniature geraniums. H. V. Wilson. il Flower Grower 52:31-2 S '65
Save those geraniums. W. Luten. il Pop Gard 16:14-15 S '65
GERARD, Claude
Solutions for problem areas. Pop Gard 16:46 Ap '65
GERARD, R. W.
Intelligence, information, and education; address, September 28, 1964. bibliog Science 148:762-5 My 7 '65
GERBER, John
Four-finger exercise. por Sports Illus 22:56+ Je 7 '65
GERBER, Merrill Joan
Approval; story. Redbook 124:44-5 F '65
Baby blues; story. Redbook 126:60-1 N '65
Chipping; story. Redbook 125:56-7 My '65
GERBER products company
How to feed profits as well as babies. il Bsns W p64-6+ Ja 8 '66
GERBILS
Here come the gerbils. il Newsweek 66:70 D 27 '65
GERCHOW, William
Acropolis; Dream like wind; Bird; poems. Nation 201:316 N 1 '65
GERDY, Robert S.
Obituary
New Yorker 41:112 Ja 8 '66
GEREN, Paul F.
Worldwide standards for color television. Dept State Bul 53:597-601 O 11 '65
GERHARDSEN, Einar
Shadowboxing. por Newsweek 66:42 S 13 '65
GERHARDT, Elena
Legend of Gerhardt. I. Kolodin. por Sat R 48:87 O 30 '65
GERHOLZ, Robert Paul
Every problem is an opportunity; interview. C. B. Seib. il pors Nation Bsns 53:40-1+ My '65
GERIATRIC research, incorporated
Non sequitur, red-on-red; FTC vs advertising of G.R.I.'s over fifty capsulets. Consumer Rep 30:226-7 My '65
GERIATRICS. See Aged—Care and hygiene
GERJUOY, E. See Fite, W. L. jt. auth.
GERLACH, Rex R.
Runny-nose brigade. por Outdoor Life 137:54-5+ Ja '66
GERM-free isolators. See Hospitals—Isolation departments
GERM warfare. See Biological warfare
GERMAN, James, and others
Chromosomal breakage in a rare and probably genetically determined syndrome of man. bibliog Science 148:506 Ap 23 '65
GERMAN atrocities. See World war, 1939-1945 —Atrocities
GERMAN automobiles. See Automobiles, Foreign
GERMAN business men. See Business men
GERMAN cookery. See Cookery, German
GERMAN fiction
Outgrowing Germany. S. Koch. Nation 200:484-6 My 3 '65
GERMAN internment camps. See Concentration camps—Germany
GERMAN measles. See Rubella
GERMAN postage stamps. See Postage stamps
GERMAN refugees. See Refugees, German
GERMAN resistance movement. See Anti-Nazi movement
GERMAN reunification question. See Germany —Union (proposed)
GERMAN war criminals. See World war, 1939-1945—War criminals
GERMAN wirehaired pointers. See Pointers (dogs)
GERMAN youth movement. See Youth movement—Germany
GERMANIUM
Germanium and silicon disulfides: structure and synthesis. C. T. Prewitt and H. S. Young. bibliog il Science 149:535-7 Jl 30 '65
High-pressure transitions of germanium and a new high-pressure form of germanium. C. H. Bates and others. bibliog il Science 147:860-2 F 19 '65
GERMANS
Sins of the fathers. D. Schorr. il Sat R 48:47-8 N 13 '65

Stirrings behind the wall: East Germany's muted revolution. W. Hangen. il Harper 230:77-83 My '65
See also
Berliners
GERMANS in Pennsylvania. See Pennsylvania Germans
GERMANY
This Germany: the story since the Third Reich, by R. W. Leonhardt. Review
Nation 200:453-6 Ap 26 '65. P. Wohl
See also
Colleges and universities—Germany
Fascism—Germany
World war, 1939-1945—Germany

Foreign relations
Russia
Russia and Germany, by W. Laqueur. Review
Nation 202:48-50 Ja 10 '66. J. Gimbel
Sat R 48:48+ N 13 '65. H. C. Wolfe

History
Bibliography
Articles and other books received; comp. by A. H. Price. See issues of American historical review

Historiography
Origins of the Institut für zeitgeschichte: scholarship, politics, and the American occupation, 1945-1949. J. Gimbel. bibliog f Am Hist R 70:714-31 Ap '65

Weimar Republic, 1918-1933
Hans Zehrer as a neoconservative elite theorist. W. Struve. bibliog f Am Hist R 70:1035-57 Jl '65

1933-1945
Belief in blood. H. Kohn. Nation 200:456-8 Ap 26 '65
See also
Anti-Nazi movement

Allied occupation, 1945-1955
Origins of the Institut für zeitgeschichte: scholarship, politics, and the American occupation, 1945-1949. J. Gimbel. bibliog f Am Hist R 70:714-31 Ap '65

Intellectual life
Hans Zehrer as a neoconservative elite theorist. W. Struve. bibliog f Am Hist R 70:1035-57 Jl '65

National socialist movement
See Fascism—Germany

Nationalism
Belief in blood. H. Kohn. Nation 200:456-8 Ap 26 '65

Politics and government
Origins of the Institut für zeitgeschichte: scholarship, politics, and the American occupation, 1945-1949. J. Gimbel. bibliog f Am Hist R 70:714-31 Ap '65

Reconstruction
Germany today. G. Astor. il Look 29:44-5+ My 4 '65
Germany: twenty years after Hitler. G. Astor. il Look 29:29-33 My 4 '65

Religious institutions and affairs
Profiles; D. Bonhoeffer. V. Mehta. New Yorker 41:65-8+ N 27 '65

Union (proposed)
Alliance and the future of Germany. F. Erler. For Affairs 43:436-46 Ap '65
Approaches to German reunification. B. G. Lall. Bul Atomic Sci 21:41-4 Ap '65
Can Germany be united? R. Steel. Commonweal 82:433-6 Je 25 '65
East-West dialogue: the one Germany question. F. Kuh. il Nation 200:579-81 My 31 '65
German unification; prospects and merits. O. Gass. bibliog Commentary 40:25-38 Jl '65
Price of German unity. H. A. Kissinger. il Reporter 32:12-17 Ap 22 '65; Reply. H. Duhnke. 32:6 My 20 '65
Unification of Germany; address, February 18, 1965. C. Schmid. Vital Speeches 31:403-5 Ap 15 '65
United States and Germany: common goals; address, February 9, 1965. G. C. McGhee. Dept State Bul 52:375-80 Mr 15 '65
GERMANY (Democratic Republic)
East Germany: stable or immobile? H. Rogger. bibliog f Cur Hist 48:135-41 Mr '65
Gains for East Germans, behind wall. il Bsns W p 188 N 20 '65

GERMANY (Democratic Republic)—*Continued*
Stirrings behind the wall; East Germany's
muted revolution. W. Hangen. il Harper
230:77-83 My '65
  See also
Berlin (East Berlin)
Elections—Germany (Democratic Republic)

Boundaries
Atlantic report. Atlan 216:14+ Ag '65
Of hope & *heimatsrecht*. il Time 86:33 D 3
'65

Commerce
Curious case of Dr Apel; trade pace with
the Soviet Union. il Time 86:20 D 31 '65
West Germany's economic romantics. **G.**
Bailey. il Reporter 33:37-41 S 23 '65

Commercial treaties and agreements
Ally's reward; E. Apel suicide; protest against
Russian-East German trade pact. News-
week 66:39-40 D 20 '65
How Russia plunders its allies. il U S News
59:47 D 27 '65

Economic conditions
Progress in purgatory. il Time 86:98 O 15 '65
Some strength & little joy. il Time 85:91-2
Mr 12 '65
Under the Berlin wall. G. Bailey. il Reporter
33:18-23 N 4 '65

Industries
Will the real Zeiss please stand up? trade-
mark controversy between Zeiss East and
Zeiss West. il Bsns W p54-6+ O 30 '65

Intellectual life
Culture commissars; Ulbricht and Honecker
attack cultural deviates. il Newsweek 67:
47 Ja 17 '66
Letter from Berlin. H. Lohr. Nation 202:51-
4 Ja 10 '66

Politics and government
Since August 13, everything's different; end
of hope for 17 millions. A. J. Olsen. il N Y
Times Mag p36-7+ S 19 '65

Religious institutions and affairs
News of the Christian world (cont) Christian
Cent 82:219-21, 752, 970, 1392-4, 1556-7 F 17,
Je 9, Ag 4, N 10, D 15 '65
  See also
Christians in Germany

GERMANY (Federal Republic)
German awakening; Time essay. Time 85:22-
3 Je 4 '65
Time for decision; free world of Germany;
address, May 30, 1965. G. C. McGhee. Vital
Speeches 31:579-80 Jl 15 '65
Time for decision; goal of world's acceptance;
address, May 30, 1965. G. C. McGhee. Dept
State Bul 53:157-60 Jl 26 '65
Twenty years after defeat, is it really a new
Germany? il Newsweek 65:56-8+ My 10
'65
What Germany has become; rediscovered
identity. A. Clément. New Repub 153:12-
14 O 23 '65
  See also
Aerospace industries—Germany (Federal Re-
public)
Airlines—Germany (Federal Republic)
Airplane industry and trade—Germany (Fed-
eral Republic)
Architecture—Germany (Federal Republic)
Astronomical observatories—Germany (Fed-
eral Republic)
Automobile industry and trade—Germany
(Federal Republic)
Bamberg
Coal mines and mining—Germany (Federal
Republic)
Education—Germany (Federal Republic)
Elections—Germany (Federal Republic)
Electronic apparatus industry and trade—
Germany (Federal Republic)
Elizabeth II, queen of Great Britain—Visit to
Germany (Federal Republic) 1965
Festivals—Germany (Federal Republic)
Labor supply—Germany (Federal Republic)
Liquor laws and regulations—Germany (Fed-
eral Republic)
Music festivals—Germany (Federal Republic)
Natural resources—Germany (Federal Repub-
lic)
Periodicals—Germany (Federal Republic)
Political campaigns—Germany (Federal Re-
public)
Political parties—Germany (Federal Repub-
lic)
Publishers and publishing—Germany (Federal
Republic)
Railroads—Germany (Federal Republic)

Research—Germany (Federal Republic)
Roads—Germany (Federal Republic)
Ruhr River
Science—Germany (Federal Republic)
Space research—Germany (Federal Republic)
Tariff—Germany (Federal Republic)
Theater—Germany (Federal Republic)
Trials—Germany (Federal Republic)
Waterways—Germany (Federal Republic)
Wuppertal, Germany (Federal Republic)
Youth—Germany (Federal Republic)

Air force
Deutschland uber Arizona. il Newsweek 65:
48 Je 14 '65

Boundaries
United States reiterates position on Polish-
German boundary; statement, April 27,
1965. Dept State Bul 52:757 My 17 '65

Commerce
West Germany's economic romantics. **G.**
Bailey. il Reporter 33:37-41 S 23 '65

Defenses
Bonn seeking additional nuclear weapon.
G. C. Wilson. il Aviation W 83:23-4 O 18 '65
Common market idea wins a role in defense;
U.S. West Germany pool talent and money
to develop tank for 1970s. Bsns W p21
Jl 3 '65
Sting of the bee in saturation parity. L.
Szilard. il Bul Atomic Sci 21:8-13 Mr '65

Economic conditions
Germany's economic requirements. K. Schil-
ler. For Affairs 43:671-81 Jl '65
Is the German miracle dimming? il Bsns
W p60+ D 18 '65
Sparkle costs more; gaudy inflation. Time
86:108+ N 12 '65

Economic policy
Erhard's free-market concepts go on trial.
Bsns W p62 D 18 '65
West Germany's economic romantics. **G.**
Bailey. il Reporter 33:37-41 S 23 '65

Foreign relations
Alliance and the future of Germany. F. Erler.
For Affairs 43:436-46 Ap '65
German problem heats up. il U S News 58:45
F 1 '65
Germany: the passing of a policy; Hallstein
doctrine. il Newsweek 65:35 Mr 8 '65
Notes from Asia and Germany. B. G. Lall.
Bul Atomic Sci 21:33-5 N '65
Under the moral sword. il Time 85:30 Mr 5
'65

Arab states
Bark and bite; Arab reaction to proposed
diplomatic relations with Israel. Newsweek
65:32 Mr 29 '65
Moves, countermoves; Arab reactions to proposed diplomatic relations with Israel. Sr
Schol 86:11 Ap 1 '65
Price of recognition. Newsweek 65:58 My 24
'65

Egypt
Bonn, Cairo, Jerusalem: the triple crisis. W.
Z. Laqueur. Commentary 39:29-38 My '65
Cairo and Bonn. Commonweal 82:37 Ap 2 '65
Caving in. il Time 85:28 F 19 '65
Dale Carnegie, help! Nat R 17:180 Mr 9 '65
Defaulting debtor. Newsweek 65:40 F 22 '65
Germany: the passing of a policy; Hallstein
doctrine. il Newsweek 65:35 Mr 8 '65
Hat trick; dispute over Ulbricht visit. News-
week 65:49 Mr 1 '65
Sincere Chancellor; concerning arms deal
with Israel. Time 85:30-1 F 26 '65
West Germany trapped in Mideast squeeze.
il Bsns W p26-7 Mr 6 '65
What to do about Germany. Time 85:35 Mr
19 '65

Europe, Eastern
Germany looks at Eastern Europe. **G.**
Schröder. For Affairs 44:15-25 O '65

France
Cooling Franco-German relations. E. M. von
Kuehnelt-Leddihn. Nat R 17:650-1 Jl 27 '65
France and Germany: divergent outlooks. A.
Grosser. For Affairs 44:26-36 O '65
Necessary guest; President de Gaulle in
Bonn. Time 85:30 Je 18 '65
New storm over Germany; de Gaulle's latest
maneuver. il U S News 59:65-6 N 8 '65
No change in Germany. G. Bailey. il Reporter
33:32-3 O 7 '65
Once burned; talks between de Gaulle and
Erhard. Newsweek 65:47-8 Je 21 '65

GERMANY (Federal Republic)—Foreign relations—*Continued*

Israel

Bark and bite; Arab reaction to proposed diplomatic relations with Israel. Newsweek 65:32 Mr 29 '65

Bonn, Cairo, Jerusalem: the triple crisis. W. Z. Laqueur. Commentary 39:29-38 My '65; Reply. M. R. Sheinberg. 40:24+ S '65

Call for wise hearts; Israel to establish diplomatic ties with West Germany. il Time 85:26 Mr 26 '65

Dale Carnegie, help! Nat R 17:180 Mr 9 '65

Defaulting debtor. Newsweek 65:40 F 22 '65

German ambassador to Israel. J. Feron. il N Y Times Mag p 102+ O 31 '65

Mideast mix-up: everybody loses. Newsweek 65:29 Mr 22 '65

Moves, countermoves: Arab reactions to proposed diplomatic relations with Israel. Sr Schol 86:11 Ap 1 '65

Price of recognition. Newsweek 65:58 My 24 '65

Remember, remember! West Germany and Israel establish diplomatic relations. Newsweek 66:40 Ag 23 '65

Sincere Chancellor; concerning arms deal with Israel. Time 85:30-1 F 26 '65

West Germany trapped in Mideast squeeze. il Bsns W p26-7 Mr 6 '65

United States

Der Alte returns. W. S. Schlamm. Nat R 17: 811-12 S 21 '65

Back in stride; U.S. visit of L. Erhard. il Newsweek 67:13 Ja 3 '66

Chancellor Erhard of Germany talks with President Johnson; joint statement, June 4, 1965. L. B. Johnson and L. Erhard. Dept State Bul 52:1051-3 Je 28 '65

German vote: meaning for U.S. il U S News 59:70 O 4 '65

West Germany's aim: closer ties with the U.S.; interview. L. Erhard. U S News 59: 36-7 D 20 '65

Whither Germany? W. Lippmann. Newsweek 66:27 O 11 '65

Industries

Boom in büstenhalter; Munich's Triumph international, largest manufacturer of foundation garments in Europe. il Time 86:84 Jl 23 '65

Communist-capitalist partnerships; company owned jointly by West Germany and Poland. Time 86:98+ O 15 '65

Rotary engine gets on the road; commercial models of NSU's little Spider powered by Wankel engine. il Bsns W p 118-20 Ap 3 '65

Teddy's bear; Margarete Steiff, ltd, 85th anniversary. il Newsweek 66:85 D 20 '65; Reply. B. F. Michtom. 67:2+ Ja 17 '66

To tell the truth; new statistics publication law. Newsweek 67:68 Ja 24 '66

West Germany. N. J. G. Pounds. il Focus 16:1-6 N '65

Will the real Zeiss please stand up? trademark controversy between Zeiss East and Zeiss West. il Bsns W p54-6+ O 30 '65

See also

Electric apparatus industry

Krupp works, Essen

Photographic apparatus industry and trade

Intellectual life

Letter from Berlin. H. Lohr. Nation 202:51-4 Ja 10 '66

Nationalism

Danger in Germany: rise of a new nationalism. J. R. Moskin. il Look 29:119-22 D 14 '65

Parliament

Autobahn stop-go; Communist harassment to protest West German parliament meeting in West Berlin. Sr Schol 86:27 Ap 29 '65

Island and the sea; Soviet harassment during Bundestag meeting in West Berlin. il Newsweek 65:38+ Ap 19 '65

Simple signpost; Bundestag session in West Berlin in defiance of Soviet wishes. il Time 85:32 Ap 16 '65

Smiles change to snarls in Berlin: the meaning; Communist harassment around Berlin to protest the meeting of the West German Parliament in West Berlin. il U S News 58:52 Ap 19 '65

Politics and government

Adenauer at ninety. K. Kellen. For Affairs 44:275-90 Ja '66

Again Franz-Josef. Newsweek 66:38 S 20 '65

At the epicenter. Newsweek 66:57-8 O 11 '65

Danger in Germany: rise of a new nationalism. J. R. Moskin. il Look 29:119-22 D 14 '65

Debate over the dark side. il Time 85:40 My 7 '65

Fighting the past. Newsweek 65:38 Ap 5 '65

Germans will vote for a stronger voice. il Bsns W p 108-11+ S 4 '65

Ghosts of Weimar; opposition of the trade unions to emergency legislation. Time 85: 39 Je 11 '65

March of oblivion; renewed feud between Erhard and Strauss. Newsweek 66:40+ N 29 '65

Nazi murders & German politics. D. Schoenbaum. Commentary 39:72-7 Je '65

Of pride & politics. il Time 85:40+ Ap 30 '65

Patching it up; birth pangs of coalition government. il Newsweek 66:46 N 1 '65

Rubber lion strikes again; Cabinet appointments. il Time 86:35 O 29 '65

See also

Elections—Germany (Federal Republic)

Political parties—Germany (Federal Republic)

Religious institutions and affairs

News of the Christian world (cont) Christian Cent 82:628-30, 1168-70 My 12, S 22 '65

Social policy

Some soul massage for *die formierte gesellschaft;* Teutonic equivalent of Great society. Time 86:47-8 N 19 '65

GERMANY, EASTERN. See Germany (Democratic Republic)

GERMANY and the United States

United States and Germany: common goals; address, February 9, 1965. G. C. McGhee. Dept State Bul 52:375-80 Mr 15 '65

GERMER, Lester H.

Structure of crystal surfaces; with biographical sketch. Sci Am 212:16, 32-41 Mr '65

GERMINATION

Germination of lily pollen: respiration and tube growth. D. B. Dickinson. bibliog il Science 150:1818-19 D 31 '65

Physiological predetermination: imbibition, respiration, and growth of lima bean seeds. L. W. Woodstock and B. M. Pollock. il Science 150:1031-2 N 19 '65

GERMS. See Microorganisms; Microorganisms, Pathogenic

GERNREICH, Rudi

Gernreich's progress; or, Eve unbound. G. Steinem. il pors N Y Times Mag p 18-22+ Ja 31 '65

Great idea boy. L. H. Lapham. il por Sat Eve Post 238:74-81 F 13 '65

GERO, Marie J. and Backster, N. V.

Keep spring at your doorstep. Pop Gard 17: 36+ Ja '66

GERONTOLOGY. See Aging

GERRYMANDER

Reapportionment and redistricting. R. C. Silva. il Sci Am 213:20-7 bibliog(p 142) N '65

GERSH, Gabriel

Books. Commonweal 82:669-70 S 17 '65

Report on poverty. Sat R 48:61 O 30 '65

GERSHON, Michael D. and others

Serotonin: synthesis and release from the myenteric plexus of the mouse intestine. bibliog Science 149:197-9 Jl 9 '65

GERSHOY, Leo

Light of the enlightenment. Sat R 48:65-6 O 23 '65

GERSTEIN, Kurt

Spy of God. L. Poliakov. Commentary 40: 67-70 Ag '65

GERSTENKORN, H.

Origin of the moon. H. Alfvén. bibliog Science 148:476-7 Ap 23 '65

GERSTNER, Karl

Op: exhibition at Staempfi gallery. New Yorker 41:29-30 F 20 '65

GERTZ, Elmer

End to all censorship. Nation 201:7-10 Jl 5 '65

GESELL Institute of child development

Folly of overplacement. J. H. Pollack. il NEA J 54:10-13 F '65

GESNERIACEAE

Gesneriads. B. Thompson. il Horticulture 43: 14-17+ S '65

GEST, Howard. See Gray, C. T. jt. auth.

GESTURE

See also

Sign language

GETCHELL, Nelson F.

Inventor of the month. S. V. Jones. il por Sci Digest 57:27 My '65

GETHMAN, M. C.

New food for sportsmen. Field & S 69:52-5 F '65

GIBSON, Gerald G.
Living with antiques. Antiques 87:716-19 Je
'65
GIBSON, John E.
How good a driver are you? Todays Health
43:34-6 My '65
GIBSON, Walker
How different we were! N Y Times Mag
p8-9+ Je 13 '65
Reunion poem, 1965. N Y Times Mag p80 Je
13 '65
GIBSON, William E. and others
Intracranial reinforcement compared with
sugar-water reinforcement. bibliog Science
148:1357-9 Je 4 '65
GIBSON Ranch County park. See Ranches
GIDDENS, Paul H.
Scramble for college athletes. Atlan 216:49-
52 D '65
GIDE, André Paul Guillaume
André Gide, his life and art, by W. Fowlie.
Review
Commentary 40:102-4 S '65. J. G. Weight-
man
Conversations with André Gide, by C.
Mauriac, tr. by M. Lebeck. Review
Sat R 49:26 Ja 1 '66. J. O'Brien
GIDEONS international (organization)
Gideons' way. Newsweek 66:61 Ag 2 '65
GIEDION, Siegfried
Books. L. Mumford. New Yorker 41:158+ Mr
6 '65
GIELGUD, Sir John
John Gielgud and Edward Albee talk about
the theater; ed by R. S. Stewart. Atlan
215:61-8 Ap '65
GIESE, Arthur C.
Blepharisma intermedium: ultraviolet resist-
ance of pigmented and albino clones. bib-
liog Science 149:540-1 Jl 30 '65
GIESE, Donald John
How to cope with crank telephone calls.
Read Digest 86:138-40 My '65
GIFFELS and Rossetti, Incorporated
How one office handles problems in specify-
ing new materials. il Arch Rec 138:104-5
S '65
GIFFEN, Daniel H.
Summer in the White Mountains. Antiques
88:195-9 Ag '65
GIFFORD, Ernest M. Jr, and Stewart, K. D.
Ultrastructure of vegetative and reproductive
apices of chenopodium album. bibliog Sci-
ence 149:75-7 Jl 2 '65
GIFFORD, Tom
Tommy Gifford's new fishing machine. il
Yachting 117:118-19+ Je '65
GIFT shops
Hallmark sells the gifts, as well as the cards.
il Bsns W p 144-6 O 23 '65
Where women's work has a golden touch;
St Thomas, Virgin Islands. il Bsns W
p 100-2 Mr 27 '65
GIFT wrappings. See Wrapping of packages
GIFTED, The. See Mentally superior
GIFTED children. See Children, Gifted
GIFTS
Bride's first kitchen; shower gifts. M. David-
son. il Ladies Home J 82:30+ Je '65
For Mother's day; For Father's day. il
Seventeen 24:138-9 My '65
Machine maids; make back-to-school work
and play, a breeze. il Seventeen 24:277 Ag
'65
To thank a weekend hostess. R. Reif. il N Y
Times Mag p24-5 Jl 4 '65
What to buy for car owners. il Consumer
Rep 30:556-7 N '65
When you give, give yourself. E. Hill. il
Read Digest 87:161-2+ D '65
See also
Books as gifts
Christmas gifts
Colleges and universities—Gifts, legacies, etc.
Wedding gifts

Taxation
For people with estates to pass on; some-
thing to watch; estate, gift and death
taxes. il U S News 58:108-9 Ap 12 '65
GIFTS, Spiritual
Charismatic strucure of the church; excerpts.
H. Kung. Cath World 201:302-6 Ag '65
GIFTS for children
See also
Christmas gifts for children
GIFTS in business
Business of giving; western Europe. Time 86:
91 D 17 '65
GIGANTES, Michael. See Deane, P. pseud.
GILA trout. See Trout
GILBERT, Bil
Bird, the vow and the child. Sports Illus
23:58-62+ Ag 30 '65
Can a girl find happiness under eighty?
Sat Eve Post 238:34-7 S 25 '65

Great wild bee safari. Sat Eve Post 238:28-9
Jl 17 '65
Moment-of-truth menace. Esquire 64:98+ D
'65
GILBERT, Douglas
Psycolorgy. il Pop Phot 56:56-7+ Mr '65
GILBERT, G. P. See Baxendale, J. H. jt.
auth.
GILBERT, George
Big world of little cameras. U S Camera 28:
62-3+ O '65
Closeups with RF & TLR. U S Camera
28:54-5+ F '65
200 flashes; new ultrablitz circuitry plus
revolutionary nickel-cadmium batteries.
U S Camera 28:66-7 Mr '65
GILBERT, Jack
It is difficult to speak of the night; Bartleby
at the wall; What is there to say; Fidelity;
Sirens again; poems. Poetry 105:252-6 Ja '65
GILBERT, James
Flying photographer. Flying 77:138-9 O '65
GILBERT, Lawrence I. See Wiens, A. W. jt.
auth.
GILBERT, Richard
Good time at UCLA; an English view. Har-
per 230:75-80+ Ap '65
GILBRETH, Frank B.
Who says newspapers are going broke? Sat
R 48:74-6 D 11 '65
GILCHRIST, Agnes
Daniel Huntington, portrait painter over
seven decades. Antiques 87:709-11 Je '65
GILDEN, Bert
Authors. H. Frankel. por Sat R 48:41-2 Mr 6
'65
Literary duet. il pors Life 58:45-6 F 5 '65
GILDEN, Katya
Authors. H. Frankel. por Sat R 48:41-2 Mr 6
'65
Literary duet. il pors Life 58:45-6 F 5 '65
GILELS, Emil
Notes from our correspondents. P. G. Davis.
il por Hi Fi 15:36 Ap '65
GILES, Avery
On coexistence; poem. Cath World 201:390
S '65
GILES, Eugene, and others
Gamma-globulin factors (Gm and Inv) in
New Guinea: anthropological significance.
bibliog Science 150:1158-60 N 26 '65
GILES, John Warren
Stop buying insurance off the shelf. Motor B
115:34+ Ap '65
GILES, Robert H. Jr
Rich Hole country. Liv Wildn 29:3-6 Sum '65
GILGAMESH
Epic of Gilgamesh. K. Rexroth. Sat R 48:19
Mr 20 '65
GILKA, Robert E.
Two men behind the scene. por Pop Phot
57:63+ Jl '65
GILKEY, Langdon
Dissolution and reconstruction in theology.
Christian Cent 82:135-9 F 3 '65
GILL, Brendan
Current cinema. See issues of New Yorker
Knife; story. Parents Mag 40:80-1 N '65
GILL, Frank
Fifty years old, and full steam ahead. Hi Fi
15:121 My '65
GILL, Jack
Vote for good service. Am City 80:96-7 My
'65
GILL, Robert
(ed) See Soyer, M. Informal portraits of
Moses Soyer
GILL, Robert L.
Negro in the Supreme court, 1940. Negro Hist
Bul 28:194+ My '65
Negro in the Supreme court, 1954-64; ad-
dress, 1964 (cont) bibliog Negro Hist Bul
28:86-8, 117-19 Ja-F '65
GILL, Theodore
Freedom to read and religious problems;
address, January 1965. por ALA Bul 59:
477-83 Je '65
GILL, Tom
Virgin Islands National Park. Am For 71:
38-41+ My '65
GILL, W. E. See Byg, D. M. jt. auth.
GILL, William J. See Stevenson, C. jt. auth.
GILL, William Jerome
Pittsburgh, pattern for progress. Nat Geog
Mag 127:342-71 Mr '65
GILLELAN, G. Howard
Archery. See issues of Outdoor life
GILLESPIE, Alfred
Evil eye; story. Sat Eve Post 239:48-57 Ja
15 '66
GILLESPIE, J. D.
Annual report on CB equipment. Pop Electr
23:67-75+ Ag '65
GILLESPIE, John
Get into the act. Library J 90:5478-81 D 15
'65

GILLESPIE, Norville
Take flower show ideas home with you.
Horticulture 43:40-1+ Mr '65
GILLETTE, Arthur
20,000 volunteer workers for progress and friendship. UNESCO Courier 18:57-9 Jl '65
GILLETTE company
Gillette hones its edge; super-stainless blade, and a razor. il Bsns W p 143 O 23 '65
GILLHAM, C. E.
Arctic adventure. Field & S 70:40-2+ Ag '65
Doves are indestructible. Field & S 70:70-2+ S '65
Just rabbits. Field & S 70:76-8+ O '65
TV fakeroo. Field & S 70:10-12+ Jl '65
GILLIATT, Penelope
Actors studio in London, or, the Broadway boiler-house abroad. Harper 231:32+ S '65
Peter Brook: a natural saboteur of order. Vogue 147:102-5 Ja 1 '66
GILLIGAN, Edmund
Books for the fisherman. Yachting 117:157 Je '65
Saving drought-stricken trout streams. Yachting 117:105+ Je '65
GILLIGAN, John J.
Forty-eight freshmen build their fences. D. S. Broder. il pors N Y Times Mag p51+ D 12 '65
GILLIGAN, Thomas R.
Who is a public official? por Time 86:73 N 26 '65
GILMORE, Bob
How to make any glue work better. Pop Sci 187:146-7 O '65
Try pebble-faced paving for new beauty underfoot. Pop Sci 187:152-4 S '65
GILMORE C. P.
Booster pump gives new life to failing hearts. Pop Sci 187:48-51+ D '65
Heart research begins to pay off. N Y Times Mag p 16-17+ Ja 16 '66
Humidify your home, and cut heating costs. Pop Sci 188:152-5 Ja '66
Must your body wear out? Sat Eve Post 238: 78+ S 25 '65
Omar Khayyam and his talking typewriter. Sat Eve Post 238:40-1 N 20 '65
They're solving the world's greatest mystery. Pop Sci 187:102-5+ N '65
Tickle talk, now you can hear with your fingers. Pop Sci 188:104-5 Ja '66
—See Luckett, H. jt. auth.
GILMORE, Ken
Project choose. Pop Electr 23:41-8 S '65
—and Luckett, Hubert
How good are those suitcase stereo systems? Pop Sci 186:90-3+ Ap '65
GILMORE, Kenneth O.
Cuba's brazen blueprint for subversion. Read Digest 87:67-75 Ag '65
Hero comes home. Read Digest 87:61-6 N '65
—See Harvey, H. jt. auth.
GILOT, Françoise
Life with Picasso. il por Newsweek 65:80-1 Mr 29 '65
People are talking about... il por Vogue 145:138-9 Ap 1 '65
GILPATRIC, Roswell L.
Will Vietnam lead to World war III? N Y Times Mag p 10-11+ My 30 '65
GILSDORF, Gordon
Two haiku for Christmas; poem. Cath World 202:143 D '65
GILSVIK, Ken
Way to get deer. por Outdoor Life 136:36-9+ N '65
GIMBEL, Bernard F.
Don't run up hills or run down people. C. Curtis. il pors N Y Times Mag p38-9+ Ap 4 '65
GIMBEL, John
Mutual misunderstanding. Nation 202:48-50 Ja 10 '66
Origins of the Institut für zeitgeschichte: scholarship, politics, and the American occupation, 1945-1949. bibliog f Am Hist R 70:714-31 Ap '65
GIMBEL, Mrs Russell
Festival of light. Recreation 58:479 D '65
GIN rummy. See Rummy (game)
GINGERBREAD cookies. See Cookies
GINGLEND, David
Discovering materials for the retarded. M. Harayda. il por Sr Schol 86:sup 10-11 My 6 '65
GINGRICH, Arnold
Publisher's page. See issues of Esquire
Strength of the light rod; excerpt from Well-tempered angler. Atlan 216:114-16 S '65
GINIGER, K. S. company
Giniger describes program; joint imprint publishing. Pub W 188:48-9 S 20 '65

GINKGO
In late autumn its leaves turn to pure gold. il Sunset 135:234+ N '65
GINOTT, Haim G.
Art of talking with children. Parents Mag 40:58-9+ O '65
GINSBERG, Allen
Discovery of a new kick; letter. por Esquire 64:151+ D '65
about
Berkeley: free speech and free verse. D. Wesling. Nation 201:338-40 N 8 '65
Ginsberg makes the world scene. R. Kostelanetz. il pors N Y Times Mag p22-3+ Jl 11 '65
GINZBERG, Eli
Needed: sense of racial pride; interview. por U S News 58:61-3 Je 28 '65
GINZBURG, Ralph
ACLU, Authors league, 111 friends urge Supreme court to hear Ginzburg. Library J 90:836 F 15 '65
Supreme court to review Ginzburg conviction. Pub W 187:68 Ap 19 '65
GIORDANO, Henry L.
Dope-smuggling diplomats; ed. by J. C. G. Conniff. por Pop Sci 186:100-3+ Je '65
GIOTTO di Bondont
Giotto and Duccio. J. Canaday. il Horizon 7:92-107 Sum '65
GIPSIES in France
Outcasts. Newsweek 65:35 Je 7 '65
GIPSIES in Ireland
Orgy, by M. Rukeyser. Review
Nation 200:282-3 Mr 15 '65. D. Johnston
GIPSON, James Herrick
James Herrick Gipson, RIP. L. H. Gipson. Nat R 17:508 Je 15 '65
GIPSON, Lawrence Henry
James Herrick Gipson, RIP. Nat R 17:508 Je 15 '65
GIRARD, Françoise
Oceania. UNESCO Courier 18:17-26 D '65
GIRARD, Stephen
Philadelphia's Negroes challenge a will. P. H. Binzen. il Reporter 33:43-5 O 21 '65
GIRARD college, Philadelphia, Pa.
Philadelphia dilemma; trouble resulting from S. Girard's will. il Time 86:65 Jl 23 '65
Philadelphia's Negroes challenge a will. P. H. Binzen. il Reporter 33:43-5 O 21 '65
GIRASOLES. See Jerusalem artichokes
GIRAUD, Françoise
After Courrèges, what future for the haute couture? N Y Times Mag p50-1+ S 12 '65
GIRAUD, Josette
Welcome new world for a son of Gauguin. D. Chapman. il por Look 29:66-70 Jl 13 '65
GIRAUDOUX, Jean
Judith. Criticism
Nation 200:403-4 Ap 12 '65
New Repub 152:23-4 Ap 10 '65
New Yorker 41:86 Ap 3 '65
Reporter 32:38-40 My 6 '65
Sat R 48:58 Ap 10 '65
Time 85:79 Ap 9 '65
Vogue 145:68 Je '65
GIRDERS
Cantilevered upper floor increases space. il Arch Rec 137:106-9 mid-My '65
Girder wall is all precast. il Arch Rec 137: 217-18 Je '65
GIRDLES. See Foundation garments
GIRL in the camel's-hair coat; story. See Gaffron, C.
GIRL of the golden West; opera. See Puccini, G.
GIRL scouts
Good scouts all; senior roundup 1965, Farragut, Idaho. P. L. Levin. il N Y Times Mag p30 Je 27 '65
GIRL to marry; story. See Corson, M.
GIRL who drew the gods; story. See Jacobs, H.
GIRLS
All girls have problems; excerpts from Way to womanhood. W. W. Bauer and F. M. Bauer. il Todays Health 43:24-7+ F '65
Doomsday calendar; with the girls. il Esquire 64:224-9 D '65
Farmer's daughter, 1965. il Farm J 89:69+ S '65
Girls of Greenwich Village. A. Geracimos and J. Ferris. Mlle 61:82-3+ Je '65
Man talk; the disguise. D. Newman and R. Benton. il Mlle 61:52 My '65
My necessary nuisance. R. R. Gogerty. il Farm J 89:48E Je '65
Nothing rotten in the states of Denmark, Norway, Sweden and Finland, especially the girls. R. Joseph. il Esquire 63:84-7 My '65

GIRLS—*Continued*
World of Janet; J. Winkler. Marshall County, Ill. il Farm J 89:80 Je '65
Young living; questions and answers. A. Wood. See issues of Seventeen
  See also
Adolescence
Coeducation
College students, Women
Debutantes
Negro youth
Young women
Youth—United States
GIRLS books. See Childrens literature
GIRLS clothing. See Clothing and dress; Clothing and dress—Children
GIRLS clubs
  See also
4-H clubs
GIRLS rooms. See Childrens rooms
GIRODIAS, Maurice
Maurice Girodias: in trouble for his d.b.'s. por Pub W 188:34-5 O 11 '65
On the fringe. H. Frankel. Sat R 48:46+ O 2 '65
GISCARD D'ESTAING, Valéry
Gallic Kennedy. il pors Newsweek 65:46+ Ap 26 '65
Golden fleece. por Time 85:94 F 19 '65
Young aristocrat of finance. il por Bsns W p 134 F 20 '65
GITLIN, Todd
Movement; poem. Nation 201:331 N 8 '65
Power and the myth of progress. New Repub 153:19-21 D 25 '65
GITLOW, Benjamin
Benjamin Gitlow, RIP. W. Herberg. Nat R 17:682 Ag 10 '65
GITTES, Ruben F. and Irvin, G. L.
Thyroid and parathyroid roles in hypercalcemia: evidence for a thyrocalcitonin-releasing factor. bibliog Science 148:1737-9 Je 25 '65
GITTINGS, John
Addendum to Why Vietnam? a basis for negotiation exists. Nation 201:111-15 S 6 '65
GIVEN names. See Names, Personal
GIVING
Abuses of sweet charity. S. Alexander. Life 58:28 My 21 '65
How much do others give? il Changing T 19:31-3 Mr '65
Money and lay rights. Commonweal 82:204 My 7 '65
One-man war on poverty. il Ebony 20:77-8+ F '65
  See also
Gifts
GIZYCKA, Felicia
Jackson Hole, 1916-65: a reminiscence. Vogue 145:200+ Ap 1 '65
GLACIAL geology
Late glacial ice-wedge casts in northern Nova Scotia, Canada. H. W. Borns, jr. bibliog il Science 148:1223-6 My 28 '65
Paleontologic technique for defining ancient ocean currents. F. G. Stehli. bibliog il Science 148:943-6 My 14 '65
Pleistocene glaciation: a criterion for recognition of its onset. D. H. Krinsley and W. S. Newman. bibliog il Science 149:442-3 Jl 23 '65
Precambrian glaciated surface beneath the Gowganda formation, Lake Timagami, Ontario. P. E. Schenk. bibliog il Science 149:176-7 Jl 9 '65
Pseudo superglacial till. A. D. Howard. bibliog il Science 148:1461-2 Je 11 '65
  See also
Geology, Stratigraphic—Pleistocene
GLACIER BAY NATIONAL MONUMENT
Glacier Bay National Monument. E. B. Flanegan. il Nat Parks Mag 39:12-15 Je '65
GLACIER NATIONAL PARK
Grizzly; story of five hikers. A. Ruffin. il Life 59:73-4+ Ag 27 '65
Guide to Glacier National Park, by G. C. Ruhle. Review
  Liv Wildn 29:33 Spr '65. N. Nadel
GLACIER PEAK
Mazama and Glacier Peak pumice glass: uniformity of refractive index after weathering. V. C. Steen and R. Fryxell. bibliog il Science 150:878-80 N 12 '65
Mazama and Glacier Peak volcanic ash layers: relative ages. R. Fryxell. bibliog il Science 147:1288-90 Mr 12 '65
Titanium dioxide in pyroclastic layers from volcanoes in the Cascade Range. G. K. Czamanske and S. C. Porter. bibliog il Science 150:1022-5 N 19 '65
GLACIERS
Alaskan glaciers: recent observations in respect to the earthquake-advance theory. A. S. Post. bibliog il Science 148:366-8 Ap 16 '65

Under the Allalin; Switzerland's worst avalanche in eighty-four years. il Newsweek 66:40+ S 13 '65
Unpredictable ice; Allalin glacier, Switzerland. il Time 86:22 S 10 '65
  See also
Moraines
GLADIOLUS
Gladiolus. J. B. Brimer. il Flower Grower 52:45-6 Ap '65
Miniature gladiolus. C. Fischer. il Horticulture 43:34-5+ Ap '65
Miniature glads. E. M. Schroeder. il Pop Gard 16:26+ Jl '65
GLANDS
Circadian rhythm in pineal serotonin: effect of monoamine oxidase inhibition and reserpine. S. H. Snyder and J. Axelrod. bibliog il Science 149:542-4 Jl 30 '65
Cyclic variations in the digestive gland and glandular oviduct of chitons (mollusca) A. L. Lawrence and others. bibliog il Science 147:508-10 Ja 29 '65
Pineal gland. R. J. Wurtman and J. Axelrod. il Sci Am 213:50-60 bibliog(p 124) Jl '65
Pineal gland: influence on gonads of male hamsters. R. A. Hoffman and R. J. Reiter. bibliog il Science 148:1609-11 Je 18 '65
  See also
Parathyroid glands

Diseases
  See also
Cystic fibrosis
GLANDS, Sebaceous. See Sebaceous glands
GLANDS, Sexual. See Gonads
GLANVILLE, Brian
Amazons. Mlle 61:166-7+ My '65
GLASER, Alice
Hair! Esquire 64:36-7+ Jl '65
Making of the president, 1968! Esquire 64:153-63 D '65
GLASER, Peter E.
Solar energy. Science 148:1127-9+ My 21 '65
GLASHAN, John
Happy hardware salesman. Holiday 38:54-9 Ag '65
Santa and the crown jewels; Christmas fable. Holiday 38:44-9 D '65
GLASS, Andrew J.
Hubert Humphrey's one-man constituency. Reporter 33:27+ N 18 '65
GLASS, Bentley
Ethical basis of science; excerpt from Science and ethical values. bibliog Science 150:1254-61 D 3 '65
Japan points a way. Science 150:1107 N 26 '65
GLASS, Bob
Crisis in water. Sat R 48:35-6 O 23 '65
GLASS, Herbert
On Angel, Klemperer's The magic flute. Am Rec G 31:700-3 Ap '65

  about
Ten Mozart symphonies. Am Rec G 31:1074+ Jl '65
GLASS
Glass for electronics. J. R. Collins. il Electr World 74:44-6+ N '65
Glitter in glass. G. J. Berkwitt. il Duns R 86:32-4+ S '65
GLASS, Cellular
Salt rejection by a porous glass. K. A. Kraus and others. bibliog il Science 151:194-5 Ja 14 '66
GLASS, Colored
Colored art glass. J. Mebane. il Bet Hom & Gard 44:54-5+ Ja '66
GLASS, Ornamental
Colored art glass. J. Mebane. il Bet Hom & Gard 44:54-5+ Ja '66
Melodies for the eye; Venetian glass sculpture. il Time 86:98-101 S 17 '65
GLASS, Porous. See Glass, Cellular
GLASS, Safety
Curbing a clear and present danger; injuries to people who barge through glass doors and panels. il Bsns W p84+ Jl 10 '65
Glass doors. il Consumer Rep 30:121-3 Mr '65
GLASS, Stained. See Glass painting and staining
GLASS as building material. See Glass construction
GLASS construction
Curbing a clear and present danger; injuries to people who barge through glass doors and panels. il Bsns W p84+ Jl 10 '65
Expression of engineering; new engineering building in Lancaster, Pa. il Arch Rec 138:169-76 O '65
GLASS cutting
Cutting glass. W. E. Burton. il Pop Mech 124:148-55+ O '65

GLASS doors. See Doors
GLASS electrodes. See Electrodes, Glass
GLASS fiber boats. See Boats—Materials
GLASS fibers
Fiberglas repairs cut pole replacement. il
  Am City 80:120-1 O '65
Fiberglassing with cellophane; the cello-finish
  process. B. Cobb, jr. il Yachting 117:60-1+
  My '65
Only the game remains the same; synthetics
  replace traditional materials of sports; with
  account by L. Smith. il Sports Illus 23:
  32-9 S 27 '65
    See also
Owens-Corning fiberglas corporation
GLASS fibers, Optical. See Fiber optics
GLASS industry
At Saint-Gobain, the first 300 years were the
  easiest. R. A. Smith. il Fortune 72:148-50+
  O '65
Glitter in glass. G. J. Berkwitt. il Duns R
  86:32-4+ S '65

              Wages and hours
Wages in pressed or blown glassware plants,
  May 1964. F. W. Mohr. il Mo Labor R 88:
  44-7 Ja '65
GLASS manufacture
Visit with the glass artist, Emil Larsen;
  Durand glass maker. I. P. Tuttle. il Hob-
  bies 70:66-7 S '65

              History
From a monarch's whim, a great corporation:
  la Compagnie de Saint-Gobain. il Fortune
  72:151-3 O '65
GLASS menagerie; drama. See Williams, T.
GLASS mosaics. See Mosaics
GLASS painting and staining
Joy of color; Notre Dame and new window.
  il Newsweek 66:64 Ag 2 '65
Through glass, brightly; modern stained glass.
  il Time 85:78-84 F 5 '65
GLASS sponges. See Sponges
GLASS walls. See Walls, Glass
GLASS world in June; story. See Henry, V.
GLASSBERG, Bert Y.
Since Malachi. PTA Mag 60:6 S '65
GLASSER, F. P. See Williamson, J. jt. auth.
GLASSER, Leo G.
Mount Cuba observatory in Delaware. Sky &
  Tel 30:4-7 Jl '65
GLASSER, William
Research frontier; SR preview of Reality
  therapy. por Sat R 48:54-6 Mr 6 '65
GLASSES for the eyes. See Eyeglasses
GLASSWARE
America sings; recorded by the glassmaker.
  T. H. Marsh. il Hobbies 70:88-9 Je '65
Bartered bride as seen on glassware; Bo-
  hemian glass, with enameled scenes from
  the opera. T. Shull. Hobbies 70:82 Ap '65
Carnival glass collectors attention. M. T.
  Hartung. Hobbies 70:83 Ap '65
Corning museum accessions in glass. R.
  Davidson. il Antiques 8:846+ D '65
Cut glass. J. Mebane. il Bet Hom & Gard
  43:41-2 S '65
Glass; dancing lights for party tables. il
  House & Gard 127:112-15 F '65
Glass; Northwest Territory. il Antiques 87:
  319-21 Mr '65
Glass-ware patents; William King (cont) A.
  G. Peterson. il Hobbies 69:72 F '65
Glassware patents of Augustus Heisey. A. G.
  Peterson. il Hobbies 70:84-5 Ja '66
Glass-ware, the Hickman pattern. A. G.
  Peterson. il Hobbies 70:82-3 Mr '65
Heesen's glass; risk and discipline. D. Smith.
  il Craft Horiz 25:34-7+ Ja '65
James B. Lyon, glassmaker & designer. il
  A. G. Peterson. il Hobbies 70:72+ Jl '65
Museum accessions in glass. il Antiques 89:
  141-2+ Ja '66

              Care
Care and safekeeping of china and glass. il
  House & Gard 128:84+ S '65
Right care for glassware. il Good H 161:140
  Ag '65

         Collectors and collecting
Melvin Billups glass collection. P. N. Perrot.
  il Antiques 88:341-6 S; 800-5 D '65

              Exhibitions
Bread plates popular window display; at
  First federal savings and loan association
  of Chicago. il Hobbies 70:72+ Mr '65

Gift of glass; Duckworth collection at Toledo
  museum of art. R. Davidson. il Antiques
  89:20 Ja '66
Sculpture in glass; exhibition at New York's
  Museum of modern art. il Craft Horiz 25:
  22-3 N '65
GLATFELTER, P. H, company
P. H. Glatfelter company dedicates new
  paper machine; first phase of expansion
  program. il Pub W 187:146-7 Je 14 '65
GLAUCOMA
Doctor's office tests urged for glaucoma.
  Sci N L 87:134 F 27 '65
GLAZE, Eleanor
One of those days; story. Redbook 125:78-9
  S '65
GLAZER, Dorothy. See Arkin, J. jt. auth.
GLAZER, Nathan
Peoples of America. Nation 201:137-41 S 20
  '65
Renewal of cities; with biographical sketch.
  Sci Am 213:32, 194-202+ bibliog(p278+) S '65
Slum dwellings do not make a slum. N Y
  Times Mag p54-5+ N 21 '65
What happened at Berkeley. Commentary 39:
  39-47 F; 84-5 Mr '65
GLAZER, Sidney
(comp) Articles and other books received;
  Near East. See issues of American histor-
  ical review
GLAZES and glazing
    See also
Salt glaze ware
GLEASON, Jackie
One man's Miami. H. Sutton. il pors Sat R
  48:36+ O 9 '65
GLEASON, Marion
Poison proof your home. Parents Mag 40:34+
  Mr '65
GLENCOE, III.
Combined service saves $35,000 a year;
  police-fire service. il Am City 80:47 Ag '65
GLENDALE, Calif.
Film sparks PR training; ed. by P. D.
  Eimon. il Am City 80:140+ Ag '65
GLENESK, William
Introducing Clive Barnes. Dance Mag 39:28-
  9 O '65
Still point. por Dance Mag 39:39-41 Ap '65
GLENN, John Herschel, 1921-
Mrs John Glenn talks about the years
  since . . . E. M. Wylie. il pors Good H 161:
  76-81+ Jl '65
GLENNAN, T. Keith
Inventing an education for engineers. Sat R
  48:72-4+ N 20 '65
GLENTON, William
Princess Margaret's other home; excerpts
  from Tony's room. por McCalls 93:132-3+
  N '65
Room on the London docks; excerpt from
  Tony's room. McCalls 93:116-19+ O '65
GLENVILLE, Peter
Great Gallic welcome. J. F. Fixx. il por Sat R
  48:17 D 25 '65
GLICK, J. Leslie, and Goldberg, A. R.
Inhibition of Li210 tumor growth by thymus
  DNA. bibliog Science 149:997-8 Ag 27 '65
GLICKMAN, Harvey
One-party system in Tanganyika. bibliog f
  Ann Am Acad 358:136-49 Mr '65
GLIDERS (aeronautics)
Climbing the wind. R Bach. il Holiday 38:
  102+ Ag '65
I cut my engine at 9000 feet, then . . . K. V.
  Brown. il Pop Mech 124:110-14+ D '65
Parafoil shows potential for spacecraft re-
  covery. R. Pay. il Miss & Roc 16:38-9 My
  10 '65
Rocket recovery system nears flight; Ger-
  many's paraglider-ground control system.
  il Miss & Roc 17:35+ Jl 12 '65
Vehicle for future spacemen? Northrop corp.'s
  M2-F2 manned lifting body research vehicle.
  il Bsns W p29 Je 19 '65
Wingless glider. il Time 85:65 Je 25 '65
GLIDING and soaring
I cut my engine at 9000 feet, then . . . K. V.
  Brown. il Pop Mech 124:110-14+ D '65
GLINOS, André D. and others
Constitution, viability, and lactate dehydro-
  genase in stationary-phase L-cell suspension
  cultures. bibliog Science 150:350-3 O 15 '65
GLIOMAS. See Tumors
GLIXON, David M.
Harold Latham's My life in publishing. Pub
  W 188:287-8 Ag 30 '65
Well, what do we know? Sat R 48:30-1+
  Mr 20 '65
—See Winterich, J. T. jt. ed.
GLOBE (Boston)
Boston book review editors express view;
  summary of addresses. H. Kenny and A.
  Duhamel. Pub W 187:39 My 17 '65
Make it deadpan, make it factual. Time
  86:57-8 O 29 '65

GLOBE and mail (Toronto)
No-enterprise system; full-time correspondent in China. Nation 201:178 O 4 '65
GLOBERSON, Amiela, and Auerbach, Robert
Primary immune reactions in organ cultures. bibliog Science 149:991-3 Ag 27 '65
GLOBULINS
Linkage in control of allotypic specificities on two different γG-immunoglobulins. R. Lieberman and others. bibliog il Science 148:640-2 Ap 30 '65
Macroglobulin-producing plasma-cell tumor in mice: identification of a new light chain. K. R. McIntire and others. bibliog il Science 150:361-3 O 15 '65
Specificity of macroglobulin antibody synthesized by the normal human fetus. W. V. Epstein. bibliog il Science 148:1591-2 Je 18 '65
GLORIA, Sister
God speaks, 1966; poem. America 114:42-3 Ja 8 '66
GLORIOSA. See Glory lilies
GLORY lilies
Gloriosa-lilies. S. Caldwell. il Flower Grower 52:8 Je '65
GLOSSBRENNER, Alfred S.
Steel settlement: now the protests; excerpts from statement. U S News 59:113 O 11 '65
GLOSSOPTERIS
Glossopteris discovered in west Antarctica. C. Craddock and others. bibliog il Science 148:634-7 Ap 30 '65
GLOUCESTER, Robert, earl of. See Robert, earl of Gloucester
GLOUCESTER, Mass.
Prayer that startled Gloucester. Read Digest 86:23-4 Ap '65
GLOVER, Everett D. See Sippel, R. F. jt. auth.
GLOVES
How to knit our chin-chin cover cap & mittens. il Good H 162:122 Ja '66
GLOWKA, Arthur
Best trout stream in the East. Field & S 70:54-7+ My '65
GLOXINIAS
Gloxinias. B. Thompson. il Horticulture 43:28-9+ F '65
GLUCK, Christoph Willibald
Iphigénie en Tauride. Criticism
New Yorker 41:131-2 O 30 '65
GLUCK, Louise
Fragment of a letter home: poem. Mlle 61:325 Ag '65
GLUCOSE
α-D-glucose: precise determination of crystal and molecular structure by neutron-diffraction analysis. G. M. Brown and H. A. Levy. bibliog il Science 147:1038-9 F 26 '65
GLUCOSE phosphatase. See Phosphatases
GLUCOSE phosphate dehydrogenases. See Dehydrogenases
GLUE
How to make any glue work better. B. Gilmore. Pop Sci 187:146-7 O '65
GLUECK, Eleanor T.
Can delinquency be predicted? J. Olsen. Sr Schol 86:sup 14 My 6 '65
—See Glueck, S. jt. auth.
GLUECK, Grace
It's not pop, it's not op, it's Marisol. N Y Times Mag p34-5+ Mr 7 '65
GLUECK, Sheldon
Can delinquency be predicted? J. Olsen. Sr Schol 86:sup 14 My 6 '65
—and Glueck, E. T.
Warning to parents: why young people go bad; interview. pors U S News 58:56-60+ Ap 26 '65
GLUECKS, Richard
Wanted: 1,000 Nazis still at large. G. Samuels. il N Y Times Mag p26-7+ F 28 '65
GLUING. See Glue
GLUTAMIC oxaloacetic transaminase
Glutamic-oxaloacetic transaminases in reticulocytes and erythrocytes. J. S. Nisselbaum and O. Bodansky. bibliog il Science 149:195-7 Jl 9 '65
GLUTAMINE
Control of glutamine synthetase in the embryonic retina in vitro. A. A. Moscona and D. L. Kirk. bibliog il Science 148:519-21 Ap 23 '65
GLUTEN
How to eat well on a gluten-free diet. il Todays Health 43:38-40+ O '65
GLYCERIDES
Medial neurosecretory cells as regulators of glycogen and triglyceride synthesis. E. Van Handel and A. O. Lea. bibliog il Science 149:298-300 Jl 16 '65
GLYCERIN
Glycerol metabolism in the human liver: inhibition by ethanol. F. Lundquist and others. bibliog il Science 150:616-17 O 29 '65

GLYCEROL. See Glycerin
GLYCOGEN
Hepatic glycogen depletion in amphiuma during induced anoxia. F. L. Rose and others. bibliog il Science 147:1467-8 Mr 19 '65
Medial neurosecretory cells as regulators of glycogen and triglyceride synthesis. E. Van Handel and A. O. Lea. bibliog il Science 149:298-300 Jl 16 '65
GLYCOLS
See also
Propylene glycol
GLYCOPROTEIN
Glycoprotein biosynthesis in human reticulocytes: a lesion in thalassemia. E. H. Eylar and G. T. Matioli. bibliog il Science 147:869-70 F 19 '65
GLYNDEBOURNE festival. See Music festivals—England
GLYNN-WARD, H.
Vancouver. Motor B 115:40-1 My '65
GLYOXYLATES
Glyoxylate in fatty-acid metabolism. R. Rabin and others. bibliog il Science 150:1548-58 D 17 '65
GNÄDIGES fräulein; drama. See Williams, T.
GOAL values. See Value (psychology)
GOAT hunting
$25 got my goat. D. D. Zietlow. il Outdoor Life 136:46-7+ S '65
See also
Rocky Mountain goat hunting
GOBEIL, Madeleine
(ed) See Sartre, J. P. Sartre talks of Beauvoir
GOBEN, Wini. See Brockman, H. E. jt. auth.
GOBI meteorite. See Meteorites
GOBLE, Emerson
Behind the record. See issues of Architectural record
GOD
God is changing. il Time 85:68+ My 7 '65
God without God. G. Vahanian. Christian Cent 82:745-6 Je 9 '65
Hidden God, by L. Goldmann. Review
Commonweal 83:352-3 D 17 '65. C. Johnson
No access to God's diaries. C. G. Rutenber. bibliog f Christian Cent 82:1570-3 D 22 '65
Problem of God, by J. C. Murray. Review
Christian Cent 82:870-1 Jl 7 '65. R. Luecke
Profiles; concerning Honest to God, by J. Robinson. V. Mehta. il New Yorker 41:63-4+ N 13; 60-2+ N 20 '65
Swallowed up by godlessness. G. Vahanian. Christian Cent 82:1505-7 D 8 '65
Unscrewing the inscrutable? A. B. Creel. Christian Cent 82:894+ Jl 14 '65
Why this non-God-talk? death-of-God theologians. Christian Cent 82:1467-8 D 1 '65; Discussion. 83:85-6 Ja 19 '66
See also
Atheism
Christianity
Jesus Christ
Natural theology
Theology
GOD and the tower and the boy; story. See Kingston, J.
GODARD, Jean Luc
Current cinema. B. Gill. New Yorker 41:99-100 Ag 21 '65
Godard est Godard. New Yorker 41:43-6 O 9 '65
GODBOUT, Oscar
New reefs for better fishing. Yachting 117:153-4 Je '65
$13,925.75 worth of guns. Esquire 63:109-11 F '65
GODDARD, James Lee
New FDA chief gets mandate. por Bsns W p33 Ja 15 '66
GODDARD, Maurice K.
Conservation critique; summary of address, February 8, 1965. por Am For 71:8-9+ Ap '65
about
Goddard named by President Johnson. por Am For 71:16 F '65
GODDARD, Robert Hutchings
This high man. W. J. Coughlin. Miss & Roc 16:46 Mr 22 '65
GODDARD space flight center. See United States—National aeronautics and space administration—Goddard space flight center
GODDEN, Rumer
Poetry in every child. Ladies Home J 82:168-70 N '65
Responsibility of writing for children; excerpts from address, November 26, 1965. Sr Schol 87:sup 14 D 9 '65
(tr) See Gasztold, C. B. de. Creatures' choir

GOLDBERG, Arthur Joseph—*Continued*
Peiping's admission to the U.N; address, November 8, 1965. Vital Speeches 32:98-102 D 1 '65
President names Justice Goldberg as U.S. Ambassador to U.N; remarks, July 20, 1965. Dept State Bul 53:240-1 Ag 9 '65
Security council urged to respond to challenge in southeast Asia; letter, July 30, 1965. Dept State Bul 53:278-80 Ag 16 '65
U.N. condemns Rhodesia's attempt to perpetuate minority rule; statement, October 12, 1965. Dept State Bul 53:762 N 8 '65
U.N. General assembly again rejects move to change representation of China; statement, November 8, 1965. Dept State Bul 53:940-7 D 13 '65
U.N. repeats call for withdrawal of Indian and Pakistan forces; statements, October 25 and November 5, 1965. Dept State Bul 53:952-7 D 13 '65
U.N. Security council demands cease-fire between armed forces of India and Pakistan; statements, September 17, 18, 20 and 22, 1965. Dept State Bul 53:602-8 O 11 '65
U.S. agrees to discuss holding of world disarmament conference; statement, November 23, 1965. Dept State Bul 53:1032-3 D 27 '65
U.S. finds U.N. majority unwilling to enforce article 19; statement, August 16, 1965. Dept State Bul 53:454-7 S 13 '65
U.S. sets record straight on position in Viet-Nam; statement, October 7, 1965. Dept State Bul 53:724-5 N 1 '65
United States supports call for India-Pakistan cease-fire; statements, September 4 and September 6, 1965. Dept State Bul 53:526-9 S 27 '65
U.S. urges Portuguese-African talks on self-determination; statements, November 11 and November 23, 1965. Dept State Bul 53:1034-8 D 27 '65
Viet-Nam: winning the peace; television interview, August 23, 1965. Dept State Bul 53:431-44 S 13 '65
White House conference on international cooperation; address, November 30, 1965. Dept State Bul 53:973-6 D 20 '65
World peace through law; address, September 17, 1965. Dept State Bul 53:544-8 O 4 '65

about

Ambassador to United Nations. America 113:127 Ag 7 '65
America's voice at the U.N. por Bsns W p27 Jl 24 '65
Clearing the slate at the U.N; with editorial comment. il por Bsns W p32-3, 144 Ag 21 '65
Conciliator challenged. por Newsweek 66:38 Ag 23 '65
Conciliator goes to the U.N. A. H. Raskin. il por N Y Times Mag p 10+ Ag 8 '65
Duty overrules Justice Goldberg. J. Neary. il pors Life 59:30B Jl 30 '65
Garlanded with good wishes. M. McGrory. America 113:131 Ag 7 '65
Goldberg and world rule by law. Life 59:4 Jl 30 '65
Goldberg at the U.N. N. McKitterick. New Repub 153:13-15 S 11 '65; Reply. H. M. Pachter. 153:38 S 25 '65
Goldberg at the U.N: an ambassador who loves a fight. por U S News 59:12-13 Ag 2 '65
Hat trick; new U.S. ambassador to the United Nations. il por Newsweek 66:25-7 Ag 2 '65
New face at the U.N. H. Brandon. Sat R 48:16 N 27 '65
New man at the U.N. por Sr Schol 87:21 S 16 '65
New man at the U.N. il por Time 86:11 Jl 30 '65
President and I... il por Newsweek 66:26-7 O 4 '65
Proconsuls and ambassadors. Nation 201:49 Ag 2 '65
We won by losing. Christian Cent 82:1053 S 1 '65
Whither Goldberg? Nation 201:205 O 11 '65
Who needs newspapers? A. H. Raskin. Reporter 33:33-5 O 21 '65
Why LBJ wants men ten feet tall. P. Lisagor. por Nations Bsns 53:23-4 O '65

GOLDBERG, Erwin
Lactate dehydrogenases in trout: evidence for a third subunit. bibliog Science 148:391-2 Ap 16 '65

GOLDBERG, Irving H. See Seed, R. W. jt. auth.

GOLDBERG, Joseph P.
Labor-management since World war II. Cur Hist 48:346-52+ Je '65

GOLDBERG, Miriam L.
Stimulus to dialogue. Sat R 48:87-9 N 20 '65

GOLDBERG, Rube
My most unforgettable character. J. Chapman. il por Read Digest 86:111-15 Je '65
New bunch of boobs by Rube. il por Life 59:143-4 O 8 '65

GOLDBERG, Samuel A.
Aquila Romana. NEA J 54:29 D '65

GOLDBLOOM, Maurice J.
Johnson so far: foreign policy. Commentary 39:47-55 Je; 40:8+ N '65

GOLDEN, Francis
Hiking away to the woods; paintings. Sports Illus 22:42-6 My 31 '65
Hunters of the sky; paintings. Sports Illus 23:46-50 N 8 '65

GOLDEN, Harry
Bobby twins revisited. Esquire 63:42-5 Je '65

GOLDEN, L. L. L.
Congressman on the move. Sat R 48:40+ S 25 '65
Public relations. See second issues of each month of Saturday review

GOLDEN, Ruth I.
How to improve sentence structure. Sr Schol 86:sup25 Ap 15 '65
Troublesome S and verb difficulties. Sr Schol 86:sup9 Mr 25 '65

GOLDEN door resort. See Health resorts. watering places, etc.

GOLDEN eagles. See Eagles

GOLDEN Gate park. See San Francisco—Parks and playgrounds

GOLDEN key award. See Rewards, prizes, etc.

GOLDEN press, incorporated
Golden press' new juveniles in shapes and blocks. il Pub W 188:95-6 D 6 '65

GOLDEN VALLEY, Minn. See Minneapolis

GOLDENSON, Leonard
Goldenson touch. il por Newsweek 65:92+ Ap 19 '65

GOLDENSON, Robert M.
Who's pressuring Johnny; home? PTA Mag 60:22-3 bibliog(p36) S '65

GOLDFARB, Robert
Voyage of the Southern Breeze. il Time 86:64 Ag 20 '65

GOLDFARB, Ronald
High price of civil rights protest. New Repub 153:11-12 O 16 '65

GOLDFINCHES
American goldfinches. J. K. Terres. il Pop Gard 16:14 Jl '65

GOLDING, William
Affection for cathedrals. Holiday 38:35-9+ D '65

about

Fables after the fall. G. Hough. por Sat R 48:17-18 Jl 31 '65
William Golding. K. Rexroth. por Atlan 215:96-8 My '65; Discussion. 216:28 Jl '65

GOLDMAN, Abe A.
Copyright law revision and music librarians. por Library J 90:1268-70 Mr 15 '65

GOLDMAN, Albert
Art as performance. Commentary 39:88-91 My '65
Comic prison. Nation 200:142-4 F 8 '65

GOLDMAN, Eric F.
Presidential scholars. por Am Ed 1:1-3 Je '65

GOLDMAN, R. and others
Papain membrane on a collodion matrix: preparation and enzymic behavior. bibliog Science 150:758-60 N 5 '65

GOLDMAN, Robert
Election slogans in Germany. New Repub 153:8 Ag 21 '65

GOLDMAN, Robert P.
Miscarriage; skin patch gives hope to victims of a medical enigma. Sat Eve Post 238:72-3+ Jl 17 '65

GOLDMAN, Sol
Quiet giants. Time 85:86 Mr 12 '65

GOLDMANN, Robert B.
Spiritless alliance. New Repub 153:13-15 O 30 '65

GOLDOVSKY, Boris
Third man. Opera N 30:26-7 Ja 15 '66

GOLDREICH, Gloria
Gradual joy; story. McCalls 93:102-3 O '65
Next year in Jerusalem. Commentary 39:70-4 Mr '65

GOLDSMITH, Arthur
Faulkner's county. Pop Phot 56:62-3+ F '65
How to get the most from one photoflood. Pop Phot 57:158-9+ N '65
Light you can bank on. il Pop Phot 56:70-3+ Mr '65
Photographer as god. Pop Phot 57:141+ D '65

GOLDSMITH, Barbara L.
Life with the new baby. Parents Mag 40:52-4+ S '65

GOLDSMITH, Harris
Beethoven sonatas, by divers hands. Hi Fi 15:58-60 My '65
Bombardment of Beethoven; concerts. Hi Fi 15:137-8+ Ap '65
For an orchestral treasure trove, a big package bargain-priced. Hi Fi 16:102 Ja '66
New art of Vladimir Horowitz. Hi Fi 15:65-6 Ag '65
Pianists in full swing. Hi Fi 16:137+ Ja '66
Serkin's Beethoven, once with Toscanini, today wth Ormandy. Hi Fi 15:80-1 O '65

GOLDSMITHING
Early American gold. P. J. Bohan. il Antiques 88:812-19 D '65
Master goldsmiths of Sitio Conte; excerpt from Sweat of the sun and tears of the moon. A. Emmerich. il Natur Hist 74:18-25 O '65

GOLDSTEIN, Allan C.
Schools, science & society. Nation 200:341-3 Mr 29 '65

GOLDSTEIN, Fred B.
Phenylketonuria: limit in capacity of preweanling rats to oxidize β-phenyllactate and other α-hydroxy acids. bibliog Science 150:1042-4 N 19 '65

GOLDSTEIN, Irwin
Irwin Goldstein: expanding the visual. il Pop Phot 57:152-3 N '65

GOLDSTEIN, Jack. See Schleich, T. jt. auth.

GOLDSTEIN, R. M.
Mars: radar observations. Science 150:1715-17 D 24 '65

GOLDSTEIN, Samuel J. Jr
Search for intergalactic hydrogen in the Virgo cluster. bibliog Science 151:71-3 Ja 7 '66

GOLDSTONE, Steven. See Michalitsanos, A. jt. auth.

GOLDTHORPE, Jack C.
Coast guard's 175th. Motor B 116:39+ Ag '65

GOLDWATER, Barry Morris
Excerpt from report, October 25, 1964. Cong Digest 44:53+ F '65
[Excerpts from address] November 11, 1965. por Nat R 17:1120-1 N 30 '65
Just what Goldwater said on Vietnam: excerpts from statements. por U S News 58:20 Mr 22 '65

about

Advice from a kamikaze; political advice to Bill Buckley. il por Time 86:70 N 19 '65
Agony of the GOP 1964, by R. D. Novak. Review
    New Repub 152:28 F 20 '65. G. W. Johnson
Apropos 1964; excerpt from National election of 1964. S. Kelley, jr. Nat R 17:1015-16 N 16 '65
Conservatism after Goldwater. D. Danzig. Commentary 39:31-7 Mr '65
Conservative mindlessness. R. H. Rovere. Commentary 39:38-42 Mr '65
Do you mean it, Mr Goldwater? J. C. Evans. Christian Cent 82:1312 O 27 '65
Goldwater rallies the troops. W. D. Burnham. Commonweal 82:552-5 Ag 6 '65
How G.O.P. rivals destroyed themselves; excerpts from making of the President—1964. T. H. White. il pors Life 58:82-4+ Je 25 '65
How many votes does Goldwater own? L. H. Bean and R. Drummond. il Look 29:75-6 Mr 23 '65
In the hearts of the right, Goldwater lives! B. H. Bagdikian. il por N Y Times Mag p6-7+ Jl 18 '65
I've been working on the doorbells. D. C. Johnston. il por Nat R 17:726-7 Ag 24 '65
LBJ for the USA: 1964 campaign evaluation: address, December 28, 1964. H. F. Harding. Vital Speeches 31:249-51 F 1 '65
Naive idealists and wanton realists. Christian Cent 82:1403-4 N 17 '65
No remorse, no grudges. il por Newsweek 66:41-2 N 15 '65
Off the back burner. por Newsweek 65:27 Je 28 '65
Requiem for a lightweight. C. Mohr. por Esquire 64:66-9+ Ag '65
Run, run, run. il por Newsweek 65:46-7 My 10 '65
What did happen in 1964? W. A. Rusher. Nat R 17:690-2 Ag 10 '65
When Goldwater launched a new group. il por U S News 58:15 Je 28 '65

GOLF
Case of the too hot golfer: F. DiPaglia. G. S. Brown. il Sports Illus 23:42-4+ N 22 '65
Five-figure exercise: Calcuttas. Time 86:59 Ag 20 '65

Game of the goff, or golf; excerpt from Hoyle's games, American edition, 1875. il Am Heritage 16:83 Ap '65
Getting the biggest bite from a dogleg. J. Nicklaus. il Sports Illus 22:78 Ap 26 '65
Glory game at Goat Hills; course at Fort Worth, Tex. D. Jenkins. il Sports Illus 23:54-62 Ag 16 '65
Golf. C. Price. Esquire 64:64+ S; 70+ D '65
Hardest-hitting Snead. J. Underwood. il Sports Illus 23:58-62+ Jl 5 '65
Heaven in the cup; a hole in one. il Time 85:80+ F 19 '65
Hitting fat? go have your head examined. J. Nicklaus. il Sports Illus 22:68 Je 7 '65
How businessmen can play smarter golf. G. Sarazen. il Nations Bsns 53:92-4+ O '65
How you can survive an explosion. J. Nicklaus. il Sports Illus 23:68 O 25 '65
I'm going to keep the money and give away Gary; D. Marr. A. Wright. Sports Illus 23:50-3 S 6 '65
Jack and Jimmy hold a bash in the Big Thicket: offer lift to amateur golf. A. Wright. il Sports Illus 22:62-3 Mr 29 '65
Joys of trouble. A. Palmer. il Sports Illus 23:26-39 Jl 26; 36-43 Ag 2; 32-8 Ag 9 '65
Long irons: tips and warnings; ed. by G. S. Brown. T. Lema. il Sports Illus 22:50-5 Mr 22 '65
Man who casts the longest shadow. A. Wright. il Sports Illus 22:40-2+ Ap 5 '65
New tradition; U.S. Open and U.S. Amateur championship format changed to enhance televising. Sports Illus 22:6 F 8 '65
New way to play long irons; ed. by G. S. Brown. T. Lema. il Sports Illus 22:40-7+ Mr 15 '65
One way of getting back to business. J. Nicklaus. il Sports Illus 22:48 Mr 1 '65
Place where gambling is proper. J. Nicklaus. il Sports Illus 22:74 My 10 '65
Revolt of the golf pros. A. Wright. il Sports Illus 23:14-17 Ag 9 '65
Save strokes by being a divot digger. J. Nicklaus. il Sports Illus 24:43 Ja 3 '66
Small chip can beat a big blast. J. Nicklaus. il Sports Illus 23:56 N 8 '65
Trouble shots by P. Hahn. Review
    Time il 85:57 Mr 5 '65
Two for Mr Clean; Doug Sanders two victories in eight days. il Time 85:44 Mr 26 '65
Warm hopes for a man with a cold touch: K. Venturi. G. S. Brown. Sports Illus 22:64-7 Mr 15 '65
    See also
Caddies (golf)
Golf courses
Swing (golf)
United States golf association

Study and teaching
Rule of thumb that strengthens your grip. J. Nicklaus. il Sports Illus 23:93 S 13 '65
Teacher. il Time 86:64-5 S 3 '65
What comes after dictates what comes first. J. Nicklaus. il Sports Illus 23:118 S 20 '65

Tournaments
All alone at the top: J. Nicklaus winner of Masters tournament. A. Wright. il Sports Illus 22:24-9+ Ap 19 '65
Arnold Palmer on the PGA; Professional golfers association tournament. A. Palmer. Newsweek 66:53 Ag 16 '65
Augusta: where old masters are on display; with photographs by N. Barr. Sports Illus 22:34-9 Ap 5 '65
Aussie menace; British Open. il Time 86:48 Jl 16 '65
Bing's bash: National pro-amateur golf championship. il Newsweek 67:78 Ja 24 '66
Byron's boys beat the British cup team: biennial Ryder cup matches at Royal Birkdale golf club. A. Wright. il Sports Illus 23:79-80+ O 18 '65
Can a girl find happiness under eighty? Ladies' professional golf association tour. B. Gilbert. il Sat Eve Post 238:34-7 S 25 '65
Carol is the ladies' Mann; winner of U.S. women's Open. G. S. Brown. il Sports Illus 23:22-3 Jl 12 '65
Delicate look at one that is no soft touch; photographs by J. Maisel; with account by A. Wright. Sports Illus 23:34-44+ Je 14 '65
Diary of a career in turmoil; D. Marr wins PGA championship, while Palmer has the worst week in his golfing career. A. Wright. il Sports Illus 23:24-6+ Ag 23 '65
Double, double toil and trouble; Bing Crosby national pro-amateur championship. B. Crampton the winner. A. Wright. il Sports Illus 22:12-17 F 1 '65

GOLF—Tournaments—*Continued*

$84,500 worth of practicality; Bing Crosby national pro-amateur golf championship. il Time 85:93 F 5 '65

Gallery had me grinning; Masters championship at Augusta national. J. Nicklaus. il Sports Illus 22:26-9 Ap 26 '65

I feel awful; U.S. open, St Louis' Bellerive country club. il Times 86:53 Jl 2 '65

It is something special U.S. Open at Bellerive country club, St Louis. J. Nicklaus. il Sports Illus 22:30-3 Je 14 '65

Joys of trouble. A. Palmer. il Sports Illus 23:26-39 Jl 26; 36-43 Ag 2; 32-8 Ag 9 '65

Kangaroo ball at Kooyonga; Australian Open. Time 86:84 N 5 '65

Laugher for the team from Texas; G. Brewer and B. Baird won PGA championship. A. Wright. il Sports Illus 23:84+ D 20 '65

Long live the king! il Time 86:60 Ag 20 '65

Man from down under laughs it up; P. Thomson winner of British Open. J. Lovesey. il Sports Illus 23:16-17+ Jl 19 '65

No affinity for the Trinity; Colonial national invitation, Fort Worth. D. Jenkins. il Sports Illus 22:76+ My 17 '65

Player and the course; Bellerive country club. il Newsweek 66:52-3 Jl 5 '65

Rock and roll in the Rockies; U.S. girls' junior championship, Evergreen, Colo. P. Ryan. il Sports Illus 23:16-19 Ag 30 '65

Short, shy and sure; British Open. il Newsweek 66:48 Jl 19 '65

Smiling Jack; Masters tournament. il Time 85:82-3 Ap 23 '65

Spanish discover golf and its Player; Canada cup matches in Madrid. A. Wright. il Sports Illus 23:69-71 O 11 '65

Sporting scene; Masters tournament. H. W. Wind. il New Yorker 41:140+ My 1 '65

Sporting scene; PGA championship at Laurel Valley club. H. W. Wind. il New Yorker 41:209-10+ N 13 '65

Sporting scene; United States open. H. W. Wind. il New Yorker 41:72+ Jl 17 '65

Sporting scene; Walker cup match at Five farms course, Baltimore country club. H. W. Wind. New Yorker 41:217-20 N 13 '65

Taste of money; D. Marr, winner of P.G.A. tournament, Ligonier, Pa. Time 86:68 Ag 27 '65

Their hungry golfers feast on us. M. McCormack. il Sports Illus 23:16-17 Jl 26 '65

Two daring ways to attack the Masters; A. Palmer vs J. Nicklaus. G. S. Brown. il Sports Illus 22:30-3 Ap 5 '65

Two foreign blokes shock the slammers. A. Wright. il Sports Illus 22:24-31 Je 28 '65

Word for the new year could be charge. A. Wright. Sports Illus 24:10-12 Ja 17 '66

You're all right, Pete; British team; Walker cup. A. Wright. il Sports Illus 23:32-5 S 13 '65

You're nobody till somebody hates you; unknowns have won five of the fifteen major tournaments. D. Jenkins. il Sports Illus 22:62+ My 3 '65

GOLF balls
Don't let your ego shorten your tee shots. J. Nicklaus. il Sports Illus 23:56 Jl 19 '65

USGA hits some hot golf balls. il Sports Illus 22:42-3 Je 14 '65

GOLF clubs (sticks)
Fiberglas fairway. Newsweek 66:76 Jl 12 '65

Gary Player tests fiberglass clubs. P. Bryan. il Pop Mech 124:86-7 Ag '65

Grip it like a club, not a rifle. J. Nicklaus. il Sports Illus 23:65 N 1 '65

Long irons; tips and warnings; ed. by G. S. Brown. T. Lema. il Sports Illus 22:50-5 Mr 22 '65

New way to play long irons; ed. by G. S. Brown. T. Lema. il Sports Illus 22:40-7+ Mr 15 '65

When a big club suits small boys. J. Nicklaus. il Sports Illus 22:74 My 31 '65

You don't need sand to use a sand wedge. J. Nicklaus. il Sports Illus 23:49 S 6 '65

GOLF courses
Best eighteen in America; great golf holes selected by J. Dey, B. Nelson and C. Coe. D. Jenkins. il Sports Illus 22:30-40+ F 15; 32-43 F 22 '65

Gallery had me grinning; Masters championship at Augusta national. J. Nicklaus. il Sports Illus 22:26-9 Ap 26 '65

Glory game at Goat Hills; course at Fort Worth, Tex. D. Jenkins. il Sports Illus 23:54-62 Ag 16 '65

Golf club that business built; Laurel Valley club. il Bsns W p48-51 Ag 28 '65

Golfing along the Gulf. V. J. Flanagan. il Travel 123:42-4 F '65

Greatest golf clubs. C. Price. il Esquire 64:112-13+ Ag '65

It is something special U.S. Open at Bellerive country club, St Louis. J. Nicklaus. il Sports Illus 22:30-3 Je 14 '65

No affinity for the Trinity; Colonial national invitation, Forth Worth. D. Jenkins. il Sports Illus 22:76+ My 17 '65

Perfect golf course. A. Palmer. il Esquire 63:89-93 Ap '65

Sporting scene. H. W. Wind. New Yorker 41:220-2+ N 13 '65

Lighting
Fun under floodlights. D. B. Warnick. il Travel 123:39-42 Ap '65

Some rules for golf-course lighting. il Am City 80:136+ Mr '65

GOLF courses, Municipal
Get your golf course out of the red. J. E. O'Connor, jr. il Am City 81:98-100 Ja '66

GOLF gambling. See Gambling

GOLFERS
Augusta; where old masters are on display; with photographs by N. Barr. Sports Illus 22:34-9 Ap 5 '65

Bluest chip on the greens; earnings. Time 86:94 O 1 '65

British plan a cup caper. J. Lovesey. il Sports Illus 23:28-9 D 20 '65

Can a girl find happiness under eighty? Ladies' professional golf association tour. B. Gilbert. il Sat Eve Post 238:34-7 S 25 '65

Carol is the ladies' Mann; winner of U.S. women's Open. G. S. Brown. il Sports Illus 23:22-3 Jl 12 '65

Double, double toil and trouble; Bing Crosby national pro-amateur championship. B. Crampton the winner. A. Wright. il Sports Illus 22:12-17 F 1 '65

Glory game at Goat Hills; course at Fort Worth, Tex. D. Jenkins. il Sports Illus 23:54-62 Ag 16 '65

Heiress apparent; K. Whitworth. il Newsweek 66:66 D 13 '65

Revolt of the golf pros. A. Wright. il Sports Illus 23:14-17 Ag 9 '65

Rock and roll in the Rockies; U.S. girls' junior championship, Evergreen, Colo. P. Ryan. il Sports Illus 23:16-19 Ag 30 '65

Sporting scene; United States open. H. W. Wind. il New Yorker 41:72+ Jl 17 '65

Their hungry golfers feast on us. M. McCormack. il Sports Illus 23:16-17 Jl 26 '65

Two daring ways to attack the Masters; A. Palmer vs J. Nicklaus. G. S. Brown. il Sports Illus 22:30-3 Ap 5 '65

Word for the new year could be charge. A. Wright. Sports Illus 24:10-12 Ja 17 '66

You're nobody till somebody hates you; unknowns have won five of the fifteen major tournaments. D. Jenkins. il Sports Illus 22:62+ My 3 '65

GOLGI apparatus
Intercisternal elements of the Golgi apparatus. F. R. Turner and W. G. Whaley. il Science 47:1303-4 Mr 12 '65

GOLIAD, Tex.
My real friend, Joe; with portrait of J. Chadwick by G. Catlin. L. Burkhalter. Am Heritage 16:44-5 Ap '65

GOLLANCZ, Victor
Victor Gollancz, publisher. Harper 230:58-9 Ap '65

GOLLOB, Herman
Life movie review. Life 58:15 My 21 '65

GOLYSHEV, M.
Soviet article raps DOD space role; summary of report. Miss & Roc 17:17 N 22 '65

GOMBRICH, Ernst H.
Painter and critic. Atlan 215:90-3 Mr '65

GOMER, Robert
ABM debate; a Soviet view. Bul Atomic Sci 21:25-6 F '65

GÓMEZ-SICRE, José
Cuzco school. Américas 17:4-11 Jl '65

GÓMEZ VALDERRAMA, Pedro A.
History, stuff of dreams. Américas 17:28-33 D '65

GOMUŁKA, Władysław
Poland takes a French lesson. P. Ben. Reporter 33:38-9 N 18 '65

Retrogression in Poland. R. F. Staar. bibliog f il Cur Hist 48:154-60+ Mr '65

GONADOTROPIC hormones. See Hormones, Sex

GONADS
Pineal gland; influence on gonads of male hamsters. R. A. Hoffman and R. J. Reiter. bibliog il Science 148:1609-11 Je 18 '65

GONCOURT prize
France presents its 1965 literary prizes. H. R. Lottman. il Pub W 188:32-7 D 27 '65

GONIOLITHON. See Algae

GONORRHEA
Why all the fuss about gonorrhea? G. E. Maxwell. Todays Health 43:26-31 D '65
GONZALES, Conrad, and Dull, H. J.
Pumps, tanks and automation. Am City 80: 95-7 Ag '65
GONZALES, Mary N.
Vote for student protest. Atlan 216:112 N '65
GONZALES, Pancho. See Gonzales, R. A.
GONZALES, Richard Alonzo
New rules enrage Pancho but excite fans. il por Life 59:52+ Ag 13 '65
GONZALEZ, Arturo F. jr, and Gonzalez, Gloria
Mad metropolis. Sat R 48:57-8+ Mr 13 '65
Oh, little town of Tokyo. Sat R 48:81-2 S 18 '65
GONZALEZ, Gloria. See Gonzalez, A. F. jr, jt. auth.
GONZALEZ, Marta
Cuba's bestseller: A gusano returns. J. Yglesias. Nation 201:251-2 O 18 '65
GOOD, G. R.
Manhattan opera company. Hobbies 70:33-4 N '65
GOOD, Paul
Beyond the bridge. Reporter 32:23-6 Ap 8 '65
Beyond the voting rights act. Reporter 33: 25-9 O 7 '65
Birmingham two years later. Reporter 33:21-7 D 2 '65
Klantown, USA. Nation 200:110-13 F 1 '65
Southern juries: white hand of justice. Nation 201:278-80 O 25 '65
Tuskegee's Negro majority. Reporter 33:18-21 Jl 1 '65
GOOD, Ruth
Jean; poem. Sat R 48:28 S 18 '65
GOOD and evil
See also
Conscience
Sin
GOOD and gallant woman; story. See Yates, R.
GOOD-by to Molly; story. See Hecht, F.
GOOD-bye, Bossy; story. See West, J.
GOOD housekeeping (periodical)
Inside GH. il Good H 160:84 My '65
GOOD housekeeping institute
Inside GH: men at work. il Good H 160:20 Ja '65
What's new at the Institute? lots of things. il Good H 161:124-7 S '65
GOOD humor corporation
Sticky business. il Time 86:62 Ag 13 '65
GOOD location; story. See O'Hara, J.
GOOD taste. See Aesthetics
GOODALL, Jane. See Van Lawick, J. G.
GOODBYE, Ady, goodbye, Joe; story. See Witting, A.
GOODGAL, Sol H. and Postel, E. H.
Nitrous acid mutation of transforming DNA: consideration of mode of action. bibliog Science 148:1095-7 My 21 '65
GOODHART, William
Generation. Criticism
America 113:508-9 O 30 '65
Commonweal 83:125-6 O 29 '65
Life 59:72A-72B N 5 '65
New Yorker 41:195-6 O 16 '65
Newsweek 66:114 O 18 '65
Sat R 48:74 O 23 '65
Time il 86:75 O 15 '65
Vogue 146:68 N 15 '65
GOODHEART, Eugene
New apocalypse. Nation 201:207-11 S 20 '65
GOODLAD, John I.
Curriculum revolution in the 'sixties; address, July 1964. por Library J 90:927-31 F 15 '65
Meeting children where they are. Sat R 48:57-9+ Mr 20 '65
—and Hunter, M. C.
Big-city school: problems and prospects. PTA Mag 59:8-10 Ap '65
GOODMAN, Andrew
My son didn't die in vain! ed. by B. Asbell. Mrs R. W. Goodman. por Good H 160:98-9+ My '65
GOODMAN, Benny
Day the King of swing met the Beatles. R. Goodman. il Esquire 64:52-3+ Jl '65
GOODMAN, DeWitt S. and Huang, H. S.
Biosynthesis of vitamin A with rat intestinal enzymes. bibliog Science 149:879-80 Ag 20 '65
GOODMAN, Ezra
Low-budget movies with pow! N Y Times Mag p42-3+ F 28 '65
GOODMAN, Harriett
Words in color. Wilson Lib Bul 40:62 S '65
GOODMAN, Joel W.
Edgewise presentation of Saturn's rings. Sky & Tel 30:128-31 S '65

GOODMAN, Mitchell
Greek islands. Atlan 215:124+ F '65
Philadelphia: the second revolution. Redbook 125:60-1+ Jl '65
GOODMAN, Morris, and others
Species and geographic differences in the transferrin polymorphism of macaques. bibliog Science 147:884-6; 148:255 F 19, Ap 9 '65
—See Syner, F. N. jt. auth.
GOODMAN, Paul
Ocean! poem. Nation 200:450 Ap 26 '65
What will the Hudson be? N Y Times Mag p42-3+ F 14 '65
about
On Paul Goodman. M. Harrington. por Atlan 216:88-91 Ag '65
GOODMAN, Rachel
Day the King of swing met the Beatles. Esquire 64:52-3+ Jl '65
GOODMAN, Mrs Robert W.
My son didn't die in vain! ed. by B. Asbell. Good H 160:98-9+ My '65
GOODMAN, Ryah Tumarkin
Lean on the wind; poem. Horn Bk 41:27 F '65
GOODMAN, Saul
Brief biographies. See issues of Dance magazine
Nora Kaye. Dance Mag 39:36-43 F; 54-8 Mr '65
GOODMAN, Walter
Abortion and sterilization: the search for answers. Redbook 125:70-1+ O '65
Doing something about TV. Commentary 39: 80+ F '65
H.U.A.C. meets the K.K.K. N Y Times Mag p48-9+ D 5 '65
Klan discovers HUAC. Nation 201:328-30 N 8; inside cover, 428 N 29 '65
What happens when life begins. Redbook 125:54-5+ Jl '65
Women's prejudices against women. Redbook 124:46-7+ F '65
GOODNOW, Earle T.
Clocks by Riley Whiting. Hobbies 70:44 O '65
GOODRICH, B. F, company
Goodrich helps Akron get a renewal project. Bsns W p29 Je 26 '65
GOODRICH, David L.
Discovery of Miss America. Sat Eve Post 238:36-41 N 6 '65
Run on nylons. N Y Times Mag p79-80 My 16 '65
GOODRICH, Gail
Best and littlest Bruin. il por Sports Illus 22:27 Mr 15 '65
Twig or treat? H. L. Masin. il por Sr Schol 86:20 F 25 '65
GOODRUM, Charles A.
Librarians to the Congress. por Library J 90:572-7 F 1 '65
GOODSELL, Jane
How to tell a man from a woman. Good H 160:12+ Mr '65; Same abr. Read Digest 86: 112-13 My '65
Parent teacher. Read Digest 86:198A+ F '65
GOODWIN, B. C. and Sizer, I. W.
Histone regulation of lactic dehydrogenase in embryonic chick brain tissue. bibliog Science 148:242-4 Ap 9 '65
GOODWIN, Richard H.
Our coastal marshes. Recreation 58:305-7 Je '65
GOODWIN, Richard Naradof
Mr Goodwin's Great society. W. F. Buckley, jr. Nat R 17:760 S 7 '65
GOODYEAR aircraft corporation
Last of the sky monsters. J. Gilbert. il Flying 78:48-52 Ja '66
GOODYEAR tire and rubber company
Goodyear gets back on the race track; Indianapolis 500. il Bsns W p 144-6+ My 22 '65
Undersea rubber under scrutiny. J. F. Judge. il Miss & Roc 17:32 S 27 '65
GOOKIN family
Gookin coat-of arms. H. K. Eilers. il Hobbies 70:126 O '65
GOOLRICK, William K.
Kingfish's son picks up the whip. Sat Eve Post 238:78+ F 27 '65
GOOSE. See Geese
GOOSE LAKE meteorite. See Meteorites
GOOSE shooting. See Geese, Wild
GOPHERS
Extermination
Man versus gopher in the western United States. il Sunset 134:102-7 Je '65
GORDEY, Michel
Don't expect de Gaulle to change. New Repub 153:16-19 D 18 '65
Paris-Moscow flirtation. New Repub 152:10-11 My 15 '65

GORDIMER, Nadine
Praise; story; excerpt from Not for publication. Atlan 215:99-105 Ap '65
Proof of love; story. Ladies Home J 82:80-1 F '65
Son-in-law; story. Reporter 32:37-40 Mr 11 '65

GORDON, Aaron David
Legacy of A. D. Gordon. R. Sanders. Commentary 39:74-6 Ap '65

GORDON, Bernard K.
Regional cooperation in southeast Asia. bibliog f Cur Hist 48:103-8+ F '65

GORDON, Cyrus H.
Greeks and the Hebrews; with biographical sketch. Sci Am 212:17, 102-6+ bibliog(p 136) F '65
World of the Phoenicians. Natur Hist 75:14-23 bibliog(p68) Ja '66

GORDON, Dave
Build a stereo bal. Pop Electr 22:48-9+ Je '65
How to buy a console. Esquire 64:115 N '65

GORDON, Ethel Edison
My enemy; story. Redbook 126:50-1 Ja '66
New neighbors; story. Redbook 126:173 N '65

GORDON, George B.
I got tne message. Outdoor Life 136:66-8+ Jl '65

GORDON, Harry
Best and best-paid amateur. N Y Times Mag p36-7+ My 16 '65
Pioneer in short white pants. N Y Times Mag p6-7+ Ja 2 '66

GORDON, Harry H.
Good news for parents of preemies; interview, ed. by M. Markham. por Parents Mag 40:46-7+ Je '65

GORDON, James Stewart-. See Stewart-Gordon, J.

GORDON, Kermit
Best of both worlds. por Newsweek 66:82-3 Jl 12 '65
Mrs Gordon's home-cooked budget. M. Gordon. Life 59:4 Jl 2 '65
Powerhouse of economic thought. il por Bsns W p 124-6+ Je 5 '65
Remarkable Mr Gordon and his quiet power center. J. Kraft. Harper 230:40+ My '65

GORDON, Linda S.
Films in review; decade of improvement. Natur Hist 74:66-8 O '65

GORDON, Margaret S.
Failures of unemployment insurance. Nation 200:610-13 Je 7 '65

GORDON, Marvin
Marvin Gordon's ballet concepts. Clark center for the performing arts. J. Maskey. Dance Mag 39:63 Jl '65

GORDON, Molly
Budgeting back home. Read Digest 87:49 O '65
Mrs Gordon's home-cooked budget. Life 59:4 Jl 2 '65

GORDON, Noah
Rabbi; story. Ladies Home J 82:56-9 Jl '65

GORDON, Robert
Wawa moves East. Time 85:40 F 5 '65

GORDON, Ruth
Very rich woman; adaptation of Les joies de la famille, by P. Hériat. Criticism
Commonweal 83:38 Ap 30 '65
New Yorker 41:184 O 9 '65
Newsweek 66:97 O 11 '65
Sat R 48:75 O 16 '65
Time il por 86:68 O 8 '65
Vogue 146:71 N 15 '65

GORDON, Thomas P. See Siegel, J. jt. auth.

GORDON, William J. J.
Synectics: inventing by the madness method. T. Alexander. Fortune 72:168+ Ag '65

GORDON-LAZAREFF, Hélène
Arbiter of the taste of France. H. Moffett. il pors Life 58:43-4+ Ap 30 '65

GORDON WALKER, Patrick
As he lay dying; defeat of Labor party in Leyton by-election. Nat R 17:89 F 9 '65
Labor party jolted. Sr Schol 86:19 F 4 '65
Setback for socialism; British vote a blow to Wilson. il por U S News 58:20 F 1 '65

GORDON research conferences
Gordon research conferences. D. Wolfle. Science 148:583 Ap 30 '65
Program for 1965. W. G. Parks. Science 147:1312-26+ Mr 12 '65
Winter Gordon research conferences. Science 150:925-6 N 12 '65

GORDY, Berry, Jr
No town like Motown. il por Newsweek 65:92 Mr 22 '65

GORE, Albert Arnold
Excerpt from debate, August 31, 1964. Cong Digest 44:80-1 Mr '65
How to be rich without paying taxes. N Y Times Mag p28-9+ Ap 11 '65

GORE, Daniel
In praise of error. Library J 90:582-5 F 1 '65
about
Saga of the cataloger; letters to the editor. Library J 90:2050+ My 1 '65

GORE, David Ormsby, 5th baron Harlech. See Harlech, D. O. G.

GORE, Lesley
Teen-age singer tops the pops; with excerpts from interviews. il pors Life 58:64-7 Ap 9 '65

GORE, Lillian L.
For young children in a changing world. Sch Life 47:4-7 D '64

GOREN, Charles Henry
Bridge. See issues of Sports illustrated
[Monthly column on bridge] See issues of McCall's to December 1965
about
Letter from the publisher. G. Valk. Sports Illus 23:4 D 13 '65

GOREY, Edward
Evil garden; poem. Holiday 38:46-9 S '65

GORHAM, B. F. See Baldwin, B. jt. auth.

GORINI, Luigi. See Old, D. jt. auth.

GORKY, Maxim
Innocents at home. J. Swan. il pors Am Heritage 16:58-61+ F '65
Prophet and a prisoner. I. Weil. por Sat R 48:44-5 Jl 24 '65
Stormy petrel, by D. Levin. Review
America 113:220-2 Ag 28 '65. H. Iswolsky

GORMAN, George C. and Dessauer, H. C.
Hemoglobin and transferrin electrophoresis and relationships of island populations of anolis lizards. bibliog Science 150:1454-5 D 10 '65

GORMAN, Katherine
Migrant workers; poem. Commonweal 82:585 Ag 20 '65

GORN, Janice L.
World history with a new look. Sat R 48:66 Jl 17 '65

GORNEY, Sondra K.
Educational exchange statistics, 1964-65. Sch & Soc 93:479-81 D 11 '65

GORNITZKA, Reuben
Ministry to millionaires. por Time 86:42 Ag 13 '65

GORR, Rita
Star quality. R. Lawrence. por Opera N 30:14-15 N 6 '65

GORSLINE, Douglas
Beat boatmen of the lazy shore; illustrations. Sports Illus 22:74-9 My 24 '65

GOSNELL, Charles F.
Copying grab-bag. bibliog f ALA Bul 60:46-55 Ja '66

GOSPEL songs. See Negro songs

GOSPELS. See Bible—New Testament—Gospels

GOSSAGE, John
As they see themselves. il Esquire 64:86-9 Jl '65

GOTA CANAL
Slow boat on the Göta Canal. P. L. Adams. il Atlan 216:82-6 N '65

GOTH, Trudy
Of orchestras, choirs, and growing festivals. Hi Fi 15:170-1 O '65

GOTHAM book mart. See Booksellers and bookselling—New York (state)

GOTLAND (island)
Sweden's twin treasures. E. J. Guerin. il Travel 124:32-5+ Ag '65

GOTTFRIED, Martin
View from Women's wear. il por Time 86:109-10 N 5 '65

GOTTLIEB, Carl A.
Upward mobility of the motorcycle. Esquire 64:138-9 N '65

GOTTLIEB, Darcy
Christmas trees after the event; poem. Mlle 62:48 D '65

GOTTLIEB, Gilbert
Prenatal auditory sensitivity in chickens and ducks. bibliog Science 147:1597-8 Mr 26 '65

GOTTLIEB, Linda
Relaxing in Gagra. Mlle 62:16+ N '65

GOTTLIEB, Robert J.
Classic comments. See issues of Motor trend

GOTTLIEB, Sanford
Road to negotiations. Sat R 48:16-17+ D 18 '65

GOTTSCHALK, Louis Moreau
Books. W. Sargeant. New Yorker 41:189-92 Ap 17 '65
Notes of pianist. R. Kammerer. por Am Rec G 31:886-7 My '65

GOTTSCHO, Samuel Herman
Backgrounds help make pictures. il Horticulture 43:18-19+ Jl '65
Visit with Edwin Way Teale. il Audubon Mag 67:164-7 My '65

GOTTSCHO, Samuel Herman—*Continued*

about

Day with Samuel Gottscho. E. W. Teale. il Audubon Mag 67:164+ My '65
Gottscho, always in love with his medium. J. Deschin. il por Pop Phot 56:28+ Ap '65
—and Schleisner, D. G.
Joy of wildflowering. il Audubon Mag 67:97-101 Mr '65

GOUDY, Frederic
Recollections of F. W. Goudy: his types, books and press. P. A. Bennett. il por Pub W 187:88+ Mr 1 '65

GOULASH. See Cookery—Meat

GOULD, George, and Gould, Thelma
Bridges with a past. Hobbies 70:124-5+ Ag '65

GOULD, George K.
Some call it Slocumania. por Motor B 116:42-3+ S '65

GOULD, Glenn
Ives fourth. Hi Fi 15:96-7 Jl '65

GOULD, Joe
Joe Gould's masterpiece. J. Epstein. New Repub 153:26-7+ O 23 '65

GOULD, Laurence M.
Antarctica, continent of international science; adaptation of address, December 28, 1965. Science 150:1775-81 D 31 '65

GOULD, Morton
Morton Gould talks to teens. por Seventeen 24:166+ My '65

GOULD, Richard Gordon
Who invented the laser? il por Bsns W p 132-7 N 27 '65

GOULD, Samuel B.
Core of conscience, core of community; excerpts from address, May 7, 1965. por Library J 90:3993-6 O 1 '65

GOULD, Thelma. See Gould, G. jt. auth.

GOULD, William B.
Portrait of a decade. Commonweal 81:767-9 Mr 12 '65

GOULD, William S. Baring-. See Baring-Gould, W. S.

GOULDING, Peter C.
Why doctors vote yes to fluoridation. Todays Health 43:8+ O '65

GOUNOD, Charles François
Faust. Criticism
  Life 59:16 O 22 '65
  New Yorker 41:231 O 9 '65
  New Yorker 41:199 O 16 '65
  Opera N 30:31 Ja 1 '66
  Sat R 48:42 O 9 '65
  Sat R 48:40 N 27 '65
  Sat R 48:54 D 18 '65
  Sat R 49:76 Ja 8 '66

GOURAS, Peter
Primate retina: duplex function of dark-adapted ganglion cells. bibliog Science 147:1593-4 Mr 26 '65

GOURDS
Anna Canatselos loofa dolls. C. H. Fawcett. il Hobbies 70:36-7 Je '65
Gourd surprise. A. V. Hancock. il Flower Grower 52:42+ Ap '65
Holiday ideas with gourds. A. V. Hancock. il Flower Grower 52:39-40 D '65
How to work with gourds; ideas for crafts projects. il Sunset 135:202 S '65
Your gourds can give many surprises. A. V. Hancock. il Flower Grower 52:14-15 O '65

GOURIN, France
Les Américains. il Time 85:33 Ap 16 '65

Le GOÛTER des généraux; drama. See Vian, B.

GOVERNMENT. See Administration, Public

GOVERNMENT, Military. See Military administration

GOVERNMENT, Resistance to
Loud little handful; wars that offended Abraham Lincoln and Mark Twain. Nation 202:2-3 Ja 3 '66
Mao's man in Harlem. il Time 86:15 D 31 '65
  See also
Revolutions

GOVERNMENT agencies. See United States—Executive departments

GOVERNMENT aid. See Grants-in-aid; Subsidies

GOVERNMENT aid to business
  See also
Industry and state

GOVERNMENT and art. See Art and state

GOVERNMENT and science. See Science and state

GOVERNMENT and the press
All Washington's a stage. J. N. Eller. America 112:847 Je 12 '65
Big city press. Nation 200:211 Mr 1 '65
Candor, credibility, confidence; techniques of feeding misinformation. Nation 201:429 D 6 '65

Cold war in Washington; President and the press. il Time 85:38+ Mr 5 '65
End of the honeymoon; LBJ's deteriorating press relations. il Newsweek 65:62-3 F 15 '65
Johnson and the press: what the grumbling is about. il U S News 58:49-51 Mr 22 '65
Lid in Vietnam: restrictions on newsmen. Newsweek 65:58-9 Mr 29 '65
L.B.J.'s man for the press. il Life 59:47-8+ S 10 '65
Mission in torment, by J. Mecklin. Review New Repub 152:24-6 My 29 '65. I. F. Stone
New press secretary. H. Brandon. Sat R 48:10-11 Ag 7 '65
Not for attribution: State department briefing on aggression from the North: the record of North Vietnam's campaign. A. Campbell. New Repub 152:7-8 Mr 13 '65
Politics of power: portrait of a master. il Newsweek 66:18-19+ Ag 2 '65
Politics of the Washington press corps. J. Kraft. Harper 230:100+ Je '65
President and the press. L. L. L. Golden. Sat R 48:65-6 My 8 '65
President and the press. W. Lippmann. Newsweek 65:17 Mr 1 '65
Top editor: L.B.J. Time 86:76 O 8 '65
Washington confidential. il Newsweek 66:18-19 Ag 16 '65
Widening no man's land: President vs. the press; with report by R. B. Stolley. il Life 58:34-9 My 7 '65
  See also
Press conferences

GOVERNMENT appropriations and expenditures
  See also subhead Appropriations and expenditures under names of countries, e.g. United States—Appropriations and expenditures

GOVERNMENT auctions. See Auctions

GOVERNMENT banking. See Postal savings banks

GOVERNMENT bonds. See Bonds, Government

GOVERNMENT budgets. See Budget

GOVERNMENT buildings. See Public buildings

GOVERNMENT centralization. See Decentralization in government

GOVERNMENT competition
Industry fears new U.S. encroachments. C. Brownlow. Aviation W 83:16-17 D 27 '65

GOVERNMENT consultants
Aim, FAIM, fire! civilians to assist ambassadors. New Repub 153:7-8 O 23 '65

GOVERNMENT contracts. See Contracts, Government

GOVERNMENT decentralization. See Decentralization in government

GOVERNMENT documents. See Government publications

GOVERNMENT employees
Collective bargaining agreements in the federal service. H. P. Cohany and H. J. Neary. il Mo Labor R 88:944-50 Ag '65
DOD research information flow studied. il Aviation W 83:114-15+ S 13 '65
Industry fears new U.S. encroachments; conversion of industry employes to civil service. C. Brownlow. Aviation W 83:16-17 D 27 '65
President asks strengthening of foreign affairs agencies; letters, May 6, 1965; with executive order. L. B. Johnson. Dept State Bul 52:930-3 Je 7 '65
Scientist in the federal service. J. W. Macy, jr. Science 148:51-4 Ap 2 '65
They go overseas for Uncle Sam; Americans in foreign countries. J. Ornstein and M. L. Lee. il Parents Mag 40:36-7+ Jl '65
Trends and outlook for employment in government. B. Yabroff. il Mo Labor R 88:285-91 Mr '65
Working for the government. C. W. Morton. Atlan 215:105-14 Je '65
Young scientists cited; winners of Arthur S. Flemming awards. Sci N L 87:116 F 20 '65
  See also
Negro government employees
Patronage, Political
Postal employees
Public officers
United States—Armed forces—Civilian employees

  Appointment, qualifications, tenure, etc.
Snoops; private lives and public service. J. Ridgeway; discussion. New Repub 152:22 Ja 2; 28-30 Ja 9; 35-6 Ja 30; 27-8 Ap 10 '65

    Pensions
See Civil service pensions

GOVERNMENT employees—*Continued*

Political activities

Merit controls, the Hatch acts, and personnel standards in intergovernmental relations. H. W. Reynolds, jr. bibliog f Ann Am Acad 359:81-93 My '65

Salaries, allowances, etc.

Does it pay to work for the government? il U S News 59:90+ D 6 '65
Government's wage policy; reprint from June 1920 issue. M. Conyngton. Mo Labor R 88: 795 Jl '65
LBJ goal: another raise for federal workers. U S News 58:14 My 24 '65
Upgrading Uncle Sam's payroll. Bsns W p 100+ Je 19 '65

Great Britain

King's friends, civil servants, or politicians; civil service in England. F. B. Wickwire. bibliog f Am Hist R 71:18-42 O '65

GOVERNMENT entertaining

Host: Lyndon Johnson's foreign guests. il Time 85:32 Ap 30 '65
It's the most fascinating job in Washington. W. T. Buchanan, jr. il Life 58:74-5 Mr 12 '65
Poppy Cannon's White House cookbook; excerpts. P. Cannon and P. K. Brooks. il Ladies Home J 82:86-9+, 108D Ag '65
See also
White House festival of the arts, 1965

GOVERNMENT ethics. See Political ethics

GOVERNMENT housing projects. See Housing projects, Government

GOVERNMENT investigations

GAO policies hit; with editorial comment. Miss & Roc 16:10, 54 Je 7 '65
High-energy politics: forces now jockeying for position as plans proceed for giant new accelerator. D. S. Greenberg. il Science 147: 1423-6 Mr 19 '65
Iranian aid story: new twists to the mystery. F. J. Cook. Nation 200:550-6 My 24 '65
John J. Williams, watchdog of the Senate. L. Stern. il Reporter 32:37-8 F 11 '65
Pollution politics: LBJ retreats on opposition to measure curbing pollution from automobile exhaust. E. Langer. Science 148: 611-13 Ap 30 '65
Quackery: Senate investigators concerned with billion-dollar business preying on elderly. E. Langer. Science 147:1119-20 Mr 5 '65
Snoopers & tappers; Edward V. Long's investigation into the invasion of privacy. F. J. Cook. il Nation 201:496-501 D 20 '65
Stink of dead stripers: Con Ed under attack over killing of fish at Hudson's bass spawning grounds. R. H. Boyle. il Sports Illus 22:81-2+ Ap 26 '65
Violence and the KKK. Nation 200:406-7 Ap 19 '65
See also
United States—President's commission to investigate the assassination of President Kennedy

Aerospace industries

Aerospace: congressional study of AF contractor raises questions about proper role of nonprofits. E. Langer. Science 149:1076-9 S 3 '65
Aerospace corp. agrees to open its books. K. Johnsen. Aviation W 82:36 My 17 '65
Aerospace elephant. W. J. Coughlin. Miss & Roc 17:50 S 27 '65
Aerospace interlocks with other firms; table. Aviation W 82:91 Ap 19 '65
House group details corporate interlocks. G. C. Wilson. Aviation W 82:92+ Ap 12 '65
House probe of Aerospace corp. begun; with editorial comment. H. M. David. Miss & Roc 16:16, 46 My 10 '65
House unit hits Aerospace corp. spending. K. Johnsen. Aviation W 82:38-9 My 10 '65
Into the think tank. Newsweek 66:56+ S 6 '65
Report blasts Aerospace violations. Miss & Roc 17:14 Ag 23 '65
Report lashes air force, Aerospace corp. K. Johnsen. Aviation W 83:34-5 Ag 23 '65

Airlines

Senate group may probe Eastern shuttle. J. R. Ashlock. Aviation W 83:27-8 Jl 26 '65

American telephone and telegraph company

AT&T; folksy octopus; Western union-AT&T-Bell battle. D. Smith. il Nation 202:16-18 Ja 3 '66
FCC gets set to push AT&T probe to finish. Bsns W p36 N 6 '65

Government and the AT&T. il U S News 59:88 N 15 '65
More light on the investigation of AT&T. il U S News 59:86-8 D 6 '65
Numbers, please; FCC to investigate financial operations of company. Newsweek 66:77 N 8 '65
To probe telephone charges; FCC orders investigation. Bsns W p25 O 30 '65
Wringing bell; FCC to investigate. Time 86: 97 N 5 '65

Baker case

Baker case: one phase ends, but-. U S News 58:18 Mr 15 '65
Comeuppance for the Pickens kid. il Time 87: 21B Ja 14 '66
Coup de grâce; FBI report. Newsweek 65:27 Mr 15 '65
Echoes of the Baker case: Williams tangles with critics. U S News 58:16 My 31 '65
Former White House aide's testimony: tie between LBJ's insurance and TV ads. il U S News 58:10 My 8 '65
Law-abiding need not apply; right of privacy. Nat R 17:140 F 23 '65
Messrs Clean. il Time 86:23 Jl 9 '65
Miss E, Mrs A and Miss C. Newsweek 66:32 Jl 12 '65
New chapter in the Baker case. il U S News 58:6 F 8 '65
Senator's insurance: question of pressure. Time 85:20 Mr 5 '65
Two years of Bobby Baker case: and now an indictment. il U S News 60:42-3 Ja 17 '66
See also
Baker, R. G.

Banks and banking

Banky panky: concerning testimony on irregularities at San Francisco national. Newsweek 65:68 Mr 29 '65
Bit of embarrassment. Time 85:95 Mr 19 '65
Con men, racketeers: links to bank failure? U S News 58:12 My 24 '65
Critical look at banking. il U S News 58:39-41 Mr 15 '65
Failing banks & sporty bankers. M. Harris. il Nation 200:442-5 Ap 26 '65; Discussion. 200:inside cover My 17; inside cover My 31 '65
Hard twelve: former president of San Francisco national bank gives evidence. il Newsweek 65:78 Ap 5 '65
Saxon on the stand; concerning testimony on failure of San Francisco national bank. il Newsweek 65:72 Mr 22 '65
Senate investigates how to buy a bank. il Bsns W p24-5 Mr 13 '65
Too many regulators in banking? why thirteen banks failed. il Bsns W p 28-9 Mr 27 '65
Trouble among the regulators; exposure of the government's own performance at supervising banks. il Time 85:79 Mr 26 '65
Warning signs bankers now see. il U S News 58:97-9 F 15 '65
Why banks failed; new testimony. U S News 58:16 Mr 22 '65

Drug trade

Bill would bar doctors from owning drug stores. Sci N L 88:226 O 9 '65
Congress and drugs: political interest in drug problems is at lowest point in five years. E. Langer. Science 147:846-8 F 19 '65
FDA: scientific, medical groups support agency in dispute with Fountain over access to drug data. E. Langer. Science 149:731-4 Ag 13 '65; Reply. W. L. Nyhan. 150:1533 D 17 '65
Healing the doctor; investigating of doctor-owned drug firms. Newsweek 66:92 O 11 '65
Real voice, by R. Harris. Review Commentary 39:75-7 F '65. D. T. Bazelon

Electric power

Blackout study points to new FPC powers. Bsns W p34 D 11 '65
More juice for the FPC? congressional hearings on Northeastern blackout. Time 86: 14 D 24 '65
Should U.S. use power on power companies? debate on whether electric utilities should be tied into national grid. Bsns W p45-6 N 13 '65

Food industry and trade

Story for our times; Truth-in-packaging bill. il Consumer Rep 30:118-20 Mr '65
Why U.S. is looking into food industry. il U S News 58:66 F 22 '65

GOVERNMENT investigation—*Continued*

Government contracts

DOD-GAO friction probed. Miss & Roc 16:11 My 17 '65

McNamara methods arousing fresh criticism in Congress; with editorial comment. M. Getler. Miss & Roc 18:15, 46 Ja 17 '66

More responsive GAO attitude seen. Miss & Roc 17:15 D 13 '65

Rivers renews drive to curb McNamara. G. C. Wilson. Aviation W 84:38 Ja 17 '66

Senate committee will examine procedures for contract appeal. K. Johnsen. Aviation W 83:48 Jl 26 '65

Statute may speed refund actions. Miss & Roc 16:13 My 24 '65

Government funded research

Congress and science: new probe by Senate unit reviews evidence on spread of government funds. E. Langer. Science 148:1573-5 Je 18 '65

Elliott postscript: Reuss to head new House subcommittee recommended by research study. D. S. Greenberg. Science 148:56-7 Ap 2 '65

Findings and recommendations of the Wooldridge study. Science 147:1556-7 Mr 26 '65

NIH study: Wooldridge committee praises past efforts, but urges major organizational revisions. D. S. Greenberg. il Science 147:1556-9 Mr 26 '65; Discussion. 149:6, 133+, 1047-8 Jl 2-9, S 3 '65

News in brief: hearings on NSF, other federal programs, announced; NAS to study accelerator site. D. S. Greenberg. Science 148:775-6 My 7 '65

Reuss committee: new probe planned into priorities for R&D. D. S. Greenberg. Science 150:1565-6 D 17 '65

Ku Klux klan

Bedside manner; Edwin Willis comment. Nation 201:515 D 27 '65

Dark days in weird week; public hearings before House un-American activities committee. Time 86:29 O 29 '65

Drive to expose Klan. il U S News 58:69 Ap 12 '65

Gambling on HUAC. Commonweal 82:101 Ap 16 '65

Grand drag: investigation by House committee on un-American activities. Reporter 33:10+ N 18 '65

H.U.A.C. meets the K.K.K. W. Goodman. il N Y Times Mag p48-9+ D 5 '65

HUAC versus the Klan. Reporter 32:9-10 Ap 22 '65

How to make a wizard talk; citations for contempt of Congress. Time 87:21B Ja 14 '66

Investigating the klans. New Repub 152:5-6 Ap 10 '65

Klan clams up. M. Kempton. New Repub 153:11-13 O 30 '65

Klan discovers HUAC; R. M. Shelton Ku Klux klan contributions. W. Goodman. il Nation 201:328-30 N 8 '65

Klan on the pan. Sr Schol 86:27 Ap 15 '65

Kurtains for the Klan. K. Crawford. Newsweek 66:34 D 13 '65

Snake pit; un-American activities committee's eye-popping evidence. Newsweek 67:29 Ja 24 '66

Unraveling secrets of the hooded Klan. il U S News 59:12 N 1 '65

Unsheeting the Klan. il Newsweek 65:29-30 Ap 12 '65

McCarthy censure

Days of shame, by C. E. Potter. Review New Repub 153:28-31 N 20 '65. I. Silver

Packaging

Story for our times; Truth-in-packaging bill. il Consumer Rep 30:118-20 Mr '65

We can't compare prices; CU's truth-in-packaging testimony. Consumer Rep 30:342-6 Jl '65

Television industry

TV's week that was; FCC probe; CBS storm. il Bsns W p28 Mr 6 '65

Traffic accidents

At stake: 48,000 lives; problem of highway safety. Bsns W p29 Mr 27 '65

GOVERNMENT labor policy. See United States —Labor policy

GOVERNMENT lending

How to make budget spending seem less; sale to investors of federal-held loans. il Bsns W p 136+ F 13 '65

GOVERNMENT owned patents. See Patents, Government owned

GOVERNMENT ownership

Statist mentality. R. Moley. Newsweek 65:108 Ap 19 '65

See also

Industry and state

Mines and mineral resources—Government ownership

Socialism

Great Britain

As Britain moves to take over steel. il U S News 58:95 My 17 '65

Britain moves further into industry ownership. Bsns W p 13 D 25 '65

Can Wilson win fight on steel? nationalization of steel. Bsns W p36 My 8 '65

Gamble in steel; vote on proposals for renationalization. Newsweek 65:52+ My 17 '65

Labor's bid for steel. Newsweek 65:92 My 10 '65

Letter from London; steel debate in the House of commons. M. Panter-Downes. New Yorker 41:123-5 My 22 '65

Nationalizing steel. America 112:703-4 My 15 '65

Plowden report supports nationalization. H. J. Coleman. Aviation W 83:25-6 D 20 '65

U.K. merger seen step to nationalization; British aircraft corp. and Hawker Siddeley aviation. H. J. Coleman. Aviation W 83:28 D 27 '65

Syria

Seizure at midnight; nine oil distribution companies nationalized. Newsweek 65:79 Mr 15 '65

United States

Chronicle of trade union positions on government ownership. P. Henle. bibliog f Mo Labor R 88:805-16 Jl '65

Yardstick illusion. R. Moley. Newsweek 65:100 F 15 '65

GOVERNMENT pensions. See Civil service pensions

GOVERNMENT printing office. See United States—Government printing office

GOVERNMENT publications

List of non-GPO materials available on need-for basis. Library J 90:2796+ Je 15 '65

See also

Congressional record

Bibliography

Congressional documents relating to foreign policy. See issues of Department of state bulletin

Publications of the Department of state. See issues of Department of state bulletin

GOVERNMENT publicity

See also

Government and the press

Press conferences

GOVERNMENT records. See Records

GOVERNMENT regulation of industry. See Industry and state

GOVERNMENT research

Antarctica: congressional urge for tidy research administration manifests itself in new proposal. D. S. Greenberg. Science 148:1304-5 Je 4 '65

DOD research information flow studied. il Aviation W 83:114-15+ S 13 '65

Lab focus changing as funds shift: plans for federal R&D spending. il Bsns W p47-8+ D 4 '65

Military objectives spur work. il Miss & Roc 16:83-4+ Mr 29 '65

Proposed changes in lab management stir debate. Miss & Roc 16:42-3 Mr 29 '65

Research backlash; Project Camelot: excerpts from remarks. J. W. Fulbright. Aviation W 83:17 Ag 30 '65

Scholars and foreign policy: varieties of research experience; address, October 21, 1965. T. L. Hughes. Dept State Bul 53:747-58 N 8 '65

GOVERNMENT security regulations. See Security classification (government documents)

GOVERNMENT service. See Civil service; Public officers

GOVERNMENT spending policy

Big accelerator: competition for AEC facility is stirring up communities throughout country. D. S. Greenberg. Science 149:730-1 Ag 13 '65

Bigger slice goes to poorer areas; geographic breakdown of federal spending made by M. L. Weidenbaum. il Bsns W p54+ N 27 '65

Budget: portrait of a growing nation; Johnson calls for $99.7-billion. il Bsns W p78-80+ Ja 30 '65

GOVERNMENT spending policy—*Continued*
Budget: total funds for R&D rise modestly to 15.4 billion; research gets most of increase. J. Walsh. il Science 147:485-6 Ja 29 '65
Burdens on the budget. il Fortune 71:32+ Je '65
Congress and science: new probe by Senate unit reviews evidence on spread of government funds. E. Langer. Science 148:1573-5 Je 18 '65
Deficits in good times and bad; around the world. U S News 58:30 F 8 '65
In year ahead: 143 billions of federal spending. il U S News 59:81-2 Ag 30 '65
New accelerator: wide open race under way across the nation to provide site for vast machine. D. S. Greenberg. Science 148: 1571-3 Je 18 '65
Plan for perpetual prosperity: more spending and tax cuts. il U S News 59:106-8 S 20 '65
Powerful society. H. C. Wallich. il Newsweek 66:84 O 4 '65
Research and development pork barrel. P. H. Abelson. Science 149:11 Jl 2 '65
Shift of signals on government spending. il U S News 59:32 D 13 '65
Some current problems of government science policy; address, April 26, 1965. H. Orlans. bibliog Science 149:37-40 Jl 2 '65
See also subhead Procurement under various subjects, e.g. United States—Armed forces—Procurement

GOVERNMENT statistics. See United States—Statistics

GOVERNORS

Succession
Filibustered. Newsweek 66:34-5 O 25 '65

GOVERNORS conference, 1965
Governors swap ideas on paying the bills; meeting in Minneapolis. il Bsns W p22-3 Jl 31 '65
Schools make news; fifty-seventh annual conference. Sat R 48:57 Ag 21 '65

GOVERNORS ISLAND
Nut island. New Yorker 41:37-8 Mr 13 '65

GOVINDJEE. See Rabinowitch, E. jt. auth.

GOWERS, Sir Ernest Arthur
Our man in Trotton. New Yorker 41:20-3 Ag 14 '65
Spitting permitted. por Newsweek 65:64+ My 17 '65

GOWLAND, Peter
Gowland (cont of Glamor) See issues of Popular photography
Gowland goes candid at the beach. il Pop Phot 57:74-5 O '65

GOYA Y LUCIENTES, Francisco José de
Books. V. S. Pritchett. New Yorker 40:157-8+ F 13 '65

GOZZI, Patricia
I want to be like everyone else; ed. by E. Miller. Seventeen 25:82-3+ Ja '66

GRABER, Richard R.
Night flight with a thrush. Audubon Mag 67:367-74 N '65

GRACE, Patricia, consort of Rainier III, prince of Monaco
What Princess Grace likes and doesn't like about the life she leads. M. Davidson. il pors Good H 160:58-63+ Ja '65

GRACE, Doris
Time out for parents. PTA Mag 59:11-13 bibliog(p35) Ap '65

GRACE, W. R, and company
Chemistry of growth. Time 85:98+ My 21 '65

GRACE, William Edwin
Fruehauf hooked up for the long haul. il por Bsns W p 74-6 D 18 '65

GRACE line, Incorporated
See also
Grace, W. R, and company

GRADING and marking (students)
Changing a student's grade. NEA J 54:62 My '65
Grades, eyeball-to-eyeball; don rag at St John's college in Annapolis. il Time 85:59 F 12 '65
In my opinion: more people would really learn if grades were abolished. M. Woodward. Seventeen 24:402 Ag '65
In so far as ... attempt to see if computers can evaluate essay style. Newsweek 65:61 Ap 5 '65
Solution to the problem of distributing course grades; using Minnesota scholastic aptitude test. R. F. Berdie. Sch & Soc 93:373-5 O 16 '65
See also
Ungraded classes

GRADING of meat. See Meat—Grading and standardization

GRADING of swine. See Swine—Grading and standardization

GRADUAL job; story. See Goldreich, G.

GRADUATE business schools. See Business education

GRADUATE fellowships. See Scholarships and fellowships

GRADUATE schools. See Colleges and universities—Graduate work

GRADUATE students
Talent and performance, by E. Ginzberg and others. Review
Sat R 48:89-90 F 20 '65. H. N. Rivlin

GRADUATE work. See Colleges and universities—Graduate work

GRADUATES, College. See College graduates, Women

GRADUATES, High school. See High school graduates

GRADUATION addresses. See Baccalaureate addresses

GRAETZ, Paul
Great Gallic welcome. J. F. Fixx. il Sat R 48:14-17 D 25 '65

GRAFF, Henry F.
Decision in Viet Nam; how Johnson makes foreign policy. N Y Times Mag p4-7+ Jl 4 '65
Isolationism again, with a difference. N Y Times Mag p26-7+ My 16 '65

GRAFFITI
Message from the Maya; Tikal, Guatemala. L. C. Walker. il Américas 17:15-19 O '65

GRAFFMAN, Gary
Notes from our correspondents. P. G. Davis. por Hi Fi 15:16+ My '65

GRAFLEX cameras
Graflex XL: camera with 1,000 faces. J. Forney. il Pop Phot 56:102-3+ Je '65
Large camera; Graflex x1 and the Koni-Omega. A. Feininger. il Mod Phot 29:32+ Ag '65

GRAFTING (surgery) See Transplantation of organs, tissues, etc.

GRAFTON, Samuel
Climate of crime. McCalls 92:92-3+ Mr '65
Crime that threatens every woman. McCalls 92:122-3+ F '65
Hard look at health insurance. McCalls 93: 110-11+ N '65
Of crime and punishment. McCalls 92:73+ Je '65
Our new drug addicts. McCalls 92:112-13+ Ap '65
Teachers who make children hate school. McCalls 93:68-9+ Ja '66
What do we want from our policemen? McCalls 92:110-11+ My '65

GRAGG, Bert A.
Automatic purchase orders. Am City 80:140+ F '65

GRAHAM, Augusta
Who's pressuring Johnny; school? PTA Mag 60:23-4 bibliog(p36) S '65

GRAHAM, Billy
Quiet talk with LBJ; excerpts from sermon at Camp David. Good H 162:186 Ja '66

about
Be specific, Mr Graham! Christian Cent 82: 1053 S 1 '65
Billy Graham's physical fitness program can help you. C. Mitchell. il pors Pop Sci 186: 61-4+ My '65; Same abr. Read Digest 87: 58-62 Jl '65
Billy heads South. Time 85:88+ Ap 30 '65
For the warriors, against the war. Christian Cent 82:1597 D 29 '65

GRAHAM, David L.
Government by freshmen; Maine's year of the donkey. Nation 202:43-5 Ja 10 '66

GRAHAM, Ford Mulford
Look at Louisiana land! J. B. Weiner. il por Duns R 86:42-4+ O '65

GRAHAM, Howard D.
Toronto exchange cleans house. Bsns W p 156+ Je 19 '65

GRAHAM, J. A. Maxtone
Here is the odd paradise of the record maniac. Sports Illus 22:54-8+ F 8 '65; Same abr. with title Book to end arguments. Read Digest 86:152-4+ My '65
Protocol at the Spotted cow. Esquire 63:110-11 My '65
Quiet day with the chavender. Harper 230: 32+ Je '65
Shopwalk. Sports Illus 23:8 S 13 '65

GRAHAM, John M. 2d
Scotia furnishings. Antiques 89:99-105 Ja '66

GRAHAM, Martha
How I became a dancer. pors Sat R 48:54 Ag 28 '65

about
Dark one; M. Graham season review. D. Hering. il Dance Mag 40:46-9+ Ja '66
Fountainhead; program at Broadway's Fifty-fourth street theatre. il por Newsweek 66: 108 N 15 '65

GRAHAM, Martha—about—*Continued*
Martha Graham, indomitable. R. Krokover. Hi Fi 16:142 Ja '66
Martha Graham's retrospective season. J. Martin. il pors Sat R 48:60+ D 11 '65
Three Graham restorations. L. Leatherman. il pors Dance Mag 39:42-6 N '65
Untamed surge of modern dance; with report by C. Barnes. il pors Life 59:96B-108 N 12 '65

GRAHAM, Philip
Go-between's memo on the wild day L.B.J. was named Vice President. por Life 58:90 Je 18 '65

GRAHAM, Robert A.
Another point of view. America 113:710-11 D 4 '65
Council, the popes and peace. America 113:365-7 O 2 '65
John Tracy Ellis on the pathetic blackout. America 112:305 Mr 6 '65

GRAIN
Storage
Used parts make a first-rate grain center. il Suc Farm 63:54 N '65

Testing
More corn growers try leaf testing. Farm J 89:48 O '65

GRAIN in photography. See Photography—Grain

GRAIN sorghums. See Sorghum

GRAIN trade
See also
Cargill, incorporated
Wheat trade

GRAINGER, Joseph W.
Loaded with morality. por Newsweek 65:38 Ap 26 '65

GRAMM, Donald
Well-spoken singer; interview, ed. by A. M. Lingg. por Opera N 30:16 D 18 '65

GRAMMAR, English. See English language—Grammar

GRAMONT, Sanche de. See De Gramont, S

GRANADA, Spain
See also
Alhambra

GRANBY, Conn.
Do-it-yourself in Granby; experiment to improve educational opportunities. E. D. Stevens. il Sat R 48:62-3 Jl 17 '65

GRAND, P. M.
Magic presences. Art N 64:24-7+ My '65
Russian delegation to Paris. Art N 64:34-5+ O '65

GRAND BAHAMA ISLAND
Burgeoning Grand Bahama. M. M. Davis. il Travel 125:32-3 Ja '66

GRAND CANYON
Attack on Grand Canyon. R. C. Bradley. il Liv Wildn 87:3-7 Wint '64
Battle of the Grand Canyon; dam builders vs. conservationists. A. Hano. il N Y Times Mag p56-7+ D 12 '65
Grand Canyon, world wonder. H. Sutton. McCalls 92:42+ Jl '65
Think big: open letter to the Secretary of the Interior to build two dams on Colorado River. B. Stewart. il Harper 231:62-3 Ag '65; Discussion. 231:8+ N '65
Time and the river flowing: Grand Canyon, by F. Leydet; ed. by D. Brower. Review
Liv Wildn 87:28 Wint '64

GRAND CANYON DAMS. See Dams

GRAND FALLS, Ariz.
Grand Falls of the Little Colorado. I. Dryer. il Nat Parks Mag 39:10-12 My '65

GRAND HAVEN STATE PARK. See Michigan—Parks and reserves

GRAND national steeplechase. See Horse racing

GRAND national stock-car racing. See Automobile racing

GRAND opera. See Opera

GRAND opera singers. See Singers

GRAND PRAIRIE, Tex.
State law aids vacant land development. C. A. Johnson. Am City 80:12+ O '65

GRAND TETON NATIONAL PARK
Mile high in Teton country. R. C. Lillie. il Motor B 115:22-5+ My '65
Seventy-two hours of terror: on Teewinot Mountain. J. Lipscomb. il Sports Illus 22:86-90+ Je 14; 64-8+ Je 21 '65

GRAND theater of opera and ballet, Warsaw. See Opera houses

GRANDE, Luke M.
Elegy for a teacher turned administrator. Cath World 202:221 Ja '66
Sisyphus: poem. Cath World 201:61 Ap '65
Youth today. por Cath World 202:41-4 O '65

GRANDINI, Luigi
Verdi's gardener; interview, ed. by M. J. Matz. por Opera N 29:28 Mr 20 '65

GRANDMOTHERS. See Grandparents

GRANDPARENTS
What two generations can do about children and their grandparents. K. B. Garner and I. V. Sperry. Farm J 89:97 My '65
When grandchildren come to visit. E. Towner. il Suc Farm 63:51+ Jl '65

GRANGER, Gale A. and Weiser, R. S.
Homograft target cells: contact destruction in vitro by immune macrophages. bibliog Science 151:97-9 Ja 7 '66

GRANT, Bruce
Cocktail party. Reporter 33:46-8+ O 21 '65

GRANT, Cary
New look of Cary Grant. il pors Good H 160:44+ Ja '65

GRANT, Mary Kent
Mystery, detective, suspense. See first issue of each month of Library journal

GRANT, Norman H. and Alburn, H. E.
Fast reactions of ascorbic acid and hydrogen peroxide in ice, a presumptive early environment. bibliog Science 150:1589-90 D 17 '65

GRANT, Ulysses Simpson, 1822-1885
Appomattox. U. S. Grant, 3d. il pors Nat Geog Mag 127:435-69 Ap '65
Grant or Greeley? the abolitionist dilemma in the election of 1872. J. M. McPherson. bibliog f Am Hist R 71:43-61 O '65
U. S. Grant, eighteenth President. F. Freidel. il pors Nat Geog Mag 127:680-5 My '65

GRANT, Ulysses Simpson, 1881-
Appomattox. por Nat Geog Mag 127:435-69 Ap '65

GRANTS, Literary. See Rewards, prizes, etc.

GRANTS-in-aid
National-state-local systems of government and intergovernmental aid. A. K. Campbell. bibliog f il Ann Am Acad 359:94-106 My '65
Trends in intergovernmental relations. G. C. S. Benson. bibliog f Ann Am Acad 359:1-9 My '65
See also
Economic assistance, Domestic

GRANTS to colleges and universities. See Colleges and universities—Gifts, legacies, etc.

GRANULOCYTOSIS. See Blood—Diseases

GRAPES
Picking
See Fruit—Picking

GRAPHIC arts
Books about bookmaking. C. B. Grannis. il Pub W 188:88-9 Ag 9 '65
Expert's expert; exhibition of modern prints currently on view at Harvard. il Time 85:72-7 F 19 '65
Interesting valuable project for graphic artists; concerning series of first-hand reports on modern masters. C. B. Grannis. Pub W 189:75 Ja 3 '66
TPG-65, Paris exposition: a production man's view. R. D. Chapman. il Pub W 188:64-8+ Ag 9 '65
See also
American institute of graphic arts
Printing

Exhibitions
Four centuries of graphic art; Metropolitan museum of art. il N Y Times Mag p 121-2 S 19 '65

GRAPHIC arts research council
R & E reviews computers and electronics in the graphic arts; annual meeting. Pub W 187:123-4+ Je 14 '65

GRAPHIC arts technical foundation
GATF: new building, research and educational projects. Pub W 187:111+ My 3 '65

GRAPHIC methods
Frequency or wavelength? letter. G. Wald. Science 150:1239 D 3 '65
Square root variations of reciprocal graphing of enzyme kinetic data. P. Stutts and I. Fridovich. il Science 149:447 Jl 23 '65; Reply. J. R. Totter and M. J. Cormier. bibliog 150:1627-9 D 17 '65
See also
Diagrams

GRAPHITE
Nondestructive testing fundamental to advanced materials development. J. F. Judge. il Miss & Roc 16:27+ F 22 '65
Screw dislocations in graphite. G. R. Hennig. bibliog il Science 147:733-4 F 12 '65
Siderite (FeCO₃): thermal decomposition in equilibrium with graphite. B. M. French and P. E. Rosenberg. bibliog il Science 147:1283-4 Mr 12 '65

GRASES, Pedro
Humanist of the Americas. Américas 17:6-10 My '65

GRASS, Günter
In the egg; poem. Nation 201:82 Ag 16 '65

about

Author. M. Stone. por Sat R 48:26 My 29 '65
Grass takes to the stump. America 113:89 Jl 24
'65
Green years for Grass; with report by D. E.
Scherman. il pors Life 58:51-2+ Je 4 '65
Günter Grass. M. Roloff. Atlan 215:94-7 Je
'65
Tumultuous indictment of man. R. Kluger.
Harper 230:110+ Je '65

GRASS clippings. See Lawn thatch

GRASS lands
Scrap woodlands, transported grassland soils.
and concept of grassland climate in the
Great Plains Region. P. V. Wells. bibliog il
Science 148:246-9 Ap '65

GRASS silage. See Silage

GRASS snow mold. See Grasses—Diseases and
pests

GRASSES
Grass. W. H. Frederick, jr. and R. A. Simon.
il Horticulture 43:14-15+ Ag '65
Grass nobody wants; annual bluegrass. R. M.
Carleton. Flower Grower 52:8-9 Ag '65
Migration of a plant; Kentucky bluegrass.
R. W. Schery. il Natur Hist 74:40-5 D '65
Plant zoysia grass for a lawn that laughs at
drought. B. C. Kilvert, jr. Flower Grower
52:10 My '65
Trans-aconitic acid in range grasses in early
spring. R. Burau and P. R. Stout. bibliog
il Science 150:766-7 N 5 '65

Diseases and pests

What causes brown patches? snowmold fungi.
R. M. Carleton. Flower Grower 52:41-2 F
'65

Seed

All around the place. J. Milton. Pop Gard 16:
59 S '65
Pick the right grass seed; home lawns. il
Changing T 19:17-18 Ag '65

GRASSHOPPERS
Desert locusts; sexual maturation delayed by
feeding on senescent vegetation. P. E. Ellis
and others. bibliog il Science 149:546-7 Jl
30 '65
Man fights swarming insects. B. Tufty. il
Sci N L 87:90-1 F 6 '65
Perception by locusts of rotated patterns.
E. T. Burtt and W. T. Catton. Science
151:224 Ja 14 '66

Control

Locust fighters; UN special fund. J. Gunther.
il Look 29:40-2 Ap 20 '65

GRASTYAN, Endre, and others
Hypothalamic motivational processes as reflected by their hippocampal electrical correlates. bibliog Science 149:91-3 Jl 2 '65

GRATUITIES. See Tipping

GRAU, C. R. and others
Degeneration of the eyes of tyrosine-deficient
chick embryos. bibliog Science 148:1743-5 Je
25 '65

GRAU, Shirley Ann
Beach party; story. Redbook 125:54-5 S '65
Vineyard is the place to go. N Y Times Mag
p26-7+ Ag 15 '65

GRAUBARD, Stephen R.
Tourist in academe. Nation 200:148 F 8 '65

GRAUMAN, Lawrence
Tough case, tough guy. New Repub 152:28+
My 15 '65

GRAUMAN, Lawrence, Jr
In your heart, you know he's president. New
Repub 153:43-5 N 27 '65
Theories of the American experience. New
Repub 153:23-6 O 2 '65

GRAVEL
You can have fun with gravel; in landscape
design. il Sunset 135:186-7 S '65

GRAVES, Charles
Man with a club; excerpts from Leather arm-
chairs. Read Digest 87:147-8+ Ag '65

GRAVES, Dorothy
Developing durable values. PTA Mag 60:10-12
bibliog(p35) D '65

GRAVES, Eleanor
Great dinners; battle plan for the feast. See
issues of Life

GRAVES, Elizabeth Minot
Selected list of children's books. Commonweal 82:327-34 My 28 '65

GRAVES, Frank H Jr.
Unspoken confession. Time 86:58 Jl 30 '65

GRAVES, Milford
Jazz concerts; performances on drums at Jud-
son Hall. W. Balliett. New Yorker 41:122-4
F 27 '65

GRAVES, Ralph
Look what's happening at my house. Life
58:77-8 F 5 '65

GRAVES, Robert
Are women more romantic than men? pors
Life 59:126-8+ O 15 '65
Change; poem. New Repub 153:21 Ag 7 '65
Eight love poems; The vow; The fetter;
Nothing now astonishes; Those who came
short; Son altesse; What do we fear? Con-
junction; Postscript. New Repub 154:30-1
Ja 1 '66
Four poems: Fortunate child; Tomorrow's
envy of today; The wedding; Iron palace.
New Repub 153:20 N 27 '65
Poems; Good-night to the old gods; Snap-
comb wilderness; Sweetshop round the
corner. Atlan 216:75 S '65
Polite lie. por Atlan 215:74-80 Je '65
Three poems; Shift of scene; When a neck-
lace breaks; Impossible. New Repub 153:
28 O 16 '65

about

Last word on the subject of love. G. P.
Hunt. por Life 59:5 O 15 '65

GRAVES, Soldiers. See Service mens graves

GRAVITATION
How to fall up; shields against gravitational
forces. B. H. Frisch. il Sci Digest 58:42-6
D '65
Orbiting potato. J. Lear. il Sat R 48:47-50 S
4 '65; Discussion. 48:92 D 4 '65
Relativity and solar evolution. Sky & Tel 30:
275-6 N '65
Zero and lunar gravity simulated by device.
il(p 193) Sci N L 87:200 Mr 27 '65
See also
Weightlessness

GRAVURE. See Photogravure

GRAY, Barry
Good evening. New Yorker 41:18-21 Jl 3 '65

GRAY, Clarke T. and Gest, Howard
Biological formation of molecular hydrogen.
bibliog Science 148:186-92 Ap 9 '65

GRAY, Francine du Plessix. See Du Plessix, F.

GRAY, J. Glenn
Salvation on the campus; why existentialism
is capturing the students. Harper 230:53-9
My '65

GRAY, Ralph
Alps; man's own mountains. por Nat Geog
Mag 128:350-95 S '65

GRAY, Wilfred
One family's strange journey. H. Champion. il
por Life 59:80-1 Jl 23 '65

GRAY, Wood
(comp) Articles and other books received;
United States. See issues of American historical review

GRAY flannel blues; drama. See Murray, J.

GRAY house, black trim; story. See Shyer, M.
F.

GRAY wolves. See Wolves

GRAYBACKS. See Alewives (fishes)

GRAYKOWSKI, Edward A. See Driscoll, E. J.
jt. auth.

GRAYLING fishing
Where grayling gang; Hatchet Lake. M.
Ellis. il Field & S 70:59-61+ S '65

GRAYSON, Esther C. See Rockwell, F. F. jt.
auth.

GRAYSON, James
Austria; art in freedom. Hi Fi 15:169 S '65

GRAZING
Saguaro problem and grazing in southwestern
national monuments. W. A. Niering and
R. H. Whittaker. bibliog il Nat Parks Mg
39:4-9 Je '65
See also
Pastures

GREAT ABACO ISLAND. See Bahama Islands

GREAT Atlantic and Pacific tea company
Weak tea; A.&P.'s earnings drop. Time 85:
94 My 21 '65

GREAT BARRIER REEF
Myriad colors in coral. B. Hunter. il Natur
Hist 75:30-3 Ja '66

GREAT BRITAIN
See also
Aerospace industries—Great Britain
Airplanes, Military—Great Britain
Automobile industry and trade—Great Britain
Banks and banking—Great Britain
Budget—Great Britain
Coal industry—Great Britain
Crime and criminals—Great Britain
Education—Great Britain
Electric power—Great Britain
Finance—Great Britain
Foreign students in Great Britain

GREAT BRITAIN—See also—*Continued*
  Gambling—Great Britain
  Government employees—Great Britain
  Government ownership—Great Britain
  Immigration and emigration—Great Britain
  Justice, Administration of—Great Britain
  Libraries—Great Britain
  Library schools and education—Great Britain
  Money—Great Britain
  National parks and reserves—Great Britain
  Newspapers—Great Britain
  Periodicals—Great Britain
  Phonograph record industry—Great Britain
  Police—Great Britain
  Poor—Great Britain
  Price regulation by government—Great Britain
  Prices—Great Britain
  Public health—Great Britain
  Publishers and publishing—Great Britain
  Roads—Great Britain
  Science—Great Britain
  Strikes—Great Britain
  Television broadcasting—Great Britain
  Theater—Great Britain
  Trade unions—Great Britain
  Wales
  West Indians in Great Britain
  World war, 1939-1945—Great Britain
  Youth—Great Britain

Armed forces

Britain shies at cost of policing the world. il Bsns W p32+ Mr 13 '65
Word from the challenger; plea for reduction of British military commitments east of Suez. il Time 86:46 O 22 '65

Appropriations and expenditures

Role for Britain; defense review. H. Brandon. Sat R 48:16-17+ D 11 '65
U.K. defense total boosted $341 million. H. J. Coleman. Aviation W 82:16-17 Mr 1 '65

Forces in Malaysia

How much can British defend? S. Hugh-Jones. New Repub 153:11-12 Ag 21 '65

Forces in the Far East

Test for tigers. il Time 85:25-9 F 26 '65

Forces in the Near East

How much can Britain defend? S. Hugh-Jones. New Repub 153:11-12 Ag 21 '65

Arts council
See Arts council of Great Britain

Cabinet
Left-right for the team. Time 86:21 D 31 '65

Colonial office
Colonial office: a final inventory. N. Mostert. il Reporter 33:24-6 Jl 1 '65

Colonies and dominions
See Commonwealth of nations

Commerce
Battle of Britain, 1965. il Newsweek 66:59-61+ S 6 '65
Buying overseas for U.S. arsenal; policy of reciprocity. il Bsns W p 142+ O 9 '65
Swallow from the Scilly Isles; import-export figures show narrowing of trade gap. il Newsweek 66:57 Ag 23 '65

Constitutional history
See also
Magna carta

Defenses
Britain looks forward. Q. Hogg. For Affairs 43:409-25 Ap '65
Britain shies at cost of policing the world. il Bsns W p32+ Mr 13 '65
Britain wields a modernizing ax. V. K. McElheny. Science 147:1429-31 Mr 19 '65
British cite savings in U.S. aircraft buys. Aviation W 83:28 Ag 9 '65
Sting of the bee in saturation parity. L. Szilard. il Bul Atomic Sci 21:8-13 Mr '65
U.K. defense total boosted $341 million. H. J. Coleman. Aviation W 82:16-17 Mr 1 '65
West is best; the Powell line. B. Wenham. New Repub 153:18-19 N 20 '65
See also
Gibraltar

Economic conditions
Atlantic report (cont) Atlan 215:16+ Mr '65
Behind Britain's economic woes. M. A. Heilperin. Fortune 71:160-1+ Je '65
Britain looks forward. Q. Hogg. For Affairs 43:409-25 Ap '65
Clouds of recession. il Time 86:76 Ag 27 '65

Enterprise is secret weapon in new battle of Britain. F. Morley. Nations Bsns 53:27-8 N '65
No road back; the welfare state. A. Lejeune. Nat R 17:418 My 18 '65
Perils of the pound. Newsweek 65:66 Je 28 '65
Swallow from the Scilly Isles; import-export figures show narrowing of trade gap. il Newsweek 66:57 Ag 23 '65
Underdeveloped British businessman. S. White. Atlan 217:75-8 Ja '66
Where the au pair girls are. A. Carthew. il N Y Times Mag p 175-6+ O 31 '65
Why Britain is the new sick man of Europe. il U S News 59:57-9 Ag 16 '65
See also
Budget—Great Britain
Money—Great Britain
Wages—Great Britain

Economic policy
Atlantic report. Atlan 216:38+ O '65
Behind Britain's economic woes. M. A. Heilperin. Fortune 71:160-1+ Je '65
Britain stands firm for the pound; with editorial comment. Bsns W p28-9, 192 Ap 17 '65
Britain takes more medicine. il Bsns W p32+ Ag 7 '65
Britain writes its long-term plan; Labor party's economic goals for 1970; with editorial comment. il Bsns W p34+, 198 S 25 '65
Britain's budget: a blow to pride and purse. il Newsweek 65:77-9 Ap 19 '65
British scan their future; economists like Wilson program. Bsns W p50+ My 15 '65
European political cooperation; address, February 11, 1965. M. Stewart. Vital Speeches 31:329-31 Mr 15 '65
How Britain plans to save the pound. il U S News 58:47 Ap 19 '65
Nation not afraid, by E. Powell. Review Nat R 17:935-7 O 19 '65. A. Lejeune
Now Britain tries a planned recession. U S News 59:96 S 6 '65
Pallid plan; five-year economic plan. il Time 86:102 S 24 '65
Plan; blueprint for revitalizing the British economy. Newsweek 66:76 S 27 '65
Pound sterling; address, April 14, 1965. H. Wilson. Vital Speeches 31:452-9 My 15 '65
Protector of the pound. il Time 85:90 F 26 '65
Ready to knock hell; concerning Harold Wilson's speech to the Economic club of New York. il Time 85:33 Ap 23 '65
Trying to make an income policy stick. Bsns W p29 Ap 17 '65

Economic relations
Britain looks forward. Q. Hogg. For Affairs 43:409-25 Ap '65
Role for Britain; defense review. H. Brandon. Sat R 48:16-17+ D 11 '65

United States
Can Commander Whitehead save Britain? J. Weingarten. il Duns R 86:42-3+ Jl '65

Foreign opinion
American
Who's o-o-ooh in America. H. J. Gans. Vogue 145:108+ Mr 15 '65

Foreign population
Back street new worlds, by E. Huxley. Review Nat R 17:736-7 Ag 24 '65. A. W. Green

Foreign relations
Anthony Eden and the cacophony of nations. H. Feis. For Affairs 44:78-89 O '65
European political cooperation; address, February 11, 1965. M. Stewart. Vital Speeches 31:329-31 Mr 15 '65
How much can Britain defend? S. Hugh-Jones. New Repub 153:11-12 Ag 21 '65
Perils of Harold. Newsweek 65:32+ Mr 22 '65
Red Sea to Singapore: new burden for U.S.? il U S News 59:72-3 N 15 '65
Tightening the screws on rebellious Rhodesia. il Bsns W p40-1 N 20 '65
See also
Munich four power agreement, 1938

France
Duck with de Gaulle; meeting with Harold Wilson. il Time 85:31 Ap 9 '65
Slightly warmer. Newsweek 65:54+ Ap 12 '65

India
Area of darkness, by V. S. Naipaul. Review Commentary 39:94-7 Je '65. J. Mander

GREAT BRITAIN—Foreign relations—*Cont.*

Palestine

Trouble in Palestine. J. Amery. New Repub 153:30-2 D 4 '65

Spain

Reporter at large; Gibraltar question. A. Reid. New Yorker 41:38-42+ Jl 31 '65

United States

Plugged in; H. Wilson's U.S. visit. il Newsweek 66:20+ D 27 '65

Silent allies; Anglo-American relations. Commonweal 82:68-9 Ap 9 '65

History

See also
Magna carta

Bibliography

Articles and other books received; comp. by L. H. Carlson. See issues of American historical review

Sources

William of Malmesbury's Robert of Gloucester: a re-evaluation of the Historia novella. R. B. Patterson. bibliog f il Am Hist R 70:983-97 Jl '65

Textbooks

History is a dangerous subject; findings of Anglo-United States team survey of secondary school textbooks. R. A. Billington. il Sat R 49:59-61+ Ja 15 '66

Norman period, 1066-1154

William of Malmesbury's Robert of Gloucester: a re-evaluation of the Historia novella. R. B. Patterson. bibliog f il Am Hist R 70:983-97 Jl '65

Eighteenth century

Decadence and decorum. L. Kronenberger. il Atlan 216:103-6 N '65

1760-1789

See also
United States—History—Revolution

20th century

English history: 1914-1945, by A. J. P. Taylor. Review
    Newsweek 67:58-9 Ja 3 '66

European war, 1914-1918

See European war, 1914-1918—Great Britain

House of lords

See Great Britain—Parliament—House of lords

Industries

Can science save Britain's industry? il Bsns W p112-14+ My 8 '65
See also
Airplane industry and trade—Great Britain
Coal industry—Great Britain
Industrial management—Great Britain
Steel industry and trade—Great Britain

Intellectual life

See also
Bloomsbury group

Moral conditions

New morality. A. Lunn. Nat R 17:836-8 S 21 '65
See also
Prostitution

National health service

Britain's angry doctors. B. Wenham. New Repub 152:9-10 Ap 10 '65
Doctor strike coming in Britain? il U S News 58:62 Mr 1 '65
Doctors in crisis. il Newsweek 65:60 Mr 1 '65
Socialized medicine: crisis grows in Britain. U S News 58:14 Mr 22 '65
What the AMA really fears. W. P. Keim. New Repub 152:11-12 F 13 '65; Discussion. 152:35-6 Mr 6; 27-9 Mr 20; 28-9 Ap 10; 44 Ap 17 '65

National library of medicine

British experiment with MEDLARS; NLM to provide tapes and training. Library J 90:2990 Jl '65

National trust

See National trust for places of historic interest on natural beauty

Nobility

See also
Great Britain—Parliament—House of lords

Parliament

Mum's 700th. il Time 86:26+ Jl 2 '65

House of commons

Hear! hear! Britons disturbed by current rowdiness. il Time 85:33 F 19 '65
Letter from London; steel debate. M. Panter-Downes. New Yorker 41:123-5 My 22 '65
Tory ambush. Newsweek 66:36 Jl 19 '65

House of lords

House of lords. S. Bedford. il Horizon 7:4-13+ Autumn '65

Rules and practice

Fair cop. Time 86:31-2 Jl 16 '65

Politics and government

Britain heads into its next 100 days. il Bsns W p29-30 Ja 30 '65
British politics in the collectivist age, by S. H. Beer. Review
    Nat R 17:988-9 N 2 '65. J. Hart
Buy American! Newsweek 65:39-40 F 22 '65
Capacity to govern. R. Moley. Newsweek 65:92 Je 28 '65
Close votes & dark omens. Time 85:36 Je 11 '65
Color in Britain. B. Wenham. New Repub 152:14-15 Mr 6 '65
Crooked road of Harold Wilson. C. Brogan. Nat R 17:1026-7 N 16 '65
Down the middle. Time 85:35-6 Mr 19 '65
Future of Rhodesia; extremes of political opinion. H. Brandon. Sat R 48:9 D 25 '65
Harold Wilson: Labour's Lloyd George? M. Foot. Nation 201:518-20 D 27 '65
Harold Wilson's new Tory challenger. H. Massingham. New Repub 153:15-16 S 4 '65
Harrying Harold; censure motion defeated. Time 85:21 F 12 '65
Heath's middle road to Downing street. L. Malkin. il Reporter 33:39+ D 16 '65
Man with a four-seat margin. il Time 85:35-39A Ap 30 '65; Same abr. with title Britain's benign socialist. Read Digest 87:121-5 Jl '65
Mr Wilson is master of the House. A. Lewis. il N Y Times Mag p24-5+ Ap 11 '65
MLF & other problems. G. Lichtheim; reply with rejoinder. D. Rush. Commentary 39:22+ My '65
Rallying the ranks; support for Wilson. Time 86:47 O 8 '65
Road to number 10, by A. Howard and R. West. Review
    Nat R 17:372-80 My 4 '65. A. Lejeune
Sir Alec loses, and wins. P. Worsthorne. il N Y Times Mag p33+ Mr 21 '65
Steel nationalization is not around the corner. B. Wenham. New Repub 152:9-10 My 22 '65
Sterling and steel sour Wilson's hopes. Bsns W p38-9 Je 12 '65
Sterling recovery puts better odds on Wilson. il Bsns W p34-5 O 9 '65
Still at Home. Newsweek 65:48+ F 15 '65
Sunshine for labor; Wilson hangs on. Newsweek 66:51-2 O 4 '65
Three times round. Newsweek 65:60+ Je 14 '65
Victory without advance. Time 86:27 Ag 13 '65
Wilson's breather. Time 86:27-8 Jl 9 '65
Wilson's unhappy hundred days. B. Wenham. New Repub 152:9-10 F 6 '65
Word from the challenger; upstaging Tories' new leader. il Time 86:46 O 22 '65
See also
Conservative party (Great Britain)
Elections—Great Britain
Great Britain—Prime ministers
Labor party (Great Britain)
Political parties—Great Britain

Popular culture

Pop goes the island. M. Richler. Commentary 39:67-70 My '65

Population

See also
West Indians in Great Britain

Prime ministers

Asquith, by R. Jenkins. Review
    Reporter 33:48-50+ D 2 '65. A. West

Prime ministers conference

See Prime ministers conferences

Race problems

Alabama, here we come. C. Brogan. Nat R 17:195-6 Mr 9 '65
Britain and race. America 112:382 Mr 20 '65
Britain: color and commonwealth. K. Haselden. Commonweal 82:327-8 Mr 17 '65
British melting pot is coming to a boil; colored immigrants. il Bsns W p88-90+ F 13 '65

GREAT BRITAIN—Race problems—_Continued_

British say they aren't prejudiced. C. E. Lincoln. il N Y Times Mag p64-5+ N 14 '65

Color in Britain. B. Wenham. New Repub 152:14-15 Mr 6 '65

Color in England. J. B. Gerald. Commonweal 83:304-6 D 10 '65

Commons debate on banning discrimination. B. Wenham. New Repub 152:7-8 My 29 '65

Dark million. il Time 85:36+ My 14 '65

James Crow, esq, comes to Britain. R. W. Howe. il Reporter 32:28-30 My 6 '65; Reply. P. W. Tripp. 32:4 Je 3 '65

Klan comes to Britain: what it's all about. il U S News 59:30-1 Jl 5 '65

Race problem in Great Britain. C. L. Sanders. il Ebony 21:146-8+ N '65

Race relations in Britain. P. Mason. Christian Cent 82:738-41 Je 9 '65

Reporter at large. C. Trillin. New Yorker 41:115-16+ D 4 '65

Religious institutions and affairs

New morality. A. Lunn. Nat R 17:836-8 S 21 '65

News of the Christian world. Christian Cent 82:1520 D 8 '65

Royal air force

U.K. weighs France's Mirage 4A as alternative to F-111A for RAF. Aviation W 83:39 Ag 16 '65

Royal Marines

So forget the Beatles; Royal Marines tattoo touring North America. il Time 86:60 O 8 '65

Social conditions

Is homosexuality a crime? J. Grigg. N Y Times Mag p6-7 Je 27 '65

See also
Crime and criminals—Great Britain
Social and economic security—Great Britain

Social life and customs

Bringing up children; the American vs. the British way. E. Wintour; discussion. Harper 229:11-12 O '64; 230:13-14 My '65

Britain's with-it society. S. Hagerty. il Newsweek 66:52-3 D 6 '65

Clubs for commoners; Wythenshawe and other workingmen's clubs. il Newsweek 67:20 Ja 3 '66

In the restaurants and at Ascot, they will never surrender; Expense account society. S. Mead. il N Y Times Mag p58-9+ Je 6 '65

Technology, Ministry of

Can science save Britain's industry? il Bsns W p 112-14+ My 8 '65

GREAT BRITAIN and the United States. See England and the United States

GREAT charter, 1215. See Magna carta

GREAT cities research council
Textbook needs in urban education; American textbook publishers institute and the Great cities research council meeting, Los Angeles; summaries of addresses. il Pub W 188:16-27 D 6 '65

GREAT LAKES
Brighter picture for the Great Lakes. H. Titus. Field & S 70:24+ S '65

Crisis in water; Great and dirty lakes. G. Hill. il Sat R 48:32-4 O 23 '65

Filth in the Great Lakes; what can be done about it; interview. G. B. Langford. il U S News 59:58-61 D 13 '65

Forecasting Great Lakes weather. F. R. Shumway. il Motor B 115:53-6+ Je '65

Great Lakes research; report on eighth conference. J. L. Hough. Science 149:327 Jl 16 '65

Great Lakes yachting; symposium. il Yachting 117:40-53+ My '65

Water crisis on the Great Lakes. A. Balk. il Read Digest 86:165-6+ Mr '65

See also
Superior, Lake

GREAT LAKES REGION
See also
Fishing—Great Lakes Region
Water supply—Great Lakes Region

Industries

One depressed area that's solving its own problems; Mesabi Range. il U S News 58:86-8 Mr 22 '65

GREAT men
Americans not everybody knows (title varies) C. W. Ferguson. See issues of PTA magazine

Let's throw a star-spangled party! R. Dunlop. il Todays Health 44:36-9+ Ja '66

100 best people in the world. il Esquire 64:64-5 Ag '65

Procession, by J. Gunther. Review
Newsweek il 66:86+ Jl 19 '65

Topic: The unreasonable man; excerpts from College entrance examination papers. P. L. Levin. il N Y Times Mag p92+ Mr 28 '65

World changers, by B. Bliven. Review
Sat R 49:36 Ja 1 '66. R. T. Elson

See also
Leadership

GREAT plague of 1665. See Plague

GREAT PLAINS REGION
Scrap woodlands, transported grassland soils, and concept of grassland climate in the Great Plains Region. P. V. Wells. bibliog il Science 148:246-9 Ap '65

See also
Radioactive fallout—Great Plains Region

GREAT powers
See also
Power (political science)

GREAT RIFT VALLEY
Journey into the Great Rift. H. Schreider and F. Schreider. il Nat Geog Mag 128:254-90 Ag '65

GREAT SALT LAKE
Disappointment or not, the lake is a must for every visitor. il Sunset 134:88-9 Ap '65

GREAT SMOKY MOUNTAINS
We took the high road. W. Hartley. il Redbook 124:70-1+ Mr '65

See also
Great Smoky Mountains National Park

GREAT SMOKY MOUNTAINS NATIONAL PARK
Bad bargain in the Smokies; destructive highways. A. W. Smith. il Nat Parks Mag 39:2 D '65

Great Smoky Mountains National Park. H. Broome. il Nat Parks Mag 39:4-7 Mr '65

Look toward the future in the TVA-Smokies region; with editorial comment. il Nat Parks Mag 39:2, 8-15 Mr '65

Rhododendron trail ride. M. Rabb. il Am For 71:50-1+ S '65

Wilderness plan for the Smokies; Wilderness recommendations; with editorial comment. Liv Wildn 29:2, 32-6 Sum '65

GREAT society. See United States—Social policy

GREAT society press, incorporated
Teacher of the unteachables; Springboards reading program. J. Tebbel. Sat R 48:72+ My 15 '65

GREAT Soviet encyclopedia. See Encyclopedias

GREAT stone face; drama. See Hackett, W.

GREAT SWAMP national wildlife refuge. See Wildlife sanctuaries

GREAT women. See Women, Famous

GREATHOUSE, Edwin A.
Dogfighting with MiGs; interview. Aviation W 83:11 Jl 26 '65

GREBANIER, Bernard
Elizabethan in the round. Sat R 48:33-4 D 25 '65

William and the scholars. Sat R 48:39 N 27 '65

GREBES
Giant grebe of Guatemala. A. L. Bowes. il Audubon Mag 67:88-90 Mr '65

GRECO, José
Jose Greco and his gypsies, Brooklyn academy of music. J. Maskey. Dance Mag 39:32 Mr '65

GRÉDY, Jean Pierre
Cactus flower; adaptation. See Burrows, A.

GREECE, Ancient
See also
Athens

Archeology

Early neolithic village in Greece; excavations at Nea Nikomedeia. R. J. Rodden. il Sci Am 212:82-8+ Ap '65

Search for Greece of the stone age. E. S. Higgs. il Natur Hist 74:18-25 N '65

See also
Pella, Greece (ancient city)

History

Athens. P. L. Fermor. il Holiday 37:40-51+ Je '65

GREECE, Modern
See also
Aegean Islands
Athens
Automobile industry and trade—Greece, Modern
Cyclades (islands)
Earthquakes—Greece, Modern
Gardens—Greece, Modern

GREECE, Modern—*Continued*

Description and travel

Sayonara, Agamemnon; initiation into the world of genuine tourism. M. Laurence. Holiday 39:21-4+ Ja '66

Travel's picture portfolio. Travel 123:50-5 My '65

See also
Peloponnesus

Foreign relations

Greece and Turkey: the second round. G. Bailey. il Reporter 33:14-18 S 9 '65

History

Athens. P. L. Fermor. il Holiday 37:40-51+ Je '65

Industries

Greece bottles a drink with a familiar shape: Tam Tam, grape-based soft drink. il Bsns W p 146+ O 16 '65

Politics and government

All the King's men; Tsirimokos defeated. il Time 86:34 S 3 '65

Bee stings and bombs. Newsweek 66:38+ S 20 '65

Commoner vs. king; Papandreou and King Constantine. Newsweek 66:42+ Jl 26 '65

Continuing crisis. Time 86:21 Ag 27 '65

Drinks at the palace. Time 86:25-6 Ag 20 '65

End in sight? il Sr Schol 87:17-18 O 14 '65

Field day for the left in Athens. G. Bailey. Reporter 33:25-7 Ag 12 '65

Government at last. il Time 86:43 O 1 '65

Greece and Turkey: the second round. G. Bailey. il Reporter 33:14-18 S 9 '65

Greek crisis. E. M. von Kuehnelt-Leddihn. Nat R 17:763 S 7 '65

If at first. il Newsweek 66:40 Ag 30 '65

Impasse in Athens. Time 86:34 Ag 6 '65

In or out? il Newsweek 66:38+ Ag 9 '65

King & the fox. il Time 86:25 Jl 23 '65

King & the orator. il Time 86:21A S 10 '65

King is on trial in Greece. C. L. Sulzberger. il N Y Times Mag p 12-13+ Ag 15 '65

Left oblique. il Newsweek 66:44 S 13 '65

Looking for a solution. il Newsweek 66:34 Ag 16 '65

No. 3: new premier named. Time 86:36 S 24 '65

Qualified confidence. Newsweek 66:52 O 4 '65

Rocks in the cradle; resurgence of Communists. Newsweek 65:40-2 Mr 8 '65

Royal dilemma. Time 86:28 Ag 13 '65

Searing days of summer. il Time 86:19 Jl 30 '65

Stretched thin; attempt of Socialist Elias Tsirimokos to form new government. A. Friendly, jr. Newsweek 66:30+ S 6 '65

Three times and out? il Newsweek 66:38+ Ag 23 '65

Victory for the king? Stephanopoulos's second attempt to form a government. Newsweek 66:51-2 S 27 '65

Violent days: Greek against Greek. il Newsweek 66:33 Ag 2 '65

What the palace fears. C. Poulos. il Nation 201:158-61 S 27 '65

Religious institutions and affairs

King & the bishops; fuss about money and bishops transfers. il Time 86:77 D 3 '65

GREEK Catholic church. See Orthodox Eastern church

GREEK civilization. See Civilization, Greek

GREEK cookery. See Cookery, Greek

GREEK drama

Man and God in dialogue; Sodom and Gomorrah, prologue, tr. by A. J. Skalafuris. N. Kazantzakis. Sat R 48:16-17+ Ag 28 '65

Sophocles: the Theban plays. K. Rexroth. Sat R 48:40 N 13 '65

See also
Aeschylus

Production, Modern

Greek theater in the country; Greek art theater's presentations in Corfu. H. Hewes. Sat R 48:33+ Ag 21 '65

GREEK letter societies. See College fraternities

GREEK literature
See also
Greek poetry

GREEK mythology. See Mythology, Greek

GREEK Orthodox church. See Orthodox Eastern church

GREEK poetry

Sappho, poet and legend. K. Rexroth. Sat R 48:27 N 27 '65

Translations into English

Archilochus not quite revived. J. Redfield. Poetry 105:329-31 F '65

GREEK sculpture. See Sculpture, Greek

GREEKS in Turkey

Imperiled patriarch. D. Peerman. Christian Cent 82:1470-1 D 1 '65

GREELEY, Andrew M.

But not the greatest movie. Reporter 32:36+ Ap 22 '65

Catholic education. America 112:522-4+ Ap 17 '65

Puppets adrift. Reporter 33:48-9 N 4 '65

Real problems of the American church. America 113:571-2+ N 13 '65

Secular city. Commonweal 83:181-4 N 12 '65

Temptation of the new breed. America 112:750-2 My 22 '65

GREELEY, Horace

Americans nobody knows. C. W. Ferguson. por PTA Mag 59:22-4 Ap '65

Grant or Greeley? the abolitionist dilemma in the election of 1872. J. M. McPherson. bibliog f Am Hist R 71:43-61 O '65

GREELEY, Colo.

Divisible cluster plan for a compact elementary school. il Arch Rec 137:176-7 Mr '65

GREEN, A. Wigfall

(ed) See Falkner, M. Day the balloon came to town

GREEN, Arnold Wilfred

Cultures at odds. Nat R 17:736-7 Ag 24 '65

GREEN, Burt

Sheet music. A. Debus. il Hobbies 70:36+ S '65

GREEN, C. See Ashworth, L. A. E. jt. auth.

GREEN, Howard. See Todaro, G. J. jt. auth.

GREEN, John Mort

Happy punter of Ally Pally. J. Olsen. il pors Sports Illus 23:52-7+ Ag 9 '65

GREEN, L. B.

Keep refuse collectors on the route. Am City 80:110-11 Je '65

We vacuum and flush our streets. Am City 80:104-5 My '65

GREEN, Louis C.

Relativistic astrophysics. Sky & Tel 29:145-9, 226-9 Mr-Ap '65

GREEN, M. S.

Critical-point phenomena. Science 150:229-32+ O 8 '65

GREEN, Marshall

Communist China as a problem in U.S. policymaking; address, February 26, 1965. Dept State Bul 52:449-53 Mr 29 '65

Thai countermeasures to Communist threat; excerpt from address, March 14, 1965. Dept State Bul 52:489-91 Ap 5 '65

about

Bitter champagne. Newsweek 66:48 Ag 9 '65

Coping with the Bung. il por Time 86:30 Ag 6 '65

GREEN, Martin

Russian science fiction. Commonweal 82:27-8 Mr 26 '65

GREEN, Maurice. See Lacy, S. jt. auth.

GREEN, Sidney L. and Nathan, Paul

It's good to know that those new mother blues are normal and short-lived. Parents Mag 40:40-1+ My '65

GREEN BAY Packers (football club) See Football clubs

GREEN giant company

Growing Green giant. il Newsweek 66:81 S 27 '65

What's new, besides ho-ho-ho. il Bsns W p 136+ O 23 '65

GREEN RIVER, Wyo.

Reporter at large. B. Rouché. New Yorker 41:105-6+ O 23 '65

Science in the small school. J. V. Bernard. Atlan 215:95-8 Ap '65; Discussion. 216:56+ S '65

GREENAWAY, Emerson

Greater division of federal taxes. por Library J 90:2080+ My 1 '65

Greenaway outlines current legislation affecting school academic libraries; excerpts from report. Library J 90:1082+ Mr 1 '65

GREENBAUM, Everett

There were pigeons in the square; story. Harper 230:94-7 Ap '65

GREENBERG, Bernard

Flies and disease; with biographical sketch. Sci Am 213:17, 92-9 Jl '65

GREENBERG, Daniel S.
Case for and case against tuberculosis vaccine. Todays Health 43:38-9+ D '65; Same abr. with title Let's use BCG to fight TB. Read Digest 87:58-62 D '65
Scientific pork barrel. Harper 232:90-2 Ja '66
There's a windmill in the attic. Sat R 48:48-50 Je 5 '65
GREENBERG, Leonard, and Field, Franklyn
Deadly heat wave of '96. Read Digest 87:39-40+ Ag '65
GREENBERG, Noah
Soft sound in the U.S.S.R. por Hi Fi 15:41-3+ My '65
GREENBERG, Pearl
Bead making. Sch Arts 65:20-2 S '65
Displaying art work. Sch Arts 64:9-11 My '65
Notes on art. Sch Arts 64:8-11 Mr '65
GREENBERG, Selig
Practice and malpractice. Nation 200:464-7+ My 3 '65
GREENBERG, Syd
Old look at Valley Forge. U S Camera 28:66-7 S '65
GREENE, Bob
Up on two wheels. See issues of Hot rod
GREENE, Daniel
Painting the feeling of autumn. il pors Design 67:36-7 N '65
GREENE, Felix
China on film. P. Velde. Commonweal 82:535-6 Jl 23 '65
Inside Hanoi. il Newsweek 66:69 D 20 '65
GREENE, George
Books. Commonweal 82:478-9 Jl 2 '65
GREENE, Graham
Invisible Japanese gentlemen; story. Sat Eve Post 238:60-1 N 20 '65
Palace of chance; story; excerpt from Comedians. Reporter 33:41-2 D 2 '65
GREENE, Lorenzo J.
Doctor Woodson prepares for Negro history week, 1930; excerpts from diary. por Negro Hist Bul 28:174-5+ My '65
GREENE, Lorne
Bonanza. R. W. Lewis. il pors Sat Eve Post 238:84-9 D 4 '65
He likes to cook. il por Bet Hom & Gard 43:80 Jl '65
GREENE, Nancy
Two Canadians raid Aspen. B. Ottum. por Sports Illus 22:50-1 F 8 '65
GREENE, S. W.
Antarcticana. New Yorker 41:33-4 Je 5 '65
GREENE, Thomas
Book of the month. Cath World 201:331-3 Ag '65
Book reviews. America 114:142+ Ja 22 '66
GREENE, Wade
Federal birth control: progress without policy. Reporter 33:35-7 N 18 '65
GREENE, Wallace Martin, 1907-
Management team. il por Time 85:22-23A F 5 '65
GREENEWALT, Crawford H.
Sensing who can command: interview. pors Nations Bsns 53:40-1+ O '65
GREENFELD, Howard
Life movie review. Life 59:18 Jl 2 '65
GREENFIELD, Edward
Anniversary for Tippett. Hi Fi 15:86T Mr '65
Best foot forward and otherwise. Hi Fi 15:135 Ag '65
Bumper Britten crop. Hi Fi 15:164-5 S '65
City of five orchestras. Hi Fi 15:51-4 Ap '65
New sound on the south bank. Hi Fi 15:141 Ap '65
Notes from our correspondents (cont) Hi Fi 15:28+ Mr; 18+ My; 18+ Jl; 14+ S; 28+ N; 16+ D '65
Period passion at Sadler's Wells. Hi Fi 15:136 Je '65
Solti's Ring, Stravinsky's Firebird. Hi Fi 15:182-3 D '65
Thirty-one by Rostropovich. Hi Fi 15:166-0 '65
GREENFIELD, Meg
After the Washington teach-in. Reporter 32:16-19 Je 3 '65
Lady in the east wing. Reporter 33:28-31 Jl 15 '65
Lost session at the U.N. Reporter 32:14-20 My 6 '65
Problem problem. Reporter 32:31-2 F 25 '65
Uhuru comes to the Senate. Reporter 33:32-7 S 23 '65
Unmistakable message. Reporter 33:10+ Ag 12 '65
What's the matter with the mails? Reporter 32:21-5 F 11 '65
GREENFIELD, Iowa
Extra electric-plant benefits. D. Moore. il Am City 80:187-8 Mr '65
GREENFIELD VILLAGE. See Henry Ford museum and Greenfield Village, Dearborn, Mich.

GREENGARD, Olga, and others
Iron accumulation in cockerel plasma after estrogen: relation to induced phosphoprotein synthesis. bibliog Science 147:1571-2 Mr 26 '65
GREENHALL, Arthur M.
Trinidad and bat research. Natur Hist 74:14-21 Je '65
GREENHILL, J. P.
Sex and pregnancy. Redbook 124:28+ Ap '65
GREENHOUSE plants
Enjoy summer all winter long. B. Francois. il Pop Gard 16:36+ N '65
GREENHOUSES
CO_2-lifesaver for greenhouse plants. R. S. Lindstrom and J. J. Marks. il Horticulture 43:24-5 D '65
Easy-to-make greenhouse. J. Simpkins. il Flower Grower 52:15-16 Mr '65
Farming under wraps. il Newsweek 65:33 Je 28 '65
Greenhouse to live in. M. Perry. il Flower Grower 52:32-3 F '65
Home greenhouse. J. Eaton. See issues of Flower grower, the home garden magazine
Keep spring at your doorstep. M. J. Gero and N. V. Backster. il Pop Gard 17:36+ Ja '66
Many faces of today's greenhouse. il House & Gard 129:116-21 Ja '66
My greenhouse is summerized. S. Caldwell. il Flower Grower 52:18-19 Je '65
Put your greenhouse to work. C. H. Potter. il Horticulture 44:32-3+ Ja '66
There's a greenhouse next door: coupling greenhouse to living quarters. il Sunset 135:114+ N '65
Thinshell greenhouses. il Farm J 89:50B O '65
See also
Hotbeds
Heating and ventilation
Step up CO_2 with greenhouse heaters. C. Johnson. Farm J 89:60H My '65
GREENING, W. E.
Crisis in French Canada. Yale R 54:375-82 Mr '65
GREENLEAF publishing company
Grove gets injunction vs. bootleg Thief's journal; edition issued by Greenleaf publishing company. Pub W 188:64 Jl 19 '65
Thief's journal copying ruled infringement. Pub W 188:26-7 O 18 '65
GREENLEE, Lyman E.
Simple 60-cycle stroboscope. Pop Electr 22:71 Je '65
GREENOUGH, Richard
New alphabets for five African languages. Sch & Soc 93:375-6 O 16 '65
GREENS, Edible
Great greens of spring. il Bet Hom & Gard 43:80-1+ My '65
They're picking weeds for supper. il Sunset 134:206+ Mr '65
GREENSBORO, N.C.
Something for everybody; new community center. O. T. Hester. il Am City 80:88-9 N '65
GREENSPAN, J. A.
Mars: compatible determinations of surface pressure through particle scattering. bibliog Science 150:1156-8 N 26 '65
GREENSTEIN, Fred I.
Personality and political socialization: the theories of authoritarian and democratic character. bibliog f Ann Am Acad 361:81-95 S '65
GREENWALD, Frank L.
Know your carburetor. Pop Sci 187:94-8 Jl '65
Motorized humidifier for your furnace. Pop Mech 124:176-80+ N '65
Straightening out a steering system. Pop Sci 186:140-3+ Ap '65
GREENWICH, Conn.
Education
Students hold a book fair: to browse, to buy, to read, and maybe earn a profit. D. DuBose. il Sr Schol 86:sup 14-15 Ap 29 '65
GREENWICH mean time. See Time measurements
GREENWICH VILLAGE, New York. See New York (city)—Greenwich Village
GREER, Rebecca
New girl in town. Seventeen 24:366+ Ag '65
GREER, Scott
Waiting for reality, birth of the megalopolis. Nation 201:98-102 S 20 '65
GREER ISLAND nature center and refuge. See Nature centers

GREETING cards
UNICEF greeting cards. il UNESCO Courier 18:32-3 N '65
See also
American greetings corporation
Christmas cards
Hallmark cards, incorporated
GREGERSON, Hans M.
Campurbia. Am For 71:18-20 Jl '65
GREGG, Charles E.
Tips on lawn care. Pop Gard 16:50 My '65
GREGG, Duane
(ed) See Sueppel, W. F. Can driver's license laws really save lives?
GREGG, Edwin H. jr, and Kovar, G. A.
Welcome Lassie. Am For 71:2-3+ Mr '65
GREGG, Frank
Wilderness and the Land and water conservation fund act. il Liv Wildn 29:25-8 Sum '65
GREGG, James H.
Centrifugal homogenizer. Science 150:1739-40 D 24 '65
GREGG, James R.
Family canoe trip. pors Field & S 70:58-60+ Je '65
Go South for camping. Field & S 69:70-3 F '65
GREGG, Richard N.
Josiah Wedgwood: Potter to the Queen. Hobbies 70:24-5+ Je '65
—and Delhom, M. M.
Wedgwood from midwestern collections. Antiques 87:705-8 Je '65
GREGO, Hal
Hal Grego jazz ballets, 92nd street Y. M. Marks. Dance Mag 39:62+ N '65
GREGOR, Arthur
Basic movements; poem. Poetry 105:379-80 Mr '65
Exiled: poem. Nation 201:479 D 13 '65
GREGOR, Harry P. and Berkowitz, J. M.
Gastric secretion: mechanism for production of hydrogen ions. bibliog Science 150:773-6 N 5 '65
GREGORIAN calendar. See Calendar
GREGORIOS, Benedict Mar, abp. See Benedict Mar Gregorios
GREGORY, Cynthia
Brief biography. S. Goodman. pors Dance Mag 39:58-9 Je '65
GREGORY, Dick
Off the deep end. Christian Cent 82:670 My 26 '65
GREGORY, John R.
Quick cuts & action shots: questions and answers. See issues of U.S. camera & travel
GREGORY, L. P.
Polonium-210 in leaf tobacco from four countries. bibliog Science 150:74-6 O 1 '65
GREHAN, Farrell
Sculptor as well as photographer. G. P. Hunt. il por Life 59:3 N 12 '65
GREISMAN, Leah D. See Weintraub, R. G. jt. auth.
GRELL, E. H. and others
Alcohol dehydrogenase in drosophila melanogaster: isozymes and genetic variants. bibliog Science 149:80-2 Jl 2 '65
GRENDON, Edith
Confessions of a monster mother. Parents Mag 40:56-7+ Mr '65
GRENE, Marjorie
Portmann's thought; adaptation of address, August 1965. Commentary 40:31-8 N '65
GRENFELL, Sir Wilfred Thomason
One man's land of romance. A. Sulley. il por Am For 71:12-15+ Jl '65
GRENFELL mission. See Missions, Medical
GRENIER, Richard
Son of Bogie. Esquire 65:66-9+ Ja '66
GRENNAN, Sister Jacqueline
One small college and research. por Am Ed 1:14-15 Je '65
GRÉPON
Reporter at large: Mummery ascent. J. Bernstein. New Yorker 41:152+ Mr 13 '65
GRÈS, Mme
When the daughter of Madame Grès married. il por Vogue 146:184-5 N 1 '65
GRESHAM, Grits
Big bucks of the Badlands. pors Outdoor Life 136:52-5+ N '65
Cajun quail. Field & S 70:43-5+ N '65
Check these hot lakes. pors Outdoor Life 136:48-9+ D '65
Chinks are bedded! Outdoor Life 135:34-5+ Mr '65
GRESHAM'S law
Remember Gresham's law. A. M. Sullivan. Duns R 86:84 Ag '65
GRESSITT, J. L. and others
Flora and fauna on backs of large papuan moss-forest weevils. bibliog Science 150:1833-5 D 31 '65

GREW, Joseph Clark
Ambassador. pors Time 85:17 Je 4 '65
Obituary
Nat R 17:496 Je 15 '65
GREWIA
It does whatever you ask; grewia caffra. il Sunset 134:261 Ap '65
GREY, Edward, viscount Grey of Fallodon.
See Grey of Fallodon, E. G.
GREY, Samuel, and Steinbach, T. B.
Zanesville and the mass-transit act. Am City 80:144+ S '65
GREY of Fallodon, Edward Grey, viscount
Great Britain and the 1914-1915 Straits agreement with Russia: the British promise of November 1914. C. J. Smith, jr. bibliog f Am Hist R 70:1015-34 Jl '65
GRIBBINS, Joseph
What's new. Motor B 115:58-9+ Je; 116-58+ Jl; 60-1 Ag; 50-1+ S; 58+ O; 54-5+ N; 54+ D '65
GRIDDLE cakes
But never for breakfast; Hungarian pancakes. il Sunset 135:100-3 Ag '65
Eye-opening pancakes; with recipes. C. Claiborne. il N Y Times Mag p45 Ja 31 '65
From one basic batter: three great pancakes. M. Kaytor. il Look 29:110-11 Mr 23 '65
Pancakes plus. il Bet Hom & Gard 43:88-9 Ap '65
Pancakes with a new twist. il Farm J 90:78-9+ Ja '66
Welsh cakes from the frying pan. il Sunset 134:147 F '65
GRIESE, Bob
Boiled by the Boilermakers. il Time 86:92+ O 1 '65
Oh, that Griese kid stuff! D. Jenkins. il Sports Illus 23:30-1+ O 4 '65
GRIEVANCE procedures
High cost of automation; strain on nation's professional arbitrators. T. R. Brooks. Duns R 85:61 F '65
GRIFFETH, W. L. and Zeman, L. E.
How to fertilize for six tons of hay per acre. Suc Farm 63:50-1+ Mr '65
GRIFFIN, C. W. jr
America's airborne garbage. Sat R 48:32-4+ My 22 '65
City slums and segregated suburbs. Sat R 49:85 Ja 8 '66
New hope for straphangers. Reporter 33:27-9 D 30 '65
Our deadly atmosphere. Reporter 33:49-50 Jl 15 '65
Slum salvage or city sacrifice? Sat R 48:30-1 F 27 '65
State of the cities. Reporter 33:52-4 D 16 '65
GRIFFIN, Ella
Building language skills. Wilson Lib Bul 40:62-3 S '65
GRIFFIN, Guy E.
Good-neighbor plant. Am City 80:99-102 Mr '65
GRIFFIN, Jack R.
TV kidnaps sports. Nation 200:336-8 Mr 29 '65
GRIFFIN, Robert P.
89th Congress in perspective; address, November 15, 1965. Vital Speeches 32:140-3 D 15 '65
Excerpt from debate, July 28, 1965. Cong Digest 44:201+ Ag '65
Right to work; address, August 9, 1965. Vital Speeches 31:702-4 S 1 '65
GRIFFIN, William D.
Instant closeups. il U S Camera 28:44-5+ My '65
GRIFFITH, Albert
Flannery O'Connor. America 113:674-5 N 27 '65
GRIFFITH, David Wark
Birth of The birth of a nation. B. Crowther. il por N Y Times Mag p24-5+ F 7 '65
GRIFFITH, Emile
Family man. il por Time 85:52-3 Ap 9 '65
GRIFFITH, F. H.
Old mechanical banks. See issues of Hobbies
GRIFFITH, L. J. and others
Drug antagonism between lincomycin and erythromycin. bibliog Science 147:746 F 12 '65
GRIFFITH, William E.
Containing communism East and West. Atlan 215:71-5 My '65
We must stop red China now! interview. Read Digest 86:67-72 F '65
GRIFFITHS, Bede
India after the Pope. Commonweal 81:641-2 F 12 '65
GRIGG, John
Is homosexuality a crime? N Y Times Mag p6-7+ Je 27 '65

GRIGGS, John
Excursion to death. Am Heritage 16:32-5+
F '65
GRIGGS, Lee
Unhappiest circus. Life 58:83 Ap 23 '65
When he wills it, things happen. Life 60:
42+ Ja 14 '66
GRILIKHES, Alexandra
Sleeping beauty wakes up in Philadelphia.
Dance Mag 40:20-1 Ja '66
GRILLS, Barbecue. See Barbecue grills
GRILLS, Picnic. See Camp stoves
GRIMES, Roger
He's too good to be false. por Sports Illus
23:55 S 20 '65
GRIMOND, Joseph
Liberal outlook. por Newsweek 66:27 S 6
'65
GRINDING machines
Band grinder smooths and sharpens. W. G.
Waggoner. il Pop Mech 124:172-4 D '65
GRINDING wheels
Wondrous evolution in abrasives. il Duns R
85:54-8 F '65
GRIS, Charles Édouard Jeanneret-. See Le
Corbusier
GRISSOM, Virgil
I'm thankful to be first; historic voices from
space; conversation. U S News 58:35 Je 14
'65
    See also
Space flight—Manned flights—Grissom-Young
flight, 1965
—and Young, John
Molly Brown was OK from the first time we
met her. pors Life 58:41-42A Ap 2 '65
GRIST, Reri
Reri Grist, toast of two continents. il pors
Ebony 20:84-6+ Mr '65
GRISWOLD, Estelle T.
Back in business. il Newsweek 65:60 Je 21
'65
GRISWOLD, S. Smith
What pollution costs. Bul Atomic Sci 21:12-16
Je '65
GRIZZLY bears. See Bears
GROBSTEIN, Clifford, and Cohen, Julia
Collagenase: effect on the morphogenesis of
embryonic salivary epithelium in vitro. bib-
liog Science 150:626-8 O 29 '65
GROCERY stores
    See also
Supermarkets
GROCERY trade
Edouard Leclerc: grocer of France. S. Berger
Yale R 55:90-106 O '65
Uncle's 1,700 grocers; Super Valu stores,
inc; Hopkins, Minn. S. Freedgood. il
Fortune 71:130-3 Mr '65
GRODDECK, Georg Walther
Wild analyst, by C. M. Grossman and S.
Grossman. Review
New Repub 152:22-4 My 1 '65. A. Watts
GROENHOFF, Hans
Flying photographer. Flying 78:84-5 Ja '66
GROLIER, incorporated
Grolier subsidiary fined $100,000 in FTC
action; action brought against the Amer-
icana corporation. Pub W 189:44 Ja 3 '66
GROMMETS. See Eyelets, Metal
GROMYKO, Andreï Andreevich
Making Gromyko smile. E. Taylor. Reporter
32:28-9 My 20 '65
GRONER, Warren
Laser measurements. Electr World 74:50-
2+ N '65
Laser; practice and applications. Electr
World 74:45-8+ S '65
Lasers. Electr World 74:31-5+ Ag '65
GRONOUSKI, John Austin
Post office deportment. Reporter 32:6+ Mr
11 '65
    about
Can he really put zip in the mails? il por
Bsns W p83-4+ Je 19 '65
People of the week. U S News 59:19 S 13 '65
Postal innovations: what Gronouski has in
mind. por U S News 58:22 F 22 '65
Welcome, unrehearsed. il por Time 86:44 D
10 '65
GROOMING. See Beauty, Personal
GROOMING, Personal. See Toilet
GROOMS, Charles
Grand pop Moses. il por Time 85:76 Ap 9 '65
GROOMS, Red. See Grooms, C.
GROPIUS, Walter
Architectural details. Arch Rec 137:133-48
F '65
GROPPER, William
Art galleries: exhibition at the ACA. R. M.
Coates. New Yorker 41:219 D 11 '65
GROSE, E. See Marinkelle, C. J. jt. auth.

GROSECLOSE, Elgin
Excerpt from testimony before House com-
mittee on foreign affairs, March 4, 1965.
Cong Digest 44:184+ Je '65
GROSPIRON, Alvin F.
Oil workers get a tougher chief. por Bsns W
p82 Ag 28 '65
GROSS, Allan
Record clubmen. J. M. Conly. Reporter 32:46+
Ap 8 '65
GROSS, Beatrice. See Gross, R. jt. auth.
GROSS, Calvin Edward
Educational politics. Reporter 32:12+ Mr 25
'65
New York city: Gross out; desegregation in.
il por Sr Schol 86:sup 1 Mr 25 '65
Nice guy's exit. por Time 85:48 Mr 12 '65
Quiet way out. Newsweek 65:79 Je 28 '65
School of hard knocks. il por Newsweek 65:
88-9 Mr 15 '65
GROSS, Elly
Elly Gross, Israeli book designer and teacher.
il Pub W 187:86-7 Ap 5 '65
GROSS, Frank
Semiconductor sweeps for large-screen TV.
Electr World 73:30-2+ Je '65
GROSS, Gerald C.
ITU and the future of International telecom-
munications. UN Mo Chron 2:75-8 My '65
GROSS, J. A.
Pressure-induced color mutation of euglena
gracilis. bibliog Science 147:741-2 F 12 '65
GROSS, John
Nay sayers. Commentary 39:77-80 F '65
GROSS, Julian D. and Caro, L. G.
Genetic transfer in bacterial mating. bibliog
Science 150:1679-84 D 24 '65
GROSS, M. Grant, and others
Radioactivity of the Columbia River effluent.
bibliog Science 149:1088-90 S 3 '65
GROSS, Marthe
How serious is teenage drinking? Parents
Mag 40:64-5+ N '65
Picking a puppy to love. Parents Mag 40:
62-3+ Je '65
GROSS, Martin
Record clubmen. J. M. Conly. Reporter 32:
46+ Ap 8 '65
GROSS, Richard E.
Social studies in British schools. Sr Schol
87:sup36-8 S 23 '65
—See Allen, D. W. jt. auth.
GROSS, Ronald
American higher education in 1980. Sch &
Soc 93:484-5 D 11 '65
—and Gross, Beatrice
Let the child teach himself. N Y Times Mag
p34-5+ My 16 '65
GROSS, Sally
Sally Gross, Elizabeth Keen, Eugene Lion,
Judson dance theatre. M. Marks. Dance
Mag 40:57 Ja '66
GROSS, Sarah Chokla
How to run a successful book fair. Sr Schol
86:sup 13 Ap 29 '65
Tumblin' Creek's cabin library. Sr Schol 87:
sup 17-19 S 30 '65
GROSS national product
Art of unbalancing the budget; potential
GNP. N. W. Chamberlain. il Atlan 217:58-
62 Ja '66
Better than anyone thought. il Time 86:73
Ag 27 '65
Big gun on poverty. E. L. Dale, jr. New
Repub 153:13-15 Ag 7 '65; Reply. R. M.
Paige. 153:29-30 S 11 '65
Booming economy with only small ifs. Life
59:4 O 22 '65
How the deflator clarifies GNP. il Bsns W
p94+ D 11 '65
More money for spending. il Bsns W p21-2
Ag 28 '65
1965: better than hoped; with editorial com-
ment. il Bsns W p33-4. 180 Mr 20 '65
Phoney baloney in welfare spending. R. A.
Freeman. il Nat R 17:823-6 S 21 '65
Pressures up and down. il Fortune 72:29-30
O '65
Profits jump sharply, on paper. il Bsns W p24
Ag 28 '65
Uncle Sam's $50,000,000,000 surplus. E. L.
Dale, jr. il N Y Times Mag p32-3+ N 7 '65;
Reply. H. Hazlitt. Nat R 17:1151-2 D 14 '65
U.S. economy gets a truer yardstick. il Bsns
W p86+ Ag 21 '65
GROSSE, Aristid V.
Viscosities of liquid sodium and potassium,
from their melting points to their criticals
points. bibliog Science 147:1438-41 Mr 19
'65
La GROSSE valise; musical comedy. See Mu-
sical comedies, revues, etc.—Criticisms,
plots, etc.
GROSSER, Alfred
France and Germany: divergent outlooks.
For Affairs 44:26-36 O '65

GROSSFELD, Muriel Davis
Fitness should be fun. C. Mangel. il pors Look 29:88-90+ Ag 24 '65
GROSSINGER, Jennie
Jennie; excerpts from Jennie went to the country, the Grossinger dream that came true. Q. Reynolds. il pors Look 29:86-8+ Jl 13 '65
GROSSINGER family
Jennie; excerpts from Jennie went to the country, the Grossinger dream that came true. Q. Reynolds. il Look 29:86-8+ Jl 13 '65
GROSSINGER'S hotel. See Hotels, taverns, etc.
GROSSMAN, Bob, and Ottum, Bob
Olds' seven-year secret: a racy front drive. Sports Illus 23:55-8 S 27 '65
GROSSMAN, Edward
Jean Shepherd: radio's noble savage. Harper 232:88-9 Ja '66
GROSSMAN, Howard J.
Deeds—not words. Am For 71:18-21+ Mr '65
Small borough's comprehensive plan. Am City 80:118-19 Je '65
GROSSMAN, N. M.
(comp) 276 used cameras compared. Mod Phot 29:73-104 D '65
GROSSMAN, Ruth. See Putnam, J. jt. ed.
GROSSMAN, Sylva
Old guy. New Yorker 41:207-8+ O 30 '65
GROSSMAN, publishers, incorporated
Orion press merges with Grossman. Pub W 187:78 Je 21 '65
GROST, Michael
Nicest young genius in the U.S. J. Howard. il pors Life 58:104-6+ My 21 '65
GROSVENOR, Elsie May Bell
First lady of the National geographic. G. H. Grosvenor. il pors Nat Geog Mag 128:100-21 Jl '65
GROSVENOR, Gilbert Hovey
First lady of the National geographic. il pors Nat Geog Mag 128:100-21 Jl '65
GROSVENOR, Melville Bell
Doorway to watery wonderlands. Nat Geog Mag 127:388-93 Mr '65
National geographic's newest adventure: a color television series. por Nat Geog Mag 128:448-52 S '65
Safe landing on Sable; isle of 500 shipwrecks. il por Nat Geog Mag 128:398-431 S '65
GROTON school. See Private schools
GROUND control approach system. See Airports—Traffic control
GROUND covers. See Cover plants
GROUND effect machines
Across land and sea on a Hovercraft ferry. W. S. Griswold. il Pop Sci 187:74-5+ Ag '65
Coast guard molding policy for GEM service. Aviation W 82:49 Je 28 '65
Floating on air; Hovercraft shuttle between Oakland and San Francisco airports. il Time 86:59 Ag 20 '65
Helicopter carrier petitions CAB for GEM trials at San Francisco. Aviation W 82:32 Mr 1 '65
Hovercraft not so zany after all. il Bsns W p94-6 Ag 21 '65
Largest Russian GEM nears completion. il Aviation W 82:69 Ap 26 '65
Leading international ground effect machines; specifications (cont) Aviation W 82:221 Mr 15 '65
Low-level observation platforms studied by Convair for army; ducted-fan observation platform. il Aviation W 83:75 Ag 16 '65
Magnetic highway proposed. il Am City 80:64 O '65
San Francisco Hovercraft trials stir interest of other U.S. cities. R. G. O'Lone. Aviation W 83:48 Ag 16 '65
SR-N5 demands skills in flying, boating; Westland Hovercraft. H. J. Coleman. il Aviation W 82:97-9+ Ap 12 '65
Tomorrow's hulls: on wings and wind. F. Rohr. il Motor B 115:32-5+ F '65
GROUND meat. See Cookery—Meat
GROUND support equipment. See Guided missiles—Equipment
GROUND temperature. See Earth temperature
GROUNDCOVERS. See Cover plants
GROUNDING (electricity) See Electric distribution—Grounding
GROUP behavior
Group structure and role behavior. J. Jackson and C. McGehee. bibliog f Ann Am Acad 361:130-40 S '65
Political integration and political development. M. Weiner. bibliog f Ann Am Acad 358:52-64 Mr '65
Seeking thrills with the in crowd. C. Sherif and M. Sherif. PTA Mag 60:5-6 S '65

GROUP life insurance. See Insurance, Group life
GROUP medicine. See Medicine—Group practice
GROUP psychotherapy
Homosexuals need help. Sci N L 87:102 F 13 '65
Therapeutic play helps; child psychiatric therapy. Sci N L 87:102 F 13 '65
300-year weekend. Time 86:55 Jl 9 '65
GROUP theater. See New York (city)—Theater
GROUPERS
Mating of groupers: hermaphroditic fish. E. Clark. il Natur Hist 74:22-5 Je '65
Rare fish, the scamp. Sports Illus 22:19-20 Ap 19 '65
GROUPING by ability. See Ability grouping in education
GROUPS (sociology)
Group decision fixed by leader's attitude. Sci N L 89:8 Ja 1 '66
Locomotives; excerpt from Fashionable savages. J. Fairchild. il Ladies Home J 82:47+ S '65
Patterns, structures, of modernization and political development. M. J. Levy, jr. Ann Am Acad 358:29-40 Mr '65
Peoples of America. N. Glazer. il Nation 201:137-41 S 20 '65
White power structure. A. Morrison. il Ebony 20:141-4+ Ag '65
GROUSE shooting
Big red. K. Davis. Esquire 65:28-30 Ja '66
Private line from London; season opens. V. Cowles. Vogue 146:34 Ag 15 '65
Who needs a grouse dog? N. Smith. il Outdoor Life 136:44-7+ O '65
GROVE, Gene
When a no. 2 applies for a job. N Y Times Mag p32-3+ S 19 '65
GROVE press
Grove gets injunction vs. bootleg Thief's journal; edition issued by Greenleaf publishing company. Pub W 188:64 Jl 19 '65
Grove publishes Sexus to counter rival edition. Pub W 187:37 My 3 '65
Thief's journal copying ruled infringement. Pub W 188:26-7 O 18 '65
GROVES, Hubert
Garden row soup. Farm J 89:90 S '65
GROWTH
See also
Maturity
Regeneration (biology)
Stature
GROWTH (plants)
Auxin transport, gibberellin, and apical dominance. W. P. Jacobs and D. B. Case. bibliog il Science 148:1729-31 Je 25 '65
See also
Geotropism (botany)
Growth promoting substances (plants)
Tree rings
GROWTH, Economic. See Economic development
GROWTH companies. See Corporations
GROWTH funds. See Investment trusts
GROWTH hormones. See Hormones
GROWTH inhibiting substances (plants)
Abscisin II: inhibitory effect on flower induction in a long-day plant. L. T. Evans. bibliog il Science 151:107 Ja 7 '66
Plant growth retardant B-995: a possible mode of action. D. J. Reed and others. bibliog il Science 148:1469-71 Je 11 '65
Tryptamine oxidation by extracts of pea seedlings: effect of growth retardant β-hydroxyethylhydrazine. D. J. Reed. bibliog Science 148:1097-9 My 21 '65
See also
Indoleacetic acid
GROWTH of cities and towns. See Cities and towns—Growth
GROWTH promoting substances (plants)
Growth factor found; chromophore, bile pigment present in certain plant proteins Sci N L 88:21 Jl 10 '65
See also
Auxins
GROWTH promoting substances (protozoa)
Probiotics: growth-promoting factors produced by microorganisms. D. M. Lilly and R. H. Stillwell. bibliog il Science 147:747-8 F 12 '65
GROWTH stock. See Stocks
GROZNY, I. L.
Tapes to choose from. Hi Fi 15:40-2+ Ag '65
GRUBB, Davis
Tree full of stars; story. Ladies Home J 82:62-3 D '65
GRUBISICH, Thomas
Transit mess. Commonweal 83:456-7 Ja 21 '66
GRUEN, Victor, associates
Upgrading downtown. il Arch Rec 137:175-90 Je '65

GRUENBERG, Selma
Wax resist. Sch Arts 64:28-9 Je '65
GRUENING, Ernest
Excerpt from address, February 24, 1965.
Cong Digest 44:119+ Ap '65
Personal note. por Nation 201:36-9 S 20 '65
Plot to strangle Alaska. Atlan 216:56-9 Jl;
52 S '65

about
Birth control. K. Crawford. Newsweek 66:32
Jl 12 '65
If we ignore the plight. . ; bill to establish
assistant secretaryships for population con-
trol. por Time 86:16 Jl 2 '65
Myth-busters. por Newsweek 66:19 Jl 5 '65
Population politics; new bill introduced by
Gruening brings birth control issues to
Congress. E. Langer. Science 148:1702-3
Je 25 '65
GRUENINGER, Walter F.
Phonograph records. See issues of Consumer
bulletin
GRUENWALD, A. and Reynolds, J. A.
Less than $3,000 per ton. Am City 80:100-1
O '65
GRUMBACH, Melvin M. See Kaplan, S. L. jt.
auth.
GRUMMAN aircraft engineering corporation
Surface of the moon; research of Grumman
scientists. il Fortune 72:191-2 Jl '65
GRUNDT, Leonard
Branch library inadequacies in a typical large
city. bibliog por Library J 90:3997-4001
O 1 '65
GRUNDY CENTER, Iowa
Start at Grundy Center; elementary school
library. D. Fistler. il Library J 90:5465-7
D 15 '65
GRUNFELD, Frederic V.
Critics' critic. Reporter 32:43-4 Je 17 '65
Men, women and music. Read Digest 87:35-6
N '65
Road to Santiago. Reporter 34:40+ Ja 13 '66
St Wanda's testament. Reporter 32:42-4 F 25
'65
Smugglers I have known. Opera N 30:8-12
N 6 '65
Touch like a paving stone. Reporter 33:38-41
Jl 15 '65
Unraveling Ravel: the great leap sideways.
Reporter 32:35-8 My 6 '65
GRÜSSER, Otto Joachim. See Finkelstein, D.
jt. auth.
GSCHEIDLE, Gertrude Elizabeth
Chicago public library under fire in pro-
longed newspaper campaign. Library J 90:
3233-4 Ag '65
GSOVSKY, Tatjana
Tatjana Gsovsky: a prayer to the deity. W.
Sorell. il Dance Mag 39:14-15 Ag '65
GUADALAJARA, Mexico
Market for travel pictures. L. Barry. il Pop
Phot 57:44+ S '65
GUADALCANAL
Guadalcanal: 1942 and 1965. R. Joseph. il
Esquire 64:54-5 Ag '65
GUADALUPE MOUNTAINS NATIONAL PARK
(proposed) See National parks and reserves
—United States
GUADELOUPE ISLAND
Butterfly wings in the Caribbean. H. Sutton.
il Sat R 48:46+ My 1 '65
Le high-life in Guadeloupe. J. Egan. il Atlan
216:120+ D '65
GUAGNINI, Bernard J.
Recreation en route. Recreation 58:403-4 O '65
GUAM
Letter from Guam. E. J. Kahn, jr. il New
Yorker 40:39-40+ F 13 '65
GUAMANIANS. See Chamorros
GUANIDINE
Chloroplast mutagenesis: effect of N-methyl-
N'-nitro-N-nitrosoguanidine and some other
agents on euglena. D. R. McCalla. bibliog
il Science 148:497-9 Ap 23 '65
GUARANTEES. See Guaranty of goods
GUARANTY. See Warranty
GUARANTY of goods
Oh, what they do with the fine print!
manufacturers' guarantees. Consumer Rep
30:379 Ag '65
GUARD rails. See Roads—Safety guards
GUARDI, Francesco
Canal chroniclers. il Time 86:76-7 S 10 '65
GUARDI, Giovanni Antonio
Canal chroniclers. il Time 86:76-7 S 10 '65
GUARDIANS of the city. See Hasidism
GUARDUCCI, Margherita
Where is St Peter buried? E. M. Jung. il
Cath World 202:107-13 N '65

GUATEMALA
See also
Antigua
Atitlán, Lake
Communism—Guatemala
Education—Guatemala
Guerrillas—Guatemala

Description and travel
Guatemala. C. Matty. il Travel 124:36-8 D '65

Industries
Expanding today for business manana; Ar-
row de Centro America, ltda. il Bsns W
p 120 S 11 '65
GUATEMALAN national science fair. See Sci-
ence fairs
GUAVAS
Pineapple guavas are ready now. il Sunset
135:235-6 O '65
GUAYANA, Venezuela
Home-grown Ruhr. Newsweek 65:48 F 22 '65
GUAZZI, Maurizio, and others
Carotid sinus and aortic reflexes in the reg-
ulation of circulation during sleep. bibliog
Science 148:397-9 Ap 16 '65
GUBERNATORIAL candidates. See Candidates,
Political
GUBERNATORIAL elections. See Elections—
United States
GUDRIDGE, Beatrice M.
Do tell; effective communications and public
relations. NEA J 54:32-3 My '65
GUEDE, Max
Nazi murders & German politics. D. Scho-
enbaum. Commentary 39:72-7 Je '65
GUELPH, University, Ontario
At the crossroads; reprint. L. Minshall. Rec-
reation 58:343-4 S '65
GUENDLING, Marie
Spot dots, 3-D. Sch Arts 65:38-9 D '65
GUERIN, Ann
Happy to be a king. Life 59:141-2 N 19 '65
Life movie review (cont) Life 58:12 Mr 5 '65
GUERIN, Etienne J.
Sweden's twin treasures. Travel 124:32-5+
Ag '65
GUERRERO, Rodrigo
Family planning. America 112:665-6 My 8 '65
GUERRILLA warfare
Battle of Dienbienphu. by J. Roy. Review
Commonweal 82:119-20 Ap 16 '65. W. C.
McWilliams
U.S. secret army: fighting reds by red meth-
ods. il U S News 58:49-50 Ap 12 '65
See also
Minutemen (organization)
GUERRILLAS
See also
Jungle warfare

Guatemala
Ideology and nerve; Yon Sosa's guerrilla
movement. il Newsweek 66:49 Ag 9 '65

Latin America
On with the war; Castroite F.A.L.N. il Time
86:46 N 12 '65
Where Castro brews new trouble for U. S.
il U S News 59:38-40 O 18 '65

Peru
Anatomy of a nightmare. Time 85:50 Je 25
'65
Escalation in the highlands. Time 86:26 Ag
27 '65
Shock of recognition. Newsweek 66:39+ Jl
19 '65

Philippines
See also
Hukbalahaps

Tibet
Tibet; Khamba tribesmen. G. Patterson. il
Reporter 32:31-3 Mr 25 '65
Where guerrillas are giving reds a lot of
trouble. il U S News 59:54 O 11 '65

Venezuela
Bravo and his boys; Venezuela's Castro-
inspired armed forces of national liberation.
M. J. Kubic. Newsweek 66:47 Jl 5 '65

Vietnam (Democratic Republic)
See also
Vietnamese war, 1957- —Guerrillas

Vietnam (Republic)
See also
Vietnamese war, 1957- —Guerrillas
GUERRINA, Carl C.
It's easy to plant trees downtown. Am City
80:108-9 Ap '65
GUESSING games. See Mathematical recre-
ations

GUEST, Cornelia Cochrane
One-year-old Cornelia Guest. il por Vogue
145:142-3 Ap 1 '65
GUEST beds. See Beds
GUEST rooms
How to make room for a guest when you
don't have a guest room. D. Popplestone.
il Bet Hom & Gard 43:54-9 Ag '65
Seven ways to find space for a guest bed.
C. T. Sigman. il Pop Sci 186:140-4 Mr '65
GUESTS
How to be a good guest on a cruise. L.
O'Brien. il Motor B 116:56+ Jl '65
        See also
Entertaining
Hospitality
GUESTS, Government. See Government enter-
taining
GUEVARA, Ernesto
Come out, come out wherever you are. por
Time 85:50 Je 25 '65
Farewell, dear hearts. il Time 86:51 O 15 '65
Guevara: out of Cuba, or just out of favor?
por U S News 59:20 O 18 '65
Petrified forest. il por Time 86:36-40 O 8 '65
Rebel without a pause. Newsweek 66:71 O 18
'65
Troublemaker on a tour of trouble spots. por
U S News 58:16 Mr 8 '65
Where's Che? Newsweek 65:44 Je 28 '65
GUEVARA, Susana
August 16, 1906; excerpt from Alvaro and
I. Américas 17:29-32 Jl '65
GUGGENHEIM, Peggy
Venerable Bohemian of Venice. por Life 58:
101-2+ Je 18 '65
GUGGENHEIM, Solomon R, museum, New
York. See Solomon R. Guggenheim mu-
seum, New York
GUGGENHEIMER, Elinor C.
Can we live with our cars? Nation 201:164-6
S 27 '65
GUGGENHEIMER, Minnie (Schafer)
Summer haven. Newsweek 66:80 Jl 5 '65
GUHL, A. M.
Sociobiology and man. Bul Atomic Sci 21:22-4
O '65
GUIDANCE. See Counseling; Personnel service
(education)
GUIDANCE, Reader. See Libraries—Readers
advisory service
GUIDANCE directors. See School counselors
GUIDANCE systems for space vehicles. See
Space vehicles—Control systems
GUIDE books. See Guidebooks
GUIDEBOOKS
Antidote to nonsense. R. Lynes. Harper 230:
44 Ap '65
Down with Michelin! K. Williams. Atlan 216:
130-3 Jl '65
Eugene Fodor-Shell oil travel guides to U.S.A.
Pub W 188:70 D 27 '65
Guiding the traveler *a la Michelin et cie,*
Guide Michelin. il Bsns W p 138 Jl 17 '65
Self-guided touring; Michelin guidebooks. il
Holiday 38:103 S '65
Traveling by book, 1965. E. Kiester, jr. il
Redbook 125:22 Jl '65
GUIDED missile bases
Is Hanoi another Havana for Soviets? ques-
tion of SAM missile installations. il U S
News 58:6 Ap 26 '65
JFK's greatest hour; Khrushchev retreats in
Cuba; excerpts from Kennedy. T. C. Soren-
sen. il Look 29:48-52+ S 21 '65
Vietnam: a matter of interpretation; missile
sites near Hanoi. il Newsweek 65:37-8
Ap 26 '65
GUIDED missile models
ASW missile test site readied; scale model
testing at NOL. M. Getler. il Miss & Roc
17:18 N 8 '65
GUIDED missiles
AF confirms ICBM improvement drive. D. L.
Zylstra. Miss & Roc 16:18 Je 14 '65
Army to begin SAM-D contract definition
phase. M. Getler. Miss & Roc 18:12 Ja 3 '66
Atomic dud; Davy Crockett weapon dropped.
il Newsweek 65:17-18 Je 7 '65
Bombers lose again to missiles; cutback of
B-52s and B-58s. Bsns W p33 D 11 '65
Competition may widen U.S.-French rift. L.
L. Doty. Aviation W 82:17 Mr 1 '65
Decision time grows shorter for Nike-X. il
Aviation W 82:147+ Mr 15 '65
Europeans pushing joint missile efforts. W. C.
Wetmore. il Aviation W 83:69-70+ Jl 5 '65
ICBM studies focus on 156-in. motors. I.
Stone. il Aviation W 82:141-3+ Mr 15 '65
Leading international missiles; specifica-
tions (cont) Aviation W 82:209-10 Mr 15
'65

LASRV gets big boost from air force. Miss
& Roc 17:15 N 15 '65
McDonnell likely choice for MAW; medium
assault weapon. Miss & Roc 18:15 Ja 10 '66
Minuteman II emplacement cost to top $1
billion. Miss & Roc 16:12 My 24 '65
Missiles and rockets astrolog; current status
of U.S. missile and space programs. See oc-
casional issues of Missiles and rockets
Missiles and rockets world missile/space en-
cyclopedia 1965. il Miss & Roc 17:37-44+ Jl
26 '65
Moscow parade features solid, liquid-fuel
ICBMs and new battlefield-class missiles;
with photographs and editorial comment.
H. J. Coleman. Aviation W 82:21, 26-31 My
17 '65
Myriad R&D problems await solution. il Miss
& Roc 16:40-3+ Mr 29 '65
New rockets unveiled in Moscow; with edi-
torial comment. il Miss & Roc 16:16-17,
74 My 17 '65
Orbiting missile; red smoke screen? il U S
News 59:6 N 22 '65
Question mark remains in missile future.
M. Yaffee. il Aviation W 82:152-5 Mr 15 '65
Rocket that tightened U.S.-Soviet tensions
anew; SAM-II, surface to air missile. il
U S News 59:8 Ag 9 '65
Russia revamps its missile might; weapons
reequipped with latest in rocketry and elec-
tronics. il Bsns W p 138+ N 20 '65
Soviet claim could spur space track. M.
Getler. il Miss & Roc 17:14-15 N 15 '65
Soviets brandish medium, long range mis-
siles; with photographs. Aviation W 82:
20-3 My 24 '65
Soviets parade medium, long range missiles;
photographs. Aviation W 83:64-5 D 6 '65
Tactical weaponry pushed by air force. il
Aviation W 82:72-5 Mr 15 '65
Technology for tomorrow's missile power;
ballistic lull; address, June 10, 1965. H. J.
Sands. Vital Speeches 31:554-7 Jl 1 '65
Titan III family may fill Atlas silos. D. L.
Zylstra. Miss & Roc 17:12-13 Jl 12 '65
TOW, Shillelagh face showdown; year of de-
cision for army's tactical missile develop-
ment program. D. L. Zylstra. Miss & Roc
16:14-15 My 10 '65
U.S. drones and target missiles; specifica-
tions (cont) Aviation W 82:222 Mr 15 '65
U.S. missiles; specifications (cont) Avia-
tion W 82:187-8 Mr 15 '65

Control

AF awaits F-111A weapons studies. D. L.
Zylstra. Miss & Roc 16:18 Je 7 '65
Air force cites good test data in first STAFF
system flight; stellar acquisition flight
feasibility guidance system. Aviation W 82:
36 Ap 19 '65
Deadline draws near in competition for F-111
digital inertial navigation unit. Miss &
Roc 17:21 Ag 2 '65
Physical failure studies could lead NAA
toward second-generation IC's. R. Pay.
Miss & Roc 17:34+ Ag 2 '65
STAFF success improves hopes for STINGS;
stellar-inertial guidance systems. Miss &
Roc 17:15 N 22 '65

Cost

Army spells out its $253.7-million missile
request. il Miss & Roc 16:13 Mr 15 '65

Defenses

Air defense featured in Soviet film on mis-
siles. il Miss & Roc 17:16-17 S 13 '65
Anti-missile defense; should Nike X be de-
ployed? L. J. Carter. il Science 150:1696-9
D 24 '65
Antimissile systems and disarmament. N. Ta-
lensky. Bul Atomic Sci 21:25-9 F '65; Dis-
cussion. 21:25-6 F; 29-30 O '65
Army weighs new air-defense system. M.
Getler. Miss & Roc 17:14 N 1 '65
Bonn seeking additional nuclear weapon. G. C.
Wilson. il Aviation W 83:23-4 O 18 '65
Chinese and ballistic missile defense. J. I.
Coffey. Bul Atomic Sci 21:17-19 D '65
Chinese nuclear threat pushes studies of
Nike-X options. Miss & Roc 16:17 My 31
'65
Containing the arms race. J. J. Stone. Bul
Atomic Sci 21:18-21 S '65
Countdown for Nike-X. G. A. W. Boehm.
il Fortune 72:132-7+ N '65
Decision nears on Nike X; antimissile de-
fense system. Bsns W p 170+ Je 12 '65
Decision time grows shorter for Nike-X. il
Aviation W 82:147+ Mr 15 '65
Defense against ballistic missiles. F. J. Dy-
son; reply with rejoinder. R. H. McMahan,
jr. Bul Atomic Sci 21:37-40 Mr '65

GUIDED missiles—Defenses—*Continued*

Defense dept. defers for year decision on Nike-X production. Aviation W 82:26 F 22 '65

Heading the other way; White House conference on international cooperation. New Repub 153:5-6 D 11 '65

Is Nike X the answer in missile defense? with editorial comment. il Bsns W p32-4, 164 D 4 '65

Naked country. W. J. Coughlin. Miss & Roc 17:46 S 20 '65

Navy firing at Redstone targets. M. Getler. il Miss & Roc 17:16-17 D 13 '65

No technical bars to deploying Nike-X. D. L. Zylstra. Miss & Roc 17:14-15 Ag 2 '65

No time for civilians. W. J. Coughlin. Miss & Roc 17:46 Ag 9 '65

Public ignorant of A-ICBM situation. D. L. Zylstra. Miss & Roc 17:32+ Ag 16 '65

Sea Sparrow eyed for point defense. D. L. Zylstra. Miss & Roc 16:14 Mr 22 '65

Space arms control. A. Frye. Bul Atomic Sci 21:30-3 Ap '65

Studies seek improved ASM guidance; reassessing air-to-surface missile guidance techniques. B. Miller. il Aviation W 83:77+ D 6 '65

Truth about our missile defense. H. O. Johansen. il Pop Sci 187:84-7+ O '65

$20 billion question; hold back on Nike-X. il Newsweek 66:60+ D 13 '65

$25 billion question; Nike-X system. il Time 85:25B Je 18 '65

U.S. pilots may face new SAM radar. G. C. Wilson. Aviation W 84:32-3 Ja 10 '66

Viet needs may delay Nike-X production. Aviation W 83:23-4 O 4 '65

Detection

Detection of ICBMs key in MOL approval. Aviation W 83:26-7 S 27 '65

Navy improves accuracy, detection range of space surveillance chain. P. J. Klass. il Aviation W 83:56-7+ Ag 16 '65

Electronic equipment

Advanced TM/MDI proposed for three-T's; Terrier, Tartar and Talos. C. D. LaFond. il Miss & Roc 16:22-3 My 24 '65

Phoenix packaging reduces size, weight. B. Miller. il Aviation W 82:67+ My 24 '65

Physical failure studies could lead NAA toward second-generation IC's. R. Pay. Miss & Roc 17:34+ Ag 2 '65

Equipment

Cubic proposes sharpening targeting; high accuracy targeting sub-system. R. Pay. Miss & Roc 16:36+ My 17 '65

Program promises better instruments; improving range support and missile design. M. Getler. il Miss & Roc 17:24-6 Ag 30 '65

Launching

Moscow TV film shows launch of ballistic missile types. il Aviation W 82:36-7+ Je 7 '65

Soviets show firings of various missile types; photographs. Aviation W 83:84-5 S 20 '65

Launching from airplanes

Advanced target missile sought for F-111. il Aviation W 82:71-2 Je 28 '65

AF seeks new tactical missile; air-to-surface weapon dubbed Maverick. M. Getler. Miss & Roc 17:14 D 6 '65

B-52 cutback won't affect SRAM. Miss & Roc 17:18 D 13 '65

Deadline draws near in competition for F-111 digital inertial navigation unit. Miss & Roc 17:21 Ag 2 '65

DOD re-evaluates tactical missiles. M. Getler. Miss & Roc 17:18+ O 18 '65

Explosive structure removal may aid designers of air-to-air missiles. M. Getler. il Miss & Roc 16:34-7 Ap 19 '65

First photos of new Sidewinder head. il Miss & Roc 17:34 N 22 '65

Navy aids search for 'copter missiles. M. Getler. il Miss & Roc 17:14-15 O 25 '65

Phoenix to give navy new air-to-air missile. D. L. Zylstra. Miss & Roc 16:34 Mr 29 '65

Scramjet flights may begin in 1967. W. E. Wilks. il Miss & Roc 17:15 S 13 '65

SRAM funding slashed by House. Miss & Roc 16:18 Je 28 '65

Studies seek improved ASM guidance; reassessing air-to-surface missile guidance techniques. B. Miller. il Aviation W 83:77+ D 6 '65

Launching from ships

Advanced TM/MDI proposed for three-T's; Terrier, Tartar and Talos. C. D. LaFond. il Miss & Roc 16:22-3 My 24 '65

Sea Sparrow eyed for point defense. D. L. Zylstra. Miss & Roc 16:14 Mr 22 '65

Launching from submarine boats

ASW missile test site readied. M. Getler. il Miss & Roc 17:18 N 8 '65

Lockheed gets go-sign for improved Polaris. il Bsns W p86+ F 20 '65

Launching pads

Nuclear-age tomb; Titan II ICBM rocket silos near Searcy, Ark. il Newsweek 66:23 Ag 23 '65

Ogden keeps Minuteman ICBM unready rate below 0.3 per cent. M. L. Yaffee. il Aviation W 83:60-2+ S 27 '65

Toll of a Titan; explosion in rocket silo near Searcy, Ark. il Time 86:23 Ag 20 '65

Launching sites

Ogden keeps Minuteman ICBM unready rate below 0.3 per cent. M. L. Yaffee. il Aviation W 83:60-2+ S 27 '65

Silos for sale. il Newsweek 66:81-2 S 20 '65

Manufacture

Defense dept. defers for year decision on Nike-X production. Aviation W 82:26 F 22 '65

Materials

Shillelagh round to boast fully combustible casing. J. F. Judge. il Miss & Roc 18:38+ Ja 10 '66

Propulsion

Air-augmented missile studies increasing. M. L. Yaffee. il Aviation W 83:49+ N 22 '65

Hercules, Thiokol win Poseidon work. Miss & Roc 17:16 O 25 '65

Recovery

Payload test vehicle contractor to be picked by BSD this month. I. Stone. il Aviation W 82:75+ Mr 22 '65

Scaling laws set by ABRES program. J. Trainor. Miss & Roc 16:10 F 8 '65

Testing

ASW missile test site readied; scale model testing at NOL. M. Getler. il Miss & Roc 17:18 N 8 '65

Army prepares Sprint pop-up flight. D. L. Zylstra. il Miss & Roc 16:22 My 17 '65

External radar on F-101B track missiles. il Aviation W 82:57-8 Je 7 '65

First Sprint flight gratifies DOD. Miss & Roc 16:12 Ap 5 '65

First Sprint pop-up test successful. il Miss & Roc 17:13 N 29 '65

French strategic missile test set; surface-to-surface strategic ballistic missile system. il Miss & Roc 17:12 Jl 5 '65

Pending shot may seal SIGS future; navy's simplified inertial guidance system. C. D. LaFond. il Miss & Roc 17:32-3 Ag 2 '65

Piston launch system favored for Sprint. G. Alexander. il Aviation W 84:54-5+ Ja 17 '66

White Sands ARTRAC network to be operational by next summer; Advanced range testing, reporting, and control system. il Miss & Roc 17:28 S 20 '65

Tracking

Air force cites good test data in first STAFF system flight; stellar acquisition flight feasibility guidance system. Aviation W 82:36 Ap 19 '65

ALOTS advances airborne tracking. R. Pay. il Miss & Roc 17:26-7 N 22 '65

First BUIC-2 begins SAGE back-up net; back-up interceptor control. il Aviation W 83:83-5 S 6 '65

GT-5 may track missiles. Miss & Roc 17:20-1 Jl 26 '65

Test stand aids Polaris mission. C. D. LaFond. il Miss & Roc 16:34-6+ F 15 '65

WSMR consolidating control center. R. Pay. Miss & Roc 16:32-4 F 1 '65

Transportation

Details of new Soviet missile container shown; with photographs. Aviation W 83:40-1+ N 29 '65

Missile carrier details seen in Soviet display; photographs. Aviation W 83:80-1 Ag 23 '65

Soviet Union displays new missile carriers; with photographs. Aviation W 83:30-1 N 15 '65

GUIDES

Guided tour of tourists in Rome. I. Shenker. il N Y Times Mag p24-5+ Jl 11 '65

See also
Mountaineering

GUILFORD, Vt.

Bijah's Luce of Guilford, Vermont. M. R. Wright. il Negro Hist Bul 28:152-3+ Ap '65

GUILLAIN, Robert
Ten years of secrecy. Bul Atomic Sci 21:24-5
F '65
GUILLEMOTS. See Murres
GUILLET, Meredith M.
Nature and man in Canyon de Chelly. Nat
Parks Mag 39:9-11 Jl '65
GUILLOT, René
René Guillot. G. Marsh. il por Horn Bk 41:
192-4 Ap '65
GUIMARÃES, João
Marvelous city. Américas 17:1-10 Mr '65
GUINEA
Economic conditions
Reason to worry. il Time 87:27-8 Ja 7 '66
GUINNESS, Arthur, son and company, limited
Here is the odd paradise of the record ma-
niac. Guinness book of records. J. A. M.
Graham. il Sports Illus 22:54-8+ F 8 '65;
Same abr. with title Book to end argu-
ments. Read Digest 86:152-4+ My '65
Stout-hearted island. il Time 87:71 Ja 21 '66
GUITAR, Mary Anne
Bennett's proper pickets. Mlle 61:112-15+
Je '65
Can't the pendulum swing this way? Am
Home 68:8 Mr '65
GUITAR
Amplifier module electrifies guitar. M. E.
McGrew and N. Fried. il Pop Electr 22:
64-6 Je '65
Big noise; the electric guitar. P. Vander-
wicken. il Esquire 64:38-9+ Jl '65
Guitars hit a cashbox crescendo. il Bsns W
p 154-6 My 8 '65
If you want to play a guitar. il Good H
160:182 Ap '65
On the upbeat; best-selling musical instru-
ment. il Newsweek 65:73 F 15 '65
Singing steel guitar. R. L. Clough. il Pop
Mech 124:129-31+ Ag '65
GUITAR music
See also
Phonograph records—Guitar music
GUITTON, Jean
Mission of the faithful; excerpts from inter-
view. Cath World 202:114-15 N '65
GULBENKIAN, Nubar
Last aristocrat. por Esquire 63:104-7+ Ap
'65
about
Man who prefers everything; with report by
J. Hicks. il pors Life 59:89-90+ O 15 '65
GULDESCA, Stanko
Middle East dilemma. Nat R 17:510-11 Je 15
'65
GULF and Western industries, incorporated
Living on breakdowns. Time 86:98+ O 8 '65
GULF INTRACOASTAL WATERWAY. See
Intracoastal Waterway
GULF OF MEXICO. See Mexico, Gulf of
GULF oil corporation
Gulf name goes nationwide; Gulftane goes
to West coast. Bsns W p31 S 18 '65
GULF states
Give the Gulf Coast a try. V. J. Flanagan.
il Motor B 115:50-1+ Ap '65
See also
Fishing—Gulf states
Florida
GULF STREAM
Dipping deep into the Gulf Stream; U.S.
launches a major survey. il Bsns W p78-80
Jl 31 '65
Gulf Stream probed. Sci N L 88:54 Jl 24 '65
GULI, Francesca
Day I proctored a religion exam to the ac-
companiment of a garbage truck; poem.
America 113:441 O 16 '65
GULLS
Brown pelican is victim of gull piracy. A. J.
Meyerriecks and R. Meyerriecks. il Natur
Hist 74:32-5 N '65
Predation's impact on penguins; skua and
Adélie predator-prey habits. W. J. Maher.
il Natur Hist 75:42-51 Ja '66
GUMMERE, Richard M. Jr
Discipline in the dark; on beating school
children. Nation 201:442-5 D 6 '65; 202:in-
side cover Ja 10 '66
GUMS (anatomy)
Diseases
Periodontal disease in developing nations.
H. S. Sinrod. bibliog Science 149:400-2 Jl
23 '65
GUN carriers, Automobile. See Automobiles—
Equipment
GUN racks
Dust-free gun cabinet. A. A. Altomare. il
Pop Mech 124:176-7 O '65
GUN sights. See Firearms—Sights

GUNDEL, Charles
Gastronomy. J. Wechsberg. Esquire 64:126-
8+ D '65
GUNDERSON, Harold. See Stockdale, H. jt.
auth.
GUNGA Din. See Mirdrekvandi, A.
GUNN, Ross
Collision characteristics of freely falling
water drops. bibliog Science 150:695-701 N 5
'65
Thunderstorm electrification and raindrop
collisions and disjection in an electric field.
Science 150:888-9 N 12 '65
GUNNE, Lars-Magnus. See Reis, D. J. jt. auth.
GUNNERY
See also
Shooting
GUNNING. See Hunting
GUNRACKS. See Gun racks
GUNS. See Ordnance
GUNS (small arms) See Firearms; Pistols;
Shotguns
GUNS, Miniature. See Miniature objects
GUNTHER, John
How America lives. Ladies Home J 82:56+
Ap '65
Locust fighters. Look 29:40-2 Ap 20 '65
Old grad returns to Chicago; excerpt from
university magazine. por Sat R 48:85-7+
O 16 '65
GUNTHER, Max
Article queries that sell. Writer 78:19-21+
Ag '65
Fraternity of crippled men. N Y Times Mag
p34-5+ S 19 '65
Secret of life. Sat Eve Post 238:25-9 Jl 3 '65
We've got to call it something. Sat Eve Post
238:60-1 S 11 '65
GUPTA, N. N. Das. See Das Gupta, N. N.
GUPTA, Sisir K.
Asian nonalignment. bibliog f Ann Am Acad
362:44-51 N '65
GURLEY, Henry T.
More life from your car battery. Pop Sci 188:
120-3+ Ja '66
Secrets of shooting color at night. Pop Sci
187:92-5 S '65
GURNEY, Edward J.
Excerpt from debate, July 28, 1965. Cong
Digest 44:203+ Ag '65
GURTOV, Melvin
Communist China's foreign aid program. bib-
liog f Cur Hist 49:150-4+ S '65
GUSSIN, Gary N. See Capecchi, M. R. jt. auth.
GUSTAFSON, Alice, and others
Christmas in the castle. Sch Arts 65:29-30
D '65
GUSTAFSON, James M.
Christian faith and moral action. Christian
Cent 82:1345-7 N 3 '65
GUSTON, Philip
Piero della Francesca: the impossibility of
painting. il Art N 64:38-9 My '65
GUSTS. See Winds
GUT DAM. See Dams
GUTETTER, Lee. See Kujawski, J. jt. auth.
GUTH, William D. and Tagiuri, Renato
Personal values and corporate strategy. bib-
liog f Harvard Bsns R 43:123-32 S '65
GUTHART, Leo A.
More companies are buying back their stock.
Harvard Bsns R 43:40-2+ Mr '65
GUTHEIM, Frederick
Declining, bewildered, frustrated. Nation 201:
225-6 O 11 '65
Foggy Bottom's dolce vita. Nation 201:395-7
N 22 '65
Townscapes and turnpikes. Nation 200:622 Je
7 '65
GUTHRIE, A. B. Jr
April in Montana; excerpts from Blue hen's
chick. Holiday 37:70-1 Mr '65
about
Big sky smiled. R. L. Perkin. por Sat R
48:28 Je 5 '65
GUTHRIE, Sir Tyrone
Two Cherry orchards; Guthrie theatre, Min-
neapolis. J. Novick. Nation 201:87-8 Ag 16
'65
GUTIERREZ, José L.
Plastic paints. N. Roukes. il por Sch Arts
64:20-4 F '65
GUTMAN, John
Lustrum for the studio. Opera N 30:26-7 D 4
'65
GUTMAN, Yehuda, and others
Micropuncture study of inulin absorption in
the rat kidney. Science 147:753-4 F 12 '65

GUTTERS
On-the-spot tests check gutter capacity; San Leandro, Calif. G. H. Hamlin and J. Bautista. il Am City 80:94-6 Ap '65

GUTTERS (roof)
Is your run-off system doing its job? il Pop Mech 124:158-64+ N '65

GUTTMACHER, Alan F.
How births can be controlled. Nat R 17:641-2 Jl 27 '65
Will it be twins? Redbook 124:20+ F '65

GUTTMAN, Irving
Vancouver's high priest; interview, ed. by F. Stevenson. por Opera N 29:29-31 F 20 '65

GUTTMANN, Allen
Spanish tragedy. Commentary 40:78-80 Ag '65; 41:21 Ja '66

GUTTRIDGE, Frank
Designs his watercolors. il por Am Artist 29:42-3 D '65

GUZMAN, Ramon M.
Six years ahead of schedule. Am City 80:132-3 F '65

GUZZARDI, Walter, Jr
Consultants: the men who came to dinner. Fortune 71:138-41+ My '65
—See McCreary, E. jr. jt. auth.

GWYNNE-JONES, Alun, baron Chalfont. See Chalfont, A. G.-J.

GYMNASIUMS
Natural, appropriate use of concrete shells; Carleton college men's gymnasium. il Arch Rec 137:129-32 F '65

GYMNASTICS
Fitness should be fun. C. Mangel. il Look 29:88-90+ Ag 24 '65
New bounce on the trampoline. P. Stewart. il Sports Illus 23:52-3 Jl 12 '65
See also
Physical education and training

GYMNODINIUM breve. See Oysters

GYNANDROMORPHISM
Nature note. Sci N L 87:271 Ap 24 '65

GYNECOLOGY. See Woman—Diseases

GYÖRGYI, Albert Szent-. See Szent-Györgyi, A.

GYPSUM panels. See Paneling

GYROSCOPE
Gyroscope: theory and application. W. Wrigley and W. M. Hollister. bibliog il Science 149:713-21 Ag 13 '65

GYROSCOPIC instruments
Gyroscope: theory and application. W. Wrigley and W. M. Hollister. bibliog il Science 149:713-21 Ag 13 '65

H

HELP (highway emergency locating plan) See Radio communication—Emergency applications

HUAC. See United States—Congress—House of representatives—Un-American activities committee

H. W. Wilson company. See Wilson, H. W. company

HAAGG, Gillis
Negative color: this mystery world. il Pop Phot 56:66-7 My '65

HABIT spasms. See Tic

HABITS, Nervous. See Nervous habits

HABITS of animals. See Animals—Habits and behavior

HACK, Margherita
Light elements in stellar atmospheres. il Sky & Tel 29:347-9; 30:9-12 Je-Jl '65

HACKER, Andrew
After the fall. Commentary 40:104+ S '65
College grad has been short-changed. N Y Times Mag p25+ Je 6 '65
Election stories; America. Commentary 40:110+ D '65
Even if they can't read, they should have the vote. N Y Times Mag p26-7+ Ap 18 '65
Pill and morality. N Y Times Mag p32-3+ N 21 '65

HACKER, Harold S.
Urban failures and crises. por Library J 90:2077-9 My 1 '65

HACKETT, Alice Payne
Hardcover best sellers of 1965 in the U.S. book trade. Pub W 189:60-4 Ja 17 '66

HACKETT, Blanche
Be my quest! Recreation 58:115+ Mr '65

HACKETT, Bobby
Jazz concerts; performance in sixth Jazz in the garden concert at the Museum of modern art. W. Balliett. New Yorker 41:68 Jl 31 '65

HACKETT, Robert A.
Harness racing (cont) Sports Illus 23:54 Ag 30 '65

HACKETT, Walter
Great stone face; dramatization of novel by N. Hawthorne. Plays 25:85-94 N '65

HADDAD, William F.
Mr Shriver and the savage politics of poverty. Harper 231:43-50 D '65

HADDON, William, Jr. See Klein, D. jt. auth.

HADEN, James C.
Books in the field: philosophy. bibliog Wilson Lib Bul 40:422-31 Ja '66

HADJ. See Pilgrimages to Mecca

HADLEY, Joseph
Abstract sculpture. Sch Arts 64:12-14 Mr '65

HAEFNER, John H.
News in the classroom. Sat R 49:71 Ja 15 '66

HAFF, Harold
Street cleaning involves more than sweeping. Am City 80:100-1 Jl '65

HAFNER, E. M. and Presswood, Susan
Strong inference and weak interactions. bibliog Science 149:503-10 Jl 30 '65

HAFS, Harold D. See Kirton, K. T. jt. auth.

HAFSTAD, L. R.
Judging research and development payoff. Aviation W 82:21 Ap 19 '65

HAGANS, Josephine F. See Coleman, J. E. jt. auth.

HAGAR, Conger Neblitt
Wondrous birds and a wondrous lady. E. W. Teale. il pors Audubon Mag 67:222-8 Jl '65

HAGE, Elizabeth B.
United planning. Wilson Lib Bul 40:250-1 N '65

HAGEL, Raymond Charles
Hagel asks for independent economic study on copyright. Pub W 188:31 Ag 9 '65

HAGEMAN factor. See Blood—Plasma

HAGEN, Dorothy
In defense of children's books: price, quality, durability; summary of address. Pub W 187:33-4 Mr 15 '65

HAGER, Bengt
Choreographic institute. por Dance Mag 39:14-15 F '65

HAGER, Gus
We vacuum-filter lime softening sludge. por Am City 80:105-7 Je '65

HAGFORS, Tor, and others
Tenuous surface layer on the moon: evidence derived from radar observations. bibliog Science 150:1153-6 N 26 '65

HAGGIN, Bernard H.
New records in review. See issues of Yale review
Records. See issues of New republic

about
Critics' critic. F. V. Grunfeld. Reporter 32:43-4 Je 17 '65

HAGIWARA, Susumu, and Nakajima, Shigehiro
Tetrodotoxin and manganese ion: effects on action potential of the frog heart. bibliog Science 149:1254-5 S 10 '65

HAGUE, The
International court of justice
See International court of justice, The Hague

HAGUE conference on private international law, 1964
Unification of the rules of private international law: report of the U.S. delegation, January 15, 1965. il Dept State Bul 52:265-73 F 22 '65

HAGY, Loleta
Fire in a paper; drama. Plays 24:79-82 My '65

HAHN, Emily
Inner workings of the atom. New Yorker 41:120+ Je 5 '65
Kathy, not me. New Yorker 41:57-62 N 13 '65
Till the well runs dry. New Yorker 41:184+ O 23 '65

HAHN, L. Albert
Keeping the dollar strong; how U.S. can avoid trouble; interview. por U S News 58:78-80 My 31 '65

HAHN, Steven
Private ear for silent TV viewing. Pop Mech 125:196-7 Ja '66

HAHN, Vera D.
Decorating newsletter (cont) Am Home 68:38 Ja; 24 Mr; 22 Ap '65

HAIDER, Michael L.
Businessmen in the news. il por Fortune 71:37 Ap '65
Change at Jersey. por Time 85:86 F 26 '65
Joining the club. Newsweek 65:74 Mr 1 '65

HAIFA, Israel
Sojourn in Haifa. W. Teller. il Atlan 215:132+ My '65

HAILE Selassie I, emperor of Ethiopia
Ethiopia: end of a dark age. C. Miller. il por
Sat R 48:38-9 Ap 10 '65
Lamb in lionskin. S. Meisler. Nation 200:510-
12 My 10 '65

**HAILSHAM, Quintin McGarel Hogg, 2d vis-
count.** See Hogg, Q. M.

HAIMBACH, David
Fresno mall. Am City 80:91-3 Ap '65

**HAIMOFF, Sandra Hirsch, and De La Fuente,
M. P.**
Speech therapy in the secondary school.
NEA J 54:52-3 N '65

HAINAN
Digging in. S. Liu. il Newsweek 66:31 Jl 19 '65

HAIR
Skin. W. Montagna. il Sci Am 212:56-66 bib-
liog(p 134-5) F '65
See also
Baldness
Hairdressing
Wigs

Anecdotes, facetiae, satire, etc.
Negro, Jewish, and Italian hair; bristly reply
to the American barber's most barbarous
complaint. M. Mayer. Harper 231:44-6 Jl '65

Care
Head start on summer. il McCalls 92:90-3+
Je '65
Project: you; how to condition your hair. il
Ladies Home J 82:51 Ag '65
Quick beauty change-over; a pair of easy
hairdos and new makeup tricks. il Good H
160:102-3+ Je '65
We know you're busy, but hair thrives on
simple care. il Good H 160:94-5+ F '65

Dyeing and bleaching
Beauty life: a compendium of hair-coloring
terms. il Mlle 60:102-3+ F '65
Semipermanent hair colorings. Consumer Rep
30:347-51 Jl '65
Temporary hair colorings. il Consumer Rep
30:134-7 Mr '65

HAIR, Removal of
Removing excess hair; questions and answers;
ed. by L. Allen. Todays Health 43:6+ S '65

HAIR curlers
Day of the roller. Time 85:71 Mr 12 '65

HAIR dressing. See Hairdressing

HAIR follicles. See Follicles

HAIR pieces. See Wigs

HAIR preparations
Aerosol hair sprays. il Consumer Bul 48:15-
18 Ag '65

HAIR rollers. See Hair curlers

HAIR sprays. See Hair preparations

HAIRCUTTING
Are home haircuts for your family? B. B.
Smith. il Parents Mag 40:122-3 O '65
Beauty bulletin. il Vogue 146:112-15 Ag 15
'65
London bob. S. Harney. il Ladies Home J
82:82-3 Mr '65
Year of the shears. il Mlle 61:118-21 O '65

HAIRDRESSING
All-American beauty book with twenty-one
lively, new hairdos. il Good H 161:96-107+
N '65
Beauty bulletin. il Vogue 146:198-203 O 1 '65
Beauty life: hairdos, the new movement. il
Mlle 60:100-1 F '65
Beauty life: Mlle guest editors make the
beauty scene. il Mlle 61:272-80+ Ag '65
Beauty life: parties. il Mlle 62:84-7 D '65
Beauty life: the disco dos. il Mlle 60:96-7+
F '65
Beauty life; '30's hair styles right, now. il
Mlle 61:76-81 Jl '65
Big sprout-out of male mop-tops; revolt
against the close-trimmed male haircut. il
Life 59:56-9+ Jl 30 '65
Born curly? born straight? il Redbook 124:
76-7+ Ap '65
Bouffants are out, Beatle cuts are in. il Ebony
20:118-19 F '65
Chic hairdos for fall wear. il Ebony 20:126+
S '65
Day of the roller. Time 85:71 Mr 12 '65
Dear beauty editor; advice to girls who wear
glasses: frame and hairdo. il Seventeen
24:341 Ag '65
Easy, breezy hairdos. il Seventeen 24:132-5
My '65
Eleventh-hour hairstyles; holiday season. il
McCalls 93:122-3 D '65
Frou frou curls. il Good H 161:92-3 D '65
Groovy Beatle-type man is an Arthur. D.
McCabe. il Mlle 62:180-1 N '65
Hair style you can wear three ways. L. D.
Kirk. il Parents Mag 40:76 Ap '65

Hair! teen-agers' hair fashions. A. Glaser.
il Esquire 64:36-7+ Jl '65
Hairdo of the month. See issues of Seventeen
Hairstyles and settings. il McCalls 92:160-1
Je '65
I wish, I wish, I wish. il Seventeen 25:70-
5+ Ja '66
Ironing hair fad. J. Shepherd. il Look 29:
104+ Ap 20 '65
Jewelry touches. il Good H 161:94-5 D '65
Keeping the hair up; creative hairdressers.
il Time 86:56 D 31 '65
Let's take a short cut. il Ebony 20:120-2
Jl '65
Mad, mad world of coifs. il Ebony 20:171-2
Ap '65
New fall hair styles. il Redbook 125:66-73+ S
'65
Night-blooming coiffures. il McCalls 92:82-5
S '65
No time for beauty; hairdos for Joanne
Smerdon's round-the-world trip. il McCalls
93:80-1+ Ja '66
Popular guiche curl. il Ebony 20:130-1 Mr
'65
Project: you; successful set. il Ladies Home J
82:48 My '65
Rockwell and rollers; with painting by N.
Rockwell. Look 30:34-5 Ja 11 '66
Sassoon and his scissors. il Life 59:67-8 Jl
9 '65
Seven ways to stay feminine afloat. H. Ham.
il Motor B 116:110 Jl '65
Short & the long of it; boys' hairdos. il Time
86:54 O 1 '65
Shortcut summer. S. Harney. il Ladies
Home J 82:44+ My '65
Slimming hair styles. il Ebony 20:149-50 Je
'65
Soft new curlier hairdos look ahead now to
fall. il Good H 161:76-9+ Ag '65
Speaking out; keep out of my kids' hair.
B. J. Friedman. il Sat Eve Post 239:6+ Ja
15 '66
Spirited styles for spring. il Ebony 20:181-2
My '65
Splitting hairs over moptops; or, How lunatic
is the fringe? il Sr Schol 87:20 O 14 '65
Spring makeup magic & twenty-one hit hair-
dos. il Good H 160:104-13+ Ap '65
Twenty years of hair styling. il Ebony 21:
205-6+ N '65
Unkindest cut for student moptops. Life
59:4 S 24 '65
Untampered look. il Ebony 20:144-6 O '65
Vogue's eye view: the Paris idea of the small
head. il Vogue 146:83 S 15 '65
Whole pretty new look in just two hours!
il Seventeen 24:158-9 S '65
Yearbook of hairdos. il Seventeen 24:208-11+
Ag '65

Anecdotes, facetiae, satire, etc.
Tyranny of hairdressers and fashion designers. M. Mannes. McCalls 93:34+ Ja '66

HAIRPIECES. See Wigs

HAITI
Crushing a country. il Time 86:25 Ag 27 '65
Emperor Duvalier? Newsweek 65:49 Mr 29 '65
Haiti: hatred without hope. H. Gold. il Sat
Eve Post 238:74-6+ Ap 24 '65
Haunted Haiti. H. Gold. il Holiday 37:64-9
Mr '65

Politics and government
Nightmare. il Newsweek 65:34+ My 31 '65

HAITIAN pottery. See Pottery, Haitian

HAITIANS
Haiti: hatred without hope. H. Gold. il Sat
Eve Post 238:74-6+ Ap 24 '65

HAJJ. See Pilgrimages to Mecca

HALABY, Najeeb E.
Jet-age expert gives some blunt answers:
interview, ed. by B. Kocivar. por Look 29:
50+ D 14 '65
Perspicacity for Pan Am. il por Newsweek
66:82 S 27 '65

HALACY, D. S. Jr
Myo-electricity; the transistorized man. Pop
Electr 22:41-4+ F '65
New survival technique: get water anywhere.
Outdoor Life 136:14-15+ Ag '65

HALBERSTAM, David
Face of the enemy in Vietnam; excerpts
from Making of a quagmire. Harper 230:62-
4+ F '65
about
Pole ax. Newsweek 67:42 Ja 10 '66

HALE, Dennis. See McWilliams, W. C. jt.
auth.

HALE, Nancy
Age for action; story. Ladies Home J 82:92-3
Mr '65
Between the dark and the daylight; story.
Parents Mag 40:62-3 O '65
Eyes and no eyes; or the art of seeing. New
Yorker 41:52-9 N 20 '65
Fiction writer faces facts. Sat R 48:23-5+
Je 12 '65
My mother's solitudes. New Yorker 41:38-42
Mr 6 '65
Sunday lunch; story. New Yorker 41:44-9 My
8 '65
HALE, Richard W. Jr
Methods of research for the amateur his-
torian. Hobbies 70:110-12+ Ag '65
HALE, S. Dennis
I saw a Negro sin in Selma; poem. Christian
Cent 82:576 My 5 '65
HALE, Sarah Josepha (Buell)
Sarah Josepha Hale. C. W. Ferguson. por
PTA Mag 60:10-12 Ja '66
HALEAKALA
Notes for a gazetteer. P. Hamburger. New
Yorker 41:172-4 S 18 '65
HALF a sixpence; musical comedy. See Musical
comedies, revues, etc.—Criticisms, plots,
etc.
HALF-frame cameras. See Cameras
HALFORD, Russ
Nakamura and his nudes. U S Camera 28:
48-9+ D '65
HALIBUT POINT, Mass.
Collect shells at Halibut Point. A. G. Melvin.
il Hobbies 70:130 Jl '65
HALITOSIS
What causes bad breath? il Good H 162:139
Ja '66
HALL, A. Rupert
Books (cont) Sci Am 212:125-6+ F '65
HALL, Albert G.
Washington lookout. See issues of American
forests
HALL, Anna C.
Language for librarians. Library J 90:3177-8
Ag '65
HALL, Sir Arnold
Who's who in foreign business. por Fortune
71:56 Ap '65
HALL, Clarence W.
Is religion banned from our schools? Read
Digest 86:49-54 F '65
Neighbors to all the world. Read Digest 87:
127-32 Ag '65
Samoa: America's showplace of the South
Seas. Read Digest 87:157-64+ N '65
To get the most out of the New York world's
fair. Read Digest 86:186-8+ My '65
Where shall we build the new canal? Read
Digest 87:213-14+ S '65
HALL, David
Dave Hall, the man who put the pink in iris.
E. J. Purcell. il por Flower Grower 52:17-18
Jl '65
Master of pink is ninety. E. J. Purcell and
J. E. Dwyer. il por Pop Gard 16:21+ Jl '65
HALL, Donald
Fifty-dollar bill. Esquire 63:106 F '65
Mr Schwartz; story. Esquire 64:88 O '65
Profiles; H. S. Moore. New Yorker 41:66-8+
D 11; 59-60+ D 18 '65
(ed) See Moore, M. Interview with Marianne
Moore
about
Three poets. M. McCloskey. Poetry 107:125 N
'65
HALL, Edward T.
Territorial needs and limits. Natur Hist 74:
12-19 bibliog(p66) D '65
HALL, Edwin H.
Amateur scientist. E. D. Sisson. il Sci Am
213:106-10 Jl '65
HALL, Elizabeth C.
Books for holiday giving. Pop Gard 16:10-
11+ N '65
HALL, Elvajean
Got anything new on Russia? bibliog por
Library J 90:5041-2+ N 15 '65
HALL, F. G.
Hemoglobin and oxygen: affinities in seven
species of sciuridae. bibliog Science 148:
1350-1 Je 4 '65
HALL, Floyd D.
Eastern's aloft again. por Bsns W p56-8+
Mr 13 '65
Sunrise at Eastern. il por Newsweek 65:
76+ Mr 15 '65
HALL, Frances
Changing generation; poem. America 112:
320 Mr 6 '65
Exuberance of shoes; poem. America 113:207
Ag 28 '65
Mountain people; poem. Commonweal 82:116
Ap 16 '65

HALL, George Bret
Verbal acrobatics. Christian Cent 82:1038-9
Ag 25 '65
HALL, George F.
Gaucho Jesus. Christian Cent 82:1419 N 17
'65
HALL, Granville Stanley
Editor's bookshelf. P. Woodring. il Sat R
48:92 O 16 '65
HALL, H. Tracy
Periodic compounds: syntheses at high pres-
sures and temperatures. bibliog Science
148:1331-3 Je 4 '65
—See Evenson, W. E. jt. auth.
HALL, J. Floyd
How Evanston passed its bond issue. por
NEA J 54:42-4 D '65
HALL, James B.
Motorcycle racing: the hot-shoe hotshots.
Holiday 38:142+ N '65
HALL, John A.
Atoms for peace, or war. For Affairs 43:602-15
Jl '65
HALL, Joseph B.
Making ideas flow; interview. pors Nations
Bsns 53:41-2+ S '65
HALL, Joyce Clyde
Photography on Fifth avenue. J. Durniak. il
Pop Phot 57:54 Jl '65
Sponsor who cares. por Newsweek 66:64 N 1
'65
HALL, Lee
Echo of his V anthem. Life 58:65-6+ F 5 '65
Garlic curtain cuts off the rock. Life 59:R2+
O 8 '65
Incident on a road, a Pakistani in chains.
Life 59:44B S 17 '65
Riches won close to the horns. Life 59:68
Ag 6 '65
HALL, Leonard Wood
What's wrong with us? por Time 85:24-5 Ap
2 '65
about
Hall appointed to commission. Nat Parks
Mag 39:20 Ag '65
HALL, Maybelle F.
How to succeed without really cleaning. Mc-
Calls 92:118-19 My '65
HALL, Nason E. Jr
Saving the trouble-prone. NEA J 54:26-8 Ap
'65
HALL, Peter
Other side; thwarted attempt to present
Schönberg's Moses and Aaron at the Royal
opera house. T. Heinitz. Sat R 48:43 Jl
31 '65
HALL, Richard L.
What to do with a highway borrow pit.
Farm J 89:60B My '65
HALL, Robert E.
Right to be well born. PTA Mag 60:13 Ja '66
HALL, Ruth T.
How to use a multiple textbook approach
in junior high social studies classes. Sr
Schol 87:sup 19 N 18 '65
HALL, William M.
Hidden persuaders. Am For 71:54-7 My '65
HALL, Willis. See Waterhouse, K. jt. auth.
HALL effect
Amateur scientist; semiconducting Hall de-
vice. E. D. Sisson. il Sci Am 213:106-10
Jl '65
HALL of fame, Cowboy. See National cowboy
hall of fame and western heritage center
HALL of science. See New York (city)—Worlds
fair, 1964-1965—Hall of science
HALLBERG, Ronald C.
Recreation afloat. Recreation 58:439-42 N '65
HALLE, Louis J.
Acheson: birth of a statesman. New Repub
153:23-4+ N 13 '65
Our war aims were wrong. N Y Times Mag
p 12-13+ Ag 22 '65
HALLER, John M.
Now's the time to save your split trees.
Pop Sci 187:148-9 O '65
HALLESY, D. W. See Layton, W. M. jr, jt.
auth.
HALLET, Jean-Pierre
Profit and loss on safari; ed. by A. Pelle.
Esquire 64:47-8+ S '65
HALLIBURTON, Richard
Halliburton: the magnificent myth, by J.
Root. Review
Newsweek il por 66:102-3 N 29 '65
HALLIDAY, Ian
Possible occultation by the planet Pluto. Sky
& Tel 29:216-17 Ap '65
HALLIDAY, Patrick
European semiconductor code. Electr World
74:62 Ag '65
Sea stations for aircraft V.H.F. coverage.
Electr World 74:36+ O '65

HALLIDAY, Russell
Halliday rides crest of demand for offset book printing. il por Pub W 188:106-8+ S 6 '65
HALLIDAY, William R.
Conservation and American caves. il Nat Parks Mag 39:17-19 D '65
HALLIDAY lithograph corporation
Halliday rides crest of demand for offset book printing. il Pub W 188:106-8+ S 6 '65
HALLINAN, Paul John, abp
One world, one word. America 113:202-4 Ag 28 '65
HALLMARK cards, Incorporated
Hallmark sells the gifts, as well as the cards. il Bsns W p 144-6 O 23 '65
HALLMARK gift shops. See Gift shops
HALLOWEEN
Stop those Halloween hollows! Halloween program, White Plains, N.Y. D. Shaw. il Recreation 58:397-8 O '65
They scare up pennies: UNICEF trick or treat program celebrates fifteenth anniversary. Recreation 58:398 O '65

Drama
Magic pumpkin patch. E. M. Thomas. Plays 25:73-8 O '65
Witch in the golden hat. F. B. Watts. Plays 25:68-72, 86 O '65
HALLS
Decorating wrongs made right. il Bet Hom & Gard 43:42 O '65
HALLSTEIN, Walter
European economic community; address, December 4, 1964. Vital Speeches 31:331-7 Mr 15 '65
European economy and European policy; address, July 8, 1965. Vital Speeches 31:654-8 Ag 15 '65
True problems of European integration; address, February 19, 1965. Vital Speeches 31: 459-67 My 15 '65
—See Johnson, L. B. jt. auth.

about
Supranational stall. Time 86:31 Jl 16 '65
HALLUCINATIONS. See Illusions and hallucinations
HALLUCINOGENIC drugs
Drug puzzle; student use of drugs. M. Herr. Mlle 61:246-7+ Ag '65
Drugs studied to aid astronauts. il Miss & Roc 16:33 Mr 15 '65
See also
Lysergic acid diethylamide
HALOID company. See Xerox corporation
HALPER, Nathan
Joyce and Eliot: a tale of Shem & Shaun. Nation 200:590-5 My 31 '65
HALPERIN, Ernst
Decline of communism in Latin America. Atlan 215:65-70 My '65
HALPERIN, Walter, and Wetherell, D. F.
Ontogeny of adventive embryos of wild carrot. bibliog Science 147:756-8 F 12 '65
HALPERN, Burton M.
New exodus: Israel's talent drain. Nation 200:497-9 My 10 '65
HALPERN, Manfred
Rate and costs of political development. bibliog f Ann Am Acad 358:20-8 Mr '65
HALPERT, Edith Gregor
I had the wild guys. por Newsweek 66:94+ S 20 '65
HALPRIN, Ann
Parades and changes, scandal and delight. R. Hartley. il pors Dance Mag 39:50-1+ O '65
HALSBAND, Robert
Man who wrote his mind. Sat R 48:46 N 13 '65
HALSEY, Elizabeth, and Porter, Lorena
Outdoor play areas; excerpts from Physical education for children. Recreation 58:189-90 Ap '65
HALSEY, Margaret
White papers and Negro readers. New Repub 153:18-20 O 16 '65
HALSEY, William D.
Your encyclopedia: tool for teaching research skills. Sr Schol 86:sup9 My 6 '65
HALSMAN, Philippe
Marilyn Monroe. il Pop Phot 58:109+ Ja '66

about
Creating surprise out of commonplace elements. R. Hattersley. il Pop Phot 56:74-5+ Ap '65
Philippe Halsman. L. Barry. il pors Pop Phot 56:47-9+ F '65
HALTRECHT, E. J. See McCormack, P. D. jt. auth.

HALYARD, Dianne
English sparrows with American accents. Audubon Mag 67:178-9 My '65
HAM, Clifford C.
Urban renewal: a case study in emerging goals in an intergovernmental setting. bibliog f Ann Am Acad 359:44-52 My '65
HAM, Helen
Seven ways to stay feminine afloat. Motor B 116:110 Jl '65
HAM, Lee
Wrested from the bay. Am City 80:102-3 Ag '65
HAM
See also
Cookery—Meat
HAM, Canned. See Meat, Canned
HAM radio stations. See Radio stations, Amateur
HAMADA, Shōji
Shoji Hamada. A. R. Park. bibliog il pors Sch Arts 64:23-7 Je '65
HAMANI, Diori
Assassination that failed. G. Comte. Nat R 17:509-10 Je 15 '65
HAMBLETONIAN race. See Harness racing
HAMBLIN, Dora Jane
Bigamy Italian style. Life 59:52A-52B Jl 23 '65
Everybody sure glad. por Life 58:69-70+ My 21 '65
Her honor bops the hoodlums. Life 59:74+ Jl 9 '65
Life movie review (cont) Life 58:10 Ap 9 '65
She puts the oomph in the opera. Life 58: 77-8+ Mr 5 '65
HAMBURG
Music
Ghiaurov's Moses, Karajan's Bohème. W. Legge. Hi Fi 15:160-1 S '65
Notes from our correspondents. K. Blaukopf. Hi Fi 15:20 Je '65
HAMBURGER, Philip
Notes for a gazetteer. See occasional issues of New Yorker to September 18, 1965
HAMBURGER stands. See Drive-in and curb services
HAMBURGER steak. See Cookery—Meat
HAMBURGERS. See Cookery—Meat
HAMER, Elizabeth E. and McCormick, Adoreen
Washington report: from the Library of Congress. See issues of ALA bulletin
HAMILL, Harold L.
Numbers game. por Library J 90:3563-7 S 15 '65
HAMILL, Katharine
Enchantment in the Louisiana marshes. Fortune 72:158-64 O '65
HAMILL, Pete
Brigitte Bardot: no place left to hide. Sat Eve Post 238:40-2+ My 8 '65
Heston: larger than life. Sat Eve Post 238:87-91 Jl 3 '65
—and Weber, David
I'm just an ordinary girl. Sat Eve Post 238: 91-7 S 25 '65
HAMILL, Robert H.
Christmas after Christmas. Christian Cent 82:1486-7 D 1 '65
HAMILTON, Alexander
Fatherly sedition. C. Kenyon. Nation 200:172-6 F 15 '65
HAMILTON, Alice
Edith and Alice Hamilton: students in Germany. Atlan 215:129-32 Mr '65
HAMILTON, Andrew
Cotton candy from Congress. New Repub 153:9-10 O 9; 37-8 N 20 '65
HAMILTON, Andrew Jackson
Here come the tutors! PTA Mag 60:7-9 D '65
How to cope with cold weather. Sci Digest 58:56-60 D '65
Matter of a piñon. Am For 71:60-1+ My '65
New science of supercold. Sci Digest 58:71-4 S '65
Report on DMSO. Sci Digest 58:78-82 Ag '65
Scientific secrets of fitness. Sci Digest 58: 60-5 Jl '65
What science knows about dolphin talk. Sci Digest 57:9-13 My '65
What we're learning about tides in the earth. Sci Digest 58:55-8 N '65
HAMILTON, Charles
From Jackie to Lady Bird. il por U S News 58:10-11 My 31 '65
HAMILTON, Charles, autographs, Incorporated
Missive that went astray; Jackie Kennedy's invitation to Lady Bird Johnson removed from auction. il Time 85:70 My 28 '65
HAMILTON, Clive, pseud. See Lewis, C. S.

HAMILTON, D. Lee
Non-western studies in liberal arts colleges. Sch & Soc 93:244+ Ap 17 '65

HAMILTON, Edith
Edith and Alice Hamilton: students in Germany. A. Hamilton. il Atlan 215:129-32 Mr '65

HAMILTON, George Heard
Gift of art: from the Greeks to the vanguard. Sat R 48:60+ D 4 '65
Life and art in bits and pieces. Sat R 48:38 N 27 '65

HAMILTON, Hamish, limited
Thomson organization buys Hamish Hamilton, ltd. Pub W 188:33 N 29 '65

HAMILTON, Harry
Washington front (cont) America 112:874 Je 19 '65

HAMILTON, Karen
Come take my hand. Seventeen 24:98-9+ D '65

HAMILTON, Richard F.
Conviction or convenience; the trap of the Great society. Nation 201:384-7 N 22 '65
Touch of tyranny. Nation 201:75-8 Ag 16 '65

HAMILTON, Robert
Guardian angel of the air well. Read Digest 88:95-8 Ja '66

HAMILTON, T. R.
Photoplasts and L-forms. Science 147:635-6+ F 5 '65

HAMILTON, William
Faith and the facts of life. Nation 200:424-6 Ap 19 '65
Shape of a radical theology. Christian Cent 82:1219-22 O 6 '65

HAMILTON, Ohio
How to attract industry. C. R. Lukens. il Am City 80:104-5 Ag '65

HAMILTON, beach division. See Scovill manufacturing company—Hamilton beach division

HAMILTON watch company
Rolling mill in miniature with a jeweler's touch. il Bsns W p 128-30 D 18 '65

HAMISH Hamilton, limited. See Hamilton, Hamish, limited

HAMLIN, Arthur T.
Signs are propitious: the current library scene in France. por Library J 90:2081-6 My 1 '65
Visiting bookmen in France. por ALA Bul 59:815-18 O '65

HAMLIN, Fred
Six rules for selling to the trade journals. Writer 78:26-7 N '65

HAMLIN, G. Homer, and Bautista, Jose
On-the-spot tests check gutter capacity. Am City 80:94-6 Ap '65

HAMLIN, Roy M. Jr, and others
Hydrogen-bonded dimers of adenine and uracil derivatives. bibliog Science 148:1734-7 Je 25 '65

HAMM, Marie Roberson
Memorable breakfasts. Parents Mag 40:71+ S '65

HAMMARSKJÖLD, Dag
Markings: excerpts from the diary of Dag Hammarskjöld. por Read Digest 86:84-6 Mr '65

about
Inner legislation. W. Stafford. Poetry 106: 356-8 Ag '65
Legacy of Dag Hammarskjöld. L. Paffrath. por Sat R 48:32-3+ Jl 24 '65
On reading Hammarskjöld. M. Ascoli. il por Reporter 32:38-40 My 20 '65
Other Hammarskjöld; posthumous publication of D. Hammarskjöld's Markings. L. Hines. Commonweal 81:606-8 F 5 '65
Spirit of holiness in men of power. Life 58:4 Ap 16 '65

HAMMEL, Lisa
Home. N Y Times Mag p30-1 Jl 18; 122-3 D 5 '65

HAMMER, Willis, Jr
Growing up on a farm. J. Star. il pors Look 29:109-14+ Je 15 '65

HAMMETT, Dashiell
Novels of Dashiell Hammett, ed. by L. Hellman. Review
New Repub 154:32-4 Ja 8 '66. L. Moss

HAMMING, R. W.
Numerical analysis vs. mathematics; address, December 29, 1964. Science 148:473-5; 149:245 Ap 23, Jl 16 '65

HAMMOND, Robert P.
Orchids for profit. Pop Gard 16:24-5 N '65

HAMPSHIRE college
Dream college; estimated opening date, September 1968. Newsweek 66:58 Ag 16 '65
New prestige college to open September 1969. Sat R 48:74 S 11 '65
School with four parents. il Time 86:49 Ag 13 '65

HAMPTON, John K. Jr, and Hampton, S. H.
Marmosets (hapiladae): breeding seasons, twinning, and sex of offspring. bibliog Science 150:915-17 N 12 '65

HAMPTON, Suzanne H. See Hampton, J. K. jr, jt. auth.

HAMS (radio) See Radio operators, Amateur

HANAYAGI, Suzushi
Japanese classical dance. Fashion institute of technology. M. Marks. Dance Mag 39:66 Je '65

HANBURY family
Hanbury coat-of-arms. H. K. Eilers. il Hobbies 70:126 Ap '65

HANCOCK, Alice V.
Gourd surprise. il Flower Grower 52:42+ Ap '65
Your gourds can give many surprises. il Flower Grower 52:14-15 O '65

HANCOCK, James
African pink-backed pelican. Natur Hist 74: 24-9 bibliog(p70) My '65

HANCOCK, Ronald. See Ryser, H. J.-P. jt. auth.

HAND, Ann
Lloyd Hand, the new U.S. protocol chief and his wife. il pors Life 58:70-3 Mr 12 '65
Mr & Mrs protocol. il por Time 85:49 Mr 5 '65

HAND, G. Othell
Church as it appears today; address, November 16, 1965. Vital Speeches 32:143-5 D 15 '65

HAND, Jackson
Boat finishes. Pop Sci 186:100-3 Mr '65
Fast-set glue gun for the home. Pop Sci 187:154-5 D '65
Interior clear finishes. Pop Sci 186:168-70 F '65
Let electricity ease your hard work. Pop Sci 187:60-3 Jl '65
Masonry finishes. Pop Sci 187:128-30 Jl '65
Metal finishes. Pop Sci 187:142-4 Ag '65
Shopping for a suburban tractor. Pop Sci 186:154-7+ Mr '65
That new flying lawn mower. Pop Sci 186: 171+ Ap '65
Three steps to installing ceramic tile anywhere. Pop Sci 187:144-7+ S '65

HAND, Lloyd Nelson
How ya gonna keep 'em down in Upper Volta after they've met Lloyd Hand? E. Wittenberg. Esquire 64:24+ D '65
Lloyd Hand, the new U.S. protocol chief and his wife. il por Life 58:70-3 Mr 12 '65
Mr & Mrs protocol. il por Time 85:49 Mr 5 '65

HAND
House of hands; rehabilitation center at Chapel Hill, N.C. il Life 58:113-14 Mr 19 '65
Housewife and her hands. E. W. Rauschkolb. il Todays Health 44:58-60 Ja '66

Surgery
Renewed hope for a special pair of hands; K. Venturi recovering from surgery at Mayo clinic. G. Crozier. il Sports Illus 23: 48-50 Jl 12 '65

HAND bells. See Bells

HAND loaded bullets. See Bullets

HAND railings
Banisters in teak and oak. il Sunset 135:118 O '65

HAND tools. See Tools

HANDBAGS
Well-stocked handbag. McCalls 93:206 N '65
Your pick of fall purses. il Good H 161:260 N '65

HÄNDEL, Georg Friedrich
Eternal Handel. H. Weinstock. Sat R 48:60 Ap 24 '65
Julius Caesar. Criticism
Opera N 30:26 S 25 '65
Opera N 30:31 Ja 1 '66
Time il 85:44 Je 4 '65
Messiah, two new versions. J. Diether. il Am Rec G 32:306-8 D '65
New York: Amor artis chorale and orchestra present Semele. E. R. Rizzo. Opera N 30: 31 Ja 1 '66
On records; Messiah. Opera N 30:34 D 11 '65
On records; Rodelinda. Opera N 29:34 Mr 6 '65
Serse. J. W. Barker. Am Rec G 32:374-5 D '65
Two feasts: Alexander's, Belshazzar's. J. W. Barker. il Am Rec G 31:616-20 Mr '65

HANDEL and Haydn society
Subduing the passions: 150th birthday. Newsweek 66:89-90 N 1 '65

HANDGUNS. See Pistols

HANDICAPPED
Handicapped girl; questions and answers. A. Wood. il Seventeen 24:102-3 D '65
These clothes are easy to put on. V. Odell. il Farm J 89:80-1 S '65
See also
Children, Handicapped
Mentally handicapped
Recreation for the handicapped

Apparatus and appliances
Housekeeping on wheels. D. Liston. il Todays Health 43:62-6+ My '65
Telephones for the deaf; reprint. G. M. Smith. il Sci Digest 57:55-9 My '65
See also
Automobiles for the disabled

Rehabilitation
See Rehabilitation

HANDICRAFT
Arts & crafts corner (cont) il Recreation 58: 257, 291, 350, 455, My-S, N '65
Fast fast fast ideas; meals, crafts, outdoor projects, decorating. il Bet Hom & Gard 43:50-75 Jl '65
You just paint faces on rocks. il Sunset 135: 120+ O '65
See also
Christmas projects
Shellwork

HANDKERCHIEFS
Elegant handkerchief. A. W. Murray. il Antiques 87:720-3 Je '65

HANDLER, Philip
National planning for medical research; adaptation of address, March 1, 1965. bibliog Science 148:1688-92 Je 25 '65

HANDLES (machines, tools, etc)
How to hang an axe. il Pop Sci 187:132 Ag '65

HANDLIN, Oscar
Americanizing our immigration laws. Holiday 39:8+ Ja '66
Making the most of leisure. Parents Mag 40:60-1+ Je '65
Reader's choice. por Atlan 216:166+ O '65

HANDLING of feed. See Feed handling

HANDMADE paper. See Paper making and trade

HANDSCREWS. See Screws

HANDWRITING. See Autographs

HANDY, Robert T.
Father Hecker, a bridge between Catholic and Protestant thought. Cath World 202: 158-9+ D '65

HANES, Ralph P.
Old Salem. Antiques 88:99 Jl '65

HANFORD works, Richland, Wash.
Town that wouldn't stay down; Richland, Wash, and its sister cities. il U S News 59: 96-7 Jl 19 '65

HANGEN, Welles
Stirrings behind the wall: East Germany's muted revolution. Harper 230:77-83 My '65

HANGERS, Clothes. See Clothes hangers

HANGING
Britain abolishes the hangman's job. U S News 59:16 N 8 '65

HANGING of pictures. See Pictures, Hanging of

HANGINGS, Wall. See Wall hangings

HANLEY, Clifford
Kilt complex. Horizon 7:30-1 Sum '65

HANLEY, Frank
Subject is houses. il Am Artist 30:66-9+ Ja '66

HANLEY, James
Say nothing. Criticism
New Yorker 40:94+ F 6 '65

HANLEY, Wayne
Nature's ways. Recreation 58:271 Je '65

HANLEY, William
Mrs Daily. Criticism
America 113:508 O 30 '65
Commonweal 83:61-2 O 15 '65
New Yorker 41:176 O 2 '65
Newsweek il 66:94 O 4 '65
Sat R 48:34 O 9 '65
Time il 86:67 O 1 '65
Slow dance on the killing ground. Criticism
America 112:231-2 F 13 '65
Reporter 32:50-1 F 11 '65

HANLON, V. T.
Coal dusting saves a lake. Outdoor Life 137: 10-11+ Ja '66

HANNA, M. A, company
Consol, Hanna sell-offs stun Street. il Bsns W p 166+ O 16 '65

HANNA mining company
Brazil: Hanna's immovable mountains. il Fortune 71:55-6+ Ap '65

HANNAN, Cecil J.
Teachers, a political force. NEA J 54:49 N '65

HANNAN, Philip Matthew, abp
Letter from the council. R. E. Tracy. America 113:432-3 O 16 '65

HANNIGAN, Ed
As I see it. See issues of U.S. camera & travel
Photo schools. U S Camera 28:56-9+ S '65

HANNON, Leslie
When royalty goes go-go; keeping up with the Armstrong-Joneses. Ladies Home J 82: 60-1+ S '65

HANNON, Michael
Chief Parker and company. Christian Cent 82:1308-9 O 27 '65
Odd cop out. por Newsweek 65:30+ Je 21 '65
One for the courts. Christian Cent 82:981 Ag 11 '65
Two good cops in bad trouble. S. Alexander. Life 59:16 Jl 30 '65

HANO, Arnold
Battle of the Grand Canyon. N Y Times Mag p56-7+ D 12 '65
John Wayne. Good H 161:82-3+ O '65
Julie Andrews: her magic, her moods. Good H 160:90-3+ My '65
TV's topmost, this is America. N Y Times Mag p 10-11+ D 26 '65

HANOI, Vietnam (Democratic Republic)
Is Hanoi another Havana for Soviets? question of SAM missile installations. il U S News 58:6 Ap 26 '65
Vietnam: a matter of interpretation; missile sites near Hanoi. il Newsweek 65:37-8 Ap 26 '65

HANS Syz collection. See Smithsonian institution—Museum of history and technology

HANSBERGER, Robert Vail
It's grow or die at Boise Cascade. T. Alexander. il por Fortune 72:180-3+ D '65

HANSBERRY, Lorraine
Sign in Sidney Brustein's window. Criticism
Nat R 17:250 Mr 23 '65

HANSBERRY, William Leo, and Johnson, E. H.
Africa's golden past (cont) Ebony 20:62-5+ F; 70-2+ Mr; 136-7+ Ap '65

HANSBURY, Edward B.
How to make perfect slide captions. R. Miller. il U S Camera 28:24-5 Ap '65

HANSEL and Gretel; drama. See Thane, A.

HANSEN, Gerald L.
Operation of a high-quality CCTV camera. Electr World 74:44-7+ D '65

HANSEN, Harry
First to speak for freedom. Sat R 48:81-2 My 22 '65
Old vision of a new South. Sat R 48:42-3 Ap 10 '65

HANSEN, John
How to buy a projection screen. Pop Sci 186:116-19+ Mr '65

HANSEN, Joseph J.
Case of the punctilious president. Harvard Bsns R 43:160-3+ N '65

HANSEN, Paul E.
Flying photographer. il Flying 77:122-3 N '65

HANSEN, Robert J.
Trains at 300 mph, what travel of future will be like; interview. por U S News 59:96-9 Jl 26 '65

HANSEN, Robert W.
Time of many fevers; address, June 10, 1965. Vital Speeches 31:603-5 Jl 15 '65

HANSEN, Woods
Success marks Thiokol 156-in. solid firing. Aviation W 82:22 Mr 8 '65

HANSEN'S disease. See Leprosy and lepers

HAN-shan
Out of China. A. Fang. Poetry 107:196-9 D '65

HANSHAW, Bruce B, and others
Radiocarbon determinations for estimating groundwater flow velocities in central Florida. bibliog Science 148:494-5 Ap 23 '65

HANSON, Carroll
First hundred years. Sat R 48:82-3 Ap 17 '65

HANSON, Dick
Across the editor's desk. See issues of Successful farming

HANSON, Earl Parker
New conquistadors in the Amazon jungle. Américas 17:1-8 S '65

HANSON, Jack
He shows you the girl; interview, ed. by M. Byers. pors Life 59:55-6+ O 8 '65

HANSON, John W. and Brembeck, C. S.
Toward a theory of education for development; excerpts from Education and the development of nations. Sch & Soc 93:499-502 D 25 '65

HANSON, Norwood Russell
Galileo's discoveries in dynamics; adaptation of address, September 10, 1964. bibliog Science 147:471-8; 149:1049 Ja 29, S 3 '65

HANSON, Pauline
We meet; poem. Poetry 106:388-93 S '65
HANSON, Wallace
Instant movies ahead? Pop Phot 58:38+ Ja '66
HAPGOOD, Robert
Stratford: a theatre in search of itself. Reporter 33:37-9 S 9 '65
HAPPER, Mary
Deed of friendship. Newsweek 65:30 Ap 26 '65
HAPPINESS
Ingredients of happiness. P. Brock. il Sci Digest 58:83-5 S '65
Overtaken by joy. A. Whitman. Read Digest 86:105-9 Ap '65
Riley's route to the eternal now. W. Amos. Read Digest 86:227-8+ F '65
True meaning of comfort. F. Du Plessix. House & Gard 128:192-3 O '65
Who's happy and why. J. Brothers. Good H 161:28+ S '65
HAPPINESS, Philosophy of. See Hedonism
HAPPY anniversary, darling; story. See Speas, J.C.
HAPPY days; drama. See Beckett, S.
HAPPY ending; drama. See Ward, D. T.
HAPTENS
Genetic control in guinea pigs of immune response to conjugates of haptens and poly-L-lysine. B. B. Levine and B. Benacerraf. bibliog il Science 147:517-18 Ja 29 '65
HAPWORTH 16, 1924; story. See Salinger, J.D.
HARA, Teruo
Teruo Hara. J. Eagle. il por Craft Horiz 25:32-4 Jl '65
HARA, Toshiaki J. and others
Electroencephalographic studies of homing salmon. bibliog Science 149:884-5 Ag 20 '65
HARABIN, Joseph
Report from Cape Kennedy. pors Seventeen 25:88-9+ Ja '66
HARARI, Manya
(tr) See Tertz, A. Makepeace experiment
HARAYDA, Marei
Discovering materials for the retarded. il Sr Schol 86:sup 10-11 My 6 '65
HARBERT, Ruth
Movie report. See issues of Good housekeeping
HARBORS
Harbor recreation; Huntington, Long Island, N.Y. F. Bickman. il Recreation 58:272-3 Je '65
See also
Ports
HARBUTT, Charles
Restless wind; photographs. Sat Eve Post 239:18-23 Ja 1 '66
HARCOURT, Brace and World, Incorporated
Harcourt launches awards for exceptional service. il Pub W 188:36 N 1 '65
On-the-spot picture sources. il Pub W 188:104-5 N 8 '65
HARDENING of the arteries. See Arteriosclerosis
HARDESTY, Nancy
Waiting for God. Christian Cent 82:683 My 26 '65
HARDINESS in plants. See Plants—Hardiness
HARDING, Florence (Kling) De Wolfe
Harding papers: how some were burned; and some were saved. K. W. Duckett; F. Russell. il Am Heritage 16:24-31+ F '65
HARDING, H. F.
LBJ for the USA; address, December 28, 1964. Vital Speeches 31:249-51 F 1 '65
HARDING, Vincent
Make mine light, please; poem. Christian Cent 82:959 Ag 4 '65
Other roads from Selma. Christian Cent 82:580-1 My 5 '65
HARDING, Warren Gamaliel
Available man, by A. Sinclair. Review
Nat R il por 17:336-8 Ap 20 '65. F. Russell
Sat R 48:43 Je 12 '65. L. W. Koenig
Harding letters: this case and library censorship. E. J. Gaines. ALA Bul 59:343-4 My '65
Harding papers: how some were burned; and some were saved. K. W. Duckett; F. Russell. il pors Am Heritage 16:24-31+ F '65
Tempest over Teapot. B. Bliven. il Am Heritage 16:20-3+ Ag '65
Twenty-ninth President 1921-1923. F. Freidel. il pors Nat Geog Mag 128:562-5 O '65
HARDMAN, William J. Jr
Medics who moonlight. R. H. Berg. il pors Look 29:28-32+ F 9 '65
HARDON, John A.
Book reviews. America 113:502+ O 30 '65
His wit against the wicked. Sat R 48:88-9 My 22 '65

HARDWARE
See also
Household appliances
HARDWICK, Bill
Poor man's tour begins to strike it rich. J. Jares. il por Sports Illus 22:112-14 Ap 19 '65
HARDWICK, Elizabeth
Movies (cont) Vogue 145:61 Mr 15; 57 Ap 15; 69 Je; 146:51 Ag 1; 52 Ag 15 '65
HARDWOOD flooring. See Flooring
HARDY, Thomas
Day with Jude the obscure. Elton. Horizon 7:62-4 Spr '65
Hardy as a modern novelist; excerpt from introd. to new edition of Jude the obscure. I. Howe. New Repub 152:19-22 Je 26 '65
HARDY oranges. See Trifoliate oranges
HARE, James A.
Charge to the jury. por Time 85:28 Ap 23 '65
HARGESHEIMER, Fred
Something belong friendship. J. Reddy. il Read Digest 86:224-8+ My '65
HARGIS, Billy James
Oh, to be in Manitou! Christian Cent 82:599 My 5 '65
HARI, Kenneth
Face to face with an impatient painter. por Seventeen 24:131 N '65
HARIJANS. See Untouchables
HARING, Bernard
Catholic church in modern America. por Cath World 201:27-31 Ap '65
Church and the world; interview, ed. by C. L. Palms. por Cath World 202:17-20 O '65
HARK, Mildred
Spring tonic; drama. Plays 24:71-6, 95 Mr '65
—and McQueen, Noel
Aladdin, incorporated; drama. Plays 24:51-60 F '65
Christmas snowman; drama. Plays 25:41-50, 96 D '65
Homecoming; drama. Plays 25:37-47, 86 O '65
Our famous ancestors; drama. Plays 25:26-36 N '65
Spring fever; drama. Plays 24:45-56 Ap '65
HARKINS, Gery
Ideas that work. Hot Rod 18:11 N '65
HARKNESS, Georgia
Father Divine's righteous government. Christian Cent 82:1259-61 O 13 '65
HARKNESS, Rebekah
Angel in tights. il por Time 85:67 Ap 2 '65
Who pays the piper? J. L. Collier. Holiday 38:168+ D '65
HARKNESS ballet (organization)
Angel in tights. il Time 85:67 Ap 2 '65
Opening scene; debut in Cannes. C. Barnes. il Dance Mag 39:27-8+ Ap '65
HARL, Neil E.
Save dollars by being tax-wise on deductions. Suc Farm 64:28+ Ja '66
—and Stoneberg, Everett
Year-end tips to lower income taxes. Suc Farm 63:34-5+ D '65
HARLAN, John Marshall
John Marshall Harlan: today's great dissenter. N. F. Busch. por Read Digest 86:201-4+ Je '65
HARLECH, David Ormsby Gore, 5th baron
Best since Bryce? New Repub 152:7 Mr 27 '65
HARLEM. See New York (city)—Harlem
HARLEM music project. See New York orchestral society
HARLEM riot, 1964. See New York (city)—Riots
HARLEM RIVER, New York
Fishing. New Yorker 41:45-6 N 13 '65
HARLEM youth opportunities unlimited, Incorporated
Growing troubles for an antipoverty plan. U S News 59:13 O 18 '65
Louis Johnson and the Har-You dancers. 92nd street Y. J. Maskey. Dance Mag 39:28 Ag '65
Mystery of Haryou. New Repub 153:7-8 D 18 '65
HARLEQUINADE; ballet. See Ballets—Criticisms
HARLESTON, Bernard W.
Higher education for the Negro. Atlan 216:139-44 N '65
HARLEY, John H. See Salter, L. P. jt. auth.
HARLOW, Francis H. and Fromm, J. E.
Computer experiments in fluid dynamics; with biographical sketches. Sci Am 212:18, 104-10 bibliog(p 140) Mr '65
—and others..
Liquid waves by computer. Science 149:1092-3 S 3 '65
HARLOW, Harry F. See Weisman, H. A. jt. auth.

HARLOW, Jean
Today is tonight; condensation of novel. pors Mlle 61:90-117 Jl '65

HARLOW, Lewis A.
Pinpoint those erase troubles. Pop Electr 23:55-6 D '65

HARLOW, Neal
Misused librarians. por Library J 90:1597-9 Ap 1 '65

HARMAN, Carter
Duke clicks in squaresville. Life 59:15 Ag 27 '65
Life music review. Life 59:29 O 15; 23 D 10 '65; 60:13 Ja 7 '66
Life theater review. Life 59:12 Jl 30 '65
Pappy, listen to Petula. Life 59:23 D 10 '65

HARMON, John J.
Life together in the city; address, February 1965. por Cath World 201:322-8 Ag '65

HARMON, Steve
Steve Harmon: actor and dancer. V. H. Swisher. il pors Dance Mag 39:135-6 D '65

HARMONOGRAPHS. See Oscillographs

HARMOUNT, James Godfrey
Art of cleanliness. Todays Health 43:49-51+ D '65

HARNACK, Curtis
Depression's late harvest. Nation 200:226-8 Mr 1 '65

HARNESS racing
America's prize stays French; Ozo, winner of Prix d'Amérique. P. Ryan. il Sports Illus 22:20-1 F 8 '65
Bond named Bret. il Time 85:81 Je 11 '65
Dream race ends in a Speedy victory; trotting race between Triple Crown winners Speedy Scot and Ayres. J. Kiser. Sports Illus 22:83-4 Je 14 '65
Fast pace in trotting. il Duns R 85:40 Mr '65
Fastest ham on four legs; Little Brown Jug week, Delaware, Ohio. P. Ryan. il Sports Illus 23:72+ O 4 '65
Hambo in the gloaming; Hambletonian. P. Ryan. il Sports Illus 23:38-9 S 13 '65
Messenger was late, but Bret was ready; at Roosevelt raceway. P. Ryan. il Sports Illus 23:74 N 29 '65
Mud in Stanley's eye; Hambletonian. il Time 86:92 S 10 '65
Odd time in Du Quoin, Illinois; Hambletonian trotting race and state fair. M. Kram. il Sports Illus 23:24-31 Ag 30 '65
Racing beneath the peaks; tracks surrounding Phoenix and Santa Anita. M. R. Werner. il Sports Illus 22:50-2+ Mr 8 '65
Set for a Noble Victory; trotting superhorse should capture the Hambletonian and the Triple crown. R. A. Hackett. Sports Illus 23:54 Ag 30 '65
Speedy son carries on the Adios tradition; Meadow Lenco at Laurel raceway. il Sports Illus 23:18-23 Jl 5 '65
Tradition battles expediency; question whether the Hambletonian will move from Du Quoin, Ill. to Phila. P. Ryan. il Sports Illus 23:22-3 N 1 '65
Treating a filly with finesse; Armbro Flight, Goshen, N.Y. P. Ryan. il Sports Illus 23: 60-1 Jl 19 '65
Trotting to the bank; opening night at New York's Roosevelt raceway. il Newsweek 67: 56 Ja 17 '66

HARNEY, Susan
London bob. Ladies Home J 82:82-3 Mr '65

HARNISCHFEGER, Walter
Excerpt from statement, March 4, 1965. Cong Digest 44:180+ Je '65

HARP
Angelic instrument; third International harp contest, Tel Aviv. Newsweek 66:95 S 27 '65
Harp famine; Welsh repair measures. il Newsweek 67:41 Ja 17 '66

HARPER, Charles
Twenty dudes in the wilderness; reprint. il Liv Wildn 87:13-15 Wint '64

HARPER, John Dickson
Harper of Alcoa. por Fortune 71:69 Je '65

HARPER, Maryon Wood
I like this side of the fence. Farm J 89:43 Jl '65

HARPER and brothers, publishers. See Harper and Row, publishers, incorporated

HARPER and Row, publishers, incorporated
Brother Harper, by E. Exman. Review Pub W il 188:38-40 Ag 2 '65. J. T. Winterich
Fitzhenry to start Harper Canadian agency. Pub W 188:69 D 27 '65
Harper Bible department sold to Zondervan. Pub W 188:40+ N 22 '65
When Harper's was young; excerpt from Brothers Harper. E. Exman. il Sat R 48: 72-4 Je 12 '65

HARPER'S magazine
Harper and Row sells 50 per cent of Harper's magazine. Pub W 187:37 My 10 '65
Harper's bazaar; change of ownership. Time 85:63 My 7 '65
New hand at Harper's; Cowles purchase. il Newsweek 65:98 My 10 '65

HARPOONING
Hot-seat angler; fishing with electric harpoon. Sports Illus 23:8 Ag 2 '65

HARPSICHORD
Kit can be a harpsichord. R. Lindstrom. il Hi Fi 15:34-8 Jl '65

HARPSICHORD music
St Wanda's testament. F. V. Grunfeld. il Reporter 32:42-4 F 25 '65
See also
Phonograph records—Harpsichord music

HARR, Karl Gottlieb
Aerospace industry; address, February 15, 1965. Vital Speeches 31:500-4 Je 1 '65

HARRAH, William F.
World's biggest gambler. R. Wernick. il pors Sat Eve Post 238:27-32 F 13 '65
World's greatest automobile collection. K. Purdy. il Atlan 216:84-92 Jl '65

HARRAR, J. George
Foundations, the new pioneers. Read Digest 87:100-1 O '65

HARRIGAN, Anthony
Letter from the Pacific. Nat R 17:546 Je 29 '65
We can win in southeast Asia. Nat R 17: 187-8+ Mr 9 '65

HARRIMAN, William Averell
Canada and U.S. mark anniversary of Joint board on defense; address, August 18, 1965. Dept State Bul 53:449-52 S 13 '65
Challenges to freedom and peace; address, October 31, 1965. Dept State Bul 53:863-7 N 29 '65
Economic responsibilities of the United States; address, February 4, 1965. Dept State Bul 52:245-50 F 22 '65
Finland and the United States, an enduring friendship; address, September 5, 1965. Dept State Bul 53:555-8 O 4 '65
My visits with Kosygin and Tito. pors Life 59:89-90 Ag 27 '65
United States and international cooperation; address, March 26, 1965. Dept State Bul 52:621-8 Ap 26 '65
Veteran diplomat looks at U.S. in today's world; interview. por U S News 59:70-2 Jl 12 '65
about
Peace seekers. por Newsweek 66:16-17 Ag 16 '65

HARRINGTON, LaMar
Northwest craftsmen's exhibition. Craft Horiz 25:12-17 My '65

HARRINGTON, Michael
New radicalism. Commonweal 82:623-7 S 3 '65
On Paul Goodman. Atlan 216:88-91 Ag '65
Radicals, old and new. New Repub 153:29 Jl 3 '65

HARRINGTON, Stephanie
Appalachia beyond free enterprise. Commonweal 82:213-16, 427+ My 7, Je 25 '65
Why the U.N. survives. Commonweal 82:527-9 Jl 23 '65

HARRIS, Barbara
Barbara Harris: Broadway's new all-female funnygirl. B. Rollin. il pors Look 29:139-42 D 14 '65
In lights it spells Harris. por Time 86:71 D 3 '65
On a clear day, a battalion of Barbaras. il pors Newsweek 66:84+ N 1 '65
Up soars her pink balloon. il pors Life 59: 79-80+ D 17 '65

HARRIS, Dale, and Harris, Elizabeth
Choice toys for Christmas. PTA Mag 60:27-9 D '65
—See Harris, E. jt. auth.

HARRIS, DeLong
Excerpt from testimony, October 24, 1963. Cong Digest 44:249+ O '65

HARRIS, Dixie Dean
And this, dear God, is what they read. Esquire 64:50-1+ Jl '65
Now you can have your hair restored ($1 a hair) your eyelids tightened ($500) Esquire 64:134-6+ N '65

HARRIS, Elizabeth, and Harris, Dale
Let's bring back children's play. PTA Mag 60:28-30 bibliog(p35) S '65
—See Harris, D. jt. auth.

HARRIS, Frank
That rascal Frank Harris. M. Kamin. Hobbies 70:110-12 Jl '65

HARRIS, John F.
Surgeon on a hot seat; colonel battles killer disease as senior medic of sixth army. il pors Ebony 20:87-90 F '65

HARRIS, Julie
In lights it spells Harris. por Time 86:71 D 3 '65

HARRIS, MacDonald
Snow and lilac; story. Redbook 125:72-3 Ag '65

HARRIS, Mark
Blau & Irving come out of the West. N Y Times Mag p 16-17+ F 21 '65
On stage in San Francisco. Holiday 38:180+ O '65

HARRIS, Michael
Failing banks & sporty bankers. Nation 200: 442-5 Ap 26; inside cover My 17; inside cover My 31 '65
—See Garrett, R. jt. auth.

HARRIS, Oren
Congressman or judge? the Oren Harris mystery por U S News 59:15 D 20 '65
Key chairmanship for an LBJ liberal. por U S News 60:10 Ja 10 '66

HARRIS, Patricia Roberts
View from the other side; address. November 23, 1965. Dept State Bul 54:16-19 Ja 3 '66

about

Ambassador is a lady. C. Sanders. il pors Ebony 21:23-6+ Ja '66
Four in one. il por Time 85:23 My 28 '65
New envoy: Negro woman; LBJ picks her for Luxembourg. por U S News 58:16 My 31 '65

HARRIS, Peter Carr-. See Carr-Harris, P.

HARRIS, Reese Harvey, 1911-
Why the next portfolio gains may come harder. por Bsns W p 152+ N 20 '65

HARRIS, Rosemary
Medley of grievous things. Mlle 60:171+ Ap '65

HARRIS, Roy
Fine arts. J. K. Waters. America 113:787 D 18 '65

HARRIS, Sydney J.
On the contrary; excerpts. Read Digest 86: 27-8+ Ap '65

HARRIS, Wade N.
Voice of industry. por Duns R 85:16+ F '65

HARRIS, William Henry
Morality, moralism and Vietnam. Christian Cent 82:1155-7 S 22 '65

HARRIS-intertype corporation
Next big jump is near in printing. il Bsns W p92+ Ap 24 '65

HARRIS, Upham and company
Reading the future in the past; technique of the chartist. il Bsns W p 107-8+ Ag 14 '65

HARRISBURG, Pa.

Water supply

Scum yields to a screw conveyor at a sewage-purification plant. L. A. Ritter. il Am City 80:108-9 Je '65

HARRISON, A. Cleveland
ABC's of excellence; address, April 6, 1965. Vital Speeches 31:565-7 Jl 1 '65

HARRISON, Benjamin
Benjamin Harrison, twenty-third President. F. Freidel. il pors Nat Geog Mag 127:704-7 My '65

HARRISON, Henry T.
Flying weather signposts. Flying 77:49-51 N '65
More flying weather signposts. Flying 77:79-81 D '65

HARRISON, Jim
Dead doe; Complaint; Return; Poem; David; poems. Poetry 106:328-30 Ag '65
Exercise; poem. Nation 200:374 Ap 5 '65
New liturgy; poem. Nation 200:374 Ap 5 '65
Northness of North. Nation 200:180 F 15 '65

HARRISON, K. C.
Hell is a city much like London. por Library J 90:4902-6 N 15 '65

HARRISON, Rex
Rich, restless life of Rex Harrison. J. Hamilton. il pors Look 29:62-6 N 2 '65

HARRISON, Ruth M.
Children in a shadow world. Parents Mag 40:52-3+ My '65

HARRISON, Wallace Kirkman
New Met. C. L. Osborne. il pors Hi Fi 15: 50-4+ S '65

HARRISON, William Henry
Hero of Tippecanoe. B. Finnegan. il Hobbies 69:118-20 F '65

HARRISON Bergeron; story. See Vonnegut, K. jr

HARROD, Henry
Wedding of the Hon Lucinda Lambton and Henry Harrod in England's North country. il por Vogue 145:140-1 Ap 1 '65

HARRY W. A. Davis, jr; story. See Maloney, R.

HARSHBARGER, Gretchen
Use iris to advantage in your garden. Horticulture 43:22-3+ My '65

HART, Henry C.
Dawn of a community-defining federalism. bibliog f Ann Am Acad 359:147-56 My '65

HART, Howard
Suddenly falling earth. J. Crawford, jr. Poetry 105:411-12 Mr '65

HART, Jeffrey
American dissent; decade of modern conservatism; excerpts. Nat R 17:A1-47 N 30 '65
Complacency ltd. Nat R 17:988-9 N 2 '65
Grenadiers in Zululand. Nat R 17:882-3 O 5 '65
Pattern of our war. Nat R 18:31-2 Ja 11 '66
Rebirth of Christ. Nat R 17:1192-6 D 28 '65

HART, Jerry
Behind the dunes. Yachting 118:58-9+ O '65
East from Florida. il Yachting 118:44-5+ S '65

HART, Mildred, and Aldrich, Dorothy
How to make a wreath. Pop Gard 16:28 N '65

HART, Moss, and Kaufman, G. S.
You can't take it with you. Criticism
America 113:762-3 D 11 '65
Life 59:16 D 17 '65
Nation 201:484 D 13 '65
New Repub 153:29 D 18 '65
New Yorker 41:106 D 4 '65
Newsweek il 66:92 D 6 '65
Sat R 48:51 D 11 '65
Time 86:54 D 3 '65

HART, Philip A.
Packagers rap Hart bill. il Bsns W p34 My 8 '65

HART, Richard
Books in the field: poetry. bibliog Wilson Lib Bul 40:440-59 Ja '66

HART, S. R. and Steinhart, J. S.
Terrestrial heat flow: measurement in lake bottoms. bibliog Science 149:1499-501 S 24 '65
—See Rama, S. N. I. jt. auth.

HART MOUNTAIN antelope and sage hen refuge, Ore. See Wildlife sanctuaries

HARTFORD, Huntington
Hartford on the rocks? il por Newsweek 65: 73-4 Je 7 '65

HARTFORD, Conn.

City planning

One city's answer to downtown decay; Constitution Plaza. J. Peter. il Look 29:44-6 S 21 '65

Education

Hartford's antismoking campaign; high schools. C. L. Towne. il Sr Schol 87:sup39+ S 23 '65

HARTIGAN, William J.
Postal service, the oldest form of international cooperation. Dept State Bul 53:840-2 N 22 '65

HARTLEY, Ellen. See Hartley, W. jt. auth.

HARTLEY, Lois
Book reviews. America 113:82 Jl 17 '65

HARTLEY, Raymond
Peace corps volunteers return. Seventeen 24: 20+ My '65

HARTLEY, Russell
Parades and changes, scandal and delight. Dance Mag 39:50-1+ O '65

HARTLEY, William
Florida's Gulf coast. Redbook 126:48-9+ Ja '66
We took the high road. Redbook 124:70-1+ Mr '65
—and Hartley, Ellen
I can be 'most anything! Good H 161:262 N '65
Seminoles' long road to victory. Read Digest 86:199-200+ F '65

HARTMAN, Chester W. See Nash, W. W. jr. jt. auth.

HARTMAN, Maxine
Department of amplification. New Yorker 40: 88+ Ja 30 '65

HARTNEY, James B.
Blood in your future. Todays Health 43:5+ D '65

HARTUNG, Marion T.
Carnival glass collectors attention. Hobbies 70:83 Ap '65

HARTUNG, Philip T.
Following the films. See issues of Senior scholastic
Screen. See issues of Commonweal

HARUNA, I. and Spiegelman, S.
Autocatalytic synthesis of a viral RNA in vitro. bibliog Science 150:884-6 N 12 '65

HARVARD conference on the new morality. See Religious conferences

HARVARD observatory. See Astronomical observatories

HARVARD university
Adaptable new tower for Harvard; William James hall of the behavioral sciences. il Arch Rec 138:138-9 O '65
Decade of Harvard university. N. M. Pusey. il Sch & Soc 93:115-20 F 20 '65
Dropouts and kickouts: expulsion from Harvard, followed by undergraduate years in Germany from 1931 through 1932. F. Russell. Nat R 17:1166-7 D 14 '65
Harvard's Midas; value of investments. Time 85:57 Ap 16 '65
Student protest and commitment; address, June 15, 1965. N. M. Pusey. Sch & Soc 93:471-4 D 11 '65
University and the high school; reprint of a 1939 article. J. B. Conant. Sch & Soc 93: 52-6 Ja 23 '65
Why Harvard still ranks first; oldest graduate economics department. il Bsns W p 118-20+ Ap 24 '65

Fogg art museum
Fogg's find; Rembrandt's Head of Christ. il Time 85:94 Ap 16 '65

Graduate school of business administration
Allen Dulles completes a non-secret mission; resident fellow at Harvard business school. il Bsns W p34-5 Ap 10 '65
Grads honor the dean of retailers; name a chair at Harvard for him. il Bsns W p 130+ Je 12 '65
Harvard's degree in the higher materialism. S. Klaw. il Esquire 64:103+ O '65
Pattern for success; Harvard business school's advanced management course. W. Wingo. il Nations Bsns 53:46-50+ S; 48-52+ O; 94-6+ N '65

Graduate school of education
Container to fit the contained; new building. il Time 87:64-6 Ja 21 '66
Harvard tweed: Roy E. Larsen Hall. il Newsweek 66:94 O 11 '65

Harvard medical school
High style at Harvard; Francis A. Countway library of medicine, Boston, Mass. R. T. Esterquest. il Library J 90:5186-8 D 1 '65
No. 1 at no. 1. il Time 86:55 Jl 9 '65

Libraries
High style at Harvard; Francis A. Countway library of medicine, Boston, Mass. R. T. Esterquest. il Library J 90:5186-8 D 1 '65

Society of fellows
Best Fellows at Harvard. M. Mayer. il Esquire 63:76-9+ Je '65

HARVARD urban design conference. See Architectural conferences

HARVEST hands. See Farm labor

HARVEST labor. See Farm labor

HARVESTING machinery
Machines take over bracero job. il Bsns W p 108-10 Ja 8 '66
Mechanical harvest: it's really rolling! J. Russell. il Farm J 89:54F Ap '65
New boost for berries; harvest for blackberries. il Farm J 89:55 F '65
Timesaving combine ideas. il Suc Farm 63:61 Je '65
See also
Corn harvesting machinery

HARVEY, Holman, and Gilmore, K. O.
Reapportionment: shall the Court or the people decide? Read Digest 86:111-16 Mr '65

HARVEY, John A. and Lints, C. E.
Lesions in the medial forebrain bundle; delayed effects on sensitivity to electric shock. bibliog Science 148:250-2 Ap 9 '65
—See Roth, B. F. jt. auth.

HARVEY, Ruth
Pleasure of your company; story. Seventeen 24:112-13 F '65

HARVEY, Van A.
Nature and function of faith. Christian Cent 82:962-6 Ag 4 '65

HARWELL, Richard
Blended simplicity for Bowdoin. Library J 90:5192-4 D 1 '65

HARWOOD, Raymond C.
Attenborough and Harwood speak on distribution; summary of address. por Pub W 187:74-5 Je 21 '65

HARWOOD, Richard
Miami super-lobby. Reporter 32:21-5 My 6 '65

HARYOU. See Harlem youth opportunities unlimited, incorporated

HAS anybody here seen Barbie? story. See Oppenheimer, J. L.

HASEGANU, Mihail
United Nations commemoration address, June 26, 1965. UN Mo Chron 2:147-9 Jl '65

HASEGAWA, Shin'ichi
Twenty-one volume Japanese novel sells 11 million copies. UNESCO Courier 18:27 S '65

HASELDEN, Kyle
Abraham's children. Christian Cent 82:455-7 Ap 14 '65
And see the land, what it is. Christian Cent 82:360-1 Mr 24 '65
E pluribus Israel. Christian Cent 82:390-2 Mr 31 '65
Israel's quest for water. Christian Cent 82: 423-5 Ap 7 '65
N.C.C. agenda. Christian Cent 82:766-7 Je 16 '65
Not for Jews only. Christian Cent 82:894 Jl 14 '65
Which South? Christian Cent 82:1055-6 S 1 '65

HASELKORN, Robert, and others
Electron microscopic and biochemical characterization of fraction I protein. bibliog Science 150:1598-601 D 17 '65
—See Dahlberg, J. E. jt. auth.

HASHEM, Nemat
Mitosis: induction by cultures of human peripheral lymphocytes. bibliog Science 150: 1460-2 D 10 '65

HASIDISM
Rabbi's shiksa. il Newsweek 66:77 Ag 9 '65
Wedding in B'nai Brak. H. Weiner. Commentary 40:39-46 Jl; Discussion. 40:12+ N '65

HASKINS, Caryl P.
Don K. Price, jr, president-elect. Science 150: 1690-1 D 24 '65
Evolution of science; adaptation from Report of the president. Science 148:737 My 7 '65

HASKINS, R. H.
Sterols and temperature tolerance in the fungus pythium. bibliog Science 150:1615-16 D 17 '65

HASKINS, Sam
Unabashed ladies of Sam Haskins; photographs. Mod Phot 30:62-73 Ja '66

HASLER, Arthur D. See Rabinowitch, V. jt. auth.

HASSAM, Childe
Muley the pragmatist. il Time 86:60-1+ S 3 '65

HASSAN II, king of Morocco
Against the tide. Newsweek 65:52 Ap 12 '65
Morocco's troubled young king. C. Sterling. il Reporter 32:21-5 Je 17 '65
Royal premier. il por Time 85:31B Je 18 '65

HASSENGER, Robert
Book reviews. America 113:342-3 S 25 '65

HASTINGS, Osbert
Catholic aggiornamento. Reporter 33:19-22 D 30 '65

HAT for mother; drama. See Phillips, M. K.

HATCH, Brainard G.
Advice for amateur painters. Motor B 115: 166-8 Je '65

HATCH, Richard
Harlem's streetcorner architects. A. Lopen. il por Arch Forum 123:50-1 D '65

HATCH, Robert
Films. See occasional issues of Nation

HATCH act. See Government employees—Political activities

HATFIELD, Mark Odom
Hard-to-forsake habit. por Time 87:20-1 Ja 21 '66

HATFIELD, Philip E.
Compactron regulated power supply. Pop Electr 22:57-9 F '65
Two-compactron stereo amplifier. Pop Electr 23:43-6 Jl '65

HATGIL, Paul Peter
Contemporary craftsman. il Sch Arts 64:36-7 Je '65

HATHAWAY, Dame Sibyl Mary (Collings) Beaumont, dame of Sark
Other Eden. il por Time 86:33 Ag 20 '65

HATPIN holders
Treasure hunt: match safes and hatpin holders. J. Mebane. il Bet Hom & Gard 43:47-8 N '65

HATS
Lift for flattops. il Time 85:62 Ap 23 '65

Anecdotes, facetiae, satire, etc.
Svetlana's Easter bonnet. J. Robbins. il Read Digest 86:137-40 Ap '65

HATTERAS ABYSSAL PLAIN. See Atlantic Ocean

HATTERAS ISLAND
Visit to Hatteras. O. S. Pettingill. jr. il Audubon Mag 67:343-4+ N '65
HATTERS, cap and millinery workers international union. See United hatters, cap and millinery workers international union
HATTERSLEY, Ralph
Creating surprise out of commonplace elements. Pop Phot 56:74-5+ Ap '65
Make pictures by candlelight. il Pop Phot 57:144-7+ D '65
(ed) Marilyn Monroe; interviews with six famous photographers. Pop Phot 58:104-9+ Ja '66
Seventy-five creative photographic assignments. Pop Phot 56:41+ Mr '65
What I learned from the pros. Pop Phot 58:122-5 Ja '66
HATTON, Duncan S.
Tinnitus: that puzzling buzzing in your ears. Todays Health 43:14+ N '65
HAUGHTON, Daniel J.
Changing aerospace market; excerpts from address. Aviation W 83:21 Ag 9 '65
HAUGHTON, G.
Moloney virus-induced leukemias of mice: measurement in vitro of specific antigen. bibliog Science 147:506-7 Ja 29 '65
—and others
Lymphoma growth in vivo: electronic discrimination between tumor and stroma cells. Science 150:769-71 N 5 '65
HAUNTED houses. See Ghosts
HAUPT, Enid A.
Seventeen book of etiquette and entertaining; excerpts (cont) Seventeen 24:175 Mr; 42 Ap; 170 My; 43 Je; 318 Ag '65
HAUSER, Ernest O.
Gold king of metals. Read Digest 87:234-8+ O '65
HAUSER, Nancy
Minneapolis muse. Dance Mag 39:48-50 Ag '65
HAUSER, Philip M.
Demography and ecology. bibliog f Ann Am Acad 362:129-38 N '65
about
Segregation crisis: Chicago's troubled schools. J. Star. Look 29:59+ My 4 '65
HAUSMAN, Jerome J.
Art education 1965; prospects and problems. Sch Arts 64:7-11 Ap '65
HAUSNER, Gideon
Nazi, come home. Esquire 63:114-17+ My '65
HAUSSAMEN, Crane
When foreign-student scholarships are misused. Sat R 48:48-50+ Ag 21 '65
HAVASU LAKE
Along the Arizona-California water border you can explore the desert leisurely by boat. il Sunset 134:34-6+ Mr '65
HAVEMANN, Ernest
Divorce, loneliness and remarriage. Ladies Home J 82:62-3+ Jl '65
How America lives. Ladies Home J 82:56-9+ My '65
Should seventeen and eighteen year-old girls marry? McCalls 92:101+ F '65
Twenty-four hours in the life of Johnny Carson. McCalls 92:58+ Mr '65
HAVERFIELD, Robert A.
Extras pay dividends. Am City 80:101-3 N '65
HAVERKAMP-BEGEMANN, Egbert
Terborch's Lady at her toilet. Art N 64:38-41+ D '65
HAVERSTICK, Iola
Brief affair with fortune. Sat R 49:82 Ja 8 '66
Bygones in Boston. Sat R 48:49-50 N 27 '65
HAVERSTOCK, Mary Sayre
(ed) Cities and people. Américas 17:20-5 Ag '65
HAVIGHURST, Robert J.
Segregation crisis: Chicago's troubled schools. J. Star. Look 29:59+ My 4 '65
HAVIS, John R.
Why do rhododendron leaves curl? Horticulture 43:17 D '65
HAWAII
Hawaii: the golden land; with account by M. Leatherbee. il Life 59:84-99, 101-2+ O 8 '65
See also
Architecture, Domestic—Hawaii
Gardens—Hawaii
Libraries—Hawaii
Maui (island)
Roads—Hawaii
Water supply—Hawaii

Description and travel
Has success spoiled Hawaii? C. B. Luce. il McCalls 93:42+ N '65
Mauna Kea caper; L. Rockefeller's resort opened. H. Sutton. Sat R 48:34+ Ag 21 '65

Travel notes. R. Joseph. Esquire 64:12+ Ag '65
Travel's picture portfolio. Travel 125:34-9 Ja '66

Hotels, restaurants, etc.
Man from room 5600; Mauna Kea Beach hotel. il Newsweek 66:44-5 Ag 2 '65

Japanese raids
See Pearl Harbor, Attack on, 1941

Social conditions
Not-so-happy Hawaiians. F. R. Schreiber and M. Herman. il Sci Digest 57:16-18 My '65

Social life and customs
Hawaiian culture and prestige. I. Taves. il Look 29:65-6+ F 23 '65
HAWAII. University, Honolulu
New tides in the Pacific. il Time 85:66 F 26 '65

Cultural center
East-West center review board holds first meeting; Department announcement, March 15, 1965, with remarks by President Johnson. Dept State Bul 52:905-7 Je 7 '65
National review board appointed for East-West center. Dept State Bul 52:383-4 Mr 15 '65

HAWAIIAN cookery. See Cookery, Hawaiian
HAWAIIAN geese. See Nenes
HAWAIIAN quilting. See Quilting
HAWAIIAN State championships. See Automobile racing
HAWAIIANS
Hawaiian culture and prestige. I. Taves. il Look 29:65-6+ F 23 '65
Not-so-happy Hawaiians. F. R. Schreiber and M. Herman. il Sci Digest 57:16-18 My '65
HAWES, Elizabeth
Leaving; poem. New Yorker 41:118 Ag 14 '65
HAWES, Evelyn
Skeleton at the feast. Writer 78:17-18+ N '65
HAWK, Julia
Night the war stopped for a moment. por Redbook 126:6+ D '65
HAWKES, Alex D.
Mahonias. Horticulture 43:14 D '65
Tigridias. Horticulture 43:61 Mr '65
HAWKES, Jacquetta
Automation and imagination. Harper 231:92-4+ O '65
HAWKES, Joan
Looking ahead to college and careers. See issues of Seventeen through March 1965
HAWKING. See Falconry
HAWKINS, Coleman
Jazz. W. Balliett. New Yorker 41:92-3 Mr 6 '65
HAWKINS, Erick
Erick Hawkins and dance company, Hunter playhouse. D. Hering. Dance Mag 39:62 N '65
HAWKINS, Gerald S.
Callanish, a Scottish Stonehenge. Science 147:127-30; 148:444 Ja 8, Ap 23 '65
about
Eighth wonder. il Time 86:98 N 12 '65
HAWKS
Hawks lose way home. Sci N L 88:132 Ag 28 '65
See also
Ospreys
HAWKSWORTH, Frank Goode, and Hinds, T. E.
Spread of a parasite. Natur Hist 74:52-7 Mr '65
—See Hinds, T. E. jt. auth.
HAWTHORNE, Nathaniel
Great stone face; dramatization. See Hackett, W
HAWTHORNE, Robert J.
Intersection: point of meeting. Christian Cent 82:1599-602 D 29 '65
HAWTHORNS
Hawthorns. R. R. Thomasson. Horticulture 43:45 Je '65
Nature note; winter king. Sci N L 87:127 F 20 '65
HAY, Alex
Unexpected assemblage! D. McDonagh. il por Dance Mag 39:42-5+ Je '65
HAY, Jacob
I dreamt I drank in marble halls. Holiday 37:92-3+ My '65
HAY
How much hay do you need? P. R. Hasbargen and L. E. Zeman. il Suc Farm 63:28-9+ Ja '65
How to fertilize for six tons of hay per acre. W. L. Griffeth and L. E. Zeman. il Suc Farm 63:50-1+ Mr '65

HAY—*Continued*
How to get really top-quality hay. D. A.
Rohweder and L. E. Zeman. il Suc Farm
63:46-7+ My '65
How to tell if hay is top quality. J. E. Bay-
lor and others. il Suc Farm 63:32-3+ Jl '65
See also
Alfalfa

Wafering

See Feeding and feeding stuffs—Pelleted
feed

HAY fever
Delayed proof; injections worth cost and dis-
comfort. Time 86:93 O 8 '65
Hay fever, allergies: latest on cause and
treatment. il U S News 59:60-3 Jl 12 '65
Hypo for allergy shots; testing effectiveness
of ragweed-pollen extract. il Newsweek 66:
92 O 11 '65

HAY making machinery
How to automate haymaking. L. E. Zeman
and W. J. Fletcher. il Suc Farm 63:39-43+
Je '65

HAY wafers. See Feeding and feeding stuffs—
Pelleted feed

HAYATSU, Ryoichi
Optical activity in the orgueil meteorite.
bibliog Science 149:443-7 Jl 23 '65

HAYDEN, Casey
Raising the question of who decides. New
Repub 154:9-10 Ja 22 '66

HAYDEN, Julie
Woman's view. Atlan 216:154-6 N '65

HAYDEN, Mike
Trophy of gold. il Outdoor Life 135:44-7+
My '65
We gambled on Poison. Outdoor Life 136:
36-9+ S '65

HAYDEN, Thomas
Ability to face whatever comes. New Repub
154:16-18 Ja 15 '66
Three characters in search of an offer. Newsweek 67:18 Ja 10 '66

HAYDN, Franz Joseph
All at once, sixteen Haydn symphonies! J.
W. Barker. Am Rec G 31:634-5+ Mr '65
Creation from Decca, an extremely fine per-
formance. J. W. Barker. il Am Rec G 32:55
S '65
Haydn's Bear and Haydn's Hen, the right
scores make all the difference. H. C. R.
Landon; reply. P. J. Smith. il Hi Fi 15:67-
9+ Mr '65
Haydn's oratorios, a simple faith, sublimest
craft. N. Broder. il Hi Fi 15:82 O '65
Helping Haydn; Landon-restored Le pesca-
trici produced at Holland festival, Amster-
dam. Time 86:58 Jl 9 '65
Janigro's Haydn, a remarkably fine achievement. J. W. Barker. Am Rec G 31:994 Je
'65
On records; Seasons. Opera N 30:34 Ja 8 '66

HAYES, Alice Margaret
Beginning teacher and professional associations. NEA J 54:31 O '65

HAYES, Bartlett H. Jr
Artist's angle of vision. Sat R 48:48 N 27 '65

HAYES, Bob
Cowboy from Olympus. il por Time 86:56+
O 8 '65
Instant success. Sports Illus 23:22+ O 11
'65

HAYES, Helen
Charlie; excerpt from A gift of joy; ed. by
L. Funke. Read Digest 87:126-9 N '65
Gift of joy; excerpts, ed. by L. Funke. Mc-
Calls 92:73-5+ S '65
My faith in prayer; excerpt from A gift of
joy, ed. by L. Funke. Read Digest 87:55-7 D
'65

about
Successful autographing tours by three personalities. il por Pub W 188:53-6 D 13 '65

HAYES, Jim
Drums along Otter Creek. Outdoor Life 137:
40-3+ Ja '66

HAYES, John D.
Our merchant marine in trouble. Reporter
34:28-31 Ja 13 '66
Weak spot in our defenses. America 113:93-5
Jl 24 '65

HAYES, Lionel
Four men alone. pors Outdoor Life 137:21-
3+ Ja '66

HAYES, Peter Lind
Aboard the 36' cruiser Queen Mary with
Peter Lind Hayes and Mary Healy. G.
Sloane. il pors Motor B 115:60-1+ '65

HAYES, Philip T.
Subways are for dancing. Atlan 216:132-3 S
'65

HAYES, Robert B.
Simulators in driver education. NEA J 54:
58 Ap '65

HAYES, Rutherford Birchard
R. B. Hayes, nineteenth President. F. Freidel.
il pors Nat Geog Mag 127:686-9 My '65

HAYLOCK, E. F.
Admiral's cup. Motor B 116:86-7+ O '65
Brave Moppie best in British bash. Motor B
116:44-5+ N '65
H. R. (Bobby) Somerset; appreciation. Motor B 115:188 My '65
Stichting stamboek ronde-en platbodemjachten
zomer-reunie te Veere. il Motor B 116:34-
6+ D '65
Twenty-five years after Dunkirk. il Motor B
115:45-7+ Je '65

HAYMAN, David
Past the wit of man. Nation 200:232-4 Mr 1
'65

HAYMAN, Lee Richard
Rejuvenation; Forest recital; poems. Liv
Wildn 87:9 Wint '64

HAYNES, Harold, and others
Visual accommodation in human infants. bibliog Science 148:528-30 Ap 23 '65

HAYNEVILLE, Ala.
Not guilty again. Sr Schol 87:8-9 N 11 '65

HAYTON, Lennie
My life with Lennie. L. Horne. il pors Ebony
21:176-8+ N '65

HAYWARD, J. F.
Galleries of nineteenth-century art in the
Victoria and Albert museum. Antiques 87:
690-5 Je '65

HAYWARD, Roger
Amateur scientist. Sci Am 213:106-7 Ag '65

HAYWARD, Calif.
Hayward issues the call; ed. by P. D. Eimon.
il Am City 80:130+ Jl '65
Water bills serve as information medium. W.
F. Mortensen. Am City 80:138+ D '65

Stores

Enclosed mall with open store fronts. il Arch
Rec 137:191-3 My '65

HAYWOOD, Lorna
Fledgling Fidelio. M. Bernheimer. Sat R 48:78
F 13 '65

HAYWORTH, Rita
Brief essay on the subject of celebrity with
numerous digressions and particular attention to the actress, Rita Hayworth. E. S.
Connell, jr. il Esquire 63:114-16 Mr '65

HAZARD, Leland
Strong medicine for India. Atlan 216:43-8 D '65

HAZARD, Ky.

Education

Men and boys on Lost Creek road. G. Norman. il Am Ed 1:8-12 Ap '65

HAZARD vocational school. See Hazard, Ky.—
Education

HAZEL, Robert
NYC; poem. Nation 201:219 S 20 '65

HAZELTON, D. R.
Marriage; poem. Nation 200:626 Je 7 '65

HAZELTON, Nika Standen
German cook book. House & Gard 127:137+
F '65
Going places, findings things in Denmark.
House & Gard 127:36+ Mr '65
Winter casserole cook book. House & Gard
129:131+ Ja '66

HAZING
Ban the bomb; student injured in hell night
initiation at Oceanside high school, Long
Island. Time 85:60 Ap 30 '65

HAZLITT, Henry
Bastiat for '65. Nat R 17:154-5 F 23 '65
Business tides. See issues of Newsweek
Confusion, not conspiracy. Nat R 17:468-9 Je
1 '65
Development of economic thought. Nat R 17:
1102+ N 30 '65
Fifty billion to play with? the fear of fiscal
drag. Nat R 17:1151-2 D 14 '65

HAZO, Robert G.
Devil is a swinger. New Repub 154:26-8 Ja
15 '66

HAZO, Samuel
Hawk in the sun; poem. Commonweal 83:442
Ja 14 '66
No echo in Judea; poem. Sat R 48:65 Ag 28
'65

HAZZARD, George W. See Cook, L. G. jt. auth.

HAZZARD, Shirley
Evening of the holiday; story. New Yorker
41:44-52 Ap 17 '65
Out of Itea; story. New Yorker 41:125-6 My 1
'65

HE loves me! story. See Cave, H.

HEAD, Agnes Kastner
Welfare frauds exposed. il por Nations Bsns
53:38-9+ Je '65

HEAD, Matthew, pseud. See Canaday, J.

HEAD
See also
Baldness

Wounds and Injuries
Elusive head injuries. il Time 86:46+ S 10 '65
HEAD noises. See Tinnitus
HEAD start, Project. See Project head start
HEADACHE
Headache: our most common malady. T. Berland. il Todays Health 43:20-1+ F '65
What to do about headaches; interview. A. P. Friedman. Read Digest 86:127-30 F '65
HEADPHONES. See Earphones
HEADS of state
In the human interest; conflict with national interest. N. Cousins. Sat R 48:28 N 27 '65
Trinity of nation-builders. E. R. F. Sheehan. Harper 230:142-4 My '65
Who's who around the world (cont) il **Sr** Schol 87:40-1+ S 30 '65

Official residences
See Official residences
HEALD, Henry Townley
Ford foundation looks for new top command. por Bsns W p30-1 O 23 '65
Ford in the future. Newsweek 67:60 Ja 17 '66
Good-by Mr Chips. por Newsweek 66:86 Jl 26 '65
HEALD, Weldon F.
Colorado queen. Travel 124:36-8 Ag '65
Guadalupe Mountains National Park. Nat Parks Mag 39:4-8 S '65
New Mexico's missions. Travel 123:36-41 F '65
Oregon's Coast highway. Travel 124:24-9 S '65
Organ Pipe Cactus National Monument. il Nat Parks Mag 39:9-12 Ap '65
San Gorgonio: Southern California's rooftop. il Liv Wildn 29:12-16 Sum '65
HEALEY, Denis Winston
Whitehall's McNamara. il por Newsweek 66:50+ D 6 '65
HEALEY, James S.
Onboard in New Bedford. Wilson Lib Bul 40:246-8 N '65
HEALEY, Robert M.
Murray and liberty. Christian Cent 82:1130-1 S 15 '65
HEALTH
Among the latest health discoveries; developments reported at AMA. U S News 59:11 Jl 5 '65
Billy Graham's physical fitness program can help you. C. Mitchell. il Pop Sci 186:61-4+ My '65; Same abr. Read Digest 87:58-62 Jl '65
Five myths about health. A. J. Snider. il Sci Digest 57:31-2 My '65
I took the Niehans treatment; cellular therapy. H. Worden. Vogue 147:76-7+ Ja 15 '66
Plain talk about family health. See issues of Better homes and gardens
Scientific secrets of fitness. A. Hamilton. il Sci Digest 58:60-5 Jl '65
Today's health news. A. L. Blakeslee. See issues of Today's health
See also
Exercise
Longevity
Sleep
HEALTH, Mental. See Mental hygiene
HEALTH and aviation. See Aviation—Physiological aspects
HEALTH benefit plans. See Insurance, Health
HEALTH centers
Complete center for the mentally retarded; Hissom memorial center, Sand Springs, Okla. il Arch Rec 137:162-5 F '65
Illinois plans zone centers for mental health. il Arch Rec 137:201-8 Je '65
See also
Medical centers
HEALTH clinics
Where the needy get free medical care; Christian medical clinics. H. G. Earl. il Todays Health 43:26-9+ Mr '65
HEALTH costs. See Medical service, Cost of
HEALTH education
Harmful habits linked to health study gap; need for school health education programs. Sr Schol 86:sup4+ Mr 18 '65
HEALTH, education and welfare, Department of. See United States—Health, education and welfare, Department of
HEALTH examinations. See Physical examinations
HEALTH insurance. See Insurance, Health

HEALTH insurance companies. See Insurance companies
HEALTH machines
See also
Quacks and quackery
HEALTH records, Children's. See Children—Care and hygiene
HEALTH resorts, watering places, etc.
Executive beauty; California's Golden door. il Newsweek 65:80 Mr 22 '65
Happiness is a bad liver; visit to French and Italian cure centers. P. Dragadze. il Life 59:95+ N 26 '65
Holiday handbook of American spas. H. Papashvily. il Holiday 37:133-8 My '65
Hot Springs havens; spa hotels. J. Heuston. il Travel 123:44-5 Mr '65
Travel well; Kamena Vourla, resort town in Greece. E. N. Dye. Travel 124:43-4 S '65
Valkyrie at the beauty ranch. S. Alexander. Life 59:29 N 5 '65
See also
Montecatini Terme, Italy
HEALTH service. See Medical service
HEALTH workers
Health careers unlimited. L. Velie. Read Digest 87:108-12 Ag '65
HEALY, John J.
Book reviews. America 113:724-5 D 4 '65
HEALY, Mary
Aboard the 36' cruiser Queen Mary with Peter Lind Hayes and Mary Healy. G. Sloane. il por Motor B 115:60-1+ Je '65
HEALY, Thomas W. See LaMer, V. K. jt. auth.
HEARING
Auditory nerve: electrical stimulation in man. F. B. Simmons and others. bibliog il Science 148:104-6 Ap 2 '65
Temperature effects on the peripheral auditory apparatus. A. C. Coats. bibliog il Science 150:1481-3 D 10 '65
See also
Deafness
HEARING aids
Big secret: federal government's consumer reports service. New Repub 152:7 My 22 '65; Discussion. 152:30 Je 5; 37 Je 26 '65
Hearing aids. il Consumer Rep 31:30-9 Ja '66
Who'd rather be deaf? E. Corbett. Atlan 216:116+ O '65
Wired for sound; substitute receptors to transmit impulses to the auditory nerve. il Newsweek 66:56 Jl 12 '65
HEARING in animals
Auditory habituation: a test of a centrifugal and a peripheral theory. W. R. Webster and others. bibliog il Science 148:654-6 Ap 30 '65
Electrical output of lizard ear: relation to hair-cell population. E. G. Wever and others. il Science 150:1172-4 N 26 '65
Hearing sensitivity in bats. J. I. Dalland. bibliog il Science 150:1185-6 N 26 '65
HEARING in insects
See also
Ear (insects)
HEARN, Norman E.
Guidance: opportunities unlimited. Sr Schol 87:sup9+ N 11 '65
HEARST, James
Close the accounts; poem. Commonweal 83:57 O 15 '65
Farmer's season; poem. America 112:550 Ap 17 '65
Hen pheasant; Forsythia; Behind the stove; poems. Poetry 106:405-7 S '65
Hog economy; poem. America 113:20 Jl 3 '65
Love in autumn; poem. America 112:772 My 22 '65
Quarrel; poem. America 113:671 N 27 '65
Wilderness ways; poem. Commonweal 82:13 Mr 26 '65
HEARST, William Randolph
Vulgar press. D. Cort. Commonweal 81:761-3 Mr 12 '65
HEART
Neurosecretory processes extending into third ventricle: secretory or sensory? C. G. Smoller. bibliog il Science 147:882-4 F 19 '65
Steroid stimulation of beating of cultured rat-heart cells. R. L. McCarl and others. bibliog il Science 150:1611-13 D 17 '65

Abnormalities and deformities
See also
Heart—Surgery

Diseases
Acid test; linseed oil to curb coronaries. Newsweek 66:48-9 S 6 '65
Boy called funny face. F. F. Kirk. Read Digest 87:93-7 O '65
Case of the cranky baby; inborn heart defects. Time 85:54 Ap 9 '65

HEATH, John Kingsley-. See Kingsley-Heath, J.

HEATING
Heat by light. il Time 86:51 Ag 6 '65
Heating the house. il Consumer Rep 30:74-80 F '65
Modern home heating systems: the ultimate in comfort. Good H 161:172+ S '65
See also
Boilers
Fuel economy
Radiant heating

HEATING, Infrared
Infra-reds harden paint and melt snow. Am City 80:26+ S '65

HEATING equipment
Heating and cooling for housing. F. H. Kluckhuhn. il Arch Rec 138:211-12 O '65
Mechanical services for a large courthouse; temperature control. A. Schroeder. il Arch Rec 138:205-8 O '65
Summerize your heating system. W. J. Fletcher. Suc Farm 63:29 Je '65
See also
Electric heaters
Heat pumps
Oil burners

HEBERT, V. Leslie
Liberty tree. Horticulture 43:38-9+ Ap '65

HEBREW education. See Jews—Education

HEBREW language
Department of amplification. C. Raphael. New Yorker 41:150+ Mr 27 '65

HEBREW literature
See also
Hebrew poetry
Talmud

HEBREW manuscripts. See Manuscripts, Hebrew

HEBREW poetry
Modern Hebrew poem itself; ed. by S. Burnshaw and others. Review
Commentary 40:88+ O '65. B. Hochman

HEBREW religion. See Judaism

HEBREW university, Jerusalem. See Colleges and universities—Israel

HEBRIDES
Man's retreat from the islands. R. Kirk. Nat R 17:107 F 9 '65

HECHINGER, Fred Michael
Head start to where? Sat R 48:58-60+ D 18 '65
Room for whom at the top? Sat R 48:70-1+ Ap 17 '65
Uncle Sam's billion dollar push for better schools. Parents Mag 40:45-7+ S '65
—See Hechinger, G. jt. auth.

HECHINGER, Grace, and Hechinger, F. M.
How much have our schools improved since Sputnik? questions and answers. McCalls 92:94 F '65
In the time it takes you to read these lines the American teen-ager will have spent $2,378.22. Esquire 64:65+ Jl '65
Parent and child. N Y Times Mag p39 Ja 31 '65
Pressures on students and teachers; questions and answers. McCalls 92:180-1 Ap '65

HECHT, Bessie M.
Science in action: students in the museum. Natur Hist 75:66-7 Ja '66

HECHT, Florence
Good-by to Molly; story. Redbook 125:68-9 O '65

HECHT, George J.
Safety features in the new 1966 cars. Parents Mag 41:51-5+ Ja '66

HECHT, Harold
Two-gun banana. il Newsweek 65:118A+ My 10 '65

HECHT company. See Washington, D.C.—Stores

HECKER, Isaac T.
Human rights: divine, fundamental, practical; reprint of June 1887. Cath World 202: 47 O '65
Spiritual guidance; reprint from Catholic world, February 1888. Cath World 202:165 D '65
Things that make for unity; reprint. Cath World 201:55 Ap '65
Why we publish what we publish; reprint of February 1868. Cath World 201:307 Ag '65
about
Father Hecker, a bridge between Catholic and Protestant thought. R. T. Handy. Cath World 202:158-9+ D '65

HECKMAN, Donald
Month's jazz. See issues of American record guide
Two views of the avant-garde repertoire at Philharmonic Hall. Am Rec G 32:354 D '65

HECKSCHER, August
Arts in a New World. por Craft Horiz 25:11 My '65
On seeing and believing. Sat R 48:125-6 Mr 13 '65
Rebels with causes. Sat R 48:42 Je 12 '65

HEDGE clippers
Electric hedge and bush trimmers. il Consumer Bul 48:22-3 Mr '65

HEDGEMAN, Anna Arnold
After the good white life. R. A. Low. Sat R 48:31 F 6 '65

HEDGES
Green walls: you have many splendid choices. il Sunset 134:248-50+ My '65

HEDGPETH, Joel W.
Bodega Head, a partisan view. Bul Atomic Sci 21:2-7 Mr '65

HEDIN, Mary
Places we lost; story. McCalls 93:120-1 O '65

HEDMAN, Frank
Notes from our correspondents (cont) Hi Fi 15:20+ Ag '65

HEDONISM
Two cheers for hedonism. M. Himmelfarb. Commentary 39:61-5 Ap '65

HEED, William B. and Kircher, H. W.
Unique sterol in the ecology and nutrition of drosophila pachea. bibliog Science 149: 758-61 Ag 13 '65

HEELS (shoes) See Shoes

HEENAN, John Carmel, cardinal
Two interventions on behalf of religious liberty. Cath World 202:176-7 D '65
about
Ecumenism and converts. America 112:798 My 29 '65

HEENEY, A. D. P. See Merchant, L. T. jt. auth.

HEESEN, Willem
Heesen's glass: risk and discipline. D. Smith. il por Craft Horiz 25:34-7+ Ja '65

HEEZEN, Bruce C. See Bourne, D. W. jt. auth.

HEFFNER, Richard
Democracy in a hurry. Sat R 48:64-5 O 23 '65
(ed) See Fromm, E. Interview with Erich Fromm

HEFNER, Hugh M.
Empire built on sex; with report by D. Lurie. il pors Life 59:68-73 O 29 '65
Plato, the penthouse, and the girl who hesitates. G. Roy. Mlle 60:199+ Mr '65

HEFNER, Philip
Horizons in science. Christian Cent 82:368-9 Mr 24 '65

HEFTMANN, Erich. See Bennett, R. D. jt. auth.

HEGEL, Georg Wilhelm Friedrich
From Hegel to Nietzsche: the revolution in nineteenth-century thought, by K. Löwith. Review
Commentary 39:100-4 Je '65. W. J. Dannhauser

HEIDEGGER, Martin
Earlier Heidegger. Christian Cent 82:453 Ap 14 '65; Discussion. 82:813 Je 23 '65
Heidegger, being, and truth, by L. Versényi. Review
Sat R 48:89-90 My 22 '65. G. W. Linden

HEIDT, Ann
3-D through tints. Design 67:24-5 N '65

HEIFERS
How do your heifers grow? Suc Farm 63:64D N '65

HEIGHT of man. See Stature

HEIKKENEN, Herman J. and Hrutfiord, B. F.
Dendroctonus pseudotsugae: a hypothesis regarding its primary attractant. bibliog Science 150:1457-9 D 10 '65

HEILBRONER, Robert L.
Power of big business. Atlan 216:89-93 S '65

HEILPERIN, Michael A.
Behind Britain's economic woes. Fortune 71: 160-1+ Je '65

HEIMBERGER, Frederic
Grass roots of campus freedom. Sat R 48:60-1+ Jl 17 '65

HEIN, Piet
Mathematical games. M. Gardner. il Sci Am 213:222+ S '65

HEINEMAN, Ben W.
Chicago's miracle. A. Schiller. Harper 232:65-8+ Ja '66

HEINEMANN, Arthur
Doctor Putney's darkest hour; story. McCalls 92:76-7 Jl '65
Family man; story. Redbook 125:48-9 Je '65
I love you, Charley, please come back; story. McCalls 92:76-7 S '65
Plan ahead. Writer 78:14-16 D '65

HEINITZ, Thomas
Retiring mezzo. Sat R 48:50 My 29 '65

HELICOPTERS—Military applications—*Cont.*
Biggest, and ugliest, chopper goes to war. il Pop Sci 187:88-9 D '65
Caps set for copters. il Time 86:43A-43B N 19 '65
Detailed analysis to affect selection of army aircraft. G. Wilson. il Aviation W 82:80-1+ Mr 15 '65
Good copters, but bum tactics; U.S. helicopter tactics in South Vietnam. J. Dille. il Life 58:34D Ap 16 '65
Helicopter research begins to pay off. D. A. Brown. il Aviation W 82:245-7 Mr 15 '65
Helicopter tactics shaped by experience; war in Vietnam. C. Brownlow. il Aviation W 82:68-9+ My 31 '65
Helicopters dominate new fund request. C. Brownlow. Aviation W 83:26+ Ag 9 '65
Hughes readies OH-6A facilities; sales seen topping 7,000. C. M. Plattner. il Aviation W 82:62-3+ Je 28 '65
IHAS program may establish precedents in concepts, technology; integrated helicopter avionics system. B. Miller. il Aviation W 82:40-1+ Je 21 '65
New lift for the whirlybirds. il Bsns W p84-6+ F 27 '65
Sikorsky plans semi-compound AAFSS; Advanced aerial fire support system. D. A. Brown. il Aviation W 82:105-6 My 10 '65
UH-2A, S-61 still vying for armed role. G. C. Wilson. il Aviation W 83:60-1+ D 20 '65
Vertol to increase helicopter production. D. E. Fink. il Aviation W 83:61-5 N 29 '65
Whirlybird academy; army's school at Fort Rucker. il Life 60:75+ Ja 14 '66

Piloting
Gone flying to Shelter Cove. R. Blodget. il Flying 78:60-2 Ja '66
Just a little squeeze, please. P. Demarest. il Flying 77:42-5 Ag '65
Once around the parking lot. R. Blodget. il Flying 77:62-6 S '65
Rotary club. R. Weeghman. il Flying 77:34-9 Jl '65

Rotors
See Rotors (helicopters)

Testing
Pilot report; the Brantly 305, B2B. R. B. Weeghman. il Flying 77:40-4 D '65
U.S. pilots try out Russian helicopters. C. M. Plattner. il Aviation W 83:36-9+ Jl 26 '65

HELICOPTERS, Business
Brantly aiming 305 at executive market. D. A. Brown. il Aviation W 82:88-9+ My 31 '65

HELICOPTERS, Freight
S-64 finishes Alpine heavy transport test. Aviation W 83:96 S 20 '65

HELICOPTERS, Jet propelled
Bell to market five-place jet helicopter. il Aviation W 83:25 O 18 '65

HELICOPTERS, Military. See Helicopters—Military applications

HELICOPTERS in fire protection
Navy tests light water airborne fire-fighting system; combating crash fires on and off airfields. il Aviation W 83:90-1 Ag 23 '65

HELICOPTERS in industry
Watch the whirlybird at work. H. Manchester. il Read Digest 87:253+ N '65

HELICOPTERS in insect control
Helicopters are found to excel in precise pesticide spraying. Aviation W 83:97+ O 11 '65

HELICOPTERS in medical service
Gamest bastards of all; medical evacuation team. il Time 86:25 Jl 2 '65

HELICOPTERS in pipe laying
Water supply line built by airlift; project on the Island of Maui, Hawaii. il Am City 81:97+ Ja '66

HELICOPTERS in prospecting
Great Alaska ore snatch. il Sci Digest 57:66-9 Ap '65

HELICOPTERS in rescue work
Crisis at Coral Creek. A. Klumph. il Outdoor Life 136:24-7+ Ag '65
Operation rescue; Fifth air rescue detachment in South Viet Nam. il Time 85:21A Mr 12 '65
Six HH-43Fs handle bulk of air rescue; war in Vietnam. C. Brownlow. il Aviation W 82:71+ My 3 '65

HELICOPTERS in surveying
Electronic surveying; platform in the sky. il Pop Electr 22:64 F '65

HELIPORTS
Future for choppers? service opens off Pan Am building. il Newsweek 67:41-2 Ja 3 '66
Heliport; top of Pan American building, New York. New Yorker 41:19-22 Ja 1 '66

Roof heliport gives copter line a lift; seven minutes from New York's Pan Am building to Kennedy airport. il Bsns W p 18-20 D 25 '65
Skyscraper airport for faster plane travel; roof of Pan Am building, New York. il U S News 60:10 Ja 3 '66
Skyscraper sky-lift; mid-Manhattan gets its first heliport. il Life 60:55-6 Ja 7 '66

HELIUM
Douglas tests helium as atmosphere. H. M. David. Miss & Roc 16:38-41 Je 28 '65
Helium and the galaxy's age. Sky & Tel 29:219 Ap '65
Helium-glow photometer for picomole analysis of alkali metals. G. G. Vurek and R. L. Bowman. bibliog il Science 149:448-50 Jl 23 '65
Helium looks feasible for use in MOL cabin. il Miss & Roc 17:38-9 D 20 '65
Where did cosmic helium originate? G. S. Mumford. Sky & Tel 29:88 F '65

HELIUM-uranium dating. See Radioactive dating

HELL
Thought of hell. C. Davis. America 112:394 Mr 20 '65

HELL in art
Modern Inferno. il Life 59:44-9 D 17 '65

HELLBENDERS. See Salamanders

HELLEBORUS niger. See Christmas roses

HELLER, Alfred, and others
5-Hydroxytryptophan decarboxylase in rat brain; effect of hypothalamic lesions. bibliog Science 147:887-8 F 19 '65

HELLER, Norman
Nine simple rules for travel photography. il U S Camera 28:56-7+ D '65

HELLER, Walter Wolfgang
What 1966 holds for business; excerpts from report. por U S News 59:110-11 S 27 '65

about
Is there a new economy? G. R. Rosen. il por Duns R 85:38-41+ Je '65

HELLMAN, H.
What is the e. m. spectrum? Sci Digest 57:69-77 Je '65

HELLO, Mr Groundhog; drama. See Miller, H. L.

HELL'S Angels. See Gangs

HELLSTRÖM, K. E. and others
Abrogation of allogeneic inhibition by cortisone. bibliog Science 149:82-4 Jl 2 '65

HELM, Everett
Adventure in Poland. Hi Fi 15:185 D '65
Aesthetic thaw in progress. Hi Fi 15:141 Ag '65
Biennale, 1965. Hi Fi 15:179 D '65
Greetings to Orff, amends to Strauss. Hi Fi 15:164-5 O '65
Mad for music. Hi Fi 15:134-5 My '65
Miraculous inventions of Heinrich Schütz. Hi Fi 15:51-5+ Ag '65
Notes from our correspondents. Hi Fi 15:24+ My '65

HELMETS
Face-saving helmet to knit for servicemen. il Good H 161:228 N '65

HELMREICH, Ernst C.
Kadar's Hungary. bibliog f Cur Hist 48:142-8 Mr '65

HELMS, Paul Hoy
When Helms went to the opera; excerpt from Biography of an idea. E. L. Bernays. por Fortune 72:139+ O '65

HELMSLEY, Harry B.
Two realty partners tackle a big one alone. por Bsns W p 105-6+ Ag 21 '65

HELPFULNESS. See Service

HELSINKI

Description
Helsinki: ice-blue and sun-white, with Arabia on its outskirts. D. Messinesi. Vogue 146:61 N 15 '65

Stores
Call Helsinki 12-181; Stockmann's. il Newsweek 66:54 Ag 2 '65

HEMENWAY, Joan
Breakthroughs: Covenant House in Philadelphia. Christian Cent 82:1316-19 O 27 '65

HEMERYTHRIN. See Pigments (biology)

HEMICHORDATE worms. See Balanoglossus

HEMINGWAY, Ernest
To Mary in London; Second poem to Mary; poems. Atlan 216:94-100 Ag '65

HEMINGWAY, Ernest—*Continued*

about

[Circumstances in which To Mary in London and Second poem to Mary were written] M. W. Hemmingway. por Atlan 216:96 Ag '65

European literary scene; Hemingway's literary reputation. R. J. Clements. Sat R 48: 21 Ag 7 '65

Footnote from Hemingway's Paris, 1965. W. A. Krauss. il Harper 231:91-5 Ag '65

Hemingway in Cuba. R. Manning. il por Atlan 216:101-8 Ag '65

Last words of E.H. K. Vanderbilt. Nation 201:284-5 O 25 '65

Legends of the old man. M. Callaghan. Sat R 48:43 Ag 28 '65

Meeting; poem; tr. by S. J. Parker. E. Evtushenko. Sat R 48:22 Ag 7 '65

Papa's poems. por Time 86:33 Jl 30 '65

To Parajiso with Papa and Pilar. M. Hemingway. il Sports Illus 23:62-8+ Jl 12 '65

HEMINGWAY, Mary (Welsh)

[Circumstances in which To Mary in London and Second poem to Mary were written] por Atlan 216:96 Ag '65

Redbook dialogue: Mary Hemingway and Robert Morley. pors Redbook 126:62-3+ N '65

To Parajiso with Papa and Pilar. Sports Illus 23:62-8+ Jl 12 '65

about

Papa's poems. por Time 86:33 Jl 30 '65

HEMINGWAY, Patrick

Chip off the old Hemingway; son in the Africa loved by both. il pors Life 59:39-40+ Ag 6 '65

HEMMING, Roy

DISCussions. See issues of Senior scholastic

With Senior's editor in Viet Nam; questions and answers. por Sr Schol 86:15-16 F 11; 17+ F 25; 12-13 Mr 4 '65

HEMOGLOBIN

Animal proteins provide a study of evolution. Sci N L 87:185 Mr 20 '65

Electrophoresis of hemoglobin in single erythrocytes. G. T. Matioli and H. B. Niewisch. bibliog il Science 150:1824-6 D 31 '65

Evolution of hemoglobin. E. Zuckerkandl. il Sci Am 212:110-18 bibliog(p 152) My '65

Hemoglobin and oxygen: affinities in seven species of sciuridae. F. G. Hall. bibliog il Science 148:1350-1 Je 4 '65

Hemoglobin and transferrin electrophoresis and relationships of island populations of anolis lizards. G. C. Gorman and H. C. Dessauer. bibliog il Science 150:1454-5 D 10 '65

Hemoglobin F$_{Texas}$: gamma-chain variant. R. G. Schneider and R. T. Jones. bibliog il Science 148:240-2 Ap 9 '65

Hemoglobin heterogeneity: embryonic hemoglobin in the duckling and its disappearance in the adult. T. A. Borgese and J. F. Bertles. bibliog il Science 148:509-11 Ap 23 '65

Hemoglobin J$_{Korat}$ in Thais. R. Q. Blackwell and others. bibliog Science 150:1614-15 D 17 '65

Hemoglobin polymerization in mice. A. Riggs. bibliog il Science 147:621-3 F 5 '65

Molecules and monkeys. J. Buettner-Janusch and R. L. Hill. bibliog il Science 147:836-42 F 19 '65

Oxygen-hemoglobin system: a model for facilitated membranous transport. D. B. Zilversmit. bibliog il Science 149:874-6 Ag 20 '65

Tension gradients accompanying accelerated oxygen transport in a membrane. P. F. Scholander. bibliog il Science 149:876-7 Ag 20 '65

HEMOLYSINS

Hemolysin of mycoplasma pneumoniae: tentative identification as a peroxide. N. L. Somerson and others. bibliog il Science 150:226-8 O 8 '65

Hemolysin production in the development of staphylococcal lesions. E. A. Foster. bibliog il Science 149:1395-6 S 17 '65

HEMOPHILIA

Clot substance isolated. Sci N L 87:259 Ap 24 '65

Coddling found to be problem of hemophiliacs. Sci N L 88:149 S 4 '65

Colony of hemophilic dogs. J. M. White and G. C. Holm. Science 150:1766 D 31 '65

Lifesaving stopgap for bleeders: antihemophilic globulin (AHG) Time 86:64 Ag 6 '65

Royal hemophilia. V. A. McKusick. il Sci Am 213:88-95 bibliog(p 120) Ag '65; Reply with rejoinder. A. L. Gram. 213:6 D '65

HEMORRHAGE, Cerebral. See Cerebral hemorrhage

HEMORRHAGIC fever

Hemorrhagic fever war rages; Bolivian hemorrhagic fever. F. Marley. il Sci N L 87:74-5 Ja 30 '65

Mosquito cause of fever outbreak in Malaysia. Sci N L 87:345 My 29 '65

HEMORRHAGIC shock. See Shock

HEMPSTEAD, N.Y.

Le Roy-on-the-spot; community center building. il Recreation 58:428-9 N '65

Street cleaning involves more than sweeping. H. Haff. il Am City 80:100-1 Jl '65

HEMSLEY, Stuart

Low moment on the high road; poem. Atlan 216:97 Jl '65

Sapphics (and why not?) from the second aisle over; poem. Atlan 216:110 Ag '65

Wistfully, from the stalls; poem. Atlan 216: 157 O '65

HEN-and-chickens. See Houseleeks

HEN houses. See Poultry houses

HENAHAN, Donal J.

Culture comes to Cherokee. Holiday 38:21-6 Jl '65

HENDERSON, Arthur

Keeping peace among allies. Sat R 48:41-2 Jl 24 '65

HENDERSON, Bonnie Jo

There's some milk in the icebox; text. Mlle 62:176-7+ N '65

HENDERSON, Everett S.

June rivals. Pop Gard 16:31+ My '65

Outstanding shrubs. Horticulture 43:48-9 O '65

Sample summer's riches. Pop Gard 16:36-7 Ap '65

Seashore gardens on the Atlantic coast. Pop Gard 16:22-3+ Jl '65

HENDERSON, Lois T.

Long steep hill to victory. Read Digest 86: 103-7 Je '65

HENDERSON, Robert

House that Jerry built; story. New Yorker 41:48-51 N 20 '65

Intruder; story. Sat Eve Post 238:44-6 Mr 13 '65

Unknown rooms; story. New Yorker 41:36-40 Je 5 '65

HENDERSON, William J.

Big four. E. H. Huneker. por Opera N 30: 11-12 D 18 '65

HENDERSON COUNTY public library, Hendersonville, N.C.

Community action. M. Seagle. Wilson Lib Bul 40:256 N '65

HENDRICKS, Donald

Cooperative growing pains. por Library J 90:4699-703 N 1 '65

HENDRICKS, Frederick Maurice

Frederick Hendrick. 1946-1965. F. Knebel. Look 29:24-5 O 5 '65

HENDRICKS family

Collection. New Yorker 41:30-2 Je 12 '65

HENKE, Esther Mae

Interlibrary cooperation in Oklahoma; address, July 1965. Wilson Lib Bul 40:162-5 O '65

HENKES, Robert

Nature, sole source of motivation. Sch Arts 65:32-5 N '65

HENKIN, Mark

How to choose and use your life insurance. Am Home 68:16+ Mr; 13+ Ap '65

HENLE, Ray

There goes a good man. Nat R 17:452 Je 1 '65

HENLEY royal regatta. See Regattas

HENLOPEN, CAPE

Living sand. W. H. Amos. il Nat Geog Mag 127:820-33 Je '65

HENLOPEN dunes. See Sand dunes

HENNEPIN, Ill.

Boom town 1965: plans for Jones & Laughlin steel mill. il Time 86:90+ Jl 9 '65

HENNESEY, James J.

U.S. representative at the Vatican? America 113:707-11 D 4 '65

HENNESSY, Maurice N.

New directions for British education? Sat R 48:58-9+ Ag 21 '65

HENNESSY, Mildred L. See Tucker, H. W. jt. auth.

HENNIG, G. R.

Screw dislocations in graphite. bibliog Science 147:733-4 F 12 '65

HENNIG, P. T.

Bird automat. Pop Mech 124:156-7 N '65

HENNIGAN, Charley

Flanker who catches too many passes. E. Shrake. il por Sports Illus 23:109-11 S 20 '65

HENNING, Paul

Country slicker. il Newsweek 66:97 D 6 '65

HENRI d'Orléans, comte de Paris

Common touch. il por Newsweek 65:52+ My 24 '65

HENRI, W. Laramie
Rams of Ural. por Field & S 70:43-5+ Ag '65
HENRIOT, Peter J.
Book reviews. America 113:345-7 S 25 '65
Convocation on Pacem in terris. America 112:223-4 F 13 '65
HENRY, Carl
Amateur scientist. Sci Am 213:108+ O '65
HENRY, David D.
Outlook: worse next fall; interview. por U S News 58:58-60 F 1 '65
HENRY, E. William
Educational television is still just a promise. por Am Ed 1:26-8 F '65
HENRY, John M.
(comp) I saw it in the paper. See issues of McCall's to June 1965
HENRY, Joseph
Americans nobody knows. C. W. Ferguson. por PTA Mag 59:25-7 Je '65
HENRY, Patrick
If this be treason. il Sr Schol 86:8 My 20 '65
HENRY, Rene A. Jr
For the garden handyman build a wishing well. Pop Gard 17:19 Ja '66
HENRY, Robert
Changing times. Newsweek 67:27 Ja 17 '66
HENRY, Vera
Family skeleton with solid gold teeth. Writer 78:14-15+ Ap '65
Glass world in June; story. Seventeen 24:90-1 Je '65
HENRY Ford community college, Dearborn, Mich.
Community college provides campus plan for two-year program. il Arch Rec 137:184-6 Mr '65
HENRY Ford museum and Greenfield Village, Dearborn, Mich.
Ford archives donated to museum; gift to Edison institute. il Hobbies 70:53 Ap '65
HENRY IV; drama. See Shakespeare, W.— Plays
HENTOFF, Nat
Books. New Yorker 41:71-4+ Jl 31 '65; 115-17 Ja 15 '66
Doctor digs jazz. Holiday 37:109-10+ My '65
Filling holes in the soul. Reporter 32:44+ Mr 11 '65
Jazz revolution. Reporter 32:42+ My 20 '65
Mature Mr Bennett. Holiday 38:158+ N '65
Processing and packaging our children. Commonweal 82:386-7 Je 11 '65
Profiles (cont) New Yorker 41:32-4+ Je 26; 32-4+ Jl 3 '65; Correction. 41:102 S 11 '65
This cat needs no Pulitzer prize. N Y Times Mag p64-6+ S 12 '65
Trial by newspaper. Commonweal 82:110-13 Ap 16 '65
What next for the civil rights movement? Commonweal 81:661-3 F 19 '65
HENZE, Hans Werner
On records: Elegy for young lovers. Opera N 29:34 F 13 '65
Stag king. Criticism
  Hi Fi il 15:198+ N '65
Young lord (Junge lord) Criticism
  Hi Fi il 15:132-3 Je '65
  Opera N il 30:26-7 S 25 '65
  Time il 85:72 Je 11 '65
HEPATIC artery. See Arteries
HEPATITIS, Infectious
What parents ask about infectious hepatitis. M. J. E. Senn. McCalls 92:54 Ap '65
HEPATITIS virus
Hepatitis breakthrough; study of viral hepatitis. Sci Digest 58:17 Ag '65
HEPATOMAS. See Tumors
HEPBURN, Andrew H.
Holiday travel; with questions and answers. Sr Schol 87:sup 12-13 S 23; sup 16-17 O 28; sup 12-13 N 11 '65
HERAKLES; drama. See MacLeish, A.
HERALD tribune, New York. See New York herald tribune
HERALDRY
At the sign of the crest. H. K. Eilers. See issues of Hobbies
HERBARIUMS
  See also
Plants—Collection and preservation
HERBER, Harold L.
Building word power. Sr Schol 86:9T F 11 '65
New trends in textbook development and use. Sr Schol 87:sup7+ N 18 '65
HERBERG, Will
Civil rights and violence. por Nat R 17:769-70 S 7 '65
Conservatism, liberalism, and religion. por Nat R 17:1087-8 N 30 '65
New estate. por Nat R 17:590 Jl 13 '65
Open season on the church? por Nat R 17:363-4 My 4 '65

HERBICIDES
3,4-Dichlorobenzyl methylcarbamate and related compounds as herbicides. R. A. Herrett and R. V. Berthold. bibliog il Science 149:191-3 Jl 9 '65
Enzyme from soil bacterium hydrolyzes phenylcarbamate herbicides. P. C. Kearney and D. D. Kaufman. Science 147:740 F 12 '65
Herbicide metabolism: N-glycoside of amiben isolated from soybean plants. S. R. Colby. bibliog il Science 150:619-20 O 29 '65
Pesty plant routed by simple chemicals. Sci N L 88:248 O 16 '65
Report on preemergence weed killers for corn and soybeans. Suc Farm 63:88-9 Mr '65
  See also
Weeds—Chemical control

Residues
How to avoid a herbicide residue problem. O. C. Burnside. Suc Farm 63:70F Ap '65
HERBS
Green flowers and herb trees. B. Mellon. il Vogue 146:208-11 D '65
Growing herbs is easy and fun. T. Merkert. il Flower Grower 52:16 My '65
Herbs for roadside plantings; ideas for beautifying America from our readers. Flower Grower 52:12 Ag '65
Herbs for summer bouquets. D. Warren. Horticulture 43:29 Jl '65
Herbs; in your garden and on your windowsill. G. B. Foster; F. F. Davis. il Horticulture 43:46-9 F '65
Herbs; sweet-scented ingredients of enchanting gardens. il House & Gard 128:98-9 Ag '65
Home garden notebook. J. B. Brimer. il Flower Grower 53:53-4 Ja '66
Pick a gift from your herb garden. M. W. Muenscher. il Pop Gard 16:12-13 N '65
Spices and herbs have an intriguing history. il Todays Health 43:31 O '65
  See also
Borages
Parsley
Potpourri
Rosemary
HERBST, Edward J. See Dykstra, W. G. jr, jt. auth.
HERCULES powder company
Hercules, Thiokol win Poseidon work. Miss & Roc 17:16 O 25 '65
HEREDITY
Double mating: its use to study heritable factors in dental caries. R. H. Larson and M. E. Simms. bibliog Science 149:982-3 Ag 27 '65
Expectant mother; whom will your baby take after? E. J. De Costa and B. R. Boylan. Redbook 126:26-7 Ja '66
Hurler's syndrome: demonstration of an inherited disorder of connective tissue in cell culture. B. S. Danes and A. G. Bearn. bibliog il Science 149:987-9 Ag 27 '65
  See also
Evolution
Genetics
Mendelism
Mutation (biology)
Variegation
HEREDITY of disease
Are the killer diseases inherited? Good H 160:165-7 Je '65
Chromosomal breakage in a rare and probably genetically determined syndrome of man. J. German and others. bibliog il Science 148:506 Ap 23 '65
Clues to disease control seen in RNA research. Sci N L 87:360 Je 5 '65
Hereditary angioneurotic edema: two genetic variants. F. S. Rosen and others. bibliog il Science 148:957-8 My 14 '65
Molecular basis of heredity; report on symposium held under the auspices of the United States-Japan cooperative science program. S. E. Luria. Science 150:80-2 O 1 '65
Risk hereditary diseases. Sci N L 88:115 Ag 21 '65
Will our baby be normal? M. J. O'Neill. il McCalls 92:64+ My '65
  See also
Heterozygosis
HEREN, Louis
King's men: a British view of the White House. Harper 230:108+ F '65
HERHOLD, Robert M.
Kirchentag 1965: call for reform; summary of conference. Christian Cent 82:1064-5 S 1 '65
HÉRIAT, Philippe
Les joies de la famille; adaptation. See Gordon, R. Very rich woman

HERING, Doris
Dance and decentralization; excerpts from interview; ed. by A. H. Reiss. Dance Mag 39:124-6 D '65
Regional ballet, USA. See issues of Dance magazine

HERING, Robert L.
Add a place to park your power equipment and garden tools. Pop Gard 16:32-4 S '65

HERLIHY, Ed
Captain Herlihy emcee of the 42' Big Jeanne. G. Sloane. il por Motor B 116:56-7+ O '65

HERLIHY, James Leo
Fright of Mrs Yeager; story. Esquire 64:108-9 O '65

HERLINE, Tom
Traffic control on a limited budget. Am City 80:183-4 Mr '65

HERMAN, Melvin. See Schreiber, F. R. jt. auth.

HERMAN, Reinhold W.
Now I set me; poem. Read Digest 87:234 N '65

HERMANN, Robert
Treating a baby before birth; reprint. Sci Digest 57:70-4 Ap '65
Why not nibble like a rat? reprint. Sci Digest 57:53-7 Mr '65

HERMAPHRODITISM
Hermaphroditic fish; report on conference. J. W. Atz. Science 150:789-92+ N 5 '65
Mating of groupers. E. Clark. il Natur Hist 74:22-5 Je '65
See also
Gynandromorphism

HERMIT; story. See Updike, J.

HERMITAGE, Leningrad
Hermitage. il Life 58:53-73 Mr 26; 62-82+ Ap 2; 43-58+ Ap 9 '65
Hermitage: Russia's fabulous art palace. J. A. Michener. il Read Digest 86:133-41 Mr '65

HERNANDEZ, José
Epic of the gaucho: Martín Fierro, with excerpts. C. E. Ward. il Américas 17:8-15 N '65

HERNANDEZ, James
Our scope of freedom. Negro Hist Bul 28:76 Ja '65

HERNDON, James
Way it spozed to be. Harper 231:79-87 S '65

HERNIA
There's only one cure for hernia. R. D. Ratcliff. il Todays Health 43:60-1 N '65; Same abr. with title Quick repair for hernia. Read Digest 87:120-2 N '65

HERO worship
Idol remembered. M. Evelyn. Esquire 64:84-5 Jl '65

HEROD I, the Great, king of Judea
Herod's anguished decision. Commonweal 83:359-60 D 24 '65

HEROES
Hero comes home. K. O. Gilmore. Read Digest 87:61-6 N '65
Sergeant Erwin and the blazing bomb; Congressional medal of honor awarded. C. Ford. il Read Digest 87:86-8 Jl '65
Thirteenth mission; A. Maynarski's gallantry. ed. by D. MacDonald. G. P. Brophy. il Read Digest 87:78-82 D '65
Twenty-eight people who count; heroes of the California rebels. il Esquire 64:97 S '65

Anecdotes, facetiae, satire, etc.
What happened to the moment of truth? M. Drogin. il Read Digest 87:39-40 O '65

HEROISM. See Courage

HEROLD, Don
Early to bed and late to rise. Read Digest 87:29-30+ Ag '65
I couldn't have stood marriage. Read Digest 87:25-6 S '65

HERON, A. deF. See Daye, J. R. jt. auth.

HERON, Charles J.
Transistor CB-AM converter. Electr World 73:76-7 Je '65

HERPES-like viruses. See Viruses

HERPES simplex virus
Virus dryer; dry air treatment for infected eye. Sci Digest 58:37 O '65

HERR, Michael
Drug puzzle. Mlle 61:246-7+ Ag '65

HERR von Hancken; opera. See Blomdahl, K. B.

HERRERA, Felipe
Regional financing. Américas 17:59-64 Ap '65

HERRERA, Philip
Structure & design. Fortune 72:179-80+ S '65

HERRESHOFF, Halsey C. and Kerwin, J. E.
Sailing yacht research. Yachting 118:51-3+ Jl '65

HERRETT, Richard A. and Berthold, R. V.
3,4-Dichlorobenzyl methylcarbamate and related compounds as herbicides. bibliog Science 149:191-3 Jl 9 '65

HERRICK, John B.
Tips on stopping scours. pors Suc Farm 63:60-1 Mr '65
Watch out, don't poison your livestock. Suc Farm 63:39 Ag '65
You can control vibriosis. Suc Farm 63:38A Mr '65

HERRING, Tod
Floyd is beginning to see the light, finally. J. Lovesey. Sports Illus 22:72-3 My 24 '65

HERRNSTEIN, Richard J.
In defense of bird brains. Atlan 216:101-4 S '65

HERRON art institute workshop. See Indianapolis—Art

HERSCHLER, Robert J.
Report on DMSO. il por Sci Digest 58:78-82 Ag '65

HERSEY, John
Master Hersey. il por Newsweek 65:52 Je 7 '65
Master novelist. il por Time 85:50 Je 4 '65

HERSEY, M. Leonard
Control points. See issues of Yachting
Current situation. Motor B 115:102+ Ap '65

HERSH, Burton
Rope-tow hill to Mascara Mountain. Holiday 37:161+ Mr '65

HERSHBERGER, H. M.
Where are they now. Hot Rod 19:78-80 Ja '66

HERSHENSON, Maurice, and others
Preference for shapes of intermediate variability in the newborn human. bibliog Science 147:630-1 F 5 '65

HERSHEY, Lewis Blaine
Draft director tells what's ahead; interview; with letter to E. Celler, and the reply. por U S News 60:38-44 Ja 10 '66
General Hershey replies. Nation 202:inside cover Ja 3 '66
about
Hershey and the draft: still going strong after twenty-five years. por U S News 59:21 Ag 16 '65
Riots, songs and fishbowls, the hullabaloo is old hat to Hershey. S. McBee. il pors Life 59:28-9 Ag 20 '65
Spanking the spanker. Newsweek 67:26 Ja 24 '66

HERSHEY chocolate corporation
Hershey millions sweeten the job; starting Milton S. Hershey medical center at Penn state. il Bsns W p 192-4+ O 16 '65

HERST, Herman, Jr
Stamps. See issues of Hobbies

HERTER, Christian Archibald
Europe, the United States, and world trade; address, February 4, 1965. Dept State Bul 52:294-9 Mr 1 '65
Importance of agricultural issues in Kennedy round; statement, February 3, 1965. Dept State Bul 52:251-2 F 22 '65
Kennedy round: a progress report; address, May 20, 1965. Dept State Bul 53:31-5 Jl 5 '65
Tabling of agricultural offers in Kennedy round announced; statement, August 19, 1965. Dept State Bul 53:452-3 S 13 '65

HERTZ corporation
More driver's seats. Newsweek 66:88 O 11 '65

HERTZBERG, Arthur
Rabbis or executives. Newsweek 67:63 Ja 17 '66

HERZFELD, Norma Krause
Disarmament inches ahead. Commonweal 82:631-5 S 3 '65

HERZOG, Arthur
He loves things to be beautiful. N Y Times Mag p34-5+ Mr 14 '65

HERZOG, Yaacov David
Britain's Irish Israeli. Newsweek 65:42 Je 7 '65

HERZOG (literary character) See Characters in literature

HESKETH, Christian Mary (McEwen) Fermor-Hesketh, baroness
Lady Hesketh and her small, perfect palace. D. McEwen. il pors Vogue 147:144-51+ Ja 1 '66

HESKETT, J. L. See Stern, L. W. jt. auth.

HESLIN, James J.
Collection. New Yorker 41:30-2 Je 12 '65

HESS, Eckhard Heinrich
Attitude and pupil size; with biographical sketch. Sci Am 212:18, 46-54 Ap '65
—See Burghardt, G. M. jt. auth.
about
Your eye can't lie. B. Davidson. il por Sat Eve Post 239:76-9 Ja 15 '66

HESS, M. Whitcomb
 Kierkegaard and Socrates. Christian Cent 82:
 736-8 Je 9 '65
 Out of the grave's dust; poem. Cath World
 202:113 N '65
HESS, Dame Myra
 Dame Myra; tribute. por Newsweek 66:90 D 6
 '65
 Notes and comment. New Yorker 41:49 D
 11 '65
HESS, Thomas B.
 De Kooning's new Women. Art N 64:36-8+
 Mr '65
 J'accuse Marcel Duchamp. Art N 63:44-5+
 F '65
 You can hang it in the hall. Art N 64:41-3+
 Ap '65
HESSE, Hermann
 God within. por Time 86:68+ Jl 30 '65
HESTER, F. Eugene
 Wood ducks for your pond! Farm J 89:D3
 F '65
HESTER, Oka T.
 Something for everybody. Am City 80:88-9
 N '65
HESTON, Charlton
 Redbook dialogue: Charlton Heston and
 Robert Hutchins. por Redbook 126:68-9+ D
 '65
   about
 Agony and the ecstasy of Michelangelo. il
 pors Look 29:41-8 My 9 '65
 Heston: larger than life. P. Hamill. il pors
 Sat Eve Post 238:87-91 Jl 3 '65
 Trying to be a genius; concerning Agony and
 the ecstasy. D. Seiberling. il pors Life
 59:75-6+ N 12 '65
HETEROCYTES. See Cells
HETEROZYGOSIS
 Red-light thresholds in heterozygote carriers
 of protanopia: genetic implications. A. E.
 Krill and E. Beutler. bibliog il Science
 149:186-8 Jl 9 '65
HEUSINGER, Adolf Ernst
 Will arms build-up in Asia cut U.S. role
 in Europe? interview. por U S News 59:64-7
 Ag 23 '65
HEUSTON, John
 Buffalo River. Travel 124:56-9 Ag '65
 Hot Springs havens. Travel 123:44-5 Mr '65
 Today's arkansas traveler is a boatman.
 Motor B 116:28-31 Jl '65
HEUTTE, Frederic
 Groundcovers for the South. Horticulture 43:
 22-3+ Je '65
HEWES, Henry
 Broadway gets the green light. Sat R 49:
 56-7 Ja 22 '66
 Broadway postscript. See issues of Saturday
 review
HEWITT, Jean
 Food (cont) N Y Times Mag p87 Mr 28; 68
 My 23; 62 Ag 29; 129-30 S 12; 109-10 N 21;
 27 D 26 '65; 56 Ja 16 '66
HEWLETT, Roger S.
 Boating. Sports Illus 23:66-7 D 13 '65
HEXAFLUORODIETHYL ether. See Indoklon
HEXAMETHYLENE tetramine
 Hexamethylenetetramine hexahydrate: a new
 type of clathrate hydrate. G. A. Jeffrey and
 T. C. W. Mak. bibliog il Science 149:178
 Jl 9 '65
HEYD, Ruth
 Introducing Windsor. por ALA Bul 59:395-6
 My '65
HEYES, Frank
 Blitzen victorious in race from Chicago.
 Yachting 118:46+ S '65
HEYM, Stefan
 I arrive at socialism by train. Nation 201:
 228-30 O 11 '65
HEYMAN, Ken
 On being a photographer of people. il Pop
 Phot 56:52-5+ F '65
HEYMAN, Wayne
 Water skiing is easier than it looks. Pop Sci
 186:110-13 Je '65
HEYMANN, John Porter
 Autumn at settlers harbor; poem. Christian
 Cent 82:1344 N 3 '65
HEYNS, Roger William
 Berkeley, one year later. por Time 86:46+ D
 3 '65
 Choices at Berkeley. il por Newsweek 66:74-5
 Ag 9 '65
 Man for tomorrow. il por Time 86:49 Ag 6 '65
HEYWORTH, Peter
 Thorn grows in Warsaw. Hi Fi 15:60-5 S '65
HIALEAH park, Miami. See Race tracks
HIBACHIS. See Braziers

HIBBEN, Frank C.
 America's oldest hunting weapon. Field & S
 70:48-50+ Jl '65
 Killers of the Magdalenas. Field & S 69:58-
 61 Mr '65
 Pack of trouble. pors Outdoor Life 136:44-7+
 N '65
HIBERNATION
 Impaired recovery from hypothermia after
 anterior hypothalamic lesions in hiber-
 nators. E. Satinoff. bibliog il Science 148:
 399-400 Ap 16 '65
 Non-hibernating animals put into winter
 sleep. Sci N L 88:227 O 9 '65
 Sleeping one of the Hopis; excerpts from
 Wandering through winter. E. W. Teale.
 il Natur Hist 74:26-9 D '65
HIBISCUS
 Stunning Chinese hibiscus. il Sunset 134:104-
 7 My '65
 Two hardy hibiscus. il Sunset 134:265 Je '65
HICCUPS
 Stopping the hiccups. Time 86:67 Jl 16 '65
HICK, John H.
 To believe or not to believe. Sat R 48:39-40
 F 6 '65
HICKEY, Doralyn J.
 Plea for selective recruitment. por ALA Bul
 59:361-3 My '65
HICKEY, James T.
 Lincolns' Globe tavern; reprint. Hobbies 70:
 110-13 Ap '65
HICKEY, K. Elaine
 Businessmen's expectations. Duns R 86:11 S;
 13 D '65
HICKMAN, Dwayne
 I was a teen-ager for ten years; ed. by E.
 Miller. pors Seventeen 24:94-5+ Je '65
HICKMAN, Ernest E.
 Car-top carrier for vacation luggage. Pop
 Sci 187:138-9 Jl '65
HICKMAN, Warren L.
 Dictatorship of the majority. Sch & Soc 93:
 346-9 O 2 '65
HICKOCK, Richard Eugene
 Annals of crime: In cold blood. T. Capote.
 New Yorker 41:58-62+ O 9; 62-4+ O 16 '65
 In cold blood; an American tragedy. il por
 Newsweek 67:59-62 Ja 24 '66
 Two killers, last faces the Clutters saw. por
 Life 60:64-5 Ja 7 '66
HICKORY farms of Ohio. See Chain stores
HICKS, Betty
 (ed) See Leverton, I. Flying the mountain
 wave
HICKS, Clifford B.
 Three giant steps to the moon. Pop Mech
 124:116-20+ N '65
 Your mysterious nose. Todays Health 43:35-
 7+ O '65
HICKS, Ed
 How America lives. E. Havemann. il pors
 Ladies Home J 82:56-9+ My '65
HICKS, Edward
 Edward Hicks: Quaker painter. S. Marsal.
 il Américas 17:5-14 D '65
HICKS, Ernest L.
 Pensions and profits. Fortune 71:69-70 My '65
HICKS, Granville
 Literary horizons. See issues of Saturday re-
 view
   about
 Pattern of days and ideas. J. Slater. Sat R
 48:18-19 Jl 31 '65
 Thirties: frayed collars and large visions. L.
 Kronenberger. Atlan 217:79-81 Ja '66
 Young in the thirties. S. Kauffmann. New
 Repub 153:17-20 S 18 '65
HICKS, Jacquie
 How America lives. E. Havemann. il pors
 Ladies Home J 82:56-9+ My '65
HICKS, Jim
 Goldie got everybody into his act. Life 58:
 90 Mr 19 '65
 Hardest rendezvous of all, on the ground.
 Life 59:113-14+ O 1 '65
 Lawn bowls and police dogs. Life 59:51-2
 N 12 '65
 Nubar's declaration of love for the art of life.
 Life 59:96+ O 15 '65
 Operation foil-a-fox-hunt. Life 58:87-8+ Ap
 2 '65
HICKS, Sir John Richard
 Purdue gives and gets a lesson. il por Bsns
 W p 186-8+ Ap 17 '65
HICKS, Louise Day
 People of the week. por U S News 59:21-2
 N 15 '65
 Vote of confidence. por Newsweek 66:36 O 4 '65
HICKS, Wilson
 Miami: too much too soon. Sat R 48:42-3 O
 23 '65
   about
 Focus on Wilson Hicks. J. Durniak. il pors
 Pop Phot 56:58-6J+ Ap '65

HICKSVILLE, N.Y.
    Monuments, statues, etc.
Aquila Romana; Pennsylvania station eagle.
    S. A. Goldberg. il NEA J 54:29 D '65
HIDDEN heart; story. See Allen, E.
HIDDEN meanings; drama. See Fisher, A.
HIERNAUX, Jean
Future of Homo sapiens. UNESCO Courier 18:
    12-15 Ap '65; Same abr. with title How man
    will evolve. Sci Digest 58:90-4 Ag '65
HIGDON, Hal
Let's tell the truth about isometrics. Todays
    Health 43:58-9+ Je '65
Troubled heart of Sigma chi. N Y Times
    Mag p48-9+ N 14 '65
HIGGINS, Alice
Horse shows (cont) Sports Illus 22:72 My 3;
    59 Je 21; 23:76 O 11; 94+ N 22 '65
HIGGINS, George
Who is adequate, Monsignor? criticism of
    current Vietnamese policy. Christian Cent
    82:668 My 26 '65
HIGGINS, Marguerite
No club for cookie-pushers. NEA J 54:15
    Mr '65
            about
Lady at war. por Time 87:61 Ja 14 '66
Maggie. por Newsweek 67:83 Ja 17 '66
Obituary
    Nat R 18:60-1 Ja 25 '66. J. Chamberlain
HIGGS, E. S.
Search for Greece of the stone age. Natur
    Hist 74:18-25 N '65
HIGGS, William Leon
Case of the missing registrars; LBJ and the
    Negro vote. Nation 201:460-2 D 13 '65
HIGH altitude, Influence of. See Altitude,
    Influence of
HIGH altitude flying. See Aviation—Altitude
    flying
HIGH ASWAN DAM. See Aswan High Dam
HIGH blood pressure. See Hypertension
HIGH commissioner for refugees. See United
    Nations—High commissioner for refugees
HIGH energy particles. See Particles (nuclear
    physics)
HIGH energy physics. See Nuclear physics
HIGH fidelity (periodical)
Roy Lindstrom, artist & art director. F.
    Johnson. il Am Artist 29:50-5+ D '65
HIGH fidelity amplifiers. See Amplifiers
HIGH fidelity music shows. See Audio fairs
HIGH fidelity sound systems
British audio establishment. N. Eisenberg.
    il Hi Fi 15:56-60+ Ap '65
Hi-fi stereo for '66, in solid. H. Fantel. il
    Pop Electr 23:47-51+ N '65
High fidelity equipment reports. See issues
    of High fidelity incorporating Musical
    America
High fidelity newsfronts. See issues of High
    fidelity incorporating Musical America
Modular music components. il House & Gard
    128:58 Jl '65
New products: 1965. N. Eisenberg. il Hi Fi
    15:55-9 O '65
        See also
Phonograph—High fidelity sound systems
Stereophonic sound systems

            History
1956-1965 hi-fi ten years later. L. Lekashman.
    il Pop Electr 23:41-6 N '65

            Noise
Antidotes for noise. E. F. McIntyre. Hi Fi
    15:39-42+ Jl '65
HIGH-intensity lamps. See Electric lamps
HIGH pressure. See Pressure
HIGH pressure oxygenation
High-pressure oxygen aids cancer treatment.
    Sci N L 87:251 Ap 17 '65
HIGH school annuals
Yearbook photo journalism, by I. Lloyd. Re-
    view
    Pop Phot il 56:100 F '65. P. Sarbin
HIGH school athletes. See Athletes
HIGH school baseball players. See Baseball
    players, High school
HIGH school buildings. See School buildings
HIGH school dropouts. See Dropouts
HIGH school football. See Football
HIGH school girls. See Girls
HIGH school graduates
Employment of high school graduates and
    dropouts in 1964. F. A. Bogan. il Mo Labor
    R 88:637-43 Je '65
Increase in high school graduates. Sch & Soc
    93:239+ Ap 17 '65

HIGH school Journalism. See College and
    school journalism
HIGH school libraries
Oregon plan; Marshall high school, Portland.
    R. Tidwell and E. Wiseblood. il Library J
    90:3686-9 S 15 '65

            Reference work
Wrap-up senior lesson; Erasmus Hall high
    school, Brooklyn. J. Sverdlik. il Library J
    90:4516-19+ O 15 '65
HIGH school publications. See College and
    school journalism
HIGH school students
Bright-D-minus kids; Upward bound. il Time
    86:55 Ag 20 '65
Coming of age in America, by E. Z. Frieden-
    berg. Review
    America 113:340+ S 25 '65. P. J. Rice
How to prepare a community code for young
    teens. il Parents Mag 40:67+ O '65
How well do you know teen-agers? J. Beck.
    il Todays Health 43:47-8+ F '65
Long and short of it; aspects of student
    dress and grooming. il Newsweek 6:64-6
    S 27 '65
Profile of a high school; New Jersey paper-
    back study. Sr Schol 87:sup22-3 O 28 '65
Splitting hairs over moptops; or, How lunatic
    is the fringe? il Sr Schol 87:20 O 14 '65
Talking it over with Gay Head; questions
    and answers. Gay Head. See issues of
    Senior scholastic
Unkindest cut for student moptops. Life 59:4
    S 24 '65
        See also
Scholastic research center
Student activities
Youth
            Clothing
    See Clothing and dress
            Dating
    See Dating
            Employment
    See Student employment
            Rating
High school students' self-rating. Sch & Soc
    93:291-2 Sum '65
            Smoking
    See Smoking
HIGH school students, Married
Do teenagers make good parents? E. S.
    Stewart. il Parents Mag 40:46-9+ F '65
Netta and Freddy married too young. D. C.
    Disney. Ladies Home J 82:34+ D '65
Should seventeen and eighteen year-old girls
    marry? E. Havemann. il McCalls 92:101+
    F '65
Teen-age marriage; love finds a way. B. Lang.
    il Ladies Home J 82:68-9+ Je '65
What happens to teen-age marriages? il
    Changing T 19:6-10 N '65
HIGH school students, Mentally superior
        See also
College entrance examination board—Ad-
    vanced placement program
HIGH school students, Negro. See Negro stu-
    dents
HIGH school students as automobile drivers.
    See Automobile drivers
HIGH school teachers. See Teachers
HIGH schools
Best place for vocational education: the com-
    prehensive high school. J. B. Zack. il NEA
    J 54:48-50 D '65
Catholic high schools today; Scholastic
    teacher interview. C. A. Koob. Sr Schol
    86:sup29-31 Ap 15 '65
New intermediate school; return to four-year
    system. P. Woodring. Sat R 48:77-8 O 16
    '65
New vigor in the urban high schools. F.
    Keppel. il PTA Mag 59:4-6 Mr '65
Our best high schools (cont) Atlan 215:89-92
    F; 120-3 Mr; 95-8 Ap; 99-102+ My '65
Quality secondary schools of the future (cont)
    O. F. Parody. Sch Life 47:24-8 D '64
What's going on in schools & colleges. See
    issues of Changing times
        See also
Negro schools
            Curriculum
America's most wanted students; Seattle's
    public schools' program of business educa-
    tion. G. B. Leonard. il Look 29:46-51 Jl
    27 '65
        See also
Colleges and universities—Entrance require-
    ments
English language—Courses of study

HILTON hotels corporation
New big-city hotel; San Francisco and Washington Hilton hotels. il Arch Rec 138:143-50 Jl '65
View from a tall glass oasis: subliminal pleasures of Hilton hotels. G. Bradshaw. Vogue 146:82+ Jl '65

HIMALAYAS
Himalayas. il Life 58:56-68 My 28 '65
See also
Ladakh

HIMBER, Charlotte
Parent and child. N Y Times Mag p59-60 Ag 29 '65

HIMMELFARB, Milton
In the community (cont) Commentary 39:61-5 Ap; 16+ Je; 40:54-7 Jl; 56-65 O '65

HIMWICH, Harold E. See Takeo, Y. jt. auth.

HINCKLEY, Anita W.
Gibson girl romance. Am Heritage 17:106-11 D '65
Wickford tales. pors Am Heritage 16:80-90 Je '65

HINCKLEY, Helen
You can change puppets to people. Writer 78:12-16 My '65

HINDEMITH, Paul
On records: Requiem for those we love (When lilacs last in the door-yard bloom'd, American requiem) Opera N 29:34 F 13 '65

HINDENBURG (airship) See Airships

HINDI language
Crisis in south India; Hindi made the official language of Indian union. P. G. Altbach. Christian Cent 82:403-4 Mr 31 '65

HINDLEY, Donald
Indonesia: pride & politics. Nation 200:636-8 Je 14 '65

HINDS, Jeanette
Journey to the store; poem. McCalls 92:119 Jl '65
Mundane mother; poem. McCalls 92:154 F '65

HINDS, Thomas E. and Hawksworth, F. G.
Seed dispersal velocity in four dwarfmistletoes. Science 148:517-19 Ap 23 '65
—See Hawksworth, F. G. jt. auth.

HINDU mythology. See Mythology, Hindu

HINDU sculpture. See Sculpture, Indian (East Indian)

HINDUISM
Kashmir: a religious war; Muslim and Hindu intolerance. J. F. Drane. Cath World 202:212-16 Ja '66

HINDUS, Milton
Harmonies. Commentary 41:76-8+ Ja '66

HINDUS
See also
India—Hindu-Moslem relations

HINE, Alvaro Cardona-. See Cardona-Hine, A.

HINES, Earl
Life with Fatha; comeback trial. por Newsweek 66:108+ O 18 '65
Rediscovery of Earl Hines. M. Williams. por Sat R 48:59 Je 26 '65

HINES, John Elbridge, bp
Conscientiously disobedient. Christian Cent 82:670 My 26 '65
Holiness through action. il por Time 85:61 F 5 '65

HINES, Leo
From nineteenth-century piety to aggiornamento. Commonweal 82:448-9 Je 25 '65
Other Hammarskjöld. Commonweal 81:606-8 F 5 '65

HINES, Milton. See Sales, S.

HINES, William
Great Boston power play. Read Digest 88:99-104 Ja '66

HINKLE, Charles L.
Strategy of price deals. Harvard Bsns R 43:75:85 Jl '65

HINMAN, Charles
Three new, cool, bright imagists. E. H. Johnson. il por Art N 64:42-4+ Sum '65

HINSHELWOOD, Sir Cyril
Science and scientists; excerpts from address, September 1, 1965. Sci N L 88:182 S 18 '65

HINT of the future in the last day program; story. See Crabb, A. L.

HINTON, Harold C.
Difference of dangers. Sat R 48:54 Ap 17 '65

HIP dysplasia. See Dogs—Diseases and pests

HIPP, Frederick
How do you talk to a parade? adaptation of address, May 1965. PTA Mag 60:13-15 O '65

HIPPOCRATIC oath. See Oaths

HIPPOPOTAMUS
Hippos. J. Nagenda. il Reporter 32:32-3 Je 3 '65

HIPSTER. See Beatniks

HIRABAYASHI, Kazuko
Triad dance company, 92nd street Y. M. Marks. Dance Mag 39:68 Je '65

HIRAM Scott college, Scottsbluff, Neb.
Tradition sprouts in a cornfield; F. Anderson of Big ten basketball helping to build brand-new college. G. Holland. il Sports Illus 24:42-5 Ja 10 '66

HIRED men. See Farm labor

HIRING. See Employment systems

HIROSHIMA
A-bomb is twenty. H. Pryor. il Sci Digest 58:20-6 Ag '65
Claimants of Hiroshima. R. A. Falk. il Nation 200:157-61 F 15 '65
Ground zero at Hiroshima twenty years later. il Life 59:32-3 Ag 20 '65
Hiroshima: 1945 and 1965. R. Joseph. il Esquire 64:62-3 Ag '65
Taste of life in Hiroshima now. A. M. Rosenthal. il N Y Times Mag p4-5+ Ag 1 '65

Monuments, statues, etc.
Girl of the paper cranes; Children's monument in the Peace park. B. J. Lifton. il N Y Times Mag p35 Ag 1 '65

HIRSCH, Walter
Knowledge for what? Bul Atomic Sci 21:28-31 My '65

HIRSCHFELD, Jan
Serologic codes: interpretation of immunogenetic systems. bibliog Science 148:968-71 My 14 '65

HIRSCHL, Milton
It's in the bag! Sch Arts 65:36-7 N '65
White on white. Sch Arts 64:5-7 Mr '65

HIRSCHMAN, Jack
Baseball poem. Poetry 106:398-9 S '65

about
World dances between our eyes. K. Irby. Poetry 105:418-20 Mr '65

HIRSCHMANN, W. B. and Brauweiler, J. R.
Investment analysis: coping with change. Harvard Bsns R 43:62-72 My '65

HIS first patient; drama. See Richmond, S. S.

HISPANIOLA
Hispaniola: a history of hate. il Time 85:30-1 My 7 '65

HISTAMINE
Histamine synthesis and gastric secretion after portacaval shunt. J. E. Fischer and S. H. Snyder. bibliog Science 150:1034-5 N 19 '65

HISTOLOGY
See also
Bone

HISTONES
Biosynthesis of histones and acidic nuclear proteins under different conditions of growth. L. S. Hnilica and others. bibliog il Science 150:1470-2 D 10 '65
Histone regulation of lactic dehydrogenase in embryonic chick brain tissue. B. C. Goodwin and I. W. Sizer. bibliog il Science 148:242-4 Ap 9 '65
Histones and basic polyamino acids stimulate the uptake of albumin by tumor cells in culture. H. J. P. Ryser and R. Hancock. bibliog il Science 150:501-3 O 22 '65

HISTOPLASMOSIS
Histoplasma capsulatum from the liver of a bat in Colombia. C. J. Marinkelle and E. Grose. bibliog Science 147:1039-40 F 26 '65
Histoplasma capsulatum: occurrence in soil from the Emilia-Romagna region of Italy. G. Sotgiu and others. bibliog Science 147:624 F 5 '65
It's a new disease; it's called histoplasmosis. il Changing T 19:29-31 S '65

HISTORIANS, American
Instant and judicial history; Schlesinger and Stevens exposures condemned. Life 59:4 Ag 13 '65
See also
Lorant, S.

HISTORIANS, Latin American
Inca Garcilaso. A. Salgado. il Américas 17:22-8 Jl '65

HISTORIC house museums
New England sea captain's home becomes a museum; Captain Robert Bennet Forbes House, Milton, Mass. R. Davidson. il Antiques 88:434+ O '65

HISTORIC houses, etc.
Historic houses, landmarks, and museums. See issues of Antiques
See also
National trust for places of historic interest or natural beauty
Official residences
also subhead Historic houses, etc. under names of countries, states, cities, etc. e.g. Vermont—Historic houses, etc.

HISTORIC houses, etc.—*Continued*

Conservation and restoration
See Architecture—Conservation and restoration

HISTORIC letters. See Letters

HISTORICAL fiction
Reader as eye-witness of the past. W. O. Steele. Writer 78:15-16+ Mr '65
Vidal to Vidal: on misusing the past. G. Vidal. il Harper 231:162-4 O '65

Technique
See Fiction—Technique

HISTORICAL handkerchiefs. See Handkerchiefs

HISTORICAL libraries
Myth of the historical society library. P. Z. Dubois. il Library J 90:4279-81 O 15 '65

HISTORICAL literature
Watch your language, you're writing for young people! J. Beatty and P. Beatty. Horn Bk 41:34-40 F '65

HISTORICAL museums
Museum village; Smith's Clove, N.Y. S. Bologna. il Travel 124:60-2 Ag '65
Old western humor preserved; Alamo Village. Tex. L. Barry. il Pop Phot 56:20+ Mr '65
See also
Milan, Ohio, historical museum

HISTORICAL research
Methods of research for the amateur historian. R. W. Hale, jr. Hobbies 70:110-12+ Ag '65

HISTORICAL society libraries. See Historical libraries

HISTORICAL villages. See Historical museums

HISTORIOGRAPHY. See History—Historiography

HISTORY
See also
Current events
Historical research
Treaties

Bibliography
History (cont) J. J. O'Connor. America 112:674-6; 113:682-4 My 8, N 27 '65
Reading, writing, and history. B. Caton. See issues of American heritage

Historiography
History by the ounce; adaptation of address, B. W. Tuchman. Harper 231:65-8+ Jl '65; Discussion. 231:8+ S '65

Philosophy
Shapes of philosophical history, by F. E. Manuel. Review
Nation 200:311-12 Mr 22 '65. H. Meyerhoff

Study and teaching
Historic myopia: a suggested cure; use of personal heritage. R. Finkbine. NEA J 55:63-4 Ja '66
Why history. H. S. Commager. il Am Ed 1:26-9 Je '65

HISTORY, Ancient
Ancient world; excerpts. L. Pareti; L. Petech; M. V. Frederiksen. il UNESCO Courier 18:24-32 My '65
See also
Greece, Ancient—History

Bibliography
Articles and other books received; comp. by T. R. S. Broughton. See issues of American historical review

HISTORY, Modern
Urban nation, 1920-1960, by G. E. Mowry. Review
Nation 201:225-6 O 11 '65. F. Gutheim
See also
Twentieth century

HISTORY, Universal. See World history

HISTORY and science. See Science and civilization

HITCH, Charles Johnston
Defense: McNamara's comptroller, Charles J. Hitch, leaves after four pioneering years at DOD. J. Walsh. por Science 149:1074-6 S 3 '65
What a whiz kid did. por Newsweek 66:21 Jl 19 '65

HITCHCOCK, Alfred Joseph
Hitchcock, master of cinema! L. Jacobs, jr. il pors U S Camera 29:72-3+ Ja '66
Hitchcock's three nightmares. il pors Newsweek 67:89-89A+ Ja 24 '66

HITCHCOCK, George
World dances between our eyes. K. Irby. Poetry 105:416-18 Mr '65

HITCHCOCK, James
Catholic universities as a cultural force. Cath World 201:233-6 Jl '65

HITCHENS, Dolores
Unloved; story. Redbook 125:175-205 O '65

HITLER, Adolf
End of the Hitler gang; excerpts from Last 100 days. J. Toland. il Look 29:70-2+ Je 1 '65
Preview of a German controversy. G. K. Romoser. Nation 201:172-4 S 27 '65

HITLER youth movement. See Youth movement—Germany

HITLERISM. See Fascism—Germany

HITREC, Joseph
Time for praise. Sat R 48:27 S 4 '65

HITT, James K.
Practical advice from a university admissions official; some ways to get into college. interview. por U S News 58:59-61 My 10 '65

HITTINGER, William C. and Sparks, Morgan
Microelectronics; with biographical sketches. Sci Am 213:14, 56-64+ N '65

HIXON, Susan
Dial F for fiction. Seventeen 24:116 Ag '65

HLAVKA, George E.
Siblings of the test ban. Bul Atomic Sci 21:24 N '65

HNILICA, Lubomir S. and others
Biosynthesis of histones and acidic nuclear proteins under different conditions of growth. bibliog Science 150:1470-2 D 10 '65

HO-chi-Minh
Inside Hanoi; impressions of J. Cameron and F. Greene. por Newsweek 66:69 D 20 '65
Jungle Marxist. il pors Time 86:24-8 Jl 16 '65
Uncle Ho defies Uncle Sam. J. Lacouture. il pors N Y Times Mag p25+ Mr 28 '65
Uncovered country. il Time 85:30-2 Ap 16 '65
View from the North. K. Crawford. Newsweek 65:34 Ap 12 '65
War or peace? Ho chi Minh had choice. il por U S News 58:20 F 22 '65
Why Ho refuses to yield to U.S. por U S News 60:21 Ja 17 '66

HOAGLAND, Edward
Wanted: a Protestant novelist. L. Kriegel. Commonweal 83:276 D 3 '65

HOAGLAND, Mahlon B. See Dresden, M. jt. auth.

HOAGLAND, Robert J.
New treatment for coma. Time 86:68 Jl 16 '65

HOARDING
Green stuff gets sticky, too; currency outside banks. il Bsns W p88 Ag 14 '65

HOARDING by animals. See Animals—Habits and behavior

HOARE, Michael
Changing guard. Time 86:30 D 17 '65
How to win wars & elections. il Time 85:30-1 Ap 2 '65
Road to Fizi. il por Time 86:43-4 O 15 '65

HOAXES
Science in action; hoaxes and half-truths. R. Silverberg. Natur Hist 74:62-5 Mr '65
Yak fat? railroad rate schedule hoax. Newsweek 66:62+ Ag 23 '65
See also
Piltdown forgery

HOBAN, Russell
New ingénue. Holiday 37:131+ Mr '65

HOBBIES
Compleat hobbyist. A. Bester. Holiday 38:140-2+ D '65
Hobby kits dads may enjoy. il Good H 161:170 D '65
How to pursue a hobby. E. N. Smith. il Suc Farm 63:119-23 F '65
Make the world more beautiful with tiny things. S. A. Parvin. Hobbies 70:120 S '65
Things to do just for fun. il Changing T 19:40-2 Jl '65
What makes a good hobby? excerpt from Today's health guide. il Todays Health 43:39-40 Jl '65
See also
Postage stamps—Collectors and collecting

HOBBS, Cecil
(comp) Articles and other books received; south Asia. See issues of American historical review

HOBBY, Oveta Culp
Houston: the race is on. Sat R 48:43-4 My 22 '65

HOBERMAN, Stuart
Tiny electric eye to guard your home. Pop Sci 187:100-2 S '65

HOBOS. See Vagabonds

HOBSBAWN, Eric
Pentagon's dilemma: Goliath and the guerrilla. Nation 201:33-8 Jl 19 '65

HOBSON, Julius Wilson
Washington's civil rights maverick. S. Booker. il pors Ebony 20:140-2+ My '65

HOCHMAN, Baruch
Translating a tradition. Commentary 40:88+
O '65
HOCHMAN, Sandra
Couple; poem. New Yorker 41:103 Ja 8 '66
Words for my mother; poem. Mlle 61:134 S
'65
HÖCHST porcelain. See Pottery, German
HOCHSTEIN, Robert A.
OE's open doors. por Am Ed 1:10-11 O '65
Tiger in Stephen's jungle. Am Ed 1:5-7 Ap
'65
HOCHSTEIN, Rollie
Pity the poor hostess. Good H 161:56+ N '65
TV's favorite comedy team breaks up. Good
H 161:30+ O '65
That cat; story. Good H 160:48 F '65
—and Sugarman, Daniel
Pleasures and problems of friendship. Seven-
teen 24:86-7+ Je '65
—See Sugarman, D. jt. auth.
HOCKEY
Aged on the rink. il Time 85:58+ Mr 19 '65
    See also
Field hockey
National hockey league
        Caricatures and cartoons
Niceties of the ice. R. McKie. Sports Illus
23:24-6+ N 1 '65
            Rules
Some changes made. Sports Illus 23:19 O 25
'65
HOCKEY players
Golden hawk of hockey; B. Hull. J. Atwater.
il Sat Eve Post 239:56-9 Ja 1 '66
In New York, hockey's house is not a home;
Ranger management trade best players.
W. Leggett. il Sports Illus 22:62-4 Mr 8 '65
    See also
Shack, E.
HOCKEY teams
Detroit flies high on beat-up old Red Wings.
M. Kram. il Sports Illus 22:66-7 Mr 29 '65
Hard Toe right to the jaw; Montreal
Canadiens beat Chicago Black Hawks to
win eleventh Stanley cup championship. M.
Kram. il Sports Illus 22:32-3 My 10 '65
In New York, hockey's house is not a home;
Ranger management trade best players.
W. Leggett. il Sports Illus 22:62-4 Mr 8 '65
Private game: no admittance! major league
hockey not interested in becoming bigger.
J. Olsen. il Sports Illus 22:64-6+ Ap 12 '65
Puck's good boy: E. Giacomin. il Newsweek
66:61 N 29 '65
Worrying is the way to win; Montreal Cana-
diens' Toe Blake. M. Kram. il Sports Illus
23:48-50+ N 22 '65
HOCKNEY, David
Play's the thing. il Time 86:86-7 D 10 '65
HOCTOR, Harriet
Don't forget the backbend, Harriet! D.
Hering pors Dance Mag 39:112-17 D '65
HODESH, Robert
Stealing their way through college. Esquire
64:96+ S '65
HODGENS, Richard M.
Movies in brief. Nat R 17:292-4, 518-19, 784-5,
993-4, 1203-4 Ap 6, Je 15, S 7, N 2, D 28
'65
HODGES, Elizabeth
New ALA officer. ALA Bul 59:654+ Jl '65
HODGINS, Maibelle Dickey
Flycatchers in the rose garden. il Flower
Grower 52:14+ Je '65
Margie's porridge, make it for the birds.
il Flower Grower 53:66 Ja '66
HODGKIN, Dorothy Crowfoot
X-ray analysis of complicated molecules; ad-
dress. December 11, 1964. bibliog Science
150:979-88 N 19 '65
HODGKIN'S disease
Control of Hodgkin's disease seen in future.
Sci N L 88:376 D 11 '65
Hodgkin's clue? Time 85:78 F 19 '65
HODOSH, Milton
Replacing teeth with plastic. il por Time 86:
57 Ag 13 '65
HOEBEL, Bartley G.
Hypothalamic lesions by electrocauteriza-
tion; disinhibition of feeding and self-
stimulation. bibliog Science 149:452-3 Jl 23
'65
HOEFFLER, Buck
R for print sharpness. il Mod Phot 29:80-1
F '65
HOEFLICH, Sherman
All the news that's fit to paint. il Am Artist
29:26-9+ D '65
HOEHN, Karl
Inventor of the month. S. V. Jones. il por
Sci Digest 58:28 N '65

HOEKSTRA, Pieter. See Anderson, D. M. jt.
auth.
HOENACK, August
Current trends in hospital architecture. Arch
Rec 138:197-9 S '65
HOES
Scuffle down the row. M. Cook. il Pop Gard
16:57 Mr '65
HOFFA, Harlan E.
Arts & humanities in the U.S. Office of edu-
cation. Sch Arts 64:52 My '65
HOFFA, James Riddle
Hoffa and the teamsters, by R. James and
E. James. Review
U S News il por 59:62+ O 25 '65
Hoffa comes under view from three sides.
Bsns W p98-100 N 27 '65
Hoffa's hookers; charges of prostitution and
prejudice in asking for new trial. Time
86:33 O 1 '65
Justice dept. keeps heat on Hoffa. Bsns W
p48 F 13 '65
Ordeal of a Hoffa victim. B. Davidson. il por
Sat Eve Post 238:23-7 Je 19 '65
Tales of Hoffa. G. W. Johnson. New Repub
154:33 Ja 15 '66
Teamsters gird for day of change. il Bsns
W p97-8 N 27 '65
Tentacles of power, by C. R. Mollenhoff.
Review
Sat R 48:65-6 N 13 '65. V. Riesel
What next, if Hoffa loses out. por Bsns W
p 142 Ap 24 '65
Who will succeed Hoffa? il por Newsweek
66:84 D 20 '65
HOFFER, Bernard K.
Trotsky in the Bronx. Esquire 63:156-7 Ap
'65
HOFFER, Eric
Automation is here to liberate us. N Y Times
Mag p48-9+ O 24 '65
Time of juveniles. Harper 230:16+ Je '65
HOFFER, J. R. See Corlett, T. B. jr. jt. auth.
HOFFMAN, Bernard
New Varigam filters. Pop Phot 57:142-3+ D
'65
HOFFMAN, Betty Hannah
Coeds in rebellion. Ladies Home J 82:82-4+
O '65
HOFFMAN, Daniel
Entering doorways; In the Republic of the
Troll King; poems. Poetry 106:209-11 Je '65
In the cove; Locust; Before the fall; poems.
Yale R 54:394-6 Mr '65
There; poem. Nation 200:228 Mr 1 '65
HOFFMAN, Donald
Annals of medicine. B. Roueché. New Yorker
41:51-2+ Ap 24 '65
HOFFMAN, Frederick J.
In search of Edmund Wilson. Nation 202:74-5
Ja 17 '66
HOFFMAN, George A.
Future city. por Sat R 48:42-4 Ag 7 '65
HOFFMAN, Jay K.
Recordings. M. Mayer. Esquire 63:52+ Mr '65
HOFFMAN, Joyce
Odd sport, and an unusual champion. G.
Rogin. il pors Sports Illus 23:94-8+ O 18
'65
HOFFMAN, Morton
As we live and breathe! letter. Nat R 17:
682 Ag 10 '65
HOFFMAN, Paul G.
Buttressing the foundations. Sat R 48:30-1+
Jl 24 '65
        about
Locust fighters. J. Gunther. il por Look 29:
40-2 Ap 20 '65
HOFFMAN, Robert
How to build a better body. A. Steinberg.
il Read Digest 86:102-5 Mr '65
HOFFMAN, Roger A. and Reiter, R. J.
Pineal gland; influence on gonads of male
hamsters. bibliog Science 148:1609-11 Je 18
'65
HOFFMAN, Ronan
Latin America in the church's global mis-
sion: what priority? America 114:68-70 Ja
15 '66
HOFFMANN, Banesh
College boards fail the test. N Y Times
Mag p52-3+ O 24 '65
HOFFMANN, E. T. A.
Tales for our time. P. J. Smith. Opera N
29:24-5 F 27 '65
HOFFMANN, Rita
Educational testing. Mlle 62:112-13+ D '65
Jobs overseas; daydreams and data. Mlle
60:178-81+ Mr '65
We're nothing, but we want to be some-
thing. Mlle 62:155-7+ N '65

HOFFMANN, Stanley
Evolutionary concept. New Repub 152:17 My
29 '65
Treading between abysses. Nation 200:198-
200 F 22 '65
HOFHEINZ, Roy
Giltfinger's golden dome. L. Smith. il por
Sports Illus 22:44-6+ Ap 12 '65
Incredible Houston dome. F. X. Tolbert. il
por Look 29:96-8 Ap 20 '65
HOFMANN, Elayne B.
Brookhurst plan. NEA J 54:50-2 S '65
HOFMANN, Erich
Reporter at large; Eskimo canneries for
Eskimo foods, results of sampling in dis-
trict of Keewatin. E. Iglauer. New Yorker
41:122+ Ap 24 '65
HOFMANN, Hans
Art galleries; exhibition of new paintings at
the Kootz gallery. R. M. Coates. New
Yorker 41:100+ F 27 '65
Hans Hofmann. H. Rosenberg. por Vogue 145:
192-5+ My '65
Mystery of Hans Hofmann. il Art N 63:39+
F '65
HOFMANN, Paul
Cuba is in Fidel's shirt pocket. N Y Times
Mag p7+ Je 13 '65
HOFMANNSTHAL, Hugo Hofmann, edler von
One who's right. P. J. Smith. por Opera N
30:24-5 D 18 '65
HOFMEYER, Hans
Judgment at Frankfurt. Time 86:22 Ag 27 '65
HOFMEYR, Jan Hendrik
South African tragedy, by A. Paton. Review
Sat R por 48:43-4 O 30 '65. J. Barkham
HOFSOMMER, Aphrodite J.
How to care for orchids in the summer. il
Horticulture 43:26-7+ Ag '65
HOFSTATTER, Lewis
Nickel-cadmium batteries. Electr World 74:
37-41 O '65
HOG cholera
Hog cholera eradication: we are making
progress. L. D. Mark. Suc Farm 63:39 Mr
'65
Key states close in on hog cholera. Farm J
89:38 Je '65
HOG houses. See Swine houses
HOGAN, Ben
Man who casts the longest shadow. A.
Wright. il por Sports Illus 22:40-2+ Ap 5 '65
HOGAN, Robert F. See Squire, J. R. jt. auth.
HOGAN'S goat; drama. See Alfred, W.
HOGARTH, Grace Allen
Transatlantic editing. Horn Bk 41:520-3 O '65
HOGE, William
Day Hitler lost the war; excerpts from Last
100 days. J. Toland. il por Look 29:36-40+
My 4 '65
HOGG, Quintin McGarel
Britain looks forward. For Affairs 43:409-25
Ap '65
HÖGLUND, B. and Mezger, P. G.
Hydrogen emission line $n_{110} \rightarrow n_{109}$: detection
at 5009 megahertz in galactic H II regions.
bibliog Science 150:339-40+ O 15 '65
HOGLUND, Ray
How to stay in the dairy business; ed. by
J. R. Borcherding. por Suc Farm 64:40-1+
Ja '66
HOGS. See Swine
HOHENBERG, John
From the big lie to the half-truth. Sat R
48:37 D 25 '65
New front page. Sat R 48:117-18+ S 18 '65
HOKE, John
Solar boat: army evaluators record a plus
for novel craft. J. Walsh. il Science 147:
1559-60 Mr 26 '65
HOKIN, Lowell E. and Hokin, M. R.
Chemistry of cell membranes; with biographi-
cal sketches. Sci Am 213:10, 78-84+ O '65
HOKIN, Mabel R. See Hokin, L. E. jt. auth.
HOLAHAN, J. F.
Colorimetry in color television. Electr World
74:21-3+ D '65
Manufacture of color picture tubes. Electr
World 74:30-2+ D '65
HOLBROOK, Weare
Hired help. Atlan 215:130+ Ap '65
HOLBROOK, Mass.
Neighborhood ecumenism: Interchurch coun-
cil. America 112:796 My 29 '65
HOLCOMB, Kan.
Annals of crime; In cold blood; murder of
H. W. Clutter family. T. Capote. New
Yorker 41:57-60+ S 25: 57-60+ O 2; 58-62+
O 9; 62-4+ O 16 '65
Horror spawns a masterpiece; T. Capote's In
cold blood inspired by Clutter family mur-
ders; excerpt; with report by J. Howard. il
Life 60:58-72+ Ja 7 '66

HOLCOMBE, Arthur N.
Social ideal, political reality. Sat R 49:41
Ja 22 '66
HOLD-ups. See Robberies and assaults
HOLDEN, John S.
Big browns in the Crystal. Atlan 216:84-7 Ag
'65
HOLDING companies
See also
Interpublic group of companies, incorporated
HOLDING devices (machine work)
Quickie saw guide for cutting big panels. V.
Kondra. il Pop Sci 187:144-5 O '65
Work-holding center for a drill press. W. G.
Waggoner. il Pop Sci 187:131 Ag '65
See also
Clamps
HOLIDAY house (firm)
Holiday house sold to John H. Briggs, jr.
Pub W 187:26 Mr 29 '65
HOLIDAY inns of America, incorporated
Southern business: the boomman. T. G. Har-
ris. il Look 29:40-4 N 16 '65
HOLIDAYS
How to solve the holiday collection problem;
Tucson, Ariz. H. L. Danforth. il Am City
80:20 Mr '65
See also
Festivals
HOLINESS
Spirit of holiness in men of power. Life 58:4
Ap 16 '65
HOLLAND, Barbara
Dreams of Rosemary; story. McCalls 93:52-3
Ja '66
World outside; story. Redbook 124:56-7 Mr
'65
HOLLAND, Gerald
Report on a mission for L.B.J. Sports Illus
23:24-6+ Jl 5 '65
Track & field. Sports Illus 23:46-7 Ag 2 '65
HOLLAND, Jerome H.
Negro and higher education. NEA J 54:22-4
Mr '65
HOLLAND, Jim
Make it pay! U S Camera 28:14+ Ap '65
HOLLAND, John A. family
Mayor picks deprived area. il Ebony 20:132-4+
Ag '65
HOLLAND, Kenneth
For knowledge and understanding. Bul
Atomic Sci 21:45-6 Ap '65
HOLLAND, V. F. and Lindenmeyer, P. H.
Dislocation networks in folded-chain poly-
ethylene crystals. bibliog Science 147:1296-7
Mr 12 '65
HOLLAND, Mich.
Windmill Island; with editorial comment. H.
Holt. il Am City 80:8, 98-9 Jl '65
**HOLLAND festival. See Music festivals—Neth-
erlands**
HOLLAND furnace company
Court catches up with Holland furnace co.
Consumer Bul 48:25-6 Ap '65
End of a thirty years' war on consumers;
FTC vs Holland furnace. Consumer Rep
30:238 My '65
HOLLANDER, John
Darryl Click; poem. Reporter 33:56 N 18 '65
Night mirror; poem. New Yorker 41:111
Ag 28 '65
Sunday evenings; poem. New Yorker 41:42 Mr
20 '65
HOLLANDER, Lawrence J.
Big blackout: whooping cranes & power
failures. Nation 202:33-6 Ja 10 '66
HOLLANDER, Lorin
Lorin Hollander: 1965 style in pianists; ed. by
R. Hemming. por Sr Schol 86:16 Mr 25 '65
HOLLENBECK, Alice
I fought against hatred among my neigh-
bors; ed. by J. N. Bell. por Good H 161:
71+ S '65
HOLLEY, Robert W. and others
Structure of a ribonucleic acid. bibliog Sci-
ence 147:1462-5 Mr 19 '65
about
Cracking the code. il por Newsweek 65:57 Mr
29 '65
HOLLIDAY, Judy
Bright girl. por Newsweek 65:87 Je 21 '65
Curtain slowly descends. G. Ace. Sat R 48:
12-13 Jl 17 '65
HOLLIDAY, S. C.
Administrative policy and book stock pro-
vision. Library J 90:4907-11 N 15 '65
**HOLLISTER, Walter M. See Wrigley, W. jt.
auth.**
HOLLISTER, William G.
Moral equivalents. PTA Mag 60:7 S '65
Setting up grievance channels. PTA Mag
59:18-19 Ap '65

HOLLOMON, J. Herbert
Future of engineering education; address, June 24, 1965. Vital Speeches 31:634-6 Ag 1 '65

HOLLOS, Steven
Medical care for the aged. America 112:309-12, 852+ Mr 6, Je 12 '65

HOLLOWAY, Sister Marcella M.
Fable of the phoebe bird. Cath World 202: 224-7 Ja '66

HOLLOWELL, Daniel
What's wrong with our students? New Repub 152:24 F 20 '65

HOLLY
Cheerful holly tree. J. P. Wood. il Read Digest 87:171-2+ D '65
Hollies for the South. I. S. Nelson. il Horticulture 43:26-7+ N '65
Holly. M. M. Leister. il Flower Grower 52: 34+ Mr '65
Let's be honest about hollies. W. H. Frederick, jr. il Horticulture 43:22-3+ D '65

HOLLYHOCKS
Hollyhock. il Horticulture 43:24-5 Je '65
Hollyhocks, the flower with old-fashioned charm. B. Brinhart. il Pop Gard 16:6-7+ Jl '65

HOLLYWOOD, Fla.

Recreation

Rejected beams span water hazards; Orange-brook golf course. W. A. Peterson. il Am City 80:98-9 My '65

HOLLYWOOD museum
Lament for a museum. A. Knight. Sat R 48: 43 Je 19 '65

HOLM, Bernard J.
(comp) Articles and other books received; medieval. See issues of American historical review

HOLM, Glen C. See White, J. M. jt. auth.

HOLM, Hanya
Copyright by Hanya Holm. il pors Dance Mag 39:44 Jl '65
Hanya Holm asks and answers. J. Anderson. il por Dance Mag 39:32-3 Ag '65
Start with the body. il por Newsweek 66:77 Ag 30 '65

HOLM, Tryggve
Saab sets up a neutral's defense. il por Bsns W p 124+ Je 19 '65

HOLMBERG, Allan R. and Dobyns, H. F.
Transformation of peasant societies. Science 147:1062+ F 26 '65

HOLMER, Paul L.
Contra the new theologies. Christian Cent 82:329-32 Mr 17 '65

HOLMES, Carl A.
When your baby catches cold. Parents Mag 41:36-7+ Ja '66

HOLMES, Charles S.
James Thurber and the art of fantasy. Yale R 55:17-33 O '65

HOLMES, Doris
Dock of the morning; poem. Sat R 48:50 Jl 17 '65
Mr Meccano; poem. Sat R 48:56 F 13 '65

HOLMES, J. B. S.
Fitzhugh and FitzHughs in the China trade. Antiques 89:130-1 Ja '66

HOLMES, John Clellon
15¢ before 6:00 PM; the wonderful movies of the 'thirties. Harper 231:51-5 D '65

HOLMES, Lowell D.
Portrait in science; Jefferson's avocation. Natur Hist 74:59-62 N '65

HOLMES, Marjorie
Do you love me in the supermarket? Todays Health 44:42-4 Ja '66
For a child adventuring; poem. McCalls 92: 93 F '65

HOLMES, Oliver Wendell, 1841-1935
Friendship of Holmes and Brandeis. F. Biddle. por Atlan 216:86-91 D '65

HOLMES, Theodore
Winter park with beeches; Woman and horse; poems. Poetry 106:283-5 Jl '65

HOLMSTEDT, Bo
Simple microcentrifuge for use in the field. bibliog Science 149:977-8 Ag 27 '65

HOLT, A. D.
This year's freshmen: more and better. NEA J 54:29-30 Ap '65

HOLT, Harold Edward
Exit burly Bob. por Newsweek 67:44 Ja 24 '66

HOLT, Herbert
Windmill Island. Am City 80:98-9 Jl '65

HOLT, John
How to help babies learn without teaching them. Redbook 126:54-5+ N '65
Why children fail in school. PTA Mag 60:14-16 bibliog(p36) Ja '66

HOLT, Rinehart and Winston, incorporated
Holt series. M. Robinson. il Wilson Lib Bul 40:56-8 S '65

HOLTER, Ruth
Stay-at-home vacation. Parents Mag 40:50-1+ Jl '65

HOLTON, Abner Linwood
Flutter in Byrdland. por Time 86:32 O 15 '65

HOLTY, Carl Robert
Other side of freedom. il por Art N 64:32-4+ Sum '65

HOLTZER, H. See De La Haba, G. jt. auth.

HOLY Cross college, Washington, D.C.
Post-seminary thoughts. M. Novak. Commonweal 83:9-12 O 8 '65

HOLY Ghost. See Holy Spirit

HOLY Innocents, Massacre of the
Herod's anguished decision. Commonweal 83: 359-60 D 24 '65

HOLY places
Road to Santiago; Spain's ancient road refurbished for modern pilgrims. F. V. Grunfeld. il Reporter 34:40+ Ja 13 '66
Roll, Jordan, roll! G. Kent. il Read Digest 87: 173-4+ O '65

HOLY Roman empire
See also
Charlemagne, king of the Franks

HOLY scriptures. See Bible

HOLY See. See Vatican

HOLY Sepulcher, Church of. See Jerusalem—Church of the Holy Sepulcher

HOLY Spirit
Word (cont) V. P. McCorry. America 112: 840-1 Je 5 '65
See also
Pentecost

HOLY week
Holy week in Seville. A. Mayor. il Holiday 37:80-5 Ap '65

HOLZER, Jane Brookenfield
Way-out Baby Jane is really in. il pors Life 58:121-2 Mr 19 '65

HÖLZLHUBER, Franz
Sketches from northwestern America and Canada. por Am Heritage 16:49-64 Je '65

HOLZMAN, Robert S.
Watch your minutes. bibliog f Harvard Bsns R 43:162-4+ Mr '65

HOMANS, George C.
Sailing with Uncle Charlie. Atlan 216:39-45 Jl '65

HOME, Alexander Frederick Douglas-Home, 14th earl of. See Douglas-Home, A. F.

HOME and the school. See School and the home

HOME bars. See Bars and barrooms

HOME building. See Building

HOME building industry. See Building industry

HOME decoration. See House decoration

HOME economics
Diary of a spring housecleaner. il McCalls 92:78 Ap '65
First things first; solving the house chore problem. D. McDonald. il Redbook 125:6+ Je '65
Housekeeping on wheels. D. Liston. il Todays Health 43:62-6+ My '65
Housework get you down? W. C. Jardine. il Farm J 89:56 Jl '65
How to keep farmyard mud out of the house. il Farm J 89:90-1 Ap '65
Keeping house with Emily Taylor. E. Taylor. See issues of Good housekeeping
Keeping up to date (cont) il Farm J 89:100 F '65
Keeping up to date in your home. il Farm J 89:68 Je; 44 Jl '65
Notes of a happy housekeeper. M. E. Falter. See issues of House & garden incorporating Living for young homemakers
120 ways to please a man. il Good H 161:104-26+ O '65
Tiredest night of the week. J. K. Lubold. il Read Digest 87:108-11 S '65
Use your eyes to clean house. Am Home 68: 96 Ap '65
What does she do all day? record of a typical day; reply. il Changing T 19:33-4 Ap '65
See also
Budget, Household
Dishwashing
Good housekeeping institute
House cleaning

Anecdotes, facetiae, satire, etc.

Where the action is! K. Nelson. il Good H 160:70+ Ap '65

Study and teaching

See also
Home economic departments

HOME economics departments
Home economics facilities. J. L. Taylor and J. Christian. il Sch Life 47:13-16 D '64

HOME fire drills. See Fire drills

HOME fire prevention. See Fire protection

HOME fires burning; story. See Wood, M.

HOME free! drama. See Wilson, L.

HOME freezers. See Freezers

HOME furnishings. See Household furnishings

HOME grounds
After the builder left. B. C. Kilvert, jr. il Flower Grower 52:34-6 Ap '65
For easy maintenance, a self-controlled landscape. B. Black. il Pop Gard 17:32-3 Ja '66
How an ugly lot in Florida was transformed. A. Rolf. Flower Grower 52:13 Je '65
Inspired fantasy, carried off with a flourish. il House & Gard 127:114-15 Je '65
Little things count. E. B. McClure. il Pop Gard 16:16-17 Jl '65
No garden is hopeless. il Bet Hom & Gard 43:64-5 Ap '65
Off-street parking, right in your own back yard. il Bet Hom & Gard 43:15-16+ Mr '65
Trees and vines for every setting. H. Mason and others. il Bet Hom & Gard 43:56-61 Mr '65

HOME libraries. See Libraries, Private

HOME life. See Family life

HOME loan bank board. See United States—Federal home loan bank board

HOME loans. See Loans, Personal

HOME management. See Home economics

HOME movies. See Moving pictures, Amateur

HOME offices. See Offices

HOME ownership
Costly mistakes home buyers can make. il Changing T 19:17-20 Ap '65
Don't plan to build trouble. il Bet Hom & Gard 43:44+ Ap '65
Home away from home; second homes. il Newsweek 67:50 Ja 3 '66
Older homes outsell the new. Bsns W p 144+ Ja 15 '66
Those homes you can buy from the VA. Good H 160:151 F '65
Want to sell your house in a hurry? P. Friggens. Read Digest 87:147-50 O '65
We leave our house; memories of ten years. C. Burch. il Good H 161:44+ Ag '65
See also
Mortgages

HOME remedies. See Medicine

HOME safety devices and measures. See Safety devices and measures

HOME sewing. See Sewing

HOME; story. See Jackson, S.

HOME study
Q. are teens overworked? pro and con discussion. il Seventeen 24:132-3+ Ap '65
Should homework be abolished? pro and con discussion. O. Arnold; B. M. Shaw. il NEA J 54:22-3+ F '65
Teaching study skills. J. Olsen. Sr Schol 86:sup24 Mr 4 '65

HOME study courses. See Correspondence schools and courses

HOME work. See Home study

HOME workshops. See Workshops

HOMECOMING; drama. See Hark, M. and McQueen, N.

HOMECOMING; drama. See Pinter, H.

HOMECOMING of Joel Bialystock; story. See Levinson, D.

HOMEMAKERS, Visiting. See Visiting housekeepers

HOMEMAKING. See Home economics

HOMER
Iliad. K. Rexroth. Sat R 48:17 Mr 27 '65
Odyssey. K. Rexroth. Sat R 48:18 Ap 3 '65

HOMES, Institutional
Special hell for children in Washington. J. W. Anderson. Harper 231:51-6 N '65; Discussion. 232:6+ Ja '66

HOMESTEAD, Pa.
Battle at Homestead; excerpt from Lockout. L. Wolff. il Am Heritage 16:64-79 Ap '65

HOMESTEAD NATIONAL MONUMENT OF AMERICA
Homestead National Monument; near Beatrice, Neb. J. Robertson. il Travel 124:48-9 S '65

HOMESTEAD strike, 1892
Lockout, by L. Wolff. Review
Time il 85:111+ My 14 '65

HOMEWORK. See Home study

HOMICIDE
See also
Euthanasia
Murder

HOMILETICS. See Preaching

HOMING instinct. See Orientation

HOMING pigeons. See Pigeons

HOMO erectus. See Man, Prehistoric

HOMO transvaalensis. See Man, Prehistoric

HOMOCYSTINURIA. See Cystathionine

HOMOGENIZERS
Centrifugal homogenizer. J. H. Gregg. il Science 150:1739-40 D 24 '65

HOMOGRAFTS. See Transplantation of organs, tissues, etc.

HOMONYMS
See also
Puns and punning

HOMOSEXUALITY
Charge of immorality; concerning Civil service commission hiring procedures. New Repub 153:6-7 Jl 3 '65
Deviance and deviates. H. S. Becker. Nation 201:115-19 S 20 '65
Do our homosexuality laws make sense? R. K. Woetzel. Sat R 48:23-5 O 9 '65
Heterosexual backlash; present position of homosexual drama. W. Sheed. Commonweal 82:289-90+ My 21 '65
Homosexual in America; Time essay. Time 87:40-1 Ja 21 '66
Homosexuals can be cured. Time 85:44+ F 12 '65
Homosexuals need help. Sci N L 87:102 F 13 '65
Is homosexuality a crime? J. Grigg. N Y Times Mag p6-7+ Je 27 '65
Justice for homosexuals. Nation 201:318-19 N 8 '65; Reply. S. H. Hofstadter. 201:428 N 29 '65
Law and homosexuality. America 113:71 Jl 17 '65
Law and the homosexual problem; New York fails to ratify revision. Life 58:4 Je 11 '65
Mothers and sons: an intimate discussion. V. T. Lathbury. Ladies Home J 82:43-5 F '65
New immoralists. W. Phillips. Commentary 39:66-9 Ap '65
"Our son was different." L. David. Good H 162:51+ Ja '66
Reappraising law on homosexuality; Wolfenden committee's recommendation. Christian Cent 82:669 My 26 '65
Their liberal lordships; House of lords vote on Private members bill. il Newsweek 65:38 Je 7 '65
See also
Lesbianism

HONAN, William H.
Merry bang-bang (and happy New Year) New Repub 153:11-12 D 25 '65

HONDA, Soichiro
Who's who in foreign business. il por Fortune 71:52 My '65

HONDA motor company. See Automobile industry and trade—Japan

HONDURAS
Honduras: problems and prospects. W. S. Stokes. Cur Hist 50:22-6+ Ja '66
See also
Economic assistance in Honduras
Elections—Honduras

Politics and government
One kind of freedom. il Newsweek 65:48 F 22 '65

HONDURAS, BRITISH. See British Honduras

HONECKER, Erich
Culture commissars. il Newsweek 67:47 Ja 17 '66

HONESTY
High cost of conscience. L. R. Young. il McCalls 93:81-2+ O '65
Honesty in the church, by D. Callahan. Review
Commonweal 82:222-3 My 7 '65
Incident at the soda fountain. L. L. Outlaw. Read Digest 88:187-8 Ja '66
Man, morals and maturity; excerpt from Sin, sex and self-control. N. V. Peale. Read Digest 87:253-6+ O '65
Nothing but the truth? H. Cecil. il Holiday 37:12+ Mr '65
300-year weekend: marathon, practice total honesty. S. Alexander. Life 59:28 S 24 '65
See also
Business ethics
Cheating in schoolwork
Integrity

HONEY, Patrick J.
Hard times in North Vietnam: hunger, failures, dissension; excerpts from address, May 13, 1965. U S News 58:56-7 My 31 '65
Here's how North Vietnam is doing in the war; interview, ed. by J. Fromm. por U S News 58:40-2 Ap 12 '65

HONEY bees. See Bees

HONEYCOMB construction. See Sandwich construction

HONEYWELL, incorporated
Executive denies computer costs force small firms into mergers. G. E. Wilson. Aviation W 83:124+ S 13 '65
Honeywell calls a computer bet; Series 200 line challenges IBM and RCA. il Bsns W p 102+ F 13 '65

HONG KONG
What goes in Hong Kong? everything. S. Topping. il N Y Times Mag p40-1+ Ap 11 '65
Why China leaves Hong Kong alone. D Kirk. Reporter 33:31-2 S 23 '65
See also
Electric power—Hong Kong
Restaurants—Hong Kong
Tourist trade—Hong Kong

Banks
Another kind of crisis; run on Chinese-owned banks. il Time 85:96 F 19 '65

Description
Hong Kong. A. Menen. il Vogue 145:204-7+ My '65
Hong Kong high life. H. Sutton. il Sat R 48:42+ S 18 '65
Hong Kong: there is a splendour about the place. G. Bradshaw. Vogue 146:74 S 15 '65
Right little island. R. Joseph. il Esquire 64: 110-13+ O '65
Well traveled camera. H. Keppler. il Mod Phot 29:105+ Ap '65

Stores
Reds reach for cash in Hong Kong; Communist China opens department store. il Bsns W p 140-2+ N 6 '65

HONIG, George R. and Rabinovitz, Marco
Actinomycin D: inhibition of protein synthesis unrelated to effect on template RNA synthesis. bibliog Science 149:1504-6 S 24 '65

HONIG, Joel
Pearl of Brazil. Opera N 30:6-7 D 25 '65

HONOLULU
Notes for a gazetteer. P. Hamburger. New Yorker 41:90+ Ap 3 '65
Women to the rescue; Outdoor circle keeps Honolulu beautiful. America 113:313 S 25 '65

Description
Fresh look at Honolulu. K. Lamott. il Holiday 38:68-73 D '65

Housing
Unusual structure boldly expressed. il Arch Rec 137:216-17 Ap '65

Music
Music at the Iolani palace. il Sunset 134:9 F '65

Sanitary affairs
For better breathing: a landfill. Y. Kunimoto. il Am City 80:62 O '65

Social life and customs
Honolulu: problems in paradise. I. Taves. il Look 29:58-61+ F 23 '65

HONOR
See also
Sportsmanship

HOOD, MOUNT
Ghosts of Gnarl Ridge. J. E. Kollas. il Am For 71:66-8 My '65

HOOFT, Willem Adolf Visser't. See Visser't Hooft, W. A.

HOOGENBOOM, Ari
Roots of hate run long and deep. Sat R 48: 48+ S 11 '65

HOOKE, Nina Warner
Sammy, the sociable seal; condensation of Seal summer. Read Digest 86:233-9+ Mr '65

HOOKER, Ruth H.
SLA awards. Library J 90:2996 Jl '65

HOOKWORM disease
Hookworm disease still plagues southeast U.S. Sci N L 88:196 S 25 '65

HOOPER, Bayard
Scuttle the jib sheets, where's my checkbook! Life 58:12+ F 12 '65

HOOVER, Helen
Big cat, the starving lynx. Audubon Mag 67: 91-2 Mr '65
Wilderness trail: autumn. Liv Wildn 87:11-12 Wint '64
Wilderness trail: winter. Liv Wildn 29:8-10 Spr '65

HOOVER, Herbert Clark
Thirty-first President 1929-1933. F. Freidel. il pors Nat Geog Mag 128:572-7 O '65

HOOVER, John Edgar
Communist gains among youths. por U S News 59:46 N 1 '65
Faith of freedom; address, October 19, 1965. Vital Speeches 32:71-4 N 15 '65
From J. Edgar Hoover: a report on campus reds; excerpts from testimony, March 4, 1965. por U S News 58:84 My 31 '65
National police force? no, says FBI chief Hoover; excerpts from statements. por U S News 58:20 Ap 12 '65
Police brutality: how much truth; how much fiction? por U S News 59:116-17+ S 27 '65
Warning from J. Edgar Hoover; reprint. por U S News 59:20 S 13 '65
We mollycoddle criminals. por U S News 59: 67 Ag 9 '65
When criminals are set free too soon. por U S News 58:21 My 17 '65

about
Chief speaks. por Time 85:26 My 28 '65
Crime is too big for the FBI. W. W. Turner. il Nation 201:322-8 N 8 '65
Heil Hoover. New Repub 153:9 S 4 '65
Hoover of the FBI. J Phelan. il pors Sat Eve Post 238:23-8+ S 25 '65
In defense of J. Edgar Hoover. Time 85:41 Mr 5 '65
J. Edgar Hoover, the compleat bureaucrat. J. Kraft. Commentary 39:59-62 F '65
Perils of omnipotence; concerning novel, Doorbell rang. Nation 201:291 N 1 '65
What's ahead for the FBI. M. Ottenberg. Look 29:27-9 F 23 '65
When Hoover corrected the record. por U S News 59:13 Ag 2 '65

HOOVER, Mary Bidgood
Anxiety; hidden threat to children's health. Parents Mag 40:74-6+ N '65
It's smart to play favorites. Parents Mag 40:48-9+ My '65

HOOWIJ, Jan H.
Paintings of Jan Hoowij. J. Lovoos. il por Am Artist 29:66-71+ Je '65

HOPE, Marjorie
Vietnam youth in revolt. Mlle 61:96-7+ Je '65
When Bonneyclaire came North. Good H 161:262b N '65

HOPE Namgyal, maharani of Sikkim
Crowning of Hope Cooke, Sarah Lawrence '63. il pors Life 58:36-8 Ap 23 '65
Hope-la in Gangtok. il por Time 85:39 Ap 16 '65

HOPE
Images of hope: imagination as healer of the hopeless, by W. F. Lynch. Review America 113:247-8 S 4 '65. J. E. Royce

HOPE diamond. See Diamonds

HOPKINS, D. M. and others
Quaternary correlations across Bering Strait. bibliog Science 147:1107-14 Mr 5 '65

HOPKINS, Gerard Manley
Hopkins the critic. M. Ochshorn. Yale R 54: 346-67 Mr '65

HOPKINS center. See Dartmouth college, Hanover, N.H.—Hopkins center

HOPPE, Fred D.
Systemic way to control pests. Flower Grower 52:52 My '65

HOPPENSTEDT, Elbert M. See Waite, H. E. jt. auth.

HOPPER, Dennis
Loved house of the Dennis Hoppers. por T. Southern. il Vogue 146:138-43+ Ag 1 '65

HOPPER, Edward
Edward Hopper. R. Squirru. il Américas 17: 11-17 My '65

HOPPER, Rex Devern
Project Camelot. Newsweek 66:18-19 Jl 5 '65

HOPPOUGH, Robert
Study corner that grows. Pop Sci 187:112-13 S '65

HORAN, Ellen
How to tie a knot! Yachting 117:236-7 Ap '65

HORATIO Seymour's house. See Middlebury, Vt.—Historic houses, etc.

HORCHLER, Richard
Paul VI: continuing enigma? Christian Cent 82:831-4 Je 30 '65

HORICON national wildlife refuge. See Wildlife sanctuaries

HORMEL, George A, and company
Processed meat, a quality convenience food. M. B. Keiser. il Parents Mag 40:26+ D '65

HORMONE creams. See Cosmetics

HORMONES
Cure for psychosis seen; adrenal hormone balance. Sci N L 88:78 Jl 31 '65
Growth hormone: important role in muscular exercise in adults. W. M. Hunter and others. bibliog il Science 150:1051-3 N 19 '65
Hormones and genes. E. H. Davidson. il Sci Am 212:36-45 bibliog(p 146) Je '65

HORMONES—*Continued*
Immunoassay for human chorionic growth
hormone-prolactin in serum and urine. S.
L. Kaplan and M. M. Grumbach. bibliog
il Science 147:751-3 F 12 '65
Men and their looks; tape-talk straight from
a famous doctor; questions and answers.
Vogue 146:118-21 N 15 '65
Permeability of a nuclear membrane: changes
during normal development and changes
induced by growth hormone. S. Ito and W.
R. Loewenstein. bibliog il Science 150:909-10
N 12 '65
See also
Aldosterone
Estrogens
HORMONES, Plant
Progesterone: biosynthesis from pregnenolone
in holarrhena floribunda. R. D. Bennett and
E. Heftmann. bibliog Science 149:652-3 Ag 6
'65
See also
Ethylene
HORMONES, Sex
Fertility experiment recalled. W. F. Windle.
Science 149:1444+ S 24 '65
Hormone helps reduce weight; chorionic go-
nadotrophin. Sci Digest 58:36-7 Jl '65
Hormone that produces quints. il Sci Digest
58:26-7 O '65
Hormones may induce sleep and epilepsy;
steroids. Sci N L 88:341 N 27 '65
Multiple-birth hormone; Lawson and Ohlsen
quintuplets. il Time 86:64 Ag 6 '65
Narrowing the odds; Lawson and Olsen
quintuplets. il Newsweek 66:78 Ag 9 '65
New harmless hormones promise fertility
control. Sci N L 89:19 Ja 8 '66
Sex hormone aids bones. il Sci Digest 58:18-
19 D '65
Steroid hormones and the pill. il Science 150:
1189-91 N 26 '65
See also
Progesterone
Testosterone
HORN, Huston
Tennis. Sports Illus 22:58-9 Mr 8 '65
HORN, Zoia
Intellectual freedom committee reports busy
year of censorship in New Jersey; excerpts
from address, May 14, 1965. Library J 90:
2774+ Je 15 '65
HORNBECK, Gene
Bow and arrow turkey. Field & S 70:70-1+
Jl '65
HORNBECK, James S.
Building in context. Arch Rec 137:125-7 F '65
HORNE, Bryant
Jackson, Mississippi's nature trail. Horticul-
ture 43:44 O '65
HORNE, Carl A.
Court upholds recent civil rights law. Nat R
17:929 O 19 '65
HORNE, Lena
My life with Lennie; excerpt from Lena.
pors Ebony 21:176-8+ N '65
about
Successful autographing tours by three
personalities. il por Pub W 188:53-6 D 13
'65
HORNE, Marilyn
Out of the shade. por Time 85:44+ F 19 '65
Presenting Marilyn Horne. G. L. Mayer.
por Am Rec G 31:706-7 Ap '65
HORNER, John E.
Education and world affairs: a search for
new techniques. Dept State Bul 53:1017-20
D 27 '65
HORNETS
Nature note; paper wasp. Sci N L 87:238 Ap
10 '65
HORNIG, Donald F.
Main competition lies ahead; address, March
1, 1965. Sci N L 87:165+ Mr 13 '65
Science and international cooperation; re-
marks, November 30, 1965. Dept State Bul
54:20-2 Ja 3 '66
Universities and federal science policies; ad-
dress, October 11, 1965. Science 150:847-51
N 12 '65
about
Doctor Hornig studies establishment of science institute in Korea. Dept State Bul 53:
172 Jl 26 '65
HORNS, Removal of. See Dehorning
HORNUNG, Clarence P.
What a way to go; excerpts from Gallery of
the American automobile. il Am Heritage
17:65-79 D '65
about
Hornung's luxurious prints of the American
automobile. il por Pub W 187:90-1 Ap 5 '65

HORNUNG, Paul
Football and the single man; excerpts. pors
Look 29:60-2+ Jl 27; 61-2+ Ag 10 '65
about
Confessions of a legend. por Time 86:78 O
29 '65
HOROSKO, Marian
Mme Anderson-Ivantzova. Dance Mag 39:54-6
Je '65
about
Dancer's second career. D. Leddick. il pors
Dance Mag 39:19-20+ Ag '65
HOROWITZ, Milton W.
For men only? por Flying 77:30-3 Ag '65
HOROWITZ, Samuel B. See Fenichel, I. R. jt.
auth.
HOROWITZ, Vladimir
Horowitz; interview, ed. by A. Chasins. il
por Hi Fi 15:50-4+ O '65
about
Boss is back! J. Lyons. il por Am Rec G
31:956-7+ Je '65
Horowitz method: listen and sing. H. Klein.
il por N Y Times Mag p32-3+ My 9 '65
Music to my ears: Horowitz return to stage
of Carnegie Hall. I. Kolodin. Sat R 48:54
My 22 '65
New art of Vladimir Horowitz. H. Goldsmith.
il Hi Fi 15:65-6 Ag '65
Return. New Yorker 41:21-3 My 29 '65
Return in triumph. il pors Life 58:121-2 My
21 '65
Return of the thunderer. por Newsweek 65:
92-3 My 17 '65
Vladimir Horowitz. A. Chasins. il por Hi Fi
15:122+ Ag '65
HORROR films. See Moving pictures—Horror
films
HORS d'oeuvres. See Appetizers
HORSE breeding
Bold is the badge of champions; Bold Ruler
racing's foremost sire. W. Tower. il Sports
Illus 22:22-4+ F 22 '65
California rancher. il Ebony 21:77-8+ Ja '66
Chromosome complement: differences between
equus caballus and equus przewalskii.
Poliakoff. K. Benirschke and others. bibliog
il Science 148:382-3 Ap 16 '65
HORSE farms
Pickles, hosses and my man from Princeton;
Greentree stable. J. Olsen. il Sports Illus
22:70-4+ Mr 15 '65
HORSE race betting
Happy punter of Ally Pally. J. Olsen. il Sports
Illus 23:52-7+ Ag 9 '65
Horse sense, by B. P. Fabricand. Review
Sports Illus 22:15 Ap 26 '65. R. Cantwell
Horseplayer's wild ride through Europe. G.
Smith. il Sat Eve Post 238:80-2 Jl 3 '65
Ministers vs. Miljay. inc. Knox County, Ill.
L. M. Martin. Christian Cent 82:679-80 My
26 '65
Morley view of sport. R. Morley. il Sports
Illus 22:52+ Ap 26 '65
Track, fast; bets, too; automated system
handling bets. il Bsns W p66-7 N 27 '65
HORSE racing
Absurd and senseless; use of whips. Sports
Illus 22:18 My 24 '65
Add this pair to your Derby list; Isle of
Greece and Tom Rolfe. W. Tower. Sports
Illus 22:69 Mr 22 '65
And then there were only two; Tom Rolfe
and Hail to All. W. Tower. il Sports Illus
23:53 Ag 30 '65
Bay and the gray were a perfect parlay;
Native Charger and Lucky Debonair for
Kentucky Derby. W. Tower. il Sports Illus
22:60+ Mr 15 '65
Bon voyage! Flag Raiser wins Wood memo-
rial. il Time 85:83 Ap 23 '65
Change of luck; Kentucky Derby, won by
Lucky Debonair. il Newsweek 65:73 My
10 '65
Derby daze; 1965 Kentucky Derby. il News-
week 65:63 My 3 '65
Diminishing returns; thoroughbred racing at-
tendance dropped. Sports Illus 24:6 Ja 3 '66
Education of a jockey; R. Turcotte wins
Preakness on Tom Rolfe. il Time 85:70 My
21 '65
Faith and form at Saratoga; Bishop Mc-
Kinstry's devotion to Kelso. W. Tower.
il Sports Illus 23:14-15 Ag 16 '65
France repels the invasion; winners of
Europe's top race at Longchamp. W. Tower.
il Sports Illus 23:32-3 O 11 '65

HORSE racing—*Continued*

French ride to the rescue; International at Laurel. W. Tower. Sports Illus 23:92 N 22 '65

Good one left is Jacinto; soundest potential Kentucky Derby favorite. W. Tower. il Sports Illus 22:55-6+ F 15 '65

Grass may not be greener; Roman Brother, best U.S. handicap horse at Laurel. W. Tower. Sports Illus 23:71 N 8 '65

Hail to Zelda! Hail to Ben! Hail to All wins Belmont Stakes. W. Tower. il Sports Illus 22:28-9 Je 14 '65

Happy punter of Ally Pally. J. Olsen. il Sports Illus 23:52-7+ Ag 9 '65

Hello, lady; Lucky Debonair wins Kentucky Derby. il Time 85:82 My 7 '65

Horses, roses and groaning boards; photographs by R. Meek; with account by L. Smith. Sports Illus 22:40-51 Ap 26 '65

Into the valley of tangles rode the forty-seven; Grand national steeplechase, Aintree, England. il Life 58:60B-61 Ap 9 '65

Invasion and retreat; victory for France in International series. Newsweek 66:66 N 22 '65

Jump that won a Grand national; Maryland-bred Jay Trump and jockey Tommy Smith. M. Kane. il Sports Illus 22:24-9 Ap 5 '65

Like father, like sons; Ribot's sons, Dapper Dan and Tom Rolfe in Preakness. W. Tower. il Sports Illus 22:30-1 My 24 '65

Little old ladies of Pasadena missed a good bet; G. Pope's Hill Rise to go off at 12-to-1 odds in the Santa Anita handicap. W. Tower. il Sports Illus 22:60-1 Mr 8 '65

Long trip in a short race; Bold Lad favorite of Kentucky Derby. W. Tower. il Sports Illus 22:30-1+ Ap 12 '65

Lucky's Shoe tries to put on the second leg; Willie Shoemaker and Lucky Debonair in Preakness. W. Tower Sports Illus 22:82 My 17 '65

Mink-lined millionaire; horse named Kelso. il Time 86:53 Jl 16 '65

Pigeon of the year, at least; Priceless Gem wins the Frizette stakes at Aqueduct. P. Ryan. Sports Illus 23:86+ O 18 '65

Prince wins a noble sum; Garden State race. W. Tower. Sports Illus 23:76+ N 29 '65

Race horses are a cash crop. S. Cady. il N Y Times Mag p26-7+ Je 13 '65

Race track. A. Minor. See issues of New Yorker

Racing beneath the peaks; tracks surrounding Phoenix and Santa Anita. M. R. Werner. il Sports Illus 22:50-2+ Mr 8 '65

Ribot and a Tom Fool lead all the rest. W. Tower. il Sports Illus 23:112-13 S 20 '65

Rise of a new star named Pia; New York's Aqueduct racetrack. W. Tower. il Sports Illus 23:16-17 Ag 2 '65

Roses for the Shoe; Shoemaker wins with Lucky Debonair. W. Tower. il Sports Illus 22:24-9 My 10 '65

Sentimental Derby; Bold Lad, trainer Winfrey and jockey Hartack. W. Tower. il Sports Illus 22:20-5 My 3 '65

Startling economics of horse racing. T. J. Murray. il Duns R 85:39-40+ Mr '65

Syndication is the new big game at the racetrack; trading thoroughbred stallions. J. McDonald. il Fortune 73:159-63+ Ja '66

Taking advantage of a lady was the way to win; Buckpasser defeats Priceless Gem, in Champagne stakes. W. Tower. il Sports Illus 23:75-7 O 25 '65

This Native never left home; California's, Native Diver. W. Tower. il Sports Illus 23:43 Jl 26 '65

True test for a world title; Tom Rolfe joins top colts for France's Prix de l'Arc de triomphe. W. Tower. Sports Illus 23:62-3 S 27 '65

Two upsets were not really upsetting; Bold Lad and Lucky Debonair suffered defeats. W. Tower. il Sports Illus 22:87+ Ap 26 '65

What price victory; France's Prix de l'Arc de triomphe. il Time 86:76-7 O 15 '65
See also
Harness racing

HORSE shows

Horse-show whodunits; series of unrelated tragedies. A. Higgins. il Sports Illus 23:38-40 S 20 '65

New horsy set; National horse show in New York. il Time 86:104 N 5 '65

New voltage for an old circuit; Florida shows. A. Higgins. Sports Illus 22:64-5 Mr 29 '65

Out-SMERSHed in San Antonio. A. Higgins. Sports Illus 22:72 My 3 '65

With all horses go, the U.S. swings into a high orbit; U.S. team in Madison Square Garden. A. Higgins. Sports Illus 23:94+ N 22 '65

Year of the dagger at Devon. A. Higgins. Sports Illus 22:59 Je 21 '65

Yes yes, three in a row for My My, and Sweetie Face, too; Kentucky state fair horse show. A. Higgins. Sports Illus 23:76 O 11 '65

HORSE training

Pickles, hosses and my man from Princeton; Greentree stable. J. Olsen. il Sports Illus 22:70-4+ Mr 15 '65

Price's horsy prep; Dorchester Equine preparatory school, Ocala, Fla. il Sports Illus 24:24-7E Ja 10 '66

HORSEBACK riding. See Horsemanship

HORSEBACK trips

Young girl, an old horse, and astonishing journey; experiences in southern Spain and France. L. Moffat. Vogue 146:16+ N 1 '65

HORSEMANSHIP

Blue ribbon girl. S. Dencklau. il Seventeen 24:136-7+ Mr '65

New horsy set. il Time 86:104 N 5 '65
See also
Horseback trips

HORSERADISH

Grow your own horseradish. L. K. Lantz. Horticulture 43:51 Mr '65

HORSES

Blue ribbon girl. S. Dencklau. il Seventeen 24:136-7+ Mr '65

Mustangs and cow horses, ed. by J. F. Dobie and others. Review
Time il '86:82 Jl 2 '65

Role of the horse in Chinese history. H. G. Creel. bibliog f Am Hist R 70:647-72 Ap '65

Terror of the pack train. D. Brown. il Outdoor Life '135:48-51+ Ap '65

Wild horses couldn't hold us back. Z. Taylor. il Motor B 115:30-3+ Ap '65
See also
Horse shows
Ponies
Race horses

        Paces, gaits, etc.

Symmetrical gaits of horses. M. Hildebrand. bibliog il Science 150:701-8 N 5 '65

        Training

See Horse training

HORSES, Miniature. See Ponies

HORSES in war. See Cavalry

HORSETAIL plant. See Equisetum

HORSFALL, Frank L. Jr

Cancer research; why a top authority is optimistic; interview. por U S News 58:57+ Ap 19 '65

HORSFALL, William R. See Anderson, J. F. jt. auth.

HORSZOWSKI, Mieczyslaw

Question of study. il por Newsweek 65:84-5 Mr 8 '65

HORTICULTURAL societies

Members' news. See issues of Horticulture

HORTICULTURE
See also
Gardening

        Bibliography

Books and reviews. See issues of Horticulture

HORTICULTURE (periodical)

Garden club yearbook contest rules. Horticulture 43:40-2 Ap '65

Garden club yearbook winners. Horticulture 43:52 Mr '65

Rules for Garden club yearbook contest. Horticulture 43:45+ O '65

HORTIN, Mellie Scott

Chickens belong in the indoor garden. Flower Grower 52:35 N '65

HORTON, Frank L.

Johannes Krause, master joiner of Salem. Antiques 88:92-3 Jl '65

Salem interiors. Antiques 88:81-91 Jl '65

HORWICH, Frances R.

Don't rob them of their childhood. NEA J 54:14-15 F '65

Roots of prejudice. PTA Mag 60:22-4 bibliog(p34) D '65

HORWITZ, Abraham

Health and development. Américas 17:54-8 Ap '65

HORWITZ, Elinor Lander

Gargoyles for Washington. Horizon 7:46-8 Sum '65

HORWITZ, Julius

Arithmetic of delinquency. N Y Times Mag p 12-13+ Ja 31 '65

Peace corpsman returns to darkest America. N Y Times Mag p74+ O 24 '65

This is the age of the aged. N Y Times Mag p25+ My 16 '65

HORWITZ, Solis
  Military members of the country team. Dept
  State Bul 53:268-71 Ag 16 '65
HOSANNA! I said; story. See Foster, M. S.
HOSIERY
  Cantrece nylons, as advertised. Consumer Rep
  30:225 My '65
  Challenge to nylon hosiery; Vectra hosiery.
  Consumer Rep 30:53-4 F '65
  New hosiery fibers; Cantrece nylon and
  Vectra olefin. il Consumer Bul 48:35-6 Je
  '65
  On making of Happy feet; faces on feet of
  stockings. il Design 67:31 S '65
  Run on nylons; debut of nylon hose twenty-
  five years ago. D. L. Goodrich. il N Y
  Times Mag p79-80 My 16 '65
  When you shop for stockings. il Good H 161:
  154 S '65
HOSIERY industry

          Wages and hours
  Wages in hosiery mills, September-October
  1964. G. L. Stelluto. il Mo Labor R 88:
  1093-5 S '65
HOSKINS, Halford L.
  U.S. in the Middle East: policy in transition.
  Cur Hist 48:257-62 My '65
HOSOKAWA, Bill
  Japan's two-mile-a-minute train. Read Di-
  gest 86:153-6+ Ap '65
HOSPITAL beds
  Floating bed relieves suffering from pres-
  sure. il(p 337) Sci N L 87:345 My 29 '65
HOSPITAL care
  New way to cut hospital costs. il U S News
  58:70-2 My 10 '65; Same abr. with title New
  look in hospital care. Read Digest 87:106-9
  Jl '65
HOSPITAL interns. See Interns (medicine)
HOSPITAL nursing. See Nurses and nursing
HOSPITAL patients. See Sick, The
HOSPITAL records
  Rx for hospitals: computers; information sys-
  tem at Massachusetts general hospital, and
  Missouri medical center. il Bsns W p 142+
  My 15 '65
HOSPITAL service, Cost of. See Medical serv-
  ice, Cost of
HOSPITAL service, State. See Medical service,
  State
HOSPITALITY
  Capsule history of hospitality. J. Clapperton.
  Holiday 37:46-7 F '65
  Race to succeed Nicole; the entries. M.
  Cheshire. il Life 59:93-4+ N 12 '65

    Anecdotes, facetiae, satire, etc.
  Gallery of hosts. F. B. Maynard and M. Main-
  waring. il Ladies Home J 82:160+ O '65
  No uncertain terms. J. Beatty, jr. Atlan 215:
  118+ Je '65
HOSPITALIZATION insurance. See Insurance,
  Hospitalization
HOSPITALS
  How to get the best treatment from your
  hospital. R. M. Cunningham, jr. il Ladies
  Home J 83:42+ Ja '66
    See also
  Children—Hospitals
  Nursing homes

          Architecture
  Building types study (cont) il Arch Rec
  137:161-80 F; 138:197-220 S '65
  Hospital designed to comfort the patients;
  American oncologic hospital, Phila. il For-
  tune 71:159 Ap '65
  Illinois plans zone centers for mental health.
  il Arch Rec 137:201-8 Je '65

       Childrens wards
  Today's hospital techniques save ailing new-
  borns. J. T. Burns and A. P. Riker. il
  Parents Mag 40:46-7+ Ap '65

       Emergency rooms
  Emergency room: solution to a problem. il
  Look 29:29 Je 29 '65
  Something will have to be done. il U S News
  58:51 Mr 15 '65

      Emergency services
  Code 99; signal for teamwork on the double;
  Pratt clinic-New England center hospital.
  il Todays Health 43:90-1 My '65
  Emergency service: medicine's newest spe-
  cialty. A. Q. Maisel. Read Digest 86:96-100
  Je '65
  New kind of doctor; emergency room of Wes-
  son memorial hospital, Springfield, Mass.
  R. H. Berg. il Look 29:22-6 Je 29 '65

          Employees
  Health careers unlimited. L. Velie. Read
  Digest 87:108-12 Ag '65

     Equipment and supplies
  Adaptable building system for progressive
  patient care; Texan A&M investigates mod-
  ules and service systems. il Arch Rec 138:
  202-4 S '65
    See also
  Hospital beds

         Federal aid
  Federal subsidies to segregated hospitals. A.
  Kopkind. New Repub 152:8 My 22 '65

        Food service
  Order, please? selective menu system. il
  Todays Health 43:15 N '65

     Isolation departments
  Germ-free bubble; airtight plastic keeps out
  infection. il Life 58:39-40+ Je 4 '65

    Management and regulation
  Research in patient care; report on seminar.
  P. J. Sanazaro. Science 148:1489-90 Je 11
  '65

         Standards
  As medicare nears: a crisis in hospital care?
  with interview with W. C. Rappleye. il
  U S News 58:50-6 Mr 15 '65

         Visitors
  When a friend is hospitalized. G. G. Greer.
  Bet Hom & Gard 43:26 F '65

         Nigeria
  Hospital that Jack & Jill built; Gusau. il
  UNESCO Courier 18:54-6 Jl '65

       United States
  As medicare nears: a crisis in hospital care?
  with interview with W. C. Rappleye. il
  U S News 58:50-6 Mr 15 '65
  Collectivizing the hospital; abolishing many
  local, voluntary, and charitable hospitals.
  R. Kirk. Nat R 17:729 Ag 24 '65
  In hospitals, patients packed into the aisles.
  il Life 59:54-5 S 3 '65
  Way to save millions on hospitals. il Chang-
  ing T 19:37-40 Ag '65
    See also
  Indians of North America—Hospitals
  United States—Veterans administration hos-
  pitals
    also subhead Hospitals under names
  of cities, e.g. Seattle—Hospitals
HOSPITALS, Indian. See Indians of North
  America—Hospitals
HOSPITALS, Military
  Battlefield readiness; portable airconditioned
  hospital. il Time 85:72 Mr 5 '65
  New army hospital travels with troops. Sci
  N L 87:152 Mr 6 '65
  Portable hospital up in thirty minutes;
  MUST. il Pop Sci 187:60-1 Ag '65
HOSPITALS, Portable. See Hospitals, Military
HOSPITALS, Prefabricated
  Hospitals in storage. Nation 201:514 D 27 '65
HOSPITALS, Psychiatric
  Coming upheaval in psychiatry. M. Pines. il
  Harper 231:54-60 O '65; Discussion. 231:6+
  D '65
  Illinois plans zone centers for mental health.
  il Arch Rec 137:201-8 Je '65
  LSD blueprint; psychedelic drugs used to
  see architecture from a psychotic viewpoint.
  Newsweek 65:69 My 24 '65
  Psychiatric vistas; day hospitals. il News-
  week 66:95+ N 29 '65
    See also
  Mentally ill—Care and treatment
HOSTAGES
  Arrows to heaven. Time 85:40 Je 11 '65
  Congo question; position of the United States;
  address, December 14, 1964. A. E. Steven-
  son. Vital Speeches 31:231-6 F 1 '65
HOSTELS. See Youth hostels
HOSTESS gifts. See Gifts
HOSTESSES. See Hospitality
HOSTESSES, Air. See Airlines—Hostesses
HOSTICK, King V.
  Autographs. See issues of Hobbies
HOT air engines. See Air engines
HOT breads. See Bread
HOT cross buns. See Bread
HOT salads. See Salads
HOT shoppes (restaurants) See Restaurants—
  United States

HOT SPRINGS NATIONAL PARK
Hot Springs havens. J. Heuston. il Travel 123:44-5 Mr '65
HOT SPRINGS spa resorts. See Health resorts, watering places, etc.
HOT weather menus. See Menus
HOTBEDS
Plastic sheeting, a useful aid; hotbed covers. S. Caldwell. il Flower Grower 52:6+ Ap '65
Portable frame you can build. R. E. Wester and W. E. Edgerley. il Horticulture 43:24-5 Mr '65
HOTCHKIN, John
New breed? old breed? half breed? America 113:318-19+ S 25 '65
HOTEL management

Study and teaching

Changing the recipe for innkeepers; New York university's course in hotel, restaurant management. il Bsns W p66-8+ F 27 '65
HOTEL Passionato; musical comedy. See Musical comedies, revues, etc.—Criticisms, plots, etc.
HOTELLING, Carole
Handle with care! Parents Mag 40:50-1+ My '65
HOTELS, taverns, etc.
Catskills: land of milk and money; Grossinger's and the Concord. M. Richler. il Holiday 38:56-63+ Jl '65
Colonial innkeepers; Treadway inns. il Time 85:85 Je 18 '65
Following the lure of the sun; resorts boom. il Bsns W p30-1 Mr 6 '65
Hotel headliners. See issues of Travel
Jennie; excerpts from Jennie went to the country, the Grossinger dream that came true. Q. Reynolds. il Look 29:86-8+ Jl 13 '65
Man who put the rhinestones on Miami. M. Mayer. il Harper 230:61-8 Mr '65
With a view of the dollar; new ways of conserving space. il Time 86:78 Ag 6 '65
Woo the secretary and win the boss; promotion of Hyatt house hotels. il Bsns W p30-1 S 11 '65
Wreckers rip into old downtown hotels. il Bsns W p63-4 Ag 21 '65
  See also
Hilton hotels corporation
Sheraton corporation of America
  also subhead Hotels, restaurants, etc. under names of cities, e.g. New York (city)—Hotels, restaurants, etc.

Designs and plans

New big-city hotel; San Francisco and Washington Hilton hotels. il Arch Rec 138:143-50 Jl '65

Hawaii

Builder's paradise. il Time 86:54 Jl 23 '65
Shocking approach to tranquillity; L. Rockefeller resort hotel, Mauna Kea, on island of Hawaii; photographs by P. Turner; with account by G. S. Brown. Sports Illus 22:68-76+ Je 28 '65

Japan

East goes West. H. Sutton. Sat R 48:52+ Je 12 '65

Kenya

New Stanley hotel. P. Vanderwicken. Esquire 63:1,6 My '65

Russia

Relaxing in Gagra; accommodations at Hotel Gagripsch. L. Gottlieb. Mlle 62:16+ N '65
  See also
Moscow—Hotels, restaurants, etc.

Scotland

Inns of the Highlands. R. Postgate. il Holiday 37:82-3+ Mr '65

West Indies

Going places, finding things in small hotels in the Caribbean. J. Wilson. il House & Gard 128:32-3+ D '65
HOTH, William E.
Paperbacks and professional growth; excerpts from address, 1965. Sr Schol 87:sup36 O 28 '65
HOTHEM, Larry L.
Curious coati. Field & S 70:47+ Ja '66
HOTHOUSES. See Greenhouses
HOTTELET, Richard C.
Same mandate, a different world. Sat R 48:26-7+ Jl 24 '65

HOTTINGER, Arnold
Keeping Nasser afloat. New Repub 153:15-16 N 20 '65
HOUCK, Carter
Best way to sew on buttons. Parents Mag 41:104 Ja '66
How to sew a fine seam. Parents Mag 40:105 Je '65
Parents' magazine's sewing circle. See issues of Parents' magazine and better home-making
Stay-stitch in time. Parents Mag 40:78 Ap '65
HOUGH, Graham
Fables after the fall. Sat R 48:17-18 Jl 31 '65
HOUGH, J. L.
Great Lakes research. Science 149:327 Jl 16 '65
HOULIHAN, H. Joseph
Sticky problem of price stickers. Pub W 187:60-1 My 24 '65
HOULIHAN, Raymond F.
Illustrations of Raymond F. Houlihan. F. Whitaker. il por Am Artist 29:47-53+ Mr '65
HOULTON, William
1066-1966. NEA J 55:57-9 Ja '66
HOUPHOUET-BOIGNY, Christiane (Hervé-Dupenher)
African scion takes a bride. il pors Ebony 20:25-8+ O '65
HOUPHOUET-BOIGNY, Guillaume
African scion takes a bride. il pors Ebony 20:25-8+ O '65
HOURS of labor
Earnings and hours; tables. See issues of Monthly labor review
Earnings and weekly hours of factory workers. J. Cocco. il Mo Labor R 88:1206-12 O '65
French resist overtime; demands for more leisure. il Bsns W p46+ Je 5 '65
Hours of work and output; reprint from July 1947 issue. M. D. Kossoris. Mo Labor R 88:801-2 Jl '65
Long hours and premium pay. J. R. Wetzel. il Mo Labor R 88:1083-8 S '65
Shorter work week: a report to wives. T. Howard. il McCalls 92:108-9+ Ap '65
  See also
Night work
Overtime
Vacations, Employee

Statistics

Wholesale trade: employee earnings and hours, 1964. H. A. Donolan. bibliog f il Mo Labor R 88:1307-12 N '65
HOUSE, J. Albert
Paging Emily Post. Nat R 17:718 Ag 24 '65
HOUSE boats
Hot-rod houseboat. J. Roe. il Pop Sci 186:108-10+ Ap '65
HOUSE building. See Building
HOUSE building materials. See Building materials
HOUSE buying. See Home ownership
HOUSE cars. See Automobiles
HOUSE cleaning
Fifty ways to save time on spring cleaning. il Good H 160:173-5 Ap '65
$500 spring house cleaning. M. Davidson. il Ladies Home J 82:128+ Ap '65
How to care for finishes and surfaces. Farm J 89:106 F '65
How to keep farmyard mud out of the house. il Farm J 89:90-1 Ap '65
Philosophy of fall housecleaning; with questions and answers. il McCalls 92:106-7+ S '65
Solutions to some pesky problems. il Good H 160:184 F '65

Anecdotes, facetiae, satire, etc.

How to clean the square. A. Menen. House & Gard 128:90-1 Jl '65
HOUSE committee on un-American activities. See United States—Congress—House of representatives—Un-American activities committee
HOUSE decoration
All these ideas, and more, in one house! il Bet Hom & Gard 43:66-7 Je '65
At home with the Arnolds; traditional warmth meets contemporary ease. il pors Good H 160:98-106+ Ja '65
Beauty treatment for blank walls. il Bet Hom & Gard 43:115 Mr '65
Better homes and gardens editors' choice houses for 1965. Bet Hom & Gard 43:47-55 Je '65

HOUSE decoration—*Continued*

Cool solutions; decorative treatments for air-conditioning units. R. Reif. il N Y Times Mag p80-1 Je 6 '65

Decorating in a new mood. il House & Gard 129:80-9 Ja '66

Decorating newsletter (cont) V. D. Hahn. Am Home 68:24 Mr '65

Decoration knows no bounds. G. O'Brien. il N Y Times Mag p86-7 Mr 21 '65

Decorators' benefit; Parke-Bernet galleries. B. Plumb. il N Y Times Mag p76-7 My 16 '65

Desert traditions, decorative riches. M. Roche. il House & Gard 128:254-9+ N '65

Fast fast fast ideas; meals, crafts, outdoor projects, decorating. il Bet Hom & Gard 43:50-75 Jl '65

Five ways to solve the long-room problem. il House & Gard 127:134-9 My '65

Great expectations; 1966 viewpoints. il House & Gard 129:100-5 Ja '66

H&G's Hallmark house for 1965: the return to absolute simplicity. il House & Gard 127:130-5+ Ap '65

H&G's house of color. il House & Gard 128:200-9 S '65

House laced with light. il House & Gard 127:122-9+ Mr '65

House of surprises; central patio in year-round house in New England. il House & Gard 128:82-95 Ag '65

House that grew and grew; Dower house, Fairfax County, Va. M. White. il Ladies Home J 82:84-9 N '65

House that pop art built. F. Du Plessix. il House & Gard 127:158-63 My '65

House that time cannot wither, nor custom stale; Casa Contenta; with editorial comment. il House & Gard 128:173-81 O '65

House with a natural point of view; built around an atrium. il Good H 161:127-36 O '65

How a single stroke can work the enchantment of change. il House & Gard 128:200-13 O '65

How to achieve that mellow, lived-in country look. R. Martens. il Farm J 90:88-9 Ja '66

In a Paris mood. E. Sverbeyeff. il N Y Times Mag p36-7 Je 27 '65

In glorious black & white. B. Plumb. il N Y Times Mag p 106-7 N 21 '65

Lighthearted pavilion; Nicholas du Pont Palm Beach house. V. Lawford. il Vogue 145:140-5+ Je '65

Living like a lord and lady; 18th-century house, London. E. Sverbeyeff. il N Y Times Mag p84-9 Ap 25 '65

Living with fling in small quarters; rooms William Baldwin decorates. il Vogue 145:142-7 Mr 15 '65

Love me, love my Duncan Phyfe. J. L. O'Neill. Am Home 68:30 Mr '65

Most effective decorating starts with the floor. A. C. Borg. il Am Home 68:48-53 Ap '65

Newer and better; symposium. il Bet Hom & Gard 43:62-83 Ap '65

100 ideas under $100. il Bet Hom & Gard 43:46-77 O '65

Portrait windows. il McCalls 92:128-33 F '65

Redecorate, yes, but plan first. il Changing T 19:43-5 Je '65

Remodeling with fabric; Celanese contemporary fibers. il House & Gard 128:276-83 N '65

Sixteen new ideas for your farm home. J. Lemmon. il Suc Farm 63:62-3 Ag '65

Stripes, checks and polka dots. il House & Gard 127:112-21+ Mr '65

That special magic of paint. il McCalls 92:120-3 My '65

This is spring's look. E. Sverbeyeff. il N Y Times Mag p94-5+ Ap 4 '65

Tradition with a grain of salt. il House & Gard 127:130-5+ F '65

Very natural approach to family living. N. Seney. il Bet Hom & Gard 44:36-9+ Ja '66

Where spring lives all year. il House & Gard 128:168-73 D '65

See also

Antiques
Apartments
Art in the home
Bathrooms
Bedrooms
Blinds
Childrens rooms
Christmas decorations
Color in house decoration
Furniture
Furniture, Arrangement of
Halls
Household furnishings
Kitchens
Laundries

Music rooms and equipment
Nurseries
Painting, Industrial and practical
Rooms
Screens (furniture)
Studios
Wall coverings
Wallpaper
Window shades
Windows

HOUSE decoration, American

Their home is their hobby. il Am Home 68:78-9 Mr '65

HOUSE decoration, Exterior

See also

House painting

HOUSE decoration, Italian

See also

Furniture, Italian

HOUSE decoration, Mediterranean

Here's why you'll like Mediterranean. il Am Home 68:86-7 Ap '65

HOUSE decoration, Spanish

Spain: Casa Dali. il Ladies Home J 82:121-5 F '65

Spain: sunny influence on decorating. M. White. il Ladies Home J 82:72-3+ F '65

HOUSE drainage. See Drainage, House

HOUSE expansion. See Houses, Remodeled

HOUSE insulation. See Insulation (heat)

HOUSE lighting. See Electric lighting

HOUSE mice. See Mice

HOUSE of commons. See Great Britain—Parliament—House of commons

HOUSE of hands. See Rehabilitation centers

HOUSE of lords. See Great Britain—Parliament—House of lords

HOUSE of representatives. See United States—Congress—House of representatives

HOUSE office building. See Washington, D.C.—Public buildings

HOUSE organs

House organs move out into a wider world. il Bsns W p 152+ D 4 '65

HOUSE painting

Sunday house painters; new color scheme. J. Peter. il Look 29:54-5+ Je 1 '65

HOUSE painting, Interior. See Painting, Industrial and practical

HOUSE plans. See Architecture, Domestic—Designs and plans

HOUSE plants

Fifteen ways to have a garden indoors. il Flower Grower 52:26-7 N '65

Green gifts. il Sunset 135:78-9 D '65

Houseplants: what to do when you vacation. Good H 16:171 Je '65

Knickknacks that grow in the spring. il Seventeen 24:34 Ap '65

Meyer lemon. A. Albohn. Horticulture 43:12-13 D '65

Most popular house plants and how to grow them. Bet Hom & Gard 43:116-19 F '65

Pest control on plants indoors. P. P. Pirone. il Horticulture 43:26-8 S '65

Pick tomatoes indoors in May. M. Helleiner. Flower Grower 52:16 F '65

Plants indoors. R. C. Hands. il Horticulture 43:18+ S '65

See also

Amaryllis
Bromeliads
Epiphyllums
Ferns
Flower boxes, planters, etc.
Gesneriaceae
Ti plant
Window gardening

HOUSE prices. See Housing—Costs

HOUSE protection

How to leave your house when you go on a long trip. Bet Hom & Gard 43:128 My '65

HOUSE rent. See Rent

HOUSE selling. See Home ownership

HOUSE that Jerry built; story. See Henderson, R.

HOUSE trailers. See Automobile trailers

HOUSE wiring. See Electric wire and wiring

HOUSECLEANING. See House cleaning

HOUSEHOLD, Geoffrey

Secret police; story. Atlan 216:57-61 D '65

HOUSEHOLD appliances

Brighteners for the home front. il Good H 161:220+ D '65

It's not only autos that are booming. il U S News 58:82-3 Mr 29 '65

Keeping up to date. il Farm J 90:85 Ja '66

New for your home. See issues of Popular mechanics

Other household aids and appliances. il Consumer Rep 30:87-166 D '65

Shopping center for party appliances. il Good H 161:184+ N '65

HOUSEHOLD appliances—*Continued*
What's new for living. See issues of House & garden incorporating Living for young homemakers
What's new in furnishings and housewares (cont) R. Martens and J. Gillies. il Farm J 89:84-5 Mr '65
What's new in homemaking. See issues of Successful farming
Electric apparatus and appliances, Domestic
  See also
Labor saving devices
Laundry equipment
Vacuum cleaners

Exhibitions
Gadgets, tools & hardware; a look at what's new. Changing T 19:6 D '65
HOUSEHOLD budget. See Budget, Household
HOUSEHOLD employees
Help wanted: maybe Mary Poppins, inc; Time essay. Time 86:42-3 Jl 9 '65
Hired help. W. Holbrook. Atlan 215:130+ Ap '65
Regular jobs for household help. S. Saben. il Mo Labor R 88:1228-9 O '65
Where the au pair girls are. A. Carthew. il N Y Times Mag p 175-6+ O 31 '65
Where the girls are; Continental au pair girls in Britain. Newsweek 65:39-40 Mr 8 '65
  See also
Visiting housekeepers

Anecdotes, facetiae, satire, etc.
Don't upset the apricot. B. Conklin. Sat Eve Post 238:18 S 25 '65
How to succeed without really cleaning. M. F. Hall. il McCalls 92:118-19 My '65
HOUSEHOLD expenses. See Domestic finance
HOUSEHOLD finance corporation
Polonius reversed. il Time 86:103A N 12 '65
HOUSEHOLD furnishings
Backward-looking forward look. B. Plumb. il N Y Times Mag p36-7 Jl 11 '65
Connoisseur's corner. See issues of House & garden incorporating Living for young homemakers
Courtly country homes. il McCalls 92:88-95 S '65
Decorating newsletter. V. D. Hahn. Am Home 68:22 Ap '65
English decorative arts at the Art institute of Chicago. A. Wardwell. il Antiques 89:78-9, 86-93 Ja '66
Fantasy finishes at work. il House & Gard 127:142-5+ Mr '65
Here's something new. M. White. il Ladies Home J 82:76-9 Mr '65
Home furnishings head toward a new design; All-industry home furnishings conference. il Bsns W p45-6+ Ag 14 '65
Home furnishings: how much people spend; guide for budgeting. il Changing T 19:13-15 Ag '65
Keeping up to date in your home (cont) il Farm J 89:68 Je; 44 Jl '65
Little decorating ideas. R. Martens. il Farm J 89:69 Ag '65
Lucky Seventeen accessories: you and your room. il Seventeen 24:316-17 Ag '65
Newer and better; symposium. il Bet Hom & Gard 43:62-83 Ap '65
100 ideas under $100. il Bet Hom & Gard 43:46-77 O '65
Other household aids and appliances. il Consumer Rep 30:87-166 D '65
Pattern plus! how to combine exciting and bold patterns. P. Rumely and E. T. Lawyer. il Bet Hom & Gard 43:40-7 Ag '65
Sleepy-time things. il Seventeen 24:176-7 S '65
Stripes, checks and polka dots. il House & Gard 127:112-21+ Mr '65
What's new for living. See issues of House & garden incorporating Living for young homemakers
Where to put the things you love to look at. il House & Gard 128:100-5 Jl '65
  See also
Color in house decoration
Furniture
Kitchen furniture
Laundry equipment
HOUSEHOLD linens. See Linens, Household
HOUSEHOLD management. See Home economics
HOUSEHOLD purchasing. See Purchasing, Household
HOUSEHOLD records
  See also
Family records

HOUSEHOLD scales. See Scales (weighing instruments)
HOUSEKEEPERS, Visiting. See Visiting housekeepers
HOUSEKEEPING. See Home economics
HOUSELEEKS
Chickens belong in the indoor garden; hen-and-chickens. M. S. Hortin. il Flower Grower 52:35 N '65
Sempervivums handsome and hardy. H. A. MacPherson. il Pop Gard 16:14-15 Mr '65
Try something different. D. E. Stebbins. il Pop Gard 16:14-15+ N '65
HOUSEMAN, John
Lost fortnight. Harper 231:55-61 Ag '65
HOUSES
Ideas in houses (cont) il Life 58:94-7+ F 26; 90-3 Ap 16; 124-7+ My 7; 88-91+ Je 4; 59: 90-3+ Jl 16 '65
Temple and the house, by Lord Raglan. Review
  Harper 230:150+ Mr '65. P. Pickrel
  See also
Building
Flashing
Home ownership
Kitchens
Rooms

Advertising
  See Real property—Advertising

Air conditioning
  See Air conditioning

Maintenance and repair
Booklets about home repairs. Consumer Bul 48:22 O '65
Can you save any money on home repair services? Bet Hom & Gard 43:6+ O '65
Does it really pay to do your own home repairs? J. H. Ingersoll. Bet Hom & Gard 43:14+ Jl '65
Home section. il Pop Mech 124:125-67 S '65
Improve your home. il Pop Sci 187:107-54+ S '65
Seven home repairs you're most likely to face: questions and answers. R. C. Whitman. il Pop Sci 187:150-2+ O '65

Prices
  See Housing—Costs

Protection
  See House protection
HOUSES, Prefabricated
Another imaginative prefab. A. C. Borg. il Am Home 68:45 Ap '65
Fun of variety and the cash savings of prefabrication; houses in Salt Lake City. il Sunset 135:100-3 N '65
Good things are happening to prefab houses. J. D. Bloodgood. il Bet Hom & Gard 43: 647+ My '65
Have house, will travel. il Time 86:84 N 19 '65
Have vacation hideout, can travel; portable vacation house. il Bsns W p66 N 6 '65
Latest in prefabricated dreams. il Fortune 72:188 Ag '65
Low-cost prefab with study plans you can buy. A. C. Borg. il Am Home 68:42-3 Ap '65
New grab bag of prefabs. il Pop Mech 124: 128-32 S '65
Personal business; summer house from factory. Bsns W p 121 Je 5 '65
Three new prefabs with a custom-built look. R. Charles. il Parents Mag 40:76-81 Ag '65
HOUSES, Protection of. See House protection
HOUSES, Remodeled
Basements can be family rooms. J. LemMon. il Suc Farm 63:52-5 Jl '65
Design your farm home addition. J. LemMon. il Suc Farm 64:108-9 Ja '66
Even the nails are 250 years old; Connecticut mill rebuilt. B. Plumb. il N Y Times Mag p58-9 Ja 16 '66
New angle on adding space; variation of the bay. il Bet Hom & Gard 44:86 Ja '66
Old house: new plan for city living; home of the Richard Newmans in New York city. M. White. il Ladies Home J 83:58-63 Ja '66
Private place; home of Frank Schlesinger, Doylestown, Pa. il Life 58:88-91+ Je 4 '65
Remodel the house you have. il House & Gard 127:88-111+ F '65
See how little changes can make a big difference. il Am Home 68:88 Ap '65
Successful farming family remodels again. J. LemMon. il Suc Farm 63:72-3 Je '65
They lost a tree, but they gained a room. il Sunset 135:110 O '65
They raised the roof for their teen-ager. il Sunset 135:106 N '65

HOUSING laws and legislation
United States
Dilemmas of urban America, by R. C. Weaver. Review
    Sat R 49:85 Ja 8 '66. C. W. Griffin, jr
Housing action: too little, not quite too late. il Arch Forum 123:90 Jl '65
Housing for the Nation's poor; are rent supplements the answer? L. E. Schaller. Christian Cent 83:44-7 Ja 12 '66
How new rent-subsidy program works. U S News 59:8 Jl 26 '65
Land-rich or land-poor schools; Open space land program, part of Housing act of 1961. D. E. Gardner. il Am Ed 1:12-14 N '65
Last days of Congress; administration's hard-won victory on rent subsidies. W. V. Shannon. Commonweal 83:140-2 N 5 '65
Long trial of public housing. E. B. Drew. il Reporter 32:15-18 Je 17 '65; Reply with rejoinder. I. S. Robbins. 33:6+ Jl 15 '65
Meat and potatoes; concerning housing message to Congress. Newsweek 65:26 Mr 15 '65
New housing act regarded as spur to apartment building. G. A. Christie. il Arch Rec 138:44 S '65
New housing bill also does this—. il U S News 59:70 Ag 2 '65
Timing the test on housing; with editorial comment. Bsns W p46+, 168 Mr 13 '65
    See also
Housing—Federal aid
HOUSING of students. See College students—Housing
HOUSING projects
Housing design: quality returns to the city; symposium. Arch Forum 123:40-69 Jl '65
Housing in the city: is this the best we can do? D. Canty. il Arch Forum 123:31 Jl '65
Housing policy: it must offer a way out of despair; excerpts from the City is the frontier. C. Abrams. il Arch Forum 123:34-9 Jl '65
Ten great places to live. Esquire 64:223+ D '65
    See also
Levitt and sons, incorporated
Site planning
Clustered development gets park as bonus. il Arch Rec 137:114-17 mid-My '65
Second-home communities. il Arch Rec 138:143-58 N '65
Super-block play areas; New York city housing project rehabilitates its recreation space. M. P. Friedberg. il Recreation 58:164-6+ Ap '65
Visit to Pihlajamäki; residential district near Helsinki. J. Barnett. il Arch Rec 138:121-8 D '65
France
Lesson from Levitt. il Time 86:108 D 10 '65
Levittown look takes on a French style: 650-unit development twenty miles from Paris. il Bsns W p64+ O 23 '65
New accent for Bill Levitt: venture in France. il Fortune 72:192 D '65
HOUSING projects, Cooperative
Union-sponsored middle-income housing: 1927-65. D. K. Lewis. il Mo Labor R 88:629-36 Je '65
HOUSING projects, Government
Can subsidies solve America's problems? an industry's answer; real estate. il Nations Bsns 53:36-7+ Ag '65
Case history of a failure: Pruitt-Igoe housing project, St Louis. J. Bailey. il Arch Forum 123:22-5 D '65
Long trial of public housing. E. B. Drew. il Reporter 32:15-18 Je 17 '65; Reply with rejoinder. I. S. Robbins. 33:6+ Jl 15 '65
Now, U.S. subsidies for rents: who gets them, how much. il U S News 59:69-70 Ag 2 '65
Who gets rent subsidies under the new law. il U S News 59:12 Ag 23 '65
HOUSING projects, Trade union
Union-sponsored middle-income housing: 1927-65. D. K. Lewis. il Mo Labor R 88:629-36 Je '65
HOUSING research
    See also
Building research
HOUSING subsidies. See Housing—Federal aid
HOUSTON, Samuel
Sam Houston's last fight. A. Castel. il por Am Heritage 17:80-7 D '65
HOUSTON, Walter Scott
Deep-sky wonders. Sky & Tel 29:186 Mr '65

HOUSTON, Tex.
And now over to Houston; Manned spacecraft center. il Newsweek 65:34-6 Je 14 '65
How a city faced an epidemic; encephalitis outbreak. B. Merson. il Good H 160:80-1+ Je '65
What Houston won when NASA came to town. il Bsns W p90-1+ S 11 '65
Air pollution
Houston: the race is on. O. C. Hobby. il Sat R 48:43-4 My 22 '65
Banks
Banking heats up in Houston. il Bsns W p88-9+ Jl 31 '65
Economic conditions
Where space race is bringing a twenty-five year boom. il U S News 59:44-7 S 6 '65
Education, Board of
Lady stirs her city's conscience. G. Zimmermann. il Look 29:66+ S 21 '65
Hospitals
Author shakes up a city; conditions at Jefferson Davis city-county charity hospital. B. Paisner. il Life 58:47-9 Mr 26 '65
Industries
Personal business: Houston: new magnet for business. Bsns W p 125-6 O 2 '65
Music
Lively accomplishments in the lively arts. H. Roussel. il Hi Fi 15:110 Jl '65
    See also
Houston grand opera association
Newspapers
    See also
Houston chronicle
Theater
Dramatic theatre for Houston. il Fortune 72:167+ O '65
Up their alley; proposed Alley theater. il Newsweek 66:74 Ag 16 '65
HOUSTON astrodome. See Stadiums
HOUSTON chronicle
Coup in Houston; Collier and Steven in and out. il Newsweek 66:61-2 S 20 '65
From mules to millions; Mecom's latest acquisition. Newsweek 66:70 D 20 '65
Modern editor gets the boot. New Repub 153:8 S 25 '65
Shot in the dark: question of M. Steakley's death. il Time 85:50 My 14 '65
Surprise package; sale of newspaper. il Time 86:80 D 17 '65
HOUSTON endowment, incorporated
From mules to millions; Mecom's latest acquisition. Newsweek 66:70 D 20 '65
HOUSTON grand opera association
Fort Worth, Houston. J. Rosenfield; A. Holmes. Opera N 30:32 Ja 15 '66
State of Texas. A. Holmes. il Opera N 30:24 S 25 '65
Texas. A. Holmes. il Opera N 30:30 D 11 '65
HOUSTON stadium. See Stadiums
HOUTZ, Patricia
Church for the hungry. Sat Eve Post 238:87-91 D 18 '65
HOVERCRAFT. See Ground effect machines
HOVEYDA, Amir Abbass
Tranquilizers for the prime minister. L. Griggs. Life 60:47 Ja 14 '66
HOW to win at cocktails; story. See DeMott, B.
HOWARD, Alan
Petronillo learns to write his name. N Y Times Mag p26-7+ F 7 '65
HOWARD, Albert
Putting jarrah wood to the test. Recreation 58:299 Je '65
HOWARD, Arthur D.
Pseudo superglacial till. bibliog Science 148:1461-2 Je 11 '65
HOWARD, Eugenia Lester. See Gibbs, V. C. jt. auth.
HOWARD, Harry N.
Changes in Turkey. bibliog f Cur Hist 48:296-300 My '65
HOWARD, Jane
Crystal ball like a TV set. Life 59:69+ O 8 '65
Down on earth, their kids plotted for bubble gum. Life 58:40B Je 18 '65
Man who paints those big eyes. Life 59:39-40+ Ag 27 '65
Nicest young genius in the U.S. Life 58:104-6+ My 21 '65
Six-year literary vigil. Life 60:70-2+ Ja 7 '66

HOWARD, Joseph H.
Drum collecting dental surgeon. il pors Ebony 20:44-6 S '65
HOWARD, Larry Dean
Track man. Newsweek 65:69 Mr 15 '65
HOWARD, Mary F.
My own favorite contest. Pub W 188:88-9 Jl 19 '65
HOWARD, Richard
Far cry after a close call; poem. New Yorker 41:107 Jl 17 '65
Karl Shapiro's anti-poem. Poetry 106:225-8 Je '65
Poetry chronicle. Poetry 106:296-305 Jl '65
Some poets in their prose. Poetry 105:397-404 Mr '65
Two against chaos. Nation 200:289-90 Mr 15 '65
(tr) See Le Clézio, J. M. G. It seems to me the boat is heading for the island
HOWARD, Robert. See Bumba, V. jt. auth.
HOWARD, Roy Wilson
Most unforgettable character I've met. L. Wood. por Read Digest 87:82-6 N '65
HOWARD, Thomas, Jr
Thomas Howard jr. Providence cabinet-maker. E. B. Monahon. il Antiques 87:702-4 Je '65
HOWARD, Toni
Shorter work week: a report to wives. Mc-Calls 92:108-9+ Ap '65
HOWARD Johnson company. See Johnson, Howard, company
HOWARD university, Washington, D.C.
More campus unrest; are reds to blame? statements. J. M. Nabrit, jr. il U S News 58:14 My 10 '65
HOWE, Harold, 2d
Our colleges aren't ready for today's students. Sat R 48:77-9+ My 15 '65

about

Doc Howe. New Repub 154:8 Ja 1 '66
Education: new commissioner champions change and reform. L. J. Carter. por Science 150:1794-6 D 31 '65
Howe to do it. por Newsweek 67:48 Ja 3 '66
Leadership for education. J. Cass. Sat R 49:57-8 Ja 15 '66
New commissioner. por Time 86:34 D 31 '65
New team to spend the billions in school aid. por U S News 60:12 Ja 3 '66
HOWE, Irving
Beleaguered professors. Atlan 216:115-18 N '65
Berkeley and beyond; excerpt from Semester of crisis. New Repub 152:14-17 My 1 '65
Path to grace. New Repub 153:23-6 S 25 '65
Writer can't keep to his attic. N Y Times Mag p43-5+ D 5 '65
HOWE, Mark Antony De Wolfe
Bygones in Boston. I. Haverstick. il Sat R 48:49-50 N 27 '65
Mr Greatheart and Mrs Grundy. E. Weeks. Atlan 216:182 N '65
HOWE, Quincy
Morgenthau essays. Bul Atomic Sci 21:36-7 Ap '65
HOWE, Richard L.
Shopping for tools. Pop Mech 124:163 D '65

about

Editor's page. por Pop Mech 124:83 N '65
HOWE, Russell Warren
Ahmed ben Bella, would be leader of the third world. New Repub 152:10-11 Je 19 '65
Eastern Congo's chaotic rebellion. Reporter 32:35-6 Mr 11 '65
How tight is the squeeze? Reporter 33:29-32 D 2 '65
James Crow, esq. comes to Britain. Reporter 32:28-30 My 6 '65
Premier Tshombe. New Repub 152:8-9 Ap 24 '65
Rebellion brews in Rhodesia. Reporter 32:26+ Je 3; 33:8 S 9 '65
Rhodesia's next government. New Repub 154:15-16 Ja 15 '66
Tshombe may seek anti-white role. New Repub 153:14-15 S 18 '65
Who and what is the real Boumedienne? New Repub 153:11-12 Jl 3 '65
Wilson's razor's edge. New Repub 153:17-18 N 20 '65
HOWELL, Ted
Old Krag. Outdoor Life 135:44-5+ Mr '65
HOWELL, Wallace E.
Notes and comment. New Yorker 40:23 F 13 '65
HOWELLS, J. Harvey
Home to Arran, Scotland's magic isle. Nat Geog Mag 128:80-99 Jl '65

HOWELLS, W. W.
Some present aspects of physical anthropology. bibliog f Ann Am Acad 357:127-33 Ja '65
HOWES, Barbara
Flight; poem. New Yorker 41:28 Jl 10 '65
For J. S; Quilt of a formal pattern; Crane chub, Barbados; Cicisbeae; Lonely box; Radar and unmarked cars; poems. Poetry 107:170-5 D '65
Ode to Poseidon. New Yorker 41:60 O 30 '65
HOWES, Robert G.
Sunday sermon: pulpit; poem, reprint. Cath World 201:301 Ag '65
HOWIE, Virginia
Some easy ways to support vines, perennials, trees. il Horticulture 43:42-3 Je '65
HOWLEY, Frank L.
Nation that tried to help itself. Read Digest 86:142-4+ Je '65
HOYER, Linda Grace
Predisposition to enchantment. New Yorker 41:40-3 Mr 13 '65
HOYER, Mildred N.
Christmas tree in Rockefeller center; poem. Am For 71:37 D '65
HOYLE, Fred
Not according to Hoyle. por Newsweek 66:77 O 25 '65
HOYLE, Graham
Nature of the excitatory sarcoplasmic reticular junction. bibliog Science 149:70-2 Jl 2 '65
HOYT, J. W. and Soli, Giorgio
Algal cultures: ability to reduce turbulent friction in flow. bibliog Science 149:1509-11 S 24 '65
HOYT, Michael P. E.
Stanleyville massacre; excerpt from 111 days in Stanleyville. D. Reed. il Read Digest 87:233-8+ S '65
HOYT, Murray
Imaginative selling in small town shop. P. Johnson, jr. il Pub W 188:51-2 Ag 9 '65
Jewels from the ocean deep. Read Digest 86:146-51 My '65
HOYT, Robert G.
Role of the press. Commonweal 82:372-3 Je 11 '65
HOYT, William D. Jr
Book review. America 113:120-1 Jl 31 '65
HROMÁDKA, Josef Luki
Doctor Hromadka and the will to peace. America 113:772 D 18 '65
HRUSKA, Roman L.
Excerpt from debate, September 2, 1964. Cong Digest 44:79+ Mr '65
HRUTFIORD, Bjorn F. See Heikkenen, H. J. jt. auth.
HSIEH, Jack J. C. and others
Autoradiography: technique for drastic reduction of exposure time to alpha particles. Science 150:1821-2 D 31 '65
HUANG, Ai
Brief biography. S. Goodman. pors Dance Mag 39:52-3 O '65
HUANG, Helen S. See Goodman, D. S. jt. auth.
HUANG, Sylvia Lee-. See Lee-Huang, S.
HUARTE, John
Battle of the QBs. por Time 86:96 S 17 '65
Star is born, about forty minutes too late. D. Jenkins. il Sports Illus 23:47-9 Ag 16 '65
What might have been. il Time 86:51 Ag 13 '65
HUAUD family
Brothers Huaud and their enameled Swiss watches. P. Verdier. il Antiques 88:829-33 D '65
HUBBARD, Orville Liscum
One million per cent; segregation in Dearborn, Mich. Newsweek 66:27-8 Jl 5 '65
HUBBELL, Catherine
Leaving out the snow on Park avenue. Writer 78:22-3+ N '65
HUBBELL, John G.
Legendary triumph of Helmer Aakvik. Read Digest 86:214-17+ Ap '65
Let's go into orbit. Read Digest 86:71-5 Je '65
Skiing's good samaritans. Read Digest 87:154-6+ D '65
—and Reed, David
Man for the job in Vietnam. Read Digest 88:55-60 Ja '66
HUBER, Kathleen
Now, tell me pray, and tell me true; story. Seventeen 25:100-1 Ja '66
HUBER, Leonard V.
Mardi gras: the golden age. Am Heritage 16:16-23 F '65
HUBER, Margaret
Poem; catch the heart of snow. Mlle 62:48 D '65
HUBERMAN, Leo
Revolution revisited. Nation 201:51-4 Ag 2 '65

HUCH, William F. See Ney, E. P. jt. auth.

HUCK, Susan
Malaysia—Singapore=trouble. Nat R 17:771+
S 7 '65
Medicare for the Dominican Republic. Nat R
18:66+ Ja 25 '66

HUDAK, Joseph
Texture is essential in the garden. il Horticulture 43:28-9+ My '65

HUDOCK, G. A. and others
Alternative forms of triosephosphate dehydrogenase in chromatium. bibliog Science 150:
776-7 N 5 '65

HUDSON, Lois Phillips
Four-lane menace to California's redwoods.
Reporter 33:34-8 Ag 12 '65
Springtime in the Rockies. Reporter 32:42-5
F 11 '65
Wasters: logging for floods. Nation 200:531-3
My 17 '65

HUDSON, Stephen, pseud.
Poor little self-pitying rich boy. R. B. Dooley.
Sat R 49:31 Ja 1 '66

HUDSON, William Henry
Two novels of the Amazon. E. S. Urbanski.
il Américas 17:33-8 Mr '65

HUDSON institute, incorporated
Strategy and conscience, by A. Rapoport.
Review
Bul Atomic Sci 21:25-30 D '65; D. G.
Brennan; with reply by A. Rapoport.
21:31-6 D '65

HUDSON RIVER
Battle of the Hudson. T. Lawrence. il Am
For 71:12-15+ Ap '65
Con Edison: the Hudson River caper. D.
Cort. il Nation 201:387-9 N 22 '65; Reply.
R. L. Ottinger. 201:inside cover D 6 '65
Fight to save Storm King on Hudson. Liv
Wildn 29:38-9 Sum '65
Hideous Hudson River; Lake Erie is dirty,
too. America 113:148 Ag 14 '65
Hudson. New Yorker 41:41-3 S 11 '65
Hudson, an open, running sewer. il News-
week 66:50-1 Ag 23 '65
Hydropower and the Hudson Highlands. P. M.
Tilden. Nat Parks Mag 39:2 Ap '65
Scenic Hudson gets attention. C. H. Callison.
Audubon Mag 67:115 Mr '65
Stink of dead stripers; Con Ed under attack
over killing of fish at Hudson's bass spawn-
ing grounds. R. H. Boyle. il Sports Illus
22:81-2+ Ap 26 '65
Storm over stripers; Commission to hold
hearings on power project's threat to Hud-
son's striped bass fishery. G. Heinold. il
Outdoor Life 135:10-12+ My '65
U.S. offers timetable on cleaning up Hudson;
conference on pollution of the Hudson River.
Bsns W p31 O 2 '65
What will the Hudson be? P. Goodman. il
N Y Times Mag p42-3+ F 14 '65
Who will save the Hudson, and how? J.
Ridgeway. New Repub 153:10-11 O 2 '65

HUDSON RIVER DAM (proposed) See New
York (city)—Water supply

HUDSON RIVER VALLEY commission. See
New York (state)—Hudson River Valley
commission

HUEBNER, Robert J.
Cure for the common cold? interview. por
U S News 58:46-8 My 3 '65

HUFF, Betty Tracy
Recipe for rain; drama. Plays 25:15-26 N
'65

HUFF, Darrell
How to travel when you can't afford to. Red-
book 126:118-19 D '65
Those amazing speed controls. Pop Sci 186:
137-9+ Mr '65
Understanding the new math? Harper 231:
134-7 S '65
Wood squares give you a luxury floor fast.
Pop Sci 187:116-18 S '65

HUFF, Frances N.
Do you get along with your teen-ager? Todays Health 43:42-3+ F '65

HUFF, Robert
How not to make a model in a bottle in a
bar in Ithaca; poem. Sat R 48:95 N 20 '65

HUFF, William H. See Brown, N. B. jt. auth.

HUGEL, Max
How big Brother trades on its own. il por
Bsns W p78 Ja 8 '66

HUGENTOBLER, Walter
Rembrandt lighting. G. Pyle. il Pop Phot 56:
68-9 My '65

HUGGINS, Charles Brenton
Vietnam: a bid to parley. il Newsweek 65:40-8
My 24 '65
—and others
Carcinogenic aromatic hydrocarbons: special
vulnerability of rats. bibliog Science 147:
1153-4 Mr 5 '65

HUGGINS, Norman
Lot of luck in one whack. por Time 86:45
N 12 '65

HUGH-JONES, Stephen
How much can Britain defend? New Repub
153:11-12 Ag 21 '65
Nonaligned Afghans. New Repub 152:10-11
Ap 17 '65

HUGHES, Emmet John
[Current events column] See issues of Newsweek
Kennedy: the blurred photograph. New Repub
153:23-7 O 9 '65

HUGHES, H. Stuart
Messianic pose; post-cold-war delusions. Nation 202:7-10 Ja 3 '66

HUGHES, Howard Robard
T.W.A: prosperity but no peace. J. McDon-
ald. il Fortune 72:122-5+ Jl '65
T.W.A: the struggle for the corporate cock-
pit. J. McDonald. il por Fortune 71:106-11+
My '65

HUGHES, Jo
Oracle to high society girls. il pors Life
58:76-8+ My 7 '65

HUGHES, Kenneth
Church and marriage in Africa. Christian
Cent 82:204-8 F 17 '65

HUGHES, Langston
Ebony's nativity; an evaluation from birth.
pors Ebony 21:40-2+ N '65
Long view: Negro; poem. Harper 230:186 Ap
'65

about
Prodigal son. Criticism
America 113:62 Jl 10 '65

HUGHES, Mary Gray
Welcome, strangers and others too; story.
Redbook 125:54-5 Je '65

HUGHES, Quentin
Perils of vision; excerpts from Seaport; archi-
tecture and townscape in Liverpool. Arch
Forum 123:48-51 N '65

HUGHES, R. Stuart
Pope John's revolution: secular or religious?
Commonweal 83:301-3 D 10 '65

HUGHES, Richard
Chinese opera walks the party line. N Y
Times Mag p62+ Mr 21 '65
My Japanese days with Ought-ought seven.
Sat R 48:38-40+ S 18 '65

HUGHES, Richard Joseph
Chance for a change in the Garden state.
J. J. Farmer. Reporter 33:27-9 Ag 12 '65
Dick to the rescue. Nation 201:345-6 N 15 '65

HUGHES, Robert E.
Powder keg in Rhodesia. Christian Cent 82:
208-10+, 240+ F 17-24 '65

HUGHES, Spike
Così is like that. Opera N 29:24-5 F 20 '65
Never a dull moment. Opera N 29:24-5 Ap 10
'65

HUGHES, Ted
Hill top; poem. New Yorker 41:103 F 27 '65
Trees; poem. New Yorker 41:30 Jl 17 '65

HUGHES, Thomas L.
Scholars and foreign policy: varieties of
research experience: address, October 21,
1965. Dept State Bul 53:747-58 N 8 '65;
Excerpt. Science 150:1430 D 10 '65

about
Foreign affairs research: review process
rises on ruins of Camelot. J. Walsh. Science
150:1429-31 D 10 '65

HUGHES tool company
Hughes readies OH-6A facilities; sales seen
topping 7,000. C. M. Plattner. il Aviation W
82:62-3+ Je 28 '65

HUGO, Richard F.
Three poets. M. McCloskey. Poetry 107:126
N '65

HUIE, William Bradford
Murder: the Klan on trial. Sat Eve Post
238:86-9 Je 19 '65
PPA press conference; summary. por(p41)
Pub W 187:43-4 Mr 22 '65

about
One southerner does the job with facts. D.
Nevin. Life 58:8+ Je 25 '65

HUIZINGA, J. H.
Which way Europe? For Affairs 43:487-500
Ap '65

HUKBALAHAPS
Huks bring terror to the Philippines; guerrillas of People's liberation army. R. Trumbull. il N Y Times Mag p28-9+ Mr 14 '65
Letter from Manila. R. Shaplen. New Yorker
41:98+ Ja 15 '66

HULETT, Bill
Amateur scientist. Sci Am 213:124-6+ N '65

HULL, Bobby
Golden hawk of hockey. J. Atwater. il pors Sat Eve Post 239:56-9 Ja 1 '66
Positive protection. Time 87:68 Ja 21 '66

HULL, C. D. and others
Cerebral temperature changes accompanying sexual activity in the male rat. bibliog Science 149:89-90 Jl 2 '65

HULL, Clinton R.
Klamath slot. Outdoor Life 136:40-3+ Jl '65

HULL, Dale O. and Petersen, E. D.
Should you own, lease, or custom hire machinery? Suc Farm 64:56-7+ Ja '66

HULL, David. See Dawkins, M. J. R. jt. auth.

HULL, Donald F.
AAU plays by international rules; reprint. Recreation 58:281-2 Je '65

HULL, Harper H.
Plain facts about planning. por Motor B 116:36-8+ Ag '65

HULL, Robert N. and others
Oncogenicity of the simian adenoviruses. bibliog Science 150:1044-6 N 19 '65

HULL, William H.
How my Saturday's bargain became a truckload of trouble. Flower Grower 52:42-3 Je '65

HULLS (naval architecture)
Hull development paces exploration. J. F. Judge. il Miss & Roc 17:27-8+ S 6 '65
Johnson's new trihedrals. A. Mikesell. il Pop Mech 124:118-21+ O '65
Plain facts about planing. H. H. Hull. il Motor B 116:36-8+ Ag '65
Sailing yacht research; use of computers in tests at MIT. H. C. Herreshoff and J. E. Kerwin. il Yachting 118:51-3+ Jl '65

HULME, William E.
Breakthroughs: Dubuque's experiment in ecumenism. Christian Cent 82:1187-90 S 29 '65

HUMAN behavior. See Behavior (psychology)

HUMAN beings. See Man

HUMAN body. See Physiology

HUMAN ecology
See also
Man—Influence on nature

HUMAN electricity. See Electrophysiology

HUMAN embryo. See Fetus

HUMAN embryology. See Embryology

HUMAN engineering
Inevitable science of human engineering. G. Berkwitt. il Duns R 86:45-7+ O '65

HUMAN equality. See Equality

HUMAN evolution. See Evolution

HUMAN figure in art
Indonesian decorative design. G. Kaler. Hobbies 69:42-5+ F '65
See also
Nude in art

HUMAN figure in photography
Art of good taste. P. Gowland. il Pop Phot 57:8+ N '65
Beyond cheesecake. C. Allen. il U S Camera 28:42-3+ My '65
Getting privacy outdoors. P. Gowland. il Pop Phot 56:12+ F '65
Nakamura and his nudes. R. Halford. il U S Camera 28:48-9+ D '65
Nude in nature. il U S Camera 28:52-3 Je '65
Two nudes. L. Solmssen. il Mod Phot 29:84-5 Je '65
Unabashed ladies of Sam Haskins; photographs, with account by H. Keppler. S. Haskins. Mod Phot 30:62-73 Ja '66

HUMAN nature
Happiest New Year of Greta Miller. J. Robbins. Good H 160:34+ Ja '65

HUMAN progress. See Progress

HUMAN race. See Man

HUMAN relations
Conformity as a tactic of ingratiation. E. E. Jones. bibliog il Science 149:144-50 Jl 9 '65
Family's role in political socialization. J. C. Davies. bibliog f Ann Am Acad 361:10-19 S '65
I want my rights. R. O. Johann. America 112:805 My 29 '65
Intergovernmental relations as seen by public officials. R. W. McCulloch. bibliog f Ann Am Acad 359:127-36 My '65
Magic of being in touch. S. Blanton. Read Digest 87:76-8 Ag '65
Power of the open heart. A. Whitman. Read Digest 86:179-80+ My '65

Say it now! M. B. Johnstone. Read Digest 87:139-42 O '65
See also
Brotherhood of man
Conversation
Friendship
Love
Marriage
Prejudice

HUMAN rights. See Civil rights

HUMAN rights day and week
Human rights day; proclamation. L. B. Johnson. Dept State Bul 53:1013 D 27 '65

HUMAN time lag. See Reaction time

HUMAN voice. See Voice

HUMAN welfare. See Social welfare

HUMANE treatment of animals. See Animals—Treatment

HUMANISM
Socialist humanism: an international symposium, ed. by E. Fromm. Review
Sat R 48:107-8 S 18 '65. H. Cox

HUMANITIES
Humanity's previous attempts... to transcend the world it inhabits; recommendation for establishment of a National humanities foundation. Sat R 48:60 F 6 '65
See also
Science and the humanities
United States—National foundation for the humanities (proposed)

Study and teaching
Experimental course in the humanities for high school students. L. C. Hyslop. il Sr Schol 87:sup9 D 2 '65
Humanities in the ninth grade introduced in project Cue; New York state. Library J 90:1999-2000 Ap 15 '65

HUMANITY (mankind) See Man

HUMASON, S. W. M.
And be my love; story. Ladies Home J 82:78-80 O '65

HUMBOLDT REDWOODS STATE PARK.
See California—Parks and reserves

HUME, James D.
Sea-level changes during the last 2000 years at Point Barrow, Alaska. bibliog Science 150:1165-6 N 26 '65

HUMENNY, Bobbie
American worker's daughter reports on workers' paradise. pors U S News 59:82-3 N 8 '65

HUMES, Lawrence
Hoop ace of Evansville. il pors Ebony 20:84-6+ Ap '65

HUMES, Leonard
Yachting asks about wooden-kit boatbuilding; interview, ed. by E. Robberson. por Yachting 117:61-4+ Mr '65

HUMIDIFIERS
Humidify your home, and cut heating costs. C. P. Gilmore. il Pop Sci 188:152-5 Ja '66
Motorized humidifier for your furnace. F. L. Greenwald. il Pop Mech 124:176-80+ N '65

HUMIDITY
Humidity, your house and your health. House & Gard 127:18+ F '65
Why Americans have sallow skins. Sci Digest 57:25 Mr '65
See also
Hygrometers

HUMIDORS
Humidors. il House & Gard 128:242-3 O '65

HUMILITY
Case for Catholic humility. M. Novak. Christian Cent 82:1406-8 N 17 '65

HUMLIKON, Switzerland
Village where people cared. O. Schisgall. il Read Digest 86:55-60 F '65

HUMM, Douglas G. and Sylvia, A. L.
Soluble proteins of a melanoma and normal skin from the swordtail, platyfish, and their hybrids. bibliog Science 150:635-6 O 29 '65

HUMMINGBIRDS
Year of the hummingbirds. J. C. Johnson. il Audubon Mag 67:186-9 My '65

HUMOR
Comic prison. A. Goldman. Nation 200:142-4 F 8 '65
Family skeleton with solid gold teeth. V. Henry. Writer 78:14-15+ Ap '65
Humor is no laughing matter. M. Shulman. Seventeen 24:110+ Je '65
Senior scholastic interview; ed. by R. Hemming. B. Cosby. Sr Schol 86:17 Mr 18 '65

HUMOR—*Continued*
Trade winds; concerning Laugh day, by B.
  Cerf. J. G. Fuller. il Sat R 48:10+ D 18
  '65
  See also
Limericks
Music—Humor
Puns and punning
Radio broadcasting—Humor
Satire
Television broadcasting—Humor
  also subhead Anecdotes, facetiae, satire,
  etc. under various subjects, e.g. Travelers—
  Anecdotes, facetiae, satire, etc.

HUMOR, American
James Thurber and the art of fantasy. C. S.
  Holmes. Yale R 55:17-33 O '65
Trade winds; humor lobbyist, Jim Atkins. J.
  Beatty, jr. Sat R 49:14 Ja 1 '66
Yiddishization of American humor. W. Mark-
  field. il Esquire 64:114-15+ O '65

HUMOR, Austrian
Vienna laughs; comp. by C. A. Farnsworth.
  N Y Times Mag p38 Mr 7 '65

HUMOR, Pictorial
Dwigs comics; post cards. R. C. Finnegan.
  il Hobbies 70:124-5+ O '65
Mix fun with glamor. P. Gowland. il Pop Phot
  56:24+ My '65
Signed with a grin. il U S Camera 28:48-9
  O '65
35mm techniques. P. Stackpole. U S Camera
  28:16-17 D '65
  See also
Comics (books, strips, etc)

HUMOR in music. See Music—Humor

HUMPERDINCK, Engelbert
On records; Hänsel und Gretel. Opera N 30:
  35 D 25 '65

HUMPHREY, Hal
Do raise your voice! NEA J 54:57 My '65

HUMPHREY, Hubert Horatio, 1911-
Alliance is a partnership. Américas 17:1-5
  My '65
America's great success story. por Read
  Digest 87:71-4 D '65
Conservation revolt; excerpt from address,
  March 8, 1965. por Audubon Mag 67:252-4
  Jl '65
Excellence in education: foundation of the
  Great society; excerpt from address, No-
  vember 24, 1964. Sch & Soc 93:175-7 Mr 20
  '65
Foundation of freedom. por NEA J 54:15 O
  '65
Future of NATO: areas of common effort;
  address, October 5, 1965. Dept State Bul
  53:650-3 O 25 '65
Humphrey vows dynamic space support; ex-
  cerpts from address, March 19, 1965. Avia-
  tion W 82:25 Mr 29 '65
Interdependence of mankind; address, June 9,
  1965. Dept State Bul 53:56-9 Jl 12 '65
Letter from the Vice President; Humphrey
  on free enterprise. por U S News 59:53 O
  25 '65
Los Angeles riots; handling the topic in
  class. Sr Schol 87:sup 16 O 7 '65; Same with
  additions. 87:9-10 O 28 '65
Making cities fit for people. Sat R 48:16-17
  Jl 3 '65
National power and the creation of a work-
  able world community; remarks, June 2,
  1965. Dept State Bul 52:1048-50 Je 28 '65
Nature of dissent in a democracy; address,
  August 23, 1965. Vital Speeches 31:741-3
  O 1 '65
Our children deserve the best in education.
  por Parents Mag 40:40+ S '65
Peace on earth: address, February 17, 1965.
  Vital Speeches 31:322-5 Mr 15 '65; Same.
  Dept State Bul 52:326-32 Mr 8 '65
75th anniversary of the Organization of
  American states: the record of the inter-
  American system; address, April 14, 1965.
  bibliog f Dept State Bul 52:726-31 My 10 '65
White House conference on international co-
  operation; address, November 29, 1965. Dept
  State Bul 53:966-70 D 20 '65

about

Ask not what became of Hubert Humphrey?
  P. Lisagor. il pors N Y Times Mag p6-7+
  Jl 25 '65
Backup man winds up Congress and has a
  few tense hours. R. B. Stolley. il pors Life
  59:38-42A O 22 '65
Bob dropped, Hubert kept dangling; excerpts
  from Making of the President—1964. T. H.
  White. il por Life 59:70-2+ Jl 2 '65
For commuter Humphrey: official home in
  town? il por U S News 59:13 Ag 23 '65
Gruntled man. Time 85:15 F 12 '65
Happy understudy. H. Brandon. Sat R 48:
  16-17 My 8 '65

Head of steam: Vice President omitted from
  delegation to Sir Winston Churchill's fu-
  neral. Newsweek 65:22-3 F 8 '65
Heir apparent. S. Alsop. por Sat Eve Post
  238:18 Ap 10 '65
Home for Hubert. il Time 86:30-1 O 1 '65
Hubert Humphrey; advance man for the
  Great society. F. Knebel. pors Look 29:80+
  Ap 6 '65
Hubert Humphrey's one-man constituency.
  A. J. Glass. por Reporter 33:27+ N 18 '65
Hubert unbound; trip abroad. il por Time
  87:22 Ja 7 '66
Humphrey. J. Deakin. New Repub 152:10-12
  My 29 '65
Humphrey: a strong no. 2. il pors Bsns W
  p 175-6+ N 13 '65
Humphrey, by W. Griffith. Review
  America 112:464-5 Ap 3 '65. F. K. Kelly
  New Repub 152:22 Ap 3 '65. G. W. John-
  son
  Sat R 48:124 Mr 13 '65. F. Freidel
Humphrey gets a summons to stand in; acting
  president, while Johnson undergoes surgery.
  por Bsns W p28-9 O 9 '65
I enjoy it. il pors Newsweek 65:28-9 Mr 15 '65
Kennedy or Humphrey: who rates higher? il
  por U S News 60:13 Ja 3 '66
Kennedys vs. Humphrey; who has gained in
  '65. il por U S News 59:52-3 N 8 '65
Memo to HHH. il pors Newsweek 67:14-15
  Ja 3 '66
New Hubert. S. McBee. por Life 59:46A Jl
  30 '65
No vacancy. Reporter 32:16+ Mr 25 '65
On the road; resumption of duties as vice
  president. Newsweek 66:30 O 25 '65
Playing second clarinet. Time 86:17 Jl 23 '65
Vice President Humphrey to head Peace corps
  advisory council; letter, January 26, 1965.
  L. B. Johnson. Dept State Bul 52:250 F 22
  '65
What Hubert said; meeting with de Gaulle
  in Paris. il por Time 86:15-16 Jl 2 '65
What Humphrey achieved in the Far East. il
  por U S News 60:17 Ja 10 '66
What's new about the new Hubert Hum-
  phrey. W. Bowen. il pors Fortune 72:142-5+
  Ag '65
When a home is not a house. il Newsweek
  66:24 Ag 23 '65
When attention turns to the Vice President.
  il por U S News 59:36-7 O 18 '65
When Humphrey heard of LBJ's illness. il
  por U S News 58:14 F 8 '65
Why Humphrey didn't go. il por U S News
  58:53-4 F 15 '65

HUMPHREY, Muriel Fay Buck
Moment of history. por McCalls 92:57+ Jl '65

about

Many talents of Mrs Hubert Humphrey. J.
  Libman. il pors Good H 160:42+ Je '65
Second lady. N. Robertson. il pors Sat Eve
  Post 238:74-5+ Jl 3 '65

HUMPHREY, Richard
VHF: an answer to marine-phone congestion? Motor B 115:48-9+ Mr '65
VHF-FM: transmit and be heard. Motor B
  116:26-7+ N '65

HUMPHREY, William
Gaudiest thing on wheels; story. Sat Eve Post
  238:60-4 Ag 28 '65

HUMPHREYS, Robert
If a man die, shall he live again? eulogy,
  October 20, 1965. E. Dirksen. por U S News
  59:124+ N 8 '65

HUMPHRIES, Rolfe
Dread; poem. Christian Cent 82:643 My 19 '65

HUMPHRY, James, 3d
Met museum turns modern. Library J 90:
  5208-9 D 1 '65

HUNDERE, Al
Al's place. A. Trammell. il por Flying 77:45-
  7 D '65

HUNDERTWASSER, Friedrich
Whirlpool of the waters. il por Time 85:74-5
  Mr 5 '65

HUNDLEY, Rod
Little slice of heaven. F. Deford. il por Sports
  Illus 23:62-4+ N 29 '65

HUNDRED dollar bills. See Paper money—
  United States

HUNEKER, Erik Hinton
Big four. Opera N 30:8-13 D 18 '65

HUNEKER, James Gibbons
America's first sophisticated critic. W. L.
  Purcell. por Am Rec G 31:1094-6 Jl '65
Big four. E. H. Huneker. por(p8) Opera N
  30:12-13 D 18 '65

James Gibbons Huneker. J. W. Freeman.
  Opera N 29:35 F 27 '65

HUNG, Frederick
Vietnam. bibliog Focus 16:1-6 D '65

HUNG, P. P.
Enrichment of serine-acceptor soluble RNA by nucleic gels. bibliog Science 149:639-40 Ag 6 '65
HUNGARIAN cookery. See Cookery, Hungarian
HUNGARIANS in the United States
Hungarians. E. Newhouse. New Yorker 41:57-64 N 27 '65
HUNGARY
See also
Airlines—Hungary
Booksellers and bookselling—Hungary
Communist party (Hungary)
Strikes—Hungary
Youth—Hungary

Antiquities
Lunar calendar from the Hungarian upper paleolithic. L. Vértes. bibliog il Science 149:855-6 Ag 20 '65

Economic conditions
For Hungary, a fairly easygoing life. il Bsns W p 186 N 20 '65
Kadar's Hungary. E. C. Helmreich. bibliog f Cur Hist 48:142-8 Mr '65
Something new in east Europe: the customer is right. A. Kucherov. il U S News 58:80-3 Je 28 '65

Economic policy
Now it's *gulyás* Gyula-style. Time 86:26 Jl 9 '65

History
Windischgraetz caper: Hungarian counterfeiting scandal of 1925-1926. G. Bailey. il Reporter 32:30-4 F 11 '65

Politics and government
Kadar's Hungary. E. C. Helmreich. bibliog f Cur Hist 48:142-8 Mr '65
Truth about Hungary. B. Fabian. America 113:749-51 D 11 '65

Religious institutions and affairs
Priests jailed for teaching. America 113:149 Ag 14 '65
Trouble with Hungary: arrest of eight Jesuit priests. America 112:181 F 6 '65
HUNGER
Lateral hypothalamic stimulation in satiated rats: T-maze learning for food. J. Mendelson and S. L. Chorover. bibliog il Science 149:559-61 Jl 30 '65
HUNLOCK family
Hunlock coat-of-arms. H. K. Eilers. il Hobbies 70:126-7+ Mr '65
HUNN, Max
State parks of Kentucky. Travel 124:22-7+ Jl '65
HUNSAKER, Gordon D.
Explorers in the surf. por Recreation 58:286-7+ Je '65
Lively art of retirement. por Recreation 58:386-8+ O '65
HUNT, Bobby
Pittsburgh Hurricane roars into wrestling. il pors Ebony 20:100-2+ Je '65
HUNT, Dorothy
Books. Commonweal 82:673-5 S 17 '65
HUNT, Edward L. and others
Humoral mediation of radiation-induced motivation in parabiont rats. bibliog Science 150:1747-8 D 24 '65
HUNT, G. Bowdon
Does get tough work? PTA Mag 59:8-10 Je '65
HUNT, Irene
Newbery runner-up. por Library J 90:1467 Mr 15 '65
HUNT, John Clark
Forest that men made. Am For 71:18-21+ N; 32-5+ D '65
Great portage. Am For 71:8-11+ Jl '65
Revolt in the provinces. Am For 71:40-1+ Je '65
Ride to remember. Am Heritage 16:80-3 Ap '65
HUNT, Morton M.
Patterns of marriage: how successful men and women arrange their married lives. Redbook 125:56-7+ S '65
HUNT, William
Winter waking; poem. Atlan 215:95 F '65
HUNT breakfasts. See Breakfasts
HUNT foods and industries, incorporated
Corporate Cézanne. il Time 85:74-6+ Je 4 '65
HUNTER, Betty P.
Four approaches to Zion: an interpretation. bibliog Negro Hist Bul 29:5-6+ O '65
HUNTER, Bruce
Myriad colors in coral. Natur Hist 75:30-3 Ja '66

HUNTER, Charlayne Alberta
Hundred-fifteenth-between-Lenox-and-Fifth. New Yorker 41:109-10+ F 20 '65
Trip to Leverton. New Yorker 41:95-6+ Ap 24 '65
HUNTER, Doris, and Hunter, Howard
Neither male nor female. Christian Cent 82:527-8+ Ap 28 '65
HUNTER, Evan
Race of hairy men! Criticism
Time 85:89 My 7 '65
HUNTER, Howard. See Hunter, D. jt. auth.
HUNTER, Jacqueline
Patricia couldn't see the board. Parents Mag 40:68-9+ Mr '65
HUNTER, Madeline C. See Goodlad, J. I. jt. auth.
HUNTER, Patricia P.
Education of handicapped children in residential schools. bibliog f Sch Life 47:9-12 D '64
HUNTER, Richard
Jamaica without gilt. Travel 123:30-5 F '65
HUNTER, Rodello
Heritage of going without. Read Digest 87:120-2 Ag '65
HUNTER, W. M. and others
Growth hormone: important role in muscular exercise in adults. bibliog Science 150:1051-3 N 19 '65
HUNTER-farmer relations. See Farmer-hunter relations
HUNTERDON COUNTY, N.J.
New way to care for the aged & infirm; Hunterdon program. il Changing T 19:22-4 Mr '65
HUNTERDON medical center. See Medical centers
HUNTERS
See also
Farmer-hunter relations
HUNTING, Constance
Conversation, late day; poem. Christian Cent 82:1248 O 13 '65
HUNTING
America's oldest hunting weapon: stone-pointed lance. F. C. Hibben. il Field & S 70:48-50+ Jl '65
Gist of it; digest of the outdoor news, ed. by H. Moore. See issues of Outdoor life
How to hit running game. J. O'Connor. il Outdoor Life 136:82+ O '65
It wasn't my time; dangerous experiences. D. M. Newell. il Field & S 70:62-5+ S '65
Luck! T. Trueblood. il Field & S 69:30+ F '65
Outdoors. T. Williams. Esquire 64:72+ S '65
Sportsman's notebook. H. G. Tapply. See issues of Field & stream
Underground animals, good targets. H. Bradshaw. il Suc Farm 63:54-5 O '65
Where to go fishing, vacationing, hunting. See issues of Outdoor life
See also
Falconry
Game
Hunting with bow and arrow
also Rabbit hunting, and similar headings

Accidents and injuries
See also
Hunting—Safety devices and measures

Safety devices and measures
Get lost! C. Elliott. il Outdoor Life 136:50-2+ Ag '65
Thing called early blur; use of color in hunting outfits. F. Woolner. il Outdoor Life 136:48-9+ N '65
Watch your step! D. M. Newell. il Field & S 70:42-5+ D '65

Statistics
Hit-or-miss statistics. H. G. Tapply. il Field & S 70:68 N '65

Study and teaching
Teenage gunners only; Oregon youngsters learn the do's and don'ts of good sportsmanship. R. O. Beatty. il Field & S 70:110-11 N '65

Africa
Big ones of Africa hit back. B. Swinehart. il Outdoor Life 135:28-31+ My '65
Safari! G. A. Kistler. il Sr Schol 86:sup 13-14 Mr 18 '65
Tale of two cats. W. Page. il Field & S 70:62-5+ My '65

Anecdotes, facetiae, satire, etc.
Profit and loss on safari; ed. by A. Pelle. J. P. Hallet. Esquire 64:47-8+ S '65

HUNTING—*Continued*

Africa, East

Day on safari. C. G. Spiegel. Reporter 33: 38+ Jl 1 '65

Alaska

Big game hunting forecast. il Field & S 70: 106-7 Ag '65

Daffy deer. F. Dufresne. il Field & S 70:34-6+ Ja '66

Day on the Slana. D. DeHart. il Outdoor Life 135:36-9+ Je '65

Eleventh hour caribou. J. R. Johnson. il Field & S 70:32-5+ Ag '65

Four men alone. L. Hayes. il Outdoor Life 137:21-3+ Ja '66

Hell on an island; interview. ed. by J. Rearden. F. C. Johnson. il Outdoor Life 136: 50-3+ S '65

Pack of trouble. F. C. Hibben. il Outdoor Life 136:44-7+ N '65

Wake up, Willie! D. DeHart. il Outdoor Life 135:48-9+ My '65

Argentina

10,000 miles from Thuringia. E. Schwiebert. il Field & S 70:67-9+ Ja '66

Arizona

Grand climax. R. V. Broadbent. il Outdoor Life 135:36-9+ My '65

Last chance at San Carlos. B. Behme. il Field & S 70:73-5 O '65

Three kinds of quail. L. Watson. il Outdoor Life 137:36-7+ Ja '66

Brazil

Meeting in the Mato Grosso. V. Kraft. il Sports Illus 22:64-8+ F 22 '65

Tight turn with a tigre. S. E. Brock. il Outdoor Life 135:36-9+ Mr '65

California

Bucks above the smog zone. L. Oertle. il Field & S 70:124-6+ S '65

Covey birds. T. Trueblood. il Field & S 70: 28+ O '65

Family affair. J. Vadon. il Outdoor Life 136: 54-5+ O '65

Game grab bag for sportsmen. T. Stimson. il Pop Mech 124:136-8+ O '65

Little cat is big stuff. J. Philbrick. il Outdoor Life 136:56-7+ D '65

There arose such a clatter. J. McFarland. il Field & S 70:65-7+ O '65

California, Lower

Man's man. W. Page. il Field & S 70:31-3 Ja '66

Canada

Big game hunting forecast. il Field & S 70: 106-7 Ag '65

Blood in his eye. H. J. Lowry. il Outdoor Life 136:28-9+ S '65

Campout for prairie ducks. J. O. Cartier. il Outdoor Life 136:60-1 O '65

Crisis at Coral Creek. A. Klumph. il Outdoor Life 136:24-7+ Ag '65

Greatest moments in hunting. H. P. Davis. il Farm J 89:42-3 N '65

Holiday moose hunt. B. Cary. il Outdoor Life 136:29-31+ D '65

Mixed bag in the Yukon. J. O'Connor. il Outdoor Life 136:60-2+ S '65

Moose in a blind alley; Newfoundland swamp. C. E. Priddle. il Outdoor Life 137:28-31+ Ja '66

My toughest trophy. C. Elliott. il Outdoor Life 135:24-7+ Mr '65

Old Krag. T. Howell. il Outdoor Life 135:44-5+ Mr '65

Sinkbox shoot; paintings by R. Cunningham; with account by D. Barnes. Sports Illus 23:40-5 O 4 '65

Thirty-minute moose. R. Starnes. il Field & S 70:29-31+ Ag '65

Want more hunting information? Suc Farm 63:100 S '65

World's rarest trophy? H. Shelley. il Outdoor Life 136:36-9+ Jl '65

Colombia

To kill a jaguar. R. Joseph. il Esquire 63:94-9 Mr '65

Colorado

Colorado's first goat hunt. J. J. Branney. il Outdoor Life 136:33-5+ O '65

Mad bull of Bristol Head. G. A. Wintz. il Outdoor Life 135:56-7+ My '65

Connecticut

Pilot was a pioneer. C. W. Bishop. il Outdoor Life 136:52-5+ D '65

We hunt the littlest big game. F. McKinley. il Outdoor Life 135:32-3+ Mr '65

Florida

All outdoors for rent. E. A. Bauer. il Outdoor Life 136:20-3+ Ag '65

Nightmare gobbler. N. Taylor. il Outdoor Life 137:46-7+ Ja '66

Opening day on doves. G. X. Sand. il Outdoor Life 136:54-7+ S '65

Spooky grays of Tate's hell. R. F. Burgess. il Outdoor Life 136:48-51+ Jl '65

Sunshine cottontails. G. X. Sand. il Field & S 70:50-1+ S '65

Idaho

Big buck on the Snake. J. O'Connor. il Outdoor Life 135:42-3+ My '65

Bull elk in the brush. J. O'Connor. il Outdoor Life 136:50-1+ O '65

Little battle of the bighorn. V. Kraft. il Sports Illus 23:56-8+ O 11 '65

We learned about elk. N. Smith. il Outdoor Life 136:44-7+ D '65

Illinois

Life in a goose pit. W. Page. il Field & S 70:80-4 N '65

India

First day tiger. J. O'Connor. il Outdoor Life 136:33-5+ N '65

Tigress of Elephantville; Eleanor O'Connor. J. O'Connor. il Outdoor Life 137:32-5+ Ja '66

Iowa

How to hunt pheasants. H. Bradshaw. il Field & S 70:41-3+ S '65

Sportiest duck hunting of all! J. Madson. il Farm J 89:50+ O '65

Iran

Ram and the silver bullet. J. O'Connor. il Outdoor Life 135:44-5+ Ap '65

Kenya

Full house on leopards. J. C. Rikhoff. il Outdoor Life 136:56-9+ O '65

Man-eater of Darajani. J. Kingsley-Heath. il Outdoor Life 136:32-5+ D '65

Louisiana

Cajun quail. G. Gresham. il Field & S 70: 43-5+ N '65

Maine

Odd fellow of the alder runs. L. Dietz. il Field & S 70:56-7+ S '65

Maryland

Gift of gabbling. T. Janes. il Outdoor Life 137:44-5+ Ja '66

Mexico

Wings over the jungle. H. Stilwell. il Field & S 70:116-18+ Jl '65

Michigan

Christmas adventure. E. A. Bauer. il Outdoor Life 136:36-9+ D '65

Foxes aren't killed by accident. J. O. Cartier. il Outdoor Life 137:52-3+ Ja '66

Michigan's first elk hunt; ed. by B. East. G. Loebrich. il Outdoor Life 135:36-9+ Ap '65

No time to climb. G. McKechnie. il Outdoor Life 136:48-9+ O '65

Where the deer are. J. Chiappetta. il Field & S 70:126-9 O '65

Whitetails can make mistakes. L. A. Anderson. il Field & S 70:70-2+ O '65

Wood ducks are special. J. O. Cartier. il Outdoor Life 136:32-3+ Ag '65

Minnesota

Way to get deer. K. Gilsvik. il Outdoor Life 136:36-9+ N '65

Montana

Big bucks of the Badlands. G. Gresham. il Outdoor Life 136:52-5+ N '65

Buck the hard way. E. A. Bauer. il Outdoor Life 136:60-3+ Jl '65

Rams of Ural. W. L. Henri. il Field & S 70:43-5+ Ag '65

$25 got my goat. D. D. Zietlow. il Outdoor Life 136:46-7+ S '65

Mozambique

Sables are hard to hit. J. O'Connor. il Outdoor Life 136:44-5+ Jl '65

Up to our necks in nyalas. J. O'Connor. il Outdoor Life 135:50-1+ Je '65

Nebraska

Bow and arrow turkey. G. Hornbeck. il Field & S 70:70-1+ Jl '65

HUNTING—*Continued*

Nepal
In the land of the tiger. V. Kraft. il Sports Illus 23:44-67 D 20 '65

New Jersey
Dig those crazy brant; New Jersey's Barnegat Bay. P. McLain. il Field & S 70:39-41 D '65
Where the woodcock are. T. Janes. il Outdoor Life 136:32-5+ S '65

New Mexico
Killers of the Magdalenas. F. C. Hibben. il Field & S 69:58-61 Mr '65
Slap a lion with your hat. J. C. Linville. il Outdoor Life 136:40-1+ Ag '65

New York (state)
Packtrain hunt in New York. D. Danaher. il Outdoor Life 136:36-9+ O '65
You've got to be crazy to hunt coot; Long Island Sound. N. Karas. il Field & S 70:66-9+ S '65

Northwestern states
Anything can happen hunt. C. Conley. il Field & S 70:47-9+ S '65

Oregon
Trophy takes more doing; mule deer head. E. Park. il Outdoor Life 136:44-7+ Ag '65
Whitetails don't hesitate. E. Park. il Outdoor Life 135:44-7+ Je '65

Patagonia
See Hunting—Argentina

Pennsylvania
Dutch country ringneck shoot. S. R. Slaymaker, 2d. il Outdoor Life 135:56-7+ N '65
Redcoats return to Bucks County. J. O'Reilly. il Sports Illus 23:78-80+ N 22 '65

Russia
Bear stroganoff; Intourist safari. il Newsweek 65:40 Mr 8 '65

Scotland
My hunt of a lifetime. W. R. Bimson. il Sports Illus 23:82-6+ O 25 '65

South Carolina
Buck at the secret crossing. A. Rutledge. il Outdoor Life 135:46-7+ Mr '65

Tanganyika
Family safari. P. Barrett. il Field & S 70:36-9+ Ag '65

Tennessee
Cottontail jungle. C. Vinson. il Outdoor Life 136:66-7+ N '65

Texas
Bring a buck to horn; antler rattling. D. Klepper. il Field & S 70:68-9+ O '65
Cat that liked cabrito. B. W. Dalrymple. il Field & S 70:37-9+ Ja '66
Mystery geese. B. Brister. il Field & S 70:44-6+ S '65
New techniques for old toms. B. W. Dalrymple. il Field & S 70:51-3+ N '65
Number one combo; bass-dove combination. B. W. Dalrymple. il Field & S 70:48-9+ O '65
Song of the coyote. B. W. Dalrymple. il Outdoor Life 135:64-5+ Je '65
Speed and the quail hunter; ed. by W. Page. il Field & S 70:138-43 My '65

Uganda
Jackson was a lady. W. Page. il Field & S 69:37-9+ Mr '65
Waterbuck by the yard. W. Page. il Field & S 70:26-7 Ag '65

United States
Best deer hunting this season; symposium. il Outdoor Life 136:65-80 O '65
Doves are indestructible. C. E. Gillham. il Field & S 70:70-2+ S '65
Field & stream 1965 hunting forecast, small & big game. il Field & S 70:53-64 O '65
How to do something about it. T. Trueblood. il Field & S 69:18+ Mr '65
Hunt with your boat. F. M. Paulson. il Field & S 69:129 F '65
I read my own stuff. T. Janes. il Outdoor Life 136:40-1+ D '65
Interview on hunting; ed. by D. Hanson. S. Udall. Suc Farm 63:6+ N '65

Just rabbits. C. E. Gillham. il Field & S 70:76-8+ O '65
To kill a cottontail. M. Ellis. il Field & S 70:44-6+ Ja '66
Want more hunting information? Suc Farm 63:100 S '65
Where do you hunt deer? W. Page. il Field & S 70:92-7 O '65

Utah
Utah, still the promised land. V. L. Oertle. il Field & S 70:10-12+ Ag '65

Vermont
Chair-lift rabbits; mountaintop rabbit hunt. H. Carroll. il Field & S 70:27-9+ D '65

Washington (state)
Lost like a goose. C. Chatfield. il Outdoor Life 136:60-3+ N '65
Wind River bear run. L. Miracle. il Outdoor Life 135:54-5+ Ap '65

Western states
Hurrah for the real elk hunter. C. Conley. il Field & S 70:50-1+ Ag '65

Wisconsin
Bonus: 500-pound bear. L. H. Johns. il Outdoor Life 137:38-9+ Ja '66
Edge of heaven; mouth of the Bois Brule River. M. Ellis. il Field & S 70:45-7 O '65

HUNTING clothes. *See* Clothing and dress—Sports clothes

HUNTING clubs
Pope and Young club; bow hunters' organization. G. H. Gillelan. il Outdoor Life 136:86+ Ag '65

HUNTING dogs
Dogs. D. M. Duffey. See issues of Outdoor life
How to save that gun-shy dog. J. M. Kelly. il Field & S 70:120-2+ Ag '65

HUNTING knives. *See* Bowie knives

HUNTING laws. *See* Game laws

HUNTING leopards. *See* Cheetahs

HUNTING lodges. *See* Lodges (architecture)

HUNTING on farm lands. *See* Farmer-hunter relations

HUNTING outfits
See also
Archery—Equipment
Hunting—Safety devices and measures

HUNTING rifles. *See* Rifles

HUNTING trophies. *See* Trophies, Sport

HUNTING with bow and arrow
Archery. G. H. Gillelan. See issues of Outdoor life
Bag it with a bow. F. Bear. il Pop Mech 124:106-9+ S '65
Big ones of Africa hit back. B. Swinehart. il Outdoor Life 135:28-31+ My '65
Bow and arrow turkey. G. Hornbeck. il Field & S 70:70-1+ Jl '65
You can't figure bears. A. Laha. il Outdoor Life 136:58-9+ N '65

HUNTINGTON, Anna (Hyatt)
Sculptor. G. Meek. il pors Américas 17:3-5 Je '65

HUNTINGTON, Daniel
Daniel Huntington, portrait painter over seven decades. A. Gilchrist. il por Antiques 87:709-11 Je '65

HUNTINGTON, David C.
Olana, the center of the world. Antiques 88:656-63 N '65

HUNTINGTON, Roger
All about gear drives. Hot Rod 18:76-8 Je '65
Automobiles, 1966 model review. Consumer Bul 48:27-32 D '65
Axle ratios, key to performance + economy. Motor T 17:58-9 My '65
Chevy's fabulous new 396. Motor T 17:52-5 Je '65
Detroit's cars and the big smog problem. Consumer Bul 48:35-7 Ap '65
Is Chevy stuck in 2nd? Motor T 17:56-7 Mr '65
Looking through the sound barrier. Hot Rod 18:42-4+ Jl '65
Toronado. Hot Rod 18:82-4+ O '65
Trophy team. Hot Rod 18:54-5+ Ag '65
Wind up with light valves. Hot Rod 18:82+ Ag '65

HUNTINGTON, N.Y.
Harbor recreation. F. Bickman. il Recreation 58:272-3 Je '65

HUNTINGTON, Vt.
Waiting for realty, death of a small town. D. Wakefield. Nation 201:92-7 S 20 '65

HUNTINGTON botanical gardens, San Marino, Calif. *See* Botanical gardens

HUNTINGTON Hartford foundation
Artists in paradise. H. Frost. il Opera N 29:6-11 F 27 '65

HUNTLEY, Chet
Executive farms: profit and pleasure. T. J. Murray. il Duns R 85:45-7+ Je '65
HUNTOON, R. D.
Status of the national standards for physical measurement. bibliog Science 150:169-78 O 8 '65
HUNTRESS; story. See Stead, C.
HUNTSVILLE, Ala.
Rocket age comes to tiny Triana. H. Bims. il Ebony 20:106-8+ Mr '65
HUPE, Robert Strausz-. See Strausz-Hupe, R.
HURLEY, John F.
Better Leyte than never. America 112:641-2 My 1 '65
HURLEY, Neil P.
Picture of the future. America 112:218-19 F 13 '65
HURRICANES
After Betsy, a cluster of hurricanes? il U S News 59:11 S 20 '65
Betsy in the Everglades report. E. T. Christensen. il Nat Parks Mag 39:22 N '65
Betsy's toll. il Newsweek 66:29 S 27 '65
Bouncing Betsy. il Newsweek 66:25-6 S 20 '65
Buildings that stood up to Betsy; prefab resort abuilding. il Bsns W p 56+ S 25 '65
Double duty for Dinner Key auditorium, Miami. W. Coburn. il Yachting 118:56+ N '65
Elements: still untamed and deadly; Betsy in Louisiana. il U S News 59:48-9 S 27 '65
Hellion hell-bent; hurricane Betsy. Time 86:37 S 17 '65
Hurricane Betsy viewed by TIROS satellites; photographs. Miss & Roc 17:18 S 20 '65
In Betsy's wake, a search for solutions; Florida, Louisiana hard hit. il Bsns W p28-9 S 18 '65
Lethal lady; Betsy. il Sr Schol 87:9 S 30 '65
Looking a hurricane in the eye; effect of cloud seeding. Bsns W p54 Ag 7 '65
Seed hurricanes to study intensity and growth. Sci N L 88:40 Jl 17 '65
September hurricane. W. Brown. il Yachting 118:38-40+ S '65
Trying to salvage Betsy's discards; Avondale shipyards. il Bsns W p 180+ O 23 '65
What made Betsy blow; energy from the sea. il Time 86:82 D 3 '65
See also
Microseisms

Anecdotes, facetiae, satire, etc.
How to help your wife cope with a hurricane. W. R. Benedetto. Harper 230:106 Mr '65
HURRICANES and building. See Building, Stormproof
HURST, Margery
One-woman show. il por Time 85:106 Mr 19 '65
HURST, Tex.
Putting a city's memory on film. D. R. Edmonds. Am City 80:96 O '65
HURT, Robert M.
Robert M. Hurt, RIP. R. M. Schuchman. Nat R 17:316 Ap 20 '65
HURTIG, M. G.
Store directories simplify stock control. Pub W 188:48-52 D 27 '65
HURWITZ, Howard L.
Book reviews. Sr Schol 86:sup21 Mr 18; 87:sup5 N 11 '65
Churchill as historian. Sr Schol 86:1T F 11 '65
Integrating the two Israels. Sr Schol 87:sup 18+ S 23 '65
Myrdal: poverty in America. Sr Schol 86:sup 12 Ap 15 '65
New books for your history shelf. Sr Schol 87:sup22-4 S 30 '65
New books for your professional shelf. Sr Schol 86:sup 16-17+ Mr 4 '65
New books in American history. Sr Schol 87:sup 17 N 18 '65
New paperbacks for high school teachers. Sr Schol 87:sup24-5+ O 28 '65
(ed) What's happening in social studies; summaries of periodical articles and reports (cont) Sr Schol 86:7T F 11; sup 19 Ap 29; 87:sup27 S 23 '65
HURWITZ, Sidney
White-ground etchings of Ron Kowalke. Am Artist 30:60-5+ Ja '66
HUS, Jan
John Hus and Vatican II. America 113:491 O 30 '65
HUSBAND and wife. See Husbands; Marriage; Wives
HUSBANDS
Art of influencing a husband. J. Brothers. Good H 160:56+ Je '65
Confidential memo to busy husbands: ten ways to satisfy a neglected wife. M. R. Feinberg. Ladies Home J 82:66+ O '65

Secret thoughts of a happy husband. E. Joseph. McCalls 92:18 Ag '65
Worlds to share. L. Strong. Am Home 68: 18 Mr '65
See also
Marriage
Wives

Anecdotes, facetiae, satire, etc.
Why can't I get more done? C. Ogburn, jr. il Read Digest 86:21-2+ My '65
HUSKE, Joseph
Church for the hungry. P. Houtz. il pors Sat Eve Post 238:87-91 D 18 '65
HUSSEIN, Mohamed Kamel
International co-operation and world peace; address. UN Mo Chron 2:59-70 Mr '65
HUSSEY, Betty
Wando, the reliable pea. Flower Grower 52: 14+ Ap '65
HUSSEY, Charles
Britain pays the victim of the crime. N Y Times Mag p 19-20+ F 21 '65
Snowdons come on a visit. N Y Times Mag p48-9+ O 31 '65
HUSTING, Nancy Evans, pseud.
World for Amy. Redbook 125:70-1+ Ag '65
HUSTON, John
Ark that John built. il por Life 59:43-4 Ag 13 '65
Giraffe in Piazza del popolo. T. Sage. il Nat R 17:105-6 F 9 '65
Noah. il pors Look 29:21-6 Jl 27 '65
Our far flung correspondents. L. Ross. New Yorker 41:185-6+ S 25 '65
HUSTON, McCready
Making nature writing pay. Writer 78:29-30 S '65
HUSTWITT, Arthur
Christian booksellers association tops convention records. por Pub W 188:38-41 S 6 '65
HUTCHENS, John K.
One thing and another. Sat R 48:27 Mr 20; 38 Ap 17; 58-9+ My 22; 25 Jl 3; 23 Ag 21 '65
Reviewer on review. Sat R 48:25-6 F 20 '65
HUTCHINS, Robert Maynard
Are we educating our children for the wrong future? Sat R 48:66-7+ S 11 '65
Redbook dialogue: Charlton Heston and Robert Hutchins. por Redbook 126:68-9+ D '65
Speaking out. por Sat Eve Post 238:10+ S 25 '65
What I have learned; first glimpses of a new world. por Sat R 48:33-5+ D 4 '65
HUTCHINSON, Franklin
Electron-spin-resonance signals and biological effects. Science 150:644+ O 29 '65
HUTCHINSON, Robert
Lives of the ancient poets: Margaret: Battle in Amherst: E.D; poems. Poetry 105: 377-8 Mr '65
HUTCHISON, Bruce
Open letter to the American people. Read Digest 87:96-100 Ag '65
HUTH, Hans
German lacquer. Antiques 87:456-60 Ap '65
HUXLEY, Aldous
Devils of Loudun; dramatization. See Whiting, J. Devils
HUXLEY, Elspeth
African affairs (cont) por Nat R 17:95-6+ F 9 '65
Australia's Aborigines step out of the stone age. N Y Times Mag p 10-11+ Je 20 '65
Bead on roos. N Y Times Mag p 119-20+ O 24 '65
HUXLEY, H. E.
Mechanism of muscular contraction; with biographical sketch. il Sci Am 213:10, 18-27 bibliog(p 126) D '65
HUXLEY, Matthew
Incompleat suicide. Nation 201:414-17 N 29 '65
HUXTABLE, Ada Louise (Landman)
Eye on the environment. por Newsweek 66: 70-1 Ag 23 '65
HUYCK, Dorothy Boyle
Job corps=human+natural conservation. Am For 71:22-5 Jl '65
Shenandoah National Park. Nat Parks Mag 39:4+ N '65
Sig Olson: wilderness philosopher. Am For 71:46-7+ My '65
HUYNH-tan-Phat
Life with the Viet Cong. Time 86:25-6 Jl 2 '65
HYACINTHS, Water. See Water hyacinths
HYALINE membrane disease
Death by reflex? il Time 85:55-6 Je 4 '65
Killer that stalks the newborn; respiratory-distress syndrome. S. M. Spencer. il Sat Eve Post 238:32-5 Ag 28 '65
New way to treat hyaline membrane disease. Time 86:70 Ag 27 '65

HYALURONIDASE
Cellular origin of hyaluronateprotein in the human synovial membrane. S. Blau and others. bibliog il Science 150:353-5 O 15 '65

HYAMS, Joe
Last days of Humphrey Bogart; excerpt from Bogie, the biography of Humphrey Bogart. Good H 162:54-7+ Ja '66
Mind and heart of Richard Burton. Good H 160:84-7+ Je '65
Samantha gets her way. Sat Eve Post 238: 32-3 Mr 13 '65

HYATT, Robert M.
Let's halt the federal land grab. Nat R 17: 984-5 N 2 '65

HYBRID amaryllis. See Amaryllis
HYBRID lilies. See Lilies
HYBRID rockets. See Rockets

HYBRIDIZATION
Blooming big business! J. N. Miller. il Read Digest 86:17-18+ Mr '65
Chromosome complement: a fertile hybrid between equus prjewalskii and equus caballus. L. Koulischer and S. Frechkop. bibliog il Science 151:93-5 Ja 7 '66
Disappearance of a genetic marker from a cytoplasmic hybrid plasmodium of a true slime mold. N. S. Kerr. bibliog il Science 147:1586-8 Mr 26 '65
Hybridization experiments: evidence of dissociation equilibrium in hemerythrin. S. Keresztes-Nagy and others. bibliog il Science 150:357-9 O 15 '65
Master of pink is ninety. E. J. Purcell and J. E. Dwyer. il Pop Gard 16:21+ Jl '65
Sex-linkage of glucose-6-phosphate dehydrogenase in the horse and donkey. J. M. Trujillo and others. bibliog il Science 148: 1603-4 Je 18 '65
When gardening is gambling. il Sunset 134: 268+ Je '65
See also subhead Hybrids under various subjects, e.g. Alfalfa—Hybrids

HYDE, H. Montgomery
Traitor and a queen. Harper 230:156-8 Mr '65

HYDE, J. F.
Chemical background of silicones. bibliog Science 147:829-36 F 19 '65

HYDE, Scott
Color alchemy of Scott Hyde; composite photographs. Pop Phot 56:64-71+ F '65

HYDE, Vance
Don't be a martyr-mother. Parents Mag 40: 38-9+ Jl '65

HYDÉN, Holger, and Lange, P. W.
Rhythmic enzyme changes in neurons and glia during sleep. bibliog Science 149:654-6 Ag 6 '65

about
Where the memory is. il Newsweek 66:70 Ag 23 '65

HYDRA (zoology)
Cell proliferation in hydra: an autoradiographic approach. R. D. Campbell. bibliog il Science 148:1231-2 My 28 '65
Cellular segregation and heterocytic dominance in hydra. H. M. Lenhoff. bibliog il Science 148:1105-7 My 21 '65
Hydra: induction of supernumerary heads by isolated neurosecretory granules. T. L. Lentz. bibliog il Science 150:633-5 O 29 '65
Nature note; somersaulting hydras; members of the phylum coelenterata. Sci N L 88: 206 S 25 '65

HYDRAULIC engineering
See also
Bridges—Foundations and piers
Flood prevention and control
Hydraulic laboratories

HYDRAULIC laboratories
Best by test; Dana Point project at Vicksburg, Miss. hydraulics testing station. C. West. il Motor B 115:32-4+ My '65

HYDROCARBONS
Carcinogenic aromatic hydrocarbons: special vulnerability of rats. C. B. Huggins and others. bibliog il Science 147:1153-4 Mr 5 '65
Hydrocarbons of biological origin in sediments about two billion years old. J. Oró and others. bibliog il Science 148:77-9 Ap 2 '65
Intermolecular forces in association of purines with polybenzenoid hydrocarbons. B. Pullman and others. bibliog il Science 147:1305-7 Mr 12 '65
Isoprenoid hydrocarbons in recent sediments: presence of pristane and probable absence of phytane. M. Blumer and W. D. Snyder. bibliog il Science 150:1588-9 D 17 '65

New chemical molecule; laboratory-produced organic compound, cubane. il Sci N L 87:131 F 27 '65
Paraffinic hydrocarbons in pasture plants. J. Oró and others. bibliog il Science 147: 870-3 F 19 '65

HYDROCORTISONE
Actinomycin D and hydrocortisone: intracellular binding in rat liver. C. W. Dingman and M. B. Sporn. bibliog il Science 149:1251-4 S 10 '65
Wasting disease induced with cortisol acetate: studies in germ-free mice. N. D. Reed and J. W. Jutila. bibliog il Science 150:356-7 O 15 '65

HYDRODYNAMICS
Air-sea interface; report on conference. R. L. Snyder. Science 149:766 Ag 13 '65
Vertical density currents. W. H. Bradley. bibliog il Science 150:1423-8 D 10 '65
See also
Vortex motion

HYDROELECTRIC plants
Battle of the Hudson. T. Lawrence. il Am For 71:12-15+ Ap '65
Fight to save Storm King on Hudson. Liv Wildn 29:38-9 Sum '65
Hydropower and the Hudson Highlands. P. M. Tilden. Nat Parks Mag 39:2 Ap '65
Rebuke to the FPC; failure to investigate Storm King Mountain project. New Repub 154:7 Ja 15 '66
Storm over stripers; Commission to hold hearings on power project's threat to Hudson's striped bass fishery. G. Heinold. il Outdoor Life 135:10-12+ My '65
World's biggest wet storage battery; Storm King Mountain. H. Walton. il Pop Sci 187: 52-3 Ag '65

HYDROELECTRIC power
President sends Congress report on New England resource program. Dept State Bul 53:215-16 Ag 2 '65
See also
Tide power

HYDROFOILS
Disco Volante, the saucer that flies; new James Bond epic Thunderball. J. Martenhoff. il Motor B 116:32-3+ D '65
I flew an outboard hydrofoil. J. Martenhoff. il Pop Sci 187:79-81 N '65
New flying pod for high-speed boating; Water Spyder. C. B. Hicks. il Pop Mech 125:48-9 Ja '66
New hydrofoil ship begins passenger runs; between Seattle, Wash. and Victoria, B.C. Sci N L 88:89 Ag 7 '65
Way out of traffic jams. B. Kocivar. il Look 29:M6-8 F 9 '65

HYDROGEN
Biological formation of molecular hydrogen. C. T. Gray and H. Gest. bibliog il Science 148:186-92 Ap 9 '65
Hydrogen emission line $n_{110} \rightarrow n_{109}$: detection at 5009 megahertz in galactic H II regions. B. Höglund and P. G. Mezger. bibliog il Science 150:339-40+ O 15 '65
Radio astronomers detect another hydrogen line. Sky & Tel 30:127+ S '65
Slush hydrogen seen as rocket engine fuel. Sci N L 89:11 Ja 1 '66

Isotopes
Exchange of carbon-bound hydrogen atoms ortho to the hydroxyl group in tyrosine. R. B. Martin and V. J. Morlino. bibliog Science 150:493 O 22 '65
See also
Tritium

HYDROGEN, Liquid
Wonderful, terrible liquid. il Time 86:59 Jl 16 '65

HYDROGEN bombs
Another Chinese bomb? A. Ewing. Sci N L 87:133 F 27 '65

Testing
See Atomic bombs—Testing

Testing, Suspension of
See Atomic bombs—Testing, Suspension of

HYDROGEN bonding. See Chemical bonds

HYDROGEN ion concentration
Electron yield in the γ-radiolysis of water vapor. J. H. Baxendale and G. P. Gilbert. bibliog il Science 147:1571 Mr 26 '65
Gastric secretion: mechanism for production of hydrogen ions. H. P. Gregor and J. M. Berkowitz. bibliog il Science 150:773-6 N 5 '65
Silica: role in the buffering of natural waters. R. M. Garrels. bibliog Science 148:69 Ap 2 '65

HYDROGEN peroxide
Fast reactions of ascorbic acid and hydrogen peroxide in ice, a presumtive early environment. N. H. Grant and H. E. Alburn. bibliog il Science 150:1589-90 D 17 '65

HYDROGEN sulfide
Nematodes: biological control in rice fields: role of hydrogen sulfide. R. Rodriguez-Kabana. bibliog il Science 148:524-6 Ap 23 '65

HYDROGRAPHY; story. See Brodeur, P.

HYDROLOGY
See also
Water

HYDRONIC waves. See Radio waves

HYDROPHIDAE. See Sea snakes

HYDROPHONES
Aid underwater hearing. Sci N L 87:389 Je 19 '65

HYDROPLANE racing. See Motor boat racing

HYDROSTATIC pressure
What's your water pressure? il Sunset 134:135-6+ My '65

HYDROSTATIC transmission. See Automobiles—Transmission

HYDROXYCINNAMYL alcohols. See Alcohols

HYDROXYETHYLHYDRAZINE. See Growth inhibiting substances (plants)

HYDROXYL
Hydroxyl radicals in space. B. J. Robinson. il Sci Am 213:26-33 bibliog(p 124) Jl '65

HYDROXYLAMINE
Mutagenic effects of hydroxylamine in vivo. I. Tessman and others. bibliog il Science 148:507-8 Ap 23 '65

HYDROXYLAPATITE
See also
Carbonate-apatite

HYDROXYMERCURIBENZOATE. See Mer-capto group

HYDROXYTRYPTAMINE. See Serotonin

HYDROXYTRYPTOPHAN decarboxylase. See Enzymes

HYDROXYUREA. See Urea

HYGIENE
See also
Children—Care and hygiene
Infants—Care and hygiene
Women—Health and hygiene

HYGROMETERS
Psychrometric measurement of leaf water potential: lack of error attributable to leaf permeability. H. D. Barrs. bibliog il Science 149:63-5 Jl 2 '65

HYLA. See Tree frogs and tree toads

HYLIN, John W. and Watson, D. P.
Ergoline alkaloids in tropical wood roses. bibliog Science 148:499-500 Ap 23 '65

HYMAN, Mervin
Basketball's week. See issues of Sports illustrated published during basketball season
Football's week. See issues of Sports illustrated published during football season

HYMAN, Sidney
Washington's Negro elite. Look 29:60+ Ap 6 '65

HYMAN, Stanley Edgar
Shirley Jackson, 1919-1965. Sat Eve Post 238:63 D 18 '65

HYMENOPTERA
See also
Wasps

HYMES, James L. Jr
Does your child act his age? Farm J 89:112 Ap '65
Who's pressuring Johnny? home and school. PTA Mag 60:24 bibliog(p36) S '65

HYMNS
Lutheran hit parade. Time 85:74 Mr 12 '65

HYNES, Ron
Go or no go. Flying 77:88+ Ag '65

HYNES, Samuel
TV's battle of Britain. Commonweal 82:564-6 Ag 6 '65

HYPERCALCEMIA
Thyroid and parathyroid roles in hypercalcemia: evidence for a thyrocalcitonin-releasing factor. R. F. Gittes and G. L. Irvin. bibliog il Science 148:1737-9 Je 25 '65

HYPERSONIC airplanes. See Airplanes, Supersonic

HYPERTENSION
Arterial hypertension elicited by subpressor amounts of angiotensin. J. W. McCubbin and others. il Science 149:1394-5 S 17 '65
Diabetes & blood pressure; adrenal-gland disorder. Time 86:59 D 3 '65
Drug usage may explain racial gap in deaths. Sci N L 88:136 Ag 28 '65

High blood pressure? it may be in your genes; experiments on rats at Brookhaven national laboratory. il Bsns W p90+ Ap 3 '65
Lactic acid metabolism in hypertensive patients. F. E. Demartini and others. bibliog il Science 148:1482-4 Je 11 '65

HYPERTHYROIDISM. See Thyroid gland

HYPNOSIS
Eye and I. J. Dotson. il Seventeen 24:140-1+ N '65

HYPNOTISM
Hypnosis no mystery anthropologist says. Sci N L 88:264 O 23 '65
Hypnosis: what it can and can't cure. A. J. Snider. il Sci Digest 58:70-6 O '65
Hypnotist in danger as well as subject. Sci N L 87:249 Ap 17 '65
Remote-control hypnosis. il Time 86:37 Jl 2 '65

HYPOCRISY
Speaking out; hypocrisy is no sin. D. W. Brogan. Sat Eve Post 238:10+ Ag 14 '65

HYPOTHALAMUS
Chemical coding of behavior in the brain. N. E. Miller. bibliog il Science 148:328-38 Ap 16 '65
5-Hydroxytryptophan decarboxylase in rat brain: effect of hypothalamic lesions. A. Heller and others. bibliog il Science 147:887-8 F 19 '65
Hypothalamic lesions by electrocauterization: disinhibition of feeding and self-stimulation. B. G. Hoebel. bibliog il Science 149:452-3 Jl 23 '65; Reply. R. W. Reynolds. 150:1322 D 3 '65
Hypothalamic motivational processes as reflected by their hippocampal electrical correlates. E. Grastyán and others. bibliog il Science 149:91-3 Jl 2 '65
Impaired recovery from hypothermia after anterior hypothalamic lesions in hibernators. E. Satinoff. bibliog il Science 148:399-400 Ap 16 '65
Increased activities of glycogenolytic enzymes in liver after splanchnic-nerve stimulation. T. Shimazu and A. Fukuda. bibliog ii Science 150:1607-8 D 17 '65
Lateral hypothalamic stimulation in satiated rats: T-maze learning for food. J. Mendelson and S. L. Chorover. bibliog il Science 149:559-61 Jl 30 '65
Lateral hypothalamus: learning of food-seeking response motivated by electrical stimulation. E. E. Coons and others. bibliog il Science 150:1320-1 D 3 '65

HYPOTHESIS
Method of multiple working hypotheses; reprint from Science, 1890. T. C. Chamberlin. Science 148:754-9 My 7 '65; Discussion. 149:246+, 1176 Jl 16, S 10 '65

HYPOXIA. See Anoxemia

HYSLOP, Beatrice F.
(comp) Articles and other books received; France. See issues of American historical review

HYSLOP, Lorin C.
Experimental course in the humanities for high school students. Sr Schol 87:sup9 D 2 '65

HYSTERECTOMY. See Uterus—Surgery

HYSTERIA
Hysteria a myth British doctor claims. Sci N L 87:393 Je 19 '65

HYYPIA, Jorma
How to build a brook. Pop Gard 16:26-7+ Mr '65

I

IACC. See Inter-American cultural council

IAEA. See International atomic energy agency

IA-ECOSOC. See Inter-American economic and social council

IAF. See International astronautical federation

IAM. See International association of machinists

IATA. See International air transport association

IBA. See Investment bankers association of America

IBM. See International business machine corporation

ICAO. See International civil aviation organization

ICBM (intercontinental ballistic missiles) See Guided missiles

ICCC. See International council of Christian churches

ICEM. See Intergovernmental commmittee for European migration

ICFTU. See International confederation of free trade unions

ICL. See International Christian leadership (organization)

ICS. See International correspondence schools

ICY. See International cooperation year

IDA. See International development association

IDB. See Inter-American development bank

IDC. See Israel development corporation

IEEE. See Institute of electrical and electronics engineers

IESC. See International executive service corps

IFALPA. See International federation of air line pilots associations

I.G. farbenindustrie a.g. See Interessengemeinschaft farbenindustrie aktiengesellschaft

IHAS (integrated helicopter avionic systems) See Aeronautic instruments

I had a ball; musical comedy. See Musical comedies, revues, etc.—Criticisms, plots, etc.

I know my love; story. See Plagemann, B.

ILA. See Illinois library association

ILAAS (integrated light attack avionics system) See Aeronautic instruments

ILC. See United Nations—International law commission

ILO. See International labor organization

ILPA. See International labor press association

ILS (instrument landing system) See Airplanes—Landing

I love you, Charley, please come back; story. See Heinemann, A.

I love you truly; story. See Stolz, M.

IMF. See International monetary fund

IMP (interplanetary monitoring platform) See Artificial satellites—Use in research

INCO. See International nickel company, incorporated

IOS. See Investors overseas services, limited

IPA. See International publishers association

IPR. See Institute of Pacific relations

IQ. See Intelligence quotient

IQSY. See International years of the quiet sun

IRA. See International reading association

IRI (Istituto per la ricostruzione industriale) See Italy—Industries

IRRI. See International rice research institute

IRS. See United States—Internal revenue service

ISPA. See International society for the protection of animals

ISSI. See International social science institute

ITA (initial teaching alphabet) See Alphabet

ITU. See International typographical union

IUCD (intra-uterine contraceptive devices) See Contraceptives

IUCN. See International union for the conservation of nature and natural resources

IUD. See American federation of labor and Congress of industrial organizations—Industrial union department

IUE. See International union of electrical, radio and machine workers

IUFO. See International union of family organizations

IUS. See International union of students

IWA. See International woodworkers of America

IYRU. See International yacht racing union

IAKOVOS, abp
Orthodox churches vis-a-vis the ecumenical movement; address, April 28, 1965. Cath World 201:237-9 Jl '65

IALONGO, Donna
Waitings; poem. America 113:671 N 27 '65

IANNI, Francis A. J. and McNeill, B. D.
Organizing for continuing change. Sat R 48:55-6+ Je 19 '65

IBISES
New Floridian: the scarlet ibis. C. F. Bundy. il Audubon Mag 67:84-5 Mr '65
See also
Wood storks

ICARUS (asteroid) See Asteroids

ICE
Activation energy of direct-current electrical conductivity of ice with HF and NH3 added. S. Y. Chai and P. O. Vogelhut. bibliog il Science 148:1595-8 Je 18 '65
Crystal multiplication without nucleation. B. Chalmers and R. B. Williamson. bibliog il Science 148:1717-18 Je 25 '65
Crystallization of clay-adsorbed water. D. M. Anderson and P. Hoekstra. bibliog il Science 149:318-19 Jl 16 '65

Fast reactions of ascorbic acid and hydrogen peroxide in ice, a presumptive early environment. N. H. Grant and H. E. Alburn. bibliog il Science 150:1589-90 D 17 '65
High-pressure single-crystal studies of ice VI. S. Block and others. bibliog il Science 148:947-8 My 14 '65
Negative crystals in ice: a method for growth. C. A. Knight and N. C. Knight. bibliog il Science 150:1819-21 D 31 '65
Reactions occur in ice. Sci N L 89:38 Ja 15 '66
Structure of ice VI. B. Kamb. bibliog il Science 150:205-9 O 8 '65

Polar Regions
Four brutal years on a floating ice island; Arlis II. H. Shuldiner. il Pop Sci 187:50-4 Jl '65

ICE age national scientific reserve (proposed) See National parks and reserves—United States

ICE algae. See Algae

ICE and snow building. See Building, Ice and snow

ICE boats and ice boating
Chill challenge of hard water sailing. R. R. Nicholas. il Motor B 116:38-9+ D '65
Ice boating. il Travel 125:45-7 Ja '66
Sledding at a mile a minute; racing Simko power sled. S. James. il Pop Mech 125:130-1 Ja '66
Winter sailors. il Newsweek 65:54 Mr 8 '65

ICE breaking vessels
Rescue in the polar ice pack; USS Glacier freeing sealer Polarhav. E. A. McDonald. il Pop Mech 124:92-6+ D '65

ICE cream, ices, etc.
America's favorite food. M. B. Keiser. il Parents Mag 40:28+ Ag '65
Here's looking at you. il Sunset 135:144 S '65
How long since you've had homemade ice cream? with recipes. il Bet Hom & Gard 43:99 Ag '65
Ice cream and ice-cream desserts. il Redbook 125:84-5+ Ag '65
Ice cream and sauces. R. Hanna. il Suc Farm 63:74-5 Je '65
Ice cream in confection cups. il Sunset 135:245 O '65
Spectaculars on ice. il McCalls 92:112-13+ Je '65
Stop by for homemade ice cream and cake. il Farm J 89:66-7+ Ag '65
When the cheering stops, explain that it's just ice cream. il Sunset 135:58-9 Ag '65
See also
Good humor corporation

ICE cream sauces. See Sauces

ICE cream sodas. See Beverages

ICE cube trays. See Refrigerators, Electric

ICE fish, Antarctic
Ice fish. J. T. Ruud. il Sci Am 213:108-14 bibliog(p 144) N '65

ICE fishing. See Fishing, Winter

ICE hazards in aviation. See Airplanes—Ice protection

ICE hockey. See Hockey

ICE islands. See Ice—Polar Regions

ICE on rivers, lakes, etc.

Control
Coal dusting saves a lake; letting sunlight through to plants that make oxygen for fish. V. T. Hanlon. il Outdoor Life 137:10-11+ Ja '66
Two de-icing systems for wet storage in winter. C. Kucyn; M. Jancsics, jr. il Motor B 116:100-2 O '65

ICE photography. See Photography of snow, ice, etc.

ICE shows

Anecdotes, facetiae, satire, etc.
At ease in absentia. C. W. Morton. Atlan 215:128 Ap '65

ICE skating rinks. See Skating rinks

ICE trays. See Refrigerators, Electric

ICEBERGS
Dyes to mark icebergs. B. Tufty. Sci N L 87:135 F 27 '65

ICEBREAKERS. See Ice breaking vessels

ICED drinks. See Beverages

ICELAND
See also
Airlines—Iceland

Description and travel
Implausible island. T. Olson. il Sat R 48:54-5 S 11 '65

ICELAND disease. See Epidemic neuromyasthenia
ICELAND poppies. See Poppies
ICELANDAIR. See Airlines—Iceland
ICELANDERS
Implausible island. T. Olson. il Sat R 48:54-5 S 11 '65
ICELANDIC literature
See also
Sagas
ICELANDIC painting. See Painting, Icelandic
ICHIKAWA, Kon
Triumph in Cannes. Sports Illus 22:17 My 31 '65
ICI, on parle what? story. See Stolz, M.
ICINGS
Make beautiful cakes your food hobby. J. Figg. il Suc Farm 63:124-5+ F '65
New toppings for angel food; with recipes. B. Pierson. il Farm J 89:92-3 F '65
IDAHO
See also
Hunting—Idaho

Religious institutions and affairs
News of the Christian world (cont) Christian Cent 82:251-2, 973-4, 1267 F 24, Ag 4, O 13 '65
IDE, Averill
Desert panorama; poem. Am For 71:47 Ag '65
IDE, Leta Foster
Youth surges, age repulses; poem. Am For 71:47 Ag '65
IDEA files. See Fiction—Technique
IDEALISM
Ideals can be disquieting; with study-discussion program, by C. Smallenburg and H. Smallenburg. W. J. Anderson; H. Long. bibliog il PTA Mag 59:14-16, 36-7 My '65
What is realism doing to American history? adaptation of address. A. MacLeish. il Sat R 48:10-12 Jl 3 '65; Discussion. 48:13-14+ Jl 3; 38 Jl 24 '65
IDEALS. See Idealism
IDEAS
Care and feeding of intellectual property. J. H. Munster, jr. and J. C. Smith. bibliog Science 148:739-43 My 7 '65
IDEAS in business
Ideas to order. il Sci Digest 59:61-3 Ja '66
Making ideas flow; interview. J. B. Hall. Nations Bsns 53:41-2+ S '65
Synectics: inventing by the madness method. T. Alexander. Fortune 72:165+ Ag '65
Ten ways to sell them. R. J. Tiernan. il Nations Bsns 53:84-6+ Je '65
Test your creativity. il Nations Bsns 53:80-3+ Je '65; Same abr. with title Are you creative? Read Digest 87:181-2 O '65
What makes a company creative; symposium. Nations Bsns 53:76-9 Je '65
IDENTIFICATION
See also
Photography in criminal investigation
IDENTIFICATION of birds. See Birds—Identification
IDENTIFICATION of infants. See Infants—Identification
IDENTIFICATION tags, bracelets, etc.
Tagged for life; emergency medical tags. D. A. Dukelow. il Todays Health 43:58-9+ D '65
IDENTITY, Personal. See Personality
IDEOLOGY
Revolt against ideology. H. D. Aiken; discussion. Commentary 38:14+ S; 69-76 O '64; 39:8+ F '65
IDIOT lights. See Automobiles—Safety devices and measures
IDIOT savant. See Mentally handicapped
IDYLL, Clarence P.
Shrimp need fresh water, too; address, June 1965. Nat Parks Mag 39:14-15 O '65
Shrimp nursery. Nat Geog Mag 127:636-59 My '65
IF one green bottle; story. See Thomas, A. C.
IGER, Martin, and Rothschild, Norman
Kodak Ektachrome infrared aero. il Pop Phot 57:158-61+ D '65
IGESZ, Bodo
From Bayreuth, via Philips, a live Tannhäuser. Am Rec G 32:108-11 O '65
IGGERS, Georg G.
Idea of progress: a critical reassessment; adaptation of paper, September 1964. bibliog f Am Hist R 71:1-17 O '65
IGLAUER, Edith
Reporter at large (cont) New Yorker 41:121-2+ Ap 24; 174+ N 6 '65
IGLOOS. See Snow houses

IGNACIO RASCO, José
Toward a Latin American parliament. Américas 17:12-17 Jl '65
IGNATOW, David
Poetry chronicle. R. Howard. Poetry 106:298-9 Jl '65
IGNEOUS rocks. See Rocks, Igneous
IGNITION, Automobile. See Automobile engines—Ignition
IGNITION, Marine. See Marine engines—Ignition
IGUANAS
Nature note; marine iguana. Sci N L 87:221 Ap 3 '65
IKEDA, Hiroshi
Interspecific transfer of the sex-ratio agent of drosophila willistoni in drosophila bifasciata and drosophila melanogaster. bibliog Science 147:1147-8 Mr 5 '65
IKEYA, Kaoru
Boy who redeemed his father's name. T. Morris. il pors Redbook 125:86-7+ O '65; Same abr. Read Digest 88:107-11 Ja '66
IKEYA comet. See Comets
IKLÉ, Frank W.
Japanese-German peace negotiations during World war I. bibliog f Am Hist R 71:62-76 O '65
IKLE, Fred Charles
Real negotiations on South Vietnam. Reporter 32:15-16 Je 3 '65
ILG, Paul
Shot down in North Vietnam, pilot tells his story of pursuit and rescue; ed. by B. Wise. por Life 59:24-5 Ag 6 '65
ILIAD. See Homer
ILL. See Sick, The
ILLEGITIMACY
Abortion and the sick mind. America 113:37-8 Jl 10 '65
Confucius' outcasts; South Korea. Time 86:43 D 10 '65
Other face of the problem: the unmarried teen father. J. Beck. il Todays Health 43:28-31+ F '65
Rights of the illegitimate; case of child conceived during the rape of a hospitalized mental patient. Time 86:64 Jl 9 '65
See also
Mothers, Unmarried
ILLINOIS
See also
Booksellers and bookselling—Illinois
Hunting—Illinois
Libraries—Illinois

Politics and government
Cleaning up the Illinois legislature; a follow-up report. P. Simon. Harper 231:125 S '65
Oiling the works; plot to bribe Illinois legislators. Newsweek 66:22+ Jl 5 '65
Shadow governor. Newsweek 65:28 Je 21 '65

Religious institutions and affairs
News of the Christian world (cont) Christian Cent 82:157-8 F 3 '65
ILLINOIS library association
Librarians, author, trustee cited in Illinois LA awards; 69th annual conference. Library J 90:4936 N 15 '65
ILLINOIS producers livestock association
New way to bargain on livestock prices. Farm J 89:64J F '65
ILLINOIS. University, Urbana
Contemporary arts at the University of Illinois; Festival of contemporary arts. P. Yates. il Hi Fi 15:128-9 Je '65
Design of residence hall units; symposium. il Arch Rec 138:114-18 Ag '65
Outlook: worse next fall; interview. U S News 58:58-60 F 1 '65

Chicago campus
By the cloverleaf; new Chicago commuter campus. il Time 87:54-5+ Ja 7 '66
Campus City, Chicago; University of Illinois' new urban campus. il Arch Forum 123:21-45 S '65
Chapter I for Chicago circle. F. G. Poole. il Library J 90:5198-200 D 1 '65
Chicago's newest showcase: U. of Illinois bookstore. E. B. Vest. il Pub W 189:32-5 Ja 3 '66
Chicago's Oxford on the rocks: new break for city youngsters. A. Schiller. il Harper 230:87-90+ My '65
City campus 1965; new $160 million campus. il Newsweek 65:58 Mr 8 '65
ILLITE
Potassium content of illite. C. E. Weaver. bibliog il Science 147:603-5 F 5 '65

ILLITERACY
Campaign for world literacy; Second committee adopted resolution. UN Mo Chron 2:96-7 D '65
For want of a word. R. L. Tobin. Sat R 48:65-6 F 13 '65
Grapes of wrath in the vineyard of illiteracy. R. F. Lucid. ALA Bul 59:525-7 Je '65
Iran's education corps and illiteracy. S. Bella. Sch & Soc 93:156-7 Mr 6 '65
Library and adult illiteracy; symposium. bibliog il Wilson Lib Bul 40:40-86+ S '65
Petronillo learns to write his name; Guatemala's literacy campaign. A. Howard. il N Y Times Mag p26-7+ F 7 '65
Rise in world illiteracy. Sch & Soc 93:492+ D 25 '65
Shah of Iran appeals to UN to fight illiteracy. Sch & Soc 93:470+ D 11 '65
Toward literacy in the United States; address, April 1965. M. C. Neff. Wilson Lib Bul 39:885-6+ Je '65
Toward world literacy; address, April 1965. L. Carnovsky. bibliog il Wilson Lib Bul 39:887-95 Je '65
Uncomprehending 40 per cent; new UNESCO project. il Time 86:67-8 N 19 '65
When jurors cannot read or write; D'Andrea case before all-Negro jury. U S News 59:12 D 6 '65
World congress on literacy appeals to UN for help. Pub W 188:34-5 N 1 '65
World congress spurs fight against illiteracy; first World congress of ministers of education on the eradication of illiteracy. UNESCO Courier 18:30-1 N '65

ILLNESS. See Sickness

ILLUMINATED manuscripts. See Illumination of books and manuscripts

ILLUMINATION of books and manuscripts
Ancient art of illumination. il Design 66:17-20 Ap '65
Base and noble metals in illumination. S. Alexander. il Natur Hist 74:30-9 bibliog (p66) D '65

ILLUSION of reality. See Trompe-l'oeil

ILLUSIONS, Optical. See Optical illusions

ILLUSIONS and hallucinations
Do-it-yourself hallucinations. il Sci Digest 57:41-3 My '65

ILLUSTRATED books
Christmas art books. H. Rosenberg. Vogue 146:148-50 D '65
Christmas avalanche; guide to the best illustrated books. il Time 86:116+ D 10 '65
Christmas on the coffee table. F. Getlein. New Repub 153:33-5 D 18 '65
Illustrated books, 1945-65 exhibited at Grolier club. P. A. Bennett. Pub W 189:104-5 Ja 17 '66

ILLUSTRATION of books and periodicals
Adrienne Adams; illustrator of children's books. D. Waugh. il Am Artist 29:54-9+ N '65
Antic disposition: a young British illustrator interviews himself; childrens literature. B. Wildsmith. il Library J 90:5035-8 N 15 '65
Artist at work (cont) il Horn Bk 41:152-7, 408-12, 651-4 Ap, Ag, D '65
Artists and books surveyed at panel discussion and exhibition; summary of panel discussion, with list of award winners. il Pub W 188:86-8+ N 8 '65
Before the act; ALA pre-conference: Cranbrook colloquium, art of children's book illustration. H. B. Quimby. il Library J 90:3694-5 S 15 '65
Children's book illustrators honor an art director. il Pub W 187:90-1 F 22 '65
How to get greater value from stock photographers. G. T. Resch. il Pub W 188:82+ Ag 9 '65
Illustrating a book in lithography; reprint. L. Ward. Am Artist 29:21+ N '65
Illustrations of Raymond F. Houlihan. F. Whitaker. il Am Artist 29:47-53+ Mr '65
Illustrations of Robert Quackenbush. J. H. Michel. il Am Artist 29:28-33+ Ap '65
Israeli illustrator, teacher discusses bookmaking; interview. J. Stern. il Pub W 188:104-5 S 6 '65
Line drawings of Thoreau MacDonald. N. Kent. il Am Artist 29:34-41+ D '65
Lots of pictures, and a few words, about the magazine. il Esquire 63:98-105 My '65
On-the-spot picture sources. il Pub W 188:104-5 N 8 '65
Robert Abbett, illustrator. F. Whitaker. il Am Artist 29:48-53+ Je '65
Roy Lindstrom, artist & art director. F. Johnson. il Am Artist 29:50-5+ D '65

Subliminal approach to illustration. L. H. Klaschik. il Design 67:6-11 N '65
Time-Life uses effective 3-D models. il Pub W 188:110-13 N 8 '65
See also
Picture books for children

ILLUSTRATORS
Artist at work (cont) il Horn Bk 41:152-7, 408-12, 651-4 Ap, Ag, D '65
Illustrating a book in lithography; reprint. L. Ward. Am Artist 29:21+ N '65
See also
Beardsley, A.
Houlihan, R. F.
Society of illustrators

I'M not going to ask you again; story. See Tyler, A.

IMAGES of loss; story. See McCord, J.

IMAGINARY cities. See Geographical myths

IMAGINARY countries. See Geographical myths

IMAGINATION
Automation and imagination. J. Hawkes. Harper 231:92-4+ O '65
Imagination and the child; symposium. bibliog il Wilson Lib Bul 40:332-58 D '65
What makes a company creative; symposium. Nations Bsns 53:76-9 Je '65
Where did you get that idea? E. H. Friermood. Horn Bk 41:655-61 D '65
See also
Creation (literary, artistic, etc)
Fantasy

IMBECILS. See Mentally handicapped

IMHOTEP
Tomb of the scientist-god. il Sci Digest 57:21 Mr '65

IMIPRAMINE
Pills for depression more effective on men. Sci N L 87:242 Ap 17 '65

IMLAY, Florence
How to make and use candied grapefruit peel. Farm J 89:97 D '65

IMMIGRANTS in Great Britain
See also
Great Britain—Foreign population

IMMIGRANTS in Israel
How Israel solves its cultural lag. E. B. Thompson. il Ebony 21:121-6+ N '65
Settling in Israel? R. Sanders. Commentary 40:37-44 Ag; Discussion. 40:24+ N '65

IMMIGRANTS in Switzerland
Everybody go home! Time 85:28+ F 19 '65

IMMIGRANTS in the United States
Nondiscrimination policy. Newsweek 66:30+ O 4 '65
Uprootedness: a Jamaican Negro. J. Anderson. Commentary 40:63-7 Ag '65
See also
Deportation
also Hungarians in the United States, and similar headings

IMMIGRATION and emigration

Law
See Immigration and emigration law

Australia
Manning the outpost. il Time 86:30 Jl 9 '65
Snatch at Sydney. Time 86:28 Ag 13 '65

Brazil
See also
Brazil—Colonization

Europe, Western
Mass migration, then and now; nineteenth-century America and twentieth century Europe. C. P. Kindleberger. For Affairs 43:647-58 Jl '65

Great Britain
Admitting foreigners: Britain closes down, U.S. acts to open up. il U S News 59:10 Ag 16 '65
British melting pot is coming to a boil; colored immigrants. il Bsns W p88-90+ F 13 '65
British say they aren't prejudiced. C. E. Lincoln. il N Y Times Mag p64-5+ N 14 '65
Color in England. J. B. Gerald. Commonweal 83:304-6 D 10 '65
Klan comes to Britain; what it's all about. il U S News 59:30-1 Jl 5 '65
Question of original sin; Britain and color discrimination. il Time 86:27 Ag 13 '65
Race relations in Britain. P. Mason. Christian Cent 82:738-41 Je 9 '65
Reporter at large. C. Trillin. New Yorker 41:115-16+ D 4 '65
See also
Great Britain—Foreign population

IMMIGRATION and emigration—*Continued*

Israel

Prejudice in Israel; Jews from north Africa and Asia. Oriental Jews. J. R. Moskin. il Look 29:67+ O 5 '65

United States

Admitting foreigners: Britain closes down, U.S. acts to open up. il U S News 59:10 Ag 16 '65

Equitable immigration. Sci Am 213:48 N '65

Ev's curve ball. il Time 86:17 S 10 '65

Foreign policy aspects of proposals to revise immigration law; statement, February 24, 1965. D. Rusk. Dept State Bul 52:384-7 Mr 15 '65

Historic homage; Senate adopts sweeping reform bill. il Time 86:27-8 O 1 '65

Hope for a new type of immigrant. Life 58:4 Mr 12 '65

How much of a limit on immigration? il U S News 59:8 S 6 '65

Immigration or jobs? address, June 23, 1965. M. M. Jones. Vital Speeches 31:629-32 Ag 1 '65

Immigration policy; policy toward potential immigrants from Latin America. Commonweal 82:713-14 O 1 '65

Immigration quotas established for Malta and Zambia; proclamation, February 5, 1965. L. B. Johnson. Dept State Bul 52: 338 Mr 8 '65

Immigration reform? Commonweal 82:340-1 Je 4 '65

Lifting the quota. Time 86:17A Ag 13 '65

Limiting immigration from the western hemisphere; pro and con discussion. Sr Schol 87:14-15 O 21 '65

More immigration? E. Van Den Haag. il Nat R 17:821-2+ S 21 '65; Discussion. 17:956+ N 2 '65

New immigration policy. A. Kopkind. New Repub 152:15-16 F 27 '65

New mix for America's melting pot. il U S News 59:55-7 O 11 '65

Problems of immigration; letter. A. P. Schwartz. New Repub 152:36-8 Mr 6 '65

Reform of our basic immigration law; address, April 19, 1965. D. Rusk. Dept State Bul 52:806-9 My 24 '65

Refugee provisions of administration's proposals to revise immigration law; statement, March 3, 1965. A. P. Schwartz. il Dept State Bul 52:471-5 Mr 29 '65

This month's feature: Congress and U.S. immigration policy. Cong Digest 44:131-41+ My '65

U.S. to take people barred by Britain? immigrants from West Indies. il U S News 59:31 Jl 5 '65

Why Castro exports Cubans. G. Samuels. il N Y Times Mag p30-1+ N 7 '65

See also

Ellis Island

Immigrants in the United States

IMMIGRATION and emigration law

Amending the Immigration and nationality act; message, January 13, 1965. L. B. Johnson. Dept State Bul 52:146-7 F 1 '65

Americanizing our immigration laws. O. Handlin. il Holiday 39:8+ Ja '66

Equitable immigration. Sci Am 213:48 N '65

Foreign policy aspects of proposals to revise immigration law; statement, February 24, 1965. D. Rusk. Dept State Bul 52:384-7 Mr 15 '65

Historic homage; Senate adopts sweeping reform bill. il Time 86:27-8 O 1 '65

In the Statue of Liberty's shadow; new bill signed into law. H. Hamilton. America 113: 431 O 16 '65

Limiting immigration from the western hemisphere; pro and con discussion. Sr Schol 87:14-15 O 21 '65

More immigration? E. Van Den Haag. il Nat R 17:821-2+ S 21 '65; Discussion. 17:956+ N 2 '65

New immigrants. New Repub 153:7 S 25 '65

New mix for America's melting pot. il U S News 59:55-7 O 11 '65

Presbyterians challenge immigration policy; laws riddled with racial discrimination. Christian Cent 82:956 Ag 4 '65

President signs immigration bill; offers asylum to Cubans; remarks, October 3, 1965. L. B. Johnson. Dept State Bul 53:661-3 O 25 '65

Quota system altered. Sr Schol 87:19 O 21 '65

Reform of our basic immigration law; address, April 19, 1965. D. Rusk. Dept State Bul 52:806-9 My 24 '65

Refugee provisions of administration's proposals to revise immigration law; statement, March 3, 1965. A. P. Schwartz. il Dept State Bul 52:471-5 Mr 29 '65

This month's feature: Congress and U.S. immigration policy. Cong Digest 44:131-41+ My '65

IMMORAL literature and pictures

Against pornography. G. P. Elliott. Harper 230:51-60 Mr '65; Discussion. 230:6+ My '65

Anti-pornographers plan court appearances. Pub W 188:35-6 N 8 '65

Banned in Boston; concerning cases brought by public prosecutors. J. Ciardi. Sat R 48: 14 Mr 6 '65

Booksellers, a summer of uncertainty; New York state censorship legislation. R. H. Smith. Pub W 188:45 Ag 2 '65

Censorship: fanatics and fallacies. N. Mark; E. Gertz. il Nation 201:5-10 Jl 5 '65

Clerical error; creator of Cindy. Newsweek 65:32-3 Ap 12 '65

Damning case against pornography. O. K. Armstrong. Read Digest 87:131-4 D '65

Fight against the smut peddlers; newsstand and mail-order pornography. O. K. Armstrong. Read Digest 87:177-8+ S '65

How can we protect our children from obscenity? B. Spock. Redbook 124:18+ Ap '65

Literature and obscenity. R. Tracy. Christian Cent 82:769-72 Je 16 '65; Discussion. 82:993 Ag 11 '65

Manner of speaking; Hubert Selby's gutter-to sewer chronicle. J. Ciardi. Sat R 48:12 Ap 3 '65

Manner of speaking; the book banners again (and again and again); trial of W. Burroughs's Naked lunch, Judge E. A. Hudson presiding. J. Ciardi. Sat R 48:21 Ag 28 '65

Massachusetts finds Fanny Hill obscene. Pub W 187:37-8 My 3 '65

Nation of peeping toms; discussion. America 112:34, 179 Ja 9, F 6 '65

New pornography; Time essay. Time 85:28-9 Ap 16 '65

N.Y. anti-obscenity laws passed to protect minors. Pub W 188:181 Jl 12 '65

Operation Yorkville: New York interdenominational project to combat traffic. Nat R 17:1146+ D 14 '65

Showdown coming on the billion-dollar smut industry. il U S News 59:38+ D 6 '65

Smut hunters; new jurisprudery; activities of Citizens for decent literature, inc. H. Junker. il Nation 201:358-60 N 15 '65

Wayward reader. P. S. Beagle. Holiday 37: 35-8 Je '65

See also

Censorship

Literature and morals

Obscenity (law)

Sex in literature

IMMORALITY. See Ethics

IMMORTALITY

Frozen Christian; cryogenic interment. R. C. W. Ettinger. Christian Cent 82:1313-15 O 27 '65; Reply. L. J. Putnam. 82:1550+ D 15 '65

New hopes for the dead. R. C. W. Ettinger; A. Cutler. il Esquire 63:63-7+ My '65

See also

Death

IMMUNITIES and privileges. See Privileges and immunities

IMMUNITY

Genetic control in guinea pigs of immune response to conjugates of haptens and poly-L-lysine. B. B. Levine and B. Benacerraf. bibliog il Science 147:517-18 Ja 29 '65

Immunization. Consumer Rep 30:94-8 F '65

Immunology may hold clue to cancer control. Sci N L 87:200 Mr 27 '65

Let's end these unnecessary deaths. J. D. Ratcliff. il Read Digest 87:124-8 S '65

What immunity to disease means to you. A. Limax. Todays Health 43:54-5+ N '65

See also

Antigens and antibodies

Complements (immunity)

Vaccination

Vaccines

IMMUNOGLOBULINS. See Serum globulins

IMPERATO, Pascal James

Specialist finds many tropical diseases on Brooklyn waterfront. il por Todays Health 43:71 Ag '65

IMPERIAL moths

Life cycle of seclusion. R. J. Donahue. il Natur Hist 74:50-1 My '65

IMPERIALISM

Can Pax Americana succeed? D. F. Fleming. Ann Am Acad 360:127-38 Jl '65

Cheer for American imperialism. H. Fairlie. il N Y Times Mag p7+ Jl 11 '65

IMPERIALISM—*Continued*
First anti-imperialists; excerpt from Proud tower; a portrait of the world before the war, 1890-1914. B. W. Tuchman. Nation 201:77-82 S 20 '65
Speaking out; long live imperialism. J. Morris. Sat Eve Post 238:10+ Jl 3 '65
See also
Colonies
IMPERIALS, Crown. See Crown imperials
IMPORT quotas
Bottles over the border; new United States restrictions on liquor imports. il Newsweek 66:36 O 4 '65
Limits terminated on imports of unmanufactured lead and zinc; statement, October 22, 1965, with proclamation. L. B. Johnson. Dept State Bul 53:795-7 N 15 '65
Oilmen jam hearings to speak up on quotas. Bsns W p 136 Mr 20 '65
IMPORTATION of books. See Books—Importation
IMPORTS. See Commerce; *also* subhead Commerce under names of countries, e.g. United States—Commerce
IMPOSSIBLE years; drama. See Fisher, B. and Marx, A.
IMPOSTERS and imposture
Doctors' dilemma; Thomas Edison Miyawaki. il Time 87:60 Ja 7 '66
Dream department; Brooklyn mechanic poses as CIA agent. Newsweek 65:27-8 Ap 26 '65
Letter from the Berkeley underground. M. Miller. Esquire 64:85-7+ S '65
Magnificent obsession of Colonel Brown. J. Phelan. il Sat Eve Post 238:98-101 My 8 '65
See also
Quacks and quackery
IMPREGNATION, Artificial. See Artificial insemination, Human
IMPRESSIONISM (art)
Art galleries; exhibition: Olympia's progeny at the Wildenstein. R. M. Coates. New Yorker 41:163-5 N 13 '65
Camille Pissarro: the unassuming eye. L. Nochlin. il Art N 64:24-7+ Ap '65
Conscience of impressionism; Pissarro's art. M. Kozloff. Nation 200:430-1 Ap 19 '65
Degas' American cousins; New Orleans acquisition. il Life 59:52-5+ Jl 2 '65
Muley the pragmatist: F. C. Hassam. il Time 86:60-1+ S 3 '65
Points in color; work of ninth grade students. E. M. Bollo. il Sch Arts 64:15-17 Mr '65
That was the era that was. il N Y Times Mag p 156-7 O 24 '65
Three new, cool, bright imagists; exhibition at Oberlin, Ohio. E. H. Johnson. il Art N 64:42-4+ Sum '65
IMPRESSIONISM (music)
Sound of infinity. Newsweek 66:94+ N 22 '65
IMPRIMATUR. See Catholic church—Discipline
IMPRINTING (animals) See Animals—Habits and behavior
IN-flight movies. See Airlines—Passenger service
IN love with a beautiful girl; story. See Jhabvala, R. P.
IN-service librarian education. See Librarians—Education in service
IN-service teacher education. See Teachers—Education in service
IN service training of employees. See Employees—Training
IN the case of J. Robert Oppenheimer; drama. See Kipphardt, H.
IN the deep sea; story. See Epstein, S.
IN the face of life; story. See Boyd, C.
IN the place of angels; story. See Epstein, S.
IN transit; story. See Gallant, M.
INADMISSIBLE evidence; drama. See Osborne, J.
INAUGURATIONS
Great day. New Yorker 40:24-5 Ja 30 '65
Great society bows in; inauguration of L. B. Johnson. il Ebony 20:66-8+ Ap '65
Inauguration: J. V. Lindsay as Mayor of New York city. New Yorker 41:20-3 Ja 8 '66
It was a warm day in Washington. J. N. Eller. America 112:185 F 6 '65
It was LBJ's great day. il U S News 58:37-40 F 1 '65
INBAU, Fred E.
Crime and the law: most of the problem comes back to the Supreme court; interview. U S News 58:40-1 Mr 22 '65
Excerpt from testimony, October 23, 1963. Cong Digest 44:246+ O '65
Lawlessness galore: address, August 26, 1965. Vital Speeches 32:95-6 N 15 '65; Excerpt. U S News 59:82 S 13 '65

INBOARD motors. See Gas and oil engines, Inboard
INBOARD-outboards. See Marine engines
INCARNATION
Story that begins and ends in joy. America 113:771 D 18 '65
See also
Jesus Christ
INCAS
See also
Machu Picchu, Peru
INCENDIARISM. See Arson
INCENTIVES in industry
Air force to charge interference by GAO as lingering feud erupts. Aviation W 82:17 My 24 '65
Incentive basis set for NAA Apollo work. Aviation W 83:79 N 29 '65
Low fees may undermine incentive goal; cost plus incentive fee. B. Backe; reply. G. C. Bannerman. Aviation W 82:67-8 Mr 1 '65
Test your leadership skill. C. A. Cerami. Nations Bsns 53:74-5 Ap '65
Titan 3 program involves five major incentive fee contracts. W. H. Gregory. il Aviation W 83:42-3+ Jl 5 '65
INCINERATORS. See Refuse incinerators
INCOME
Measure of personal income (title varies) tables. See issues of Business week
Poor grow fewer; Census bureau reports. Bsns W p64 Jl 17 '65
Psychology of a guaranteed income; excerpt from Guaranteed income: next step in economic evolution? E. Fromm. Nation 201: 439-42 D 6 '65
Trends in average annual earnings and income. A. Sackley. il Mo Labor R 88:1302-6 N '65
See also
Consumption (economics)
Gross national product
Retirement income
Royalties
Salaries
INCOME tax
Subject: tax time; comp. by E. F. Murphy. N Y Times Mag p49 Ap 4 '65

Capital gains tax

Books and the tax laws; Rules for inventors to get capital gains treatment. H. F. Pilpel. Pub W 189:39-40 Ja 3 '66
Investment nobody knows about. T. J. Murray. il Duns R 85:40-3+ Ap '65
Tax rules you should know before you sell property. F. Bailey, jr. Suc Farm 63:34+ F '65
Taxpayer got nowhere with his capital gains plea; case of Ruth McKenney. Pub W 187: 52-3 Je 28 '65
Your investments and taxes: what to do before year-end. il U S News 59:111-14 N 15 '65

Collection

See Withholding tax

Deductions

Drive for simpler tax laws. il U S News 59:107-8 D 13 '65
Giving away 10.6 billion dollars; tax-deductible gifts. U S News 59:114 O 18 '65
Here are ways to save on your 1964 taxes. il U S News 58:112-14 F 22 '65
How to be tax-wise on livestock. B. Brantley. Suc Farm 63:40-1+ N '65
Maybe it's deductible: entertainment expenditure. B. Mills. Motor B 115:50+ Mr '65
Next: a tax break for lower incomes? il U S News 58:101-3 Ap 19 '65
Personal business. Bsns W p 137-8 Mr 6; p 179-80 S 25 '65
Personal business; deductible charities. Bsns W p 133 Jl 17 '65
Save dollars by being tax-wise on deductions. N. E. Harl. Suc Farm 64:28+ Ja '66
Tax help for parents. R. Moley. Newsweek 66:132 O 18 '65
Tax proposal to help states. U S News 59: 117-18 N 1 '65
Tax row revives price-fixing case. Bsns W p76 F 27 '65
Ten common tax puzzlers. il Changing T 19:41-2 D '65
What records should you keep for your income tax? Bet Hom & Gard 44:6+ Ja '66
What you can do now to save 1965 tax dollars. Farm J 89:66A+ D '65
When tax agent asks for more: many fight, and win; IRS appeals division. il U S News 58:99-100 Mr 15 '65

INCOME tax—Deductions—*Continued*
Will incorporation reduce taxes? il Suc Farm 63:90 Ap '65
Your income tax: check those exemptions. il Changing T 19:19-21 Mr '65
Your income tax: what you can deduct. il Changing T 19:15-18 F '65
Your 1965 tax; with chart. U S News 58:95 Mr 1 '65
    See also
Depletion allowances
Expense accounts (business)
Tax planning

Estimates
Personal business; estimated income tax. Bsns W p 145 Ap 3 '65

Forms
    See Tax forms

Returns
    See Tax returns

Canada
Canadians get their taxes cut. Bsns W p27 My 1 '65

United States
Computed & uncomputed bonus; $1.6 billion more received than estimated. Time 86:74 Jl 2 '65
How tax cut is melting away. il U S News 59:87-8 Ag 16 '65
How to be rich without paying taxes. A. Gore. il N Y Times Mag p28-9+ Ap 11 '65
Income tax that pays the poor; subsidies to those too poor to pay taxes. il Bsns W p 105-6 N 13 '65
New big rich, a postscript. S. Alsop. Sat Eve Post 238:16 Jl 31 '65
Personal business; potential pitfalls in trusts. Bsns W p 117 Ja 30 '65
Postmortem on April 15. il Sat Eve Post 238:96 My 22 '65
Profiles. J. Brooks. il New Yorker 41:52-4+ Ap 3; 51-2+ Ap 10 '65
Still more ideas for cutting taxes; negative tax to people on low incomes. U S News 59:93-6 Jl 12 '65
What income is tax-free? il Changing T 19: 13-15 Ap '65
Your 1965 guide to federal income taxes. N. Kuehnl and G. Bush. il Bet Hom & Gard 43:7-8+ F '65

INCOMPARABLE chapeau; story. See Sherris. R.

INCORPORATED farms. See Farms, Incorporated

INCREASE of population. See Population, Increase of

INCURABLES
Brutal truth. M. M. Shideler. Christian Cent 82:1375-8 N 10 '65

INDECENT exposure
Legal libertarianism; bare-breasted waitresses declared not guilty. il Time 85:70+ My 28 '65
Topless triumph; topless-bathing-suit wearer acquitted in French court. Time 85:73 Mr 12 '65

INDEPENDENCE, Political. See Autonomy

INDEPENDENT moving picture producers. See Moving picture production and direction

INDEPENDENT regulatory commissions
Abuse of power. D. Lawrence. U S News 58:116 My 3 '65; Same abr. with title Erosion of freedom. Read Digest 87:143-4 Jl '65
Ordeal by law; regulatory agencies. Duns R 85:37 Je '65
Renascent role of the regulatory agencies. J. F. Olesky. Duns R 85:pt2 96-7+ Je '65
Watchdog agencies soften the bark; shift in viewpoint among federal regulators. il Bsns W p 132+ O 30 '65

INDEPENDENT television authority. See Television broadcasting—Great Britain

INDEX librorum prohibitorum
French authors and Roman indexers. H. M. Watson. America 114:79-83 Ja 15 '66
Morality of Catholic censorship. B. A. Curtis. Christian Cent 82:772-5 Je 16 '65

INDEX numbers
Coinage, commodities, and Count Carli. A. Sackley. il Mo Labor R 88:817-21 Jl '65

INDEXES
Department of amplification; setting of lines in index of Bartlett's familiar quotations to resemble poetry. M. Hartman. New Yorker 40:88+ Ja 30 '65

Why catalog books? W. Brahm. Library J 90: 2510-11 Je 1 '65
    See also
Mental health book review index
Public affairs information service
Social sciences and humanities index

INDIA
Atlantic report. Atlan 215:14+ My '65
Pride & reality. il Time 86:18-26B Ag 13 '65
    See also
Agriculture—India
Air travel—India
Architecture—India
Arts and crafts—India
Astronomical observatories—India
Atomic power—India
Benares
Book industries and trade—India
Calcutta
Christmas—India
Cutch, Rann of
Economic assistance in India
Food supply—India
Hunting—India
Irrigation—India
Kashmir
Kerala
New Delhi
Periodicals—India
Research—India
Taxation—India

Antiquities
    See also
Indus Valley—Antiquities

Boundaries
Himalayas; disputed border between India and Tibet. Life 58:68 My 28 '65
Salt in the wounds; dispute over Great Rann of Kutch. Newsweek 65:40 Ap 26 '65

Cabinet
Tough times for T.T.K; Finance minister leaves. Time 87:40 Ja 14 '66

Description and travel
Taj, the Raj, and I. S. Karnow. il Sat R 48: 56+ S 18 '65
Travel's picture portfolio. Travel 124:50-5 Jl '65
Two descriptions of the elephant. S. Rama Rau. Reporter 33:40+ S 9 '65
Well traveled camera. H. Keppler. il Mod Phot 29:52 Jl; 38+ Ag; 15 S '65

Economic conditions
Mountain of troubles piles up for India. il U S News 59:105-6 N 22 '65
Strong medicine for India. L. Hazard. Atlan 216:43-8 D '65

Economic policy
Has India an economic future? C. E. Lindblom. For Affairs 44:239-52 Ja '66
India's crisis; Community development program. S. Menefee and A. Menefee. New Repub 153:6-7 Ag 7 '65
India's lonely road. H. C. Wallich. Newsweek 65:80 Ap 5 '65
Undeclared war; businessmen attack government's policy. il Newsweek 65:68+ Ap 5 '65

Foreign relations
First report from India; reaction to ceasefire. E. Taylor. Reporter 33:14+ O 7 '65
Shastri-Pearson talks. Nation 200:686 Je 28 '65
    See also
    Pakistan
Cutch, Rann of
Kashmir
    Russia
Neutral attitude. il Time 85:38 My 28 '65

Hindu-Muslim relations
Kashmir: a religious war; Muslim and Hindu intolerance. J. F. Drane. Cath World 202: 212-16 Ja '66
Why Hindu and Moslem speak hate. K. Singh. il N Y Times Mag p27-9+ S 19 '65

History
Black hole of Calcutta. by N. Barber. Review Time 87:86 Ja 21 '66

Languages
Communications problem. Newsweek 65:38 F 8 '65
Crisis in south India; Hindi made the official language of Indian union. P. G. Altbach. Christian Cent 82:403-4 Mr 31 '65
Force of words; non-Hindi ministers demand that English be recognized as an official language. Time 85:35 F 19 '65

INDIA—Languages—*Continued*
Hindi imposition. Time 85:34+ F 5 '65
India's linguistic dilemma. S. Rajan. il Reporter 32:31-2 My 6 '65
Retreat to English. Time 85:31 Mr 5 '65
War of tongues; riots over adoption of Hindi as official language. il Newsweek 65:42 Mr 1 '65

Nationalism

First report from India; reaction to ceasefire. E. Taylor. Reporter 33:14+ O 7 '65

Politics and government

Bangalore torpedo. il Time 86:34 Ag 6 '65
India: downhill toward disaster. S. Karnow. il Sat Eve Post 238:78-83 Je 5 '65
India looks for a new leader; death of Prime Minister Shastri. Bsns W p27 Ja 15 '66
India without Nehru. N. D. Palmer. Cur Hist 48:69-74 F '65
India's civil war. G. Woodcock. Commonweal 82:352-5 Je 4 '65
Nehru's *munshi* comes out of Nehru's shadow. J. A. Lukas. il N Y Times Mag p54-5+ N 28 '65
Passing through fire. Time 86:34 S 3 '65
Politicians, bureaucrats, and development in India. W. Wilcox. bibliog f Ann Am Acad 358:114-22 Mr '65
Process of change. il Time 87:22-5 Ja 21 '66
Shade of the banyan; Shastri's first year in office. Newsweek 65:55 My 17 '65
Shastri: hard to follow, too. Life 60:4 Ja 21 '66
Strong medicine for India. L. Hazard. Atlan 216:43-8 D '65
Under a caretaker; can India keep going? U S News 60:42 Ja 24 '66
War in a windblown waste called the Rann of Kutch. il Life 58:30-6 Je 11 '65
Who next? il Newsweek 67:38-9 Ja 24 '66
See also
Communism—India
Elections—India
India—Cabinet
India—Hindu-Muslim relations
Political parties—India

Population

See also
Birth control—India
Birth rate—India

Religious institutions and affairs

People of God. E. J. Martin. America 113: 186-8 Ag 21 '65
See also
Christians in India
Hinduism
India—Hindu-Moslem relations

Social conditions

Angry young Indian; interview, ed. by S. Oberbeck. V. S. Naipaul. Newsweek 65: 103-103A+ Ap 19 '65
Has India an economic future? C. E. Lindblom. For Affairs 44:239-52 Ja '66
India's crisis; Community development program. S. Menefee and A. Menefee. New Repub 153:6-7 Ag 7 '65
They are staring at me; excerpt from Area of darkness. V. S. Naipaul. il Sat Eve Post 238:82-4 Ap 10 '65
Two descriptions of the elephant. E. Rama Rau. Reporter 33:40+ S 9 '65
Why Go Matha is loved. R. K. Narayan. il N Y Times Mag p 12-13+ My 30 '65
See also
Untouchables

Social life and customs

Families are different in India. S. Rama Rau. Read Digest 87:167-8+ Ag '65
See also
Untouchables

INDIA and the United States
India is centuries away; Wisconsin undergraduate year in India; a student recalls. M. C. Vander Wal. il Sat R 48:51-2+ Ag 21 '65

INDIA-Pakistan dispute. See Cutch, Rann of; Kashmir

INDIAN affairs, Bureau of. See United States —Indian affairs, Bureau of

INDIAN arrow points. See Arrowheads

INDIAN arts and crafts. See Indians of North America—Industries

INDIAN baskets. See Baskets

INDIAN boy without a name; drama. See Vahl, R.

INDIAN-Chinese border dispute, 1957-. See Sino-Indian border dispute, 1957-

INDIAN claims commission. See United States —Indian claims commission

INDIAN cookery (East Indian) See Cookery, Indian (East Indian)

INDIAN costumes. See Indians of North America—Costume and adornment

INDIAN dancing (East Indian) See Dancing, Indian (East Indian)

INDIAN HEAD mills, incorporated
Perilous quest for acquisitions. J. B. Weiner. il Duns R 86:32-5+ Jl '65

INDIAN international film festival. See Moving picture festivals

INDIAN OCEAN
Decision east of Suez. C. J. Creekmore. il Nat R 17:457-9 Je 1 '65
Igneous rocks of the Indian Ocean floor. C. G. Engel and others. bibliog il Science 150: 605-10 O 29 '65
Indian Ocean floor may have sunk a mile. Sci N L 88:308 N 13 '65
See also
Diego Garcia (atoll)
International Indian Ocean expedition
Seychelles (islands)

INDIAN-Pakistan dispute. See Cutch, Rann of; Kashmir

INDIAN poetry. See Indians of North America —Poetry

INDIAN reservations. See Indians of North America—Reservations

INDIAN rice. See Wild rice

INDIAN schools. See Indians of North America —Education

INDIAN sculpture (East Indian) See Sculpture, Indian (East Indian)

INDIAN summer
Peripatetic reviewer; origin of the term. E. Weeks. Atlan 216:180+ N '65

INDIAN uprising; story. See Barthelme, D.

INDIAN women. See Indians of North America —Women

INDIANA, Robert
Second fame. N. Lyon. il Vogue 145:184-6 Mr 1 '65

INDIANA
See also
Booksellers and bookselling—Indiana
Fishing—Indiana

Parks and reserves

Indiana's state parks. F. M. Simison. il Travel 123:48-9 My '65

Race problems

Long, hot summer in Indiana; 1924. W. E. Wilson. il Am Heritage 16:56-64 Ag '65

Religious institutions and affairs

News of the Christian world (cont) Christian Cent 82:1042-3 Ag 25 '65

INDIANA. University, Bloomington
Bloomington; I. U. music school. Q. Eaton. il Opera N 30:26-30 Ja 8 '66
Crescendo on the campus; our new music centers; Indiana university's school of music. H. Pleasants. il Reporter 33:52-6 S 23 '65

INDIANAPOLIS

Art

Summer ceramics; workshop for all ages and vocations at the Herron art institute, Indianapolis. il Design 66:24-6 My '65

City planning

Most forgettable city. Reader's digest ever met. J. Bailey. il Arch Forum 123:56-7 S '65

Education

Allisonville shapes up; Knapp project school works toward ALA standards. D. L. Barnes. il Library J 90:942-4 F 15 '65

Music

Chipper new chip off the old Met; opening in Indianapolis. il Life 59:90-1 O 1 '65
Met goes west. il Newsweek 66:91-2 O 4 '65
Met national company; opera on the road. C. L. Osborne. il Hi Fi 15:199+ N '65

Newspapers

Death of a newspaper; Indianapolis times. A. Randall. New Repub 153:29 O 30 '65
Not well enough; Scripps-Howard kills Indianapolis times. il Time 86:86 O 22 '65
Shade of difference; death of Indianapolis times. il Newsweek 66:96 O 25 '65

Sanitary affairs

TV plus grout; bargain repairs for leaking sewer systems. il Am City 80:112-13 Ap '65

INDIANAPOLIS automobile races. See Automobile racing

INDIANS

Art

See also
Indians of North America—Art
Indians of South America—Art
Petroglyphs

Origin

Radiocarbon age of a Nevada mummy. P. C. Orr and R. Berger. bibliog il Science 148: 1466-7 Je 11 '65

Pottery

See also
Pottery, Ecuadorian

INDIANS. Treatment of

Submerged dynamite; Latin American discrimination against Indians. il Newsweek 66:60-1 D 6 '65

INDIANS in art

Eyes in the wilderness; Catlin exhibition at the Smithsonian. F. Getlein. New Repub 153:24+ S 18 '65

INDIANS of Brazil. See Indians of South America—Brazil

INDIANS of Central America

Antiquities

See also
Mayas

Guatemala

Complex ancient society puzzles archaeologists; Tikal, Guatemala. Sci N L 87:280 My 1 '65
Tikal, Guatemala, and emergent Maya civilization. W. R. Coe. bibliog il Science 147: 1401-19 Mr 19 '65

Art

Master goldsmiths of Sitio Conte; excerpt from Sweat of the sun and tears of the moon. A. Emmerich. il Natur Hist 74:18-25 O '65
Thousand and one characters from the human comedy; pre-Columbian figurines. il UNESCO Courier 18:32-4 D '65

INDIANS of Mexico

Antiquities

Ancient U.S.-Mexico cultural bridge dated; dating of ceramic fragments. Sci N L 88: 233 O 9 '65
Mexican pyramids show signs of early writing. Sci N L 87:347 My 29 '65
New marvel; Mexico's pyramids. H. M. Kovar. il Sci Digest 57:62-8 Je '65
Pox pottery; earliest identified Mexican ceramic. C. F. Brush. bibliog il Science 149: 194-5 Jl 9 '65
Radiocarbon dates from a tomb in Mexico. P. T. Furst. bibliog il Science 147:612-13 F 5 '65
Supernatural forces; exhibition of Olmec art at Museum of primitive art, New York. il Newsweek 65:86 Mr 8 '65
See also
Mayas

Art

Masterpieces of ancient Mexico. il UNESCO Courier 18:30-1+ D '65
Pre-Columbian America. H. Lehmann. il UNESCO Courier 18:27-30 D '65

INDIANS of North America

Europo-American block; the truly native Americans. C. Miles. Hobbies 70:114+ Ag '65
First Americans; the evidence of mud. P. Colinvaux. Yale R 54:397-410 Mr '65
Goals of the group; last days of the Plains Indians. D. McNickle. Nation 201:167-8 S 27 '65
Indian in a cultural trap. L. E. Barry. America 112:482-4 Ap 10 '65; Discussion. 112:736-7 My 22 '65
Requests probe of Indian slaying; white racists in Maine. Christian Cent 83:37 Ja 12 '66
Three apostles to the Indians. P. W. Schmidtchen. il Hobbies 70:106+ Ag '65
Who's in the trap? T. E. Connolly. America 113:716 D 4 '65
See also
Chumash Indians
Dakota Indians
Menominee Indians
Navaho Indians
Nez Percé Indians
Pawnee Indians
Potawatomi Indians
Pueblo Indians
Seminole Indians

Agriculture

Corn, beans, squash. B. C. Kilvert, jr. il Flower Grower 52:32-4 Jl '65

Antiquities

Cradleboard hoods, not corsets. R. L. Carlson and G. J. Armelagos. bibliog il Science 149:204-5 Jl 9 '65
Indian relics. C. Miles. See issues of Hobbies

Arizona

Oldest canals in America; Snaketown, Ariz. il Sci Digest 58:38 Jl '65
Split-twig figurines from northern Arizona; new radiocarbon dates. R. C. Euler and A. P. Olson. bibliog il Science 148:368-9 Ap 16 '65
Travel far and near; the Kinishba Pueblo ruins. J. E. Ransom. il Natur Hist 74: 58-60+ My '65

Nevada

Radiocarbon age of a Nevada mummy. P. C. Orr and R. Berger. bibliog il Science 148: 1466-7 Je 11 '65

Architecture

See also
Pueblo architecture

Art

American Indian student; two educational programs. A. Thorpe; M. Libhart. il Craft Horiz 25:12-13+ Jl '65
Ladies launch a gallery; sculpture and paintings by American Indians. I. Moore. il Am For 71:22-5 Mr '65
Pablita Velarde; Pueblo painters. W. T. Le Viness. il Am Artist 29:40-5+ Ap '65

Boats

Science in action; winter bark, slow fire; excerpt from The woods and the sea. D. C. Lunt. Natur Hist 74:57-8 Ap '65

Claims

See also
United States—Indian claims commission

Costume and adornment

Clothes and the Indians. C. Miles. il Hobbies 70:115-17+ My '65

Culture

Culture areas among the Eskimos and Indians of North America. C. Miles. il Hobbies 70:112-14 S '65

Dwellings

See also
Pueblo architecture

Education

Institute of American Indian arts. Santa Fe. A. Thorpe. il Craft Horiz 25:12-13+ Jl '65
One generation to another; experiences teaching at a reservation school in 1915. H. H. Shoen. il Sat R 49:68-70+ Ja 15 '66
Schools for the first Americans. J. Crow. il Am Ed 1:15-22 O '65

Fiction

Light in the forest. C. Richter. il Read Digest 87:207-10 Ag '65

Government relations

Constitution & Mrs Colliflower; curb power of tribal courts. il Time 86:72 S 3 '65
See also
Indians of North America—Education
Indians of North America—Reservations
Indians of North America—Treaties
United States—Indian claims commission

Health and hygiene

Saturday night bath, Navajo style; sweat bath. F. W. Lewis. il Am For 71:6 Mr '65

History

What happened to the Indians. C. Miles. Hobbies 70:114 Ap '65

Hospitals

For healthier little Indians. il Todays Health 43:12-14 Jl '65

Industries

Corn husk bags of the Nez Perce. L. L. Quihuis. il Hobbies 70:114-16+ Mr '65
See also
Basket making

Languages

Indian singer helps in Catawba study. Sci N L 87:147 Mr 6 '65

INDIANS of North America—_Continued_

Legal status, laws, etc.

See Indians of North America—Government relations

Medicine

Indian birth control plant holds clues to glands. Sci N L 87:281 My 1 '65

Missions

Investiture controversy; F. Stadtmueller v. the pagans. America 113:88 Jl 24 '65

White father is heap bad medicine; Monsignor Stadtmuller thrown off the reservation at Isleta, N.Mex. il Life 59:40B Jl 16 '65

Poetry

Selected poems by students at the Institute of American Indian arts. Craft Horiz 25: 14-15 Jl '65

Reservations

American Indian: citizen in captivity; plight of Navajo Indians and a land sale case. B. W. Young. il Sat R 48:25-6 D 11 '65; Discussion. 49:21 Ja 1; 34 Ja 22 '66

Be my guest! Apache Indian reservation open to campers. B. Hackett. il Recreation 58: 115+ Mr '65

Off the reservation; Red Cliff ousts VISTA workers. il Newsweek 66:27-8 D 27 '65

Two new booklets promote tourism on Indian reservations. Am For 71:53 Jl '65

Transportation

See also
Indians of North America—Boats

Treaties

Most satisfactory council; excerpts from Nez Perce Indians and the opening of the Northwest. A. M. Josephy, jr. il Am Heritage 16:26-31+ O '65

Three and a half centuries of accord and conflict. il Sr Schol 86:5 Mr 18 '65

Wars

New England frontier: Puritans and Indians, 1620-1675, by A. T. Vaughan. Review
    Nation 202:22-3 Ja 3 '66. W. Eastlake

Women

Deadlier than the male. J. C. Ewers. il Am Heritage 16:10-13 Je '65

Arizona

Very unusual vacation; among the Pueblo ruins at Grasshopper. Ariz. L. B. Johnson. il McCalls 92:58+ S '65

New Mexico

New Mexico's missions. W. F. Heald. il Travel 123:36-41 F '65

INDIANS of Peru. See Indians of South America—Peru

INDIANS of South America

Antiquities

Ancient ills in clay; collection of Dr Abner I. Weisman. il Life 59:99-100 Jl 16 '65

Gold of the Indies; excerpts from introduction to Sweat of the sun and tears of the moon. A. Emmerich. Américas 17:23-9 My '65

Ecuador

Archaeological travels in the long ago; prehistoric contacts between Indians and natives of Asiatic islands. Hobbies 69:115 F '65

Transpacific contact in 3000 B.C; Jomonlike pottery unearthed at Valdivia. Ecuador. B. J. Meggers and C. Evans. il Sci Am 214:28-35 Ja '66

Peru

Early man in Peru. E. P. Lanning. il Sci Am 213:68-76 bibliog(p 127) O '65

Art

Figurines of the Carajá; photographs by K. Severin. Natur Hist 74:54-5 Ap '65

Treatment

See Indians, Treatment of

Brazil

Figurines of the Carajá; photographs by K. Severin. Natur Hist 74:54-5 Ap '65

Waurá: Brazilian Indians of the hidden Xingu. H. Schultz. il Nat Geog Mag 129:130-52 Ja '66

Colombia

Chocós of the Taparal. J. W. L. Robinson. il Natur Hist 74:46-51 Je '65

Peru

Gunboat diplomacy; gunboats of Peruvian navy with crews of physicians, dentists, and nurses treat jungle Indians. il Time 86:59 S 17 '65

Transformation of peasant societies; report on symposium on Vicos, Peru, project. A. R. Holmberg and H. F. Dobyns. Science 147:1062+ F 26 '65

INDIGESTION. See Dyspepsia

INDIUM telluride

Indium telluride (II'): transitory intermediate phase in the transformation InTe(II) to InTe(I) C. B. Sclar and others. bibliog il Science 147:1569-71 Mr 26 '65

INDIVIDUAL and society

Assumptions about the learning of political values. R. Sigel. bibliog f Ann Am Acad 361:1-9 S '65

Coming of age in America, by E. Z. Friedenberg. Review
    Nation 201:254-5 O 18 '65. M. V. Miller

False faces for the real me. L. Wainwright. Life 58:21 Ap 30 '65

INDIVIDUAL and state

America will be different because of you; address, May 6, 1965. A. N. Booth. Vital Speeches 31:537-9 Je 15 '65

And still our enemy. W. F. Rickenbacker. Nat R 17:1082-3 N 30 '65

Eisenhower on the choice Americans must make; interview. D. D. Eisenhower. il Nations Bsns 53:34-7+ O '65

INDIVIDUAL instruction

Individualized instruction; symposium, ed. by M. P. Archer. bibliog il Library J 90:1977-90 Ap 15 '65

INDIVIDUAL liberty. See Liberty

INDIVIDUALISM

Coming of age in America, by E. Z. Friedenberg. Review
    Nation 201:254-5 O 18 '65. M. V. Miller

Pillars of privacy. B. W. Overstreet. il PTA Mag 59:28-30 Ap '65
    See also
Conformity

INDIVIDUALITY

In each of us. M. J. Gadfield. il Sch Arts 65:35-7 S '65

Seven-year Cinderella. R. Peters. Seventeen 24:146+ F '65
    See also
Personality
Self

INDIVIDUALIZED instruction. See Individual instruction

INDOCHINA, FRENCH

History

Civil war, 1946-1954

Battle of Dienbienphu, by J. Roy. Review
    Commonweal 82:119-20 Ap 16 '65. W. C. McWilliams
    Nation 200:539-40 My 17 '65. D. Ford
    Newsweek 65:104+ Mr 15 '65

Civil war, 1946-1954—American participation

1956 warning on land war in Asia; excerpts from Soldier, ed. by H. H. Martin. M. B. Ridgway. il U S News 60:32-3 Ja 3 '66

Civil war, 1946-1954—Peace and mediation

    See also
Council of foreign ministers, Geneva, 1954

INDOCTRINATION

How sharp are the dragon's claws? People's liberation army. C. Johnson. il N Y Times Mag p22-3+ F 28 '65
    See also
Brainwashing

INDOKLON

Now, shock therapy by chemistry. F. R. Schreiber and M. Herman. il Sci Digest 58: 28-31 S '65

INDOLE

Indole compounds: isolation from pineal tissue. W. M. McIsaac and others. bibliog il Science 148:102-3 Ap 2 '65

INDOLEACETIC acid

Hormone-induced stabilization of soluble RNA in pea-stem tissue. F. E. Bendaña and A. W. Galston. bibliog il Science 150: 69-70 O 1 '65

Inhibitory oxidation products of indole-3-acetic acid; enzymic formation and detoxification by pea seedlings. C. C. Still and others. bibliog il Science 149:1249-51 S 10 '65

INDONESIA

Indonesia: a dissent. S. Lens; reply. S. Kelman. Commonweal 81:650 F 19 '65

Indonesia today. H. P. Van Dusen. Christian Cent 82:584-8, 616-17 My 5-12 '65

Indonesia: united against progress. B. R. Anderson. Cur Hist 48:75-81 F '65

Sukarno: headman to a nation. il Newsweek 65:40-4 F 15 '65; Same abr. with title Sukarno: the other Asian problem. Read Digest 86:97-102 My '65

See also

Anti-Communist movements—Indonesia
Communism—Indonesia

Army

Indonesia: the reds are on the run, but . . . S. W. Sanders. il U S News 59:63-4 N 1 '65

Red paper tiger: failure in Indonesia; interview. S. W. Sanders. il U S News 59:82+ N 22 '65

Economic conditions

Cutting edge of Koti. il Time 86:22 D 24 '65

Economic relations

Sukarno method; form of expropriation. Time 85:32 Mr 5 '65

Expropriation policy

U.S. survivors await Sukarno's ax. il Bsns W p52+ Je 26 '65

Foreign relations

Ambassador Bunker concludes meetings with Indonesian leaders; joint communique, April 15, 1965. Dept State Bul 52:654-5 My 3 '65

Another Asian country in a weird war with reds; conflict between Indonesia and Malaysia. R. P. Martin. il U S News 58:74-6 My 3 '65

Bitter champagne; U.S. to maintain open diplomatic line to Djakarta and Sukarno. Newsweek 66:48 Ag 9 '65

Blowup in Indonesia: what it means to U.S. and reds. il U S News 59:43-4 O 11 '65

Coping with the Bung. il Time 86:30 Ag 6 '65

End of the road for U.S. in Indonesia. U S News 58:49 Mr 15 '65

Indonesia: pride & politics. D. Hindley. il Nation 200:636-8 Je 14 '65

Indonesia talks big about nuclear club. Bsns W p32 F 6 '65

Message from Morning Star; Ratna Sari Dewi's trip to Japan. il Time 87:40 Ja 14 '66

Old game. il Newsweek 65:38 F 8 '65

On the southern flank. J. Burnham. Nat R 17:146 F 23 '65

Peking-Djakarta axis. D. Warner. il Reporter 33:25-7 S 23 '65

Sukarno's Indonesia. il N Y Times Mag p36-9 Mr 21 '65

Sukarno's war against Malaysia. J. Jacquet-Francillon. New Repub 152:16-18 Ap 10 '65

U.S. and Indonesia, a tragedy in diplomacy. F. N. Trager. il N Y Times Mag p26-7+ Ag 29 '65

What is Sukarno up to in southeast Asia? Sr Schol 86:8-11 F 25 '65

China (People's Republic)

No substitute. Newsweek 66:69 N 15 '65

History

Decolonization in Indonesia: the problem of continuity and change. H. J. Benda. bibliog f Am Hist R 70:1058-73 Jl '65

Politics and government

After an evening with Morning Star; revolt. il Time 86:41-2 O 8 '65

Atlantic report; contributing factors of coup failure. Atlan 217:12+ Ja '66

La bombe; celebrations for tenth anniversary of the birth of the Afro-Asian bloc. il Time 85:43 Ap 30 '65

Coup in Jakarta. Commonweal 83:78 O 22 '65

Fumbling juggler; new appointments to the Supreme operation command. il Newsweek 66:41 D 27 '65

Gathering in the paddies; Communist resistance. il Time 86:40 N 12 '65

In the midst of *musharawah*. il Time 86:49 N 5 '65

Indonesia: generals who got away. D. Warner. Reporter 33:39-40 O 21 '65

Indonesia: pride & politics. D. Hindley. il Nation 200:636-8 Je 14 '65

Indonesia: the confused coup. il Newsweek 66:51-4 O 11 '65

Indonesia's Communists: down but not out. D. Warner. il Reporter 33:23-6 N 18 '65

Just a pinprick? Sukarno orders halt to anti-Communist and anti-Chinese demonstrations. il Newsweek 66:53 N 1 '65

Light that fails. Time 86:35 D 3 '65

Long live America; after the latest crisis. il Newsweek 66:57-8 O 18 '65

Losing face; post-coup conditions. il Newsweek 66:53 O 25 '65

On the southern flank. J. Burnham. Nat R 17:146 F 23 '65

Peking-Djakarta axis. D. Warner. il Reporter 33:25-7 S 23 '65

Question of unanimity; Sukarno Heroes' day speech. Newsweek 66:54+ N 22 '65

Reference for privacy. il Time 87:25B Ja 21 '66

Smoldering struggle. il Newsweek 66:56 N 8 '65

Still swinging. F. Sully. il Newsweek 66:53-4 D 13 '65

Sukarno struts as Chen Yi snoozes; during anniversary parade. il Life 59:36-36A S 3 '65

Surprising news from Asia. il Sat Eve Post 238:90 D 4 '65

Wanted: a magician; after the coup. il Time 86:37-8 O 15 '65

INDONESIAN art. See Art, Indonesian

INDOOR gardening. See House plants; Window gardening

INDOOR gardens. See Gardens, Indoor

INDOOR plants. See House plants

INDOOR tennis. See Tennis

INDOOR tennis courts. See Tennis courts, Indoor

INDUCTANCE

Improved switching of inductive loads. J. P. Reed. il Electr World 74:35+ S '65

INDULGENCES

Indulgences at the council. G. Baum. Commonweal 83:307+ D 10 '65

Indulgences made easy. Time 86:51 D 31 '65

Pious bookkeeping; Vatican council's views on proposed reform. il Time 86:68+ N 26 '65

Streamlining the merit machine. D. Peerman. Christian Cent 82:1503-4 D 8 '65

INDUS VALLEY

Antiquities

Water, history, and the Indus Plain. G. C. Taylor, jr. il Natur Hist 74:40-9 bibliog(p70) My '65

See also

Mohenjo-Daro

INDUSTRIAL arbitration. See Arbitration, Industrial

INDUSTRIAL arts

Study and teaching

Conversation on industrial arts and vocational education; interviews. K. E. Dawson; L. A. Burkett. NEA J 54:25-8 N '65

INDUSTRIAL buildings

For a newspaper plant: a glass showcase. il Arch Rec 138:174-5 S '65

INDUSTRIAL control. See Industry and state

INDUSTRIAL cooperation

NATO common market; excerpts from address. H. J. Kuss. Aviation W 83:11 O 18 '65

INDUSTRIAL design. See Design, Industrial

INDUSTRIAL disputes. See Labor disputes

INDUSTRIAL districts

Industrial park gives rare plants a showcase; Sunshine State industrial park, Fla. il Bsns W p 122-4 Ja 15 '66

INDUSTRIAL diversification. See Diversification in industry

INDUSTRIAL education

See also

Vocational education

INDUSTRIAL efficiency. See Efficiency, Industrial

INDUSTRIAL employment. See Employment

INDUSTRIAL espionage. See Spies, Industrial

INDUSTRIAL exhibitions. See Exhibitions

INDUSTRIAL expansion

Business spending: a strong pattern; spending for new plant and equipment. il Newsweek 66:82 D 6 '65

Expansion gets larger share of spending; survey; vith editorial comment. il Bsns W p24-6, 138 My 1 '65

See also

Capital investments

INDUSTRIAL films. See Moving pictures in industry

INDUSTRIAL forecasting. See Business forecasting

INDUSTRIAL gases. See Gases—Industrial applications

INDUSTRIAL instruments. See Instruments

INDUSTRIAL laboratories. See Research laboratories

INDUSTRIAL landscaping. See Landscape gardening

INDUSTRIAL location. See Location in business and industry

INDUSTRIAL management and organization
Case for a consistent company labor policy. J. A. Belford. Mo Labor R 88:148 F '65
Exporting U.S. standards to underdeveloped countries. J. C. Shearer. Mo Labor R 88: 145-7 F '65
Famous firsts: author of management's bible: Principles of industrial organization, published 1913. Bsns W p 134+ Ag 14 '65
Imperatives of authority; excerpt from Managers for tomorrow. Duns R 85:49-50+ F '65
Man with too many hats; product manager, long on duties, short on authority. il Bsns W p43-4 My 22 '65
Modular production, a new concept. M. K. Starr. il Harvard Bsns R 43:131-2+ N '65
Tracking conformity to its business lair; Porter survey. Bsns W p74 F 27 '65
When workers manage themselves; permissive management. il Bsns W p93-4 Mr 20 '65
    See also
Business management and organization
Personnel management

Study and teaching
Training Europe's executives; Institut Européen d'administration des affaires, Fontainebleau. il Time 85:100 Ap 9 '65
    See also
Executives—Training
Harvard university—Graduate school of business administration

Great Britain
Underdeveloped British businessman. S. White. Atlan 217:75-8 Ja '66

INDUSTRIAL migration. See Migrant labor

INDUSTRIAL mobilization
Arms orders on the rise; who's in line for business. il U S News 59:73-4 Ag 16 '65
Buildup without strain: Viet Nam. il Time 86:75 Ag 6 '65
Business feels first pressures. il Bsns W p24-5 Jl 24 '65
Mobilization outlook: effect on business and people. il U S News 59:20-3 Ag 2 '65
Ready for escalation. il Time 86:63-4 Jl 30 '65

INDUSTRIAL organization. See Industrial management and organization

INDUSTRIAL parks. See Industrial districts

INDUSTRIAL pensions. See Pensions, Industrial

INDUSTRIAL production. See Production

INDUSTRIAL property
Legal protection of computer programs. M. R. Wessel. Harvard Bsns R 43:97-106 Mr '65
Moscow to sign patent agreement. Bsns W p42 Mr 20 '65

INDUSTRIAL relations
Another worry for employers; union pledge cards. W. J. Sandler. U S News 58:86-9 Mr 15 '65
Change or consequences; address, October 27, 1964. R. J. Anton. Vital Speeches 31:274-9 F 15 '65
Coalitions versus consumers in the analysis of power. Mo Labor R 88:655-7 Je '65
Communicator; employer, employee relations; address, June 24, 1965. L. A. Townsend. Vital Speeches 31:670-2 Ag 15 '65
Developments in industrial relations. See issues of Monthly labor review
For Texas employers, word from other side; union and government speakers at labor-management conference. il Bsns W p 122-4 N 6 '65
Industrial relations in the next decade; address, October 13, 1965. D. A. Morse. Vital Speeches 32:60-4 N 1 '65
Industrial relations policy and action-oriented research. S. Barkin. Mo Labor R 88:142-3 F '65
Labor-management: symposium. bibliog f il Cur Hist 48:321-60+; 49:1-44+; 65-105+ Je-Ag '65
Labor relations in the Common market. C. W. Summers. il Harvard Bsns R 43:148-50+ Mr '65
Liberal NLRB faces tougher road; Supreme court upsets three rulings. Bsns W p78+ Ap 3 '65

Limits on labor & management. il Time 85:66-7 Ap 9 '65
Moving day; how General foods prepared its employees. L. L. L. Golden. Sat R 49:107 Ja 8 '66
Right to manage. D. Lawrence. U S News 59:120 N 1 '65
Significant decisions in labor cases. See issues of Monthly labor review
State of the unionists: griping, but living well. il Bsns W p24-6 F 20 '65
Strike vs. lockout; Supreme court decision. Newsweek 65:82 Ap 12 '65
This month's feature: U.S. policy on labor-management relations. Cong Digest 44:193-224 Ag '65
Union representation election. J. E. Drotning. bibliog f il Mo Labor R 88:938-43 Ag '65
Unions act on threats to privacy. il Bsns W p87-8 Mr 13 '65
    See also
Collective bargaining
Communication in management
Industrial management and organization
Open and closed shop
Spies, Industrial
United States—National labor relations board

Bibliography
Readings on labor-management. M. C. Shebesta. Cur Hist 49:46-9+, 108-11+ Jl-Ag '65

INDUSTRIAL relations research association
Papers from the IRRA annual meeting; excerpts (cont) Mo Labor R 88:141-9, 292-7 F-Mr '65

INDUSTRIAL research
Amazing alchemy of ultrahigh pressure. G. A. W. Boehm. Read Digest 86:144E-144F+ Mr '65
Atlantic report: science and industry. Atlan 215:28+ My '65
Company budgets for basic research; letter. J. F. G. Hicks. Science 147:985 F 26 '65
Five firms top field in achievement; applications of fluidics. il Miss & Roc 16:36+ F 8 '65
One big race U.S. is winning: new products. il U S News 59:84-7 S 27 '65
R&D entrepreneur: profile of success. H. Schrage. bibliog f il Harvard Bsns R 43:56-69 N '65
Selling R&D to the government. S. F. Divita. il Harvard Bsns R 43:62-75 S '65
Where GE peers far into future. il Bsns W p45-6+ S 11 '65
    See also
Battelle memorial institute of Columbus, Ohio
Engineering research
National research corporation
Petroleum research
Research laboratories
Wood research

INDUSTRIAL research laboratories. See Research laboratories

INDUSTRIAL revenue bonds. See Municipal bonds

INDUSTRIAL secrets. See Trade secrets

INDUSTRIAL sociology. See Sociology, Industrial

INDUSTRIAL union department. See American federation of labor and Congress of industrial organizations—Industrial union department

INDUSTRIAL waste. See Trade waste

INDUSTRIAL workers of the world
Rebel voices, ed. by J. L. Kornbluh. Review Commonweal 82:361-2 Je 4 '65. T. R. Brooks
    Nation 200:371-3 Ap 5 '65. H. Zinn

INDUSTRIALIZATION
    See also
Economic development
Underdeveloped areas

INDUSTRY
    See also
Cities and towns—Industries
Location in business and industry

Charitable contributions
    See Corporations—Charitable contributions

Location
    See Location in business and industry

Social aspects
    See Sociology, Industrial

INDUSTRY, Nationalization of. See Government ownership

INDUSTRY and art. See Art and industry

INDUSTRY and education. See Business and education

INDUSTRY and state

Atomic insurance: the ticklish statistics. D. E. Pesonen. il Nation 201:242-5 O 18 '65

Big business & the Democrats; excerpts from What is power? D. T. Bazelon. Commentary 39:39-46 My '65

BMI; government concern, industry outlook, 1966; summaries of addresses at 33rd annual convention. il Pub W 188:68-70+ D 6 '65

Briefing the brass: Business council meets with Cabinet members. il Bsns W p30-1 My 8 '65

Business and the balance of payments; top executives discuss administration's voluntary program. il Duns R 86:37-9+ S '65

Business and the G.O.P. J. Berry. il Duns R 86:34-6+ D '65

Business role in the Great society. J. Terhorst; W. Welch. il Reporter 33:26-32 O 21 '65

Capitalism today. B. B. Seligman. Commentary 39:88-90 Ap '65

Changing balance power; with views of leading business executives. il Bsns W p84-5+ Jl 17 '65

Collective coercion? D. Lawrence. U S News 59:120 S 20 '65; Same abr. with title Must collective bargaining be sabotaged? Read Digest 87:113-14 D '65

Commitment for expansion. il Time 86:80 Jl 23 '65

Congress and business: Senators Mansfield and Dirksen debate outlook; ed. by J. W. Bunting. M. Mansfield and E. M. Dirksen. il Nations Bsns 53:76-80+ Mr '65

Coordination. D. Lawrence. U S News 59:124 S 27 '65

Face in the mirror. Duns R 85:31 Mr '65

Faith in the individual; address, December 9, 1964. D. D. Eisenhower. Vital Speeches 31:228-31 F 1 '65

First thirty-five years of Fortune; with editorial comment. H. R. Luce. il Fortune 71:115-16, 136-7+ F '65

Gaining a clearer view of the top; Brookings' dialogue for bureaucrats and corporate brass. il Bsns W p84-6 Ag 7 '65

Government and the food industry; domestic food marketing; address, September 17, 1965. G. L. Mehren. Vital Speeches 31:755-8 O 1 '65

Government-business partnership on balance-of-payments problem; remarks, February 18, 1965. L. B. Johnson. Dept State Bul 52:335-7 Mr 8 '65

Government-by-guideline; address. G. Champion. Duns R 86:17-18+ Jl '65

Governing by guideline; indirect controls. il Time 86:89 N 26 '65

Industrial relations in the next decade; address, October 13, 1965. D. A. Morse. Vital Speeches 32:60-4 N 1 '65

Is shale-oil boom on the way at last? il U S News 58:100 My 31 '65

Johnson and the businessmen. G. R. Rosen. il Duns R 85:40-3+ My '65

Labor-management: symposium. bibliog f il Cur Hist 48:321-60+; 49:65-105+ Je, Ag '65

Labor policies jolt British industry. H. J. Coleman. il Aviation W 82:265-7 Mr 15 '65

LBJ's program and the investor. il Duns R 85:99-100 Mr '65

Mexico's auto makers switch to home brew. il Bsns W p68-70 Jl 31 '65

Mobilization outlook; what business can expect in controls from Washington; interview. B. Ellington. il U S News 59:24-6 Ag 2 '65

New phase? Newsweek 65:70-1 Je 7 '65

New threat to economic freedom; address, May 25, 1965. G. Champion. Vital Speeches 31:521-4 Je 15 '65

News lines. See issues of U.S. news & World report

Our dilapidating language; voluntary vs. mandatory controls. Nat R 17:963-4 N 2 '65

Political economy of the Great society. O. Gass. bibliog f Commentary 40:31-6 O '65

Public-private enterprise; effects of technology; address, November 1, 1965. W. M. Allen. Vital Speeches 32:112-15 D 1 '65

Rash of mergers: new crackdown? il U S News 58:72 Mr 29 '65

Rule by guideline. H. Hazlitt. Newsweek 66:76 S 13 '65

Saboteurs at work; reprint from Wall Street journal, September 20, 1965. J. E. Evans. U S News 59:120 O 4 '65

Shale oil: the cartel's ace in the hole. R. Fleming. il Nation 200:274-6 Mr 15 '65

Some questions about mergers; attitude of government; address, September 27, 1965. G. H. Love. Vital Speeches 32:9-12 O 15 '65

Still a mirage. Nation 200:350-1 Ap 5 '65

Tax-free municipal industrial bonds; address, December 1, 1964. F. L. Magee. Vital Speeches 31:300-14 Mr 1 '65

Trends in intergovernmental relations. G. C. S. Benson. bibliog f Ann Am Acad 359: 1-9 My '65

Two on the aisle. W. J. Coughlin. Miss & Roc 16:46 Mr 15 '65

U.S. oil: a giant caught in its own web. G. Burck. il Fortune 71:113-19+ Ap '65; Discussion. 71:82 My; 130 Je '65

Voice for business in U.S. policy. il Bsns W p96-8+ Mr 13 '65

Wages and prices by formula? address. A. F. Burns. Harvard Bsns R 43:55-64 Mr '65

Washington desk. J. R. Slevin. See issues of Dun's review and modern industry

Watchdog agencies soften the bark; shift in viewpoint among federal regulators. il Bsns W p 132+ O 30 '65

What business wants from Lyndon Johnson. E. K. Faltermayer. il Fortune 71:122-5+ F '65

Will government slow business in 1966? U S News 59:87-8 Ag 9 '65

Your kids when they grow up; interview. D. N. Michael. il Changing T 19:7-13 Mr '65

See also

Government competition
Government ownership
Industrial mobilization
Interstate commerce
Price regulation by government
Strikes—United States—Government intervention
Sugar industry and trade—Regulation
United States—Commerce, Department of
United States—Federal trade commission

Anecdotes, facetiae, satire, etc.

Silvertoe; financial adventure of James Debenture. W. L. Safire. il Harvard Bsns R 43:110-18 My '65

INDUSTRY wide collective bargaining. See Collective bargaining, Industry wide

INERTIAL guidance systems

Airlines to test British inertial system. il Aviation W 83:67-8 D 20 '65

Celestial simulator is major advance. il Miss & Roc 16:28+ Mr 15 '65

Deadline draws near in competition for F-111 digital inertial navigation unit. Miss & Roc 17:21 Ag 2 '65

Flight data system applies new concepts. B. Miller. il Aviation W 83:101+ S 20 '65

Inertial Navaid yields improved accuracy. P. J. Klass. Aviation W 83:46 N 22 '65

Low-cost inertial design tested. il Aviation W 82:63 Mr 8 '65

Multi-sensor navaid test planned; stellar inertial Doppler system. Aviation W 83:31 Jl 12 '65

Pending shot may seal SIGS future; navy's simplified inertial guidance system. C. D. LaFond. il Miss & Roc 17:32-3 Ag 2 '65

Situation display offers wide data range. il Aviation W 83:91 Ag 2 '65

Strapped inertial techniques show gains. P. J. Klass. il Aviation W 83:79+ S 6 '65

USAF to test suitcase Navaid for F-111. B. Miller. il Aviation W 83:52-3+ Ag 23 '65

INEXPERIENCED ghost; drama. See Nolan, P. T.

INFALLIBILITY. See Catholic church—Infallibility

INFANT carriers. See Carriers (infants)

INFANT mortality

Three new miracle treatments to keep babies alive. B. Merson. Good H 161:68-9+ Jl '65

We must lower our infant death rate. H. Jacobziner. Parents Mag 40:56+ N '65
See also
Death

INFANT psychology. See Child study

INFANTE, Anthony A. See Nemer, M. jt. auth.

INFANTS

Buttercup meets the baby. J. R. Moskin. il Look 29:114-16+ Mr 23 '65

There are babies and babies. P. L. Levin. il N Y Times Mag p 132+ S 12 '65
See also
Embryology
Fetus
Nurseries

Care and hygiene

Baby's skin in summer. Parents Mag 40:96 Jl '65

Better health for every baby; fourteen major medical centers from Oregon to New York participating in unique child development project. T. Wilson and K. Niehans. il Parents Mag 40:59-61+ N '65

INFANTS—Care and hygiene—*Continued*
Dr Spock answers. B. Spock. il Redbook 124: 24+ Mr '65
Pacifiers: useful or harmful for the young? il Good H 161:155 Jl '65
Toilet training need not be a battle. S. M. Chess and A. Thomas. il Parents Mag 40: 54-5+ F '65
When your baby catches cold. C. A. Holmes. il Parents Mag 41:36-7+ Ja '66
See also
Baby sitters
Children—Care and hygiene
Colic
Infants—Clothing

Clothing
All dressed up and rarin' to go. J. W. Parks. il Parents Mag 40:62-3+ Mr '65
What every new mother should know about washing baby clothes. Redbook 125:46+ O '65
See also
Diapers, Infants

Crying
How to interpret your baby's cries. F. R. Schreiber. il Todays Health 43:41-5 Ag '65

Diseases
See Children—Diseases

Growth and development
Time when time stands still. P. La Farge. Redbook 124:43+ F '65
Train your baby to be a genius. G. Doman and C. Delacato. McCalls 92:65+ Mr '65
Two-year-olds take their time. M. Albrecht. il Parents Mag 40:48-9+ Ag '65

Identification
I took the wrong baby home from the hospital; case in Scheibbs, Austria. F. Spelman. il McCalls 92:62+ Ap '65

Immunity
See Immunity

Language
See Children—Language

Nutrition
Breast feeding made easy. M. A. Wessel. il Parents Mag 40:70-1+ N '65
New ways to feed the baby. H. F. Meyer. il Todays Health 43:49-50 Je '65
To nurse or not to nurse? Time 85:68 Ap 23 '65

Sight
See Sight

Surgery
See Children—Surgery

INFANTS, Deformed. See Deformities

INFANTS, Newborn
Electroretinography in newborn human infants. A. B. Barnet and others. bibliog il Science 148:651-4 Ap 30 '65
Fighting staph with staph. il Time 86:46 S 10 '65
Galvanic skin reflex in newborn humans. D. H. Crowell and others. bibliog il Science 148:1108-11 My 21 '65
Killer that stalks the newborn; respiratory-distress syndrome. S. M. Spencer. il Sat Eve Post 238:32-5 Ag 28 '65
Our daughter Ivan the Terrible. E. Thompson. il Redbook 125:8+ O '65
Sex chromatin in newborns: presumptive evidence for external factors in human nondisjunction. A. Robinson and T. T. Puck. bibliog il Science 148:83-5 Ap 2 '65
Stimulus variables determining space perception in infants. T. G. R. Bower. bibliog il Science 149:88-9 Jl 2 '65
Today's hospital techniques save ailing newborns. J. T. Burns and A. P. Riker. il Parents Mag 40:46-7+ Ap '65
Visual accommodation in human infants. H. Haynes and others. bibliog il Science 148: 528-30 Ap 23 '65

INFANTS, Premature
Fewer premature babies in USSR than in USA. Sci N L 87:377 Je 12 '65
Good news for parents of preemies; interview, ed. by M. Markham. H. H. Gordon. il Parents Mag 40:46-7+ Je '65
New way to treat hyaline membrane disease. Time 86:70 Ag 27 '65

INFANTS furniture. See Furniture, Childrens

INFECTION
First aid. C. J. Potthoff. Todays Health 43: 64-6+ D '65

INFECTIOUS hepatitis. See Hepatitis, Infectious

INFECTIOUS mononucleosis. See Mononucleosis, Infectious

INFELD, Leopold
As I see it. por Bul Atomic Sci 21:7-14 F '65

INFERNO. See Dante Alighieri

INFERTILITY. See Sterility

INFLATABLE dams. See Dams

INFLATABLE furniture. See Furniture, Inflatable

INFLATION (finance)
Balance of economy cools fear of inflation. il Bsns W p 104+ S 25 '65
Brazil: land of massive problems. R. H. Bolton; reply. A. R. Kratz. Christian Cent 82: 748 Je 9 '65
End of the French miracle. il U S News 58:81 Je 7 '65
Europe's boom in trouble? how real the signs are. il U S News 58:74-6 Mr 22 '65
Guidelines won't do it alone. Bsns W p 148 Ja 15 '66
Harsh curbs generate growing discontent; in Brazil. il Bsns W p56+ Mr 27 '65
How real is inflation in the U.S? il U S News 60:78-80 Ja 24 '66
Inflated globe. il Newsweek 66:76 D 20 '65
Inflation: is U.S. in Europe's footsteps? A. Zanker. U S News 59:98 N 22 '65
Inflation talk starts again. Bsns W p 198 S 25 '65
Is inflation a threat again? Bsns W p 116 Ag 7 '65
Is your dollar in trouble again? Outlook for inflation; what to do about it. il U S News 59:42-4+ S 20 '65
Money illusion. H. C. Wallich. Newsweek 66: 58 D 27 '65
One black cloud: inflation; interview. C. H. Madden. Nations Bsns 53:34-5 N '65
Other war in Vietnam; fight against inflation. il U S News 59:32-3 Ag 30 '65
Skilled labor shortage holds down the gains; industrial nations fear inflation. il Bsns W p84+ F 6 '65
Vietnam or California; spectrum of inflation; address, December 11, 1965. T. E. Dewey. Vital Speeches 32:170-3 Ja 1 '66
Washington desk. J. R. Slevin. Duns R 86: 5-6 O '65
What helps the U.S. stave off inflation. il Bsns W p28-9 Je 26 '65
Whither inflation? H. C. Wallich. Newsweek 65:80 My 3 '65
Why workers don't mind a little inflation. il U S News 59:99-100 O 4 '65

INFLUENCE of altitude. See Altitude, Influence of

INFLUENCE of music. See Music, Influence of

INFLUENZA
Warns of more flu coming next season. Sci N L 88:56 Jl 24 '65

Vaccines
How good are flu vaccines? Sci Digest 57:32 F '65

INFORMATION, Freedom of
Finding out about red China; need for exchange of information. L. H. Evans. il Sat R 48:17-18 Je 26 '65
Freedom of information. W. J. Coughlin. Miss & Roc 16:46 Ap 26 '65
See also
Freedom of the press
Government and the press
Television broadcasting—Censorship

INFORMATION agency (United States) See United States—Information agency

INFORMATION libraries, Overseas. See American libraries abroad

INFORMATION service, Public affairs. See Public affairs information service

INFORMATION storage and retrieval systems
Big information mess. B. H. Frisch. il Sci Digest 58:23-7 S '65
British experiment with MEDLARS; NLM to provide tapes and training. Library J 90: 2990 Jl '65
Changing role of libraries: need for efficient network of national information systems in science and technology; address, July 1965. W. T. Knox. ALA Bul 59:720-5 S '65; Reply. W. H. Carlson. 60:11 Ja '66
Computer reference system speeds bibliographies; Universal reference system. Pub W 187:42 My 3 '65
Copyright debate clarified on computer uses. Pub W 188:36-7 O 11 '65
Data library will aid scientists and doctors. Sci N L 88:153 S 4 '65
Flexible display system gaining users. C. D. LaFond. il Miss & Roc 17:36-7 S 27 '65

INFORMATION storage and retrieval systems
—*Continued*
Good-by to Gutenberg; concepts incubating in laboratories. il Newsweek 67:85 Ja 24 '66
How to organize information systems. J. Dearden. bibliog f il Harvard Bsns R 43:65-73 Mr '65
Information explosion in the factory. H. E. Klein. Duns R 85:pt2 112-13+ Mr '65
Information storage and retrieval. il Duns R 86:pt2 162-3+ S '65
Intelligence, information, and education; address, September 28, 1964. R. W. Gerard. bibliog Science 148:762-5 My 7 '65
Librarians' Pugwash, or INTREX on the Cape; conference on MIT's program, Woods Hole, Mass. J. H. Shera. bibliog Wilson Lib Bul 40:359-62 D '65
Libraries of the future, by J. C. R. Licklider. Review
　Wilson Lib Bul 39:813-14 Je '65
Long John Nebel and the woodlouse; science-fiction writer looks at information science, address, December 8, 1964. F. Pohl. Library J 90:4704-8 N 1 '65
MEDLARS in operation; letter to the editor. M. M. Cummings. Library J 90:1218+ Mr 15 '65; Discussion. 90:1580+, 2450+ Ap 1, Je 1 '65
Office: the era of total information. il Duns R 86:pt2 132-5 S '65
Post-mortems can be fun; the cost analysis of information systems. H. Wooster. il Library J 90:2968-73 Jl '65
Universal reference system. Wilson Lib Bul 39:826+ Je '65
Vision of university library of 1975 emerges from Woods Hole conference; MIT's project INTREX (Information transfer experiments) Library J 90:4024 O 1 '65
What's ahead in information technology. J. Diebold. il Harvard Bsns R 43:76-82 S '65
When a computer needs a friend; thinking machines vs. human judgment. il Bsns W p 146+ Mr 6 '65
　See also
Electronic data processing
Information systems, Management
Libraries—Automation
Programming (computers)

INFORMATION systems, Management
Meshing managers and computers; Deering Milliken's new total information center. il Bsns W p82-3 Jl 3 '65
What's ahead in information technology. J. Diebold. il Harvard Bsns R 43:76-82 S '65

INFORMATION tests
Animal behavior quiz. J. Daugherty and M. Daugherty. il Sci Digest 58:87-9 N '65
Bird quiz. J. Daugherty and M. Daugherty. il Sci Digest 58:83-5 Ag '65
Can you answer these questions about blood? L. Galton. il Pop Sci 186:122-5+ Mr '65
Changing times quiz (cont) Changing T 19:48 Ag; 46 Ag; 43 D '65
Contemporary affairs test (cont) il Sr Schol 87:26 S 16 '65
Do you act your age? questions and answers. J. Daugherty and M. Daugherty. il Sci Digest 57:92-4 My '65
Do you know your metals? questions and answers. J. Daugherty and M. Daugherty. il Sci Digest 57:88-90 Je '65
Do you smell something? questions and answers. J. Daugherty and M. Daugherty. il Sci Digest 58:89-91 Jl '65
Electricity and magnetism quiz. J. Daugherty and M. Daugherty. il Sci Digest 58:91-4 D '65
Family quiz game. See issues of Parents' magazine and better homemaking
How do you figure? questions and answers. J. Daugherty and M. Daugherty. il Sci Digest 57:95-7 F '65
Inventors quiz. J. Daugherty and M. Daugherty. Sci Digest 57:93-4 Mr '65
Plants that cure, quiz. J. Daugherty and M. Daugherty. il Sci Digest 58:92-4 O '65
Quiz: how we use rocks and minerals. J. Daugherty and M. Daugherty. il Sci Digest 57:89-91 Ap '65
Senior scholastic end-term review test (cont) il Sr Schol 86:23-4 My 13 '65
Senior scholastic mid-semester review test. il Sr Schol 86:21-2 Mr 25 '65
Spider quiz. J. Daugherty and M. Daugherty. il Sci Digest 58:90-2 S '65
Trivia, anyone? N Y Times Mag p64 O 31 '65
Which is older, the earth or the sun? quiz. J. Daugherty and M. Daugherty. il Sci Digest 59:92-4 Ja '66

You may be smarter than you think; excerpt from Miracle ahead. G. Gallup. Read Digest 86:145+ My '65
Your literary I.Q; ed. by J. T. Winterich and D. M. Glixon. See issues of Saturday review

INFORMATION transfer experiments. See Information storage and retrieval systems
INFORMATIONAL media guaranty program. See United States—Information agency
INFRARED films. See Photography—Films
INFRARED photography. See Photography, Infrared
INFRARED rays
Infrared astronomy. B. C. Murray and J. A. Westphal. il Sci Am 213:20-9 bibliog(p 118) Ag '65
　See also
Photography, Infrared
INFRASONIC waves. See Sound waves
INGERSOLL, John H.
Brick. Pop Gard 16:18-21 N '65
Create your own private world. Pop Gard 16:30-2 Ap '65
Does it really pay to do your own home repairs? Bet Hom & Gard 43:14+ Jl '65
Garden teahouse. Pop Gard 17:30-1+ Ja '66
Hot new ideas in home heaters! Pop Mech 124:110-14+ N '65
New roofing: better than ever. Pop Sci 187:126-9 S '65
Plastic pipe cuts plumbing costs. Pop Sci 188:148-50+ Ja '66
Use less water. Pop Gard 16:34-7 My '65
—and Rhine, C. E.
How to save up to 25 per cent on your fuel-oil bill. Pop Sci 187:148-51 S '65
INGLE, David J.
Interocular transfer in goldfish: color easier than pattern. bibliog Science 149:1000-2 Ag 27 '65
INGLIS, David R.
Chinese bombshell. Bul Atomic Sci 21:19-21 F '65
INGLIS, Ruth Langdon
Pilots who saved England. Harper 231:52-7 S '65
INGRAHAM, Leonard W.
Realistic A-V content; excerpts from address, November 1965. Sr Schol 87:sup9 D 9 '65
INGRAO, Hector C.
Harvard observatory's new patrol cameras. Sky & Tel 29:200-4 Ap '65
INHERITANCE
Please send one billion dollars; J. Perring's nine-year search for a fortune. R. K. Massie. il Sat Eve Post 238:76-8+ D 4 '65
　See also
Estate planning
Wills
INHERITANCE (biology) See Heredity
INHERITANCE of disease. See Heredity of disease
INHERITANCE tax
For people with estates to pass on; something to watch; estate, gift and death taxes. il U S News 58:108-9 Ap 12 '65
INHIBITING substances, Growth. See Growth inhibiting substances
INITIAL teaching alphabet. See Alphabet
INITIALS
P.J.s: bars and other businesses with these initials on Third avenue between Forty-second and Eighty-sixth streets. New Yorker 41:35-6 Mr 13 '65
INITIATIONS (into trades, societies, etc)
　See also
Hazing
INJECTIONS, Hypodermic
　Anecdotes, facetiae, satire, etc.
Baudelaire in three injections. L. Simpson. Harper 230:48-50 Je '65
INJURIES (law) See Damages
INLAND navigation
　See also
Canals
River trips
INLAND sea
Inland Sea of Japan, dose of splendour. G. Bradshaw. Vogue 146:151 D '65
INLAND waterway. See Intracoastal Waterway
INLAND waterways. See Waterways—United States
INLAY
Do-it-yourself wood mosaics. il Design 67:9 S '65
INNESS, George
George Inness, painter of landscapes. L. Ireland. il Antiques 88:820-3 D '65

INNIS, Pauline
National seashore or a national loss? Audubon Mag 67:86-7 Mr '65
Painting swans for science. Audubon Mag 67:292-5 S '65

INNOCENTS, Massacre of the Holy. See Holy Innocents, Massacre of the

INOCULATION
Measles prevention easy: one-shot vaccination. F. Marley. Sci N L 87:87 F 6 '65
See also
Immunity
Vaccination

INÖNÜ, Ismet
Who profits? Newsweek 65:42 Mr 1 '65

INOSITOL
Inositol deficiency resulting in death: an explanation of its occurrence in neurospora crassa. P. Matile. bibliog il Science 151:86-8 Ja 7 '66
Myoinositol kinase: partial purification and identification of product. P. D. English and others. bibliog il Science 151:198-9 Ja 14 '66

INOZEMSTEV, N. N.
Alternative to war: address, February 18, 1965. Vital Speeches 31:421-4 My 1 '65

INPUT-output equipment. See Computers—Input-output equipment

INQUISITION
Spanish inquisition. H. Kamen. il Horizon 7:28-31+ Autumn '65

INSANE, Criminal and dangerous
See also
Forensic psychiatry

INSANITY
Madness and civilization, by M. Foucault. Review
Commentary 40:93-4+ O '65. P. Gay
See also
Hysteria
Mental illness
Psychology, Pathological

INSCRIPTIONS
See also
Graffiti

INSECT baits and repellents
Devices sold for getting rid of flying insects. Consumer Bul 48:35 Ag '65
Insect repellents. il Consumer Rep 30:352-5 Jl '65
One man's meat; catnip. Sci Am 212:54 F '65

INSECT biochemistry. See Biochemistry

INSECT bites and stings
How to treat insect and pest bites. il Good H 161:151 Jl '65
Tips for your home and family; guard against dangerous insect stings. E. Maxwell. Todays Health 43:71-2 Jl '65

INSECT calls. See Insect sounds

INSECT camouflage. See Mimicry (biology)

INSECT control. See Insects, Injurious and beneficial—Control

INSECT flight. See Insects—Flight

INSECT mating behavior. See Courtship of insects

INSECT muscles. See Muscles

INSECT nests. See Nests

INSECT repellents. See Insect baits and repellents

INSECT resistant plants. See Plants—Insect resistance

INSECT sex attractants
American cockroach sex attractant. M. Jacobson and M. Beroza. bibliog Science 147:748-9 F 12 '65
Metarchons; insect control through recognition signals. R. H. Wright. il Bul Atomic Sci 21:28-30 Mr '65

INSECT songs. See Insect sounds

INSECT sounds
Moths and ultrasound. K. D. Roeder. il Sci Am 212:94-102 Ap '65
Stridulation in leaf-cutting ants. H. Markl. bibliog il Science 149:1392-3 S 17 '65

INSECTICIDES
Chemical turmoil results in: new recommendations for controlling forage insects. il Suc Farm 63:58 Ap '65
Corn insects, here's how to control them. Suc Farm 63:84-5 Mr '65
New insecticides seen; organophosphate and carbamate insecticides. Sci N L 87:71 Ja 30 '65
Systemic way to control pests. F. D. Hoppe. il Flower Grower 52:52 My '65
See also
DDT (insecticide)
Malathion
Pesticides

Injurious effects
Food safety program: endrin monitoring in the Mississippi River. A. F. Novak and M. R. R. Rao. bibliog il Science 150:1732-3 D 24 '65

INSECTIVOROUS plants
See also
Sundew

INSECTS
Books in review; studies in entomology. S. Radinovsky. Natur Hist 74:8+ Ag '65
See also
Color of insects
Fertilization of plants
Insect sounds
also names of insects. e.g. Bees

Collection and preservation
One million insects; Australian national insect collection. il Sci Digest 57:82 Mr '65
Preserved insects; entomologist embeds specimens in permanent plastic cases. il Design 66:11-13 My '65
See also
Butterflies—Collection and preservation

Control
See Insects, Injurious and beneficial—Control

Development
Diapause induction in daphnia requires two stimuli. R. G. Stross and J. C. Hill. bibliog il Science 150:1462-4 D 10 '65

Ear
See Ear (insects)

Eyes
See Eye (insects)

Flight
Flight muscles of insects. D. S. Smith. il Sci Am 212:76-82+ Je '65
Machine that flies but shouldn't; beetle aerodynamics. il Sci Digest 57:24-5 Ap '65

Food
Feeding stimulants for the female house fly, musca domestica linneaus. W. E. Robbins and others. bibliog il Science 147:628-30 F 5 '65

Habits and behavior
Chemical communication in the social insects. E. O. Wilson. bibliog il Science 149:1064-71 S 3 '65
Living sand; Cape Henlopen. Del. W. H. Amos. il Nat Geog Mag 127:820-33 Je '65
Man fights swarming insects. B. Tufty. il Sci N L 87:90-1 F 6 '65
See also
Courtship of insects

Molting
See Molting

Nests
See Nests

Physiology
Neurosecretory supply to the epidermis of an insect. S. H. P. Maddrell. bibliog il Science 150:1033-4 N 19 '65

Protective equipment
See Defense mechanisms (biology)

Sight
See Sight (insects)

Wings
Flight muscles of insects. D. S. Smith. il Sci Am 212:76-82+ Je '65
Machine that flies but shouldn't; beetle aerodynamics. il Sci Digest 57:24-5 Ap '65

INSECTS, Injurious and beneficial
Insect morticians; decomposition of dead bodies. il Time 87:77 Ja 21 '66
See also
Plant quarantine

Control
Banish these garden pests. B. C. Kilvert, jr. il Flower Grower 52:46-9 My '65
Books in review; man against the insects. R. C. Murphy. Natur Hist 74:4 My '65
Control Japanese beetle. il Sci N L 88:187 S 18 '65
Feeding stimulants for the female house fly, musca domestica linneaus. W. E. Robbins and others. bibliog il Science 147:628-30 F 5 '65
France halts forest insects; using biological controls. R. Maury. il Audubon Mag 67:384-5 N '65

INSECTS, Injurious and beneficial—Control
—Continued
Here's how to identify and control beef
cattle insects. R. E. Roselle. il Suc Farm
63:48-9+ My '65
How to cut down on pesticides. J. Ridgeway.
New Repub 152:11-12 Mr 27 '65
Insect control calendar. P. P. Pirone. il Pop
Gard 17:20-1 Ja '66
Integrated pest control in California. R. Van
Den Bosch. Bul Atomic Sci 21:22-6 Mr '65
Is spraying necessary? C. Westcott. il Horti-
culture 43:20-1+ N '65
Man fights swarming insects. B. Tufty. il
Sci N L 87:90-1 F 6 '65
1965 weed and insect control guide; sym-
posium. il Suc Farm 63:69-74+ Mr '65
Pest destroyers; excerpt from Beneficial in-
sects (cont) L. A. Swan. bibliog il Audu-
bon Mag 67:172-7 My '65
Powerful paper. Sci Am 213:39 O '65
Stop these insects this year. H. B. Petty
and L. E. Zeman. il Suc Farm 63:56-7+
Ap '65
Substance in newspapers may aid insect
control; hormonally active factor in Amer-
ican paper pulp. Sci N L 88:152 S 4 '65
Tiny parasitic ant may curb dread fire ant.
Sci N L 87:318 My 15 '65
U.S. ready for fruit fly. Sci N L 87:294 My 8
'65
Walter Lippmann & the sex life of bugs;
hormonelike chemical in newspapers. Time
86:95 S 17 '65
See also
Flies—Extermination
Insect sex attractants
Insecticides
Pesticides
Spraying and dusting
INSECTS as carriers of infection
See also
Flies as carriers of infection
Mosquitoes as carriers of infection
Tsetse flies
INSECTS in literature
See also
Pets in literature
INSEMINATION, Artificial. See Artificial in-
semination, Human
INSOMNIA
Can't sleep? the medical facts about insom-
nia may put your mind at ease. Bet Hom
& Gard 43:36 N '65
See also
Sleep
INSPECTION of poultry. See Poultry inspec-
tion
INSPIRATION
Defense of the bedside pad. W. Brown.
Writer 78:15-17 S '65
Have faith in your subconscious. C. Mercer.
Writer 78:12-14 Mr '65
Off the cuff. L. Conger. Writer 78:7-8 Ap '65
INSTALMENT plan
Better arithmetic needed for effective in-
stallment buying. Consumer Bul 48:31-2 Jl
'65
Consumer loans: delinquencies rise.   U S
News 58:101 My 3 '65
Financing: the not-so-tender trap; excerpt
from How to get the best car deal, every
time. N. C. Thompson. il Motor T 17:36-8 Je
'65
Installment credit soars to a record; with
table. Bsns W p46+ Ja 8 '66
What it costs to say charge it; new kinds
of accounts, revolving account. il Chang-
ing T 19:17-19 Je '65
See also
Credit

Laws and regulations
Auto buying headaches; lesson in the high
cost of borrowing. J. Osborne. New Repub
152:15-18 Mr 27 '65; Reply. A. J. Man-
zano. 152:42+ Ap 17 '65
Expert views credit bill. W. F. Kelly. Na-
tions Bsns 53:104+ Je '65
SEC prods accountants; ruling how install-
ment sales shall be carried on balance
sheets. Bsns W p 102 Ja 15 '66
INSTAMATIC cameras. See Cameras
INSTANT idiot; story. See Malaret, N.
INSTANT loading moving picture cameras.
See Moving picture cameras
INSTINCT
See also
Animals—Habits and behavior
INSTITUTE for biomedical research. See
American medical association—Institute for
biomedical research

INSTITUTE for research in animal behavior
Rockefeller university II: designs on behav-
ioral biology. J. Walsh. il Science 150:1791-4
D 31 '65
INSTITUTE for technical economics (proposed)
Institute for technical economics. W. Leon-
tief. Bul Atomic Sci 21:46 S '65
INSTITUTE of aerospace sciences. See Ameri-
can institute of aeronautics and astro-
nautics
INSTITUTE of American Indian arts, Santa Fe
Institute of American Indian arts, Santa Fe.
A. Thorpe. il Craft Horiz 25:12-13+ Jl '65
INSTITUTE of electrical and electronics en-
gineers
IC lines increase, prices decrease. M. Getler.
il Miss & Roc 16:32-3+ Ap 5 '65
I.E.E.E. and N.E.W. shows. W. A. Stocklin.
Electr World 73:6 Je '65
IEEE lays groundwork for aerospace group;
Aerospace and electronic systems conven-
tion to replace major electronic confer-
ences. C. D. Lafond. Miss & Roc 17:31 Jl
5 '65
INSTITUTE of logopedics, Wichita, Kan.
Speech defects treated. Sci N L 87:119 F 20
'65
INSTITUTE of Pacific relations
Nobody but us agrarians: A. L. Strong. I. Ep-
stein, F. Coe. J. Burnham. Nat R 17:684
Ag 10 '65
INSTITUTE of reconstructive plastic surgery.
See New York university—Medical center
INSTITUTE on social change in a democratic
society
Spotlight on change. K. Haselden. Christian
Cent 82:638-9 My 19 '65
INSTITUTE of sound
Sound, preserved & pirated; sound stealers.
il Time 86:100 N 19 '65
INSTITUTES, Library. See Library institutes
and workshops
INSTITUTES, Teachers. See Teachers insti-
tutes
INSTITUTIONAL bonds. See Bonds, Institu-
tional
INSTITUTIONAL investors. See Stockholders
INSTRUCTIONAL materials. See Teaching—
Aids and devices
INSTITUTIONS, State. See State institutions
INSTRUCTIONAL materials centers
Function before form; Central-University
high school, Madison, Wis. library program,
with bibliography. K. I. Taylor. Library J
90:5481-3 D 15 '65
See also
School libraries
INSTRUCTORS, College. See College professors
and instructors
INSTRUMENT boards (automobiles) See Auto-
mobiles—Dashboards
INSTRUMENT boards (space vehicles)   See
Space vehicles—Instrument boards
INSTRUMENT landing. See Airplanes—Landing
INSTRUMENTAL music
See also
Chamber music
Phonograph records—Instrumental music
INSTRUMENTS
Sixth sense on the production line. H. E.
Klein. il Duns R 85:57-9+ My '65
INSTRUMENTS, Testing. See Testing instru-
ments
INSULATING materials
See also
Glass fibers
INSULATION (electric)
See also
Dielectrics
INSULATION (heat)
How much insulation? il Consumer Rep 30:
79-80 F '65
New way to insulate a cold basement. il Pop
Sci 187:168-9 O '65
INSULATION (sound) See Soundproofing
INSULIN
Antibodies against the component polypeptide
chains of bovine insulin. Y. Yagi and
others. bibliog il Science 147:617-19 F 5 '65
Human insulin made. Sci N L 89:35 Ja 15
'66
Human insulin synthesis reported to be im-
minent. Sci N L 88:258 O 23 '65
Insulin: inducer of pyruvate kinase. G. Weber
and others. bibliog il Science 149:65-7 Jl
2 '65
Lower insulin doses urged for children. Sci
N L 88:25 Jl 10 '65
Protein synthesis by ribosomes from heart
muscle: effect of insulin and diabetes. O.
R. Rampersad and I. G. Wool. bibliog il
Science 149:1102-3 S 3 '65

INSURANCE

Russia tries insurance. R. J. Myers. Nation 200:113-14 F 1 '65
See also
Estate planning

All risk policies

How to insure your valuables. il Changing T 19:37-9 Jl '65

Catastrophe coverage

Insurance trade gets off easy; losses from storms, floods, and quake were not covered. Bsns W p62+ My 8 '65
Underwriting the underwriters; Zurich's Swiss reinsurance co. il Time 86:56-7 D 24 '65

Reinsurance

Underwriting the underwriters; Zurich's Swiss reinsurance co. il Time 86:56-7 D 24 '65

INSURANCE, Accident

School accident insurance: worth buying? il Changing T 19:14 S '65
See also
Insurance, Liability

INSURANCE, Agricultural

Guides in insuring your 1965 crops. Suc Farm 63:29 F '65

INSURANCE, Automobile

Are car insurance extras worth the money? Bet Hom & Gard 43:145+ Ap '65
Automobile liability insurance: address, October 21, 1965. G. E. Mann. Vital Speeches 32:93-5 N 15 '65
Car insurance you may need. il Good H 161:170 S '65
Crisis in auto insurance; what can be done about it. il U S News 58:112-14 Je 14 '65
Every driver should know these auto insurance terms. Bet Hom & Gard 43:120+ S '65
Have you overlooked these ten ways to save money on your car insurance? Bet Hom & Gard 43:25-6 Ag '65
How to buy auto insurance. il Changing T 19:25-8 Mr '65
Your auto insurance: why it will cost more. il U S News 58:72-5 F 8 '65

INSURANCE, Aviation

Airplanes abroad: crashes and consequences. K. M. Ruppenthal. il Nation 201:408-10 N 29 '65
Dropping the pact; damages for death outdated. Newsweek 66:68+ N 1 '65
Congress lashes Hague protocol, protests airline liability limit. W. Wright. Aviation W 83:47 Ag 16 '65
IATA members vote liability limit raise. J. R. Ashlock. il Aviation W 83:36-7 N 8 '65
What is a life worth? U.S. proposes raise of liability limit. Time 86:98 O 29 '65
See also
Warsaw convention

INSURANCE, Dental

Coming next: dental insurance. G. G. Greer. Bet Hom & Gard 43:19+ Je '65
Insurance for dental bills. il Changing T 19:13-14 O '65
What you should know about dental insurance. D. Z. Meilach. Suc Farm 63:86B F '65

INSURANCE, Disability

Policy for the judge; life of pondering judge insured. Time 86:88+ O 8 '65

INSURANCE, Fire

See also
Arson

INSURANCE, Group life

New benefits under ALA group insurance. R. N. Foulk. ALA Bul 59:110-11 F '65

INSURANCE, Health

AMA hits free care for merchant seamen. Sci N L 88:41 Jl 17 '65
Consumer expenditures for health purposes. L. S. Reed. il Mo Labor R 88:168-70 F '65
Hard look at health insurance. S. Grafton. il McCalls 93:110-11+ N '65
Your medical dollar. L. R. Chevalier. il Ladies Home J 83:40-1 Ja '66
See also
Insurance, Dental

Canada

Health-care fight: how it's going in Canada. U S News 58:10 Mr 1 '65
How medicare grows: Canada's story. U S News 58:46 Ap 12 '65
One medical-care plan that's in trouble; Vancouver, British Columbia. il U S News 58:16 F 1 '65
Two and a half years later: Canada's doctor strike; surprise ending to Saskatchewan's bitter battle over socialized medicine. J. Star. il Look 29:101+ Mr 23 '65

New York (state)

Hospital insurance for all, here's a new plan. il U S News 58:89-90 Ap 26 '65

Sweden

Where medicare is in trouble. il U S News 60:61 Ja 24 '66

United States

ABC's of coming medicare. il U S News 59:44-7 Ag 2 '65
AMA and the Catholic press. B. L. Masse. America 113:583+ N 13 '65
AMA asks hospital aid; changing status of four specialty services under medicare. Sci N L 88:167 S 11 '65
AMA: doctors' organization faces growing outside criticism, wide range of policy problems. E. Langer. Science 149:282-3+ Jl 16 '65
AMA in disarray. New Repub 153:7 Jl 10 '65
At last: the details on bigger pensions, medicare. il U S News 58:98+ Ap 5 '65
Biggest change since the New deal; Mills medicare bill. il Newsweek 65:88-90 Ap 12 '65
Burnham on medicare; letters to the editor. Nat R 17:750 S 7 '65
Business of health insurance. T. R. Brooks. Duns R 86:47-8 Ag '65
Crisis ahead in medical care? with interview with R. E. Trussell. il U S News 59:33-7 Jl 26 '65
Dead red herring; medicare funds for reds barred. Reporter 33:10+ D 30 '65
Doctor Ward's last words; AMA opposition to medicare bill. Time 85:28-9 My 21 '65
Doctors' debate: what to do when medicare comes is main topic of stormy AMA session. E. Langer. Science 149:164-7 Jl 9 '65
Doctors' revolt in U.S? the battle over medicare; meeting of the American medical association. il U S News 59:26-8 Jl 5 '65
Eldercare v. medicare. Time 85:22 F 19 '65
Expanding health care. America 112:386-7 Mr 20 '65
Health care for the aged: now Democratic and Republican plans compare. U S News 58:64 F 22 '65
Health insurance bill, pluses and minuses. H. H. Miller. New Repub 152:10-11 Ap 24 '65
Health program attacked. Sci N L 87:284 My 1 '65
How eldercare protects the elderly in need of medical care. D. F. Ward. Todays Health 43:67+ Mr '65
How medicare will affect medicine. il Bsns W p 144+ Jl 10 '65
How to choose and use your health insurance. M. Henkin. Am Home 68:13+ Ap '65
Impact of medicare. S. Meisler. il Nation 200:479-81 My 3 '65
It hurts right here, doctor; new medicare bill. Nat R 17:681 Ag 10 '65
It's what's happening, Barry; Republican efforts to sabotage medicare bill. J. N. Eller. America 113:92 Jl 24 '65
Just a minute, doctor; eldermedicare synthesis, sponsored by AMA. K. Crawford. Newsweek 65:34 Mr 15 '65
Latest answers to questions about medicare. il U S News 59:48+ D 20 '65
Latest plan for medicare: cover doctor bills, too. U S News 58:44 Mr 22 '65
Medical care for the aged. S. Hollos. il America 112:309-12 Mr 6 '65; Discussion. 112:442-3, 470, 501-2, 622, 850-2+ Ap 3-17, My 1, Je 12 '65
Medicare. H. C. Wallich. Newsweek 65:72 My 31 '65
Medicare and negotiated health insurance for workers. Mo Labor R 88:III-IV S '65
Medicare: bonanza or burden for drugs? il Bsns W p 174+ S 11 '65
Medicare costs analyzed. F. Marley. Sci N L 88:99 Ag 14 '65
Medicare, how it will work; with chart. Bsns W p51+ Jl 31 '65
Medicare is launched into a shambles; with benefits guide. il Life 59:52B-58 S 3 '65
Medicare, or medical care? W. H. Judd. Read Digest 86:97-102 F '65
Medicare passes. Commonweal 82:516 Jl 23 '65
Medicare prescription. il Newsweek 66:27 Ag 2 '65
Medicare: the major defects. F. Van Dyke. il Nation 200:697-700 Je 28 '65
Medicare vs. the AMA's latest substitute. Consumer Rep 30:148-9 Mr '65
Medicare: what it means to you. F. Bailey, jr. Suc Farm 63:36 O '65
Medicoup; medicare bill. Newsweek 65:28-9 Ap 5 '65

INSURANCE, Health—United States—*Cont.*
Mr Mills's elder-medi-bettercare. H. B. Meyers. il Fortune 71:166-8+ Je '65
More for more; Senate version of the Johnson administration's medicare bill. Time 86:16-17 Jl 16 '65
New welfare state; passing of medicare and aid-to-education bills. il Time 85:21 Ap 16 '65
No rush to hospitals seen. Sci N L 88:114 Ag 21 '65
Note medicare deadline. Sci N L 89:36 Ja 15 '66
Old medicare plan that's growing. il U S News 59:74 S 20 '65
Partnership of promise; private companies fiscal intermediaries for medicare. Time 87:69A-69B Ja 21 '66
Pension plan: up, cost plan: up; major changes in pension-and-medicare bill. U S News 58:95 Je 28 '65
Personal business; medicare. Bsns W p85 Jl 31 '65
Personal business; what medicare will do to retirement plans. Bsns W p 109-10 F 6 '65
Premium from medicare; insurance industry anxious to help. Time 86:105-6 O 22 '65
Rx: medicare. il Sr Schol 87:21-2 S 16 '65
Rhetoric and medicare. J. Burnham. Nat R 17:720 Ag 24 '65; Discussion. 17:794+, 877 S 21, O 5 '65
Russell Long's capers; medicare bill amendments. New Repub 153:6 Jl 3 '65
Senior citizens organize. America 113:519 N 6 '65
Simple facts about medicare. Bet Hom & Gard 43:158+ O '65
This month's feature: controversy in Congress over medicare. Cong Digest 44:67-77+ Mr '65
Three health-care plans most talked about in Congress. U S News 58:6 F 8 '65
Three-in-one care; rival schemes. Time 85:23 Ap 2 '65
Unions see windfall from medicare. Bsns W p 116+ Ag 21 '65
Wait & see; how to oppose medicare, question facing A.M.A. il Time 86:36 Jl 2 '65
What medicare will be like. U S News 59:74 Jl 5 '65
What medicare will do. Time 85:22 Ap 16 '65
What will the doctor charge under medicare? il U S News 59:53 Ag 16 '65
• Why the medical profession is opposed to medicare; adaptation of address. D. F. Ward. Todays Health 43:8+ F '65
Wrapping up medicare; biggest social security measure in history. Bsns W p25 Jl 3 '65
Wrapping up the medicare bill; House ways & means committee reports. Bsns W p32 Mr 27 '65
Your doctor and the A.M.A. J. Bird. il Sat Eve Post 239:13-17+ Ja 1 '66

INSURANCE, Hospitalization
Hospital insurance for all, here's a new plan; including Blue cross, Blue shield and New York state insurance. il U S News 58:89-90 Ap 26 '65
Medicare: what it means to you. F. Bailey, jr. Suc Farm 63:36 O '65
This month's feature: controversy in Congress over medicare. Cong Digest 44:67-77+ Mr '65
Wrapping up the medicare bill; House ways & means committee reports. Bsns W p32 Mr 27 '65

INSURANCE, Liability
Liability insurance your family may need. il Good H 160:154 F '65
Liability revolution. P. Vanderwicken. Esquire 64:88+ Ag '65
See also
Insurance, Automobile
Insurance, Aviation

INSURANCE, Library
Model insurance policy approved. Wilson Lib Bul 39:621 Ap '65

INSURANCE, Life
Cutting their own mortality rate. il Bsns W p 148+ S 25 '65
Insurance: decision for life? il Sr Schol 87: 13-14 O 28 '65
Is life insurance a good investment? F. Bailey, jr. Suc Farm 63:58 S '65
Personal business. Bsns W p 125-6 Ag 21 '65
Policy for the judge; life of pondering judge insured. Time 86:88+ O 8 '65
Should your wife have life insurance? Suc Farm 63:31 F '65
Today's best buy in life insurance. Changing T 19:30 N '65
What life insurance should a young man buy? il Changing T 19:7-12 Ag '65
See also
Insurance, Group life

Policies
How to choose and use your life insurance. M. Henkin. il Am Home 68:16+ Mr '65
$10 million man. Newsweek 67:70 Ja 17 '66
What's the best life insurance for a young father? N. Kuehnl and G. Bush. Bet Hom & Gard 43:8+ S '65

Rates
How your health affects your life insurance rates. Bet Hom & Gard 44:28 Ja '66

War risks
See also
Insurance, Soldiers and sailors

INSURANCE, Marine
Are you covered? A. R. Mansfield, jr. Yachting 117:67+ Je '65
Stop buying insurance off the shelf. J. W. Giles. Motor B 115:34+ Ap '65

INSURANCE, Medical. See Insurance, Health

INSURANCE, Military. See Insurance, Soldiers and sailors

INSURANCE, Property
In riot areas, an insurance cutback. il U S News 59:16 S 13 '65
Insurance: when things go wrong. il Sr Schol 87:21-2 N 4 '65

INSURANCE, Sickness. See Insurance, Health

INSURANCE, Social
Is social security a sacred cow? F. S. Meyer. Nat R 17:463 Je 1 '65

United States
One tax that will go up and up; Social security tax. il U S News 59:104 Jl 12 '65
Pensions, benefits, taxes; how they go up under the new social security law. il U S News 59:48-9 Ag 2 '65
Poor need money. E. M. Burns. il Nation 200:613-15 Je 7 '65
Private insurance gets ready to adjust to medicare. il U S News 59:82-3 O 18 '65
Social security: a growing giant; Congress to boost benefits and taxes. il Bsns W p76-7+ F 6 '65
Two approaches to welfare. O. A. Ornati. bibliog f Mo Labor R 88:296-7 Mr '65
Two sides of social security. America 114:4 Ja 1 '66
Welfare frauds exposed. il Nations Bsns 53: 38-9+ Je '65
Welfare programs in evolution. E. M. Burns. Mo Labor R 88:294-5 Mr '65
See also
Insurance, Health—United States
Insurance, Unemployment—United States
Old age, survivors' and disability insurance trust fund

INSURANCE, Soldiers and sailors
Pru drafts a GI policy; military insurance program. Bsns W p77 O 23 '65

INSURANCE, Unemployment

United States
Affluent poor. J. Burgess. il Esquire 63:82-7+ Ap '65
Failures of unemployment insurance. M. S. Gordon. il Nation 200:610-13 Je 7 '65
Unemployment insurance. J. M. Becker. America 113:73-6 Jl 17 '65
Unemployment insurance legislation in 1965. G. H. Rubin. il Mo Labor R 88:1325-30 N '65
Welfare frauds exposed. il Nations Bsns 53: 38-9+ Je '65
What's happened to the will to work? il Nations Bsns 53:56-8+ My '65
See also
Supplemental unemployment benefits

INSURANCE, War Risk. See Insurance, Soldiers and sailors

INSURANCE actuaries
Those uncertain actuaries. T. A. Wise. il Fortune 72:154-7+ D '65; 73:164-6+ Ja '66

INSURANCE companies
Cutting their own mortality rate. il Bsns W p 148+ S 25 '65
Insurance trade gets off easy; losses from storms, floods, and quake were not covered. Bsns W p62+ My 8 '65
Is insurance the next big antitrust target? Bsns W p52 Je 19 '65
Partnership of promise; private companies fiscal intermediaries for medicare. Time 87: 69A-69B Ja 21 '66
Premium from medicare; insurance industry anxious to help. Time 86:105-6 O 22 '65
Rash of new life insurance companies. il Changing T 19:35-8 My '65
Year of catastrophe; casualty companies. il Time 87:80 Ja 14 '66
See also names of insurance companies, e.g. Travelers insurance company

INTER-AMERICAN music festivals. See Washington, D.C.—Music

INTER-AMERICAN relations
Inter-American conference: Rio meeting seeks to strengthen OAS; with report by J. A. Mora. Américas 17:43-4 My '65
Inter-American systems; address, November 22, 1965. D. Rusk. Vital Speeches 32:130-5 D 15 '65
José Cecilio del Valle, Pan Americanist. P. F. Lavin. il Américas 17:7-9 Ag '65
Recommendations of Secretary General; address, 1965. J. A. Mora. Américas 17:40-1 D '65
Special issue in honor of the seventy-fifth anniversary of the inter-American system; symposium. il Américas 17:1-65 Ap '65
See also
Latin America and the United States
Organization of American states

INTER-AMERICAN specialized conference to deal with problems relating to the conservation of renewable natural resources in the western hemisphere
Conservation; OAS-sponsored meeting. il Américas 17:42 D '65
Inter-American conference on renewable natural resources; Mar del Plata, Argentina. il Nat Parks Mag 40:20 Ja '66

INTER-AMERICAN trade center project, Miami. See Inter-American cultural and trade center, Miami

INTER-AMERICANISM. See Inter-American relations

INTERCHANGE of teachers. See Teachers, Interchange of

INTERCITY transportation. See Transportation—United States

INTERCOLLEGIATE athletics. See College athletics

INTERCOLLEGIATE rowing association regatta. See Regattas

INTERCOMMUNICATING systems
What can an intercom system do for you? Bet Hom & Gard 43:28 Ag '65

INTERCOMMUNION. See Lords Supper

INTERCONNECTION of power systems. See Electric plants—Interconnection

INTERCUTTING of moving pictures. See Moving pictures—Editing

INTERESSENGEMEINSCHAFT farbenindustrie aktiengesellschaft
In the footsteps of Farben. Time 85:96 F 19 '65

INTEREST
Ahead: tighter money, higher interest rates? U S News 59:87-9 S 6 '65
Battle of interest; banks and savings and loan associations. il Time 87:81 Ja 7 '66
Behind the tug of war on money; administration, lenders clash on need for higher rates; with editorial comment. il Bsns W p51-2+, 198 O 16 '65
Brokers find loans costlier; banks raise lending rates. Bsns W p 150 Ap 24 '65
Fed keeps street guessing. Bsns W p 154 N 20 '65
Fed puts quiet hand on interest rates; U.S. monetary policy; with editorial comment. il Bsns W p 104+, 180 Mr 27 '65
Fixing interest rates. H. Hazlitt. Newsweek 66:86 D 20 '65
Higher cost of borrowing; what it means. il U S News 59:38-40 D 20 '65
It will cost more to borrow; here's the word from bankers. il U S News 59:110+ O 18 '65
Latest on boost in interest rates. U S News 59:75 D 27 '65
Make your savings earn more. il Changing T 19:7-10 S '65
Manipulating interest. H. Hazlitt. Newsweek 65:84 Mr 15 '65
Manipulating money. H. Hazlitt. Newsweek 67:47 Ja 3 '66
Markets feel the pressure; question of interest rates. Bsns W p27-8 O 9 '65
Pressure goes on Fed not to tighten credit. Bsns W p40 N 13 '65
Rate rise sharpens savings battle; Fed's boost of interest ceiling on time deposits. il Bsns W p56-8 D 18 '65
Savers come out ahead in big drive for their money. il U S News 60:67-9 Ja 3 '66
Wages of money. D. Lawrence. U S News 60:112 Ja 17 '66
What it costs to borrow money abroad. il U S News 59:115-17 N 1 '65
Why bank shares are lagging; investors fear profit squeeze. il Bsns W p68-9 D 25 '65
Why money is a little harder to borrow. il U S News 58:76 Mr 8 '65

Why the Federal reserve raised interest rates; excerpts from address, December 8, 1965. W. M. Martin, jr. U S News 59:92-4 D 20 '65
See also
Instalment plan

INTERFERENCE, Radio. See Radio interference

INTERFERENCE, Television. See Television interference

INTERFEROMETERS
Infrared spectroscopy with an interferometer. P. B. Boyce and W. M. Sinton. il Sky & Tel 29:78-80 F '65
Light wave measures heat and density. il Sci N L 87:246 Ap 17 '65

INTERFEROMETERS, Sonic
Acoustical thermometer: ultrasonic interferometer. H. H. Plumb and G. Cataland. bibliog il Science 150:155-61 O 8 '65

INTERFERON
New light on an old mystery: the common cold. M. J. E. Senn. il McCalls 93:136-7+ N '65
Wanted, drugs to fight the new viruses. B. Slaton and N. Slaton. il Sci Digest 57:81-4 F '65
Warming up for attack on the common cold; Purdue university research report. Bsns W p55 N 6 '65

INTERGOVERNMENTAL committee for European migration
U.S. participates in meeting of migration committee; statement, December 1, 1965. A. P. Schwartz. Dept State Bul 54:39-41 Ja 3 '66

INTERGOVERNMENTAL commodity agreements. See Commodity control

INTER-GOVERNMENTAL maritime consultative organization
Breakthrough in the facilitation of international maritime traffic. J. Roullier. UN Mo Chron 2:58-62 F '65

INTERIOR, Department of. See United States—Interior, Department of

INTERIOR decoration
How architects practice interior design; summary of interviews (cont) W. B. Foxhall. il Arch Rec 137:105+ Ap '65
See also
Electric lighting
House decoration
Mural painting and decoration

INTERLIBRARY loans
Acknowledgments from an author; address, July 3, 1965. G. Carson. Wilson Lib Bul 40:271-4+ N '65

INTERLOCKING directorates
Outside directors under attack; proposed legislation against interlocks in corporate management. A. R. Towl. il Harvard Bsns R 43:135-47 S '65

INTERMARRIAGE of races
Does amalgamation work in Brazil? E. B. Thompson. il Ebony 20:27-30+ Jl; 33-42 S '65 (to be cont)
Intermarriage and the Court. A. C. Brownfeld. Commonweal 81:609-10 F 5 '65
Interracial marriage and the law. W. D. Zabel. Atlan 216:75-9 O '65
Is a mixed race inevitable? excerpt from The pace is important. V. Dabney. U S News 58:67 My 10 '65
Miscegenation test case; Virginia law. America 112:183 F 6 '65
Mixed marriages: next trend in race problem? with interviews with S. M. Garn and E. Ginzberg. il U S News 58:58-63 Je 28 '65
Test interracial marriage bans; case of Mr and Mrs Richard P. Loving, Va. Christian Cent 82:164 F 10 '65
Trials of an interracial couple; V. and T. Wright of East Meadow, Long Island. il Ebony 20:66-8+ O '65
Would you want your daughter to marry one? H. J. Massaquoi. il Ebony 20:82-4+ Ag '65

INTERMARRIAGES, Religious. See Marriages, Mixed

INTERMEDIC, incorporated
Doubtful bargain for tourists. Consumer Rep 30:272-3 Je '65

INTERMISSIONS
See also
Basketball—Intermissions

INTERNAL migration. See Migration, Internal

INTERNAL revenue. See Excise tax

INTERNAL revenue service. See United States—Internal revenue service

INTERNAL security
New security risks: disloyalty to the leader. W. F. Buckley, jr. Nat R 17:863 O 5 '65
Security practices: nonmilitary agencies still hold to vestiges of procedures developed in 1950's. D. S. Greenberg. Science 148:773-5 My 7 '65

INTERNAL structure of the earth. See Earth
—Internal structure
INTERNATIONAL advisory committee on bibliography, documentation and terminology.
See United Nations educational, scientific
and cultural organization—International
advisory committee on bibliography, documentation and terminology
INTERNATIONAL aeroclassic. See Aviation—
Exhibitions
INTERNATIONAL agencies
Law and survival; address, March 24, 1965.
W. O. Douglas. il Vital Speeches 31:400-3
Ap 15 '65
See also
International cooperation
International organization
INTERNATIONAL air and space show. See
Aviation—Exhibitions
INTERNATIONAL air transport association
Airline talks fail to end movie deadlock. J.
W. Carter. Aviation W 82:29 F 8 '65
Airlines' movie war. New Repub 152:7 My 8
'65
Big fight over the Atlantic. il Duns R 86:43-
4+ S '65
Board refuses to back inflight movie ban.
J. R. Ashlock. Aviation W 82:28 Je 7 '65
Fare slash talks set for IATA meeting. J. R.
Ashlock. Aviation W 83:40 Ag 23 '65
IATA Atlantic fares to get CAB approval.
Aviation W 83:38-9 N 8 '65
IATA carriers report 64.5 per cent cargo
gain. Aviation W 82:43 My 17 '65
IATA members vote liability limit raise. J. R.
Ashlock. il Aviation W 83:36-7 N 8 '65
IATA simplifies conference procedures. J. R.
Ashlock. Aviation W 83:24-5 N 1 '65
IATA slashes group, excursion tariffs. il Aviation W 83:38 O 11 '65
Justice dept. may block IATA movie ban.
J. W. Carter. Aviation W 82:40-1 My 10 '65
Movies up in the air; agreement to end inflight showings on transatlantic flights.
Bsns W p 164 Ap 24 '65
Warsaw move seen threat to cooperation.
J. R. Ashlock. Aviation W 83:35 D 6 '65
World cargo rate structure seen continuing
after IATA session. L. L. Doty. Aviation W
82:27 My 31 '65
INTERNATIONAL airlines. See Aviation—International aspects
INTERNATIONAL airways. See Aviation—International aspects
INTERNATIONAL association of machinists
St Louis blues; McDonnell aircraft strike.
Newsweek 66:72 N 29 '65
INTERNATIONAL association of universities
Shop talk. Newsweek 66:82+ S 13 '65
INTERNATIONAL astronautical congress
Booster revolution foreseen at IAF. Miss &
Roc 17:21-2 S 27 '65
Soviets at Athens detail Voskhod training.
W. C. Wetmore. Aviation W 83:35 S 20
'65
INTERNATIONAL astronautical federation
Booster revolution foreseen at IAF. Miss &
Roc 17:21-2 S 27 '65
INTERNATIONAL atomic energy agency
Atomic energy agency's reports noted; General assembly. UN Mo Chron 2:96 D '65
Atoms for peace: concern growing that program is spreading means for more nations
to build weapons. D. S. Greenberg. Science
147:843-4 F 19 '65; Reply. F. J. Bradley.
148:733 My 7 '65
Atoms for peace, or war. J. A. Hall. For
Affairs 43:602-15 Jl '65
Civilizing the atom. J. Lear. il Sat R 48:
63-6 O 2 '65
Henry Seligman's Sisters of mercy; the research mission of the isotopes. S. White.
il Sat R 48:68-71 O 2 '65
International cooperation on the peaceful uses
of atomic energy; statement. September 22,
1965. G. T. Seaborg. Dept State Bul 53:677-
82 O 25 '65
New center for physics; International center
for theoretical physics. A. Salam. Bul
Atomic Sci 21:43-5 D '65
Nuclear power and proliferation; address.
November 17, 1965. H. D. Smyth. Dept
State Bul 54:31-5 Ja 3 '66
President sends message to IAEA conference.
Dept State Bul 53:678 O 25 '65
INTERNATIONAL automobile show. See Automobiles—Exhibitions
INTERNATIONAL balance of payments. See
Balance of payments
**INTERNATIONAL bank for reconstruction and
development**
Can 102 nations agree on a new reserve
unit? IMF and World bank meet in Washinton. il Bsns W p29-30 S 25 '65

World bank issues six-month financial statement. Dept State Bul 52:273-4 F 22 '65
World bank setting up a court for investors;
plan to settle disputes in developing countries. Bsns W p46 Ap 3 '65
INTERNATIONAL banking. See Banks and
banking, International
INTERNATIONAL book programs. See Books
and reading—International aspects
INTERNATIONAL brigades. See Spain—History—Civil war, 1936-1939—Volunteers
**INTERNATIONAL brotherhood of electrical
workers**
Electrical fusion ahead. Bsns W p 126 Je
26 '65
**INTERNATIONAL brotherhood of teamsters,
chauffeurs, warehousemen and helpers of
America**
Aviation industry teamster ranks swell. J.
W. Carter. Aviation W 83:35 N 22 '65
Hoffa and the teamsters, by R. James and
E. James. Review
U S News il 59:62+ O 25 '65
Is Hoffa getting set to raid? brewery workers
challenge to Toledo teamsters. Bsns W p55
Mr 27 '65
Ordeal of a Hoffa victim; S. Baron. B.
Davidson. il Sat Eve Post 238:23-7 Je 19 '65
Teamsters gird for day of change; question
of Hoffa's legal appeals. il Bsns W p97-8
N 27 '65
What next, if Hoffa loses out? Bsns W p 142
Ap 24 '65
Who will succeed Hoffa? il Newsweek 66:84
D 20 '65
INTERNATIONAL business machines corporation
IBM buys its own sales pitch; System 360
computers in six plants. il Bsns W p 140-2+
O 30 '65
IBM sends computers on air tour. Aviation
W 83:30 O 18 '65
IBM's answer to time-sharing. Bsns W p50
Mr 13 '65
Peace on earth; Christmas exhibit at I.B.M.'s
display center, New York. New Yorker 41:
22-3 Ja 1 '66
Specialists try a wider track; management
development problem. il Bsns W p56-7 Jl
31 '65
INTERNATIONAL center for theoretical physics. See International atomic energy agency
INTERNATIONAL children's emergency fund.
See United Nations children's fund
INTERNATIONAL Chopin piano competition.
See Music—Competitions
INTERNATIONAL Christian leadership (organization)
Power of prayer; Presidential prayer breakfast. A. Kopkind. New Repub 152:19-20 Mr
6 '65
INTERNATIONAL civil aviation organization
Cooperation, the cornerstone of international
civil aviation. R. P. Boyle. Dept State Bul
53:820-7 N 22 '65
ICAO seeks improved techniques for testing
air navigation devices. J. R. Ashlock. Aviation W 83:26 Jl 5 '65
Pilot group disputes separation rule. J. R.
Ashlock. Aviation W 83:38-9 D 13 '65
INTERNATIONAL code signals. See Signals
and signaling
INTERNATIONAL coffee council
Big stir in coffee. J. M. Salazar. Read
Digest 87:31-2+ D '65
President assigns functions for participation
in coffee group; executive order. June 14,
1965. L. B. Johnson. Dept State Bul 53:87-8
Jl 12 '65
INTERNATIONAL commodity control. See Commodity control
**INTERNATIONAL confederation of free trade
unions**
Labor takes a harder line overseas; AFL-
CIO is threatening to boycott two top international labor groups. Bsns W p 139-
40 Ap 24 '65
INTERNATIONAL conferences
Calendar of international conferences. See
occasional issues of Department of state
bulletin
Can we talk to Marxian atheists? opening
attempt; conference in Salzburg, Austria.
D. I. MacLean. America 113:115-17 Jl 31 '65
Quiet place fosters U.S.-British harmony;
meeting of U.S. senators and representatives and British officials to discuss
world's most disturbing problems. il
Bsns W p32-3 F 13 '65
Summit diplomacy; next test for LBJ. P.
Lisagor. il Nations Bsns 53:23-4 Mr '65

INTERNATIONAL conferences—*Continued*
United States delegations to international conferences. See issues of Department of state bulletin
  See also
Conference of the Eighteen nation committee on disarmament, Geneva, 1962-
Council of foreign ministers, Geneva, 1954
Inter-American conferences
Peace conferences
Pugwash conferences on science and world affairs

INTERNATIONAL congress on air technology. See Aviation—International aspects

INTERNATIONAL cookery. See Cookery, International

INTERNATIONAL cooperation
Building blocks of world order; address, March 23, 1965. H. Cleveland. Dept State Bul 52:566-9 Ap 19 '65
Great revolution; address. W. Lippmann. UN Mo Chron 2:66-72 Ap '65; Same. il UNESCO Courier 18:20-4 O '65
International cooperation, a necessity of our age; statement, November 29, 1965. L. B. Johnson. Dept State Bul 53:969 D 20 '65
International cooperation: a realistic appraisal; address, March 23, 1965. M. Bundy. Dept State Bul 52:562-5 Ap 19 '65
International co-operation and world peace; address. M. K. Hussein. U N Mo Chron 2: 59-70 Mr '65
International co-operation: man's new dimension; address. G. M. d'Arboussier. UN Mo Chron 2:74-84 F '65
International co-operation: the three periods of co-operation; address. E. Faure. UN Mo Chron 2:47-58 Mr '65
International co-operation: twenty years after the San Francisco conference; address. A. Lleras Camargo. UN Mo Chron 2:63-73 F '65
National power and the creation of a workable world community; remarks, June 2, 1965. H. Humphrey. Dept State Bul 52:1048-50 Je 28 '65
Problem of international co-operation in the contemporary world; address. A. K. Brohi. UN Mo Chron 2:71-88 Mr '65
Regional cooperation in southeast Asia. B. K. Gordon. bibliog f il Cur Hist 48:103-8+ F '65
Science must serve the cause of peace; address. M. D. Millionshchikov. UN Mo Chron 2:53-65 Ap '65
Strengthening the international development institutions; statement. July 9, 1965. A. E. Stevenson. Dept State Bul 53:142-51 Jl 26 '65; Same with title International development. Vital Speeches 31:610-15 Ag 1 '65
United Nations commemoration address, June 25, 1965. P. Tremblay. UN Mo Chron 2: 88-91 Jl '65
United States and international cooperation; address, March 26, 1965. W. A. Harriman. Dept State Bul 52:621-8 Ap 26 '65
Unseen search for peace; address, October 16, 1965. D. Rusk. Dept State Bul 53:690-9 N 1 '65
  See also
Antarctic treaty, 1959
Banks and banking, International
Economic planning, International
Education—International cooperation
Inter-American relations
International agencies
Internationalism
Science—International aspects
United Nations
White House conference on international cooperation

INTERNATIONAL cooperation year
Committees set up for International cooperation year. Dept State Bul 52:382-3 Mr 15 '65
How to live together. H. Cleveland. il Am Ed 1:1-5 My '65
International cooperation year. H. Bowser. Sat R 48:20 Mr 6 '65
ICY; report on the White House conference on International cooperation year. A. Balk. Sat R 49:24-8 Ja 22 '66
International co-operation year: statement. Thant. UN Mo Chron 2:1 F '65
International cooperation year: symposium. Dept State Bul 53:383-423 S 6; 811-47 N 22 '65
1965: International co-operation year. il UNESCO Courier 18:2 Mr '65
Peace comes in parcels; address, March 31, 1965. H. Cleveland. Dept State Bul 52:613-18 Ap 26 '65
Teaching about International cooperation year. D. DuBose. bibliog Sr Schol 86:sup6 Ap 1 '65

To the young people of the world; for the New Year 1965. R. Maheu. UNESCO Courier 18:37 Ja '65
U.S. reports to United Nations on ICY activities; letter, May 20, 1965, with U.S. note to Secretary-General, May 17, 1965. A. E. Stevenson. Dept State Bul 52:1067-9 Je 28 '65

INTERNATIONAL copyright. See Copyright

INTERNATIONAL corporations. See Corporations, International

INTERNATIONAL correspondence schools
Educating yourself. H. Shuldiner. il Pop Sci 186:84-6+ My '65

INTERNATIONAL council of Christian churches
Those who don't want it. Time 86:59-60 Ag 27 '65

INTERNATIONAL council of community churches
Council of community churches. R. H. Taylor. Christian Cent 82:1136 S 15 '65

INTERNATIONAL council of scientific unions
  See also
International geophysical year

Committee on space research
COSPAR meet stresses cooperation. W. S. Beller. Miss & Roc 16:16-17 My 24 '65

INTERNATIONAL court of arbitration, The Hague
Two members named to Permanent court of arbitration. Dept State Bul 53:885 N 29 '65

INTERNATIONAL court of justice, The Hague
International court of justice; concerning public hearings in the South West Africa and South Africa cases. UN Mo Chron 2:50-2 Ap '65
New blow at Connally; U.S. chamber of commerce calls for repeal of the Connally reservation. Time 85:24 My 7 '65

INTERNATIONAL criminal police organization
Interpol: theft warnings alert police in ninety-five countries. il UNESCO Courier 18:8-9 N '65

INTERNATIONAL development association
AID means service. America 113:197 Ag 28 '65

INTERNATIONAL drag festival. See Motorcycle racing

INTERNATIONAL economic planning. See Economic planning, International

INTERNATIONAL education
Dichotomies in American education. J. J. Van Patten. Sch & Soc 93:474-5 D 11 '65
International education; symposium, ed. by N. L. Beach. il Sr Schol 86:sup 1, 9-14 My 20 '65
New program in comparative international education. Sch & Soc 93:496+ D 25 '65
New program in international education. Sch & Soc 93:340+ O 2 '65
  See also
Area studies
International relations—Study and teaching
Salzburg seminar in American studies
Teachers, Interchange of
Travel study courses
United Nations educational, scientific and cultural organization

INTERNATIONAL educational exchanges. See Educational exchanges

INTERNATIONAL emergency children's fund. See United Nations children's fund

INTERNATIONAL executive service corps
Executive peace corps: it works; retired U.S. businessmen as volunteer executives. il Bsns W p84+ O 9 '65

INTERNATIONAL exhibition of paper, printing and graphic arts industries, Paris, 1965
TPG-65, Paris exposition: a production man's view. R. D. Chapman. il Pub W 188:64-8+ Ag 9 '65

INTERNATIONAL federation for documentation
It's a wise child; FID congress. J. Berry. Library J 90:4724 N 1 '65

INTERNATIONAL federation of air line pilots associations
International pilots federation supports heads-up flight displays. Aviation W 83:32 N 1 '65
Pilot group disputes separation rule. J. R. Ashlock. Aviation W 83:38-9 D 13 '65

INTERNATIONAL festival of contemporary music, Zagreb. See Music festivals—Yugoslavia

INTERNATIONAL festival of contemporary music, Warsaw. See Music festivals—Poland

INTERNATIONAL festival of music and drama, Edinburgh
Transplants in Edinburgh. J. W. Stedman; F. Aprahamian. Opera N 30:23 N 6 '65

INTERNATIONAL film festival, Cannes. See Cannes international film festival

INTERNATIONAL finance. See Finance, International

INTERNATIONAL franchise association
Franchising finds it's an industry; franchisers conference at Boston. il Bsns W p72+ Je 19 '65
INTERNATIONAL games for the deaf
1965 Olympics for the deaf. il Ebony 20:76-80 O '65
INTERNATIONAL geophysical year
Antarctica, continent of international science; adaptation of address December 28, 1965. L. M. Gould. il Science 150:1775-81 D 31 '65
INTERNATIONAL government. See International organization
INTERNATIONAL horse race. See Horse racing
INTERNATIONAL index. See Social sciences and humanities index
INTERNATIONAL Indian Ocean expedition
Effects of the Indian Ocean expedition. V. K. McElheny. il Science 149:957-8 Ag 27 '65; Reply. W. S. Wooster. 150:290+ O 15 '65
INTERNATIONAL industrial conference
Peace: common stock for business; San Francisco meeting of top executives from sixty-six nations. il Bsns W p80-2 S 25 '65
Thinking internationally. Newsweek 66:81 S 27 '65
INTERNATIONAL inventors and new products exhibition. See Exhibitions
INTERNATIONAL joint commission (United States and Canada)
IJC recommendations approved for Rainy River pollution control. Dept State Bul 54:36 Ja 3 '66
INTERNATIONAL labor movement. See Trade unions—International aspects
INTERNATIONAL labor organization
Labor takes a harder line overseas; AFL-CIO is threatening to boycott two top international labor groups. Bsns W p 139-40 Ap 24 '65
Man as a beast of burden; I.L.O. recommendations for maximum load carrying. R. L. Tobin. Sat R 48:22 Ag 28 '65
INTERNATIONAL labor press association
Off the barricades; U.S. unions' 1,000 publications. il Time 85:48+ My 14 '65
INTERNATIONAL language. See Language, Universal
INTERNATIONAL latex corporation
Design verification under way on Apollo suit backpack; Block 2 Apollo suit tests. D. E. Fink. il Aviation W 83:52-3+ D 13 '65
INTERNATIONAL law
Breakdown of international law and order; address, October 11, 1965. F. Nogueira. Vital Speeches 32:81-4 N 15 '65
Diplomatic escape hatch; inconsistency of sovereign immunity. Time 86:74 S 17 '65
Dominican situation in the perspective of international law; address, June 9, 1965. L. C. Meeker. Dept State Bul 53:60-5 Jl 12 '65
For a worldwide judiciary; World peace through law center, Washington, D.C. il Time 85:62-3 My 28 '65
Law and survival; address, March 24, 1965. W. O. Douglas. il Vital Speeches 31:400-3 Ap 15 '65
There's a will; is there a way? gathering of international jurists. il Time 86:48 S 24 '65
What is world law? N. Cousins. Sat R 48:24-5 Ag 14 '65
See also
Claims
Extradition
Fishery laws and legislation
Geneva conventions
Intervention
Rule of law
Sanctions (international law)
Space law
United Nations—Charter
United Nations—International law commission
United Nations—Legal committee
INTERNATIONAL law, Private
Unification of the rules of private international law; report of the U.S. delegation, January 15, 1965, to the 10th session of the Hague conference on private international law. il Dept State Bul 52:265-73 F 22 '65
INTERNATIONAL law commission. See United Nations—International law commission
INTERNATIONAL loans. See Loans, Foreign
INTERNATIONAL longshoremen's association
Dock peace leaves some question marks. il Bsns W p90+ Mr 13 '65
How to damage the economy. il Time 85:90 F 19 '65
INTERNATIONAL minerals and chemical corporation
I.M.C: the miner who shook the fertilizer market. R. J. Whalen. il Fortune 71:108-13+ Mr '65
They make things grow at IMC. J. B. Weiner. il Duns R 85:32-5+ F '65

INTERNATIONAL monetary fund
Breaking the ice. il Time 86:102 O 8 '65
Can 102 nations agree on a new reserve unit? IMF and World bank meet in Washington. il Bsns W p29-30 S 25 '65
Closed shop for monetary reform. N. McKitterick. New Repub 153:9-10 S 25 '65
Cry for change. il Time 85:90+ Ap 16 '65
Edging closer to monetary reform; with editorial comment. il Bsns W p68+, 160 Je 26 '65
International monetary problems; strong, sound and stable dollar; address, July 10, 1965. H. H. Fowler. Vital Speeches 31:646-9 Ag 15 '65
Light on liquidity. il Fortune 72:57-8+ Ag '65
Money reformers start bargaining; IMF conference, Washington; with editorial comment. il Bsns W p25-6, 144 O 2 '65
Pin-pointing problems in payments reform; highlights of Ossola group study. il Bsns W p87 Ag 14 '65
President recommends increase of U.S. quota in monetary fund; letter, March 17, 1965, with proposed amendment. L. B. Johnson. Dept State Bul 52:507-8 Ap 5 '65
U.S. gets break on IMF gold. Bsns W p 139-40 F 13 '65
Why the dollar is in danger. J. Daniel and J. B. Shuman. Read Digest 87:130-4 N '65
World money plan. H. Hazlitt. Newsweek 66:95 O 25 '65
World money shortage: five cures. il U S News 58:127 Ap 26 '65
INTERNATIONAL nickel company, incorporated
International nickel: the quiet sensation. J. Perham. il Duns R 86:51-4 O '65
INTERNATIONAL nickel company of Canada
France bets millions on nickel; Societe le nickel. Bsns W p 110+ Ap 24 '65
INTERNATIONAL organization
Cardinal Ottaviani on world unity; speech. A. Ottaviani. Cath World 202:242-3 Ja '66
Key to peace. J. S. Clark. Sat R 49:28 Ja 15 '66
Ottaviani favors world government. America 113:454-5 O 23 '65
INTERNATIONAL organization, Regional
Address to non-governmental organizations; annual conference May 27, 1965. Thant. UN Mo Chron 2:68-70 Je '65
American regionalism and the United Nations; address, April 10, 1965, with questions and answers. C. Gibson. Ann Am Acad 360:120-4 Jl '65
Malaise of sovereignty. A. Weill-Tuckerman. il Nation 200:690-1 Je 28 '65
Regional organization: a planner's perspective. W. W. Rostow. Dept State Bul 52:994-1000 Je 21 '65
See also names of international organizations, e.g. Organization of American states
INTERNATIONAL organizations. See International agencies
INTERNATIONAL patent convention. See Patents—International aspects
INTERNATIONAL PEN club. See PEN club
INTERNATIONAL plastics exhibition, London. See Exhibitions
INTERNATIONAL postal union. See Universal postal union
INTERNATIONAL professional pilots association
Gone flying with the NPA to Basin Harbor, Vermont. E. D. Muhlfeld. il Flying 77:96-101 O '65
INTERNATIONAL publishers association
Brochure, registration mailed for IPA congress. il Pub W 187:36 Mr 8 '65
Dean Rusk, at IPA, cites international role of books. Pub W 187:75-7 Je 14 '65
Hjalmar Pehrsson: Secretary General of IPA; interview. H. Pehrsson. Pub W 187:24-6 My 31 '65
IPA congress hits U.S. on copyright and foreign policies. Pub W 187:141-3 Je 7 '65
IPA education section: ways sought for international publishing aid; meeting in Frankfurt. il Pub W 188:32-8 N 22 '65
IPA reports and proceedings given to Melcher library. Pub W 187:55 Je 28 '65
International publishers congress in Washington. D. C; symposium. il Pub W 187:30-42 Je 28 '65
International publishers congress to be held in US for first time. Library J 90:597 F 1 '65
Take a bow: Storer Lunt. Pub W 187:22-3 My 31 '65
See also
Publishers and publishing—International aspects

INTERNATIONAL publishers congress. See
    International publishers association
INTERNATIONAL reading association
    Meeting, 1965. Sr Schol 86:sup 1-2 My 20 '65
INTERNATIONAL Red cross. See Red cross
INTERNATIONAL relations
    All in one life's span. il U S News 58:46-8 F
        1 '65
    America's place in the world. D. D. Eisen-
        hower. Read Digest 87:75-81 O '65
    As the world struggles against war and
        famine. il U S News 60:30-2 Ja 10 '66
    Building a decent world order; address, June
        5, 1965. D. Rusk. Dept State Bul 53:27-30
        Jl 5 '65
    Can science prevent war? A. Larson. Sat R
        48:15-17+ F 20 '65; Reply. J. J. Agria. 48:
        25 Mr 13 '65; Rejoinder. 48:27 Ap 3 '65
    Catalytic China; U.S. and U.S.S.R. peace
        depends on peril. Christian Cent 82:1307-8
        O 27 '65
    Churchill on America; a legacy in words;
        quotations. W. L. S. Churchill. il U S News
        58:38-9 F 8 '65; Same abr. with title
        Churchill legacy in words. Read Digest
        86:214B-214C My '65
    Communists never give up; condensation of
        address, December 1, 1964. T. J. Dodd. Read
        Digest 86:61-6 Mr '65
    Facts, fallacies and foreign policy; address,
        May 4, 1965. H. M. Jackson. Vital Speeches
        31:515-18 Je 15 '65
    Foreign affairs. W. Pfaff. Commonweal 81:
        685-6; 82:6-7, 135-7, 520-1, 683-4 F 26, Mr 26,
        Ap 23, Jl 23, S 24 '65
    Geography and foreign affairs. G. E. Pearcy.
        Dept State Bul 52:1035-41 Je 28 '65
    Hard realities of power demand that we must
        fight on. E. V. Rostow. il Life 59:40B-40C Jl
        2 '65
    Ideology of foreign policy; equal opportunities
        for all people; address, December 1, 1965.
        P. Dean. Vital Speeches 32:173-5 Ja 1 '66
    Moscow returns to the attack as Mansfield
        reaches Moscow. America 113:699 D 4 '65
    Nonalignment in foreign affairs; symposium,
        ed. by C. V. Crabb, jr. bibliog f Ann Am
        Acad 362:1-138 N '65
    Partnership in world affairs; address, June
        17, 1965. A. E. Stevenson. Dept State Bul
        53:123-8 Jl 19 '65
    Society of man, by L. J. Halle. Review
        Sat R 49:41 Ja 22 '66. A. N. Holcombe
    Someday, a real Christmas; excerpts from
        editorial, December 23, 1955. D. Lawrence.
        U S News 59:84 D 27 '65
    Soviet leaders on the move. il Newsweek
        67:36+ Ja 24 '66
    State of affairs (cont) H. Brandon. Sat R
        48:16-17 F 13; 14+ F 27; 22-3 Ap 10 '65
    U.S. and world affairs annual, 1965-66; ed.
        by E. R. Floyd and others. il Sr Schol
        87:12-41+ S 30 '65
    Uses of flexibility; adaptation of address.
        J. W. Fulbright. Sat R 48:19-21+ My 8
        '65; Discussion. 48:21 My 29 '65
    Vacuum diplomacy. G. Lichtheim. Commen-
        tary 41:49-53 Ja '66
    Way U.S. leaders size up the world now.
        U S News 59:42-4 N 15 '65
    Why? lack of ability to transmit will to peace
        to others. D. Lawrence. U S News 59:144 O
        11 '65
    With what little wisdom the world is ruled.
        G. Myrdal. il N Y Times Mag p20-1+ Jl
        18 '65
    World in a mess. il U S News 59:38-42 D
        6 '65
    World is a campus; recommendations by
        committees on aviation, transportation, and
        cultural exchange. W. D. Patterson. Sat
        R 49:20 Ja 1 '66
        See also
    Agriculture—International aspects
    Atlantic community
    Crimea conference, Yalta, Russia, 1945
    Diplomacy
    Disarmament
    Imperialism
    International law
    International organization
    International security
    Internationalism
    Intervention
    League of Nations
    Monroe doctrine
    Nationalism
    Neutrality

Peace
Power (political science)
United Nations
War
War, Declaration of
War, Prevention of
World politics
    also subhead Foreign relations under
    names of countries, regions, etc., e.g.
    United States—Foreign relations

Bibliography

International relations, 1960-1964. H. J. Mor-
    genthau. bibliog f Ann Am Acad 360:163-71
    Jl '65
Recent books on international relations;
    comp. by H. L. Roberts. See issues of For-
    eign affairs
World affairs bibliography chaotic according
    to ISSI research project. Library J 90:4314
    O 15 '65
World scene. F. Canavan. America 112:681-3
    My 8 '65
World scene. V. S. Kearney. America 113:
    676-7+ N 27 '65

Study and teaching

Book fair exhibit for international under-
    standing. M. F. Taylor. il Sr Schol 86:sup
    18 Ap 29 '65
Education and world affairs; a search for
    new techniques. J. E. Horner. Dept State
    Bul 53:1017-20 D 27 '65
Raising children to know their neighbors,
    near and far. C. W. Yost. Parents Mag
    40:46 O '65
INTERNATIONAL rice research institute
    Our far-flung correspondents. E. J. Kahn, jr.
        il New Yorker 41:154+ O 23 '65
INTERNATIONAL rostrum of composers
    Composers on the rostrum. R. McMullen. Hi
        Fi 15:133+ Ag '65
INTERNATIONAL science fair. See Science
    fairs
INTERNATIONAL scientific and technological
    affairs, Office of. See United States—State,
    Department of—International scientific and
    technological affairs, Office of
INTERNATIONAL security
    Nuclear fallout. Newsweek 66:29 D 6 '65
    Problem of international co-operation in the
        contemporary world; address. A. K. Brohi.
        UN Mo Chron 2:71-88 Mr '65
    20th anniversary of V-E day; address, May
        7, 1965. L. B. Johnson. Dept State Bul 52:
        790-3 My 24 '65
        See also
    Atomic power—International aspects
    International organizations
    International relations
    War, Prevention of
INTERNATIONAL settlements, Bank for. See
    Bank for international settlements
INTERNATIONAL social cooperation. See In-
    ternational cooperation
INTERNATIONAL social science institute
    World affairs bibliography chaotic according
        to ISSI research project. Library J 90:4314
        O 15 '65
INTERNATIONAL society for the protection
    of animals
    Surinam animal rescue. J. R. Smith. il Natur
        Hist 75:24-9 Ja '66
INTERNATIONAL sugar agreement
    Sugar conference; asked second session be
        convened to continue negotiations for new
        International sugar agreement. UN Mo
        Chron 2:47 N '65
INTERNATIONAL sugar conference
    Sugar conference; meeting in Geneva. UN
        Mo Chron 2:38 O '65
INTERNATIONAL telecommunication union
    Cooperation in international communications.
        L. Loevinger. Dept State Bul 53:828-34 N
        22 '65
    ITU and the future of International telecom-
        munications. G. C. Gross. UN Mo Chron
        2:75-8 My '65
    Telecommunications: 1865-1965. il UNESCO
        Courier 18:4-9 My '65
INTERNATIONAL telecommunications satel-
    lite consortium
    Apollo, commercial net endorsed by Interna-
        tional consortium vote. Aviation W 83:34
        N 8 '65
INTERNATIONAL telephone and telegraph-
    American broadcasting company merger.
        See Business consolidations and mergers
INTERNATIONAL telephone and telegraph
    corporation
    Hardware limitation leads to ITT spinoff.
        Aviation W 82:73 F 8 '65
    ITT: can profits be programed? J. B. Weiner.
        il Duns R 86:38-41+ N '65

INTERNATIONAL television. See Television broadcasting—International aspects

INTERNATIONAL theatre institute
International theatre institute; congress in Tel Aviv. H. Popkin. Nation 201:127-8 S 6 '65

INTERNATIONAL tin agreement
See also
United Nations tin conference

INTERNATIONAL tin council
International tin agreement. UN Mo Chron 2:64-6 My '65

INTERNATIONAL trade. See Commerce

INTERNATIONAL trade fair, Tokyo. See Exhibitions

INTERNATIONAL trade fairs. See Exhibitions

INTERNATIONAL traffic in arms. See Munitions

INTERNATIONAL travel. See Travel

INTERNATIONAL typographical union
Death of a craft? automation in the printing industry. T. R. Brooks. Commonweal 82: 46-9 Ap 2 '65
New York newspapers under the gun again. il Bsns W p111-12 Mr 20 '65
Newsmen v. printers; typographers defiance of automation. Time 86:74 S 3 '65
Presses keep rolling; shutdown averted. Bsns W p 146 Ap 10 '65
Settlement in New York. Time 85:60 Ap 16 '65
Solidarity forever; Baltimore sunpapers strike ends. Newsweek 65:22 Je 7 '65
Strike in New York? issue of automation. il Newsweek 65:88 Mr 22 '65
Why printers broke strike; Sunpapers, Baltimore. U S News 58:77 Je 7 '65

INTERNATIONAL understanding. See Internationalism

INTERNATIONAL union for the conservation of nature and natural resources
International nature union needs U.S.A. C. W. Buchheister. Audubon Mag 67:284 S '65
To save our natural resources; Latin American committee on national parks. M. Buchinger. il Américas 17:28-31 Ag '65

INTERNATIONAL union of electrical, radio and machine workers
Carey's comeuppance; fraudulent election. Time 85:26 Ap 16 '65
Carey's fall causes union quake; Labor dept. report of misconduct on IUE's election. il Bsns W p 140+ Ap 10 '65
Counted out. M. Kempton. New Repub 152: 16-18 Ap 24 '65
Electrical fusion ahead. Bsns W p 126 Je 26 '65
Great vote steal; president resigns after vote-counting irregularities. il Newsweek 65:82-3 Ap 19 '65
Interim report on the IUE election. W. W. Wirtz. Mo Labor R 88:562-5 My '65
New IUE chief tries to heal the wounds. Bsns W p52+ Ap 17 '65
Rebuilding the IUE. Newsweek 66:80-1 N 1 '65
Reuther pushes toward an old goal; merger of UAW and IUE. Bsns W p 128 F 20 '65
Reuther's offer to IUE: one stronger union; UAW-IUE merger proposal. Bsns W p28 F 13 '65
Why the electrical workers union turned against its president. U S News 58:94 Ap 19 '65

INTERNATIONAL union of family organizations
For the world's children; IUFO conference. J. Moorhead. il PTA Mag 60:16-18 N '65

INTERNATIONAL union of mine, mill and smelter workers
National embarrassment; government's harassment. Nation 201:150 S 27 '65

INTERNATIONAL union of students
Two Communist fronts at work. L. M. Taubinger and S. Musulin. Nat R 17:328 Ap 20 '65

INTERNATIONAL university choral festival. See Music festivals

INTERNATIONAL volunteer service. See Volunteer service, International

INTERNATIONAL whaling commission
Of whales and whaling. N. Simon. Science 149:943-6 Ag 27 '65
Senseless slaughter. Nation 200:574-5 My 31 '65
South Atlantic: death of the whales. J. Hillaby. il Nation 200:245-7 Mr 8 '65

INTERNATIONAL woodworkers of America
Bargaining in the western lumber industry. J. L. Dana. il Mo Labor R 88:925-31 Ag '65

INTERNATIONAL yacht racing union
Changes in the racing rules. R. N. Bavier, jr. Yachting 117:51 Mr '65
IYRU design competition winners. O. J. Stephens, 2d. il Yachting 117:54-7+ Mr '65
Look out for Tempest; two-man keel boat. R. N. Bavier, jr. il Yachting 118:46-7+ Jl '65

INTERNATIONAL year for human rights
International year for human rights. UN Mo Chron 2:38-9 Mr '65
International year for human rights; concerning the committee's report. UN Mo Chron 2:39-41 Ap '65
International year for human rights; working party adopts report. UN Mo Chron 2:60 Jl '65

INTERNATIONAL years of the quiet sun
Quiet eclipse. il Sci Digest 57:45-6 Je '65
Solar activity during the first fourteen months of the International years of the quiet sun. H. W. Dodson and others. bibliog il Science 184:1328-31 Je 4 '65

INTERNATIONAL yellow pages. See Business —Directories

INTERNATIONALISM
Cardinal Ottaviani on world unity; speech. A. Ottaviani. Cath World 202:242-3 Ja '66

INTERNMENT camps. See Concentration camps

INTERNS (medicine)
Intern, by Dr X. Review
Life 59:19 Jl 9 '65. L. Wainwright
Newsweek il 66:54 Jl 19 '65

INTERNSHIP teaching. See Student teaching

INTEROCEANIC canal commission. See United States—Interoceanic canal commission

INTERPERSONAL relations. See Human relations

INTERPLANETARY dust. See Matter, Interstellar

INTERPLANETARY monitoring platform. See Artificial satellites—Use in research

INTERPLANETARY navigation. See Navigation (space flight)

INTERPOL. See International criminal police organization

INTERPRETERS and interpretation. See Translations and translating

INTERPUBLIC group of companies, incorporated
Simon & Schuster to issue Interpublic books line. il Pub W 188:35-6 D 6 '65

INTERRACIAL adoption. See Adoption

INTERRACIAL cooperation
Interracial etiquette. America 112:796 My 29 '65
Mississippi: after violence a ray of hope. il Ebony 20:109-10+ Je '65
Spirit of '76 in the 1960's. R. Wilkins. Seventeen 24:150+ O '65
We like the suburbs but. E. Simonds. il Parents Mag 40:54-5+ D '65
What you can do for human rights in your own home town. D. Klein. il Seventeen 24: 130-1+ My '65

INTERRACIAL marriages. See Intermarriage of races

INTERRACIAL relations. See Race relations

INTERREGNUM, Presidential. See Presidents —United States

INTERSECTION, San Francisco. See Coffee houses

INTERSEXUALITY. See Hermaphroditism

INTERSTATE commerce
Curbing the states' tax reach; taxes on out-of-state companies and on interstate sales. Bsns W p85-6+ S 11 '65
Monumental muddle in state taxes. J. F. Olesky. il Duns R 86:61+ N '65
New U.S. agency urged to run some state taxes; sales and use levies on out-of-state companies. Bsns W p58-9 Jl 3 '65

INTERSTATE commerce commission. See United States—Interstate commerce commission

INTERSTATE highway system. See Express highways; Roads—United States

INTERSTATE mobility. See Migration, Internal

INTERSTELLAR matter. See Matter, Interstellar

INTERVENTION
International law, morality and American interventions. W. V. O'Brien. Cath World 201:388-93 S '65
U.N.'s gobbledygook. D. Lawrence. U S News 60:82 Ja 3 '66

INTERVIEWING
Delicate art of asking questions. J. K. Lagemann. Read Digest 86:87-91 Je '65
Finding a job; excerpt from Seventeen book of etiquette and entertaining. E. A. Haupt. Seventeen 24:42 Ap '65

INTERVIEWING—*Continued*
Testing daze. il Newsweek 65:111-111A+ Je
14 '65
What a man looks for when he hires a girl;
a candid view. N. Breckenridge. Mlle 60:
146+ F '65
What every job hunter should know. il Good
H 161:139 Ag '65
Your college interview. D. Klein. Seventeen
24:56+ O '65
See also
Applications for positions
INTESTINES
Serotonin: synthesis and release from the
myenteric plexus of the mouse intestine.
M. D. Gershon and others. bibliog il Science
149:197-9 Jl 9 '65

Diseases
Cystinuria: effect of D-penicillamine on
plasma and urinary cystine concentrations.
J. C. Crawhall and C. J. Thompson. bibliog
il Science 147:1459-60 Mr 19 '65
See also
Appendicitis
INTOLERANCE. See Prejudice
INTOLERANCE, 1960; opera. See Nono, L.
INTOLLERANZA 1960; opera. See Nono, L.
INTOXICATION. See Alcoholism
INTRACOASTAL WATERWAY
Behind the dunes; Inland waterway south-
ward from Norfolk, Va. J. Hart. il Yacht-
ing 118:58-9+ O '65
Going south. J. Emmett. Yachting 118:154-6
D '65
West coast of Florida wakes up. W. H.
Kendall. il Motor B 115:45-9+ Ap '65
INTRA-UTERINE contraceptive devices. See
Contraceptives
INTRAVENOUS anesthesia. See Anesthesia
INTREX (Information transfer experiments)
See Information storage and retrieval sys-
tems
INTROVERSION and extroversion
See also
Autism
INTRUDER; story. See Henderson, R.
INULIN
Micropuncture study of inulin absorption in
the rat kidney. Y. Gutman and others. il
Science 147:753-4 F 12 '65
INVALIDITY insurance. See Insurance, Health
INVENTIONS
Can we use Russian inventions? S. V. Jones.
il Sci Digest 58:44-8 S '65
Can you invent a million-dollar fad? W. S.
Griswold. il Pop Sci 188:78-81+ Ja '66
Here's your guide to successful inventing:
questions and answers; excerpts from The
successful inventor's guide. N. Carlisle and
K. O. Kessler. il Pop Sci 186:89-93 Mr '65
How much of your job belongs to you? H.
Shuldiner. il Pop Sci 187:98-100 D '65
Inventions, patents, processes. See issues of
Science digest
Inventors' utopia; Limited war laboratory.
D. Francis. il Pop Sci 187:54-7+ S '65
James Bond's weird world of inventions;
zany gimmicks for James Bond movies. H.
Shuldiner. il Pop Sci 188:60-3+ Ja '66
New ideas from the inventors. See issues of
Popular science monthly
1965 science review. Sci N L 88:396-7 D 18 '65
Pop! flick! zaaap! first International inventors
and new products exhibition, New York. il
Newsweek 66:106-106A+ S 27 '65
Sensing of time in China; J. Needham's con-
clusions on Chinese priority in clockmak-
ing. J. Lear. il Sat R 49:95-100 Ja 1 '66
Speed of change. R. Calder. Bul Atomic Sci
21:2-5 D '65
U.S. patent policy and government research.
R. L. Wright; discussion. Bul Atomic Sci
20:32-4 O '64; 21:34 F '65
See also
Patent laws and legislation
Patents

Exhibitions
New help for free-lance inventors. il Chang-
ing T 19:13-15 My '65
INVENTORIES
Big turn in inventories. il Fortune 72:28+
Ag '65
Inventories go volatile. Fortune 71:30+ F '65
Inventory climax. il Fortune 71:28+ My '65
Less for inventory. il Fortune 72:48+ N '65
Taking inventory: when? how? any short
cuts? suggestions of booksellers. Pub W
187:43-5 Mr 29 '65

INVENTORS
Inventor of the month. S. V. Jones. See is-
sues of Science digest
Inventors quiz. J. Daugherty and M.
Daugherty. Sci Digest 57:93-4 Mr '65
New help for free-lance inventors. il Chang-
ing T 19:13-15 My '65
INVERTEBRATES
See also
Arthropods
INVERTEBRATES, Fossil
Wormlike fossil from the Pennsylvanian of
Illinois; tullimonstrum gregarium. E. S.
Richardson, jr. il Science 151:75-6 Ja 7 '66
INVERTERS, Electric. See Electric inverters
INVESTMENT. See Investments
INVESTMENT bankers association of America
Anatomy of a bond campaign. il Am City 80:
126+ F '65
INVESTMENT banking
See also
Development banks
INVESTMENT companies. See Investment
trusts
INVESTMENT counselors. See Investments—
Advisers
INVESTMENT trusts
Changing pattern for funds. il Bsns W p95-6
Jl 24 '65
Closed-end funds gaining strength. il U S
News 59:89-90 S 6 '65
Dreyfus corp. going public. Bsns W p 176
O 9 '65
Europe's funds have a long way to go. Bsns
W p 158 Ap 17 '65
Executives and mutual funds. T. J. Murray.
il Duns R 86:59-61+ O '65
Foreign beachhead on U.S. funds. Bsns W
p 146+ Je 12 '65
Fresh face in money management; Fidelity
capital fund's G. Tsai. Bsns W p54+ F 20
'65
Have you looked into no-load mutual funds?
il Changing T 19:21-3 F '65
How to turn mutual funds into income. il
Changing T 19:41-3 Ag '65
Life among the no-loads. C. J. Loomis. il
Fortune 72:86+ O '65
Luring big investors with a success story;
swap or exchange fund. il Bsns W p 148+
Ap 24 '65
More gains coming, but pace will lag. Bsns W
p 148+ Ap 10 '65
Mutual funds, a modern way to invest. E.
Turner. NEA J 54:24-5 S '65
Mutual funds: latest trends, new ideas; with
charts. il U S News 60:80-3 Ja 17 '66
Once-hurt managers still careful; mutual
funds vs. the averages. il Bsns W p 106+
Ja 30 '65
Personal business; mutual funds. Bsns W
p 151-2 Mr 20 '65
Playing with trains for profit; French in-
vestment company, Algeco. il Time 86:78+
Ag 27 '65
Rush to swap. Fortune 71:64+ My '65
Stocks the investment funds are buying now.
il U S News 59:77-9 Ag 23 '65
Tokyo upsurge buoys Japan fund; closed-end
investment company. il Bsns W p93-4+ D
18 '65
When change hits a billion-dollar fund; An-
chor corp, Elizabeth, N.J. il Bsns W p
158+ O 23 '65
Where is the big money? institutional in-
vestors. il Time 86:73-4 Jl 2 '65
Where mutual funds are putting their money
now. il U S News 59:106 N 8 '65
See also
Hanna, M. A. company
INVESTMENTS
Executive investor. See issues of Dun's re-
view and modern industry
How to buy stocks. il Changing T 19:7-11
O '65
Is real estate a smart investment? il Chang-
ing T 19:7-12 My '65
More companies are buying back their stock.
L. A. Guthart. il Harvard Bsns R 43:40-2+
Mr '65; Discussion. 43:31+ Jl '65
Most common investing mistakes. il Good H
161:178 O '65
Off the beaten track. il Time 85:100 Mr 19 '65
Personal investing. See issues of Fortune
Repurchase stock to revitalize equity. C. D.
Ellis. il Harvard Bsns R 43:119-28 Jl '65
Syndication is the new big game at the
racetrack; trading thoroughbred stallions.
J. McDonald. il Fortune 73:159-63+ Ja '66
What the new year holds for investors and
savers. il U S News 60:78-80 Ja 10 '66

INVESTMENTS, Foreign (in Thailand)
Takeoff in Thailand; foreign investments welcomed. il Fortune 73:88+ Ja '66
INVESTMENTS, Foreign (in Turkey)
Doing business abroad: a top businessman's view; excerpts from address, January 13, 1965. L. A. Townsend. U S News 58:94-5 F 1 '65
INVESTMENTS, Foreign (in underdeveloped areas)
U.S. tightens screws on overseas investing; less developed countries exempted. il Bsns W p 110-11 N 27 '65
World bank setting up a court for investors; plan to settle disputes in developing countries. Bsns W p46 Ap 3 '65
INVESTMENTS, Foreign (in United States)
Foreign beachhead on U.S. funds. Bsns W p 146+ Je 12 '65
INVESTMENTS, Foreign (in Vietnam [Republic])
Business enlists in South Vietnam. il Bsns W p 114 Je 12 '65
Danger, drama, maybe profit; U.S. construction projects. il Newsweek 66:75-6+ N 1 '65
Why French pay off to the Viet Cong. il U S News 59:39 Jl 19 '65
INVESTORS. See Stockholders
INVESTORS overseas services, limited
Foreign beachhead on U.S. funds. Bsns W p 146+ Je 12 '65
Return of Bernie Cornfeld. il Time 85:98+ Ap 23 '65
INVESTORS planning corporation of America
Return of Bernie Cornfeld. il Time 85:98+ Ap 23 '65
INVISIBLE Japanese gentlemen; story. See Greene. G.
INVITATION to the voyage; story. See Miller, W.
INVITATIONAL masters angling tournament. See Fishing—Competitions
INYALA hunting. See Antelope hunting
IO (satellite) See Satellites
IODINE
Isotopes
Alkyl iodide-iodine exchange and the Szilard-Chalmers effect. E. D. Cohen and C. N. Trumbore. bibliog Science 148:1460-1 Je 11 '65
Meteorological evaluation of the sources of iodine-131 in pasteurized milk. R. J. List and others; reply. E. A. Martell. bibliog Science 148:1756-7 Je 25 '65
IODINE in the body
Iodination in relation to thyroglobulin maturation and subunit aggregation. R. W. Seed and I. H. Goldberg. bibliog il Science 149:1380-2 S 17 '65
Iodine: accumulation by balanoglossus gigas. F. B. De Jorge and others. bibliog il Science 150:1182-3 N 26 '65
IODOACETAMIDE
Complement: increased efficiency of the second component after treatment with iodoacetamide. M. J. Polley and H. J. Müller-Eberhard. bibliog il Science 148:1728-9 Je 25 '65
IOKU, Masahiko, and others
Parkinsonism: electromyographic studies of monosynaptic reflex. bibliog Science 150:1472-5 D 10 '65
IOLANTHE; opera. See Tchaikovsky, P. I.
ION engines
Atoms and ions in orbit; nuclear generator and ion engine in space. il Bsns W p 105-6 Ap 10 '65
EOS advances ion engine art. J. F. Judge. il Miss & Roc 16:22-3 Ap 5 '65
Ion engine decision due this week. Miss & Roc 16:17 Ap 19 '65
Ion engine interferes with Snap 10A data. Aviation W 82:30 Ap 12 '65
Ion engine runs 2,610 hours. il Miss & Roc 17:22+ Jl 26 '65
ION exchange
Alkyl iodide-iodine exchange and the Szilard-Chalmers effect. E. D. Cohen and C. N. Trumbore. bibliog Science 148:1460-1 Je 11 '65
IONESCO, Eugène
Literature of the absurd. G. P. Nemes. il por Américas 17:6-10 F '65
Rhinoceros. Criticism
Américas il por 17:6-10 F '65
IONIAN ISLANDS
See also
Corfu (island)
IONIZATION of gases
AF lets pact for measuring plasma microinstability; TOPSY. il Miss & Roc 17:36 Ag 2 '65
Ionizing waves of potential gradient. L. B. Loeb. bibliog il Science 148:1417-26 Je 11 '65

IONOSPHERE. See Atmosphere. Upper
IOOSS, Walter, Jr
Rise and fall of the fabulous Phillies; photographs. Sports Illus 22:52-6 Mr 1 '65
IOWA
See also
Hunting—Iowa
Law—Iowa
Social life and customs
Culture comes to Cherokee. D. J. Henahan. Holiday 38:21-6 Jl '65
IOWA CITY, Ia.
Recreation center; with song of praise by third-grade students. E. A. Scholer. il Recreation 58:436 N '65
IOWA state university of science and technology, Ames
How we feed college cows. A. Coletti. il Suc Farm 63:106+ F '65
IOWA. University, Iowa City
Paul Engle: poet-grower to the world; University of Iowa. T. G. Harris. il Look 29:95-7 Je 1 '65
IPHIGÉNIE en Tauride; opera. See Gluck, C. W.
IRAN
Dilemma in Iran. M. Jabri. Cur Hist 48:277-80+ My '65
Modern monarch on the peacock throne; with report by L. Griggs. il Life 60:38-40+ Ja 14 '66
See also
Economic assistance in Iran
Education—Iran
Hunting—Iran
Land tenure—Iran
Marriage—Iran
Description and travel
Iran. L. Blanch. il Vogue 146:130-9+ Ag 15 '65
Foreign relations
Darius Canal; clash of interests between Egypt and Iran. Newsweek 65:45 F 22 '65
Shots across the border; Iraq and Iran. il Time 87:30+ Ja 7 '66
History
Iran celebrates a 2,500th birthday. A. S. Mehdevi. il N Y Times Mag p50-1+ O 31 '65
Politics and government
Billion-dollar mystery; with editorial comment. F. J. Cook. il Nation 200:377-8, 380-97 Ap 12 '65
Coming crisis in Iran. H. Mahdavy. For Affairs 44:134-46 O '65
Politics of distrust in Iran. A. F. Westwood. Ann Am Acad 358:123-35 Mr '65
Shah and his exasperating subjects: a report from Iran. J. Fischer. Harper 230:24+ Ap '65
Succession: new premier appointed. Newsweek 65:38+ F 8 '65
Unholy alliance: Communists and fanatical Moslems. il Time 85:39 F 5 '65
Reconstruction
Perils of reform; attempted assassination of the Shah. Time 85:38 Ap 23 '65
Social conditions
Land of charming anarchists: a report from Iran. J. Fischer. il Harper 230:22+ Mr '65
Social life and customs
Persian lions, Persian lambs, by C. Harnack. Review
Nation 200:178-80 F 15 '65. F. M. Esfandiary
Take a lesson from a pasha. A. S. Mehdevi. Harper 230:97-9 My '65
IRANIANS
Iran celebrates a 2,500th birthday. A. S. Mehdevi. il N Y Times Mag p50-1 O 31 '65
IRAQ
Description and travel
Marsh Arabs, by W. Thesiger. Review
New Yorker 41:126-8 My 29 '65. N. Bliven
Foreign relations
Shots across the border; Iraq and Iran. il Time 87:30+ Ja 7 '66
Native races
Marsh Arabs, by W. Thesiger. Review
Commonweal 82:669-70 S 17 '65. G. Gersh
New Yorker 41:126-8 My 29 '65. N. Bliven
Politics and government
Coup de Razzak. Time 86:42 S 24 '65
From Razzak to Bazzaz; new premier. Time 86:40 O 1 '65

IRAQ—Politics and government—*Continued*
Historical accident. il Newsweek 66:44 Jl 26 '65
Iraq: seven years of revolution. G. Lenczowski. bibliog f Cur Hist 48:281-9+ My '65
Serpentine politics in latter-day Eden; September coup. C. Sterling. Reporter 33:30-2 D 30 '65

IRAZU. See Volcanoes

IRBY, Kenneth
World dances between our eyes. Poetry 105: 414-20 Mr '65

IRELAND, Leroy
George Inness, painter of landscapes. Antiques 88:820-3 D '65

IRELAND, William Henry
Great Shakespeare forgery, by B. Grebanier. Review
Sat R 48:61+ O 23 '65. H. T. Moore

IRELAND
Building a bridge? meeting of the two states. Sr Schol 86:20 F 11 '65
Ireland: appetite for success. S. Hagerty. il Newsweek 65:40+ Ap 19 '65
Letter from Ireland. J. Navone. il Cath World 200:364-9 Mr '65
Lopsided country. H. F. Woodhouse. Christian Cent 82:901 Jl 14 '65
Subject: Ireland; comments in honor of St Patrick's day, comp. by G. Flatley. il N Y Times Mag p42 Mr 14 '65
Writers and politics, by C. C. O'Brien. Review
New Repub 153:21+ S 11 '65. P. O'Donovan
See also
Censorship—Ireland
Country estates—Ireland
Gardens—Ireland
Gipsies in Ireland
Yachts and yachting—Ireland

Description and travel
Irish time; with photographs by H. Cartier-Bresson. Lord Kilbracken. Horizon 7:42-9 Autumn '65
Jaunty Ireland. G. Clark. il Travel 123:24-8 Mr '65
See also
Gardens—Ireland

Foreign relations
Herring war; Ireland vs Northern Ireland. Newsweek 67:40 Ja 17 '66

History
Bibliography
Articles and other books received; comp. by L. H. Carlson. See issues of American historical review

Religious institutions and affairs
News of the Christian world (cont) Christian Cent 82:442, 1268-9 Ap 7, O 13 '65

IRIARTE, Braulio, and others
Five-color photometry of bright stars. Sky & Tel 30:21-4 Jl '65

IRION, Mary Jean
Who's afraid of Franz Gruber? poem. Christian Cent 82:1569 D 22 '65

IRISES
Are you using iris for all they are worth? M. Price. il Flower Grower 52:22-3+ Je '65
Award winning iris. il Pop Gard 16:12+ My '65
Blue grows the iris. D. F. Stebbins. il Pop Gard 16:28-9 My '65
Dave Hall, the man who put the pink in iris. E. J. Purcell. il Flower Grower 52:17-18 Jl '65
Dutch iris. E. F. Steffek. il Horticulture 43: 34 Mr '65
Grow a rainbow of iris. il Pop Gard 16:22+ Ap '65
Iris in July? yes! with the fabulous, fantastic Japanese iris. O. A. Reid. il Flower Grower 52:37 Jl '65
Iris that are different. il Pop Gard 16:15 My '65
Japanese iris. E. Westmeyer. il Horticulture 43:14-15+ Jl '65
Louisiana iris North and South. Mrs T. Nesmith; C. W. Davis. il Horticulture 43: 26-7+ Mr '65
Plant next year's iris blooms now. Flower Grower 52:11 Je '65
Spuria iris. M. Redford. il Horticulture 43:48 Ap '65
Use iris to advantage in your garden. G. Harshbarger. il Horticulture 43:22-3+ My '65

IRISH, Clair Galbraith
Squires at large. il por Esquire 65:107 Ja '66

IRISH, Jerry A.
New and old theologies. Christian Cent 82: 742 Je 9 '65

IRISH cookery. See Cookery, Irish

IRISH free state. See Ireland

IRISH literature
Celtic heritage in Ireland. A. Moray. il Horizon 7:32-9 Spr '65

IRISH moss. See Carrageen

IRIZARRY, Carmen
La afición. Hi Fi 15:142-3 Ap '65
Search for the Spanish soul. Hi Fi 15:186-7 D '65

IRON
Isotopes
Iron-55 in humans and their foods. H. E. Palmer and T. M. Beasley. bibliog il Science 149:431-2 Jl 23 '65

IRON-clad vessels. See Armored vessels

IRON deficiency anemia. See Anemia

IRON in the body
Iron accumulation in cockerel plasma after estrogen: relation to induced phosphoprotein synthesis. O. Greengard and others. bibliog il Science 147:1571-2 Mr 26 '65
Unusual arthritis type linked to excess iron. Sci N L 88:46 Jl 17 '65

IRON industry and trade
Brazil
Brazil: Hanna's immovable mountains. il Fortune 71:55-6+ Ap '65
Mexico
Cheaper to build, cheaper to run; Mexico's Monterrey plant. il Bsns W p 142+ F 27 '65

IRON metallurgy
Cheaper to build, cheaper to run; Mexico's Monterrey plant. il Bsns W p 142+ F 27 '65
Pellet gives iron ore industry shot in the arm; upgrading of taconite. il Bsns W p 106-8+ D 4 '65

IRON mines and mining
Australia
Great iron treasure; international scramble for Australian iron. il Fortune 72:69-70+ O '65
Brazil
National solution. Time 86:68 D 31 '65

IRON ores
Siderite ($FeCO_3$): thermal decomposition in equilibrium with graphite. B. M. French and P. E. Rosenberg. bibliog il Science 147:1283-4 Mr 12 '65
See also
Taconite
Transportation
See also
Ore handling

IRON workers
See also
Blacksmiths

IRONCLADS. See Armored vessels

IRONING
It's easier now. il Redbook 126:52-3+ Ja '66
Press as you sew for best results. C. Houck. il Parents Mag 40:92 N '65

IRONS, Flat. See Flatirons

IROQUOIS Indians
Corn, beans, squash. B. C. Kilvert jr. il Flower Grower 52:32-4 Jl '65

IRRADIATED food. See Food, Effect of radiation on

IRRADIATION of diamonds. See Diamonds

IRRELIGION
Varieties of unbelief, by M. E. Marty. Review
Christian Cent 82:142 F 3 '65. W. J. Ong

IRRIGATION
Irrigation accomplished by automatic control. Sci N L 88:105 Ag 14 '65
See also
Arid regions
Reclamation of land
India
Water, history, and the Indus Plain. G. C. Taylor, jr. il Natur Hist 74:40-9 bibliog(p70) My '65
Israel
Jordan Valley plan. M. A. Garbell. il Sci Am 212:23-31 Mr '65

IRRIGATION—*Continued*

Pakistan

Water, history, and the Indus Plain. G. C. Taylor, jr. il Natur Hist 74:40-9 bibliog(p70) My '65

Western states

Water poachers; large landowners in western desert areas fight to keep subsidized irrigation. J. L. Vizzard. il America 112:220-3 F 13 '65

IRVIN, George L. See Gittes, R. F. jt. auth.

IRVING, Florence
Coffee cup conversions. Design 66:10-11 Mr '65

IRVING, John
Winter branch; story. Redbook 126:56-7 N '65

IRVING, Jules
Blau & Irving come out of the West. M. Harris. il por N Y Times Mag p 16-17+ F 21 '65
Enter the gadflies. Newsweek 65:82-3 F 8 '65
People are talking about... por Vogue 146: 204-5 O 1 '65

IRVING, Laurence
Adaptations to cold; with biographical sketch. Sci Am 214:15, 94-101 bibliog(p 135-6) Ja '66

IRVING P. Krick associates
Your weather. See issues of Farm journal

IRVING, Robert
On the podium: Robert Irving. D. McDonagh. il pors Dance Mag 39:55-7 F '65

IRVING, Washington
Instinct for misanthropy; concerning J. Quidor's paintings. H. Cohen. Reporter 33: 51-2 D 16 '65

IRWIN, Louis Neal. See Tinkle, D. W. jt. auth.

IRWIN, Theodore
Dangers of being your own doctor. Read Digest 86:91-4 My '65
Electronic lifeline on the high seas. Pop Sci 187:86-8+ S '65
How to invent the wheelbarrow or the wheel. Pop Sci 187:162-3 D '65
They're selling you with subtle smells. Pop Sci 186:60-1+ Je '65

IRWIN, Wallace
Mothers; story. Parents Mag 40:44-5 Jl '65

IS it a vice or a talent? story. See Amft, M. J.

IS there a monster in the house? drama. See Fontaine, R.

IS there life on other planets? drama. See Lane, M.

ISAAC, Erich
Forbidden foods. Commentary 41:36-41 Ja '66

ISAACS, Harold R.
Portrait of a revolutionary. Commentary 40: 67-71 Jl '65

ISAACS, John D. and Schwartzlose, R. A.
Migrant sound scatterers: interaction with the sea floor. bibliog Science 150:1810-13 D 31 '65

ISAACS, Norman E.
Louisville: law or license? Sat R 48:44-5 My 22 '65

ISAACSON, Julie
Mouth and the mitt. T. Maule. il por Sports Illus 22:30-2+ Mr 1 '65

ISAKOVIĆ, Katarina, and others
Immunologic tolerance in thymectomized, irradiated rats grafted with thymus from tolerant donors. bibliog Science 148:1333-5 Je 4 '65

ISBELL, Harold
Shrine; poem. Commonweal 82:555 Ag 6 '65

ISENBERG, I. and others
Quenching of DNA phosphorescence. bibliog Science 150:1179-81 N 26 '65

ISICA, Carl
Hitch & go. See issues of Motor trend

ISLAM
Moslem world's struggle to modernize. il Time 85:66-73 Ap 16 '65
See also
Pilgrimages to Mecca

ISLAM and Christianity. See Christianity and other religions

ISLANDIA NATIONAL MONUMENT (proposed) See National monuments

ISLANDS
Avifauna: turnover on islands. E. Mayr. bibliog il Science 150:1587-8 D 17 '65
Canada: islands galore. N. D. Ford. il Travel 124:26-31 Ag '65
White Island; owner's reminiscences. R. B. Fosdick. il Atlan 216:110-12+ O '65
See also names of islands, e.g. Corsica

ISLANDS of the Pacific
Great society comes to the Pacific Isles. il U S News 60:48-51 Ja 17 '66
Pacific Orient dinner: 1944 and 1965. R. Joseph. il Esquire 64:58-9 Ag '65
See also
Oceania
Solomon Islands

ISLE ROYALE NATIONAL PARK
Isle Royale: laboratory of Lake Superior. L. D. Mech. il Nat Parks Mag 39:4-8 D '65

ISOENZYMES. See Enzymes

ISOLATION, Social
Babies harmed in solitary. Sci N L 87:291 My 8 '65

ISOLATIONISM (United States) See United States—Foreign relations

ISOMERS
Zamene, isomeric C_{19} monoolefins from marine zooplankton, fishes, and mammals. M. Blumer and D. W. Thomas. bibliog il Science 148:370-1 Ap 16 '65

ISOMETRIC contraction. See Exercise

ISOPODA
Entrainment of a tidal rhythm. J. T. Enright. bibliog il Science 147:864-7 F 19 '65

ISOPRENOID hydrocarbons. See Hydrocarbons

ISOTOPE separation
Neon isotope fractionation during transient permeation. S. N, I. Rama and S. R. Hart. bibliog Science 147:737-8 F 12 '65

ISOTOPES
Chemistry of isotopes; adaptation of address, October 16, 1963. J. Bigeleisen. bibliog il Science 147:463-71 Ja 29 '65
See also
Radioisotopes
also subhead Isotopes under various subjects, e.g. Iron—Isotopes

ISOZYMES. See Enzymes

ISRAEL
Abraham's children. K. Haselden. Christian Cent 82:455-7 Ap 14 '65
Israel: land of promise. J. Scofield. il Nat Geog Mag 127:394-434 Mr '65
Israel: the state of siege. D. J. Simpson. il Cur Hist 48:263-8 My '65
Israeli notebook, updated. G. Kennedy. Christian Cent 82:237-8 F 24 '65
Modern Israel. A. Eban. America 112:896-7 Je 26 '65
Notes on Israel. D. M. Friedenberg; discussion. Commonweal 81:554-5, 626-7+ Ja 29, F 12 '65
See also
Achziv
Americans in Israel
Arabs in Israel
Civil rights—Israel
Collective settlements—Israel
Education—Israel
Elections—Israel
Foreign students in Israel
Haifa
Immigrants in Israel
Immigration and emigration—Israel
Investments, Foreign (in Israel)
Jerusalem
Jordan River
Music—Israel
Research—Israel
United Nations—Israel
Water supply—Israel
Zionism

Civilization

Facts of Jewish exile; excerpt from Ben Gurion looks back. D. Ben Gurion. Harper 231:47-51 S '65; Reply. E. Berger. 231:6+ N '65
New exodus: Israel's talent drain. B. M. Halpern. Nation 200:497-9 My 10 '65

Description and travel

And see the land, what it is. K. Haselden. Christian Cent 82:360-1 Mr 24 '65
Dearth of dromedaries. L. Barry. il Pop Phot 58:24+ Ja '66
E pluribus Israel. K. Haselden. Christian Cent 82:390-2 Mr 31 '65

Economic conditions

Search for identity; Eshkol victory. il Newsweek 66:64+ N 15 '65
Under threats, Israel booms. il U S News 58:62-3 Mr 15 '65

Economic policy

Israel worries about its applied research. V. K. McElheny. il Science 147:1123-4+ Mr 5 '65
See also
Israel development corporation

ITALY—*Continued*

Industries

Giant shapes Italy's future; state-owned IRI holding company stresses industrial development. il Bsns W p 102-4 Jl 10 '65
Italy's new empire; construction industry. il Fortune 72:74+ O '65
Natural; merger of Società Montecatini and Società Edison. Newsweek 66:51 D 27 '65
Place in the sun for Italy's south; Cassa per il Mezzogiorno. il Newsweek 65:77-80 Mr 22 '65
See also
Olivetti

Moral conditions

See also
Prostitution

Politics and government

Atlantic report; scandals nourish cynicism of voters. Atlan 216:23-4+ D '65
Closing the socialist ranks. Newsweek 67: 41-2 Ja 24 '66
Italy's Catholic-Communist dialogue. C. Sterling. il Reporter 32:18-22 Ap 22 '65
Motor quits; Fanfani resignation. Newsweek 67:28 Ja 10 '66
See also
Communist party (Italy)
Fascism—Italy
Political parties—Italy
Public officers—Italy

Religious institutions and affairs

See also
Protestants in Italy

Social conditions

Matter of blood. il Time 85:35 F 19 '65

ITCHING
Itch and vibration. R. Melzack and B. Schecter. bibliog il Science 147:1047-8 F 26 '65

ITEK corporation
Many tricks in Itek's new bag; new material called RS (recording system) il Bsns W p60-2 Ja 30 '65

ITHACA college, Ithaca, N.Y.
How to buy a campus. il Time 85:61 My 14 '65

ITO, S. and Loewenstein, W. R.
Permeability of a nuclear membrane: changes during normal development and changes induced by growth hormone. bibliog Science 150:909-10 N 12 '65

ITOH, S. See Sargent, F. 2d, jt. auth.

IUSUPOV, Feliks Feliksovich, knîaz'
Killing the mad monk. il por Newsweek 66: 38 N 1 '65

IVANOV, Razumnik Vasil'evich
Prophet and a prisoner. I. Weil. Sat R 48: 44-5 Jl 24 '65

IVANTZOVA, Elizaveta Anderson-. See Anderson-Ivantzova, E.

IVERSON, Andrina
With a little wand. Writer 78:16-19 Je '65

IVES, Burl
Dear wayfarers. por Seventeen 24:264+ Ag '65

IVES, Charles Edward
Cantankerous Yankee; world première of Fourth symphony. por Time 85:56 My 7 '65
Divine document, the Ives Fourth. A. Cohn. Am Rec G 32:220-2 N '65
Ives fourth. G. Gould. por Hi Fi 15:96-7 Jl '65
Ives's Fourth symphony, an unplayable work gets played. A. Frankenstein. il Hi Fi 15: 83-4 N '65
Music to my ears; Stokowski's performance with the American symphony orchestra of C. Ives's Fourth symphony. I. Kolodin. Sat R 48:32+ My 15 '65
Musical events; Fourth symphony performed by American symphony orchestra. W. Sargeant. New Yorker 41:169 My 8 '65
On five labels simultaneously, more music by Chas. E. Ives. A. Cohn. il por Am Rec G 31:958-61 Je '65
Postscript on Ives's Fourth. R. Franceschini. Am Rec G 32:223 N '65
Transcendentalist. il por Newsweek 65:101-2 My 10 '65

IVES, Ronald L.
High-Q detector and noise-limiter system. Electr World 73:74-5 Mr '65

IVORIES
Eskimo ivory carving. il Design 66:34-6 Ja '65

IVORY-billed woodpecker. See Woodpeckers

IVORY COAST
Ivory Coast. T. E. Hilton. bibliog il Focus 16:1-6 O '65
On the threshold of take-off. E. Behr. il Newsweek 66:46-8 Ag 9 '65

IVY-leaved geraniums. See Geraniums

IWAMOTO, David
Student violence and rebellion. NEA J 54:10-13 D '65

IWO JIMA
Iwo Jima revisited; ex-residents pay homage to ancestors buried on the island. J. M. Truitt. il Newsweek 65:40 My 31 '65

IWO JIMA, Battle of, 1945
Japanese remembers Iwo Jima. T. Ohno. il N Y Times Mag p26-7+ F 14 '65

IZARD, Anne
Children's libraries. Wilson Lib Bul 39:689 Ap '65

IZENBERG, Jerry
Town where the Mets are champs. Sat Eve Post 238:84+ Ap 24 '65

J

J. C. Penney company. See Penney, J. C. company

JCS. See United States—Joint chiefs of staff

J. G. Ferguson, associates. See Ferguson, J. G. associates

J. M. Smucker company. See Smucker, J. M. company

JO (justitieombudsman) See Administrative remedies

JOIDES (Joint oceanographic institutions' deep earth sampling program) See Underwater drilling

J. P. Morgan and company. See Morgan guaranty trust company

J. P. Stevens and company. See Stevens, J. P. and company

JABLIN, Julian N. See Dobrof, A. jt. auth.

JABLONSKI, Edward
Unlikely corners. See issues of American record guide
V.W. Am Rec G 31:882-4 My '65

JABRI, Marwan
Dilemma in Iran. Cur Hist 48:277-80+ My '65

JACCOUX, Claude
Reporter at large. J. Bernstein. il New Yorker 41:122+ Mr 20 '65

JACK, Homer A.
Disarmament at the U.N. Christian Cent 82: 991-2 Ag 11 '65
UNDC: for a world disarmament conference. Bul Atomic Sci 21:39-40 S '65

JACK fishing. See Crevallé fishing

JACK-the-Ripper. See Murder

JACKETS, Life saving. See Life saving suits

JACKETS, Mens. See Clothing and dress—Men

JACKLET, Jon W. See Cohen, M. jt. auth.

JACKSON, Barbara (Ward) lady. See Ward, B.

JACKSON, Bruce
Who goes to prison. Atlan 217:52-7 Ja '66

JACKSON, Charles
Lady Julia; story. McCalls 92:110-11 Ap '65

JACKSON, Charlotte
Books for children. Atlan 216:152-60 D '65

JACKSON, David. See Press, F. jt. auth.

JACKSON, Donald
How lost was Zebulon Pike? Am Heritage 16: 10-15+ F '65

JACKSON, Edna Burke
Book review. Negro Hist Bul 28:95 Ja '65

JACKSON, Eleanor. See Jackson, J. jt. auth.

JACKSON, Gabriel
Spanish students rebel. Commonweal 83: 469-71 Ja 21 '66

JACKSON, Gardner
Death of a liberal. W. V. Shannon. Commonweal 82:341-2 Je 4 '65
Gardner Jackson 1897-1965. A. Schlesinger, jr. New Repub 152:17 My 1 '65

JACKSON, Gene L.
Field-effect transistor. Electr World 74:81-4 N '65

JACKSON, Harry
Last first. Am Artist 29:6 D '65
Range burial. F. Getlein. il por Am Artist 29:60-4+ N '65

JACKSON, Henry M.
Facts, fallacies and foreign policy; address, May 4, 1965. Vital Speeches 31:515-18 Je 15 '65
Will to stay the course; address, November 23, 1965. Vital Speeches 32:138-40 D 15 '65

JACKSON, James P.
Conservation and the population explosion.
Am For 71:30-1+ D '65
Small footsteps on the trail. il por Nat Parks
Mag 39:10-13 O '65
Visit to a primeval woods. Am For 71:36-7+
Ag '65
JACKSON, Jay and McGehee, Charles
Group structure and role behavior. bib-
liog f Ann Am Acad 361:130-40 S '65
JACKSON, Jean
What makes a salable confession? Writer
78:17-22 Mr '65
JACKSON, Julian, and Jackson, Eleanor
Dentistry 100 years ago; excerpts from Den-
tists to the world. Todays Health 43:20-1+
Mr '65
JACKSON, Katherine Gauss
Books in brief. See issues of Harper's maga-
zine
JACKSON, Maud
Glories I've seen! Read Digest 87:95-8 S '65
JACKSON, Morton B.
Second Civil war: a closer look at Los An-
geles riots; excerpts from address, August
1965. por U S News 59:80-2+ S 20 '65
JACKSON, Philip W.
Way teaching is; excerpts from address. NEA
J 54:10-13+ N '65
JACKSON, Ray D. and Van Bavel, C. H. M.
Solar distillation of water from soil and plant
materials: a simple desert survival tech-
nique. Science 149:1377-9 S 17 '65
JACKSON, Ronald W. See Torgesen, J. L.
jt. auth.
JACKSON, Shirley
Bus; story. Sat Eve Post 238:62-3 Mr 27 '65
Home; story. Ladies Home J 82:64-5 Ag '65
Possibility of evil; story. Sat Eve Post 238:
61-4 D 18 '65

about

Obituary
Pub W por 188:70 Ag 23 '65
School of one. Newsweek 66:83B Ag 23 '65
Shirley Jackson, 1919-1965. S. E. Hyman. por
Sat Eve Post 238:63 D 18 '65
JACKSON, William M. and Scheer, M. D.
Xenon-photosensitized formation of metas-
table nitrogen. bibliog Science 148:1718-19
Je 25 '65
JACKSON, Miss.
Public may be heard; FCC investigation of
station WLBT. R. L. Shayon. Sat R 48:
44 Je 26 '65
Total parish; St Richard's. C. J. McNaspy.
America 113:465 O 23 '65

Churches
It happened in Jackson. B. L. Williams.
Christian Cent 82:1366 N 3 '65
JACKSON HOLE VALLEY
Jackson Hole, 1916-65: a reminiscence. F.
Gizycka. Vogue 145:200+ Ap 1 '65
Mile high in Teton country. R. C. Lillie. il
Motor B 115:22-5+ My '65
JACKSONVILLE, Fla.

Education
Poor rich county. il Newsweek 65:86-7 Je 21
'65
JACOB, Dorothy
Witch's garden. Pop Gard 16:32-3+ N '65
JACOB, François
1965 Nobel laureates in medicine or physiol-
ogy. G. S. Stent. por Science 150:462-4 O
22 '65
Nobel prize awarded. F. Marley. por Sci N L
88:261 O 23 '65
Revolution in the cell. Newsweek 66:77 O
25 '65
JACOB, Sir Ian
His finest hour. Atlan 215:81-4 Mr '65
JACOBINIAS
Favorite indoor plants. G. R. Robinson. il
Horticulture 43:53 Je '65
JACOBOVSKI and the colonel; opera. See
Klebe, G.
JACOBS, Emanuel J.
Social dance: an aid to rehabilitation. por
Recreation 58:494-6 D '65
JACOBS, Harvey
Girl who drew the gods; story. Mlle 61:174-5
My '65
JACOBS, Hayes B.
At home and afraid. Reporter 33:62-3 O 21
'65
How to turn Bartók into a fruit bowl. New
Yorker 41:199-200+ My 15 '65
Tahiti learns about the bomb. N Y Times
Mag p46-7+ D 5 '65
JACOBS, Jay
At the Metropolitan: good history, indifferent
art. Reporter 32:36-7 Je 3 '65

JACOBS, Lou, Jr
Hitchcock, master of cinema! U S Camera 29:
72-3+ Ja '66
Jordy has his tonsils out. Parents Mag 40:
77-9 N '65
Stoboard makes movie editing faster, easier.
Mod Phot 29:86-7+ Jl '65
You need long lens, high flying camera to
film an eagle. Mod Phot 29:89+ Mr '65
JACOBS, Louis
Faith & reason. Commentary 40:20+ S '65
JACOBS, Marian B. and Ewing, Maurice
Mineralogy of particulate matter suspended
in sea water. bibliog Science 149:179-80 Jl
9 '65
JACOBS, Paul
America's schizophrenic view of the poor.
Nation 201:191-7 S 20 '65
Our friends, the poor. Commonweal 81:722-
3 Mr 5 '65
That man, those years. Nation 201:368 N 15
'65

about

From rebellion to responsibility. E. Capouya.
por Sat R 48:45 O 30 '65
JACOBS, William Jay
Frontier faith revisited. Horn Bk 41:464-73
O '65
JACOBS, William P. and Case, D. B.
Auxin transport, gibberellin, and apical dom-
inance. bibliog Science 148:1729-31 Je 25 '65
JACOB'S Pillow dance festival
Nederlands Dans theater at Jacob's Pillow.
D. Hering. il Dance Mag 39:31-2+ S '65
JACOBSEN, Josephine
Interrupted; poem. Commonweal 83:12 O 8
'65
Sea fog; poem. New Yorker 41:60 N 6 '65
Water; poem. New Yorker 41:54 O 2 '65
JACOBSON, Allan
Where the memory is. il Newsweek 66:70 Ag
23 '65
—and others
Differential-approach tendencies produced by
injection of RNA from trained rats. Science
150:636-7 O 29 '65
Somnambulism: all-night electroencephalo-
graphic studies. bibliog Science 148:975-7
My 14 '65
JACOBSON, Bernard
Bach's Forty-eight, on the piano as a piano
should sound. Hi Fi 16:76-7 Ja '66
Cheltenham comes of age. Sat R 48:44 Jl 31
'65
Mozart and Haydn in Holland. Hi Fi 15:167
S '65
La Scala requiem. Sat R 48:59 D 25 '65
JACOBSON, Dan
Apprenticeship; story. Parents Mag 40:66-7
Mr '65
Problem of Isaac Bashevis Singer. Com-
mentary 39:48-52 F '65
Sonia; story. Commentary 39:47-50 My '65
JACOBSON, Jerry H.
Common fallacies about your child's eyes.
Parents Mag 40:62-3+ N '65
JACOBSON, Martin, and Beroza, Morton
American cockroach sex attractant. bibliog
Science 147:748-9 F 12 '65
JACOBSON, Rovena. See Comen, P. jt. auth.
JACOBZINER, Harold
We must lower our infant death rate. por
Parents Mag 40:56+ N '65
JACOPETTI, Gualtiero
Too much realism? il por Newsweek 65:48
Ap 19 '65
JACQUELINE Grennan, Sister. See Grennan,
J.
JACQUET-FRANCILLON, Jacques
Sukarno's war against Malaysia. New Repub
152:16-18 Ap 10 '65
JADE
Four jade carvings of the Ch'ien Lung pe-
riod. L. F. Reals. il(p 1) Hobbies 70:32 Ja
'66
JADOT, Jean
Church in the Congo; tr. by E. O'Gorman.
Cath World 201:247-53 Jl '65
JADWIN, Mrs Stanley P.
Kind lady. il Newsweek 65:54 Mr 1 '65
JAEGER, Celso Paulo
Giant snail is used for muscle studies. Natur
Hist 74:26-7 N '65
JAEGER, Edmund C.
Sleeping one of the Hopis; excerpt from
Wandering through winter. E. W. Teale. il
Natur Hist 74:26-9 D '65
JAFFA, Harry V.
Open question. Nat R 17:827-8+ S 21 '65

about

Strange bedfellows. G. Kateb. Commentary
40:71-3 Ag '65

JAFFE, Dan
Of love, of death, of sudden understanding;
poem. Sat R 48:73 F 13 '65
JAFFE, Frederick S. See Best, W. jt. auth.
JAFFE, Morris H.
Monocular for 2¼. U S Camera 28:34 Ag '65
JÄGERSTÄTTER, Franz
Conscience and religion. J. F. Powers. Commentary 40:89-92 Jl '65
In solitary witness, by G. C. Zahn. Review
America 112:81 Ja 16 '65. A. T. Sheehan;
Discussion. 112:209, 340 F 13, Mr 13 '65
Nation 200:426-8 Ap 19 '65. T. Roszak
JAGUAR cave, Idaho. See Caves
JAGUAR hunting
Meeting in the Mato Grosso; Brazil. V.
Kraft. il Sports Illus 22:64-8+ F 22 '65
Tight turn with a tigre. S. E. Brock. il Outdoor Life 135:36-9+ Mr '65
To kill a jaguar. R. Joseph. il Esquire 63:
94-9 Mr '65
JAI alai. See Pelota (game)
JAI Singh II, maharaja of Jaipur
Stones of Jaipur speak of astronomy. S.
Singh. UNESCO Courier 18:34 N '65
JAILS. See Prisons
JAIPUR, India
Stones of Jaipur speak of astronomy. il
UNESCO Courier 18:18-21 Je '65; Reply. S.
Singh. 18:34 N '65
JAM. See Jelly, jam, etc.
JAM can curling. See Curling
JAMAICA
Two sides of an island. P. Siekman. il Fortune
71:51-2+ My '65
We can learn to be color-blind. P. Abrahams.
il N Y Times Mag p38+ Ap 11 '65
See also
Airlines—Jamaica

Description and travel
Jamaica without gilt. R. Hunter. il Travel
123:30-5 F '65
U-drive's the way to see Jamaica. il Sunset
134:79 My '65

Religious institutions and affairs
World around us. Christian Cent 83:58+ Ja
12 '66

JAMES, Bartholomew
We was amazingly fortunate; excerpts from
journal, ed. by T. J Fleming. Am Heritage 16:32-5+ O '65
JAMES, Carl
Ultimate weapon in war on poverty. il pors
Nations Bsns 53:36-7+ F '65
JAMES, Ewing S.
Baptists' conscience. por Newsweek 66:65
O 25 '65
JAMES, Henry
Washington square; dramatization. See Olfson, L.
about
Edith Wharton and Henry James, by M.
Bell. Review
Reporter 33:44+ Ag 12 '65. A. Kazin
Edith Wharton and Henry James: the story
of their friendship, by M. Bell. Review
Commonweal 82:417-18 Je 18 '65. J. R.
Mellow
New Repub 152:21-4 My 29 '65. J. L.
Featherstone
Henry James and the Nation. L. Edel. Nation 201:237-40 S 20 '65
Henry James, Edith Wharton, and the age
of leisure. W. Andrews. Harper 230:137-
40 My '65
JAMES, Jesse, Jr
Case against pesticides. por Field & S 70:
10-11+ Ja '66
JAMES, L. Eldon
American merchant marine; address, September 29, 1965. Vital Speeches 32:51-3 N 1 '65
JAMES, Laurie
Curtain going up! Parents Mag 40:46-7+
Ag '65
JAMES, Pat
Conimbriga the Roman city in Portugal. U S
Camera 28:62 Ap '65
JAMES, Stuart
Snowless skiing on tank treads. Pop Mech
124:140-1 O '65
JAMES, William
William James and alcoholics anonymous.
R. J. Roth. America 113:48-50 Jl 10 '65
JAMES Bond (literary character) See Spies
in literature
JAMES Noble conifer collection. See Conifers
JAMESTOWN, N.Y.
Parade of lighting progress. M. W. Smedberg. Am City 80:130+ O '65

JAMMU and Kashmir (native state) See Kashmir
JANÁČEK, Leoš
Deutsche grammophon presents the first
stereo recordings of the two ultra-Moravian
vocal works by Janáček. J. Diether. il por
Am Rec G 31:710-14 Ap '65
Great Glagolitic mass, pagan, Christian, intensely personal. A. Rich. por Hi Fi 15:66-7
Ag '65
Janáček. R. Ellsworth. por Am Rec G 31:900-
2 My '65
On records; Slavonic mass. Opera N 30:30
N 6 '65
JANCSICS, M. Jr
Air system. Motor B 116:101 O '65
JANECEK, Blanche
Chicago U's laboratory school. Library J
90:5468-71 D 15 '65
JANEL, Emil
Lumberjack artist; ed by I. Moore. por Am
For 71:20-3+ Ag '65
about
Emil Janel: lumberjack artist. il por Design
67:26-9 N '65
JANER, Albert Christ-. See Christ-Janer, A.
JANES, Kelly
Blessed are the meek; poem. Christian Cent
82:1121 S 15 '65
JANES, Ted
Gift of gabbling. pors Outdoor Life 137:
44-5+ Ja '66
Horseshoe bass. por Outdoor Life 136:56-7+
Jl '65
I read my own stuff. pors Outdoor Life 136:
40-1+ D '65
Where the woodcock are. Outdoor Life 136:
32-5+ S '65
JANGADAS. See Rafts
JANIS, Sidney
Cash expressionism. por Newsweek 65:96 Ap
12 '65
JANITORS
Let's make the most of our school custodians.
R. N. Finchum. Sch Life 47:29-31 D '64
JANKUS, E. V. See Barr, S. jt. auth.
JANSEN, Jan K. S. and Rudjord, Torstein
Dorsal spinocerebellar tract: response pattern
of nerve fibers to muscle stretch. bibliog
Science 149:1109-11 S 3 '65
JANSKY, Karl Guthe
Karl Jansky: his career at Bell telephone
laboratories. H. T. Friis. Science 149:841-
2 Ag 20 '65
JANSON, Donald
State dept. on campus: sit down and shut up.
Nation 200:547-50 My 24 '65
JANSSEN, David
The Fuge. por Newsweek 65:94 Ap 26 '65
TV's longest chase. S. Gordon. il pors Look
29:M10+ My 18 '65
JANSSEN, Peter A.
Threads of fashion. por Am Ed 1:9-11 N '65
JANUSCH, John Buettner-. See Buettner-
Janusch, J.
JANUSZ, Natalie
Curl up and read. Seventeen 24:188 N '65
JAPAN
See also
Aerospace industries—Japan
Agriculture—Japan
Airlines—Japan
Airplane industry and trade—Japan
Automobile industry and trade—Japan
Ballet—Japan
Baseball—Japan
Bonin Islands
Costume—Japan
Earthquakes—Japan
Electronic apparatus industry and trade—
Japan
Hiroshima
Hotels, taverns, etc.—Japan
Investments, Foreign (in Japan)
Missions—Japan
Moving pictures—Japan
Nagasaki
Okinawa
Osaka
Photographic apparatus industry and trade
Political parties—Japan
Publishers and publishing—Japan
Railroads—Japan
Recreation—Japan
Restaurants—Japan
Ryukyu Islands
Shipbuilding
Space research—Japan
Strikes—Japan
Tokyo
World war, 1939-1945—Japan
Youth—Japan

JAPAN—*Continued*

Armed forces
Letter from Guam; search for more stragglers: Japanese soldiers still hidden since end of the war. E. J. Kahn, jr. New Yorker 40:50+ F 13 '65

Civilization
Living relics. Newsweek 65:56 Je 14 '65

Commerce
Death for the dummies; trade with the Communists. Newsweek 66:86 O 18 '65
Hands across the China Sea. il Fortune 71:54+ Mr '65
Japan's giant web of world traders; trading companies serve as export-import agents for manufacturers. il Bsns W p76-8 Ja 8 '66
Political price of Japan's China trade. J. Schecter. il Reporter 33:28-30 S 23 '65
Salesmen san on safari; challenging area: Africa. il Time 86:78-9 Jl 2 '65

Commercial treaties and agreements
U.S. and Japan amend bilateral cotton textile arrangement; joint announcement, May 19, 1965, with U.S. note. Dept State Bul 52:980-1 Je 14 '65

Defenses
Growing defense force. Time 86:40+ D 10 '65
Japan's non-military buildup. A. Axelbank. il Reporter 34:35-7 Ja 13 '66
Should we give Japan some bombs? Nat R 17:908+ O 19 '65

Description and travel
Japan. R. S. Eisley. il U S Camera 28:42-5+ Je '65
Kimono mind, by B. Rudofsky. Review
    Sat R il 48:38-9 My 29 '65. H. Bristol
My Japanese days with Ought-ought seven. R. Hughes. il Sat R 48:38-40+ S 18 '65
Travel's picture portfolio. il Travel 124:52-7 O '65

Economic conditions
As Japan's miracle begins to fade. il U S News 58:113-14 My 24 '65
Asia's giant begins to groan. America 114:63 Ja 15 '66
Bumps in a boom. Time 85:90+ F 26 '65
Canada rides a crest, Japan fights recession; inflation worries Latin America. il Bsns W p48-9 Ja 1 '66
Danger of dominoes; economy short of capital. il Newsweek 65:80 Ap 26 '65
End to pessimism. il Time 86:102+ O 8 '65
In Japan, it's a money problem. il U S News 59:80 Jl 26 '65
Japan. F. Gibney. il Look 29:17-20 Ag 10 '65
Japan begins to regain its balance. Bsns W p74 F 20 '65
Japan's role in south Asia. T. McNelly. il Cur Hist 49:284-93 N '65
Pause for repairs. il Fortune 72:57-8+ Jl '65

Economic relations
Change in *moodo*; Japanese-South Korean accord. il Time 85:28 Ap 2 '65
Japan and the future. A. Harrigan. Nat R 17:546 Je 29 '65
Japan puts out small welcome mat. il Bsns W p 116+ F 27 '65
    See also
Joint United States-Japan committee on trade and economic affairs

Foreign relations
Japan's rockets: a future nuclear threat? il U S News 59:12 S 6 '65
U.S.-Japanese trends and prospects; address, October 30, 1965. W. P. Bundy. Dept State Bul 53:770-7 N 15 '65

China (People's Republic)
Japan: the reluctant ally against China. New Repub 154:12-13 Ja 15 '66

Korea (Republic)
Complex affair. Newsweek 66:34-5 Jl 5 '65
Japan-Korea accords. G. K. Chapman. Christian Cent 82:1612+ D 29 '65

United States
Direct hit; using Okinawa as a launching pad for Vietnam-bound bombers. il Newsweek 66:40+ Ag 16 '65
Japan and the future. A. Harrigan. Nat R 17:546 Je 29 '65

Japan and the United States: the essentials of partnership; address, October 25, 1965. W. P. Bundy. Dept State Bul 53:777-80 N 15 '65
Japan: the reluctant ally against China. New Repub 154:12-13 Ja 15 '66
President Johnson and Prime Minister Sato of Japan exchange views on matters of mutual interest; exchange of greetings, with joint communique, January 13, 1965. L. B. Johnson; E. Sato. Dept State Bul 52:133-6 F 1 '65

History
Onward and upward with technology; varying interest in guns from mid-sixteenth century on. N. Perrin. New Yorker 41:211-16+ N 20 '65

European war, 1914-1918
See European war, 1914-1918—Japan

Allied occupation, 1945-1952
Honorable conquerors, by W. Sheldon. Review
    Sat R 48:36 N 6 '65. J. M. Allison

Imperial palace
See Palaces

Industries
As Osaka goes, so goes Japan. il Bsns W p75-7+ Ag 21 '65
How big Brother trades on its own; Brother industries, and Brother international corp. il Bsns W p78 Ja 8 '66
How good is Japanese equipment? il U S Camera 28:56-9+ Je '65
How to succeed in business in Japan. il Newsweek 65:80-2 My 17 '65
Japan's giant web of world traders; trading companies serve as export-import agents for manufacturers. il Bsns W p76-8 Ja 8 '66
Mister Japan in the U.S.A; Japanese photographic industry. E. Bennett. U S Camera 28:18+ Je '65
Suntory brews a drive for its beer in Japan. il Bsns W p 118:20 S 4 '65
Super shipbuilders. il Newsweek 65:74-5 F 15 '65
Willing hands on Japanese watches; K. Hattori & co. il Fortune 72:144-8 Jl '65

Intellectual life
Japan. F. Gibney. il Look 29:17-20 Ag 10 '65

Moral conditions
Missing farmers; abandoning families for city life. Newsweek 66:53-4 D 6 '65
Troubled Japan. H. Ehrlich. il Look 29:21-7 Ag 10 '65

National Diet library
Japan's Library of congress. il Travel 123:41-3 Mr '65

Nationalism
Oh what a lovely war? nostalgia. il Time 86:45-6 O 8 '65

Politics and government
Criticism at the polls. il Time 86:33 Jl 16 '65
Demo in the damp; leftists hope to pull down Sato. il Time 86:34 N 26 '65
Political movements in Japan. N. Kishi. For Affairs 44:90-9 O '65
    See also
Japan—Nationalism

Religious institutions and affairs
News of the Christian world (cont) Christian Cent 82:152-4, 315-16, 816+, 1458-10 F 3, Mr 10, Je 23, N 24 '65
    See also
Missions—Japan
Soka Gakkai (sect)

Social conditions
Letter from Tokyo. M. Evans. Nation 201:203-4 O 4 '65
    See also
Caste

Social life and customs
Shibui & hade; Japan is a land of paradoxes. L. L. Smith. il U S Camera 28:60-3+ Je '65
    See also
Caste
Christmas—Japan
Geishas

JAPAN—*Continued*

Treaties
New treaty in Asia that will help U.S. il
U S News 59:108 N 29 '65
Treaty for tomorrow; Japan and South
Korea sign a normalization treaty. il Time
86:23 Jl 2 '65

JAPAN air lines. See Airlines—Japan

JAPAN and the United States
Jap and the fierce American conqueror; ed.
by L. Rosten. M. Nagal. il Look 29:38 Ag
10 '65
Japan in neutral. P. W. Quigg. For Affairs
44:253-63 Ja '66
Japanese view of America. M. Kosaka. il
Harper 230:18+ My '65
Yankees and samurai, by F. R. Dulles. Review
Sat R il 48:35 N 6 '65. D. M. Brown

JAPAN current. See Ocean currents

JAPAN Tupperware company
Tupperware brings home party to Japan;
marketing polyethylene containers. il Bsns
W p 162-4 N 20 '65

JAPAN-United States cooperative science program. See Science—International aspects

JAPANESE
Japan. F. Gibney. il Look 29:17-20 Ag 10 '65

JAPANESE AMERICANS
Closing the books; case of K. Koda family.
il Newsweek 66:50-1 O 18 '65
Success story, Japanese-American style. W.
Petersen. il N Y Times Mag p20-1+ Ja 9
'66

JAPANESE art. See Art, Japanese

JAPANESE artificial satellites. See Artificial
satellites, Japanese

JAPANESE attack on Hawaii. See Pearl Harbor, Attack on, 1941

JAPANESE baseball. See Baseball—Japan

JAPANESE beetles
Control Japanese beetle. il Sci N L 88:187
S 18 '65

JAPANESE cherry trees. See Oriental flowering cherry

JAPANESE dancing. See Dancing, Japanese

JAPANESE drama
No theater; ancient dramatic art bears many
similarities to opera. F. Bowers. il Opera N
30:8-13 Ja 1 '66
Soap opera, Japanese style. J. Nathan. il
N Y Times Mag p 12-13+ D 19 '65

JAPANESE economic assistance. See Economic
assistance, Japanese

JAPANESE flowering cherry. See Oriental
flowering cherry

JAPANESE imperial palace. See Palaces

JAPANESE in foreign countries
Japanese zoologists abroad; letter. A. Gorbman and T. Fujii. il Science 147:1395-6
Mr 19 '65

JAPANESE in the United States
See also
Japanese Americans

JAPANESE irises. See Irises

JAPANESE literature
Tale of Genji; concerning A. Waley's translation. K. Rexroth. Sat R 48:27 D 11 '65

JAPANESE maple
Airy, delicate Japanese marvels. il Sunset
135:92-5 N '65

JAPANESE music. See Music, Japanese

JAPANESE netsukes. See Netsukes

JAPANESE newspapers. See Newspapers—Japan

JAPANESE persimmons. See Persimmons

JAPANESE pottery. See Pottery, Japanese

JAPANESE securities. See Securities

JAPANESE spurge. See Pachysandra

JAPANESE students
Bashful revolutionary; a Japanese student's
war against war. il Look 29:34-5+ Ag 10
'65

JAPANESE students in the United States. See
Foreign students in the United Sees

JAQUA, Richard A. See Nicklas, R. B. jt.
auth.

JAQUES-DALCROZE, Émile
Lessons with Monsieur Jaques. E. Findlay.
il por Dance Mag 39:40-5 Ag '65

JARCHO, Saul
Paleopathology. Science 147:1160+ Mr 5 '65

JARDINE, Winnifred C.
Housework get you down? Farm J 89:56 Jl
'65

JARES, Joe
Bowling. Sports Illus 22:112-14 Ap 19 '65
Track & field (title varies) Sports Illus 22:
56+ Je 28 '65

JARGON
See also
Slang

JAROSZEWICZ, Mark
Mark Jaroszewicz says something; excerpts
from address. por Arch Forum 123:64 D '65

JARRAH wood. See Wood

JARRELL, Randall
Augsburg adoration; poem. New Yorker
41:56 D 11 '65
Man who loved children; excerpt from introduction to C. Stead's Man who loved
children. Atlan 215:166-71 Mr '65

about
Finding the lost world. S. Moon. Poetry 106:
425-6 S '65
Obituary
Pub W 188:57 O 25 '65
Randall Jarrell, RIP. Nat R 17:968 N 2 '65

JARRETT, Emmett
Directions; poem. Nation 200:458 Ap 26 '65

JARRETT, James L.
College students: the new breed. Sat R 48:
64-5+ Mr 20 '65

JARRY, Alfred
Books. J. Updike. New Yorker 41:216+ O 2
'65
Godot's grandfather. H. Kramer. Reporter
32:40 Je 3 '65
How absurd to be absurd. G. Rogoff. Nation
200:649-50 Je 14 '65
Plain scoundrels and pataphysics. H. Popkin. Sat R 48:37-8 My 8 '65

JARVIS, Kenneth W.
Why Mr Jarvis deserves torture. L. H. Lapham. il por Sat Eve Post 238:80+ D 18 '65

JARVIS, Woodie
Cheerful chickadee. Field & S 70:10+ O '65
Wired for walleyes. Outdoor Life 136:34-5+
Ag '65

JASMINE
Star jasmine. il Pop Gard 17:58 Ja '66

JASPER, H. H. and others
Amino acids released from the cerebral
cortex in relation to its state of activation.
bibliog Science 147:1448-9 Mr 19 '65

JASPER ware. See Wedgwood ware

JASTROW, Robert
Intuition in science: why cover it up? address. Sat R 48:55 My 1 '65

JAVELINA hunting. See Peccary hunting

JAVITS, Jacob Koppel
Paradox of Jacob Javits. W. Weaver, jr. il
pors N Y Times Mag p34-5+ Ap 4 '65

JAVORONKOV, Vadim A.
Engineers in the new India. UNESCO Courier
18:14-17+ My '65

JAVORSKY, Emil
Easy-to-make redwood baskets. il Flower
Grower 52:36-7 F '65
Weed is where you find it; photographs.
Natur Hist 74:22-5 Ap '65

JAWARA, David Kairaba
Newest, smallest. il Time 85:32+ F 26 '65

JAY, John
Let's travel: N.America ski-lands. Mlle 62:
204-10+ N '65

JAYCEE awards. See United States junior
chamber of commerce

JAYNE, John Franklin
Burglar alarm for boats. Motor B 115:175+
Je '65
How to handle a twin screw boat. Yachting
117:54-5+ My '65

JAYS
Audubon stamp bird moves to the U.S;
collie's magpie-jay. L. S. Uren. il Audubon Mag 67:101-2 Mr '65

JAZY, Michel
Big three are miles apart. J. Underwood. por
Sports Illus 22:26-7+ Je 21 '65
Jazy records. il por Newsweek 66:52 Jl 5 '65
Jug of wine, and pow! por Time 85:69 Je 18
'65
Vas-y, Ja-zy! and he went. E. Shrake. il
pors Sports Illus 23:32-4+ Ag 30 '65

JAZZ bands. See Bands (music)

JAZZ dance. See Dancing

JAZZ festivals. See Music festivals

JAZZ music
Doctor digs jazz. N. Hentoff. il Holiday 37:
109-10+ My '65
Doctor jazz. il Newsweek 66:94 S 27 '65
Ecumenical Ellington; concert in San Francisco's Grace cathedral. S. Dance. il Sat R
48:70-1 O 16 '65
Hear that big sound; with report by T.
Thompson. il Life 58:82-94+ My 21 '65
Hierarchy of the jazz anarchy; symposium,
ed. by L. Feather. il Esquire 64:123-5+
S '65
Hot, cool, and all that jazz. R. Hemming. il
Sr Schol 86:20-1 My 6 '65
Jazz; C. Hawkins' music. W. Balliett. New
Yorker 41:92-3 Mr 6 '65

JENNISON, Keith Warren
Keith Jennison starts book series in large type. Pub W 187:33 My 31 '65
JENNISON, Peter S.
National service organization proposes a nationwide survey. por ALA Bul 59:89-90 F '65
Take a bow: Virginia Mathews. Pub W 187: 32-3 My 24 '65
JENSEN, Erik Allerslev
Denmark's new Public libraries act. Wilson Lib Bul 39:567-71 Mr '65
JENSEN, J. Hans D.
History of the theory of structure of the atomic nucleus; address, December 12, 1963. bibliog Science 147:1419-23 Mr 19 '65
JENSEN, L. H. See Sundaralingam, M. jt. auth.
JENSEN, M. Anthony, and others
Electron density and electronic properties in noble-metal transition elements. bibliog Science 150:1448-50 D 10 '65
JENSEN, Oliver
Vinland the good emerges from the mists. Am Heritage 16:5+ O '65
JENSEN, T. E. See Bowen, C. C. jt. auth.
JEREMY, Sister Mary. See Mary Jeremy, Sister
JERNICK, W. J.
Cycle-basis billing. Am City 80:104+ O '65
JEROME, Judson
Not even a bridge; poem. Sat R 48:25 Ag 14 '65
St. Thomas: January; poem. Harper 231:46 Jl '65
JEROME, Sister Marie
Four fascinating worlds. Sr Schol 86:sup26-7 Ap 15 '65
JERSEY CITY, N.J.

Lighting
Fight crime with light. il Am City 80:123+ My '65

Politics and government
Slide-rule Caesar. Time 86:15A D 31 '65
JERSILD, Arthur T.
Voice of the self. por NEA J 54:23-5 O '65
JERUSALEM
Jerusalem. F. J. Kiesler. Vogue 145:187 My '65
Mandelbaum gate: way to peace? P. E. Lapide. Christian Cent 82:239-40 F 24 '65

Antiquities
Ancient Jerusalem. K. M. Kenyon. il Sci Am 213:84-91 Jl '65

Church of the Holy Sepulcher
Church of the Holy Sepulcher: toward an ecumenical symbol. R. H. Smith. Yale R 55:34-56 O '65

Description
Holy City. N. Kotker. il Horizon 7:4-19 Spr '65

Galleries and museums
See also
Israel museum

History
Ancient Jerusalem. K. M. Kenyon. il Sci Am 213:84-91 Jl '65
Holy City. N. Kotker. il Horizon 7:4-19 Spr '65

Hospitals
Artificial kidney center to be established in Israel; grant by U.S. government. Dept State Bul 53:448 S 13 '65
JERUSALEM artichokes
Three unusual vegetables. R. Gannon. il Flower Grower 52:54-5 My '65
JERUSALEM university. See Colleges and universities—Israel
JESSEN, Hans
I just can't afford low pasture yields; ed. by L. E. Zeman. pors Suc Farm 63:30-1+ Ag '65
JESSICA, Sister Mary. See Mary Jessica, Sister
JESSOP, E. Jean
Red sweater; story; adaptation from Suffer the little children. NEA J 54:41-2 S '65
JESSUP, John K.
Answer to what Vietniks call a moral issue. Life 59:40D O 29 '65
New currents swirling around Peter's rock. Life 59:27-9+ D 17 '65
Pope Paul's magnificent risk. Life 59:56A-56B O 15 '65
Search for something more than a community of fear. Life 58:34-36A+ Mr 5 '65
Two most eminent and strikingly different columnists. Life 58:40-1 My 7 '65

JESUITS
Choosing the Black Pope. il Newsweek 65: 60+ My 17 '65
Father Pedro Arrupe, new Father General of Jesuits. R. C. Dressman. America 112: 818-19 Je 5 '65
Jesuit aggiornamento. F. McCool. Commonweal 82:349-51 Je 4 '65
Like a dead body. America 112:741 My 22 '65
New Black Pope. Time 85:88 My 28 '65
Renewal among the Jesuits. il Time 85:80 My 21 '65
Shintoist Jesuit; Father Arrupe elected Superior General. Newsweek 65:74 My 31 '65
Trouble with Hungary; arrest of eight Jesuit priests. America 112:181 F 6 '65

Education
Jesuits and Catholic gentlemen; Beaumont college for boys, thirteen to eighteen, at Runnymede, England. Nat R 17:807 S 21 '65

Missions
They asked me why I came; missionary in Japan. J. Blewett. America 113:469-70 O 23 '65
JESUS, Society of. See Jesuits
JESUS CHRIST
Child who is God. V. P. McCorry. America 114:27-8 Ja 1 '66
Christian natural theology and Christian existence. J. B. Cobb, jr. Christian Cent 82: 265-7 Mr 3 '65
Christ's sexuality. il por Time 85:59 Ap 9 '65
Gaucho Jesus; concerning Creole gospel of Amado Anzi. G. F. Hall. Christian Cent 82:1419 N 17 '65
Jocund with Christ. V. P. McCorry. il America 113:733-4 D 4 '65
Man nobody knows; condensation. B. Barton. il pors Read Digest 86:215-18+ Mr; 247-50+ Je '65
Place of Jesus in theological reconstruction. D. T. Rowlingson. Christian Cent 82:1034-6 Ag 25 '65
We Jews and Jesus, by S. Sandmel. Review Commentary 40:107-8+ S '65. P. Winter
Word; Christ's hidden life. V. P. McCorry. America 112:205-6 F 6 '65
See also
Bible—New Testament
Christianity
Sacred Heart, Devotion to

Art
Message for the millions from the Pietà. il(cover) America 113:428 O 16 '65

Biography
Trial of Jesus. P. Winter; discussion. Commentary 39:10+ Mr '65

Chronology
History of Jesus Christ, by R. B. Bruckberger. Review
Christian Cent 82:1039 Ag 25 '65. P. J. Cahill
Commonweal 83:247-9 N 26 '65. J. Ratte

Crucifixion
Did Christ die on the cross? il por Time 86:96-7 D 10 '65
From his death comes our life. J. R. Nelson. Christian Cent 82:355 Mr 24 '65
Good Friday. Christian Cent 82:451 Ap 14 '65
Who kills Christ now? Christian Cent 82:571-2 My 5 '65

Divinity
Child who is God. V. P. McCorry. America 114:27-8 Ja 1 '66

Incarnation
See Incarnation

Kingdom
Word. V. P. McCorry. America 113:509-10 O 30 '65

Nativity
Greatest news story; excerpt from Christmas stocking. B. Considine. il Todays Health 43:18-19 D '65
Saviour is born. V. P. McCorry. America 113:788 D 18 '65
See also
Holy Innocents, Massacre of the
Incarnation

Passion
Herzog and the passion. R. F. Capon. America 112:425-7 Mr 27 '65
Word (cont) V. P. McCorry. America 112: 468-9, 497 Ap 3-10 '65

JESUS CHRIST—*Continued*

Resurrection and ascension

Did Christ die on the cross? il por Time 86:96-7 D 10 '65
  See also
Easter

Teaching

New words of Jesus? Coptic prayer book discovered. il Time 87:70 Ja 7 '66

Transfiguration

Meaning of transfiguration. J. C. Evans. Christian Cent 82:291 Mr 10 '65
Word. V. P. McCorry. America 112:375-6 Mr 13 '65

JET air travel. See Air travel
JET airplane engines
Snecma develops four versions of M 45 jet engine. W. C. Wetmore. il Aviation W 82: 230-2 Je 14 '65

Design

General electric designs SST powerplant for afterburner operation. M. L. Yaffee. il Aviation W 82:24-7 Je 7 '65

Maintenance and repair

TBO fading as guide to reliability concept; time-between-overhauls on jet engines. M. L. Yaffee. Aviation W 83:36-7+ D 27 '65
TWA reliability program quickens lengthening of jet engine TBOs. Aviation W 82:41 F 22 '65

JET airplane fares. See Airlines—Fares
JET business planes. See Airplanes, Business
JET cargo planes. See Airplanes, Freight
JET engine noise. See Airplanes—Noise
JET helicopters. See Helicopters, Jet propelled
JET pilots. See Air pilots
JET propelled airplanes. See Airplanes, Jet propelled
JET propelled automobiles. See Automobiles, Jet propelled
JET propelled motor boats. See Motor boats, Jet propelled
JET propulsion
New propulsion vistas; excerpts from remarks at symposium on advanced propulsion concepts. B. A. Schriever. Aviation W 82:21 My 10 '65
Scramjet flights may begin in 1967. W. E. Wilks. il Miss & Roc 17:15 S 13 '65
Scramjet tests showing high promise; supersonic combustion ramjet. Miss & Roc 17:16 O 11 '65
  See also
Jet airplane engines
JET propulsion laboratory
He keeps the space shots zooming; W. H. Pickering, director of JPL. il Bsns W p 118-20 Ag 14 '65
JPL debating alternate methods for contacting Mariner 4 in 1967. H. D. Watkins. il Aviation W 83:32 Ag 2 '65
JPL to manage Voyager lander. H. Taylor. Miss & Roc 16:14 My 3 '65
Man behind our mission to Mars; Mariner IV. B. Kocivar. il Look 29:36-8+ Jl 13 '65
Portrait of a planet; flight of Mariner IV. il Time 86:36-8+ Jl 23 '65
Voyager procurement plans uncertain. H. Taylor. Miss & Roc 17:13 Jl 5 '65

JETS (football club) See Football clubs
JEWEL thefts. See Burglary and burglars
JEWELRY
All that glitters; Lalique masterpieces. il Time 86:68-71 Jl 23 '65
Cloisonné; collaboration between modern U.S. painters and craftsmen. J. McDevitt. il Craft Horiz 25:32-5 N '65
Jewelry by Margaret DePatta. Y. Uchida. il Craft Horiz 25:22-5 Mr '65
Jewelry touches. il Good H 161:94-5 D '65
Mistletoe touch. il Seventeen 24:150 D '65
Old jewelry. Hobbies 70:45+ O '65
Pomodoro; the jewelry of Arnaldo and Gió. E. Ritter. il Craft Horiz 25:8-11 Jl '65
Silver band rings. B. Proese. il Sch Arts 64:18-19 Mr '65
Take a fashion lesson. il Seventeen 24:198 My '65
Time for a treasure trove. il Seventeen 24: 148-9 My '65

Exhibitions

International jewelry show in Darmstadt. il Craft Horiz 25:28-9 Ja '65
Object: adornment; current show at Museum of contemporary crafts. W. Berkson. il Craft Horiz 25:12-25 S '65

JEWELRY, Ancient
Gold of Alexander. P. Davidson. il Art N 64:32-5+ D '65
JEWISH American authors. See American literature—Jewish authors
JEWISH-Arab relations
Abraham's children. K. Haselden. Christian Cent 82:455-7 Ap 14 '65
Ancient hatred builds toward war; struggle for water. G. De Carvalho. il Life 58:44+ Je 18 '65
Arab refugees; a zionist view. M. Syrkin. Commentary 41:23-30 Ja '66
Arab refugees after eighteen years. E. Ben-Horin. Christian Cent 83:28-30 Ja 5 '66
Arab voice for peace. Life 58:4 My 7 '65
Arabs thirst for revenge. Israel stands to its arms; Arabs tap a disputed stream. il Life 58:45-9 Je 18 '65
Disputed Jordan waters. E. Monroe. New Repub 153:15-16 Ag 7 '65
E pluribus Israel. K. Haselden. Christian Cent 82:390-2 Mr 31 '65
Eye for an eye. Newsweek 65:57 Je 14 '65
Formula for peace? il Sr Schol 86:20 My 13 '65
Heresy in Cairo; views of Nasser given at Palestine liberation organization's National assembly, Cairo. il Time 85:41 Je 11 '65
Jordan waters conflict. K. B. Doherty. bibliog f il Int Concil 553:3-66 My '65
Man to anger Nasser. Time 85:42+ My 7 '65
Mandelbaum gate; way to peace? P. E. Lapide. Christian Cent 82:239-40 F 24 '65
Maverick kicks up; Bourguiba proposes Israeli settlement. Newsweek 65:46+ My 3 '65
Middle East; temperature rising. R. D. Heinl, jr. New Repub 152:9-11 Mr 20 '65; Reply. R. L. Cleveland. New Repub 152:28 My 8 '65
New war coming? pressure rises in Mideast. il U S News 58:61-2 Mr 15 '65
Reality and vision in the Middle East; Israeli view. A. Eban. For Affairs 43:626-38 Jl '65
Storm troopers; terrorist group of Palestinian Arabs. Time 85:31A-31B Je 18 '65
JEWISH-Arab war, 1947-1949. See Israel-Arab war, 1948-1949
JEWISH art. See Art, Jewish
JEWISH chronic disease hospital. See Brooklyn—Hospitals
JEWISH cookery. See Cookery, Jewish
JEWISH education. See Jews—Education
JEWISH language. See Yiddish language
JEWISH literature (American)
Decolonization of American literature; address. April 1965. K. Shapiro. il Wilson Lib Bul 39:846-53 Je '65; Discussion. 40: 172-5 O '65
Jews and Americans, by I. Malin. Review Nat R 17:556+ Je 29 '65. M. Geltman
JEWISH parochial schools. See Jews—Education
JEWISH periodicals
  See also
Menorah journal
JEWISH philosophy. See Philosophy, Jewish
JEWISH question. See Anti-Semitism
JEWISH rabbis. See Rabbis
JEWISH sects
Lost leader; Guardians of the city. il Time 86:73 S 10 '65
  See also
Hasidism
JEWS
Facts of Jewish exile; excerpt from Ben Gurion looks back. D. Ben Gurion. Harper 231:47-51 S '65; Reply. E. Berger. 231:6+ N '65
Higher freedom, by D. Polish. Review Christian Cent 82:894 Jl 14 '65. K. Haselden; Reply. E. Berger. 82:1040 Ag 25 '65
Jews, by R. Peyrefitte. Review Newsweek 66:35 Jl 19 '65
This people Israel, by L. Baeck. Review Commonweal 82:600-2 Ag 20 '65. M. D. Zeik
Two cheers for hedonism. M. Himmelfarb. Commentary 39:61-5 Ap '65
  See also
Anti-Semitism
Catholic church—Relations—Jews
Israel
Zionism

Dietary laws

Forbidden foods; kashruth doctrine. E. Isaac. Commentary 41:36-41 Ja '66

Education

Education for survival. il Time 86:51 D 31 '65

JEWS—*Continued*

History

History of the Jews, by P. Borchsenius. Review
　Commentary 40:110-12 N '65. L. S. Dawidowicz
Trial of Jesus. P. Winter; discussion. Commentary 39:10+ Mr '65

Persecutions

Absolving the Christians; Harry Golden urges Jewish ecumenical council. Newsweek 66:68 N 8 '65
Anguish of the Jews, by E. H. Flannery. Review
　Commonweal 82:542-3 Jl 23 '65. G. Baum
Journal of the Warsaw ghetto; excerpts. C. A. Kaplan. Commentary 40:42-58 N '65
Kind of survivor. G. Steiner. Commentary 39: 32-8 F '65; Discussion. 40:20+ Jl '65
Last return; tr. by A. Schwartz. E. Wiesel. Commentary 39:43-9 Mr '65
Scapegoat in need. R. Kluger. Harper 231: 126+ O '65
Trees that need no stars; tree-lined avenue in Jerusalem, dedicated to those who risked their lives to save Jews. A. Eisenberg and H. Eisenberg. il McCalls 93:30+ D '65

Religion

See Judaism

Rites and ceremonies

Forbidden foods; kashruth doctrine. E. Isaac. Commentary 41:36-41 Ja '66

Sects

See Jewish sects

JEWS and Catholics. See Catholic church—Relations—Jews
JEWS and Negroes
　Freedom meals; Negroes invited to share Passover meal. W. M. Abbott. America 112:883 Je 19 '65
JEWS and the world war. See World war, 1939-1945—Jews
JEWS in Germany
　Beyond Bonhoeffer? H. Cox. Commonweal 83:227+ N 26 '65
　Rabbi asks: isn't it time we forgave the Germans? J. Asher. il Look 29:84-6+ Ap 20 '65
JEWS in Isreal
　Facts of Jewish exile; excerpt from Ben Gurion looks back. D. Ben Gurion. Harper 231:47-51 S '65; Reply. E. Berger. 231:6+ N '65
　Lady in the dark; investigation of citizenship of R. Eitani. Time 85:65 F 12 '65
　Modern Israel. A. Eban. America 112:896-7 Je 26 '65
　Notes on Israel. D. M. Friedenberg; discussion. Commonweal 81:554-5, 626-7+ Ja 29, F 12 '65
JEWS in literature
　Jew as protagonist. A. P. Klausler. Christian Cent 82:941 Jl 28 '65
　Jews and Americans, by I. Malin. Review Nat R 17:556+ Je 29 '65. M. Geltman
　Rothschilds & the mind. Time 86:31 Jl 16 '65
JEWS in Palestine
　Legacy of A. D. Gordon. R. Sanders. Commentary 39:74-6 Ap '65
　Shemittah & sham; land owned by Jews in Palestine must lie fallow. il Time 86:73 O 8 '65
See also
Jewish-Arab relations
JEWS in Poland
　Ashes and irony. W. Coffey. Commentary 39: 82+ Ap '65; Reply. A. Donat. 40:6 Jl '65
　Forgive them not, for they knew what they did; Warsaw ghetto. A. M. Rosenthal. il N Y Times Mag p50-1+ O 24 '65; Discussion. p22 N 7 '65
　Journal of the Warsaw ghetto; excerpts. C. A. Kaplan. Commentary 40:42-58 N '65
　Scapegoat in need. R. Kluger. Harper 231: 126+ O '65
　Scroll of agony: Warsaw diary of C. A. Kaplan, tr. by A. I. Katsh. Review. Sat R 48:68 D 4 '65. L. Meyer
JEWS in Rumania
　Last return; tr. by A. Schwartz. E. Wiesel. Commentary 39:43-9 Mr '65
JEWS in Russia
　Cultural genocide in Russia. H. E. Fey Christian Cent 82:914-16 Jl 21 '65
　Plight of Soviet Jews. America 112:216-17 F 13 '65
JEWS in Spain
　Not since 1492: meeting between representatives of Spanish Jewry and Spanish chief of state. Newsweek 65:81 F 8 '65

JEWS in the United States
　Assimilation & the sociologists. M. Sklare. Commentary 39:63-7 My '65; Discussion. 40: 16-17 Ag '65
　Baltimore boy. R. Kotlowitz. Harper 231:62-6+ D '65
　Bandstand synagogues; New Year in the Catskills. il Newsweek 66:86-7 O 4 '65
　Break in the ranks; Union of Orthodox Jewish congregations of America disassociate itself from National community relations advisory council. America 113:392 O 9 '65
　Dilemmas of American Jewry; address, February 9, 1965. L. R. Sussman. Vital Speeches 31:340-5 Mr 15 '65
　How we are. M. Himmelfarb; discussion. Commentary 39:26 My; 12+ Je '65
　Jew and Christmas; to observe or not? from a new generation, a new answer. L. Gross. il Look 29:22-4 D 28 '65
　Jew: subject or object? M. Himmelfarb. Commentary 40:54-7 Jl '65
　Kind of survivor. G. Steiner. Commentary 39:32-8 F '65; Discussion. 40:20+ Jl '65
　Negroes & Jews; the new challenge to pluralism. N. Glazer; discussion. Commentary 39:8 My; 6+ Je '65
　New American Jew; Time essay. Time 85: 34-5 Je 25 '65
　Peddlers in Eldorado. L. Berg. Commentary 40:63-7 Jl '65
　Tithe that binds; Jewish fund-raising techniques. il Newsweek 66:86-7 D 13 '65
　Who's vanishing? Time 85:61 Je 4 '65
JHABVALA, R. Prawer
　In love with a beautiful girl; story. New Yorker 41:31-9 Ja 15 '66
JIGS
　Notched jigs for your table saw. R. J. De Cristoforo. il Pop Sci 187:112-14 Ag '65
　Thingamajig for cutting tapers. R. J. De Cristoforo. il Pop Sci 188:128-31 Ja '66
JIGSAW puzzles. See Puzzles
JILLSON, Joyce
　Face to face: with a mettlesome actress. por Seventeen 24:161 S '65
JIMÉNEZ, Josefa Ventosa. See Ventosa Jiménez, J.
JIMÉNEZ, Marcos Pérez. See Pérez Jiménez, M.
JIMSON weed
　Annals of medicine. B. Roueché. New Yorker 41:180+ My 15 '65
JINNAH, Fatima
　Ayub's basic democracy. R. Knox. il Reporter 32:34-6 F 11 '65
JIŘÍ Z Poděbrad, king of Bohemia. See George of Poděbrad
JIUDICE, Joseph
　Family courts at work; ed. by M. R. Sherwin. Parents Mag 40:64-6+ Ag '65
JIU-Jitsu
See also
Judo
JOAN of Arc, Saint
　Miracle of Saint Joan. L. R. Peattie. pors Read Digest 86:239-40+ My '65
JOB corps. See United States—Job corps
JOB corps for women. See United States—Job corps
JOB discrimination. See Discrimination in employment
JOB instruction training. See Employees—Training
JOB interviews. See Interviewing
JOB placement guidance. See Vocational guidance
JOB satisfaction
　How to get out of a dead-end job. H. Levinson. il Pop Sci 186:104-5+ Ap '65
JOB security. See Employment systems—Guaranty of employment
JOB training. See Employees—Training
JOB transfers
　Manpower planning at an electric and gas utility; displaced employees due to extensive technological changes. R. W. Riche. Mo Labor R 88:965-7 Ag '65
JOBS. See Employment; Occupations
JOCKEY club of Paris. See Paris—Clubs
JOCKEYS
　Well-helmeted jockey; insuring jockeys against injury. Sports Illus 22:8+ F 1 '65
See also
Longden, J.
Sellers, J.
JODRELL bank telescope. See Radio telescope
JOE, Gloria
　On decoration. Design 67:38-9 S '65
JOFFE, J. M.
　Genotype and prenatal and premating stress interact to affect adult behavior in rats. bibliog Science 150:1844-5 D 31 '65

JOFFREY, Robert
Who pays the piper? J. L. Collier. Holiday 38:168+ D '65
JOFFREY, Robert, ballet. See Ballet companies
JOHANN, Robert O.
Creativity without guilt. America 113:165 Ag 14 '65
Philosopher's notebook (cont) America 112: 287, 487 F 27, Ap 10 '65
JOHANNES, R. E. and Webb, K. L.
Release of dissolved amino acids by marine zooplankton. bibliog Science 150:76-7 O 1 '65
JOHANNOT, Louis
I couldn't care less about their fathers; interview, ed. by N. Liber. Life 58:60 My 7 '65
JOHN XXIII, pope
Convocation on Pacem in terris. P. J. Henriot. America 112:223-4 F 13 '65
From nineteenth-century piety to aggiornamento. L. Hines. Commonweal 82:448-9 Je 25 '65
Guidelines to peace. M. Frakes. Christian Cent 82:294-6 Mr 10 '65
How the Jews changed Catholic thinking. J. Roddy. il Look 30:18-23 Ja 25 '66
Lasting vision of Pope John. por Time 85: 37 F 26 '65
Letter from Vatican City (cont) X. Rynne. New Yorker 41:34-6+ D 25 '65
Pacem in terris; symposium. il por Sat R 48:19-30 F 13 '65
Peace and pathos. N. O'Gorman. Commonweal 81:783-5 Mr 19 '65
Peace on earth; address, February 17, 1965. H. H. Humphrey. Vital Speeches 31:322-5 Mr 15 '65; Same. Dept State Bul 52:326-32 Mr 8 '65
Peace on earth? New York convocation discusses encyclical Pacem in terris; with report by J. K. Jessup. il Life 58:32-36A+ Mr 5 '65
Pope John and his revolution, by E. E. Y. Hales. Review
  Commonweal 83:300 D 10 '65. J. O'Gara
Pope John and Luther. C. Welch. Christian Cent 82:244+ F 24 '65
Pope John's revolution: secular or religious? R. S. Hughes. Commonweal 83:301-3 D 10 '65
Recollections in tranquillity. W. J. Ong. il por Sat R 48:37-8+ Ap 10 '65
Requirements of peace. il Time 85:36-8 F 26 '65
St John and St Pius? por Newsweek 66:86 N 29 '65
Spirit of holiness in men of power. Life 58:4 Ap 16 '65
Under way: sainthood for two former popes U S News 59:10 N 29 '65
United Nations in a changing world; address, February 1965. Thant. UN Mo Chron 2:41-2 Mr '65
Vatican council ends: reform on borrowed time? F. E. Cartus. Harper 231:100-3+ S '65
When the world's peoples talked peace. il Sat R 48:22-6+ My 1 '65

Bibliography
Pope of renewal. E. C. Bianchi. Cath World 202:178-9 D '65
JOHN, king of England
Day for the rights of man. S. D. Smith. il por N Y Times Mag p29-30+ Je 13 '65
Magna charta: forerunner of the U.S. Constitution. H. G. Earl. il Todays Health 43: 54-7 Je '65
JOHN, E. Roy
Brain and how it changes; adaptation of address, April 1964. Bul Atomic Sci 21:12-14 N '65
JOHN, Sister Patricia. See Patricia John, Sister
JOHN Birch society
Birch policemen; reply. D. W. Bullock. Commonweal 81:594 F 5 '65
Birch society's two faces. Christian Cent 82: 1212-13 O 6 '65
Birchers have birthday party. America 113: 457 O 23 '65; Reply. R. F. Drinan. 113:657 N 27 '65
Birchers settle in; Washington headquarters. R. Stolley. Life 58:43 Je 18 '65
Bouquet for Buckley. Christian Cent 82:1028 Ag 25 '65
Going public. Newsweek 65:26 Mr 8 '65
GOP attacks the John Birch society. F. Knebel. il Look 29:74-6 D 28 '65
Guerrilla warfare, U.S.A. Nation 200:405 Ap 19 '65
How to beat a good congressman. N. Freeman. il Nat R 17:547-50 Je 29 '65; Discussion. 17:672-3 Ag 10 '65

John Birch society and the conservative movement; editors of National review; symposium. Nat R 17:914-20+ O 19 '65; Discussion. 17:1141 D 14 '65
John Birch versus PTA. Nation 200:156 F 15 '65
Livy's ghost; Republican party and John Birch society. Newsweek 66:26-7 D 27 '65
Looking at the Birchers. R. L. Shayon. Sat R 48:41 Ag 14 '65
Night crawlers; Meadville, Pa. Christian Cent 82:763 Je 16 '65
No comfort for Birchers. il Time 86:12 D 24 '65
Plot to take over the PTA. E. Dunbar. il Look 29:27-31 S 7 '65
Poor Karl Mundt, poor GOP! Nation 201: 261 O 25 '65
Republicans blast Birch society. Christian Cent 82:1244 O 13 '65
They never give up. Christian Cent 82:516 Ap 28 '65
We Birchers are trained to look for patterns. J. Witcover. New Repub 152:8-9 My 8 '65
Welch's new bid for power; drive to repeal the Civil rights act of 1964. Christian Cent 82:1004 Ag 18 '65
Why I can't join the John Birch society; letter. R. G. Bacon. il Look 28:76+ N 3 '64; Correction. 29:14+ Mr 23 '65; Discussion. 28:10+ D 15 '64
JOHN Cotton Dana publicity awards
Six libraries share top honors in John Cotton Dana awards. Library J 90:2993-4 Jl '65
JOHN Coy dance company. See Dance companies
JOHN Eaton school. See Washington, D.C.—Education
JOHN F. Kennedy airport. See New York (city)—Airports
JOHN F. Kennedy Center for the performing arts, Washington, D.C.
John F. Kennedy Center for the performing arts. R. L. Stevens. il Opera N 30:11-12 O 23 '65
JOHN F. Kennedy library, Cambridge, Mass.
EB gives $100,000 to JFK memorial library. il Pub W 187:50 Mr 22 '65
He loves things to be beautiful; designer of the Kennedy library at Harvard. A. Herzog. il N Y Times Mag p34-5+ Mr 15 '65
NLW presentation made to Kennedy memorial library. Pub W 187:36-7 My 10 '65
NLW presentation of notable books to Kennedy memorial library. Library J 90:2515 Je 1 '65
Voices of history; Kennedy library oral-history project. il Newsweek 66:72 Ag 23 '65; Same. Hobbies 70:110-11 N '65
JOHN F. Kennedy memorial regatta. See Regattas
JOHN Foster Dulles international airport. See Washington, D.C.—Airports
JOHN Hancock mutual life insurance company
Hancock bets on postwar babies; long-range expansion program. il Bsns W p92-3+ Ja 15 '66
JOHN Hay fellows programs. See John Hay Whitney foundation
JOHN Hay Whitney foundation
Seventy teachers win John Hay fellowships. Sr Schol 86:sup 1-2 Ap 8 '65
JOHN LaFarge institute
LaFarge institute charter. il America 112: 853-6 Je 12 '65
JOHN Tracy clinic. See Deaf—Education
JOHN Wiley and sons. See Wiley, John, and sons, incorporated
JOHNBOATS. See Boats and boating
JOHNNIE Brewer: story. See Warner, S. T.
JOHNS, Jasper
New old masters. L. Lerman. il por Mlle 60:120-3 F '65
Oh, say can you see? il Time 87:70-1 Ja 14 '66
JOHNS, Lawrence H.
Bonus; 500-pound bear. Outdoor Life 137: 38-9+ Ja '66
JOHNSGARD, Paul A.
Elusive musk ducks. Natur Hist 74:26-9 O '65
JOHNSON, Albert W. and Packer, J. G.
Polyploidy and environment in Arctic Alaska. bibliog Science 148:237-9 Ap 9 '65
JOHNSON, Andrew
Andrew Johnson, seventeenth President. F. Freidel. il pors Nat Geog Mag 127:676-9 My '65
Day a president stood trial. il Sr Schol 86: 5 F 18 '65
JOHNSON, Betsey
Betsey's world; a tale about what a lot of talent can do. il pors Mlle 62:178+ N '65
JOHNSON, Carl M. See Srihongse, S. jt. auth.

JOHNSON, Carol
Books. Commonweal 83:352-3 D 17 '65

JOHNSON, Chalmers
How sharp are the dragon's claws? N Y Times Mag p22-3+ F 28 '65

JOHNSON, Charles Earl
Quiet triumph of a gentle man. C. Farnsworth. il pors Ebony 20:124-6+ Jl '65

JOHNSON, Charley
Cards unscramble the East. T. Maule. il Sports Illus 23:36-9 O 18 '65
Charley green giant. H. L. Masin. por Sr Schol 87:28 O 7 '65
Quiet quarterback. il Newsweek 66:80-1 O 18 '65

JOHNSON, Charlotte Buel
Gallery for young people. See issues of School arts

JOHNSON, Claudia Alta (Taylor)
First lady talks about her mother-in-law. por McCalls 93:8+ N '65
More beautiful America. por NEA J 54:33 N '65
Ways to beautify America; interview. por U S News 58:72-6+ F 22 '65; Same abr. with title Let's beautify America! Read Digest 86:131-4 My '65

about

Beauty, politics, romance. il por Newsweek 66:26 S 20 '65
Chance to roam; Lady Bird and Cabinet wives tour landscapes and landmarks of Virginia. il por Time 85:27 My 21 '65
Claudia the beautician; beautifying of cities. il por Time 86:29 O 1 '65
First lady's Lady Boswell. N. Robertson. il pors N Y Times Mag p 130-1+ Ap 11 '65
From Jackie to Lady Bird; letter that caused an uproar. il U S News 58:10-11 My 31 '65
How Lady Bird watches LBJ's health. D. Kiker. pors Good H 160:96-7+ My '65
Johnsons' financial empire; up a million, branching out. il U S News 58:44-5 My 31 '65
Lady Bird Johnson writes her own picture story; with introd. by deRosset Morrissey. il pors Life 59:56B-65 Ag 13 '65
Lady Bird's Washington. il por Newsweek 66:92-3 N 22 '65
Lady in the east wing. M. Greenfield. il por Reporter 33:28-31 Jl 15 '65
Lady looks at the First lady. M. McGrory. America 112:242 F 20 '65
LBJ as a determined suitor; excerpts from letter. T. J. Taylor. il por U S News 58:51 F 15 '65
Mrs Lyndon B. Johnson: a new kind of First lady? M. Mead. il por Redbook 125:12+ Jl '65
Now, White House help for tourists. il U S News 59:14-15 Ag 16 '65
Rhubarb in the kitchen. il por Newsweek 66:24 D 27 '65
Still talkin' about the Tetons. D. Fleeson. il por Am For 71:22-5 N '65
With Lady Bird in the White House. il por U S News 58:33 F 1 '65

JOHNSON, Clinton B.
Dogfighting with MiGs; interview. Aviation W 83:11 Jl 26 '65

JOHNSON, Deron
Deron who? il por Newsweek 66:58+ S 13 '65

JOHNSON, DeWayne B.
Easy-to-make back yard fire pit. Pop Gard 16:45 Jl '65

JOHNSON, E. Harper. See Hansberry, W. L. jt. auth.

JOHNSON, Edwin, family
Village blacksmiths; Japhia interiors. il Ebony 21:96-8+ D '65

JOHNSON, Electa. See Johnson, I. jt. auth.

JOHNSON, Ellen H.
Three new, cool, bright imagists. Art N 64:42-4+ Sum '65

JOHNSON, Eric W.
When bright children fail. Parents Mag 40:48-9+ S '65

JOHNSON, Everene (Cooper)
My daughter, the policeman. il pors Ebony 20:82-4+ O '65

JOHNSON, F. S.
Atmosphere of Mars. bibliog Science 150:1445-8 D 10 '65

JOHNSON, Frank C.
Hell on an island; interview. ed. by J. Rearden. por Outdoor Life 136:50-3+ S '65

JOHNSON, Frank Minis, Jr
No immunity. Time 86:15-15A Ag 13 '65

JOHNSON, Franklyn A.
Misuses of the university; address, June 17, 1965. Vital Speeches 31:586-8 Jl 15 '65

JOHNSON, Fridolf
Art of the bookplate. Am Artist 29:48-53+ My '65
Roy Lindstrom, artist & art director. Am Artist 29:50-5+ D '65
2,000 years of calligraphy. Am Artist 29:40-5+ O '65

JOHNSON, G. Griffith
Trade and the balance of payments; statement, March 16, 1965. Dept State Bul 52:502-7 Ap 5 '65

JOHNSON, Gerald W.
In the shadow of the presidency. New Repub 153:26-7 Jl 3 '65
Little liberal, or a little conservative. New Repub 152:28 F 20 '65
Phenomenon called Mencken. New Repub 152:32-3 Ap 17 '65
That close to the presidency. New Repub 152:22 Ap 3 '65

JOHNSON, Harold
Less than a plumber; ed. by B. E. Burk. Flying 77:83 S '65

JOHNSON, Harold Keith
Defense of freedom in Viet-Nam; address, January 14, 1965. Dept State Bul 52:176-80 F 8 '65
New war in Vietnam; address, July 23, 1965. Vital Speeches 31:676-9 S 1 '65
Vietnam: problems and progress; address, January 14, 1965. Vital Speeches 31:262-5 F 15 '65

about

Management team. il por Time 85:22-23A F 5 '65
Renaissance in the ranks. il pors Time 86:30-4 D 10 '65
Winning instead of wishing. il por Time 86:31-31A N 5 '65

JOHNSON, Harriett
(ed) See Schneider-Siemssen, G. Light touch

JOHNSON, Harry G.
Common market for U.S. and Canada? interview. por U S News 58:98-101 F 8 '65
Paying for basic research; some economic issues. Bul Atomic Sci 21:12-16 D '65

JOHNSON, Howard
Building from scratch; interview. por Nations Bsns 53:40-2+ N '65

JOHNSON, Howard, company
HoJo challenges the giants. J. F. Olesky. il Duns R 86:59+ S '65

JOHNSON, Howard Wesley
Manager for MIT. por Newsweek 67:48 Ja 3 '66
MIT goes to social sciences for a boss. il por Bsns W p62-3 Ja 8 '66

JOHNSON, Hugh
Bitters, the tangy mixers. House & Gard 127:152+ Je '65
Choosing wine for a casserole. House & Gard 129:130+ Ja '66
Corkscrew (cont) House & Gard 127:160+
Corkscrew: light, summery wines of Alsace. House & Gard 128:116+ Ag '65
London's villages. House & Gard 127:22+ Je '65

JOHNSON, Irving, and Johnson, Electa
Yankee cruises the storied Nile. pors Nat Geog Mag 127:583-633 My '65

JOHNSON, James C.
Year of the hummingbirds. Audubon Mag 67:186-9 My '65

JOHNSON, James Ralph
Eleventh hour caribou. Field & S 70:32-5+ Ag '65
Secrets of camping pleasure; excerpt from Anyone can camp in comfort. Field & S 69:48-51 F '65

JOHNSON, Junior
Last American hero is Junior Johnson, yes! T. Wolfe. il pors Esquire 63:68-75+ Mr '65

JOHNSON, K. M. and others
Chronic infection of rodents by machupo virus. bibliog Science 150:1618-19 D 17 '65

JOHNSON, Lady Bird. See Johnson, C. A. T

JOHNSON, Louis
Louis Johnson and the Har-You dancers, 92nd street Y. J. Maskey. Dance Mag 39:28 Ag '65

JOHNSON, Louise
Plastic to the rescue. Pop Gard 16:10 My '65

JOHNSON, Luci Baines
Luci Baines Johnson; interview. ed. by E. Vexler. pors Ebony 20:40-2+ F '65

about

After Luci Johnson was baptized. il U S News 59:16 Jl 19 '65
Another Catholic in the White House. V. Eller. Christian Cent 82:1007-8 Ag 18 '65; Discussion. 82:1194-5; 1388-9 S 29, N 10 '65

JOHNSON, Luci Baines—about—*Continued*

Baptism of fire. il por Time 86:73 Jl 16 '65

Catholic priest stubs ecumenical toe. Christian Cent 82:932 Jl 28 '65

Do they or don't they? Christian Cent 82:909 Jl 21 '65

For Luci Johnson: instruction in Catholic faith. por U S News 58:14 F 8 '65

How to deal with daddy. il por Newsweek 67:21 Ja 10 '66

Luci Johnson and history, by K. J. Atchity. America 113:334+ S 25 '65

Luci Johnson's religion: she joins the Catholic church. por U S News 59:20 Jl 12 '65

Rites and wrongs. il por Newsweek 66:79 Jl 19 '65

Taking instruction: in the Roman Catholic faith. Newsweek 65:80-1 F 8 '65

Why the President's daughter turned to the Catholic church. N. Robertson. por Ladies Home J 82:76+ Ag '65

JOHNSON, Lynda Bird

I see America first: diary of the President's daughter. pors Nat Geog Mag 128:874-904 D '65

My life in the White House. Look 29:98+ My 18 '65

Very unusual vacation. McCalls 92:58+ S '65

about

Beauty, politics, romance. il por Newsweek 66:26 S 20 '65

Wilderness White House. por Time 86:52 Ag 6 '65

JOHNSON, Lyndon Baines

Address at the White House conference on education, July 20 and July 21, 1965. pors Am Ed 1:28 Jl '65

Advisory group reports on study of science institute in Korea; White House announcement; with remarks, August 5, 1965. Dept State Bul 53:322-3 Ag 23 '65

Alliance for progress; four years of forward movement; address, August 17, 1965. Dept State Bul 53:426-30 S 13 '65; Excerpts. Cur Hist 49:362 D '65

Amending the Immigration and nationality act; message, January 13, 1965. Dept State Bul 52:146-7 F 1 '65

Amending U.N. charter to enlarge Security council and ECOSOC; message, April 6, 1965. Dept State Bul 52:678-81 My 3 '65

America's commitment to social justice and progress for all; excerpt from address, June 1, 1965. Dept State Bul 52:1005-6 Je 21 '65

Anniversary of sovereignty of German Federal Republic; message, May 5, 1965. Dept State Bul 52:814 My 24 '65

Annual report of National science foundation sent to Congress; message, February 15, 1965. Dept State Bul 52:434-6 Mr 22 '65

Arms control and disarmament; some sober truths; remarks, May 27, 1965. Dept State Bul 52:973-4 Je 14 '65

Assessment of the situation in the Dominican Republic; statement, June 17, 1965. Dept State Bul 53:19-21 Jl 5 '65

At the center of our concerns. por Bsns W p25-6 Ja 15 '65

Automotive products agreement with Canada becomes effective; statements, October 22, 1965, with texts of the proclamation and the order. Dept State Bul 53:793-5 N 15 '65

Bill authorizing new embassy at Saigon signed by President; statement, My 25, 1965. Dept State Bul 52:974 Je 14 '65

Boy scouts visit White House on 55th anniversary of scouting; remarks, February 8, 1965. Dept State Bul 52:289-90 Mr 1 '65

Budget of the United States government for the fiscal year ending June 30, 1966; excerpts from message to Congress, January 25, 1965. Dept State Bul 52:207-11 F 15 '65

Congress approves appropriations for Inter-American bank; statement, March 25, 1965. Dept State Bul 52:537-8 Ap 12 '65

Congress approves supplemental appropriation for Viet-Nam; remarks, May 4, 1965, with message to Congress. Dept State Bul 52:816-26 My 24 '65

Conquering the ancient enemies of mankind; remarks, July 22, 1965. Dept State Bul 53:236-8 Ag 9 '65

Dominican Republic; address, May 2, 1965. Vital Speeches 31:450-2 My 15 '65

East-West center review board holds first meeting; remarks, May 13, 1965. Dept State Bul 52: 906-7 Je 7 '65

Effectiveness of U.S. delegation to U.N. enhanced by new law; statement, September 28, 1965. Dept State Bul 53:641 O 18 '65

Exchange of greetings; exchange of toasts with President Mohammed Ayub Khan. December 14, 1965. Dept State Bul 54:2-5 Ja 3 '66

Food for peace program and the challenge of the future; message, March 31, 1965. Dept State Bul 52:682-4 My 3 '65

Forecast: change; summaries of inaugural address and messages to Congress. por Sr Schol 86:18-19 F 4 '65

Foreign aid, an investment in man's future; remarks, January 11, 1965. Dept State Bul 52:132 F 1 '65

Foreign aid appropriations act signed into law; statement, October 20, 1965. Dept State Bul 53:760 N 8 '65

Foreign aid; message to the Congress, January 14, 1965. Dept State Bul 52:126-32 F 1 '65

Foreign assistance act of 1965 signed by President; statement, September 6, 1965. Dept State Bul 53:525 S 27 '65

From LBJ: why he moved into Caribbean; excerpts from news conference, June 1, 1965 por U S News 58:6 Je 14 '65

Full educational opportunity; key points of President's message. Sat R 48:84-5 F 20 '65

Government-business partnership on balance-of-payments problem; remarks, February 18, 1965. Dept State Bul 52:335-7 Mr 8 '65

Historic occasion; address, September 29, 1965. por Dance Mag 39:34 N '65

Improving the world's monetary system; remarks, October 1, 1965. Dept State Bul 53:614-17 O 18 '65

International cooperation, a necessity of our age; statement, November 29, 1965. Dept State Bul 53:969 D 20 '65

Interview with LBJ; ed. by J. Cannon and C. Roberts. por Newsweek 66:20-1 Ag 2 '65

Johnson on southeast Asian aid; statement, with excerpts from special message, June 1, 1965. Cur Hist 49:303-4+ N '65

Justice Goldberg sworn in as representative to U.N; remarks, July 26, 1965. Dept State Bul 53:265-6 Ag 16 '65

Legacy of James Smithson; address, September 16, 1965. Dept State Bul 53:550-2 O 4 '65; Same with title Smithsonian honored; remarks, September 16, 1965. Sci N L 88:199 S 25 '65; Same with title President Johnson on international education. Sch & Soc 93:481+ D 11 '65

Lincoln's birthday, 1965; remarks, February 12, 1965. Dept State Bul 52:334-5 Mr 8 '65

LBJ keynote: a prosperous, great and mighty nation; inaugural address, January 20, 1965. pors U S News 58:102-3 F 1 '65; Same. Vital Speeches 31:258-9 F 15 '65; Dept State Bul 52:162-4 F 8 '65

LBJ praises the revolution of the Negro American; address, June 4, 1965. por U S News 58:50-2 Je 14 '65; Excerpts. Newsweek 65:36-7 Je 14 '65; Summary. U S News 58:52-3 Je 21 '65

LBJ's funny stories about his family; excerpt from Warm, wonderful wit and humor of Lyndon B. Johnson; comp. by B. Adler. por Good H 161:74-5 Ag '65

LBJ's views on big pay raises in industry, government; excerpts from news conference, August 25, 1965. U S News 59:75 S 6 '65

Message from the President of the United States, February 8, 1965; excerpt. Liv Wildn 87:2 Wint '64; Recreation 58:107 Mr '65

Message from the President to all who work with youth. Am Ed 1:27 S '65

Morality of nations; address, June 6, 1965. Dept State Bul 52:1026-9 Je 28 '65

OAS achieves reconciliation in Dominican Republic; statements, September 1, 1965. Dept State Bul 53:477 S 20 '65

Other side of the Vietnam war; excerpts from address, May 13, 1965. por U S News 58:22 My 24 '65

Peace of mankind; address, June 3, 1965. Dept State Bul 52:986-9 Je 21 '65; Excerpts. U S News 58:4 Je 14 '65

Peace or war: the Johnson plan; address, April 7, 1965. por U S News 58:76-8 Ap 19 '65; Same. Vital Speeches 31:386-8 Ap 15 '65; Dept State Bul 52:606-10 Ap 26 '65

President and Mr Black discuss Asian economic progress; statement, April 20, 1965. Dept State Bul 52:719 My 10 '65

President asks authority to remove duties on Canadian auto products; letter, March 31, 1965. Dept State Bul 52:638-9 Ap 26 '65

President asks strengthening of foreign affairs agencies; letters, May 6, 1965; with executive order. Dept State Bul 52:930-3 Je 7 '65

President calls for full use of resources in overseas programs; statement, March 25, 1965. Dept State Bul 52:538 Ap 12 '65

President calls Gemini-5 flight a journey of peace; statement, August 29, 1965. Dept State Bul 53:475 S 20 '65

JOHNSON, Lyndon Baines—*Continued*

President comments on several foreign policy developments; statement, August 29, 1965. Dept State Bul 53:476 S 20 '65

President gratified by report on U.S.-Japan health program; statement, April 29, 1965. Dept State Bul 52:761 My 17 '65

President inaugurates commercial telephone service by satellite; remarks, June 28, 1965. Dept State Bul 53:117 Jl 19 '65

President Johnson and Prime Minister Sato of Japan exchange views on matters of mutual interest; greeting, January 12, 1965. Dept State Bul 52:133 F 1 '65

President Johnson and Secretary McNamara review situation in Viet-Nam; statement, April 27, 1965. Dept State Bul 52:748-9 My 17 '65

President Johnson asks four-year extension of ACDA authorization; letter to Congress, January 15, 1965. Dept State Bul 52:144-5 F 1 '65

President Johnson discusses Viet-Nam, Dominican Republic, disarmament; statements, July 13, 1965. Dept State Bul 53:182-3 Ag 2 '65

President Johnson features libraries in $1.5 billion educational proposal; excerpts from message to Congress, January 12, 1965. Library J 90:596, 946 F 1-15 '65; ALA Bul 59:94-5, 183-4 F-Mr '65; Summary. Sr Schol 86:1T+ F 4 '65

President Johnson meets with Antarctic policy group; statement, My 1, 1965 and remarks, My 20, 1965. Dept State Bul 52:1013-15 Je 21 '65

President Johnson on education; text of remarks, July 2, 1965. Sch & Soc 93:351-4 O 2 '65

President Johnson on employment; excerpt from news conference, April 1, 1965. Cur Hist 49:45+ Jl '65

President Johnson on the economy; address, January 28, 1965. Cur Hist 48:362-3+ Je '65

President Johnson receives book on the Magna carta; remarks, July 22, 1965. Dept State Bul 53:235 Ag 9 '65

President Johnson receives report on increasing trade with U.S.S.R; remarks, January 7, 1965. Dept State Bul 52:102-3 Ja 25 '65

President Johnson recommends expansion of Peace corps; letter, February 25, 1965. Dept State Bul 52:433-4 Mr 22 '65

President Johnson to the Secretary-General of the United Nations; letter, July 28, 1965. Dept State Bul 53:275 Ag 16 '65

President Johnson's message to the Detroit conference; letter to ALA. ALA Bul 59:590 Jl '65

President meets winners; remarks, March 1, 1965. Sci N L 87:163+ Mr 13 '65

President names Justice Goldberg as U.S. Ambassador to U.N; remarks, July 20, 1965. Dept State Bul 53:240-1 Ag 9 '65

President notes anniversary of American specialist program; letter, April 15, 1965. Dept State Bul 52:725 My 10 '65

President outlines objectives for disarmament talks; message, July 27, 1965. Dept State Bul 53:335 Ag 23 '65

President pays tribute to Ambassador Stevenson; statement, July 14, 1965. Dept State Bul 53:229 Ag 9 '65

President reaffirms U.S. goal of peace in southeast Asia; statement, March 20, 1965. Dept State Bul 52:488-9 Ap 5 '65

President recommends increase of U.S. quota in monetary fund; letter, March 17, 1965. Dept State Bul 52:507-8 Ap 5 '65

President reiterates U.S. policy on Viet-Nam; statement, March 25, 1965. Dept State Bul 52:527-8 Ap 12 '65

President reports on progress of negotiations with Panama; statement, September 24, 1965. Dept State Bul 53:624-5 O 18 '65; Excerpts. Cur Hist 50:49 Ja '66

President sends Congress reports on cultural and exhibits programs; letters, October 6, 1965. Dept State Bul 53:673-4 O 25 '65

President sends Congress report on cultural exchange program; letter, February 1, 1965. Dept State Bul 52:263-4 F 22 '65

President signs immigration bill; offers asylum to Cubans; remarks, October 3, 1965. Dept State Bul 53:661-3 O 25 '65

President signs Wilderness and Conservation acts; remarks, September 3, 1964. Liv Wildn 86:44 Spr '64

President submits promotion list, asks FSO appointments for USIA; letter, April 13, 1965. Dept State Bul 52:733 My 10 '65

President urges implementation of Florence agreement; statement, with letter, June 1, 1965. Dept State Bul 52:1015 Je 21 '65

President Yameogo of Upper Volta visits the United States; greetings, March 29, 1965. Dept State Bul 52:618-19 Ap 26 '65

President's days of crisis and decision: in LBJ's own words; excerpts from statements, May 4, 1965. il pors U S News 58:43 My 17 '65

President's message to Congress on labor; address, May 18, 1965. Cur Hist 49:106-7+ Ag '65

Protocol amending double-taxation convention with Germany; message, September 29, 1965. Dept State Bul 53:722-3 N 1 '65

Pulaski memorial day, 1965; statement, October 11, 1965. Dept State Bul 53:708 N 1 '65

Purpose that binds America and Australia; a toast in honor of Sir R. Menzies, June 7, 1965. Dept State Bul 52:1050-1 Je 28 '65

Review of international balance of payments and our gold position; message to Congress, February 10, 1965. Dept State Bul 52:282-8 Mr 1 '65

Right to vote; address, March 15, 1965. Vital Speeches 31:354-7 Ap 1 '65; Excerpts. por U S News 58:110-11 Mr 29 '65; Sr Schol 86:9 Ap 1 '65

Saved! excerpts from address, September 21, 1965. Am For 71:4-5 N '65

Search for a durable peace in the Dominican Republic; address, May 28, 1965. Dept State Bul 52:989-92 Je 21 '65

Search for steps to improve international monetary system; statement, August 25, 1965. Dept State Bul 53:452 S 13 '65

Southeast Asia aid program; statement, June 1, 1965, and message to Congress. Dept State Bul 52:1054-6 Je 28 '65

State of our defenses; message to Congress, January 18, 1965. Dept State Bul 52:211-18 F 15 '65

State of the Union; address to the Congress, January 4, 1965. Dept State Bul 52:94-100 Ja 25 '65; Excerpts. Cur Hist 48:176-8+ Mr '65

Teacher corps proposed by LBJ; summary of address, July 1965. por Sr Schol 86:sup 1 S 16 '65

To the Soviet people, an LBJ appeal for peace; excerpts from address, June 3, 1965. U S News 58:4 Je 14 '65

Tragedy, disappointment, and progress in southeast Asia; statement, April 17, 1965. Dept State Bul 52:650-2 My 3 '65

Transcendent issues in today's world; address, February 22, 1965. Dept State Bul 52:372-4 Mr 15 '65

Twentieth anniversary of the United Nations; address, June 25, 1965. Dept State Bul 53:98-101 Jl 19 '65; Excerpts. por U S News 59:8 Jl 5 '65

20th anniversary of V-E day; address, May 7, 1965. Dept State Bul 52:790-3 My 24 '65

United Nations commemoration address, June 25, 1965. UN Mo Chron 2:84-8 Jl '65

U.S. acts to meet threat in Dominican Republic; statements, April 28-May 2, 1965. bibliog f Dept State Bul 52:738, 742-8 My 17 '65

United States and Italy reaffirm close ties of friendship; greetings, April 20, 1965. Dept State Bul 52:809-10 My 24 '65

U.S. and Japan begin program of cooperation in medical science; statement, April 8, 1965. Dept State Bul 52:667-8 My 3 '65

United States and Korea reaffirm strong bonds of friendship; greetings, May 17, 1965. Dept State Bul 52:950 Je 14 '65

U.S. and Mexico agree on measures to solve Lower Colorado River salinity problem; statement, March 22, 1965. Dept State Bul 52:555-6 Ap 12 '65

U.S. defense: the changes Johnson wants; summary of special message. U S News 58:14 F 1 '65. Excerpts Sci N L 87:67 Ja 30 '65

U.S. embassy at Saigon damaged: funds for new building requested; statement, March 30, and letter, April 1, 1965, with bill. Dept State Bul 52:571-2 Ap 19 '65

U.S. goals in Vietnam as set by the President; excerpts from news conference, July 28, 1965. por U S News 59:50-1 Ag 9 '65

U.S. interest in free trade and peaceful commerce; remarks, June 9, 1965. Dept State Bul 53:30-1 Jl 5 '65

U.S.-Japan cabinet committee on trade and economic affairs holds fourth meeting at Washington; remarks, July 14, 1965, with joint communique. Dept State Bul 53:244-6, 247-9 Ag 9 '65

JOHNSON, Lyndon Baines—*Continued*

U.S. loan to support economic integration of Central America; remarks, July 29, 1965. Dept State Bul 53:330-1 Ag 23 '65

U.S., Mexico, IAEA agree on joint saline water feasibility study; remarks, October 7, 1965. Dept State Bul 53:720-2 N 1 '65

U.S. recognizes new Dominican government; offers aid; statement, September 4, 1965. Dept State Bul 53:514 S 27 '65

Unity, the legacy of American democracy; address, February 3, 1965. Dept State Bul 52:242-4 F 22 '65

Vice President Humphrey to head Peace corps advisory council; letter, January 26, 1965. Dept State Bul 52:250 F 22 '65

Viet-Nam: the third face of the war; address, May 13, 1965. Dept State Bul 52:838-41 My 31 '65

Voting rights law; address, August 6, 1965. Vital Speeches 31:642-3 Ag 15 '65

War, taxes, labor, rights: LBJ's plans for 1966; State of the Union message, January 12, 1966. por U S News 60:62-6+ Ja 24 '66

Washington report; excerpts from address, March 1, 1965, ed. by J. Lloyd. Sr Schol 86:sup21 Mr 18 '65

We will stand in Viet-Nam; statement. July 28, 1965. Dept State Bul 53:262-5 Ag 16 '65

What the President says now about U.S. role in Vietnam; news conference, April 27, 1965. por U S News 58:73 My 10 '65

Why we are in Viet-Nam; excerpts from remarks, December 9, 1965. Dept State Bul 53:1014 D 27 '65

Works of peace; remarks, April 10, 1965. Dept State Bul 52:652-4 My 3 '65

World law day; remarks, July 8, 1965, with proclamation. Dept State Bul 53:216-17 Ag 2 '65

World peace through law; address, September 16, 1965. Dept State Bul 53:542-4 O 4 '65

—and Erhard, Ludwig

Chancellor Erhard of Germany talks with President Johnson; joint statement, June 4, 1965. Dept State Bul 52:1051-3 Je 28 '65

—and Hallstein, W.

President of EEC commission meets with President Johnson; joint communique, March 18, 1965. Dept State Bul 52:491-2 Ap 5 '65

about

After fifteen months, what businessmen think of LBJ. il por U S News 58:98-102 F 22 '65

Amateur. K. Crawford. Newsweek 66:25 Ag 23 '65

. . . And this is what they have to say; ed. by S. V. Roberts. il Esquire 64:90-3+ N '65

Anti-Johnson underground. S. Alsop. por Sat Eve Post 238:18 Ag 14 '65

As LBJ starts his third year, new problems, bigger plans. il por U S News 59:58-60 D 6 '65

Atlantic report. Atlan 215:6+ Mr; 6+ Ap; 4+ My; 216:6+ S; 6+ O; 6 D '65

Author's view on how Johnson was chosen; excerpt from Thousand days. A. M. Schlesinger, jr. il por Life 59:68-9 Jl 16 '65

Awaiting Johnson's word on labor. Bsns W p52 My 1 '65

Back home; foreign opinion of American role in Vietnam. M. Ascoli. Reporter 32:20 Mr 25 '65

Beatnik unrest baffles LBJ. P. Lisagor. il Nations Bsns 53:23-4 Je '65

Big change in Washington; symposium. il por Look 29:21-34+ Ap 6 '65

Bill Movers: Johnson's good angel. T. Wicker. por Harper 231:41-9 O '65; Same abr. with title Remarkable rise of Bill D. Moyers. Read Digest 88:72-7 Ja '66

Business as usual. Newsweek 65:21-2 F 22 '65

Campaign document. Newsweek 66:108 O 18 '65

Close to his vest; concerning press conference of July 28, 1965. Nat R 17:680 Ag 10 '65

Cold war in Washington. il por Time 85:38+ Mr 5 '65

Concern about LBJ. J. Osborne. New Repub 153:12-14 Jl 24 '65

Continuing battle. New Repub 152:5-6 Mr 27 '65

Cool of consensus. K. Crawford. Newsweek 65:22 Je 7 '65

Dangers of the consensus. H. Brandon. Sat R 48:14+ F 27 '65

Days and nights of the Great Persuader. E. T. Folliard. America 112:655 My 8 '65

Decision in Viet Nam; how Johnson makes foreign policy. H. F. Graff. il pors N Y Times Mag p4-7+ Jl 4 '65

Defending the dollar: latest moves by LBJ; concerning message to Congress. il U S News 58:47-50 F 22 '65

Diplomacy a la Johnson. Nation 200:461 My 3 '65

Disrobing the king. K. Crawford. Newsweek 66:26 Jl 19 '65

Dry society. il Time 86:22 Ag 20 '65

E pluribus unum. il por Newsweek 66:21 Ag 30 '65

Economy under new management; with editorial comment. L. Banks. il Fortune 71:90-1, 96-9+ My '65

Election year to remember. M. L. Coit. il por Sat R 48:29-31 Jl 10 '65

End of the honeymoon; LBJ's deteriorating press relations. il Newsweek 65:62-3 F 15 '65

Family album; by R. B. Johnson. Review Time il por 86:36-7 N 5 '65

Family album; excerpt, with editorial comment. R. B. Johnson. il pors McCalls 93:4, 103-7+ N '65

For a more beautiful U.S; the President asks this; with interview with C. A. T. Johnson. il por U S News 58:71-6+ F 22 '65

Ford's future? il Time 86:17 Ag 13 '65

Forgotten in abundance? concerning the inaugural address. Nation 200:97 F 1 '65

French press warms up to LBJ. E. Taylor. Reporter 32:29-30 Au 22 '65

From dissent to opposition. Nation 200:629 Je 14 '65

From the Professor's notebook; concerning A. M. Schlesinger's account. il Time 86:22 Jl 23 '65

From White House to Capitol, how things get done; interview. L. F. O'Brien. il por U S News 59:68-73 S 20 '65

Gallup poll: Johnson's popularity; an upturn after a dip. il U S News 58:19 F 15 '65

Gallup poll; President Johnson's popularity, down again, after a rise. il U S News 59:21 Ag 16 '65

Great day; inaugural ball. New Yorker 40:24-5 Ja 30 '65

Great society. S. Booker. il pors Ebony 20:148-50+ Ag '65

Great society bows in. il pors Ebony 20:66-8+ Ap '65

Greyer, graver, and growing. Time 86:18 S 3 '65

Growing burden for convalescent LBJ. il por U S News 59:8 D 20 '65

Growing ordeal of LBJ. il U S News 58:29-30 Mr 15 '65

Hard limits of government by consensus. L. W. Koenig. il por N Y Times Mag p 26-7+ Mr 7 '65

His mother's story of LBJ; excerpts from manuscript. R. B. Johnson. il pors U S News 58:48-52 F 15 '65

Home front. K. Crawford. Newsweek 66:34 Ag 9 '65

How businessmen size up LBJ, outlook, spending, hiring. il U S News 58:94-5 My 10 '65

How Europe sees the President. H. Brandon. Sat R 48:22-3 Ap 10 '65

How fares the Lyndon image? V. Gold. il Nat R 17:414-15 My 18 '65

How Johnson meets the challenge. il por Bsns W p28-9 Mr 13 '65

How Johnson uses his Cabinet. il por Bsns W p 180+ My 22 '65

How LBJ picks his men; interview. J. W. Macy, jr. il por Nations Bsns 53:36-7+ Jl '65

How LBJ was chosen: Robert Kennedy's version; interview. R. F. Kennedy. por U S News 59:15 S 6 '65

How LBJ wins at the budget game; with editorial comment. il Bsns W p30-1 Je 26 '65

How the President eases his cares. il pors U S News 60:16 Ja 24 '66

How unions are adding to Johnson's worries. U S News 58:76+ Je 14 '65

How world reacted to LBJ's speech. il U S News 58:32 F 1 '65

How ya gonna keep 'em down in Upper Volta after they've met Lloyd Hand? E. Wittenberg. Esquire 64:24+ D '65

Hundred-day mark. Newsweek 65:26 Ap 19 '65

If Goldwater had won; A. Buchwald on President Johnson's policy in Vietnam. Time 85:72 Mr 19 '65

If Kennedy hadn't picked LBJ. il U S News 59:50-2 Ag 2 '65

I'm devoted to him; Freedman and LBJ. por Newsweek 66:54 Jl 12 '65

In the Statue of Liberty's shadow. H. Hamilton. America 113:431 O 16 '65

Inner-directed mood. S. Alsop. il por Sat Eve Post 238:18 Mr 13 '65

JOHNSON, Lyndon Baines—about—*Continued*

Inner inner circle around Johnson. B. H. Bagdikian. il por N Y Times Mag p21+ F 28 '65

Inside the White House. il pors Newsweek 65:27-9+ Mr 1 '65

Is it to be the Kennedy brothers vs. LBJ? il U S News 59:50-2 Jl 12 '65

It was a warm day in Washington; inauguration as 36th President. J. N. Eller. America 112:185 F 6 '65

It was LBJ's great day. il pors U S News 58:37-40 F 1 '65

It's still a one-way budget: up. il U S News 58:75-8 F 1 '65

Johnson abroad. New Repub 152:5-6 Je 12 '65

Johnson and 14(b) Nat R 17:714 Ag 24 '65

Johnson and the businessmen. G. R. Rosen. il por Duns R 85:40-3+ My '65

Johnson & the intellectuals. H. Fairlie. Commentary 40:49-55 O '65; Discussion. 41:4+ Ja '66

Johnson and the press; what the grumbling is about. il pors U S News 58:49-51 Mr 22 '65

Johnson at San Francisco. Nation 200:685-6 Je 28 '65

Johnson charts his economics; with editorial comment. il pors Bsns W p25-6, 136 Ja 30 '65

Johnson era starts; What's ahead now under LBJ? il pors U S News 58:29-34 F 1 '65

Johnson gives the cheerful earful. por Bsns W p26-7 Je 26 '65

Johnson message. New Repub 152:1+ F 6 '65

Johnson oversell. W. V. Shannon. Commonweal 81:777-8 Mr 19 '65; Reply. Time 85:76 Ap 2 '65

Johnson so far; symposium. Commentary 39:37-55 Je '65

Johnsons' financial empire: up a million branching out. il U S News 58:44-5 My 31 '65

Johnson's road starts getting bumpier. il por Bsns W p38-9 F 27 '65

Johnson's talent hunt. J. Kraft. Harper 230:40+ Mr '65

Kennedy legend & the Johnson performance; Time essay. Time 86:30-1 N 26 '65

Labor-management under the Johnson administration. J. R. Wason. Cur Hist 49:65-70+ Ag '65

Laws. then what next? R. Moley. Newsweek 66:116 O 11 '65

Leading from strength: LBJ in action. D. Brinkley. Atlan 215:49-54 F '65

Letter from Washington (cont) R. H. Rovere. New Yorker 41:177-8+ Mr 20; 160+ Ap 17; 204+ My 15; 143-50 Je 12; 108-10+ Ag 14 '65

Liberal break with Johnson. U S News 58:35-6 My 24 '65

Lights! cameras! action! the LBJ news conference. il pors U S News 59:66-7 S 20 '65

Loyal lieutenant views LBJ; excerpts from address. J. Valenti. por Newsweek 66:16-17 Jl 12 '65

Lyndon B. attitudes; jokes at L.B.J.'s expense. Time 86:18 S 10 '65

LBJ and business now: not quite so friendly. U S News 58:82 Je 14 '65

LBJ and businessmen; climate gets cooler. il por U S News 59:39-41 N 29 '65

LBJ and Congress: after a fast start. harder tests ahead. il U S News 58:52-3 Mr 1 '65

LBJ and Congress: secrets of a briefing. il pors U S News 59:30-1 Ag 23 '65

LBJ and the unions; an uneasy honeymoon. il U S News 58:69-71 Mr 8 '65

LBJ country. L. M. Rhodes. Travel 123:29-32+ Mr '65

LBJ directive: he says spread the research money. D. S. Greenberg. Science 149:1483-5 S 24 '65; Reply. P. H. Abelson. 150:11 O 1 '65

LBJ for the USA: 1964 campaign evaluation; address. December 28, 1964. H. F. Harding. Vital Speeches 31:249-51 F 1 '65

LBJ image. what's happening. il pors U S News 59:35-7 Jl 19 '65

LBJ is asking for all this. il U S News 58:35-6 F 1 '65

LBJ, JFK & route 66. R. Moley. Newsweek 66:88 Jl 5 '65

LBJ phenomenon: a whirlwind pace. il Bsns W p26-8 Je 5 '65

LBJ: political gamester. Pyrrho. por Nat R 18:67-9 Ja 25 '66

LBJ: rights are not enough. il por Newsweek 65:36-7 Je 14 '65

LBJ under pressure. K. Crawford. Newsweek 65:26 Mr 29 '65

LBJ vs. Reserve board: who gets last word on money. U S News 59:47 D 20 '65

LBJ's decision: guns and butter; concerning State-of-the Union message. il por U S News 60:27-8 Ja 24 '66

LBJ's feel for science. F. R. Schreiber. il por Sci Digest 57:9-11 Ap '65

L.B.J.'s foreign policy; manner and matter. S. Alsop. por Sat Eve Post 238:18 Je 19 '65

LBJ's Great society, what will it be? Read Digest 86:136-9 F '65

LBJ's heart. C. Mitchell. il por Pop Sci 186:74-7+ F '65

L.B.J.'s inner circle, by C. Roberts. Review Sat R 48:51 D 4 '65

LBJ's new budget. Nat R 17:91-2 F 9 '65

LBJ's new experiment in government. il pors U S News 58:64-8+ Ap 5 '65

LBJ's 100 days: a record piling up: Way LBJ runs Congress. il pors U S News 58:41-4 Ap 26 '65

LBJ's plan for roads: beauty; or no money. il U S News 58:62-3 Je 7 '65

LBJ's revolution: the big changes. il por U S News 59:46-9 O 11 '65

LBJ's strategy: room to maneuver. il por Newsweek 65:21-2 Mr 8 '65

Lyndon Johnson and the paradox of the presidency. C. P. Magrath. Yale R 54:481-93 Je '65

Lyndon Johnson is ten feet tall. T. Wicker. il N Y Times Mag p23+ My 23 '65

Lyndon Johnson vs the ghost of Jack Kennedy. T. Wicker. Esquire 64:87+ N '65

Lyndon Johnson's religion. J. Bird. il pors Sat Eve Post 238:80-1+ Mr 27 '65

Lyndon Johnson's school days. il pors Time 85:56-8 My 21 '65

Lyndon Johnson's time of trial. por Newsweek 65:19-20 My 31 '65

Lyndon's lobbyists: how they get what he wants. il Nations Bsns 53:38-9+ Ap '65

Majority leader. New Repub 152:5-6 Ap 24 '65

Making of the President-1964, by T. H. White. Review Commentary 40:110+ D '65. A. Hacker Harper 231:110-12 Ag '65. W. V. Shannon Time 86:17 Jl 2 '65

Making of the President—1964; excerpts. T. H. White. il pors Life 58:86-7+ Je 18; 59:70-2+ Jl 2 '65

Making of the veep. il Newsweek 66:23 Jl 26 '65

Man behind our Latin-American actions. L. Gross. il por Look 29:35-7 Je 15 '65

Measure of the man; two years in office. H. Sidey il por Life 59:53+ D 3 '65

Meat and potatoes; concerning housing message to Congress. por Newsweek 65:26 Mr 15 '65

Meeting of history & fate. il por Time 85:20-2 Mr 26 '65

Messianic pose; post-cold-war delusions. H. S. Hughes. il Nation 202:7-10 Ja 3 '66

More heat and light. H. Brandon. Sat R 48:10 Je 5 '65

More on inside story of how JFK picked LBJ; statement. G. M. Williams. U S News 59:9 Ag 9 '65

Nation surges to join the Negro on his march: President speaks to Congress on Negro voting rights; with report by R. B. Stolley. il pors Life 58:30-7 Mr 26 '65

Not the sort of place to live in. E. T. Folliard. America 112:797 My 29 '65

Nothing personal, Mr. President. Christian Cent 82:667-8 My 26 '65

Now campus liberals denounce LBJ. U S News 58:36 My 24 '65

Of extra glands, giant agony and the grey stone mountain; excerpts from address. J. Valenti. Time 86:19-20 Jl 9 '65

One year of L.B.J. T. Wicker. il New Repub 153:13-22 N 13 '65

Our no-nonsense President. M. Ascoli. Reporter 32:18 My 20 '65

Out of the past; President's voting record as a congressman. il Newsweek 66:21 Jl 26 '65

Path for reasonable men; concerning President's address at John Hopkins university. il pors Newsweek 65:25-6 Ap 19 '65

People curious to know what he's really like. P. Lisagor. pors Nations Bsns 53:23-4 Ap '65

Pleiku and Qui Nhon: decision points. il Newsweek 65:32-5 F 22 '65

Plugged in. il pors Newsweek 66:20+ D 27 '65

Politics of power: portrait of a master. il por Newsweek 66:18-19+ Ag 2 '65

Pope and President at the UN? America 113:179-80 Ag 21 '65

Power narcotic. R. Moley. Newsweek 66:84 Ag 9 '65

Presidency. See issues of Time

President. See occasional issues of Newsweek

JOHNSON, Lyndon Baines—about—*Continued*
President and the press. L. L. L. Golden. Sat R 48:65-6 My 8 '65
President and Vietnam. N. Cousins. Sat R 48:22 My 15 '65
President as picture editor. J. Durniak. Pop Phot 56:46 Ap '65
President: in a week of crisis. il por U S News 58:20 F 22 '65
President Johnson and the Negroes. M. McGrory. America 112:893 Je 26 '65
President Johnson vs. the intellectuals. Life 58:4 Je 25 '65
President Johnson's magic formula. M. McGrory. America 112:600 Ap 24 '65
President Lyndon B. Johnson awarded Parents' magazine medal for outstanding service to children. il por Parents Mag 40:38 D '65
President outlines housing and arts subsidy programs, names National council on arts. Arch Rec 137:20+ Ap '65
President's chance. Nation 201:233 O 18 '65
President's urban package. Am City 80:7 Ap '65
President's year; estimation of his work in 1965. Commonweal 83:424 Ja 14 '66
Probable visit of Pope Paul. E. T. Folliard. America 113:237 S 4 '65
Real reason LBJ was irked. por U S News 59:41 Ag 16 '65
Reassuring the neighbors. il Time 86:25 Ag 27 '65
Relevancies and irrelevancies; problem of his public image. Nation 201:30 Jl 19 '65
Reply to the critics. il Time 85:23-4 Ap 16 '65
Report to the stockholders. Nation 200:545 My 24 '65
Revolutionizing the U.S, the changes Congress is making. il U S News 59:29-32 Jl 26 '65
Selma and Saigon. Nat R 17:270-1 Ap 6 '65
Shift of focus. LBJ looks abroad. il por Newsweek 66:23-4 D 20 '65
Southeast Asia: the waiting game. Newsweek 65:25-6 Mr 15 '65
Space: a White House endorsement and a NASA view on the attitudes of scientists toward the program. D. S. Greenberg. Science 147:1269-70 Mr 12 '65
Spoiled spring; leadership and methods of LBJ. E. J. Hughes. Newsweek 65:17 My 31 '65
Squeeze. Nation 201:1 Jl 5 '65
Starry heavens; the moral law; concerning address on the Negro's right to vote. il por Newsweek 65:19-20 Mr 29 '65
State of LBJ; concerning State of the Union address. K. Crawford. Newsweek 67:35 Ja 24 '66
State of the Union. America 114:113 Ja 22 '66
State of the Union. R. Hotz. Aviation W 84:21 Ja 17 '66
State of the Union, and the war. il por Newsweek 67:15-16 Ja 17 '66
Super Lyndon. il Newsweek 66:25-6 S 27 '65
T.R.B. from Texas. New Repub 153:4 Ag 21 '65
Tale of wine and the rose garden. J. N. Eller. America 112:385 Mr 20 '65
Tell it to the President. J. Osborne. New Repub 153:12-13 O 9 '65
Thank you, Mr President. Nat R 17:802+ S 21 '65
Thanks, without enthusiasm. il por Time 86:30 O 8 '65
Their master's voice. New Repub 152:8-9 Ap 17 '65
There is no one else; Press conference: Mover of men. il pors Time 86:17-22 Ag 6 '65
Third bird. K. Crawford. Newsweek 65:32 Mr 8 '65
Thirty-sixth President 1963-. F. Freidel. il pors Nat Geog Mag 129:110-19 Ja '66
This is really war; White House press conference, July 28, 1965. il por Bsns W p 15-16 Jl 31 '65
This may be LBJ's Achilles' heel. P. Lisagor. il Nations Bsns 53:23-4 N '65
To build, to help, and to fight; concerning President's State of the Union message. il por Newsweek 67:21-3 Ja 24 '66
Top aide's close-up of a President who never says I'm tired. J. Valenti. por U S News 59:22 Jl 12 '65
Two hours with LBJ. L. Rosten. Look 29:16 N 16 '65
Two presidents. E. J. Hughes. Newsweek 66:13 S 6 '65
Two views of Lyndon Johnson; excerpts. J. Reston; S. Alsop. por U S News 58:34 F 1 '65

Uneasy alliance. H. Brandon. Sat R 48:8 Jl 3 '65
Unhappy birthday; principal guest at 20th anniversary celebration of United Nations in San Francisco. por Time 86:15 Jl 2 '65
Union & the war; concerning State of the Union address. il por Time 87:19-19B Ja 21 '66
Union organizer looks at Texas, LBJ and the future. U S News 59:91 D 13 '65
Unmaking of a vice president; excerpts from Making of the President—1964. T. H. White. por U S News 59:15 Jl 5 '65
Unmistakable message. M. Greenfield. Reporter 33:10 Ag 12 '65
Vietnam: new policy in the making. H. W. Baldwin. il Reporter 33:16-20 Ag 12 '65
Wartime leader. il por Time 85:23-4+ My 14 '65
Washington desk. J. R. Slevin. Duns R 86:5-6 N '65
Washington desk; remarkable progress of domestic program. J. R. Slevin. Duns R 85:7-8 Je '65
Washington wire; cold eye on Johnson. R. G. Sherrill. Nation 202:4-7 Ja 3 '66
Washington's top banana. L. L. King. Nation 201:282-3 O 25 '65
Wave of the past. New Repub 152:1+ My 15 '65
West wing story. J. Kraft. Harper 230:106-10 Ap '65
What business wants from Lyndon Johnson. E. K. Faltermayer. il por Fortune 71:122-5+ F '65
What LBJ can expect from Congress now. il U S News 60:59-1 Ja 10 '66
What price liberalism? J. Burnham. Nat R 17:456 Je 1 '65
What unions asked of LBJ; and what they got. U S News 58:67-9 My 31 '65
What's ahead for the FBI. M. Ottenberg. Look 29:27-9 F 23 '65
What's happened to the LBJ image? il pors U S News 60:39-41 Ja 17 '66
When Johnson does the unexpected. il U S News 58:15 My 31 '65
When Johnson said yes in 1960, was Kennedy surprised? il pors U S News 59:20-1 Jl 26 '65
White House on the Pedernales. R. B. Semple, jr. il pors N Y Times Mag p54-5+ O 31 '65
Who is Lyndon Johnson? L. H. Lapham. il pors Sat Eve Post 238:21-5+ S 11 '65
Who the President listens to. C. B. Seib. il pors Nations Bsns 53:32-3+ Ap '65
Who's writing LBJ's speeches. il por U S News 58:57 Je 28 '65
Why Humphrey didn't go. il por U S News 58:53-4 F 15 '65
Why liberals grumble about LBJ. il por U S News 59:40-2 Jl 5 '65
Why LBJ has trouble with his image. P. Lisagor. il por Nations Bsns 53:21-2 Ag '65
Why our allies are seeing ghosts. P. Lisagor. il por Nations Bsns 53:21-2 My '65
Why should open dealing be suspect? L. Wainwright. Life 60:20 Ja 14 '66
Why White House troubles mount. por U S News 58:31-3 Je 28 '65
Widening no man's land: President vs. the press; with report by R. B. Stolley. il pors Life 58:34-9 My 7 '65
World's size-up of LBJ now. il pors U S News 59:26-9 D 27 '65
You can be humble when you're number one. P. Lisagor. il por Nations Bsns 53:23-4 F '65

Anecdotes, facetiae, satire, etc.
Here we go a-wassailing with LBJ; poems. W. H. Von Dreele. il Nat R 17:1191 D 28 '65

Caricatures and cartoons
Artists and model. Newsweek 65:96 My 24 '65

Health
As LBJ gets back his strength. il U S News 60:14 Ja 3 '66
As LBJ regains his strength. por U S News 59:22 N 15 '65
Cold that sent a tremor through the Nation; President Johnson's medical history. il por U S News 58:33-4 F 8 '65
Doctors who took care of LBJ. il U S News 59:18 O 18 '65
Health: normal range. il por Time 86:28 D 10 '65
How Lady Bird watches LBJ's health. D. Kiker. pors Good H 160:96-7+ My '65
Hurting good; recuperation. por Time 86:23 O 29 '65
I think I'm in good shape. Sr Schol 87:17 O 21 '65

JOHNSON, Lyndon Baines—Health—_Continued_
In the glow of an Indian summer sun; convalescence after surgery. il pors Newsweek 66:29 O 25 '65
Latest on how LBJ has been feeling. il pors U S News 59:21 D 13 '65
Letter from Washington. R. H. Rovere. New Yorker 41:233 O 16 '65
Log of the President's operation; When the White House moves to a hospital. il U S News 59:6 O 18 '65
Loud and soft; working convalescent. il por Newsweek 66:32 N 8 '65
LBJ and the fabulous 89th go home. S. Shaffer. il por Newsweek 66:21-3 N 1 '65
LBJ is fit; but is his pace too fast? il por U S News 58:15 Mr 29 '65
LBJ wants a rest, too. il pors U S News 59:36-7 O 25 '65
LBJ'S week: the work load grows. U S News 59:22 N 22 '65
Not a usual man; gallbladder operation. il pors Time 86:27-9 O 15 '65
Operation; details on doctors and LBJ prepared the nation for Presidential surgery. Newsweek 66:23 N 1 '65
President: his own pacemaker now; Why doctors didn't remove one of LBJ's kidney stones. il pors U S News 59:24 N 1 '65
President is not a usual man. il pors Newsweek 66:31-4 O 18 '65
Presidential cholecystectomy. il Time 86:59 O 15 '65
President's health: its meaning to the Nation; with medical history. il pors U S News 59:33-7 O 18 '65
Recuperating on the ranch, LBJ style. il pors U S News 59:26 N 8 '65
State of LBJ's health. pors Newsweek 67:57 Ja 10 '66
Tapioca & sympathy. il por Time 86:23 O 22 '65
Thinner look; recovery trail as expected. il por Newsweek 66:28 D 13 '65
Two operations for the price of one. il pors Life 59:104-5 O 29 '65
Valenti's valentine. Reporter 33:18 Jl 15 '65
View from the ranch; recuperating with work. il por Newsweek 66:42 N 15 '65

JOHNSON, Lyndon Baines, family
Johnson by-line. il Newsweek 66:70 S 27 '65
Luci-Lynda beat; H. Thomas and White House coverage. il Newsweek 66:89 D 6 '65
LBJ's borrowing; and clues to his income. U S News 58:18 Ap 12 '65
LBJ's funny stories about his family; excerpt from Warm, wonderful wit and humor of Lyndon B. Johnson; comp. by B. Adler. L. B. Johnson. il Good H 161:74-5 Ag '65
My life in the White House. L. B. Johnson. il por Look 29:98+ My 18 '65

JOHNSON, Martha Sherwood
Invitation; poem. Harper 231:101 D '65

JOHNSON, Napoleon Bonaparte
Cash-and-carry justice. por Newsweek 65:37-8 My 24 '65

JOHNSON, Nicholas
Bailing out the fleet. por Time 86:84+ Jl 16 '65
Charting a new course. il por Bsns W p 166+ Ap 24 '65
Merchant marine: wilderness of tigers. H. Junker. il Nation 202:71-3 Ja 17 '66

JOHNSON, Orval C.
Death rode the surf. por Outdoor Life 136:52-5+ Jl '65

JOHNSON, Pamela Hansford
Young Dylan Thomas; excerpts from The life of Dylan Thomas. C. Fitzgibbon. Atlan 216:66-72 N '65

JOHNSON, Paul
Atlanticism. Commentary 40:110-12 S '65
What did it mean? Sat R 48:67-8 Jl 17 '65

JOHNSON, Paul Burney, 1916?-
Vote for reason. por Time 86:13 Ag 27 '65

JOHNSON, Pauline
Fold-dye paper designs. Sch Arts 64:4-6 Je '65

JOHNSON, Philip Cortelyou
Down with art? G. O'Brien. il por N Y Times Mag p70-1 F 28 '65
House of glass today. il House & Gard 128:184-7 O '65
Second fame: good food. N. Lyon. il por Vogue 146:166-8 S 15 '65

JOHNSON, Pyke, jr
Area meeting of booksellers held in Denver. Pub W 188:14 N 29 '65
Bookshop with a belfry. Pub W 187:98-100 F 15 '65
Imaginative selling in small town shop. Pub W 188:51-2 Ag 9 '65

Paperbacks for the elementary school. por Library J 90:5054-5 N 15 '65
Personal touch in Vermont. Pub W 188:58-60 S 6 '65

JOHNSON, Rafer
New role for Rafer. il pors Ebony 21:181-4 D '65

JOHNSON, Rebekah (Baines)
Family album; excerpt. por McCalls 93:103-7+ N '65
His mother's story of LBJ; excerpts from manuscripts. por U S News 58:48-52 F 15 '65

about
First lady talks about her mother-in-law; with editorial comment. C. A. T. Johnson. il por McCalls 93:4, 8+ N '65
Lyndon Johnson's mother. l. Shelton. il pors Sat Eve Post 238:94+ My 8 '65

JOHNSON, Robert F.
Aboard Big Ti in the Transpac. Yachting 118:95-7 S '65
Victorious skipper to ship designer; letter. Esquire 64:151+ D '65

JOHNSON, Robin
Interrupted space; poem. Horn Bk 41:661 D '65

JOHNSON, Ronald
From The book of the green man; poem. Poetry 106:37-52 Ap '65

JOHNSON, Russell H.
City of water and ice. por Recreation 58:161-2 Ap '65

JOHNSON, Samuel
Man who wrote his mind. R. Halsband. il Sat R 48:46 N 13 '65
Samuel Johnson, poems, ed. by E. L. McAdam, jr. Review
Commonweal 83:379-80 D 24 '65. G. Wills
Withering wit of Samuel Johnson. W. H. Chamberlin. por Sat R 48:14-15+ S 4 '65

JOHNSON, Samuel Ealy, family
His mother's story of LBJ; excerpts from manuscripts. R. B. Johnson. il por U S News 58:48-52 F 15 '65

JOHNSON, U. Alexis
Viet-Nam today; address, September 16, 1965. Dept State Bul 53:626-35 O 18 '65

JOHNSON, W. MacLean
Obituary
Pub W por 188:77 N 15 '65

JOHNSON, William A.
Schleiermacher today. Christian Cent 82:439-41 Ap 7 '65

JOHNSON, William Weber
Baja, the other California. Holiday 38:112-15 Ag '65

JOHNSON family
President Johnson and his family tree. il U S News 58:50 F 15 '65

JOHNSON grass
Whip Johnsongrass with chemicals, good management. J. Everly. il Suc Farm 63:102 Ap '65

JOHNSON publishing company
Twenty years of Ebony. il Ebony 21:58-60+ N '65

JOHNSTON, D. Bruce
Use of turntables in buildings. Arch Rec 138:235-6 S '65

JOHNSTON, David C.
I've been working on the doorbells. Nat R 17:726-7 Ag 24 '65

JOHNSTON, Denis
Goat's minions. Nation 200:282-3 Mr 15 '65

JOHNSTON, Francis E.
American association of physical anthropologists. Science 149:1526 S 24 '65

JOHNSTON, W. T.
Dictionaries. Consumer Bul 48:13-18 Je '65

JOHNSTON, Walter
Suggested preliminary steps for organizing a conference; excerpt from Pilot conference on student use of libraries. ALA Bul 59:735 S '65

JOHNSTONE, M. S. See Chow, T. J. jt. auth.

JOHNSTONE, Margaret Blair
Say it now! Read Digest 87:139-42 O '65

JOHNSTONE, William C.
United States in southern Asia. Cur Hist 48:65-8+ F '65

Les JOIES de la famille; drama. See Gordon, R.

JOINT adventures
Goodrich, Gulf ready to end tie; joint synthetic rubber venture. Bsns W p33 O 9 '65
Japan puts out small welcome mat. il Bsns W p 116+ F 27 '65

JOINT chiefs of staff. See United States—Joint chiefs of staff

JOINT oceanographic institutions' deep earth sampling program. See Underwater drilling

JOINT ownership. See Community property

JOINT United States-Japan committees on scientific cooperation
Mechanical translation: U.S.-Japan joint conference. F. L. Alt. Science 147:1599-600 Mr 26 '65
Molecular basis of heredity; report on symposium held under the auspices of the United States-Japan cooperative science program. S. E. Luria. Science 150:80-2 O 1 '65

JOINT United States-Japan committee on trade and economic affairs
U.S.-Japan cabinet committee on trade and economic affairs holds fourth meeting at Washington; remarks, July 12 and July 14, 1965; with joint communique. D. Rusk; E. Shiina; L. B. Johnson. Dept State Bul 53:242-9 Ag 9 '65
U.S. Japan hold second meeting on use of natural resources. Dept State Bul 52:1052-3 Je 28 '65

JOINTS (carpentry)
Secrets of drill-press mortising. R. J. De Cristoforo. il Pop Sci 187:146-50 D '65

JOINTS (metal work)
See also
Flanges

JOKES. See Humor

JOKES, American. See Humor, American

JOKES, Practical. See Practical jokes

JOMON pottery. See Pottery, Japanese

JONAS, Gerald
Foghorn on East End avenue; poem. Atlan 216:94 S '65
Poem before dawn. Sat R 48:50 O 30 '65
Revival; poem. New Yorker 41:164 S 18 '65
Winter: the city: a ballad. New Yorker 40: 92 F 13 '65

JONATHAN, Sister Mary. See Mary Jonathan, Sister

JONES, Alan Pryce-. See Pryce-Jones, A.

JONES, Alice Eleanor
Ones that got away. Writer 78:17-18+ My '65

JONES, Alun Gwynne-, baron Chalfont. See Chalfont, A. G.-J.

JONES, Antony Charles Robert Armstrong-, 1st earl of Snowdon. See Snowdon, A. C. R. A.-J.

JONES, Ashton Bryan
Ashton Jones freed. Christian Cent 82:732 Je 9 '65
Epic of Ashton Jones. C. Brown. il pors Ebony 20:45-8+ O '65

JONES, Barbara A.
Home, sweet home; poem. Read Digest 87: 58 S '65

JONES, Bob
Golf. C. Price. Esquire 64:64+ S '65

JONES, David Pryce-. See Pryce-Jones, D.

JONES, David R.
This Republican for 1968? N Y Times Mag p28-9+ F 28 '65

JONES, E. Stanley
New wine in wineskins. Christian Cent 82: 1160-2+ S 22 '65

JONES, Edward E.
Conformity as a tactic of ingratiation. bibliog Science 149:144-50 Jl 9 '65

JONES, Elena
Bright new spirit in Tonyville. B. Asbell. il por Good H 162:60-1+ Ja '66

JONES, Galen E.
Living economy of the sea. Bul Atomic Sci 21:13-17 Mr '65

JONES, Gordon P.
Coastwise in a museum ship. Yachting 117: 45-7+ Mr '65

JONES, Harry W.
Law. NEA J 54:42-5 Ap '65

JONES, Howard Mumford
Meaning of a university. Atlan 216:157-60 N '65

JONES, J. Benton, Jr
Molybdenum content of corn plants exhibiting varying degrees of potassium deficiency. Science 148:94 Ap 2 '65

JONES, James
Why they invade the sea. por N Y Times Mag p47+ Mr 14 '65

JONES, James Earl
James Earl Jones, actor still climbing. il pors Ebony 20:98-100+ Ap '65

JONES, Jenkin Lloyd
Excerpt from Tulsa tribune column. Cong Digest 44:159 My '65
Message from a dead city; reprint. Am For 71:34 Mr '65

JONES, Larry
Bright new spirit in Tonyville. B. Asbell. il por Good H 162:60-1+ Ja '66

JONES, LeRoi
Black bourgeoisie; poem. Harper 230:158 Ap '65
In one battle; poem. Harper 230:68 Je '65
about
Demagogy of Le Roi Jones. G. Dennison. Commentary 39:67-70 F '65
Slave. Criticism
Nat R 17:249 Mr 23 '65
Some poets in their prose. R. Howard. Poetry 105:403-4 Mr '65
Tax funds for a hate the whites project. por U S News 59:16-17 D 13 '65
Toilet. Criticism
Nat R 17:249 Mr 23 '65
Two against chaos. R. Howard. Nation 200: 289-90 Mr 15 '65

JONES, Marie
Industrial and biological microscopy: new paths. Science 148:986+ My 14 '65

JONES, Marjorie
Difference of more than opinion. Redbook 124:6+ Ap '65

JONES, Mark M.
Immigration or jobs? address, June 23, 1965. Vital Speeches 31:629-32 Ag 1 '65

JONES, Sister Mary Roberta
Sister considers chastity. America 112:488-90 Ap 10 '65

JONES, Pamela
Happy ways of doing things. Am Home 68: 33+ Mr '65

JONES, Phil B. and Mutti, R. J.
Seven ways to handle livestock feed, which one for you? Suc Farm 63:37-9 O '65

JONES, Phillip L.
Serendipity. Sr Schol 86:sup24-5 Ap 15 '65

JONES, Richard T. See Schneider, R. G. jt. auth.

JONES, Robert
Feast of piano music by Bartók. Am Rec G 32:22-5+ S '65
Resistor noise graphs. Electr World 73:42-3 Ap '65

JONES, Robert A. See Seagrave, S. jt. auth.

JONES, Stacy V.
Can we use Russian inventions? Sci Digest 58:44-8 S '65
How to beat the traffic mess. Sci Digest 57: 77-9 My '65
Inventor of the month. See issues of Science digest

JONES, Stephen Hugh-. See Hugh-Jones, S.

JONES, Sue
Discovery. Sch Arts 64:23-4 Ap '65

JONES, T. O.
Life at Antarctic U. por Am Ed 1:29-32 N '65

JONES, Tom
Lonely responsibility of Tom Jones. il por Bsns W p 164 O 23 '65

JONES, Tom (singer)
My name is, Tom Jones? A. Carthew. il pors N Y Times Mag p67+ N 14 '65

JONES, Tony Ray-. See Ray-Jones, T.

JONES, Virginia Lacy
Library in the South: educational problems; address, April 1965. por Wilson Lib Bul 39:878-84 Je '65

JONES, William R.
Our first national park: Yellowstone or Yosemite? Audubon Mag 67:382-4 N '65
Yosemite's hundredth birthday. Nat Parks Mag 39:14-17 Ap '65

JONES, Wyman
Administrative conscience. por Library J 90: 3539-41 S 15 '65

JONES and Laughlin steel corporation
Boom town 1965; plans for Jones & Laughlin steel mill. il Time 86:90+ Jl 9 '65
J&L bets big on Midwest. il Bsns W p94-6+ My 1 '65

JONQUILS. See Narcissus

JONSEN, Albert R.
Of note: Protestant-Catholic ethics. Commonweal 81:613-15 F 5 '65

JONSON, Ben
O rare Ben Jonson. P. W. Schmidtchen. il por Hobbies 69:106 F '65

JORDAN, Eileen Herbert
Car-sitter; story. McCalls 92:74-5 Je '65
Wanderer; story. McCalls 92:124-5 F '65

JORDAN, James N. and others
Aftershocks of the 4 February 1965 Rat Island earthquake. bibliog Science 148:1323-5 Je 4 '65

JORDAN, Robert Paul
New spirit soars in Mid-America's proud old city. Nat Geog Mag 128:605-41 N '65

JORDAN
See also
Jerusalem
National parks and reserves—Jordan
Petra

Antiquities

Ancient Jordan secrets to be probed again; Tell es-Sa'idiyeh believed to be Biblical city of Zarethan. Sci N L 87:185 Mr 20 '65
Scroll search controlled by Jordan government. Sci N L 87:178 Mr 20 '65

Politics and government

Two to watch; new crown prince. il Time 85:29 Ap 9 '65

JORDAN RIVER
Ancient hatred builds toward war; Arab-Israeli struggle for water. G. De Carvalho. il Life 58:44+ Je 18 '65
Arabs thirst for revenge, Israel stands to its arms; Arabs tap a disputed stream. il Life 58:45-9 Je 18 '65
Atlantic report; dividing the waters. Atlan 216:24+ Ag '65
Disputed Jordan waters. E. Monroe. New Repub 153:15-16 Ag 7 '65
Israel's quest for water. K. Haselden. Christian Cent 82:423-5 Ap 7 '65
Jordan Valley plan. M. A. Garbell. il Sci Am 212:23-31 Mr '65
Jordan waters conflict. K. B. Doherty. bibliog f il Int Concil 553:3-66 My '65
Roll, Jordan, roll! G. Kent. Read Digest 87:173-4+ O '65

JORIS, Françoise Mallet-. See Mallet-Joris, F.

JOSEPH, Elliott
Secret thoughts of a happy husband. McCalls 92:18 Ag '65

JOSEPH, Lou
Now they're transplanting teeth! Todays Health 43:70-1+ My '65

JOSEPH, Richard
Before Ava Gardner arrived, Tartessians, Iberians, Phoenicians, Romans, Visigoths, Moors and Spaniards all lived there. Esquire 63:98-103+ Ap '65
Fastest way to the other side of time. Esquire 65:98+ Ja '66
From America with love. Esquire 64:62 Jl '65
How to live like a European in Europe. Esquire 64:121+ S '65
Iron curtain going up. Esquire 63:118-19+ Je '65
Nothing rotten in the states of Denmark, Norway, Sweden and Finland, especially the girls. Esquire 63:84-7 My '65
Right little island. Esquire 64:110-13+ O '65
To kill a jaguar. Esquire 63:94-9 Mr '65
Travel notes. See issues of Esquire

about

Half the fun of travel is reading Richard Joseph. A. Gingrich. Esquire 64:6 Ag '65

JOSEPH of Arimathea, Saint
Abstentionists and morticians. H. Schomer. Christian Cent 82:419 Ap 7 '65

JOSEPHS, Wilfred
La Scala requiem. B. Jacobson. Sat R 48:59 D 25 '65

JOSEPHY, Alvin M. Jr
Most satisfactory council; excerpts from Nez Perce Indians and the opening of the Northwest. Am Heritage 16:26-31+ O '65

JOSEY, E. J.
Giant step in Georgia; letter to the editor. Library J 90:5320 D 15 '65
In defense of academic freedom. por Wilson Lib Bul 40:173-5 O '65
Reading and the disadvantaged. por Negro Hist Bul 28:156-7+ Ap '65

JOSIE, Edith
Everybody sure glad. D. J. Hamblin. por Life 58:69-70+ My 21 '65

JOSLIN, Holly
Dewy morning; poem. Horn Bk 41:530 O '65

JOUGHIN, Louis
Is freedom academic? Nation 201:176-82 S 20 '65

Le JOUR de la tortue; musical comedy. See Musical comedies, revues, etc.—Criticisms, plots, etc.

JOURNALISM
Hail to the cliché; Associated press computer assesses use of clichés. R. L. Tobin; discussion. Sat R 48:66 F 13; 66 Ap 10; 68 My 8 '65

Mass man and mass media; adaptation of address. H. Brucker. il Sat R 48:14-16+ My 29 '65
See also
Catholic press
Editors and editing
Freedom of the press
Libel and slander
News letters
Newspaper court reporting
Reporters and reporting
Women as editors

Anecdotes, facetiae, satire, etc.

Adversaria. Esquire 64:128-9 N '65
Always worse than I had thought. C. W. Morton. il Atlan 215:118+ F '65

Study and teaching

Journalism education: myth and reality; comment on Boroff report. J. Tebbel. Sat R 48:92+ N 13 '65
Journalism's mounting storms; comment on E. W. Barrett's speech before the association for education in journalism. R. L. Tobin. Sat R 48:36 D 4 '65
What Africa reads; International press institute training programs in Africa. il Newsweek 65:97-8 My 17 '65
What ails the journalism schools. D. Boroff. Harper 231:77-8+ O '65; Discussion. 231:8+ D '65
Where are tomorrow's journalists? A. Balk. Sat R 49:105-6 Ja 8 '66

France

See also
Newspapers—France

Great Britain

See also
Newspapers—Great Britain

Russia

See also
Newspapers—Russia

United States

Behold the grass-roots press, alas! B. H. Bagdikian; discussion. Harper 230:14 F '65
See also
Newspapers—United States

History

American journalism from essay to assay. P. Kimball. il Nation 201:72-6 S 20 '65

JOURNALISTIC ethics
Trial by newspaper. I. Ross. Atlan 216:63-8 S '65

JOURNALISTIC photography. See Photography, Journalistic

JOURNALISTS
More than color; top Negro syndicated columnist. Time 86:60 Ag 13 '65
Where are tomorrow's journalists? A. Balk. Sat R 49:105-6 Ja 8 '66
Young publisher with problems; Brooklyn Peace corps volunteer puts out Spanish newspaper in slum of Lima, Peru. il Ebony 21:101-2+ N '65
See also
Women as journalists

JOURNALS. See Periodicals

JOURNALS, Personal. See Diaries

JOURNEY for love; story. See Knowlton, R. A.

JOVANOVICH, William
Call for meaningful cooperation for bookstores; excerpts from article in American scholar. Pub W 188:42 O 11 '65

JOWITT, Deborah
Dance theatre workshop, inc. works by Valerie Bettis, Anna Sokolow, Deborah Jowitt; East 74th street theatre. J. Maskey. Dance Mag 39:160-1 D '65

JOY. See Happiness

JOY manufacturing company
Joy digs from under its burden of coal. il Bsns W p100-2+ Ja 8 '66

JOY to the whole wide world; story. See Scovel, C.

JOYCE, James
In the echo chamber. J. Wain. New Repub 153:20-2 Ag 7 '65
Joyce and Eliot: a tale of Shem & Shaun. N. Halper. por Nation 200:590-5 My 31 '65
Odyssey of a unique book: Ulysses. R. Ellmann. il pors N Y Times Mag p56-7+ N 14 '65
Re Joyce, by A. Burgess. Review
Sat R por 48:34-5 D 25 '65. A. M. Sullivan
Tidings from Pound to Joyce; letter. E. Pound. Esquire 40:152+ D '65

JOYCE, James Avery
Peace-keeping: a new chapter? Christian Cent 82:306-8 Mr 10 '65

JUNGLE
New conquistadors in the Amazon jungle. E.
P. Hanson. il Américas 17:1-8 S '65; Correction. 17:48 N '65
Two novels of the Amazon: J. E. Rivera's
La vorágine (The vortex) and W. H. Hudson's Green mansions. E. S. Urbanski. il
Américas 17:33-8 Mr '65

JUNGLE warfare
When G.I. Joe meets ol' Charlie. J. Raymond. il N Y Times Mag p4-5+ Jl 25 '65

JUNGMANN, Stephanie
Wait! il Pop Phot 57:156-7 D '65

JUNIOR chambers of commerce. See United
States junior chamber of commerce

JUNIOR colleges
After high school: the role of the community
college. T. E. O'Connell; reply. New Repub
152:36 F 20 '65
Best place for vocational education: the two-
year community college. T. Urich and J.
Mauck. NEA J 54:51-2 D '65
Community college provides campus plan for
two-year program; Henry Ford community
college, Dearborn, Mich. il Arch Rec 137:
184-6 Mr '65
Community college's learning laboratory. E.
T. Brown. Wilson Lib Bul 40:80-3 S '65
Crossing the college threshold. M. W. Raines.
il Am Ed 1:30-2 Jl '65
Deprived student in the two-year college:
new breed with a new need; summary of
speeches at Conference on the teaching
of remedial English and math. il Pub W
189:26-31 Ja 3 '66
Do junior college transfers make the grade?
survey findings. J. H. Nelson. il NEA J
54:55-7 O '65
Junior colleges: students' hope for the future.
il U S News 58:66-8 My 17 '65; Same abr.
Read Digest 87:51-2+ O '65
School for all through the age of twenty. il
Time 85:60-5 Mr 5 '65
See also names of junior colleges, e.g.
Asheville-Biltmore college, Asheville, N.C.

JUNIOR fellows of Harvard university. See
Harvard university—Society of fellows

JUNIOR high school buildings. See School
buildings

JUNIOR librarians. See Librarians

JUNIOR rocketeers. See Rockets—Amateur experiments

JUNIOR village, Washington, D.C. See Homes,
Institutional

JUNK
See also
Scrap metal

JUNK cars. See Automobiles—Wrecking

JUNK yards. See Junkyards

JUNKER, Howard
Andy Warhol, movie maker. Nation 200:
206-8 F 22 '65
Editor as artist. Nation 200:655-6 Je 14 '65
Free university; academy for mavericks. Nation 201:78-80 Ag 16 '65
LSD: contact high. Nation 201:25-6 Jl 5 '65
Merchant marine: wilderness of tigers. Nation
202:71-3 Ja 17 '66
Résumé of the young man as a non-generation. Esquire 64:169 D '65
Smut hunters; new jurisprudery. Nation 201:
358-60 N 15 '65
TV programming: the fight for prime time.
Nation 200:279-81 Mr 15 '65
Underground renaissance. Nation 201:539-40
D 27 '65

JUNKYARDS
Orders to clean up those junkyards. E. T.
Folliard. America 112:215 F 13 '65
See also
Automobile graveyards

JUPITER (planet)
Clue to Jupiter's decametric radiation. Sky
& Tel 30:275 N '65
Jupiter as a star. Sci Am 214:47-8 Ja '66
Observation of a partial occultation of Jupiter. Sky & Tel 30:250 O '65
Radio Jupiter, right on time. il Sci Digest
57:27 Mr '65
Storms on a mixed-up planet. il Time 86:
62+ D 17 '65

Atmosphere
Hot shadows of Jupiter. R. L. Wildey. il
Science 147:1035-6 F 26 '65
Jovian atmospheric feature of special interest. B. A. Smith and E. J. Reese. il
Sky & Tel 29:118-19 F '65
More about ammonia and Jupiter's rotation.
G. S. Mumford. Sky & Tel 29:88 F '65

Satellites
See Satellites

Spectra
See Planets—Spectra

Temperature and radiation
See Planets—Temperature and radiation

JUPITER probe. See Space probes

JURISDICTIONAL disputes. See Trade unions
—Jurisdictional disputes

JURY
After Hayneville; exclusion of Negroes from
jury box. Reporter 33:16+ O 21 '65
Breathes there a jury with soul so pure?
trial of U.S. Communist party for failing to
register as agent of Soviet Union. il Time
86:37 N 12 '65
Compulsory jury trial. Time 85:72 Mr 12 '65
If you are called to jury service. il Good H
162:136 Ja '66
Illiterate peers; Florida's jury. il Time 86:40
Ag 27 '65
Justice in the South. New Repub 153:7 N 6
'65
Legal miscarriage of justice. L. Wainwright.
Life 59:30 D 3 '65
Opening a second front; drive to reform
southern justice. Newsweek 66:33-4 N 8 '65
Silence of the bar; all-white southern jury.
Nation 201:291-2 N 1 '65
Southern juries: white hand of justice. P.
Good. il Nation 201:278-80 O 25 '65
When jurors cannot read or write; D'Andrea
case before all-Negro jury. U S News 59:12
D 6 '65
See also
Youth jury

JUST a friendly little game; story. See Fox,
W. P.

JUST before dawn; story. See Baldwin, B.
and Gorham, B. F.

JUST the man for you; story. See Shyer, M. F.

JUSTICE, Donald
Dreams of water; poem. New Yorker 41:233
N 20 '65
For the suicides of two years ago; Evening
of the mind; About my poems; At a rehearsal of Uncle Vanya; Memory of a
porch; poems. Poetry 105:349-54 Mr '65

about
Vision, celebration, and testimony. M. Van
Duyn. Poetry 105:266-7 Ja '65

JUSTICE, Administration of
Justice for the poor; Public defender system. M. T. Bloom. il Read Digest 86:126-30
Ap '65
See also
Criminal law
Criminal procedure
Judges
Legal aid
Trials

Algeria
Saved for the sand; death sentence commuted. Time 85:37 Ap 23 '65

Great Britain
British verdict on trial-by-press. A. Lewis. il
N Y Times Mag p 14-15+ Je 20 '65
Her Majesty's incorruptible, imperturbable,
incomparable judges. S. Bedford. il Esquire
64:78-82+ O '65
Speedier justice in Britain; we reformed our
laws in the 19th century and U.S. didn't;
interview. J. Foster. U S News 58:42-3
Mr 22 '65

Oklahoma
Cash-and-carry justice. Newsweek 65:37-8 My
24 '65

Southern states
Guilty verdicts in the South. America 113:768
D 18 '65
How to reform southern justice. il Time 86:
76 N 19 '65
Justice in the South. Commonweal 83:227-8
N 26 '65
Justice in the South. New Repub 153:7 N 6
'65
Let us now praise southern justice! R.
Nicole. Christian Cent 82:145-6 F 3 '65
No federal case? lynch-murder of three civil-
rights workers. Newsweek 65:25 Mr 8 '65
Opening a second front; drive to reform
southern justice. Newsweek 66:33-4 N 8
'65
Rule of law in the South. H. Burns. Commentary 40:80+ S '65
Silence of the bar; all-white southern jury.
Nation 201:291-2 N 1 '65
Southern juries: white hand of justice. P.
Good. il Nation 201:278-80 O 25 '65
Southern justice; with painting by N. Rockwell. C. Morgan, jr. Look 29:72-3 Je 29 '65
Turn in a dark road. il Time 86:27-8 D 10
'65

JUSTICE, Administration of—Southern States
  —*Continued*
Two faces of Sheriff Rainey; Neshoba County,
  Miss. R. Cleghorn. il N Y Times Mag p 10-
  11+ F 21 '65
Uncolored justice; racial slayings, Alabama;
  white juries convict whites. Newsweek 66:
  34 D 13 '65
Unprecedented turn of justice in the South;
  trial of Damon Strange. J. Neary. il Life
  59:34 D 17 '65

Sweden
Our far-flung correspondents; ombudsman, or
  J.O. J. Bainbridge. New Yorker 40:136+
  F 13 '65

United States
Beyond the law; pathetic tale of Joe B.
  Driver. New Repub 153:7-8 O 2 '65; Reply.
  A. M. Brannon and J. M. Read, jr. 153:39-
  40 N 6 '65
Crime in the streets and the new McCarthy-
  ism; accusing people in high places of
  being soft on criminals. J. S. Wright. New
  Repub 153:10-11 O 9 '65; Discussion. 153:
  38 O 23; 28 O 30; 37-8 N 13 '65
Free press and fair trial; address, April 15,
  1965. N. deB. Katzenbach. Vital Speeches
  31:518-21 Je 15 '65
How the government won the third Liuzzo
  trial. A. Clymer. Reporter 33:25-6 D 30 '65
Innocents, by E. D. Radin. Review
  Nation 200:262-3 Mr 8 '65. M. Polner
Men may come, and men may go; attempt
  to save a man from the electric chair in
  Pennsylvania. W. F. Buckley, jr. Nat R
  17:683 Ag 10 '65
Police find lawyer friends; right of law-abid-
  ing citizens to freedom from criminal mole-
  station. Life 59:4 Ag 20 '65
Sentencing mess. il Time 86:52 D 31 '65
Serviceman's rights; Uniform code of mili-
  tary justice. il Time 86:36+ Ag 13 '65
Should confessions be outlawed? A. Poinsett.
  il Ebony 20:173-4+ My '65
Turn in the cycle? trend to push safety of
  society ahead of rights of individuals. Nat R
  17:715 Ag 24 '65
Unbounded bondsmen; Tyrone Collins seized
  by Alabama bondsmen in Philadelphia. il
  Time 87:74 Ja 7 '66
Union tactics stall justice thirteen years. il
  Nations Bsns 53:31-3 N '65
  See also
Courts—United States
Jury
Trials
United States—Justice, Department of
JUSTICE, Department of. See United States—
  Justice, Department of
JUSTICES. See Judges
JUSTICES of the peace
Philadelphia's magisterial mess. il Time 86:
  59 O 1 '65
JUSTIFICATION
Justification, by H. Kung. Review
  Commonweal 81:618-19 F 5 '65. J. F.
  McCue
Justification: the doctrine of Karl Barth and
  a Catholic reflection, by H. Küng. Review
  America 112:787-8 My 22 '65. J. H. Wright
JUSTIN K. Thannhauser collection. See Art—
  Private collections
JUSTITIEOMBUDSMAN. See Administrative
  remedies
JUSTMAN, Joseph
Educational values in disorder. Sch & Soc
  93:147-50 Mr 6 '65
JUTILA, J. W. See Reed, N. D. jt. auth.
JUVENILE courts
Does get tough work? G. B. Hunt. il PTA
  Mag 59:8-10 Je '65
Her honor bops the hoodlums. D. J. Ham-
  blin. il Life 59:74+ Jl 9 '65
  See also
Juvenile delinquency
JUVENILE delinquency
Arithmetic of delinquency. J. Horwitz. il
  N Y Times Mag p 12-13+ Ja 31 '65
Can delinquency be predicted? J. Olsen. Sr
  Schol 86:sup 14 My 6 '65
Can reading affect delinquency? address, Jan-
  uary 1965. W. C. Kvaraceus. bibliog f ALA
  Bul 59:516-22 Je '65
Cool world; controversial movie changes
  lives of N.Y. delinquents. il Ebony 20:43-
  4+ Jl '65
Does get tough work? G. B. Hunt. il PTA
  Mag 59:8-10 Je '65
Early identification of delinquency. Sch &
  Soc 93:388+ O 30 '65
Hijinks that can haunt your life. J. M. Lasky.
  Read Digest 86:92-5 Je '65

Improbable successes of Ettie Lee; Ettie Lee
  homes, inc. S. W. Taylor. Read Digest 87:
  187-8+ D '65
My name is barbarian; incident in Mamaro-
  neck, N.Y. G. Ace. Sat R 48:18 N 13 '65
Predelinquent behavior hostile and aggressive. Sci N L 88:323 N 20 '65
Warning from J. Edgar Hoover; reprint. J.
  E. Hoover. U S News 59:20 S 13 '65
Warning to parents: why young people go
  bad; interview. S. Glueck and E. T. Glueck.
  il U S News 58:56-60+ Ap 26 '65
World side story; excerpts from Juvenile
  delinquency, a problem for the modern
  world. W. C. Kvaraceus; discussion.
  UNESCO Courier 18:33 Mr '65
Youth crime: some suggested treatments;
  statements. H. L. Edwards; J. E. Winters.
  il U S News 59:46-7 N 15 '65
  See also
Gangs

Prevention
Delinquency and recreation: fact and fiction!
  R. G. Kraus. bibliog il Recreation 58:382-5
  O '65
  See also
Boys brotherhood republic of New York, in-
  corporated
JUVINALL, Andrew
Ten corporations and automation. Christian
  Cent 82:271-3 Mr 3 '65

K

KKK. See Ku Klux klan
KLM (airline) See Airlines—Netherlands
KAARTO, Timothy
Using diodes to protect circuits. Electr World
  73:82 F '65
KABANA, Rodrigo Rodriguez-. See Rodriguez-
  Kabana, R.
KABAT, Luke
My friend in Mississippi. New Repub 152:18-
  20 My 29 '65
KABDEBO, Thomas
  (tr) See Kosztolányi, D.   Barkokhba
KABOBS. See Cookery—Meat
KABUKI
Letter from Paris; Kabuki theatre of Tokyo,
  at Odèon-Thèâtre de France. Genêt. New
  Yorker 41:130-1 O 30 '65
  See also
Japanese drama
KACHINSKOYE military aviation high school,
  Russia. See Aviation schools
KADAR, János
Cutting the chain. Newsweek 66:44 Jl 12 '65
KAEL, Pauline
Life movie review. Life 59:12 Ag 13; 10 S 24;
  10 O 29 '65
Movies. Vogue 146:180 S 1; 168 O 1, 147 D '65
Old movies never die. Mlle 61:63+ Jl '65
Spoofing and schtik. Atlan 216:84-5 D '65

about
Films. D. Macdonald. Esquire 64:27-30 Ag '65
KAFKA, Franz
Amerika; dramatization. See Barrault, J. L.
  L'amérique
  about
European literary scene. R. J. Clements. Sat
  R 48:57 O 23 '65
KAHANA, Robert J.
Semipro game: football in the rough. W. J.
  McKean. il pors Look 29:90-6 N 30 '65
KAHIN, George McT. and Lewis, J. W.
United States in Vietnam. bibliog f Bul
  Atomic Sci 21:28-40 Je '65
KAHL, Fritz O.
Fiber optics in electronics. Electr World 73:
  25-8+ My '65
KAHN, Ely Jacques, 1916-
Abe Burrows: what he does to earn $2,000
  a day. McCalls 92:116-17+ F '65
Letter from Guam. New Yorker 40:39-40+
  F 13 '65
Our far-flung correspondents (cont) New
  Yorker 41:154+ O 23 '65
There's no gambling like show gambling.
  Vogue 147:12b+ Ja 1 '66
KAHN, Herman
Bigger wars ahead? interview. por U S News
  58:42-9 Je 7 '65

KAHN, Herman—*Continued*
Escalation as a strategy; excerpts from On escalation: metaphors and scenarios. Fortune 71:110-12+ Ap '65
On Herman Kahn; interview. por Newsweek 65:54-5 Je 7 '65

about
Herman's ladder. Nation 200:405 Ap 19 '65
Onward and upward with Herman Kahn. A. Buchan. New Repub 152:19-21 Je 5 '65

KAHN, Reuben Leon
Manner of speaking. J. Ciardi. Sat R 48:18+ D 11 '65

KAHN, Roger
C=(Frank Ryan)÷2. Sat Eve Post 238:92+ N 20 '65
Case of the dead bookie. Sat Eve Post 238: 34-8+ Mr 13 '65
House of Adolph Ochs. Sat Eve Post 238: 32-8+ O 9 '65

KAHN, Tom. See Rustin, B. jt. auth.

KAHNWEILER, Daniel Henry
Man who invented modern art dealing. J. Russell. il pors Vogue 146:146-9+ S 15 '65

KAIN, Margaret
Working one's way through the ABA trade show. Pub W 187:58-60 My 24 '65

KAISER, Edgar Fosburgh
Kaiser's spreading empire. il por Time 85:79 Mr 26 '65

KAISER, Henry J.
Kaiser's spreading empire. il Time 85:79 Mr 26 '65

KAISER, Walter H.
Inquiring librarian's guide. Library J 90: 2761-5 Je 15 '65

KALAMAZOO, Mich.
Wildflowers in an asphalt jungle. il Recreation 58:112-14 Mr '65

KALB, Bernard
Asia: a measure and a memoir. Sat R 48: 36-7+ S 18 '65

KALB, Marvin
Kremlin dilemma over Vietnam. Reporter 33: 22-3 Jl 1 '65
Kremlin: evolution or extinction? Sat R 48: 35-6 My 8 '65

KALCKAR, Herman M.
Galactose metabolism and cell sociology. bibliog Science 150:305-13 O 15 '65

KALEDIN, Arthur
Books. Commonweal 83:377-9 D 24 '65

KALER, Grace
Old metals. See issues of Hobbies

KALKSTEIN, Shawn
Oklahoma's education war. Look 30:80+ Ja 25 '66

KALLIKREIN
Bradykinin: effect on ureteral peristalsis. P. Catacutan-Labay and S. Boyarsky. bibliog il Science 151:78-9 Ja 7 '66

KALLMANN, Hartmut P.
One man's adventures with a shiny suit. G. M. Spruch. por Sat R 48:88-90 D 4 '65

KÁLMÁN, Charles
Bitters in the sweet. por Opera N 29:8-11 F 20 '65

KÁLMÁN, Emmerich
Bitters in the sweet. C. Kalman. il por Opera N 29:8-11 F 20 '65

KALMANOFF, Martin
Getting opera on. Opera N 30:8-12 Ja 8 '66

KALS, William S.
Do-them-in-your-head navigation tricks. Pop Mech 124:184-6 S '65
Going overboard for maintenance and fun por Yachting 118:52-3+ N '65
Polynesian navigation. Motor B 116:28-31 Ag '65

KALTENBORN, Hans V.
Man of convictions. il por Time 85:67 Je 25 '65

KALTHUM, Om
Voice of the Arabs. por Newsweek 67:31-2 Ja 10 '66

KALVAR process. See Copying processes

KALVODA, Josef
Communist strategy in Latin America. Yale R 55:191-208 D '65

KAMAT, Virendra B. and Wallach, D. F. H.
Separation and partial purification of plasma-membrane fragments from Ehrlich ascites carcinoma microsomes. bibliog Science 148: 1343-5 Je 4 '65

KAMB, Barclay
Clathrate crystalline form of silica. bibliog Science 148:232-4 Ap 9 '65
Structure of ice VI. bibliog Science 150:205-9 O 8 '65

KAMEN, Henry
Spanish inquisition. Horizon 7:28-31+ Autumn '65

KAMENA VOURLA resort. See Health resorts, watering places, etc.

KAMENTSKY, Louis A. and others
Spectrophotometer: new instrument for ultra-rapid cell analysis. bibliog Science 150:630-1 O 29 '65

KAMIN, Martin
That rascal Frank Harris. Hobbies 70:110-12 Jl '65

KAMINETZKY, Harold A.
Expectant mother; ed. by D. Mellach. Redbook 125:30 S '65

KAMINSTEIN, Abraham Louis
Senate opens hearings on copyright revision. Pub W 188:289-90 Ag 30 '65

KAMISAR, Yale
When the cops were not handcuffed. N Y Times Mag p34-5+ N 7 '65

KAMMEN, Michael G.
Colonial court records and the study of early American history: a bibliographical review. bibliog f Am Hist R 70:732-9 Ap '65

KAMMERER, Paul
Science in action; hoaxes and half-truths. R. Silverberg. Natur Hist 74:62-4 Mr '65

KAMMERER, Rafael
Especially for pianophiles. Am Rec G 31:914-16 My '65
Liszt piano music: five discs. Am Rec G 32: 58-9 S '65
Mighty Forty-eight. Am Rec G 32:214-15 N '65
Notes of a pianist. Am Rec G 31:886-7 My '65

KAMPEN, Irene
Europe with some reservations; excerpts from Europe without George. McCalls 92:124-5+ My '65
Last year at Sugarbush. McCalls 93:74+ O '65

KANDEL, I. L.
Danger of complacency: reprint of a 1952 article. Sch & Soc 93:58-63 Ja 23 '65

Obituary
Sch & Soc por(p385) 93:387 O 30 '65. W. W. Brickman

KANDRA, George A.
Tire failure no longer a problem. Am City 80:104-5 Mr '65

KANE, Art
Songs of freedom; photographs. Look 29:83-9 N 16 '65
Zoom in on the city; photographs. Life 59: 24-35 D 24 '65

about
Art Kane. J. Deschin. Pop Phot 57:70-9+ S '65
Kane. P. Caulfield. il por Mod Phot 29:74-83+ Ap '65

KANE, Harnett Thomas
Twenty-fifth anniversary party for Harnett Kane in Louisiana. il por Pub W 188:60 N 22 '65

KANE, Martin
Boxing. Sports Illus 23:89-90 N 22 '65

KANE, Robert S.
Corsica. Travel 124:47-9 N '65
North of the border; Bob Kane's Canada. il Pop Phot 56:88-91+ Je '65

KANGAROOS
Australia's gray kangaroo; danger of extinction. Nat Parks Mag 39:21 Je '65
Bead on roos; Australia's emblem being exterminated. E. Huxley. il N Y Times Mag p 119:20+ O 24 '65
Flying start made on kangaroo count; New South Wales. Sci N L 88:79 Jl 31 '65
Goodby, kangaroos. V. Kraft. il Sports Illus 22:76-80+ My 31 '65

KANIN, Garson
Money man; story. McCalls 92:94-7 Ap '65

KANSAS
See also
Crime and criminals—Kansas

KANSAS CITY, Mo.
Kansas City: new medical complex, university should complement Midwest research institute. J. Walsh. Science 148:1202-4 My 28 '65

Libraries
See also
Linda Hall library

Music
C.C.C. in K.C.; U.S. première of Händel's Julius Caesar. il Time 85:44 Je 4 '65
Everything's up to date; American première of Handel's Julius Caesar. il Newsweek 65: 76-7 My 31 '65

KANSAS CITY, Mo.—Music—*Continued*
Everything's up to date in. . . R. C. Marsh.
Hi Fi 15:126 Ag '65
Kansas City perspective; position in the
jazz story. S. Dance. Sat R 48:36-7 Jl
31 '65
See also
Kansas City lyric theater

Newspapers
See also
Kansas City star

KANSAS CITY, Mo, public library
Children's libraries; public library and the
school book fair. J. A. Merrill. Wilson Lib
Bul 39:913 Je '65

KANSAS CITY Athletics (baseball) See Baseball clubs

KANSAS CITY lyric theater
Kansas City. J. Haskins. Opera N 30:31 D 11
'65

KANSAS CITY star
End of one-man rule. il Time 86:68 O 1 '65

KANTOR, MacKinlay
Why I believe in flying saucers. por Pop Sci
188:72-4+ Ja '66

KANZLER, Hal
Big-game hunting with camera. Field & S
70:37-9 N '65

KAO, Ch'i
Out of China. A. Fang. Poetry 107:196-9 D
'65

KAPITZA, Peter Leonidovich
Letters. S. A. Colgate. Sci Am 213:6 Jl '65

KAPLAN, Chaim A.
Journal of the Warsaw ghetto; excerpts.
Commentary 40:42-58 N '65

KAPLAN, Edgar
Up-and-down week in San Francisco. C.
Goren. il Sports Illus 23:100+ D 6 '65

KAPLAN, Ethel, and Kaplan, Jules
Who is healthy and why? Todays Health
43:22-3+ F '65

KAPLAN, Jules. See Kaplan, E. jt. auth.

KAPLAN, Selna L. and Grumbach, M. M.
Immunoassay for human chorionic growth
hormone-prolactin in serum and urine.
bibliog Science 147:751-3 F 12 '65

KAPLOW, Jeffry
At home with the Caudillo. Sat R 49:36-7 Ja
15 '66

KAPPEL, Frederick R.
Where are tomorrow's leaders? excerpt from
address. por Read Digest 87:123-5 N '65

KAPPEL, Philip
Philip Kappel, etcher & engraver. E. M. Ettenberg. il por Am Artist 29:36-41+ N '65

KAPPLER, Frank
Divine poet's totality. Life 59:51+ D 17 '65
Italian beauty's maiden voyage. Life 58:109-
10 Je 18 '65
Wise old teacher of I-thou. Life 58:97-8 Je 25
'65
about
As Kappler prowls the haunts of Dante. G. P.
Hunt. por Life 59:3 D 17 '65

KARAJAN, Herbert von
Music to my ears; Karajan's Nine; per-
formance of First and Ninth symphonies
of Beethoven by the Berlin Philharmonic
in Carnegie Hall. I. Kolodin. Sat R 48:34+
F 13 '65
Musical events; performances of Beethoven
cycle with Berlin philharmonic in Carnegie
Hall. W. Sargeant. New Yorker 40:64-5
Ja 30; 98 F 6 '65

KARAS, Nicholas
Cold-sport hotspot. Field & S 70:52-3+ D '65
Expressways to the north. por Field & S
69:61-3+ Ap '65
You've got to be crazy to hunt coot. Field
& S 70:66-9+ S '65

KARASEK, Marvin. See Gates, A. H. jt. auth.

KAREL, Leonard and others
Computerized bibliographic services for biomedicine. bibliog Science 148:766-72 My 7
'65

KARIBA LAKE
Kariba case: manmade lakes and resource
development in Africa. T. Scudder. il Bul
Atomic Sci 21:6-11 D '65

KARL, Jean
Cry of the curlew, call to freshness. Pub W
188:176-8 Jl 12 '65
Maia Wojciechowska; Beni Montresor. Library J 90:1464-6 Mr 15 '65

KARLEN, Arno
Notes of a bad American. Holiday 38:8+
Jl '65
Surviving Ireland. Nation 200:486-8 My 3 '65
Walk through Málaga. Holiday 37:26+ Ap
'65
Yugoslavia. Holiday 38:42-55+ N '65

KARLIKOW, Abe
Binding with vat-made papers. Craft Horiz
25:12-15+ Mr '65

KARNOW, Stanley
Bill Cosby: variety is the life of spies. Sat
Eve Post 238:86+ S 25 '65
India: downhill toward disaster. Sat Eve Post
238:78-83 Je 5 '65
Taj, the Raj, and I. Sat R 48:56+ S 18 '65
Vietnam: where do we go from here? Sat
Eve Post 238:28-30+ Mr 27 '65

KARP, Irwin
House copyright hearings: education and fair
use. Pub W 188:291 Ag 30 '65

KARP, Ivan
Gargoyle snatchers. il Time 85:74 Mr 5 '65
Man from AARS. il Newsweek 65:75 My 31

KARP, Richard
Steel city stage. Q. Eaton. il por Opera N
30:29-32 Ja 22 '66

KARP, Tony
Don't get hooked buying a camera. Mod Phot
29:67+ D '65
Tony Karp on 35mm. por Mod Phot 30:38+
Ja '66

KARR, P. S.
Tennis on top of the tank. Am City 80:108-9
O '65

KARRAS, Alex
Detroit Lions' remarkable screwball; Alex
Karras; excerpt from Paper lion. G.
Plimpton. por Harper 232:76-82 Ja '66

KARRE, Wilma
String painting. Sch Arts 65:10-11 O '65

KARSTEN, C. F.
Should Europe restrict U.S. investments?
Harvard Bsns R 43:53-61 S '65

KART racing. See Karting

KARTEN, Barbara
Face to face: with an architect of the future.
por Seventeen 24:339 Ag '65

KARTING
Glove. T. Medley. il Hot Rod 18:115 Ag '65

KARTS (midget cars)
Glove. T. Medley. il Hot Rod 18:115 Ag '65

KARZMARK, C. J. and others
Luminescence dosimetry. Science 150:391-2+
O 15 '65

KASAVUBU, Joseph
But he has survived. J. Lelyveld. il pors N Y
Times Mag p52-3+ N 28 '65
View from the terrace. il por Time 86:40+
O 22 '65

KASBERG, K. G.
Martin Luther; poem. Christian Cent 82:1312
O 27 '65

KASER, Tom
Classroom TV comes to Samoa. Sat R 48:58-
9+ Je 19 '65

KASEY, Elizabeth H.
Safety is a way of living. PTA Mag 60:22-4
Ja '66

KASH, Don E.
Is good science good politics? Bul Atomic
Sci 21:34-6 Mr 27 S '65

KASHMIR
At a Russian table Shastri made peace with
an old enemy. il Life 60:22-5 Ja 21 '66
Behind Asia's new war: years of fear, hate.
il Bsns W p28-9 S 11 '65
Big war in Asia? with report by F. B.
Stevens. il U S News 59:37-41 S 20 '65
Cease-fire and backdown. il Newsweek 66:
42+ O 4 '65
Cease-fire of sorts. il Time 86:50 N 5 '65
China the peacemaker; behind India and
Pakistan's cease-fire. Nation 201:177 O 4
'65
China threatens war. il Sr Schol 87:10-11 S
30 '65
China's presence at the UN; decay of old
alliances, birth of new alignments. P. Ben.
New Repub 153:9-10 O 2 '65
Cold wind from Moscow; detente illusions
die hard; Radio Moscow commentary on
ceasefire. A. Brumberg. il Reporter 33:40-2
O 21; 10 D 2 '65
Conflict between India and Pakistan; address,
September 15, 1965. B. K. Nehru. Vital
Speeches 32:5-7 O 15 '65
Decrease-fire. Time 86:45 O 8 '65
Encirclement in Asia. il Time 86:35-6 S 17
'65
Ending the suspense. il Time 86:44-8 S 17 '65
First report from India; reaction to cease-
fire. E. Taylor. Reporter 33:14+ O 7 '65
Harsh testing ground for the faith of hardy
pilgrims. il Life 58:64-7 My 28 '65
Hawks. A. de Borchgrave; E. G. Martin.
il Newsweek 66:54-5 O 11 '65
Himalayan rumbles. Nat R 17:856-8 O 5 '65
If there is no cease-fire soon. . . S. Barber.
New Repub 153:22 S 25 '65

KASHMIR—*Continued*

India and Pakistan at war. C. B. Marshall. New Repub 153:19-21 S 25 '65

India vs. Pakistan: who won? who lost? il U S News 59:33-5 O 4 '65

Indian hara-kiri; Indian-Pakistani war. Christian Cent 82:1243 O 13 '65; Discussion. 82:1515-16 D 8 '65

Indo-Pakistan frustration. P. G. Altbach. Christian Cent 82:1512 D 8 '65

Kashmir: a religious war; Muslim and Hindu intolerance. J. F. Drane. Cath World 202:212-16 Ja '66

Kashmir: blindfolded war. il Newsweek 66:35 Ag 30 '65

Kashmir: dilemma of a people adrift. A. B. Tourtellot. il Sat R 48:16-19 Mr 6 '65; Discussion. 48:25 My 8; 23-4+ My 15; 44 My 29; 21-2 Jl 17 '65

Kashmir dispute; address, October 2, 1965. M. Ayub Khan. Vital Speeches 32:8-9 O 15 '65

Kashmir, India and Pakistan. M. Abdullah. For Affairs 43:528-35 Ap '65

Kashmir: on the escalator. il Newsweek 66:39 S 13 '65

Kashmir: Shastri's time for decision. S. Rajan. Reporter 33:41-3 S 23 '65

Kashmir the beautiful, torn by war; with reports by G. De Carvalho and L. Hall. il Life 59:40-44B S 17 '65

Kashmir: tinderbox of Asia. J. E. Frazer. Read Digest 87:91-6 D '65

Kosygin in Tashkent. America 114:113-14 Ja 22 '66

Kutch and Kashmir, how the war started. G. Woodcock. Commonweal 82:724-6 O 1 '65

Limit to patience. il Time 86:20 Ag 27 '65

Matter of honor; brink of all-out war. il Time 86:21 S 10 '65

New hope, new purpose; emergency meeting on the India-Pakistan war. il Newsweek 66:25-7 O 4 '65

New threat of big war; red China goes to the brink. il U S News 59:38-9 S 27 '65

New war for world; new worry for U.S. il U S News 59:33-4 S 13 '65

No give. il Newsweek 66:64+ O 18 '65

One conflict that got to the conference table. il U S News 60:21 Ja 17 '66

Passing through fire. Time 86:34 S 3 '65

Pistol-proud pupils; India and Pakistan. C. Northcott. Christian Cent 82:1215 O 6 '65

Playing the honest broker; Kosygin mediates at Tashkent conference. il Newsweek 67:36+ Ja 17 '66

Senseless war on the subcontinent: Nations war under the spell of Kashmir. il Newsweek 66:33-7 S 20 '65

Soviet bid for India; hate America campaign. E. Taylor. il Reporter 33:18-23 N 18 '65

Strong young men; fighting between Indians and Pakistanis. F. Melville; A. de Borchgrave. il Newsweek 66:43-4 S 27 '65

Talk in Tashkent. Time 87:26-7 Ja 7 '66

Tightening the screws; Hazratbal mosque incident. il Newsweek 66:54+ N 8 '65

Tortured Kashmir. E. Taylor; R. Critchfield. il Reporter 33:24-30 N 4 '65

U.N. repeats call for withdrawal of Indian and Pakistan forces; statements, October 25 and November 5, 1965; with text of resolution. A. J. Goldberg. Dept State Bul 53:952-7 D 13 '65

U.N. Security council demands cease-fire between armed forces of India and Pakistan; statements, September 17, 18, 20 and 22, 1965; with text of resolution. A. J. Goldberg. Dept State Bul 53:602-8 O 11 '65

United States supports call for India-Pakistan cease-fire; statements, September 4 and September 6, 1965, with texts of resolutions. A. J. Goldberg. Dept State Bul 53:526-9 S 27 '65

View from India. W. D. Patterson. il Sat R 48:38-9+ O 30 '65

Violence in the Vale. il Time 86:31 Ag 20 '65

Voice from the mountains. il Time 86:32-3 S 24 '65

War ends in Kashmir, but issues still simmer. il Bsns W p31 S 25 '65

War in Asia; religious issue. Commonweal 82:679-80 S 24 '65; Reply. D. Chakkalakal. 83:76 O 22 '65

Who said irrational? reductio ad absurdum of war. Nation 201:149 S 27 '65

Why not let them fight it out? Nat R 17:802 S 21 '65

See also

United Nations—Kashmir

KASLIK, Václav

Magic lantern. D. Stevens. il por Opera N 29:12-13 F 27 '65

KASPER, John S. and others

Clathrate structure of silicon Na_8Si_{46} and $Na_x Si_{136}$. bibliog Science 150:1713-14 D 24 '65

KASS, Judie

Give them a chance to dance. Parents Mag 40:55-7+ S '65

KASSAN, Peter

Statement; poem. Seventeen 24:72 My '65

KASSAN, Roberta

Talk to me; story. Seventeen 24:112-13 S '65

KASSMAN, Shirley

Summer art workshop for high school students. Sch Arts 64:18-22 Ap '65

KASTON, Henryk

Metropolitan miniature. F. Stevenson. il por Opera N 30:inside back cover N 20 '65

KASTOR, Hilton, Chesley, Clifford and Atherton, incorporated

Regimen & responsibility; judgment against ad agency promoting a fraudulent product. Time 85:92 My 14 '65

KASUGAMYCIN

Kasugamycin effective against urinary infection. Sci N L 88:274 O 30 '65

KASZA, William J.

Research in art education. Sch Arts 64:24-6 My '65

KATAHDIN, MOUNT

Mister Maine and the mountain. E. W. Smith. il Field & S 70:10-11+ D '65

KATANGA

Crisis in the Congo, by E. W. Lefever. Review

America 112:863-4 Je 12 '65. V. S. Kearney

Katanga's comeback: bright spot in Africa. A. J. Meyers. il U S News 58:70-1 My 24 '65

KATEB, George

Beyond decadence. Commentary 41:84-7 Ja '66

Revising the unthinkable. Commentary 40:101-2+ N '65

KATEB, George

Strange bedfellows. Commentary 40:71-3 Ag '65

KATERINA Ismailova; opera. See Shostakovich, D. D.

KATRIN'S crusade; story. See Rohde, B.

KATY (railroad) See Missouri-Kansas-Texas railroad

KATZ, Alex

Domesticated hipster; exhibition at Fischbach gallery. il por Newsweek 66:88 D 13 '65

Katz cocktail; grand and cozy; exhibition at Fischbach, N.Y. S. Tillim. il Art N 64:46-9+ D '65

KATZ, Joseph, and Sanford, Nevitt

Causes of the student revolution. Sat R 48:64-6+ D 18 '65

KATZ, Loren B.

Some guidelines in teaching American Negro history. Negro Hist Bul 28:190-1 My '65

KATZ, Menke

In retrospect; poem. Atlan 215:81 My '65

KATZ, Robert

Russia's cars. Motor T 17:36-9 Jl '65

KATZENBACH, Nicholas deBelleville

Attorney General of the United States, talks; statements ed. by J. R. Moskin. pors Look 29:27-33 Je 1 '65

Attorney General on draft dodging; excerpts from interview. por U S News 59:41 N 1 '65

Courts too soft on criminals? a warning by Attorney General; excerpts from letter. U S News 59:66-7 Ag 16 '65

Excerpt from testimony, February 10, 1965. Cong Digest 44:146+ My '65

Free press and fair trial; address, April 15, 1965. Vital Speeches 31:518-21 Je 15 '65

Voting rights act of 1965; address, March 18, 1965. Vital Speeches 31:391-8 Ap 15 '65

about

Antitrust policy gets a long, hard look. il por Bsns W p45-6+ My 8 '65

Daily dilemmas of the Attorney General. D. Oberdorfer. il pors N Y Times Mag p28-9+ Mr 7 '65

Equality v. deterrence. il por Time 86:41 Ag 13 '65

Katzenbach and Kennedy; how their methods differ. por U S News 58:20 Mr 22 '65

Katzenbach's commission. A. Kopkind. New Repub 154:7-8 Ja 15 '66

New Attorney General. por U S News 58:14+ F 8 '65

New title. por Time 85:23B F 5 '65

Police find lawyer friends. Life 59:4 Ag 20 '65

Trigger of hope. il Time 86:19-20 Ag 20 '65

When Hoover corrected the record. por U S News 59:12 Ag 2 '65

KAUAI NATIONAL PARK (proposed) See National parks and reserves—United States
KAUFFMAN, Draper L.
Irregular. pors Newsweek 65:33 F 15 '65
KAUFFMANN, Stanley
Can culture explode? notes on subsidizing the arts. Commentary 40:19-28 Ag '65
Films. See issues of New republic
Focus on film criticism. Harper 230:113-16 Je '65
Greatness as a literary standard. Harper 231:151-6 N '65
Life book review. Life 58:10+ My 14 '65
Literature of the early sixties; reprint from Great ideas today, 1964. annual to Great books of the western world. bibliog Wilson Lib Bul 39:748-56+ My '65
Maximum Max. New Repub 152:19-22 Ap 10 '65
Young in the thirties. New Repub 153:17-20 S 18 '65

about

New man on the aisle. il por Newsweek 66:92 D 20 '65
KAUFMAN, Arnold S.
Teach-ins: new force for the times. Nation 200:666-70 Je 21 '65
KAUFMAN, Bel
Real world of the beginning teacher; adaptation of address. por NEA J 54:16-19 O '65
Teaching in triplicate. H. Frankel. Sat R 48:36 Ap 10 '65
KAUFMAN, Betty
Art. See issues of Commonweal
KAUFMAN, Donald D. See Kearney, P. C. jt. auth.
KAUFMAN, George S. See Hart, M. jt. auth.
KAUFMAN, John W. See Weber, J. N. jt. auth.
KAUFMAN, Shirley
There she goes; poem. Nation 200:510 My 10 '65
KAUFMANN, Walter
Superfluity of uncertainty. Sat R 48:86+ My 22 '65
KAUL, Balkrishena, and Staba, E. J.
Visnagin: biosynthesis and isolation from ammi visnagi suspension cultures. bibliog Science 150:1731-2 D 24 '65
KAUNDA, Kenneth David
After while, crocodile. il por Time 85:30 Ap 2 '65
Another Suez? Newsweek 66:52 D 13 '65
Colored rulers. G. C. Turner. bibliog por Negro Hist Bul 28:134-5 Mr '65
Five colors. il por Time 86:25 S 10 '65
Imperiled president. il Newsweek 66:40+ D 20 '65
Independence comes to Zambia. il pors Ebony 20:27-30+ F '65
Some planes arrive. il Time 86:39-40 D 10 '65
KAUPER, Paul G.
Areas of Catholic-Protestant conflict. por Cath World 201:375-81 S '65
KAVADLO, Abraham
Teacher of the unteachables. J. Tebbel. por Sat R 48:72+ My 15 '65
KAVANAGH, Patrick
Life at work. R. Skelton. Poetry 106:234-6 Je '65
Verse. L. Bogan. New Yorker 41:193-4+ Ap 10 '65
KAVANAUGH, James J.
Missing dimension. America 112:604-5+ Ap 24 '65
KAVANAUGH, Robert E.
Dialogue with campus agnostics. America 114:126-8 Ja 22 '66
KAWAMURA, Hiroshi, and Sawyer, C. H.
Elevation in brain temperature during paradoxical sleep. bibliog Science 150:912 N 12 '65
KAY, Hubert
Two-billion-dollar company that lives by the cent. Fortune 72:166-9+ D '65
Warrior from Patman's switch. Fortune 71:154-6+ Ap '65
KAY, Jane H.
Reviews: Boston. Art N 63:17+ S '64; 21 F; 64:23 Sum '65
KAYE, Gordon E.
Mercury batteries. Electr World 74:46-8 O '65
KAYE, Gordon I. and others
Electron microscopy: sodium localization in normal and ouabain-treated transporting cells. bibliog Science 150:1167-8 N 26 '65
KAYE, Nora
Nora Kaye: with photos from her scrapbook and captions by her. S. Goodman. il pors Dance Mag 39:63-43 F; 54-8 Mr '65
KAYIRA, Legson
Good will odyssey. por Time 85:118+ Ap 30 '65

KAYSEN, Carl, and Stone, J. J.
Keeping the lid on nuclear weapons. New Repub 154:13-14 Ja 15 '66
KAZAKHSTAN
Dust bowl Khrushchev created. U S News 60:9 Ja 3 '66
KAZAMIAS, Andreas M. and Massialas, B. G.
Recent educational tendencies in Greece; excerpt from Tradition and change in education: a comparative study. bibliog f Sch & Soc 93:275-80 My 1 '65
KAZAN, Elia
How to succeed in the theatre without really being successful. E. Dundy. il Esquire 63:88-9+ My '65
KAZAN, Lainie
Do stars grow in Brooklyn? por Time 85:64 F 19 '65
KAZANTZAKIS, Nikos
Man and God in dialogue; Sodom and Gomorrah, prologue, tr. by A. J. Skalafuris. Sat R 48:16-17+ Ag 28 '65

about

Cretan glance. G. Davenport. Nat R 17:937-8 O 19 '65
Kazantzakis report. K. Friar. pors Sat R 48:34 Ag 14 '65
Last testament. il por Time 86:77-8 Ag 13 '65
Old man from Crete. P. Deane. New Repub 153:26-7 O 2 '65
KAZAZIAN, H. H. Jr, and others
X-linked 6-phosphogluconate dehydrogenase in drosophila: subunit associations. bibliog Science 150:1601-2 D 17 '65
KAZIN, Alfred
Literary mind. Nation 201:203-6 S 20 '65
Republic of the spirit. Reporter 33:44+ Ag 12 '65
Useful critic. Atlan 216:73-4+ D '65

about

In that dawn to be alive. R. Bendiner. Reporter 33:57-8 D 2 '65
Literary radical. L. Marx. Commentary 40:118+ D '65
Thirties: frayed collars and large visions. L. Kronenberger. Atlan 217:79-81 Ja '66
To America, with some regret. E. Capouya. por Sat R 48:101 S 18 '65
Young in the thirties. S. Kauffmann. New Repub 153:17-20 S 18 '65
KEANE, Johnny
Boss of the Yankees. il por Newsweek 65:60 Mr 29 '65
Redbirds on the grapefruit. il por Time 85:58 Mr 19 '65
Word for Johnny Keane is: patience. E. Asinof. il pors N Y Times Mag p24-8 My 30 '65
KEANE, Kevin
Cost of the arms race. America 113:372-4 O 2 '65
KEANE, Margaret
Man who paints those big eyes. J. Howard. il por Life 59:39-40+ Ag 27 '65
KEANE, Walter
Man who paints those big eyes. J. Howard. il pors Life 59:39-40+ Ag 27 '65
KEARNEY, Paul W.
Have you checked your tires lately? Read Digest 87:103-5 Jl '65
Tailgating, invitation to tragedy. Read Digest 87:103-6 O '65
To keep your car from being stolen. Read Digest 87:249-50+ N '65
Your eyes, your auto and your life. Read Digest 87:115-18 D '65
KEARNEY, Philip C. and Kaufman, D. D.
Enzyme from soil bacterium hydrolyzes phenylcarbamate herbicides. Science 147:740 F 12 '65
KEARNEY, Vincent S.
Katanga revisited. America 112:863-4 Je 12 '65
Little war in Laos. America 112:250-1 F 20 '65
Prince of the Khmers. America 112:715-16 My 15 '65
Vietnam background. America 113:8-11 Jl 3 '65
World scene. America 113:676-7+ N 27 '65
KEARNS, Francis E.
Kearns case. J. Leo; discussion. Commonweal 81:718-19, 774-5+; 82:31, 34-5+, 178-9+ Mr 5, 19-Ap 2, 30 '65
KEATING, Edward M.
Of many things; what has happened to Catholicism and editorial censorship. T. N. Davis. America 113:173 Ag 21 '65

KEATING, Kenneth Barnard
Not Bonanza, not Peyton Place, but the U.S. Senate! N Y Times Mag p66-7+ Ap 25 '65

about

Kennedy vs. Keating: was Bobby unfair? U S News 58:14 Ap 26 '65
People of the week. por U S News 59:21-2 N 15 '65
Population committee formed. Nat Parks Mag 39:20 Je '65

KEATS, John, 1920-
Girls, gold and beasts on wheels. Life 58:12 Ap 30 '65
Great grad school gold rush. Life 58:107-8+ Je 11 '65
On running away. Holiday 37:8+ Je '65

KEATTS, Margret E.
Kiki, the personality mousebird. Audubon Mag 67:386-7 N '65

KEBABIAN, Eleanor
Librarian talks to teachers. Sr Schol 87:sup 12-13 S 30 '65

KECK, George E.
United charts a new flight plan. il por Bsns W p 128-30+ Ag 14 '65

KEEFE, Frederick L.
Woman who stayed where she was. New Yorker 41:208+ N 6 '65

KEEFE, John C.
Human-rights committee in action. Am City 80:116-18 O '65

KEELER, Marston W.
Motorboating in the Mediterranean. il Yachting 117:42-4+ Mr; 82-4+ Ap '65

KEEN, Elizabeth
Sally Gross, Elizabeth Keen, Eugene Lion, Judson dance theatre. M. Marks. Dance Mag 40:57 Ja '66

KEENE, L. C. and Pierson, T. E.
Astrovision: an in-flight entertainment system. Electr World 73:42-3+ Mr '65

KEENEY, Barnaby C.
Proposal for a national foundation for the humanities; adaptation of address, August 31, 1964. Sch & Soc 93:211-14 Ap 3 '65
Why we need a national humanities foundation. Sat R 48:68-70 Mr 20 '65

KEENEY, Eugene Adams
Call for full investigation of the Labor relations board; excerpts from testimony, September 16, 1965. por U S News 59:106-7 O 11 '65

KEEP America beautiful, incorporated
Litterbugs are expensive. Nat Parks Mag 40:22 Ja '66

KEEP-America-green campaign. See Forest fire protection

KEEP moving, please; story. See Streeter, E.

KEEPSAKES
Place for sentiment; home displays. N. Mandelbaum. il McCalls 92:104-9 My '65

KEFAUVER, Estes
Kefauver memorial. W. A. Geier. Christian Cent 82:595 Mv 5 '65
Real voice, by R. Harris. Review Commentary 39:75-7 F '65. D. T. Bazelon

KEFFORD, N. P. and Rijven, A. H. G. C.
Gibberellin and growth in isolated wheat embryos. bibliog Science 151:104-5 Ja 7 '66

KEGLEY, Charles W.
Talks with Tillich. Christian Cent 82:1012 Ag 18 '65

KEHLET, Niels
Brief biography. S. Goodman. pors Dance Mag 39:52-3 N '65
High & the mighty. il por Time 86:62 D 10 '65

KEIFFER, Elisabeth
(ed) See Lombroso, C. T. Living with epilepsy

KEIM, William P.
What the AMA really fears. New Repub 152:11-12 F 13 '65

KEINO, Kipchoge
Sophisticate & the natural. por Time 86:37 D 24 '65

KEISER, Marjorie
Consumer service bureau report. See issues of Parents' magazine and better homemaking

KEITH, Agnes Newton
Sahara holiday; excerpt from Children of Allah. il Atlan 216:92-4+ D '65

KEITH, G. Stuart
Science in action; the sounds of singing. Natur Hist 74:61-4 Je '65

KEITH, H. D. and others
Intercrystalline links in bulk polyethylene. Science 150:1026-7 N 19 '65

KEITH, James A.
Guidance bookshelf. Sr Schol 87:sup4+ N 11 '65

KEITH, M. L. and Weber, J. N.
Systematic relationships between carbon and oxygen isotopes in carbonates deposited by modern corals and algae. bibliog Science 150:498-501 O 22 '65

KELLEN, Konrad
Adenauer at ninety. For Affairs 44:275-90 Ja '66
Opinion: on gluttony. por Mlle 61:25+ O '65
Reminiscences of Thomas Mann. Yale R 54:383-91 Mr '65

KELLEY, James B.
Book reviews. America 113:244-5 S 4 '65
Youth wants to work. America 112:428-30 Mr 27 '65

KELLEY, Lora
Library burns in the Los Angeles riot; report. E. T. Moore. ALA Bul 59:983-6 D '65

KELLEY, Reeve Spencer
Afraid; poem. Sat R 48:24 D 18 '65
Inevitable wreck; poem. Sat R 48-38 F 6 '65

KELLEY, Stanley, Jr
Apropos 1964; excerpt from National election of 1964. Nat R 17:1015-16 N 16 '65

KELLEY, Thomas F.
Polonium-210 content of mainstream cigarette smoke. bibliog Science 149:537-8 Jl 30 '65

KELLEY, Virginia
New college. Mlle 61:148+ O '65

KELLEY, William Melvin
American in Rome. Mlle 60:202+ Mr '65

KELLY, Anthony
Fiber-reinforced metals; with biographical sketch. Sci Am 212:16, 28-37 F '65

KELLY, Ellsworth
Gallery for young people. C. B. Johnson. il Sch Arts 64:46-7 Ap '65

KELLY, Faye M.
Circus comes to town. Sch Arts 65:34 S '65

KELLY, Frank K.
Book reviews. America 113:81 Jl 17 '65

KELLY, Gene
Some notes for young dancers. por Dance Mag 39:49 S '65

about

Dancing in the dark. il pors Dance Mag 39:103-7 D '65

KELLY, Grace. See Grace Patricia, consort of Rainier III, prince of Monaco

KELLY, J. Michael
How to save that gun-shy dog. Field & S 70:120-2+ Ag '65

KELLY, Sister Suzanne
Putting sisters in their place. America 114:10-11 Ja 1 '66

KELLY, Thomas A.
Ethics in business. America 113:716 D 4 '65

KELLY, Tom
Catch a bigot by the toe. Nation 200:169-70 F 15 '65

KELLY, William Cody
Kelly caper. il por Newsweek 66:20-1 Jl 5 '65

KELLY, William F.
Expert views credit bill. por Nations Bsns 53:104+ Je '65

KELLY; musical comedy. See Musical comedies, revues, etc.—Criticisms, plots, etc.

KELLY'S girl; story. See Fritz, J.

KELP
Foresters look after underwater trees. Sci N L 87:201 Mr 27 '65

KELSEY-Hayes company
Anyone for survival? A. Balk. il Sat Eve Post 238:72+ Mr 27 '65

KELVIN temperature scale. See Low temperature research

KELVINATOR division. See American motors corporation—Kelvinator division

KEMAL, Mustafa. See Atatürk, K.

KEMMERER, Jack B.
Iron colts in the back yard. Pop Mech 124:80-4 Ag '65
R for automobiles. Motor T 17:30-5 Mr '65

KEMPE, C. Gordon. See McCann, R. W. jt. auth.

KEMPER, James S.
Doctor King's policy; invitation to racial violence? excerpts from address, September 21, 1965. por U S News 59:22 O 4 '65

KEMPNER, Mary Jean
Unicorn in the pool. Harper 231:57-61 N '65

KEMPTON, Murray
Bundy-Gruening debate. New Repub 152:9-10 My 8 '65
Crisis in American culture; address. por Wilson Lib Bul 39:746-7 My '65
Life TV review. Life 58:16 Mr 5 '65
Lucky Lindsay. New Repub 154:10-11 Ja 15 '66
Sorensen's Kennedy. Atlan 216:71-4 O '65
Trial of the Klansman. New Repub 152:10-13 My 22 '65

KENNEDY, Robert Francis—About—*Cont.*
Saying it & not saying it; speech. Time 86:
19 Jl 16 '65
To honor JFK: brother Robert climbs a peak.
il U S News 58:8 Ap 5 '65
Two senators named Kennedy. il pors News-
week 67:17-20+ Ja 17 '66
Unmaking of a vice president; excerpts from
Making of the President—1964. T. H. White.
por U S News 59:15 Jl 5 '65
What Americans expect from Robert Ken-
nedy; excerpts from Dear Senator Ken-
nedy, ed. by B. Adler. il Ladies Home J
82:71+ O '65
What burned Bobby; charge of planting in
Life magazine a derogatory story about
Jimmy Hoffa. por Time 85:23-23A Mr 12 '65
What liberty means. il Newsweek 66:26 N
29 '65
When will Bobby make his play? Cato.
Nat R 18:11 Ja 11 '66
Where toys are locked away. Christian Cent
82:1179 S 29 '65
Will the real Robert Kennedy stand up? W.
Weaver, jr. il pors N Y Times Mag p8-9+
Je 20 '65
KENNEDY, Robert Francis, family
Kennedys in New York; excerpts. G. Gard-
ner. il McCalls 92:100-3+ Ag '65
KENNEDY, Rose (Fitzgerald)
Full happy life of John F. Kennedy; com-
ments on paintings by J. Duhême. Ladies
Home J 82:100-5 N '65
KENNEDY, Ted. See Kennedy, E. M.
KENNEDY, William V.
Danger of labels. America 113:717-18 D 4 '65
KENNEDY brothers
As showdown came on a Kennedy aide. il
por U S News 59:23 N 1 '65
Is it to be the Kennedy brothers vs. LBJ?
il U S News 59:50-2 Jl 12 '65
Kennedy brothers: rallying point for the
liberals. il U S News 58:20 My 24 '65
Kennedys vs Humphrey; who has gained in
'65. il U S News 59:52-3 N 8 '65
KENNEDY, CAPE
Amazing new Cape Kennedy. H. Pryor. il Sci
Digest 57:47-51 Je '65
New look at the Cape. il Time 85:86-94+
Mr 26 '65
Report from Cape Kennedy. J. Harabin. il
Seventeen 25:88-9+ Ja '66
KENNEDY, MOUNT
Canada's Mount Kennedy; discovery and first
ascent. B. Washburn; R. F. Kennedy; J. W.
Whittaker. il Nat Geog Mag 128:1-33 Jl '65
How did I get myself into this? B. Kennedy
climbs Yukon mountain. D. Connelly. il
Sports Illus 22:56-8+ Ap 5 '65
Our climb up Mt Kennedy. R. F. Kennedy. il
Life 58:22-7 Ap 9 '65
KENNEDY international airport. See New
York (city)—Airports
KENNELS
Anatomy of a kennel. J. Stetson. il Field &
S 70:116-17 Ja '65
KENNER, Hugh
Art. Nat R 17:160-2 F 23 '65
Ode from the echo chamber. bibliog f por
Nat R 17:1084-6+ N 30 '65
KENNEY, Ann D.
(ed) Family movie guide. See issues of
Parents' magazine and better homemaking
KENNEY, Dick
Barefoot in the driver's seat. il por Sports
Illus 23:28-9 N 8 '65
KENNEY, Nathaniel T.
Ethiopian adventure. por Nat Geog Mag 127:
548-82 Ap '65
KENNY, Delbert J.
Church bonds ride the population wave. il
por Bsns W p 138+ Mr 13 '65
KENNY, Herbert A.
Geese and the phoenix; poem. Commonweal
82:536 Jl 23 '65
KENOSHA, Wis.

Water supply

Capacity doubled, manpower unchanged.
O. F. Nelson. il Am City 80:118-19+ Ap '65
KENT, Allen
Electronic information handling. Science 148:
540-3 Ap 23 '65
KENT, George
Case of the golden turkey eggs. Read Digest
87:148:51 N '65
Count down for Pisa. Travel 123:58-60 F '65;
Same abr. with title Pisa's problem tower.
Read Digest 86:237-8+ F '65
Faith that moved a church. Read Digest 86:
61-5 Ap '65
He made beauty his business. Read Digest
87:260-5 N '65

Roll, Jordan, roll! Read Digest 87:173-4+
O '65
Titian: master painter of Venice. Read Di-
gest 87:198-202 D '65
—and Reddy, John
Master of the mountain peaks. Read Digest
87:102-7 S '65
KENT, Sister Mary Corita
Peace on earth. New Yorker 41:22-3 Ja 1 '66
KENT, Norman
Line drawings of Thoreau MacDonald. Am
Artist 29:36-41+ D '65
Warren Baumgartner, 1894-1963. Am Artist
29:46-7+ Ap '65
KENTFIELD, Calvin
California coast. Holiday 38:80-91+ O '65
Nob Hill festival. Nation 201:398+ N 22 '65
KENTUCKY
Louisville: law or license? contamination of
land and water. N. E. Isaacs. il Sat R
48:44-5 My 22 '65
See also
Education—Kentucky
Paleontology—Kentucky

Economic conditions

Tyranny of charity; furniture makers plight
in east Kentucky. W. Berry. il Nation
201:161-4 S 27 '65

Historic houses, etc.

Old Kentucky home; My old Kentucky home
state park, Bardstown. R. H. Woodward.
il Hobbies 70:120 My '65

Parks and reserves

In the valley of ice age wildlife; Big Bone
Lick State Park; excerpt from Wandering
through winter. E. W. Teale. il Audubon
Mag 67:286-91 S '65
State parks of Kentucky. M. Hunn. il Travel
124:22-7+ Jl '65

Religious institutions and affairs

News of the Christian world (cont) Christian
Cent 82:1428-9 N 17 '65
KENTUCKY bluegrass. See Grasses
KENTUCKY Derby. See Horse racing
KENTUCKY mountaineers. See Mountaineers
(southern states)
KENTUCKY opera association
Kentucky's King. W. Mootz. Opera N 29:32
Ap 10 '65
KENTUCKY state fair. See Agricultural ex-
hibitions
KENTUCKY state fair horse show. See Horse
shows
KENTUCKY. University
Gathering on the bluegrass; comp. by R.
Brown. il Sat R 48:58-9+ My 22 '65
KENTUCKY university press
Gathering on the bluegrass; comp. by R.
Brown. il Sat R 48:58-9+ My 22 '65
University of Kentucky press celebrates an
anniversary. il Pub W 187:27-31 Ap 12 '65
KENYA
Thicker than water. Nat R 17:408 My 18 '65
See also
Hotels, taverns, etc.—Kenya
Hunting—Kenya

Foreign relations

Casual correspondent; Wang Te-ming expelled from Nairobi. Newsweek 66:45 Ag 2
'65

Politics and government

Arms & Odinga. Time 85:39 Ap 23 '65
Different direction. il Time 85:47 My 7 '65
Double O loses. il Newsweek 65:58 Je 14 '65
Harambee, says Kenyatta, let's all pull to-
gether. L. Fellows. il N Y Times Mag p36-
7+ N 7 '65
Why we reject communism. Time 85:40 Je 11
'65
KENYATTA, Jomo
Colored rulers. G. C. Turner. Negro Hist Bul
28:89-90 Ja '65
Farewell to arms. Time 85:30 Je 4 '65
Harambee, says Kenyatta; let's all pull to-
gether. L. Fellows. il pors N Y Times Mag
p36-7+ N 7 '65
Why we reject communism. Time 85:40 Je 11
'65
KENYON, Cecelia
Fatherly sedition. Nation 200:172-6 F 15 '65
KENYON, Kathleen M.
Ancient Jerusalem. Sci Am 213:84-91 Jl '65
KEOHEN, Gerald
Ode to Saint Raphael. America 112:462 Ap 3
'65
KEPES, Gyorgy
Visual arts and the sciences: a proposal for
collaboration. il Arch Rec 137:145-56 My '65

KEPES, Juliet
Color separation II: the use of photostats.
Horn Bk 41:651-4 D '65
KEPLER, Johann
Kepler's dream. by J. Lear. Review
Nation 200:343-4 Mr 29 '65. W. Miller
Sat R il por 48:41 Ap 3 '65. W. D. Stahlman
KEPPEL, Francis
Are we turning away from talent? excerpt
from address. Sat R 48:66 My 15 '65
Civil rights and education. por Ebony 20:
110-12+ S '65
Education and international understanding.
Dept State Bul 53:812-15 N 22 '65
Impact of educational technology; excerpts
from address, July 1965. por Sr Schol 87:
sup4 O 7 '65
Keppel speaks out on education bill; excerpts from interview. Sr Schol 86:1T F 18
'65
New vigor in the urban high schools. PTA
Mag 59:4-6 Mr '65

about

Education's muddled bureaucracy. J. Spivak.
il Reporter 32:33-6 Ap 8 '65
Head of the class. il por Time 86:60-2+ O 15
'65
Leadership for education. J. Cass. Sat R 49:
57-8 Ja 15 '66
New team to spend the billions in school
aid. por U S News 60:12 Ja 3 '66
Pilot for school aid, into uncharted areas.
pors Bsns W p30-2 F 6 '65
Schools make news. Sat R 48:57 Ag 21 '65
KEPPLER, Herbert
Keppler on the SLR. See issues of Modern
photography
KEPPLER, Philip
Sparkle of sound. Opera N 29:24-5 Mr 13 '65
KERALA, India
Kerala: agricultural slum. Benedict Mar
Gregorios. America 112:701 My 15 '65
KERALA election. See Elections—India
KERATIN
Hereditary absence of sebaceous glands in the
mouse. A. H. Gates and M. Karasek. bibliog
il Science 148:1471-3 Je 11 '65
KERENSKY, Alexander
Man who lost Russia. H. Schwartz. por Sat R
48:38 N 20 '65
KERESZTES-NAGY, Steven, and others
Hybridization experiments: evidence of dissociation equilibrium in hemerythrin. bibliog
Science 150:357-9 O 15 '65
KERKAM, Earl Cavis
Earl Kerkam, 1890-1965. L. Finkelstein. il por
Art N 64:28-31+ My '65
KERLAN, Robert
Ben Casey at the ball park. J. Murphy. il por
N Y Times Mag p 18-19+ Ag 22 '65
KERLINGER, Fred N.
Mythology of educational research: the descriptive approach. bibliog f Sch & Soc
93:222-5 Ap 3 '65
KERMIT, Mark
Rumble strips jar dreamy drivers. Am City
80:94-5 N '65
KERMODE, Frank
Novel as Jerusalem; analysis of M. Spark's
Mandelbaum gate. Atlan 216:92-4+ O '65
KERN COUNTY land company
Gleaning new ventures from farming profits.
il Bsns W p89-90+ O 23 '65
KERN COUNTY museum
Bakersfield's museum is a twelve acre village. il Sunset 135:56+ O '65
KEROUAC, Jack
On the road with Memére. Holiday 37:74-5
My '65

about

Jack Kerouac comes home. D. Wakefield. por
Atlan 216:69-72 Jl '65
KERR, Anna B.
Pringle-Claggett House in Hastings, Minnesota. Antiques 89:112-15 Ja '66
KERR, Clark
Berkeley affair: Mr Kerr vs. Mr Savio &
co. A. H. Raskin. il por N Y Times Mag
p24-5+ F 14 '65
How campus discord forced a university
president to resign. il por U S News 58:
22 Mr 22 '65
Lesson of Clark Kerr. il por Newsweek 65:53
Mr 22 '65
On the campus: a troubled reflection of the
U.S. M. Ways. il por Fortune 72:130-5+
S '65
Stiffening the spine. il por Time 85:48 Mr 19
'65

Trouble again at Cal and Kerr calls it quits.
il por Life 58:43 Mr 19 '65
Why campus crisis flares again. il por Bsns
W p38-9 Mr 20 '65
KERR, Deborah
Redbook dialogue: Deborah Kerr, Peter
Viertel and Miguel Dominguin. por Redbook
125:50-1+ My '65

about

Deborah Kerr; the lady is a scamp. J.
Wilkie. por Good H 160:86-7+ F '65
KERR, Ed
For sale: vacation sites from Uncle Sam.
Pop Sci 186:138-40 Je '65
KERR, Jean
Why mommy can't read. McCalls 93:51+
Ja '66

about

Poor Richard. Criticism
Look il 29:67-70 Mr 9 '65
KERR, Norman S.
Disappearance of a genetic marker from a
cytoplasmic hybrid plasmodium of a true
slime mold. bibliog Science 147:1586-8 Mr
26 '65
KERR, Sophie
Obituary
Pub W 187:52 Mr 1 '65
KERR, Walter
TV talk shows, great conversation killers.
McCalls 92:74-5+ Jl '65
KERR-Mills act. See Insurance, Health—United
States
KERSHNER, William K.
Follow me through. Flying 77:130+ S; 91
N; 110 D '65
KERWIN, Justin E. See Herreshoff, H. C.
jt. auth.
KESA in barter. See Barter
KESSEL, David, and others
Uptake as a determinant of methotrexate
response in mouse leukemias. bibliog Science 150:752-4 N 5 '65
KESSEL, Dmitri
His Excellency Dmitri Kessel. G. P. Hunt.
por Life 59:3 D 3 '65
KESSLER, Edward
In a Williamsburg backyard; poem. Sat R
48:25 N 6 '65
KESSLER, Jane W.
Preparation for puberty. PTA Mag 59:25-7
bibliog(p36) My '65
KESSLER, Jascha
Cannibals; poem. Sat R 48:126 Mr 13 '65
Still life; poem. Sat R 48:46 Je 12 '65
KESSLER, K. O. See Carlisle, N. jt. auth.
KETCHES. See Sailing vessels
KETCHUM, Philip
Plots and plans. Writer 78:23-5 Je '65
KETCHUM, Richard M.
Faces from the past (cont) Am Heritage 16:
62-3 F; 60-1 Ap; 96-7 Ag '65
KETOGENIC diet
Now dairymen squirt away ketosis. il Farm
J 89:48 Ap '65
KETONES
Electron spin resonance spectroscopy: application to proof of structure of organic
ketones. G. A. Russell and E. R. Talaty.
bibliog il Science 148:1217-18 My 28 '65
See also
Ketogenic diet
KETOSIS. See Ketogenic diet
KETTLE of brains; drama. See Williams,
G. M.
KETTLEWELL, H. B. D.
Insect survival and selection for pattern.
bibliog Science 148:1290-6 Je 4 '65
KEYES, Frances Parkinson
Love letter to Spain. Ladies Home J 82:68-
9+ F '65
KEYNES, John Maynard Keynes, 1st baron
Keynes revolution. por Newsweek 65:66 My 31
'65
New orthodoxy. H. Hazlitt. Newsweek 65:82
Je 21 '65
Slippery path of prosperity. il Bsns W p70-3
Ja 1 '66
We are all Keynesians now. il pors Time
86:64-67B D 31 '65
KEYS. See Locks and keys
KEYS, FLORIDA. See Florida Keys
KEYSERLING, Leon H.
Great society. New Repub 152:11-14 Je 12 '65
Poverty and the economy. Nation 200:615-17
Je 7 '65

about

Diehard on the left. por Duns R 85:41 Je '65
KHABELE, Paseka E.
Book reviews. America 113:188 Ag 21 '65

KHAMA, Seretse
  Walking the tightrope; Bechuanaland's first prime minister. il por Time 85:29 Mr 12 '65
KHAN, Khaibar
  Billion-dollar mystery; with editorial comment. F. J. Cook. il Nation 200:377-8, 380-97 Ap 12 '65
  Iranian aid story: new twists to the mystery. F. J. Cook. Nation 200:550-6 My 24 '65
  Khan game. por Newsweek 65:28 Ap 19 '65
KHAN, Khan Abdul Hameed
  Kashmir debate. Sat R 48:21-2 Jl 17 '65
KHAN, Mohammad Ayub. See Ayub Khan, M.
KHAN, Sadruddin. See Sadruddin Khan
KHANH, Nguyen. See Nguyen Khanh
KHARCHEV, Anatolii Georgievich
  Sex under socialism, E. Pawel. Commentary 40:90+ S '65
KHATCHADOURIAN, Sylvia
  Flagstad's winner. il por Opera N 29:33 Mr 13 '65
KHEEL, Theodore Woodrow
  Kheel: the artist as optimist. por Newsweek 66:78-9 Jl 12 '65
  What makes Teddy Kheel run. A. H. Raskin. il pors N Y Times Mag p52-3+ D 5 '65
KHIOS. See Chios
KHOMAN, Thanat. See Thanat Khoman
KHRUSHCHEV, Nikita Sergeevich
  After the fall. il por Time 85:24 Mr 26 '65
  Cults, coups and collective leaderships. H. R. Swearer. bibliog f il Cur Hist 49:193-200+ O '65
  Dear Nikita; L'Europeo publishes supposed interview with Khrushchev. il Newsweek 65:58 Mr 29 '65
  Khrushchev votes. Commonweal 82:4 Mr 26 '65
  Kremlin mood: strain and anxiety. il por Newsweek 65:31 Mr 29 '65
  One year, two views. R. J. Korengold; L. Volkov. il Newsweek 66:56-7 O 18 '65
  Pensioner's life; interview, ed. by R. J. Korengold. il por Newsweek 65:42+ Ap 19 '65
  Reporter at large. R. Blum. New Yorker 41: 40-2+ Ag 28; 32-6+ S 4; 168+ S 11 '65
  Soviet Union today. il por Sr Schol 86:12-16 F 4 '65
  What the world owes Khrushchev. H. E. Salisbury. il pors N Y Times Mag p 16-17+ Ap 25 '65
KIBBUTZIM. See Collective settlements— Israel
KICK, Judith
  I asked them to draw. Sch Arts 65:21-4 D '65
KICKAPOO. See Beverages
KIDD, Billy
  Bullet in the Rockies. D. Jenkins. il por Sports Illus 22:26-31 Mr 8 '65
KIDD, Charles V.
  Research on research in Venezuela. bibliog Science 149:727-9 Ag 13 '65
KIDD, William Winston
  Killy & the Kidd. il por Time 87:68 Ja 21 '66
KIDDE, Walter, and company
  To reorganize, turn bottom up. il Bsns W p81-2+ Ap 10 '65
KIDDER, Ann
  Woman who stayed. J. Robbins. il pors McCalls 92:96-7+ S '65
KIDNAPING
  Kidnaping for more than money; cases in Colombia. Time 85:44 Mr 19 '65
  Missing the cue; attempt to kidnap L. Firestone. il Time 87:21 Ja 21 '66
  One family's strange journey; Champion family's ordeal. H. Champion. il Life 59: 80-1 Jl 23 '65
  Operation hammer; wave of kidnaping in Colombia. il Newsweek 65:56-7 My 3 '65
  St-Germain caper; Mehdi Ben Barka kidnaped in Paris. Newsweek 66:61-2 N 15 '65
  Shaking the throne; French press points to Gen. M. Oufkir, as instigator of Ben Barka plot. Newsweek 66:39 N 29 '65
  Snatch that failed; L. K. Firestone. il Newsweek 67:31+ Ja 24 '66
    See also
  Brigands and robbers
KIDNEY stones. See Calculi, Urinary
KIDNEYS
  Micropuncture study of inulin absorption in the rat kidney. Y. Gutman and others. il Science 147:753-4 F 12 '65
  Renin production by organ cultures of renal cortex. A. L. Robertson and others. bibliog il Science 149:650-1 Ag 6 '65
    See also
  Urinary organs
  Urine

Diseases
  Plain facts about kidney disease. Todays Health 43:82+ My '65
KIDNEYS, Artificial
  Freezer manufacturer builds a life saver; H. Swenson of Sweden freezer. il Bsns W p88+ Mr 6 '65
KIDNEYS, Transplantation of. See Transplantation of organs, tissues, etc.
KIENHOLZ, Edward
  Beanery built for art. il por Life 60:78-80+ Ja 14 '66
  Beanery; on view at Dwan gallery, New York city. il por Newsweek 66:103-4 D 20 '65
  Crossing the bar. S. Gablik. il por Art N 64:22-5 O '65
KIEPPER, Allan F. and others
  Punched-card votes meet with instant success. Am City 80:110-12 S '65
KIERKEGAARD, Søren Aabye
  Kierkegaard and Socrates. M. W. Hess. Christian Cent 82:736-8 Je 9 '65
KIESLER, Frederick J.
  Jerusalem. Vogue 145:187 My '65
  Kiesler by Kiesler. il Arch Forum 123:64-72 S '65
                about
  Endless search. il por Newsweek 67:60 Ja 10 '66
KIESSEL, William C.
  Wily prisoner of war. Sat R 48:66 O 23 '65
KIESTER, Edwin, Jr
  How to rent a vacation. Redbook 124:46+ Mr '65
  Traveling by book, 1965. Redbook 125:22 Jl '65
KIKER, Douglas
  How Lady Bird watches LBJ's health. Good H 160:96-7+ My '65
KILANDER, H. Frederick
  Adolescents fail on food facts. PTA Mag 59: 7-8 My '65
KILBRACKEN, John Raymond Godley, 3d baron
  Irish time. Horizon 7:42-9 Autumn '65
KILBURN, Kaye H. and Salzano, J. V.
  Respiratory cilia. Science 148:1618-19; 149:1176 Je 18, S 10 '65
KILBURN, Paul D.
  Floras of the tundra. Natur Hist 74:52-9 Ag '65
KILGALLEN, Dorothy
  Newsman in a $500 dress. il por Newsweek 66:68 N 22 '65
  Triple threat. por Time 86:70 N 19 '65
KILGORE, William J.
  Freedom and unity in the Americas; with bibliography. Américas 17:1-4 D '65
KILHAM, Lawrence, and Margolis, George
  Cerebellar disease in cats induced by inoculation of rat virus. bibliog Science 148: 244-6 Ap 9 '65
KILLEN, James S.
  New partner; replacing director of the U.S. aid mission in South Vietnam. il por Newsweek 66:33 Ag 16 '65
  Squaring the circle. il por Newsweek 65:54+ Je 14 '65
KILLENS, John Oliver
  Black man's burden; excerpts. Ebony 20:173-5 Ag '65
  Hollywood in black and white. Nation 201: 157-60 S 20 '65
KILLER whales. See Whales
KILLIAN, James R. Jr
  Lift the human spirit! excerpts from address. por Sat R 48:58-60 My 1 '65
  Science in the State department: a practical imperative; adaptation of address. Bul Atomic Sci 21:12-17 My '65
  Teaching is better than ever. Atlan 216:53-6 D '65
KILLING, Mercy. See Euthanasia
KILMER, Frances Frieseke
  Green Hedges. Horn Bk 41:598-601 D '65
KILMER, Miriam
  Streams deserve to have willows; poem. Horn Bk 41:673 D '65
KILMER, Rosamond
  Books my father read to me. Horn Bk 41: 319-20 Je '65
KILNS
  Workshop: a kiln is built. P. Soldner. il Craft Horiz 25:38-9 Ja '65
    See also
  Cement kilns

KILPATRICK, James Jackson
Conservative prophecy: peace below, tumult above. Harper 230:160-4 Ap '65
Must we lose this freedom? Read Digest 86: 221-2 Ap '65
Must we repeal the Constitution to give the Negro the vote? Nat R 17:319-22, 350+ Ap 20-My 4 '65

about

Spoofing the despots. il por Time 87:47 Ja 21 '66

KILPATRICK, William Heard
Philosophy of the New education; reprint of a 1941 article. Sch & Soc 93:56-8 Ja 23 '65

about

Obituary
  Pub W 187:52 Mr 1 '65
  Sr Schol por 86:sup 1 Mr 11 '65
William Heard Kilpatrick, 1871-1965. F. Parker. bibliog por(p357) Sch & Soc 93: 368-71 O 16 '65

KILRAVEN castle; story. See Crowe, C. T.

KILROY, Jim
Jim Kilroy on steering. Yachting 117:206+ Je '65

KILTS
Kilt complex. C. Hanley. il Horizon 7:30-1 Sum '65

KILVERT, B. Cory, Jr
After the builder left. il Flower Grower 52:34-6 Ap '65
Banish these garden pests. Flower Grower 52: 46-9 My '65
Basic care of the four-cycle engine. il Flower Grower 52:42 Jl '65
Corn, beans, squash. Flower Grower 52:32-4 Jl '65
Get your soil in shape. il Flower Grower 52:44-7 Mr '65
It's easy to prolong the life of a lawn spreader. il Flower Grower 52:48-9 Ap '65
More dahlias for your money. Pop Gard 16: 37 Mr '65
Winner. Flower Grower 52:33-5 D '65

KIM, Il Sung
Change of course for the flying red horse. il por Time 86:45 O 8 '65

KIM, Po Sung
Seventh century Korean observatory. Sky & Tel 29:229-30 Ap '65

KIM, Yong Ik
Book-writing venture. Writer 78:28-30 O '65

KIMBA, Evariste
Kind of progress. por Newsweek 66:48 O 25 '65

KIMBALL, Dexter Simpson
Famous firsts: author of management's bible. por Bsns W p 134+ Ag 14 '65

KIMBALL, Penn
American journalism from essay to assay. Nation 201:72-6 S 20 '65

KIMBALL, Ruth Putnam
Racketty-packetty house; dramatization of story by F. H. Burnett. Plays 24:54, 75-8 My '65
Where is Phronsie Pepper? dramatization of Five little Peppers midway, by M. Sidney. Plays 24:51-9 Mr '65

KIMBERLY-CLARK corporation
Industry combats pollution. G. Hill. Bul Atomic Sci 21:42-3 D '65

KIMES, Charles
On a wing & a prayer. il por Time 86:23-4 Jl 9 '65
Sight few have seen and lived to tell about. il pors Life 59:22-7 Jl 9 '65

KIMNACH, Myron
Huntington botanical gardens, San Marino, Calif. Horticulture 43:34-6+ S '65

KINCAID, Alan
Tracers for shotguns. Outdoor Life 135:118-20 My '65

KIND, Joshua
Art news from Chicago (cont) Art N 64:52 Ap 52-4 Sum; 52+ D '65

KINDERGARTEN
Why kindergarten is so important. il Good H 160:149 F '65
  See also
Montessori method of education

KINDLEBERGER, Charles P.
Integration vs. nationalism in the European economy. Reporter 33:38-40 D 2 '65
Mass migration, then and now. For Affairs 43: 647-58 Jl '65
Trends in international economics. bibliog f Ann Am Acad 358:170-9 Mr '65

KINDNESS
Can we keep on being neighborly? H. Stieve. Farm J 89:C2 S '65

KINETIN
Kinetin-induced chloroplast maturation in cultures of tobacco tissue. D. A. Stetler and W. M. Laetsch. bibliog il Science 149: 1387-8 S 17 '65

KING, Alan
Offend institutions. por Newsweek 66:118 N 15 '65

KING, Alexander
Memoirs of a mouse; story McCalls 92:86-7 S '65
Obituary
  Pub W 188:42 N 29 '65

KING, Cecil Harmsworth
King of England. il por Newsweek 66:112+ N 15 '65

KING, Cecil R.
Excerpt from remarks, January 4, 1965. Cong Digest 44:84+ Mr '65

KING, Elizabeth R. and others
Genesis of the Arctic Ocean Basin. bibliog Science 144:1551-7; 147:1055-6 Je 26 '64, F 26 '65

KING, James
Homecoming; interview, ed. by E. Davidson. por Opera N 30:12 Ja 22 '66

KING, James W. Jr. See Benson, S. W. jt. auth.

KING, Larry L.
Requiem for a west Texas town. Harper 232:46-53 Ja '66
Sugar: down but not quite out. Sports Illus 23:58-66 S 6 '65
Washington's money birds. Harper 231:45-54 Ag '65
Washington's top banana. Nation 201:282-3 O 25 '65

KING, Martin Luther, 1929-
Behind the Selma march. Sat R 48:16-17+ Ap 3 '65
Civil right no. 1: the right to vote. por N Y Times Mag p26-7+ Mr 14 '65
Dreams of brighter tomorrows. por Ebony 20:34-5 Mr '65
Let justice roll down. Nation 200:269-74 Mr 15 '65
Next stop: the North. Sat R 48:33-5+ N 13 '65
Un-Christian Christian. por Ebony 20:76-80 Ag '65

about

American tragedy; state troopers charge marching Negroes at Selma, Ala. il por Newsweek 65:18-21 Mr 22 '65
Atlanta rose to the occasion. Christian Cent 82:164 F 10 '65
Beyond the bridge. P. Good. il Reporter 32: 23-6 Ap 8 '65
Central point. il pors Time 85:23-8 Mr 19 '65
Confusing the cause; civil rights groups U.S. foreign policy. Time 86:20 Jl 16 '65
Crackdown; US policy dissenter. Nation 201: 205-6 O 11 '65
Doctor King and the Paris press. America 113:560 N 13 '65
Doctor King's closed session set the strategy. il pors Life 58:35 Mr 19 '65
50,000 march on Montgomery. S. Booker. il pors Ebony 20:46-8+ My '65
How Martin Luther King won the Nobel peace prize. il pors U S News 58:76-7 F 8 '65
Is Vietnam to become a civil rights issue? U S News 59:12 Jl 19 '65
It looks like a hot summer; with Selma the beginning. il por U S News 58:32-3 Mr 22 '65
King. New Yorker 41:35-7 My 1 '65
King acts for peace. Christian Cent 82:1180 S 29 '65
King comes to Chicago. Christian Cent 82:979 Ag 11 '65
King moves North. il por Time 85:32-3 Ap 30 '65
Letter from Selma. R. Adler. New Yorker 41:121-2+ Ap 10 '65
Letter from the publisher. B. M. Auer. pors Time 85:21 Mr 19 '65
Martin Luther King: who he is. . .what he believes. il pors U S News 58:18 Ap 5 '65
Men behind Martin Luther King. il pors Ebony 20:164-6+ Je '65
No peace for winner of peace prize. il por U S News 58:19 F 1 '65
Now, Dr King's marchers turn north. il por U S News 58:8 My 3 '65
On to Montgomery. il por Newsweek 65:21-2 Mr 29 '65
Rare tribute; civic dinner in Atlanta. il por Time 85:24 F 5 '65
Rebuke to Dr King? Negro official speaks out; excerpts from address, August 19, 1965. G. Weaver. U S News 59:16 Ag 30 '65
Remarkable dinner: Atlanta celebrates Nobel award; with editorial comment. il pors Life 58:4, 34-34A F 12 '65

KING, Martin Luther—About—*Continued*
Search for a new Selma. Newsweek 66:29-30 D 20 '65
Selma campaign. Nat R 17:227 Mr 23 '65
Siege of Selma. Nation 200:154+ F 15 '65
Summer strategy. Newsweek 65:28-9 Ap 12 '65
Tortuous road to Oslo. C. L. Sanders. il pors Ebony 20:36+ Mr '65
Tough years ahead. L. Beachy. il por Newsweek 66:19-20 Ag 30 '65
Victory in jail. il por Time 85:16-17 F 12 '65
Violence of nonviolence. F. S. Meyer. Nat R 17:327 Ap 20 '65
Violence versus non-violence. il Ebony 20:168-9 Ap '65
Why they riot. Nat R 17:178-80 Mr 9 '65
KING, Nicholas
Reporter at large; Watts towers, Los Angeles. C. Trillin. il New Yorker 41:72+ My 29 '65
KING, Seth S.
Singapore's restless Chinese. Reporter 33:20-2 Ag 12 '65
KING, Stella
Housewife at no. 10. N Y Times Mag p43+ F 7 '65
KING, Terry Johnson
Compleat boat. Yachting 118:152 S '65
KING, William C.
Glass-ware patents; William King (cont) A. G. Peterson. il Hobbies 69:72 F '65
KING family
Queen of the little Kings. H. Ehrlich. il Look 29:80-4 Je 29 '65
KING-Anderson bill. See Insurance, Health—United States
KING Lear; drama. See Shakespeare, W.—Plays
KING Merrily's Merry Christmas; story. See Tichenor, T.
KING snakes. See Snakes
KINGDOM of God
See also
Jesus Christ—Kingdom
KINGS PEAK, Utah
Climb up Utah's tallest. il Sunset 135:35-6 Ag '65
KINGSLEY-HEATH, John
Man-eater of Darajani. por Outdoor Life 136:32-5+ D '65
KINGSPORT press, incorporated
NLRB dismisses unfair labor charges against Kingsport. Pub W 188:32-3 Ag 9 '65
Three unions certified in Kingsport strike. Pub W 187:48 Mr 1 '65
Wrong approach; two year strike. C. B. Grannis. Pub W 187:54 Mr 22 '65
KINGSTON, Jeremy
God and the tower and the boy; story. Atlan 216:80-7 O '65
KINGSTON, N.Y, city library
Interning in Kingston. D. J. Sager. il Wilson Lib Bul 40:252-4 N '65
KINGWOOD center. See Gardens—Ohio
KININS. See Peptides
KINMONT, Jill
Never look back in sorrow. K. Baskette. pors Good H 160:66-7+ Ja '65
KINNANE, Mary
Some reflections on graduate school enrollments. Sch & Soc 93:114 F 20 '65
KINNE, Russ
Critics at large. Pop Phot 56:100 Ap '65
Flying photographer. Flying 77:110 S '65
Ten daylight color films & how they perform. Pop Phot 57:68-73+ O '65
KINNE, Sharon
I'm just an ordinary girl. P. Hamill and D. Weber. il pors Sat Eve Post 238:91-7 S 25 '65
KINNEAR, Lynn, and Kinnear, Willis
Confusing rock. Nat Parks Mag 39:17-19 N '65
KINNEAR, Willis. See Kinnear, L. jt. auth.
KINNELL, Galway
Fossils; poem. New Yorker 41:58 O 16 '65
Mystic river; poem. Poetry 106:53-69 Ap '65
about
Vision, celebration, and testimony. M. Van Duyn. Poetry 105:264-5 Ja '65
KINNEY, Cle. See Kinney, J. jt. auth.
KINNEY, Jean, and Kinney, Cle
Newborn is a picture star. Parents Mag 40:62-3 F '65
KINNEY service corporation
Trojan horse. Newsweek 66:74 Jl 5 '65
KINO, Eusebio Francisco
Kino in bronze; statue in Capitol building, Washington, D.C. America 112:277 F 27 '65

KINSOLVING, Arthur
Morals on the campus. NEA J 54:23-4 Ap '65
KINTNER, E. E.
Atomic sub no. 1. N Y Times Mag p30+ F 21 '65
KINTNER, Robert Edmonds
Broadcasting and the news. Harper 230:49-55 Ap '65 (to be cont)
Televising the real world. Harper 230:94-6+ Je '65
Television and the world of politics. Harper 230:121-3+ My; 231:8 Jl '65
about
Man who had it made. por Newsweek 66:94 D 20 '65
KINTNER, William R.
Dialectic of force. Sat R 48:29-30 Je 26 '65
KINZER, H. M.
(ed) See Uelsmann, J. I like to present a problematical situation, and let the viewer come to grips with it
KINZUA DAM. See Dams
KIPNIS, Igor
Landowska on music. Am Rec G 31:1012-14 Je '65
Mendelssohn revisited. Am Rec G 31:888+ My '65
about
Again on Epic. J. W. Barker. il por Am Rec G 31:1135 Ag '65
KIPPHARDT, Heinar
In the case of J. Robert Oppenheimer. Criticism Vogue 146:296-8+ S 1 '65
KIRBY, George
George Kirby: mammoth of mimicry. il pors Ebony 20:57-60+ Je '65
KIRCHENTAG. See Religious conferences
KIRCHER, Henry W. See Heed, W. B. jt. auth.
KIRCHWEY, Freda
Personal note. por Nation 201:27-35 S 20 '65
KIRK, David L. See Moscona, A. A. jt. auth.
KIRK, Donald
Why China leaves Hong Kong alone. Reporter 33:31-2 S 23 '65
KIRK, Florence F.
Boy called funny face. Read Digest 87:93-7 O '65
KIRK, John T.
Sources of some American regional furniture. Antiques 88:790-8 D '65 (to be cont)
KIRK, Kathleen L. and Bitterman, M. E.
Probability-learning by the turtle. bibliog Science 148:1484-5 Je 11 '65
KIRK, Lucile D.
Good looks. See issues of Parents' magazine and better homemaking
KIRK, Robert N.
Educating slum children in London. Sch & Soc 93:180-2 Mr 20 '65
Social service projects in English schools. Sch & Soc 93:476-7 D 11 '65
KIRK, Russell
From the academy. See issues of National review
KIRK, Ruth
Olympic reverie. il Nat Parks Mag 39:4-7 My '65
KIRKLAND, Douglas
Marilyn Monroe. il Pop Phot 58:141-2+ Ja '66
KIRKLEY, Henry B.
Fluorescent light fixture design. il Horticulture 43:18-19+ N '65
KIRKPATRICK, John
I want to make money, not records; ed. by J. Bickers. Farm J 89:34-5+ Je '65
KIRKUS, Virginia, service, incorporated
Best-sellers, bombs, and Q tips; Virginia Kirkus book service. D. Dempsey. Sat R 48:30-1 Ag 28 '65
KIRKWOOD, Robert Campbell
Changing world of Woolworth. T. J. Murray. il por Duns R 86:46-7+ N '65
KIRSCH, Robert R.
Case of the busy bookwright. N Y Times Mag p89+ Mr 21 '65
Custodians, eunuchs, and lovers; excerpts from address, November 2, 1964. por Wilson Lib Bul 39:647-50 Ap '65
KIRSCHENMANN, Fred
Boosting Bushnell. Christian Cent 82:176 F 10 '65
KIRST, Hans Hellmut
Germany '45: the day the Americans came. N Y Times Mag p26-7+ My 2 '65
KIRSTEIN, George
Personal note. por Nation 201:18-21 S 20 '65
Statements to our readers. Nation 202:3 Ja 3 '66
KIRSTEIN, Lincoln
Poetry chronicle. R. Howard. Poetry 106:296-7 Jl '65

KIRSTEN, Dorothy
Stars at home. il pors Opera N 29:14-16 Mr 27 '65
KIRSTEN Flagstad memorial fund. See Memorial funds
KIRTLAND, Susanne
Fashions for castle hopping. Holiday 38:78-83 N '65
KIRTLAND'S warblers. See Warblers
KIRTON, Kenneth T. and Hafs, H. D.
Sperm capacitation by uterine fluid or beta-amylase in vitro. bibliog Science 150:618-19 O 29 '65
KIRVAN, John J.
Newman apostolate is not enough. por Cath World 201:308-11+ Ag '65
KIRWAN, Judy
America's most wanted students. G. B. Leonard. il pors Look 29:46-51 Jl 27 '65
KISER, Jack
Harness racing. Sports Illus 22:83-4 Je 14 '65
KISHI, Nobusuke
Political movements in Japan. For Affairs 44:90-9 O '65
KISMET; musical comedy. See Musical comedies, revues, etc.—Criticisms, plots, etc.
KISS me Kate; musical comedy. See Musical comedies, revues, etc.—Criticisms, plots, etc.
KISSIMMEE, Fla.
On-site meter testing. C. B. Tyson. il Am City 80:113 S '65
KISSING disease. See Mononucleosis
KISSINGER, Henry A.
Illusionist: why we misread de Gaulle. Harper 230:69-70+ Mr '65
Price of German unity. Reporter 32:12-17 Ap 22 '65
KISTER, Kenneth
Yank in Sherwood Forest. bibliog por Library J 90:4914-20 N 15 '65
KISTLER, Geraldine A.
Safari! Sr Schol 86:sup 13-14 Mr 18 '65
KIT boatbuilding. See Boatbuilding
KIT boats. See Boatbuilding
KIT building
Kits, kits, kits! il Changing T 19:46 My '65
KITAGAWA, Daisuke
Comparative missiology. Christian Cent 82:1323 O 27 '65
Faulty identification. Christian Cent 83:50 Ja 12 '66
Ubiquitous frontier. Christian Cent 82:214+ F 17 '65
KITAJ, Ronald B.
Art. M. Kozloff. Nation 200:263-4 Mr 8 '65
Art galleries; exhibition at the Marlborough-Gerson. R. M. Coates. New Yorker 40:132+ F 13 '65
Literary collage. il por Time 85:72 F 19 '65
KITCHEN cabinets
Bring glamour to kitchen cabinets. il Bet Hom & Gard 43:70-1 Ap '65
Job-proven ideas for better kitchen cabinets. R. S. Wilkes. il Pop Sci 186:152-4 F '65
Kitchen storage. il House & Gard 128:92-5 Jl '65
Kitchen storage, more than meets the eye. il Bet Hom & Gard 43:93+ My '65
KITCHEN closets. See Closets
KITCHEN furniture
Remodel your kitchen this easy way. R. Charles il. Parents Mag 40:71-3+ O '65
Today's wonderful, workable kitchens, and how to plan one into your new or present house! H. A. Dawson and G. V. Young. il Bet Hom & Gard 43:62-73+ Mr '65
What a good mixing center should have. il Bet Hom & Gard 43:104 F '65
See also
Kitchen cabinets
KITCHEN garbage grinders. See Refuse grinders
KITCHEN gardening. See Vegetable gardening
KITCHEN knives. See Knives
KITCHEN storage. See Storage in the home
KITCHEN utensils
Bride's first kitchen; shower gifts. M. Davidson. il Ladies Home J 82:30+ Je '65
Good cooks tell us their favorite tools. il Sunset 134:108-9 Mr '65
How to get out of the kitchen after dinner. il Redbook 126:76-7+ N '65
How to make cooking a carnival. il McCalls 92:48+ F '65
Pots and pans; non-stick cookware. il Consumer Bul 48:43+ My '65

Shopping center for cookware. il Good H 161:166-7 Ag '65
Western kitchen. See issues of Sunset
See also
Cookie press
Knives
KITCHEN ventilators. See Ventilators
KITCHENS
All set for action. il Good H 161:114-15 S '65
Architect's notes on kitchen and bathroom planning. P. M. Bolton. il Arch Rec 137:15-16+ mid-My '65
Bright ideas for borrowing. il House & Gard 128:194-5 O '65
Deeper colors move into the kitchen. il House & Gard 127:154-7 Mr '65
Doll house kitchen; storage on display stretches the available space. il House & Gard 127:200 My '65
Eating areas that don't eat up space! il Bet Hom & Gard 43:106 O '65
Five on one side, the cook on the other. il Sunset 134:126 Ap '65
For American independents. M. Davidson. il Ladies Home J 82:78-80 Jl '65
Get more kitchen from your old farm home. J. Holmstrand. il Suc Farm 63:112-13 Ap '65
His office and her kitchen. J. Gillies. il Farm J 89:86 Mr '65
How to control noise in your kitchen. il House & Gard 127:152-3 Ap '65
How to make your kitchen a personal joy. il House & Gard 128:68-81 Ag '65
How to survive a kitchen remodeling. Bet Hom & Gard 43:106-7 Ap '65
In this family kitchen almost everybody cooks. il Sunset 136:70 Ja '66
Inside kitchen that's open and airy. il Sunset 134:94 F '65
Kitchen for big family meals. J. Gillies. il Farm J 89:98-9 O '65
Kitchen for people who entertain big! H. A. Dawson. il Bet Hom & Gard 43:44 Je '65
Kitchen of anyone's dream. il Good H 160:112-13+ Je '65
Kitchen of surprises for families with a passion for cruising and fishing. il House & Gard 129:122-9 Ja '66
Making the kitchen a decorator's dream; Kelvinator originals. il Bsns W p 116-17+ N 20 '65
New kitchen the painless way! G. V. Young. il Bet Hom & Gard 43:76-7 Ap '65
New materials bring elegance to a kitchen. il Am Home 68:56-7 Mr '65
New pantry kitchen, more than meets the eye. M. Davidson. il Ladies Home J 83:78-9+ Ja '66
Not an inch wasted. J. Gillies. il Farm J 89:62-3 Ag '65
Now they have an open or shut kitchen. il Sunset 134:123 My '65
Provincial, pretty, and practical! il McCalls 92:122-3 Mr '65
Quest for a better kitchen. il House & Gard 127:108-11+ F '65
Remodel your kitchen this easy way. R. Charles. il Parents Mag 40:71-3+ O '65
Same space: two kitchens. il House & Gard 127:140-3 My '65
So you plan to remodel your farm kitchen. J. LemMon. il Suc Farm 63:81-5 O '65
Spain: new warmth for the kitchen. M. Davidson. il Ladies Home J 82:74-6 F '65
Successful farming family remodels again. J. LemMon. il Suc Farm 63:72-3 Je '65
They didn't have to do very much. il Sunset 135:154 O '65
This farm family needed a good kitchen. J. LemMon. il Suc Farm 63:64-5 Ag '65
This farm family planned their own kitchen, too. il Suc Farm 63:116-17 S '65
This kitchen means business. il Good H 160:130-1 Mr '65
Three kitchens with character. il Good H 162:100-4+ Ja '66
Today's wonderful, workable kitchens, and how to plan one into your new or present house! H. A. Dawson and G. V. Young. il Bet Hom & Gard 43:62-73+ Mr '65
Very distinctive small kitchen. il Bet Hom & Gard 43:118 S '65
Well-planned kitchen at low cost. J. Gillies. il Farm J 89:108-9 Ap '65
Why settle for a bad house? il Bet Hom & Gard 43:63-5+ N '65
KITES
Go fly a fishing kite. W. Yolen. il Todays Health 43:58-61+ Mr '65
Jet-fighter kite. R. L. Clough, jr. il Pop Sci 186:134-5 Mr '65
Kites; work by students of Herron school of art. il Design 66:40-1 Mr '65
Letter from Stan Delaplane. S. Delaplane. Todays Health 43:3 F '65
Season for kites. New Yorker 41:44-5 S 18 '65

KITES (birds)
Nature note; Everglade kite. Sci N L 88:142
Ag 28 '65
KITMAN, Marvin
My wife, the critic. Sat Eve Post 238:18 My
22 '65
Should women give men the vote? Sat Eve
Post 238:20 Jl 17 '65
To heck in a handcar. Sat Eve Post 238:16
D 18 '65
KITT PEAK national observatory. See Astronomical observatories
KITTLER, Glenn D.
They rebuild broken faces. Read Digest 87:
195-6+ S '65
KITTO, H. D. F.
Summer in Greece. Sat R 48:75-6+ F 20 '65
KIWANIS clubs
Whitewash in Whitewater; letter to the
editor. S. D. Robertson; reply. D. Goddard.
Library J 90:414 F 1 '65
KLABER, Doretta
How to succeed with saxifrages. il Horticulture 43:16-17 Ag '65
KLASCHIK, Lothar H.
Subliminal approach to illustration. Design
67:6-11 N '65
KLAUSLER, Alfred P.
Architecture's servant function. Christian
Cent 82:680-1 My 26 '65
Bedsheet terrorists. Christian Cent 82:967 Ag
4 '65
Jew as protagonist. Christian Cent 82:941 Jl
28 '65
Russia and religion. Christian Cent 82:276+
Mr 3 '65
Scandal of particularity. Christian Cent 82:
563-6 Ap 28 '65
KLAUSMEIER, Herbert J.
Research and development center for learning and re-education. Sch & Soc 93:182-3
Mr 20 '65
KLAW, Barbara
James Thurber, doodler extraordinary. Am
Heritage 16:56-7 F '65
KLAW, Spencer
Harvard's degree in the higher materialism.
Esquire 64:103+ O '65
Is Ogilvy a genius? Fortune 71:142-3+ Ap '65
KLEBE, Giselher
Jacobovski and the colonel. Criticism
Opera N il 30:31-2 D 18 '65
KLEE, Manfred R. and others
Cross-correlation analysis of electroencephalographic potentials and slow membrane transients. bibliog Science 147:519-21
Ja 29 '65
KLEE, Paul
At the feet of Klee. H. Kramer. il Reporter
32:56+ F 11 '65
Fire and water: obscurities in the late Paul
Klee; exhibition in Basel. W. Ueberwasser.
il Art N 64:40-1+ Sum '65
KLEIN, Carole. See Lazar, E. jt. auth.
KLEIN, Cornelis, Jr. See Frondel, C. jt. auth.
KLEIN, David
College & careers. Seventeen 24:104-5 Ap;
216-17 My; 166-7 Je; 20+ Jl; 30+ Ag; 246-
8 S; 56+ O; 20+ N; 32+ D '65
How to run away from home. Seventeen
24:150-1+ Mr '65
Sometime during your teen years someone is
likely to urge you to drink: what will you
say? Seventeen 24:140-1+ S '65
What you can do for human rights in your
own home town. Seventeen 24:130-1+ My '65
—and Haddon, William, Jr
Prospects for safer autos. Consumer Rep
30:176-81 Ap '65
KLEIN, Eloise
Funny war; poem. America 113:441 O 16 '65
KLEIN, Eugene Victor
King of intermissions. il por Time 86:93-4
Jl 9 '65
KLEIN, Herbert E.
New challenger to electronics. Duns R 85:48-
50 Je '65
Numerical control: from class to mass market.
Duns R 86:34-5+ Ag '65
KLEIN, Howard
At white heat. Opera N 30:24-5 D 4 '65
Horowitz method: listen and sing. N Y Times
Mag p32-3+ My 9 '65
KLEIN, Lawrence R.
Coat of many colors. Mo Labor R 88:749-51 Jl
'65
KLEIN, LeRoy. See Bensusan, H. B. jt. auth.
KLEIN, Martin J.
Books. Sci Am 212:129-32+ Mr '65
Einstein, specific heats, and the early quantum theory; address, December 29, 1964.
bibliog Science 148:173-80 Ap 9 '65

KLEIN, Woody
Housing the poor. Commonweal 82:377-9 Je
11 '65
KLEINSORGE, Paul L. and Smith, R. E.
Compulsory arbitration: a broad view. bibliog f Cur Hist 49:97-105+ Ag '65
KLEMENT, Alfred W. Jr. See Bierly, E. W.
jt. auth.
KLEMPERER, Otto
Decades of Klemperer. N. Cardus. il pors Sat
R 48:45-7+ My 29 '65
Early days with Klemperer. W. Steinberg.
il pors Sat R 48:47-8+ My 29 '65
KLEPPER, Dan
Bring a buck to horn. Field & S 70:68-9+
O '65
KLICK, Clifford C.
Point defects in insulators. bibliog Science
150:451-6 O 22 '65
KLIEWER, Warren
Dramatic perception in the liturgy. Christian
Cent 82:459-61 Ap 14 '65
KLIMT, Gustav
Women of Klimt and Schiele. A. Werner.
il Reporter 32:44+ F 25 '65
KLINCK, Richard E.
Teaching the fifth essence. NEA J 54:38-9 N
'65
    about
Johnson presents award to Teacher of the
year. il por Sr Schol 86:sup 1 My 6 '65
Richard Klinck: teacher of the year. J.
Poppy. il pors Look 29:47-50+ Ap 20 '65
KLINE, Charles H.
(ed) Case of the diversification dilemma. por
Harvard Bsns R 43:12-14+ My '65
KLINE, Nancy Ann
Children abroad. il Yachting 118:148-9 S '65
KLING, Arthur, and Orbach, J.
Stump-tailed macaque; a promising laboratory
primate. bibliog Science 139:45-6; 148:1173
Ja 4 '63, My 28 '65
KLIORE, Arvydas, and others
Occultation experiment: results of the first
direct measurement of Mars's atmosphere
and ionosphere. bibliog Science 149:1243-8
S 10 '65
KLOETZLI, Walter
Church and city. Christian Cent 82:711 Je 2
'65
KLUCKHUHN, Fred H.
Heating and cooling for housing. Arch Rec
138:211-12 O '65
KLUGE, John Werner
Metromedia's creative financier. J. F. Olesky.
il por Duns R 86:49-52 D '65
KLUGER, Richard
Pied Piper of Davis, California. New Repub
153:30-1 Ag 7 '65
Scapegoat in need. Harper 231:126+ O '65
Tumultuous indictment of man. Harper 230:
110+ Je '65
KLUMPH, Alfred
Crisis at Coral Creek. Outdoor Life 136:24-7+
Ag '65
KNAKE, Ellery
Report on postemergence weed killers for
corn. Suc Farm 63:79 Mr '65
—and Reece, F. N.
Report on flame cultivation; questions and
answers. Suc Farm 63:95 Mr '65
KNAPP, Pauline Park Wilson. See Osborn,
D. K. jt. auth.
KNAPP, Robert P. Jr
Of war, time, and generals. Reporter 34:49-53
Ja 13 '66
KNAPP school libraries project
Allisonville shapes up; Knapp project school
works toward ALA standards. D. L. Barnes.
il Library J 90:942-4 F 15 '65
In full swing: end of Knapp project's second
year, start of Phase III. P. Sullivan. il
Library J 90:2328-30 My 15 '65
Knapp school libraries project; address, July
1965. M. V. Gaver. il(cover) ALA Bul 59:
806-9 O '65
Three high schools chosen for Knapp foundation grants. Library J 90:2342 My 15 '65
KNAPPERTSBUSCH, Hans
Obituary
Opera N 30:33 D 18 '65
KNATHS, Karl
Knaths and Morris in Washington. F.
Getlein. New Repub 152:30-1 My 15 '65
KNEBEL, Fletcher
Changing face of southern politics. Look 29:
50+ N 16 '65
GOP attacks the John Birch society. Look
29:74-6 D 28 '65
Hubert Humphrey: advance man for the
Great society. Look 29:80+ Ap 6 '65

KNEE
Knee & the board; surfer's knobs. il Time 85:75 My 7 '65

Surgery
$400,000 knee. il Time 85:53 F 5 '65
Joint for next season; J. Namath's knee operation; Lenox Hill hospital. G. Cant. il Sports Illus 22:38-41 F 8 '65

KNELLER, George F.
Education in modern and primitive societies; excerpt from Educational anthropology. bibliog f Sch & Soc 93:158-63 Mr 6 '65

KNESSE, Allen V.
New directions in water management. Bul Atomic Sci 21:2-8 My '65

KNETSCH, Jack L. See Davis, R. K. jt. auth.

KNICKERBOCKER, Conrad
Life book review. Life 58:6+ Ap 9 '65; 60:8+ Ja 14 '66
No one's in charge. Life 59:37-8+ D 24 '65
Not wanted on the voyage; story. Esquire 63:104 Je '65
Spies who come in from next door. Life 58:13 Ap 30 '65

KNICKERBOCKER, Suzy, pseud. See Mehle, A.

KNIEF, Christopher
Beauty life: girl into model. il pors Mlle 60:194-7 Mr '65

KNIFE sharpening. See Sharpening

KNIFE; story. See Gill, B.

KNIGHT, Arthur
Literary life in Las Vegas. Sat R 48:25 N 6 '65
Meanwhile, back in Hollywood. Sat R 48:21 D 25 '65
SR goes to the movies. See issues of Saturday review

KNIGHT, Charles A. and Knight, N. C.
Negative crystals in ice: a method for growth. bibliog Science 150:1819-21 D 31 '65

KNIGHT, Nancy C. See Knight, C. A. jt. auth.

KNIGHT, O. A.
Another union changes the guard. il por Bsns W p124+ Jl 17 '65

KNIGHT, Pamela
Design for sport. Sports Illus 22:68-9 Je 14; 23:64-6 N 8 '65

KNIGHTS and dragons; story. See Spencer, E.

KNIGHTS of Columbus
Knights and windmills. il Newsweek 66:56-7 Ag 30 '65

KNIGHTS of the square table; drama. See Dias, E. J.

KNIPHOFIA. See Torch lilies

KNIT goods
Knitwear for school togs. M. B. Keiser. il Parents Mag 40:28+ S '65
More girl than sweater; newest knitted look. il Life 58:59-60 My 14 '65

KNITTING
How to knit our chin-chin cover cap & mittens. il Good H 162:122 Ja '66
Mary Walker Phillips. A. Adams. il Craft Horiz 25:24-7 Ja '65

KNITWEAR. See Knit goods

KNIVES
Carving path to a top market spot; electric knife as sales leader. il Bsns W p78+ Ja 15 '66
Electric carving knife keeps the peace. Am Home 68:77 Mr '65
Electric carving knives. il Changing T 19:38 D '65
Electric slicing knives. il Consumer Rep 30:296-8 Je '65
Heated knife for frozen foods; Osrow electric heat knife. il Consumer Rep 30:110-11 Mr '65
Knife know-how. il Bet Hom & Gard 43:136-7 My '65
Le-Mir miracle kitchen knife. Consumer Bul 48:32 Ap '65

KNOEDEL, Jerome
It is now the hour... America 113:666-9 N 27 '65

KNOEDLER company. See Art dealers

KNOEPFLE, John
Mother of the hero; poem. Commonweal 81:642 F 12 '65

KNOLL, Erwin
Revolt of the professors. Sat R 48:60-1+ Je 19 '65
Ten years of deliberate speed. por Am Ed 1:1-3 D '64
—and Witcover, Jules
Fighting poverty and city hall. Reporter 32:19-22 Je 3 '65
—See Witcover, J. jt. auth.

KNOPF, Alfred A.
Alfred Knopf keepsake. W. Caxton, jr. il Am Artist 29:38-43+ S '65
Golden anniversary of excellence; with reminiscences about their illustrious authors. il pors Life 59:37-8+ Jl 23 '65
How Alfred Knopf saw his authors. M. R. Weiss. il Sat R 48:26-8 Je 12 '65
Keepsake for Alfred A. Knopf. P. A. Bennett. il Pub W 188:72-4+ Ag 9 '65

KNOPF, Alfred, incorporated
Borzoi anniversary marked at Knopf dinner. il Pub W 188:36 N 8 '65
Fifty years of the Borzoi. il Pub W 187:48-54 F 1 '65
Golden anniversary. il Newsweek 65:106-7+ My 17 '65
Golden anniversary of excellence. il Life 59:37-8 Jl 23 '65

KNOTS, Macramé. See Macramé

KNOTS and splices
Back splice; you don't stop at the bitter end. G. S. Smith. il Motor B 115:57 Je '65
How to tie a knot! E. Horan. il Yachting 117:236-7 Ap '65

KNOTT, Lawson Beasley, 1912-
Lawson B. Knott, jr. named administrator of General services. Arch Rec 138:365+ S '65

KNOTT, Sarah Gertrude
Many songs, many dances. Américas 17:27-33 F '65

KNOTTING. See Macramé

KNOWLAND park zoo, Oakland, Calif. See Zoological gardens

KNOWLEDGE
See also
Learning and scholarship

KNOWLEDGE, Theory of
Discipline that needs some. Life 59:4 S 24 '65
See also
Education—Philosophy
Objectivity

KNOWLES, Everett
Good right arm; fracture of reattached arm. il por Newsweek 66:78 Ag 9 '65

KNOWLES, Ruth Sheldon
They lead small business to bigger markets. Read Digest 87:107-10 O '65

KNOWLTON, Kenneth C.
Computer-produced movies. Science 150:1116-20 N 26 '65

KNOWLTON, Murray
Cook in any storm. Motor B 115:44-5+ My '65

KNOWLTON, Robert A.
After all these years; story. Good H 160:90-1 Mr '65
Journey for love; story. Good H 161:82-3 D '65
Man who learned to listen; story. Good H 161:72-3 S '65
North of Boston; story. McCalls 92:114-15 F '65
Second nature; story. Good H 160:56-7 Ja '65
Someone to care; story. Good H 161:70-1 Ag '65

KNOX, Rawle
Ayub's basic democracy. Reporter 32:34-6 F 11 '65

KNOX, William T.
Changing role of libraries; address, July 1965. por ALA Bul 59:720-5 S '65

KNUDSEN, Edwin J.
Ice boating: watch it grow. See issues of Motor boating
Midwest watch. See issues of Motor boating to May 1965

KNUDSEN, Semon
Pontiac's chiefs. por Motor T 17:76-9 F '65

KNUDSEN, Thomas W.
Batiks. il Sch Arts 64:3-8 My '65

KOBAYASHI, Koji
Nippon electric does it the U.S. way. il pors Bsns W p70-2+ D 11 '65

KOBLER, John
Four deadly minutes. Sat Eve Post 238:42-4 N 6 '65
Torment of Alberto Giacometti. Sat Eve Post 238:68-71 Jl 31 '65

KOBRIN, Jerry
Pocketful of golumpkis. Sat Eve Post 238:22 N 20 '65

KOÇ, Vehbi
Who's who in foreign business. il por Fortune 72:58 Ag '65

KOCH, Albert
Science in action: hoaxes and half-truths. R. Silverberg. Natur Hist 74:64-5 Mr '65

KOCH, Christopher
Enemy: 20,000 missions later. Newsweek 66:44-8 O 11 '65

about
In Hanoi a show of fists by Ho & co. il Life 59:34-5 O 1 '65

KOCH, Kenneth
  From Seine; poem. Poetry 106:70-80 Ap '65
KOCH, Stephen
  Outgrowing Germany. Nation 200:484-6 My
  3 '65
KODA, Keisaburo
  Closing the books. Newsweek 66:50-1 O 18
  '65
KODACHROME films. See Photography—Films
KODAK Bimat process. See Photography—Developing and developers
KODAK recording film 2475. See Photography—Films
KODÁLY, Zoltán
  Lives of Kodály. A. L. Ringer. il pors Sat R
  48:33-4 Jl 31 '65
KODL, Francis
  What new mothers worry about. Parents
  Mag 40:52-3+ D '65
KOEGLER, Horst
  Great opera houses: Berlin. Opera N 29:26-
  30 Mr 13 '65
KOEHLER, Charles R.
  Cape Cod's Marconi station site. il Nat Parks
  Mag 39:18 S '65
KOEHLER, Walter O.
  Truth about multigrade oils. Pop Sci 188:
  106-8+ Ja '66
KOEHLER, Wolfgang
  Auf wiedersehen; departure from Washington.
  il pors Am For 71:56 S '65
KOEHRING company
  Koehring co. digs out its share. il Bsns W
  p 148-50 D 4 '65
KOEMPEL, Leslie
  Speaking out. por Sat Eve Post 238:10+ F
  13 '65; Same abr. Read Digest 86:55-7 My
  '65
KOENIG, Louis W.
  Hard limits of government by consensus.
  N Y Times Mag p26-7+ Mr 7 '65
  Through myth, smoke, and scandal. Sat R
  48:43 Je 12 '65
  View from Capitol Hill. Sat R 48:32 Jl 10 '65
KOENIG, Richard E.
  Rebuking existentialism. Christian Cent 82:
  1098+ S 8 '65
KOERNER, Henry
  Letter from the publisher. B. M. Auer. il por
  Time 86:21 O 22 '65
KOFRANEK, Anton M.
  Help your lawn spring back to life. Am Home
  68:34 Ap '65
KOFYAR (native race) See Nigeria—Native
  races
KÖHLER, J. W. L.
  Stirling refrigeration cycle; with biographical
  sketch. Sci Am 212:20, 119-25+ bibliog(p
  160) Ap '65
KOHLER company
  Eleven years later. Newsweek 66:56-7 D 27 '65
KOHLER strike. See Strikes—United States
KOHN, Hans
  Belief in blood. Nation 200:456-8 Ap 26 '65
KOHN, Pamela
  Book shop in Aurora, Ill: personality plus.
  Pub W 187:60-3 My 10 '65
KOHNER, Frederick
  Writing for the in-betweenster. Writer 78:
  22-4 Ag '65
KOKOSCHKA, Oskar
  Psychological document in sadness; portrait
  of O. Kokoschka by H. Erfurth. G. M.
  Mayer. Pop Phot 56:50-1+ F '65
KOLBE, Helmuth
  Notes from our correspondents. K. Blaukopf.
  Hi Fi 15:18+ Ag '65
KOLCUM, Edward H.
  Voskhod 2 expands Soviet space lead. Avia-
  tion W 82:23 Mr 22 '65
KOLESKE, Joseph V. See Faucher, J. A. jt.
  auth.
KOLFF, Willem J.
  Artificial heart inside the body; with
  biographical sketch. Sci Am 213:14, 38-46
  bibliog(p 142) N '65
KOLKWITZIA. See Beauty bush
KOLLAS, Joseph E.
  Ghosts of Gnarl Ridge. Am For 71:66-8 My '65
KOLM, Henry H. and Freeman, A. J.
  Intense magnetic fields; with biographical
  sketches. Sci Am 212:18, 66-74+ Ap; 213:6
  Jl '65
KOLODIN, Irving
  Education on the Menuhin plan. Sat R 48:
  57-8+ N 27 '65
  Future of the performing arts. Sat R 48:
  21-2+ Mr 13 '65
  Music to my ears. See issues of Saturday
  review
  Philharmonic in the park. Sat R 48:56-7 S 11
  '65
KOMAN, Bill
  Tormented life of a pro linebacker. J. At-
  water. il pors Sat Eve Post 238:26-31 D 18
  '65

KOMIDAR, Joseph S.
  Tufts steps down a slope. Library J 90:5189-
  91 D 1 '65
KOMINZ, David R.
  Mercurial-induced transformation of myosin
  prevented by adenosine triphosphate and
  pyrophosphate. bibliog Science 149:1374-5 S
  17 '65
KOMPFNER, R.
  Optical communications. bibliog Science 150:
  149-55 O 8 '65
KONDRA, Victor
  Quickie saw guide for cutting big panels. Pop
  Sci 187:144-5 O '65
KONDRASHIN, Kiril
  Moscow philharmonic; New York concerts. A.
  Chasins. por Hi Fi 16:131+ Ja '66
  Pursuing the U.S. ideal. por Time 86:71 O 29
  '65
KONECKY, Edith
  Chastity of Magda Wickwire; story. Sat Eve
  Post 238:58-60 Jl 31 '65
KONER, Pauline
  Old and new, new and old. il pors Dance
  Mag 39:51 Ag '65
KONINGSBERGER, Hans
  Poland's new far west. Harper 231:86-93 Jl
  '65
KONI-Omega cameras. See Cameras
KONVITZ, Milton R.
  Definition of a nation. Sat R 49:37 Ja 15 '66
el-KONY, Mohamed Awad
  United Nations commemoration address,
  June 26, 1965. UN Mo Chron 2:163-5 Jl '65
KOOB, C. Albert
  Catholic high schools today; Scholastic
  teacher interview. por Sr Schol 86:sup29-31
  Ap 15 '65
  Washington report; interview, ed. by J.
  Lloyd. Sr Schol 86:sup 13 Ap 15 '65
KOONTZ, Elizabeth
  Education's lady on the go. il pors Ebony 21:
  29-32+ D '65
  Six weeks in Russia. NEA J 54:51 My '65
KOPAL, Zdeněk
  Luminescence of the moon; with biographical
  sketch. Sci Am 212:18, 28-37 bibliog(p 150)
  My '65
KOPECKI, Ernest
  Stainless steel surprises. Motor B 115:56-9
  My '65
KOPIT, Arthur
  Day the whores came out to play tennis.
  Criticism
    Nation 200:374 Ap 5 '65
    New Repub 152:24 Ap 10 '65
    New Yorker 41:146-7 Mr 27 '65
    Newsweek 65:82 Mr 29 '65
    Time il 85:58+ Mr 26 '65
    Vogue 145:142 My '65
  Sing to me through open windows. Criticism
    Nation 200:373-4 Ap 5 '65
    New Repub 152:24 Ap 10 '65
    Newsweek 65:82 Mr 29 '65
KOPKIND, Andrew D.
  Alabama unbound. New Repub 153:12-16 N
  27; 36 D 18 '65
  Baseball, pure and undefiled. New Repub
  153:9-10 Ag 7 '65
  Birth of a bill. New Repub 152:11-13 My
  15 '65
  Boycotting Alabama. New Repub 152:11-13
  Ap 17 '65
  Bureaucracy's long arm. New Repub 153:19-
  22 Ag 21 '65
  Connally's Texas. New Repub 153:9-12 N 20
  '65
  Federal subsidies to segregated hospitals.
  New Repub 152:8 My 22 '65
  FDR's prophet to gloom. New Repub 152:
  25-6 F 20 '65
  Hooray for the red, white and blue. New
  Repub 152:23-4 My 8 '65
  Modern times in Phoenix. New Repub 153:
  14-16 N 6 '65
  New immigration policy. New Repub 152:15-
  16 F 27 '65
  New radicals in Dixie. New Repub 152:13-16
  Ap 10; 34 My 1 '65
  Of, by and for the poor. New Repub 152:15-19
  Je 19; 153:29-30 Jl 3 '65
  Politics of avoiding politics. New Repub 152:
  20-2 Mr 20 '65
  Power of prayer. New Repub 152:19-20 Mr 6
  '65
  Race rule in Washington. New Repub 152:
  18-20 Mr 27 '65
  Radicals on the march. New Repub 153:15-19
  D 11 '65
  Republicans at sea. New Repub 153:12-14 S
  25; 37 O 9 '65
  Running wild. New Repub 153:15-19 O 30 '65
  Selma. New Repub 152:7-9 Mr 20 '65
  Teach-in on Vietnam. New Repub 152:15-16
  My 29 '65

KOPP, Larry J.
Identification test for bird enthusiasts. il Nat Parks Mag 39:22-3+ My '65

KOPP, Leonard L.
We chose three-stage sewage purification. Am City 80:89-91 D '65

KOPPETT, Leonard
Busch, beer and baseball. N Y Times Mag p32-3+ Ap 11 '65

KOPROWSKI, Hilary, and others
New science city in Siberia. il Science 149: 947-9 Ag 27 '65

KORATRON company
Crease & increase. il Time 86:88 D 17 '65

KORBONSKI, Andrzej
U.S. policy in east Europe. bibliog f Cur Hist 48:129-34+ Mr '65

KORDAN, Herbert A.
Fluorescent contaminants from plastic and rubber laboratory equipment. bibliog Science 149:1382-3 S 17 '65

KOREA
See also
Astronomical observatories—Korea

KOREA (People's Democratic Republic)
Change of course for the flying red horse; emphasis on independence. il Time 86:45 O 8 '65
Progress in the North. J. M. Truitt. il Newsweek 66:54+ D 6 '65
See also
Education—Korea (People's Democratic Republic)

Air force
Marauders. Time 85:39 My 7 '65

KOREA (Republic)
Korea 1965. D. N. Rowe. Nat R 17:184 Mr 9 '65
Striking parallel: South Viet Nam and South Korea. il Time 85:35-6 My 21 '65
See also
Economic assistance in Korea (Republic)
Japan—Foreign relations—Korea (Republic)
Korea and the United States
Science—Korea (Republic)

Commercial treaties and agreements
U.S. and Korea conclude cotton textile agreement; Department announcement, January 26, 1965, with agreement and related letters. il Dept State Bul 52:274-8 F 22 '65

Description and travel
Come to carefree Korea. H. Sutton. Sat R 48: 20-1 Jl 3 '65

Economic conditions
See also
Economic assistance in Korea (Republic)

Economic relations
Change in moodo; Japanese-South Korean accord. il Time 85:28 Ap 2 '65

Foreign relations
Complex affair. Newsweek 66:34-5 Jl 5 '65
Japan-Korea accords. G. K. Chapman. Christian Cent 82:1612+ D 29 '65
Korean foreign minister holds talks with Secretary Rusk; joint statement, March 17, 1965. T. W. Lee and D. Rusk. Dept State Bul 52:491 Ap 5 '65
United States and Korea reaffirm strong bonds of friendship; exchange of greetings, with joint communique, May 18, 1965. L. B. Johnson; C. H. Park. Dept State Bul 52:950-4 Je 14 '65
U.S. welcomes dispatch of Korean division to South Viet-Nam; statement, August 13, 1965, with letter. B. D. Moyers; L. B. Johnson. Dept State Bul 53:448 S 13 '65

Politics and government
Unlearned lesson of Korea. Nation 200:322 Mr 29 '65

Religious institutions and affairs
News of the Christian world (cont) Christian Cent 82:718-19, 1104, 1554+ Je 2, S 20, D 15 '65

Riots
Echo of history? student riots. Time 85:39 Ap 23 '65
Old hatreds, new mobs; student opposition to pact with Japan. Time 86:34 S 3 '65
School days. il Newsweek 66:30 S 6 '65

Social conditions
Confucius' outcasts; South Korea. Time 86: 43 D 10 '65

Treaties
New treaty in Asia that will help U.S. il U S News 59:108 N 29 '65
Treaty for tomorrow; Japan and South Korea sign a normalization treaty. il Time 86:23 Jl 2 '65

KOREA, NORTHERN. See Korea (People's Democratic Republic)

KOREA and the United States
Korea, a free-world partner in the Far East; address, September 20, 1965. W. P. Bundy. Dept State Bul 53:593-6 O 11 '65

KOREAN armistice. See Korean war, 1950-1953—Peace and mediation

KOREAN GI bill of rights. See Servicemen, Discharged—Education

KOREAN poetry
Ever white mountain, ed. by I. K. Pai. Review
Time 86:127+ O 22 '65

KOREAN war, 1950-1953
Viet Nam & Korea: a comparison. Time 86: 16 Jl 23 '65

Peace and mediation
Unfinished conflict; periodic meetings of the Military armistice commission at Panmunjom. il Time 86:19 Jl 2 '65
Vietnam: once truce talks start; Korean example. il U S News 59:35 S 13 '65

Statistics
Korea and Vietnam: how two wars compare; table. il U S News 59:6 D 6 '65

KORENGOLD, Robert J.
One year, two views. por Newsweek 66:56-7 O 18 '65

KORIN, Pavel Dimitrievich
People's artist. il por Newsweek 65:100-1 My 24 '65

KORNS, William A.
Reforming the House of representatives. New Repub 152:23-4+ F 13 '65

KORSAKOV, Nikolai Andreevich Rimskii-. See Rimskii-Korsakov, N. A.

KOSAKA, Masataka
Japanese view of America. Harper 230:18+ My '65

KOSHER food. See Jews—Dietary laws

KOSLOFF, Theodore
Baldina; interview, by D. Leddick. A. Baldina. il pors Dance Mag 39:21-3 N '65

KOSSORIS, Max D.
Hours of work and output; reprint from July 1947 issue. Mo Labor R 88:801-2 Jl '65

KOSTANECKI, Andrew. See Sutphen, J. jt. auth.

KOSTELANETZ, Richard
Books. Commonweal 82:420 Je 18 '65
Ginsberg makes the world scene. N Y Times Mag p22-3+ Jl 11 '65
Literature in the Soviet Union. Commonweal 81:740+ Mr 5 '65
Men of the '30s. Commonweal 83:266-9 D 3 '65

KOSYGIN, Aleksei Nikolaevich
Russia's new five year plan; address, September 28, 1965. Vital Speeches 32:115-28 D 1 '65
Sort of dialogue; excerpts from interview, ed. by Lord Thomson. por Newsweek 66: 40 S 20 '65
To catch a planner; excerpts from address. Newsweek 65:43+ My 3 '65

about
Kremlin mood: strain and anxiety. il por Newsweek 65:31 Mr 29 '65
Kremlin on the Black Sea. R. J. Korengold. il Newsweek 66:56 N 15 '65
My visits with Kosygin and Tito. W. A. Harriman. il Life 59:89-90 Ag 27 '65
New look for Kremlin leadership. por U S News 58:22 Mr 15 '65
New style. il por Newsweek 65:46 Mr 15 '65
One conflict that got to the conference table. il por U S News 60:21 Ja 17 '66
One year, two views. R. J. Korengold; L. Volkov. il Newsweek 66:56-7 O 18 '65
Playing the honest broker. il por Newsweek 67:36+ Ja 17 '66
Russia puts a new spur to output. Bsns W p32 O 2 '65
Soviet Union today. il Sr Schol 86:12-16 F 4 '65
Vietnam: Mr Kosygin goes calling. il por Newsweek 65:36+ F 15 '65

KOSZTOLANYI, Dezsö
Barkokhba; story, tr. by T. Kabdebo. Commentary 39:56-60 Ap '65

KOTKER, Norman
Holy City. Horizon 7:4-19 Spr '65
Thinking man's lake. Horizon 7:64-79 Autumn '65

KOTLER, Philip
  Diagnosing the marketing takeover; excerpt from Marketing management: analysis, planning, and control. Harvard Bsns R 43:70-2 N '65
  Phasing out weak products. bibliog f Harvard Bsns R 43:107-18 Mr '65
KOTLER, Yuri
  Generation of builders. UNESCO Courier 18: 62-5 Jl '65
KOTLOWITZ, Robert
  Baltimore boy. Harper 231:62-6+ D '65
  Happenings on Upper Broadway: a comparative dig. Harper 231:30+ Ag '65
  He calls the tunes at the City Center. N Y Times Mag p44-5+ My 2 '65
  Writer's life; foreword. Harper 231:142 O '65
KOUBA, Maria
  Music to my ears: role of Salome. I. Kolodin. Sat R 48:39 F 27 '65
KOUFAX, Sandy
  Sportsman of the year; interview, ed. by J. Olsen. por Sports Illus 23:34-8+ D 20 '65

about

  Best; perfect game. por Time 86:96 S 17 '65
  Down to the wire and then Sandy Koufax settled it all. J. Lake il Newsweek 66:68-70 O 11 '65
  Final strength was Sandy. W. Leggett. por Sports Illus 23:28-9 O 25 '65
  Just perfect. il por Newsweek 66:84 S 20 '65
  Mr Cool & the pros. il por Time 86:93+ O 22 '65
  $100,000 for Sandy. Time 86:61 Ag 20 '65
  Sandy makes a pitch for posterity. J. Jares. il pors Sports Illus 23:10-13 Ag 2 '65
  Sandy's series. por Newsweek 66:60 O 25 '65
  Strikes and strokes. il Newsweek 66:68-9 Ag 23 '65
  With trauma, stress & it. il por Time 86:56 Jl 30 '65
KOULISCHER, Lucien, and Frechkop, Serge
  Chromosome complement: a fertile hybrid between equus prjewalskii and equus caballus. bibliog Science 151:93-5 Ja 7 '66
KOUWENHOVEN, John A.
  Cars coming faster and faster. Harper 232: 97-9 Ja '66
KOVAC, Frank J.
  Kelly caper. il Newsweek 66:20-1 Jl 5 '65
KOVACH, Bill
  Air-conditioned sweatshop. Reporter 33:29-31 O 7 '65
KOVAR, Glenn A. See Gregg, E. H. jr. jt. auth.
KOVAR, Helen M.
  New marvel: Mexico's pyramids. Sci Digest 57:62-8 Je '65
KOVNER, Milton
  Soviet trade and aid. bibliog f Cur Hist 49:227-34 O '65
KOWALKE, Ron
  White-ground etchings of Ron Kowalke. S. Hurwitz. il Am Artist 30:60-5+ Ja '66
KOWALSKI, Piotr
  Explosive forms of Piotr Kowalski; interview, ed. by B. P. Spring. pors Arch Forum 123:30-5 D '65
KOWITZ, Gerald T. and Armstrong, C. M.
  Patterns of academic achievement. Sch & Soc 93:91-2 F 6 '65
KOZLOFF, Max
  Art. See issues of Nation
KOZLOW, Richard
  Landscape paintings of Richard Kozlow. L. Bruner. il por Am Artist 29:54-9+ My '65
KRAAR, Louis
  I am in fact a very ordinary human. Life 58:37 Je 11 '65
KRACHMALNICK, Samuel
  Maestros on the road; interview, ed. by Q. Eaton. por Opera N 30:20 O 23 '65
KRADITOR, Aileen S.
  Slave South: beyond economics. Nation 201: 390-2 N 22 '65
KRAFT, Christopher Columbus, jr
  Conductor in a command post. il Time 86: 48-54 Ag 27 '65
  Man at the switch with no time to argue. M. Durham. il pors Life 58:74-6 Je 18 '65
  Weight of space is on his shoulders. il pors Bsns W p64+ Je 12 '65
  When the countdown is one, his pulse is 135. G. Bylinsky. il pors N Y Times Mag p 14-15+ Ag 15 '65
KRAFT, Ivor
  Are we overselling the pre-school idea? por Sat R 48:63 D 18 '65
KRAFT, Joseph
  J. Edgar Hoover, the compleat bureaucrat. Commentary 39:59-62 F '65
  Washington insight. See issues of Harper's magazine

KRAFT, Virginia
  Dogs (cont) Sports Illus 22:71+ Ap 26 '65
  Fishing. Sports Illus 23:92+ N 15 '65
  Goodby, kangaroos. Sports Illus 22:76-80+ My 31 '65
  In the land of the tiger. por Sports Illus 23: 44-67 D 20 '65
  Shooting. Sports Illus 24:46-8 Ja 17 '66
KRAGEN, Jinx, and Perry, Judy
  Saucepans and the single girl; excerpts. pors Ladies Home J 82:36+ My; 90+ Je; 86+ Jl; 94+ Ag; 90+ S '65
KRAINIS, Bernard
  Recordings. M. Mayer. Esquire 64:62+ D '65
KRAM, Mark
  Day the Cowboys got lassoed for a loss. Sports Illus 22:82-4 Ap 5 '65
  Detroit flies high on beat-up old Red Wings. Sports Illus 22:66-7 Mr 29 '65
  Odd time in Du Quoin, Illinois. Sports Illus 23:24-31 Ag 30 '65
  Soccer. Sports Illus 22:60-1 Je 21 '65
  Wrestling. Sports Illus 22:82-4 Ap 5 '65
KRAMER, Dale
  Jungle law in the farm belt. Nation 200:587-9 My 31 '65
KRAMER, Hilton
  At the feet of Klee. Reporter 32:56+ F 11 '65
  Godot's grandfather. Reporter 32:40+ Je 3 '65
  How good is Israeli art? Commentary 39: 62-4 F '65
KRAMER, Irma L. See Ashby, L. W. jt. auth.
KRAMER, Jack
  Cinnamon scented orchid. Flower Grower 52: 28 O '65
  Spice orchid for spring. Flower Grower 52:44 Ap '65
KRAMER, Larry
  Transatlantic view. por Pub W 188:26-9 N 29; 38-41 D 27 '65
KRAMER, Norman
  Norman Kramer, painter & potter. il Am Artist 29:30-5+ My '65
KRAMER, Rita
  Parent and child (cont) N Y Times Mag p77-8 F 14; 65-6+ My 23; 129-30 O 24; 128+ D 5 '65
KRAMER, Robert
  Don't let big western feed lots run you out of business. Suc Farm 63:32-3+ O '65
  —and Malena, Dave
  Good feed lot ideas to help you compete. Suc Farm 63:32-3+ N '65
KRAMER, Stanley
  Movies & messages. M. Decter. Commentary 40:77-8 N '65
KRASKE, Robert
  Fall of Galloping Gertie. Sci Digest 58:61-5 D '65
KRASNE, Franklin B. See Lawrence, P. A. jt. auth.
KRASOVETZ, Mary
  Brief encounter. Seventeen 24:132 Jl '65
KRASSOVSKA, Nathalie
  Ballet romantique, High school of printing. M. Marks. il Dance Mag 39:66 Mr '65
KRATZ, Daniel G.
  Town with too many churches. N. M. Lobsenz. il por Redbook 126:70-1+ N '65
KRAUS, Barbara
  (comp) Holiday handbook. Holiday 38:95-100 S '65
KRAUS, C. Norman
  Church universal. Christian Cent 82:1132+ S 15 '65
KRAUS, K. A. and others
  Salt rejection by a porous glass. bibliog Science 151:194-5 Ja 14 '66
KRAUS, Richard G.
  Delinquency and recreation: fact and fiction! bibliog por Recreation 58:382-5 O '65
KRAUSE, Herbert
  Black Hills of South Dakota; excerpt from The bird watcher's America. ed. by O. Pettingill. por Audubon Mag 67:140+ My '65
KRAUSE, Johannes
  Johannes Krause, master joiner of Salem. F. L. Horton. il Antiques 88:92-3 Jl '65
KRAUSHAR, Leon
  House that pop art built. F. Du Plessix. il House & Gard 127:158-63 My '65
KRAUSKOPF, John, and Srebro, Richard
  Spectral sensitivity of color mechanisms: derivation from fluctuations of color appearance near threshold. bibliog Science 150:1477-9 D 10 '65
KRAUSS, William A.
  Footnote from Hemingway's Paris, 1964. Harper 231:91-5 Ag '65
KRAUSZ, N. G. P.
  Protect your liabilities when your animals get on the road. Suc Farm 63:64 Jl '65
KRAWITZ, Herman E.
  New Met. C. L. Osborne. il pors Hi Fi 15:50-4+ S '65

KRECH, Hilda Sidney
Identity of modern woman. Nation 201:125-8 S 20 '65
KREH, Lefty
New way to fly cast. por Outdoor Life 135: 28-31+ Mr '65
KREHBIEL, Henry Edward
Big four. E. H. Huneker. por Opera N 30: 9-10 D 18 '65
KRELL, Nancy
Report from Appalachia. pors Seventeen 25: 92-3+ Ja '66
KRELOVE, Lillian
Your state flower (cont) Flower Grower 52:39 Je; 38 Jl; 45 Ag '65
KREMEN, Bennett
Fourth-grade course in color. Holiday 37:24+ Mr '65
KREMLIN chimes; drama. See Pogodin, N.
KRENEK, Ernst
Dartmouth's congregation. O. Daniel. por Sat R 48:35+ Jl 31 '65
Krenek on campus. C. L. Osborne. il por Hi Fi 15:148-9 O '65
KRESPAN, C. G
Organic fluorine chemistry. bibliog Science 150:13-18 O 1 '65
KRESS, Stephen W.
Bullfrogs sing along with jets. Audubon Mag 67:93-6 Mr '65
KRETTEK, Germaine, and Cooke, E. D.
ALA Washington notes. See issues of Wilson library bulletin
Washington report: from the ALA Washington office. See issues of ALA bulletin
KRETZ, Thomas
Friday's work; poem. Christian Cent 82:458 Ap 14 '65
Journey toward truth. Christian Cent 82:1513 D 8 '65
Transfiguration; poem. Christian Cent 82:1033 Ag 25 '65
KREUGER, Miles
Broadway on records; Capitol at twenty-three. Am Rec G 32:112-17+ O '65
Broadway on records: Columbia, six decades of innovation. Am Rec G 32:322-3+ D '65
Broadway on records: Decca, where it all started. Am Rec G 32:6-11 S '65
Discography of RCA Victor LP original-cast albums. Am Rec G 31:1044-6 Jl '65
RCA Victor's notable new reissue program. Am Rec G 31:1040-3 Jl '65
KREVITSKY, Nik
Developmental approach to crafts. Sch Arts 64:30-5 Je '65
KRICK, Irving P, associates. See Irving P. Krick associates
KRIEGEL, Leonard
Wanted: a Protestant novelist. Commonweal 83:273+ D 3 '65
KRILL, Alex E. and Beutler, Ernest
Red-light thresholds in heterozygote carriers of protanopia: genetic implications. bibliog Science 149:186-8 Jl 9 '65
KRINSLEY, David H. and Newman, W. S.
Pleistocene glaciation: a criterion for recognition of its onset. bibliog Science 149:442-3 Jl 23 '65
KRIPS, Josef
Music to my ears; Krips on Bruckner's Ninth. I. Kolodin. Sat R 48:39 F 27 '65
KRISHNAYYA, Jaswant
Prescription for progress. Horn Bk 41:202-5 Ap '65
KRISTOL, Irving
Few kind words for Uncle Tom. Harper 230: 95-9 F '65
20th century began in 1945. N Y Times Mag p25+ My 2 '65
What's bugging the students. Atlan 216:108-11 N '65
KRITZECK, James
Books. Commonweal 82:672-3 S 17 '65
KRIZEK, Donald T. and others
Photoperiodic induction of senescence in xanthium plants. bibliog Science 151:95-6 Ja 7 '66
KROC, Ray
Hamburger king. por Newsweek 66:74-5 S 13 '65
KROCK, Arthur
Critical look at U.S. policy; excerpts from television broadcast. U S News 58:29 Mr 1 '65
KROENING, John L.
Stratosphere and troposphere: transport of material between them. Science 147:862-4 F 19 '65
KROGER company
Kroger co. adds data to its wares; Product movement index. Bsns W p38 S 4 '65

KROHN, Mildred L.
Lomond learning center. Library J 90:5463-4 D 15 '65
Study in self-reliance. Library J 90:4520-2 O 15 '65
KROKOVER, Rosalyn
American ballet theatre. Hi Fi 15:120+ Je '65
Balanchine's Don Quixote. Hi Fi 15:123 Ag '65
Martha Graham, indomitable. Hi Fi 16:142 Ja '66
Royal ballet. Hi Fi 15:99+ Jl '65
KROL, John J. abp
Walking the road together; excerpt from address, April 21, 1965. Cath World 201: 329-30 Ag '65
KROLL, Ernest
Stone bridge inn; poem. Sat R 48:37 My 1 '65
View from the bridge; poem. Sat R 48:23 Ap 3 '65
KROMER, William
Bill Kromer's miniature railroad. S. A. Parvin. il por Hobbies 70:122-3 Mr '65
KRONENBERGER, Louis
Adventures in book keeping. Vogue 146:273-4+ O 1 '65
Decadence and decorum. Atlan 216:103-6 N '65
How not to write, what not to say. Atlan 216:97-100 S '65
Staggered culture. Nation 201:67-71 S 20 '65
Thirties: frayed collars and large visions. por Atlan 217:79-81 Ja '66
KROPP, Sister Maura Christine
Credo of three articles; poem. Commonweal 81:637 F 12 '65
Love; poem. Wilson Lib Bul 40:362 D '65
KROSS, Anna M.
Social problem of sexual assault. Sat R 48: 23-5+ Ag 7 '65
KRUCENISCA, Salomea
Her name was Salome. E. Arnosi. por Opera N 29:31 Mr 13 '65
KRUG, Judith F.
ALA library research clearinghouse. ALA Bul 60:72 Ja '66
KRUG, Julius
Wood keeps him warm. R. H. Lysager. il pors Am For 71:25+ F '65
KRUIJFF, Jan de
Notes from our correspondents (cont) Hi Fi 15:22+ O '65
KRULAK, Victor Harold
Brute Krulak of the marines. D. Moser. il pors Life 58:77-8+ Ap 30 '65
KRUMMEL, Donald W.
Bibliography's stepchild: the printed note. por Library J 90:1248-52+ Mr 15 '65
KRUPP family
House of Krupp (cont) W. Manchester. Holiday 37:60-1+ F '65
KRUPP works, Essen
Idea; plan for industrial complex in Poland. Newsweek 65:68+ F 15 '65
Krupp forges a new German trade weapon; partnership with Polish government. il Bsns W p92-4 F 6 '65
Krupp looks east. Time 85:100 Ap 9 '65
Share of Krupp. il Newsweek 66:68 Jl 19 '65
Sharing the empire. il Time 87:70 Ja 21 '66
KRUSE, Richard H.
Step by step to a finished basement. Bet Hom & Gard 43:68-9+ N '65
KRUTCH, Joseph Wood
Calipers on the human mind. Sat R 48:22-5 Je 19 '65
Walking's back in fashion. Read Digest 86: 19-20 F '65
What does violence say about man? Sat R 48:18-19 Mr 27 '65
Why I am not going to the moon. Sat R 48: 29-31 N 20 '65
KU KLUX klan
AFL-CIO fights Klan infiltration. Bsns W p47-8 O 23 '65
Anatomy of the Klan. S. M. Lipset. Commentary 40:74+ O '65
Englishman goes to a Klan meeting; Durham, N.C. rally. H. Fairlie. il N Y Times Mag p26-7+ My 23 '65
FBI's secret war against the Ku Klux klan. J. Barron. il Read Digest 88:87-92 Ja '66
Gathering of the Klan. J. M. Arisman. Commonweal 82:373-4 Je 11 '65
Haters among us. R. N. Baldwin. il Sat R 48:36 Je 19 '65
Hooded Americanism, by D. M. Chalmers. Review
    Christian Cent 82:967 Ag 4 '65. A. P. Klausler
Hooded horsemen gallop out of the past in a sudden revival of the KKK. il Life 58: 28-35 Ap 23 '65

KU KLUX Klan—*Continued*
If ever a devil . . . il Time 86:109 N 5 '65
Kashing in; B. Shelton's tax evasion trial.
  Newsweek 66:34+ N 1 '65
Klan comes to Britain: what it's all about.
  il U S News 59:30-1 Jl 5 '65
Klansman's secret; New York times story.
  Time 86:54 N 12 '65
Klantown, USA. P. Good. il Nation 200:110-
  13 F 1 '65
Konstitutional rites; educational program of
  violence. Newsweek 66:34 N 8 '65
Ku Klux klan, a century of infamy, by W. P.
  Randel. Review
    America 112:884 Je 19 '65. W. F. Minor
Ku Klux klan: the violent history of a
  hooded society. il Sr Schol 87:5-8 D 2 '65
Long, hot summer in Indiana; 1924. W. E.
  Wilson. il Am Heritage 16:56-64 Ag '65
Murder: the Klan on trial; L. Penn case.
  W. B. Huie. il Sat Eve Post 238:86-9 Je 19
  '65
Nobody turn me 'round; anti-Klan demon-
  strations in Natchez, Miss. Time 86:31-2
  O 15 '65
Same old HUAC. Nation 201:290-1 N 1 '65
Sending a goose to catch a fox; HUAC to
  investigate K.K.K. Christian Cent 82:453
  Ap 14 '65; Reply. 82:1435 N 24 '65
Shooting at the Klan but wounding the
  Negro; clergyman denounce H.U.A.C.'s im-
  pending investigation of KKK. Christian
  Cent 82:1149 S 22 '65
Various shady lives of the Ku Klux klan.
  il Time 85:24-5 Ap 9 '65
WBOX and the KKK; Bogalusa, La. il News-
  week 66:75 Ag 16 '65
    See also
Government investigations—Ku Klux klan
KUBITSCHEK, Juscelino
Back to exile. Time 86:59 N 19 '65
Man from Ipanema. il por Newsweek 66:71
  O 18 '65
Out of the past. il por Time 86:52 O 15 '65
KUBRICK, Stanley
Beyond the stars. New Yorker 41:38-9 Ap 24
  '65
Offbeat director in outer space. H. Alpert.
  il pors N Y Times Mag p 14-15+ Ja 16 '66
KUCH, Dick
Triad dance company, 92nd street Y.
  M. Marks. Dance Mag 39:68 Je '65
KUCHEL, Thomas Henry
Kuchel's quandary. por Newsweek 66:28 S
  27 '65
Smear. Time 85:23 Mr 5 '65
Victim strikes back. Sr Schol 86:20 Mr 18 '65
Where are the new Republicans? Reporter
  33:16+ O 7 '65
KUCHNOW, Karl P. See Fox, D. L. jt. auth.
KUCKUCK, F. D.
Designed for the people who use it. Am City
  80:108-10 Ag '65
KUCYN, Chet
Stop that noise. Motor B 116:46-7+ Jl '65
Water system. Motor B 116:100+ O '65
KUEGELGEN, E. von
Wall: three years later. Nat R 17:764-5 S 7
  '65
KUEHNELT-LEDDIHN, Erik Maria, ritter von
Cooling Franco-German relations. por Nat R
  17:650-1 Jl 27 '65
European's impressions. por Nat R 17:986
  N 2 '65
Letter from Brazil. por Nat R 17:191 Mr 9
  '65
Letter from the Continent. See occasional
  issues of National review
KUEHNL, Neil
How to talk about money with a doctor. Bet
  Hom & Gard 43:44 O '65
—and Bush, George
Family money management; questions and
  answers. See issues of Better homes and
  gardens
KUH, Frederick
East-West dialogue: the one Germany ques-
  tion. Nation 200:579-81 My 31 '65
Prospects in Vietnam. Nation 200:213 Mr 1
  '65
KUH, Katharine
Los Angeles: salute to a new museum. Sat R
  48:29-35 Ap 3 '65
KUHLMAN, David L.
Water worries disappear with the old plant.
  Am City 81:110-11 Ja '66
KUHN, Allan Dale
Beachboy caper. J. Roth. Esquire 64:118-19+
  S '65
KUHN, Edward W.
A.B.A.'s no. one issue. por Time 86:46 Ag
  20 '65
KUHN, Irene Corbally
Mountain-top Shangri-las. Travel 124:28-35 O
  '65

KUIPER, Gerard Peter
Lunar results from Rangers 7 to 9. bibliog
  Sky & Tel 29:293-308 My '65
    about
Where a moon landing takes place every
  night; Arizona's Lunar & planetary lab.
  il por Bsns W p68-70+ Ja 15 '66
KUJAWSKI, John, and Gutetter, Lee
Art motivation from music. Design 66:20-3
  My '65
KULA. See Barter
KUMAKIRI, Keisuke
China: the grand tour. il Newsweek 67:36-8
  Ja 17 '66
KUMBLE, Vrinda
Root-room for delight. Horn Bk 41:247-51 Je
  '65
KUMIN, Maxine W.
Appointment; poem. Sat R 48:93 F 20 '65
KUMLIEN, Gunnar D.
Catholics left and right. Commonweal 82:
  16-17 Mr 26 '65
Marxist's Christ. Commonweal 82:471-2 Jl 2
  '65
KUNCEWICZ, Maria
Letter from Poland. Nation 201:537-8 D 27 '65
KUNDSIN, Ruth B.
Why nobody wants women in science; re-
  print. por Sci Digest 58:60-5 O '65
KÜNG, Hans
And after the council? Commonweal 82:619-23
  S 3 '65
Charismatic structure of the church; ex-
  cerpts. por Cath World 201:302-6 Ag '65
Council: end or beginning? tr. by H. R.
  Bronk. Commonweal 81:631-7 F 12 '65
What has the council done? tr. by J. Dwyer
  and H. Bronk. Commonweal 83:461-8 Ja 21
  '66
**KUNHARDT, Dorothy Meserve, and Kunhardt,
  P. B. Jr**
Assassination! excerpt from Twenty days.
  Am Heritage 16:4-35 Ap '65
Hundred years ago; excerpts from Twenty
  days. Life 58:66C-75 Ap 16 '65
Mr Lincoln at last comes home to Spring-
  field. Life 58:76-80+ Ap 16 '65
KUNHARDT, Philip B. Jr. See Kunhardt, D. M.
  jt. auth.
KUNIMOTO, Yoshio
People wanted this plant. Am City 80:89-90
  My '65
KUNKLE, James R.
Traction-bars: why and how. Hot Rod 18:
  110-11 D '65
KUNSTLER, William M.
Mob against the outsider. Life 59:15 D 3
  '65
KUPCHAN, S. Morris, and others
Beta-solamarine: tumor inhibitor isolated
  from solanum dulcamara. bibliog Science
  150:1827-8 D 31 '65
KUPER, Hilda
Prisons of apartheid. Nation 202:76-8 Ja 17 '66
KUPFERBERG, Herbert
Record reviews. See issues of Atlantic
They shall have music. See issues of Atlantic
KURLAND, Norman D.
Integrated schools: a progress report. Parents
  Mag 40:60-1+ S '65
KURODA, P. K. and others
Fallout from the nuclear explosion of 16
  October 1964. bibliog Science 147:1284-6 Mr
  12 '65
Strontium isotopes: global circulation after
  the Chinese nuclear explosion of 14 May
  1965. bibliog Science 150:1289-90 D 3 '65
KUROSAWA, Akira
Films and faces of Akira Kurosawa. B. Or-
  tolani. il America 113:368-71 O 2 '65
Japanese screen. H. Alpert. il Sat R 48:35
  D 25 '65
KUROSHIO current. See Ocean currents
KURU. See Diseases
KUSS, Henry J. 1922?-
NATO common market; excerpts from ad-
  dress. Aviation W 83:11 O 18 '65
    about
Buying overseas for U.S. arsenal. il por Bsns
  W p 142+ O 9 '65
KUTCH, Rann of. See Cutch, Rann of
KUTNER, Luis
Let habeas corpus be worldwide. Life 59:4
  S 3 '65
KUTSCHBACH, Hans F.
At last! a home TV tape recorder kit! Pop
  Electr 22:44+ Ap '65
KUWAIT
Everything's up to date in Kuwait. G. De
  Carvalho. il Life 59:96-8+ S 17 '65
How to use $2.5 billion. il Fortune 71:65-6+
  F '65

KUWAIT—*Continued*
Kuwait: economic kingpin of the Arab world.
il Sr Schol 87:13-15+ N 4 '65
Man for all Arabs. il Time 86:39 D 3 '65
Trouble in the garden. Time 86:96 Jl 9 '65
Where people are getting richer fast. il
U S News 59:19 D 6 '65
See also
Investments, Foreign (by Kuwait)

KUWAYAMA, George
Yamato-e time-machine. Art N 64:40-3+ N
'65

KUYPERS, Henricus G. J. M. See Lawrence,
D. G. jt. auth.

KUZNETSOV, Nikolai Gerasimovich
Polishing the escutcheons. Time 85:31A Je 18
'65

KVARACEUS, William C.
Can reading affect delinquency? address,
January 1965. bibliog f por ALA Bul 59:
516-22 Je '65
Ten ways to upgrade your PTA. Parents
Mag 40:45+ F '65

KY, Nguyen-cao-. See Nguyen-cao-Ky

KYLE, Jim
Decibel wheel. Electr World 73:29 F '65
Eliminating impulse noise. Electr World 73:
36-8+ Mr '65
Low-noise r.f. amplifiers. Electr World 74:71-
4 D '65
Selective audio amplifiers. Electr World 74:84-
8 Jl '65
Spectrum analyzers. Electr World 73:51-4+
My '65

KYODAN. See United church of Christ in
Japan

L

**LACNP (Latin American committee on national
parks)** See International union for the conservation of nature and natural resources

LAFTA. See Latin American free trade association

**LAINS (low altitude inertial navigation sys-
tem)** See Inertial guidance systems

LAPL. See Los Angeles public library

LASA (large-aperture seismic array) See
Atomic bombs—Testing, Detection of

**LASRV (low altitude supersonic research
vehicle)** See Guided missiles

LEM (lunar excursion module) See Space
vehicles—Landing systems—Moon

LES (Lincoln experimental satellite) See Communications satellites

LIL (lunar international laboratory) See Space
stations

LPD (landing platform dock) See Landing craft

LRS. See United States—Library of Congress—
Legislative reference service

LSA (library services act) See Library laws
and legislation

LSD. See Lysergic acid diethylamide

LTP. See American library association—Library technology project

LAATSCH, Barbara
Colonial kaleidoscope. Sr Schol 86:sup22-3 Ap
15 '65

LABANOTATION. See Dance notation

LABAY, Peregrina Catacutan-. See Catacutan-
Labay, P.

LABELS
Caution: cigarette smoking may be hazardous
to your health; warning to be on every
cigarette pack and carton. Consumer Rep
30:488-91 O '65
Cigarette label battle: death warning on pack-
ages. C. A. Betts. Sci N L 87:223 Ap 3 '65
Cigarette warning: too late and too little.
Christian Cent 82:1118 S 15 '65
Convenient label maker; Dymo labelmaker. il
Consumer Bul 48:19 Ag '65
Deadlock looms ahead on tobacco control;
health warning labels on cigarette pack-
ages. Sci N L 88:25 Jl 10 '65
Jar of hope; concerning Mrs Neuberger's drive
for labeling cosmetics. Newsweek 65:64 My
31 '65
Label makers; Label-mate and Dymo label-
maker. il Consumer Bul 49:30 Ja '66
Lavish labels for your gourmet gifts. il
McCalls 93:126-7 D '65
Questions about labels. E. Weston. McCalls
92:34 Ap '65
Read the label on the fertilizer sack. F. E.
Bear. Horticulture 44:22-3+ Ja '66

Sticky issues; latest car bumper stickers. il
Newsweek 66:104B+ N 22 '65
10,000,000 bottles; mistakes in labeling intravenous drugs at Abbott laboratories. J.
Ridgeway. New Repub 153:12-14 N 6 '65
Toadying to tobacco. New Repub 152:7 Ap 10
'65
Warning labels ordered; drugs harmful to an
unborn child. Sci N L 88:293 N 6 '65

LABOR, Earle
Life was always worth the living. Sat R 48:
38-9 S 25 '65

LABOR (obstetrics) See Childbirth

LABOR, Migrant. See Migrant labor

LABOR agreements. See Trade agreements

LABOR and laboring classes
Labor front. T. R. Brooks. See issues of
Dun's review and modern industry
Push for full employment. T. R. Brooks.
Duns R 85:83+ My '65
Skilled labor shortage holds down the gains;
industrial nations fear inflation. il Bsns W
p84+ F 6 '65
Workers' market. il Time 86:78 Jl 2 '65
See also
Age and employment
Church and labor
Employment
Hours of labor
Migrant labor

Bibliography
Book reviews and notes. See issues of
Monthly labor review

Education
Educational attainment of workers, March
1964. D. F. Johnston. bibliog f il Mo Labor
R 88:517-27 My '65
Rising levels of education among young work-
ers. J. D. Cowhig and C. L. Beale. il Mo
Labor R 88:625-8 Je '65

International aspects
See Trade unions—International aspects

Non-wage payments
See Non-wage payments

Periodicals
See also
Monthly labor review

Political activities
See Trade unions—Political activities

Statistics
Current labor statistics. See issues of
Monthly labor review

Europe, Western
European limitations on employee dismissal.
K. Braun. Mo Labor R 88:67-8 Ja '65
European slogan, go North, young man. I.
Ross. il N Y Times Mag p34-6+ My 9 '65;
Same abr. with title Europe's workers on
the move. Read Digest 87:49-50+ N '65
Labor *omnia vincit*. il Time 85:82 Je 4 '65
Labor relations abroad; American business
overseas. T. R. Brooks. Duns R 86:75-6 N
'65
Labor relations in the Common market. C.
W. Summers. il Harvard Bsns R 43:148-
50+ Mr '65
Retraining programs in western Europe. M.
S. Gordon. Mo Labor R 88:292-3 Mr '65

Florida
Shortage of Florida crops? U S News 58:82-3
Mr 1 '65

France
French resist overtime; demands for more
leisure. il Bsns W p46+ Je 5 '65
Great craftsmen of Paris; tr. by A. White.
V. Leduc. Vogue 145:80-3+ Mr 15 '65

Germany (Federal Republic)
How foreign workers bolster German boom.
il Bsns W p44-6 My 1 '65
Savings incentives offered to West German
workers. K. Braun. Mo Labor R 88:971-3
Ag '65

Great Britain
See also
Immigration and emigration—Great Britain
Strikes—Great Britain
Trade unions—Great Britain
Wages—Great Britain

Japan
See also
Strikes—Japan

LABOR laws and legislation—United States—
Continued

Taft-Hartley law

Awaiting Johnson's word on labor. Bsns W
p52 My 1 '65
Battle over 14(b) Taft-Hartley act's contro-
versial clause. C. M. Cook; W. J. Fannin.
Christian Cent 82:937-40 Jl 28 '65
Bracing to keep T-H intact. il Bsns W p 120+
My 15 '65
Changes in Taft-Hartley act? right-to-work.
T. R. Brooks. Duns R 85:87-90 Ap '65
Congress and the right to work; labor's fight
to repeal section 14 (b) A. Kopkind. New
Repub 152:11-12 Je 5 '65
End of a battle; exit 14(B) Newsweek 66:
30 Ag 9 '65
Ev's extendalong. Time 86:30 O 15 '65
Fate of 14(b); aid for the unions. S. Lens.
Commonweal 82:662-5 S 17 '65
14(b) defeat: who's to blame? U S News 59:
100-1 N 8 '65
14(b) filibuster; mildest in history. A. Kop-
kind. New Repub 153:8 O 16 '65
Fourteen B or fight. Fortune 71:129-30 Je '65
14(b) pending. Commonweal 82:712 O 1 '65
Fulfilling the pledge; President urges repeal
of section of the Taft-Hartley law. il Time
85:23-4 My 28 '65
Has labor a case against 14(b)? summary of
arguments against repeal of right-to-work
clause. S. Petro. Nat R 17:535-6 Je 29 '65
Johnson and 14(b); right to work clause.
Nat R 17:714 Ag 24 '65
Labor-management since World war II.
J. P. Goldberg. Cur Hist 48:346-52+ Je '65
Labor message promises storms; repeal of
right-to-work laws. Bsns W p 170 My
22 '65
Leave-taking time? Dirksen's filibuster forces
prepared to battle repeal of 14(B) News-
week 66:42 O 11 '65
Let right-to-work remain a right. Life 59:8
O 8 '65
New controls over strikes; what will Johnson
ask? concerning State-of-the-Union mes-
sage. U S News 60:86 Ja 24 '66
Non-crisis he should skip. Life 58:4 My 14 '65
One-sided compulsion; section 14 (B) of Taft-
Hartley act. H. Hazlitt. Newsweek 66:76 Jl
5 '65
Polls find consensus: people want right to
work; Opinion research corporation survey.
Nations Bsns 53:33 Jl '65
Rammed right on through; bill to repeal sec-
tion 14(b) of Taft-Hartley act passed by
House. Time 86:22-3 Ag 6 '65
Right to choose; section 14 (B) H. Hazlitt.
Newsweek 65:77 Je 7 '65
Right to vote: against repeal of the contro-
versial section 14(B) of the Taft Hartley
act. Newsweek 66:83 Jl 26 '65
Right to work; best that section 14 (B) of
Taft-Hartley act be repealed. H. C. Wal-
lich. Newsweek 65:74 Je 28 '65
Right to work laws; religious objection to
proposed repeal of section 14 (b) of Taft-
Hartley act. America 112:817 Je 5 '65
Right-to-work laws; retain or repeal?
section 14(b) pro and con discussion. Sr
Schol 87:10-12 N 4 '65
Right to work; political skullduggery; address,
August 9, 1965. R. P. Griffin. Vital
Speeches 31:702-4 S 1 '65
Right-to-work repeal hits a roadblock; im-
peding of civil rights according to New
York's Representative Powell. Bsns W p58
Je 19 '65
Roses, for courage; Rosemary, for remem-
brance; need to hang onto section 14(b),
right to work clause. Nat R 17:856 O 5 '65
Senate stalls repeal of 14(b) Bsns W p 163-
4+ O 9 '65
Squaring off over 14(b) il Time 86:30 O 1 '65
Storm over 14(B) K. Crawford. Newsweek 66:
53 O 18 '65
Strange case against fourteen-B; right-to-
work clause. J. Chamberlain. il Nat R 17:
500-2+ Je 15 '65
This month's feature: U.S. policy on labor-
management relations. Cong Digest 44:193-
224 Ag '65
Through a glass clearly; Senate's rejection of
bill to repeal 14(b) il Time 86:22-3 O 22
'65
Transit tie-up hurts labor's fight on 14(b),
New York city subway-bus tie-up. Bsns W
p31 Ja 15 '66
Union lobby gets the word to fight; attempt
to repeal section of Taft-Hartley act. il
Bsns W p 134-6 My 8 '65
**Unions seek second round on 14(b) Bsns W
p54 O 23 '65**

We got ours, then they got theirs; proposed repeal of section 14 (B) il Newsweek
65:63-4 My 31 '65
What unions asked of LBJ: and what they
got, repeal of right to work laws AFL-
CIO's no. 1 goal. U S News 58:67-9 My
31 '65
Why labor didn't get all it wanted from
Congress; repeal of 14 (b) U S News 59:
93-4+ O 25 '65
Will organizing be made easier? NLRB reviewing rules governing drives for representation. Bsns W p 111 My 29 '65
Will right to work live on? repeal of 14(b)
by no means certain. U S News 59:95 S 20
'65

LABOR leaders. See Trade unions—Officials
LABOR-management cooperation. See Em-
ployees representation in management
LABOR-management relations. See Industrial
relations
LABOR-management reporting and disclosure
act of 1959. See Labor laws and legislation
—United States
LABOR officials. See Trade unions—Officials
LABOR output. See Labor productivity
LABOR party (Great Britain)
And then there were two; three-vote margin
in Parliament to two. Time 86:30+ S 3 '65
Letter from London (cont) M. Panter-
Downes. New Yorker 41:135-7 Je 5 '65
Plan; blueprint for revitalizing the British
economy. Newsweek 66:76 S 27 '65
Steel nationalization is not around the
corner. B. Wenham. New Repub 152:9-10
My 22 '65
Sterling and steel sour Wilson's hopes.
Bsns W p38-9 Je 12 '65
Taming of the shrews. Newsweek 66:56 O 11
'65
Trouble for another Socialist experiment. il
U S News 58:42-3 Je 14 '65
Wilson's unhappy hundred days. B. Wenham.
New Repub 152:9-10 F 6 '65
LABOR press. See Trade unions—Publications
LABOR productivity
Cost trends in nine industrial nations; with
charts. J. H. Chandler and P. C. Jackman.
il Mo Labor R 88:1062-8 S '65
Hours of work and output; reprint from July
1947 issue. M. D. Kossoris. Mo Labor R
88:801-2 Jl '65
Labor-management in World war II. M.
Derber. Cur Hist 48:340-5 Je '65
Line still holds on unit labor costs; Census
bureau's revised index. il Bsns W p26-7
O 30 '65
Model for the prediction of manpower require-
ments; excerpt from address, April 15, 1965.
E.R.F.W Crossman. bibliog f Mo Labor R
88:669-71 Je '65
Output per man-hour, gas and electric utili-
ties. J. E. Dragonette and P. W. Jaynes.
il Mo Labor R 88:34-9 Ja '65
Productivity in an expanding industry;
aluminum industry. J. M. Cleaver. il Mo
Labor R 88:373-7 Ap '65
Recent unit cost trends in U.S. manufactur-
ing; with charts. J. A. Mark and E. Kahn.
bibliog f il Mo Labor R 88:1056-62 S '65
What helps the US. stave off inflation. il
Bsns W p28-9 Je 26 '65
See also
Work measurement
LABOR relations. See Industrial relations
LABOR relations board, National. See United
States—National labor relations board
LABOR requirements (for production)
Employment effects of construction expendi-
tures. C. M. Ball. il Mo Labor R 88:154-8
F '65
Labor and material required for college hous-
ing. S. F. Miller. il Mo Labor R 88:1100-4 S
'65
LABOR saving devices
How much leisure can you stand? B. Forker.
il Suc Farm 63:89+ My '65
LABOR shortage. See Labor supply
LABOR statistics, Bureau of. See United
States—Labor statistics, Bureau of
LABOR supply
Workers' market; labor shortages throughout
the world. il Time 86:78 Jl 2 '65
See also
Manpower
Unemployment

Europe, Western
Shorthanded Europe. il Fortune 71:91-2+
Je '65

Germany (Federal Republic)
Let Hans do it; shortage of workers. il
Newsweek 66:80+ O 4 '65

LABOR supply—*Continued*

United States

Avalanche of youth into the labor force. H. C. Taylor. Mo Labor R 88:544-6 My '65

Business widens its hiring range; stockpiling of employees. il Bsns W p 125-6 D 4 '65

Growing worry: jobs with nobody to fill them. il U S News 59:66-7 Jl 5 '65

Help wanted almost everywhere; shortage of skilled workers. il Bsns W p28-9 O 16 '65

Help wanted: the great manpower shortage. il Newsweek 66:78-80 N 29 '65

Interindustry employment requirements; with input-output tables. J. Alterman. Mo Labor R 88:841-50 Jl '65

Labor force and employment in 1964. S. S. Holland and J. R. Wetzel. il Mo Labor R 88:384-95 Ap '65

Labor force projections for 1970-80. S. Cooper and D. F. Johnston. il Mo Labor R 88:129-40 F '65

Labor force status of youth, 1964. H. R. Hamel. il Mo Labor R 88:932-7 Ag '65

Labor shortage: worse in 66? U S News 60:72 Ja 3 '66

Manpower needs by industry to 1975. H. Stambler. Mo Labor R 88:279-84, 378-83 Mr-Ap '65

Skilled labor pinch gets tighter. Bsns W p32-3 Ja 15 '66

LABOR turnover

Labor turnover; tables. See issues of Monthly labor review

LABOR union scholarship programs. See Scholarships and fellowships

LABOR unions. See Trade unions

LABORATORIES

Building types study. il Arch Rec 138:173-96 N '65

  See also

Atomic research laboratories
Hydraulic laboratories
Medical laboratories
Research laboratories
Underwater laboratories

Air conditioning

Air conditioning matches laboratory loads. il Arch Rec 137:188-92 F '65

Distribution of laboratory services. il Arch Rec 138:186-90 N '65

Architecture

American castle in Japan; Teijin ltd.'s textile research institute. il Fortune 71:136-9 My '65

Building types study. il Arch Rec 138:173-96 N '65

Campus City, Chicago; the labs. il Arch Forum 123:36-7 S '65

For a laboratory: a precast concrete curtain wall. il Arch Rec 138:176 S '65

For a laboratory; precision, flexibility. il Arch Rec 138:167 S '65

Formal facades for Annapolis; Naval academy laboratories. by John Carl Warnecke. il Arch Rec 137:156-7 Je '65

New architecture for the research laboratory; Agronomy building for the New York state college of agriculture at Cornell. il Arch Rec 137:153-60 Ap '65

Equipment

Fluorescent contaminants from plastic and rubber laboratory equipment. H. A. Kordan. bibliog Science 149:1382-3 S 17 '65

Laboratory furniture and equipment. il Arch Rec 138:191-4 N '65

LABORATORY animals

Ages of experimental animals. N. O. Calloway. Science 150:1771 D 31 '65

Lost pets that stray to the labs; unscrupulous dognappers. C. Phinizy. il Sports Illus 23:36-8+ N 29 '65

Use of animals in research and teaching. Science 150:147 O 8 '65

White miniature hogs used to test drugs. Sci N L 89:41 Ja 15 '66

  See also

Animal experimentation
Monkeys

LABORIT, Henri

Killer for all pains. Time 86:62+ N 12 '65

LABOUISSE, Henry R.

Peace prize. New Yorker 41:44-7 N 6 '65

UNICEF executive director. por UN Mo Chron 2:81 Ap '65

LABOULBENIALES. See Ascomycetes

LABRADOR

One man's land of romance; Grenfell mission throughout Labrador and Newfoundland. A. Sulley. il Am For 71:12-15+ Jl '65

  See also

Fishing—Labrador

LABRADOR dogs

Bargain. D. M. Duffey. il Outdoor Life 135: 148-50+ My '65

LABRADOR retriever trial. See Field trials (dogs)

LABRADOR retrievers. See Labrador dogs

LABROIDES dimidiatus. See Wrasses

LABYRINTH (ear)

Outer space and the inner ear. il Bsns W p45-6+ Ja 30 '65

LACE and lace making

Two centuries of needle lace. C. C. Mayer. il Antiques 87:176-81 F '65

  See also

Macramé

LACERDA, Carlos

That man in Rio. il por Time 85:45 Je 11 '65

LACHANCE, Roland

Snow removal from skating areas. Recreation 58:452 N '65

LACONIA, N.H.

Bikies' fun; Weirs Beach, N.H. il Newsweek 66:21 Jl 5 '65

Come to the riot. See Weirs Beach burn. M. Mok. il Life 59:88-9 Jl 2 '65

LACOSTE, René

Lacoste tries for an ace with a steel racket. por Bsns W p70+ O 30 '65

LACOUTURE, Jean

Bourguiba: portrait of a nonconformist. N Y Times Mag p26-7+ Je 6 '65

Military situation in Vietnam; excerpt. New Repub 152:20 My 22 '65

Uncle Ho defies Uncle Sam. N Y Times Mag p25+ Mr 28 '65

Viet Cong; who are they, what do they want? New Repub 152:21-4 Mr 6 '65

LACQUER and lacquering

German lacquer. H. Huth. il Antiques 87: 456-60 Ap '65

LACROSSE

Home of the braves; Baltimore's Mt Washington club. il Time 85:66 Ap 30 '65

Hopkins lost a title and maybe a tradition; Navy lacrosse team wins on Homecoming at Johns Hopkins. R. Cantwell. il Sports Illus 22:70+ My 17 '65

LACTIC acid

Lactic acid metabolism in hypertensive patients. F. E. Demartini and others. bibliog il Science 148:1482-4 Je 11 '65

LACTIC dehydrogenases. See Dehydrogenases

LACY, Dan

Censorship and obscenity; address, January 1965. por ALA Bul 59:471-6 Je '65

Copyright revision and the writer; reprint. Writer 78:19-21 My '65

Federal foundations for arts & humanities; condensation of testimony before Senate subcommittee. Pub W 187:14-18 Mr 29 '65

LACY, Gene

About face. Design 66:8-12 Ja '65

Double talk. Design 67:22-3 S '65

LACY, Herman E.

How I use futures to up beef profits. por Suc Farm 63:26 Mr '65

LACY, Robert

Win a few, lose a few; story. Sat Eve Post 238:70-5 D 18 '65

LACY, S. and Green, Maurice

Adenovirus multiplication: genetic relatedness of tumorigenic human adenovirus types 7, 12, and 18. bibliog Science 150: 1296-8 D 3 '65

LADAKH

Temples and towns huddled in the high places. il Life 58:60-1 My 28 '65

LADD, Everett C. Jr

Civil rights: the continuing revolution. Yale R 55:1-16 O '65

Negro as cause. Nation 200:161-5 F 15 '65

LADDERS

How to buy the right ladder. P. McCafferty. il Pop Sci 186:158-61+ Je '65

LADENSON, Alex

Twenty years of library legislation. ALA Bul 59:125-31 F '65

LADER, Lawrence

Scandal of abortion laws. N Y Times Mag p32+ Ap 25 '65

LADERMAN, Ezra

BBC symphony orchestra. Hi Fi 15:114+ Ag '65

Contemporary music comes to town. Hi Fi 15:118+ Je '65

LADIES
See also
Woman
LADIES and gentlemen; story. See Spark, M.
LADU, Tora T.
Innovations in foreign language instruction.
Sr Schol 87:sup 16-17 O 14 '65
LADY in blue; story. See Turner, C.
LADY Julia; story. See Jackson, C.
LADY Macbeth of Mtsensk; opera. See Shos-
takovich, D. D.
LADY-slippers. See Ladys slippers
LADYS slippers
You can grow lady slippers indoors or under
glass. il Sunset 136:126-7 Ja '66
LAETSCH, W. M. See Stetler, D. A. jt. auth.
LA FARGE, Henry A.
Archetypical China. Art N 63:32-5+ F '65
LAFARGE, John
LaFarge legacy. America 113:663 N 27 '65
LAFARGE, John, institute. See John LaFarge
institute
LAFARGE, Phyllis
Time when time stands still. Redbook 124:
43+ F '65
LAFAY, Gloria
Inter-American music festival. Hi Fi 15:124
Ag '65
Variety in the capital. Hi Fi 15:114 Jl '65
LA FAY, Howard
Be ye men of valour. Nat Geog Mag 128:
158-95 Ag '65
Portugal at the crossroads. Nat Geog Mag
128:453-501 O '65
LAFEAN, Richard
Ceramics by twelve artists. Craft Horiz 25:
30-3+ Ja '65
LAFOND, Richard
Amateur scientist. Sci Am 212:126-7+ Je '65
LA FONTAINE, Barbara
He's just got that look. Sports Illus 22:32-4+
Ap 26 '65
There is a doctor on the ice. Sports Illus
22:28-30+ F 8 '65
LAGEMANN, John Kord
Delicate art of asking questions. Read Digest
86:87-91 Je '65
Drowned wearing life preserver. Read Digest
87:215-18+ Jl '65
LAGERKVIST, Pär
Lazarus as hero: the novels of Lagerkvist.
W. Weathers. Commonweal 81:688-91 F
26 '65
LA GUARDIA, Fiorello Henry
When La Guardia took over. A. Mann. il pors
N Y Times Mag p22-3+ Ja 2 '66
LA GUARDIA airport. See New York (city)—
Airports
LAGUNA, Ismael
Shark ran into a tiger. M. Kram. il por Sports
Illus 22:32-4+ Ap 19 '65
LAGUNA BEACH, Calif.
Vagabond camera; Pageant of the masters.
W. Lane. il Travel 123:66-7 Je '65
LAHA, Art
You can't figure bears. por Outdoor Life 136:
58-9+ N '65
LAHAINA, Hawaii
Notes for a gazetteer. P. Hamburger. New
Yorker 41:166+ S 18 '65
LAHAYE, Jim
Little parcel of commitment. L. Wainwright.
Life 58:28 Je 11 '65
LAIDLAW, Angus
Can you beat the trouble-shooting champs?
Pop Sci 187:146-9 Ag '65
How to cure an oil hog. Pop Sci 186:168-71
My '65
Keep your lights beaming. Pop Sci 187:136-9
N '65
LAING, Alexander
Nation and its poets. Nation 201:212-18 S 20
'65
LAING, Douglas
Stuff a darkroom in a closet. Mod Phot
29:106 Je '65
LAING, Gerald
Hot-rod heraldry. il por Time 86:86 N 12 '65
LAITIN, Joseph
Right hand for Reedy. por Newsweek 65:62
Mr 8 '65
LAITY
Charter for laymen, 1822. G. Traynor; dis-
cussion. Commonweal 81:555+, 750 Ja 29,
Mr 12 '65
Constitution on the church and the laity;
question of free and responsible laity in a
hierarchical church. D. Callahan. Cath World
202:21-5 O '65
Decree on the laity. Commonweal 83:262-3
D 3 '65

Erosion of rational debate; authority of
church and state; address, June 10, 1965.
W. J. Baroody. Vital Speeches 31:720-4 S 15
'65
Laity today and tomorrow. J. Cogley. Cath
World 201:32-40 Ap '65
Mission of the faithful; excerpts from inter-
view. J. Guitton. Cath World 202:114-15
N '65
Real sleeper; concerning address of Dr Albert
C. Outler. America 112:704 My 15 '65
Responsible laymen; letter. J. T. Ellis. Com-
monweal 81:651+ F 19 '65; Reply. P. A.
Lockrey. 82:95 Ap 9 '65
Rise up ye Catholic rebels! J. B. Sheerin.
Cath World 201:286-9 Ag '65
Toward a responsible laity; discussion. Com-
monweal 81:650-1+ F 19 '65
LAKE, Albert C.
Pursuing a policy; excerpts from Library
reaches out, ed. by K. Coplan and E.
Castagna. por Library J 90:2491-4 Je 1 '65
LAKE, Alice
Andrea: a nurse who cares. Ladies Home J
82:74-5+ Ag '65
Empty days. McCalls 92:78-81+ S '65
Medical lab tests: dangerous mistakes. Mc-
Calls 92:116-17+ My '65; Same abr. with
title Laboratory test: medicine's Achilles
heel. Read Digest 87:70-4 O '65
Menopause: is it necessary? Good H 160:85+
Ap '65
Redbook's guide to the major diseases and
handicaps of children. Redbook 125:33-40
Je '65
LAKE, Carlton
(ed) See Giacometti, A. Wisdom of
Giacometti
LAKE BOSOMTWE. See Meteorite craters
LAKE central airlines
Nord 262 battles competition from auto. D. A.
Brown. il Aviation W 83:57+ N 8 '65
LAKE ERIE. See Erie, Lake
LAKE GENEVA. See Geneva, Lake
LAKE GEORGE opera festival. See Music fes-
tivals—New York (state)
LAKE LEMAN. See Geneva, Lake
LAKE-lover; story. See Rieth, M.
LAKE of the Rain. See Rainy Lake
LAKE SUPERIOR. See Superior, Lake
LAKE WASHINGTON. See Washington, Lake
LAKELAND, Fla.
Colorful trailers serve as mobile libraries.
W. H. Murphy. il Am City 80:106-7 Jl '65
LAKES
Stability of lakes near the temperature of
maximum density. H. Eklund. il Science
149:632-3 Ag 6 '65
See also
Great Lakes

Cleaning
Our own dredge proved best; Rochester, Minn.
W. M. Van Hook. il Am City 80:155+ O '65

Clearing
Fight to save Lake Erie. H. Titus. il Field &
S 69:10-12+ Mr '65
Water weeds give way to simple treatment.
il Am City 81:106-7 Ja '66

Temperature
Terrestrial heat flow: measurement in lake
bottoms. S. R. Hart and J. S. Steinhart.
bibliog il Science 149:1499-501 S 24 '65
LAKES, Artificial
Soil sealant plugs a leak; Lower Lake
Pleasant, Ariz. il Am City 80:106-7 Ag '65
See also
Kariba Lake
LAKEWOLD, Kenton
Line design with pen and ink. Sch Arts 64:32
Mr '65
Weaving. Sch Arts 64:33 Mr '65
LAKONIA fire. See Ships—Fires and fire pro-
tection
LALL, Arthur S.
Political effects of the Chinese bomb. Bul
Atomic Sci 21:21-4 F '65
LALL, Betty Goetz
Approaches to German reunification. Bul
Atomic Sci 21:41-4 Ap '65
Government sponsored research for disarma-
ment. Bul Atomic Sci 21:44-6 F '65
Notes from Asia and Germany. Bul Atomic
Sci 21:33-5 N '65
Perspectives on inspection for arms control.
Bul Atomic Sci 21:51-3 Mr '65
LAM, William M. C.
Lighting of cities. Arch Rec 137:210-14 Je:
138:173-80 Jl '65

LA MARCHINA, Robert
Maestros on the road; interview. ed. by Q.
Eaton. por Opera N 30:20 O 23 '65
LAMB (meat)
See also
Cookery—Meat
LAMBARÉNÉ, Gabon
Schweitzer method hit. Sci N L 88:180 S 18
'65
Schweitzer: reverence for life. Newsweek
66:62 S 13 '65
White wizard's 90th. H. Moffett. il Life 58:
82-92+ F 19 '65
LAMBERT, Betty Joe
Moonlighting in Kanawha County. NEA J
54:21 D '65
LAMBERT, Darwin
Let's outgrow the growth mania. Nat Parks
Mag 39:4-8 Ap '65
You meet such wonderful people. Field & S
70:46-7+ Je '65
LAMBERT, Léon, baron
Modern Medici. il Time 86:44-7 Ag 13 '65
LAMBERT, William. See Oulahan, R. jt. auth.
LAMBS
How to get two lamb crops a year. C. Ran-
dolph. il Suc Farm 63:102 S '65

Feeding
How to glean cornfields with feeder lambs.
il Suc Farm 63:43 Ag '65
LAMBTON, Lucinda
Wedding of the Hon Lucinda Lambton and
Henry Harrod in England's North country.
il por Vogue 145:140-1 Ap 1 '65
LAMER, Victor K. and Healy, T. W.
Evaporation of water: its retardation by
monolayers. bibliog Science 148:36-42 Ap 2
'65
LAMINATED construction. See Sandwich
construction
LAMINATED plastics. See Plastics, Laminated
LAMINATED prints. See Photography—Print-
ing processes
LAMMEY, W. Clyde
Backyard & birdbath R.R. Pop Mech 124:
118-28+ Ag '65
Homeowners' clinic. Pop Mech 124:16-17 D '65;
125:38+ Ja '66
Pattern your shotgun. Pop Mech 124:172-5+
N '65
LAMONT, Thomas Stilwell
When private news is public. Time 86:86 Jl
16 '65
LAMOTT, Kenneth
Cityscape at Tahoe. Nation 201:252-4 O 18 '65
Fresh look at Honolulu. Holiday 38:68-73+
D '65
People of Seattle. Holiday 38:44-51+ Ag '65
LAMP bulbs. See Electric lamps
LAMP shades
How to clean a lamp shade. Bet Hom &
Gard 43:117 My '65
Map lights up. il Sunset 134:120+ F '65
Non-electric, and it's also non-glare; make
white fiberglass shades. il Sunset 135:111
N '65
LAMPERT, James B.
Army makes a new Point. il por Bsns W
p 130-2+ Mr 27 '65
LAMPHIER, Walter C.
Plastic-film capacitors. Electr World 74:42-4
Jl '65
LAMPMAN, Robert J.
Historical approach. Nation 200:606-9 Je 7 '65
LAMPORT, Felicia
Das ist Alice; poem. Harper 230:20 My '65
LAMPREYS
Nature note; sea lamprey. Sci N L 87:317
My 15 '65
LAMPS
Non-electric, and it's also non-glare; make
white fiberglass shades. il Sunset 135:111
N '65
LAMPSHADES. See Lamp shades
LANAHAN, Scottie (Fitzgerald)
Fitzgerald touch. il por Newsweek 66:110 N 15
'65
LANCASTER, Donald
Build the Li'l Dusker; the light watchman.
Pop Electr 23:73-6+ S '65
Build your own dual-throttle power-tool speed
control. Pop Sci 187:128-30 N '65
Dymwatt. Pop Electr 22:71-3+ My '65
Integrated circuits: what's available? Electr
World 74:47-9+ N '65
Low-cost hi-fi color organ. Pop Electr 22:
43-7 Mr '65
Optical link: a new circuit tool. Electr World
74:36-9 S '65
Parts profiles. Pop Electr 23:56-8+ S; 72-3+
O; 76-7+ N '65

Put your best meter face forward. Pop Electr
22:71-2+ F '65
Solid-state dimmers & power controls. Electr
World 73:34-6+ My; 41-4+ Je '65
Tools for the electronic hobbyist. Pop Electr
22:65-70+ Mr '65
LANCASTER, Nancy
English dream: with account by V. Lawford.
il pors Vogue 146:112-21+ Jl '65
LANCASTER COUNTY, Pa.
Amish folk; plainest of Pennsylvania's plain
people. R. Gehman. il Nat Geog Mag 128:
226-53 Ag '65
LANCER books, incorporated
Both Lancer and Putnam injunctions denied.
Pub W 187:132-3 F 22 '65
LAND
See also
Land utilization
Prices
See Land values
Taxation
See also
Property tax
California
Destruction of California, by R. F. Dasmann.
Review
Nation 201:252-4 O 18 '65. K. Lamott
Florida
Land in the sun. il Time 85:96 Mr 5 '65
Seminoles' long road to victory; right to
compensation for loss of lands. W. Hartley
and E. Hartley. Read Digest 86:199-200+
F '65
United States
How private are private lands? summary of
speeches at conference sponsored by Amer-
ican forest products industries, inc. J. B.
Craig. il Am For 71:22-3+ D '65
See also
Public lands—United States
LAND auctions. See Auctions
LAND BETWEEN THE LAKES NATIONAL
RECREATION AREA. See Wilderness
areas
LAND cameras. See Polaroid Land cameras
LAND fills. See Filling (earthwork); Municipal
dumps
LAND grants
See also
School lands
LAND management, Bureau of. See United
States—Land management, Bureau of
LAND planning. See Land utilization
LAND pollution. See Soil pollution
LAND reform. See Land tenure
LAND retirement program. See Agricultural
administration—United States
LAND sailboats
Sailing the seas of sand; wheeled boats by
Nu-sport mfg. co. il Bsns W p32-3 Je 19 '65
LAND speculation
Bubble in the sun; Florida real estate boom.
G. B. Tindall. il Am Heritage 16:76-83+
Ag '65
LAND tenure
Iran
Coming crisis in Iran. H. Mahdavy. For Af-
fairs 44:134-46 O '65
Latin America
Urban and rural development in Latin Amer-
ica; with questions and answers. J. P.
Powelson and A. A. Solow. bibliog f Ann
Am Acad 360:56-62 Jl '65
Peru
Dreaming big. il Newsweek 65:44 Je 28 '65
Rocky road to reform. Time 86:24+ D 31 '65
United States
Crusade against gringos; Federal alliance of
land grants claims original Spanish land. il
Newsweek 67:17-18 Ja 3 '66
Vietnam (Republic)
Bold proposal for Vietnam; agrarian reform.
G. T. Robinson. Look 29:93-4 O 19 '65
LAND utilization
Making American cities more livable; sym-
posium. with introd. by F. B. Wilde. il
Sat R 49:37-41+ Ja 8 '66
Natural beauty and conservation. P. H. Abel-
son. Science 147:1245 Mr 12 '65
Open-space planning process; excerpt from
address, 1964. A. A. Davis. il Recreation
58:400-2 O '65

LAND utilization—*Continued*
President proposes programs supporting planning, the arts and natural beauty; with editorial comment. il Arch Rec 137:9, 23 F '65
Realistic development plan; Monrovia, Calif. G. W. Miller. il Am City 80:100-1 My '65
Santa Clara: the bulldozer crop. J. P. Degnan. il Nation 200:242-5 Mr 8 '65
Saturation: a problem evaded in planning land use. G. Macinko. bibliog il Science 149:516-21 Jl 30 '65
Site reading. N. Morris; R. Laudenslayer. Recreation 58:167-8 Ap '65
Uses of land in cities. C. Abrams. il Sci Am 213:150-6+ bibliog(p277) S '65

LAND values
Are we going land crazy? B. Brantley. il Suc Farm 63:43+ Ap '65
Back of the boom in land prices; with charts. il U S News 58:110-12 My 17 '65
What about land prices now? Suc Farm 63: 62 N '65

LANDABURU, Ricardo H. and others
Peptides attached to thrombin: their influence on proteolysis. bibliog Science 148: 380-1 Ap 16 '65

LANDAU, Elliott D.
Literary adventure in educational television. Horn Bk 41:28-33 F '65
Preparing for a teacher-parent conference. PTA Mag 60:13-15 bibliog(p34) N '65

LANDAU, Lev Davidovich
Persistent Russian. A. Cutler. il Esquire 63: 66-7+ My '65

LANDECK, Ron
This Tiger is not in the tank. J. Underwood. por Sports Illus 23:28-31 N 15 '65

LANDERMAN, Peter
My life as a Soviet prisoner. pors Sat Eve Post 239:32-6+ Ja 15 '66
Tell my parents not to worry. G. Feiffer. il pors Sat Eve Post 238:33-4+ F 13 '65

LANDERS, Ann
Going steady, who needs it? Read Digest 87: 88-90 D '65

LANDES, Edward
Black-box plant is coming. Duns R 85:pt2 114-17+ Mr '65

LANDFILLS. See Filling (earthwork); Municipal dumps

LANDING craft
Experimental air-jet landing craft. L. Evans. il Yachting 118:160 D '65
Our one-package landing force; USS Raleigh, landing platform dock. G. F. Eliot. il Pop Sci 187:40-3+ Jl '65

LANDING platform dock. See Landing craft
LANDING strips. See Airports—Runways
LANDING systems for space vehicles. See Space vehicles—Landing systems

LANDLORD and tenant
See also
Farm tenancy
Leases
Rent

LANDMARKS, Historic. See United States—Historic houses ,etc.
LANDMARKS, Literary. See Literary landmarks

LANDON, Alfred Mossman
Liveliest Republican of them all. P. Engle. il pors N Y Times Mag p 141-3 Ap 4 '65

LANDON, H. C. Robbins
Honorable tradition of Englishmen. Hi Fi 15: 44-50 Ap '65
Mozart on the eighteenth-century stage. Hi Fi 15:62-4+ N '65

about
Helping Haydn; Landon-restored Le pescatrici produced at Holland festival, Amsterdam. Time 86:58 Jl 9 '65
Question of function. P. J. Smith. il Hi Fi 15:67-9+ Mr '65

LANDON, Michael
Bonanza. R. W. Lewis. il pors Sat Eve Post 238:84-9 D 4 '65

LANDOWSKA, Wanda
Landowska on music. I. Kipnis. Am Rec G 31:1012-14 Je '65
St Wanda's testament. F. V. Grunfeld. il por Reporter 32:42-4 F 25 '65

LANDS, Public. See Public lands

LANDSBURG. Robert E.
Spring salmon ring the bell. por Outdoor Life 135:40-3+ Ap '65

LANDSCAPE
Landscaping rural America. F. C. Edminster. il Travel 124:30-5 D '65

LANDSCAPE architecture. See Landscape gardening

LANDSCAPE gardening
Cacti and succulents in the garden. L. Cutak. il Horticulture 43:18-21+ O '65
Case for one total profession. A. Mayer. il Arch Rec 138:189-94 O '65
Eight landscape tricks for plastic pools. C. Sigman. il Pop Sci 187:132-5 Jl '65
Ideas to profit by; planting for a boundary. J. A. Brimer. il Flower Grower 52:33 My '65
Industrial park gives rare plants a showcase; Sunshine State industrial park, Fla. il Bsns W p 122-4 Ja 15 '66
Landscape for casual living. R. W. Schery. il Pop Gard 16:10-11+ Jl '65
Landscaping with cobbles and boulders. il Sunset 135:146 Ag '65
Leased landscapes put bloom on business. il Bsns W p 158 F 27 '65
Marx brother; R. B. Marx, landscape architect. New Yorker 41:19 My 29 '65
Planting at the base of a tree. il Sunset 135: 152 Jl '65
Portfolio of plans for little gardens. il Flower Grower 52:20-3 S '65
Shopping center with take-home ideas; Oakbrook, Ill. L. Burgess. il Flower Grower 53:34-5 Ja '66
Taste for placement. M. C. Ohlander. il Flower Grower 52:44-5 My '65
Up the walk to the door. il Sunset 135: 94-5 O '65
See also
Back yards
Gardening—Planting plans and tables
Walks (paths)

LANDSCAPE improvement
Citizen action for a beautiful America. L. Perlis. il Recreation 58:482-3 D '65
Monthly review of events and ideas. Arch Forum 123:1 Jl; 13-16+ O; 11-14+ N; 9-12+ D '65
Special journal feature on beautification; symposium. il NEA J 54:33-40 N '65
See also
Roadside improvement

LANDSCAPE painting
American romantic landscapes. W. K. Sturges il Antiques 88:689-93 N '65
George Inness, painter of landscapes. L. Ireland. il Antiques 88:820-3 D '65
Landscape painting composition and its relation to abstract design. D. Frantz. il Design 67:31-3 N '65
Landscape paintings of Richard Kozlow. L. Bruner. il Am Artist 29:54-9+ My '65
Paintings; people and places of the old Northwest Territory. il Antiques 87:302-9 Mr '65
Total immersion in landscape; selection of Constable's prophetic sketches on loan from London, touring the U.S. G. Reynolds. il Art N 64:42-5+ O '65
Trove of Doughtys. T. N. Maytham. il Antiques 88:681-5 N '65

LANDSCAPE protection
America the ugly. C. B. Luce. il McCalls 92:20+ Je '65
Don't be a wreckreator. M. Robarge. il Recreation 58:274-6 Je '65
Duty to the future. S. L. Udall. Sat R 48: 48+ My 22 '65
Fighting fire with fire; saving wooded neighborhoods from developers bulldozers. Am For 71:9 N '65
Fouling of the American environment; symposium. il Sat R 48:31-48+ My 22 '65; Discussion. 48:21 Je 26 '65
Junk-car plague. Nation 200:630 Je 14 '65
Let's keep our natural beauty. P. F. Frese. Flower Grower 52:15 S '65
Quality of environment; excerpts from remarks, May 21, 1965. L. S. Rockefeller. Am For 71:11 Je '65
Still talkin' about the Tetons; Johnsons hailed on conservation. D. Fleeson. il Am For 71:22-5 N '65
Strip mining: Kentucky begins to close the reclamation gap. J. Walsh. il Science 150: 36-9 O 1 '65
Strip mining: TVA in middle in reclamation controversy. J. Walsh. il Science 150: 194-8 O 8 '65
Townscapes and turnpikes. F. Guthelm. Nation 200:622 Je 7 '65
What has happened to America the beautiful? R. Bendiner. il Redbook 125:50-1+ Je '65

LANDSLIDES
Dangerous dirt; some damage in Anchorage earthquake caused by landslides. Sci Am 213:42 D '65
Don't water the daisies! damaged homes of Pacific Palisades, suburban Los Angeles. il Time 85:43 Je 18 '65

LANDY, Maurice, and others
Involvement of thymus in immune response of rabbits to somatic polysaccharides of gram-negative bacteria. bibliog Science 147: 1591-2 Mr 26 '65
LANE, Elizabeth
Call her mister. por Time 86:40 Ag 27 '65
LANE, Laura
Want to stretch your mind? Farm J 89:82-3 Mr '65
LANE, Marion
Is there life on other planets? drama. Plays 24:60 Mr '65
LANE, Robert E.
Need to be liked and the anxious college liberal. bibliog f Ann Am Acad 361:71-80 S '65
LANE, Thomas A.
Unseen epic. Nat R 17:246-7 Mr 23 '65
When do we seize the initiative? Nat R 17:384-5 My 4 '65
LANE, Will
Vagabond camera. See issues of Travel
LANE magazine and book company
New Lane building nearing completion. il Pub W 187:68-9 F 15 '65
LANE publishing company. See Lane magazine and book company
LANG, Barbara
Teen-age marriage: love finds a way. Ladies Home J 82:68-9+ Je '65
Truth about college weekends; excerpt from Boys and other beasts. McCalls 92:32-3 Ap '65
LANG, Daniel
Greatest discovery; excerpt from Inquiry into enoughness. Sat R 48:28 Ap 17 '65
LANG, Pearl
Pearl Lang and dance company, Hunter college playhouse. M. Marks. Dance Mag 39: 33+ Je '65
LANG, Thomas G. and Smith, H. A. P.
Communication between dolphins in separate tanks by way of an electronic acoustic link. bibliog Science 150:1839-44 D 31 '65
LANGBAUM, Robert
Publish or perish, why Prof. Edelweiss has little time for junior. N Y Times Mag p74-5+ N 14 '65
LANGE, Juel
Memorable Mount Rainier. Travel 124:48-9 Ag '65
LANGE, P. W. See Hydén, H. jt. auth.
LANGE, Victor
Challenge of the myth and mask. Sat R 48: 43 Mr 6 '65
Worlds of desolation. New Repub 153:36-8 N 27 '65
L'ANGE de feu; opera. See Prokof'ev, S. S.
LANGENHEIM, Jean H. and Beck, C. W.
Infrared spectra as a means of determining botanical sources of amber. bibliog Science 149:52-5 Jl 2 '65
LANGER, Elinor
Scientists and policy at ground zero. Nation 201:124-7 S 6 '65
LANGER, Howard J.
(ed) See Foshay, A. W. Scholastic teacher interview
(ed) See Spock, B. Scholastic teacher interview
LANGEWIESCHE, Wolfgang
Our car-strangled cities. Read Digest 87:71-6 Jl '65
What water shortage? Read Digest 88:51-4+ Ja '66
LANGFORD, George B.
Filth in the Great Lakes: what can be done about it; interview. por U S News 59:58-61 D 13 '65
LANGGUTH, Jack
Ambush! N Y Times Mag p4-5+ Je 27 '65
Saigon tries to live in a hurry. N Y Times Mag p 12-13+ Ag 8 '65
They are not jolly in the foxholes. N Y Times Mag p26-7+ My 9 '65
War in Vietnam can be won, but—. N Y Times Mag p30-1+ S 19 '65
LANGLAND, Joseph
Singing in late summer; poem. Poetry 105:237 Ja '65
LANGLEY, Bobby
Champion of champions. D. Wells. il Hot Rod 18:82-3+ F '65
LANGNER, Lawrence
Shakespeare explosion. J. Reddy. Read Digest 87:198+ Ag '65
LANGUAGE, Universal
Undoing Babel. P. Rónai. il Américas 17:26-30 Je '65
LANGUAGE and languages
Hidden politics of words; colonialism of language. M. Pei. Sat R 49:22-4 Ja 15 '66
Language conflicts: can they be defused? il Sr Schol 86:12-16+ Ap 8 '65

Mother tongue, by L. Hogben. Review
Time 85:98 Ap 2 '65
Well-traveled camera? the well-spoken camera! with set of phrases, in four languages. R. Burgess. Mod Phot 29:14+ Je '65
World languages. il Sr Schol 87:16-17 S 30 '65
See also
Alphabet
Communication (speech, writing, etc)
Languages, Modern
Semantics
Translations and translating

Psychology
Classroom incident; symposium. NEA J 54: 40-1 F '65

Study and teaching
Non-western studies in liberal arts colleges. D. L. Hamilton. Sch & Soc 93:244+ Ap 17 '65
See also
Languages, Modern—Study and teaching
LANGUAGE arts
New curriculum in English, speech, and communications. S. Simonson. Sch & Soc 93: 394-5 O 30 '65

Bibliography
Book reviews: history and language arts. H. L. Hurwitz. Sr Schol 86:sup21 Mr 18 '65

Study and teaching
New tool for English teachers; concerning Annotated recording list in the language arts. M. Schreiber. il Sr Schol 87:sup5 O 7 '65
Ode from the echo chamber. H. Kenner. bibliog f il Nat R 17:1084-6+ N 30 '65
LANGUAGE of animals. See Animal communication
LANGUAGES. See Language and languages
LANGUAGES, Modern

Study and teaching
Foreign language curriculum and its shifting foundations. R. L. Politzer. bibliog f Sch & Soc 93:249-52 Ap 17 '65
Foreign language summer camps for children. T. O. Brandt. Sch & Soc 93:372-3 O 16 '65
Foreign language teaching: Inter-American program in linguistics and language teaching: letter to the editor. F. G. de Matos. Américas 17:48 N '65
Innovations in foreign language instruction; North Carolina. T. T. Ladu. il Sr Schol 87:sup 16-17 O 14 '65
Language for librarians; working knowledge in foreign languages at Graduate school of library and information sciences, University of Pittsburgh. A. C. Hall. il Library J 90:3177-8 Ag '65
Trump plan applied to modern language teaching. J. L. Trump. il NEA J 54:50-4 Ap '65
Why should we learn foreign languages? C. B. Luce. McCalls 93:41+ O '65
See also
Portuguese language—Study and teaching
LANHAM, T. J.
Nip in the air. Flying 77:110 O '65
LANNING, Edward P.
Early man in Peru; with biographical sketch. Sci Am 213:10, 68-76 bibliog(p 127) O '65
LANSDALE, Edward G.
Appointment that led to questions. U S News 59:15 S 6 '65
Old lover; special assistant to Ambassador H. C. Lodge. il por Newsweek 66:29-30 Ag 30 '65
True test. il por Newsweek 67:34-5 Ja 17 '66
LANSDALE, Nelson
Three centuries of the art of Niagara Falls. Am Artist 29:34-9+ Ap '65
LANTZ, Louise K.
Be lavish with lavender. Flower Grower 52: 74 F '65
Grow your own horseradish. Horticulture 43: 51 Mr '65
LAOS
See also
Economic assistance in Laos
United States—Air force—Forces in Laos

Air force
Bombing reds' lifeline in Laos: eyewitness report, Ho Chi Minh trail. S. W. Sanders. il U S News 60:37-9 Ja 24 '66
Silver lining: no pilots killed in explosion at Vientiane's Wattay airport. T. Arbuckle. Newsweek 65:37 F 8 '65

LAOS—*Continued*

Neutrality

More troublesome trail; Ho Chi Minh trail. il Time 86:28-9 D 17 '65
Neutralization experiment in Laos. A. J. Dommen. Cur Hist 48:89-94+ F '65
United States reaffirms support of Geneva agreements on Laos; statement, January 18, 1965. R. J. McCloskey. Dept State Bul 52:167 F 8 '65

Politics and government

Battle of the neckerchiefs. Time 85:20-1 F 12 '65
Cautionary report on Laos. D. Warner. il Reporter 33:35-8 D 2 '65
Now it's Laos where war erupts. il U S News 58:8 F 15 '65
Our secret war in Laos. D. Warner. il Reporter 32:23-6 Ap 22 '65
Progress amid the potholes. Time 86:39 O 1 '65
Silent sideshow. il Time 85:35-6 Je 11 '65
Whose coup? Newsweek 65:38 F 15 '65

LAPCHICK, Joe
Joe Lapchick: basketball's biggest man. T. Cohane. il pors Look 29:95-6+ Mr 9 '65
LAPCHICK, Joseph Bohumiel. See Lapchick, J.
LAPHAM, Lewis
Great idea boy. Sat Eve Post 238:74-81 F 13 '65
Has anyone here seen Kelly? Sat Eve Post 238:32-4+ Ap 24 '65
Mirage of beautiful air. Sat Eve Post 238: 34-6+ Mr 27 '65
Who is Lyndon Johnson? Sat Eve Post 238: 21-5+ S 11 '65
Why Mr Jarvis deserves torture. Sat Eve Post 238:80+ D 18 '65
LAPIDARY carving. See Carving (art industries)
LAPIDE, Pinchas E.
Mandelbaum gate; way to peace? Christian Cent 82:239-40 F 24 '65
LAPIDUS, Morris
Man who put the rhinestones on Miami. M. Mayer. il Harper 230:61-8 Mr '65
LAPIERRE, Dominique. See Collins, L. jt. auth.
LAPINSKI, Susan
Toast to pop music. Seventeen 25:12 Ja '66
LA PIRA, Giorgio
Amateur hour. Newsweek 66:19 D 27 '65
LAPORTE, Roger Allen
Catholic worker. il por Newsweek 66:71 N 22 '65
Human voice means more. por Time 86:118 N 19 '65
Immolations in U.S. Sr Schol 87:15 D 2 '65
In witness to man's oneness. B. Reynolds. Christian Cent 83:81 Ja 19 '66
LAPP, Ralph E.
5:29 a.m. and the world was changed forever. Life 59:14+ Jl 16 '65
Nuclear power of China. Life 58:86-90+ My 28 '65; Same abr. with title Does red China understand the bomb? Read Digest 87:49-53 S '65
LAPPALAINEN, Kalevi
Night in the woods; poem. Nation 200:152 F 8 '65
LAPWORTH, Bill
Bill Lapworth on design. Yachting 117:204+ Je '65
Yachting interviews: Bill Lapworth; ed. by B. Robinson. por Yachting 117:45+ Je '65
LAQUEUR, Walter Z.
Bonn, Cairo, Jerusalem: the triple crisis. Commentary 39:29-38 My '65
LARDNER, Rex
Rugby. Sports Illus 22:65-6+ My 10 '65
Winter madmen on the courts. N Y Times Mag p44-5+ N 21 '65
LARDNER, Susan
Current cinema. New Yorker 41:102+ Je 12; 114 Je 19 '65
LAREDO, Tex.

Anti-poverty program

Laredo: case history in war on poverty. il U S News 59:74-6 N 8 '65
LA RETAMA public library, Corpus Christi, Tex.
Project opportunity in Corpus Christi. P. S. Burson. il Wilson Lib Bul 40:257-61 N '65
LAREW, Lee O.
Boats! camera! action! il por Motor B 115: 26-9+ Je '65
LAREZ, Jess
College serves the community. Recreation 58: 485 D '65

LARGE families. See Family, Size of
LARGEMOUTH bass fishing. See Bass fishing
LARGENT, Robert E.
To catch a butterfly. il U S Camera 28:50-1 Jl '65
LARKIN, Philip
Losses, engagements, privacies. W. Stafford. Poetry 106:294 Jl '65
Poetry of commonplaces. J. L. Featherstone. New Repub 152:27-9 Mr 6 '65
Solitary sensibility. por Time 85:E5+ F 19 '65
Verse. L. Bogan. New Yorker 41:193-4+ Ap 10 '65
LARNEN, Brendan
Patrick—the first. Criticism America 112:440 Mr 27 '65
LARNER, Jeremy
College drug scene. Atlan 216:127-30+ N '65
New improved drug scene. Nation 201:120-4 S 20 '65
Young drug addict: can we help him? excerpt from Addict in the street. Atlan 215:75-80 F '65
LA ROCHELLE, Pierre Drieu. See Drieu La Rochelle, P.
LARRABEE, Eric
Jazz notes. See issues of Harper's magazine
Pursuit of peace. Atlan 216:61-5 N '65
Time to kill, automation, leisure and jobs. Nation 201:198-202 S 20 '65
LARRICK, Nancy
All-white world of children's books. Sat R 48:63-5+ S 11 '65
Letter to parents. por Sr Schol 86:sup 15 Mr 4 '65
New phonetic alphabets. Parents Mag 40: 49-53+ O '65
Summer reading programs pay big dividends. Sr Schol 86:sup21-2 Mr 4 '65
LARROCHA, Alicia de
Music to my ears; performance of Mozart piano concerto in A, with Philharmonic orchestra. I. Kolodin. Sat R 49:30 Ja 15 '66
LARSEN, Ellouise Baker, collection. See Smithsonian institution—Museum of history and technology
LARSEN, Emil
Visit with the glass artist, Emil Larsen. I. P. Tuttle. il por Hobbies 70:66-7 S '65
LARSEN, Jack Lenor
Arts and architecture; functionalism versus decoration; condensation of debate. Craft Horiz 25:56+ My '65
LARSEN, Leonard
Where Negroes keep out other Negroes; reprint. U S News 59:62-3 O 18 '65
LARSEN, Roy E.
Arts committee reports progress on cultural presentations; letter of transmittal, December 29, 1964. Dept State Bul 52:108-11 Ja 25 '65
LARSON, Arthur
Can science prevent war? Sat R 48:15-17+ F 20; 27 Ap 3 '65
Future of peacekeeping. Sat R 48:22-3+ Jl 24 '65
—See Larson, D. R. jt. auth.
LARSON, Carl H.
Sand cast sculpture: fine art in fine sand. il Design 66:6-9 Mr '65
LARSON, Don R. and Larson, Arthur
Plan for peace in Vietnam. Sat R 48:21-4 Ap 24 '65
LARSON, Don W.
Magic month for fishing. Outdoor Life 136: 30-1+ S '65
LARSON, James E.
Operation brainstorm. NEA J 54:41 N '65
LARSON, Rachel H. and Simms, M. E.
Double mating: its use to study heritable factors in dental caries. bibliog Science 149:982-3 Ag 27 '65
LARUS, Joel
To reduce the possibility of nuclear catastrophe. Bul Atomic Sci 21:33-6 Ap '65
LARYNX cancer. See Cancer
LASAGNA. See Cookery, Italian
LASALLE, Pierre
Radiocarbon date from the Lake St John area, Quebec. bibliog Science 149:860-2 Ag 20 '65

LA SALLE college, Philadelphia
Drop in dropouts. America 112:512 Ap 17 '65

LASCA, Moises
Exclusive! Cuban education: on-the-spot interview; ed. by W. Johnson. Sr Schol 87: sup2 N 18 '65

LA SCALA museum. See Music museums

LASCH, Christopher
Explosion that froze the world. Nation 201: 123-4 S 6 '65
Getting out of power. Commentary 40:116+ N '65
Magazines of dissent thrive on unpopularity. N Y Times Mag p 10-11+ Jl 18 '65
New curriculum for teach-ins. Nation 201: 239-41 O 18 '65
—and Spitzer, A. B.
Unthinkable target. Nation 201:74-5+ Ag 16 '65

LASER altimeters. See Altimeters

LASER communication systems. See Light communication systems

LASER photography. See Lasers—Photographic applications

LASERS
Amateur scientist; homemade laser. C. L. Stong. il Sci Am 213:108-13 D '65
Chemical lasers. Sci Am 212:58 Ap '65
Gemini laser test may speed future use. B. Miller. il Aviation W 83:71+ D 13 '65
Laser, a three-step device. W. H. Murray. il Electr World 73:49+ F '65
Laser advances affect communications, radar. Miss & Roc 17:31 S 20 '65
Laser coherence problems reduced. C. D. LaFond. il Miss & Roc 16:35-6 Ap 5 '65
Laser communication qualified success; optical-frequency communications system. C. D. LaFond. il Miss & Roc 17:18+ Jl 12 '65
Laser measurements. W. Groner. il Electr World 74:50-2+ N '65
Laser; practice and applications. W. Groner. il Electr World 74:45-8+ S '65
Laser precautions. W. A. Stocklin. Electr World 74:6 Ag '65
Laser R&D spending soars. Miss & Roc 17: 10 Ag 30 '65
Lasers. W. Groner. il Electr World 74:31-5+ Ag '65
Lasers; adaptation of address, December 28 1963. A. L. Schawlow. bibliog il Science 149:13-22 Jl 2 '65
Lidar observation of cloud. R. T. H. Collis. il Science 149:978-81 Ag 27 '65
Optical communications. R. Kompfner. bibliog il Science 150:149-55 O 8 '65; Reply. H. Malamud. 150:1484 D 10 '65
Optical imaging unit shown feasible. C. D. LaFond. il Miss & Roc 16:32-3+ Je 7 '65
Production of coherent radiation by atoms and molecules; address, December 11, 1964. C. H. Townes. bibliog il Science 149:831-41 Ag 20 '65
Retina: pathology of neodymium and ruby laser burns. M. L. Wolbarsht and others. bibliog il Science 150:1453-4 D 10 '65
Selective mitochondrial damage by a ruby laser microbeam: an electron microscopic study. R. L. Amy and R. Storb. bibliog il Science 150:756-8 N 5 '65
Semiconductor lasers; address, December 11, 1964. N. G. Basov. bibliog il Science 149: 821-7 Ag 20 '65
Single laser beam relays seven channels. Sci N L 87:131 F 27 '65
Two-quantum maser; obtaining two-quantum emission in optical maser. Sci Am 213:40-1 O '65
Varied tactical uses developing for laser. B. Miller. il Aviation W 82:39+ My 31 '65
Who invented the laser? C. H. Townes' and A. L. Schawlow's patent rights challenged. il Bsns W p 132-7 N 27 '65

Medical applications
Laser light beam can heal or damage eyes. Sci N L 87:357 Je 5 '65
Laser on the cancer frontier; with account by M. Steinmann. il Life 59:70-1+ Jl 9 '65
Laser to relieve cancer. Sci N L 88:52 Jl 24 '65
New world of surgery: hottest heat and coldest cold perform operating-room miracles. R. Berg. il Look 29:78-82+ My 4 '65

Photographic applications
Air reconnaissance aided by line-scanning laser camera. B. Miller. il Aviation W 82: 80-1+ Ap 26 '65
Dark is light enough; Perkin-Elmer corporation's laser camera for TV. Newsweek 66:98 D 20 '65
NOL uses laser light to get clear test pictures. il Miss & Roc 17:22 N 8 '65

Photography by laser. E. N. Leith and J. Upatnicks. il Sci Am 212:24-35 Je '65
True 3-D image from laser photography. E. N. Leith and J. Upatnieks. il Electr World 74:34-5+ O '65

LASKER, Mary (Woodard)
Unforgettable character of Dusty Rhoads. Read Digest 86:163-4+ Ap '65

about
Beautifier. por Time 85:43 Je 4 '65

LASKER awards. See Albert Lasker awards

LASKI, Marghanita
Her daughter, the princess. Sat R 48:24 Ap 3 '65

LASKY, Jerome M.
Hijinks that can haunt your life. Read Digest 86:92-5 Je '65

LASKY, Victor
Mature (i.e. liberal) JFK. Nat R 17:1029-30 N 16 '65

LASS, Herbert
Gauguin woodblocks rediscovered. Am Artist 29:36-41+ My '65

LASSEN, Peter
War of the Never Sweats. T. St George. il por Nat Parks Mag 39:16-17 S '65

LASSEN VOLCANIC NATIONAL PARK
War of the Never Sweats. T. St George. il Nat Parks Mag 39:16-17 S '65

LASSUS, Roland de
Nonesuch has hit the bull's-eye again. J. W. Barker. Am Rec G 31:1163 Ag '65

LAST jack-o'-lantern; story. See Schaeling, M.

LAST rites; story. See Vivante, A.

LAST stop; drama. See Cable, H.

LAST time I saw Petrograd; story. See Argus, M. K.

LAST tree; story. See Madrid-Malo, N.

LASTER, Leonard
Stones people get: causes, treatment; interview. por U S News 59:37-8 O 25 '65

LASTRA, Luis
Unknown treasure. Américas 17:18-26 F '65

LAS VEGAS, Nev.
What Del Webb is up to in Nevada. T. Alexander. il Fortune 71:130-2+ My '65

Description
Vacation in Las Vegas. il Ebony 20:180-2 Je '65

Education
Las Vegas' impressive Newcomer. Time 86: 94+ D 17 '65

LATEINER, Jacob
Lateiner's Beethoven. J. M. Conly. il Reporter 32:46+ F 11 '65

LATENESS. See Tardiness

LATHAM, Harold Strong
Harold Latham's My life in publishing. D. M. Glixon. Pub W 188:287-8 Ag 30 '65
Peripatetic reviewer. E. Weeks. Atlan 216: 162+ O '65
Way it was. J. F. Fixx. Sat R 48:53+ Ag 14 '65

LATHBURY, Vincent T.
Mothers and sons: an intimate discussion. Ladies Home J 82:43-5 F '65

LATHES
Tricks for milling on a lathe. C. W. Woodson. il Pop Sci 188:144-5 Ja '66

LATIES, Victor G. See Weiss, B. jt. auth.

LATIN AMERICA
Breakthrough in South America. W. Lippmann. Newsweek 67:11 Ja 3 '66
Four views of Latin America; symposium. Yale R 55:161-208 D '65
Latin America tomorrow; report on annual meeting of the American academy of political and social science. F. L. Phelps. il Américas 17:13-15 Je '65
Latin America tomorrow; symposium, ed. by J. C. Charlesworth. bibliog f Ann Am Acad 360:1-138 Jl '65
See also
Arts and crafts—Latin America
Automobile industry and trade—Latin America
Birth control—Latin America
Booksellers and bookselling—Latin America
Catholic church in Latin America
Church and state in Latin America
Communism—Latin America
Cooperation—Latin America
Economic assistance in Latin America
Education—Latin America
Food relief—Latin America
Food supply—Latin America
Guerrillas—Latin America
Housing—Latin America

LATIN AMERICA—See also—*Continued*
  Libraries—Latin America
  Natural resources—Latin America
  Nutrition problems—Latin America
  Opera—Latin America
  Political parties—Latin America
  Protestants in Latin America
  Publishers and publishing—Latin America
  Research—Latin America
  Sports—Latin America
  Technical assistance in Latin America
  Trade unions—Latin America
  United Nations—Latin America

Antiquities
See also
Indians of South America—Antiquities

Bibliography
Readings on Latin America. M. H. Sable.
  Cur Hist 49:363-6 D '65

Civilization
Culture we share; American hemisphere as
  single cultural entity. R. Squirru. il Américas 17:42-9 Ap '65

Commerce
Common market for Latin America? il U S
  News 58:93-4 My 3 '65
Community for prosperity. Time 85:40 Ap 16
  '65
Facts and figures of the Americas; coffee
  and banana exports, 1963. Américas 17:47
  Mr '65
Facts and figures of the Americas; meat and
  sugar exports, 1963. il Américas 17:45 Jl '65
  See also
Coffee trade

Defenses
Latin America reacts. D. D. Ranstead.
  Commonweal 82:613-15 S 3 '65

Description and travel
Bettina: the adventures of a passionate
  traveller; excerpts from journal; tr. by F.
  Frenaye. S. Bodin. il Vogue 147:138-43+ Ja
  1 '66
Land of mule trains and monasteries. J.
  Mirsky. il Sat R 48:73 My 22 '65
Why you need to know about South America.
  C. P. Streeter. il Farm J 89:34-6+ S '65

Economic conditions
Canada rides a crest, Japan fights recession;
  inflation worries Latin America. il Bsns W
  p48-9 Ja 1 '66
Challenge of development in Latin America,
  by V. L. Urquidi. Review
    Cath World 201:406+ S '65. W. J. Gibbons
Inter-American development bank: investing
  in Latin America, 1965; address, February
  3, 1965. T. G. Upton. il Vital Speeches 31:
  375-80 Ap 1 '65
Latin America: myth and reality, by P.
  Nehemkis. Review
    Américas 17:39-40 Mr '65. L. R. Scheman
Latin example for growth. Life 58:4 Ap 9
  '65
New conquest. il Time 85:32-42 Mr 12 '65
New conquistadors in the Amazon jungle.
  E. P. Hanson. il Américas 17:1-8 S '65;
  Correction. 17:48 N '65
'64 balance sheet and '65 prospectus. R.
  Peter. Nat R 17:194 Mr 9 '65
Sudden development; growth patterns. R. N.
  Adams. il Américas 17:3-6 Ag '65
Three on the go: off the crisis list; Nicara-
  gua, Honduras, Paraguay. il Time 86:43
  N 26 '65
U.S. trade policy in Latin America; state-
  ment, September 10, 1965. J. H. Vaughn.
  Dept State Bul 53:559-67 O 4 '65
Warning signals. Time 85:32 Je 4 '65
What's wrong in Latin America. J. N. Wal-
  lace. il U S News 58:40-4 My 24 '65
Written large and clear. Farm J 89:106 Je '65
  See also
Poor—Latin America
United Nations—Economic commission for
  Latin America

Economic integration
Latin American integration; its legal and
  institutional aspects. F. V. García-Amador.
  il Américas 17:50-3 Ap '65

Economic policy
Chapter that Keynes never wrote; address,
  February 24, 1965. W. W. Rostow. Dept
  State Bul 52:454-9 Mr 29 '65
Common goal; economic and social progress.
  W. J. Sedwitz. il Américas 17:10-15 Ap '65

Common quest for freedom and prosperity in
  the American republics; address, November 22, 1965; with texts of resolutions
  adopted at Rio de Janeiro conference.
  D. Rusk. bibliog f Dept State Bul 53:985-
  95, 996-8 D 20 '65
Social science and development; excerpt from
  Social sciences in Latin America, ed. by
  M. Diégues, jr. and B. Wood. L. E. Cerda.
  il Américas 17:1-7 N '65

Foreign relations
Diplomatic asylum, by C. N. Ronning. Re-
  view
    Américas 17:36 N '65. C. G. Fenwick
Latin America and neutralism. N. de S. Sam-
  paio. Ann Am Acad 362:62-70 N '65
  See also
Monroe doctrine

United States
Dominican crisis: issue is nonintervention.
  D. D. Ranstead. New Repub 152:8-9 My
  29 '65
Latin American mission, by deL. S. Morri-
  son. Review
    Sat R 48:29-30 Ag 21 '65. A. A. Berle
New man in Rio: J. H. Vaughn. il News-
  week 66:48-9 N 29 '65

History
Bibliography
Articles and other books received; comp. by
  W. N. Simonson. See issues of American
  historical review

War of independence, 1806-1830
Liberators of the South. E. Correas. il
  Américas 17:14-21 S '65

Industries
Deeper roots for the Alliance; national mar-
  kets for economic development. W. W.
  Rostow. il Américas 17:37-41 Ap '65

Maps
Map of Latin America (cont) Sr Schol 87:
  25 S 30 '65

Politics
Burning fuses: violence and unrest. il News-
  week 65:37 My 31 '65
Changing South America; symposium. bib-
  liog f il Cur Hist 49:321-61+ D '65
Freedom and unity in the Americas; with
  bibliography. W. J. Kilgore. il Américas 17:
  1-4 D '65
Hopes rise south of the border; Communists
  losing ground. il Bsns W p97-8 My 29 '65
Latin America and revolution. J. A. Mackay.
  Christian Cent 82:1409-12 N 17 '65
Latin America: myth and reality, by P.
  Nehemkis. Review
    Américas 17:39-40 Mr '65. L. R. Scheman
Latin America reacts. D. D. Ranstead.
  Commonweal 82:613-15 S 3 '65
Latin America: the fear within. F. J. Mo-
  reno. Yale R 55:161-8 D '65
Our good neighbors should come first. J.
  Plank. il N Y Times Mag p30-1+ Je 6 '65
Soldier as reformer. il Newsweek 66:45 Ag
  23 '65
Toward a Latin American parliament. J.
  Ignacio Rasco. il Américas 17:12-17 Jl '65
What hope for Latin America? W. S. Stokes.
  il Nat R 17:591-4 Jl 13 '65
What's wrong in Latin America. J. N. Wal-
  lace. il U S News 58:40-4 My 24 '65

Population
Population program; world-wide American
  population control policy. America 112:216
  F 13 '65; Reply. R. M. Fahey. 112:408 Mr
  27 '65
What hope for Latin America? W. S. Stokes.
  il Nat R 17:591-4 Jl 13 '65

Religious institutions and affairs
World around us. Christian Cent 83:90-1 Ja
  19 '66
  See also
Catholic church in Latin America

Social conditions
Alliance for progress: failures and opportu-
  nities. T. J. Draper. Yale R 55:182-90 D '65
Revolution in Latin America. G. C. Lodge.
  For Affairs 44:173-97 Ja '66
Sudden development; growth patterns. R. N.
  Adams. il Américas 17:3-6 Ag '65

LATIN AMERICA—*Continued*

Social policy

Common quest for freedom and prosperity in the American republics; address, November 22, 1965; with texts of resolutions adopted at Rio de Janeiro conference. D. Rusk. bibliog f Dept State Bul 53:985-95. 996-8 D 20 '65

Pattern of development in Latin America; with questions and answers. R. N. Adams. il Ann Am Acad 360:1-10 Jl '65

Social science and development; excerpt from Social sciences in Latin America, ed. by M. Diégues, jr. and B. Wood. L. E. Cerda. il Américas 17:1-7 N '65

LATIN AMERICA and the United States
On thinking Latin American. K. J. Pollinger. America 113:214-15 Ag 28 '65

Our good neighbors should come first. J. Plank. il N Y Times Mag p30-1+ Je 6 '65

United States and Latin America; special ties of interest and affection; address, January 30, 1965. E. Bunker. Dept State Bul 52:301-4 Mr 1 '65

What liberty means; reactions to visits of D. Rusk and R. Kennedy. il Newsweek 66: 26 N 29 '65

See also
Inter-American relations

LATIN AMERICAN art. See Art, Latin American

LATIN AMERICAN baseball players. See Baseball players

LATIN AMERICAN book programs, incorporated
Nonprofit inter-American book program is projected. Pub W 189:45-6 Ja 3 '66

LATIN AMERICAN committee on national parks. See International union for the conservation of nature and natural resources

LATIN AMERICAN folk art. See Folk art

LATIN AMERICAN free trade association
Common market for Latin America? il U S News 58:93-4 My 3 '65

Latin American free trade association; with text of Montevideo treaty. M. S. Wionczek. bibliog f il Int Concil 551:3-80 Ja '65

LATIN AMERICAN historians. See Historians, Latin American

LATIN AMERICAN literature
In praise of Guimaraes Rosa; U.S. critical neglect of Latin American writers. E. Rodriguez-Monegal. Commentary 41:65-7 Ja '66

Latin America's neglected literature. R. J. Clements. il Sat R 48:60-1 My 22 '65

LATIN AMERICAN Lutheran conference. See Religious conferences

LATIN AMERICAN painting. See Painting, Latin American

LATIN AMERICAN times
Southward venture; first U.S. daily devoted exclusively to news from south of the border. Time 86:45 Jl 16 '65

LATIN AMERICANS in the United States
Crusade against gringos; Federal alliance of land grants claims original Spanish land. il Newsweek 67:17-18 Ja 3 '66

LATIN historians
See also
Livy (Titus Livius)

LATTIMER, John K.
Sword hilts by early American silversmiths. Antiques 87:196-9 F '65

LATTIMORE, Richmond
Bathtubs; poem. New Yorker 41:30 Jl 31 '65
Of seven sins; Sticks; poems. Poetry 106:185-9 Je '65

LAUE, James H.
Changing character of Negro protest. bibliog f Ann Am Acad 357:119-26 Ja '65

LAUGHING gulls. See Gulls

LAUGHING sickness. See Diseases

LAUGHLIN, James
Those old gods; Saxo cere; poems. Nation 200:654 Je 14 '65

LAUGHTER
See also
Humor

LAUGHTON, Floyd R.
Test your soil. Pop Gard 16:6+ Mr '65

LAUNCHING pads for missiles. See Guided missiles—Launching pads

LAUNCHING pads for space vehicles. See Space vehicles—Launching pads

LAUNCHING sites for space vehicles. See Space vehicles—Launching sites

LAUNDRIES
It takes very little to make your laundry pretty. il House & Gard 128:222-5 O '65
This laundry was designed for farm living. J. LemMon. il Suc Farm 63:114-15 S '65

LAUNDRY
Solutions to your laundry quandary. B. Strawn. Bet Hom & Gard 43:112-13 Mr '65
Washday tips for children's clothes. B. G. Wadsworth. Parents Mag 40:148 S '65
What every new mother should know about washing baby clothes. Redbook 125:46+ O '65

LAUNDRY equipment
Complete laundry; do-it-yourself plans. il Ladies Home J 82:104+ S '65
What's the word on farm home laundries? J. LemMon. il Suc Farm 64:106-7 Ja '66
See also
Clothes dryers
Flatirons
Washing machines

LAUNDRY workers
Stomping on the Savoy. Newsweek 67:46 Ja 3 '66

LAURA Ingalls Wilder award. See Wilder award

LAUREL international. See Horse racing

LAUREL-Langley agreement. See Philippines—Commercial treaties and agreements

LAUREL VALLEY club course. See Golf courses

LAURENCE, Margaret
Epic love of Elmi Bonderi. Holiday 38:35+ N '65
Sayonara, Agamemnon. Holiday 39:21-4+ Ja '66

LAURENCE, William L.
Alamogordo, mon amour. Esquire 63:118-21+ My '65
(ed) Would you make the bomb again? N Y Times Mag p8-9 Ag 1 '65

LAURENT, Robert
Robert Laurent, master carver. N. Kent. il por Am Artist 29:42-7+ My '65

LAURENTIIS, Dino de
Giraffe in Piazza del Popolo. T. Sage. il Nat R 17:105-6 F 9 '65
Our far-flung correspondents. L. Ross. New Yorker 41:185-6+ S 25 '65

LAUYANS, Sherry
Curl up and read. il Seventeen 24:174 F '65

LAVA BEDS NATIONAL MONUMENT
Petroglyphs. I. Reed. il Nat Parks Mag 39: 9-10 S '65
They're exploring a lava cave. il Sunset 134: 77+ Je '65

LAVA tubes (caves) See Caves

LAVALLEE, John E.
Gas-driven drywasher. por Pop Mech 125:170-3 Ja '66

LAVENDER
Be lavish with lavender. L. K. Lantz. Flower Grower 52:74 F '65

LAVER, James
What will fashion uncover next? Read Digest 87:142-5 S '65

LAVER, Rod
Rocket off the pad. il por Time 85:81-2 My 14 '65

LAVIN, Mary
One summer; story. New Yorker 41:50-8 S 11 '65

LAVIN, Pablo F.
José Cecilio del Valle, Pan Americanist. Américas 17:7-9 Ag '65

LAVINE, Harold
Between rebels and rightists. Sat R 48:36 N 27 '65
Mercurial Fidel. Sat R 48:28-9 Ag 21 '65

LAVON, Pinhas
Old man the young Sabras. C. Sterling. il Reporter 33:35-8 N 4 '65

LAW, G, R. J. and Munro, S.S.
Inheritance of two alkaline phosphatase variants in fowl plasma. bibliog Science 149:1518 S 24 '65

LAW, John H. and others
Biochemical polymorphism in ants. bibliog Science 149:544-6 Jl 30 '65

LAW
U.S. tourist's legal sampler: foreign laws. il Time 85:84-5 My 7 '65
See also
Civil rights
Confession (law)
Copyright
Justice, Administration of
Lawyers
Libel and slander
also special branches of law, e.g. Criminal law; *also* law on special subjects e.g. Boats and boating—Laws and regulations; Game laws; etc

Bibliography
Laying down the law. M. Feldman. Sat R 48:70-2 My 22 '65

LAW—*Continued*

Curiosa and miscellany
Codes of ethics. A. M. Sullivan. Duns R 85: 146 Ap '65
Recent rulings; comp. by H. Helfer. il N Y Times Mag p63 My 23: 83 Je 6; 67 Ag 29; 40 N 21 '65

History
Colonial court records and the study of early American history: a bibliographical review. M. G. Kammen. bibliog f Am Hist R 70: 732-9 Ap '65

Philosophy
Morality and policy. America 112:747 My 22 '65
See also
Law and ethics

Study and teaching
Prodigious professor; new breed of young law professors. Time 86:68 D 10 '65

Alabama
Brave politician in the South: Attorney General R. M. Flowers. Life 59:4 N 5 '65

California
Compensating the victim; first laws go into effect. Newsweek 67:16 Ja 3 '66
Fire safety around your country place. Sunset 135:120+ S '65
Psychotherapeutic abortion; bill under consideration. R. P. Vaughan. America 113: 436-8 O 16 '65
Round one to Proposition fourteen. il Time 85:74 F 12 '65

Connecticut
Catholic agency opposes birth control ban; Catholic council on civil liberties. Christian Cent 82:262 Mr 3 '65
Now, legal family planning; Connecticut birth control law unconstitutional. H. G. Lewis. Christian Cent 82:970+ Ag 4 '65
Some of your best friends will go to court for you; amicus curiae brief, attacking law that bans sale of contraceptives. il Time 85:50 F 26 '65

Georgia
Justice, southern style; Ashton Jones vs Atlanta's First Baptist church. J. Gillies; discussion. Christian Cent 81:270-2; 82:732 F 26 '64. Je 9 '65

Great Britain
Britain pays the victim of the crime; state compensation for victims of criminal violence. C. Hussey. il N Y Times Mag p 19-20+ F 21 '65
Is homosexuality a crime? J. Grigg. N Y Times Mag p6-7+ Je 27 '65
See also
Divorce—Great Britain

Iowa
Death penalty abolished. P. B. Mather. Christian Cent 82:382 Mr 24 '65

Israel
Lady in the dark; investigation of citizenship of R. Eitani. Time 85:65 F 12 '65

Maryland
God & courts in Maryland. Time 86:67 D 10 '65
God & man in Maryland; religious test oaths. Time 86:94 O 22 '65

Mississippi
Impeach Judge Cox. A. M. Bickel. New Repub 153:13 S 4 '65

North Carolina
Academic casualty; North Carolina speaker-ban law. C. N. Degler. New Repub 153:10 Jl 10 '65
Speaker-ban law; North Carolina's law barring Communists and pleaders of the Fifth amendment from speaking at state-supported educational institutions. W. M. Wells, jr. Christian Cent 82:902 Jl 14 '65

Ohio
Mother's right & duty; case involving sex instruction and free speech. Time 87:75 Ja 7 '66

Russia
Russia shoots its business crooks; executions for economic crimes. G. Feifer. il N Y Times Mag p32-3+ My 2 '65

United States
Colonial court records and the study of early American history: a bibliographical review. M. G. Kammen. bibliog f Am Hist R 70: 732-9 Ap '65
Education of Tom Brady. Time 86:94+ O 22 '65
Interstate relations, some emergent trends. P. Monypenny. bibliog f Ann Am Acad 359: 53-9 My '65
It's against the law! il Ebony 20:138-9 Ag '65
Law. H. W. Jones. il NEA J 54:42-5 Ap '65
Policeman. il Sat Eve Post 238:100 Mr 13 '65
Why slap a helping hand? Life 58:4 Ap 30 '65
See also
Courts—United States
Justice, Administration of—United States
Law enforcement
Legislation—United States
United States—Constitution

Virginia
Spoofing the despots; Richmond news leader's Beadle bumble fund. Time 87:47 Ja 21 '66

LAW, Maritime. See Maritime law

LAW, Natural. See Natural law

LAW, Sunday. See Sunday legislation

LAW and ethics
Good Samaritans: law and the golden rule. L. Wille. il Nation 200:447-9 Ap 26 '65
Morality and policy. America 112:280, 351, 450 F 27, Mr 13, Ap 3 '65

LAW and mental illness. See Mental health laws

LAW enforcement
Attorney General of the United States, talks; statements ed. by J. R. Moskin. N. deB. Katzenbach. il Look 29:27-33 Je 1 '65
Crime in the cities: an unnecessary crisis. W. Bowen. il Fortune. 72:140-5+ D '65
Criminal is living in a golden age; excerpts from address, October 11, 1965. Shawcross. il U S News 59:80-2 N 1 '65
Crisis in crime control. G. R. Blakey. America 113:238-40 S 4 '65
Eisenhower's views on the breakdown in law and order; excerpts from address, September 1, 1965. D. D. Eisenhower. U S News 59:20 S 13 '65
Harsh words about coddling of criminals; summary of statement, June 24, 1965. J. L. McClellan. U S News 59:16 Jl 5 '65
Lawlessness galore; address, August 26, 1965. F. E. Inbau. Vital Speeches 32:95-6 N 15 '65; Excerpt. U S News 59:82 S 13 '65
Police brutality: fact or fiction? FBI statistics show civilian brutality against police practiced widely. il U S News 59:37-40 S 6 '65
Police brutality: how much truth; how much fiction? J. E. Hoover. il U S News 59:116-17+ S 27 '65
Right to loot? D. Lawrence. U S News 59. 100 S 6 '65
Rule of law in the South. H. Burns. Commentary 40:80+ S '65; Discussion. 40:22+ D '65
Shift in the wind in Washington; violent defiance of law and order gone too far. il U S News 59:27-8 S 6 '65
This month's feature: moves to strengthen law enforcement. Cong Digest 44:225-56 O '65
Violence and the KKK. Nation 200:406-7 Ap 19 '65
Welcome back! Nat R 17:756 S 7 '65
When the cops were not handcuffed. Y. Kamisar. il N Y Times Mag p34-5+ N 7 '65
See also
Police

LAW libraries
See also
American association of law libraries
United States—Library of Congress—Law library

LAW making. See Legislation

LAW reports, digests, etc.
See also
Copyright—Law reports, digests, etc.

LAW students civil rights research council
Learning by doing. il Time 85:64 My 21 '65

LAW suits. See Lawsuits

LAWFORD, Valentine
English dream. Vogue 146:121+ Jl '65
Lighthearted pavilion. Vogue 145:140-5+ Je '65
Museum of wine in art. Vogue 145:172-83+ Mr 1 '65

LAWLER, Justus George
Problem of priests in the world. Commonweal 82:105-9, 394-5+ Ap 16, Je 18 '65
Time is now. Commonweal 82:691-4 S 24 '65

LAWN bowling. See Bowling on the green

LAWN furniture. See Furniture, Outdoor

LAWN mowers
Electric lawn mowers. il Consumer Rep 30:286-90 Je '65
How to stay friends with your lawn mower. D. Seim. il Farm J 89:34E Jl '65
Power lawn mowers reel type. il Consumer Bul 48:20-4 Ag '65
Rotary power lawn mowers. il Consumer Bul 48:2+ Jl '65
Shopping for a riding mower. S. M. Gallager. il Pop Sci 186:172-5+ Ap '65
That new flying lawn mower. J. Hand. il Pop Sci 186:171+ Ap '65
To reduce grass mowing hazards. il Consumer Bul 48:22-4 Ap '65

LAWN sprinklers. See Sprinklers

LAWN sweepers
It sure beats raking! leaf blowers. M. Banister. il Pop Mech 124:170-3 S '65
Lawn sweepers. il Consumer Rep 30:385-7 Ag '65

LAWN tennis. See Tennis

LAWN thatch
Lawn thatch, what is it, how to get rid of it. B. C. Kilvert, jr. il Flower Grower 52:53 Ap '65

LAWNER, Lynne
Autumn come; poem. Atlan 216:86 N '65
March; poem. Atlan 215:171 Mr '65

LAWNS
Fallacy of civil disobedience. Read Digest 52:18-19 S '65
First aid for winter-scarred lawns. B. Brinhart. il Pop Gard 16:44-5+ Ap '65
Guide to lawn problems and how to solve them. H. Mason and L. Grove. Bet Hom & Gard 43:40+ Ap '65
Help your lawn spring back to life. A. M. Kofranek. Am Home 68:34 Ap '65
Here is one way to walk on a wet lawn. il Sunset 134:176 F '65
Home garden notebook. J. B. Brimer. il Flower Grower 52:33-4 S '65
How to keep your lawn loyal. C. B. Hicks. il Pop Mech 124:68-75+ Ag '65
Latest news about lawns. R. W. Schery. Horticulture 44:34-5+ Ja '66
Rebuild your lawn this quick way. Bet Hom & Gard 43:12 S '65
Solutions for problem areas. C. Gerard. Pop Gard 16:46 Ap '65
This spring have a good lawn. il Flower Grower 52:40-1 Ap '65
Tips on lawn care. C. E. Gregg. il Pop Gard 16:50 My '65
See also
Grasses

LAWRENCE, A. L. and others
Cyclic variations in the digestive gland and glandular oviduct of chitons (mollusca) bibliog Science 147:508-10 Ja 29 '65

LAWRENCE, Barbara
Distinctions; poem. New Yorker 40:126 F 6 '65

LAWRENCE, David
Abuse of power. U S News 58:116 My 3 '65; Same abr. with title Erosion of freedom. Read Digest 87:143-4 Jl '65
Fallacy of Civil disobedience. Read Digest 87:111-12 O '65
Must collective bargaining be sabotaged? Read Digest 87:113-14 D '65
Our unbalanced federal budget. Read Digest 86:103-4 Ap '65
Reducing take-home pay. U S News 59:108 Jl 19 '65
World united? poem. U S News 60:88 Ja 10 '66

LAWRENCE, David Herbert
Cast of characters: a Bloomsbury memoir; excerpt from Taken care of. E. Sitwell. Reporter 32:44-5 Ap 8 '65
Reflections on Lawrence. A. Rich. Poetry 106:218-25 Je '65

LAWRENCE, Donald G. and Kuypers, H. G. J. M.
Pyramidal and non-pyramidal pathways in monkeys: anatomical and functional correlation. bibliog Science 148:973-5 My 14 '65

LAWRENCE, H. C.
Get the most from your radio. Motor B 115:26-9+ F '65
Installing a depth sounder inside and out. Motor B 115:124-6 Mr '65

LAWRENCE, H. Lea
Backwoods browns. Field & S 69:12-14+ F '65

LAWRENCE, Harding Luther
Braniff refuels on razzle-dazzle. il Bsns W p 110+ N 20 '65
New course for Braniff. por Time 85:92 F 19 '65

LAWRENCE, Joan
Parent and child. N Y Times Mag p52+ Ag 15 '65

LAWRENCE, Peter A. and Krasne, F. B.
Annelid ciliary photoreceptors. bibliog Science 148:965-6 My 14 '65

LAWRENCE, Robert
Berlioz by Ormandy, and others. Sat R 48:82 O 30 '65
Cascade of jewels. Opera N 30:6-7 N 6 '65
Caviar from opera workshops. Hi Fi 15:115 Ag '65
Connoisseur's Tosca. Opera N 29:24-5 Ap 17 '65
Debussyist Pelléas. Sat R 48:59 Je 12 '65
Festival at Caramoor. Hi Fi 15:147+ S '65
French-American festival. Hi Fi 15:147+ O '65
French opera. Opera N 29:29 Ap 17 '65
Hoffmann's tales retold. Sat R 48:51 D 25 '65
Parsifal from Bayreuth. Sat R 48:52 Mr 27 '65
Professor Bernstein's required readings. Hi Fi 15:164 D '65
Schoenberg's Gurrelieder, an event for a generation. Hi Fi 15:79-80 O '65
South American scene. Hi Fi 15:208-13 N '65
Star quality. Opera N 30:14-15 N 6 '65
Tosca at last. Hi Fi 15:113-14 Je '65

LAWRENCE, T. E.
Tragic and the epic in T. E. Lawrence. J. A. Notopoulos. Yale R 54:331-45 Mr '65

LAWRENCE, Turner
Battle of the Hudson. Am For 71:12-15+ Ap '65

LAWRENCE Ernest Orlando memorial awards. See Ernest Orlando Lawrence memorial awards

LAWRENCE radiation laboratory, Berkeley, Calif.
High-energy politics: forces now jockeying for position as plans proceed for giant new accelerator. D. S. Greenberg. il Science 147:1423-6 Mr 19 '65

LAWRENSON, Helen
Androgyne, you're a funny valentine. Esquire 63:80-1+ Mr '65
Is it true what they say about Otto? McCalls 92:106-7+ Mr '65
Letter home. Esquire 64:20+ N; 132+ D '65

LAWS of nature. See Nature, Laws of

LAWSON, Katheryn
Scientific couple finds success in Albuquerque. il pors Ebony 20:67-70+ Je '65

LAWSON, Kenneth
Progressive design ideas cancel corrosion. Am City 81:90-1 Ja '66

about
Scientific couple finds success in Albuquerque. il pors Ebony 20:67-70+ Je '65

LAWSON, Shirley Ann
Fantastic drug that creates quintuplets. il pors Life 59:24-6 Ag 13 '65

LAWSON quintuplets. See Quintuplets

LAWSUITS. See Actions and defenses

LAWTON, William K.
In good company. Flying 77:50-3 O '65

LAWYER (Indian chief)
Most satisfactory council; excerpts from Nez Perce Indians and the opening of the Northwest. A. M. Josephy, jr. il por Am Heritage 16:28-31+ O '65

LAWYERS
A.B.A.'s no. one issue. Time 86:46 Ag 20 '65
Colleagues in conscience; lawyers for indigent defendants in felony cases. Time 85:60-1 Je 11 '65
Every family needs a lawyer. F. L. Remington. il Parents Mag 40:48-9+ Jl '65
Independence of the bar: its meaning and its future; address, November 13, 1965. R. F. Drinan. Vital Speeches 32:102-5 D 1 '65
Non-discussion in Alabama; lawyers attitude to Supreme court. Time 85:70-1 F 5 '65
Serving the poor. Time 86:35 Jl 2 '65
When you need a lawyer. il Good H 168:182 My '65
See also
Legal aid
Negro lawyers

LAWYERS in politics
Abe, help! LBJ; Johnson's right-hand man. C. B. Seib and A. L. Otten. il Esquire 63:86-8+ Je '65

LAY apostolate. See Catholic action

LAY missionaries. See Missionaries

LAYCOCK, George
Gator poachers. Field & S 70:40-3+ Jl '65
Land between the Lakes. Field & S 69:130-3+ Mr '65
Old fish eater. Field & S 70:54+ D '65
Ten sure tips to catch bass. Farm J 89:68-9 My '65
We found the hidden char. Field & S 70:49-51+ My '65

LAYMEN. See Laity

LAY-off bonuses. See Wages—Dismissal wage

LAYS, Nancy Jane
Tiki Nui of Tahiti. Motor B 116:80-1 D '65

LAYTON, W. M. jr, and Hallesy, D. W.
Deformity of forelimb in rats: association with high doses of acetazolamide. bibliog Science 149:306-8; 150:79 Jl 16, O 1 '65

LAZAR, Eve, and Klein, Carole
Parent and child. N Y Times Mag p63-4 F 7 '65

LAZAREFF, Hélène Gordon-. See Gordon-Lazareff, H.

LAZARUS, Arnold
Three for the road; poem. Christian Cent 82: 1008 Ag 18 '65

LAZARUS, George
Chicago: doing something about it. Sat R 48:41-2 My 22 '65
Madison avenue (cont) Sat R 48:148 Mr 13; 77 Je 12; 59-60 Ag 14; 77-8 D 11 '65

LAZARUS, Ralph
Surviving the age of the city. Sat R 49:44 Ja 8 '66
Time on our hands. por NEA J 54:15 My '65

LAZEGA, Max
Israel has still to find its way. Cath World 202:84-90 N '65

LAZO, Mario
Reversible revolution. Nat R 17:656-8 Jl 27 '65

LEA, Arden O. See Van Handel, E. jt. auth.

LEACH, Frederic B.
Man whose praise we sing; summary of Trappers of New York, by J. R. Simms. Am Heritage 16:62-3+ Ap '65

LEACH, Richard H.
Department of urban affairs. America 112: 388-91 Mr 20 '65

LEACHMAN, R. B.
Nuclear fission; with biographical sketch. Sci Am 213:11, 49-56+ bibliog(p 119) Ag '65

LEACOCK, Stephen
My fishpond; excerpt from Here are my lectures. Read Digest 86:244B-244E Ap '65
You have to say something; excerpt from Hohenzollerns in America. Read Digest 86: 226B-226C F '65

LEAD
Limits terminated on imports of unmanufactured lead and zinc; statement, October 22, 1965, with proclamation. L. B. Johnson. Dept State Bul 53:795-7 N 15 '65

Isotopes
Lead isotopes in gasoline and aerosols of Los Angeles basin, California. T. J. Chow and M. S. Johnstone. bibliog il Science 147: 502-3 Ja 29 '65

LEADERSHIP
Economic factors and political development. W. Malenbaum. bibliog f Ann Am Acad 358:41-51 Mr '65
Human relations or human resources? theories of participative leadership. R. E. Miles. il Harvard Bsns R 43:148-9 Jl '65
Intellectual royalty; address, August 4, 1965. J. R. Palmer. Vital Speeches 31:696-9 S 1 '65
Lessons of leadership; symposium. il Nations Bsns 53:34-5+ Je; 40-1+ Jl; 46-8+ Ag; 40-2+ S: 40-1+ O: 40-2+ N '65
Negro now; excerpts from Who speaks for the Negro? with quotations by four Negro leaders. R. P. Warren. il Look 29:23-31 Mr 23 '65
Parties and the masses. K. H. Silvert. bibliog f Ann Am Acad 358:101-8 Mr '65
Political socialization and leadership selection. K. Prewitt. bibliog f il Ann Am Acad 361:96-111 S '65
Rise and role of charismatic leaders. A. R. Willner and D. Willner. bibliog f Ann Am Acad 358:77-88 Mr '65
Success has four price tags; excerpts from address. October 2, 1964. L. S. Bickmore. Read Digest 86:69-70 Mr '65
What is leadership? D. D. Eisenhower. Read Digest 86:49-54 Je '65
Where are tomorrow's leaders? excerpt from address. F. R. Kappel. Read Digest 87:123-5 N '65

LEAF blowers. See Lawn sweepers

LEAF design. See Design, Decorative—Plant forms

LEAF prints
Technique
See Prints—Technique

LEAGUE for industrial democracy
Radicals, old and new. M. Harrington. New Repub 153:29 Jl 3 '65

LEAGUE of Nations
League of Nations treaties; recommendations of Sixth committee. UN Mo Chron 2:54-5 N '65

LEAGUE of women voters of the United States
Anecdotes, facetiae, satire, etc.
Manner of speaking; notes of a beleagured husband. J. Ciardi. Sat R 48:24+ N 13 '65
Should women give men the vote? M. Kitman. il Sat Eve Post 238:20 Jl 17 '65

LEAHY, Emmett J. and Cameron, C. A.
Paperwork explosion: can we control it? excerpts. Nations Bsns 53:102-4+ S '65

LEAK detectors. See Detectors

LEAKAGE in water pipes. See Water pipes—Leakage

LEAKEY, Louis Seymour Bazett
Battle of the bones. Newsweek 65:57-8 Ap 19 '65
Man evolved like animals; Third species questioned. C. A. Betts. il(p241) Sci N L 87:243 Ap 17 '65
Man's tree, a new root? C. A. Betts. il por Sci N L 87:346-7 My 29 '65

LEAKEY family
Leakeys of Africa; family in search of prehistoric man. M. M. Payne. il Nat Geog Mag 127:194-231 F '65

LEAKPROOF fuel tanks. See Airplanes—Fuel tanks

LEAKS in roofs. See Roofs—Leakage

LEAN, David
David Lean recipe: a whack in the guts. H. Alpert. il pors N Y Times Mag p32-3+ My 23 '65
Dr Zhivago: the making of a movie. R. S. Stewart. il por Atlan 216:58-64 Ag '65
Epic of beauty and terror: Dr Zhivago; with report by R. Schickel. il Life 60:48-59+ Ja 21 '66

LEAPER, Rae
Traveling with Mlle; camping in Europe. Mlle 61:121-2 Je '65

LEAR, Edward
With birds in his beard. A. White. il Sat R 49:26-7 Ja 15 '66

LEAR, Evelyn
Mephisto's musings. Hi Fi 15:160 D '65

LEAR, John
Crisis in water; what brought it on? Sat R 48:24-8+ O 23; 29 N 27 '65
Gardner appointment. Sat R 48:46 Ag 21 '65
Patient's right to know. Sat R 48:20 Je 26 '65

LEAR, Martha Weinman
How now, Shangri-La? N Y Times Mag p26-7+ Ja 31 '65
She is tough, she is earthy, she is kicky. N Y Times Mag p 10-11+ Jl 4 '65
Winging it with Jonathan Winters. N Y Times Mag p36-7+ Mr 28 '65

LEAR, William Powell
Is Bill Lear taking off again? il por Fortune 72:138-40+ Jl '65

LEAR Jet corporation
Lear jet designing twin-engine, single-propeller pusher aircraft. Aviation W 83:32 N 22 '65
Lear liner sales to near 500 in decade. D. A. Brown. il Aviation W 83:86-7+ N 1 '65

LEARNED Journals. See Periodicals

LEARNING, Maze. See Maze tests

LEARNING, Psychology of
Brain and how it changes; adaptation of address, April 1964. E. R. John. Bul Atomic Sci 21:12-14 N '65
Elevator rat. il Sci Digest 57:24-5 Je '65
Family business in brief. P. L. Levin. il N Y Times Mag p99 Ap 4 '65
How to help babies learn without teaching them. J. Holt. il Redbook 126:54-5+ N '65
Intelligence, information, and education; address, September 28, 1964. R. W. Gerard. bibliog Science 148:762-5 My 7 '65
Judgments of sameness and difference: experiments on decision time. D. Bindra and others. bibliog il Science 150:1625-7 D 17 '65
Learning to read; adaptation of address. October 31, 1963. E. J. Gibson. bibliog il Science 148:1066-72 My 21 '65; Reply with rejoinder. D. Elkind. 149:1325-6 S 17 '65
Observable changes of hypotheses under positive reinforcement. P. Suppes and M. Schlag-Rey. bibliog il Science 148:661-2 Ap 30 '65
Power of effective thinking. A. P. Farrell. America 112:517 Ap 17 '65
Signal detection in fixed-ratio schedules. M. Rilling and C. McDiarmid. bibliog il Science 148:526-7 Ap 23 '65
What I have learned; learning how to learn. C. A. Doxiadis. Sat R 49:16-18+ Ja 1 '66
See also
Attention
Transfer of training

LEARNING, Psychology of—*Continued*

Anecdotes, facetiae, satire, etc.

Notes from an empty room; reprint. J. V. McConnell. il Horizon 7:42-7 Spr '65

LEARNING and scholarship

ABC's of excellence: ability not equality; address, April 6, 1965. A. C. Harrison. Vital Speeches 31:565-7 Jl 1 '65
   See also
Humanities
Intellectuals

LEARNING materials. See Teaching—Aids and devices

LEARY, John P.
Morality and the public school; address, March 18, 1965. Vital Speeches 31:427-30 My 1 '65

LEARY, Virginia
Aggiornamento in vocations. America 112:548-51 Ap 17 '65

LEASES
Look how leases are changing! B. Brantley. Suc Farm 63:58+ N '65
Read that lease; before you sign. il Changing T 19:11-13 Jl '65
   See also subhead Leasing under various subjects, e.g. Airplanes—Leasing

LEASING of equipment. See Agricultural machinery—Leasing

LEASK, Ada Longfield
Excise marks on English and Irish wallpapers. Antiques 88:216-19 Ag '65

LEASON, James
Doctor Love strikes again; story. Vogue 146:183 N 1 '65

LEATHERBEE, Mary
Happy flights of an island hopper. por Life 59:101-2+ O 8 '65
Lively jaunt around the big state. por Life 59:81-2+ O 1 '65
Majestic grotto for the gods and a Mack Sennett act. Life 60:54A Ja 7 '66
Road to Goulimine. Life 58:74+ Mr 19 '65
Scary climb and shish kebab from the sea. Life 58:125-6 Mr 5 '65

LEATHERMAN, Leroy
Three Graham restorations. Dance Mag 39:42-6 N '65

LEAVENS, Peter A.
Space astronomy at the World's fair. Sky & Tel 30:68-70 Ag '65

LEAVES
Autumn foliage; few of this fall's opportunities. il Changing T 19:24 S '65
Psychrometric measurement of leaf water potential: lack of error attributable to leaf permeability. H. D. Barrs. bibliog il Science 149:63-5 Jl 2 '65
Texture is essential in the garden. J. Hudak. il Horticulture 43:28-9+ My '65
Why do rhododendron leaves curl? J. R. Havis. Horticulture 43:17 D '65
   See also
Color of leaves
Stomata

LEAVITT, Hunt
Art of trading up for a song. Motor B 116:48+ N '65

LEAVITT, Scot
Life TV review. Life 58:22 Je 11 '65

LEBANON
New cedars of Lebanon. il UNESCO Courier 18:18-19 O '65
   See also
Beirut—Description
Natural resources—Lebanon

Description and travel

West went thataway, East; with report by M. Leatherbee. il Life 60:46-53 Ja 7 '66

Industries

Lebanon. P. P. Vouras and A. Taylor. bibliog il Focus 15:1-6 Je '65

Politics and government

Excess of apples. Newsweek 66:53 N 1 '65

LEBLANC, Richard
Thief-proofing our art museums. UNESCO Courier 18:4-7+ N '65

LEBO, G. R. and others
Jupiter's decametric emission correlated with the longitudes of the first three galilean satellites. bibliog Science 148:1724-5 Je 25 '65

LEBOW, Victor
What price discount? Nation 201:255-6 O 18 '65

LEBRÓN-PUMAROL, Alfredo
Four sensations. Américas 17:31-4 Je '65

LECANUET, Jean
Also running. Newsweek 66:50+ N 8 '65
Instant image. por Newsweek 66:38 D 20 '65

LE CARRÉ, John, pseud. See Cornwell, D. J. M.

LE CHEVALLIER, Jacques
Joy of color. il Newsweek 66:64 Ag 2 '65

LECHLITNER, Ruth
Sunflower; poem. Commonweal 82:379 Je 11 '65

LECHTRECK, Roy
Myth of American conservatism. America 114:44-6 Ja 8 '66

LECLER, René
England's firebrand princess. Good H 160:20+ My '65

LECLERC, Édouard
Edouard Leclerc; grocer of France. S. Berger. Yale R 55:90-106 O '65

LE CLÉZIO, J. M. G.
It seems to me the boat is heading for the island; story. tr. by R. Howard. por Vogue 145:102-3 F 15 '65

LE CORBUSIER
Le Corbusier, a tribute. il pors Arch Forum 123:17-64 O '65
Le Corbusier, 1887-1965; a tribute. A. Malraux. Art N 64:21 O '65
Letter from Paris. Genêt. New Yorker 41:137-8+ S 18 '65
Master builder. il por Newsweek 66:63-4 S 6 '65
   Obituary
Arch Rec il por 138:35 O '65
Open hand in Venice. il Time 85:82 Ap 30 '65
Revolutionary. il por Time 86:63 S 3 '65
Soaring legacy of a titan; tribute by V. Scully. il Life 59:118-21 S 24 '65

LECTURE halls. See Auditoriums

LEDDICK, David
Dancer's second career. Dance Mag 39:19-20+ Ag '65
(ed) See Baldina, A. Baldina

LEDDIHN, Erik Maria, ritter von Kuehnelt-. See Kuehnelt-Leddihn, E. M. von

LEDERMAN, Leon M.
Anti-mirror on the anti-wall. il por Time 85:64+ Je 25 '65

LEDOGAR, Robert J.
Liturgy, Asian style. Commonweal 82:43-5 Ap 2 '65

LEDUC, Violette
Balenciaga; tr. by A. White. Vogue 145:82-3+ Ap 15 '65
La bâtarde; excerpt. tr. by D. Coltman. Vogue 146:238-9+ O 1 '65
Courrèges. Vogue 145:208-9+ My '65
Great craftsmen of Paris; tr. by A. White. Vogue 145:80-3+ Mr 15 '65
I went on location with Zhivago. Vogue 146:114-21+ S 15 '65

about

Author. P. Meras. Sat R 48:47 O 30 '65
[Biographical sketch] por Vogue 145:80-1 Mr 15 '65
Girl who wrote the wrong book. T. Foote. Life 59:25 O 15 '65
Passions of a Gallic Sappho. H. Peyre. por Sat R 48:46-7 O 30 '65

LEE, Al
Scope of seas; poem. Yale R 55:252-3 D '65

LEE, Ann
Six on a honeymoon. Parents Mag 41:42-3+ Ja '66

LEE, Calvin B. T.
Classroom learning is not enough. B. B. Stretch. il Sat R 48:62-3+ Je 19 '65

LEE, Charles
Washington at Monmouth; with painting. Am Heritage 16:14-17 Je '65

LEE, David B.
Don't blame the ghetto. Read Digest 86:145-8 Ap '65

LEE, Deborah
Works by Deborah Lee, Carol Marcy, and James Waring; Judson memorial church. J. Anderson. Dance Mag 39:158 D '65

LEE, Dorris May
What can the schools do? NEA J 54:25-7 F '65

LEE, Ettie
Improbable successes of Ettie Lee; Ettie Lee homes, inc. S. W. Taylor. Read Digest 87:187-8+ D '65

LEE, Gypsy Rose
Cut short. por Time 86:38 Ag 27 '65

LEE, Harper
When children discover America. McCalls 92:76-9 Ag '65

LEE, Kuan-yew
Atlantic report. Atlan 216:48+ N '65
Blasting off. il por Time 86:21B S 10 '65
Brand-new baby for the U.N. R. Morse. il por Life 59:65+ Ag 20 '65
Brilliant, but a bit of a thug; report and interview by R. Morse. il pors Life 59:43-4+ Jl 16 '65
Lee Kuan Yew is Singapore. S. Topping. il pors N Y Times Mag p66-7+ O 31 '65

LEE, Kuan-yew—*Continued*
Malaysia: my dream is shattered. il por Newsweek 66:33-4 Ag 23 '65
One of our islands is missing. il por Time 86:26+ Ag 20 '65
People of the week. por U S News 59:14 Ag 23 '65
Promise threatened. il por Newsweek 65:43 Je 21 '65
Shaky domino. il por Newsweek 66:44-5 S 13 '65
Singapore's restless Chinese. S. S. King. il Reporter 33:20-2 Ag 12 '65

LEE, Laurie
Love: what is? where fails? Mlle 62:100-1 D '65

LEE, Marjorie
Did I say it was funny? story. Redbook 126: 52-3 N '65

LEE, Miriam Lubitow. See Ornstein, J. jt. auth.

LEE, Peggy
Red hot blama. il por Newsweek 65:92-3 Mr 15 '65

LEE, Peter E. and Wilkes, A.
Polymorphic spermatozoa in the hymenopterous wasp dahlbominus. bibliog Science 147:1445-6 Mr 19 '65

LEE, Philip Randolph
HEW: running the Great society. E. Langer. por Science 150:1272-4 D 3 '65

LEE, Rex
Classroom TV comes to Samoa. T. Kaser. il Sat R 48:58-9+ Je 19 '65
Samoa: America's showplace of the South Seas. C. W. Hall. il por Read Digest 87: 157-64+ N '65

LEE, Robert Edward
Appomattox. U. S. Grant, 3d. il pors Nat Geog Mag 127:435-69 Ap '65
Lee, by C. Dowdey. Review
Sat R 49:34 Ja 1 '66. F. Vandiver

LEE, Susan
Widening of horizons. por Recreation 58:473-4 D '65

LEE-HUANG, Sylvia, and Cavalieri, L. F.
Nucleic acid polymerases: possible subunit structure. bibliog Science 148:1474-6 Je 11 '65

LEEDHAM, Charles
Chip revolutionizes electronics. N Y Times Mag p56-7+ S 19 '65; Same abr. with title Chip newest marvel in electronics. Read Digest 88:173-4+ Ja '66
Driving tests should be tougher. N Y Times Mag p40+ F 14 '65

LEEDY, Gene Robert
Bold structures enclose large spaces at low cost. il Arch Rec 138:177-88 O '65

LEENHOUTS, Keith J.
Royal Oak aids its problems youth. J. A. Morris. il Read Digest 87:163-7 O '65

LEERHØY, J.
Cytopathic effect of rubella virus in a rabbit-cornea cell line. bibliog Science 149:633-4 Ag 6 '65

LEES, Hannah
Look what I brought back from ancient Egypt. Atlan 215:174-5 Mr '65
Vertical drinking in the Soviet Union. Atlan 216:164-6 N '65
VISTA: a new kind of public service. Reporter 32:31-2 Ap 22 '65

LEETE, Edward
Biosynthesis of alkaloids. bibliog Science 147: 1000-6 F 26 '65

LEEWARD ISLANDS
See also
Guadeloupe Island

LEFF, Jay C.
Exotic. New Yorker 41:23-4 Je 19 '65

LEFRAK, Samuel J.
This is total living? il por Newsweek 66: 101-2 N 8 '65

LEFT and right (political science) See Right and left (political science)

LEFT wing (politics) See Right and left (political science)

LEFTOVERS
See also
Cookery—Leftovers

LEFTWICH, Marvin R.
Coin collecting police clerk. il pors Ebony 21:126-8+ D '65

LEG
Big girl's notes on little girls' legs. B. Comden. Esquire 63:41 Je '65
Case of the restless legs. Time 85:54 Ap 9 '65

LEG exercises. See Exercise

LEGAL aid
Equal justice: need for adequate legal assistance for the poor. America 112:275 F 27 '65
Expanding sense of justice. Nation 200:519 My 17 '65

Law corps? how to overcome injustices of legal apparatus to the poor. Commonweal 82:396-7 Je 18 '65
Missionaries; supplement legal-aid societies with storefront neighborhood law offices. il Time 86:59 N 12 '65
Poverty's neglected battlefront. Sat R 48: 29-30 S 11 '65

LEGAL aid societies
Missionaries; supplement legal-aid societies with storefront neighborhood law offices. il Time 86:59 N 12 '65

LEGAL confession. See Confession (law)

LEGAL education. See Law—Study and teaching

LEGAL history. See Law—History

LEGAL profession. See Lawyers

LEGAULT-DEMARE, Jean. See Weiss, S. B. jt. auth.

LEGG, Carol Dee
Layette for mother of a new baby. Farm J 89:79+ O '65

LEGGE, Walter
Festival 1965. Hi Fi 15:204-7+ N '65
Ghiaurov's Moses, Karajan's Bohème. Hi Fi 15:160-1 S '65
Kokoschka Flute and a new regime. Hi Fi 16:147+ Ja '66
Three at La Scala. Hi Fi 15:132-3 My '65
World premieres at La Scala. Hi Fi 15:135 Je '65

LEGGETT, Stanton
New views of schools. Sat R 48:93-4 O 16 '65

LEGGETT, William
Baseball (cont) Sports Illus 22:70+ Je 14 '65
Hockey. Sports Illus 22:62-4 Mr 8 '65

LEGIBILITY of printing. See Printing—Legibility

LEGION of decency. See National Catholic office for motion pictures

LEGION of honor. See Decorations of honor

LEGIONARY ants. See Ants

LEGISLATION

New York (state)

See also
Labor laws and legislation—New York (state)

United States

Big fish that get away; conflict of quality vs. political expediency. J. Ridgeway. New Repub 153:15-17 O 23 '65
Bills already enacted; bills not yet enacted, and their outlook. U S News 58:33 Je 28 '65
Congressional scorecard; bills and acts of interest to recreation. Recreation 58:264-5 Je '65
Domestic record. Commonweal 83:111-12 O 29 '65
Hard act to follow; record in carrying out the recommendations of the President. Newsweek 65:26 Ap 26 '65
How to out-fox the majority. J. Deakin. New Repub 152:13-14 F 27 '65
How you can get into the acts. T. L. Moses. Sr Schol 87:sup4+ O 14 '65
Johnson message; first seven messages to Congress. New Repub 152:1+ F 6 '65
Laws you may have missed. il U S News 59: 77 N 22 '65
Laying down the law; scoreboard for the 89th. il Newsweek 66:20 Jl 19 '65
Legislative process, address, January 1965. R. W. Frase. bibliog ALA Bul 59:276-81 Ap '65
LBJ and the fabulous 89th go home; achievements and future implications. S. Shaffer. il Newsweek 66:21-3 N 1 '65
LBJ's 100 days: a record piling up; Way LBJ runs Congress. il U S News 58:41-4 Ap 26 '65
LBJ's third veto. Reporter 33:10+ S 9 '65
Scant rest in sight for weary Congress; with editorial comment. Bsns W p27-8, 196 O 23 '65
Uhuru comes to the Senate; deterioration of the Senate club. M. Greenfield. il Reporter 33:32-7 S 23 '65
Work done. Time 85:23-4 Ap 2 '65
See also
Agricultural laws and legislation
Labor laws and legislation—United States
Social legislation—United States
United States—Congress
United States—Supreme court

Washington (state)

I spent a winter in politics; confessions of farmer. S. Bledsoe. il Farm J 90:38+ Ja '66

LEGISLATIVE bodies
United States
See also
State legislatures
United States—Congress
also subhead Legislature under names of
states, e.g. New York (state)—Legislature
LEGISLATIVE reference service. See United
States—Library of Congress—Legislative
reference service
LEGISLATORS
See also
Negro legislators
LEGISLATURES, State. See State legislatures
LEGLER, Philip
Suddenly falling earth. J. Crawford, jr. Poetry
105:412-14 Mr '65
LEGS. See Leg
LEGUM, Colin
Darkest Africa. Commentary 40:112-14+ N '65
LEHMAN, Donald J. and Corrigan, J. E.
Self-denial. America 112:391-3 Mr 20 '65
LEHMAN CAVES NATIONAL MONUMENT
Conservation and American caves. W. R.
Halliday. il Nat Parks Mag 39:17-19 D '65
LEHMANN, A. F.
Why sewage effluents must be chlorinated;
summary of Masters thesis. bibliog Am City
80:79-81 Jl '65
LEHMANN, Gary A.
Magnetic reed switches and relays. Electr
World 74:23-6+ S '65
LEHMANN, Henri
Pre-Columbian America. UNESCO Courier
18:27-30 D '65
LEHMANN, John
Very old party. New Repub 154:23-4 Ja 8 '66
LEHMANN, Lilli
Empress of song. A. M. Lingg. il pors Opera
N 29:26-8 F 20 '65
LEHMBRUCK, Wilhelm
Tender monumentality of Wilhelm Lehm-
bruck. A. Werner. il Am Artist 29:54-9+
Je '65
LEHRBAUMMER, A. L.
Mixing purchasing and public relations. Am
City 80:104-5 S '65
LEHRER, Stanley
School and society: the vision and the vital-
ity. Sch & Soc 93:33-4 Ja 23 '65
LEHRER, Tom
Sabbatical satirist. por Time 85:61 Je 25 '65
LEHRMAN, Hal
Dark Continent in a different light. Sat R
48:29-30 S 4 '65
Salute to Israel's grand old man. Sat R 48:
39-40 Ap 10 '65
LEIBER, Fritz
Homes for men in the stars. Sci Digest 58:
53-7 S '65
LEIBERT, Julius A.
Books. A. Nebolsine. Commonweal 82:476 Jl
2 '65
LEIBIK, Leon J.
Correct usage for he and I. Sr Schol 86:sup4
Mr 25 '65
LEIBY, Paul D.
Cestode in North Dakota: echinococcus in
field mice. bibliog Science 150:763 N 5 '65
LEICA gallery. See Photography—Galleries and
museums
LEICAFLEX cameras. See Single-lens reflex
cameras
LEICH, Alexander, and Leich, Roland
Cole, the old king. Motor T 17:42-5 Jl '65
LEICH, Roland. See Leich, A. jt. auth.
LEIF Ericsson
New light on discovery of the New World. il
U S News 59:8-9 O 25 '65
Windblown Leif. il Time 86:25B O 22 '65
LEIGH, Carma R.
Interlibrary cooperation in California; ad-
dress, July 1965. Wilson Lib Bul 40:157-61
O '65
LEIGHTON, Alexander H.
Poverty and social change; with biographical
sketch. Sci Am 212:18, 21-7 bibliog(p 150)
My '65
LEIGHTON, Bonnie
She only cried once. L. David. il Good H
161:74-5+ S '65
LEIGHTON, Robert B. and others
Mariner IV photography of Mars: initial re-
sults. Science 149:627-30 Ag 6 '65
LEINSDORF, Erich
Genius of Richard Strauss. Atlan 216:79-83
Ag '65
Maestro demands brilliance. il pors Life 59:
39-40+ Jl 9 '65
LEINWOLL, Stanley
Predicted radio receiving conditions. See oc-
casional issues of Popular electronics to
November 1965

LEIOMYOMAS. See Tumors
LEIPZIG
Music
Upward swing. P. Moor. Hi Fi 15:126-7 My
'65
LEIPZIG trade fair. See Exhibitions
LEIRIS, Michel
Africa. UNESCO Courier 18:10-16 D '65
LEISER, Dorothy
Sea noise; poem. Christian Cent 82:637 My
19 '65
LEISHMANIA enriettii. See Protozoa
LEISTER, Mary McFarland
Cactus for Christmas. Flower Grower 52:
26-7+ D '65
Dwarf dahlias. il Flower Grower 52:37+ Ap
'65
Holly. il Flower Grower 52:34+ Mr '65
Put fragrance in your summertime living.
Flower Grower 52:32-3+ Je '65
LEISURE
Automation is here to liberate us. E. Hoffer.
il N Y Times Mag p48-9+ O 24 '65
Getting the most out of your leisure time;
excerpt from Today's health guide. Todays
Health 43:37-9 Jl '65
How much leisure can you stand? B. Forker.
il Suc Farm 63:89+ My '65
Making the most of leisure; with discussion
group program, by E. G. Neisser. O. Hand-
lin. il Parents Mag 40:22+, 60-1+ Je '65
Time on our hands. R. Lazarus. NEA J 54:
15 My '65
Time to kill, automation, leisure and jobs.
E. Larrabee. Nation 201:198-202 S 20 '65
Work that play built. L. Velie. Read Digest
86:151-2+ Je '65
- *See also*
Hobbies

Anecdotes, facetiae, satire, etc.
New American leisure and how to beat it. il
Esquire 63:76 F '65
LEITÃO DA CUNHA, Vasco Tristão
Common quest for freedom and prosperity in
the American republics; eulogy, November
22, 1965. Dept State Bul 53:995 D 20 '65
LEITER, Sarah L.
Guidance in the elementary school. NEA J
54:49+ S '65
LEITH, Emmett N. and Upatnieks, Juris
Photography by laser; with biographical
sketches. Sci Am 212:20, 24-35 Je '65
True 3-D image from laser photography.
Electr World 74:34-5+ O '65
LEJEUNE, Anthony
Africa without fear or favor. Nat R 17:833-5
S 21 '65
Can Britain stop Rhodesia? Nat R 18:22-3
Ja 11 '66
Green icing on the cake. Nat R 17:379-80 My
4 '65
Letter from London (cont) Nat R 17:418, 723-
4, 1071-2 My 18, Ag 24, N 30 '65
To Valhalla with twin exhausts. Nat R 17:
776-7 S 7 '65
Virtues of the market. Nat R 17:935-7 O 19
'65
LEKACHMAN, Robert
Defense economy. Commentary 41:80-2 Ja '66
Faces of five decades. Commonweal 81:731-
3 Mr 5 '65
Fashions in liberalism. Nation 201:62-6 S 20
'65
Great society. Commentary 39:37-42 Je '65
Ryan and Lindsay. New Repub 153:8-9 Jl 24
'65
Steel: no longer the bellwether? Duns R 85:
56-7+ Ap '65
LEKASHMAN, Lawrence
1956-1965 hi-fi ten years later. Pop Electr
23:41-6 N '65
LELAND, Dorothy E.
Award-winning children's books. Parents Mag
40:153 N '65
Books for boys & girls. See issues of Parents'
magazine and better homemaking
LELASH, Marjorie
From Angel, the first in stereo. Am Rec G
32:218-19 N '65
Massenet Thais. Am Rec G 31:964-5 Je '65
LELYVELD, Joseph
But he has survived. N Y Times Mag p52-3+
N 28 '65
Grim siesta of Stanleyville. N Y Times Mag
p28-9+ My 16 '65
Mr Smith draws the line in Africa. N Y Times
Mag p22+ Ag 22 '65
LEMA, Tony
Long irons: tips and warnings; ed. by G. S.
Brown. pors Sports Illus 22:50-5 Mr 22 '65
New way to play long irons; ed. by G. S.
Brown. pors Sports Illus 22:40-7+ Mr 15
'65

LEMAN, LAKE. See Geneva, Lake

LEMASS, Seán Francis
Ireland: appetite for success. S. Hagerty. il
por Newsweek 65:40+ Ap 19 '65

LE MAT percussion revolver. See Revolvers

LEMAY, Curtis E.
LeMay's warning; excerpts from address.
Aviation W 82:21 Ap 5 '65
U.S. air force: power for peace. pors Nat
Geog Mag 128:291-7 S '65

about

Changes for air force: new chief; new tactics.
por U S News 58:16 F 8 '65
Collier trophy. B. Kocivar. il pors Look 29:
77+ N 2 '65

LEMAY, Georges
Slippery worm. il por Newsweek 66:35 O 4 '65

LEMMON, Jack
My husband, Jack Lemmon; ed. by M. Davidson. F. Farr. il por Good H 160:58+ Ap
'65

LEMON, A. Neil
Hearing, lost and found. Todays Health 43:
49-50 Jl '65

LEMON, Bernard
Sign talk. Motor B 116:84 D '65

LEMON, Richard
Anne Bancroft: hey ma, I can do that! Sat
Eve Post 238:86-8+ N 20 '65
Good-bye to a second banana. Sat Eve Post
238:94-5+ N 6 '65
Mobiles: the soaring art of Alexander Calder.
Sat Eve Post 238:30-5 F 27 '65

LEMONADE
Old-fashioned lemonade with variations. il
Farm J 89:70 Ag '65

LEMONE, Evelyn
Records for teachers. See issues of Dance
magazine

LEMONS, Lawrence A.
Education courses. NEA J 54:26-8 O '65

LEMONS
Meyer lemon. A. Albohn. Horticulture 43:12-
13 D '65

LEMURS
Lemur may be stand-in for human allergy
tests; bush babies may be ideal test animals il(p 17) Sci N L 89:24 Ja 8 '66

LENCZOWSKI, George
Iraq: seven years of revolution. bibliog f
Cur Hist 48:281-9+ My '65

LENG, Russell J.
Reductio ad Vietnam. Nation 200:445-7 Ap
26 '65

LENGTH of life. See Longevity

LENHOFF, Howard M.
Cellular segregation and heterocytic dom-
inance in hydra. bibliog Science 148:1105-7
My 21 '65

LENIN, Vladimir Il'ich
No short cut to Soviet paradise. M. Nomad.
il por Sat R 48:39+ N 20 '65
Was Lenin necessary? L. Schapiro; discussion. Commentary 39:16+ My '65

Tomb

Loved one; mausoleum closed for repairs. por
Time 86:48 N 19 '65

LENINGRAD

Galleries and museums
See also
Hermitage

Music

In Russia, music for May day. P. Moor. il
Hi Fi 15:120-1 Jl '65

LENINGRAD, Siege of, 1941-1944
Leningrad 1941. by D. V. Pavlov. Review
Nation 202:50-1 Ja 10 '66. A. Werth
Sat R 48:42 D 11 '65. G. Feifer

LENK, Thomas T.
Making a wider cast to lure the customers.
il pors Bsns W p94-6+ Ap 10 '65

LENNON, John
Toy boy; poem. por McCalls 93:68 D '65

about

In the echo chamber. J. Wain. New Repub
153:20-2 Ag 7 '65

LENOX ware. See Pottery, American

LENS, Sidney
American labor abroad: Lovestone diplomacy.
Nation 201:10-16+ Jl 5 '65
Fate of 14(b) Commonweal 82:662-5 S 17 '65
Revolt of the left-outs. Commonweal 82:441-
4, 514 Je 25, Jl 23 '65
Russia's new economy. Christian Cent 82:236
F 24 '65

LENSES, Photographic
A's to your Q's about camera lenses. P.
McCafferty. il Pop Sci 187:120-3 O '65
Auxiliary lenses. Pop Phot 57:109-10 N '65
Build a mirror lens? it's not easy, but. il
Mod Phot 29:64-5+ Ag '65
Close-up which lenses? M. Edelson and H.
Keppler. il Mod Phot 29:76-9 Mr '65
Come in with a long lens. il U S Camera
28:60-1 F '65
Converters double tele length, but. B. Sher-
man. il Mod Phot 29:36+ Ag '65
Do converters equal teles? H. Keppler. il Mod
Phot 29:56-9 Ag '65
Enna auto-magic interchangeable-lens sys-
tem. M. Bernam. il Pop Phot 56:82-3 Ap '65
500-mm mirror lens now has T mount. J.
Forney. il Pop Phot 57:52+ O '65
Get closer than close with a + 10 lens. N.
Rothschild. il Pop Phot 56:76-7+ Ap '65
Having a problem focusing on your SLR
ground glass? M. A. Matzkin. il Mod Phot
29:20+ Mr '65
Jewel in the junkbox. K. Poli. il Pop Phot
56:104-5+ Je '65
Keppler on the SLR; mirror lenses. H. Kep-
pler. il Mod Phot 29:46+ Ag '65
Large camera; using swings and tilts. A.
Feininger. il Mod Phot 29:48+ Jl '65
Lens guide for 35-mm and 2¼ cameras. Pop
Phot 57:97-108 N '65
Micro-Nikkor auto f/3.5. A. Francekevich. il
Pop Phot 56:72-3+ F '65
Monocular for 2¼. M. H. Jaffe. il U S Camera
28:34 Ag '65
1965 interchangeable lense guide; comp. by
D. L. Miller. Mod Phot 29:95-110 O '65
Nonexistent best lens; IPEX, New York. N.
Rothschild. Pop Phot 57:16+ Ag '65
Odd effects with Aetna Trix lenses. M. A.
Matzkin. il Mod Phot 29:104-5 Je '65
Techniques tomorrow. B. Sherman. il Mod
Phot 29:46+ Jl '65
Techniques tomorrow; eliminating ultimate
lens flare due to diffraction. B. Sherman.
il Mod Phot 29:30+ Mr '65
Techniques tomorrow; lenses should be neu-
tral in color. B. Sherman. il Mod Phot 29:
20+ S '65
Techniques tomorrow; photographic lenses
which can resolve more than 400 lines per
millimeter on film. B. Sherman. Mod Phot
29:18 Je '65
Think wide. M. Morrison. il U S Camera
28:54-5+ Ap '65
See also
Zoom lenses

Testing

How to test a lens, and you should! C. W.
Kennedy. il Pop Phot 57:38+ O; 166+
D '65
How to test your tele lens. il Mod Phot
29:14 Ag '65
Keppler on the SLR; behind-the-lens meter
camera quandary. H. Keppler. Mod Phot
29:140+ D '65
Techniques tomorrow. B. Sherman. il Mod
Phot 29:16+ F '65
Techniques tomorrow; use of the auto-
collimator. B. Sherman. il Mod Phot 29:38+
My '65
35mm; Modern's lens tests compared with
those of the National bureau of standards.
J. Wolbarst. il Mod Phot 29:14+ O '65

LENSHINA, Alice
Question of theology. por Newsweek 65:46+
Ap 19 '65

LENT, Blair
Cardboard cuts. Horn Bk 41:408-12 Ag '65

LENT
Called to servanthood. J. A. Pike. Christian
Cent 82:387 Mr 31 '65
Catholics and Lent. M. Novak. Christian Cent
82:323 Mr 17 '65
Lenten reading in the age of Christian re-
newal. V. Kendall. Cath World 200:356-7 Mr
'65
Lenten yoke. G. S. Shockley. Christian Cent
82:259 Mr 3 '65
Quick Lent? il Time 85:74 Mr 12 '65
Word. V. P. McCorry. America 112:297-8 F
27 '65

LENTEN menus
Favor fish for Lenten dishes. il Parents Mag
40:30 Mr '65
Lenten menus unlimited. il Ladies Home J
82:96-8+ Mr '65
Sea food for Lent. il Ebony 20:138+ Mr
'65

LENTZ, John J.
Feeling no pain. Todays Health 43:60-3+
D '65
Get rid of those worn-out medicines. Todays
Health 43:88 F '65

LESTER, Henry M.
Focus on Henry M. Lester: photography's Ben Franklin. D. S. Gelatt. il por Pop Phot 56:60-3+ My '65

LESTER, Richard
Knack of being Richard Lester. A. Carthew. il pors N Y Times Mag p 16-17+ Ag 8 '65
People are talking about. . . por Vogue 146: 112-13 S 15 '65

LESTER, William
Capital punishment. America 112:484-6 Ap 10 '65

LESUK, Alex, and others
Crystalline human urokinase: some properties. bibliog Science 147:880-2 F 19 '65

LESURE, Thomas B.
South American cruise. Travel 124:28-32+ N '65
Spanning Europe. Travel 124:47-9 Jl '65
U.S. retirement cities. Travel 123:36-40 Mr '65

LET sleeping beauties lie; drama. See Fontaine, R.

LET the rest of the world go by; story. See O'Brien, E.

LETERMAN, Elmer G.
What makes Elmer run. por Newsweek 65: 78+ Je 21 '65

LETICIA, Colombia
For South America travelers, here is detour to adventure. il Sunset 135:34-6+ N '65

LETTER boxes. See Mail boxes

LETTER paper. See Stationery

LETTER sorting. See Mail handling

LETTER writing
Why doesn't he write? L. Benedict. il Seventeen 24:326+ Ag '65

LETTERING
Double talk. G. Lacy. il Design 67:22-3 S '65

LETTERS
Other people's mail. Esquire 64:149-52+ D '65
See also
Letter writing

LETTERS by children
Dear Santa; ed. by B. Adler. Ladies Home J 82:59+ D '65

LETTERS from service men
Christmas letters from Vietnam; excerpts. Look 29:29 D 28 '65

LETTERS of complaint. See Complaints

LETTERS of the alphabet. See Alphabet

LETTERS patent; story. See Barr, S.

LETTERS to children
C/O Camp hill-and-dale; parents' letters to campers. E. S. Oshin. il N Y Times Mag p48-9+ Ag 8 '65

LETTERS to the editor. See Periodicals—Letters to the editor

LEUCINE
Protein synthesis in enucleated eggs of rana pipiens. L. D. Smith and R. E. Ecker. bibliog il Science 150:777-9 N 5 '65

LEUCOCYTES
Chediak-Higashi syndrome: hereditary gigantism of cytoplasmic organelles. D. B. Windhorst and others. bibliog il Science 151:81-3 Ja 7 '66
Interferon-like virus-inhibitor induced in human leukocytes by phytohemagglutinin. E. F. Wheelock. bibliog il Science 149:310-11 Jl 16 '65

LEUKEMIA
Adenosylmethionine elevation in leukemic white blood cells. R. J. Baldessarini and P. P. Carbone. bibliog il Science 149:644-5 Ag 6 '65
Indicting a virus; affinity between Burkitt's tumor and leukemia. il Time 87:68 Ja 14 '66
Inhibition of L1210 tumor growth by thymus DNA. J. L. Glick and A. R. Goldberg. bibliog il Science 149:997-8 Ag 27 '65
Last year of little Sal; case of Salvatore Tabile. E. M. Wylie. il Good H 161:12+ N '65
Leukemia in husbands and wives. S. Milham, jr. bibliog il Science 148:98-100 Ap 2 '65
Leukemia not contagious for husbands and wives. Sci N L 87:245 Ap 17 '65
Leukocyte alkaline phosphatase: electrophoretic variants associated with chronic myelogenous leukemia. J. C. Robinson and others. bibliog il Science 150:58-60 O 1 '65
Nuclear mitochondria? D. Brandes and others. il Science 149:1373-4 S 17 '65
Uptake as a determinant of methotrexate response in mouse leukemias. D. Kessel and others. bibliog il Science 150:752-4 N 5 '65
Viral diseases related; infectious mononucleosis and leukemia. Sci N L 87:260 Ap 24 '65
Zeroing in on a cancer cure. Bsns W p 142+ Ap 17 '65

Therapy
Radiation outside the body. il Time 85:54 Ap 9 '65

Vaccines
Immunization against Rauscher mouse leukemia with tissue culture material. G. Barski and K. Y. Jung. bibliog il Science 149:751-2 Ag 13 '65

LEUKEMIA viruses
Human leukemia may also be virus caused. Sci N L 88:261 O 23 '65
Immunization against Rauscher mouse leukemia with tissue culture material. G. Barski and K. Y. Jung. bibliog il Science 149:751-2 Ag 13 '65
Immunodiffusion: detection of a murine leukemia virus. Rauscher. M. A. Fink and C. A. Cowles. bibliog il Science 150:1723-5 D 24 '65
Mice give disease and antibody to offspring. Sci N L 87:249 Ap 17 '65
Moloney virus-induced leukemias of mice: measurement in vitro of specific antigen. G. Haughton. bibliog il Science 147:506-7 Ja 29 '65

LEUKOCYTES. See Leucocytes

LEUSCHNER observatory. See Astronomical observatories

LEUTZE, Emanuel
Upstaging history; Washington rallying the troops at Monmouth. il Time 85:74 F 26 '65
Washington at Monmouth; with painting. Am Heritage 16:14-17 Je '65

LEVANT, Oscar
Anatomizing Oscar: a friend looks at Levant. C. Fadiman. Holiday 38:27+ N '65
Books. M. Muggeridge. Esquire 64:26+ O '65

LEVEAU, Carl Walter
Anti-fouling paints for aluminum hulls. Yachting 117:223-4 Ap '65

LEVENBOOK, Leo
Insect biochemistry. Science 150:643-4 O 29 '65

LEVERETT, Christie Kirk
Columbus' voyage; poem. Horn Bk 41:530 O '65

LEVERTON, Irene
Flying the mountain wave; ed. by B. Hicks. Flying 77:68-73 Ag '65

LEVERTOV, Denise
Man; poem. Nation 201:220 S 20 '65
Monster with melopoeia. Nation 200:618-19 Je 7 '65
Olga poems. Poetry 106:81-9 Ap '65
Some notes on organic form. Poetry 106:420-5 S '65
To write is to listen. Poetry 105:326-9 F '65
—See Dimock, E. C. jr, jt. auth.

about
Informal epic. H. Carruth. Poetry 105:259-61 Ja '65

LEVEY, A. B. See Martin, I. jt. auth.

LEVI, Leslie
Why a motor-sailer? Motor B 116:34-5+ Ag '65

LEVIN, Harold A.
Soviet adherence to International patent convention. Dept State Bul 52:758-61 My 17 '65

LEVIN, Harry, and Meltzer, N. S.
This reading thing. pors Am Ed 1:30-2 Ap '65

LEVIN, Kim
Wild beast of high life. Art N 64:28-9+ D '65

LEVIN, Martin
(ed) Phoenix nest. See issues of Saturday review

LEVIN, Meyer
Last thorn. Sat R 48:68 D 4 '65

about
Facts behind the fiction. H. Frankel. Sat R 48:31 N 6 '65

LEVIN, Phyllis Lee
Parent and child (cont) N Y Times Mag p47 F 21; 65-6 F 28; 68+ Mr 7; 72+ Mr 14; 79 Mr 21; 92+ Mr 28; 99 Ap 4; 93-4 Ap 11; 94+ Ap 18; 79+ Ap 25; 100+ My 2; 65-6 My 9; 69-70 My 16; 30 Je 27; 132+ S 12; 118+ N 28 '65

LEVIN, Robert J.
Twelve angry young men. Sat R 49:84 Ja 8 '66

LEVIN, Tom
Bureaucracy's long arm. A. Kopkind. New Repub 153:19-22 Ag 21 '65

LEVINE, Bernard B.
Antigen-antibody reaction: nature of complex initiating delayed hypersensitivity. bibliog Science 149:205-7 Jl 9 '65

—and Benacerraf, Baruj
Genetic control in guinea pigs of immune response to conjugates of haptens and poly-L-lysine. bibliog Science 147:517-18 Ja 29 '65

LEVINE, Leo
Auto racing: Detroit fights it out. Nation 200:559-61 My 24 '65

LEVINE, Milton I.
What to do for the colicky baby. Parents Mag 40:54-5+ O '65

LEVINE, Neil A.
(ed) See Newman, B. New York school question

LEVINE, Philip
Book; Common entrances; poems. Poetry 106:400-2 S '65

LEVINE, Robert A.
Open letter from a military intellectual to a sophisticated liberal leader. Bul Atomic Sci 20:24-7 S '64; 21:33 Mr '65

LE VINESS, W. Thetford
Pablita Velarde; Pueblo painter. Am Artist 29:40-5+ Ap '65

LEVINSON, Deirdre
Homecoming of Joel Bialystock; story. Commentary 39:78-82 Je '65

LEVINSON, Harry
How good is your mental health? Read Digest 87:54-8 S '65
How to get out of a dead-end job. por Pop Sci 186:104-5+ Ap '65
Who is to blame for maladaptive managers? Harvard Bsns R 43:143-6+ N '65

LEVITAS, Mitchel
It was the greatest secret. N Y Times Mag p2+ Ag 1 '65
Vietnam comes to Oregon U. N Y Times Mag p24-5+ My 9 '65

LEVITEN, David
October; poem. Nation 201:197 O 4 '65
With the fall; poem. Nation 200:312 Mr 22 '65

LEVITSKY, Serge L.
Book review. America 113:416-17 O 9 '65

LEVITT, Helen
Way of seeing; photographs. Horizon 7:49-59 Sum '65

LEVITT, Theodore
Exploit the product life cycle; excerpt from Marketing vision. Harvard Bsns R 43:81-94 N '65

LEVITT, William Jaird
Levittown look takes on a French style. il por Bsns W p64+ O 23 '65

LEVITT and sons, incorporated
New accent for Bill Levitt: venture in France. il Fortune 72:192 D '65
New look of Mr Levitt's towns. il Newsweek 66:72-4 S 13 '65

LEVY, Alan
Day JFK died; what people remember now. Good H 161:84-7+ N '65
Doc Simon's R for comedy. N Y Times Mag p42-3+ Mr 7 '65
Great escapo-vision in the sky. Life 59:57-8+ O 29 '65
How Jackie Kennedy & other young widows have rebuilt their lives. Good H 160:96-9+ Mr '65
Lost in the bookshops of New York. Harper 231:148-52 O '65
Muzak men. Horizon 7:39-45 Sum '65
Peekaboo sex, or How to fill a drive-in. Life 59:81-2+ Jl 16 '65
So why is this Bobby Vinton? Life 58:76-8+ Mr 12 '65
Voice of the underground cinema. N Y Times Mag p70+ S 19 '65
What every woman should know about the Beatles. Good H 161:12+ Jl '65

LEVY, David
Case of the missing testimony. R. L. Shayon. Sat R 48:42 F 27 '65

LEVY, Henri A. See Brown, G. M. jt. auth.

LEVY, Herbert
Wirewound power resistors. Electr World 73:47-51 Ap '65

LEVY, Marion J. jr
Patterns, structures, of modernization and political development. Ann Am Acad 358:29-40 Mr '65

LEVY, Marvin David
Mourning becomes Electra. Criticism
Opera N il por 29:26-7 Ap 10 '65

LEWANIKA, Sir Mwanawina III. See Mwanawina III

LEWENTHAL, Raymond
Mystery man; Alkan; reprint. H. C. Schonberg. Am Rec G 31:1132-4 Ag '65
Rebirth of an old romantic: Alkan revival. R. Eyer. Life 59:22 N 26 '65

LEWICKY, George I.
New appointment. por Wilson Lib Bul 40:294 N '65

LEWIN, Katie
Jigsaw puzzles go full circle. il Bsns W p68+ Jl 10 '65

LEWIS, Andrew M. Jr, and others
Lymphocytic-choriomeningitis virus in hamster tumor: spread to hamsters and humans. bibliog Science 150:363-4 O 15 '65

LEWIS, Anthony
British verdict on trial-by-press. N Y Times Mag p 14-15+ Je 20 '65
Mr Wilson is master of the House. N Y Times Mag p24-5+ Ap 11 '65
Tough lawyer goes to the Court. N Y Times Mag p 11+ Ag 8 '65

LEWIS, C. Day-. See Day-Lewis, C.

LEWIS, Charles
Color perfection with tuberous begonias. Horticulture 43:18-19+ Mr '65
—See Moore, C. B. jt. auth.

LEWIS, Clarence E.
Wisteria. Horticulture 43:18-20 Je '65

LEWIS, Clive Staples
Men and morals in space. J. M. Phelan. America 113:405-7 O 9 '65
Rebirth of Christ. J. Hart. il Nat R 17:1192-6 D 28 '65

LEWIS, Don
How to make handsome duck silhouettes. Pop Sci 188:134-5 Ja '66

LEWIS, Donald W.
Emerging specialty: adolescent medicine. Todays Health 43:38-41 F '65

LEWIS, Doris E.
High rise at Waterloo. Library J 90:5210-12 D 1 '65

LEWIS, Elsie M.
Book review. Negro Hist Bul 28:202+ My '65

LEWIS, F. W.
Saturday night bath, Navajo style. Am For 71:6 Mr '65

LEWIS, Gertrude, and Mackintosh, H. K.
Headstart for children in slums. pors Am Ed 1:30, inside back cover D '64

LEWIS, Gordon F.
New breed; reply to J. L. Jarrett. Sat R 48:75-6 S 11 '65

LEWIS, Gordon K.
Tidying up the unjust kingdom. Nation 201:449-50 D 6 '65

LEWIS, Henry
Top face. il por Time 86:49 D 31 '65

LEWIS, Howard R.
With every breath you take; excerpt. Read Digest 87:63-8+ S '65

LEWIS, Ida
Black mask of angry Africa. Life 58:111-12+ Ap 2 '65

LEWIS, Janet
Breakable cup; story. Sat Eve Post 238:60-1 F 27 '65

LEWIS, Joel
Roof over your head with *viager*. Atlan 215:120+ F '65

LEWIS, John
Senior scholastic interview; ed. by R. Hemming and G. Berg. por Sr Schol 86:21-2 My 6 '65

LEWIS, John W. See Kahin, G. M. jt. auth.

LEWIS, Meriwether
Meriwether Lewis, by R. Dillon. Review
Sat R il por 48:27 F 20 '65. B. Capps
Time il por 85:100+ F '19 '65

LEWIS, Oscar
Mother and son in a Puerto Rican slum; excerpt from In the life. Harper 231:71-6+ D '65
Portrait of Gabriel: Puerto Rican family in San Juan and New York; excerpt from In the life. Harper 232:54-9 Ja '66

about

Silencing the children of Sanchez. J. Sommers. il Nation 201:530-3 D 27 '65

LEWIS, Ramsey
View from the inside. Time 87:62 Ja 7 '66

LEWIS, Richard S.
Masterminds of Mars. Bul Atomic Sci 21:39-41 Ap '65
Message from Mariner 4. Bul Atomic Sci 21:38-40 N '65
Nawapa: water for the year 2000. Bul Atomic Sci 21:9-11 My '65

LEWIS, Richard Warren
Bonanza. Sat Eve Post 238:84-9 D 4 '65
Carroll Baker: the lady was a tramp. Sat Eve Post 238:36-8+ F 27 '65
Those swinging beach movies. Sat Eve Post 238:83-7 Jl 31 '65

LEWIS, Sinclair
Arrowsmith's American dream. J. K. Hutchens. por Sat R 48:25 Jl 3 '65

LEWIS, Theophilus
Theatre. See issues of America

LEWIS, Wyndham
Some poets in their prose. R. Howard. Poetry 105:397-8 Mr '65

LEWIS acidity. See Acidity

LEWIS and Clark expedition
By boat on Lewis and Clark's water highway; Missouri River. il Sunset 134:34-6+ Je '65
Great portage. J. C. Hunt. il Am For 71:8-11+ Jl '65
Lewis and Clark expedition's botanical discoveries. R. D. Burroughs. il Natur Hist 75:56-62 Ja '66

LEWIS AND CLARK NATIONAL WILDERNESS WATERWAY (proposed)
Whither the wide Missouri? conflict of interest between National park service and Army corps of engineers. G. F. Stucker. il Nat Parks Mag 39:10-15 Ag '65
Wilderness waterway problems. Nat Parks Mag 39:21 S '65

LEWIS-Wadhams school. See Schools, Experimental

LEWISOHN stadium concerts. See New York (city)—Music

LEWISTON, Me.
Big fight moves to small town: Liston-Clay fight. J. Underwood. il Sports Illus 22:22-3 My 17 '65

LEXINGTON, Ky.

Education

School for the future; Garden Springs elementary school. C. Brossard. il Look 29:55-6+ Mr 9 '65

Sanitary affairs

Tepee refuse burner has extension dome. W. M. Moore. il Am City 80:165 Ag '65

LEXINGTON, Mass.
Best weapon in the fight for better education. B. Asbell. Redbook 125:135-8 My '65

LEXINGTON, Miss.
Eleven year siege of Mississippi's lady editor. T. G. Harris. il Look 29:121-2+ N 16 '65

L'HEUREUX, John
Omen; poem. Commonweal 82:493 Jl 9 '65
Quince; poem. Commonweal 82:284 My 21 '65
Window; poem. Atlan 216:83 Ag '65

LI, Kwan-ming
Ciguatera fish poison: a cholinesterase inhibitor. bibliog Science 147:1580-1 Mr 26 '65

LI, Tsung-jen
Prize defector. Time 86:18 Jl 30 '65
Propaganda coup. Newsweek 66:36+ Ag 2 '65

LIABILITY (law)
Big stick for consumers; new legal pressures on U.S. auto manufacturers. il Time 86:42 Ag 6 '65
Corvair's second case. il Time 86:37 S 10 '65
Good & bad Samaritans. il Time 85:47 Ap 23 '65
Good Samaritans: law and the golden rule. L. Wille. il Nation 200:447-9 Ap 26 '65
Parishioners v. church; damage suits of Chicago's Our Lady of the Angels' fire. il Time 86:48-9 S 24 '65
Strict liability suits pile up for auto makers. Bsns W p30+ Ag 28 '65
U.S. may renounce pact: airline liability. Sr Schol 87:10+ N 11 '65
Verdict for Corvair; G.M. vs. D. Collins. il Time 86:46+ Ag 20 '65
Who pays when a visitor gets hurt on your property? Bet Hom & Gard 43:8 O '65
Your liability for student accidents. F. S. Shapiro. NEA J 54:46-7 Mr '65
See also
Damages

Anecdotes, facetiae, satire, etc.

Nothing beats money. Time 86:77 N 19 '65

LIABILITY insurance. See Insurance, Liability

LIBBY, Willard F.
Man's place in the physical universe. Bul Atomic Sci 21:12-17 S '65

LIBEL and slander
Controversial issues should be debated; concerning New York times decision. H. F. Pilpel. Pub W 187:18-19 Mr 29 '65
Decision is affirmed; we deplore it again; Warren Spahn right of privacy decision. H. F. Pilpel. Pub W 188:28-9 Jl 26 '65

I fought against hatred among my neighbors; ed. by J. N. Bell A. Hollenbeck. il Good H 161:71+ S '65
Libel and privacy lines are now diverging. Pub W 188:33 N 1 '65
Public officials & public men; right of free speech shield against state libel law. Time 86:90 O 8 '65
Satisfaction for Kuchel. Newsweek 65:23 Mr 8 '65
Statement to the friends of National review; concerning remarks by A. Shaw. W. F. Buckley, jr. Nat R 17:448 Je 1 '65
That was New York; scandal column of Town topics, weekly magazine. A. Logan. il New Yorker 41:37-8+ Ag 14; 41-2+ Ag 21 '65
Victim strikes back. Sr Schol 86:20 Mr 18 '65
Walker wins again; segregationist sues A.P. Time 86:110 N 5 '65
Who is a public official? concerning collections of libel damages. il Time 86:73 N 26 '65
See also
Trials (libel)

LIBEN, Meyer
CCNY; a memoir. Commentary 40:64-70 S '65

LIBER, Nadine
That way, the film is mine. Life 59:54 Ag 27 '65
(ed) See Courrèges, A. I warned my house, no Duchess

LIBERACE, Wladziu Valentino
What ever happened to Buster Keys? il por Time 86:89 O 1 '65

LIBERAL arts colleges. See Liberal education

LIBERAL education
New design for the college of liberal arts and sciences. G. D. Stoddard. il Sch & Soc 93:265-7 My 1 '65
Plight of the small college. W. A. Wallis. Atlan 216:124-6 N '65; Discussion. 217:38 Ja '66
Task of the liberal arts college; summary of report. C. H. Plimpton. Sch & Soc 93:264 My 1 '65
See also
Humanities

LIBERAL party (United States)
Fusion & confusion. Reporter 33:14+ Jl 15 '65

LIBERAL theology. See Modernism

LIBERALISM
Bankruptcy of the liberals; address, November 27, 1965; with reply by P. Steinfels. C. Oglesby. Commonweal 83:396-401 Ja 7 '66
Conservatism, liberalism, and religion. W. Herberg. il Nat R 17:1087-8 N 30 '65
Death of a liberal. W. V. Shannon. Commonweal 82:341-2 Je 4 '65
Fashions in liberalism. R. Lekachman. il Nation 201:62-6 S 20 '65
Liberal establishment, by M. S. Evans. Review
Esquire 64:28+ S '65. M. Muggeridge
Nat R 17:832 S 21 '65. W. F. Rickenbacker
Liberalism; excerpts from American dissent; decade of modern conservatism. J. Hart. il Nat R 17:A8-18 N 30 '65
Muffled voice of Russian liberalism: Novy mir, Russia's distinguished literary magazine. D. Brown. il N Y Times Mag p 10-11+ D 19 '65
Need to be liked and the anxious college liberal. R. R. Lane. bibliog f Ann Am Acad 361:71-80 S '65
Open letter from a military intellectual to a sophisticated liberal leader. R. A. Levine; discussion. Bul Atomic Sci 21:31 Ja; 31-3 Mr; 28-9 O '65
Robert Kennedy and the liberals. S. Alsop. Sat Eve Post 238:18 Ag 28 '65
Vietnam protest; are the liberals listening? W. C. McWilliams and D. Hale. Commonweal 83:333-6 D 17 '65
What price liberalism? J. Burnham. Nat R 17:456 Je 1 '65
Whereas—a judge's premises, by C. E. Wyzanski, jr. Review
Nat R 17:1201-3 D 28 '65. J. D. Mahoney
White liberal. L. E. Lomax. il Ebony 20:60-2+ Ag '65
Why liberals grumble about LBJ. il U S News 59:40-2 Jl 5 '65
See also
Conservatism
Right and left (political science)

LIBERMAN, Evsel
Borrowing from the capitalists. il por Time 85:23-6+ F 12 '65
Russia discovers the customer is always right. D. Crankshaw. il por N Y Times Mag p26-7+ Mr 28 '65
Russia's new economy. S. Lens. Christian Cent 82:236 F 24 '65

LIBERTY

Academic freedom and political liberty. A. Lepawsky. bibliog Science 150:1559-63 D 17 '65

Bill of rights: its origin and meaning, by I. Brant. Review
New Repub 153:38-40 N 27 '65. I. Dilliard

Equality and liberty, by H. V. Jaffa. Review
Nat R il 17:606-7 Jl 13 '65. S. Parry

Foundation of freedom. H. H. Humphrey. NEA J 54:15 O '65

Four simple words: the right to choose. W. McMillen. Read Digest 86:24B F '65

Freedom and unity in the Americas; with bibliography. W. J. Kilgore. il Américas 17:1-4 D '65

Road to peace and freedom. A. W. Munk. Bul Atomic Sci 21:30-1 O '65

Toward the therapeutic state; involuntary mental hospitalization. T. S. Szasz. New Repub 153:26-9 D 11 '65; Reply. Mrs W. A. Anthony. 153:30 D 25 '65

View from up there; address, July 2, 1965. H. Cleveland. Dept State Bul 53:151-6 Jl 26 '65

See also
Democracy
Equality
Intellectual liberty
Magna carta

LIBERTY, Religious. See Religious liberty

LIBERTY of conscience
See also
Religious liberty

LIBERTY of speech. See Free speech

LIBERTY tree. See Trees, Historic

LIBHART, Myles
Alaska's designer-craftsman training project. Craft Horiz 25:16+ Jl '65

LIBRARIANS
Better class of mouse. J. Shera. Wilson Lib Bul 39:677 Ap '65

Future too, is prologue. J. Shera. Wilson Lib Bul 39:253 N '64; Correction. 39:636 Ap '65

Great land of libraries; address, July 1965. L. C. Powell. il ALA Bul 59:643-8 Jl '65; Reply. D. M. Broderick. Library J 90: 4532-3 O 15 '65

Kinder, kueche, und bibliotheken; dangers of employing part-time librarians. J. Shera. Wilson Lib Bul 40:365 D '65

Lifeblood of the profession: junior librarians. J. Shera. Wilson Lib Bul 39:785 My '65

Misused librarians. N. Harlow. Library J 90: 1597-9 Ap 1 '65

My career as a "librain." Library J 90:4538-9 O 15 '65

New member and ALA; address, July 1965. F. H. Wagman. ALA Bul 59:995-1002 D '65

Of wine, waiters, and librarians. J. Shera. Wilson Lib Bul 39:903+ Je '65

Role for librarians in the relevant war against poverty; address, May 15, 1965. K. B. Clark. il Wilson Lib Bul 40:42-7 S '65

Sex and the stuffy librarian. E. De Grazia. il Library J 90:2483-5 Je 1 '65

Special librarian. P. Wasserman; J. Harvey; A. M. Rees; discussion. Library J 89:4840+; 90:796+ D 15 '64, F 15 '65
See also
Catalogers
Library staffs
School librarians

Education
See Library schools and education

Education in service
In-service training for subprofessionals; division of library extension, Maryland state department of education. H. T. Walker. il ALA Bul 59:134-8 F '65

This old gal went back to college; student at Graduate school of library service at Rutgers; and trainee at Montclair free public library. M. Bartley. il Library J 90: 5351-3 D 15 '65

Political activities
Hearing: testimony in support of the President's higher education bill by ALA. S. Smith. ALA Bul 59:329 My '65

Qualifications
See also
School librarians—Qualifications

Recruiting
Hole in the network: delay in reaching local level from ALA Office for recruitment. J. Berry. Library J 90:590-1 F 1 '65; Reply. H. V. Deale. 90:2052 My 1 '65

Librarian-for-a-day 1964; state-wide student recruitment; Pennsylvania library association. C. A. Vogel. il Library J 90:1468-70 Mr 15 '65

Namath system; bonus for beginning professional. E. Moon. Library J 91:68 Ja 1 '66

One public library; Rochester, N.Y. public library. M. E. Cashman. ALA Bul 59:147-50 F '65

Plea for selective recruitment. D. J. Hickey. ALA Bul 59:361-3 My '65; Discussion. 59:594 Jl '65

Recruitment (cont) M. Ricking. ALA Bul 59:750-2, 835 S-O '65

Unorthodox recruiting: science librarians; letter to the editor. S. W. Hilyard. Library J 90:3830+ O 1 '65

What does the local representative do? address, July 1964. E. E. Budell. ALA Bul 59: 303-5 Ap '65

Anecdotes, facetiae, satire, etc.
Recruitment release. F. J. Anderson. Library J 90:829 F 15 '65

Salaries
Sixty-one forty-five in nineteen sixty-four. D. E. Strout and R. B. Strout. il Library J 90:2741-9 Je 15 '65

Supply and demand
See also
Librarians—Recruiting

Tenure
Defending the freedom to read in the courts. E. de Grazia. ALA Bul 59:507-15 Je '65

Legal defenses for public librarians; suggested insurance fund to support librarians forced out of their positions for defending freedom of expression. E. J. Gaines. ALA Bul 59:343 My '65

LIBRARIANS, Negro. See Negro librarians

LIBRARIANSHIP
As you wished you were; concerning the symposium, sponsored by Syracuse university library school. J. Shera. Wilson Lib Bul 40:179 O '65

Don't give us your tired, your poor. M. Bennett. il Atlan 215:93-5 My '65

Fire from the maddened crowd; librarianship a profession? E. Moon. Library J 90:578-81 F 1 '65

Future too, is prologue. J. Shera. Wilson Lib Bul 39:253 N '64; Correction. 39:636 Ap '65

Great land of libraries; address, July 1965. L. C. Powell. il ALA Bul 59:643-8 Jl '65; Reply. D. M. Broderick. Library J 90:4532-3 O 15 '65

Interview with Verner Clapp; ed. by K. Molz. Wilson Lib Bul 40:150-6 O '65

Library council? E. N. Waters. Library J 90: 4002-4 O 1 '65
See also
Library science as a profession

International aspects
International scene: possibilities in children's service. M. L. Batchelder. Library J 90:5039-40 N 15 '65

LIBRARIES
See also
American libraries abroad
Books and reading
College libraries
Historical libraries
School libraries

Acquisitions
Book acquisition costs. R. D. Franklin. il Library J 90:1612-13 Ap 1 '65

Cost indexes for library materials. M. Chicorel. il Wilson Lib Bul 39:896-900+ Je '65

Great manuscript rush. D. Dempsey. Sat R 48:28-9 My 1 '65
See also
College libraries—Acquisitions

Administration
See Library administration

Architecture
See Library architecture

Automation
Automation in the Detroit public library. C. M. Mohrhardt. il ALA Bul 59:829-33 O '65

Computerized bibliographic services for biomedicine. L. Karel and others. bibliog il Science 148:766-72 My 7 '65

Data processing equipment in libraries (cont) J. Becker. il ALA Bul 59:293-6, 823-6 Ap, O '65

How not to waste knowledge. il Time 86: 52-7 S 3 '65

Keeping up with mechanization. S. A. Artandi. il Library J 90:4715-17 N 1 '65

LIBRARIES—Automation—*Continued*
Let's all tell the truth; Univac at World's fair, Department of agriculture report of task force; letter to the editor, with editorial comment. R. R. Shaw. ALA Bul 59: 594-7 Jl '65
See also
Information storage and retrieval systems
United States—Library of Congress—Automation

Book drives
See Book and periodical giving campaigns

Book losses
See also
Book thefts

Book mutilation
See Books—Mutilation, defacement, etc.

Book selection
See Book selection

Branches and stations
Branch library inadequacies in a typical large city. L. Grundt. bibliog Library J 90:3997-4001 O 1 '65

Censorship
Full freedom of expression; symposium. bibliog il Wilson Lib Bul 39:638-72 Ap '65
Intellectual freedom. E. J. Gaines. See issues of ALA bulletin
Library and librarian attacked in California censorship case. Library J 90:1683 Ap 1 '65
More than lip service. E. Geller. Library J 90:3640 S 15 '65
National service organization proposes a nationwide survey. P. S. Jennison. ALA Bul 59:89-90 F '65; Discussion. 59:239 Ap '65
Ordeal at Long Beach. B. Collins. il Library J 90:2486-90+ Je 1 '65
Right to read. Christian Cent 82:1244-5 O 13 '65
Sex and the stuffy librarian. E. De Grazia. il Library J 90:2483-5 Je 1 '65
Stand on censorship: statement of position of California library association and California association of school librarians. Wilson Lib Bul 39:720+ My '65
Supporting the Library bill of rights; proceedings of midwinter conference sponsored by ALA Intellectual freedom committee. bibliog ALA Bul 59:469-533 Je '65
Teaching librarians to fight back. D. Dempsey. il Sat R 48:20-1+ F 27 '65; Reply. E. Moon. 48:22 Mr 20 '65
They play it safe; North Carolina public libraries, report of survey. E. W. Tamblyn. il Library J 90:2495-8 Je 1 '65; Reply. E. Moon. 90:2980-1 Jl '65
This was 1965: censorship at all levels. il Library J 91:44-6 Ja 1 '66
To right-thinking people; letter to the editor. B. L. Andrew. Library J 90:2048+ My 1 '65
Whitewash in Whitewater; Wisconsin state college vs Kiwanis club; letter to the editor. S. D. Robertson; reply. D. Goddard. Library J 90:414 F 1 '65
See also
American library association—Intellectual freedom committee
School libraries—Censorship

Charging systems
Efficiency and individuality. W. J. Biehl. il Library J 90:586-9 F 1 '65

Circulation, loans, etc.
Efficiency and individuality. W. J. Biehl. il Library J 90:586-9 F 1 '65
See also
Interlibrary loans

Cooperative service
See Library cooperation

Directories
See also
American library directory

Extension work
See Library extension

Federal aid
See Libraries and state

Finance
Book acquisition costs. R. D. Franklin. il Library J 90:1612-13 Ap 1 '65
Numbers game: performance budgeting; Los Angeles public library. H. L. Hamill. il Library J 90:3563-7 S 15 '65
See also
Libraries and state
School libraries—Finance

Fines
Common fine; report of survey by Akron public library. J. H. Rebenack; discussion. Library J 90:412+ F 1 '65
Nickel-a-day addiction: Anoka County library, Spring Lake Park, Minn. J. Challman; discussion. Library J 90:412+ F 1 '65

Gifts, legacies, etc.
America's future promotes library gift book package. Library J 90:2800+ Je 15 '65
See also
Book and periodical giving campaigns

History
Renaissance in library history? new publication of Florida state university library school. J. Shera. Wilson Lib Bul 40:281 N '65

Information service
See Libraries—Reference work

Instruction in use
Individualized instruction; symposium. ed. by M. P. Archer. bibliog il Library J 90:1977-90 Ap 15 '65
TV or the herded tour: teaching large numbers of entering freshmen; California state college, Los Angeles. C. M. Brown. il Library J 90:2214-18 My 15 '65
Temples & confessional booths. J. Weatherford. Library J 91:70 Ja 1 '66

Intermediate departments
See also
Libraries—Work with young people

International aspects
International exchange. Wilson Lib Bul 39: 567-71, 778-82 Mr, My '65

Legislation
See Library laws and legislation

Manuscript collections
Great manuscript rush. D. Dempsey. Sat R 48:28-9 My 1 '65

Microfilm collections
National register of microform masters to be issued. E. Hamer and A. McCormick. ALA Bul 59:791-2 O '65
Preservation of deteriorating books; excerpts from report. G. R. Williams. bibliog Library J 91:51-6 Ja 1 '66

Music collections
Music in libraries; symposium; ed. by G. Stevenson. bibliog il Library J 90:1243-70 Mr 15 '65
See also
School libraries—Music collections

Organization
See Library administration

Paperback books
Public libraries in metro Toronto automate reordering of paperbacks. Library J 90: 2232 My 15 '65

Periodical collections
Boast of Englishmen: project to microfilm British periodicals from the Restoration to the death of Queen Victoria. D. Fader. bibliog il Library J 90:1841-3 Ap 15 '65
South Carolina undertakes project to increase P.L. periodical holdings. Library J 90:1850-1 Ap 15 '65

Public relations
Antibodies in the civic bloodstream: keeping the community informed about basic values of intellectual freedom. E. J. Gaines. ALA Bul 59:177 Mr '65
Professional publicity services: a 1965 checklist. A. Norton. il Library J 90:3392-6 S 1 '65
See also
Adult education—Library participation

Readers advisory service
Return of the reader's adviser; pre-conference institute at University of Wisconsin. E. T. Smith. il Library J 90:3215-16 Ag '65

Reading rooms
Divisional reading room; college and university libraries. G. Fitzgerald. Wilson Lib Bul 39:565-6+ Mr '65

Reference work
On library panic; reference work with students; excerpt from address, February 1965. E. Tripp. il Library J 90:4514-16 O 15 '65

LIBRARIES—Reference work—*Continued*
Providence pioneer: William E. Foster. J. L. Wheeler. il Wilson Lib Bul 40:275-8 N '65
Reference encounter; discussion with Lj editors. W. J. Bonk; T. J. Galvin. il Library J 90:1818-24 Ap 15 '65; Discussion. 90:2696+ Je 15 '65
See also
Reference books

Registration

Appendectomy: nonresident fee. W. Brahm. Library J 90:4726 N 1 '65; Reply. W. S. Eddy. 91:2+ Ja 1 '66

Science collections

Orne surveys eighty-five academic libraries, finds science facilities inadequate; excerpts from report. J. Orne. Library J 90:2108 My 1 '65

Security measures
See Library protection systems

Special collections
See also
United States—Library of Congress—Special collections

Standards

Break for the blind; preview of a forthcoming set of standards. E. Moon. il Library J 90:830-3 F 15 '65; Reply. R. R. Shaw. 90:1766 Ap 15 '65
See also
School libraries—Standards

Statistics

Numbers game: performance budgeting; Los Angeles public library. H. L. Hamill. il Library J 90:3563-7 S 15 '65

Student assistants
See Library assistants

Technical processes

Cooperative growing pains: Oak Park, Ill. book processing center. D. Hendricks. Library J 90:4699-703 N 1 '65

Trustees, boards, committees, etc.

Trustees in the age of consensus. K. Nyren. Library J 90:3550-2 S 15 '65
Trustee's thoughts on censorship. C. E. Reid. ALA Bul 59:527-8 Je '65
See also
American library trustee association

Vandalism
See Vandalism

Work with blind

Break for the blind; preview of a forthcoming set of standards. E. Moon. il Library J 90:830-3 F 15 '65; Reply. R. R. Shaw. 90:1766 Ap 15 '65
See also
School libraries—Work with blind

Work with groups

Education vs. culture: strange case of the Burbank public library. T. Schoenman. ALA Bul 60:27-30 Ja '66

Work with schools
See Libraries and schools

Work with young people

Age of the acronym: Boston public library, address, February 1965. J. Manthorne. Wilson Lib Bul 40:84-6 S '65
Fair garden and the swarm of beasts; address, December 1964. M. A. Edwards. il Library J 90:3379-83 S 1 '65
National library week; and work with youth. C. A. Vogel; R. Lindenmeyer. il Library J 90:1468-71 Mr 15 '65
Twelve-year-old adult reader. D. M. Broderick. il Library J 90:2321-7 My 15 '65
See also
Libraries and students

Arizona
See also
Tucson, Ariz. public library

California

Interlibrary cooperation in California; address, July 1965. C. R. Leigh. Wilson Lib Bul 40:157-61 O '65

Stand on censorship: statement of position of California library association and California association of school librarians. Wilson Lib Bul 39:720+ My '65
See also
Burbank, Calif. public library
Coalinga, Calif. district library
Long Beach, Calif. public library
Los Angeles County public library
Los Angeles public library
Riverside, Calif. public library
Sausalito, Calif. public library

Canada

Rugged stupidity; rugged individualism in cataloging practices. E. Moon. Library J 90:3406 S 1 '65
See also
Canadian library association

Denmark

Denmark's new Public libraries act. E. A. Jensen. Wilson Lib Bul 39:567-71 Mr '65

England
See also
Libraries—Great Britain
London—Libraries
Nottingham, England, public library

Florida
See also
Miami, Fla. public library

France

Signs are propitious: the current library scene in France. A. T. Hamlin. il Library J 90:2081-6 My 1 '65

Great Britain

Administrative policy and book stock provision; excerpts. S. C. Holliday. il Library J 90:4907-11 N 15 '65
Here and there: differences between American and British attitudes and practices. E. Moon. Library J 90:4929 N 15 '65
Library explosion: British librarianship in the sixties. F. M. Gardner. il Library J 90:4897-901 N 15 '65
New deal on an old frontier. R. Stokes. il Library J 90:1608-11 Ap 1 '65
See also
Library association
National lending library for science and technology, Boston Spa, Yorkshire

Hawaii

Hawaii governor's committee report recommends statewide library system. Library J 90:3228 Ag '65

Illinois

Cooperative growing pains: Oak Park, Ill. book processing center. D. Hendricks. Library J 90:4699-703 N 1 '65
See also
Belleville, Ill. public library
Chicago public library
Wheaton, Ill. public library

Japan
See also
Japan—National Diet library

Latin America

Aid to libraries in Latin America. M. D. Shepard. il Wilson Lib Bul 39:778-82 My '65

Maryland

Maryland starts new cooperative library project. Pub W 187:68 F 15 '65
Peopleless town surveyed for library needs; plans for Columbia, Md. Pub W 188:92 S 27 '65
See also
Baltimore County, Md. public library
Prince George's County memorial library, Hyattsville
Washington County free library, Hagerstown

Massachusetts
See also
New Bedford, Mass. free public library

Michigan
See also
Detroit—Libraries
Detroit public library

Minnesota
See also
Minneapolis public library
St Paul—Libraries

LIBRARIES—*Continued*

Mississippi

Freedom libraries; program of Council of federated organizations. F. W. Heinze. il Library J 90:1991-3 Ap 15 '65; Reply. R. B. Layton. 90:2308+ My 15 '65

Mississippi summer; libraries in freedom schools. M. Braverman. il Library J 90:5045-7 N 15 '65

Missouri

Interlibrary cooperation in Missouri; address, July 1965. G. Martin. il Wilson Lib Bul 40:166-71 O '65

See also

Columbia, Mo. public library

Kansas City, Mo, public library

New Jersey

See also

Montclair, N.J. free public library

New Jersey library association

New York (state)

See also

Buffalo and Erie County, N.Y. public library

Kingston, N.Y. city library

New York library association

New York public library

Rochester, N.Y. public library

Yonkers, N.Y. public library

North Carolina

They play it safe: report of survey. E. W. Tamblyn. il Library J 90:2495-8 Je 1 '65; Reply. E. Moon. 90:2980-1 Jl '65

See also

Henderson County public library, Hendersonville

Oklahoma

Interlibrary cooperation in Oklahoma; address, July 1965. E. M. Henke. il Wilson Lib Bul 40:162-5 O '65

Pakistan

Peace corps in perspective. N. Barron; reply. K. S. Diehl. Library J 90:988 Mr 1 '65

Pennsylvania

See also

Norristown, Pa. public library

Pennsylvania state library, Harrisburg

Philadelphia—Free library

Scranton, Pa. public library

Rhode Island

See also

Providence, R.I. public library

South Carolina

South Carolina undertakes project to increase P.L. periodical holdings. Library J 90:1850-1 Ap 15 '65

Southern states

Library in the South: educational problems; address, April 1965. V. L. Jones. il Wilson Lib Bul 39:878-84 Je '65

Library in the South: socioeconomic and cultural aspects; address, April 1965. A. L. McNeal. bibliog il Wilson Lib Bul 39:867-8+ Je '65

Switzerland

American books for American children in Switzerland; Children's library of Zurich. E. V. Epstein. il Pub W 189:64-5 Ja 10 '66

Tennessee

See also

Memphis, Tenn. public library

Nashville, Tenn. public library

Texas

See also

La Retama public library, Corpus Christi

United States

ALA conference focuses on libraries for a Great society. il Pub W 188:24-30 Ag 9 '65

Cooperation in action. E. Yungmeyer and others. ALA Bul 59:733-44 S '65

Equalization of opportunity; address, October 1964. R. Blasingame, jr. il Library J 90:2071-5 My 1 '65; Discussion. 90:2076-80+, 3336+ My 1, S 1 '65

Form and the substance; address, 1964. R. R. Shaw. Library J 90:567-71 F 1 '65; Discussion. 90:1214+, 1580, 1764+ Mr 15-Ap 15 '65

Here and there: differences between American and British attitudes and practices. E. Moon. Library J 90:4929 N 15 '65

How not to waste knowledge. il Time 86:52-7 S 3 '65

National inventory of library needs. ALA Bul 59:621 Jl '65

Simplifying work in small public libraries, by D. D. Dennis. Review

Wilson Lib Bul 39:911 Je '65. G. K. Schenk

This was 1965: selective review of the library news. il Library J 91:41-50 Ja 1 '66

See also

Center for research libraries, Chicago

Council on library resources, incorporated

Library surveys

National library week

Special libraries association

Washington (state)

See also

Washington state library

Wisconsin

See also

Madison, Wis. public library

LIBRARIES (rooms)

Room for books and music. il House & Gard 127:100-1 F '65

LIBRARIES, Business

How to start a business library; in one easy lesson. C. Georgi. il Library J 90:1058-62 Mr 1 '65

LIBRARIES, Childrens

American books for Americans children in Switzerland; Children's library of Zurich. E. V. Epstein. il Pub W 189:64-5 Ja 10 '66

Case against childhood. R. H. Viguers. Horn Bk 41:139 Ap '65

Children's libraries. Wilson Lib Bul 39:689, 913 Ap, Je '65

International scene. M. L. Batchelder. Library J 90:5039-40 N 15 '65

See also

Story telling

Book selection

See Book selection

Caricatures and cartoons

Library coloring sheet. E. Norton and G. Billington. Library J 90:4534-5 O 15 '65

Projects

Dropouts or readers? need for summer reading programs. M. C. Austin. bibliog f il Sr Schol 86:sup26-7 Mr 4 '65

Summer reading programs pay big dividends. N. Larrick. il Sr Schol 86:sup 21-2 Mr 4 '65

LIBRARIES, Church

Mormon genealogical library establishing branch system. Library J 90:1853-4 Ap 15 '65

LIBRARIES, College. See College libraries

LIBRARIES, County

See also

Los Angeles County public library

Washington County free library, Hagerstown, Md.

LIBRARIES, Deposit

See also

Center for research libraries, Chicago

LIBRARIES, Depository

Implementing the depository law; proposal for the distribution of non-GPO publications to depository libraries, 1962 statute. C. Brock. bibliog il Library J 90:1825-33 Ap 15 '65

LIBRARIES, documentation and archives, Division of Unesco. See United Nations educational, scientific and cultural organization—Division of libraries, documentation and archives

LIBRARIES, Historical. See Historical libraries

LIBRARIES, Hospital

See also

United States—Veterans administration hospitals—Libraries

LIBRARIES, Instruction in use of. See Libraries—Instruction in use

LIBRARIES, Moving of. See Moving of libraries

LIBRARIES, Phonograph record. See Phonograph record libraries

LIBRARIES, Private

Adventures in book keeping; care and collecting of the personal library. L. Kronenberger. Vogue 146:273-4+ O 1 '65

Tumblin' Creek's cabin library; Tennessee mountains. S. C. Gross. il Sr Schol 87:sup 17-19 S 30 '65

See also

Book collecting

LIBRARIES, School. See School libraries

LIBRARIES, Special

Special librarian. P. Wasserman; J. Harvey; A. M. Rees; discussion. Library J 89:4840+; 90:796+ D 15 '64; F 15 '65

See also

Libraries, Business

Newspapers—Libraries

Special libraries association

LIBRARIES, State
See also
Pennsylvania state library, Harrisburg
LIBRARIES, Thefts from. See Book thefts
LIBRARIES, Traveling
See also
Bookmobiles
LIBRARIES, University. See College libraries
LIBRARIES and adult education. See Adult education—Library participation
LIBRARIES and audio-visual materials
Radio active library; Oakland university, Rochester, Mich. F. M. Cammack. il Library J 90:4300-2 O 15 '65
LIBRARIES and authors
Acknowledgments from an author; address, July 3, 1965. G. Carson. Wilson Lib Bul 40:271-4+ N '65
LIBRARIES and booksellers
Visiting bookmen in France. A. T. Hamlin. ALA Bul 59:815-18 O '65
LIBRARIES and music
Music in libraries; symposium; ed. by G. Stevenson. bibliog il Library J 90:1243-70 Mr 15 '65
LIBRARIES and Negroes
In defense of academic freedom; reply to newspaper article by R. Martin. E. J. Josey. Wilson Lib Bul 40:173-5 O '65
Library burns in the Los Angeles riot; Willowbrook branch; report. E. T. Moore. il ALA Bul 59:983-6 D '65
New Jersey, Nebraska, and Detroit feature Negro history projects. Library J 90:1278 Mr 15 '65
Reading and the disadvantaged. E. J. Josey. Negro Hist Bul 28:156-7+ Ap '65
See also
New York public library—135th Street branch
LIBRARIES and publishers
Books, not copying machines, are the long-term answer; address, March 1964. L. C. Deighton. il Library J 90:2087-92 My 1 '65
Library promotion: an Adclub seminar. Pub W 187:29-33 Mr 8 '65
LIBRARIES and readers
Core of conscience, core of community; excerpts from address, May 7, 1965. S. B. Gould. il Library J 90:3993-6 O 1 '65
Home runs needed: library service to adults and children at home. W. Brahm. Library J 90:4022 O 1 '65
No sale; libraries and Gateway to ideas program. R. L. Shayon. Sat R 48:34 Mr 20 '65
Of wine, waiters, and librarians. J. Shera. Wilson Lib Bul 39:903+ Je '65
Very serious matter: regional libraries vs. keeping in touch with the readers. G. K. Schenk. Wilson Lib Bul 39:911 Je '65
LIBRARIES and research
Acknowledgments from an author; address, July 3, 1965. G. Carson. Wilson Lib Bul 40:271-4+ N '65
Basic book courses for prospective teachers: young adult literature, bibliography, reference. H. R. Sattley. Wilson Lib Bul 39:797 My '65
Changing role of libraries; need for efficient network of national information systems in science and technology; address, July 1965. W. T. Knox. ALA Bul 59:720-5 S '65; Reply. W. H. Carlson. 60:11 Ja '66
Divisional reading room; college and university libraries. G. Fitzgerald. Wilson Lib Bul 39:565-6+ Mr '65
Libraries and the inquiring mind; address, July 9, 1965. R. G. Vosper. ALA Bul 59:709-17 S '65
See also
American library association—Research and development, Office of
LIBRARIES and schools
Children's libraries; public library and the school book fair, Kansas City public library. J. A. Merrill. Wilson Lib Bul 39:913 Je '65
See also
School libraries
LIBRARIES and social and economic problems
Books for the Job corps; with excerpts from guidelines by J. M. Carroll. J. Manthorne. il Library J 90:932-4 F 15 '65
Equalization of opportunity; address, October 1964. R. Blasingame, jr. il Library J 90:2071-5 My 1 '65; Discussion. 90:2076-80+, 3336+ My 1, S 1 '65
Federal financing for library personnel; provided by Economic opportunity act, 1964; symposium. il Wilson Lib Bul 40:242-61 N '65
Good books and easy discipline; school library, Lansing, Mich. P. Anderson. Library J 90:5048-50 N 15 '65

Head start programs; New York, Brooklyn and Queens public libraries. il Library J 90:2338-40 My 15 '65
Library and adult illiteracy; symposium. bibliog il Wilson Lib Bul 40:40-86+ S '65
Library service for the undereducated topic of one-day conference at Drexel. Library J 90:3239-40 Ag '65
Materials for the underprivileged, theme of New books preview dinner. Library J 90:4536 O 15 '65
Poverty programs; divisional meetings at Detroit. J. Berry. il Library J 90:3196-200 Ag '65
Precious irrelevance; poverty programs. J. Berry. Library J 90:2772 Je 15 '65
Preparation for war: use of experience in poverty service points abroad in serving poverty service points at home. E. Moon. Library J 90:834 F 15 '65
What happened in Watts? letter to the editor. C. M. Weisenberg. Library J 90:5018+ N 15 '65
LIBRARIES and state
ALA conference focuses on libraries for a Great society. il Pub W 188:24-30 Ag 9 '65
Assistance for medical libraries approved by House and Senate. Library J 90:4732-3 N 1 '65
Equalization of opportunity; address, October 1964. R. Blasingame, jr. il Library J 90:2071-5 My 1 '65; Discussion. 90:2076-80+, 3336+ My 1, S 1 '65
Federal financing for library personnel; provided by Economic opportunity act, 1964; symposium. il Wilson Lib Bul 40:242-61 N '65
Federal grants and loans in 1965 support 648 library building projects. Library J 91:72 Ja 1 '66
First work of these times; features of Elementary and secondary education act, relating to library service. il Library J 90:3671-3 S 15 '65
Hands-off policy continues; expanded NDEA and pending legislation without federal edict. E. Geller. Library J 90:916+ F 15 '65
Higher education act approved. G. Krettek and E. D. Cooke. ALA Bul 59:988-9 D '65
Higher education act approved, but no funds appropriated for library title. Library J 90:4930 N 15 '65
Higher education act passed by Senate. G. Krettek and E. D. Cooke. Wilson Lib Bul 40:191 O '65
Higher education bill granted rule. G. Krettek and E. D. Cooke. ALA Bul 59:789 O '65
Higher education bills voted with $70 million for libraries. Library J 90:4026 O 1 '65
How the Elementary and secondary education act will operate; Higher education act. G. Krettek. ALA Bul 59:778-9 O '65
Laws, law-makers, and libraries. J. E. Fogarty. ALA Bul 59:269-73 Ap '65
LSCA and higher education grants total $110 million for construction. Library J 90:2986+ Jl '65
Legislation and the schools; new legislation of NDEA, ALA midwinter report. E. Geller. il Library J 90:1481-2 Mr 15 '65
Medical library aid. G. Krettek and E. D. Cooke. Wilson Lib Bul 40:291 N '65
Myth of federal control. W. Brahm. Library J 90:2106 My 1 '65
Texas Title II plan approved by OE; other states have tentative breakdowns. Library J 90:5486 D 15 '65
This was 1965: selective review of the library news. il Library J 91:41-50 Ja 1 '66
Two more library bills pass; Higher education and Medical library assistance acts. G. Krettek and E. D. Cooke. Wilson Lib Bul 40:375+ D '65
What's happening in education? money from the new federal education act. W. D. Boutwell. PTA Mag 60:11-12 O '65
Why Title 2? Elementary and secondary education act of 1965; address, May, 1965. J. Lorenz. Library J 90:3674-5 S 15 '65
Your guide to Title 2; Elementary and secondary education act of 1965: materials, eligible schools, local project applications. Library J 90:3675-80 S 15 '65
LIBRARIES and students
Airlie House conference: education and the Nation's libraries; sponsored by ALA. E. Geller. il Library J 90:2331-3 My 15 '65
Airlie House conference; sponsored by ALA. C. Carner. ALA Bul 59:441 Je '65
Clean, well-lighted place; West African students in London libraries; reprint. J. Wakeman. Library J 90:4912-13 N 15 '65
Education and the Nation's libraries: invitational conference at Airlie House, Warrenton, Va. sponsored by ALA. K. Molz. Wilson Lib Bul 39:729-30 My '65

LICENSES
See also
Automobile drivers—Licenses
LICHENS
Air pollution affects pattern of photosynthesis in parmelia sulcata a corticolous lichen. L. Pearson and E. Skye. bibliog il Science 148:1600-2 Je 18 '65; Reply. R. H. Linnell. 149:1267 S 10 '65
Artificial reestablishment of the lichen cladonia cristatella. V. Ahmadjian. bibliog il Science 151:199-201 Ja 14 '66
LICHT, Fred
Winter in Berlin; story. Reporter 33:34-9 D 30 '65
LICHTENBERGER, Edgar W.
Verdict. NEA J 54:48-50 Mr '65
LICHTENSTEIN, Eugene
Our silver dolors. Fortune 71:126-9+ Mr '65
LICHTHEIM, George
All the news that's fit to print, reflections on the New York times. Commentary 40: 33-46 S; 19-20+ D '65
Public affairs (cont) Commentary 39:62-6 Mr; 26, 56-9 My; 40:58-62 Jl '65; 41:49-53 Ja '66
LICKONA, Thomas
Another priest, another ban. Commonweal 83:298-9 D 10 '65
LICORICE
Licorice & ulcers. Time 85:77 F 26 '65
LIDAR (light detection and ranging) See Lasers
LIDDELL, Alice
Millions in wonderland. G. L. Potter. il Horn Bk 41:593-7 D '65
LIDSTONE, John
We want to make something. Sch Arts 65: 11-15 S '65
Whole secret is feeling. Sch Arts 64:22-8 Mr '65
LIE detectors
Lie detection at a distance. A. Ewing. il Sci N L 88:106-7 Ag 14 '65
Lie detector investigated. Sci Am 212:50 My '65
Unions act on threats to privacy. il Bsns W p87-8 Mr 13 '65
LIEBELT, R. A. See Delmonte, L. jt. auth.
LIEBER, Joel
Bikinis in the desert. Sat R 48:68+ Mr 13 '65
Kibbutzing in Israel. Travel 123:48-51+ F '65
Land of Hope and yaks. Sat R 48:60+ S 18 '65
LIEBERMAN, Henry R.
Everyday life in Liu Ling. Reporter 33:33-4+ Jl 1 '65
LIEBERMAN, Herbert
Matty and the moron and madonna. Criticism New Yorker 41:84 Ap 10 '65
LIEBERMAN, J. Ben
Printing's do-it-yourselfers. Sat R 48:70-2+ O 9 '65
LIEBERMAN, Myron
Teachers on the march: the militant mice. Nation 200:107-10 F 1 '65
Who speaks for teachers? Sat R 48:64-6+ Je 19 '65
LIEBERMAN, Rose, and others
Linkage in control of allotypic specificities on two different γG-immunoglobulins. bibliog Science 148:640-2 Ap 30 '65
LIEBERSON, Goddard
Return; V. Horowitz. New Yorker 41:21-3 My 29 '65
LIECHTENSTEIN
Letter from Liechtenstein. J. Bainbridge. il New Yorker 41:68+ Ag 7 '65
LIECHTENSTEIN collection. See Art—Private collections
LIEM, Karel F.
Fish that walks, breathes, changes sex. por Sci Digest 57:12-13 Ap '65
LIES. See Lying
LIFE
Teaching of reverence for life, by A. Schweitzer. Review Sat R il 48:52-3 Ap 24 '65
See also
Conduct of life
Death
Immortality
LIFE (biology)
Aging and everyman. N. J. Berrill. il Atlan 217:86-90 Ja '66
Beyond Darwinism. A. Portmann; M. Grene. Commentary 40:31-41 N '65
Control of life. il Life 59:59-69 S 10; 94-6+ O 1 '65
Life 2.7 billion years old. Sci N L 87:339 My 29 '65
Nearer the secret of life. il Sci Digest 57:15-16 Je '65

New man; what will he be like? A. Rosenfeld. Life 59:94-6+ O 1 '65; Same abr. with title Will man direct his own evolution? Read Digest 88:37-42 Ja '66
Notes and comment; synthetic creation of life. New Yorker 41:43 O 9 '65
Older than ever: forms of life older than recognized before. Time 86:100 N 12 '65
Physical basis of life and learning; adaptation of address, April 23, 1965. F. O. Schmitt. bibliog Science 149:931-6 Ag 27 '65
Still-earlier life. Sci Am 212:58 Je '65
Test tube life, a step forward; production of self-duplicating ribonucleic acid. Bsns W p 137-8 O 9 '65
What happens when life begins. W. Goodman. Redbook 125:54-5+ Jl '65
Where there's life... il Newsweek 65:100 My 10 '65
Will man create life? F. Marley. Sci N L 88: 227 O 9 '65

Origin

Can science produce life? R. Platt. il Read Digest 87:189-90+ Jl '65
Life from chemicals. il Sci Digest 58:40-1 D '65
Life may have begun without preexisting life. Sci N L 89:25 Ja 8 '66
New evidence for early life. G. S. Mumford. Sky & Tel 30:84 Ag '65
New evidence reported on origin of life. Sci N L 87:168 Mr 13 '65
Organisms and molecules in evolution; adaptation from paper. G. G. Simpson; reply. J. Moor-Jankowski and A. S. Wiener. bibliog Science 148:255-6 Ap 9 '65
Secret of life; today's most fascinating mystery story. M. Gunther. il Sat Eve Post 238:25-9 Jl 3 '65

LIFE (periodical)
Catholic abortions; Life's admission of falsehood. America 113:273 S 18 '65
Day at the studio, or Why the cook quit. G. P. Hunt. il Life 59:3 Jl 30 '65
1938: Birth of a baby. 1965: Drama of life; reaction to picture journalism. G. P. Hunt. il Life 58:3 My 21 '65
Problem: to make the ordinary extraordinary concerning year's end issue. G. P. Hunt. il Life 59:5 D 24 '65
Putting Life to bed at 33,000 feet; airplane fitted out as a flying editorial office. G. P. Hunt. il Life 58:3 F 5 '65
Quick look over there; selection of photographs from miscellany section. Read Digest 87:146-53 D '65
Think big, that's Life. G. Silk. il Mod Phot 29:19+ My '65
Trapped in a skyscraper; carrying on during power blackout. G. P. Hunt. il Life 59:3 N 19 '65
LIFE and love upstairs; story. See Shyer, M. F.
LIFE expectancy. See Longevity
LIFE in other worlds. See Life on other planets
LIFE insurance. See Insurance, Life
LIFE insurance companies. See Insurance companies
LIFE of Joseph; drama. See Rej, M.
LIFE of your own; story. See O'Connor, F.
LIFE on other planets
Ames exobiologists provide major link in understanding origin of life on earth. il Miss & Roc 17:38-9 Ag 16 '65
Anatomy of a man from Mars. I. Asimov. il Esquire 64:113-17+ S '65
Automated lab will search for Mars life. H. D. Watkins. il Aviation W 83:61+ Ag 2 '65
Big question about Mars, is there life on it? A. P. Armagnac. il Pop Sci 187:86 Jl '65
Biological material in meteorites: a review. H. C. Urey. bibliog il Science 151:157-66 Ja 14 '66
Does life exist on Mars? Sci N L 87:292 My 8 '65
Eight eyes on strange new worlds; opinions of science-fiction writers. il Esquire 65: 56-9 Ja '66
End to the myths about men on Mars. il U S News 59:4 Ag 9 '65
Finding life on Mars may depend on season. Sci N L 87:168 Mr 13 '65
Homes for men in the stars. F. Leiber. il Sci Digest 58:53-7 S '65
Is anybody out there? Mars-bound Mariner IV. S. M. Spencer. il Sat Eve Post 238: 44-6 Je 19 '65
Is there life on Mars? J. Eberhart. il Sci N L 88:74-5 Jl 31 '65
Is there life on Mars or earth? comparison of photographs. il Time 87:44 Ja 7 '66

LIFE on other planets—*Continued*
Is there vegetation on Mars? R. Smoluchowski. bibliog Science 148:946-7 My 14 '65
Life in an ammonia-rich atmosphere. G. S. Mumford. Sky & Tel 30:84-5 Ag '65
Mariner IV could not see life forms on Mars. il Sci N L 87:245 Ap 17 '65
Mars as a laboratory for the study of life. New Repub 152:12-13 My 8 '65
Mars, tantalizing question mark in the sky. W. Sullivan. il N Y Times Mag p 12-13+ Jl 11 '65
Martian environment. P. H. Abelson. Science 147:683 F 12 '65; Discussion. 148: 1042; 149:135, 813 My 21, Jl 9, Ag 20 '65
Martian life; a darkening wave. il Newsweek 66:56-7 Jl 26 '65
Mathematical games; communication with intelligent organisms on other worlds. M. Gardner. il Sci Am 213:96-100 bibliog(p 120) Ag '65
Message from Mariner 4. R. S. Lewis. Bul Atomic Sci 21:38-40 N '65
Meteoritic life studied. Sci N L 88:259 O 23 '65
New evidence of intelligent life on other worlds. il Sci Digest 57:8-10 F '65
Obituary of a planet. B. H. Frisch. il Sci Digest 58:8-9 O '65
Quarantine for space travelers? il Time 85: 70 Je 4 '65
Science in search of a subject; exobiology. I. Asimov. il N Y Times Mag p52-3+ My 23 '65
Search for Martian life. il Time 85:78+ My 7 '65
Some earth life seen adaptable to Mars. R. D. Hibben. il Aviation W 82:71+ Ap 12 '65
What we'll see on Mars. B. H. Frisch. il Sci Digest 58:44-53 Jl '65
Where there's hope there may be life: Mars. Time 86:67 O 8 '65
Where there's life... il Newsweek 65:100 My 10 '65

LIFE preservers
How much do you know about your life preservers? W. Andrews. il Yachting 118:66-8+ Ag '65
Life jackets: some are safe, some aren't. il Changing T 19:46-7 Jl '65

LIFE saving. See Rescue work

LIFE saving equipment
Lifesaving surfboard designed by surgeon. Sci N L 89:8 Ja 1 '66
Look to your lifelines. H. H. Cappel. il Motor B 116:102-3+ N '65

LIFE saving jackets. See Life saving suits

LIFE saving suits
Drowned wearing life preserver; life jackets and other safety devices. J. K. Lagemann. il Read Digest 87:215-18+ Jl '65
Life jackets: some are safe, some aren't. il Changing T 19:46-7 Jl '65

LIFE span. See Longevity

LIFE support systems (space environment)
Apollo suit substantially redesigned. H. M. David. il Miss & Roc 16:26+ Ap 26 '65
Biosatellite hardware nearly ready; first U.S.-spacecraft to carry a mixed oxygen-nitrogen atmosphere at sea-level pressure. H. M. David. il Miss & Roc 16:34+ F 22 '65
Carbon dioxide changed to breathable oxygen. Sci N L 88:105 Ag 14 '65
Depth problems yielding to research. H. M. David. il Miss & Roc 17:56-9 S 6 '65
Design verification under way on Apollo suit backpack; Block 2 Apollo suit tests. D. E. Fink. il Aviation W 83:52-3+ D 13 '65
Douglas tests helium as atmosphere. H. M. David. Miss & Roc 16:38-41 Je 28 '65
Early start on Mars systems urged. H. M. David. Miss & Roc 17:22 Jl 12 '65
Helium looks feasible for use in MOL cabin. il Miss & Roc 17:38-9 D 20 '65
LTV flight-testing astronaut maneuvering unit. Miss & Roc 17:19 S 27 '65
LEM system readied for checkout. H. M. David. il Miss & Roc 16:22-3 My 3 '65
Lunar suit and backpack design selected. D. E. Fink. Aviation W 83:37 N 15 '65
MSC initiates design of two-gas AA system. H. M. David. Miss & Roc 17:39-40 O 25 '65
Nose may sniff out systems problems. R. Hawkes. il Miss & Roc 16:26-7 F 1 '65
Refined Apollo suit nearing final form. R. D. Hibben. il Aviation W 82:56-7+ F 1 '65
Scientist hopes for Mars ice layer; with bio-astronomical data table. Miss & Roc 17:37 Jl 19 '65
Shirtsleeve garb eases tasks in Gemini 7. E. J. Bulban. il Aviation W 83:30-1 D 13 '65

Space simulation: man-rated testing and vacuum generation; report on second national Space simulation testing conference. A. C. Bond Science 147:523-7 Ja 29 '65
White House push seen in excursion decision. G. Alexander. Aviation W 82:17 My 31 '65

LIFELINES. See Life saving equipment

LIFTING. See Weight lifting

LIFTON, Betty Jean
Anne and the sand dobbies. Horn Bk 41:80 F '65
Girl of the paper cranes. N Y Times Mag p35 Ag 1 '65

LIGHT
Interaction between light and minerals. P. E. Desautels. il Natur Hist 74:52-7 O '65
    See also
Lasers
Optical illusions

Physiological effects

Catalase: kinetics of photooxidation. S. Aronoff. bibliog il Science 150:72-3 O 1 '65
Catalase photoinactivation. R. L. Mitchell and I. C. Anderson. bibliog il Science 150:74 O 1 '65
Day length and food caches; photoperiods cue the flying squirrel. I. Muul. il Natur Hist 74:22-7 Mr '65
Lizard reproduction: refractory period and response to warmth in Uta stansburiana females. D. W. Tinkle and L. N. Irwin. bibliog il Science 148:1613-14 Je 18 '65
Pineal gland: influence on gonads of male hamsters. R. A. Hoffman and R. J. Reiter. bibliog il Science 148:1609-11 Je 18 '65
Where is science taking us? D. J. C. Friend. Sat R 48:61-2 My 1 '65

LIGHT, Zodiacal. See Zodiacal light

LIGHT amplification by stimulated emission of radiation. See Lasers

LIGHT amplifiers. See Lasers

LIGHT bulbs. See Electric lamps

LIGHT communication systems
Communication by laser. S. E. Miller. il Sci Am 214:19-27 bibliog(p 134) Ja '66
Gemini laser test may speed future use. B. Miller. il Aviation W 83:71+ D 13 '65
Laser communication qualified success; optical-frequency communications system. C. D. LaFond il Miss & Roc 17:18+ Jl 12 '65
Optical communications. R. Kompfner. bibliog il Science 150:149-55 O 8 '65; Reply. H. Malamud. 150:1484 D 10 '65

LIGHT filters
Filters. Pop Phot 58:80 Ja '66
How to get the most out of Polacolor. H. M. Kinzer. il Pop Phot 57:78-9+ Jl '65
How to get the most out of polarizers; they're especially valuable with today's SLR's. M. Bernam. il Pop Phot 56:84-7+ Je '65
Instant color correction! color filter nomography. il Mod Phot 29:60-1 O '65
Techniques tomorrow; eliminating ultimate lens flare due to diffraction. B. Sherman. il Mod Phot 29:30+ Mr '65

LIGHT in the forest; story. See Richter, C.

LIGHT meters. See Exposure meters; Photometers

LIGHT projection
How to get the most from one photo-flood. A. Goldsmith. il Pop Phot 57:158-9+ N '65

LIGHT towers. See Lighthouses

LIGHT water. See Fire protection

LIGHTHOUSES
Jack-in-the-box lighthouse becomes world's tallest. D. Scott. il Pop Sci 187:108-9 D '65
San Pedro's antique lighthouse. il Sunset 135: 44 N '65

LIGHTING
Heat by light. il Time 86:51 Ag 6 '65
High light from the sky is marvelous indoors. il Sunset 134:110-16 Mr '65
House laced with light. il House & Gard 127: 122-9+ Mr '65
How to choose the right lamps. C. Murphy. il Redbook 124:32+ Ap '65

Exhibitions

Light: fifth National lighting exposition and world lighting forum at the Coliseum. New Yorker 41:19-20 Je 26 '65

LIGHTING, Outdoor
Breakthrough in exterior lighting. il Bet Hom & Gard 43:28 Je '65
Fun under floodlights. D. B. Warnick. il Travel 123:39-42 Ap '65
Improving your home wiring; how to wire your yard. G. Daniels. il Pop Sci 187:122-7+ Ag '65

LIGHTING, Outdoor—*Continued*
Lighting a water tank; Massena, N.Y. il Am City 81:124 Ja '66
Outdoor lighting. See issues of American city
    See also
Airports—Lighting
Christmas decorations, Outdoor
Gardens—Lighting
Golf courses—Lighting
Roads—Lighting
Street lighting
    also subhead Lighting under names of cities, e.g. New York (city)—Lighting
LIGHTING fixtures
Danforth's toadstools; Tucson, Ariz. H. L. Danforth. il Am City 80:132 Ag '65
Improving your home wiring. G. Daniels. il Pop Sci 187:138-42 S: 154-9+ O '65
Three smart light fixtures. il Pop Mech 124: 164-5 S '65
    See also
Street lighting fixtures
LIGHTING of cities. See Street lighting
LIGHTNING
Bomb radiation similar to that of lightning. Sci N L 88:121 Ag 21 '65
Lightning: nature's deadly fireworks. C. Conley. il Field & S 70:52-3+ My '65
Nature note. Sci N L 88:79 Jl 31 '65
No thundercloud needed; volcanic lightning. il Time 85:102 Je 11 '65
Research in America; relation of lightning to rain. J. Lear. il Sat R 48:50-1 S 4 '65
    See also
Aviation—Lightning hazards
Photography of lightning
LIGHTNING bugs. See Fireflies
LIGHTNING conductors
Truth about lightning rods. il Farm J 89: D12 Ap '65
LIGHTNING rods. See Lightning conductors
LIGHTS, Warning. See Signals and signaling
LIGNIN
Lignin: its constitution and formation from p-hydroxycinnamyl alcohols; adaptation of address. May 25, 1964. K. Freudenberg. bibliog il Science 148:595-600 Ap 30 '65
LIGUUS. See Snails
LIKE a bad dream; story. See Böll, H.
LILEY, A. William
Expectant mother. Redbook 126:38+ N '65
LILEY, Margaret, and Day, Beth
New discoveries about an old miracle. McCalls 92:92-3+ Ag '65; Same abr. with title Secret world of the unborn. Read Digest 87:74-7 N '65
LILIENTHAL, David E.
300,000,000 Americans would be wrong. N Y Times Mag p24-5+ Ja 9 '66

    about

Journals, by D. E. Lilienthal. Review Bul Atomic Sci 21:42-3 Mr '65. C. P. Anderson
LILIES
"Consider the (new-style) lilies. . ." F. J. Taylor. il Read Digest 87:154-9 Ag '65
Coral lily. J. Antonitis. Horticulture 43:16-17+ Je '65
Hybrid lilies indoors. J. De Graaff. il Horticulture 44:24-5+ Ja '66
Lilies need other plants. C. M. Fitch. il Flower Grower 52:32-3+ Ag '65
Madonna lilies. R. C. Hands. Horticulture 43:7 Jl '65
Madonna lilies, plant them early. B. Brinhart. il Flower Grower 52:18-19 Ag '65
    See also
African lilies
Belladonna lilies
Day lilies
Glory lilies
LILJEDAHL, J. B.
What is a hydrostatic transmission? Suc Farm 63:51 O '65
LILLARD, Richard G.
Life in the parking lot. Nation 201:435-7 D 6 '65
LILLIE, Raymond C.
Mile high in Teton country. Motor B 115: 22-5+ My '65
LILLY, Daniel M. and Stillwell, R. H.
Probiotics: growth-promoting factors produced by microorganisms. bibliog Science 147:747-8 F 12 '65
LILLY, Othelia
Hounds of pleasure; poem. Christian Cent 83:77 Ja 19 '66
In the Black Forest; poem. Christian Cent 82:1569 D 22 '65
When vision touches; poem. Christian Cent 82:1312 O 27 '65

LILY pools. See Garden pools
LIMA, Francisco Negrão de. See Negrão de Lima, F.
LIMA, Frank
Four young poets. M. Bell. Poetry 106:371 Ag '65
LIMA, Peru
Young publisher with problems: Brooklyn Peace corps volunteer puts out Spanish newspaper in slum of Lima, Peru. il Ebony 21:101-2+ N '65

    Description
Lima today; drawings. S. Perl. Opera N 30: 13-15 D 25 '65
    Riots
Twenty minutes of horror; disaster at National stadium. J. P. Blank. Read Digest 86:141-4 Ap '65
LIMAX, Andy
What immunity to disease means to you. Todays Health 43:54-5+ N '65
LIMBACHER, James L.
Recorded word. See second issue of each month of Library journal
(ed) Recordings for young people. Library J 90:4526-8 O 15 '65
(ed) Records for young people. Library J 90: 1483-4 Mr 15 '65
LIME
Let's take a new look at lime. S. R. Aldrich and J. J. Feight. il Suc Farm 63:42-3+ O '65
LIME trees
Which lime for you? Sunset 134:262-3 Ap '65
LIMERICKS
Ten new limericks. O. Nash. il Holiday 38: 56-7 N '65
With birds in his beard; how the limerick was born. A. White. il Sat R 49:26-7 Ja 15 '66
LIMES
Which lime for you? Sunset 134:262-3 Ap '65
LIMESTONE
Double duty from hidden assets; rich vein of limestone in Kansas City, Kan. il Fortune 73:175-6 Ja '66
LIMITATION of actions
Bonn may extend statute on war criminals. Christian Cent 82:292-3 Mr 10 '65
Fighting the past; deadline for trying Nazi crimes extended to 1970. Newsweek 65:38 Ap 5 '65
German statute of limitations applies to Berlin; text of note delivered to Soviet ministry of foreign affairs on October 11, 1965. Dept State Bul 53:746 N 8 '65
Nazi murders & German politics. D. Schoenbaum. Commentary 39:72-7 Je '65
Time runs out on Germany's war-crimes trials. D. L. Schoenbaum. Reporter 32:30-2 Mr 11 '65
LIMITATION of armaments. See Disarmament
LIMITATION of population. See Population
LIMITED editions. See Publishers and publishing—Limited editions
LIMITED lone ranger; story. See Flannery, J.
LIMITED war laboratory. See United States—Army research office
LIMON, José
Interview about trimming, toning. Mlle 60: 137+ F '65

    about

Jose Limon and company, lecture-demonstration, Hunter playhouse. D. Hering. Dance Mag 39:59+ Mr '65
LIMOUSINE renting. See Automobiles—Renting
LIMPETS
Nature note; dunce-cap limpet. Sci N L 88: 382 D 11 '65
LIMULUS eye. See Eye (crustacea)
LIN, Piao
Blueprint for conquest. Newsweek 66:37 S 20 '65
LIN, T. Y.
Tall buildings in prestressed concrete. Arch Rec 138:165-70 D '65
LINCK, Tony
Flying photographer. il Flying 77:103-4 Jl '65
LINCOCIN. See Antibiotics
LINCOLN, Abraham
Abraham Lincoln, sixteenth President. F. Freidel. il pors Nat Geog Mag 127:664-75 My '65
Great man theory of emancipation. C. H. Wesley. por Negro Hist Bul 28:101-2+ F '65
If Lincoln lived today. il pors U S News 58: 74-6 F 15 '65
In pursuit of Honest Abe; Lincoln heritage trail. T. J. Fleming. il Good H 160:138+ F '65

LINCOLN, Abraham—*Continued*

Lincoln, man of steel and velvet; excerpts from address, February 12, 1959. C. Sandburg. por Read Digest 86:61-4 F '65

Lincoln without rhetoric. F. S. Meyer. Nat R 17:725 Ag 24 '65; Discussion. 17:827-8+, 850+, 898+; 18:71+ S 21-O 19 '65 Ja 25 '66

Lincolniana in 1964. B. E. Wheeler. il Hobbies 69:28-9+ F '65 (to be cont)

Lincoln's birthday, 1965; remarks, February 12, 1965. L. B. Johnson. Dept State Bul 52:334-5 Mr 8 '65

Miniatures pertaining to Lincoln. S. A. Parvin. il Hobbies 69:122 F '65

Religion of Abraham Lincoln. R. Niebuhr. Christian Cent 82:172-5 F 10 '65

Three generations of research. G. P. Hunt. Life 58:3 Ap 16 '65

Voyage to the Marquesas; cannibals, whalermen and A. Lincoln's timepiece. R. Thales. il Motor B 115:22-5+ F '65

World did note and long remember; Gettysburg address. P. W. Schmidtchen. il por Hobbies 70:106-8 Mr '65

Assassination

Assassination! excerpt from Twenty days. D. M. Kunhardt and P. B. Kunhardt, jr. il pors Am Heritage 16:4-35 Ap '65; Discussion. 16:7 Ap; 93 O '65

He belongs to the ages. Sr Schol 86:5 Ap 8 '65

Hundred years ago; excerpts from Twenty days. D. M. Kunhardt and P. B. Kunhardt, jr. il por Life 58:66C-75 Ap 16 '65

It was on Good Friday. J. E. Frazer. il Read Digest 86:76-8 Ap '65

Mask for treason: Lincoln murder trial, by V. Shelton. Review

Sat R il 48:32-3 Je 26 '65. H. Mitgang

Drama

Present from Abe. D. Newman. Plays 24:75-8 F '65

Funeral journey to Springfield

Mr Lincoln at last comes home to Springfield. D. M. Kunhardt and P. B. Kunhardt, jr. il Life 58:76-80+ Ap 16 '65

LINCOLN, C. Eric

Absent father haunts the Negro family. N Y Times Mag p60+ N 28 '65

British say they aren't prejudiced. N Y Times Mag p64-5+ N 14 '65

Meaning of Malcolm X. Christian Cent 82: 431-3 Ap 7 '65

LINCOLN, Evelyn

My twelve years with Kennedy; excerpts. pors Sat Eve Post 238:23-7+ Ag 14; 36-40+ Ag 28 '65

LINCOLN, Marjorie

Contemporary contrast for Wheaton. Library J 90:5176-8 D 1 '65

LINCOLN, Mary (Todd)

Assassination! excerpt from Twenty days; with editorial comment. D. M. Kunhardt and P. B. Kunhardt, jr. il por Am Heritage 16:7-35 Ap '65

LINCOLN back country wilderness area (proposed) See Wilderness areas

LINCOLN Center for the performing arts, New York

Heroic bather: H. Moore's Reclining figure. il Time 86:60 S 3 '65

Lincoln Center. W. McQuade. Nation 200: 204+ F 22 '65

Lincoln Center: tomb of the future. B. Boretz. il Nation 200:299-304+ Mr 22 '65

Library and museum of the performing arts

Archives of recorded sound; Rodgers and Hammerstein collection to be at Lincoln Center; with editorial comment. P. L. Miller. il Hi Fi 15:33, 38-41+ Je '65

Lincoln Center library opened. il Wilson Lib Bul 40:319 D '65

NYPL's performing arts library opens in new Lincoln Center home. Library J 90:5224 D 1 '65

Performing arts library set for dedication. Pub W 188:37 N 8 '65

Toscanini archives. J. W. Freeman. il Opera N 30:30-1 Ja 15 '66

Opera house

Endowing the future; Seat endowment program. il Opera N 29:30 Ap 17 '65

Metropolitan's new house. H. Kupferberg. il Atlan 216:158+ O '65

New Met. C. L. Osborne. il Hi Fi 15:50-4+ S '65

New Met. il Newsweek 66:98 N 8 '65

Philharmonic Hall

French-American festival. R. Lawrence. il Hi Fi 15:147+ O '65

Promenade concerts at Lincoln Center. M. Schafer. Hi Fi 15:144+ S '65

Scenario for inexactness; good acoustics achieved. il Time 86:83-4 O 15 '65

Two views of the avant-garde repertoire at Philharmonic Hall. D. Heckman; A. Cohn. il Am Rec G 32:354-6 D '65

Vivian Beaumont theater

All the marbles. il Newsweek 66:100 S 27 '65

Collaborators; opening. il Time 86:60-3 O 29 '65

How now, Herb Blau? G. Weales. il Reporter 34:43-5 Ja 13 '66

Impossibilities are limited. H. Hewes. Sat R 48:41-2 N 6 '65

New regime at Lincoln Center. W. S. Smith. Christian Cent 82:1578-9 D 22 '65

Possible theater. H. Hewes. il Sat R 48:28+ O 2 '65

LINCOLN Center repertory theater company

All the marbles. il Newsweek 66:100 S 27 '65

California wine in New York bottles. R. Brustein. New Repub 153:37-8 N 6 '65

How now, Herb Blau? G. Weales. il Reporter 34:43-5 Ja 13 '66

Lincoln Center: act II; Danton's death presentation. J. Richardson. Commentary 41: 55-6+ Ja '66

Possible theater. H. Hewes. il Sat R 48:28+ O 2 '65

Repertory in New York; Association of performing artists, Lincoln Center repertory theater. N. Cohen. Nat R 17:660 Jl 27 '65

LINCOLN experimental satellite. See Communications satellites

LINCOLN park zoo, Chicago

Rural spot in an urban complex; new Farm-in-the-zoo. il Am City 80:51 Jl '65

LINCOLN tunnel. See New York (city)—Tunnels

LINCOMYCIN. See Antibiotics

LIND, Jakov

Nazis on trial; pages from a journal. tr. by W. J. Dannhauser. Commentary 39:69-72 Ap '65

LIND, Jenny

Audubon and the Swedish nightingale. E. Gaines. il por Antiques 88:526-7 O '65

LINDA Hall library, Kansas City, Mo.

Linda Hall library: Kansas City institution builds a reputation with operations outside its region. J. Walsh. il Science 148:1073-5 My 21 '65

LINDBECK, Violette

Needed: a new status for the single woman. Cath World 202:151-7 D '65

LINDBERG, Marv

Safe trapshooting with a .22. Pop Sci 187: 134-5 Ag '65

Take along your own campfire. Pop Sci 186: 152-5 Je '65

LINDBERG, Pete

Why see a doctor when you're healthy? Bet Hom & Gard 43:16+ S '65

LINDBERGH, Jon

Deepest days. R. Sténuit. il pors Nat Geog Mag 127:534-47 Ap '65

LINDBLAD, Bertil

Great Swedish astronomer. T. L. Page. il pors Sky & Tel 30:142-3 S '65

LINDBLOM, Charles E.

Has India an economic future? For Affairs 44:239-52 Ja '66

LINDEMAN, Bard

Riddle of the nice killer. Sat Eve Post 238:98+ O 23 '65

—See Heinz, W. C. jt. auth.

LINDEMAN, Jack

Hermit of a singular thought; poem. Commonweal 83:374 D 24 '65

LINDEMAN, Joan

Borage. Horticulture 43:55 My '65

Impatiens for the shady garden. Horticulture 43:19 F '65

LINDEMAN, Lee

Pictures to make and feel. Design 66:25-7 Ja '65

LINDEN, George W.

Begin in wonder. Sat R 48:89-90 My 22 '65

Business of being human. Sat R 48:39 S 11 '65

LINDEN, N.J.

Art in the park. M. Poston. il Recreation 58:278-9 Je '65

LINDENMEYER, P. H.

Crystallization and molecular folding. bibliog Science 147:1256-62 Mr 12 '65

—See Holland, V. F. jt. auth.

LINDENMEYER, Ruth

That Knapp film catches on. Library J 90: 1470-1 Mr 15 '65

LINDER, David, and Gartler, S. M.
Glucose-6-phosphate dehydrogenase mosaicism: utilization as a cell maker in the study of leiomyomas. bibliog Science 150: 67-9 O 1 '65

LINDGREN, Nilo
Day on the Runeberg. Travel 124:28-30 Jl '65

LINDHEIM, Judy. See Putnam, J. jt. ed.

LINDQUIST, Clarence B. See Abel, R. B. jt. auth.

LINDSAY, John Vliet
Can New York be saved? pors Sat Eve Post 238:78-80 O 9 '65
Congressman looks at the arts. Sat R 48:23+ Mr 13 '65
Future of the American city. Sat R 49:70 Ja 8 '66
We talk to. . ; interview. por Mlle 61:229 Ag '65
Why city government must be nonpartisan. por Look 29:162+ O 19 '65

about

Atlantic report. Atlan 216:24+ O '65
Big gamble of John Vliet Lindsay. W. Weaver, jr. il pors N Y Times Mag p30-1+ My 23 '65
British press postscript. J. Fletcher. il Nat R 18:25-6 Ja 11 '66
Can John Lindsay lick New York's problems? with editorial comment. por Bsns W p28, 192 N 6 '65
Can Lindsay make it? M. Kempton. New Repub 152:17-18 Je 5 '65
Can New York find a cure for urban ills? il por Bsns W p34-8 D 25 '65
Candidate & the clamor. il por Time 85:29-30 My 21 '65
Coming seven years' war. E. J. Hughes. Newsweek 66:27 N 15 '65
Congressman on the move. L. L. L. Golden. por Sat R 48:40+ S 25 '65
Crush baptizes the new mayor. il pors Life 60:32-3 Ja 14 '66
Elected. New Yorker 41:46-9 N 13 '65
Fresh style at city hall. il por Time 87:27-8 Ja 14 '66
Fusion & fightin'. Time 86:23 Jl 9 '65
GOP hope; Lindsay of N Y. il pors Newsweek 65:23-4+ My 31 '65
Inauguration. New Yorker 41:20-3 Ja 8 '66
Incitement to excellence. il pors Time 86: 28-33 N 12 '65
John Lindsay: new GOP hope. G. Astor. il pors Look 29:M6-M8 Ap 6 '65
John V. Lindsay: less than meets the eye. N. E. Parmentel, jr. il pors Esquire 64: 100-2+ O '65
Letter from Washington. R. H. Rovere. New Yorker 41:205-6 N 20 '65
Liberals and John Lindsay. A. M. Bickel. New Repub 153:16-18 Jl 3 '65
Lindsay and New York's needs. Life 59:4 O 29 '65
Lindsay: campaign in Brooklyn and Queens. New Yorker 41:47-9 O 16 '65
Lindsay candidacy. Nation 200:546 My 24 '65
Lindsay, fusion and the future. Life 59:4 N 12 '65
Lindsay miracle. C. McWilliams. Nation 201: 348-50 N 15 '65
Lindsay on the line. Newsweek 66:20 Jl 12 '65
Lindsay test. Nation 202:29-30 Ja 10 '66
Lindsay the daring young man. G. W. Johnson. New Repub 153:29+ O 16 '65
Lindsay-Woolsey. Nat R 17:629 Jl 27 '65
Lindsay's future: bright or dim? il por U S News 59:21 N 15 '65
Loner Lindsay's New York triumph; with report by R. Ajemian. il pors Life 59:42-5 N 12 '65
Lucky Lindsay. M. Kempton. New Repub 154:10-11 Ja 15 '66
Mayor John Lindsay: new GOP hope? il pors Newsweek 66:31-6 N 15 '65
Mischievous Robert Wagner. J. Desmond. il por Nation 200:688-90 Je 28 '65
New York: a long week's walk into chaos. il por Newsweek 67:28-31 Ja 17 '66
New York election. M. Ascoli. Reporter 33:14 N 4 '65
Now that Lindsay is elected: how he plans to help New York. por U S News 59:32-3 N 15 '65
Odd-man-in. il pors Newsweek 65:32 My 24 '65
On the move. Newsweek 66:42 N 22 '65
One of the world's toughest jobs. il por U S News 60:16 Ja 10 '66
Picture of a mayor in deep trouble. il por U S News 60:46-7 Ja 17 '66

Prince charming to the fore. M. McGrory. America 113:621 N 20 '65
Representative Lindsay steps to the fore. M McGrory. America 112:820 Je 5 '65
Republican wins in New York city. Christian Cent 82:1406 N 17 '65
Running away from them. il por Time 85:19 Je 4 '65
Speaking for ourself. John. Nat R 17:451-2 Je 1 '65
Special election supplement; symposium. Il Nat R 17:937-82 N 2 '65
Statement sent to the press, November 3, 1965. W. F. Buckley, jr. Nat R 17:1014 N 16 '65
This Tuesday's winner, and loser. W. Weaver, jr. il por N Y Times Mag p 46-7+ O 31 '65
Trouble for Democrats; Lindsay campaign is gaining. U S News 58:22 Jl 12 '65
Underdog issue. il por Newsweek 66:47 O 18 '65
Untold tale. E. J. Hughes. il por Newsweek 66:18-19 Jl 12 '65
Victory for honest John. Newsweek 67:29-31 Ja 24 '66
Voters' own urban renewal. Fortune 72:134+ D '65
Walking. New Yorker 41:26-7 Ja 15 '66
What New York mayor's race can mean. por U S News 58:20 My 24 '65
Why the G.O.P. is smiling again: Lindsay is running; with report by R. Ajemian. il pors Life 58:32-5 My 28 '65

LINDSAY, Mary (Harrison)
She will not vegetate in Gracie mansion. G. Steinem. il pors N Y Times Mag p22-3+ Ja 9 '66

LINDSAY, Wesley N.
Novel dual-field 8-inch telescope. por Sky & Tel 29:112-17 F '65

LINDSEY, Robert
Recorders slash time base error. Miss & Roc 17:40-1 O 4 '65
UTC solves Scout stage spin problem. Miss & Roc 17:28+ Ag 30 '65
Vandenberg begins expanding for MOL. Miss & Roc 18:35-6 Ja 10 '66

LINDSLEY, Donald B. See Rose, G. H; Velasco, M. jt. auths.

LINDSLEY, E. F.
Build a gas-powered mulcher. Pop Sci 187: 136-40 O '65
Central vacuum system for your home? por Pop Sci 186:160-2 Ap '65
Copper tubing: key to easy plumbing. Pop Sci 187:134-7+ S '65

LINDSTROM, Richard S. and Marks, J. J.
CO₂-lifesaver for greenhouse plants. pors Horticulture 43:24-5 D '65

LINDSTROM, Roy
Kit can be a harpsichord. Hi Fi 15:34-8 Jl '65

about

Roy Lindstrom, artist & art director. F. Johnson. il Am Artist 29:50-5+ D '65

LINDSTROM, Sherrill
Ostriches, parents and television. Parents Mag 40:20+ O '65

LINEAWEAVER, Marion
Barn owl; poem. Harper 230:98 My '65

LINEN, Household
Bed linens; guide to the best. il Good H 160: 162 F '65
Your own touch on sheets, pillowcases, and towels. M. Garrity. il Bet Hom & Gard 43:124+ My '65
See also
Table linen

LINEN closets. See Closets

LINERS. See Ocean liners

LING, James J.
Splitting to grow faster. il por Bsns W p75-6+ F 13 '65

LING-Temco-Vought, Incorporated
LTV rejoins civilian ranks; plans to buy Okonite co. Bsns W p96 O 23 '65
Navy/LTV A-7A vendors listed. Aviation W 83:87 N 15 '65
Splitting to grow faster; Project redeployment for reorganizing. il Bsns W p75-6+ F 13 '65

LINGELBACH, D. D.
Electromagnetic relays; report on 13th annual national relay conference. Science 149:1004 Ag 27 '65

LINGEMAN, Richard R.
Pop sex; some sex symbols of the sixties. Mlle 62:184-5+ N '65

LINGERIE. See Underwear

LINGG, Ann M.
Cio-Cio-San arrives. Opera N 30:24-5 Ja 1 '66

LINGG, Ann M.—*Continued*
Empress of song. Opera N 29:26-8 F 20 '65
Ladies and gentlemen. Opera N 29:12-16 Mr 20 '65
Stout-hearted men. Opera N 29:12-13 F 6 '65
Support from the state. Opera N 30:13-15 Ja 15 '66
LINHART, Jim
Tall man takes a long chance. C. Goren. il Sports Illus 23:116 S 20 '65
LINK, Edwin A.
Outpost under the ocean. pors Nat Geog Mag 127:530-3 Ap '65
LINK, Mark J.
Challenge to modern catechetics. America 113:42-4 Jl 10 '65
LINK trainers. See Flight simulators
LINN, Edward
Last angry old man. Sat Eve Post 238:75-8 Jl 31 '65
(ed) See Barnette, A. Black Muslims are a fraud
—See Veeck, B. jt. auth.
LINOFILM. See Photocomposing machines
LINOLEIC acid
Inheritance of linoleic and oleic acids in maize. C. G. Poneleit and D. E. Alexander. bibliog il Science 147:1585-6 Mr 26 '65
LINTON, David
H.R. 4347 and you. Pop Phot 57:51+ S '65
Mirages. Natur Hist 74:36-9 Ap '65
Nature and photography. Natur Hist 74:59-61 Mr '65
LINTS, Carlton E. See Harvey, J. A. jt. auth.
LINVILLE, J. C.
Slap a lion with your hat. por Outdoor Life 136:40-1+ Ag '65
LION, Eugene
Sally Gross, Elizabeth Keen, Eugene Lion, Judson dance theatre. M. Marks. Dance Mag 40:57 Ja '66
LION fish. See Lionfish
LION hunting
Jackson was a lady. W. Page. il Field & S 69:37-9+ Mr '65
Man-eater of Darajani. J. Kingsley-Heath. il Outdoor Life 136:32-5+ D '65
See also
Puma hunting
LION to lamb: drama. See Boiko, C.
LIONEL, Daniel L.
Advertising's little giants. Sat R 48:61+ My 8 '65
LIONFISH
Instant ocean plus care keep fragile fish alive. il Sci N L 87:391 Je 19 '65
LIONS
Siesta time, or royalty out on a limb. S. A. Thompson. il Natur Hist 74:34-7 O '65
LIOTARD, Jean Étienne
Liotard: the painter who drew the truth from the mythic East. F. Fosca. il Vogue 145:112-15+ Ap 15 '65
LIP make-up. See Make-up
LIPASE
Lipase: localization in adipose tissue. M. S. Moskowitz and A. A. Moskowitz. bibliog il Science 149:72-3 Jl 2 '65
LIPCHITZ, Jacques
Mythmaker in bronze. por Time 86:112 N 5 '65
New bronze portrait of John Fitzgerald Kennedy. il por Vogue 145:96-7 Je '65
LIPETZ, Jacques
Crown-gall tumorigenesis: effect of temperature on wound healing and conditioning. bibliog Science 149:865-7 Ag 20 '65
LIPIDES
Epinephrine-induced normalization of lipid metabolism in adrenalectomized rats. M. Friedman and S. O. Byers. bibliog il Science 148:644-6 Ap 30 '65
Protein synthesis inhibition: mechanism for the production of impaired fat absorption. S. M. Sabesin and K. J. Isselbacher. bibliog il Science 147:1149-51 Mr 5 '65
Repellency of skin-surface lipids of humans to mosquitoes. W. A. Skinner and others. il Science 149:305 Jl 16 '65
Stability of the myelin membrane. J. S. O'Brien. bibliog il Science 147:1099-107 Mr 5 '65
LIPIN, Carl
Near or far, catch 'em candidly. il U S Camera 28:46-7 My '65
LIPOPROTEINS
Double beta-lipoprotein: a new genetic variant in man. W. Seegers and others. bibliog il Science 149:303-4 Jl 16 '65
LIPOVIRUSES. See Viruses
LIPPINCOTT, Barbara B. See Lippincott, J. A. jt. auth.

LIPPINCOTT, James A. and Lippincott, B. B.
Agrobacterium tumefaciens: thermal inactivation of tumor-inducing ability. bibliog Science 147:1578-9 Mr 26 '65
LIPPINCOTT, Sarah Lee, and Worth, M. D.
Double star Sirius. Sky & Tel 31:4-6 Ja '66
LIPPINCOTT and Margulies, incorporated
Turnaround boys. il Time 86:84 Jl 16 '65
LIPPITT, Ronald O. and Flanders, M. P.
Sharing good teaching practices. NEA J 54:30-2 D '65
LIPPMANN, Gabriel
Perfect color film. L. Lipton. il Pop Phot 56:62-3+ Mr '65
LIPPMANN, Walter
[Current events column] See issues of Newsweek
Great revolution; address. UN Mo Chron 2:66-72 Ap '65; Same UNESCO Courier 18:20-4 O '65
about
Lippmann, East & West; U.S. foreign policy. Time 86:52+ Ag 6 '65
Talk is for TV. H. J. Morgenthau. por Sat R 48:48 Ag 28 '65
Two most eminent and strikingly different columnists. J. K. Jessup. por Life 58:40-1 My 7 '65
LIPS
Whose lips are perfect? il Seventeen 24:150-1 Ap '65
LIPSCOMB, James
Seventy-two hours of terror. Sports Illus 22:86-90+ Je 14; 64-8+ Je 21 '65
LIPSET, Seymour Martin
Anatomy of the Klan. Commentary 40:74+ O '65
LIPSKY, Yuri N.
Zond-3 photographs of the moon's far side; tr. by M. P. Lopez-Morillas. Sky & Tel 30:338-41 D '65
LIPSTICK
Whose lips are perfect? il Seventeen 24:150-1 Ap '65
LIPTAY, Alberto
Undoing Babel. P. Rónai. il Américas 17:26-30 Je '65
LIPTON, Leonard
Movie test reports. Pop Phot 56:125 F '65
Movies super 8 & other goodies. Pop Phot 57:98-100 Ag '65
Perfect color film. Pop Phot 56:62-3+ Mr '65
LIPTON, Seymour
Seriousness of Seymour Lipton. F. Getlein. New Repub 152:24+ Ap 10 '65
LIQUEFIED petroleum gas
Laclede adds propane to keep a customer. Bsns W p 158 F 20 '65
LIQUID assets. See Liquidity (economics)
LIQUID propellant rockets
USAF gives aerojet ares engine contract; hypergolic liquid-fueled rocket engine. Aviation W 83:19 Jl 5 '65
LIQUIDITY (economics)
As good as gold? plan to hike international liquidity with new reserve asset. Bsns W p 178+ S 11 '65
Light on liquidity. il Fortune 72:57-8+ Ag '65
Problem of international liquidity; address, April 29, 1965. F. L. Deming. Dept State Bul 52:955-63 Je 14 '65
LIQUIDITY, International
Washington desk; ways to bolster the free world payments system. J. R. Slevin. Duns R 86:5-6 Jl '65
LIQUIDS
Ultrasound chemical effects on pure organic liquids. A. Weissler and others. bibliog Science 150:1288-9 D 3 '65
LIQUOR habit. See Alcoholism
LIQUOR industry
Liquor men uncork a new sales mix, liquor sales patterns. il Bsns W p48-9 F 20 '65
Macy's toasts its price war; brand name liquor. il Bsns W p32-3 F 27 '65
LIQUOR laws and regulations

Germany (Federal Republic)
End of an oasis; West Berlin liquor prices to climb. Time 86:68 D 31 '65

United States
In my opinion; laws against teen-age drinking defeat their purpose. K. Goff. Seventeen 24:146 Jl '65
LIQUOR problem
See also
Alcoholism
Temperance

Russia
Such are the joys. il Newsweek 66:32 S 6 '65

LIQUOR problem—*Continued*

United States

How serious is teenage drinking? with discussion group program, by E. G. Neisser. M. Gross. il Parents Mag 40:24, 64-5+ N '65

In my opinion; laws against teen-age drinking defeat their purpose. K. Goff. Seventeen 24:146 Jl '65

Margaret Mead answers; teen-age drinking. M. Mead. Redbook 125:24 O '65

Should you offer teen-agers drinks in your home? S. Wilson. Read Digest 86:100-2 Ap '65

Sometime during your teen years someone is likely to urge you to drink; what will you say? D. Klein. il Seventeen 24:140-1+ S '65

Teen-age drinking. B. Davidson. il Sat Eve Post 238:23-7 Ap 10 '65

Toward a B.A. in alcohol? proposal to provide students with group experiences in drinking. il Time 87:64+ Ja 21 '66

Whatever happened to the temperance movement? R. Burgess. Christian Cent 82:984-7 Ag 11 '65; Discussion. 82:1166 S 22 '65

See also
Liquor traffic—United States

LIQUOR traffic

Great Britain

See also
Bars and barrooms

United States

Moriarty's wonderful saloon: speakeasy operating as gentleman's club. L. Beebe. il Am Heritage 16:65-9+ Ag '65

LIQUORS

Liquor men uncork a new sales mix, liquor sales patterns. il Bsns W p48-9 F 20 '65

Mixed-up drinks. Newsweek 65:96+ Ap 19 '65

Nine new pop party drinks. il Esquire 65: 104-5 Ja '66

White spirits. H. Johnson. House & Gard 127:160+ Mr '65

See also
Cocktails
Rum

LISAGOR, Peter

Ask not what became of Hubert Humphrey? N Y Times Mag p6-7+ Jl 25 '65

Trends: Washington mood. See issues of Nation's business

LISBON, Portugal

Inside Lisbon's Coach museum. il Sunset 135:8 S '65

Bridges

U.S. builders tie Portugal together; span across Tagus River at Lisbon. il Bsns W p28-9 Ag 14 '65

Description

Wonderama finds a wonderland. L. Barry. il Pop Phot 57:28+ Ag '65

Music

Lisbon quartet. F. Teixeiro Direito. Opera N 29:31 Ap 10 '65

LISI, Virna

La Lisi. por Time 85:47 Ap 2 '65

Sunniness on sight: Virna Lisi. por Vogue 145:156-7 Ap 1 '65

Virna Lisi: experiment in star making. J. Hamilton. il pors Look 29:60-6+ My 18 '65

LISLE, Clifton

Dusty dimmers. Pop Gard 16:8 Ap '65

Evergreens keep their good looks. Flower Grower 52:30-1+ Ap '65

LISSAJOUS patterns. See Oscillographs

LISTENING. See Attention

LISTENING devices, Electronic. See Electronics in criminal investigation, espionage, etc.

LISTER, Philip Cunliffe-, 1st earl of Swinton. See Swinton, P. C.-L.

LISTER, Richard Percival

Fault is in our stars. Mlle 60:146+ Ap '65

Great Britain; poem. New Yorker 41:61 D 25 '65

On losing touch; poem. Atlan 216:45 Jl '65

Short history of mankind; poem. Atlan 215: 175 Mr '65

Sunday afternoon; poem. New Yorker 41:26 Ja 8 '66

LISTON, Charles. See Liston, S.

LISTON, Dorothy

Housekeeping on wheels. pors Todays Health 43:62-6+ My '65

LISTON, Sonny

Cassius to win a thriller. T. Maule. il por Sports Illus 22:22-5 My 24 '65

He's just got that look. B. La Fontaine. il pors Sports Illus 22:32-4+ Ap 26 '65

No phantom punch; with account by J. Murray. il pors Sports Illus 22:48-53 Je 7 '65

Quick, hard right and a needless storm of protest. T. Maule. il Sports Illus 22:22-5 Je 7 '65

Theater of the absurd. il Time 85:68-9 Je 4 '65

LISZT, Franz

Liszt piano music: five discs. R. Kammerer. Am Rec G 32:58-9 S '65

LITANIES

Agony and the wild cry; worship service, Chicago's First congregational church. Christian Cent 82:910 Jl 21 '65; Discussion. 82:1070-2, 1211-12, 1516 S 1, O 6, D 8 '65

LITCHFIELD, Edward Harold

Big dreams or pipe dreams? chancellor of the University of Pittsburgh. por Time 86: 49 Ag 6 '65

Off balance. il por Newsweek 66:74 Ag 9 '65

Pitt's juggler fumbles. Time 86:65+ Jl 2 '65

What happened at Pitt? il pors Fortune 72: 48 S '65

LITERACY. See Illiteracy

LITERACY tests (election law)

Amendment by civil disobedience; Voting rights bill. Nat R 17:268-9 Ap 6 '65

Challenge to 4(e); Federal district court rules amendment unconstitutional. Time 86:26 N 26 '65

Even if they can't read, they should have the vote. A. Hacker. il N Y Times Mag p26-7+ Ap 18 '65

Fever in the air; voting bill. Newsweek 65: 20-1 Mr 29 '65

If voting is the problem: a look outside the South. il U S News 58:39-41 Ap 5 '65

Immoral law; excerpts from editorials in Wall Street journal, March 22 and March 24, 1965. U S News 58:116+ Ap 5 '65

Kennedy-Javits voting amendment. A. M. Bickel. New Repub 152:10 Je 5 '65

Lynching the states; proposed Voting rights act of 1965. D. Lawrence. U S News 58: 124 Ap 12 '65

Right to vote: small fruit of a bold promise. W. W. Van Alstyne. il Nation 200:411-13 Ap 19 '65

Voting rights bill speeded. Sr Schol 86:8 Ap 1 '65

LITERARY ability. See Creation (literary, artistic, etc)

LITERARY agents

Rights and permissions; agents relatively scarce in most countries. P. Nathan. Pub W 188:56 N 22 '65

Should every writer have an agent? excerpts from Writing and selling of fiction. P. R. Reynolds; reply. G. Hackel. Sat R 48:67 F 13 '65

LITERARY censorship. See Censorship

LITERARY characters. See Characters in literature

LITERARY clubs

Some recollections of the Poetry club at the University of Chicago. G. Campbell. Poetry 107:110-17 N '65

See also
Pen club

LITERARY criticism

Authors league panel: book reviews and reviewers. il Pub W 187:38-41 Mr 22 '65

Books in the field: poetry. R. Hart. bibliog il Wilson Lib Bul 40:440-59 Ja '66

Computer critic's Christmas. B. L. Burman. il Sat R 48:44-5 D 4 '65

Dilemma of success. J. D. Adams; reply with rejoinder. R. Kluger. Sat R 48:21 Mr 6 '65

Edmund Wilson, Lionel Trilling, Philip Rahv. P. Pickrel. Harper 232:95-6 Ja '66

Greatness as a literary standard. S. Kauffman. il Harper 231:151-6 N '65

Hopkins the critic. M. Ochshorn. Yale R 54: 346-67 Mr '65

Literature and obscenity. R. Tracy. Christian Cent 82:769-72 Je 16 '65; Discussion. 82:993 Ag 11 '65

Myth and the powerhouse, by P. Rahv. Review
Sat R 48:55 O 2 '65. E. Capouya

New American poets. K. Rexroth. Harper 230:65-7+ Je '65; Discussion. 231:6 Ag '65

See also
Book reviews
Critics

LITERARY critics. See Critics

LITERARY fads. See Fads

LITERARY fantasies. See Fantasies, Literary

LITERARY forgeries and mystifications

Great Shakespeare forgery, by B. Grebanier. Review
Sat R 48:61+ O 23 '65. H. T. Moore

LITERARY form. See Style, Literary

LITERARY grants. See Rewards, prizes, etc.

LITERARY inspiration. See Inspiration

LITERARY landmarks
Thinking man's lake. N. Kotker. il Horizon 7:64-79 Autumn '65

LITERARY piracy. See Copyright—Unauthorized reprints

LITERARY prizes. See Rewards, prizes, etc.

LITERARY property. See Copyright

LITERARY research
Fiction writer faces facts. N. Hale. il Sat R 48:23-5+ Je 12 '65
Research for the mystery writer. F. Crane. Writer 78:15-17 F '65
Skeleton at the feast. E. Hawes. Writer 78:17-18+ N '65
There's a dividend in mysteries. P. McGerr. Writer 78:9-11 Ap '65

LITERARY selections. See Literature—Collections

LITERARY style. See Style, Literary

LITERARY symposium, Esquire. See Esquire literary symposium

LITERARY topics. See Literature—Themes

LITERATURE
Letter from Rome; fourth international congress of the European community of writers. E. M. Borgese. Nation 201:313-16 N 1 '65
Next step forward is back; modern writing. R. G. G. Price. Atlan 216:127-8 Jl '65
Your literary I.Q; ed. by J. T. Winterich and D. M. Glixon. See issues of Saturday review
See also
Anthologies
Authors
Biography
Books and reading
Censorship
Literary criticism
Plagiarism
Quotations
Translations and translating
also national literature, e.g. French literature; *also* literature of special subjects, e.g. Scientific literature

Appreciation and interpretation
Classics revisited. K. Rexroth. Sat R 48:19 Mr 20 '65
See also
Poetry—Appreciation

Collections
Modern tradition, ed. by R. Ellmann and C. Feidelson, jr. Review
Nat R il 17:938-40 O 19 '65. V. Miller

Moral and religious aspects
See Literature and morals

Periodicals
European literary scene. R. J. Clements. Sat R 48:30-1 Jl 17 '65
See also
Dial (periodical)

Study and teaching
American reading problem. S. Fraiberg. bibliog f Commentary 39:56-65 Je '65; Discussion. 40:30 S; 16+ O '65

Bibliography
Book reviews for teachers of English. J. Mersand. Sr Schol 87:sup8-9 N 4 '65

Technique
See also
Fiction—Technique

Textbooks
Pony boom: the object is to pass, isn't it? il Newsweek 66:101-2+ N 22 '65

Themes
Bigger than life. E. Downes. il Opera N 30:24-5 Ja 22 '66
Kind of magic. C. Gaffron. Writer 79:12-14 Ja '66
Literature of the early sixties; reprint from Great ideas today, 1964, annual to Great books of the western world. S. Kauffmann. bibliog il Wilson Lib Bul 39:748-56+ My '65
New apocalypse. E. Goodheart. Nation 201:207-11 S 20 '65
On being, reluctantly, a capitalist. J. Ciardi. Sat R 48:21 Ap 10 '65
On the grave. C. Brooks. Yale R 55:275-9 D '65
To ranch life, with love. J. Jeffers. Writer 78:17-19+ D '65
Two novels of the Amazon: J. E. Rivera's La vorágine (The vortex) and W. H. Hudson's Green mansions. E. S. Urbanski. il Américas 17:33-8 Mr '65

Where did you get that idea? E. H. Friermood. Horn Bk 41:655-61 D '65
Willa Cather and The professor's house; anti-Semitism in American literature of the 1920's. J. Schroeter. Yale R 54:494-512 Je '65
See also
Jews in literature
Nature in literature
Negroes in literature
New England in literature
Sex in literature

LITERATURE, Catholic. See Catholic literature

LITERATURE, Childrens. See Childrens literature

LITERATURE, Comparative

English and American
Anglo-American attitudes. D. Lodge. Commonweal 83:84-7 O 22 '65

English and Russian
Russian literature and modern English fiction. ed. by D. Davie. Review
Nation 202:47-8 Ja 10 '66. A. Field

LITERATURE, Immoral. See Immoral literature and pictures

LITERATURE, Influence of
See also
Books and reading—International aspects

LITERATURE, Japanese. See Japanese literature

LITERATURE and morals
Anglo-American attitudes; decorum in British and American fiction. D. Lodge. Commonweal 83:84-7 O 22 '65
Gargantua and Pantagruel. K. Rexroth. Sat R 48:20 Ag 28 '65
German court clears Sex and the office. Pub W 188:32 Ag 9 '65

LITERATURE and science
Poets and scientists. M. K. McCorquodale. Bul Atomic Sci 21:18-20 N '65
See also
Science fiction

LITERATURE as a profession. See Authorship

LITHIUM
See also
Perlithiopropyne

LITHOCHOLIC acid
Gallstones produced experimentally by lithocholic acid in rats. R. H. Palmer. bibliog il Science 148:1339-40 Je 4 '65
Lithocholic acid in human-blood serum. J. B. Carey, jr. and G. Williams. bibliog il Science 150:620-2 O 29 '65

LITHOGRAPHIC technical foundation, incorporated. See Graphic arts technical foundation

LITHOGRAPHY
Illustrating a book in lithography; reprint. L. Ward. Am Artist 29:21+ N '65
See also
Photolithography
Printing, Offset

LITIGATION. See Actions and defenses

LITRICO, Angelo
Tailor to king, premier, president. I. Shenker. il por N Y Times Mag p60 Mr 28 '65

LITT, Edgar
Education and political enlightenment in America. bibliog f Ann Am Acad 361:32-9 S '65

LITTEN, Larry. See Forsdale, J. R. jt. auth.

LITTER. See Refuse and refuse disposal

LITTER (bedding)
See also
Feeding and feeding stuffs—Poultry house litter

LITTLE, Floyd
Floyd Little on the run. il pors Ebony 21:86-8+ D '65
Ghostly power of old 44. il por Life 59:111-12 N 26 '65
Little bit goes a long way. H. L. Masin. por Sr Schol 87:20 O 21 '65

LITTLE, John B. and Chang, R. S.
Radiation resistance in lipovirus-altered human cells. bibliog Science 148:1746-7 Je 25 '65

LITTLE, Malcolm. See Malcolm X

LITTLE, Nina Fletcher
Engraved sources for American overmantel panels. Antiques 88:494-501 O '65
Identification of Staffordshire ladles. Antiques 88:212-15 Ag '65

LITTLE, Robert T.
Amateur scientist. il Sci Am 213:106-9 D '65

LITTLE, Thomas F.
Modern legion and its modern outlook. America 113:744-6 D 11 '65

LITTLE, W. A.
Superconductivity at room temperature; with biographical sketch. Sci Am 212:16, 21-7 bibliog(p 134) F '65

LITTLE COLORADO RIVER
See also
Grand Falls, Ariz.

LITTLE people of America, incorporated
Little people: tiny minority with big problems. A. Adams. il Ebony 20:104-6+ O '65

LITTLE; story. See Rukeyser, M.

LITTLEJOHN, David
Books. Commonweal 82:358-60 Je 4 '65

LITTON industries, incorporated
Champagne case; E. Steele vs Litton industries. Time 85:103 Ap 30 '65
Fastest billion in U.S. business. il Newsweek 66:60-2 Ag 23 '65
Get it in writing. Newsweek 65:78-9 My 3 '65
Into the $1 billion club. Time 86:69 Ag 20 '65
Perilous quest for acquisitions. J. B. Weiner. il Duns R 86:32-5+ Jl '65

LITURGICAL art. See Christian art and symbolism

LITURGICAL language
Better off in Latin? translating Roman Catholic mass into vernacular languages. il Time 86:53 Jl 30 '65
One world, one word; preparatory steps to English text for Mass. P. J. Hallinan. America 113:202-4 Ag 28 '65
Ritual and meaning. C. Davis. America 113:284 S 18 '65
Switch from Latin and some experiments. America 113:701 D 4 '65
Wisdom of the East; letter. E. M. Sheehan. America 112:179 F 6 '65

LITURGICAL movement

Catholic church
Liturgical week, 1965. Commonweal 82:579-80 Ag 20 '65
No time to stop; the beginning of liturgical reform. H. A. Reinhold. il Commonweal 82:583-5 Ag 20 '65
Post-Waugh insight. J. M. Cameron. Commonweal 83:114-15 O 29 '65; Reply. E. Waugh. 83:391 Ja 7 '66

Protestant Episcopal church
Liturgy seeking daily life. K. B. Cully. Christian Cent 82:714-15 Je 2 '65

LITURGICAL week
Chicago and charism. C. J. McNaspy. America 113:351-3 S 25 '65
Liturgical week, 1965. Commonweal 82:579-80 Ag 20 '65

LITURGIES
Dramatic perception in the liturgy. W. Kliewer. Christian Cent 82:459-61 Ap 14 '65
Liturgy as political event. W. Stringfellow. Christian Cent 82:1573-5 D 22 '65

LITURGY, Catholic. See Catholic church—Liturgy and ritual

LITWAK, Leo E.
Fantasy that paid off. N Y Times Mag p22-3+ Je 27 '65
Ronald Reagan story; or, Tom Sawyer enters politics. N Y Times Mag p46-7+ N 14 '65
Visit to a town of the mind. N Y Times Mag p46-7+ Ap 4 '65

LIU, Chieh
United Nations commemoration address, June 25, 1965. UN Mo Chron 2:105-8 Jl '65

LIU, Dan
Famous chief fights new crimes. il por Look 29:64 F 23 '65

LIU, Han-shou, and O'Keefe, J. A.
Theory of rotation for the planet Mercury. bibliog Science 150:1717 D 24 '65

LIUZZO, Viola Gregg
Freedom march ends in a murder. il por Life 58:45 Ap 2 '65
How the government won the third Liuzzo trial. A. Clymer. Reporter 33:25-6 D 30 '65
Hung jury. il Newsweek 65:40-2 My 17 '65
Murder in Alabama. L. Tornabene. il por Ladies Home J 82:42+ Jl '65
Protest on route 80. il por Time 85:22 Ap 2 '65
Rally, and tragedy. il Sr Schol 86:18-19 Ap 8 '65
Road from Selma: hope and death. il por Newsweek 65:23, 26-7 Ap 5 '65
Trial. il Time 85:27-9 My 14 '65
Trial by jury. Newsweek 66:36 N 1 '65
Uncolored justice. Newsweek 66:34 D 13 '65

LIVE bait. See Bait

LIVE like pigs; drama. See Arden, J.

LIVER
Glycerol metabolism in the human liver; inhibition by ethanol. F. Lundquist and others. bibliog il Science 150:616-17 O 29 '65

Major urinary protein complex of normal mice: origin. J. S. Finlayson and others. bibliog il Science 149:981-2 Ag 27 '65

Diseases
Happiness is a bad liver; visit to French and Italian cure centers. P. Dragdze. il Life 59:95+ N 26 '65
Lithocholic acid in human-blood serum. J. B. Carey, jr. and G. Williams. bibliog il Science 150:620-2 O 29 '65
Pig liver: new spare for humans. il Ebony 20:57-8+ S '65
Saved by perfusion: using porcine liver. il Newsweek 65:78 Je 28 '65
Stand-in liver: pig's liver used for perfusion technique. Newsweek 65:68 My 24 '65
Toward a substitute liver; pig's liver used for perfusion. il Time 85:62 Je 11 '65
See also
Hepatitis, Infectious

Surgery
Tie-up to a pig liver. il Life 59:68-9 S 24 '65

LIVER as food
See also
Cookery—Meat

LIVERPOOL
Letter from Liverpool, almost. B. Comden. Vogue 146:120+ D '65
Perils of vision; excerpts from Seaport: architecture and townscape in Liverpool. Q. Hughes. il Arch Forum 123:48-51 N '65

Crime
Television eyes catch criminals in the act. D. Scott. il Pop Sci 187:102-3 D '65

LIVERPOOL ware. See Pottery, English

LIVESTOCK
Beef news. See issues of Farm journal

Diseases and pests
See also
Abortion, Vibrionic
Anthrax

Judging
See also
Swine—Judging

Marketing
NFO's new market push. R. C. Black. Farm J 89:36-7+ Ap '65
Taming the cattle of the future. Fortune 71:92 F '65

Poisoning
Watch out, don't poison your livestock. J. B. Herrick. Suc Farm 63:39 Ag '65

Prices
See also
Swine—Prices

LIVESTOCK, Cooling of
How to help livestock beat the heat. D. Malena and others. il Suc Farm 63:29-31 Jl '65
Two ways to cool cows. il Farm J 89:52D Ag '65

LIVESTOCK shows
Look what's happening to hog shows. R. C. Black. il Farm J 89:32-3+ S '65
Ranchmen have their big fling in Denver; nine-day National western stock show. il Bsns W p 120-2 Ja 30 '65

LIVING. See Conduct of life; Life

LIVING rooms
Family room under $800. il Bet Hom & Gard 43:79 Ap '65
How to make room for a guest when you don't have a guest room. D. Popplestone. il Bet Hom & Gard 43:54-9 Ag '65
Light pyramids add drama to flexible spaces. il Arch Rec 137:98-101 mid-My '65
One great room. il House & Gard 127:102-3 F '65
Rooms for entertaining. il House & Gard 128:197-9 O '65
'Round the clock family room. il Good H 161:140 O '65
Small living rooms with big ideas. il Good H 160:136-43 Mr '65
Talking points; settings to promote conversation. il McCalls 93:76-9 Ja '66
They added a new living room. il Sunset 134:164 Ap '65
Treetop living pavilion of steel and glass. il Arch Rec 137:66-9 mid-My '65
Young couple's first living room. il House & Gard 127:164-5+ My '65

LIVING rooms, Outdoor. See Outdoor rooms

LIVING underground. See Underground living

LIVINGSTON, W. and others
Sodium D lines in comet Ikeya-Seki. il Sky & Tel 31:24-5 Ja '66
LIVY (Titus Livius)
Livy's early Rome. K. Rexroth. por Sat R 48:17 My 29 '65
LIZARDS
Electrical output of lizard ear: relation to hair-cell population. E. G. Wever and others. il Science 150:1172-4 N 26 '65
Hemoglobin and transferrin electrophoresis and relationships of island populations of anolis lizards. G. C. Gorman and H. C. Dessauer. bibliog il Science 150:1454-5 D 10 '65
Lizard reproduction: refractory period and response to warmth in Uta stansburiana females. D. W. Tinkle and L. N. Irwin. bibliog il Science 148:1613-14 Je 18 '65
Triploidy in parthenogenetic species of the teiid lizard, genus cnemidophorus. L. A. Pennock. bibliog il Science 149:539-40 Jl 30 '65
LIZASO, Félix
Martí in Central park. Américas 17:1-3 Je '65
LIZZIE Borden; opera. See Beeson, J.
LLAMAS
Bedside llama: visits to childrens hospital from Zurich zoo. E. Gurewitsch. il Look 29:55-6 Ag 10 '65
LLERAS CAMARGO, Alberto
International co-operation: twenty years after the San Francisco conference; address. UN Mo Chron 2:63-73 F '65
LLOYD, G. Stephen, and McCann, Raymond
Waging war on abandoned autos. Am City 80:98-100 N '65
LLOYD, James E.
Aggressive mimicry in photuris: firefly femmes fatales. bibliog Science 149:653-4 Ag 6 '65
LLOYD, John
Washington report. See issues of Senior scholastic
LLOYD, Lewis E.
Excerpt from testimony before House committee on foreign affairs, March 4, 1965. Cong Digest 44:186+ Je '65
LOADING and unloading
See also
Freight handling
LOADING cameras. See Cameras—Loading
LOAN associations. See Savings and loan associations
LOANS
Different & cheaper way to borrow. Changing T 20:42 Ja '66
See also
Credit
Interest
Mortgages
Student loans
LOANS, Art. See Art loans
LOANS, Bank
Bankers learn to live with foreign loan limits; lending abroad. il Bsns W p40-1 Jl 3 '65
Business borrowing rises again; boom year for bankers. il Bsns W p47-8 My 15 '65
How to stay ahead of your lender; handbook for bankers. B. Brantley. il Suc Farm 63:74 N '65
Perpetual money machine? il Changing T 19:27-8 Jl '65
Spending abroad, lending at home; loan demand up. Time 86:93 O 15 '65
LOANS, Foreign
To build abroad, borrow abroad. Newsweek 67:41 Ja 3 '66
LOANS, Government. See Government lending
LOANS, Interlibrary. See Interlibrary loans.
LOANS, Mortgage. See Mortgages
LOANS, Personal
What home loans cost now. il Changing T 19:24 Ag '65
See also
Household finance corporation
LOANS, Student. See Student loans
LOBBIES (architecture)
Prosperous lobbyist; design and decoration of apartment house lobbies. il Fortune 72:194 D '65
LOBBYING
Bracing to keep T-H intact. il Bsns W p 120+ My 15 '65
Miami super-lobby; Inter-American cultural and trade center. H. Harwood. il Reporter 32:21-5 My 6 '65
Quiet victory of the cigarette lobby. E. B. Drew. Atlan 216:76-80 S '65
Sad day for lobbyists. J. N. Eller. America 113:7 Jl 3 '65
Sugar stick-up. Nation 201:206 O 11 '65
Sweet talk; hearings on sugar legislation. Reporter 33:10 S 9 '65

Union lobby gets the word to fight; attempt to repeal section of Taft-Hartley act. il Bsns W p 134-6 My 8 '65
Washington's money birds; guide to lobbyist Americanus and his predatory pursuits. L. L. King. il Harper 231:45-54 Ag '65; Discussion. 231:8 O '65
See also
Pressure groups
LOBBYISTS
Dale Miller: the President's favorite lobbyist. D. S. Broder. il Look 29:66-8 Ap 6 '65
Lobbyists: cloud of doubt; Findley plan to amend Sugar act. Newsweek 66:34 O 25 '65
Our ex-congressmen; seven register as lobbyists. New Repub 153:8 D 25 '65
Trade winds; humor lobbyist, Jim Atkins. J Beatty, jr. Sat R 49:14 Ja 1 '66
Washington's money birds; guide to lobbyist Americanus and his predatory pursuits. L. L. King. il Harper 231:45-54 Ag '65; Discussion. 231:8 O '65
LOBELIAS
Wild flowers for fall. G. A. Krueger. Flower Grower 52:41 D '65
LOBOS, Heitor Villa-. See Villa-Lobos, H.
LOBSENZ, Norman M.
Town with too many churches. Redbook 126:70-1+ N '65
—See Cranin, A. N. jt. auth.
LOBSTER tails. See Cookery—Fish
LOBSTER trapping
H.C.L. makes the lobsterman happy; high cost of lobster. E. Hill. il N Y Times Mag p 18-19+ Ap 25 '65
LOBSTERS
See also
Cookery—Fish
LOCAL finance
How to watchdog a town budget. J. N. Miller. il Read Digest 86:125-9 Mr '65
State-local finances. R. Moley. Newsweek 65:100 My 3 '65
LOCAL girl makes good; story. See Temple, W. H.
LOCAL government
See also
Metropolitan areas
State and local relations

United States

Dawn of a community-defining federalism. H. C. Hart. bibliog f Ann Am Acad 359:147-56 My '65
Where are the new Republicans? Reporter 33:16+ O 7 '65
LOCAL government officers. See Public officers
LOCAL service airlines
High-density routes still locals' goal. il Aviation W 82:166-7 Mr 15 '65
Mohawk blazes a trail. il Bsns W p74+ Je 26 '65
San Jose hearings will begin this week. R. G. O'Lone. Aviation W 83:31 O 18 '65
Short-medium versions proliferating as traffic swells. C. M. Plattner. il Aviation W 83:148-52 O 25 '65
Stability sought for supplemental carriers. R. G. O'Lone. Aviation W 82:30-1 Mr 29 '65
Vast local service growth seen by emphasizing public interest. Aviation W 83:40 D 6 '65

Federal aid

Flying porkbarrels; subsidy paid to the Nation's small feeder airlines. R. Burkhardt. New Repub 153:11 Ag 7 '65
LOCAL taxation
ABCs of space-age MPR. P. D. Eimon. il Am City 80:144+ Ap '65
Allocation of responsibilities and resources among the three levels of government. J. C. Charlesworth. il Ann Am Acad 359:71-80 My '65
Great urban tax tangle. Fortune 71:106-7+ Mr '65
Non-property taxes. M. Walker. Am City 81:42+ Ja '66
States dig for new revenues. il Bsns W p 108-10+ My 1 '65
Tax rises that are snowballing. U S News 59:121 O 11 '65
Where taxes keep going up and up. il U S News 59:100+ O 25 '65
Your city taxes, compare them with others. il Changing T 19:25-8 My '65
LOCATION in business and industry
Boom town 1965; plans for Jones & Laughlin steel mill. il Time 86:90+ Jl 9 '65
Factory sites in rural areas. B. L. Masse. America 113:440 O 16 '65
Good schools attract industry. R. A. Will. NEA J 54:28 Mr '65

LOCATION in buiness and industry—*Cont.*
How to attract industry; Hamilton, Ohio.
C. R. Lukens. il Am City 80:104-5 Ag '65
Rural-urban balance; relocation of industry;
address, September 20, 1965. W. B. Murphy.
Vital Speeches 32:53-7 N 1 '65
Science in the mountains: NRAO astronomers
to leave for city. E. Langer. il Science
150:722-4 N 5 '65
Site selection: a tough job gets tougher.
il Duns R 85:pt2 118-21+ Mr '65
Steel turns to the Midwest, back of big expansion. il U S News 59:101-3 Jl 19 '65
See also
Cities and towns—Industries
LOCATIONS. See Moving pictures—Setting
and scenery
LOCATORS, Target. See Target locators
LOCHER, David A.
Gull; poem. Liv Wildn 87:21 Wint '64
Oxford bells; poem. America 113:207 Ag 28 '65
Time in another season; poem. America 113:
776 D 18 '65
LOCK, Frank R.
Expectant mother. Redbook 125:48+ O '65
LOCK HAVEN, Pa.
How a strike looks to a computer. il U S
News 59:98-100 N 15 '65
LOCKABEY, Almon
Largest and fastest Transpac. Yachting 118:
41-3+ S '65
LOCKE, Edith Raymond
Styles, the stylers, the stylish Sat R 48:69
N 13 '65
LOCKE, Michael, and others
Molt and intermolt activities in the epidermal cells of an insect. bibliog Science
149:437-8 Jl 23 '65
LOCKE, Octavia
Silk screen. Sch Arts 64:17-19 F '65
LOCKHEED aircraft corporation
C-5A: Lockheed's path to the future: giant
military cargo plane contract to Lockheed-
Georgia co. il Bsns W p32-3 O 9 '65
Keeping ahead on real time. il Bsns W
p 166-8+ Mr 27 '65
Lockheed begins freezing SST features.
J. R. Ashlock. il Aviation W 84:43+ Ja 10
'66
Lockheed holds a steady lead; heads defense
contractor list. il Bsns W p35 N 27 '65
Lockheed retains top contract rank. il Aviation W 83:24 N 29 '65
Lockheed scrambles for the battle of the
primes. C. J. V. Murphy. il Fortune 71:
148-52+ F '65
Lockheed sees management key to C-5A. C.
Brownlow. Aviation W 83:55-7+ O 18 '65
Lockheed tops DOD contractor list. il Miss
& Roc 17:14 N 29 '65
Lockheed's big victory: winning contract for
world's largest airplane, C-5A. il Newsweek
66:80 O 11 '65
Pentagon tests one-stop bidding. il Bsns W
p99-100+ N 6 '65
See also
Lockheed propulsion company
LOCKHEED-Georgia company. See Lockheed
aircraft corporation
LOCKHEED propulsion company
LPC big solids R&D leads to interest in volume-limited motor production. J. F. Judge.
il Miss & Roc 16:28+ Mr 1 '65
LOCKRIDGE, C. P.
Opinion, please: from New York. Mlle 60:44+
F '65
LOCKS and keys
Key maker Cole sharpens its vision; largest
vendor of replacement keys. il Bsns W
p84+ Ja 15 '66
LOCKWOOD, David E.
U.S. aid program in Asia. bibliog f Cur Hist
49:257-61+ N '65
LOCKWOOD, Lee
Cuba's new beat: a communication. New
Repub 153:36-7 D 11 '65
LOCOMOTION
Plasticity in sensory-motor systems. R. Held.
il Sci Am 213:84-8+ N '65
LOCOMOTIVE firemen
Rail firemen fuel fight. Bsns W p52+ O 23 '65
Trainmen yank brakes on featherbed label;
AAR demands reforms in union work
rules. il Bsns W p 102+ N 27 '65
LOCOMOTIVE models. See Railroad models
LOCOMOTIVES
For travelers east, here are three rides behind steam. il Sunset 135:20-1 Ag '65
LOCOMOTIVES, Atomic powered
Atomic locomotives seen for high-speed
freight. Sci N L 87:217 Ap 3 '65
LOCUSTS. See Grasshoppers
LODEESEN, Marius
Final approach. Writer 78:12-13 Jl '65

LODGE, David
Anglo-American attitudes. Commonweal 83:
84-7 O 22 '65
LODGE, Edith
Arlington April; poem. Christian Cent 82:526
Ap 28 '65
LODGE, George C.
Revolution in Latin America. For Affairs 44:
173-97 Ja '66
LODGE, Henry Cabot, 1902-
Excerpt from address, January 16, 1965.
Cong Digest 44:124+ Ap '65
Go on fighting in Vietnam? interview. pors
U S News 58:62-7 F 15 '65; Excerpts. 59:
66-7 Jl 19 '65
about
Behind Lodge's reappointment. R. Stolley.
Life 59:32B Jl 23 '65
Case of jitters; appointment of ambassador
to South Vietnam. il Newsweek 66:29-30
Ag 23 '65
Cat out of the bag. Nation 201:90 Ag 30 '65
Dog that didn't bite. il por Newsweek 66:23+
S 6 '65
For Lodge: an old job grown tougher. il por
U S News 59:19 Jl 19 '65
Hello, David! trouble over Dolly troupe in
South Vietnam. il Newsweek 66:36+ O 25
'65
How two officials size up Vietnam. por U S
News 58:26 My 17 '65
Lodge returns to Saigon. Christian Cent 82:
908 Jl 21 '65
To have a part in it. por Time 86:15 Jl 16
'65
Trouble shooter for LBJ; Lodge gets a tough
new job. il por U S News 58:29 Ap 26 '65
War by any other name. Nat R 17:625-7 Jl 27
'65
Worse before it gets better; H. C. Lodge
returns to Saigon. il por Newsweek 66:17-
18 Jl 19 '65
LODGE, James P. See Dixon, J. P. jt. auth.
LODGES (architecture)
Shooting lodge high on a volcano; Mauna
Kea, dormant volcano of Hawaii. P. Knight.
il Sports Illus 22:64-6 N 8 '65
360-degree view of life; round houses built
for sport. il Sports Illus 22:26-9 Mr 1 '65
LOEB, John N. and others
Turnover of ribosomal RNA in rat liver.
bibliog Science 149:1093-5 S 3 '65
LOEB, Leonard B.
Ionizing waves of potential gradient. bibliog
Science 148:1417-26 Je 11 '65
LOEBRICH, Gary
Michigan's first elk hunt; ed. by B. East.
por Outdoor Life 135:36-9+ Ap '65
LOESER, Katinka
Brothers and sisters have I none; story. New
Yorker 41:44-50 My 1 '65
Don't give my body to science, the dying
mother said; story. New Yorker 41:57-62
O 30 '65
LOEVINGER, Lee
Cooperation in international communications.
Dept State Bul 53:828-34 N 22 '65
LOEWE, Carl
Now on Vox: Brahms, Loewe, and Wolf
lieder by Prey, magnificent. H. Glass. Am
Rec G 31:526-7 F '65
LOEWE, Erhard
Eurospace views space program needs. por
Aviation W 82:74-5+ My 10 '65
LOEWENSTEIN, Werner R. and others
Intercellular communication: renal, urinary
bladder, sensory, and salivary gland cells.
bibliog Science 149:295-8 Jl 16 '65
—See Ito, S.; Penn, R. D. jt. auths.
LOEWY, Raymond
Twenty years from now. Atlan 216:93-7 Jl
'65
LOFTLEIDIR Icelandic airlines. See Airlines—
Iceland
LOFTS, Norah
Throw your heart over. Writer 78:11-13+ D
'65
LOFTUS, Sister Mary Malachy
Students strike in Colombia. America 113:
98 Jl 24 '65
LOGAN, Andy
That was New York. New Yorker 41:41-2+
F 27; 37-8+ Ag 14; 41-2+ Ag 21 '65
LOGAN, Giuseppi
Jazz concerts; performance at Judson Hall.
W. Balliett. New Yorker 41:123-4 F 27 '65
LOGAN, Innes
Church of Scotland assembly. Christian Cent
82:811-12 Je 23 '65
LOGAN, John
Prison poem. Nation 201:390 N 22 '65
LOGAN, John A.
Crisis on our campuses; excerpts from address. Read Digest 86:124-6 F '65

LOGAN, M. D.
Caladiums for color. Pop Gard 16:21+ Mr '65

LOGIC
Multiple choice and the either-or fallacy.
P. DePue. Sch & Soc 93:154-6 Mr 6 '65
This is right; that must be wrong. Brother
F. Joseph. America 112:430 Mr 27 '65
See also
Hypothesis

LOGIC, Symbolic and mathematical
Games, logic and computers. H. Wang. il
Sci Am 213:98-104+ N '65

LOGSDON, Eugene H.
How to tell if you should be farming. Farm J
89:14 My '65
When doctors take over farming. Farm J
89:53 F '65

LOGUE, Edward J.
Bold Boston gladiator, Ed Logue. il pors
Life 59:126-34 D 24 '65
What's happening to proper old Boston? il
por Newsweek 65:77-9 Ap 26 '65

LOHENGRIN; opera. See Wagner, R.

LOHMAN, Joseph D.
Expose, don't impose. NEA J 55:24-6 Ja '66

LOHR, Helga
Letter from Berlin. Nation 202:51-4 Ja 10 '66

LOIRE, Gabriel
Through glass, brightly. il Time 85:78-84 F 5
'65

LOMASK, Milton
Sergeant Bates' march. Am Heritage 16:12-17
O '65

LOMAX, Louis E.
Georgia boy goes home. Harper 230:152-9 Ap
'65
White liberal. por Ebony 20:60-2+ Ag '65

LOMBARDO, Guy
Past, present and yet to come. W. K.
Zinsser. il por Life 59:82+ D 17 '65

LOMBROSO, Cesare T.
Living with epilepsy; interview, ed. by E.
Keiffer. Parents Mag 40:72-3+ N '65

LONDON, George
George London, searing intensity, blazing
intellectuality. M. Lelash. Am Rec G 31:
1173 Ag '65
Second fame: good food. N. Lyon. por Vogue
146:276-8 S 1 '65

LONDON, Jack
Life was always worth the living. E. Labor.
por Sat R 48:38-9 S 25 '65

LONDON, Nora
Second fame: good food. N. Lyon. por Vogue
146:276-8 S 1 '65

LONDON, Perry
Psychoanalysis and morality. L. H. Farber.
Commentary 40:69-74 N '65

LONDON
Letter from London. M. Panter-Downes. See
issues of New Yorker
London: lovable Dickensian cliché. G. Sherman. il Sat R 49:44+ Ja 1 '66
Private line from London; Little Venice community, Paddington. V. Cowles. Vogue 146:
148 S 1 '65
Soho synthesis. K. Tynan. il Holiday 37:54-
9 F '65

Air raids
Way it was in the blitz. J. Beavan. il N Y
Times Mag p 12-13+ S 5 '65

Architecture
In London, belief in social ideals shapes an
urban setting of rare distinction. P. Blake.
il Arch Forum 123:42-7 Jl '65

Art
Art news from London. J. Russell. See is-
sues of Art news
London: from imperium to maniac. J. Russell.
Art N 64:48-9+ N '65

Churches
See also
London—Westminster abbey

City planning
How Europe's biggest city hopes to handle
its problems. il U S News 59:80-3 O 11 '65
Letter from London; reconstruction of City
of London. M. Panter-Downes. New Yorker
41:137-9 Je 5 '65

Clubs
Man with a club; excerpts from Leather arm-
chairs. C. Graves. il Read Digest 87:147-8+
Ag '65

Covent Garden
Recordings. M. Mayer. Esquire 64:12+ O '65

Description
London's villages. H. Johnson. il House &
Gard 127:22+ Je '65
Long wait for night. L. Wainwright. Life 58:
25 F 5 '65
Teen travel talk. il Seventeen 24:172 Mr '65

Anecdotes, facetiae, satire, etc.
Happy hardware salesman. J. Glashen. il
Holiday 38:54-9 Ag '65

Gardens
Chelsea flower show. W. Feinberg. il Horticulture 43:38-9+ My '65

Hotels, restaurants, etc.
Of bangers, blighters, and bloaters. H. Sut-
ton. il Sat R 48:43-5 Jl 17 '65
Simpson's in the Strand. R. Postgate. il
Holiday 38:68-70+ S '65

Housing
In London, belief in social ideals shapes an
urban setting of rare distinction. P. Blake.
il Arch Forum 123:42-7 Jl '65

Intellectual life
See also
Bloomsbury group

Libraries
Clean, well-lighted place; West African stu-
dents; reprint. J. Wakeman. Library J
90:4912-13 N 15 '65
Hell is a city much like London. K. C. Har-
rison. il Library J 90:4902-6 N 15 '65
Hornsey goes long and low; Central library.
W. B. Stevenson. il Library J 90:5215-17
D 1 '65
Spencerian style for Hampstead central li-
brary. W. R. Maidment. il Library J 90:
5213-15 D 1 '65

Music
Anniversary for Tippett. E. Greenfield. Hi Fi
15:86T Mr '65
Bumper Britten crop; Aldeburgh festival.
E. Greenfield. Hi Fi 15:164-5 S '65
City of five orchestras. E. Greenfield. il
Hi Fi 15:51-5 Ap '65
High fidelity newsfronts. N. Eisenberg. il
Hi Fi 15:40+ Ap '65
Honorable tradition of Englishmen. H. C. R.
Landon. il Hi Fi 15:44-50 Ap '65
London letter. D. Shawe-Taylor. il Opera N
29:33 F 27 '65
New sound on the south bank. E. Greenfield.
il Hi Fi 15:141 Ap '65
Notes from our correspondents. R. Wimbush.
Hi Fi 16:22+ Ja '66
Notes from our correspondents (cont) E.
Greenfield. Hi Fi 15:28+ Mr; 18+ My; 18+
Jl; 14+ S; 28+ N; 16+ D '65
Period passion at Sadler's Wells. E. Green-
field. il Hi Fi 15:136 Je '65
Solti's Ring. Stravinsky's Firebird. E. Green-
field. il Hi Fi 15:182-3 D '65
Thirty-one by Rostropovich. E. Greenfield.
Hi Fi 15:166 O '65

Newspapers
See also
Sun (newspaper)

Politics and government
London's answer to big-city sprawl; pattern
for U.S? il U S News 58:61-2 Je 21 '65

Reconstruction
See London—City planning

Stores
Moss bros. suits the British. J. Stewart-
Gordon. il Read Digest 86:188-90+ Je '65

Street traffic
Letter from London. M. Panter-Downes. New
Yorker 41:56 Ja 1 '66

Streets
Our far-flung correspondents: knowledge-of-
London test for taxi-drivers. J. Bain-
bridge. New Yorker 41:62+ Jl 3 '65

Theater
Actors studio in London, or, the Broadway
boiler-house abroad. P. Gilliatt. Harper 231:
32+ S '65
England's summer season. H. Hewes. Sat R
48:45 Ag 14 '65
Letter from London (cont) M. Panter-
Downes. New Yorker 41:227-8+ D 11 '65
London's the place for playgoing. il Sunset
134:34-5 F '65

LONDON—Theater—*Continued*
New plays in London. W. S. Smith. Christian Cent 82:1066-7, 1096-7 S 1-8 '65
Notes from afar. H. Clurman. Nation 201:105-6 Ag 30 '65
Period passion at Sadler's Wells. E. Greenfield. il Hi Fi 15:136 Je '65
Theater in London. R. Brustein. New Repub 152:30-3 My 29 '65
Theatre; Peter Shaffer's The royal hunt of the sun. Vogue 146:49 Ag 1 '65

Traffic problems
See London—Street traffic

Westminster abbey
Royal peculiar. il Time 86:38-42 D 24 '65
LONDON plague, 1665. See Plague
LONDON zoological gardens
Elephants are such architectural animals; elephant and rhinoceros house. il Arch Forum 123:36-9 N '65
LONE, Jacqueline V.
Journey into wilderness. Liv Wildn 29:9-11 Sum '65
LONELINESS. See Solitude
LONERT, A. C.
Amateur scientist. Sci Am 214:116-19+ Ja '66
LONEY, Glenn
Cult and myth on the green hill. Hi Fi 15:160-1 O '65
LONG, Clarence D.
Double pay for overtime. Nations Bsns 53:84-6 Jl '61
LONG, Don
Project; 200 MPH. E. Dahlquist. il pors Hot Rod 18:78-83+ Mr; 44-7+ Ap '65
LONG, E. John
Giant wave of wood. Am For 71:31+ Ag '65
LONG, Edward M.
Long-hand printed circuits. Electr World 74:40-1 Ag '65
LONG, Edward V.
Speaking out. por Sat Eve Post 238:10+ N 20 '65
LONG, Henry, pseud.
Toughest armor. PTA Mag 59:16 bibliog(p37) My '65
LONG, Inez
Church of the Brethren; new involvement. Christian Cent 82:924-6 Jl 21 '65
LONG, John Luther
Butterfly's cocoon. A. N. Fischer. por Opera N 29:13 Mr 27 '65
LONG, Russell Billiu
Excerpt from address, September 15, 1965. Cong Digest 44:268+ N '65
Foreign-policy changes? Fulbright has some in mind; statements. U S News 58:20 F 1 '65

about

Drive for simpler tax laws. por U S News 59:107-8 D 13 '65
Growing power for Louisiana's Long. por U S News 59:20 N 29 '65
Kingfish's son picks up the whip. W. K. Goolrick. il pors Sat Eve Post 238:78+ F 27 '65
Long battle. New Repub 153:6 Jl 10 '65
Long's two hats. Time 86:26 N 26 '65
Princefish comes into his own. L. M. Stern. il Reporter 32:34-6 Mr 25 '65
Russell Long's capers. New Repub 153:6 Jl 3 '65
Son of the Kingfish. T. Wicker. il pors N Y Times Mag p76-7+ Ap 4 '65
U.S. patent policy. R. Moley. Newsweek 67:68 Ja 10 '66
LONG BEACH, Calif.
Wealth for a riviera; reservoir of untapped oil sits under Long Beach to be drilled. il Time 85:88 F 26 '65
LONG BEACH, Calif. public library
Ordeal at Long Beach. B. Collins. il Library J 90:2486-90+ Je 1 '65
LONG ISLAND, N.Y.
Home, sweet home, for seven million people. C. Morrison. il Look 29:71-3 S 7 '65
Long Island. C. Crandall. il Look 29:61-9 S 7 '65
See also
Architecture, Domestic—Long Island, N.Y.
Montauk, N.Y.
LONG ISLAND center, Stony Brook. See New York state university—Long Island center, Stony Brook
LONG ISLAND college hospital

Tropical disease clinic
See Brooklyn—Hospitals

LONG ISLAND daily
Letters from Steinbeck; H. F. Guggenheim hires J. Steinbeck. Newsweek 66:68 N 22 '65
LONG ISLAND rail road
8:02 to history; state ownership. Time 86:15 D 31 '65
Man from L.I.R.R. tells a few. C. B. Palmer. il N Y Times Mag p 154+ N 28 '65
LONG ISLAND SOUND
Cruising through history on Long Island Sound. L. A. Solomon. il Motor B 115:22-9+ Ap '65
Current situation. M. L Hersey. il Motor B 115:102+ Ap '65
LONG playing record catalog. See Phonograph records—Catalogs
LONG playing records. See Phonograph records
LONG range navigation. See Loran
LONG way to go; story. See Deal, B.
LONGARONE, Italy
Night the mountain fell; Vaiont Dam disaster. G. Gaskill. il Read Digest 86:59-67 My '65
LONGDEN, Johnny
Tough old man in the saddle. J. Stewart-Gordon. il Read Digest 87:19-20+ Jl '65
LONGEVITY
Facts and figures of the Americas; life expectancy at birth. il Américas 17:37 S '65
How long you'll live; questions and answers. Sci Digest 58:36 N '65
Who is healthy and why? E. Kaplan and J. Kaplan. il Todays Health 43:22-3+ F '65
See also
Aging
LONGORIA, Peggy
Peggy was dying. W. S. Ross. il por Ladies Home J 82:50-1+ Jl '65
LONGSHOREMEN
Hiring practices for longshoremen; Labor department study of ten East and Gulf Coast ports. P. Groom. Mo Labor R 88:1289-96 N '65
Latin dockers join Castro boycott. Bsns W p50+ My 1 '65
Report on a study of British posts; excerpt. Mo Labor R 88:1335-45 N '65
See also
Strikes—United States—Maritime workers
LONGSTRETH, T. Morris
Weather. Horticulture 43:26-8+ Ap '65
LONGWORTH, Alice Roosevelt
Sharpest wit in Washington; interview, ed. by J. V. Heuvel. pors Sat Eve Post 238:30-3 D 4 '65
LONIE, D. D. Jr
Build a tool-shed fort. Pop Gard 17:14-15 Ja '66
LONSDALE, Gordon Arnold
Good gray spy. il por Newsweek 66:104+ D 20 '65
Honest-to-badness. por Time 86:44-5 N 12 '65
I stole America's secrets. il por Newsweek 65:33 Ap 12 '65
LOOK (periodical)
Fast-changing South; symposium; with paintings by A. Briggs. il Look 29:33-44+ N 16 '65
Johnson presents award to Teacher of the year. il Sr Schol 86:sup 1 My 6 '65
Richard Klinck; teacher of the year. J. Poppy. il Look 29:47-50+ Ap 20 '65
See also
All-America cities
Collier trophy
LOOKING glass war; novel. See Cornwell, D. J. M.
LOOKING glasses. See Mirrors
LOOKOUTS, Forest. See United States—Forest service
LOOMIS, Alfred F.
Men overboard; in the Atlantic. Yachting 118:60+ O '65
LOOMIS, Carol J.
Personal investing. Fortune 72:85-6+ O '65
Should companies promote their own stocks? Fortune 72:184-6+ D '65
LOOMIS, Daniel P.
Great railroads for the Great society; address, April 1, 1965. Vital Speeches 31:424-7 My 1 '65
LOOMIS, Frederic
Who shall be the judge? excerpt from Consultation room. Read Digest 86:91-4 Ap '65
LOOMIS, Mahlon
Real inventor of wireless. T. Appleby. il Pop Electr 23:64-6+ O '65
LOONEY, Joe Don
Bad boy of the pros. M. Smith. il pors Life 59:85-6+ O 22 '65
LOONEY, Ralph
Georgia O'Keeffe. Atlan 215:106-10 Ap '65
LOONS
Dead loon mystery. J. Van Coevering. il Audubon Mag 67:229-30 Jl '65

LOOTING. See Pillage

LOOY, Rik van
Five against the gods. R. Daley. il Esquire 64:100+ N '65

LOPEN, Andrea
Harlem's streetcorner architects. Arch Forum 123:50-1 D '65

LOPEZ, Alfonso Ramon
Garter on the Sox. il por Time 85:56 My 28 '65
Valiant Yankee-chaser. G. Rogin. il pors Sports Illus 22:36-8+ Mr 22 '65

LOPEZ, Hank
(ed) See Porter, K. A. Country and some people I love

LÓPEZ ARELLANO, Osvaldo
His master's voice. por Newsweek 65:50 Mr 1 '65

LÓPEZ CISNEROS, Alberto
Up from the slums. il por Newsweek 66:70 N 15 '65

LOPEZ-MORILLAS, Martin P.
(tr) See Lipsky, Y. N. Zond-3 photographs of the moon's far side

LÓPEZ RODÓ, Laureano
Spain and the E.E.C. For Affairs 44:127-33 O '65

LOPEZ TIJERINA, Reies. See Tijerina, R. L.

LOPEZ ISLAND. See San Juan Islands, Wash.

LORAN
Loran-D designed as limited war navaid. P. J. Klass. il Aviation W 83:71-2 Jl 26 '65

LORANT, Stefan
Trade winds. J. Beatty, jr. il Sat R 49:12+ Ja 15 '66

LORCA, Federico García. See García Lorca, F.

LORD, James
Giacometti said, I'm giving up painting for good. Vogue 146:85+ Ag 1 '65

LORD, Mary Helen
School libraries: reflections. Wilson Lib Bul 39:587 Mr '65

LORD, Walter
Mississippi: the past that has not died. Am Heritage 16:4-9+ Je '65

LORDEN, Peter
Salute to the tall violin; poem. Christian Cent 82:1252 O 13 '65

LORDS Supper
Beyond transubstantiation: new theory of the real presence. il Time 86:68+ Jl 2 '65; Reply. America 113:90 Jl 24 '65
Celebration of a hope; worldwide communion Sunday. Christian Cent 82:1182 S 29 '65
Lord's Supper: summary of discussion of Faith and order conference. L. Webb. Christian Cent 82:1063-4 S 1 '65
Toward one table. Christian Cent 82:909 Jl 21 '65
See also
Catholic church—Eucharist
Mass

LOREN, Sophia
Bigamy Italian style. D. J. Hamblin. por Life 59:52A-52B Jl 23 '65
Concubinage, Italian style. por Time 85:56 F 19 '65
Name is Ponti, not Mr Loren. I. Shenker. il pors N Y Times Mag p32-3+ Je 6 '65
Viva Sophia! Christian Cent 82:695 My 26 '65

LORENZ, John G.
Why Title 2? Elementary and secondary education act of 1965; address. May, 1965. por Library J 90:3674-5 S 15 '65
—and Muirhead, P. P.
Campus library. pors Am Ed 1:12-19 My '65

LORRINSON, Leverret
Washington front (cont) America 113:493 O 30 '65

LOS ALAMOS, N.Mex.
Secret city on the magic mountain. D. Masters. il Sat Eve Post 238:36-40+ Ag 14 '65
Suburb without the urb. il Time 86:31 O 1 '65

LOS ANGELES
Angel city, burning bright; portfolio. Fortune 71:102-5 Mr '65
Day before Easter on Olvera street. il Sunset 134:40+ Ap '65
Mining-camp megalopolis; sprawling, brawling, galling Los Angeles. C. Fadiman. il Holiday 38:8+ O '65
Pressure switches monitor electrical distribution system. il Am City 80:117 Je '65
See also
Stock exchange—Los Angeles

Air pollution
Breath of life, by D. E. Carr. Review
New Repub 152:36 Ap 17 '65. J. Ridgeway
CO on the highway. Sci Am 212:52+ My '65
Los Angeles: no end in sight. P. Bart. il Sat R 48:39-40 My 22 '65
Poison air around us. D. E. Carr. il Sat R 48:17-19+ F 27 '65; Discussion. 48:21 Mr 27; 29 Ap 10; 29 Ap 17 '65

Smog today & smog tomorrow; main offender: motor vehicles. M. Neiburger. il Nation 201:432-5 D 6 '65
When a smog blanket smothers a city. il U S News 59:18 N 15 '65

Airports
S-64 sky lounge demonstration sought. H. D. Watkins. Aviation W 83:43 N 8 '65

Anti-poverty program, 1964-
Fruits of fire; federal help for riot-torn area. Time 86:21 S 3 '65
Ticktock, ticktock; end of stalemate over poverty program. Newsweek 66:18-19 S 6 '65
Watts and the welfare riot. Nat R 17:1146 D 14 '65
When the poor are powerless. New Repub 153:7 S 4 '65

Art
Art news from Los Angeles. J. Coplans. il Art N 63:51-4 F; 64:52+ D '65
Los Angeles: the scene. J. Coplans. il Art N 64:28-9+ Mr '65
Reviews: Los Angeles. F. A. Danieli. Art N 64:65 My '65

Banks
Bank robber sees his picture and gives up; United California bank. il Life 58:39 Mr 12 '65
Expanding the unusual; Union bank of Los Angeles. il Bsns W p68-70+ Ag 28 '65
Split-second record of a bank robbery; Western-Manchester branch of the United California bank. il Life 58:34-5 F 26 '65
Two round floors on a sunken plaza. il Arch Rec 137:194 Je '65

Center for the performing arts
Johann Strauss on the freeway. I. Kolodin. Sat R 48:44 Ag 21 '65
Something for everyone; popularity of new Music pavilion. Newsweek 65:81-2 Mr 1 '65

City planning
Los Angeles, prototype of supercity. R. A. Smith. il Fortune 71:98-101+ Mr '65
Troubled Los Angeles; race is only one of its problems. il U S News 59:58-62 Ag 30 '65

Crime
Summer job: ordeal of girl selling magazine subscriptions. il Newsweek 66:21-2 Jl 19 '65

Description
Foamrubbersville. J. Ciardi. Sat R 48:20 Je 19 '65
Personal business; businessman's guide. Bsns W p 141 F 20 '65
Two-hour walk through the heart of downtown L.A. il Sunset 134:84-95 Mr '65

Education
Brains, newts, legs, eggs, and sea shells; science center of the Los Angeles school system. D. Turpin. il Am Ed 1:1-4 Ap '65
De facto integration in Bel Air. A. M. Clark. il Sat R 49:72-3 Ja 15 '66
Meeting children where they are; non-graded classes at University elementary school, University of California. J. I. Goodlad. il Sat R 48:57-9+ Mr 20 '65

Elections
Wins by ins; Yorty re-elected mayor. Newsweek 65:26-7 Ap 19 '65
Yorty's chortle. Time 85:27 Ap 16 '65

Electric power
Cheviot Hills goes underground. Sunset 134:157-8 Mr '65

Galleries and museums
Los Angeles has a piano museum. il Sunset 134:58 F '65
Westsonian west wing: Westsonian institution's exhibit and workshop. H. D. Brown. il Hobbies 70:113+ Jl; 113+ Ag '65
See also
Los Angeles County museum of art

Hospitals
Screams, slaps and love; new treatment for withdrawn children at UCLA Neuropsychiatric institute; with report by D. Moser. il Life 58:90A-96+ My 7 '65

Libraries
See also
Los Angeles public library

LOS ANGELES—*Continued*

Music

Johann Strauss on the freeway. I. Kolodin.
Sat R 48:44 Ag 21 '65
Kenton at the Pavilion; Los Angeles neo-
phonic orchestra. H. Siders. il Sat R 48:
62-3 F 13 '65
See also
Los Angeles philharmonic orchestra

Negroes

Does anyone really care? Negroes who rioted
in Los Angeles. Christian Cent 82:1148 S
22 '65
Far country: Watts. il Time 86:23-4 S 24 '65
Hard lesson for the law. M. L. Schwartz. Sat
R 48:35-7+ N 13 '65
Loneliest road; quietness in Negro ghetto
of Watts. il Time 86:9-10 Ag 27 '65
Los Angeles: a city still facing trouble. il
U S News 59:58-60+ N 15 '65
Los Angeles: tragedy and opportunity. E. C.
Bianchi. America 113:260-1 S 11 '65
Search for why's. il Sr Schol 87:23-4+ S
23 '65
Tough years ahead; Los Angeles riot, and
proposed remedial measures. L. Beachy. il
Newsweek 66:19-20 Ag 30 '65
Trigger of hate. il Time 86:13-19 Ag 20 '65
Watts: the forgotten slum. C. McWilliams.
Nation 201:89-90 Ag 30 '65
Watts today: brave plans and a sick psyche.
Newsweek 66:31 D 13 '65

Newspapers

See also
Los Angeles times

Parks and playgrounds

Parks and politics in Los Angeles. F. M.
Brodie. il Reporter 32:39-42 F 11 '65

Police

Mafia can't crack Los Angeles. B. Davidson.
il Sat Eve Post 238:23-7 Jl 31 '65
One for the courts. Christian Cent 82:981
Ag 11 '65
Terror in Los Angeles; interview with a
policeman assigned to the Watts area.
Nat R 17:773-4 S 7 '65
There's no easy place to pin the blame. D.
Moser. il Life 59:30-3 Ag 27 '65
This would never have happened, police ac-
tion ignites fiery L.A. riot. L. Robinson.
il Ebony 20:114-24 O '65
Two good cops in bad trouble; M. Hannon
and T. O'Neal. S. Alexander. Life 59:16 Jl
30 '65

Police department

Chief Parker and company; John Birch society members. Christian Cent 82:1308-9
O 27 '65

Politics and government

Jimmy for mayor. il Time 85:22 Mr 5 '65
Parks and politics in Los Angeles. F. M.
Brodie. il Reporter 32:39-42 F 11 '65
Somebody out there hates the Mayor. A.
Costy. New Repub 153:8-9 S 4 '65

Public library

See Los Angeles public library

Religious institutions and affairs

Vacuum in Los Angeles. Newsweek 66:43
S 6 '65

Riots

After the blood bath. il Newsweek 66:13-19
Ag 30 '65
Are we listening? Commonweal 82:612 S 3 '65;
Reply. C. P. Boyer. 82:711+ O 1 '65
Beyond the Los Angeles riots. M. L. King;
M. L. Schwartz. Sat R 48:33-7+ N 13 '65
Chief Parker and company; John Birch so-
ciety members. Christian Cent 82:1308-9 O
27 '65
Dispute over blame for the Los Angeles
riots; statements. S. W. Yorty; S. Shriver.
U S News 59:16 Ag 30 '65
End of a quiet summer; a flare-up of riots.
il U S News 59:6 Ag 23 '65
For shocked Los Angeles: now the morning
after. il U S News 59:34 S 6 '65
Innuendo and accusation; public hearings on
Negro riots. il Newsweek 66:30-1 S 27 '65
Library burns in the Los Angeles riot; Wil-
lowbrook branch; report. E. T. Moore. il
ALA Bul 59:983-6 D '65
Loneliest road; quietness in Negro ghetto
of Watts. il Time 86:10-11 Ag 27 '65
Los Angeles: and now what? America 113:
199 Ag 28 '65

Los Angeles riots: handling the topic in class;
symposium. il Sr Schol 87:sup8-10+ O 7;
sup5 O 14; sup5 O 21 '65; Excerpts. 87:9-
12+ O 28 '65
Los Angeles searches for answer to riots. il
Bsns W p28-9 Ag 21 '65
Los Angeles: the fire this time. il Newsweek 66:15-17 Ag 23 '65
LA: three who died; F. M. Hendricks, F. M.
George and C. P. Fizer. F. Knebel; S. Gor-
don; T. G. Harris. il Look 29:23-7 O 5 '65
McWhat report; reactions to McCone report.
il Newsweek 66:28-9 D 20 '65
Mrs Frye's fuse. il Time 86:36 N 12 '65
My friend in Watts; S. Sanders. S. Alex-
ander. Life 59:18 Ag 27 '65
No panacea. Christian Cent 82:1027 Ag 25
'65; Discussion. 82:1294+ O 20 '65
Out of a cauldron of hate, arson and death;
in Watts; with reports by M. Crawford
and D. Moser. il Life 59:20-34 Ag 27 '65
Psychiatrists analyze the Los Angeles riots.
F. R. Schreiber and M. Herman. il Sci
Digest 58:18-22 N '65
Race friction; now a crime problem? with
interview with W. H. Parker. il U S News
59:21-4 Ag 30 '65
Report on Watts; McCone commission's re-
port. il Newsweek 66:29-30+ D 13 '65
Riot as a weapon; the language of Watts.
S. Sanders. il Nation 201:490-3 D 20 '65
Search for why's. il Sr Schol 87:23-4+ S 23 '65
Second civil war; a closer look at Los An-
geles riots; excerpts from address, August
1965. M. B. Jackson. il U S News 59:80-2+
S 20 '65
Some Negroes riot but most go forward
Life 59:4 Ag 27 '65
TV's riot squad; bias in news coverage. J. G.
Dunne. New Repub 153:27-9 S 11 '65
Terror in Los Angeles; interview with a
policeman assigned to the Watts area.
Nat R 17:773-4 S 7 '65
This would never have happened, police ac-
tion ignites fiery L.A. riot. L. Robinson.
il Ebony 20:114-24 O '65
Trigger of hate. il Time 86:13-19 Ag 20 '65
Violence in Los Angeles. M. Boyd. Christian
Cent 82:1093-5 S 8 '65
Watts. E. Geller. il Library J 90:4388 O 15
'65
Watts: the fire next time. S. Alsop. il Sat
Eve Post 238:20 N 6 '65
Watts: the forgotten slum. C. McWilliams.
Nation 201:89-90 Ag 30 '65
Watts: the sad litany; report of McCone com-
mission. Nation 201:487 D 20 '65
What happened in Watts? letter to the edi-
tor. C. M. Weisenberg. Library J 90:5018+
N 15 '65
Who are the guilty ones? W. Herberg.
Nat R 17:769-70 S 7 '65
Why Negroes rioted in Watts; official report;
excerpts. il U S News 59:54 D 20 '65
Why's of Watts; report of commission to find
reasons for six-day uprising. Time 86:21 D
17 '65

Social conditions

Troubled Los Angeles; race is only one of
its problems. il U S News 59:58-62 Ag 30
'65

Stores

Sense of space in a small store; Flax build-
ing. il Arch Rec 137:200-1 My '65
Shopping in little Tokyo. il Sunset 135:46+
O '65

Water supply

Increase water supply, don't allocate shortages; plan for Colorado River. S. B. Nelson. il Am City 80:96-8 Mr '65

LOS ANGELES Angels (baseball) See Baseball
clubs

LOS ANGELES archdiocese. See Catholic church
—Dioceses

LOS ANGELES COUNTY, Calif.

Finance

Instant money for small-order purchases. V.
W. Quam. il Am City 80:118-19 My '65

LOS ANGELES COUNTY museum of art
Art wagon; Dr R. Brown's resignation. Nation 201:459-60 D 13 '65
Broken harness; trustees vote to dismiss director. il Time 86:76+ N 26 '65
Colossus in L.A. il Newsweek 65:84+ Ap 5
'65
Drawing the line in L.A; trustee interference
causes R. Brown's resignation. il Newsweek 66:98 N 22 '65
For $10 a burst of civic pride; a visit on
opening day. S. Alexander. Life 58:21 Ap
9 '65
Happy New Year. Dr Brown. S. Alexander.
Life 60:20 Ja 7 '66

LOS ANGELES COUNTY museum of art
—*Continued*
How to visit a museum: masterpieces to be exhibited. il McCalls 92:116-27 Ap '65
L.A. has a beautiful new art museum. il Sunset 134:42+ My '65
Los Angeles: salute to a new museum. K. Kuh. il Sat R 48:29-35 Ap 3 '65
Los Angeles: the new museum. A. Frankfurter. il Art N 64:30-4+ Mr '65
Los Angeles: the scene. J. Coplans. il Art N 64:28-9+ Mr '65
New York school question; interview, ed. by N. A. Levine. B. Newman. il Art N 64:38-42+ S '65
Temple on the tar pits. il Time 85:70-3 Ap 2 '65
Wondrous temple of art in L.A. il Life 58:30-1 Ap 9 '65

LOS ANGELES COUNTY public library
Library burns in the Los Angeles riot: Willowbrook branch; report. E. T. Moore. il ALA Bul 59:983-6 D '65

LOS ANGELES Dodgers (baseball) See Baseball clubs

LOS ANGELES-Honolulu race. See Yacht racing

LOS ANGELES Lakers (basketball team) See Basketball teams

LOS ANGELES neophonic orchestra. See Orchestras

LOS ANGELES philharmonic orchestra
Flashing music of Zubin Mehta. W. Malloch. Hi Fi 15:129 Ag '65

LOS ANGELES public library
EOA and LAPL. A. F. Mafrica. il Wilson Lib Bul 40:243-5 N '65
Numbers game: performance budgeting. H. L. Hamill. il Library J 90:3563-7 S 15 '65
Watts. E. Geller. il Library J 90:4388 O 15 '65

Branches
What happened in Watts? letter to the editor. C. M. Weisenberg. Library J 90:5018+ N 15 '65

LOS ANGELES times. See Times. Los Angeles

LOS ANGELES times Grand prix. See Automobile racing

LOSCUITO, Ned N. jr
Letters from a soldier; ed. by R. G. Deindorfer. pors Good H 161:68-9+ D '65

LOSS of memory. See Amnesia

LOST children. See Missing persons

LOST city of the Incas. See Machu Picchu, Peru

LOST days; story. See Lyons, R.

LOST persons. See Missing persons

LOST, strayed, stolen; story. See Fisher, M. F. K.

LOST wax process
Men, beeswax, and molten metal. P. J. Baus. il Natur Hist 74:18-25 bibliog(p74) Ag '65

LOTTERIES
Look at legalized gambling. V. W. Peterson. Christian Cent 82:675-9 My 26 '65
Second thoughts in New Hampshire. Christian Cent 82:1028 Ag 25 '65

LOTTMAN, Herbert R.
Christmas in France: selling books in English. Pub W 188.22-4 D 13 '65
France presents its 1965 literary prizes. Pub W 188:32-7 D 27 '65
Splendors and miseries of the literary cafe. Sat R 48:34-5+ Mr 13 '65
Third fall of Paris. N Y Times Mag p46-7+ N 28 '65
Venice: no one asks, gondola? Sat R 49:47+ Ja 1 '66
Warsaw book fair. Pub W 188:24-7 Jl 26 '65

LOTZ, Waltrud Klara Martha
Mayhem by mail; Israeli terrorist campaign against the West German scientists working on Nasser's rocket-development program. Newsweek 66:38 Ag 16 '65

LOTZ, Wolfgang
Mayhem by mail; Israeli terrorist campaign against the West German scientists working on Nasser's rocket-development program. Newsweek 66:38 Ag 16 '65
Price of success. il por Newsweek 66:32 S 6 '65

LOUD speaking apparatus
Bantam hi-fi speaker systems ride on air cushion. H. Fantel. il Pop Electr 22:40-3+ My '65
Build a stereo bal. D. Gordon. il Pop Electr 22:48-9+ Je '65
Compact loudspeaker systems. il Consumer Rep 30:210-16 Ap '65
Compact speaker you build from a kit. R. Benrey. il Pop Sci 187:127 N '65
Designing the hi-fi loudspeaker. A. B. Cohen. il Electr World 73:61-4+ Ap '65

Extension speakers. L. Buckwalter. il Hi Fi 15:70-3 Mr '65
Fantastic coneless loudspeaker! L. Steckler. il Pop Mech 124:36+ D '65
Haunted: sequence of notes of unknown cause, over public-address system in Penn station. New Yorker 41:42-4 S 18 '65
Interflex; hi-fi and stereo speaker system. E. Stowell. il Pop Mech 124:194-8 S '65
Magnificent monsters; report on large speakers. N. Eisenberg. il Hi Fi 15:55-9+ S '65
Phasing speaker systems. J. A. Dewar. il Pop Electr 23:66+ S '65
Placing the speakers. H. Fantel. Opera N 29:35 F 6 '65
Sound advice; auxiliary speakers for tape recorders. R. N. Angus. Mod Phot 29:12+ Jl '65

Cabinets
Build the Cinderella; hi-fi speaker enclosure. D. B. Weems. il Pop Electr 23:49-52 O '65
Mr Thursas' magic box. D. B. Weems. il Pop Electr 22:45-9 Ap '65
Unique 99¢ speaker enclosure. J. N. Ayres. il Pop Electr 23:52-3 N '65

Testing
How good is the new breed of compact speakers? H. Luckett and C. P. Gilmore. il Pop Sci 186:104-7 Mr '65
Transformerless multi-impedance test speaker. H. L. Davidson. il Pop Electr 23:59 S '65

LOUGHMILLER, Henry C.
I studied with Duveneck. Am Artist 29:40-5+ Mr '65

LOUGHRAN, Charles P.
Book reviews. America 113:296 S 18 '65

LOUIS, Arthur M.
Friendly Britannica. Nation 200:224-5 Mr 1 '65

LOUIS, Murray
Murray Louis and company, Henry street playhouse. D. Hering. il pors Dance Mag 39:24-6 F '65

LOUIS M. Rabinowitz foundation, incorporated
And in this corner... Nat R 17:406 My 18 '65

LOUISIANA
See also
Architecture, Domestic—Louisiana
Booksellers and bookselling—Louisiana
Hunting—Louisiana

Description and travel
Lessons in bayoumanship. H. Sutton. Sat R 49:92+ Ja 8 '66
Trembling prairie; great salt marshes of Louisiana. L. Dietz. il Field & S 69:57-9+ F '65

Race problems
Man in the middle. il Time 86:19 Jl 23 '65
Visit Bogalusa and you will look for me; Deacons for defense and justice. S. Alexander. Life 59:28 Jl 2 '65

LOUISIANA land and exploration company
Look at Louisiana land! J. B. Weiner. il Duns R 86:42-4+ O '65

LOUISIANA purchase
How lost was Zebulon Pike? D. Jackson. il Am Heritage 16:10-15+ F '65

LOUISIANA state university and agricultural and mechanical college, Baton Rouge

School of medicine at New Orleans
Residence hall. il Arch Rec 138:124-5 Ag '65

LOUISIANA state university press
La. state univ. to do Jefferson Davis papers. Pub W 187:51 Mr 1 '65

LOUISVILLE
Ambulance is not a hearse; police-operated system. R. H. Berg. il Look 29:40-2+ D 14 '65
Ham and hominy in Bourbon Town. L. Smith. il Sports Illus 22:47-51 Ap 26 '65

City planning
Progress in programming: a renewal scheme based on the problems of people. il Arch Forum 123:76-9 Jl '65

Education
NEA report on Louisville schools. Sch & Soc 93:342 O 2 '65

Music
In the Bluegrass: music new and old. W. Mootz. Hi Fi 15:155+ O '65
See also
Kentucky opera association

Newspapers
See also
Courier-journal

LOURDES, France
Behold thy mother, by S. Burden. Review
Pop Phot il 57:192-3 D '65. J. Barnett
LOURIE, Richard
English; poem. Nation 201:259 O 18 '65
LOURMAIS, Louis
Five against the gods. R. Daley. il por
Esquire 64:100-1+ N '65
LOUTH, John D.
Management's forgotten sales forecast. Duns
R 86:69+ O '65
LOUVRE, Paris
Red faces at the Louvre; cultural exchange
from Russia's hermitage and Pushkin col-
lections. il Time 86:74 O 29 '65
LOVE, Edmund G.
Hometown USA; excerpt from The situation
in Flushing. pors Sat Eve Post 238:32-6+
S 11 '65
LOVE, George H.
Some questions about mergers; address, Sep-
tember 27, 1965. Vital Speeches 32:9-12 O 15
'65
LOVE
Are you really in love? questions and an-
swers. L. David. il Read Digest 86:33-4+
Je '65
Are women more romantic than men? R.
Graves. il Life 59:126-8+ O 15 '65
Can love last forever? J. Brothers. Good H
160:68+ Mr '65
Do our children know you love them? P.
Popenoe. il Parents Mag 40:43-5+ D '65
First love, first heartbreak. L. Stinnett. il
McCalls 93:26+ O '65
Good advice from the social scientists. R. L.
Dean. Cath World 202:80-3 N '65
Grandad. P. M. Tate. il Read Digest 87:66-9
O '65
How to know when a child is happy. J.
Scott. Bet Hom & Gard 43:40+ F '65
Longing years; parents' love. P. Mozena.
Redbook 126:12+ N '65
Love is the only measure; with reply by
H. McCabe. J. Fletcher. Commonweal
83:427-32, 439-40 Ja 14 '66
Love: what is? where fails? L. Lee. Mlle 62:
100-1 D '65
Of love, etc. for Valentine's day; quotations,
comp. by E. F. Murphy. il N Y Times
Mag p14+ F 14 '65
What love is and isn't. S. de Beauvoir. il Mc-
Calls 92:71+ Ag '65
See also
Jealousy
LOVE (charity) See Charity
LOVE (theology)
Love is not enough. R. O. Johann. America
113:404 O 9 '65
Validity of absolutes; with reply by
J. Fletcher and rejoinder. H. McCabe.
Commonweal 83:432-7, 439-40 Ja 14 '66
LOVE, Maternal
Boy called funny face. F. F. Kirk. Read
Digest 87:93-7 O '65
Why babies love their mothers; reprint. il
Sci Digest 57:73-6 My '65
See also
Mothers
LOVE and wisdom; story. See Mountzoures,
H. L.
LOVELAND, Colo.
Brickwork piers form structural facade. il
Arch Rec 137:193 Je '65
LOVELESS, B. G.
Capital surroundings. Travel 124:42-4 Ag '65
LOVELL, Sir Bernard
He keeps score for the space race. il pors
Bsns W p96-8+ O 30 '65
LOVELL, Colin Rhys
Republic of South Africa. Cur Hist 48:226-31
Ap '65
LOVELL, James A. Jr
We felt content, cozy and safe and never got
bored. il pors Life 60:68-72 Ja 14 '66
about
Countdown for an astronaut's baby. M. Lov-
ell. il pors Life 59:48 D 3 '65
See also
Space flight—Manned flights—Borman-Lovell
flight, 1965
LOVELL, Marilyn
Countdown for an astronaut's baby. por Life
59:48 D 3 '65
LOVELORN columns. See Newspapers—Advice
columns
LOVELY, Walter G.
One treatment controls rootworm and corn
borer. Suc Farm 63:92 Mr '65
LOVERING, J. F. and Andersen, C. A.
Electron microprobe analysis of oxygen in an
iron meteorite. bibliog Science 147:734-6
F 12 '65
LOVE'S labour's lost; drama. See Shakespeare,
W.—Plays

LOVESEY, John
Automobiles. Sports Illus 23:68-70 N 8 '65
Boxing (cont) Sports Illus 22:72-3 My 24 '65
Track & field. Sports Illus 22:108+ Ap 19 '65
LOVESTONE, Jay
American labor abroad; Lovestone diplomacy;
with editorial comment. S. Lens. il Nation
201:2, 10-16+ Jl 5 '65
Unions briefed on red goals; ex-Communist
J. Lovestone says that Russia's aim is still
world domination. Bsns W p 127 My 15 '65
LOVETT, William
Rock-a-bye turkey. Field & S 70:8-9 D '65
LOVEY; drama. See Morganstern, J.
LOVIN, Carole Ann
Curl up and read. Seventeen 24:30 Ap '65
LOVOOS, Janice
Paintings of Jan Hoowij. Am Artist 29:66-71+
Je '65
Watercolors by James Couper Wright. Am
Artist 29:52-7+ O '65
LOW, Sir David
Cartoons; best of Winston Churchill. il Atlan
215:85 Mr '65
LOW, Robert A.
After the good white life. Sat R 48:31 F 6 '65
LOW altitude inertial navigation system. See
Inertial guidance systems
LOW altitude supersonic research vehicle. See
Guided missiles
LOW atmospheric pressure. See Atmospheric
pressure
LOW fat diet. See Diet in disease
LOW temperature research
Acoustical thermometer; ultrasonic interfero-
meter. H. H. Plumb and G. Cataland. bib-
liog il Science 150:155-61 O 8 '65
Chemical-biochemical signal and noise; adap-
tation of address, September 23, 1964. S.
Freed. bibliog il Science 150:576-84 O 29 '65
New science of supercold. A. Hamilton. il
Sci Digest 58:71-4 S '65
Ultraviolet damage to bacteria and bacterio-
phage at low temperatures. M. J. Ashwood-
Smith and others. bibliog il Science 149:
1103-5 S 3 '65
LOW temperatures
Can deep freeze conquer death? cryogenic
interment. R. C. W. Ettinger. il Ebony
21:60-1+ Ja '66
Cryogenic cooling by noncondensible-gas in-
jection. F. W. Lytle and J. T. Stoner. bib-
liog il Science 148:1721-3 Je 25 '65
Cryogenics in electronics. W. Nelson. il Electr
World 74:28-9+ D '65
Frozen Christian; cryogenic interment. R. C.
W. Ettinger. Christian Cent 82:1313-15 O
27 '65; Reply. L. J. Putnam. 82:1550+ D 15
'65
LOWDEN, Merle S.
From firefighting to revolution in three days.
Am For 71:16-19+ Ag '65
LOWE, David G.
House that Sam built. Am Heritage 16:67 O
'65
LOWE, George E.
Congress and scientific advice. Bul Atomic Sci
21:39-42 D '65
LOWELL, Robert
Applause for a prize poet; with excerpts
from his poems and statements. il pors
Life 58:49-50+ F 19 '65
Festival guest here beat his breast; refusal of
invitation to participate in White House
arts festival. il por Time 85:29 Je 11 '65
Freedom and style. H. Carruth. Poetry 106:
358-60 Ag '65
Lowell refuses to attend White House arts
festival. Pub W 187:77 Je 14 '65
Occasion for protest. Nation 200:658 Je 21 '65
Robert Lowell's Benito Cereno. C. J. Luten.
il por Am Rec G 31:806-7 My '65
Verse. L. Bogan. New Yorker 41:193-4+ Ap
10 '65
White House festival. S. Maloff. Commonweal
82:485-7 Jl 9 '65
LOWELL observatory, Flagstaff, Ariz. See
Astronomical observatories
LÖWENBRÄU brewery. See Breweries
LOWENFELS, Walter
World and self; instances. G. Sorrentino.
Poetry 106:307 Jl '65
LOWENS, Irving
Future of music librarianship. por Library J
90:1263-7 Mr 15 '65
Thirty world premieres. Américas 17:18-21
Jl '65
LOWENTHAL, Richard
Can we make common cause with Russia?
N Y Times Mag p34-5+ N 21 '65
Kremlin's difficult choice. Atlan 215:76-83
Ap '65
Soviets change their foreign policy. N Y
Times Mag p30-1+ Ap 4 '65
LOWER CALIFORNIA. See California, Lower

LOWRENCE, Mara
Cynthia and Mara. Carnegie recital hall. J. Maskey. Dance Mag 39:161-2 D '65

LOWRY, Elizabeth C.
Snob sidelines: chess sets, jigsaw puzzles, literary dolls. Pub W 187:100-4 Ap 26 '65

LOWRY, Howard J.
Blood in his eye. por Outdoor Life 136:28-9+ S '65

LOWRY, Malcolm
Harrowing hell. por Newsweek 66:105 D 20 '65
Lowry's subjective equipment. J. Wain. New Repub 154:23-4 Ja 15 '66
One great statement. G. Hicks. Sat R 48: 39-40 D 4 '65
One man's volcano. por Time 86:79+ D 31 '65
Tortured life is key to a masterwork. J. Davenport. Life 59:12+ D 10 '65

LOXTON, Howard
(ed) See De Mille, A. Viewpoint: Agnes De Mille

LOYALTY
See also
Patriotism

LOYALTY, Oaths of
Challenge to Georgia's loyalty oath law. Sch & Soc 93:363-4 O 16 '65
Loyalty oaths. Commonweal 82:396 Je 18 '65
Notes and comment. New Yorker 41:19 Ja 8 '66

LOYALTY investigations
Wanted: more political gadflies; Congressman C. E. Gallagher opposes government's psychological testing. Christian Cent 82:668 My 26 '65

LUBBERT, Carl A.
Trial at Tippecanoe. Recreation 58:130-1 Mr '65

LUBIN, Germaine
Lubin revisited. M. De Schauensee. il pors Opera N 30:26-8 Ja 22 '66

LUBOLD, Joyce Kissock
Feminine mistake; excerpt from This half of the apple is mine. Read Digest 86:55-7 Je '65
My love affair with the washing-machine man. Read Digest 87:60-2 Ag '65
Tiredest night of the week. Read Digest 87: 108-11 S '65
Two's company; or, What every woman knows; excerpt from This half of the apple is mine. Read Digest 87:135-6 D '65

LUBRICATION and lubricants
Motor oils. il Consumer Bul 48:16-17 D '65
Truth about multigrade oils. W. O. Koehler. il Pop Sci 188:106-8+ Ja '66
See also
Automobiles—Lubrication
Gas turbines, Aircraft—Lubrication

LUCA, Mark
Poetic license for all. Sch Arts 65:38 S '65

LUCAS, F. L.
Art of proverbs. Holiday 38:8+ S '65

LUCAS, Lawrence E.
Play of the month (cont) Cath World 201:215-16 Je '65

LUCAS, Victoria, pseud. See Plath, S.

LUCE, Clare (Boothe)
Crisis in the United Nations; address, December 10, 1964. Vital Speeches 31:236-41 F 1 '65
We do not all celebrate this occasion for the same reasons; excerpts from address, November 11, 1965. pors Nat R 17:1118 N 30 '65
Without portfolio. See issues of McCall's

about
Women. Criticism
Time il 86:94 N 12 '65

LUCE, Henry Robinson
First thirty-five years of Fortune. por Fortune 71:136-7+ F '65

LUCE, Phillip Abbott
Why I quit the extreme left. por Sat Eve Post 238:32-3 My 8 '65

LUCET, Charles E.
Changing the guard. il por Newsweek 66:49 S 27 '65

LUCEY, Robert E. abp
Southwest poverty. America 112:183 F 6 '65

LUCEY, William L.
Book review. America 113:412-13 O 9 '65
Home scene. America 113:680-2 N 27 '65

LUCID, Robert F.
Grapes of wrath in the vineyard of illiteracy. ALA Bul 59:525-7 Je '65

LUCIENTES, Francisco José de Goya y. See Goya y Lucientes, F. J. de

LUCIER, Josiah
Doc Lucier, who fights his war with a tin washbasin. M. Mok. il pors Life 59:64-9+ N 26 '65

LUCK, David J. and Nowak, Theodore
Product management, vision unfulfilled. Harvard Bsns R 43:143-50+ My '65

LUCK
See also
Superstition

LUCKETT, Hubert, and Gilmore, C. P.
How good is the new breed of compact speakers? Pop Sci 186:104-7 Mr '65

LUDWIG, Jack
Exile from the Emerald Isle. Nation 200: 287-8 Mr 15 '65

LUECKE, Richard
Sitting on a rainbow. Christian Cent 82:870-1 Jl 7 '65

LUELLEN, David E.
Vietnamese tragedy. NEA J 54:18 Ap '65

LUFFA cylindrica. See Gourds

LUFTHANSA. See Airlines—Germany (Federal Republic)

LUGGAGE
Choosing your luggage. A. Eisenberg and H. Eisenberg. il Holiday 38:131-6 D '65
Highly totable gifts for travelers. il House & Gard 128:324-5 N '65
New soft touch. il Seventeen 24:152 D '65
Samsonite: on land, in the air, on the sea. il Bsns W p98+ F 27 '65
Space race. il Seventeen 24:234-5 Ag '65
Travelers' aids. il Seventeen 24:146-7 My '65
See also
Packing of luggage

LUKACS, John A.
Battle that began a 100-year peace. N Y Times Mag p 10-11+ Je 13 '65
It's halfway to 1984. N Y Times Mag p8-9+ Ja 2 '66
Magyar wedding, Irish funeral. Esquire 64: 34+ Ag '65

LUKAS, J. Anthony
Congo is Kibweta not Leopoldville. por N Y Times Mag p24-5+ Mr 7 '65
Nehru's *munshi* comes out of Nehru's shadow. N Y Times Mag p54-5+ N 28 '65

LUKE, Saint
Greatest news story; excerpt from Christmas stocking. B. Considine. Todays Health 43: 18-19 D '65

LUKE, Sister Mary
Council and sisters' renewal. por Cath World 201:41-3+ Ap '65

LUKE, Robert A.
Operation alphabet. Wilson Lib Bul 40:54-6 S '65

LUKENS, C. R.
How to attract industry. Am City 80:104-5 Ag '65

LUKENS steel company
How Lukens turned out Titan plates. il Miss & Roc 17:35 Ag 30 '65
Whatever happened to Lukens steel? small company thriving among the giants. il Duns R 86:39+ Jl '65

LUKSUS, Tzaims
How Tzaims Luksus became a Vermont industrialist. por Life 60:54A Ja 14 '66

LULL, Howard W. See Reinhart, K. G. jt. auth.

LULU; opera. See Berg, A.

LUMB, H. C.
Excerpt from monograph, Three's a crowd. Cong Digest 44:213+ Ag '65

LUMBER

Drying
How to season green wood. Sunset 134:160+ Je '65

Grading
Nailing down lumber's ability to take stress; new machines grade wood strength faster. Bsns W p 150+ F 27 '65

Grading and standardization
Lumber standards dispute: when the bomb went off in the sawdust pile. il Am For 71:38-41 Jl '65
Whittling away at lumber size standards. Consumer Rep 31:5-6 Ja '66

Standards
See Lumber—Grading and standardization

LUMBER and lumbering
See also
United States—Forest products laboratory

LUMBER and sawmill workers (trade union)
Bargaining in the western lumber industry. J. L. Dana. il Mo Labor R 88:925-31 Ag '65

LUMBER industry and trade
Bargaining in the western lumber industry. J. L. Dana. il Mo Labor R 88:925-31 Ag '65
See also
National lumber manufacturers association
Teton studs, incorporated

Computer installations
Computers point way to profits in lumber. il Bsns W p80-1 Ja 1 '66

LUMBER industry and trade—*Continued*

Wages and hours

Wages in West Coast sawmills, June 1964. J. L. Dana. il Mo Labor R 88:678-80 Je '65

LUMBER workers

Wages in West Coast sawmills, June 1964. J. L. Dana. il Mo Labor R 88:678-80 Je '65

LUMBERING

Logging plant operated by data processing. il(p 193) Sci N L 88:201 S 25 '65

Tongass timber sale; Alaska's Tongass national forest. V. Metcalfe. il Am For 71:42+ S '65

Wasters: logging for floods; California, 1964. L. P. Hudson. il Nation 200:531-3 My 17 '65

See also

Boise Cascade corporation

LUMBERING machinery

New logging system like field artillery; Sund timber. il Sci N L 87:117 F 20 '65

LUMBYE, Hans Christian

Copenhagen pops! J. W. Barker. il Am Rec G 32:216-17 N '65

LUMINAIRES. See Street lighting fixtures

LUMINESCENCE

Ionizing waves of potential gradient. L. B. Loeb. bibliog il Science 148:1417-26 Je 11 '65

Paleotemperatures and chronology at archeological cave site revealed by thermoluminescence; Jaguar cave, Idaho. W. Dort, jr. and others. bibliog il Science 150:480-1 O 22 '65

LUMINESCENCE, Biological

Bioelectric control of bioluminescence in the dinoflagellate noctiluca. R. Eckert. bibliog il Science 147:1140-5 Mr 5 '65

Glowing report on that weird light of the sea; bioluminescence. F. A. Montgomery, jr. il Motor B 115:52-5 F '65

Optical second-harmonic generation in crystalline amino acids. K. E. Rieckhoff and W. L. Peticolas. bibliog il Science 147: 610-11 F 5 '65

See also

Fireflies

LUMINESCENCE dosimeters. See Radiometers

LUMPA sect (Zambia)

Question of theology. Newsweek 65:46+ Ap 19 '65

LUMUMBA, Patrice Emergy

Stanleyville massacre; excerpt from 111 days in Stanleyville. D. Reed. il Read Digest 87:233-8+ S '65

LUMUMBA university, Moscow. See Colleges and universities—Russia

LUNACY. See Insanity

LUNAR bases

Crowded moon forseen. J. Eberhart. il(p305) Sci N L 87:309 My 15 '65

Earthlings on moon must support selves. Sci N L 88:328 N 20 '65

LUNAR environment chamber. See Simulators

LUNAR international laboratory. See Space stations

LUNAR landing systems. See Space vehicles—Landing systems—Moon

LUNAR models. See Astronomical models

LUNAR orbiter photo craft. See Space vehicles

LUNAR probes

Apollo crater landing seen possible; Ranger IX photos. W. E. Wilks. Miss & Roc 16: 26+ Mr 29 '65

Atlas-Centaur shot bolsters Surveyor. Miss & Roc 17:16 Ag 16 '65

Boost for U.S: Ranger 8 flight. Sr Schol 86:23 Mr 11 '65

Centaur ready for critical launching. H. Taylor. Miss & Roc 16:11 Mr 1 '65

Drama from the moon: flight of Ranger IX. il Time 85:48 Ap 2 '65

Launch conflict to delay Surveyor again. Aviation W 83:32 D 6 '65

Lunar orbiter nears final configuration. H. D. Watkins. il Aviation W 82:42-3+ F 1 '65

Lunar orbiter perilune lowered. Aviation W 83:21 N 1 '65

Lunar results from Rangers 7 to 9. G. P. Kuiper. bibliog il Sky & Tel 29:293-308 My '65

Lunar surface structure probes studied. I. Stone. il Aviation W 82:46-8 F 8 '65

Mapping the moon; Ranger VIII. il Time 85: 58-9 F 26 '65

Mid-course change puts Ranger on target. Aviation W 82:34 F 22 '65

Moon men: conference at Goddard space flight center reporting on the pictures transmitted by Rangers VII, VIII. New Yorker 41:35-7 My 8 '65

Moon struck. W. J. Coughlin. Miss & Roc 16:46 Ap 12 '65

NASA hopes for surveyor launch in fall, despite failure of AC-5. G. Alexander. Aviation W 82:19 Mr 8 '65

New clues about the moon: fiery within, but safe on the surface? Ranger IX. il U S News 58:36 Ap 5 '65

Plan reflector on moon. Sci N L 87:355 Je 5 '65

Planners alter lunar orbiter trajectory. D. E. Fink. il Aviation W 83:49+ O 4 '65

Ranger 8 lunar reconnaissance. il Sky & Tel 29:205-9 Ap '65

Ranger hits the spot with its moon photos. il Bsns W p36-7 F 27 '65

Ranger missions to the moon. H. M. Schurmeier and others. il Sci Am 214:52-67 bibliog(p 134-5) Ja '66

Ranger IX may shoot Surveyor site; with editorial comment. W. E. Wilks. il Miss & Roc 16:18+, 46 Mr 1 '65

Ranger program ends in success. R. N. Watts, jr. Sky & Tel 29:280-1 My '65

Ranger program exceeds expectations. W. E. Wilks. il Miss & Roc 16:28+ Ap 5 '65

Rangers confirm moon landing areas. W. E. Wilks. Miss & Roc 16:22-3 Ap 12 '65

Rangers 8, 9 readied for flights to moon. Aviation W 82:52 F 15 '65

Ranger's-eye view. il Sci N L 87:149 Mr 6 '65

Report raps Surveyor management. H. M. David. Miss & Roc 17:16 N 1 '65

Soft landing on the moon. W. S. Griswold. il Pop Sci 187:102-5+ O '65

Still a big secret: is the moon a mantrap? results of Ranger VIII shot. il U S News 58:33-4 Mr 8 '65

Surveyor program procedures revamped. D. E. Fink. Aviation W 82:66-7+ Mr 22 '65

Surveyor unit permits live TV broadcast from Ranger 9. H. D. Watkins. il Aviation W 82:26-7 Mr 29 '65

Target for '66: a look around the moon. B. Frisch. il Sci Digest 59:16-17 Ja '66

Three steps to the moon: two US and one Russian achievement in space. il Bsns W p 144-6+ Mr 27 '65

To the moon, softly. W. J. Coughlin. Miss & Roc 17:46 N 1 '65

Via Ranger, rills and dimples; Ranger 8. il Newsweek 65:64-5 Mr 1 '65

Zond designed to transmit photos repeatedly from extreme ranges. il Aviation W 83:32 Ag 23 '65

LUNAR probes, Russian

Moonstruck; Lunik 5 failure. Newsweek 65: 103 My 24 '65

Russians hit moon again; Lunik-5 crashes. il Bsns W p25-6 My 15 '65

Soft landing the hard way; Lunik V. Time 85:72 My 21 '65

Soviet moon failure, a very near miss; Luna-7 crashes. Bsns W p 132+ O 16 '65

Zond 3 photographs moon. R. N. Watts, jr. il Sky & Tel 30:215-16 O '65

LUNAR research. See Moon

LUNAR roving vehicle. See Lunar vehicles

LUNAR simulators. See Simulators

LUNAR tides. See Tides

LUNAR vehicles

Grumman testing surface mobility; studying MOLAB operation. Miss & Roc 17:22 D 6 '65

Lunar crews to navigate by watching the stars; mobile lunar laboratory. Sci N L 87:264 Ap 24 '65

Lunar exploration systems advance. H. Taylor. Miss & Roc 17:10 Jl 12 '65

Lunar rover cabin space examined. il Miss & Roc 17:30+ O 4 '65

LUNCH boxes

Tiffin boxes from India. G. Kaler. il Hobbies 70:46+ D '65

LUNCHEONS

Craft-bazaar luncheon. il Bet Hom & Gard 43:82-3+ N '65

Happy marriage; the bride gives a party luncheon. il McCalls 92:38 Je '65

Luncheon for the girls. il Ebony 20:182+ Ap '65

Mom-daughter spring hat luncheon. il Farm J 89:88-9 My '65

See also

Brunches

LUNCHES

Lunch notes. See issues of Parents' magazine and better homemaking

Lunches kids like. il Parents Mag 41:84 Ja '66

Turn-table lunches; lunchbox and table! with recipes. il Seventeen 24:183-4 Ap '65

See also

Outdoor meals

LUNCHES, Employees

Meal ticket; employees at British firms enjoying free lunches. Newsweek 66:68 Ag 9 '65

LUNCHES, School. See School lunches

LUND, R. D.
Uncrossed visual pathways of hooded and albino rats. bibliog Science 149:1506 S 24 '65
LUND, Susan
Here comes a chopper. Vogue 145:68+ Ap 1 '65
LUNDAHL, Björn
Führer exposed. il por Time 85:85-6 Je 4 '65
LUNDBERG, B. K. O.
Supersonic adventure. Bul Atomic Sci 21:29-33 F '65
LUNDBERG, Trilby
Classical music swings. Seventeen 25:14 Ja '66
LUNDQUIST, Frank, and others
Glycerol metabolism in the human liver: inhibition by ethanol. bibliog Science 150:616-17 O 29 '65
LUNDY, Frank A. and Enerson, L. A.
Nebraska mounts a podium. Library J 90:5195-7 D 1 '65
LUNDY, Victor
In pursuit of diversity. il Time 86:56-8 Jl 2 '65
LUNG cancer. See Cancer
LUNGFISHES
Lungfish burrows from the Michigan coal basin. R. L. Carroll. bibliog il Science 148:963-4 My 14 '65
LUNGS
Fatty change of the granular pneumocyte. E. Valdivia and others. bibliog il Science 151:213-14 Ja 14 '66
Lung surfactants, counterions, and hysteresis. E. M. Scarpelli and others. bibliog il Science 148:1607-9 Je 18 '65
See also
Respiratory organs

Diseases

See also
Cystic fibrosis
Emphysema

Surgery

Extended effort; excerpts from Climate is hope, ed. by W. Ross. J. M. Chamberlain. il Todays Health 44:62-6+ Ja '66
LUNIK probes. See Lunar probes, Russian
LUNN, Sir Arnold
London scene. Nat R 17:836-8 S 21 '65
Reflections on Vatican II: Christianity in a secularized world. Nat R 18:19-21 Ja 11 '66
LUNT, Dudley C.
Science in action: winter bark, slow fire; excerpt from The woods and the sea. Natur Hist 74:57-8 Ap '65
LUNT, Storer Boardman
Take a bow. Pub W 187:22-3 My 31 '65
LURIA, S. E.
Molecular basis of heredity. Science 150:80-2 O 1 '65
LURIE, Diana
In Hefnerland. Women are status symbols. Life 59:70-3 O 29 '65
LURKIS, Alexander
How to cut your city's electric bill. Am City 80:53+ Je '65
LUSBY, Christopher Columbus
Ultimate weapon in war on poverty. il pors Nations Bsns 53:90+ F '65
LUSHER, David W.
Forecaster for the forecasters. il por Bsns W p 158+ Ap 3 '65
LÜST, R.
European space research organization. Science 149:394-7 Jl 23 '65
LUTEN, C. J.
Furtwängler Bruckner. Am Rec G 31:1052-3 Jl '65
Götterdämmerung. Am Rec G 31:952-5 Je '65
Juilliard string quartet: Bartók string Quartets nos. 1-6. Am Rec G 31:772-4 My '65
Pas de deux. Am Rec G 31:500-1 F '65
LUTHER, Martin
Pope John and Luther. C. Welch. Christian Cent 82:244+ F 24 '65
LUTHER; story. See Neugeboren, J.
LUTHERAN church in the United States
Hope for alcoholics; Lutheran institute of human ecology. A. P. Klausler. Christian Cent 82:221 F 17 '65
Lutheran church-Missouri synod in triennial session. D. Runge. Christian Cent 82:922-4 Jl 21 '65
Mission in the making: the missionary enterprise among Missouri synod Lutherans, 1846-1963, by F. D. Lueking. Review
Christian Cent 82:622+ My 12 '65. J. A. Scherer
Needed: a Lutheran profile of courage: rightist attacks against singers and speakers appearing at church conventions. Christian Cent 82:356 Mr 24 '65
Turning in the never buttons. Time 86:68 Jl 2 '65

LUTHERAN institute of human ecology. See Lutheran church in the United States
LUTHERER, Lorenz O. See Blatteis, C. M. jt. auth.
LÜTHY, Herbert
De Gaulle: pose and policy. For Affairs 43:561-73 Jl '65
LUTT, Bob
Music in the redwoods. J. Scott. il Am For 71:19+ Je '65
LUV; drama. See Schisgal, M.
LUXEMBOURG
View from the other side; address, November 23, 1965. P. R. Harris. Dept State Bul 54:17 Ja 3 '66
LWOFF, André
1965 Nobel laureates in medicine or physiology. G. S. Stent. por Science 150:462-4 O 22 '65
Nobel prize awarded. F. Marley. por Sci N L 88:261 O 23 '65
Revolution in the cell. Newsweek 66:77 O 25 '65
LYDON, Christopher
(ed) See Brenner, P. D. I believe
LYE, Len
Timehenge. il por Newsweek 65:94 Mr 22 '65
LYING
Truth about children's lying; excerpt from Life among the giants. L. R. Young. McCalls 93:186+ N '65
Web of lies. il Good H 160:44+ Mr '65
LYMPHOCYTES
Allograft survival: effect of antiserums to thymus glands and lymphocytes. H. Nagaya and H. O. Sieker. bibliog il Science 150:1181-2 N 26 '65
Defective RNA synthesis in lymphocytes from patients with primary agammaglobulinemia. M. J. Cline and H. H. Fudenberg. bibliog il Science 150:1311-12 D 3 '65
Lymphocyte lifetime in women. A. Norman and others. bibliog Science 147:745 F 12 '65
Lymphocytes of small mammals: spontaneous transformation in culture of blastoids. S. M. Sabesin. bibliog il Science 149:1385-7 S 17 '65
Mitosis: induction by cultures of human peripheral lymphocytes. N. Hashem. bibliog il Science 150:1460-2 D 10 '65
LYMPHOID cells
Contact-induced cytotoxicity by lymphoid cells containing foreign isoantigens. E. Möller. bibliog il Science 147:873-4+ F 19 '65
Focal antibody production by transferred spleen cells in irradiated mice. J. H. L. Playfair and others. bibliog il Science 149:998-1000 Ag 27 '65
LYMPHOMAS. See Tumors
LYNCH, Daniel
Confessions of a speechwriter. Duns R 86:42-3+ N '65
LYNCH, G. Leslie
Evaluation of concept. Recreation 58:236 My '65
Meeting recreation area standards (title varies) (cont) Recreation 58:80-1, 126-7 F-Mr '65
LYNCH, Jack
Last of the outlaw wolves. R. K. Massie. il por Sat Eve Post 239:71-4 Ja 15 '66
LYNCH, Kevin
City as environment: with biographical sketch. Sci Am 213:32, 209-14+ bibliog(p280) S '65
LYNCH, Kevin A.
Book of the month. Cath World 201:64+ Ap '65
LYNCHBURG, Va.
Future in retrospect! fiftieth birthday of Recreation department. M. F. Patterson. Recreation 58:486-7 D '65
LYNCHING
Little girl is dead, by H. Golden. Review
Life 59:15 D 3 '65. W. M. Kunstler
LYND, Staughton
And now the nouvelle gauche. il por Time 87:23 Ja 7 '66
Three characters in search of an offer. por Newsweek 67:18 Ja 10 '66
LYNDHURST (manor house) See New York (state)—Historic houses, etc.
LYNDON, Donlyn
In Canada, the continent's first single-structure campus. Arch Forum 123:13-21 D '65
LYNDS, Beverly T.
Notes on some planetary problems. Sky & Tel 30:80-3 Ag '65
LYNES, Russell
Antidote to nonsense. Harper 230:44 Ap '65
Auction by Early bird. Harper 231:28+ Ag '65

LYNES, Russell—*Continued*
Delightful provincialism of Portugal. Harper 231:32+ N '65
Goodbye to World's fairs. Harper 231:28+ O '65
Mrs Johnson's cultural cookout. Harper 231: 28+ S '65
Persia on the Hudson. Harper 230:30+ F '65
Two-a-day circuit in Virginia colleges. Harper 230:26+ Je '65

LYNN, John C.
Excerpt from testimony before Committee on foreign affairs, March 24, 1965. Cong Digest 44:176+ Je '65

LYNN, Kenneth S.
How bad was reconstruction? Reporter 32:48 Ap 22 '65

LYNNE, James Broom
Trigon. Criticism
New Yorker 41:196-7 O 16 '65

LYNXES
Big cat, the starving lynx. H. Hoover. il Audubon Mag 67:91-2 Mr '65

LYON, James B.
James B. Lyon, glassmaker & designer. A. G. Peterson. il Hobbies 70:72+ Jl '65

LYON, Ninette
Second fame: good food. See issues of Vogue

LYON, Peter
Ballad of Pete Seeger. Holiday 38:83-4+ Jl '65

LYONS, Daniel
Automation and mankind. por Cath World 201:126-31 My '65

LYONS, Eugene
Is a new revolution brewing in the U.S.S.R? Read Digest 87:213-14+ O '65

LYONS, J, and company
From tea to tease. il Time 86:97-8 O 29 '65

LYONS, Leonard
Practice! practice! Vogue 146:160+ D '65

LYONS, Nathan
Meaning must come from the picture itself. Pop Phot 57:60-1+ S '65

LYONS, Ruth
Lost days; story. McCalls 92:102-3 My '65
Something nice; story. Seventeen 24:138-9 N '65

LYREBIRDS
Changes in the tail feathers of the adolescent lyrebird. L. H. Smith. il Science 147: 510-13 Ja 29 '65; Correction. 149:565 Jl 30 '65

LYRIC opera of Chicago
Chicago. G. McElroy and J. Stedman. il Opera N 30:23 N 20; 32 D 25 '65; 30-1 Ja 1 '66

LYSAGER, Rachel Hope
Forestry's scientific U.N. Am For 71:28-30+ Ag '65
Wood keeps him warm. Am For 71:25+ F '65

LYSENKO, Trofim Denisovich
Final defeat for Comrade Lysenko. por Time 85:51 F 12 '65
Lysenko: Soviet science writes finis to geneticist's domination of nation's biological research. D. S. Greenberg. Science 147:716-17 F 12 '65
Rise and fall of Lysenko. E. W. Caspari and R. E. Marshak. Science 149:275-8 Jl 16 '65; Discussion. 149:1443-4+; 150:435 S 24, O 22 '65

LYSERGIC acid diethylamide
Drug puzzle; student use of drugs. M. Herr. Mlle 61:246-7+ Ag '65
Hearing color, smelling music, touching a scent; bizarre reactions become normal under the influence of LSD. L. W. Robinson. il N Y Times Mag p 14-15+ Ag 22 '65
How to use LSD. F. R. Schreiber and M. Herman. il Sci Digest 58:48-51 Ag '65
LSD and the anguish of dying. S. Cohen. Harper 231:69-72+ S '65; Reply. H. L. Wenger. 231:16+ D '65
LSD: contact high; effects of psychedelics. H. Junker. Nation 201:25-6 Jl 5 '65

LYSIS (bacteriology) See Bacteriolysis

LYSOSOMES
Lysosomal and free acid phosphatase in salivary glands of chironomus tentans. K. S. Schin and U. Clever. bibliog il Science 150:1053-5 N 19 '65
Primary lysosomes in tetrahymena pyriformis. A. M. Elliott. bibliog il Science 149:640-1 Ag 6 '65

LYSOZYME
Enzyme in three dimensions. Sci Am 213:46-8 Jl '65

LYTLE, Farrel W. and Stoner, J. T.
Cryogenic cooling by noncondensible-gas injection. bibliog Science 148:1721-3 Je 25 '65

M

M. A. Hanna company. See Hanna, M. A. company

MAC. See United States—Military airlift command

MCA incorporated
How to win star billing for an S&L. il Bsns W p90-2 My 1 '65

MDTA (Manpower development and training act) See Labor laws and legislation—United States

MFDP. See Mississippi freedom democratic party

MGIC. See Mortgage guarantee insurance corporation

MILA (Merritt Island launch area) See Proving grounds

MIT. See Massachusetts institute of technology, Cambridge

MKT. See Missouri-Kansas-Texas railroad

MLA. See Modern language association of America; Music library association

MLD. See Brain—Diseases

MMSW. See International union of mine, mill and smelter workers

MOL (manned orbiting laboratory) See Space stations

MRA. See Moral rearmament

MSTS. See United States—Military sea transportation service

MSU. See Michigan state university of agriculture and applied science, East Lansing

MUST (medical unit self-contained, transportable) See Hospitals, Military

MAAZEL, Lorin
Maazel era begins. P. Moor. il por Hi Fi 15: 180+ D '65
Music to my ears; Haydn's Seasons under L. Maazel. I. Kolodin. Sat R 48:32 My 1 '65
Musical events; concert performed by New York philharmonic. W. Sargeant. New Yorker 41:170+ Ap 17 '65

MACACA mulatta. See Monkeys

MACADAMIAS
See also
Cookery—Nuts

MCALEER, John J.
Book review. America 113:444-5 O 16 '65

MCALISTER, Clare
Commemorating Wagner. Opera N 29:17 F 13 '65

MCALISTER, Lyle N.
Changing concepts of the role of the military in Latin America; with questions and answers. bibliog f Ann Am Acad 360:85-98 Jl '65

MCALLISTER, Claire
Inventing to discover. L. Turco. Poetry 106: 369-70 Ag '65

MCALLISTER, William W.
Mac the Fac's last mission. por Time 85:31 Ap 30 '65

MACAO
Chip of old China. H. Sutton. il Sat R 48:56+ N 20 '65
Well traveled camera. H. Keppler. il Mod Phot 29:54+ My; 114+ Je '65

MACAPAGAL, Diosdado
Macapagal looks at Philippine problems; interview. por U S News 58:71 Je 14 '65

about
He gave the voters cut-rate food at the treasury's expense; with report by G. De Carvalho. il por Life 59:78A-80+ N 26 '65
Letter from Manila (cont) R. Shaplen. il New Yorker 41:84+ Ja 15 '66

MACAQUES. See Monkeys

MCARDLE, Kenneth
Behind the image. Sat R 48:72 O 9 '65

MACARONI
Great pasta dish from a 30-minute sauce. M. Kaytor. il Look 29:68-9 Ag 24 '65
Hurry-up luncheon dishes. M. B. Keiser. il Parents Mag 40:30+ O '65
Pass the pasta, please. B. M. Stover. il Parents Mag 40:110 O '65

MACARTHUR, Charles
Charlie; excerpt from A gift of joy; ed. by L. Funke. H. Hayes. por Read Digest 87: 126-9 N '65
Gift of joy; excerpts; ed. by L. Funke. H. Hayes. McCalls 92:73-5+ S '65

MACARTHUR, Douglas, 1880-1964
Soldier's prayer for his son. Read Digest 86:41 My '65
about
Of war, time, and generals. R. P. Knapp, jr. il Reporter 34:49-53 Ja 13 '66
Old soldier's rhetoric. C. B. Marshall. New Repub 153:26+ N 20 '65
Two fighting generals: Patton and MacArthur. J. M. Gavin. Atlan 215:58-61 F '65; Reply with rejoinder. H. E. Scott. 215:40 Je '65
MACARTHUR, Douglas, 1909-
America and Belgium; a community of interests; address, June 16, 1965. Dept State Bul 53:118-22 Jl 19 '65
MCARTHUR, Edwin
Kirsten Flagstad I knew; excerpt from Flagstad: a personal memoir. il Sat R 48:55-6+ S 25 '65
MACAULAY, Thomas Babington Macaulay, 1st baron
Magnificent middlebrow. W. H. Chamberlin. por Sat R 48:28-9+ O 9 '65
MACAULEY, Pauline
Creeper. Criticism
Christian Cent 82:1097 S 8 '65
MCBEE, Susanna
L.B.J. was worried about hollering judges. Life 59:62+ N 12 '65
New Hubert. Life 59:46A Jl 30 '65
Riots, songs and fishbowls, the hullabaloo is old hat to Hershey. Life 59:28-9 Ag 20 '65
MACBETH, George
Return; poem. New Yorker 41:26 Ja 1 '66
MCBRIDE, C. R.
Are agricultural missions out of date? Christian Cent 82:1606-7 D 29 '65
MCBROOM, Patricia
Compressed speech helps. Sci N L 88:214 O 2 '65
MCCABE, Bernard
Guises of love. Commonweal 83:270-3 D 3 '65
Taking Dickens seriously. Commonweal 82:244-7 My 14 '65
MCCABE, David
Groovy Beatie-type man is an Arthur. Mlle 62:180-1 N '65
MCCABE, Herbert
Validity of absolutes. Commonweal 83:432-7 Ja 14 '66
MCCAFFERTY, Phil
A's to your Q's about camera lenses. Pop Sci 187:120-3 O '65
Car air conditioner you install yourself. Pop Sci 186:126-8 Mr '65
How to buy the right ladder. Pop Sci 186:158-61+ Je '65
You can make wrought-iron furniture. Pop Sci 186:122-5 Je '65
MCCAFFREY, Austin J.
What's ahead in educational publishing? por Sr Schol 87:sup 13 N 18 '65
MCCAFFREY, Stanley
San Francisco: telling the Bay area story. Sat R 49:52+ Ja 8 '66
MCCAGUE, Bob
Brooklyn daily eagle and its post cards. Hobbies 70:118-19 Mr '65
MCCAIN, James A.
Goodness is as goodness does; address, May 30, 1965. Vital Speeches 31:598-600 Jl 15 '65
MCCALEB, B. M.
Abstract art; poem. Christian Cent 82:1542 D 15 '65
MCCALL, Wallace. See Mullaney, J. jt. auth.
MCCALLA, D. R.
Chloroplast mutagenesis: effect of N-methyl-N'-nitro-N-nitrosoguanidine and some other agents on euglena. bibliog Science 148:497-9 Ap 23 '65
MCCALL'S (periodical)
Golden mike awards. il McCalls 92:36+ My '65
MCCALLUM, David
Spy who'd rather not be known; ed. by E. Miller. por Seventeen 24:116-17 S '65
about
Man called I-I-l-y-a. B. Wolfe. il pors N Y Times Mag p56-7+ O 24 '65
U.N.C.L.E.'s Illya: new kind of TV idol. C. Brossard. il pors Look 29:79-82 Jl 27 '65
MCCAMPBELL, Beth
Curl up and read. Seventeen 24:288 Ag '65
MCCANDLESS, J. H.
Letter to an American adviser; poem. Christian Cent 82:398 Mr 31 '65
MACCANN, Donnarae
Wells of fancy, 1865-1965. por Wilson Lib Bul 40:334-43 D '65
MCCANN, G. D.
Nervous system research with computers. bibliog Science 148:1565-71 Je 18 '65

MCCANN, Raymond. See Lloyd, G. S. jt. auth.
MCCANN, Richard W. and Kempe, C. G.
Small-water-works automation earnings. Am City 80:91-2 My '65
MCCANN, William
Current U.S. patents. Sci N L 87:286, 302, 335, 349, 381, 398; 88:14, 61, 77, 109, 141 My 1-8, 22-29, Je 12-19, Jl 3, 24-31, Ag 14, 28 '65
MCCARL, Richard L. and others
Steroid stimulation of beating of cultured rat-heart cells. bibliog Science 150:1611-13 D 17 '65
MCCARRAN act. See Communism—United States—Anti-Communist measures
MCCARRAN-Walter immigration act. See Immigration and emigration law
MCCARRICK, Theodore E.
Top priority: a reply. America 114:70-1 Ja 15 '66
MCCARTEN, John
Theatre. See issues of New Yorker
MCCARTHY, Cormac
Bounty; story. Yale R 54:368-74 Mr '65
MCCARTHY, Glenn
Wildcatter's return. il por Newsweek 65:82-3 Mr 15 '65
MCCARTHY, Joe
Bar Harbor. Holiday 38:46-53+ Jl '65
(ed) See Allen, F. Quiet please; Mr Allen is back on the air.
MCCARTHY, Joseph Raymond
Days of shame, by C. E. Potter. Review
  Life 59:18 O 8 '65. D. Nevin
  Nat R 17:912 O 19 '65. W. F. Buckley, jr
  New Repub 153:28-31 N 20 '65. I. Silver
  Newsweek il por 66:109-10 O 11 '65
  Sat R 48:49 O 16 '65. N. S. Finney
Point of order; T. McIntyre's part in downfall of Sen. J. R. McCarthy. Newsweek 66:62 N 8 '65
MCCARTHY, Mary
Group on: The group. L. Lerman. il Mlle 61:166-8 S '65
MCCARTY, Maclyn. See Freimer, E. H. jt. auth.
MCCARVER, James Timothy
McCarver of the Cardinals: masked menace. T. Cohane. il pors Look 29:99-100+ Je 15 '65
MCCAUGHEY, Alex
Soup up your bounce shots. por U S Camera 28:18 Jl '65
MCCAULEY, James Emmit
What I have saw. por Time 86:80 Ag 20 '65
MCCAULEY, Robert H. collection. See Smithsonian institution—Museum of history and technology
MCCAY, Winsor
And a merry Christmas from Little Nemo! il Redbook 126:70-1 D '65
MCCLANE, A. J.
Angling in Austria. por Field & S 69:39-41+ Ap '65
Caliph of caviar. Field & S 70:36-8+ D '65
Cobras of the sea. Field & S 69:74+ F '65
(ed) Fishing. See issues of Field & stream
From aawa to zooplankton; concerning the compilation of the Fishing encyclopedia. Field & S 70:46-7 N '65
Guide to violence. Field & S 70:74-8+ My '65
Real savoy. Esquire 63:92-4+ F '65
Seafood freezer. Field & S 69:52-5+ Mr '65
Spring tide plugging. Field & S 69:100 Ap '65
Wyoming roundup. por Field & S 70:48-52+ Je '65
MCCLARREN, Robert R.
Volunteer for the cavalry. por Library J 90:2079-80 My 1 '65
MCCLELLAN, John Little
Harsh words about coddling of criminals; summary of statement, June 24, 1965. por U S News 59:16 Jl 5 '65
about
Iranian aid story: new twists to the mystery. F. J. Cook. Nation 200:550-6 My 24 '65
MCCLELLAND, Charles A.
Where is science taking us? excerpt from Nature of human conflict. por Sat R 48:45-6 Je 5 '65
MCCLELLAND, David C.
Achievement motivation can be developed. Harvard Bsns R 43:6-8+ N '65
MCCLELLAND, Keith
Piano lessons begin with a good teacher. Parents Mag 41:48-50+ Ja '66
MCCLINTOCK, Barbara
Making room for bold, new ideas. Todays Health 43:56-9 N '65
MCCLOSKEY, Margaret (Durand)
Our fair lady! Horn Bk 41:481-6 O '65
MCCLOSKEY, Mark
Change for the better; poem. Poetry 105:245 Ja '65
Seven poets. Poetry 105:270-3 Ja '65

MCCLOSKEY, Mark—*Continued*

about

Three poets. Poetry 107:125-7 N '65

MCCLOSKEY, Robert J.
U.S.-Italian exchange on North Viet-Nam contacts released; introductory statement, December 17, 1965. Dept State Bul 54:10-11 Ja 3 '66
United States reaffirms support of Geneva agreements on Laos; statement, January 18, 1965. Dept State Bul 52:167 F 8 '65

MCCLOY, John Jay
Ford foundation looks for new top command. por Bsns W p30-1 O 23 '65

MCCLURE, Alan, and Robinson, L. J.
Convention highlights from Reno. Sky & Tel 30:206-10 O '65

MCCLURE, Claude
Cardinal rule. por Newsweek 67:25 Ja 10 '66
On parole. por Newsweek 66:37-8 D 13 '65

MCCLURE, Eleanor
Little things count. Pop Gard 16:16-17 Jl '65
Lots of garden in a small space. Pop Gard 16:30 My '65

MCCLURG, A. C, and company
McClurg merchandise unit sold to Chicago group. Pub W 188:91 S 27 '65

MCCLURG, Jean
Trouble with my parents. Farm J 89:75 Ag '65

MCCLUSKEY, Elwood S.
Circadian rhythms in male ants of five diverse species. bibliog Science 150:1037-9 N 19 '65

MCCOLLOUGH, Celeste
Color adaptation of edge-detectors in the human visual system. bibliog Science 149:1115-16 S 3 '65

MACCOLLUM, Donald W.
Face maker. il Newsweek 67:52 Ja 24 '66

MCCOLLUM, L. F.
Importance of self confidence; address, February 26, 1965. Vital Speeches 31:441-4 My 1 '65

MCCOMB, Miss.
How it is in Mississippi. W. Rowland. Christian Cent 82:340+ Mr 17 '65
Meanwhile, in Mississippi. B. L. Smith. Commonweal 82:39-42 Ap 2 '65

MCCOMBE, John H.
(comp) Prayers for everyday. Read Digest 87:153-4 S '65

MCCOMBS, Nancy. See Cleland, R. jt. auth.

MCCOMBS, Philip A.
New American revolution. Nat R 17:766-8+ S 7 '65

MCCONE, John
Search for someone to fill the cloak. por Time 85:26 Ap 9 '65

MCCONKEY, James
Every day requires an atlas and more. New Yorker 41:64-8+ D 4 '65

MCCONKEY, Thomas W.
(ed) Library buying guide 1965. Library J 90:1624+ Ap 1 '65
(ed) Products & equipment. See first issue of each month of Library journal

MCCONNAUGHEY, Janet
It took two; poem. Horn Bk 41:674 D '65

MCCONNELL, Gene
Our rural schools aren't half good enough! por Farm J 89:70D Ap '65

MCCONNELL, Grant
P.R. in the forests. Nation 201:522-4 D 27 '65

MCCONNELL, James V.
Notes from an empty room; reprint. Horizon 7:42-7 Spr '65

MCCONNELL, John
New Lincoln letter: Lincoln aids John McConnell. W. C. Temple. Hobbies 69:110-11 F '65

MCCONNELL, John Paul
Lesson of Vietnam; address, December 6, 1965. Vital Speeches 32:182-4 Ja 1 '66; Excerpts. Aviation W 83:21 D 13 '65; U S News 59:24 Ja 17 '66
Role of airpower in Viet-Nam; address, September 16, 1965. Vital Speeches 32:12-15 O 15 '65

about

Changes for air force; new chief; new tactics. por U S News 58:16 F 8 '65
Management team. il por Time 85:22-23A F 5 '65

MCCONNELL, T. R.
Revolution in British higher education? NEA J 54:55-6+ My '65

MCCOOL, Francis
Jesuit aggiornamento. Commonweal 82:349-51 Je 4 '65

MCCORD, Jean
Every day is yesterday; story. Seventeen 24:142-3 My '65

Images of loss; story. Seventeen 24:246-7 Ag '65

MCCORD, William M.
We ask the wrong questions about crime. N Y Times Mag p27+ N 21 '65

MCCORKLE, Donald M.
Musical life in Salem. Antiques 88:65-8 Jl '65

MCCORKLE, George. See Melcher, D. jt. auth.

MCCORMAC, Billy M.
Radiation trapped in earth's magnetic field. Science 150:785-6 N 5 '65

MCCORMACK, Arthur
Books. Commonweal 82:477-8 Jl 2 '65
Economics of aid. Commonweal 81:227-30, 751+ N 13 '64, Mr 12 '65

MCCORMACK, James
Businessmen in the news. il por Fortune 72:81 D '65
New boss for Comsat. por Time 86:108+ O 22 '65

MCCORMACK, John William
Protecting the freshmen. New Repub 153:10-11 S 4 '65

MCCORMACK, Mark
Their hungry golfers feast on us. Sports Illus 23:16-17 Jl 26 '65

MCCORMACK, P. D. and Haltrecht, E. J.
Two-stage paired-associate learning and eye movements. bibliog Science 148:1749-50 Je 25 '65

MCCORMICK, Adoreen. See Hamer, E. E. jt. auth.

MCCORMICK, Richard A.
Abortion. America 112:877-81 Je 19 '65
Toward a new sexual morality? por Cath World 202:10-16 O '65

MCCORMICK, Tom
Tips for busy beginners. Writer 78:29-31 F '65

MCCORQUODALE, Marjorie K.
Poets and scientists. Bul Atomic Sci 21:18-20 N '65

MCCORRY, Vincent P.
Having a go at grog. America 112:225 F 13 '65

MCCORRY, Vincent P.
Letter from Lusaka. America 113:528-30 N 6 '65
Letter from Nairobi. America 114:20-1 Ja 1 '66
Report from Africa; from Lusaka, with love. America 112:881-2 Je 19 '65
Word. See issues of America

MCCOY, Joan
Hymn, a praise. Commonweal 83:317 D 10 '65

MCCOY, Paul S.
You don't belong to me; drama. Plays 24:15-28 Ap '65

MCCRACKEN, James
Economics of singing. Opera N 30:8-11 N 20 '65

MCCRACKEN, Paul W.
Outlook for 1966; address, September 23, 1965. Vital Speeches 32:15-18 O 15 '65
Three experts on the outlook. por Newsweek 67:52-3 Ja 10 '66

MCCRACKEN, Robert J.
Magic of Christmas. por Parents Mag 40:40 D '65

MCCRACKIN, Maurice
McCrackin, again. Christian Cent 82:452-3 Ap 14 '65
McCrackin reprise. F. Stauffer. Christian Cent 82:186 F 10 '65

MCCRAW, Harry Wells
Music in the Bayou. Hi Fi 15:130-1 Je '65

MCCREADY, Frank
No light meter. il pors U S Camera 28:58-9+ D '65

MCCREARY, Edward, Jr. and Guzzardi, Walter jr
Customer is a company's best friend. Fortune 17:180-2+ Je '65

MCCUBBIN, James W. and others
Arterial hypertension elicited by subpressor amounts of angiotensin. Science 149:1394-5 S 17 '65

MCCUE, G. A. and others
Western satellite research network. Sky & Tel 30:88-90 Ag '65

MCCULLOCH, Robert W.
Intergovernmental relations as seen by public officials. bibliog f Ann Am Acad 359:127-36 My '65

MCCUNE, Shannon
Ryukyu Islands. bibliog Focus 15:1-6 Mr '65

MCCUNE, Wesley
Freedom to read and the political problem; address, January 1965. ALA Bul 59:500-6 Je '65

MCCUTCHEON, Steve
Atomic blast vs otter? il Audubon Mag 67:376-81 N '65
Water highway to the top of the world. Pop Mech 124:102-5 Ag '65

MACDANIELS, L. H.
Gather walnuts, filberts, chestnuts and hickories in your garden. Horticulture 43: 22-3+ S '65
MCDAVID, Raven I.
Topping the okus in Bates' left prat. Nation 200:261-2 Mr 8 '65
MCDERMOTT, John J.
Books. Commonweal 82:731-2 O 1 '65
MCDERMOTT, John R.
Draft central, N.F.L.'s secret HQ. Life 59: 40-1 D 10 '65
Everybody's tripped up by the light fantastic. Life 58:78 Ag 23 '65
Last innings of greatness. Life 59:46B-53 Jl 30 '65
Life TV review. Life 58:18 Mr 26 '65
New breed of bronc buster. Life 59:60+ Ag 20 '65
Pros throw the book at Butkus and a rookie is blooded. Life 59:74S+ N 5 '65
Wait till this year. Life 58:75-6+ Mr 26 '65
MCDEVITT, Jan
Cloisonné. Craft Horiz 25:32-5 N '65
MCDIARMID, Colin. See Rilling, M. jt. auth.
MCDIVITT, James Alton
I'm thankful to be first; historic voices from space; conversation. U S News 58:35 Je 14 '65
What a real thrill it was to zap up. por Life 58:25-7+ Je 25 '65

about

Closing the gap. il por Time 85:24-8 Je 11 '65
How they shot the space walk. il U S Camera 28:68-9+ S '65
Men, the wives, the kids. il Newsweek 65: 32 Je 14 '65
Tumult on earth; series of tumultuous receptions. il por Time 85:33 Je 25 '65
See also
Space flight—Manned flights—McDivitt-White flight. 1965
MCDIVITT, James Alton, family
Down on earth, their kids plotted for bubble gum. J. Howard. il Life 58:40B Je 18 '65
MCDONAGH, Donald
On the podium: Robert Irving. Dance Mag 39:55-7 F '65
Unexpected assemblage! Dance Mag 39:42-5+ Je '65
MACDONALD, Bernice
Libraries and literacy activities; excerpts from report of the Study of services to adult illiterates. por Wilson Lib Bul 40:48-50 S '65
MACDONALD, David
Saga of Moby Doll. Read Digest 86:95-9 Ap '65
(ed) See Brophy, G. P. Thirteenth mission
MCDONALD, David J.
After steel election, the strike outlook now. il por U S News 58:37-8 F 22 '65
Battle for leadership: a major revolt in steel union. U S News 58:22 F 22 '65
Campaign '65: men of steel. il por Newsweek 65:64+ F 8 '65
Chances of avoiding a steel strike. U S News 58:93-4 Ap 26 '65
Photo finish in USW? il pors Bsns W p98-100 Ja 30 '65
Pressure on steel union to extend May 1 deadline for strike. por U S News 58:72 Mr 8 '65
Revolt of the left-outs; union malaise. S. Lens. Commonweal 82:441-4 Je 25 '65
Say a prayer. il por Time 85:24 My 28 '65
U.S. sweats out the steel vote. il por Newsweek 65:77-8 F 22 '65
USW may escape family fight. il Bsns W p49-50 My 1 '65
MCDONALD, David Lamar
Management team. il por Time 85:22-23A F 5 '65
MCDONALD, Dorothy
First things first. por Redbook 125:6+ Je '65
MACDONALD, Dwight
Crisis in American culture; address. por Wilson Lib Bul 39:740-4 My '65
Critique of the Warren report. Esquire 63: 59-63+ Mr '65
Films. See issues of Esquire
MCDONALD, Edwin A.
Rescue in the polar ice pack. por Pop Mech 124:92-6+ D '65
MCDONALD, James P.
One-man refuse collection. Am City 80:93 S '65
MCDONALD, John
Comsat compromise starts a revolution. Fortune 72:128-9 O '65
Syndication is the new big game at the racetrack. Fortune 73:159-63+ Ja '66
T.W.A: the struggle for the corporate cockpit. Fortune 71:106-11+ My '65

MCDONALD, Katherine Griffith
Three under stress. Opera N 29:24-5 F 6 '65
Wayward daughter. Opera N 30:22-3 D 25 '65
MCDONALD, Lucy
Stopping the hiccups. por Time 86:67 Jl 16 '65
MCDONALD, Martha Grayson
But, mom, all the other kids do it! Parents Mag 40:66-7+ O '65
MCDONALD, Shirley Louise Mendelson
Portrait of a racing lady. E. Crimmin. por Motor B 116:115-16 Ag '65
MCDONALD, Thoreau
Line drawings of Thoreau MacDonald. N. Kent. il Am Artist 29:36-41+ D '65
MCDONALD, Wesley L.
Navy war in Vietnam. S. Castin. il pors Look 29:28-31 N 30 '65
MACDONALD-WRIGHT, Stanton
Out there in the universe; exhibition at Knoedler gallery. il por Newsweek 66:88 N 1 '65
MCDONNELL, Gerald J, incorporated
New firm will finance educational technology. Pub W 188:30-1 Jl 26 '65
MCDONNELL, James Smith
He builds for space explorers. por Newsweek 66:65-7 Ag 16 '65
MCDONNELL, Thomas
Lark over a wheatfield; poem. America 112: 772 My 22 '65
MCDONNELL aircraft corporation
He builds for space explorers. il Newsweek 66:65-7 Ag 16 '65
St Louis blues; strike. Newsweek 66:72 N 29 '65
MCDONOUGH, James
Notes of a peace corps reject. Esquire 65:90+ Ja '66
MACDOUGALL, Allister
Christmas cactus. Horticulture 43:29+ D '65
MACDOUGALL, Ruth Doan
Man to marry; story, excerpt from Lilting house. Redbook 125:161 S '65
MCDOWELL, Bart
Changing face of Old Spain. por Nat Geog Mag 127:291-339 Mr '65
MCDOWELL, Roddy
Living for today. il pors Newsweek 66:98+ N 29 '65
MACDOWELL memorial colony, Peterboro, N.H.
Artists in paradise. H. Frost. il Opera N 29:6-11 F 27 '65
MCELHENY, Victor K.
Israel worries about its applied research. Science 147:1123-4+ Mr 5 '65
Research climate in Italy. II. Science 148:205-7 Ap 9 '65
MCENTEE, Howard G.
Battery-powered fluorescent light. Pop Sci 186:116-18 Je '65
Build your own capacitor-discharge ignition system. Pop Sci 186:94-7+ My '65
—and Walton, Harry
Be your own weatherman. Pop Sci 187:116-20+ Ag '65
MACEOIN, Gary
Book reviews. America 113:99 Jl 24 '65
MACER, George A.
Fluids in pregnancy. Redbook 125:28+ My '65
MACES, Ceremonial
Wood research in a hymn to Hippocrates. F. A. Strenge. il Am For 71:42-5+ My '65
MCEVOY, J. P.
To my son on his wedding day. Read Digest 86:160F-160G Je '65
MACEWAN, Gwendolyn
Poem for Gabriel. Atlan 215:165 Mr '65
MCEWEN, David
Lady Hesketh and her small, perfect palace. Vogue 147:144-51+ Ja 1 '66
MCEWEN, John
Australia: investors' paradise? summary of statements. U S News 58:83 Ap 5 '65
MCFADDEN, Dorothy
Gardens to visit. Pop Gard 16:40-4 Jl '65
MCFALL, Russell W.
Western union hums with data. il por Bsns W p 150-2+ F 20 '65
MCFARLAND, Gary
Jazz records. W. Balliett. New Yorker 41: 172-4 My 8 '65
Young art of Gary McFarland. R. F. Thompson. por Sat R 48:58-9 F 13 '65
MCFARLAND, James, Jr
In and out. Hot Rod 18:78-80 Ag '65
MCFARLAND, Jim
There arose such a clatter. Field & S 70:65-7+ O '65
MCFARLAND, Marvin W.
Service to an infinite public. por Library J 90:1053-7 Mr 1 '65

MCFARLAND, William N. and Munz, F. W.
Codominance of visual pigments in hybrid fishes. bibliog Science 150:1055-7 N 19 '65

MCFARLIN, D. E. and others
Immunoglobulin A production in ataxia telangiectasia. bibliog Science 150:1175-7 N 26 '65

MACFARQUHAR, Roderick
China goes it alone. Atlan 215:69-75 Ap '65

MCFEGGAN, James
Integrate your patching components. Am City 80:93-5 My '65

MCGAHERN, John
Irish censors deny entry to John McGahern novel. Pub W 188:40, 48 O 11 '65

MCGEE, Frank
Frank talk. Newsweek 67:52 Ja 3 '66

MCGEE, Gale W.
Excerpt from address, March 1, 1965. Cong Digest 44:122+ Ap '65

MCGEHEE, Charles. See Jackson, J. jt. auth.

MCGEHEE, Helen
Helen McGehee, 92nd street Y. M. Marks. Dance Mag 39:60-1 Je '65

MCGEOCH, Charlotte
Props from my farm. il Flower Grower 52:35 S '65

MCGERR, Patricia
There's a dividend in mysteries. Writer 78: 9-11 Ap '65

MCGHEE, George C.
Atlantic partnership and European unity; address, March 9, 1965. Dept State Bul 52: 582-8 Ap 19 '65
Frank look at some current issues in German-American relations; address, October 22, 1965. Dept State Bul 53:902-7 D 6 '65
Tasks of the free-world community; address, July 14, 1965. Dept State Bul 53:324-30 Ag 23 '65
Time for decision; address, May 30, 1965. Vital Speeches 31:579-80 Jl 15 '65; Dept State Bul 53:157-60 Jl 26 '65
United States and Germany: common goals; address, February 9, 1965. Dept State Bul 52:375-80 Mr 15 '65

MCGHEE, Peter S.
Thailand, next Asian domino? New Repub 153:11-12 Jl 10 '65

MCGIFFIN, Lee
Carefree years; story. Redbook 124:159 Ap '65

MCGILL, Ralph
Atlanta: the waiting game. Sat R 48:42-3 My 22 '65
W. E. B. DuBois. Atlan 216:78-81 N '65

MCGILL university, Montreal
We're nothing, but we want to be something; attitudes of students at University of Montreal, and McGill. R. Hoffmann. il Mlle 62:155-7+ N '65

MACGILLIVRAY, Leo
Puppets in wonderland. Recreation 58:73-5 F '65

MCGILLIVRAY, R. K.
No monopoly on snow-fighting. Am City 80: 102-3 D '65

MCGINLEY, Phyllis
Dinner party in Connecticut; poem. Atlan 216: 79 Jl '65
For better, for worse, but not for lunch. Ladies Home J 82:34+ F '65
What every (mother of the) bride should know. Ladies Home J 82:57+ Je '65

about

Poet's garden. M. E. O'Brien. il pors Pop Gard 16:20-3 S '65
Telltale hearth. il pors Time 85:74-6+ Je 18 '65; Same abr. with title Wit, wisdom and Phyllis McGinley. Read Digest 87:105-8 N '65

MCGINN, Lawrence C.
Problem child for both Schiller and Verdi, Don Carlo. Opera N 30:24-5 D 11 '65

MCGLINN, William D.
Symmetry principles at high energy. Science 148:671-2 Ap 30 '65

MCGLOIN, John Bernard
Archbishop comes home. America 112:360-1 Mr 13 '65

MCGOVERN, George S.
Excerpt from address, February 17, 1965. Cong Digest 44:121+ Ap '65
We can solve the Vietnam dilemma; excerpt from address, July 27, 1965. Sat R 48:37-8 O 16 '65

about

McGovern versus Nixon. Nation 200:126-7 F 8 '65

MCGOWAN, Jane
Matter of health; drama. Plays 24:70-6 Ap '65

MCGRATH, Lee Parr
Living with antiques. Antiques 87:208-11 F '65

MCGRATH, Mark G. bp
Impressions of the council. America 113:182-3 Ag 21 '65

MCGRAW-Hill, incorporated
Expansion gets larger share of spending; survey; with editorial comment. il Bsns W p24-6, 138 My 1 '65
McGraw-Hill delays merger with Standard & Poor's. Pub W 188:67 D 27 '65
McGraw-Hill set to acquire Standard & Poor's. Pub W 188:55 O 25 '65
Putting facts together; Standard & Poors to merge with McGraw-Hill. Time 86:92 O 29 '65
Relating to ETV. C. G. Benjamin. Pub W 187:15-17 Ap 5 '65

MCGRAW-Hill book company. See McGraw-Hill, incorporated

MCGRAW-Hill publishing company. See McGraw-Hill, incorporated

MCGREGOR, Janet
It was a beautiful wedding, but... Good H 161:90-1+ N '65

MCGREGOR, Tex.
Don't have one? we'll build it. L. H. Muegge. il Am City 80:116-17 Ag '65

MCGREW, M. E. and Fried, Norm
Amplifier module electrifies guitar. Pop Electr 22:646 Je '65

MCGRORY, Mary
Washington front. See occasional issues of America

MCGUIRE, Alice Brooks
New wing at Casis. Library J 90:5460-2 D 15 '65

MCGUIRE, Barry
Children of Bobby Dylan. il pors Life 59:43-4+ N 5 '65

MCGUIRE, F. E.
First computer center billing. Am City 80: 102-3 My '65

MACH, Bernard, and Vassalli, Pierre
Template activity of RNA from antibody-producing tissues. bibliog Science 150:622-6 O 29 '65

MACH, Ernst
Ernst Mach; biographical notes. H. W. Pittenger. bibliog il por Science 150:1120-2 N 26 '65

MCHALE, Jane
Mademoiselle's guest editors: 1965. Mlle 61: 224-5 Ag '65

MACHEN, Eddie
No place to wear his crown. T. Maule. il por Sports Illus 22:28-9 Mr 15 '65

MACHIAVELLI, Niccolò
Machiavelli. K. Rexroth. Sat R 48:25 O 2 '65
Machiavelli speaks; comp. by R. Block. por N Y Times Mag p57-8 Mr 14 '65
Two great Florentines. R. Moley. Newsweek 65:88 My 31 '65

MACHINE age
See also
Technology and civilization

MACHINE tool industry and trade
Most frustrating industry of all. il Duns R 85:52-4+ My '65
See also
Simmons machine tool corporation

MACHINE tools
Shop talk. S. M. Gallager. See issues of Popular science monthly
Which power tool to buy? Bet Hom & Gard 43:40+ Mr '65
Workshop and garden equipment. il Consumer Rep 30:166-202 D '65
See also
Grinding machines
Lathes
Planing machines

Control

Cheaper automatic machining; numerical controls. il Bsns W p58-60 Ap 10 '65
Finding new ways to make autos. il Bsns W p 190-2+ S 11 '65
Ford lifts lid on secret; numerical control in auto production. il Bsns W p 140+ Ja 15 '66
Numerical control: from class to mass market. H. H. E. Klein. il Duns R 86:34-5+ Ag '65
Prospects for numerical control of machine tools. J. J. Macut. il Mo Labor R 88:403-6 Ap '65

Exhibitions

Machine tools gear for steady rise; show in Chicago's International amphitheatre. il Bsns W p47-8+ S 25 '65
Machine tools go onstage in biggest show; National machine tool builders association show, Chicago. il Bsns W p26-7 S 11 '65

Numerical control
See Machine tools—Control

MACHINE translators. See Translating machines

MACHINE works

Employees
See also
Machinery industry—Wages and hours

MACHINERY
See also
Agricultural machinery
Bookbinding machinery

Stands
Sander stand swallows its own dust; combining belt-disk sander and shop vacuum. J. Copeland.. il Pop Sci 186:158-61 My '65

MACHINERY, Automatic
Black-box plant is coming. E. Landes. il Duns R 85:pt2 114-17+ Mr '65
Finding new ways to make autos. il Bsns W p 190-2+ S 11 '65
Inevitable science of human engineering. G. Berkwitt. il Duns R 86:45-7+ O '65
See also
Automation
Packaging machinery

MACHINERY in industry
See also
Automation
Unemployment, Technological

MACHINERY industry

Wages and hours
Earnings in the machinery industries, March-May 1964. F. W. Mohr. il Mo Labor R 88: 174-7 F '65

MACHINES, Copying. See Copying processes

MACHINISTS union. See International association of machinists

MACHU PICCHU, Peru
Message from a dead city; reprint. J. L. Jones. Am For 17:34 Mr '65

MCHUGH, Keith Stratton
How New York pushes its wares overseas. il por Bsns W p32 S 11 '65

MCHUGH, Vincent
Holiday handbook. Holiday 38:141-6 O '65

MACHUPO virus. See Viruses

MCILHENNY, Walter S.
Enchantment in the Louisiana marshes. K. Hamill. il por Fortune 72:158-64 O '65

MCILHENNY company
Sweet and hot; island history and resources. H. Sutton. il Sat R 49:46-7 Ja 15 '66

MCINERNY, Ralph M.
Thomism in an age of renewal. America 113: 258-60 S 11 '65

MACINKO, George
Saturation: a problem evaded in planning land use. bibliog Science 149:516-21 Jl 30 '65

MACINNES, Colin
Old English music hall songs are new. N Y Times Mag p62-3+ N 28 '65

MCINTIRE, Carl
Liberal intolerance. por Time 85:65 F 12 '65
Who's afraid of McIntire; discussion. Christian Cent 82:344 Mr 17 '65

MCINTIRE, K. R. and others
Macroglobulin-producing plasma-cell tumor in mice: identification of a new light chain. bibliog Science 150:361-3 O 15 '65

MCINTYRE, Edward F.
Antidotes for noise. Hi Fi 15:39-42+ Jl '65

MCINTYRE, James Francis, cardinal
With such friends . . charges against the Cardinal. Christian Cent 82:1052 S 1 '65

MCINTYRE, John P.
Library cooperation in Dade County. por ALA Bul 59:540-2 Je '65

MCINTYRE, Robert L.
What you should know about depth in pictures. Pop Phot 56:60 Je '65

MCINTYRE, Thomas J.
Excerpt from debate, August 30, 1965. Cong Digest 44:242+ O'65

MCINTYRE, Tommy
Point of order; T. McIntyre's part in downfall of Sen. J. R. McCarthy. por Newsweek 66:62 N 8 '65

MACINTYRE, Walter M.
Charge-transfer self-complex formed by 8-azaguanine. bibliog Science 147:507-8 Ja 29 '65

MCISAAC, William M. and others
Indole compounds: isolation from pineal tissue. bibliog Science 148:102-3 Ap 2 '65

MCJENKIN, Virginia
(ed) Service to students; joint responsibility of school and public libraries. bibliog il ALA Bul 59:540-2, 649-52, 733-44; 60:63-72 Je-S '65, Ja '66

MACK, Richard
Hiking away to the woods; paintings by F. Golden; with account by D. Barnes. Sports Illus 22:42-9 My 31 '65

MACK, Ruth. See Ponnamperuma, C. jt. auth.

MCKAIN, David
Neighbor; Monologue; poems. Poetry 107:91-2 N '65

MACKAY, Colin, and Wolfgang, Richard
Free carbon atom chemistry. bibliog Science 148:899-907 My 14 '65

MACKAY, John A.
Latin America and revolution. Christian Cent 82:1409-12, 1439-43 N 17-24 '65

MCKECHNIE, Gene
No time to climb. pors Outdoor Life 136:48-9+ O '65

MCKEE, William F.
McKee confirmation follows quiet hearing. Aviation W 83:25 Jl 5 '65

MCKEEN, John E.
Pfizer's self-prescribed tonic. il por Fortune 72:152-5+ Ag '65

MCKEITHEN, John J.
Man in the middle. il por Time 86:19 Jl 23 '65

MCKELVEY, Blake
City historian. Am City 80:40d My '65

MCKELWAY, St Clair
Close to mom; story. New Yorker 41:28-31 Ag 21 '65
Mr Whitweeks' massive tone; whistlers rampant in Robinson opera; other notes. New Yorker 41:144+ Mr 6 '65
Paris at long last. Holiday 38:16+ S '65
Princeton pond. New Yorker 41:48+ Ja 1 '66
This world we live in. New Yorker 41:155-6+ S 11 '65

MCKENDRICK, Norman G.
Stroll; poem. America 113:671 N 27 '65

MCKENNA, Joseph
Supreme court justice steps down. D. J. Danelski. Yale R 54:411-25 Mr '65

MCKENNA, Malcolm C.
Undersea history of America; reprint. Sci Digest 57:80-3 Ap '65

MCKENNA, Tatiana
Wedding cook book. House & Gard 127:175+ My '65

MCKENTY, Neil
Last hurrah as the power failed. America 113:665 N 27 '65

MACKENZIE, Fred T. and Garrels, R. M.
Silicates: reactivity with sea water. bibliog Science 150:57-8 O 1 '65

MACKENZIE RIVER, Canada
Arctic adventure. C. E. Gillham. il Field & S 70:40-2+ Ag '65

MCKEON, William
No inferences, please. il por Time 85:25 F 5 '65

MCKEOWN, Raymond M.
How AMA research into smoking will help you. Todays Health 43:12-13 Ag '65

MCKEOWN, William Taylor
This boat is looking for trouble. Esquire 63: 102-5+ Mr '65
Ultimate motorboat tour. Esquire 63:110-11+ Je '65

MACKEREL fishing
Pint-size speedster. G. Heinold. il Outdoor Life 136:14-15 N '65
To catch a king. E. Buckow. il Field & S 70: 96-8+ D '65

MCKERVILL, Hugh W.
Most unforgettable character I've met. Read Digest 87:223-4+ O '65

MACKEY, Ernan
First farewell; story. Redbook 125:58-9 S '65

MACKEY, Jerome
Mr Judo. C. S. Wren. il pors Look 29:64-5 Mr 9 '65

MACKEY of Appalachia; musical comedy. See Musical comedies, revues, etc.—Criticisms, plots, etc.

MACKIE, Romaine P.
Special education reaches nearly 2 million children. Sch Life 47:8-9 D '64

MCKIE, Roy
Niceties of the ice. il Sports Illus 23:24-6+ N 1 '65

MCKIERNAN, Joseph
Anniversary; poem. America 113:441 O 16 '65

MACKINAC race. See Yacht racing

MCKINLEY, Fred
We hunt the littlest big game. Outdoor Life 135:32-3+ Mr '65

MCKINLEY, Georgia
Fragile heaven; story. Redbook 125:58-9 Ag '65

MCKINLEY, William
William McKinley, twenty-fifth President. F. Freidel. il por Nat Geog Mag 127:708-11 My '65

MCKINLEY NATIONAL PARK. See Mount McKinley National Park

MCKINNON, James
  Book reviews. America 113:58 Jl 10 '65
MCKINSEY and company
  Patchwork quilt of pension programs. il Bsns
    W p46-8 S 4 '65
MCKINSEY foundation
  It's the men up front that count. il Bsns W
    p73-5 My 1 '65
  Prize books for management shelf. Bsns W
    p75 My 1 '65
MCKINSTRY, Arthur Raymond
  Faith and form at Saratoga. W. Tower. il
    Sports Illus 23:14-15 Ag 16 '65
MACKINTOSH, Helen K. See Lewis, G. jt.
    auth.
MACKINTOSH, Malcolm
  Military aspects of the Sino-Soviet dispute.
    Bul Atomic Sci 21:14-17 O '65
MCKITTERICK, Nathaniel
  Closed shop for monetary reform. New Repub
    153:9-10 S 25 '65
  Diplomatic logjam. New Repub 152:8-11 Mr
    27 '65
  Fragments of a dream. New Repub 152:22-3
    My 15 '65
  Goldberg at the UN. New Repub 153:13-15
    S 11 '65
  Marshall plan for east Europe? New Repub
    152:26-7 Je 26 '65
  Perking up the Nation's parks. New Repub
    153:15-16 S 18 '65
  Plumbing our leaky payments balance. New
    Repub 152:10-11 F 27 '65
MCKNEW, Thomas W.
  Four-ocean navy in the nuclear age. por Nat
    Geog Mag 127:145-87 F '65
MCKUSICK, Victor A.
  Royal hemophilia; with biographical sketch.
    Sci Am 213:11, 88-95 bibliog(p 120) Ag; 6 D
    '65
MCLAIN, James
  Trade! trade! who'll hoss trade? por Rec-
    reation 58:187-8 Ap '65
MACLAIN, Jon
  Angel's Il Trovatore. Am Rec G 31:1048-50
    Jl '65
  Book review. Am Rec G 32:132+ O '65
  Helge Roswaenge, apparent eternal youth.
    Am Rec G 31:624-5 Mr '65
  Life and loves of La Nordica. Am Rec G
    31:884-5 My '65
  Maria Callas returns to Tosca. Am Rec G
    31:688-90+ Ap '65
MCLAIN, Pete
  Dig those crazy brant. por Field & S 70:39-41
    D '65
  Stealthy approach for stripers. Field & S 70:
    18-20+ Je '65
MCLANE, Charles B.
  U.S.S.R. policy in Asia. Cur Hist 49:214-20+
    O '65
MACLANE, Saunders
  Can we buy quality in science? Bul Atomic
    Sci 21:6-11 N '65
MCLAREN, Norman
  Paint a movie on film! E. Davis. il Pop Phot
    56:120 My '65
MCLAUCHLIN, W. A.
  Castle Frank high school: new concept in
    secondary education. Sr Schol 86:sup 10
    My 20 '65
MCLAUGHLIN, David J. See Foote, G. H. jt.
    auth.
MCLAUGHLIN, John
  Movie of the month (cont) Cath World 202:
    190-2 D '65
MCLAUGHLIN, Lorrie
  Can you learn to write? Writer 78:31-3 D '65
MCLAUGHLIN, Marya
  Legwomen. il por Newsweek 65:58 Je 21 '65
MCLAUGHLIN, Mignon
  Neurotic's notebook (cont) Atlan 215:134 Ap;
    216:129 Jl; 118 D '65
MCLAUGHLIN, William
  Killers; poem. Nation 200:404 Ap 12 '65
MCLEAN, David A.
  Death and the law in Bena Kanyoka. Re-
    porter 33:44-5 D 2 '65
MACLEAN, Donald I.
  Can we talk to Marxian atheists? opening
    attempt. America 113:115-17 Jl 31 '65
MACLEAN, F. I. and others
  Photosynthetic phosphorylation: stimulation
    by pteridines and a comparison with phos-
    phodoxin. bibliog Science 149:636-8 Ag 6 '65
MCLEAN, Herbert E.
  Jet age camping. il Am For 71:16-17+ Jl '65
MCLEAN, Paul
  How to match your money to your dreams.
    Parents Mag 40:58-9+ F '65
MACLEAN, Paul D.
  Mirror display in the squirrel monkey, saimiri
    sciureus. bibliog Science 146:950-2; 147:1157
    N 13 '64, Mr 5 '65

MCLEAN, Wilmer
  Tale of a table. M. A. Benjamin. il Am
    Heritage 16:100-1 Ap '65
MACLEISH, Archibald
  Eleanor Roosevelt; excerpt from script of
    film. McCalls 92:98-101+ My '65
  Former librarian of Congress questions US
    foreign policy. Library J 90:2984 Jl '65
  Talent for joy. Sat R 48:25-6 N 27 '65
  United Nations hold memorial ceremony for
    Ambassador Stevenson; remarks, July 19,
    1965. Dept State Bul 53:231-3 Ag 9 '65
  What is realism doing to American history?
    adaptation of address. por Sat R 48:10-12
    Jl 3 '65

                        about
  Brush of a comet. F. Frankfurter; D. C.
    Mearns. por Atlan 215:90-2 My '65
  Herakles. Criticism
    Life 59:10 D 3 '65
MACLEISH, Kenneth
  Land of Galilee. Nat Geog Mag 128:832-65
    D '65
MCLEMORE, W. P.
  History; poem. Negro Hist Bul 28:140 Mr '65
MACLENNAN, Hugh
  Canada. Am Heritage 17:6-45+ D '65
MCLEOD, G. R.
  How the RTCM helps boatmen. por Motor B
    115:52-3 Ap '65
MACLEOD, Margaretha Geertruida (Zelle) See
    Mata Hari
MAC LOW, Jackson
  From the pronouns, forty dances for the
    dancers; poem. Nation 200:150 F 8 '65
MCLUHAN, Herbert Marshall
  Books. H. Rosenberg. New Yorker 41:129-36
    F 27 '65
  McLuhan metaphor. New Yorker 41:43-4 My
    15 '65
  Marshall McLuhan: Canada's intellectual
    comet. R. Schickel. Harper 231:62-8 N '65
MCMAHAN, Ida, and Whitehorn, Ethel
  Motion picture previews. See issues of PTA
    magazine
MCMAHON, Frances E.
  Orestes Brownson. Commonweal 83:260 D 3
    '65
MCMILLEN, Wheeler
  Four simple words. Read Digest 86:24B F
    '65
MCMULLEN, Roy
  Composers on the rostrum. Hi Fi 15:133+
    Ag '65
  Crisis in all Gaul. Hi Fi 15:128-9 My '65
  Festival à la mode; Aix report. Hi Fi 15:167
    O '65
  Marais festival. Hi Fi 15:162 S '65
  Michelangeli and the machine. Hi Fi 16:46-9
    Ja '66
  New look for the Opera-comique. Hi Fi 15:
    116-17 Jl '65
  Notes from our correspondents. See issues
    of High fidelity incorporating Musical
    America
  Prestige of the organ. Hi Fi 15:181 D '65
  Season strangely flavored. Hi Fi 15:138 Je '65
  Ubiquitous flutist. Hi Fi 15:34-7+ My '65
  Uproar at the Champs-Elysées. Hi Fi 15:
    143-4 Ap '65
  Wieland Wagner's Fidelio. Hi Fi 16:148-9 Ja
    '66
MACMURRAY, Fred
  He likes to cook. por Bet Hom & Gard 43:
    30+ Ap '65
MCMURRY, Robert N.
  Clear communications for chief executives.
    Harvard Bsns R 43:131-2+ Mr '65
MCMURTRY, Larry
  Texas: good times gone, or here again?
    Holiday 38:58-9+ S '65
MCNAIR, Barbara
  I'm gonna make it. por Newsweek 67:64 Ja 10
    '66
MCNAIR, Donald
  Yachting asks about wooden-kit boatbuild-
    ing; interview, ed. by E. Robberson. por
    Yachting 117:61-4+ Mr '65
MCNAIR, Malcolm P.
  Grads honor the dean of retailers. il pors
    Bsns W p 130+ Je 12 '65
MCNALLY, Robert E.
  Books. Commonweal 83:221-2 N 19 '65
MCNALLY, Terrence
  And things that go bump in the night.
    Criticism
    Commonweal 82:290+ My 21 '65
    Sat R 48:24 My 15 '65
    Time il 85:88-9 My 7 '65
MCNAMARA, Eugene
  Certain gestures; poem. America 113:20 Jl
    3 '65

MCNAMARA, Robert Strange
Buildup of U.S. forces in Viet-Nam; statement, August 4, 1965. Dept State Bul 53: 369-74 Ag 30 '65
Excerpt from testimony before Committee on foreign affairs, March 11, 1965. Cong Digest 44:179+ Je '65
Is Russia slowing down in arms race? interview. pors U S News 58:52-6+ Ap 12 '65
Memorandum for the President; allocation of additional appropriation for military requirements in Vietnam. Dept State Bul 52: 896-7 Je 7 '65
Political and military aspects of U.S. policy in Viet-Nam; interview, August 9, 1965. Dept State Bul 53:342-56 Ag 30 '65
President Johnson and Secretary McNamara review situation in Viet-Nam; news conference, April 26, 1965. Dept State Bul 52:749-57 My 17 '65; Excerpts. Aviation W 82:20 My 3 '65
Secretary McNamara discusses buildup of forces in Viet-Nam; news conference, June 16, 1965. Dept State Bul 53:12-19 Jl 5 '65
Secretary McNamara discusses U.S. operations in Viet-Nam; questions and answers, July 14, 1965. Dept State Bul 53:190-1 Ag 2 '65
So? Communist China's nuclear development; summary of address; December 15, 1965. Nat R 18:12-13 Ja 11 '66
Strategic problems detailed by McNamara; testimony before the House armed services committee. Aviation W 82:62-6 Mr 1 '65; Excerpts. por Time 85:20 F 26 '65
Strongest peace force in the world. Read Digest 86:83-7 F '65
United States and South Vietnamese forces launch retaliatory attacks against North Viet-Nam; statement, February 7, 1965. Dept State Bul 52:239-40 F 22 '65

about

Argentina's friend. Nation 201:234 O 18 '65
Bombers vs. missiles: showdown ahead. il U S News 59:30-2 D 27 '65
Brilliant administrator or human I.B.M. machine? J. Raymond. il pors N Y Times Mag p30-1+ Ap 11 '65
Downhill path. W. J. Coughlin. Miss & Roc 18:50 Ja 10 '66
Foil for the critics. il por Time 86:24 D 3 '65
He's gone. Mr Secretary. Time 85:25A-25B Je 18 '65
McNamara and Vietnam: sharp questions; statements. por U S News 59:32 D 27 '65
McNamara at the bar. W. F. Buckley, jr. Nat R 17:361 My 4 '65
McNamara line. J. Burnham. Nat R 17:104 F 9 '65
McNamara methods arousing fresh criticism in Congress. M. Getler. Miss & Roc 18:15 Ja 17 '66
McNamara shuffles Pentagon managers. Bsns W p31 S 18 '65
McNamara's management revolution. D. Seligman. il por Fortune 72:116-20+ Jl '65
McNamara's many wars; investigations of policies. il por Time 87:19C-19D Ja 21 '66
Man for all problems. il por Time 86:35-6 N 19 '65
New House foe fires on McNamara. Bsns W p24-5 Jl 3 '65
New profits for the primes. C. J. Loomis. il Fortune 17:76+ Ap '65
Power in the Pentagon. il pors Newsweek 66: 30-4 D 6 '65
Rivers renews drive to curb McNamara. G. C. Wilson. Aviation W 84:38 Ja 17 '66
Rough days ahead for Secretary McNamara? il por U S News 59:24 N 8 '65
Secretary of defense. A. Campbell. New Repub 152:13-15 Je 26 '65
Secretary of defense McNamara explains how things are going in Vietnam. Nat R 17: 1182-3 D 28 '65
Strongest & longest. Time 86:32-3 O 8 '65
Two powerful men who stayed. R. Dudman. por Esquire 64:95+ N '65

MCNASPY, Clement J.
Fine arts. See occasional issues of America
Forgotten five million. America 113:531 N 6 '65
Jottings from a pilgrim diary. America 113: 243-4 S 4 '65
More changes at mass. America 112:281 F 27 '65
Music. See issues of America
Roundup of some new liturgical works. America 113:216 Ag 28 '65
Total parish. America 113:465 O 23 '65

MCNAUGHTON, S. J.
Differential enzymatic activity in ecological races of typha latifolia L. bibliog Science 150:1829-30 D 31 '65

MCNEAL, Archie L.
Conference background. por ALA Bul 59:469-70 Je '65
Library in the South: socioeconomic and cultural aspects; address, April 1965. bibliog por Wilson Lib Bul 39:867-8+ Je '65

MCNEAL, Martha
Anomaly's eyes; story. Harper 230:91-4 F '65

MCNEICE, Louis
Ends and means. S. F. Morse. Poetry 105: 404-6 Mr '65

MCNEIL, Virginia A.
I'm glad I tried to help! ed. by L. David. por Good H 160:92-3+ Ap '65

MCNEILL, Barbara D. See Ianni, F. A. J. jt. auth.

MCNEILL, Robert B.
Return to Georgia. por Look 29:95-6 N 16 '65

MCNELLY, Theodore
Japan's role in south Asia. Cur Hist 49:284-93 N '65

MCNESKY, Robert
Sculptor's secret tool. Design 66:14-17 My '65

MCNICKLE, D'Arcy
Goals of the group. Nation 201:167-8 S 27 '65

MCPARTLIN, Charlie
Lonely stand on a peak in Danang. G. P. Hunt. il por Life 58:3 Ap 9 '65

MACPEEK, Walter
Five notions I won't buy; address, December 15, 1964. Vital Speeches 31:247-9 F 1 '65

MACPHEADRIS-Warner House. See Portsmouth, N.H.—Historic houses, etc.

MCPHEE, Walter T.
Duquesne, Pa, breaks precedent. Am City 80: 93-6 O '65

MCPHERSON, Archibald T.
Synthetic food for tomorrow's billions. Bul Atomic Sci 21:6-11 S '65

MACPHERSON, H. A.
Sempervivums handsome and hardy. Pop Gard 16:14-15 Mr '65

MACPHERSON, Ian
Reversion in hamster cells transformed by Rous sarcoma virus. Science 148:1731-3 Je 25 '65

MCPHERSON, James M.
Grant or Greeley? the abolitionist dilemma in the election of 1872. bibliog f Am Hist R 71:43-61 O '65

MCQUADE, Walter
Architects: a chance for greatness. Fortune 73:151-8+ Ja '66
Architecture (cont) Nation 200:204+; 201:86-7 F 22, Ag 16 '65
[Monthly column] Arch Forum 123:92 Jl; 76 S; 68 O; 70 N; 64 D '65
Structure & design. See issues of Fortune

MCQUEEN, Mildred Hark. See Hark, M.

MCQUEEN, Noel. See Hark, M. jt. auth.

MACRAE, Donald A.
Explorer of the Milky way. Sky & Tel 30:7-8 Jl '65

MACRAMÉ
Spencer Depas and knotting. N. Znamierowski. il Craft Horiz 25:32-3+ Mr '65

MACROGLOBULIN. See Globulins

MACROPHAGES
Homograft target cells: contact destruction in vitro by immune macrophages. G. A. Granger and R. S. Weiser. bibliog il Science 151:97-9 Ja 7 '66

MACSHANE, Frank
Horrors at Berkeley, or did architecture make students riot? Art N 64:30-3+ S '65

MCSHERRY, Elizabeth Melissa
Elizabeth McSherry, M.D. il pors Good H 161:54-5+ S '65

MCSWEEN, Cirilo A.
How I sold $1,000,000 worth of insurance in a single month. por Ebony 20:208-9 My '65

MACURDY, Jack
Redbook's guide to Italian furniture. Redbook 125:82-90 My '65

MACUT, John J.
Prospects for numerical control of machine tools. Mo Labor R 88:403-6 Ap '65

MCVEA, Warren
Look out, man, he went thataway. por Sports Illus 23:80 S 20 '65

MCVEY, Frank L.
University of Kentucky press celebrates an anniversary. il Pub W 187:27-31 Ap 12 '65

MCWHAN, D. B. and others
Superconducting gallium antimonide. bibliog Science 147:1441-2 Mr 19 '65

MCWHIRTER, William
(ed) See Murphy, F. D. New voices on campus

MCWILLIAMS, Carey
Anatomy of indignation. Nation 200:428-30 Ap 19 '65
Lindsay miracle. Nation 201:348-50 N 15 '65

MCWILLIAMS, Carey—*Continued*
Personal note. por Nation 201:21-7 S 20 '65
Poland's perennial problem. Nation 201:118-21
S 6 '65

about

Personal note. G. Kirstein. Nation 201:18-21
S 20 '65

MCWILLIAMS, Wilson Carey
Books. Commonweal 83:126-8 O 29 '65
How we bungled our way in. Commonweal
82:537-8 Jl 23 '65
What the French learned the first time
around. Commonweal 82:119-20 Ap 16 '65
—and Hale, Dennis
Vietnam protest. Commonweal 83:333-6 D 17
'65

MACY, John Williams, 1917-
How LBJ picks his men; interview. por
Nations Bsns 53:36-7+ Jl '65
Scientist in the federal service. Science 148:
51-4 Ap 2 '65

about

Talent hunter Macy. por Bsns W p20 Jl 31
'65
Talent scout. por Time 85:26 My 7 '65

MACY, R.H, and company
Macy's puts its stamp on every store it owns;
fifty department stores span the continent.
il Bsns W p64+ O 2 '65
Macy's toasts its price war. il Bsns W p32-3
F 27 '65
Retail reorganization. W. H. Bingham and
D. L. Yunich. il Harvard Bsns R 43:129-
32+ Jl '65
Wanted: concern for the customer; address,
September 29, 1965. J. I. Straus. Vital
Speeches 32:109-12 D 1 '65
Well-rounded shopping center; store in
Queens. il Fortune 72:189 D '65

MAD show; revue. See Musical comedies, revues, etc.—Criticisms, plots, etc.

MADAME Butterfly; opera. See Puccini, G.

MA'DAN. See Iraq—Native races

MADDEN, Carl H.
One black cloud; inflation; interview. Nations
Bsns 53:34-5 N '65

MADDEN, Henry Miller
Fire from the maddened crowd. E. Moon. Library J 90:578-81 F 1 '65

MADDOW, Ben
Psalm of twelve Fridays. Poetry 105:355-7
Mr '65

MADDOX, Gaynor
Better nutrition through research and edu-
cation. Todays Health 43:42-5+ O '65
Bread and rolls baked at home add flavor to
your family meal. Todays Health 43:52-7
F '65
Colonial recipes for the jet age. Todays
Health 43:52-7 D '65
Delectable cheese dishes. Todays Health 43:
52-7 Mr '65
Enjoy outdoor eating modern style. Todays
Health 43:60-5 Je '65
Exciting chicken recipes to delight the taste.
Todays Health 44:52-7 Ja '66
Flowers that bloom in the spring signal
added freshness for recipes. Todays Health
43:49-55 Ap '65
Good nutrition can be spiced by variety. To-
days Health 43:54-9 O '65
How to celebrate Thanksgiving in ten lan-
guages. Todays Health 43:70-5 N '65
Main-course salads add sparkle to meals.
Todays Health 43:60-5 Jl '65
Vegetable season offers tasty dishes. Todays
Health 43:56-61 Ag '65
Where to dine out in New York. Todays
Health 43:18-23+ My '65

MADDOX, Paul
Kentucky doctor: one man's war against
southern poverty. L. Bergquist. il pors Look
29:76-80 N 16 '65

MADDRELL, S. H. P.
Neurosecretory supply to the epidermis of an
insect. bibliog Science 150:1033-4 N 19 '65

MADDY, A. H. and Malcolm, B. R.
Protein conformations in the plasma membrane. bibliog Science 150:1616-18 D 17 '65

MADEIRA

Description and travel
Shape of Madeira. D. Messinesi. Vogue 145:
82 Mr 1 '65

MADEMOISELLE (periodical)
All in all, a most enlightening happening.
G. Buckman. il Mlle 61:162-3+ O '65
Mademoiselle's guest editors; 1965. J. Mc-
Hale. il Mlle 61:224-5 Ag '65
Memo from the editor; thirtieth birthday.
B. T. Blackwell. il Mlle 60:85-7 F '65

Success story; the all-American girl enters
Mademoiselle's college competitions. il Mlle
62:130-1 N '65

MADERO, Luis Eduardo Sánchez. See
Sánchez Madero, L. E.

MADIGAN, Francis C.
Problems of world population; interview. ed.
by F. Canavan. America 113:524-6 N 6 '65

MADIGAN, Lawrence M.
Church, unity and community. Cath World
202:91-5 N '65

MADILL, Jean
Enameling. por Sch Arts 64:14-16 F '65

MADISON, James
Monumental amends. il por Time 86:32 O 8 '65

MADISON, Wis.

Education
Function before form; Central-University
high school library program, with bibliography. K. I. Taylor. Library J 90:5481-3 D
15 '65

MADISON, Wis, public library
Madison cuts a corner. B. Schwab. il Library J 90:5170-2 D 1 '65

MADISON Square Garden. See New York (city)
—Madison Square Garden

MADNESS. See Insanity

MADOCS, Rita
Fandango; story. Ladies Home J 83:66-7
Ja '66

MADONNA lilies. See Lilies

MADRID

Music
La afición. C. Irizarry. Hi Fi 15:142-3 Ap '65

MADRID-MALO, Néstor
Last tree; story. Américas 17:35-7 S '65

MADRIGALS
See also
Phonograph records—Madrigals

MADSON, John
Sportiest duck hunting of all! Farm J 89:50+
O '65

MAEGHT, Aimé
Stones for the spirit. il por Time 86:70-1
Jl 16 '65

MAEGHT museum. See Art—Galleries and
museums

MAENTEL, Jacob
Folk art in New York. R. Davidson. il Antiques 88:150+ Ag '65

MAERKI, Vic
Vermont House gets remodeled. Reporter 33:
38-9 O 7 '65

MAFFEI, Lamberto, and others
Geniculate unit responses to sine-wave photic
stimulation during wakefulness and sleep.
bibliog Science 149:563-4 Jl 30 '65

MAFIA
Crime is too big for the FBI. W. W. Turner.
il Nation 201:322-8 N 8 '65; Discussion.
201:inside cover D 20 '65
Lying, thieving, murdering, upper-middle
class, respectable crook. N. Pileggi. il
Esquire 65:50-2+ Ja '66
Mafia can't crack Los Angeles. B. Davidson.
il Sat Eve Post 238:23-7 Jl 31 '65
Underworld links. Newsweek 66:26+ Ag 16
'65

MAFRICA, Anthony
EOA and LAPL. Wilson Lib Bul 40:243-5
N '65

MAGAZINE advertising. See Advertising mediums—Periodicals

MAGAZINE art. See Illustration of books and
periodicals

MAGAZINE articles. See Periodical literature

MAGAZINE editors. See Editors and editing

MAGAZINE fiction. See Fiction in periodicals
and newspapers

MAGAZINE publishing. See Periodicals, Publishing of

MAGAZINE stands, racks, etc.
Magazine racks; a miscellany. il House &
Gard 128:72+ S '65

MAGAZINES. See Periodicals—United States

MAGAZINES, Childrens. See Childrens periodicals

MAGEE, Frank L.
Tax-free municipal industrial bonds; address, December 1, 1964. Vital Speeches 31:
300-4 Mr 1 '65

MAGGIO musicale fiorentino. See Music festivals—Italy

MAGI
See also
Holy Innocents, Massacre of the

MAGIC
Antiquity's undercover magicians; reconstruc-
tion of the Sefar ha-razim. H. Nelson. il
Sat R 48:21+ F 6 '65
Power of juju; magic to overthrow govern-
ment. il Time 86:36 S 3 '65

MAGIC—*Continued*
Some enchanting evening; supper club devoted to magicians and magic lovers. il Time 86:88 S 24 '65
MAGIC flute; opera. See Mozart, J. C. W. A.
MAGIC pumpkin patch; drama. See Thomas, E. M.
MAGID, Marion
Death of hip. Esquire 63:89-103+ **Je '65**
MAGINI-COLETTI, Antonio
Antonio Magini-Coletti. A. Favia-Artsay. Hobbies 69:30 F '65
MAGISTRATES. See Justices of the peace
MAGMA. See Rocks, Igneous
MAGNA carta
Cornerstone of liberty. il Sr Schol 86:7 My 20 '65
Day for the rights of man. S. D. Smith. il N Y Times Mag p29-30+ Je 13 '65
Magna charta; forerunner of the U.S. Constitution. H. G. Earl. il Todays Health 43:54-7 Je '65
President Johnson receives book on the Magna carta; remarks, July 22, 1965. P. Dean; L. B. Johnson. Dept State Bul 53:235 Ag 9 '65
What happened at Runnymede. il Time 85:56 Je 25 '65
MAGNANI, Anna
Anna is everything! por Newsweek 65:81 Je 7 '65
MAGNER, Jeanadele. See Magner, K. jt. auth.
MAGNER, Ken, and Magner, Jeanadele
Gone flying to Virginia. por Flying 77:52-6 Ag '65
Gone flying to Washington. pors Flying 77:62-7 N '65
MAGNESIUM
Strontium and magnesium in water and in crassostrea calcite. A. Lerman. bibliog il Science 150:745-6+ N 5 '65
See also
Brucite
MAGNESIUM in the body
Glycerinated skeletal and smooth muscle: calcium and magnesium dependence. R. S. Filo and others. bibliog il Science 147:1581-3 Mr 26 '65
MAGNETIC field
Intense magnetic fields. H. H. Kolm and A. J. Freeman. il Sci Am 212:66-74+ Ap '65; Discussion. 213:6 Jl; 6 N '65
Ultrastrong magnetic fields. F. Bitter. il Sci Am 213:64-73 Jl '65
MAGNETIC field (cosmic physics)
Faint ring around the spiral galaxy M82. H. Arp. bibliog Science 148:363-4 Ap 16 '65
Magnetic field measurements near Mars. E. J. Smith and others. bibliog Science 149:1241-2 S 10 '65
Magnetic field of the galaxy. G. L. Berge and G. A. Seielstad. il Sci Am 212:46-54 bibliog(p 146) Je '65
Magnetic fields in interplanetary space. L. J. Cahill, jr. bibliog il Science 147:991-1000 F 26 '65
Search for trapped electrons and a magnetic moment at Mars by Mariner IV. J. J. O'Gallagher and J. A. Simpson. bibliog il Science 149:1233-9 S 10 '65
Sector structure of the quiet interplanetary magnetic field. N. F. Ness and J. M. Wilcox. bibliog il Science 148:1592-4 Je 18 '65
Solar magnetic fields. V. Bumba and R. Howard. bibliog il Science 149:1331-7 S 17 '65
MAGNETIC memory (computers)
Many tricks in Itek's new bag: new optical memory system computer will use RS material. il Bsns W p60-2 Ja 30 '65
MAGNETIC recorders and recording
Basics for the tape recordist; bonus manual. A. Sterling. il Hi Fi 15:43-50 Ag '65
Battery-operated tape recorder guide. M. A. Matzkin. il Mod Phot 29:108-9 Je '65
Bird song; the anatomy of a miracle. D. J. Borror. il Audubon Mag 67:159-63 My '65
Compatible couple; tape recorder with photos & movies. R. Miller. il U S Camera 28:63-5+ Ap '65
Dashboard tape player for highway hi-fi. il Pop Sci 187:103 S '65
Five ways to tape your sound. M. Matzkin and H. Manoogian. il Mod Phot 29:88-9 Jl '65
High fidelity newsfronts; electronic music console at School of music, University of Illinois, Urbana. N. Eisenberg. il Hi Fi 15:31 Ag '65
High fidelity newsfronts; model 150 Carry-Corder tape recorder. N. Eisenberg. il Hi Fi 15:46+ N '65
Inflight engine-data recording evaluated. il Aviation W 83:71+ N 1 '65

Inside the new tape recorders. R. M. Benrey. il Pop Sci 187:104-6+ S '65
Midget tape recorder that thinks for itself. R. Benrey. il Pop Sci 186:119 Je '65
Pictures in sound; tape recorders. J. Arthur. il Pop Phot 57:116-17 D '65
Riding gain; how to get best results. I. B. Berger. Sat R 48:59 Ag 28 '65
Science in action; the sounds of singing; East Africa. G. S. Keith. Natur Hist 74:61-4 Je '65
Sight and sound. R. Miller. il U S Camera 28:62-3+ My '65
Sound advice; how to prevent or cure sound distortion. L. Zide. Mod Phot 29:58+ Je '65
Sound advice; putting sound on wheels with an inverter. R. Angus. Mod Phot 29:80+ O '65
Sound advice; tape deck or complete tape recorder? R. Flanzraich. Mod Phot 29:21+ S '65
Sound advice; tape recorders for cars. H. Manoogian. il Mod Phot 29:24+ My '65
Tape for turnpikes; dashboard tape players. L. Buckwalter. il Hi Fi 15:42-4+ Je '65
Tape recorder guide. M. A. Matzkin. il Mod Phot 29:97-116 N '65
Tape recorder trends. H. Fantel. Opera N 30:47 O 23 '65
Taping off the air; tapes of radio performances. H. H. Fantel. Opera N 29:35 Mr 20; 35 Ap 3 '65
Three airlines and Boeing order Fairchild cockpit voice recorders. il Aviation W 83:75 Ag 30 '65
Tips to keep your tape recorder trouble free. il Bet Hom & Gard 43:38 S '65
Will stereo tapes bring music to Detroit ears? il Bsns W p34 N 6 '65
See also
Tape recordings
Video tape recorders and recording

Aeronautic applications

Inflight engine-data recording evaluated. il Aviation W 83:71+ N 1 '65
ICAO unit adopts rule requiring recorders on all turbine aircraft. Aviation W 83:47 D 13 '65

Competitions

Contest winners; Portrait in sound. T. Schwartz. Pop Phot 56:18 Je '65

Control

Tape recorder remote switch. H. L. Davidson. il Pop Electr 23:53 D '65

Educational applications

How to teach typewriting with tape recorders; Hammond, Ind. high school. J. H. Nichols. Sr Schol 87:sup7 N 4 '65

Equipment

Inside tips from the pros. B. G. Wels. il Pop Electr 23:51-3 D '65
New slant on recording; inclined base. G. F. Stillwell. il Pop Electr 23:50 D '65

Industrial applications

Recorders slash time base error. R. Lindsey. il Miss & Roc 17:40-1 O 4 '65

Repairing

Quick cures for sick recorders. G. F. Stillwell. il Pop Electr 23:57-8+ D '65

Stereophonic recorders

Carnegie Hall on wheels; dashboard stereotape player in 1966 models. Time 85:98+ Ap 30 '65

Visual recordings

See Video tape recorders and recording
MAGNETIC recorders and recording, Portable
Big year for small recorders. P. Geraci. il Pop Electr 23:47-9 D '65
MAGNETIC resonance
Electron spin resonance characteristics of some normal tissues; effect of microwave power. H. M. Swartz and R. P. Molenda. bibliog il Science 148:94-5 Ap 2 '65
Electron spin resonance of irradiated DNA. P. S. Pershan and others. bibliog il Science 148:378-80 Ap 16 '65
Electron-spin-resonance signals and biological effects; report on meeting to discuss recent work. F. Hutchinson. il Science 150:644+ O 29 '65
Electron spin resonance spectroscopy: application to proof of structure of organic ketones. G. A. Russell and E. R. Talaty. bibliog il Science 148:1217-18 My 28 '65

MAIL order business—*Continued*
Shopping scout; Spencer gifts, Atlantic City. A. M. Gallagher. il Parents Mag 41:114-16 Ja '66
Weathervane; plants and garden supplies by mail. R. G. Miner. Flower Grower 53:8 Ja '66
What are these mail-order shopping clubs? Changing T 19:43-4 Jl '65
What to do if you shop by mail. il Good H 161:182 N '65
  See also
Catalogs, Mail order

MAIL order catalogs. See Catalogs, Mail order

MAILER, Norman
Cities higher than mountains. N Y Times Mag p 16-17+ Ja 31 '65
PPA press conference; summary. por(p42) Pub W 187:44-5 Mr 22 '65
    about
Always the challenger. B. Brower. il pors Life 59:94-6+ S 24 '65; Reply. W. F. Buckley, jr. Nat R 17:969 N 2 '65
Morbid-mindedness. R. Poirier. Commentary 39:91-4 Je '65
Thing of darkness. P. Pickrel. Harper 230:116-17 Ap '65

MAINBOCHER
Second fame: good food. N. Lyon. por Vogue 146:154-6 N 15 '65

MAINE
  See also
Allagash River
Fishing—Maine
Hunting—Maine
White Island
Zoology—Maine

    Description and travel
Cruising down east. A. W. Moffat. il Yachting 118:38-40+ Jl; 57-9+ Ag '65 (to be cont)

    Legislature
Government by freshmen: Maine's year of the donkey. D. L. Graham. il Nation 202:43-5 Ja 10 '66

    Parks and reserves
Mister Maine and the mountain. E. W. Smith. il Field & S 70:10-11+ D '65

    Race problems
Requests probe of Indian slaying; white racists. Christian Cent 83:37 Ja 12 '66

MAINICHI (newspaper) See Newspapers—Japan

MAINTENANCE men. See Repairmen

MAINWARING, Marion. See Maynard, F. jt. auth.

MAINWARING, W. C.
Why fear the future? address, June 28, 1965. Vital Speeches 31:691-6 S 1 '65

MAIR, Beveridge J. See Douglas, A. G. jt. auth.

MAISEL, Albert Q.
Emergency service: medicine's newest specialty. Read Digest 86:96-100 Je '65
Facts about fluoridation. Read Digest 87:87-92 N '65

MAISEL, Jay
Delicate look at one that is no soft touch; photographs. Sports Illus 22:34-9 Je 14 '65
35-mm in night-town. il Pop Phot 57:60-5+ Ag '65

MAISEL, Sherman J.
People of the week. por U S News 58:20 Ap 12 '65

MAIZE. See Corn

MAIZE dwarf mosaic. See Viruses, Plant

MAJOR, John
Almain and Major: conciliar theory on the eve of the reformation. F. Oakley. bibliog f Am Hist R 70:673-90 Ap '65

MAJORCA
Majorca: an island haven. E. Dahlberg. il Holiday 37:48-51 F '65
Smugglers I have known. F. V. Grunfeld. il Opera N 30:8-12 N 6 '65

MAK, T. C. W. See Jeffrey, G. A. jt. auth.

MAKARIOS III, abp
New bloodletting? Newsweek 65:36 Mr 29 '65

MAKE-up
Beauty bulletin; up: brilliance. il Vogue 146:194-7 O 1 '65
Beauty life: girl into model. il Mlle 60:194-7 Mr '65
Beauty life: parties. il Mlle 62:84-7 D '65
Beauty with a brush. il Seventeen 24:116-17 F '65
Big fade; the pale pale look. il Time 86:79 Jl 16 '65
Face the light. il Vogue 146:142-5 O 15 '65
Here's art in your eye. il Life 59:98-101+ O 29 '65
How can you find the perfect makeup shades without trying them all? B. Lee. il McCalls 92:112-13+ My '65
Make-up step that makes the difference; foundations. il Redbook 124:66-7+ F '65
New guide to make-up. il Redbook 125:90-3+ O '65
New role of the makeup man. G. Plaut. il Look 29:54-6 F 23 '65
Newest makeup of the season; Scheherazade leg. il Vogue 146:176-9 D '65
Newsmaking makeups. il Mlle 61:114-17 O '65
Personal makeup color chart. Good H 161:106 N '65
Spring makeup magic & twenty-one hit hairdos. il Good H 160:104-13+ Ap '65
Wide-eyed look. il McCalls 92:114-15 Ap '65
  See also
Beauty, Personal

MAKEPEACE experiment; story. See Tertz, A.

MAKIGUCHI, Tsunesaburo
Soka Gakkai brings absolute happiness. I. Morris. il N Y Times Mag p8-9+ Jl 18 '65

MAKSIMOVIĆ, Ivan
Constitutional socialism in Yugoslavia. bibliog f Ann Am Acad 358:159-69 Mr '65

MALAGA
Walk through Málaga. A. Karlen. Holiday 37:26+ Ap '65

MALAMUD, Herbert
Kick the scientist. Bul Atomic Sci 21:34-5 My '65

MALANGA, Gerard
Some thoughts on bottom and after I's. Poetry 107:60-4 O '65

MALAPROPISMS. See Blunders

MALARET, Niso
Instant idiot; story. Américas 17:34-7 F '65

MALARIA
Anopheles balabacensis balabacensis identified as vector of simian malaria in Malaysia. W. H. Cheong and others. bibliog Science 150:1314-15 D 3 '65
Malaria flares on a new front; health hazard in Vietnam. Bsns W p32 D 4 '65
More action, more malaria. il Time 86:92 D 10 '65
Naturally acquired quotidian-type malaria in man transferable to monkeys. W. Chin and others. bibliog Science 149:865 Ag 20 '65
New health hazard for GI's in Vietnam. U S News 59:18 D 13 '65
Quinine-resistant plasmodium berghei in mice. P. E. Thompson and others. bibliog il Science 148:1240-1 My 28 '65
Similar malaria danger. F. Marley. Sci N L 88:149 S 4 '65
Susceptibility of the gibbon hylobates lar to felciparum malaria. R. A. Ward and others. bibliog il Science 150:1604-5 D 17 '65
  See also
Blackwater fever

    Prevention and control
Aerial spray studied to combat malaria; measures for South Vietnam. Aviation W 83:31 D 6 '65
Malaria in Viet Nam. Time 86:43 Ag 20 '65
  See also
Quinine

MALATHION
Fastest way yet to kill bugs; Farm Journal staff report; ed. by R. D. Wennblom. il Farm J 89:34-5+ O '65

MALAWI
Colored rulers. G. C. Turner. bibliog Negro Hist Bul 28:107-8 F '65
Good-by, Mr Chips? il Newsweek 65:40+ Ap 26 '65
Lay training center opens. B. Boston. Christian Cent 82:848 Je 30 '65
Price of stability. B. Boston. Christian Cent 83:26 Ja 5 '66
Stormy first year. Christian Cent 82:1074+ S 1 '65

MALAYA
  See also
Arts and crafts—Malaya
Malaysia

MALAYS
Expulsion of Singapore. C. P. FitzGerald. il Nation 201:208-12 O 11 '65

MALAYSIA
Another Asian country in a weird war with reds; conflict between Indonesia and Malaysia. R. P. Martin. il U S News 58:74-6 My 3 '65

MALAYSIA—*Continued*
Anti-red bulwark weakens; secession of Singapore. il Bsns W p26 Ag 14 '65
Art of dispelling anxiety. Time 86:20 Ag 27 '65
As Jakarta and Peiping rejoice; Singapore's eviction from Malaysia. America 113:200 Ag 28 '65
Atlantic report. Atlan 215:11-12+ Je '65
Bad day in a rear area of Asia; Singapore leaves federation. Life 59:4 Ag 20 '65
Brand-new baby for the U.N; secession of Singapore. R. Morse. Life 59:65+ Ag 20 '65
Endurance contest. R. K. McCabe. Newsweek 65:44+ F 15 '65
Expulsion of Singapore. C. P. FitzGerald. il Nation 201:208-12 O 11 '65
Federal idea; Singapore to secede from the Federation of Malaysia. Christian Cent 82:1028-9 Ag 25 '65
Malaysia: key area in southeast Asia. A. T. Rahman. For Affairs 43:659-70 Jl '65
Malaysia: my dream is shattered. il Newsweek 66:33-4 Ag 23 '65
Malaysia—Singapore=trouble. S. Huck. Nat R 17:771+ S 7 '65
Malaysia's first year. C. P. Bradley. bibliog f Cur Hist 48:82-8+ F '65
More bad news for U.S. from Asia. il U S News 59:21-3 Ag 23 '65
More cracks in Malaysia. D. Warner. il Reporter 33:40-2 O 7 '65
One of our islands is missing. il Time 86:26+ Ag 20 '65
Second fall of Singapore. D. Warner. il Reporter 33:27-9 S 9 '65
Singapore's restless Chinese. S. S. King. i! Reporter 33:20-2 Ag 12 '65
Still good friends. Newsweek 66:37 Ag 30 '65
Sukarno steps up the war. Time 86:30 Jl 9 '65
Sukarno's war against Malaysia. J. Jacquet-Francillon. New Repub 152:16-18 Ap 10 '65
See also
Architecture—Malaysia
Communism—Malaysia
Recreation—Malaysia
Singapore

Race problems
More cracks in Malaysia. D. Warner. il Reporter 33:40-2 O 7 '65
Promise threatened. il Newsweek 65:43 Je 21 '65

MALCOLM X
Brief return from Mecca. E. Capouya. il pors Sat R 48:42+ N 20 '65
Delinquent's progress. T. Nelson. Nation 201:336-8 N 8 '65
Journey toward truth. T. Kretz. Christian Cent 82:1513 D 8 '65
Malcolm X. Nation 200:239 Mr 8 '65
Meaning of Malcolm X. C. E. Lincoln. Christian Cent 82:431-3 Ap 7 '65
Peking and Malcolm X. New Repub 152:8 Mr 27 '65; Reply. L. M. Edwards. 152:44 Ap 17 '65
Satan in the ghetto. il por Newsweek 66:130+ N 15 '65
Violence versus non-violence. il por Ebony 20:168-9 Ap '65
Who was Malcolm X? C. W. Wiley. Nat R 17:239-40 Mr 23 '65

Assassination
Death and transfiguration. il por Time 85:23-5 Mr 5 '65
Death of a desperado. il por Newsweek 65:24-5 Mr 8 '65
Now it's Negroes vs. Negroes in America's racial violence. il U S News 58:6 Mr 8 '65
Tragedy of Malcolm X. America 112:303 Mr 6 '65
Vendetta by rivals feared. il por Sr Schol 86:21 Mr 11 '65
Violent end of the man called Malcolm X; with report by G. Parks. il pors Life 58:26-31 Mr 5 '65
Who killed Malcolm X? A. Morrison. il pors Ebony 20:135-6+ O '65
MALCOLM, B. R. See Maddy, A. H. jt. auth.
MALCOLM; drama. See Albee, E.
MALDIVE ISLANDS
New & happy era. il Time 86:35 Ag 6 '65
See also
United Nations—Maldive Islands
MALDONADO, A. W.
New man in La Fortaleza. Reporter 33:32-3 N 4 '65
MALE coiffure. See Hairdressing
MALENBAUM, Wilfred
Economic factors and political development. bibliog f Ann Am Acad 358:41-51 Mr '65

MALEV Hungarian airlines. See Airlines—Hungary
MALFORMATIONS. See Deformities
MALI (Republic)
Mission from Mali concludes visit to United States; joint statement, July 14, 1965. Dept State Bul 53:192 Ag 2 '65
See also
Timbuktu
MALIGNANT melanomas. See Cancer
MALIGNANT tumors. See Cancer
MALIK, Charles Habib
New era in world development. America 113:496-8 O 30 '65
MALITSON, Harriet H.
Solar energy spectrum. Sky & Tel 29:162-5 Mr '65
MALKIN, Lawrence
Heath's middle road to Downing street. Reporter 33:39+ D 16 '65
el MALLAKH, Ragaei
Cloudy future for foreign aid. New Repub 153:10-11 Ag 21 '65
MALLAN, Lloyd
Can you see the moon in 3-D? Pop Phot 57:52-5 S '65
MALLARD ducks. See Ducks, Wild
MALLET-JORIS, Françoise
Breaking it off; story. Mlle 61:108-9 Je '65
MALLINCKRODT chemical works
Chemical maker finds the formula. il Bsns W p93-4+ N 13 '65
MALLOCH, William
Flashing music of Zubin Mehta. Hi Fi 15:129 Ag '65
MALLS, Shopping. See Business districts
MALMESBURY, William of. See William of Malmesbury
MALMQUIST, Eve
IRA focus: reading instruction in transition; statements. por Sr Schol 86:sup 1-2 My 20 '65
MALO, Néstor Madrid-. See Madrid-Malo, N.
MALOCCLUSION. See Teeth
MALOFF, Saul
Books. Commonweal 82:638-9, 730-1 S 3, O 1 '65
Teaching Johnny to cop out. Commonweal 82:321-3 My 28 '65
White House festival. Commonweal 82:485-7 Jl 9 '65
MALONE, E. V.
Lure of Tollymore. Am For 71:30-1 F '65
MALONE, John R.
UNIFON system. Wilson Lib Bul 40:63-5 S '65
MALONE, Vivian
She came through. il pors Newsweek 65:37-8 Je 14 '65
MALONEY, Elbert S.
Boating's best bargains. Motor B 115:92+ Ap '65
Rich delights of Tidewater, Virginia. bibliog Motor B 116:22-7+ S '65
MALONEY, Jim
Eye opener; 187 pitches, no hits. il por Newsweek 66:54 Ag 30 '65
Practice makes perfect. por Time 86:69 Ag 27 '65
MALONEY, Ralph
Gallantry; story. Atlan 216:73-7 N '65
Harry W. A. Davis, jr; story. Atlan 215:58-62 Je '65
MALORY, Sir Thomas
Le morte d'Arthur. K. Rexroth. il Sat R 48:19 Jl 10 '65
MALOZEMOFF, Plato
Newmont mining's fourth generation of gamblers. il pors Fortune 72:132-7+ O '65
MALPASS, Eric
All's right with the world; story. Redbook 126:119-45 Ja '66
MALPRACTICE
Practice and malpractice. S. Greenberg. il Nation 200:464-7+ My 3 '65
Tragic case: Deutsch suit against Doctor's hospital. N.Y. Newsweek 66:86 S 20 '65
See also
Quacks and quackery
MALRAUX, André
Le Corbusier, 1887-1965; a tribute. Art N 64:21 O '65
about
Malraux's fate. M. Turnell. Commonweal 82:410-13 Je 18 '65
Mysterious visitor. il por Time 86:26B-27 Ag 13 '65
MALTBY, P. and Moffet, A. T.
Spectrum of the intensity variations in 3C 273B. bibliog Science 150:63-4 O 1 '65
MAMELLES de Tirésias; opera. See Poulenc, F.

MAMMALS
Bibliography
Books in review; dedicated to mammals. R. G. Van Gelder. Natur Hist 74:4+ Ap '65

MAMMALS, Fossil
Cretaceous mammals from Montana. R. E. Sloan and L. Van Valen. bibliog il Science 148:220-7 Ap 9 '65
Miocene mammals and Central American seaways. F. C. Whitmore, jr. and R. H. Stewart. bibliog il Science 148:180-5 Ap 9 '65

MAMMARY glands
See also
Breast

MAMMARY tumor virus. See Tumor viruses

MAMOULIAN, Rouben
Shatouni the Magnificent. Read Digest 87: 170-2+ Jl '65

MAN
Creativity without guilt; man's relation to God. R. O. Johann. America 113:165 Ag 14 '65
Denatured man; address, November 24, 1964. R. T. Eubanks. bibliog Vital Speeches 31: 241-3 F 1 '65
Education, democracy, and the human condition. B. O. Wireman. Sch & Soc 93:366-8 O 16 '65
Future of Homo sapiens; biologist's view. J. Hiernaux. il UNESCO Courier 18:12-15 Ap '65; Same abr. with title How man will evolve. Sci Digest 58:90-4 Ag '65
Greatest discovery; excerpt from Inquiry into enoughness. D. Lang. Sat R 48:28 Ap 17 '65
Images in the lonely crowd; awareness of self; address, April 3, 1965. J. A. Dyal. Vital Speeches 31:729-35 S 15 '65
Report on the earthmen. N. Cousins. Sat R 48:40 O 16 '65
Special position of man in the realm of the living; tr. by W. J. Dannhauser. A. Portmann. Commentary 40:38-41 N '65
See also
Civilization
Evolution
Woman

Influence of environment
Medical geology and geography; report on interdisciplinary symposium. H. V. Warren. il Science 148:534-7+ Ap 23 '65

Influence on nature
Man and his habitat; symposium. il Bul Atomic Sci 21:18-30 Mr; 16-26 Ap; 2-11 My; 6-25 Je '65
Man's place in the physical universe. W. F. Libby. Bul Atomic Sci 21:12-17 S '65

Origin and antiquity
Artifact from deposits of mid-Wisconsin age in Illinois. P. J. Munson and J. C. Frye. bibliog il Science 150:1722-3 D 24 '65
Battle of the bones; differing interpretations of discoveries made by L. S. B. Leakey. Newsweek 65:57-8 Ap 19 '65
How man began. J. D. Ratcliff. il Read Digest 87:129-33 O '65
Problem of man's emergence. Sci Am 212: 50+ My '65
Recognizing the emergence of man. R. Ascher and M. Ascher; discussion. Science 148: 167-8 Ap 9 '65
See also
Man, Prehistoric
Neanderthal race

Periodicity
See Periodicity

Survival
Staying alive to solve the problems. K. W. Thompson. Sat R 48:22-3 Ap 3 '65
Whose Sputnik? reprint. D. Lawrence. U S News 59:100 Ag 16 '65

MAN, Effect of altitude on. See Altitude, Influence of

MAN, Effect of submersion on. See Submersion

MAN, Prehistoric
Ancient skulls found; discovery by Yale university archaeologists in the Kom Ombo area, Egypt. Sci N L 88:66 Jl 31 '65
Early man in East Africa; recent excavations in Olduvai Gorge, Tanzania. P. V. Tobias. bibliog il Science 149:22-33 Jl 2 '65; Discussion. 149:918 Ag 27 '65
Leakeys of Africa; family in search of prehistoric man. M. M. Payne. il Nat Geog Mag 127:194-231 F '65

Man evolved like animals; Third species questioned. C. A. Betts. il(p241) Sci N L 87:243 Ap 17 '65
Man's tree, a new root? discoveries by L. S. B. Leakey, at Olduvai Gorge, Tanzania, East Africa. C. A. Betts. il Sci N L 87:346-7 My 29 '65
New species name of homo suggested; homo transvaalensis. Sci N L 87:73 Ja 30 '65
Paleolithic funeral. Sci Am 212:53-4 F '65
Skull of apeman named most ancient human; Lantien skull. Sci N L 88:297 N 6 '65
When man first stood up. J. Pfeiffer. il N Y Times Mag p70-1+ Ap 11 '65
See also
Man—Origin and antiquity
Missing link
Neanderthal race

MAN amplifiers
Man amplifiers; machines that let you carry a ton; Cornell's exoskeleton. W. Cloud. il Pop Sci 187:70-3+ N '65

MAN-hour requirements. See Labor requirements (for production)

MAN of affairs; story. See Davis, C.

MAN of La Mancha; musical comedy. See Musical comedies, revues, etc.—Criticisms, plots, etc.

MAN power. See Manpower

MAN to marry; story. See MacDougall, R. D.

MAN who learned to listen; story. See Knowlton, R. A.

MANAGEMENT, Business. See Business management and organization

MANAGEMENT, Industrial. See Industrial management and organization

MANAGEMENT education. See Industrial management and organization—Study and teaching

MANAGEMENT of children. See Children—Management and training

MANAGERIAL sociology. See Sociology, Industrial

MANAGERS. See Executives

MANAGERS, Concert. See Concert managers

MANAUS, Brazil
Floating community of Amazonas. F. D. de A. Pires. il Natur Hist 74:12-17 O '65
Pearl of Brazil; Teatro Amazonas, Manaus. J. Honig. il Opera N 30:6-7 D 25 '65

MANCHESTER, Harland
France's magic castle in the sea. Read Digest 86:185-6+ Ap '65
News about electric light bulbs. Read Digest 87:102-4 N '65
They're turning salt water into sweet. Read Digest 86:15-16+ Ap '65
Watch the whirlybird at work. Read Digest 87:253+ N '65

MANCHESTER, William
House of Krupp (cont) Holiday 37:60-1+ F '65

MANCINI, Marlene R. and Someroski, J. M.
Crafts classes for children. Sch Arts 65:32-5 O '65
Saturday classes in the creative arts. Sch Arts 64:27-34 F '65

MANDEL, George
Day the time changed; story. Sat Eve Post 238:56-61 N 6 '65

MANDEL, Paul
Fine but farcical British balloon race. Life 58:49-52+ Je 11 '65
Obituary
Life por 60:3 Ja 7 '66. G. P. Hunt

MANDELA, Nelson
Prisons of apartheid. H. Kuper. Nation 202: 76-8 Ja 17 '66

MANDELBAUM gate; story. See Spark, M.

MANDELLI, Enrique F. See Burkholder, P. R. jt. auth.

MANDEL'SHTAM, Osip Emil'evich
From the noise of time; excerpt from The prose of Osip Mandelstam. Commentary 40:37-41 O '65
about
Posthumously rehabilitated. D. Fanger. Nation 202:46-7 Ja 10 '66
Raspberry in Stalin's mouth. por Time 87: 90+ Ja 7 '66
Wild parabolas. por Newsweek 67:58 Ja 3 '66

MANDER, John
Anglo-Indian theme. Commentary 39:94-7 Je '65
Election stories; England. Commentary 40: 114+ D '65

MANDRIOTA, Frank J. and others
Classical conditioning of electric organ discharge rate in mormyrids. bibliog Science 150:1740-2 D 24 '65

MANET, Édouard
Eternal Olympia. A. Werner. il por **Am Artist** 29:48-53+ Ap '65
MANEUVERS, Military. See Military maneuvers
MANGAN, J. and others
Protein synthesis and the mitotic apparatus. bibliog Science 147:1575-8 Mr 26 '65
MANGANARO, Charles A.
Vaults combine with biennial conduit cleaning. por Am City 80:126-8 Je '65
MANGANESE
  Isotopes
Tetrodotoxin and manganese ion; effects on action potential of the frog heart. S. Hagiwara and S. Nakajima. bibliog il Science 149:1254-5 S 10 '65
Thermal neutron activation: measurement of cross section for manganese-53. H. T. Millard, jr. bibliog il Science 147:503-4 Ja 29 '65
MANGIERI, A. A.
Transistor and diode curve tracer. Electr World 73:65-8 Je '65
MANGUM, Garth L.
Education: what kind, for whom, how much? PTA Mag 60:4-7 bibliog(p34-5) N '65
MANGUS, Marlyn. See Schaeffer, B. jt. auth.
MANHATTAN, Kan.
Mile of runway to everywhere. D. C. Wesche. il Am City 80:148 Jl '65
MANHATTAN opera company
Manhattan opera company; second season, 1907-1908. G. R. Good. il Hobbies 70:33-4 N '65
MANHATTAN project. See Atomic bombs—Manufacture
MANHATTAN school of music
Miracle in Manhattan; J. Brownlee's opera theater. Q. Eaton. il Opera N 30:14-15 D 18 '65
Musical events; performance of Berlioz's Beatrice and Benedict. W. Sargeant. New Yorker 41:122+ My 29 '65
Musical events; performance of Puccini's Le Villi. W. Sargeant. New Yorker 41:52 D 25 '65
MANHOFF, Bill
Owl and the pussycat. Criticism
America 112:232-3 F 13 '65
MANIC 5 DAM. See Dams—Canada
MANICURING
Battery-powered manicure sets. Consumer Rep 30:225-6 My '65
Project; you. il Ladies Home J 82:73 N '65
MANILA, Quijano de, pseud.
Are Americans more comfortable with Lyndon Johnson? Nat R 17:552-4+ Je 29 '65
MANIPULATORS
Hope for amputees seen in use of nuclear tools. Sci N L 88:360 D 4 '65
MANISTEE and Northeastern railroad. See Railroads, Short line
MANITÉ international. See Photography—Societies
MANITOBA
  Description and travel
Magnificent Manitoba. K. Ferguson. il Motor B 116:34-7 Jl '65
MANKATO, Minn.
No longer decrepit and dull. il Am City 80: 124 O '65
MANLEY, John H.
Back in history. Bul Atomic Sci 21:26-7 O '65
MANN, Arthur
When La Guardia took over. N Y Times Mag p22-3+ Ja 2 '66
MANN, Carol
Carol is the ladies' Mann. G. S. Brown. il por Sports Illus 23:22-3 Jl 12 '65
MANN, Charles August
New partner; replacing director of the U.S. aid mission in South Vietnam. Newsweek 66:33 Ag 16 '65
MANN, David
(tr) See Yevtushenko, Y. Chicken-god
MANN, Guy E.
Automobile liability insurance; address, October 21, 1965. Vital Speeches 32:93-5 N 15 '65
MANN, Horace
Americans not everybody knows. C. W. Ferguson. por PTA Mag 60:8-10 N '65
MANN, Jack
Baseball. Sports Illus 22:66-8+ My 24; 23:54-6 Jl 5; 45-7 Jl 26; 114-15 S 20 '65
Decline and fall of a dynasty. Sports Illus 22:20-5 Je 21 '65
Destiny's whipping boys. Sports Illus 22:68-70+ Ap 5 '65

MANN, Martin
Amazing new power sources. Pop Sci 186: 100-3+ Ap '65
Are you in more danger in a small car? yes. Pop Sci 186:72+ F '65
Fast-reflex school for patrolmen. Pop Mech 124:96-100 Ag '65
MANN, Paul
Dotography. Design 67:40 N '65
MANN, Stanley J. and Straile, W. E.
Tylotrich (hair) follicle: association with a slowly adapting tactile receptor in the cat. bibliog Science 147:1043-5 F 26 '65
MANN, Thomas
Essays on Thomas Mann, by G. Lukács. Review
  Sat R 48:39-40+ N 6 '65. E. M. Potoker
Reminiscences of Thomas Mann. K. Kellen. Yale R 54:383-91 Mr '65
MANN, Thomas Clifton
Department supports bill to carry out auto agreement with Canada; statement, April 27, 1965. Dept State Bul 52:830-3 My 24 '65
Disparities in progress among nations. Ann Am Acad 360:63-7 Jl '65
Disparities in progress between nations; address, April 9, 1965. Dept State Bul 52:720-4 My 10 '65
Dominican crisis: correcting some misconceptions; address, October 12, 1965. Dept State Bul 53:730-8 N 8 '65; U S News 59:19 O 25 '65
Improving the world's monetary system; statement, September 28, 1965. Dept State Bul 53:617-19 O 18 '65
International trade; address, March 31, 1965. Dept State Bul 52:665-7 My 3 '65
Repeal of restrictive trade clause in transportation act urged; statement, March 30, 1965. Dept State Bul 52:636-7 Ap 26 '65
  about
Dominican crisis. T. Draper. Commentary 40: 33-68 D '65
Man behind our Latin-American actions. L. Gross. il por Look 29:35-7 Je 15 '65
Mann on the move. por Time 85:21 F 19 '65
Mann to watch. A. Campbell. New Repub 152: 13-15 Je 5 '65
Mann's divided mind. New Repub 153:6-7 O 23 '65
Rising star at State; LBJ promotes Mann. por U S News 58:22 F 22 '65
Tough U.S. diplomat Mann runs Dominican policy. por U S News 58:22 My 24 '65
MANN, William d'Alton
That was New York. A. Logan. il por New Yorker 41:37-8+ Ag 14; 41-2+ Ag 21 '65
MANNED orbiting space stations. See Space stations
MANNED space flight, Office of. See United States—National aeronautics and space administration—Manned space flight, Office of
MANNED space flights. See Space flight—Manned flights
MANNED spacecraft center. See United States—National aeronautics and space administration—Manned spacecraft center
MANNEQUINS. See Models (persons)
MANNERISM (art)
What is mannerism? exhibitions of 16th-century European art in Paris. A. Chastel. il Art N 64:22-5+ D '65
MANNERS, Gail
Togetherness; interview, ed. by F. Stevenson. por Opera N 30:13 Ja 22 '66
MANNERS. See Courtesy; Etiquette
MANNERS and customs
All girls have problems; excerpts from Way to womanhood. W. W. Bauer and F. M. Bauer. il Todays Health 43:24-7+ F '65
Exotic and the erotic. L. Blanch. il Vogue 145:106-11+ Ap 15 '65
Happy ways of doing things. P. Jones. Am Home 68:33+ Mr '65
Let's face it; what is vulgar? who is vulgar? M. Mannes. McCalls 82:16+ Ag '65
Pop sex; some sex symbols of the sixties. R. R. Lingeman. il Mlle 62:184-5+ N '65
  See also
Clothing and dress
Dating
Drinking customs
Hairdressing
Tipping
MANNES, Marya
But, M. Courrèges, what about Mrs Bottomley? N Y Times Mag p34-5+ Mr 28 '65
I, Mary, take thee, John, as...what? N Y Times Mag p52-3+ N 14 '65

MANNES, Marya—*Continued*
  Let's face it. por McCalls 92:18+ Je; 14+ Jl;
    16+ Ag; 18+ S; 93:92+ O; 34+ N '65; 34+
    Ja '66
  Life radio review. Life 58:12 F 5 '65
  Status cymbal. New Repub 153:12 D 18 '65
  Threatening crowd. Read Digest 86:173-4+
    F '65

MANNES college of music, New York
  Manhattan Olympiad. Q. Eaton. Opera N 29:
    31 Mr 20 '65

MANNIK, Mart. and Metzger, Henry
  Hybrid antibody molecules with allotypically
    different L-polypeptide chains. bibliog Sci-
    ence 148:383-5 Ap 16 '65

MANNING, Gordon P.
  Easily built dish rack. Motor B 116:43 N '65
  Easy to make cockpit panels. Motor B 116:
    42 N '65
  Sailaway, sailaway, sailaway home. Motor B
    116:30-4+ S '65

MANNING, Robert
  Hemingway in Cuba. Atlan 216:101-8 Ag '65

MANNING, Rosemary
  Garland of friendship; story. Mlle 61:140-1
    O '65
  Our dreams are tales. Horn Bk 41:24-7 F '65

MANNING, S. F.
  Dandiest dock in Darien. il Yachting 118:146
    S '65

MANNITOL
  Thin-layer chromatography of plant pigments
    on mannitol or sucrose. L. W. Smith and
    others. il Science 148:508-9 Ap 23 '65

MANNIX, Daniel P.
  Horses in the living room. Sat Eve Post
    238:36-7 Je 5 '65

MANOOGIAN, Haig
  Sound advice. Mod Phot 29:24+ My '65

MANOU, Rallou
  Meeting with Rallou Manou. S. J. Cohen. il
    por Dance Mag 39:57 Je '65

MANPOWER
  Manpower implications of technological
    change. Mo Labor R 88:III-IV F '65
  Toward an integrated manpower policy. G. L.
    Mangum. Mo Labor R 88:547-9 My '65
    See also
  Labor supply

MANPOWER development and training act.
  See Labor laws and legislation—United
  States

MANRY, Robert Neal
  Aboard Tinkerbelle on her run to glory. il
    pors Life 59:30-9 S 17 '65

    about
  Brave self far at sea. L. Wainwright. Life
    59:18 S 3 '65
  Conquering copyreader. il por Time 86:61
    S 10 '65
  Reluctant ocean-going hero. G. P. Hunt.
    il por Life 59:3 S 17 '65
  Scoop at sea. il Time 86:48 Ag 20 '65
  Seventy-eight days to fame. il por Time
    86:22 Ag 27 '65
  Suburbanite's saga. M. Lydon. il Newsweek
    66:37-8 Ag 30 '65

MANSFIELD, A. Rulon, Jr
  Are you covered? Yachting 117:67+ Je '65

MANSFIELD, Lewis P.
  Rubber dollars; address, June 28, 1965. Vital
    Speeches 31:735-6 S 15 '65

MANSFIELD, Michael Joseph
  How to end the war: Mansfield's five points;
    excerpts from statements. por U S News
    59:19 S 13 '65
  Congress and business: Senators Mansfield
    and Dirksen debate outlook; ed. by J. W.
    Bunting. pors Nations Bsns 53:76-80+ Mr
    '65

    about
  Charity begins abroad. M. Ascoli. Reporter
    33:24 O 7 '65
  Small something for Hanoi. por Time 86:19
    S 10 '65
  Two key senators who question LBJ's policy
    on Vietnam. por U S News 58:17 My 3 '65

MANSFIELD, Ohio
  Kingwood center. J. M. Martin. il Horticul-
    ture 43:44-7 Ap '65

MANSLAUGHTER. See Murder

MANSUR, Hassan Ali
  Two premiers felled. por Sr Schol 86:18 F
    11 '65

MANTHORNE, Jane
  Age of the acronym: address, February 1965.
    por Wilson Lib Bul 40:84-6 S '65
  Books for the Job corps. por(p 934) Library J
    90:932-3 F 15 '65

MANTLE, Mickey
  Decline and fall of a dynasty; with editorial
    comment. J. Mann. il por(cover) Sports
    Illus 22:4, 20-5 Je 21 '65
  Last innings of greatness. J. R. McDermott.
    il pors Life 59:46B-53 Jl 30 '65
  Mickey Mantle: Oklahoma to Olympus. G.
    Astor. il pors Look 29:70-5 F 23 '65
  $100,000 invalid. Newsweek 66:63 D 27 '65
  Vulgar tribute to greatness. L. Wainwright.
    Life 59:25 O 1 '65
  Yank. il por Newsweek 66:92-3 S 27 '65

MANTZ, Paul
  I'll put on one hell of a show. T. Taylor
    and J. Atwater. il por Sat Eve Post 238:74-7
    O 9 '65

MANUEL, Michael
  At least 130 people in love; interview. ed. by
    L. Lerman. por Mlle 61:146-7+ O '65

MANUFACTURED houses. See Houses, Prefabricated

MANUFACTURERS

Wages and hours

Wage developments in manufacturing. R. W.
  Benny. il Mo Labor R 88:1182-8 O '65
MANUFACTURERS, National association of.
  See National association of manufacturers
MANUFACTURERS excise tax. See Excise tax
MANUFACTURERS guarantees. See Guaranty
  of goods
MANUFACTURERS Hanover trust company.
  See New York (city)—Banks
MANUFACTURES
  Labor turnover; tables. See issues of Monthly
    labor review
    See also
  Private brands

Statistics

Ratios of manufacturing; with table. il
  Duns R 86:62-5 N '65
MANURE odors. See Odors
MANURES. See Fertilizers and manures
MANUS tribe. See New Guinea—Native races
MANUSCRIPT division. See United States—
  Library of Congress—Manuscript division
MANUSCRIPTS
  Great manuscript rush. D. Dempsey. Sat R
    48:28-9 My 1 '65
  Manuscripts at Sotheby's. K. V. Hostick.
    Hobbies 70:110-11 D '65
  Off the cuff. L. Conger. Writer 78:7-8 My '65
  Testaments of time. by L. Devel. Review
    Sat R il 48:32 D 18 '65. J. B. Pritchard
    See also
  Dead Sea scrolls

Collection and preservation

Manuscripts make history. R. L. Brubaker.
  Hobbies 70:110-11+ Ja '66

Photographic reproduction and
projection

New center for coordination of foreign manu-
  script copying. ALA Bul 59:701 S '65
MANUSCRIPTS, Coptic (papyri)
  New words of Jesus? Coptic prayer book
    discovered. il Time 87:70 Ja 7 '66
MANUSCRIPTS, Hebrew
  Antiquity's undercover magicians; recon-
    struction of the Sefar ha-razim. H. Nel-
    son. il Sat R 48:21+ F 6 '65
MANUSCRIPTS, Illuminated. See Illumination
  of books and manuscripts
MANUSCRIPTS, Illumination of. See Illumina-
  tion of books and manuscripts
MANUSCRIPTS, Rejected. See Editors and
  editing
MANZANITAS. See Bearberries
MANZELLA, David
  R.I.S.D. hypotheses. Sch Arts 65:31-3 S '65
MANZER, Helen C.
  Are color photographers born or made? R.
    Miller. il U S Camera 28:26 O '65
MANZONI, Giacomo
  Atomtod. Criticism
    Hi Fi 15:135 Je '65
MANZÙ, Giacomo
  Relief from drabness. il Time 85:86 My 7 '65
MAO, Tse-tung
  Interview with Mao, ed. by E. Snow. New
    Repub 152:17-23 F 27 '65; Reply. M. Lind-
    say. 152:27 Mr 13 '65. Summary. por News-
    week 65:36+ F 22 '65

    about
  China goes it alone. R. MacFarquhar. Atlan
    215:69-75 Ap '65

MAO, Tse-tung—about—*Continued*
China's strategy; a critique. D. S. Zagoria.
Commentary 40:61-6 N '65
It doesn't matter who succeeds Mao. J.
Marcuse. il pors N Y Times Mag p8-9+
Jl 11 '65
Leadership and succession in Communist
China. W. F. Dorrill. bibliog f Cur Hist 49:
129-35+ S '65
Mao and the Chinese revolution, by J. Ch'en.
Review
Nation 200:703-4 Je 28 '65. C. P. Fitz-
gerald
Mao at 72. S. Liu. il por Newsweek 67:37 Ja 10
'66
Mao Tse-tung industry. F. Nossal. il Sat R
49:108-9 Ja 8 '66
Mind of Mao. S. Alsop. il por Sat Eve Post
239:14 Ja 15 '66
Old, old order. il por Newsweek 65:56 Je 14
'65
On translating Mao's poetry. D. Davie. Na-
tion 200:704-5 Je 28 '65
To Mao we are the prime enemy. M. Gayn.
il N Y Times Mag p46-7+ O 24 '65

MAP making. See Cartography

MAPES, John G.
Public relations; address, March 4, 1965. Vital
Speeches 31:362-5 Ap 1 '65

MAPHAM, Neville W.
Battery-operated fluorescent lamp. Electr
World 74:68 O '65

MAPLE
Autumn color you can count on; bigleaf
maple. il Sunset 135:72 O '65
Maple gives New York a first. N. Ashby. il
Am For 71:16-19+ Ap '65; Discussion. 71:53
Je '65

MAPLE, Japanese. See Japanese maple

MAPLE syrup
Maple gives New York a first. N. Ashby. il
Am For 71:16-19+ Ap '65; Discussion. 71:53
Je '65
New money from old maples. D. K. O'Brien.
il Farm J 89:56B-56C F '65

MAPPING, Aerial
Better maps; Pittsburgh new aerial mapping
program. C. B. Genrich, jr. il Am City 80:
166+ Jl '65
Infrared maps spot fresh water. Sci N L 87:
168 Mr 13 '65
See also
Artificial satellites—Mapping applications
Photogrammetry

MAPS
Good maps & where to get them. il Chang-
ing T 19:21-3 O '65
See also
Cartography
World maps

MARA
Princess Qua-Qua. 92nd street Y. M. Marks.
Dance Mag 39:162 D '65

MARANTZ, Kenneth
Books. See issues of School arts

MARAT/Sade; drama. See Weiss, P.

MARATHON oil company
Up from the old mill stream. il Time 86:66
Ag 13 '65

MARATHON running. See Running

MARBACH, Ethel
Will the real Pollyanna please stand up?
Farm J 89:71+ N '65

MARBERRY, M. M.
Overloved one. Am Heritage 16:84-7+ Ag
'65

MARBLE CANYON DAM (proposed) See Dams

MARBLE House. See Newport, R.I.—Historic
houses

MARBLE MOUNTAIN wilderness area. See
Wilderness areas

MARBLING
Binding with vat-made papers; C. Delpierre
and K. Vinding revive centuries-old art.
A. Karlikow. il Craft Horiz 25:12-15+ Mr
'65

MARBURGER, Carl L. See Sorenson, R. jt.
auth.

MARCEAU, Marcel
Who am I? pors Dance Mag 39:49-51 N '65
about
Marcel Marceau New York city center. M.
Marks. Dance Mag 40:18 Ja '66

MARCEL Dekker, incorporated. See Dekker,
Marcel, incorporated

MARCELLA M. Holloway, Sister. See Holloway, M. M.

MARCH
In March; few of the dates, memorable and
not so, coming up next month (title varies)
(cont) il N Y Times Mag p33+ F 28 '65

MARCH on Washington. See Civil rights demonstrations

MARCHANT, William
Copenhagen. Holiday 38:30-43+ S '65
December. in Naples. Holiday 39:54-9+ Ja
'66

MARCHETTI, John
Silk-screened circuit boards. Electr World
73:46-8+ Je '65

MARCHOWSKY, Marie
Marie Marchowsky, 92nd st. Y. J. Maskey.
Dance Mag 39:65 My '65

MARCO, Guy A.
After Grove's, what? por Library J 90:1259-
62 Mr 15 '65

MARCONI, Guglielmo
Cape Cod's Marconi station site. C. R.
Koehler. il Nat Parks Mag 39:18 S '65

MARCOS, Ferdinand
Demand for heroes. il por Time 87:26 Ja
7 '66
Go Marcos. il por Newsweek 66:54 N 22 '65
He promised them everything except for my
wife; with report by G. De Carvalho. il
pors Life 59:78A-80+ N 26 '65
Letter from Manila. R. Shaplen. il New
Yorker 41:84+ Ja 15 '66
Marcos elected. Sr Schol 87:20 D 9 '65
Surprise in Manila. il por Time 86:52 N 19 '65

MARCUCCI, Robert P.
Image polished. P. Bart. por Esquire 64:
80-1+ Jl '65

MARCUS, Leon, and others
Polysomes from yeast: distribution of
messenger RNA and capacity to support
protein synthesis in vitro. bibliog Science
147:615-17 F 5 '65

MARCUS, Leonard
Munich Bach chorus and orchestra. Hi Fi
15:102-3 Jl '65
Posthumous career of J. S. Bach. Hi Fi 16:
56-8+ Ja '66
Tomorrow's grand old men. Hi Fi 15:119
'65

MARCUS, Paul, and Zide, Larry
Solid-state designs for hi-fi amplifiers. Electr
World 73:49-52+ Je '65

MARCUS, Philip I. and Carver, D. H.
Hemadsorption-negative plaque test: new assay for rubella virus revealing a unique interference. bibliog Science 149:983-6 Ag 27
'65

MARCUS, Ruth
Small wonders. See issues of Good housekeeping

MARCUSE, Jacques
How to talk to the Chinese in Peking. N Y
Times Mag p24-5+ My 23 '65
It doesn't matter who succeeds Mao. N Y
Times Mag p8-9+ Jl 11 '65

MARCY, Carl
Burdens of power. Sat R 48:11-13 S 4 '65

MARCY, Carol
Works by Deborah Lee, Carol Marcy, and
James Waring; Judson memorial church
J. Anderson. Dance Mag 39:158 D '65

MARDI gras. See Carnival

MARDI gras! musical comedy. See Musical
comedies, revues, etc.—Criticisms, plots,
etc.

MARDON, Allan
Once around the clock swiftly rolling; paintings. Sports Illus 22:28-34 Mr 22 '65

MAREK, George R.
Michelin for museums. Sat R 48:44+ Mr 13
'65

MARETT, Lynn
Double duty for dad. Parents Mag 40:52-5 Je
'65

MARGAIN, Hugo B.
Mexican economic and social development.
Ann Am Acad 360:68-77 Jl '65

MARGALIOTH, Mordecai
Antiquity's undercover magicians. H. Nelson. il Sat R 48:21+ F 6 '65

MARGARET, princess of Great Britain
Beyond the great divide; trip to the U.S.
il Time 86:38 N 12 '65
Fun party; hostess, Lydia Katzenbach. il por
Newsweek 66:26-7 N 29 '65
H.R.H. the Princess Margaret, Countess of
Snowdon and the Earl of Snowdon, on an
official visit to the United States. por Vogue
146:82-3 N 15 '65
Margaret: the British princess with American
tastes. D. Eisenberg. il pors Look 29:68-70+
N 30 '65
Meg & Tony show. il por Time 86:29 N 26 '65
Princess in Washington. il pors U S News
59:48-9 N 29 '65
Princess looks us over. il pors Life 59:110A-
11 N 19 '65

MARGARET, princess of Great Britain—
Continued
Princess Margaret's other home; excerpts from Tony's room. W. Glenton. il por McCalls 93:132-3+ N '65
Radiant interlude in history; White House dinner and dance. il pors Life 59:32-41 D 3 '65
Room on the London docks; excerpt from Tony's room. W. Glenton. il por McCalls 93:116-19+ O '65
Royal doll; San Francisco press club reception. il por Newsweek 66:42+ N 15 '65
Snowdons come on a visit. C. Hussey. il pors N Y Times Mag p48-9+ O 31 '65
Snowdons come to call. il pors Newsweek 66:44-6+ N 22 '65
Two worlds of Princess Margaret. J. Morris. il pors Sat Eve Post 238:27-31 N 20 '65
When royalty goes go-go; keeping up with the Armstrong-Joneses. L. Hannon. il pors Ladies Home J 82:60-1+ S '65

MARGE, Michael
Gift of speech. por Am Ed 1:23-5 N '65

MARGIN requirements, Stock. See Stock exchange—Regulation

MARGIOTTA, Mike
Look at me. il U S Camera 29:54-5 Ja '66

MARGOLIN, Paul
Bipolarity of information transfer from the salmonella typhimurium chromosome. bibliog Science 147:1456-8 Mr 19 '65

MARGOLIS, Frank L. and Russell, E. S.
Delta-aminolevulinate dehydratase activity 'n mice with hereditary anemia. bibliog Science 150:496-7 O 22 '65

MARGOLIS, George. See Kilham, L. jt. auth.

MARGOLIS, Howard
From Washington: McNamara's new budget. Bul Atomic Sci 21:54-6 Mr '65
From Washington: notes on defense matters. Bul Atomic Sci 21:36-8 S '65
From Washington: notes on gas and disarmament. Bul Atomic Sci 21:30-2 N '65
From Washington: notes on Vietnam. Bul Atomic Sci 21:2-3+ Ap '65
From Washington: some problems in Vietnam. Bul Atomic Sci 21:40-3 My '65
From Washington: the air force in space and peacekeeping assessments. Bul Atomic Sci 21:34-7 O '65
From Washington: the spring lull. Bul Atomic Sci 21:26-7+ Je '65

MARGOLIS, Richard J.
Integration: the problems nobody talks about. Redbook 124:68-9+ Ap '65
Trouble with textbooks. Redbook 124:64-5+ Mr '65

MARGOSIAN, George
Suggestions for the college supervisor. NEA J 54:39 Ap '65

MARGUERITE Thomas, Sister
Nuns at Selma. America 112:454-6 Ap 3 '65

MARIAN Frances, Sister
Christmas card verse '65. Commonweal 83:374 D 24 '65
Discipline is. . . NEA J 54:26-8 S '65

MARICHAL, Juan Antonio
Bat day. il por Newsweek 66:44 S 6 '65
Battle of San Francisco. J. Mann. il Sports Illus 23:12-15 Ag 30 '65
Time for tension. il por Time 86:64 S 3 '65
Weirdest race rolls on. W. Leggett. Sports Illus 23:36-7 S 13 '65

MARIE Aimée Carey, Mother. See Carey, M. A.

MARIE Jerome, Sister. See Jerome, M.

MARIE LAURIE, vicomtesse de Noailles. See Noailles, M. L.

MARIGOLDS
Marigolds help kill tiny worms in fields. Sci N L 88:110 Ag 14 '65

MARIHUANA
Pot-picking time; boys arrested for growing marijuana in Carpinteria, Calif. Newsweek 65:42 My 1 '65
Pot problem; college students use of marijuana. il Time 85:49 Mr 12 '65

MARIJUANA. See Marihuana

MARIN, Luis Muñoz. See Muñoz Marín, L.

MARIN, Pedro Antonio
Return of sure shot. Time 85:37 Ap 9 '65

MARIN COUNTY, Calif.
Gold in the hills of California. il Fortune 72: 162-4 Ag '65
Marin-on-the-Bay. il Sunset 134:87-97 My '65

MARINA city, Chicago. See Chicago—Housing

MARINAS
Boatman's haven. il Newsweek 65:90+ Je 21 '65

Models
Best by test; marina at Dana Point, Calif. C. West. il Motor B 115:32-4+ My '65

MARINE aquariums. See Aquariums

MARINE biological laboratory, Woods Hole. See Woods Hole, Mass, marine biological laboratory

MARINE biology
See also
Marine resources

MARINE cookery. See Cookery, Marine

MARINE corps. See United States—Marine corps

MARINE corrosion. See Corrosion and anticorrosives

MARINE deposits. See Deep sea deposits

MARINE engines
Big stern-drive cruise handles like outboard. J. Roe. il Pop Sci 186:96-8 Mr '65
How to build your own sea engine. il Pop Sci 188:114-15 Ja '66
New for '65, as seen at the Chicago trade show. Yachting 118:164-6 O '65
New small-boat stern drive: Merc goes miniature. J. Roe. il Pop Sci 186:100-2 F '65
1965 success story; with list of new stern drive manufacturers; ed. by F. M. Paulson. il Field & S 70:130-4 My '65
'66 power profile. il Motor B 116:49-53 N '65
Wankel engine. H. G. Strepp. il Motor B 116: 28-31 D '65
See also
Gas and oil engines, Inboard
Gas and oil engines, Outboard

Ignition
Transistor ignitions, good? bad? and how can you tell? G. M. Galster. il Motor B 115:82-3+ Mr '65

MARINE fauna
Schlieren technique for studying water flow in marine animals. J. A. Westphal. il Science 149:1515-16 S 24 '65
Science in action: mixing oceans and species. I. Rubinoff. Natur Hist 74:69-72 Ag '65
See also
Plankton
Sponges

Collection and preservation
Amateur scientist; on collecting and preserving animals that live along the edge of the sea. J. J. Rudloe. il Sci Am 212:119-20+ Mr '65

MARINE iguanas. See Iguanas

MARINE insurance. See Insurance, Marine

MARINE microorganisms. See Microorganisms

MARINE military academy, Harlingen, Tex. See Military schools

MARINE paint. See Paint

MARINE painting
By the beautiful sea; artist and the sea. F. Getlein. New Repub 154:34-5 Ja 8 '66

MARINE photography. See Photography—Marines

MARINE resources
Living economy of the sea. G. E. Jones. Bul Atomic Sci 21:13-17 Mr '65
Oceanography: a wet and wondrous journey. A. Spilhaus; reply. G. Pontecorvo. Bul Atomic Sci 21:33 My '65
Race for riches under the sea. B. H. Frisch. il Sci Digest 59:48-56 Ja '66
See also
Fisheries

MARINE sediments. See Sedimentation and deposition

MARINE snails. See Snails

MARINE spark plugs. See Spark plugs

MARINE worms
Pogonophora: living species found off the coast of Florida. C. Nielsen. bibliog Science 150:1475 D 10 '65

MARINER probes. See Space probes

MARINKELLE, C. J. and Grose, E.
Histoplasma capsulatum from the liver of a bat in Colombia. bibliog Science 147:1039-40 F 26 '65

MARIO, Jessie Meriton White
Jessie White Mario: Victorian in Italy. E. A. Daniels. il Nation 202:13-16 Ja 3 '66

MARION, John
Auction by Early bird. R. Lynes. il Harper 231:28+ Ag '65

MARION, Ala.
Eulogy for a woodchopper; Negro shot by state police. Time 85:23B Mr 12 '65
Freedom fever; civil rights violence. Time 85:23 F 26 '65

MARISOL
Dollmaker. il por Time 85:80-1 My 28 '65
It's not pop, it's not op, it's Marisol. G. Glueck. il pors N Y Times Mag p34-5+ Mr 7 '65

MARITAL Infidelity. See Sexual ethics

MARITAL separation. See Domestic relations

MARITIME college, Fort Schuyler, N.Y.
Maritime remodels. J. N. Whitten. il Library J 90:5201-3 D 1 '65

MARITIME commission. See United States—Maritime commission

MARITIME law
Change on the high seas. M. Penzer. il Motor B 115:54-5+ Ap '65
Neglected sea power; US navy patrolling coast of South Vietnam. R. Moley. Newsweek 65:112 My 17 '65
See also
Blockade
Boats and boating—Laws and regulations
Pilots and pilotage
Territorial waters

MARITIME meteorology. See Meteorology, Maritime

MARITIME PROVINCES, Canada
Vacation bargain. C. W. Morton. il Atlan 216:110+ D '65

MARITIME unions. See Trade unions—United States

MARITIME workers
Shipping all at sea; government silence on policy blamed. Bsns W p 142 Je 12 '65
See also
Longshoremen
Strikes—United States—Maritime workers

MARK, Barry R.
Hiring and training personnel for the bookstore. Pub W 187:68-71 Mr 1 '65

MARK, Larry D.
Hog cholera eradication: we are making progress. Suc Farm 63:39 Mr '65

MARK, Mary Ellen
Discovery. P. Caulfield. il Mod Phot 30:82-3+ Ja '66

MARK, Norman
Censorship: fanatics and fallacies. Nation 201:5-7 Jl 5 '65

MARK Twain, pseud. See Clemens, S. L.

MARKEL, Helen
(ed) See Phillips, I. Every woman's life is a soap opera
(ed) See Von Hess, M. I teach famous men to talk

MARKEL, Lester
Public opinion and the war in Vietnam. N Y Times Mag p9+ Ag 8 '65

MARKER, Leonard
Wozzeck at forty. Opera N 30:6-7 N 20 '65

MARKER, Richard
Opinion, please from New York. Mlle 61:38+ Je '65

MARKET carts. See Carts

MARKET hunting. See Poaching

MARKET research
Diagnosing the marketing takeover; excerpt from Marketing management: analysis, planning, and control. P. Kotler. il Harvard Bsns R 43:70-2 N '65
Grass roots market research. L. W. Stern and J. L. Heskett. bibliog f il Harvard Bsns R 43:83-96 Mr '65
How to measure marketing performance. R. A. Feder. il Harvard Bsns R 43:132-42 My '65
Leverage in the product life cycle. D. K. Clifford, jr. il Duns 85:62-4+ My '65
Must advertising communicate to sell? C. K. Ramond. bibliog f il Harvard Bsns R 43:148-56+ S '65

MARKET surveys
See also
Consumers preferences
Youth market

MARKETING
Business lectures professors; Monsanto woos chemistry graduates to marketing by teaching their teachers. il Bsns W p65-6 Jl 10 '65
Concept of a national market; address, September 1, 1965. W. W. Rostow. Vital Speeches 31:717-20 S 15 '65
Deeper roots for the Alliance; developing nations of Latin America. W. W. Rostow. il Américas 17:37-41 Ap '65
Exploit the product life cycle; excerpt from Marketing vision. T. Levitt. il Harvard Bsns R 43:81-94 N '65
Man with too many hats; product manager, long on duties, short on authority. il Bsns W p43-4 My 22 '65
More sense about market segmentation. W. H. Reynolds. bibliog f il Harvard Bsns R 43:107-14 S '65
Multi-agency marketing. G. Lazarus. Sat R 48:59-60 Ag 14 '65

To reorganize, turn bottom up; more markets for Walter Kidde & company. il Bsns W p81-2+ Ap 10 '65
See also
Advertising
Booksellers and bookselling
Dealer relations
Exclusive agencies
Packaging
Price cutting
Sales promotion
Supermarkets

Cost
Next place for paring costs. il Bsns W p 132+ My 1 '65

Study and teaching
Marketing strategy brings higher sales. il Nations Bsns 53:94-6+ N '65

MARKETING, Cooperative
What bargaining power can, and can't do; excerpt from address. D. Paarlberg. Farm J 89:77 Mr '65

MARKÉVITCH, Igor
Second fame: good food. N. Lyon. por Vogue 145:190-2 Ap 1 '65

MARKFIELD, Wallace
Yiddishization of American humor. Esquire 64:114-15+ O '65

MARKHAM, Margaret
Arthritis. Parents Mag 40:60-1+ D '65
Scientists use new techniques to study the complex activity called sleep. Parents Mag 40:60-1+ Ag '65
(ed) See Gordon, H. H. Good news for parents of preemies

MARKL, Hubert
Stridulation in leaf-cutting ants. bibliog Science 149:1392-3 S 17 '65

MARKLEY, Edith
Peanuts from start to finish. Flower Grower 52:68-71 F '65

MARKOS, Joanne
Blue and white paper silhouettes. Design 67:17 S '65

MARKOVA, Dame Alicia
Dancer's life. por Seventeen 24:126+ D '65
about
On their toes. E. H. Palatsky. il Opera N 29:12-16 Ap 10 '65

MARKOWITZ, Marvin D. and Weiss, H. F.
Rebellion in the Congo. Cur Hist 48:213-18+ Ap '65

MARKOWITZ, Rubin
Case of the dead bookie. R. Kahn. il por Sat Eve Post 238:34-8+ Mr 13 '65

MARKS, Frank H.
Microfilm your records and save. Am City 80:152+ Je '65

MARKS, Joseph J. See Lindstrom, R. S. jt. auth.

MARKS, Margaret
Re-verses; poem. McCalls 92:117 S '65

MARLBORO festival of music. See Music festivals—Vermont

MARLBOROUGH-Gerson gallery. See New York (city)—Galleries and museums

MARLEY, C. F.
Easy way to move feed, blow it! il Suc Farm 63:64A N '65
Eighty litters per year, the low-cost way. Suc Farm 63:34A Jl '65
Need water? build a cistern. il Suc Farm 63:73 N '65

MARLIN fishing
And sometimes the marlin win. D. Phillips. il Motor B 116:48-51 Ag '65
Billfish West. C. West. il Motor B 116:36+ S '65
To Parajiso with Papa and Pilar. M. Hemingway. il Sports Illus 23:62-8+ Jl 12 '65

MARLOWE, Christopher
Christopher Marlowe: his life and work, by A. L. Rowse. Review
Nation 200:115+ F 1 '65. A. Burgess
In search of Christopher Marlowe, by A. D. Wraight and V. F. Stern. Review
Sat R por 48:33-4 D 25 '65. B. Grebanier

MARMOSET twins. See Twins

MARMOTS
Great sleeper. S. F. Arno. il Nat Parks Mag 39:20 O '65
Olympic reverie. R. Kirk. il Nat Parks Mag 39:4-7 My '65

MAROF, Achkar
United Nations commemoration address, June 25, 1965. UN Mo Chron 2:113-18 Jl '65

MAROS, Rudolf
Find, the music of Rudolf Maros. A. Cohn. por Am Rec G 31:729 Ap '65

MARQUAND, John Phillips
Young John Marquand. J. P. Driver. por Atlan 216:69-72 Ag '65

MARQUÉS, René
Blue kite; story. Américas 17:30-3 My '65

MARQUESAS ISLANDS
Sailing through the Marquesas. S. A. Simpson. il Travel 125:48-54 Ja '66

Voyage to the Marquesas. R. Thales. il Motor B 115:22-5+ F '65

MARQUETTE, Jacques
Three apostles to the Indians. P. W. Schmidtchen. il Hobbies 70:106+ Ag '65

MARQUIS, Don
Don Marquis to the young; letter. ed. by C. O'Neill. Esquire 63:77+ My '65

MARQUIS, William C.
What is a small businessman? address, September 13, 1965. Vital Speeches 32:21-4 O 15 '65

MARR, Dave
I'm going to keep the money and give away Gary. A. Wright. por Sports Illus 23:50-3 S 6 '65

Sporting scene. H. W. Wind. il New Yorker 41:209-10+ N 13 '65

Taste of money. il por Time 86:68 Ag 27 '65

MARRIAGE
Can love last forever? J. Brothers. Good H 160:68+ Mr '65

Can this marriage be saved? case histories; ed. by D. C. Disney. See issues of Ladies home journal

Couples must bargain. Sci N L 88:29 Jl 10 '65

Difference of more than opinion: conflicting temperaments. M. Jones. Redbook 124:6+ Ap '65

For newlyweds & soon-to-weds; hints and advice. il Changing T 19:24-5 Je '65

I love you; and I like you! ed. by M. Longwell. H. D. Schalock. Farm J 89:75+ O '65

I, Mary, take thee, John, as...what? concerning research by H. Lopata of Roosevelt university, Chicago. M. Mannes. il N Y Times Mag p52-3+ N 14 '65

Infidelity: a growing problem in American marriages. J. Callwood. Ladies Home J 82:76-7+ Ap '65

Long, hard look at love and marriage. M. Drury. il McCalls 92:93+ Ap '65

Man talk; improvised marriage. D. Newman and R. Benton. il Mlle 61:16+ Je '65

Marriage, neurotic and otherwise. F. R. Schreiber and M. Herman. il Sci Digest 57:26-30 Je '65

Marriage's best and worst prospects. F. R. Schreiber and M. Herman. il Sci Digest 57:16-18 Mr '65

Patterns of marriage: how successful men and women arrange their married lives. M. M. Hunt. Redbook 125:56-7 S '65

Reproduction and the whole man. F. W. Carney. il America 112:245-7 F 20 '65

Secret; excerpt from In my father's court. I. B. Singer. Commentary 40:72+ O '65

Should you try to remodel your mate? Farm J 89:65+ Je '65

Speaking out; why get married? L. Koempel. il Sat Eve Post 238:10+ F 13 '65; Same abr. Read Digest 86:55-7 My '65

Time out for parents; with study-discussion program, by R. Strang. D. Grace. bibliog il PTA Mag 59:11-13, 35 Ap '65

To my son on his wedding day. J. P. McEvoy. Read Digest 86:160F-160G Je '65

What every (mother of the) bride should know. P. McGinley. Ladies Home J 82:57+ Je '65

What young husbands really think about marriage. S. Blum and S. Welles. il Redbook 125:60-1+ Ag '65

What young wives have learned about husbands. D. Siegel. il Redbook 126:58-9+ N '65

When a marriage is in trouble. il Changing T 19:43-5 My '65

When the ideal wife marries the absolutely perfect husband. R. Baker. Ladies Home J 82:66-7 S '65

Young wife's world. H. Valentine. See issues of Good housekeeping

See also
Alimony
Divorce
Dowry
High school students, Married
Husbands
Intermarriage of races
Love
Physical examinations, Premarital
Weddings
Wives
Woman

Anecdotes, facetiae, satire, etc.
Bachelor's guide to marriage. C. Ford. Read Digest 86:229-32 Ap '65

I couldn't have stood marriage; a humorist-artist's account. D. Herold. il Read Digest 87:25-6 S '65

Marrying kind. E. Kendall. Mlle 61:122-3+ O '65

Annulment
Legal facts about divorce, separation and annulment. il Good H 160:180 Mr '65

Handbooks, manuals, etc.
Priest with a breezy way; Father Capon writes about wine, food and marriage. il Life 59:79-80 D 3 '65

Sex manuals: how not to ... il Newsweek 66:100-1 O 18 '65

Statistics
Prop for business in '66; increase in the number of newlyweds. il U S News 58:82 Ap 19 '65

Africa
Church and marriage in Africa. K. Hughes. Christian Cent 82:204-8 F 17 '65; Reply. L. Andrews. 82:497 Ap 21 '65

Iran
Take a lesson from pasha. A. S. Mehdevi. Harper 230:97-9 My '65

Russia
Sex under socialism. E. Pawel. Commentary 40:90+ S '65; Reply with rejoinder. J. Weber. 41:14+ Ja '66

United States
See Marriage

MARRIAGE brokers
Courtship by computer; German matchmakers. il Newsweek 65:34+ Mr 29 '65

MARRIAGE counseling
Can this marriage be saved? case histories; ed. by D. C. Disney. See issues of Ladies home journal

How marriage counseling helps children; Juvenile welfare board, Pinellas County, Fla. C. Foster. il Parents Mag 40:42-3+ My '65

Letters to Karen; excerpt. C. W. Shedd. il Read Digest 88:211-16+ Ja '66

Man to marry; excerpt from Way to womanhood. W. W. Bauer and F. M. Bauer. il Todays Health 43:38-9+ Ap '65

When a marriage is in trouble. il Changing T 19:43-5 My '65

MARRIAGE law
See also
Community property

Italy
Bigamy Italian style; Ponti-Loren muddle. D. J. Hamblin. il Life 59:52A-52B Jl 23 '65

Marriage Italian style. il Newsweek 65:40+ F 8 '65

MARRIAGE manuals. See Marriage—Handbooks, manuals, etc.

MARRIAGE of Figaro; opera. See Mozart, J. C. W. A.

MARRIAGE settlements. See Dowry

MARRIAGES, Interracial. See Intermarriage of races

MARRIAGES, Mixed
Catholic-Protestant marriages still a problem. Christian Cent 82:860 Jl 7 '65

Clash of cultures. D. C. Disney. Ladies Home J 82:54+ Mr '65

Dialogue on marriage; Protestant-Catholic. E. Gibson. Christian Cent 82:297-300 Mr 10 '65

Mixed marriages; laws of the Catholic church. Commonweal 81:719-20 Mr 5 '65; Discussion. 82:66, 202 Ap 9, My 7 '65

MARRIED college students. See College students, Married

MARRIED women

Employment
Case against full-time motherhood. A. Rossi. Redbook 124:51+ Mr '65

Come back to the work force, mother! L. Velie. Read Digest 87:201-2+ S '65

Identity of modern woman. H. S. Krech. il Nation 201:125-8 S 20 '65

Marital and family characteristics of workers in March 1964. V. C. Perrella. il Mo Labor R 88:260-5 Mr '65

Married women returning. PTA Mag 59:18 My '65

MARS (planet)—Surface—*Continued*
Scientist hopes for Mars ice layer; with bio-astronautical data table. Miss & Roc 17:37 Jl 19 '65
Where there's hope there may be life; Mars. Time 86:67 O 8 '65

Temperature
Mariner 4 data yields Martian temperatures. Sci N L 89:37 Ja 15 '66
Temperature measurements of Mars. Sky & Tel 30:213 O '65

MARS landing systems. See Space vehicles—Landing systems—Mars
MARS probe. See Space probes
MARSAL, Sonia
Edward Hics: Quaker painter. Américas 17:5-14 D '65
MARSCHALL, John P.
Thread of renewal. America 113:622-5 N 20 '65
MARSDEN, Brian G.
Great comet of 1965. Sky & Tel 30:332-7 D '65
Strange story of comet de Vico-Swift. Sky & Tel 30:139-40 S '65
MARSH, Bernard L.
Skokie Swift, the answer to a commuter's prayer. Am City 80:122-3 Je '65
MARSH, George Perkins
George Perkins Marsh: conservation's forgotten man. C. E. Randall. por Am For 71:20-3 Ap '65
MARSH, Gwen
René Guillot. Horn Bk 41:192-4 Ap '65
MARSH, Reginald
In the American grain. K. Kuh. il Sat R 48:68-70 O 30 '65
MARSH, Robert C.
Art before virtuosity, and chamber music as it's meant to be. Hi Fi 15:57-8 Je '65
Everything's up to date in... Hi Fi 15:126 Ag '65
Opera in a bonanza town. Hi Fi 15:153+ O '65
Quality in several forms. Hi Fi 15:156 S '65
Sense of tradition. Hi Fi 15:128+ Ag '65
Two seasons by Martinon. Hi Fi 15:111 Jl '65
MARSH, Tracy H.
America sings: recorded by the glassmaker. Hobbies 70:88-9 Je '65
Tea and the teapot story. Hobbies 70:82-3+ Ag '65
MARSH Arabs. See Iraq—Native races
MARSHAK, Robert E. See Caspari, E. W. jt. auth.
MARSHALL, Armina
Loveless start in life. Sat R 49:80-1 Ja 8 '66
MARSHALL, Charles Burton
Eisenhower's second term. New Repub 153:25-7 N 6 '65
India and Pakistan at war. New Repub 153:19-21 S 25 '65
Old soldier's rhetoric. New Repub 153:26+ N 20 '65
MARSHALL, E. G.
He likes to cook. il por Bet Hom & Gard 43:88 Ag '65
MARSHALL, Eleanor M.
Early starter: Christmas in America. Travel 124:42-4 N '65
MARSHALL, George Catlett
Marshall papers: volume II; Pearl Harbor blunders; excerpt from George C. Marshall: the war years. F. C. Pogue. il pors Look 29:34-9 D 14 '65
MARSHALL, Jack
Bacon's Van Gogh; poem. Poetry 106:208 Je '65
MARSHALL, John
Two-day torture on wheels. H. Peterson. il Sports Illus 23:32-4+ O 4 '65
MARSHALL, Ray
Prospects for equal employment: conflicting portents. Mo Labor R 88:650-3 Je '65
MARSHALL, S. L. A.
Chimeras in Viet Nam. Time 85:63 Mr 12 '65
MARSHALL, Thurgood
Advocate for U.S; report by S. McBee. il pors Life 59:57-8+ N 12 '65
Battler from Baltimore. por Newsweek 66:22 Jl 26 '65
From robe to swallowtail. il por Time 86:18 Jl 23 '65
Solicitor General. P. Pierce. il pors Ebony 21:67-9+ N '65
Stirring controversy, two LBJ nominations. U S News 59:10 Jl 26 '65
Tenth member. il por Time 86:94 O 22 '65

Thurgood Marshall takes a new tush-tush job. S. E. Zion. por N Y Times Mag p 11+ Ag 22 '65
Up from slavery. por Newsweek 66:41 O 18 '65
MARSHALL space flight center. See United States—National aeronautics and space administration—Marshall space flight center
MARSHES
Marsh Arabs, by W. Thesiger. Review
New Yorker 41:126-8 My 29 '65. N. Bliven
MARSHES, Salt. See Salt marshes
MARSICANO, Merle
Peril and delight; interview, ed. by W. Como. il por Dance Mag 39:25-7+ My '65

about

Merle Marsicano and company, 92nd street Y. J. Maskey. Dance Mag 39:62-3 Jl '65
MARSTON, Red
Disaster at Cat Cay. Yachting 117:196+ Je '65
World of Tampa Bay. Yachting 118:47-9+ N '65
MARSTON, Robert Quarles
HEW: running the Great society. E. Langer. por Science 150:1272-4 D 3 '65
MARSTON, William Moulton
Put your mind on the spot. Read Digest 86:68-71 My '65
Try everything once. Read Digest 86:93-6 F '65
MARSUPIALS
Chromosomes of American marsupials. J. D. Biggers and others. bibliog il Science 148:1602-3 Je 18 '65
MARTENHOFF, Jim
Disco Volante, the saucer that flies. il Motor B 116:32-3+ D '65
How to be happy though outdoors. Outdoor Life 136:58-9+ Jl '65
How to tackle torque. Pop Sci 187:78+ Jl '65
I flew an outboard hydrofoil. Pop Sci 187:79-81 N '65
Outboard know-how. Motor B 115:38-9+ Ap '65
Research rules the waves. il Motor B 115:40-2+ Ap '65
Tricks with trailers. Pop Sci 187:7-7 Jl '65
What sort of power next? See issues of Motor boating
Winds of the world. Motor B 115:45-7+ Mr '65
MARTENS, Anne Coulter
My swinging swain; drama. Plays 25:1-12 O '65
Over the river; drama. Plays 25:1-14, 26 N '65
MARTENS
America's most beautiful animal. C. A. Wheeler. il Field & S 70:58+ S '65
MARTHA'S VINEYARD
Vineyard is the place to go. S. A. Grau. il N Y Times Mag p26-7+ Ag 15 '65
MARTÍ, Jorge Luis
Beginnings of industrialism in Latin America. Américas 17:1-7 O '65
MARTÍ, José
Martí in Central park. F. Lizaso. il Américas 17:1-3 Je '65
MARTIAL law
See also
Courts martial
Military law
MARTIN, pseud.
Return of fire; poem. America 112:462 Ap 3 '65
MARTIN, Allie Beth, and Ward, C. W.
Tulsa in orbit. Library J 90:5164-7 D 1 '65
MARTIN, Archer N.
Glass dielectric capacitors. Electr World 74:54-6 Jl '65
MARTIN, Carol
Christmas tree for the children; excerpts from diary during West Coast flood, December 1964. Am For 71:17 Mr '65
MARTIN, David
Life movie review. Life 58:17 Ap 23; 12 Je 4; 59:8 Ag 20 '65
Life TV review (cont) Life 58:17 F 19 '65
Powerhouse in the attic. Life 59:98+ N 19 '65
MARTIN, Donald K.
You must use brains. Am City 80:95+ D '65
MARTIN, Edward J.
People of God. America 113:186-8 Ag 21 '65
MARTIN, Frank
On records; Jedermann. Der sturm; excerpts. Opera N 29:34 F 20 '65
MARTIN, Gene
Interlibrary cooperation in Missouri; address. July 1965. pors Wilson Lib Bul 40:166-71 O '65
MARTIN, George
How to make a quality print. G. Martin. il U S Camera 28:52-3+ S '65

MARTIN, Harold H.
American minister. Sat Eve Post 238:19-23+
　Ap 24 '65
New era for the old South. Sat Eve Post
　238:23-5+ O 9 '65
Two loves of Doctor Zhivago. Sat Eve Post
　239:26-31 Ja 15 '66
(ed) See Ridgway, M. B. 1965. warning on
　land war in Asia
MARTIN, Irene, and Levey, A. B.
Efficiency of the conditioned eyelid response.
　bibliog Science 150:781-3 N 5 '65
MARTIN, James M.
Kingwood center. Horticulture 43:44-7 Ap '65
MARTIN, Jean
Hospitals without nurses. Nation 201:245-6
　O 18 '65
MARTIN, John
Martha Graham's retrospective season. Sat R
　48:60+ D 11 '65
MARTIN, John Bartlow
Struggle to bring together two sides torn by
　killing. pors Life 58:28-31+ My 28 '65; Same
　abr. with title Assignment Santo Domingo.
　Read Digest 87:94-102 Jl '65
MARTIN, John Stuart
Rebirth of the shad. Atlan 215:90-3 Je '65
MARTIN, Lawrence
From Guzzle Down to the Tah. Sat R 48:52+
　Mr 13 '65
MARTIN, Lee
Rail cruise encore. Travel 123:10 Ap '65
MARTIN, Lowell
Ski resorts and glass branches. por Library J
　90:2076-7 My 1 '65
MARTIN, Lucy M.
Ministers vs. Miljay, inc. Christian Cent 82:
　679-80 My 26 '65
MARTIN, Mary
Broadway show in a theater of war. S.
　Alexander. Life 59:30 O 22 '65
Hello, Dolly, and hellish ambush. il pors Life
　59:32-3 O 22 '65
MARTIN, Mildred Crowl
Pied Piper of suburbia. Parents Mag 40:
　60-1+ Mr '65
MARTIN, Paul
If you wonder how the U.S. got into the
　war in Vietnam. por U S News 59:56-62
　S 13 '65
MARTIN, R. Bruce, and Morlino, V. J.
Exchange of carbon-bound hydrogen atoms
　ortho to the hydroxyl group in tyrosine.
　bibliog Science 150:493 O 22 '65
MARTIN, Ray
Here 'n' there; National library week: sour
　notes, questions; reprint. por Wilson Lib
　Bul 40:172 O '65
MARTIN, Robert
What you don't see can hurt you! Todays
　Health 43:42-7 N '65
MARTIN, Ruth, and Martin, Thomas
Good libretto. Opera N 29:12-15 F 20 '65
MARTIN, Ruth P.
Take advantage of leftover egg whites.
　Parents Mag 40:70-1+ My '65
MARTIN, Thomas. See Martin, R. jt. auth.
MARTIN, W. Edgar
Children be seated. por Am Ed 1:4-6 Je '65
MARTIN, Warren Bryan
American values in a revolutionary world;
　address, April 24, 1965. Vital Speeches 31:
　588-92 Jl 15 '65
MARTIN, William McChesney, 1906–
Does monetary history repeat itself? address,
　June 1, 1965. Vital Speeches 31:580-3 Jl 15
　'65; Excerpts. por U S News 58:84-6 Je 14
　'65; Summary. Newsweek 65:79 Je 14 '65
Why the Federal reserve raised interest
　rates; excerpts from address, December 8,
　1965. por U S News 59:92-4 D 20 '65

about

Bill Martin's red flag. il por Time 85:83 Je 11
　'65
Caution signal. Duns R 86:31 Jl '65
FRB Chairman Martin: a clash developing
　with the President? il por U S News 58:14
　Je 14 '65
Federal reserve's Martin: no to LBJ. il por
　U S News 59:15 D 20 '65
Growing fight over money. il por U S News
　58:91 Je 21 '65
Just a hint of chill; no recession in sight;
　with editorial comment. il Bsns W p23-6,
　140 Je 5 '65
LBJ vs. Reserve board: who gets last word
　on money. U S News 59:47 D 20 '65
Market rides a roller coaster. il Bsns W p25-7
　Je 19 '65
Monetary cassandra. B. L. Masse. America
　112:873 Je 19 '65
Patman vs. Martin: new clash on money. por
　U S News 59:20 Jl 19 '65

Up go the rates and the roof. il por News-
　week 66:75-6 D 20 '65
Wall Street goes into a mood of caution.
　Bsns W p28-9 Je 5 '65
What is the lesson of 1929? J. Tobin. New
　Repub 152:11-12 Je 19 '65; Reply with re-
　joinder. C. C. Killingsworth. 153:37-8 Jl 24
　'65
Why Martin spoke out; with editorial com-
　ment. il por Bsns W p36-7, 188 Je 12 '65
**MARTIN company. See Martin-Marietta cor-
　poration**
MARTIN-Marietta corporation
Major aircraft role sought by Martin co.
　M. L. Yaffee. il Aviation W 84:97+ Ja 17 '66
Martin aiming at spacecraft field. D. L. Zyl-
　stra. Miss & Roc 17:16 Jl 19 '65

Aerospace division

Move up in space, win points; Martin co.
　steering Titan III program toward a profit.
　il Bsns W p92-4+ S 25 '65
MARTINEZ, C. G.
Cocktail lore and legend. House & Gard 127:
　174+ Ap '65
MARTINEZ, R. E.
Europe's What is man? exhibit; tr. by A.
　Rosin. Pop Phot 56:8+ Je '65
**MARTINEZ, Rafael Arévalo. See Arévalo Mar-
　tínez, R.**
MARTINEZ MONTERO, Homero
Republic of Central America. Américas 17:
　18-23 Mr '65
MARTINI, Karl Heinz
How Abu Simbel is being saved; reprint.
　Sci Digest 57:48-54 Ap '65
MARTINON, Jean
Queen of Chicago. Newsweek 65:84-5 Ap 26
　'65
Two seasons by Martinon. R. C. Marsh. por
　Hi Fi 15:111 Jl '65
MARTINSON, William D. and others
Summer study-skills program for minority
　group pupils. Sch & Soc 93:300-2 Sum '65
MARTY, Martin E.
M.R.A.: the new Druseanism. Christian Cent
　82:399-401 Mr 31 '65
On primacy: thinking the unthinkable. por
　Cath World 202:26-31 O '65
Script-writers take over. Christian Cent 82:
　733-5 Je 9 '65
MARTYNIA. See Unicorn plants
MARUYAMA, Magoroh
Computer that psychoanalyzes you. Sci Di-
　gest 59:70-5 Ja '66
MARVEL, David Thomas
One man's hobby. il U S Camera 28:50-3 Ap
　'65
MARVICK, Dwaine
Political socialization of the American Negro.
　bibliog f Ann Am Acad 361:112-27 S '65
MARVIN, Lee
Drunkest gun in the West. il pors Life 58:
　121-2+ Je 11 '65
Man for vicaries. il por Time 85:58 Je 4 '65
MARX, Anne
Heady adventure; poem. Good H 161:216 O
　'65
MARX, Arthur. See Fisher, B. jt. auth.
MARX, Harpo
Gift of laughter; excerpt. A. Sherman. il por
　Read Digest 87:82-6 O '65
MARX, Karl
Can we talk to Marxian atheists? P. Ehlen;
　D. I. MacLean. America 113:112-17 Jl 31
　'65
Karl Marx's theories need reevaluation. Sci
　N L 88:165 S 11 '65
Little-known chapter in American history;
　column for Horace Greeley's Tribune. M.
　Geltman. il Nat R 17:865-7 O 5 '65
Marxism: 100 years in the life of a doctrine,
　by B. D. Wolfe. Review
　Cath World 202:122-3 N '65. N. D. Rood-
　kowsky
　Commonweal 82:733-4 O 1 '65. W. Conyng-
　ham
　Nat R 17:990+ N 2 '65. M. Geltman
　Sat R 48:38-9 Je 12 '65. R. Strausz-Hupe
Socialist humanism; an international sym-
　posium, ed. by E. Fromm. Review
　Sat R 48:107-8 S 18 '65. H. Cox
MARX, Leo
America's first anarchist snob. Nation 200:
　171-2 F 15 '65
Literary radical. Commentary 40:118+ D '65
Tyranny of the unplenishable self. Nation
　201:102-5 Ag 30 '65
MARX, Roberto Burle
Marx brother. New Yorker 41:19 My 29 '65

MARX, Wesley
At the end of the yo-yo, the federal city.
Bul Atomic Sci 21:48-50 Mr '65
Case of the vanishing beaches. Am For 71:
10-13+ N '65
MARXISM. See Communism; Socialism
MARY, Virgin

Art

Sittow Assumption. C. T. Eisler. il Art N
64:34-7+ S '65

Theology

Mary, mother of the redemption, by E.
Schillebeeckx. Review
Commonweal 81:792-4 Mr 19 '65. G. H.
Tavard; Reply with rejoinder. W.
Kuhns. 82:98 Ap 16 '65
Pope on Mary. America 112:239 F 20 '65
MARY, queen of Scots
Casket letters, by M. H. A. Davison. Review
Time 86:106+ N 26 '65
MARY Stuart, queen of the Scots. See Mary,
queen of Scots
MARY, Mother Cecilia. See Cecilia Mary,
Mother
MARY-ALICE, Sister
My mentor, Flannery O'Connor. Sat R 48:
24-5 My 29 '65
MARY Anthony, Mother
Fragment: poem. Commonweal 82:320 My 28
'65
MARY Cecile, Mother
Regina medal presentation. por Horn Bk 41:
477-8 O '65
M. Christina, Sister
Research papers in high school English.
NEA J 54:43-4 N '65
MARY Claude, Sister
Crisp celery; poem. Commonweal 82:191 Ap
30 '65
First grade poems. Sch Arts 65:38 N '65
Poems in the dust. Christian Cent 82:1255
O 13 '65
MARY Corita Kent, Sister. See Kent, M. C.
MARY Emmanuel, Sister
Convent canticle; poem. Commonweal 81:640
F 12 '65
Northeast of Gaza; poem. Commonweal 83:
374 D 24 '65
MARY Faith, Sister
Message to a silent friend; poem. America
112:772 My 22 '65
MARY Helene, Sister
Into today; poem. America 112:320 Mr 6 '65
MARY Jeremy, Sister
Some fruit in cold weather; poem. Common-
weal 81:608 F 5 '65
MARY Jessica, Sister
Christ blooded in red wine; poem. America
112:775 My 22 '65
MARY Jonathan, Sister
Audience; poem. Commonweal 82:42 Ap 2 '65
MARY Judith, Sister
Watching SML die; poem. Commonweal 82:
55 Ap 2 '65
MARY Malachy Loftus, Sister. See Loftus,
M. M.
MARY Mercy, Sister
Decorated mink boards. Sch Arts 65:10-11
N '65
MARY Michael, Sister
Devot Christ; poem. Cath World 201:387 S
'65
MARY Roberta Jones, Sister. See Jones, M. R.
MARY Stephanie, Sister
Ferris wheel, anyone? Commonweal 82:14-16
Mr 26 '65
MARY Thérèse, Sister
Child's world; poem. America 112:320 Mr 6
'65
Letter to Avila; poem. Cath World 202:39
O '65
There is a night; poem. America 113:776 D
18 '65
MARY Xavier, Sister. See Xavier, M.
MARYLAND
See also
Colleges and universities—Maryland
Education—Maryland
Hunting—Maryland
Law—Maryland
Libraries—Maryland
Montgomery County

Education, Department of

In-service training for subprofessionals. H.
T. Walker. il ALA Bul 59:134-8 F '65

Historic houses, etc.

Maryland pilgrimage spotlights historic homes.
il Hobbies 70:52 My '65

Maps

Marvel of maps. G. Cross. il Holiday 38:106+
Jl '65

Religious institutions and affairs

News of the Christian world (cont) Chris-
tian Cent 82:156 F 3 '65
MARYLAND academy of sciences, Baltimore
Events of 1966 in the graphic time table.
Sky & Tel 31:33-5 Ja '66
MARYLAND. University, College Park
Maryland U.'s global classrooms. F. V. Rum-
mell. Read Digest 86:245-8+ Ap '65
New library school at Maryland starts
classes under Wasserman. Library J 90:
3570+ S 15 '65
Protesting the protesters; Collegiate anti-
protest organization group. Time 85:77 My
28 '65
MASCHMANN, Melita
Memories of a brownshirt girlhood. L. Segal.
New Repub 153:23-8 Ag 21 '65
MASCOTS, Automobile. See Automobiles—
Equipment
MASERS
Production of coherent radiation by atoms
and molecules; address, December 11, 1964.
C. H. Townes. bibliog il Science 149:831-41
Ag 20 '65
Two-quantum maser; obtaining two-quantum
emission in optical maser. Sci Am 213:40-1
O '65
MASERS, Optical. See Lasers
MASIN, Herman L.
Sports. See issues of Senior scholastic
MASINA, Giulietta
First the pasta, then the play. M. S. Davis.
il pors N Y Times Mag p 10-11+ Ja 2 '66
Profiles; F. Fellini. L. Ross. New Yorker
41:63-6+ O 30 '65
Second fame: good food. N. Lyon. il por
Vogue 147:152-4 Ja 1 '66
MASK netsukes. See Netsukes
MASKS (for the face)
Secret of creative mask design; fifth grade.
L. S. Roe. il Design 67:28-30 S '65
MASKS, Oxygen. See Oxygen apparatus
MASOCHISM
Immolations and consensus: the justification
of innocence. A. Towne. Christian Cent
83:72-5 Ja 19 '66
MASON, Brian
Feldspar in chondrites. bibliog Science 148:
943 My 14 '65
MASON, Edwin A.
Attract birds to your garden. Horticulture
43:20-1+ D '65
MASON, Elizabeth
Lucile Droege Mauntel: swinging on a star.
Am For 71:10+ S '65
MASON, James Hocker
Natural history book reviews. Sr Schol 86:
sup34-5 Mr 4 '65
MASON, Ken
New things in ice fishing. Outdoor Life 137:
24-7+ Ja '66
MASON, Philip
Race relations in Britain. Christian Cent 82:
738-41 Je 9 '65
MASON, Rossie L. and Ruthven, Courtney
Bone density measurements in vivo: im-
provement of X-ray densitometry. bibliog
Science 150:221-2 O 8 '65
MASON, Stewart C.
Leicestershire plan: breakthrough in British
education. Sr Schol 86:sup 11 My 20 '65
MASON NECK, Va. See Wilderness areas
MASONIC orders. See Freemasons
MASONRY
American masonry; portfolio. W. Evans. For-
tune 71:150-3 Ap '65
Care and safekeeping of masonry floors.
House & Gard 128:75-6+ O '65
High-rise apartment structures of masonry.
R. M. Gensert. il Arch Rec 137:182-7 F '65
Interior and exterior masonry finishes. il Con-
sumer Rep 30:138-41 Mr '65
Masonry finishes. J. Hand. Pop Sci 187:128-30
Jl '65
MASONS, Free. See Freemasons
MASS
Exclusivist liturgy. America 112:654 My 8 '65
More changes at mass. C. J. McNaspy. Amer-
ica 112:281 F 27 '65
No time to stop; the beginning of liturgical
reform. H. A. Reinhold. il Commonweal
82:583-5 Ag 20 '65
Poll on English mass. America 112:304 Mr 6
'65
Post-tribal worship; benefits of liturgical re-
form in English language. J. J. Ryan. Com-
monweal 82:586-9 Ag 20 '65; Discussion.
82:648-9+; 83:4 S 17, O 8 '65

MASS—*Continued*
Traditionalist manifesto; objections to the church's current reforms in the liturgy. America 112:477-8 Ap 10 '65; Discussion. 112:697 My 15 '65
What is to be done. L. T. Mahon. Commonweal 82:590-2+ Ag 20 '65
See also
Liturgical language

MASS (music)
Changes in church music. C. J. McNaspy. America 112:373-4 Mr 13 '65
See also
Phonograph records—Mass

MASS communication. See Mass media

MASS culture. See Popular culture

MASS media
Combining all channels to reach a mass public; J. W. Kluge's Metromedia. il Bsns W p80-2+ S 18 '65
Education by electronics; address, December 3, 1965. R. Brent. Vital Speeches 32:175-8 Ja 1 '66
Good-by to Gutenberg; concepts incubating in laboratories. il Newsweek 67:85-8 Ja 24 '66
Mass man and mass media; adaptation of address. H. Brucker. il Sat R 48:14-16+ My 29 '65
Mass media calmed U.S; catharsis for national grief over President John F. Kennedy's death. Sci N L 88:260 O 23 '65
One-world concept of mass communication; General Sarnoff's forecast. R. L. Tobin. Sat R 49:101-2 Ja 8 '66
Spoofing and schtik; gimmicks used to attract new generation. P. Kael. Atlan 216:84-5 D '65
Understanding media, by M. McLuhan. Review
New Yorker 41:129-36 F 27 '65. H. Rosenberg
Pop Phot 58:100 Ja '66. J. Durniak

MASS transit. See Rapid transit

MASSACHUSETTS
See also
Architecture, Domestic—Massachusetts
Booksellers and bookselling—Massachusetts
Crime and criminals—Massachusetts
Education—Massachusetts
Gardens—Massachusetts
Martha's Vineyard
Merrimack River
Nantucket Island

Historic houses, etc.
See also
Medford, Mass.—Historic houses, etc.
Salem, Mass.—Historic houses, etc.

Legislation
Balancing imbalances; Massachusetts outlaws de facto segregation. Newsweek 66:74 Ag 30 '65

Politics and government
Free for all; contenders for Saltonstall's seat. il Newsweek 67:20-1 Ja 10 '66
Last Brahmin. Time 87:22 Ja 7 '66
Massachusetts: rogues and reformers in a state on trial. E. R. F. Sheehan. il Sat Eve Post 238:25-32+ Je 5 '65
Political chowder. il Newsweek 65:23 F 22 '65
Running Brooke. Reporter 34:12+ Ja 13 '66
Saltonstall's successor. M. F. Nolan. New Repub 154:8 Ja 22 '66

Religious institutions and affairs
News of the Christian world (cont) Christian Cent 82:498 Ap 21 '65

MASSACHUSETTS   BAY   transportation authority
To keep Boston's wheels turning; new regional transit authority for seventy-seven neighboring towns. il Bsns W p 144+ F 20 '65

MASSACHUSETTS Institute of technology, Cambridge
Gone with the wind; new Cecil and Ida Green earth-sciences building. Newsweek 65:56 Mr 8 '65
Librarians' Pugwash, or INTREX on the Cape; conference on MIT's program, Woods Hole, Mass. J. H. Shera. bibliog Wilson Lib Bul 40:359-62 D '65
Manager for MIT. Newsweek 67:48 Ja 3 '66
MIT goes to social sciences for a boss. il Bsns W p62-3 Ja 8 '66
Revolution at M.I.T. il Sci Digest 58:48-55 D '65

Vision of university library of 1975 emerges from Woods Hole conference; MIT's project INTREX (information transfer experiments) Library J 90:4024 O 1 '65

MASSACRE of the Innocents. See Holy Innocents, Massacre of the

MASSACRES
See also
Congo massacre, 1964

MASSAMBA-DEBAT, Alphonse
To burn, to bury or to hang? Time 86:35 Ag 6 '65

MASSAQUOI, Hans J.
Mission of mercy. Ebony 20:149-52+ My '65
Would you want your daughter to marry one? Ebony 20:82-4+ Ag '65

MASSE, Benjamin Louis
American capitalists, go home! America 112:190-2 F 6 '65
Churches and the war on poverty. America 113:208-9+ Ag 28 '65
Commerce with Communists. America 112:639-41 My 1 '65
Factory sites in rural areas. America 113:440 O 16 '65
Highlights of Title VII. America 113:23 Jl 3 '65

MASSÉ, Victor
For very special attention. J. Maclain. por Am Rec G 31:550 F '65

MASSENET, Jules
Don Quichotte. Criticism
Opera N 29:33 Mr 20 '65
Massenet Thais. M. Lelash. il Am Rec G 31:964-5 Je '65
On records; Thais. Opera N 30:35 D 25 '65

MASSEY competition. See Architecture—Competitions

MASSIALAS, Byron G. See Kazamias, A. M. jt. auth.

MASSIE, Robert K.
Last of the outlaw wolves. Sat Eve Post 239:71-4 Ja 15 '66
Please send one billion dollars. Sat Eve Post 238:76-8+ D 4 '65
Sub that sails in the sky. Sat Eve Post 239:52-4 Ja 1 '66

MASSIE, Suzanne
Mr B: God creates, I assemble. Sat Eve Post 238:34-7 O 23 '65

MASSILLON, Ohio
Go, Massillon, go! cradle of football. C. Davis. il Esquire 64:206-7+ D '65

MASSINGHAM, Hugh
Harold Wilson's new Tory challenger. New Repub 153:15-16 S 4 '65
That earthy man. Atlan 215:50-3 Mr '65

MASSON, André
Wanderer. il por Newsweek 66:106 N 15 '65

MASTECTOMY. See Breast—Surgery

MASTER, Michiel the Fleming. See Sittow, M.

MASTERS, Dexter
Secret city on the magic mountain. Sat Eve Post 238:36-40+ Ag 14 '65

MASTERS, Roger
US option in Europe: a pro-French policy. New Repub 153:7-9 D 4 '65
What about a nuclear guarantee for India? New Repub 153:9-10 D 25 '65

MASTERS, William Howell
Nature of sexual response. il por Time 87:65 Ja 7 '66
Secrets of sex. il por Newsweek 65:58+ Ap 26 '65

MASTERS, incorporated
Riot sale; New York post error sells TV sets at $8.98. il Newsweek 66:81 D 13 '65

MASTERS golf tournament. See Golf—Tournaments

MASTITIS
Chase mastitis with hot water? Farm J 89:66F Mr '65
How one vet controls mastitis. Suc Farm 63:95 Ap '65
Mastitis crackdown is here. N. Reeder. il Farm J 89:76+ F '65

MASTROIANNI, Marcello
Italy for Barbra Streisand. Esquire 63:68-70 F '65

about
Man who made apathy irresistible. I. Shenker. il pors N Y Times Mag p54-5+ D 12 '65
Mastroianni the man, the actor, the reluctant lover. L. Barzini. il pors Vogue 146:96-9+ O 15 '65
Redbook dialogue: Barbra Streisand and Marcello Mastroianni. pors Redbook 125:50-1+ Jl '65

MASTS and rigging
Roller wings. W. Britton. il Yachting 118:54-6+ Ag '65

MASTS and rigging—*Continued*
Tune up! a new look at an old problem. W. Britton. il Motor B 115:42+ My '65
See also
Sails

MATA Hari
Mata Hari, by S. Waagenaar. Review
Newsweek por 66:103-5 O 4 '65

MATADORS. See Bullfighters

MATCH, Richard
Your voice is you. Read Digest 87:135-7 N '65

MATCH safes
Treasure hunt: match safes and hatpin holders. J. Mebane. il Bet Hom & Gard 43:47-8 N '65

MATERIALS
Composite materials offer vast potential for structures; aerospace applications. M. L. Yaffee. il Aviation W 82:38-9+ My 3 '65
Materials and the development of civilization and science; adaptation of seminar, September 1963. C. S. Smith. bibliog il Science 148:908-17 My 14 '65; Reply. L. F. Trueb. 149:246 Jl 16 '65
Science used to analyze what art has discovered. Sci N L 87:399 Je 19, '65

Testing
See Testing

MATERIALS, Strength of. See Strength of materials

MATERIALS centers. See Instructional materials centers

MATERIALS handling
Materials handling enjoying a big lift; automation. il Bsns W p60-1+ My 29 '65
Materials handling, from field to market (cont) il Suc Farm 63:50-1 F '65
Nobody neglects materials management. il Duns R 85:pt2 134-7+ Mr '65
See also
Freight handling

MATERIALS of instruction. See Teaching—Aids and devices

MATERIALS research
Composite materials offer vast potential for structures; aerospace applications. M. L. Yaffee. il Aviation W 82:38-9+ My 31 '65
Corrosion hampers AF development; comprehensive materials symposium. J. F. Judge. il Miss & Roc 16:26-7+ Je 14 '65
Where is science taking us? composite materials for the future. A. G. H. Dietz. il Sat R 49:104-5 Ja 1 '66

MATERNAL love. See Love, Maternal

MATHEMATICAL instruments
See also
Slide rule

MATHEMATICAL recreations
How many beans in the jar? E. O. Thorp. il Pop Mech 124:96-7+ N '65
Mathematical games. M. Gardner. See issues of Scientific American

MATHEMATICS
How do you figure? questions and answers. J. Daugherty and M. Daugherty. il Sci Digest 57:95-7 F '65
Mathematical sciences; report on third anniversary symposium of the Institute of mathematical sciences, Madras, India. A. Ramakrishnan. Science 149:209-10 Jl 9 '65
Numerical analysis vs. mathematics; address, December 29, 1964. R. W. Hamming. Science 148:473-5 Ap 23 '65; Discussion. 149:243-5, 1049-50 Jl 16, S 3 '65
See also
Algebra
Games, Theory of
Numerical calculations
Topology

Philosophy
Mathematical games: infinite regress in philosophy, literature and mathematical proof. M. Gardner. il Sci Am 212:128-30+ bibliog(p 160) Ap '65

Study and teaching
Adding up the new math; with study-discussion program, by E. Harris and D. Harris. P. Suppes. bibliog PTA Mag 60:8-10, 36 O '65
Mathematics for the low achiever. I. Adler. il NEA J 54:28-30+ F '65
New math: does it really add up? il Newsweek 65:112+ My 10 '65
New math your children may be learning. il Good H 160:132-3 Ja '65
Progress report on the mathematics revolution. E. Sharp. il Sat R 48:62-3+ Mr 20 '65

Recent developments in mathematics education. H. E. Bowie. Sch & Soc 93:252-4 Ap 17 '65
Spreading the word on the new math: use of telephone lines and the Electrowriter. il Bsns W p 110-12 Ap 10 '65
See also
Mathematics laboratories

Textbooks
New math book sales add up. il Bsns W p 117-18+ Ap 10 '65

Bibliography
Understanding the new math? D. Huff. Harper 231:134-7 S '65

MATHEMATICS and art. See Art and mathematics

MATHEMATICS as a profession
Emotional perils of mathematics; letter. D. R. Weidman. Science 149:1048 S 3 '65

MATHEMATICS laboratories
Mathematics laboratory. H. L. Phillips. il Am Ed 1:1-3 Mr '65

MATHES, William
Saint-Exupéry's posthumous testament. New Repub 152:22-3 Je 12 '65

MATHEWS, Ross
Excerpt from address, July 13, 1965. Cong Digest 44:209+ Ag '65

MATHEWS, Thomas
West Indies after the federation. bibliog f Cur Hist 50:27-31+ Ja '66

MATHEWS, Virginia H.
Take a bow: Virginia Mathews. P. S. Jennison. il por Pub W 187:32-3 My 24 '65
Virginia H. Mathews receives Constance Lindsay Skinner award. por Library J 90:2348 My 15 '65
Virginia Mathews wins WNBA's Skinner award. Pub W 187:37 Ap 12 '65

MATHIS, Johnny
Johnny Mathis: millionaire with problems. L. Robinson. il pors Ebony 20:99-102+ Mr '65

MATHIS, Louie E.
Be somebody. por Am Ed 1:28-32 My '65

MATILE, P.
Inositol deficiency resulting in death: an explanation of its occurrence in neurospora crassa. bibliog Science 151:86-8 Ja 7 '66

MATIN, Leonard, and Pearce, D. G.
Visual perception of direction for stimuli flashed during voluntary saccadic eye movements. bibliog Science 148:1485-8 Je 11 '65

MATING behavior. See Sex behavior

MATING behavior (insects) See Courtship of insects

MATING instinct. See Courtship of animals

MATIOLI, Gastone T. and Niewisch, H. B.
Electrophoresis of hemoglobin in single erythrocytes. bibliog Science 150:1824-6 D 31 '65
—See Eylar, E. H. jt. auth.

MATISSE, Henri
Henri Matisse; University of California Dickson art center exhibition. il por Newsweek 67:50-3 Ja 17 '66

MATLOCK, Jean
Black and white. V. Scott. il Ladies Home J 82:92-3+ N '65

MATLOCK, Robert
Black and white. V. Scott. il Ladies Home J 82:92-3+ N '65

MATRIMONY. See Marriage

MATS for pictures. See Pictures—Mounting

MATSON, James Randel
BMOC. il por Newsweek 65:60+ My 3 '65
Busting the seventy-foot barrier. il pors Life 58:80A-80B My 21 '65
Champ from Pampa. il por Time 85:65 Ap 30 '65
Record-slinging in the rain. E. Shrake. il por Sports Illus 22:26-7 My 3 '65

MATSUI, Akira
United Nations commemoration address, June 25, 1965. UN Mo Chron 2:118-20 Jl '65

MATSUSHITA, Konosuke
Anything worth doing is worth 10 per cent por Bsns W p80 Ag 21 '65

MATTE, Tom
Tommy's terrible surprise. T. Maule. il por Sports Illus 24:16-17 Ja 17 '66

MATTER, Mercedes
Giacometti: in the vicinity of the impossible. Art N 64:26-31+ Sum '65

MATTER
Matter created on loan due in 80 billion years. Sci N L 88:72 Jl 31 '65
See also
Gravitation
Particles (nuclear physics)

MATTER, Interstellar
Annihilation of matter seen source of quasars. Sci N L 87:310 My 15 '65
Atmospheric noble gases: solar-wind bombardment of extraterrestrial dust as a possible source mechanism. D. Tilles. bibliog Science 148:1085-8 My 21 '65
Atoms span galactic space. Sci N L 87:295 My 8 '65
Dynamics of interplanetary dust. M. J. S. Belton. bibliog il Science 151:35-44 Ja 7 '66
Extraterrestrial dust as a source of atmospheric argon. R. A. Schmidt. bibliog il Science 151:223 Ja 14 '66
Milky way mysterium; study of the radiation given off by hydroxyl radical. Newsweek 66:104 O 18 '65
New look at the universe. Sci Digest 59:24-5 Ja '66
Zodiacal dust: measurements by Mariner IV. W. M. Alexander and others. Science 149:1240-1 S 10 '65
See also
Plasma (ionized gases)
MATTER of health; drama. See McGowan, J.
MATTERHORN
Reporter at large; Whymper's ascent. J. Bernstein. New Yorker 41:134+ Mr 13 '65
Three days on a rope; north face of the Matterhorn attempted by Italy's W. Bonatti. il Time 85:82 F 26 '65
MATTESICH, Rudolph
Ski touring. Travel 125:42-4 Ja '66
MATTHAU, Walter
That wonderful what's-his-name. por Time 85:52 Mr 26 '65
MATTHEW, Eileen Holm
Five water skills every child should know. Parents Mag 40:53-5+ Ag '65
Ten pointers for new article writers. Writer 79:29-30 Ja '66
MATTHEW, Gospel of. See Bible—New Testament—Matthew
MATTHEWS, Adam
Packaging for productivity. Duns R 86:pt2 99-100+ D '65
MATTHEWS, Bernard
Case of the golden turkey eggs. G. Kent. il Read Digest 87:148-51 N '65
MATTHEWS, Desmond S.
Irish phone call. America 112:395-6 Mr 20 '65
MATTHEWS, Howard A.
Most delicious career. por Am Ed 1:23-5 My '65
MATTHEWS, M. M.
Teacup; a basic-basic sailboat. Pop Mech 125:146-51+ Ja '66
MATTHEWS, T. S.
He tries to answer her; poem. Mlle 61:110 O '65
It isn't the game that's impossible, it's the people. Vogue 146:154 D '65
(ed) See Eliot, T. S. Interview with Eliot
MATTHIESSEN, George C.
Tidemarshes; a vanishing resource. Recreation 58:271+ Je '65
MATTHIESSEN, Peter
Reporter at large. New Yorker 41:116+ Ap 3 '65
MATTRESSES
Facts you should know before buying a mattress. Good H 162:128 Ja '66
MATTY, Carol
Guatemala. Travel 124:36-8 D '65
MATTY and the moron and madonna: drama. See Lieberman, H.
MATURANA, H. R. and Frenk, S.
Synaptic connections of the centrifugal fibers in the pigeon retina. bibliog Science 150:359-61 O 15 '65
MATURITY
Dear wayfarers. B. Ives. Seventeen 24:264+ Ag '65
How to run away from home. D. Klein. il Seventeen 24:150-1+ Mr '65
How well do you handle your worries and fears? D. Sugarman and H. Hochstein. il Seventeen 24:120-1+ F '65
Josh White talks to teens. J. White. Seventeen 24:172+ Ap '65
Morton Gould talks to teens. M. Gould. Seventeen 24:166+ My '65
That big word: integrity. C. E. Shain. Seventeen 24:94-5+ D '65
Whatever became of the class of '55? seven high school boys' planned careers in '55 and actual careers in '65. J. Star. il Look 29:112-14+ My 18 '65
When is old enough? questions and answers. A. Wood. il Seventeen 24:160-1 F '65
Will the real Dutch uncle please stand up? R. Serling. Seventeen 24:110+ Jl '65

MATUTE, Ana María
Wounded generation. Nation 201:420-4 N 29 '65
MATZ, Mary Jane
Opera-lover's guide to Venice. Opera N 30:14-17 D 11 '65
MATZKIN, Myron A.
Movie maker. See issues of Modern photography
MAUCH, Gene
Mean man named Mauch sounds off. J. Mann. por Sports Illus 23:45-7 Jl 26 '65
Rise and fall of the fabulous Phillies; photographs by W. Iooss, jr; with account by W. Leggett. il por Sports Illus 22:52-63 Mr 1 '65
Wait till this year. J. R. McDermott. il pors Life 58:75-6+ Mr 26 '65
MAUCK, Joe. See Urich, T. jt. auth.
MAUDLING, Reginald
Could Maudling win for the Tories? P. Worsthorne. il pors N Y Times Mag p28-9+ F 14 '65
MAUGHAM, William Somerset
Confidential question. por NEA J 54:19 Ap '65
about
Better than most. por Newsweek 66:33 D 27 '65
In the great tradition. H. Smith. por Sat R 49:25 Ja 15 '66
Maugham never forgot the day I trumped his ace. C. Goren. il por Sports Illus 24:50-1 Ja 17 '66
Notes and comment. New Yorker 41:17 D 25 '65
Obituary
Nat R 18:16 Ja 11 '66. G. Davenport
Pub W 188:74+ D 27 '65
Reporter 33:13 D 30 '65
Sat R 49:13+ Ja 8 '66. C. Amory
Time 86:58 D 24 '65
Very old party. J. Lehmann. New Repub 154:23-4 Ja 8 '66
MAUI (island)
You are welcome to try; Buddhist graveyard. il Sunset 134:74 Je '65
See also
Haleakala
MAUL, Ray C.
NEA research division looks at secondary school class size. NEA J 54:44-5 Mr '65
MAULDIN, Bill
Attack. New Repub 152:8-9 F 20 '65
1965 as it looked to Mauldin. il New Repub 154:17-19 Ja 8 '66
Vivid picture of the attack on Pleiku; and who ordered it. il por Life 58:32-3 F 19 '65
about
Back up front. il por Newsweek 65:56 F 22 '65
Up front once more. il por Time 85:50-1 F 19 '65
MAULDIN, William Henry. See Mauldin, B.
MAULE, Tex
Quick, hard right and a needless storm of protest. Sports Illus 22:22-5 Je 7 '65
MAUNA KEA Beach hotel. See Hawaii—Hotels, restaurants, etc.
MAUNTEL, Lucile Droege
Lucile Droege Mauntel: swinging on a star. E. Mason. por Am For 71:10+ S '65
MAUPIN, T. I.
Now you can read the signs. Am City 80:114-15 Ag '65
MAURA Christine Kropp, Sister. See Kropp, M. C.
MAURIAC, Claude
Immobilization of time. V. Mercier. Nation 200:119-21 F 1 '65
MAURITIUS
Toward chaos; question of independence. P. Webb. il Newsweek 65:40-1 My 31 '65
MAURO, Alexander
Osmotic flow in a rigid porous membrane. bibliog Science 149:867-9 Ag 20 '65
MAURY, René
France halts forest insects. Audubon Mag 67:384-5 N '65
MAVROS, Louis A.
Gemini fuel filtration solved. Miss & Roc 17:26-8 Ag 2 '65
MAX, Jerome
Exhaustion of our son's love. Criticism
New Yorker 41:110 O 30 '65
Newsweek 66:97 N 22 '65
MAX, Peter
Realistic hallucinations. il Horizon 7:116-20 Spr '65
MAXIM, Hiram H.
Piloting blooper. Yachting 117:193-4 Ap '65

MAXIMS
    Age and the adage. A. M. Sullivan. Duns R
    85:104 Mr '65
        See also
    Aphorisms and apothegms
MAXWELL, Emily
    Books (cont) New Yorker 41:217-20+ D 4 '65
MAXWELL, G. Edward
    Safari for science. Todays Health 43:22-31
    N '65
    Ski East by Northeast. Todays Health 44:50-
    1+ Ja '66
    They jump to save lives. Todays Health
    43:42-5+ Mr '65
    Why all the fuss about gonorrhea? Todays
    Health 43:26-31 D '65
    Why the rise in teen-age venereal disease?
    Todays Health 43:18-23+ S '65
MAXWELL, Rhoda Specht
    Planning makes perfect. Pop Gard 16:24-7 My
    '65
MAXWELL, William
    Further tales about men and women. New
    Yorker 41:22-7 Ag 7; 50-4 O 16; 51-6 N 13;
    54-60 D 11; 26-33 D 25 '65
MAXWELL street, Chicago. See Chicago—
    Streets
MAY, Catherine
    Every man should have his say; address,
    June 17, 1965. Vital Speeches 31:622-4 Ag
    1 '65
MAY, Edgar
    Mountain of books for mountain children.
    PTA Mag 60:8-10 S '65
MAY, Ernest R.
    Man behind the grin. Sat R 48:48-9 O 16 '65
MAY, Gladys E.
    Have you met Miss May? il pors Mlle 61:152-
    5 My '65
MAY, Jurgen
    Sophisticate & the natural. por Time 86:37
    D 24 '65
MAY, Marjorie Merriweather (Post)
    World unique and magnificent. il pors Life
    59:54-71 N 5 '65
MAY, Morton D.
    Remaking the image. il por Time 86:98 N 5
    '65
MAY, William F.
    Management in the coming decade; address,
    October 23, 1964. Vital Speeches 31:285-8
    F 15 '65
        about
    Businessmen in the news. il por Fortune
    72:47 S '65
    Philosophy, American can, and William May.
    J. F. Olesky. por Duns R 86:73+ O '65
MAY
    In May; few of the dates, memorable and
    not so, coming up this month (title varies)
    (cont) il N Y Times Mag p39 My 2 '65
MAY department stores company
    Flexible prototype for a western chain;
    Buena Park, Calif. il Arch Rec 137:208 My
    '65
    May-D&F, Denver, combines sale of original
    art and art books. Pub W 188:61 N 22 '65
    Remaking the image. il Time 86:98 N 5 '65
MAY festival of contemporary music. See
    Music festivals—Ohio
MAYAS
    Barre duplicates Mayan prints, dating to
    1842. il Pub W 189:94+ Ja 3 '66
    Complex ancient society puzzles archaeolo-
    gists; Tikal, Guatemala. Sci N L 87:280 My
    1 '65
    Message from the Maya; Tikal, Guatemala.
    L. C. Walker. il Américas 17:15-19 O '65
    Rubbings of Maya monuments. D. Nichols. il
    Am Artist 29:54-7 Ap '65
    Tikal, Guatemala, and emergent Maya civ-
    ilization. W. R. Coe. bibliog il Science 147:
    1401-19 Mr 19 '65
    U.S. explorers seek Mayan cities in Yucatan.
    Sci N L 88:263 O 23 '65
MAYDAY (signal) See Signals and signaling
MAYER, Albert
    Case for one total profession. Arch Rec 138:
    189-94 O '65
MAYER, Christa C.
    Two centuries of needle lace. Antiques 87:
    176-81 F '65
MAYER, Frederick
    Education for Democracy; address, Novem-
    ber 14, 1964. Vital Speeches 31:254-6 F 1
    '65
MAYER, George Louis
    Age of bel canto. Am Rec G 31:514-16 F '65
    From Bayreuth (and Philips), a stunning
    stereo, Parsifal. Am Rec G 31:684-7 Ap '65

MAYER, Giselle
    Hawaii, here we come. por Motor B 116:48-
    50+ Jl '65
MAYER, Grace M.
    Psychological document in sadness. Pop Phot
    56:50-1+ F '65
        about
    Grace Mayer. J. Deschin. il por Pop Phot 56:
    41+ My '65
MAYER, Jean
    Best diet is exercise. N Y Times Mag p34-5+
    Ap 25 '65
    Doctor's first job: preventing sickness. N Y
    Times Mag p48-9+ N 28 '65
MAYER, Manfred M. See Willoughby, W. F.
    jt. auth.
MAYER, Martha Hazzard
    Nervous breakdown; poem. Christian Cent
    82:837 Je 30 '65
MAYER, Martin
    Best Fellows at Harvard. Esquire 63:76-9+
    Je '65
    Close to midnight for the New York schools.
    N Y Times Mag p34-5+ My 2 '65
    Governor at work at the U.N. N Y Times
    Mag p22-3+ F 7 '65
    In the face of odds; operas. Hi Fi 15:86E-86F
    Mr '65
    Madison avenue: the big invisible sell. Sat
    Eve Post 238:23-31 Mr 13 '65
    Man who put the rhinestones on Miami.
    Harper 230:61-8 Mr '65
    Nilsson's own Elektra. Hi Fi 15:134 Ag '65
    Recordings. See issues of Esquire
    Thirty years' war. Opera N 30:10-12 S 25 '65
    Who's afraid of the Furtwängler Ring?
    Hi Fi 15:32+ O '65
MAYER, Milton
    Negro, Jewish, and Italian hair. Harper 231:
    44-6 Jl '65
    Peace! peace! in Budapest. Christian Cent
    82:1448-9 N 24 '65
MAYER, Moshe
    Israel's peripatetic builder. il por Fortune
    73:94 Ja '66
MAYER, Ralph
    Ralph Mayer's technical question & answer
    page. See issues of American artist
MAYER, Tom
    So you want to be a dropout. Atlan 216:151-3
    N '65
MAYES, Herbert R.
    Notes on creative editing; excerpt from ad-
    dress. Writer 78:18-19+ F '65
MAYFIELD, Eugene Andrew
    From Cincinnati, with love. Newsweek 65:90
    Ap 12 '65
MAYHEW, Alice
    Beauvoir's reflections on her middle years.
    Commonweal 82:728-9 O 1 '65
    Books. Commonweal 82:540-2 Jl 23 '65
    Sartre as Western cheerleader for the East.
    Commonweal 82:194-6 Ap 30 '65
MAYNARD, Fredelle
    How to buy without money. Good H 160:146+
    Mr '65
—and Mainwaring, Marion
    Gallery of hosts. Ladies Home J 82:160+ O
    '65
MAYNARD, Olga
    (ed) See Bruhn, E. Interview with Erik
    Bruhn
MAYNARD, Rona
    Paper flowers; story. Ladies Home J 82:74-6
    O '65
MAYO, Lida
    Miss Adams in love. Am Heritage 16:36-49+
    F '65
MAYO clinic, Rochester, Minn.
    Calories still count; Mayo clinic disclaims
    any association with diets. il Time 86:102
    N 19 '65
    Mayo's magic: the human touch. il Bsns W
    p 104-7+ D 11 '65
MAYOR, A. Hyatt
    Aquatint views of our infant cities. Antiques
    88:314-18 S '65
MAYORS, Negro. See Negro municipal officers
MAYORS wives
    She will not vegetate in Gracie mansion.
    G. Steinem. il N Y Times Mag p22-3+
    Ja 9 '66
MAYR, Ernst
    Avifauna: turnover on islands. bibliog Sci-
    ence 150:1587-8 D 17 '65
MAYS, Willie
    Giant. il por Newsweek 66:92 S 27 '65
    They love Herman and Willie. J. Mann.
    il pors Sports Illus 23:24-6+ S 27 '65
    Willie the virtuoso hurtles on to the finish.
    il pors Life 59:26-33 O 1 '65

MEAT industry and trade—*Continued*

Securities

Packers' year of plenty. il Fortune 71:90+ F '65

MEAT inspection

They safeguard the Nation's meat supply. il Todays Health 43:60-3 O '65

What that meat inspection stamp really means. Bet Hom & Gard 43:134-5 My '65

MEAT loaf, pies, etc. See Cookery—Meat

MEAT packing industry. See Meat industry and trade

MEAT prices. See Meat—Prices

MEATBALLS. See Cookery—Meat

MEBANE, John

Treasure hunt. Bet Hom & Gard 43:25+ My; 82-3 Je; 96 Ag; 41-2 S; 10+ O; 47-8 N '65; 44:54-5+ Ja '66

MECCA, Pilgrimages to. See Pilgrimages to Mecca

MECH, Dave

Meanwhile, back at the lab. . . Outdoor Life 136:16-17+ N '65

MECH, L. David

Isle Royale: laboratory of Lake Superior. il Nat Parks Mag 39:4-8 D '65

MECHANICAL aids in education. See Teaching—Aids and devices

MECHANICAL banks. See Banks, Coin

MECHANICAL drawing

See also

Drawing instruments

MECHANICAL handling

See also

Ore handling

MECHANICAL hearts. See Heart, Artificial; Heart-lung machines

MECHANICAL inventions. See Inventions

MECHANICAL models

Models of Leonardo da Vinci's automobile, helicopter, aeroplane. il UNESCO Courier 18:18-20 Mr '65

See also

Automatons

MECHANICAL translating. See Translating machines

MECHANICS

See also

Torque

MECHANICS, Household

Housekeeping on wheels. D. Liston. il Todays Health 43:62-6+ My '65

Make your house free and easy. il Bet Hom & Gard 43:136-7 Mr '65

MECKLIN, John

Biggest, cheapest lift ever. Fortune 72:179-80+ N '65

Ordeal of the plane makers: the C-5. Fortune 72:158-9+ D '65

MECOM, Harvey

From mules to millions. Newsweek 66:70 D 20 '65

MECOM, John Whitfield

Surprise package. il por Time 86:80 D 17 '65

MECREDY, Alice

Home fire drills may save your family. Parents Mag 40:87+ Ap '65

MEDAL of honor (United States)

Beyond the call of duty; Congressional medal of honor. il Sat Eve Post 238:110 O 23 '65

Freedom fighters. J. W. Blassingame. bibliog Negro Hist Bul 28:105-6 F '65

Sergeant Erwin and the blazing bomb; Congressional medal of honor awarded. C. Ford. il Read Digest 87:86-8 Jl '65

MEDALS

See also names of medals. e.g. Caldecott medal

MEDELMAN, John

Gear and flaps man; story. Esquire 63:94 My '65

Illusion of a future. Esquire 64:137+ N '65

MEDFORD, Mass.

Historic houses, etc

History in houses; Royall House. A. L. Cummings. il Antiques 88:506-10 O '65

MEDIASTINOSCOPE. See Medical instruments and apparatus

MEDIATION, Industrial. See Arbitration, Industrial

MEDIC-alert bracelets. See Identification tags, bracelets, etc.

MEDICAL art. See Medicine in art

MEDICAL buildings

Medical buildings that work two ways. il Fortune 73:178 Ja '66

Small buildings for group medical practice. il Arch Rec 138:159-66 Ag '65

MEDICAL care. See Medical service

MEDICAL centers

Aim to conquer killers; network of regional medical complexes for heart disease, cancer and stroke. Sci N L 87:151 Mr 6 '65

Elements of progressive patient care; Greenville, S. C. il Arch Rec 138:200-1 S '65

First phase of a medical center; training hospital for the Medical mission sisters of Philadelphia. il Arch Rec 138:205-7 S '65

Government in medicine; now one more step; regional centers. il U S News 59:59-60 S 27 '65

How LBJ's network of medical centers would work. il U S News 58:58-9 F 8 '65

New way to care for the aged & infirm; Hunterdon program. il Changing T 19:22-4 Mr '65

See also

New York university—Medical center

Pennsylvania. University—Medical centers

MEDICAL clinics. See Health clinics

MEDICAL colleges

AMA: the restrictive power. E. Rayack. il Nation 200:470-9 My 3 '65

How the U.S. doctors its MD crisis; multimillion dollar program to expand medical education. il Bsns W p 182+ O 16 '65

Older than the U.S. Constitution; first medical school in U.S. H. Earl. il Todays Health 43:38-40+ N '65

On giving oneself away. E. T. Harris; discussion. Harper 230:8+ F '65

MEDICAL education

Education: the forgotten patient. G. A. Silver. il Nation 200:467-70 My 3 '65

From student to doctor. il Todays Health 43:34-7+ Mr '65

Team approach urged in medical education. Sci N L 88:24 Jl 10 '65

Who should govern medicine? J. Lear. il Sat R 48:39-42 Je 5 '65: Discussion. 48:43-5 Jl 3; 56-8 S 4 '65

See also

Medical colleges

Federal aid

AAMC: a broader leadership role in health education prescribed for Association of medical colleges. J. Walsh. Science 148:1700-2 Je 25 '65; Discussion. 150:554, 1666 O 29, D 24 '65

How the U.S. doctors its MD crisis; multimillion dollar program to expand medical education. il Bsns W p 182+ O 16 '65

MEDICAL electronics

Switching off the pain; electrodes placed in the brain. Time 86:62 O 1 '65

MEDICAL ethics

How doctors use patients as guinea pigs. W. B. Furlong. Good H 161:79+ O '65

Is martyrdom ethical? Sci N L 87:214 Ap 3 '65

Who shall be the judge? excerpt from Consultation room. F. Loomis. Read Digest 86:91-4 Ap '65

MEDICAL examinations. See Physical examinations

MEDICAL fakers. See Quacks and quackery

MEDICAL fees. See Medical service, Cost of

MEDICAL genetics. See Heredity of disease

MEDICAL hypnosis. See Hypnotism

MEDICAL instruments and apparatus

At the core of life. il Fortune 71:214+ Je '65

Camera probes stomach. Sci N L 88:373 D 11 '65

Day I swallowed a camera; stomach camera. R. Gannon. il Pop Sci 187:56-7 Jl '65

Diagnose uterine cancer; fluorospectrophotometers. Sci N L 87:341 My 29 '65

Electronic detectives of medicine. J. R. Thomson. il Todays Health 43:22-5+ Mr '65

Electronic pacemaker for kidney. Sci Digest 57:33 F '65

Is that chest operation necessary? using mediastinoscope as diagnostic tools. Sci Digest 58:37 S '65

Middle ear examined with new device; endotoscope. Sci N L 87:152 Mr 6 '65

Must your body wear out? new electronic devices. C. P. Gilmore. il Sat Eve Post 238:78+ S 25 '65

New heart pacemaker. Sci N L 87:114 F 20 '65

New in the world of medicine. il Todays Health 43:80-1 Ap '65; 44:14-15 Ja '66

New model heart pacer gets energy from heart. Sci N L 87:311 My 15 '65

Pacemaker corrects backflow of urine. Sci N L 88:233 O 9 '65

MEDICAL instruments and apparatus—*Cont.*
Pacemaker problems; high-frequency interference. il Time 85:79 Je 25 '65
Pacemakers, plus and minus. Sci Digest 57:21 Je '65
Pocket heart pacemaker. il Sci Digest 57:23 My '65
Pump sustains life in liver cancer patients. Sci N L 87:217 Ap 3 '65
Radio, neon can upset vital heart pacemaker. Sci N L 88:9 Jl 3 '65
This stuff is to keep him from getting hurt, it doesn't always work. il Esquire 64:74-5 O '65
Tiny heart pacemaker takes up small space. il(p 161) Sci N L 88:169 S 11 '65
To stimulate the heart, electricity from the heart; Pacemakers. W. Cloud. il Pop Sci 187:19-20 Jl '65
See also
Heart-lung machines
Respiratory apparatus
Surgical instruments
MEDICAL insurance. See Insurance, Health
MEDICAL inventions. See Inventions
MEDICAL laboratories
Medical lab tests: dangerous mistakes. A. Lake. McCalls 92:116-17+ My '65; Same abr. with title Laboratory test: medicine's Achilles' heel. Read Digest 87:70-4 O '65
Testing the testers; question of competence. il Newsweek 65:92+ Mr 22 '65
MEDICAL libraries
See also
Medical library center of New York
United States—National library of medicine
MEDICAL libraries and state. See Libraries and state
MEDICAL library association
History will creep in; a report on the annual conference. M. E. Feeney. Library J 90:2978-9 Jl '65
MEDICAL library center of New York
Medical library center of New York. E. Moon. bibliog il Library J 90:2952-7 Jl '65
MEDICAL literature analysis and retrieval system. See Information storage and retrieval systems
MEDICAL missions. See Missions, Medical
MEDICAL photography. See Photography, Medical
MEDICAL practice. See Medicine—Practice
MEDICAL profession. See Medicine—Practice; Physicians
MEDICAL radiology. See Radiology, Medical
MEDICAL relief work

Vietnam (Republic)

A.I.D. a symbol of help. il Todays Health 43:14 D '65

British Guiana

They stopped a tropical epidemic. J. Winchester. il Todays Health 43:32-3+ D '65
MEDICAL research
Brain revolution. J. B. Sheerin. Cath World 201:223-6 Jl '65
Ethics in new medicine: tissue transplants. F. D. Moore. Nation 200:358-62 Ap 5 '65
How to make a bequest. Todays Health 43:88 My '65
New boost for pediatric research; Detroit's Children's hospital of Michigan. il Ebony 20:93-4+ O '65
1965 science review. Sci N L 88:395-6 D 18 '65
Research with the brakes off; symposium. Todays Health 43:41-59 N '65
Trends in some areas of Soviet biomedical research. E. Simonson and J. Brožek. bibliog Science 150:1687-9 D 24 '65
We tamed penicillin; ed. by J. D. Ratcliff. E. B. Chain. Read Digest 86:89-93 Mr '65
Zeroing in on three killer diseases: heart disease, cancer, and stroke. Bsns W p 170+ O 23 '65
See also
Animal experimentation
Autopsy
Cancer research
Computers—Medical applications
Laboratory animals
Ophthalmology
Physiological research
Rockefeller university
United States—National institutes of health

Experimentation on man

How doctors use patients as guinea pigs. W. B. Furlong. Good H 161:79+ O '65
Is martyrdom ethical? Sci N L 87:214 Ap 3 '65

Law on human guinea pigs; experiments at the Jewish chronic disease hospital. J. Lear. Sat R 48:56 Ap 3 '65
LSD and the anguish of dying. S. Cohen. Harper 231:69-72+ S '65; Reply. H. L. Wenger. 231:16+ D '65
Patient's right to know; experiments at Jewish chronic disease hospital. J. Lear. Sat R 48:20 Je 26 '65

Federal aid

National planning for medical research; adaptation of address, March 1, 1965. P. Handler. bibliog Science 148:1688-92 Je 25 '65; Reply. J. D. Cooper. 149:1173 S 10 '65

International aspects

See Science—International aspects
MEDICAL schools. See Medical colleges
MEDICAL service
Doctors, patients & society; symposium. il Nation 200:464-81+ My 3 '65
Does the U.S. really have the world's finest medical care? Consumer Rep 30:146-50 Mr '65
How to get good medical care. Nation 200:490 My 10 '65
Making modern medicine work better for you and your family; symposium. il Ladies Home J 83:33-5+ Ja '66
Summoning medical help. C. J. Potthoff. Todays Health 43:74 My '65
Talking turkey to doctors. America 113:704 D 4 '65
Where is science taking us? W. Darley. Sat R 48:55-6 S 4 '65
Where the needy get free medical care; Christian medical clinics. H. G. Earl. il Todays Health 43:26-9+ Mr '65
See also
Ambulances
Helicopters in medical service
Hospitals
Radio in medicine
Television in medicine

Peru

Gunboat diplomacy; gunboats of Peruvian navy with crews of physicians, dentists, and nurses treat jungle Indians. il Time 86:59 S 17 '65
MEDICAL service, Cost of
Advice from Europe's doctors to U.S. doctors. il U S News 59:40 Jl 26 '65
Doctors get a guide in setting their fees. il U S News 59:14 N 29 '65
How eldercare protects the elderly in need of medical care. D. F. Ward. Todays Health 43:67+ Mr '65
How much does it cost to have a baby? il Good H 160:175 Je '65
How to talk about money with a doctor. N. Kuehnl. Bet Hom & Gard 43:44 O '65
New way to cut hospital costs. il U S News 58:70-2 My 10 '65; Same abr. with title New look in hospital care. Read Digest 87:106-9 Jl '65
Way to save millions on hospitals. il Changing T 19:37-40 Ag '65
What will the doctor charge under medicare? il U S News 59:53 Ag 16 '65
Your medical dollar. L. R. Chevalier. il Ladies Home J 83:40-1 Ja '66
MEDICAL service, Radio. See Radio in medicine
MEDICAL service, State
Advice from Europe's doctors to U.S. doctors. il U S News 59:40 Jl 26 '65
Government in medicine; now one more step; regional centers. il U S News 59:59-60 S 27 '65
Heart, cancer, stroke: rising opposition from doctors may slow passage of Johnson program. E. Langer. Science 149:843-5 Ag 20 '65
How LBJ's network of medical centers would work. il U S News 58:58-9 F 8 '65
Medical services: federal grants for medical programs. New Repub 153:7 O 30 '65
New health act: AMA criticism reflected in adoption of bill on heart, cancer, and stroke. E. Langer. Science 150:323-4 O 15 '65
Two and a half years later: Canada's doctor strike; surprise ending to Saskatchewan's bitter battle over socialized medicine. J. Star. il Look 29:101+ Mr 23 '65
See also
Great Britain—National health service
MEDICAL supplies
Health and grooming. Consumer Rep 30:353-5 D '65
See also
Abbott laboratories

MEDICAL ultrasonics. See Ultrasonic waves
—Medical applications
MEDICARE. See Insurance, Health—United
States
MEDICINAL plants. See Botany, Medical
MEDICINE
Dangers of being your own doctor. T. Irwin.
Read Digest 86:91-4 My '65
Facts about prescribing drugs for yourself.
Good H 161:167-8 O '65
Healthy new world of 2015? Newsweek 66:62
D 27 '65
Keep up with medicine. B. Yuncker. See is-
sues of Good housekeeping
Medical news of the month. M. Fishbein. See
issues of McCall's
Medicine today. See issues of Ladies' home
journal
On the frontiers of medicine. il Life 59:59-
77+ S 10 '65
Progress of medicine. A. J. Snider. See issues
of Science digest
See also
Biomedical engineering
Drugs
Indians of North America—Medicine
Medical research
Nurses and nursing
Radio in medicine
Television in medicine

Bibliography
Medical books for the public library; comp.
by V. S. Flandorf. Library J 90:4718-23 N
1 '65
Scientific, technical, and medical books to
come; ed. by J. Putnam and R. Grossman. Library J 90:1160-201, 3083-119, 4820-
65 Mr 1, Jl, N 1 '65

Exhibitions
Medicine and art in Philadelphia; exhibition
at the Philadelphia museum of art. R.
Davidson. il Antiques 88:594+ N '65

Group practice
New kind of doctor; emergency room of
Wesson memorial hospital, Springfield,
Mass. R. H. Berg. il Look 29:22-6 Je 29
'65
Small buildings for group medical practice.
il Arch Rec 138:159-66 Ag '65
When your doctor is part of a group prac-
tice. il Good H 161:150-1 Jl '65

History
Medicine and art in Philadelphia; exhibition
at the Philadelphia museum of art. R.
Davidson. il Antiques 88:594+ N '65
Physician who healed himself. il Todays
Health 43:5+ Ap '65
Surgeons and ships in gold rush days; ex-
cerpt from Doctors on the American fron-
tier. R. Dunlop. il Todays Health 43:50-1+
Mr '65

International aspects
See Science—International aspects

Practice
Day in the life of a family doctor. T. Gal-
lagher. Good H 160:78-81+ F '65
Doctor's first job: preventing sickness. J.
Mayer. il N Y Times Mag p48-9+ N 28 '65
Doctors, patients & society; symposium. il
Nation 200:464-81+ My 3 '65
Embattled nurse of Jackrabbit Flats; P.
Gardelius on trial for practicing medicine
without a license. J. G. Dunne. il Sat Eve
Post 238:42-4+ N 20 '65
Medicine in the year 2000; report on sixth
annual conference on graduate medical
education. S. Y. Botelho. Science 147:1164+
Mr 5 '65
Trial of Patricia Gardelius; practical nurse
charged with practicing medicine without
a license. B. Asbell. il Redbook 126:46-8+
D '65
Who should govern medicine? J. Lear. il
Sat R 48:39-42 Je 5 '65; Discussion. 48:
43-5 Jl 3; 56-8 S 4 '65
See also
Diagnosis
Medical service
Physicians
Physicians and patients

Study and teaching
See also
Medical colleges
Medical education

Terminology
Heart attack terms confuse the layman. Sci
N L 88:340 N 27 '65

Burma
Burma surgeon's last battle. S. Seagrave.
il Sat Eve Post 238:38-40+ Jl 3 '65

Europe, Western
Biomedical science in Europe. R. P. Grant
and others; reply. R. K. Appleyard. Science 147:556-7 F 5 '65

Russia
Persistent Russian. A. Cutler. il Esquire
63:66-7+ My '65
Soviet search for viruses that cause chronic
neurologic diseases in the U.S.S.R. J. A.
Brody and others. bibliog Science 147:
1114-16 Mr 5 '65

United States
Colds, gout, overweight: what's new; meet-
ing of American medical association. U S
News 59:12 D 13 '65
Doctors, patients & society; symposium. il
Nation 200:464-81+ My 3 '65
Healthy outlook; predictions of Surgeon
General. Newsweek 65:68 F 22 '65
New health act: AMA criticism reflected in
adoption of bill on heart, cancer, and stroke.
E. Langer. Science 150:323-4 O 15 '65
Troubled calling crisis in the medical estab-
lishment, by S. Greenberg. Review
New Repub 153:26-8 S 4 '65. M. Alderman
MEDICINE, Military
See also
Vietnamese war, 1957- —Medical and sanitary
affairs
MEDICINE, Popular
What's wrong with self-medication? Todays
Health 43:8+ My '65
See also
Chiropractors
MEDICINE, Preventive
Ben Casey at the ball park; R. Kerlan of
Los Angeles Dodgers. J. Murphy. il N Y
Times Mag p 18-19+ Ag 22 '65
See also
Immunity
Public health
MEDICINE, Primitive
See also
Medicine men
MEDICINE, Psychosomatic
Why cancer may be psychosomatic; reprint.
il Sci Digest 58:75-8 S '65
MEDICINE, State. See Medical service, State
MEDICINE cabinets
Some new medicine cabinets are almost
child-proof. il Consumer Bul 48:43+ Jl '65
Your medicine chest. Parents Mag 40:106 N
'65
MEDICINE in art
Ancient ills in clay; collection of Dr Abner
I. Weisman. il Life 59:99-100 Jl 16 '65
Case histories in clay; Dr Weisman's col-
lection of pre-Columbian figures. il Time
86:75-6 Jl 9 '65
Medical sculpture: Weisman collection of pre-
Columbian medical sculpture. New Yorker
41:15-16 Jl 10 '65
MEDICINE men
On the rounds with a witch doctor. M.
Gelfand. il N Y Times Mag p44-5+ Mr 14
'65
Witch doctors and psychiatry. J. Randal. il
Harper 231:56-61 D '65
MEDICINES. See Drugs
MEDICINES, Patent, proprietary, etc.
Cold tablet for children; congespirin. M. B.
Keiser. il Parents Mag 41:18+ Ja '66
No easy cure for a sore throat. il Consumer
Bul 48:21-2 O '65
Personal business; self-medication can be
dangerous. Bsns W p 147 F 13 '65
MEDICO (organization)
New Tom Dooleys; with pictures. Sci Digest
57:60-3 My '65
MEDIEVAL art. See Art, Medieval
MEDIEVAL music. See Music, Medieval
MEDIOCRITY
Retreat from excellence; need for men of
moderation; address, June 25, 1965. E. F.
Scoutten. Vital Speeches 31:761-5 O 1 '65
MEDITATION
See also
Retreats, Spiritual
Spiritual exercises
MEDITERRANEAN anemia. See Anemia
MEDITERRANEAN cookery. See Cookery,
Mediterranean
MEDITERRANEAN house decoration. See
House decoration, Mediterranean

MEDITERRANEAN REGION
See also
Middle East

Description and travel
Europe's Mediterranean coast. V. S.
Pritchett. il Holiday 39:32-51+ Ja '66
Holiday handbook: Mediterranean pleasure-
spots. N. Barry. il Holiday 39:93-8 Ja '66

MEDITERRANEAN SEA
Motorboating in the Mediterranean. M. W.
Keeler. il Yachting 117:42-4+ Mr; 82-4+
Ap '65
See also
Corsica

MEDLARS (medical literature analysis and retrieval system) See Information storage
and retrieval systems

MEDVED, Ron
Halfback married, off on honeymoon, sitter
too. il pors Life 59:42-5 D 10 '65

MEDWIN family
Keep spring at your doorstep. M. J. Gero
and N. V. Backster. il Pop Gard 17:36+
Ja '66

MEE, Charles L. Jr
Discotheque man. N Y Times Mag p92+
Ja 9 '66
For Joan, the woe must go on. N Y Times
Mag p 137+ O 31 '65
That's the truth, and other Cosby stories.
N Y Times Mag p96-7 Mr 14 '65

MEEHAN, Thomas
Are we losing East Frambesia to the Com-
munists? New Yorker 41:50-1 O 2 '65
Big deal on tiny wheels. Sat Eve Post 238:
78-9 D 18 '65
Fantasy, flesh and Fellini. Sat Eve Post 239:
24-8+ Ja 1 '66
In the far-off land of ennui, etc. New Yorker
41:49-50 N 6 '65
Not good taste, not bad taste, it's camp. N Y
Times Mag p30-1+ Mr 21 '65
Please don't call me Fireball. Sat Eve Post
238:18 Jl 31 '65
Public writer no. 1? N Y Times Mag p44-5+
D 12 '65
Where did all women go? Sat Eve Post 238:26-
31 S 11 '65

MEEK, Richard
Horses, roses and groaning boards; photographs. Sports Illus 22:40-6 Ap 26 '65

MEEKER, Leonard C.
Dominican situation in the perspective of international law; address, June 9, 1965. Dept
State Bul 53:60-5 Jl 12 '65
Excerpts from statements, July 8 and July
12, 1965. Cong Digest 44:304+ D '65
Prospects of law in a world of conflict; address, April 29, 1965. Dept State Bul 52:
900-5 Je 7 '65

MEERLOO, Joost A. M.
Freedom to choose one's death. Nation 200:
344-5 Mr 29 '65

MEESKE, Marilyn
Memoirs of a female pornographer. Esquire
63:112-15 Ap '65

MEET the Pilgrims! drama. See Boiko, C.

MEETINGS
Something should be done about meetings.
J. Fithian. il Suc Farm 63:77+ N '65
See also
Business meetings
Chairmen

MEGGERS, Betty J. and Evans, Clifford
Transpacific contact in 3000 B.C; with bio-
graphical sketches. Sci Am 214:14, 28-35
Ja '66

MEGGITT, William, and Richardson, E. C.
New way to control weeds in sugar beets.
Suc Farm 63:82 Ap '65

MEGIVERN, James J.
Students talk of their faith. America 112:
636-8 My 1 '65

MEHDEVI, Anne Sinclair
Iran celebrates a 2,500th birthday. N Y Times
Mag p50-1+ O 31 '65
Take a lesson from a pasha. Harper 230:
97-9 My '65

MEHL, Bernard
Standards in teacher education and the new
image makers. Sch & Soc 93:81-2 F 6 '65

MEHLE, Aileen
Kidding the social setup. por Time 86:54 S 24
'65

MEHREN, George L.
Government and the food industry; address,
September 17, 1965. Vital Speeches 31:755-
8 O 1 '65

MEHRLICH, Ferdinand P.
Radiation preservation of foods. Science 147:
1600+ Mr 26 '65

MEHTA, Ved
All found in London. New Yorker 41:144+
S 18 '65
Books. New Yorker 41:193-4+ Mr 13 '65
Companion of St Michael and St George. New
Yorker 41:205-8+ D 11 '65
Music master. New Yorker 41:42-50 Ap 24 '65
Profiles; concerning Honest to God, by J.
Robinson. New Yorker 41:63-4+ N 13; 60-
2+ N 20 '65
Profiles; D. Bonhoeffer. New Yorker 41:65-
8+ N 27 '65

MEHTA, Zubin
Afternoon with an autocrat; interview. ed.
by F. Stevenson. por Opera N 30:27 Ja 1
'66

about
Flashing music of Zubin Mehta. W. Malloch.
por Hi Fi 15:129 Ag '65
Mehta at the Met. por Newsweek 67:64 Ja
10 '66
Mehta at the Metropolitan. I. Kolodin. Sat
R 49:30 Ja 15 '66
Musical events; performance of Bruckner's
Ninth symphony by Philadelphia orchestra.
W. Sargeant. New Yorker 41:236 N 13 '65

MEILACH, Dona Z.
What you should know about dental insurance. Suc Farm 63:86B F '65
(ed) See Kaminetzky, H. A. Expectant mother

MEINERS, Norm
Now is the time for prop repair. Motor B
115:30-1 F '65
Removable stern light. il Motor B 116:37
D '65

MEINSCHEIN, W. G.
Soudan formation: organic extracts of early
Precambrian rocks. bibliog Science 150:
601-5 O 29 '65

MEINWALD, Jerrold, and others
Cyclopentanoid terpene biosynthesis in a
phasmid insect and in catmint. bibliog Science 151:79-80 Ja 7 '66

MEINWALD, Yvonne C. See Eisner, T. jt.
auth.

MEISCON corporation. See Control data corporation

MEISLER, Stanley
. . .And a cold eye. Nation 201:200-2 O 4 '65
Impact of medicare. Nation 200:479-81 My 3
'65
Lamb in lionskin. Nation 200:510-12 My 10
'65
Our stake in apartheid. Nation 201:71-3 Ag 16
'65
—See Duke, P. jt. auth.

MEISTER, Alton. See Wellner, D. jt. auth.

MEISTER, Hans
Brief biography. S. Goodman. pors Dance
Mag 39:52-3 Ap '65

MEKAS, Jonas
Voice of the underground cinema. A. Levy.
il por N Y Times Mag p70+ S 19 '65

MEKONG RIVER
Hopes for harnessing the Mekong. il Bsns W
p 113 Ap 17 '65
Lower Mekong River development. UN Mo
Chron 2:73-4 Je '65
Mekong work in Cambodia. UN Mo Chron
2:106 D '65
Mekong work progresses. UN Mo Chron 2:47-
8 Ag '65
On the Mekong; Mr Johnson's billion dollar
offer. J. Ridgeway. New Repub 152:13-14
Ap 24 '65
Southeast Asia's old man river; development
progress. il Sat R 48:36-7 O 30 '65
Vietnam: the fourth course; international
cooperation in science. G. F. White; reply.
H. Newcombe. Bul Atomic Sci 21:29-30 S
'65

MELADY, Margaret Badum. See Melady, T. P.
jt. auth.

MELADY, Thomas Patrick
Needed: Afro-Asian studies. America 112:709-
10+ My 15 '65
Nonalignment in Africa. bibliog f Ann Am
Acad 362:52-61 N '65
Spain's new role in Africa. America 114:17-
19 Ja 1 '66
—and Melady, M. B.
Teilhard de Chardin and the Afro-Asian
world. pors Cath World 202:102-6 N '65

MELAMED, Monte
Choosing your day camp site. Recreation 58:
122-3 Mr '65

MELANIN
Reversible, light-screening pigment of elasmobranch eyes: chemical identity with
melanin. D. L. Fox and K. P. Kuchnow.
bibliog il Science 150:612-14 O 29 '65

MELANOMA
Soluble proteins of a melanoma and normal skin from the swordtail, platyfish, and their hybrids. D. G. Humm and A. L. Sylvia. bibliog il Science 150:635-6 O 29 '65

MELARO, Constance L.
R U there? ed. by M. Levin. Sat R 48:6+ Ag 14 '65; Same. Read Digest 87:199-200+ N '65

MELBOURNE, Australia
Music
Sutherland comes home. R. Covell. il Hi Fi 15:162-3 O '65

MELBY, John F.
Philippines: a unique effort. Cur Hist 49:278-83+ N '65

MELCHER, Daniel
Notes on authors alterations and the new technology. Pub W 187:35-6 My 3 '65
—and McCorkle, George
ABPC: planning for profits in publishing; report of conference at Princeton inn. Pub W 187:32-5 My 10 '65

MELCHERT, Thomas E. and Alston, R. E.
Flavonoids from the moss mnium affine bland. bibliog Science 150:1170-1 N 26 '65

MELE, Sabath
No more Mr Nice Guy: manager of Minnesota Twins. por Newsweek 66:62 Jl 26 '65

MELHADO, Ruth
Following the films. Sr Schol 86:23 Mr 25 '65

MELLEN, James G.
Drew dismisses dissenter. D. Macleod. Christian Cent 82:1490 D 1 '65

MELLERS, Wilfrid
Books. R. Kostelanetz. Commonweal 82:420 Je 18 '65

MELLO, Nancy K.
Interhemispheric reversal of mirror-image oblique lines after monocular training in pigeons. bibliog Science 148:252-4; 149:1519-20 Ap 9, S 24 '65

MELLON, Bunny
Green flowers and herb trees. Vogue 146:208-11 D '65

MELLOW, James R.
Books. Commonweal 82:417-18 Je 18 '65
Father Coughlin & the New deal. Commonweal 82:121-2, 335 Ap 16, My 28 '65

MELMAN, Seymour
Behind the mask of success; excerpt from Our depleted society. Sat R 48:8-10+ Jl 31 '65
Three anxieties; excerpt from Our depleted society. Sat R 48:14-15 Ap 3 '65

MELNICK, Norman
San Francisco quake. Opera N 30:8-12 D 25 '65

MELONS
New cantaloupe variety extends season. Farm J 89:60H My '65
See also
Muskmelons

MELPHALAN therapy. See Cancer—Therapy

MELTZER, Nancy S. See Levin, H. jt. auth.

MELVILLE, Herman
Man who wrote Moby Dick. M. Eastman. il Read Digest 86:182-4+ Mr '65

MELVIN, A. Gordon
Natural history. See issues of Hobbies

MELVIN, Elizabeth
Traveler's choice. Travel 124:13 N '65

MELVIN, Glen E.
Get more hours between valve jobs. Suc Farm 64:76D Ja '66
Install a vacuum gauge for top tractor efficiency. Suc Farm 63:68 S '65

MELZACK, Ronald, and Schecter, Bayla
Itch and vibration. bibliog Science 147:1047-8 F 26 '65
—and Wall, P. D.
Pain mechanisms: a new theory. bibliog Science 150:971-9 N 19 '65

MEMBRANE equilibrium. See Donnan equilibrium

MEMBRANES (biology)
Cellular origin of hyaluronateprotein in the human synovial membrane. S. Blau and others. bibliog il Science 150:353-5 O 15 '65
Chemistry of cell membranes. L. E. Hokin and M. R. Hokin. il Sci Am 213:78-84+ O '65
Erythrocyte membrane: chemical modification. H. C. Berg and others. bibliog il Science 150:64-7 O 1 '65
Membrane role in cell metabolism discussed. Sci N L 88:243 O 16 '65

Permeability of a nuclear membrane: changes during normal development and changes induced by growth hormone. S. Ito and W. R. Loewenstein. bibliog il Science 150:909-10 N 12 '65
See also
Plasma membranes

MEMBRANES (technology)
Animals breathe own air; teflon membrane for underwater breathing. Sci N L 88:101 Ag 14 '65

MEMENTOS. See Keepsakes

MEMOIRS of a mouse; story. See King, A.

MEMORIAL fountains. See Fountains

MEMORIAL funds
Flagstad's winner; Kirsten Flagstad memorial fund. il Opera N 29:33 Mr 13 '65

MEMORIALS
See also
Kennedy, J. F.—Memorials
Roosevelt, T.—Statues, portraits, etc.
Stone Mountain memorial

MEMORY
Animal memory varies. Sci N L 87:134 F 27 '65
Brain stores same data in many different places. Sci N L 88:120 Ag 21 '65
Calendar-calculating twins; idiot savants. Sci Am 213:46 Ag '65
Chemistry of the brain. F. R. Schreiber and M. Herman. Sci Digest 57:33-4 Ap '65
Drug improves memory; Cylert. Sci N L 89:6 Ja 1 '66
Fish aid memory study; puromycin effect. Sci N L 89:3 Ja 1 '66
Information and control processes in living systems; report on first of a projected series of conferences. D. Ramsey. Science 149:459 Jl 23 '65
Jot it down. B. Day. il Read Digest 87:31-2+ Jl '65
Learning in the octopus. B. B. Boycott. il Sci Am 212:42-50 bibliog(p 138) Mr '65
Memory may use proteins. Sci N L 87:391 Je 19 '65
Memory transfer seen. Sci N L 88:114 Ag 21 '65
Memory transferred? Sci N L 89:39 Ja 15 '66
Molecule for memory? boosting the supply of RNA. il Time 87:66 Ja 7 '66
One octopus brain has two memory stores. Sci N L 87:194 Mr 27 '65
Site of short-term memory. Sci Am 212:52-3 F '65
Transfer of a response to naive rats by injection of ribonucleic acid extracted from trained rats. F. R. Babich and others. bibliog il Science 149:656-7 Ag 6 '65; Discussion. 150:228, 1749 O 8, D 24 '65
Where the memory is; ribonucleic acid, storehouse of experience. il Newsweek 66:70 Ag 23 '65
See also
Reminiscence

MEMORY, Loss of. See Amnesia

MEMORY devices (computers) See Magnetic memory (computers)

MEMPHIS, Tenn.
Southern business: the boomman. T. G. Harris. il Look 29:40-4 N 16 '65

Banks
Notable low budget building; First national bank of Memphis. il Arch Rec 137:149-56 F '65

MEMPHIS, Tenn, public library
Too much ado about too little? letter. C. L. Wallis. ALA Bul 59:100 F '65

MEN
Men who deliver the male. il Mlle 61:116-17+ Je '65
See also
Bachelors
Cookery by men
Fathers
Husbands
Young men

Anecdotes, facetiae, satire, etc.
Brief rebellion of the American male. A. M. Auerbach. il Harper 230:85-7 F '65
How to tell a man from a woman. J. Goodsell. il Good H 160:12+ Mr '65; Same abr. Read Digest 86:112-13 My '65

Clothing
See Clothing and dress—Men

Health and hygiene
Animal man needs to hike. W. O. Douglas. il N Y Times Mag p34-5 Mr 21 '65

MEN—Health and hygiene—*Continued*
Executive beauty; beauty treatments for tired businessmen. il Newsweek 65:30 Mr 22 '65
How to preserve a husband. J. A. Nimrod. il Farm J 89:81+ Mr '65
Men and their looks; tape-talk straight from a famous doctor; questions and answers. Vogue 146:118-21 N 15 '65
Personal business; executive ulcer. Bsns W p 187 S 18 '65
Personal business; middle years. Bsns W p 125-6 Ag 14 '65
Sturdy gray line; physical aptitude testing at West Point. Sports Illus 22:16 My 24 '65
Sugarcoating the executive's health checkup. il Bsns W p68-9 Je 19 '65
See also
Beauty, Personal

Psychology
Flight from woman, by K. Stern. Review America 113:289-90 S 18 '65. F. J. Braceland
Smokers seek masculinity. C. A. Betts. Sci N L 87:373 Je 12 '65
What kind of men cry? symposium. il Ebony 20:47+ Je '65

Anecdotes, facetiae, satire, etc.
Marrying kind. E. Kendall. Mlle 61:122-3+ O '65
MEN and women. See Women and men
MENASHE, Samuel
Sheen; poem. New Yorker 41:212 S 25 '65
MENCKEN, Henry Louis
Overplaying it. D. Smith. Nation 200:566-7 My 24 '65
Phenomenon called Mencken. G. W. Johnson. New Repub 152:32-3 Ap 17 '65
MENDEL, Gregor Johann
Johann Gregor Mendel. J. Rostand. il por UNESCO Courier 18:16-19 Ap '65
MENDELISM
Johann Gregor Mendel. J. Rostand. il UNESCO Courier 18:16-19 Ap '65
MENDELS, Ora
End of world scourge. Sci Digest 57:36 F '65
MENDEL'S law. See Mendelism
MENDELSON, Joseph, and Chorover, S. L.
Lateral hypothalamic stimulation in satiated rats: T-maze learning for food. bibliog Science 149:559-61 Jl 30 '65
MENDELSSOHN, Felix
Mendelssohn revisited. I. Kipnis. por Am Rec G 31:888+ My '65
MENDENHALL, Joseph A.
Department officers discuss Viet-Nam situation. Dept State Bul 52:291-4 Mr 1 '65
MENDING
Iron-on patches for mending. il Consumer Bul 48:34 Ag '65
With today's miracle adhesives, you can mend anything. R. C. Whitman. Am Home 68: 98-9 Ap '65
MENEFEE, Audrey. See Menefee, S. jt. auth.
MENEFEE, Selden, and Menefee, Audrey
India's crisis. New Repub 153:6-7 Ag 7 '65
MENEMENCIOGLU, Turgut
United Nations commemoration address, June 26, 1965. UN Mo Chron 2:156-9 Jl '65
MENEN, Aubrey
French town, an American base, a frontier. N Y Times Mag p 14-15+ Ja 31 '65
Hong Kong. Vogue 145:204-7+ My '65
How to clean the square. House & Gard 128: 90-1 Jl '65
On the way to Nirvana. Holiday 37:144+ Mr '65
Real citizens of Rome. Holiday 38:50-1+ S '65
Singapore. Vogue 145:200-3+ My '65
Two views of Rome. Holiday 37:68-73+ My '65
MENGELE, Josef
Wanted: 1,000 Nazis still at large. G. Samuels. il por N Y Times Mag p26-7+ F 28 '65
MENINGITIS
Surgeon on a hot seat; colonel battles killer disease as a senior medic of sixth army. il Ebony 20:87-90 F '65
MENKE, John L.
Amateur scientist. Sci Am 213:106-8 O '65
MENNINGER, Edwin A.
Gardener's guide to Florida. Horticulture 43: 30-3+ D '65
MENNINGER, Karl Augustus
New approach to mental illness. Read Digest 86:71-3 Mr '65
MENNINGER, Robert
When should you see a psychiatrist? por(p34) Ladies Home J 83:50-1 Ja '66

MENNONITES
Amish, an old order flourishes; Pennsylvania Dutch country. il Bsns W p30-1 My 22 '65
Amish folk; plainest of Pennsylvania's plain people. R. Gehman. il Nat Geog Mag 128: 226-53 Ag '65
Cease-fire in a church-school dispute; Amish farmers, Buchanan County, Ia. il U S News 59:15 D 6 '65
Frankness on Vietnam. M. Shelly. Christian Cent 82:1018-20 Ag 18 '65
Old Order; Amish families defy Iowa education authorities. il Newsweek 66:38 D 6 '65
On the current scene; Mennonite church's general conference. P. Erb. Christian Cent 82:1172 S 2 '65
MENOMINEE Indians
Lost Indians. J. Ridgeway. New Repub 153: 17-20 D 4 '65
MENON, M. A. K.
Universal postal union. bibliog f Int Concil 552:3-64 Mr '65
MENOPAUSE
Age, postponement: a doctor speaks; questions and answers. il Vogue 146:62-5+ Ag 15 '65
How I took the menace out of menopause. M. N. Dunne. Farm J 89:101+ Mr '65
Key to staying young; excerpts from Feminine forever. R. A. Wilson. il Look 30:66+ Ja 11 '66
Menopause: is it necessary? A. Lake. Good H 160:85+ Ap '65
MENORAH Journal
Epitaph for a Jewish magazine. R. Alter. Commentary 39:51-5 My '65; Discussion. 40:6+ O '65
MENOTTI, Gian Carlo
Menotti & Pound. C. A. Matz. por Opera N 30:14-15 N 20 '65
Musica é martini dry. il por Time 86:62 Jl 16 '65
On records; Death of the Bishop of Brindisi. Opera N 29:34 Ap 3 '65
Saint of Bleecker street. Criticism New Yorker 41:172 Mr 27 '65
Spilling the beans. por Newsweek 66:79-80 Jl 5 '65
MENOYO, Eloy Gutiérrez
Man for one season. por Newsweek 65:49 F 8 '65
MENS clothes. See Clothing and dress—Men
MENS clothing industry. See Clothing industry
MENS shirts. See Shirts
MENS shoes. See Shoes
MENSTRUATION
What you and your daughter should know about menstruation. H. Puner. Parents Mag 40:36+ F '65

Disorders
Now doctors can end monthly problems. L. R. Chevalier. Ladies Home J 82:44+ Ag '65
MENSTRUATION, Cessation of. See Menopause
MENTAL chronometry. See Time perception
MENTAL deficiency
See also
Mentally handicapped
Phenylketonuria
MENTAL depression. See Depression, Mental
MENTAL derangements. See Insanity
MENTAL development of children. See Children —Growth and development
MENTAL development of infants. See Infants —Growth and development
MENTAL healing
See also
Christian Science
MENTAL health book review index
Bibliographical challenges in the age of the computer; excerpts from editorial. I. Bry and L. Afflerbach. il Library J 90:813-18 F 15 '65
MENTAL health laws
Mental patient's rights; commitment laws. Time 86:49-50 S 24 '65
Toward the therapeutic state; involuntary mental hospitalization. T. S. Szasz. New Repub 153:26-9 D 11 '65; Reply. Mrs W. A. Anthony. 153:30 D 25 '65
MENTAL health literature. See Psychological literature
MENTAL hospitals. See Hospitals, Psychiatric
MENTAL hygiene
Far right's fight against mental health. D. Robinson. il Look 29:30-2 Ja 26 '65; Correction. 29:12 Mr 9 '65
How good is your mental health? H. Levinson. Read Digest 87:54-8 S '65
Inside psychiatry today. See issues of Science digest

MENTAL hygiene—*Continued*
Keeping mentally fit; excerpts from Today's health guide. Parents Mag 40:38+ N '65
  See also
Adjustment, Social
Relaxation
Social psychiatry

MENTAL illness
Bigger hospitals or bigger people? H. H. Ashbury. il Sat R 48:59-60 N 6 '65
Image of hope; imagination as healer of the hopeless, by W. F. Lynch. Review
    America 113:247-8 S 4 '65. J. E. Royce
When should you see a psychiatrist? R. Menninger. il Ladies Home J 83:50-1 Ja '66
  See also
Insanity
Psychiatry
Psychoses
Schizophrenia

Terminology
  See also
Psychiatry—Terminology

Therapy
Injections for depression. Time 85:75 My 7 '65
Long hospitalization hit. Sci N L 89:14 Ja 1 '66
Psychiatric vistas; day hospitals. il Newsweek 66:95+ N 29 '65
Witch doctors and psychiatry. J. Randal. il Harper 231:56-61 D '65
  See also
Dance therapy
Recreation for the handicapped
Shock therapy

Africa
Witch doctors and psychiatry. J. Randal. il Harper 231:56-61 D '65

MENTAL illness and law. See Mental health laws

MENTAL processes. See Thought and thinking

MENTAL telepathy. See Telepathy

MENTALLY handicapped
Calendar-calculating twins; idiot savants. Sci Am 213:46 Ag '65
Help for the retarded; Senator Kennedy's proposals. Nation 201:151 S 27 '65
My daughter Laure. S. M. Chassier. il Redbook 124:8+ Mr '65
They speed up slow minds; Connecticut's Seaside regional center for mentally retarded. S. Schuler. Todays Health 44:40-1+ Ja '66; Same. Read Digest 88:177-80 Ja '66

MENTALLY handicapped children
Attention in infancy may halt retardation. Sci N L 88:249 O 16 '65
Where toys are locked away; Senator R. F. Kennedy's indictment of New York state's institutions for mentally retarded children. Christian Cent 82:1179 S 29 '65
  See also
Slow learning children

Education
  See also
Slow learning children—Education

MENTALLY ill

Care and treatment
Be brothers keepers; program of mental health centers. Sci N L 87:147 Mr 6 '65
Brink of suicide; fifteen year old. Good H 161:12+ O '65
Coming upheaval in psychiatry. M. Pines. il Harper 231:54-60 O '65; Discussion. 231:6+ D '65
Dangerous ones; help for children with twisted minds. A. Ribicoff. Harper 230:88-90 F '65
How jobless are retrained to work in mental hospitals. H. G. Earl. il Todays Health 43:8-9+ Ap '65
Illinois plans zone centers for mental health. il Arch Rec 137:201-8 Je '65
Mental health act; what community services will now be available through the use of federal funds. P. R. Sullivan. America 112:773-5 My 22 '65
Mental health and the poor; summary of address, March 15, 1965. S. F. Yolles. America 112:449 Ap 3 '65
Mental health of the poor; ed. by F. Riessman and others. Review
    Commonweal 82:87-8 Ap 9 '65. K. Stern
Psychiatric vistas; day hospitals. il Newsweek 66:95+ N 29 '65

Treating the mentally ill; study of southern children. R. Coles. New Repub 152:17-20 F 20 '65
  See also
Dance therapy

Legal status, laws, etc.
  See Mental health laws

MENTALLY superior
Are aptitude tests valid for the highly able? H. Chauncey and T. L. Hilton. bibliog il Science 148:1297-304 Je 4 '65; Discussion. 149:245-6, 583, 708; 150:553-4 Jl 16, Ag 6-13, O 29 '65

MENTALLY superior children. See Children, Gifted

MENUHIN, Yehudi
Education on the Menuhin plan. I. Kolodin. il Sat R 48:57-8+ N 27 '65
Music to my ears; Menuhin trio; latest appearance in New York with Hephzibah and M. Gendron. I. Kolodin. Sat R 48:56 D 11 '65

MENUS
Cook it cool. C. Claiborne. il N Y Times Mag p41 Ag 1 '65
Dinner-in-a-jiffy; with recipes. il Good H 160:112-29+ Mr '65
Fifteen-minute meals with a flair. il Redbook 124:78-9+ Ap '65
Ladies' home journal party portfolio. il Ladies Home J 82:95-124+ O '65
Menu treasures from Good housekeeping. C. Brock. See issues of Good housekeeping
[Month] menus; with recipes. See issues of Sunset
Party brioche and many more new party foods. il McCalls 92:124-5+ Mr '65
Party file. il Ladies Home J 82:100-1 Ap; 90-1 My; 98-9 Je '65
Taste of spring. il McCalls 92:140-1+ Ap '65
  See also
Breakfasts
Buffet meals
Camp cookery
Dinners and dining
Lunches
Meals
Suppers
Thanksgiving dinners

MENZIES, Sir Robert Gordon
Exit burly Bob. por Newsweek 67:44 Ja 24 '66

MERAS, Phyllis
Author: V. Leduc. Sat R 48:47 O 30 '65

MERCAPTO group
Complement and hemolytic antibody: changes in their activity induced by mercaptoethanol. M. M. Frank and others. bibliog il Science 147:742-3 F 12 '65
Complement: inactivation of second component by p-hydroxymercuribenzoate. M. A. Leon. bibliog il Science 147:1034-5 F 26 '65

MERCAPTOETHANOL. See Mercapto group

MERCER, Charles
Have faith in your subconscious. Writer 78:12-14 Mr '65

MERCER, David
Ride a cock horse. Criticism
    Christian Cent 82:1067 S 1 '65

MERCER, Jinx
Agena re-use in orbit considered. Miss & Roc 17:18 S 13 '65
Agena tests key to April Gemini shot. Miss & Roc 17:16-17 D 6 '65
Gemini 6 flight could last five days. Miss & Roc 17:16-17 O 4 '65
NASA cranking up for Gemini 6 & 7. Miss & Roc 17:14-15 S 6 '65
New suit to be worn aboard Gemini 7. Miss & Roc 17:17 O 18 '65
Rendezvous, EVA conditions may extend Gemini flights. Miss & Roc 18:16 Ja 17 '66
Star-sighting difficulties could alter Apollo guidance system. Miss & Roc 18:17-18 Ja 10 '66

MERCER, Mabel
Durable underground doyenne. il pors Life 59:123-4+ O 15 '65

MERCER ISLAND, Wash.
How Mercer Island got its kids' forest wonderland. il Sunset 134:96-9 Mr '65

MERCHANDISE, Quality of. See Quality of products

MERCHANDISING
Bond market; James Bond label of 007. il Time 85:92 F 26 '65
Bonanza; 007 products boom. il Newsweek 65:92+ My 10 '65
  See also
Television broadcasting—Merchandising tie-in

MERCHANDISING clubs
What are these mail-order shopping clubs? Changing T 19:43-4 Jl '65

MERCHANT, Livingston T. and Heeney, A. D. P.
Canada and the United States, principles for partnership; report, June 28, 1965. Dept State Bul 53:193-208 Ag 2 '65

MERCHANT marine

Czechoslovakia
Landlocked fleets sail the seas. il Bsns W p83 F 27 '65

Russia
Cold, wet war; American merchant fleet declines while Soviet fleet increases. R. Moley. Newsweek 65:100 Ap 5 '65

Switzerland
Landlocked fleets sail the seas. il Bsns W p83 F 27 '65

United States
American merchant marine: fourth arm of our defense; address, September 29, 1965. L. E. James. Vital Speeches 32:51-3 N 1 '65
Automation goes to sea. J. H. Winchester. il Read Digest 86:119-22 My '65
Bailing out the fleet. il Time 86:84+ Jl 16 '65
Charting a new course; U.S. shipping. il Bsns W p 166+ Ap 24 '65
Cold, wet war; American merchant fleet declines while Soviet fleet increases. R. Moley. Newsweek 65:100 Ap 5 '65
Hard astern. il Time 86:20 S 10 '65
Is our merchant fleet really afloat? il Bsns W p 128+ S 25 '65
Lifeline to the war; shippers object to operate for Military sea transport service. il Newsweek 66:79 D 6 '65
Merchant fleet hopes its ships will come in. il Bsns W p 121-2 Je 26 '65
Merchant marine: wilderness of tigers. H. Junker. il Nation 202:71-3 Ja 17 '66
Of ships, subsidies, and seamen. Mo Labor R 88:III-IV O '65
Our merchant marine in trouble. J. D. Hayes. il Reporter 34:28-31 Ja 13 '66
Radical reform, some day. Time 86:96 O 15 '65
Sink or swim for U.S. ships; Marine engineers strike. Life 59:4 Jl 30 '65
SOBIGM sent me; low state of the U.S. merchant marine. il Newsweek 65:74 Mr 1 '65
Strong medicine; new prescription for ailing fleet. Newsweek 66:95 O 18 '65
Weak spot in our defenses. J. D. Hayes. America 113:93-5 Jl 24 '65
See also
Maritime workers
Merchant ships
Shipping—United States

MERCHANT ships
Lay-up fleet: not all shipshape; National defense reserve fleet. il Bsns W p 142-4 S 25 '65
Maritime plan riding out storm; overhaul program of US maritime industry. Bsns W p36 O 16 '65
Shipping blueprint shapes up; overhaul of U.S. merchant fleet. Bsns W p27 O 2 '65

MERCIER, Vivian
Immobilization of time. Nation 200:119-21 F 1 '65

MERCOURI, Melina
Melina Mercouri and Salvador Dali match wits in a discussion of love, wealth, fidelity and death. por Redbook 124:52-3+ F '65

MERCURY (planet)
Mercurial Mercury; new evidence on period of rotation. il Newsweek 65:83-4 My 3 '65
Mercury rotation found. A. Ewing. Sci N L 87:277 My 1 '65
Mercury rotation set. A. Ewing. il Sci N L 88:291 N 6 '65
Spin of Mercury. Sci Am 212:58 Je '65
Theory of rotation for the planet Mercury. H. S. Liu and J. A. O'Keefe. bibliog il Science 150:1717 D 24 '65

MERCURY batteries. See Storage batteries
MERCURY probe. See Space probes
MERCURY vapor lamps. See Electric lamps, Mercury vapor
MERCY, Sister Mary. See Mary Mercy, Sister
MERCY killing. See Euthanasia

MEREDITH, William
Auden as critic. Poetry 107:118-20 N '65
Queen of spades; poem. Opera N 30:18 Ja 15 '66

MERGARD, Jean Carpenter
Christmas in the Southwest; poem. Farm J 89:107 D '65

MERGERS. See Business consolidations and mergers; Railroads—Consolidations and mergers; Trusts, Industrial—Law

MERINGUE
Easily, you invent your own; meringue torte. il Sunset 135:166 S '65
For the snowy season. C. Claiborne. il N Y Times Mag p 115-16 N 28 '65
Snow-peaked frozen torte. V. V. Voboril. il Good H 161:140 S '65

MERISTEMS. See Plant cells and tissues
MERIT scholarship program. See National merit scholarship corporation
MERIT system (civil service) See Government service

MERIWETHER, David
Bad old days. Time 86:E3-4 D 24 '65

MERKERT, Tilde
Growing herbs is easy and fun. Flower Grower 52:16 My '65

MERKLING, Frank
Importance of Bing. Opera N 29:8-11 Ap 17 '65

MERLIN, Angelina
Italy: house and home. il Newsweek 66:53 N 8 '65

MERRELL, William S, company
More about thalidomide. J. Ridgeway. New Repub 154:12-15 Ja 8 '66

MERRIAM, Eve
View from the West side. Nation 200:620-2 Je 7 '65
We're teaching our children that violence is fun. Read Digest 86:39+ F '65

MERRICK, David
Broadway show in a theater of war. S. Alexander. Life 59:30 O 22 '65
Hello, David! trouble over Dolly troupe in South Vietnam. il Newsweek 66:36+ O 25 '65

MERRICK, T. R.
CB antennas then, now, and tomorrow. Pop Electr 22:62-7 My '65

MERRIFIELD, R. B.
Automated synthesis of peptides. bibliog Science 150:178-85 O 8 '65

MERRIHUEITE
Merrihueite, a new alkali-ferromagnesian silicate from the Mezö-Madaras chondrite. R. T. Dodd, jr. and others. bibliog il Science 149:972-4 Ag 27 '65

MERRILL, James
Broken homes; poem. New Yorker 41:55 O 30 '65
Current; poem. New Yorker 41:140 Je 12 '65
From the cupola; poem. Poetry 107:143-58 D '65

MERRILL, Jean A.
Children's libraries. Wilson Lib Bul 39:913 Je '65

MERRILL Lynch, Pierce, Fenner and Smith, incorporated
Wall Street's thundering herd. il Newsweek 65:75-8 Mr 1 '65

MERRIMACK RIVER
Cleaning up the Merrimack. L. Wolf. Bul Atomic Sci 21:16-18 Ap '65

MERRIMAN, Nan
Retiring mezzo. T. Heinitz. il por Sat R 48:50 My 29 '65

MERRITT, Clifton R.
(ed) House warming; excerpts from statements during the floor debate of the Wilderness bill. Liv Wildn 86:36-8 Spr '64

MERRITT ISLAND launch area. See Proving grounds

MERRY-go-rounds
Back-yard merry-go-round. R. E. Londgren. il Pop Sci 187:111 Jl '65

MERSAND, Joseph
Book review. Sr Schol 87:sup6+ S 30; sup6 D 2 '65
Book reviews for teachers of English. Sr Schol 87:sup8-9 N 4 '65

MERSON, Ben
How a city faced an epidemic. Good H 160:80-1+ Je '65
Three new miracle treatments to keep babies alive. Good H 161:68-9+ Jl '65

MERTON, Thomas
Challenge of responsibility. Sat R 48:28-30 F 13 '65
Few questions and fewer answers; extracts from a monastic notebook. Harper 231:79-81 N '65
Rain and the rhinoceros. Holiday 37:8+ My '65
about
Unwordly wisdom. D. J. Callahan. Commentary 39:90+ Ap '65

MERTZ, Edwin T. and others
Growth of rats fed on opaque-2 maize. bibliog Science 148:1741-2 Je 25 '65

MERWIN, W. S.
December night; poem. Atlan 216:91 D '65
Glimpse of the ice; poem. Atlan 217:74 Ja '66
Herds; poem. New Yorker 41:36 Ja 15 '66
In autumn; After the solstice; Crows on the
North slope; Cold before the moonrise; New
moon in November; December among the
vanished: poems. Nation 201:364 N 15 '65
On the bestial floor. Nation 200:313-14 Mr
22 '65
Wave; poem. New Yorker 41:176 N 27 '65

MERYMAN, Richard
(ed) See Wyeth, A. Andrew Wyeth

MESERVE, Frederick Hill
Three generations of research. G. P. Hunt. il
por Life 58:3 Ap 16 '65

MESONS
Lost force; fifth force in addition to four
known forces: nuclear, electromagnetic,
weak and gravitational. Sci Am 212:56-8 Ap
'65
New headache for physicists; fifth force
and CPT. B. H. Frisch. il Sci Digest 58:
28-32 Jl '65

MESOPOTAMIA

History
Ancient life was hard. Sci N L 87:199 Mr 27
'65
Ecology of early food production in Mesopotamia. K. V. Flannery. bibliog il Science
147:1247-56 Mr 12 '65

MESOZOIC period. See Paleobotany—Mesozoic

MESQUITE, Tex.
Park-school facilities do double duty. G.
Schrader and R. Poteet. il Am City 80:110-
11 D '65

MESSAGES, Bottle. See Bottle messages

MESSENGER; story. See Ford, J. H.

MESSERLY, Wayne
Here's proof that diversified farming isn't
dead! Suc Farm 63:72 N '65
Six good truck ideas on one truck. il Suc
Farm 63:107 S '65

MESSERSMITH, Fred
Francis Chapin: an exuberant painter. Am
Artist 29:28-33+ Mr '65

MESSIAH (oratorio)
Christmas, the Messiah and the small town.
J. Sittler. Christian Cent 82:1576-7 D 22 '65

MESSINESI, Despina
Travel (cont) Vogue 145:82 Mr 1; 149 Ap 15;
255+ My; 66 Je; 146:178 S 1; 164-5 O 1;
118+ N 1; 61 N 15; 152-3+ D '65

MESTA, Perle
[Monthly column] See issues of McCall's
to May 1965

MESTHENE, Emmanuel G.
Learning to live with science. Sat R 48:14-17
Jl 17 '65

MESTROVIC, Matthew
Paunchy revolution. Commonweal 83:336-9 D
17 '65

METABOLISM
Biological feedback control at the molecular
level. D. E. Atkinson. bibliog il Science
150:851-7 N 12 '65
Epinephrine-induced normalization of lipid
metabolism in adrenalectomized rats. M.
Friedman and S. O. Byers. bibliog il Science 148:644-6 Ap 30 '65
Glycerol metabolism in the human liver: inhibition by ethanol. F. Lundquist and others. bibliog il Science 150:616-17 O 29 '65
Glyoxylate in fatty-acid metabolism. R. Rabin
and others. bibliog il Science 150:1548-58 D
17 '65
Hurler's syndrome: demonstration of an inherited disorder of connective tissue in cell
culture. B. S. Danes and A. G. Bearn.
bibliog il Science 149:987-9 Ag 27 '65
Metabolic controls in cultured mammalian
cells; adaptation of address, June 2, 1964.
H. Eagle. bibliog il Science 148:42-51 Ap 2
'65
Metabolism of iodine-131-labeled thyroxine-
binding prealbumin in man. J. H. Oppenheimer and others. bibliog il Science 149:
748-51 Ag 13 '65
Regulation of cockroach fat-body metabolism
by the corpus cardiacum in vitro. A. W.
Wiens and L. I. Gilbert. bibliog il Science
150:614-16 O 29 '65
Retinoyl beta-glucuronic acid: a major metabolite of vitamin A in rat bile. P. E. Dunagin, jr. and others. bibliog il Science 148:86-
7 Ap 2 '65
When nature errs; genetic disorders in children. Newsweek 65:78 Je 28 '65
See also
Fat metabolism
Galactose metabolism

METABOLISM (herbicides)
Herbicide metabolism: N-glycoside of amiben
isolated from soybean plants. S. R. Colby.
bibliog il Science 150:619-20 O 29 '65

METABOLISM (plants) See Plants—Metabolism

METACHROMATIC leukodystrophy. See Brain
—Diseases

METAL, Scrap. See Scrap metal

METAL castings
Metal casting for the grades. J. Burgner. il
Design 67:32-7 S '65

METAL cleaning
Care and safekeeping of stainless steel,
chromium, and aluminum. House & Gard
129:29-30+ Ja '66
Copper, brass, and pewter. House & Gard 128:
52-3+ N '65

METAL coloring
Chemical color coating is promising. Miss &
Roc 16:56 My 17 '65

METAL construction
Curved roof elements make use of metal
lath. il Arch Rec 138:179-80 Ag '65

METAL cutting
How to cut metal with woodworking power
tools. J. Burroughs. il Pop Sci 186:128-30
Je '65
See also
Electric cutting
Electrochemical cutting

METAL eyelets. See Eyelets, Metal

METAL finishing
Industry study produces a designation system
for aluminum finishes. il Arch Rec 137:199-
200 Mr '65
Metal finishes. J. Hand. Pop Sci 187:142-4 Ag
'65
See also
Metal coloring

METAL furniture. See Furniture, Metal

METAL polishes. See Polishing materials

METAL powders
Solid parts from a powdered start; portfolio.
Fortune 72:148-51 Ag '65

METAL sculpture
Anyone can sculpt. il Design 66:20-1 Mr '65

METAL work
Escalating war in metalworking: machining
and casting. G. Berkwitt. il Duns R 86:
44-6+ Jl '65
June Schwarcz: electroforming and enamel.
A. Ventura. il Craft Horiz 25:36-7+ N '65
Silver, pewter, and other metals: old North-
west Territory. il Antiques 87:322-3 Mr '65
See also
Art metal work
Dies (metal work)
Flanges

Projects
Three projects for a child's room; plywood
rocker; trumpet lamp; drum toy box. il
Pop Sci 187:124-5 D '65

METALIOUS, Grace
Tragedy of Grace Metalious and Peyton
Place. M. Miller. il Ladies Home J 82:58-
9+ Je '65

METALLIZED textile fabrics. See Textile
fabrics, Metallized

METALLURGICAL research
Glide mechanisms in experimentally de-
formed minerals. C. B. Raleigh. bibliog il
Science 150:739-41 N 5 '65

METALS
Do you know your metals? questions and
answers. J. Daugherty and M. Daugherty.
il Sci Digest 57:88-90 Je '65
Electron density and electronic properties in
noble-metal transition elements. M. A.
Jensen and others. bibliog il Science 150:
1448-50 D 10 '65
See also
Alkali metals
Mineralogy
also names of metals, e.g. Molybdenum

Analysis
Analysis of copper and brass coins of the
early Roman empire. G. F. Carter. bibliog
il Science 151:196-7 Ja 14 '66

Coloring
See Metal coloring

Irradiation
Xenon-photosensitized formation of metastable nitrogen. W. M. Jackson and M. D.
Scheer. bibliog il Science 148:1718-19 Je 25
'65

Prices
Why the lid will stay on prices for metals;
stockpile sales. il Bsns W p32-3 N 27 '65
See also
Copper—Prices

METEOROLOGY, Aeronautic
Flying weather signposts. H. T. Harrison. il Flying 77:49-51 N '65
More flying weather signposts H. T. Harrison. il Flying 77:79-81 D '65
See also
Mountain waves
Radar meteorology

METEOROLOGY, Maritime
Forecasting Great Lakes weather. F. R. Shumway. il Motor B 115:53-6+ Je '65
Weather while you wait. A. E. Sik. il Motor B 116:42-5+ O '65
Winds of the world. J. Martenhoff. il Motor B 115:45-7+ Mr '65

METEORS
Huge meteors may have created continents. Sci N L 87:297 My 8 '65
Late-1964 meteor shower roundup; Taurids; Leonids; Geminids. L. J. Robinson. il Sky & Tel 29:120-1 F '65
Two summer meteor showers. il Sky & Tel 30:248-9 O '65
Unexpected increase in meteor counts. G. S. Mumford, 3d. il Sky & Tel 29:156 Mr '65

METER reading
Modern water rates; meter reading and billing frequency. Am City 80:102-4+ F '65

METERS
What you should know about feed meters. P. B. Jones. il Suc Farm 63:40-1 N '65
See also
Electric meters
Voltmeters
Water meters

METERS, Exposure. See Exposure meters

METHADONE
Anti-heroin. Sci Am 212:62+ Ap '65
Breaking the habit. il Newsweek 65:60+ Je 21 '65
Case history of an addict-patient. il Look 29:25-7 N 30 '65
New hope for drug addicts. R. H. Berg. il Look 29:23-4 N 30 '65
Now, a drug that cures drug addicts. J. Reinert. Sci Digest 58:38-41 N '65
One answer to heroin. Time 86:44 S 3 '65

METHANOL
Wood alcohol seen as electricity source. Sci N L 88:185 S 18 '65

METHODIST bishops. See Bishops

METHODIST church
Union without renewal? critique of the Methodist-E.U.B. negotiations. J. E. Will. Christian Cent 82:588+ My 5 '65; Discussion. 82:809-11, 815 Je 23 '65
See also
World Methodist council

METHODIST church in England
Methodism, 1784-1970; plans to heal Anglican-Methodist breach. il Newsweek 65:74 My 31 '65

METHODIST church in the United States
Integrating Methodism; elimination of central jurisdiction. Christian Cent 83:3-4 Ja 5 '66
Join, consolidate, or drift? Time 86:42 Ag 13 '65
Methodism's three alternatives. Christian Cent 82:933-4 Jl 28 '65
Methodism's way. J. C. Evans. Christian Cent 82:1005 Ag 18 '65
Methodist merger maneuvers; Methodist-E.U.B. merger. J. C. Evans. Christian Cent 82:1246-7 O 13 '65; Reply. J. S. Thomas. 82:1518 D 8 '65
Methodists in Mississippi. America 113:3 Jl 3 '65
Methodists merge; conferences. Christian Cent 82:133 F 3 '65
Methodists on evangelism. P. B. Mather. Christian Cent 82:282 Mr 3 '65
Move toward church unity; Methodists appoint Negroes to Jersey, Iowa bishoprics. il Ebony 20:54-60 F '65
Some relevant religion; Night call changes format and widens audience. R. L. Shayon. Sat R 48:41 Ag 21 '65

METHOTREXATE
Uptake as a determinant of methotrexate response in mouse leukemias. D. Kessel and others. il Science 150:752-4 N 5 '65

METHOTREXATE therapy. See Cancer—Therapy

METHVIN, Eugene H.
Behind those campus demonstrations. Read Digest 88:43-8 Ja '66

METHYL sulfoxide
DMSO future dimmed. Sci N L 89:19 Ja 8 '66
End of a wonder drug? Newsweek 66:94 N 22 '65
Limited wonder. Time 86:82+ S 17 '65
Oxidation of dimethyl sulfoxide to dimethyl sulfone in the rabbit. K. I. H. Williams and others. bibliog il Science 149:203-4 Jl 9 '65
Preservation of mammalian cells in a chemically defined medium and dimethylsulfoxide. B. L. Brown and S. C. Nagle, jr. bibliog il Science 149:1266-7 S 10 '65
Promise and perils of the miraculous DMSO. L. David. il Good H 161:68-9+ Ag '65
Report on DMSO; dimethyl sulphoxide. A. Hamilton. il Sci Digest 58:78-82 Ag '65
Too good to be true; strange medicinal properties. il Newsweek 65:109-10 My 10 '65

METHYLACETYLENE. See Propyne

METHYLPHENIDATE. See Analeptics

METRIC system
Adoption of the metric system. D. Wolfle. Science 149:139 Jl 9 '65
'Alf a liter, luv; Britain to convert to metric system. Time 85:24-5 Je 4 '65
Give an inch, get a centimeter; British conversion. Bsns W p34 Je 5 '65
If all the rules do change—. il U S News 58:97 Je 28 '65
Inches or meters. Am City 80:37+ Ag '65
Inches, pounds, pints: the case for changing them all. L. L. Strauss. U S News 58:96-7 Je 28 '65
Measured response; Britain to abandon imperial standard. Newsweek 65:37 Je 7 '65
Metric conversion: petition to Congress; resolution by the American institute of nutrition. R. W. Engel. Science 148:1670 Je 25 '65
Metric system; letter. J. L. Gressitt. Science 149:814 Ag 20 '65
Should the U.S. go metric? pro and con discussion. il Sr Schol 87:18-19 O 28 '65
We're going to go on the metric system. il Changing T 19:29-32 D '65
Why not meters and kilos? A. Smith. il Sci Digest 58:90-3 N '65
See also
Weights and measures

METROMEDIA, incorporated
Combining all channels to reach a mass public; J. W. Kluge's Metromedia. il Bsns W p80-2+ S 18 '65
Metromedia's creative financier. J. F. Olesky. il Duns R 86:49-52 D '65

METRONIDAZOLE
Accidental help for alcoholics. Time 86:67 N 12 '65
Pill for alcoholism. Newsweek 66:82 N 15 '65

METRONOME
Tonal darkroom timer or metronome. F. W. Chesson. il Pop Electr 23:95-6 N '65

METROPOLITAN areas
Modern metropolis. H. Blumenfeld. il Sci Am 213:64-74 bibliog(p276) S '65
Mutli-tiered cities; stringing out. il Life 59:164-5 D 24 '65
Problem of metropolis. D. J. Curran. America 114:38-40 Ja 8 '66
Supplemental wage benefits in metropolitan areas, 1963-64. J. E. Buckley. il Mo Labor R 88:550-4 My '65
Upward thrust for Lower California: The City. il Fortune 71:185-6 Je '65
See also
Cities and towns
Urban renewal
also subhead Metropolitan district under names of cities, e.g. New York (city)—Metropolitan district

METROPOLITAN museum of art, New York
American art at the Metropolitan. A. T. Gardner. il Antiques 87:434-8 Ap '65
Cinderella question; museum's purchase of controversial bust. il Time 86:112 N 5 '65
Looking forward with the Metropolitan; expansion plans. R. Davidson. Antiques 88:18+ Jl '65
Met looks homeward; Three centuries of American painting exhibition. J. Gerassi. il Newsweek 65:86-7 Ap 19 '65
Met museum turns modern; Thomas J. Watson library. J. Humphry, 3d. il Library J 90:5208-9 D 1 '65
Metropolitan's new library. Am Artist 29:6 Ap '65
Muses' marble acres. il Time 85:80-5 Mr 19 '65
Nation's past in paint; historic exhibition of American painting, at the Metropolitan museum. K. Kuh. il Sat R 48:40-2 Ap 24 '65
Recently acquired American paintings at the Metropolitan. S. P. Feld. il Antiques 87:439-43 Ap '65
Wandering patio; Blumenthal patio. New Yorker 40:23-4 F 6 '65
Winging away; plans for a $4,000,000 wing for American art. il Time 85:78 F 5 '65

METROPOLITAN national company. See Metropolitan opera national company

METROPOLITAN opera association
Endowing the future; Seat endowment program. il Opera N 29:30 Ap 17 '65

METROPOLITAN opera auditions. See Singing
—Competitions

METROPOLITAN opera ballet
Ballet evening, Metropolitan opera. D. Her-
ing. Dance Mag 39:30 Je '65
Metropolitan opera ballet. Lewisohn stadium.
D. Hering. Dance Mag 39:86 S '65
On their toes. E. H. Palatsky. il Opera N 29:
12-16 Ap 10 '65

METROPOLITAN opera club
Metropolitan opera club. P. J. Smith. il Opera
N 29:6-7 Ap 3 '65

METROPOLITAN opera company
At the Met: the unadventurous, repeated. G.
Rogoff. il Hi Fi 15:170-1 D '65
Challenge of the new Met. Hi Fi 15:49 S '65
Don Carlo with Schippers and Bumbry. I.
Kolodin. Sat R 48:54 O 23 '65
First comes the singing. H. C. Schonberg.
il N Y Times Mag p54-5+ O 24 '65
Home stretch at the Met. C. L. Osborne. il
Hi Fi 15:111-12 My '65
Importance of Bing; appraisal of the general
manager. F. Merkling. il Opera N 29:8-11 Ap
17 '65
Last debuts; pre-Lincoln Center season. il
Newsweek 66:96 N 22 '65
Lewisohn stadium: the Met moves in; con-
certs. C. L. Osborne. Hi Fi 15:146+ S '65
Maestro remembers; excerpt from It's all in
the music, by D. G. Monteux. P. Monteux.
Opera N 30:26-7 D 25 '65
Met: some outstanding performances. G.
Rogoff. il Hi Fi 16:132-3 Ja '66
Metropolitan calendar. See issues of Opera
news published during opera season
Metropolitan opera 1965-66: roster, repertory,
schedule. il Opera N 30:17-20 S 25 '65
Metropolitan spring tour, 1965. Opera N 29:
32-3 Mr 13 '65
Met's new pact with Lucifer; last Faust at
the old Met. R. Eyer. Life 59:16 O 22 '65
Music to my ears; devil of a Faust opens the
Met under J. L. Barrault direction. I.
Kolodin. Sat R 48:42 O 9 '65
Music to my ears; Resnik as a regal Pique
dame; Freni. I. Kolodin. Sat R 48:39+
O 16 '65
Music to my ears; return of Nilsson. I.
Kolodin. Sat R 49:48 Ja 22 '66
Musical events; opening of outdoor opera in
concert form, at Lewisohn stadium. W. Sar-
geant. New Yorker 41:70+ Jl 3 '65
On their toes; Metropolitan opera ballet.
E. H. Palatsky. il Opera N 29:12-16 Ap
10 '65
Opera sampler; Metropolitan opera and New
York city opera productions. D. Hering.
il Dance Mag 39:25-6 Ap '65
Preem; opening-night. New Yorker 41:46-7
O 9 '65
Spring tour casts. Opera N 29:31 Mr 27 '65
Star-gazing at the Lewisohn observatory. I.
Kolodin. Sat R 48:22 Jl 10 '65
Tosca at last; R. Crespin. R. Lawrence. il
Hi Fi 15:113-14 Je '65
Under the stars; Lewisohn stadium concerts.
D. J. Soria. il Opera N 29:8-12 My 1 '65

METROPOLITAN opera guild
Banner luncheon; annual membership lunch-
eon at Waldorf-Astoria. il Opera N 30:31
Ja 8 '66
Last evening; photographs. Opera N 30:12-13
N 20 '65
Out of Mourning; discussion of opera. Mourn-
ing becomes Electra. F. Merkling. il
Opera N 29:26-7 Ap 10 '65
Reaching for the young; Guild's student per-
formance. R. A. Tuggle. il Opera N 29:27
F 13 '65
Thirty years' war; appraisal of Guild's first
three decades. M. Mayer. il Opera N 30:
10-12 S 25 '65
See also
Metropolitan opera studio

METROPOLITAN opera house, New York
Family circle; word and picture story. N.
Ross. Opera N 29:11-13 Mr 13 '65
First comes the singing. H. C. Schonberg.
il N Y Times Mag p54-5+ O 24 '65
Flower boy; interview, ed. by A. M. Lingg.
A. Weidhaas. il Opera N 29:12-13 Ap 3
'65
Gilding the horseshoe; Metropolitan book
party; photographs. Opera N 30:13 D 4 '65
Golden horseshoe; pictorial history book. A.
Rich. Opera N 30:6 O 23 '65
Last stand at the Met. il Newsweek 66:99-
100 O 11 '65
Mementos. New Yorker 41:25-6 Ja 15 '66
Opening night; cartoons. J. Stevenson. Opera
N 30:16-18 N 6 '65
Why save the old Met? Hi Fi 15:47 D '65

METROPOLITAN opera national company
At least 130 people in love; interviews, ed.
by L. Lerman. R. Stevens; M. Manuel. il
Mlle 61:146-7+ O '65
Cast of tour. il Opera N 30:29-31 O 23 '65
Chipper new chip off the old Met; opening
in Indianapolis. il Life 59:90-1 O 1 '65
Cinderella ball; dance after New York debut,
sponsored by the Metropolitan opera guild.
il Opera N 30:27-9 D 11 '65
Hands across the land. F. Merkling. Opera
N 30:48 O 23 '65
Mephisto's musings. il Hi Fi 15:190 N '65
Met goes west. il Newsweek 66:91-2 O 4 '65
Met national company; opera on the road;
Indianapolis report. C. L. Osborne. il Hi Fi
15:199+ N '65
Metropolitan opera national company. F.
Merkling. Opera N 30:29 D 18 '65
Musical events; performance of Rossini's Cin-
derella. W. Sargeant. New Yorker 41:237-8
N 13 '65
National company tour; cities and dates. il
Opera N 30:16-19 O 23 '65
Niska; last repertory production in New York
state theater. I. Kolodin. Sat R 48:40 N 27
'65
Off & running. il Time 86:80 O 1 '65
Reaching for the young; Guild's student per-
formance. R. A. Tuggle. il Opera N 29:27
F 13 '65
This week. F. Merkling. Opera N 30:2 O 23
'65
Two cheers for the Met national co; first
week of first New York season. I. Kolodin.
Sat R 48:64+ N 20 '65

METROPOLITAN opera on the air. See Radio
broadcasting—Music

METROPOLITAN opera orchestra. See Orchestras

METROPOLITAN opera studio
Lustrum for the studio. J. Gutman. il
Opera N 30:26-7 D 4 '65

METS (baseball) See Baseball clubs

METS farm club (Minor league baseball) See
Baseball

METZ, Clinton E.
Super engine puts a plus in power distribution. Am City 80:106-7 N '65

METZGER, Henry. See Mannik, M. jt. auth.

MEVALONIC acid. See Dihydroxymethyl
valeric acid

MEXICAN architecture. See Architecture,
Mexican

MEXICAN cookery. See Cookery, Mexican

MEXICAN engravings. See Engravings, Mexican

MEXICAN honey bears. See Coatis

MEXICAN oranges
Mexican orange as a screen. il Sunset 134:
282 Je '65

MEXICAN pottery. See Pottery, Mexican

MEXICAN sunflower. See Tithonia

MEXICAN visitors in the United States. See
Foreign visitors in the United States

MEXICO
Country and some people I love; interview,
ed. by H. Lopez. K. A. Porter. Harper
231:58-62+ S '65
That very special neighbor: Mexico. il For-
tune 72:140-8 S '65
See also
Acapulco
Agriculture—Mexico
Architecture, Domestic—Mexico
Automobile industry and trade—Mexico
Automobile touring—Mexico
Botany—Mexico
California, Lower
Camping—Mexico
Crime and criminals—Mexico
Divorce—Mexico
Ensenada
Fishing—Mexico
Guadalajara
Hunting—Mexico
Iron industry and trade—Mexico
Michoacán
Paleontology—Mexico
Poor—Mexico
Silver mines and mining—Mexico
Sonoran Desert
Sulfur mines and mining—Mexico
Teotihuacán
Tijuana
Zoology—Mexico

Antiquities
See Indians of Mexico—Antiquities

MEXICO—*Continued*

Commerce

New octopus; Mexico's trade with CACM. il Newsweek 67:38 Ja 10 '66
See also
United States—Commerce—Mexico

Commercial treaties and agreements

U.S. and Mexico agree on measures to solve Lower Colorado River salinity problem; statement, March 22, 1965; with joint State-Interior department announcement. L. B. Johnson. Dept State Bul 52:555-7 Ap 12 '65

Description and travel

By railroad to Mexico city. Sunset 134:68-9 My '65
Crossing the Rio Grandely. L. Barry. il Pop Phot 57:28+ O '65
Five secret clues to Mexico. C. Fuentes. il Vogue 147:108-9+ Ja 1 '66
Let's travel: Mexico. J. Bush. il Mlle 61:123-6 Je '65
Mexican trio; Guaymas, Alamos and Hermosillo. M. Atwater. il Travel 124:44-6 O '65
Mexico. L. Barry; N. Rothschild; J. M. Zanutto. il Pop Phot 57:86-97+ O '65
Mexico: manana land today. A. H. Hepburn. il Sr Schol 87:sup 12-13 N 11 '65
New approach to Mexico. T. Stabile. il Redbook 125:28+ Ag '65
Travel notes. R. Joseph. Esquire 64:70+ N '65

Economic conditions

Atlantic report. Atlan 216:41-2+ N '65
Mexico: a model for Latin America? il U S News 60:58-60 Ja 24 '66
Mexico and the United States; address, February 1, 1965. B. Pagliai. Vital Speeches 31:472-5 My 15 '65

Economic policy

Boomland south of the border. E. Tomlinson. il Read Digest 86:201-2+ Mr '65
Mexican economic and social development. H. B. Margain. Ann Am Acad 360:68-77 Jl '65
We're bullish on Mexico. E. K. Faltermayer. il Fortune 72:149-51+ S '65

Foreign relations

Soothing words from a new colossus; new good-neighbor policy with Central America. il Time 87:39 Ja 21 '66

History

1821-1861

Sam Houston's last fight. A. Castel. il Am Heritage 17:80-7 D '65

Politics and government

Consensus. il Time 86:28+ S 10 '65
Mexico: a model for Latin America? il U S News 60:58-60 Ja 24 '66
Mexico: 1966 and beyond. F. Brandenburg. bibliog f Cur Hist 50:32-7+ Ja '66
See also
Elections—Mexico

Relief work

Amigo Americans; Project Amigos. il Time 85:49 Ap 30 '65

Religious institutions and affairs

News of the Christian world (cont) Christian Cent 82:755, 1017-18, 1138+ Je 9, Ag 18, S 15 '65

Social conditions

Urban concentration, agriculture, and agrarian reform; with questions and answers. G. J. Eder. bibliog f Ann Am Acad 360:27-47 Jl '65
See also
Poor—Mexico

Social history

Mexican economic and social development. H. B. Margain. Ann Am Acad 360:68-77 Jl '65

United States air agreement

See Aviation—International aspects

MEXICO (city)
Mexico city: roses on the Reforma. D. Weber. il Sat R 49:52+ Ja 1 '66

Galleries and museums

Living temple; National museum of anthropology. il Time 85:76-8 Je 25 '65
Mexico city has a stunning new museum; Museum of anthropology. il Sunset 135:54+ N '65

Museum with a mission; Anthropología. W. Buehr. il Horizon 7:32-5 Autumn '65
New museum in Mexico; National museum of anthropology. J. Didion. Vogue 146:48 Ag 1 '65

Music

Mexico city. L. Frick. Opera N 30:33 D 11 '65

MEXICO, GULF OF
Pliocene-pleistocene boundary, northern Gulf of Mexico. W. H. Akers. bibliog il Science 149:741-2 Ag 13 '65
See also
Gulf states

MEXICO and the United States
Bottles over the border; new United States restrictions on liquor imports. il Newsweek 66:36 O 4 '65
See also
United States—Foreign opinion—Mexican

MEYER, Albert Gregory, cardinal
Obituary
Christian Cent 82:485 Ap 21 '65
Commonweal 82:135 Ap 23 '65
Voice is stilled. America 112:603 Ap 24 '65

MEYER, Carl S.
Proto-Puritans. Christian Cent 82:1159 S 22 '65

MEYER, Charles R.
Stripers are my downfall! pors Yachting 117:120-1+ Je '65

MEYER, Daniel
Build a miniature R/Ceiver. Pop Electr 22:39-41+ Ap '65
FM wireless microphone. Pop Electr 22:35-8 My '65
R/C transmitter. Pop Electr 22:67-70 Je '65

MEYER, Eldon Mike
We are legion. il por PTA Mag 59:21-2 F '65

MEYER, Frank S.
Growth of conservative thought. Nat R 17:1097-8 N 30 '65
Open question. por Nat R 17:725, 888; 18:71+ Ag 24, O 5 '65, Ja 25 '66
Principles and heresies. See issues of National review

MEYER, Garson
Voluntarism in retirement; address, 1964. por Recreation 58:219+ My '65

MEYER, Guilhermo
New West. M. J. Kubic. il por Newsweek 66:48 Ag 16 '65

MEYER, Herbert G.
School gardens in Cleveland. Horticulture 43:24-5+ Ap '65

MEYER, Herman F.
New ways to feed the baby. Todays Health 43:49-50 Je '65

MEYER, Howard N.
Books. Commonweal 82:388-91 Je 11 '65

MEYER, June
Instant slum clearance. Esquire 63:108-11 Ap '65

MEYER, Karl, and others
Extracellular matrices. Science 147:760-1 F 12 '65

MEYER, Lewis
Some hardy perennials and important annuals for the coming holiday season. Pub W 188:58-9 N 8 '65
Wednesday is biddy day; excerpt from Customer is always. Pub W 187:56-7 Mr 8 '65

MEYER, Marshall T.
Tucker at the Colon. Sat R 48:63 Ag 28 '65

MEYER, Robert, Jr
SR/1966 world travel calendar. Sat R 49:55-6+ Ja 1 '66

MEYER, Roy W.
Theodore Roosevelt Memorial Park. Nat Parks Mag 39:17-20 My '65

MEYER, Ruth E.
Family story told by dolls. Hobbies 70:40+ S '65

MEYERHOFF, Arthur E.
War of words; address, June 21, 1965. Vital Speeches 31:600-3 Jl 15 '65

MEYERHOFF, Erich
Medical library center of New York. E. Moon. bibliog il por Library J 90:2952-7 Jl '65

MEYERHOFF, Hans
History's grand designs. Nation 200:311-12 Mr 22 '65

MEYERINK, Victoria Paige
Big push for Danny's charmer. il pors Life 58:57-8+ Mr 19 '65

MEYERKORD, Harold Dale
In search of a Vietnam hero. L. Wainwright. Life 58:23-4 My 28 '65

MEYERRIECKS, Andrew J. and Meyerriecks, Robert
Brown pelican is victim of gull piracy. Natur Hist 74:32-5 N '65

MEYERRIECKS, Robert. See Meyerriecks, A. J. jt. auth.

MEYERS, Harold B.
Commuter railroads can be saved. Fortune 71:100-5+ My '65
Mr Mills's elder-medi-bettercare. Fortune 71:166-8+ Je '65
Monument to power. Fortune 71:122-5+ Mr '65
Professor Turner's turn at antitrust. Fortune 72:168-71+ S '65
—See Alexander, H. E. jt. auth.

MEYERS, Juno
Redemption centers; story. Esquire 65:73 Ja '66

MEZEI, Louis. See Rokeach, M. jt. auth.

MEZEY, Robert
Back; poem. Harper 230:99 F '65
Late afternoon, riverhouse; poem. New Yorker 41:189 Ap 24 '65

MEZGER, P. G. See Baars, J. W. M. jt. auth; Höglund, B. jt. auth

MIAMI, Fla.
No place like it; Miami's little Havana. il Time 86:36-7 N 12 '65

Description
Miami, and its beach. E. Scully. il U S Camera 29:56-7+ Ja '66

Music
Miami firsts. D. Reno. Opera N 29:36 My 1 '65

MIAMI, Fla, public library
Filling the gap in Miami. F. B. Sessa. Wilson Lib Bul 40:255-6 N '65
Library cooperation in Dade County. J. P. McIntyre. ALA Bul 59:540-2 Je '65

MIAMI-Bahamas race. See Motor boat racing

MIAMI BEACH, Fla.
Coming on down. il Time 85:41 Ap 2 '65

Hotels, restaurants, etc.
Man who put the rhinestones on Miami. M. Mayer. il Harper 230:61-8 Mr '65

Politics and government
Elliott for mayor too. il Time 85:22 Mr 5 '65
Like father; E. Roosevelt elected mayor. il Newsweek 65:38+ Je 14 '65
Mayor of the Beach. il Time 85:32 Je 11 '65

MIAMI BEACH rod and reel club. See Sports clubs

MIAMI-Nassau race. See Motor boat racing

MIAMI university, Oxford, Ohio
Real Miami stands up. F. Deford. il Sports Illus 22:50+ F 1 '65

MICA
Mica polytypes: systematic description and identification. M. Ross and others. bibliog il Science 151:191-3 Ja 14 '66
See also
Biotite

MICE
Mus musculus: experimental induction of territory formation. P. K. Anderson and J. L. Hill. bibliog il Science 148:1753-5 Je 25 '65

MICHAEL, Sister Mary. See Mary Michael, Sister

MICHAEL, Donald N.
Your child and the world of tomorrow; questions and answers. NEA J 55:33-48 Ja '66
Your kids when they grow up; interview. Changing T 19:7-13 Mr '65

MICHAEL I and Michael II; story. See Amft, M. J.

MICHAELS, Marilyn
Girl next door. por Newsweek 66:81 Jl 19 '65

MICHALITSANOS, Andrew, and Goldstone, Steven
Observing the eclipse from Peru. por Sky & Tel 30:76-7 Ag '65

MICHALSON, Carl
Carl Michalson dies in plane crash. Christian Cent 82:1435 N 24 '65
Obituary
Pub W 188:37 D 13 '65

MICHAUD, Marguerite
Air battles close to home. Audubon Mag 67:116-20 Mr '65

MICHEL, Joan Hess
Illustrations of Robert Quackenbush. Am Artist 29:28-33+ Ap '65
Lewis Brown, artist in the theater. Am Artist 30:47-53+ Ja '66

MICHELANGELI, Arturo Benedetti
Diamond touch; New York concerts. il por Newsweek 67:81 Ja 24 '66
First, Horowitz, now, Michelangeli returns. R. Kammerer. il por Am Rec G 31:1131 Ag '65

Letter from Paris; concert with Conservatoire orchestra. Genêt. New Yorker 40:114 F 6 '65
Michelangeli and the machine. R. McMullen. il pors Hi Fi 16:46-9 Ja '66
Music to my ears; New York appearance. I. Kolodin. Sat R 49:48 Ja 22 '66
Reluctant master. il por Time 86:58 Jl 9 '65

MICHELANGELO Buonarroti
Agony and the ecstasy of Michelangelo. il Look 29:41-8 Mr 9 '65
Last giant. por Sr Schol 87:28 D 9 '65
Letter from London; exhibition of sculpture: Virgin and child. M. Panter-Downes. New Yorker 41:125-6 My 22 '65
Pietà safe. Am Artist 30:6 Ja '66
Trying to be a genius; concerning Agony and the ecstasy. D. Seiberling. il Life 59:75-6+ N 12 '65

MICHELANGELO (ship) See Ocean liners

MICHELIN and company, France. See Tire industry and trade

MICHELIN guide. See Guidebooks

MICHELSON, Albert Abraham
Michelson honored by naval academy. Sci N L 87:313 My 15 '65

MICHELSON, Arnold. See Raup, D. M. jt. auth.

MICHENER, James A.
Hermitage: Russia's fabulous art palace. Read Digest 86:133-41 Mr '65
Miracles of Santiago. Read Digest 87:228-34 Jl '65
On the fringe; ed. by H. Frankel. Sat R 48:62 Jl 24 '65
One near-square who doesn't knock the rock. por N Y Times Mag p56-7+ O 31 '65
Writer's public image; letter. por Esquire 64:150+ D '65

MICHIEL, Master. See Sittow, M.

MICHIGAN
See also
Camping—Michigan
Education—Michigan
Fishing—Michigan
Hunting—Michigan
Paleontology—Michigan

Description and travel
Michigan's Upper Peninsula. G. Caesar. Holiday 37:68-9+ Je '65

Parks and reserves
Campurbia; crowded tent and trailer cities. H. M. Gregerson. il Am For 71:18-20 Jl '65

Politics and government
Three up; victory over Democrat-dominated legislature. Time 86:12 D 24 '65

Religious institutions and affairs
News of the Christian world (cont) Christian Cent 82:506-8, 1074, 1586-7 Ap 21, S 1, D 22 '65

Social conditions
Royal Oak aids its problem youth. J. A. Morris. il Read Digest 87:163-7 O '65

MICHIGAN state university of agriculture and applied science, East Lansing
Lesson of Jackie Brant; Student education corps. il Newsweek 65:62 F 22 '65
Rim of hell; How the United States got involved. Nation 201:110 S 6 '65

Libraries
Sound of history; story of the National voice library. G. R. Vincent. il Library J 90:4282-90 O 15 '65

MICHIGAN technological university, Houghton
GM in their future; MTU draws engineering head-hunters. il Newsweek 67:80 Ja 24 '66

MICHIGAN. University, Ann Arbor
Diamond in the college press; University of Michigan's Daily celebrates its seventy-fifth anniversary. R. L. Tobin. Sat R 48:115-16 S 18 '65

MICHOACÁN, Mexico
Going places, finding things in Michoacán, Mexico. E. Sheridan. il House & Gard 128:60+ S '65

MICKELSON, Merlyn Francis
Memory man. il por Time 86:90 D 3 '65

MICOCCI, Antonio A.
New life for Cuban exiles. por Am Ed 1:29-32 Mr '65

MICROALGAE. See Algae

MICROARTHROPODS. See Arthropods

MICROBES. See Microorganisms

MICROBIOLOGY, Soil. See Soil microbiology

MICROCENTRIFUGES. See Centrifuges

MICROCIRCUITS. See Electronic circuits

MICROELECTRONICS. See Miniature electronic equipment

MICROELECTROPHORESIS. See Electrophoresis

MICROFILMS
Microfilm and electronics. D. M. Costigan. il Electr World 74:37-9 Ag '65
Microfilm your manuals. B. G. Wels. il Pop Electr 23:80 D '65
USOE contract to put school programs on microfiche. Pub W 189:42 Ja 3 '66
See also
Libraries—Microfilm collections
Municipal records on microfilm
Newspapers on microfilm
University microfilms, Ann Arbor, Mich.

MICROMETEOROLOGY
Micrometeorology; report on first national conference on micrometeorology. S. Barr and E. V. Jankus. Science 148:108+ Ap 2 '65

MICROMINIATURIZATION. See Miniature electronic equipment

MICRO-Nikkor lens. See Lenses, Photographic

MICROORGANISMS
All about bugs. I. Asimov. il Sci Digest 58:84-5 N '65
Marine microorganisms; report on conference held in Berkeley, Calif. M. B. Allen. Science 147:638-9 F 5 '65
See also
Bacteria
Soil microbiology
Staphylococci

MICROORGANISMS, Pathogenic
Elusive PPLO. il Time 86:62 O 1 '65
Hemolysin of mycoplasma pneumoniae: tentative identification as a peroxide. N. L. Somerson and others. bibliog il Science 150:226-8 O 8 '65
Lability of host-cell DNA in growing cell cultures due to mycoplasma. C. C. Randall and others. bibliog il Science 149:1098-9 S 3 '65
Lysis of pleuropneumonia-like organisms by staphylococcal and streptococcal toxins. A. W. Bernheimer and M. Davidson. bibliog il Science 148:1229-31 My 28 '65
Nucleoside incorporation into strain L cells: inhibition by pleuropneumonia-like organisms. R. M. Nardone and others. bibliog il Science 149:1100-1 S 3 '65
What you don't see can hurt you! R. Martin. il Today's Health 43:42-7 N '65

MICROPALEONTOLOGY
Electron microscopy of fossil bacteria two billion years old. J. W. Schopf and others. bibliog il Science 149:1365-7 S 17 '65
Fossil bacteria in pyrite. E. G. Ehlers and others. il Science 148:1719-21 Je 25 '65
Microorganisms from the late Precambrian of central Australia. E. S. Barghoorn and J. W. Schopf. bibliog il Science 150:337-9 O 15 '65

MICROPHONES
FM wireless microphone. D. Meyer. il Pop Electr 22:35-8 My '65
Microphone as a lens. T. Schwartz. il Pop Phot 57:32+ S '65

MICROPHOTOGRAPHY
Art in science; chemical reactions. P. Caulfield. il Mod Phot 29:56-7 O '65
Microelectrophoresis with alternating electric fields. L. D. Sher and H. P. Schwan. bibliog il Science 148:229-31 Ap 9 '65
Putting a library in a shoe box; photochromic micro-images. il Pop Sci 186:77 Mr '65

MICROSACCADES. See Eye—Movements

MICROSCOPE and microscopy
Finding rare beauty in common rocks. L. G. Collins. il Nat Geog Mag 129:120-9 Ja '66
Industrial and biological microscopy: new paths; report on biennial symposium. M. Jones. Science 148:986+ My 14 '65
Nature and the microscope (cont) J. D. Corrington. Natur Hist 74:61-6 Ap '65
See also
Field ion microscope

MICROSEISMS
Microseisms from hurricane Hilda. J. C. De Bremaecker. bibliog il Science 148:1725-7 Je 25 '65

MICROWAVE amplification by stimulated emission of radiation. See Masers

MICROWAVE electronics corporation
MEC turning out TWT's with increased power. Miss & Roc 17:42+ O 18 '65

MICROWAVE ovens. See Electronic ovens

MICROWAVES
Crystal diode gains as microwave source. P. J. Klass. il Aviation W 83:68+ N 8 '65

Microwave radiation laboratory to cost $5.9 million by FY '68; ERC's Electromagnetic research division. Miss & Roc 16:68 My 31 '65
Radar, ECM gains seen with Sperry delay line. M. Getler. Miss & Roc 16:34-6 Ap 26 '65
Waves hit high frequency. Sci N L 89:38 Ja 15 '66

MIDAS (satellite) See Artificial satellites—Military applications

MID-ATLANTIC ridge. See Ocean bottom

MIDDLE aged workers. See Age and employment

MIDDLE ages
See also
Art, Medieval
Renaissance

History
Bibliography
Articles and other books received; comp. by B. J. Holm. See issues of American historical review

MIDDLE classes
Teen-age aristocracy. F. Musgrove. il Nation 200:439-42 Ap 26 '65

MIDDLE EAST
Middle East, 1965; symposium. il Cur Hist 48:257-301+ My '65
Nature of modernization; the Middle East and north Africa. W. R. Polk. For Affairs 44:100-10 O '65
See also
Great Rift Valley
Music—Middle East
Saudi Arabia

Antiquities
Deities and dolphins: the story of the Nabataeans, by N. Glueck. Review
  Sat R il 48:21-2 S 4 '65. F. G. Bratton

Defenses
Raiding the coop; L. Eshkol denounces Arab leaders for arms purchases. il Newsweek 67:42+ Ja 24 '66

Description and travel
Finds and surprises in the Middle East; impressions of Vogue cast. D. Messinesi. il Vogue 146:152-3+ D '65
Journey into the Great Rift. H. Schreider and F. Schreider. il Nat Geog Mag 128:254-90 Ag '65
Match me such marvel! rhapsody on Middle Eastern themes. L. Blanch. il Vogue 146:180-201+ D '65
Traveling with Mlle: North Africa and the Middle East. D. Beal. il Mlle 61:205-6 S '65

History
Bibliography
Articles and other books received; comp. by S. Glazer. See issues of American historical review

Maps
Map of the Middle East (cont). Sr Schol 87:32 S 30 '65

Politics
Atlantic report: dividing the waters. Atlan 216:24+ Ag '65
Middle East; address, April 21, 1965. P. H. Nitze. Vital Speeches 31:504-9 Je 1 '65
One more notch. Newsweek 65:46 Ap 19 '65
Shifting scales. Newsweek 65:57 Mr 15 '65
Swing from the left. Time 86:52+ N 19 '65
See also
Arab states—Politics
Jewish-Arab relations

MIDDLE EASTERN cookery. See Cookery, Middle Eastern

MIDDLE schools. See Education—United States

MIDDLE WEST
Reapers of the dust, a prairie chronicle, by L. P. Hudson. Review
  Nation 200:226-8 Mr 1 '65. C. Harnack
See also
Canals—Middle western states
Colleges and universities—Middle western states
Great Lakes

Economic conditions
Research and development pork barrel. P. H. Abelson. Science 149:11 Jl 2 '65
Why Midwest is happy again. il U S News 59:78 Jl 5 '65

Industries
Steel turns to the Midwest, back of big expansion. il U S News 59:101-3 Jl 19 '65

MIDDLE WEST—*Continued*

Tornadoes

See Tornadoes

MIDDLEBURY, Vt.

Historic houses, etc.

Beauty of imperfection; Seymour House.
M. D. Smith. il Am For 71:32-5+ Ag '65

MIDDLEBURY college, Middlebury, Vt.
Babeling in Vermont; Middlebury's foreign
language schools. il Newsweek 66:58 Ag 16
'65

MIDDLEBURY'S foreign language schools. See
Middlebury college, Middlebury, Vt.

MIDDLETON, Drew
U.N. tries hard, but—. N Y Times Mag p28-
9+ Ja 9 '66

MIDDLETON, John T.
Man and his habitat: problems of pollution.
Bul Atomic Sci 21:18-22 Mr '65

MIDGET airplane racing. See Airplane racing

MIDGET horses. See Ponies

MIDGETS. See Dwarfs

MID-INDIAN OCEAN ridge. See Ocean bottom

MIDLAND, Mich.
Small town, big company. L. L. L. Golden.
Sat R 48:57 Jl 10 '65

MIDORIKAWA, Yoichi
Inland sea. il U S Camera 28:54-5 Je '65

MIDSUMMER night's dream; drama. See
Shakespeare, W.—Plays

MIDSUMMER night's dream; opera. See
Britten, B.

MIDWEST inter-library center. See Center
for research libraries, Chicago

MIDWEST research institute
Kansas City: new medical complex, university should complement Midwest research
institute. J. Walsh. Science 148:1202-4 My
28 '65

MIDWEST stock exchange, Chicago. See Stock
exchange—Chicago

MIGRANT labor
Asparagus aspersions; dispute over employment of domestic or foreign workers. Newsweek 65:34 Ap 5 '65
Bracero blunder. R. Moley. Newsweek 66:88
Jl 19 '65
Bring back the braceros; shortage of do-
mestic farm workers in California. News-
week 65:78 Mr 8 '65
How a government policy conflicts; problems
from keeping braceros. il Nations Bsns 53:
33+ My '65
How foreign workers bolster German boom.
il Bsns W p44-6 My 1 '65
I picked apples with the unemployed; with
editorial comment. G. Logsdon. il Farm J
89:36-7+, 118 N '65
Machines take over bracero job. il Bsns W
p 108-10 Ja 8 '66
Old myth fades; bracero program's end in
California. Nation 201:31 Jl 19 '65
Our brother the migrant. J. L. Corker. Christian Cent 82:1192-3 S 29 '65
Report from the National farm labor conference. P. Groom. Mo Labor R 88:275-8 Mr
'65
Slaves for rent: the shame of American farming; excerpt from Slaves we rent. T. Moore.
il Atlan 215:109-22 My '65; Discussion. 216:
28 Jl; 34-6 Ag '65
Stoop labor; California farm workers. Com-
monweal 81:596-7 F 5 '65
Stoop labor furor; bracero system. il Sr
Schol 86:18-19 My 6 '65
When U.S. barred foreign workers from
farms; bracero ban. il U S News 58:73-5
My 31 '65
Who'll pick the strawberries? problem of
braceros, minimum wage, and immigration
laws. Time 85:19 Je 4 '65
Will growers get Mexican labor? bracero
program. U S News 58:93-4 Ap 5 '65
See also
Church work with migrants

MIGRANT laborers, Children of. See Children
of migrant laborers

MIGRATION, Internal
Americans discover the West again; Moun-
tain West. il U S News 58:80-2 Je 21 '65
How U.S. is changing: people on the move.
il U S News 59:74-8 N 15 '65
Ultimate weapon in war on poverty. il Na-
tions Bsns 53:86-8+ F '65
See also
Negroes in the United States—Migration

MIGRATION of animals. See Animals—Migration

MIGRATION of birds. See Birds—Migration

MIGRATION of fishes. See Fishes—Migration

MIGRATION of Negroes. See Negroes in the
United States—Migration

MIGRATION of plants. See Plants—Migration

MIGRATORY workers. See Migrant labor

MIHAJLOV, Mihajlo
Capitalist exploitation; excerpt from Moscow
summer. Sat R 48:41 D 11 '65
Now it can be told, by the Russians. N Y
Times Mag p25+ Mr 14 '65
Revolution coming in Russia? a Yugoslav
says this; summary of report. por U S
News 59:72-3 Jl 19 '65

about

Intellectual travelogue. P. Viereck. Sat R
48:41-2 D 11 '65
Quiet, please. Time 85:40+ My 7 '65
Thin red line. Newsweek 65:56 My 10 '65
Ungentle ways of Marshal Tito. T. Molnar.
Nat R 17:595+ Jl 13 '65

MIKHAIL, grand duke of Russia
Gibson girl romance. A. W. Hinckley. il
Am Heritage 17:106-11 D '65

MIKODA, Philip M.
Mikoda, peacocks, astronauts, and Vikings.
J. Deschin. il pors Pop Phot 56:26+ Mr '65

MIKOIAN, Anastas Ivanovich
Who's on third? por Newsweek 66:38-9 D 20
'65

MIKSCH, W. F.
No-sweat garden guide for spring. Atlan
215:126+ My '65
Shunpiking on the moon. Atlan 215:176-7 Mr
'65

MILAN, Italy

Music

Boxing match at La Scala. W. Weaver. il Hi
Fi 15:86U Mr '65
Ghiaurov's Moses, Karajan's Bohème. W.
Legge. Hi Fi 15:160-1 S '65
Three at La Scala; Rossini, Bellini, and
Donizetti. W. Legge. Hi Fi 15:132-3 My '65

MILAN, Ohio, historical museum
Milan, Ohio, museum has large doll family.
il Hobbies 70:43 My '65

MILANO, Aldo da
Faith and a friar. Newsweek 65:40+ Je 28 '65

MILANOV, Zinka
From the heart. J. Ardoin. por Opera N 29:
14-15 My 1 '65

MILASHKINA, Tamara
Music to my ears; production of Tchaikovsky's Pique dame, by Concert opera association. I. Kolodin. Sat R 48:30 Mr 6 '65

MILEAGE indicators. See Odometers

MIL-E-CON. See Military electronics conference

MILES, Bebe
Small gems for your rock garden. Pop Gard
16:22-3+ N '65
Three months of tulips. il Flower Grower
52:30+ O '65

MILES, Betty
What youngsters learn from foreign lands.
Parents Mag 40:52-3+ Ap '65

MILES, Charles
Indian relics. See issues of Hobbies

MILES, Dick
Spongers seldom chisel. Sports Illus 23:102-4+
N 15 '65

MILES, Josephine
First; poem. Atlan 215:121 Ap '65
Height; poem. Nation 201:420 N 29 '65

MILES, Raymond E.
Human relations or human resources? Harvard Bsns R 43:148-9 Jl '65

MILES, Sarah
I'll never go to Hollywood; ed. by E. Miller.
pors Seventeen 24:144-5+ My '65

MILES laboratories, incorporated
For that great feeling. il Time 85:92+ Ap
23 '65

MILGRAM, Morris
Builder who makes integration pay. A. Balk.
Harper 231:94-9 Jl '65

MILHAM, Samuel, jr
Leukemia in husbands and wives. bibliog
Science 148:98-100 Ap 2 '65

MILHAUD, Darius
Pope John set to music. J. Davis. Am Rec G
32:60 S '65

MILITARISM
Changing concepts of the role of the military
in Latin America; with questions and an-
swers. L. N. McAlister. bibliog f Ann Am
Acad 360:85-98 Jl '65
Whatever happened to the State department?
C. W. Tait. il Nation 201:137-41 S 13 '65

MILITARY administration
Changing concepts of the role of the military in Latin America; with questions and answers. L. N. McAlister. bibliog f Ann Am Acad 360:85-98 Jl '65
Soldiers and the nation-state. D. B. Bobrow. bibliog f il Ann Am Acad 358:65-76 Mr '65
MILITARY airlift command. See United States —Military airlift command
MILITARY airplanes. See Airplanes, Military
MILITARY art and science
Air mobility boosts army effectiveness. il Aviation W 82:70-1+ Je 7 '65
Escalation as a strategy; excerpts from On escalation: metaphors and scenarios, with editorial comment. H. Kahn. Fortune 71: 105, 110-12+ Ap '65
On escalation, by H. Kahn. Review
Commentary 40:101-2+ N '65. G. Kateb
On escalation: metaphors and scenarios, by H. Kahn. Review
Nat R il 17:601-3 Jl 13 '65. S. T. Possony
See also
Chemical warfare
Guerrilla warfare
Military research
Strategy
MILITARY assistance
Senseless war on the subcontinent; Nations war under the spell of Kashmir. il Newsweek 66:33-7 S 20 '65
MILITARY assistance, American
Alliance for reaction; Latin American program. E. Flores. Nation 200:659-62 Je 21 '65
Argentina's friend. Nation 201:234 O 18 '65
Arms diplomacy. Nation 201:149-50 S 27 '65
Arms embargo could blunt war in air. C. Brownlow. Aviation W 83:26-7 S 13 '65
As world leaders come to LBJ: what they ask, what they offer. il U S News 59:22-3 D 27 '65
Break it up! Nation 200:153-4 F 15 '65
Foreign aid; message to the Congress, January 14, 1965. L. B. Johnson. Dept State Bul 52:126-32 F 1 '65
Foreign aid program for 1966; statement, February 4, 1965. D. E. Bell. Dept State Bul 52:343-8 Mr 8 '65
Foreign assistance act of 1965 signed by President; statement, September 6, 1965. L. B. Johnson. Dept State Bul 53:525 S 27 '65
Ft. Riley shipping them out; for the war in Vietnam. il Newsweek 65:20-1 Je 28 '65
Give them the tools. W. J. Coughlin. Miss & Roc 16:46 My 24 '65
Great debate over American military interventions. W. V. O'Brien. Cath World 201: 316-21 Ag '65
History unleashed; policy in southeast Asia. K. Crawford. Newsweek 66:27 Ag 30 '65
Open up! Nation 200:377-8 Ap 12 '65
Thai countermeasures to Communist threat; excerpt from address, March 14, 1965. M. Green. Dept State Bul 52:489-91 Ap 5 '65
United States aid in Asia; symposium. bibliog f il Cur Hist 49:257-99+ N '65
U.S. intervention in Latin America, 1900-1965. il Sr Schol 87:8-9+ S 16 '65
U.S. to sell or lend eleven warships to friendly foreign countries. Dept State Bul 53:871-2 N 29 '65
Vietnam war pace strains C-141 program. Aviation W 83:30-1 S 13 '65
War's widening ripples; U.S. commitment in Vietnam. il Newsweek 66:51-3 Ag 2 '65
Where U.S. is pledged to defend more than forty other nations around the world. il U S News 58:36-7 My 10 '65
Who needs enemies? Commonweal 82:371-2 Je 11 '65
MILITARY assistance, British
Arms embargo could blunt war in air. C. Brownlow. Aviation W 83:26-7 S 13 '65
MILITARY assistance, Communist
Red arsenals arm the Simbas; with eyewitness reports from Life correspondents. il Life 58:26-33 F 12 '65
MILITARY assistance, Russian
Dogfighting with MiGs; interview. E. A. Greathouse; C. B. Johnson. Aviation W 83:11 Jl 26 '65
Stronger hand for Russia in Vietnam? il U S News 60:11 Ja 17 '66
MILITARY attaches. See United States—Foreign service
MILITARY aviators. See Air pilots
MILITARY bases
Bad news, good news; cutback of bases. il Newsweek 66:25 D 20 '65
Bigger war. Nation 201:233 O 18 '65
U.S. and Philippines amend military bases agreement. Dept State Bul 53:358 Ag 30 '65

MILITARY bases, British
New beginning? Britain gaining atoll of Diego Garcia. il Time 86:45-6 N 19 '65
MILITARY budget. See United States—Armed forces—Appropriations and expenditures
MILITARY capitulations. See Capitulations, Military
MILITARY chaplains. See Chaplains, Military
MILITARY-civilian relations. See United States —Armed forces—Relations with civilians
MILITARY construction. See Building
MILITARY contracts. See Contracts, Government
MILITARY cooperation (United States) See Military assistance, American
MILITARY discharge. See Discharge, Military
MILITARY education
See also
United States military acedemy, West Point
MILITARY electronics conference
MIL-E-CON told space program spurring general electronics R&D. Miss & Roc 17: 20 S 27 '65
MILITARY engineering
See also
Electronics—Military applications
MILITARY evacuation. See Evacuation, Military
MILITARY expenditures. See United States— Armed forces—Appropriations and expenditures
MILITARY installations. See Military bases
MILITARY intelligence
According to informed sources; unanswered questions about Vietnam. New Repub 152: 6-7 F 20 '65
MILITARY inventions. See Inventions
MILITARY law
Alive again; precedent setting decision concerning dishonorable discharge. il Time 87: 74 Ja 7 '66
Servicemen's Gideon? right to counsel means trained lawyer. Time 86:49 O 29 '65
See also
Capitulations, Military
Courts martial
MILITARY maneuvers
Arctic maneuvers; the gimmicks of war. R. J. Reguly. il Nation 200:333-6 Mr 29 '65
How NATO works when politics is left out: U.S. troops with Turks and Greeks. il U S News 59:8 O 4 '65
War games with a political angle; plans to involve the armed forces of Greece and Turkey in separate-but-joint maneuvers. il U S News 59:8 S 27 '65
MILITARY miniatures
Toys to train army tankmen for battle; Armor school, Fort Knox, Ky. A. Whitman. il Pop Mech 124:142-6 O '65
MILITARY mobilization. See United States— Armed forces—Mobilization
MILITARY models. See Military miniatures
MILITARY parades. See Parades
MILITARY pensions. See Pensions, Military
MILITARY purchasing. See United States— Armed forces—Procurement
MILITARY reconnaissance
See also
Aerial reconnaissance
Artificial satellites—Military applications
MILITARY research
DOD to overhaul internal R&D policies; laboratory improvement program. K. Johnsen. Aviation W 83:28-9 S 27 '65
Military objectives spur work. il Miss & Roc 16:83-4+ Mr 29 '65
Project hindsight to isolate gains of DOD's fundamental research. K. Johnsen. Aviation W 83:47-8+ O 18 '65
Recent arms control research in Europe. J. B. Teeple. Bul Atomic Sci 21:37-9 O '65
See also
Hudson institute, incorporated
MILITARY schools
More boot camp than campus; Marine military academy, Harlingen, Tex. il Life 59: 51-2+ O 22 '65
MILITARY sea transportation service. See United States—Military sea transportation service
MILITARY secrets. See Defense information. Classified
MILITARY service, Compulsory
Modest proposal; draft at sixty-five. F. L. Redefer. New Repub 154:37+ Ja 8 '66

Deferments and exemptions
V for Vietnam; students and deferments. il Newsweek 66:59+ D 27 '65

MILITARY service, Compulsory—*Continued*

United States

ABC's of draft dodging. il Newsweek 66:32 N 1 '65

As draft calls rise: changes to expect. il U S News 59:35 Ag 9 '65

As draft calls rise: who'll be taken now. il U S News 58:33-4+ D 13 '65

As draft calls rise; your chances. and choices. il U S News 60:40-1 Ja 24 '66

As high school students see it! how fair is the draft? Institute of student opinion. il Sr Schol 87:16 D 2 '65

Available for service; some students reclassified 1-A since participating in Vietnam protest. New Repub 153:9 D 11 '65

Burning advice; concerning S. Casady's statement on burning of draft cards. Time 86:33 O 1 '65

December draft call; eligibility standards. New Repub 153:8 N 13 '65

Demonstrators: why? how many? anti-Vietnam movement. il Newsweek 66:25-6+ N 1 '65

Dodging the draft: how big a problem? excerpts from televised report. U S News 59:6 O 25 '6F

Doubling the draft: when they tag you 1-A; with report by J. Frook. il Life 59:22-7 Ag 20 '65

Draft board tyrants; draft boards in Michigan reclassified as I-A student demonstrators. Christian Cent 82:1565 D 22 '65

Draft boards escalate; experience of Asbury Park draft board. F. J. Cook. il N Y Times Mag p54-5+ S 12 '65

Draft director tells what's ahead; interview; with letter to E. Celler. and the reply. L. B. Hershey. il U S News 60:38-44 Ja 10 '66

Draft is unfair. J. Raymond. il N Y Times Mag p5+ Ja 2 '66

Draft prospect as war speeds up; Department of defense answers questions. il U S News 59:40-1 Jl 19 '65

Draft resisters 1965. C. Brossard. il Look 29 13-17 D 28 '65

Draft riots on college campuses? Sch & Soc 93:420+ N 13 '65

Draft scandal; reclassifying of student peace demonstrators. New Repub 153:7 D 25 '65

Draft should be on a fair footing. Life 59:6 O 15 '65; Same abr. with title Let's put the draft on a fair footing. Read Digest 88:171-2 Ja '66

Draft sit-ins: a clash of views. U S News 60:10 Ja 24 '66

Draft steps up, what it means. il U S News 58:39 Ap 12 '65

Drafting dissenters. New Repub 153:8 N 6 '65

Ending the draft. Commonweal 82:680 S 24 '65

Facing draft soon; thousands of married men, college students. U S News 59:11 N 8 '65

G.I. and the draft. il Sr Schol 87:6-8 O 28 '65

Great draft-card hubbub. Nation 201:373-4 N 22 '65

Hershey and the draft: still going strong after twenty-five years; Selective service. U S News 59:21 Ag 16 '65

How to end the draft. R. Wilhelm. il Nation 201:350-2 N 15 '65; Reply. F. Lundberg. 201:inside cover N 29 '65

Keeping the draft. New Repub 152:7 My 29 '65

Limited objectors. J. M. Swomley, jr. Christian Cent 82:1541-2 D 15 '65

Marriage and the draft. New Repub 153:9 S 11 '65

Out of the kitchen into the soup; draft-card burning. il Time 86:35 N 5 '65

Outlook now for draft, reserves, armed force build-up; interview. N. S. Paul. il U S News 59:36-40 Ag 16 '65

Personal business; military manpower situation. Bsns W p 113-14 D 18 '65

Personal business; Uncle Sam may want you. Bsns W p97 Ag 7 '65

Protests on principle and some practical options. il Life 59:30-1 Ag 20 '65

Punishment by conscription; General Hershey's big stick. C. Cohen. il Nation 201:520-2 D 27 '65; Reply with rejoinder by editors. L. Hershey. 202:inside cover. 28 Ja 3 '66

Rash of student riots aimed at the draft? excerpts from statements. R. Wilhelm. U S News 59:18 S 20 '65

Riots, songs and fishbowls, the hullabaloo is old hat to Hershey; America's Mr Draft. S. McBee. il Life 59:28-9 Ag 20 '65

Spanking the spanker: General Hershey admonition from Department of justice. Newsweek 67:26 Ja 24 '66

Storm at home: anti-draft and anti-Viet demonstrations; with press comments. il Sr Schol 87:18-20 N 4 '65

T.R.B. from Washington: unjust draft. New Repub 152:4 Ap 10 '65

Today's draft dodgers: how big a problem; with excerpts from interview with N. deB. Katzenbach. U S News 59:40-1 N 1 '65

Vietnam: growing war and campus protests threaten student deferments. E. Langer. Science 150:1567-70 D 17 '65

When a nation held its breath for a draft. il Sr Schol 87:5 S 16 '65

Why the protests? demonstrations. New Repub 153:6-7 O 30 '65

Your son's draft chances now. il U S News 58: 39 Je 21 '65

See also
Conscientious objectors

Vietnam (Republic)

Asiatic teach-ins: opposition to draft law. Time 86:29 S 3 '65

MILITARY slang. See Slang

MILITARY strategy. See Strategy

MILITARY supplies

See also
United States—Army—Equipment and supplies
Vietnamese war, 1957- —Equipment and supplies

MILITARY surgery. See Surgery, Military

MILITARY tanks. See Tanks, Military

MILITARY toys. See Toys

MILITARY training

Here I am, back at Alcatraz East; return to marine boot camp, Parris Island, S.C. A. Buchwald. il Life 59:70-4+ Ag 13 '65

I survived a jungle survival test, could you? R. Gannon. il Pop Sci 187:62-5+ Ag '65

Renaissance in the ranks. il Time 86:30-4 D 10 '65

Toys to train army tankmen for battle; Armor school, Fort Knox, Ky. A. Whitman. il Pop Mech 124:142-6 O '65

MILITARY training camps

Then the old sarge says, you're all mine now; report from Fort Knox, Ky. induction center. J. Frook. il Life 59:26-7 Ag 20 '65

Training for the front-all-around-you war; training for guerrilla warfare. W. B. Furlong. il N Y Times Mag p 184+ O 24 '65

MILITARY transport airplanes. See Airplanes. Military transport

MILITARY transportation. See Transportation, Military

MILITARY trials. See Courts martial

MILK

Fresh milk faces a new struggle. Farm J 89: 58 Mr '65

See also
Dairy inspection
Dairying

Fat content

Soda, magnesium oxide boost fat test Farm J 89:32 Ag '65

Marketing

Tale of two markets; one with quotas, one with federal order. G. Lorang. il Farm J 89:28-9+ S '65

Prices

He full-feeds grain, with $3.50 milk! D. Hagen. il Farm J 89:34-5+ N '65

Tale of two markets; one with quotas, one with a federal order. G. Lorang. il Farm J 89:28-9+ S '65

Production

Beef calves wear diapers; experiment to learn about beef cow milk production. Suc Farm 63:40 My '65

Ten-ton cows, without pampering. N. Reeder. il Farm J 89:A4-6 Jl '65

MILK containers

Tempest in a milk carton; plastic container. L. Rich. il Duns R 86:pt2 101-6+ D '65

MILK contamination

Meteorological evaluation of the sources of iodine-131 in pasteurized milk. R. J. List and others; reply E. A. Martell. bibliog Science 148:1756-7 Je 25 '65

Radioactive milk cleansed, peril eased. Sci N L 87:168 Mr 13 '65

MILK delivery. See Milk industry and trade

MILK drinks. See Beverages

MILK industry and trade
See also
Milk—Marketing

Employees
See also
Milk industry and trade—Wages and hours

Wages and hours
Earnings in the fluid milk industry in 1964.
F. L. Bauer. il Mo Labor R 88:1096-9 S '65
MILK inspection. See Dairy inspection
MILK is good for skinny kids; story. See
Stein, G.
MILK production. See Milk—Production
MILK wagon drivers. See Milk industry and
trade

MILKING
Make sure your cows are completely milked
out. Suc Farm 63:38G My '65
MILKING parlors
Half a herringbone. J. D. Boyd. il Farm J
89:D11 Ap '65

Equipment
Cow spreaders speed milking. F. L. Elam and
R. J. Wyndham. il Farm J 89:48L Je '65
MILKY way
Explorer of the Milky way. D. A. MacRae. il
Sky & Tel 30:7-8 Jl '65
Heart of the Milky way. G. S. Mumford.
Sky & Tel 29:282 My '65
MILLARD, Hugh T. Jr
Thermal neutron activation: measurement of
cross section for manganese-53. bibliog Sci-
ence 147:503-4 Ja 29 '65
MILLER, Alden H.
Remaining California condors menaced by
dams. il Nat Parks Mag 39:22 Mr '65
MILLER, Arjay R.
Easy problems have been solved; excerpts
from testimony, July 1965. por U S News
59:101-2 Ag 9 '65
Industry leader looks at the auto boom and
its future; interview. por U S News 58:78-
9 Ap 5 '65
MILLER, Arthur
PEN pals. J. Blocker. il por Newsweek 66:92
Jl 26 '65
Revival of a salesman. W. Sheed. Common-
weal 81:670 F 19 '65
View from the bridge. Criticism
Commonweal 81:670 F 19 '65
New Yorker 40:94 F 6 '65
Newsweek il 65:93 Mr 15 '65
Vogue 145:56 Ap 15 '65
MILLER, Arthur Selwyn
Engineering of change in the U.S. Constitu-
tion; excerpt from Technology, social
change, and the Constitution. Sat R 48:52-5
F 6 '65
Fluoridation vs. the Constitution. Sat R 48:49-
53 Ap 3 '65
MILLER, Charles
Africa: a clash of empires. Sat R 48:27-8
S 4 '65
Ethiopia: end of a dark age. Sat R 48:38-9
Ap 10 '65
Freedom that comes with liberty. Sat R
48:28-9 F 20 '65
Horror in the Congo. Sat R 48:37-8 D 11 '65
Independence through calculus. Sat R 48:27
Mr 6 '65
Judo: mayhem with a gentle touch. Read
Digest 87:137-41 S '65
MILLER, Dale
Dale Miller: the President's favorite lobbyist.
D. S. Broder. il por Look 29:66-8 Ap 6 '65
MILLER, David
Crime of David Miller. J. O'Gara. Common-
weal 83:174 N 12 '65
Out of the kitchen into the soup. por Time
86:35 N 5 '65
MILLER, David L.
Downward to wisdom. Christian Cent 82:
656-9 My 19 '65
False prophets in the Secular city. Chris-
tian Cent 82:1417-18 N 17 '65
MILLER, Edwin
At the movies. See issues of Seventeen
Hollywood scene. See issues of Seventeen
Spotlight! See issues of Seventeen, April
1965-
Teens are listening to... See issues of
Seventeen
MILLER, Frank J.
Salt water in the sewers. Am City 80:112+
D '65
MILLER, Fred Springer-. See Springer-Miller,
F.
MILLER, George, Jr
Dirksen amendment. New Repub 153:30 Jl 3
'65

MILLER, Gifford W.
Realistic development plan. Am City 80:100-1
My '65
MILLER, Greta
Happiest New Year of Greta Miller. J. Rob-
bins. Good H 160:34+ Ja '65
MILLER, Heather Ross
Youth is not an age. Vogue 145:84 Mr 1 '65
MILLER, Helen Hill
College presidents look at the students. New
Repub 153:9-10 O 23 '65
Health insurance bill, pluses and minuses.
New Repub 152:10-11 Ap 24 '65
MILLER, Helen Louise
Birds' Christmas carol; dramatization of
story by K. D. Wiggin. Plays 25:87-96 D
'65
Call Washington 1776; drama. Plays 24:3-16
F '65
Case of the forgetful Easter rabbit; drama.
Plays 24:63-9 Ap '65
Hello, Mr Groundhog; drama. Plays 24:65-74
F '65
Miss Frankenstein; drama. Plays 25:13-22 O
'65
Mother for mayor; drama. Plays 24:31-44 My
'65
One to grow on; drama. Plays 24:35-44 Ap
'65
Paper bag mystery; drama. Plays 25:47-55
N '65
Shirley Holmes and the FBI; drama. Plays
24:45-54 My '65
Valentine for Kate; drama. Plays 24:29-40 F
'65
MILLER, Henry
Grove publishes Sexus to counter rival edi-
tion. Pub W 187:37 My 3 '65
More Miller; publishing of Sexus. America
112:819 Je 5 '65
Transcendentalist in the basement. W.
Winters. por Sat R 48:39 Je 19 '65
We two, the world and the whale. W. Win-
ters. por Sat R 48:27-8 My 15 '65
MILLER, Herman P.
Millionaires are a dime a dozen. N Y Times
Mag p50-1+ N 28 '65
Who are the poor? Nation 200:609-10 Je 7 '65
MILLER, J. Jefferson, 2d
Larsen and McCauley collections at the
Smithsonian institution. Antiques 85:522-5
O '65
MILLER, Jack
Coming to Washington? por Suc Farm 63:
111+ Ap '65
Excerpt from debate, September 2, 1964.
Cong Digest 44:87+ Mr '65
MILLER, James Nathan
Agriculture's fantastic new machines. Read
Digest 86:117-21 F '65
Art of intelligent listening. Read Digest 87:
83-6 S '65
Blooming big business! Read Digest 86:17-
18+ Mr '65
How to watchdog a town budget. Read Di-
gest 86:125-9 Mr '65
It's a dead-end road for the dropout. Read
Digest 86:125-30 My '65
Our horse-and-buggy state legislatures. Read
Digest 86:49-54 My '65
Railroads are fighting back! Read Digest
87:153-6+ O '65
MILLER, Jason
Square in Savannah; poem. Nation 201:24 Jl 5
'65
MILLER, John B.
Selection of hunting bullets. Consumer Bul
48:16-18 O '65
MILLER, Karl
Opinion, please from London. Mlle 60:84+
Mr '65
MILLER, L. Keith
Activity in mammalian peripheral nerves dur-
ing supercooling. bibliog il Science 149:74-5
Jl 2 '65
MILLER, Loren
Protest against housing segregation. bibliog
f Ann Am Acad 357:73-9 Ja '65
MILLER, Lucille Marie
Double indemnity. Newsweek 65:33-4 Mr
15 '65
MILLER, Margaret
Management, distribution, planning: new
Russian revolution. Nation 201:437-9+ D 6
'65
MILLER, Margaretha Brohmer
Animal forms. il Sch Arts 64:15-17 My '65
MILLER, Marianne T.
Book review. America 113:760 D 11 '65
MILLER, Mary Lou
City; stained glass wall panel. il por Sch
Arts 65:14-15 O '65
MILLER, Mary Susan
Confessions on a teen-age son. McCalls 92:27
F '65

MILLER, Merle
Tragedy of Grace Metalious and Peyton Place.
Ladies Home J 82:58-9+ Je '65
MILLER, Michael Vincent
Journey to identity. Nation 201:254-5 O 18 '65
Letter from the Berkeley underground. Esquire 64:85-7+ S '65
Lovers; poem. Atlan 216:94 S '65
MILLER, Neal E.
Chemical coding of behavior in the brain.
bibliog Science 148:328-38 Ap 16 '65
MILLER, Philip L.
Anna Moffo: RCA Victor's Luisa Miller. Am
Rec G 32:118-19+ O '65
Archives of recorded sound. Hi Fi 15:38-41+
Je '65
Joan Sutherland as Norma. Am Rec G 31:604-5 Mr '65
La Forza del destino. Am Rec G 31:798-9+
My '65
Looking backward. Sat R 48:68 N 27 '65
(ed) Recorded music. See issues of Library
journal
Reissued by Angel: Gerhardt's Hugo Wolf,
perhaps the greatest of all collector's items.
Am Rec G 32:126-9 O '65
Very beginning. Am Rec G 31:1128-30+ Ag
'65
MILLER, R. C. and Rychlewski, T. V.
Rare-earth phosphors for color-TV tubes.
Electr World 74:48 D '65
MILLER, Ralph
Color slides. See issues of U.S. camera &
travel
Compatible couple. U S Camera 28:63-5+
Ap '65
MILLER, Richard I.
Looking ahead in teaching about communism; excerpt from Teaching about
communism. bibliog f Sch & Soc 93:502-5
D 25 '65
MILLER, Roger
King of the road. il pors Life 58:105-6 My 7
'65
Unhokey Okie. il por Time 85:55 Mr 19 '65
MILLER, Sharol, family
Come alive, America. C. Remsberg and B.
Remsberg. il pors Esquire 63:102-5+ F '65
MILLER, Shirley
Our young people (cont) Audubon Mag 67:
130 Mr '65
MILLER, Stewart E.
Communication by laser; with biographical
sketch. Sci Am 214:14, 19-27 bibliog(p 134)
Ja '66
MILLER, Vincent
Chunks of existence. Nat R 17:938-40 O 19
'65
Science in the grand tradition. Nat R 17:243-4 Mr 23 '65
Who are the Americans? Nat R 17:1035-7
N 16 '65
MILLER, Warren
Invitation to the voyage; story. Sat Eve
Post 238:54-6 Ap 24 '65
One score in Harlem. Sat R 48:49 Ag 28 '65
Secession to the moon. Nation 200:343-4 Mr
29 '65
MILLER, William Lee, and Appleby, L. T.
You shove out the poor to make houses for
the rich. N Y Times Mag p36+ Ap 11 '65
MILLER House. See New York (state)—Historic houses, etc.
MILLET, Jean François
The sower. il Am Artist 30:4+ Ja '66
MILLFIELD school, Somerset. See Public
schools (endowed)—England
MILLIONAIRES
America's new big rich; with editorial comment. S. Alsop. il Sat Eve Post 238:23-7+,
82 Jl 17; 16 Jl 31 '65
Brazil's rich feel the tax man's bite. il Bsns
W p60-2+ Mr '65
How they do it; six men under forty. il Time
86:88-92+ D 3 '65
How to become a millionaire. il Time 86:87-8+
Jl 9 '65
Millionaires are a dime a dozen. H. P. Miller.
il N Y Times Mag p50-1+ N 28 '65
Nigerian millionaires. il Time 86:122 S 17 '65
Now there are 90,000 millionaires in U.S. il
U S News 59:119-20 O 11 '65
Speaking out; the world is mean to millionaires. J. P. Getty. Sat Eve Post 238:10+
My 22 '65
MILLIONSHCHIKOV, Mikhail Dmitrievich
Science, a new social force. UNESCO Courier
18:24-6 O '65
Science must serve the cause of peace; address. UN Mo Chron 2:53-65 Ap '65
MILLIPEDS
Mystery of a millipede; hydrogen cyanide
produced by apheloria corrugata. T.
Eisner and H. E. Eisner. il Natur Hist 74:
30-7 Mr '65

MILLNER, Esther A.
Six sure-fire perennials. Flower Grower 52:
20-1 Mr '65
MILLS, Bert
Maybe it's deductible. Motor B 115:50+ Mr
'65
MILLS, Billy
What the men can do for an encore. G. S.
Brown. il Sports Illus 22:45-7 Mr 1 '65
MILLS, Ernest M.
Control of tree squirrels. Consumer Bul 48:
43+ S '65
MILLS, H. B.
Out of a storm; story. Redbook 124:62-3
Mr '65
MILLS, James
Detective. Life 59:90D-101+ D 3 '65
Drug addiction. Life 58:66B-82+ F 26; 92B-103+ Mr 5 '65; Same abr. with title We are
all animals. Read Digest 86:226-30+ Je '65
World of Needle park. Life 58:82+ F 26 '65

about

Junkie's life. Newsweek 65:63 Mr 8 '65
MILLS, John
People are talking about J. Mills; like Henry
the Eighth in mufti. por Vogue 145:150-1
Mr 1 '65
MILLS, Ralph J. Jr
Edith Sitwell: prophetess to an age. Christian Cent 82:652+ My 19 '65
MILLS, Steve
Comic. New Yorker 41:37-9 Ap 17 '65
MILLS, Tom
Repos & rentals. Motor T 17:39 Je '65
MILLS, Wilbur Daigh
Drive for simpler tax laws. por U S News
59:107-8 D 13 '65
Mr Mills's elder-medi-bettercare. H. B.
Meyers. il por Fortune 71:166-8 +Je '65
MILLSPAUGH, Frank
Should students go South? Commonweal 82:
406-9 Je 18 '65
MILLSTEIN, Gilbert
Number one melody man. Sat Eve Post 238:
95-9 Mr 13 '65
MILO
How to feed milo in the finishing ration. D.
Malena. Suc Farm 63:68 N '65
MILTON, John
All around the place. See issues of Popular
gardening & living outdoors
Wonderful wacky willow. Flower Grower 52:
17 S '65
MILTOWN. See Tranquilizing drugs
MILWAUKEE
Atlanta you can have the rest, leave us
Eddie Mattress, our hero. W. Leggett. il
Sports Illus 22:24-5+ Ap 26 '65

Architecture

Making precast concrete do more for less;
new IBM headquarters. J. Bailey. il Arch
Forum 123:52-5 N '65

Education

Education for industry. H. S. Vincent. il
Sat R 49:58+ Ja 8 '66
Freedom of conscience; civil rights boycott
of public schools. D. A. Runge. Christian
Cent 82:1525-6 D 8 '65
Milwaukee: a fair deal; Voluntary equal employment opportunity council activities. E.
L. Winter. il Sat R 49:54+ Ja 8 '66
Race crisis hits another northern city. il
U S News 59:75 N 1 '65
Twin billing at Nicolet high: Wibracht and
the F-wing libraries. J. O. Reiels. il Library J 90:5472-5 D 15 '65

Industries

Education for industry. H. S. Vincent. il
Sat R 49:58+ Ja 8 '66
Milwaukee: a fair deal; Voluntary equal employment opportunity council activities. E.
L. Winter. il Sat R 49:54+ Ja 8 '66

Labor and laboring classes

Found! summer jobs for teen-agers; Youthpower, inc. M. A. Robertson. Bet Hom &
Gard 43:31 My '65

Lighting

Guide for parking-lot lighting. L. C. Odry. Am
City 80:128 O '65

Negroes

Milwaukee: a fair deal; Voluntary equal employment opportunity council activities. E.
L. Winter. il Sat R 49:54+ Ja 8 '66

MILWAUKEE—*Continued*

Newspapers

Competition in Milwaukee; after merger of Sentinel and Journal. il Time 85:71-2 F 12 '65

Sanitary affairs

Soil fumigants control roots in sewers. G. Z. Rayner. il Am City 80:135-6 Je '65

Stations

Putting Milwaukee on a new track. il Bsns W p 182 Je 19 '65

Streets

Snow-fighting by careful design. W. J. Rheinfrank. il Am City 80:98-101 Ag '65

Theater

Theater that made Milwaukee famous; Milwaukee repertory theater. H. Hewes. Sat R 48:53 F 13 '65

MILWAUKEE Braves (baseball) See Baseball clubs

MILWAUKEE journal. See Milwaukee—Newspapers

MILWAUKEE repertory theater. See Milwaukee—Theater

MILWAUKEE sentinel. See Milwaukee—Newspapers

MIME

Polish mime theatre, New York city center. D. Hering. il Dance Mag 39:30-1 Mr '65

Who am I. M. Marceau. il Dance Mag 39:49-51 N '65

MIMICRY

George Kirby: mammoth of mimicry. il Ebony 20:57-60+ Je '65

MIMICRY (biology)

Aggressive mimicry in photuris: firefly femmes fatales. J. E. Lloyd. bibliog Science 149:653-4 Ag 6 '65

Asian insects in disguise. E. S. Ross. il Nat Geog Mag 128:432-9 S '65

Insect survival and selection for pattern. H. B. D. Kettlewell. bibliog il Science 148:1290-6 Je 4 '65

See also

Mind and body

Beyond Darwinism. A. Portmann; M. Grene. Commentary 40:31-41 N '65

Science and antiscience; address. December 27, 1964. W. R. Brain. bibliog Science 148:192-8 Ap 9 '65; Reply. D. J. Pletsch. 149:926 Ag 27 '65

See also

Medicine, Psychosomatic

Mental hygiene

Nervous system

MINDSZENTY, Jozsef, cardinal

Four men: four stories. America 112:449-50 Ap 3 '65

MINE, mill and smelter works union. See International union of mine, mill and smelter workers

MINER, Jak

Marine law enforcement. il Yachting 118:63-5+ Ag '65

MINER, Lisbeth

Community junior training. il Yachting 118:41-3+ Jl '65

MINER, Robert G.

Weathervane. See issues of Flower grower, the home garden magazine

MINER, Virginia Scott

On Mother's day; poem. Good H 160:148 My '65

MINERAL resources in submerged lands

Vast potential seen in sea minerals. R. Lindsey. il Miss & Roc 17:34-5+ Ag 9 '65

MINERALOGY

Interaction between light and minerals. P. E. Desautels. il Natur Hist 74:52-7 O '65

Quiz; how we use rocks and minerals. J. Daugherty and M. Daugherty. il Sci Digest 57:89-91 Ap '65

See also

Meteorites

MINERALS. See Mineralogy

MINERALS in sea water. See Sea water

MINERS

Ultimate weapon in war on poverty. il Nations Bsns 53:86-8+ F '65

MINERS and Eskimos; story. See Evans, J. M.

MINES, Robert

How your body can shape your personality. Sci Digest 57:79-83 Je '65

MINES and mineral resources

See also

Mica

Mineral resources in submerged lands

Mineralogy

Newmont mining corporation

Quarries and quarrying

Salt

Government ownership

President Frei and the copper goose. M. Adams. New Repub 153:10-12 D 18 '65

Australia

Australia stumbles onto new Golconda. il Bsns W p68-72 Ag 7 '65

Opal miners of Lightning Ridge; New South Wales. B. L. Burman. il Read Digest 86:171-6 Je '65

Bolivia

See also

Tin mines and mining—Bolivia

Brazil

Devil's digs; white crystal found near Cristalina. il Time 85:37 Ap 9 '65

Mexico

See also

Silver mines and mining—Mexico

Nevada

Just an old hole in the ground; azur-malachite mine. H. D. Brown. il Hobbies 70:113+ Je '65

Southwest Africa

See also

Diamond mines and mining

United States

See also

Oil shales

Washington (state)

Okanogan country. H. D. Brown. il Hobbies 70:116 N '65

Silver Ridge minerals. H. D. Brown. il Hobbies 70:116-17 O '65

MING, Chou

China's largest meteorite. Sky & Tel 30:347 D '65

MINGUS, Charlie

Mingus by mail. M. Williams. por Sat R 48:55 My 29 '65

MINH, Ho-chi-. See Ho-chi-Minh

MINIATURE cameras. See Cameras

MINIATURE chapels. See Chapels, Miniature

MINIATURE electronic equipment

Chip revolutionizes electronics. C. Leedham. il N Y Times Mag p56-7+ S 19 '65; Same abr. with title Chip newest marvel in electronics. Read Digest 88:173-4+ Ja '66

Coming: two-inch TV; microminiaturization. S. L. Englebardt. il Sci Digest 57:55-9 Ap '65

Microelectronics. W. C. Hittinger and M. Sparks. il Sci Am 213:56-64+ N '65

Tiny chip brings a big payoff. il Bsns W p85-6+ Ap 17 '65

MINIATURE geraniums. See Geraniums

MINIATURE lamps. See Electric lamps

MINIATURE objects

Arsenal in miniature. B. Sweeney. il Hobbies 70:122 Je '65

Ira Renoll's indoor farm. S. A. Parvin. il Hobbies 70:120 O '65

Make the world more beautiful with tiny things. S. A. Parvin. Hobbies 70:120 S '65

Master modeler of midget guns. E. Nanas. il Pop Mech 124:88-90 D '65

Miniatures pertaining to Lincoln. S. A. Parvin. il Hobbies 69:122 F '65

See also

Models

MINIATURE rooms. See Rooms, Miniature

MINIATURE trees. See Trees, Dwarf

MINIATURES (models) See Models

MINIATURES, Military. See Military miniatures

MINIMAX

Yankee marketeers; Italy's largest supermarket. il Time 85:97 Ap 23 '65

MINIMUM wage

United States

Effects of minimum wage on employment and business. il Mo Labor R 88:541-3 My '65

Higher minimum wage in 1966? U S News 60:71 Ja 10 '66

If minimum wage moves up to $1.75 an hour. il U S News 59:75-6 Ag 16 '65

Is boost in minimum wage near? Bsns W p34+ Jl 3 '65

Where wage-fixing keeps kids idle. il Nations Bsns 53:34-5+ Jl '65

MINISTERS of the gospel. See Clergy

MINNEAPOLIS

Don't splinter the dance! J. Brin. Dance Mag 39:34-5 Ag '65

MINNEAPOLIS—*Continued*

Architecture

Lofty portico, a termination and a transition; insurance company office building. M. Yamasaki. il Arch Rec 138:146-9 D '65

Description

Beautiful Minneapolis. il Recreation 58:78-9 F '65

Libraries

Minneapolis-St Paul opinion survey reveals high public library use. Library J 90:2790+ Je 15 '65

See also

Minneapolis public library

Music

Bold ambition on the open stage. J. K. Sherman. il Hi Fi 15:140 Ap '65

Recreation

City of water and ice. R. H. Johnson. il Recreation 58:161-2 Ap '65

Stores

Trend-setting store imports, fiesta from Mexico; Dayton's of Minneapolis. il Bsns W p62 Jl 31 '65

Streets

Flush before sweeping for cleaner streets. L. C. Pratt. il Am City 80:118-20 Mr '65

Theater

Guthrie's getaway season; new productions of Minnesota theatre company at Tyrone Guthrie theatre. H. Hewes. Sat R 48:34 Ag 7 '65

Search for style; Minnesota theatre company. Newsweek 66:65 Ag 2 '65

Two Cherry orchards; Guthrie theatre, Minneapolis, and Shakespearean festival theatre, Stratford, Ont, productions. J. Novick. Nation 201:87-8 Ag 16 '65

Water supply

Pilot plant points the way to a rate decrease. T. B. Corlett, jr. and J. R. Hoffer. il Am City 80:113-15 O '65

Three suburbs team up for better water; Crystal, New Hope and Golden Valley. F. G. Goff. il Am City 80:76-8 F '65

MINNEAPOLIS center opera company
Twin city four. A. B. Cutts. il Opera N 29:32 Mr 20 '65

MINNEAPOLIS public library
Summer storms in Minnesota; censorship. E. J. Gaines. ALA Bul 59:693-4 S '65

MINNEAPOLIS-St Paul theater. See Minneapolis—Theater

MINNELLI, Liza
On stage; ed. by E. Miller. por Seventeen 24:14 Je '65

about

Red mackerel. por Newsweek 65:99 My 24 '65

Theatre. America 113:121-2 Jl 31 '65

Triumph of Judy's Liza. il pors Life 58:82-4 My 28 '65

MINNESOTA
See also
Architecture, Domestic—Minnesota
Booksellers and bookselling—Minnesota
Camping—Minnesota
Geology—Minnesota
Paleontology—Minnesota

Description and travel

Try Paul Bunyan country for vacation size; northern Minnesota. J. Engh. il Todays Health 43:18-23 Jl '65

Historic houses, etc.

Pringle-Claggett House in Hastings, Minnesota. A. B. Kerr. il Antiques 89:112-15 Ja '66

Religious institutions and affairs

News of the Christian world (cont) Christian Cent 82:189-90, 500+, 724-6, 1043-4, 1362-4 F 10, Ap 21, Je 2, Ag 25, N 3 '65

MINNESOTA mining and manufacturing company
Nolo contendere given a fresh treatment; Judge Juergens' decision of 3M's no contest plea. Bsns W p88 Ja 15 '66

MINNESOTA multiphasic personality inventory. See Personality tests

MINNESOTA scholastic aptitude test. See Aptitude tests

MINNESOTA theatre company. See Minneapolis—Theater

MINNESOTA Twins (baseball) See Baseball clubs

MINOAN writing. See Writing, Minoan

MINOR, Audax, pseud.
Race track. See issues of New Yorker

MINOR, W. F.
Book review. America 112:884 Je 19 '65

MINOR league baseball. See Baseball

MINOR planets. See Asteroids

MINORITIES
Assimilation & the sociologists. M. Sklare. Commentary 39:63-7 My '65; Discussion. 40:16-17 Ag '65

How about the non-Negro poor? an untold story. il U S News 59:66-8 O 4 '65

Success story, Japanese-American style. W. Petersen. il N Y Times Mag p20-1+ Ja 9 '66

MINSHALL, Lloyd
At the crossroads; reprint. Recreation 58:343-4 S '65

MINSHEW, Velon H.
Potassium-argon age from a granite at Mount Wilbur, Queen Maud Range, Antarctica. bibliog Science 150:741-3 N 5 '65

MINTER, Jim
Mayor surrenders Atlanta. Sports Illus 23:14-17 Jl 12 '65

MINTZ, Beatrice
Genetic mosaicism in adult mice of quadriparental lineage. bibliog Science 148:1232-3 My 28 '65

MINTZ, David A.
Techniques to improve lighting effects. Arch Rec 138:199-202 N '65

MINUS, Paul M. jr
Pioneering for Christian unity. America 114:117 Ja 22 '66

MINUTEMAN (guided missile) See Guided missiles

MINUTEMEN (organization)
Waiting for Armageddon; proposed bill to outlaw paramilitary private armies in California. il Newsweek 65:33 Ap 26 '65

MIOCENE period. See Paleontology—Miocene

MIRACLE, Leonard
Wind River bear run. Outdoor Life 135:54-5+ Ap '65

MIRACLE, Roland
New shielded twin-lead for color TV & U.H.F. Electr World 74:29+ O '65

MIRAGES
Mirages. D. Linton. il Natur Hist 74:36-9 Ap '65

MIRDREKVANDI, Ali
Heavenly homer from an Iranian batman. J. Sayre. Life 59:6 S 24 '65

Protest march on purgatory. E. Capouya. por Sat R 48:41-2 S 25 '65

MIRET, Gil
Two woodcut artists. il Am Artist 29:68-70+ O '65

MIRÓ, Joan
Gallery for young people. C. B. Johnson. il Sch Arts 64:46-7 F '65

MIROLLI, Maurizio
Tritium: distribution in busycon canaliculatum (L.) injected with labeled reserpine. bibliog Science 149:1503-4 S 24 '65

MIRROR lenses. See Lenses, Photographic

MIRRORS
For stealing peeks or serious looking. il Sunset 134:176-7 My '65

Picture worth a thousand words; mirror with landskip painting in Tryon Palace, New Bern, N.C. G. Z. Thomas. il Antiques 88:686-8 N '65

Reflections of the past; decorated mirrors. il McCalls 93:104-7 D '65

MIRRORS for cameras
New design: Pellix-fixed-mirror BSR- and fast load 35. il Pop Phot 56:141 Je '65

MIRRORS for telescopes
In-shop or on-site figuring of large telescope mirrors? D. S. Brown. il Sky & Tel 29:350-2 Je '65

MIRSKY, Jeanette
Land of mule trains and monasteries. Sat R 48:73 My 22 '65

MIRVISH, Edwin
Mix discounts and art and make sales jump. il pors Bsns W p50-2 F 20 '65

MISCARRIAGE. See Abortion

MISCEGENATION. See Intermarriage of races

MISCH, Robert Jay
Curious Catalonians. Sat R 48:48+ Mr 13 '65

MISHAWAKA, Ind.
Maggie modernizes Mishawaka's methods. W. H. Smith. il Am City 80:124-5 Je '65

MISHAWAKA rubber company
Improved foot comfort ahead. M. B. Keiser.
il Parents Mag 40:14+ My '65
MISKEL, John A. See Bonner, N. A. jt. auth.
MISNER, David E.
Physical activity aids the three R's. bibliog
Sr Schol 86:sup6 My 6 '65
MISREPRESENTATION. See Quacks and
quackery
MISS America contests. See Beauty contests
MISS Frankenstein; drama. See Miller, H. L.
MISS Julie; opera. See Rorem, N.
MISS teen-age America contests. See Beauty
contests
MISSALS
Don't burn your missals. C. J. McNaspy.
America 113:718-20 D 4 '65
MISSILE command, Army. See United States—
Army—Materiel command
MISSILE ranges. See Proving grounds
MISSILE sleds. See Rocket sleds
MISSILE support. See Guided missiles—Equipment
MISSILES, Guided. See Guided missiles
MISSING link
Is there a missing link? D. Cohen. il Sci
Digest 58:96-7 S '65
See also
Neanderthal race
MISSING persons
Dead or alive? case of L. J. Bader. il Newsweek 65:29 F 22 '65
Get lost! C. Elliott. il Outdoor Life 136:50-2+
Ag '65
Haunted man's perilous search; quest for
missing pilot in Vietnam; with report by
D. Moser. il Life 58:26-35+ Mr 12 '65
I finally met the Vietcong and became their
prisoner; with introduction. D. Dawson. il
Life 59:121-2+ O 8 '65
Outdoors; concerning two boys lost in the
woods. T. Williams. Esquire 64:50+ D '65
MISSION BAY PARK, San Diego. See San
Diego, Calif.—Parks and playgrounds
MISSIONARIES
New missionary; liberal, practical, secular.
J. W. Egerton. Christian Cent 82:1507-9
D 8 '65
Pilgrims of peace. il Sr Schol 86:16-17 Mr 11
'65
Praise the Lord and pass the lug wrench;
missionary technicians accepted for missions. K. Engh. il Pop Mech 124:82-5+
D '65
Teaching missionaries expelled from Rhodesia.
Christian Cent 82:1003 Ag 18 '65
Yankees in Roman collars. J. Bishop. Commonweal 82:469-71 Jl 2 '65
See also
Missions
MISSIONARY conferences
Missionary cooperation on an ecumenical level; churches of Germany and Japan. Christian Cent 82:1533 D 15 '65
MISSIONARY technicians. See Missionaries
MISSIONS
Are agricultural missions out of date? C. R.
McBride. Christian Cent 82:1606-7 D 29 '65
Cross and crucifix in mission, by N. A.
Horner. Review
America 113:604 N 13 '65. W. J. Richardson
Cath World 202:246 Ja '66. H. D. Noyes
Christian Cent 82:1323 O 27 '65. D.
Kitagawa
Men make the mission; Bishop Sheen commends Protestant stewardship. Christian
Cent 82:1029 Ag 25 '65; Discussion. 82:1294
O 20 '65
Ubiquitous frontier. D. Kitagawa. Christian
Cent 82:214+ F 17 '65
See also
Catholic church—Missions
Missionaries
Student volunteer movement

California
See California—Missions

Indians of North America
See Indians of North America—Missions

Japan
Missionary exodus from Japan? R. H. Drummond. Christian Cent 82:672-4 My 26 '65;
Discussion. 82:892, 943-4; 83:19-20+ Jl 14,
28 '65, Ja 5 '66
MISSIONS, Medical
One man's land of romance; Grenfell mission throughout Labrador and Newfoundland. A. Sulley. il Am For 71:12-15+ Jl
'65

MISSISSIPPI
See also
Law—Mississippi
Libraries—Mississippi
Prohibition—Mississippi

Constitution
Vote for reason; Mississippi's new voting law.
Time 86:13 Ag 27 '65

Description and travel
Mississippi Gulf coast; unsung Riviera. H.
Ehrlich. il Look 29:133-6 N 16 '65

Economic conditions
Mississippi; summer of discontent. E. Sutherland. il Nation 201:212-15 O 11 '65
Mississippi; the past that has not died. W.
Lord. il Am Heritage 16:4-9+ Je '65

Industries
Space age comes to Mississippi. il U S News
58:78-80 F 15 '65

Newspapers
Appreciation day; editor of four Holmes
County weeklies suggests Negro boycott
to keep papers alive. Newsweek 66:70 D 13
'65

Politics and government
Challenge is real. Nation 200:659 Je 21 '65
Five seats in Congress; Mississippi challenge.
G. Slaff. il Nation 200:526-9 My 17 '65
Letter from Washington; Mississippi challenge; by members of Freedom democratic
party. R. H. Rovere. New Yorker 41:233-4+
O 16 '65
See also
Mississippi—Constitution

Race problems
Beauty for ashes; Committee of concern organized to rebuild Negro churches bombed
and burned in Mississippi. il Time 85:61
F 5 '65
Behind the magnolia curtain; Yankee in
Mississippi. R. Boeth. Atlan 216:46-52 Ag
'65; Discussion. 216:53+ O '65
How it is in Mississippi. W. Rowland. Christian Cent 82:340+ Mr 17 '65
Integration at Ole Miss. by R. H. Barrett.
Review
Sat R 48:43 Ap 10 '65. E. M. Yoder, jr
Interpretation, anyone? public hearings concerning tests for voter registration in Mississippi. il Time 85:23-4 F 26 '65
Let us now praise southern justice! R. Nicole.
Christian Cent 82:145-6 F 3 '65
Letters from Mississippi. Review
Newsweek il 65:22 My 31 '65
Meanwhile, in Mississippi. B. L. Smith. Commonweal 82:39-42 Ap 2 '65
Mississippi; after violence a ray of hope. il
Ebony 20:109-10+ Je '65
Mississippi business plans for integration.
Bsns W p32 Ap 17 '65
Mississippi; summer of discontent. E. Sutherland. il Nation 201:212-15 O 11 '65
Mississippi; the past that has not died. W.
Lord. il Am Heritage 16:4-9+ Je '65
My friends in Mississippi. L. Kabat. New
Repub 152:18-20 My 29 '65
My son didn't die in vain! ed. by B. Asbell.
Mrs R. W. Goodman. Good H 160:98-9+
My '65
No federal case? lynch-murder of three civilrights workers. Newsweek 65:25 Mr 8 '65
Obsolete Negro. R. G. Sherrill. il Nation 202:
59-61 Ja 17 '66
Reconciliation through anger; Delta ministry.
il Time 86:70-1 Jl 2 '65
Speaking out; integration could destroy rural
Mississippi; with editorial comment. C.
Sullivan. Sat Eve Post 238:10+, 100 Ap 10
'65
Voices in Mississippi. Time 85:23 F 19 '65

Bibliography
Hope and sorrow in the South. C. Shapiro.
il Sat R 48:31-3 Ag 14 '65

Religious institutions and affairs
Church in Mississippi. S. Sicotte. Commonweal 82:487-8 Jl 9 '65

Social conditions
Behind the magnolia curtain; Yankee in
Mississippi. R. Boeth. Atlan 216:46-52 Ag
'65; Discussion. 216:53+ O '65
Mississippi; the fallen paradise. W. Percy.
il Harper 230:166-72 Ap '65

MISSISSIPPI freedom democratic party
Mississippi challengers; failure to unseat the state's congressmen. New Repub 153:8 O 2 '65
Seat belts for Mississippi's five. A. Kopkind. New Repub 153:17-18 Jl 24 '65

MISSISSIPPI in art
Second invasion; my experiences in Mississippi. T. Sugarman. il Am Artist 20:48-53+ N '65

MISSISSIPPI RIVER
Cruel beauty of the ravages of flood; Mississippi bursts its banks. il Life 58:34-5 Ap 30 '65
Food safety program: endrin monitoring in the Mississippi River. A. F. Novak and M. R. R. Rao. bibliog il Science 150:1732-3 D 24 '65
Old Man River recedes, leaving its mud behind. il Bsns W p32-3 My 8 '65

MISSISSIPPI. University
Integration at Ole Miss. by R. H. Barrett. Review
    Sat R 48:43 Ap 10 '65. E. M. Yoder. jr
Of many things; Professor Silver's transfer. T. N. Davis. America 113:145 Ag 14 '65

MISSISSIPPI VALLEY
History
    See also
Louisiana purchase

MISSOULA, Mont.
Extras pay dividends; Missoula's water-pollution-control plant. R. A. Haverfield. il Am City 80:101-3 N '65

MISSOURI
    See also
Fishing—Missouri
Forests and forestry—Missouri
Libraries—Missouri

MISSOURI-Kansas-Texas railroad
Katy puts an old hand in the cab; retired railroad president J. Barriger. il Bsns W p 192+ O 9 '65

MISSOURI RIVER
By boat on Lewis and Clark's water highway. il Sunset 134:34-6+ Je '65
Missouri barges, dams ready for record thaw. Bsns W p67 Mr 13 '65
Whither the wide Missouri? conflict of interest between National park service and Army corps of engineers. G. F. Stucker. il Nat Parks Mag 39:10-15 Ag '65

Flood control projects
Mighty Missouri: river that was finally tamed; Pick-Sloan plan. il U S News 59:70-2+ S 13 '65

MISSOURI. University, Columbia
Laurels for lensmen: Pictures-of-the-year competition. M. R. Weiss. il Sat R 48:62-3 My 8 '65

MISTAKES. See Errors, Popular

MR Acarius; story. See Faulkner, W.

MR Schwartz; story. See Hall, D.

MR Travel award
Eleventh annual Mr Travel award: Conrad Hilton elected. il Travel 124:34-6 Jl '65

MISTLETOE
Seed dispersal velocity in four dwarfmistletoes. T. E. Hinds and F. G. Hawksworth. il Science 148:517-19 Ap 23 '65
Spread of a parasite: dwarfmistletoe. F. C. Hawksworth and T. E. Hinds. il Natur Hist 74:52-7 Mr '65

MRS 'Arris goes to Parliament; story. See Gallico, P.

MRS Dally; drama. See Hanley, W.

MITCHELL, Anne
Crux of the matter. por Sat R 49:66 Ja 15 '66

MITCHELL, Carleton
Finisterre sails the Windward Islands. por Nat Geog Mag 128:755-801 D '65
Handy Pied-à-Terre for a sailorman. Sports Illus 22:79-80+ My 24 '65
It burst upon us like a star shell. il Sports Illus 23:35-6 Jl 12 '65
Time turns back in picture-book Portofino. Nat Geog Mag 127:232-53 F '65

MITCHELL, Curtis
Billy Graham's physical fitness program can help you. Pop Sci 186:61-4+ My '65; Same abr. Read Digest 87:58-62 Jl '65
LBJ's heart. Pop Sci 186:74-7+ F '65
Your aching back, and what to do about it. Read Digest 88:78-82 Ja '66

MITCHELL, Frank
Couple of whizzes go to Washington. il pors Ebony 20.75-8 Je '65

MITCHELL, H. C. and Thaemert, J. C.
Three dimensions in fine structure. bibliog Science 148:1480-2 Je 11 '65

MITCHELL, Helene A.
Our puppenhaus. Hobbies 70:40-1 Je '65

MITCHELL, Herschel K. and Weber, U. M.
Drosophila phenol oxidases. bibliog Science 148:964-5 My 14 '65

MITCHELL, Jere H. See Chapman, C. B. jt. auth.

MITCHELL, Joan
Expressionist in Paris. J. Ashbery. il por Art N 64:44-5+ Ap '65

MITCHELL, Joseph McDowell
Catch a bigot by the toe. T. Kelly. Nation 200:169-70 F 15 '65
Is nothing sacred? Reporter 32:10+ F 11 '65

MITCHELL, Margaret
Margaret Mitchell of Atlanta, by F. Farr. Review
    Nat R 18:33-4 Ja 11 '66. P. L. Buckley
Woman who wrote Gone with the wind; excerpt from Margaret Mitchell of Atlanta. F. Farr. il pors McCalls 92:84-7+ Jl '65

MITCHELL, Roger L. and Anderson, I. C.
Catalase photoinactivation. bibliog Science 150:74 O 1 '65

MITCHELL, Thomas
Where does Chile go from here? Nat R 17:275-7 Ap 6 '65

MITCHELL and Giurgola associates
Mitchell/Giurgola win A.I.A. competition; design of headquarters building. il Arch Rec 137:10 F '65

MITFORD, Jessica
Disease that Dr Kildare couldn't cure. McCalls 92:102-3+ S '65
Formaldehyde frolics. Holiday 38:174+ D '65
Good grief. Nation 201:533-5 D 27 '65
Have the undertakers reformed? Atlan 215:63-73 Je '65
Raising kids without fear or Freud. Life 59:10 N 19 '65

MITGANG, Herbert
Conspiracy or coincidence? Sat R 48:32-3 Je 26 '65
Hot property. Sat R 48:39-40 O 2 '65

MITOCHONDRIA
Nuclear mitochondria? D. Brandes and others. il Science 149:1373-4 S 17 '65
Selective mitochondrial damage by a ruby laser microbeam: an electron microscopic study. R. L. Amy and R. Storb. bibliog il Science 150:756-8 N 5 '65

MITOSIS. See Cell division (biology)

MITROPOULOS, Dimitri, International music competition. See Music—Competitions

MITROVICH, George S.
Punishment of a priest. Christian Cent 82:782+ Je 16 '65

MITSUBISHI shipbuilding and engineering company. See Shipbuilding

MITTENS. See Gloves

MITTERRAND, François
Letter from Paris. Genêt. New Yorker 41:61-2+ Ja 1 '66
Man who . . . Newsweek 66:51 O 4 '65
Other candidate in France. K. Botsford. il pors N Y Times Mag p8-9+ D 19 '65
Survival expert. por Newsweek 66:38 D 20 '65

MITTY, Glenn O.
Safety gun holder. Field & S 70:101 N '65

MIXED marriages. See Marriages, Mixed

MIXING
Personality of the month: J. H. Rushton. il Sci Digest 57:38-40 My '65

MIXING utensils
Summer coolers; blending equipment. B. G. Wadsworth. il Parents Mag 40:24 Jl '65

MIZENER, Arthur
Path to promotion. Atlan 216:135-8 N '65

MOAS
Bird that stood 10 feet tall. R. A. Caras. il Sci Digest 59:57-60 Ja '66

MOATS, Alice-Leone
Some of the Pope's problems. Nat R 17:367 My 4 '65

MOB violence
    See also
Lynching

MOBILE homes. See Automobile trailers; Campers and coaches, Truck

MOBILE hospitals. See Hospitals, Traveling

MOBILE libraries. See Bookmobiles

MOBILE lunar laboratory. See Lunar vehicles

MOBILE transmitters. See Radio transmitters, Portable

MOBILES
Calder the pioneer; exhibitions at the Guggenheim and at Milwaukee. F. Getlein. New Repub 152:31-2 Mr 27 '65

MODERNISM (art)—*Continued*
Variables of energy. M. Kozloff. Nation 200: 513-14 My 10 '65
Visual arts 1955-1965. G. Davenport. Nat R 17:1111-12 N 30 '65
What is this thing called op? D. Chu. il Sr Schol 86:18-21 Ap 1 '65
Why do they paint like that? some ins and outs of modern art. W. Johnson. il Sr Schol 86:20-1 Ap 1 '65
You bought it now live with it; pop are collectors and their collections. il Life 59:56-61 Jl 16 '65
You can hang it in the hall; op art. T. B. Hess. il Art N 64:41-3+ Ap '65
See also
Cubism
Impressionism (art)

Anecdotes, facetiae, satire, etc.
Broads were very skinny, or Pop art, shmop art, leave me alone. L. Rosten. Harper 231: 90-1 O '65; Same abr. with title Pop art, shmop art, leave me alone. Read Digest 87: 75-7 D '65

Caricatures and cartoons
Op art. Stevenson. New Yorker 41:44-8 Ap 3 '65
Op goes the artist; with drawings by Erich Sokol. Holiday 38:66-9 N '65
MODERNISM in music. See Music
MODERNIZATION. See Social change
MODERNIZATION, Housing. See Houses, Remodeled
MODESTO, Calif.
Human-rights committee in action. J. C. Keefe. il Am City 80:116-18 O '65
MODULAR design
Modular scheme provides disciplined variety. il Arch Rec 137:90-3 mid-My '65
MODULAR production. See Production
MOFFAT, Alex W.
Cruising down east. Yachting 118:38-40+ Jl; 57-9+ Ag '65 (to be cont)
MOFFAT, Lorna
Young girl, an old horse, and astonishing journey. por Vogue 146:16+ N 1 '65
MOFFET, Alan T.
Argelander and the BD. Sky & Tel 29:276-8 My '65
—See Maltby, P. jt. auth.
MOFFETT, Hugh
Arbiter of the taste of France. Life 58: 43-4+ Ap 30 '65
Pack den tiger in dem tank. Life 59:43-4 O 1 '65
White wizard's 90th. Life 58:82-92+ F 19 '65
MOFFITT, John
Greeting; poem. America 112:520 Ap 17 '65
Joseph in Bethlehem; poem. America 113: 777 D 18 '65
Musings of a poetry editor. America 113:262, 485 S 11, O 30 '65
MOGOLLON, N.Mex.
Muggy-own, a New Mexico ghost. il Sunset 135:49+ N '65
MOHAMMED
Moslem world's struggle to modernize. il Time 85:66-73 Ap 16 '65
MOHAMMED el Badr, king of the Yemen
Yemen's desert fox. G. De Carvalho. il por Life 58:97-8+ F 19 '65
MOHAMMED Reza Pahlevi, shah of Iran
Billion-dollar mystery; with editorial comment. F. J. Cook il por Nation 200:377-8, 380-97 Ap 12 '65
Modern monarch on the peacock throne; with report by L. Griggs. il pors Life 60:38-40+ Ja 14 '66
Shah and his exasperating subjects. J. Fischer. Harper 230:24+ Ap '65
MOHAMMED Zahir, king of Afghanistan
Kingly accomplishment. il por Time 86:36 D 3 '65
MOHAMMEDANISM. See Islam
MOHAWK airlines
High flight of Mohawk. J. F. Olesky. il Duns R 86:67-8 N '65
Mohawk blazes a trail. il Bsns W p74+ Je 26 '65
Mohawk presses jet, turboprop training. J. W. Carter. il Aviation W 82:32-3 Je 7 '65
Mohawk to begin BAC 111 service in July. J. W. Carter. il Aviation W 82:28 My 31 '65
MOHENJO-DARO
City of the dead; mystery of Mahenjo-Daro. M. Brion. il UNESCO Courier 18:27-31 Je '65
Mohenjo-Daro; 5,000-year old heritage menaced by destruction. H. J. Plenderleith and others. il UNESCO Courier 18:22-6 Je '65

MOHN, Einar O.
Who will succeed Hoffa? il por Newsweek 66:84 D 20 '65
MOHN, Reinhard
Many-titled tycoon. por Time 86:65 Jl 30 '65
MOHOLE project
Building a platform for Project Mohole. il Bsns W p 122+ S 25 '65
Crust's origin indicated; mixture of rare-earth metals. Sci N L 88:195 S 25 '65
Mighty hole in the earth. B. Tuffy. il Sci N L 88:26 Jl 10 '65
Mohole: drilling site in Pacific favored as time nears to award construction contract for vessel. D. S. Greenberg. Science 147: 487 Ja 29 '65
Mohole finds a site at last: area off Hawaiian Islands. il Bsns W p52 Ja 30 '65
Mohole: last-minute opposition turned aside. D. S. Greenberg. Science 150:195 O 8 '65
Place for the Mohole. Sci Am 212:54 Mr '65
MOHOLY-NAGY, Sibyl
In Barcelona, an architectural heritage is transformed into a modern tradition. Arch Forum 123:52-7 Jl '65
MOHR, Charles
Requiem for a lightweight. Esquire 64:66-9+ Ag '65
War only lasts a lifetime. Nation 200:536-7 My 17 '65
MOHRHARDT, Charles M.
Automation in the Detroit public library. por ALA Bul 59:829-33 O '65
Nation's new leader among convention cities. ALA Bul 59:547-51 Je '65
MOISEYEV dance company
Moiseyev dance company, Metropolitan opera house. J. Maskey. Dance Mag 39:61-2 Jl '65
Music to my ears; new Moiseyev. I. Kolodin. Sat R 48:29 Je 5 '65
Proud ones; in New York. il Newsweek 65:77 My 31 '65
MOISTURE
Convection plumes from ulmus americana L. E. B. Peterson and A. W. H. Damman. bibliog il Science 148:392-3 Ap 16 '65; Discussion. 149:764; 150:783, 1629 Ag 13, N 5, D 17 '65
See also
Dampness in buildings
MOK, Michael
Come to the riot. See Weirs Beach burn. Life 59:88-9 Jl 2 '65
Day his funny friends frolicked in grief. Life 58:40B-40C Ap 30 '65
Dog-walking dolls. Life 58:65-6 Je 11 '65
In they go to the reality of this war. Life 59:50-69+ N 26 '65
Plot to behead the Statue of Liberty. Life 58:38-9 F 26 '65

about
Our man Mok with the marines. G. P. Hunt. por Life 59:3 N 26 '65
MOLAB (mobile lunar laboratory) See Lunar vehicles
MOLDS (botany)
See also
Fungi
MOLECULAR beams
Molecular beams. O. R. Frisch. il Sci Am 212:58-72+ My '65
New accelerator extends molecular beam's energy. il Sci N L 87:295 My 8 '65
MOLECULAR binding energy. See Chemical bonds
MOLECULAR biochemistry. See Biochemistry
MOLECULAR dynamics
See also
Molecular beams
MOLECULAR hydrogen. See Hydrogen
MOLECULAR interactions. See Molecules
MOLECULES
Crystal packing of molecules. D. E. Williams. bibliog Science 147:605-6 F 5 '65
Crystallization and molecular folding. P. H. Lindenmeyer. bibliog il Science 147:1256-62 Mr 12 '65
Hard-sphere fluid. H. L. Frisch. bibliog il Science 150:1249-54 D 3 '65
Hybrid antibody molecules with allotypically different L-polypeptide chains. M. Mannik and H. Metzger. bibliog il Science 148:383-5 Ap 16 '65
Intermolecular forces in association of purines with polybenzenoid hydrocarbons. B. Pullman and others. bibliog il Science 147:1305-7 Mr 12 '65

MOLECULES—*Continued*
Lattice formation in complement fixation: studies with univalent rabbit antibody. H. H. Fudenberg and others. bibliog il Science 148:91-3 Ap 2 '65
Molecular transitions and chemical reaction rates. B. Widom. bibliog Science 148:1555-60 Je 18 '65
Organisms and molecules in evolution; adaptation from paper. G. G. Simpson; reply. J. Moor-Jankowski and A. S. Wiener. bibliog Science 148:255-6 Ap 9 '65
Ultrasound chemical effects on pure organic liquids. A. Weissler and others. bibliog Science 150:1288-9 D 3 '65
X-ray analysis of complicated molecules; address, December 11, 1964. D. C. Hodgkin. bibliog il Science 150:979-88 N 19 '65
See also
Atoms

MOLENDA, Robert P. See Swartz, H. M. jt. auth.

MOLES (dermatology)
Pigmented nevi and malignant melanomas as studied with a specific fluorescence method. B. Falck and others. bibliog Science 149:439 Jl 23 '65
See also
Melanoma

MOLEY, Raymond
Perspective. See Issues of Newsweek

MOLIÈRE, Jean Baptiste Poquelin
Tartuffe; tr. by R. Wilbur. Criticism
America 112:336 Mr 6 '65
Commonweal 81:611-12 F 5 '65
Nation 200:122 F 1 '65
Sat R 48:44 F 6 '65
Vogue 145:95 Mr 1 '65

MOLINA, José
José Molina bailes espanoles. 92nd street Y. J. Maskey. Dance Mag 39:62 Mr '65

MOLINA, Rafael Leonidas Trujillo. See Trujillo Molina, R. L.

MOLISKE, M. B.
Cats, Christmas lights and line maintenance. Am City 81:112-13 Ja '66

MÖLLER, Erna
Contact-induced cytotoxicity by lymphoid cells containing foreign isoantigens. bibliog Science 147:873-4+ F 19 '65

MOLLUSKS
Classification of mollusks. A. G. Melvin. il Hobbies 70:130 Ap '65
See also
Chitons
Limpets
Sea hares
Shells (conchology)
Snails

MOLNAR, Thomas
Europe of Charles de Gaulle. Nat R 17:108-9 F 9 '65
Ideology of aggiornamento. Nat R 17:365-6 My 4 '65
Rhodesia at the crossroads. Nat R 17:971-2 N 2 '65
Sartre and the cancelation. Nat R 17:270 Ap 6 '65
Ungentle ways of Marshal Tito. Nat R 17:595+ Jl 13 '65

MOLNO, Carl N.
Carl N. Molno stresses design principles; with biographical sketch. il por Am Artist 29:54-5+ Mr '65

MOLODY, Kenon Trofimovich. See Lonsdale, G. A.

MOLOKAI CHANNEL
Honolulu race nemesis. F. N. Rothwell. il Yachting 117:64+ My '65

MOLONEY virus. See Leukemia virus

MOLTING
Life cycle of seclusion. R. J. Donahue. il Natur Hist 74:50-1 My '65
Molt and intermolt activities in the epidermal cells of an insect. M. Locke and others. bibliog il Science 149:437-8 Jl 23 '65

MOLUCELLA laevis. See Shell flowers

MOLYBDENUM
Getting there the hot way; molybdenum drill bit. Time 85:52 F 12 '65
Molybdenum content of corn plants exhibiting varying degrees of potassium deficiency. J. B. Jones, jr. il Science 148:94 Ap 2 '65

MOLYBDENUM corporation of America
Demands of color TV push rare ore process; europium oxide. Bsns W p71 Jl 24 '65

MOMENT of force. See Torque

MOMMAERTS, W. F. H M. and O'Malley, C. D.
Vesalius commemoration at Brussels. Science 147:1603-5 Mr 26 '65

MOMMSEN, Ernst Wolf
Some advice for Americans who do business in Europe; interview. por U S News 59:76-7 Jl 5 '65

MONA LISA (painting) See Leonardo da Vinci

MONACO, Anthony P. and others
Adult thymectomy: effect on recovery from immunologic depression in mice. bibliog Science 149:432-5 Jl 23 '65

MONACO
See also
Gardens—Monaco

Economic conditions
Monarch & the magnate. il Time 86:43 O 1 '65
Monarch vs. millionaire; feud between Onassis and Rainier. il Newsweek 65:78 Mr 8 '65

Royal family
New princess in Monaco. il Look 29:43-8 Je 1 '65

MONAHAN, Harry
They work together. Yachting 117:48-9+ Je '65

MONAHON, Eleanore Bradford
Providence cabinetmakers of the eigtheenth and early nineteenth centuries. Antiques 87:573-9 My '65
Thomas Howard jr, Providence cabinetmaker. Antiques 87:702-4 Je '65

MONASH, Paul
Triple jeopardy. il Time 86:65 Ag 20 '65

MONASTERIES
Visit to Taizé. P. Nobile. America 114:21-2 Ja 1 '66

MONCRIEFF, Donald
In a Christmas universe; poem. America 113:776 D 18 '65

MONDAY, Rick
Red-hot baseball in the Valley of the Sun. J. Mann. por Sports Illus 22:66-8+ My 24 '65

MONDRIAAN, Pieter Cornelis
Squares over curves; paintings turned into dresses. il por Time 86:76 S 10 '65

MONEGAL, Emir Rodriguez-. See Rodriguez-Monegal, E.

MONESTIME, S. F.
Doctor gets call to mayor's chair. il pors Ebony 20:171-2+ O '65

MONETARY fund. See International monetary fund

MONETARY stabilization. See Money

MONEY
Carry money safely while vacationing. il Good H 161:156 Jl '65
See also
Barter
Coins
Gold as money
Gresham's law
Hoarding
Inflation (finance)
Liquidity (economics)

International aspects
See Finance, International

Argentina
Addict's agony; peso devalued. Newsweek 65:56 My 3 '65

Australia
Aussies ring up currency change; switch from pound to decimal currency. il Bsns W p58+ Ja 15 '66

Brazil
Brazil tries a new cruzeiro. il U S News 59:86 O 11 '65

France
Heading for a new monetary unit? dollar and pound under fire. il Bsns W p 132+ F 20 '65
Mixed-up money. Time 85:22 F 12 '65

Great Britain
Battle for the pound. Fortune 72:123-4 S '65
Battle to defend the pound. Bsns W p 144 Ag 14 '65
Breather for Britain. il Fortune 72:97-8+ N '65
Britain stands firm for the pound; with editorial comment. Bsns W p28-9, 192 Ap 17 '65
Business hedges on British pound. Bsns W p 117-18 F 13 '65
More heat on the pound; sterling crisis. il Bsns W p23-4 Ap 3 '65

MONEY—Great Britain—*Continued*
More pressure on the pound. Time 85:94 F 19 '65
Perils of the pound. il Sr Schol 87:12-13 O 21 '65
Pound sterling; address, April 14, 1965. H. Wilson. Vital Speeches 31:452-9 My 15 '65
Sterling recovery puts better odds on Wilson. il Bsns W p34-5 O 9 '65
Sterling signs: good & bad. il Time 85:91 Je 11 '65

Russia
Russians have gold problems, too. il U S News 59:111 N 8 '65

United States
Battle the U.S. is winning; recovery for the dollar. il U S News 58:46-8 Ap 19 '65
Change in change. Newsweek 65:88+ Je 14 '65
Defending the dollar: latest moves by LBJ; concerning message to Congress. il U S News 58:47-50 F 22 '65
Do we need money? H. Hazlitt. Newsweek 66:58 Ag 2 '65
Dollar drought. Time 85:80 Mr 26 '65
Dollar: is it still as good as gold? il U S News 59:110-11 N 8 '65
Experts' verdict on LBJ's cure for dollar: not enough. U S News 58:50 F 22 '65
Growing fight over money. il U S News 58:91 Je 21 '65
How real is inflation in the U.S.? erosion of dollar. il U S News 60:78-80 Ja 24 '66
Inside story of our new silver-saving coins. A. P. Armagnac. il Pop Sci 187:64-6 S '65; Same abr. with title Those new sandwich coins. Read Digest 87:21-2+ D '65
Inside story of the dollar and its future; interview. R. V. Roosa. il U S News 58:48-53+ F 8 '65
Keeping the dollar strong; how U.S. can avoid trouble; interview. L. A. Hahn. il U S News 58:78-80 My 31 '65
Mr Dollar goes abroad. il Time 86:84-84B+ S 10 '65
Monetary reform: blood will be spilled. il Newsweek 66:70-3 Jl 5 '65
Monetary talks get go-ahead. Bsns W p26-7 Jl 17 '65
New dam for the dollar drain; new voluntary restraints on overseas spending. il Time 86:99 D 10 '65
Nobody can pay bills with bottle caps. F. Morley. Nations Bsns 53:27-8 Jl '65
Prestige abroad can be no stronger than dollar. F. Morley. Nations Bsns 53:25-6 My '65
Puzzle: where's the cash going? U S News 59:100+ S 27 '65
Rubber dollars; address, June 28, 1965. L. P. Mansfield. Vital Speeches 31:735-6 S 15 '65
Scare over money: what's back of it. il U S News 59:37-9 Jl 12 '65
Silver coin plan: a bit for everyone; plan to eliminate silver from dimes and quarters, leave some in half-dollars. il Bsns W p57-8+ Je 12 '65
Spending abroad, lending at home. Time 86:93 O 15 '65
Steps toward a new monetary agreement. Bsns W p96 Jl 31 '65
U.S. dollar: can it stand its popularity? il Sr Schol 86:12+ Ap 15 '65
Watch the coin bills in Congress. C. French. Hobbies 70:102 S '65
What is money, anyway? answers to your questions. il U S News 58:48-51 Ap 19 '65
See also
Paper money—United States
Silver as money
United States—Engraving and printing. Bureau of

History
Establishing our first national coinage. C. French. Hobbies 70:102 Ja '66
Small change shortage: conditions in the 1860's. C. French. Hobbies 70:102 N '65
MONEY, Counterfeit. See Counterfeits and counterfeiting
MONEY brokers. See Brokers
MONEY man; story. See Kanin, G.
MONEY management. See Budget, Household; Budget, Personal
MONEY market
Sharing the dollar's burden; Europe to share world's capital burden. il Bsns W p54+ Je 5 '65
MONEY raising campaigns. See Fund raising
MONEY rates. See Interest

MONGIN, Alfred
Forgotten founding fathers. Antiques 88:516-21 O '65
MONGOLIA
Journey to Mongolia; Seminar on participation of women in public life. G. A. Tillett. Dept State Bul 53:918-23 D 6 '65
MONGOLISM
Intelligent mongoloid. Sci Am 213:48 Jl '65
MONGOLOIDS. See Mongolism
MONK, Elizabeth Graham
Enemy: love; story. Seventeen 24:118-19 F '65
MONK, Marion S. Jr
$20 million footnote. Am For 71:24-7 Ap '65
MONK, Thelonious Sphere
Thelonious Monk and some others. R. De Toledano. Nat R 17:940-2 O 19 '65
MONKEY of his own; story. See Berger, T.
MONKEY trial. See Tennessee evolution controversy
MONKEYS
Field studies of Old World monkeys and apes. S. L. Washburn and others. bibliog Science 150:1541-7 D 17 '65
Jackson was a lady. W. Page. il Field & S 69:37-9+ Mr '65
Molecules and monkeys. J. Buettner-Janusch and R. L. Hill. bibliog il Science 147:836-42 F 19 '65
Monkey business; experiment suggesting psychosexual behavior determined chemically in the fetus. il Newsweek 66:84 N 15 '65
Pyramidal and non-pyramidal pathways in monkeys: anatomical and functional correlation. D. G. Lawrence and H. G. J. M. Kuypers. bibliog il Science 148:973-5 My 14 '65
Safari for science. G. E. Maxwell. il Todays Health 43:22-31 N '65
Social ways of monkeys. il Life 58:62-76B+ F 19 '65
Species and geographic differences in the transferrin polymorphism of macaques. M. Goodman and others. bibliog il Science 147:884-6 F 19 '65; Reply with rejoinder. J. Fooden. 148:255 Ap 9 '65
Spontaneous opiate addiction in rhesus monkeys. J. L. Claghorn and others. bibliog il Science 149:440-1 Jl 23 '65
Stump-tailed macaque: a promising laboratory primate. A. Kling and J. Orbach; discussion. bibliog il Science 148:1173-4 My 28 '65
Why babies love their mothers; reprint. il Sci Digest 57:73-6 My '65
See also
Gibbons
Primates

Training
See Animals—Training
MONKEYS, Experiments on. See Animal experimentation
MONKEYS as carriers of infection
Naturally acquired quotidian-type malaria in man transferable to monkeys. W. Chin and others. bibliog Science 149:865 Ag 20 '65
MONMOUTH COUNTY, N.J.
Overhead projector aids property sales. M. H. Worth. Am City 80:155 Ag '65
MONOAMINE oxidase
Circadian rhythm in pineal serotonin: effect of monoamine oxidase inhibition and reserpine. S. H. Snyder and J. Axelrod. bibliog il Science 149:542-4 Jl 30 '65
MONOD, Jacques
Jacques Monod: further comments on French universities. V. K. McElheny. Science 150:1701 D 24 '65
1965 Nobel laureates in medicine or physiology. G. S. Stent. por Science 150:462-4 O 22 '65
Nobel prize awarded. F. Marley. por Sci N L 88:261 O 23 '65
Revolution in the cell. Newsweek 66:77 O 25
MONOGRAMS
Monogramming Rx for writing paper. il House & Gard 127:150-1 My '65
MONONUCLEOSIS, Infectious
Mono: the medical mimic. J. Beck. il Todays Health 43:36-7+ F '65
They call it the students' disease. Seventeen 24:244-5 S '65
Viral diseases related; infectious mononucleosis and leukemia. Sci N L 87:260 Ap 24 '65
MONOPOLIES
In a few hands: monopoly power in America, by E. Kefauver and I. Till. Review
Sat R 48:29-30 F 27 '65. P. H. Douglas

MONOPOLIES—*Continued*
UAW mounts campaign against monopsony; vs Detroit's Big three. Bsns W p43-4 Jl 24 '65
MONOPOLY. See Monopolies
MONOPSONY. See Monopolies
MONOPTERUS
Fish that walks, breathes, changes sex. Sci Digest 57:12-13 Ap '65
MONORAIL railroads. See Railroads, Single rail
MONROE, Elizabeth
Disputed Jordan waters. New Repub 153:15-16 Ag 7 '65
MONROE, Harriet
Some recollections of the Poetry club at the University of Chicago. G. Campbell. Poetry 107:110-17 N '65
MONROE, Lynne C.
Should foreign aid include secondary education in Nigeria? por Negro Hist Bul 28: 128-9+ Mr '65
MONROE, Marilyn
Losers. por Newsweek 66:67-8 Jl 5 '65
Marilyn Monroe; interviews with six famous photographers, ed. by R. Hattersley. il pors Pop Phot 58:104-9+ Ja '66
Marilyn Monroe versus Uncle Sam; financial career. por Sat Eve Post 238:88 Jl 31 '65
MONROE community college, Rochester, N.Y.
Recreation supervision crisis. J. M. Caverly. il Recreation 58:342-3 S '65
MONROE doctrine
Johnson corollary; legality and morality of U.S. intervention in foreign states. il Time 85:24-5 My 14 '65
Protecting a hemisphere. il Sr Schol 87:4 D 2 '65

MONROVIA, Calif.

City planning
Realistic development plan. G. W. Miller. in Am City 80:100-1 My '65
MONSANTO company
Business lectures professors; Monsanto woos chemistry graduates to marketing by teaching their teachers. il Bsns W p65-6 Jl 10 '65
Customers rush for the ammonia. il Bsns W p70-1 Jl 24 '65
Monsanto moves into farmers' backyard. il Bsns W p60-2 F 6 '65
MONSOONS
Monsoon may alter war. Sci N L 87:287 My 1 '65
MONSTERS
Monster season; Michigan. il Newsweek 66: 22+ Ag 30 '65
MONSTERS, Mechanical. See Automatons
MONT SAINT MICHEL, France
France's magic castle in the sea. H. Manchester. il Read Digest 86:185-6+ Ap '65
1,000 years of sieges and seclusion. il Life 59:44A S 24 '65
MONTAGE
Color alchemy of Scott Hyde; composite photographs. S. Hyde. Pop Phot 56:64-71+ F '65
How David Attie creates montages in his darkroom. L. Solmssen. il Mod Phot 29: 80-5 Mr '65
Incredible photoons of Masatoshi Naito. M. Naito. il Mod Phot 29:86-91 F '65
See also
Collage
MONTAGNA, William
Skin; with biographical sketch. Sci Am 212: 16, 56-66 bibliog(p 134-5) F '65
MONTAGNARDS
Surrender. il Time 86:34 S 24 '65
Thunder in the mountains; United front for the struggle of the oppressed race, dedicated to achieving political autonomy for the Montagnards. M. Perry. il Newsweek 66:47 S 20 '65
Vietnam convoy. D. Ford. New Repub 152: 11-12 F 6 '65
MONTAGU, Ashley
Every day is father's day. Parents Mag 40: 43+ Je '65
MONTAGUE, John
All legendary obstacles; poem. Poetry 106: 408 S '65
MONTAGUE, Joseph Franklin
Tea: from medicine to beverage. Todays Health 43:30-5 Ap '65
MONTAIGNE, Michel Eyquem de
Invisible man. P. Zweig. Nation 201:307-8+ N 1 '65
Montaigne, by D. M. Frame. Review
Sat R por 48:50-1 O 16 '65. R. J. Clements
MONTALVO, Rafael. See Wheeler, O. H. jt. auth.

MONTANA, Edward J. Jr. See Carroll, J. M. jt. auth.
MONTANA
April in Montana; excerpts from Blue hen's chick. A. B. Guthrie, jr. Holiday 37:70-1 Mr '65
See also
Flathead River
Glacier National Park
Hunting—Montana
Paleontology—Montana

Description and travel
Montana between two battlefields. K. N. Anderson. il Todays Health 43:48-55+ Ag '65
Northern Montana loop. K. N. Anderson. il Todays Health 43:41-5+ S '65

Religious institutions and affairs
News of the Christian world (cont) Christian Cent 82:688-9 My 26 '65
MONTAUK, N.Y.
Fishing for peace. B. Wisner. il Motor B 115:50-1+ My '65
MONTCLAIR, N.J, free public library
This old gal went back to college. M. Bartley. il Library J 90:5351-3 D 15 '65
MONTE CARLO rally See Automobile racing
MONTE ROSSO, Antonio da
Undoing Babel. P. Rónai. il Américas 17: 26-30 Je '65
MONTECATINI TERME, Italy
Taking the cure at Montecatini. L. Moorehead. Vogue 146:47+ S 15 '65
MONTEITH college. See Wayne state university, Detroit—Monteith college
MONTEREY, Calif.
In Monterey: shopping and sightseeing along Cannery row. il Sunset 135:3 N '65
MONTEREY COUNTY, Calif.
What this is is picnic country; Hunter-Liggett military reservation and Los Padres national forest. il Sunset 134:46-8+ Ap '65
MONTEREY cypress. See Cypress
MONTEREY jazz festival. See Music festivals —California
MONTERO, Carlos
On the gypsy circuit. W. Como. por Dance Mag 39:140-1 D '65
MONTERO, Homero Martínez. See Martínez Montero, H.
MONTESSORI, Maria
Let the child teach himself. R. Gross and B. Gross. il por N Y Times Mag p34-5+ My 16 '65
MONTESSORI method of education
Let the child teach himself. R. Gross and B. Gross. il N Y Times Mag p34-5+ My 16 '65
Montessori expands; teaching of brain-damaged children. P. McBroom. Sci N L 88:375 D 11 '65

Bibliography
Yesterday's prophet: Maria Montessori. P. Pinson. Parents Mag 40:18 S '65
MONTEUX, Pierre
Maestro remembers; excerpt from It's all in the music, by D. G. Monteux. por Opera N 30:26-7 D 25 '65
MONTEVERDI, Claudio
Monteverdi: Il ritorno d'Ulisse in patria. J. W. Barker. il Am Rec G 31:782-5 My '65
On records: Coronation of Poppaea. Opera N 29:40 My 1 '65
MONTEZ, Lola
What was Lola? por Newsweek 66:40 D 20 '65
MONTGOMERY, Charlotte
Speaker for the house. See issues of Good housekeeping
MONTGOMERY, Elizabeth
Samantha gets her way. J. Hyams. pors Sat Eve Post 238:32-3 Mr 13 '65
MONTGOMERY, Frank A. Jr
Glowing report on that weird light of the sea; bioluminescence. Motor B 115:52-5 F '65
MONTGOMERY, George Granville
Gleaning new ventures from farming profits. il por Bsns W p89-90+ O 23 '65
MONTGOMERY, George Samuel
Obituary
Nat R 18:61 Ja 25 '66. W. F. Buckley, jr
MONTGOMERY, Marion
Sincerity in poetry. Writer 78:20-2 Ap '65
MONTGOMERY, Ruth
Crystal ball; condensation from Gift of prophecy. por Read Digest 87:235-42+ Jl '65
MONTGOMERY, Suzanne
Early bird going into business. Miss & Roc 16:24 Je 28 '65

MONTGOMERY, Ala.
On to Montgomery; decision on right to march from Selma to Montgomery. il Newsweek 65:21-2 Mr 29 '65
This was Montgomery; racial attitudes in the Deep South. G. H. Dunne. il America 112:660-1+ My 8 '65; Discussion. 113:78-9 Jl 17 '65

Newspapers
Fifty-fifty in the South; Southern courier's civil rights news. Time 86:110+ O 15 '65

Sanitary affairs
Keep refuse collectors on the route. L. B. Green. il Am City 80:110-11 Je '65
We vacuum and flush our streets. L. B. Green. il Am City 80:104-5 My '65

MONTGOMERY COUNTY, Md.
Church in the Wildwood; Mt Zion Baptist church. C. West. il Am For 71:8-9 Je '65
Maryland's Montgomery County: the changing suburban dream. T. Coffin. Holiday 38:54-5+ Jl '65

MONTHLY labor review
Fifty years of the MLR; symposium. Mo Labor R 88:749-802 Jl '65

MONTI, Eugenio
One winner, two victories. il pors UNESCO Courier 18:22-5 Jl '65

MONTICELLO (historic house)
Monticello swag. il House & Gard 127:38-9 Je '65

MONTLEY, Patricia
Other signs; poem. America 112:547 Ap 17 '65

MONTREAL
Architecture
In New Delhi and Montreal, cellular solutions for high-density living. il Arch Forum 123:68-9 Jl '65

Subways
Montreal's silent subway; rubber-tired wheels. il Am City 80:89 Jl '65

Worlds fair, 1967
Montreal touts Expo 67. il Bsns W p44+ Je 12 '65
Pavilion designs begin to shape Montreal exhibition. il Arch Rec 138:42-3 S '65

MONTREAL. University
We're nothing, but we want to be something; attitudes of students at University of Montreal, and McGill. R. Hoffmann. il Mlle 62: 155-7+ N '65

MONTREALER, The (periodical) See Periodicals—Canada

MONTRESOR, Beni
Caldecott award acceptance; address, July 6, 1965. Horn Bk 41:368-74 Ag '65

about
Beni Montresor. J. Karl. il por Library J 90:1465-7 Mr 15 '65
Beni Montresor. V. V. Varner. il pors Horn Bk 41:374-9 Ag '65
Newbery and Caldecott winners: Wojciechowska, Montresor. il por Pub W 187:27-8 Mr 8 '65
Newbery-Caldecott awards. por Wilson Lib Bul 39:627 Ap '65

MONUMENTS
See also
National monuments
Washington monument, Washington, D.C.
also subhead Monuments, statutes, etc. under names of cities, e.g. Washington, D.C.—Monuments, statues, etc.

MONYPENNY, Phillip
Interstate relations, some emergent trends. bibliog f Ann Am Acad 359:53-9 My '65

MOODY, Howard R.
Way-out minister of Washington square. L. Tornabene. il por N Y Times Mag p 116-17+ Je 6 '65

MOODY, Joseph
Insects: art class. Sch Arts 64:35 F '65

MOODY, Mark
Tactiles. P. Barron. il Design 67:24-6 S '65

MOODY, R. Bruce
Water; story. New Yorker 41:24-31 Je 26 '65

MOON, Eric
Benefit of the doubt; address, May 2, 1963. por Wilson Lib Bul 39:663-7+ Ap '65

about
Lj editor elected to Bowker board. por Library J 90:842 F 15 '65

MOON, Samuel
Dialogue of poets; What is love? Moment of turning; Composing an eclogue; Shape of space; poems. Poetry 105:366-70 Mr '65
Finding the lost world. Poetry 106:425-6 S '65

MOON
After the manned lunar landing? P. H. Abelson. Science 150:557 O 29 '65
Enigma of the moon, how did it get there? P. Stubbs. il N Y Times Mag p30-1+ Mr 28 '65
Kepler's dream, by J. Lear. Review
Nation 200:343-4 Mr 29 '65. W. Miller
Lighthearted moon. Time 85:57 Ap 30 '65
Meteorites and the moon. H. C. Urey. bibliog Science 147:1262-5 Mr 12 '65
Moon may give evidence on how stars are born. Sci N L 87:309 My 15 '65
Origin of the moon. H. Alfvén. bibliog Science 148:476-7 Ap 23 '65
Research in America; speculation about the makeup of the moon. J. Lear. il Sat R 48:54 My 1 '65
Sun, moon, and planets this month. See issues of Sky and telescope
See also
Moonlight
Space flight to the moon
Space vehicles—Landing systems—Moon
Tides

Anecdotes, facetiae, satire, etc.
Shunpiking on the moon. W. F. Miksch. il Atlan 215:176-7 Mr '65

Atlases
Fauth moon atlas. J. Ashbrook. il Sky & Tel 30:202+ O '65

Orbit
Moon's orbit computed. A. Ewing. il Sci N L 87:261 Ap 24 '65
New computation of moon's orbit. G. S. Mumford. Sky & Tel 31:25 Ja '66
Research in America; speculation about the makeup of the moon. J. Lear. il Sat R 48:54 My 1 '65

Photographs, maps, etc.
Australian scientist challenges interpretation of Ranger photos. Aviation W 83:59-60 S 6 '65
Can you see the moon in 3-D? L. Mallan. Pop Phot 57:52-5 S '65
In focus (cont) Sky & Tel 29:91+, 364+ F, Je '65
Lunar results from Rangers 7 to 9. G. P. Kuiper. bibliog Sky & Tel 29:293-308 My '65
Ranger 8 lunar photos appear to confirm Ranger 7 data. Aviation W 82:20-3 Mr 1 '65
Ranger 8 lunar reconnaissance. Sky & Tel 29:205-9 Ap '65
Ranger hits the spot with its moon photos. Bsns W p36-7 F 27 '65
Surveyor unit permits live TV broadcast from Ranger 9. H. D. Watkins. il Aviation W 82:26-7 Mr 29 '65
Zond-3 photographs of the moon's far side; tr. by M. P. Lopez-Morillas. Y. N. Lipsky. Sky & Tel 30:338-41 D '65
See also
Moon—Atlases

Surface
Australian scientist challenges interpretation of Ranger photos. Aviation W 83:59-60 S 6 '65
Better cratering extrapolation seen: simulation of moon's surface. il Miss & Roc 16: 23-4 Mr 1 '65
Icy-conglomerate moon. il Sky & Tel 29:143-4 Mr '65
IR studies show moon surface makeup varies. Miss & Roc 16:41 My 17 '65
Long night of selenography. J. Ashbrook. il Sky & Tel 29:92-4 F '65
Luminescence of the moon. Z. Kopal. il Sci Am 212:28-37 bibliog(p 150) My '65
Lunar blindness; porous layer of moon's crust. Time 86:91 N 19 '65
Lunar debate still rages despite Ranger; designs of LEM and Surveyor landing gear may be redesigned. Aviation W 82: 34 Ap 26 '65
Lunar experiments: the moon as a site for certain physical measurements. R. D. Hill. bibliog Science 151:195-6 Ja 14 '66
Lunar fossil tracks to answer many puzzles. Sci N L 88:89 Ag 7 '65
Lunar questions discussed at Pasadena. J. A. O'Keefe. il Sky & Tel 31:10-12 Ja '66
Lunar results from Rangers 7 to 9. G. P. Kuiper. bibliog il Sky & Tel 29:293-308 My '65
Lunar surface controversy rekindled. W. S. Beller. Miss & Roc 16:16 Ap 26 '65

MOON—Surface—*Continued*
Moon glow will aid in mapping. il Miss & Roc 16:25-6 Mr 1 '65
Moon has hot spots. Sci N L 87:197 Mr 27 '65
Moon miners to find many new obstacles. il(p97) Sci N L 88:102 Ag 14 '65
Moon still mysterious after Ranger photos. Sci N L 87:181 Mr 20 '65
Moon surface safe? il Sci N L 87:279 My 1 '65
Moon's skin. G. S. Mumford. Sky & Tel 29:345 Je '65
Observing the moon; Beer and Feuillée. A. K. Herring. il Sky & Tel 31:58 Ja '66
Observing the moon; Kepler. A. K. Herring. il Sky & Tel 30:50-1 Jl '65
Observing the moon, Milichius. A. K. Herring. il Sky & Tel 29:252 Ap '65
Observing the moon, Piton. A. K. Herring. il Sky & Tel 30:251 O '65
Radiation sintering of lunar dust. R. Smoluchowski. bibliog Science 150:1025-6 N 19 '65
Ranger 8 lunar photos appear to confirm Ranger 7 data. il Aviation W 82:20-3 Mr 1 '65
Ranger missions to the moon. H. M. Schurmeier and others. il Sci Am 214:52-67 bibliog(p 134-5) Ja '66
Ranger 9 data promises basic insights on lunar surface. H. D. Watkins. il Aviation W 82:84-9 Ap 5 '65
Ranger IX may shoot Surveyor site; with editorial comment. W. E. Wilks. il Miss & Roc 16:18+, 46 Mr 1 '65
Ranger program exceeds expectations. W. E. Wilks. il Miss & Roc 16:28+ Ap 5 '65
Ranger's answer. il Newsweek 65:56-7 Mr 8 '65
Rangers confirm moon landing areas. W. E. Wilks. Miss & Roc 16:22-3 Ap 12 '65
Ranger's-eye view. il Sci N L 87:149 Mr 6 '65
Research in America; Ranger 8 findings. J. Lear. il Sat R 48:47-8 Ap 3 '65
Rock degradation by alkali metals: a possible lunar erosion mechanism. J. J. Naughton and others. bibliog il Science 149:630-2 Ag 6 '65
Rock samples match lunar properties; upwelling or expanding magma in high order vacuums. J. F. Judge. il Miss & Roc 16:31 My 10 '65
Scan of eclipsed moon finds more hot spots. Aviation W 82:48+ F 8 '65
Scientists argue: what is the moon made of? B. H. Frisch. il Sci Digest 58:10-16 O '65
Surface of the moon; research of Grumman scientists. il Fortune 72:191-2 Jl '65
Tenuous surface layer on the moon: evidence derived from radar observations. T. Hagfors and others. bibliog il Science 150:1153-6 N 26 '65
Tests set to define landing hazard. W. E. Wilks. il Miss & Roc 17:36-7 D 20 '65
Unusual observation of Plato. A. K. Herring. il Sky & Tel 30:184 S '65
Via Ranger, rills and dimples: Ranger 8. il Newsweek 65:64-5 Mr 1 '65
What will the moon feel like? D. Cohen. il Sci Digest 57:30 My '65
Where a moon landing takes place every night: Arizona's Lunar & planetary lab. il Bsns W p68-70+ Ja 15 '66
Young craters best for landing on moon. il Sci N L 87:277 My 1 '65
Zond-3 photographs of the moon's far side; tr. by M. P. Lopez-Morillas. Y. N. Lipsky. il Sky & Tel 30:338-41 D '65

Temperature
Moon has hot spots. Sci N L 87:197 Mr 27 '65
Nonuniform cooling of the eclipsed moon: a listing of thirty prominent anomalies. R. W. Shorthill and J. M. Saari. bibliog il Science 150:210-12 O 8 '65

MOON, Distance to. See Astronomical distances
MOON, Flight to the. See Space flight to the moon
MOON bases. See Lunar bases
MOON jellyfish. See Jellyfish
MOON landing systems. See Space vehicles—Landing systems—Moon
MOON models. See Astronomical models
MOON probes. See Lunar probes
MOON vehicles. See Lunar vehicles
MOONEY, Stephen
After Selma; poem. New Repub 152:23 My 15 '65

MOONEY aircraft, incorporated
Mooney's air circus. R. Blodget. il Flying 77:53-9 D '65
Two new light twins planned by Mooney. E. J. Bulban. il Aviation W 83:101+ D 6 '65
MOONLIGHT
Luminescence of the moon. Z. Kopal. il Sci Am 212:28-37 bibliog(p 150) My '65
MOONLIGHT is when; drama. See Arthur, K.
MOONLIGHTING. See Supplementary employment
MOONSHINING
Moonshine war. il Time 85:72 Mr 12 '65
MOOR, Paul
Festive spring. Hi Fi 15:132 Ag '65
Hanze's The young lord. Hi Fi 15:132-3 Je '65
In Russia, music for May day. Hi Fi 15:120-1 Jl '65
Maazel era begins. Hi Fi 15:180+ D '65
Notes from our correspondents. Hi Fi 15:22+ Ap; 16+ Jl; 12+ S '65
Opera East and West. Hi Fi 15:86X-86Y Mr '65
Russian winter. Hi Fi 15:86R-86S Mr '65
Twentieth spring. Hi Fi 15:144-6 Ap '65
Upward swing. Hi Fi 15:126-7 My '65
MOORE, Barbara
Vietnam crisis: what happens when war separates a young family. W. C. Heinz. il por Ladies Home J 82:74-5+ S '65
MOORE, Bernice Milburn
Mothers, homemakers, and wage earners. NEA J 54:22-3 My '65
MOORE, Brian
Exile from the Emerald Isle. J. Ludwig. Nation 200:287-8 Mr 15 '65
MOORE, Carleton B.
Meteorites. Science 147:1061-2 F 26 '65
—and Lewis, Charles
Carbon abundances in chondritic meteorites. bibliog Science 149:317 Jl 16 '65
MOORE, Charles W.
In San Francisco, a renewal effort based on civic pride falls short of expectation. Arch Forum 123:58-63 Jl '65
San Francisco skyline: hard to spoil, but they're working on it. Arch Forum 123:40-7 N '65
MOORE, Clement Clarke
Night before Christmas; poem. Redbook 126:49-61 D '65
MOORE, Dan H.
Mammary tumor virus in mice. Science 147:1158-60 Mr 5 '65
—See Das Gupta, N. N. jt. auth.
MOORE, Det
Extra electric-plant benefits. Am City 80:187-8 Mr '65
MOORE, Dorothy Stanley
Family approach to regional planning. Nat Parks Mag 39:19 S '65
MOORE, Douglas
Vietnam crisis: what happens when war separates a young family. W. C. Heinz. il por Ladies Home J 82:74-5+ S '65
MOORE, Edward W. and Ross, J. W.
Cationic glass electrode response in aqueous solutions of sodium chloride and potassium chloride. bibliog Science 148:71-2 Ap 2 '65
MOORE, Emily C.
Approach to Mr Everest; letter. Am Heritage 16:112 Ap '65
MOORE, Everett T.
Library burns in the Los Angeles riot; report. ALA Bul 59:983-6 D '65
MOORE, Francis D.
Ethics in new medicine: tissue transplants. Nation 200:358-62 Ap 5 '65
MOORE, George
Yankee 300. Motor T 17:73-5 Jl '65
MOORE, Harry T.
Boy who played the Bard. Sat R 48:61+ O 23 '65
Far lands and fairy tales. Sat R 49:31 Ja 8 '66
Time pardons him for writing well. Sat R 48:39+ D 11 '65
While revolutions came and went. Sat R 48:76 My 22 '65
MOORE, Henry
(ed) Gist of it. See Issues of Outdoor life
MOORE, Henry Spencer
Henry Moore, sculptor. Harper 230:59-61 Ap '65
Heroic bather. il Time 86:60 S 3 '65
Profiles. D. Hall. New Yorker 41:66-8+ D 11; 59-60+ D 18 '65
MOORE, Hubert D.
Teacher's right arm. Library J 90:1984-6 Ap 15 '65
MOORE, Hugh L.
Current-limiting power supply. Electr World 74:85 O '65

MOORE, I. M. See Craig, J. B. jt. auth.
MOORE, Irene
Ladies launch a gallery. Am For 71:22-5 Mr '65
(ed) See Janel, E. Lumberjack artist
MOORE, Jack
Mary Anthony; Jack Moore and companies. East 74th street theatre. J. Maskey. Dance Mag 40:18 Ja '66
MOORE, James W.
Moore on movies. See issues of U.S. camera & travel
MOORE, Lillian
La Sylphide. Dance Mag 39:42-7 Mr '65
What's different about the Danes? Dance Mag 39:44-9 O '65
MOORE, Marianne
Dream; poem. New Yorker 41:52 O 16 '65
Interview with Marianne Moore; ed. by D. Hall. pors McCalls 93:74+ D '65
Mind, intractable thing; poem. New Yorker 41:60 N 27 '65
MOORE, Mary Louise
Freedom; poem. Negro Hist Bul 28:85 Ja '65
MOORE, Mary Tyler
How to succeed though married. por Time 85:62 Ap 9 '65
MOORE, Mette Christina
When grandma was a girl. Parents Mag 40:54+ Jl '65
MOORE, Omar Khayyam
Omar Khayyam and his talking typewriter. C. P. Gilmore. il por Sat Eve Post 238:40-1 N 20 '65
MOORE, Paul, Jr, bp
Bishop Moore: a leader of the new breed. por Newsweek 65:77 Mr 29 '65
MOORE, Richard
Poet who needs his poem. Sat R 48:29-31 D 25 '65
Willy; poem. Reporter 33:43 Ag 12 '65
Winter reflections; poem. Atlan 216:80 D '65
MOORE, Sam
Life radio review. Life 59:22 N 12 '65
Life review. Life 58:12 Ap 9 '65
MOORE, Theodore C. Jr. See Heath, G. R. jt. auth.
MOORE, Thomas
Secrets of good brazing. Pop Sci 186:150-3+ Ap '65
MOORE, Thomas W.
Picture pointers. Motor B 115:26-31+ My '65
MOORE, Truman
Slaves for rent: the shame of American farming; excerpt from Slaves we rent. por Atlan 215:109-22 My '65
MOORE, W. M.
Tepee refuse burner has extension dome. Am City 80:165 Ag '65
MOORE-McCormack line. See Steamship lines
MOOREHEAD, Alan
Procession marches through history he had made. Life 58:29-31 F 5 '65
MOOREHEAD, Lucy
Taking the cure at Montecatini. Vogue 146:47+ S 15 '65
MOORER, Thomas Hinman
Admiral Moorer appointed Supreme allied commander, Atlantic. Dept State Bul 52:299 Mr 1 '65
Three hats for a hero. por Time 85:21 F 26 '65
MOORHEAD, Jennelle
Danger of extremism. por NEA J 54:17 S '65
For the world's children. PTA Mag 60:16-19 N '65
Key is cooperation. por Sr Schol 87:sup9 O 21 '65
President's message. See issues of PTA magazine

about

John Birch versus PTA. Nation 200:156 F 15 '65
MOORHEAD, William S.
H.R. 334; text of bill. Sch & Soc 93:214-18 Ap 3 '65
Legislation to create a national foundation for the arts and humanities. Sch & Soc 93:256-7 Ap 17 '65
MOORING of boats. See Boats—Mooring
MOOSE
His magnificence, the moose. J. D. Scott. il Read Digest 87:118-22 O '65
MOOSE hunting
Blood in his eye. H. J. Lowry. il Outdoor Life 136:28-9+ S '65
Holiday moose hunt. B. Cary. il Outdoor Life 136:29-31+ D '65
Moose in a blind alley; Newfoundland swamp. C. E. Priddle. il Outdoor Life 137:28-31+ Ja '66
Thirty-minute moose. R. Starnes. il Field & S 70:29-31+ Ag '65

MOOTZ, William
In the Bluegrass: music new and old. Hi Fi 15:155+ O '65
MORA, Douglas Bravo
Bravo and his boys; Venezuela's Castro-inspired armed forces of national liberation. M. J. Kubic. Newsweek 66:47 Jl 5 '65
MORA, José A.
Foundations for tomorrow. Américas 17:1-3 Ap '65
Recommendations of Secretary General; address, 1965. Américas 17:40-1 D '65
Secretary General's report. Américas 17:44 My '65
MORA, Peter T. and others
Reduction-like effect of carbohydrates on cytochrome c. bibliog Science 149:642-4 Ag 6 '65
MORAES, Frank
Indian looks at Africa. T. Sterling. Reporter 32:55+ Mr 25 '65
MORAINES
Late-Wisconsin end moraines in northern Canada. G. Falconer and others. bibliog il Science 147:608-10 F 5 '65
MORAL attitudes
Hard lesson for the law. M. L. Schwartz. Sat R 48:35-7+ N 13 '65
Love in place of law? gathering at Harvard divinity school to ponder the new morality and its significance for the church. Time 85:42 Mr 5 '65
Man, morals and maturity; excerpt from Sin, sex and self-control. N. V. Peale. Read Digest 87:253-6+ O '65
Morality of nations; address, June 6, 1965. L. B. Johnson. Dept State Bul 52:1026-9 Je 28 '65
Notes on the Toronto teach-in: the irrelevance of morality. R. H. Welker. il Nation 201:301-4 N 1 '65
Toward a new sexual morality? R. A. McCormick. Cath World 202:10-16 O '65
MORAL codes. See Ethics
MORAL conditions
Are student moral values slipping? round-table discussion from 1965 student burgesses at Williamsburg. il Sr Schol 86:14-16+ Ap 29 '65
MORAL education
Developing durable values; with study-discussion program, by E. Harris and D. Harris. D. Graves. bibliog il PTA Mag 60:10-12, 35 D '65
See also
Honesty
MORAL philosophy. See Ethics
MORAL rearmament
Breakthrough for peace? H. E. Fey. Christian Cent 82:1119 S 15 '65
M.R.A: the new Druseanism. M. E. Marty. Christian Cent 82:399-401 Mr 31 '65
MRA's new crisis. America 112:347 Mr 13 '65
Morally rearmed? W. Peabody. Christian Cent 82:756 Je 9 '65
MORAL sense. See Ethics
MORAL theology. See Christian ethics
MORAL values. See Worth
MORALE, National

Europe, Western
Vietnam, LBJ, good times: what Europeans are saying. il U S News 59:70-4 Ag 9 '65

United States
America's mood today. L. Gross. il Look 29:15-21 Je 29 '65
Changing mood of America; what a nation-wide survey shows. il U S News 58:36-43 My 31 '65
I'm glad I tried to help! ed. by L. David. V. A. McNeil. il Good H 160:92-3+ Ap '65
Nation apathetic. Nation 200:321-2 Mr 29 '65
MORALES, Henry
From their hands, a feast. por Am Ed 1:1-5 N '65
MORALES, Herbert
Diffusing knowledge among men. Am Ed 1:1-5 S '65
MORALITY. See Ethics
MORALS. See Ethics
MORALS and law. See Law and ethics
MORALS and literature. See Literature and morals
MORALS and war. See War—Moral aspects
MORAN, Ronald
So simply means the rain; poem. Commonweal 82:526 Jl 23 '65

MORAN, William E. Jr
National population policy. Cath World 202: 138-43 D '65

MORANDI, Gianni
Show on the road. il Newsweek 66:63 Jl 26 '65

MORANDI, Riccardo
Bridges that span three continents. il por Fortune 72:154-7 N '65

MORANT, Ricardo B. and Beller, H. K.
Adaptation to prismatically rotated visual fields. bibliog Science 148:530-1 Ap 23 '65

MORAVIA, Alberto
When art becomes propaganda; excerpt from Man as an end. Sat R 48:23-5+ Ap 17 '65

about

Born to suffer and to serve. C. Simmons. Sat R 49:40 Ja 22 '66

MORAVIAN church in the United States
Moravians of Salem. C. Davis. il Antiques 88:60-4 Jl '65

MORAVIANS
Moravians of Salem. C. Davis. il Antiques 88:60-4 Jl '65

MORAY, Ann
Celtic heritage in Ireland. Horizon 7:32-9 Spr '65

MORE, Paul Elmore
Paul Elmer More: the Nation's conservative editor. F. X. Duggan. por Nation 200:248-51 Mr 8 '65

MORE, Sir Thomas, Saint
Born for friendship, by B. Bassett. Review Cath World 202:187-8 D '65. G. Blatt
Wanted: more men for all seasons, and women too. G. Blatt. Cath World 201:56-61 Ap '65

MORE the merrier; story. See Boyd, C.

MOREA. See Peloponnesus

MOREAU, Jeanne
Les girls in Mexico. il pors Life 58:53-4+ Ap 2 '65
Jeanne Moreau. M. Duras. por Vogue 146: 100-1+ N 15 '65
Jeanne Moreau: death, suffering, love. C. R. Jennings. il pors Sat Eve Post 238:86-8 Ap 10 '65
Making the most of love. il pors Time 85:78-83 Mr 5 '65
Name is Moreau (not Bardot) L. Collins and D. Lapierre. il pors N Y Times Mag p46-7+ Mr 21 '65
On the set with Moreau and Bardot. C. Brossard. il pors Look 29:64-6+ My 4 '65

MORELIA, Mexico
Going places, finding things in Michoacán, Mexico. E. Sheridan. il House & Gard 128: 60+ S '65

MORELLO, Ted
New world of teaching machines or Brave new teaching machines? UNESCO Courier 18:10-16 Mr '65

MORENO, Frank Jay
Latin America: the fear within. Yale R 55: 161-8 D '65

MORENO, Hugo, and others
Photometry at Cerro Tololo, Chile: effects of Mount Agung eruption. bibliog Science 148:364-6 Ap 16 '65

MORENO, Rita
Getting out from under an image. A. Bermel. il Harper 230:38+ Ap '65

MOREY, Marion
New for your home. Pop Mech 124:116-17 Ag; 144-5 N; 116-17 D '65; 125:140-1 Ja '66

MORGAN, Charles, Jr
Freedom to read and racial problems; address, January 1965. por ALA Bul 59:484-90 Je '65

about

Opening a second front. por Newsweek 66: 33-4 N 8 '65

MORGAN, Charlie
Another Morgan sails the sea for treasure. H. Whall. il por Sports Illus 22:72+ Mr 22 '65

MORGAN, Derek
Absolutely ripping! Reporter 33:54-5 N 18 '65
When the cows came home. Reporter 32:41-2 My 20 '65

MORGAN, Franke
You know how it is with a mother. Good H 160:160 F '65

MORGAN, J. P., and company. See Morgan guaranty trust company

MORGAN, John
Older than the U.S. Constitution. H. Earl. il Todays Health 43:38-40+ N '65

MORGAN, Murray
College-bred fish for man's delight. Harper 231:47-51 Jl '65; Same abr. Read Digest 87:193-5+ O '65
Most powerful governor in the U.S.A. Harper 231:98+ O '65

MORGAN, Neal
State as a campus. Holiday 38:78-9+ O '65
WLB biography (cont) Wilson Lib Bul 39: 695, 920 Ap, Je '65

MORGAN, Thomas B.
American war game. Esquire 64:71-2+ O '65
He wants to keep his people steeped in struggle. Life 58:63-4+ F 12 '65
Julie, baby. Look 29:47-51+ D 28 '65

MORGAN, Thomas Ellsworth
Bedside manner. por Time 85:18 Je 4 '65

MORGAN, William
Starting a successful practice. il Arch Rec 138:133-42 Jl '65

MORGAN guaranty trust company
Banking the blue chips. Time 85:94+ My 14 '65
New master at Morgan; T. S. Gates to be chairman and chief executive officer. Newsweek 65:74+ My 17 '65

MORGANTI, Helen
Putting out the school newspaper. NEA J 54: 41-2 Mr '65

MORGENSTERN, Joseph
Lovey. Criticism
New Yorker 41:86+ Ap 3 '65

MORGENTHAU, Hans J.
Globalism; Johnson's moral crusade. New Repub 153:19-22 Jl 3 '65
International relations, 1960-1964. bibliog f Ann Am Acad 360:163-71 Jl '65
Jewish declaration. Commonweal 83:142-4 N 5 '65
Russia, the US and Vietnam. New Repub 152:12-13 My 1 '65
Stevenson, tragedy and greatness. New Repub 153:17-19 Ag 7 '65
Talk is for TV. Sat R 48:48 Ag 28 '65
U.N. of Dag Hammarskjöld is dead. N Y Times Mag p32-3+ Mr 14 '65
Vietnam crisis and China. Bul Atomic Sci 21:27 Je '65
War with China? New Repub 152:11-14 Ap 3 '65
We are deluding ourselves in Vietnam. N Y Times Mag p24-5+ Ap 18 '65
Where consensus breaks down. New Repub 154:16-18 Ja 22 '66

about

Politics in the twentieth century, by H. J. Morgenthau. Review
Bul Atomic Sci 21:36-7 Ap '65. Q. Howe.

MORGENTHAU, Henry, 1891-
From the Morgenthau diaries: years of urgency, 1938-1941, by J. M. Blum. Review
Harper 230:118+ F '65. J. M. Burns
New Repub 152:25-6 F 20 '65. A. Kopkind

MORGENTHAU, Henry, 3d
Undercover job. R. L. Shayon. Sat R 48:50 Jl 24 '65

MORI, Hanae
Ah, sew. il por Newsweek 67:50-1 Ja 3 '66

MORIARTY brothers
Moriarty's wonderful saloon. L. Beebe. il Am Heritage 16:65-9+ Ag '65

MORILLAS, Martin P. Lopez-. See Lopez-Morillas, M. P.

MORIN, Milt
Caught in the draught. H. L. Masin. por Sr Schol 87:40 N 11 '65

MORISON, Samuel Eliot
PPA press conference: summary. por Pub W 187:41-3 Mr 22 '65
Sons of liberty; excerpt from The Oxford history of the American people. por Read Digest 87:281-6+ N '65

about

Elder of the tribe. por Newsweek 65:100+ Ap 26 '65

MORKOS, Joanne
Sponge painting. Design 66:33 My '65

MORLEY, Charles
(comp) Articles and other books received; eastern Europe. See issues of American historical review

MORLEY, Christopher Darlington
Singular set of people. Watson. W. S. Baring-Gould. il Esquire 65:92-5+ Ja '66

MORLEY, Felix
Trends: the state of the Nation. See issues of Nation's business

MORLEY, Robert
Morley view of sport. pors Sports Illus 22: 52+ Ap 26 '65
Redbook dialogue: Mary Hemingway and Robert Morley. pors Redbook 126:62-3+ N '65

MORLINO, Vito J. See Martin, R. B. jt. auth.

MORMONS and Mormonism
Mormon genealogical library establishing branch system. Library J 90:1853-4 Ap 15 '65

Mormon missionaries and the race question; condemned by NAACP. G. W. Davidson. Christian Cent 82:1183-6 S 29 '65; Discussion. 82:1452 N 24 '65

Serendipity; camping trip with thirty teen-agers. P. L. Jones. il Sr Schol 86:sup24-5 Ap 15 '65

She who shall be nameless. M. Cable. il Am Heritage 16:50-5 F '65

Unique gospel in Utah; religious and civil doctrines of Church of Jesus Christ of Latter-day saints. D. L. Foster. Christian Cent 82:890-2 Jl 14 '65; Discussion 82:1041 Ag 25 '65

MORMONS and Mormonism, Negro
Black saints of Nigeria. Time 85:56 Je 18 '65

Saints and race. Christian Cent 82:756 Je 9 '65

MORNING glories
Glory in the morning. R. C. Hands. il Horticulture 43:24-5 S '65

Soon as high as an elephant's eye. il Sunset 134:269 Mr '65

MORO, Aldo
United States and Italy reaffirm close ties of friendship; greetings, April 20, 1965. Dept State Bul 52:810-11 My 24 '65

MOROCCO
See also
Moulay Idris
Natural resources—Morocco

Description and travel
In Morocco, a new pocket of tranquility. D. Messinesi. Vogue 146:178 S 1 '65
Morocco: Marrakech and South; with report by M. Leatherbee. il Life 58:64-74+ Mr 19 '65

Foreign relations
Bridge over the River Kiss. il Time 85:42 My 21 '65
J'accuse! chill into Franco-Moroccan relations following Barka kidnaping. Time 86:54 N 19 '65

History
Morocco. I. W. Zartman. bibliog il Focus 15:1-6 F '65

Politics and government
Morocco's troubled young king. C. Sterling. il Reporter 32:21-5 Je 17 '65
Royal premier. il Time 85:31B Je 18 '65
Shaking the throne; French press points to Gen. M. Oufkir, as instigator of Ben Barka plot. Newsweek 66:39 N 29 '65
Voice of the mob. il Time 85:28-9 Ap 9 '65

Riots
Against the tide. Newsweek 65:52 Ap 12 '65

MOROSOV, Ivan Abramovich
Celebrated choices of Ivan Morosov. il por(p44) Life 58:45-8 Ap 9 '65

MORPHINE
How opiates change behavior. J. R. Nichols. il Sci Am 212:80-6+ bibliog(p 135) F '65

MORPHOGENESIS. See Morphology

MORPHOLOGY
Collagenase: effect on the morphogenesis of embryonic salivary epithelium in vitro. C. Grobstein and J. Cohen. bibliog il Science 150:626-8 O 29 '65
Morphogenetic effects of 6-azauracil and 6-azauridine. R. M. Rizki and T. M. Rizki. bibliog il Science 150:222-3 O 8 '65

MORRIS, Andrea
Andrea: a nurse who cares. A. Lake. il pors Ladies Home J 82:74-5+ Ag '65

MORRIS, Arval A.
McCarran act: new lease on malignancy. Nation 200:295-9 Mr 22 '65

MORRIS, Eddie, and Stewart, Paul
How to float the fluff. il Sports Illus 23:61-5 N 15 '65

MORRIS, Everett
Lifetime contribution. B. Robinson. por Yachting 117:60+ Mr '65
Vineyard race. Yachting 118:173-5 O '65

MORRIS, George L. K.
Knaths and Morris in Washington. F. Getlein. New Repub 152:30-1 My 15 '65

MORRIS, Ivan
Theatre (cont) Vogue 145:95 Mr 1; 68 Je; 38 Jl; 146:179 S 1 '65

MORRIS, Ivan I.
Soka Gakkai brings absolute happiness. N Y Times Mag p8-9+ Jl 18 '65

MORRIS, James, 1926-
In praise of a folly. Horizon 7:16-19 Sum '65
Oxford's magnificent oddballs. Harper 231:69-74 N '65
Speaking out. por Sat Eve Post 238:10+ Jl 3 '65
Two worlds of Princess Margaret. Sat Eve Post 238:27-31 N 20 '65
Unquiet genius of Egypt. por Atlan 216:126-30+ O '65
Violent past. Holiday 37:68-9+ Ap '65

MORRIS, James, 1938?-
Ambush. il Esquire 64:76-7+ Ag '65

MORRIS, Joe Alex
Royal Oak aids its problem youth. Read Digest 87:163-7 O '65

MORRIS, Jonus V.
House cleaning. Nation 200:600 My 31 '65

MORRIS, Joseph B.
How two janitors bought white bank in Texas. L. Robinson. il pors Ebony 20:119-22+ Je '65

MORRIS, Monique Peer-. See Peer-Morris, M.

MORRIS, Norval
Reflections on gaols. Nation 201:168-9+ S 27 '65

MORRIS, Richard B.
Americans loyal to the crown. Sat R 48:30-1 D 18 '65
Paradoxical pragmatist. Sat R 48:63 N 13 '65

MORRIS, Robert
Unexpected assemblage! D. McDonagh. il por Dance Mag 39:42-5+ Je '65
Yvonne Rainer and Robert Morris, Judson memorial church. J. Maskey. Dance Mag 39:64 My '65

MORRIS, Roger
Russia's stake in Vietnam. New Repub 152:13-15 F 13 '65
Saturday in Suzdal. Reporter 33:42+ Jl 15 '65

MORRIS, Taylor
Retreat from the sea; story. New Yorker 41:45-53 My 22 '65

MORRIS, Terry
Boy who redeemed his father's name. Redbook 125:86-7+ O '65; Same abr. Read Digest 88:107-11 Ja '66

MORRIS, Willie
(ed) South today. Harper 230:126-84+ Ap '65

MORRISON, Allan
Adam Powell returns to Harlem. Ebony 20:80-2+ Jl '65
New look for the Urban league. Ebony 21:164-6+ N '65
White power structure. Ebony 20:141-4+ Ag '65
Who killed Malcolm X? Ebony 20:135-6+ O '65

MORRISON, Jack S.
Building tomorrow's audience. por Am Ed 1:24-7 O '65

MORRISON, Lillian
Ode to extremities; poem. Atlan 215:145 Ap '65

MORRISON, Morton
Darkroom on a shoestring. U S Camera 28:64-5+ O '65
Films & formats, where are we headed? U S Camera 28:55-7+ My '65
Should you join a camera club? U S Camera 29:24+ Ja '66
Think wide. U S Camera 28:54-5+ Ap '65

MORRISON, Norman
Drop the baby. Newsweek 66:44+ N 15 '65
Fiery pangs of conscience. L. Wainwright. Life 59:34 N 12 '65
Giving and taking one's life. Christian Cent 82:1404 N 17 '65; Discussion. 83:84 Ja 19 '66
Immolations in U.S. Sr Schol 87:15 D 2 '65
In witness to man's oneness. B. Reynolds. Christian Cent 83:81 Ja 19 '66
Pacifists. il por Time 86:68 N 12 '65

MORRISON, Philip
Books. Sci Am 213:257-8+ S '65
Mandate of heaven. Nation 200:339-41 Mr 29 '65

MORRISSEY, deRosset
Our girl at the White House. G. P. Hunt. il por Life 59:3 Ag 13 '65

MORRISSEY, Francis Joseph Xavier
As showdown came on a Kennedy aide. il por U S News 59:23 N 1 '65
From pillory to post. por Time 86:24-5 O 22 '65
How judges are made. New Repub 153:5-6 O 23 '65
Is loyalty enough? Newsweek 66:32 O 25 '65
Kennedy backs away. New Repub 153:7 O 30 '65
Kennedy friend rebuffed. Sr Schol 87:9 N 11 '65
Last days of Congress. W. V. Shannon. Commonweal 83:140-2 N 5 '65

MORRISSEY, Francis Joseph Xavier—*Cont.*
Lowering the bench. New Repub 153:6 O 9 '65
LBJ and Edward Kennedy: their nominee under fire. il por U S News 59:16 O 11 '65
Make it deadpan, make it factual; investigative journalism in Morrissey case. Time 86:57-8 O 29 '65
Morrissey case. R. Moley. Newsweek 66:100 N 1 '65
One for Old Joe. il por Newsweek 66:33-4 O 11 '65
Profile in brinkmanship. Time 86:28-9 O 29 '65
Report on Washington. Atlan 216:13 D '65
Sergeant's reward. il por Time 86:33-4 O 8 '65
Too high a price. il por Newsweek 66:23-4 N 1 '65

MORROW, Sherman L.
In crowd and the out crowd. N Y Times Mag p 12-14+ Jl 18 '65

MORROW, Susan
Promise; story. Good H 160:94-5 My '65

MORSE, Carl
Agile man who built Third avenue. il pors Fortune 71:145-6 My '65

MORSE, David A.
Industrial relations in the next decade; address, October 13, 1965. Vital Speeches 32:60-4 N 1 '65

MORSE, F. Bradford
Third annual meeting of Inter-American economic and social council. Dept State Bul 52:640-3 Ap 26 '65

MORSE, Gerry E.
Pendulum of management control; adaptation of address, February 10, 1965. bibliog Harvard Bsns R 43:158-60+ My '65

MORSE, Grant A.
There soars the condor. Am For 71:22-4+ F '65

MORSE, Ralph
Story of a photograph. G. P. Hunt. il Life 60:3, 22-33 Ja 7 '66

MORSE, Robert
Brand-new baby for the U.N. Life 59:65+ Ag 20 '65
I could hear their cries and it was terrible. Life 59:119 O 15 '65

MORSE, Samuel French
Ends and means. Poetry 105:404-9 Mr '65
Remembering the innocents; poem. Horn Bk 41:601 D '65
Speaking to the imagination. Horn Bk 41:255-9 Je '65

about
Three poets. M. McCloskey. Poetry 107:126-7 N '65

MORSE, Wayne
Excerpt from address, January 15, 1965. Cong Digest 44:174+ Je '65
Excerpt from address, January 6, 1965. Cong Digest 44:111+ Ap '65
Excerpt from debate, August 30, 1965. Cong Digest 44:245+ O '65
Protests against Vietnam policy; address, October 19, 1965. Vital Speeches 32:74-8 N 15 '65

MORSE, Wilbur A.
What a perfect friendship. G. Weller. il Sports Illus 22:42-6 Je 21 '65

MORSE, William B.
Ann Webb, girl forester. Am For 71:28-9+ Ap '65
Old men and tired legs. il Am For 71:38-41 S '65

MORSELL, John A.
National association for the advancement of colored people and its strategy. Ann Am Acad 357:97-101 Ja '65

MORTENSEN, W. F.
Water bills serve as information medium. Am City 80:138+ D '65

MORTGAGE guarantee insurance corporation
How home loans are guaranteed. il Changing T 19:26 D '65

MORTGAGES
Beware this get-out-of-debt scheme; 2nd mortgage financing. il Changing T 19:29-30 F '65
Facts about second mortgages for homeowners. il Good H 161:146 Ag '65
Living high on the old homestead; refinancing mortgages. il Bsns W p47-8 Ap 24 '65
Ways to finance a vacation home. il Sunset 134:146-8+ Je '65
What home loans cost now. il Changing T 19:24 Ag '65
See also
United States—Federal housing administration

MORTICIANS. See Undertakers and undertaking

MORTILLITO, Domenico
New medium for sculpture. pors Am Artist 29:44-9+ D '65

MORTIMER, Charles G.
Purposeful pursuit of profits and growth in business; address, April 7, 1965. Vital Speeches 31:636-40 Ag 1 '65

about
It's the men up front that count. il Bsns W p73-5 My 1 '65

MORTISE and tenon joints. See Joints (carpentry)

MORTON, Charles W.
Accent on living. See issues of Atlantic
How to tell a fishing story. Read Digest 87:201-2 Jl '65
Magazine of the year. Atlan 215:62-3 F '65
Solo in Wyoming. Atlan 217:91-102 Ja '66
Working for the government. por Atlan 215:105-14 Je '65

MORTON, Donald
That stardust malady. il Time 86:67 Jl 16 '65

MORTON, Frederic
Palace in St Moritz. Holiday 38:76-7+ N '65

MORTON, Syria
We are legion. il por PTA Mag 59:21 F '65

MORTON, W. W., and company, incorporated
Some welcome fresh air in the subsidiary rights field; 50-50 royalty split. R. H. Smith. Pub W 188:45 N 29 '65

MORTON salt company
When it rains, it shines. il Time 85:96 My 7 '65

MOSAICS
City; stained glass wall panel. M. L. Miller. il Sch Arts 65:14-15 O '65
Do-it-yourself wood mosaics. il Design 67:9 S '65
Group mosaics by elementary students. I. Beaudoin. il Design 66:16-18 Mr '65
Mosaic art. L. Argiro. il Sch Arts 64:10-14 Je '65
Mosaics take the floor. J. Lerman. il Recreation 58:246-7 My '65
Mosaics with eggshells. T. Sasano. il Design 66:13-15 Ja '65
See also
Tiles

MOSAICS, Genetic. See Variegation

MOSBY, Aline
Moscow: Tolstoy and troika rides. Sat R 49:51+ Ja 1 '66

MOSCONA, A. A. and Kirk, D. L.
Control of glutamine synthetase in the embryonic retina in vitro. bibliog Science 148:519-21 Ap 23 '65

MOSCONI, Willie
Return of Willie. il por Time 86:59 O 8 '65

MOSCOW
Western village in Moscow. J. Wolfenden. il N Y Times Mag p21+ F 7 '65

Airports
Domodedovo airport integrates surface transit; photographs. Aviation W 83:52-3 S 13 '65

Description
Moment of history; trip to Moscow for signing of nuclear test ban treaty. M. F. B. Humphrey. McCalls 92:57+ Jl '65
Moscow: Tolstoy and troika rides. A. Mosby. il Sat R 49:51+ Ja 1 '66
Wan cold of a bright sight. L. Wainwright. Life 58:28 F 19 '65

Hotels, restaurants, etc.
Up in Ivan's room; Hotel Ukraina. J. Carroll. Holiday 38:62-3+ D '65

Music
David and Isaac: joint concert by I. Stern and D. Oistrakh. Newsweek 65:102 My 10 '65
Notes from our correspondents. P. Moor. Hi Fi 15:22+ Ap '65
Russian winter. P. Moor. il Hi Fi 15:86R-86S Mr '65

Riots
Anti-U.S. riots. Commonweal 81:776 Mr 19 '65
Down with the Cossacks! Moscow students protest against the U.S. air raids on North Viet Nam. il Time 85:24-5 Mr 12 '65
New tool; Moscow students protest U.S. air attacks on North Vietnam. il Newsweek 65:46+ Mr 15 '65
New twist to anti-U.S. riots: reds vs. reds. il U S News 58:11 Mr 15 '65
U.S. embassies are under siege. il Life 58:38-9 Mr 19 '65

Theater
See also
Moscow art theatre

MOSCOW art theatre
Lively visitors. H. Hewes. Sat R 48:43 F 20 '65
MATmen; visit to New York. il Newsweek 65:84 F 15 '65
Moscow art theatre. H. Clurman. Nation 200: 235-6, 291-2 Mr 1, 15 '65
Moscow art theatre. H. Popkin. Vogue 145:59 Mr 15 '65
Moscow art theatre; surprises after Stanislavski. G. Rogoff. il Reporter 32:49-50 Mr 25 '65
Off Broadway; performance of Chekhov's Cherry orchard. E. Oliver. New Yorker 41: 54+ F 20 '65
Off Broadway; performance of Chekhov's Three sisters. E. Oliver. New Yorker 41: 96+ F 27 '65
Off Broadway; performance of Dead souls. E. Oliver. New Yorker 40:76+ F 13 '65
Off Broadway; performance of Pogodin's Kremlin chimes. E. Oliver. New Yorker 41: 80+ Mr 6 '65
Russian evenings; New York visit. R. Brustein. New Repub 152:26-8 F 27 '65
Stanislavsky's ghosts. il Time 85:78 F 12 '65
Yellowed pages; New York visit. Newsweek 65:93-4 F 22 '65
MOSCOW film festival. See Moving picture festivals
MOSCOW philharmonic orchestra
Flying high; first visit to America. il Newsweek 66:89 N 1 '65
Moscow philharmonic; New York concerts. A. Chasins. Hi Fi 16:131+ Ja '66
Music to my ears; concerts in Carnegie Hall. I. Kolodin. Sat R 48:71 O 30 '65
Musical events; concerts in Carnegie Hall. W. Sargeant. New Yorker 41:149 O 23; 137-8+ O 30 '65
Pursuing the U.S. ideal. Time 86:71 O 29 '65
MOSCOW small displacement automobile plant. See Automobile industry and trade—Russia
MOSER, Charles M. and Bester, J. F.
Anesthetize pest birds. Am City 80:30+ My '65
MOSER, Don
Brute Krulak of the marines. Life 58:77-8+ Ap 30 '65
Eight dedicated men marked for death. Life 59:30-3+ S 3 '65
Nightmare of life with Billy. Life 58:96+ My 7 '65
There's no easy place to pin the blame. Life 59:30-3 Ag 27 '65
Where will the bullet come from? pors Life 58:32-5+ Mr 12 '65
MOSER, Lida
Excitement on 20th street. il Dance Mag 39: 30-1 N '65
MOSES, Robert
Two for SNCC; interviews, excerpts from Who speaks for the Negro? ed. by R. P. Warren. Commentary 39:38-42 Ap '65
MOSES, Robert, 1888-
Fair fights back on financing. Bsns W p34+ Ja 30 '65
NYPL restrictions on Moses' papers queried in Herald tribune report; summary. J. Zukosky. Library J 90:1088+ Mr 1 '65
There's no business like no business. G. Ace. Sat R 48:12 My 29 '65
MOSES and Aaron; opera. See Schönberg, A.
MOSHER, Charles A.
Invitation to revolt; address. Vital Speeches 31:596-8 Jl 15 '65
Scientists and congressmen; address, August 17, 1965. Vital Speeches 31:709-13 S 15 '65
MOSKOWITZ, Audrey A. See Moskowitz, M. S. jt. auth.
MOSKOWITZ, Merle S. and Moskowitz, A. A.
Lipase: localization in adipose tissue. bibliog Science 149:72-3 Jl 2 '65
MOSKOWITZ, Saul
Instruments for the new celestial navigation. Sky & Tel 30:348-51 D '65
MOSKVICH-408. See Automobile industry and trade—Russia
MOSLEM brotherhood
Plot to kill Nasser. il Time 86:53 S 17 '65
MOSLEMS. See Muslims
MOSQUES
Mosque for tomorrow; Malaysia's National mosque. il Time 86:70-3 O 8 '65
MOSQUITOES
Dimorphic development of transplanted juvenile gonads of mosquitoes. J. F. Anderson and W. R. Horsfall. bibliog il Science 147:624-5 F 5 '65
Mosquito-proof man. il Sci Digest 58:32-3 N '65
Repellency of skin-surface lipids of humans to mosquitoes. W. A. Skinner and others. il Science 149:305 Jl 16 '65

Extermination
Yellow fever, a new airborne threat. D. A. Dukelow and R. Alden. il Todays Health 43:30-1+ Mr '65
See also
Malaria—Prevention and control
MOSQUITOES as carriers of infection
Anopheles balabacensis balabacensis identified as vector of simian malaria in Malaysia. W. H. Cheong and others. bibliog Science 150:1314-15 D 3 '65
Dengue type 2 virus in naturally infected aedes albopictus mosquitoes in Singapore. A. Rudnick and Y. C. Chan. bibliog il Science 149:638-9 Ag 6 '65
Mosquito gives cancer. F. Marley Sci N L 87:371 Je 12 '65
Mosquito transmission of a reticulum cell sarcoma of hamsters. W. G. Banfield and others. bibliog il Science 148:1239-40 My 28 '65
MOSS, Don
Champ for all time!!! R. H. Boyle. il Sports Illus 22:120-4+ Ap 19 '65
MOSS, Frank T.
Summer fishing in the Bahamas. il Yachting 117:102-4+ Je '65
Yachtsmen and marine science. il Yachting 117:44-5+ F '65
MOSS, Howard
Breakwater; poem. New Yorker 41:42 F 20 '65
Fall; poem. New Yorker 40:32 F 6 '65
History; poem. Sat R 48:58 Mr 6 '65
In Colorado; poem. New Yorker 41:50 Ap 3 '65
Lu; poem. Christian Cent 82:643 My 19 '65
Robinson; poem. New Yorker 41:42 Mr 13 '65
Semblances; poem. Harper 230:77 Mr '65
Tree surgeon in New York; poem. New Repub 152:19 Ap 10 '65
MOSS, Leonard
Hammett's heroic operative. New Repub 154: 32-4 Ja 8 '66
MOSS, Norman
Building a shrine for disarmament. Reporter 33:33-5 O 7 '65
Where have all the young men gone? Sat R 48:26-7+ Ap 17 '65
MOSS, Stanley
Prayer; poem. Nation 201:534 D 27 '65
Two fishermen; poem. New Repub 153:24 Ag 21 '65
Valentine's day sketch of Negro slaves, Jews in concentration camps, and unhappy lovers; poem. Nation 201:451 D 6 '65
Winter in Vermont; poem. Nation 202:74 Ja 17 '66
MOSS brothers and company. See London—Stores
MOSS pink. See Phlox
MOSSES
Antarcticana. New Yorker 41:33-4 Je 5 '65
Flavonoids from the moss mnium affine bland. T. E. Melchert and R. E. Alston. bibliog il Science 150:1170-1 N 26 '65
See also
Carrageen
MOSSLER, Candace
Bonded blonde. il por Time 86:47 Ag 20 '65
MOSSMAN, A. S. See Child, G. jt. auth.
MOSTERT, Noel
Colonial office: a final inventory. Reporter 33:24-6 Jl 1 '65
MOTELS
Motel walls angled to view serve also to resist wind; Howard Johnson motor hotel on Cleveland's lakefront. il Arch Rec 137: 226-7 Ap '65
See also
Holiday inns of America, incorporated
MOTHER-child relationship. See Parent-child relationship
MOTHER Courage and her children; drama. See Brecht, B.
MOTHER for mayor; drama. See Miller, H. L.
MOTHER Goose's Christmas surprise; drama. See Boiko, C.
MOTHER in Mannville; story. See Rawlings, M. K.
MOTHERHOOD. See Mothers
MOTHERS
Answer to the attacks on motherhood. E. K. Shriver. il McCalls 92:88-9+ Je '65
Bill of rights for wives and mothers. J. Brothers. Good H 160:48+ Ap '65
Case for the caboose. Z. J. Aranow. il McCalls 92:42+ Mr '65
Come back to the work force, mother! L. Velie. Read Digest 87:201-2+ S '65
Don't be a martyr-mother. V. Hyde. il Parents Mag 40:38-9+ Jl '65
Empty days; adjusting to when children leave home. A. Lake. il McCalls 92:78-81+ S '65

MOTHERS—*Continued*

First things first; solving the house chore problem. D. McDonald. il Redbook 125:6+ Je '65

Happiness is a baby's laugh; a jeepful of kids. P. Coffin. il Look 30:46-53 Ja 11 '66

It's good to know that those new mother blues are normal and short-lived. S. L. Green and P. Nathan. il Parents Mag 40:40-1+ My '65

Mature married woman. S. C. Callahan. Cath World 201:102-6 My '65

Murder in Alabama; American wives think Viola Liuzzo should have stayed home. L. Tornabene. il Ladies Home J 82:42+ Jl '65

Reward the years bring. C. Seton. il Redbook 125:67+ O '65

What every (mother of the) bride should know. P. McGinley. Ladies Home J 82:57+ Je '65

What new mothers worry about. F. Kodl. il Parents Mag 40:52-3+ D '65

Young mothers story. See issues of Redbook

See also

Love, Maternal

Anecdotes, facetiae, satire, etc.

Every day is mother's day. M. Brophy. See issues of Good housekeeping

Employment

See Married women—Employment

MOTHERS, Unmarried

Other face of the problem: the unmarried teen father. J. Beck. il Todays Health 43:28-31+ F '65

Teenage mother. il Good H 160:8+ F '65

Unwed mother and her job. America 113:68 Jl 17 '65

MOTHERS and daughters. See Parent-child relationship

MOTHERS and sons. See Parent-child relationship

MOTHERS day

For Mother's day; gifts. il Seventeen 24:138-9 My '65

Drama

All about mothers. C. Boiko. Plays 24:71-4, 86 My '65

Hat for mother. M. K. Phillips. Plays 24:65-70, 86 My '65

MOTHERS helpers. See Household employees

MOTHERS-in-law

Clash of cultures. D. C. Disney. Ladies Home J 82:54+ Mr '65

How mothers-in-law disrupt marriages: an old problem in new forms; symposium, ed. by B. Bettelheim. il Redbook 124:54-5+ Mr '65

What our daughters-in-law didn't tell you; an unexpected response from a group of mothers-in-law; symposium, ed. by B. Bettelheim. il Redbook 124:66-7+ Ap '65

MOTHERS; story. See Irwin, W.

MOTHERWELL, Robert

Grand manner of Motherwell. F. O'Hara. il por Vogue 146:206-9+ O 1 '65

Lochinvar's return. il por Time 86:84-5+ O 8 '65

Motherwell; exhibition at Museum of modern art. M. Kozloff. Nation 201:256-8 O 18 '65

Motherwell retrospective; exhibit at Museum of modern art. B. Kaufman. Commonweal 83:383 D 24 '65

Satisfactions of Robert Motherwell. N. Edgar. il por Art N 64:38-41+ O '65; Reply. R. Motherwell. 64:6 D '65

What a gesture! exhibition at New York's Museum of modern art. il por Newsweek 66:98-9 O 11 '65

MOTHS

Caterpillar feeding on a sundew plant. T. Eisner and J. Shepherd. bibliog il Science 150:1608-9 D 17 '65

Moths that behave like hummingbirds; sphinx moths. T. Davidson. il Nat Geog Mag 127:770-5 Je '65

See also

Imperial moths

Ear

See Ear (insects)

MOTION of solar system in space. See Solar system—Motion in space

MOTION pictures. See Moving pictures

MOTION sickness

Travel well. E. N. Dye. il Travel 123:59-60 Mr '65

MOTIVATION (education)

Motivating the slow learner; interests of teen-agers; excerpt from an address. April 1965. W. D. Boutell. Wilson Lib Bul 40:75-7+ S '65

MOTIVATION (psychology)

Achievement motivation can be developed; recent experiments. D. C. McClelland. il Harvard Bsns R 43:6-8+ N '65

Dynamics of subordinacy; excerpt. A. Zalenznik. il Harvard Bsns R 43:119-31 My '65

Productive environment for innovation. D. Wolfie. Science 149:501 Jl 30 '65

MOTIVATION in literature. See Fiction—Technique

MOTOR ability

Ability to move should be in physical fitness test. Sci N L 88:200 S 25 '65

MOTOR boat racing

Behind the scenes in a Gold cup race, 1964; photographs. D. Rosenfeld. Yachting 118:24-5 S '65

Brave Moppie best in British bash; Cowes-Torquay offshore powerboat race. E. F. Haylock. il Motor B 116:44-5+ N '65

Donsy, baby, this is your Sam; second annual Sam Griffith memorial powerboat race. L. Evans. Sports Illus 22:60-2 F 15 '65

Electrifying race; Electric cup race. T. Burrier. il Motor B 115:60 F '65

First to Nassau. M. Crook. il Yachting 117:53-4+ Je '65

Gold cup. E. Crimmin. il Motor B 116:116-17 S '65

Halfway there; Gold cup. Time 86:60-1 Ag 20 '65

He drives a hairy race; Florida's J. Wynne. B. Ottum. il Sports Illus 23:30-5 Ag 2 '65

Hey, what happened to the Hudson? third Hudson River marathon. M. Penzer. il Motor B 116:74-5 Ag '65

Long happy life of the phenomenal outboard motor; search for speed. C. D. Strang. il Motor B 116:43-5+ Jl '65

Month in yachting. See issues of Yachting

More power to you. M. Crook. See issues of Yachting

NDBA hot water battle. J. McFarland. il Hot Rod 18:42-5 D '65

No spray, no sweat; Miami-to-Nassau powerboat race. Time 85:98 Ap 16 '65

Offshore powerboat racing, and a great man. R. H. Bertram. il Yachting 117:58-9+ Mr '65

Power on the southern circuit; Miami-Nassau race. M. Penzer. il Motor B 115:174-5+ My '65

Proving ground for fast boats and tough men; Sam Griffith memorial ocean race, Miami to Bahamas race. il Bsns W p28-30 F 20 '65

Research rules the waves; Miami-Nassau race. J. Martenhoff. il Motor B 115:40-2+ Ap '65

Rooster tales. E. Rickman. See issues of Hot rod

Skip, skip, skip, and thwack! Miami-Nassau race. H. Whall. il Sports Illus 22:30-1 Ap 19 '65

1320 feet of speed, drag racers. G. Engle. il Motor B 116:40-1+ Ag '65

Thumping around two islands. T. Burrier; P. Paran. il Motor B 116:26-7+ Jl '65

Union international motorboating. E. H. Nabb. il Yachting 118:160 Ag '65

World championship powerboat race; Miami to Key West classic. il Motor B 116:20a-20b D '65

MOTOR boat shows. See Motor boats—Exhibitions

MOTOR boats

Goin' show boats. il Hot Rod 18:76-9 F '65

Rich rush of a Rybo; Florida's John Rybovich and sons. H. Whall. il Sports Illus 23:22-4 Ag 2 '65

What's new in boating for 1965. J. Roe. il Pop Sci 186:112-15 F '65

Why a motor-sailer? L. Levi. il Motor B 116:34-5+ Ag '65

Accidents

See Boats and boating—Accidents

Design

Boats we meet: Captain Handy, Camulin IV. J. Emmett. il Yachting 118:51-3+ D '65

Designs. W. H. deFontaine. See issues of Yachting

Floating patio does 40 m.p.h. J. Roe. il Pop Sci 186:106-8 Je '65

Hatteras fifty. il Motor B 116:40-1 N '65

New boat, a new venture; Baja California. E. Newmark. il Yachting 118:61-4+ D '65

New boats for 1966. J. A. Emmett. il Outdoor Life 137:60-2+ Ja '66

Sixty feet of style; Connie IV. il Motor B 116:74 S '65

Slim and seakindly outboard. il Motor B 116:104-5 O '65

MOTOR boats—Design—*Continued*
This boat is looking for trouble. W. T. Mc-Keown. il Esquire 63:102-5+ Mr '65
Tommy Gifford's new fishing machine. il Yachting 117:118-19+ Je '65

Electronic equipment

Electronics goes boating. J. Roe and R. M. Benrey. il Pop Sci 187:84-8 Ag '65
Stop that noise. C. Kucyn. il Motor B 116:46-7+ Jl '65

Equipment

Controlling twins, twin-screw boat. M. Crook. il Yachting 118:64-6+ N '65
New boating accessories (cont) Outdoor Life 137:65 Ja '66
Outboard yachting in the Bahamas. R. Smythe and J. W. Smythe. il Yachting 118:58-9+ N '65
This boat is looking for trouble. W. T. Mc-Keown. il Esquire 63:102-5+ Mr '65

Exhibitions

New York boat show; National motor boat show. il Motor B 115:84+ Mr '65
Scuttle the jib sheets, where's my check-book! 55th National motor boat show. B. Hooper. Life 58:12+ F 12 '65
Ship shopping; fifty-fifth National motor boat show. New Yorker 40:21-2 Ja 30 '65

Hatches

Build bigger engine hatches. H. Clark. il Motor B 116:120-1 N '65

Steering gear

How to handle a twin screw boat. J. F. Jayne. il Yachting 117:54-5+ My '65
How to tackle torque. J. Martenhoff. il Pop Sci 187:78+ Jl '65

Testing

Johnson's new trihedrals. A. Mikesell. il Pop Mech 124:118-21+ O '65
Research rules the waves. J. Martenhoff. il Motor B 115:40-2+ Ap '65

MOTOR boats, Jet propelled
Pros and cons of jet power for small boats. J. Roe. il Pop Sci 187:86-9+ N '65
World's fastest man on water. L. Taylor. il Pop Sci 187:96-9+ Ag '65

MOTOR boats, Outboard
Five tips for better outboarding. il Pop Sci 186:103 F '65
Got the bigger-boat bug? J. A. Emmett. il Outdoor Life 135:112+ Mr '65
Outboard yachting in the Bahamas. R. Smythe and J. W. Smythe. il Yachting 118:58-9+ N '65

MOTOR bus drivers
See also
Strikes—United States—Transportation workers

MOTOR bus lines
Dixie bus company at a crossroads; Safe bus, inc. il Ebony 21:70-4 D '65
Zanesville and the mass-transit act; Zanesville, Ohio. S. Grey and T. B. Steinbach. Am City 80:144+ S '65

Employees

Worst censorship; refusal of bus drivers balked to transport passengers to SANE demonstration. Nation 201:459 D 13 '65

MOTOR bus travel
On the road with Memére. J. Kerouac. Holiday 37:74-5 My '65

MOTOR buses
Bus competitor GM helped build; Flxible co. il Bsns W p 172+ D 11 '65
GM bus suit settled. Bsns W p34 D 4 '65
See also
Advertising mediums—Motor buses

MOTOR buses, Electric. See Electric vehicles
MOTOR caravans
Global trailer travel; Wally Byam around the world caravan. W. Thoms. il Travel 123:26-31+ My '65

MOTOR cultivators. See Cultivators
MOTOR cycle racing. See Motorcycle racing
MOTOR cycles. See Motorcycles
MOTOR mounts. See Electric motors—Mounting
MOTOR oils. See Lubrication and lubricants
MOTOR sailers. See Motor boats
MOTOR scooters
If you really hanker for a cycle or a scooter... il Changing T 19:45-7 Mr '65
Motor scooter pressure; banning of vehicles matter of law under the new Wilderness act. Liv Wildn 87:29 Wint '64

Sit-down skiing; snowmobiles. il Time 85:55 F 19 '65
Trail scooter tips. Liv Wildn 29:39 Spr '65
Two scooters you can build. J. McBride; J. M. Harris. il Pop Sci 186:164-9 Mr '65

MOTOR sleds
Hodag endurance run; snowmobile shakedown. S. James. il Pop Mech 125:127-9+ Ja '66
New winter fun. . . a 10-horse open sleigh. B. Hardy. il Farm J 90:66-7 Ja '66
Ski-scooters, how you can go-go-go in snow; world championship of snowmobiling at Lake Placid, N.Y, Winter carnival. H. Shuldiner. il Pop Sci 188:116-18 Ja '66
Snow cruising; snowmobiles. F. Donatien. il Travel 125:40-1 Ja '66
See also
Ice boats and ice boating

MOTOR trend award
Motor trend award to the 1965 Pontiacs. il Motor T 17:26-7 F '65

MOTOR truck drivers
See also
Strikes—United States—Truck drivers

MOTOR truck engines
More pull at lower revs. D. Scott. il Pop Sci 187:92-4 Ag '65
See also
Gas turbines, Automotive

MOTOR truck industry and trade
Gains for truck sales zip past rise in autos; sale of camper coaches. il Bsns W p25 Mr 6 '65
Making it big and small; shatter records. Time 86:97A+ N 5 '65
See also
White motor company

MOTOR truck lines
See also
Denver Chicago trucking company

Consolidations and mergers

Did Yale express go too fast? Yale express system acquired Republic carloading & distributing co. Bsns W p78 Mr 27 '65
Trucking rolls into an age of giants. il Bsns W p 174-6+ Je 12 '65

MOTOR truck tires. See Tires, Motor truck
MOTOR truck trailers
See also
Fruehauf trailer company

MOTOR trucking. See Trucking
MOTOR trucks
Hauling Ranchero; pickup with classy styling and passenger-car comfort. B. McVay. il Motor T 17:40-1 Jl '65
How to buy the right truck for the job. W. J. Fletcher. Suc Farm 63:64 N '65
New pickups carry six up front. il Pop Sci 187:73 Jl '65
New trucks for '66. il Farm J 89:50 N '65
Suddenly pickup trucks are in. J. P. Norbye. il Pop Sci 186:94-9 Je '65
Switching the charge on batteries. il Bsns W p 132+ Mr 13 '65

Equipment

Six good truck ideas on one truck. W. E. Messerly. il Suc Farm 63:107 S '65

Springs and suspension

Inventor of the month; at seventy-five, trucker's friend; demonstrating rubber torsion suspensions. S. V. Jones. il Sci Digest 57:31 Je '65

MOTOR trucks, Amphibious
Fire truck that swims. il Pop Sci 187:89 S '65

MOTOR trucks, Armored
Armored truck battles against bandits. il Pop Sci 187:82-3 Ag '65

MOTOR trucks, Fire. See Fire apparatus, Motor

MOTOR vehicle drivers
See also
Automobile drivers

MOTOR vehicle industry. See Motor truck industry and trade

MOTOR vehicles
Enter the Bronco; four-wheel drive vehicle. il Newsweek 66:62 Ag 23 '65
Ford's agile new Bronco; lightweight four-wheel-drive. J. P. Norbye. il Pop Sci 187:47-9+ S '65
Four-wheel drives; they're great in the boondocks; Ford's new Bronco and Wagoneer. A. Markovich. il Pop Mech 124:104-5+ O '65
Leapin' lizzies! sand buggies. S. James. il Pop Mech 124:122-3 D '65

MOTOR vehicles—*Continued*
Missing link in transportation. J. Doblin. il Pop Mech 124:84-7+ N '65
My love affair with sand and wheels. E. S. Gardner. il Pop Sci 187:112-17+ N '65
New vehicle for country driving; 4-wheel drive Bronco. il Suc Farm 63:74 S '65
They call it a sport now, sarge; four-wheel driving vehicles. B. Gilbert. il Sports Illus 24:50-6+ Ja 10 '66
See also
Electric vehicles

Design
Grand-Sander. il Hot Rod 18:74-7 Ap '65

Renting
Guided growth of leasing. il Duns R 85:pt2 132-3+ Je '65

Testing
Test-driving the ruggeds: cars with four-wheel drive. J. P. Norbye. il Pop Sci 187:46-50+ Ag '65

MOTOR vehicles, Amphibious
Chevy's Sidewinder. D. Wells. il Hot Rod 18:80-2 Je '65

MOTOR vehicles, Military
Chevy's Sidewinder. D. Wells. il Hot Rod 18:80-2 Je '65

MOTOR vehicles, Municipal
Tire failure no longer a problem; Batavia, N.Y. G. A. Kandra. il Am City 80:104-5 Mr '65

MOTOR vehicles, Police
Patrol wagon that doubles as an ambulance. J. Trainer. il Am City 81:104 Ja '66

MOTORCYCLE clubs
Hell's Angels; outlaw motorcycle club in Calif. W. Murray. il Sat Eve Post 238:32-9 N 20 '65
Varoom at the top: the Madison avenue motorcycle club. M. Sumner. il Esquire 64:141 N '65

MOTORCYCLE racing
Bikies' fun; racing at Loudon, N.H. il Newsweek 66:21 Jl 5 '65
Come to the riot. See Weirs Beach burn. M. Mok. il Life 59:88-9 Jl 2 '65
I hit the ground at 150 mph; ed. by J. E. Boykin. E. J. Potter. il Pop Mech 124:104-5+ S '65
Lion's share; First international drag festival. L. Wineland. il Hot Rod 18:84-7 Mr '65
Motorcycle racing: the hot-shoe hotshots. J. B. Hall. Holiday 38:142+ N '65

MOTORCYCLES
Civilized cycles: everybody rides 'em now. E. Arctander. il Pop Sci 187:68-72 Jl '65
Festival flyer. R. Renstrom. il Hot Rod 18:84-5 Je '65
If you really hanker for a cycle or a scooter... il Changing T 19:45-7 Mr '65
Spotlight on the commuter cycle. A. Markovich. il Pop Mech 124:50-3 N '65
Suzuki town and country 80. B. Greene. il Hot Rod 18:88-9+ Jl '65
Tiger, here's your meat! B. Greene. il Hot Rod 18:75-7+ D '65
Up on two wheels. B. Greene. See issues of Hot rod
Upward mobility of the motorcycle. C. A. Gottlieb. il Esquire 64:138-9 N '65
Zingy lightweights zoom in. il Life 58:111-13 Ap 23 '65

Maintenance and repair
Winter tune-up for your cycle. M. J. Schultz. il Pop Mech 125:152-5+ Ja '66

Safety devices and measures
How to avoid killing yourself. il Esquire 64:140 N '65

MOTORCYCLING
See also
Motorcycle clubs
Motorcycle racing

MOTORING. See Automobile touring
MOTORISTS. See Automobile drivers
MOTOROLA, Incorporated
Hiring tests wait for the score. Bsns W p45-6+ F 13 '65
MOTORS. See Diesel engines
MOTORS, Outboard. See Gas and oil engines, Outboard
MOTORSAILERS. See Motor boats
MOTOWN record corporation
No town like Motown; Motown records. il Newsweek 65:92 Mr 22 '65
MOTT, John R.
John R. Mott, Christian statesman; tribute. Christian Cent 82:795 Je 23 '65

John R. Mott remembered. J. R. Nelson. Christian Cent 82:671 My 26 '65
Postville, Iowa, remembers. Christian Cent 82:165 F 10 '65
MOTT, Kenneth
Grouping the gifted is the best way. NEA J 54:10-11 Mr '65
MOTT, Newcomb
Tourist trap, Soviet style. Life 59:4 D 10 '65
MOTT, William Penn, jr
Creative approach to parks and recreation. por Recreation 58:340-1 S '65
MOULAY IDRIS, Morocco
Reader's choice. F. R. Smith. Travel 123:9 Je '65
MOULINEX. See France—Industries
MOULTON, Warren L.
Apocalypse in a casket? Christian Cent 82:1412-14 N 17 '65
MOUND, Minn.
We chose three-stage sewage purification. L. L. Kopp. il Am City 80:89-91 D '65
MOUNT BLANC tunnel. See Tunnels and tunneling
MOUNT ETNA. See Etna, Mount
MOUNT FUJI. See Fuji, Mount
MOUNT HOOD. See Hood, Mount
MOUNT KATAHDIN. See Katahdin, Mount
MOUNT KENNEDY. See Kennedy, Mount
MOUNT MCKINLEY NATIONAL PARK
Roadbuilding in Mount McKinley National Park. A. Murie. il Nat Parks Mag 39:4-8 Jl '65
MOUNT PLEASANT, N.Y.
Don't make it look like a garage. M. L. Rovello. il Am City 80:114-15 Mr '65
MOUNT RAINIER. See Rainier, Mount
MOUNT RAINIER NATIONAL PARK
Around Rainier's back side. il Sunset 135:39 Jl '65
MOUNT RUSHMORE NATIONAL MEMORIAL
Good fun in the Badlands. B. Ballantine. il Holiday 37:20+ Je '65
MOUNT VERNON (historic house)
George Washington, businessman; excerpt from George Washington: the forge of experience, with editorial comment. J. T. Flexner. il Am Heritage 16:94-8 O '65
Visit to Mount Vernon; excerpts from Travels through America; tr. and ed. by M. J. E. Budka. J. U. Niemcewicz. il Am Heritage 16:64-71 F '65
MOUNT WOLF, Pa.
Refuse sacks are in. il Am City 80:96-7 D '65
MOUNTAIN climbing. See Mountaineering
MOUNTAIN flying. See Aviation—Mountain flying
MOUNTAIN goat hunting. See Rocky Mountain goat hunting
MOUNTAIN goats. See Rocky Mountain goats
MOUNTAIN lion hunting. See Puma hunting
MOUNTAIN lions. See Pumas
MOUNTAIN madness; drama. See Dias, E. J.
MOUNTAIN men. See Trappers
MOUNTAIN pine beetle. See Pine—Diseases and pests
MOUNTAIN plants. See Alpine flora
MOUNTAIN sculpture
See also
Stone Mountain memorial
MOUNTAIN sheep hunting
Grand climax. R. V. Broadbent. il Outdoor Life 135:36-9+ My '65
Little battle of the bighorn. V. Kraft. il Sports Illus 23:56-8+ O 11 '65
Old Krag. T. Howell. il Outdoor Life 135:44-5+ Mr '65
Pack of trouble. F. C. Hibben. il Outdoor Life 136:44-7+ N '65
Ram and the silver bullet. J. O'Connor. il Outdoor Life 135:44-5+ Ap '65
Rams of Ural. W. L. Henri. il Field & S 70:43-5+ Ag '65
MOUNTAIN states. See West
MOUNTAIN waves
Flying the mountain wave; ed. by B. Hicks. I. Leverton. il Flying 77:68-73 Ag '65
MOUNTAINEERING
Above the clouds. A. C. Schmidt. il Reporter 32:38+ Ap 22 '65
Because it was there; R. Kennedy's climb of Mount Kennedy. il Time 85:25 Ap 2 '65
Canada's Mount Kennedy; discovery and first ascent. B. Washburn; R. F. Kennedy; J. W. Whittaker. il Nat Geog Mag 128:1-33 Jl '65
Climb up Utah's tallest. il Sunset 135:35-6 Ag '65
Climber; climbing of Mount Kennedy. il Newsweek 65:29 Ap 5 '65

MOUNTAINEERING—*Continued*

Five against the gods. R. Daley. il Esquire 64:96-7+ N '65

How did I get myself into this? B. Kennedy climbs Yukon mountain. D. Connelly. il Sports Illus 22:56-8+ Ap 5 '65

Kennedy on top of Mt Kennedy. il Life 58:46-7 Ap 2 '65

Master of the mountain peaks: W. Bonatti. G. Kent and J. Reddy. il Read Digest 87: 102-7 S '65

Old men and tired legs. W. B. Morse. il Am For 71:38-41 S '65

Our climb up Mt Kennedy. R. F. Kennedy. il Life 58:22-7 Ap 9 '65

Reporter at large; Chamonix, France. J. Bernstein. il New Yorker 41:43-6+ Mr 6; 109-10+ Mr 20 '65

Reporter at large; Whymper and Mummery: Matterhorn and Grépon. J. Bernstein. il New Yorker 41:130+ Mr 13 '65

Seventy-two hours of terror; on Teewinot Mountain in Grand Teton National Park. J. Lipscomb. il Sports Illus 22:86-90+ Je 14: 64-8+ Je 21 '65

Three days on a rope; north face of the Matterhorn attempted by Italy's W. Bonatti. il Time 85:82 F 26 '65

MOUNTAINEERS (southern states)

Happy pappies of Handshoe Holler. il Time 86:38-9 N 5 '65

Is there a future for yesterday's people? excerpt from Yesterday's people; life in contemporary Appalachia. J. E. Weller. il Sat R 48:33-6 O 16 '65

Kentucky doctor: one man's war against southern poverty. L. Bergquist. il Look 29: 76-80 N 16 '65

Tumblin' Creek's cabin library; Tennessee mountains. S. C. Gross. il Sr Schol 87:sup 17-19 S 30 '65

Yesterday's people, by J. Weller. Review
Sat R 48:60 O 30 '65. D. M. Potter

MOUNTAINS

Journey into wilderness. J. V. Lone. il Liv Wildn 29:9-11 Sum '65

See also

Mountain waves

also names of mountain ranges and peaks, e.g. Alps

MOUNTBATTEN, Louis, 1st earl Mountbatten of Burma. See Mountbatten of Burma, L. M.

MOUNTBATTEN of Burma, Louis Mountbatten, 1st earl

Dickie strikes his flag. il pors Newsweek 66:38 Jl 19 '65

MOUNTBATTEN family

Mountbattens, by A. Hatch. Review
Life 58:15 My 28 '65. S. E. Morison

MOUNTING of butterflies. See Butterflies—Collection and preservation

MOUNTING of insects. See Insects—Collection and preservation

MOUNTING of motors. See Electric motors—Mounting

MOUNTING of pictures. See Pictures—Mounting

MOUNTZOURES, H. L.

Love and wisdom; story. New Yorker 41:50-7 S 18 '65

Music of the tree; story. New Yorker 41:24-6 Ja 8 '66

MOURNING becomes Electra; opera. See Levy, M. D.

MOURNING customs

Death, grief and mourning, by G. Gorer. Review
Nation 201:533-5 D 27 '65. J. Mitford

MOURNING dove shooting

Doves are indestructible. C. E. Gillham. il Field & S 70:70-2+ S '65

Opening day on doves. G. X. Sand. il Outdoor Life 136:54-7+ S '65

MOURNING doves

Energy intake of the mourning dove zenaidura macroura marginella. W. D. Schmid. bibliog il Science 150:1171-2 N 26 '65

MOUSE salivary glands. See Salivary glands

MOUSEBIRDS

Kiki, the personality mousebird. M. E. Keatts. il Audubon Mag 67:386-7 N '65

MOUSSE. See Desserts

MOUSSORGSKY, Modest Petrovich. See Musorgskii, M. P.

MOUTH

Diseases

What parents ask about infections of the mouth. M. J. E. Senn. McCalls 93:46+ O '65

MOUTHBREEDERS

Tricky tilapia. G. X. Sand. il Field & S 70:70-1+ Ja '66

MOUTON, Musée de. See Museums

MOVEMENT of fish. See Animal locomotion

MOVIE censorship. See Moving picture censorship

MOVIE parties. See Entertaining

MOVING

If you are planning a move. Sunset 135:124-5 S '65

Moving-day blues. Sci Digest 57:19 My '65

Moving? the special care children may need. il Good H 160:175 My '65

New wheels for the nomads. il Newsweek 65:90+ My 10 '65

Planning and making the move to a new store. E. Young. Pub W 188:56-60 O 11 '65

MOVING and storage companies

New wheels for the nomads. il Newsweek 65:90+ My 10 '65

MOVING of libraries

NYPL music, theatre, dance divisions have budget and removal problems. Library J 90:2792+ Je 15 '65

MOVING picture acting

Carroll Baker: the lady was a tramp; preparation for role in Sylvia. R. W. Lewis. il Sat Eve Post 238:36-8+ F 27 '65

MOVING picture actors and actresses

Ages of man; aging stars. Time 86:90 O 1 '65

007 girls. il Time 86:53 S 10 '65

Hamlet who wants to play clowns; V. Gassman. M. S. Davis. il N Y Times Mag p46-7+ S 19 '65

Heston: larger than life. P. Hamill. il Sat Eve Post 238:87-91 Jl 3 '65

Hollywood scene. E. Miller. See issues of Seventeen through March 1965

Hooray for Hollywood; symposium. il Mlle 61:4+ Jl '65

How movies break up marriages. il Ebony 20:98-100+ S '65

Jean Simmons: the mouse becomes a cat. C. R. Jennings. Sat Eve Post 238:77-8 Ag 28 '65

Jeanne Moreau: death, suffering, love. C. R. Jennings. il Sat Eve Post 238:86-8 Ap 10 '65

John Wayne: a love song. J. Didion. il Sat Eve Post 238:76-9 Ag 14 '65

Man who made apathy irresistible; Italy's M. Mastroianni. I. Shenker. il N Y Times Mag p54-5+ D 12 '65

Me? a movie about me? Manny, it's a natural. il Esquire 65:48-9 Ja '66

Mirage of beautiful air. L. H. Lapham. il Sat Eve Post 238:34-6+ Mr 27 '65

Name is Moreau (not Bardot) L. Collins and D. Lapierre. il N Y Times Mag p46-7+ Mr 21 '65

Of stars and men. A. Croce. Nat R 17:1104-5+ N 30 '65

Son of Bogie. R. Grenier. Esquire 65:66-9+ Ja '66

Spotlight! E. Miller. See issues of Seventeen, April 1965-

Two loves of Doctor Zhivago; J. Christie and G. Chaplin. H. H. Martin. il Sat Eve Post 239:26-31 Ja 15 '66

Why Barbara Stanwyck grinned all the way to the bank. V. Scott. il McCalls 92:82 Mr '65

See also

Academy awards (moving pictures)

Children as actors

also names of moving picture actors and actresses, e.g. B. Bardot

MOVING picture adaptations. See Film adaptations

MOVING picture advertising. See Moving picture industry—Advertising

MOVING picture authorship

Life of a wordsmith. Time 85:76+ Ap 16 '65

My word is his bond: a view from the back room; writing and producing Thunderball. R. Maibaum. Esquire 63:73+ Je '65

Secret mind; excerpt from Afterword to Anthem sprinters and others antics. R. Bradbury. Writer 78:13-16 N '65

MOVING picture cameras

Advantages of having your own 8mm camera. R. H. Burgert. Sr Schol 87:sup 10 N 4 '65

Are 8mm movie finder images bright enough? M. A. Matzkin. il Mod Phot 29:91-2 My '65

Bolex P4 zoom reflex; test report. H. Everngam. il Pop Phot 57:113 Jl '65

8-mm dream: the Fairchild 900. L. Lipton. il Pop Phot 56:116-17+ My '65

Flash: more Super 8 coming. il Pop Phot 56:73 Je '65

Fuji Single 8. il U S Camera 28:66-7+ Je '65

Here's super 8. il U S Camera 28:56-7 Ag '65

Home movie cameras now generally automated. il Consumer Bul 48:27-32 Ap '65

Instant-loading cameras make it big. il Bsns W p50-2+ My 8 '65

MOVING picture cameras—_Continued_
Movie cameras; super 8 to 16. H. Everngam. il Pop Phot 57:70-1 D '65
Movie maker; the super 8 and others. M. A. Matzkin. il Mod Phot 29:134+ O '65
Movie test report. See issues of Popular photography
Movies super 8 & other goodies. L. Lipton. il Pop Phot 57:98-100 Ag '65
Photography. il Consumer Rep 30:326-38 D '65
Super 8: how does it stack up? M. A. Matzkin. il Mod Phot 29:78-81 Ag '65

Loading
Movie maker; Fuji single-8 cartridge may bring back small, lightweight 8mm movie cameras. M. A. Matzkin. il Mod Phot 29:12+ Ag '65

Sound equipment
Fairchild Professional Sound 900. il U S Camera 28:66-7+ My '65

MOVING picture cameras on space vehicles. See Space vehicles—Equipment

MOVING picture cartoons. See Moving pictures—Animated cartoons

MOVING picture censorship
ABPC again files amicus brief for John Goldfarb. Pub W 187:51 Mr 22 '65
Appellate court reverses John Goldfarb decision. Pub W 187:133-4 F 22 '65
Burden on the censor. Newsweek 65:88 Mr 29 '65
Censoring the censors. Time 85:72 Mr 12 '65
Court of appeals OK's John Goldfarb. Pub W 187:25 Mr 29 '65
Morality crisis. il Newsweek 65:98+ Ap 19 '65
Toward Christian film criteria. J. M. Wall. Christian Cent 82:775-8 Je 16 '65; Discussion. 82:994+ Ag 11 '65

MOVING picture criticism. See Moving picture plays—Criticisms, plots, etc.

MOVING picture directors
At the movies: Southern way of death. M. Barrett. Reporter 33:40-2 N 18 '65
Headstrong directors. H. Alpert. Sat R 48:63 O 16 '65
Of stars and men. A. Croce. Nat R 17:1104-5+ N 30 '65
See also
Fellini, F.
Hitchcock, A.
Kubrick, S.
Lester, R.

MOVING picture editing. See Moving pictures—Editing

MOVING picture festivals
Are we doomed to festivals? New York film festival. S. Kauffmann. New Repub 153:30-2 O 2 '65
Berlin film festival. L. A. Murray. America 113:118-19 Jl 31 '65
Even the old are young; New York film festival report. R. Hemming and B. Johnson. il Sr Schol 87:28-9 O 14 '65
Festival; New York film festival. il Newsweek 66:95-6 S 27 '65
Godard est Godard; third New York film festival. New Yorker 41:43-6 O 9 '65
Letter home; International film festival, Moscow. H. Lawrenson. Esquire 64:20+ N '65
Lost opportunity in India; American entries for third Indian international film festival. A. Knight. Sat R 48:52 F 13 '65
Nob Hill festival; San Francisco's ninth International and North Beach. C. Kentfield. Nation 201:398+ N 22 '65
Old movies are better than ever. A. Knight. Sat R 48:32 S 18 '65
Quarrelsome festival; New York film festival. H. Alpert. Sat R 48:33 O 9 '65
Rotten to the corpse; New York film festival. A. Knight. Sat R 48:75 O 23 '65
Screen; third New York film festival. P. T. Hartung. Commonweal 82:666 S 17 '65
Student filmmakers; UCLA's festival. il Newsweek 66:114+ O 25 '65
That Masque at Lincoln Center; third New York film festival. D. Macdonald. Esquire 64:82+ D '65
Third festival; the New York film festival. R. Hatch. Nation 201:175-6 S 27 '65
Tolstoi bomb; Moscow film festival. Newsweek 66:66 Ag 2 '65
See also
Cannes international film festival

MOVING picture films
Double super 8 is here! il Pop Phot 58:48 Ja '66
Fast load for movies; new 8-mm movie pack. il Bsns W p 130 Ap 24 '65

Instant movies ahead? W. Hanson. il Pop Phot 58:38+ Ja '66
Kodak's revolution in home movies; new 8mm movie film. E. H. Ortner. il Pop Sci 186:50-4+ Je '65
Matzkin on movies; 100-ft. double super 8 spools are on the way. M. A. Matzkin. il Mod Phot 30:100 Ja '66
Movie maker; Super-8. M. A. Matzkin. Mod Phot 29:26+ Je; 34 Jl; 12 S '65
Shapes of 8 to come. H. V. Fondiller. il Pop Phot 58:42-3+ Ja '66
Still & movie films. Pop Phot 58:71-9 Ja '66
Straight facts; super 8. L. Lipton. il Pop Phot 57:42+ D '65
Super 8: how does it stack up? M. A. Matzkin. il Mod Phot 29:78-81 Ag '65
Super 8 movies and you. D. B. Eisendrath, jr. Pop Phot 57:8+ O '65
War of the photo systems; 8mm movies, American Super 8. E. H. Ortner. il Pop Sci 187:88-92+ Jl '65

MOVING picture industry
See also
Moving picture production and direction

Advertising
Censoring sex; Los Angeles times screening board. il Time 85:71 F 12 '65
SR goes to the movies; showmanship; Warner brothers studio tours. A. Knight. Sat R 48:37 Je 5 '65
Virna Lisi: experiment in star making. J. Hamilton. il Look 29:60-6+ My 18 '65

Finance
Gross is greener; Sound of music a financial success. Time 87:46 Ja 14 '66

Regulation
See Moving picture laws and regulations

Brazil
Hollywood producers go rolling down to Rio. il Bsns W p32-3 S 25 '65

France
Great come-&-see-it day. Time 85:62+ Ap 9 '65

Italy
Fantasy, flesh and Fellini. T. Meehan. il Sat Eve Post 239:24-8+ Ja 1 '66
Horse, Italian style. il Newsweek 65:87D-88 Je 28 '65

Japan
Films and faces of Akira Kurosawa. B. Ortolani. il America 113:368-71 O 2 '65

Russia
Russian studios steal a scene from Hollywood. il Bsns W p22-3 Jl 3 '65

United States
Great Gallic welcome; American films and film makers take over Paris. J. F. Fixx. il Sat R 48:14-17 D 25 '65
Hollywood in black and white. J. O. Killens. Nation 201:157-60 S 20 '65
Meanwhile, back in Hollywood. A. Knight. Sat R 48:21 D 25 '65
Peekaboo sex, or How to fill a drive-in; Peter Pan syndrome and beach pictures. A. Levy. il Life 59:81-2+ Jl 16 '65
Retrospective; fifteen years of movie-going. H. Alpert. Sat R 48:45 N 27 '65
Underground renaissance. H. Junker. Nation 201:539-40 D 27 '65
Voice of the underground cinema. A. Levy. il N Y Times Mag p70+ S 19 '65

MOVING picture laws and regulations
Toward Christian film criteria. J. M. Wall. Christian Cent 82:775-8 Je 16 '65; Discussion. 82:994+ Ag 11 '65

MOVING picture locations. See Moving pictures—Setting and scenery

MOVING picture music. See Moving pictures—Music

MOVING picture photography
Filming in the studio; amateur dance films. F. De Langrange. il Dance Mag 39:52-3+ S '65
Fps creativity. W. P. Banner. il U S Camera 28:72-3+ Jl '65
Making movies through your windshield. K. Brooks. il Pop Sci 186:120 Mr '65
Moore on movies. J. W. Moore. See issues of U.S. camera & travel
Movie maker. M. A. Matzkin. See issues of Modern photography
Nature and photography; movie problems in public aquariums. S. Dunton. Natur Hist 74:58-60 D '65

MOVING picture photography—*Continued*
New but muddy wave. R. Christgau. il Pop Phot 56:118-19+ My '65
No light meter; F. McCready's hobby. il U S Camera 28:58-9+ D '65
Super 8 movies and you. D. B. Eisendrath, jr. Pop Phot 57:8+ O '65
Ten keys to movie quality. M. A. Matzkin. il Mod Phot 29:94-5 Ap '65
You need long lens, high flying camera to film an eagle. L. Jacobs, jr. il Mod Phot 29:89+ Mr '65

Apparatus and supplies
Easy way. H. V. Fondiller. il Pop Phot 56: 122-3 F '65
Movie maker; equipment for a European trip. M. A. Matzkin. Mod Phot 29:64 Ap '65

Renting
If you can't buy, rent! H. V. Fondiller. Pop Phot 56:116+ F '65

Lighting
Movie lighting: direct or bounce? M. A. Matzkin. il Mod Phot 30:86+ Ja '66
MOVING picture photography in criminal investigation. *See* Photography in criminal investigation
MOVING picture plays
See also
Film adaptations
Television broadcasting—Moving pictures

Criticisms, plots, etc.
At the movies. E. Miller. See issues of Seventeen to March 1965
Critical eye. Holiday 38:120+ S '65
Current cinema. B. Gill. See issues of New Yorker
007 knows what to do; Thunderball. il Life 60:79-81 Ja 7 '66
Family movie guide; ed. by A. D. Kenney. See issues of Parents' magazine and better homemaking
Films. D. Macdonald. See issues of Esquire
Films. M. Walsh. See issues of America
Films. R. Hatch. See occasional issues of Nation
Films. S. Kauffmann. See issues of New republic
Following the films. P. T. Hartung; M. Ronan. See issues of Senior scholastic
Goings on about town. See issues of New Yorker
I lost it at the movies, by P. Kael. Review Esquire 64:27-30 Ag '65. D. Macdonald Harper 230:113-16 Je '65. S. Kauffmann Life movie review. See issues of Life
Motion picture previews. I. McMahan and E. Whitehorn. See issues of PTA magazine
Movie of the month (cont) Cath World 201: 76+, 279-80 Ap, Jl '65
Movie report. R. Harbert. See issues of Good housekeeping
Movies. See issues of Consumer reports
Movies. See issues of National review
Movies. E. Hardwick. Vogue 145:61 Mr 15 '65
Movies. R. Blum. Vogue 146:64 O 15 '65
Movies in brief. R. M. Hodgens. Nat R 17: 292-4, 518-19, 784-5, 993-4, 1203-4 Ap 6, Je 15, S 7, N 2, D 28 '65
New movies. F. Somers. See issues of Redbook
New movies. M. Ronan. il Sr School 87:sup 18 O 14; sup 10 N 18 '65
Ratings of current motion pictures. See issues of Consumer bulletin
SR goes to the movies. A. Knight. See issues of Saturday review
SR's annual survey of the movies; symposium. il Sat R 48:10-22+ D 25 '65
Screen. P. T. Hartung. See issues of Commonweal
Sight & sound. L. Benjamin; L. Hershey. See issues of McCall's
Spotlight! E. Miller. See issues of Seventeen beginning April 1965
Ten best. P. T. Hartung. Commonweal 83: 409 Ja 7 '66
Those swinging beach movies. R. W. Lewis. il Sat Eve Post 238:83-7 Jl 31 '65
When the school desk is a theatre seat; courses in movie appreciation. W. Johnson. il Sr Schol 86:26 My 6 '65

Anecdotes, facetiae, satire, etc.
Surfside sex; script for sequel to The sandpiper.
Christian Cent 82:1079 S 1 '65

Single works
Across the river
Newsweek 65:97 My 3 '65

Agent 8¾
Redbook 125:26 S '65
Time 86:76 Ag 20 '65
Agony and the ecstasy
America 113:448 O 16 '65
Cath World 202:127-8 N '65
Christian Cent 82:1548 D 15 '65
Commonweal 83:61 O 15 '65
Life 59:19 O 15 '65
Life il 59:75-6+ N 12 '65
Look il 29:41-8 Mr 9 '65
New Repub 153:31 N 6 '65
New Yorker 41:228-9 O 16 '65
Sat R 48:50 S 25 '65
Sr Schol 87:44 N 11 '65
Time il 86:117+ O 15 '65
Alphaville
America 113:694-5 N 27 '65
Commonweal 83:192-3 N 12 '65
New Repub 153:31-2 N 20 '65
New Yorker 41:116+ Je 12 '65
Newsweek 66:109+ N 8 '65
Sat R 48:73 N 13 '65
Amorous adventures of Moll Flanders
America 112:887 Je 19 '65
Life 58:17 Je 11 '65
New Repub 152:26 Je 5 '65
New Yorker 41:68+ My 29 '65
Newsweek il 65:85 My 31 '65
Time il 85:67 Je 4 '65
Andy
Nation 200:152 F 8 '65
New Repub 152:26-8 F 6 '65
Art of love
Time 86:94 Jl 16 '65
Baby the rain must fall
America 112:231 F 13 '65
Time 85:64 F 5 '65
Backfire
New Yorker 41:120 My 1 '65
Newsweek il 65:118 My 10 '65
Sat R 48:34 My 15 '65
Time 85:107 My 7 '65
Bambole!
New Yorker 41:60-1 Jl 17 '65
Time 86:96 Jl 9 '65
Banana peel
Life 58:15 F 12 '65
New Repub 152:28 F 6 '65
Battle of the bulge
America 114:52 Ja 8 '66
Newsweek il 67:62 Ja 10 '66
Time 86:77-8 D 31 '65
Battle of the Villa Fiorita
Commonweal 82:414-15 Je 18 '65
Time il 85:67 Je 4 '65
Bedford incident
America 113:609-10 N 13 '65
Life 59:22 N 5 '65
New Yorker 41:122 N 6 '65
Newsweek 66:108+ N 22 '65
Redbook 126:48 N '65
Sat R 48:73 N 13 '65
Sat R 48:75 D 4 '65
Before the revolution
Life 59:12 Ag 13 '65
Newsweek il 66:66-7 Ag 2 '65
Billie
Newsweek il 66:99 S 27 '65
Birth of a nation
N Y Times Mag il p24-5+ F 7 '65
Black fox
Commonweal 82:503 Jl 9 '65
Blue beast
Newsweek 65:91A-91B F 15 '65
Boeing Boeing
Newsweek il 67:62 Ja 10 '66
Time 87:80 Ja 21 '66
La Bohème
Life 59:23 O 29 '65
Opera N il 30:42 O 23 '65
Boy ten feet tall
Life 58:19 Mr 12 '65
Brainstorm
Time 85:102 Je 18 '65
Bunny Lake is missing
America 113:542+ N 6 '65
Commonweal 83:100 O 22 '65
Life 59:20 D 3 '65
New Repub 153:31 N 6 '65
New Yorker 41:229-30 O 16 '65
Newsweek 66:120+ O 18 '65
Sat R 48:75 O 30 '65
Bus Riley's back in town
Commonweal 82:192 Ap 30 '65
Newsweek 65:110+ Ap 12 '65
Sat R 48:39-40 Ap 24 '65
Time il 85:C9+ Ap 23 '65
Carpetbaggers
Esquire 64:34 O '65

MOVING picture plays—Criticisms, plots, etc.—
Single works——*Continued*
Casanova 70
America 113:224-6 Ag 28 '65
Commonweal 82:599 Ag 20 '65
Esquire 64:34+ O '65
Life 59:8 Ag 20 '65
New Repub 153:36-8 Ag 7 '65
New Yorker 41:56+ Jl 31 '65
Newsweek il 66:79 Ag 9 '65
Sat R 48:44 S 4 '65
Time il 86:85 Ag 6 '65
Cat Ballou
Commonweal 82:192 Ap 30 '65
Esquire 64:40 S '65
Life il 58:121-2+ Je 11 '65
Nation 201:68 Ag 2 '65
New Repub 152:27-8 My 22 '65
New Yorker 41:78+ Je 26 '65
Newsweek il 65:118A My 10 '65
Sat R 48:34 My 15 '65
Sr Schol 86:36 My 13 '65
Time il 146:180 S 1 '65
Le ciel sur la tête. See Sky falls in, below
Cincinnati kid
America 113:544 N 6 '65
Commonweal 83:217 N 19 '65
Life 59:15 N 19 '65
New Yorker 41:235 N 13 '65
Newsweek il 66:113 N 8 '65
Vogue 146:116 N 1 '65
Circle of love
Commonweal 82:157 Ap 23 '65
New Yorker 41:104+ Ap 3 '65
Newsweek 65:112 Ap 12 '65
Sat R 48:30 Ap 10 '65
Time 85:105-6 Ap 9 '65
Collector
America 112:905-6 Je 26 '65
Commonweal 82:446 Je 25 '65
Life 58:153-4+ My 14 '65
New Repub 152:26-7 Je 19 '65
Newsweek il 65:96+ Je 21 '65
Sat R 48:57 Je 12 '65
Time il 85:103-4 Je 25 '65
Vogue 146:52 Ag 15 '65
Contempt
Commonweal 81:611 F 5 '65
Sat R 48:43 F 6 '65
Cool world
Ebony il 20:43-4+ Jl '65
Crack in the world
Vogue 145:143 My '65
Crooked road
Time 85:91 F 12 '65
Darling
America 113:190-1 Ag 21 '65
Cath World 202:190-2 D '65
Christian Cent 83:17 Ja 5 '66
Commonweal 82:598 Ag 20 '65
Esquire 64:32+ N '65
Life 59:10 Ag 27 '65
Mlle il 61:62 O '65
Nation 201:108 Ag 30 '65
New Repub 153:29-31 S 4 '65: Reply.
  N. A. Renton. 153:37-8 S 25 '65
New Yorker 41:66 Ag 7 '65
Newsweek 66:79 Ag 16 '65
Sat R 48:40+ Ag 21 '65
Sr Schol il 87:sup 18 O 14 '65
Time il 86:74 Ag 13 '65
Vogue 146:168 O 1 '65
Dear Brigitte
Time il 85:64 F 5 '65
Dear heart
Commonweal 81:733 Mr 5 '65
Life 58:18 F 5 '65
Newsweek il 65:90D+ Mr 8 '65
Sat R 48:123 Mr 13 '65
Time il 95:97-8 Mr 12 '65
Diary of a chambermaid
Life 58:15 Mr 26 '65
New Repub 152:23 Ap 3 '65
Time 85:110 Mr 19 '65
Die! die! my darling!
Life 58:10 Ap 9 '65
Newsweek il 65:95 Ap 5 '65
Sat R 48:57 Je 12 '65
Time 85:97 Ap 2 '65
Dingaka
Time 86:80 Jl 2 '65
Do not disturb
Newsweek 67:62 Ja 10 '66
Time 87:89 Ja 14 '66
Doctor Zhivago
America 114:94 Ja 15 '66
Commonweal 83:441-2 Ja 14 '66
Esquire 64:132+ D '65
Life 60:48-59+ Ja 21 '66
New Repub 154:34+ Ja 15 '66
New Yorker 41:46-7 Ja 1 '66
Newsweek il 67:54-5 Ja 3 '66
Sat Eve Post il 239:26-31 Ja 15 '66
Sat R 49:43 Ja 15 '66
Time il 86:77 D 31 '65

Eva
New Repub 152:23 Ap 3 '65
New Yorker 41:102+ Je 12 '65
Newsweek il 65:116 Je 14 '65
Sat R 48:44 F 20 '65
Time 85:108 Je 11 '65
Eye of the needle
Commonweal 82:385 Je 11 '65
New Yorker 41:58+ Jl 3 '65
Face of Fu Manchu
Newsweek 66:111 N 22 '65
Fascist
New Yorker 41:58 Jl 3 '65
Time il 86:98 Jl 9 '65
Finnegans wake
Vogue 145:69 Je '65
Flight of the Phoenix
Newsweek 66:90+ Jl 12 '65
Fool killer
Commonweal 82:218 My 7 '65
New Repub 152:26 My 1 '65
Sat R 48:34 My 15 '65
Sr Schol 86:28 My 6 '65
Time 85:106 My 14 '65
Genghis Khan
Newsweek il 65:117 Je 14 '65
Time il 85:105 Je 25 '65
Girl happy
Sat R 48:30 My 29 '65
Goldfinger
Nat R 17:116 F 9 '65
New Yorker 41:165-7 Mr 20 '65
Goldstein
New Yorker 41:214-15 My 15 '65
Sat R 48:31 My 29 '65
Time 85:104+ My 7 '65
Goodbye, Charlie
New Repub 152:27 F 13 '65
Gospel according to Matthew
Commonweal 82:471-2 Jl 2 '65
Grand substitution
Newsweek 66:109 D 6 '65
Great race
America 113:349-51 S 25 '65
Commonweal 82:699-700 S 24 '65
Good H il 161:50 O '65
Life 59:8 S 17 '65
Life il 59:84-5+ Jl 9 '65
New Repub 153:31 N 6 '65
New Yorker 41:126 S 18 '65
Newsweek il 66:67 Ag 2 '65
Redbook 126:48 N '65
Sat R 48:24 Jl 17 '65
Sr Schol 87:22 O 7 '65
Time 86:106 S 24 '65
Greatest story ever told
America 112:296-7 F 27 '65
Cath World 201:76+ Ap '65
Christian Cent 82:492-5 Ap 21 '65
Commonweal 81:765 Mr 12 '65
Esquire 64:120-2 Jl '65
Life 58:25 F 26 '65
Nat R 17:430-2 My 18 '65
Nation 200:234 Mr 1 '65
New Repub 152:32+ Mr 6 '65
New Yorker 41:137 F 20 '65
Newsweek il 65:96B+ F 22 '65
Reporter 32:36+ Ap 22 '65
Sat R 48:41 F 27 '65
Sr Schol 86:28 Mr 18 '65
Sr Schol 86:sup 10 Ap 8 '65
Time il 85:96 F 26 '65
Vogue 145:57 Ap 15 '65
Group
Esquire 64:234-7+ D '65
Look il 29:32-6 S 7 '65
Mlle 61:166-8 S '65
Guide
Time 85:99 F 19 '65
Hallelujah trail
Commonweal 82:534 Jl 23 '65
Newsweek 66:90 Jl 26 '65
Time il 86:94 Jl 16 '65
Harlow (Levine production)
America 112:791-2 My 22 '65
America 113:123-4 Jl 31 '65
Nat R 17:738 Ag 24 '65
Newsweek il 66:89-90 Jl 26 '65
Sat R 48:37 Je 5 '65
Time il 86:88 Jl 23 '65
Harlow (Sargent production)
Sat R 48:37 Je 5 '65
Time 85:109 My 28 '65
Harvey Middleman, fireman
Esquire 64:43-4 S '65
New Repub 153:32 Jl 24 '65
New Yorker 41:87-8 Jl 24 '65
Newsweek il 66:83 Jl 19 '65
Sat R 48:31 Jl 31 '65
Time il 86:88 Jl 23 '65
Having a wild weekend
New Repub 153:35 S 25 '65
Newsweek il 66:86+ S 13 '65
Seventeen il 24:90-1 Jl '65
Time il 86:84 S 3 '65

MOVING picture plays—Criticisms, plots, etc.—
   Single works—*Continued*
Help!
   New Repub 153:34-5 S 25 '65
   New Yorker 41:101 Ag 28 '65
   Sat R 48:28 Ag 28 '65
   Seventeen il 24:230-1+ Ag '65
   Sr Schol 87:52 S 30 '65
   Time il 86:84 S 3 '65
High infidelity
   Time il 86:88 Jl 23 '65
High wind in Jamaica
   Commonweal 82:415 Je 18 '65
   New Repub 152:26 Je 5 '65
   Newsweek il 66:91 Jl 12 '65
   Sat R 48:30 My 29 '65
   Time il 86:80 Jl 2 '65
Hill
   America 113:419 O 9 '65
   Christian Cent 82:1548 D 15 '65
   Commonweal 83:25-6 O 8 '65
   Nation 201:288 O 25 '65
   New Repub 153:29-30+ O 9 '65
   New Yorker 41:189-90 O 9 '65
   Newsweek il 66:113-14 O 25 '65
   Sat R 48:30 O 2 '65
   Vogue 146:64 O 15 '65
How not to rob a department store
   Life 60:10 Ja 21 '66
   Time il 87:89 Ja 14 '66
How to murder your wife
   America 112:202-4 F 6 '65
   Commonweal 81:643 F 12 '65
   New Repub 152:27 F 13 '65
   New Yorker 40:114 Ja 30 '65
   Newsweek 65:86 F 8 '65
Hush . . . hush, sweet Charlotte
   Commonweal 81:734 Mr 5 '65
   New Repub 152:27 Mr 20 '65
   New Yorker 41:168 Mr 13 '65
   Newsweek il 65:98 Mr 15 '65
   Time 85:109 Mr 19 '65
Hysteria
   Newsweek 66:96+ S 20 '65
I saw what you did
   Redbook 125:26 S '65
   Sat R 48:44 S 4 '65
   Time il 86:67 Jl 30 '65
In harm's way
   America 112:588 Ap 17 '65
   Commonweal 82:117 Ap 16 '65
   New Repub 152:41 Ap 17 '65
   New Yorker 41:158 Ap 17 '65
   Newsweek il 65:110 Ap 12 '65
   Sat R 48:39 Ap 24 '65
   Time il 85:101-2 Ap 9 '65
Ipcress file
   Commonweal 82:637 S 3 '65
   Nation 201:108 Ag 30 '65
   New Repub 153:33 Jl 24 '65
   New Yorker 41:92 Ag 14 '65
   Newsweek 66:79 Ag 9 '65
   Sat R 48:31 Jl 31 '65
   Sr Schol 87:32 S 23 '65
   Time 86:74 Ag 13 '65
Italiano brava gente
   Newsweek 66:125D N 15 '65
   Sat R 48:75 O 30 '65
John Goldfarb, please come home
   New Yorker 41:103-4 Ap 3 '65
   Time 85:101 Ap 9 '65
Joy house
   New Yorker 41:114 F 27 '65
   Time 85:100 F 26 '65
Joy in the morning
   Commonweal 82:385 Je 11 '65
   Sat R 48:51 My 8 '65
   Time 85:108+ Je 11 '65
Judith
   Sat R 49:49 Ja 22 '66
Juliet of the spirits
   America 113:784+ D 18 '65
   Commonweal 83:244+ N 26 '65
   Life 59:18+ N 26 '65
   Nation 201:371-2 N 15 '65
   New Repub 153:28-30+ N 13 '65
   New Yorker 41:120-2 N 6 '65
   Newsweek il 66:124-124A+ N 15 '65
   Reporter 33:45-6 D 16 '65
   Sat R 48:55 N 20 '65
   Time il 86:114+ N 12 '65
   Vogue 147:70 Ja 1 '66
Ken Murray's Hollywood
   New Repub 152:34 My 29 '65
King and country
   Commonweal 83:26 O 8 '65
   Life 59:21 O 1 '65
   Sat R 48:30 O 2 '65
   Time il 86:113 O 1 '65
King Rat
   America 113:608-9 N 13 '65
   Commonweal 83:148-9 N 5 '65
   Life 59:15 N 12 '65
   New Repub 153:35 D 4 '65
   New Yorker 41:203 O 30 '65
   Newsweek 66:113 N 8 '65
   Sat R 48:46 N 6 '65
   Sr Schol 87:32 N 18 '65
   Time il 86:115+ N 5 '65

Kiss me, stupid
   Christian Cent 82:144-5 F 3 '65
   Vogue 145:97 Mr 1 '65
Knack
   America 113:103 Jl 24 '65
   Christian Cent 82:1547-8 D 15 '65
   Commonweal 82:473 Jl 2 '65
   Esquire 64:36+ O '65
   Nat R 17:886+ O 5 '65
   Nation 201:68 Ag 2 '65
   New Repub 153:29-30 Jl 10 '65
   New Yorker 41:82+ Je 26 '65
   New Yorker 41:54 Jl 10 '65
   Newsweek 66:82 Jl 5 '65
   Redbook 126:48 N '65
   Reporter 33:64 S 23 '65
   Sat R 48:24 Jl 17 '65
   Time il 86:98 Jl 9 '65
   Vogue 146:52 Ag 15 '65
Kwaidan
   New Yorker 41:233 N 27 '65
   Newsweek 66:112 N 22 '65
   Sat R 48:55 N 20 '65
   Sr Schol 87:33 D 9 '65
Laurel and Hardy's Laughing 20's
   Time il 86:113 D 10 '65
Leather boys
   America 113:761 D 11 '65
   Commonweal 83:280 D 3 '65
   Life 59:20 D 10 '65
   New Repub 153:32 N 20 '65
   New Yorker 41:233 N 13 '65
   Newsweek 66:108 N 22 '65
   Sat R 48:55 N 20 '65
   Time 86:130+ N 19 '65
Life at the top
   Commonweal 83:376 D 24 '65
   New Repub 153:32-3 D 18 '65
   New Yorker 41:162-3 D 18 '65
   Newsweek 66:71A-71B D 27 '65
   Sat R 48:42 D 18 '65
Life upside down
   Commonweal 82:666 S 17 '65
   New Repub 153:25-6 S 11 '65
   Newsweek 66:70B S 6 '65
   Time il 86:95+ S 10 '65
Little ones
   Life 59:15 O 22 '65
Lonely boy
   Vogue 145:69 Je '65
Lord Jim
   America 112:375 Mr 13 '65
   Commonweal 81:791-2 Mr 19 '65
   Life 58:15 Mr 19 '65
   Nation 200:315 Mr 22 '65
   New Repub 152:22-3+ Mr 13 '65
   New Yorker 41:94+ Mr 6 '65
   Newsweek il 65:91-2 Mr 8 '65
   Reporter 32:46-8 Je 17 '65
   Sat R il 48:39 Mr 6 '65
   Sr Schol 86:33 Ap 29 '65
   Time 85:98 Mr 5 '65
   Vogue 145:57 Ap 15 '65
Love à la carte
   Time il 85:91 F 12 '65
   Vogue 145:52 F 15 '65
Love has many faces
   Commonweal 81:611 F 5 '65
   Newsweek 65:99 Mr 15 '65
   Sat R 48:43 F 6 '65
   Time il 85:E7 Mr 5 '65
Loved one
   America 113:481-2 O 23 '65
   Holiday 38:174+ D '65
   Life 59:34 O 8 '65
   Life 59:10 O 29 '65
   Nation 201:316 N 1 '65
   New Repub 153:32-4 O 23 '65
   New Yorker 41:198 O 23 '65
   Newsweek 66:122+ O 18 '65
   Reporter 33:40-2 N 18 '65
   Sat R 48:75 O 23 '65
   Sr Schol il 87:sup 10 N 18 '65
   Time il 86:121 O 22 '65
   Vogue 146:69 N 15 '65
Magnificent cuckold
   Time il 85:97 Ap 2 '65
Major Dundee
   Commonweal 82:118 Ap 16 '65
   New Repub 152:40 Ap 17 '65
   Newsweek 65:94 My 3 '65
   Sat R 48:30 Ap 10 '65
   Time il 85:101 Ap 16 '65
   Vogue 145:99 Ap 1 '65
Male companion
   Time il 87:80 Ja 21 '66
Male hunt
   Commonweal 82:293 My 21 '65
   Life 58:16 My 7 '65
   New Yorker 41:120 My 1 '65
   Time il 85:109+ Ap 30 '65
Marriage—Italian style
   America 112:202-4 F 6 '65
   Sr Schol 86:10T F 11 '65

MOVING picture plays—Criticisms, plots, etc.—
  Single works—*Continued*
Married woman
    Commonweal 82:637-8 S 3 '65
    Nation 201:259 O 18 '65
    New Repub 153:26-7 S 11 '65
    New Yorker 41:100 Ag 21 '65
    Newsweek 66:79-80 Ag 30 '65
    Sat R 48:28 Ag 28 '65
    Time il 86:82 Ag 27 '65
Masquerade
    America 112:809 My 29 '65
    Commonweal 82:292 My 21 '65
    Life 58:15 My 21 '65
    New Yorker 41:168 My 22 '65
    Time il 85:106+ My 14 '65
Mickey One
    Commonweal 83:99-100 O 22 '65
    Nation 201:259 O 18 '65
    New Repub 153:29-30+ O 9 '65
    New Yorker 41:211 O 2 '65
    Newsweek il 66:94 O 4 '65
    Sat R 48:63 O 16 '65
Mirage
    America 112:887 Je 19 '65
    Commonweal 82:357 Je 4 '65
    Life 58:15 Je 18 '65
    New Repub 152:25 Je 5 '65
    New Yorker 41:118-19 Je 5 '65
    Sat R 48:31 Jl 31 '65
    Time il 85:104+ My 28 '65
Mister Moses
    America 112:809 My 29 '65
    Commonweal 82:292 My 21 '65
    New Repub 152:34 My 29 '65
    Time il 85:106+ My 28 '65
Moment of truth
    America 113:226 Ag 28 '65
    Life 59:10 S 24 '65
    New Yorker 41:92 Ag 14 '65
    Newsweek 66:81 Ag 23 '65
    Sat R 48:51 S 11 '65
    Time il 86:76 Ag 20 '65
Monsieur Verdoux
    Esquire 63:18+ Ap '65
Morituri
    America 113:265 S 11 '65
    Commonweal 82:637 S 3 '65
    Life 59:10 S 3 '65
    Newsweek il 66:81+ Ag 23 '65
    Sat R 48:40 Ag 21 '65
    Time 86:84 S 3 '65
    Vogue 146:76 S 15 '65
Murder most foul
    Time 85:110 Je 11 '65
My fair lady
    Esquire 63:44+ F '65
Nanny
    America 113:542+ N 6 '65
    Commonweal 83:217 N 19 '65
    Life 59:20 D 3 '65
    New Repub 153:34 D 11 '65
    Time 86:101+ O 29 '65
    Vogue 146:147 D '65
Never too late
    America 113:733 D 4 '65
    New Yorker 41:234 N 13 '65
    Newsweek il 66:125A+ N 15 '65
Night walker
    Time 85:64 F 5 '65
Nine days of one year
    Esquire 63:18+ My '65
Nobody waved goodbye
    America 112:646-7 My 1 '65
    Cath World 201:279-80 Jl '65
    Christian Cent 82:839-40 Je 30 '65
    Commonweal 82:218+ My 7 '65
    Life 58:12 Je 4 '65
    Nation 200:516 My 10 '65
    New Repub 152:32 My 15 '65
    New Yorker 41:163-4 Ap 24 '65
    Sat R 48:31 My 29 '65
    Sr Schol 86:sup 10 Ap 8 '65
    Time il 85:110+ Ap 30 '65
    Vogue 145:69 Je '65
None but the brave
    Commonweal 82:84 Ap 9 '65
    Newsweek il 65:92 F 15 '65
    Time 85:96+ F 26 '65
Not on your life!
    America 112:690-1 My 8 '65
    Commonweal 82:157 Ap 23 '65
    Nation 200:432 Ap 19 '65
    New Repub 152:24+ My 1 '65
    New Yorker 41:158 Ap 17 '65
    Newsweek 65:94+ My 3 '65
    Time 85:102 Ap 16 '65
Nothing but a man
    Ebony il 20:198-201 Ap '65
    Life 58:15 F 19 '65
    Vogue 145:52 F 15 '65
Once a thief
    Commonweal 82:727 O 1 '65
One way pendulum
    New Repub 152:25 Mr 20 '65
    Newsweek 65:99 Mr 15 '65
    Time Il 85:97 Mr 12 '65

Onibaba
    Nation 200:234 Mr 1 '65
    New Yorker 41:113 F 27 '65
    Newsweek 65:86+ F 8 '65
Operation crossbow
    America 112:587 Ap 17 '65
    Commonweal 82:118 Ap 16 '65
    Life 58:18 Ap 16 '65
    New Repub 152:40 Ap 17 '65
    New Yorker 41:158-9 Ap 17 '65
    Newsweek 65:95 Ap 5 '65
    Sat R 48:39 Ap 24 '65
    Time il 85:102+ Ap 9 '65
Othello
    Newsweek il 67:85 Ja 17 '66
Overcoat
    Commonweal 81:705 F 26 '65
    Nation 200:316 Mr 22 '65
    Newsweek il 65:87+ F 8 '65
Paris secret
    Time il 86:130 S 17 '65
Patch of blue
    America 114:158 Ja 22 '66
    Commonweal 83:376 D 24 '65
    Commonweal 83:478 Ja 21 '66
    New Yorker 41:58+ D 25 '65
    Newsweek il 66:71 D 27 '65
    Sat R 49:97 Ja 8 '66
    Time 86:98+ D 17 '65
    Vogue 147:36 Ja 15 '66
Pawnbroker
    America 112:838-9 Je 5 '65
    Christian Cent 82:942-3 Jl 28 '65
    Commonweal 82:255-6 My 14 '65
    Life 58:16 Ap 2 '65
    Nation 200:515-16 My 10 '65
    New Repub 152:23 Ap 24 '65
    New Yorker 41:164-5 Ap 24 '65
    Newsweek il 65:96+ Ap 26 '65
    Sat R 48:37 Ap 3 '65
    Time il 85:103+ Ap 23 '65
    Vogue 146:37 Jl '65
Quick, before it melts
    Commonweal 81:643 F 12 '65
Rage to live
    Vogue 146:116 N 1 '65
Railroad man
    America 113:693-4 N 27 '65
    Commonweal 83:217 N 19 '65
    Nation 201:372 N 15 '65
Rapture
    America 113:297 S 18 '65
    Commonweal 82:666 S 17 '65
    New Repub 153:35 S 25 '65
    New Yorker 41:86 S 4 '65
    Newsweek il 66:88 S 13 '65
    Sat R 48:51 S 11 '65
    Time 86:82 Ag 27 '65
Red beard
    Esquire 64:84+ D '65
Red desert
    Christian Cent 82:713 Je 2 '65
    Commonweal 81:704-5 F 26 '65
    Life 58:12 Mr 5 '65
    New Repub 152:30-4 F 20 '65
    New Yorker 40:88+ F 13 '65
    Newsweek il 65:96+ F 22 '65
    Sat R 48:44 F 20 '65
    Time il 85:99 F 19 '65
Red dust
    Nation 200:234 Mr 1 '65
Red line 7000
    Newsweek il 66:71A D 27 '65
    Sat R 48:74 D 4 '65
    Time il 87:89 Ja 14 '66
Repulsion
    Commonweal 83:124-5 O 29 '65
    Life 59:23 O 8 '65
    New Repub 153:31-2+ O 16 '65
    New Yorker 41:190 O 9 '65
    Sat R 48:63 O 16 '65
    Time il 86:115+ O 8 '65
    Vogue 146:147 D '65
Return from the ashes
    Commonweal 83:315 D 10 '65
    Newsweek il 66:104+ D 6 '65
    Time il 86:104 N 26 '65
Reward
    America 113:351 S 25 '65
    Commonweal 82:727 O 1 '65
    Time il 86:114+ O 1 '65
Rotten to the core
    Newsweek 66:87A+ S 13 '65
    Sat R 48:51 Jl 24 '65
    Time il 86:76 Ag 20 '65
Rounders
    New Repub 152:26 Mr 20 '65
    Newsweek 65:95 Ap 5 '65
    Time il 85:104 My 7 '65
Saboteur
    New Yorker 41:102 Ag 28 '65
Sallah
    America 113:482 O 23 '65
    Sat R 48:43 Mr 27 '65
    Sat R 48:50 S 25 '65

MOVING picture plays—Criticisms, plots, etc.—
Single works—*Continued*
Salt of the earth
Nation 201:372 N 15 '65
Samurai assassin
New Repub 152:23 Ap 3 '65
New Yorker 41:168-9 Mr 27 '65
Newsweek 65:88+ Mr 29 '65
Sandpiper
America 113:103 Jl 24 '65
Life 59:22 Jl 16 '65
New Repub 153:33 Jl 24 '65
New Yorker 41:87 Jl 24 '65
Newsweek 66:89 Jl 26 '65
Sat R 48:51 Jl 24 '65
Time il 86:94 Jl 16 '65
Sands of the Kalahari
Commonweal 83:315 D 10 '65
Newsweek il 66:104 D 6 '65
Time il 86:103+ D 3 '65
Satan bug
Newsweek il 65:94 My 3 '65
Time 85:110 Ap 30 '65
Secret of my success
Commonweal 83:315 D 10 '65
Time 86:103 N 26 '65
Sex and the single girl
Commonweal 81:643 F 12 '65
She
New Yorker 41:100+ S 11 '65
Newsweek 66:98+ S 20 '65
Sat R 48:51 My 8 '65
Time il 86:127+ S 17 '65
Shenandoah
America 113:170 Ag 14 '65
Commonweal 82:384 Je 11 '65
Newsweek 66:81B Ag 23 '65
Sat R 48:51 My 8 '65
Sr Schol 86:36 My 13 '65
Time 86:74 Ag 13 '65
Ship of fools
America 113:170 Ag 14 '65
Christian Cent 82:1262 O 13 '65
Commentary 40:77-8 N '65
Commonweal 82:563-4 Ag 6 '65
Holiday 38:120+ S '65
Life 59:11 Ag 6 '65
New Repub 153:36-8 Ag 7 '65
New Yorker 41:56 Jl 31 '65
Newsweek 66:80 Ag 16 '65
Reporter 33:48-9 N 4 '65
Sat R 48:19+ Jl 3 '65
Time 86:85 Ag 6 '65
Vogue 146:51 Ag 1 '65
Shocking old party. See La vieille dame
indigne, below
Shop on Main Street
Sat R 49:49 Ja 22 '66
Signpost to murder
Commonweal 81::610 F 5 '65
Time 85:106 My 28 '65
Situation hopeless but not serious
America 113:482 O 23 '65
New Repub 153:32 N 6 '65
Sky falls in
Newsweek 65:44 F 8 '65
Slender thread
America 114:158 Ja 22 '66
Commonweal 83:478 Ja 21 '66
New Yorker 41:71 Ja 15 '66
Newsweek 67:61-2 Ja 10 '66
Sat R 49:97 Ja 8 '66
Time 87:89 Ja 14 '66
Soft skin
Esquire 63:22+ My '65
Sons of Katie Elder
America 113:296-7 S 18 '65
Newsweek il 66:70B S 6 '65
Sat R 48:44 S 4 '65
Time 86:84 S 3 '65
Sound of music
America 112:374-5 Mr 13 '65
Commonweal 82:24 Mr 26 '65
Life il 58:52 Mr 12 '65
New Repub 152:26 Mr 20 '65
New Yorker 41:96 Mr 6 '65
Newsweek il 65:100 Mr 15 '65
Sat R 48:36 Mr 20 '65
Sr Schol 86:23 Mr 25 '65
Time il 85:98+ Mr 5 '65
Vogue 145:143 My '65
Spy who came in from the cold
America 114:94 Ja 15 '66
Life 60:8+ Ja 7 '66
Nation 202:84 Ja 17 '66
New Repub 154:32-3 Ja 1 '66
New Yorker 41:46 Ja 1 '66
Newsweek il 67:56 Ja 3 '66
Sat R 49:44 Ja 15 '66
Time il 86:46 D 24 '65
Stagecoach
Newsweek il 66:79 Ag 30 '65
Strange bedfellows
Time 85:98 Mr 12 '65

Stranger knocks
Commonweal 82:157 Ap 23 '65
Nation 200:432 Ap 19 '65
New Yorker 41:106 Ap 3 '65
Newsweek 65:110 Ap 12 '65
Il successo
Commonweal 82:293 My 21 '65
Newsweek il 65:104 My 17 '65
Time il 85:105 My 14 '65
Sylvia
Commonweal 81:610 F 5 '65
New Yorker 40:90+ F 13 '65
Newsweek il 65:96D F 22 '65
Sat R 48:36 Mr 20 '65
Time 85:99 F 19 '65
Symphony for a massacre
Commonweal 82:357 Je 4 '65
New Repub 153:28-9 Jl 3 '65
New Yorker 41:102 Je 12 '65
Newsweek 65:116+ Je 14 '65
Synanon
America 112:810 My 29 '65
Commonweal 82:320 My 28 '65
Life 58:19 My 14 '65
New Repub 152:33-4 My 29 '65
Newsweek 65:104 My 17 '65
Sat R 48:51 My 1 '65
Time 85:108 My 14 '65
Taxi for Tobruk
Commonweal 82:84 Ap 9 '65
Life 58:17 Ap 23 '65
New Yorker 41:159 Ap 10 '65
Time 85:99+ F 26 '65
Tenth victim
Commonweal 83:478 Ja 21 '66
Esquire il 65:81 Ja '66
Nation 202:27 Ja 3 '66
New Yorker 41:56 D 25 '65
Newsweek 67:55 Ja 3 '66
Time 86:46 D 24 '65
Terra trema
New Repub 153:31-2 O 23 '65
That darn cat
America 113:760 D 11 '65
Commonweal 83:349 D 17 '65
New Yorker 41:232-3 D 11 '65
Sr Schol il 87:28 D 2 '65
Time il 86:113+ D 10 '65
That funny feeling
Time 86:118 N 5 '65
These are the damned
Time 86:67 Jl 30 '65
Third day
Time 86:67 Jl 30 '65
36 hours
America 112:230 F 13 '65
New Yorker 40:120 F 6 '65
Newsweek il 65:86 F 8 '65
Time 85:64 F 5 '65
Those Calloways
America 112:619 Ap 24 '65
Newsweek 65:90B+ Mr 8 '65
Sr Schol 86:18 F 25 '65
Time 85:C10 Ap 23 '65
Those magnificent men in their flying ma-
chines
Cath World 202:64 O '65
Commonweal 82:534 Jl 23 '65
Life 58:15 Je 25 '65
New Repub 152:27 Je 19 '65
New Yorker 41:114 Je 19 '65
Newsweek 66:83 Jl 5 '65
Redbook 125:26 S '65
Sat R 48:22 Je 26 '65
Sr Schol 87:30-1 S 16 '65
Time il 85:100+ Je 18 '65
Vogue 146:37 Jl '65
Thousand clowns
Commonweal 83:349 D 17 '65
Life 60:10 Ja 14 '66
New Repub 153:33-4 D 11 '65
New Yorker 41:162 D 18 '65
Newsweek 67:55 Ja 3 '66
Sat R 48:42 D 18 '65
Time il 86:101+ D 17 '65
Thunderball
America 114:52-3 Ja 8 '66
Esquire il 63:62-73 Je '65
Life 60:8+ Ja 7 '66
Look il 29:45-50+ Jl 13 '65
New Yorker 41:101-3 Ja 8 '66
Newsweek 67:56 Ja 3 '66
Sat R 49:43 Ja 15 '66
Time 86:46 D 24 '65
La Tía Tula
Life 59:18 Jl 2 '65
New Repub 153:28 Jl 3 '65
Newsweek 65:98 Je 21 '65
Time il 85:106+ Je 11 '65
Tomb of Ligeia
Newsweek 65:88 Mr 1 '65
Time il 85:110 My 21 '65

MOVING picture plays—Criticisms, plots, etc.—
    Single works—*Continued*
Train
    America 112:466 Ap 3 '65
    Commonweal 82:52-3 Ap 2 '65
    Nation 200:376 Ap 5 '65
    New Repub 152:25 Mr 20 '65
    New Yorker 41:152-3 Mr 20 '65
    Newsweek il 65:97-97A Mr 22 '65
    Sat R 48:123 Mr 13 '65
    Sr Schol 86:sup38 Mr 4 '65
    Sr Schol il 86:26 Mr 4 '65
    Time il 85:98+ Mr 26 '65
    Vogue 145:57 Ap 15 '65
Trial of Joan of Arc
    Commonweal 81:671 F 19 '65
    New Repub 152:26 F 13 '65
    New Yorker 41:138 F 20 '65
    Newsweek il 65:90+ F 15 '65
    Time il 85:91 F 12 '65
Les vampires
    Sat R 48:32 S 18 '65
Variety lights
    New Repub 152:33 My 15 '65
    New Yorker 41:167 My 8 '65
    Newsweek 65:104 My 17 '65
Very special favor
    Newsweek 66:87A S 13 '65
Vice and virtue
    Newsweek il 65:92+ Ap 5 '65
La vieille dame indigne
    New Yorker 41:185-6 Ap 17 '65
Viva Maria
    Commonweal 83:478 Ja 21 '66
    Look il 29:64-6+ My 4 '65
    Nation 202:27-8 Ja 3 '66
    New Yorker 41:56+ D 25 '65
    Newsweek 67:56 Ja 3 '66
    Time il 86:77 D 31 '65
Von Ryan's express
    America 112:888 Je 19 '65
    Life 59:16 Jl 23 '65
    New Yorker 41:59-60 Jl 17 '65
    Newsweek 66:90D-90E Jl 12 '65
    Sat R 48:24 Jl 17 '65
    Time 85:104 Je 25 '65
War lord
    Commonweal 83:315 D 10 '65
    Newsweek il 66:106+ D 6 '65
    Time il 86:103 N 26 '65
What's new pussycat?
    America 113:27 Jl 3 '65
    Commonweal 82:473 Jl 2 '65
    Esquire 64:34+ N '65
    Life 59:12 Jl 9 '65
    Nation 201:68 Ag 2 '65
    New Repub 153:30-1 Jl 10 '65
    New Yorker 41:78 Je 26 '65
    Newsweek il 66:90E+ Jl 12 '65
    Sat R 48:25 Jl 17 '65
    Time il 86:80 Jl 2 '65
When the boys meet the girls
    Time il 87:80 Ja 21 '66
White voices
    Commonweal 82:158 Ap 23 '65
    New Repub 152:29-30 Mr 27 '65
    Sat R 48:43 F 6 '65
    Time il 85:102+ Ap 16 '65
Why bother to knock
    Time 85:91 F 12 '65
Wild seed
    Sat R 48:40 Ap 24 '65
Winner
    Cath World 201:411-12 S '65
    Commonweal 82:502 Jl 9 '65
    New Repub 153:32 Jl 24 '65
    Newsweek il 66:90 Jl 26 '65
Yellow Rolls-Royce
    America 112:809 My 29 '65
    Commonweal 82:319 My 28 '65
    New Repub 152:24 Ap 24 '65
    New Yorker 41:167 My 22 '65
    Sat R 48:30-1 My 29 '65
Young Cassidy
    America 112:466-7 Ap 3 '65
    Commonweal 82:53 Ap 2 '65
    Life il 58:93-5 F 12 '65
    New Repub 152:29-30 Mr 27 '65
    New Yorker 41:169-70 Mr 27 '65
    Newsweek 65:97A Mr 22 '65
    Reporter 32:46-8 Je 17 '65
    Time il 85:97 Ap 2 '65
    Vogue 145:99 Ap 1 '65
Young lovers
    Newsweek 65:91B F 15 '65
Your cheatin' heart
    Time 85:67 Je 4 '65
Zebra in the kitchen
    Time il 87:80 Ja 21 '66
Zorba the Greek
    Christian Cent 82:216-18 F 17 '65
    Vogue 145:52 F 15 '65
MOVING picture production and direction
Agony and the ecstasy of Michelangelo. il
    Look 29:41-8 Mr 9 '65

All for the love of Mike; filming of Virginia
    Woolf. C. R. Jennings. il Sat Eve Post 238:
    83-7 O 9 '65
Andy Warhol, movie maker. H. Junker. Na-
    tion 200:206-8 F 22 '65
Ark that John built; J. Huston's new ver-
    sion of The Bible. il Life 59:43-4 Ag 13 '65
Big build-up and a no-name cast for the
    Group. I. Mothner. il Look 29:32-6 S 7 '65
Call me Elizabeth; filming Who's afraid of
    Virginia Woolf? il Newsweek 66:86 S 13 '65
Celluloid syllabus. D. C. Stewart. il Am Ed
    1:29-32 S '65
David Lean recipe: a whack in the guts.
    H. Alpert. il N Y Times Mag p32-3+ My
    23 '65
Day with Disney. F. Whitaker. il Am Artist
    29:44-8+ S '65
Defeat of Hitler's order to burn Paris;
    filming of Is Paris burning? il Look 30:
    40-5 Ja 25 '66
Disco Volante, the saucer that flies; new
    James Bond epic Thunderball. J. Marten-
    hoff. il Motor B 116:32-3+ D '65
Dr Zhivago: the making of a movie. R. S.
    Stewart. il Atlan 216:58-64 Ag '65
007-the spy with the golden touch; creation
    of James Bond. J. Stewart-Gordon. Read
    Digest 87:113-17 O '65
Epic of beauty and terror; Dr Zhivago; with
    report by R. Schickel. il Life 60:48-59+ Ja
    21 '66
Fantasy, flesh and Fellini. T. Meehan. il Sat
    Eve Post 239:24-8+ Ja 1 '66
First the pasta, then the play; G. Masina and
    F. Fellini. M. S. Davis. il N Y Times Mag
    p 10-11+ Ja 2 '66
Giraffe in Piazza del Popolo; D. de Laurentiis'
    story of the Bible. T. Sage. il Nat R
    17:106-6 F 9 '65
Good drizzle after a big sizzle; shooting The
    reward. D. Zeitlin. il Life 57:45-6+ F 26 '65
Greatest pie fight ever creates a horrendous
    splaat! scene in Great race. D. Zeitlin. il
    Life 59:84-5+ Jl 9 '65
Group on: The group. L. Lerman. il Mlle
    61:166-8 S '65
Hitchcock's three nightmares. il Newsweek
    67:89-89A+ Ja 24 '66
Hollywood's heedless horseman. J. G. Dunne.
    il Holiday 38:111-12+ D '65
I went on location with Zhivago. V. Leduc.
    il Vogue 146:114-21+ S 15 '65
James Bond conquers all in Thunderball. G.
    Zimmermann. il Look 29:45-50+ Jl 13 '65
James Bond's weird world of inventions;
    zany gimmicks for James Bond movies. H.
    Shuldiner. il Pop Sci 188:60-3+ Ja '66
Letter from Paris; filming of Is Paris burn-
    ing? Genêt. New Yorker 41:142-3 S 18 '65
Letter home; filming of Doctor Zhivago.
    H. Lawrenson. Esquire 64:132+ D '65
Lot to learn; Electronovision used to film
    W. Sargent's Harlow. il Newsweek 65:83+
    My 31 '65
Low-budget movies with pow! E. Goodman.
    il N Y Times Mag p42-3+ F 28 '65
Luis Buñuel: an eye in the wilderness. R.
    Carson. il Holiday 37:123-4+ Ap '65
Man you hate to love; filming of Is Paris
    burning? il Time 86:94 N 12 '65
My word is his bond: a view from the back
    room; writing and producing Thunderball.
    R. Maibaum. Esquire 63:73+ Je '65
New fantasy by the 8½ man; with report
    by N. Liber. il Life 59:50-4 Ag 27 '65
New role for Rafer. il Ebony 21:181-4 D '65
Noah; literal view of the Bible in Huston's
    new movie, The Bible. il Look 29:21-6 Jl
    27 '65
Offbeat director in outer space; S. Kubrick.
    H. Alpert. il N Y Times Mag p 14-15+
    Ja 16 '66
On the scene with the Beatles; movie num-
    ber two: Help! ed. by E. Miller. il Seven-
    teen 24:230-1+ Ag '65
On the set with Moreau and Bardot; filming
    of Viva Maria. C. Brossard. il Look 29:64-
    6+ My 4 '65
Oscar bound: Doctor Zhivago. il Time 86:
    44-5 D 24 '65
Our far-flung correspondents; filming of The
    Bible. L. Ross. New Yorker 41:185-6+ S 25
    '65
Pall of the wild; filming of Tarzan and the
    big river. il Time 86:60 O 29 '65
Profiles; F. Fellini. L. Ross. New Yorker 41:
    63-6+ O 30 '65
Reign of Spain. il Time 85:60+ F 26 '65
Sean Connery takes over Rock Point; shoot-
    ing of Thunderball. B. Allen. il Mlle 62:
    127+ D '65
Senior scholastic interview: choreographing a
    spy thriller, Arabesque; ed. by M. Ronan.
    S. Donen. il Sr Schol 87:20 D 2 '65

MOVING picture production and direction
    —*Continued*
Step right this way to movieland; Studio
    tour of Universal and visit to Warlord set.
    B. Owen. il Sr Schol 86:34 My 13 '65
Up anchor! Otto's navy; Lilliputian version
    of the battle of Leyte Gulf for a movie
    called In harm's way. il Life 58:73-4 Mr
    5 '65
What I did last summer; acting in The group.
    C. Bergen. il Esquire 64:234-7+ D '65
Where the action is; symposium. il Sat R 48:
    10-22+ D 25 '65
Wyler's wiles; The collector. il Time 85:92
    Je 18 '65
        See also
Moving picture directors

MOVING picture projection
Flash: more Super 8 coming. il Pop Phot
    56:73 Je '65
How to put that zing in your screenings!
    I. Watson. il Pop Phot 56:122+ Ap '65
Much belabored reverse projection results
    in a wonderfully amusing motion picture.
    M. A. Matzkin. Mod Phot 29:92 Mr '65
Now: instant-projection super 8. J. S. Forney.
    il Pop Phot 58:44 Ja '66
        See also
Projection apparatus

MOVING picture projectors. See Projection
    apparatus

MOVING picture scripts. See Moving picture
    authorship

MOVING picture societies
Movies on the campus. D. C. Stewart. il
    Sat R 48:82-3 F 20 '65

MOVING picture sound recording
8-mm optical sound arrives! H. V. Fondiller.
    il Pop Phot 58:46+ Ja '66

MOVING picture studios
Hollywood changes script on sightseers; Uni-
    versal City tours. il Bsns W p30-1 Jl 10 '65
Step right this way to movieland; Studio
    tour of Universal and visit to Warlord set.
    B. Owen. il Sr Schol 86:34 My 13 '65

MOVING picture theaters
King of intermissions. il Time 86:93-4 Jl 9
    '65
        See also
New York (city)—Radio City music hall

MOVING pictures
Are movies going to pieces? P. Kael; dis-
    cussion. Atlan 215:42 Mr '65
Festival 1: experiments of Film-makers'
    Cinematheque. New Yorker 41:52-4 D 4 '65
Films '65. C. Reynolds. Pop Phot 56:126+ F;
    123 Ap; 57:129 O '65
Gross is greener; Sound of music a financial
    success. Time 87:46 Ja 14 '66
Movie you feel and smell as well as see.
    il Pop Sci 187:44-5 Jl '65
Two Harlows; deluxe and quickie. il Life 58:
    118+ My 7 '65
        See also
Academy awards (moving pictures)
Moving picture plays
Moving picture production and direction
Moving picture theaters
Television broadcasting—Moving pictures

Advertising
        See Moving picture industry—Advertising

Animated cartoons
Computer-produced movies. K. C. Knowlton.
    il Science 150:1116-20 N 26 '65
Five ideas to animate. L. Lipton. il Pop
    Phot 56:124 F '65
Paint a movie on film! E. Davis. il Pop Phot
    56:120 My '65
Put a panther in your tank; back in the
    cartoon business. il Time 86:90 O 1 '65
VanDerBeek: master of animation. R. Christ-
    gau. il Pop Phot 57:106-11 S '65
        See also
Disney, Walt, productions

Bibliography
Books for your summer reading. C. Reynolds.
    il Pop Phot 57:108-9+ Jl '65

Censorship
        See Moving picture censorship

Collectors and collecting
Show the world's greatest movies. C. Reyn-
    olds. il Pop Phot 56:108-14 F '65

Comedy
Films; present day vs. old-time comedies.
    D. Macdonald. Esquire 63:14+ Je '65
Laughter needs a renaissance. R. A. Duprey.
    Cath World 202:63-4 O '65
Out is in. il Look 29:18-19 Mr 9 '65
Return of Batman. Time 86:60+ N 26 '65

Rise and fall and rise of slapstick. M. Ronan.
    il Sr Schol 87:21 O 7 '65
Vacuous comedies. M. Walsh. America 112:
    437-8 Mr 27 '65
When in doubt, spoof. M. Walsh. America
    113:83-5 Jl 17 '65

Dance films
1965 directory of dance films. il Dance Mag
    39:58-64+ S '65
Poisoned half loaf. C. Barnes. il Dance Mag
    40:36-7 Ja '66
Special issue. il Dance Mag 39:22-6+ S '65

Dancing
Senior scholastic interview; ed. by M. Ronan.
    S. Donen. il Sr Schol 87:20 D 2 '65

Detective and mystery films
Big Bond bonanza; Thunderball production.
    W. K. Zinsser. il Sat Eve Post 238:76-81
    Jl 17 '65
Bondomania; popularity of James Bond films.
    il Time 85:59 Je 11 '65

Documentary films
ABC's of filming bees. W. D. Woodson. il
    Pop Phot 56:120-1+ Ap '65
Films about patriotism. V. M. Falconer. Sr
    Schol 86:13T F 4 '65
Films and filmstrips (cont) V. Falconer. Sr
    Schol 86:22T F 18; sup22 Mr 18; sup34 Ap
    15 '65
Films and filmstrips for literature units.
    V. M. Falconer. Sr Schol 86:sup34 Mr 4 '65
Films and filmstrips for teachers and parents.
    V. M. Falconer. Sr Schol 86:sup 11 My 13 '65
Films beget films. by J. Leyda. Review
    Nation 200:655-6 Je 14 '65. H. Junker
Focus on Willard Van Dyke. A. Zuckerman.
    il Pop Phot 56:118-19+ Ap '65
New films. Am For 71:55 Jl '65
New films and filmstrips (cont of) Films and
    filmstrips. V. M. Falconer. Sr Schol 87:
    sup24 S 23; sup4 O 21; sup 10-11 O 28; sup
    16 N 4 '65
Red line 7000. il Hot Rod 18:112-13 O '65
Three kinds of dance film. A. F. Snyder.
    il Dance Mag 39:34-9 S '65

Criticisms, plots, etc.

Bus
    America 112:618-19 Ap 24 '65
    Commonweal 82:84 Ap 9 '65
    Sat R 48:43 Mr 27 '65
    Sr Schol 86:38+ Ap 15 '65
China!
    Commonweal 82:535-6 Jl 23 '65
    Esquire 64:44+ S '65
    New Repub 152:25 Je 5 '65
    Newsweek il 65:96 Je 21 '65
Chronicle of a summer
    New Repub 152:33 My 15 '65
    New Yorker 41:167 My 8 '65
Eleanor Roosevelt story
    Commonweal 83:216-17 N 19 '65
    Esquire 64:42-3 S '65
    Life 59:10 D 3 '65
    New Repub 153:34-5 D 4 '65
    New Yorker 41:231-3 N 20 '65
    Sat R 48:74 D 4 '65
Evening with the Royal ballet
    Dance Mag il 40:36-7 Ja '66
Guns of August
    Sr Schol 86:42 F 18 '65
Islands of green
    Am For 71:55 Jl '65
    Audubon Mag il 67:317-19 S '65
Love goddesses
    Commonweal 82:22+ Mr 26 '65
    New Repub 152:25 Mr 20 '65
    New Yorker 41:167-8 Mr 13 '65
    Newsweek 65:90B Mr 8 '65
    Sat R 48:36 Mr 20 '65
    Time il 85:E5+ Mr 19 '65
Mediterranean holiday
    Sr Schol 86:29-30 F 11 '65
South African essay
    Sat R 48:50 Jl 24 '65
To die in Madrid
    Commonweal 83:25 O 8 '65
    Esquire 64:40-2 S '65
    Life 59:16 S 10 '65
    Nation 201:288 O 25 '65
    New Repub 153:27 Jl 3 '65
    New Yorker 41:168 S 25 '65
    Newsweek 66:96 S 20 '65
    Sat R 48:32 S 18 '65
    Time 86:117 O 1 '65
Tokyo Olympiad
    Newsweek il 66:106+ O 11 '65
    Sat R 48:50 D 11 '65
World without sun
    Seventeen 24:56 F '65
    Vogue 145:97 Mr 1 '65

MOVING pictures—*Continued*

Editing

Much belabored reverse projection results in a wonderfully amusing motion picture. M. A. Matzkin. Mod Phot 29:92 Mr '65

Sporting spirit; Tokyo Olympiad; J: Douglas version changes Japanese epic into news-reel. A. Knight. Sat R 48:50 D 11 '65

You need long lens, high flying camera to film an eagle. L. Jacobs, jr. il Mod Phot 29:89+ Mr '65

Educational aspects

See Moving pictures in education

Educational films

See Moving pictures in education

History

Birth of The birth of a nation. B. Crowther. il N Y Times Mag p24-5+ F 7 '65

15¢ before 6:00 PM: the wonderful movies of the, 'thirties. J. C. Holmes. il Harper 231: 51-5 D '65

Hooray for Hollywood; symposium. il Mlle 61:4+ Jl '65

Horror films

Letter from Paris. Genêt. New Yorker 41: 171-2 My 15 '65

Industrial applications

See Moving pictures in industry

International aspects

Mecca for film trade; Film centrum, Brussels. Bsns W p80 Ap 17 '65

Where the action is; symposium. il Sat R 48: 10-22+ D 25 '65

Medical films

See Moving pictures in medicine

Moral aspects

After nudity, what? J. Roddy. il Look 29:36+ Mr 9 '65

Dirty joke. J. M. Wall. Christian Cent 82:144-5 F 3 '65

Four for foolery: Bambole. Time 86:96 Jl 9 '65

Lost ladies and bad logic. M. Walsh. America 112:334 Mr 6 '65

Morality crisis. il Newsweek 65:98+ Ap 19 '65

Must our movies be obscene? O. K. Armstrong. Read Digest 87:154-6 N '65

Nudity in films. America 112:895 Je 26 '65

Out is in. il Look 29:18-19 Mr 9 '65

Rising sun is blue; erotic productions. il Time 86:93 N 5 '65

To those of you who remember Eric Linden in Are these our children? I say: are these our parents? B. Comden. Esquire 65:12+ Ja '66

See also

Moving picture censorship

National Catholic office for motion pictures

National legion of decency

Music

Aboard the bandwagon. il Time 87:62+ Ja 14 '66

Catch up with; Decca's 50 years of movie music. L. Lerman. Mlle 61:24 Jl '65

Recordings reports: stage and screen. R. Sherman. Sat R 48:58 D 25 '65

See also

Phonograph records—Moving picture music

Musical films

100 lighted violins; Tribute to Busby Berkeley, at New York's Gallery of modern art. il Newsweek 66:104+ D 13 '65

Tuning U.S. musicals to overseas box office. T. Thompson. il Life 58:55+ Mr 12 '65

Winning friends for opera. S. Spaeth. il Opera N 30:8-11 D 11 '65

Natural history films

Films in review; decade of improvement. L. S. Gordon. Natur Hist 74:66-8 O '65

Opera films

See Moving pictures—Musical films

Religious films

Who speaks for the church? M. Boyd. Christian Cent 82:493-5 Ap 21 '65; Discussion. 82:815 Je 23 '65

Science fiction

Beyond the stars. New Yorker 41:38-9 Ap 24 '65

Imagination of disaster; excerpt from Against interpretation. S. Sontag. Commentary 40: 42-8 O '65

Setting and scenery

Where the action is; symposium. il Sat R 48:10-22+ D 25 '65

Sex films

See Moving pictures—Moral aspects

Social aspects

Portrait of a man; Negro life and culture in US. M. Boyd. Christian Cent 82:336-7 Mr 17 '65

Sports films

Triumph in Cannes; color movie of 1964 Olympics, Tokyo Olympiad. Sports Illus 22: 17 My 31 '65

Study and teaching

Celluloid syllabus. D. C. Stewart. il Am Ed 1:29-32 S '65

Movies on the campus. D. C. Stewart. il Sat R 48:82-3 F 20 '65

Movies students make new wave on campus. D. C. Stewart. il Harper 231:66-72 O '65

Reasons of the eye; course at Museum of modern art. New Yorker 40:25-7 F 13 '65

When the school desk is a theatre seat; courses in movie appreciation. W. Johnson. il Sr Schol 86:26 My 6 '65

Suspense films

See Moving pictures—Detective and mystery films

Themes

Movies students make new wave on campus. D. C. Stewart. il Harper 231:66-72 O '65

Westerns

Yockenee-poo! Stagecoach is being remade. J. Nugent. il Newsweek 66:79 Ag 30 '65

France

Letter from Paris; horror films. Genêt. New Yorker 41:171-2 My 15 '65

Italy

Profiles; F. Fellini. L. Ross. New Yorker 41:63-6+ O 30 '65

Seduced & amended; Socialists amendment to a bill providing subsidies to Italian film makers. il Time 85:39 Je 11 '65

This is Doris Day? censorship issue. il Newsweek 65:48+ Je 21 '65

Too much realism? Africa addio enquiry. il Newsweek 65:48 Ap 19 '65

Japan

Japanese screen. H. Alpert. il Sat R 48:35 D 25 '65

Rising sun is blue; erotic productions. il Time 86:93 N 5 '65

Russia

Saturday night at the movies; Trotsky and Stalin portrayed. Time 86:44 N 12 '65

Spain

Something for everyone. W. S. Ross. il Sat R 48:18-20 D 25 '65

United States

Beach-blanket babies; teen-age beach movies. J. Ransom. il Esquire 64:90-5+ Jl '65

Hooray for Hollywood; symposium. il Mlle 61:4+ Jl '65

Ken Murray's Hollywood. T. Lewis. America 112:811 My 29 '65

Movies: the big flick kick; symposium. il Look 29:17-28+ Mr 9 '65

See also

Disney, Walt, productions

Moving picture industry—United States

MOVING pictures, Amateur

Boats! camera! action! L. O. Larew. il Motor B 115:26-9+ Je '65

8-mm. Fellinis. Newsweek 67:58-9 Ja 17 '66

Fps creativity. W. P. Banner. il U S Camera 28:72-3+ Jl '65

Kodak's revolution in home movies: new 8mm movie film. E. H. Ortner. il Pop Sci 186:50-4+ Je '65

Living-room spectaculars; home movies. J. Peter. il Look 29:50 Mr 9 '65

Movie making in high school; Lillis high school, Kansas City, Mo. B. Sullivan. il Sr Schol 87:sup 13-14 N 4 '65

MTSHALI, Benedict Vulindlela
Crisis in Rhodesia. America 113:712-13 D 4 '65
MUCH ado about nothing; drama. See Shakespeare, W.—Plays
MUD hen shooting. See Coot shooting
MUEGGE, L. H.
Don't have one? we'll build it. Am City 80: 116-17 Ag '65
MUELLER, George E.
How U.S. plans to conquer the moon; interview. por U S News 59:33-7 D 27 '65
MUELLER, John H.
Cultural explosion and musical myths. bibliog por Library J 90:1243-7 Mr 15 '65
MUFFIN pans. See Kitchen utensils
MUFFINS
Our best blueberry muffins. il Bet Hom & Gard 43:153 O '65
MUGGERIDGE, Malcolm
Books. See issues of Esquire
Down with sex! Esquire 63:72-4 F '65

about

Mugger at large. por Newsweek 66:62 Jl 19 '65
Muggeridge, as seen from Winston-Salem. A. Gingrich. Esquire 63:8 F '65
MUHAMMAD Ali. See Clay, C.
MUHLFELD, Edward D.
Publisher's memo. See issues of Flying
MUIR, E. A.
Gulls; poem. Harper 230:136 My '65
MUIR, Jean
Blooped out. Nation 202:30 Ja 10 '66
MUIR, John
Faces from the past. R. M. Ketchum. por Am Heritage 16:62-3 F '65
MUIR, Karen
Strikes and strokes. il por Newsweek 66:68-9 Ag 23 '65
MUIRHEAD, Peter P. See Lorenz, J. G. jt. auth.
MULCHERS. See Garden tools, equipment and supplies
MULCHING
All around the place. J. Milton. Pop Gard 16:15 Jl '65
Black plastic mulch to the rescue. il Flower Grower 52:28 Je '65
Mulching just makes your gardening easier. Sunset 135:167 Jl '65
Use less water. J. Ingersoll. il Pop Gard 16: 34-7 My '65
MULDER, Marie
Near miss. por Newsweek 66:52 Ag 16 '65
This is the way the girls go. J. Underwood. il por Sports Illus 22:34-6+ My 10 '65
MULE deer hunting. See Deer hunting
MULE racing
Hijinks at the hee-haw derby; Chagrin Valley Mule point-to-point. L. Smith. il Sports Illus 22:34-6+ Je 21 '65
MULFORD, Carolyn. See Eiss, A. F. jt. auth.
MULFORD, Don
Nonstudent left. H. S. Thompson. il Nation 201:154-8 S 27 '65
MULLAN, John Francis
New way to relieve pain within minutes; reprint. L. Getz. por Sci Digest 58:80-3 O '65
MULLANEY, James, and McCall, Wallace
Finest deep-sky objects. Sky & Tel 30:280-3, 356-8; 31:13-16 N '65-Ja '66
MULLER, A. C.
(comp) Can flash synchronization be added to a used camera? Mod Phot 29:104 D '65
MÜLLER, Erwin W.
Field ion microscopy. bibliog Science 149: 591-601 Ag 6 '65
MÜLLER, Heinrich
Wanted: 1,000 Nazis still at large. G. Samuels. il por N Y Times Mag p26-7+ F 28 '65
MULLER, Hermann Joseph
Uses of tolerance. Sat R 48:23-5 F 13 '65
MULLER, Steven
NATO: the entangled alliance. Bul Atomic Sci 21:26-8 N '65
MÜLLER-EBERHARD, Hans J. See Polley, M. J. jt. auth.
MULLIGAN, Evelyn S.
To Banzai with love. Motor B 115:36-7+ F '65
MULLIKEN, Nathaniel
Rare Nathaniel Mulliken clock. L. W. Slaughter. il Hobbies 69:50-1 F '65
MULLINS, Helene
Three dimensions of love; poem. Commonweal 82:505 Jl 9 '65

MULLINS, J. Thomas, and Raper, J. R.
Heterothallism in biflagellate aquatic fungi: preliminary genetic analysis. bibliog Science 150:1174-5 N 26 '65
MULLINS, Sue
Hey, mom, it's party time! Farm J 89:61+ Ag '65
MULTIFOCAL leukoencephalopathy. See Brain —Diseases
MULTILEVEL house. See Architecture, Domestic
MULTIPLE access computer. See Computers— Cooperative use
MULTIPLE choice tests. See Educational tests and measurements
MULTIPLE jobholding. See Supplementary employment
MULTIPLE sclerosis. See Sclerosis, Multiple
MULTIVIBRATORS
Design of transistor multivibrators. L. E. Frenzel, jr. il Electr World 73:52-4 F '65
MULVOY, Mark
Baseball's week. See issues of Sports illustrated during the baseball season
MUMFORD, George S. 3d
Distance modulus. Sky & Tel 29:274-5 My '65
News notes. See issues of Sky and telescope
MUMFORD, L. Quincy
New ALA officer. ALA Bul 59:655-8 Jl '65
MUMFORD, Lewis
Books (cont) New Yorker 41:158+ Mr 6 '65
New regional plan to arrest megalopolis. Arch Rec 137:147-54 Mr '65
New world promise; excerpts from address, June 1965. Américas 17:22-3 Ag '65

about

Political troubles jar American academy. Pub W 187:32 My 31 '65
MUMMERY, A. F.
Reporter at large. J. Bernstein. New Yorker 41:152+ Mr 13 '65
MUMS. See Chrysanthemums
MUNCH, Edvard
Art galleries; exhibition at the Guggenheim museum. R. M. Coates. New Yorker 41: 219-20 O 30 '65
Cry of anguish. A. Werner. il Reporter 33: 51-3 O 21 '65
Rhythmic furor; exhibition at the Guggenheim museum. M. Kozloff. Nation 201:342-4 N 8 '65
MUNDT, Karl Earl
Poor Karl Mundt, poor GOP! Nation 201:261 O 25 '65
MUNICH
Efficiency in its country of origin. A. Page. il Atlan 217:105-6 Ja '66
Practical planner, Yugoslavia and Munich Holiday 38:120+ N '65

Description

Mad metropolis. A. Gonzalez and G. Gonzalez. il Sat R 48:57-8+ Mr 13 '65
MUNICH Bach chorus. See Choral groups and societies
MUNICH festival. See Music festivals—Germany (Federal Republic)
MUNICH four power agreement, 1938
Dreamer wide awake; letter with editorial comment. J. F. Kennedy. il Am Heritage 16:77-81 O '65
MUNICH opera festival. See Music festivals— Germany (Federal Republic)
MUNICIPAL accounting
Computer that puts the budget in order every day; Oakland, Calif. A. A. Brizee. il Am City 80:116-17 Mr '65
Watch dog accounts for every gallon of gas; Gastonia, N.C. H. L. Parker. il Am City 80:48 Mr '65
See also
Billing
MUNICIPAL administration. See Municipal government
MUNICIPAL advertising
Cincinnati wins clean-up contest; expanded National cleanest town contest. il Am City 80:105-7 Ap '65
City tells its story; ed. by P. D. Eimon. See issues of American city
MUNICIPAL and federal relations. See Federal and municipal relations
MUNICIPAL bands. See Bands (music)
MUNICIPAL bonds
Anatomy of a bond campaign. il Am City 80: 126+ F '65

MUNICIPAL bonds—*Continued*
Tax-free municipal industrial bonds; address, December 1, 1964. F. L. Magee. Vital Speeches 31:300-4 Mr 1 '65
See also
Bonds, Revenue

MUNICIPAL buildings
Designed for the people who use it; Wauwatosa, Wis. F. D. Kuckuck. il Am City 80:108-10 Ag '65
Don't make it look like a garage; Mount Pleasant, N.Y. M. L. Rovello. il Am City 80:114-15 My '65
Municipal buildings. il Arch Rec 137:169-76 My '65
Small-village hall; East Hazel Crest, Ill. il Am City 81:145-6 Ja '66
See also
City halls

MUNICIPAL centers
Mies designs Federal center; plan for Chicago's Loop. il Arch Rec 137:125-34 Mr '65

MUNICIPAL Christmas decorations. See Christmas decorations, Outdoor

MUNICIPAL contracts
Lowest responsible bidder, who is he? F. N. Benevelli. Am City 80:146+ Mr '65

MUNICIPAL corporations
Legal notes and decisions; prepared by National institute of municipal officers. See issues of American city

MUNICIPAL debts. See Municipal finance

MUNICIPAL dumps
For better breathing; a landfill; Honolulu. Y. Kunimoto. il Am City 80:62 O '65
See also
Filling (earthwork)
Refuse and refuse disposal

MUNICIPAL elections
See also
New York (city)—Elections

MUNICIPAL employees
See also
Strikes—United States—Municipal employees

MUNICIPAL equipment
Cats, Christmas lights and line maintenance; hydraulic aerial lift, owned by Oglesby, Ill. M. B. Moliske. il Am City 81:112-13 Ja '66
Don't have one? we'll build it; McGregor, Tex. L. H. Muegge. il Am City 80:116-17 Ag '65
Integrate your patching components; Rolling Meadows, Ill. J. McFeggan. il Am City 80:93-5 My '65
New hope for old streets; Santa Rosa, Calif. il Am City 80:90-1 N '65
See also
Street cleaning apparatus

MUNICIPAL finance
Credit problem; one more trouble for cities. U S News 59:64-6 Ag 2 '65
See also
Municipal bonds

MUNICIPAL garages. See Garages, Municipal

MUNICIPAL government
City tells its story; ed. by P. D. Eimon. See issues of American city
Our municipal notebook. See issues of American city
See also
Cities and towns
Police
also subhead Politics and government under names of cities, e.g. New York (city)—Politics and government

City manager plan
See City manager plan

United States
Mayor's exciting view from city hall. Life 59:6-7 D 24 '65
See also
Boss rule

MUNICIPAL improvement
Beautification from sea to shining sea. il NEA J 54:34-7 N '65
Blueprint for blightproof neighborhoods; association of home owners maintaining common properties and other neighborhood facilities. il Am City 80:78 F '65
Business can save America's cities. L. Smith. il Nations Bsns 53:38-9+ N '65
Citizen action for a beautiful America. L. Perlis. il Recreation 58:482-3 D '65
Claudia the beautician; beautifying of cities. il Time 86:29 O 1 '65
For a de-uglified America; call to the churches for action. Christian Cent 82:228-9 F 24 '65

For a more beautiful America; excerpts from remarks, February 8, 1965. L. B. Johnson. Recreation 58:107-8+ Mr '65
Half-finished society. E. K. Faltermayer. il Fortune 71:96-7+ Mr '65
Make a charming entrance. L. F. Betts. il Am City 81:94-5 Ja '66
President Johnson outlines programs for realization of the Great society. il Arch Rec 137:23+ Mr '65
President proposes programs supporting planning, the arts and natural beauty; with editorial comment. il Arch Rec 137:9, 23 F '65
President's urban package. Am City 80:7 Ap '65
Still talkin' about the Tetons; Johnsons hailed on conservation. D. Fleeson. il Am For 71:22-5 N '65
To break the old patterns. E. Goble. Arch Rec 137:9 Mr '65
Ugliness and the law. I. Silver. Commonweal 83:144-6 N 5 '65
Villains are greed, indifference, and you. P. Ylvisaker. il Life 59:92-4+ D 24 '65
What has happened to America the beautiful? R. Bendiner. il Redbook 125:50-1+ Je '65
White House conference on natural beauty. C. H. Callison. Audubon Mag 67:250-1 Jl '65
World society for the study of human settlements. Arch Rec 137:358+ Ap '65
See also
Billboards
Landscape protection
Playgrounds
Refuse and refuse disposal
Trees in cities
Urban renewal

MUNICIPAL incinerators. See Refuse incinerators

MUNICIPAL industrial bonds. See Municipal bonds

MUNICIPAL officers
See also
New York (city)—Public officers

MUNICIPAL ordinances
Legal notes and decisions; prepared by National institute of municipal officers. See issues of American city

MUNICIPAL publications

Bibliography
Municipal and civic publications. See issues of American city

MUNICIPAL purchasing. See Purchasing, Municipal

MUNICIPAL radio communication. See Radio in municipal government

MUNICIPAL records on microfilm
Microfilm your records and save; Fort Lauderdale, Fla. F. H. Marks. Am City 80:152+ Je '65
Putting a city's memory on film; Hurst, Tex. D. R. Edmonds. Am City 80:96 O '65
Records protection system with a plus; El Dorado, Kan. R. D. Thomas. il Am City 80:109 S '65

MUNICIPAL supplies
Bags vs bulk; savings and storage; how communities store de-icing chemicals in bulk. il Am City 81:108-9 Ja '66

MUNICIPAL taxation. See Local taxation

MUNICIPAL universities. See Colleges and universities, Municipal

MUNITIONS
Argentina's friend. Nation 201:234 O 18 '65
Business is booming. Nation 200:602 Je 7 '65
Hard-sell arms race, U.S. style. il Newsweek 65:59 Je 14 '65
Have gun, will sell; international traffic in arms. New Repub 152:5-6 Je 5 '65
Military common market sought. Miss & Roc 16:17 Je 7 '65
Why U.S. is pushing the sale of weapons. il U S News 59:122 O 11 '65
See also
Atomic weapons
Weapons

MUNITIONS industries
NATO common market; excerpts from address. H. J. Kuss. Aviation W 83:11 O 18 '65

United States
DOD broadening plans of action for faster weapon production. C. Brownlow. Aviation W 83:25-6 Jl 26 '65
DOD overhauls procedures for export. C. Brownlow. Aviation W 84:26-7 Ja 17 '66
Our way of life. Nation 201:69-70 Ag 16 '65
Questions and answers. W. J. Coughlin. Miss & Roc 17:54 N 8 '65

MUNITIONS works
Radford is largest ordnance plant. J. F.
Judge. il Miss & Roc 16:29-30+ Je 28 '65
MUNK, Arthur W.
Objectivity in the college classroom. bib-
liog f Sch & Soc 93:297-8 Sum '65
Road to peace and freedom. Bul Atomic Sci
21:30-1 O '65
MUÑOZ, Julio
Europe's bank scandal: the meaning. il U S
News 58:108 Je 21 '65
MUÑOZ MARIN, Luis
Farewell to Muñoz Marin. K. Botsford. Com-
mentary 39:86-9 Je '65; Discussion. 40:8+
O '65
MUNRO, Elisabeth C.
New look in Santa Fe. Opera N 30:14-16 S
25 '65
MUNRO, S. S. See Law, G. R. J. jt. auth.
MUNSINGWEAR, incorporated
Knitwear for school togs. M. B. Keiser. il
Parents Mag 40:28+ S '65
MUNSON, Fred C.
Trade union as an organization. Mo Labor R
88:497-501 My '65
MUNSON, Gorham
Workshops for writers. Sat R 48:46-9+ Ap
24 '65
MUNSON, Patrick J. and Frye, J. C.
Artifact from deposits of mid-Wisconsin age
in Illinois. bibliog Science 150:1722-3 D 24 '65
MUNSTER, J. H. Jr, and Smith, J. C.
Care and feeding of intellectual property.
bibliog Science 148:739-43 My 7 '65
MURAL painting and decoration
Making a rug mural; interview. C. R. Perrin.
il Am Artist 30:38-41+ Ja '66
Mural of copper repoussé for our school. S. L.
Dieffenbach. il Sch Arts 64:19-21 Je '65
Mural panels for a publisher's office; decora-
tive scheme for the foyer of the Thomas Y.
Corwell company offices. A. A. Watson. il
Am Artist 29:46-51+ O '65
Six days of creation; panel by third and
fourth graders. A. Geisert. il Sch Arts 65:
5-8 D '65
There's good money in art by the acre. il
Bsns W p 150-2+ Ap 3 '65
See also
Benton, T. H.
Cave drawings and paintings
Mosaics
Panels, Decorative
Walls
MURASAKI shikibu, ca 978-1030
Tale of Genji. K. Rexroth. Sat R 48:27 D 11
'65
MURAY, Nickolas
Nickolas Muray, time for a leisurely lunch.
J. Deschin. por Pop Phot 57:40+ O '65
MURDER
After Hayneville; T. Coleman acquitted of
Daniels murder. Reporter 33:16+ O 21 '65
Annals of crime; In cold blood; murder of
H. W. Clutter family. T. Capote. New
Yorker 41:57-60+ S 25; 57-60+ O 2; 58-62+
O 9 '65
Blame pep pills for murder; murder of F. A.
Christiansen by three teenage Chicago boys.
Christian Cent 82:199 F 17 '65
Bonded blonde. il Time 86:47 Ag 20 '65
Chicago on the Charles; Chicago-style mur-
ders. Time 86:27 N 26 '65
College football hero's postgraduate course in
horror; D. Pope's Big Springs bank killings.
il Life 58:30-30A Je 25 '65
Death sails west on the Seven Seas. il Life
59:68-71 Ag 20 '65
Dream and reality; violent death of Baroness
de Courtry. Newsweek 66:49-50 S 27 '65
End of the façade; Sammy Younge shot to
death. Time 87:29 Ja 14 '66
Four lives to Flagstaff; ex-convict Donald
Melvin Boggs. Time 86:40 S 17 '65
Ghosts on the moors; children's murders in
Great Britain. il Time 86:54 N 5 '65
Horror spawns a masterpiece; T. Capote's In
cold blood inspired by Clutter family mur-
ders; with report by J. Howard. il Life 60:
58-72+ Ja 7 '66
I'm just an ordinary girl; three murder
charges for S. Kinne. P. Hamill and D.
Weber. il Sat Eve Post 238:91-7 S 25 '65
In cold blood, an American tragedy; concern-
ing T. Capote's book. il Newsweek 67:
59-63 Ja 24 '66
In cold blood, by T. Capote. Review
America 114:142+ Ja 22 '66. T. Greene
Sat R 49:35-6 Ja 22 '66. G. Hicks
Kurtains for the Klan. K. Crawford. News-
week 66:34 D 13 '65
Little girl is dead, by H. Golden. Review
Life 59:15 D 3 '65. W. M. Kunstler
Newsweek il 66:104 N 29 '65

Model boy; sniper on California highway. il
Newsweek 65:46 My 10 '65
Model community; S. Younge murder. News-
week 67:25-6 Ja 17 '66
Nightmare afloat; five murdered on the Seven
Seas. Newsweek 66:23-4 Ag 23 '65
On England's misty moors, a grisly search;
case of multiple murder. il Life 59:46-7 N
12 '65
Riddle of the nice killer; D. Pope. B. Linde-
man. il Sat Eve Post 238:98+ O 23 '65
Scoreboard on civil-rights killings. U S News
59:6+ O 11 '65
Secrets in the sand; murder of three Tucson
girls. il Time 86:27 N 26 '65
Slaughter on the Seven Seas. il Time 86:35
Ag 20 '65
Stranger in Big Springs; Nebraska bank
robbery. il Newsweek 65:29-30 Je 21 '65
Trial by headline? Charles H. Schmid, jr.
charged with murdering three Tucson teen-
agers. il Newsweek 66:70 D 13 '65
When London walked in terror, by T. A.
Cullen. Review
Newsweek il 66:98 F+ S 20 '65
Reporter 33:54-5 N 18 '65. D. Morgan
Who killed the clown? P. Jung of Ringling
bros murdered in New York. Newsweek
65:34-5 My 3 '65
Why Tim killed Todd; Nicholson twins. il
Newsweek 65:30 Je 21 '65
See also
Capital punishment
Trials (murder)
MURDER trials. See Trials (murder)
MURDERERS. See Murder
MURDICK, Olin J.
Parish school board. America 114:132-6 Ja 22
'66
Preparing for change in parochial schools.
America 112:282-4 F 27 '65
MURDOCH, Ian
John Fulton, artist & matador. Am Artist
29:22-7+ Ap '65
MURDOCH, Iris
Guises of love. B. McCabe. Commonweal 83:
270-3 D 3 '65
MURDOCH, Rupert
Beating the bush for subscribers. il por
Bsns W p 102 Je 26 '65
MURIE, Adolph
Roadbuilding in Mount McKinley National
Park. il Nat Parks Mag 39:4-8 Jl '65
MURILLO, Gerardo
Doctor Atl, 1875-1964. M. Brand. il por Amér-
icas 17:35-7 Ag '65
MURPHY, Abbie M.
Dwarf dahlias. Horticulture 43:53 F '65
MURPHY, B. F.
Photographing sewers doesn't cost a cent.
Am City 80:112-13 Mr '65
MURPHY, Bob, Jr
Jolly Bob finds his game. A. Wright. il por
Sports Illus 23:22-3 S 27 '65
MURPHY, C. B.
Thermal analysis. Science 151:111 Ja 7 '66
MURPHY, Charles J. V.
Lockheed scrambles for the battle of the
primes. Fortune 71:148-52+ F '65
Strategy for the Pacific. Fortune 73:167-8+
Ja '66
Thailand's fight to the finish. Fortune 72:
122-7+ O '65
Traveler in a small utopia; excerpts from
letters. Fortune 71:92+ My '65
Traveler on the rim of Asia. Fortune 71:264+
Je '65
Traveler to the Pacific wars; letter. Fortune
72:132-4+ Ag '65
MURPHY, Charles S.
U.S. travel push. Aviation W 83:11 N 29 '65
about
CAB chairman pledges firm fare limits. J.
R. Ashlock. Aviation W 83:37 S 13 '65
CAB chairman sees no reason for immediate
over-all fare cuts. W. Wright. Aviation
W 83:37-8 N 8 '65
Will CAB get tough now? por Bsns W p34
Ag 7 '65
MURPHY, Cicero
Saga of Cicero Murphy. Sports Illus 22:20
Ap 5 '65
MURPHY, Claire
How to choose the right lamps. Redbook 124:
32+ Ap '65
MURPHY, David M.
Plea for uniformity in the liturgy. por Cath
World 201:296-300 Ag '65

MURPHY, Edward F.
(comp) Famous. N Y Times Mag p62 O 31 '65
(comp) Final say. N Y Times Mag p80 Mr 21 '65
(comp) Fools day. N Y Times Mag p71 Mr 28 '65
(comp) Game time. N Y Times Mag p 101 My 16 '65
(comp) Of love, etc. N Y Times Mag p 14+ F 14 '65
(comp) Reading matter. N Y Times Mag p 102 Ap 25 '65
(comp) Subject: tax time. N Y Times Mag p49 Ap 4 '65

MURPHY, Francis X.
New Constitution on the church: a new approach. Cath World 200:346-53 Mr '65

MURPHY, Franklin D.
New voices on campus; interview, ed. by W. McWhirter. por Mlle 61:302+ Ag '65

MURPHY, Jack
Ben Casey at the ball park. N Y Times Mag p 18-19+ Ag 22 '65
Better mouse beats a path. Sat Eve Post 238:72-3 O 9 '65

MURPHY, John J.
Report from Vietnam. pors Seventeen 25:91+ Ja '66

MURPHY, Kenneth B.
Do they really want to die? Todays Health 43:48-9+ Ap '65

MURPHY, Matt
My kountry: Klonsel's kreed. por Newsweek 65:41 My 17 '65

MURPHY, Michael
Hard fight by a spunky cripple. Life 58:87-8+ F 5 '65
If I had to live in here I'd go nuts. Life 58:54-5 Mr 19 '65

about

Court & the cop. por Time 86:74 S 17 '65

MURPHY, Paul L.
Labor-management relations: constitutional assumptions. bibliog f Cur Hist 48:353-60+ Je '65

MURPHY, Robert
Are the days of the Arctic's king running out? N Y Times Mag p38-40 Mr 28 '65

MURPHY, Robert Cushman
Books in review. Natur Hist 74:4 My '65
First flight: a golden eagle evades capture; excerpt from Golden eagle. Audubon Mag 67:244-8 Jl '65

MURPHY, W. B.
Rural-urban balance; address. September 20, 1965. Vital Speeches 32:53-7 N 1 '65

MURPHY, Walter H.
Colorful trailers serve as mobile libraries. Am City 80:106-7 Jl '65

MURRAY, Anne Wood
Elegant handkerchief. Antiques 87:720-3 Je '65

MURRAY, Bruce C. and Westphal, J. A.
Infrared astronomy; with biographical sketches. Sci Am 213:11, 20-9 bibliog(p 118) Ag '65

MURRAY, Don, 1924-
Condition critical: cause unknown. Read Digest 86:145-8+ F '65

MURRAY, Donald J. See Donley, M. O. jt. auth.

MURRAY, Geoffrey
Enugu: second thoughts. Christian Cent 82:167-8 F 10 '65

MURRAY, Jim
Drubbing. Sports Illus 22:53 Je 7 '65

MURRAY, John
Gray flannel blues; drama. Plays 24:1-14 My '65
Take my advice; drama. Plays 25:23-35 O '65
Two for the money; drama. Plays 24:17-30 Mr '65

MURRAY, John Courtney
Murray and liberty. R. M. Healey. Christian Cent 82:1130-1 S 15 '65
Religious freedom: intrinsic or fortuitous? A. F. Carrillo de Albornoz. bibliog f Christian Cent 82:1122-6 S 15 '65

MURRAY, Ken
Three tips for happy hosing. Flower Grower 52:5 Ag '65

MURRAY, Leo A.
Berlin film festival. America 113:118-19 Jl 31 '65

MURRAY, Madalyn E.
20th century witch hunt. Christian Cent 82: 1340 N 3 '65

MURRAY, Michele
Books. Commonweal 82:477 Jl 2 '65

MURRAY, Pauli
Protest against the legal status of the Negro. bibliog f Ann Am Acad 357:55-64 Ja '65

MURRAY, Spencer, and Poole, Ralph
Cruising the West coast of Mexico. il Yachting 117:50-2+ Je; 118:54-6+ Jl '65

MURRAY, William
Go West. young writer. Holiday 38:20+ O '65
Hell's Angels. Sat Eve Post 238:32-9 N 20 '65

MURRAY, William H.
Laser, a three-step device. Electr World 73:49+ F '65

MURRAY Ohio manufacturing company
Wheels for tykes and teens. M. B. Keiser. il Parents Mag 40:15-16 Je '65

MURRES
Life and death on the Funks. F. Russell. il Horizon 7:32-8 Sum '65

MURROW, Edward R.
Ed Murrow dies. por Sr Schol 86:20-1 My 13 '65
Edward R. Murrow: noblesse oblige. M. McGrory. America 112:702 My 15 '65
Edward R. Murrow, RIP. Nat R 17:410 My 18 '65
Johnson's farewell to a gallant reporter. il pors Life 58:42-42A My 7 '65
Murrow's lost fight. R. L. Shayon. por Sat R 48:94 My 22 '65
Voice of a generation. pors Newsweek 65:77-8 My 10 '65
Voice of crisis. il por Time 85:63 My 7 '65

MURTAGH, William J.
Architecture of Salem. Antiques 88:69-80 Jl '65

MURTON, Jessie Wilmore
Mountain people; poem. Liv Wildn 87:21 Wint '64

MURVILLE, Maurice Couve de. See Couve de Murville, M.

MUS musculus. See Mice

MUSCLE
Anaphylactic reaction of denervated skeletal muscle in the guinea pig. F. Alonso-De-Florida and others. bibliog il Science 147: 1155-6 Mr 5 '65
Giant snail is used for muscle studies; research in the physiology of strophocheilidae. C. P. Jaeger. il Natur Hist 74:26-7 N '65
Glycerinated skeletal and smooth muscle: calcium and magnesium dependence. R. S. Filo and others. bibliog il Science 147:1581-3 Mr 26 '65
Muscle volume changes: relation to the active state. R. J. Baskin and P. J. Paolini. bibliog il Science 148:971-2 My 14 '65
Nature of the excitatory sarcoplasmic reticular junction. G. Hoyle. bibliog il Science 149:70-2 Jl 2 '65
Nonelectrolyte transport in muscle during induced protein loss. I. R. Fenichel and S. B. Horowitz. bibliog il Science 148:80-3 Ap 2 '65
Nuclear magnetic resonance studies of living muscle. C. B. Bratton and others. bibliog Science 147:738-9 F 12 '65
Rabbit muscle lactate dehydrogenase 5; a regulatory enzyme. P. J. Fritz. bibliog il Science 150:364-6 O 15 '65
Sarcolemma: transmitter of active tension in frog skeletal muscle. S. F. Street and R. W. Ramsey. bibliog il Science 149:1379-80 S 17 '65; Reply with rejoinder. H. Lamport. 150: 1846 D 31 '65
Sarcoplasmic reticulum. K. R. Porter and C. Franzini-Armstrong. il Sci Am 212:72-8+ bibliog(p 139) Mr '65
Sarcoplasmic reticulum: ultrastructure of the triadic junction. W. H. Fahrenbach. bibliog il Science 147:1308-10 Mr 12 '65
Smooth muscle: an ultrastructural basis for the dynamics of its contraction. J. Rosenbluth. bibliog il Science 148:1337-9 Je 4 '65
Sodium pump: its electrical effects in skeletal muscle. A. S. Frumento. bibliog il Science 147:1442-3 Mr 19 '65

MUSCLES
Flight muscles of insects. D. S. Smith. il Sci Am 212:76-82+ Je '65
Mechanism of muscular contraction. H. E. Huxley. il Sci Am 213:18-27 bibliog(p 126) D '65
Sarcoplasmic reticulum. K. R. Porter and C. Franzini-Armstrong. il Sci Am 212:72-8+ bibliog(p 139) Mr '65
Structure of smooth muscle. Sci Am 213:86 S '65

Diseases

Neuromuscular diseases. il Todays Health 43:33-7 Ag '65
See also
Dystrophy, Muscular

MUSCULAR dystrophy. See Dystrophy, Muscular

MUSÉE de l'homme. See Paris—Galleries and museums

MUSÉE de Mouton. See Museums

MUSEUM loans. See Art loans

MUSEUM of early American folk arts, New York
Folk art in New York; exhibitions. R. Davidson. il Antiques 88:150+ Ag '65

MUSEUM of famous people. See New York (city)—Galleries and museums

MUSEUM of history and technology. See Smithsonian institution—Museum of history and technology

MUSEUM of modern art, New York
His men look like survivors of a shipwreck; Giacometti's sculpture. P. E. Schneider. il N Y Times Mag p34-5+ Je 6 '65
Photo essay exhibition traces development of a medium. il Pub W 187:84-5 Ap 5 '65

MUSEUM of natural history. See American museum of natural history, New York

MUSEUM of primitive art, New York
Supernatural forces; exhibition of Olmec art. il Newsweek 65:86 Mr 8 '65

MUSEUM of the city of New York
In old New Amsterdam. R. Davidson. il Antiques 88:842+ D '65

MUSEUM workers
Science in action; confessions of a curator. S. Anderson. Natur Hist 74:60-4 O '65

MUSEUMS
All for science; West Germany's oddball museums. Newsweek 65:38+ Je 28 '65
Collectors. il Newsweek 66:100+ O 11 '65
Inside Lisbon's Coach museum. il Sunset 135: 8 S '65
Museum of wine in art; Musee de Mouton. V. Lawford. il Vogue 145:172-83+ Mr 1 '65
Museum world. J. L. Stoutenburgh, jr. See issues of Hobbies
New life for museums; proposed National museum act of 1965. B. Tufty. il Sci N L 88:122-3 Ag 21 '65
Oldest store; Hamblen and company, St Augustine, Fla. il Travel 124:39-41 D '65
Try Christmas shopping at the museum. il Changing T 19:46-7 N '65
Vandalism. N. Kent. Am Artist 29:3+ Ap '65
See also
Aeronautic museums
Anthropological museums
Art—Galleries and museums
Music museums

Architecture
Down with art? underground art gallery, Conn. G. O'Brien. il N Y Times Mag p70-i F 28 '65
Spatial variety in two museums. il Arch Rec 138:129-34 D '65

MUSEUMS, Wax. See Wax museums

MUSGRAVE, R. A.
Tax-cut habit. Nation 200:643-5 Je 14 '65

MUSGROVE, Frank
Teen-age aristocracy. Nation 200:439-42 Ap 26 '65

MUSHROOM sauce. See Sauces

MUSHROOMS
Bizarre world of the fungi. P. A. Zahl. il Nat Geog Mag 128:502-27 O '65
Hunting the wild mushroom. J. Cerruti. il Holiday 38:96-100 Ag '65
Lure of the mushroom; recent poison and death cases. il Newsweek 66:67 O 4 '65
Most dangerous game; wild-mushroom collecting. B. Gilbert. il Sports Illus 22:76-8+ Mr 22 '65
Non-drinking man's mushrooms; inky caps Time 85:54 Ap 9 '65
See also
Truffles

MUSIAL, Stan
What makes Stan Musial The Man? B. Broeg. il pors Pop Sci 187:126-8+ O '65

MUSIC
Artist life. D. J. Soria. See issues of High fidelity incorporating Musical America
Classical music swings. T. Lundberg. Seventeen 25:14 Ja '66
Here & there. Hi Fi 16:144-5 Ja '66
Letter from Paris; performance of K. Stockhausen's Gruppen für drei orchester. Genêt. New Yorker 41:111-12 Je 12 '65
Life music review. Life 59:16 O 22; 22 N 26; 23 D 10 '65
Lorin Hollander: 1965 style in pianists; ed. by R. Hemming. L. Hollander. il Sr Schol 86:16 Mr 25 '65

Mephisto's musings. il Hi Fi 15:109-10+ My; 110-12+ Je; 92-3+ Jl; 112-13 Ag; 142+ S; 142+ O; 188+ N; 160-1 D '65; 16:124-5+ Ja '66

Music. C. J. McNaspy. America 112:730; 113:82-3 My 15, Jl 17 '65

[Musical events] il Hi Fi 15:86C-86D+ Mr '65

Musical events: avant-garde concert performed by BBC symphony orchestra in Carnegie Hall. W .Sargeant. New Yorker 41: 173-4 My 15 '65

Profiles; G. Szell: foremost interpreter of clasical music. J. Wechsberg. New Yorker 41:59-62+ N 6 '65

You call that music? big lie of modernism. A. Chasins. il McCalls 92:76+ Ap '65; Same abr. Read Digest 87:141-4 Ag '65
See also
Bands (music)
Chamber music
Church music
Computers—Musical applications
Handel and Haydn society
Impressionism (music)
Jazz music
Moving pictures—Music
Musical instruments
Opera
Orchestras
Phonograph records
Television broadcasting—Music
Tone

Acoustics and physics
Music moves outdoors. F. Bowers. House & Gard 127:40+ Je '65
Sound conditioning for music. House & Gard 127:192-3 Ap '65
See also
Musical pitch

Analysis, interpretation, etc.
Music observed, by B. H. Haggin. Review Commentary 39:88-91 My '65. A. Goldman; Discussion. 40:6+ S; 26+ O '65
Twentieth-century music in western Europe, by A. Cohn. Review
Am Rec G 32:4-5+ S '65. N. Slonimsky

Anecdotes, facetiae, satire, etc.
Men, women and music. F. V. Grunfeld. il Read Digest 87:35-6 N '65

Appreciation
Cultural explosion and musical myths J. H. Mueller. bibliog il Library J 90:1243-7 Mr 15 '65
High-brows vs no-brows. A. Chasins. il McCalls 92:42+ S '65
Music for non-listening. L. Rich. il Hi Fi 15:34+ N '65
Winning friends for opera. S. Spaeth. il Opera N 30:8-11 D 11 '65

Arrangement
See Musical arrangement

Bibliography
Four ages of music, by W. Wiora. Review America 113:58 Jl 10 '65. J. McKinnon

Competitions
Battle of Warsaw; Chopin international piano competition. Newsweek 65:78-9 Mr 29 '65
Dark victor; seventh International Chopin piano competition. il Time 85:64 Mr 26 '65
Mitropoulos competition. Américas 17:45 S '65
One near-square who doesn't knock the rock; rock 'n' roll world championship. Lambertville, N.J. J. A. Michener. il N Y Times Mag p56-7+ O 31 '65

Criticism
See Music—History and criticism

History and criticism
Big four; music critics of the golden age: H. E. Krehbiel, H. T. Finck, W. J. Henderson and J. G. Huneker. E. H. Huneker. il Opera N 30:8-13 D 18 '65
40,000 years of music, by J. Chailley; tr. by R. Myers. Review
New Yorker 41:181-4 S 25 '65. W. Sargeant
Is our music different? C. J. McNaspy. America 113:142-4 Ag 7 '65
Music observed, by B. H. Haggin. Review Commentary 39:88-91 My '65. A. Goldman; Discussion. 40:6+ S; 26+ O '65

MUSIC—History and criticism—*Continued*
Public vs. modern music. M. Rudolf. il Opera
N 30:8-11 Ja 22 '66
Question of function; music critic making
mountains out of musicologists' molehills.
P. J. Smith. il Hi Fi 15:67-9+ Mr '65
    See also
Jazz music

Anecdotes, facetiae, satire, etc.
Mr Whitweeks' massive tone; whistlers
rampant in Robinson opera; other notes.
S. McKelway. New Yorker 41:144+ Mr 6
'65

Humor
Jazz records; D. Wells' music. W. Balliett.
New Yorker 41:156+ N 20 '65
Properly neglected; creations of P. Schickele.
il Time 87:62 Ja 7 '66

Instruction and study
Bernac and Lehmann: pupils in public. C. L.
Osborne. il Hi Fi 15:104-5 Jl '65
Do schools teach art and music all wrong?
il Changing T 19:37-40 Je '65
Grade schoolers strike up the rhythm band.
il Todays Health 43:32-3+ S '65
Opening the door to music for the musically
shy adult. F. Bowers. il House & Gard
128:196-7 S '65
Want to play a musical instrument, again?
Bet Hom & Gard 43:26 S '65
    See also
Music camps
Musical education
Organ—Instruction and study
Piano—Instruction and study

Moving pictures
See Moving pictures—Music

Notation
See Musical notation

Periodicals
Opera serials; information on several foreign
opera publications. R. E. Pfeiffer. Opera N
30:32-3 Ja 8 '66

Philosophy
    See also
Style, Musical

Study and teaching
See Music—Instruction and study

Argentina
    See also
Buenos Aires—Music
Musicians, Argentine

Australia
    See also
Melbourne, Australia—Music

Austria
    See also
Salzburg festivals

Belgium
    See also
Brussels—Music

Brazil
    See also
Opera—Brazil

Canada
L'esprit de jeunesse, et de corps, et d'art;
Arctic report. H. von Hochmeister. Hi Fi 15:
188-90 D '65

Czechoslovakia
    See also
Prague—Music

Denmark
    See also
Copenhagen—Music

Europe, Western
Twentieth-century music in western Europe,
by A. Cohn. Review
    Am Rec G 32:4-5+ S '65. N. Slonimsky

Finland
    See also
Opera—Finland

France
    See also
Paris—Music

Germany (Democratic Republic)
    See also
Berlin—Music

Germany (Federal Republic)
    See also
Berlin—Music
Berlin (West Berlin)—Music
Frankfort on the Main—Music
Hamburg—Music
Leipzig—Music

Hawaii
    See also
Honolulu—Music

Hungary
    See also
Budapest—Music

Ireland
    See also
Dublin—Music

Israel
Of orchestras, choirs, and growing festivals.
T. Goth. il Hi Fi 15:170-1 O '65

Italy
    See also
Milan, Italy—Music
Opera—Italy
Opera, Italian
Rome (city)—Music

Latin America
    See also
Opera—Latin America

Mexico
    See also
Mexico (city)—Music

Middle East
Notes from the Middle East. C. J. McNaspy.
il America 113:82-3 Jl 17 '65

Netherlands
    See also
Amsterdam, Netherlands—Music

Poland
Mephisto's musings. Hi Fi 15:142 O '65
    See also
Warsaw—Music

Portugal
    See also
Lisbon, Portugal—Music

Rumania
Abundance and high standards in Rumania.
F. Mahler. il Hi Fi 15:134 Je '65

Russia
Soft sound in the U.S.S.R: New York pro
musica in the Soviet Union. N. Greenberg.
il Hi Fi 15:41-3+ My '65
Sound of the thaw. il Newsweek 65:108B-
108D Je 14 '65
    See also
Leningrad—Music
Moscow—Music

Scandinavia
    See also
Opera—Scandinavia

Spain
Search for the Spanish soul; series of courses
on the interpretation of Spanish music. C.
Irizarry. il Hi Fi 15:186-7 D '65

Switzerland
Music from the cantons; discs, by Swiss
composers. O. Daniel. Sat R 48:49-50 D 25
'65
    See also
Opera—Switzerland
Winterthur, Switzerland—Music

United States
Here & there, U.S.A. il Hi Fi 15:86N-86O
Mr '65
Hills are alive: summer camps, schools, fes-
tivals. R. Hemming. il Sr Schol 86:32 My
20 '65
New music, big money; Schuller-Columbia
activities, Rutgers project and others.
B. Boretz. Nation 201:47-8 Jl 19 '65
Orchestras U.S.A. season's forecast. Hi Fi
15:150-3 S '65
Very too bad; Pulitzer prize for music not
awarded. Newsweek 65:93-4 My 17 '65
    See also
Folk songs, American
Jazz music
    also subhead Music under names of
cities, e.g. Central City, Colo.—Music

Wales
Harp famine: Welsh repair measures. il
Newsweek 67:41 Ja 17 '66

MUSIC, African
See also
Phonograph records—African music
MUSIC, American
Musical life in Salem. D. M. McCorkle. il
Antiques 88:65-8 Jl '65
See also
Folk songs, American
Jazz music
Music—United States
MUSIC, Argentine
See also
Musicians, Argentine
MUSIC, Baroque
See also
Phonograph records—Baroque music
MUSIC, Chamber. See Chamber music
MUSIC, Church. See Church music
MUSIC, Electronic
Research in music with electronics. L. Hiller
and J. Beauchamp. bibliog il Science 150:
161-9 O 8 '65
This man is composing music; electronic
music. B. H. Frisch. il Sci Digest 57:72-7
F '65
MUSIC, English
See also
Songs, English
MUSIC, Influence of
Muzak men. A. Levy. il Horizon 7:39-45 Sum
'65
See also
National association for music therapy
MUSIC, Italian
See also
Phonograph records—Italian music
MUSIC, Japanese
Filling a lacuna: the music of Japan. W. L.
Purcell. Am Rec G 31:910-12 My '65
MUSIC, Latin American
Music. See issues of Américas
MUSIC, Medieval
Looking backward; Purcell's songs. P. L.
Miller. il Sat R 48:68 N 27 '65
See also
Phonograph records—Medieval music
MUSIC, Modern. See Music
MUSIC, Popular (songs, etc)
Children of Bobby Dylan; boom in protest
songs with a rock beat. il Life 59:43-4+
N 5 '65
London scene; pop music. F. Gannon. Nat R
17:838-40 S 21 '65
Old English music hall songs are new. C.
Macinnes. il N Y Times Mag p62-3+ N
28 '65
Onward and upward with the arts; new
sound, with discography. R. Adler. il New
Yorker 41:63-4+ F 20 '65
Pop's bad boys: the Rolling Stones. il News-
week 66:92 N 29 '65
Popular records (cont) D. Watt. New Yorker
40:65+ Ja 30 '65
Sound of music? P. L. Levin. il N Y Times
Mag p72+ Mr 14 '65
Where's it at? pop groups and the new
sound. L. Lerman. il Mlle 61:74-7 Je '65
MUSIC, Spanish
Musical events; Promenade concert at Phil-
harmonic Hall. W. Sargeant. New Yorker
41:128+ Je 12 '65
MUSIC and children
Education on the Menuhin plan; Yehudi
Menuhin school. Stoke d'Abernon, Surrey,
England and plans for U.S. school. I.
Kolodin. il Sat R 48:57-8+ N 27 '65
Life with music. H. L. Gardner. Opera N
30:6 Ja 22 '66
MUSIC and libraries. See Libraries and music
MUSIC and state
Next on the subsidy list: plays, opera, or-
chestras. il U S News 58:64-5 Mr 15 '65
Performing arts; excerpts concerning opera
from Performing arts: problems and
prospects. il Opera N 29:6-10 Mr 20 '65
Something for the arts; findings of Rocke-
feller panel. M. Straight. New Repub 152:
11-15 Mr 13 '65; Reply. H. Green. 152:28
Ap 3 '65
MUSIC as a profession
Overture to a future; jobs in the music
world. C. Schwalberg. il Mlle 60:194-5+
Ap '65
MUSIC as recreation
Opening the door to music for the musically
shy adult. F. Bowers. il House & Gard
128:196-7 S '65
MUSIC camps
Music in the redwoods; Cazadero music camp,
Calif. J. Scott. il Am For 71:19+ Je '65

MUSIC collections in libraries. See Libraries—
Music collections
MUSIC collections in school libraries. See
School libraries—Music collections
MUSIC copyright. See Copyright—Music
MUSIC criticism. See Music—History and cri-
ticism
MUSIC critics. See Critics
MUSIC education. See Musical education
MUSIC festivals
Guide to European music festivals: 1965;
preliminary forecast. H. D. Jellinek. Sat R
48:132-3 Mr 13 '65
International university choral festival. J.
Roddy. Hi Fi 15:174-5 D '65

Austria
Austria: art in freedom; Vienna festival. J.
Grayson. il Hi Fi 15:169 S '65
See also
Salzburg festivals

California
At Stanford, eight weeks of Mozart; Summer festival of the arts, Stanford university. il Sunset 134:27-8 Je '65
Baroque on the peninsula; Stanford university summer festival. I. Kolodin. Sat R
48:46 Ag 14 '65
Jazz concerts; eighth annual Monterey jazz
festival. W. Balliett. New Yorker 41:185-90
O 2 '65
Mozart era: Stanford university, summer
festival. R. Commanday. il Hi Fi 15:156+
O '65

Canada
Music festivals. H. D. Jellinek. Sat R 48:49
Jl 17 '65

Colorado
Manon on a mountaintop; Central City festival performance and season's forthcoming events. I. Kolodin. Sat R 48:33 Ag
7 '65
Tippett in the Rockies; Aspen report. A.
Young. il Hi Fi 15:152 O '65

Czechoslovakia
Man without; Prague spring festival of
music. Time 85:44 Je 4 '65

England
Best foot forward and otherwise; Glynde-
bourne report. E. Greenfield. il Hi Fi 15:
135 Ag '65
Bumper Britten crop; Aldeburgh festival. E.
Greenfield. Hi Fi 15:164-5 S '65
Cheltenham comes of age. B. Jacobson. Sat
R 48:44 Jl 31 '65
Chilly Glyndebourne. E. Downes; R. A. Tug-
gle. il Opera N 30:25-6 S 25 '65
Letter from London; Glyndebourne festival's
new production of Donizetti's Anna Bolena.
M. Panter-Downes. New Yorker 41:86 Je 26
'65
New blood for Glyndebourne. T. Heinitz.
Sat R 48:61 Je 26 '65

Europe, Western
Happy plague. il Time 85:72-3 Je 11 '65
Music for summer; a guide to festivals
abroad. Hi Fi 15:130-2+ Ap '65
Summer evenings (cont) Opera N 29:31-2 Ap
17 '65
Tips for tourists. M. E. Peltz. Opera N 29:13
My 1 '65

France
Festival à la mode; Aix report. R. McMullen.
Hi Fi 15:167 O '65
Festivals of France; in Strasbourg and Aix-
en Provence. M. E. Davies. Opera N 30:26
N 6 '65
Springs of Provence; Aix prepares for its
annual festival. il Opera N 29:23-5 My 1
'65

Germany (Federal Republic)
Bavarian bounty; Munich opera festival. E.
D. Echols. Opera N 30:25 N 20 '65
Festival rich in music and beauty; Wies-
baden festival. F. Stevenson. il Hi Fi 15:
139 Ag '65
Greetings to Orff amends to Strauss; Munich
festival. E. Helm. il Hi Fi 15:164-5 O '65
Hamburg and Berlin. J. H. Sutcliffe. il
Opera N 30:31-2 D 18 '65
Maazel era begins; Berlin report. P. Moor. il
Hi Fi 15:180+ D '65
See also
Bayreuth festival

MUSIC festivals—*Continued*

Illinois

Contemporary arts at the University of Illinois; Festival of contemporary arts. P. Yates. il Hi Fi 15:128-9 Je '65

Italy

Battling bards; International poetry week at the annual Spoleto festival of two worlds. C. G. Pepper. il Newsweek 66:42+ Jl 12 '65

Biennale, 1965; Venice report. E. Helm. il Hi Fi 15:179 D '65

Boboli blues; Maggio musicale. Newsweek 66:84-5 Jl 12 '65

Florence magpie and jazz. P. Affelder. il Opera N 30:22-3 S 25 '65

In Italy, festivals old and new; Florence's Maggio musicale, and Spoleto's Festival of two worlds. W. Weaver. Hi Fi 15:163 S '65

Intimate festivals. W. Weaver. il Hi Fi 15:178+ D '65

Molto Presleyoso; San Remo festival and RCA Italia anti-festival. il Newsweek 65:86-7 F 15 '65

Musica é martini dry; Festival of two worlds, Spoleto. il Time 86:62 Jl 16 '65

Naples; Autumn music festival. F. Nuzzo. il Opera N 30:34 D 25 '65

Massachusetts

See also
Berkshire symphonic festival

Netherlands

Dutch perspectives; Holland festival. F. Stevenson. il Opera N 30:27 N 6 '65

New York (state)

Empire state circuit. R. D. Daniels; F. Stevenson; M. Lelash. il Opera N 30:27-8 S 25 '65

Festival at Caramoor. R. Lawrence. il Hi Fi 15:147+ S '65

Summer nights at the Philharmonic; French-American festival of the New York philharmonic orchestra. I. Kolodin. Sat R 48:41 Jl 31 '65

Ohio

On campus, an educator's dream; Festival of contemporary music. S. Fleming. il Hi Fi 15:120 My '65

Sense of tradition; May festival. R. C. Marsh. Hi Fi 15:128+ Ag '65

Poland

Adventure in Poland; Warsaw report. E. Helm. Hi Fi 15:185 D '65

Thorn grows in Warsaw. P. Heyworth. il Hi Fi 15:60-5 S '65

Rhode Island

Jazz concerts; eleventh Newport jazz festival. W. Balliett. New Yorker 41:92-5 Jl 17 '65

Sweden

Stockholm launching. J. W. Stedman. il Opera N 30:23 N 6 '65

Texas

San Antonio's skill. J. Rosenfield. Opera N 29:32 My 1 '65

United States

Guide to summer festivals on our continent. il Hi Fi 15:122-4 My '65

Music festivals U.S.A. H. D. Jellinek. Sat R 48:46-9 Jl 17 '65

Singing the way; New York's first folk festival at Carnegie Hall. il Newsweek 65:84 Je 28 '65

Summer evenings (cont) Opera N 29:32 Ap 17 '65

Vermont

Sweet sounds in the woods; Marlboro festival. il Time 86:46+ Jl 23 '65

Yugoslavia

Aesthetic thaw in progress; Zagreb biennale. E. Helm. il Hi Fi 15:141 Ag '65

MUSIC for children
Little orchestra society, Philharmonic Hall. M. Marks. Dance Mag 39:63 Mr '65

See also
Phonograph records—Childrens records

MUSIC history. See Music—History and criticism

MUSIC in industry. See Music, Influence of

MUSIC in the home
Music for non-listening. L. Rich. il Hi Fi 15:34+ N '65

MUSIC libraries
See also
Music library association
New York public library—Music library

MUSIC library association
Future of music librarianship. I. Lowens. il Library J 90:1263-7 Mr 15 '65

MUSIC man; musical comedy. See Musical comedies, revues, etc.—Criticisms, plots, etc.

MUSIC museums
La Scala's treasures: Museo della Scala. il Opera N 29:28-30 Ap 10 '65

MUSIC of the tree; story. See Mountzoures, H. L.

MUSIC research. See Musicology

MUSIC rooms and equipment
How to build a sing-around music bar. H. Walton. il Pop Sci 186:164-7 Ap '65

Music room is dominant feature of house. il Arch Rec 137:74-7 mid-May '65

Place for music, for conversation, for dining. il Sunset 135:83 Jl '65

Portfolio and stereo décor, 1965. il Hi Fi 15:54-61 Mr '65

Room for books and music. il House & Gard 127:100-1 F '65

MUSIC schools
See also
Juilliard school of music, New York
Manhattan school of music

MUSIC service, Planned. See Muzak corporation

MUSIC shells. See Orchestra shells

MUSIC subsidies. See Music and state

MUSIC teachers
Bernac and Lehmann; pupils in public. C. L. Osborne. il Hi Fi 15:104-5 Jl '65

MUSIC therapy
Doctor jazz. il Newsweek 66:94 S 27 '65

MUSIC writing. See Composition (music)

MUSICAL appreciation. See Music—Appreciation

MUSICAL arrangement
Jazz records; composer-arrangers are the diametrically opposed G. Evans and G. McFarland. W. Balliett. New Yorker 41:171-4 My 8 '65

Swing low, sweet Siegfried; Stan Kenton's jazz innovations on great Wagnerian themes. R. Schoenstein. Sat R 48:91 Ap 10 '65

MUSICAL comedies, revues, etc.
See also
Phonograph records—Musical comedies, revues, etc.
Television broadcasting—Musical comedies, revues, etc.

Anecdotes, facetiae, satire, etc.

Making of the president, 1968! a musical extravaganza. A. Glaser. il Esquire 64:153-63 D '65

Stop the greasepaint, I want to smell the crowd! E. Beauchamp. New Yorker 41:68+ Jl 17 '65

Criticisms, plots, etc.

Anya
Dance Mag 40:17 Ja '66
New Yorker 41:142+ D 11 '65
Time 86:78 D 10 '65

Baker street
America 112:589 Ap 17 '65
Commonweal 82:21-2 Mr 26 '65
Dance Mag 39:18-19 Ap '65
Life il 58:133-4 Ap 2 '65
Nat R 17:561 Je 29 '65
New Yorker 41:94+ F 27 '65
Newsweek il 65:84 Mr 1 '65
Sat R 48:22 Mr 6 '65
Time il 85:78 F 26 '65
Vogue 145:100 Ap 1 '65

Ben Franklin in Paris
Sr Schol il 86:21 Mr 4 '65

Carousel
America 113:266-7 S 11 '65
Dance Mag 39:16-17 O '65

Day of the tortoise. See Le jour de la tortue, below

Decline and fall of the entire world as seen through the eyes of Cole Porter, revisited
Life 59:12 Jl 30 '65
Nat R 17:561 Je 29 '65
Newsweek il 65:98 Ap 12 '65
Sat R 48:44 Ap 17 '65

Do I hear a waltz?
America 112:590-1 Ap 17 '65
Commonweal 82:85-6 Ap 9 '65
Dance Mag 39:28-9 My '65
New Yorker 41:144 Mr 27 '65
Newsweek 65:82 Mr 29 '65
Sat R 48:36 Ap 3 '65
Time 85:60 Mr 26 '65

MUSICAL comedies, revues, etc.—Criticisms, plots, etc.—*Continued*
Drat! the cat!
  Dance Mag 39:138 D '65
  Sat R 48:74 O 30 '65
Fiddler on the roof
  Commentary 38:73-5 N '64; Discussion. 39:12+ Ap '65
Flora, the red menace
  America 113:121-2 Jl 31 '65
  Dance Mag il 39:23 Jl '65
  Nat R 17:561-2 Je 29 '65
  New Yorker 41:114 My 22 '65
  Newsweek 65:99 My 24 '65
  Sat R il 48:50 My 8 '65
  Time il 85:69 My 21 '65
  Vogue 146:38 Jl '65
La grosse valise
  New Yorker 41:50 D 25 '65
Half a sixpence
  America 113:63 Jl 10 '65
  Commonweal 82:383-4 Je 11 '65
  Dance Mag il 39:22-3 Jl '65
  New Yorker 41:120 My 8 '65
  Newsweek 65:100 My 10 '65
  Sat R 48:24 My 15 '65
  Time il 85:88 My 7 '65
Hotel Passionato
  New Yorker 41:116 N 6 '65
I had a ball
  America 112:335-6 Mr 6 '65
Le jour dé la tortue
  New Yorker 41:220-2 O 16 '65
Kelly
  New Yorker 40:76 F 13 '65
  Sat Eve Post il 238:32-4+ Ap 24 '65
  Time 85:64 F 19 '65
Kismet
  America 113:122 Jl 31 '65
  Dance Mag 39:24 Ag '65
Kiss me Kate
  New Yorker 41:130+ Je 12 '65
Leonard Bernstein's theatre songs
  America 113:122 Jl 31 '65
  Life 59:12 Jl 30 '65
Mackey of Appalachia
  America 113:384-5 O 2 '65
Mad show
  Newsweek il 67:82 Ja 24 '66
Man of La Mancha
  America 114:53 Ja 8 '66
  Dance Mag il 40:16 Ja '66
  Nation 201:484 D 13 '65
  New Yorker 41:106+ D 4 '65
  Sat R 48:51 D 11 '65
  Time 86:54 D 3 '65
  Vogue 147:34 Ja 15 '66
Mardi gras!
  America 113:190 Ag 21 '65
Music man
  Dance Mag 39:24 Ag '65
On a clear day you can see forever
  Dance Mag il 39:138-9 D '65
  Holiday 39:118+ Ja '66
  Nation 201:398 N 22 '65
  New Yorker 41:108 O 30 '65
  Newsweek il 66:84+ N 1 '65
  Sat R 48:41-2 N 6 '65
  Time 86:84 O 29 '65
Pickwick
  America 113:509 O 30 '65
  Dance Mag 39:24 N '65
  New Yorker 41:195 O 16 '65
  Newsweek 66:114 O 18 '65
  Sat R 48:74 O 23 '65
  Time 86:75 O 15 '65
  Vogue 146:71 N 15 '65
Roar of the greasepaint—The smell of the crowd
  America 112:867-8 Je 12 '65
  Cath World il 201:151-2 My '65
  Dance Mag il 39:22-3 Jl '65
  New Yorker 41:56 My 29 '65
  Newsweek 65:76 My 31 '65
  Reporter 32:45-6 Ap 8 '65
  Sat R il 48:38 Je 5 '65
  Time il 85:83 My 28 '65
Skyscraper
  Commonweal 83:316 D 10 '65
  Dance Mag 40:16 Ja '66
  Holiday 39:118+ Ja '66
  New Yorker 41:149 N 20 '65
  Newsweek il 66:91 N 29 '65
  Sat R 48:76 D 4 '65
  Time 86:67 N 26 '65
South Pacific
  New Yorker 41:130+ Je 12 '65
That thing at the Cherry lane
  New Yorker 41:58+ My 29 '65
West side story
  Dance Mag il 39:35-8 Ap '65
  Dance Mag il 39:40-1 N '65
Wet paint
  New Yorker 41:85-6 Ap 24 '65
World of Charles Aznavour
  Time 86:102+ O 22 '65

MUSICAL comedy production. See Theatrical production
MUSICAL comedy, revue, etc.
Broadway: mid-winter. D. Hering. il Dance Mag 39:30-2 F '65
Goings on about town. See issues of New Yorker
Number one melody man. G. Millstein. il Sat Eve Post 238:95-9 Mr 13 '65
RCA Victor's notable new reissue program, back to Broadway. M. Kreuger. il Am Rec G 31:1040-3 Jl '65
Same old tune; turning old plays into new musical comedies. Newsweek 66:78 Ag 23 '65
MUSICAL criticism. See Music—History and criticism
MUSICAL education
Crescendo on the campus; our new music centers; Indiana university's school of music. H. Pleasants. il Reporter 33:52-6 S 23 '65
Education on the Menuhin plan; Yehudi Menuhin school, Stoke d'Abernon, Surrey England and plans for U.S. school. I. Kolodin. il Sat R 48:57-8+ N 27 '65
  See also
Music—Instruction and study
MUSICAL instruments
Mephisto's musings. il Hi Fi 15:160-1 D '65
New designs for musical instruments. il Design 66:34-7 My '65
Of shapes and sounds; Baschet-Lasry instruments. W. Buehr. il Horizon 7:60-3 Sum '65
Sound shaper; exhibition of F. Baschet's structures. il Newsweek 66:112-13 O 18 '65
World in tune. il Recreation 58:61 F '65
  See also
Drum
MUSICAL museums. See Music museums
MUSICAL notation
Musical events; attempts to give specific meanings to chords, or other musical phenomena. W. Sargeant. New Yorker 41:143 Je 5 '65
MUSICAL pitch
Musical events; method of measuring the precise pitches of notes. W. Sargeant. New Yorker 41:173 Ap 17 '65
MUSICAL research. See Musicology
MUSICAL societies
  See also
Handel and Haydn society
Metropolitan opera club
MUSICAL style. See Style, Musical
MUSICAL trade unions. See Trade unions—United States
MUSICIANS
Artist life. D. J. Soria. See issues of High fidelity incorporating Musical America
Debuts and reappearances; New York concerts. Hi Fi 15:173 D '65
Here & there. Hi Fi 16:144-5 Ja '66
Musical whirl; photographs. See issues of High fidelity incorporating Musical America
  See also
Composers
Jazz musicians

Anecdotes, facetiae, satire, etc.
My uncle, the violinist. A. Sherman. il Sat Eve Post 238:16 S 11 '65

Salaries
Unions, legislation, and the courts. L. E. Lunden. Mo Labor R 88:1177-81 O '65
MUSICIANS, American
  See also
American federation of musicians
Coleman, O.
Ellington, D.
Foss, L.
Garner, E.
Gottschalk, L. M.
Hawkins, C.
Russell, C. E.
Stern, I.
MUSICIANS, Argentine
Argentine panorama. il Américas 17:45 Ag '65
MUSICIANS, French
  See also
Rampal, J. P.
MUSICIANS, Israeli
  See also
Perlman, I.
MUSICIANS, Italian
  See also
Michelangeli, A. B.
Paganini, N.

MUSICIANS, Polish
   See also
Horszowski, M.
Rubinstein, A.
MUSICIANS, Russian
   See also
Rostropovich, M.
MUSICIANS, Swiss
   Music from the cantons; discs, by Swiss composers. O. Daniel. Sat R 48:49-50 D 25 '65
MUSICIANS contracts. See Contracts
MUSICOGENIC epilepsy. See Epilepsy
MUSICOLOGY
   Musical treasure hunt; Juilliard repertory project. V. Giannini. il Am Ed 1:23-6 D '64
   Research in music with electronics. L. Hiller. and J. Beauchamp. bibliog il Science 150: 161-9 O 8 '65
MUSIL, Karl
   Brief biographies. S. Goodman. pors Dance Mag 39:48-9 Mr '65
MUSK ducks. See Ducks, Wild
MUSK oxen
   Musk ox domesticated. il Sci N L 87:370 Je 12 '65
MUSKAT, Irving Elkin
   Interama (continued) Reporter 33:20 O 7 '65
   Miami super-lobby. H. Harwood. il Reporter 32:21-5 My 6 '65
MUSKELLUNGE fishing
   Muskie explosion. E. A. Bauer. il Outdoor Life 135:18-23+ Mr '65
MUSKETS
   See also
Rifles
MUSKIE, Edmund S.
   Air pollution: federal standards likely unless states and localities take early action. L. J. Carter. por Science 150:467-8+ O 22 '65
   Pollution politics: LBJ retreats on opposition to measure curbing pollution from automobile exhaust. E. Langer. por Science 148:611-13 Ap 30 '65
MUSKMELONS
   Cantaloupes are versatile; with recipes. il Sunset 134:228 Je '65
MUSLIMS
   Kashmir: a religious war; Muslim and Hindu intolerance. J. F. Drane. Cath World 202: 212-16 Ja '66
   See also
Islam
Pilgrimages to Mecca
MUSLIMS, Black. See Black Muslim movement
MUSLIMS in Egypt
   See also
Moslem brotherhood
MUSLIMS in India
   See also
India–Hindu–Moslem relations
MUSORGSKII, Modest Petrovich
   Boris Godunov. Criticism
     Opera N il 30:27-8 N 6 '65
   On records: Songs & dances of death. Opera N 30:38 Ja 15 '66
MUSSELMAN, Maxine Treesh
   Among the books: Standing up country. Liv Wildn 29:29-31 Sum '65
MUSSELMAN, Virginia
   Retirement to leisure: adaptation of address, September 1964. Recreation 58:239-40+ My '65
   Save our children's playgrounds. por Parents Mag 40:40+ Ag '65
   Your playground manual. por Recreation 58: 185 Ap '65
MUSSELS
   Preferential settling of the sea anemone stomphia coccinea on the mussel modiolus modiolus. D. M. Moss. bibliog il Science 148:527-8 Ap 23 '65
   Serotonin and adenosine triphosphate: synergistic effect of the beat frequency of cilia of mussel gills. S. L. Schor. bibliog il Science 148:500-1 Ap 23 '65
MUSSOLINI, Benito
   Twilight of a tyrant; excerpts from Last 100 days. J. Toland. il pors 29:38-40+ My 18 '65
   When the trains ran on time. il por Time 85:40 Ap 30 '65
MUSSON, Ron
   Halfway there. Time 86:60-1 Ag 20 '65
MUSTANG. See Nepal
MUSTANGS. See Horses
MUSTARD gas
   Sulfur mustard: reaction with L-cells treated with 5-fluorodeoxyuridine. I. G. Walker. bibliog il Science 151:99-101 Ja 7 '66
MUSULIN, Stella. See Taubinger, L. M. jt. auth.

MUSURILLO, Herbert
   Book review. America 114:87 Ja 15 '66
MUTATION (bacteria)
   Genetics of a bacterial virus. R. S. Edgar and R. H. Epstein. il Sci Am 212:70-8 F '65
MUTATION (biology)
   Cellular segregation and heterocytic dominance in hydra. H. M. Lenhoff. bibliog il Science 148:1105-7 My 21 '65
   Conditional-lethal mutants of an animal virus: identification of two cistrons. B. W. Burge and E .R. Pfefferkorn. bibliog il Science 148:959-60 My 14 '65
   Double beta-lipoprotein: a new genetic variant in man. W. Seegers and others. bibliog il Science 149:303-4 Jl 16 '65
   Electrophoretic variation in enzymes. C. R. Shaw. bibliog Science 149:936-43 Ag 27 '65
   Hereditary absence of sebaceous glands in the mouse. A. H. Gates and M. Karasek. bibliog il Science 148:1471-3 Je 11 '65
   Neurological mutants of the mouse; report on conference. R. L. Sidman and others. Science 150:153-14+ O 22 '65
   Nitrous acid mutation of transforming DNA: consideration of mode of action. S. H. Goodgal and E, H. Postel. bibliog Science 148:1095-7 My 21 '65
   Odorous secretion of normal and mutant tribolium confusum. M. Engelhardt and others. bibliog il Science 150:632-3 O 29 '65
   Spontaneous mutation rates at five coatcolor loci in mice. G. Schlager and M. M. Dickie. bibliog il Science 151:205-6 Ja 14 '66
   Suppression in vitro: identification of a serine-sRNA as a nonsense suppressor. M. R. Capecchi and G. N. Gussin. bibliog il Science 149:417-22 Jl 23 '65
   See also
Heterozygosis
MUTATION (botany)
   Chloroplast mutagenesis: effect of N-methyl-N'-nitro-N-nitrosoguanidine and some other agents on euglena. D. R. McCalla. bibliog il Science 148:497-9 Ap 23 '65
   Mutagenic effects of hydroxylamine in vivo. I. Tessman and others. bibliog il Science 148:507-8 Ap 23 '65
   Mutagenicity of a monofunctional alkylating agent derivative of acridine in neurospora. H. E. Brockman and W. Goben. bibliog il Science 147:750-1 F 12 '65
   Mutation of the blue-green alga, anacystis nidulans. C. Van Baalen. bibliog Science 149:70 Jl 2 '65
   Phosphatase mutants in aspergillus nidulans. G. Dorn. bibliog il Science 150:1183-4 N 26 '65
   Pressure-induced color mutation of euglena gracilis. J. A. Gross. bibliog il Science 147: 741-2 F 12 '65
   Second mutant gene affecting the amino acid pattern of maize endosperm proteins. O. E. Nelson and others. bibliog il Science 150: 1469-70 D 10 '65
   Tricarboxylic acid cycle mutants in saccharomyces: comparison of independently derived mutants. M. Ogur and others. bibliog Science 147:1590 Mr 26 '65
MUTCHMOR, James Ralph
   More church union in Canada? Christian Cent 82:1090-3 S 8 '65
   Salute across the border. Christian Cent 82:517 Ap 28 '65
MUTILATED; drama. See Williams, T.
MUTILATION of books. See Books—Mutilation, defacement, etc.
MUTINY
   Great mutiny, by J. Dugan. Review
     New Repub 153:23-5 N 6 '65. J. Featherstone
     Time il 86:104+ O 29 '65
MUTTI, R. J. See Jones, P. B. jt. auth.
MUTUAL funds. See Investment trusts
MUTUAL trust funds. See Investment trusts
MUUL, Illar
   Day length and food caches. Natur Hist 74: 22-7 Mr '65
MUZAK corporation
   Muzak men. A. Levy. il Horizon 7:39-45 Sum '65
MUZII, E. O. and Skinner, H. C. W.
   Calcite deposition during shell repair by the aragonitic gastropod murex fulvescens. bibliog Science 151:201-3 Ja 14 '66
MUZZEY, David Saville
   Obituary
     Pub W 187:81 Ap 26 '65
MUZZLE-loading rifles. See Rifles

MWAMBUTSA IV, king of Burundi
Josy and the king. il por Newsweek 67:41 Ja 24 '66
MWANAWINA III, paramount chief of Barotseland
After while, crocodile. il por Time 85:30 Ap 2 '65
MY enemy; story. See Gordon, E. E.
MY first love; story. See O'Brien, E.
MY lover has dirty fingernails; story. See Updike, J.
MY most unforgettable experience of last summer; story. See Amft, M. J.
MY mother and Joey; story. See Criswell, M .
MY Oedipus complex; story. See O'Connor, F.
MY swinging swain; drama. See Martens, A. C.
MYASTHENIA gravis
Critical junction found in muscle disease. Sci N L 87:182 Mr 20 '65
Muscle disease victim allergic to himself. Sci N L 87:104 F 13 '65
MYCOPLASMA. See Microorganisms, Pathogenic
MYDANS, Carl
Bush pilot of Angel Falls. il Life 59:80-2+ O 15 '65
MYELIN. See Nerves
MYELOGENOUS leukemia. See Leukemia
MYELOMA. See Cancer
MYERS, Charles F. Jr
Weaving a profit pattern. il por(cover) Bsns W p72-4+ Mr 6 '65
MYERS, Fred
Movies. Christian Cent 82:492-3 Ap 21 '65
MYERS, George R.
Achieving quality. NEA J 54:37 Ap '65
MYERS, Judith Maguire
Linnet on the leaf. McCalls 92:20+ F '65
MYERS, L. S. Jr, and others
Radiolysis of thymine in aqueous solutions: change in site of attack with change in pH. bibliog Science 148:1234-5 My 28 '65
MYERS, Leonore
To an old doll in an antique shop; poem. Hobbies 70:40 My '65
MYERS, Lloyd E.
Evaporation retardants: application by means of a water-soluble matrix. Science 148:70-1 Ap 2 '65
MYERS, Max H. See Schneiderman, M. A. jt. auth.
MYERS, Richard. See Someroski, J. M. jt. auth.
MYERS, Robert J.
Russia tries insurance. Nation 200:113-14 F 1 '65
MYLECRAINE, Walter E.
Public domain. por Am Ed 1:7-8 N '65
MYNARSKI, Andy
Thirteenth mission; ed. by D. MacDonald. G. P. Brophy. il Read Digest 87:78-82 D '65
MYOINOSITOL. See Inositol
MYOPIA
Good look at the mystery of nearsightedness. il Good H 161:165 S '65
Is nearsightedness hereditary? Sci Digest 58: 28 S '65
MYOSIN
Mercurial-induced transformation of myosin prevented by adenosine triphosphate and pyrophosphate. D. R. Kominz. bibliog il Science 149:1374-5 S 17 '65
MYRBERG, Arthur A. Jr, and others
Sound production by cichlid fishes. bibliog Science 149:555-8 Jl 30 '65
MYRDAL, Gunnar
Will we prevent mass starvation? New Repub 152:14-15 Ap 24 '65
With what little wisdom the world is ruled. N Y Times Mag p20-1+ Jl 18 '65
World famine ahead? Gunnar Myrdal's warning; excerpts from address, March 15, 1965. U S News 58:16 Mr 29 '65
MYRDAL, Jan
(ed) Village life in Communist China; excerpts from Report from a Chinese village. Sat R 48:24-6+ Ap 10 '65
MYRER, Anton
Cornerstone of fiction. Writer 78:9-11+ O '65
WLB biography. N. Morgan. por Wilson Lib Bul 39:920 Je '65
MYRISTICIN
Myristicin in cigarette smoke. I. Schmeltz and others. bibliog Science 151:96-7 Ja 7 '66
MYRTLE
For a green garden wall: Pacific wax myrtle. il Sunset 135:212 S '65
MYRTLE, Crape. See Crape myrtle

MYSTERY stories. See Detective and mystery stories
MYSTERY writers of America
Candidates for MWA Edgars announced. Pub W 187:37 Mr 15 '65
MYSTIC, Conn.
It still is yesterday in Mystic. il Sunset 134: 35-6+ My '65
MYTHOLOGY, Assyro-Babylonian
See also
Gilgamesh
MYTHOLOGY, Classical
See also
Mythology, Greek
MYTHOLOGY, Greek
Mythological geography of the Mediterranean. il Holiday 39:100-1 Ja '66
MYTHOLOGY, Hindu
Gods, demons, and others, by R. K. Narayan. Review
New Yorker 41:193-4 Mr 13 '65. V. Mehta
MYTHOLOGY, Norse
See also
Sagas
MYTILENE
Two Greek islands. E. Perényi. Vogue 146: 269+ O 1 '65
MYXOMYCETES
Amateur scientist; how to cultivate the slime molds and perform experiments on them. A. C. Lonert. il Sci Am 214:116-19+ Ja '66
Disappearance of a genetic marker from a cytoplasmic hybrid plasmodium of a true slime mold. N. S. Kerr. bibliog il Science 147:1586-8 Mr 26 '65

N

NAACP. See National association for the advancement of colored people
NAB. See National association of broadcasters
NACS. See National association of college stores
NAE. See National academy of engineering
NAFBRAT. See National association for better radio and television
NAM. See National association of manufacturers
NATC. See National air taxi conference
NATO. See North Atlantic treaty organization
NAYRU. See North Atlantic yacht racing union
NBA. See National basketball association; National book awards
NBAA. See National business aircraft association
NBC. See National book committee; National broadcasting company
NCACLU. See National capital area civil liberties union
NCAWE. See National council of administrative women in education
NCC. See National council of the churches of Christ in the United States of America
NCCE. See National center for citizens in education
NCCM. See National council of Catholic men
NCEA. See National Catholic educational association
NCGE. See National council for geographic education
NCOA. See National council on the aging
NCSC. See National council of senior citizens
NCSS. See National council for the social studies
NCTE. See National council of teachers of English
NDEA (National defense education act) See School laws and legislation—United States
NEA. See National education association
NEA Journal
Editor's notebook (cont) M. S. Fenner. NEA J 54:72 Mr '65
NERVA (nuclear engine for rocket vehicle application) See Rockets, Atomic powered
NET. See National educational television and radio center
NFL. See National football league
NFO. See National farmers organization
NHL. See National hockey league
NIH. See United States—National institutes of health
NLM. See United States—National library of medicine
NLRB. See United States—National labor relations board
NLW. See National library week

NRA. See United States—National recovery administration

NRECA. See National rural electric cooperative association

NSA. See United States—National security agency; United States national student association

NSC. See United States—National security council

NSCF. See National student Christian federation

NSF. See United States—National science foundation

NSIA. See National security industrial association

NSU-Wankel engines. See Automobile engines

NSVP (National school volunteer program) See Teachers aides

NYPL. See New York public library

NABB, Edward H.
Union international motorboating. Yachting 118:160 Ag '65

NABOKOV, Vladimir
Nabokov's Eugene Onegin. R. Conquest. Poetry 106:236-8 Je '65

NABORS, Jim
Gomer Pyle: country boy next door. S. Gordon. il pors Look 29:99-102 Je 1 '65

NABRIT, James M. Jr
More campus unrest: are reds to blame? statements. por U S News 58:14 My 10 '65

NABRIT, S. M.
Removing the stereotype. Sat R 48:69 Je 19 '65

NABUCO, Janio
Dead end in Portugal; tr. by J. Drury. Commonweal 83:240-2 N 26 '65

NADAR
Letter from Paris; retrospective exhibition of his original photographs at the Bibliothèque nationale. Genêt. New Yorker 41:165-6 My 1 '65

NADEL, Michael
Areas subject to study within next ten years for possible inclusion in the National wilderness preservation system. Liv Wildn 86:26-30 Spr '64
Grand Canyon. Liv Wildn 87:28 Wint '64
Great guide to Glacier. Liv Wildn 29:33 Spr '65

NADEL, Norman
Gentle adventure: from Lake Erie to the sea. il Yachting 118:44-6+ Ag; 48-9+ S '65

NADER, Ralph
Profits vs. engineering: the Corvair story; excerpts from Unsafe at any speed. Nation 201:295-301 N 1 '65

NADJARI, Maurice
Beachboy caper. J. Roth. Esquire 64:118-19+ S '65

NADWORNY, Milton J.
State right to work laws. Cur Hist 49:85-90+ Ag '65

NAESS, Ragnar D.
Another '29? no chance of anything like that; interview. por U S News 58:44-6 Je 28 '65

NAGAI, Michio
World of Leo Rosten; ed. by L. Rosten. Look 29:38 Ag 10 '65

NAGASAKI
Nagasaki; H. Kosasa family. il Look 29:28-9 Ag 10 '65

NAGAYA, Hiroshi, and Sieker, H. O.
Allograft survival: effect of antiserums to thymus glands and lymphocytes. bibliog Science 150:1181-2 N 26 '65

NAGENDA, John
Hippos. Reporter 32:32-3 Je 3 '65
Sketches of Uganda. Reporter 33:46-9 O 7 '65

NAGLE, Kel
Two foreign blokes shock the slammers. A. Wright. il por Sports Illus 22:24-31 Je 28 '65

NAGLE, Stanley C. Jr. See Brown, B. L. jt. auth.

NAGLE, William J.
Next council. Commonweal 82:688-91 S 24 '65

NAGRIN, Daniel
Daniel Nagrin 92nd street Y. M. Marks. Dance Mag 39:67 Je '65

NAGY, Bartholomew
Optical activity in the orgueil meteorite. bibliog Science 150:1846 D 31 '65

about

Optical activity in the orgueil meteorite. R. Hayatsu. bibliog il Science 149:443-7 Jl 23 '65

NAGY, Jill
Head start in suburbia. Sat R 48:62+ D 18 '65

NAGY, Sibyl Moholy-. See Moholy-Nagy, S.

NAGY, Steven Keresztes-. See Keresztes-Nagy, S.

NAHAS, G. G. See Triner, L. jt. auth.

NAILS
Ordinary nails and extraordinary. il Sunset 135:144+ N '65

NAILS (anatomy)
See also
Manicuring

NAIPAUL, V. S.
Angry young Indian; interview. ed. by S. Oberbeck. por Newsweek 65:103-103A+ Ap 19 '65
East Indian, West Indian. Reporter 32:35-7 Je 17 '65
They are staring at me; excerpt from Area of darkness. Sat Eve Post 238:82-4 Ap 10 '65

NAIROBI, Kenya
Letter from Nairobi. V. P. McCorry. America 114:20-1 Ja 1 '66

NAISMITH, Grace
Speaking of feminine hygiene. Todays Health 43:22-3+ D '65
When the sap begins to flow. Todays Health 43:44-6+ F '65

NAITO, Masatoshi
Incredible photoons of Masatoshi Naito. il Mod Photo 29:86-91 F '65

NAITO, Tatsuro. See Yamamoto, N. jt. auth.

NAKAJIMA, Shigehiro. See Hagiwara, S. jt. auth.

NAKAMURA, Masaya
Nakamura and his nudes. R. Halford. il U S Camera 28:48-9+ D '65
Nude in nature. il U S Camera 28:52-3 Je '65

NAKAS, M. and others
Uncoupling of an epithelial cell membrane junction by calcium-ion removal. bibliog Science 151:89-91 Ja 7 '66

NAKASA, Nathaniel
Mr Nakasa goes to Harlem. pors N Y Times Mag p40-7+ F 7 '65

NAKEDNESS. See Nudism

NAKIAN, Reuben
Portraits in paganism. K. Kuh. il Sat R 48:28-9 Jl 31 '65

NAMATH, Joe
Another good Joe for the AFL. J. Underwood. il Sports Illus 23:46-9 Ag 9 '65
Battle of the QBs. por Time 86:96 S 17 '65
Countdown for Joe Namath. W. C. Heinz. por Life 59:37+ Ag 20 '65
$400,000 knee. il por Time 85:53 F 5 '65
Joint for next season. G. Cant. il Sports Illus 22:38-41 F 8 '65

NAM DONG, Battle of. See Vietnamese war, 1957- —Campaigns and battles

NAME of Patrick Henry; story. See Cope, J.

NAMES, Astronomical. See Astronomy—Nomenclature

NAMES, Geographical
Gotham: nickname for New York. New Yorker 41:19-20 Ag 7 '65
Of many things; name game in old Kentucky. T. N. Davis. America 112:407 Mr 27 '65

Pronunciation

From Guzzle Down to the Tah. L. Martin. il Sat R 48:52+ Mr 13 '65

NAMES, Personal
Don't tread on Harvey. Newsweek 66:75-6 Ag 30 '65
Qu'y a-t-il dans un nom? France's permissible first names. il Time 87:29-30 Ja 7 '66
What's in a name? Latin American and Chinese names; letter to the editor. Sr Schol 86:28 My 13 '65

NAMES of boats. See Boats—Names

NAMES of products. See Trade names

NAMIAS, Jerome
Drought in East, floods in West, why the strange weather; interview. por U S News 59:48-50 D 27 '65
Short-period climatic fluctuations. bibliog Science 147:696-706 F 12 '65

NAMING contests. See Competitions

NAMUTH, Hans
Architects: a chance for greatness; photographs. Fortune 73:152-7 Ja '66

NANAS, Ed
Master modeler of midget guns. Pop Mech 124:88-90 D '65

NANCE, Paul K. See Deering, E. C. jt. auth.

NANDA, Gulzarilal
Under a caretaker: can India keep going? por U S News 60:42 Ja 24 '66

NANOLITER pipette. See Biological apparatus and supplies

NANTUCKET ISLAND
World & Nantucket. N. Benchley. il Am Heritage 16:28-31+ Je '65

NAPA, Calif.
Banking pavilion of wood and glass. il Arch Rec 137:192 Je '65

NAPERVILLE, Ill.
People like cul-de-sacs. D. Wiegand. il Am City 80:108 Mr '65

NAPHTHALENE
Device rids impurities. Sci N L 88:228 O 9 '65

NAPLES
Description
December in Naples. W. Marchant. il Holiday 39:54-9+ Ja '66

NAPOLEON I, emperor of the French
Battle that began a 100-year peace. J. A. Lukacs. il N Y Times Mag p 10-11+ Je 13 '65
Napoleon's eighty days, by D. J. Goodspeed. Review
　Sat R por 48:57 O 2 '65. J. H. Plumb
Waterloo: 1815. T. N. Carmichael. il pors Life 58:68-87 Je 11 '65

NARAYAN, R. K.
Why Go Matha is loved. N Y Times Mag p 12-13+ My 30 '65

NARCISSUS
Getting to know the daffodils. M. J. Dietz. il Flower Grower 52:24-5 S '65

NARCOTIC addicts
Anti-heroin; methadone, transitional drug for addicts. Sci Am 212:62+ Ap '65
Army of the lost. F. R. Schreiber and M. Herman. il Sci Digest 58:23-7 D '65
Breaking the habit; new treatment with methadone. il Newsweek 65:60+ Je 21 '65
Case history of an addict-patient; methadone program. il Look 29:25-7 N 30 '65
Children of the poppy. H. S. Peyser. New Repub 152:19-20 F 13 '65; Reply. J. Benjamin. 152:28-9 F 27 '65
Deviance and deviates. H. S. Becker. Nation 201:115-19 S 20 '65
Drug addiction. J. Mills. il Life 58:66B-82+ F 26; 92B-103+ Mr 5 '65; Same abr. with title We are all animals. Read Digest 86: 226-30+ Je '65
How Bill Eppridge photographed the world of junkies. B. Eppridge. il Mod Phot 29: 22+ Je '65
Junkie's life; concerning Life magazine article. Newsweek 65:63 Mr 8 '65
Mom is the villain. il Time 85:83 My 21 '65
My son was a drug addict. L. David. Good H 160:53+ Ja '65
Narcotics: slum to suburb. il Newsweek 65: 68A-68C F 22 '65
New hope for drug addicts; methadone. R. H. Berg. il Look 29:23-4 N 30 '65
New improved drug scene. J. Larner. il Nation 201:120-4 S 20 '65
Now, a drug that cures addicts. J. Reinert. Sci Digest 50:38-41 N '65
Our new drug addicts. S. Grafton. McCalls 92:112-13+ Ap '65
Profiles: Dr M. Nyswander. N. Hentoff. New Yorker 41:32-4+ Je 26; 32-4+ Jl 3 '65; Correction. 41:102 S 11 '65
Reporter at large; gang of teen-age drug addicts in rehabilitation program sponsored by Mobilization for youth. R. Rice. New Yorker 41:50-2+ Mr 27 '65
Terror in the streets? W. Sparks. Commonweal 82:345-8 Je 4 '65
War on addiction. D. R. Campion. il America 112:356-9 Mr 13 '65; Reply. L. H. Burke. 112:650 My 8 '65
Young drug addict: can we help him? excerpt from Addict in the street. J. Larner. il Atlan 215:75-80 F '65

NARCOTIC habit
College drug scene. J. Larner. Atlan 216:127-30+ N '65
Drug addiction. J. Mills. il Life 58:66B-82+ F 26; 92B-103+ Mr 5 '65; Same abr. with title We are all animals. Read Digest 86: 226-30+ Je '65
Drug addiction studied. Sci N L 88:87 Ag 7 '65
How opiates change behavior. J. R. Nichols. il Sci Am 212:80-6+ bibliog(p 135) F '65
Junkie's life; concerning Life magazine article. Newsweek 65:63 Mr 8 '65
Narcotics: slum to suburb. il Newsweek 65: 68A-68C F 22 '65
New hope for drug addicts: methadone. R. H. Berg. il Look 29:23-4 N 30 '65

One answer to heroin. Time 86:44 S 3 '65
Pill addicts; amendments to the U.S. food and drug laws. il Newsweek 66:64 D 20 '65
Playmates in the narcotics game. H. E. Barnes. il Sat R 48:25+ Mr 6 '65
Profiles: Dr M. Nyswander. N. Hentoff. New Yorker 41:32-4+ Je 26; 32-4+ Jl 3 '65; Correction. 41:102 S 11 '65
Spontaneous opiate addiction in rhesus monkeys. J. L. Claghorn and others. bibliog il Science 149:440-1 Jl 23 '65
Thrill-pill menace. B. Davidson. il Sat Eve Post 238:23-7 D 4 '65
Tunnel back, by L. Yablonsky. Review
　Nation 200:256-61 Mr 8 '65. E. Friedenberg
Where junkies learn to hang tough. G. Samuels. il N Y Times Mag p30-1+ My 9 '65
Young drug addict: can we help him? excerpt from Addict in the street. J. Larner. il Atlan 215:75-80 F '65

NARCOTIC laws
Addict and the law, by A. R. Lindesmith. Review
　Commentary 40:76-8 Ag '65. H. S. Becker
Profiles: Dr M. Nyswander. N. Hentoff. New Yorker 41:32-4+ Je 26; 32-4+ Jl 3 '65; Correction. 41:102 S 11 '65
Realities we must face but won't. J. Mills. il Life 58:105-6+ Mr 5 '65

NARCOTIC trade. See Narcotics, Control of

NARCOTIC traffic. See Narcotics, Control of

NARCOTICS
　See also
Marihuana
Morphine

NARCOTICS, Bureau of. See United States —Narcotics, Bureau of

NARCOTICS, Control of
Dope-smuggling diplomats; ed. by J. C. G. Conniff. H. L. Giordano. il Pop Sci 186:100-3+ Je '65
Drug addiction. J. Mills. il Life 58:92B-103+ Mr 5 '65
Narcotics: slum to suburb. il Newsweek 65: 68A-68C F 22 '65
Stupefying Sam; biggest single haul of heroin captured in the U.S. il Time 86:15B D 31 '65
　See also
Narcotic addicts

NARDONE, Roland M. and others
Nucleoside incorporation into strain L cells: inhibition by pleuropneumonia-like organisms. bibliog Science 149:1100-1 S 3 '65

NARRAGANSETT BAY
Dirty-clam caper; Great Narragansett Bay quahog war. J. Skow. il Sat Eve Post 238:44+ F 27 '65

NASH, Curtis E. and others
They lead two lives in Central Michigan university's five-year teacher intern program. NEA J 54:12-14 My '65

NASH, Gerald D.
Industry and the federal government: 1850-1933. Cur Hist 48:321-7+ Je '65

NASH, Mary
Teaching by delight. Horn Bk 41:158-60 Ap '65

NASH, Ogden
Backward, turn backward, O commentator, in thy flights; poem. New Yorker 41:48 S 18 '65
I'm no saint, but I have my doubts about Valentine, too; poem. Ladies Home J 82: 79 F '65
Just Holmes and me, and Mnemosyne, makes three; poem. New Yorker 41:42 Ap 17 '65
Let's have a look at your license! por McCalls 92:48 Jl '65
Strange case of Mrs Moodus's second honeymoon; poem. Sat Eve Post 238:20 D 4 '65
Ten new limericks. Holiday 38:56-7 N '65
They don't read De Quincey in Philly or Cincy; poem. Harper 231:78 S '65
To my valentine; poem. Read Digest 86:76-7 F '65
Vice-President of Kenya; poem. New Repub 153:23 N 6 '65
Wrongs of spring; poem. New Yorker 41:44 Mr 27 '65

NASH, William W. Jr, and Hartman, C. W.
Laissez-faire in the slums. Reporter 32:49-50+ F 25 '65

NASHVILLE, Ind.
Greenish village. il Design 66:30-2 My '65

NASHVILLE, Tenn.
Lighting
Updating the lighting report. E. E. Parks. Am City 80:116+ Jl '65

NASHVILLE, Tenn, public library
Nashville respects tradition. D. M. Stewart.
il Library J 90:5167-9 D 1 '65
NASSAU, Jason John
Explorer of the Milky way. D. A. MacRae. il
pors Sky & Tel 30:7-8 Jl '65
NASSAU, Bahama Islands
See also
Tourist trade—Bahama Islands
NASSER, Gamal Abdel
Arab world in ferment. il por Sr Schol 86:
14-16+ My 6 '65
Diplomatic farce in Yemen. S. Guldesca. il
Nat R 17:510-11 Je 15 '65
Forgotten war in the desert: a first-hand
report. J. Law. il por U S News 58:67-9
My 24 '65
Journey to Jedda. il por Time 86:20-1 Ag 27
'65
Nasser's Egypt. G. H. Torrey. il Cur Hist
48:290-5+ My '65
New war coming? pressure rises in Mideast.
il por U S News 58:61-2 Mr 15 '65
Nonalignment in the Arab world. D. Peretz.
bibliog f Ann Am Acad 362:36-43 N '65
Plot to kill Nasser. il por Time 86:53 S 17
'65
Reprieve for Nasser. G. Comte. Nat R 17:
728 Ag 24 '65
Sudden freeze. A. Higbee. il por Newsweek
66:36 Ag 2 '65
Tale of two autocrats. il pors Time 85:25-6
Mr 26 '65
They call him El Rayis, the boss. H. Smith.
il por N Y Times Mag p32-3+ My 16 '65
Unquiet genius of Egypt. J. Morris. Atlan
216:126-30+ O '65
Willie Sutton and Abdel Nasser. W. S.
Schlamm. por Nat R 17:238 Mr 23 '65
NASSIKAS, James
How to tip just enough; interview. Changing
T 19:33-6 S '65
NASUA narica. See Coatis
NASUTION, Abdul Haris
Indonesia: generals who got away. D. Warner.
Reporter 33:39-40 O 21 '65
Strong man who cracked down on reds. por
U S News 60:14 Ja 3 '66
NATAL plums
It does nicely in the Bay area. il Sunset
134:258+ Je '65
NATCHEZ, Miss.
Natchez boycott. Reporter 33:18 D 2 '65
Nobody turn me 'round. Time 86:31-2 O 15
'65
Twilight zone. il Newsweek 66:48 O 18 '65
NATHAN, John
Soap opera, Japanese style. N Y Times Mag
p 12-13+ D 19 '65
NATHAN, Leonard E.
Guardian angels; poem. New Repub 153:23
D 11 '65
Translation from the wind of Guadalajara;
Thoughts like hawks; I would write more;
poems. Poetry 106:395-7 S '65
NATHAN, Paul
Quiet, please! Parents Mag 40:56-7+ O '65
Rights and permissions. See issues of Pub-
lishers' weekly
—See Green, S. L. jt. auth.
NATHAN, Ruth. See Ellis, A. jt. auth.
NATHANS, M. W. and others
Iron minerals formed by a nuclear explosion
in salt bed. bibliog Science 150:1027 N 19
'65
NATION (periodical)
Change of charity. Time 87:41 Ja 7 '66
Charles Sanders Peirce & The nation. R. J.
Bernstein. Nation 200:308-10 Mr 22 '65
Fiduciary of this trust; new publisher. il
Newsweek 67:42 Ja 10 '66
Henry James and the Nation. L. Edel. Na-
tion 201:237-40 S 20 '65
Media. Pub W 189:24 Ja 3 '66
Nation and its poets. A. Laing. Nation 201:
212-18 S 20 '65
Nation at 100; compilation of birthday greet-
ings. Nation 201:17-21 Jl 5 '65
Norton and Godkin: launching The nation.
K. Vanderbilt. Nation 200:165-9 F 15 '65
One hundred years of 'The Nation', ed. by
H. M. Christman. Review
America 113:413-14 O 9 '65. R. A. Schroth
100th anniversary issue. bibliog il Nation 201:
14-242+ S 20 '65
Paul Elmer More: the Nation's conservative
editor. F. X. Duggan. Nation 200:248-51 Mr
8 '65
State of the Nation: 200th anniversary. H.
Nelson. Sat R 48:53 Jl 10 '65
Statements to our readers. G. G. Kirstein;
J. J. Storrow, jr. Nation 202:3-4 Ja 3 '66
Two Nation portraits: F. L. Olmsted, J. M.
W. Mario. R. Fridlington; E. A. Daniels.
il Nation 202:10-16 Ja 3 '66

NATIONAL academy of education
Education: scholars organize a national acad-
emy intended to advance educational schol-
arship. J. Walsh. Science 148:202-4 Ap 9
'65
Education's elite; with list of charter mem-
bers. P. Woodring. Sat R 48:49-50 Je 19 '65;
Discussion. 48:52 Jl 17 '65
Nat'l academy of education formed by U.S.
scholars. Pub W 187:42 Ap 12 '65
New establishment in education. W. W.
Brickman. Sch & Soc 93:442 N 27 '65
NATIONAL academy of engineering
Academy of engineers. Sci Am 212:50-1 F '65
Advice to a new academy; address, April 27,
1965. J. A. Stratton. Science 149:1206-8 S
10 '65
Building the American dream. J. Lear. il
Sat R 48:49-51 F 6 '65; Discussion. 48:55
Ap 3 '65
NATIONAL academy of medicine. See United
States—National academy of medicine
NATIONAL academy of sciences
Abstracts of papers presented at meetings,
1965. Science 148:663-70 Ap 30 '65
Abstracts of papers presented at the autumn
meeting. Science 150:368-90 O 15 '65
Academy and Congress: NAS panel completes
its first assignment in new relationship
with Congress. D. S. Greenberg. Science
148:608-9 Ap 30 '65
Academy of engineers. Sci Am 212:50-1 F '65
Academy reelects Seitz. Sci N L 87:132 F 27
'65
Basic research and national goals. P. H.
Abelson. Science 148:897 My 14 '65
Brooks succeeds Kistiakowsky as head of
NAS committee on public policy. Science
149:953 Ag 27 '65
$15-billion question brings complex reply;
National academy of sciences' answer to
Congress concerning allocation of research
funds. Bsns W p 122+ My 8 '65
Mars as a laboratory for the study of life;
exploration advocated. New Repub 152:12-13
My 8 '65
NAS urges increase in chemistry program.
Sci N L 89:24 Ja 8 '66
National academy: Seitz elected to full-time,
six year presidency amidst signs of greater
activity. D. S. Greenberg. Science 147:715-
16 F 12 '65
News in brief: hearings on NSF, other federal programs, announced; NAS to study
accelerator site. D. S. Greenberg. Science
148:775-6 My 7 '65
Thirty-five elected to Academy. Sci N L 87:
290 My 8 '65

History
Advice to a new academy; address. April 27,
1965. J. A. Stratton. Science 149:1206-8 S
10 '65
NATIONAL account manager. See Sales man-
agers
NATIONAL achievement scholarship program
Awards for outstanding Negro students. Sch
& Soc 93:173 Mr 20 '65
NATIONAL advisory council on the arts. See
United States—National council on the arts
NATIONAL aeronautic association
See also
Collier trophy
NATIONAL air and space museum. See Smith-
sonian institution—National air and space
museum
NATIONAL air taxi conference
Air taxi. R. Shippee. il Flying 77:60-1 D '65
NATIONAL airlines, incorporated
Maytag sees continued growth in traffic.
Aviation W 82:41 My 17 '65
National expects to exercise jet options. H.
D. Watkins. il Aviation W 82:34 F 8 '65
NATIONAL archives. See United States—Na-
tional archives
NATIONAL art education association
National art education association confer-
ence. F. Schwartz. il Craft Horiz 25:8-9
My '65
NATIONAL arts and humanities foundation.
See United States—National arts and
humanities foundation (proposed)
**NATIONAL association for better radio and
television**
Tune out the bad, tune in the good on TV.
F. Orme. il Parents Mag 40:56-7+ F '65
Watch out for children; inclusive critique
of all prime-time TV, judged on its po-
tential value, or harm, to children. Time
85:96 F 5 '65
NATIONAL association for music therapy
Music therapy. C. J. McNaspy. America 112:
730 My 15 '65

NATIONAL association for retarded children
Forgotten five million. C. J. McNaspy. America 113:531 N 6 '65
NATIONAL association for the advancement of colored people
Golden age of the NAACP. il Ebony 20:127-8+ My '65
Legal action; Cleveland N.A.A.C.P. chapter contemplating court action to obtain copies of voter lists. O. M. Walton. Christian Cent 82:626 My 12 '65
Moment of history; headquarters. New Yorker 41:38-9 Mr 27 '65
Mormon missionaries and the race question. G. W. Davidson. Christian Cent 82:1183-6 S 29 '65
National association for the advancement of colored people and its strategy. J. A. Morsell. Ann Am Acad 357:97-101 Ja '65
Negro self-help; new focus. America 112:186-7 F 6 '65
NATIONAL association of broadcasters
FCC stirs new TV program clash; proposes tougher programming rule. Bsns W p27-8 Mr 27 '65
NATIONAL association of business economists
Forecasters look again, upward; opinion of business economists. il Bsns W p58+ O 9 '65
Value of practical eggheads. il Bsns W p52+ F 13 '65
NATIONAL association of college stores
NACS annual meeting; books, education and the college store. il Pub W 187:52-4 Je 14 '65
NACS merchandising awards presented at NACS convention. Pub W 187:89-90 Je 14 '65
When planning a college store, call in an expert; sessions at annual meeting. il Pub W 188:36-40 Jl 5 '65
NATIONAL association of convenience stores
Snaring sales while others sleep; convenience stores. il Bsns W p 128+ N 6 '65
NATIONAL association of independent schools
NAIS chooses ten best adult books of 1964. Pub W 187:30 Mr 29 '65
NATIONAL association of manufacturers
Laughter at the Waldorf; NAM convention. M. Kempton. New Repub 153:19-20 D 18 '65
NATIONAL association of photo-lithographers
Photo-lithographers meet in Chicago, 10,000 strong; equipment shown at NAPL exhibit. J. B. Goetz. il Pub W 188:94-5 O 4 '65
NATIONAL associations. See Associations
NATIONAL automation commission. See United States—National commission on technology, automation and economic progress
NATIONAL ballet of Canada
Toronto: excitement. il Dance Mag 39:22-3 F '65
NATIONAL banks. See Banks and banking—United States
NATIONAL Baptist convention, USA,, incorporated. See Baptists in the United States
NATIONAL basketball association
Wheels within wheels; prize to most valuable player in All-star game. il Time 87:68 Ja 21 '66
NATIONAL book awards
More news of NBA week program. Pub W 187:44 Mr 1 '65
National book awards. Library J 90:1307 Mr 15 '65; Same. il Wilson Lib Bul 39:628 Ap '65
NBA, 1965. il Newsweek 65:99 Mr 22 '65
National book awards judges appointed in five categories. Library J 90:4730+ N 1 '65
National book awards, 1965; with statements by the winners. il Sr Schol 86:sup9 Ap 8 '65
National book awards: that was the week that was. il Pub W 187:34-45 Mr 22 '65
NBA's to Bellow, Clark, Fischer, Roethke, Wiener. il Pub W 187:35 Mr 15 '65
Program of the week for National book awards; Leading contenders for 16th National book awards. Pub W 187:94-5 F 8 '65
NATIONAL book committee
Book committee urges survey of bookstores; annual meeting. Pub W 188:66 D 27 '65
See also
National medal for literature
NATIONAL book council. See National book league
NATIONAL book league
Salute to the National book league. Pub W 188:77 D 27 '65
NATIONAL broadcasting company
Back to work; exposition of American foreign policy since the end of World war II. R. L. Shayon. Sat R 48:40 S 4 '65
Disease that Dr Kildare couldn't cure: NBC cancels TV film on syphilis. J. Mitford. McCalls 92:102-3+ S '65
Man who had it made; exit of R. E. Kintner. Newsweek 66:94 D 20 '65
Winner & now champion; NBC. Time 85:68 Ap 30 '65

NATIONAL budget. See Budget—United States
NATIONAL business aircraft association
NBAA display reflects international flavor. il Aviation W 83:90-1 N 1 '65
NBAA, old chap. J. Fricker. il Flying 78:63-6 Ja '66
NBAA panel urges executive status for corporation pilots. Aviation W 83:93-5 N 1 '65
NBAA seeks meeting on New York jetport. Aviation W 83:38-9 N 15 '65
New aircraft, sales drives mark NBAA. il Aviation W 83:19-20 O 18 '65
NATIONAL camera repair school, Englewood, Colo. See Photography—Study and teaching
NATIONAL capital area civil liberties union
Trash-tapping; segregating the trash of special individuals into separate bundles. Reporter 32:7-8 Je 3 '65
NATIONAL capital grotto rescue team. See Rescue work
NATIONAL cash register company
Famous firsts; how personnel relations was born. il Bsns W p92+ Je 26 '65
Noiseless printer, pocket library shown by NCR. Pub W 188:116 O 4 '65
NATIONAL Catholic book awards
Finalists in Catholic book awards contest. Pub W 187:41 My 10 '65
NATIONAL Catholic conference on interracial justice
Project equality is growing; San Antonio joins. America 113:233 S 4 '65
NATIONAL Catholic educational association
Laymen of the future. America 112:277 F 27 '65
Meeting, 1965. il Sr Schol 86:sup 1 My 13 '65
Spirit of Sixth avenue; 62nd annual convention. il Newsweek 65:85 My 3 '65
NATIONAL Catholic office for motion pictures
Changing Legion of decency; sophisticated appraiser of adult films. il Time 86:77-8+ D 3 '65
Films: condemnation of The pawnbroker. M. Walsh. America 112:838-9 Je 5 '65
Lost ladies and bad logic. M. Walsh. America 112:334 Mr 6 '65
Modern legion and its modern outlook; new title for National legion of decency. T. F. Little. America 113:744-6 D 11 '65
Sexy nights didn't last; influence of Legion of decency in British Guiana. America 113:149 Ag 14 '65
NATIONAL Catholic reporter. See Catholic press
NATIONAL Catholic welfare conference
CRS, Leopoldville. America 112:742 My 22 '65
Sermon for Labor day. America 113:235-6 S 4 '65
NATIONAL center for atmospheric research
Atmospheric research: a powerful concept emerges. W. O. Roberts. il Science 147:1093-8 Mr 5 '65
NATIONAL center for citizens in education
U.S. education chief asks for innovation in books; official announcement of the formation of a new private, non-profit educational service agency. Pub W 188:36+ N 29 '65
NATIONAL championship drag races. See Automobile racing
NATIONAL childrens book week. See Book week
NATIONAL city bank. See New York (city)—Banks
NATIONAL clay pipe institute
NCPI awards for pollution control. Am City 80:28 My '65
NATIONAL collection of fine arts, Washington, D.C. See Smithsonian institution—National collection of fine arts
NATIONAL collegiate athletic association
Open season on the Wolverine; NCAA championship pairings. F. Deford. il Sports Illus 22:24-7 Mr 15 '65
Whole team touched by stardust; Princeton winner of Eastern title, NCAA tournament. F. DeFord. il Sports Illus 22:20-3 Mr 22 '65
NATIONAL commission on technology, automation and economic progress. See United States—National commission on technology, automation and economic progress
NATIONAL committee for a sane nuclear policy
Getting serious; SANE Thanksgiving demonstration at White House. Nat R 17:1143-4 D 14 '65
NATIONAL company of the Metropolitan opera. See Metropolitan opera national company
NATIONAL conference of Christians and Jews
Books for brotherhood. il Commonweal 81:698-700 F 26 '65

NATIONAL conference on church architecture
Architecture's servant function. A. P.
Klausler. Christian Cent 82:680-1 My 26 '65
NATIONAL conference on poverty in the South-west
Faces of poverty. J. L. Vizzard. America 112:
552 Ap 17 '65
Our friends, the poor; Welcome anti-poverty
conference. P. Jacobs. Commonweal 81:722-3 Mr 5 '65
NATIONAL conference on South African crisis and American action
Vehicle for concern. V. E. Lowder. Christian
Cent 82:508-10 Ap 21 '65
NATIONAL conventions (political)
See also
Television in politics
NATIONAL conventions, Republican
Horror show. il Newsweek 66:20 Jl 12 '65
NATIONAL council for civic responsibility
Council drops truth-telling program; lack of
funds. Christian Cent 82:261 Mr 3 '65
Who's responsible now? Nat R 17:224-6 Mr 23
'65
NATIONAL council for geographic education
Convention previews. Sr Schol 87:sup 1-2 N
11 '65
Meeting, 1965. il Sr Schol 87:sup6-7 D 9 '65
NATIONAL council for the social studies
Convention previews. Sr Schol 87:sup 1 N
11 '65
Meeting, 1965. il Sr Schol 87:sup8 D 9 '65
New perspectives in world history, ed. by
S. H. Engle. Review
Sr Schol 87:sup27 S 23 '65. H. L. Hurwitz
NATIONAL council of administrative women
in education
Needed: more women in school administra-tion. Sr Schol 86:sup 1 Ap 8 '65
NATIONAL council of Catholic men
New lay responsibilities. J. C. Evans. Chris-tian Cent 82:819-20 Je 23 '65
NATIONAL council of churches. See National
council of the churches of Christ in the
United States of America
NATIONAL council of senior citizens
Senior citizens organize. America 113:519 N 6
'65
NATIONAL council of state garden clubs, in-corporated
Lucile Droege Mauntel: swinging on a star.
E. Mason. Am For 71:10+ S '65
NATIONAL council of teachers of English
Censorship as seen by English teachers.
E. M. Olson. ALA Bul 59:525 Je '65
Convention previews. Sr Schol 87:sup 1 N
11 '65
Meeting, 1965. il Sr Schol 87:sup4-5+ D 9 '65
NATIONAL council of the churches of Christ
in the United States of America
Christian consensus on Vietnam. Christian
Cent 82:1083-4 S 8 '65
Churches and the airwaves; with editorial
comment. D. Smith. Christian Cent 82:355-6, 364-6, Mr 24 '65; Discussion. 82:496-7,
681-2 Ap 21, My 26 '65
Coordinated for mission. B. Thompson. Chris-tian Cent 82:370+ Mr 24 '65
Council & its critics. il Time 85:42 Mr 5 '65
N.C.C. agenda. K. Haselden. Christian Cent
82:766-7 Je 16 '65
N.C.C. and the economic scene. Christian
Cent 82:1053 S 1 '65
Nat'l council of churches. Paulist press co-publish. Pub W 188:36 D 6 '65
Old wounds reopened; southern churchmen
attack integration activities of the NCC.
America 112:239 F 20 '65
Peace and Protestantism. Nation 201:513-14
D 27 '65
See also
World order study conference

Commission on international affairs
On foreign policy; appeal to NCC by Christian
century and Christianity and crisis. Christ-ian Cent 82:863 Jl 7 '65

Commission on religion and race
Delta ministry. E. D. Blanchard. Christian
Cent 82:337-8 Mr 17 '65

Division of Christian education
Grueling schedule; National council of
churches' annual drama workshop. F.
Myers. Christian Cent 82:1300-2 O 20 '65

Division of home missions
Why so much secrecy? consultation on the
role of the churches in urban organization
and development. Christian Cent 82:163 F 10
'65; Discussion. 82:376-7 Mr 24 '65

Division of overseas ministries
New division meets. W. A. Geier. Christian
Cent 82:1360 N 3 '65
NATIONAL council of the Metropolitan opera
association
Council convenes. A. M. Lingg. il Opera N 30:
28-30 D 25 '65
NATIONAL council on the aging
New plans for older workers. C. A. Betts. il
Sci N L 87:298-9 My 8 '65
NATIONAL council on the arts. See United
States—National council on the arts
NATIONAL cowboy hall of fame and western
heritage center
National cowboy hall of fame. il Hobbies
70:28 S '65
NATIONAL crime commission. See United
States—National crime commission
NATIONAL debt (United States) See Debts,
Public—United States
NATIONAL defense
See also subhead Defenses under names
of countries, e.g. United States—Defenses
NATIONAL defense education act. See School
laws and legislation—United States
NATIONAL Diet library, Japan. See Japan—
National Diet library
NATIONAL education association
AASL plans its programs for ALA, NEA
conferences. Library J 90:2346-8 My 15 '65
Building on a legacy of change; Development
project. L. W. Ashby and I. L. Kramer.
NEA J 54:52-4 O '65
Children's books of 1964-65. NEA J 54:65-8
N '65
Education's lady on the go; president of
classroom teacher's section. il Ebony 21:
29-32+ D '65
Financial report to members. il NEA J 54:66
O '65
Helping teachers stand tall; Million dollar
fund for protection of all teachers. T. M.
Stinnett. il NEA J 55:19 Ja '66
NEA and Negro teacher displacement prob-lem. Sch & Soc 93:365+ O 16 '65
NEA time to teach project. M. M. Provus.
il NEA J 54:8-10 Ap '65
NEA's civil rights school project. Sch & Soc
93:239 Ap 17 '65
NEA's panic button. Nation 202:30-1 Ja 10 '66
New NEA. il Newsweek 66:83 Jl 12 '65
Oklahoma's education war; NEA sanctions.
S. Kalkstein. il Look 30:80 +Ja 25 '66
Proposed amendments to NEA bylaws and
rules. NEA J 54:62-5 Ap '65
Should teachers join a union? H. Rudoff;
G. Hillman. Parents Mag 40:60-1+ O '65
Teachers give Oklahoma a lesson; NEA sanc-tions against state. B. Carter. Reporter 33:
34-7 S 9 '65
Teacher's unions: rift without differences. S.
Elam. il Nation 201:247-9 O 18 '65
Thirty-three NEA departments. NEA J 54:
61-3 N '65
Travel the NEA way; with list of summer
tours. il NEA J 55:60-1 Ja '66
Washington report; project to resolve teacher
displacement problems. J. Lloyd. Sr Schol
87:sup4 S 30 '65
See also
American association of school adminis-trators
Educational policies commission
National council of administrative women in
education

Meeting, 1965
Big meeting in the big town. L. V. Edinger.
il NEA J 54:20-1 My '65
Nation's teachers speak out. il NEA J 54:14-16 S '65
Our New York city convention. L. V.
Edinger. il NEA J 54:42 F '65
Summer '65. Sr Schol 87:sup 1-2 S 16 '65

Department of elementary
school principals
Meeting, 1965. Sr Schol 86:sup3 My 20 '65

Department of higher education
See Association for higher education

Research division
NEA research division looks at secondary
school class size. R. C. Maul. il NEA J
54:44-5 Mr '65
What teachers say about evaluation of teach-ers. H. Davis. il NEA J 54:37-9 F '65
NATIONAL educational television and radio
center
Educational TV loves dance. J. Venza. il
Dance Mag 39:43-5+ S '65

NATIONAL educational television and radio center—*Continued*

Educational TV; the timid crusaders. R. M. Elman. il Nation 200:217-21 Mr 1 '65

Minority TV should cultivate. Life 59:8 O 1 '65

Not so educational TV. J. Ridgeway. New Repub 153:16-18 Ag 21 '65

NATIONAL electronics week show. See Electronics—Exhibitions

NATIONAL farmers organization

NFO's new market push. R. C. Black. Farm J 89:36-7+ Ap '65

New NFO plan. Farm J 89:150 Ap '65

NATIONAL food marketing commission

Price of meat. New Repub 152:8 F 27 '65

NATIONAL football league

Bigger than all of us; agreement between CBS and the N.F.L. il Time 87:68 Ja 7 '66

Confrontations and contrasts at the summit; Browns vs Packers. Sports Illus 24:14-15 Ja 3 '66

NFL-CBS pact nails prime time, top cash. il Bsns W p 17 Ja 1 '66

Pride of old pro quarterbacks; in NFL. il Sports Illus 23:22-6 Ag 16 '65

Scouting reports. T. Maule and M. H. Sharnik. il Sports Illus 23:456-71 S 13 '65

Separate but equal. il Time 86:74 D 17 '65

Upstaging the AFL. Newsweek 67:44 Ja 10 '66

NATIONAL forests

Along Kaiser Ridge fourteen fishing lakes are waiting. il Sunset 135:20+ S '65

Boundary waters canoe area decision: Superior national forest, Minn. il Liv Wildn 29:20-6 Spr '65

Desert walk near Tucson; Sabino Canyon. il Sunset 136:40+ Ja '66

Jet age camping; cabin camping in Alaska's Tongass national forest. H. E. McLean. il Am For 71:16-17+ Jl '65

Night comes to Admiralty! Tongass national forest, Admiralty Island, Alaska. R. Starnes. il Field & S 70:18-22+ Ag '65

Ski-touring the national parks and forests. C. M. Ouellette. il Nat Parks Mag 40:8-11 Ja '66

Story of Sylvania; Michigan's Gogebic County. Nat Parks Mag 39:22 Ag '65

Timber in the Tetons: the dangerous Mr D; dendroctonus monticolae, mountain pine beetle. il Am For 71:54-5+ S '65

Tongass timber scale; Alaska's Tongass national forest. V. Metcalfe. il Am For 71:42+ S '65

Wildlife and multiple use. V. Metcalfe. il Am For 71:30-1+ N '65

See also

National parks and reserves—United States

NATIONAL foundation for neuromuscular diseases, incorporated

When nature errs; genetic disorders in children. Newsweek 65:78 Je 28 '65

NATIONAL foundation for the arts and humanities. See United States—National foundation for the arts and humanities

NATIONAL funeral directors association

Funeral industry, some harbingers of change? Consumer Rep 30:283-4 Je '65

NATIONAL gallery of art, Washington, D.C.

Chester Dale collection. F. Getlein. New Repub 152:27-8 Je 5 '65

Chesterdale the custodian. il Time 85:70-5 My 14 '65

For the people. il Newsweek 65:103-7 My 10 '65

How great is the Dale collection? A. Frankfurter. il Art N 64:40-3+ My '65

John Singleton Copley exhibition. il Newsweek 66:92-3 O 4 '65

Museum accessions in painting. R. Davidson. il Antiques 88:636+ N '65

NATIONAL general corporation

King of intermissions. il Time 86:93-4 Jl 9 '65

NATIONAL geographic magazine

National geographic. Pop Phot 57:63+ Jl '65

National geographic; new, neat, & quality-oriented. il Pop Phot 57:104-7 Jl '65

National geographic newest adventure: a color television series. M. B. Grosvenor. il Nat Geog Mag 128:448-52 S '65

Who knows more about color than the National geographic? D. B. Eisendrath, jr. il Pop Phot 57:58-63 Jl '65

NATIONAL geographic society

First lady of the National geographic. G. H. Grosvenor. il Nat Geog Mag 128:100-21 Jl '65

Water, prey, and game birds: a new singing book. Review

Nat Geog Mag il 128:528-35 O '65. M. B. Grosvenor

NATIONAL goals commission. See United States—President's commission on national goals

NATIONAL guard (United States) See United States—National guard

NATIONAL health service (Great Britain) See Great Britain—National health service

NATIONAL highway traffic safety center (proposed) See United States—Commerce, Department of

NATIONAL historical wax museum. See Washington, D.C.—Galleries and museums

NATIONAL hockey league

Niceties of the ice. R. McKie. il Sports Illus 23:24-6+ N 1 '65

Private game: no admittance! major league hockey not interested in becoming bigger. J. Olsen. il Sports Illus 22:64-6+ Ap 12 '65

Survival of the biggest. Sports Illus 23:10+ N 1 '65

NATIONAL horse show. See Horse shows

NATIONAL hot rod association

National scene. See issues of Hot rod

NATIONAL income. See Income

NATIONAL industrial conference board

Corporate charts go global. Bsns W p52+ S 11 '65

How thirteen leading economists see the '66 business outlook; symposium. il U S News 60:52-9 Ja 10 '66

NATIONAL institutes of health. See United States—National institutes of health

NATIONAL interest. See Nationalism

NATIONAL labor relations board. See United States—National labor relations board

NATIONAL legion of decency. See National Catholic office for motion pictures

NATIONAL lending library for science and technology, Boston Spa, Yorkshire

Model of simplicity. D. J. Urquhart. bibliog il Library J 90:4926-8 N 15 '65

NATIONAL library of medicine. See United States—National library of medicine

NATIONAL library of medicine, Great Britain. See Great Britain—National library of medicine

NATIONAL library week

All-out, fifty-state promotion for National library week. il Pub W 187:75-7 Ap 26 '65

In defense of academic freedom; reply to newspaper article by R. Martin. E. J. Josey. Wilson Lib Bul 40:173-5 O '65

Keep growing—read is 1966 library week theme. Pub W 188:55 O 25 '65

National library week; and work with youth. C. A. Vogel; R. Lindenmeyer. il Library J 90:1468-71 Mr 15 '65

NLW 1965. Wilson Lib Bul 39:821-2+ Je '65

National library week 1965 most comprehensive ever, including presentation to Kennedy library. Library J 90:2514-15 Je 1 '65

National service organization proposes a nationwide survey. P. S. Jennison. ALA Bul 59:89-90 F '65

1966 National library week committees appointed. Pub W 188:75 N 15 '65

Steering committee and advisory board appointed for 1966 NLW program. Library J 90:4730 N 1 '65

Whitewash in Whitewater; Wisconsin state college vs Kiwanis club; letter to the editor. S. D. Robertson; reply. D. Goddard. Library J 90:414 F 1 '65

NATIONAL lumber manufacturers association

Lumber standards dispute: when the bomb went off in the sawdust pile. il Am For 71:38-41 Jl '65

NATIONAL Lutheran council

Creed and witness; meeting of Catholic bishops and Lutherans in Baltimore. America 112:445 Ap 3 '65

NATIONAL manufacturers association. See National association of manufacturers

NATIONAL maritime union of America

SOBIGM sent me; low state of the U.S. merchant marine. il Newsweek 65:74 Mr 1 '65

NATIONAL medal for literature

Thornton Wilder wins first National medal for literature. Pub W 187:36 My 10 '65

NATIONAL medal of science

President names 1965 Medal of science winners. Sci N L 88:404 D 25 '65

NATIONAL merit scholarship corporation

Equalizing the race for scholarships. Christian Cent 82:164 F 10 '65

Financial status of National merit finalists. R. C. Nichols. bibliog il Science 149:1071-4 S 3 '65; Reply. A. Thorne. 150:827 N 12 '65

Merit exam tests reasoning. Ebony 20:44 Ap '65

Presidential scholars. E. F. Goldman. il Am Ed 1:1-3 Je '65

See also

National achievement scholarship program

NATIONAL monuments
Fossil beds of Florissant. E. E. Gamer. il Nat Parks Mag 39:16-19 Jl '65
We endorse a Florida Keys national monument; proposed Coral Reefs-Islandia National Monument. C. W. Buchheister. il Audubon Mag 67:356 N '65
See also names of national monuments, e.g. Lava Beds National Monument

NATIONAL motor boat show. See Motor boats —Exhibitions

NATIONAL motor company of Athens. See Automobile industry and trade—Greece, Modern

NATIONAL municipal league
See also
All-America cities

NATIONAL museum of anthropology, Mexico city. See Mexico (city)—Galleries and museums

NATIONAL observer (newspaper)
Wall Street and religion. Christian Cent 82: 357 Mr 24 '65

NATIONAL opera of Finland. See Opera—Finland

NATIONAL opinion research center
Editorial dissent: articles on the NORC report. J. O'Gara. Commonweal 81:657 F 19 '65; Reply. P. A. Lockrey. 82:95 Ap 9 '65

NATIONAL parachuting championships. See Parachuting

NATIONAL park service. See United States—National park service

NATIONAL parks and reserves

Roads

Question of national interest; California lax in protecting its natural resources. Nat Parks Mag 39:21 Ag '65
Roadbuilding in Mount McKinley National Park. A. Murie. il Nat Parks Mag 39:4-8 Jl '65
Roads in human refuges. P. M. Tilden. Nat Parks Mag 39:2 My '65
Toward quieter trails. Nat Parks Mag 39:20 Mr '65

Trails

Small footsteps on the trail. J. P. Jackson. il Nat Parks Mag 39:10-13 O '65

Canada

What Yoho means is wonderful; Yoho National Park. il Sunset 134:41-2 Je '65

Great Britain

England's Peak Park. J. Foster. il Am For 71:40-3 Ag '65

Jordan

National park for Jordan? Nat Parks Mag 39:25 N '65

United States

Concerning the parks. P. M. Tilden. Natur Hist 75:13 Ja '66
Conservation docket. See issues of National parks magazine
Ecology of man and the land ethic. S. L. Udall. il Natur Hist 74:32-41 Je '65
From Yellowstone to Canyonlands, the story of the West's great parks; concerning Sunset book, National parks of the West. il Sunset 135:96-9 N '65
Guadalupe Mountains National Park. W. F. Heald. Nat Parks Mag 39:4-8 S '65
How private are private lands? Redwoods Park proposal. J. B. Craig. il Am For 71: 22-3+ D '65
Ice age national scientific reserve. il Nat Parks Mag 39:19 F '65
In the national parks; considering Guadalupe Mountains National Park, Tex. and Redwood National Park, Calif. P. M. Tilden. Natur Hist 74:62+ Ap '65
Let's talk parks. il Am For 71:26-9 Mr '65
Looking forward. A. W. Smith. Nat Parks Mag 40:2 Ja '66
New Hawaiian park? Kauai National Park on Island of Kauai. Nat Parks Mag 40:20 Ja '66
New lakeshore proposal; Apostle Islands National Lakeshore (proposed) Nat Parks Mag 39:22 N '65
Nothing but the best! directors of AFA recommend establishment of Redwood National Park in northern Calif. Am For 71: 37 My '65
Oregon Dunes Seashore. Nat Parks Mag 39: 20 S '65
Our wilderness Alps; North Cascades. il Sunset 134:84-97 Je '65

Perking up the Nation's parks. N. M. McKitterick. New Repub 153:15-16 S 18 '65; Discussion. 153:36-7 O 2; 35-6 O 9 '65
Pictured Rocks National Lakeshore. H. A. Raup. il Nat Parks Mag 39:14-18 F '65
Preserving vegetation in parks and wilderness. E. C. Stone. bibliog il Science 150: 1261-7 D 3 '65
Redwood National Park. R. D. Butcher. il Nat Parks Mag 39:4-9 F '65
Redwood National Park, but where, and how much? R. D. Butcher. il Liv Wildn 29:11-15 Spr '65
Redwoods and parks. S. T. Dana and K. B. Pomeroy. bibliog f il Am For 71:1-32 My '65
Redwoods face a race against time. R. D. Butcher. il Audubon Mag 67:234-9 Jl '65
Report of president and general counsel to the general membership of National parks association; May 20, 1965. Nat Parks Mag 39:I-IV My '65
Seeds for agreement; AFA for Humboldt. K. B. Pomeroy. il Am For 71:16-18+ Je '65
Ski-touring the national parks and forests. C. M. Ouellette. il Nat Parks Mag 40:8-11 Ja '66
Trail scooter tips. Liv Wildn 29:39 Spr '65
Vanishing redwoods; an album; ancient trees fall fast in proposed national park. il Audubon Mag 67:358-63 N '65
Very special redwoods. G. Collins. il Liv Wildn 87:22-6 Wint '64
Wilderness in the parks; need for new wilderness bill. A. W. Smith. Nat Parks Mag 39:2 O '65
See also
National forests
National monuments
United States—National park service
also names of national parks and reserves, e.g. Grand Teton National Park

NATIONAL parks association
NPA's annual meeting. Nat Parks Mag 39:21 Jl '65
Report of president and general counsel; May 20, 1965. Nat Parks Mag 39:I-IV My '65
Summary of National parks association study and comment to the National park service on the proposed Redwood National Park. il Nat Parks Mag 39:12-13 F '65

NATIONAL pilots association. See International professional pilots association

NATIONAL planning
National planning of science and technology in France; adaptation of address. October 1964. J. B. Quinn. bibliog il Science 150: 993-1003 N 19 '65

NATIONAL portrait gallery, Washington, D.C. See Smithsonian institution—National portrait gallery

NATIONAL radio astronomy observatory, Green Bank, W.Va.
First observations at short wavelengths with the 140-foot radio telescope. J. W. M. Baars and P. G. Mezger. il Sky & Tel 31: 7-10 Ja '66
New 140-foot radio telescope. M. M. Small. il Sky & Tel 30:267-74 N '65
Science in the mountains; NRAO astronomers to leave for city. E. Langer. il Science 150:722-4 N 5 '65

NATIONAL recovery administration. See United States—National recovery administration

NATIONAL recreation and park association
New organization now a reality. il Recreation 58:315-17 S '65

NATIONAL recreation association
Highlights of public recreation, 1964; field reports. A. Todd. il Recreation 58:283-4 Je '65
Introducing NRA board of trustees. il Recreation 58:110-11 Mr '65
Your spring conferences. il Recreation 58:116-18 Mr '65

NATIONAL recreation congress
Highlights of the 47th National recreation congress, Minneapolis, October 3-8, 1965. il Recreation 58:330-2 S '65
Make no little plans! il Recreation 58:280 Je '65
Scene and heard at the 47th National recreation congress. il Recreation 58:467-70+ D '65

NATIONAL recreation month
Nation on wings and wheels. il Recreation 58:241 My '65

NATIONAL research corporation
Norton gives itself a selling lesson; advertising and marketing program directed toward consumers. il Bsns W p70 Ja 8 '66

NATIONAL responsibility. See Responsibility

NATURAL resources—*Continued*

United States

LBJ gives Udall wider role; Secretary of natural resources. il Bsns W p98-100+ Ap 3 '65

300,000,000 Americans would be wrong. D. E. Lilienthal. il N Y Times Mag p24-5+ Ja 9 '66

Washington lookout. A. G. Hall. See issues of American forests
See also
Water supply—United States

NATURAL scenery. See Landscape

NATURAL science. See Natural history

NATURAL steam. See Steam, Natural

NATURAL theology

Christian natural theology and Christian existence. J. B. Cobb, jr. Christian Cent 82:265-7 Mr 3 '65; Discussion. 82:496 Ap 21 '65

Christian natural theology: based on the thought of Alfred North Whitehead, by J. B. Cobb, jr. Review
Christian Cent 82:712-13 Je 2 '65. F. Ferré

NATURALISTS

Augusto Ruschi's Garden of Eden. A. Rankin. il Read Digest 86:216-18+ Je '65

NATURE

On the bestial floor. W. S. Merwin. Nation 200:313-14 Mr 22 '65

What nature teaches man. I. Ross. il Sci Digest 59:89-91 Ja '66
See also
Man—Influence on nature
Nature study
Science
Winter

Bibliography

Books. A. Clampitt. See issues of Audubon magazine

Books in review (title varies) See issues of Natural history incorporating Nature magazine

Recent nature books received. Liv Wildn 29:34-5 Spr '65

Try just looking. A. Dalgliesh. il Sat R 48:47-8 Jl 24 '65

NATURE (aesthetics)

Nature, sole source of motivation. R. Henkes. il Sch Arts 65:32-5 N '65

NATURE, Human. See Human nature

NATURE, Laws of

Violations of symmetry in physics. E. P. Wigner. il Sci Am 213:28-36 bibliog(p 126) D '65

NATURE and art. See Nature (aesthetics)

NATURE centers

Birth of a nature center; Greer Island nature center and refuge. J. R. Preston. il Audubon Mag 67:78 Mr '65

Guideposts to a nature center. B. L. Ashbaugh. Audubon Mag 67:148-51 My '65

Nature center grows in the Land between the Lakes. J. J. Shomon. il Audubon Mag 67:212-14 Jl '65

Wildflowers in a asphalt jungle; Kalamazoo's nature center and Baltimore's Cylburn project. il Recreation 58:112-14 Mr '65

NATURE in art

Bohdan D. Osyczka strives for the elusive moment. B. D. Osyczka. il Am Artist 29:56-7 S '65

NATURE in literature

Siskins under the skin; nature novels. H. F. Ellis. New Yorker 41:40-1 Ap 24 '65

NATURE literature

Making nature writing pay. M. Huston. Writer 78:29-30 S '65

NATURE of man. See Man

NATURE photography

ABC's of filming bees. W. D. Woodson. il Pop Phot 56:120-1+ Ap '65

Dennis Stock. P. Caulfield. il Mod Phot 29:66-9 S '65

Nature and photography. D. Linton. Natur Hist 74:59-61 Mr '65

Nature and photography. J. Couffer. Natur Hist 74:66-9 Je '65

Nature and photography (cont) S. Dunton. Natur Hist 74:58-60 D '65

Photographing nature, by D. Linton. Review Pop Phot 56:100 Ap '65. R. Kinne
See also
Photography of fishes
Photography of snow, ice, etc.

NATURE study

Our kids collect butterflies. J. D. Rossio. il Parents Mag 40:62-3+ Ag '65

Sense of wonder; excerpts. R. Carson. il McCalls 92:76-83+ Je '65

Spring: a time to grow. P. L. Levin. il N Y Times Mag p 100+ My 2 '65

Teaching the fifth essence. R. E. Klinck. il NEA J 54:38-9 N '65
See also
Audubon nature camps
Bird study
Nature centers
Plants

NATURE trails. See Trails

NATWAR-SINGH, K.

He dignified our political dialogue. Sat R 49:35 Ja 1 '66

NAUDE, C. F. Beyers

Onlookers and others. J. Squire. Christian Cent 82:1524-5 D 8 '65

NAUGHTON, Bill

All in good time. Criticism
America 112:438-9 Mr 27 '65
Commonweal 81:790-1 Mr 19 '65
Nation 200:319 Mr 22 '65
Newsweek 65:84 Mr 1 '65
Sat R 48:22 Mr 6 '65
Time 85:78 F 26 '65
Vogue 145:56 Ap 15 '65

NAUGHTON, J. J. and others

Rock degradation by alkali metals: a possible lunar erosion mechanism. bibliog Science 149:630-2 Ag 6 '65

NAUGHTON, William A.

Rails that linked the oceans. Américas 17:11-17 F '65

NAURU (island)

Tight little isle, with life-insured style. Time 86:26 Jl 2 '65

Visiting mission to New Guinea and Nauru. UN Mo Chron 2:48-50 Ap '65

NAUTICAL astronomy

Practical astronomy from shipboard. W. S. Von Arx. bibliog il Sky & Tel 29:340-5 Je '65

NAUTICAL charts

Boating's best bargains. E. S. Maloney. il Motor B 115:92+ Ap '65

Where to get charts; information from the states; general cruising information. E. Preiss. Motor B 115:58-60 Ap '65

NAUTICAL instruments
See also
Compass

NAUTICAL training schools. See United States—Navy—Education

NAUTILUS (submarine boat) See Submarine boats, Atomic powered

NAVAHO Indian reservations. See Indians of North America—Reservations

NAVAHO Indians

American Indian: citizen in captivity. B. W. Young. il Sat R 48:25-6 D 11 '65; Discussion. 49:21 Ja 1; 34 Ja 22 '66

Navajoland. C. C. Pepper. il Travel 124:38-40 O '65

NAVAL architecture

Sailing yacht research; use of computers in tests at MIT. H. C. Herreshoff and J. E. Kerwin. il Yachting 118:51-3+ Jl '65
See also
Yachts—Design

NAVAL art and science
See also
Blockade

NAVAL bases. See Navy yards and naval stations

NAVAL observatory (United States) See United States—Naval observatory

NAVAL officers (United States) See United States—Navy—Officers

NAVAL oil reserve scandal. See Teapot Dome case

NAVAL ordnance laboratory. See United States—Navy department—Weapons, Bureau of

NAVAL propellant plant. See United States—Naval propellant plant

NAVAL radio communication. See Radio communication, Naval

NAVAL space surveillance system. See Guided missiles—Detection

NAVAL submarine school, New London, Conn. See United States—Navy—Education

NAVAL training schools. See United States—Navy—Education

NAVAL weapons test laboratory, Dahlgren, Va. See Navy yards and naval stations

NAVARETTA, Emanuel

Centering: toward a new humanism. Craft Horiz 25:37+ Mr '65

NAVCOM systems. See Aeronautic instruments

NAVIGATION

Change on the high seas. M. Penzer. il Motor B 115:54-5+ Ap '65

Do-them-in-your-head navigation tricks. W. S. Kals. il Pop Mech 124:184-6 S '65

NAVIGATION—*Continued*
For whom do storm signals fly? T. Cofield. il Motor B 116:46-7+ O '65
Jim Kilroy on steering. J. Kilroy. Yachting 117:206+ Je '65
Outboard in fog. B. Whittier. il Yachting 117:66-7 My '65
Piloting blooper and the lesson it taught. H. H. Maxim. Yachting 117:193-4 Ap '65
Skiing team; skiboat driving. C. Ward. il Motor B 116:40-2+ Jl '65
Solving current problems by VTV; vector triangles of velocity. E. L. Slepian. il Motor B 115:48-51 Je '65
What is this thing called seamanship? R. M. Clancy. il Motor B 116:24-6+ D '65
See also
Artificial satellites—Navigational applications
Computers—Navigational applications
Lighthouses
Nautical astronomy
Radar in navigation
Voyages
Winds

Competitions
Control points. M. L. Hersey. See issues of Yachting
Predicted logger's '65 preview. J. D. Paris. Motor B 115:52 Je '65

History
Polynesian navigation. W. S. Kals. il Motor B 116:28-31 Ag '65

NAVIGATION (space flight)
Instruments for the new celestial navigation. S. Moskowitz. il Sky & Tel 30:348-51 D '65
New navigation system developed for Apollo. Sci N L 88:18 Jl 10 '65
Sextant studies scheduled for Gemini-4. il Aviation W 82:63-4 My 31 '65
Star-sighting difficulties could alter Apollo guidance system. J. Mercer. Miss & Roc 18:17-18 Ja 10 '66
See also
Inertial guidance systems

NAVIGATION, Aerial
See also
Airplanes—Piloting
Decca navigation
Helicopters—Piloting
Inertial guidance systems
Loran
Radio in aviation

NAVIGATION, Interplanetary. See Navigation (space flight)

NAVIGATOR, Aerial. See Aeronautic instruments

NAVONE, John
Letter from Ireland. Cath World 200:364-9 Mr '65

NAVSPASUR (naval space surveillance system) See Guided missiles—Detection

NAVY officers (United States) See United States—Navy—Officers

NAVY yards and naval stations
A look inside a secret U.S. base: Chichi-jima, Bonin Is. il U S News 59:62-3 Ag 23 '65
Navy to build huge blast tube; Naval weapons test laboratory, Dahlgren, Va, to simulate high-altitude blasts. il Miss & Roc 16:17 Ap 26 '65

NAWAPA See North American power and water alliance

NAWRACAJ, Edward, and Forman, Fred
Build a fail-safe transistor power supply. Pop Electr 23:74-6 O '65

NAZI war criminals. See World war, 1939-1945—War criminals

NAZISM. See Fascism—Germany

NE Win
Behind closed doors. il por Newsweek 67:20+ Ja 3 '66

NEA, Margaret
Meet Mrs Nea. il pors NEA J 54:31 Mr '65

NEAL, Fred Warner
Convocation. New Yorker 41:31-2 Mr 6 '65

NEAL, Harry
Music goes round. il por Newsweek 65:102 My 24 '65

NEAL, James
Slight case of contempt. il Time 86:58 Jl 3 '65

NEAL, Patricia
Gallant fight of Pat Neal. B. Farrell. il pors Life 59:92-103+ O 22 '65
Her best performance; recovery after three strokes. il por Newsweek 65:55 My 31 '65
My wife, Patricia Neal. R. Dahl. il pors Ladies Home J 82:53-5+ S '65
Patricia Neal: a woman's fight to live. S. Frank. il pors Good H 161:64-5+ Ag '65
Road back. il por Time 85:37 Mr 26 '65

NEANDERTHAL race
Past, modern man linked. Sci N L 88:359 D 4 '65

NEAPOLITANS
System; bargaining. F. Steegmuller. New Yorker 41:181-4 Mr 13 '65

NEAR EAST. See Middle East

NEARSIGHTEDNESS. See Myopia

NEBOLSINE, Arcadi
Books. Commonweal 82:476 Jl 2 '65

NEBRASKA
See also
Homestead National Monument of America
Hunting—Nebraska

NEBRASKA CITY, Neb.
One lighting project leads to another. V. Livingston. Am City 80:127 O '65

NEBRASKA national forest. See Forests and forestry—Nebraska

NEBRASKA state historical society, Lincoln
Charnley's fabulous guns. K. D. Curtis. il Hobbies 70:116-17+ Ap '65

NEBRASKA. University, Lincoln

Libraries
Nebraska mounts a podium; C. Y. Thompson library. East campus. F. A. Lundy and L. A. Enersen. il Library J 90:5195-7 D 1 '65

NEBULAE
Age of the Orion nebula. P. O. Vandervoort. il Sci Am 212:90-6+ bibliog(p 136) F '65
Nuclei of planetary nebulae. G. S. Mumford. Sky & Tel 29:281 My '65
Organic compounds in carbonaceous chondrites. M. H. Studier and others. bibliog il Science 149:1455-9 S 24 '65
Supernova of 1054, a double star? G. S. Mumford. Sky & Tel 30:140 S '65

NECKING. See Dating

NECKTIE racks
Lazy-susan tie rack. H. Hilton. il Pop Mech 124:196 N '65

NECKTIES
How to select neckties men will wear. Good H 161:253 D '65

NEDERLANDS Dans theater. See Dance companies

NEEDLEWORK
Enrichment of a famous textile collection; aquisitions of Museum of fine arts, Boston. R. Davidson. il Antiques 88:534+ O '65
Many kinds of needlework. il Good H 160:174-5 Ap '65
She does it with wet string; free-form design. il Sunset 135:127-8 O '65
Stitchcraft! beautiful accessories made on your sewing machine. M. Garrity. il Bet Hom & Gard 43:70-3+ S '65
See also
Crewel work
Knitting
Macramé
Quilting
Sewing

NEFF, Monroe C.
Toward literacy in the United States; address, April 1965. por Wilson Lib Bul 39:885-6+ Je '65

NEFF, Muriel
Forty centuries of consistency. Art N 63:46-9+ F '65

NEGATIVE lenses. See Lenses, Photographic

NEGOTIATION, International. See Diplomacy

NEGOVSKY, Vladimir, and Soboleva, Valentina
How to delay death. Sci Digest 57:60-5 Ap '65

NEGRÃO DE LIMA, Francisco
Riding the tiger. il por Newsweek 66:50 D 20 '65

NEGRO actors and actresses
Owl and the pussycat. il Ebony 20:98-103 F '65
See also
Cosby, B.
Dawn, M.
Jones, J. E.
Kirby, G.
Sands, D.

NEGRO air pilots
Breakthrough on the airlines. il Ebony 21:112-14+ N '65
Whirlybird whiz of the coast guard; R. C. Wilks. il Ebony 20:26-8+ My '65

NEGRO ambassadors
Ambassador is a lady; P. R. Harris. C. Sanders. il Ebony 21:23-6+ Ja '66
Four in one; first Negro woman to head an American embassy. il Time 85:23 My 28 '65

NEGRO astronauts. See Astronauts

NEGRO athletes
Entertaining athletes; Negro sports stars. il
Ebony 21:39-40+ D '65
Illinois' unheralded champions. il Ebony 20:
125-8 Mr '65
Low and inside; views from the arena. W.
Ward. Nation 200:508-10 My 10 '65
See also
Ashe, A.
Beard, A.
Edwards, F.
Samples, K.

NEGRO authors
See also
Baldwin, J.
Ellison, R.
Jones, L.
Negro poets

NEGRO bachelors. See Bachelors

NEGRO bands. See Bands (music)

NEGRO bankers
How two janitors bought white bank in
Texas. L. Robinson. il Ebony 20:119-22+
Je '65

NEGRO baseball players. See Baseball players

NEGRO basketball players. See Basketball
players

NEGRO bishops. See Negro clergy

NEGRO business men
Computer company president. il Ebony 21:
95-8 Ja '66
Village blacksmiths; Japhia interiors. il
Ebony 21:96-8+ D '65
See also
Gaston, A. G.

NEGRO chemists. See Chemists

NEGRO children
Fourth-grade course in color; experience of a
white teacher in Harlem. B. Kremen. Holiday 37:24+ Mr '65
Happy homes for foster children; Women's
Christian alliance. il Ebony 20:29-32+ Ap
'65
That they might learn; Chicago college
students' SWAP program offers tutoring
help to children of ghetto schools. il Ebony
20:93-4+ Mr '65

NEGRO children, Handicapped. See Children,
Handicapped

NEGRO church. See Negroes in the United
States—Religion

NEGRO civil rights organizations. See Civil
rights organizations

NEGRO clergy
Appoints Negro bishop; Louisiana-born. H.
R. Perry. Christian Cent 82:1277-8 O 20 '65
Historic bishop; first American-born Negro
Catholic bishop. Time 86:70 O 8 '65
Move toward church unity; Methodists ap-
point Negroes to Jersey, Iowa bishoprics.
il Ebony 20:54-60 F '65
Negro bishop in the South. America 113:425
O 16 '65
Plight of the colored clerisy; incidents at
Selma, Ala. R. Kirk. Nat R 17:551 Je 29 '65

NEGRO colleges. See Negroes in the United
States—Education

NEGRO comedians
They have overcome. il Time 85:94 F 5 '65
See also
Cosby, B.

NEGRO conductors. See Conductors (music)

NEGRO congressmen
First Negro in Congress. il Sr Schol 87:7 D 9
'65
Key congressman dares not go home. U S
News 58:21 Mr 15 '65

NEGRO cowboys. See Cowboys

NEGRO criminals. See Negroes in the United
States—Crime

NEGRO diplomats
Alex Quaison-Sackey; UN's first black president. il Ebony 20:198-200+ My '65

NEGRO education. See Negroes in the United
States—Education

NEGRO entertainers
Entertaining athletes; Negro sports stars. il
Ebony 21:39-40+ D '65
See also
Bradley, H.
Davis, S.

NEGRO executives. See Executives

NEGRO family life. See Family life; Negroes in
the United States—Social conditions

NEGRO farmers
California rancher. il Ebony 21:77-8+ Ja '66
Negro farmers get unfair deal. Farm J 89:78
Ap '65

On the outside looking out. E. Peter, jr. New
Repub 152:18 Je 26 '65
Unrepresented Negro farmers in the South;
Department of agriculture's Agricultural
stabilization and conservation service. P.
Wieck. New Repub 153:8-9 D 25 '65

NEGRO football players. See Football players

NEGRO government employees
Customs clears way to progress; Negro personnel moves up in U.S. agency. il Ebony
21:104-6+ D '65
Employment of Negroes in the federal government. B. E. Anderson. il Mo Labor R
88:1222-7 O '65
How Negroes fare in getting federal jobs.
U S News 59:14 N 15 '65

NEGRO history. See Negroes in the United
States—History

NEGRO history week
Association's 50th year witnesses increased
interest in Negro history; pace-setting ob-
servances in New York and Detroit. il
Negro Hist Bul 28:124-5+ Mr '65
Doctor Woodson prepares for Negro history
week, 1930; excerpts from diary. L. J.
Greene. Negro Hist Bul 28:174-5+ My '65
Make Negro history week an open-end
activity in '65. C. W. Thomas. il Negro Hist
Bul 28:75 Ja '65
More about Negro history week observances.
il Negro Hist Bul 28:148 Ap '65
State governors proclaiming Negro history
week 1965. Negro Hist Bul 28:122 Mr '65

NEGRO journalism. See Negro press

NEGRO journalists. See Journalists

NEGRO judges
Colored judges. J. H. Roy. Negro Hist Bul
28:135-7, 158+ Mr-Ap '65
Negro judges in the United States. J. H.
Roy. Negro Hist Bul 28:108-11 F '65
Unfrightened crusader; J. K. Stout. Time 85:
47 Ap 16 '65
See also
Marshall, T.

NEGRO labor. See Negroes in the United States
—Employment

NEGRO lawyers
Law student overcomes handicap to win
point. il Ebony 20:119-20+ My '65

NEGRO legislators
Beyond the voting rights act. P. Good il
Reporter 33:25-9 O 7 '65
Georgia legislature's new look for 1966. il
Ebony 20:48-50+ S '65
Legislative change; Georgia legislature. Time
85:33 Je 25 '65
States boast record number of Negro law-
makers. pors Ebony 20:191-2+ Ap '65
Things to come; Negroes in the Georgia
House of representatives. New Repub 152:
7 My 22 '65
Times have changed; Negro members in
Georgia's House. il Newsweek 65:24+ Je
28 '65

NEGRO librarians
Discrimination at Detroit; ALA conference.
E. Moon. Library J 90:3224 Ag '65; Discus-
sion. 90:4648+ N 1 '65
Movement in Mobile. E. Moon. Library J 90:
2519 Je 1 '65; Reply. E. J. Josey. 90:5320
D 15 '65
Opinions in black and white. D. M. Broder-
ick. il Library J 90:1994-5 Ap 15 '65

NEGRO literature
Decolonization of American literature; ad-
dress, April 1965. K. Shapiro. il Wilson
Lib Bul 39:842-53 Je '65; Discussion. 40:172-
5 O '65
Ebony book shelf. See issues of Ebony

NEGRO mayors. See Negro municipal officers

NEGRO ministers. See Negro clergy

NEGRO Mormons. See Mormons and Mormonism, Negro

NEGRO municipal officers
Changing times; R. Henry sworn in as mayor
of Springfield, Ohio. Newsweek 67:27 Ja 17
'66
Doctor gets call, to mayor's chair; Mattawa.
Ontario. il Ebony 20:171-2+ O '65

NEGRO music
Filling holes in the soul; blues singers.
N. Hentoff. Reporter 32:44+ Mr 11 '65
See also
Jazz music

NEGRO musicians
Preservation Hall; New Orleans. il Ebony
20:64-6+ My '65
See also
Coleman, O.
Ellington, D.
Hines, E.
Shirley, G.

NEGRO newspaper readers. See Newspapers—
Readers
NEGRO newspapers. See Negro press
NEGRO nurses
Impact of integration on the nursing profes-
sion; historical sketch. M. E. Carnegie. bib-
liog Negro Hist Bul 28:154-5+ Ap '65
NEGRO pastors. See Negro clergy
NEGRO periodicals
See also
Ebony (periodical)
NEGRO physicians
See also
Monestime, S. F.
Norman, J. C.
NEGRO poets
Bijah's Luce of Guilford, Vermont. M. R.
Wright. il Negro Hist Bul 28:152-3+ Ap '65
Paul Laurence Dunbar; a new perspective.
W. Phillips. bibliog Negro Hist Bul 29:7-8
O '65
NEGRO police
My daughter, the policeman. il Ebony 20:82-
4+ O '65
NEGRO press
Full of grace; first appearance in nine news-
papers of Sunday supplement called Tues-
day. New Yorker 41:42 S 18 '65
It's Tuesday on Sundays; Negro's newest
magazine. W. Sullivan. il Sat R 48:90-1
N 13 '65; Discussion. 48:66 D 11 '65
New Negro supplement; Tuesday. il Time
86:80 S 17 '65
Tuesday every Sunday; Negro newspaper
supplement. R. Ross. il Newsweek 66:62
S 20 '65
NEGRO professors. See College professors and
instructors
NEGRO schools

Alabama

Education for Negroes in the space capital;
William H. Councill school, Huntsville, Ala.
B. Patterson. New Repub 153:9 Jl 3 '65
NEGRO scientists
Committee for professional opportunity; let-
ter. T. Hayashi. Science 148:1411 Je 11 '65
Negroes in science. J. Viorst. il Sci N L 87:
218-19 Ap 3 '65
See also
Carver, G. W.
NEGRO service men and women
Military ordeal of Sammy Davis jr; excerpt
from Yes I can. S. Davis. il Ebony 21:151-
4+ D '65
Negroes in Vietnam; we, too, are Americans.
S. Booker. il Ebony 21:89-90+ N '65
NEGRO singers
Filling holes in the soul; blues singers.
N. Hentoff. Reporter 32:44+ Mr 11 '65
Leading man at the Met: G. Shirley. il Ebony
21:84-6+ Ja '66
Supremes make it big. il Ebony 20:80-2+ Je
'65
Why I am returning to show business. M. H.
Cole. il Ebony 21:45-50+ Ja '66
See also
Anderson, M.
Brown, J.
Cole, N. K.
Grist, R.
Mathis, J.
Pittman, E.
Staples, Roebuck, family
NEGRO soldiers. See United States—Army—
Negroes
NEGRO songs
First family of gospel; Staple singers. il Ebony
20:79-81+ S '65
Moment of history; development of We shall
overcome. New Yorker 41:37-8 Mr 27 '65
NEGRO students
Child seller; with account by R. Stolley. il
Life 59:109-10+ O 8 '65
Equalizing the race for scholarships. Chris-
tian Cent 82:164 F 10 '65
Higher education for the Negro; obstacles.
B. W. Harleston. Atlan 216:139-44 N '65;
Reply. W. D. Berkeley. 217:40 Ja '66
In Chicago no, Negro students exceed whites.
U S News 59:18 N 1 '65
School and the Negro child. C. Stewart.
Negro Hist Bul 29:9-10 O '65
See also
Colleges and universities—Desegregation
National achievement scholarship program
NEGRO suffrage. See Negroes in the United
States—Politics and suffrage
NEGRO superstitions
See also
Voodooism

NEGRO surgeons
See also
Williams, D. H.
NEGRO teachers
Burl Toler blows a whistle. il Ebony 21:142-7
D '65
Discriminatory dismissals of Negro teachers.
Sch & Soc 93:338 O 2 '65
Displaced teachers. Commonweal 82:613 S 3
'65
Education's lady on the go; E. D. Koontz. il
Ebony 21:29-32+ D '65
Integrating the Negro teacher out of a job;
dilemma in Munday. B. Carter. il Re-
porter 33:31-3 Ag 12 '65; Discussion. 33:
10+ S 23 '65
Integration and dismissals of southern Negro
teachers. Sch & Soc 93:468+ D 11 '65
Is integration a must for faculties, too?
conditions in southern areas. U S News 58:
14-15 Je 7 '65
Most displaced teachers find new positions.
Sr Schol 87:sup2 O 14 '65
NEA and Negro teacher displacement prob-
lem. Sch & Soc 93:365+ O 16 '65
NEA's panic button. Nation 202:30-1 Ja 10
'66
New Negro casualties; where do the teachers
go? J. M. Arisman. il Commonweal 83:372-
3 D 24 '65
Segregation by integration; problem of Negro
teachers. Time 85:58+ Je 18 '65
Talofa, Norma! N. Anderson. il Ebony 21:
54-6+ Ja '66
Washington report; project to resolve teacher
displacement problems. J. Lloyd. Sr Schol
87:sup4 S 30 '65
NEGRO tennis players. See Tennis players
NEGRO theater. See Theater, Negro
NEGRO voters, Registration of. See Voters,
Registration of
NEGRO-white intermarriage. See Intermar-
riage of races
NEGRO-white relations. See Race relations
NEGRO women
Bennett's proper pickets. M. A. Guitar. il
Mlle 61:112-15+ Je '65
Woman fills man-size union job. il Ebony 20:
91-2+ Ap '65
NEGRO women as journalists. See Women as
journalists
NEGRO youth
Three girls who were born again. E. Selby
and A. Selby. Read Digest 87:133-6 S '65
Watch out, whitey; Negro youth gangs and
violence. L. Yablonsky. New Repub 154:10-
12 Ja 1 '66; Reply. T. J. Cummins. 154:29-30
Ja 22 '66
See also
Negro students
NEGROES
Negro biography neglected in children's en-
cyclopedias. Library J 90:2002 Ap 15 '65

Colonization

Four approaches to Zion; an interpretation.
B. P. Hunter. bibliog Negro Hist Bul 29:
5-6+ O '65

Libraries
See Libraries and Negroes

Religion
See also
Mormons and Mormonism, Negro
NEGROES and advertising. See Advertising and
Negroes
NEGROES and Jews. See Jews and Negroes
NEGROES as farmers. See Negro farmers
NEGROES as soldiers. See United States—
Army—Negroes
NEGROES in Africa
Black mask of angry Africa. I. Lewis. il Life
58:111-12+ Ap 2 '65
Glorious age in Africa, by D. Chu and E.
Skinner. Review
Negro Hist Bul 28:160+ Ap '65
See also
Africa—Race problems
South Africa—Race problems
NEGROES in art
Second invasion; my experiences in Missis-
sippi. T. Sugarman. il Am Artist 29:48-53+
N '65
NEGROES in drama. See Negroes in literature
NEGROES in Italy
Americans in Rome. W. M. Kelley. Mlle 60:
202+ Mr '65

NEGROES in literature
All-white world of children's books. N. Larrick. il Sat R 48:63-5+ S 11 '65; Discussion. 48:78-9 O 16 '65
Atlanta institute makes proposals on library materials on the Negro. Library J 90:5225 D 1 '65
Color me brown, I'm integrated. T. B. Dolmatch. Sat R 48:73 S 11 '65
Ebony book shelf. See issues of Ebony
Freedom to read and racial problems; address, January 1965. C. Morgan, jr. ALA Bul 59:484-90 Je '65
Shakespeare and the Harlem clowns: illusion and comic form in Genet's The blacks. H. D. Swander. Yale R 55:209-26 D '65
See also
Uncle Tom

NEGROES in South Africa
See also
South Africa—Race problems

NEGROES in the United States
After freedom; conditions a year after passage of law. New Repub 153:5-6 Jl 10 '65
American dream and the American Negro; condensed transcript of Baldwin-Buckley debate at Cambridge, England. J. Baldwin; W. F. Buckley, jr. il N Y Times Mag p32-3+ Mr 7 '65
Black and white: two worlds of Robert Matlock. V. Scott. il Ladies Home J 82:92-3+ N '65
Don't blame the ghetto. D. B. Lee. Read Digest 86:145-8 Ap '65
Few kind words for Uncle Tom. I. Kristol. Harper 230:95-9 F '65; Discussion. 230:12+ Ap '65
Historical notes. C. W. Thomas. Negro Hist Bul 28:149+ Ap '65
Integration: opportunity and obligation. W. M. Young, jr. Parents Mag 41:30 Ja '66
Inward and the outward ear. B. Galphin. Sat R 48:22 Je 5 '65
Journey in misery. D. L. Dumond. Sat R 48:30 Mr 13 '65
Little richer and better educated; findings of Census bureau study. il Bsns W p 136+ N 6 '65
LBJ: rights are not enough. il Newsweek 65:36-7 Je 14 '65
Manchild in the promised land, by C. Brown. Review
Commentary 41:82-4 Ja '66. G. Dennison
New Yorker 41:242+ N 13 '65. W. Balliett
Reporter 33:53-5 N 4 '65. D. Pinck
Sat R 48:49 Ag 28 '65. W. Miller
Meeting of history & fate: the President addresses Congress on civil rights legislation, with excerpts from speech. il Time 85:20-2 Mr 26 '65
My problem and how I solved it; a southern family's trials due to friendship with Negroes. il Good H 160:62+ Ja '65
Negro after Watts; Time essay. Time 86:16-17 Ag 27 '65
Negro and the American dream; concerning Cambridge union debate with J. Baldwin. W. F. Buckley, jr. Nat R 17:273 Ap 6 '65
Negro as cause. E. C. Ladd, jr. il Nation 200:161-5 F 15 '65
Negro in America 1965. il Newsweek 65:24-7 F 15 '65
Negro in America '65: progress. Newsweek 66:32 O 25 '65
Negro protest: symposium; ed. by A. M. Rose. bibliog f Ann Am Acad 357:1-133 Ja '65
Negroes & Jews; the new challenge to pluralism. N. Glazer; discussion. Commentary 39:8 My; 6+ Je '65
Peoples of America. N. Glazer. il Nation 201:137-41 S 20 '65
Positive side of the racial story: advances of the Negro citizen; address, May 31, 1965. W. M. Young, jr. Vital Speeches 31:572-6 Jl 1 '65
Progress report 1965; year of the vote. il Ebony 21:35-6+ Ja '66
Riot as a weapon: the language of Watts. S. Sanders. il Nation 201:490-3 D 20 '65
Robert Penn Warren and Ralph Ellison: dialogue; excerpt from Who speaks for the Negro? R. P. Warren; R. Ellison. il Reporter 32:42-6+ Mr 25 '65
Some Negroes riot but most go forward. Life 59:4 Ag 27 '65
This is my country too, by J. A. Williams. Review
Reporter 33:62-3 O 21 '65. H. B. Jacobs
Through black glasses. J. O'Gara. Commonweal 82:38 Ap 2 '65
Uprootedness: a Jamaican Negro. J. Anderson. Commentary 40:63-7 Ag '65

White problem in America; symposium. il Ebony 20:27+ Ag '65
Who speaks for the Negro? by R. P. Warren. Review
Commentary 40:101-5 O '65. J. Epstein
New Repub 152:21-3 My 22 '65. C. V. Woodward
Whose society is this? C. Cobb. New Repub 153:13-15 D 18 '65
Why Negro suicides are increasing. J. N. Woodford. il Ebony 20:89-90+ Jl '65
Why Negroes riot; excerpt from The making of the President, 1964. T. H. White. Read Digest 87:67-73 N '65
See also
Black Muslim movement
Congress of racial equality
Interracial cooperation
National association for the advancement of colored people
National urban league
Negro history week
Slavery—United States
also subhead Negroes under names of cities, e.g. Washington, D.C.—Negroes

Bibliography
Negro in history. I. J. Sloan. Sat R 48:90-2 F 20 '65

Civil rights
After Alabama; Negroes' next battlegrounds. il U S News 58:37-8 Ap 5 '65
Are we listening? Commonweal 82:612 S 3 '65
Armed justice? administration of justice in the South. Commonweal 82:517 Jl 23 '65
At home: a racial revolution. il Sr Schol 87:18-19+ S 30 '65
Beware the day they change their minds! C. E. Silberman. il Fortune 72:150-3+ N '65
Beyond civil rights; dealing with President Johnson's address at Howard university. America 112:875 Je 19 '65
Biased broadcaster put on probation; United church of Christ petition to F.C.C. Christian Cent 82:732-3 Je 9 '65
Birmingham two years later. P. Good. il Reporter 33:21-7 D 2 '65
Boundaries of the permissible. M. Ascoli. Reporter 32:22 Ap 8 '65
Civil rights. B. Rustin and T. Kahn. Commentary 39:43-6 Je '65
Civil rights; continuing confrontation. Time 85:23-5 Ap 9 '65
Civil rights: the continuing revolution. E. C. Ladd, jr. Yale R 55:1-16 O '65
Civil rights: what's in the wind now. U S News 59:8 N 29 '65
Climax near in Negro revolt. il U S News 58:27-9 Mr 29 '65
Communists and civil rights: how closely linked? Chicago and Montgomery, Ala. il U S News 59:12 Jl 12 '65
Confrontation: black and white, by L. Bennett, jr. Review
Sat R 48:60-1 O 16 '65. K. B. Clark
Confusing the cause; civil rights groups U.S. foreign policy. Time 86:20 Jl 16 '65
Continuing battle. New Repub 152:5-6 Mr 27 '65
Crisis in American culture: address. W. M. Young, jr. il Wilson Lib Bul 39:744-6 My '65
Demagogy of Le Roi Jones. G. Dennison. Commentary 39:67-70 F '65
Dreams of brighter tomorrows. M. L. King, jr. il Ebony 20:34-5 Mr '65
Embattled South: now, it's how? instead of never! il U S News 59:57-9 Jl 12 '65
Federal step-up in rights enforcement? U S News 60:8 Ja 10 '66
Half-century of struggle for equal rights: 1915-1965. E. A. Toppin. bibliog Negro Hist Bul 28:176-7+ My '65
Harlem priest reports on Selma; interview, ed. by C. L. Palms. E. T. Dugan. Cath World 201:171-6 Je '65
Katzenbach's commission. A. Kopkind. New Repub 154:7-8 Ja 15 '66
King; concerning address at headquarters of the Association of the bar of the city of New York. New Yorker 41:35-7 My 1 '65
Let justice roll down. M. L. King, jr. il Nation 200:269-74 Mr 15 '65
LBJ praises the revolution of the Negro American; address, June 4, 1965. L. B. Johnson. il U S News 58:50-2 Je 14 '65; Excerpts. Newsweek 65:36-7 Je 14 '65; Summary. U S News 58:52-3 Je 21 '65
Moderates speak; voice of southern businessmen. Newsweek 65:79 Ap 26 '65

NEGROES in the United States—Civil rights —*Continued*

Natchez boycott. Reporter 33:18 D 2 '65

Nation aroused. Nation 200:321 Mr 29 '65

Negro aims; meeting of Negro leaders at the Interchurch center, New York city. America 112:210-11 F 13 '65

Negro and the vote; here's LBJ's address to Congress; March 15, 1965; excerpts. L. B. Johnson. il U S News 58:110-11 Mr 29 '65; Sr Schol 86:9 Ap 1 '65

Negro in the Supreme court, 1954-64; address, 1964 (cont) R. L. Gill. bibliog Negro Hist Bul 28:86-8, 117-19 Ja-F '65

Negro now; excerpts from Who speaks for the Negro? with quotations by four Negro leaders. R. P. Warren. il Look 29:23-31 Mr 23 '65

Negro problem; excerpts from American dissent; decade of modern conservatism. J. Hart. il Nat R 17:A19-24 N 30 '65

Negroes sharpen call for real equality; southern justice as main target. il Bsns W p46 N 20 '65

Now the era of complexities. il Newsweek 65:27-8 F 15 '65

Our scope of freedom. T. Hernandez. Negro Hist Bul 28:76 Ja '65

Planners and civil rights; planning session for the White House conference, mid-November. A. Kopkind. New Repub 153: 13-14 D 4 '65

Portrait of a decade, by A. Lewis. Review
  Commonweal 81:767-9 Mr 12 '65. W. B. Gould

President Johnson and the Negroes; concerning address at Howard university. M. McGrory. America 112:893 Je 26 '65

Professional radical moves in on Rochester; conversations with S. Alinsky, ed. by M. K. Sanders. il Harper 231:52-9 Jl '65

Protest against the legal status of the Negro. P. Murray. bibliog f Ann Am Acad 357: 55-64 Ja '65

Reflections on the first decade of the freedom movement (1955-1965) address, July 20 1965. R. F. Drinan. Vital Speeches 31: 619-22 Ag 1 '65

Right to vote; address, March 15, 1965. L. B. Johnson. Vital Speeches 31:354-7 Ap 1 '65; Excerpts. il U S News 58:110-11 Mr 29 '65; Sr Schol 86:9 Ap 1 '65

Rule of law in the South. H. Burns. Commentary 40:80+ S '65; Discussion. 40:22+ D '65

Search for a new Selma. Newsweek 66:29-30 D 20 '65

Second civil war: a closer look at Los Angeles riots; excerpts from address, August 1965. M. B. Jackson. il U S News 59:80-2+ S 20 '65

Selma campaign; justification of non-violence. Commonweal 81:684-5 F 26 '65

Selma, contd; woman beaten by sheriff during registration drive in Selma, Ala. Time 85:24 F 5 '65

Shifting patterns in race problem; what Negro leaders want now. il U S News 59: 32-4+ Ag 23 '65

Spotlight on change. K. Haselden. Christian Cent 82:638-9 My 19 '65

Starry heavens; the moral law; concerning address on the Negro's right to vote. il Newsweek 65:19-20 Mr 29 '65

SNCC: rebels with a cause; southern freedom movement. L. Bennett, jr. il Ebony 20:146-53 Jl '65

Ten years after Montgomery. America 113: 619 N 20 '65

Trip to Leverton. C. Hunter. New Yorker 41: 95-6+ Ap 24 '65

Unfinished business of the Civil war; true freedom for the Negro; excerpt from the Centennial history of the Civil war. B. Catton. il N Y Times Mag p28-9+ Ap 4 '65

Waving the red flag; fear of Communist infiltration of civil rights movement. il Newsweek 65:30-1 Ap 12 '65

What next for the civil rights movement? N. Hentoff. Commonweal 81:661-3 F 19 '65

What now for civil rights? America 113:70 Jl 17 '65

What to do next? conference of top civil rights leaders. il Newsweek 66:27-8 N 29 '65

Wheel of history rolls on. E. T. Folliard. America 112:415 Mr 27 '65

Who are the guilty ones? W. Herberg. Nat R 17:769-70 S 7 '65

Who speaks for the Negro? by R. P. Warren. Review
  Commonweal 83:377-9 D 24 '65. A. Kaledin

Will success spoil civil rightists? Christian Cent 83:35-6 Ja 12 '66
  See also
Civil rights act of 1964
Civil rights demonstrations

Anecdotes, facetiae, satire, etc.

Court upholds recent civil rghts law; 1983. C. A. Horne. Nat R 17:929 O 19 '65

History

General Benjamin Franklin Butler and the Negro: the evolution of the racial views of a practical politician. N. Weiss. bibliog Negro Hist Bul 29:3-4+ O '65

Crime

Death penalty for rape. Nation 200:156-7 F 15 '65

Race friction: now a crime problem? il U S News 59:21-4 Ag 30 '65

Economic conditions

Economic forces serving the ends of the Negro protest. A. B. Batchelder. bibliog f Ann Am Acad 357:80-8 Ja '65

From protest to politics: the future of the civil rights movement. B. Rustin. Commentary 39:25-31 F '65; Discussion. 40:16+ Jl '65

Mixed marriages: next trend in race problem? with interviews with S. M. Garn and E. Ginzberg. il U S News 58:58-63 Je 28 '65
  See also
Negroes in the United States—Migration

Education

Bennett's proper pickets. M. A. Guitar. il Mlle 61:112-15+ Je '65

Cash for college careers. il Ebony 20:40-2+ Ap '65

Civil rights and education. F. Keppel. il Ebony 20:110-12+ S '65

Exchange faculties to aid Negro colleges, paid by Hill family foundation grant. Christian Cent 82:606 My 12 '65

Good try in Alabama; Selma university. il Time 85:67 F 26 '65

Higher education for the Negro; obstacles. B. W. Harleston. Atlan 216:139-44 N '65; Reply. W. D. Berkeley. 217:40 Ja '66

I.Q. increases in educationally deprived children; testing of Negro youngsters in Prince Edward County, Va. Sch & Soc 93:388 O 30 '65

Mixed marriages: next trend in race problem? with interviews with S. M. Garn and E. Ginzberg. il U S News 58:58-63 Je 28 '65

Negro and higher education. J. H. Holland. il NEA J 54:22-4 Mr '65

Negro history; basis for the new freedom; address, July 12, 1965. L. W. Neyland. Vital Speeches 31:765-8 O 1 '65

New approach to educating Negro children in gray area schools (cont) W. A. Parris. bibliog Negro Hist Bul 28:91+ Ja '65

Perils of integration. il Newsweek 65:61 Ap 5 '65

Predominantly Negro colleges and universities in transition, by E. J. McGrath. Review Sat R 48:69 Je 19 '65. S. M. Nabrit

Reading and the disadvantaged. E. J. Josey. Negro Hist Bul 28:156-7+ Ap '65

Slow deliberate speed. America 112:345 Mr 13 '65

Ten years of deliberate speed. E. Knoll. il Am Ed 1:1-3 D '64

Textbooks, civil rights and the education of the American Negro; concerning conference in New York, sponsored by American textbook publishers institute, and National urban league, with editorial comment. il Pub W 187:26-32, 45 My 10 '65

That they might learn; Chicago college students' SWAP program offers tutoring help to children of ghetto schools. il Ebony 20:93-4+ Mr '65

They closed their schools, by B. Smith. Review
  Sat R 48:67-8 Jl 17 '65. P. Johnson

Urgent concern. D. W. Dodson. Sat R 48:82-3 My 15 '65

When Bonnyeclaire came North. M. Hope. il Good H 161:262b N '65

When school stopped; case of Prince Edward County, Va. Newsweek 66:81 N 15 '65

NEGROES in the United States—Education—
Continued
Who is qualified? S. Carmichael. New Re-
pub 154:20-2 Ja 8 '66
See also
Colleges and universities—Desegregation
Freedom schools
Howard university, Washington, D.C.
Private schools
Public schools—Desegregation

Employment
Behind Los Angeles: jobless Negroes & the
boom. D. P. Moynihan. Reporter 33:31 S 9
'65; Reply with rejoinder. E. L. Dale, jr.
33:6+ O 7 '65
Industry plugs positive Negro job message;
Opportunity center. il Bsns W p34 Je 26 '65
Job consultant for big business. il Ebony
20:115-16+ Ap '65
LBJ works for cool summer. il Bsns W p26
Ap 3 '65
Sweeney's miracle; janitor into a computer
expert. il Look 29:117-18 N 16 '65
Ten best cities for Negro employment. il
Ebony 20:115-16+ Mr '65
Unfinished business of Negro jobs; Title VII
of Civil rights act. il Bsns W p82-4+ Je 12
'65
We help ourselves; job-training courses.
Philadelphia project. P. Friggens. Read
Digest 87:134-8 O '65
When a no. 2 applies for a job. G. Grove.
il N Y Times Mag p32-3+ S 19 '65
When equality is not enough. L. Zimpel.
Christian Cent 82:1060-3 S 1 '65
Will Negroes really get more jobs under new
law? il U S News 59:83-4 Jl 19 '65
See also
Discrimination in employment
Negro government employees
United States—President's committee on
equal employment opportunity

Health and hygiene
Indecent exposure. Nation 200:323 Mr 29 '65

History
Capsule history: 1945-65. il Ebony 21:160-3
N '65
Derogatory images of the Negro and Negro
history. G. E. Cunningham. Negro Hist
Bul 28:126-7+ Mr '65
Flight from history, the heritage of the Negro.
C. V. Woodward. Nation 201:142-6 S 20 '65
Negro history; basis for the new freedom;
address, July 12, 1965. L. W. Neyland.
Vital Speeches 31:765-8 O 1 '65
New Jersey, Nebraska, and Detroit feature
Negro history projects. Library J 90:1278 Mr
15 '65
Pioneers in protest. L. Bennett, jr. See is-
sues of Ebony
Some guidelines in teaching American Negro
history. L. B. Katz. Negro Hist Bul 28:190-1
My '65
Worth fighting for: a history of the Negro
in the United States during the Civil war
and reconstruction, by A. McCarthy and
L. Reddick. Review
Negro Hist Bul 28:202 My '65. E. A.
Toppin
You are part of his past. il Ebony 20:120-1
F '65

Housing
Builder who makes integration pay. A. Balk.
Harper 231:94-9 Jl '65
For freedom of residence. E. Norquist. Chris-
tian Cent 82:596-7 My 5 '65
Housing for the Nation's poor. L. E. Schaller.
Christian Cent 83:10-13 Ja 5 '66
New landlords; churches and other non-profit
groups enter housing market. il Ebony 20:
113-19 Jl '65
See also
Discrimination in housing
Housing—Desegregation

Migration
Down on the farm. K. Crawford. Newsweek
66:22 S 6 '65
Negro migration from Georgia; reprint from
January 1924 issue. Mo Labor R 88:797 Jl
'65
Negro's journey to the city. D. K. Newman.
bibliog f il Mo Labor R 88:502-7, 644-9 My-
Je '65

Occupations
Speaking of people. See issues of Ebony

Politics and suffrage
Amendment by civil disobedience; Voting
rights bill. Nat R 17:268-9 Ap 6 '65
Barrier falls: the U.S. Negro moves to vote;
Voting rights act of 1965. il Newsweek 66:
15-16 Ag 16 '65

Behind the magnolia curtain; Yankee in
Mississippi. R. Boeth. Atlan 216:46-52 Ag
'65
Black power; reconstruction of the South,
1867-1877. L. Bennett, jr. il Ebony 21:28-9+
N; 51-2+ D '65; 116-22 Ja '66 (to be cont)
Challenge is real. Nation 200:659 Je 21 '65
Civil right no. 1: the right to vote. M. L.
King, jr. il N Y Times Mag p26-7+ Mr 14
'65
Deluge; Negro registration in the South. il
Newsweek 66:17-18 Ag 23 '65
Effective Negro voting. America 113:615 N
20 '65
Fever in the air; voting bill. Newsweek 65:
20-1 Mr 29 '65
Five seats in Congress: Mississippi challenge.
G. Slaff. il Nation 200:526-9 My 17 '65
Flamboyant Mr Powell. J. Q. Wilson. Com-
mentary 41:31-5 Ja '66
From protest to politics: the future of the
civil rights movement. B. Rustin. Com-
mentary 39:25-31 F '65; Discussion. 40:16+
Jl '65
If voting is the problem: a look outside
the South. il U S News 58:39-41 Ap 5 '65
Immoral law; excerpts from editorials in
Wall Street journal, March 22 and March
24, 1965. U S News 58:116+ Ap 5 '65
Issue at Selma. W. F. Buckley, jr. Nat R 17:
183 Mr 9 '65
Legal action; Cleveland N.A.A.C.P. chapter
contemplating court action to obtain copies
of voter lists. O. M. Walton. Christian
Cent 82:626 My 12 '65
Letter from Washington; Mississippi chal-
lenge: by members of Freedom democratic
party. R. H. Rovere. New Yorker 41:233-
4+ O 16 '65
LBJ works for cool summer. il Bsns W p26
Ap 3 '65
LBJ's reply to Selma: this time, no delay,
President asks for law to guarantee vote to
Negroes. il Bsns W p36-7 Mr 20 '65
Meaning of the Selma march: great day at
Trickem Fork. W. C. Heinz and B. Linde-
man. il Sat Eve Post 238:30-1+ My 22 '65
Million more Negro voters; what happens
on Election day? il U S News 59:63-4 S 20
'65
Must we repeal the Constitution to give the
Negro the vote? with editorial comment.
J. J. Kilpatrick. il Nat R 17:312, 319-22,
350+ Ap 20-My 4 '65
Nation surges to join the Negro on his
march: President speaks to Congress on Ne-
gro voting rights; with report by R. B.
Stolley. il Life 58:30-7 Mr 26 '65
Negro leader's advice to Republicans; in-
terview. E. W. Brooke. U S News 58:66-70
F 1 '65
Negroes move toward power. J. O'Shea. il
Atlan 216:90-2+ N '65
Negro's new force. Time 86:33-4 N 12 '65
Negro's strange bedfellows. Nation 201:346
N 15 '65
New pattern for the Negro vote? il U S
News 59:49 N 22 '65
New voting law goes into action. il Life 59:
34-34A Ag 20 '65
Other roads from Selma. V. Harding. Chris-
tian Cent 82:580-1 My 5 '65
Other side of the voting-rights bill; ex-
cerpts from statement. H. F. Byrd. U S
News 58:86-8 Ap 12 '65
Political socialization of the American Negro.
D. Marvick. bibliog f il Ann Am Acad 361:
112-27 S '65
President's voting bill. America 112:411 Mr 27
'65
Protest against the political status of the
Negro. A. P. Sindler. Ann Am Acad 357:
48-54 Ja '65
Real stakes in Negro-vote drive. il U S News
58:37-8 Mr 8 '65
Right to vote. K. Crawford. Newsweek 65:39
Mr 1 '65
Right to vote: small fruit of a bold promise.
W. W. Van Alstyne. il Nation 200:411-13
Ap 19 '65
Rising Negro vote: what it will mean to the
South. il U S News 59:46-7 N 29 '65
Seat belts for Mississippi's five. A. Kopkind.
New Repub 153:17-18 Jl 24 '65
South's new Negro voters: can they swing
an election? with chart. il U S News 59:
38-40 Ag 23 '65
Tuskegee's Negro majority. P. Good. il Re-
porter 33:18-21 Jl 1 '65
Voting rights act of 1965; address, March 18,
1965. N. deB. Katzenbach. Vital Speeches
31:391-8 Ap 15 '65

NEGROES in the United States—Politics and suffrage—*Continued*

Voting rights bill is tough. A. M. Bickel. New Repub 152:16-18 Ap 3 '65

Voting rights bill speeded. Sr Schol 86:8 Ap 1 '65

What the Negro vote will do to South; what southern editors say about the Negro vote. il U S News 58:30-8 Mr 29 '65

Who is qualified? S. Carmichael. New Repub 154:20-2 Ja 8 '66

Who's afraid of those new Negro voters? J. Witcover. New Repub 153:10 O 30 '65

Year of the vote: the how and whither. Life 58:4 Mr 26 '65

See also
Election laws—United States

Religion

Mississippi: after violence a ray of hope. il Ebony 20:109-10+ Je '65

New landlords; churches and other non-profit groups enter housing market. il Ebony 20:113-19 Jl '65

Vacuum in Los Angeles. Newsweek 66:43 S 6 '65

Segregation

Delusions of the white liberal; excerpt from Dark ghetto. K. B. Clark. il N Y Times Mag p27+ Ap 4 '65

Dying white South; denial and repression beneath the racial quietude. J. Osborne. New Repub 154:10-12 Ja 22 '66

Hollywood in black and white. J. O. Killens. Nation 201:157-60 S 20 '65

Hospital discrimination; HEW criticized by civil rights groups. E. Langer. Science 149:1355-7 S 17 '65

I was always mad at the world. J. Rechy. Nation 200:254-6 Mr 8 '65

Inevitable questions. il Ebony 21:86-7 N '65

It's against the law! il Ebony 20:138-9 Ag '65

James Baldwin's jeremiad. A. B. Southwick. Christian Cent 82:362-4 Mr 24 '65

Low and inside; views from the arena. W. Ward. Nation 200:508-10 My 10 '65

Negro on TV; case of Jackson, Miss. station, WLBT. Nation 201:374 N 22 '65

Residential segregation. K. E. Taeuber. il Sci Am 213:12-19 Ag '65

Take another look at us. il Ebony 20:128-9 Je '65

World champion is refused a meal; C. Clay in Yulee, Ga. G. Plimpton. il Sports Illus 22:24-7 My 17 '65

See also
Church and race problems
Public schools—Desegregation
Segregation in education

Segregation, Resistance to

After Watts, where is the Negro revolution headed? C. V. Woodward. il N Y Times Mag p24-5+ Ag 29 '65

At home; a racial revolution. il Sr Schol 87:18-19+ S 30 '65

Beyond the bridge; race relations in Selma, Ala. P. Good. il Reporter 32:23-6 Ap 8 '65

Changing character of Negro protest. J. H. Laue. bibliog f Ann Am Acad 357:119-26 Ja '65

Home to roost; violence between white and black in America. Commonweal 81:752 Mr 12 '65

Law and morality in race relations. A. T. Davies. Christian Cent 82:1256-8 O 13 '65

Looks like a hot summer. Christian Cent 82:259-60 Mr 3 '65

Negro protest against segregation in the South. T. C. Cothran. bibliog f il Ann Am Acad 357:65-72 Ja '65

No immunity; violation of the law in the name of civil rights. Time 86:15-15A Ag 13 '65

Reflections on the first decade of the freedom movement (1955-1965) address, July 20, 1965. R. F. Drinan. Vital Speeches 31:619-22 Ag 1 '65

Ringers; Prince Georges County, Md. White citizens' council. Newsweek 65:24+ F 8 '65

Rise of the Negro protest. D. C. Thompson. bibliog f Ann Am Acad 357:18-29 Ja '65

Sit-ins prove effective. E. Lederer. Sci N L 87:215 Ap 3 '65

Violence of nonviolence. F. S. Meyer. Nat R 17:327 Ap 20 '65

Violence or nonviolence in the Deep South? M. Boyd. Christian Cent 82:1126-8 S 15 '65

Violence versus non-violence. il Ebony 20:168-9 Ap '65

White folk, wake up! il Ebony 20:170-1 My '65

Worker hits the freedom road. J. Shepherd. il Look 29:M16+ N 16 '65

See also
Civil rights demonstrations
Civil rights workers

Social conditions

Absent father haunts the Negro family. C. E. Lincoln. il N Y Times Mag p60+ N 28 '65

American Negro family. America 113:492 O 30 '65

American Negro problem in the context of social change; excerpts from Negro in America. A. M. Rose. Ann Am Acad 357:1-17 Ja '65

Beware the day they change their minds! C. E. Silberman. il Fortune 72:150-3+ N '65

Bitter and insistent plague; misery of the house on Hough; with report by P. Welch. il Life 59:106-17+ D 24 '65

Blackout on the Moynihan report; with editorial comment. M. McGrory. America 113:738, 742 D 11 '65

Church and the reliefers; urban Negro slum-dwellers. D. G. Cater. Christian Cent 82:232-5 F 24 '65

Civil rights; the continuing revolution. E. C. Ladd, jr. Yale R 55:1-16 O '65

Danger facing big cities; equal rights not complete answer to Negro problems. il U S News 59:29-33 S 6 '65

Dark ghetto, by K. B. Clark. Review
Reporter 33:59-62 O 21 '65. R. Coles

Georgia boy goes home. L. E. Lomax. il Harper 230:152-9 Ap '65

In search of Bisco. E. Caldwell. il Esquire 63:120-1+ Ap '65

License to murder. il Ebony 21:148-9 D '65

Long, cold winter. il Ebony 20:102-3 O '65

Los Angeles riots: handling the topic in class; symposium. il Sr Schol 87:sup8-10+ O 7; sup5 O 14; sup5 O 21 '65; Excerpts. 87:9-12+ O 28 '65

Man around the house. il Ebony 21:92-3 Ja '66

Moynihan report: Negro family, the case for national action. Christian Cent 82:1531-2 D 15 '65

Moynihan report. New Repub 153:8-9 S 11 '65

Negro family. Commonweal 82:649-50 S 17 '65

Negro family, by D. P. Moynihan. Review
New Yorker 41:116+ S 11 '65. R. H. Rovere

Negro family life. Commonweal 83:229 N 26 '65

Negro family; reflections on the Moynihan report. H. J. Gans. Commonweal 83:47-51 O 15 '65

Negro family: visceral reaction; D. P. Moynihan report. Newsweek 66:38-40 D 6 '65

Negro poverty decried. Sci N L 88:36 Jl 17 '65

New crisis: the Negro family. il Newsweek 66:32+ Ag 9 '65

Of many things; what has come to be called the Moynihan report. T. N. Davis. America 114:inside cover Ja 1 '66

Savage discovery; the Moynihan report. W. Ryan. il Nation 201:380-4 N 22 '65; Discussion. 201:inside cover, 526 D 27 '65

T.R.B. from Washington: Negro breakdown; family collapse. New Repub 153:4 Jl 24 '65; Reply. T. N. Stern. 153:30 S 11 '65

This U.S.A, by B. J. Wattenberg and R. M. Scammon. Review
U S News il 59:68-72 D 13 '65

Two for SNCC; interviews, excerpts from Who speaks for the Negro? ed. by R. P. Warren. R. Moses; S. Carmichael. Commentary 39:38-48 Ap '65

Wonder is there have been so few riots. K. B. Clark. il N Y Times Mag p 10-11+ S 5 '65

Statistics

This U.S.A, by B. J. Wattenberg and R. M. Scammon. Review
U S News 59:68-72 D 13 '65

Suffrage

See Negroes in the United States—Politics and suffrage

Trade union membership

See Trade unions—Negro membership

NEGROES in the United States—*Continued*

North

Bijah's Luce of Guilford, Vermont. M. R. Wright. il Negro Hist Bul 28:152-3+ Ap '65
New York state and New York city, by M. Glassman. Review
  Negro Hist Bul 28:138-9 Mr '65. E. C. Brooks
  See also
  New York (city)—Harlem
  also subhead Negroes under names of cities, e.g. Springfield, Mass.—Negroes

South

Beyond the voting rights act. P. Good il Reporter 3:25-9 O 7 '65
Black power; reconstruction of the South, 1867-1877. L. Bennett, jr. il Ebony 21:28-9+ N; 51-2+ D '65; 116-22 Ja '66 (to be cont)
Civil rights; continuing confrontation. Time 85:23-5 Ap 9 '65
Conscience of the South. Nation 200:295 Mr 22 '65
Conservative prophecy: peace below, tumult above. J. J. Kilpatrick. il Harper 230:160-4 Ap '65
Deacons, too, ride by night. R. Reed. il N Y Times Mag p 10-11+ Ag 15 '65
Deep South's other venerable tradition. E. Caldwell. il N Y Times Mag p 10-11+ Jl 11 '65
Dying white South; denial and repression beneath the racial quietude. J. Osborne. New Repub 154:10-12 Ja 22 '66
Embattled South: now, it's how? instead of never! il U S News 59:57-9 Jl 12 '65
Encounters in Virginia; freedom teacher & gentle ladies. E. Newmark. il Nation 200: 193-7 F 22 '65
Federal courts practice racial exclusion. Christian Cent 82:605 My 12 '65
In search of Bisco. E. Caldwell. il Esquire 63:120-1+ Ap '65
In search of Bisco, by E. Caldwell. Review New Yorker 41:174-7 My 22 '65. W. Balliett
Mind and soul of the South. G. B. Leonard. il Look 29:140+ N 16 '65
Negro protest against segregation in the South. T. C. Cothran. bibliog f il Ann Am Acad 357:65-72 Ja '65
Negroes' future in the South; interview, with statements from southern governors. H. E. Talmadge. U S News 59:66-8+ O 11 '65
New era for the old South. H. H. Martin. il Sat Eve Post 238:23-5+ O 9 '65
Old vision of a new South. H. Hansen. il Sat R 48:42-3 Ap 10 '65
Other South; Time essay. Time 85:48-9 My 7 '65; Same abr. Read Digest 87:173-4+ Ag '65
Registering Negro voters in the South; necessity for federal voting referees. A. M. Bickel. New Repub 152:9-10 F 20 '65
Reporter at large; attempts of Negroes to register in Tuskegee, Ala. B. Taper. New Yorker 41:58+ Jl 24 '65
Return to Georgia; southern minister. R. B. McNeill. Look 29:95-6 N 16 '65
Selma campaign; justification of non-violence. Commonweal 81:684-5 F 26 '65
South as it is: 1865-1866, by J. R. Dennett. Review
  Sat R 48:48+ S 11 '65. A. Hoogenboom
South revisited. H. Zinn. Nation 201:147-53 S 20 '65
South today; symposium, ed. by W. Morris. il Harper 230:126-84+ Ap '65; Discussion. 230:4+ Je '65
Southern justice, ed. by L. Friedman. Review
  Nation 201:366-8 N 15 '65. G. Felfer
South's option. Christian Cent 82:483-4 Ap 21 '65
Speaking out: integration could destroy rural Mississippi; with editorial comment. C. Sullivan. Sat Eve Post 238:10+, 100 Ap 10 '65
This was Montgomery; racial attitudes in the Deep South. G. H. Dunne. il America 112:660-1+ My 8 '65; Discussion. 113:78-9 Jl 17 '65
Unexpected dividend for the South. P. M. Stern. Harper 230:66-72 My '65
Violence or nonviolence in the Deep South? M. Boyd. Christian Cent 82:1126-8 S 15 '65

Who is Jimmie Lee Jackson? D. Riley. New Repub 152:8 Ap 3 '65
Worker hits the freedom road. J. Shepherd. il Look 29:M16+ N 16 '65
  See also
  Negroes in the United States—Politics and suffrage
  also subhead Negroes under names of cities, e.g. Birmingham, Ala.—Negroes

Bibliography

Hope and sorrow in the South. C. Shapiro. il Sat R 48:31-3 Ag 14 '65

History

1865: the South as it is. J. R. Dennett. Nation 201:153-6 S 20 '65

NEGROES in the United States armed forces. See United States—Armed forces—Negroes

NEGROES in the United States army. See United States—Army—Negroes

NEHAMKIN, Lester
Bonneville. il Hot Rod 18:84-5 D '65
—and Rickman, Eric
Baby bottle bomb. il Hot Rod 18:60-1 D '65

NEHMER, Stanley
U.S. pledged to cooperate in solving commodity problems; statement, July 22, 1965. Dept State Bul 53:530-2 S 27 '65

NEHRU, Braj Kumar
Conflict between India and Pakistan; address, September 15, 1965. Vital Speeches 32:5-7 O 15 '65

NEHRU, Jawaharlal
He left his country a future. V. M. Dean. por Sat R 48:26-7 Mr 27 '65
Legacy of Nehru, ed. by K. Natwar-Singh. Review
  Sat R por 48:27 S 4 '65. J. Hitrec
Nehru: a view from the embassy. C. A. Galbraith. por Harper 231:76-80 Jl '65
Nehru: a visual biography; exhibition in New York's Union carbide building. K. Kuh. il pors Sat R 48:41-2 F 20 '65
Nehru: sixty years to power. A. Campbell. New Repub 152:20+ My 1 '65
Nehru: the first sixty years, ed. by D. Norman. Review
  Nation 200:707-8 Je 28 '65. J. T. Crown

NEIBURGER, Morris
Smog today & smog tomorrow. Nation 201: 432-5 D 6 '65
Where is science taking us? por Sat R 48: 40-2 Jl 3 '65

NEIGHBORHOOD law office plan. See Legal aid

NEIGHBORHOOD; story. See O'Hara, J.

NEIGHBORHOOD youth corps. See United States—Job corps

NEIL, J. P.
Universal SSB converter. Electr World 74: 82-4 O '65

NEIMAN-Marcus company. See Dallas—Stores

NEISSER, Edith G.
Children like simple pleasures best. Parents Mag 40:58-9+ Je '65
—See Sklansky, M. A. jt. auth.

NELL-BREUNING, Oswald von
Social philosopher. America 112:446-7 Ap 3 '65

NELSON, Allison
Music goes round. il por Newsweek 65:102 My 24 '65

NELSON, B. H.
Book reviews. Negro Hist Bul 28:138 Mr '65

NELSON, Byron
Byron's boys beat the British cup team. A. Wright. il Sports Illus 23:79-80+ O 18 '65

NELSON, Claud
Protestant surveys schema thirteen. por Cath World 201:394-9 S '65

NELSON, Ed
Detroit listening post. See issues of Popular mechanics to September 1965

NELSON, Gaylord Anton
Appalachian trail: most famous footpath in the world. Am For 71:24-7 D '65
Congress and science: new probe by Senate unit reviews evidence on spread of government funds. E. Langer. por Science 148: 1573-5 Je 18 '65

NELSON, Helen
Antiquity's undercover magicians. Sat R 48: 21+ F 6 '65
State of the Nation. Sat R 48:53 Jl 10 '65

NELSON, Ira S.
Hollies for the South. Horticulture 43:26-7+ N '65

NELSON, J. L.
Radar imagery. Electr World 74:42-3+ Ag '65

NELSON, J. Robert
Concord at Lexington. Christian Cent 82:
575-6 My 5 '65
Deicide, theothanasia, or what do you mean?
Christian Cent 82:1414-17 N 17 '65
From his death comes our life. Christian
Cent 82:355 Mr 24 '65
John R. Mott remembered. Christian Cent
82:671 My 26 '65
New Catholicism. Christian Cent 82:1068-9 S
1 '65
Resolutionary Christianity? Christian Cent
82:639-40 My 19 '65
NELSON, James H.
Do junior college transfers make the grade?
NEA J 54:55-7 O '65
NELSON, John Byron. See Nelson, B.
NELSON, Kay
Where the action is! Good H 160:70+ Ap '65
NELSON, L. S.
Explosion of burning zirconium droplets
caused by nitrogen. bibliog Science 148:
1594-5 Je 18 '65
NELSON, O. Fred
Capacity doubled, manpower unchanged. Am
City 80:118-19+ Ap '65
NELSON, Oliver E. and others
Second mutant gene affecting the amino acid
pattern of maize endosperm proteins. bib-
liog Science 150:1469-70 D 10 '65
NELSON, Robert A.
Future of mass transportation; address. por
Duns R 85:pt2 158A-158C+ Je '65
NELSON, Roy Paul
Unshelling peanuts. Christian Cent 82:276 Mr
3 '65
NELSON, Samuel B.
Increase water supply, don't allocate short-
ages. Am City 80:96-8 Mr '65
NELSON, Truman
Delinquent's progress. Nation 201:336-8 N 8
'65
NELSON, Walter Henry
Mixed bag of gimmicks. Pub W 188:34-7 Ag
2 '65
NELSON, William
Cryogenics in electronics. Electr World 74:28-
9+ D '65
NELSON, William H.
Revolutionary character of the American
revolution. bibliog f Am Hist R 70:998-
1014 Jl '65
NEMATODES
Genetic adaptation of caenorhabditis elegans
(nematoda) to high temperatures. J. Brun.
il Science 150:1467 D 10 '65
Nematodes: biological control in rice fields:
role of hydrogen sulfide. R. Rodriguez-
Kabana. bibliog il Science 148:524-6 Ap 23
'65
Plant parasitic nematodes: a new mecha-
nism for injury of hosts. D. R. Vig-
lierchio and P. K. Yu. bibliog il Science
147:1301-3 Mr 12 '65
See also
Roundworms
NEMER, Martin, and Infante, A. A.
Messenger RNA in early sea-urchin embryos;
size classes. bibliog Science 150:217-21 O
8 '65
—See Spirin. A. S. jt. auth.
NEMEROV, Howard
Companions; poem. New Yorker 41:30 Ag 21
'65
Relation of art and life; poem. Reporter 33:
54-5 S 23 '65
Some poets in their prose. R. Howard.
Poetry 105:400-3 Mr '65
NEMES, Graciela (Palau)
Literature of the absurd. Américas 17:6-10 F
'65
NENES
Nature note; Hawaii's nene. Sci N L 88:11
Jl 3 '65
Saving the nene. Nat Parks Mag 39:22 S '65
Saving the nene, world's rarest goose. S. D.
Ripley. il Nat Geog Mag 128:744-54 N '65
NENNI, Pietro
Pietro & Paul. il por Time 85:33-4 Ap 23
'65
NEOLITHIC period. See Stone age
NEON
Isotopes
Neon isotope fractionation during transient
permeation. S. N. I. Rama and S. R. Hart.
bibliog Science 147:737-8 F 12 '65
NEON art. See Modernism (art)
NEON lamps. See Electric lamps, Neon
NEOPLASIA. See Tumors
NEOPLASIA, Malignant. See Cancer

NEOPLASMS. See Tumors
NEOSHO, Mo.
Put your leaves to work. C. W. Bell. il
Am City 80:112-13 Ag '65
NEPAL
See also
Hunting—Nepal

Description and travel
Mustang, remote realm in Nepal. M. Peissel.
il Nat Geog Mag 128:578-604 O '65

Politics and government
Back is forward. D. Van Praagh. il Newsweek
67:32+ Ja 10 '66
NEPTUNE (planet)
Closest approaches of Pluto and Neptune.
G. S. Mumford, 3d. Sky & Tel 29:157-8
Mr '65
NERO Wolfe (literary character) See Charac-
ters in literature
NERPEL, Charles
Editor's auto-graphs. See issues of Motor
trend
NERVE cells
Dorsal spinocerebellar tract: response pattern
of nerve fibers to muscle stretch. J. K. S.
Jansen and T. Rudjord. bibliog il Science
149:1109-11 S 3 '65
Mammalian retina: associational nerve cells
in ganglion cell layer. A. Gallego and J.
Cruz. bibliog il Science 150:1313-14 D 3
'65
Medial neurosecretory cells as regulators of
glycogen and triglyceride synthesis. E. Van
Handel and A. O. Lea. bibliog il Science
149:298-300 Jl 16 '65
Nerve repair possible? Sci N L 87:291 My
8 '65
Neurons of insects: RNA changes during in-
jury and regeneration. M. Cohen and J. W.
Jacklet. bibliog il Science 148:1237-9 My 28
'65
Neurosecretory processes extending into third
ventricle: secretory or sensory? C. G.
Smoller. bibliog il Science 147:882-4 F 19 '65
Uncoupling of a nerve cell membrane junc-
tion by calcium-ion removal. R. D. Penn
and W. R. Loewenstein. bibliog il Science
151:88-9 Ja 7 '66
NERVE gases. See Gases in warfare
NERVES
Activity in mammalian peripheral nerves
during supercooling. L. K. Miller. bibliog il
Science 149:74-5 Jl 2 '65
Myelin membrane: a molecular abnormality.
J. S. O'Brien and E. L. Sampson. bibliog il
Science 150:1613-14 D 17 '65
Stability of the myelin membrane. J. S.
O'Brien. bibliog il Science 147:1099-107 Mr 5
'65
NERVOUS habits
See also
Tic
NERVOUS system
Annelid ciliary photoreceptors. P. A. Law-
rence and F. B. Krasne. bibliog il Science
148:965-6 My 14 '65
Botulinum toxin, type A: effects on central
nervous system. E. H. Polley and others.
bibliog il Science 147:1036-7 F 26 '65
Dorsal spinocerebellar tract: response pattern
of nerve fibers to muscle stretch. J. K. S.
Jansen and T. Rudjord. bibliog il Science
149:1109-11 S 3 '65
Hydra: induction of supernumerary heads by
isolated neurosecretory granules. T. L.
Lentz. bibliog il Science 150:633-5 O 29 '65
Information processing in the nervous system. D. E. Broadbent. bibliog Science 150:
457-62 O 22 '65
Neural stage of adaptation between the receptors and inner nuclear layer of monkey
retina. K. T. Brown and K. Watanabe. bibliog il Science 148:1113-15 My 21 '65
Neurological mutants of the mouse; report
on conference. R. L. Sidman and others.
Science 150:513-14+ O 22 '65
Parkinsonism: electromyographic studies of
monosynaptic reflex. M. Ioku and others.
bibliog il Science 150:1472-5 D 10 '65
Physical basis of life and learning; adaptation of address, April 23, 1965. F. O. Schmitt. bibliog Science 149:931-6 Ag 27 '65
Plasticity in sensory-motor systems. R. Held.
il Sci Am 213:84-8+ N '65
Pyramidal and non-pyramidal pathways in
monkeys: anatomical and functional correlation. D. G. Lawrence and H. G. J. M.
Kuypers. bibliog il Science 148:973-5 My
14 '65

NERVOUS system—*Continued*

Diseases

Absence of taste-bud papillae in familial dysautonomia. A. Smith and others. bibliog il Science 147:1040-1 F 26 '65

Functional studies of cultured brain tissues as related to demyelinative disorders. M. B. Bornstein and S. M. Crain. bibliog il Science 148:1242-4 My 28 '65

Soviet search for viruses that cause chronic neurologic diseases in the U.S.S.R. J. A. Brody and others. bibliog Science 147:1114-16 Mr 5 '65

See also
Ataxia
Mental illness

Surgery

See also
Spinal cord—Surgery

NERVOUS system, Sympathetic

Noradrenaline stores in nerve terminals of the spleen: changes during hemorrhagic shock. A. B. Dahlström and B. E. M. Zetterström. bibliog il Science 147:1583-4 Mr 26 '65

Prostaglandin: release from the rat phrenic nerve-diaphragm preparation. P. W. Ramwell and others. bibliog il Science 149:1390-1 S 17 '65

Synaptic connections of the centrifugal fibers in the pigeon retina. H. R. Maturana and S. Frenk. bibliog il Science 150:359-61 O 15 '65

Tylotrich (hair) follicle: association with a slowly adapting tactile receptor in the cat. S. J. Mann and W. E. Straile. bibliog il Science 147:1043-5 F 26 '65

NERVOUS tension. See Stress (physiology)

NESBITT, Dorothy
Outdoors in North Carolina. Dance Mag 39:31 Ag '65

NESMITH, Mrs Thomas
Louisiana iris in North. Horticulture 43:26 Mr '65

NESS, Frederic W.
Case of the lingering degree. Sat R 49:64-5+ Ja 15 '66

NESS, Norman F. and Wilcox, J. M.
Sector structure of the quiet interplanetary magnetic field. bibliog Science 148:1592-4 Je 18 '65

NEST builder; story. See Pritchett, V. S.

NESTS
Evolution of nest building. N. E. Collias. il Natur Hist 74:40-7 bibliog(p74) Ag '65

Nest sites of 400 eastern species. Audubon Mag 67:258-9 Jl '65

Tree ants build a nest. il Natur Hist 75:64-5 Ja '66

Whooper nest sits for a rare portrait. L. H. Walkinshaw. il Audubon Mag 67:299-301 S '65

NET book agreement. See Books—Prices

NETHERLANDS
See also
Airlines—Netherlands
Airplane industry and trade—Netherlands
Dams—Netherlands
Electronic apparatus industry and trade—Netherlands
Music festivals—Netherlands
Petroleum industry and trade—Netherlands
Reclamation of land—Netherlands
Television broadcasting—Netherlands

Description and travel

Canal boat with a photo deck. L. Barry. il Pop Phot 57:36+ Jl '65

History
Bibliography

Articles and other books received; comp. by H. H. Rowen. See issues of American historical review

Industries

Dutch computers hit the European market; Holland's Electrologica. il Bsns W p 110+ Jl 10 '65

Politics and government

Because of a tube; government crisis over commercial TV. il Newsweek 65:50 Mr 15 '65

Television crisis. Time 85:25B Mr 12 '65

Religious institutions and affairs

See also
Catholic church in the Netherlands

Royal family

Toast to Beatrix and her betrothed. il Life 59:30-30A Jl 9 '65

NETHERLANDS INDIES. See Indonesia

NETHERLANDS WEST INDIES
Personal business; winter vacation on ABC islands. Bsns W p 171-2 N 13 '65
See also
Bonaire (island)

NETSCH, Walter Andrew, 1920-
By the cloverleaf. il por Time 87:54-5+ Ja 7 '66

Campus City, Chicago; the concept. il por Arch Forum 123:26-9 S '65

NETSUKES
Netsuke. W. Buehr. il Horizon 7:14-17 Autumn '65

NETTING, Robert M.
Heritage of survival. Natur Hist 74:14-21 Mr '65

NETUREI karta. See Hasidism

NEUBAUER, Henrik
Visitor from Yugoslavia. J. Anderson. Dance Mag 39:18-20 Jl '65

NEUBAUER, John
Has tax cut aided photographers? Pop Phot 57:59+ N '65

How Congress can save photographers $28,000,000. Pop Phot 56:51+ My '65

President's choice: photography can show that government is personal. Pop Phot 57:59+ N '65

NEUBERGER, Linda, and Neuberger, Roy
Life as a fire lookout in Crater Lake National Park. il por Nat Parks Mag 39:16-19 Ag '65

NEUBERGER, Maurine Brown
Jar of hope. il por Newsweek 65:64 My 31 '65

NEUBERGER, Roy. See Neuberger, L. jt. auth.

NEUGEBOREN, Jay
Graduate speed-up. Commonweal 83:8 O 8 '65
Luther; story. Commentary 41:42-8 Ja '66

NEUMANN, Alfred, and others
War and peace; dramatization of novel by L. N. Tolstoi. Criticism
Life 58:10 F 26 '65
Nation 200:121-2 F 1 '65
Sat R 48:44 F 6 '65
Vogue 145:95 Mr 1 '65

NEURAIRTOME. See Surgical instruments

NEURALGIA, Trigeminal
Hot water cures tic. F. Marley. il Sci N L 88:371 D 11 '65

NEURONS. See Nerve cells

NEUROPHYSIOLOGY. See Nervous system

NEUROPSYCHIATRIC institute at UCLA. See Los Angeles—Hospitals

NEUROSES
Combat fatigue lasts. Sci N L 87:343 My 29 '65

Margaret Mead answers. M. Mead. Redbook 125:20+ O '65
See also
Phobias

NEUROSPORA
Inositol deficiency resulting in death: an explanation of its occurrence in neurospora crassa. P. Matile. bibliog il Science 151:86-8 Ja 7 '66

Mutagenicity of a monofunctional alkylating agent derivative of acridine in neurospora. H. E. Brockman and W. Goben. bibliog il Science 147:750-1 F 12 '65

NEUROTICS. See Neuroses

NEUSTADT, Richard E.
Lawyer's brief before the bar of history. Harper 231:120+ O '65

NEUTRALITY
Nonalignment in foreign affairs; symposium, ed. by C. V. Crabb, jr. bibliog f Ann Am Acad 362:1-138 N '65

UN power shifts; decline of the unaligned. A. Weill-Tuckerman. Nation 201:488-90 D 20 '65

NEUTRINOS
Finding the natural neutrino. Time 86:67 S 10 '65

Gilt-edged neutrinos; detection of naturally produced neutrinos in gold mine near Johannesburg. Sci Am 213:38 O '65

Natural neutrinos found in South African mine. Sci N L 88:168 S 11 '65

NEUTRINOS—*Continued*
Neutrino identified. il Sci N L 88:230 O 9 '65
Neutrino trap. Sci Am 212:53 F '65
New method to detect neutrinos proposed.
  Sci N L 87:89 F 6 '65
Now you see it: neutrino catching in East
  Rand proprietary mine, South Africa. News-
  week 66:57 S 13 '65

NEUTRON activation analysis. See Radioactivation analysis

NEUTRONS
Close-packed-spheron theory and nuclear fis-
  sion. L. Pauling. bibliog il Science 150:297-
  305 O 15 '65
Forces in atom core are weak and strong.
  Sci N L 87:137 F 27 '65
High flux beam research reactor in operation.
  Sci N L 88:312 N 13 '65
Neutron affects heredity more than pre-
  dicted. Sci N L 88:217 O 2 '65

NEVADA
  See also
Lehman Caves National Monument
Mines and mineral resources—Nevada

Antiquities
  See Indians of North America—Antiquities—Nevada

Religious institutions and affairs
News of the Christian world (cont) Christian
  Cent 82:348-50 Mr 17 '65

NEVADA. University, Reno
Reno offers you the weather; Atmospherium
  at University of Nevada. il Sunset 134:28
  Mr '65

NEVELSON, Louise
Personal backgrounds. il por House & Gard
  128:180 D '65

NEVER let a cat go hungry; story. See Stewart,
E.

NEVI. See Birthmarks; Moles (dermatology)

NEVIN, David
Life book review. Life 59:18 O 8 '65
Outward bound from Miami on a shabby
  ocean liner. Life 59:30-5 N 26 '65

NEVIS (island)
Traveler's choice. F. R. Smith. Travel 124:7 D
  '65

NEW, Edward F. Jr
Slight case of contempt. il por Time 86:58
  Jl 30 '65

NEW BEDFORD, Mass, free public library
Onboard in New Bedford. J. S. Healey. il
  Wilson Lib Bul 40:246-8 N '65

NEW books preview. See Book exhibits

NEW BRITAIN (island)
Something belong friendship; Airmen's
  memorial school on island of New Britain.
  J. Reddy. il Read Digest 86:224-8+ My '65

NEW business enterprises
Building from scratch; interview. H. Johnson. Nations Bsns 53:40-2+ N '65

NEW Catholic encyclopedia
Making of an encyclopedia. H. C. Gardiner.
  America 112:668-9 My 8 '65

NEW college, Sarasota, Fla.
New college; profile. V. Kelley. il Mlle 61:
  148+ O '65

NEW deal. See United States—Economic policy

NEW DELHI, India
In New Delhi and Montreal, cellular solutions for high-density living. il Arch Forum 123:68-9 Jl '65

NEW ENGLAND
  See also
Fishing—New England

History
  Colonial period
  See also
Puritans

Religious institutions and affairs
News of the Christian world (cont) Christian
  Cent 82:1589 D 22 '65

NEW ENGLAND book show. See Book exhibits

NEW ENGLAND in literature
Fiction writer faces facts; research for an
  edited anthology. N. Hale. il Sat R 48:23-
  5+ Je 12 '65

NEW ENGLANDERS
Puritan promenade, by M. Bacon. Review
  New Repub 152:22-4+ Mr 27 '65. W. J.
  Smith

NEW frontiersmen. See Public officers

NEW GUINEA
  See also
New Britain (island)

Bibliography
Books in review; life in an alien culture.
  H. M. Van Deusen. Natur Hist 75:6 Ja
  '66

Description and travel
Behind New Guinea's masks. G. Thomas. il
  Sat R 48:68+ S 18 '65

Native races
Gamma-globulin factors (Gm and Inv) in
  New Guinea; anthropological significance.
  E. Giles and others. bibliog il Science 150:
  1158-60 N 26 '65
High valley, by K. E. Read. Review
  Life 59:10 Ag 13 '65. L. C. Eiseley
New Guinea revisited. M. Mead. il Redbook
  124:6+ F '65
Stone-age men go modern; Manus people.
  W. Cloud. il Pop Sci 186:29-30 F '65

NEW GUINEA, TERRITORY OF
Visiting mission to New Guinea and Nauru.
  UN Mo Chron 2:48-50 Ap '65

NEW HAMPSHIRE
  See also
Fishing—New Hampshire
Merrimack River

History
Summer in the White Mountains. D. H.
  Giffen. il Antiques 88:195-9 Ag '65

NEW HAVEN, Conn.
You shove out the poor to make houses
  for the rich; urban renewal means Negro
  removal. W. L. Miller and L. T. Appleby.
  il N Y Times Mag p36+ Ap 11 '65

Architecture
In Nîmes and New Haven, continuous forms
  broken into human-sized units. Arch Forum 123:64-5 Jl '65

City planning
Lighting of cities. W. M. C. Lam. il Arch
  Rec 138:173-80 Jl '65

Clubs
Ingenious use of a narrow site. il Arch Rec
  138:161-4 N '65

Education
How to get into college; Hillhouse high
  school's unusual marking system. il Time
  86:56 Ag 27 '65

Lighting
Lighting of cities. W. M. C. Lam. il Arch
  Rec 138:173-80 Jl '65

NEW HAVEN and Hartford railroad. See New
  York, New Haven and Hartford railroad
  company

NEW HOPE, Minn. See Minneapolis

NEW JERSEY
  See also
Architecture, Domestic—New Jersey
Booksellers and bookselling—New Jersey
Colleges and universities—New Jersey
Education—New Jersey
Fishing—New Jersey
Hunting—New Jersey
Raritan River

Historic houses, etc.
Domestic architecture of New Jersey. J. E.
  Boucher. il Antiques 88:184-9 Ag '65
History in houses; Dey mansion, Wayne,
  N.J. E. Stillinger. il Antiques 88:190-4 Ag
  '65

Politics and government
Chance for a change in the Garden state.
  J. J. Farmer. Reporter 33:27-9 Ag 12 '65
Dick to the rescue; Nixon's reactions to
  New Jersey election. Nation 201:345-6 N 15
  '65
Genovese campaign; issue in gubernatorial
  race. il Time 86:25 O 22 '65
Getting the Garden growing; Hughes' victory.
  il Time 86:33 N 12 '65
Sit down, you're rocking the boat. E. J.
  Bell. Nat R 17:983+ N 2 '65
Study in academic freedom; Genovese case.
  A. Beichman. il N Y Times Mag p 14-15+
  D 19 '65

Religious institutions and affairs
News of the Christian world (cont) Chris-
  tian Cent 82:718, 1042, 1490 Je 2, Ag 25,
  D 1 '65

NEW JERSEY library association

Intellectual freedom committee

Intellectual freedom committee reports busy year of censorship in New Jersey; excerpts from address, May 14, 1965. Z. Horn. Library J 90:2774+ Je 15 '65

NEW JERSEY turnpike. See Roads—New Jersey

NEW Lincoln school, New York. See New York (city)—Education

NEW MEXICO
See also
Booksellers and bookselling—New Mexico
Fishing—New Mexico
Hunting—New Mexico
Pueblo Indians
Rio Grande Valley

Churches
See Churches—United States

Description and travel

Desert traditions, decorative riches. M. Roche. il House & Gard 128:254-9+ N '65

Largest volcanic crater? Valle Grande. il Sunset 135:66+ N '65

New Mexico's crater country. J. V. Young. il Travel 124:30-4 S '65

New Yorker's report on New Mexico. D. Boroff. il Harper 230:72-8 F '65

Religious institutions and affairs

News of the Christian world (cont) Christian Cent 82:945, 1491 Jl 28, D 1 '65

NEW MEXICO. University, Albuquerque

Enchantment in the land of the Lobos. G. S. Brown. il Sports Illus 22:66-7 My 31 '65

Fine sound in the Fine arts center. P. G. Davis. il Hi Fi 15:202 N '65

Five immovable objects stood fast; New Mexico's Lobos vs Brigham Young and Utah. F. Deford. il Sports Illus 22:52+ F 22 '65

NEW mirror; story. See Petry, A.

NEW neighbors; story. See Gordon, E. E.

NEW ORLEANS

New Orleans gets a piece of the action; economic breakthrough for Louisiana metropolis. il Bsns W p 160-2+ Ap 10 '65

Solace for a stricken city; havoc wrought by hurricane Betsy. il Time 86:36-7 S 17 '65

Up from the deluge; aftermath of hurricane Betsy. il Time 86:24-5 S 24 '65

Description

New Orleans and all that jazz. H. Sutton. Sat R 48:38-9+ Ap 3 '65

Vieux Carré, just the right size for walkers. il Sunset 134:78+ Mr '65

Education

Community leadership and education in a crisis. T. L. Patrick. Sch & Soc 93:403-4 O 30 '65

Hotels, restaurants, etc.

New Orleans and all that jazz. H. Sutton. Sat R 48:38-9+ Ap 3 '65

Music

Music in the Bayou. H. W. McCraw. il Hi Fi 15:130-1 Je '65

Preservation Hall. il Ebony 20:64-6+ My '65
See also
New Orleans opera house association

Sanitary affairs

Hurricane clean-up brings biggest sewer-cleaning contract. il Am City 81:13 Ja '66

NEW ORLEANS Mardi gras. See Carnival

NEW ORLEANS opera house association

New Orleans; revival of Samson et Dalila. J. Belsom. il Opera N 30:30 D 4 '65

New Orleans spring. J. Belsom. Opera N 29:30 My 1 '65

NEW ORLEANS philharmonic-symphony orchestra

Music to my ears; this, too, is New Orleans; Rockefeller foundation finances performance of contemporary music. I. Kolodin. Sat R 48:30 Ap 17 '65

Music to my ears; two reports for the price of one. I. Kolodin. Sat R 48:30 Ap 24 '65

NEW products. See Products, New

NEW realism. See Modernism (art)

NEW republic (periodical)

Faces of five decades. R. Lekachman. Commonweal 81:731-3 Mr 5 '65

NEW sources of food supply. See Food supply—New sources

NEW statesman (periodical)

Maintaining the proper tone; Paul Johnson and Catholicism. America 113:4 Jl 3 '65

NEW stock issues. See Stocks

NEW testament. See Bible—New testament

NEW Thought

New developments in New Thought. C. A. Anderson. bibliog f Christian Cent 83:78-80 Ja 19 '66

NEW Tokaido line. See Railroads—Japan

NEW towns

Case for building 350 new towns. W. Von Eckardt. il Harper 231:85-8+ D '65

Rural ring; satellite for Washington, D.C. il Life 59:166-7 D 24 '65

Ten great places to live. Esquire 64:223+ D '65

Visit to Pihlajamäki; residential district near Helsinki. J. Barnett. il Arch Rec 138:121-8 D '65
See also
Ciudad Guayana
Columbia, Md
Foster City, Calif
Guayana, Venezuela
Reston, Va.

NEW words. See Words, New

NEW World. See America

NEW World in literature. See America in literature

NEW YEAR decorations. See Decoration and ornament

NEW YORK (city)

New York proclaimed, by V. S. Pritchett. Review
Commentary 39:80-2+ My '65. J. Epstein
Commonweal 82:247-50 My 14 '65. J. Finn
Reporter 32:48-50 My 20 '65. E. Wensberg

New York, site unseen; drawings. J. M. Folon. Horizon 7:116-20 Sum '65

Sound of sounds that is New York. H. C. Schonberg. il N Y Times Mag p38+ My 23 '65

Summer festival. New Yorker 41:24 Je 19 '65

Zoom in on the city; photographs. A. Kane. Life 59:24-35 D 24 '65
See also
Harlem River, New York
Lincoln Center for the performing arts

Air pollution

New York: too little, too late? C. G. Bennett. il Sat R 48:45-6 My 22 '65

Sewer in the sky. il Newsweek 66:59 Jl 5 '65

Airports

BOAC may expand JFK cargo terminal. il Aviation W 83:39-41 N 22 '65

Collision spurs New York airport dispute. J. W. Carter. Aviation W 83:33-4 D 20 '65

Halaby, Tobin clash on New York airports. R. D. Hibben. Aviation W 82:30 Mr 1 '65

New runways built on stilts; LaGuardia airports. il Pop Sci 188:94-5 Ja '66

Reverse-bent blades skim over the bumps. il Am City 80:30 Ag '65

Surface tension. R. B. Parke. Flying 78:30 Ja '66

Ten carriers' New York area plan discounts need for new jetport. J. W. Carter. Aviation W 83:28 N 1 '65

Twenty-nine general aviation fields urged for N.Y. Aviation W 82:31 My 3 '65

Architecture

Cost of the good environment. il Fortune 72:184+ Ag '65

Eye on the environment. Newsweek 66:70-1 Ag 23 '65

Showcase on the Square; Allied chemical corp. opens office building. il Newsweek 66:79 D 13 '65

Tower; Allied chemical building, Times square. New Yorker 41:49-50 D 11 '65

Art

Art galleries. R. M. Coates. See issues of New Yorker

Banks

Antitrust chaos; Manufacturers and Hanover merger. H. Hazlitt. Newsweek 65:74 Mr 29 '65

Bank weighs appeal against breakup order; Justice dept. anti-trust suit against Manufacturers Hanover trust co. il Bsns W p35 Mr 20 '65

NEW YORK (city)—Banks—*Continued*
Bank with the boardinghouse reach; First
national city. T. A. Wise. il Fortune 72:
136-9+ S '65

Chase goes national. il Time 86:80 Jl 23 '65

First national's full house. il Time 86:102+
O 1 '65

How to lose $8-million on sterling; New
York's First national city bank tells how.
Bsns W p96+ Jl 24 '65

Making risk-taking pay at U.S. trust. il
Bsns W p 138-40+ Mr 20 '65

Saxon charm draws Chase bank; Chase Manhattan to switch to national charter from
state charter. il Bsns W p 121+ Jl 24 '65

Two big banking rivals meet in another
arena; Chase Manhattan and First national
city come to Wall Street to raise money.
Bsns W p 154 Je 19 '65

Unscrambling an egg? antitrust suit by
Justice department against Manufacturers
Hanover trust company. Newsweek 65:72
Mr 22 '65
See also
Morgan guaranty trust company

Bibliography
NEA in New York and the World's fair;
guidebook. P. P. Coleman. Sr Schol 86:sup
10 My 13 '65

Bookstores
See Booksellers and bookselling—New
York (state)

Bridges
Bridges. New Yorker 41:51 N 27 '65
See also
Brooklyn bridge

Buildings
See New York (city)—Architecture

Carnegie Hall
Boss is back! J. Lyons. il Am Rec G 31:956-
7+ Je '65

Charities
See also
Charity organization society of the city of
New York

Churches
Way-out minister of Washington square;
H. R. Moody of Judson memorial church.
L. Tornabene. il N Y Times Mag p16-17+
Je 6 '65
See also
New York (city)—St John the Divine, Ca-
thedral of

City planning
Computer produces 120-volume planning reference. W. F. R. Ballard. il Am City 80:
110+ Jl '65

Progress in strategy; New York turns to
invisible renewal to save its West side.
D. Dennehy. il Arch Forum 123:72-5 Jl '65
See also
New York (city)—Metropolitan district

Clubs
Princeton pond; water from rain and dew on
roof of the Princeton club. S. McKelway.
New Yorker 41:48+ Ja 1 '66

Singular set of people. Watson; Baker street
irregulars. W. S. Baring-Gould. il Esquire
65:92-5+ Ja '66

Strictly for laughs; Thursday literature and
luncheon society. il Newsweek 66:50 S 6 '65

Crime
Arithmetic of delinquency. J. Horwitz. il
N Y Times Mag p 12-13+ Ja 31 '65

Crime underground; increase in serious
crimes on the subways. Time 85:55 F 19 '65

Detective: G. Barrett, hunter of men. J.
Mills. il Life 59:90D-101+ D 3 '65

They no longer bop. they jap. G. Samuels.
il N Y Times Mag p40+ Mr 7 '65

Deputy mayors
See New York (city)—Public officers

Description
Beautiful, anarchic, always on the make.
V. S. Pritchett. il N Y Times Mag p63+
Ap 18 '65

Miss Streisand's New York for Marcello
Mastroianni. B. Streisand. Esquire 63:56+
My '65

Three days afoot in New York. R. Dunlop. il
Todays Health 43:42-9 My '65
See also
New York (city)—Streets

Economic conditions
Can New York find a cure for urban ills? il
Bsns W p34-8 D 25 '65

Chaos in New York; trouble of almost every
kind. il U S News 58:8+ F 1 '65

Does New York city have a future? il U S
News 60:44-7 Ja 24 '66

New York's bid for a way out. U S News
59:51 D 13 '65

Why New York city is deeper in trouble. il
U S News 58:40-2 F 8 '65

Education
Breaking up the big systems; plans to decentralize authority. P. Woodring. Sat R
48:51-2 Jl 17 '65

Challenging the gifted; Bronx high school of
science. A. Taffel. Atlan 215:99-102+ My '65

Close to midnight for the New York schools.
S. Mayer. il N Y Times Mag p34-5+ My 2
'65

Dancing words; correlation of music and
reading at P.S. 77. il Time 86:64 O 22 '65

Integrated schools; a progress report; with
discussion group program, by M. Smart.
N. D. Kurland. il Parents Mag 40:32+, 60-
1+ S '65

Negro & the New York schools. M. Decter;
discussion. Commentary 39:16 Ja; 13-14 F
'65

New intermediate school; return to four-
year system. P. Woodring. Sat R 48:77-8
O 16 '65

NYC to abolish all junior highs. Sr Schol
86:sup4 My 13 '65

New York's avant-garde school; New Lincoln.
il Ebony 20:34-6+ My '65

New York's take-charge man. Time 85:57
Ap 16 '65

Room for whom at the top? F. M. Hechinger.
il Sat R 48:70-1+ Ap 17 '65

School of performing arts dance concert.
auditorium. High school of printing. D.
Hering. Dance Mag 39:64-5 Jl '65
See also
Free university of New York
New York (city) City university of New
York

Education, Board of
Educational politics; Gross asked to resign.
Reporter 32:12+ Mr 25 '65

New York city; Gross out; desegregation in.
il Sr Schol 86:sup 1 Mr 25 '65

Nice guy's exit; Superintendent C. Gross
asked to resign. Time 85:48 Mr 12 '65

School of hard knocks; school superintendent
Gross asked to resign. il Newsweek 65:88-9
Mr 15 '65

Elections
Big city faces its decisive moment. T. H.
White. il Life 59:34-40A+ O 29 '65

Buckleyism forever? K. Crawford. Newsweek
66:49 N 15 '65

Elected. New Yorker 41:46-9 N 13 '65

Lindsay, fusion and the future. Life 59:4
N 12 '65

Lindsay, Kennedy, and the power struggle
in New York. W. V. Shannon. Harper 232:
37-45 Ja '66

Lindsay miracle. C. McWilliams. Nation 201:
348-50 N 15 '65

Loner Lindsay's New York triumph; with
report by R. Ajemian. il Life 59:42-5 N 12
'65

Mayor John Lindsay; new GOP hope? il
Newsweek 66:31-6 N 15 '65

New York and the GOP. Nat R 17:1014
N 16 '65

New York election; Reporter supports J. V.
Lindsay. M. Ascoli. Reporter 33:14 N 4 '65

News & views; analysis of returns in mayoral
election. J. Leo. Commonweal 83:202 N 19 '65

Running against Buckley, Lindsay beats
Beame. M. Kempton. New Repub 153:9-10
N 13 '65

Electric power
Big city lived by the light of the moon;
with report by T. H. White. il Life 59:
36-46B+ N 19 '65

Dark night to remember. L. Wainwright.
Life 59:35 N 19 '65

Disaster that wasn't; Northeast blackout. il
Time 86:36-43 N 19 '65

NEW YORK (city)—Electric power—*Cont.*
Lighting up the blackout. il Newsweek 66:92
N 22 '65
Longest night. il Newsweek 66:27-8+ N 22 '65
Night they unplugged society; power failure,
November 9, 1965. J. Lear. il Sat R 48:81-4
D 4 '65; Discussion. 49:106 Ja 1 '66
Notes and comment; blackout. New Yorker
41:43-7 N 20 '65
Signs and portents; paralysis. J. Burnham.
Nat R 18:70 Ja 25 '66
See also
Consolidated Edison company of New York

Finance

Computerize your purchases and save. G.
A. Wechsler. il Am City 80:86-7 N '65
How to cut your city's electric bill. A.
Lurkis. Am City 80:53+ Je '65
See also
New York (city)—Taxation

Foreign population
See also
Puerto Ricans in the United States

Galleries and museums

Break's over, Mac, Mac! Mac! Museum of
famous people, New York. il Life 60:39-40+
Ja 21 '66
For more than art's sake; New York Marl-
borough-Gerson gallery exploits modern
selling methods. il Bsns W p 150-2+ My
15 '65
Museums as living newspapers; current fare
in the Guggenheim and Modern museums
in New York. F. Getlein. New Repub 152:
21-3 Ap 24 '65
Out there in the universe; exhibition at
Knoedler gallery. il Newsweek 66:88 N 1 '65
Personal business; touring New York's art
world. Bsns W p77-8 D 25 '65
Reviews and previews. See issues of Art
news
See also
American museum of natural history, New
York
Frick collection
Metropolitan museum of art
Museum of early American folk arts, New
York
Museum of primitive art
Museum of the city of New York
Solomon R. Guggenheim museum
Whitney museum of American art

Gardens

World's fair blooms again. il Flower Grower
52:28-9 My '65
See also
Brooklyn botanic garden
New York botanical garden

Greenwich Village

Girls of Greenwich Village. A. Geracimos
and J. Ferris. Mlle 61:82-3+ Je '65

Harlem

Books; Negro and Spanish Harlem. N. Hen-
toff. New Yorker 41:71-4+ Jl 31 '65
Cool world; controversial movie changes lives
of N.Y. delinquents. il Ebony 20:43-4+ Jl
'65
Cry from Harlem. C. Brossard. il Look 29:
125-6+ D 14 '65
Dark ghetto, by K. B. Clark. Review
Commonweal 83:67-9 O 15 '65. J. Stanley
Newsweek il 65:78+ My 31 '65
Don't blame the ghetto. D. B. Lee. Read
Digest 86:145-8 Ap '65
Harlem is in New York city. W. F. Buckley,
jr. Nat R 17:978-9 N 2 '65
Harlem LSCA project begun by New York
public library. Library J 90:2512 Je 1 '65
Harlem's streetcorner architects; Architects
renewal committee in Harlem. A. Lopen.
il Arch Forum 123:50-1 D '65
Hundred-fifteenth-between-Lenox-and-Fifth.
C. Hunter. New Yorker 41:109-10+ F 20 '65
In Harlem and Pittsburgh, limited gains in
the fight against rules and red tape. il
Arch Forum 123:66-7 Jl '65
Instant slum clearance. J. Meyer. il Esquire
63:108-11 Ap '65
Mr Nakasa goes to Harlem; contrast with
Johannesburg. N. Nakasa. il N Y Times
Mag p40-1+ F 7 '65
Nobody wants to hear that nonsense in
Harlem; excerpts from television discus-
sion. C. Brown; N. Podhoretz. New Repub
153:20 O 16 '65

Saturday night in Harlem; a memoir; ex-
cerpt from Manchild in the promised land.
C. Brown. Commentary 40:47-53 Jl '65
Way of seeing; excerpts. J. Agee. il Horizon
7:49-59 Sum '65
See also
New York public library—135th Street branch

History

Boss Tweed's New York, by S. J. Mandel-
baum. Review
Newsweek il 65:122 Je 14 '65
Gotham. New Yorker 41:19-20 Ag 7 '65

Hotels, restaurants, etc.

Dining in/out with Esquire; Rainbow room
and Rainbow grill. il Esquire 64:124+ Ag
'65
Famous foods from famous places; three restaurants in Manhattan's Pan-American
building. il Bet Hom & Gard 43:78-9 Jl
'65
Goings on about town. See issues of New
Yorker
Manhattan's highest paid headwaiter. W.
McQuade. il Arch Forum 123:76 S '65
Past, present and yet to come; G. Lombardo,
ghost of New Year's. W. K. Zinsser. il Life
59:82+ D 17 '65
Plaza fights to stay elegant, and profitable.
il Bsns W p32-3 D 18 '65
Special list for New York world's fair visi-
tors. Holiday 38:72 Jl '65
Where to dine out in New York. G. Maddox.
il Todays Health 43:18-23+ My '65
See also
Night clubs

Housing

55,000 neighbors; Co-op city project. News-
week 65:92 F 22 '65
Instant slum clearance. J. Meyer. il Esquire
63:108-11 Ap '65
New York tries a new approach. T. C.
Wheeler. Reporter 32:18-20 Je 17 '65
This is total living? S. Lefrak's utopia in
Queens. il Newsweek 66:101-2 N 8 '65

Industries

How the strike cost New York $800 million.
il Newsweek 67:70-1+ Ja 24 '66
New York printing week salutes graphic arts.
Pub W 187:126 F 1 '65
Rags to riches on Seventh avenue; garment
business. J. Weingarten. il Duns R 86:52-
4+ N '65

Lewisohn stadium

Summer haven. Newsweek 66:80 Jl 5 '65

Libraries

Head start programs; New York, Brooklyn
and Queens public libraries. il Library J
90:2338-40 My 15 '65
See also
New York metropolitan reference and research library agency, incorporated
New York public library

Lighting

Famous Fifth takes on a new glow at night.
il Am City 80:128 O '65
Shedding light. New Yorker 41:16-18 Jl 10
'65

Madison Square Garden

That was New York; building on Madison
Square. A. Logan. il New Yorker 41:41-2+
F 27 '65

Markets

Hey, Leach! driver of last horse truck in the
old Washington market area. New Yorker
41:24-7 Je 19 '65
Where the treasure is for the finding; flea
market, Avenue of the Americas and 25th
street. il Bsns W p34-5 O 16 '65

Mayors

Dropout? Wagner may not run for re-elec-
tion. Newsweek 65:18 Je 7 '65
Man who ran the show; R. Price, manager
of Lindsay campaign. Newsweek 66:34 N 15
'65
New York election; Reporter supports J. V.
Lindsay. M. Ascoli. Reporter 33:14 N 4 '65
See also
LaGuardia, F.
New York (city)—Politics and government
Wagner, R. F.

NEW YORK (city)—*Continued*

Medical and health centers
See also
New York university—Medical center

Metropolitan district
New York: a metropolitan region. B. Chinitz. il Sci Am 213:134-8+ bibliog(p277) S '65

Metropolitan museum of art
See Metropolitan museum of art

Monuments, statues, etc.
Martí in Central Park. F. Lizaso. il Américas 17:1-3 Je '65

Moral conditions
This flood of filth; New York city citizens' anti-pornography commission's steps to curb pornography. E. F. Cavanagh. jr. America 113:184-5 Ag 21 '65
See also
New York (city)—Crime

Music
Avant-garde; minister's daughter recalls the daring Wagnerism of her youth. N. Dana. il Opera N 29:8-13 F 13 '65
Black tie from heaven; operas. C. Osborne. Hi Fi 15:86G Mr '65
Bombardment of Beethoven; concerts. H. Goldsmith. Hi Fi 15:137-8+ Ap '65
B.B.C. in New York. B. Boretz. Nation 200: 682-3 Je 21 '65
BBC symphony orchestra. E. Laderman. Hi Fi 15:114+ Ag '65
Caviar from opera workshops; Benjamin Britten's Albert Herring, and Hector Berlioz's Béatrice et Benedict. R. Lawrence. il Hi Fi 15:115 Ag '65
Contemporary music comes to town. E. Laderman. Hi Fi 15:118+ Je '65
Debuts and reappearances; concerts. S. Fleming. Hi Fi 15:138-9 Ap; 118-19 My '65
Debuts and reappearances; concerts. Hi Fi 15:118-19 My; 121-3 Je; 106-7+ Jl; 116-17 Ag; 173 D '65; 16:138-41 Ja '66
Five-part harmony at Philharmonic Hall; Bach festival. D. Stevens. Hi Fi 16:136 Ja '66
French-American festival. R. Lawrence. il Hi Fi 15:147+ O '65
From France: classic and romantic. P. J. Smith. Hi Fi 15:115 Je '65
Henze's Elegy for young lovers: production by Juilliard opera theatre. C. L. Osborne. il Hi Fi 15:95+ Jl '65
Home stretch at the Met. C. L. Osborne. il Hi Fi 15:111-12 My '65
In the face of odds; operas. M. Mayer. il Hi Fi 15:86E-86F Mr '65
Ives fourth; in Carnegie Hall. G. Gould. Hi Fi 15:96-7 Jl '65
Lewisohn stadium: the Met moves in; concerts. C. L. Osborne. Hi Fi 15:146+ S '65
Little Vivaldi festival; Carnegie Hall. S. Fleming. Hi Fi 15:172 D '65
Metropolitan opera presents summer concerts at Lewisohn stadium; calendar. il Opera N 29:19-22 My 1 '65
Month of mezzos; concerts. C. L. Osborne. Hi Fi 15:135-6 Ap '65
Moscow philharmonic. A. Chasins. Hi Fi 16: 131+ Ja '66
Munich Bach chorus and orchestra; Karl Richter's Munich Bach chorus and orchestra at Carnegie Hall. L. Marcus. Hi Fi 15: 102-3 Jl '65
Music to my ears. I. Kolodin. See issues of Saturday review
Music to my ears: Mahler completed Tenth symphony. I. Kolodin. Sat R 48:34 Je 12 '65
Musical events. W. Sargeant. See issues of New Yorker
Musical whirl. il Hi Fi 15:114-15 My; 124-5 Je; 120-1 Ag; 154-5 S '65
Musical Yuletide in New York; concerts. D. Stevens. Hi Fi 15:86H-86I Mr '65
New York. F. Merkling. Opera N 30:33 D 25 '65
New York novelties. F. Merkling; R. D. Daniels. il Opera N 30:22 S 25 '65
Notes from our correspondents. P. G. Davis. il Hi Fi 15:36 Ap; 16+ My; 24+ Je; 22+ Jl; 14+ D '65; 16:16+ Ja '66
Of Spades and Turks; operas. P. J. Smith. il Hi Fi 15:116 My '65
Philharmonic in the park. I. Kolodin. il Sat R 48:56-7 S 11 '65
Pianists in full swing. H. Goldsmith. Hi Fi 16:137+ Ja '66

Presence of cellos; concerts. J. Roddy. il Hi Fi 15:86J-86K Mr '65
Professor Bernstein's required readings; New York concerts. R. Lawrence. Hi Fi 15:164 D '65
Right place for a party; New York philharmonic concert in Central park. il Time 86:38 Ag 20 '65
Rubinstein, adventurer and elder statesman. A. Chasins. il Hi Fi 15:113+ My '65
Sing unto the Lord; concerts. J. Roddy. il Hi Fi 15:117 My '65
Star-gazing at the Lewisohn observatory. I. Kolodin. Sat R 48:22 Jl 10 '65
Summer haven. Newsweek 66:80 Jl 5 '65
Summer nights at the Philharmonic; French-American festival of the New York philharmonic orchestra. I. Kolodin. Sat R 48: 41 Jl 31 '65
Sviatoslav Richter returns; Carnegie Hall recitals. A. Chasins. Hi Fi 15:100-1 Jl '65
Tomorrow's grand old men. L. Marcus. Hi Fi 15:119 Je '65
Tosca at last; R. Crespin. R. Lawrence. il Hi Fi 15:113-14 Je '65
Total theatre, part-time; operas. G. Rogoff. il Hi Fi 15:133-4 Ap '65
Two views of the avant-garde repertoire at Philharmonic Hall. D. Heckman; A. Cohn. il Am Rec G 32:354-6 D '65
Under the stars; Lewisohn stadium concerts. D. J. Soria. il Opera N 29:8-12 My 1 '65
Vladimir Horowitz; concert at Carnegie Hall, May 9. A. Chasins. il Hi Fi 15:122+ Ag '65
See also
Lincoln Center for the performing arts
Manhattan opera company
Metropolitan opera club
Metropolitan opera company
Metropolitan opera house
New York city center of music and drama
New York city opera company
New York orchestral society
Philharmonic-symphony society of New York

Anecdotes, facetiae, satire, etc.
Mr Whitweeks' massive tone; whistlers rampant in Robinson opera; other notes. S. McKelway. New Yorker 41:144+ Mr 6 '65

Negroes
Black man, go South. F. Powledge. il Esquire 64:72-4+ Ag '65
New York state and New York city, by M. Glassman. Review
Negro Hist Bul 28:138-9 Mr '65. E. C. Brooks

Newspapers
And then there were; merger rumors. Newsweek 65:51 Je 28 '65
Another newspaper strike possible in New York city. Pub W 187:37 Mr 15 '65
Another strike in Manhattan? Time 85:52+ F 26 '65
Automation, printers and publishers. R. Severo. New Repub 152:16 Mr 13 '65
Deadline in New York; strike averted. il Newsweek 65:75 Ap 12 '65
Dear John; Herald tribune withdraws from association, resumes publishing. il Newsweek 66:62 O 4 '65
Death of a craft? automation in the printing industry. T. R. Brooks. Commonweal 82: 46-9 Ap 2 '65
Great Manhattan newspaper duel. A. H. Raskin. il Sat R 48:58-60+ My 8 '65
It didn't fit to print; concerning Saturday review article by A. H. Raskin. Newsweek 65:94 My 17 '65
Manhattan mergers. il Time 85:66 Je 25 '65
Mergers: latest edition; New York metropolitan newspapers may pool their printing facilities. Bsns W p31 Je 19 '65
New York newspapers at the brink again. il Fortune 71:231-2+ Mr '65
New York newspapers under the gun again. il Bsns W p 111-12+ Mr 20 '65
New York's newspapers; need for continuing discussion industry's problems. Nation 201: 262 O 25 '65
Papers back in New York. Bsns W p70 O 16 '65
Presses keep rolling; shutdown averted. Bsns W p 146 Ap 10 '65
Reporter at large. F. C. Shapiro. New Yorker 41:161-4+ Ap 10 '65
Settlement in New York. Time 85:60 Ap 16 '65
Strike in New York? issue of automation. il Newsweek 65:88 Mr 22 '65

NEW YORK (city)—Newspapers—*Continued*
Trouble in New York city. Bsns W p 138
S 11 '65
Unsettling settlement. Newsweek 65:64 Ap
19 '65
See also
Brooklyn eagle
New York herald tribune
New York times
Strikes—United States—Newspapers
El Tiempo (newspaper)

Parks and playgrounds

Bridge to the future; Verrazano Narrows
bridge playground. N. Morris. il Recreation
58:167 Ap '65
Concert; performance in Sheep Meadow, Central park, by N.Y. philharmonic. New
Yorker 41:26-7 Ag 21 '65
Escape from buildings; Central park. New
Yorker 41:20 My 29 '65
Recipe for city playgrounds. il Recreation
58:173 Ap '65
Super-block play areas; New York city housing project rehabilitates its recreation
space. M. P. Friedberg. il Recreation 58:
164-6+ Ap '65
See also
New York (city)—Washington square
New York zoological park

Police

Aftermath to Harlem riot; Epton anarchy
trial. F. J. Donner. il Nation 201:355-8+
N 15 '65
Detective; G. Barrett, hunter of men. J.
Mills. il Life 59:90D-101+ D 3 '65
Good cop and crime prevention; concerning
Thank God for the George Barretts letters
to editors. Life 60:4 Ja 7 '66
I hadda shoot; case of Detective J. Devlin.
M. Kempton. New Repub 152:13-15 Mr 20
'65; Reply. A. Deutsch. 152:42 Ap 17 '65
New York's finest. T. R. Brooks. Commentary
40:29-36 Ag; Discussion. 40:22+ N '65
Police emergency number; visit to Manhattan
communications unit. New Yorker 41:37-9
My 8 '65
Suspect confesses, but who believes him?
G. Whitmore affair. S. E. Zion. il N Y
Times Mag p30-1+ My 16 '65

Politics and government

After you; question of Republican candidate
for mayor. Newsweek 65:29-30 Mr 8 '65
As New York goes. Nat R 17:859 O 5 '65
Atlantic report. Atlan 216:24+ O '65
Best-kept secret; Wagner will not seek reelection. il Newsweek 65:27-8 Je 21 '65
Big city faces its decisive moment. T. H.
White. il Life 59:34-40A+ O 29 '65
Big gamble of John Vliet Lindsay. W. Weaver, jr. il N Y Times Mag p30-1+ My 23
'65
Bill Buckley, how to have a certain amount
of fun. Newsweek 66:28-9 S 20 '65
Bobby Kennedy and the fight for New York.
R. Armstrong. il Sat Eve Post 238:29-31+
N 6 '65
Can anybody run New York city? il U S
News 58:57-60 Je 21 '65
Can John Lindsay lick New York's problems?
with editorial comment. Bsns W p28, 192
N 6 '65
Can Lindsay make it? M. Kempton. New
Repub 152:17-18 Je 5 '65
Can New York be saved? J. V. Lindsay. il
Sat Eve Post 238:78-80 O 9 '65
Candidate & the clamor; J. V. Lindsay announces candidacy for mayor against
Democrat Robert Wagner. il Time 85:29-30
My 21 '65
Candidates: Democrats for Mayor of New
York. New Yorker 41:26-7 Ag 28 '65
Coming seven years' war. E. J. Hughes.
Newsweek 66:27 N 15 '65
Different kind of candidate: W. F. Buckley.
Time 86:18 Jl 2 '65
Does New York city have a future? il U S
News 60:44-7 Ja 24 '66
Frank O'Connor takes the high road; City
council president. S. E. Zion. il N Y Times
Mag p9+ Ja 16 '66
From Tammany to Tiffany; Lindsay's first
round of appointments. il Time 86:36 D 10
'65
Fusion & confusion. Reporter 33:14+ Jl 15 '65
GOP hope; Lindsay of N.Y. il Newsweek 65:
23-4+ My 31 '65
Ill-kept city. R. Moley. Newsweek 66:106
O 4 '65
Incitement to excellence. il Time 86:28-33
N 12 '65

Lesson for a liberal? il U S News 59:20 O
25 '65
Letter from Washington; effect of Lindsay's
candidacy and victory. R. H. Rovere. New
Yorker 41:205-6 N 20 '65
Liberals and John Lindsay. A. M. Bickel.
New Repub 153:16-18 Jl 3 '65
Lindsay and New York's needs. Life 59:4 O
29 '65
Lindsay candidacy. Nation 200:546 My 24 '65
Lindsay, Kennedy, and the power struggle
in New York. W. V. Shanon. Harper 232:37-
45 Ja '66
Lucky Lindsay; New York city finds its
avenger. M. Kempton. New Repub 154:10-11
Ja 15 '66
Mischievous Robert Wagner. J. Desmond. il
Nation 200:688-90 Je 28 '65
More polyphyletic than profound; mayoral
campaign. il Time 86:29-30 O 29 '65
New York city; is it governable? il Newsweek 65:24-5 My 31 '65
New York: dispirited city. A. H. Armitstead.
Christian Cent 82:1319-21 O 27 '65
New York election. Nation 201:130 S 13 '65
New York, now that Wagner says no. M.
Kempton. New Repub 152:10 Je 26 '65
Now for the dialogue; mayoral campaign.
il Time 86:25-6 S 24 '65
Now that Lindsay is elected: how he plans
to help New York. U S News 59:32-3 N 15
'65
Odd-man-in; J. V. Lindsay to run for mayor.
il Newsweek 65:32 My 24 '65
Old math; mayoral campaign. il Newsweek
66:29 Ag 2 '65
On the move; J. V. Lindsay's government-
in-exile. Newsweek 66:42 N 22 '65
One man, one candidate. Newsweek 66:21-2
Jl 5 '65
One of the world's toughest jobs. il U S
News 60:16 Ja 10 '66
Ryan and Lindsay. R. Lekachman. New
Repub 153:8-9 Jl 24 '65
Shouting for help; internal Democratic struggle. M. Kempton. New Repub 153:11-12 S
25 '65
Special election supplement; symposium. il
Nat R 17:973-82 N 2 '65
Statement by Wm. F. Buckley jr, announcing
his candidacy for mayor of New York,
June 24, 1965; with questions and answers. W. F. Buckley, jr Nat R 17:586-9
Jl 13 '65
Switcheroo; Primary day in New York city.
il Newsweek 66:29-30 S 27 '65
This Tuesday's winner, and loser. W. Weaver, jr. il N Y Times Mag p46-7+ O 31 '65
Tongue-in-cheek candidate; with excerpts
from conversations with W. Buckley, ed.
by S. Angeloff. il Life 59:49-50+ S 17 '65
Tough day in new York. L. Gross. il Look
29:99-101+ N 2 '65
Trying, trying; candidates positions. il Newsweek 66:36-7 N 1 '65
Underdog issue; Lindsay image. il Newsweek
66:47 O 18 '65
Untold tale; Lindsay's drive for the mayoralty. E. J. Hughes. il Newsweek 66:18-19 Jl 12
'65
Victory for honest John; Lindsay's present
image. Newsweek 67:29-31 Ja 24 '66
Voters' own urban renewal. Fortune 72:134+
D '65
What a new mayor faces in New York city.
il U S News 59:40-2 N 8 '65
What New York mayor's race can mean.
U S News 58:20 My 24 '65
What the New York primary shows. il U S
News 59:16 S 27 '65
When La Guardia took over. A. Mann. il
N Y Times Mag p22-3+ Ja 2 '66
Who's ahead for mayor of New York. il U S
News 59:51 O 4 '65
Why city government must be nonpartisan.
J. Lindsay. Look 29:162+ O 19 '65
Why the G.O.P. is smiling again; Lindsay is
running; with report by R. Ajemian. il
Life 58:32-5 My 28 '65
William F. Buckley, jr. M Kempton. New
Repub 153:9 Jl 10 '65
With Wagner out of the New York race.
U S News 58:8 Je 21 '65

Anecdotes, facetiae, satire, etc.

Mayor, anyone? W. F. Buckley, jr. Nat R
17:498 Je 15 '65
Notes and comment; political water-sports
season. New Yorker 41:41 S 18 '65

Public buildings

House that Tweed built; New York County
courthouse. A. B. Callow, jr. il Am Heritage 16:64-9 O '65

NEW YORK (city)—*Continued*

Public officers

Second man at City hall: Deputy Mayor R. Price. R. Armstrong. il N Y Times Mag p 12-14+ D 26 '65

Publicity

Wanted: one lovely monster. R. Bongartz. il Sat Eve Post 238:22 Jl 3 '65

Purchase, Department of

Fragile: 28 million eggs; ed. by P. D. Eimon. il Am City 80:138+ S '65

Radio City music hall

Music hall: still the no. 1 hit; last of the motion picture palaces. il Bsns W p46-9 D 25 '65

Recreation

See also
New York (city)—Parks and playgrounds

Religious institutions and affairs

News of the Christian world (cont) Christian Cent 82:282-5, 345, 504-6, 898, 1170-2, 1360-2, 1426+, 1588-9, 1615 Mr 3, 17, Ap 21, Jl 14, S 22, N 3, 17 D 22, 29 '65

Restaurants

See New York (city)—Hotels, restaurants, etc.

Riots

Aftermath to Harlem riot: Epton anarchy trial. F. J. Donner. il Nation 201:355-8+ N 15 '65

Rockefeller center

Relief from drabness; bronze plaques at Rockefeller center. il Time 85:86 My 7 '65

St John the Divine, Cathedral of

Heavy cost of Christian witness. America 113:559 N 13 '65

Sanitary affairs

Spring cleaning begins with a bang. il Am City 80:35 My '65

School board

See New York (city)—Education, Board of

Schools

See New York (city)—Education

Social conditions

Can anybody run New York city? il U S News 58:57-60 Je 21 '65

Tough day in New York. L. Gross. il Look 29:99-101+ N 2 '65

What a new mayor faces in New York city. il U S News 59:40-2 N 8 '65

Why New York city is deeper in trouble. il U S News 58:40-2 F 8 '65

World of Needle park. J. Mills. il Life 58: 82+ F 26 '65
See also
New York (city)—Harlem

Social life and customs

In crowd and the out crowd. S. L. Morrow. il N Y Times Mag p12-14+ Jl 18 '65

That was New York; scandal column of Town topics, weekly magazine. A. Logan. il New Yorker 41:37-8+ Ag 14; 41-2+ Ag 21 '65
See also
Night clubs

Social work

Can the Job corps do the job? B. Carter. il Reporter 32:21-6 Mr 25 '65

Reporter at large; gang of teen-age drug addicts in rehabilitation program sponsored by Mobilization for youth. R. Rice. New Yorker 41:50-2+ Mr 27 '65

War on poverty: are the poor left out? R. A. Cloward. il Nation 201:55-60 Ag 2 '65
See also
New York city mission society

Stations

Haunted: sequence of notes of unknown cause, over public-address system in Penn station. New Yorker 41:42-4 S 18 '65

Penn station: arriving on schedule. il Bsns W p32-3 O 30 '65

Stock exchange

See Stock exchange—New York (city)

Stores

Bloomingdale's intermingles paperbacks, modern library with hardbound books. il Pub W 188:53-4 D 27 '65

Golden one: government-of-India-sponsored handicraft shop in Corning glass building. New Yorker 41:20-1 Je 26 '65

New York transit tieup jams business gears; department store losses. il Bsns W p30-1 Ja 8 '66

Oracle to high society girls; super-saleswoman at De Pinna. il Life 58:76-8+ My 7 '65

Trade winds; Bloomingdale's delicacy department. J. Beatty, jr. il Sat R 48:10+ S 25 '65
See also
Abercrombie and Fitch company
Alexander's department stores, incorporated
Macy, R. H, and company

Street traffic

Are you a traffic expert? H. A. Barnes. il Am City 80:140+ Mr '65

Can computers call the signals? il Bsns W p30-1+ N 20 '65

Public service; traffic reports over radio station WOR, relayed from helicopter. New Yorker 41:44-5 S 11 '65

World's largest traffic-control system. il Am City 80:129 N '65

Streets

P.J.s; bars and other businesses with these initials on Third avenue between Forty-second and Eighty-sixth streets. New Yorker 41:35-6 Mr 13 '65

Revolution on Third avenue. I. Taves. il Look 29:34-9 Ap 20 '65

What a Citizens committee can do; Citizens committee to keep New York clean. Recreation 58:143 Mr '65

Subways

New hope for straphangers. C. W. Griffin, jr. il Reporter 33:27-9 D 30 '65

Riding shotgun; police ride subway trains. Newsweek 65:27 Ap 19 '65

Taxation

New York's bid for a way out. U S News 59:51 D 13 '65

Theater

Bad days on Broadway. G. P. Gates. Holiday 39:118+ Ja '66

Blau & Irving come out of the West; assume directorship of Lincoln Center repertory theater. M. Harris. il N Y Times Mag p 16-17+ F 21 '65

Enter the gadflies; directors of San Francisco's Actors workshop appointed to direct Lincoln Center repertory theater. Newsweek 65:82-3 F 8 '65

Fall'n angels; Broadway season. Sat R 48: 50 S 11 '65

Happenings on Upper Broadway: a comparative dig; New York's First theater rally. R. Kotlowitz. Harper 231:30+ Ag '65

How to succeed in the theatre without really being successful. E. Dundy. il Esquire 63:88-9+ My '64

Obscene or pleistocene? Broadway's current obscenity trend. America 112:239 F 20 '65

Off Broadway; Theater 1965; four plays by unknown dramatists. E. Oliver. New Yorker 41:56+ F 20 '65

Off have I traveled; Theatre 1965's New playwrights series at the Cherry Lane. H. Hewes. Sat R 48:35 Mr 20 '65

Pass-the-hat theater circuit; Off off Broadway theater. E. Lester. il N Y Times Mag p90+ D 5 '65

Plight of the out-of-town theatergoer, ticket problems; with round-up of opinion by critics, and report by H. Hewes. J. F. Wharton. il Sat R 49:29-31+ Ja 22 '66

Reviewer's notebook; reflections on the past season. T. Lewis. America 113:267-8 S 11 '65

Shakespeare for the people. J. Novick. Nation 201:146-8 S 13 '65

Shape-up; coming season. il Time 86:37 Ag 27 '65

Spotlight! E. Miller. See issues of Seventeen beginning April 1965

Survival of the hittest. Time 86:63 Jl 2 '65

Theatre 1965. H. Clurman. Nation 200:318-19 Mr 22 '65

Theater 1965. J. Marris. Vogue 145:100 Ap 1 '65

NEW YORK (city)—Theater—*Continued*
Trouble with inbreeding; off-Broadway's Theater 1965. il Time 85:58 Mr 12 '65
What makes some run; current season, on and off Broadway. Time 85:67 My 14 '65
See also
Lincoln Center for the performing arts
Lincoln Center repertory theater company
New York city center of music and drama

Times square
Showcase on the Square; Allied chemical corp. opens office building. il Newsweek 66:79 D 13 '65

Traffic problem
See New York (city)—Street traffic

Transportation
Never a kind word; TWU strike threat. il Newsweek 66:27-8 D 20 '65
Spectacle New Yorkers hope never to see again. il Life 60:62D-67 Ja 21 '66
Urban neurosis. Commonweal 83:456 Ja 21 '66
See also
New York (city)—Subways
Strikes—United States—Transportation workers

Tunnels
Asphalt planing precedes tunnel resurfacing; Lincoln tunnel. il Am City 80:44 S '65

Washington square
Tree: sapling from G. Washington's estate planted for opening of City parks week. New Yorker 41:44-6 My 15 '65

Water supply
Blimp trip; inspection of reservoirs. New Yorker 41:23-4 Jl 31 '65
Drip, drip, drip; emergency program for four drought-plagued northeastern states. Newsweek 66:22 Ag 30 '65
Leak; methods of dealing with leakage. New Yorker 41:19-20 S 4 '65
N.Y. discovers the Hudson. Nation 201:1-2 Jl 5 '65
On the rocks. Time 86:15 Ag 27 '65
People-water crisis. il Newsweek 66:48-50+ Ag 23 '65
Put a price on water. H. Hazlitt. Newsweek 66:71 Ag 30 '65
Rain is free, water isn't. Life 59:4 S 3 '65
Silly water. il Newsweek 66:19 S 6 '65
Water, water, anywhere? Northeast drought. il Newsweek 66:59 Ag 2 '65

Anecdotes, facetiae, satire, etc.
Notes and comment; political water-sports season. New Yorker 41:41 S 18 '65

Welfare, Department of
Eclipse of social work. Nation 200:99 F 1 '65

Worlds fair, 1939-1940
Time capsule
See Civilization—Preservation of records

Worlds fair, 1964-1965
Another look at the World's fair. il Good H 160:178 Ap '65
Around our fair world. E. Scully. il U S Camera 28:56-9+ Ap '65
At the fair, beer garden is heady surprise; Lowenbrau beer gets back $750,000 sunk in promotion at World's fair. il Bsns W p56-7+ Ag 21 '65
Biggest in history. il Newsweek 66:76+ S 20 '65
Changes you'll find at the fair this year. il U S News 58:16 Ap 26 '65
Children's world, Library/USA. S. Shaw. il Library J 90:1996-7 Ap 15 '65
De Soto and the fair. C. J. McNaspy. America 112:790-1 My 22 '65
Education at the N.Y. world's fair. il Sr Schol 86:sup5 Ap 15 '65
Electronic magic at the World's fair. A. Zuckerman. il Pop Electr 23:63-5+ Jl '65
European looks at the New York world's fair. R. Bosc. il America 113:77 Jl 17 '65
Exhibitors give a lift to fair beset by feuds. il Bsns W p26 Mr 13 '65
Fair draws to an end, the last of its kind? il Bsns W p32-3 O 16 '65

Fair: low on customers, and cash. il U S News 58:12 My 31 '65
Fair: New York's spectacle opens again. G. Zimmermann. il Look 29:27-33 Ap 20 '65
Fair reopens; photograph by J. P. Blair; with account by C. B. Patterson. Nat Geog Mag 127:504-29 Ap '65
Fantastic photographic nights at the fair. A. Rothstein. U S Camera 28:16+ Ap '65
Farewell to the fair. R. Kirk. Nat R 17:987 N 2 '65
Farewell to the fair. il Newsweek 66:34 O 25 '65
First of the month; how Animal kingdom at Worlds fair came to be. C. Amory. Sat R 48:6+ Ag 7 '65
Going to the fair this year? il Changing T 19:39-40 Mr '65
Goodbye to World's fairs. R. Lynes. il Harper 231:28+ O '65
Great souvenir sale; sale of surplus goods. il Time 86:96 O 8 '65
Hall of presidents. New Yorker 41:38-40 My 22 '65
How do children view the fair? Parents Mag 40:100 Jl '65
Irish Moses; policy disagreements. Newsweek 65:72 F 8 '65
It's not the money. Newsweek 66:80+ N 29 '65
Library/USA staff, 1964. ALA Bul 59:300-2 Ap '65
Library/USA's first season; view from the inside. F. M. Cammack. il ALA Bul 59:115-19 F '65
Meaning of the fair. R. Moley. Newsweek 66:92 Jl 12 '65
Mosaic pattern; Indonesia's seized pavilion. il Time 85:22 Ap 9 '65
New New York fair. E. Scully. il U S Camera 28:66-7+ O '65
N.Y. world's fair 1965. il Sr Schol 86:sup 10-11 Ap 15 '65
People problem; second year attendance lagging. il Newsweek 65:89 My 24 '65
Reopening. New Yorker 41:37 My 1 '65
Salute; tribute by Broadway to the fair. New Yorker 41:36-8 Ap 24 '65
Second time around. il Time 85:76+ Ap 30 '65
Summer festival. New Yorker 41:24 Je 19 '65
To get the most out of the New York world's fair. C. W. Hall. il Read Digest 86:186-8+ My '65
To the bitter end; closed. il Time 86:52 O 29 '65
Upbeat fair; second season. il Newsweek 65:88-90 Ap 26 '65
Well-rounded; fair members and board of directors. New Yorker 40:26-7 F 6 '65
What the matter can be. il Time 86:78 Jl 16 '65
What to look for; a guide to exhibits. il N Y Times Mag p55-8+ Ap 18 '65
What's new at the fair. Holiday 38:112-13 Jl '65
World of sound at the fair. T. Schwartz. il Pop Phot 56:58-9+ My '65
World's fair. R. F. Wagner; V. S. Pritchett; J. Canaday. il N Y Times Mag p52-61+ Ap 18 '65
World's fair blooms again. il Flower Grower 52:28-9 My '65
World's fair picture-taking & exposure guide. C. Burger. il Pop Phot 56:62-7+ Ap '65
World's fair revisited. il Sr Schol 86:26-9 Ap 1 '65
World's fare to enjoy at the World's fair or to savor at home. B. M. Stover. il Parents Mag 40:81+ Mr '65

Architecture
Fair had no patent on absence of design. E. Goble. Arch Rec 138:9 D '65

Art
Critics' choice=chaos? H. Keppler. il Mod Phot 29:88-91 S '65

Finance
Big bash that is running short of cash. C. Welles. il Life 58:136-8+ My 14 '65
Fair fights back on financing. Bsns W p34+ Ja 30 '65
Foul-up at the fair. M. Kempton. New Repub 152:13-14 F 20 '65
Post-mortem on why the fair ran in the red. il U S News 60:8 Ja 3 '66
There's no business like no business. G. Ace. Sat R 48:12 My 29 '65
Wanted: one lovely monster. R. Bongartz. il Sat Eve Post 238:22 Jl 3 '65

NEW YORK (city)—World's fair, 1964-1965—
Continued

Hall of science

Space astronomy at the World's fair. P. A. Leavens. il Sky & Tel 30:68-70 Ag '65
World's fair tries the impossible: kidproof exhibit. Todays Health 43:6 Ag '65

Time capsule

See Civilization—Preservation of records

Zoological park

See New York zoological park

NEW YORK (city) City university of New York
Crisis at CUNY. il Newsweek 66:69 D 6 '65

City college

CCNY; a memoir; something special in the 1930's. M. Liben. Commentary 40:64-70 S '65
Kind of proletarian Harvard. D. Boroff. il N Y Times Mag p 28-9+ Mr 28 '65

NEW YORK (state)
New regional plan to arrest megalopolis; New York state's development program. L. Mumford. il Arch Rec 137:147-54 Mr '65
See also
Adirondack Mountains
Booksellers and bookselling—New York (state)
Education—New York (state)
Festivals—New York (state)
Finger Lakes, N.Y.
Hudson River
Hunting—New York (state)
Insurance, Health—New York (state)
Labor laws and legislation—New York (state)
Water supply—New York (state)

Commerce, Department of

How New York pushes its wares overseas. il Bsns W p32 S 11 '65

Council on the arts

Support from the state. A. M. Lingg. il Opera N 30:13-15 Ja 15 '66

Description and travel

Inside New York state. F. Fitzgerald. il Mlle 61:199+ My '65
New York's Adirondack trail. W. L. Wessels. il Travel 124:38-9 S '65
While you're in New York; trips you can make in a day or two. S. Robinson. il McCalls 92:56+ Ag '65

Elections

See New York (state)—Politics and government

Historic houses, etc.

A. J. Davis' greatest Gothic: Lyndhurst. J. N. Pearce. il Antiques 87:684-9 Je '65
Living with antiques; Hudson Valley home of Mrs Henry M. Sage. N. S. Rice. il Antiques 88:806-11 D '65
Olana, the center of the world. D. C. Huntington. il Antiques 88:656-63 N '65
Persia on the Hudson; Olana, home of Frederic E. Church. R. Lynes. il Harper 230:30+ F '65
Washington at White Plains; headquarters at Miller House. il Travel 124:41-3 O '65

History

Man whose praise we sing; summary of Trappers of New York, by J. R. Simms. F. B. Leach. il Am Heritage 16:62-3+ Ap '65

Hudson River Valley commission

Who will save the Hudson, and how? J. Ridgeway. New Repub 153:10-11 O 2 '65

Legislature

A+B+C+D=NY²; New York state reapportionment case. M. Greenfield. il Reporter 33:32-5 D 2 '65

Politics and government

Albany hippodrome: Wagner, Rocky and the Kennedy act. J. Desmond. il Nation 200:184-5 F 22 '65
Bobby twins revisited; R. Kennedy charged with ruthlessness in campaign issues. H. Golden. Esquire 63:42-5 Je '65
Business as usual. Newsweek 65:30+ Ap 26 '65

Can Wagner stop Kennedy in New York? il U S News 58:59-60 F 22 '65
How not to succeed. Sr Schol 86:34 F 18 '65
No room at the top. Newsweek 65:39 My 17 '65
Up Bob, down Bobby. il Time 85:18 F 12 '65
Victory's losers; Republicans join Wagner forces to pick leaders for the Democratic majorities. il Newsweek 65:23 F 15 '65
Warren's monkey wrench: one man, one vote principle. Nat R 17:628-9 Jl 27 '65

Religious institutions and affairs

News of the Christian world (cont) Christian Cent 82:410, 720, 1398 Mr 31, Je 2, N 10 '65

NEW YORK airways, incorporated
CAB cool to airline aid for NY airways. Aviation W 83:28 Jl 5 '65
NY airways faces financial crisis. Aviation W 82:41 Ap 19 '65
NY airways reports loan arrangements. Aviation W 82:27 Je 7 '65
Pan American, TWA agree to aid NY airways in survival effort. Aviation W 82:34 Je 21 '65
Roof heliport gives copter line a lift; seven minutes from New York's Pan Am building to Kennedy airport. il Bsns W p 18-20 D 25 '65

NEW YORK blood center
One number for all types; world's biggest computerized inventory for human blood. Time 85:72 Mr 5 '65

NEW YORK botanical garden
New York botanical garden. P. Clark. il Horticulture 43:38-41 Je '65

NEW YORK bus advertising, incorporated
Sponsorless; New Yorker bus riders digest posters. New Yorker 41:49-50 O 23 '65

NEW YORK central railroad-Pennsylvania merger. See Railroads—Consolidations and mergers

NEW YORK city ballet
About Don Quixote. E. Denby. il Dance Mag 39:33-7 Jl '65; Reply. D. Vaughan. 39:30+ Ag '65
Balanchine dances; role of Don Quixote. il N Y Times Mag p39-40 My 16 '65
Balanchine's Don Quixote; ballet. R. Krokover. il Hi Fi 15:123 Ag '65
Don Quixote, New York city ballet, New York state theater. D. Hering. Dance Mag 39:32-3+ N '65
Happenings on Upper Broadway; a comparative dig; New York's First theater rally. R. Kotlowitz. Harper 231:30+ Ag '65
I cannot wait; M. Tallchief's decision. il Newsweek 66:100 O 25 '65
Mr B: God creates, I assemble. S. Massie. il Sat Eve Post 238:34-7 O 23 '65
Music to my ears; performance of Don Quixote. I. Kolodin. Sat R 48:34+ Je 12 '65
Musical events; performance of Balanchine's Don Quixote. W. Sargeant. New Yorker 41:184 O 2 '65
Musical events; performance of George Balanchine's Harlequinade. W. Sargeant. New Yorker 40:154 F 13 '65
New York city ballet in A midsummer night's dream. New York state theater. D. Hering. Dance Mag 39:29+ Ag '65
New York city ballet, New York state theater. D. Hering. Dance Mag 39:99+ D '65
New York city ballet, New York state theater. J. Maskey. Dance Mag 39:31 Jl '65
New York city ballet, three premieres, New York state theater. D. Hering. il Dance Mag 39:67-70 Mr '65
No lousy little stories; back in London. Time 86:104 S 17 '65
Nutcracker, New York city ballet, New York state theatre. D. Hering. il Dance Mag 39:26+ F '65
Project Buffalo; workshops, seminars, lecture-demonstrations. J. P. Dwyer. il Dance Mag 40:54-5 Ja '66
Quixote and pure art; G. Balanchine's new version. America 113:450-1 O 16 '65

NEW YORK city center of music and drama
He calls the tunes at the City Center. R. Kotlowitz. il N Y Times Mag p44-5+ My 2 '65
Spring comes to City Center. C. L. Osborne. Hi Fi 15:116-17 Je '65

NEW YORK city mission society
Summer camp education for underprivileged children; Edgewater creche, 1884-1964. F. M. Cordasco and J. G. Redd. bibliog f Sch & Soc 93:299 Sum '65

NEW YORK stock exchange. See Stock exchange—New York (city)

NEW YORK times
All the news that's fit to print; reflections on the New York times. G. Lichtheim. Commentary 40:33-46 S '65; Discussion. 40: 8+ D '65
Britannica joins N.Y. times in social studies program. Pub W 188:69 D 27 '65
Differences at the Times. Time 86:60 Jl 23 '65
Dishing it up in the Times: food editor. il Time 86:57 O 29 '65
Fitzgerald touch. il Newsweek 66:110 N 15 '65
Ghost writers; reporters assigned to cover Pope Paul VI's visit to New York. Newsweek 66:71 O 11 '65
House of Adolph Ochs. R. Kahn. il Sat Eve Post 238:32-8+ O 9 '65
New York times. Newsweek 66:59 N 29 '65
NY times book program. il Pub W 188:23-5 O 18 '65
Pole ax; Warsaw correspondent expelled. Newsweek 67:42 Ja 10 '66
Preserving the news that's fit to print. J. Rothman. Sat R 48:89+ N 13 '65
Taking on the Times; foreign reporting criticized by G. Lichtheim. Newsweek 66: 78 S 13 '65
Trade winds; lightning publication of book on Sir Winston Churchill. J. G. Fuller. il Sat R 48:10 F 20 '65
Year and a half too late; reporting of political turmoil in South Vietnam. America 112:412 Mr 27 '65

NEW YORK times index
Preserving the news that's fit to print. J. Rothman. Sat R 48:89+ N 13 '65

NEW YORK transit strike. See Strikes—United States—Transportation workers

NEW YORK university
Changing the recipe for innkeepers; New York university's course in hotel, restaurant management. il Bsns W p66-8+ F 27 '65
NYU: mecca for transfers. D. Boroff. il Sat R 48:68-9+ Ap 17 '65

Medical center
They rebuild broken faces; Institute of reconstructive plastic surgery, N.Y. G. D. Kittler. Read Digest 87:195-6+ S '65

NEW YORK world
This world we live in; experiences as reporter on the old New York world. S. McKelway. New Yorker 41:155-6+ S 11 '65

NEW YORK Yankees (baseball) See Baseball clubs

NEW YORK zoological park
Turning day into night; Bronx zoo. il Sci Digest 58:inside back cover O '65
Zoo party; Bronx zoo's annual garden party. New Yorker 41:17-18 Je 26 '65
See also
Institute for research in animal behavior

NEW YORKER (periodical)
Department of amplification; reaction to article on New Yorker in New York herald tribune. Newsweek 65:82-3 My 3 '65
New Yorker at forty. il Newsweek 65:62-4 Mr 1 '65
Talk of the town; concerning T. Wolfe article in New York herald tribune. Nat R 17:359-60 My 4 '65
Whisperer; W. Shawn's objection to T. Wolfe's article for Trib's Sunday magazine. il Time 85:60 Ap 16 '65
William and the Wolfe; concerning article in New York herald tribune. il Newsweek 65:62+ Ap 19 '65

NEW YORKERS
Heat wave N.Y. L. Rosten. Look 29:18 S 21 '65
Long-winded lady (cont) New Yorker 41:17-19 Ag 7 '65
One Saturday in Brooklyn. W. Alfred. New Yorker 41:42-6 D 18 '65
Teen-ager tames the city; Karen Koscuik. D. R. Maxey. il Look 29:99-101+ S 21 '65
Tough day in New York. L. Gross. il Look 29:99-101+ N 2 '65

NEW ZEALAND
Traveler in a small utopia; excerpts from letters. C. J. V. Murphy. Fortune 71:92+ My '65
See also
Birds—New Zealand
Parks—New Zealand

Description and travel
Opening up the underneath. G. Chaplin. il Sat R 48:74+ S 18 '65
Travel's picture portfolio. Travel 124:50-5 D '65

Economic conditions
Sooner than *apopo*; creation of a steel industry and a tourist trade. il Time 85:104+ Mr 19 '65

Religious institutions and affairs
News of the Christian world. Christian Cent 82:1611-12 D 29 '65

NEWARK, N.J.

Anti-poverty program
Poverty plums; anti-poverty operations. Reporter 32:16+ Mr 11 '65

Negroes
Negroes move toward power. J. O'Shea. il Atlan 216:90-2+ N '65

NEWARK museum
Current and coming; new acquisitions. R. Davidson. il Antiques 87:638+ Je '65

NEWBERY medal
Children's Pulitzers; 1965 winners. il Newsweek 65:102+ Mr 15 '65
Mia Wojciechowska. J. Karl. Library J 90: 1464-6 Mr 15 '65
Newbery and Caldecott award winners. il ALA Bul 59:238 Ap '65
Newbery and Caldecott winners: Wojciechowska. Montresor. il Pub W 187:26-8 Mr 8 '65
Newbery-Caldecott awards. Wilson Lib Bul 39:627 Ap '65
Newbery runner-up. Library J 90:1467 Mr 15 '65
Say I'm eccentric. H. Frankel. Sat R 48:25 Mr 27 '65
Spring brings the winners. A. Dalgliesh. il Sat R 48:32-3 Mr 27 '65
Teaching Johnny to cop out. S. Maloff. Commonweal 82:321-3 My 28 '65

NEWBORN infants. See Infants, Newborn

NEWBURGH, N.Y.
Progress report; city to build sewage plant. il Newsweek 66:37 N 8 '65

NEWCOMB, Robinson
Why recessions are obsolete. Nations Bsns 53:62-4 My '65

NEWCOMBE, Sylvia C.
Trojan horse tactics. por Recreation 58:234-5+ My '65

NEWCOMER, Leland Byerly
Las Vegas' impressive Newcomer. por Time 86:94+ D 17 '65
Mr '65

NEWELL, David M.
It wasn't my time. Field & S 70:62-5+ S '65
Watch your step! Field & S 70:42-5+ D '65
What scares a deer? Field & S 69:46-8+
Why does a fish? Field & S 70:66-8+ My '65

NEWFIELD, Jack
Question of SNCC. Nation 201:38-40 Jl 19 '65
Revolt without dogma: the student left. Nation 200:491-5 My 10 '65
Student left; idealism and action. Nation 201: 330-3 N 8 '65
There sits Mayor Wagner. Nation 200:267-9 Mr 15 '65

NEWFOUNDLAND
One man's land of romance; Grenfell mission throughout Labrador and Newfoundland. A. Sulley. il Am For 71:12-15+ Jl '65
See also
Fishing—Newfoundland
Funk Island

NEWHOUSE, Edward
Hungarians. New Yorker 41:57-64 N 27 '65

NEWICK, Dick
High speed in the Caribbean. D. Teague. il por Yachting 117:58-9+ Je '65

NEWLEY, Anthony
Poppycocky. il Time 85:83 My 28 '65

NEWLIN, Louisa
Our last day in Venice; story. Atlan 216: 121-4 O '65

NEWMAN, Arnold
Arnold Newman's Europe. pors Pop Phot 56:50-5+ Mr '65

NEWMAN, Barnett
New York school question; interview, ed by N. A. Levine. Art N 64:38-42+ S '65

NEWMAN, Clarence
News for nose. Esquire 64:192-3 D '65

NEWMAN, David, and Benton, Robert
Basic library of trash. Esquire 63:78-9+ F '65
Cal kid. Esquire 64:81-4 S '65
Man talk. See issues of Mademoiselle

NEWMAN, Deborah
Present from Abe; drama. Plays 24:75-8 F '65

NEWMAN, Howard A.
Finding the right combination. por Bsns W p49-50+ Ag 21 '65

NEWMAN, J. Wilson
Longtime credit-rater figures its own future. il pors Bsns W p70+ Ap 10 '65

NEWMAN, James Roy
Books (cont) Sci Am 213:114-17+ D '65

NEWMAN, John Henry, cardinal
Newman: patristics, liberalism and ecumenism. T. Tredway. Christian Cent 82: 987-9 Ag 11 '65; Reply. A. Atkins. 82:1222 O 6 '65
Newman's Apologia, 1965. W. T. Noon. America 112:631-3+ My 1 '65

NEWMAN, L. Hugh
Churchill's interest in animal life. por Audubon Mag 67:240-3 Jl '65
When Churchill brought butterflies to Chartwell. Audubon Mag 67:154-8 My '65

NEWMAN, Louis E.
Man who got the owner's job. il por Bsns W p86+ Je 26 '65

NEWMAN, Marvin E.
High-mountain down; photographs. Sports Illus 23:68-72 N 15 '65
Week to remember. il Sports Illus 22:44-9 Ap 19 '65

NEWMAN, Montgomery
Face of the enemy. New Yorker 41:132-7 My 22 '65

NEWMAN, Paul
Second fame: good food. N. Lyon. il por Vogue 146:144-6 Ag 1 '65

NEWMAN, Paul B.
Knight of infinite resignation; poem. Christian Cent 82:706 Je 2 '65
Radical doubt; poem. Christian Cent 82:1477 D 1 '65
South; poem. Christian Cent 82:1030 Ag 25 '65

NEWMAN, Walter S. and Rusnak, G. A.
Holocene submergence of the eastern shore of Virginia. bibliog Science 148:1464-6 Je 11 '65
—See Krinsley, D. H. jt. auth.

NEWMAN clubs
Crash program for the Newman apostolate. J. L. Quinn. Cath World 202:166-70 D '65
End of the Newman club; golden jubilee congress of the Newman apostolate. R. Butler. Commonweal 82:627-30 S 3 '65
Newman apostolate is not enough. J. J. Kirvan. Cath World 201:308-11+ Ag '65
Newman Apostolate jubilee. America 112:345 Mr 13 '65
Newman jamboree. R. Ellinger. Commonweal 82:632-3 S 24 '65; Discussion. 83:42-3+ O 15 '65

NEWMARK, Esther
New boat, a new venture. il Yachting 118: 61-4+ D '65 (to be cont)

NEWMARK, Eva
Encounters in Virginia; freedom teacher & gentle ladies. Nation 200:193-7 F 22 '65

NEWMONT mining corporation
Newmont mining's fourth generation of gamblers. il Fortune 72:132-7+ O '65

NEWPORT, R.I.
Anyone care to play some VASSS? Van Alen simplified scoring system. F. Deford. il Sports Illus 23:20-2+ Jl 19 '65

Description

Newport, out of season. A. Pryce-Jones. Vogue 145:58 Mr 15 '65

Historic houses

Marble cottages; the Breakers and Marble House. M. Cable. il Horizon 7:18-27, Autumn '65

NEWPORT, R.I. Jazz festival. See Music festivals—Rhode Island

NEWQUIST, Roy
(ed) See Porter, K. A. Interview

NEWS
Tell it to the President; internal news operation to serve the President. J. Osborne. New Repub 153:12-13 O 9 '65
See also
Currents events
Government and the press
Journalism
Radio broadcasting—News
Television broadcasting—News

NEWS agencies
Supplements to the diet; six main supplemental services. Time 87:58+ Ja 14 '66
What passes for American news in Africa. J. Strohmeyer. Harper 231:98+ N '65; Reply with rejoinder. G. Long. 232:8+ Ja '66

NEWS broadcasts. See Radio broadcasting—News

NEWS commentators. See Radio broadcasting—News; Television broadcasting—News

NEWS conferences. See Press conferences

NEWS letters
Newsletters; the ubiquitous medium. J. Tebbel. Sat R 48:57-8 Ag 14 '65

NEWS magazines. See Periodicals

NEWS photography. See Photography, Journalistic

NEWSDAY (newspaper)
Little giant of Nassau County. J. Tebbel. il Sat R 48:68-70 F 13 '65

NEWSLETTERS. See News letters

NEWSOM, David D.
North Africa: active crossroads. Dept State Bul 53:315-22 Ag 23 '65

NEWSOM, John B.
Why a city turned down federal dollars. il por Nations Bsns 53:38-9+ O '65

NEWSPAPER advertising. See Advertising mediums—Newspapers

NEWSPAPER and periodical wholesalers
Large magazine distributors charged by Justice dept. Pub W 187:76 Je 21 '65

NEWSPAPER columns. See Newspapers—Sections, columns, etc.

NEWSPAPER correspondents. See Reporters and reporting

NEWSPAPER court reporting
British verdict on trial-by-press. A. Lewis. il N Y Times Mag p 14-15+ Je 20 '65
Free press vs. fair trial. New Repub 153:7 S 25 '65; Reply. N. Horrock. 153:38 O 16 '65
Trial by newspaper; free press versus the rights of the defendant. N. Hentoff. il Commonweal 82:110-13 Ap 16 '65

NEWSPAPER guild. See American newspaper guild

NEWSPAPER libraries. See Newspapers—Libraries

NEWSPAPER mergers. See Newspapers—Consolidations and mergers

NEWSPAPER publishing
Chicago inheritance. il Time 86:69 O 1 '65
Collector; R. Thomson. il Time 86:53 N 26 '65
Mergers: latest edition; New York metropolitan newspapers may pool their printing facilities. Bsns W p31 Je 19 '65
Money, merger, and monopoly. R. L. Tobin. Sat R 48:45-6 Jl 10 '65
Newspapers fight a dollar deadline. il Bsns W p 136+ S 11 '65
What's wrong with the press? il Newsweek 66:55-8+ N 29 '65
Who says newspapers are going broke? F. B. Gilbreth. Sat R 48:74-6 D 11 '65

Automation

Troubled tide of automation. il Time 86:42+ Jl 16 '65

NEWSPAPER strikes. See Strikes—United States—Newspapers

NEWSPAPERS
City room sagas. J. K. Hutchens. Sat R 48: 27 Mr 20 '65
New life for the Cheshire cat; the small-town weekly. J. Tebbel. Sat R 48:64-5 My 8 '65; Reply. G. H. Danzberger. 48:67 Je 12 '65
Press in developing countries. R. F. Rankin. il Sat R 48:124-5 S 18 '65
Why the Monitor changed. E. D. Canham. il Sat R 48:78-9 Ap 10 '65; Discussion. 48:57+ My 8 '65
See also
Journalism
Publicity
Religious newspapers and periodicals
also names of newspapers, e.g. Times, Los Angeles

Advice columns

Very Dear Abby; abandons McNaught for Chicago tribune-New York news syndicate. Newsweek 66:62 N 8 '65

Animal stories

How to write animal stories. J. O'Reilly. il Sat R 48:54-6 Ag 14 '65

Book reviews

See Book reviews

Consolidations and mergers

Merger in San Francisco; Chronicle and Examiner. il Newsweek 66:61 S 20 '65
Out West, two more papers bite the dust; shake up and consolidation in San Francisco. il Bsns W p30 S 18 '65

NEWSPAPERS and politics
Patriotism of protest; rousing speeches during March on Washington for peace in Vietnam not covered by press. R. G. Sherrill. il Nation 201:463-6 D 13 '65; Correction. 202:inside cover, 45 Ja 10 '66

NEWSPAPERS on microfilm
Preserving the news that's fit to print. J. Rothman. Sat R 48:89+ N 13 '65

NEWSPRINT paper. See Paper

NEWSWRITERS. See Reporters and reporting

NEWTON, Derek A.
Advertising agency services: make or buy? Harvard Bsns R 43:111-18 Jl '65

NEWTON, Douglas
Books in review. Natur Hist 74:6+ O '65

NEWTON, Sir Isaac
Spectrum: all colors of the rainbow. il Sci Digest 57:85-7 Ap '65

NEWTON, Stella Mary
Study of dress in the works of the old masters. Antiques 88:650-5 N '65

NEWTON, Mass.

Education
Newton: pipeline from Harvard. P. Shrag; reply. D. P. Adam. Sat R 48:67 Ap 17 '65

NEWTS eyes. See Eye (amphibia)

NEY, E. P. and Huch, W. F.
Gemini V experiments on zodiacal light and gegenschein. bibliog Science 150:53-6, 1629 O 1, D 17 '65

NEYLAND, Leedell W.
Negro history; address, July 12, 1965. Vital Speeches 31:765-8 O 1 '65

NEZ Percé Indians
Most satisfactory council; excerpts from Nez Perce Indians and the opening of the Northwest. A. M. Josephy, jr. il Am Heritage 16:26-31+ O '65
Nez Perce Indians and the opening of the Northwest, by A. M. Josephy, jr. Review Time il 86:136+ N 19 '65

NGENDANDUMWE, Pierre
Two premiers felled. por Sr Schol 86:18 F 11 '65

NGO-dinh-Diem
Last of the Mandarins, by A. T. Bouscaren. Review
Sat R 48:63 My 22 '65. J. M. Allison
Mission in torment, by J. Mecklin. Review Time 85:95 Je 11 '65
Tragedy of Diem and the paradox of Asia: interview, ed. by D. L. Flaherty. M. L. West. America 112:352-6 Mr 13 '65
Vietnam: in and out of focus. Pyrrho. por Nat R 17:1161-3 D 14 '65

NGUYEN-cao-Ky
General Nguyen Cao Ky: we've got to go fast; interview, ed. by R. Chelminski. pors Life 59:58-60 Jl 23 '65

about
Bust week for Ky and troops. Newsweek 66:44+ S 20 '65
Buy me a coffin. Nat R 17:581-2 Jl 13 '65
Dog that didn't bite. il por Newsweek 66:23+ S 6 '65
Getting to know them. il por Time 86:19 Ag 27 '65
Ky: who rules Vietnam? il pors Newsweek 66:32+ S 27 '65
Playboy to premier. il por Newsweek 66:34+ Jl 12 '65
Ten days of action. il Time 86:24 Jl 2 '65

NGUYEN-duy-Trinh
Tough foe for U.S. Hanoi's new foreign chief. U S News 58:22+ Ap 19 '65

NGUYEN Khanh
From crisis to crisis in Saigon. il U S News 58:28-9 Mr 8 '65
General is back. Time 85:33B-34 F 5 '65
Khanh's farewell. il Newsweek 65:36 Mr 8 '65

NIAGARA FALLS
Let's go again to Niagara. il Time 85:42-3 Je 18 '65
Three centuries of the art of Niagara Falls. N. Lansdale. il Am Artist 29:34-9+ Ap '65

NIAGARA FALLS aquarium. See Aquariums

NIARCHOS, Charlotte (Ford) See Ford, Charlotte

NIARCHOS, Stavros
Yes and no; marriage. il por Newsweek 66: 29 D 27 '65

NICARAGUA
See also
Fishing—Nicaragua

Politics and government
In quest of Sandino, imperialism still rides. C. Beals. Nation 201:83-7 S 20 '65

NICE, France
Embattled Nice: headquarters of the Riviera underworld. Newsweek 66:46 Jl 26 '65
Quick look at Nice's carnival. D. Dodge. Holiday 39:60-1 Ja '66

NICHOLAS, Robert R.
Chill challenge of hard water sailing. il Motor B 116:38-9 D '65

NICHOLS, Beverly
Nature thought of them first. House & Gard 128:96-7 Ag '65

NICHOLS, Dale
Rubbings of Maya monuments. Am Artist 29: 54-7 Ap '65

NICHOLS, Jeannette
Fast run in the junkyard; poem. Atlan 215:68 F '65
Last one in; poem. Sat R 48:68 N 13 '65
Man I know; poem. Sat R 48:41 My 1 '65
Moment; poem. Sat R 48:75 S 25 '65
Return; poem. Harper 231:84 O '65

NICHOLS, John H.
How to teach typewriting with tape recorders. Sr Schol 87:sup7 N 4 '65

NICHOLS, John R.
How opiates change behavior; with biographical sketch. Sci Am 212:16, 80-6+ bibliog(p 135) F '65

NICHOLS, Mike
All for the love of Mike. C. R. Jennings. il pors Sat Eve Post 238:83-7 O 9 '65
View from the penthouse. por Newsweek 65: 89 Ap 5 '65

NICHOLS, Robert C.
Financial status of National merit finalists. bibliog Science 149:1071-4 S 3 '65

NICHOLS, William I.
Youth explosion; address, May 3, 1965. Vital Speeches 31:524-7 Je 15 '65

NICHOLSON, James Hartford
Peekaboo sex, or How to fill a drive-in. A. Levy. il por Life 59:81-2+ Jl 16 '65

NICHOLSON, Jessie
Teapot trouble; drama. Plays 24:61-9 Mr '65

NICHOLSON, Thomas D.
Sky reporter. See issues of Natural history incorporating Nature magazine

NICHOLSON, Timothy
Why Tim killed Todd. il por Newsweek 65:30 Je 21 '65

NICKEL
See also
International nickel company, incorporated
International nickel company of Canada

NICKEL cadmium batteries. See Storage batteries

NICKEL mines and mining
France bets millions on nickel; Societe le nickel. Bsns W p 110+ Ap 24 '65

NICKEL trade
End of the war; banning imports from France containing Cuban nickel. Time 86: 57 D 24 '65

NICKERSON, Albert L.
Dollar's future: what companies will do; interview. por Nations Bsns 53:32-3+ My '65

NICKLAS, R. Bruce, and Jaqua, R. A.
X chromosome DNA replication: developmental shift from synchrony to asynchrony. bibliog Science 147:1041-3 F 26 '65

NICKLAUS, Jack
Gallery had me grinning. por Sports Illus 22:26-9 Ap 26 '65
Golf. See issues of Sports illustrated
It is something special. Sports Illus 22:30-3 Je 14 '65
One way of getting back to business. Sports Illus 22:48 Mr 1 '65

about
All alone at the top. A. Wright. il pors Sports Illus 22:24-9+ Ap 19 '65
Hello, Arnie! il Newsweek 65:88 My 17 '65
Jack Nicklaus: power vs. Palmer. il pors Newsweek 65:82B-85 Je 21 '65
Long live the king! il por Time 86:60 Ag 20 '65
Red tape on the green. Sports Illus 23:8 N 1 '65
Smiling Jack. il por Time 85:82-3 Ap 23 '65
Sporting scene. H. W. Wind. il New Yorker 41:140+ My 1 '65
Virtuoso of three clubs. T. Flaherty. il pors Life 58:115-18 Ap 23 '65

NICKNAMES
See also
Uncle Sam (nickname)
NICOLAI, Otto
On records; Merry wives of Windsor. Opera N
30:30 N 6 '65
NICOLE, Roger
Let us now praise southern justice! Christian
Cent 82:145-6 F 3 '65
NICOLL, William
William Nicoll and Edit. inc. P. A. Bennett.
il por Pub W 188:88-92 D 6 '65
NICOLOFF, Philip
Wildest ride; story. Sat Eve Post 238:48-54
Jl 17 '65
NICOTINE
Nicotine: effect on the sleep cycle of the cat.
E. F. Domino and K. Yamamoto. bibliog il
Science 150:637-8 O 29 '65
Nicotine stimulates cats while they sleep.
Sci N L 88:310 N 13 '65
NIEBERDING, C. B.
Let kids take their own pictures! il Pop Phot
57:144-5 N '65
NIEBERL, Helen R.
From rich homes or poor. NEA J 54:45-6
O '65
NIEBUHR, Reinhold
Lessons of the Detroit experience. Christian
Cent 82:487-90 Ap 21 '65
Martin Buber: in memoriam. Sat R 48:37
Jl 24 '65
Religion of Abraham Lincoln. Christian Cent
82:172-5 F 10 '65
Sex crimes in the spotlight. Harper 231:137-8
S '65
Some things I have learned. por Sat R 48:
21-4+ N 6 '65

about
In perspective. por Newsweek 66:68 N 8 '65
Taking inventory. por Time 86:79 N 5 '65
Taking man's measure. M. Wreszin. Nation
202:19-22 Ja 3 '66
NIEBUHR, Richard R.
Power and a goodness. Christian Cent 82:
1472-5 D 1 '65
NIEDECKER, Lorine
Five poems: To my pressure pump; Consider
at the outset; March; Spring stood there
all body; Park a darling walk for the mind;
poems. Poetry 106:341-4 Ag '65
NIEDERS, H.
Electrolytic capacitors. Electr World 74:57-60
Jl '65
NIEHANS, Ken. See Wilson, T. jt. auth.
NIEHANS, Paul
I took the Niehans treatment. H. Worden.
por Vogue 147:76-7+ Ja 15 '66
NIEHUIS, Dave
Art of varmint calling. pors Outdoor Life
136:36-9+ Ag '65
NIELSEN, Carl
Nielsen centennial. F. Stevenson. il Hi Fi
15:138 Ag '65
Nielsen centennial recording of Bernstein's
Espansiva. J. W. Barker. il por Am Rec
G 32:18-21 S '65
Unmelancholy Dane. S. A. K. Roewade. por
Opera N 29:6-7 My 1 '65
NIELSEN, Charles M.
Loneliness of Protestantism. Christian Cent
82:1120-1 S 15 '65
NIELSEN, Claus
Pogonophora; living species found off the
coast of Florida. bibliog Science 150:1475 D
10 '65
NIELSEN, Sivert A.
United Nations commemoration address, June
25, 1965. UN Mo Chron 2:133-5 Jl '65
NIELSEN rating system. See Television broad-
casting—Program rating
NIEMCEWICZ, Julian Ursyn
Visit to Mount Vernon; excerpts from Travels
through America; tr. and ed. by M. J. E.
Budka. por Am Heritage 16:64-71 F '65
NIERENBERG, William A.
Nato science program. Bul Atomic Sci 21:
45-8 My '65
NIERING, W .A. and Whittaker, R. H.
Saguaro problem and grazing in southwestern
national monuments. bibliog Nat Parks Mag
39:4-9 Je '65
NIETZSCHE, Friedrich Wilhelm
Nietzsche. by K. Jaspers. Review
New Repub 152:24-6 Je 26 '65. N. S. Care
Sat R por 48:36+ My 22 '65. W. Kauf-
mann
NIEUWERKERK, H. T. M. See Bekkum, D.
W. van. jt. auth.
NIEWISCH, Helgard B. See Matioli, G. T. jt.
auth.

NIEWOEHNER, Carl
Low cost bird feeding. Audubon Mag 67:257
Jl '65
NIGER
Assassination that failed. G. Comte. Nat R
17:509-10 Je 15 '65

History
Niger Republic. R. J. H. Church. bibilog il
Focus 16:1-6 S '65
NIGERIA
King at work; Deji of Akure. il N Y Times
Mag p99-100 Ap 25 '65
Nigerian millionaires. il Time 86:122 S 17 '65
See also
Agriculture—Nigeria
Airlines—Nigeria
Church unity—Nigeria
Economic assistance in Nigeria
Elections—Nigeria
Hospitals—Nigeria

Economic conditions
Men who build Nigeria's big business. il
Bsns W p 116+ S 18 '65
On the threshold of take-off. E. Behr. il
Newsweek 66:46-8 Ag 9 '65

History
Yoruba warfare in the 19th century, by J. F.
Ade Ajayi and R. S. Smith. Review
Negro Hist Bul 28:139-40 Mr '65. A. C.
Hill

Native races
Heritage of survival; Kofyar terraces pre-
serve soil and water. R. M. Netting. il
Natur Hist 74:14-21 Mr '65

Politics and government
Essentials for Nigerian survival. N. Azikiwe.
For Affairs 43:447-61 Ap '65
Flickering light; election rigging causes riots.
Newsweek 66:52+ N 22 '65
Fragile stability. Time 87:22 Ja 21 '66
Nigerian tragedy. Newsweek 67:39-40 Ja 24
'66
Power of juju; magic to overthrow govern-
ment. il Time 86:36 S 3 '65
Way the West was won; post-election
violence. Time 86:54 N 19 '65

Religious institutions and affairs
See also
Church unity—Nigeria

Social conditions
Day they banned the mammy wagons. il Time
85:41 Je 11 '65
NIGERIA airways. See Airlines—Nigeria
NIGERIAN millionaires. See Millionaires
NIGERIANS
Men who build Nigeria's big business. il
Bsns W p 116+ S 18 '65
NIGHT airglow. See Airglow
NIGHT call. See Radio broadcasting—Religious
programs
NIGHT clubs
And another who never went away; J.
Durante at the Copacabana in New York.
S. Moore. Life 58:12 Ap 9 '65
Discothèque. N. Poirier. il Sat Eve Post
238:21-7 Mr 27 '65
Empire built on sex; with report by D. Lurie.
il Life 59:68-73 O 29 '65
Everything was coming up Arthur; New
York night life. il Time 85:67 My 14 '65
Fall of the velvet rope; Manhattan's Stork
club, closed. il Time 86:70 O 15 '65
Go-go, and hurry; it's later than you think.
P. Bogdanovich. il Esquire 63:86-91 F '65
Instant discotheque; just add dancers. il
Bsns W p 108-10 F 27 '65
I.T.S.C.A. International theatre and supper
clubs association convention. New Yorker
41:48-9 O 30 '65
Meet you at the . . .? Stork club closed. il
Newsweek 66:42+ O 18 '65
Merry Bonenkai; Tokyo's nightspots. il Time
86:18 D 31 '65
Package: discotheque. promotion of Seeburg
corporation. New Yorker 41:26-7 F 27 '65
Some enchanting evening; supper club de-
voted to magicians and magic lovers. il
Time 86:88 S 24 '65
Starecase; Daisy, Beverly Hills. il Time 85:
60 Ap 23 '65
Summer camp; High camp, Squaw Valley.
il Time 86:62 Ag 13 '65
Wild scene at Arthur. L. Bergquist. il Look
29:40-2+ N 30 '65

NIGHT clubs—*Continued*

Employees

Playboy of the western night world; night manager of Playboy club. il Ebony 20:103-4+ Jl '65

NIGHT crawlers. See Earthworms

NIGHT driving, Automobile. See Automobile driving

NIGHT for celebration; story. See White, V. R.

NIGHT labor. See Night work

NIGHT photography. See Photography, Night

NIGHT sky. See Sky

NIGHT walk; story. See Ballvé, J.

NIGHT watch; story. See Boles, P. D.

NIGHT work

Provisions for late shifts in manufacturing industries. A. Strasser. il Mo Labor R 88:511-16 My '65

NIGHTCLUBS. See Night clubs

NIGHTGLOW. See Airglow

NIGHTINGALE, E. M.

Ariadne exposed; drama. Plays 25:15-20 Ja '66

NIKE X. See Guided missiles—Defenses

NIKOLAIS, Alwin

Alwin Nikolais, Henry street playhouse. J. Maskey. Dance Mag 39:61 My '65

NIKTON, N. N.

Movies. Vogue 146:69 N 15 '65

NILAND, John

Caught in the draught. H. L. Masin. por Sr Schol 87:40 N 11 '65

NILE RIVER

Yankee cruises the storied Nile. I. Johnson and E. Johnson. il Nat Geog Mag 127:583-633 My '65

See also

Aswan High Dam

NILE VALLEY

Maps

Society maps the river of Pharaohs. il Nat Geog Mag 127:634-5, sup(folded map) My '65

NILES, Fred

Divorce, loneliness and remarriage. E. Havemann. il pors Ladies Home J 82:62-3+ Jl '65

NILES, Marye

Divorce, loneliness and remarriage. E. Havemann. il pors Ladies Home J 82:62-3+ Jl '65

NILSSON, Birgit

Moon girl; role of Salome. il por Newsweek 65:86 F 15 '65

Musical events; performance of title role in R. Strauss's Salome. W. Sargeant. New Yorker 40:152-3 F 13 '65

Nilsson's own Elektra. M. Mayer. por Hi Fi 15:134 Ag '65

Salome in silver. il por Time 85:57 F 12 '65

NILSSON, Lennart

Drama of life before birth; photographs. Life 58:54-69 Ap 30 '65

Remarkable photographic feat. G. P. Hunt. por Life 58:3 Ap 30 '65

NILSSON, Nils

Please don't eat the oleander. Pop Mech 124:112-14+ Ag '65

NIMBUS (satellite) See Artificial satellites—Meteorological applications

NIMES, France

In Nimes and New Haven, continuous forms broken into human-sized units. Arch Forum 123:64-5 Jl '65

NIMNI, Marcel E. and Bavetta, L. A.

Collagen defect induced by penicillamine. bibliog Science 150:905-7 N 12 '65

NIMROD, Jean Ann

How to preserve a husband. il Farm J 89:81+ Mr '65

NINETEEN hundred and eighty-four

It's halfway to 1984; concerning G. Orwell's novel. J. Lukacs. il N Y Times Mag p8-9+ Ja 2 '66

NINETEEN hundred and forty

How different we were! 25th reunion at Yale. W. Gibson. il N Y Times Mag p8-9+ Je 13 '65

NINETEEN hundred and sixties

Literature of the early sixties; reprint from Great ideas today, 1964, annual to Great books of the western world. S. Kauffmann. bibliog il Wilson Lib Bul 39:748-56+ My '65

NINETEEN hundred and sixty-five

Esquire's fifth annual dubious achievement awards 1965. il Esquire 65:74-9 Ja '66

Letter from the editor. W. J. Coughlin. Miss & Roc 17:48 D 20 '65

1965 as it looked to Mauldin; cartoons. W. H. Mauldin. New Repub 154:17-19 Ja 8 '66

Summing up. Christian Cent 82:1595 D 29 '65

Unhappy new year. K. Crawford. Newsweek 67:23 Ja 10 '66

Vintage year. il Sat Eve Post 238:92 D 18 '65

Year's best, or There is room at the top; Time essay. Time 86:16-17 D 31 '65

NINETEEN hundred and sixty-six

Greater challenge of 1966. America 114:7 Ja 1 '66

1966: the year of the big if. il Newsweek 67:26+ Ja 10 '66

1966: year of decision. il U S News 60:23-8+ Ja 10 '66

Three experts on the outlook; promises and problems of 1966. P. W. McCracken; P. Samuelson; R. J. Saulnier. Newsweek 67:52-3 Ja 10 '66

NINETEEN hundred and thirties

Starting out in the thirties, by A. Kazin. Review

Newsweek il 66:101+ S 20 '65

Thirties: frayed collars and large visions. L. Kronenberger. Atlan 217:79-81 Ja '66

NINETEEN hundred and twenties

Twenties; symposium. il Am Heritage 16:2-112 Ag '65

NINETY-Nines, incorporated (organization) See Women as air pilots

NINTH amendment. See United States—Constitution—Bill of rights

NIPPON electric company. See Electronic apparatus industry—Japan

NIPSON, Herb

Camera safari to East Africa. il por Ebony 20:148-50+ O '65

NIRENBERG, Marshall W. See Bernfield, M. R. jt. auth.

NISBET, Robert A.

What is an intellectual? Commentary 40:93-4+ D '65

NISEI. See Japanese Americans

NISSELBAUM, J. S. and Bodansky, Oscar

Glutamic-oxaloacetic transaminases in reticulocytes and erythrocytes. bibliog Science 149:195-7 Jl 9 '65

NISSENSON, Hugh

God breaks through. America 112:821 Je 5 '65

NITEHAWK (rocket) See Rockets, Sounding

NITRATES

See also

Silver nitrate

Soils—Nitrogen content

Water supply—Nitrate content

Physiological effects

Excessive nitrate making water unsafe. Sci N L 88:41 Jl 17 '65

NITROGEN

Explosion of burning zirconium droplets caused by nitrogen. L. S. Nelson. bibliog il Science 148:1594-5 Je 18 '65

See also

Plants, Effect of nitrogen on

Industrial applications

Work in the cold. il Fortune 71:213 Je '65

Isotopes

Xenon-photosensitized formation of metastable nitrogen. W. M. Jackson and M. D. Scheer. bibliog il Science 148:1718-19 Je 25 '65

NITROGEN, Liquid

Work in the cold. il Fortune 71:213 Je '65

NITROGEN content of soils. See Soils—Nitrogen content

NITROGEN mustards

Inactivation by nitrogen mustard of single- and double-stranded DNA and RNA bacteriophages. N. Yamamoto and T. Naito. bibliog il Science 150:1603-4 D 17 '65

NITROGEN oxides

Nitrogen: formation by photooxidation of ethylene in the presence of its oxides. J. J. Bufalini and J. C. Purcell. bibliog il Science 150:1161 N 26 '65

NITROSOGUANIDINE. See Guanidine

NITROUS acid

Nitrous acid mutation of transforming DNA: consideration of mode of action. S. H. Goodgal and E. H. Postel. bibliog Science 148:1095-7 My 21 '65

NITZE, Paul H.

Middle East; address, April 21, 1965. Vital Speeches 31:504-9 Je 1 '65

NIU, M. C.

Glucose-6-phosphatase: reexamination of the RNA-induced activity in mouse ascites tumor cells. bibliog Science 148:513-16 Ap 23 '65

NIVOLA, Costantino
Horsy set. il por Time 85:68 F 12 '65

NIX, Lucile
Read! open your future and theirs. bibliog
PTA Mag 59:32-4 Ap '65

NIXON, Howard
Major Abbey's modern bookbindings. Craft
Horiz 25:28-31 Jl '65

NIXON, John, Jr
End of the metal season; poem. Mlle 62:134
N '65

NIXON, Richard Milhous
Facing the facts in Vietnam; address, January 26, 1965. Vital Speeches 31:337-40 Mr
15 '65; Excerpt. Cong Digest 44:110+ Ap '65
Why not negotiate in Vietnam? Read Digest
87:49-54 D '65

about

Dick to the rescue. Nation 201:345-6 N 15 '65
McGovern versus Nixon. Nation 200:126-7 F 8
'65
Next chief of the GOP. E. J. Hughes. News-
week 66:19 N 29 '65
Nixon on the move; is his eye on '68 cam-
paign? U S News 59:19 S 27 '65
Nixon on Vietnam. R. Moley. Newsweek 65:
120 Ap 12 '65
Now, we can. Time 85:21 F 5 '65
On the road. il por Newsweek 66:27-8 S 27 '65
Over-nominated under-elected, still a promis-
ing candidate. R. J. Donovan. il pors N Y
Times Mag p 14-15+ Ap 25 '65

NIXON, Robert E.
Profile of normality; reprint. Sr Schol 87:sup8
N 18 '65

NKRUMAH, Kwame
When Nkrumah bit the hand that fed him;
summary of Neocolonialism: the last stage
of imperialism. por U S News 59:19 D 6 '65

about

Conflict of summits. Time 86:21 Ag 27 '65
Eliminating the frills. Newsweek 65:43-4 Je
21 '65
Fateful moment at the Maginot Hilton. Time
86:37 O 29 '65
Host with the most. Newsweek 66:43 N 1 '65
Loneliness of Kwame Nkrumah. J. K. Sale. il
pors N Y Times Mag p20-1+ Je 27 '65
Lord high everything. il Newsweek 65:51 Ap
12 '65

NO drama. See Japanese drama
NO game for children; story. See Gaines, D.
NO more roses; story. See Seager, A.
NO one kicks cans any more; story. See
Randall, F. E.
NO quarter asked; story. See Fontaine, R.

NOAH, Harold J.
Soviet education's unsolved problems. Sat R
48:54-6+ Ag 21 '65

NOAH'S ark
Noah; literal view of the Bible in Huston's
new movie, The Bible. il Look 29:21-6 Jl 27
'65

NOAILLES, Marie Laure, vicomtesse de
Second fame: good food. N. Lyon. por Vogue
145:148-50 Mr 15 '65

NOBEL foundation
How Nobel prize fund pays way. il Bsns W
p36 D 11 '65

NOBEL prizes
France considers significance of Nobel awards.
V. K. McElheny. il Science 150:1013-15
N 19 '65
How Martin Luther King won the Nobel
peace prize; with list of recent winners.
il U S News 58:76-7 F 8 '65
How Nobel prize fund pays way. il Bsns W
p36 D 11 '65
Is the Nobel prize for literature political?
R. J. Clements. il Sat R 48:41-2+ D 4 '65
Just what is a Nobel prize? Good H 161:176
O '65
Mikhail Sholokhov awarded Nobel prize in
literature. Pub W 188:53 O 25 '65
Nobel peace prize for the love of children;
award to UNICEF. il Life 59:30-7 N 5 '65
Nobel prize awarded; three French scientists
sharing prize in physiology or medicine.
F. Marley. il Sci N L 88:261 O 23 '65
Nobel prize winners; physics and chemistry
awards. il Sci N L 88:279 O 30 '65
Nobel prizes. Sci Am 213:38-40 D '65
Peace prize to UNICEF. Sr Schol 87:10 N 11
'65
Peace prize: UNICEF. New Yorker 41:44-7
N 6 '65

Synthesizers; awards in science. Newsweek
66:56 N 1 '65
Three Americans win Nobel science prizes.
Pub W 188:74-5 N 15 '65
Three men & a messenger; prize in phys-
iology and medicine. il Time 86:101 O 22 '65
Tomonga, Schwinger, and Feynman awarded
Nobel prize for physics. F. J. Dyson. il
Science 150:588-9 O 29 '65
Tortuous road to Oslo. C. L. Sanders. il
Ebony 20:36+ Mr '65
See also
Jacob, F.
Lwoff, A.
Monod, J.
Woodward, R. B.

NOBILE, Philip
Visit to Taizé. America 114:21-2 Ja 1 '66

NOBIS, Tommy
Nobis oblige. il pors Newsweek 66:63 D 27 '65
Nobis roamer of them all. H. L. Masin. por
Sr Schol 87:24 O 14 '65
1-A in football draft; with report by J. R.
McDermott. il pors Life 59:36-41 D 10 '65
There's no show biz like Nobis. D. Jenkins.
il pors Sports Illus 23:40-2+ O 18 '65

NOBLE, James, conifer collection. See Conifers

NOBLE, Mary
Seeds of success. il Flower Grower 53:27
Ja '66

NOBLE, Richard
When the sun is low. il U S Camera 28:62-3
Mr '65

NOBLE and Noble publishers, incorporated
Dell publishing acquires Noble & Noble. Pub
W 187:34 My 24 '65

NOBLE gases. See Gases, Rare
NOBLE metals. See Metals
NOBODY believes in witches! drama. See Wat-
kins, M. S.
Les NOCES; ballet. See Ballets—Criticisms

NOCHLIN, Linda
Camille Pissarro: the unassuming eye. Art N
64:24-7+ Ap '65

NOCTILUCA miliaris. See Dinoflagellates
NOCTILUCENT clouds. See Clouds

NODEL, Sol
Ancient art of illumination. il pors Design 66:
17-20 Ja '65

NOEL, Lois Jones Pierre-. See Pierre-Noel,
L. J.

NOETHER, Emiliana P.
(comp) Articles and other books received;
Italy. See issues of American historical
review

NOGA, Helen
Johnny Mathis: millionaire with problems.
L. Robinson. il por Ebony 20:99-102+ Mr
'65

NOGEE, Joseph L.
Neutralist world and disarmament negotia-
tions. bibliog f Ann Am Acad 362:71-80
N '65

NOGUEIRA, Franco
Breakdown of international law and order;
address, October 11, 1965. Vital Speeches
32:81-4 N 15 '65

NOISE
It's not the noise, it's the annoyance. il
House & Gard 127:148-55+ Ap '65
Just a shimmy, no bang-bang; pile driver in
Schenectady, N.Y. il Am City 80:24 S '65
Law of noise. Time 86:37-8 S 10 '65
Let's take the din out of living. W. R.
Vath. il Todays Health 43:6-7+ F '65
Noise pollutes air. Sci N L 87:389 Je 19 '65
Quiet, please! P. Nathan. il Parents Mag
40:56-7+ O '65
Sound of sounds that is New York. H. C.
Schonberg. il N Y Times Mag p38+ My 23
'65
See also
Electric resistors—Noise
Electronic apparatus and appliances—Noise

Physiological effects
Infrasound tests human tolerance. H. M.
David. Miss & Roc 17:31+ O 11 '65

NOISE, Radio. See Radio interference
NOISE generator. See Sound—Apparatus
NOISE suppressors. See Sound suppressors
NOISES, Head. See Tinnitus

NOLAN, Martin F.
Saltonstall's successor. New Repub 154:8 Ja
22 '66

NOLAN, Paul T.
Birthday of the infanta; dramatization of story by O. Wilde. Plays 24:85-95 Ap '65
Inexperienced ghost; dramatization of story by H. G. Wells. Plays 25:87-96 O '65
View of the sea; drama. Plays 24:31-42 Mr '65

NOLDAN, Henry
BLM's tenor in the timber. F. Bradford. il pors Am For 71:32-3+ Je '65

NOLL, Bink
Ralph Jones' pain; poem. Sat R 48:64 N 6 '65
That windworthy house; poem. Commonweal 82:440 Je 25 '65

NOLTE, Charles
Do not pass go. Criticism
Commonweal 82:290+ My 21 '65
New Yorker 41:122 My 8 '65

NOMAD, Max
No rules but their own rules. Sat R 48:34-5 Ap 24 '65
No short cut to Soviet paradise. Sat R 48:39+ N 20 '65

NOMOGRAPHY. See Charts, Calculating

NONALIGNMENT. See Neutrality

NONCONFORMIST; story. See Bell, E.

NONCONFORMITY See Conformity

NONDESTRUCTIVE testing. See Testing

NON-GOVERNMENTAL organizations of the United Nations. See United Nations—Nongovernmental organizations

NONGRADED classes. See Ungraded classes

NON-LETHAL gases in warfare. See Gases in warfare

NON-LINEAR systems, incorporated
When workers manage themselves; permissive management. il Bsns W p93-4 Mr 20 '65

NON-MUSICAL phonograph records. See Phonograph records—Spoken records

NONO, Luigi
Firebrand of Venice. M. J. Matz. il pors Opera N 29:6-7 F 13 '65
Intolerance, 1960 (Intolleranza, 1960) Criticism
Newsweek il 65:84 Mr 8 '65
Opera N 29:34 My 1 '65
Time il 85:66 Mr 5 '65

NONPROFIT corporations. See Corporations, Nonprofit

NONRESIDENT borrowers. See Libraries—Registration

NON-SELF governing territories. See Colonies

NONSTICK cookware. See Kitchen utensils

NON-VIOLENT non-cooperation. See Passive resistance to government

NON-WAGE payments
Fringe benefits: why, when and how. M. Starr. bibliog f Cur Hist 49:29-35 Jl '65
Fringe binge: how much it's costing now. il U S News 59:89-90 S 27 '65
Supplemental wage benefits in metropolitan areas, 1963-64. J. E. Buckley. il Mo Labor R 88:550-4 My '65
Where raises are headed now; fringe benefits. U S News 59:81-2 Ag 9 '65

NON-WESTERN studies. See Area studies

NOODLES
She's serving green noodles. il Sunset 134:228+ Mr '65

NOON, William T.
Newman's Apologia, 1965. America 112:631-3+ My 1 '65

NORAD. See North American air defense command

NORADRENALINE. See Adrenalin

NORDBERG, William
Geophysical observations from Nimbus I. bibliog Science 150:559-72 O 29 '65

NORDELL, Roderick
Superman revisited. Atlan 217:104-5 Ja '66

NORDICA, Lillian
Yankee diva, by I. Glackens. Review
Am Rec G il por 31:884-5 My '65. J. Maclain

NORDLING, Raoul
General who defied Hitler. H. Ehrlich. il Look 30:48+ Ja 25 '66

NORDQUIST, Edwin C.
Why a complete soil analysis is important. Arch Rec 137:215-16 Je '65

NORDSTROM, Ursula
In defense of children's books: price, quality, durability; summary of address. Pub W 187:33-4 Mr 15 '65

NOREPINEPHRINE
Acidosis: effect on lipolytic activity of norepinephrine in isolated fat cells. L. Triner and G. G. Nahas. bibliog il Science 150:1725-7 D 24 '65

NORFOLK and Western railway-Chesapeake and Ohio merger. See Railroads—Consolidations and mergers

NORMAN, Amos, and others
Lymphocyte lifetime in women. bibliog Science 147:745 F 12 '65

NORMAN, Anthony W.
Actinomycin D and the response to vitamin D. bibliog Science 149:184-6 Jl 9 '65

NORMAN, Gurney
Men and boys on Lost Creek road. por Am Ed 1:8-12 Ap '65

NORMAN, Guy
Take my hand; story. Good H 161:88-9 N '65

NORMAN, John C.
Pig liver: new spare for humans. il pors Ebony 20:57-8+ S '65

NORODOM Sihanouk, king of Cambodia (abdicated 1955)
Atlantic report. Atlan 216:20+ Jl '65
Close-up of a red sanctuary; Cambodia and its leaky border. S. W. Sanders. il por U S News 60:48-9 Ja 3 '66
Embattled prince. Time 87:25B Ja 21 '66
Prince of the Khmers. V. S. Kearney. America 112:715-16 My 15 '65
Real reason why Prince Sihanouk broke with America. por U S News 58:24 My 17 '65
Scuttled hopes. il Newsweek 65:56+ My 17 '65
Sihanouk, stay home. Newsweek 66:53 N 1 '65
Snookie's snub. il por Time 85:36 My 7 '65
We don't live in the clouds. B. Krisher. il por Newsweek 65:46-7 Ap 5 '65
When a prince got a kick in the pants. il por U S News 59:26 N 8 '65

NORRIS, Charles W.
Fresh raspberries. Pop Gard 16:21+ Ap '65

NORRIS, Hoke
Two kinds of censorship. PTA Mag 59:10-12 bibliog(p36) Mr '65

NORRIS, Kenneth S.
Trained porpoise released in the open sea. bibliog Science 147:1048-50 F 26 '65

NORRISH, R. G. W.
Kinetics and analysis of very fast chemical reactions; address, January 14, 1965. bibliog Science 149:1470-82 S 24 '65

NORRISTOWN, Pa.
Solving land-use determinations electronically. D. B. Witwer. il Am City 80:90-1 F '65

NORRISTOWN, Pa, public library
Avenues of cooperation. Mrs H. Frankenfield. ALA Bul 59:744-5 S '65

NORTH, Arthur A.
Book review. America 113:446-8 O 16 '65

NORTH, Henry Ringling
Resurgence. New Yorker 41:38-9 Ap 10 '65

NORTH, Myles E. W. See Thorpe, W. H. jt. auth.

NORTH, Sterling
Frog's-eye view at Walden Pond. Sat R 49:39 Ja 15 '66

NORTH AMERICA
See also
Birds—North America

NORTH AMERICAN air defense command
Come visit the village inside a mountain. D. Francis. il Pop Sci 187:96-9+ N '65
Finally: an attack-proof center for U.S. defense; NORAD's Combat operations center at Cheyenne Mountain, Colo. il U S News 60:54-7 Ja 24 '66
Navy improves accuracy, detection range of space surveillance chain. P. J. Klass. il Aviation W 83:56-7+ Ag 16 '65
Norad operations center. P. J. Klass. il Aviation W 82:66+ F 1; 65-8 F 8 '65

NORTH AMERICAN aviation, incorporated
Incentive basis set for NAA Apollo work. Aviation W 83:79 N 29 '65
North American accelerates COIN work. D. E. Fink. il Aviation W 82:20-2 F 8 '65
NAA easily repeats as top contractor. Miss & Roc 16:18 F 15 '65
North American continues to lead NASA contractors in fiscal 1965. Aviation W 83:34 D 13 '65
NAC-100 decision awaits new surveys. il Aviation W 83:29 Jl 5 '65
R&D needs outlined; NAA transportation study to go on. Miss & Roc 18:23 Ja 17 '66

Ocean systems division
North American sets up Ocean systems facility. Miss & Roc 17:28 N 1 '65

Space and information systems division
North American prepares report on paraglider flight test results. Aviation W 83:34 N 15 '65

NORTH AMERICAN bicycle championship race.
See Bicycle racing

NORTH AMERICAN Indians. See Indians of
North America

NORTH AMERICAN newspaper alliance
Long, hard night of the TV commercial;
nationwide poll on television programing
and commercials. R. L. Tobin. Sat R 48:
65-6 Ap 10 '65; Discussion. 48:55-7 My 8;
66-7 Je 12 '65

NORTH AMERICAN power and water alliance
Nawapa: water for the year 2000. R. S.
Lewis. il Bul Atomic Sci 21:9-11 My '65

NORTH AMERICAN wildlife and natural re-
sources conference
Conference finds renewed hope. H. Titus.
Field & S 70:32+ Je '65

NORTH ATLANTIC council. See North Atlantic
treaty organization

NORTH ATLANTIC treaty organization
And then there were two: American-German
alliance. W. Pfaff. Commonweal 82:683-4
S 24 '65
Atlanticism. P. Johnson. Commentary 40:110-
12 S '65
Books. R. Steel. Commonweal 83:104-6 O 22
'65
Competition may widen U.S.-French rift. L.
L. Doty. Aviation W 82:17 Mr 1 '65
Function of the Atlantic alliance; address,
October 4, 1965. M. Brosio. Vital Speeches
32:41-6 N 1 '65
Future of NATO: areas of common effort; ad-
dress, October 5, 1965. H. H. Humphrey.
Dept State Bul 53:650-3 O 25 '65
Grand frustrations; annual spring meeting.
Newsweek 65:51-2 My 24 '65
How NATO works when politics is left out:
U.S. troops with Turks and Greeks. il U S
News 59:8 O 4 '65
How sick is NATO? Time 85:23B Mr 12 '65
If France pulls out, the future of NATO. M.
S. Johnson. il U S News 59:40-2 S 27 '65
Impact of change in eastern Europe on the
Atlantic partnership; address, April 3, 1965.
J. R. Schaetzel. Dept State Bul 53:161-71
Jl 26 '65
Military common market sought. Miss & Roc
16:17 Je 7 '65
Mr Ball discusses U.S. relations with Europe
on BBC; interview, ed. by A. Burnet, Octo-
ber 2, 1965. G. W. Ball. Dept State Bul 53:
653-60 O 25 '65
Much to talk about in 1966. America 114:35-6
Ja 8 '66
Must anything be done about Europe? will-
fulness of Charles de Gaulle; Time essay.
Time 86:28-9 D 3 '65
National networks complicate NADGE. Avia-
tion W 82:77-8 Je 14 '65
North Atlantic council meets at London; text
of communique, May 13, 1965, with annex.
Dept State Bul 52:926-8 Je 7 '65
North Atlantic council meets at Paris; text
of communique, December 16, 1965, and list
of the members of the U.S. delegation.
Dept State Bul 54:7-10 Ja 3 '66
NATO after sixteen years: an anniversary
assessment. D. H. Popper. il Dept State
Bul 52:518-27 Ap 12 '65
NATO common market; excerpts from ad-
dress. H. J. Kuss. Aviation W 83:11 O
18 '65
NATO conference to discuss role of civil
aviation in emergency. Dept State Bul 53:
609 O 11 '65
NATO defense ministers meet at Paris;
June 1, 1965. Dept State Bul 52:993 Je 21
'65
Nato science program. W. A. Nierenberg.
Bul Atomic Sci 21:45-8 My '65
NATO strategy: what is past is prologue.
H. Owen. For Affairs 43:682-90 Jl '65
NATO: the entangled alliance. S. Muller. Bul
Atomic Sci 21:26-8 N '65
Nato tomorrow. H. A. Crosby. Bul Atomic
Sci 21:18-21 My '65
NATO without France? Time 86:50+ N 5 '65
NATO's cohesiveness continues to ebb. L. L.
Doty. Aviation W 82:95+ Mr 15 '65
NATO's end. Nat R 17:492 Je 15 '65
NATO's uneven steps toward integration. H.
W. Baldwin. Reporter 32:32-4 Mr 11 '65
Other end of the telescope; address, October
21, 1965. H. Cleveland. Dept State Bul 53:
781-7 N 15 '65
Our Atlantic policy; address, March 6, 1965.
D. Rusk. Dept State Bul 52:427-31 Mr
22 '65
Palmerstonian America. G. Lichtheim. Com-
mentary 40:58-62 Jl '65
Red world vs. the West, which is stronger?
il U S News 60:34-6 Ja 10 '66

Secretary Rusk's news conference of Novem-
ber 5, 1965. D. Rusk. Dept State Bul 53:
854-62 N 29 '65
Tidying the war room. il Time 85:36+ Je 11
'65
Tomorrow's Atlantic alliance. G. C. Smith.
America 113:132-5 Ag 7 '65
Troubled partnership, by H. A. Kissinger.
Review
Nat R 17:512-13 Je 15 '65. M. S. Evans
Reporter 33:57-9 S 23 '65. B. Brodie
Sat R 48:41-2 Jl 24 '65. A. Henderson
Twilight of NATO. M. Frankel. il N Y Times
Mag p54-5+ D 5 '65
United States, France, and NATO: a com-
parison of two approaches; address, Janu-
ary 21, 1965. D. H. Popper. Dept State
Bul 52:180-7 F 8 '65
US option in Europe: a pro-French policy.
R. Masters. New Repub 153:7-9 D 4 '65
Veto by France? two rumors. Newsweek 46:
44+ N 1 '65
Watch their smoke! meeting of Defense min-
isters. Newsweek 65:58+ Je 14 '65
West's mission is now in east Europe. Life
58:4 My 28 '65
What to watch for in Europe. F. Morley. il
Nations Bsns 53:27-8 Ap '65
Who is the real realist? constructive role
of de Gaulle. A. de Borchgrave. il News-
week 66:47-8+ D 13 '65
See also
Atlantic community
Supreme headquarters, Allied powers, Europe

Meetings, 1965
Old problems never die: Paris three-day review of state of alliance. il Newsweek 66:
31 D 27 '65
Special committee of NATO defense ministers
meets at Paris; final communique; November 27, 1965. Dept State Bul 53:939 D 13 '65

Multilateral force (proposed)
MLF & other problems. G. Lichtheim; reply
with rejoinder. D. Rush. Commentary 39:
22+ My '65

NORTH ATLANTIC yacht racing union
Changes in the racing rules. R. N. Bavier,
jr. Yachting 117:51+ Mr '65

NORTH BORNEO
More cracks in Malaysia. D. Warner. il Reporter 33:40-2 O 7 '65

NORTH CAROLINA
See also
Architecture, Domestic—North Carolina
Birds—North Carolina
Education—North Carolina
Fishing—North Carolina
Law—North Carolina
Libraries—North Carolina
Winston-Salem

Capitol
1840 North Carolina capitol and its furniture.
J. Craig. il Antiques 88:205-7 Ag '65

Historic houses, etc.
1840 North Carolina capitol and its furniture.
J. Craig. il Antiques 88:205-7 Ag '65

NORTH CAROLINA arts and crafts. See Arts
and crafts—United States

NORTH CAROLINA pageants. See Pageants

NORTH CAROLINA, University, Chapel Hill
Academic casualty; North Carolina speaker-
ban law. C. N. Degler. New Repub 153:10
Jl 10 '65

Futile bans on ideas; protest against state
law barring Communist lecturers. Time 85:
74+ Je 11 '65

Speaker ban: North Carolina law. L. J.
Carter. il Science 150:589-91, 725-8 O 29-N 5
'65

Speaker ban: State assembly kills law denying forum to Communists: U.N.C.'s status
is believed safe. L. J. Carter. Science 150:
1141+ N 26 '65

Who's for academic freedom? K. L. Penegar.
New Repub 153:15-17 D 4 '65

Charlotte campus
School Miss Bonnie built. il Time 86:56 Jl 16
'65

NORTH CASCADES NATIONAL PARK (proposed) See National parks and reserves—
United States

NORTH CASCADES primitive area. See Wilderness areas

NORTH CHANNEL
North Channel cruise. C. H. Vilas. il Yachting
117:46-8+ My; 60-2+ Je '65

NORTH DAKOTA
North Dakota runs down. A. Stern. Nation 201:41 Jl 19 '65
See also
Geology—North Dakota

NORTH DAKOTA. University, Grand Forks
Univ. of North Dakota library ends statewide loan service. Library J 90:2520 Je 1 '65

NORTH KOREA. See Korea (People's Democratic Republic)

NORTH MIAMI, Fla.
Salt water in the sewers. F. J. Miller. il Am City 80:112+ D '65

NORTH of Boston; story. See Knowlton, R. A.

NORTH star. See Pole star

NORTH star all steel drum band. See Bands (music)

NORTH TONAWANDA, N.Y.
Sanitary fill supermechanized. il Am City 80:20 D '65

NORTH VIETNAM. See Vietnam (Democratic Republic)

NORTHCOTT, Cecil
Evanston after eleven years. Christian Cent 82:1005-6 Ag 18 '65
Gambling on God. Christian Cent 82:765-6 Je 16 '65
Pistol-proud pupils. Christian Cent 82:1215 O 6 '65
Punctures balloon words. Christian Cent 82:134 F 3 '65
Reasonable instrument. Christian Cent 82:1265 O 13 '65
Will Rome take the pill? Christian Cent 82:518 Ap 28 '65

NORTHEAST airlines, Incorporated
New course for Northeast? Storer broadcasting co. of Miami, Fla. il Newsweek 65:90+ Je 14 '65
Northeast asks fares geared to seat needs. Aviation W 82:45 Ap 19 '65
Northeast keys Florida bid to new jets. W. Wright. Aviation W 83:45 Ag 23 '65
Northeast may have a buyer; Storer broadcasting co, Miami. Bsns W p31 Je 5 '65
Northeast's next pilot? il Bsns W p39-40 Je 12 '65
Northeast's $100-million gamble; moneymaking route: New York-Florida. Bsns W p34 Ag 14 '65

NORTHEAST regional ballet festival. See Dance festivals

NORTHEASTERN states
See also
Gardens—Northeastern states
Water supply—Norteastern states

NORTHERN IRELAND
See also
Elections—Northern Ireland
Investments, Foreign (in Northern Ireland)
Ireland

Industries
How to import jobs. il Fortune 72:62+ Ag '65

NORTHERN lights. See Auroras

NORTHMEN
See also
Vikings

NORTHWEST
See also
Frontier and pioneer life—United States
Hunting—Northwestern states

History
Mosquitoes, mules, and men: Pacific Northwest; with sketches by A. Downing. B. Le Roy. Am Heritage 16:102-7 Ap '65

Industries
Tightening trade ties with Japan; Pacific Northwest products at industrial fair in Tokyo. il Bsns W p 104-6+ Ap 24 '65

NORTHWEST, Old
Old Northwest Territory; symposium. il Antiques 87:300-31 Mr '65

Historic houses, etc.
Furniture and interiors. il Antiques 87:310-18 Mr '65

Maps
Old Northwest Territory. Antiques 87:287-8 Mr '65

NORTHWEST airlines, Incorporated
Northwest thrives on uncommon policies. W. H. Gregory. il Aviation W 83:36-7+ O 4 '65

NORTHWEST craftsmen's exhibition. See Arts and crafts—Exhibitions

NORTHWEST Orient airlines. See Northwest airlines, incorporated

NORTHWEST TERRITORY, United States.
See Northwest, Old

NORTON, Alice
Professional publicity services: a 1965 checklist. por Library J 90:3392-6 S 1 '65

NORTON, Charles Eliot
Norton and Godkin: launching The nation. K. Vanderbilt. por Nation 200:165-9 F 15 '65

NORTON, Elliot
Doctor in the house. il por Newsweek 65:76 Ap 12 '65

NORTON, Eloise
Time for a special lesson. bibliog por Library J 90:1987-8 Ap 15 '65
—and Billington, Grace
Library coloring sheet. il Library J 90:4534-5 O 15 '65

NORTON, John K.
Score on school finance. PTA Mag 59:4-6 My '65

NORTON, O. Richard
Thoughts about constellation figures. Sky & Tel 30:203-5 O '65

NORTON-TAYLOR, Duncan
What on earth is happening to Protestantism? Fortune 72:170-3+ D '65

NORTON, W. W. and company, Incorporated
Norton raises authors' cut on paperback reprints. Pub W 188:72 N 15 '65

NORTON company
Distributors fight for their take; manufacturers of grinding wheels. Bsns W p33 Ja 8 '66
Norton gives itself a selling lesson; advertising and marketing program directed toward consumers. il Bsns W p70 Ja 8 '66

NORWALK, Calif.
Barnyard serenade; park and recreation district operates popular small animal farm. B. Avenatti. il Recreation 58:425-6 N '65

NORWAY
Description and travel
Last great empty slopes. E. Schwiebert. il Esquire 65:88-9+ Ja '66

Politics and government
Cautious revolt; Labor government replaced by non-Socialist coalition. Newsweek 66:52+ S 27 '65
End of Labor. il Time 86:35 S 24 '65
See also
Political campaigns—Norway

NORWELL, Mass.
North River, town of Norwell, Plymouth County, Mass. W. O. Douglas. Bul Atomic Sci 21:11 My '65

NORWICH, Diana (Manners) Cooper, viscountess. See Cooper, D. M.

NOSE
And so perfumed that the winds were lovesick with them. L. Blanch. Vogue 146:127-8+ N 15 '65
Why do we have noses? H. Downs. il Sci Digest 57:85-7 My '65
See also
Smell

Surgery
Nasal surgery improved. Sci N L 88:98 Ag 14 '65

NOSSAL, Frederick
Mao Tse-tung industry. Sat R 49:108-9 Ja 8 '66

NOSSITER, Bernard D.
Is General de Gaulle that alarming? New Repub 153:13-15 O 9 '65
Reporter on poverty turns to bad prophecy. Life 59:11 Ag 20 '65
US corporations, go home. New Repub 152:10-12 Ap 10 '65

NOT for every eye; story. See Waltham, C.

NOT wanted on the voyage; story. See Knickerbocker, C.

NOTABLE books council. See American library association—Adult services division

NOTABLES. See Great men

NOTATION (music) See Musical notation

NOTE paper. See Stationery

NOTEBOOKS
Fellow photographers, do you need a little black book? K. Poli. il Pop Phot 57:98-9 O '65

NOTHING box; story. See Brooks, T. E.

NOTHNAGLE, John T.
Giving the picture to home buyers. il por Bsns W p87-8 My 29 '65

NOTOPOULOS, James A.
Tragic and the epic in T. E. Lawrence. Yale R 54:331-45 Mr '65

NOTRE DAME, Ind. University
ABPC again files amicus brief for John Goldfarb. Pub W 187:51 Mr 22 '65
Appellate court reverses John Goldfarb decision. Pub W 187:133-4 F 22 '65
Bring on the dancing girls; injunction prohibiting showing of John Goldfarb, please come home, reversed. America 112:276-7 F 27 '65
Court of appeals OK's John Goldfarb. Pub W 187:25 Mr 29 '65
Rockne, Parseghian and the Fighting Irish. T. Cohane. il Look 29:88-9+ N 2 '65
NOTRE DAME cathedral, Paris
Joy of color; Notre Dame and new window. il Newsweek 66:64 Ag 2 '65
NOTROM, Henry B.
Winterize your outboard. Pop Mech 124:186-9 O '65
NOTT, Kathleen
Little bourgeois. Commentary 39:82-6 F '65
Mortal statistics. Commentary 38:64-8 O '64; 39-8 Ap '65
NOTTINGHAM, England, public library
Yank in Sherwood Forest. K. Kister. bibliog il Library J 90:4914-20 N 15 '65
NOTTINGHAM conference. See Church unity—Great Britain
NOTTINGHAMSHIRE COUNTY, England, library
Yank in Sherwood Forest. K. Kister. bibliog il Library J 90:4914-20 N 15 '65
NOVA SCOTIA
Scouting around Nova Scotia: treasure of early French trade materials at Mic-Mac treasure museum, Pictou. A. Brown. il Hobbies 70:114 O '65
See also
Fishing—Nova Scotia
Geology—Nova Scotia
Sable Island
NOVACULITE
See also
Chert
NOVAK, Arthur F. and Rao, M. R. R.
Food safety program: endrin monitoring in the Mississippi River. bibliog Science 150:1732-3 D 24 '65
NOVAK, Michael
American Catholicism after the council. Commentary 40:50-8 Ag '65
Books. Commonweal 82:56-7 Ap 2 '65
Catholic imprint. Christian Cent 82:990 Ag 11 '65
Catholics and Lent. Christian Cent 82:323 Mr 17 '65
Ecclesiology of birth control. Christian Cent 82:454-5 Ap 14 '65
Grape strike. Commonweal 83:366-9 D 24 '65
Post-seminary thoughts. Commonweal 83:9-12 O 8 '65
Secular city. Commonweal 83:184-6 N 12 '65
Timidity crisis; temptation to slow down. Commonweal 82:685-8 S 24 '65
Where is theology going? Christian Cent 82:1342-3 N 3 '65
NOVAK, Robert. See Evans, R. jt. auth.
NOVAK, Vincent M.
Christian commitment and Catholic schools. America 112:40-2 Jl 10 '65
NOVAKOWSKI, N. S.
Day we rescued a whooping crane. Audubon Mag 67:230-3 Jl '65
NOVELISTS
First novelists, spring 1965; statements by the writers, ed. by B. Pearlman. pors Library J 90:671-85 F 1 '65
First novelists, summer-fall 1965; statements by the writers, ed. by I. Stokvis. il Library J 90:2589-97+, 4119-25+ Je 1, O 1 '65
Must the novelist crusade? E. Welty. Atlan 216:104-8 O '65
Seventh literary symposium at Chapel Hill. A. Gingrich. Esquire 64:6 Jl '65
See also
Women as authors
NOVELISTS, American
Black humorists. il Time 85:94+ F 12 '65
Notes on the new style. W. Phillips. Nation 201:232-6 S 20 '65
Pioneers and caretakers, by L. Auchincloss. Review
Harper 231:112 Ag '65. P. Pickrel
What happened to the postwar authors? J. W. Aldridge. Sr Schol 87:sup 16-17+ S 23 '65
See also
Bellow, S.
Bongartz, R.
Cain, J. M.
Cather, W.
Cheever, J.
Clark, W. V. T.
Cormier, R.

Elliott, G. P.
Ellison, R.
Faulkner, W.
Fiedler, L. A.
James, H.
Lewis, S.
Metalious, G.
Mitchell, M.
Porter, K. A.
Rosskam, E.
Stead, C.
Swanberg, W. A.
Updike, J.
Wharton, E. N. J.
NOVELISTS, Catholic. See Catholic authors
NOVELISTS, Colombian
See also
Rivera, J. E.
NOVELISTS, English
See also
Lessing, D. M.
Powell, A.
Waugh, E.
NOVELISTS, French
See also
Beyle, M. H.
Peyrefitte, R.
NOVELISTS, German
See also
Böll, H.
Grass, G.
NOVELISTS, Irish
See also
Moore, B.
O'Brien, E.
West, A. C.
NOVELISTS, Italian
See also
Bassani, G.
Pratolini, V.
NOVELISTS, Mexican
See also
Fuentes, C.
NOVELISTS, Russian
See also
Ehrenburg, I. G.
NOVELS. See Fiction
NOVELS, American. See American fiction
NOVEMBER
In November; few of the dates, memorable and not so, coming up next month (title varies) (cont) il N Y Times Mag p60 O 31 '65
NOVENAS
No more novenas? Time 87:55 Ja 21 '66
NOVICK, Julius
Theatre. Nation 201:146-8 S 13 '65
NOVITSKI, E. and others
Cytological basis of sex ratio in drosophila pseudoobscura. bibliog Science 148:516-17 Ap 23 '65
NOVY mir (new world) periodical. See Periodicals—Russia
NOW, tell me pray, and tell me true; story. See Huber, K.
NOWAK, Joe
Ski-jumpers paradise. Recreation 58:65+ F '65
NOWAK, Theodore. See Luck, D. J. jt. auth.
NOWELL, Peter C. and Cole, L. J.
Hepatomas in mice: incidence increased after gamma irradiation at low dose rates. bibliog Science 148:96-7 Ap 2 '65
—See Cole, L. J. jt. auth.
NOYES, Henry Drury
New books. Cath World 202:246 Ja '66
NOYES, Judith
Currents from the Chinook: putting a bookstore on the map. por Pub W 187:58-60 Ap 12 '65
Paperbacks for childen win sales. Pub W 188:202-4 Jl 12 '65
NOYES, R. W. and others
Pronuclear ovum from a patient using an intrauterine contraceptive device. bibliog Science 147:744 F 12 '65
Le NOZZE di Figaro; opera. See Mozart, J. C. W. A.
NOZZLES, Rocket engine. See Rocket engines
NUBIA
Antiquities
Yankee cruises the storied Nile. I. Johnson and E. Johnson. il Nat Geog Mag 127:583-633 My '65
NUCLEAR bombs. See Atomic bombs
NUCLEAR detection satellites. See Atomic bombs—Testing, Detection of
NUCLEAR energy. See Atomic power
NUCLEAR excavation. See Atomic blasting
NUCLEAR explosion simulators. See Simulators

NUCLEAR fission
Close-packed-spheron theory and nuclear fission. L. Pauling. bibliog il Science 150:297-305 O 15 '65
Kink-bands: shock deformation of biotite resulting from a nuclear explosion. D. Cummings. bibliog il Science 148:950-2 My 14 '65
Nuclear fission. R. B. Leachman. il Sci Am 213:49-56+ bibliog(p 119) Ag '65
Trinitite: cobalt-60, cesium-137, and europium-152. L. P. Salter and J. H. Harley. bibliog il Science 148:954-5 My 14 '65

NUCLEAR fuels
  See also
Plutonium

NUCLEAR laboratories. See Atomic research laboratories

NUCLEAR medicine. See Radiology, Medical

NUCLEAR physics
Books; Lord Rutherford and the origins of nuclear physics at Manchester. M. J. Klein. Sci Am 212:129-32+ Mr '65
Electronic and atomic collisions; report on fourth international conference. W. L. Fite and E. Gerjuoy. Science 150:516-18+ O 22 '65
$.5 billion/year market possible result of planned high-energy physics effort. W. S. Beller. il Miss & Roc 17:26-8 O 11 '65
Nuclear physics: a status report. A Zucker and D. A. Bromley. il Science 149:1197-205 S 10 '65
Strong inference and weak interactions. E. M. Hafner and S. Presswood. bibliog il Science 149:503-10 Jl 30 '65
Symmetry principles at high energy; report on second Coral Gables conference. W. D. McGlinn. Science 148:671-2 Ap 30 '65
  See also
Cosmic rays
Particles (nuclear physics)
Time reversal

NUCLEAR power plants. See Atomic power plants

NUCLEAR reactions
Analytical chemistry in nuclear technology; report on eighth Conference on analytical chemistry in nuclear technology. C. D. Susano and others. Science 147:523 Ja 29 '65

NUCLEAR reactors
Burgeoning reactors. Sci Am 213:80 S '65
Cheapest atomic power. Sci Am 213:46 Jl '65
Computing methods applied to reactor problems; report on international conference at Argonne national laboratory. W. Sangren. Science 149:1268+ S 10 '65
Decisions on nuclear power. V. K. McElheny. Science 149:407-9 Jl 23 '65
Enough power to run Chicago; TRIGA research reactor. il Sci Digest 57:11 F '65
How breeder reactors work. I. Asimov. il Sci Digest 59:84-5 Ja '66
Labor and the Savannah River AEC project; reprint from June 1952 issue. M. M. Smith. Mo Labor R 88:799-800 Jl '65
Nuclear reactors: the between generation. il Fortune 71:219 Je '65
Where is science taking us? excerpt from the 1964 report of the director of Oak Ridge national laboratory. A. M. Weinberg. il Sat R 48:56-7 F 6 '65

        Accidents and explosions
Four deadly minutes; accident at the Boris Kidrič institute of nuclear sciences, Yugoslavia. J. Kobler. il Sat Eve Post 238:42-4 N 6 '65

NUCLEAR research. See Atomic research
NUCLEAR rockets. See Rockets, Atomic powered
NUCLEAR test ban treaty, 1963
Moment of history; trip to Moscow. M. F. B. Humphrey. McCalls 92:57+ Jl '65
Siblings of the test ban. G. E. Hlavka. Bul Atomic Sci 21:24 N '65

NUCLEAR warfare. See Atomic warfare
NUCLEAR weapons. See Atomic weapons

NUCLEIC acids
Enrichment of serine-acceptor soluble RNA by nucleic acid gels. P. P. Hung. bibliog il Science 149:639-40 Ag 6 '65
Nucleic acid and protein changes in wheat leaf nuclei during rust infection. P. K. Bhattacharya and others. bibliog il Science 150:1605-7 D 17 '65
Nucleic acid polymerases: possible subunit structure. S. Lee-Huang and L. F. Cavalieri. bibliog il Science 148:1474-6 Je 11 '65
  See also
Deoxyribonucleic acid
Nucleoproteins
Ribonucleic acid

NUCLEOPROTEINS
Configuration of inactive and active polysomes of the developing down feather. E. Bell and others. bibliog il Science 148:1739-41 Je 25 '65
Functional ribosomal unit of gamma-globulin synthesis. M. D. Scharff and J. W. Uhr. bibliog il Science 148:646-8 Ap 30 '65
Polyribosomes from escherichia coli: enzymatic method for isolation. M. Dresden and M. B. Hoagland. bibliog il Science 149:647-9 Ag 6 '65
Polysomes from yeast: distribution of messenger RNA and capacity to support protein synthesis in vitro. L. Marcus and others. bibliog il Science 147:615-17 F 5 '65
Protein synthesis by ribosomes from heart muscle: effect of insulin and diabetes. O. R. Rampersad and I. G. Wool. bibliog il Science 149:1102-3 S 3 '65
Ribosomal-RNA synthesis in the absence of ribosome synthesis in germinating cotton seeds. L. Waters and L. Dure, 3d. bibliog il Science 149:188-91 Jl 9 '65
Ribosomes: analysis by cesium sulfate gradient centrifugation. F. M. DeFilippes. bibliog il Science 150:610-12 O 29 '65
Ribosomes from escherichia coli: lack of specificity for viral RNA. J. E. Dahlberg and R. Haselkorn. bibliog il Science 149:78-80 Jl 2 '65
Turnover of ribosomal RNA in rat liver. J. N. Loeb and others. bibliog il Science 149:1093-5 S 3 '65
  See also
Interferon

NUCLEOSIDES
Nucleoside incorporation into strain L cells: inhibition by pleuropneumonia-like organisms. R. M. Nardone and others. bibliog il Science 149:1100-1 S 3 '65
Nucleoside phosphatases of fetal and maternal blood cells: electron microscope study. R. S. Connell and R. L. Bacon. bibliog il Science 150:503-4 O 22 '65

NUCLEOTIDES
Antibodies to DNA and a synthetic polydeoxyribonucleotide produced by oligodeoxyribonucleotides. O. J. Plesca and others. bibliog Science 148:1102-3 My 21 '65
Base specificity in the interaction of polynucleotides with antibiotic drugs. D. C. Ward and others. bibliog il Science 149:1259-63 S 10 '65
Enzymatic synthesis of tri- and tetranucleotides of defined sequence. R. E. Thach and P. Doty. bibliog il Science 148:632-4 Ap 30 '65
Nucleotide synthesis under possible primitive earth conditions. C. Ponnamperuma and R. Mack. bibliog il Science 148:1221-3 My 28 '65
Synthesis of block oligonucleotides. R. E. Thach and P. Doty. bibliog il Science 147:1310-11 Mr 12 '65

NUDE culture. See Nudism

NUDE in art
Eternal Olympia. A. Werner. il Am Artist 29:48-53+ Ap '65

NUDISM
Naked defeat; Saint-Tropez, France. il Newsweek 66:38 Ag 9 '65
Naked discrimination; case of Tennessee nudists. Time 86:36 N 12 '65

NUGENT, Elliott
Wild ride. Newsweek 66:110 D 13 '65

NUGENT, John Peer
Seychelles; really away from it all. Atlan 216:154+ O '65

NUGENT, Patrick
How to deal with daddy. il por Newsweek 67:21 Ja 10 '66

NUISANCES
  See also
Odors

NUMBER games. See Mathematical recreations
NUMBERS, Symbolism. See Symbolism of numbers
NUMBERS game. See Gambling

NUMERICAL calculations
Numerical analysis vs. mathematics; address, December 29, 1964. R. W. Hamming. Science 143:473-5 Ap 23 '65; Discussion. 149:243-5, 1049-50 Jl 16, S 3 '65

NUMERICALLY controlled machine tools. See Machine tools—Control

NUMEROLOGY. See Symbolism of numbers
NUMISMATICS. See Coins

NUNCIOS, Papal
Diplomacy Vatican style. il Newsweek 67:62 Ja 17 '66

NUNNALLY, G. Lloyd
Value analysis in purchasing. Am City 80:
162+ Je '65

NUNNERY, Michael Y.
Effective cooperative decision-making in education. Sch & Soc 93:151-2 Mr 6 '65

NUNS. See Sisterhoods

NUREEV, Rudolf
Un-Anglo-Saxon attitudes. Nat R 17:607-9
Jl 13 '65

about

Man in motion. il pors Time 85:48-52 Ap 16
'65
Man of the hour. il por Time 85:52 Ap 30 '65
Musical events; performances with Royal bal-
let. W. Sargeant. New Yorker 41:173 My 22
'65
Nureyev: Tartar of the dance. il pors Newsweek 65:88-91 Ap 19 '65; Same abr. with
title He lives to dance. Read Digest 87:
139-42 Jl '65
Nureyevniks. il pors Newsweek 65:52 My 31
'65
People are talking about . . . pors Vogue 146:
80-1 Jl '65
Royal ballet's eighth New York season,
Metropolitan opera house. D. Hering. Dance
Mag 39:29-30+ Jl '65
Secret of the Nureyev spell. C. Barnes. il
pors N Y Times Mag p 30-1+ Ap 18 '65
Toronto: excitement. il por Dance Mag 39:22-
3 F '65

NURSERIES
Making room for baby. il Good H 162:78-81
Ja '66

NURSERIES (horticulture)
Idea collecting in specialty nurseries; spe-
cial needs of San Francisco gardeners. il
Sunset 134:184+ F '65
See also
Conard-Pyle company

NURSERY schools
For young children in a changing world;
education facilities in Scandinavia. L. L.
Gore. il Sch Life 47:4-7 D '64
Headstart for children in slums. G. Lewis
and H. Mackintosh. il Am Ed 1:30, inside
back cover D '64

NURSES and nursing
Andrea: a nurse who cares. A. Lake. il Ladies
Home J 82:74-5+ Ag '65
Embattled nurse of Jackrabbit Flats; P.
Gardelius on trial for practicing medicine
without a license. J. G. Dunne. il Sat Eve
Post 238:42-4+ N 20 '65
Hospitals without nurses. J. Martin. Nation
201:245-6 O 18 '65
Nurse shortage; another headache for hos-
pitals. il U S News 58:52 Mr 15 '65
Trial of Patricia Gardelius; practical nurse
charged with practicing medicine without
a license. B. Asbell. il Redbook 126:46-8+
D '65
See also
American nurses association

Training

Gray heads for white caps; Quo Vadis nursing
school, Toronto. il Life 59:41-2+ Jl 30 '65
How to choose a nursing school. F. M.
Alexander. il Todays Health 44:45-9 Ja '66
LPN: the gentle people. H. Powers. il Am
Ed 1:12-14 O '65
More glamor, pay, glory needed to attract
nurses. Sci N L 88:89 Ag 7 '65

NURSES and nursing, Public health
Nurse who comes to the house. Good H 161:
164 N '65

NURSING education. See Nurses and nursing—
Training

NURSING homes
Diverse programs for three nursing homes.
il Arch Rec 137:166-9 F '65
Dreary reality in nursing homes, and ma-
chines cranking up. Life 59:56-7 S 3 '65
Get up & live; Dr J. L. Whitaker's Issaquah
villa. il Time 86:59 N 26 '65
Good news about nursing homes; joint com-
mission on accreditation of hospitals to
check nursing homes. Consumer Rep 30:474
O '65
How to pick a home for mother or dad.
Farm J 89:66G Mr '65

NUSSBAUM, Ernest
Let the computer plan your traffic program.
Am City 80:102-4 Jl '65

NUT trees
Fruits and nuts of the South. C. M. Bruce. il
Horticulture 43:38-9+ F '65
Gather walnuts, filberts, chestnuts and
hickories in your garden. L. H. MacDaniels.
il Horticulture 43:22-3+ S '65

NUTLEY, N.J.
Cycle-basis billing. W. J. Jernick. il Am City
80:104+ O '65

NUTRITION
•Eating low on the hog. A. B. Spalding. il
Harper 230:139-40+ Mr '65
Food and nutrition; special issue; symposium.
il Todays Health 43:18-24+ O '65
Helping your teen-agers to better nutrition.
H. G. Earl. il Todays Health 43:49-51+ F
'65
Let's talk about food; ed. by P. L. White.
See issues of Today's health
More myths about nutrition. E. Weston.
McCalls 92:36 Je '65
Turista; bane of travelers abroad and at
home. Consumer Bul 48:16-17 Mr '65
See also
Children—Nutrition
Diet
Proteins
Vitamins

Study and teaching

See Nutrition education

NUTRITION education
Better nutrition through research and education. G. Maddox. il Todays Health 43:42-
5+ O '65
Family of twelve trained to improve family
diet. Sci N L 88:313 N 13 '65

NUTRITION foundation
Better nutrition through research and education. G. Maddox. il Todays Health 43:42-
5+ O '65

NUTRITION problems

Latin America

More children; more hunger. G. M. Schultz.
il Todays Health 43:18-23+ O '65

NUTRITION research
Battler against hidden starvation. Todays
Health 43:18 F '65
Better nutrition through research and edu-
cation. G. Maddox. il Todays Health 43:42-
5+ O '65
Why not nibble like a rat? reprint. R. Her-
mann. il Sci Digest 57:53-7 Mr '65

NUTS
Mixed nuts mostly peanuts. il Consumer Bul
48:32 Je '65
What to look for in buying nuts. il Good H
161:174 N '65

NUTT, Mary E.
All my yesterdays; story. Good H 160:86-7
Ap '65
Beckoning hand. Writer 78:9-11+ Mr '65

NUTT, Patrick A.
How to over-winter aquatic plants. Horticulture 43:34-5+ N '65

NYALA hunting. See Antelope hunting

NYANGIRA, Nicholas
Africans don't go to Russia to be brainwashed. por N Y Times Mag p52+ My 16
'65

NYASALAND. See Malawi

NYERERE, Julius Kambarage
Adding fuel. il Newsweek 66:34+ D 27 '65
Albatross. il Newsweek 65:43-4 Mr 1 '65
Nation that tried to help itself. F. L. Howley.
Read Digest 86:142-4+ Je '65
Why we guard against subversion. il por
Time 85:40 Je 11 '65

NYLON hosiery. See Hosiery

NYLON sails. See Sails

NYREN, Karl
Trustees in the age of consensus. por Library
J 90:3550-2 S 15 '65

NYSWANDER, Marie
Profiles. N. Hentoff. por New Yorker 41:
32-4+ Je 26; 32-4+ Jl 3 '65; Correction.
41:102 S 11 '65

O

OAR. See United States—Air force—Aerospace
research, Office of

OART (Office of advanced research and technology) See United States—National aeronautics and space administration—Advanced research and technology, Office of

OAS. See Organization of American states

OASDI. See Old age, survivors' and disability
insurance trust fund

OAU. See Organization of African unity

OCAW. See Oil, chemical and atomic workers
international union

OEA. See Overseas education association

OECD. See Organization for economic cooperation and development

OEP. See United States—Emergency planning, Office of

OGO (orbiting geophysical observatory) See Artificial satellites—Astronomical applications

OH radicals. See Hydroxyl

OMEP (organisation mondial pour l'education préscolaire) See World organization for early childhood education

OPEC. See Organization of petroleum exporting countries

OTS (optical technology satellite) See Artificial satellites—Use in research

OV (orbital vehicle) See Artificial satellites— Use in research

OAHU (island)
People wanted this plant; first major sewage-treatment plant built on island since 1927. Y. Kunimoto. il Am City 80:89-90 My '65

OAHU oceanarium. See Aquariums

OAK RIDGE, Tenn.
Oak Ridge: twenty years after, diversification is the goal. J. Walsh. Science 150:863-5 N 12 '65

OAK RIDGE national laboratory
AEC unlocks some files for business; Y-12 facilities near Oak Ridge. il Bsns W p50+ O 2 '65
Oak Ridge national laboratory: aim is change along with growth. J. Walsh. il Science 150:1133-6 N 26 '65
Oak Ridge: twenty years after, diversification is the goal. J. Walsh. Science 150:863-5 N 12 '65
Where is science taking us? excerpt from the 1964 report of the director of Oak Ridge national laboratory. A. M. Weinberg. il Sat R 48:56-7 F 6 '65

OAKLAND, Calif.

Finance
Computer that puts the budget in order every day. A. A. Brizee. il Am City 80:116-17 Mr '65

Labor and laboring classes
Can subsidies solve America's problems? a city's answer. il Nations Bsns 53:32-3+ Ag '65

Negroes
Danger signals. il Newsweek 67:32 Ja 17 '66

Parks and playgrounds
Walk on the wild side; Knowland park zoo. Am City 80:20 N '65

OAKLAND, N.J.
Oakland, N.J. proving ground for cathodic protection. N. D. Fagerlund. il Am City 80: 106-8 S '65

OAKLAND Raiders (football club) See Football clubs

OAKLAND university, Rochester, Mich.
Radio active library. F. M. Cammack. il Library J 90:4300-2 O 15 '65

OAKLEY, Francis
Almain and Major: conciliar theory on the eve of the reformation. bibliog f Am Hist R 70:673-90 Ap '65

OATES, James F. jr
Thinking ahead in federal tax policy; address, November 9, 1965. Vital Speeches 32:105-9 D 1 '65

OATES, Joyce Carol
Sweet enemy. Criticism
   Commonweal 81:764 Mr 12 '65

OATHS
God & courts in Maryland; religious test oaths. Time 86:67 D 10 '65
God & man in Maryland; religious test oaths. Time 86:94 O 22 '65
Wood research in a hymn to Hippocrates. F. A. Strenge. il Am For 71:42-5+ My '65

OATHS of loyalty. See Loyalty, Oaths of

OBATA, Gyo
Architectural details. Arch Rec 138:143-58 Ag '65

OBER, Harry
Occupational wage differentials, 1907-47. Mo Labor R 88:787-9 Jl '65

OBERBECK, S. K.
Underground letters. Reporter 33:58 O 21 '65

OBERDORFER, Don
Common noun spelled f-u-l-b-r-i-g-h-t. N Y Times Mag p79-80+ Ap 4 '65
Daily dilemmas of the Attorney General. N Y Times Mag p28-9+ Mr 7 '65
Filibuster's best friend. Sat Eve Post 238: 90+ Mr 13 '65

Man who speaks for L.B.J. Sat Eve Post 238: 32-3 O 23 '65
Proliferating Appalachias. Reporter 33:22-3+ S 9 '65
Rivers delivers. N Y Times Mag p30-1+ Ag 29 '65
Uncle Sam's wonderful tax machine. Sat Eve Post 238:28-9 Ap 10 '65
Washington insight. Harper 231:108+ O '65

OBERLIN college, Oberlin, Ohio
Discontinue Oberlin school of theology. Christian Cent 82:861 Jl 7 '65
On campus, an educator's dream; Festival of contemporary music. S. Fleming. il Hi Fi 15:120 My '65

OBERLIN graduate school of theology. See Oberlin college, Oberlin, Ohio

OBERMAN, Heiko A.
Lonely pope or first of the brethren? Christian Cent 82:835-7 Je 30 '65

OBESITY. See Corpulence

OBJECTIVES in education. See Education— Aims and objectives

OBJECTIVISM
Ayn Rand: a voice in the wilderness. B. Cook. Cath World 201:119-24 My '65

OBJECTIVITY
Objectivity in the college classroom. A. W. Munk. bibliog f Sch & Soc 93:297-8 Sum '65

OBJECTS, Miniature. See Miniature objects

OBOTE, Milton
Colored rulers. G. C. Turner. Negro Hist Bul 28:201 My '65
Farewell to arms. Time 85:30 Je 4 '65

OBOURN, Ellsworth S.
India trains teachers for a new age. por Am Ed 1:16-22 Mr '65

O'BRIEN, B. J.
Auroral phenomena. bibliog Science 148:449-60 Ap 23 '65

O'BRIEN, Bonaventure
Another priest, another ban. T. Lickona. Commonweal 83:298-9 D 10 '65

O'BRIEN, Conor Cruise
Neurosis of colonialism. Nation 200:674-6 Je 21 '65
President's constituency. New Repub 153:28-31 Ag 21 '65

about
Chipping away. R. Owen. Commentary 40: 99-100+ S '65

O'BRIEN, Dennis
Adlai Stevenson: politician. Christian Cent 82:1009-11 Ag 18 '65

O'BRIEN, Donald K.
New money from old maples. Farm J 89: 56B-56C F '65
Why we switched to soft corn. il Farm J 89:36-7+ D '65

O'BRIEN, Edna
Let the rest of the world go by; story. Ladies Home J 82:48-9 Jl '65
My first love; story. Ladies Home J 82:60-1 Je '65
Woman at the seaside; story. Mlle 60:168-9 Mr '65

about
Books. W. J. Smith. Commonweal 82:507 Jl 9 '65

O'BRIEN, Harry R.
Pop Gardener says. See issues of Popular gardening & living outdoors

O'BRIEN, James H. See Fox, S. S. jt. auth.

O'BRIEN, John S.
Stability of the myelin membrane. bibliog Science 147:1099-107 Mr 5 '65
—and Sampson, E. L.
Myelin membrane: a molecular abnormality. bibliog Science 150:1613-14 D 17 '65

O'BRIEN, Justin
Appearances in Paris. Sat R 49:26 Ja 1 '66

O'BRIEN, Lawrence Francis
From White House to Capitol, how things get done; interview. pors U S News 59:68-73 Jl 20 '65
Presidential system; summary of television interview. Nat R 17:627-8 Jl 27 '65

about
Back-room boy up front. il por Time 86:18-19 S 10 '65
Farley mold. por Newsweek 66:21 S 13 '65
Now O'Brien delivers the mail. P. Anderson. il pors N Y Times Mag p54-5+ N 14 '65

O'BRIEN, Lincoln
How to be a good guest on a cruise. Motor B 116:56+ Jl '65

O'BRIEN, Trevor
Swing now, madam! story. Sports Illus 22: 96-8 Ap 26 '65

O'BRIEN, William V.
Great debate over American military interventions. por Cath World 201:316-21 Ag '65
International law, morality and American interventions. Cath World 201:388-93 S '65

OBSCENE literature. See Immoral literature and pictures

OBSCENITY (law)
ALA, ACLU, and US Justice department oppose federal obscenity commission; hearings before Select subcommittee on education. Library J 90:4317-18 O 15 '65
Booksellers, a summer of uncertainty; New York state censorship legislation. R. H. Smith. Pub W 188:45 Ag 2 '65
Censorship and obscenity; address, January 1965. D. Lacy. ALA Bul 59:471-6 Je '65
Colin Wilson novel cleared of obscenity charges; Conn. Pub W 189:101 Ja 17 '66
Connecticut appeals court reverses obscenity ruling; case of magazine Keyhole. Pub W 188:59 S 13 '65
Defending the freedom to read in the courts. E. de Grazia. ALA Bul 59:507-16 Je '65
Fight against the smut peddlers; newsstand and mailorder pornography. O. K. Armstrong. Read Digest 87:177-8+ S '65
High court review asked on Mass. Fanny Hill ruling. Pub W 188:31-2 Ag 9 '65
In the mill. E. J. Gaines. ALA Bul 59:452-4 Je '65
Mail snooping. New Repub 153:6-7 Ag 21 '65
May it please the Court. A. Kopkind. New Repub 153:9-10 D 18 '65
N.Y. state protects minors with new anti-obscenity laws. Library J 90:3704 S 15 '65
Obscenity chore. il Time 86:36+ D 17 '65
Obscenity legislation: Cunningham, Mundt, Zablocki bills. Wilson Lib Bul 39:693+ Ap '65
Supreme court and obscenity; censorship a defensive weapon; address, May 2, 1965. J. J. Regan. Vital Speeches 31:592-5 Jl 15 '65
Supreme court to hear Fanny Hill case; may attempt legal definition of obscene. Library J 90:5356 D 15 '65
Supreme court to review Mass. Fanny Hill ruling. Pub W 188:73 N 15 '65
This flood of filth; New York city citizens' anti-pornography commission's steps to curb pornography. E. F. Cavanagh, jr. America 113:184-5 Ag 21 '65
U.S. Supreme court reexamines precedents in hearings on three book censorship cases; allegedly obscene books. Pub W 188:61-6 D 27 '65; Discussion 189:48-9 Ja 17 '66
What are national or community standards? H. F. Pilpel. Pub W 188:55-6 S 12 '65
Witchcraft and obscenity: twin superstitions; excerpts from address, November 2, 1964. S. Fleishman. il Wilson Lib Bul 39:640-6 Ap '65

OBSERVATIONS, Astronomical. See Astronomy—Observations

OBSERVATORIES
See also
Astronomical observatories

OBSTETRICS
Miscarriage; skin patch gives hope to victims of a medical enigma. R. P. Goldman. il Sat Eve Post 238:72-3+ Jl 17 '65
See also
Childbirth

O'CASEY, Sean
Bald primaqueera. por Atlan 216:69-74 S '65
Sean O'Casey: the man I knew, by G. Fallon. Review
America 113:444 O 16 '65. S. P. Ryan

OCCULT sciences
See also
Magic

OCCULTATIONS
Close tracking of Mariner continues. il Miss & Roc 17:14-15 Jl 19 '65
Extreme grazing occultations. T. C. Van Flandern. il Sky & Tel 29:386-7 Je '65
1966 occultation supplement. il Sky & Tel 30:291-8 N '65
Observation of a partial occultation of Jupiter. Sky & Tel 30:250 O '65
Occultation highlights, September-February, 1965-66. D. W. Dunham. il Sky & Tel 30:186, 394 S, D '65
Possible occultation by the planet Pluto. I. Halliday. il Sky & Tel 29:216-17 Ap '65

OCCUPATIONAL education. See Vocational education

OCCUPATIONAL guidance. See Vocational guidance

OCCUPATIONAL literature. See Vocational literature

OCCUPATIONAL psychology. See Vocational psychology

OCCUPATIONAL therapy
Making hospital rounds with the science lady. J. H. Pollack. il Todays Health 43:37-41 My '65

OCCUPATIONS
Careers without college: plenty of good ones. il U S News 59:68-70 N 29 '65
Executive job hunters get a guide; with editorial comment. il Bsns W p45-6+, 129-30 Ja 15 '66
Fifty best paying jobs today. Changing T 19:12 O '65
Focusing on careers with a purpose. il Sr Schol 87:11-22+ N 11 '65
Getting ahead; questions and answers. L. R. Fibel. See issues of Popular science monthly
How does religion influence job choice? Harvard study. il Bsns W p 178+ Ap 17 '65
How to choose your job, and land it; questions and answers. L. Velie. Read Digest 87:140-3 N '65
How to get out of a dead-end job. H. Levinson. il Pop Sci 186:104-5+ Ap '65
If you're wondering about a career for your son; table. U S News 58:80 Mr 29 '65
Is business letting young people down? P. F. Drucker. Harvard Bsns R 43:49-55 N '65
Like a good second marriage; switching careers. il Time 86:89 N 12 '65
Manpower needs in 1975. H. Stambler. Mo Labor R 88:378-83 Ap '65
Non-academic profile of college freshmen. Sch & Soc 93:292-3 Sum '65
Occupational wage differentials, 1907-47. H. Ober. Mo Labor R 88:787-9 Jl '65
Peace corps volunteers return; what are they doing now? R. Hartley. il Seventeen 24:20+ My '65
Ranking of U.S. occupations by earnings. M. A. Rutzick. bibliog f il Mo Labor R 88:249-55 Mr '65
Take charge of your career. R. Dunlop. Pop Mech 124:20+ Ag; 30+ S '65
Ultimate weapon in war on poverty. il Nations Bsns 53:34-7+ F '65
Whatever became of the class of '55? seven high school boys' planned careers in '55 and actual careers in '65. J. Star. il Look 29:112-14+ My 18 '65
Where jobs are going begging. il U S News 59:85-7 N 29 '65
Your career barometer (title varies) C. Peet. il Pop Mech 124:32+ O; 44+ N; 20+ D '65; 125:22+ Ja '66
See also
Business
Woman—Occupations

OCCUPATIONS, Choice of. See Vocational guidance

OCCUPATIONS for children
Help your children get the most out of summer. il Good H 160:173 Je '65
How many chores should your kids do? R. Gogerty. il Farm J 89:66 F '65

OCEAN
See also
Diving, Submarine
Meteorology, Maritime
Oceanographic research
Tides

Economic aspects
See Marine resources

OCEAN bottom
Genesis of the Arctic Ocean Basin. E. R. King and others; reply with rejoinder. N. A. Ostenso. bibliog il Science 147:1052-6 F 26 '65
Igneous rocks of the Indian Ocean floor. C. G. Engel and others. bibliog il Science 150:605-10 O 29 '65
Magnetic anomalies over a young oceanic ridge off Vancouver Island. F. J. Vine and J. T. Wilson. bibliog il Science 150:485-9 O 22 '65
Migrant sound scatterers: interaction with the sea floor. J. D. Isaacs and R. A. Schwartzlose. bibliog il Science 150:1810-13 D 31 '65
Morphology and sediments of a portion of the Mid-Atlantic ridge. T. H. van Andel and others. bibliog il Science 148:1214-16 My 28 '65
Ocean-bottom topography: the divide between the Sohm and Hatteras Abyssal Plains. R. M. Pratt. bibliog il Science 148:1598-9 Je 18 '65
Sands of the Mid-Atlantic Ridge. P. J. Fox and B. C. Heezen. bibliog il Science 149:1367-70 S 17 '65

OCEAN bottom—*Continued*

Surtsey, child of an expanding earth? J. Lear. il Sat R 48:33-9 Jl 3 '65; Discussion. 48:45 Ag 7 '65

Transform faults, oceanic ridges, and magnetic anomalies southwest of Vancouver Island. J. T. Wilson. bibliog il Science 150:482-5 O 22 '65

Underwater landslides discovered near Hawaii. il Sci N L 88:143 Ag 28 '65

Wandering enteropneust from the abyssal Pacific, and the distribution of spiral tracks on the sea floor. D. W. Bourne and B. C. Heezen. bibliog il Science 150:60-3 O 1 '65

What's going on down there? J. Dugan. il Holiday 37:70-9+ Je '65

See also

Deep sea deposits

Rift valleys

Submarine geology

OCEAN currents

Current situation; Long Island Sound. M. L. Hersey. il Motor B 115:102+ Ap '65

Gulf Stream of the Pacific; Kuroshio, or Japan current. K. Fedorov. il UNESCO Courier 18:36-8 D '65

Ocean currents studied. Sci N L 87:278 My 1 '65

Paleontologic technique for defining ancient ocean currents. F. G. Stehli. bibliog il Science 148:943-6 My 14 '65

Solving current problems by VTV; vector triangles of velocity. E. L. Slepian. il Motor B 115:48-51 Je '65

See also

Bottle charts

Gulf Stream

OCEAN fishing. See Salt water fishing

OCEAN in art

See also

Marine painting

OCEAN liners

Double feature; sentimental directors of the state-run Italian line's new luxury liners. Time 85:101 My 28 '65

Italian beauty's maiden voyage; Michelangelo. F. Kappler. il Life 58:109-10 Je 18 '65

Let's travel; on the high seas. J. Bush. il Mlle 61:183-6 O '65

Michelangelo sails in. il Newsweek 65:78+ My 24 '65

Michelangelo study in the art of ship design. il Bsns W p30-1 Mr 13 '65

S.S. United States. G. Bradshaw. Vogue 145:138-40 My '65

See also

Steamship lines

OCEAN science and ocean engineering conference

Oceanography spending seen soaring. W. S. Beller. Miss & Roc 16:15 Je 21 '65

OCEAN sounds

Sea noises upset studies. Sci N L 88:229 O 9 '65

OCEAN spray cranberries, incorporated

Spreading sassamanesh; broader base for industry. il Time 86:104 N 12 '65

OCEAN systems, incorporated

How Jon Lindbergh works on the ocean floor. G. Soule. il Pop Sci 187:50-3 S '65

Race for riches under the sea. B. H. Frisch. il Sci Digest 59:48-56 Ja '66

OCEAN systems division. See North American aviation, incorporated—Ocean systems division

OCEAN travel

Florida, by sea. M. A. Scott. il Travel 124:36-7 O '65

Michelangelo sails in. il Newsweek 65:78+ My 24 '65

Trip abroad; go by freighter, fun, different, a bargain. il Changing T 19:35-6 F '65

See also

Ocean liners

Voyages

OCEANARIUMS. See Aquariums

OCEANIA

See also

Islands of the Pacific

Antiquities

Oceania; sculpture. F. Girard. il UNESCO Courier 18:17-26 D '65

OCEANOGRAPHIC buoys

Sea stations for aircraft V.H.F. coverage. P. Halliday. il Electr World 74:36+ O '65

OCEANOGRAPHIC institution, Woods Hole. See Woods Hole, Mass, oceanographic institution

OCEANOGRAPHIC instruments

Oceanography promising market for microcircuit manufacturers. Miss & Roc 16:37 Ap 5 '65

OCEANOGRAPHIC research

Deepest days. R. Sténuit. il Nat Geog Mag 127:534-47 Ap '65

Dipping deep into the Gulf Stream; U.S. launches a major survey. il Bsns W p78-80 Jl 31 '65

Economic benefits from oceanographic research. P. H. Abelson. Science 147:461 Ja 29 '65

Grappler for life's clues in the world's oceans; M. Ewing of Lamont geological observatory. il Bsns W p68-70+ My 22 '65

House passes bill to expand oceanographic effort. Miss & Roc 17:18 S 27 '65

Inner space, sea of opportunity; with editorial comment. R. B. Abel and C. B. Lindquist. il Am Ed 1:inside cover, 4-8 Mr '65

Man in the sea. A. F. Spilhaus; discussion. Science 146:471, 1113; 147:1396 O 23, N 27 '64, Mr 19 '65

North American sets up Ocean systems facility. Miss & Roc 17:28 N 1 '65

Oceanography; House subcommittee encourages use of merchant ships to gather data on the high seas. J. Walsh. Science 148:349-50 Ap 16 '65

Oceanology; symposium. il Miss & Roc 17:23-5+ S 6 '65; Discussion. 17:6 S 27 '65

Race for riches under the sea. B. H. Frisch. il Sci Digest 59:48-56 Ja '66

Surtsey, child of an expanding earth? J. Lear. il Sat R 48:33-9 Jl 3 '65; Discussion. 48:45 Ag 7 '65

Talk with Cousteau; ed. by E. Miller. J. Y. Cousteau. Seventeen 24:56 F '65

Urge sea-grant colleges to benefit from sea. Sci N L 88:312 N 13 '65

Vast potential seen in sea minerals. R. Lindsey. il Miss & Roc 17:34-5+ Ag 9 '65

Yachtsmen and marine science. F. T. Moss. il Yachting 117:44-5+ F '65

See also

International Indian Ocean expedition

United States—Commerce, Department of—Institute of oceanography

Woods Hole, Mass, oceanographic institution

Equipment

Disposables scan sea. W. McCann. Sci N L 87:213 Ap 3 '65

Divers' agenda; Underwater society of America convention. il Life 59:41-2 S 3 '65

Industry struggles to meet demand; building submerged platforms. C. D. LaFond. il Miss & Roc 17:47-8+ S 6 '65

Lack of definition slows progress. M. Getler. il Miss & Roc 17:34-5+ S 6 '65

Navy hunts test debris; cable-controlled underwater research vehicle. Sci N L 88:309 N 13 '65

Outpost under the ocean. E. A. Link. il Nat Geog Mag 127:530-3 Ap '65

Sea spider installed for deep-sea research. il(p241) Sci N L 88:249 O 16 '65

Searchers beneath the seas; Deepstar. il Newsweek 66:84-5 S 27 '65

Tools for the ocean depths. il Fortune 72:213-14 Ag '65

OCEANOGRAPHY

Crisscross grid surveys urged for ocean study. Sci N L 88:24 Jl 10 '65

Inner space, sea of opportunity; with editorial comment. R. B. Abel and C. B. Lindquist. il Am Ed 1:inside cover, 4-8 Mr '65

Man can dwell undersea. B. Tuffy. Sci N L 87:405 Je 26 '65

Oceanography spending seen soaring. W. S. Beller. Miss & Roc 16:15 Je 21 '65

Russian oceanography making great gains. Sci N L 87:405 Je 26 '65

Soviet surge since World war II challenges U.S. oceanography lead. D. L. Zylstra and C. D LaFond il Miss & Roc 17:60-7 S 6 '65

See also

United States—Commerce, Department of—Institute of oceanography

Instruments

See Oceanographic instruments

OCHS, Adolph Simon

House of Adolph Ochs. R. Kahn. il por Sat Eve Post 238:32-8+ O 9 '65

OCHSHORN, Myron

Hopkins the critic. Yale R 54:346-67 Mr '65

O'CONNELL, Adelyn

Christmas prodigal; poem. America 113:777 D 18 '65

Epilogue; Rich young man; Matthew; poems. America 113:530 N 6 '65

Even now this woman; poem. Cath World 202:104 N '65

O'CONNELL, Adelyn—*Continued*
Experience of Easter; poem. Cath World 201:
21 Ap '65
Man born blind; poem. America 112:669 My 8
'65
Physician to Lazarus; poem. Commonweal 83:
98 O 22 '65
O'CONNELL, Genevieve
Man and his boat. B. Crabtree. il por Yacht-
ing 118:55-7+ O '65
O'CONNELL, John
Man and his boat. B. Crabtree. il pors Yacht-
ing 118:55-7+ O '65
O'CONNELL, Marvin R.
Gnostics on a train. Nat R 17:151-3 F 23 '65
O'CONNER, Norman
Movie of the month. Cath World 201:279-80
Jl '65
O'CONNOR, Edwin
How to cook without baloney. Life 59:21 Jl
16 '65
O'CONNOR, Flannery
Parker's back; story. Esquire 63:76-8 Ap '65
about
Books. J. P. Degnan. Commonweal 82:510-11
Jl 9 '65
Cold, hard look at humankind. G. Hicks.
il pors Sat R 48:23-4 My 29 '65
Flannery O'Connor. A. Griffith. America 113:
674-5 N 27 '65
Flannery O'Connor. W. Coffey. Commentary
40:93-9 N '65
Flannery O'Connor: faith's stepchild. W.
Schott. Nation 201:142-4+ S 13 '65
God breaks through. America 112:821 Je 5
'65
My mentor, Flannery O'Connor. Sister Mary-
Alice. Sat R 48:24-5 My 29 '65
O'CONNOR, Frank
Cheat; story. Sat Eve Post 238:78-80 My 8 '65
Life of your own; story. Sat Eve Post 238:
40-1 F 13 '65
My Oedipus complex; story. Parents Mag 40:
64-8 F '65
Willie is so silly. Vogue 145:122+ Mr 1 '65
O'CONNOR, Frank Daniel
Frank O'Connor takes the high road. S. E.
Zion. il por N Y Times Mag p9+ Ja 16 '66
O'CONNOR, J. E. Jr
Get your golf course out of the red. por
Am City 81:98-100 Ja '66
O'CONNOR, Jack
Big buck on the Snake. por Outdoor Life 135:
42-3+ My '65
Big change in guns. Outdoor Life 136:61-76
D '65
Bull elk in the brush. pors Outdoor Life 136:
50-1+ O '65
First day tiger. pors Outdoor Life 136:33-5+
N '65
Getting the range. See issues of Outdoor life
Mixed bag in the Yukon. Outdoor Life 136:
60-2+ S '65
Ram and the silver bullet. por Outdoor Life
135:44-5+ Ap '65
Sables are hard to hit. por Outdoor Life 136:
44-5+ Jl '65
(ed) Shooters' problems. See issues of Out-
door life
Shooting. See issues of Outdoor life
Tigress of Elephantville. pors Outdoor Life
137:32-5+ Ja '66
Up to our necks in nyalas. pors Outdoor Life
135:50-1+ Je '65
O'CONNOR, James
What is a Socialist? Nation 201:195-6 O 4 '65
O'CONNOR, John Joseph, 1904-
Books to be noted; history (cont) America
112:674-6 My 8 '65
History. America 113:682-4 N 27 '65
O'CONNOR, Norman
New songs unto the Lord. Sat R 48:88-9+
Ap 10 '65
O'CONNOR, Patrick
Two views of Vietnam. America 113:240-3,
735 S 4, D 11 '65
Vietnam background. America 113:11-13+ Jl
3 '65
OCTOBER
October splendor; excerpt from Sundial of the
seasons. H. Borland. il Read Digest 87:25-6
O '65
OCTOBER house, incorporated
Dispute over publication of Yevtushenko
poems. Pub W 187:36-7 Mr 15 '65
OCTOPUS
Learning in the octopus. B. B. Boycott. il
Sci Am 212:42-50 bibliog(p 138) Mr '65
Nature note; blushing devil. Sci N L 88:399
D 18 '65
One octopus brain has two memory stores.
Sci N L 87:194 Mr 27 '65

OCULISTS. See Ophthalmologists
ODD couple; drama. See Simon, N.
ODE to joy; ballet. See Ballets—Criticisms
ODEGAARD, Charles E.
Iron man at Washington. il por Time 86:69
N 5 '65
ODELL, Arthur Gould, 1913-
Architect as leader in a golden age? E.
Goble. Arch Rec 138:9 Ag '65
ODELL, Bruce Taylor
Interrupted lunch. il por Time 86:35 Ag 6 '65
ODELL, Luis E. and others
How Latin America sees it. Christian Cent
82:805-6 Je 23 '65
ODELL, Van Davis
These clothes are easy to put on. Farm J
89:80-1 S '65
ODEN, Thomas C.
Overview of Tillich. Christian Cent 82:1481
D 1 '65
ODER-Neisse line. See Germany (Democratic
Republic)—Boundaries; Poland—Boundaries
ODINGA, Oginga
Double O loses. il por Newsweek 65:58 Je 14
'65
Why we reject communism. Time 85:40 Je
11 '65
O'DOHERTY, Barbara Novak
Copley: eye & idea. Art N 64:22-7+ S '65
O'DOHERTY, Brian
Life movie review. Life 58:15 F 19; 59:21 O
1 '65
O'DOHERTY, Kieran. See Mahoney, J. D. jt.
auth.
ODOMETERS
Attack on Detroit. J. Ridgeway. New Repub
152:13-14 Mr 6 '64
Does your car lie about its mileage? Changing
T 20:32 Ja '66
O'DONOGHUE, Joseph
Elections in the church. Commonweal 82:281-
4 My 21 '65
O'DONOVAN, Patrick
Lord Avon's vantage point. New Repub 152:
24-5 My 15 '65
Right way to wear the green. New Repub
153:21+ S 11 '65
ODORS
Manure odors can land you in court! J.
Russell. Farm J 89:19+ Ag '65
No nose knows; nothing smells the way it
used to. Time 86:89 S 24 '65
Odor identifies disease. Sci N L 87:341 My
29 '65
You and your olfactronics; classifying
instrument developed by Dr A. Dravnieks.
il Life 59:103-4 D 10 '65
See also
Perfumery
Smell
ODYSSEY. See Homer
OEHSER, Paul H.
Footnote to the philosophy of wilderness.
Liv Wildn 86:5 Spr '64
Land of no Sunday. Liv Wildn 29:31-3 Spr '65
OERTLE, V. Lee
Bucks above the smog zone. Field & S 70:
124-6+ S '65
Fat truck tires for farm hauling. Suc Farm
63:65 Je '65
Look before you leap! Motor T 17:30-3 Je '65
Super tires for sportsmen. Field & S 69:145+
Ap '65
Utah, still the promised land. Field & S
70:10-12+ Ag '65
Which vacation-on-wheels is best for you?
Pop Sci 186:112-17 Ap '65
OETTINGER, Katherine Brownell
Day care centers for children with no place
to go. Parents Mag 40:42 F '65
O'FAOLAIN, Sean
Don Juan in Dublin; story. Sat Eve Post
238:48-51 Je 19 '65
In search of Sardinia. Holiday 39:52-3+
Ja '66
Three shapes of love; story. Atlan 215:124-8
Mr '65
OFF-Broadway theater. See New York (city)
—Theater
OFF-campus love story; story. See Dursin, M.
OFFENBACH, Jacques
From Angel, the first in stereo. M. Lelash.
Am Rec G 32:218-19 N '65
On records: Les contes d'Hoffman. Opera N
29:34 F 27 '65
On records; La Perichole. Opera N 30:35 D
25 '65
La Perichole. Criticism
Opera N il 30:17-20 D 25 '65
Opera N il 30:22-3 D 25 '65
Sat R 49:76 Ja 8 '66

OFFENBACH, Jacques—*Continued*
Tales of Hoffmann (Les contes d'Hoffmann)
Criticism
New Yorker 41:150+ O 23 '65
Opera N 29:24-5 F 27 '65
Opera N il 29:14-16 F 27 '65
Opera N il 29:17-20 F 27 '65
OFFERING; story. See Cavanaugh, A.
OFFICE appliances
Communication aids; telephone aids, intercoms, telescribers, pneumatic tubes and document conveyors. il Duns R 86:pt2 164-5+ S '65
General office machines. il Duns R 86:pt2 140-2+ S '65
See also
Computers—Business applications
Exhibitions
Automating chores in the office; Business equipment exposition at New York's Coliseum. il Bsns W p 104+ O 30 '65
OFFICE buildings
Campus plan for an office complex; California water service company offices in San Jose, Calif. il Arch Rec 137:167-70 Je '65
Chicago builds a new skyline for business. il Bsns W p 126-8+ My 1 '65
Expression of engineering; new engineering building in Lancaster, Pa. il Arch Rec 138:169-76 O '65
Fuse is lit for another office building boom. il Bsns W p28+ Jl 24 '65
Invisible architecture in the Paris underground; UNESCO three-story underground building. il Fortune 73:176 Ja '66
Small offices with a lot to say; ed. by W. McQuade. il Fortune 71:178-9 F '65
Solar shield in Norfolk; new municipal office building. il Fortune 72:184 Ag '65
See also
Bank buildings
New York (city)—Architecture
Designs and plans
Bearing wall expressed in a skyscraper; IBM building, Seattle; with account by J. S. Hornbeck. il Arch Rec 137:123-8 F '65
Bold solution to a difficult problem; new offices for the Housing and home finance agency. il Arch Rec 137:136-9 Mr '65
Building types study. il Arch Rec 138:139-62 D '65
Office complex bridges new mall; Washington, D.C. il Arch Rec 137:143-6 Mr '65
Saarinen's skyscraper: Columbia broadcasting system's office tower, New York city. il Arch Rec 138:111-18 Jl '65
Heating and ventilation
Let your lights heat your building; high-intensity lighting. il Bsns W p 136-8 Ag 21 '65
Lighting
Let your lights heat your building; high-intensity lighting. il Bsns W p 136-8 Ag 21 '65
OFFICE for recruitment. See American library association—Library administration division
OFFICE furniture
Space planning, furniture and interior design. il Duns R 86:pt2 138-9+ S '65
OFFICE holders. See Public officers
OFFICE machines. See Office appliances
OFFICE management
Office report. il Duns R 86:pt2 132-43+ S '65
Paperwork explosion: can we control it? excerpts from Modern records management; a basic guide to records control, filing, and information retrieval. E. J. Leahy and C. A. Cameron. il Nations Bsns 53:102-4+ S '65
OFFICE of aerospace research. See United States—Air force—Aerospace research, Office of
OFFICE of criminal justice. See United States—Justice, Department of—Office of criminal justice
OFFICE of economic opportunity. See United States—Economic opportunity, Office of
OFFICE of education. See United States—Education, Office of
OFFICE of science and technology. See United States—Science and technology, Office of
OFFICE parties. See Business entertaining
OFFICE seekers. See Patronage, Political
OFFICE workers
Desk work gets faster countdown; work measurement programs. Bsns W p91-2+ O 30 '65

Salaries
Pay raises: how white-collar workers are faring now. il U S News 59:93 N 22 '65
Training
Polishing up the office boy; Speedwriting company's personality improvement program. Bsns W p98+ N 13 '65
OFFICES
Agreeable office. il Esquire 64:219 D '65
His office and her kitchen. J. Gillies. il Farm J 89:86 Mr '65
Starting a successful practice. il Arch Rec 138:133-42 Jl '65
These places are offices at home. il Sunset 135:116-17 O '65
Working environment. il Duns R 86:pt2 136-7+ S '65
Designs and plans
Space planning, furniture and interior design. il Duns R 86:pt2 138-9+ S '65
OFFICIAL entertaining. See Government entertaining
OFFICIAL grievance man. See Administrative remedies
OFFICIAL residences
Kremlin on the Black Sea; Kosygin's dacha at Pitsunda. R. J. Korengold. il Newsweek 66:56 N 15 '65
Living is easier for the heads of governments in other lands. il U S News 58:52 My 24 '65
OFFICIAL secrets
See also
Government and the press
OFFICIALISM. See Bureaucracy
OFFNER, Richard
For Richard Offner, at seventy-five. A. Frankfurter. Art N 64:23+ My '65
OFFSET printing. See Printing, Offset
OFFSHORE boundaries. See Territorial waters
OFFSHORE oil fields. See Petroleum in submerged lands
OFFSHORE oil well drilling. See Oil well drilling, Submarine
O'FLAHERTY, Terrence
Critic's choice; a newspaperman feathers his aerie. il House & Gard 128:272-5 N '65
O'GALLAGHER, J. J. and Simpson, J. A.
Search for trapped electrons and a magnetic moment at Mars by Mariner IV. bibliog Science 149:1233-9 S 10 '65
O'GARA, James
All things considered. See issues of Commonweal
OGBURN, Charlton, Jr
Trials of a word-watcher. Harper 230:88-90+ Ap '65
Why can't I get more done? Read Digest 86:21-2+ My '65
OGDEN, Schubert M.
Faith and truth. Christian Cent 82:1057-60 S 1 '65
OGILVY, Benson and Mather, incorporated
Back to the kitchen; David Ogilvy returns to old job. il Newsweek 66:85 D 20 '65
OGILVY, David
Confessions of a picture man? J. Durniak. Pop Phot 56:38 Mr '65
Is Ogilvy a genius? S. Klaw. por Fortune 71:142-3+ Ap '65
OGLE, Alice
Revolution in the vineyards. America 113:747-8 D 11 '65
OGLESBY, Carl
Bankruptcy of the liberals; address, November 27, 1965. Commonweal 83:396-400 Ja 7 '66
Bourgeois gentlemen of Saigon. Nation 201:352-5 N 15 '65
about
Patriotism of protest. R. G. Sherrill. il Nation 201:463-6 D 13 '65
OGLESBY, T. W.
Spanish modern city hall. Am City 80:84-5 F '65
O'GORMAN, Mother Eileen
(tr) See Jadot, J. Church in the Congo
O'GORMAN, Ned
Peace and pathos. Commonweal 81:783-5 Mr 19 '65
O'GRADY, Desmond
Poor: French vs. American viewpoint. Cath World 201:177-82 Je '65
OGUR, M. and others
Tricarboxylic acid cycle mutants in saccharomyces: comparison of independently derived mutants. bibliog Science 147:1590 Mr 26 '65

OHANA, Maurice
People are talking about. . . por Vogue 146: 155 N 1 '65

O'HANLON, James F. Jr
Adrenaline and noradrenaline; relation to performance in a visual vigilance task. bibliog Science 150:507-9 O 22 '65

O'HARA, Frank
Grand manner of Motherwell. Vogue 146:206-9+ O 1 '65

O'HARA, John
Assistant; story. New Yorker 41:22-8 Jl 3 '65
Gambler; story. New Yorker 41:40-2 My 1 '65
Good location; story. New Yorker 41:29-31 S 4 '65
Memoirs of a sentimental duffer. Holiday 37: 66-7+ My '65
Neighborhood; story. New Yorker 41:49-53 My 15 '65

about
Mr Peeve; column canceled. Time 86:74 O 8 '65
O'Hara's farewell; unemployed newspaperman to write weekly column for syndicate of Newsday. por Newsweek 66:71 O 11 '65

O'HARA, William T.
President Kennedy and education; excerpt from John F. Kennedy on education. bibliog f Sch & Soc 93:444-50+ N 27 '65

O'HIGGINS, Bernardo
Liberators of the South. E. Correas. il por Américas 17:14-21 S '65

OHIO
See also
Booksellers and bookselling—Ohio
Chagrin Valley
Law—Ohio
Music festivals—Ohio

Politics and government
Forty-eight freshmen build their fences; Democrat from Republican district who won with LBJ. D. S. Broder. il N Y Times Mag p51+ D 12 '65

Religious institutions and affairs
News of the Christian world (cont) Christian Cent 82:312+, 1020-1, 1109-10, 1396-8 Mr 10, Ag 18, S 8, N 10 '65

OHIO oil company. See Marathon oil company

OHIO RIVER VALLEY
Golden industry on a golden thread; photographs, with account by C. Burck. Fortune 73:124-31 Ja '66

Industries
Valley's lopsided boom. C. Burck. Fortune 73:131 Ja '66

OHIO state university, Columbus
Free speech at Ohio state. E. Solomon. il Atlan 216:119-23 N '65; Discussion. 217:34+ Ja '66

OHNO, Susumu, and others
Sex-linkage of erythrocyte glucose-6-phosphate dehydrogenase in two species of wild hares. bibliog Science 150:1737-8 D 24 '65

OHNO, Toshihiko
Japanese remembers Iwo Jima. pors N Y Times Mag p26-7+ F 14 '65

OHRNING, Rudolph
Water color page; with biographical sketch. il por Am Artist 29:40-1+ Je '65

OIL birds
Birds that see in the dark with their ears. E. S. Ross. il Nat Geog Mag 127:282-90 F '65

OIL burners
How to save up to 25 per cent on your fuel-oil bill; using firebox liner. J. Ingersoll and C. E. Rhine. il Pop Sci 187:148-51 S '65

OIL changes, Automobile. See Automobiles—Lubrication

OIL, chemical and atomic workers international union
Another union changes the guard; J. Knight of Oil, chemical & atomic workers retires. il Bsns W p 124+ Jl 17 '65
Oil workers get a tougher chief. Bsns W p82 Ag 28 '65
Prospects rise for pact in oil; money gap narrow, strike may be averted. il Bsns W p 120-1 O 2 '65

OIL companies. See Petroleum industry and trade—United States

OIL fields, Offshore. See Petroleum in submerged lands

OIL filters
50,000 miles without an oil change; Bergstrom purifier. D. Francis and D. Sneigr. il Pop Sci 186:57-61+ Mr '65

OIL fuel
See also
Fuel economy

OIL gages. See Gages

OIL industries
See also
Petroleum industry and trade

OIL pollution of coastal waters. See Oil pollution of rivers, harbors, etc.

OIL pollution of rivers, harbors, etc.
Operation oil; accident at Cannes. il Newsweek 66:44+ Jl 26 '65

OIL shales
Is shale-oil boom on the way at last? il U S News 58:100 My 31 '65
New ways to squeeze oil out of a stone; pilot plant in Colorado extracting oil from shale. il Bsns W p78-9+ Jl 10 '65
Oil rush; shale extraction experiment at Rifle, Colo. R. Fleming. New Repub 153:11 S 18 '65
Shale oil; the cartel's ace in the hole. R. Fleming. il Nation 200:274-6 Mr 15 '65

OIL tankers. See Tank ships

OIL well drilling, Submarine
Plumbing the seas for oil. il Fortune 71:131-5 F '65
Worldwide boom in offshore oil; contract drillers tap a money field. il Bsns W p 120-2+ Mr 13 '65
See also
Petroleum in submerged lands

OIL workers. See Petroleum workers

OIL workers union. See Oil, chemical and atomic workers international union

OILS, Lubricating. See Lubrication and lubricants

OISTRAKH, David
David and Isaac. Newsweek 65:102 My 10 '65

OJEMANN, Ralph H.
What do they need to play with? PTA Mag 59:37-9 bibliog(p44) F '65

OJHA, R. J. See Pal, N. L. jt. auth.

OKA, Takashi
Vietnam's young generals face the old problems. Reporter 33:36-8 Jl 15 '65

OKADA, Koyo
Magic mountain. il U S Camera 28:50-1 Je '65

OKAMURA, Akihiko
Back from a Vietcong hellhole in the jungle. por Life 59:56D-63 Jl 2 '65

about
Life with the Viet Cong. por Time 86:25-6 Jl 2 '65

O'KEEFE, John A.
Lunar questions discussed at Pasadena. Sky & Tel 31:10-12 Ja '66
—See Liu, H. S. jt. auth.

O'KEEFE, Patricia
Who's who in American dogs. McCalls 92:202 F '65

O'KEEFE, Patrick E.
Reporting session four. America 113:19 Jl 3 '65

O'KEEFFE, Georgia
Georgia O'Keeffe. R. Looney. il pors Atlan 215:106-10 Ap '65
Personal backgrounds. il por House & Gard 128:176-7 D '65

OKELLO, John
Black mask of angry Africa. I. Lewis. il pors Life 58:111-12+ Ap 2 '65

OKINAWA
Okinawa; 1945 and 1965. R. Joseph. il Esquire 64:60-1 Ag '65
Troubled keystone. J. M. Truitt. il Newsweek 66:35-7 Ag 30 '65

OKLAHOMA
See also
Courts—Oklahoma
Education—Oklahoma
Festivals—Oklahoma
Justice, Administration of—Oklahoma
Libraries—Oklahoma
Ozark Mountains

OKLAHOMA CITY
See also
National cowboy hall of fame and western heritage center

Airports
Learning to love the boom. Time 85:64+ My 7 '65

OKLAWAHA RIVER
Across Florida by outboard. E. White. il Yachting 117:62-3+ F '65
Oklawaha, natural river or canal? C. W. Buchheister. Audubon Mag 67:284 S '65

OKONITE company
LTV rejoins civilian ranks; plans to buy Okonite co. Bsns W p96 O 23 '65
OKTOBERFEST. See Festivals—Germany (Federal Republic)
OLAH, Franz
Tales of the Vienna hoods. G. Bailey. il Reporter 32:36-40 Mr 25 '65
OLANA (historic house) See New York (state) —Historic houses, etc.
OLAND (island)
Sweden's twin treasures. E. J. Guerin. il Travel 124:32-5+ Ag '65
OLD, David, and Gorini, Luigi
Amino acid changes provoked by streptomycin in a polypeptide synthesized in vitro. bibliog Science 150:1290-2 D 3 '65
OLD age
Harvest in May: promises of age. il Am Ed 1:20-1 My '65
Splendid old. G. Fielding. Harper 230:104-6 F '65
See also
Aged
OLD age homes
See also
Nursing homes
Retirement, Places of
OLD age pensions
See also
Pensions, Industrial
Retirement income
United States
At last: the details on bigger pensions, medicare. il U S News 58:98+ Ap 5 '65
Bigger checks for old people: who gets how much and when. il U S News 58:94-5 F 22 '65
New rules for self-pensioning? U S News 58:122 Je 21 '65
Why pension plans boost savings; concerning G. Katona's book Private pensions and individual savings. Bsns W p98+ D 11 '65
See also
Social security act amendments
OLD age, survivors' and disability insurance trust fund
Ruminations on social security. J. Brookner. il Nat R 17:868-9 O 5 '65
OLD automobile museums. See Automobile museums
OLD automobiles
Collectors and collecting
See Automobiles—Collectors and collecting
OLD Faithful (geyser) See Geysers
OLD irreplaceable me; story. See Rudo, R. M.
OLD NORTHWEST. See Northwest, Old
OLD Order, Amish. See Mennonites
OLD people. See Aged
OLD priest; story. See Cullinan, E.
OLD SALEM, N.C. See Winston-Salem, N.C.
OLDENBURG, Claes
Object: still life; interview. por Craft Horiz 25:31-2+ S '65
OLDERSHAW, C. F.
About that carburetor. Flying 77:104+ S '65
OLDHAM, C. H. G.
How red China is taking science to its peasants; ed. by J. Lear. Sat R 48:45-6 Mr 6 '65
Science in mainland China: a tourist's impressions. bibliog Science 147:706-14 F 12 '65
OLDSMOBILE division. See General motors corporation—Oldsmobile division
O'LEARY, K. Basil
Brother. Commonweal 82:142-6 Ap 23 '65
OLEFINS
Phytadienes in zooplankton. M. Blumer and D. W. Thomas. il Science 147:1148-9 Mr 5 '65
OLEIC acid
Inheritance of linoleic and oleic acids in maize. C. G. Poneleit and D. E. Alexander. bibliog il Science 147:1585-6 Mr 26 '65
OLENGA, Nicolas
111 days in Stanleyville, by D. Reed. Review
Sat R il 48:37-8 D 11 '65
Stanleyville massacre; excerpt from 111 days in Stanleyville. D. Reed. il por Read Digest 87:233-8+ S '65
OLFACTORY nerves
Electroencephalographic studies of homing salmon. T. J. Hara and others. bibliog il Science 149:884-5 Ag 20 '65

OLFSON, Lewy
Washington square; dramatization of novel by H. James. Plays 24:85-94 Mr '65
(ed) See Shakespeare, W. Julius Caesar
(ed) See Shakespeare, W. Macbeth
OLIGONUCLEOTIDES. See Nucleotides
OLIN Mathieson chemical corporation
Ammonia's new world: more plant, less crew; largest synthetic ammonia plant, Lake Charles, La. il Bsns W p 134-6+ N 13 '65
Tidying up the house. il Time 86:92+ N 26 '65
OLITSKI, Jules
Frankenthaler & Olitski. M. Kozloff. Nation 200:374-6 Ap 5 '65
OLIVA, Tony
Tony Oliva: Twins' lonely star. T. Cohane. il pors Look 29:83+ Je 1 '65
Twins' blessed event. H. L. Masin. por Sr Schol 86:34 My 20 '65
OLIVEIRA SALAZAR, António de. See Salazar, A. de O.
OLIVER, Edith
Current cinema (cont) New Yorker 41:78+ Je 26; 58+ Jl 3; 54 Jl 10 '65
Off Broadway. See issues of New Yorker
OLIVER, Margaretta (Wood)
Obituary
Sr Schol 86:sup2 Mr 11 '65
OLIVER, Robert T.
Influence of public speaking in American history; address, August 20, 1965. Vital Speeches 31:759-61 O 1 '65
OLIVER Twist; drama. See Side, R. K.
OLIVETTI
Olivetti hits the keys of revival; Italy's office machine manufacturer. Bsns W p70+ N 20 '65
OLMEC INDIANS. See Indians of Mexico
OLMSTED, Frederick Law
Frederick Law Olmsted: launching the Nation. R. Fridlington. por Nation 202:10-12 Ja 3 '66
Yosemite's hundredth birthday. W. R. Jones. il por Nat Parks Mag 39:14-17 Ap '65
OLSEN, Arthur J.
Man who holds the mirror to Germany. N Y Times Mag p30-1+ F 7 '65
Since August 13, everything's different. N Y Times Mag p36-7+ S 19 '65
OLSEN, Jack
Island asylum for mad fishermen. Sports Illus 23:74-6+ N 8 '65
OLSEN, James
Can delinquency be predicted? Sr Schol 86:sup 14 My 6 '65
Teaching study skills. Sr Schol 86:sup24 Mr 4 '65
Trouble with programmed teaching. por Library J 90:935-6+ F 15 '65
Where kids are kings. Sr Schol 86:sup 10-11 Mr 4 '65
OLSEN, Tillie
Silences, when writers don't write; adaptation of address. Harper 231:153-6+ O '65
OLSON, Alan P. See Euler, R. C. jt. auth.
OLSON, Allen Dale
Teachers: partners in progress. NEA J 55: 62 Ja '66
OLSON, Charles
Grandfather-father poem; Cole's island; poems. Poetry 106:90-9 Ap '65
about
Berkeley: free speech and free verse. D. Wesling. Nation 201:338-40 N 8 '65
OLSON, Edwin A. and Chatters, R. M.
Carbon-14 and tritium dating. Science 150: 1488-92 D 10 '65
OLSON, Enid M.
Censorship as seen by English teachers. ALA Bul 59:525 Je '65
OLSON, John F.
Inexpensive alerting system brings fire safety to private buildings. Am City 80:119+ O '65
OLSON, Sigurd F.
Sig Olson: wilderness philosopher. D. B. Huyck. pors Am For 71:46-7+ My '65
OLSON, Ted
Booked for travel. Sat R 48:54-5 S 11 '65
Esthete contemplates nature and finds it derivative; poem. Sat R 48:95 N 13 '65
OLTER, Bailey
Trust Territory of the Pacific Islands; statement, June 2, 1965. Dept State Bul 53:295-7 Ag 16 '65
OLYMPIA press
Maurice Girodias: in trouble for his d.b.'s. Pub W 188:34-5 O 11 '65
On the fringe. H. Frankel. Sat R 48:46+ O 2 '65

OLYMPIC games
AAU plays by international rules; reprint. D. F. Hull. il Recreation 58:281-2 Je '65
Anyone for golf? Sports Illus 22:11 F 15 '65
See also
International games for the deaf
OLYMPIC games, 1964
Sporting spirit; Tokyo Olympiad; J. Douglas version changes Japanese epic into newsreel. A. Knight. Sat R 48:50 D 11 '65
OLYMPIC games, 1968
Getting high in Mexico city; high altitude's effect on athletes. B. Ottum. il Sports Illus 23:30-1 O 25 '65
In the high, thin air; Mexico city. il Time 86:70 D 31 '65
Olympics without oxygen? predictions of disaster in Mexico city. Newsweek 66:63 N 1 '65
Trouble in the snow; International Olympic committee to recognize East Germany as an Olympic nation. Sports Illus 22:17 Ap 26 '65
OLYMPIC NATIONAL PARK
Olympic reverie. R. Kirk. il Nat Parks Mag 39:4-7 My '65
Spring in July on Hurricane Ridge. il Sunset 135:48 Jl '65
O'MALLEY, C. D. See Mommaerts, W. F. H. M. jt. auth.
O'MALLEY, Patrick Lawrence
Where profits are really food and drink; Automatic canteen co. of America. il Bsns W p88-90 Jl 3 '65
OMAN
See also
United Nations—Oman
OMBUDSMAN. See Administrative remedies
OMEGA cameras. See Cameras
OMELETS
It's a puffy Swedish omelet. il Sunset 135:240+ O '65
ON a clear day you can see forever; musical comedy. See Musical comedies, revues, etc. —Criticisms, plots, etc.
ON the edge of Arcadia; story. See Cole, T.
ON the edge; story. See Feeley, C.
ON-the-job training. See Employees—Training
ON the waves; story. See Brodkey, H.
ON trial; drama. See Rice, E.
ONASSIS, Aristotle Socrates
Monarch & the magnate. il por Time 86:43 O 1 '65
ONCE upon a midnight; story. See Ernst, P.
ONE Christmas in Montana; story. See Richard, A.
ONE of those days; story. See Glaze, E.
ONE-room schools. See Rural schools—One-teacher schools
ONE summer; story. See Lavin, M.
ONE sunny morning; story. See Boyle, K.
ONE to grow on; drama. See Miller, H. L.
O'NEAL, Shirley
Summer job. il por Newsweek 66:21-2 Jl 19 '65
O'NEAL, Thomas
Two good cops in bad trouble. S. Alexander. Life 59:16 Jl 30 '65
O'NEIL, Paul
Bradley: good man and true. Life 58:93-4+ Ap 2 '65
Flag or rag, it's still grand. Life 58:19 My 7 '65
Grand old king of the Senate. Life 58:88-90+ Mr 26 '65; Same abr. Read Digest 87:84-8 Ag '65
Little queen Hollywood deserved. Life 58:72-6+ Je 4 '65
O'NEILL, Charles
(ed) See Marquis, D. Don Marquis to the young
O'NEILL, Charles Edwards
Book reviews. America 113:100 Jl 24 '65
O'NEILL, Colman
What is transignification all about? por Cath World 202:204-10 Ja '66
O'NEILL, Eugene Gladstone
Vulgarity of O'Neill. T. F. Curley. Commonweal 83:443-6 Ja 14 '66
O'NEILL, Jeanne Lamb
Love me, love my Duncan Phyfe. Am Home 68:30 Mr '65
Under the spreading chestnut tree, the shopping center stands. Am Home 68:16 Ap '65
O'NEILL, Michael J.
Will our baby be normal? McCalls 92:64+ My '65
O'NEILL, Thomas P.
Excerpt from remarks, July 28, 1965. Cong Digest 44:200 Ag '65

ONG, Walter J.
Recollections in tranquillity. Sat R 48:37-8+ Ap 10 '65
Ungodly world. Christian Cent 82:142 F 3 '65
ONIONS
How to spot untreated onions. B. Hardy. il Farm J 89:56F F '65
Onions. il Ladies Home J 82:84 Jl '65
See also
Shallots
ONSAGER, Lars
Life of a theoretical scientist. E. J. Sozanski. por Sci Digest 57:28-31 F '65
ONTARIO
See also
Geology—Ontario
North Channel
Paleontology—Ontario

Description and travel

Triangle of cruising contrasts; Ontario's Golden triangle. B. Koelbel. il Motor B 115:22-5+ Je '65

Religious institutions and affairs

News of the Christian world (cont) Christian Cent 82:347-8, 821-2, 1583 Mr 17, Je 23, D 22 '65
ONTARIO, LAKE
U.S. and Canada sign agreement on claims relating to Gut Dam; Department statement, March 25, 1965, with text of agreement. Dept State Bul 52:643-6 Ap 26 '65
OP art. See Modernism (art)
OP photography. See Photography
OPAL
Opal miners of Lightning Ridge; New South Wales. B. L. Burman. il Read Digest 86:171-6 Je '65
OPAQUE-2 maize. See Corn
OPEN air church services. See Church services
OPEN and closed shop
Inviting strikes; automation and union shop are issues in New York newspaper strike. H. Hazlitt. Newsweek 66:90 O 11 '65
Workers vs. unions. il Nations Bsns 53:60-2+ Ap '65
OPEN-end investment trusts. See Investment trusts
OPERA
Bravo Bacchus! drinking in opera; reprint. G. Jellinek. il Opera N 30:8-9 O 23 '65
Mozart on the eighteenth-century stage. H. C. R. Landon. il Hi Fi 15:62-4+ N '65
No theater; ancient dramatic art bears many similarities to opera. F. Bowers. il Opera N 30:8-13 Ja 1 '66
Singing in a tree. J. Sutherland. Seventeen 24:164+ S '65

Appreciation

See Music—Appreciation

Chorus

Ladies and gentlemen. A. M. Lingg. il Opera N 29:12-16 Mr 20 '65

History and criticism

About Four saints; libretto by G. Stein. V. Thomson. Am Rec G 31:520-1 F '65
Beautiful dreamer; sleep in opera. G. Jellinek. Opera N 29:12 Mr 6 '65
Bigger than life; in Fidelio Beethoven wrote more than an opera. E. Downes. il Opera N 30:24-5 Ja 22 '66
Connoisseur's Tosca. R. Lawrence. Opera N 29:24-5 Ap 17 '65
Cosi is like that. S. Hughes. il Opera N 29:24-5 F 20 '65
Erminie, a Victorian extravaganza. H. Birdoff. il Hobbies 70:35 D '65
Never a dull moment; Ernani. S. Hughes. Opera N 29:24-5 Ap 10 '65
New and enlarged treasury of grand opera, by. H. W. Simon. Review
New Yorker 41:236-7 D 11 '65. W. Sargeant
Non-traveling opera. A. Dorati. Opera N 29:6-7 Ap 17 '65
One who's right; Arabella, Hofmannsthal's fairy tale. P. J. Smith. Opera N 30:24-5 D 18 '65
Outlaw as hero; opera, Ernani. H. Peyre. il Opera N 29:8-11 Ap 10 '65
Perfect achievement; Ring of the Nibelung. H. Bailey. Opera N 29:24-5 Mr 6 '65
Problem child for both Schiller and Verdi, Don Carlo. L. C. McGinn. Opera N 30:24-5 D 11 '65
Tales for our time. P. J. Smith. Opera N 29:24-5 F 27 '65

OPERA—History and criticism—*Continued*

To weep and remember; Barber's nostalgic score mirrors Vanessa's backward glances. J. W. Freeman. il Opera N 29:24-6 Ap 3 '65

Wayward daughter; Perichole. K. McDonald. il Opera N 30:22-3 D 25 '65

Wings of the storm; Wagner's first music drama Der fliegende Holländer. E. Downes. il Opera N 29:24-6 F 13 '65

Instruction and study

Miracle in Manhattan: J. Brownlee's opera theater. Q. Eaton. il Opera N 30:14-15 D 18 '65
  See also
College operas, revues, etc.

Language

American bel canto. J. Raskin. Opera N 30:6 Ja 15 '66
Good libretto. R. Martin and T. Martin. il Opera N 29:12-15 F 20 '65
Non-traveling opera. A. Dorati. Opera N 29: 6-7 Ap 17 '65

Stage scenery

Light touch; interview, ed. by H. Johnson. G. Schneider-Siemssen. il Opera N 29:6 Mr 6 '65

Man engaged; interview, ed. by P. J. Smith. R. Heinrich. il Opera N 29:14-15 Mr 13 '65

Opera urbanized; designer, director, architect, J. Urban revolutionized the stage. Q. Eaton. il Opera N 29:26-30 F 27 '65

Australia

Sutherland back home. T. Durdin. il Opera N 30:36+ O 23 '65

Brazil

Pearl of Brazil; Teatro Amazonas, Manaus. J. Honig. il Opera N 30:6-7 D 25 '65

Canada

Canadian east. R. D. Daniels. Opera N 30:25 N 20 '65

Czechoslovakia

Brno. C. N. Welsh. il Opera N 30:31 D 4 '65

Finland

Northern country. Opera N 29:14-16 Ap 3 '65

France

Rouen, Paris. D. Stevens. Opera N 29:29 My 1 '65

Germany (Democratic Republic)

News from Germany. J. H. Sutcliffe. il Opera N 29:30-1 My 1 '65

Germany (Federal Republic)

News from Germany. E. D. Echols; H. Koegler. Opera N 29:30-1 My 1 '65
  See also
Bayreuth festival

Italy

First nights in Italy. F. Nuzzo. il Opera N 29:32-3 F 27 '65
Spoleto, Naples, Rome. F. Nuzzo. il Opera N 30:24 N 6 '65
Year for Rossini. W. Weaver. Hi Fi 15:119 Jl '65

Latin America

South American scene. R. Lawrence. il Hi Fi 15:208-13 N '65

Scandinavia

Scandinavian spring. F. Stevenson. il Opera N 30:24 S 25 '65

Switzerland

Swiss hits. D. A. Mackinnon. il Opera N 29: 32 Ap 10 '65

United States

California's Mozart era. P. Emerson. il Opera N 30:30 S 25 '65
Donizetti's Lucrezia Borgia; concert performance in Carnegie Hall. P. J. Smith. il Hi Fi 15:98 Jl '65
From France; classic and romantic. P. J. Smith. Hi Fi 15:115 Je '65
Great opera houses: the ghosts; from Albany to Buffalo. Q. Eaton. il Opera N 29:26-9 Mr 27 '65
Home stretch at the Met. C. L. Osborne. il Hi Fi 15:111-12 My '65
Ladies on the loose; itinerant prima donnas. Q. Eaton. il Opera N 30:32-4 O 23 '65
Lustrum for the studio. J. Gutman. il Opera N 30:26-7 D 4 '65

Manon on a mountaintop; Central City festival performance and season's forthcoming events. I. Kolodin. Sat R 48:33 Ag 7 '65

Opera: con amore; Time essay. Time 86:54-5 O 8 '65

Spring comes to City Center. C. L. Osborne. Hi Fi 15:116-17+ Je '65

Spring tour casts (cont) Opera N 29:31 Mr 27 '65

Tosca at last; R. Crespin. R. Lawrence. il Hi Fi 15:113-14 Je '65

Total theatre, part-time; operas. G. Rogoff. il Hi Fi 15:133-4 Ap '65

U.S. calendar (cont) Opera N 30:32-3 S 25; 28-9 N 6; 33 D 4; 35 D 11 '65

U.S. calendar; New York city opera season of 20th-century works. Opera N 29:33 Mr 6 '65

U.S. opera survey: a new wave. F. Merkling. il Opera N 30:16-19 N 20 '65

Winning friends for opera. S. Spaeth. il Opera N 30:8-11 D 11 '65
  See also
American opera society
Associated opera companies of America
Central City opera association, Colo.
Central opera service
Cincinnati summer opera association
Clarion music society
Connecticut opera association
Metropolitan opera company
Metropolitan opera house, New York
Metropolitan opera national company
New York city opera company
Opera guilds
Pittsburgh opera company
Santa Fe opera association

OPERA, Chinese

Chinese opera walks the party line. R. Hughes. il N Y Times Mag p62+ Mr 21 '65

OPERA, French

French opera, by N. Demuth. Review Opera N 29:29 Ap 17 '65. R. Lawrence

OPERA, Italian

Don't call me maestro; interview with librettist of two Puccini operas, ed. by B. Fischer-Williams. G. Forzano. Opera N 30:6-7 Ja 1 '66
World premieres at La Scala. W. Legge. Hi Fi 15:135 Je '65

OPÉRA, Paris. See Opera houses

OPERA, Russian

Richnesses of Russian opera; Oprichnik, Maiden of Orleans; Cherivichki, and Queen of spades. C. L. Osborne. Hi Fi 16:74-6 Ja '66

OPERA and state. See Music and state

OPERA audiences. See Audiences

OPERA ballet. See Ballet

OPERA broadcasts. See Radio broadcasting—Music

OPERA club, Metropolitan. See Metropolitan opera club

OPÉRA-comique, Paris. See Opera houses

OPERA dancing. See Dancing

OPERA guilds

Affiliated guilds report (cont) il Opera N 29: 32-3 Mr 27 '65
Winning the West; San Francisco's opera guild. P. J. Smith. il Opera N 30:6-7 D 18 '65
  See also
Metropolitan opera guild

OPERA house, Lincoln Center. See Lincoln Center for the performing arts, New York —Opera house

OPERA houses

Brno. C. N. Welsh. il Opera N 30:31 D 4 '65
Great opera houses (cont) il Opera N 29:26-30 Mr 13 '65
Great opera houses: the ghosts; from Albany to Buffalo. Q. Eaton. il Opera N 29:26-9 Mr 27 '65
New look for the Opera-comique. R. McMullen. Hi Fi 15:116-17 Jl '65
New look in Santa Fe; opera theater underwent a face-lifting. E. C. Munro. il Opera N 30:14-16 S 25 '65
Pearl of Brazil; Teatro Amazonas, Manaus. J. Honig. il Opera N 30:6-7 D 25 '65
Renaissance in Warsaw; Grand theater of opera and ballet reopened. V. C. Gibbs and E. L. Howard. il Opera N 30:28-9 Ja 1 '66
South American scene. R. Lawrence. il Hi Fi 15:208-13 N '65
  See also
London—Covent Garden
Metropolitan opera house, New York

OPERA mundi, incorporated

Rights and permissions. P. Nathan. Pub W 188:57 N 1 '65

OPERA singers. See Singers
OPERA society of Washington
Natalia in Washington. M. E. Peltz. il
Opera N 29:34 My 1 '65
Roots for Washington. Q. Eaton. il Opera N
29:28-31 F 13 '65
Washington, D.C. F. C. Smith. Opera N 30:
31 Ja 1 '66
OPERA translation. See Opera—Language
OPERA workshops. See Opera—Instruction and
study
OPERAS
Cold steel, hot blood; operatic crimes. M. E.
Geib. il Opera N 29:6-7 Mr 27 '65
See also
Phonograph records—Operas

Bibliography
Operas on American subjects, by H. E. John-
son. Review
Opera N il 29:26-8 My 1 '65. Q. Eaton

Criticisms, plots, etc.
See name of composer for full entry
Aida. G. Verdi
L'ange de feu. See Flaming angel, below
Angel of fire. See Flaming angel, below
Arabella. R. Strauss
Atomtod. G. Manzoni
Barber of Seville. G. Rossini
Il barbiere di Siviglia. See Barber of Seville,
above
Beatrice and Benedict. H. Berlioz
Billy Budd. B. Britten
La Bohème. G. Puccini
Boris Godunov. M. P. Musorgskiĭ
Capriccio. R. Strauss
Carmen. G. Bizet
Cinderella. G. Rossini
Clitennestra. I. Pizzetti
Les contes d'Hoffmann. See Tales of Hoff-
mann, below
Cosi fan tutte. J. C. W. A. Mozart
Don Carlo. G. Verdi
Don Giovanni. J. C. W. A. Mozart
Don Quichotte. J. Massenet
Die dreigroschenoper. See Threepenny opera,
below
L'elisir d'amore. See Elixir of love, below
Elixir of love. G. Donizetti
Entführung aus dem serail. J. C. W. A.
Mozart
Ernani. G. Verdi
Fairy queen. H. Purcell
La fanciulla del West. See Girl of the golden
West, below
Faust. C. F. Gounod
Fidelio. L. van Beethoven
Flaming angel. S. S. Prokof'ev
Der fliegende Holländer. See Flying Dutch-
man, below
Flying Dutchman. R. Wagner
Force of destiny. See La forza del destino,
below
La forza del destino. G. Verdi
Four saints in three acts. V. Thomson
Girl of the golden West. G. Puccini
Herr von Hancken. K. B. Blomdahl
Intolerance, 1960. L. Nono
Intolleranza 1960. See Intolerance, 1960, above
Iolanthe. P. I. Tchaikovsky
Iphigénie en Tauride. C. W. Gluck
Jacobovski and the colonel. G. Klebe
Julius Caesar. G. F. Handel
Lohengrin. R. Wagner
Junge lord. See Young lord, below
Katerina Ismailova. D. D. Shostakovich
Lady Macbeth of Mtsensk. See Katerina
Ismailova, above
Lizzie Borden. J. Beeson
Lohengrin. R. Wagner
Lulu. A. Berg
Madame Butterfly. G. Puccini
Magic flute. J. C. W. A. Mozart
Mahagonny. K. Weill
Mamelles de Tirésias. F. Poulenc
Marriage of Figaro. J. C. W. A. Mozart
Midsummer night's dream. B. Britten
Miss Julie. N. Rorem
Moses and Aaron. A. Schoenberg
Mourning becomes Electra. M. D. Levy
Le nozze di Figaro. See Marriage of Figaro,
above
Pelléas et Mélisande. C. Debussy
La Perichole. J. Offenbach
Pique dame. See Queen of spades, below
Queen of spades. P. I. Tchaikovsky
Ring of the Nibelung. R. Wagner
Rise and fall of the city of Mahagonny.
See Mahagonny, above
Saint of Bleecker street. G. C. Menotti
Salome. R. Strauss
Samson and Delilah. C. Saint-Saëns
Stag king. H. W. Henze
Susannah. C. Floyd

Tales of Hoffmann. J. Offenbach
Threepenny opera. K. Weill
Tosca. G. Puccini
Il Trovatore. G. Verdi
Vanessa. S. Barber
Le Villi. G. Puccini
Die Walküre. R. Wagner
Wozzeck. A. Berg
Yolanta. See Iolanthe, above
Young lord. H. W. Henze

Scores
Sparkle of sound; score of Salome. P.
Keppler. il Opera N 29:24-5 Mr 13 '65
OPERATIC acting. See Acting
OPERATIC composition. See Composition
(music)
OPERATIC production
All of them do it; photographs of Metropoli-
tan Cosi fan tutte. Opera N 29:21-3 F 20 '65
Ballad of a glad cafe; photographs of Offen-
bach's Perichole. Opera N 30:21 D 25 '65
Belle of the ball; photographs of Arabella.
Opera N 30:21-3 D 18 '65
Betrayal of faith; photographs of Metropolitan
Don Carlo. Opera N 30:21-3 D 11 '65
Conquering hero; pictures of Metropolitan
Aida. il Opera N 29:21-3 Mr 20 '65
Ernani's rivals; photographs of Metropolitan
Ernani. Opera N 29:21-3 Ap 10 '65
Fact and fancy; photographs of Metropoli-
tan's La forza del destino. il Opera N 29:
21-3 F 6 '65
Fatal decision; photographs of Madama But-
terfly. Opera N 30:21-3 Ja 1 '66
Germ and the virus. H. Weinstock. il Sat R
48:47-9 D 25 '65
Getting opera on. M. Kalmanoff. il Opera N
30:8-12 Ja 8 '66
Great lady; photographs of Metropolitan's
Vanessa. Opera N 29:21-3 Ap 3 '65
Gypsy's son; photographs of Metropolitan
Il Trovatore. Opera N 30:21-3 D 4 '65
Happiest girl in the world; photographs of
Madame Butterfly. Opera N 29:21-3 Mr 27
'65
Her mother's child; photographs of Salome.
Opera N 29:21-3 Mr 13 '65
Lady general: M. Wallmann. il Time 85:50
Mr 12 '65
Love or money; photographs of Queen of
spades. Opera N 30:23-5 Ja 15 '66
Love triumphant; photographs of Fidelio.
Opera N 30:21-3 Ja 22 '66
Nightmare world; photographs of Tales of
Hoffmann. Opera N 29:21-3 F 27 '65
Of fortune and faro; gambling in opera. A.
Boucher. il Opera N 30:8-12 Ja 15 '66
Opera urbanized; designer, director, architect.
J. Urban revolutionized the stage. Q. Eaton.
Opera N 29:26-30 F 27 '65
Other side; Peter Hall's production of Moses
and Aaron. T. Heinitz. Sat R 48:43 Jl 31 '65
Preparing a performance; ed. by A. M. Lingg.
G. Schick. il Opera N 29:8-12 Mr 27 '65
Recognition; photographs of Die Walküre.
Opera N 29:21-3 Mr 6 '65
Richard und Ludwig; a new Tristan und
Isolde at Munich's National theater. Time
85:73 Je 18 '65
Salvation; photographs of the Flying Dutch-
man. Opera N 29:21-3 F 13 '65
She puts the oomph in the opera. D. J.
Hamblin. il Life 58:77-8+ Mr 5 '65
Some challenges. C. J. McNaspy. America
113:786 D 18 '65
Teamwork in Indianapolis; Metropolitan opera
national company productions; photographs.
Opera N 30:13-15 O 23 '65
To the rescue, photographs of Girl of the
golden West. Opera N 30:21-3 Ja 8 '66
Tosca's kiss; photographs of Metropolitan
production. Opera N 29:21-3 Ap 17 '65
Touch of magic; interview, ed. by P. J. Smith.
J. L. Barrault. Opera N 30:8-9 S 25 '65
See also
College operas, revues, etc.
Opera—Chorus
OPERATION long shot. See Atomic bombs—
Testing, Underground
OPERATION silver lance. See United States
—Marine corps—Maneuvers
OPERATIONS, Surgical. See Children—Surgery;
Surgery
OPHTHALMOLOGISTS
Making spectacles. New Repub 153:6 D 25 '65
OPHTHALMOLOGY
Need more eye research. Sci N L 87:182 Mr 20
'65
See also
Ophthalmologists
OPIE, John, Jr
Modernity of fundamentalism. Christian Cent
82:608-11 My 12 '65

OPINION, Public. See Public opinion

OPINION, Student. See Student opinion

OPINIONS, Personal. See Attitudes

OPIUM
See also
Morphine

OPPEN, George
Guest room; People, the people; poems.
Poetry 105:387-91 Mr '65

OPPENHEIMER, Jack H. and others
Metabolism of iodine-131-labeled thyroxine-
binding prealbumin in man. bibliog Science
149:748-51 Ag 13 '65

OPPENHEIMER, Joan L.
Has anybody here seen Barbie? story. Seventeen 24:104-5 Jl '65

OPPENHEIMER, Julius Robert
Controversial European play. H. Popkin.
Vogue 146:296-8+ S 1 '65
Oppenheimer: the story of a friendship, by
H. Chevalier. Review
America 113:244-5 S 4 '65. J. B. Kelley
Nat R 17:806 S 21 '65
New Repub 153:25-7 D 18 '65. T. Wilson,
jr
Newsweek il por 66:80-1 Ag 30 '65
Sat R por 48:102+ S 18 '65. N. S. Finney

OPTICAL art. See Modernism (art)

OPTICAL communication systems. See Light
communication systems

OPTICAL glass fibers. See Fiber optics

OPTICAL illusions
Balls o' fire! PM tracks down Ozark Spook-
light. R. Gannon. il Pop Mech 124:116-19+
S '65
Illusions. Design 66:2-3 Ja '65

OPTICAL instruments
See also
Range finding
Telescope

OPTICAL masers. See Lasers

OPTICAL reading machines. See Reading machines

OPTICAL scanners. See Reading machines

OPTICAL stimulus. See Stimulus and response

OPTICAL technicians. See Technicians in industry

OPTICS
See also
Fiber optics
Light
Photographic optics

Terminology
Glossary of optical terms. Electr World 73:
28 My '65

ORAL English. See English language

ORAL history
Voices of history. il Newsweek 66:72 Ag 23 '65

ORANGE soufflé; drama. See Bellow, S.

ORANGES
Orange men get caught in squeeze; Florida's
citrus problem. il Bsns W p 156+ D 4 '65
See also
Cookery—Fruit

ORANS, Martin
U.S.-Soviet Kula. Bul Atomic Sci 21:44-5
Mr '65

ORANS, Muriel
Geraniums bring a new look to your summer
garden picture. Pop Gard 16:18-20 Jl '65
Geraniums new for 1965. il Flower Grower
52:19 Mr '65

ORATORIOS
See also
Phonograph records—Oratorios

ORBACH, J. See Kling, A.; Schuckman, H. jt.
auths.

ORBELO, William R.
Colt model 1849 pocket revolver. Hobbies 69:
127 F '65
Underhammer pistols. Hobbies 70:115+ Ja
'66

ORBITAL rendezvous (space flight)
After a failure, a space spectacular? il U S
News 59:18 N 8 '65
Agena ready for new rendezvous role. J. F.
Judge. il Miss & Roc 17:35-6 O 18 '65
Agena target effort pushed for Gemini 8. R.
G. O'Lone. il Aviation W 83:59-60 D 27 '65
Docking last big goal as Gemini reaches
halfway point. W. J. Normyle. il Aviation
W 83:22-6 D 27 '65
Four men who met in space. il U S News
59:12 D 27 '65
Gemini-5 may attempt rendezvous with sepa-
rately launched Agena. Aviation W 82:26
Je 21 '65
Gemini-5, pod to rendezvous after three hr.
P. J. Klass. il Aviation W 83:22-3 Jl 19 '65

Gemini rendezvous hinges on countdown. G.
Alexander. Aviation W 83:74+ O 18 '65
Gemini 7/6 demonstrate Apollo feasibility;
with editorial comment. W. J. Normyle. il
Aviation W 83:11, 16-18 D 20 '65
GTA-6 plan includes for docking attempts.
Miss & Roc 17:15 O 25 '65
GT-5 will test rendezvous system. C. D. La-
Fond. il Miss & Roc 16:22-3 Je 28 '65
Gemini to rendezvous with Pegasus vehicle.
Aviation W 83:37 Jl 12 '65
Gemini triumphs; what's next? il U S News
59:19-21 D 27 '65
Gemini ²; new NASA proposal. il Newsweek
66:72 N 8 '65
Longest journey; Gemini 7/6 mission. il
Newsweek 66:60 D 13 '65
Memorable Gemini triumphs. il Life 60:24-31
Ja 7 '66
Moon in their grasp; first manned rendezvous.
il Time 86:32-6 D 24 '65
NASA to try rendezvous of Gemini 6,7. Avia-
tion W 83:17 N 1 '65
185 miles high, Gemini meets Gemini. il
Newsweek 66:42-6 D 27 '65
Rendezvous, formation mission profile evolves
for Gemini 7/6. Aviation W 83:24 N 22 '65
Rendezvous in space. W. Von Braun. il Pop
Sci 187:58-9+ Jl '65
Russia may attempt space rendezvous next.
Aviation W 82:28-9 Je 28 '65
Still all go for space meeting; Gemini-6 to
rendezvous with Gemini-7. il Bsns W
p 150+ D 11 '65
Success spells change in Gemini plans. H.
Taylor; C. D. LaFond; J. Mercer. il Miss
& Roc 17:15-17 D 20 '65
Two for rendezvous; Gemini 6 preview. il
Newsweek 66:56 N 1 '65
We did it, nose-to-nose in orbit for a space
first; Gemini 7 and Gemini 6. il Bsns W
p30 D 18 '65
Year the moon came closer; space accomplish-
ment topped by Gemini rendezvous. il Bsns
W p 14-15 D 25 '65

ORBITING astronomical observatory. See Artificial satellites—Astronomical applications

ORBITING geophysical observatory. See Artificial satellites—Astronomical applications

ORBITING radio astronomy observatory. See
Artificial satellites—Astronomical applications

ORBITING solar observatory. See Artificial
satellites—Astronomical applications

ORBITS
See also
Moon—Orbit

ORCAS ISLAND. See San Juan Islands, Wash.

ORCHARD sprayers. See Spraying and dusting
apparatus

ORCHARDS. See Fruit trees

ORCHESTRA shells
Philharmonic in the park. I. Kolodin. il Sat
R 48:56-7 S 11 '65

ORCHESTRAL music
See also
Phonograph records—Orchestral music

ORCHESTRAS
Again, the Ford millennium; foundation grant
to American orchestras. B. Boretz. Nation
201:368-70 N 15 '65
City of five orchestras; London. E. Green-
field. il Hi Fi 15:51-5 Ap '65
L'esprit de jeunesse, et de corps, et d'art;
Arctic report. H. von Hochmeister. Hi Fi
15:188-90 D '65
Ford in their future; grants to U.S. orchestras. Time 86:71 O 29 '65
Giving an upbeat to orchestra finances. Bsns
W p31 O 23 '65
Kenton at the Pavilion; Los Angeles neo-
phonic orchestra. H. Siders. il Sat R 48:
62-3 F 13 '65
Letter from Paris; two concerts performed
by Vermont's Marlboro festival group,
in Théâtre des Champs-Elysées. Genêt.
New Yorker 41:205-6 O 2 '65
Mephisto's musings; movement toward year-
round contracts, higher salaries, and in-
creased benefits for players. il Hi Fi 15:
188+ N '65
Music to my ears; the other Richter. M.
Bernheimer. Sat R 48:48 My 8 '65
Orchestra at work; photographs. Opera N
29:27-9 Ap 3 '65
Orchestras second to none. R. Hemming. Sr
Schol 86:22 My 6 '65
Orchestras U.S.A. season's forecast. Hi Fi
15:150-3 S '65
See also names of orchestras, e.g. BBC
symphony orchestra

ORCHIDS
Cinnamon scented orchid. J. Kramer. il
Flower Grower 52:28 O '65

ORCHIDS—*Continued*

Hardy orchids. K. S. Taylor. il Horticulture 43:20-3 Ap '65

How to care for orchids in the summer. A. J. Hofsommer. il Horticulture 43:26-7+ Ag '65

Living with orchids. J. A. Eaton. il House & Gard 128:290-1+ N '65

Orchids. J. Arditti. il Sci Am 214:70-8 bibliog (p 135) Ja '66

Orchids for profit. R. P. Hammond. il Pop Gard 16:24-5 N '65

Should you try cymbidiums? il Sunset 134:256+ Ap '65

Spice orchid for spring. J. Kramer. il Flower Grower 52:44 Ap '65

See also
Ladys slippers

ORD, Edward Otho Cresap

Tale of a table. M. A. Benjamin. il por Am Heritage 16:100-1 Ap '65

ORDAZ, Gustavo Díaz. See Díaz Ordaz, G.

ORDNANCE

Small-caliber weapons get new look. il Miss & Roc 16:94-6+ Mr 29 '65

Materials

Pyrofuze finds ordnance application: palladium and aluminum in a bimetallic composite. J. F. Judge. il Miss & Roc 16:32-4 My 24 '65

ORDNANCE plants. See Munitions works

ORE handling

Processing ore to suit the customers; Port ore processing co, Phila. il Bsns W p 138-40 My 22 '65

OREAR, Jay, and Wolfenstein, Lincoln

European scientists speak. Bul Atomic Sci 21:44-5 Ap '65

OREGON

See also
Architecture, Domestic—Oregon
Crater Lake National Park
Education—Oregon
Fishing—Oregon
Hood, Mount
Hunting—Oregon
Santiam River

Description and travel

Oregon loop for beachcombers; Cape Meares loop road. il Sunset 134:28 My '65

Oregon's Coast highway. W. F. Heald. il Travel 124:24-9 S '65

Politics and government

Mark's other woman. Time 86:37 N 5 '65

OREGON CAVES NATIONAL MONUMENT

Going underground in Oregon. il Sunset 134:44 Je '65

OREGON Coast highway. See Roads—Oregon

OREGON DUNES NATIONAL SEASHORE (proposed) See National parks and reserves—United States

OREGON. University

Holiday U; Vacation college, an eight-day session for adults. il Newsweek 66:74 Ag 30 '65

O'REILLY, John

Conservation. Sports Illus 22:70+ Je 7 '65

How to write animal stories. Sat R 48:54-6 Ag 14 '65

Nature (cont) Sports Illus 22:46-7 F 1 '65

Redcoats return to Bucks County. Sports Illus 23:78-80+ N 22 '65

O'REILLY, Peter

Academic revolution at St John's. F. Canavan. America 113:137-40 Ag 7 '65

ORGAN

Answers please: Heathkit electronic organ. il Pop Electr 23:53-5 S '65

Consumer study of electronic organs. il Consumer Bul 48:19-29 S '65

Piano and organ glossary at your finger tips. House & Gard 127:8+ F '65

You build this electronic organ from a kit. H. P. Luckett. il Pop Sci 186:158-61 Mr '65

Instruction and study

Five fast ways to learn the organ! Bet Hom & Gard 43:12 Jl '65

ORGAN music

Prestige of the organ; Paris report. R. McMullen. Hi Fi 15:181 D '65

ORGAN PIPE CACTUS NATIONAL MONUMENT

Organ Pipe Cactus National Monument. W. F. Heald. il Nat Parks Mag 39:9-12 Ap '65

Winter visit to Organ Pipe. Sunset 134:24 F '65

ORGANIC chemistry. See Chemistry, Organic

ORGANIC compounds

Organic compounds in carbonaceous chondrites. M. H. Studier and others. bibliog il Science 149:1455-9 S 24 '65

See also
Cyclobutadiene

ORGANIC evolution. See Evolution

ORGANIC ketones. See Ketones

ORGANIZATION for economic cooperation and development

Agreed minute provides for exchange of shipping information. Dept State Bul 52:188-90 F 8 '65

Economic hassle for de Gaulle; OECD advice to scrap economic stabilization plan. Bsns W p98+ Ag 14 '65

Europeans frustrated in space hopes; OECD study. W. S. Beller. il Miss & Roc 18:34-5 Ja 3 '66

New plan for older workers. C. A. Betts. il Sci N L 87:298-9 My 8 '65

OECD ministerial council meets at Paris; text of communique, November 26, 1965, and U.S. delegation. Dept State Bul 53:1038-9 D 27 '65

ORGANIZATION for European nuclear research. See European organization for nuclear research

ORGANIZATION in industry. See Industrial management and organization

ORGANIZATION of African unity

Adding fuel; OAU ultimatum over British Rhodesia policy. il Newsweek 66:34+ D 27 '65

Conflict of summits. Time 86:21 Ag 27 '65

Fateful moment at the Maginot Hilton. Time 86:37 O 29 '65

General assembly adopts resolution; co-operation with OAU. UN Mo Chron 2:17 N '65

Host with the most. Newsweek 66:43 N 1 '65

Looking for votes; meeting of the Organization of African unity. Time 85:26+ Mr 12 '65

Organization of African unity. il Dept State Bul 52:669-77 My 3 '65

Organization of African unity; excerpts from Nation-building in Africa. A. Rivkin. bibliog f Cur Hist 48:193-200+ Ap '65

Resolutions on the Congo; excerpts from the O.A.U. resolution, September 10 and text of the Security council resolution, December 30, 1964. Cur Hist 48:237-8 Ap '65

ORGANIZATION of American states

Common quest for freedom and prosperity in the American republics; address, November 22, 1965; with texts of resolutions adopted at Rio de Janeiro conference. D. Rusk. bibliog f Dept State Bul 53:985-95, 996-8 D 20 '65; Same with title Inter-American systems. Vital Speeches 32:130-5 D 15 '65

Council considers situation; conditions in the Dominican Republic. UN Mo Chron 2:11-16 Ag '65

Dialogue begins; second special Inter-American conference. il Time 86:40 N 26 '65

Dominican crisis: help from the OAS. il Newsweek 65:44+ My 17 '65

Dominican intervention: forward or backward for Uncle Sam? with press comments. il Sr Schol 87:6-8, 10-11 S 16 '65

Dominican Republic: force for conciliation. il Time 85:32-3 My 14 '65

Johnson corollary; legality and morality of U.S. intervention in foreign states. il Time 85:24-5 My 14 '65

Letter from Washington. R. H. Rovere. New Yorker 41:206-10+ My 15 '65

Only a beginning; concerning OAS foreign minister's meeting in Rio. Time 86:40+ D 3 '65

OAS achieves reconciliation in Dominican Republic; statements, September 1, 1965; with declaration to the Dominican people. L. B. Johnson. Dept State Bul 53:477-80 S 20 '65

OAS approves peace force; Dominican Republic. il Sr Schol 86:14 My 20 '65

OAS foreign ministers provide for establishment of inter-American force in Dominican Republic; statements May 1-14, 1965, with texts of resolutions and Act of Santo Domingo. E. Bunker. Dept State Bul 52:854-69 My 31 '65

OAS in action. See issues of Américas

OAS in Rio. Commonweal 83:263-4 D 3 '65

OAS informed of U.S. move to help Cuban refugees; statement, October 6, 1965. W. P. Allen. Dept State Bul 53:663-4 O 25 '65

OAS moves in, slowly; Dominican turmoil. il Bsns W p36 My 15 '65

ORGANIZATION of American states—*Cont.*
O.A.S. on the Dominican Republic resolution,
May 6, 1965. Cur Hist 50:50+ Ja '66
OAS Secretary General to represent meeting
of consultation in Dominican Republic;
Brazilian to command inter-American
force; statements and notes, May 15-22,
1965, with resolutions adopted by the meet-
ing E. Bunker. Dept State Bul 52:908-13
Je 7 '65
OAS to help restore democratic order in
Dominican Republic; statement, June 2,
1965, with text of resolution. D. Rusk. Dept
State Bul 52:1017-18 Je 21 '65
OAS: trying to hold the Americas together.
Time 85:33 My 14 '65
O.A.S. turns a corner; peace-keeping in Santo
Domingo. Life 58:4 Je 11 '65
Principles of U.N.-OAS relationship in Do-
minican Republic; statements, May 22 and
May 24, 1965. A. E. Stevenson. Dept State
Bul 52:975-80 Je 14 '65
Q&A on the OAS: what it is, how strong,
what it can do. il U S News 58:39-40 My
17 '65
Relief operation; Dominican Republic. Amér-
icas 17:41 O '65
Responsibility & deadlock; OAS military
force in Santo Domingo. il Time 85:42+ Je
11 '65
Resurgent OAS? Commonweal 83:360 D 24 '65
Secretary discusses situation in Dominican
Republic interview, ed. by J. Hightower.
D. Rusk. Dept State Bul 52:842-4 My 31 '65
Secretary Rusk's news conference of May 26,
1965; with questions and answers. D. Rusk.
Dept State Bul 52:938-47 Je 14 '65
Security council authorizes U.N. representa-
tive in Dominican Republic; statements,
May 3-5, 1965, with text of resolution adopt-
ed May 14, 1965. A. E. Stevenson. bibliog f
Dept State Bul 52:869-85 My 31 '65
75th anniversary of the Organization of
American states: the record of the inter-
American system; address, April 14, 1965.
H. H. Humphrey. bibliog f Dept State Bul
52:726-31 My 10 '65
Special issue in honor of the seventy-fifth
anniversary of the Inter-American system;
symposium. il Américas 17:1-65 Ap '65
Stalemate of hate; role of OAS team in the
Dominican Republic. il Time 86:30-1 Jl 2
'65
Success of sorts; foreign ministers meeting.
Newsweek 66:54 D 13 '65
Uncertain solution. Time 86:34-5 Ag 20 '65
U.N. Security council considers situation in
Dominican Republic; statements, May 19-21,
1965. A. E. Stevenson. Dept State Bul 52:
913-19 Je 7 '65
U.S. acts to meet threat in Dominican Re-
public; statements and letter, April 28-
May 2, 1965, with texts of three resolutions.
L. B. Johnson; A. E. Stevenson; E. Bunker.
bibliog f Dept State Bul 52:738-48 My 17 '65
U.S. steps into another hornet's nest; sending
troops to Santo Domingo. il Bsns W p28-9
My 8 '65
U.S. submits to U.N. security council OAS
documents on Dominican Republic; state-
ment, June 18, 1965. A. E. Stevenson. Dept
State Bul 53:132-5 Jl 19 '65
When it comes to getting action out of OAS.
il U S News 58:38 My 24 '65
Yankee go home? stay home? intervene?
J. P. Davies, jr. il N Y Times Mag p28-9+
My 23 '65
See also
Inter-American cultural council
ORGANIZATION of petroleum exporting coun-
tries
Libya acts to bolster the price for its oil.
Bsns W p 16 Ja 1 '66
ORGANIZATIONS. See Associations
ORGANIZATIONS for peace. See Peace con-
ferences
ORGANIZED crime. See Crime and criminals
—United States
ORGANOMETALLIC compounds. See Organic
compounds
ORGANS. See Organ
ORGANS, Artificial. See Prosthesis
ORGUEIL meteorite. See Meteorites
ORIENT. See Far East
ORIENT and Occident. See East and West
ORIENT express. See Railroads—Europe
ORIENTAL dolls. See Dolls
ORIENTAL flowering cherry
Nature note; Japanese cherry tree. Sci N L
87:207 Mr 27 '65
ORIENTAL poppies. See Poppies

ORIENTAL rugs. See Rugs and carpets, Orien-
tal
ORIENTATION
Hawks lose way home. Sci N L 88:132 Ag
28 '65
Navigation of the green turtle. A. Carr. il
Sci Am 212:78-86 bibliog(p 151) My '65
ORIENTATION (architecture)
House planned for leisure, easy care and re-
tirement. il Arch Rec 137:62-5 mid-My '65
ORIENTATION of teachers. See Teachers—Ad-
justment
ORIGIN of man. See Man—Origin and antiquity
ORIGINALITY. See Creation (literary, artistic,
etc)
ORIGO, Iris
Marguerite Caetani. Atlan 215:81-8 F '65
ORING, Stuart
Elementary art experience. il Sch Arts 65:9-
12 D '65
ORIOLES
Air battles close to home. M. Michaud. il
Audubon Mag 67:116-20 Mr '65
ORION nebula. See Nebulae
ORION press incorporated
Orion press merges with Grossman. Pub W
187:78 Je 21 '65
ORKNEY ISLANDS
Man's retreat from the islands. R. Kirk.
Nat R 17:107 F 9 '65
ORLANDO, Fla.

City planning

Why a city turned down federal dollars. il
Nations Bsns 53:38-9+ O '65

Street traffic

City gets the green light. W. L. Thomas. il
Am City 80:123-4 S '65
ORLANS, Harold
Some current problems of government science
policy; address, April 26, 1965. bibliog Sci-
ence 149:37-40 Jl 2 '65
ORLOVITZ, Gil
Median eighteen; poem. New Repub 153:17
S 18 '65
ORMANDY, Eugene
Hungarian's rhaposdy. por Time 86:83 O 15
'65
ORME, Frank
Tune out the bad, tune in the good on TV.
Parents Mag 40:56-7+ F '65
ORMSBEE, Thomas H.
Antiques; questions & answers. See issues
of House & garden incorporating Living
for young homemakers
ORMSBY, Virginia H.
Ricardo. NEA J 54:24-5 Ap '65
ORMSBY GORE, David, 5th baron Harlech.
See Harlech, D. O. G.
ORNAMENTAL cookery. See Cookery, Orna-
mental
ORNAMENTAL glass. See Glass, Ornamental
ORNAMENTAL grasses. See Grasses
ORNAMENTAL tiles. See Tiles
ORNATI, Oscar A.
Two approaches to welfare. bibliog f Mo
Labor R 88:296-7 Mr '65
ORNE, Jerrold
Orne surveys eighty-five academic libraries,
finds science facilities inadequate; excerpts
from report. Library J 90:2108 My 1 '65
ORNITZ, Don
Perils of picture making. M. Ornitz. il U S
Camera 29:42-3+ Ja '66
ORNITZ, Marguerite
Perils of picture making. U S Camera 29:
42-3+ Ja '66
ORNSTEIN, Jacob, and Lee, M. L.
They go overseas for Uncle Sam. Parents
Mag 40:36-7+ Jl '65
ORÓ, J. and Tornabene, T.
Bacterial contamination of some carbona-
ceous meteorites. bibliog Science 150:1046-8
N 19 '65
—and others
Hydrocarbons of biological origin in sedi-
ments about two billion years old. bibliog
Science 148:77-9 Ap 2 '65
Paraffinic hydrocarbons in pasture plants.
bibliog Science 147:870-3 F 19 '65
OROVAN, Mary
Bag of tricks and talent. U S Camera 28:60-
1+ Ap '65
Mama, you've gone too far! U S Camera
28:40-1 F '65
Mountains of misery. U S Camera 28:58-61+
My '65
OROZCO, José Clemente
Man of fire. il Time 86:86 O 1 '65
We are all victims; exhibition at the gallery
of modern art. il por Newsweek 66:102A-
104 S 27 '65

ORPHANS and orphan asylums
  See also
  Adoption
  Girard college, Philadelphia, Pa.
ORPHANS' progress; story. See Gallant, M.
ORR, Glenn L.
  Old men of the sea. C. Phinizy. il por Sports
    Illus 23:72-4+ Ag 23 '65
ORR, Phil C. and Berger, Rainer
  Radiocarbon age of a Nevada mummy. bib-
    liog Science 148:146-7 Je 11 '65
ORSHANSKY, Mollie
  Identification of the poor. bibliog f Mo La-
    bor R 88:300-9 Mr '65
ÖRSY, Ladislas M.
  Collegiality; its meaning. America 112:705-9
    My 15 '65
  Decree on religious life. America 114:12-13+
    Ja 1 '66
ORTEGA Y GASSET, José
  Ortega y Gasset. E. Ardura. il por Américas
    17:15-19 D '65
ORTH, Herbert
  Darkroom that went 600 mph. Pop Phot 56:
    64-5+ My '65
ORTHOCARPUS densiflorus. See Parasitic
  plants
ORTHODONTICS
  Why the high cost of braces for teeth? A.
    Toffler. il Good H 160:87+ My '65
ORTHODOX Eastern church
  King & the bishops; fuss about money and
    bishops transfers. il Time 86:77 D 3 '65
  Social consciousness in Eastern orthodoxy;
    long hampered by subservience to Islamic
    rule. C. S. Calian. Christian Cent 82:1284-
    6 O 20 '65
  Soul of Greece. by R. Etteldorf. Review
    Christian Cent 82:334 Mr 17 '65. J. S.
    Romanides
**ORTHODOX Eastern church in the United
States**
  Orthodox church wants federal recognition.
    Christian Cent 82:1004-5 Ag 18 '65
ORTHODOX Eastern church in Turkey
  Bishop in check. Commonweal 82:205 My 7 '65
  Sidelight on Cyprus: fate of a patriarch. T.
    E. Bird. Commonweal 82:374-5 Je 11 '65;
    Reply. R. Harper. 82:482-3+ Jl 9 '65
  Turkey threatens to expel Orthodox patri-
    archate. Christian Cent 82:573 My 5 '65;
    Reply. R. G. Stephanopoulos. 82:840 Je 30
    '65
ORTHOPEDIA
  Calf bones to mend people. il Life 58:41+ F
    26 '65
  Cutting her down to size; Ann Rowston's
    operation in England. il Time 85:62+ Je 11
    '65
  New techniques may cut leg amputations.
    Sci N L 87:104 F 13 '65
ORTHOPEDIC surgery. See Orthopedia
ORTIZ, Carlos
  Carlos and the king of con. M. Kram. il
    por Sports Illus 24:28-31 Ja 10 '66
  Shark ran into a tiger. M. Kram. il pors
    Sports Illus 22:32-4+ Ap 19 '65
ORTIZ, Elizabeth Lambert de
  Mexican cook book. House & Gard 128:219+
    S '65
ORTIZ, Michael
  Purely biological; letter. America 112:195-6
    F 6 '65
ORTIZ, Miguel Angel Zavala. See Zavala
  Ortiz, M. A.
ORTMAN, George
  Object is symbol. M. Friedman. il por Art N
    64:32-5+ N '65
ORTOLANI, Benito
  Films and faces of Akira Kurosawa. America
    113:368-71 O 2 '65
ORTON, Joe
  Entertaining Mr Sloane. Criticism
    New Yorker 41:94 O 23 '65
    Newsweek 66:102 O 25 '65
    Reporter 33:48+ N 18 '65
    Sat R 48:74 O 30 '65
    Time 86:103A O 22 '65
ORTONVILLE, Minn.
  Trickling filter overcomes shock loads. R. L.
    Smith and T. N. Rodeberg. il Am City 80:
    29 O '65
ORTUÑO, René Barrientos. See Barrientos Or-
  tuño. R.
ORVIETO, Italy
  Mother church. Orvieto. R. M. Coates. il
    Horizon 7:76-95 Spr '65
ORVIETO cathedral. See Cathedrals—Italy
ORVILLE, Richard E.
  Lightning through a lens. Natur Hist 75:34-
    41 bibliog(p68) Ja '66
ORWELL, George, pseud.
  It's halfway to 1984. J. Lukacs. il N Y Times
    Mag p8-9+ Ja 2 '66

ORYE, R. V. and others
  Lewis acidity of polar organic solvents from
    thermodynamic measurements. bibliog Sci-
    ence 148:74-5 Ap 2 '65
OSAKA, Japan
  As Osaka goes, so goes Japan. il Bsns W
    p75-7+ Ag 21 '65
OSBORN, D. Keith, and Knapp, P. P. W.
  Sing and tell. PTA Mag 59:7-9 bibliog(p34)
    Mr '65
OSBORN, Robert Chesley
  Art gets the tag end of Friday. il por Am
    Ed 1:5-7 F '65; Same abr. with title Cheat-
    ing our children out of beauty. McCalls 93:
    78+ N '65
  Cars & what they are doing to us! Atlan
    216:98-101 Jl '65
OSBORNE, Conrad L.
  Berg's Wozzeck, all made lucid and urgent.
    Hi Fi 15:75-7 D '65
  Bernac and Lehmann: pupils in public. Hi
    Fi 15:104-5 Jl '65
  Black tie from heaven; operas. Hi Fi 15:86G
    Mr '65
  City Center's Flaming angel. Hi Fi 15:168-
    9 D '65
  Henze's Elegy for young lovers. Hi Fi 15:95+
    Jl '65
  Home stretch at the Met. Hi Fi 15:111-12
    My '65
  Krenek on campus. Hi Fi 15:148-9 O '65
  Lewisohn stadium: the Met moves in: con-
    certs. Hi Fi 15:146+ S '65
  Luisa Miller in new stereo dress. Hi Fi
    15:84-5 N '65
  Met national company: opera on the road.
    Hi Fi 15:199+ N '65
  Miss Julie at City Center. Hi Fi 16:126-7+
    Ja '66
  Month of mezzos; concerts. Hi Fi 15:135-6
    Ap '65
  New Met. Hi Fi 15:50-4+ S '65
  Operas of Mozart on microgroove. Hi Fi
    15:65-72+ N '65
  Pelléas in stereo, with Ansermet in brilliant
    form. Hi Fi 15:72-3 Ap '65
  Peter Pears and Julian Bream: in a word.
    musicality. Hi Fi 15:58-9 Je '65
  Richnesses of Russian opera. Hi Fi 16:74-6
    Ja '66
  Spring comes to City Center. Hi Fi 15:116-
    17+ Je '65
  Stereo Parsifal for the faithful and new
    converts. Hi Fi 15:85-6+ Mr '65
  Stupendous stereo for the Gods in Twilight.
    Hi Fi 15:57-8 Jl '65
  Whole of Rusalka; lovable, touching, uniquely
    atmospheric. Hi Fi 15:77-8 S '65
OSBORNE, John
  Auto buying headaches. New Repub 152:15-18
    Mr 27 '65
  Concern about LBJ. New Repub 153:12-14 Jl
    24 '65
  Dying white South. New Repub 154:10-12
    Ja 22 '66
  Speaking to the Russians in a new voice.
    New Repub 153:9-10 N 6 '65
  Tell it to the President. New Repub 153:12-
    13 O 9 '65
OSBORNE, John, 1929-
  Entertainer. Criticism
    America 114:54 Ja 8 '66
  Inadmissible evidence. Criticism
    Christian Cent 82:1066 S 1 '65
    Commonweal 83:375 D 24 '65
    Life 60:17 Ja 14 '66
    Nation 201:508-9 D 20 '65
    New Repub 154:34-5 Ja 1 '66
    New Yorker 41:176+ Ap 17 '65
    New Yorker 41:142 D 11 '65
    Newsweek il 66:90 D 13 '65
    Reporter 33:38-40+ N 4 '65
    Sat R 49:96 Ja 8 '66
    Sat R 48:31 My 29 '65
    Sat R 48:43 D 18 '65
    Time il por 86:76+ D 10 '65
    Vogue 147:34 Ja 15 '66
    Vogue 146:51-2 Ag 15 '65
  Patriot for me. Criticism
    Christian Cent 82:1067 S 1 '65
    New Yorker 41:59-60 Jl 31 '65
    Reporter 33:38-40+ N 4 '65
    Sat R 48:45 Ag 14 '65
    Vogue 146:179 S 1 '65
OSBORNE, Karl
  Anyway you look at cobia. Outdoor Life 135:
    50-2+ Mr '65
  June blues. por Field & S 70:124-7 Je '65
OSCAR B. Cintas collection. See Art—Private
  collections
OSCAR III (artificial satellite) See Com-
  munications satellites
OSCARS (prizes) See Academy awards (mov-
  ing pictures)

OSCILLATORS
Light-coupled oscillator. M. S. Robbins. il
  Pop Electr 22:68 F '65
Versatile oscillator. il Electr World 74:85 S
  '65

OSCILLOGRAHS
Amateur scientist; mechanical devices draw
  figures known as harmonograms. il Sci Am
  212:128-30+ My '65
Oscilloscope calibrator. L. E. Frenzel, jr.
  il Electr World 74:58-9 Ag '65
Recording Lissajous figures. I. L. Finkle. il
  Science 148:1541-2 Je 18 '65; Reply.
  J. Potzick. 149:1446 S 24 '65
Scope-trace quiz; lissajous patterns. R. P.
  Balin. il Pop Electr 22:71+ Mr '65

OSGOOD, Lawrence
Pigeons. Criticism
  New Yorker 41:108 Mr 13 '65

O'SHEA, John
Negroes move toward power. Atlan 216:90-2+
  N '65

OSHIN, Edith Sonn
Delights of a small guest list. House & Gard
  128:56+ O '65
How to escape the serviceman syndrome.
  House & Gard 127:140-1+ Je '65
Littlest traditions. House & Gard 128:45+
  D '65
Parent and child. N Y Times Mag p48-9+
  Ag 8 '65

OSMOSIS
Desalted water builds up steam; with list of
  saline water conversion plants. il Bsns W
  p 120+ O 16 '65
Reverse osmosis purifies; Desalination advances. B. Tufty. il Sci N L 88:247 O 16 '65

OSMOTIC pressure
Osmotic flow in a rigid porous membrane.
  A. Mauro. bibliog il Science 149:867-9 Ag
  20 '65

OSMUNDSEN, John A.
Brain control by radio. Pop Mech 124:130-3+
  N '65

OSPREYS
Old fish eater. G. Laycock. il Field & S 70:
  54+ D '65

OSSAKA, Joyo. See Tetsuya, T. jt. auth.

OSSOLI, Sarah Margaret (Fuller) marchesa d'
Americans not everybody knows. C. W.
  Ferguson por PTA Mag 60:14-16 S '65

OSSORIO, Alfonso
Personal backgrounds. il por House & Gard
  128:182-3 D '65

OSTEOMYELITIS
Condition critical: cause unknown. D. Mur-
  ray. il Read Digest 86:145-8+ F '65
Osteomyelitis checked by effective new drug;
  Lincocin. Sci N L 88:313 N 13 '65

OSTEOPOROSIS. See Bones—Diseases

OSTER, Gerald
Density gradients; with biographical sketch.
  Sci Am 213:11, 70-6 Ag '65

about
And you see when you don't. il por Time
  87:70 Ja 14 '66
Op (cont.) exhibition at the Howard Wise
  gallery; Oster's magic moirés. New Yorker
  41:24-6 F 27 '65

OSTERBERG, Charles, and others
Chromium-51 as a radioactive tracer of Columbia River water at sea. bibliog Science
  150:1585-7 D 17 '65

OSTROM, Elinor. See Ostrom, V. jt. auth.

OSTROM, Vincent, and Ostrom, Elinor
Behavioral approach to the study of inter-
  governmental relations. bibliog f Ann Am
  Acad 359:137-46 My '65

OSTWALD, Peter F.
Acoustic methods in psychiatry; with
  biographical sketch. Sci Am 212:17, 82-9+
  bibliog (p 139) Mr '65

O'SULLIVAN, A. Don
Pity the poor coots; story. Mlle 60:151-3
  Mr '65

O'SULLIVAN, Christopher J.
Hero comes home. K. O. Gilmore. Read Digest 87:61-6 N '65

O'SULLIVAN, Maureen
Many lives of Maureen O'Sullivan. J. L.
  Block. il pors Good H 161:28+ N '65

OSWALD, Genevieve
Towards a dance film library. J. Anderson.
  il por Dance Mag 39:40-2 S '65

OSWALD, James R.
ABC's of editing. U S Camera 28:28-9+ Mr
  '65

OSWALD, Lee Harvey
Clearing the air. S. T. Possony. Nat R 17:
  113-14+ F 9 '65
Critique of the Warren report. D. Macdonald. Esquire 63:59-63+ Mr '65

Cursed gun, the track of C2766. K. Wheeler.
  il Life 59:62-5 Ag 27 '65
Lee Oswald's guilt; how science nailed Kennedy's killer. L. Snyder. il por Pop Sci
  186:68-73 Ap '65
Strange world of Marguerite Oswald; interview, ed. by J. Stafford. M. Oswald. il
  McCalls 93:112-13+ O '65

OSWALD, Marguerite
Strange world of Marguerite Oswald; interview, ed. by J. Stafford. por McCalls 93:
  112-13+ O '65

OSWALD, Marina
Love story. il por Newsweek 65:43+ Je 14 '65

OSYCZKA, Bohdan D.
Bohdan D. Osyczka strives for the elusive
  moment. il por Am Artist 29:56-7 S '65

OTEPKA, Otto F.
Ordeal of Otto Otepka. C. Stevenson and
  W. J. Gill. Read Digest 87:55-9 Ag '65

OTERO, Caroline
Suivez-moi, jeune homme. il por Time 85:37
  Ap 23 '65

OTHER Chanukahs; story. See Skir, L.

OTIS, Denise
Going places, finding things in Portugal.
  House & Gard 127:156-63+ Ap '65

O'TOOLE, Edward T.
Ambitious men of Europe house. Reporter 32:
  24-6 F 25 '65

OTT, Joseph K.
John Brown House loan exhibition of Rhode
  Island furniture. Antiques 87:564-71 My '65
Notes on Rhode Island cabinetmakers. An-
  tiques 87:572 My '65

OTTAVIANI, Alfredo, cardinal
Cardinal Ottaviani on world unity; address.
  Cath World 202:242-3 Ja '66

about
Ottaviani favors world government. America
  113:454-5 O 23 '65

OTTAWA national forest. See National forests

OTTEN, Alan L. See Seib, C. B. jt. auth.

OTTENBERG, Miriam
Anatomy of bank robbery. Look 29:124+ O
  19 '65
In the Nation's capital, crisis in crime; excerpts from article in Washington Sunday
  star. U S News 58:58-60 My 24 '65
What's ahead for the FBI. Look 29:27-9 F 23
  '65

OTTENSMEYER, Hilary
Blueprint for seminaries. America 113:780-1 D
  18 '65

OTTERS
Culture of animals, a lesson in evolution;
  excerpt from Wild heritage. S. Carrighar.
  il Sat R 48:56-7 My 1 '65
See also
Sea otters

OTTINGER, Richard L.
Mr Ottinger sees it through. Nation 200:518
  My 17 '65
Who will save the Hudson, and how? J.
  Ridgeway. New Repub 153:10-11 O 2 '65

OTTO, Celia Jackson
Nineteenth-century contour chairs. Antiques
  87:193-5 F '65
Rococo style in nineteenth-century American
  furniture; excerpts from American furniture of the nineteenth century. Antiques
  88:325-9 S '65

OTTUM, Bob
Fiery 500 for a cool Scot. Sports Illus 22:
  18-21 Je 7 '65
Motor sports (title varies) (cont) Sports Illus
  22:60 My 3 '65
Skiing. Sports Illus 22:50-1 F 8; 48-50 F 15;
  23:64+ Ag 23 '65

OUABAIN
Electron microscopy; sodium localization in
  normal and ouabain-treated transporting
  cells. G. I. Kaye and others. bibliog il
  Science 150:1167-8 N 26 '65

OUELLETTE, Cecil M.
Ski-touring the national parks and forests.
  il Nat Parks Mag 40:8-11 Ja '66

OUKHTOMSKY, Wladimir
Classicism, romanticism, and color; Ballet
  classique, new touring group, on the West
  coast. V. H. Swisher. il por Dance Mag
  39:118-19+ D '65

OULAHAN, Richard
Life movie review (cont) Life 58:15 F 12;
  15 Mr 26; 16 Ap 2 '65
—and Lambert, William
Real Ronald Reagan stands up. Life 60:70-
  2+ Ja 21 '66
Tyrant's fall that rocked the TV world Life
  59:90-2+ S 10 '65

OUR famous ancestors; drama. See Hark, M.
  and McQueen, N.

OUR last day in Venice; story. See Newlin, L.

OUT of a storm; story. See Mills, H. B.

OUT of Itea; story. See Hazzard, S.

OUT-of-towner; story. See Tuttle, A.

OUTBOARD motor boats. See Motor boats, Outboard

OUTBOARD motors. See Gas and oil engines, Outboard

OUTDOOR advertising. See Advertising, Outdoor

OUTDOOR bowling. See Bowling

OUTDOOR Christmas decorations. See Christmas decorations, Outdoor

OUTDOOR church services. See Church services

OUTDOOR cookery. See Cookery, Outdoor

OUTDOOR fireplaces. See Fireplaces, Outdoor

OUTDOOR furniture. See Furniture, Outdoor

OUTDOOR life
Six slick tips for vacation trips. il Pop Sci 186:156-7 Je '65
Strange places I have slept. E. W. Smith. il Field & S 70:58-61+ My '65
  See also
Hunting
Outdoor meals

OUTDOOR lighting. See Lighting, Outdoor

OUTDOOR meals
Chowder at the beach; with fish and shellfish; recipes. il Sunset 135:90-1 N '65
Dinners that take to the outdoors; cool drinks that go along. il Good H 161:82-98+ Ag '65
For the young and hungry; with recipes. J. Hewitt. il N Y Times Mag p62 Ag 29 '65
House & garden's outdoor menu cook book. P. S. Brown. il House & Gard 128:117+ Jl '65
Movable feast. il McCalls 92:88-9+ Jl '65
Outdoor dining oriental style. K. Smith. il Pop Gard 16:48-9 Mr '65
Outdoor family meal. il Pop Gard 16:52-3 Jl '65
Party; outdoor breakfast. il Ladies Home J 82:102-5+ O '65
Patio sandwich party. il Pop Gard 16:58+ My '65
Skier's lunch. M. Kaytor and others. il Look 29:96-7 D 14 '65
Time out for a portable feast; with recipes. il McCalls 93:142-3+ N '65
  See also
Barbecue cookery
Picnics

OUTDOOR recreation. See Recreation

OUTDOOR rooms
Add to the pleasure of outdoor living. il Pop Gard 16:26-9 Ap '65
Comfortable and complete outdoor room. il Pop Gard 16:32 Jl '65
Decks simple to build on any lot. il Bet Hom & Gard 43:82-3 Ap '65
How-to for wooden decks. il Bet Hom & Gard 43:35 Je '65
How to live outdoors and enjoy it. H. Mason. il Bet Hom & Gard 43:48-9 Ag '65
Ideas to profit by; the outdoor living room. J. B. Brimer. il Flower Grower 52:36 Je '65
Look to your terrace for all-season pleasure. M. C. Ohlander. il Flower Grower 52:22-5 N '65
New face on the place. E. Logsdon. il Farm J 89:65 Ag '65
Outdoor floor expands this house. il Sunset 134:100-1 Je '65
Outdoor rooms treble space in builder house. il Arch Rec 137:70-3 mid-My '65
Patio pockets & paving. il Pop Gard 16:16-17 N '65
Patios around development house add privacy. il Arch Rec 137:86-9 mid-My '65
Paving walks & terraces. J. B. Brimer. il Flower Grower 52:49 Mr '65
Sliding roof gives house year round use of patio. il Arch Rec 137:157-60 F '65
Small courtyard with a spacious look. il Pop Gard 16:41 Mr '65
Tradition with a grain of salt. il House & Gard 127:130-5+ F '65

OUTDOOR tennis, Winter. See Tennis

OUTER BANKS (island) See Hatteras Island

OUTING at Sant' Erasmo; story. See Barolini, A.

OUTLAW, Louise Lee
Incident at the soda fountain. Read Digest 88:187-8 Ja '66

OUTLETS, Electric. See Electric wire and wiring

OUTPUT of workers. See Labor productivity

OUTRAM, Richard
Hunter delirious with an infected wound; In her mirror sinister; Wineglass and candelabra; poems. Poetry 105:300-3 F '65

OUTRIGGERS. See Fishing boats—Equipment

OVEN cleaners. See Cleaning compositions

OVEN thermometers. See Thermometers, Cooking

OVENS, Carol B.
Liberal arts seminars for high school pupils. Sch & Soc 93:350-1 O 2 '65

OVENS
  See also
Electronic ovens

OVER-the-counter market. See Stocks—Marketing

OVER the river; drama. See Martens, A. C.

OVERDRIVE transmission. See Automobiles—Transmission

OVEREATING. See Eating, Psychology of

OVERHANGS. See Screens (sun)

OVERHEAD screens. See Screens (sun)

OVERHEAD wires. See Electric wire and wiring

OVERMANTEL panels. See Panels, Decorative

OVERPOPULATION. See Population—Overpopulation

OVERPROTECTION of children by parents. See Parent-child relationship

OVERSEAS education association
All for one, one for all; Overseas education association pledge to million dollar fund for teacher rights. C. Driver. il NEA J 54:45 N '65

OVERSEAS educational program. See Maryland. University, College Park

OVERSEAS extension. See Colleges and universities—Overseas extension

OVERSEAS information libraries. See American libraries abroad

OVERSEAS spending. See Investments, Foreign

OVERSTREET, Bonaro W.
Words that are ours (cont) PTA Mag 59:15-16 F; 26-8 Mr; 28-30 Ap; 28-9 My; 16-18 Je '65

OVERTIME
Big debate about double pay for overtime. il U S News 59:73-4 Jl 26 '65
Long hours and premium pay. J. R. Wetzel. il Mo Labor R 88:1083-8 S '65
Would double-time pay make jobs? U S News 59:85 Jl 19 '65

OVERWEIGHT. See Corpulence

OVIEDO, Spain
Doña Franco comes to town. J. Yglesias. Holiday 37:44+ Ap '65

OVUM
Pronuclear ovum from a patient using an intrauterine contraceptive device. R. W. Noyes and others. bibliog il Science 147:744 F 12 '65

OWEN, David
Fifteen years and 150,000 skills. UN Mo Chron 2:105-9 Je '65
Technical co-operation in a world of change. UNESCO Courier 18:12-14+ O '65

OWEN, Dwight
Honors course in the jungle. por Time 86:23 D 17 '65

OWEN, Henry
NATO strategy: what is past is prologue. For Affairs 43:682-90 Jl '65

OWEN, Lynn
Fresh valkyries; interview, ed. by R. D. Daniels. por Opera N 29:13 Mr 6 '65

OWEN, Roger
Chipping away. Commentary 40:99-100+ S '65
Good man is hard to find. Commentary 39:79-82 Ap '65

OWEN, Tobias
Saturn's ring and the satellites of Jupiter: interpretations of infrared spectra. bibliog Science 149:974-5 Ag 27 '65

OWEN, Wilfred
Transportation on earth; address, October 20, 1964. Vital Speeches 31:292-7 Mr 1 '65

OWENS, James H.
Good try in Alabama. il por Time 85:67 F 26 '65

OWENS-Corning fiberglas corporation
New edge in glass; computer runs glass furnace by itself. Bsns W p60+ Ap 10 '65

OWENS VALLEY radio observatory, Calif. See Astronomical observatories

OWETT, Trudy
Fall '65: season of contrasts. Ladies Home J 82:68-71 S '65

OWINGS, Margaret Wentworth
They're still shooting the tule elk. Audubon Mag 67:296-8 S '65

OWL and the pussycat; drama. See Manhoff, B.

OWLS
Bird that thinks it's a rabbit. B. W. Dalrymple. il Field & S 70:53+ Je '65
Notes and comments; Acadian or saw-whet owls at Tobay beach. New Yorker 41:49-50 D 4 '65

Sight
See Sight (birds)

OWNERSHIP. See Property

OWREN, Paul A.
Acid test. por Newsweek 66:48-9 S 6 '65

OXENBERG, Mrs Howard
New role of the makeup man. G. Plaut. il pors Look 29:54-6 F 23 '65

OXFORD AND ASQUITH, Herbert Henry Asquith, 1st earl of
Asquith, by R. Jenkins. Review
Nat R 17:883-4 O 5 '65. S. Leslie
Nation 200:708-10 Je 28 '65. C. Sykes
Reporter 33:48-50+ D 2 '65. A. West
Great Britain and the 1914-1915 Straits agreement with Russia: the British promise of November 1914. C. J. Smith, jr. bibliog f Am Hist R 70:1015-34 Jl '65

OXFORD, England
Our far-flung correspondents; road and the meadow. A. Bailey. il New Yorker 41:129-30+ My 8 '65

OXFORD, Miss.
Day the balloon came to town; excerpt from William Faulkner of Oxford. ed. by J. W. Webb and A. W. Green. M. Falkner. il Am Heritage 17:46-9 D '65

OXFORD-Cambridge boat race. See Rowing

OXFORD group. See Moral rearmament

OXFORD, University
Oxford is at its very best on a sunny day in May. il Sunset 134:52+ My '65
Oxford's magnificent oddballs. J. Morris. Harper 231:69-74 N '65
Unconfident Oxford. il Newsweek 65:84-85A+ F 8 '65

Oxford union society
For queen and country. Newsweek 65:47 My 31 '65
For queen & country; resolution defeated. il Time 85:33 My 28 '65

OXIDASES
α-Hydroxy acid oxidase: localization in renal microbodies. J. M. Allen and M. E. Beard. bibliog il Science 149:1507-9 S 24 '65
See also
Monoamine oxidase

OXIDATION, Physiological
Altered effect of potassium ions on cerebral respiration in vitro following subcortical lesions. B. F. Roth and J. A. Harvey. bibliog il Science 148:1463-7 Je 4 '65
Respiratory chains and sites of coupled phosphorylation. A. F. Brodie and J. Adelson. bibliog il Science 149:265-9 Jl 16 '65

OXIDATION ponds. See Sewage lagoons

OXIDATION reduction reaction
Drosophila phenol oxidases. H. K. Mitchell and U. M. Weber. bibliog il Science 148:964-5 My 14 '65
Magnetite oxidation: a proposed mechanism. U. Colombo and others. bibliog Science 147:1033 F 26 '65
Nitrogen: formation by photooxidation of ethylene in the presence of its oxides. J. J. Bufalini and J. C. Purcell. bibliog il Science 150:1161 N 26 '65
Oxidation of dimethyl sulfoxide to dimethyl sulfone in the rabbit. K. I. H. Williams and others. bibliog il Science 149:203-4 Jl 9 '65
Tryptamine oxidation by extracts of pea seedlings; effect of growth retardant β-hydroxyethylhydrazine. D. J. Reed. bibliog Science 148:1097-9 My 21 '65

OXIDATIVE phosphorylation. See Phosphorylation

OXTOBY-Smith, Incorporated
Who pays to watch the video show? report on study. il Bsns W p32 Ja 30 '65

OXYCHLORIDE cement floors. See Floors, Cement

OXYDENDRUM arboreum. See Sourwood

OXYGEN
Electron microprobe analysis of oxygen in an iron meteorite. J. F. Lovering and C. A. Andersen. bibliog il Science 147:734-6 F 12 '65
Oxygen consumption rate and electroencephalographic stage of sleep. D. R. Brebbia and K. Z. Altshuler. bibliog il Science 150:1621-3 D 17 '65

Physiological effects
Succinate: protective agent against hyperbaric oxygen toxicity. A. P. Sanders and others. bibliog Science 150:1830-1 D 31 '65

OXYGEN apparatus
O₂ fly in the troposphere. A. Trammell. il Flying 77:36-40 S '65

OXYGEN deficiency. See Antoxemia

OXYGEN in the body
Oxygen-hemoglobin system: a model for facilitated membranous transport. D. B. Zilversmit. bibliog il Science 149:874-6 Ag 20 '65
Tension gradients accompanying accelerated oxygen transport in a membrane. P. F. Scholander. bibliog il Science 149:876-7 Ag 20 '65

OYARZABAL, Beatrice (Lodge) de
Connecticut Yankee finds her destiny in Spain. M. Daly. il pors Ladies Home J 82:60-1+ F '65

OYSTER plant. See Salsify

OYSTERS
Nature note. Sci N L 89:11 Ja 1 '66
Strontium and magnesium in water and in crassostrea calcite. A. Lerman. bibliog il Science 150:745-6+ N 5 '65
See also
Cookery—Fish

OYSTERS as carriers of infection
Gymnodinium breve: induction of shellfish poisoning in chicks. S. M. Ray and D. V. Aldrich. bibliog il Science 148:1748-9 Je 25 '65

OZARK MOUNTAINS
Balls o' fire! PM tracks down Ozark Spooklight. R. Gannon. il Pop Mech 124:116-19+ S '65

OZARK NATIONAL SCENIC RIVERWAYS
New Ozark scenic riverways. E. J. Wilhelm, jr. il Nat Parks Mag 39:12-15 Jl '65

OZICK, Cynthia
Contraband life. Commentary 39:89-90+ Mr '65

P

PAGEOS (passive geodetic earth orbiting satellite) See Artificial satellites—Mapping applications
PAHO. See Pan American health organization
PAIS. See Public affairs information service
PARC (predator and rodent control) See United States—Fish and wildlife service
PASB. See Pan American sanitary bureau
PAU. See Pan American union
PBA. See Professional bowlers association
PCM (pulse code modulation) See Space telemetry
PEN club
June PEN congress to draw 500 writers to New York. Pub W 189:100-1 Ja 17 '66
PEN congress in Bled forecasts '66 session in U.S. J. Watson. Pub W 188:14-15 Ag 16 '65
PEN pals: International PEN meeting in Dubrovnik, Yugoslavia. il Newsweek 66:92 Jl 26 '65
PERT (program evaluation and review technique) See Critical path analysis
PGA. See Professional golfers' association of America
pH. See Hydrogen ion concentration
PHS. See United States—Public health service
PIA. See Printing industries of America, incorporated
PKI (Indonesian Communist party) See Communist party (Indonesia)
PKU. See Phenylketonuria
PLA (People's liberation army) See China (People's Republic)—Armed forces
POAU. See Protestants and other Americans united for separation of church and state
POINT (project for the orientation and induction of new teachers). See Education—Washington (state)
PSI. See Programming and systems, incorporated
PTA. See Parents and teachers associations
PX. See United States—Armed forces—Post exchanges
PAAR, Jack
Paar's last tape. il por Time 86:63 Jl 2 '65

PAARLBERG, Don
Everyone else can set his price, farmers should, too. Suc Farm 63:31+ N '65
Everyone else is organized; farmers should be, too. Suc Farm 63:31+ O '65
Farmers need a unified voice. Suc Farm 64:33 Ja '66
Great myths of agricultural policy. Suc Farm 63:29+ Ag; 41+ S '65
What bargaining power can, and can't do; excerpt from address. Farm J 89:77 Mr '65

PACEM in terris. See Encyclicals

PACEMAKER, Heart. See Medical instruments and apparatus

PACHANIK, Irene
Intelligent girl's lament; poem. McCalls 93:137 Ja '66

PACHYSANDRA
Fruiting pachysandra. H. Rohrbach. il Horticulture 43:15 D '65

PACIFIC air lines, incorporated
Pacific air lines buys four Boeing 737s. R. G. O'Lone. Aviation W 83:40 S 20 '65
San Jose hearings will begin this week. R. G. O'Lone. Aviation W 83:31 O 18 '65

PACIFIC airmotive corporation
PAC, the friendly octopus. R. Baehler. il Flying 77:41-3 S '65

PACIFIC cleaner wrasses. See Wrasses

PACIFIC coast
California coast. C. Kentfield. il Holiday 38:80-91+ O '65
See also
Fishing—Pacific coast

PACIFIC Coast flood. See Floods—United States

PACIFIC Coast stock exchange. See Stock exchange—Pacific coast

PACIFIC countries
[Pacific region.] R. Joseph. il Esquire 64:50-63 Ag '65
Strategy for the Pacific. C. J. V. Murphy. il Fortune 73:167-8+ Ja '66
See also
ANZUS council

PACIFIC gas and electric company
Bodega Head, a partisan view. J. W. Hedgpeth. Bul Atomic Sci 21:2-7 Mr '65

PACIFIC ISLANDS. See Islands of the Pacific

PACIFIC NORTHWEST conference on faith and order. See Religious conferences

PACIFIC OCEAN
Dolomitization of the mid-Pacific atolls. R. A. Berner. bibliog il Science 147:1297-9 Mr 12 '65
East Pacific rise: the magnetic pattern and the fracture zones. M. Talwani and others. bibliog il Science 150:1109-15 N 26 '65
Magnetic anomalies over a young oceanic ridge off Vancouver Island. F. J. Vine and J. T. Wilson. bibliog il Science 150:485-9 O 22 '65
Subbottom profile of abyssal sediments in the central equatorial Pacific. G. R. Heath and T. C. Moore, jr. bibliog il Science 149:744-6 Ag 13 '65
Transform faults, oceanic ridges, and magnetic anomalies southwest of Vancouver Island. J. T. Wilson. bibliog il Science 150:482-5 O 22 '65
See also
Oceania

PACIFIC science center. See Seattle—Pacific science center

PACIFIC Southwest airlines
San Jose hearings will begin this week. R. G. O'Lone. Aviation W 83:31 O 18 '65

PACIFIC SOUTHWEST conference on faith and order. See Religious conferences

PACIFIC SOUTHWEST water plan. See Colorado River

PACIFIC telephone and telegraph company
Attorney & his client; A. Garrett awarded $1,500,000 for punitive damages. Time 86:35 Jl 2 '65

PACIFIC wax myrtle. See Myrtle

PACIFISM
Catholic worker; R. A. LaPorte burns self to death. il Newsweek 66:71 N 22 '65
Demonstrators: why? how many? anti-Vietnam movement. il Newsweek 66:25-6+ N 1 '65
New American revolution. P. A. McCombs. il Nat R 17:766-8+ S 7 '65
Now the pacifists turn to picketing. il U S News 59:8 Ag 23 '65
On war and peace; War/Peace report vs. National review. Nat R 17:90 F 9 '65
Pacifists; N. Morrison burns self to death. il Time 86:68 N 12 '65
Political equivalent of war, civilian defense. G. Sharp. bibliog f il Int Concil 555:5-67 N '65

Storm at home: anti-draft and anti-Viet demonstrations; with press comments. il Sr Schol 87:18-20 N 4 '65
Students move for peace. Sci N L 88:302 N 6 '65
Vietnam protests. Commonweal 83:113-14 O 29 '65
Whose peace? J. Burnham. Nat R 17:541 Je 29 '65
See also
Conscientious objectors
Vietnamese war, 1957- —Protests, demonstrations, etc. against

PACIFISTS. See Pacifism

PACKAGE foods
Chow mein king spices up market drive; packaged Chinese-American foods. il Bsns W p 100-2+ Mr 6 '65

PACKAGE goods
Power of proper packaging; special report. il Bsns W p90-2+ F 20 '65

PACKAGE tours. See Travel

PACKAGES, Wrapping of. See Wrapping of packages

PACKAGING
Finishing touch: the package. il Esquire 64:168 O '65
Food forum. E. Weston. il McCalls 92:38 Mr '65
Heat 'n' eat, packaging treat. G. Lazarus. Sat R 48:77 Je 12 '65
Not necessarily cheaper by the dozen. Consumer Rep 30:52 F '65
Packagers rap Hart bill; Fair packaging & labeling act. il Bsns W p34 My 8 '65
Power of proper packaging; special report. il Bsns W p90-2+ F 20 '65
Special report on packaging; symposium. il Duns R 86:pt2 86-92+ D '65
See also
Advertising mediums—Packaging
Government investigations—Packaging
Wrapping of packages

Materials
Clear field for PVC; polyvinyl chloride. il Bsns W p90+ Ap 17 '65
Materials: the battle rages. J. Perham. il Duns R 86:pt2 88-9+ D '65

PACKAGING machinery
Machinery revolution: automation of the packaging line. L. A. Blumenthal. il Duns R 86:pt2 95-7+ D '65

PACKARD, George R.
They were born when the bomb dropped. N Y Times Mag p28-9+ Ag 29 '65

PACKARD, Vance
Bargain basements upstairs. Sat R 48:22 Jl 31 '65

PACKER, Herbert L.
Policing the police. New Repub 153:17-21 S 4 '65

PACKER, John G. See Johnson, A. W. jt. auth.

PACKER, Nancy Huddleston
Front man in line; story. Yale R 55:107-17 O '65

PACKING for shipment
Packaging for productivity; industrial packaging. A. Matthews. il Duns R 86:pt2 99-100+ D '65

PACKING industry. See Meat industry and trade

PACKING of luggage
Don't forget these items when you pack. il Good H 161:141 Ag '65
How to pack a suitcase. il Good H 160:170-1 Je '65
Unsolicited advice for travelers. M. B. Tucker. NEA J 54:58 F '65

Anecdotes, facetiae, satire, etc.
How to complicate a trip. S. Wright. il Harper 230:84-7 Ap '65

PACKS
Pleasures of family backpacking. D. Barnes. il Sports Illus 22:47-9 My 31 '65

PADDINGTON. See London

PADDOCK, Paul. See Paddock, W. C. jt. auth.

PADDOCK, William C. and Paddock, Paul
Backward nations: aid and resources. Nation 200:414-17 Ap 19 '65
They can't eat our know-how; excerpt from Hungry nations. Read Digest 86:83-6 Je '65

PADEN, J. Fred
Plywood sculptor. J. J. Rea. il por Design 67:20-3 N '65

PADGETT, Ron
Travel; poem. Poetry 105:372 Mr '65

PADUCAH, Ky.
City hall should be a show place. T. Wilson. il Am City 80:106-7 My '65

PAFFRATH, Leslie
Legacy of Dag Hammarskjöld. Sat R 48:32-3+ Jl 24 '65

PAGANINI, Niccolò
Fiddling devil. J. W. Stedman. il por Opera N 29:14-16 F 27 '65
Op Epic, a first of rich importance; Paganini: the twenty-four caprices played on the viola by Emanuel Vardi. A. Cohn. il por Am Rec G 31:966-7 Je '65
Profiles; I. Stern. J. Wechsberg. New Yorker 41:50+ Je 5 '65

PAGE, Alex
Efficiency in its country of origin. Atlan 217:105-6 Ja '66

PAGE, Ellis B.
In so far as... Newsweek 65:61 Ap 5 '65

PAGE, Irvine H.
Priority. Science 151:33 Ja 7 '66
Where's the doctor? excerpt from Modern medicine. Sat R 48:59-60 F 6 '65

PAGE, Joseph A.
In search of Afro-Brazil. Reporter 33:44-7 N 4 '65

PAGE, Thornton
Evolution of galaxies (cont) il Sky & Tel 29:81-4 F '65
Great Swedish astronomer. Sky & Tel 30:142-3 S '65

PAGE, Warren
Guessing the giants. Field & S 70:79-81+ O '65
Jackson was a lady. pors Field & S 69:37-9+ Mr '65
Man's man. pors Field & S 70:31-3 Ja '66
Riflemen prefer pronghorns. Field & S 70:46-7+ Ag '65
(ed) Shooting. See issues of Field & stream
Shooting questions. Field & S 69:116 F '65
Tale of two cats. Field & S 70:62-5+ My '65
Waterbuck by the yard. Field & S 70:26-7 Ag '65
Whether you walk or sit or stand. Field & S 70:60-3 N '65

PAGE, Wilber Allen
Tribute to Dr Charles H. Wesley. Negro Hist Bul 28:104 F '65

PAGEANT of the masters. See Pageants

PAGEANTS
Festival of light. Mrs R. Gimbel. il Recreation 58:479 D '65
Outdoors in North Carolina; history recreated in summer pageants. D. Nesbitt. il Dance Mag 39:31 Ag '65
Vagabond camera; Pageant of the masters. W. Lane. il Travel 123:66-7 Je '65
See also
Festivals

PAGLIAI, Bruno
Mexico and the United States; address, February 1, 1965. Vital Speeches 31:472-5 My 15 '65

PAGLIAI, Merle Oberon de
Travel. Vogue 147:56-7 Ja 1 66

PAHLEVI, Mohammed Reza, shah of Iran. See Mohammed Reza Pahlevi

PAID holidays. See Vacations, Employee

PAIGE, Leroy. See Paige, S.

PAIGE, Nancy
Goals for service. por Library J 90:937-41 F 15 '65
about
Patricia Allen heads Lj cards. Nancy Paige joins SLJ. por Library J 90:1492-3 Mr 15 '65

PAIGE, Ronald F.
Planning tomorrow's parks; address. Recreation 58:295-6 Je '65

PAIGE, Satchel
Conversation with Satchel Paige. W. P. Fox, jr. Holiday 38:18+ Ag '65

PAIN
Attenuation of aversive properties of peripheral shock by hypothalamic stimulation. V. C. Cox and E. S. Valenstein. bibliog il Science 149:323-5 Jl 16 '65
Control of pain motivation by cognitive dissonance. P. G. Zimbardo and others. bibliog il Science 151:217-19 Ja 14 '66
Electrical relief of pain. Time 86:57 Ag 13 '65
Killer for all pains: Ag 246. Time 86:62+ N 12 '65
Pain clinic; University of Washington hospital and school of medicine. E. Crimmin. il Sci Digest 57:66-70 F '65
Pain mechanisms: a new theory. R. Melzack and P. D. Wall. bibliog il Science 150:971-9 N 19 '65
Switching off the pain; electrodes placed in the brain. Time 86:62 O 1 '65

PAINE, Philbrook
Birth of a yacht club. Atlan 216:110-11 Ag '65

PAINE, Thomas O.
1980. il New Yorker 41:37-8 My 22 '65

PAINE, Wingate
Wingate Paine: notes from a book in the making. il Pop Phot 56:100-1 Je '65

PAINT
Anti-fouling paints for aluminum hulls. C. W. Leveau. Yachting 117:223-4 Ap '65
Boat finishes. J. Hand. il Pop Sci 186:100-3 Mr '65
Guide to the use of acrylic paints. G. Allyn. Arch Rec 138:217-18 O; 211-12 N '65
How to choose the best outdoor finish. Bet Hom & Gard 43:38 Je '65
Interior clear finishes. J. Hand. il Pop Sci 186:168-70 F '65
Masonry finishes. J. Hand. Pop Sci 187:128-30 Jl '65
Nearly flat-finish wall enamel; Sherwin-Williams Kem-Glo Velvet enamel. Consumer Rep 30:54-5 F '65
Planning to paint? il Consumer Bul 48:26 Je '65
Plastic paints. N. Roukes. il Sch Arts 64:20-4 F '65
Semigloss wall paints. il Consumer Rep 30:336-9 Jl '65

PAINT, Protective
Rust-resistant paints for metals. il Consumer Bul 48:33-4 Je '65

PAINT brushes
New tools for painters. il Consumer Rep 31:40-1 Ja '66

PAINTED furniture. See Furniture, Painted

PAINTED rocks. See Petroglyphs

PAINTED ROCKS HISTORIC PARK. See Arizona—Parks and reserves

PAINTER, George D. See Skelton, R. A. jt. auth.

PAINTING
See also
Cubism
Impressionism (art)
Mural painting and decoration
Realism in art
Water color painting

Bibliography
All the paintings of... J. H. Beck. il Art N 64:45+ My '65

Study and teaching
3-D through tints; work of eighth graders. A. Heidt. il Design 67:24-5 N '65

Technique
All the news that's fit to paint. S. Hoeflich. il Am Artist 29:26-9+ D '65
I just paint. M. Zukmann. il Am Artist 29:42-6 N '65
Importance of method in art. W. M. Gaugler. il Am Artist 29:42-7+ Je '65
Painting impressions. R. Barrio. il Design 66:6-10 My '65
Painting on burlap. J. Cramer. il Design 67:34-5 N '65
Painting with tissue paper. R. P. Benson. il Design 67:6-8 S '65
Uses a mixed aqueous technique. B. M. Bowes. il Am Artist 29:34-5+ O 30 '65
What a painting reflects. E. Sloane. il Am Artist 29:56-61+ Mr '65

PAINTING, American
American art at the Metropolitan. A. T. Gardner. il Antiques 87:434-8 Ap '65
American romantic landscapes. W. K. Sturges. il Antiques 88:689-93 N '65
Americans. M. Kozloff. Nation 200:541-3, 569-71 My 17-24 '65
Americans at the Met; 300 years of American painting. F. Getlein. New Repub 152:28+ My 1 '65
Art galleries; annual exhibition of contemporary American painting (cont) R. M. Coates. New Yorker 41:52+ Ja 1 '66
Art galleries: exhibition at the Metropolitan museum: Three centuries of American painting. R. M. Coates. New Yorker 41:172+ My 1 '65
Art galleries: exhibition: Women artists of America, 1707-1964 at Newark museum. R. M. Coates. New Yorker 41:94+ Ap 10 '65
At the Metropolitan: good history, indifferent art; Three centuries of American painting. J. Jacobs. il Reporter 32:36-7 Je 3 '65
Castle under siege; campaign to keep Olana, home of F. Church intact. K. Kuh. il Sat R 48:46-7 N 27 '65
Engraved sources for American overmantel panels. N. F. Little. il Antiques 88:494-501 O '65

PAINTING, American—*Continued*
Finances and the Eight. F. Getlein. New
  Repub 152:38-9 Ap 17 '65
In the American grain; W. Benton's art col-
  lection. K. Kuh. il Sat R 48:68-70 O 30 '65
Met looks homeward; Three centuries of
  American painting exhibition. J. Gerassi.
  il Newsweek 65:86-7 Ap 19 '65
Met moves in; 300 years of American paint-
  ing. F. Getlein. New Repub 152:26-8 My 8
  '65
National quest; America by Americans. il
  Time 86:76-82 S 24 '65
Nation's past in paint; historic exhibition of
  American painting, at the Metropolitan mu-
  seum. K. Kuh. il Sat R 48:40-2 Ap 24 '65
New York school question; exhibition at Los
  Angeles museum; interview, ed. by N. A.
  Levine. B. Newman. il Art N 64:38-42+ S
  '65
Out there in the universe; exhibition at
  Knoedler gallery. il Newsweek 66:88 N 1 '65
Paintings; people and places of the old
  Northwest Territory. il Antiques 87:302-9
  Mr '65
Recently acquired American paintings at the
  Metropolitan. S. P. Feld. il Antiques 87:439-
  43 Ap '65
School of old paint; the cowboy painters. il
  Newsweek 66:107-8 N 8 '65
Summer's day; exhibitions. il Life 59:76-8
  Jl 23 '65
Three centuries of American painting; ex-
  hibition to be shown at the Metropolitan
  museum, New York. R. Davidson. il An-
  tiques 87:252 Mr '65
Three new, cool, bright imagists; exhibition
  at Oberlin, Ohio. E. H. Johnson. il Art N
  64:42-4+ Sum '65
Well-painted decade: twenties; with paint-
  ings. Am Heritage 16:7-17 Ag '65
    See also
Albright, I. L.
Audubon, J. J.
Avery, M.
Ballinger, H. R.
Baziotes, W.
Bellows, G. W.
Benton, T. H.
Catlin, G.
Chapin, F.
Church, F. E.
Copley, J. S.
Dabney, B. W.
Davis, S.
De Kooning, W.
Dickinson, E.
Diebenkorn, R.
Doughty, T.
Duveneck, F.
Eisenstat, B.
Freilicher, J.
Grooms, C.
Gropper, W.
Hassam, C.
Hicks, E.
Hofmann, H.
Holty, C.
Hopper, E.
Huntington, D.
Inness, G.
Jackson, H.
Katz, A.
Keane, W.
Kelly, E.
Kerkam, E. C.
Kitaj, R. B.
Leutze, E.
Mitchell, J.
Morris, G. L. K.
Motherwell, R.
O'Keeffe, G.
Ortman, G.
Quidor, J.
Rauschenberg, R.
Reinhardt, A.
Rivers, L.
Rockwell, N.
Sander, L. R.
Short, J. F.
Synchromism
Tobey, M.
Velarde, P.
Whistler, J. A. M.
Wyeth, N. C.
Youngerman, J.
PAINTING, Argentine
    See also
Berni, A.
PAINTING, Australian (aboriginal) See Art,
  Australian (aboriginal)
PAINTING, Austrian
    See also
Hundertwasser, F.
Klimt, G.
Schiele, E.
Waldmueller, F. G.

PAINTING, Belgian
    See also
Alechinsky, P.
Magritte, R.
PAINTING, British
    See also
Constable, J.
Laing, G.
Turner, J. M. W.
PAINTING, Byzantine. See Art, Byzantine
PAINTING, Dutch
    See also
Borch, G. ter
Dongen, K. van
Hoowij, J. H.
Rembrandt Hermanszoon van Rijn
Terbrugghen, H.
PAINTING, Flemish
Century of Rubens; exhibition at Brussels'
  Royal museums of fine arts. il Newsweek
  66:93 D 6 '65
    See also
Rubens, P. P.
PAINTING, French
French paintings from Russia at the Louvre.
  M. E. Davies. il Antiques 88:584+ N '65
Independence through interdependence; mas-
  ters of impressionism and post-impression-
  ism at Wildenstein, N.Y. H. A. La Farge.
  il Art N 64:50-1+ N '65
Letter from Paris; exhibition in Louvre of
  French paintings collected by Russia, from
  Catherine the Great until 1917. Genêt. New
  Yorker 41:218+ O 16 '65
Russian delegation to Paris. P. M. Grand.
  il Art N 64:34-5+ O '65
    See also
Bonnard, P.
Bouguereau, W. A.
Cézanne, P.
Dega, E.
Duchamp, M.
Dufy, R.
Gilot, F.
Manet, E.
Masson, A.
Pissarro, C.
Poussin, N.
Prud'hon, P. P.
Rouault, G.
Staël, N. de
PAINTING, German
    See also
Antes, H.
Bauermeister, M.
Dürer, A.
PAINTING, Icelandic
Art galleries; exhibition at the Gallery of
  the American federation of arts. R. M.
  Coates. New Yorker 41:228+ N 27 '65
PAINTING, Industrial and practical
Basic guide to do-it-yourself room painting.
  il Good H 160:177 Ap '65
Easy way to paint a room. R. C. Whitman.
  Am Home 68:80+ Mr '65
Helpful, timesaving tips for your home and
  workshop. il Bet Hom & Gard 43:145-6 O
  '65
    See also
Boats—Painting
Metal finishing
PAINTING, Italian
Some Venetian *vedute* painters in the Wads-
  worth atheneum. W. G. Constable. il An-
  tiques 88:669-73 N '65
    See also
Baruchello, G.
Caravaggio, M. M. da
Chirico, G. de
Duccio di Buonisegna
Feraboli, M.
Giotto di Bondone
Guardi, F.
Guardi, G. A.
Piero della Francesca
Romanino, G.
Signorelli, L.
Titian
PAINTING, Latin American
New pictorial language; exhibition of selec-
  tions from second American biennial of art
  in Córdoba, at Pan American union. D.
  Suro. il Américas 17:9-13 S '65
PAINTING, Manuscript. See Illumination of
  books and manuscripts
PAINTING, Marine. See Marine painting
PAINTING, Mexican
    See also
Murillo, G.
Orozco, J. C.
Rivera, D.
PAINTING, Modern. See Modernism (art)
PAINTING, Norwegian
    See also
Munch, E.

PAINTING, Polish
See also
Topolski, F.

PAINTING, Russian
See also
Chagall, M.

PAINTING, Spanish
See also
Dali, S.
Goya y Lucientes, F. J. de
Picasso, P.
Vicente, E.

PAINTING, Swiss
See also
Klee, P.
Liotard, J. E.

PAINTING, Uruguayan
See also
Torres-García, J.

PAINTING as recreation. See Recreation—Activities

PAINTING materials. See Artists materials

PAINTINGS
Hermitage. il Life 58:53-73 Mr 26; 62-82+
Ap 2; 43-58+ Ap 9 '65
How to visit a museum: masterpieces to be
exhibited in the Los Angeles County museum of art. il McCalls 92:116-27 Ap '65
In the museums: paintings; acquisitions of
American museums. R. Davidson. il Antiques 89:134-6+ Ja '66
Noble remnants: masterpieces of Rudolf II's
collection at the Hradčany, Prague. il
Time 85:70-1 Je 18 '65
Power of a good painting. House & Gard
127:111 Mr '65
Recent museum acquisitions in paintings. R.
Davidson. il Antiques 87:468+ Ap '65
See also
Costume in art
Forgery of works of art

Appreciation
See Art—Appreciation

Circulation, loans, etc.
See Art loans

Collections
See Art—Private collections

Conservation and restoration
Care of old paintings. il UNESCO Courier
18:14-17 Ja '65

Prices
See Art—Prices

Transportation
See Transportation of works of art

PAINTINGS, Lending of. See Art loans

PAINTINGS, Reproductions of. See Reproductions of works of art

PAINTINGS, Theft of. See Art thefts

PAINTINGS in the home. See Art in the home

PAIS, Abraham
Search for symmetry. il por Newsweek 65:
58 F 8 '65

PAISNER, Bruce
Author shakes up a city. Life 58:47-9 Mr
26 '65

PAK, Chung Hi. See Park, C. H.

PAKISTAN
Terrible twins: airplane crash and a cyclone.
Time 85:38+ My 28 '65
See also
Air travel—Pakistan
Economic assistance in Pakistan
Irrigation—Pakistan
Kashmir
Paleontology—Pakistan
Political campaigns—Pakistan

Antiquities
See also
Mohenjo-Daro

Boundaries
Run-in on the Rann. il Time 85:39 My 7 '65
Salt in the wounds: dispute over Great Rann
of Kutch. Newsweek 65:40 Ap 26 '65
Tiny war: fighting over Great Rann of Kutch.
il Newsweek 65:52 My 10 '65
War where U.S. is caught in the middle:
skirmishing in Rann of Cutch. il U S News
58:12 My 10 '65

Commercial treaties and agreements
U.S. and Pakistan conclude cotton textile
agreement; Department announcement, with
text of U.S. note, February 26, 1965. G. G.
Johnson. il Dept State Bul 52:391-4 Mr 15 '65

Economic policy
Promising country risks its future. il U S
News 59:64 N 29 '65

Foreign relations
Cry of the hawks; anti-American attitudes.
Time 86:38 O 15 '65
Grand tour: President Mohammed Ayub Khan
visits Peking, Moscow and Poland. Time
85:39 Ap 16 '65
Kosygin in Tashkent. America 114:113-14 Ja
22 '66
Search for a mantle; new-found Chinese
Communist friends. Time 85:25 Mr 12 '65
U.S. and Pakistan agree on need for peaceful settlement of Asian conflicts; exchange
of greetings and exchange of toasts, December 14, 1965; with joint communiqué. M.
Ayub Khan; L. B. Johnson. Dept State
Bul 54:2-7 Ja 3 '66

Politics and government
Ayub's basic democracy. R. Knox. il Reporter
32:34-6 F 11 '65
Building an image. il Time 85:28-9 Ap 2 '65
New experiment in democracy in Pakistan.
M. Ayub Khan. Ann Am Acad 358:109-13
Mr '65

PAKISTANI students in the United States. See
Foreign students in the United States

PAL, N. L. and Ojha, R. J.
Tobacco seedlings: damage by excessive nitrogen lessened by added phosphorus. Science 151:106 Ja 7 '66

PALACE of chance; story. See Greene, G.

PALACES
Emperor's new palace. il Time 86:72 Jl 9 '65
See also
Versailles, Palace of

PALATSKY, Eugene H.
On their toes. Opera N 29:12-16 Ap 10 '65

PALAU DE NEMES, Graciela. See Nemes,
G. P.

PALDEN Thondup Namgyal, maharaja of Sikkim
Hope-la in Gangtok. il por Time 85:39 Ap
16 '65

PALEOBOTANY
Infrared spectra as a means of determining
botanical sources of amber. J. H. Langenheim and C. W. Beck. bibliog il Science 149:
52-5 Jl 2 '65
Precambrian flora: fossil-rich Gunflint cherts
of Ontario. Sci Am 212:60+ Ap '65
Prehistoric maize in southeastern Virginia.
D. R. Whitehead. bibliog il Science 150:881-
3 N 12 '65

Mesozoic
Massive extinctions in biota at the end of
Mesozoic time. M. N. Bramlette. bibliog
Science 148:1696-9 Je 25 '65; Discussion.
149:922+; 150:1240 Ag 27, D 3 '65

Paleozoic
Glossopteris discovered in west Antarctica.
C. Craddock and others. bibliog il Science
148:634-7 Ap 30 '65

Precambrian
Significance of the Gunflint, Precambrian
microflora. P. E. Cloud, jr. bibliog il Science 148:27-35 Ap 2 '65

PALEOCLIMATOLOGY
Origin of ice ages: pollen evidence from
Arctic Alaska. P. A. Colinvaux; reply with
rejoinder. W. L. Donn and M. Ewing. il
Science 147:632-3 F 5 '65

PALEOLITHIC period. See Stone age

PALEOMAGNETISM. See Magnetism, Terrestrial

PALEONTOLOGY
Oldest great ape jaws found in Sahara
Desert; Advanced animals lived earlier than
believed. il Sci N L 88:359 D 4 '65
Organic pigments: their long-term fate. M.
Blumer. bibliog il Science 149:722-6 Ag 13
'65
Paleontologic technique for defining ancient
ocean currents. F. G. Stehli. bibliog il Science 148:943-6 My 14 '65
Strontium in fossil bones and the reconstruction of food chains. H. Toots and
M. R. Voorhies. bibliog il Science 149:854-5
Ag 20 '65
See also
Brachiopods, Fossil
Man, Prehistoric
Micropaleontology

Cretaceous
Cretaceous mammals from Montana. R. E.
Sloan and L. Van Valen. bibliog il Science
148:220-7 Ap 9 '65

PALEONTOLOGY—*Continued*

Devonian
Fossil search aided by U.S. public roads; Cuyahoga County, Ohio. Sci N L 87:231 Ap 10 '65

Eocene
Fossil lakes from the eocene; Green River formation. B. Schaeffer and M. Mangus. il Natur Hist 74:10-21 Ap '65

Miocene
Endemism in middle Miocene Caribbean molluscan faunas. W. P. Woodring. bibliog il Science 148:961-3 My 14 '65

Miocene mammals and Central American seaways. F. C. Whitmore, jr. and R. H. Stewart. bibliog il Science 148:180-5 Ap 9 '65

Paleozoic
Paleozoic reef in Pakistan. C. Teichert and K. W. Stauffer. bibliog il Science 150:1287-8 D 3 '65

Pleistocene
First Americans: the evidence of mud. P. Colinvaux. Yale R 54:397-410 Mr '65

Precambrian
Hydrocarbons of biological origin in sediments about two billion years old. J. Oró and others. bibliog il Science 148:77-9 Ap 2 '65

Microorganisms from the Gunflint chert; Precambrian fossils from Ontario. E. S. Barghoorn and S. A. Tyler. bibliog il Science 147:563-77 F 5 '65; Reply. Time 85:56 Mr 12 '65

Microorganisms from the late Precambrian of central Australia. E. S. Barghoorn and J. W. Schopf. bibliog il Science 150:337-9 O 15 '65

Most ancient life found in Canada. Sci N L 87:169 Mr 13 '65

Paleobotany of a Precambrian shale. E. S. Barghoorn and others. bibliog il Science 148:461-72 Ap 23 '65

Precambrian flora; fossil-rich Gunflint cherts of Ontario. Sci Am 212:60+ Ap '65

Precambrian graphitic compressions of possible biologic origin from Canada. B. L. Stinchcomb and others. il Science 148:75-6 Ap 2 '65

Significance of the Gunflint, Precambrian microflora. P. E. Cloud, jr. bibliog il Science 148:27-35 Ap 2 '65

Soudan formation: organic extracts of early Precambrian rocks. W. G. Meinschein. bibliog il Science 150:601-5 O 29 '65

Australia
Microorganisms from the late Precambrian of central Australia. E. S. Barghoorn and J. W. Schopf. bibliog il Science 150:337-9 O 15 '65

Canada
Precambrian graphitic compressions of possible biologic origin from Canada. B. L. Stinchcomb and others. il Science 148:75-6 Ap 2 '65

Caribbean Region
Endemism in middle Miocene Caribbean molluscan faunas. W. P. Woodring. bibliog il Science 148:961-3 My 14 '65

Colorado
Fossil lakes from the eocene; Green River formation. B. Schaeffer and M. Mangus. il Natur Hist 74:10-21 Ap '65

Kentucky
In the valley of ice age wildlife; Big Bone Lick State Park; excerpt from Wandering through winter. E. W. Teale. il Audubon Mag 67:286-91 S '65

Mexico
Human skeletons of Tehuacán. J. E. Anderson. bibliog il Science 148:496-7 Ap 23 '65; Reply. E. A. Sweeney. 149:1118 S 3 '65

Michigan
Lungfish burrows from the Michigan coal basin. R. L. Carroll. bibliog il Science 148:963-4 My 14 '65

Minnesota
Soudan formation: organic extracts of early Precambrian rocks. W. G. Meinschein. bibliog il Science 150:601-5 O 29 '65

Montana
Cretaceous mammals from Montana. R. E. Sloan and L. Van Valen. bibliog il Science 148:220-7 Ap 9 '65

Ontario
Microorganisms from the Gunflint chert; Precambrian fossils from Ontario. E. S. Barghoorn and S. A. Tyler. bibliog il Science 147:563-77 F 5 '65; Reply. Time 85:56 Mr 12 '65

Precambrian flora; fossil-rich Gunflint cherts of Ontario. Sci Am 212:60+ Ap '65

Pakistan
Paleozoic reef in Pakistan. C. Teichert and K. W. Stauffer. bibliog il Science 150:1287-8 D 3 '65

Panama
Miocene mammals and Central American seaways. F. C. Whitmore, jr. and R. H. Stewart. bibliog il Science 148:180-5 Ap 9 '65

Spain
Acheulian occupation sites at Torralba and Ambrona, Spain: their geology. K. W. Butzer. bibliog il Science 150:1718-22 D 24 '65

Utah
Fossil lakes from the eocene; Green River formation. B. Schaeffer and M. Mangus. il Natur Hist 74:10-21 Ap '65

Wyoming
Fossil lakes from the eocene; Green River formation. B. Schaeffer and M. Mangus. il Natur Hist 74:10-21 Ap '65

PALEOPATHOLOGY
Paleopathology; report on symposium on human paleopathology. S. Jarcho. Science 147:1160+ Mr 5 '65

PALEOZOIC period. See Paleobotany—Paleozoic; Paleontology—Paleozoic

PALERMO
Polyphemus unbound. R. M. Coates. il Reporter 33:49-51 D 16 '65

Music
Boxing match at La Scala. W. Weaver. il Hi Fi 15:86U Mr '65

PALESTINE
See also
Galilee
Holy places
Israel
Jews in Palestine

Jewish-Arab conflict
See also
Israel-Arab war, 1948-1949

Jewish-Arab problems
See Jewish-Arab relations

Partition
Ancient hatred builds toward war. G. De Carvalho. il Life 58:54+ Je 18 '65
See also
Jewish-Arab relations

PALESTINE refugees. See Refugees, Arab

PALEVSKY, Max
New computer prodigy? J. F. Olesky. Duns R 86:71-2 N '65
Only no. 7, so it tries harder. il pors Bsns W p 172+ Mr 20 '65

PALEY, Jeffrey
Nazi crimes and the statute of limitations. New Repub 152:6-7 Mr 6 '65

PALEY, William Samuel
CBS: the money machine. il por Newsweek 65:60-2 F 22 '65
Manhattan's highest paid headwaiter. W. McQuade. il por Arch Forum 123:76 S '65

PALFREY, John G.
Atoms for peace and the effort to halt the spread of nuclear weapons. Dept State Bul 53:393-7 S 6 '65

PALKA, John
Diffraction and visual acuity of insects. bibliog Science 149:551-3 Jl 30 '65

PALLADIUM
Pyrofuze finds ordnance application; palladium and aluminum in a bimetallic composite. J. F. Judge. il Miss & Roc 16:32-4 My 24 '65

PALM BEACH, Fla.

Clubs
Connie's club for homeless glitterbugs; Palm Bay club. A. Wright. il Sports Illus 23:40-2+ D 13 '65

PALM SPRINGS, Calif.
Palm Springs, gold-plated mirage. S. Birmingham. il Holiday 37:32-45 F '65
PALM trees. See Palms

PALMARES, Brazil
Palmares: a Negro state in colonial Brazil. S. Warren, jr. Negro Hist Bul 28:79-80 Ja '65

PALMER, Arnold
Arnold Palmer on the PGA. Newsweek 66:53 Ag 16 '65
Joys of trouble. pors Sports Illus 23:26-39 Jl 26; 36-43 Ag 2; 32-8 Ag 9 '65
Perfect golf course. Esquire 63:89-93 Ap '65

about
Diary of a career in turmoil. A. Wright. pors Sports Illus 23:24-6+ Ag 23 '65
Happiness is winning; Los Angeles Open. Time 87:68A Ja 21 '66
Hello, Arnie! il por Newsweek 65:88 My 17 '65
Long live the king! il por Time 86:60 Ag 20 '65
Welcome back, Arnie; with account by A. Wright. il pors Sports Illus 24:8-13 Ja 17 '66

PALMER, C. B.
Man from L.I.R.R. tells a few. N Y Times Mag p 154+ N 28 '65

PALMER, David
Chiropractic: science or swindle? excerpt from Health hucksters. R. L. Smith. il Todays Health 43:56-61 My '65

PALMER, Harvey E. and Beasley, T. M.
Iron-55 in humans and their foods. bibliog Science 149:431-2 Jl 23 '65
—and others
Radioactivity measured in Alaskan natives, 1962-1964. bibliog Science 147:620 F 5 '65

PALMER, J. Richard
Intellectual royalty; address, August 4, 1965. Vital Speeches 31:696-9 S 1 '65

PALMER, Norman D.
India and Pakistan: the major recipients. bibliog f Cur Hist 49:262-70+ N '65
India without Nehru. Cur Hist 48:69-74 F '65

PALMER, Orville
How to make the college of daddy's choice without really knowing anything. Nation 200:251-3 Mr 8 '65
Those college boards! Seventeen 24:136-7+ S '65
What to do when children cheat. Parents Mag 41:38-9+ Ja '66

PALMER, Robert H.
Gallstones produced experimentally by lithocholic acid in rats. bibliog Science 148:1339-40 Je 4 '65

PALMS, Charles L.
New books. Cath World 201:68+; 202:249-50 Ap '65, Ja '66
(ed) See Ball, W. B. New era for public and private schools
(ed) See Dugan, E. T. Harlem priest reports on Selma
(ed) See Haring, B. Church and the world

PALMS
Palms yes? or palms no? il Sunset 134:100-5 Ap '65
Your choice in palms is wide and wonderful. il Sunset 134:250-2+ Ap '65

PALOS VERDES, Calif.
Formal invitation to quality shopping; Buffums' department store. il Arch Rec 137:202-3 My '65

PALOS VERDES HILLS, Calif.
Looking back at Los Angeles. il Sunset 134:74-5 F '65

PALSY, Cerebral. See Paralysis

PALTRIDGE, Shane
Australia and the defense of southeast Asia. For Affairs 444:49-61 O '65

PAMPHLETS
Best in booklets. See issues of House & garden incorporating Living for young homemakers
Booklets about home repairs. Consumer Bul 48:22 O '65
Booklets worth writing for. See issues of Good housekeeping
Books & booklets. See issues of American home
Free or inexpensive. See issues of NEA journal
Things to write for. See issues of Changing times
Write for these. See issues of Wilson library bulletin

PAMPHLETS, Political. See Political literature
PANAGRA. See Pan American Grace airways
PANAIR do Brasil. See Airlines—Brazil

PANAMA
See also
Paleontology—Panama
Panama Canal
Railroads—Panama

Native races
See also
Indians of Central America

Politics and government
Challenge in Panama. L. L. Pippin. Cur Hist 50:1-7+ Ja '66

PANAMA (city)

Religious institutions and affairs
Parish of the future. J. P. Fitzpatrick. America 113:521-3 N 6 '65

PANAMA and the United States
Canal settlement. Time 86:46 O 1 '65
U.S.-Panama pact: a double gain. Bsns W p29 O 2 '65

PANAMA CANAL
Canal hitch. il Time 85:32 F 12 '65
Canal settlement. Time 86:46 O 1 '65
Challenge in Panama. L. L. Pippin. Cur Hist 50:1-7+ Ja '66
President reports on progress of negotiations with Panama; statement, September 24, 1965. L. B. Johnson. Dept State Bul 53:624-5 O 18 '65; Excerpts. Cur Hist 50:49 Ja '66
Sea-level canal: how and where. J. H. Stratton. For Affairs 43:513-18 Ap '65
U.S.-Panama pact: a double gain. Bsns W p29 O 2 '65
Where shall we build the new canal? C. W. Hall. il Read Digest 87:213-14+ S '65

PANAMA CANAL ZONE
President: revisionist; treaty revised. Newsweek 66:27-8 O 4 '65

PAN AMERICAN conferences. See Inter-American conferences

PAN AMERICAN congress of architects
Cities and people; Cities of the New World conference, symposium, ed. by M. S. Haverstock. il Américas 17:20-5 Ag '65

PAN AMERICAN day and week
Pan American day. G. de Zéndegui. Américas 17:inside cover My '65
Pan American day and Pan American week, 1965; proclamation, March 1, 1965. L. J. Johnson. Dept State Bul 52:432 Mr 22 '65

PAN AMERICAN Grace airways
Panagra disputes CAB bureau on South American route awards. Aviation W 83:39 N 8 '65

PAN AMERICAN health organization
Directing council; sixteenth meeting. Américas 17:45-6 N '65
See also
Pan American sanitary bureau

Headquarters
Sculpture in light and concrete. J. Villaverde. il Américas 17:22-8 S '65

PAN AMERICAN highway
Frayed, but still holding together. il Bsns W p 116 S 11 '65

PAN AMERICAN petroleum corporation
Great Alaska ore snatch. il Sci Digest 57:66-9 Ap '65

PAN AMERICAN sanitary bureau
Health and development. A. Horwitz. il Américas 17:54-8 Ap '65

PAN AMERICAN union
Aid to libraries in Latin America. M. D. Shepard. il Wilson Lib Bul 39:778-82 My '65
Art. See issues of Américas
Music. See issues of Américas
Young art of the Americas: exhibit at the Pan American union. F. Getlein. il Américas 17:20-5 Je '65

PAN AMERICAN world airways
Duty hours major issue in Pan Am strike. Aviation W 82:45 Ap 5 '65
Pan Am asks lower DC-8 limits. Aviation W 82:30 Mr 1 '65
Pan Am expected to purchase Boeing-Bendix landing system. Aviation W 82:34 My 31 '65
Pan Am planning 727s for Berlin. Aviation W 82:32 Mr 29 '65
Pan Am proposes cut in fares from Europe. Aviation W 82:52 My 10 '65
Pan American seeking to force inflight entertainment decision. Aviation W 83:34 O 18 '65
Perspicacity for Pan Am. il Newsweek 66:82 S 27 '65

PAN AMERICANISM. See Inter-American relations

PANARINFO, Joseph
Package: discotheque, promotion of Seeburg corporation. New Yorker 41:26-7 F 27 '65

PANATOMIC-X films. See Photography—Films

PANCAKES. See Griddle cakes

PANCREAS
Secretions
Pancreatic secretion induced by stimulation of the pyloric gland area of the stomach. R. M. Preshaw and others. bibliog il Science 148:1347-8 Je 4 '65

PANCZKO brothers
Brotherly boom in burglaries; Panczko brothers criminal career. K. Wheeler. il Life 59:71-2+ Ag 6 '65

PANELING
How to choose wood paneling and flooring. Bet Hom & Gard 43:33+ My '65
Wood: what the new flooring, paneling and furniture can do for a room! D. Popplestone and D. Jordan. il Bet Hom & Gard 43:50-63 My '65

PANELS, Decorative
Engraved sources for American overmantel panels. N. F. Little. il Antiques 88:494-501 O '65

PANHANDLE agricultural and mechanical college, Goodwell, Okla.
College called Panhandle. G. Holland. il Sports Illus 22:26+ F 1 '65

PANHANDLING. See Begging and beggars

PANICS. See Stock exchange—Crisis, October 1929

PANNING, Gold. See Gold panning

PANSIES
Best pansies. il Flower Grower 52:10-11 Ag '65

PANTELL, Dora F.
Basic adult education: a study. por Wilson Lib Bul 40:71-4+ S '65

PANTER-DOWNES, Mollie
Empty place; story. New Yorker 41:42-9 Mr 27 '65
Letter from London. See issues of New Yorker

PANTOMIME
See also
Mime
Shadow pantomimes and plays

PANTRIES
New pantry kitchen, more than meets the eye. M. Davidson. il Ladies Home J 83:78-9+ Ja '66
These pantries store plenty! il Bet Hom & Gard 43:116+ Mr '65
This pantry solves the space-pinch. il Bet Hom & Gard 44:84 Ja '66

PANTRY. See Pantries

PANTRY kiss; story. See Shyer, M. F.

PAOLINI, P. J. See Baskin, R. J. jt. auth.

PAOLUCCI, Henry
Are nations washed up? Nat R 17:873-5 O 5 '65

PAP, Michael S.
Permanent crisis within Soviet Union; address, March 7, 1965. Vital Speeches 31:405-10 Ap 15 '65

PAPA, C. M.
Baldness. L. R. Chevalier. por Ladies Home J 82:34+ Je '65

PAPACY
Almain and Major: conciliar theory on the eve of the reformation. F. Oakley. bibliog f Am Hist R 70:673-90 Ap '65
Bishops of Rome. E. T. Dell, jr. Christian Cent 82:244 F 24 '65
Ecumenical criticism. K. R. Bridston. Christian Cent 82:1608 D 29 '65
On primacy: thinking the unthinkable. M. E. Marty. Cath World 202:26-31 O '65
See also
Vatican

PAPAGO Indian baskets. See Baskets

PAPAIN
Papain membrane on a collodion matrix: preparation and enzymic behavior. R. Goldman and others. bibliog il Science 150:758-60 N 5 '65

PAPAL audiences
Pietro & Paul; Pope gives audience to P. Nenni. il Time 85:33-4 Ap 23 '65

PAPAL nuncios. See Nuncios, Papal

PAPANDREOU, Andreas George
Greece and Turkey: the second round. G. Bailey. il Reporter 33:14-18 S 9 '65
His father's son. por Newsweek 66:35 Ag 16 '65

PAPANDREOU, George
Field day for the left in Athens. G. Bailey. Reporter 33:25-7 Ag 12 '65
Greece and Turkey: the second round. G. Bailey. il Reporter 33:14-18 S 9 '65
King & the fox. il por Time 86:25 Jl 23 '65

Rocks in the cradle. Newsweek 65:40-2 Mr 8 '65
Violent days: Greek against Greek. il por Newsweek 66:33 Ag 2 '65
What the palace fears. C. Poulos. il Nation 201:158-61 S 27 '65

PAPASHVILY, Helen
Holiday handbook of American spas. Holiday 37:133-8 My '65

PAPAYAS
Pleasures of papayas. il Bet Hom & Gard 43:104-5 Mr '65

PAPER
Notes and comment; chemical compound in newsprint paper effective source of insect control. il New Yorker 41:47 O 30 '65
Powerful paper; wood pulp paper effective in insect control. Sci Am 213:39 O '65
See also
Marbling

PAPER, Decorative
These papers are made by dip-and-dye. il Sunset 134:143-4 My '65

PAPER, Handmade. See Paper making and trade

PAPER bag mystery; drama. See Miller, H. L.

PAPER bag players. See Theater, Childrens

PAPER books. See Paperback books

PAPER clips
Gem of the gizmos. Time 86:52 D 3 '65

PAPER cutters (tools)
New paper trimmer. il Consumer Bul 48:31 Ag '65

PAPER flowers; story. See Maynard, R.

PAPER making and trade
Home brew: fine paper from a tub. L. Aigner. il Pop Mech 124:112-14 S '65
They see a market for all they can make. il Bsns W p50-3 Ag 7 '65
See also
Boise Cascade corporation
Crown Zellerbach corporation
Glatfelter, P. H. company

PAPER money
United States
Mystery of the $100 bills; why the flood of them. il U S News 59:78-80 D 20 '65
When the railroads printed money. il Fortune 72:172-3 S '65

PAPER sculpture
Insects: art class. J. Moody. il Sch Arts 64:35 F '65

PAPER tiger, burning bright; story. See Williams, G.

PAPER trimmers. See Paper cutters (tools)

PAPER work
Blue and white paper silhouettes. J. Markos. il Design 67:17 S '65
Cardboard contrivances. il Design 66:32-3 Ja '65
Cartonnage; the art of making paper decorations. il House & Gard 127:170-1 Ap '65
Fold-dye paper designs. P. Johnson. il Sch Arts 64:4-6 Je '65
In the manner of Matisse; fourth grade project. L. S. Roe. il Design 67:40-1 S '65
One pattern makes all three; Christmas decorations. il Sunset 135:80 D '65
Paper doll people. B. Coats and K. Wood. Parents Mag 40:93 Jl '65
Parties with paper. E. D. Craster. il Bet Hom & Gard 43:25-6 Mr '65
Poetic license for all; Spring, subject of cut paper project. M. Luca. il Sch Arts 65:38 S '65
See also
Papier-mâché
Silhouettes

PAPER work, Office. See Office management

PAPERBACK book covers. See Book covers

PAPERBACK books
Conference in October on paperbacks in education. Pub W 187:37 Mr 8 '65
Paperback books grade school through high school. Sat R 48:74 S 11 '65
Paperbacks. See issues of Publishers' weekly
Paperbacks as textbooks. R. Rahtz. Sr Schol 87:sup 18 N 18 '65
Paperbacks for children win sales. J. Noyes. il Pub W 188:202-4 Jl 12 '65
Pony boom: the object is to pass, isn't it? il Newsweek 66:101-2+ N 22 '65
Progress report on World university library. Pub W 187:58 Je 28 '65
Revolution in books. R. Escarpit. il UNESCO Courier 18:4-10 S '65
Role of paperback books in education examined in depth; summary of conference at Teachers college, Columbia university; with editorial comment. il Pub W 188:13-27, 40 N 1 '65

PAPERBACK books—*Continued*
Role of the paperback in science teaching; summaries of addresses at Teachers college, Columbia university, conference. Pub W 188:68-71 N 15 '65
Trade winds; concerning The Guinness book of world records. J. G. Fuller. il Sat R 48:8 N 27 '65
See also
Booksellers and bookselling—Paperback books
Libraries—Paperback books
Pocket books, incorporated
Publishers and publishing—Paperback books

Bibliography
Education paperbacks issue; symposium. Sr Schol 87:sup6+ O 28 '65
I/t/a paperback series. W. D. Boutwell. il Sr Schol 86:sup 18 Mr 4 '65
Keeping pace with the news in paperbacks; roundup of important new titles. America 113:532+ N 6 '65
List of paperback books. il Pub W 187:95-6+ F 1 '65
Paperback bookshelf. See issues of Changing times
Paperbacks for curriculum enrichment. D. E. Carline. il Sr Schol 86:sup 12 Mr 4 '65
Paperbacks to come; ed. by J. Putnam and R. Grossman. Library J 90:2355-70+, 3725-6+ My 15, S 15 '65
Pick of the paperbacks. R. W. Saal. See issues of Saturday review

Statistics
Data on paperbacks in religious book publishing. C. B. Grannis. Pub W 187:103 F 8 '65
1965 paperback best sellers in the bookstores. il Pub W 189:64-7, 90-3 Ja 17 '66

PAPERWEIGHTS
Metropolitan miniature; proscenium. F. Stevenson. il Opera N 30:inside back cover N 20 '65

PAPIER-MACHÉ
Animal forms. M. B. Miller. il Sch Arts 64:15-17 My '65
Pictures to make and feel. L. Lindeman. il Design 66:25-7 Ja '65

PAPILIO machaon. See Butterflies
PAPOVA viruses. See Viruses
PAPP, Joseph
Mugging the Bard in Central park. J. Simon. Commonweal 82:635-6 S 3 '65; Reply. S. Bernard. 82:678-9+ S 24 '65
Shakespeare for the people. J. Novick. Nation 201:146-8 S 13 '65

PAPPAS, George
Art. pop. Sch Arts 64:40-1 Ap '65

PARABLES
Backward bird; graphic lesson for disabled kindergarten children. A. Carilli and others. il Good H 161:156-7 D '65
Fairy princess. D. Acheson. il Reporter 33:44-5 O 7 '65

PARACHUTE jumping. See Parachuting
PARACHUTES
Steerable parasail tests point to use in Vietnam. il Miss & Roc 17:28 D 6 '65

PARACHUTING
Fall guys; National parachuting championships. R. B. Weeghman. il Flying 78:44-7 Ja '66
Look back and smile. L. Steckler. il Pop Mech 124:92-4+ Ag '65
They jump to save lives. G. E. Maxwell. il Todays Health 43:42-5+ Mr '65

PARADE wagons, Circus. See Circus equipment
PARADES
Early starter: Christmas in America. E. M. Marshall. il Travel 124:42-4 N '65
Ruffle of colors, flourish of brass; with photographs by T. Ray-Jones. Sat Eve Post 238:30-5 Jl 3 '65
Skin: container of an idea. J. Ciardi. Sat R 48:18 Mr 13 '65

PARADOXICAL sleep. See Sleep
PARAFFINIC hydrocarbons. See Hydrocarbons
PARAFOIL. See Gliders (aeronautics)
PARAGLIDER. See Gliders (aeronautics)
PARAKEETS
Keeping company with a parakeet. M. Courtney. il Harper 230:30+ My '65; Same abr. with title Petie, the perplexing parakeet. Read Digest 87:123-6 Ag '65

PARALLAX, Stellar
See also
Stars—Distance

PARALYSIS
Cat lady of Philadelphia: S. DePaur. A. Peters. il Ebony 21:76-8+ D '65

Law student overcomes handicap to win point. il Ebony 20:119-20+ My '65
Linnet on the leaf: therapy for child with cerebral palsy. J. M. Myers. McCalls 92:20+ F '65
Parkinsonism: electromyographic studies of monosynaptic reflex. M. Ioku and others. bibliog il Science 150:1472-5 D 10 '65
Parkinson's disease. il Todays Health 43:34-6 Ag '65
Secret conquest; successful operation on C. Bowles for Parkinson's disease. il Newsweek 66:19-20 Ag 23 '65
She only cried once. L. David. il Good H 161:74-5+ S '65
TV distortion compared to symptoms of palsy. Sci N L 88:185 S 18 '65

PARAMETERS
Micrometeoroid measurements. J. H. Wujek, jr. il Electr World 74:42-3+ N '65

PARAMOUNT pictures corporation
Raid on Paramount; business syndicate bid for control. Newsweek 65:72 My 31 '65

PARAN, Pat
Around Long Island marathon. Motor B 116:27+ Jl '65

PARAPETS
Solving leakage problems of parapets. H. Edwards. il Arch Rec 137:222 3 Ap '65

PARAPLEGIA. See Paralysis
PARAPSYCHOLOGY
Pseudo experience in parapsychology; letter. L. W. Alvarez. Science 148:1541 Je 18 '65
Discussion. 149:910; 150:436 Ag 27, O 22 '65
Science gets serious about E.S.P. D. Cohen. il Sci Digest 58:62-72 N '65

PARASAILS. See Parachutes
PARASITES
See also
Fleas
Nematodes
Plasmodium (parasite)
Protozoa, Pathogenic

Arthropods
Study in specificity; minute fungi parasitize living arthropods. R. K. Benjamin. il Natur Hist 74:42-9 Mr '65

Insects
Flora and fauna on backs of large papuan moss-forest weevils. J. L. Gressitt and others. bibliog il Science 150:1833-5 D 31 '65

PARASITIC plants
Angiosperm parasite and host: coordinated dispersal. P. R. Atsatt. bibliog il Science 149:1389-90 S 17 '65
See also
Mistletoe

PARATHYROID glands
Thyroid and parathyroid roles in hypercalcemia: evidence for a thyrocalcitonin-releasing factor. R. F. Gittes and G. L. Irvin. bibliog il Science 148:1737-9 Je 25 '65

PARDEE, W. D.
If you grow sweet corn, try super-sweet. Suc Farm 63:58B My '65
Report on hybrid soybeans. Suc Farm 63:46 Ag '65
Report on new soybean varieties. Suc Farm 63:52 Ap '65

PARENT-child relationship
ABC's of getting along with teenage daughters. J. Brothers. Good H 161:56+ O '65
Adventures of a peeping mom. S. Alexander. Life 58:25 Mr 12 '65
Are you a good mother? K. Gallant. Parents Mag 40:154-5 N '65
Confessions of a monster mother. E. Grendon. il Parents Mag 40:56-7+ Mr '65
Confessions on a teen-age son. M. S. Miller. McCalls 92:27 F '65
Dear, dear teen-agers. R. Russell. Seventeen 24:156+ N '65
Do you get along with your teen-ager? F. N. Huff. il Todays Health 43:42-3+ F '65
Empty days; adjusting to when children leave home. A. Lake. il McCalls 92:78-81+ S '65
Every day is father's day. A. Montagu. il Parents Mag 40:43+ Je '65
Familial colloquies. il Esquire 64:54-7 Jl '65
Family communication; with study-discussion program. by C. Smallenburg and H. Smallenburg. C. B. Broderick. bibliog il PTA Mag 60:4-6, 35-6 D '65
Fathers without children. E. T. Eberhart. il Parents Mag 40:66-7+ Ap '65
Five steps in the growth of a parent; with discussion group program. by E. J. LeShan. M. Smart. bibliog il Parents Mag 40:20+, 56-7+ D '65

PARENT-child relationship—*Continued*
From the end spring new beginnings; endings children wrote for the NEA journal's Unfinished stories. D. Waleski. il NEA J 54:14-18 Ap '65

High-brows vs no-brows. A. Chasins. il McCalls 92:42+ S '65

How marriage counseling helps children; Juvenile welfare board, Pinellas County, Fla. C. Foster. il Parents Mag 40:42-3+ My '65

How to know when a child is happy. J. Scott. Bet Hom & Gard 43:40+ F '65

How to run away from home. D. Klein. il Seventeen 24:150-1+ Mr '65

I can say no to my teenagers. D. Van Ark. il Parents Mag 40:58-9+ S '65

Ideals can be disquieting; with study-discussion program, by C. Smallenburg and H. Smallenburg. W. J. Anderson; H. Long. bibliog il PTA Mag 59:14-16, 36-7 My '65

It's smart to play favorites. M. B. Hoover. il Parents Mag 40:48-9+ My '65

Making of a man. P. Wylie. il Read Digest 87:63-8 D '65

Mistakes many mothers make: will your children ever be friends? R. W. Bacmeister. il Parents Mag 40:54-5+ Ap '65

Mothers and sons: an intimate discussion. V. T. Lathbury. Ladies Home J 82:43-5 F '65

Parental overprotection and political distrust. F. A. Pinner. bibliog f il Ann Am Acad 361:58-70 S '65

Questions for young people, and for parents. L. David. Read Digest 86:213-14 Mr '65

Responsible parenthood; unwanted child. America 113:199-200 Ag 28 '65

So he hates baseball. C. Himber. il N Y Times Mag p59-60 Ag 29 '65

Speaking out; children are a waste of time. N. Balchin. Sat Eve Post 238:10+ O 9 '65

Subtle dangers in mother-daughter talks about sex. R. Wilkenson. il McCalls 93:58-9+ Ja '66

These gifts will last. J. Shoemaker. Farm J 89:40 Jl '65

Time out for parents; with study-discussion program, by R. Strang. D. Grace. bibliog il PTA Mag 59:11-13, 35 Ap '65

Vanishing American father. M. Lerner. McCalls 92:95+ My '65; Same abr. Read Digest 87:116-18 Jl '65

War between mother and daughter. V. G. Damon and I. Taves. Look 30:30+ Ja 11 '66

What makes parents repulsive. E. A. Lazar and C. Klein. il N Y Times Mag p63-4 F 7 '65

Why can't my mother grow up? questions and answers. A. Wood. il Seventeen 24:98-9+ Jl '65

Why can't parents stop.. ? P. L. Levin. il N Y Times Mag p69-70 My 16 '65

Why your parents don't understand you. D. Sugarman and R. Hochstein. Seventeen 24:134-5+ O '65
See also
Family life
Fathers
Love, Maternal
Mothers

PARENT education
World is shaped anew; programs of parent education and home-school cooperation. J. Moorhead. PTA Mag 60:2-3 Ja '66

PARENT-helpers. See Teachers aides

PARENT-teacher associations. See Parents and teachers associations

PARENT-teacher cooperation. See School and the home

PARENTAL love. See Love

PARENTAL overprotection. See Parent-child relationship

PARENTE, Pietro, abp
What does the Note mean? America 112:707 My 15 '65

PARENTEAU, Shirley
Take them back to the farm. Nat Parks Mag 39:12-13 N '65

PARENTS
Do teenagers make good parents? E. S. Stewart. il Parents Mag 40:46-9+ F '65

How far is a parent responsible? adaptation of address, 1965. W. C. Ellzey. il PTA Mag 60:28-30 N '65

Trouble with my parents. J. McClurg. Farm J 89:75 Ag '65

Unsung underdog. R. Baker. Read Digest 87:92 Ag '65
See also
Fathers
Mothers

PARENTS and teachers associations
Congratulations and challenges to the PTA; symposium. PTA Mag 59:25-8 F; 19 Mr '65

Day the phone rang false; vicious attack on the PTA. PTA Mag 60:31-2 N '65

Dial-a-diatribe; attack on the PTA over recording service. New Repub 153:7 O 16 '65

From strength to greater strength. J. Moorhead. PTA Mag 60:2-3 S '65

How do you talk to a parade? adaptation of address, May 1965. F. Hipp. il PTA Mag 60:13-15 O '65

Invitation to the Nation: join the PTA. J. Moorhead. il PTA Mag 60:2-3 O '65

John Birch versus PTA. Nation 200:156 F 15 '65

Keeping pace with the PTA. See issues of PTA magazine

Key is cooperation. J. Moorhead. Sr Schol 87:sup9 O 21 '65

Mountain of books for mountain children; PTA project. Books for Appalachia. E. May. il PTA Mag 60:8-10 S '65

New Scholastic paperback fosters teacher-parent discussions; concerning PTA guide to What's happening in education. Sr Schol 87:sup6 O 21 '65

News and views from National PTA chairmen. PTA Mag 59:16 Je; 60:37 D '65

PTA and critical issues in education. J. Moorhead. PTA Mag 59:2-3 Je '65

PTA in 1965. PTA Mag 59:23-4 F '65

PTA members of the month (title varies) il PTA Mag 59:14-15 Ap; 60:32 O '65

Plot to take over the PTA. E. Dunbar. il Look 29:27-31 S 7 '65

President's message. J. Moorhead. PTA Mag 59:17-18 F '65

Ten ways to upgrade your PTA. W. C. Kvaraceus. Parents Mag 40:45+ F '65

We are legion. il PTA Mag 59:19-22 F '65

What's happening in education? role of PTA's in other parts of the world. W. D. Boutwell. PTA Mag 60:13-14 D '65

World is shaped anew; programs of parent education and home-school cooperation. J. Moorhead. PTA Mag 60:2-3 Ja '66

PARENTS and teachers conferences. See School and the home

PARENTS league of New York
Code for teens, updated. A. P. Eliasberg. N Y Times Mag p 112+ N 21 '65

PARENTS letters to children. See Letters to children

PARENTS magazine
President Lyndon B. Johnson awarded Parents' magazine medal for outstanding service to children. il Parents Mag 40:38 D '65
See also
Youth group achievement awards

PARETI, Luigi
Ancestors of the ball-point pen. UNESCO Courier 18:25-7 My '65

PARHAM, John G.
Vote yes for parks. por Recreation 58:405+ O '65

PARIS, James D.
Predicted logger's '65 preview. Motor B 115:52 Je '65

PARIS
Letter from Paris. Genêt. See issues of New Yorker

Paris at long last. S. McKelway. Holiday 38:16+ S '65

Paris: the Cisco kid speaks French. T. Q. Curtiss. il Sat R 49:46-7+ Ja 1 '66

Art
Art news from Paris. J. Ashbery. il Art N 64:52-3+ O; 37+ D '65

Atelier crisis. il Time 86:62 Ag 27 '65

Banks
Paris-Bas gets around. il Fortune 72:102+ N '65

City planning
Business à la U.S. now the mode in Paris. il Bsns W p58-60+ O 23 '65

Letter from Paris; Paris in the year 2000: eight new satellite towns. Genêt. New Yorker 41:72-4 Jl 10 '65

Clubs
World's most exclusive club; Jockey club of Paris. P. Feldkamp. il Horizon 7:92-6+ Autumn '65

Description
Personal business; guide to Europe's business centers: Paris. Bsns W p 177-8 O 23 '65

Third fall of Paris. H. R. Lottman. il N Y Times Mag p46-7+ N 28 '65

PARIS—*Continued*

Galleries and museums

Paris: from pre-history to outer space; Musée de l'homme. J. Ashbery. il Art N 64:45-7 Sum '65

Hotels, restaurants, etc.

I'm going to Maxim's; interview, ed. by P. Dragadze. il pors Life 60:39-42 Ja 7 '66
Lemonader extraordinary; proprietors of Chez Lipp. il Newsweek 66:54+ O 25 '65
Letter from Paris; plans for Tour Montparnasse hotel. Genêt. New Yorker 41:126+ O 30 '65
Splendors and miseries of the literary cafe. H. R. Lottman. il Sat R 48:34-5+ Mr 13 '65

Housing

City of art; Paris studio complex nears completion. Newsweek 66:93 O 4 '65

Intellectual life

City of art; Paris studio complex nears completion. Newsweek 66:93 O 4 '65
Third fall of Paris. H. R. Lottman. il N Y Times Mag p46-7+ N 28 '65

Music

Crisis in all Gaul. R. McMullen. Hi Fi 15:128-9 My '65
Marais festival. R. McMullen. Hi Fi 15:162 S '65
New look for the Opera-comique. R. McMullen. Hi Fi 15:116-17 Jl '65
Notes from our correspondents. R. McMullen. See issues of High fidelity incorporating Musical America
Paris. D. Stevens. il Opera N 30:32 D 11 '65
Paris fall. D. Stevens. il Opera N 29:30 Mr 20 '65
Prestige of the organ. R. McMullen. Hi Fi 15:181 D '65
Season strangely flavored. R. McMullen. Hi Fi 15:138 Je '65
Uproar at the Champs-Elysées. R. McMullen. il Hi Fi 15:143-4 Ap '65

Newspapers

La Croix's 25,000th. America 112:413 Mr 27 '65

Social life and customs

Très snob; craze for things British. il Newsweek 67:29 Ja 10 '65
Weekend in Moscow; *Le Tout-Paris* with report by E. Peer. il Newsweek 65:55-6 My 10 '65

Stores
History

Paris *marchands-merciers* and French eighteenth-century taste; adaptation of address, May 1964. F. J. B. Watson. il Antiques 88:347-51 S '65

Theater

America on the Paris stage. N. Biel. Nation 200:652-3+ Je 14 '65
Letter from Paris (cont) Genêt. New Yorker 41:220-3 O 16 '65

PARIS, Battle of, 1944
Defeat of Hitler's order to burn Paris; filming of Is Paris burning? il Look 30:40-5 Ja 25 '66
General who defied Hitler. H. Ehrlich. il Look 30:46+ Ja 25 '66
Is Paris burning? by L. Collins and D. Lapierre. Review
America 113:141-2 Ag 7 '65. R. L. Carol
Life 58:15 Je 4 '65. B. Frizell
Sat R il 48:27 Jl 3 '65. H. C. Wolfe
Time 85:38 Je 4 '65
Is Paris burning? condensation. L. Collins and D. Lapierre. il Read Digest 86:269-73+ Ap '65
Is Paris burning? excerpts. L. Collins and D. Lapierre. il Ladies Home J 82:89-90+ O '65

PARIS air and space show. See Aviation—Exhibitions
PARIS edition, New York Times. See New York times
PARIS international air show. See Aviation—Exhibitions
PARIS-presse (newspaper) See Newspapers—France
PARISH missions
Total parish; St Richard's, Jackson, Miss. C. J. McNaspy. America 113:465 O 23 '65

PARISHES
Parish of the future; San Miguelito, Panama City. J. P. Fitzpatrick. America 113:521-3 N 6 '65
Parish school board. O. J. Murdick. America 114:132-6 Ja 22 '66
PARISIANS
Great craftsmen of Paris; tr. by A. White. V. Leduc. Vogue 145:80-3+ Mr 15 '65
People of Paris. H. Gold. il Holiday 38:50-61 D '65
PARITY, Principle of. See Symmetry
PARITY conservation. See Wave functions
PARITY prices. See Farm produce—Prices
PARK, Arthur R.
Shoji Hamada. bibliog Sch Arts 64:23-7 Je '65
PARK, Chung Hee
Striking parallel. il por Time 85:35-6 My 21 '65
United States and Korea reaffirm strong bonds of friendship; greetings. May 17, 1965. Dept State Bul 52:951 Je 14 '65
PARK, Clara Claiborne
Loneliness can be a treasure. Ladies Home J 82:58+ Mr '65
PARK, Ed
Trophy takes more doing. pors Outdoor Life 136:44-7+ Ag '65
Whitetails don't hesitate. por Outdoor Life 135:44-7+ Je '65
PARK roads. See National parks and reserves—Roads
PARK vandalism. See Vandalism
PARKAS. See Clothing and dress—Sports clothes
PARKE-Bernet galleries, incorporated
Auction by Early bird. R. Lynes. il Harper 231:28+ Ag '65
Auction prices of the last season. R. Davidson. il Antiques 88:172+ Ag '65
Champagne and Chagall. il Newsweek 65:86-7 Ap 26 '65
Doubleheader; auction of modern art works a record for the western hemisphere. il Time 85:66 Ap 23 '65
$4,000,000 auction. il Time 86:88 O 22 '65
Odd ball in; Parke-Bernet auction of paintings by modern Americans. Newsweek 66:104 O 25 '65
Parke-Bernet has second highest season. Hobbies 70:111+ S '65
PARKER, Charlie
Jazz concerts; performance in his memory at Carnegie Hall. W. Balliett. New Yorker 41:116-18 Ap 10 '65
PARKER, David F.
Long look at city planning. Am City 80:90-2+ Jl '65
PARKER, Ellen
Beaupre; letters from a camper. por Dance Mag 39:22-4 Mr '65
PARKER, Everett C.
Papal visit. Christian Cent 82:1278-9 O 20 '65
PARKER, Franklin
1965 as a centennial year in the history of education. Sch & Soc 93:85-6 F 6 '65
White House conference on education and the emergence of the new guard. Sch & Soc 93:425-8 N 13 '65
William Heard Kilpatrick, 1871-1965. bibliog Sch & Soc 93:368-71 O 16 '65
PARKER, Garland G.
Statistics of attendance in American universities and colleges, 1965-66. Sch & Soc 94:7-22 Ja 8 '66
PARKER, Harry
Never before, at Harvard or in history. H. Whall. il pors Sports Illus 22:36-8+ Je 28 '65
Think, feel, win. il por Time 85:68 Je 18 '65
PARKER, John L.
Now we're drilling for steam. Sci Digest 57:78-80 F '65
PARKER, Louise
Big flood. Am For 71:14-17+ Mr '65
PARKER, Patrick L. and Leo, R. F.
Fatty acids in blue-green algal mat communities. bibliog Science 148:373-4 Ap 16 '65
PARKER, Stephen Jan
(tr) See Hemingway, E. Meeting
PARKER, William Henry
Are courts to blame? or police? or society? interview. por U S News 59:68-9 Ag 9 '65
Back of riots: discontent, illiteracy, criminal element; interview. por U S News 59:22-3 Ag 30 '65
Tough top cop of L.A; excerpts from remarks. por Newsweek 66:17 Ag 30 '65

PARKER, William Henry—*Continued*

about

Chief Parker and company. Christian Cent 82:1308-9 O 27 '65

Outspoken police chief; his target: untrained judges; statement. por U S News 59:22 Jl 12 '65

There's no easy place to pin the blame. D. Moser. il por Life 59:30-3 Ag 27 '65

Who's to blame? il por Time 86:10-11 Ag 27 '65

PARKER'S back; story. See O'Connor, F.

PARKHURST, Henry M.

Inventiveness of Henry Parkhurst. J. Ashbrook. por Sky & Tel 29:217+ Ap '65

PARKIN. See Cake

PARKING, Automobile. See Automobile parking

PARKING decks. See Automobile parking

PARKING lots. See Automobile parking

PARKINSON'S disease. See Paralysis

PARKS, Gordon

I was a zombie then; like all Muslims, I was hypnotized. Life 58:28-31 Mr 5 '65

PARKS, Joan W.

All dressed up and rarin' to go. Parents Mag 40:62-3+ Mr '65

PARKS, R. D.

Quantum effects in superconductors. Sci Am 213:57-62+ bibliog(p 127) O '65

PARKS, W. George

Program for 1965. Science 147:1312-26+ Mr 12 '65

PARKS

Changing functions of parks; adaptation of St Cloud, Minn. park and recreation departments annual report. il Recreation 58:225-6 My '65

Parks and playgrounds. See issues of American city

Care

Multipurpose equipment for all seasons; excerpts from address. 1964. W. F. Bruning. Recreation 58:493 D '65

Europe, Western

European parks too formal. R. R. Fleming. il Am City 80:100-3+ S '65

Ireland

Lure of Tollymore. E. V. Malone. il Am For 71:30-1 F '65

New Zealand

Playground in Kiwiland. E. A. Scholer. il Recreation 58:392-3 O '65

United States

Planning tomorrow's parks; address. R. F. Paige. Recreation 58:295-6 Je '65

See also

National parks and reserves—United States

also subhead Parks and reserves under names of states, e.g. Kentucky—Parks and reserves; *also* subhead Parks and playgrounds under names of cities, e.g. New York (city)—Parks and playgrounds

PARKS, Roadside. See Roadside improvement

PARLIAMENTARY elections. See Elections—Great Britain

PARLOR games. See Games

PARMELIA sulcata. See Lichens

PARMENTEL, Noel E. Jr

John V. Lindsay: less than meets the eye. Esquire 64:100-2+ O '65

PAROCHIAL schools

Washington report; interview, ed. by J. Lloyd. A. C. Koob. Sr Schol 86:sup 13 Ap 15 '65

Federal aid

See Federal aid to education

PAROCHIAL schools, Catholic

Back to the schools. J. O'Gara. Commonweal 82:183 Ap 30 '65

Catholic high schools today; Scholastic teacher interview. C. A. Koob. Sr Schol 86:sup 29-31 Ap 15 '65

Catholic schools in Britain. M. P. Fogarty. Commonweal 83:13-14+ O 8 '65

Catholic schools in Scotland. E. W. Schott. America 113:45 Jl 10 '65

Christian committment and Catholic schools. V. M. Novak. America 113:40-2 Jl 10 '65

Criticizing the schools. J. O'Gara. Commonweal 82:138 Ap 23 '65

Further proposal for federal aid to Catholic schools. E. A. Smith. Cath World 201:162-9 Je '65

Of many things. P. K. Cuneo. America 114:101 Ja 22 '66

One year later; further thoughts on Are parochial schools the answer? M. P. Ryan. Commonweal 82:139-41 Ap 23 '65; Reply. L. L. Routhier. 82:306-7+ My 28 '65

Pennsylvania school bus fight; public aid for parochial schools. C. W. Zunkel. Christian Cent 82:1036-7 Ag 25 '65; Discussion. 82:1322 O 27 '65

Preparing for change in parochial schools. O. J. Murdick. America 112:282-4 F 27 '65; Reply. R. Luka. 112:409 Mr 27 '65

Schools. D. Callahan; discussion. Commonweal 81:594-5+ F 5 '65

Federal aid

See Federal aid to education

Finance

Money and lay rights. Commonweal 82:204 My 7 '65

PAROCHIAL schools, Jewish. See Jews—Education

PARODY. Ovid F.

Big ideas for small schools. por Am Ed 1:1-3 Jl '65

Quality secondary schools of the future (cont) Sch Life 47:24-8 D '64

PAROLE

When criminals are set free too soon. J. E. Hoover. U S News 58:21 My 17 '65

PARQUET flooring. See Flooring

PARR, A. E.

City and psyche. Yale R 55:71-85 O '65

PARRATT, Gertrude Gray

Evil eye. Atlan 216:152 O '65

PARREÑO, Francisco de Arango y. See Arango y Parreño, F. de

PARRETT, Pat

Spotlight on the Wayne 100. Pop Mech 124:38-40 S '65

PARRIS, Wendell A.

New approach to educating Negro children in gray area schools (cont) bibliog Negro Hist Bul 28:91+ Ja '65

PARRISH, John B.

Employment of women chemists in industrial laboratories. bibliog Science 148:657-8 Ap 30 '65

PARRY, Jack

Return to the Winnipeg. por Outdoor Life 135:66-8+ Je '65

PARRY, Stanley

Dilemmas of equality. Nat R 17:606-7 Jl 13 '65

PARSEGHIAN, Ara

Rockne, Parseghian and the Fighting Irish. T. Cohane. il pors Look 29:88-9+ N 2 '65

PARSLEY

Parsley. il Ladies Home J 82:84 My '65

PARSONS, D. F.

Electron microscope and its future development. Science 148:988-91 My 14 '65

PARSONS, J. L. and Zeman, L. E.

During year of seeding grow three to five tons of forage per acre. Suc Farm 63:46-7+ F '65

PARSONS, Louella O.

Little queen Hollywood deserved. P. O'Neil. il pors Life 58:72-6+ Je 4 '65

PART time employment

Jingle bells ring out call for part-time help. il Bsns W p38+ N 27 '65

PART time farming

Executive farms: profit and pleasure. T. J. Murray. il Duns R 85:45-7+ Je '65

PART time librarians. See Librarians

PARTHASARATHY, S. See Ramachandran, G. N. jt. auth.

PARTHENOCARPY

Kinin-induced parthenocarpy in the fig, ficus carica. L. J. C. Crane and J. Van Overbeek. bibliog il Science 147:1468-9 Mr 19 '65

PARTHENOGENESIS

Triploidy in parthenogenetic species of the teiid lizard, genus cnemidophorus. L. A. Pennock. bibliog il Science 149:539-40 Jl 30 '65

PARTICLES

Microelectrophoresis with alternating electric fields. L. D. Sher and H. P. Schwan. bibliog il Science 148:229-31 Ap 9 '65

PARTICLES (nuclear physics)

Amateur scientist; how the amateur can identify subatomic particles from their tracks in photographs. E. M. Dulberg. il Sci Am 212:136-8+ Ap '65

Anti-mirror on the anti-wall; discovery of the anti-deuteron. il Time 85:64+ Je 25 '65

PARTICLES (nuclear physics)—*Continued*
Anti-world may exist; discovery of anti-particle called antideuteron, largest known particle of antimatter. Sci N L 87:402 Je 26 '65
Electricity in volcanic clouds. R. Anderson and others. bibliog il Science 148:1197-89 My 28 '65
Extended symmetry. Sci Am 212:52-4 Mr '65
Is there a second universe? B. H. Frisch. il Sci Digest 58:10-12 S '65
Mars: compatible determinations of surface pressure through particle scattering. J. A. Greenspan. bibliog il Science 150:1156-8 N 26 '65
Nature of matter; purposes of high energy physics; excerpts. Science 147:1548-55 Mr 26 '65; Discussion. 149:584-6 Ag 6 '65
Nucleation phenomena; report on international symposium at Case institute of technology. A. G. Walton. Science 148:1490+ Je 11 '65
Nucleus action probed; SU-6 theory. Sci N L 87:85 F 6 '65
Quantum theory and elementary particles; address, April, 23, 1965. V. F. Weisskopf. il Science 149:1181-9 S 10 '65
Search for symmetry. il Newsweek 65:58 F 8 '65
Tracks of charged particles in solids. R. L. Fleischer and others. bibliog il Science 149:383-93 Jl 23 '65
Tritium and phosphorous-32 in high-resolution autoradiography. L. G. Caro and M. Schnös. bibliog il Science 149:60-2 Jl 2 '65
Way-out world of antimatter. J. R. Berry. il Pop Mech 124:98-102+ D '65
See also
Mesons
Neutrinos
Van Allen radiation belts
PARTICLES, Elementary. See Particles (nuclear physics)
PARTIES. See Childrens parties; Entertaining
PARTITIONS
How two can live happily in the same room. C. Sigman. il Pop Sci 187:120-3 D '65
Inexpensive magic using tight hollow-core doors. il Sunset 134:106-8 Ap '65
See-through room divider you can build. il Pop Sci 187:111 S '65
PARTITIONS, Movable
How two can live happily in the same room. C. Sigman. il Pop Sci 187:120-3 D '65
PARTNERSHIP
See also
Joint adventures
PARTON, Ethel
Ethel Parton. R. L. Elphick. il Horn Bk 41:307-14 Je '65
PARTRIDGE shooting
Anything can happen hunt. C. Conley. il Field & S 70:47-9+ S '65
PARTY costumes. See Costume
PARTY furniture. See Furniture
PARTY luncheons. See Luncheons
PARTY menus. See Menus
PARVIN, Stuart A.
Miniaturia. See issues of Hobbies
PASADENA. Calif.

Galleries and museums
Gallery spaces defined by varied widths and heights; Carmelita cultural center. il Arch Rec 138:129-31 D '65
PASADENA art museum
California design nine; triennial juried exhibition of the Pasadena art museum. P. Soldner. il Craft Horiz 25:18-23 My '65
PASARELL, Charles, 1943?-
Charlito at twenty-one. Sports Illus 23:9 Ag 2 '65
PASHLEY, Robert
Rediscovery of Crete. M. I. Finley. il Horizon 7:64-75 Sum '65
PASOLINI, Pier Paolo
Marxist's Christ. G. D. Kumlien. Commonweal 82:471-2 Jl 2 '65
PASS-throughs
Indoor-outdoor pass-throughs. il Sunset 134:134+ Je '65
PASSALACQUA, David
Search for the big swords; paintings. Sports Illus 23:30-4 Jl 19 '65
PASSAMAQUODDY Indians. See Indians of North America
PASSENGER fares. See Airlines—Fares
PASSENGER pigeons
Silent sky, by A. W. Eckert. Review
Time il 86:125+ O 15 '65

PASSENGER service in airlines. See Airlines—Passenger service
PASSENGER traffic (railroads) See Railroads—Passenger service
PASSIFLORA. See Passionflowers
PASSION music
See also
Phonograph records—Passion music
PASSION of Daisy Hall; story. See Barrett, B. L.
PASSIONFLOWERS
Lush, vigorous, and good-looking. il Sunset 135:198 S '65
PASSIVE resistance to government
Book of Ammon, by A. Hennacy. Review
Commonweal 82:224-5 My 7 '65. E. Capouya
Dangers of mass disobedience. C. E. Whittaker. Read Digest 87:121-4 D '65
Fallacy of civil disobedience. D. Lawrence. Read Digest 87:111-12 O '65
Nonviolence and creative disorder. A. I. Waskow. Christian Cent 82:1253-5 O 13 '65
Seeds of liberation, ed. by P. Goodman. Review
New Repub 152:20-2 Mr 20 '65. A. Kopkind
Why not hang them and be done with it? stiff penalties for the willful mutilation or burning of a draft registration card. Christian Cent 82:1085-6 S 8 '65
See also
Negroes in the United States—Segregation, Resistance to
PASSLOFF, Aileen
Aileen Passloff and company, Judson memorial church. D. Hering. Dance Mag 39:22+ My '65
PASSMAN, Otto Ernest
Tartar tamed. por Time 86:37-8 S 17 '65
PASSOVER
Freedom meals; Negroes invited to share Passover meal. W. M. Abbott. America 112:883 Je 19 '65
PASSOW, A. Harry
Diagnosis and prescription. Sat R 48:81-2 My 15 '65
PASSPORTS
Right to travel; question of passport restrictions. Reporter 32:12+ My 20 '65
PAST, The
You take progress, I'll take tooth powder. J. L. Collier. Read Digest 88:197-200 Ja '66
PASTA. See Cookery, Italian; Macaroni
PASTED pictures. See Collage
PASTEL drawing
Painting the feeling of autumn. D. Greene. il Design 67:36-7 N '65
PASTERNAK, Boris Leonidovich
Poems of Doctor Zhivago, by D. Davie. Review
New Repub 153:17-19 N 27 '65. J. Wain
PASTEURELLA pestis
Pasteurella pestis: role of pesticin I and iron in experimental plague. R. R. Brubaker and others. bibliog il Science 149:422-4 Jl 23 '65
PASTORAL conferences. See Clergy conferences
PASTORAL counseling. See Counseling
PASTORE, Arthur R. Jr
Pennsylvania's Poconos. Travel 123:36-8 Ap '65
Presidential libraries. Travel 124:50-1+ O '65
PASTRANO, Willie
Champion of nonviolence. M. Cope. il pors Sat Eve Post 238:84-7 Mr 27 '65
Liver trouble and high living. E. Shrake. il por Sports Illus 22:28-9+ Ap 12 '65
PASTRY
Add quiche to pour repertoire. il Ladies Home J 82:80-1+ My '65
Come for coffee and ... il Sunset 135:168 D '65
Destination: delight; Paris-brest. C. Claiborne. il N Y Times Mag p62 Je 13 '65
Greeks call them honey puffs; loukoumades. il Sunset 134:190 Mr '65
It gets its name from the patron saint of bakers; Gateau St Honoré. il Sunset 134:175-6+ Mr '65
It's a pie to start arguments; Quiche Lorraine. il Sunset 134:80-1 F '65
Making your own Chinese pastries; with recipes. il Sunset 134:192+ Je '65
Napoleon and friends; millefeuilles; with recipes. il McCalls 93:88-90+ Ja '66
Nut-filled and honey-flavored; kadaife. il Sunset 134:236 My '65
Pick-up pastries for parties. N. Nichols. il Farm J 89:70-1 Je '65
Presto! pastry. C. Claiborne. il N Y Times Mag p79-80 Mr 14 '65

PASTRY—*Continued*
She's serving apple *fluden*. Sunset 134:152+
F '65
Shopping for *fun, go, ha gow, jin dui*, and
other Chinese pastry treats. il Sunset 134:
98-9 Je '65
Try a main-dish custard pie; French call it
quiche. S. Sarvis. il Farm J 89:84-5 O '65
Two bites each; flaky cheese tarts. il Sunset
134:190 Ap '65
When you slice the first slice, watch their
faces; pâté en croûte. il Sunset 135:156 D
'65
See also
Pie
Tarts

PASTURE plants. See Plants

PASTURES
I just can't afford low pasture yields; ed.
by L. E. Zeman. H. Jessen. il Suc Farm
63:30-1+ Ag '65

PATCH, Harry
CRI explores the universe of Harry Patch.
R. Ellsworth. il pors Am Rec G 31:606-8
Mr '65

PATCHEN, Kenneth
Choices and risks. M. Benedikt. Poetry 105:
332-4 F '65

PATCHING. See Mending

PATE, John S.
Roots as organs of assimilation of sulfate.
bibliog Science 149:547-8 Jl 30 '65

PATE, Maurice
UNICEF fights on for the world's children.
por Parents Mag 40:50+ Mr '65

about
Tributes to Maurice Pate, executive director of UNICEF. por UN Mo Chron 2:85 F
'65

PATENT laws and legislation
Antitrust, patents lead Court list. Bsns W
p30-1 O 2 '65
Patent law comes under fire. il Bsns W
p 132+ S 18 '65
Raising the price for being inventive; patent
application fees. Bsns W p80 Jl 31 '65
See also
Industrial property

PATENT medicine. See Medicines, Patent,
proprietary, etc.

PATENT office (United States) See United
States—Patent office

PATENT rights. See Patents

PATENTS
Care and feeding of intellectual property.
J. H. Munster, jr. and J. C. Smith. bibliog
Science 148:739-43 My 7 '65
Current U.S. patents. See issues of Science
news letter
Fruits of research; patents ownership con-
troversy. America 113:107 Jl 31 '65
Long battle; patents policy of federally spon-
sored research. New Repub 153:6 Jl 10 '65
U.S. patent policy. R. Moley. Newsweek 67:
68 Ja 10 '66
U.S. patent policy and government research.
R. L. Wright; discussion. Bul Atomic Sci
20:32-4 O '64; 21:34 F '65
Who invented the laser? C. H. Townes' and
A. L. Schawlow's patent rights challenged.
il Bsns W p 132-7 N 27 '65
See also
Industrial property
Inventions
United States—Patent office

Anecdotes, facetiae, satire, etc.
How to invent the wheelbarrow or the wheel.
T. Irwin. il Pop Sci 187:162-3 D '65

International aspects
Can we use Russian inventions? S. V. Jones.
il Sci Digest 58:44-8 S '65
Soviet adherence to International patent convention. H. A. Levin. Dept State Bul 52:
758-61 My 17 '65
Surrender of a pirate; Russians join the Paris
convention of 1883. Time 85:81 Mr 26 '65

PATENTS, Government owned
Patents and coyprights: Congress moves toward comprehensive policy on federally
financed research. J. Walsh. Science 148:54-
6 Ap 2 '65
Rights to research. Commonweal 83:172-3 N
12 '65
Senate weighs three patent measures. Miss
& Roc 17:15 Jl 12 '65

PATERSON, N.J.
Upgrading downtown. il Arch Rec 137:190 Je
'65

Music
Paterson, N.J. M. Lelash. Opera N 30:33
D 25 '65

PATES, John, and Malena, Dave
They fill silo all year around. Suc Farm 63:
44-5 Je '65

PATHOGENIC bacteria. See Bacteria, Pathogenic

PATHOGENIC microorganisms. See Microorganisms, Pathogenic

PATHOLOGY
See also
Diagnosis
Paleopathology

PATHS. See Walks (paths)

PATIENTS, Hospital. See Sick, The

PATIENTS and physicians. See Physicians and
patients

PATIOS. See Outdoor rooms

PATMAN, Wright
Hanky-panky in the House. J. Ridgeway.
New Repub 153:8 O 30 '65
Patman on the warpath. il Newsweek 66:51
D 27 '65
Patman vs. Martin: new clash on money. por
U S News 59:20 Jl 19 '65
Warrior from Patman's switch. H. Kay. il
Fortune 71:154-6+ Ap '65
When Chairman Patman faced a revolt. por
U S News 59:16 N 1 '65

PATNODE, Winton
Green algae divide to multiply. Natur Hist
74:28-9 Mr '65

PATON, Alan
Beloved country 1965. Commonweal 82:311-15
My 28 '65

PATRIARCHS and patriarchate
Red hats as red flags. T. E. Bird. Commonweal 82:9-13 Mr 26 '65; Discussion. 82:274-
5+ My 21 '65

PATRICIA John, Sister
Failure; poem. America 113:207 Ag 28 '65

PATRICK, T. L.
Community leadership and education in a
crisis. Sch & Soc 93:403-4 O 30 '65

PATRICK—the first; drama. See Larnen, B.

PATRIOT for me; drama. See Osborne, J.

PATRIOTISM
Hard kind of patriotism; reprint. A. E.
Stevenson. Harper 231:102 S '65
Patriotic dissenters. R. H. Rovere. NEA J
54:31 F '65
Patriots who aren't. M. Mannes. McCalls
93:92+ O '65
See also
Nationalism

Study and teaching
Special issue on patriotism; symposium. ed.
by I. Starr. bibliog il Sr Schol 86:9T-13T
F 4 '65

PATRONAGE, Art. See Art patronage

PATRONAGE, Political
New issue on postal jobs; government secrecy.
U S News 59:12 S 27 '65
New political non-job. D. Oberdorfer. il Har-
per 231:108+ O '65
Poisoning the judicial system. D. Lawrence.
U S News 59:140 O 25 '65
Row over federal jobs for students. U S
News 59:14 S 20 '65
Spoils system in Congress. America 113:252
S 11 '65

PATTERN making
See also
Templets

PATTERSON, Barbara
Education for Negroes in the space capital.
New Repub 153:9 Jl 3 '65

PATTERSON, Bryan
Alfred Sherwood Romer, president-elect. Science 147:891-2 F 19 '65

PATTERSON, Carolyn Bennett
Final tribute. Nat Geog Mag 128:199-225
Ag '65

PATTERSON, Delbert, family
No time for tears. il Ebony 20:75-8+ Ap '65

PATTERSON, Floyd
Cassius Clay must be beaten. por Sports
Illus 23:78-80+ O 11 '65

about
Baddest of all looks over the universe. T.
Maule. il por Sports Illus 22:20-3 F 15 '65
Champion as long as he wants. G. Rogin. il
por Sports Illus 23:20-5 N 29 '65
Croatian candidate. G. Rogin. il Sports Illus
22:54-60 F 1 '65
Floyd is beginning to see the light, finally.
J. Lovesey. Sports Illus 22:72-3 My 24 '65
400 blows. il pors Newsweek 66:64 D 6 '65

PATTERSON, Floyd—About—Continued
Giant they love to hate; with account by
G. Rogin. il pors Sports Illus 23:40-5+ D 6
'65
Greatest meets the grimmest. M. Kane. il
por Sports Illus 23:36-8+ N 15 '65
Lunch for a lion. il Time 86:73 D 3 '65
Okay, but don't bring on Clay. T. Maule.
il por Sports Illus 22:18-19 F 8 '65
Patterson's glass jaw; with report by D.
Brown. il por Life 59:115-16+ N 19 '65
Rabbit hunt in Vegas. G. Rogin. il por
Sports Illus 23:34-9 N 22 '65
Sickening spectacle in a ring. il pors Life
59:42-42A D 3 '65
While Ali babbled. il por Newsweek 65:60 F
15 '65

PATTERSON, George
Tibet. Reporter 32:31-3 Mr 25 '65

PATTERSON, Gwen Dudley
Academic year abroad. Sat R 48:67-8+ F
20 '65

PATTERSON, John Henry
Famous firsts: how personnel relations was
born. il por Bsns W p92+ Je 26 '65

PATTERSON, Myrtle F.
Future in retrospect! por Recreation 58:486-7
D '65

PATTERSON, Robert B.
William of Malmesbury's Robert of Gloucester: a re-evaluation of the Historia novella.
bibliog f il Am Hist R 70:983-97 Jl '65

PATTERSON, W. L.
Why water rates go up. Am City 80:118-20+
Ag '65

PATTERSON, William Allan
High-flying airlines soar higher. il por News-
week 66:50-1 D 27 '65
United charts a new flight plan. il por Bsns
W p 128-30+ Ag 14 '65

PATTERSON, William D.
Keeping faith with the traveler. Sat R 48:
30 S 18 '65
SR's businessman of the year. Sat R 49:72+
Ja 8 '66
SR's thirteenth annual advertising awards.
Sat R 48:69-74+ Ap 10 '65
View from India. Sat R 48:38-9+ O 30 '65

PATTI, Adelina
Patti at Craig-y-Nos. C. Reid. il por Hi Fi
15:43-7+ Jl '65

PATTON, Arch
Deterioration in top executive pay. Harvard
Bsns R 43:106-18 N '65

PATTON, George Smith, 1885-1945
Two fighting generals; Patton and Mac-
Arthur. J. M. Gavin. il Atlan 215:55-8
F '65

PATTON, James G.
Office of economic opportunity. New Repub
153:38 D 11 '65

PATTON, Robert D.
Education is for thinking. Sch & Soc 93:
429-30 N 13 '65

PATTON, W. H.
Eimeria tenella: cultivation of the asexual
stages in cultured animal cells. bibliog Science 150:767-9 N 5 '65

PAUL VI, pope
Ecumenical council; address, September 15,
1965. Vital Speeches 31:738-41 O 1 '65
Here's Pope Paul's historic message to the
United Nations; tr. of address, October 4,
1965. pors U S News 59:84-8 O 18 '65; Same
with title Message for humanity. Vital
Speeches 32:2-4 O 15 '65; Same with title
Address of Pope Paul VI to the United Nations. UN Mo Chron 2:65-70 N '65; Excerpts. New Repub 153:14 O 16 '65
Pope Paul VI on religious liberty. Cath World
201:400 S '65

about

Arms race: chicken or egg? America 113:361
O 2 '65
Balancing act. D. Peerman. Christian Cent
82:1534-5 D 15 '65
Catholic revolution. J. Roddy. il por Look
29:21-7 F 9 '65; Reply. America 112:213 F
13 '65
Changes for Catholics? Pope has some new
plans. por U S News 58:21 Je 21 '65
Compassionate pontiff. W. A. Quanbeck.
Christian Cent 83:16-17 Ja 5 '66
Encyclical on the eucharist; mystery of faith.
America 113:308 S 25 '65
How life will be different for Catholics. il
por U S News 59:52-3 D 20 '65
How the Jews changed Catholic thinking. J.
Roddy. il Look 30:18-23 Ja 25 '66
Letter from Vatican City (cont) X. Rynne.
New Yorker 41:135-6+ S 11; 34-6+ D 25 '65
Letter to the Pope; concerning proposed
visit to U.S. Christian Cent 82:1052 S 1
'65

Lonely pope or first of the brethren? H. A.
Oberman. Christian Cent 82:835-7 Je 30 '65
Mood of the Pope. Commonweal 82:275-6 My
21 '65
Mysterium fidei. Commonweal 82:681 S 24
'65; Discussion. 83:42, 44-5 O 15 '65
New trend in encyclicals? D. R. Campion.
Commonweal 82:714-15 O 1 '65
News & views; press changes opinion of
Pope. J. Leo. Commonweal 83:110 O 29
'65
Papal call for peace. America 112:302 Mr 6 '65
Paul VI: continuing enigma? R. Horchler.
Christian Cent 82:831-4 Je 30 '65
Paul VI to the Rotarians. America 112:445
Ap 3 '65
Paul to the U.N. Time 86:106 S 17 '65
Paul's journey. il Newsweek 66:55 S 20 '65
Paul's second encyclical. Nat R 17:408 My 18
'65
Paul's urgent cry. America 112:698 My 15 '65
Placet! Christian Cent 82:1563-4 D 22 '65
Pocket books presents Pope with luxurious
paperback. il Pub W 188:28-30 O 18 '65
Pope and President at the UN? America
113:179-80 Ag 21 '65
Pope and the Jews. M. D. Zeik. Common-
weal 82:181-2 Ap 30 '65; Reply. M. Mc-
Crimmon. 82:482 Jl 9 '65
Pope-baiting. S. J. Adamo. America 113:
382-3 O 2 '65
Pope is clearly worried. America 113:177 Ag
21 '65
Pope is not pontifical. J. Cogley. il pors N Y
Times Mag p44-7+ S 12 '65
Pope John and his revolution, by E. E. Y.
Hales. Review
America 113:542 N 6 '65. C. E. Ronan
Pope on Mary. America 112:239 F 20 '65
Pope Paul and the 2,000,000 cameras. B. C.
Brown. il pors Pop Phot 58:96-8+ Ja '66
Pope Paul: liberal, conservative, or com-
promiser? por U S News 59:19 S 27 '65
Pope Paul VI. S. de Gramont. por Atlan
216:99-103 O '65
Pope Paul VI on urbanization. America 113:
107 Jl 31 '65
Pope Paul's Christmas plea for peace. Amer-
ica 114:35 Ja 8 '66
Pope Paul's contribution. Commonweal 83:
392 Ja 7 '66
Pope to UN? America 112:891 Je 26 '65
Pope's keynote; synod of bishops. America
113:358 O 2 '65
Probable visit of Pope Paul. E. T. Folliard.
America 113:237 S 4 '65
Question of tone. J. O'Gara. Commonweal
82:716 O 1 '65
Reluctant revolutionary. il pors Time 86:62-4+
S 24 '65
Road from Rome. E. J. Hughes. Newsweek
66:21 S 20 '65
Some of the Pope's problems. A. L. Moats.
Nat R 17:367 My 4 '65
They must be kidding. America 113:232-3 S 4
'65
Vatican council ends: reform on borrowed
time. F. E. Cartus. Harper 231:100-3+ S
'65; Reply. T. N. Davis America 113:inside
cover S 11 '65
Wall and the Pope. L. Wainwright. Life 58:
28 Mr 19 '65

Visit to New York (city) 1965
Ceremony of innocence. E. J. Hughes. News-
week 66:29 O 18 '65
Covering the Pope. il Newsweek 66:106 O 18
'65
Further step toward peace. America 113:454
O 23 '65
Humble man, our brother. L. Wainwright.
Life 59:38 O 15 '65
Instrument of the peace; peace pilgrimage
to United Nations. America 113:393 O 9 '65
Main reason behind Pope Paul's decision to
visit U.S. il por U S News 59:23 O 11 '65
Moment of reflection; visit to the United Na-
tions; with text of papal brief presented
to the Secretary-General and text of ad-
dress. il pors UN Mo Chron 2:57-70 N '65
N.Y. trip for Pope. Sr Schol 87:11 S 30 '65
Notes and comment. New Yorker 41:45-7 O 16
'65
Papal visit; with editorial comment. E. C.
Parker. por Christian Cent 82:1277, 1278-9
O 20 '65
Paul VI at the U.N. M. Ascoli. Reporter
33:14+ O 21 '65
Pilgrim. il pors Time 86:86-91 O 15 '65
Pope among us. M. Kempton. New Repub
153:13-14 O 16 '65
Pope and the UN. Nat R 17:905-6 O 19 '65
Pope at the U.N. Commonweal 83:5-6 O 8 '65

PAUL VI, pope—Visit to New York (city) 1965
—*Continued*
Pope in New York. J. Leo. Commonweal
83:80-2 O 22 '65. Reply with rejoinder. V. L.
Broderick. 83:222-3 N 19 '65
Pope in New York; itinerary. il Newsweek
66:86 O 4 '65
Pope: live and help live. il pors Newsweek
66:34-41 O 18 '65
Pope Paul at the United Nations: a historic
day. America 113:428 O 16 '65
Pope Paul in New York. il por Newsweek
66:31-3 O 11 '65
Pope Paul VI in our midst. America 113:312
S 25 '65
Pope Paul's historic day in America; with
report by J. K. Jessup. il pors Life 59:40-
54+ O 15 '65
Pope Paul's historic trip to New York; with
press comments. il pors Sr Schol 87:18-19
O 21 '65
Pope's UN visit in retrospect. America 113:
458 O 23 '65
Pope's visit may be step to universal symbols.
Sci N L 88:248 O 16 '65
When in New York. il Time 86:30-1 O 8 '65
PAUL, Leslie
Elusive genius of T. S. Eliot. Reporter 32:
33-5 Ap 22 '65
PAUL, Norman S.
Outlook now for draft, reserves, armed force
build-up; interview. por U S News 59:36-40
Ag 16 '65
PAUL, Steve
In search of Steve Paul. il por Newsweek
66:116+ O 18 '65
PAUL Singer collection of early Chinese art.
See Art—Private collections
PAUL Taylor dance company. See Ballet com-
panies
PAULDING, Gouverneur
Gouverneur Paulding; a tribute. M. Ascoli.
por Reporter 33:12 S 9 '65
Gouverneur Paulding; appreciation. Common-
weal 82:611 S 3 '65
PAULING, Linus
Close-packed-spheron theory and nuclear
fission. bibliog Science 150:297-305 O 15 '65
about
Linus Pauling v. National review. Nat R
17:962 N 2 '65
PAULIST press
Nat'l council of churches, Paulist press co-
publish. Pub W 188:36 D 6 '65
PAULL, John
West side story in Japan. Dance Mag 39:
35-8 Ap '65
PAULS, Rolf Friedmann
German ambassador to Israel. J. Feron. il
pors N Y Times Mag p 102+ O 31 '65
PAULSON, F. M.
(ed) Boating. See Issues of Field & stream
Build a floating drydock. Field & S 70:84-7
Jl '65
Cruising Puget Sound. Field & S 70:65-9+
Jl '65
Cruising the Rideau. Field & S 70:40-3 Ja '66
Field & stream boatman's handbook. Field &
S 70:51-66 Ja '66
Hunt with your boat. Field & S 69:129 F
'65
PAULUCCI, Jeno F.
Chow mein king spices up market drive. il
pors Bsns W p 100-2+ Mr 6 '65
PAUWAERT, Maurice
Union international motorboating. E. H.
Nabb. il por Yachting 118:160 Ag '65
PAVEMENT markings. See Traffic markings
PAVEMENTS
Lisbon is paved with good ideas. il Sunset
135:108 O '65
What good is paving anyway? Phoenix, Ariz.
R. N. Taylor. il Am City 80:102-3 O '65
WAM builds a street in one day; Wood-
bridge, N.J. C. Beagle. il Am City 80:86-8
D '65
See also
Airports—Runways
Airports—Surfaces
Maintenance and repair
Linseed oil cuts spalling damage; Connect-
icut state highway department. R. L.
Booth. il Am City 80:96-7 S '65
Surface treatment
Asphalt planing precedes tunnel resurfacing;
Lincoln tunnel. il Am City 80:44 S '65
Beefy seal coats work best; road mainten-
ance in King County, Wash. W. F. Winters.
il Am City 81:92-3 Ja '66
New hope for old streets; Santa Rosa, Calif.
il Am City 80:90-1 N '65

Put new life in old streets; Stockton, Calif.
F. Fargo. il Am City 80:93-5 Mr '65
Seal and surface successfully in cool weather;
San Francisco-Oakland Bay bridge. il Am
City 80:112-13 Je '65
Slurry seal drops costs, boosts quality; Santa
Clara, Calif. S. Cristofano. il Am City 80:
96-8 F '65
Slurry waterproofs 'em all; streets of Fos-
toria, Ohio. H. Bradner. il Am City 80:86-8
Jl '65
Stabilizatiton solves dirt-street problems;
Erie, Pa. H. P. Wozniak. il Am City 80:60
O '65
Testing
Roughness is the key to pavement life; first
results of the Purdue study. Am City 80:
56 Je '65
PAVEMENTS, Concrete
Don't let salt do this to your driveway.
il Pop Mech 124:181 N '65
Easy way to raise sunken concrete slabs. R.
Day. il Pop Sci 186:146-9 Je '65
Tips on working with concrete. il Bet Hom
& Gard 43:30 Je '65
PAVESE, Cesare
Night thoughts from Olympus. L. Casson. Sat
R 48:25 Je 5 '65
PAVILIONS
To take advantage of the view. il Sunset 136:
140 Ja '66
PAVING bricks. See Bricks
PAVLOVA, Anna
New tastes and tests. L. Joel. por Dance
Mag 39:33 S '65
PAVONE, Rita
Show on the road. il por Newsweek 66:63
Jl 26 '65
PAWEL, Ernst
Sex under socialism. Commentary 40:90+ S
'65; 41:16 Ja '66
PAWNEE Indians
Goals of the group. D. McNickle. Nation
201:167-8 S 27 '65
PAX Romana
Students talk of their faith; Joint consulta-
tion of Pax Romana and the World student
Christian federation at Taizé. J. J.
Megivern.. America 112:636-8 My 1 '65
PAY-as-you-see television. See Television
broadcasting—Subscription programs
PAY differentials. See Wage differentials
PAYES, Rachel Cosgrove
Editors are helpful ogres.   Writer 78:27-8
Mr '65
PAYMENTS, Balance of. See Balance of pay-
ments
PAYNE, Jerry A.
Nature's morticians. Sci Am 214:51 Ja '66
PAYNE, Marty
Teen-age driver sets precedent. il pors Ebony
20:49-50+ Jl '65
PAYNE, Max
Those silly outriggers. Yachting 117:106-7+
Je '65
PAYNE, Melvin M.
Leakeys of Africa: family in search of pre-
historic man. por Nat Geog Mag 127:194-231
F '65
PAZERESKIS, John
Charm of small boats. Yachting 117:174+
F '65
PEABODY, Larry D.
Taking self-inventory. Writer 78:26-8 Ag '65
PEABODY, Mary Elizabeth
My most unforgettable character. F. Fitz-
gerald. il Read Digest 87:165-6+ S '65
PEACE
Convocation on Pacem in terris; world lead-
ers study Pope John's words. P. J. Hen-
riot. America 112:223-4 F 13 '65
Guidelines to peace; Pacem in terris. M.
Frakes. Christian Cent 82:294-6 Mr 10 '65
Here's Pope Paul's historic message to the
United Nations; tr. of address. October 4,
1965. Paul VI. il U S News 59:84-8 O 18
'65; Same with title Message for human-
ity. Vital Speeches 32:2-4 O 15 '65; Same
with title Address of Pope Paul VI to the
United Nations. UN Mo Chron 2:65-70 N
'65
History waits upon us. J. Moorhead. il PTA
Mag 60:3 D '65
International co-operation and world peace;
address. M. K. Hussein. UN Mo Chron
2:59-70 Mr '65
Letter from the council. R. E. Tracy. America 113:706 D 4 '65
Limit of hope; summary of address on Pacem
in terris. P. Tillich. Time 85:38 F 26 '65
One world; views of D. Sarnoff. Nation 201:
207 O 11 '65

PEACE—*Continued*

Pacem in terris; international conference of scholars and statesmen. Newsweek 65:24 Mr 1 '65

Pacem in terris; symposium. il Sat R 48:19-30 F 13 '65

Peace and pathos; study of Pope John's encyclical Pacem in terris. N. O'Gorman. Commonweal 81:783-5 Mr 19 '65

Peace and reality; convocation on Pacem in terris. P. Steinfels. Commonweal 81:785-6 Mr 19 '65

Peace at the Hilton; convocation on Pacem in terris. G. Wills. il Nat R 17:233-6 Mr 23 '65

Peace: common stock for business; San Francisco meeting of top executives from sixty-six nations. il Bsns W p80-2 S 25 '65

Peace of mankind; address, June 3, 1965. L. B. Johnson. Dept State Bul 52:986-9 Je 21 '65; Excerpts. U S News 58:4 Je 14 '65

Peace on earth; address, February 17, 1965. H. H. Humphrey. Vital Speeches 31:322-5 Mr 15 '65; Same. Dept State Bul 52:326-32 Mr 8 '65

Peace on earth? New York convocation discusses Pope John XXIII's encyclical Pacem in terris; with report by J. K. Jessup. il Life 58:32-36A+ Mr 5 '65

Peace prospects, as Rusk sees them; excerpts from address, October 5, 1965. D. Rusk. U S News 59:20 O 18 '65

Peace: the central task of foreign policy; address, June 8, 1965. W. W. Rostow. Dept State Bul 53:21-7 Jl 5 '65

Pope John speaks again; International convocation on Peace on earth. America 112:307-8 Mr 6 '65

Pope Paul's Christmas plea for peace. America 114:35 Ja 8 '66

Problems of peace-making; address, September 9, 1965. Thant. UN Mo Chron 2:118-22 O '65

Requirements of peace; conference on Pope John XXIII's encyclical Pacem in terris (Peace on earth) il Time 85:36-8 F 26 '65

Road to peace and beyond. A. W. Munk. Bul Atomic Sci 21:30-1 O '65

Tasks of the free-world community; address, July 14, 1965. G. C. McGhee. Dept State Bul 53:324-30 Ag 23 '65

Two strategies for peace. I. Amdur. Bul Atomic Sci 21:31 O '65

United Nations in a changing world; address, February 1965. Thant. UN Mo Chron 2:41-6 Mr '65

Unseen search for peace; address, October 16, 1965. D. Rusk. Dept State Bul 53:690-9 N 1 '65

Unseen search for peace; involvement in world affairs; address, October 16, 1965. D. Rusk. Vital Speeches 32:66-71 N 15 '65

Vatican II and U.S. peace aims. America 113:701 D 4 '65

What can I do for peace? eight young mothers discuss the question; ed. by M. Mead. il Redbook 125:68-9+ Ag '65

When the world's peoples talked peace; excerpts from speeches at the Pacem in terris convocation, with list of participants. il Sat R 48:22-6+ My 1 '65

Working together for peace; remarks, February 11, 1965. L. B. Johnson. Dept State Bul 52:333 Mr 8 '65

World conscience. D. Lawrence. U S News 58:128 Je 21 '65

World peace through the law never tried; address, May 1965. A. R. Cecil. Vital Speeches 31:557-61 Jl 1 '65
See also
Disarmament
International education
International relations
Pacifism
Vietnamese, war, 1957- —Peace and mediation
War
World war, 1939-1945—Peace and mediation

PEACE conferences

Context for peace; private conference, arranged by the Stanley foundation on how to make the United Nations work. N. Cousins. il Sat R 48:36-7 Jl 24 '65

Doctor Hromadka and the will to peace; Communist peace propaganda through Christian peace conference. America 113:772 D 18 '65

It also happened in San Francisco; unofficial meeting of world federalists, at the same time as twentieth anniversary meeting of UN. N. Cousins. il Sat R 48:20 Jl 10 '65

Let habeas corpus be worldwide; World peace through law conference agenda. Life 59:4 S 3 '65

Peace in an age of revolution. J. Riha. Bul Atomic Sci 21:39-40 O '65

Peace! peace! in Budapest; Christian peace conference. M. Mayer. Christian Cent 82:1448-9 N 24 '65

Rapid expansion; Christian peace conference. P. Peachey. Christian Cent 82:598 My 5 '65

PEACE corps. See United States—Peace corps

PEACE research institute, incorporated

Can science prevent war? A. Larson. Sat R 48:15-17+ F 20 '65

PEACE societies
See also
Catholic association for international peace

PEACE; story. See Böll, H.

PEACEFUL coexistence. See World politics, 1945-

PEACEFUL uses of atomic power. See Atomic power—Economic aspects

PEACH, Robert English

High flight of Mohawk. J. F. Olesky. por Duns R 86:67-8 N '65

PEACHES
See also
Cookery—Fruit

PEACOCK, Andrew C. and others

Serum protein electrophoresis in acrylamide gel: patterns from normal human subjects. bibliog Science 147:1451-3 Mr 19 '65

PEALE, Norman Vincent

Man, morals and maturity; excerpt from Sin, sex and self-control. Read Digest 87:253-6+ O '65

about

Doctor Peale: convert to a cause. Christian Cent 82:325 Mr 17 '65

Not positive enough? por Newsweek 65:64 Mr 15 '65

Power of positive action. Christian Cent 82:388 Mr 31 '65

PEANUT butter

Sticky issue; FDA decree. il Newsweek 66:70 N 1 '65

PEANUTS

Aflatoxins: environmental factors governing occurrence in Spanish peanuts. L. J. Ashworth, jr. and others. bibliog il Science 148:1228-9 My 28 '65

Broken pods dangerous; peanuts analyzed for presence of aflatoxin. Sci N L 87:375 Je 12 '65

Peanuts from start to finish. E. Markley. Flower Grower 52:68-71 F '65

PEARCE, Douglas G. See Matin, L. jt. auth.

PEARCE, John N.

A. J. Davis' greatest Gothic. Antiques 87:684-9 Je '65

PEARCY, G. Etzel

Geographic aspects of the struggle in Viet-Nam. Dept State Bul 53:487-96 S 20 '65

Geography and foreign affairs. Dept State Bul 52:1035-41 Je 28 '65

PEARL, Arthur

As a psychologist sees pressures on disadvantaged teen-agers. NEA J 54:18-19+ F '65

PEARL, Sherman

Stone flowers for posterity. Am For 71:40-2 F '65

PEARL HARBOR

Pearl Harbor: 1941 and 1965. R. Joseph. il Esquire 64:52-3 Ag '65

PEARL HARBOR, Attack on, 1941

Cuba and Pearl Harbor: hindsight and foresight. R. Wohlstetter. For Affairs 43:691-707 Jl '65

Marshall papers: volume II; Pearl Harbor blunders; excerpt from George C. Marshall: the war years. F. C. Pogue. il Look 29:34-9 D 14 '65

Notes for a gazetteer; P. Hamburger. New Yorker 41:96+ Ap 3 '65

PEARLMAN, Beverly G.

(ed) First novelists, spring 1965. Library J 90:671-85 F 1 '65

PEARSE, Benjamin H.

America is summer. por Am Ed 1:16-23 Je '65

PEARSON, Clinton J.

From backyard boats to yachts. il Bsns W p28-9 Ag 28 '65

PEARSON, Everett A.

From backyard boats to yachts. il por Bsns W p28-9 Ag 28 '65

PEARSON, Harold

Modern lighting helps to fight blight. Am City 80:140+ Je '65

PEARSON, James B.

Excerpt from debate, August 31, 1964. Cong Digest 44:89+ Mr '65

PEARSON, Lester Bowles

U.S. and Canada sign agreement on trade in automotive products; remarks, January 16, 1965. Dept State Bul 52:191 F 8 '65

PENN, Lemuel A.
Murder: the Klan on trial. W. B. Huie. il por
Sat Eve Post 238:86-9 Je 19 '65
PENN, Richard D. and Loewenstein, W. R.
Uncoupling of a nerve cell membrane junction
by calcium-ion removal. bibliog Science 151:
88-9 Ja 7 '66
PENNEY, J. C, company
Changes for a Penney. il Time 85:95-6 My
28 '65
PENNING, Fred
My father walked with me; poem. America
112:546 Ap 17 '65
PENNOCK, Lewis A.
Triploidy in parthenogenetic species of the
teiid lizard, genus cnemidophorus. bibliog
Science 149:539-40 Jl 30 '65
PENNSALT chemicals corporation
Where Pennsalt got its new pep. il Bsns W
p 170-2+ Je 19 '65
PENNSYLVANIA
See also
Booksellers and bookselling—Pennsylvania
Courts—Pennsylvania
Geology—Pennsylvania
Hunting—Pennsylvania
Lancaster County
Pocono Mountains

Description and travel
Going places, finding things in the Pennsyl-
vania Dutch country. J. Wilson. il House
& Gard 128:8+ Jl '65

Historic houses, etc.
Paintings and antiques; Stoke Poges on the
Main Line. B. M. Wintersteen. il Antiques
88:644-9 N '65

Politics and government
Building a base. il Time 87:28 Ja 14 '66

Race problems
Brotherly love? H. W. Fry. Christian Cent
82:692 My 26 '65

Religious institutions and affairs
News of the Christian world (cont) Chris-
tian Cent 82:950, 1394-5 Jl 28, N 10 '65
PENNSYLVANIA avenue. See Washington,
D.C.—Streets
PENNSYLVANIA ballet company
Sleeping beauty wakes up in Philadelphia. A.
Grilikhes. il Dance Mag 40:20-1 Ja '66
PENNSYLVANIA Dutch. See Pennsylvania
Germans
PENNSYLVANIA Germans
Going places, finding things in the Pennsyl-
vania Dutch country. J. Wilson. il House
& Gard 128:8 Jl '65
PENNSYLVANIA library association
Librarian-for-a-day 1964: state-wide student
recruitment. C. A. Vogel. il Library J 90:
1468-70 Mr 15 '65
PENNSYLVANIA railroad-New York central
merger. See Railroads—Consolidations and
mergers
PENNSYLVANIA railroad station, New York.
See New York (city)—Stations
PENNSYLVANIA state library, Harrisburg
Day at State library. J. N. Berry, 3d. il Li-
brary J 90:4013-18 O 1 '65; Reply. R. Blasin-
game. 90:5322+ D 15 '65
PENNSYLVANIA state university
Hershey millions sweeten the job; starting
Milton S. Hershey medical center at Penn
state. il Bsns W p 192-4+ O 16 '65
PENNSYLVANIA. University

Medical center
Older than the U.S. Constitution; first medical school in U.S. H. Earl. il Todays Health
43:38-40+ N '65

Wharton school of finance and commerce
Teaching the school teachers; Wharton fo-
cuses on secondary schools; with editorial
comment. il Bsns W p63-4, 144 Ag 14 '65
PENROSE, Lee Miller
Second fame: good food. N. Lyon. il por
Vogue 145:138-40 Ap 15 '65
PENROSE, Roland
Second fame: good food. N. Lyon. il por
Vogue 145:138-40 Ap 15 '65
PENROSE annual
Books about bookmaking. C. B. Grannis. il
Pub W 188:88-9 Ag 9 '65
PENS
Metal scriber from pen; tungsten tip pen. M.
Brenish. il Pop Mech 125:192 Ja '66
PENSION funds. See Pensions—Finance

PENSION trusts
Eye on the states; public pension funds move
into stocks. il Fortune 71:87+ F '65
PENSIONS
See also
Civil service pensions
Old age pensions

Finance
New rules for your pension plan? private
pension funds. il U S News 58:106 F 15 '65
Pensions getting better: more money, and
sooner. U S News 59:102-4 D 6 '65
Retirement bill for authors introduced in
Congress. Pub W 187:35 Mr 8 '65
Still growing: pension funds. U S News 58:93-
4 Je 14 '65
Tighter rules to regulate pensions? report
of President's committee on corporate pen-
sion funds. il Bsns W p26-7 F 6 '65
Wary now, bullish for later; corporate pen-
sion funds. il Bsns W p 160+ N 13 '65

Laws and regulations
Tighter rules to regulate pensions? report
of President's committee on corporate pen-
sion funds. il Bsns W p26-7 F 6 '65
PENSIONS, Industrial
Changes in negotiated pension plans, 1961-64.
H. E. Davis. il Mo Labor R 88:1215-18 O
'65
Common stocks make the big difference. il
Bsns W p 132+ Je 26 '65
Drift to early retirement. E. K. Faltermayer.
il Fortune 71:112-15+ My '65
Early retirement plan scores big; Big three-
UAW pension innovations. il Bsns W
p 166+ My 22 '65
How workers feel about early retirement.
il U S News 58:78+ Mr 29 '65
Medicare and negotiated health insurance for
workers. Mo Labor R 88:III-IV S '65
Normal benefits under private pension plans.
D. J. Staats. il Mo Labor R 88:857-63 Jl '65
Patchwork quilt of pension programs; Mc-
Kinsey study. il Bsns W p46-8 S 4 '65
Pension plans: growth, future. U S News
58:82-3 F 8 '65
Pensions and profits. Fortune 71:69-70 My '65
President's stake in pension planning; as
costs mount and pressures multiply. G. H.
Foote and D. J. McLaughlin. il Harvard
Bsns R 43:91-106 S '65
Still a mirage. Nation 200:350 Ap 5 '65
Storm brewing over pensions. T. R. Brooks.
Duns R 85:47+ Mr '65
Union pressures for pension changes. H. G.
Crook. Mo Labor R 88:402 Ap '65
Vesting of private pensions: implications for
public policy; excerpt from report by Pres-
ident's committee on corporate pension
funds. Mo Labor R 88:310-11 Mr '65
Why labor is calling for portable pensions.
Bsns W p66 N 13 '65
See also
United mine workers of America welfare and
retirement fund
PENSIONS, Military

United States
Veteran against veteran: dollars wasted. J. E.
Booth. il Atlan 216:88-91 O '65; Discussion.
216:38+ D '65
PENSO, Leonard E.
Live and let live. Yachting 118:60-2+ Ag '65
PENTECOST
Statement for Pentecost. America 112:845-6 Je
12 '65
You will receive power; Pentecost message
from the presidents of the World council of
churches. Christian Cent 82:699 Je 2 '65
PENTECOSTAL churches
Pentecostal fury: meaning and beginnings of
Pentecostalism. P. Damboriena. Cath World
202:217-23 Ja '66
PENTECOSTAL movement. See Pentecostal
churches
PENTHOUSES. See Apartments
PEONIES
Peonies for permanence. P. Shedesky. il Pop
Gard 16:12-13 S '65
Tree peonies. J. C. Wister and G. S. Wister.
il Horticulture 43:30-1+ My '65
PEOPLE to people international sportfishing
championships. See Fishing—Competitions
PEOPLE-to-people program
College diplomats at work: People-to-people
university program. J. Poling. Read Digest
86:197-8+ My '65
Look at the People-to-people program. Good H
160:179 Mr '65
PEOPLE-to-people university program. See
People-to-people program

PEOPLE'S liberation army. See China (People's Republic)—Armed forces

PEORIA, III.

Industries

Is a new plant in town always a blessing? il Bsns W p 124+ N 13 '65

PEP, Willie

Willie Pep's art of self-defense. S. Gelman. il pors Esquire 64:194-5+ D '65

PEP pills. See Amphetamines

PEPIN, Robert O. and Signer, Peter

Primordial rare gases in meteorites. bibliog Science 149:253-65 Jl 16 '65

PEPPER, Choral C.

Navajoland. por Travel 124:38-40 O '65

PEPSI-COLA company

Come alive, America; family to keep all the groceries it can snatch from a supermarket in thirty minutes. C. Remsberg and B. Remsberg. il Esquire 63:102-5+ F '65

Fizz & chips; Pepsi-Cola to merge with Frito-Lay, inc. Time 85:88+ Mr 5 '65

PEPTIC ulcers

Histamine synthesis and gastric secretion after portacaval shunt. J. E. Fischer and S. H. Snyder. bibliog Science 150:1034-5 N 19 '65

Licorice & ulcers. Time 85:77 F 26 '65

Personal business; executive ulcer. Bsns W p 187 S 18 '65

Ulcer treatment: blow up. Sci Digest 57:16 Ap '65

PEPTIDES

Amino acid changes provoked by streptomycin in a polypeptide synthesized in vitro. D. Old and L. Gorini. bibliog il Science 150:1290-2 D 3 '65

Antibodies against the component polypeptide chains of bovine insulin. Y. Yagi and others. bibliog il Science 147:617-19 F 5 '65

Automated synthesis of peptides. R. B. Merrifield. bibliog il Science 150:178-85 O 8 '65

Collagen: structural studies based on the cleavage of methionyl bonds. P. Bornstein and K. A. Piez. bibliog il Science 148:1353-5 Je 4 '65

Cytokinins; letter. F. Skoog and others. Science 148:532-3 Ap 23 '65; Reply. R. D. Dedolph. 149:658 Ag 6 '65

Dicyandiamide possible role in peptide synthesis during chemical evolution. G. Steinman and others. bibliog Science 147:1574 Mr 26 '65

Genetic factors and polypeptide chain subclasses of human immunoglobulin G detected in chimpanzee serums. F. P. Alepa and W. D. Terry. bibliog il Science 150:1293-4 D 3 '65

Human transferrins C and D₁: chemical difference in a peptide. A. C. Wang and H. E. Sutton. bibliog il Science 149:435-7 Jl 23 '65

Hybrid antibody molecules with allotypically different L-polypeptide chains. M. Mannik and H. Metzger. bibliog il Science 148:383-5 Ap 16 '65

Immunoglobulin structure: amino- and carboxyl-terminal peptides of type I Bence Jones proteins. K. Titani and F. W. Putnam. bibliog Science 147:1304-9 Mr 12 '65

Kinin-induced parthenocarpy in the fig, ficus carica L. J. C. Crane and J. Van Overbeek. bibliog il Science 147:1468-9 Mr 19 '65

Peptide synthesis from amino acids in aqueous solution. C. Ponnamperuma and E. Peterson. bibliog il Science 147:1572-4 Mr 26 '65

Peptides attached to thrombin: their influence on proteolysis. R. H. Landaburu and others. bibliog il Science 148:380-1 Ap 16 '65

Polypeptide chains of antibody: effective binding sites require specificity in combination. O. A. Roholt and others. bibliog il Science 147:613-15 F 5 '65

See also

Kallikrein

PERCEPTION

Detection thresholds as a function of interval separation between two successive targets. H. Schuckman and J. Orbach. bibliog il Science 150:1623-5 D 17 '65

Help young eyes identify form; kindergarten animals. D. Perkins. il Sch Arts 65:40-1 D '65

On seeing and believing. A. Heckscher. Sat R 48:125-6 Mr 13 '65

Perception by locusts of rotated patterns. E. T. Burtt and W. T. Catton. Science 151:224 Ja 14 '66

Seeing is deceiving. il Newsweek 65:56-7 F 15 '65

Texture and visual perception. B. Julesz. il Sci Am 212:38-48 bibliog (p 134) F '65

Anecdotes, facetiae, satire, etc.

Note on man-animal, animal-man, and animal perception. J. H. Slate. il Atlan 215:84-7 Ap '65

PERCEPTION, Extrasensory. See Extrasensory perception

PERCH fishing

Wired for walleyes; trolling sinkers. W. Jarvis. il Outdoor Life 136:34-5+ Ag '65

PERCUSSION instruments

See also

Drum

PERCY, Charles Harting

Challenge for the prof. por Time 86:12 D 24 '65

Chuck Percy; politico from the boardroom. il por Duns R 86:36 D '65

Chuck's challenge. por Newsweek 66:26 D 27 '65

Parallel for Percy? Time 86:43A N 19 '65

Shadow governor. por Newsweek 65:28 Je 21 '65

PERCY, Walker

Mississippi: the fallen paradise. Harper 230:166-72 Ap '65

PERCY, William Alexander

Poem for spring. Read Digest 86:144 My '65

PEREA, Florence

Yugoslavia's coast. Travel 123:62-4 Je '65

PERELMAN, Sidney Joseph

Afternoon with a pint-sized faun. New Yorker 41:55-7 D 4 '65

Are you decent, mem-sahib? story. New Yorker 41:28-31 Ag 28 '65

Caution, beware of excess prophets. New Yorker 41:53-5 O 23 '65

Caveat emptor, fortissimo ex Philadelphia. New Yorker 41:28-30 Je 19 '65

Flatten your wallet; high style ahead. New Yorker 41:34-6 F 20 '65

No autographs, please, I'm invisible. New Yorker 41:46-9 S 18 '65

Sex and the single boy. New Yorker 41:40-3 My 8 '65

Six daggers East. New Yorker 41:28-31 F 27 '65

Tell me clear, parachutist dear, are you man or mouse? New Yorker 41:22-4 D 25 '65

PERENNIALS

Good mixers: tulips & perennials. R. M. Peters. il Pop Gard 16:42-4 S '65

Perennials for spring, summer and fall. il Flower Grower 52:32-3+ Ap '65

Six sure-fire perennials. E. A. Millner. il Flower Grower 52:20-1 Mr '65

Two reliable perennials. D. Klaber. il Pop Gard 16:19 S '65

When you plan, think of perennials by twos and threes. M. C. Ohlander. il Flower Grower 52:34-5 My '65

See also

Bulbs

also names of perennials, e.g. Lavender

PERÉNYI, Eleanor

Sicily by summer. Vogue 146:46-7 Ag 1 '65

Two Greek islands. Vogue 146:269+ O 1 '65

PERETZ, Don

Nonalignment in the Arab world. Ann Am Acad 362:36-43 N '65

PEREYASLAVEC, Valentina

Class with Mme Pereyaslavec. L. Joel. il pors Dance Mag 39:24-7 Jl '65

PÉREZ JIMÉNEZ, Marcos

P.J.'s day in court. il por Time 85:40 Ap 16 '65

P.J.'s return. il pors Newsweek 65:52 Ap 19 '65

PERFECTION

Perfectionism. F. R. Schreiber and M. Herman. Sci Digest 59:22 Ja '66

PERFORMING animals. See Animals—Training

PERFORMING arts

Arts: crash program. Nation 200:294 Mr 22 '65

Arts in America. H. Taylor. il Dance Mag 39:35-9+ N '65

Congressman looks at the arts. J. V. Lindsay. Sat R 48:23+ Mr 13 '65

Crusade for the arts in Britain. M. Wechsler. New Repub 154:23-4 Ja 1 '66

Culture fizzle; Rockefeller brothers fund report. Newsweek 65:82 Mr 8 '65

Future of the performing arts; concerning the Rockefeller panel report. I. Kolodin. Sat R 48:21-2+ Mr 13 '65

Performing arts find an angel in business. il Bsns W p52+ Mr 13 '65

Something for the arts; findings of Rockefeller panel. M. Straight. New Repub 152:11-15 Mr 13 '65; Reply. H. Green. 152:28 Ap 3 '65

World travel issue 1966; world in winter; symposium. il Sat R 49:41-4+ Ja 1 '66

Year's best or, There is room at the top; Time essay. Time 86:16-17 D 31 '65

PERFORMING arts—*Continued*
Study and teaching
Artist on the campus. il Time 85:58+ **Ap 2**
'65
World for the lonely piper; projects in Winston Salem, N.C. D. Hering. il Dance Mag 39:38-41 Mr '65

PERFUMERY
And so perfumed that the winds were lovesick with them. L. Blanch. Vogue 146:127-8+ N 15 '65
Beauty bulletin; how not to be a perfume loser. il Vogue 145:220-1+ My '65
Capsule history of perfume. J. E. Cox. Holiday 38:44-5 S '65
Flattery of fragrance: enjoy it every day. Good H 160:148 Ap '65
Fragrance hall of fame. **M. Watts. Mlle 61:147** My '65
Fragrances for father. il Seventeen 24:119 Je '65
Introduction to fragrance. il Redbook 126:72-3+ N '65
News for nose. C. Newman. il Esquire 64:192-3 D '65
Open December 25; scents, from $2. il Seventeen 24:126-7 N '65
Perfume: the nose knows. il Mlle 61:138-9 O '65
Perfumes for girls on the go-go-go! il Seventeen 24:74+ My '65

PERGOLAS
Pergola is also a screen-baffle. il Sunset 135:238 N '65

PERHAM, John
International nickel: the quiet sensation. Duns R 86:51-4 O '65
Materials: the battle rages. Duns R 86.pt2 88-9+ D '65

La PERICHOLE; opera. See Offenbach, J.

PERIDOTITE
Oldest rocks? Sci Am 212:56 Mr '65

PERIODIC compounds
Periodic compounds: syntheses at high pressures and temperatures. H. T. Hall. bibliog il Science 148:1331-3 Je 4 '65

PERIODICAL advertising. See Advertising mediums—Periodicals
PERIODICAL columns. See Periodicals—Sections, columns, etc.

PERIODICAL covers
Letter from the publisher; B. Artzybasheff's Time covers. B. M. Auer. il Time 86:13 Jl 23 '65

PERIODICAL distributors. See Newspaper and periodical wholesalers
PERIODICAL libraries. See Periodicals—Libraries

PERIODICAL literature
Editor's notebook. M. S. Fenner. NEA J 54:72 Mr '65
In defense of editing. N. Podhoretz. il Harper 231:143-7 O '65
Musings of a poetry editor; choosing poems for America. J. Moffitt. America 113:262 S 11 '65; Discussion. 113:484-5 O 30 '65
Route to magazine article sales. H. D. Steward. Writer 78:19-21+ N '65
Ten pointers for new article writers. E. H. Matthew. Writer 79:29-30 Ja '66
See also
Fiction in periodicals and newspapers
Trade journals

PERIODICALS
Notes on the teen-age beat. T. Peterson. Sat R 48:76 F 13 '65
Scholarly journals: some business aspects; summary of panel discussion at AAUP convention. Pub W 188:43-4 Jl 19 '65
300 years of storing words: scientific communication; excerpt from address. J. R. Porter. il Sat R 48:92-5 Ja 2 '65; Reply. J. H. Wood. 48:56 Ap 3 '65
See also
House organs
Libraries—Periodical collections
  also subhead Periodicals under various subjects, e.g. Art—Periodicals; *also* names of periodicals, e.g. Time (periodical)
Bibliography
New periodicals. See issues of Library journal
Indexes
See also
Public affairs information service
Social sciences and humanities index
Letters to the editor
Anecdotes, facetiae, satire, etc.
Kooky questions, nasty answers. L. Rosten. il Look 30:8 Ja 11 '66

Libraries
Libraries behind the news. P. J. Zimmerman. il Library J 90:4291-5 O 15 '65; Correction. 90:5124 D 1 '65
Prices
Cost indexes for library materials. M. Chicorel. il Wilson Lib Bul 39:896-900+ Je '65
Cost indexes for 1965: U.S. periodicals and serial services. H. M. Welch; N. B. Brown and W. H. Huff. il Library J 90:2964-7 Jl '65
Sections, columns, etc.
That was New York; scandal column of Town topics, weekly magazine. A. Logan. il New Yorker 41:37-8+ Ag 14; 41-2+ Ag 21 '65
Storage
Ways to store and use old Sunsets. il Sunset 134:139-40+ Mr '65
See also
Magazine stands, racks, etc.
Canada
Fiction, humor and cartoons for the Montrealer. G. Taaffe. Writer 78:26-7 My '65
France
Arbiter of the taste of France; Elle. H. Moffett. il Life 58:43-4+ Ap 30 '65
Letter from Paris; Arts: List of ten greatest artists over last twenty years, poll of one hundred personalities of Paris art world. Genêt. New Yorker 41:84+ Ag 7 '65
Germany (Federal Republic)
End of the scandal; vindication for Der Spiegel. Time 85:34 My 28 '65
How Der Spiegel wins profits and enemies. il Bsns W p 132-4 Ja 30 '65
Man who holds the mirror to Germany; R. Augstein, publisher of Der Spiegel. A. J. Olsen. il N Y Times Mag p30-1+ F 7 '65
War of the illustrateds. il Time 86:48 Ag 20 '65
Great Britain
Boast of Englishmen: project to microfilm British periodicals from the Restoration to the death of Queen Victoria. D. Fader. bibliog il Library J 90:1841-3 Ap 15 '65
National review: 1883-1960. E. J. Bell. Nat R 17:1117+ N 30 '65
See also
Economist (London)
Penrose annual
India
Prescription for progress. J. Krishnayya. il Horn Bk 41:202-5 Ap '65
Italy
Dear Nikita; L'Europeo publishes supposed interview with Khrushchev. il Newsweek 65:58 Mr 29 '65
Latin America
Two magazines; Diálogos and Z. R. Squirru. il Américas 17:37-8 My '65
Russia
Muffled voice of Russian liberalism: Novy mir, Russia's distinguished literary magazine. D. Brown. il N Y Times Mag p 10-11+ D 19 '65
Taiwan
See also
Christian tribune (periodical)
United States
Alarm bells in the city; city magazines. il Time 86:48 D 24 '65
And this, dear God, is what they read; teenagers magazine preferences. D. D. Harris. il Esquire 64:50-1+ Jl '65
Collier's affair: a rueful memoir; excerpt from personal file. P. C. Smith; reply. W. Wirsig. Esquire 63:150+ Je '65
Lots of pictures, and a few words, about the magazine. il Esquire 63:98-105 My '65
Magazines of dissent thrive on unpopularity. C. Lasch. il N Y Times Mag p 10-11+ Jl 18 '65
What to read till the doctor comes; Doctors and dentists magazine service. D. Dempsey. il Sat R 48:29 Jl 17 '65
Where to sell manuscripts. See issues of Writer
See also
Communist periodicals
Negro periodicals
  also names of periodicals, e.g. Nation (periodical)

PERIODICALS—United States—*Continued*

Anecdotes, facetiae, satire, etc.

Marriage, periodical. il Esquire 64:83-7 Ag '65
PERIODICALS, Comic. See Comics (books, strips, etc)
PERIODICALS, Immoral. See Immoral literature and pictures
PERIODICALS, Publishing of
First ten years are the hardest; National review. W. A. Rusher. Nat R 17:1116 N 30 '65
PERIODICALS, Trade. See Trade journals
PERIODICALS for women
Fashion beat. il Time 86:58 Ag 13 '65
See also
McCall's (periodical)

Anecdotes, facetiae, satire, etc.

Invitation to the harvest; Exquise, incorporating Exquise-teens. C. Brooks. New Yorker 41:86+ Ap 10 '65
PERIODICITY
Circadian rhythm in pineal serotonin: effect of monoamine oxidase inhibition and reserpine. S. H. Snyder and J. Axelrod. bibliog il Science 149:542-4 Jl 30 '65
Circadian rhythms in male ants of five diverse species. E. S. McCluskey. bibliog il Science 150:1037-9 N 19 '65
Circadian rhythms in man. J. Aschoff. bibliog il Science 148:1427-32 Je 11 '65
Diurnal cycles studied; physiological data from Gemini 5. Sci N L 88:181 S 18 '65
Entrainment of a tidal rhythm. J. T. Enright. bibliog il Science 147:864-7 F 19 '65
Light and dark may help man adjust to jet flight. Sci N L 88:24 Jl 10 '65
Nature's built-in clocks. E. M. Steindler. il Todays Health 43:48-53+ N '65
Photoreception and entrainment of cockroach activity rhythms. S. K. Roberts. bibliog il Science 148:958-9 My 14 '65
Those circadin rhythms; what really happens to jet-age travelers. il Time 86:66 D 17 '65
PERIODONTAL disease. See Gums (anatomy)—Diseases
PERIPHERAL nerves. See Nerves
PERISCOPES
Test stand aids Polaris mission. C. D. LaFond. il Miss & Roc 16:34-6+ F 15 '65
PERIWINKLES
They do nicely on steep banks. il Sunset 134:257 My '65
PERJURY
See also
Trials (perjury)
PERKIN-Elmer corporation
To see & analyze; scientific instrument industry. il Time 86:116 S 17 '65
PERKINS, Anne
Are women people? Christian Cent 82:917-18 Jl 21 '65
PERKINS, Charles
Snatch at Sydney. Time 86:28 Ag 13 '65
PERKINS, Dale
Help young eyes identify form. Sch Arts 65:40-1 D '65
PERKINS, Frances
Lady secretary. il por Newsweek 65:37 My 24 '65
Last leaf. il por Time 85:31 My 21 '65
PERKINS, James A.
Should the artist come to the campus? adaptation of address. Sat R 48:54-6+ Jl 17 '65
PERKINS, James E.
Doctor looks at pollutants. Sat R 48:33 My 22 '65
PERKINS, John A.
Which college is best? Sat R 48:71-2+ S 11 '65
PERL, Susan
Lima today. il Opera N 30:13-15 D 25 '65
PERLEMUTER, Vlado
Other side; recording of Chopin recital at the Royal festival hall, London. T. Heinitz. Sat R 49:51 Ja 15 '66
PERLES, Paul
Now there is a choice. Pub W 187:132-3+ Je 14 '65
PERLIS, Leo
Citizen action for a beautiful America. Recreation 58:482-3 D '65
PERLITHIOPROPYNE
New field of chemistry offered by compound. Sci N L 88:184 S 18 '65
PERLMAN, D. See Lepper, M. H. jt. auth.
PERLMAN, Itzhak
Musical events; performance of Sibelius violin concerto, with Detroit symphony orchestra. W. Sargeant. New Yorker 41:132 N 6 '65

PERLMUTTER at the East Pole; story. See Elkin, S.
PERMANENT court of arbitration. See International court of arbitration. The Hague
PERMANENT joint board on defense, United States and Canada
Canada and U.S. mark anniversary of Joint board on defense; White House statement; with address by A. Harriman. Dept State Bul 53:449-52 S 13 '65
PERMEABILITY
Permeability of a nuclear membrane; changes during normal development and changes induced by growth hormone. S. Ito and W. R. Loewenstein. bibliog il Science 150:909-10 N 12 '65
PERMISSIVE management. See Industrial management and organization
PERÓN, Isabel
Fading image. il por Time 86:38 O 29 '65
Third woman. Newsweek 66:56 O 25 '65
PERÓN, Juan Domingo
Argentina; reconciliation with the Peronists. S. L. Baily. Cur Hist 49:356-60+ D '65
Third woman. Newsweek 66:56 O 25 '65
PERONISM. See Argentina—Politics and government
PEROXIDES
See also
Hydrogen peroxide
PERRIN, C. Robert
Making a rug mural; interview. il por Am Artist 30:38-41+ Ja '66
PERRIN, Noel
Answers to poets' questions. New Yorker 41:23 Je 26 '65
Four academic fantasies; story. New Yorker 41:205-6 D 4 '65
Onward and upward with technology. New Yorker 41:211-16+ N 20 '65
PERRING, John
Please send one billion dollars. R. K. Massie. il pors Sat Eve Post 238:76-8+ D 4 '65
PERROT, Paul N.
Melvin Billups glass collection. Antiques 88:341-6 S; 800-5 D '65
PERROTTA, A. J. and Stephenson, D. A.
Clinoenstatite; high-low inversion. bibliog Science 148:1090-1 My 21 '65
PERRY, Edward Caswell
Education vs. culture. T. Schoenman. ALA Bul 60:27-30 Ja '66
PERRY, Eleanor
Life movie review. Life 58:18 F 5; 15 Mr 19; 17 Je 11; 59:22 Jl 16; 15 O 22 '65; 60:10 Ja 21 '66
PERRY, George L.
'66 budget. New Repub 153:12-15 D 25 '65
PERRY, Glen
Du Pont team. L. L. L. Golden. Sat R 48:78 Je 12 '65
PERRY, Harold R. bp
Appoints Negro bishop. Christian Cent 82:1277-8 O 20 '65
Historic bishop. por Time 86:70 O 8 '65
Negro bishop in the South. America 113:425 O 16 '65
PERRY, John D. Jr
Coffee house ministry. Christian Cent 82:180-1+ F 10 '65
PERRY, Judy. See Kragen, J. jt. auth.
PERRY, Margaret
Home grown Christmas shop. il Flower Grower 52:40-1 N '65
PERRY, T. W.
Should you feed hogs a new way? Suc Farm 63:52-3 My '65
PERRY, Ia.
Welcome to Happy Hollow. R. C. Davids. il Farm J 89:82-3 My '65
PERSECUTION
See also
Jews—Persecutions
PERSHAN, P. S. and others
Electron spin resonance of irradiated DNA. bibliog Science 148:378-80 Ap 16 '65
PERSIA. See Iran
PERSIANS. See Iranians
PERSIMMONS
Elegant Oriental persimmons; if you plant. il Sunset 135:248+ N '65
See also
Cookery—Fruit
PERSINGER, Lawrence
Ultimate weapon in war on poverty. il pors Nations Bsns 53:86-8+ F '65
PERSONAL airplanes. See Airplanes—Private ownership
PERSONAL beauty. See Beauty, Personal
PERSONAL finance. See Finance, Personal
PERSONAL liberty. See Liberty
PERSONAL names. See Names, Personal
PERSONAL opinions. See Attitudes

PERSONAL property. See Property
PERSONAL property insurance, All risk. See
Insurance—All risk policies
PERSONAL records
How to protect those valuable papers. M. T.
Bloom. Read Digest 87:127-30 D '65
PERSONAL rights. See Civil rights
PERSONALITY
False faces for the real me. L. Wainwright.
Life 58:21 Ap 30 '65
Personality and political socialization: the
theories of authoritarian and democratic
character. F. I. Greenstein. bibliog f Ann
Am Acad 361:81-95 S '65
Rise and role of charismatic leaders. A. R.
Willner and D. Willner. bibliog f Ann Am
Acad 358:77-88 Mr '65
Teenagers in search of themselves. G. B.
Blaine, jr. il Parents Mag 40:46-8+ D '65
See also
Human relations
Self
PERSONALITY, Disorders of
See also
Autism
PERSONALITY tests
Peace corps test hit: Minnesota multiphasic
personality inventory. E. Lederer. Sci N L
87:404 Je 26 '65
Personality tests queried; Minnesota multi-
phasic personality inventory. Sci N L 88:
183 S 18 '65
Psychological testing and the invasion of
privacy. D. Wolfle. Science 150:1773 D 31
'65
Who are you? and who are all those others?
color and psychic makeup. R. Warfield. il
Vogue 146:84-5+ S 15 '65
Yes, I believe I am being followed; Minnesota
multiphasic personality inventory; sample
questions. Time 85:25A Je 18 '65
PERSONALITY training and development
Charm for the men; German charm schools.
il Newsweek 66:40+ Ag 9 '65
PERSONNEL management
Case of the punctilious president. J. J. Han-
sen. il Harvard Bsns R 43:160-3+ N '65
Clear communications for chief executives.
R. N. McMurry. il Harvard Bsns R 43:131-
2+ Mr '65
Company that runs family style; Schramm,
inc. of West Chester, Pa. il Bsns W p60+
Jl 24 '65
Dynamics of subordinacy; excerpt. A.
Zaleznik. il Harvard Bsns R 43:119-31 My
'65
Famous firsts: how personnel relations was
born. il Bsns W p92+ Je 26 '65
Hiring and training personnel for the book-
store. B. R. Mark. Pub W 87:68-71 Mr 1 '65
How to keep from going out of style; ex-
ecutive's problems of job obsolescence. S.
Schuler. il Nations Bsns 53:66+ F '65
Labor front. T. R. Brooks. Duns R 85:61-4
F '65
Office services; everything from laundromat
and on-line data centers to temporary-
help and employee food services. il Duns R
86:pt2 166-7+ S '65
Test your leadership skill. C. A. Cerami.
Nations Bsns 53:74-5 Ap '65
Who is to blame for maladaptive managers?
H. Levinson. Harvard Bsns R 43:143-6+ N
'65
See also
Business management and organization
Communication in management
Employees
Employment systems
Foremen
Industrial relations
Job transfers
Leadership
PERSONNEL records in education
Accounting for every pupil. J. F. Putnam.
Sch Life 47:31-3 D '64
Data link. W. O. Reed. il Am Ed 1:31-2 Je
'65
PERSONNEL selection. See Employment sys-
tems
PERSONNEL service (education)
Crossing the college threshold. M. W. Raines.
il Am Ed 1:30-2 Jl '65
PERSPECTIVE
Creating perspective. E. Wildi. il U S
Camera 28:66-7+ N '65
Illusion of depth. il Design 66:42-3 Ja '65
Line thickness can produce depth. T. S.
Dahood. il Design 66:18-19 My '65
PERSPECTIVES (periodical)
Two views of Viet Nam; new magazines.
Time 86:52-3 N 26 '65

PERSPIRATION
Sweating: direct influence of skin tempera-
ture. W. Van Beaumont and R. W. Bul-
lard. bibliog il Science 147:1465-7 Mr 19 '65
PERSUASION. See Argument
PERTUSSIS. See Whooping cough—Vaccines
PERU
See also
Cuzco
Economic assistance in Peru
Guerrillas—Peru
Land tenure—Peru
Lima
Machu Picchu
Medical service—Peru
Antiquities
See Indians of South America—Antiquities
—Peru
Economic conditions
New conquest. il Time 85:32-42 Mr 12 '65
Economic policy
New conquest. il Time 85:32-42 Mr 12 '65
Peru: encouraging new spirit. J. C. Carey.
bibliog f Cur Hist 49:321-7 D '65
Industries
Fishing for meal. D. S. Stroetzel. il Américas
17:18-22 My '65
Peru nets a boom in fishmeal. il Bsns W p64-
5+ F 20 '65
Politics and government
Architect of progress. il Time 85:45-6 F 5
'65
Harassed by cattle rustlers; Belaúnde's lead-
ership. Time 86:44 S 24 '65
Peru: encouraging new spirit. J. C. Carey.
bibliog f Cur Hist 49:321-7 D '65
Riots
See also
Lima, Peru—Riots
PERUVIAN art. See Art, Peruvian
PERUVIAN Indians. See Indians of South
America—Peru
PESONEN, David E.
Atomic insurance: the ticklish statistics. Na-
tion 201:242-5 O 18 '65
PESTA, John
Overnight; poem. America 112:546 Ap 17 '65
PESTICIDES
Be safe when you use pesticides. Consumer
Bul 48:43 Je '65
Case against pesticides. J. James, jr. Field
& S 70:10-11+ Ja '66
Government regulation of pesticides. Bul
Atomic Sci 21:27 Mr '65
Here's the right way to use pesticides. H. B.
Petty. Suc Farm 63:82 Mr '65
Pests and pesticides. Nat Parks Mag 40:22
Ja '66
See also
Spraying and dusting
Injurious effects
Is food really being poisoned? concerning
Silent spring, by R. Carson. il U S News
58:12 My 3 '65
Pesticide users advised of poisoning dangers;
compounds parathion and methyl parathion.
Sci N L 87:280 My 1 '65
Read and heed-those pesticide labels; re-
print. B. Willetts. Consumer Rep 30:324 Jl
'65
Relax controls over pesticides on food? U S
News 59:10 Ag 2 '65
Residues
New drive to head off meat residues. Farm
J 89:44 Ap '65
Pesticide residues in total-diet samples. R.
E. Duggan and others. bibliog il Science
151:101-4 Ja 7 '66
PESTICINS
Pasteurella pestis: role of pesticin I and iron
in experimental plague. R. R. Brubaker and
others. bibliog il Science 149:422-4 Jl 23 '65
PET milk company
New look at Pet milk. J. B. Weiner. il Duns
R 85:36-8+ Mr '65
Pet milk spills over into other pastures. il
Bsns W p58-60+ Jl 31 '65
PETACCI, Claretta
Twilight of a tyrant; excerpts from Last 100
days. J. Toland. Look il por 29:38-40+ My
18 '65
PÉTANQUE. See Bowling

PETECH, Luciano
Wooden ox: the world's first wheelbarrow. UNESCO Courier 18:28-9 My '65
PETER, Saint
Where is St Peter buried? E. M. Jung. il Cath World 202:107-13 N '65
PETER, Emmett, Jr
On the outside looking out. New Repub 152:18 Je 26 '65
PETER, Robert
Letter from Latin America (cont) Nat R 17:194, 876 Mr 9, O 5 '65
PETER, Simon
Musical life in Salem. D. M. McCorkle. il Antiques 88:65-8 Jl '65
PETER Bent Brigham hospital. See Boston—Hospitals
PETERS, Art
Cat lady of Philadelphia. Ebony 21:76-8+ D '65
PETERS, Edward H.
Book of the month. Cath World 202:52-3 O '65
Movie of the month. Cath World 201:76+ Ap '65
New books. Cath World 201:206-7, 403-6; 202:56-8 Je, S-O '65
PETERS, F. G.
Electronic equipment speeds survey work. Am City 80:122-4 Mr '65
PETERS, Roberta
Seven-year Cinderella. por Seventeen 24:146+ F '65
PETERS, Stan
Youth officials association. Recreation 58:381 O '65
PETERSEN, Donald
Poetry chronicle. C. Urdang. Poetry 105:338-40 F '65
PETERSEN, Errol D. See Hull, D. O. jt. auth.
PETERSEN, Howard C.
Philadelphia: the economics of social problems. Sat R 49:46+ Ja 8 '66
PETERSEN, William
Success story, Japanese-American style. N Y Times Mag p20-1+ Ja 9 '66
PETERSON, Arthur G.
Famous salt-shaker case. Hobbies 70:72 My '65
Glassware patents of Augustus Heisey. Hobbies 70:84-5 Ja '66
Glass-ware patents; William King (cont) Hobbies 69:72 F '65
Glass-ware, the Hickman pattern. Hobbies 70:82-3 Mr '65
James B. Lyon, glassmaker & designer. Hobbies 70:72+ Jl '65
PETERSON, Carl H.
Freedom project. NEA J 54:40 N '65
PETERSON, Esther
Education for consumers. NEA J 55:15 Ja '66
about
Truly a consumer council. Consumer Rep 30:456 S '65
USDA's role as the consumer's adviser. Consumer Bul 48:39-40 N '65
PETERSON, Etta. See Ponnamperuma, C. jt. auth.
PETERSON, Everett B. and Damman, A. W. H.
Convection plumes from ulmus americana L. bibliog Science 148:392-3 Ap 16 '65
PETERSON, Franklynn
Peg 'n' dowel record rack. Pop Electr 22:56 F '65
PETERSON, Harold
Two-day torture on wheels. Sports Illus 23:32-4+ O 4 '65
PETERSON, M. N. A. and Von Der Borch, C. C.
Chert: modern inorganic deposition in a carbonate-precipitating locality. bibliog Science 149:1501-3 S 24 '65
PETERSON, Mendel
Underwater thesaurus. Antiques 88:319-24 S '65
PETERSON, Olive
Tribute to a longtime friend. C. Goren. il Sports Illus 22:50 Mr 1 '65
PETERSON, Peter G.
Help wanted for the brave new world; address, May 28, 1965. Vital Speeches 31:724-7 S 15 '65
PETERSON, Robert
Colleges now teach recreation; excerpt from column Life begins at forty. Recreation 58:450 N '65
PETERSON, Roger Tory
Pribilofs; excerpt from The bird watcher's America; ed. by O. S. Pettingill. por Audubon Mag 67:72-7 Mr '65

Walk with the Birdman. J. Roddy. il por Look 29:106+ My 18 '65
PETERSON, Theodore
Golden glow of Sunset. Sat R 48:146-7 Mr 13 '65
Madison avenue (cont) Sat R 48:76 F 13 '65
PETERSON, Virgil W.
Look at legalized gambling. Christian Cent 82:675-9 My 26 '65
PETERSON, W. A.
Rejected beams span water hazards. Am City 80:98-9 My '65
PETICOLAS, Warner L. See Rieckhoff, K. E. jt. auth.
PETITE, Irving
Five little pigs; excerpt from The elderberry tree. Read Digest 87:225-6+ N '65
PETRA, Jordan
Journey to Jordan's Petra. J. W. Ryan. il Travel 123:48-51 Ap '65
PETRIE, Paul
From under the hill of night; poem. New Yorker 41:30 Ja 8 '66
PETRIFIED FOREST NATIONAL PARK
Petrified Forest National Park; northeastern Arizona. il Nat Parks Mag 40:4-7 Ja '66
PETRIFIED forests
See also
Trees, Fossil
PETRIFIED wood. See Trees, Fossil
PETRILLI, Giuseppe
Giant shapes Italy's future. il por Bsns W p 102-4+ Jl 10 '65
PETRO, Sylvester
Has labor a case against 14(b)? Nat R 17:535-6 Je 29 '65
Law professor spells out: dangers in more forced unionism; interview. por Nations Bsns 53:31-3+ Mr '65
PETROCHEMICALS. See Petroleum chemicals
PETROGLYPHS
Petroglyphs; California's Lava Beds National Monument. I. Reed. il Nat Parks Mag 39:9-10 S '65
Rest stop at the Painted Rocks. il Sunset 135:67-8 O '65
PETROGRAPHIC microscope. See Microscope and microscopy
PETROGRAPHY. See Rocks—Analysis
PETROLEUM
See also
Oil shales

Chemistry
Sulfur: role in genesis of petroleum. A. G. Douglas and B. J. Mair. bibliog il Science 147:499-501 Ja 29 '65

Geology
Oil in ancient earth allays shortage fears. Sci N L 87:216 Ap 3 '65

International aspects
Boiling world of oil. G. Burck. il Fortune 71:126-31+ F '65
Esso gains in British oil switch; Italy's ENI bows out. Bsns W p36 O 23 '65
Oiling an alliance; France's stake in Algerian oil. Time 86:82+ Jl 23 '65
Udall sparks another oil battle; decision to relax import quotas. Bsns W p36 Jl 17 '65

Pipe lines
Alpian way. il Time 85:105-6 F 5 '65

Production methods
See Petroleum engineering

Prospecting
Oil: Sahara to the North Sea. il Newsweek 66:66-8 Ag 9 '65
Stepping up the pace on last oil frontier; Florida's hopes high. il Bsns W p64+ Ap 10 '65
See also
Louisiana land and exploration company
Tideland development
See Petroleum in submerged lands

Transportation
See also
Petroleum—Pipe lines

California
Fierce bids for rich oil prize; Long Beach, Calif. il Bsns W p36 F 13 '65
Wealth for a riviera; reservoir of untapped oil sits under Long Beach to be drilled. il Time 85:88 F 26 '65

Florida
Stepping up the pace on last oil frontier. il Bsns W p64+ Ap 10 '65

PETROLEUM—*Continued*

Kentucky

Boondocks bonanza; Sulphur Lick boom. Newsweek 67:76+ Ja 17 '66

PETROLEUM chemicals

Rumanian deal settled amid fuss over another; Universal oil products case. Bsns W p71 Jl 31 '65

PETROLEUM engineering

Dry wells yield vast new oil supplies; secondary recovery. Sci N L 88:43 Jl 17 '65

Huff and puff; thermal recovery. Newsweek 65:79-80 Ap 26 '65

Secondary recovery of petroleum. N. De Nevers. il Sci Am 213:34-42 bibliog(p 124) Jl '65

PETROLEUM in submerged lands

Fierce bids for rich oil prize; Long Beach, Calif. il Bsns W p36 F 13 '65

Fueling the offshore oil rigs. il Bsns W p 101-2+ O 23 '65

Personal business; investing in oil and gas wildcat ventures. Bsns W p 173-4 N 6 '65

Where oil and ships don't mix; offshore oil and shipping in Gulf of Mexico. il Bsns W p 178+ Je 19 '65

Worldwide boom in offshore oil; contract drillers tap a money field. il Bsns W p 120-2+ Mr 13 '65

See also

Oil well drilling, Submarine

PETROLEUM industry and trade

See also

Royal Dutch-Shell group

Consolidations and mergers

Building an empire in oil, with leverage; Octane oil co. deal with Tidewater. il Bsns W p 119-20+ Mr 6 '65

Pure oil journeys a rocky merger road. il Bsns W p 122+ F 27 '65

Pure's stockholders ask for more. il Bsns W p58-60 Ap 17 '65

Finance

Analysts take a brighter view; international oil giants. il Bsns W p 165-6+ My 15 '65

International aspects

See Petroleum—International aspects

Wages and hours

See also

Collective bargaining—Petroleum industry

Italy

Esso gains in British oil switch; Italy's ENI bows out. Bsns W p36 O 23 '65

Libya

Libya acts to bolster the price for its oil. Bsns W p 16 Ja 1 '66

Netherlands

Dutch gas discovery sets off a boom; natural gas in Groningen. il Bsns W p97-8+ F 13 '65

Puerto Rico

Growth amid the sugar cane; Puerto Rico. Time 87:82+ Ja 7 '66

Russia

Stilt city; oil city of Neftyanye Kamni on the Caspian Sea. R. J. Korengold. il Newsweek 66:43 N 29 '65

United States

Are gas price wars at an end? marketing technology seems to be maturing. il Bsns W p 134-6+ My 29 '65

Oilmen jam hearings to speak up on quotas. Bsns W p 136 Mr 20 '65

Striking it big in oil without drilling a well; DeGolyer & MacNaughton, petroleum consulting concern. il Bsns W p60+ N 20 '65

Udall sparks another oil battle; decision to relax import quotas. Bsns W p36 Jl 17 '65

U.S. oil; a giant caught in its own web. G. Burck. il Fortune 71:113-19+ Ap '65; Discussion. 71:82 My; 130 Je '65

Up from the old mill stream. il Time 86:66 Ag 13 '65

See also

Collective bargaining—Petroleum industry

Standard oil company (New Jersey)

PETROLEUM pipe lines. See Petroleum—Pipe lines

PETROLEUM research

Protein from petroleum. A. Champagnat. il Sci Am 213:13-17 O '65

Proteins from petroleum. B. H. Frisch. Sci Digest 57:40 Ap '65

PETROLEUM workers

Stilt city; oil city of Neftyanye Kamni on the Caspian Sea. R. J. Korengold. il Newsweek 66:43 N 29 '65

PETRONIUS, Arbiter

Satyricon. K. Rexroth. il Sat R 48:15 Je 5 '65

PETROULAS, Sotirios

Field day for the left in Athens. G. Bailey. Reporter 33:25-7 Ag 12 '65

PETROV, Ivan

Music to my ears. I. Kolodin. Sat R 48:47 N 6 '65

PETROW, Richard

Eight boating crises. Pop Sci 186:114-18 My '65

PETRY, Ann

Common ground; adaptation of address, November 16, 1964. Horn Bk 41:147-51 Ap '65

New mirror; story. New Yorker 41:28-36 My 29 '65

PETRY, Terence M.

British Guiana's future. America 113:51 Jl 10 '65

Gamble worth taking. America 113:743 D 11 '65

Spooks, ghosts, poltergeists. America 113:501-2 O 30 '65

PETS

Curious gift. T. Capote. il Redbook 125:52-3+ Je '65

Pet news. See issues of Ladies' home journal

Unloading the ark; exotic pets. il Time 85:86 F 5 '65

What to know about purebred pets. il Good H 161:167 D '65

When kindness can hurt a pet. il Good H 161:162 S '65

See also

Travel with pets

Care

Cold weather care tips for your pet. il Good H 162:134 Ja '66

Keeping pets cool in summer. il Good H 160:169 Je '65

PETS, Stealing of. See Animal stealing

PETS in literature

Crickets, raccoons, and writers. M. L. Simon. il Library J 90:2336-7 My 15 '65

PETTEE, Ginger

In spring; poem. Horn Bk 41:315 Je '65

PETTET, Joanna

Bad moment on Broadway. C. Brossard. il pors Look 29:67-70 Mr 9 '65

PETTING. See Sexual ethics

PETTINGILL, Olin Sewall, Jr

Bird finding. See issues of Audubon magazine

PETTY, H. B.

Here's the right way to use pesticides. Suc Farm 63:82 Mr '65

—and Zeman, L. E.

Stop these insects this year. Suc Farm 63:56-7+ Ap '65

PETTY, Lee. See Petty, R. jt. auth.

PETTY, Richard

Petty's powder keg. il Hot Rod 18:48-51 F '65

—and Petty, Lee

It was a great race, what happened? interview; ed. by R. Crossley. pors Pop Mech 124:112-15+ O '65

PETUNIAS

Nothing else really splashes like petunias. il Sunset 134:264-5 Ap '65

PEUGEOT. See Automobile industry and trade—France

PEWTER

Silver, pewter, and other metals; old Northwest Territory. il Antiques 87:322-3 Mr '65

PEYRE, Henri

France transformed; seven years of de Gaulle. N Y Times Mag p50-1+ N 14 '65

Outlaw as hero. Opera N 29:8-11 Ap 10 '65

Painter's painter to the age. Art N 63:24-7+ F '65

Passions of a Gallic Sappho. Sat R 48:46-7 O 30 '65

PEYREFITTE, Roger

Rothschilds & the mind. por Time 86:31 Jl 16 '65

PEYSER, Herbert S.

Children of the poppy. New Repub 152:19-20 F 13 '65

PFAFF, William

Congo. Commonweal 81:599-601 F 5 '65

Foreign affairs. Commonweal 81:685-6; 82:2, 6-7, 135-7, 520-1, 683-4, F 26, Mr 26, Ap 23, Jl 23, S 24 '65

Yankees vs. Latins. Commonweal 82:309-10 My 28 '65

PFAU, Hugo

Salon era. Motor T 17:92-5 F '65

PFEFFERKORN, E. R. See Burge, B. W. jt.
auth.
PFEIFFER, Eric
Seven poets. M. McCloskey. Poetry 105:270-3
Ja '65
PFEIFFER, George, 3d
George Pfeiffer starts new publishing company. il por Pub W 187:97-8 F 8 '65
PFEIFFER, John
How computers will change your life. McCalls
92:34 My '65
When man first stood up. N Y Times Mag
p70-1+ Ap 11 '65
PFEIFFER, Robert E.
Opera serials. Opera N 30:32-3 Ja 8 '66
PFISTER, Herbert R.
Five ways to find space for a dishwasher.
Pop Sci 187:108-10 S '65
Tool shed houses the dog, too. Pop Sci 187:
128-30 Ag '65
PFIZER, Charles, and company
Crown for the conqueror; J. J. Powers named
president of Chas. Pfizer & co. il Bsns W
p 124+ My 22 '65
Internationalism at the top. Time 85:92+
My 14 '65
Pfizer's self-prescribed tonic. il Fortune 72:
152-5+ Ag '65
PHAM-ngoc-Thao
Man behind the coup. il por Newsweek 65:
22 Mr 1 '65
PHAN-huy-Quat
Physician among warriors. il por Time 85:33
My 7 '65
PHARMACEUTICAL research
New enzyme discovered by Vermont scientist;
esteroproteolytic enzyme. Sci N L 88:6 Jl
'65
Toxicology and the biomedical sciences. B. B.
Brodie and others. bibliog Science 148:1547-
54 Je 18 '65
PHARMACISTS
What it's like to be a pharmacist. il Changing T 19:39-41 My '65
PHAT, Huynh-tan-. See Huynh-tan-Phat
PHEASANT shooting
Dutch country ringneck shoot. S. R. Slaymaker, 2d. il Outdoor Life 136:56-7+ N '65
How to hunt pheasants. H. Bradshaw. il
Field & S 70:41-3+ S '65
My hunt of a lifetime. W. R. Bimson. il
Sports Illus 23:82-6+ O 25 '65
Outdoors. V. Bourjaily. Esquire 63:48+ F '65
PHELAN, James
Hoover of the FBI. Sat Eve Post 238:23-8+
S 25 '65
Magnificent obsession of Colonel Brown. Sat
Eve Post 238:98-101 My 8 '65
PHELAN, John M.
Men and morals in space. America 113:
405-7 O 9 '65
PHELPS, Orme W.
Excerpt from article Compulsory arbitration:
some perspectives. Cong Digest 44:210+ Ag
'65
PHELPS, Robert
Auden: a poet's joy in a new home. Life
59:17 Ag 13 '65
Life book review. Life 60:8+ Ja 21 '66
PHENOLS
Drosophila phenol oxidases. H. K. Mitchell
and U. M. Weber. bibliog il Science 148:
964-5 My 14 '65
PHENOTHIAZINE
Homograft rabbit skin protection by phenothiazine derivatives. Z. Eyal and others.
bibliog il Science 148:1468-9 Je 11 '65
PHENYLALANINE
Experimental phenylketonuria in infant monkeys. H. A. Waisman and H. F. Harlow.
bibliog il Science 147:685-95 F 12 '65; Reply
with rejoinder. R. Karrer. 148:579 Ap 30 '65
PHENYL carbamic acid. See Carbanilic acid
PHENYLKETONURIA
Experimental phenylketonuria in infant monkeys. H. A. Waisman and H. F. Harlow.
bibliog il Science 147:685-95 F 12 '65; Reply
with rejoinder. R. Karrer. 148:579 Ap 30
'65
New insight into mental illness: philosophical implications. D. W. Woolley. Atlan 216:
46-50 Jl '65
Phenylketonuria in rats: reversibility of behavioral deficit. V. J. Polidora and others.
bibliog il Science 151:219-21 Ja 14 '66
Phenylketonuria: limit in capacity of preweanling rats to oxidize β-phenyllactate
and other α-hydroxy acids. F. R. Goldstein. bibliog il Science 150:1042-4 N 19 '65
PKU test kit price hit. F. Marley. Sci N L 87:
357 Je 5 '65
Retardation disease produced in monkeys.
Sci N L 87:136 F 27 '65

What is PKU testing? Parents Mag 40:108
N '65
PHEROMONES
Chemical communication in the social insects. E. O. Wilson. bibliog il Science 149:
1064-71 S 3 '65
PHILADELPHIA
Anti-poverty program
Electing the generals. Newsweek 65:19-20 Je
7 '65
Philadelphia polls the poor. J. Ridgeway. New
Repub 152:8-9 Je 5 '65
Voice for the poor. Nation 200:631 Je 14 '65
When the poor voted on the poverty war. U S
News 58:10 Je 7 '65
Architecture
Unusual structure for an unusual plan; IBM
tower. il Arch Rec 138:158-9 D '65
Art
History
Views of Philadelphia, 1750-1770. M. P.
Snyder. il Antiques 88:674-80 N '65
City planning
City's future takes shape. il Life 59:168-74
D 24 '65
Philadelphia. H. C. Petersen; M. Duane; W.
H. Wilcox. il Sat R 49:46+ Ja 8 '66
Philadelphia report: a long wait for the
renaissance. M. F. Schmertz. il Arch Rec
138:119-32 Jl '65
Where urban renewal brings history to life;
Society Hill, Philadelphia. il Bsns W p78-
9+ O 23 '65
Description
Philadelphia: the second revolution. M. Goodman. il Redbook 125:60-1 Jl '65
Stroll through Ben Franklin's Philadelphia.
R. Dunlop. il Todays Health 43:32-7 N '65
Free library
Creative dramatics in Philadelphia; program
in the children's room. C. W. Field. il Wilson Lib Bul 40:344+ D '65
Housing
Homebuilders try to sell a city; Philadelphia-
area builders woo families to be transferred
by Defense dept. il Bsns W p60+ Ap 3 '65
Libraries
See also
Philadelphia—Free library
Music
Debuts and reappearances; concerts. il Hi Fi
16:138-41 Ja '66
Philadelphia. M. De Schauensee. Opera N
30:31 D 11 '65
Negroes
We help ourselves; job-training courses. P.
Friggens. Read Digest 87:134-8 O '65
Politics and government
Justice must begin in the lowest courts;
corrupt practices of magistrates. Life 59:8
O 8 '65
Parallel pattern; first Republican victory in
twelve years. il Newsweek 66:36 N 15 '65
Social work
Breakthroughs: Covenant House in Philadelphia. J. Hemenway. Christian Cent 82:
1316-19 O 27 '65
Street traffic
Aerial film helps to solve traffic problems.
il Am City 80:120+ S '65
Theater
Off-broad theater; Theatre of the living arts.
H. Hewes. Sat R 48:38 Ap 24 '65
PHILADELPHIA, Miss.
Two faces of Sheriff Rainey; Neshoba
County, Miss. R. Cleghorn. il N Y Times
Mag p 10-11+ F 21 '65
PHILADELPHIA and Reading corporation
Finding the right combination. Bsns W p49-
50+ Ag 21 '65
PHILADELPHIA aquarama. See Aquariums
PHILADELPHIA area restaurants. See Restaurants—United States
PHILADELPHIA lyric opera company
Philadelphia, Hartford, Baltimore. G. Fitzgerald. il Opera N 30:29-30 D 4 '65
Philadelphia tenors. M. De Schauensee.
Opera N 29:33 F 20 '65
Philadelphia war horses. M. De Schauensee.
Opera N 29:36 My 1 '65

PHILADELPHIA orchestra
Musical events; B. Bartok concert in Philharmonic Hall. W. Sargeant. New Yorker 41:149 O 23 '65
Musical events; performance of Mahler's Tenth symphony in Carnegie Hall. W. Sargeant. New Yorker 41:174 N 27 '65

PHILADELPHIA Phillies (baseball) See Baseball clubs

PHILADELPHIA 76ers (basketball team) See Basketball teams

PHILADELPHIA society (organization)
Philadelphia society; regional meeting. E. M. von Kuehnelt-Leddihn. Nat R 17:986 N 2 '65

PHILANTHROPIC foundations. See Foundations, Charitable and educational

PHILATELY. See Postage stamps

PHILBRICK, Jerry
Little cat is big stuff. por Outdoor Life 136: 56-7+ D '65

PHILCO corporation
To succeed in Europe, Philco goes European; introduces multinational line with music and dancing. il Bsns W p 132-3+ O 2 '65

PHILHARMONIC Hall. See Lincoln Center for the performing arts, New York—Philharmonic Hall

PHILHARMONIC-symphony society of New York
Concert; performance in Sheep Meadow, Central park. New Yorker 41:26-7 Ag 21 '65
Music to my ears; Krips on Bruckner's Ninth. I. Kolodin. Sat R 48:39 F 27 '65
Music to my ears; L. Bernstein conducts Mahler's Symphony no 7 and Webern's Symphony 1928. I. Kolodin. Sat R 48:26+ D 18 '65
Musical events; concert performed by New York philharmonic conducted by L. Maazel. W. Sargeant. New Yorker 41:170+ Ap 17 '65
Musical events; Ives' Third and Mahler's Ninth symphonies, performed by New York philharmonic. New Yorker 41:200-1 D 4 '65
Musical events; opening of season at Philharmonic Hall. W. Sargeant. New Yorker 41:232 O 9 '65
Musical events; performance of Bruckner's Fifth symphony. W. Sargeant. New Yorker 41:121-2 My 29 '65
Musical events; performance of Bruckner's Ninth symphony. W. Sargeant. New Yorker 41:150 F 20 '65
Musical events; performance of Mahler's Seventh symphony and A. von Webern's Symphony. W. Sargeant. New Yorker 41: 236 D 11 '65
Musical events; performance of Sibelius's Seventh symphony and new Concerto for violin and orchestra by C. Chavez. W. Sargeant. New Yorker 41:201 O 16 '65
Philharmonic in the park. I. Kolodin. il Sat R 48:56-7 S 11 '65
Right place for a party; New York philharmonic concert in Central park. il Time 86:38 Ag 20 '65

PHILIP, consort of Elizabeth II, queen of Great Britain
Dontopediatrist. Newsweek 66:36+ Jl 19 '65
Outspoken Prince Philip in hot water again. il por U S News 59:20 Jl 19 '65
Princely philippic; controversy over Duke's view of the Rhodesian problem. por Time 86:32 Jl 16 '65

PHILIPPINES
Island landing: 1944 and 1965. R. Joseph. il Esquire 64:56-7 Ag '65
Lovely island pearl suddenly erupts: Alas-as village, Volcano Island; with report by R. Morse. il Life 59:108-16+ O 15 '65
See also
Communism—Philippines
Concentration camps—Philippines
Crime and criminals—Philippines
Economic assistance in the Philippines
Education—Philippines
Hukbalahaps
Technical assistance in the Philippines

Commercial treaties and agreements
United States expresses views on Laurel-Langley agreement; statement, March 8, 1965. W. P. Bundy. Dept State Bul 52:664 My 3 '65

Description and travel
To Baguio and beyond. R. Trumbull. il Sat R 48:52+ S 18 '65
Travel's picture portfolio. il Travel 124:50-5 S '65

Foreign relations
Now: an old friend turning away from U.S? with interview with D. Macapagal. il U S News 58:68-71 Je 14 '65

Sukarno makes trouble in the Philippines. O. S. Villadolid. Reporter 33:22-4 Ag 12 '65

Politics and government
Demand for heroes. il Time 87:26 Ja 7 '66
Letter from Manila (cont) R. Shaplen. il New Yorker 41:84+ Ja 15 '66
Philippines: a unique effort. J. F. Melby. Cur Hist 49:278-83+ N '65
Sukarno makes trouble in the Philippines. O. S. Villadolid. Reporter 33:22-4 Ag 12 '65
See also
Elections—Philippines

Religious institutions and affairs
World around us (cont of) News of the Christian world. Christian Cent 82:690, 1141-2; 83:55+ My 26, S 15 '65, Ja 12 '66

PHILIPPINES and the United States
Look what's happening at my house; anti-American demonstration outside the U.S. embassy in Manila. R. Graves. il Life 58:77-8 F 5 '65
To be watched; anti-American demonstrations. Time 85:39-40 F 5 '65

PHILLIPS, Bert E.
Teamwork and corporate goals; address, November 11, 1964. Vital Speeches 31:509-11 Je 1 '65

PHILLIPS, Carrie
Harding letters: this case and library censorship. E. J. Gaines. ALA Bul 59:343-4 My '65
Harding papers; how some were burned; and some were saved. K. W. Duckett; F. Russell. il por Am Heritage 16:24-31+ F '65

PHILLIPS, Donald W.
Linking up a chain, while you wait. il por Bsns W p 148+ O 9 '65

PHILLIPS, Harry L.
Mathematics laboratory. por Am Ed 1:1-3 Mr '65

PHILLIPS, Irna
Every woman's life is a soap opera; ed. by H. Markel. McCalls 92:116-17+ Mr '65

PHILLIPS, Jackson
Trend of business. See issues of Dun's review and modern industry

PHILLIPS, John
Italian portfolio; excerpts from Italians: face of a nation. il Holiday 38:32-41 Ag '65

PHILLIPS, John Randolph
Family matter; story. Redbook 125:52-3 Jl '65

PHILLIPS, McCandlish
Jewish Nazi. il Newsweek 66:110-12 N 15 '65
Klansman's secret. Time 86:54 N 12 '65

PHILLIPS, Marguerite Kreger
Hat for mother; drama. Plays 24:65-70, 86 My '65

PHILLIPS, Mary Walker
Mary Walker Phillips. A. Adams. il Craft Horiz 25:24-7 Ja '65

PHILLIPS, Pauline Esther (Friedman) See Van Buren, A. pseud.

PHILLIPS, Robert
Reston. Am Home 68:34 Mr '65

PHILLIPS, Waldo
Paul Laurence Dunbar: a new perspective. bibliog Negro Hist Bul 29:7-8 O '65

PHILLIPS, William
Fashions of revolt. Commentary 40:85-6+ O '65
New immoralists. Commentary 39:66-9 Ap '65
Notes on the new style. Nation 201:232-6 S 20 '65

PHILLIPS petroleum company
Growth amid the sugar cane. Time 87:82+ Ja 7 '66
Udall sparks another oil battle; decision to relax import quotas. Bsns W p36 Jl 17 '65

PHILOSOPHERS
What (if anything) to expect from today's philosophers; Time essay. Time 87:24-5 Ja 7 '66

PHILOSOPHICAL literature
Books in the field: philosophy. J. C. Haden. bibliog il Wilson Lib Bul 40:422-31 Ja '66

PHILOSOPHY
Beyond the outsider, by C. Wilson. Review Sat R 48:28-9 Mr 20 '65. E. Capouya
What (if anything) to expect from today's philosophers; Time essay. Time 87:24-5 Ja 7 '66
See also
Existentialism
Life
Political philosophy
Thomism
Truth
Worth

Bibliography
See also
Philosophical literature

PHILOSOPHY, American
American values in a revolutionary world; address, April 24, 1965. W. B. Martin. Vital Speeches 31:588-92 Jl 15 '65

PHILOSOPHY, German
From Hegel to Nietzsche: the revolution in nineteenth-century thought, by K. Löwith. Review
Commentary 39:100-4 Je '65. W. J. Dannhauser

PHILOSOPHY, Greek
See also
Plato

PHILOSOPHY, Jewish
Ancient Jewish philosophy, by I. I. Efros. Review
Commentary 40:84+ Jl '65. M. Fox; Reply. I. I. Efros. 40:20+ N '65

PHILOSOPHY, Moral. See Ethics

PHILOSOPHY, Political. See Political philosophy

PHILOSOPHY, Russian
Russian philosophy, ed. by J. M. Edie and others. Review
New Repub 153:30-1 S 25 '65. N. S. Care

PHILOSOPHY and religion
World of Wilhelm Reich. P. Rieff; discussion. Commentary 39:18+ F '65

PHILOSOPHY and science
Two cheers for hedonism. M. Himmelfarb. Commentary 39:61-5 Ap '65

PHILOSOPHY of education. See Education—Philosophy

PHILPOTT, Emalee E.
Once upon a time. ALA Bul 59:810-14 O '65

PHINIZY, Coles
Old men of the sea. Sports Illus 23:72-4+ Ag 23 '65

PHIPARD, Harvey
Inventor of the month. S. V. Jones. il por Sci Digest 58:44 O '65

PHIPPEN family
Phippen coat-of-arms. H. K. Eilers. il Hobbies 70:126 D '65

PHIPPS, Mrs Henry Carnegie
Bold is the badge of champions. W. Tower. il por Sports Illus 22:22-4+ F 22 '65

PHIPPS family
Bold is the badge of champions; Bold Ruler racing's foremost sire. W. Tower. il Sports Illus 22:22-4+ F 22 '65

PHLOEM. See Plant cells and tissues

PHLOX
For summer color phlox. P. Shedesky. il Pop Gard 16:12 Jl '65
Happy-go-lucky phlox. il Flower Grower 52:43 Ap '65

PHOBIAS
Fears that can make you sick. Good H 160:137 Ja '65

PHOENICIANS
World of the Phoenicians. C. H. Gordon. il Natur Hist 75:14-23 bibliog(p68) Ja '66

PHOENIX, Ariz.
Automatic purchase orders. B. A. Gragg. Am City 80:140+ F '65
Modern times in Phoenix. A. Kopkind. New Repub 153:14-16 N 6 '65
Phoenix annexations. il Am City 81:34 Ja '66

Newspapers
Fairness in Phoenix; new look of Arizona republic and Phoenix gazette. il Time 87:41 Ja 7 '66

Parks and playgrounds
Tom Sawyer approach; annual contest of the Phoenix bricklaying joint apprenticeship committee. L. C. Austin. il Am City 80:52 O '65

Stores
Spanish-Indian theme for a Phoenix store; Saks Fifth avenue. il Arch Rec 137:210 My '65

Streets
What good is paving anyway? R. N. Taylor. il Am City 80:102-3 O '65

PHOENIX (missile) See Guided missiles—Launching from airplanes

PHOENIX art museum
New wing for the Phoenix. Time 86:79 N 26 '65

PHOENIX gazette. See Phoenix, Ariz.—Newspapers

PHONE call; story. See Rouché, B.

PHONETIC alphabet. See Alphabet

PHONIC method. See Reading—Study and teaching

PHONO amplifiers. See Amplifiers

PHONOGRAPH
Good tone but not stereo: Columbia 360. il Consumer Rep 30:320-1 Jl '65
How to buy a console. D. Gordon. il Esquire 64:115 N '65
How to choose a record player. R. Burgert. Sr Schol 87:sup20 O 7 '65
Sound ideas. L. Zide. See issues of American record guide
Sweetest sounds; consoles. I. B. Berger. il Esquire 64:112-13+ N '65
See also
Loud speaking apparatus

Care
Maintenance. H. Fantel. Opera N 30: inside back cover D 25; 33 Ja 8 '66

High fidelity sound systems
How to hook up hi-fi. I. B. Berger. Sat R 48:62 Je 26 '65
Intent of our cover. il(cover) Hi Fi 16:45 Ja '66
Small-fi. Time 86:81-2 O 8 '65

Pickup
New semiconductor phono transducer. J. F. Wood. il Electr World 73:50-1+ F '65

Record changers
Record changers. il Consumer Rep 30:412-14 Ag '65
Turntables and changers. N. Eisenberg. il Hi Fi 15:34-7 Je '65

Stereophonic equipment
Best stero your money can buy. il Changing T 19:21-3 Jl '65
How good are those suitcase stereo systems? K. Gilmore and H. Luckett. il Pop Sci 186:90-3+ Ap '65
Stereo accessories under $50. il Hi Fi 15:54-5 D '65
Stereo question box; expert answers to recurrent queries. N. Eisenberg. Hi Fi 15:61-5+ D '65
Stereo receivers. H. Fantel. Opera N 30:31 N 20 '65
Survey of solid-state stereo receivers. R. Angus. il Hi Fi 16:50-5 Ja '66
See also
Television receiving apparatus—Radio, stereophonograph and tape recorder combination

Stereophonic pickup
Updating your stereo system; change of cartridge. H. H. Fantel. il Pop Electr 22:57-60+ Mr '65

Tone arm
No stick on a swivel. H. Fantel. il Pop Electr 23:35-9+ Jl '65
Tone arm. H. Fantel. Opera N 30:33 D 11 '65

Turntables
Garrard Lab 80 automatic turntable. H. Luckett. il Pop Sci 187:115 Jl '65
Turntables and changers. N. Eisenberg. il Hi Fi 15:34-7 Je '65

PHONOGRAPH, Portable
How good are those suitcase stereo systems? K. Gilmore and H. Luckett. il Pop Sci 186:90-3+ Ap '65
New ways to make a vacation happier. Bet Hom & Gard 43:142+ My '65
Stereo FM-AM radio phonographs and portable record players. il Consumer Bul 48:10-14 D '65

PHONOGRAPH amplifiers. See Amplifiers

PHONOGRAPH in education
Recordings for the teaching of English; discography. il Sr Schol 87:sup20-1 N 18 '65

PHONOGRAPH record cabinets
First berths for your first records. il House & Gard 127:179 Mr '65
Hideaways for your records. il Seventeen 24:158+ N '65

PHONOGRAPH record clubs
Record clubmen; Record club of America and Citadel record club. J. M. Conly. Reporter 32:46+ Ap 8 '65

PHONOGRAPH record industry
One channel for the price of two; reprocessing mono origins for stereo. il Consumer Rep 30:111 Mr '65
Records: the whole funky grown-up bit. il Newsweek 66:85-6+ O 11 '65
See also
Capitol records, incorporated
Composers recordings, incorporated
Motown record corporation

France
Notes from our correspondents. R. McMullen. Hi Fi 15:18+ O '65

PHONOGRAPH records—Catalogs—*Continued*

From the editor: reply to letter concerning World's encyclopaedia of recorded music. J. Lyons. Am Rec G 31:704 Ap '65

Sad valedictory; announcement of work stoppage of The world's encyclopaedia of recorded music. F. F. Clough and G. J. Cuming. Hi Fi 15:8 Je '65

Very beginning. P. L. Miller. il Am Rec G 31:1128-30+ Ag '65

Chamber music

Art before virtuosity, and chamber music as it's meant to be; Stern, Rose, Istomin trio. R. C. Marsh. il Hi Fi 15:57-8 Je '65

Princeton chamber orchestra; Decca records. J. W. Barker. il Am Rec G 32:51 S '65

Scherchen's superabundant Musical offering. H. Glass. Am Rec G 31:1147 Ag '65

Three programs featuring guitar music not for guitars. J. W. Barker. il Am Rec G 32:262-5 N '65

Childrens records

Christmas records for the young, 1965. Sat R 48:70-2 D 4 '65

Recordings for young people; ed. by J. L. Limbacher. il Library J 90:4526-8 O 15 '65

Records for young people; ed. by J. L. Limbacher. Library J 90:1483-4 Mr 15 '65

What records can do for your child. Bet Hom & Gard 43:29 O '65

What's new in records; good buys for children. C. Brown. Redbook 125:64 O '65

Choral music

Almost terrifying dynamic contrasts: Verdi from DGG; Four sacred pieces. J. Diether. Am Rec G 32:74-5 S '65

At last in stereo, Schoenberg's Gurre lieder. J. Diether. il Am Rec G 32:208-12 N '65

Creation from Decca, an extremely fine performance of Haydn's Die schöpfung. J. W. Barker. il Am Rec G 32:55 S '65

New life for Gurre-lieder. R. Ericson. Sat R 48:85 O 30 '65

Nonesuch has hit the bull's eye again; Lassus. J. W. Barker. Am Rec G 31:1163 Ag '65

Pope John set to music; Pacem in terris choral symphony. J. Davis. Am Rec G 32:60 S '65

Schuetz, indispensable and otherwise. J. W. Barker il Am Rec G 31:1084-7 Jl '65

Christmas music

Especially for Christmas (cont) il Am Rec G 32:298-300+ D '65

Good tidings from Hong Kong; and other countries. I. Kolodin. Sat R 48:50-1 D 18 '65

Harvest of hosannas. P. G. Davis. Hi Fi 15:28+ D '65

Other side; prices and products; English recordings. T. Heinitz. Sat R 48:73 D 4 '65

Recordings for Christmas 1965. il Am Rec G 32:296-7 D '65

Collectors and collecting

Archives of recorded sound; Rodgers and Hammerstein collection to be at Lincoln Center; with editorial comment. P. L. Miller. il Hi Fi 15:33, 38-41+ Je '65

Collection cornerstone from Music guild; Monteverdi, Mozart, Nielsen, Prokofiev. Am Rec G 32:152-4+ O '65

Concertos

Brandenburgs, so musical a discourse. N. Broder. il Hi Fi 15:76-7 D '65

From Angelicum, a recording of great musical and pedagogical value. H. Glass. Am Rec G 31:534 F '65

Gilt-edged Chopin by Gilels and Ormandy. C. J. Luten. il Am Rec G 31:797 My '65

Interpretation like no other; Brandenburg concerti. H. Glass. Am Rec G 31:822 My '65

Italian Baroque. B. Schwarz. Sat R 48:63+ Ap 24 '65

Karajan: after the Beethovens, the Brahmses; Four symphonies, and Violin concerto in D. C. J. Luten. Am Rec G 31:720 Ap '65

Kogan's Tchaikovsky; violin Concerto in D. E. Belov. Am Rec G 31:1088 Jl '65

Muza imports: from Poland, Karlowicz, Lipinski, Lessel, Beethoven. C. J. Luten Am Rec G 32:38-9 S '65

Real sleeper, this one! Corrette. J. W. Barker. Am Rec G 31:1154-5 Ag '65

Serkin: Beethoven, Fourth piano concerto. E. Belov. il Am Rec G 32:120-1 O '65

Serkin's Beethoven, once with Toscanini, today with Ormandy. H. Goldsmith. il Hi Fi 15:80-1 O '65

Szell and Beethoven on Epic; Nine symphonies. J. Lyons. il Am Rec G 32:48 S '65

Thanks to Decca, the Cincinnati returns to records; Saint-Saëns violin concertos. A. Cohn. il Am Rec G 31:698-9 Ap '65

They shall have music; Casals conducts Bach's Brandenberg concertos. H. Kupferberg. il Atlan 217:113 Ja '66

Dance music

Copenhagen pops! waltzes, galops & polkas by H. C. Lumbye. J. W. Barker. il Am Rec G 32:216-17 N '65

From Antal Dorati via Mercury, the best Miraculous mandarin yet. J. Diether. Am Rec G 31:978+ Je '65

Pas de deux; ballet music by Drigo, Minkus, Auber, and Helsted. C. J. Luten. il Am Rec G 31:500-1 F '65

Records for teachers. E. LeMone. See issues of Dance magazine

Sweet and swinging. F. Reynolds. See issues of American record guide

See also
Phonograph records—Ballet music

Educational applications

See Phonograph in education

Folk music

Folk music (cont) O. B. Brummell. Hi Fi 15:121-2 Mr; 95 My; 81 Jl; 123-4 S; 54 N '65; 16:42 Ja '66

Folk music. H. Yurchenco. See issues of American record guide

Recordings reports: folk and blues LPs (cont) L. Cohn. Sat R 48:134 Mr 13; 62 Ag 28 '65

Guitar music

Three programs featuring guitar music not for guitars. J. W. Barker. il Am Rec G 32:262-5 N '65

Harpsichord music

Again on Epic: Igor Kipnis. J. W. Barker. il Am Rec G 31:1135 Ag '65

Scarlatti by Landowska. C. J. Luten. il Am Rec G 31:510 F '65

Soul of an era; Baroque masterpieces for the harpsichord. R. Sabin. Am Rec G 31:791 My '65

History

Early Zon-o-phone record catalogs. J. Walsh. il Hobbies 70:37-8 Ja '66 (to be cont)

It wa hi-fi to grandma; University of New Hampshire's cylinder recordings. R. B. Stone. il Hobbies 70:31-3 Ag '65

Performers who remade two-minute Edison cylinders. J. Walsh. il Hobbies 70:33-6 S; 35-6+ O '65

Quiz on the phonograph's early days. J. Walsh. il Hobbies 70:34+ Ap; 34+ My; 32-3+ Je; 34-6+ Jl '65

Some mysterious Edison diamond discs. J. Walsh. il Hobbies 70:34-6 Ag '65

Victor double-faced records that were remade. J. Walsh. il Hobbies 70:35-6 N '65

Instrumental music

Italian Baroque. B. Schwarz. Sat R 48:63+ Ap 24 '65

Italian music

Italian Baroque. B. Schwarz. Sat R 48:63+ Ap 24 '65

Jazz music

Bossa up to date. R. F. Thompson. il Sat R 48:80-1 N 13 '65

Henderson, Basie, and big-band jazz. R. De Toledano. Nat R 17:385-7 My 4 '65

Jazz. J. S. Wilson. See issues of High fidelity incorporating Musical America

Jazz in stained glass; jazz suite on the mass texts. C. Harman. Life 59:29 O 15 '65

Jazz in the twenties. S. Dance. il Sat R 48:136 Mr 13 '65

Jazz notes. E. Larrabee. See issues of Harper's magazine

Jazz records. W. Balliett. See occasional issues of New Yorker

Month's jazz. D. Heckman. See issues of American record guide

Mostly modernists. M. Williams. See issues of Saturday review

Recordings reports: jazz LPs. S. Dance. See issues of Saturday review

Resurgence of Pee Wee Russell. M. Williams. Sat R 48:59 F 27 '65

Thelonious Monk and some others. R. De Toledano. Nat R 17:940-2 O 19 '65

PHONOGRAPH records—*Continued*

Madrigals

Monteverdi: Il ritorno d'Ulisse in patria; Concertato madrigal. J. W. Barker. il Am Rec G 31:782-5 My '65

Marketing

When records reached the supermarket; excerpt from The fabulous phonograph. R. Gelatt. il Hi Fi 15:56-60+ D '65

Mass

Bruckner; from Lyrichord, the E minor Mass. J. Diether. il Am Rec G 31:788-90 My '65
Deutsche grammophon presents the first stereo recordings of the two ultra-Moravian vocal works by Janáček. J. Diether. il Am Rec G 31:710-14 Ap '65
Great Glagolitic mass, pagan, Christian, intensely personal. A. Rich. Hi Fi 15:66-7 Ag '65
On records; Slavonic mass. Opera N 30:30 N 6 '65

Medieval music

Carmina Burana (but not by Orff) A. Rich. Hi Fi 15:88 Mr '65
Where the Carmina Burana came from. J. W. Barker. il Am Rec G 31:708-9 Ap '65

Mexican music

Mexico in sight and sound. R. Freed. Sat R 48:92 Ap 10 '65

Moving picture music

Kisses and pistons. il Newsweek 65:108+ Je 14 '65

Musical comedies, revues, etc.

Broadway on records; Capitol at twenty-three; with discography. M. Kreuger. il Am Rec G 32:112-17+ O '65
Broadway on records; Columbia, six decades of innovation; with discography. M. Kreuger. il Am Rec G 32:322-3+ D '65
Broadway on records; Decca, where it all started; with discography. M. Kreuger. il Am Rec G 32:6-11, 76-7 S '65
Cradle still rocks. I. Kolodin. il Sat R 48:58-9 My 15 '65
Discography of RCA Victor LP original-cast albums. M. Kreuger. Am Rec G 31:1044-6 Jl '65
Marc Blitzstein's The cradle will rock. T. Brown. il Am Rec G 31:800-5 My '65
Recordings reports: stage and screen. R. Sherman. Sat R 48:58 D 25 '65

Negro music

Recordings reports: folk and blues LPs (cont) L. Cohn. Sat R 48:134 Mr 13 '65

Operas

Angel's Il Trovatore. J. Maclain. il Am Rec G 31:1048-50 Jl '65
Anna Moffo: RCA Victor's Luisa Miller. P. L. Miller. Am Rec G 32:118-19+ O '65
As never before, London's Pelléas et Mélisande. H. Glass. il Am Rec G 31:694-6 Ap '65
Barber from London. H. Weinstock. Sat R 48:59 S 11 '65
Believable and ingratiating Don Pasquale. H. Glass. il Am Rec G 31:968-9 Je '65
Berg's Wozzeck, all made lucid and urgent. C. L. Osborne. il Hi Fi 15:75-7 D '65
Berlioz by Toscanini; Roméo et Juliette. P. L. Miller. il Am Rec G 31:962-3 Je '65
Birgit Nilsson as London's Lady Macbeth. P. L. Miller. Am Rec G 31:780-1+ My '65
BSO plays Lohengrin. H. Kupferberg. il Atlan 216:174+ N '65
British and American operas. H. Kupferberg. See issues of Atlantic
Callas Carmen. I. Kolodin. il Sat R 48:55 F 27 '65
Cherevichki (Little slippers) R. Sabin. Am Rec G 31:1006 Je '65
Concert records; Stravinsky's Rake's progress. D. Watt. New Yorker 41:134+ Je 12 '65
Culture from Patagonia; Period recordings. J. Ardoin. Sat R 48:53 Je 26 '65
DGG's extraordinary Daphne. R. Sabin. il Am Rec G 31:776-9 My '65
Dawn of opera; Glyndebourne festival version of Monteverdi's L'incoronazione di Poppea. H. Weinstock. il Sat R 48:53 Mr 27 '65
Debussyist Pelléas; Pelléas et Mélisande. R. Lawrence. Sat R 48:59 Je 12 '65
Double Donizetti; L'aio nell'imbarazzo, and Betly. H. Weinstock. Sat R 48:58 My 29 '65

First, and beautiful, recording of Rusalka. R. Zarbock. il Am Rec G 32:348-9 D '65
For very special attention; Les noces de Jeannette. J. Maclain. Am Rec G 31:550 F '65
La Forza del destino; with Price, Tucker and Merrill. P. L. Miller. Am Rec G 31:798-9+ My '65
Four saints in three acts. J. Lyons. il Am Rec G 31:518-19 F '65
From Angel, the first in stereo, Offenbach, the Tales of Hoffmann. M. Lelash. Am Rec G 32:218-19 N '65
From Bayreuth (and Philips), a stunning stereo, Parsifal. G. L. Mayer. il Am Rec G 31:684-7 Ap '65
From Bayreuth, via Philips, a live Tannhäuser. B. Igesz. il Am Rec G 32:108-11 O '65
From ultraphone, Anton Rubinstein's, The demon. R. Jones. Am Rec G 31:649 Mr '65
Golden twilight; Götterdämmerung under direction of G. Solti. R. Gelatt. Reporter 33: 48 S 9 '65
Götterdämmerung. C. J. Luten. il Am Rec G 31:952-5 Je '65
Hi-fi hit for Wagner's masterwork; Götterdämmerung. E. Coleman. Life 59:22 Jl 2 '65
Hoffmann's tales retold. R. Lawrence. Sat R 48:51 D 25 '65
Inside Wozzeck; Deutsche grammophon gesellschaft recording. I. Kolodin. Sat R 48: 63 N 27 '65
Joan Sutherland as Norma. P. L. Miller. Am Rec G 31:604-5 Mr '65
Klemperer and the Flute. M. Bernheimer. il Sat R 48:50 Mr 27 '65
Late Strauss from Vienna; recording of Vienna State opera's production of Daphne. M. Bernheimer. il Sat R 48:57-8 Ap 24 '65
London's Albert Herring. Am Rec G 31:1060-3 Jl '65
Luisa Miller in new stereo dress. C. L. Osborne. il Hi Fi 15:84-5 N '65
Maria Callas returns to Tosca. J. Maclain. il Am Rec G 31:688-90+ Ap '65
Massenet Thais. M. Lelash. il Am Rec G 31:964-5 Je '65
Monteverdi: Il ritorno d'Ulisse in patria; Concertato madrigal. J. W. Barker. il Am Rec G 31:782-5 My '65
Notes from our correspondents; Boston symphony orchestra's collaboration in recording Lohengrin. P. G. Davis. il Hi Fi 15:26+ N '65
Off the beaten track. R. Gelatt. Reporter 33: 41-2 D 30 '65
On Angel, Klemperer's The magic flute. H. Glass. il Am Rec G 31:700-3 Ap '65
On records. See issues of Opera news
Opera at the Goosemarket. J. Ardoin. Sat R 48:85 N 13 '65
Operas of Mozart on microgroove: discography-in-depth. C. L. Osborne. Hi Fi 15: 65-72+ N '65
Parsifal from Bayreuth. R. Lawrence. il Sat R 48:52 Mr 27 '65
Pelléas in stereo, with Ansermet in brilliant form. C. L. Osborne. Hi Fi 15:72-3 Ap '65
Rake's progress. R. Sabin. il Am Rec G 31: 496-8 F '65
Recordings. M. Mayer. Esquire 63:40+ F '65
Serse and Samson. H. Weinstock. Sat R 48: 53 D 18 '65
Serse; from Westminster. J. W. Barker. Am Rec G 32:374-5 D '65
Shaporin and Shebalin. B. Schwarz. Sat R 48:54-5 F 27 '65
Stereo Parsifal for the faithful and new converts. C. L. Osborne. il Hi Fi 15:85-6+ Mr '65
Stupendous stereo for the Gods in Twilight; B. Nilsson in Götterdämmerung. C. L. Osborne. il Hi Fi 15:57-8 Jl '65
Sutherland's noble druid; Bellini's Norma. I. Kolodin. Sat R 48:51 Mr 27 '65
Teresa Berganza as Rosina; London's Il barbiere di Siviglia. P. L. Miller. Am Rec G 32:122-4 O '65
Two new recordings of Rigoletto. P. L. Miller. Am Rec G 31:561-3 F '65
Two nights at the opera. Discus. Harper 230: 121-2 Ap '65
Verdi's Luisa and Lady; Luisa Miller and Macbeth. R. Lawrence. Sat R 48:72+ S 25 '65
Whole of Rusalka; lovable, touching, uniquely atmospheric. C. L. Osborne. il Hi Fi 15:77-8 S '65
Who's afraid of the Furtwängler Ring? M. Mayer. Hi Fi 15:32+ O '65
Why record opera? J. Culshaw. il Opera N 30:8-12 D 4 '65

PHONOGRAPH records—Operas—*Continued*

Wozzeck; from DGG marvelously cast, lovingly prepared, flawlessly recorded. A. Sperber. il Am Rec G 32:338-41 D '65

Wozzeck strikes back. Discus. Harper 232: 102-3 Ja '66

You cannot lose, DGG's Die zauberflöte; Magic flute. A. Sperber. il Am Rec G 32:14-17 S '65

Oratorios

Book with seven seals. P. L. Miller. il Am Rec G 31:524-5 F '65

Haydn's oratorios, a simple faith, sublimest craft. N. Broder. il Hi Fi 15:82 O '65

Messiah, two new versions; Richter and Klemperer. J. Diether. il Am Rec G 32: 306-8 D '65

Messiahs via Munich and Berlin; Richter and Forster recordings. M. Bernheimer. Sat R 48:51 My 29 '65

On records; Easter oratorio. Opera N 29:34 Ap 10 '65

On records; Messiah. Opera N 30:34 D 11 '65

On records; Seasons. Opera N 30:34 Ja 8 '66

Richter and Christmas; Munich Bach choir and orchestra's Christmas oratorio. J. Ardoin. Sat R 48:53 D 18 '65

Two feasts; Alexander's, Belshazzar's. J. W. Barker. il Am Rec G 31:616-20 Mr '65

Year round bargain from the Musical heritage society; Christmas oratorio. H. Glass. Am Rec G 31:511 F '65

Orchestral music

Americans from Vienna; Wiener symphoniker recordings. O. Daniel. il Sat R 48:51-3 Je 26 '65

J. Strauss: all in the family; new recordings devoted to music of the Strauss family. R. Freed. il Sat R 48:54+ Je 26 '65

More Strauss: again the Festival prelude. J. Diether. Am Rec G 31:779 My '65

On five labels simultaneously, more music by Chas. E. Ives. A. Cohn. il Am Rec G 31:958-61 Je '65

Records. B. Boretz. Nation 200:458-60 Ap 26 '65

See also

Phonograph records—Symphonies

Organ music

Another pair of Kings from Aeolian-Skinner. R. Kammerer. Am Rec G 32:169 O '65

E. Power Biggs documents; the art of Arp Schnitger. R. Kammerer. Am Rec G 31: 660 Mr '65

Great recording by that other Richter. R. Kammerer. Am Rec G 31:998 Je '65

Passion music

On records; St John passion. Opera N 29:34 Ap 10 '65

On records; St Matthew passion. Opera N 30:34 D 11 '65

Passion according to Saint Mark; more Telemann, and especially Musique de Table. J. W. Barker. Am Rec G 31:792-6 My '65

Piano music

Bach's Forty-eight, on the piano as a piano should sound. B. Jacobson. il Hi Fi 16:76-7 Ja '66

Brilliant Busonian tour de force; Indian fantasy. R. Kammerer. Am Rec G 31:722 Ap '65

Feast of piano music by Bartók. R. Jones. il Am Rec G 32:22-5+ S '65

Liszt piano music: five discs. R. Kammerer. Am Rec G 32:58-9 S '65

Marvelous good time with Mozart; Quartets for piano and strings. H. Glass. Am Rec G 31:730 Ap '65

Mighty Forty-eight; with João Carlos Martins. R. Kammerer. il Am Rec G 32:214-15 N '65

Mystery man: Alkan; reprint. H. C. Schonberg. Am Rec G 31:1132-4 Ag '65

New art of Vladimir Horowitz. H. Goldsmith. il Hi Fi 15:65-6 Ag '65

Piano discoveries. Discus. Harper 230:130+ F '65

Rubinstein's potent art vs. the critical faculties. C. J. Luten. Am Rec G 32:143 O '65

Vladimir Ashkenazy and Malcolm Frager: as duo-pianists. C. J. Luten. il Am Rec G 31:815 My '65

Young Vladimir Horowitz. R. Kammerer. Am Rec G 32:129 O '65

Poetry

See Phonograph records—Spoken records

Preservation and storage

Peg 'n' dowel record rack. F. Peterson. il Pop Electr 22:56 F '65

Prices

Latest in low-price records. il Changing T 19:21-2 N '65

Latest on the low-price record racks. il Changing T 19:29-30 My '65

Prices and products; English market. T. Heinitz. Sat R 48:66+ S 25 '65

Recorder music

Gaggle of compatible (mono/stereo) recorders. J. Diether. Am Rec G 32:170-1 O '65

Recording

Age of the patchwork. il Time 86:90+ S 24 '65; Same abr. with title Patchwork recordings, art or artifice? Read Digest 87: 143-5 D '65

Americans from Vienna; Wiener symphoniker recordings. O. Daniel. il Sat R 48: 51-3 Je 26 '65

Notes from our correspondents. P. Moor. Hi Fi 15:16+ Jl '65

Notes from our correspondents; Boston symphony orchestra's collaboration in recording Lohengrin. P. G. Davis. il Hi Fi 15: 26+ N '65

Notes from our correspondents; Callas recording Tosca. R. McMullen. il Hi Fi 15: 20+ Mr '65

Sonic showcase. R. D. Darrell. See issues of High fidelity incorporating Musical America

Welcome back, maestri. J. M. Conly. Reporter 33:41-2 Jl 1 '65

Why record opera? J. Culshaw. il Opera N 30:8-12 D 4 '65

Religious music

Offerings to the gods. Discus. il Harper 231: 136-8 O '65

Requiems

Berlioz by Ormandy, and others. R. Lawrence. Sat R 48:82 O 30 '65

Dread day of wrath, and the whisper of compassion; Berlioz requiem. R. D. Darrell. il Hi Fi 15:86-7 N '65

Karajan's Brahms requiem, visionary eloquence. R. Sabin. Am Rec G 31:983 Je '65

On records; German requiem. Opera N 30:30 N 20 '65

On records; Requiem for those we love. Opera N 29:34 F 13 '64

Sonatas

Amazing man, Rubinstein. C. J. Luten. Am Rec G 31:1149 Ag '65

Beethoven sonatas, by divers hands. Goldsmith. il Hi Fi 15:58-60 My '65

Curzon's orchestrated Schubert. C. J. Luten. Am Rec G 31:871 My '65

Disc for history, knowledge enhanced, esteem confirmed; J. Szigeti, violin; B. Bartók, piano. A. Rich. il Hi Fi 15:60 Je '65

First, Horowitz; now, Michelangeli returns. R. Kammerer. il Am Rec G 31:1131 Ag '65

From Columbia, a Bloch, Stern, Zakin triumph. il Am Rec G 31:1067 Jl '65

Glenn Gould, some of today's finest Beethoven playing. R. Kammerer. Am Rec G 31:980 Je '65

Horowitz's Scarlatti; a really new experience. C. J. Luten. Am Rec G 31:621 Mr '65

Musical gold from Washington, D.C; Szigeti recitals with Bartók and Arrau. A. Cohn. il Am Rec G 31:1136-7 Ag '65

Muza imports: from Poland, Karlowicz, Lipinski, Lessel, Beethoven. C. J. Luten. Am Rec G 32:38-9 S '65

Scarlatti by Landowska. C. J. Luten. il Am Rec G 31:510 F '65

Songs

Again, the Abbey singers. J. W. Barker. il Am Rec G 31:727 Ap '65

Age of bel canto; singing by Joan Sutherland, Marilyn Horne, and Richard Conrad. G. L. Mayer. il Am Rec G 31:514-16 F '65

American vocal music of today and yesterday. P. L. Miller. Am Rec G 31:808-9+ My '65

Criticism disarmed, or the art of Maggie Teyte. A. Rich. Hi Fi 15:57-8 My '65

Fischer-Dieskau's Kindertotenlieder; the finest recording since Rehkemper's. J. Diether. il Am Rec G 31:506-8 F '65

Four Americans. M. Mayer. Esquire 63:36+ Ap '65

PHONOGRAPH records—Songs—*Continued*

From Odeon, the first recording by Montserrat Caballé. P. L. Miller. Am Rec G 32: 125 O '65

From Peter Pears, his third and best Britten Serenade. J. Diether. Am Rec G 31:1150-2 Ag '65

George London, searing intensity, blazing intellectuality. M. Lelash. Am Rec G 31: 1173 Ag '65

Helge Roswaenge, apparent eternal youth. M. Maclain. Am Rec G 31:624-5 Mr '65

In Angel's Great recordings of the century series: Gigli and Tetrazzini. il Am Rec G 31:658-9 Mr '65

Listen to the most exciting instrument, the human voice. Am Home 68:29+ Ap '65

Low F to high C; variety of arias. Discus. Harper 230:148+ My '65

New and novel song cycle by Ned Rorem. P. L. Miller. Am Rec G 32:158 O '65

New soprano from Spain. C. L. Osborne. Hi Fi 15:106 O '65

Now on Vox: Brahms, Loewe, and Wolf lieder by Prey, magnificent. H. Glass. Am Rec G 31:526-7 F '65

On records:
Age of bel canto. Opera N 29:39 My 1 '65
Anthology of veristic melodrama; assortment of post-Verdian Italian opera. Opera N 29:34 Mr 27 '65
Bell canto tenors. Opera N 29:34 Ap 17 '65
Diary of one who vanished. Opera N 30:38 Ja 15 '66
Dietrich Fischer-Dieskau. Opera N 30:30 N 6 '65
Eileen Farrell. Opera N 29:34 F 20 '65
Four serious songs. Opera N 30:38 Ja 15; 34 Ja 22 '66
Helge Roswange. Opera N 29:40 My 1 '65
Italian song book. Opera N 30:34 Ja 22 '66
Jennie Tourel; Songs by Rossini and Poulenc. Opera N 29:34 Mr 20 '65
Kindertotenlieder; Des knaben wunderhorn. Opera N 29:34 F 6 '65
Maureen Forrester. Opera N 29:34 F 20 '65
Montserrat Caballé. Opera N 30:34 D 4 '65
More souvenirs; of opera and song. M. De Schauensee. Opera N 29:34 F 27 '65
Die schöne müllerin. Opera N 29:34 Mr 6 '65
Shirley Verrett. Opera N 30:38 Ja 15 '66
Song recitals. Opera N 29:34 Mr 13 '65
Songs. Opera N 29:34 Ap 17 '65
Songs & dances of death. Opera N 30:38 Ja 15 '66
Die winterreise. Opera N 29:34 F 6 '65

Peter Pears and Julian Bream: in a word, musicality. C. L. Osborne. il Hi Fi 15:58-9 Je '65

Presenting Marilyn Horne. G. L. Mayer. Am Rec G 31:706-7 Ap '65

Reissued by Angel: Gerhardt's Hugo Wolf, perhaps the greatest of all collectors' items. P. L. Miller. il Am Rec G 32:126-9 O '65

Schoenberg's Gurrelieder, an event for a generation. R. Lawrence. il Hi Fi 15:79-80 O '65

Something new for Joan Baez, Villa-Lobos. J. Diether. il Am Rec G 31:502-4 F '65

Take me to your lieder; American compositions. O. Daniel. il Sat R 48:84-5 O 30 '65

Unlikely corners. E. Jablonski. See issues of American record guide

See also
Phonograph records—Arias
Phonograph records—Musical comedies, revues, etc.
Phonograph records—Operas

Spoken records

All the Nile's a stage: Caesar and Cleopatra, by B. Shaw. J. Ciardi. Sat R 48:60 S 11 '65

Armchair theatergoing. C. Brown. Redbook 124:46 Ap '65

Churchill by Churchill, and Murrow. Am Rec G 31:671 Mr '65

Churchill: his greatest utterances; twelve-record album by London. H. Kupferberg. il Atlan 215:184-6 Mr '65

Churchill records. P. J. Smith. Hi Fi 15:71-2 Ap '65

Five English poets; Argo record company project. J. Ciardi. Sat R 48:73 O 16 '65

John Fitzgerald Kennedy . . . as we remember him. W. Styron. il Hi Fi 16:38+ Ja '66

J.F.K. remembered; book and records. H. Brandon. il Sat R 48:58-9 D 11 '65

Last words of E.H; Ernest Hemingway reading. K. Vanderbilt. Nation 201:284-5 O 25 '65

Long play's the thing. il Newsweek 66:87-8 Jl 12 '65

New recordings for young adults; with discography. J. Muri. Sr Schol 86:sup 12 Ap 1 '65

New records for English and social studies; with discography. J. Muri. il Sr Schol 87:13-14 O 7 '65

New records; with discography. J. Muri. Sr Schol 87:sup 15 N 4; sup 15 D 2 '65

New tool for English teachers; concerning Annotated recording list in the language arts. M. Schreiber. il Sr Schol 87:sup5 O 7 '65

Paul Scotfield's Lear. J. Ciardi. Sat R 48:37+ Jl 31 '65

Reading, dronings, etc; releases from Spoken arts. J. Ciardi. Sat R 49:48-9 Ja 15 '66

Recorded word. J. L. Limbacher. See second issue of each month of Library journal

Recordings for English and history units; with discography. J. Muri. Sr Schol 86: sup36-7 Mr 4 '65

Recordings for teaching patriotism. J. Muri. Sr Schol 86:11T F 4 '65

Recordings for the teaching of English; discography. il Sr Schol 87:sup20-1 N 18 '65

Recordings for young people; ed. by J. L. Limbacher. il Library J 90:4526-8 O 15 '65

Records for young people; ed. by J. L. Limbacher. Library J 90:1483-4 Mr 15 '65

Robert Lowell's Benito Cereno. C. J. Luten. il Am Rec G 31:806-7 My '65

Sound of history; story of the National voice library. G. R. Vincent. il Library J 90:4282-90 O 15 '65

Splice is right; comedy album. Welcome to the L.B.J. ranch. il Time 86:75 N 19 '65

Spotlight on American history. J. Muri. Sr Schol 86:sup21 Ap 29 '65

Theology in sound; Marlowe's Dr Faustus read by J. Sandoe. J. Ciardi. Sat R 48:72 D 4 '65

Tragedie of Othello, the Moore of Venice. J. Diether. Am Rec G 31:739+ Ap '65

Voices of yesterday. R. L. Tobin. Sat R 48: 84 N 13 '65

W. S. C. S. Potter. il Am Rec G 31:600-3+ Mr '65

Words only. S. Potter. See issues of American record guide

See also
Talking books

Stereophonic records

Phonograph records. W. F. Grueninger. See issues of Consumer bulletin

Record reviews. See issues of Consumer reports

String quartet music

Juilliard string quartet: Bartók string Quartets nos. 1-6. C. J. Luten. il Am Rec G 31:772-4 My '65

Vox boxful of Brahms and Schumann quartets. A. Cohn. Am Rec G 32:233-4 N '65

Suites

From Philips, the best complete recording of L'histoire du soldat. J. Diether. il Am Rec G 31:610-1+ My '65

Scheherazade by Stokowski. J. Lyons. il Am Rec G 31:622-3 Mr '65

Stokowski's Scheherazade. R. D. Darrell. il Hi Fi 15:87-8 Mr '65

Symphonies

All at once, sixteen Haydn symphonies! J. W. Barker. Am Rec G 31:634-5+ Mr '65

Divine document, the Ives Fourth. A. Cohn. Am Rec G 32:220-2 N '65

Dorati's early Tchaikovsky on Mercury. C. J. Luten. il Am Rec G 32:381 D '65

Find, the music of Rudolf Maros. A. Cohn. Am Rec G 31:729 Ap '65

From Furtwängler; the true Brucknerian affinity. A. Rich. il Hi Fi 15:78-9 S '65

Furtwängler Bruckner; the Seventh and Eighth symphonies. C. J. Luten. Am Rec G 31:1052-3 Jl '65

Haydn's Bear and Haydn's Hen, the right scores make all the difference. H. C. R. Landon; reply. P. J. Smith. il Hi Fi 15:67-9+ Mr '65

Ives's Fourth symphony, an unplayable work gets played. A. Frankenstein. il Hi Fi 15: 83-4 N '65

Janigro's Haydn, a remarkably fine achievement. J. W. Barker. Am Rec G 31:994 Je '65

Karajan: after the Beethovens, the Brahmses; Four symphonies, and Violin concerto in D. C. J. Luten. Am Rec G 31:720 Ap '65

PHONOGRAPH records—Symphonies—*Cont.*
Mozart's last six from the indefatigable Klemperer. N. Broder. Hi Fi 15:59 Jl '65
Nielsen centennial recording of Bernstein's Espansiva. J. W. Barker. il Am Rec G 32:18-21 S '65
Schubert symphonies; a revisionist view. D. Vaughan. il Hi Fi 15:60-3 O '65
Schubert symphonies; from RCA Victor, complete edition. J. W. Barker. il Am Rec G 32:342-3+ D '65
Schubert's symphonies, the scores corrected and a finish for the Unfinished. A. Rich. Hi Fi 16:73-4 Ja '66
Szell and Beethoven on Epic; Nine symphonies. J. Lyons. il Am Rec G 32:48 S '65
Szell's Brahms, an outstanding release. C. J. Luten. Am Rec G 31:632 Mr '65
Ten Mozart symphonies. H. Glass. Am Rec G 31:1074+ Jl '65
They shall have music; D. Vaughan's Schubert and G. Szell's Beethoven. H. Kupferberg. il Atlan 217:112-13 Ja '66
To awake in paradise; Schubert symphonies performed by D. Vaughan and the orchestra of Naples. R. Gelatt. il Reporter 33:45-6+ D 2 '65

Violin music
See also
Phonograph records—Concertos

Violoncello music
Britten's new cello symphony. J. Diether. il Am Rec G 31:1056-8 Jl '65

Wind ensembles
On a new label, five new works for brass ensemble. J. Diether. Am Rec G 31:816 My '65
Recordings. M. Mayer. Esquire 64:62+ D '65

PHONOVID. See Video records

PHOSPHATASES
Glucose-6-phosphatase: reexamination of the RNA-induced activity in mouse ascites tumor cells. M. C. Niu. bibliog il Science 148:513-16 Ap 23 '65
Heat stabilities of acid phosphatases from pinto bean leaves. R. C. Staples and others. bibliog il Science 149:1248-9 S 10 '65
Inheritance of two alkaline phosphatase variants in fowl plasma. G. R. J. Law and S. S. Munro. bibliog il Science 149:1518 S 24 '65
Leukocyte alkaline phosphatase: electrophoretic variants associated with chronic myelogenous leukemia. J. C. Robinson and others. bibliog il Science 150:58-60 O 1 '65
Lysosomal and free acid phosphatase in salivary glands of chironomus tentans. K. S. Schin and U. Clever. bibliog il Science 150: 1053-5 N 19 '65
Nucleoside phosphatases of fetal and maternal blood cells: electron microscope study. R. S. Connell and R. L. Bacon. bibliog il Science 150:503-4 O 22 '65
Phosphatase mutants in aspergillus nidulans. G. Dorn. bibliog il Science 150:1183-4 N 26 '65

PHOSPHATES
Late word on corn rootworm controls. Farm J 89:47 Ap '65
Phosphate bonanza ready to be tapped; Beaufort County, N.C. il Bsns W p88+ Mr 27 '65

PHOSPHATES in the body
Mercurial-induced transformation of myosin prevented by adenosine triphosphate and pyrophosphate. D. R. Kominz. bibliog il Science 149:1374-5 S 17 '65

PHOSPHATIDES
Chemistry of cell membranes. L. E. Hokin and M. R. Hokin. il Sci Am 213:78-84+ O '65
Crystal and molecular structure of a phospholipid component: L-α-glycerophosphorylcholine cadmium chloride trihydrate. M. Sundaralingam and L. H. Jensen. il Science 150:1035-6 N 19 '65

PHOSPHENES
And you see when you don't; op art. il Time 87:70 Ja 14 '66

PHOSPHOLIPIDES. See Phosphatides

PHOSPHORESCENCE
Quenching of DNA phosphorescence. I. Isenberg and others. bibliog il Science 150:1179-81 N 26 '65

PHOSPHORESCENT substances
Rare-earth phosphors for color TV-tubes. R. C. Miller and T. V. Rychlewski. il Electr World 74:48 D '65

PHOSPHORS. See Phosphorescent substances

PHOSPHORUS
Isotopes
Tritium and phosphorus-32 in high-resolution autoradiography. L. G. Caro and M. Schnös. bibliog il Science 149:60-2 Jl 2 '65

PHOSPHORYLATION
Photosynthetic phosphorylation: stimulation by pteridines and a comparison with phosphodoxin. F. I. Maclean and others. bibliog il Science 149:636-8 Ag 6 '65
Respiratory chains and sites of coupled phosphorylation. A. F. Brodie and J. Adelson. bibliog il Science 149:265-9 Jl 16 '65

PHOTINUS fireflies. See Fireflies

PHOTO aerial reconnaissance. See Aerial reconnaissance

PHOTO timers. See Timing devices

PHOTOBIOLOGY. See Light—Physiological effects

PHOTOCELLS. See Photoelectric cells

PHOTOCHEMISTRY
Where is science taking us? D. J. C. Friend. Sat R 48:61-2 My 1 '65

PHOTOCHROMICS. See Microphotography

PHOTOCOMPOSING
Notes on authors alterations and the new technology. D. Melcher. Pub W 187:35-6 My 3 '65
Now there is a choice. P. Perles. il Pub W 187:132-3+ Je 14 '65
Photo-composing room, N.Y. demonstrates monophoto book setting. il Pub W 187: 108+ My 3 '65

PHOTOCOMPOSING machines
Books printed with a camera. il UNESCO Courier 18:18-20 S '65
Computer and photosetter linked commercially. Pub W 187:130 F 1 '65
Computerized setting: interest runs high; Research & engineering council seminar. Pub W 187:52+ Ap 5 '65
Electronic typesetting. Sci Am 214:51 Ja '66
Low-cost IBM computer sets 12,000 lines per hour. il Pub W 187:118+ Mr 1 '65
Next big jump is near in printing. il Bsns W p92+ Ap 24 '65
Publishers learn about Linofilm in Quinn & Boden plant tours. Pub W 187:102+ Mr 1 '65

PHOTOCOPYING. See Photomechanical processes

PHOTOELECTRIC cells
Writing with light. J. G. Rabinowitz. il Electr World 74:31 N '65

Control applications
Build the Li'l Dusker; the light watchman. D. E. Lancaster. il Pop Electr 23:73-6+ S '65
Optical link: a new circuit tool. D. Lancaster. il Electr World 74:36-9 S '65
Tiny electric eye to guard your home. S. Hoberman. il Pop Sci 187:100-2 S '65

PHOTOELECTRIC devices. See Photoelectric cells

PHOTOELECTRIC typesetting machines. See Photocomposing machines

PHOTOGRAPHER and artist representatives, Society of. See Society of photographer and artist representatives

PHOTOGRAPHERS
Fellow photographers, do you need a little black book? K. Poli. il Pop Phot 57:98-9 O '65
First for Fleet Street's cameras; Victoria and Albert museum's acquisition of contemporary press photos. M. R. Weiss. il Sat R 48:122-3 S 18 '65
Flying photographer. See issues of Flying
Japanese approach. il U S Camera 28:49-55 Je '65
National geographic. Pop Phot 57:63+ Jl '65
New but muddy wave. R. Christgau. il Pop Phot 56:118-19+ My '65
Photographer as god. A. Goldsmith. Pop Phot 57:141+ D '65
Turning point; eight top pros tell why they chose photography. il Pop Phot 56:106-7 Je '65
Twelve international photographers; exhibition at the New York Gallery of modern art. il U S Camera 28:56-9+ Jl '65
See also
Vietnamese war, 1957- —War correspondents
also names of photographers, e.g. D. Attie

PHOTOGRAPHIC apparatus industry and trade
Don't get hooked buying a camera. T. Karp. Mod Phot 29:67+ D '65
Fuji single 8 system; Fuji photo film co, ltd. il Pop Phot 56:74-5 Je '65

PHOTOGRAPHIC apparatus industry and trade
—*Continued*
How good is Japanese equipment? il U S
Camera 28:56-9+ Je '65
Mister Japan in the U.S.A; Japanese pho-
tographic industry. E. Bennett. U S Cam-
era 28:18+ Je '65
Nikon crowds into Leica's picture. il Bsns
W p49-50+ D 11 '65
What's new at Honeywell? N. Rothschild.
Pop Phot 56:34+ My '65
See also
Eastman Kodak company

PHOTOGRAPHIC chemistry
Is silver necessary? N. Rothschild. il Pop
Phot 57:76-9+ O '65

PHOTOGRAPHIC composing machines. See
Photocomposing machines

PHOTOGRAPHIC equipment. See Photography
—Apparatus and supplies

PHOTOGRAPHIC exhibitions. See Photography—Exhibitions

PHOTOGRAPHIC finishing
Color clinic; salvaging lost transparencies.
D. B. Eisendrath, jr. Pop Phot 56:10+
Ap '65
See also
Photography—Retouching

PHOTOGRAPHIC humor. See Humor, Pic-
torial

PHOTOGRAPHIC illustration. See Illustration
of books and periodicals

PHOTOGRAPHIC industry. See Photographic
apparatus industry and trade

PHOTOGRAPHIC lenses. See Lenses, Photographic

PHOTOGRAPHIC notebooks. See Notebooks

PHOTOGRAPHIC optics
Photography by laser. E. N. Leith and
J. Upatnicks. il Sci Am 212:24-35 Je '65
See also
Perspective

PHOTOGRAPHIC paper
Variable contrast papers; are they? P. R.
Farber. il U S Camera 28:54-7+ O '65

Testing
Printing papers; personal report on 106. D.
Vestal; discussion. Pop Phot 56:4+ My '65

PHOTOGRAPHIC reproduction. See Photography—Copying

PHOTOGRAPHIC supplies. See Photography—
Apparatus and supplies

PHOTOGRAPHS
Amateurs; backbone of American photog-
raphy. il U S Camera 28:54-7 N '65
Closeup gallery. il U S Camera 28:44-51 F
'65
Eleven great photographs; selections from
Kodak pavilion at the World's fair. N.
Kent. il Am Artist 29:31-7+ S '65
Fotografi from Norway; Manité international.
U S Camera 28:48-53+ Mr '65
Gift of photography. D. S. Gelatt. il Pop
Phot 57:148-9+ D '65
How to get greater value from stock
photographers. G. T. Resch. il Pub W 188:
82+ Ag 9 '65
Put up or shut up; pictures by Modern's
editors. Mod Phot 29:66-77 Je '65
35mm gallery. il U S Camera 28:36-41 Ap
'65
W. Eugene Smith. H. M. Kinzer. il Pop Phot
56:74-9 F '65

Editing
Editing color, from many to a select few.
A. Rothstein. U S Camera 28:22+ O '65

Retouching
See Photography—Retouching

Trimming, mounting, etc.
Cropping can save it, sometimes. M. Orovan. il U S Camera 28:42-3 F '65

PHOTOGRAPHS, Composite. See Montage

PHOTOGRAPHY
Art of photography in 1965. B. Downes. Pop
Phot 56:20 F '65; Reply. R. Downes. 56:
32+ My '65
Black & white. W. Clark. il U S Camera
29:40-1 Ja '66
Camera angles (cont) il Sr Schol 86:43 F 18;
34 Ap 15; 87:36 O 14 '65
Command performance: newest one-act cam-
eras. H. F. Bruce. House & Gard 128:72+
N '65
Foto facts. P. Farber. See issues of U.S.
camera & travel
Hanson/Rothschild/Pierce report. B. Pierce;
W. Hanson; N. Rothschild. il Pop Phot 58:
34+ Ja '66

How far have we come? M. Edelson. il U S
Camera 28:32-3+ Ap '65
I dreamed I went on a photo safari with
Betty Bruce & my Nikon F; interview. ed.
by K. Burroughs. B. Bruce. il Mod Phot
29:36+ O '65
Illusion of sharpness. A. Francekevich. Pop
Phot 57:14+ S '65
ISFTPOBAWP; black-and-white photography.
L. Barry. il Pop Phot 57:57+ Jl '65
Irwin Goldstein: expanding the visual. il Pop
Phot 57:152-3 N '65
Is silver necessary? N. Rothschild. il Pop
Phot 57:76-9+ O '65
Keppler on the SLR; creativity vs the me-
chanics. H. Keppler. il Mod Phot 29:112+
O '65
Look without prejudging; interview, ed. by
J. Deschin. D. Vestal. Pop Phot 57:34+
N '65
LBJ pushes photography in his first 365
days; symposium. il Pop Phot 57:58-60+
N '65
Nine simple rules for travel photography.
N. Heller. il U S Camera 28:56-7+ D '65
On the go. L. Barry. See issues of Popular
photography
Op photography. P. Farber. il U S Camera 28:
60-1+ Jl '65
Photo tips. See issues of Popular photog-
raphy
Photographic safari to East Africa. A. Roth-
stein. U S Camera 28:8+ D '65
Photography for inept sophisticates. H. Wolf.
il Esquire 65:62-4 Ja '66
Photography in America; symposium. il U S
Camera 28:44-63+ N '65
Plan for pictures as you plan your trip. Bet
Hom & Gard 43:122 Je '65
Pleasures of photography. R. C. Craig. il Pop
Phot 56:110-12 My '65
President as picture editor. J. Durniak. Pop
Phot 56:46 Ap '65
Quick cuts & action shots; questions and
answers. J. R. Gregory. See issues of U.S.
camera & travel
Rothschild reports. N. Rothschild. See issues
of Popular photography
Say it with your camera, by J. Deschin.
Review
Pop Phot 57:30+ S '65. B. Downes.
Shoot for quality. M. Edelson. il U S Camera
28:52-3+ My '65
Silver crisis; what it can mean to photo-
graphers. A. Wolfman. Mod Phot 29:16+ S
'65
Siskind's one-man show; George Eastman
house, Rochester. N.Y. A. Siskind. il Pop
Phot 57:74-5+ Ag '65
Six modern conveniences and how to over-
come them. K. Poli. il Pop Phot 56:72-3+
Ap '65
Six tips for photographers. il Pop Sci 188:
110-11 Ja '66
Stamp out the enemies of 35-mm. E. Stein-
bicker. il Pop Phot 57:76-7+ Ag '65
Sweep of creative power; new techniques of
film and lens which transform color and
shape. il Life 59:70-1+ D 24 '65
Take better vacation pictures the easy way.
il Good H 160:167 Je '65
Tele, why, when; with photographs. P.
Caulfield. Mod Phot 29:70-7 Ag '65
35mm gallery. il U S Camera 28:36-41 Ap '65
Tools & techniques. C. W. Kennedy. il Pop
Phot 58:18 Ja '66
Travel & camera. See issues of U.S. camera
& travel
Tricks for taking better pictures. il Chang-
ing T 19:46-7 Je '65
Vagabond camera. W. Lane. See issues of
Travel
Very model of model amateur. P. Stackpole.
U S Camera 28:22-3+ Ag '65
Well traveled camera. See issues of Modern
photography
Well-traveled camera? the well-spoken cam-
era! with set of phrases. in four lan-
guages. R. Burgess. Mod Phot 29:14+ Je
'65
What's more versatile than an SLR? selec-
tion of photographs. P. Caulfield. il Mod
Phot 29:74-81 S '65
What's there? analysis of three Bernstein
photographs. E. Siegel; L. Bernstein. il
Mod Phot 29:91+ O '65
Your wife may be right. J. Faber. il U S
Camera 28:52-3+ O '65
See also
Art and photography
Human figure in photography
Humor, Pictorial
Lasers—Photographic applications

PHOTOGRAPHY—Developing and developers
—*Continued*
Photosolubilization, anyone? N. Rothschild.
il Pop Phot 56:30+ Mr '65
Rodinal: still spry at seventy. A. France-
kevich. Pop Phot 56:14+ F '65
Speed demons. P. Farber. il U S Camera 28:
68-9+ Je '65
Super booster for developers; Crone addi-
tive C. B. Pierce. il Pop Phot 56:78-9+
My '65
Techniques tomorrow; new Du Pont system.
B. Sherman. Mod Phot 29:30+ Ap '65
35mm: Kodak Versamat film processor. J.
Wolbarst. il Mod Phot 29:50+ Ap '65
35mm; way to develop film, its own metal
cartridge. J. Wolbarst. il Mod Phot 29:34+
My '65

Distortion

Large camera. A. Feininger. il Mod Phot 29:
22+ My '65 (to be cont)
Large camera; swings and tilts. A. Feininger. Mod Phot 29:60 Je '65
Twisted easel. P. Farber. il U S Camera 28:
60-1+ Mr '65

Economic aspects

How Congress can save photographers
$28,000,000. J. Neubauer. Pop Phot 56:51+
My '65

Educational applications

See Photography in education

Enlarging

Enlargers. il Pop Phot 58:82-9 Ja '66
Free, your own darkroom meter! P. Farber.
U S Camera 28:20+ Ag '65
Full-size results from half-frame. J. S.
Forney. Pop Phot 57:34-5+ O '65
Large camera; modular enlarger. A. Fein-
inger. il Mod Phot 29:44 N '65
Marvel of marvels, Fotoval now programs for
skin tones! P. Farber. il U S Camera 28:
14+ Jl '65
Modern's enlarger guide $23.85 to $150. D. L.
Miller. il Mod Phot 29:76-9+ F '65
R for print sharpness. il Mod Phot 29:80-1
F '65
Spin away your black & white blues. W. A.
Bonner and H. C. Benedict. il U S Camera
28:54-5+ D '65
Visit with Simmon; Xenomega. N. Rothschild.
il Pop Phot 57:22+ D '65

Exhibitions

Avedon show. J. Durniak. il Pop Phot 56:52-5
My '65
Catskill photo center. L. Barry. Pop Phot 56:
42+ Je '65
Contests & exhibits. U S Camera 28:10+ Mr;
29+ Jl; 2+ Ag '65; 29:10 Ja '66
Critics' choice=chaos? H. Keppler. il Mod
Phot 29:88-91 S '65
Eleven great photographs; selections from
Kodak pavilion at the World's fair. N.
Kent. il Am Artist 29:31-7+ S '65
Europe's What is man? exhibit; tr. by A.
Rosin. R. E. Martinez. Pop Phot 56:8+
Je '65
Exhibitions; their opportunities and prob-
lems. A. Rothstein. U S Camera 28:12+ S
'65
Facts, film cleaners & flatteners; IPEX,
New York. A. Francekevich. Pop Phot 57:
24+ Ag '65
Grace Mayer; on the level of fine art. J.
Deschin. il Pop Phot 56:41+ My '65
IPEX is packed with photo attractions; In-
ternational photographic exposition in New
York Coliseum. R. Miller. il U S Camera
28:32+ My '65
IPEX: more on latest equipment. Mod Phot
29:94+ Jl '65
IPEX '65. il U S Camera 28:74-7 Je '65
IPEX '65 guide. il Mod Phot 29:87-102 Je
'65
IPEX: the very last roundup (we hope) new
equipment. il Mod Phot 29:26+ S '65
IPEX time, New York conference, workshop,
exhibitions scheduled. Mod Phot 29:64 Je
'65
Nonexistent best lens; IPEX, New York.
N. Rothschild. Pop Phot 57:16+ Ag '65
OEO sponsors photo exhibit on poverty. il
Pop Phot 57:59-60 N '65
Photo essay exhibition traces development of
a medium; Museum of modern art, New
York. il Pub W 187:84-5 Ap 5 '65
Photography on Fifth avenue; Hallmark
gallery. J. Durniak. il Pop Phot 57:54 Jl '65
Salon calendar. See occasional issues of
Modern photography

Show windup; 1965 IPEX. M. A. Matzkin
and others. il Mod Phot 29:66-7+ Ag '65
Sick or sweet? World exhibition of pho-
tography. H. Keppler and P. Caulfield.
il Mod Phot 29:78-85 My '65
Twelve international photographers; New
York Gallery of modern art. il U S Camera
28:56-9+ Jl '65
Yes, Pittsburgh; Three rivers arts festival.
J. Durniak. Pop Phot 56:44 F '65

Exposure

A's to your Q's about exposure. H. Luckett.
il Pop Sci 186:140-1 F '65
Autoradiography; technique for drastic reduc-
tion of exposure time to alpha particles.
J. J. C. Hsieh and others. il Science 150:
1821-2 D 31 '65
Caulfield on color. P. Caulfield. Mod Phot
29:48 F; 36+ Jl '65
Color clinic; why not double-expose? D. B.
Eisendrath, jr. Pop Phot 56:10+ Mr '65
Doscher exposure system. A. L. Dorn. il U S
Camera 28:44-7+ Mr '65
Exposure. H. Keppler. il Mod Phot 29:68-77
Jl '65
Images etched in time; double exposure and
blending of texture with person. J. Mor-
ris. il U S Camera 28:46-9+ Jl '65
Is it true? H. N. Todd and R. D. Zakia.
Pop Phot 56:26 My '65
Keep it warm. il U S Camera 28:42-5 Jl
'65
Nature and photography; varying exposure
for desired effect. J. Couffer. Natur Hist
74:66-9 Je '65
Now; automatic speedlight: Strobonar 660.
W. Clark. il U S Camera 28:46-7+ O '65
On the beach. il U S Camera 28:38-41 My '65
Shooting the works (fire) D. B. Eisendrath,
jr. Pop Phot 57:10+ Jl '65
Spot meters? great if you know how to use
them. E. Meyers. il Mod Phot 29:64-5+ Jl
'65
T Flex converter. N. Rothschild. il Pop Phot
57:164-5+ D '65
Unusual zoom. il Mod Phot 29:74-5 Mr '65

Films

Accentuate the negative. P. Farber. il U S
Camera 28:48-51+ My '65
Caulfield on color; improved Anscochrome
200. P. Caulfield. Mod Phot 29:41+ S '65
Caulfield on color; way to standardization
on a single negative color film. P. Caulfield.
Mod Phot 30:24+ Ja '66
Color films they don't make. N. Rothschild.
il Pop Phot 57:26+ S '65
Creative color; new photographic products
from 3M. A. Rothstein. U S Camera 28:
10+ My '65
Dynachrome vs Kodachrome. H. Keppler. il
Mod Phot 29:82-5+ F '65
Evolution of the Bluejays. L. Lipton. il Pop
Phot 56:68-70+ Je '65
Facts about film. Pop Phot 57:105 O '65
Films & formats, where are we headed? M.
Morrison. il U S Camera 28:55-7+ My '65
Films for the unusual. D. B. Eisendrath,
jr. Pop Phot 57:14+ N '65
Films you should know more about. N.
Rothschild. Pop Phot 57:80-1+ O '65
How accurate are the nine color films? il
Mod Phot 29:66-7 O '65
How do the nine color films compare? H.
Keppler. il Mod Phot 29:88-91+ Ap '65
How to get the most out of Kll. il Pop
Phot 56:60-1+ Mr '65
How to get the most out of tungsten films.
N. Rothschild. il Pop Phot 58:110-13+ Ja
'66
Improved Anscochrome 50. H. Keppler. il
Mod Phot 29:64-5 S '65
Improved high speed Ektachrome: is it really?
H. Keppler. il Mod Phot 29:70-3+ Mr '65
Is Super-8 the filmsize of the future?
E. Wildi. U S Camera 28:74+ Jl '65
Kodak Ektachrome infrared aero; two-part
test report. M. Iger and N. Rothschild. il
Pop Phot 57:158-61+ D '65
Large camera; roll film vs. sheet film. A.
Feininger. Mod Phot 29:52 O '65
Mexico. N. Rothschild; J. M. Zanutto. il Pop
Phot 57:90-7+ O '65
1965-'66 color films compared! D. L. Miller.
Mod Phot 29:58-9 O '65
Now 15 sec prints! B. Pierce. il Pop Phot 58:
34+ Ja '66
Perfect color film. L. Lipton. il Pop Phot
56:62-3+ Mr '65
Photosolubilization, anyone? N. Rothschild.
il Pop Phot 56:30+ Mr '65
Pictures in a moment; Kodak film packs. J.
Wolbarst. il Mod Phot 29:42 Ap '65

PHOTOGRAPHY—Films—*Continued*

Pictures in a moment; Polaroid color film. J. Wolbarst. Mod Phot 29:50+ F '65

RCA high-speed film processor to aid ASW; Bimat film. M. Getler. il Miss & Roc 16: 34-6 Mr 1 '65

Rapid arrives. M. Edelson. il U S Camera 28:54-5+ Ag '65

Still & movie films. Pop Phot 58:71-9 Ja '66

Super-duper 8; improved version of 8-millimeter film. Newsweek 65:76+ My 3 '65

Ten daylight color films & how they perform. R. Kinne. il Pop Phot 57:68-73+ O '65

35mm color films. M. Edelson. il U S Camera 28:60-3+ S '65

35mm; Kodak Panatomic-X. J. Wolbarst. Mod Phot 29:42+ Je '65

35mm or 4x5? J. Wolbarst. il Mod Phot 29: 84-7 N '65

35mm; Rapid cameras. J. Wolbarst. Mod Phot 29:40 Ag '65

35mm; Tri-X Pan film. J. Wolbarst. il Mod Phot 29:16+ N '65

220: twice as many shots per roll. J. Forney. il Pop Phot 56:87-8+ F '65

This is it! the Super-8 cartridge. il Pop Phot 56:94 My '65

Tri-X pan challenged; Ilford HP3 film. E. Meyers. il Mod Phot 30:98 Ja '66

2475 film: it's fast and red-sensitive too! P. Leonian. il U S Camera 28:66-7+ Ag '65

2475-world's fastest 35-mm film! B. Pierce. il Pop Phot 56:82-3+ My '65

Vagabond camera; super 8mm cameras use special film. W. Lane. il Travel 124:62-3 Jl '65

We wonder where the 220 went. M. A. Matzkin. il Mod Phot 29:52+ N '65

Which films are best for making dupes? Mod Phot 29:87 Ap '65

See also
Cameras—Loading
Moving picture films

Testing

Improved Panatomic-X. P. Farber. il U S Camera 28:46-7+ D '65

Test report: Ektachrome improved. P. Leonian. il U S Camera 28:56+ Mr '65

Focusing

Caulfield on color; differences in using RFDR and SLR cameras with color and with black-and-white films. P. Caulfield. il Mod Phot 29:40+ My '65

Closeups with RF & TLR. G. Gilbert. il U S Camera 28:54-5+ F '65

How to get the most out of available light. C. W. Kennedy. il Pop Phot 56:68-9+ Mr '65

Is the rangefinder more precise? B. Sherman. il Mod Phot 29:66-7+ My '65

Keppler on the SLR. H. Keppler. il Mod Phot 29:22+ Mr '65

Large camera; how to use swings to extend the sharply covered zone in depth. A. Feininger. il Mod Phot 29:44+ F '65

Large camera; using swings and tilts. A. Feininger. il Mod Phot 29:48+ Jl '65

Optical donuts? out of focus effects. L. Solmssen. il Mod Phot 29:62-3 Ag '65

Right way to zoom. B. Campbell. il U S Camera 28:66-7+ Ap '65

Think wide. M. Morrison. il U S Camera 28:54-5+ Ap '65

Tools of selective focus. B. Randall and N. Zabarsky. il U S Camera 28:44-5+ Ja '66

Unhappy with your groundglass? C. W. Kennedy. il Pop Phot 57:50-3 Ag '65

What you should know about depth in pictures. R. L. McIntyre. il Pop Phot 56: 60 Je '65

Why are some SLRs brighter? B. Sherman. il Mod Phot 29:68-9+ Mr '65

Galleries and museums

Catskill photo center. L. Barry. Pop Phot 56: 42+ Je '65

George Eastman house. R. Fichter. il U S Camera 28:74-5+ N '65

Helen Wright; a way of responding; Leica gallery exhibitions. J. Deschin. Pop Phot 57:36+ S '65

What a photography center should be. J. Deschin. il Pop Phot 57:32+ D '65

Grain

How to get the most grain in 35-mm. J. Stamp. il Pop Phot 57:66-7+ Ag '65

History

History of Japanese photography. E. Bennett and F. Saito. il U S Camera 28:64-5+ Je '65

Judging

See Photography—Exhibitions

Landscapes

Design your scenics. il U S Camera 28:58-61 O '65

Large camera. A. Feininger. Mod Phot 29: 24+ Ap '65

Large camera; 4x5 camera. A. Feininger. Mod Phot 29:30+ D '65

Magic mountain. il U S Camera 28:50-1 Je '65

Making the scenic. P. Caulfield. il Mod Phot 29:64-73 N '65

Sharp eye plus tight technique. P. Caulfield. il Mod Phot 29:62-5 My '65

When the moon is high. L. L. Smith. il U S Camera 28:64-5+ Mr '65

Light

Using your Christmas camera; direct sources of strong light. il Sunset 136:32+ Ja '66

When the sun is low. il U S Camera 28:62-3 Mr '65

Lighting

Color picture ideas for the winter season. A. Rothstein. U S Camera 29:16+ Ja '66

Control the contrast. J. Burroughs. il Pop Sci 186:120-4 My '65

How to get the most from one photoflood. A. Goldsmith. il Pop Phot 57:158-9+ N '65

How to get the most out of available light. C. W. Kennedy. il Pop Phot 56:68-9+ Mr '65

I learned lighting in nursery school! D. Reed. il Pop Phot 56:61 Je '65

Images by the dozen; with lights. H. Shaman. il Pop Phot 58:120-1+ Ja '66

Light it; photographs with descriptions by P. Caulfield. Mod Phot 30:48-55 Ja '66

Lighting on the run. E. Steinbicker. il Pop Phot 57:156-7+ N '65

Lighting: present and future. N. Rothschild. Pop Phot 56:34+ Ap '65

Make pictures by candlelight. R. Hattersley. il Pop Phot 57:144-7+ D '65

New approach, new problems. D. B. Eisendrath, jr. Pop Phot 58:6+ Ja '66

Reflectors for small-object photography. C. W. Kennedy il Pop Phot 56:76 Mr '65

Rembrandt lighting. G. Pyle. il Pop Phot 56:68-9 My '65

Marines

Inland sea. il U S Camera 28:54-5 Je '65

Picture pointers. T. W. Moore. il Motor B 115:26-31+ My '65

35mm; annual Aqua-Cat national championships. J. Wolbarst. il Mod Phot 29:13+ Mr '65

Vagabond camera; rules for filming afloat. W. Lane. il Travel 124:64-5 S '65

Negatives

Accentuate the negative. P. Farber. il U S Camera 28:48-51+ My '65

Pictures in a moment; Polaroid negative. J. Wolbarst. il Mod Phot 29:18+ Jl '65

Spin away your black & white blues. W. A. Bonner and H. C. Benedict. il U S Camera 28:54-5+ D '65

Take a negative view. J. Wolbarst. il Mod Phot 29:70-5 F '65

Variations on two negatives. L. Solmssen. il Mod Phot 29:66-9 F '65

Wolfman on printing; dust-free negatives. A. Wolfman. il Mod Phot 30:20+ Ja '66

Wolfman on printing; dust on negatives. A. Wolfman. il Mod Phot 29:28+ D '65

Periodicals

See also
Modern photography (periodical)

Portraits

Amateur's world. U S Camera 28:80-3 My '65

Arnold Newman's Europe. A. Newman. il Pop Phot 56:50-5+ Mr '65

Art Kane. J. Deschin. il Pop Phot 57:70-9+ S '65

Carl Van Vechten: memorial album of opera singers photographs. Opera N 29:14-16 F 13 '65

Faces at the races. M. Orovan. il U S Camera 28:68-9 O '65

Focus on: you; self-portraiture. C. W. Kennedy. il Pop Phot 56:98-9 Je '65

Gowland (cont of Glamor) P. Gowland. See issues of Popular photography

Gowland goes candid at the beach. P. Gowland. il Pop Phot 57:74-5 O '65

Hometown faces. il U S Camera 28:68-71 Ag '65

PHOTOGRAPHY—Portraits—*Continued*

How to take your own picture. H. T. Sigler. il Field & S 69:100 Mr '65

Look at me. il U S Camera 29:54-5 Ja '66

Marilyn Monroe; interviews with six famous photographers ed. by R. Hattersley. il Pop Phot 58:104-9+ Ja '66

Marvel of marvels, Fotoval now programs for skin tones! P. Farber. U S Camera 28:14+ Jl '65

New colors in your prints. il U S Camera 28:42-5 Ap '65

New Polaroid Land portrait camera. N. Rothschild. il Pop Phot 56:56-7+ Ap '65

On being a photographer of people. K. Heyman. Pop Phot 56:52-5+ F '65

On the beach. U S Camera 28:38-41 My '65

One man's hobby. il U S Camera 28:50-3 Ap '65

Op art rides again; use of moiré patterns in portraiture. P. Farber. U S Camera 28:14-15 O '65

Pictures in a moment; Polaroid's six-shooter. J. Wolbarst. il Mod Phot 29:36-8 Je '65

Portraits simply made. H. Keppler. il Mod Phot 29:92-3 F '65

Private view; excerpts. Snowdon. Vogue 146:84-95 N 15 '65

Psychological document in sadness; portrait of O. Kokoschka by H. Erfurth. G. M. Mayer. Pop Phot 56:50-1+ F '65

Printing processes

Color alchemy of Scott Hyde; composite photographs. S. Hyde. Pop Phot 56:64-71+ F '65

Convert your B&W darkroom for color printing. E. Meyers. Mod Phot 29:22+ F '65

Delville siphon. A. Francekevich. il Pop Phot 56:22+ Je '65

Dotography. P. Mann. il Design 67:40 N '65

Drying prints can be fun; Beseler Glossomatt. P. Farber. il U S Camera 29:28 Ja '66

How pros edit contact sheets. M. Edelson. il U S Camera 28:62-5+ Ag '65

How to make a quality print. G. Martin. il U S Camera 28:52-3+ S '65

In the darkroom; to gloss or not to gloss. A. Francekevich. Pop Phot 56:26 Ap '65

Is it true? H. N. Todd and R. D. Zakia. Pop Phot 57:103 Jl '65

Is this print ruined? B. C. Brown. il Pop Phot 56:122-3 Je '65

Mail-order color-film processors. il Consumer Bul 48:28-30 Mr '65

New Varigam filters; Du Pont's latest development in variable contrast printing. B. Hoffman. il Pop Phot 57:142-3+ D '65

Photography; dye transfer color. G. Arnold. il Sch Arts 65:23-6 S '65

Printing materials. Pop Phot 58:81 Ja '66

Prints by the thousands. A. Francekevich. il Pop Phot 57:20+ Jl '65

Record-keeper for color printing. A. Francekevich. il Pop Phot 57:16+ O '65

Try tone lines. P. Farber. il U S Camera 28:72-3+ Ag '65

Weird ways of posterization. P. Farber. il U S Camera 28:64-5+ S '65

White sails in the darkroom. il Pop Phot 56:60-1 F '65

Wolfman on printing. A. Wolfman. il Mod Phot 29:30+ N; 28+ D '65; 30:20+ Ja '66

Retouching

How to bleach, if you must. C. W. Kennedy. il Pop Phot 56:108 Ap '65

More about bleaching. C. W. Kennedy. il Pop Phot 56:84 My '65

More on salvaging transparencies; improving off-color. D. B. Eisendrath, jr. Pop Phot 56:20+ My '65

Scientific applications

Questing camera. M. R. Weiss. il Sat R 48:33-9 Ag 28 '65

Societies

Fotografi from Norway; Manité international. U S Camera 28:48-53+ Mr '65

Still life

Experiment: take a dozen objects. G. Pyle. il Pop Phot 56:68-9 Ap '65

Is your sight asleep? H. D. Wieck. il U S Camera 29:62-5 Ja '66

Studios and darkrooms

Apartment darkroom. C. W. Kennedy. il Pop Phot 58:18 Ja '66

Darkroom aids and short cuts. T. Runge and W. Forbes. il Pop Phot 56:126-7 Je '65

Darkroom on a shoestring. M. Morrison. il U S Camera 28:64-5+ O '65

Darkroom that went 600 mph; Life converts a jet to meet its color deadline. H. Orth. il Pop Phot 56:64-5+ My '65

Home darkroom par excellence. P. Stackpole. U S Camera 28:10+ Ap '65

Stuff a darkroom in a closet. D. Laing. il Mod Phot 29:106 Je '65

Think big, that's Life. G. Silk. il Mod Phot 29:19+ My '65

35mm; dangers of static electricity in the darkroom. J. Wolbarst. Mod Phot 29:24 F '65

35mm techniques. P. Stackpole. U S Camera 28:14-15 Mr '65

Tribute to the darkroom. Pop Phot 57:14+ O '65

Wolfman on printing; setting up a compact, efficient, inexpensive darkroom. A. Wolfman. il Mod Phot 29:30+ N '65

Study and teaching

Are color photographers born or made? R. Miller. il U S Camera 28:26 O '65

Color workshop produces sparkling results; Syracuse color workshop. A. Rothstein. U S Camera 28:12+ Ag '65

Doctor Albert Freed; teaching photography at the Educational alliance, New York. J. Deschin. il Pop Phot 57:33-4+ Ag '65

Photo school. E. Hannigan. il U S Camera 28:56-9+ S '65

Rothschild on repairs; National camera repair school, Englewood, Colo. N. Rothschild. il Pop Phot 56:74-7+ My '65

Terminology

What means what in SLR? Mod Phot 29:105 Ag '65

Themes

Any room a studio. il U S Camera 28:72-3 O '65

Discovery; C. Bruno. P. Caulfield. il Mod Phot 29:62-3+ O '65

Popular places. il U S Camera 28:62-3 N '65

Seventy-five creative photographic assignments. R. Hattersley. Pop Phot 56:41+ Mr '65

Shoot it from your car. E. Scully. il U S Camera 28:72-5+ Mr '65

There's no place like home for taking good pictures. Am Home 68:97 Ap '65

PHOTOGRAPHY, Aerial

Air reconnaissance aided by line-scanning laser camera. B. Miller. il Aviation W 82:80-1+ Ap 26 '65

Flying photographer. See issues of Flying

See also
Aerial reconnaissance
Photogrammetry
Photography in agriculture

PHOTOGRAPHY, Artistic

Art Kane. J. Deschin. il Pop Phot 57:70-9+ S '65

Compelling images of Akira Sato. il Pop Phot 56:70-3 My '65

Creative color; art through photography. A. Rothstein. U S Camera 28:10-11 F '65

Creative color; cultural influences in Japanese photography. A. Rothstein. U S Camera 28:24-5 Je '65

Critic's choice. N. Rothschild. il Pop Phot 57:72-3+ Ag '65

David Attie. il Pop Phot 56:92-7+ Je '65

Painting with film. J. Foldes. il U S Camera 28:50-1+ O '65

Photography's mock simplicity. Pop Phot 56:32 Ap '65

See also
Composition (photography)

PHOTOGRAPHY, Astronomical. See Astronomical photography

PHOTOGRAPHY, Close-up

ABC's of filming bees. W. D. Woodson. il Pop Phot 56:120-1+ Ap '65

Close-up on close-ups. E. Wildi. il Pop Phot 56:104-7+ Mr '65

Close-up which lenses? M. Edelson and H. Keppler. il Mod Phot 29:76-9 Mr '65

Close-ups, down-stage center. J. Foldes. il Pop Phot 56:74-5+ Mr '65

Closemanship. N. Rothschild. il Pop Phot 58:64-5 Ja '66

Copying and close-up equipment. il Pop Phot 58:66-8 Ja '66

Get closer than close with a + 10 lens. N. Rothschild. il Pop Phot 56:76-7+ Ap '65

Instant closeups. W. D. Griffin. il U S Camera 28:44-5+ My '65

Is your camera shy? symposium. il U S Camera 28:39-61 F '65

PHOTOGRAPHY, Trick—*Continued*
How Norman Rothschild made the cover pictures. il Pop Phot 56:82 Mr '65
Images by the dozen. N. Rothschild; H. Shaman. il Pop Phot 58:118-21+ Ja '66
Incredible photoons of Masatoshi Naito. M. Naito. il Mod Phot 29:86-91 F '65
Odd effects with Aetna Trix lenses. M. A. Matzkin. il Mod Phot 29:104-5 Je '65
Op photography. P. Farber. il U S Camera 28:60-1+ Jl '65
Philippe Halsman. L. Barry. il Pop Phot 56:47-9+ F '65
What is it? it's music. il U S Camera 28:14+ My '65

PHOTOGRAPHY and art. See Art and photography

PHOTOGRAPHY as a profession
Photography is his business. E. Bennett. il U S Camera 28:78+ N '65

PHOTOGRAPHY by children. See Children as photographers

PHOTOGRAPHY centers. See Recreation centers

PHOTOGRAPHY clubs. See Camera clubs

PHOTOGRAPHY in advertising
Confessions of a picture man? J. Durniak. Pop Phot 56:38 Mr '65

PHOTOGRAPHY in agriculture
Infrared aids agriculture. Sci N L 89:21 Ja 8 '66

PHOTOGRAPHY in archeology
Photographic documentation in archeological research: increasing the information content. C. A. Erskine. bibliog il Science 148:1089 My 21 '65

PHOTOGRAPHY in criminal investigation
Bank robber sees his picture and gives up; United California bank. il Life 58:39 Mr 12 '65
Cameras to trap crooks. A. J. Maher. il Pop Mech 125:142-5+ Ja '66
Split-second record of a bank robbery; Western-Manchester branch of the United California bank, Los Angeles. il Life 58:34-5 F 26 '65

PHOTOGRAPHY in education
Advantages of having your own 8mm camera. R. H. Burgert. Sr Schol 87:sup 10 N 4 '65
Shadow designs. W. Bock. il Sch Arts 65:18-20 N '65

PHOTOGRAPHY in science. See Photography—Scientific applications

PHOTOGRAPHY models. See Models (persons)

PHOTOGRAPHY of animals
Big-game hunting with camera. H. Kanzler. il Field & S 70:37-9 N '65
Playful dolphins can be fun. P. Stackpole. U S Camera 28:22-3+ S '65
Quick, look over there: selection of Life magazine's miscellany section. il Read Digest 87:146-53 D '65
Stalking winter wildlife. E. A. Bauer. il Outdoor Life 137:48-51+ Ja '66

PHOTOGRAPHY of boats. See Photography of ships

PHOTOGRAPHY of buildings and structures
Absence of gray. il Pop Phot 56:58-9 F '65
Photographing sewers doesn't cost a cent; Westfield, N.J. B. F. Murphy. il Am City 80:112-13 Mr '65
Wait! il Pop Phot 57:156-7 D '65
World's fair picture-taking & exposure guide. C. Burger. il Pop Phot 56:62-7+ Ap '65

PHOTOGRAPHY of children
Best subject. il U S Camera 28:42-9 Ag '65
Birthday party. E. Weck. il U S Camera 28:52-3 Jl '65
I learned lighting in nursery school! D. Reed. il Pop Phot 56:61 Je '65
Impressions; Carole Thomas' Japanese pictures. il U S Camera 28:54-5 Jl '65
Let kids take their own pictures! C. B. Nieberding. il Pop Phot 57:144-5 N '65
Making the moment. il U S Camera 29:52-3 Ja '66
Near or far, catch 'em candidly. C. Lipin. il U S Camera 28:46-7 My '65
Newborn is a picture star. J. Kinney and C. Kinney. il Parents Mag 40:62-3 F '65

PHOTOGRAPHY of fishes
Nature and photography; movie problems in public aquariums. S. Dunton. Natur Hist 74:58-60 N '65
Nature and photography; taking movies of a home aquarium. P. Villiard. il Natur Hist 74:64-6 N '65
They taught me 35-mm underwater and then I soloed with a shark. H. Shaman. il Pop Phot 57:54-7+ Ag '65

PHOTOGRAPHY of flowers, plants, trees, etc.
Focusing on the flower shows. il Pop Gard 16:18 Ap '65

Springtime photographs outdoors & indoors. J. J. Simpkins. il Flower Grower 52:33 Mr '65
Tools of selective focus. B. Randall and N. Zabarsky. il U S Camera 29:44-5+ Ja '66
Wild flower's fleeting moment of perfection. il Pop Gard 16:30-1 N '65

PHOTOGRAPHY of insects
Mantis madness; with photographs by Larry Fritz. U S Camera 28:38 S '65
To catch a butterfly. R. E. Largent. il U S Camera 28:50-1 Jl '65

PHOTOGRAPHY of lightning
Lightning through a lens. R. E. Orville. il Natur Hist 75:34-41 bibliog(p68) Ja '66

PHOTOGRAPHY of mountains. See Photography—Landscapes

PHOTOGRAPHY of moving objects
Can't move? zoom! P. Caulfield. il Mod Phot 30:76-7 Ja '66
Lighting on the run. E. Steinbicker. il Pop Phot 57:156-7+ N '65
Make it move! M. Orovan. il U S Camera 28:44-51+ S '65
Precise moment. P. Caulfield and H. Keppler. il Mod Phot 29:67-73 Ap '65
World's fair picture-taking & exposure guide. C. Burger. il Pop Phot 56:62-7+ Ap '65

PHOTOGRAPHY of rivers
Bookmaker to a river. B. Smith. il Field & S 70:52-5 Ag '65

PHOTOGRAPHY of ships
Boats! camera! action! L. O. Larew. il Motor B 115:26-9+ Je '65
Picture pointers. T. W. Moore. il Motor B 115:26-31+ My '65
See also
Photography—Marines

PHOTOGRAPHY of snow, ice, etc.
It's an icicle world up close. D. E. Burgderfer. il U S Camera 28:16+ F '65
Vagabond camera. W. Lane. il Travel 125:64 Ja '66
When fall and winter meet. il U S Camera 28:44-5 D '65

PHOTOGRAPHY of sports
Barrel of fun on ice. M. Adler. il U S Camera 28:16-17 Mr '65
Make it pay! baseball pictures. J. Holland. U S Camera 28:14+ Ap '65
New Spotmatic; a tryout at the Tokyo Olympics. F. Springer-Miller. il Pop Phot 56:70-1+ Ap '65

PHOTOGRAPHY schools. See Photography—Study and teaching

PHOTOGRAVURE
Quality gravure printing at the price of lithography; sheet-fed press operation. il Pub W 187:137-41+ Je 14 '65

PHOTOJOURNALISM. See Photography, Journalistic

PHOTOLITHOGRAPHY
Photo-lithographers meet in Chicago, 10,000 strong; equipment shown at NAPL exhibit. J. B. Goetz. il Pub W 188:94-5 O 4 '65

PHOTOMECHANICAL processes
Books, not copying machines, are the long-term answer; address, March 1964. L. C. Deighton. il Library J 90:2087-92 My 1 '65

PHOTOMETERS
BTL meters for the SLR. il U S Camera 28:46-8 Je '65
Helium-glow photometer for picomole analysis of alkali metals. G. G. Vurek and R. L. Bowman. bibliog il Science 149:448-50 Jl 23 '65
Pictures in a moment. J. Wolbarst. il Mod Phot 30:30+ Ja '66

PHOTOMETRY, Astronomical
Five-color photometry of bright stars. B. Iriarte and others. il Sky & Tel 30:21-4 Jl '65

PHOTON machine. See Photocomposing machines

PHOTONS
Double forces. Sci Am 212:51-2 F '65
Photon and electron impact; report on symposium. V. H. Dibeler. Science 150:786-7 N 5 '65

PHOTOPERIODISM. See Light—Physiological effects

PHOTOSCAN system. See Photography, Aerial

PHOTOSOLUBILIZATION. See Photography—Developing and developers

PHOTOSTAT
Color separation II: the use of photostats. J. Kepes. il Horn Bk 41:651-4 D '65

PHOTOSYNTHESIS
Biophysical problems of photosynthesis. R. K. Clayton. bibliog il Science 149:1346-54 S 17 '65

PHOTOSYNTHESIS—*Continued*

Ferredoxin and photosynthesis. D. I. Arnon. bibliog il Science 149:1460-70 S 24 '65

Key to photosynthesis found in ferredoxin. Sci N L 88:248 O 16 '65

Role of chlorophyll in photosynthesis. E. I. Rabinowitch and Govindjee. il Sci Am 213:74-83 Jl '65

PHOTOTYPESETTING. See Photocomposing

PHOTOTYPESETTING machines. See Photocomposing machines

PHOTURIS fireflies. See Fireflies

PHRASING of questions. See Questioning

PHYSICAL adsorption. See Adsorption

PHYSICAL astronomy. See Astrophysics

PHYSICAL directors

Coach; death of A. Stagg. il Time 85:45 Mr 26 '65

Colorado football's galloping disaster; memoirs of a big-time coach. B. Davis. il Harper 231:50-3 O '65

Don't get Duffy mad; Michigan state. il Time 86:75 N 12 '65

Man; Red Auerbach. Time 87:75 Ja 14 '66

Mr Bubas' business; Duke's Blue Devils. il Time 86:71 D 31 '65

Organization man: B. Devaney. Newsweek 66:60 O 4 '65

Southern football: the Bear of Alabama. G. Astor. il Look 29:101+ N 16 '65

Twelve flew out of the pressure cooker; college basketball coaches. J. Underwood. il Sports Illus 22:70-1 Mr 22 '65

Twins' miracle coach. M. Smith. il Life 59:83-4+ S 10 '65

See also names of physical directors, e.g. J. Lapchick

PHYSICAL education and training

Health, physical education, and academic achievement. C. A. Bucher. il NEA J 54:38-40 My '65

Individualized physical activity; program at the primary level in Pontiac, Mich. schools. J. M. Young. il NEA J 54:22-3 D '65

Physical activity aids the three R's. D. E. Misner. bibliog Sr Schol 86:sup6 My 6 '65

Putting muscle into marks. P. L. Levin. il N Y Times Mag p118+ N 28 '65

Scientific secrets of fitness. A. Hamilton. il Sci Digest 58:60-5 Jl '65

See also

Exercise

School athletes

Sports

PHYSICAL examinations

Sugarcoating the executive's health checkup. il Bsns W p68-9 Je 19 '65

Why get sick when you don't have to? E. Day. il Ladies Home J 83:46+ Ja '66

Why see a doctor when you're healthy? P. Lindberg. Bet Hom & Gard 43:16+ S '65

PHYSICAL examinations, Premarital

Premarital counseling: what's discussed? il Good H 161:177 O '65

PHYSICAL exercise. See Exercise

PHYSICAL fitness. See Health; Men—Health and hygiene

PHYSICAL geography

See also

Continents

Geography

Man—Influence on nature

Topography

PHYSICAL instruments

Amateur scientist; electrometer, a temperature-control apparatus and a simple electric motor. J. L. Menke; C. Henry; H. E. Stockman. il Sci Am 213:106-8+ O '65

PHYSICAL measurements

Status of the national standards for physical measurement. R. D. Huntoon. bibliog il Science 150:169-78 O 8 '65

PHYSICAL science. See Science

PHYSICAL training. See Physical education and training

PHYSICALLY handicapped. See Handicapped

PHYSICIANS

Britain's angry doctors. B. Wenham. New Repub 152:9-10 Ap 10 '65

Busy, busy ski doctor; he sets 350 fractures a winter. il Life 58:111-12 F 19 '65

Day in the life of a family doctor. T. Gallagher. il Good H 160:78-81+ F '65

Doctors in crisis; GP's revolt against Britain's National health service. il Newsweek 65:60 Mr 1 '65

Expectant mother: which doctor should I call? A. C. Posner. Redbook 125:16+ Je '65

How to pick a doctor. V. Cohn. il Ladies Home J 83:34-5 Ja '66

Kentucky doctor: one man's war against southern poverty. L. Bergquist. il Look 29:76-80 N 16 '65

Many doctors take drugs. Sci N L 87:307 My 15 '65

Physician warns about incompetent doctors. U S News 60:10 Ja 3 '66

Practice and malpractice. S. Greenberg. il Nation 200:464-7+ My 3 '65

Traveler's guide; Intermedic service lists English-speaking doctors abroad. Time 85:78 Mr 12 '65

Troubled calling, crisis in the medical establishment, by S. Greenberg. Review Sci Digest il 58:16-17 S '65. D. Lewis

Why are doctors out of step? L. Lasagna; reply. E. L. Young. New Repub 152:29 F 6 '65

Your doctor and the A.M.A. J. Bird. il Sat Eve Post 239:13-17+ Ja 1 '66

See also

American medical association

Medical ethics

Medical service

Medicine—Group practice

Medicine—Practice

Pediatricians

Specialization in medicine

Women as physicians

Anecdotes, facetiae, satire, etc.

When doctors take over farming. E. H. Logsdon. Farm J 89:53 F '65

History

Columbus' doctors. L. H. Roddis. il Américas 17:35-7 Je '65

Salaries, fees, etc.

Medics who moonlight. R. H. Berg. il Look 29:28-32+ F 9 '65

See also

Medical service, Cost of

Supply and demand

AMA: the restrictive power. E. Rayack. il Nation 200:470-9 My 3 '65

As medicare nears: a crisis in hospital care? with interview with W. C. Rappleye. il U S News 58:50-6 Mr 15 '65

From student to doctor. il Todays Health 43:34-7+ Mr '65

Heart, cancer, stroke: rising opposition from doctors may slow passage of Johnson program. E. Langer. Science 149:843-5 Ag 20 '65

Main solution: many more doctors. il Life 59:58 S 3 '65

PHYSICIANS and patients

Do doctors still care about their patients? S. Blum. Redbook 126:51+ N '65

Education: the forgotten patient. G. A. Silver. il Nation 200:467-70 My 3 '65

How to get the most from your doctor. V. Cohn. il Ladies Home J 83:39 Ja '66

Physician's image. R. E. Westlake. Sat R 48:84 D 4 '65

Research in patient care; report on seminar. P. J. Sanazaro. Science 148:1489-90 Je 11 '65

Tell me, doctor. M. E. Debakey. Ladies Home J 82:30 Ap '65

Trouble with doctors is me. J. West. Ladies Home J 82:42 Mr '65

Where is science taking us? W. Darley. Sat R 48:55-6 S 4 '65

Your doctor as a disease detective. T. Berland. Todays Health 43:62-5 S '65

Anecdotes, facetiae, satire, etc.

Ordeal to choke a sword-swallower. S. Alexander. Life 60:17 Ja 21 '66

PHYSICIANS strike (Canada) See Strikes—Canada

PHYSICISTS

Education of professional physicists; report on international conference. R. Geballe. Science 150:1752+ D 24 '65

Recollections of Max Born. M. Born. Bul Atomic Sci 21:3-6 S; 9-13 O; 3-6 N '65

PHYSICS

Theoretical physics conference; report on annual Eastern United States theoretical physics conference. E. J. Woods. Science 148:107-8 Ap 2 '65

See also

Astrophysics

Quantum theory

Apparatus and instruments

See Physical instruments

Experiments

Amateur scientist; how to measure raindrops, make snowflakes and simulate subatomic particle scatterings. N. J. Wilder; R. W. Wahl; R. Hayward. il Sci Am 213:102-7 Ag '65

PHYSICS—*Continued*

History

Einstein, specific heats, and the early quantum theory; address, December 29, 1964. M. J. Klein. bibliog Science 148:173-80 Ap 9 '65

International aspects

See Science—International aspects

Research

1965 science review. Sci N L 88:391-2 D 18 '65

Study and teaching

Physics course planned for non-college students. Sci N L 88:66 Jl 31 '65

PHYSIOGNOMY
See also
Nose

PHYSIOLOGICAL apparatus
Brain telestimulator with solar cell power supply. B. W. Robinson and others. il Science 148:1111-13 My 21 '65
Eatometer; a device for continuous recording of free-feeding behavior; experiment with rats. D. Fallon. bibliog il Science 148:977-8 My 14 '65; Reply with rejoinder. P. B. Porter. 149:764 Ag 13 '65
Electrical connections between visual cells in the ommatidium of limulus. T. G. Smith and others. bibliog il Science 147:1446-8 Mr 19 '65
Electronic separation of biological cells by volume. M. J. Fulwyler. bibliog il Science 150:910-11 N 12 '65
Glass-coated tungsten microelectrodes. H. A. Baldwin and others. bibliog il Science 148:1462-4 Je 11 '65

PHYSIOLOGICAL chemistry. See Biochemistry

PHYSIOLOGICAL effect of light. See Light—Physiological effects

PHYSIOLOGICAL effects of noise. See Noise—Physiological effects

PHYSIOLOGICAL effects of radioactivity. See Radioactivity—Physiological effects

PHYSIOLOGICAL effects of ultraviolet rays. See Ultraviolet rays—Physiological effects

PHYSIOLOGICAL research
Billy Graham's physical fitness program can help you. C. Mitchell. il Pop Sci 186:61-4+ My '65; Same abr. Read Digest 87:58-62 Jl '65
Birds aid space study. Sci N L 88:34 Jl 17 '65
Cell research gets NIH grant of $1.2 million. Sci N L 88:361 D 4 '65
Lung surfactants, counterions, and hysteresis. E. M. Scarpelli and others. bibliog il Science 148:1607-9 Je 18 '65
Moderate physical tolerance curve urged. R. D. Hibben. Aviation W 82:81+ My 17 '65
Nervous system research with computers. G. D. McCann. bibliog il Science 148:1565-71 Je 18 '65
Physiology of exercise. C. B. Chapman and J. H. Mitchell. il Sci Am 212:88-94+ My '65
Sprinters burn oxygen. Sci N L 87:311 My 15 '65
See also
Space flight—Physiological aspects

PHYSIOLOGY
Human body. il Sci Digest 57:68-81 Mr '65
You're tougher than you think. R. Gannon. il Pop Sci 186:78-81 Ap '65
See also
Dehydration (physiology)
Longevity
Psychology, Physiological
Respiration
Underwater physiology
Weight (physiology)

PHYTADIENES. See Olefins

PHYTANE. See Hydrocarbons

PHYTOHEMAGGLUTININS. See Agglutinins

PHYTOPHTHORA
Bacterial stimulation of sporangium production in phytophthora cinnamomi. G. A. Zentmyer. bibliog Science 150:1178-9 N 26 '65

PHYTOTOXINS. See Toxins and antitoxins

PIANISTS
Especially for pianophiles. R. Kammerer. Am Rec G 31:914-16 My '65
Jazz concerts; eight pianists at Hunter college. W. Balliett. New Yorker 41:190-2 Mr 13 '65
Pianists in full swing. H. Goldsmith. Hi Fi 16:137+ Ja '66

Theme team; duo-pianists Ferrante and Teicher. il Time 85:72 F 5 '65
See also
Barenboim, D.
Browning, J.
Ellington, D.
Horowitz, V.
Michelangeli, A. B.
Rubinstein, A.
Serkin, P.
Taylor, C.

PIANO
How to live with your piano. Bet Hom & Gard 43:46 Mr '65
Los Angeles has a piano museum. il Sunset 134:58 F '65
Physics of the piano. E. D. Blackham. il Sci Am 213:88-96+ bibliog(p 128) D '65
Piano and organ glossary at your finger tips. House & Gard 127:8+ F '65
Piano on the half shell; design for curved keyboard. il Time 85:52 Ap 30 '65

History

Piano in the parlor; excerpts from Polite Americans. G. Carson. il Am Heritage 17:54-9+ D '65

Instruction and study

Piano lessons begin with a good teacher. K. McClelland. il Parents Mag 41:48-50+ Ja '66
Practice! practice! L. Lyons. Vogue 146:160+ D '65
Why they don't teach piano the way they used to. Bet Hom & Gard 43:44 N '65

PIANO competitions. See Music—Competitions

PIANO music
Especially for pianophiles. R. Kammerer. Am Rec G 31:914-16 My '65
See also
Phonograph records—Piano music

PIANOFORTE. See Piano

PIATIGORSKY, Gregor
Wandmanship. il por Time 85:72+ F 5 '65

PICASSO, Jacqueline (Roque)
Jacqueline by Picasso and Picasso by Jacqueline. il por Look 29:58-9+ N 30 '65

PICASSO, Pablo
Art galleries; exhibition at the Perls. R. M. Coates. New Yorker 41:165-6 N 13 '65
Golden Picasso. C. Beaton. il pors Vogue 146:142-5+ S 15 '65
Jacqueline by Picasso and Picasso by Jacqueline. il pors Look 29:58-9+ N 30 '65
Life with Picasso, by F. Gilot and C. Lake. Review
Esquire 63:38+ Mr '65. M. Muggeridge
Picasso's theater period. il Time 86:44 Ag 13 '65

PICK-Sloan plan. See Missouri River—Flood control projects

PICKARD, Tom
Street cleaner with his 18th cent. muck cart; Poem: Sitting in firelight; Poem: Fingers of a hand that whisper softly. Poetry 105:374-6 Mr '65

PICKEREL fishing
Gamefish worth knowing. W. Davis. il Outdoor Life 136:108+ S '65
Pirate of the pads. A. W. Prince. il Outdoor Life 136:48-9+ Ag '65
Water wolves. D. J. Anderson. il Field & S 70:40-2+ Je '65

PICKERELL, Jim
Peasant Pieta; Vietnamese war photograph. il por Newsweek 66:44-5 S 20 '65

PICKERING, William Hayward
He keeps the space shots zooming. il pors Bsns W p 118-20 Ag 14 '65

PICKETT, Clarence Evan
Clarence E. Pickett. H. E. Snyder. por Sat R 48:25+ Ap 24 '65
Clarence Pickett. Nation 200:379 Ap 12 '65
Obituary
Christian Cent 82:389 Mr 31 '65

PICKING of fruit. See Fruit—Picking

PICKLES and relishes
Choose chutney, the versatile condiment. il Bet Hom & Gard 43:108-9 Mr '65
Harvest of relishes; with recipes. il McCalls 92:112-13+ S '65
How a dill pickle gets that way. Good H 160:182 Mr '65
Mango isn't the only chutney. Sunset 135:116-17 Ag '65
Put-up jobs. C. Claiborne. il N Y Times Mag p59 Ag 22 '65
To give with relish. il Ladies Home J 82:64-5+ D '65
Two good ways to use all those tomatoes. B. L. Henry. il Farm J 89:88-9 S '65

PICKPOCKETS. See Thieves

PICKREL, Paul
Edmund Wilson, Lionel Trilling, Philip Rahv.
Harper 232:95-6 Ja '66
New books. See issues of Harper's magazine
Two novelists: outsider and insider. Harper
230:116-18 Je '65
PICKUP campers. See Campers and coaches,
Truck
PICKUP trucks. See Motor trucks
PICKWICK; musical comedy. See Musical
comedies, revues, etc.—Criticisms, plots,
etc.
PICNICS
Bandana birthday. il Pop Gard 17:16 Ja '66
Before the outdoor concert begins, why not
a picnic? il Sunset 135:112+ Ag '65
Here are picnic ideas, if you travel by bike.
il Sunset 135:114+ Jl '65
Keep a picnic in your freezer. il Bet Hom &
Gard 43:82 Jl '65
Party, tail-gate picnic. il Ladies Home J 82:
112-13+ O '65
Turning a picnic into a feast. C. Claiborne.
il N Y Times Mag p76+ Je 6 '65
PICÓN-SALAS, Mariano
Humanist of the Americas. P. Grases. il por
Américas 17:6-10 My '65
PICOTT, J. Rupert
Displacement of experienced teachers with-
out due process. NEA J 54:41 D '65
PICTORIAL history of the United States. See
United States—History, Pictorial
PICTORIAL humor. See Humor, Pictorial
PICTORIAL photography. See Photography,
Artistic
PICTURE books
Boom in picture books. E. Bennett. il U S
Camera 28:68-71+ Mr '65
Wingate Paine: notes from a book in the
making. il Pop Phot 56:100-1 Je '65
PICTURE books for children
Writing the picture book story. M. Calhoun.
il Writer 78:16-19 Ap '65
See also
Caldecott medal
PICTURE frames
Carving more profits out of antique frames;
Mario Broeders. il Bsns W p 190-1 O 9 '65
How to mount and frame a print. S. Kaiser.
il Farm J 89:97 N '65
Making your own picture frames. il Sunset
135:118 N '65
Print framing the easy, inexpensive way.
C. W. Kennedy. il Pop Phot 56:112 Je '65
PICTURE post cards. See Post cards
PICTURE signs. See Signs and signboards
PICTURE tube testers. See Testing instru-
ments
PICTURE tubes. See Television receiving ap-
paratus—Picture tubes
PICTURE windows. See Windows
PICTURED ROCKS NATIONAL LAKESHORE
(proposed) See National parks and reserves
—United States
PICTUREPHONE. See Telephone—Television
combination
PICTURES
See also
Illustration of books and periodicals
Photographs
Mounting
How to mount and frame a print. S. Kaiser.
il Farm J 89:97 N '65
One way to mount a print collection. il Sun-
set 134:92 F '65
Prices
See Art—Prices
PICTURES, Framing of. See Picture frames
PICTURES, Hanging of
How to hang your treasures on the wall. il
House & Gard 127:18-20 My '65
PICTURES, Immoral. See Immoral literature
and pictures
PICTURES, Pasted. See Collage
PICTURES, Theft of. See Art thefts
PICTURES-of-the-year competition. See Pho-
tography—Competitions
PIE
All in favor say: apple pie! il Bet Hom &
Gard 43:88 O '65
Best cream pies you ever tasted. N. Nich-
ols. il Farm J 89:98-9 Ap '65
Crumbs on top, pears inside. il Sunset 135:
238 O '65
Easy as pies; recipes. il Ladies Home J 82:
112-13+ N '65
Farm journal's complete pie cookbook. N.
Nichols. il Farm J 89:90-3 Mr '65
Fresh fruit pie to end a summer supper; chif-
fon pies. il Sunset 134:180 Je '65

Glamorize your pies with new crusts, fancy
edges. N. Nichols. il Farm J 89:83-5+ My
'65
Happy marriage; old-fashioned apple pie;
with recipe. il McCalls 93:28 Ja '66
Holiday pies; with recipes. il McCalls 93:146-
8+ N '65
How to make the pie on the cover; citrus-
cheese. il Bet Hom & Gard 43:89 S '65
Intriguing all around: kahlua pie.   V. V.
Voboril. il Good H 161:132 Ag '65
Mincemeat and apples inside; fruit pudding.
il Sunset 134:185 Mr '65
Old-fashioned apple pie. B. L. Henry. il
Farm J 89:97 Mr '65
Party-best recipe: sunshine pie. Seventeen
24:164 Mr '65
Pumpkin pies. il Bet Hom & Gard 43:101-2
O '65
Successful recipes; different fruit pies. il Suc
Farm 63:121-2 S '65
Why not have apple? with recipes. il Sun-
set 135:76-7 N '65
Winter fruit pies. il Bet Hom & Gard 44:
79-80 Ja '66
PIE, Frozen. See Food, Frozen
PIED-billed grebes. See Grebes
PIEGE pour un homme seul; drama. See Wein-
stock, J.
PIERCE, Bessie
Christmas gifts children can make. Todays
Health 43:40-5 D '65
PIERCE, Bill
Now 15-sec prints! Pop Phot 58:34+ Ja '66
PIERCE, Edith G.
You'll see red when you see these annuals.
Pop Gard 17:24-5+ Ja '66
PIERCE, Edith Lovejoy
Adlai Stevenson; poem. Christian Cent 82:
1010 Ag 18 '65
Ninety-one; poem. Christian Cent 82:199 F 17
'65
To Sviatoslav Richter, Soviet pianist; poem.
Christian Cent 82:889 Jl 14 '65
PIERCE, J. R.
What are we doing to engineering? Science
149:397-9 Jl 23 '65
PIERCE, Noel
Two World's fair rooms your children will
love. Parents Mag 40:78-9+ S '65
PIERCE, Ponchitta
Crime in the suburbs. Ebony 20:167-72 Ag '65
Is it true what they say about twins? Ebony
20:148-50+ S '65
Solicitor General. Ebony 21:67-9+ N '65
PIERCE, R. MacMillan
Trees for the states. Am For 71:4-5+ Ap '65
PIERCED ear earrings. See Earrings
PIERO della Francesca
Piero della Francesca: the impossibility of
painting. P. Guston. il Art N 64:38-9 My
'65
PIERRE-NOEL, Lois Jones
Haitian ceramics celebrates twenty years. il
Negro Hist Bul 28:203-4 My '65
PIERS
How to build piers, floats, boathouses. G.
Daniels. il Pop Sci 186:104-7 F '65
PIERSON, Robert L.
Envoy. New Yorker 40:24-5 F 13 '65
PIERSON, Robert M.
Centralized cataloging: its implications to
personnel; address, November 1963. por Li-
brary J 90:826-8 F 15 '65
PIERSON, T. E. See Keene, L. C. jt. auth.
PIES. See Pie
PIES, Meat. See Cookery—Meat
PIES, Vegetable. See Cookery—Vegetables
PIESTANY, Czechoslovakia
May day in Piešt'any. D. Pryce-Jones. Vogue
145:53+ My '65
PIETA, Transportation of. See Transportation
of works of art
PIEZ, Gladys T.
Library technology. See issues of ALA bul-
letin
PIEZ, Karl A. See Bornstein, P. jt. auth.
PIGEON as food. See Cookery—Poultry
PIGEON racing
Sam's pigeons don't have nuthin' for no-
body; S. De Lucia of Wappingers Falls.
R. H. Boyle. il Sports Illus 23:102-4+ N 22
'65
PIGEONS
Interhemispheric reversal of mirror-image
oblique lines after monocular training in
pigeons. N. K. Mello. bibliog il Science
148:252-4 Ap 9 '65; Discussion. 149:1518-20
S 24 '65
What are we, statues? G. Ace. Sat R 48:16
My 1 '65

PIGEONS—*Continued*
Why a homing pigeon hurries home. C. Morrison. il Look 29:M6-8 F 23 '65
See also
Passenger pigeons
Pigeon racing
    Anecdotes, facetiae, satire, etc.
Manner of speaking; pigeon mail: about banishing pigeons. J. Ciardi. Sat R 48:15 D 18 '65
PIGEONS; drama. See Osgood, L.
PIGMENTS
See also
Carotenoids
PIGMENTS (biology)
Blepharisma intermedium: ultraviolet resistance of pigmented and albino clones. A. C. Giese. bibliog il Science 149:540-1 Jl 30 '65
Hybridization experiments: evidence of dissociation equilibrium in hemerythrin. S. Keresztes-Nagy and others. bibliog il Science 150:357-9 O 15 '65
Organic pigments: their long-term fate. M. Blumer. bibliog il Science 149:722-6 Ag 13 '65
PIGMENTS, Visual. See Retina
PIGORS, Paul
They teach business how to make decisions. il por Bsns W p72+ S 18 '65
PIGS, Wild. See Woods hogs
PIKE, James Albert, bp
Called to servanthood. Christian Cent 82:387 Mr 31 '65
    about
Another Catholic in the White House. V. Eller. Christian Cent 82:1007-8 Ag 18 '65; Discussion. 82:1194-5: 1388-9 S 29, N 10 '65
Attorney for the defense. por Time 86:106 S 17 '65
Bishop Lickfield attacks Bishop Pike. Christian Cent 82:1214 O 6 '65
Pike: heretic or iconoclast? Christian Cent 82:1051 S 1 '65
Pike off the hook. Newsweek 66:56 S 20 '65
Pyrannosaurus Rex; F. M. Brunton charging Bishop Pike with heresy. il por Newsweek 66:56 Ag 30 '65
PIKE, Zebulon Montgomery
How lost was Zebulon Pike? D. Jackson. il por Am Heritage 16:10-15+ F '65
PIKE fishing
Land of record breakers. B. Warner. il Field & S 69:152-4+ Ap '65
PIKES PEAK race. See Automobile racing
PILEGGI, Nicholas
Lying, thieving murdering, upper-middleclass, respectable crook. Esquire 65:50-2+ Ja '66
PILFERING. See Stealing
PILGRIMAGES to Mecca
Moslem world's struggle to modernize. il Time 85:66-73 Ap 16 '65
PILGRIMS and pilgrimages
Harsh testing ground for the faith of hardy pilgrims. il Life 58:64-7 My 28 '65
Miracles of Santiago. J. A. Michener. il Read Digest 87:228-34 Jl '65
Road to Santiago; Spain's ancient road refurbished for modern pilgrims. F. V. Grunfeld. il Reporter 34:40+ Ja 13 '66
PILLAGE
Right to loot? D. Lawrence. U S News 59:100 S 6 '65
PILLOW cases
Pretty pillow projects. C. Houck. il Parents Mag 40:78 Jl '65
PILLOWS
Animal pillows made by you. il Seventeen 24:168 N '65
PILOTING, Airplane. See Airplanes—Piloting
PILOTING, Helicopter. See Helicopters—Piloting
PILOTS and pilotage
Getting there and back; learn piloting. J. A. Emmett. il Outdoor Life 136:94-6 Jl '65
PILPEL, Harriet F.
But you can do that? See last issue of each month of Publishers' weekly
PILTDOWN forgery
Is there a missing link? D. Cohen. il Sci Digest 58:96-7 S '65
PIÑATAS
Piñatas for parties. il Recreation 58:501 D '65
PINAY, Antoine
Bourgeois candidate. il por Newsweek 66:28-9 S 6 '65
PINBALL machines
Wheels and bells of wills and mills: portfolio. Fortune 71:133-5 My '65
PINCK, Dan
Survivor from hell. Reporter 33:53-5 N 4 '65

PINCUS, Walter
Discriminating TV in Jackson, Mississippi. New Repub 152:7-8 Je 5 '65
PINE
Ghosts of Gnarl Ridge. J. E. Kollas. il Am For 71:66-8 My '65
Matter of a piñon. A. Hamilton. il Am For 71:60-1+ My '65
Rare evergreen defies extinction; Torrey pine. H. Bedford. il Audubon Mag 67:182-3 My '65
    Diseases and pests
Timber in the Tetons: the dangerous Mr D; dendroctonus monticolae, mountain pine beetle. il Am For 71:54-5+ S '65
PINE nuts. See Piñon nuts
PINEAL body
Indole compounds: isolation from pineal tissue. W. M. McIsaac and others. bibliog il Science 148:102-3 Ap 2 '65
PINEAL gland. See Glands
PINEAPPLES
See also
Cookery—Fruit
PIÑEIRO, Armando Alonso. See Alonso Piñeiro, A.
PINES, Maya
Coming upheaval in psychiatry. Harper 231: 54-60 O '65
What the talking typewriter says. N Y Times Mag p23+ My 9 '65
PINES. See Pine
PING pong. See Table tennis
PINK-backed pelicans. See Pelicans
PINKERTON'S national detective agency
Battle at Homestead; excerpt from Lockout. L. Wolff. il Am Heritage 16:64-79 Ap '65
PINKS
Carnations and the pinks. il Sunset 135:258 O '65
PINNER, Frank A.
Parental overprotection and political distrust. bibliog f Ann Am Acad 361:58-70 S '65
PIÑON nuts
Matter of a piñon. A. Hamilton. il Am For 71:60-1+ My '65
PIÑON trees. See Pine
PINSON, Penelope
(comp) Books for parents. See issues of Parents' magazine and better homemaking
Yesterday's prophet; Maria Montessori. Parents Mag 40:18 S '65
PINSPOTTERS. See Bowling alleys—Equipment and supplies
PINTAURO, Joseph
Meditation on a scene from the Bergman movie Through a glass darkly, a lonely ocean house; poem. Cath World 201:107 My '65
PINTCHMAN, Charles
Reader's digest gardens. Horticulture 43:34-6 Ag '65
PINTER, Harold
Homecoming. Criticism
    Christian Cent 82:1096-7 S 8 '65
    New Repub 152:29-30 Je 26 '65
    New Yorker 41:50 Jl 31 '65
    Vogue 146:75 S 15 '65
Room. Criticism
    Commonweal 82:193 Ap 30 '65
Slight ache. Criticism
    Commonweal 82:194 Ap 30 '65
PINTOFF, Ernest
Wild, wild East. Newsweek 65:58 Je 21 '65
PINZUTI, Don Mario
Vitamins restore old books at Vatican City laboratory. il Pub W 188:79+ Ag 9 '65
PIONEER probes. See Space probes
PIONEERS
How gold-rush-day doctors battled scurvy. il Todays Health 43:52-3+ O '65
PIPAL, Frank B.
Carbon-zinc batteries. Electr World 74:42-5 O '65
PIPE laying
See also
Helicopters in pipe laying
PIPE lines
See also
Gas, Natural—Pipe lines
Petroleum pipe lines
PIPER, David
I am well, who are you? Esquire 64:80-4+ N '65
PIPER, William Thomas
Man who makes me think young. R. N. Buck. il por Read Digest 86:259-60+ Ap '65
PIPER aircraft corporation
Cost of a seven-week strike: the story told by a computer. U S News 59:64 D 27 '65
How a strike looks to a computer. il U S News 59:98-100 N 15 '65
Man who makes me think young; W. T. Piper. R. N. Buck. il Read Digest 86:259-60+ Ap '65

PIPER aircraft corporation—*Continued*
  Mr Piper's club. J. Gilbert. il Flying 77:30-5 S '65
PIPES, Copper
  Copper tubing: key to easy plumbing. E. F. Lindsley. il Pop Sci 187:134-7+ S '65
PIPES, Plastic
  Plastic pipe cuts plumbing costs. J. H. Ingersoll. il Pop Sci 188:148-50+ Ja '66
PIPES, Water. See Water pipes
PIPPEN, David L.
  Ceramic i.f. filters. Electr World 74:34-5+ N '65
  Line-of-sight nomogram. Electr World 73:27 Mr '65
PIPPIN, Larry L.
  Challenge in Panama. Cur Hist 50:1-7+ Ja '66
PIQUE dame; opera. See Tchaikovsky, P. I.
PIRANHAS
  What's eating them? Newsweek 65:88 Ap 26 '65
PIRATED editions. See Copyright—Unauthorized reprints
PIRELLI, Leopoldo
  New-style Pirelli takes charge. por Fortune 72:104 N '65
PIRES, Fernando Dias de Avila
  Floating community of Amazonas. Natur Hist 74:12-17 O '65
PIRIE, Peter J.
  Unfashionable generation. Hi Fi 16:59-62 Ja '66
PIRO, Joe
  Discothèque. N. Poirier. il por Sat Eve Post 238:21-7 Mr 27 '65
  Discothèque man. C. L. Mee, jr. il por N Y Times Mag p92+ Ja 9 '66
  You start to smile. New Yorker 41:18-19 Jl 10 '65
PIROLO, Charles A.
  Neon lamp wonder. Pop Electr 22:61-4+ Ap '65
PIRONE, P. P.
  How, when and what of spraying roses. Horticulture 43:36-7 Ap '65
  Insect control calendar. Pop Gard 17:20-1 Ja '66
  Pest control on plants indoors. Horticulture 43:26-8 S '65
  Spray schedule for the flower garden. Horticulture 43:34-5 My '65
  Spray schedule for vegetables. Horticulture 43:32-4 Je '65
  Spraying evergreens. Horticulture 43:34-7 F '65
  Spraying small fruits. Horticulture 43:38-9 Mr '65
PIROVANO, Ignacio
  Parthenon and the bull. Américas 17:33-5 Jl '65
PISA
    Campanile (leaning tower)
  Count down for Pisa. G. Kent. il Travel 123:58-60 F '65; Same abr. with title Pisa's problem tower. Read Digest 86:237-8+ F '65
PISSARRO, Camille Jacob
  Camille Pissarro: the unassuming eye; exhibition at Wildenstein's, New York. L. Nochlin. il por Art N 64:24-7+ Ap '65
  Conscience of impressionism; retrospective at Wildenstein gallery. M. Kozloff. Nation 200:430-1 Ap 19 '65
  Impressionist patriarch. J. Canaday. il por N Y Times Mag p 122-3+ Mr 21 '65
  Patriarch. por Newsweek 65:86 Ap 2 '65
PISTOLS
  Elgin knife-pistols. C. G. Worman. il Hobbies 70:124+ S '65
  .45 liberator or underground pistol. C. Worman. il Hobbies 70:114 My '65
  How that new rocket gun works; Gyrojet handgun. K. Warner. il Pop Mech 124:105 N '65
  Remington rolling-block pistol. C. G. Worman. il Hobbies 70:122-3 N '65
  Underhammer pistols. W. R. Orbelo. il Hobbies 70:115+ Ja '66
    See also
    Revolvers
PISTON engines. See Automobile engines
PISTONS
  New engine for space does down-to-earth jobs. H. Walton. il Pop Sci 187:100-5+ Jl '65
PITCH, Musical. See Musical pitch
PITCH, pass and dribble; story. See Rieth, M.
PITCH, Vocal. See Voice
PITCHERS, Baseball. See Baseball players
PITCHING. See Baseball
  Survivor from hell. Reporter 33:53-5 N 4 '65

PITHECANTHROPUS erectus. See Man, Prehistoric
PITKIN, Walter, Jr
  Klein's, Westport, Conn. expands. Pub W 188:58-9 N 29 '65
PITMAN, Sir James
  Our far-flung correspondents; G. B. Shaw's interest in phonetic and initial teaching alphabets. J. Bainbridge. New Yorker 41:164+ N 6 '65
PITOT, Henry C. and others
  Effect of gamma radiation on dietary and hormonal induction of enzymes in rat liver. bibliog Science 150:901-3 N 12 '65
PITTENGER, H. W.
  Ernst Mach: biographical notes. bibliog il Science 150:1120-2 N 26 '65
PITTENWEEM, Scotland
  House among the fisherfolk. R. Kirk. Nat R 18:30 Ja 11 '66
PITTMAN, Eliana
  Eliana Pittman; newest bombshell from Brazil. il pors Ebony 21:62-4+ D '65
PITTOSPORUM
  It's a utility infielder. il Sunset 134:268 My '65
PITTSBURGH
  Golden clean-up. il Life 59:78-9 D 24 '65
  In Harlem and Pittsburgh, limited gains in the fight against rules and red tape. il Arch Forum 123:66-7 Jl '65
  Pittsburgh, pattern for progress. W. J. Gill. il Nat Geog Mag 127:342-71 Mr '65
    Air pollution
  Pittsburgh: how one city did it. T. O. Thackrey. il Sat R 48:46-7 My 22 '65
    Education
  Ford foundation aids Pittsburgh schools. Sr Schol 86:1T-2T F 11 '65
    Housing
  Notable use of light in town houses. il Arch Rec 137:212-13 Ap '65
    Maps
  Better maps; new aerial mapping program. C. B. Genrich, jr. il Am City 80:166+ Jl '65
    Music
  Pittsburgh four. R. J. Croan. Opera N 29:31 My 1 '65
    See also
    Pittsburgh opera company
    Theater
  Upon your imaginary forces. ACT! American conservatory theatre. H. Hewes. Sat R 48:43 S 4 '65
PITTSBURGH opera company
  Pittsburgh. R. J. Croan. il Opera N 30:31 D 11 '65
  Pittsburgh fare. R. J. Croan. Opera N 29:33 F 20 '65
  Steel city stage. Q. Eaton. il Opera N 30:29-32 Ja 22 '66
PITTSBURGH. University
  Fifth year makes the difference. C. P. Williams. il Am Ed 1:6-8 My '65
  Off balance. il Newsweek 66:74 Ag 9 '65
  Pitt's juggler fumbles. Time 86:65+ Jl 2 '65
  What happened at Pitt? il Fortune 72:48 S '65
    Allegheny observatory
    See Astronomical observatories
    Graduate school of library and information sciences
  Kinder, kueche, und bibliotheken; scholarships for women out of school for some time to study for Master's degree in library science. J. Shera. Wilson Lib Bul 40:365 D '65
  Language for librarians; working knowledge in foreign languages. A. C. Hall. il Library J 90:3177-8 Ag '65
PITTSFIELD, Mass.
    Newspapers
  Rare bird; Berkshire Eagle. il Newsweek 66:81 Jl 26 '65
PITUITARY body
  Adrenaline synthesis: control by the pituitary gland and adrenal glucocorticoids. R. J. Wurtman and J. Axelrod. bibliog il Science 150:1464-5 D 10 '65
  Pituitary gland: enzymic formation of methanol from S-adenosylmethionine. J. Axelrod and J. Daly. bibliog il Science 150:892-3 N 12 '65
PITY the poor coots; story. See O'Sullivan, A. D

PITZ, Henry C.
    Ben Eisenstat finds personality in buildings.
        Am Artist 29:56-61+ D '65
    N. C. Wyeth. Am Heritage 16:36-55+ O '65
    Pictures in search of a subject. Am Artist
        29:28-33 N '65
PITZER college, Claremont, Calif.
    Pitzer; profile. M. Franklin. il Mlle 61:148+
        O '65
PIUS XII, pope
    John Tracy Ellis on the pathetic blackout.
        R. A. Graham. America 112:305 Mr 6 '65
    St John and St Pius? por Newsweek 66:86
        N 29 '65
    Under way: sainthood for two former popes.
        U S News 59:10 N 29 '65
PIVER, Arthur
    (ed) See George, M. B. Handling the multi-
        hull
PIZZETTI, Ildebrando
    Clitennestra. Criticism
        Hi Fi por 15:135 Je '65
PLACE for Jimmy; story. See Strauss, T.
PLACEMENT of teachers. See Teachers—Se-
    lection and appointment
PLACENTA
    Clues from the placenta. il Time 85:58-9 Ap
        16 '65
    Pushed out into a hostile world. A. Rosen-
        feld. Life 58:70+ Ap 30 '65
PLACES of retirement. See Retirement, Places
    of
PLACES we lost; story. See Hedin, M.
PLAFKER, George
    Tectonic deformation associated with the
        1964 Alaska earthquake. bibliog Science
        148:1675-87 Je 25 '65
PLAGEMANN, Bentz
    Beautiful to behold; story. Good H 161:70-1
        Jl '65
    I know my love; story. Good H 160:76-7 F
        '65
    Short stories, preface to an episode in life.
        Writer 78:14-15+ Je '65
PLAGIARISM
    Award-winning book proves to be plagiarism;
        Arthur Koestler award competition for
        books written by prison inmates. Pub W
        188:73 N 15 '65
    Peripatetic reviewer. E. Weeks. Atlan 217:
        115-16 Ja '66
PLAGUE
    When black death stalked in London; Great
        plague of 1665. C. V. Wedgwood. il N Y
        Times Mag p92+ S 12 '65
    Year of terror; 300th anniversary of the
        great plague of London. L. M. Rhodes. il
        Todays Health 43:46-8+ D '65
PLAGUE bacilli. See Pasteurella pestis
PLAINS Indians. See Indians of North Amer-
    ica
PLANARIANS
    Nature note; flatworms. Sci N L 88:267 O 23
        '65
    Tail that remembers. il Sci Digest 57:20-1
        My '65
PLANE trees
    Tree grows in Boston; transplant from Cos
        thrives at Harvard medical school. Todays
        Health 43:70 S '65
PLANERS. See Planing machines
PLANETARIUMS
    Planetarium notes. Sky & Tel 30:151-4 S '65
PLANETS
    Astronomy. J. Stokley. See issues of Science
        news letter
    Planetary systems associated with main-se-
        quence stars. H. Brown; reply. A. T.
        Young. Science 148:532 Ap 23 '65
    Sun, moon, and planets this month. See
        issues of Sky and telescope
        See also
    Life on other planets
    Occultations
        also names of planets, e.g. Pluto (planet)

            Temperature and radiation
    Absence of Martian radiation belts and im-
        plications thereof. J. A. Van Allen and
        others. bibliog il Science 149:1228-33 S 10 '65
    Centimeter radiation from planets. il Sky
        & Tel 29:218 Ap '65
    Jupiter's decametric emission correlated with
        the longitudes of the first three galilean
        satellites. G. R. Lebo and others. bibliog
        il Science 148:1724-5 Je 25 '65
PLANETS, Minor. See Asteroids
PLANING machines
    Tool that cuts lumber costs; Belsaw planer.
        R. J. De Cristoforo. il Pop Sci 188:140-1+
        Ja '66

PLANK, John
    Caribbean: intervention, when and how. For
        Affairs 44:37-48 O '65
    Our good neighbors should come first. N Y
        Times Mag p30-1+ Je 6 '65
PLANKTON
    Migrant sound scatterers: interaction with the
        sea floor. J. D. Isaacs and R. A. Schwartz-
        lose. bibliog il Science 150:1810-13 D 31 '65
    Phytadienes in zooplankton. M. Blumer and
        D. W. Thomas. il Science 147:1148-9 Mr 5
        '65
    Predation, body size, and composition of
        plankton. J. L. Brooks and S. I. Dodson.
        bibliog il Science 150:28-35 O 1 '65
    Release of dissolved amino acids by marine
        zooplankton. R. E. Johannes and K. L.
        Webb. bibliog Science 150:76-7 O 1 '65
PLANKTON, Fossil
    Massive extinctions in biota at the end of
        Mesozoic time. M. N. Bramlette. bibliog il
        Science 148:1696-9 Je 25 '65
PLANNED music service. See Muzak corpora-
    tion
PLANNED parenthood. See Birth control
PLANNED parenthood federation of America
    Contraception and morals; concerning ad-
        dress given by Donald B. Straus. America
        112:741 My 22 '65
PLANNERS, City. See City planners
PLANNING, Business. See Business manage-
    ment and organization
PLANNING, Land. See Land utilization
PLANNING of cities. See City planning
PLANT, Richard
    Teaching in triplicate. H. Frankel. Sat R
        48:36-7 Ap 10 '65
PLANT alkaloids. See Alkaloids
PLANT boxes. See Flower boxes, planters, etc.
PLANT breeding
        See also
    Hybridization
PLANT catalogs. See Catalogs, Seed and plant
PLANT cells and tissues
    Callose: lateral movement of assimilates from
        phloem. D. B. Webster and H. H. Currier.
        bibliog Science 150:1610-11 D 17 '65
    Intercisternal elements of the Golgi appa-
        ratus. F. R. Turner and W. G. Whaley.
        il Science 147:1303-4 Mr 12 '65
    Ultrastructure of vegetative and reproductive
        apices of chenopodium album. E. M. Gif-
        ford, jr. and K. D. Stewart. bibliog il Sci-
        ence 149:75-7 Jl 2 '65
        See also
    Chromosomes (botany)
    Stomata

            Culture
    Differentiation of tobacco plants from single,
        isolated cells in microcultures. V. Vasil and
        A. C. Hildebrandt. bibliog il Science 150:
        889-92 N 12 '65
    Visnagin: biosynthesis and isolation from
        ammi visnagi suspension cultures. G. Kaul
        and E. J. Staba. bibliog il Science 150:
        1731-2 D 24 '65
PLANT diseases. See Plants—Diseases and
    pests
PLANT domestication. See Domestication
PLANT equipment. See Factories—Equipment
PLANT holders. See Flower boxes, planters,
    etc.
PLANT lice
    Aphids pose problems for farmers, research-
        ers. Sci N L 88:136 Ag 28 '65
PLANT location. See Location in business and
    industry
PLANT migration. See Plants—Migration
PLANT poisoning. See Poisonous plants
PLANT polysaccharides. See Polysaccharides
PLANT propagation
    Best pansies. il Flower Grower 52:10-11 Ag
        '65
    Growing wildflowers from seed; excerpt from
        Wild flowers and how to grow them.
        E. F. Steffek. il Horticulture 43:40-2 O '65
    Increase chrysanthemums the quick way. B.
        Brinhart. il Flower Grower 52:32 My '65
    Plants indoors. R. C. Hands. il Horticulture
        43:18+ S '65
    Root plants quickly under constant mist.
        J. Simpkins. il Flower Grower 52:20-1 Jl '65
    Ways with dahlias. il Flower Grower 52:30-1
        My '65
PLANT proteins
    Electron microscopic and biochemical charac-
        terization of fraction I protein. R. Hasel-
        korn and others. bibliog il Science 150:
        1598-601 D 17 '65
    Heat stabilities of acid phosphatases from
        pinto bean leaves. R. C. Staples and others.
        bibliog il Science 149:1248-9 S 10 '65

PLANT proteins—*Continued*
Nucleic acid and protein changes in wheat leaf nuclei during rust infection. P. K. Bhattacharya and others. bibliog il Science 150:1605-7 D 17 '65
See also
Ferredoxin

PLANT quarantine
Battle against insects and diseases of plants. B. Black. il Horticulture 43:26-7+ Jl '65
If you are moving plants interstate. B. Black. il Horticulture 43:32-3+ O '65

PLANT relocation. See Location in business and industry

PLANT shelves. See Shelves

PLANTATIONS
Plantation country. P. Deutsch and R. Deutsch. il Holiday 37:30+ My '65

PLANTERS (farm machines)
One-trip sugar beet planters. il Farm J 89:66E Mr '65
See also
Seeding machinery

PLANTERS (flower boxes) See Flower boxes, planters, etc.

PLANTING. See Floriculture; Gardening; Landscape gardening; Plants, Space arrangement of; Seeding; Shrubs—Planting; Tree planting

PLANTING, Roadside. See Roadside improvement

PLANTS
Best plants; symposium. See issues of Flower grower, the home garden magazine
Canadian plant physiology; report on Canadian society of plant physiologists meeting. J. A. Webb. Science 150:787+ Jl '65
For 1966. il Horticulture 44:18-21+ Ja '66
Knowing look at fifty annuals new this year. Sunset 134:236-7 Mr '65
[Month] in your garden. See issues of Sunset
More new plants for 1965. il Horticulture 43:40-2+ F '65
New plants for 1966. M. Ohlander. Flower Grower 53:51-2+ Ja '66
Paraffinic hydrocarbons in pasture plants. J. Oró and others. bibliog il Science 147:870-3 F 19 '65
This is my favorite. See issues of Popular gardening & living outdoors
See also
Annuals (plants)
Bulbs
Flowers
Forcing (plants)
Herbs
House plants
Parasitic plants
Perennials
Sap
Shrubs
Vegetables

All America selections
All-America flowers for 1966. il Flower Grower 53:28-9 Ja '66
All-America roses for 1966. Flower Grower 52:15 Jl '65
All-America roses for 1966. il Horticulture 43:34-5 Jl '65
All-America winners 1966; newest in annuals. H. R. O'Brien. il Pop Gard 17:26-9 Ja '66
Here's the news in new roses; All-America annuals for 1966 are stunners. il Sunset 136:121-3 Ja '66
Next year's champions; All-America roses for 1966. il Pop Gard 16:24-5 Jl '65
Trio of new roses comes to the fore. il House & Gard 128:170 S '65

Assimilation
See also
Photosynthesis

Collection and preservation
Lewis and Clark expedition's botanical discoveries. R. D. Burroughs. il Natur Hist 75:56-62 Ja '66

Diseases and pests
Danger signs in plants. F. E. Bear. il Horticulture 43:26-7 Je '65
Density-gradient centrifugation: non-ideal sedimentation and the interaction of major and minor components. M. K. Brakke and J. M. Daly. bibliog il Science 148:387-9 Ap 16 '65
H&G's 1965 guide to plant protection; comp. by C. Westcott. il House & Gard 127:210-14 Ap '65
See also
Crown gall
Nematodes
Plant quarantine

Spraying and dusting
also subhead Diseases and pests under names of plants. e.g. Corn—Diseases and pests

Drought resistance
Plants to beat drought. il Flower Grower 52:34-5 Ag '65

Electrophysiology
See Electrophysiology of plants

Fertilization
See Fertilization of plants

Fire resistance
Plants resistant to fire; replacing highly inflammable chaparral with fire-resistant plants. Sci N L 88:124 Ag 21 '65

Hardiness
What causes plant hardiness? G. J. Buck. Horticulture 43:22-3 O '65
See also
Plants—Drought resistance

Insect resistance
Marigolds help kill tiny worms in fields. Sci N L 88:110 Ag 14 '65

Metabolism
Roots as organs of assimilation of sulfate. J. S. Pate. bibliog il Science 149:547-8 Jl 30 '65
Transhydrogenation in root tissue: mediation by carbon dioxide. I. P. Ting and W. M. Dugger, jr. bibliog il Science 150:1727-8 D 24 '65

Migration
Migration of a plant; Kentucky bluegrass. R. W. Schery. il Natur Hist 74:40-5 D '65

Nutrition
See also
Photosynthesis

Physiology
See Botany—Physiology

Quarantine
See Plant quarantine

Reproduction
Biology of reproduction in ferns. K. A. Wilson. il Natur Hist 74:52-9 Je '65
Ontogeny of adventive embryos of wild carrot. W. Halperin and D. F. Wetherell. bibliog il Science 147:756-8 F 12 '65
See also
Parthenocarpy

Sodium content
Transport of sodium in plant tissue. D. W. Rains and E. Epstein. bibliog il Science 148:1611 Je 18 '65

Soilless culture
How to grow plants without soil. il Good H 161:140 Ag '65

Sulfur content
Roots as organs of assimilation of sulfate. J. S. Pate. bibliog il Science 149:547-8 Jl 30 '65

Temperature
Heat transfer in plants. D. M. Gates. il Sci Am 213:76-84 bibliog(p 128) D '65

Translocation
Density-gradient centrifugation: non-ideal sedimentation and the interaction of major and minor components. M. K. Brakke and J. M. Daly. bibliog il Science 148:387-9 Ap 16 '65
Transport of sodium in plant tissue. D. W. Rains and E. Epstein. bibliog il Science 148:1611 Je 18 '65
See also
Botany—Physiology

Transpiration
Convection plumes from ulmus americana L. E. B. Peterson and A. W. H. Damman. bibliog il Science 148:392-3 Ap 16 '65; Discussion. 149:764; 150:783, 1629 Ag 13, N 5, D 17 '65
Heat transfer in plants. D. M. Gates. il Sci Am 213:76-84 bibliog(p 128) D '65
Sap pressure in vascular plants. P. F. Scholander and others. bibliog il Science 148:339-46, 1488 Ap 16, Je 11 '65; Reply with rejoinder. W. R. Gardner and S. L. Rawlins. 149:920+ Ag 27 '65
Transpiration and the stomata of leaves. P. E. Waggoner and I. Zelitch. bibliog il Science 150:1413-20 D 10 '65

PLANTS—*Continued*

Water requirements

How to make plants less thirsty. S. V. Jones. Sci Digest 58:35 D '65

If your plants aren't healthy, check your water supply. G. Arthur. il Flower Grower 52:35 O '65

PLANTS, Age of. See Age (plants)

PLANTS, Climbing. See Climbing plants

PLANTS, Cover. See Cover plants

PLANTS, Effect of air pollution on

Air pollution affects pattern of photosynthesis in parmelia sulcata a corticolous lichen. L. Pearson and E. Skye. bibliog il Science 148:1600-2 Je 18 '65; Reply. R. H. Linnell. 149:1267 S 10 '65

PLANTS, Effect of aluminum on

DNA synthesis in aluminum-treated roots of barley. M. Sampson and others. bibliog il Science 148:1476-7 Je 11 '65

PLANTS, Effect of carbon dioxide on

CO_2-lifesaver for greenhouse plants. R. S. Lindstrom and J. J. Marks. il Horticulture 43:24-5 D '65

PLANTS, Effect of chemicals on

Tobacco seedlings: damage by excessive nitrogen lessened by added phosphorus. N. L. Pal and R. J. Ojha. Science 151:106 Ja 7 '66

PLANTS, Effect of climate on

Climate and plants. W. C. Steere. il Horticulture 43:26-7+ F '65

Letter from Paris; effect of chilly June and hot July on peach regions of the Rhône-Alpes area. Genêt. New Yorker 41:118+ Ag 21 '65

Ways to make dry weather hurt less. R. E. Geyer. Suc Farm 63:28+ Jl '65

PLANTS, Effect of drought on. See Plants—Drought resistance

PLANTS, Effect of light on

Abscisin II: inhibitory effect on flower induction in a long-day plant. L. T. Evans. bibliog il Science 151:107 Ja 7 '66

Fluorescent light fixture design. H. B. Kirkley. il Horticulture 43:18-19+ N '65

PLANTS, Effect of nitrogen on

Snatch nitrogen from air. Sci N L 87:68 Ja 30 '65

PLANTS, Effect of radiation on

Bacteria on leaf surfaces and in intercellular leaf spaces. E. H. Barnes. il Science 147:1151-2 Mr 5 '65

Harm in irradiated sugar? Sci N L 89:43 Ja 15 '66

PLANTS, Effect of radioactivity on

Alamogordo, mon amour. W. L. Laurence. il Esquire 63:118-21+ My '65

Relative radiosensitivities of woody and herbaceous spermatophytes. R. C. Sparrow and A. H. Sparrow. bibliog il Science 147:1449-51 Mr 19 '65

PLANTS, Effect of solar radiation on

Heat transfer in plants. D. M. Gates. il Sci Am 213:76-84 bibliog(p 128) D '65

PLANTS, Effect of temperature on

Crown-gall tumorigenesis: effect of temperature on wound healing and conditioning. J. Lipetz. bibliog il Science 149:865-7 Ag 20 '65

Physiological predetermination: inhibition, respiration, and growth of lima bean seeds. L. W. Woodstock and B. M. Pollock. il Science 150:1031-2 N 19 '65

Polyploidy and environment in Arctic Alaska. A. W. Johnson and J. G. Packer. bibliog il Science 148:237-9 Ap 9 '65

PLANTS, Flowering of

Abscisin II: inhibitory effect on flower induction in a long-day plant. L. T. Evans. bibliog il Science 151:107 Ja 7 '66

Ultrastructure of vegetative and reproductive apices of chenopodium album. E. M. Gifford, jr. and K. D. Stewart. bibliog il Science 149:75-7 Jl 2 '65

PLANTS, Food

Gourmet botanist. New Yorker 41:43 N 6 '65

See also
Greens, Edible
Vegetables

PLANTS, Indoor. See House plants

PLANTS, Medical. See Botany, Medical

PLANTS, Medicinal. See Botany, Medical

PLANTS, Ornamental

Accent on foliage. D. Biddle. il Pop Gard 16:14+ Ap '65

Accent on foliage: rhubarb, caladiums, and bergenia. il Flower Grower 52:31 F '65

Small trees for big effect. H. Mason. il Bet Hom & Gard 43:56-9 Je '65

PLANTS, Poisonous. See Poisonous plants

PLANTS, Potted

How to select pots for your plants. il Good H 160:151 F '65

Pot plants with a modern touch. W. Radcliffe. il Pop Gard 16:45 My '65

Pot spring bulbs now for color and fragrance this winter. J. Shiels. il Horticulture 43:24-5+ O '65

Put your greenhouse to work. C. H. Potter. il Horticulture 44:32-3+ Ja '66

Small ones into big ones; repotting. Sunset 134:280 Mr '65

Small trees for big effect. H. Mason. il Bet Hom & Gard 43:56-9 Je '65

You get to know them if you grow them in containers. il Sunset 134:108-11 Je '65

See also
Flower boxes, planters, etc.
House plants

PLANTS, Protection of

Gardening inside a cage; protection from birds and animals. il Sunset 134:287 My '65

Home garden notebook. J. B. Brimer. il Flower Grower 52:33-4 N '65

How to over-winter aquatic plants. P. A. Nutt. il Horticulture 43:34-5+ N '65

Plastic to the rescue. L. Johnson. il Pop Gard 16:10 My '65

See also
Mulching
Wilt pruf

PLANTS, Rare

Plant collector's corner. See issues of Sunset to May 1965

Plants out-of-the-ordinary. C. W. Wood. See issues of Flower grower, the home garden magazine to March 1965

PLANTS, Rock garden

See also
Saxifrages

PLANTS, Shade

Beauty for your shady spots. il Am Home 68:54-5 Ap '65

Plants that brighten the shade. il Bet Hom & Gard 43:72-3 My '65

PLANTS, Space arrangement of

Corn soybeans sorghum: how thick should you plant? W. L. Colville and L. E. Zeman. il Suc Farm 64:36-7+ Ja '66

Here come those thirty-inch corn rows. D. Seim. il Farm J 89:32-3+ My '65

PLANTS, Training of

Here is how to cascade chrysanthemums. il Sunset 134:265 My '65

Some easy ways to support vines, perennials, trees. V. Howie. il Horticulture 43:42-3 Je '65

PLANTS, Watering of. See Watering of plants

PLANTS for shady places. See Plants, Shade

PLANTS in design. See Design, Decorative—Plant forms

PLANTS in house decoration

White House flowers. il Good H 162:64-7 Ja '66

PLANTS on other planets. See Life on other planets

PLAQUES, plaquettes

Animal pinup plaques. D. Swartwout. il Pop Mech 124:156-9 O '65

Fancy frame-ups: wooden wall plaques with any paper picture. il Seventeen 24:128 Je '65

PLASMA (ionized gases)

Where is science taking us? excerpt from Trieste symposium published under title, Plasma physics. W. B. Thompson. il Sat R 48:72 O 2 '65

PLASMA, Blood. See Blood—Plasma

PLASMA arc scalpel. See Surgical instruments

PLASMA membranes

Plasma membranes: phospholipid and sterol content. L. A. E. Ashworth and C. Green. bibliog il Science 151:210-11 Ja 14 '66

Separation and partial purification of plasma-membrane fragments from Ehrlich ascites carcinoma microsomes. V. B. Kamat and D. F. H. Wallach. bibliog il Science 148:1343-5 Je 4 '65

PLASMODIUM (parasite)

Disappearance of a genetic marker from a cytoplasmic hybrid plasmodium of a true slime mold. N. S. Kerr. bibliog il Science 147:1586-8 Mr 26 '65

PLASMODIUM infection. See Malaria

PLASTER and plastering

Time-proven tips for installing plasterboard. C. E. Rhine. il Pop Sci 187:120-3 S '65

PLASTIC boats. See Boats—Materials

PLASTIC domes. See Domes

PLASTIC fabrics

Some new stick-down materials. il Consumer Bul 48:36-7 My '65

PLASTIC isolators. See Hospitals—Isolation departments
PLASTIC mulch. See Mulching
PLASTIC paint. See Paint
PLASTIC panels. See Paneling
PLASTIC pipes. See Pipes, Plastic
PLASTIC roofs. See Roofs
PLASTIC sheeting
Break in the making for acrylic sheet; production process developed by Swedlow, inc. il Bsns W p 186+ O 23 '65
PLASTIC surgery. See Surgery, Plastic
PLASTIC swimming pools. See Swimming pools
PLASTIC teeth. See Teeth, Artificial
PLASTICS
Anyone can sculpt. il Design 66:20-1 Mr '65
Bigger profits with plastic tunnels. B. Hardy. il Farm J 90:52H Ja '66
Clear field for PVC; polyvinyl chloride. il Bsns W p90+ Ap 17 '65
Copper's competitors race for its markets; aluminum, plastics, and clad metals. il Bsns W p86+ D 11 '65
New stretchy plastic can cover wires, cables; made of polyethylene plastic and butadiene. Sci N L 87:265 Ap 24 '65
Only the game remains the same; synthetics replace traditional materials of sport; with account by L. Smith. il Sports Illus 23:32-9 S 27 '65
Plastics: the outdoor type. il Good H 161:158 Jl '65
Protect corn with plastic. P. W. Rexroat. il Suc Farm 63:74 O '65
    See also
Polyethylene
Resinous products
Thermoplastics
Wilt pruf

Exhibitions

New world of plastic; Interplas 65 exhibition, London's Olympia hall. B. Plumb. il N Y Times Mag p66-7 Je 13 '65

Metal coating

Plated plastics hit a big market; uses in autos, radios, and appliances. il Bsns W p 103-4+ O 16 '65
PLASTICS, Cellular
Ingenuity in building an elliptical roof. il Arch Rec 138:177-8 Ag '65
PLASTICS, Laminated
Putting new life in old volumes; interview. R. I. Boak. il Pub W 188:115-18 Jl 19 '65
PLASTICS, Reinforced
New medium for sculpture. il Design 66:15 Mr '65
PLASTICS, Transparent
Break in the making for acrylic sheet; production process developed by Swedlow, inc. il Bsns W p 186+ O 23 '65
Preserved insects; entomologist embeds specimens in permanent plastic cases. il Design 66:11-13 My '65
PLASTICS industry and trade
Plastics show takes the train; U.S. exhibitor operates from four railroad cars International plastics exhibition in London. il Bsns W p92-4 Jl 3 '65
Why Polymer curbs its ingenuity. il Bsns W p42-4 Jl 3 '65
    See also
Tupperware home parties, incorporated

Wages and hours

Earnings in miscellaneous plastics products, June 1964. G. L. Stelluto. il Mo Labor R 88:558-61 My '65
PLATES, Glass. See Glassware
PLATH, Sylvia
November graveyard; poem. Mlle 62:134 N '65
    about
Dying is an art. G. Steiner. Reporter 33:51-4 O 7 '65
PLATING
    See also
Electroplating
PLATING on plastics. See Plastics—Metal coating
PLATO
Trial and death of Socrates; concerning four dialogues. K. Rexroth. il Sat R 48:31+ S 11 '65
PLATON, Nicholas
Kato Zakro: rediscovered palace. Horizon 7:76-9 Sum '65
PLATT, John R.
Step to man; excerpt. Science 149:607-13 Ag 6 '65
Step to man; excerpt. UNESCO Courier 18:4-9+ D '65

PLATT, June
Iced food cook book. House & Gard 128:117+ Ag '65
PLATT, Rutherford
Can science produce life? Read Digest 87:189-90+ Jl '65
Invisible multitudes in your life. Read Digest 86:213-14+ F '65
PLAUT, Fred
Portraits simply made. H. Keppler. il Mod Phot 29:92-3 F '65
PLAY
Let's bring back children's play; with study-discussion program, by R. Strang. E. Harris and D. Harris. bibliog il PTA Mag 60:28-30, 35 S '65
Play is more than fun and games. R. W. Bacmeister. il Parents Mag 40:62-3+ D '65
What do they need to play with? with study-discussion program by D. Harris and E. Harris. R. H. Ojemann. bibliog il PTA Mag 59:37-9, 43-4 F '65
PLAY houses. See Playhouses
PLAY of Daniel. See Drama, Medieval
PLAY of Herod. See Drama, Medieval
PLAY on words. See Puns and punning
PLAY production. See Theatrical production
PLAY writing. See Drama—Technique
PLAYBOY (periodical)
Empire built on sex; with report by D. Lurie. il Life 59:68-73 O 29 '65
"It", up to date; photograph of a nude actress. Time 85:58 Je 4 '65
PLAYBOY clubs. See Night clubs
PLAYER, Gary
I feel awful. il por Time 86:53 Jl 2 '65
Player and the course; Bellerive country club. por Newsweek 66:52-3 Jl 5 '65
Spanish discover golf and its Player. A. Wright. il por Sports Illus 23:69-71 O 11 '65
Two foreign blokes shock the slammers. A. Wright. il por Sports Illus 22:24-31 Je 28 '65
PLAYER piano
Player piano is back in a popular key. il Bsns W p 148+ O 23 '65
PLAYFAIR, John H. L. and others
Focal antibody production by transferred spleen cells in irradiated mice. bibliog il Science 149:998-1000 Ag 27 '65
PLAYGROUND activities
Events that are special; symposium. il Recreation 58:174-6 Ap '65
PLAYGROUND manuals. See Recreation—Administration
PLAYGROUNDS
For young children in a changing world; education facilities in Scandinavia. L. L. Gore. il Sch Life 47:4-7 D '64
Parks and playgrounds. See issues of American city
Playground in Kiwiland; Wanganui, New Zealand. E. A. Scholer. il Recreation 58:392-3 O '65
Playground issue. il Recreation 58:cover+ Ap '65
Save our children's playgrounds. V. Musselman. Parents Mag 40:40+ Ag '65
What parents ask about children's playgrounds. M. J. E. Senn. il McCalls 92:46+ Je '65
    See also
Recreation
    also subhead Parks and playgrounds under names of cities, e.g. New York (city)—Parks and playgrounds

Equipment

Horsy set; cast-stone horsies. il Time 85:68 F 12 '65
Junkyard playgrounds. il Time 85:63 Je 25 '65
Outdoor play areas; excerpts from Physical education for children. E. Halsey and L. Porter. il Recreation 58:189-90 Ap '65
Planning play areas. D. Bridgeman. il Recreation 58:169-70 Ap '65
Tot area on a shoe string; Albuquerque, N.Mex. V. L. Bedford. il Recreation 58:171-2 Ap '65
Yankee slicker; infield rain-covers. il Recreation 58:195-6 Ap '65

Safety devices and measures

Let's make our playgrounds safer. R. Charles. il Parents Mag 40:80-1+ S '65

Surface treatment

Playground surfing; Tampa. D. M. Barksdale. il Recreation 58:183-4 Ap '65
PLAYGROUNDS, Home

Equipment
    See also
Merry-go-rounds

PLAYGROUNDS, School. See School grounds

PLAYHOUSES
Build a Hansel and Gretel playhouse. E. W. Flemming. il Parents Mag 40:146 N '65
Fort: building from driftwood and seaweed on Connecticut shore. New Yorker 41:27-8 Jl 31 '65
House without a tree: designed for W. S. Robinson of Eugene, Ore. il Sunset 135:103-4 S '65
How you can build an A-frame playhouse. R. S. Wilkes. il Pop Sci 187:124-6 Jl '65
It has an outdoors, an indoors, an upstairs, and a downstairs. il Sunset 135:60-1 Jl '65

PLAYING cards. See Cards

PLAYMATES
Friendships are for growing. S. H Fraiberg. il Parents Mag 40:66-8+ D '65
When to interfere with children's friendships. D. Siegel. il Parents Mag 40:56-8+ My '65

PLAYRIGHT. See Copyright

PLAYROOM; drama. See Drayton, M.

PLAYS. See Dramas

PLAYS on records. See Phonograph records—Spoken records

PLAYWRITING. See Drama—Technique

PLAZA hotel. See New York (city)—Hotels, restaurants, etc.

PLEASANTS, Henry
Crescendo on the campus: our new music centers. Reporter 33:52-6 S 23 '65

PLEASANTS, Julian
Gas warfare. Commonweal 82:209-12, 455 My 7, Je 25 '65

PLEASANTVILLE, N.Y.
Reader's digest gardens. C. Pintchman. il Horticulture 43:34-6 Ag '65

PLEASURE
See also
Happiness

PLEASURE of your company; story. See Harvey, R.

PLEIADES
Pleiades form is analyzed. T. D. Nicholson. il Natur Hist 74:46-8 D '65

PLEISTOCENE period. See Geology, Stratigraphic—Pleistocene; Paleontology—Pleistocene; Stone age

PLENDERLEITH, Harold J.
New science of art conservation. UNESCO Courier 18:7-10 Ja '65
—and others
Mohenjo-Daro. UNESCO Courier 18:22-6 Je '65

PLENUM press
How can I find out? il Sci Digest 57:36-7 My '65

PLESCA, Otto J. and others
Antibodies to DNA and a synthetic polydeoxyribonucleotide produced by oligodeoxyribonucleotides. bibliog Science 148:1102-3 My 21 '65

PLEUROPNEUMONIALIKE organisms. See Microorganisms, Pathogenic

PLIMMER, Charlotte, and Plimmer, Denis
Remarkable new life of John Profumo. McCalls 92:60-1+ Jl '65

PLIMMER, Denis. See Plimmer, C. jt. auth.

PLIMPTON, Francis T. P.
Preserving the peacekeeping powers of the General assembly; statement, June 15, 1965. Dept State Bul 53:218-20 Ag 2 '65
U.N. peacekeeping committee meets; U.S. refutes charges on Viet-Nam; statement, March 26, 1965. Dept State Bul 52:598-600 Ap 19 '65
United States announces pledge for Palestine refugees; statement, February 17, 1965. Dept State Bul 52:390-1 Mr 15 '65
U.S. calls for deeds, not words, in U.N. committee on defining aggression; statements, April 5 and April 8, 1965. Dept State Bul 52:775-85 My 17 '65

PLIMPTON, George
But why me, coach? Sports Illus 23:18-21 D 13 '65
Celestial hell of the superfan. Sports Illus 23:104-6+ S 13 '65
Detroit Lions' remarkable screwball: Alex Karras; excerpt from Paper lion. Harper 232:76-82 Ja '66
World champion is refused a meal. Sports Illus 22:24-7 My 17 '65

PLITVICE LAKES
Traveler's choice. F. R. Smith. Travel 125:58 Ja '66

PLOTS (drama, novel, etc)
Back to beginnings; reprint. P. M Daltry. Writer 78:14-15 Jl '65

Plot, a pattern created by people. P. S. Curry. Writer 78:20-6+ F '65
Plots and plans. P. Ketchum. Writer 78:23-5 Je '65
Slick pattern. M. F. Shyer. Writer 78:12-14 Ag '65

PLOTTING (graphs) See Graphic methods

PLOVERS
Nature note; Kittlitz's sand plover. Sci N L 87:303 My 8 '65

PLOWDEN, David
Solemn journey. il U S Camera 28:58-61 N '65

PLOWMAN, Marilyn
Hand of God; poem. Christian Cent 82:1569 D 22 '65
Two gardens; poem. Christian Cent 82:910 Jl 21 '65

PLOWSHARE project. See Atomic blasting

PLUMB, Barbara
Home. See occasional issues of New York times magazine

PLUMB, Harmon H. and Cataland, George
Acoustical thermometer. bibliog Science 150:155-61 O 8 '65

PLUMB, J. H.
Enemies of his early years. Sat R 48:33 My 29 '65
Harbingers of holocaust. Sat R 49:33 Ja 15 '66
He came to claim his empire. Sat R 48:57 O 2 '65
Literary Churchill. Sat R 48:17-20+ F 6 '65
Minister's report on the past. Sat R 48:27-8 Mr 27 '65

PLUMBING
Copper tubing: key to easy plumbing. E. F. Lindsley. il Pop Sci 187:134-7+ S '65
Distribution of laboratory services. il Arch Rec 138:186-90 N '65
Is your plumbing double-crossing you? danger of cross-connections. R. Day. il Pop Mech 124:160-3+ Ag '65
Water: visual, aural and salutary delight. il House & Gard 127:150-3+ Mr '65
Where's that drain stoppage? L. Weaver. il Pop Sci 187:126-7 D '65

PLUME moths. See Moths

PLURALITY of worlds. See Life on other planets

PLUTARCH
Classics revisited. A. Rexroth. Sat R 48:29 Je 12 '65

PLUTO (planet)
Closest approaches of Pluto and Neptune. G. S. Mumford, 3d. Sky & Tel 29:157-8 Mr '65
Pluto larger than previously estimated. Sci N L 87:261 Ap 24 '65
Pluto's diameter. il Sky & Tel 30:213 O '65
Pluto's rotation and diameter. il Sky & Tel 29:141 Mr '65
Possible occultation by the planet Pluto. I. Halliday. il Sky & Tel 29:216-17 Ap '65

PLUTONIUM
isotopes
NASA sees rising need for isotopes. H. Taylor. Miss & Roc 16:12 Ap 26 '65

PLYFOAM. See Thermoplastics

PLYWOOD
How to use plywood on ceilings and walls. il Suc Farm 63:86A F '65
Workshop: vacuum forming of plywood. D. Bjorkman. il Craft Horiz 25:38-40 S '65

PLYWOOD industry
See also
Georgia-Pacific corporation
United States plywood corporation

PLYWOOD paneling. See Paneling

PNEUMATIC passenger transportation. See Transportation, High speed

PNEUMATIC trains. See Railroads—Trains

POACHING
Gator poachers. G. Laycock. il Field & S 70:40-3+ Jl '65

POCKET billiards. See Billiards

POCKET books, incorporated
Doctor Spock loses first round in Pocket books suit. Pub W 188:67 D 27 '65
Doctor Spock sues pocket books for ruling to end inserts. Pub W 188:52 O 25 '65
Pocket books' art direction committee of consultants to the art director. Pub W 189:90 Ja 3 '66
Pocket books presents Pope with luxurious paperback; Pacem in terris. il Pub W 188:28-30 O 18 '65

POCKET gophers. See Gophers

POCONO MOUNTAINS, Pa.
Pennsylvania's Poconos. A. R. Pastore, jr. il Travel 123:36-8 Ap '65

POETS, Somali
See also
Bonderi, E.

POETS, Welsh
See also
Thomas, D.

POETS manuscripts. See Manuscripts

POGODIN, Nikolai
Kremlin chimes. Criticism
New Yorker 41:80+ Mr 6 '65

POGONOPHORA. See Marine worms

POGUE, Forrest C.
Marshall papers: volume II; Pearl Harbor blunders; excerpt from George C. Marshall: the war years. Look 29:34-9 D 14 '65

POHL, Frederik
Long John Nebel and the woodlouse; address, December 8, 1964. por Library J 90:4704-8 N 1 '65

POINSETT, Alex
Poverty amidst plenty. Ebony 20:104-6+ Ag '65
Should confessions be outlawed? Ebony 20:173-4+ My '65
Tragedy of a compulsive gambler. Ebony 21:133-4+ D '65

POINT. See Education—Washington (state)

POINT, Critical. See Critical point

POINT REYES PENINSULA. See Reyes, Point, Calif.

POINTERS (dogs)
Some grousing about no grouse; Grand national grouse championship, Allegheny national forest, Pa. D. Barnes. Sports Illus 23:79-80 D 13 '65
This all-around dog idea. D. M. Duffey. il Outdoor Life 135:170+ Ap '65

POINTILLISM. See Impressionism (art)

POINTY shoes; story. See Saroyan, W.

POIRIER, Normand
Discothèque. Sat Eve Post 238:21-7 Mr 27 '65

POIRIER, Richard
Morbid-mindedness. Commentary 39:91-4 Je '65

POISONING. See Poisons

POISONOUS gases in warfare. See Gases in warfare

POISONOUS mushrooms. See Mushrooms

POISONOUS plants
All around the place. J. Milton. Pop Gard 16:49 Ap '65
Annals of medicine; jimson weed poisoning. B. Roueché. New Yorker 41:180+ My 15 '65
Careful, the lovely plant may be a killer. il Consumer Bul 48:2+ My '65
Don't eat the rhododendrons. T. Sterne. il Am For 71:40-1+ Mr '65
Please don't eat the oleander. N. Nilsson. il Pop Mech 124:112-14+ Ag '65
Watch out, don't poison your livestock. J. B. Herrick. Suc Farm 63:39 Ag '65
Witch's garden. D. Jacob. il Pop Gard 16:32-3+ N '65
See also
Mushrooms

POISONOUS snakes. See Snakes

POISONS
Menace of childhood poisoning; first aid advice. G. G. Greer. Bet Hom & Gard 43:34 My '65
Poison proof your home. M. Gleason. Parents Mag 40:34+ Mr '65
Poison-proof your home, first-aid for poisoning. G. E. Maxwell. Todays Health 43:77-8 Mr '65
Poisonings: their prevention and treatment. L. W. Sauer. il PTA Mag 60:33-4 O '65
What do you know about accidental poisoning? H. L. Verhulst. il PTA Mag 59:29-31 Mr '65
See also
Drugs
Fish poisons
Insecticides
Triazolo pyrimidin amino

POKER
Poker. J. Richardson. Esquire 64:144+ D '65

POL, Therese
Angelica Balabanoff: 1878-1965. Nation 201:482-3 D 13 '65

POLANCO-ABREU, Santiago
Economic development of Puerto Rico; address, February 24, 1965. Vital Speeches 31:418-21 My 1 '65

POLAND
Half-way approach stalls Poland's drive. il Bsns W p 192 N 20 '65

Retrogression in Poland. R. F. Staar. bibliog f il Cur Hist 48:154-60+ Mr '65
See also
Agriculture—Poland
Bialowieza Forest
Concentration camps—Poland
Crime and criminals—Poland
Economic assistance in Poland
Jews in Poland
Music—Poland
Publishers and publishing—Poland
Science—Poland
United States—Commerce—Poland
Youth—Poland

Boundaries
Atlantic report. Atlan 216:14+ Ag '65
Of hope & *heimatsrecht*. il Time 86:33 D 3 '65
Poland's new far west. H. Koningsberger. il Harper 231:86-93 Jl '65
United States reiterates position on Polish-German boundary; statement, April 27, 1965. Dept State Bul 52:757 My 17 '65

Civilization
Polish scene; excerpt from Under pressure. A. Alvarez. Commentary 39:75-9 Mr '65

Description and travel
Poland's new far west. H. Koningsberger. il Harper 231:86-93 Jl '65

Economic conditions
Atlantic report. Atlan 216:14+ Ag '65
Poland's perennial problem. C. McWilliams. Nation 201:118-21 S 6 '65

Foreign relations
Beginning of a dialogue? Polish-German relations. il Time 86:18-19 D 24 '65
Poland takes a French lesson. P. Ben. Reporter 33:38-9 N 18 '65

Industries
Butchers on the block. Newsweek 66:56+ N 15 '65
Poland's perennial problem. C. McWilliams. Nation 201:118-21 S 6 '65

Politics and government
Atlantic report. Atlan 216:14+ Ag '65
Poland takes a French lesson. P. Ben. Reporter 33:38-9 N 18 '65
Poles apart. F. Y. Blumenfeld. Newsweek 65:65 Je 14 '65
Rebuilding the bridge to Poland. T. Atkins. il Reporter 32:39-41 F 25 '65

POLAND and the United States
Invitation to a conversation; art and congressmen exchange. Nation 201:515 D 27 '65

POLANSKI, Roman
Headstrong directors. H. Alpert. Sat R 48:63 O 16 '65

POLAR bears. See Bears

POLAR ice. See Ice—Polar Regions

POLAR lights. See Auroras

POLAR REGIONS
See also
Antarctic Regions
Ice—Polar Regions

POLAR research
Antarctica: congressional urge for tidy research administration manifests itself in new proposal. D. S. Greenberg. Science 148:1304-5 Je 4 '65
Antarctica: world's most fascinating icebox. I. Wolfert. Read Digest 87:119-23 S '65
Four brutal years on a floating ice island; Arlis II. H. Shuldiner. il Pop Sci 187:50-4 Jl '65
Life at Antarctic U. T. O. Jones. il Am Ed 1:29-32 N '65
Science probes Antarctica. B. Tufty. il Sci N L 87:358-9+ Je 5 '65

POLAR strike. See Military maneuvers

POLARIS. See Pole star

POLARIS submarines. See Submarine boats, Atomic powered

POLARIZATION (fluorescence) See Polarization (light)

POLARIZATION (light)
Fluorescence polarization: measurement with ultraviolet-polarizing filters in a spectrophotofluorometer. R. F. Chen and R. L. Bowman. bibliog il Science 147:729-32 F 12 '65
How to get the most out of polarizers. M. Bernam. il Pop Phot 56:84-7+ Je '65

POLAROID color film. See Photography—Films

POLAROID corporation
Swinging Polaroid. il Time 86:95-6 S 24 '65

POLAROID Land cameras
Fully manual: Polaroid Land 180. C. W. Kennedy. il Pop Phot 58:126-7 Ja '66
In close with Polaroid. il U S Camera 28:56 F '65
Kids aid Kennedy fund; picture taking with Polaroid Land camera and initiative. D. Barry. il Pop Phot 56:22+ F '65
New Polaroid Land close-up camera. N. Rothschild. Pop Phot 56:84+ Ap '65
New Polaroid Land portrait camera. N. Rothschild. il Pop Phot 56:56-7+ Ap '65
Newest Polaroid Land cameras. il Consumer Bul 48:2+ O '65
Pictures in a moment. J. Wolbarst. See issues of Modern photography
Polaroid in lower price range with two new ones. J. Wolbarst. il Mod Phot 29:33 Je '65
Polaroid's new $20 camera swings! J. Wolbarst. il Mod Phot 29:96-7+ S '65
Polaroid's Swinger, it does and it doesn't. il Consumer Rep 30:521-2 N '65
Polaroid's $20 Swinger. H. M. Kinzer. il Pop Phot 57:66-7+ S '65
Swinger. il U S Camera 28:18-19 S '65
Swinger, new $20 Polaroid. E. H. Ortner. il Pop Sci 187:76-8 Ag '65
Swinging Polaroid; first low-priced model. il Time 86:95-6 S 24 '65
Three photographers try the Swinger. G. Pyle; C. Reynolds; J. Durniak. il Pop Phot 57:68-9+ S '65

POLAROID wraparound sunglasses. See Sun glasses

POLE star
Orbital motion of Polaris. G. S. Mumford. Sky & Tel 30:218 O '65

POLE vaulting. See Vaulting (sport)

POLECATS
See also
Skunks

POLES
See also
Electric lines—Poles

POLES, Telegraph. See Electric lines—Poles

POLES, Telephone. See Electric lines—Poles

POLESTAR. See Pole star

POLI, Kenneth
Fellow photographers, do you need a little black book? Pop Phot 57:98-9 O '65
Jewel in the junkbox. Pop Phot 56:104-5+ Je '65
Six modern conveniences and how to overcome them. Pop Phot 56:72-3+ Ap '65

POLIAKOV, Léon
Spy of God. Commentary 40:67-70 Ag '65

POLICE

Equipment
Soon: new weapons for policemen. il U S News 59:9 Ag 2 '65

Forms, blanks, etc.
Revised report speeds police work; Chula Vista, Calif. V. H. Seiveno. il Am City 80: 42 F '65

Public relations
Police under pressure. D. Clark. Cath World 202:228-32 Ja '66
Special unit revives police-community relations; San Francisco. T. J. Cahill. il Am City 80:166+ Je '65

Salaries
Trends in salaries of firemen and policemen. A. Sackley. il Mo Labor R 88:159-63 F '65

Great Britain
Crime does pay because we do not back up the police. Shawcross. il N Y Times Mag p44-5+ Je 13 '65

United States
Birch policemen; reply. D. W. Bullock. Commonweal 81:594 F 5 '65
By the book; police role in racial conflicts. Newsweek 65:34+ Mr 1 '65
Cheers and death; law enforcement problem. Commonweal 82:134-5 Ap 23 '65
Cops as robbers. R. L. Smith. il Nation 200: 102-7 F 1 '65
Cops, guns and homicides. S. Rubin. il Nation 201:527-9 D 27 '65
Courts vs the police. Life 58:4 My 21 '65
Crime in the cities: an unnecessary crisis. W. Bowen. il Fortune 72:140-5+ D '65
Crisis in crime control. G. R. Blakey. America 113:238-40 S 4 '65
How-to; books on race attitudes of police. Reporter 32:14-15+ My 20 '65
Is crime in U.S. out of hand? why LBJ worries; with interview with F. E. Inbau. il U S News 58:38-43 Mr 22 '65

Letter from Los Angeles. D. A. Elliott. Nat R 17:862-3 O 5 '65
Necessary force, or police brutality? T. R. Brooks. il N Y Times Mag p60-1+ D 5 '65
Police brutality: fact or fiction? FBI statistics show civilian brutality against police practiced widely. il U S News 59:37-40 S 6 '65
Police brutality: how much truth; how much fiction? J. E. Hoover. il U S News 59: 116-17+ S 27 '65
Police departments next in line for federal aid? il U S News 59:58 S 20 '65
Police find lawyer friends; right of law-abiding citizens to freedom from criminal molestation. Life 59:4 Ag 20 '65
Police neutral in riots. Sci N L 88:135 Ag 28 '65
Police under pressure. D. Clark. Cath World 202:228-32 Ja '66
Policeman. il Sat Eve Post 238:100 Mr 13 '65
Policing the police; undesirable restrictions by Supreme court. H. L. Packer. New Repub 153:17-21 S 4 '65; Reply. J. R. Piland. 153:38 O 16 '65
Remarks to the New York police department Holy name society, April 4, 1965. W. F. Buckley, jr. Nat R 17:324-6 Ap 20 '65
This month's feature: moves to strengthen law enforcement. Cong Digest 44:225-56 O '65
U.S. judge would restrict police; excerpts from letter with reply by N. B. Katzenbach. D. L. Bazelon. U S News 59:66-7 Ag 16 '65
What do we want from our policemen? S. Grafton. il McCalls 92:110-11+ My '65
When the cops were not handcuffed. Y. Kamisar. il N Y Times Mag p34-5+ N 7 '65
Who polices the police? disagreement concerning civilian police review boards. il Time 85:58 Ap 30 '65
See also subhead Police under names of states, cities, etc. e.g. Chicago—Police

Vietnam (Republic)
Powerful white mice; South Viet Nam's national police. Time 86:38 D 10 '65

POLICE, State

Training
Fast-reflex school for patrolmen; California highway patrol academy. M. Mann. il Pop Mech 124:96-100 Ag '65

POLICE ambulances. See Ambulances

POLICE communication systems
Police and fire reporting on a single circuit; Tarrytown, N.Y. il Am City 80:103 Mr '65

POLICE dogs
See also
Watchdogs

POLICE motor vehicles. See Motor vehicles, Police

POLICE radio
Radio, data processing speed police work. Am City 81:51 Ja '66

POLICE state. See Totalitarianism

POLICE stations
Police building for a suburban area; borough of Paramus, N.J. il Arch Rec 137:169 My '65

POLICE uniforms. See Uniforms, Police

POLICEMEN. See Police

POLICEWOMEN
My daughter, the policeman. il Ebony 20: 82-4+ O '65

POLIDORA, V. J. and others
Phenylketonuria in rats: reversibility of behavioral deficit. bibliog Science 151:219-21 Ja 14 '66

POLIKOFF, Barbara
Think of them; story. Redbook 125:60-1 My '65

POLING, Irving
What's Watts? Hot Rod 18:108-9 Je '65

POLING, James
College diplomats at work. Read Digest 86: 197-8+ My '65

POLIOMYELITIS
They stopped a tropical epidemic. J. Winchester. il Todays Health 43:32-3+ D '65

Prevention and control
Polio now conquered. Sci N L 87:258 Ap 24 '65

Vaccines
Are you immune to polio? Todays Health 43: 67 Ag '65
Salk says man is challenge. il Sci N L 87: 258-9 Ap 24 '65

POLISH, David
Statement on the Jews: an inadequate document. Christian Cent 82:1475-7 D 1 '65

POLISH visitors in the United States. See Foreign visitors in the United States

POLISHING materials
Care and safekeeping of stainless steel, chromium, and aluminum. House & Gard 129:29-30+ Ja '66
Copper, brass, and pewter. House & Gard 128: 52-3+ N '65
How to keep your silver shining. il Consumer Bul 48:19-20 Mr '65
Metal polishes. il Consumer Rep 30:255-7 My '65
POLISTES. See Hornets
POLITBURO. See Communist party (Russia) —Political bureau
POLITE, Frank
Black butterflies; poem. Nation 200:116 F 1 '65
In silver spring; poem. Reporter 32:36 Ap 22 '65
Letter from Duluth; poem. Poetry 106:279-81 Jl '65
POLITENESS. See Courtesy
POLITICAL activators. See Pressure groups
POLITICAL asylum. See Asylum, Right of
POLITICAL attitudes
Danger of labels. W. V. Kennedy. America 113:717-18 D 4 '65
On being tough. W. Pfaff. Commonweal 82: 430-1 Je 25 '65
Political socialization: its role in the political process; symposium, ed. by R. Sigel. bibliog f il Ann Am Acad 361:1-140 S '65
See also
Public opinion
POLITICAL bosses. See Boss rule
POLITICAL campaigns
Bobby twins revisited; R. Kennedy charged with ruthlessness in campaign issues. H. Golden. Esquire 63:42-5 Je '65
Bobby's image. T. Smith. Esquire 63:62-3+ Ap '65
Kennedys in New York; excerpts. G. Gardner. il McCalls 92:100-3+ Ag '65
Man who ran the show; R. Price, manager of Lindsay campaign. Newsweek 66:34 N 15 '65
Rabbi as candidate. Newsweek 66:63 S 13 '65
See also
Campaign funds
Candidates, Political
Television in politics

Anecdotes, facetiae, satire, etc.
Pocketful of golumpkis. J. Kobrin. il Sat Eve Post 238:22 N 20 '65

Ceylon
More like a thorn. il Newsweek 65:44 Mr 29 '65

France
Circus star. Newsweek 66:35-6 Ag 16 '65
French elections: Gaullism after de Gaulle. C. Sterling. il Reporter 33:33-6 D 16 '65
Shedding the shell; de Gaulle's belated campaign. Time 86:32 D 3 '65
Stooping to conquer; de Gaulle and other campaigners. Newsweek 66:50 D 6 '65

Germany (Federal Republic)
Intimations of immortality. Newsweek 66:44 S 27 '65
Knocking eggheads together. il Time 86:26 Jl 23 '65
Last weeks. il Time 86:30 S 3 '65
Making of the chancellor 1965. il Newsweek 66:26 S 6 '65
Neck und neck; Erhard's C.D.U. as Willy Brandt's Socialist party. il Time 86:27 Jl 9 '65
Non-campaigners. J. Dornberg. il Newsweek 66:32+ Jl '65
Piglet for onkel; election campaign. il Time 86:33 Ag 20 '65
They're off! il Newsweek 66:35 Ag 23 '65

Norway
Shadowboxing; electing new Parliament. Newsweek 66:42 S 13 '65

Pakistan
Ayub's basic democracy. R. Knox. il Reporter 32:34-6 F 11 '65
POLITICAL candidates. See Candidates, Political
POLITICAL cartoons. See Caricatures and cartoons
POLITICAL clubs and associations
ACU: a statement of principle. Nat R 17: 177 Mr 9 '65
Growing up right; Young Republican national federation. Newsweek 65:27-8 Je 28 '65
Liberals strike back at Goldwater win; Young Republicans. M. S. Evans. Nat R 17:584+ Jl 13 '65

Republicans after the debacle; Wednesday club. P. Duke and S. Meisler. Reporter 32: 26-8 F 11 '65
Ripon report: on Republican presidential campaign. il Time 85:24-5 F 19 '65
See also
Free society association
Freedom house (organization)
POLITICAL conventions
See also
National conventions
POLITICAL corruption. See Politics, Corruption in
POLITICAL economy. See Economics
POLITICAL education. See Political science —Study and teaching
POLITICAL ethics
Historian looks at our political morality. H. S. Commager. Sat R 48:16-18 Jl 10 '65
Treason of the experts. E. Bentley. Nation 201:466-70 D 13 '65
Whistle blowing in the dark. Reporter 33:22 S 23 '65
POLITICAL forecasts
Look ahead by the Republicans; interview. E. M. Dirksen. U S News 60:70-4 Ja 17 '66

Anecdotes, facetiae, satire, etc.
Political almanac for '66. W. V. Shannon. Commonweal 83:393-5 Ja 1 '66
POLITICAL indoctrination. See Indoctrination
POLITICAL interest groups. See Pressure groups
POLITICAL kidnaping. See Kidnaping
POLITICAL liberty. See Liberty
POLITICAL literature
Liberal establishment, by M. S. Evans. Review
Nat R 17:832 S 21 '65. W. F. Rickenbacker
See also
Political science—Periodicals
POLITICAL parties
Parties and the masses. K. H. Silvert. bibliog f Ann Am Acad 358:101-8 Mr '65

Austria
Tales of the Vienna hoods; downfall of F. Olah. G. Bailey. il Reporter 32:36-40 Mr 25 '65

Canada
Where socialism failed close to home; Cooperative commenwealth federation. T. Drury. il Nations Bsns 53:66-8+ O '65

Chile
Breakthrough in Chile. D. D. Ranstead. Commonweal 82:82-3 Ap 9 '65
Chile's Christian democrats. New Repub 152: 6 Mr 20 '65
Where does Chile go from here? Christian democratic party. T. Mitchell. il Nat R 17: 275-7 Ap 6 '65

France
French elections: Gaullism after de Gaulle. C. Sterling. il Reporter 33:33-6 D 16 '65
French politics at the municipal level. E. Taylor. il Reporter 32:31-2 Ap 8 '65
Hanging together. Newsweek 65:46 Je 21 '65
Letter from Paris: Municipal elections in metropolitan France and its overseas départements. Genêt. New Yorker 41:167-8+ Mr 20 '65
See also
Communist party (France)

Germany (Federal Republic)
At stake in the German elections. E. M. von Kuehnelt-Leddihn. Nat R 17:813 S 21 '65
Atlantic report. Atlan 216:41-2+ S '65
Fragile china; Christian democrats annual convention. Time 85:31 Ap 9 '65
German elections. E. M. von Kuehnelt-Leddihn. Nat R 17:913 O 19 '65

Great Britain
British politics in the collectivist age, by S. H. Beer. Review
Nat R 17:988-9 N 2 '65. J. Hart
Liberal outlook. Newsweek 66:27 S 6 '65
See also
Conservative party (Great Britain)
Labor party (Great Britain)

India
Suicide of the Indian left. P. G. Altbach. Christian Cent 82:1190-2 S 29 '65

Italy
Bigger opposition; Social democratic party vote to merge with the Socialists of Pietro Nenni. Time 87:25B Ja 21 '66

POLITICAL parties—Italy—*Continued*
Catholics left and right. G. D. Kumlien. Commonweal 82:16-17 Mr 26 '65
Closing the socialist ranks. Newsweek 67: 41-2 Ja 24 '66
Florentines: hope of Italy? G. Natoli. il Cath World 200:339-45 Mr '65
Italy: a lay state? role of the Christian democratic party. R. A. Graham. America 112:241 F 20 '65

Japan
Political movements in Japan. N. Kishi. For Affairs 44:90-9 O '65

Latin America
Communists, Socialists, and Christian democrats; with questions and answers. T. Szulc. Ann Am Acad 360:99-109 Jl '65
Democratic revolutions; growth of Christian democracy. R. Caldera. il Commonweal 83: 120-4 O 29 '65

Peru
Peru: encouraging new spirit. J. C. Carey. bibliog f Cur Hist 49:321-7 D '65

Puerto Rico
When violence struck at the Capitol; congressman in House shot by members of Nationalist party, March 1, 1954. il Sr Schol 86:4 F 25 '65

Russia
See also
Communist party (Russia)

Tanganyika
One-party system in Tanganyika. H. Glickman. bibliog f Ann Am Acad 358:136-49 Mr '65

United States
Grant or Greeley? the abolitionist dilemma in the election of 1872. J. M. McPherson. bibliog f Am Hist R 71:43-61 O '65
How to rebuild the two-party system. S. M. Lipset; discussion. Harper 230:6+ F '65
Politics and federalism: party or anti-party? W. Buchanan. bibliog f il Ann Am Acad 359:107-15 My '65
What is wrong with both parties. D. Lawrence. U S News 59:128 S 13 '65
See also
Communist party (United States)
Democratic party
Liberal party (United States)
Republican party

Venezuela
Democratic revolution in Venezuela. R. J. Alexander. Ann Am Acad 358:150-8 Mr '65
How Castro spreads the revolution; FALN goals. R. S. Strother. Read Digest 87:205-6+ N '65
Letter from Caracas; tactics of F.A.L.N. B. Taper. il New Yorker 41:111-12 +Mr 6 '65
Political experiment in Venezuela. R. J. Alexander. Cur Hist 49:336-41+ D '65

POLITICAL patronage. See Patronage, Political

POLITICAL philosophy
Consciencism, by K. Nkrumah. Review
Sat R 48:27 Mr 6 '65. C. Miller
Founding of new societies, by L. Hartz and others. Review
Nation 200:562-4 My 24 '65. H. Zinn
Hans Zehrer as a neoconservative elite theorist. W. Struve. bibliog f Am Hist R 70:1035-57 Jl '65
Problems of dictatorship; the Russian experience. J. R. Strayer. For Affairs 44:264-74 Ja '66
Recent trends in political theory and political philosophy. K. W. Deutsch and L. N. Rieselbach. bibliog f il Ann Am Acad 360: 139-62 Jl '65
Revolt against ideology. H. D. Aiken; discussion. Commentary 38:14+ S; 69-76 O '64; 39: 8+ F '65
Teilhard de Chardin and the Afro-Asian world. T. P. Melady and M. B. Melady. Cath World 202:102-6 N '65
See also
Liberalism
Political thought

POLITICAL power. See Power (political science)

POLITICAL pressure. See Pressure groups

POLITICAL prisoners
They fight to free the world's prisoners of conscience. I. Ross. Read Digest 86:131-5 F '65

POLITICAL prisoners, Exchange of
More refugees, more blackmail; Fidel style swap. il Time 86:38+ O 29 '65

POLITICAL public speaking. See Public speaking

POLITICAL publicity. See Television in politics

POLITICAL reporting. See Reporters and reporting

POLITICAL responsibility. See Responsibility

POLITICAL science
New nations: the problem of political development; symposium, ed. by K. Von Vorys. bibliog f il Ann Am Acad 358:1-179 Mr '65
Political and sociological theory and its applications, by G. E. G. Catlin. Review
Nat R 17:884-5 O 5 '65. C. Bauman
See also
Conservatism
Equality
Liberalism
Liberty
Nations
Political philosophy
Power (political science)
Socialism
Statism

Bibliography
See also
Political science literature

Periodicals
Magazines of dissent thrive on unpopularity. C. Lasch. il N Y Times Mag p 10-11+ Jl 18 '65

Study and teaching
Young America's newest vocation; awakening the disadvantaged and the disinterested to their political opportunities and responsibilities. A. I. Waskow. il Sat R 48:12-14+ Je 5 '65

POLITICAL science literature
Books in the field: political science. N. W. Polsby. bibliog il Wilson Lib Bul 40:432-9 Ja '66

POLITICAL theory. See Political philosophy; Political science

POLITICAL thought
Accidental century, by M. Harrington. Review
Commentary 41:84-7 Ja '66. G. Kateb
American directions; a forecast. P. F. Drucker. Harper 230:39-45 F '65; Reply. E. A. Menuez. 230:6 My '65
Child's image of government. D. Easton and J. Dennis. bibliog f il Ann Am Acad 361: 40-57 S '65
Japan in neutral. P. W. Quigg. For Affairs 44:253-63 Ja '66
New dimension in political thinking, by W. J. Thorbecke. Review
Sat R 48:36 D 18 '65. K. W. Thompson
New look on the left; solidarity forever? il Newsweek 65:29-32 My 24 '65
Nonalignment as a diplomatic and ideological credo. K. I. Babaa and C. V. Crabb, jr. bibliog f Ann Am Acad 362:6-17 N '65
Recent trends in political theory and political philosophy. K. W. Deutsch and L. N. Rieselbach. bibliog f il Ann Am Acad 360:139-62 Jl '65
Socialism and capitalism; an international misunderstanding. R. K. White. il For Affairs 44:216-28 Ja '66
Terror in the streets? W. Sparks. Commonweal 82:345-8 Je 4 '65

POLITICS
New nations: the problem of political development; symposium, ed. by K. Von Vorys. bibliog f il Ann Am Acad 358:1-179 Mr '65
Politics of ambiguity. E. J. Hughes. Newsweek 66:13 Ag 23 '65
See also
Conservatism
Economics and politics
Lawyers in politics
Liberalism
Lobbying
Political clubs and associations
Political science
Right and left (political science)
Scientists—Political activities
Teachers—Political activities
Television in politics
Women and politics
World politics
also subhead Politics and government under names of countries, e.g. France—Politics and government

Terminology
Words in the news (cont) Sr Schol 87:51 S 30 '65

POLITICS, Corruption in
  All for love; full pardon to F. Boykin. Time 86:15A D 31 '65
  Atlantic report; Italy; scandals nourish cynicism of voters. Atlan 216:23-4+ D '65
  Billion-dollar mystery; with editorial comment, F. J. Cook. il Nation 200:377-8, 380-97 Ap 12 '65
  Cleaning up the Illinois legislature: a follow-up report. P. Simon. Harper 231:125 S '65
  Despoilers of democracy, by C. R. Mollenhoff. Review
    Sat R 48:45 N 20 '65. N. S. Finney
  Florida's legislature: the pork chop state of mind. R. Sherrill. Harper 231:82+ N '65
  Justice must begin in the lowest courts; corrupt practices of Philadelphia's magistrates. Life 59:8 O 8 '65
  Scandal in Ottawa. il Time 86:34 Jl 9 '65
    See also
  Boss rule
  Bribery
  Lobbying
  Patronage, Political
  Teapot Dome case
POLITICS and art. See Art and politics
POLITICS and authors. See Authors and politics
POLITICS and business. See Business—Political aspects
POLITICS and education
  Political control in the state colleges of Pennsylvania. M. Anello. bibliog f Sch & Soc 93:83-5 F 6 '65; Reply with rejoinder. R. E. Heiges. 93:236-6 Ap 17 '65
  Political socialization: its role in the political process; symposium, ed. by R. Sigel. bibliog f il Ann Am Acad 361:1-140 S '65
    See also
  College students—Political activities
POLITICS and newspapers. See Newspapers and politics
POLITICS and religion. See Church and politics
POLITICS and science. See Science and state
POLITZER, Robert L.
  Foreign language curriculum and its shifting foundations. bibliog f Sch & Soc 93:249-52 Ap 17 '65
POLK, William R.
  Nature of modernization; the Middle East and north Africa. For Affairs 44:100-10 O '65
POLL tax
  Congress and the poll tax. A. M. Bickel. New Repub 152:11-12 Ap 24 '65; Reply. J. L. Rauh, jr. 152:28-9 My 8 '65
  Kennedy amendment. Nation 200:631+ Je 14 '65
  Teddy's triumph; Kennedy amendment to voting-rights bill. Newsweek 65:27-8 My 24 '65
  Voting rights bill, third edition. A. M. Bickel. New Repub 152:13-14 My 22 '65
POLLACK, Jack Harrison
  Folly of overplacement. NEA J 54:10-13 F '65
  Making hospital rounds with the science lady. Todays Health 43:37-41 My '65
POLLACK, Joan Diehl. See Crescitelli, F. jt. auth.
POLLARD, Ernest C. and others
  Ionizing radiation: effect of irradiated medium or synthetic processes. bibliog Science 147:1045-7 F 26 '65
POLLARD, G. F.
  Objections to Thomism. America 112:842 Je 12 '65
POLLARD, James
  Our far-flung correspondents. H. W. Wind. il New Yorker 41:138-46+ My 22 '65
POLLEN
  Germination of lily pollen: respiration and tube growth. D. B. Dickinson. bibliog il Science 150:1818-19 D 31 '65
POLLEN, Fossil
  Origin of ice ages: pollen evidence from Arctic Alaska. P. A. Colinvaux; reply with rejoinder. W. L. Donn and M. Ewing. il Science 147:632-3 F 5 '65
  Prehistoric maize in southeastern Virginia. D. R. Whitehead. bibliog il Science 150:881-3 N 12 '65
POLLEY, E. H. and others
  Botulinum toxin, type A: effects on central nervous system. bibliog Science 147:1036-7 F 26 '65
POLLEY, Margaret J. and Müller-Eberhard, H. J.
  Complement: increased efficiency of the second component after treatment with iodoacetamide. bibliog Science 148:1728-9 Je 25 '65
POLLINATION. See Fertilization of plants

POLLINGER, Kenneth J.
  On thinking Latin American. America 113:214-15 Ag 28 '65
POLLOCK, B. M. See Woodstock, L. W. jt. auth.
POLLUTION, Air. See Air pollution
POLLUTION, Water. See Water pollution
POLLUTION of streams. See Water pollution
POLNER, Murray
  Need for suburban planning. America 112:188-90 F 6 '65
  Prisoners by due process. Nation 200:262-3 Mr 8 '65
POLONIUM
  Amount of polonium 210 in tobacco differs. Sci N L 88:249 O 16 '65
  Polonium-210 analyses of vegetables, cured and uncured tobacco, and associated soils. K. C. Berger and others. bibliog il Science 150:1738-9 D 24 '65
  Polonium-210 content of mainstream cigarette smoke. T. F. Kelley. bibliog il Science 149:537-8 Jl 30 '65
  Polonium-210 in leaf tobacco from four countries. L. P. Gregory. bibliog il Science 150:74-6 O 1 '65
POLSBY, Nelson W.
  Books in the field: political science. bibliog Wilson Lib Bul 40:432-9 Ja '66
  Representing the House. Reporter 32:40+ My 6 '65
POLTERGEISTS. See Ghosts
POLYAMINO acids. See Amino acids
POLYARTHRITIS. See Arthritis
POLYDEOXYRIBONUCLEOTIDES. See Nucleotides
POLYETHYLENE
  Intercrystalline links in bulk polyethylene. H. D. Keith and others. Science 150:1026-7 N 19 '65
  Plastic sheeting, a useful aid; hotbed covers. S. Caldwell. il Flower Grower 52:6+ Ap '65
POLYGAMY
  Church and marriage in Africa. K. Hughes. Christian Cent 82:204-8 F 17 '65
    See also
  Mormons and Mormonism
POLYGRAPHS
    See also
  Lie detectors
POLYIMIDES. See Resinous products
POLYLYSINE
  Genetic control in guinea pigs of immune response to conjugates of haptens and poly-L-lysine. B. B. Levine and B. Benaceraaf. bibliog il Science 147:517-18 Ja 29 '65
POLYMER corporation
  Why Polymer curbs its ingenuity. il Bsns W p42-4 Jl 3 '65
POLYMERIZATION
  Hemoglobin polymerization in mice. A. Riggs. bibliog il Science 147:621-3 F 5 '65
POLYMERS
  Crystallization and molecular folding. P. H. Lindenmeyer. bibliog il Science 147:1256-62 Mr 12 '65
  Dislocation networks in folded-chain polyethylene crystals. V. F. Holland and P. H. Lindenmeyer. bibliog il Science 147:1296-7 Mr 12 '65
    See also
  Silicones
POLYMORPHISM (biology)
  Autosomally determined polymorphism of glucose-6-phosphate dehydrogenase in peromyscus. C. R. Shaw and E. Barto. bibliog il Science 148:1099-100 My 21 '65
  Biochemical polymorphism in ants. J. H. Law and others. bibliog il Science 149:544-6 Jl 30 '65
  Polymorphic spermatozoa in the hymenopterous wasp dahlbominus. P. E. Lee and A. Wilkes. bibliog il Science 147:1445-6 Mr 19 '65
  Polymorphism of human lactate dehydrogenase isozymes E. S. Vesell. bibliog il Science 148:1103-5 My 21 '65
  Polymorphism of lactate dehydrogenase in gelada baboons. F. N. Syner and M. Goodman. bibliog il Science 151:206-8 Ja 14 '66
  Species and geographic differences in the transferrin polymorphism of macaques. M. Goodman and others. bibliog il Science 147:884-6 F 19 '65
POLYNESIA
  Landfalls in Polynesia. P. Fleming. il Holiday 37:62-3+ Mr '65
    See also
  Marquesas Islands
POLYNESIAN sculpture. See Sculpture, Polynesian

POLYNESIANS. See Hawaiians

POLYOMA virus. See Tumor viruses

POLYPEPTIDES. See Peptides

POLYPLOIDY. See Chromosomes (botany)

POLYRIBOSOMES. See Nucleoproteins

POLYSACCHARIDES
Callose: lateral movement of assimilates from phloem. D. B. Webster and H. H. Currier. bibliog Science 150:1610-11 D 17 '65
Involvement of thymus in immune response of rabbits to somatic polysaccharides of gram-negative bacteria. M. Landy and others. bibliog il Science 147:1591-2 Mr 26 '65

POLYSOMES. See Nucleoproteins

POLYTECHNIC institute, Brooklyn
Big, little Brooklyn Poly. il Sci Digest 58:78-83 N '65

POLYTETRAFLUORETHYLENE. See Teflon

POLYVINYL chloride. See Plastics

POMERANCE, Josephine W.
Meeting U.N. crises: let us seek basic solutions. Bul Atomic Sci 21:31-2 My '65

POMEROY, Kenneth B.
Seeds for agreement. Am For 71:16-18+ Je '65
—See Dana, S. T. jt. auth.

POMEROY, Laurence
Contrasts in Europe. Atlan 216:106-8+ Jl '65

POMODORO, Arnaldo
Dissatisfied Aristotle. il Time 86:74-5 D 3 '65
Pomodoro: the jewelry of Arnaldo and Giò. E. Ritter. il por Craft Horiz 25:8-11 Jl '65

POMODORO, Giò
Pomodoro: the jewelry of Arnaldo and Giò. E. Ritter. il por Craft Horiz 25:8-11 Jl '65

POMPANO BEACH, Fla.
Make a charming entrance. L. F. Betts. il Am City 81:94-5 Ja '66

POMPIDOU, Georges
Policy of France; address, June 17, 1965. Vital Speeches 31:617-19 Ag 1 '65

about
De Gaulle's dauphin. por Newsweek 66:38 Ag 9 '65
Find another de Gaulle. E. Behr. il por Sat Eve Post 238:28-9 D 4 '65
Letter from Paris. Genêt. New Yorker 41:83-4 Ag 7 '65

PONCE, Puerto Rico

Galleries and museums
Hexagons under the sun. il Time 87:59 Ja 7 '66

PONCET, Andre Francois-. See Francois-Poncet, A.

PONCET, Tony
Notes from our correspondents. R. McMullen. Hi Fi 15:24+ Jl '65

PONCIRUS trifoliata. See Trifoliate oranges

POND, Elizabeth
Vulnerability; poem. Seventeen 24:200 My '65

PONDS
First aid for leaky ponds. R. D. Wennblom. il Farm J 89:26-7+ Ag '65

PONELEIT, C. G. and Alexander, D. E.
Inheritance of linoleic and oleic acids in maize. bibliog Science 147:1585-6 Mr 26 '65

PONIES
Chromosome complement: a fertile hybrid between equus prejawalskii and equus caballus. L. Koulischer and S. Frechkop. bibliog il Science 151:93-5 Ja 7 '66
Compact-size ponies. il Look 29:M8 N 16 '65
Horses in the living room; A. and T. Assael of Long Island. D. P. Mannix. il Sat Eve Post 238:36-7 Je 5 '65
Swimming pony. J. S. Doty. il Look 29:M8-10 Je 1 '65

PONNAMPERUMA, Cyril
Ames exobiologists provide major link in understanding origin of life on earth. il por Miss & Roc 17:38-9 Ag 16 '65
—and Mack, Ruth
Nucleotide synthesis under possible primitive earth conditions. bibliog Science 148:1221-3 My 28 '65
—and Peterson, Etta
Peptide synthesis from amino acids in aqueous solution. bibliog Science 147:1572-4 Mr 26 '65

PONSELLE, Rosa
Stars at home: Villa Pace, Green Spring Valley, Md. il pors Opera N 29:14-16 F 6 '65

PONSONBY, Sir Frederic Cavendish
Harrowing ordeal of Colonel Ponsonby. T. N. Carmichael. il por Life 58:89+ Je 11 '65

PONTI, Carlo
Bigamy Italian style. D. J. Hamblin. por Life 59:52A-52B Jl 23 '65
Concubinage, Italian style. por Time 85:56 F 19 '65
Name is Ponti, not Mr Loren. I. Shenker. il pors N Y Times Mag p32-3+ Je 6 '65

PONTIAC, Mich.

Education
Individualized physical activity; program at the primary level. J. M. Young. il NEA J 54:22-3 D '65

Hospitals
Lethal ether. il Time 86:92+ D 10 '65

PONTIAC motor division. See General motors corporation—Pontiac motor division

PONTOON boats. See Boats and boating

POOL (game) See Billiards

POOL tables. See Billiard tables

POOLE, Frazer G.
Chapter I for Chicago circle. Library J 90:5198-200 D 1 '65

POOLE, Ralph. See Murray, S; Spencer, M. jt. auths.

POOLE, Stafford
American seminary education. America 113:288-9 S 18 '65
Diocesan priest and the intellectual life; excerpt from Seminary in crisis. Commonweal 82:78-81 Ap 9 '65

POOLS. See Garden pools; Swimming pools

POONS, Larry
Three new cool, bright imagists. E. H. Johnson. il por Art N 64:42-4+ Sum '65

POOR
Exploding poor; findings at the White House conference on international cooperation. H. C. Wallich. Newsweek 66:84 D 13 '65
See also
Legal aid
Poverty
Standard of living

Great Britain
Poverty vs. inequality: diagnosis. R. Titmuss. il Nation 200:130-3 F 8 '65

Latin America
Crisis to the South. J. O'Gara. Commonweal 81:754 Mr 12 '65
Real enemy. J. O'Gara. Commonweal 82:400 Je 18 '65

Mexico
Painful truth; furor in Mexico over Children of Sanchez, by Oscar Lewis. Newsweek 65:46+ Mr 8 '65
Silencing the children of Sanchez; controversy over translation and publication. J. Sommers. il Nation 201:530-3 D 27 '65

United States
Across the editor's desk; rural nonfarm problem. D. Hanson. il Suc Farm 63:8 My '65
Children Santa forgot; cases of seventeen children. il Ladies Home J 82:48+ D '65
CAP is born; plight of the people of Appalachia. E. M. Raabe. America 112:608-10 Ap 24 '65
Church for the hungry; Epiphany Episcopal church, Sherwood, Tenn. P. Houtz. il Sat Eve Post 238:87-91 D 18 '65
Federal birth control: progress without policy. W. Greene. il Reporter 33:35-7 N 18 '65
Gadfly of the poverty war. R. Young. Newsweek 66:30+ S 13 '65
Housing the poor. W. Klein. Commonweal 82:377-9 Je 11 '65; Reply. T. E. Kristopeit. 82:515+ Jl 23 '65
How about the non-Negro poor? an untold story. il U S News 59:66-8 O 4 '65
Income tax that pays the poor; subsidies to those too poor to pay taxes. il Bsns W p 105-6 N 13 '65
Is there a future for yesterday's people? excerpt from Yesterday's people: life in contemporary Appalachia. J. E. Weller. il Sat R 48:33-6 O 16 '65
LBJ's war at home; helping the poor increase their earning power. L. J. Walinsky. il New Repub 154:19-22 Ja 15 '66
Mental health of the poor, ed. by F. Riessman and others. Review
New Repub 152:21-3 F 6 '65. R. Coles
Of, by and for the poor: new generation of student organizers. A. Kopkind. New Repub 152:15-19 Je 19 '65; Reply with rejoinder. M. Harrington. 153:29-30 Jl 3 '65
Poor amidst prosperity; Time essay. Time 86:34-5 O 1 '65

POOR—United States—*Continued*
Poor don't want to be middle-class. R. Coles. il N Y Times Mag p7+ D 19 '65; Discussion. p 10+ Ja 9 '66
Poor grow fewer; Census bureau reports. Bsns W p64 Jl 17 '65
Poverty amidst affluence; excerpts from papers delivered at Conference on poverty amidst affluence, May 3-7, 1965. Mo Labor R 88:836-40 Jl '65
Poverty amidst plenty. A. Poinsett. il Ebony 20:104-6+ Ag '65
Poverty and the size of families. Am City 80:34+ Ap '65
Poverty in America, ed. by L. A. Ferman and others. Review
America 114:88-9 Ja 15 '66. J. L. Vizzard
Poverty: our enemy at home; symposium. il Nation 200:606-17 Je 7 '65
Poverty: the word and the reality. H. H. Lamale. bibliog f il Mo Labor R 88:822-7 Jl '65
Poverty vs. inequality: diagnosis. R. Titmuss. il Nation 200:130-3 F 8 '65
Problem of poverty. America 113:361-2 O 2 '65
Raising the question of who decides. C. Hayden. New Repub 154:9-10 Ja 22 '66
Realistic view of poverty; Effect on poverty war. America 114:5-6 Ja 1 '66
Roster of poverty. M. Orshansky. bibliog f il Mo Labor R 88:951-6 Ag '65
Specter of the poor; psychological defenses. J. P. Sisk. Commonweal 82:437-40 Je 25 '65
When the war is over; mass job program and negative income tax. New Repub 154:7 Ja 1 '66
Who started the war on poverty? report on the two strikingly different books. R. Bendiner. il Redbook 124:48-9+ F '65
See also
Anti-poverty program, 1964-
Church and social problems
Economic assistance, Domestic
National conference on poverty in the Southwest
History
America's schizophrenic view of the poor. P. Jacobs. Nation 201:191-7 S 20 '65
POOR relief. See Public welfare
POOR Richard; drama. See Kerr, J.
POORWILLS
Sleeping one of the Hopis; excerpt from Wandering through winter. E. W. Teale. il Natur Hist 74:26-9 D '65
POP art. See Modernism (art)
POPE, Alexander
Portraits of Alexander Pope. W. K. Wimsatt. il pors Antiques 87:188-92 F '65
POPE, Duane Earl
All-American boy. por Newsweek 66:33 D 13 '65
College football hero's postgraduate course in horror. il pors Life 58:30-30A Je 25 '65
Riddle of the nice killer. B. Lindeman. il pors Sat Eve Post 238:98+ O 23 '65
Stranger in Big Springs. il por Newsweek 65:29-30 Je 21 '65
POPE, Fergus
Last days of Albert Schweitzer. McCalls 93: 76+ D '65
POPE, George Andrew, 1901-
Little old ladies of Pasadena missed a good bet. W. Tower. il Sports Illus 22:60-1 Mr 8 '65
POPE, Woodrow
Electronic coin tosser. Pop Electr 22:50-3 Ap '65
Super-X pulse power pack for HO railroading. Pop Electr 23:41-6+ D '65
POPE and Young club. See Hunting clubs
POPECKI, Joseph T.
Bibliographic information exchange: address, November 1963. por Library J 90:823-6 F 15 '65
POPENOE, Paul
Do your children know you love them? Parents Mag 40:43-5+ D '65
POPES
See also
Papacy
Primacy
Catholic revolution; authority of bishops and supremacy of the pope. J. Roddy. il Look 29:21-7 F 9 '65; Reply. America 112:213 F 13 '65
POPKIN, Henry
Controversial European play. Vogue 146: 296-8+ S 1 '65
Critic's holiday: a theatre fling in Europe. Vogue 145:42+ Mr 15 '65

International theatre institute. Nation 201: 127-8 S 6 '65
Plain scoundrels and pataphysics. Sat R 48: 37-8 My 8 '65
Ring up that iron curtain. Life 59:19 S 17 '65
Theatre (cont) Vogue 145:50 F 15; 59 Mr 15; 56 Ap 15; 142 My; 146:169 O 1; 65 O 15; 71 N 15 '65; 147-72 Ja 1 '66
What so proudly we hailed. Nation 200:647-9 Je 14 '65
about
Guthrie's production of Groucho the III. Life 58:8+ Je 4 '65
POPKIN, Roy
Night watch. Read Digest 87:81-2 S '65
POPOFF, Yvan
Beatniks' friend. il Newsweek 66:36+ Ag 23 '65
POPOVERS. See Bread
POPOWSKI, Bert
Decoys for diving ducks. Outdoor Life 136: 50-1+ D '65
POPPER, David H.
NATO after sixteen years: an anniversary assessment. Dept State Bul 52:518-27 Ap 12 '65
United States, France, and NATO: a comparison of two approaches; address, January 21, 1965. Dept State Bul 52:180-7 F 8 '65
POPPER, Hermine I.
Universe of Thornton Wilder. Harper 230: 72-8+ Je '65
POPPIES
Iceland poppies. M. Buttner. il Pop Gard 16: 27-9 Jl '65
Oriental poppy. F. M. Abbey. il Horticulture 43:24-5+ My '65
POPULAR culture
Camp, religious style. Christian Cent 82:479 Ap 14 '65
Not good taste, not bad taste, it's camp. T. Meehan. il N Y Times Mag p30-1+ Mr 21 '65
With-it boys in England. B. DeMott. il Reporter 33:55-7 O 21 '65
See also
United States—Popular culture
POPULAR errors. See Errors, Popular
POPULAR mechanics (periodical)
Editor's page; new faces on the PM staff. il Pop Mech 124:83 N '65
POPULAR music. See Music, Popular (songs, etc)
POPULAR photography (periodical)
1966 photography directory & buying guide. il Pop Phot 57:63-126 N; 69-88+ D '65
POPULAR singers. See Singers
POPULAR songs. See Music, Popular (songs, etc)
POPULARITY
Need to be liked and the anxious college liberal. R. E. Lane. bibliog f Ann Am Acad 361:71-80 S '65
POPULATION
Demography and ecology. P. M. Hauser. bibliog f Ann Am Acad 362:129-38 N '65
Early population checked. Sci N L 87:231 Ap 10 '65
Health and population. C. E. Taylor. For Affairs 43:475-86 Ap '65
1964 world population: 3.3 billion. Am City 80: 134 F '65
World population to double by end of century. il UNESCO Courier 18:13-14 F '65
See also
Birth control
United Nations—Population commission
World population conference, Belgrade, 1965
also subhead Population under names of countries, states, cities, e.g. United States—Population
Overpopulation
Birth control; Gruening bill. K. Crawford. Newsweek 66:32 Jl 12 '65
Birth rate. W. F. Buckley, jr. Nat R 17:231 Mr 23 '65
Disaster from overcrowding. B. H. Frisch. il Sci Digest 58:69-73 Jl '65
Famine is here. New Repub 153:6 S 18 '65
Fighting world famine. New Repub 153:7-8 Ag 7 '65
Hidden crisis. J. D. Rockefeller, 3rd. il Look 29:75-6+ F 9 '65
Middle-class litters. Nation 200:687 Je 28 '65
More than a bad dream. Christian Cent 82:861 Jl 7 '65
Population and food. Nat Parks Mag 39:22 F '65
Population explosion: how much of a menace? il Sr Schol 86:6-9 Mr 18 '65

POPULATION—Overpopulation—*Continued*
Population explosion; symposium. Nat R 17:
633-48 Jl 27 '65; Discussion. 17:706 Ag 24 '65
Population growth seen as sparking nuclear
war. Sci N L 87:315 My 15 '65
Population politics; new bill introduced by
Gruening brings birth control issues to Congress. E. Langer. Science 148:1702-3 Je 12 '65
Population program; world-wide American
population control policy. America 112:216
F 13 '65; Reply. R. M. Fahey. 112:408 Mr 27
'65
Threatening crowd. M. Mannes. Read Digest
86:173-4+ F '65
We help build the population bomb. W. Vogt.
il N Y Times Mag p32+ Ap 4 '65
World choice: limit population or face
famine. il U S News 58:64-6 Je 14 '65
World population: menace of the P-bomb. il
Sr Schol 87:14 S 30 '65
See also
Population increase of

POPULATION, Increase of
Billion Indians by 2000 A.D? S. Chandrasekhar. il N Y Times Mag p32-3+ Ap 4 '65
Birth control: academy report stresses burdens of high birth rate among the impoverished here. E. Langer. Science 148:
1205-6+ My 28 '65
Conservation and the population explosion.
J. P. Jackson. il Am For 71:30-1+ D '65
Intelligent woman's guide to the population
explosion. G. Cant. McCalls 92:32+ F '65;
Same abr. with title What the population
explosion really means. Read Digest 86:103-
6 My '65
Is the pill the answer? K. N. Anderson.
il Todays Health 43:28-34+ Je '65
Let's outgrow the growth mania. D. Lambert. il Nat Parks Mag 39:4-8 Ap '65
Population explosion and anti-baby-ism. Life
58:6 Ap 23 '65
Population explosion; symposium. Nat R 17:
633-48 Jl 27 '65; Discussion. 17:706 Ag 24 '65
60 quadrillion is a crowd. H. Downs. il Sci
Digest 57:92-4 Ap '65
300,000,000 Americans would be wrong. D. E.
Lilienthal. il N Y Times Mag p24-5+ Ja 9
'66
Too little food and too much fertility; UN
demographers report in Population bulletin.
Christian Cent 82:1405 N 17 '65
Where were the churches? public hearings on
bill S.1676 to deal with population growth.
Christian Cent 82:1565-6 D 22 '65
Will markets develop as hoped? population
explosion taking new twists. il Bsns W
p32-4 My 15 '65
World's biggest problem: how experts see it.
il U S News 59:52-5 O 4 '65
See also
Population—Overpopulation

POPULATION, Limitation of. See Population

POPULATION pressure. See Population—Overpopulation

POPULATIONS, Animal. See Animal populations

PORCELAIN. ﾟSee Pottery

PORCELAIN, Chinese. See Pottery, Chinese

PORCHES
Big change in porches. il House & Gard 127:
142-7 Je '65
It's a veranda wrapped in glass. il Sunset
134:94-5 Ap '65
What a difference a porch makes! R. Charles.
il Parents Mag 40:75-7 Mr '65
See also
Outdoor rooms

PORIFERA. See Sponges

PORK
See also
Cookery—Meat

PORK barrel legislation. See United States—Appropriations and expenditures

PORNOGRAPHY. See Immoral literature and pictures; Obscenity (law)

POROUS glass. See Glass, Cellular

PORPOISE. See Dolphins (mammals)

PORSCHE (automobile) See Automobiles, Foreign

PORT ARTHUR, Tasmania
It's a Tasmanian ghost town; ruins of former
penal colony. il Sunset 134:55 F '65

PORT of New York authority
Halaby, Tobin clash on New York airports.
R. D. Hibben. Aviation W 82:30 Mr 1 '65

PORT-OF-SPAIN, Trinidad
Letter from Port Of Spain. B. Taper. il New
Yorker 41:203-4+ O 23 '65

PORT workers. See Longshoremen

PORTABLE electric heaters. See Electric heaters

PORTABLE electric tools. See Electric tools,
Portable

PORTABLE hospitals. See Hospitals, Traveling

PORTABLE pensions. See Pensions, Industrial

PORTABLE phonograph. See Phonograph,
Portable

PORTABLE radio receivers. See Radio receiving apparatus, Portable

PORTABLE radio transmitters. See Radio
transmitters, Portable

PORTABLE typewriters. See Typewriters

PORTACAVAL anastomosis
Histamine synthesis and gastric secretion
after portacaval shunt. J. E. Fischer and
S. H. Snyder. bibliog Science 150:1034-5 N
19 '65

PORTACAVAL shunt. See Portacaval anastomosis

PORTAGES
Newest thing on wheels. B. Cary. il Outdoor Life 135:25-7+ My '65

PORTAL vein. See Veins

PORTER, Cole
Musical show minus the show. C. Harman.
Life 59:12 Jl 30 '65

PORTER, Ellen J. Lorenz
Parties that ring bells. Recreation 58:477-8
D '65

PORTER, Katherine Anne
Author: interview; ed. by H. Frankel. por Sat
R 48:36 S 25 '65
Country and some people I love; interview,
ed., by H. Lopez. por Harper 231:58-62+
S '65
Interview; ed. by R. Newquist. por McCalls
92:88-9+ Ag '65

about
Eye of the story. E. Welty. Yale R 55:265-74
D '65
Katherine Anne Porter and the art of rejection, by W. L. Nance. Review
Christian Cent 82:656-9 My 19 '65. D. L.
Miller
Katherine Anne Porter's harvest. J. Featherstone. New Repub 153:23-6 S 4 '65
Misanthrope. por Time 86:122+ N 5 '65
On the grave. C. Brooks. Yale R 55:275-9
D '65
Tradition of storytelling. G. Hicks. Sat R 48:
35-6 S 25 '65
Uncorrupted consciousness: the stories of
Katherine Anne Porter. R. P. Warren.
Yale R 55:280-90 D '65

PORTER, Keith R. and Franzini-Armstrong,
Clara
Sarcoplasmic reticulum; with biographical
sketches. Sci Am 212:17, 72-8+ bibliog(p 139)
Mr '65

PORTER, Lorena. See Halsey, E. jt. auth.

PORTER, Lyman W.
Tracking conformity to its business lair. por
Bsns W p74 F 27 '65

PORTER, ﾟMarina Oswald. See Oswald, M.

PORTER, Stephen C. See Czamanske, G. K. jt.
auth.

PORTER, Sylvia
Spending your money; questions and answers. por Ladies Home J 82:52 O; 62 N;
42+ D '65; 83:24 Ja '66

PORTILLO, Chile
Much too much snow for Portillo, Chile
1966 F.I.S. competition canceled. B. Ottum.
il Sports Illus 23:64+ Ag 23 '65

PORTILLO avalanche. See Avalanches

PORTLAND, Ore.
Portland's municipal navy acts as harbor
hosts for VIPs. il Am City 80:131-3 D '65

Architecture
Concerned with old-fashioned qualities; headquarters for the Equitable savings and
loan association. P. Belluschi. il Arch Rec
138:144-5 D '65
To suppress the visual impact of the automobile; office complex. il Arch Rec 138:
160-2 D '65

Education
Oregon plan; Marshall high school. R. Tidwell and E. Wiseblood. il Library J 90:3686-
9 S 15 '65

Lighting
Everything but the light pole goes underground; system in Somerset West. R. T.
Pintar. il Am City 80:114 Jl '65

PORTLAND, Ore.—_Continued_

Newspapers

Story of a five-year strike: cost to company and unions; Oregonian, and Oregon journal. il U S News 58:90+ Ap '65

Sanitary affairs

This plant can do tricks. il Am City 80:110-12 O '65

Water supply

New refinements in meter maintenance. T. Suderburg. il Am City 80:114-16 Je '65

PORTLAND state college

Out of the slough. il Time 85:46 Mr 26 '65

PORTMANN, Adolf

Special position of man in the realm of the living; tr. by W. J. Dannhauser. Commentary 40:38-41 N '65

about

Portmann's thought; adaptation of address, August 1965. M. Grene. Commentary 40:31-8 N '65

PORTMEIRION. See Follies (architecture)

PORTOFINO, Italy

Time turns back in picture-book Portofino. C. Mitchell. il Nat Geog Mag 127:232-53 F '65

PORTRAIT painting

Daniel Huntington, portrait painter over seven decades. A. Gilchrist. il Antiques 87:709-11 Je '65

Informal portraits of Moses Soyer: interview, ed. by R. Gill. M. Soyer. il Am Artist 29:50-5+ S '65

Painter to the New York poets. T. Berrigan. il Art N 64:44-7+ N '65

Paintings of Jan Hoowij. J. Lovoos. il Am Artist 29:66-71+ Je '65

Portraits of Alexander Pope. W. K. Wimsatt. il Antiques 87:188-92 F '65

Unlikely likenesses. il Time 85:70-3 Mr 26 '65

See also

Copley, J. S.

PORTRAIT sculpture

Break's over, Mac, Mac! Mac! Museum of famous people, New York. il Life 60:39-40+ Ja 21 '66

Football portraits in bronze. J. Worthington. il Am Artist 29:58-61 O '65

Nijinsky; M. Brofsky's Nijinsky studies. M. Marks. il Dance Mag 39:28-9 Je '65

PORTRAITS

How to crystallize basic plastic organic unity; seventeen contemporary artists experiment with self-portraits and explanations. il Esquire 63:72-5 My '65

Letter from the publisher; Time covers. B. M. Auer. Time 85:25 Ap 30 '65

Exhibitions

Private faces in public places; two New York exhibitions. il Art N 63:36-8+ F '65

PORTRAITS, American

Forgotten founding fathers. A. Mongin. il Antiques 88:516-21 O '65

New Yorkers at home; Three hundred years of New York city families, exhibition at the Wildenstein galleries. il Antiques 89:106-11 Ja '66

Paintings; people and places of the old Northwest Territory. il Antiques 87:302-9 Mr '65

PORTS

Report on a study of British ports; excerpt. Mo Labor R 88:1335-45 N '65

Tempest in Tampa; Port Manatee plans. il Newsweek 66:86+ N 22 '65

PORTSMOUTH, N.H

Historic houses, etc.

History in houses; Macpheadris-Warner House. W. G. Wendell. il Antiques 87:712-15 Je '65

PORTSMOUTH, Va.

Portsmouth's jigsaw puzzle. il Am City 81:136+ Ja '66

PORTUGAL

See also
Censorship—Portugal
Coimbra
Fishing—Portugal
Lisbon
United Nations—Portugal

Colonies

U.S. urges Portuguese-African talks on self-determination; statements, November 11 and November 23, 1965. A. J. Goldberg. Dept State Bul 53:1034-8 D 27 '65

Description and travel

Delightful provincialism of Portugal. R. Lynes. il Harper 231:32+ N '65

Going places, finding things in Portugal. D. Otis. il House & Gard 127:156-63+ Ap '65

Portugal. L. Wibberley. il Travel 123:30-5 Ap '65

Portugal at the crossroads. H. La Fay. il Nat Geog Mag 128:453-501 O '65

Foreign relations

Senegals complaint against Portugal. UN Mo Chron 2:21-7 Je '65

History
Bibliography

Articles and other books received; comp. by C. J. Bishko. See issues of American historical review

Maps

Lands of the bold captains mapped anew. il Nat Geog Mag 127:340-1, sup(folded map) Mr '65

Politics and government

Against the situation. il Time 86:39 N 12 '65

Dead end in Portugal; tr. by J. Drury. J. Nabuco. Commonweal 83:240-2 N 26 '65

Portugal awakened; Catholic laymen denounce authoritarian regime. America 113:618 N 20 '65

Portugal, imperialism on credit. A. de Figueiredo. il Nation 201:134-7 S 13 '65

Who murdered General Delgado? S. De Gramont. il Sat Eve Post 239:49-51 Ja 1 '66

PORTUGUESE cookery. See Cookery, Portuguese

PORTUGUESE fishermen. See Fishermen

PORTUGUESE GUINEA

Quiet little war. B. Rice. il Newsweek 66:36+ Jl 5 '65

PORTUGUESE language

Study and teaching

Fala-se Português? Portuguese language development group. F. P. Ellison. il Américas 17:16-21 N '65

PORTUGUESE language in Brazil

Fala-se Português? Portuguese language development group. F. P. Ellison. il Américas 17:16-21 N '65

PORTUGUESE refugees. See Refugees, Portuguese

POSADA, Jaime

Adlai E. Stevenson: voice for humanity. Américas 17:1-2 Ag '65

Three pillars of progress; education, science, culture. Américas 17:24-9 Ap '65

POSADA, José Guadalupe

José Guadalupe Posada: engraver of Mexican life. C. A. Echánove. il por Américas 17:28-35 N '65

POSEY, Cecil W. and Wessling, L. E.

We're for unified membership. NEA J 54:47 O '65

POSIES for the potentate; drama. See Swintz, M.

POSNER, A. Charles

Expectant mother. Redbook 125:16+ Je '65

POSNER, David

Algerian summer; poem. Poetry 106:100-8 Ap '65

Campus; poem. New Yorker 41:64 D 11 '65

Death of Ulysses; Pageant for François Villon; poems. Yale R 55:88-9 O '65

Mr Bridges' nightingales; poem. Nation 200:116 F 1 '65

POSNER, Donald

Baroque revolution in Italy. Art N 64:32-4+ Ap '65

POSSIBILITY of evil; story. See Jackson, S.

POSSONY, Stefan T.

Are campus radicals more red than the reds? excerpts from testimony. por U S News 59:10 S 6 '65

Campus Communists: America's time bomb? interview. por U S News 59:42-5 N 1 '65

Clearing the air. Nat R 17:113-14+ F 9 '65

War of maneuver. Nat R 17:601-3 Jl 13 '65

POST, Austin S.

Alaskan glaciers: recent observations in respect to the earthquake-advance theory. bibliog Science 148:366-8 Ap 16 '65

POST, Marjorie Merriweather. See May, M. M. P.

POST cards

Cards from Caruso; ed. by Q. Eaton. E. Caruso. il Opera N 30:14-16 Ja 8 '66

Picture post card. B. Finnegan. See issues of Hobbies

POST cards—*Continued*
Sir Winston Churchill; card showing Churchill. B. Finnegan. il Hobbies 70:118-19 Ap '65
World war I. B. Finnegan. il Hobbies 70: 124-5+ Ja '66

Anecdotes, facetiae, satire, etc.
I hate winter postcards. H. A. Smith. il Travel 125:55-7 Ja '66
POST exchanges. See United States—Armed forces—Post exchanges
POST office department (United States) See United States—Post office department
POSTAGE stamp printing
Nonprofit money-makers; Bureau of engraving and printing. W. McCann. il Sci N L 87:138-9 F 27 '65
POSTAGE stamps
Commemorating Wagner. C. McAlister. il Opera N 29:17 F 13 '65
Stamps. H. Herst, jr. See issues of Hobbies
See also
Postage stamp printing

Collectors and collecting
Stamps around the world. H. Herst, jr. Hobbies 70:99+ S '65
Stamps around the world; two national stamp societies. H. Herst, jr. Hobbies 70: 99+ D '65
POSTAL censorship
For freer speech; intercepting Communist propaganda mail found unconstitutional. Newsweek 65:16 Je 7 '65
Free mail & free speech; Supreme court decision to end censoring of Communist political propaganda. Time 85:52 Je 4 '65
Freedom of the mails; statute concerning Communist political propaganda declared unconstitutional by Supreme court. New Repub 152:6 Je 5 '65
House repasses bill to stop morally offensive mail. Pub W 187:69 Ap 19 '65
Mail-tapping. America 112:344 Mr 13 '65
New attacks on postal censorship. R. H. Smith. Pub W 187:63 F 1 '65
Showdown coming on the billion-dollar smut industry. il U S News 59:38+ D 6 '65
Snooping through the mails. J. Ridgeway. New Repub 152:11-13 Mr 20 '65
POSTAL employees
Meet the men who guard your mail; postal inspectors. F. Sondern, jr. il Read Digest 87:186-8+ O '65
POSTAL laws and regulations. See Postal service—Laws and regulations
POSTAL savings banks
Postal savings: America's poorest buy. R. L. Smith; reply. Nation 200:184 F 22 '65
POSTAL service
See also
Postal savings banks
Universal postal union

International aspects
Postal service, the oldest form of international cooperation. W. J. Hartigan. Dept State Bul 53:840-2 N 22 '65

Laws and regulations
What you can do about unwanted mail. il Good H 160:150 F '65

United States
Postal innovations: what Gronouski has in mind. U S News 58:22 F 22 '65
What's the matter with the mails? M. Greenfield. il Reporter 32:21-5 F 11 '65; Discussion. 32:6+ Mr 11 '65
What's wrong with the mails and what's being done about it. il U S News 58:64-6 Ap 12 '65
Zip codes pre-sorting and the book business. C. B. Grannis. Pub W 187:33 Mr 29 '65
Zip mail hits a snag; mandatory conversion to zip coding by all second- and third-class mailers. Bsns W p33 Ja 30 '65
See also
Air mail service
Mail handling
Postal censorship
Postal employees
United States—Post office department
POSTAL union, Universal. See Universal postal union
POSTCARDS. See Post cards
POSTEL, Edith Horn. See Goodgal, S. H. jt. auth.
POSTERIZATION. See Photography—Printing processes

POSTERS
La belle epoque. il Horizon 7:97-104 Autumn '65
Pop! goes the poster; pop art portraits of comic-book favorites. il Newsweek 65:72 Mr 29 '65
See also
Billboards
POSTGATE, Raymond
Inns of the Highlands. Holiday 37:82-3+ Mr '65
Recent European vintages. Holiday 38:125-30 N '65
Simpson's in the Strand. Holiday 38:68-70+ S '65
POSTGRADUATE education. See Colleges and universities—Graduate work
POSTMASTER General. See United States—Post office department
POSTMORTEMS. See Autopsy
POSTNATAL exercises. See Exercise
POSTON, Margaret
Art in the park. Recreation 58:278-9 Je '65
POSTS, Fence. See Fence posts
POSTS, Wooden
How to set posts. il Bet Hom & Gard 43: 36 Je '65
POSTURE
Sit, stand, walk and work with grace. L. D. Kirk. il Parents Mag 40:120 S '65
You can have a far slimmer figure if you stand up straight! il Seventeen 24:132-3 Mr '65
See also
Stature
POT merigolds. See Calendulas
POTASSIUM
Molybdenum content of corn plants exhibiting varying degrees of potassium deficiency. J. B. Jones, jr. il Science 148:94 Ap 2 '65
Potassium content of illite. C. E. Weaver. bibliog il Science 147:603-5 F 5 '65
Terrestrial ratio of potassium to rubidium and the composition of earth's mantle. P. W. Gast. bibliog il Science 147:858-60 F 19 '65
Viscosities of liquid sodium and potassium, from their melting points to their critical points. A. V. Grosee. bibliog il Science 147: 1438-41 Mr 19 '65

Isotopes
Exchangeable mass: determination without assumption of isotopic equilibrium. P. E. E. Bergner. bibliog Science 150:1048-50 N 19 '65
POTASSIUM-argon dating. See Radioactive dating
POTASSIUM chloride
Cationic glass electrode response in aqueous solutions of sodium chloride and potassium chloride. E. W. Moore and J. W. Ross. bibliog il Science 148:71-2 Ap 2 '65
POTASSIUM in the body
Altered effect of potassium ions on cerebral respiration in vitro following subcortical lesions. B. F. Roth and J. A. Harvey. bibliog il Science 148:1356-7 Je 4 '65
Exchangeable mass: determination without assumption of isotopic equilibrium. P. E. E. Bergner. bibliog Science 150:1048-50 N 19 '65
Potassium-40 content as a basis for the calculation of body cell mass in man. W. Burmeister. bibliog Science 148:1336-7 Je 4 '65
POTASSIUM iodide
Drug helps asthmatics. Sci N L 87:260 Ap 24 '65
POTATO chips
Great potato-chip war. il Newsweek 66:71 Jl 26 '65
POTATOES
Undercutting speeds spud harvest. G. Lorang. il Farm J 89:66A Mr '65
See also
Cookery—Vegetables
POTAWATOMI Indians
Status substitute sought. Sci N L 88:29 Jl 10 '65
POTEET, Ralph. See Schrader, G. jt. auth.
POTOK, Chaim
Provisional absolutes. Commentary 39:76-8+ My; 40:22+ S '65
POTOKER, Edward M.
Conscience of a culture. Sat R 48:39-40+ N 6 '65
Desire that leads to despair. Sat R 49:25-6 Ja 1 '66
POTOMAC RIVER
Potomac again in danger. A. W. Smith. Nat Parks Mag 39:2+ Jl '65
Question of good taste; Theodore Roosevelt memorial island in the Potomac River. Nat Parks Mag 39:20 F '65
Walkin' and hollerin'; 11th reunion hike of C. & O. Canal association. C. Ritter. il Am For 71:6-7+ Je '65

POTPOURRI
Fragrance that lasts and lasts. R. Almquist. il Flower Grower 52:24-5 Je '65
POTS and pans. See Kitchen utensils
POTSDAM conference, 1945. See Berlin conference, 1945
POTTED plants. See Plants, Potted
POTTER, Beatrix
Aliveness of Peter rabbit; address, June 1965. M. Sendak. il Wilson Lib Bul 40:345-8 D '65
POTTER, Charles Edward
Insider's memoir of a sinister era. D. Nevin. Life 59:18 O 8 '65
POTTER, Charles H.
Put your greenhouse to work. Horticulture 44:32-3+ Ja '66
—See Wood, E. A. jt. auth.
POTTER, David M.
Civil war: the whole story. Sat R 48:58 O 2 '65
High cost of human values. Sat R 48:60 O 30 '65
Right to defend the wrong reasons. Sat R 49:33 Ja 1 '66
POTTER, E. J.
I hit the ground at 150 mph; ed. by J. E. Boykin. Pop Mech 124:104-5+ S '65
POTTER, Frank
Conscience of an art colony. Nation 201:410-14 N 29 '65
POTTER, Fred H.
Book wholesaling and supply in California. Pub W 188:57-9 N 22 '65
POTTER, Greta Lagro
Millions in wonderland. Horn Bk 41:593-7 D '65
POTTER, Paul Edwin
Sedimentary origins of rock layering. Natur Hist 74:50-5 bibliog(p66) D '65
POTTER, Stephen
Short monograph on the uses of frailty in physical competition. Nation 200:506-8 My 10 '65
Words only. See issues of American record guide
POTTER, Van Rensselaer
Council on the future. Nation 200:133-6 F 8 '65
POTTERY
What goes with what? choosing china and silver patterns. il Seventeen 24:114-15 S '65
See also
Salt glaze ware

Care
Care and safekeeping of china and glass. il House & Gard 128:84+ S '65

Exhibitions
Ceramics by twelve artists. R. Lafean. il Craft Horiz 25:30-3+ Ja '65
European porcelains in San Francisco. R. Davidson. il Antiques 88:604+ N '65
Haitian ceramics celebrates twenty years; exhibit at Howard university gallery of art. L. J. Pierre-Noel. il Negro Hist Bul 28:203-4 My '65
Object: still life; exhibition of new work by ten young artists. Museum of contemporary crafts. B. Breckenridge. il Craft Horiz 25:33-5 S '65
23rd ceramic international. il Sch Arts 64:34-6 Mr '65
Twenty-third ceramic national. D. Rhodes. il Craft Horiz 25:18-23 Ja '65
Wedgwood from midwestern collections. R. N. Gregg and M. M. Delhom. il Antiques 87: 705-8 Je '65

Study and teaching
Summer ceramics; workshop for all ages and vacations at the Herron art institute, Indianapolis. il Design 66:24-6 My '65

Technique
Peter Voulkas. D. Cyr. il Sch Arts 65:27-30 S '65
POTTERY, American
Ann Stockton's porcelain. J. Pugliese. il Craft Horiz 25:34-6 Mr '65
Ceramics; Northwest Territory. il Antiques 87:324-6 Mr '65
Constant craftsmen; Lenox china. il Mlle 61: 196-7 My '65
Norman Kramer, painter & potter. N. Kramer. il Am Artist 29:30-5+ My '65
Twenty-third ceramic national. D. Rhodes. il Craft Horiz 25:18-23 Ja '65
POTTERY, Chinese
Fitzhugh and FitzHughs in the China trade. J. B. S. Holmes. il Antiques 89:130-1 Ja '66

POTTERY, Ecuadorian
Transpacific contact in 3000 B.C; Jomon-like pottery unearthed at Valdivia, Ecuador. B. J. Meggers and C. Evans. il Sci Am 214:28-35 Ja '66
POTTERY, English
Eighteenth-century porcelain at the Smithsonian; the Hans Syz collection. P. V. Gardner. il Antiques 88:336-40 S '65
English earthenware in the Chorley collection. Mrs K. Chorley. il Antiques 87:182-7 F '65
Larsen and McCauley collections at the Smithsonian institution. J. J. Miller, 2d. il Antiques 88:522-5 O '65
See also
Staffordshire ware
Wedgwood ware
POTTERY, French
Faïence de Nevers. R. Davidson. il Antiques 88:162+ Ag '65
In the museums; French porcelain and pottery from the Norweb collection at Cleveland museum of art. R. Davidson. il Antiques 89:134-6+ Ja '66
Large groups and figures in the soft-paste biscuit of Vincennes-Sèvres. W. J. Sainsbury. il Antiques 87:430-3 Ap '65
Small figures and groups in the soft-paste biscuit of Vincennes-Sèvres. W. J. Sainsbury. il Antiques 88:824-8 D '65
POTTERY, German
Pittsburgh collection of Höchst. Z. D. Alberts. il Antiques 89:122-6 Ja '66
POTTERY, Haitian
Haitian ceramics celebrates twenty years; exhibit at Howard university gallery of art. L. J. Pierre-Noel. il Negro Hist Bul 28:203-4 My '65
POTTERY, Italian
Doccia museum. R. Davidson. il Antiques 88: 540+ O '65
POTTERY, Japanese
Japanese pottery; a report. D. Rhodes. il Craft Horiz 25:38-40+ Mr '65
Teruo Hara. J. Eagle. il Craft Horiz 25:32-4 Jl '65
Transpacific contact in 3000 B.C; Jomon-like pottery unearthed at Valdivia, Ecuador. B. J. Meggers and C. Evans. il Sci Am 214:28-35 Ja '66
POTTERY, Mexican
Pot-shopping on the Ensenada road. il Sunset 135:61 N '65
POTTERY, Portuguese
Vista Alegre. R. C. Smith. il Antiques 87: 444-7 Ap '65
POTTERY kilns. See Kilns
POTTHOFF, Carl J.
First aid. See issues of Today's health
POUGHKEEPSIE, N.Y.
Rehabilitating a century-old fountain. R. E. Laper. il Am City 80:20 Ag '65
POULENC, Francis
Mamelles de Tirésias. Criticism
,Opera N il 30:26 N 20 '65
POULICAKOS, Paul
Giant stride. Recreation 58:131+ Mr '65
POULOS, Constantine
Discovery of politics. Nation 201:378-80 N 22 '65
What the palace fears. Nation 201:158-61 S 27 '65
Who cares about Cyprus? Nation 201:493-6 D 20 '65
POULSON, Thomas L.
Countercurrent multipliers in avian kidneys. bibliog Science 148:389-91 Ap 16 '65
POULTRY
Bursa of Fabricius in chickens; possible humoral factor. R. L. St Pierre and G. A. Ackerman. bibliog il Science 147:1307-8 Mr 12 '65
Poultry news. See issues of Farm journal
What's new. See issues of Successful farming
See also
Cookery—Poultry
Poultry houses

Carcasses
See Carcass disposal

Culling
Cull poultry flock faster with hurdles. il Suc Farm 63:34C Jl '65
Two ways to boost profits by culling. H. C. Jordan. il Farm J 89:42A Ag '65

Egg production
Birds without headaches lay more eggs. B. Fowler. Farm J 89:56J F '65
Six ways to boost egg profits. Suc Farm 63: 70A Ad '65

POULTRY—*Continued*

Feeding
Homemade feeder cuts chore time. G. Lorang. il Farm J 89:60D My '65
POULTRY dressing. See Cookery—Poultry
POULTRY houses
Bigger profits from better broiler houses. J. Bickers. il Farm J 89:50G Mr '65
They get a dozen fresh eggs every day. il Sunset 135:124 O '65

Equipment
Labor savers for your laying house. il Farm J 89:60L My '65

Heating and ventilation
More eggs with controlled climate housing! B. Fowler. il Farm J 89:60D My '65

Litter
See also
Feeding and feeding stuffs—Poultry house litter
POULTRY industry and trade
Loner can compete. J. Bickers. il Farm J 89:60K My '65
POULTRY inspection
What that meat inspection stamp really means. Bet Hom & Gard 43:134-5 My '65
POUND, Ezra
Tidings from Pound to Joyce; letter. por Esquire 64:152+ D '65

about
Menotti & Pound. C. A. Matz. por Opera N 30:14-15 N 20 '65
New works on Pound. M. L. Rosenthal. Poetry 106:361-5 Ag '65
Pound at Spoleto. L. Ferlinghetti. Sat R 48:20 S 4 '65
Reading the Cantos. M. Reck. Commonweal 83:93-5 O 22 '65
POUND sterling. See Money—Great Britain
POUNDS, Norman J. G.
West Germany. Focus 16:1-6 N '65
POSSIN, Nicolas
Painter's painter to the age. H. Peyre. il Art N 63:24-7+ F '65
POVERTY
Historical approach. R. J. Lampman. il Nation 200:608-9 Je 7 '65
Identification of the poor. M. Orshansky. bibliog f il Mo Labor R 88:300-9 Mr '65
Poverty vs. inequality: diagnosis. R. Titmuss. il Nation 200:130-3 F 8 '65
Sermon for Labor day. America 113:235-6 S 4 '65
Two approaches to welfare. O. S. Ornati. bibliog f Mo Labor R 88:266-7 Mr '65
Ultimate weapon in war on poverty. il Nations Bsns 53:34-7+ F '65
War on rural poverty. Christian Cent 82:731 Je 9 '65
World apartheid. T. Balasuriya. il Commonweal 83:363-6 D 24 '65
Would you fight poverty this way? Willow Run association for neighborhood development. il Nations Bsns 53:104+ Ap '65
See also
Anti-poverty program, 1964-
Poor
Slums

Quotations, maxims, etc.
Of want; comp. by R. Block. N Y Times Mag p25+ Jl 25 '65
POWDER metallurgy. See Metal powders
POWDERED metals. See Metal powders
POWELL, Adam Clayton, 1908-
Adam Powell returns to Harlem. A. Morrison. il pors Ebony 20:80-2+ Jl '65
Black is his way of thinking. S. Alexander. Life 58:27 Ap 23 '65
Congress: higher Education act including scholarship for needy passed in final days of session. J. Walsh. Science 150:591-2+ O 29 '65
Counterattack. por Newsweek 65:37 Mr 1 '65
Fiesta of politics. il por Newsweek 65:29-30 Ap 26 '65
Flamboyant Mr Powell. J. Q. Wilson. Commentary 41:31-5 Ja '66
Hooking a catfish. Newsweek 66:29-30 D 27 '65
Key congressman dares not go home. por U S News 58:21 Mr 15 '65
Man may come, and man may go (but Powell goes on forever) W. F. Buckley, jr. Nat R 17:540 Je 29 '65

Mr Powell and OEO. America 112:658 My 8 '65
Monstrous mackerel; Justice Maurice Wahl's orders. Time 86:31 D 24 '65
Old Adam. M. Kempton. New Repub 152:16-18 Mr 6 '65
On the lam. por Time 85:23 F 26 '65
Right-to-work repeal hits a roadblock. Bsns W p58 Je 19 '65
What about Rev Powell, gentlemen? Nat R 17:181-2 Mr 9 '65
POWELL, Alexis
Hole in the heart. il por Newsweek 66:54 Ag 16 '65
POWELL, Anthony
Music of time. New Yorker 41:17-18 Jl 3 '65
POWELL, Art
Works of Art. H. L. Masin. por Sr Schol 87:28 S 23 '65
POWELL, Bernard W.
Earthquake detector. Pop Sci 187:135-8+ D '65
POWELL, Buttercup
Big-hearted Buttercup. il pors Ebony 20:47-8+ F '65
POWELL, Dawn
Staten Island. I love you. Esquire 64:120-5 O '65
Obituary
Pub W 188:42-3 N 29 '65
POWELL, Enoch
West is best. B. Wenham. New Repub 153:18-19 N 20 '65
POWELL, John Enoch. See Powell, E.
POWELL, Lawrence Clark
Great land of libraries; address, July 1965. por ALA Bul 59:643-8 Jl '65
about
Confessions of a fellow traveler. R. Dillon. Library J 90:5484-5 D 15 '65
Profile: Lawrence Clark Powell; renaissance man in a flip-top age. R. H. Dillon. il pors Library J 90:5341-3 D 15 '65
POWELL, Lewis F. Jr
Citizens vs. criminals; whose rights come first? excerpts from address, August 9, 1965. por U S News 59:14 Ag 23 '65
POWELL, Ralph L.
China's bomb: exploitation and reactions. For Affairs 43:616-25 Jl '65
Communist China as a military power. bibliog f Cur Hist 49:136-41+ S '65
POWELL, Richard
That lively corpse: the novel. Writer 78:12-14+ O '65
POWELL, Robert Stephenson Smyth Baden-Powell, 1st baron Baden-. See Baden-Powell, R. S. S. B.-P.
POWELL, Y. Marjorie (Flores)
Man may come, and man may go (but Powell goes on forever) W. F. Buckley, jr. Nat R 17:540 Je 29 '65
$19,000 yearly now for lawmaker's wife. il por U S News 58:12 Ap 5 '65
POWELSON, John P. and Solow, A. A.
Urban and rural development in Latin America; with questions and answers. bibliog f Ann Am Acad 360:48-62 Jl '65
POWER, B. A. and Power, R. F.
Vanillin, cis-terpin hydrate, and cis-terpin as ice nucleators. bibliog Science 148:1088 My 21 '65
POWER, Crawford
Path to grace. I. Howe. New Repub 153:23-6 S 25 '65
POWER, Eugene Barnum
University microfilm head requests inquiry. Pub W 188:34-5 N 29 '65
POWER, R. F. See Power, B. A. jt. auth.
POWER (political science)
Burdens of power. C. Marcy. Sat R 48:11-13 S 4 '65
People or personnel: decentralizing and the mixed system, by P. Goodman. Review Commentary 40:116+ N '65. C. Lasch
Political integration and political development. M. Weiner. bibliog f Ann Am Acad 358:52-64 Mr '65
Politics of distrust in Iran. A. F. Westwood. Ann Am Acad 358:123-35 Mr '65
Raising the question of who decides. C. Hayden. New Repub 154:9-10 Ja 22 '66
White power structure. A. Morrison. il Ebony 20:141-4+ Ag '65
World politics of responsibility. O. Gass. Commentary 40:85-90 D '65
See also
Executive power
POWER (psychology)

Anecdotes, facetiae, satire, etc.
Power and the glory: Great Britain. A. Coren. il Atlan 216:130-2 S '65

POWER amplifiers. See Amplifiers
POWER boat racing. See Motor boat racing
POWER boats. See Motor boats
POWER failures. See Electric power
POWER garden tools. See Garden tools, equipment and supplies
POWER lawn mowers. See Lawn mowers
POWER of attorney
Power of attorney, what, when, why. Changing T 19:44 Mr '65
POWER plants
Energy plants and systems. F. J. Walsh. il Arch Rec 137:212-17 My '65 (to be cont)
  See also
Hydroelectric plants
POWER pools. See Electric plants—Interconnection
POWER resources
Utilities and appointments come of age. L. Blumenthal. il Duns R 85:pt2 138-41+ Mr '65
  See also
Solar energy
POWER saws. See Saws
POWER; story. See Cope, J.
POWER tools. See Electric tools, Portable; Machine tools
POWER transmission
  See also
Belting
POWERS, Bertram A.
Concession to Dolly. il por Time 86:59 Jl 2 '65
Reporter at large. F. C. Shapiro. New Yorker 41:167-70+ Ap 10 '65
POWERS, Helen
LPN: the gentle people. por Am Ed 1:12-14 O '65
POWERS, J. F.
Conscience and religion. Commentary 40: 89-92 Jl '65
POWERS, John G.
Powers sues P-H to get his share in profit-sharing. Pub W 187:59 F 1 '65
POWERS, John James, 1912-
Change, challenge and the drug industry; address, October 12, 1965. Vital Speeches 32:57-60 N 1 '65
  about
Crown for the conqueror. il por Bsns W p 124+ My 22 '65
Pfizer's self-prescribed tonic. il por Fortune 72:152-5+ Ag '65
POWERS, Joshua B.
New communism in South America; address, January 6, 1965. Vital Speeches 31:318-20 Mr 1 '65
POWERS, Melvin
Bonded blonde. il Time 86:47 Ag 20 '65
POWERS of attorney. See Power of attorney
POWILLS, Dorothy
Playing cards. See issue of Hobbies
POWLEDGE, Fred
Black man, go South. Esquire 64:72-4+ Ag '65
New fraternity. Esquire 64:88-9+ S '65
POX pottery. See Indians of Mexico—Antiquities
POYSKY, Frank. See Eklund, M. W. jt. auth.
PRACTICAL joker; story. See Davenport, G.
PRACTICAL jokes
Apotheosis of the practical joke. il Esquire 64:99 S '65
PRACTICAL nurses

Training
  See Nurses and nursing—Training
PRACTICAL nursing. See Nurses and nursing
PRACTICE (music) See Piano—Instruction and study
PRACTICE teaching. See Student teaching
PRAEGER, Frederick A, incorporated
Praeger observes double anniversary. Pub W 188:40 O 11 '65
PRAGER, Denis J.
Instruments at the FASEB show. Science 148:1366+ Je 4 '65
—and others
Constant volume, self-filling nanoliter pipette construction and calibration. Science 147: 606-8 F 5 '65
PRAGUE
Footloose in Prague: a Marxist Bohemia. C. Cate. il Atlan 215:100-4+ F '65

Art
Noble remnants; masterpieces of Rudolf II's collection at the Hradcany. il Time 85:70-1 Je 18 '65

Spectacular rediscovery in old Prague. il Art N 64:35 Sum '65

Description
You're welcome to walk in Prague. il Sunset 135:21 Jl '65

Music
Festive spring. P. Moor. Hi Fi 15:132 Ag '65
Notes from our correspondents. P. Moor. Hi Fi 15:12+ S '65
Twentieth spring. P. Moor. il Hi Fi 15:144-6 Ap '65

Theater
Avant-garde in Prague; Prague theatre on the Balustrade. V. Blackwell. Nation 200:650-2 Je 14 '65
PRAGUE spring festival. See Music festivals—Czechoslovakia
PRAGUE theatre on the Balustrade. See Prague—Theater
PRAIRIE chickens
Attwater prairie chicken; preservation of unbroken prairie only hope to save species from extinction. Nat Parks Mag 39:20 F '65
Attwater prairie chicken; vanishing American bird. W. S. Boardman. il Nat Parks Mag 39:16-17 Mr '65
PRAIRIE CREEK REDWOODS STATE PARK. See California—Parks and reserves
PRAIRIE dogs
Glad tidings for prairie dogs. Nat Parks Mag 39:20 S '65
PRAISE; story. See Gordimer, N.
PRAKASH, Om
Dilemmas of publishing in south-east Asia. UNESCO Courier 18:23-7 S '65
PRAMER, David. See Gandek, L. J. jt. auth.
PRASNIEWSKI, Margaret
Come back, Peter... come back, Paul; story. Redbook 125:46-7 Jl '65
PRATOLINI, Vasco
Growing up Italian. L. Barzini. Nation 200: 482-3 My 3 '65
PRATT, Christopher J.
Chemical fertilizers; with biographical sketch. Sci Am 212:20, 62-72 Je '65
PRATT, L. C.
Flush before sweeping for cleaner streets. Am City 80:118-20 Mr '65
PRATT, Richard M.
Ocean-bottom topography; the divide between the Sohm and Hatteras Abyssal Plains. bibliog Science 148:1598-9 Je 18 '65
PRATT, Winifred Sealy
Member of the month. il por PTA Mag 60:32 O '65
PRATT and Whitney aircraft division. See United aircraft corporation—Pratt and Whitney aircraft division
PRATT clinic-New England center hospital. See Boston—Hospitals
PRAY, Glenn
Is America ready for the Cord? J. Atwater. il por Sat Eve Post 238:58-60 Ag 14 '65
PRAYER
God's encounter with man: a contemporary approach to prayer, by M. Nédoncelle. Review
  Cath World 201:143-4 My '65. J. V. Gallagher
Hollow tree. J. V. McDonnell. America 112: 859 Je 12 '65
Letter from the council; prayer service for promoting Christian unity at St Paul's basilica. R. E. Tracy. America 113:774-5 D 18 '65
My faith in prayer: excerpt from A gift of joy, ed. by L. Funke. H. Hayes. il Read Digest 87:55-7 D '65
Prayermongering at the public library. D. A. Edman. Christian Cent 82:462-6 Ap 14 '65; Discussion. 82:746-7 Je 9 '65
Prayers of women, ed. by L. Sergio. Review
  Christian Cent 82:918 Jl 21 '65. M. H. Bro
What prayer means to me; personal reflections. M. Davidson. il Good H 160:90-1 Je '65
  See also
Prayers
PRAYER books
  See also
Church of England—Book of common prayer
PRAYER in the schools. See Public schools and religion

PRAYERS
Pop prayer. Time 86:70 N 26 '65
Prayer that startled Gloucester. Read Digest 86:23-4 Ap '65
Prayers for everyday; comp. by J. H. McCombe. Read Digest 87:153-4 S '65
Soldiers prayer for his son. D. MacArthur. il Read Digest 86:41 My '65

PRAZ, Mario
Books. E. Wilson. New Yorker 41:152-4+ F 20 '65

PREACHING
Manner of speaking; explanation of a homily. J. Ciardi. Sat R 48:18+ D 11 '65
Priests and preachers. K. Haselden. Christian Cent 82:830 Je 30 '65
Sermon seminar in a parish church; laymen participation. M. M. Eakin. Christian Cent 83:75-7 Ja 19 '66
Trouble with the church. by H. Thielicke. Review
    Christian Cent 82:1324 O 27 '65. W. B. Cate

PREAKNESS race. See Horse racing

PREALBUMINS. See Albumins

PREBELAKES, Panteles
Cretan glance. G. Davenport. Nat R 17:937-8 O 19 '65

PRECAMBRIAN period. See Geology, Stratigraphic—Precambrian; Paleobotany—Precambrian: Paleontology—Precambrian

PRECIPITATION (chemistry)
Nucleation of crystals from solution. A. G. Walton. bibliog il Science 148:601-7 Ap 30 '65

PRECISION casting. See Lost wax process

PRECOGNITION. See Extrasensory perception

PRE-COLLEGE guidance. See Educational guidance

PRE-COLUMBIAN art. See Art, Pre-Columbian

PRECOOKED food, Frozen. See Food, Frozen

PREDATOR and rodent control. See United States—Fish and wildlife service

PREDATORY animals. See Animals, Predatory

PREDICTED log competitions. See Navigation—Competitions

PREDICTIONS. See Forecasts

PREFABRICATED bridges. See Bridges, Iron and steel

PREFABRICATED cabins. See Cabins

PREFABRICATED hospitals. See Hospitals, Prefabricated

PREFABRICATED houses. See Houses, Prefabricated

PREFABRICATED stormproof buildings. See Building, Stormproof

PREGNANCY
Attack on the unborn; dangers of German measles during pregnancy. S. M. Spencer. il Sat Eve Post 238:82-4 Mr 13 '65
Better health for every baby; fourteen major medical centers from Oregon to New York participating in unique child development project. T. Wilson and K. Niehans. il Parents Mag 40:59-61+ N '65
Expectant mother; how husbands can help with pregnancy blues. F. R. Lock. Redbook 125:48+ O '65
Expectant mother; walking during pregnancy. J. H. Ferguson. Redbook 125:32+ Jl '65
Expectant mother; what does due date really mean? M. E. Davis. Redbook 125:33+ Ag '65
Having the first baby: the way it is today. il Newsweek 66:70 O 25 '65
Pregnancy: then, now; excerpt from Mothers are funnier than children. B. Rollin. Redbook 124:43 Ap '65
Right to be well born. R. E. Hall. il PTA Mag 60:13 Ja '66
Sex and pregnancy. J. P. Greenhill. Redbook 124:28+ Ap '65
Vaccinating against Rh. Time 86:92-3 O 8 '65
What every mother-to-be should know. V. Apgar. il Todays Health 44:35+ Ja '66
    See also
Abortion
Childbirth
Fetus
Prenatal influences

Signs and diagnosis
Those new quickie pregnancy tests; ed. by V. Cohn. P. M. Wright. Ladies Home J 82:24 S '65

PREGNANCY, Complications of
Expectant mother; what the Rh factor is. A. W. Liley. Redbook 126:38+ N '65
Expectant mother; which doctor should I call? A. C. Posner. Redbook 125:16+ Je '65

Fluids in pregnancy. G. A. Macer. Redbook 125:28+ My '65
Pregnancy & heart disease. G. C. Schauffler. il McCalls 92:42+ Je '65
    See also
Abortion

PREGNANCY tests. See Pregnancy—Signs and diagnosis

PREISS, Eleanor
Where to get charts. Motor B 115:58-60 Ap '65

PREJUDICE
Conscience of an art colony: Anatomy of prejudice, symposium at Rockport, Mass. F. Potter. il Nation 201:410-14 N 29 '65
History is a dangerous subject; findings of Anglo-United States team survey of secondary school textbooks. R. A. Billington. il Sat R 49:59-61+ Ja 15 '66
How to hate in one easy lesson. L. Rosten. il Look 29:26 D 14 '65
On the roots of prejudice. W. S. Coffin, jr. Mlle 60:176-7 Ap '65
Pshaw! Christian Cent 82:879 Jl 7 '65
Roots of prejudice; with study-discussion program, by R. Strang. F. R. Horwich. bibliog il PTA Mag 60:22-4, 34 D '65
Why nobody wants women in science; reprint. R. B. Kundsin. il Sci Digest 58:60-5 O '65
    See also
Race prejudice

PRE-KINDERGARTEN schools. See Nursery schools

PRELUTSKY, Burt
Sampling the new season. Holiday 38:176+ O '65

PREMARITAL physical examinations. See Physical examinations, Premarital

PREMATURE infants. See Infants, Premature

PREMINGER, Otto
Is it true what they say about Otto? H. Lawrenson. por McCalls 92:106-7+ Mr '65

PREMIUM pay. See Overtime

PREMIUMS
    See also
Trading stamps

PRENATAL care. See Pregnancy

PRENATAL influences
Every year 3.5 million miracles. il Newsweek 66:67-70+ O 25 '65

PRENDERGAST, Joseph
Recreation, government, and the arts. por Recreation 58:377 O '65

PRENTICE, Perry
Taxes and the death of cities. Arch Forum 123:56-7 N '65

PRENTICE-Hall, Incorporated
Powers sues P-H to get his share in profitsharing. Pub W 187:59 F 1 '65

PREPACKAGING. See Packaging

PREPARATION for college. See Colleges and universities—Entrance requirements

PREPARATORY schools. See Private schools

PREPAREDNESS, Military
    See also
United States—Defenses

PRESBYTERIAN church in Canada
Individual but ecumenical. Christian Cent 82: 846-7 Je 30 '65

PRESBYTERIAN church in the United States
Dissent on a new creed. Time 86:70-1 Ag 6 '65
    See also
United Presbyterian church in the United States of America

PRESBYTERIAN church in the United States (South)
Conflict of concerns; old hostilities rekindled. J. H. Smylie. Christian Cent 82:1602-6 D 29 '65
Presbyterians, U.S: search for unity. J. A. Womeldorf. Christian Cent 82:660-2 My 19 '65
Southern Presbyterians move forward. Christian Cent 82:573 My 5 '65
Way open to union. M. A. Vance. Christian Cent 82:842+ Je 30 '65

PRESCHOOL children
Are we overselling the pre-school idea? I. Kraft. Sat R 48:63 D 18 '65
Head start to where? F. M. Hechinger. il Sat R 48:58-60+ D 18 '65
How to learn a secret name. B. Spacks. il Am Ed 1:7-12 Je '65
New kind of school; prekindergarten school. M. J. E. Senn. il McCalls 92:48+ S '65
    See also
Kindergarten
Nursery schools
Readiness for school
Socially handicapped children

PRESCHOOL education. See Education of children; Project head start

PRESCOTT, Mrs William F.
Summer care of African violets. Horticulture 43:36-7 My '65
PRESENT from Abe; drama. See Newman, D.
PRESENTS. See Gifts
PRESERVATION Hall concerts. See New Orleans—Music
PRESERVATION of food. See Canning and preserving
PRESERVATION of landmarks, scenery, etc.

United States

Cranberry Glades; scenic area. J. C. Behrens. il Am For 71:12-13+ D '65
Keep your town's historic landmarks. il Changing T 19:11-13 S '65
PRESERVATION of paintings. See Paintings—Conservation and restoration
PRESERVATION of tissues. See Tissues—Culture
PRESERVATION of works of art. See Art objects—Conservation and restoration
PRESHAW, R. M. and others
Pancreatic secretion induced by stimulation of the pyloric gland area of the stomach. bibliog Science 148:1347-8 Je 4 '65
PRESIDENT Cleveland, where are you? story. See Cormier, R.
PRESIDENTIAL advisers. See Public officers
PRESIDENTIAL campaigns
See also
National conventions, Republican
Television in politics

Anecdotes, facetiae, satire, etc.

Making of the president, 1968! a musical extravaganza. A. Glaser. il Esquire 64:153-63 D '65

1964

Bob dropped, Hubert kept dangling; excerpts from Making of the President—1964. T. H. White. il Life 59:70-2+ Jl 2 '65
Book reviews. F. K. Kelly. America 113:81 Jl 17 '65
Election year to remember. M. L. Coit. il Sat R 48:29-31 Jl 10 '65
How G.O.P. rivals destroyed themselves; excerpts from Making of the President—1964. T. H. White. il Life 58:82-4+ Je 25 '65
How not to make presidents. E. J. Hughes. Newsweek 66:17 Jl 26 '65
LBJ for the USA: 1964 campaign evaluation; address, December 28, 1964. H. F. Harding. Vital Speeches 31:249-51 F 1 '65
Making of the President-1964, by T. H. White. Review
Commentary 40:110+ D '65. A. Hacker
Requiem for a lightweight. C. Mohr. Esquire 64:66-9+ Ag '65
Speaking out; presidential campaigns are a sham. D. Burch. Sat Eve Post 238:12+ Mr 27 '65

PRESIDENTIAL candidates

1972

Kennedy for president; a buildup starts for '72. il U S News 58:49-50 My 10 '65
PRESIDENTIAL elections. See Presidents—United States—Election
PRESIDENTIAL entertaining. See Government entertaining
PRESIDENTIAL government. See Presidents—United States
PRESIDENTIAL succession. See Presidents—United States—Succession
PRESIDENTIAL veto. See Presidents—United States—Powers and duties
PRESIDENTIAL yachts. See Yachts and yachting
PRESIDENTS

France

Oracles on the Seine. il Newsweek 66:63 O 18 '65

United States

Gentlemen's agreement; problems of presidential disability. Newsweek 65:23 F 8 '65
Lyndon Johnson and the paradox of the presidency; concerning president as nonpartisan leader. C. P. Magrath. Yale R 54:481-93 Je '65
Making of the President, 1964, by T. H. White. Review
Atlan 216:123-4 Ag '65. W. Barrett
New Repub 153:17-21 Jl 10 '65. T. Wicker
New Repub 153:38 Ag 7 '65. H. Pekar
Making of the President—1964; excerpts. T. H. White. il Life 58:86-7+ Je 18; 82-4+ Je 25; 59-70-2+ Jl 2 '65
One year of L.B.J. T. Wicker. il New Repub 153:13-22 N 13 '65

Profiles of the presidents (cont) F. Freidel. il Nat Geog Mag 127:660-711; 128:536-77; 129:66-119 My, O '65, Ja '66
Shadow presidency. J. M. Burns. il Nation 201:115-18 S 6 '65; Reply. B. M. Goldwater. 201:inside cover O 4 '65
Sharpest wit in Washington; interview, ed. by J. V. Heuvel. A. R. Longworth. il Sat Eve Post 238:30-3 D 4 '65
View from Capitol hill. L. W. Koenig. il Sat R 48:32 Jl 10 '65
See also
United States—Executive office of the president
Vice-presidents—United States
White House

Assassination

Bill for an assassin. Time 85:29 Mr 19 '65
Question of value; death penalty in case of assassination of president or vice president. Time 86:16-17 Jl 2 '65

Election

How many votes does Goldwater own? L. H. Bean and R. Drummond. il Look 29:75-6 Mr 23 '65
Real story the '64 election returns tell. il U S News 58:50-2 Je 7 '65
See also
Presidential campaigns—1964

Health

When presidents have been disabled. U S News 59:34 O 18 '65
World at his bedside. il Time 86:29 O 15 '65
See also
Johnson, L. B.—Health

Homes

See United States—Historic houses, etc.

Powers and duties

Congressional checkpoints; brakes on presidential power. Sr Schol 86:9 F 18 '65
Diplomacy a la Johnson. Nation 200:461 My 3 '65
Hard limits of government by consensus. L. W. Koenig. il N Y Times Mag p26-7+ My 7 '65
How Johnson meets the challenge. il Bsns W p28-9 Mr 13 '65
King's men: a British view of the White House. L. Heren. Harper 230:108+ F '65
People curious to know what he's really like. P. Lisagor. Nations Bsns 53:23-4 Ap '65
Power narcotic. R. Moley. Newsweek 66:84 Ag 9 '65
When the President's veto was vetoed. il Sr Schol 86:5 Mr 4 '65
Who the President listens to. C. B. Seib. il Nations Bsns 53:32-3+ Ap '65
You can be humble when you're number one. P. Lisagor. il Nations Bsns 53:23-4 F '65

Protection

Price of protection; question of specially armored limousines. il Newsweek 65:28 Ap 26 '65
Two more armored cars to help protect LBJ? il U S News 58:10 Ap 19 '65
When Johnson does the unexpected. il U S News 58:15 My 31 '65
See also
Secret service—United States

Public relations

Johnson and the businessmen. G. R. Rosen. il Duns R 85:40-3+ My '65
Nothing personal, Mr President. Christian Cent 82:667-8 My 26 '65
Politics of power; portrait of a master. il Newsweek 66:18-19+ Ag 2 '65
Putting presidents in the picture. il Sr Schol 86:5 Ap 29 '65
Washington's latest, most improbable gap. P. Lisagor. il Nations Bsns 53:21+ Jl '65
What the people really think. S. Alsop. il Sat Eve Post 238:27-31 O 23 '65
What's happened to the LBJ image? il U S News 60:39-41 Ja 17 '66
Why LBJ has trouble with his image. P. Lisagor. il Nations Bsns 53:21-2 Ag '65

Relations with Congress

Atlantic report. Atlan 216:6+ S '65
Boots, sneakers & crutches. Time 86:26 S 24 '65
Breaking down the old order; Johnson Congress. Bsns W p25-6 S 18 '65
Congress and the President. il Sr Schol 86:7-9 F 18 '65

PRESIDENTS—United States—Relations with Congress—*Continued*

89th Congress in perspective; what LBJ wants, LBJ gets; address, November 15, 1965. R. P. Griffin. Vital Speeches 32:140-3 D 15 '65

End of the affair? President Johnson and the 89th Congress. Newsweek 65:25-6 Je 21 '65

From White House to Capitol, how things get done; interview. L. F. O'Brien. il U S News 59:68-73 S 20 '65

Home front. K. Crawford. Newsweek 66:34 Ag 9 '65

Just as dangerous as the left; right wing criticism and condemnation of U.S. policy in southeast Asia. America 114:118 Ja 22 '66

Laws, then what next? R. Moley. Newsweek 66:116 O 11 '65

LBJ and Congress: after a fast start, harder tests ahead. il U S News 58:52-3 Mr 1 '65

LBJ and Congress: secrets of a briefing. il U S News 59:30-1 Ag 23 '65

LBJ is asking for all this. il U S News 58:35-6 F 1 '65

LBJ's new experiment in government. il U S News 58:64-8+ Ap 5 '65

LBJ's 100 days: a record piling up; Way LBJ runs Congress. il U S News 58:41-4 Ap 26 '65

Lyndon's lobbyists: how they get what he wants. il Nations Bsns 53:38-9+ Ap '65

Near miss; edginess between Congress and LBJ. Newsweek 65:21-2 Je 28 '65

Politics of power: portrait of a master. il Newsweek 66:18-19+ Ag 2 '65

Prospect for Congress. H. Brandon. Sat R 48:16 Mr 13 '65

Putting Congress through hoops. Bsns W p32 Ap 3 '65

They twist arms without hurting; liaison men between the White House and Capitol hill. il Bsns W p82+ Ap 24 '65

Washington desk. J. R. Slevin. Duns R 86:5-6 N '65

Washington's latest, most improbable gap. P. Lisagor. il Nations Bsns 53:21+ Jl '65

What LBJ can expect from Congress now. il U S News 60:50-1 Ja 10 '66

Relations with the press
See Government and the press

Succession

Art of amending: giving full power to vice-president during a president's disability. il Time 85:49 F 26 '65

Filling a void. Sr Schol 86:30-1 F 18 '65

If a president dies or is disabled. il U S News 58:34 F 8 '65

If a president is disabled. il U S News 58:8 Ap 26 '65

Objections to the Bayh amendment. New Repub 152:7-8 F 13 '65

Plan for a stand-in president. U S News 59:10 Jl 19 '65

Presidential succession and responsible government. D. Lawrence. U S News 59:144 O 18 '65

Presidential succession: forethought or afterthought? with text of proposed 25th amendment. il Sr Schol 87:10-13 O 14 '65

Starting to settle the succession question. Time 85:28-9 Ap 23 '65

Succession and disability. R. L. Tobin. Sat R 48:20+ F 20 '65

Succession to the presidency; with text of proposed 25th amendment. Time 86:18 Jl 16 '65

Suggestions for succession: President Johnson's recommendation. il Time 85:21 F 5 '65

25th amendment, we hope: replacing a disabled president. Life 59:6 Jl 16 '65

When a president is disabled. il U S News 59:25 Jl 5 '65

Who leads if a president falters. il U S News 59:37 O 18 '65

Wives

Lady in the east wing. M. Greenfield. il Reporter 33:28-31 Jl 15 '65

With Lady Bird in the White House. il U S News 58:33 F 1 '65

See also
Johnson, C. A. T.

PRESIDENTS addresses. See Speeches, addresses, etc.

PRESIDENT'S commission on heart disease, cancer and stroke. See United States—President's commission on heart disease, cancer and stroke

PRESIDENT'S commission on national goals; President's equal employment opportunity commission; etc; See United States—President's commission on national goals; United States—President's equal employment opportunity commission; etc.

PRESIDENTS press conferences. See Press conferences

PRESIDING officers. See Chairmen

PRESLEY, Elvis
Forever Elvis. il por Time 85:61 My 7 '65
There'll always be an Elvis. C. R. Jennings. il pors Sat Eve Post 238:76-9 S 11 '65

PRESS, Frank
Resonant vibrations of the earth; with biographical sketch. Sci Am 213:14, 28-37 bibliog(p 142) N '65

—and Jackson, David
Alaskan earthquake, 27 March 1964; vertical extent of faulting and elastic strain energy release. bibliog Science 147:867-8 F 19 '65

PRESS. See Journalism; Newspapers

PRESS, Catholic. See Catholic press

PRESS and crime. See Crime and the press

PRESS and government. See Government and the press

PRESS conferences
Invitation to a hard time ahead: press conference on Vietnam policy. L. Wainwright. Life 59:21 Jl 23 '65

Johnson and the press; what the grumbling is about. il U S News 58:49-51 Mr 22 '65

Lights! cameras! action! the LBJ news conference. il U S News 59:66-7 S 20 '65

No. 898; President Johnson and the press. il Time 85:38 Mr 26 '65

Plants and digs; B. D. Moyers indictment of Washington press corps. il Newsweek 67:56 Ja 24 '66

Press conference: high school editors meet top news correspondents; sponsored by It's academic. il Seventeen 24:32 Ap '65

That's why I asked you; that's why I told you; presidential press conference. Time 87:47 Ja 21 '66

PRESS photographers. See Photographers

PRESS photography. See Photography, Journalistic

PRESS relations. See Publicity

PRESS releases
See also
Government and the press

PRESSED glass. See Glassware

PRESSES
Workshop: vacuum forming of plywood. D. Bjorkman. il Craft Horiz 25:38-40 S '65

PRESSURE
Amazing alchemy of ultrahigh pressure. G. A. W. Boehm. Read Digest 86:144E-144F+ Mr '65

High-pressure technology. A. Zeitlin. il Sci Am 212:38-46 bibliog(p 150) My '65

High-pressure transitions of germanium and a new high-pressure form of germanium. C. H. Bates and others. bibliog il Science 147:860-2 F 19 '65

Periodic compounds: syntheses at high pressures and temperatures. H. T. Hall. bibliog il Science 148:1331-3 Je 4 '65

Pressure dependence of the alpha-beta transition temperature in silver selenide. M. D. Banus. bibliog Science 147:732-3 F 12 '65

Room temperature slip in titanium diboride produced by high pressure. F. W. Vahldiek and others. bibliog il Science 149:747-8 Ag 13 '65

Sex conversion induced by hydrostatic pressure in the marine copepod tigriopus californicus. V. D. Vacquier and W. L. Belser. bibliog il Science 150:1619-21 D 17 '65

Volume measurements on chromium to pressure of 30 kilobars. W. E. Evenson and H. T. Hall. bibliog il Science 150:1164-5 N 26 '65

PRESSURE, Atmospheric. See Atmospheric pressure

PRESSURE, Political. See Pressure groups

PRESSURE cooking
When the pressure's on; with recipes. il McCalls 92:76+ Mr '65

PRESSURE groups
Constellations of lobbies. I. Deutscher. Nation 200:352-4 Ap 5 '65

Lobbying for peace. Commonweal 82:548 Ag 6 '65

Nation apathetic. Nation 200:321-2 Mr 29 '65

Pressure groups and intergovernmental relations. T. J. Anderson. bibliog f Ann Am Acad 359:116-26 My '65

When extremists attack the press. J. F. Fixx. Sat R 48:72-3 F 13 '65

PRESSURE groups—*Continued*
Young America's newest vocation; awakening the disadvantaged and the disinterested to their political opportunities and responsibilities. A. I. Waskow. il Sat R 48:12-14+ Je 5 '65

PRESSURE of population. See Population—Overpopulation

PRESSWOOD, Susan. See Hafner, E. M. jt. auth.

PRESTHUS, Robert
University bosses. New Repub 152:20-4 F 20 '65

PRESTON, John R.
Birth of a nature center. Audubon Mag 67: 78 Mr '65

PRESTON, Robert
Senior scholastic interviews; ed. by R. Hemming. pors Sr Schol 86:21 Mr 4 '65

PRETZELS
For salty snacking: soft pretzels and salt sticks; recipes. il Sunset 135:175-6 O '65

PREVEDI, Bruno
Manhattan Manrico; interview, ed. by F. Stevenson. por Opera N 30:15 D 4 '65

PREVELAKIS, Pandelis. See Prebelakés, P.

PREVENTION of accidents. See Accidents—Prevention

PREVENTION of cruelty to animals. See Animals—Treatment

PREVENTION of war. See War, Prevention of

PREVENTIVE medicine. See Medicine, Preventive

PREWITT, C. T. and Young, H. S.
Germanium and silicon disulfides: structure and synthesis. bibliog Science 149:535-7 Jl 30 '65

PREWITT, Kenneth
Political socialization and leadership selection. bibliog f Ann Am Acad 361:96-111 S '65

PREY, Hermann
Now on Vox: Brahms, Loewe, and Wolf lieder by Prey, magnificent. H. Glass. por Am Rec G 31:526-7 F '65

PRIBILOF ISLANDS
Pribilofs: excerpt from The bird watcher's America; ed. by O. S. Pettingill. R. T. Peterson. il Audubon Mag 67:72-7 Mr '65

PRICE, Arnold H.
(comp) Articles and other books received; Germany, Austria, and Switzerland. See issues of American historical review

PRICE, C. Warner
Evergreens. Horticulture 43:36-7+ Je '65

PRICE, Carter
Why it's dangerous to get mad. Farm J 89: D6 Mr '65

PRICE, Charles
Golf. Esquire 64:64+ S: 70+ D '65
Greatest golf clubs. Esquire 64:112-13+ Ag '65

PRICE, Derek John de Solla
Networks of scientific papers; adaptation of address, March 17, 1964. bibliog Science 149:510-15 Jl 30 '65
Science of science. Bul Atomic Sci 21:2-8 O '65

PRICE, Don K.
Escape to the endless frontier; excerpt from Scientific estate. bibliog Science 148:743-9 My 7 '65

about

Don K. Price, jr, president-elect; with editorial comment. C. P. Haskins. por Science 150:1669, 1690-1 D 24 '65

PRICE, George
Let George do it. Newsweek 65:60 Mr 15 '65

PRICE, Jack
Price's horsy prep. il por Sports Illus 24:24-7 Ja 10 '66

PRICE, Molly
Are you using iris for all they are worth? Flower Grower 52:22-3+ Je '65

PRICE, Nancy
Common emperor; poem. Commonweal 82:243 My 14 '65
Naming the bones; poem. Reporter 32:44 My 20 '65
Ten-toed signature; poem. Atlan 215:88 F '65

PRICE, Paxton P. and Carl, H. A.
Washington report: from the Library services branch. See issues of ALA bulletin

PRICE, R. G. G.
Ménage à trois. Atlan 215:123 F '65
Next step forward is back. Atlan 216:127-8 Jl '65
Rage in the lab. Atlan 216:116-18 D '65

PRICE, Robert
Man who ran the show. por Newsweek 66:34 N 15 '65

Second man at City hall. R. Armstrong. il pors N Y Times Mag p 12-14+ D 26 '65

PRICE cutting
Macy's toasts its price war; brand name liquor. il Bsns W p32-3 F 27 '65
Mixed bag of gimmicks. W. H. Nelson. Pub W 188:34-7 Ag 2 '65
Price cut is no cure for declining demand; Hinkle study. Bsns W p 111 Ag 7 '65
See also
Discount houses (retail trade)

PRICE-earnings ratio. See Stocks

PRICE fixing, Resale. See Price maintenance by industry

PRICE fixing by industry
Chaotic antitrust. H. Hazlitt. Newsweek 66:73 Ag 16 '65

PRICE indexes
Calculation of average retail food prices. D. P. Rothwell. il Mo Labor R 88:61-6 Ja '65
Can you believe that cost-of-living index? il Changing T 19:45-6 Ap '65
Consumer and wholesale prices; tables. See issues of Monthly labor review
Consumer expenditures for health purposes. L. S. Reed. il Mo Labor R 88:168-70 F '65
Food expenditures of urban families, 1950 to 1960-61. L. M. Webb. il Mo Labor R 88:150-3 F '65
Industry and sector price indexes. B. R. Moss. il Mo Labor R 88:974-82 Ag '65
Note on hedonic price indexes. H. Anderson. bibliog Mo Labor R 88:658-60 Je '65
Prices since the tax cut. Mo Labor R 88:IV Ja '65
Relative importance of CPI items. G. P. Green. il Mo Labor R 88:1346-9 N '65
Trading stamps and the CPI. E. D. Hoover and M. L. Drake. bibliog f il Mo Labor R 88:429-33 Ap '65

PRICE maintenance by industry
Bread upon the waters; steel executives indicted under Sherman antitrust act. Time 86:104 O 1 '65
High cost of price fixing; suits against electrical companies. Time 86:82 S 10 '65
One more try to show price-fixing in oil. Bsns W p26 Ap 17 '65
Quality stabilization bill reintroduced in Senate; with editorial comment. Pub W 187: 48. 54 Mr 22 '65
Steel makes peace with Justice. Bsns W p 18-19 Jl 31 '65
Tax row revives price-fixing case. Bsns W p76 F 27 '65
UAW mounts campaign against monopsony; vs Detroit's Big three. Bsns W p43-4 Jl 24 '65

PRICE marks
Price tag tempest; decisions of New York's Markets Commissioner, Albert S. Pacetta. Newsweek 66:72 Ag 16 '65

PRICE policies
How business keeps prices down. R. Dreyfack. il Nations Bsns 53:34-5+ S '65
Strategy of price deals. C. L. Hinkle. Harvard Bsns R 43:75-85 Jl '65

PRICE regulation by government

Brazil

Taking the pledge. Time 85:102 My 21 '65

Great Britain

Britain's plan to control wages. U S News 58:96 Ap 26 '65

United States

Aluminum: battle over prices. il Sr Schol 87: 17-18 D 2 '65
And now, wheat. Newsweek 66:79 D 6 '65
Businessmen size up lesson on aluminum; top executive opinion concerning wage-price guideposts. il Bsns W p37-8 N 20 '65
Garroting by guideline. H. Hazlitt. Newsweek 66:86 D 6 '65
More federal controls? what Fowler sees ahead; excerpts from address, November 19, 1965. H. Fowler. U S News 59:20 D 6 '65
Steel-price dispute: a lesson for business. U S News 60:88-9 Ja 17 '66
That wrong war on aluminum. Fortune 72: 133-4 D '65
To hold price line: a new crackdown; aluminum prices. il U S News 59:37-9 N 22 '65
Unguided guidelines. il Time 87:69 Ja 21 '66
Wage-price guidelines; anti-inflationary weapon? address, August 31, 1965. T. B. Curtis. Vital Speeches 31:727-9 S 15 '65
Washington desk. J. R. Slevin. Duns R 86: 5-6 D '65

PRICE regulation by government—United States—*Continued*
Will the guideposts hold? wage-price guidepost policy. il Bsns W p35-6 N 20 '65
Without benefit of law; excerpts from editorials: New York times and Washington post, November 10, 1965. U S News 59:132 N 22 '65

PRICE supports, Agricultural. See Agricultural administration—United States; Farm produce—Prices

PRICE tags. See Price marks

PRICES
Can stability be put in commodity prices? Bsns W p32 F 20 '65
Trouble on the plantations; prices of commodities. il Time 86:80 Ag 6 '65
See also
Inflation (finance)
Price cutting
also subhead Prices under various subjects, e.g. Milk—Prices

Government regulation
See Price regulation by government

Cuba
Money and goods. il Sr Schol 87:14-15 N 18 '65

Great Britain
Whisky galore; price war raging. Newsweek 65:68-9 Mr 29 '65

United States
Big jump, but no inflation. il Time 86:75-6 Ag 6 '65
Consumer and wholesale prices; tables. See issues of Monthly labor review
Flurry in prices. il Fortune 72:28+ S '65
For 1966, an easing of pressure on prices; opinion of top corporate buyers interviewed. il Bsns W p26-7 S 25 '65
How real is inflation in the U.S? il U S News 60:78-80 Ja 24 '66
Is your dollar in trouble again? Outlook for inflation; what to do about it. il U S News 59:42-4+ S 20 '65
No inflation, yet. il Time 86:101 O 1 '65
Question of stability. il Time 86:77 S 3 '65
Steadier course ahead. il Bsns W p23-4 My 22 '65
Strange story told by prices. il U S News 59:52-4 D 6 '65
See also
Cost of living—United States
Price regulation by government—United States

PRIDDLE, Charles E.
Moose in a blind alley. por Outdoor Life 137:28-31+ Ja '66

PRIDEAUX, Tom
Cohen's coddled public. Life 58:137-8 Ap 2 '65
Life review. Life 59:10 D 3 '65
Life TV review (cont) Life 58:19 Ap 2 '65
Life theater review (cont) Life 58:10 F 26; 20 Mr 19; 18 Ap 23; 59:20 N 19; 134-5+ D 10; 16 D 17 '65; 60:17 Ja 14 '66

PRIEST workers. See Worker priests

PRIESTS
Fallen priests: Via Coeli refuse in N.Mex. S. De Gramont. il Sat Eve Post 238:99-103 N 20 '65
Missing dimension. J. J. Kavanaugh. America 112:604-5+ Ap 24 '65
Peace, priests and the missions. G. Baum. Commonweal 83:175-8 N 12 '65
Peace priests muzzled. Christian Cent 82:1500-1 D 8 '65
Problem of priests in the world. J. G. Lawler. Commonweal 82:105-9 Ap 16 '65; Discussion. 82:203+, 236-7+, 338-9+, 394-5+ My 7-14, Je 4, 18 '65
Question of freedom. Time 86:43 D 24 '65
Serra and Newman clubs; encouragement of priestly vocations. America 112:872 Je 19 '65
Should priests march? America 112:629-30 My 1 '65
Vocationless Venezuela; shortage of native born priests. P. J. Cunningham. Cath World 201:189-93 Je '65
Whisky priests. il Newsweek 67:58 Ja 10 '66
See also
Theological students
Women as priests
Worker priests

PRIESTS in literature
New priests, a controversial French novel. R. Barrat. Commonweal 82:49-51 Ap 2 '65
Vision; Father Cawder in Crawford Power's The encounter. R. A. Schroth. America 114:41 Ja 8 '66

PRIETO, Gregorio
Sketches of the banned. il Time 86:50 Ag 20 '65

PRIMA donnas. See Singers

PRIMARIES
Switcheroo; Primary day in New York city. il Newsweek 66:29-30 S 27 '65

PRIMARY education. See Education, Elementary

PRIMATES
Earliest primates. L. Van Valen and R. E. Sloan. bibliog il Science 150:743-5 N 5 '65
Primate behavior. Review
Sci Digest il 58:29-30 N '65. J. Reinert
Primate biology; planning meeting; report on meeting of scientists to discuss the possibility and desirability of cooperative efforts between the United States and Japan in the study of primates. L. Carmichael and A. J. Riopelle; reply. J. Moor-Jankowski. Science 148:734 My 7 '65
Primates: communication and social interaction; report on international symposium. S. A. Altmann. Science 149:886-7 Ag 20 '65
Private life of primates. il Life 58:48-61 F 12; 62-76B+ F 19 '65

PRIME ministers
See also
Great Britain—Prime ministers

PRIME ministers conferences
Foggy day in Londontown; plan to do something about Viet Nam. il Time 85:38 Je 25 '65
Heads I win; Conference of commonwealth prime ministers. il Newsweek 65:34+ Je 28 '65
Some questions for a friend; leaders of nineteen of the British Commonwealth's nations meet in Lagos. il Time 87:25 Ja 21 '66
Win some, lose some; Lagos conference on Rhodesian crisis. il Newsweek 67:39 Ja 24 '66

PRIMERS
Senior-made primers. E. Silverman. il NEA J 54:32-3 O '65

PRIMITIVE art. See Art, Primitive

PRIMITIVE religion. See Religion, Primitive

PRIMITIVE sculpture. See Sculpture, Primitive

PRIMROSES
In praise of primroses F. H. McGarvie. Flower Grower 52:43 D '65

PRIMUS, Pearl
Black rhythms. Circle in the square theatre. J. Maskey. Dance Mag 39:32+ Jl '65

PRINCE, Alain Wood
Pirate of the pads. pors Outdoor Life 136:48-9+ Ag '65
We had a wild time. pors Outdoor Life 136:33-5+ Jl '65

PRINCE, Bob
Prince of Pittsburgh. M. Cope. il por Sports Illus 23:84+ S 13 '65

PRINCE, Harold Smith
Businessman-showman. por Time 86:89 D 3 '65

PRINCE, Lucy Terry
Bijah's Luce of Guilford, Vermont. M. R. Wright. il Negro Hist Bul 28:152-3+ Ap '65

PRINCE EDWARD COUNTY, Va.
Encounters in Virginia; freedom teacher & gentle ladies. E. Newmark. il Nation 200:193-7 F 22 '65
Real commencement. Reporter 33:10+ Jl 1 '65
They closed their schools, by B. Smith. Review
Sat R 48:67-8 Jl 17 '65. P Johnson
When school stopped. Newsweek 66:81 N 15 '65

PRINCE GEORGE'S COUNTY memorial library, Hyattsville, Md.
United planning. E. B. Hage. il Wilson Lib Bul 40:250-1 N '65

PRINCE GEORGES COUNTY white citizens council. See White citizens councils

PRINCETON, N.J.
Princeton: the enlightened exurbia. B. Thielen. il Holiday 38:58-65+ N '65

PRINCETON (warship) See Warships—United States

PRINCETON chamber orchestra. See Chamber orchestras

PRINCETON club, New York. See New York (city)—Clubs

PRINCETON university
Formality and colonnades for Princeton; Woodrow Wilson school of public and international affairs. il Arch Rec 138:140-3 O '65
Kind lady; two new bequests. il Newsweek 65:54 Mr 1 '65
Princeton: the enlightened exurbia. B. Thielen. il Holiday 38:58-65+ N '65
Undergraduate dormitories. il Arch Rec 138:126-7 Ag '65

Libraries
$3.5 million bequest to Princeton allocated to support of library. Library J 90:2785 Je 15 '65

PRINCETON university press
Princeton university press opens new, modern plant. il Pub W 189:76-8+ Ja 3 '66
Princeton U.P. to get new printing plant, warehouse. Pub W 187:48 Mr 1 '65

PRINGLE-Claggett House. See Minnesota—Historic houses, etc.

PRINT dryers. See Photography—Apparatus and supplies

PRINTED circuits
Long-hand printed circuits. E. M. Long. il Electr World 74:40-1 Ag '65
New machine speeds diagram production. P. J. Klass. il Aviation W 83:77+ O 18 '65
Printed-circuit repair. L. E. Frenzel, jr. Electr World 74:57 O '65
Silk-screened circuit boards. J. Marchetti. il Electr World 73:46-8+ Je '65

PRINTERS
New York printers win wage increase. Pub W 188:30 D 13 '65
Print unions cast mold for merger. il Bsns W p84+ S 4 '65
See also
International typographical union
Strikes—United States—Printers

PRINTING
AAUP: two aspects of production: computers and fine design; summaries of discussions at annual convention. Pub W 188:120-5 Jl 19 '65
Bodoni's Manuale Tipografico is reproduced in Parma, Italy. il Pub W 188:129-30 Jl 19 '65
Creative color; advantages and disadvantages of printing methods; gravure, letterpress, litho. A. Rothstein. U S Camera 28:8 Mr '65
Focus on elegance. C. B. Grannis. Pub W 188:103 Jl 19 '65
Meyer Miller analyzes the state of typography; cold type and filmsetting. Pub W 189:104 Ja 3 '66
Swift advances cited in printing of covers; summary of discussion at panel held by Women's national book association. il Pub W 187:90 My 3 '65
See also
Color printing
Computers—Printing applications
Lithography
Photogravure
Photomechanical processes
Type and typefounding
Typesetting

Design
About face. G. Lacy. il Design 66:8-12 Ja '65
Recollections of F. W. Goudy: his types, books and press. P. A. Bennett. il Pub W 187:88+ Mr 1 '65
Tools of the trade. il Pub W 188:103-4 O 4 '65
See also
Type and typefounding

Exhibitions
New York printing week salutes graphic arts. Pub W 187:126 F 1 '65
Typomundus 20 exhibit is burned in Toronto. Pub W 187:58 F 1 '65

History
About face. G. Lacy. il Design 66:8-12 Ja '65
William Gaxton, master printer. P. W. Schmidtchen. il Hobbies 70:106-7+ N '65

Legibility
Thinking big; Keith Jennison books for visually handicapped. D. Dempsey. Sat R 49:38 Ja 22 '66

Private presses
Alfred Knopf keepsake. W. Caxton, jr. il Am Artist 29:38-43+ S '65
James Herrick Gipson, RIP; Caxton printers ltd, Caldwell, Idaho. L. H. Gipson. Nat R 17:508 Je 15 '65
Keepsake for Alfred A. Knopf. P. A. Bennett. il Pub W 188:72-4+ Ag 9 '65
Leonard Baskin, graphic artists; Gehenna press. P. A. Bennett. il Pub W 187:70-1+ Ap 5 '65
Printing's do-it-yourselfers. J. B. Lieberman. il Sat R 48:70-2+ O 9 '65

PRINTING, Offset
Halliday rides crest of demand for offset book printing. il Pub W 188:106-8+ S 6 '65

PRINTING industries of America, incorporated
PIA convention, publisher as printer; electronics house to become typesetting house; summaries of speeches. il Pub W 188:97-8+ N 8 '65

PIA's annual meeting looks at labor; summaries of speeches at convention. il Pub W 188:76-8+ O 4 '65
PIA's web offset section concludes annual meeting; May 26-28. Pub W 188:136-8 Jl 19 '65
Publishers and printers win awards; Graphic arts awards. il Pub W 188:84+ O 4 '65

PRINTING industry
PIA convention; publisher as printer; electronics house to become typesetting house; summaries of speeches. il Pub W 188:97-8+ N 8 '65
PIA's annual meeting looks at labor; summaries of speeches at convention. il Pub W 188:76-8+ O 4 '65
R & E reviews computers and electronics in the graphic arts; annual meeting. Pub W 187:123-4 Je 14 '65
See also
Edwards brothers, incorporated, lithographers
Halliday lithograph corporation

Consolidations and mergers
J. W. Clement company acquired by syndicate. Pub W 188:43-4 S 6 '65

PRINTING machinery
TPG-65, Paris exposition: a production man's view. R. D. Chapman. il Pub W 188:64-8+ Ag 9 '65
Tools of the trade. il Pub W 188:97-9 Ag 9 '65
See also
Photocomposing machines

PRINTING paper (photography) See Photographic paper

PRINTING presses
Electronic composing room: how near is it? J. Tebbel. il Sat R 48:75-6 Je 12 '65

PRINTS
Expert's expert; exhibition of modern prints currently on view at Harvard. il Time 85:72-7 F 19 '65
Printmaker. S. Chafetz. il Sch Arts 64:27-30 My '65
Views of Philadelphia 1750-1770. M. P. Snyder. il Antiques 88:674-80 N '65
See also
Aquatints

Technique
Elementary teacher. G. Barlow. il Sch Arts 64:34-5 My '65
Philip Kappel, etcher & engraver. E. M. Ettenberg. il Am Artist 29:36-41+ N '65
Spatter prints. M. M. Ridenour. il Flower Grower 52:20-2 Ag '65
Tempera and starch; project for the upper elementary and junior high school pupil. S. A. Batzka. il Sch Arts 64:29 Mr '65
White-ground etchings of Ron Kowalka. S. Hurwitz. il Am Artist 30:60-5+ Ja '66
White on white. M. Hirschl. il Sch Arts 64:5-7 Mr '65

PRIORITIES and allocations, Industrial
How Washington controls critical defense materials. Bsns W p24 Ag 7 '65

PRISM lenses. See Lenses, Photographic

PRISM rangefinder. See Photography—Apparatus and supplies

PRISMS
Images by the dozen; with prisms. N. Rothschild. il Pop Phot 58:118-19 Ja '66

PRISON chaplains. See Chaplains, Prison

PRISONERS
See also
Prisons

Rehabilitation
Captive class; computer programming course at the Atlanta federal penitentiary. Newsweek 66:78 N 8 '65
GE opens a prison door with computer training; teaching programming to inmates of Atlanta penitentiary. il Bsns W p96+ N 20 '65
Maximum security prison that emphasizes rehabilitation; United States penitentiary, Marion, Ill. il Arch Rec 137:187-92 Ap '65
Prison culture, from the inside; Federal correctional institutions. M. Arc. il N Y Times Mag p52-3+ F 28 '65
Working their way through jail; Work furlough programs in Santa Clara County prison. G. Samuels. il N Y Times Mag p 160+ N 14 '65

Russia
My life as a Soviet prisoner. P. Landerman. il Sat Eve Post 239:32-6+ Ja 15 '66

Spain
Twenty-three years in Franco's jails; tr. by G. Rabassa. M. Amblard. il Nation 200:305-7 Mr 22 '65

PRISONERS, Discharged
See also
Parole

Employment
Must they return? J. F. Fixx. Sat R 48:24
My 8 '65; Discussion. 48:18 Je 5; 33 Je 12;
26 O 2 '65

Rehabilitation
New life for Ron Sturrup. H. Bims. il Ebony
21:115-20+ D '65
PRISONERS, Political. See Political prisoners
PRISONERS as authors
Award-winning book proves to be plagiarism;
Arthur Koestler award competition for
books written by prison inmates. Pub W
188:73 N 15 '65
Writing the hard way. Sat R 48:34 S 11 '65
PRISONERS of war
Arctic maneuvers; the gimmicks of war.
R. J. Reguly. il Nation 200:333-6 Mr 29 '65
Red cross calls for application of convention
to war prisoners; statement, October 7,
1965, with text of U.S.-sponsored resolu-
tion. R. F. Woodward. Dept State Bul 53:
725-6 N 1 '65
See also
Geneva conventions
Vietnamese war, 1957- —Prisoners and prisons
PRISONERS of war, Returned
I am well, who are you? D. Piper. Esquire
64:80-4+ N '65

Rehabilitation
Dreams, the dreams; German ex-POW's a
decade later. J. Dornberg. il Newsweek
66:46+ N 1 '65
PRISONS
Maximum security prison that emphasizes
rehabilitation; United States penitentiary,
Marion, Ill. il Arch Rec 137:187-92 Ap '65
See also
Reformatories

Construction
Calculated compassion in prison design. il
Fortune 72:185-6 N '65

California
Working their way through jail; Work furlough programs in Santa Clara County
prison. G. Samuels. il N Y Times Mag
p 160+ N 14 '65

Colorado
Chair that scares them; delinquent boys tour
Colorado state prison; with report by M.
Murphy. il Life 58:51-2+ Mr 19 '65

Cuba
Imprisoned by Castro. G. de los Reyes. Read
Digest 86:114-18 My '65

France
On the penitentiary system in the United
States and its application in France, by
G. de Beaumont and A. de Tocqueville.
Review
Nation 201:168-9+ S 27 '65. N. Morris

Georgia
See also
Atlanta—Prisons and reformatories

South Africa
Courage in South Africa; exposé of prison
conditions in Rand daily mail. il Time 86:
60 Jl 23 '65
Crime and punishment; brutality in prisons;
government campaign to discredit Rand
daily mail articles. Newsweek 66:58 N 8 '65
How to lose friends. Time 86:36 S 3 '65
Prison scandal. il Newsweek 66:45 Ag 9 '65
There is no such thing as regulations here.
H. Strachan. il N Y Times Mag p 10-11+
Jl 25 '65
Who's lying? concerning prison brutality
story by Rand daily mail. Newsweek 66:40+
Ag 30 '65

United States
On the penitentiary system in the United
States and its application in France, by G.
de Beaumont and A. de Tocqueville. Re-
view
Nation 201:168-9+ S 27 '65. N. Morris
See also subhead Prisons and reforma-
tories under names of cities, e.g. Atlanta—
Prisons and reformatories
PRISTANE. See Hydrocarbons
PRITCHARD, James B.
They came, they saw, they testified. Sat R
48:32 D 18 '65

PRITCHETT, Victor Sawdon
Beautiful, anarchic, always on the make.
N Y Times Mag p63+ Ap 18 '65
Books. New Yorker 40:157-8+ F 13 '65
Canada: land of contrast and diversity. Read
Digest 86:200-2+ Ap '65
Discernments. Commentary 40:104+ N '65
Europe's Mediterranean coast. Holiday 39:
32-51+ Ja '66
Nest builder; story. New Yorker 41:61-5 D 11
'65
Soul of Spain. Holiday 37:52-67+ Ap '65
PRIVACY
Decision is affirmed; we deplore it again;
Warren Spahn right of privacy decision.
H. F. Pilpel. Pub W 188:28-9 Jl 26 '65
Desperate hours and the right of privacy;
concerning the limiting of freedom of
speech and the press to protect privacy of
private individuals. H. F. Pilpel. Pub W
188:32 N 1 '65
Forgotten amendment; Griswold v. Connec-
icut, right to marital privacy and redis-
covery of Ninth amendment. J. D. Carroll.
Nation 201:121-2 S 6 '65
Libel and privacy lines are now diverging.
Pub W 188:33 N 1 '65
New life for a forgotten amendment; Ninth,
involving right to privacy. il U S News
59:14 Jl 5 '65
Our right to privacy. M. Mead. Redbook
124:15-16 Ap '65
Patios around development house add pri-
vacy. il Arch Rec 137:86-9 mid-My '65
Peephole problem; gaping holes in wall of
privacy. Time 86:59+ N 12 '65
Private place; home of Frank Schlesinger,
Doylestown, Pa. il Life 58:88-91+ Je 4 '65
Snoopers & tappers; Edward V. Long's in-
vestigation into the invasion of privacy.
F. J. Cook. il Nation 201:496-501 D 20 '65
U shaped wings radiate from central core.
il Arch Rec 137:118-21 mid-My '65
Unions act on threats to privacy. il Bsns W
p87-8 Mr 13 '65
What we need is a law; invasion of privacy.
W. F. Buckley, jr. Nat R 17:455 Je 1 '65
Will there be a place for individuality? E.
Goble. Arch Rec 137:9 Ap '65
See also
Wire tapping
PRIVATE airplanes. See Airplanes—Private
ownership
PRIVATE brands
Private brands: the inside story. il Chang-
ing T 19:25-9 N '65
PRIVATE enterprise. See Free enterprise
PRIVATE flying
Fly-it-yourself; nowhere to go but up. il
Newsweek 66:98-100 N 15 '65
Gone flying to Europe. R. B. Parke. il Fly-
ing 77:36-9 D '65
Rising above it; California's Sierra sky park
commuters. il Newsweek 66:93C+ S 20 '65
Surface tension. R. B. Parke. Flying 78:30
Ja '66
Weekend pilot. F. K. Smith. See issues of
Flying
See also
Airplanes in business
PRIVATE libraries. See Libraries, Private
PRIVATE ownership. See Property
PRIVATE presses. See Printing—Private
presses
PRIVATE property. See Property
PRIVATE rights. See Civil rights
PRIVATE schools
Change at Groton. il Newsweek 65:79 Je 28
'65
Cradle-to-college struggle; New York schools.
il Time 86:40-1 Jl 30 '65
Personal business; preparatory schools.
Bsns W p85 Jl 3 '65
St Marksmanship; St Mark's school, South-
borough, Mass. il Newsweek 65:78 My 31 '65
Summer seminars; International seminars
program sponsored by the St Albans school,
Washington, D.C. il Newsweek 66:86+ Jl
26 '65
See also
Military schools

Desegregation
Child seller; with account by R. Stolley.
il Life 59:109-10+ O 8 '65

Australia
Toughening Charles at Timbertop. il Time
86:64 O 29 '65
PRIVATE schools, Experimental. See Schools,
Experimental
PRIVILEGES and immunities
King can do wrong. G. G. Coughlin. Read
Digest 87:31+ O '65

PRIX Goncourt. See Goncourt prize

PRIZE contests. See Competitions

PRIZEFIGHTING. See Boxing

PROBABILITIES
How chance affects your life; with questions and answers. G. S. Fay. Sci Digest 58:71-7 Ag '65; Discussion. 58:95-6 N '65
See also
Chance

PROBATE law and practice
See also
Estates, Decedents

PROBATION system
See also
Parole

PROBES, Space. See Space probes

PROBLEM children
Can this marriage be saved? Ava and Tracy had a problem child. D. C. Disney. Ladies Home J 82:24+ Je '65
Family courts at work; New York state's family court; ed. by M. R. Sherwin. J. Jiudice. il Parents Mag 40:64-6+ Ag '65
Problem of our early school dropouts; emotionally disturbed children at Irving Schwartz institute for children and youth, Philadelphia. J. Hamilton. il Look 29:34-8 Je 1 '65
Saving the trouble-prone. N. E. Hall, jr. il NEA J 54:26-8 Ap '65
Why good parents have problem children. A. Whitman. Read Digest 87:144-7 N '65
See also
Juvenile delinquency

PROBLEM solving
Can you analyze this problem? management exercise. P. Stryker. Harvard Bsns R 43:73-8 My '65
Every problem is an opportunity; interview. C. B. Seib. il Nations Bsns 53:40-1+ My '65
How to analyze that problem; management exercise. P. Stryker. il Harvard Bsns R 43:99-110 Jl '65

PROCEDURE (law)
See also
Criminal procedure

PROCESS control equipment. See Automatic control

PROCLAMATION of emancipation. See Emancipation proclamation

PROCRASTINATION
Mistakes many mothers make: dawdling is a necessary nuisance. R. Thomas. il Parents Mag 40:70-1+ Mr '65

PROCTER and Gamble company
Company in a quandary; competing too aggressively. Time 86:54-5 D 24 '65

PRODIGAL son; drama. See Hughes, L.

PRODIGIES. See Children, Gifted

PRODUCE exchanges. See Exchanges

PRODUCT liability. See Liability (law)

PRODUCT management. See Production control

PRODUCTION
Modular production, a new concept. M. K. Starr. il Harvard Bsns R 43:131-2+ N '65
Mood versus reality; industrial production. il Fortune 72:47-8 N '65
See also
Efficiency, Industrial
Supply and demand

PRODUCTION, Agricultural
Private investment in world agriculture. S. Williams. Harvard Bsns R 43:95-105 N '65

PRODUCTION, Theatrical. See Theatrical production

PRODUCTION code, Motion picture. See Moving picture censorship

PRODUCTION control
Man with too many hats; product manager, long on duties, short on authority. il Bsns W p43-4 My 22 '65
Product management, vision unfulfilled. D. J. Luck and T. Nowak. il Harvard Bsns R 43:143-50+ My '65
See also
Critical path analysis

PRODUCTION standards
USA seal of approval could upgrade products; creation of a USA standards institute. Sci N L 88:28 Jl 10 '65
See also
Work measurement

PRODUCTS, Commercial. See Commercial products

PRODUCTS, New
Exploit the product life cycle; excerpt from Marketing vision. T. Levitt. il Harvard Bsns R 43:81-94 N '65
Inventions, patents, processes. See issues of Science digest

Inventors peddle their wares; International inventors and new products exhibition. M. J. Pederson. il Pop Mech 124:54-7 N '65
New. B. C. Brown and C. W. Kennedy. il Pop Phot 56:108-11+ Je '65
New in the world of medicine. il Todays Health 43:80-1 Ap '65
New products. See issues of Business week
New products. See issues of Popular eletronics
New products. Time 85:63 Je 25 '65
One big race U.S. is winning. il U S News 59:84-7 S 27 '65
Pop! flick! zaaap! first International inventors and new products exhibition, New York. il Newsweek 66:106-106A+ S 27 '65
Product management, vision unfulfilled. D. J. Luck and T. Nowak. il Harvard Bsns R 43:143-50+ My '65
Products & procsses. See issues of Fortune
Products and processes. See issues of Missiles and rockets
Products you can use to improve your home. il Pop Sci 186:162-3 Mr '65
Space magic in the marketplace. il Time 86:95 S 24 '65
What's newest. See issues of Newsweek

PRODUCTS, Quality of. See Quality of products

PROESE, Bill
Silver band rings. Sch Arts 64:18-19 Mr '65

PROFESSION, Choice of. See Vocational guidance

PROFESSIONAL and scientific sales group
Technical book sales associates changes name. Pub W 188:45 Jl 5 '65

PROFESSIONAL bowlers association
Poor man's tour begins to strike it rich; Firestone tournament of champions. J. Jares. il Sports Illus 22:112-14 Ap 19 '65

PROFESSIONAL ethics
See also
Business ethics
Teachers ethics

PROFESSIONAL football clubs. See Football clubs; Football players

PROFESSIONAL golf. See Golf

PROFESSIONAL golfers' association championship. See Golf—Tournaments

PROFESSIONAL golfers' association of America
Golf in the stone age. Sports Illus 23:19 N 8 '65
Red tape on the green; PGA ruling for U.S. Ryder cup team. Sports Illus 23:8 N 1 '65
Revolt of the golf pros. A. Wright. il Sports Illus 23:14-17 Ag 9 '65

PROFESSIONAL sanctions. See Sanctions, Professional

PROFESSIONAL tennis. See Tennis

PROFESSIONS
Non-academic profile of college freshmen. Sch & Soc 93:292-3 Sum '65
See also
Occupations
Self employed

PROFESSORS. See College professors and instructors

PROFIT
America's most profitable company? Duns R 85:43 Ap '65
Cresting profits. il Fortune 71:30+ Ap '65
Fair practices and fair profits: union monopolies; address, February 20, 1965. C. R. Sligh, jr. bibliog Vital Speeches 31:430-4 My 1 '65
Fine art of high-yield management. J. B. Weiner. il Duns R 86:38-41+ O '65
Pinch on margins. il Fortune 72:52+ N '65
Profits jump sharply, on paper. il Bsns W p24 Ag 28 '65
Profits make for growth; excerpts from address. R. C. Tyson. Read Digest 86:99-101 Mr '65
Tiny flame; competition and profit; address, October 26, 1965. R. G. Wingerter. Vital Speeches 32:158-60 D 15 '65
Who pays the profit? G. R. Vila. il Duns R 86:50-2+ S '65
See also
Corporations—Finance
Recreation, Rural—Finance

PROFIT sharing
See also
Bonus system

PROFUMO, John Dennis
Remarkable new life of John Profumo. C. Plimmer and D. Plimmer. il por McCalls 92:60-1+ Jl '65

PROGESTERONE
Progesterone: biosynthesis from pregnenolone in holarrhena floribunda. R. D. Bennett and E. Heftmann. bibliog Science 149:652-3 Ag 6 '65

PROGRAM chairmen. See Chairmen

PROGRAM evaluation and budget committee.
See American library association—Program
evaluation and budget committee

PROGRAM evaluation and review technique.
See Critical path analysis

PROGRAM in humanities and the arts. See
Ford foundation

PROGRAMERS, Computer. See Computer
workers

PROGRAMMED teaching
Claims for programmed instruction of facts
and reasoning. W. W. Brickman. Sch &
Soc 93:467 D 11 '65
New course for canned teaching; teaching
machines used in industrial training.
Bsns W p67-9 Jl 24 '65
New world of teaching machines or Brave
new teaching machines? T. Morello. il
UNESCO Courier 18:10-16 Mr '65
Programed instruction: promising aid for
students, teachers, and parents. D. A. Sohn.
il PTA Mag 60:17-19 S '65
Survey of programmed materials. P. P. Cole-
man. Sr Schol 86:20T-21T F 18 '65
Trouble with programmed teaching. J. Olsen.
Library J 90:935-6+ F 15 '65
See also
Teaching machines

PROGRAMMETRY
Laser altimeter may aid photo mapping. B.
Miller. il Aviation W 82:60-1+ Mr 29 '65

PROGRAMMING (computers)
Captive class; GE course at the Atlanta
federal penitentiary. Newsweek 66:78 N 8
'65
GE opens a prison door with computer train-
ing; teaching programming to inmates of
Atlanta penitentiary. il Bsns W p96+ N 20
'65
Legal protection of computer programs. M.
R. Wessel. Harvard Bsns R 43:97-106 Mr
'65
Natural language game. J. Lear. Sat R 48:
53-4 My 1 '65
Programming learned at home. Bsns W p 140
My 22 '65

PROGRAMMING and systems, incorporated
Computer services for smaller publishers. il
Pub W 188:32-6 S 6 '65

PROGRESS
Let's invest in buggy whips. H. Downs. Sci
Digest 59:80-3 Ja '66
Mechanized monsters! S. A. Reed. il Liv
Wildn 29:17-19 Spr '65
See also
Civilization
Inventions
Science and civilization
Social progress

PROGRESSIVE education
New York's avant-garde school; New Lin-
coln. il Ebony 20:34-6+ My '65
William Heard Kilpatrick, 1871-1965. F.
Parker. Sch & Soc 93:368-71 O 16 '65

PROHIBITED books
See also
Index librorum prohibitorum

PROHIBITION
See also
Temperance

Mississippi
Prohibition's last stand. K. Vinson. New
Repub 153:10-11 O 16 '65

PROJECT Amigos. See Mexico—Relief work

PROJECT Apollo. See Space flight to the moon

PROJECT Camelot
Camelot spells controversy. Christian Cent
82:1138 S 15 '65
Decline of State. Nation 201:129 S 13 '65
Episode in intercultural misunderstanding.
C. H. Savage, jr. America 113:778-9 D 18
'65
Foreign affairs research: review process rises
on ruins of Camelot. J. Walsh. Science 150:
1429-31 D 10 '65
From Washington: notes on defense matters.
H. Margolis. Bul Atomic Sci 21:36-8 S '65
Research backlash; excerpts from remarks.
J. W. Fulbright. Aviation W 83:17 Ag 30 '65
Social science research and international re-
lations. D. Wolfle. Science 151:155 Ja 14 '66
Social sciences: cancellation of Camelot after row in Chile brings research under
scrutiny. J. Walsh. Science 149:1211-13 S
10 '65; Discussion. 150:289, 1770 O 15, D
31 '65

PROJECT for the orientation and induction
of new teachers. See Education—Washington (state)

PROJECT Gemini. See Space flight—Manned
flights

PROJECT head start
Are we overselling the pre-school idea? I.
Kraft. Sat R 48:63 D 18 '65
Bold experiment. il Newsweek 66:80-1 Jl 19
'65
Bureaucracy's long arm; too heady a start
in Mississippi? A. Kopkind. New Repub
153:19-22 Ag 21 '65
Come take my hand. B. L. Wilkinson; K.
Hamilton; S. Wolf. il Seventeen 24:98-9+
D '65
Fast start for Head start. il Time 86:64 Jl
2 '65
Getting a Head start. L. Hunt. il Sr Schol
87:sup 14-15 S 23 '65
Great society: a man with a problem; anti-
poverty project, Head start. B. Carter. il
Reporter 32:32-3 My 20 '65; Reply. S. Shri-
ver. 33:6 S 9 '65
Head start for a boy in a cubby; Hector's
experiences. il Life 59:91-2 S 24 '65
Headstart for children in slums. G. Lewis
and H. Mackintosh. il Am Ed 1:30, inside
back cover D '64
Head start programs; New York, Brooklyn
and Queens public libraries. il Library J
90:2338-40 My 15 '65
Hopeful Head start. il Time 86:17-18 S 10 '65
How helpful is Project head start? U S News
59:17 N 15 '65
Let's make Head start regular start. il Ebony
20:96-7 S '65
New kind of school; prekindergarten school.
M. J. E. Senn. il McCalls 92:48+ S '65
Pre-school program. F. M. Hechinger; F.
François; J. Nagy. il Sat R 48:58-62+ D
18 '65
Project head start. il NEA J 54:58-9 O '65
Project head start. il Seventeen 24:218-19
My '65
Six years old is too late. B. Asbell. il Redbook
125:53+ S '65

PROJECT INTREX. See Information storage
and retrieval systems

PROJECT Mohole. See Mohole project

PROJECT plowshare. See Atomic blasting

PROJECT Ranger. See Lunar probes

PROJECT Rover. See Rockets, Atomic powered

PROJECTILES
Tracers for shotguns. A. Kincaid. il Outdoor
Life 135:118-20 My '65

PROJECTION, Television. See Television projection

PROJECTION apparatus
Buying guide to slide projectors. il Good H
161:174-5 N '65
Cartridge sound projector. il U S Camera 28:
64-5 My '65
Caulfield on color. P. Caulfield. il Mod Phot
29:50+ D '65
Caulfield on color; mattee screens. P. Caul-
field. Mod Phot 29:54 Ap '65
Compact and clever, rear projection is a hit;
SOLO projection system. R. Miller. il U S
Camera 28:14+ Je '65
Evolution of Pointers; Super 8. il Pop Phot
56:72+ Je '65
Exciting inventions: Octarama and Dissol-
votron. R. Miller. il U S Camera 28:32+ Jl
'65
Films, projector, and a silencer. T. W. Mc-
Conkey. il Library J 90:1100 Mr 1 '65
Full-size results from half-frame. J. S. For-
ney. il Pop Phot 57:84-5+ O '65
Honeywell Rondelle 100. il U S Camera 28:28
O '65
Honeywell's Rondelle 100 slide projector. J.
Forney. il Pop Phot 57:100-1+ O '65
How to buy a movie projector. H. V. Fon-
diller. il Pop Phot 57:91-2 D '65
How to buy a projection screen. J. Hansen.
il Pop Sci 186:116-19+ Mr '65
Matzkin on movies; dual-purpose projector.
M. A. Matzkin. il Mod Phot 29:134+ N '65
Movies super 8 & other goodies. L. Lipton.
il Pop Phot 57:98-100 Ag '65
Quiet revolution in slide projectors. A. Ahlers.
il Pop Phot 56:64-7 Mr '65
Show side: slide projectors. A. Ahlers. il
Pop Phot 57:101-3 D '65
Slide projectors. il Consumer Rep 30:562-8
N '65
Take your slide show with you. H. Walton.
il Pop Sci 187:132-5 N '65
Tests of slide projectors. il Consumer Bul
48:43+ N '65

Phonograph combination
For children: GE's phono-viewer; combina-
tion record player-filmstrip projector. il
Consumer Rep 30:378-9 Ag '65

PROJECTION of transparencies. See Transparencies—Projection

PROJECTORS. See Projection apparatus

PROJECTS (teaching)
Batch of winners; USOE approve 216 of the
first PACE applications. il Newsweek 67:79
Ja 24 '66
See also
Art—Study and teaching—Projects
Science—Study and teaching—Projects
PROKHOROV, Aleksandr M.
Quantum electronics; address, December 11,
1964. bibliog Science 149:828-30 Ag 20 '65
PROKOF'EV, Sergei Sergeevich
Flaming angel (L'ange de feu) Criticism
Hi Fi 15:168-9 D '65
New Yorker 41:180+ O 2 '65
Opera N il 29:30 Mr 20 '65
Opera N il 30:24-5 N 6 '65
Sat R 48:42 O 9 '65
Time il 86:80 O 1 '65
PROMENADE concerts. See Concerts
PROMISCUITY. See Sexual ethics
PROMISE; story. See Morrow, S.
PROMOTERS and promoting
Man in the champ's corner; A. Dundee, a
combination psychologist, engineer and sur-
geon to Clay. G. Rogin. Sports Illus 22:
32-6+ My 24 '65
Secrets of a master showman. W. L. Veeck
and E. Linn. il Sports Illus 22:48-50+ Je
14 '65
See also
Isaacson, J.
PROMOTION, Sales. See Sales promotion
PRO MUSICA (organization) See New York
pro musica antiqua (organization)
PRONE and speechless dialect; story. See Jen-
ning, M. B.
PRONENESS to accidents. See Accidents—Psy-
chological aspects
PRONGHORN hunting
Buck the hard way. E. A. Bauer. il Outdoor
Life 136:60-3+ Jl '65
Riflemen prefer pronghorns. W. Page. il
Field & S 70:46-7+ Ag '65
PRONUNCIATION
See also
Names, Geographical—Pronunciation
PROOF of love; story. See Gordimer, N.
PROPAGANDA
From the big lie to the half-truth. J. Hohen-
berg. Sat R 48:37 D 25 '65
Now U.S. has one propaganda voice in Viet-
nam. U S News 58:22 Ap 19 '65
Strategy of persuasion, by A. F. Meyerhoff.
Review
Nation 200:118-19 F 1 '65. D. Cort
War of words; America's un-used weapon;
address, June 21, 1965. A. E. Meyerhoff.
Vital Speeches 31:600-3 Jl 15 '65
See also
Vietnamese war, 1957- —Propaganda
Voice of America (radio program)
PROPAGANDA, American. See Propaganda
PROPAGANDA, Chinese
Mao Tse-tung industry; when news is con-
traband. F. Nossal. il Sat R 49:108-9 Ja
8 '66
PROPAGANDA, Communist
New Communist propaganda strategy; French
anti-Americanism. E. Taylor. il Reporter
33:27-9 Jl 1 '65
People's wars. New Repub 153:7-8 S 18 '65
Police brutality: how much truth; how much
fiction? J. E. Hoover. il U S News 59:116-
17+ S 27 '65
What passes for American news in Africa.
J. Strohmeyer. Harper 231:98+ N '65
PROPAGANDA, Russian
Africans don't go to Russia to be brain-
washed. N. Nyangira. il N Y Times Mag
p52+ My 16 '65
PROPAGATION of plants. See Plant propaga-
tion
PROPANE
See also
Liquefied petroleum gas
PROPELLERS
Are you getting the outboard performance
you paid for? L. Eppel. il Motor B 116:32-
3+ Jl '65
Emergency prop. C. D. Wertman. il Field
& S 69:40 F '65
Get the pitch. R. W. Carrick. il Yachting
117:63+ Je '65
How to handle a twin screw boat. J. F.
Jayne. il Yachting 117:54-5+ My '65
Repairing
Now is the time for prop repair. N. Meiners.
il Motor B 115:30-1 F '65
PROPER, Datus C.
Rainbows in a strange land. Outdoor Life
136:40-3+ O '65

PROPER motions of the stars. See Stars—
Motions
PROPERTY
Schema thirteen and private property. Amer-
ica 113:394 O 9 '65
See also
Air rights
Community property
Real estate
PROPERTY in foreign countries. See Invest-
ments, Foreign
PROPERTY insurance. See Insurance, Property
PROPERTY rights. See Real property
PROPERTY tax
Property tax reform. R. Moley. Newsweek
65:128 My 10 '65
PROPERTY values. See Land values
PROPHECIES
Gift of prophecy, by R. Montgomery. Review
Life il 59:69+ O 8 '65. J. Howard
Jeane Dixon predicts the future. B. David-
son. Ladies Home J 82:74+ N '65
Seer in Washington. il Time 86:59-60 Ag 13
'65
See also
Prophets
PROPHETS
Jeane Dixon: psychic star of the year. il D.
Cohen. Nation 201:470-3 D 13 '65
PROPULSION, Jet. See Jet propulsion
PROPULSION, Rocket. See Rocket propulsion
PROPYLENE glycol
Now dairymen squirt away ketosis. il Farm
J 89:48 Ap '65
PROPYNE
New field of chemistry offered by compound.
Sci N L 88:184 S 18 '65
PROSPECTING
New methods could aid search for silver.
Sci N L 87:232 Ap 10 '65
See also
Helicopters in prospecting
Petroleum—Prospecting
PROSPERITY
Can prosperity go on and on? il U S News
59:54-7 N 15 '65
See also
Business conditions
United States—Economic conditions
PROSTAGLANDIN
Prostaglandin: release from the rat phrenic
nerve-diaphragm preparation. P. W. Ram-
well and others. bibliog il Science 149:1390-1
S 17 '65
PROSTHESIS
Brains without bodies. B. H. Frisch. il Sci
Digest 58:10-14 N '65
Control of life. il Life 59:66-83+ S 24 '65
Hope for amputees seen in use of nuclear
tools. Sci N L 88:360 D 4 '65
New ear for Susan. il Todays Health 43:43
Je '65
Plastic parts for the human body. Read
Digest 86:135-7 My '65
PROSTITUTION
Hostel is not a house; West Germany's
quarters for prostitutes. il Time 86:26+ Jl
23 '65
Italy: house and home; move to amend Mer-
lin law. il Newsweek 66:53 N 8 '65
Let's face it. M. Mannes. McCalls 92:18+ Je
'65
Murphy man misses, then scores at last.
J. Mills. il Life 59:94-5 D 3 '65
Streetwalking, theory and practice. V. L.
Bullough. Sat R 48:52-4 S 4 '65
PROTANOPIA. See Color blindness
PROTECTION against radiation. See Radiation
—Safety devices and measures
PROTECTION of animals. See Animals—Pro-
tection
PROTECTION of books. See Books—Conserva-
tion and restoration
PROTECTION of houses. See House protection
PROTECTION of plants. See Plants, Protec-
tion of
PROTECTION of the president. See Presidents
—United States—Protection
PROTECTIVE clothing. See Clothing, Pro-
tective
PROTECTIVE coloration. See Color of insects
PROTECTIVE mechanisms (biology) See De-
fense mechanisms (biology)
PROTECTIVE mimicry. See Mimicry (biology)
PROTEINS
Animal protein from plants; opaque-2 maize.
Sci Am 213:44 Ag '65
Anomalous dispersion method: its power for
protein structure analysis. G. N. Ra-
machandran and S. Parthasarathy. bibliog
il Science 150:212-14 O 8 '65

PROTEINS—*Continued*

Biosynthesis of histones and acidic nuclear proteins under different conditions of growth. L. S. Hnilica and others. bibliog il Science 150:1470-2 D 10 '65

Chondroitin sulfate: inhibition of synthesis by puromycin. G. De La Haba and H. Holtzer. bibliog il Science 149:1263-5 S 10 '65

Disulfide-bond cleavage and formation in proteins. O. Smithies. bibliog il Science 150:1595-8 D 17 '65

Dynein: a protein with adenosine triphosphatase activity from cilia. I. R. Gibbons and A. J. Rowe. bibliog il Science 149:424-6 Jl 23 '65

Immunoglobulin structure: amino- and carboxyl-terminal peptides of type I Bence Jones proteins. K. Titani and F. W. Putnam. bibliog Science 147:1304-5 Mr 12 '65

Immunoglobulin structure: partial amino acid sequence of a Bence Jones protein. K. Titani and others. bibliog il Science 149:1090-2 S 3 '65; Reply with rejoinder. D. W. Talmage. 150:1484-5 D 10 '65

Inhibition of protein synthesis by spectinomycin. J. Davies and others. bibliog il Science 149:1096-8 S 3 '65

Iodination in relation to thyroglobulin maturation and subunit aggregation. R. W. Seed and I. H. Goldberg. bibliog il Science 149:1380-2 S 17 '65

Major urinary protein complex of normal mice: origin. J. S. Finlayson and others. bibliog il Science 149:981-2 Ag 27 '65

Nonelectrolyte transport in muscle during induced protein loss. I. R. Fenichel and S. B. Horowitz. bibliog il Science 148:80-3 Ap 2 '65

Properties of bursicon: an insect protein hormone that controls cuticular tanning. G. Fraenkel and others. bibliog il Science 151:91-3 Ja 7 '66

Protein conformations in the plasma membrane. A. H. Maddy and B. R. Malcolm. bibliog il Science 150:1616-18 D 17 '65

Protein from coal. Sci Am 213:52 N '65

Protein from petroleum. A. Champagnat. il Sci Am 213:13-17 O '65

Protein solutions: concentration by a rapid method. W. F. Blatt and others. bibliog il Science 150:224-6 O 8 '65

Protein synthesis and the mitotic apparatus. J. Mangan and others. bibliog il Science 147:1575-8 Mr 26 '65

Protein synthesis by ribosomes from heart muscle: effect of insulin and diabetes. O. R. Rampersad and I. G. Wool. bibliog il Science 149:1102-3 S 3 '65

Protein synthesis in enucleated eggs of rana pipiens. L. D. Smith and R. E. Ecker. bibliog il Science 150:777-9 N 5 '65

Protein synthesis in rat liver: influence of amino acids in diet on microsomes and polysomes. A. Fleck and others. bibliog il Science 150:628-9 O 29 '65

Protein synthesis inhibition: mechanism for the production of impaired fat absorption. S. M. Sabesin and K. J. Isselbacher. bibliog il Science 147:1149-51 Mr 5 '65

Proteins by machine. Sci Am 213:44+ Ag '65

Proteins from petroleum. B. H. Frisch. Sci Digest 57:40 Ap '65

RNA codewords and protein synthesis. M. R. Bernfield and M. W. Nirenberg. bibliog il Science 147:479-84 Ja 29 '65

Soluble proteins of a melanoma and normal skin from the swordtail, platyfish, and their hybrids. D. G. Humm and A. L. Sylvia. bibliog il Science 150:635-6 O 29 '65

What's so important about proteins? D. G. Cooley. il Todays Health 43:46-51+ O '65

See also
Amino acids
Collagen
Ferredoxin
Interferon
Nucleoproteins
Plant proteins
Proteolysis
Tryptophan

PROTEOLYSIS

Peptides atached to thrombin: their influence on proteolysis. R. H. Landaburu and others. bibliog il Science 148:380-1 Ap 16 '65

PROTEST songs. See Music, Popular (songs, etc)

PROTESTANT church-owned publishers association

Church-owned publishers topics: management, new theology. il Pub W 187:46-7 Mr 22 '65

PROTESTANT churches

See also
Church unity
Ecumenical movement

Clergy
See Clergy

Missions
See Missions

Theology
See Theology

Africa
What are Protestants doing in Africa? Christian Cent 82:198 F 17 '65

England
See also
British council of churches

Indonesia
Indonesia today. H. P. Van Dusen. Christian Cent 82:616-17 My 12 '65

Japan
See also
Missions—Japan

Latin America
Latin America and revolution; new mood in the churches. J. A. Mackay. Christian Cent 82:1439-43 N 24 '65

Taiwan
Centenary of Protestantism in Formosa. D. H. Rayner. Christian Cent 82:1021-2 Ag 18 '65

United States
Church for unbelievers? renewal movement within American Protestantism. Newsweek 65:62 Ap 26 '65

Church on trial. D. A. Easton. Christian Cent 82:582 My 5 '65

Mindless and mute; inability of any person or group to speak authoritatively for a Protestant denomination. Christian Cent 82:1371-2 N 10 '65

Town with too many churches; Schellsburg, Pa. votes for United church. N. M. Lobsenz. il Redbook 126:70-1+ N '65

U.S. Protestantism: time for a second reformation. il Newsweek 67:33-7 Ja 3 '66

PROTESTANT churches and international relations. See Church and international relations

PROTESTANT churches and race problems. See Church and race problems

PROTESTANT churches and social problems. See Church and social problems

PROTESTANT council of the city of New York
Not positive enough? Dr N. V. Peale elected president. Newsweek 65:64 Mr 15 '65

PROTESTANT Episcopal church
Attorney for the defense. Time 86:106 S 17 '65

Bells in the Delta; Episcopal civil rights activists. Time 85:71 F 26 '65

Council rescinds restrictions; clergymen's participation in racial justice projects. Christian Cent 82:293 Mr 10 '65

Holiness through action; induction of Presiding bishop of the Protestant Episcopal church. il Time 85:61 F 5 '65

Secession in Savannah; St John's Episcopal church refuses integration. il Time 85:70 My 7 '65

Second thoughts; support for National council of churches civil-rights work. Newsweek 65:55 Mr 1 '65

See also
Liturgical movement—Protestant Episcopal church

Converts
Catholic leakage; Chicago survey findings. America 112:846 Je 12 '65

PROTESTANT missions. See Missions

PROTESTANT monasteries. See Monasteries

PROTESTANT newspapers and periodicals. See Religious newspapers and periodicals

PROTESTANT reformation. See Reformation

PROTESTANTISM

Catholic and Protestant renewal. W. B. Blakemore. Cath World 201:183-8 Je '65

Faith and the facts of life. W. Hamilton. Nation 200:424-6 Ap 19 '65

Protestant deformation. H. O. J. Brown. il Nat R 17:464-6 Je 1 '65

Protestantism in American sociology. R. L. Means; reply. R. T. Wolcott. Christian Cent 82:146-7 F 3 '65; Rejoinder. 82:470-1+ Ap 14 '65

PROTESTANTISM—*Continued*
Protestantism in an ecumenical age, by O.
A. Piper. Review
    Christian Cent 82:1450-1 N 24 '65. D. G.
    Bloesch
Protestantism: mid-decade assessment. Christian Cent 83:67-8 Ja 19 '66
What on earth is happening to Protestantism. D. Norton-Taylor. il Fortune 72:
170-3+ D '65
    See also
Evangelicalism
Fundamentalism
Reformation

Anecdotes, facetiae, satire, etc.
Loneliness of Protestantism. C. M. Nielsen.
    Christian Cent 82:1120-1 S 15 '65
Power and the glory. Christian Cent 82:1239
    O 6 '65

PROTESTANTS and other Americans united
for separation of church and state
Audiatur et altera pars: charge of censorship by POAU against librarian of Belleville, Ill, public library. Wilson Lib Bul
40:9+ S '65
Church, state, and freedom to read, charge
of censorship by POAU against librarian
of Belleville, Ill, public library E. J.
Gaines. ALA Bul 59:785-6 O '65
IRS: please note! tax-exempt POAU. Nat R
17:681-2 Ag 10 '65
PROTESTANTS in Italy
Getting ahead in Italy. il Time 85:62 Je 4 '65
PROTESTANTS in Latin America
Conversion in Latin America. il Time 86:72
    Jl 23 '65
How Latin America sees it. L. E. Odell and
others. Christian Cent 82:805-6 Je 23 '65;
Discussion. 82:797, 1292+, 1552 Je 23, O 20,
D 15 '65
Witness in Latin America. Christian Cent
82:699-700 Je 2 '65
PROTESTANTS in Spain
Rights for Spanish Protestants? Franco
pledged broadening of religious liberty. S.
F. Wexler. Christian Cent 82:867-9 Jl 7 '65
PROTESTANTS in the United States
U.S. Protestantism: time for a second reformation. il Newsweek 67:33-7 Ja 3 '66
PROTESTS against Vietnamese war. See Vietnamese war, 1957- —Protests, demonstrations, etc, against
PROTOCOL, Diplomatic. See Diplomatic etiquette
PROTON accelerators. See Accelerators (electrons, etc)
PROTONS
Faraday society discussion: proton transfer
processes; report on meeting. M. R. Crampton. Science 149:208 Jl 9 '65
Forces in atom core are weak and strong.
    Sci N L 87:137 F 27 '65
Radiation sintering of lunar dust. R. Smoluchowski. bibliog Science 150:1025-6 N 19
'65
PROTOZOA
Invisible multitudes in your life. R. Platt.
    il Read Digest 86:213-14+ F '65
Isolation and characterization of DNA from
kinetoplasts of leishmania enriettii. H. G.
Du Buy and others. bibliog il Science 147:
754-6 F 12 '65
Primary lysosomes in tetrahymena pyriformis.
A. M. Elliott. bibliog il Science 149:640-1
Ag 6 '65
    See also
Euglena
Growth promoting substances (protozoa)

Culture mediums
Eimeria tenella: cultivation of the asexual
stages in cultured animal cells. W. H.
Patton. bibliog il Science 150:767-9 N 5 '65
PROTOZOA, Pathogenic
Eimeria tenella: cultivation of the asexual
stages in cultured animal cells. W. H.
Patton. bibliog il Science 150:767-9 N 5 '65
PROUST, Marcel
Letter from Paris; exhibition around his
life and works at the Bibliothèque. Genêt.
New Yorker 41:92+ Je 26 '65
Proust: the later years, by G. D. Painter.
Review
    Newsweek il por 67:65+ Ja 10 '66
    Sat R il por 48:58-9 O 23 '65. L. LeSage
PROUTY, Winston L.
Excerpt from debate, August 30, 1965. Cong
Digest 44:238+ O '65
PROVERBS
Art of proverbs. F. L. Lucas. il Holiday 38:
8+ S '65
    See also
Maxims

PROVIDENCE, R.I.

Historic houses, etc.
John Brown House. A. F. Downing. il Antiques 87:556-63 My '65
Living with antiques; Providence home of
Mrs R. H. Ives Goddard. B. Snow. il Antiques 87:580-5 My '65
PROVIDENCE, R.I, public library
Providence pioneer: William E. Foster. J. L.
Wheeler. il Wilson Lib Bul 40:275-8 N '65
PROVING grounds
Air force expands range dominance; takeover of control at Point Arguello for Western test range. D. L. Zylstra. il Miss &
Roc 16:33-5 Mr 8 '65
Amazing new Cape Kennedy. H. Pryor. il Sci
Digest 57:47-51 Je '65
As U.S. moonport takes shape; John F. Kennedy space center, Merritt Island launch
area. il U S News 59:27-30 Ag 30 '65
Base where MOL will be born; air force's
Vandenberg. il Bsns W p70-2+ N 13 '65
Cosmic room to stagger the mind; Apollo
project's Vehicle assembly building. J. Atwater. il Sat Eve Post 238:30-1 Ap 24 '65
ETR antennas gets wide-range ability; updating of the Eastern test range to handle
spacecraft S-band telemetry. R. Pay. il
Miss & Roc 16:26-7 My 24 '65
Guidance, control studies under way; ERC's
Guidance and control div. il Miss & Roc
16:32-5 My 31 '65
MILA construction delays cramping space
agency's launch schedulers; Merritt Island
launch area. M. Getler. il Miss & Roc 16:
26-7 Mr 15 '65
Our fantastic moonport; John F. Kennedy
space center, Merritt Island launch area.
il Bsns W p76-80+ Je 5 '65
Program promises better instruments; improving range support and missile design. M. Getler. il Miss & Roc 17:24-6 Ag
30 '65
Space age comes to Mississippi. il U S News
58:78-80 F 15 '65
Space training flights in NF-104A near; Aerospace research pilot school, Edwards AFB,
Calif. C. M. Plattner. il Aviation W 83:80-
1+ Ag 9 '65
Top this; Merritt Island's vehicle assembly
building. il Newsweek 65:65 Ap 26 '65
White Sands ARTRAC network to be operational by next summer; Advanced range
testing, reporting, and control system. il
Miss & Roc 17:28 S 20 '65
WSMR consolidating control center. R. Pay.
Miss & Roc 16:32-4 F 1 '65
PROVUS, Malcolm M.
NEA time to teach project. NEA J 54:8-10
Ap '65
Self-direction for teachers. NEA J 55:49 Ja '66
PRUDDEN, T. M.
Salvage. Yachting 118:157-9 D '65
PRUDEN, Don
Reporter at large; return to George River.
E. Iglauer. il New Yorker 41:174+ N 6 '65
PRUDEN, Gwen
Reporter at large; return to George River.
E. Iglauer. il New Yorker 41:174+ N 6 '65
PRUDENTIAL insurance company of America
Pru drafts a GI policy; military insurance
program. Bsns W p77 O 23 '65
PRUD'HON, Pierre Paul
Prud'hon's The union of love and friendship.
A. Brookner. il Art N 64:36-8+ N '65
PRUITT-Igoe housing development. See St
Louis—Housing
PRUNING
Importance of spring pruning. il Bet Hom &
Gard 43:134-5 Mr '65
PRYBYLA, Jan S.
Paris-Peking trade; Marianne & the dragon.
Nation 200:99-102 F 1 '65
PRYCE-JONES, Alan
Edith Sitwell. Commonweal 82:241-3 My 14 '65
How to act like a writer in New York and
London. Harper 231:146-50 N '65
Mixture as never before. House & Gard 127:
146-7 Mr '65
Newport, out of season. Vogue 145:58 Mr 15
'65
Reality of real people. Commonweal 83:88-
9+ O 22 '65
PRYCE-JONES, David
May day in Piešt'any. Vogue 145:53+ My '65
PRYOR, Frances
What shall I write about? NEA J 54:54-5
N '65
PRZYBYLSKI, A.
Spectrum of satellite Echo I. Sky & Tel 30:
217 O '65
PSEUDO medicine. See Quacks and quackery

PSEUDOMONAS
Staphylolytic substance from a species of pseudomonas. J. W. Zyskind and others. bibliog il Science 147:1458-9 Mr 19 '65

PSEUDOURIDINE. See Uridine

PSOMIADES, Harry J.
Cyprus dispute. bibliog f Cur Hist 48:269-76+ My '65

PSYCHIATRY
Acoustic methods in psychiatry. P. F. Ostwald. il Sci Am 212:82-9+ bibliog(p 139) Mr '65
Inside psychiatry today. See issues of Science digest
Research frontier; SR preview of Reality therapy. W. Glasser. Sat R 48:54-6 Mr 6 '65; Discussion. 48:64 My 1 '65
See also
Mental illness
Social psychiatry

Terminology
New approach to mental illness. K. Menninger. Read Digest 86:71-3 Mr '65

PSYCHIATRY, Forensic. See Forensic psychiatry

PSYCHIATRY and religion
Church and the couch. P. Rowley. Nation 200:203-4 F 22 '65

PSYCHICAL research
See also
Hypnosis
Parapsychology

PSYCHOANALYSIS
Computer that psychoanalyzes you. M. Maruyama. il Sci Digest 59:70-5 Ja '66
Ethics of psychoanalysis, by T. S. Szasz. Review
Nat R 17:1031-2 N 16 '65. E. Van Den Haag
New Repub 153:31-3 Ag 7 '65. Z. Teplitz; Reply. J. D. W. Andrews. 153:38 S 4 '65
Freudian slip; no monuments for Freud in Vienna. J. Wechsberg. il N Y Times Mag p 105-8 Je 6 '65
Freud's theories tested. P. McBroom. Sci N L 88:278 O 30 '65
Primary thinking. F. R. Schreiber and M. Herman. Sci Digest 59:23 Ja '66
Psychoanalysis and contemporary American culture, ed. by H. M. Ruitenbeek. Review
Commentary 39:72-4 Ap '65. H. Rosenberg
Psychoanalysis and morality. L. H. Farber. Commentary 40:69-74 N '65
Research frontier; SR preview of Reality therapy. W. Glasser. Sat R 48:54-6 Mr 6 '65; Discussion. 48:64 My 1 '65
Wild analyst; the life and work of Georg Groddeck, by C. M. Grossman and S. Grossman. Review
New Repub 152:22-4 My 1 '65. A. Watts
See also
Dreams

PSYCHOANALYSIS and religion. See Psychiatry and religion

PSYCHOLOGICAL examinations
Adventures of a test taker. J. Zola; discussion. Nat R 17:86+ F 9 '65
Rage in the lab; Feshback experiment. R. G. G. Price. il Atlan 216:116-18 D '65
Sharper tools for the talent hunt; psychological tests for potential executives. il Bsns W p70+ Mr 27 '65
Test bans; government tightening regulations over use of psychological tests. New Repub 152:8 Je 19 '65
Testing daze. il Newsweek 65:111-111A+ Je 14 '65
Who's fit to serve? J. Ridgeway. New Repub 152:9-11 Mr 13 '65
See also
Personality tests

PSYCHOLOGICAL experiments. See Psychological examinations

PSYCHOLOGICAL literature
Bibliographical challenges in the age of the computer; excerpts from editorial in Mental health book review index. I. Bry and L. Afflerbach. il Library J 90:813-18 F 15 '65

PSYCHOLOGICAL stress. See Stress (physiology)

PSYCHOLOGICAL tests. See Psychological examinations

PSYCHOLOGICAL warfare
Air force U-10Bs play key role in psychological warfare tactics. C. Brownlow. Aviation W 82:69 Je 7 '65
See also
Vietnamese war, 1957- —Psychological aspects

PSYCHOLOGY
See also
Anxiety
Behavior (psychology)
Hypnotism
Motivation (psychology)
Parapsychology
Self
Sleep
Television broadcasting—Psychological aspects
Woman—Psychology

PSYCHOLOGY, Abnormal. See Psychology, Pathological

PSYCHOLOGY, Applied
See also
New Thought

PSYCHOLOGY, Criminal. See Criminal psychology

PSYCHOLOGY, Educational
Way teaching is; excerpts from address. P. W. Jackson. il NEA J 54:10-13+ N '65
Why children fail in school; with study-discussion program by E. Harris and D. Harris. bibliog il PTA Mag 60:14-16, 36 Ja '66
See also
Thought
Thought and thinking

PSYCHOLOGY, Experimental
Ethology and experimental psychology; report on an international conference in Rome. W. N. Schoenfeld and S. H. Baron. Science 147:634-5 F 5 '65
Your eye can't lie; psychology called pupillometrics. B. Davidson. il Sat Eve Post 239:76-9 Ja 15 '66
See also
Stimulus and response

PSYCHOLOGY, Pathological
Presidential disease; presidential assassination syndrome. il Newsweek 65:67 My 17 '65
See also
Criminal psychology
Hysteria
Medicine, Psychosomatic
How your body can shape your personality. R. Mines. il Sci Digest 57:79-83 Je '65

PSYCHOLOGY, Religious. See Religion, Psychology of

PSYCHOLOGY, Social. See Social psychology

PSYCHOLOGY, Vocational. See Vocational psychology

PSYCHOLOGY of color. See Color—Psychology

PSYCHOLOGY of eating. See Eating, Psychology of

PSYCHOSES
Cure for psychosis seen; adrenal hormone balance. Sci N L 88:78 Jl 31 '65

PSYCHOSOMATIC medicine. See Medicine, Psychosomatic

PSYCHOSURGERY. See Brain—Surgery

PSYCHOTHERAPY
Milieu therapy, a new approach to treatment. F. R. Schreiber and M. Herman. il Sci Digest 57:16-18 Mr '65
See also
Group psychotherapy

PSYCHROMETERS. See Hygrometers

PTERIDINES
Photosynthetic phosphorylation: stimulation by pteridines and a comparison with phosphodoxin. F. I. Maclean and others. bibliog il Science 149:636-8 Ag 6 '65

PUBERTY
Preparation for puberty; with study-discussion program. by E. Harris and D. Harris. J. W. Kessler. bibliog il PTA Mag 59:25-7, 35-6 My '65
See also
Adolescence

PUBLIC address systems. See Loud speaking apparatus

PUBLIC administration. See Administration, Public

PUBLIC affairs information service
Esoteric indexing crusade: inclusion of Superintendent of documents number with each government document entry; letter to the editor. R. B. Dennis; reply. M. Lopez. Library J 90:1220 Mr 15 '65

PUBLIC buildings
Base for smoke jumpers given roof-like forms; Redmond air center, Ore. il Arch Rec 138:195-8 O '65
See also
County buildings
Library architecture
Municipal buildings

PUBLIC buildings service. See United States
—Public buildings service

PUBLIC debt (United States)   See Debts,
Public—United States

PUBLIC defenders
Justice for the poor. M. T. Bloom. il Read
Digest 86:126-30 Ap '65

PUBLIC domain. See Public lands

PUBLIC health
See also
Air pollution
Meat inspection
Water pollution

International aspects

International cooperation for health: a modern imperative. J. Watt. Dept State Bul
53:412-18 S 6 '65
See also
World health organization

Great Britain

Too health-conscious? Newsweek 66:42 Ag 2
'65
See also
Great Britain—National health service

Latin America

See also
Pan American sanitary bureau

Puerto Rico

Up by the bootstraps; disease and death rates
cut. Time 86:77 O 29 '65

Underdeveloped areas

Economic growth brings industrial diseases.
Sci N L 88:280 O 30 '65

United States

Aim to conquer killers; network of regional
medical complexes for heart disease, can-
cer and stroke. Sci N L 87:151 Mr 6 '65
Doctor's first job: preventing sickness. J.
Mayer. il N Y Times Mag p48-9+ N 28 '65
Prevent early deaths. Sci N L 88:180 S 18
'65
See also
United States—Public health service

Vietnam (Democratic Republic)

Viet Cong immune to variety of viruses. il
Sci N L 89:2 Ja 1 '66

Vietnam (Republic)

Viet Cong immune to variety of viruses. il
Sci N L 89:2 Ja 1 '66

PUBLIC health Indian hospitals. See Indians
of North America—Hospitals

PUBLIC high schools. See High schools

PUBLIC houses (Great Britain) See Bars and
barrooms

PUBLIC housing. See Housing

PUBLIC housing projects. See Housing projects, Government

PUBLIC industries. See Public service industries

PUBLIC institutions. See State institutions

PUBLIC interest (periodical)
In the Public interest; first issue of new
quarterly. Newsweek 66:90 N 1 '65

PUBLIC land law review commission.   See
United States—Public land law review
commission (proposed)

PUBLIC lands

United States

For a more beautiful U.S; the President asks
this; with interview with C. A. T. Johnson.
il U S News 58:71-6+ F 22 '65
For sale: vacation sites from Uncle Sam.
E. Kerr. il Pop Sci 186:138-40 Je '65
Let's halt the federal land grab. R. M.
Hyatt. il Nat R 17:984-5 N 2 '65
Natural lands: the big country. D. B. Stough.
il Am For 71:64-5+ My '65
Public land review. M. Clawson. il Am For
71:10-13+ Mr; 34-9+ Ap; 50-3+ My; 20-3+
Je; 26-9+ Jl; 12-15+ Ag '65; Discussion. 71:9
Mr; 2-3 Je '65
See also
National parks and reserves—United States
United States—Land management, Bureau of

PUBLIC libraries. See Libraries

PUBLIC meetings
See also
Chairmen

PUBLIC officers
Abe, help! LBJ; Johnson's right-hand man.
C. B. Seib and A. L. Otten. il Esquire 63:
86-8+ Je '65

Administrators in the county of tomorrow;
address, November 24, 1964. B. F. Hillen-
brand. Vital Speeches 31:243-7 F 1 '65
Always a bridesmaid; case of A. Yarmolin-
sky. Newsweek 66:32 N 8 '65
As LBJ moves his own men into top spots.
il U S News 58:19-20 My 10 '65
As the White House views revolt of the
liberals. U S News 59:41 Jl 5 '65
Bundy and beyond. H. Brandon. Sat R 49:18
Ja 22 '66
Bureaucrats and citizens. D. E. Ashford.
bibliog f Ann Am Acad 358:89-100 Mr '65
Change & chatter; administration changes. il
Time 86:15-16 Jl 16 '65
Crisis solver for LBJ; J. Califano. Bsns W
p34+ Ja 15 '66
Filling the gaps; presidential appointments.
il Newsweek 66:21-2 Jl 26 '65
Four get new posts from LBJ. Bsns W p27-8
My 1 '65
Historic picture of the New frontier, and
this is what they have to say; symposium,
ed. by S. V. Roberts. il Esquire 64:88-95+
N '65
How Johnson fills jobs at the top; stress on
intelligence and skill in government. il Bsns
W p20-2 Jl 31 '65
How LBJ picks his men; interview. J. W.
Macy, jr. il Nations Bsns 53:36-7+ Jl '65
How the State department baffled him; ex-
cerpts from A thousand days. A. M.
Schlesinger, jr. il Life 59:18-27 Jl 30 '65
Importance of being Bundy. M. Frankel.
il N Y Times Mag p32-3+ Mr 28 '65
Inner, inner circle around Johnson. B. H.
Bagdikian. il N Y Times Mag p21+ F 28 '65
Inside the White House; LBJ aides. il News-
week 65:27-9+ Mr 1 '65
Intergovernmental relations as seen by public
officials. R. W. McCulloch. bibliog f Ann
Am Acad 359:127-36 My '65
JFK's private opinions of prominent people.
il U S News 59:53-4 Ag 9 '65
Johnson taps his financial team; appoint-
ment of four men for fiscal and monetary
policy team. il Bsns W p26-7 Ap 24 '65
Johnson's talent hunt. J. Kraft. Harper 230:
40+ Mr '65
L.B.J.'s inner circle, by C. Roberts. Review
Sat R 48:51 D 4 '65. B. Cochran
L.B.J.'s young man in charge of everything.
il Time 86:24-8 O 29 '65
Lyndon Johnson presents eight new adminis-
tration appointees. il Time 85:25 My 7 '65
Men around Johnson; how well off they are.
il U S News 58:46-7 My 24 '65
Men closest to the President; Johnson's
White House staff. il Bsns W p34+ Je 19
'65
Most happy dropouts; former presidential
assistants make good. il Time 86:29 S 24 '65
Musical chairs season: Johnson administra-
tion. il Sr Schol 87:16 O 7 '65
New line-up; White House staff. il Time 86:
28-9 S 24 '65
New press secretary. H. Brandon. il Sat R
48:10-11 Ag 7 '65
Nine key aides; who does what for LBJ. il
U S News 59:13 D 27 '65
Of power, men, and politics. il Newsweek
65:32-4 My 17 '65
Politics of power; portrait of a master. il
Newsweek 66:18-19+ Ag 2 '65
President calls for full use of resources in
overseas programs; statement, March 25,
1965. L. B. Johnson. Dept State Bul 52:538
Ap 12 '65
They twist arms without hurting; liaison
men between the White House and Capitol
hill. il Bsns W p82+ Ap 24 '65
To administer does not always mean to rule;
men who handle money for Johnson's new
domestic program. il Fortune 73:122-3 Ja '66
Who the President listens to. C. B. Seib.
il Nations Bsns 53:32-3+ Ap '65
Who's minding the kitchen these days? White
House employees. J. N. Eller. America
113:153 Ag 14 '65
Why LBJ wants men ten feet tall. P. Lisagor.
il Nations Bsns 53:23-4 O '65
See also
Cabinet officers
Government employees
Political ethics
also subhead Public officers under names
of cities, e.g. New York (city)—Public
officers

Anecdotes, facetiae, satire, etc.

When in Washington: hang up while you're
talking; excerpt from My appointed round.
J. E. Day. il Nations Bsns 53:38-9+ Jl '65

PUBLIC officers—*Continued*

Appointment, qualifications, tenure, etc.

Boyd role to bolster Commerce office. R. G. O'Lone. Aviation W 82:27 My 3 '65

New security risks; disloyalty to the leader. W. F. Buckley, jr. Nat R 17:863 O 5 '65

White House years; waging peace: 1956-1961, by D. D. Eisenhower. Review U S News il 59:64-5 O 18 '65

Families

L.B.J.'s grass widows; wives of presidential assistants. P. Cavin. Ladies Home J 82:64+ N '65

History

King's friends, civil servants, or politicians; civil service in England. F. B. Wickwire. bibliog f Am Hist R 71:18-42 O '65

Italy

Atlantic report; scandals nourish cynicism of voters. Atlan 216:23-4+ D '65

PUBLIC opinion

How world reacted to LBJ's speech. il U S News 58:32 F 1 '65

Morality and policy. America 112:747 My 22 '65

1938: Birth of a baby, 1965: Drama of life; reaction to picture journalism. G. P. Hunt. il Life 58:3 My 21 '65

Occasion for protest. Nation 200:658 Je 21 '65

Public opinion and the war in Vietnam; Great debate. L. Markel. il N Y Times Mag p9+ Ag 8 '65

U.S. & world opinion; Time essay. Time 85:30-1 My 28 '65; Same abr. with title United States and world opinion. Read Digest 87:59-62 S '65

Whose opinion is world opinion? reprint, July 14, 1964. J. Burnham. Nat R 17:1070 N 30 '65

See also
Attitudes
United States—Foreign opinion
Vietnamese war, 1957- —Public opinion

Africa

See also
United States—Foreign opinion—African

China (People's Republic)

See also
China (People's Republic)—Foreign opinion

Cuba

See also
United States—Foreign opinion—Cuban

Europe, Western

Europe's schizophrenia. H. Brandon. Sat R 48:16 S 25 '65

Vietnam: European viewpoints. B. B. Fall. New Repub 153:13-15 Ag 21 '65

Vietnam, LBJ, good times: what Europeans are saying. il U S News 59:70-4 Ag 9 '65

See also
United States—Foreign opinion—European

France

Letter from Paris; Goldfinger a hit with the French. Genêt. New Yorker 41:165-7 Mr 20 '65

Opinion in Paris; China won't fight. P. Ben. New Repub 153:18 S 25 '65

See also
United States—Foreign opinion—French

Great Britain

1966 and all that. J. M. Cameron. Commonweal 83:459-60 Ja 21 '66

See also
United States—Foreign opinion—British

Japan

See also
United States—Foreign opinion—Japanese

Mexico

Silencing the children of Sanchez; controversy over translation and publication. J. Sommers. il Nation 201:530-3 D 27 '65

See also
United States—Foreign opinion—Mexican

Russia

See also
United States—Foreign opinion—Russian

South Africa

What it means to be an American. T. Roszak. Nation 201:277 O 25 '65

United States

America's mood today. L. Gross. il Look 29: 15-21 Je 29 '65

Are Americans more comfortable with Lyndon Johnson? Q. de Manila. Nat R 17:552-4+ Je 29 '65

Bundy-Gruening debate. M. Kempton. New Repub 152:9-10 My 8 '65

Changing mood of America; what a nationwide survey shows. il U S News 58:36-43 My 31 '65

Christmas, 1965; antagonisms. M. Ascoli. Reporter 33:10 D 30 '65

Crisis in the United Nations; address, December 10, 1964. C. B. Luce. Vital Speeches 31:236-41 F 1 '65

Duty of Congress; representatives organize public discussions in own districts. Nation 201:457-8 D 13 '65

Foreign policy fever. Commonweal 82:307-8 My 28 '65

From dissent to opposition. Nation 200:629 Je 14 '65

Gallup poll; President Johnson's popularity, down again, after a rise. il U S News 59:21 Ag 16 '65

Glimpse inside an LBJ stag dinner; discussions with President and selected Cabinet officers. U S News 59:10 Ag 30 '65

Great debate on Viet Nam. Sr Schol 87:6-9 S 23 '65

Great debate over American military interventions. W. V. O'Brien. Cath World 201: 316-21 Ag '65

Hearing: called locally and unofficially by W. F. Ryan in his district on Vietnam war. New Yorker 41:23-6 Ag 28 '65

Honor and the hazard; protest parades and demonstrations. Nation 201:289 N 1 '65

Liberal break with Johnson. U S News 58: 35-6 My 24 '65

LBJ's Vietnam policy; what the polls show. U S News 58:11 My 10 '65

Morality, moralism and Vietnam. W. H. Harris. Christian Cent 82:1155-7 S 22 '65; Discussion. 82:1452+ N 24 '65

Mover of men; opinions about President Johnson. il Time 86:18-22 Ag 6 '65

Professor votes for Mr Johnson; intellectual community, anti-administration. J. P. Roche. il N Y Times Mag p45+ O 24 '65; Discussion. p22+ N 7; 16+ N 21 '65

Public opinion and Vietnam. Nat R 17:678-9 Ag 10 '65

Shift in the wind in Washington; violent defiance of law and order gone too far. il U S News 59:27-8 S 6 '65

Spectrum on Viet Nam; campus activity in support of U.S. policy. il Time 86:67 N 19 '65

State dept. on campus: sit down and shut up. D. Janson. il Nation 200:547-50 My 24 '65

Vietniks: self-defeating dissent; Time essay. Time 86:44-5 O 29 '65

Vox Vietnik fires a volley of protest; with report by J. K. Jessup. il Life 59:40B-40D O 29 '65

What people say about the mails. il U S News 58:65 Ap 12 '65

What people think about college. W. C. Eckerman and A. Campbell. il Am Ed 1: 30-2 F '65

What senators' mail says about Vietnam. U S News 59:9 Ag 23 '65

What the people really think; views on President Johnson and his policies in Vietnam. S. Alsop. il Sat Eve Post 238:18, 27-31 O 23 '65

Where consensus breaks down; Great society. H. J. Morgenthau. New Repub 154:16-18 Ja 22 '66

Why liberals grumble about LBJ. il U S News 59:40-2 Jl 5 '65

Why the protests? demonstrations against war in Vietnam. New Repub 153:5-7 O 30 '65

Vietnam (Republic)

See also
United States—Foreign opinion—Vietnamese

PUBLIC opinion polls

Morals of a teen; poll of PTA presidents; with study-discussion program, by C. Smallenberg and H. Smallenberg. R. Squires. bibliog il PTA Mag 59:4-7, 36-7 Ap '65

What the people really think. S. Alsop. il Sat Eve Post 238:27-31 O 23 '65

See also
Scholastic research center

PUBLIC ownership. See Government ownership

PUBLIC parking facilities. See Automobile parking

PUBLIC prayer. See Prayer

PUBLIC relations
Image in the marketplace. E. Dundy. il Esquire 64:82-3+ Jl '65
Public relations. L. L. L. Golden. See second issue of each month of Saturday review
Public relations; address, March 4, 1965. J. G. Mapes. Vital Speeches 31:362-5 Ap 1 '65
P.R. goes continental; new figure in European business. il Time 86:115 O 22 '65
See also
Business—Public relations
Customer relations
School and the community

Bibliography
Books in communications. J. F. Fixx. See second issue of each month of Saturday review

PUBLIC relations directors
Where do they come from? L. L. L. Golden. Sat R 48:60-1 Ag 14 '65

PUBLIC relations society of America
PR takes over history. G. Ace. Sat R 48:16 S 11 '65

PUBLIC relief. See Unemployment—Relief measures

PUBLIC schools
How to judge your children's schools. il Good H 160:176-7 Mr '65
Morality and the public school; address, March 18, 1965. J. P. Leary. Vital Speeches 31:427-30 My 1 '65
What's going on in schools & colleges. See issues of Changing times
Who runs our big city schools? F. M. Hechinger; P. Binzen. il Sat R 48:70-3+ Ap 17 '65; Discussion. 48:67 My 15 '65
See also
Negro schools

Desegregation
Beyond tokenism. il Time 86:45 S 10 '65
Big-city schools in trouble? resegregation in North. il U S News 59:44-7 S 27 '65
Biggest push yet for school integration; threat to cut off aid. il U S News 58:50-1 Mr 1 '65
Brookses and the Gowsters. S. Alsop. il Sat Eve Post 238:16 D 4 '65
Chicago a racial battleground; what the fight is about. il U S News 59:54-5 Ag 2 '65
Civil rights and education. F. Keppel il Ebony 20:110-12+ S '65
Civil rights compliance bars U.S. aid loss. Sr Schol 86:sup2 Mr 25 '65
Close to midnight for the New York schools. M. Mayer. il N Y Times Mag p34-5+ My 2 '65
Compliance. L. Baker. il Am Ed 1:24-6 S '65
Constitution: it's gone! D. Lawrence. U S News 58:104 My 31 '65
De facto decision; question of northern school segregation resulting from Negro neighborhoods. Newsweek 65:28 Mr 15 '65
De facto integration in Bel Air. A. M. Clark. il Sch R 49:72-3 Ja 15 '66
De facto segregation; excerpt from American education and the search for equal opportunity. il NEA J 54:34-6+ O '65
Desegregation; tables. Sat R 48:70 S 11 '65
Discrimination in Chicago. Newsweek 66:94 O 11 '65
Dixie disunity; government threat to noncompliant states. Reporter 32:8-9 Je 3 '65
Federal crackdown starts on local schools; Chicago case. il U S News 59:57-8 O 18 '65
How to produce a demonstration; trouble over speech tournaments in Dallas. J. C. Evans. Christian Cent 82:134 F 3 '65
How to say N-e-g-r-o; integration at two Deep South schools. M. Frady and F. Moore. il Newsweek 66:64 S 27 '65
How U.S. pressure is speeding mixed schools; conditions in southern and border states. U S News 58:14 Je 21 '65
Integrated parochial schools. America 112:346 Mr 13 '65
Integrated schools; a progress report; with discussion group program, by M. Smart. N. D. Kurland. il Parents Mag 40:32+, 60-1+ S '65
Integrating the Negro teacher out of a job; dilemma in Munday. B. Carter. il Reporter 33:31-3 Ag 12 '65; Discussion. 33:10+ S 23 '65
Integration roundup: North and South. Sr Schol 87:sup2 N 4 '65
Integration takes hold in southern schools. il U S News 59:40 S 13 '65
Is integration a must for faculties, too? conditions in southern areas. U S News 58:14-15 Je 7 '65
It pays to desegregate. Time 85:60 F 12 '65

Lady stirs her city's conscience; Houston, Tex. G. Zimmerman. il Look 29:66+ S 21 '65
Mississippi's kickouts. Newsweek 66:94 O 11 '65
Negro & the New York schools. M. Decter; discussion. Commentary 39:16 Ja; 13-14 F '65
Neighborhood schools: a new Court victory. U S News 58:16 Mr 15 '65
New attack on de facto. Time 85:70 F 5 '65
New Negro casualties; where do the teachers go? J. M. Arisman. il Commonweal 83:372-3 D 24 '65
New plan to get more mixed classes. il U S News 59:8 Ag 2 '65
Progress in school integration. Sch & Soc 93:468 D 11 '65
Race crisis hits another northern city; Milwaukee. il U S News 59:75 N 1 '65
Segregation crisis: Chicago's troubled schools. J. Star. Look 29:59+ My 4 '65
Segregation issue; Supreme court decisions. Sr Schol 86:19 Mr 18 '65
Slow deliberate speed. America 112:345 Mr 13 '65
Southern political culture and school desegregation. R. E. Cleary. bibliog f Sch & Soc 93:392-4 O 30 '65
Speeding up school integration. A. M. Bickel. New Repub 152:14-16 My 15 '65
Status of southern public school desegregation. Sch & Soc 93:73+ F 6 '65
Ten years of deliberate speed. E. Knoll. il Am Ed 1:1-3 D '64
Title VI: southern education faces the facts; guidelines to school authorities. G. W. Foster, jr. il Sat R 48:60-1+ Mr 20 '65
U.S. government policies on desegregation of elementary and secondary schools. Sch & Soc 93:377-80+ O 16 '65
U.S. wields big stick on integration. U S News 58:12 My 10 '65
Who's deprived? E. Geller. Library J 90:2306 My 15 '65
Why a big northern city faces a crisis in schools; Chicago; excerpts from testimony, July 27, 1965. B. C. Willis. il U S News 59:62-3 Ag 9 '65
Year of compliance. Newsweek 66:19-20 S 6 '65

Finance
See School finance

Standards
See Education—Standards

United States
Can the public school foster creativity? R. J. Mueller; reply. J. O. Goodsell. Sat R 48:96 F 20 '65
One campus for all schools: is this your city's solution? educational parks or school villages. il U S News 58:53-6 Je 14 '65
Public school and the private vision. by M. Greene. Review
Sat R 48:73-4 D 18 '65. F. G. Jennings
Public schools for private enterprise. E. Z. Friedenberg. Nation 201:171-5 S 20 '65
Scholar in an age of conflicts; reprint of a 1936 article. C. A. Beard. Sch & Soc 93:43-4+ Ja 23 '65
School where children teach themselves; Valley Winds school, St Louis. H. Black. il Sat Eve Post 238:80-1+ Je 19 '65
Uncle Sam's billion dollar push for better schools. F. M. Hechinger. il Parents Mag 40:45-7+ S '65
U.S. schools getting better? a look at what billions buy. il U S News 59:77-80 S 13 '65
Where a school of the future is holding classes today; complete education on one campus, South Florida education center, Broward County. il U S News 59:36-9 Jl 5 '65
See also
Rural schools—One-teacher schools
School year

Political control
See Politics and education
PUBLIC schools (endowed)

England
Public school that jumps; Millfield school, Somerset. il Sports Illus 23:16-21 Ag 16 '65

Great Britain
New directions for British education? M. N. Hennessy. il Sat R 48:58-9+ Ag 21 '65
PUBLIC schools and religion
Continuing the war against the First amendment. Christian Cent 82:909 Jl 21 '65

PUBLIC schools and religion—*Continued*
Inherit the wind production barred in up-state New York; Vestal high school. Library J 90:5486 D 15 '65
Is a prayer amendment coming? C. E. Rice. Nat R 17:597-9 Jl 13 '65
Is religion banned from our schools? C. W. Hall. Read Digest 86:49-54 F '65
Law of church and state; freedom of the mind; address, October 13, 1965. P. W. Bruton. Vital Speeches 32:149-54 D 15 '65
Schools don't have to ban the Bible! R. C. Davids. Farm J 89:50+ S '65
Voluntary prayer? Time 86:31 D 24 '65

PUBLIC schools and the community. See School and the community

PUBLIC service
New political non-job. D. Oberdorfer. il Harper 231:108+ O '65

PUBLIC service commissions
See also
Independent regulatory commissions

PUBLIC service industries
Behavioral approach to the study of inter-governmental relations. V. Ostrom and E. Ostrom. bibliog f Ann Am Acad 359:137-46 My '65

PUBLIC speaking
How to be a better speaker. H. P. Zelko. il Nations Bsns 53:88+ Ap '65
Influence of public speaking in American history; address, August 20, 1965. R. T. Oliver. Vital Speeches 31:759-61 O 1 '65
See also
Preaching
Speech education

PUBLIC spirit. See Patriotism

PUBLIC utilities
Warning strips protect underground spaghetti; Wheaton, Ill. S. J. Kennedy. il Am City 80:98 Mr '65
See also
Electric utilities—Finance
Public service industries

Securities
All-purpose utility stocks. il Fortune 72:90+ S '65

PUBLIC welfare

California
California's jackpot for the jobless. E. Selby and A. Selby. Read Digest 86:67-70 Je '65

Canada
If you think welfare costs are high in America... il U S News 58:102 Mr 1 '65

Europe, Western
If you think welfare costs are high in America... il U S News 58:101-2 Mr 1 '65

United States
Can subsidies solve America's problems? a U.S. senator's answer. R. C. Byrd. il Nations Bsns 53:30-1+ Ag '65
How it pays to be poor in America. il U S News 59:65-8 N 1 '65
How welfare provisions of the civil-rights act will be enforced; questions and answers. U S News 58:43 My 3 '65
Reclaiming the American dream, by R. C. Cornuelle. Review
Nat R 17:1030-1 N 16 '65. M. S. Evans
Size of the jungle; Great society killing charitable activities of service clubs. Christian Cent 83:5 Ja 5 '66
Welfare frauds exposed. il Nations Bsns 53:38-9+ Je '65
Why must the taxpayer subsidize immorality? J. K. Stout. Read Digest 86:66-9 Ap '65
Why the dole doesn't work. E. Selby and A. Selby. Read Digest 86:79-83 Mr '65

Washington, D.C.
Johnson's model city; the poverty program in Washington. J. Ridgeway. New Repub 152:15-18 F 13 '65

Washington (state)
Triumph of a stubborn lady. J. Poppy. il Look 29:64-6+ F 9 '65

PUBLIC works

Federal aid
Billions for boondoggles. il Nations Bsns 53:70-3 Ag '65
President sends Congress report on New England resource program. Dept State Bul 53:215-16 Ag 2 '65
Priming the pump of area growth; combining public works with regional planning. il Bsns W p96-8+ O 9 '65

PUBLICITY
Overloved one. M. M. Marberry. il Am Heritage 16:84-7+ Ag '65
Personal business; dealing with the press. Bsns W p 179-80 O 16 '65
You mean I'm the publicity chairman? il Changing T 19:24 My '65
See also
Advertising
Television in politics
Theater—Advertising

PUBLISHERS adclub
Publishers' adclub elects new officers. Pub W 187:67-8 Ap 19 '65

PUBLISHERS and libraries. See Libraries and publishers

PUBLISHERS and publishing
ABPC: planning for profits in publishing; report on conference at Princeton inn. D. Melcher and G. McCorkle. Pub W 187:32-5 My 10 '65
Are authors obsolete? proof correction cost dispute. J. Tebbel. Sat R 48:68-9 D 11 '65
Bowker plans new edition of Publishers' world. Pub W 188:32 D 13 '65
Publishers should put more effort on their staple stock. B. Schweid. il Pub W 187:45 My 31 '65
Revolution in books; symposium. bibliog il UNESCO Courier 18:4-32 S '65
Up for grabs; Putnam's suit against Lancer books over publishing of Candy. il Newsweek 65:88+ F 8 '65
See also
Authors and publishers
Best sellers
Books—Advertising
Copyright
International publishers association
Literary agents
Newspaper publishing
Periodicals, Publishing of
Royalties

Business literature
Are business books really necessary? T. O'Hanlon. il Duns R 85:44-5+ Ap '65
Publishers' addresses. Library J 90:1062 Mr 1 '65

Catholic literature
Catholic book production declined 13 per cent in 1964. Pub W 187:38 Mr 15 '65

Childrens literature
Getting a children's book published. F. Watts. Writer 78:21-2 O '65
Learning about children's books in translation; address, July 1965. M. L. Batchelder. il ALA Bul 60:33-42 Ja '66
New services from book publishers. il Sr Schol 87:sup20+ S 30 '65
Royalties: religious and children's book publishers. Pub W 187:39-42 Mr 1 '65

Computer installations
Are authors obsolete? proof correction cost dispute. J. Tebbel. Sat R 48:68-9 D 11 '65
Computer services for smaller publishers. il Pub W 188:32-6 S 6 '65
IBM computer will speed Fawcett book distribution. il Pub W 187:41-2 Mr 8 '65
Survey shows computer use more than doubles in year. Pub W 188:125 N 8 '65

Consolidations and mergers
Orion press merges with Grossman. Pub W 187:78 Je 21 '65
Wall Street notes, 1965: book publishing stock prices, mergers and acquisitions. il Pub W 189:84-9 Ja 17 '66

International aspects
Challenge of the sixties; congress of the International publishers association. D. Dempsey. il Sat R 48:27-8+ Je 26 '65
International co-publishing; panel. Pub W 187:56-7 Je 28 '65
IPA education section: ways sought for international publishing aid; meeting in Frankfurt. il Pub W 188:32-8 N 22 '65
Nonprofit inter-American book program is projected. Pub W 189:45-6 Ja 3 '66
Toward international aid for educational publishing. R. H. Smith. Pub W 188:46 N 22 '65
U.S. and Rumania exchange publishing delegations. Pub W 188:34 N 1 '65

Limited editions
Book as an artist's medium: Theobald's bestiary. il Pub W 187:114+ F 1 '65

Paperback books
Exhibit highlights at the Paperback conference; Role of paperback books in Education. J. Foster. Sr Schol 87:sup6 O 28 '65

PUBLISHERS and publishing—Paperback books—*Continued*

Is this edition really necessary? C. B. Grannis. Pub W 188:40 N 1 '65

Paperbacks for the elementary school. P. Johnson, jr. Library J 90:5054-5 N 15 '65

Revolution in books. Sch & Soc 93:494 D 25 '65

Revolution in books. R. Escarpit. il UNESCO Courier 18:4-10 S '65

Where the money lies. il Time 85:99 Mr 12 '65

Public relations

Danish campaign promotes books in your budget; Gyldendal launches an institutional public relations campaign. il Pub W 188:74 N 15 '65

MIT tech coop honors Wiley authors on campus. il Pub W 188:90 N 15 '65

Religious literature

Data on paperbacks in religious book publishing. C. B. Grannis. Pub W 187:103 F 8 '65

Royalties: religious and children's book publishers. Pub W 187:39-42 Mr 1 '65

Scholarly religious book: editing, pricing, marketing; Religious publishers group meeting. Pub W 187:20-4 Mr 29 '65

Some trends in religious books for the fall. C. B. Grannis. Pub W 188:95 S 27 '65

Scientific literature

Royalties: current practices affecting scientific and technical books. Pub W 187:65-6 Ap 19 '65

Science books. D. Wolfle. Science 148:317 Ap 16 '65

See also
Publishers and publishing—Technical literature

Securities

Book publishing stock prices: a monthly report. See issues of Publishers' weekly

Wall Street notes 1965: book publishing stock prices, mergers and acquisitions. il Pub W 189:84-9 Ja 17 '66

Statistics

American book title output January through June 1965. Pub W 188:101 Jl 19 '65

American book title output January through September 1965. il Pub W 188:73 O 4 '65

American book title output 1965; Subject analysis of American book title output. il Pub W 189:50-9 Ja 17 '66

Technical literature

Royalties: current practices affecting scientific and technical books. Pub W 187:65-6 Ap 19 '65

Translator and publisher: the popular technical book. T. E. Burton. Pub W 187:62-4 Ap 19 '65

Textbooks

ATPI and the textbook: a coming of age; annual meeting. il Pub W 187:22-35 My 17 '65

Color me brown, I'm integrated. T. B. Dolmatch. Sat R 48:73 S 11 '65

Commercial textbooks and urban education. R. H. Smith. Pub W 188:39 D 6 '65

Feffer and Simons launches overseas textbook program; reprints of American college texts. Pub W 188:42-3 O 4 '65

Immediate future of textbook publishing; summary of address by Darrel E. Peterson. Pub W 188:78-9 N 8 '65

It sometimes helps if you're an educational publisher. R. H. Smith. Pub W 187:43 My 17 '65

Textbook needs in urban education: American textbook publishers institute and the Great cities research council meeting. Los Angeles; summaries of addresses. il Pub W 188:16-27 D 6 '65

Textbooks, civil rights and the education of the American Negro; concerning conference in New York, sponsored by American textbook publishers institute, and National urban league; with editorial comment. il Pub W 187:26-32, 45 My 10 '65

What's ahead in educational publishing? A. J. McCaffrey. Sr Schol 87:sup 13 N 18 '65

See also
Textbooks

Africa

Continent in quest of a publishing industry; Unesco survey in Africa. C. M. Fyle. il UNESCO Courier 18:28-31 S '65

Asia

Dilemmas of publishing in south-east Asia. O. Prakash. il UNESCO Courier 18:23-7 S '65

Australia

Australian merger joins Horwitz and Ure Smith. Pub W 188:57 Ag 23 '65

Denmark

Danish campaign promotes books in your budget; Gyldendal launches an institutional public relations campaign. il Pub W 188:74 N 15 '65

Finland

Finnish author, publisher prosecuted for blasphemy. Pub W 187:100 F 8 '65

France

Report on French publishing. G. Borchardt. Pub W 187:27-9 My 31 '65

Germany (Federal Republic)

Many-titled tycoon; R. Mohn, head of C. C. Bertelsmann publishing company. Time 86:65 Jl 30 '65

Great Britain

Attenborough and Harwood speak on distribution; summary of address. J. Attenborough. Pub W 187:73-4 Je 21 '65

King of England. il Newsweek 66:112+ N 15 '65

Transatlantic view. L. Kramer. Pub W 188:26-9 N 29; 38-41 D 27 '65

Italy

Fabbri of Milan small rise in book sales. Pub W 189:69-70 Ja 10 '66

Italian publisher opens giant printing plant; Fabbri company. il Pub W 189:100-1 Ja 3 '66

Skira joins Fabbri to publish art books. il Pub W 187:24 Ap 5 '65

Trade winds; bookstore boom on Fifth avenue; Rizzoli international bookstore. J. Beatty, jr. Sat R 48:14+ O 9 '65

Japan

Twenty-one volume Japanese novel sells 11 million copies. S. Hasegawa. il UNESCO Courier 18:27 S '65

Latin America

Growth of the Hispanic book market. il UNESCO Courier 18:16-17 S '65

Poland

Warsaw book fair. H. R. Lottman. Pub W 188:24-7 Jl 26 '65

South America

See Publishers and publishing—Latin America

Spain

Growth of the Hispanic book market. il UNESCO Courier 18:16-17 S '65

United States

ABA regionals: exhibits feature many California book publishers; imprints exhibited, with some of the featured books. il Pub W 188:46-51 O 25 '65

Attenborough and Harwood speak on distribution; summary of address. R. C. Harwood. Pub W 187:74-5 Je 21 '65

Book publishers' '65 sales expected to reach $2 billion. il Pub W 187:35 Mr 8 '65

California regional publishing; report of session at ABA Los Angeles meeting. il Pub W 188:31-4 O 25 '65

Double-jointed imprint; how small, independent operators team up with large firms to preserve identity. D. Dempsey. Sat R 48:45-6 O 16 '65

Hagel asks for independent economic study on copyright. Pub W 188:31 Ag 9 '65

Hard-covering the news; newspapers in the book business. il Newsweek 65:56 My 31 '65

House can be a home. G. Buckman. il Mlle 61:148-9 S '65

January books; major campaigns. il Pub W 188:26-34 N 8 '65

Keeping up with knowledge. J. Tebbel. Sat R 48:52-3 Jl 10 '65

Lasser report; distribution of books by publishers. J. A. Duffy. Pub W 188:51-2 D 13 '65

More than regional; California book publishers. C. B. Grannis. Pub W 188:58 O 25 '65

My life in publishing, by H. S. Latham. Review
Pub W 188:287-8 Ag 30 '65. D. M. Glixon
Sat R 48:53+ Ag 14 '65. J. F. Fixx

PUBLISHERS and publishing—United States
—*Continued*
OP publishing: the new look in reprints; with selected list of OP publishers. D. Dempsey. Sat R 48:37-8+ Je 12 '65
Package deal. D. Dempsey. Sat R 48:45 Ap 17 '65
Publishers' executives review order-time survey; Lasser survey report; summary of discussion at ABPC luncheon. Pub W 188: 29-30 D 13 '65
Thinking big; Keith Jennison books for visually handicapped. D. Dempsey. Sat R 49:38 Ja 22 '66
Trade winds; lightning publication of book on Sir Winston Churchill. J. G. Fuller. il Sat R 48:10 F 20 '65; Reply. A. F. Gonzales, jr. 48:21 Mr 27 '65
Warsaw book fair. H. R. Lottman. Pub W 188:24-7 Jl 26 '65
When Harper's was young; excerpt from Brothers Harper. E. Exman. il Sat R 48:72-4 Je 12 '65
Will bookstore machinery be adequate for 1975-1985? C. B. Grannis. Pub W 187:152 Je 7 '65
   See also
American book publishers council
Protestant church-owned publishers association
University presses
PUBLISHERS book advertisements. See Books—Advertising
PUBLISHERS catalogs. See Catalogs, Publishers
PUBLISHERS company
   See also
Books, incorporated
PUBLISHERS' publicity association
New reviewers address PPA luncheon. Pub W 188:36-7 N 1 '65
PUBLISHING. See Publishers and publishing
PUBLISHING of periodicals. See Periodicals, Publishing of
PUBS (Great Britain) See Bars and barrooms
PUCCINI, Giacomo
La Bohème. Criticism
   Life 59:23 O 29 '65
   Opera N 29:29-30 My 1 '65
   Sat R 48:39+ O 16 '65
   Sat R 48:26+ D 18 '65
Connoisseur's Tosca. R. Lawrence. Opera N 29:24-5 Ap 17 '65
Girl of the golden West (La fanciulla del West) Criticism
   New Yorker 41:235 D 11 '65
   Opera N il 30:17-20 Ja 8 '66
   Opera N il 30:24-5 Ja 8 '66
   Sat R 48:26+ D 18 '65
   Sat R 49:48 Ja 22 '66
Madame Butterfly. Criticism
   Opera N 29:24-5 Mr 27 '65
   Opera N 30:27 O 23 '65
   Opera N 30:30 D 18 '65
   Opera N il 29:17-20 Mr 27 '65
   Opera N il 30:18-20 Ja 1 '66
   Opera N il por 30:24-5 Ja 1 '66
   Sat R 48:64 N 20 '65
   Sat R 48:69 D 4 '65
Maria Callas returns to Tosca. J. Maclain. il Am Rec G 31:688-90+ Ap '65
On records; La fanciulla del West. Opera N 30:34 Ja 8 '66
On records; Madame Butterfly. Opera N 30:44 O 23 '65
On records; Madame Butterfly. Opera N 29:34 Mr 27 '65
On records; Madame Butterfly. Opera N 30:34 Ja 1 '66
On records; Tosca. Opera N 29:34 Ap 17 '65
Tosca. Criticism
   New Yorker 41:162+ Mr 20 '65
   New Yorker 41:171-2 Mr 27 '65
   Newsweek 65:78 Mr 29 '65
   Opera N 29:24-5 Ap 17 '65
   Opera N il 29:17-20 Ap 17 '65
Le Villi. Criticism
   New Yorker 41:52+ D 25 '65
PUCK, Theodore T. See Robinson, A. jt. auth.
PUDDINGS
Tall cool one for dessert. il Sunset 135:120-1 Ag '65
PUEBLO architecture
Travel far and near: the Kinishba Pueblo ruins. J. E. Ransom. il Natur Hist 74: 58-60+ My '65
PUEBLO BONITO, N.Mex.
Confusing rock. L. Kinnear and W. Kinnear. il Nat Parks Mag 39:17-19 N '65
PUEBLO bread. See Bread
PUEBLO Indians
Investiture controversy; F. Stadtmueller v. the pagans. America 113:88 Jl 24 '65

Pablita Velarde: Pueblo painter. W. T. Le Viness. il Am Artist 29:40-5+ Ap '65
Visit to the living Pueblos. il Sunset 135:64-71 S '65
White feather is heap bad medicine; Monsignor Stadtmuller thrown off the reservation at Isleta, N. Mex. il Life 59:40B Jl 16 '65
PUERTO RICANS
Mother and son in a Puerto Rican slum; excerpt from In the life. O. Lewis. il Harper 231:71-6+ D '65
Portrait of Gabriel: Puerto Rican family in San Juan and New York; excerpt from In the life. O. Lewis. Harper 232:54-9 Ja '66
PUERTO RICANS in the United States
Portrait of Gabriel: Puerto Rican family in San Juan and New York; excerpt from In the life. O. Lewis. Harper 232:54-9 Ja '66
Puerto Ricans. R. M. Elman. Commonweal 83:405-8 Ja 7 '66
PUERTO RICO
Farewell to Muñoz Marin. K. Botsford. Commentary 39:86-9 Je '65; Discussion. 40:8+ O '65
   See also
Political parties—Puerto Rico
Public health—Puerto Rico
Trials—Puerto Rico

Economic conditions
Economic development of Puerto Rico; address, February 24, 1965. S. Polanco-Abreu. Vital Speeches 31:418-21 My 1 '65

History
Administration of a revolution: executive reform in Puerto Rico under Governor Tugwell, 1941-1946, by C. T. Goodsell. Review
   Nation 201:449-50 D 6 '65. G. K. Lewis

Industries
Big money comes to rescue of Puerto Rico's boom. il U S News 58:90-2 Mr 15 '65

Politics and government
New man in La Fortaleza. A. W. Maldonado. il Reporter 33:32-3 N 4 '65

Social conditions
Cracks in the showcase. K. Wagenheim. New Repub 153:15-16 O 16 '65; Reply. G. Laguardia. 153:36-7 D 4 '65
PUERTO RICO and the United States
Administration of a revolution: executive reform in Puerto Rico under Governor Tugwell, 1941-1946, by C. T. Goodsell. Review
   Nation 201:449-50 D 6 '65. G. K. Lewis
PUFF pastry. See Pastry
PUGET SOUND
Cruising Puget Sound. F. M. Paulson. il Field & S 70:65-9+ Jl '65
   See also
San Juan Islands, Wash.
PUGH, James E. Jr
Taking temperatures. Field & S 70:92-6 Je '65
PUGLIESE, Joseph
Ann Stockton's porcelain. Craft Horiz 25:34-6 Mr '65
PUGWASH conferences on science and world affairs
About Pugwash. E. Rabinowitch. Bul Atomic Sci 21:9-15 Ap '65
Pugwash XIV. E. Rabinowitch. Bul Atomic Sci 21:41 S '65
PUKAPUKA (island) See South Sea Islands
PUKU. See Antelopes
PUŁASKI, Kazimierz
Pulaski memorial day, 1965; statement, October 11, 1965. L. B. Johnson. Dept State Bul 53:708 N 1 '65
PULITZER prizes
Honoring the concensus. Nation 200:518 My 17 '65
Music to my ears; no duke for the Duke; justification of Ellington's rejection. I. Kolodin. Sat R 48:22 My 29 '65
New front page. J. Hohenberg. il Sat R 48: 117-18+ S 18 '65
1965 Pulitzer prizes; drama letters awards all bestowed. il Pub W 187:37-9 My 10 '65
Out of the jury box; two members of music jury resign. Newsweek 65:102 My 24 '65
Prize for hungry horse. il Newsweek 65:94+ My 17 '65
Pulitzer for community service? R. L. Tobin. Sat R 48:63-4 O 9 '65
Pulitzer prizes. New Repub 152:8 My 15 '65
Pulitzers in perspective. Time 85:48 My 14 '65
Very too bad; no prize awarded in music. Newsweek 65:93-4 My 17 '65

PULLIAM, Eugene Collins
Fairness in Phoenix. il por Time 87:41 Ja 7 '66

PULLMAN, Bernard, and others
Intermolecular forces in association of purines with polybenzenoid hydrocarbons. bibliog Science 147:1305-7 Mr 12 '65

PULSE techniques (electronics)
Pulse radiolysis of dioxane solutions. J. H. Baxendale and others. bibliog il Science 148:637 Ap 30 '65

PUMA hunting
Killers of the Magdalenas. F. C. Hibben. il Field & S 69:58-61 Mr '65
My toughest trophy. C. Elliott. il Outdoor Life 135:24-7+ Mr '65
Slap a lion with your hat. J. C. Linville. il Outdoor Life 136:40-1+ Ag '65

PUMAROL, Alfredo Lebrón-. See Lebrón-Pumarol, A.

PUMAS
Cougars in the U.S. are barely holding their own; excerpt from Preliminary study of distribution and numbers of cougar, grizzly and wolf in North America. V. H. Cahalane. il Audubon Mag 67:108-9 Mr '65

PUMPING engines See Fire apparatus, Motor
PUMPING stations, Sewage. See Sewage pumping

PUMPS, Fuel. See Fuel pumps

PUNCH (beverage)
Cheers. il Ladies Home J 82:72-3+ D '65
Christmas gathering. il Good H 161:132-3+ D '65
Fruit, wine, and bubbles. il Sunset 134:242 Je '65

PUNCH; story. See Friedman, B. J.

PUNCHED card systems
Accounting machines and punched-card processing. il Duns R 86:pt2 149+ S '65

PUNCTUALITY
See also
Tardiness

Anecdotes, facetiae, satire, etc.
Early bird. S. Weeks. Atlan 215:135-6 Ap '65

PUNCTUATION
Apostrophobia. G. Ace. Sat R 48:12 Mr 27 '65

PUNER, Helen
What you and your daughter should know about menstruation. Parents Mag 40:36+ F '65

PUNISHMENT
Moral indignation and middle class psychology, by S. Ranulf. Review
Nation 200:428-30 Ap 19 '65. C. McWilliams
See also
Capital punishment
Corporal punishment

PUNISHMENT of children. See Children—Management and training

PUNJAB, India
Queen of the hill stations. il Life 58:62-3 My 28 '65

PUNS and punning
Confessions of a pun addict. J. Skow. il Sat Eve Post 238:20 Je 19 '65

PUPIL (eye)
Attitude and pupil size. E. H. Hess. il Sci Am 212:46-54 Ap '65
Your eye can't lie; psychology called pupillometrics. B. Davidson. il Sat Eve Post 239: 76-9 Ja 15 '66

PUPIL data. See Personnel records in education

PUPIL self evaluation. See Self evaluation

PUPPETS and puppet plays
Inventor of the month; she built a better mouse. S. V. Jones. il Sci Digest 59:32 Ja '66
Puppets in wonderland; Garden of Wonders, Montreal's children's zoo. L. MacGillivray. il Recreation 58:73-5 F '65
Theater of the string puppet. H. Bedford. il Sch Arts 64:25-32 Ap '65
See also
Shadow pantomimes and plays

PURCELL, Edna Jean
Dave Hall, the man who put the pink in iris. Flower Grower 52:17-18 Jl '65
—and Dwyer, J. E.
Master of pink is ninety. Pop Gard 16:21+ Jl '65

PURCELL, Francis
What's wrong with Job corps; interview. por U S News 59:54-5 D 27 '65

PURCELL, Henry
Fairy queen. Criticism
Time 86:71 O 29 '65
Hipster among the ancients. C. Harman. Life 60:13 Ja 7 '66
Looking backward. P. L. Miller. il Sat R 48: 68 N 27 '65

PURCELL, J. C. See Bufalini, J. J. jt. auth.

PURCELL, William L.
America's first sophisticated critic. Am Rec G 31:1094-6 Jl '65
Filling a lacuna; the music of Japan. Am Rec G 31:910-12 My '65

PURCHASING
See also
Consumer education
Consumers
Instalment plan

PURCHASING, Government
Buying overseas for U.S. arsenal; policy of reciprocity. il Bsns W p 142+ O 9 '65
Value analysis in purchasing; Virginia. G. L. Nunnally. Am City 80:162+ Je '65
See also
Contracts, Government
United States—Armed forces—Procurement

PURCHASING, Household
How to deal with appliance dealers. Good H 161:234 O '65
See also
Food—Prices

PURCHASING, Municipal
Automatic purchase orders; Phoenix, Ariz. B. A. Gragg. Am City 80:140+ F '65
California group advocates standardized purchasing. Am City 80:156 Ag '65
Computerize your purchases and save; use of computers by Department of purchase, New York city. G. A. Wechsler. il Am City 80: 86-7 N '65
Instant money for small-order purchases; Los Angeles County, Calif. V. W. Quam. il Am City 80:118-19 My '65
Lowest responsible bidder, who is he? F. N. Benevelli. Am City 80:146+ Mr '65
Maintenance contracts; Chicago buy best value rather than low bid. il Am City 80:101+ D '65
Mixing purchasing and public relations. A. L. Lehrbaummer. il Am City 80:104-5 S '65
Old purchasing system takes on a new look; Fulton County, Atlanta, Ga. F. T. Farran. il Am City 80:126+ Jl '65
Pros and cons of pre-bid conferences. J. M. Robertson. Am City 81:96 Ja '66
Prudent equipment purchasing; Fresno, Calif. M. J. Carozza. il Am City 80:107+ O '65
Research programs can solve purchasing problems, reduce costs; Chicago, Ill. R. H. Vlerick. Am City 80:150+ Ap '65

PURCHASING agents
For 1966, an easing of pressure on prices; opinion of top corporate buyers interviewed. il Bsns W p26-7 S 25 '65

PURDUE university, Lafayette, Ind.
Purdue gives and gets a lesson. il Bsns W p 186-8+ Ap 17 '65

PURDY, James
Dame Edith Sitwell's sad, witty farewell. Life 58:8+ Ap 30 '65
Malcolm; dramatization. See Albee, E.

PURDY, Ken W.
At ten tenths of capacity. Atlan 216:102-5 Jl '65
Out of the orchard and up a tantalizing hill. Sports Illus 22:42-4+ My 3 '65
World's greatest automobile collection. Atlan 216:84-92 Jl '65

PURE oil company
Curious pursuit of Pure oil. T. A. Wise. il Fortune 72:112-15+ Jl '65
Prize union; merger negotiations with California's Union oil co. Time 85:86+ F 26 '65
Pure oil journeys a rocky merger road. il Bsns W p 122+ F 27 '65
Pure's stockholders ask for more. il Bsns W p58-60 Ap 17 '65

PUREBRED pets. See Pets

PURIFICATION of air. See Air purification

PURIFICATION of water. See Water purification

PURINES
Immunoadsorbent for the isolation of purine-specific antibodies. H. H. Weetall and N. Weliky. bibliog il Science 148:1235-7 My 28 '65
Intermolecular forces in association of purines with polybenzenoid hydrocarbons. B. Pullman and others. bibliog il Science 147:1305-7 Mr 12 '65

PURITANISM
See also
Puritans

PURITANS
New England frontier: Puritans and Indians, 1620-1675, by A. T. Vaughn. Review
Nation 202:22-3 Ja 3 '66. W. Eastlake
PURMA Special cameras. See Cameras
PUROMYCIN
Chondroitin sulfate: inhibition of synthesis by puromycin. G. De La Haba and H. Holtzer. bibliog il Science 149:1263-5 S 10 '65
Fish aid memory study; puromycin effect. Sci N L 89:3 Ja 1 '66
Puromycin: effect on messenger RNA synthesis and β-galactosidase formation in escherichia coli 15T-. B. H. Sells. bibliog il Science 148:371-3 Ap 16 '65
PURPLE foxglove. See Foxgloves
PURRINGTON, Bruce R.
100 to grow on: core music collection. bibliog por Library J 90:4523-5 O 15 '65
PURSES
    See also
Handbags
PUSEY, Nathan M.
Decade of Harvard university. Sch & Soc 93:115-20 F 20 '65
Student protest and commitment; address, June 15, 1965. Sch & Soc 93:471-4 D 11 '65
PUSHKIN, Aleksandr Sergeevich
Pushkin and the lepidopterist. G. Daniels. New Repub 152:19-21 Ap 3 '65
Third man. B. Goldovsky. Opera N 30:26-7 Ja 15 '66
PUTNAM, Frank W. See Titani, K. jt. auth.
PUTNAM, John F.
Accounting for every pupil. Sch Life 47:31-3 D '64
PUTNAM, Judith, and Grossman, Ruth
(eds) Books to come. Library J 90:2598-600+ Je 1 '65
(eds) Business books to come. Library J 90:1150-8, 3078-82 Mr 1, Jl '65
(eds) Paperbacks to come. Library J 90:2355-70+, 3725-6+ My 15, S 15 '65
(eds) Religious books to come. Library J 90:3482-97 S 1 '65
(eds) Scientific, technical, and medical books to come. Library J 90:1160-201, 3083-119 Mr 1, Jl '65
—and Lindheim, Judy
(eds) Business books to come. Library J 90:4810-19 N 1 '65
(eds) Religious books to come. Library J 91:134-48 Ja 1 '66
(eds) Scientific, technical, and medical books to come. Library J 90:4820-65 N 1 '65
—and others
(ed) Books to come. Library J 90:4126-247 O 1 '65
—See Stokvis, I. E. jt. ed.
PUTNAM, Leon J.
Death of death? Christian Cent 82:1550+ D 15 '65
PUTNAM, Tex.
Requiem for a west Texas town. L. L. King. Harper 232:46-53 Ja '66
PUTNAM art collection. See San Diego, Calif. —Galleries and museums
PUTNAM'S, G. P, sons
Both Lancer and Putnam injunctions denied. Pub W 187:132-3 F 22 '65
PUTTY
Versatile adhesive putty; epoxybound. Consumer Rep 30:472 O '65
PUYA
Flower cluster is five feet high. il Sunset 134:283 Ap '65
PUZZLES
Jigsaw puzzles go full circle; K. Lewin of Springbok editions. il Bsns W p68+ Jl 10 '65
New jag in jigsaws. Time 85:67 Mr 26 '65
Puzzle fun for everyone. See issues of Parents' magazine and better homemaking
    See also
Crossword puzzles
PYE, Lucian W.
Concept of political development. Ann Am Acad 358:1-13 Mr '65
Real story of Vietnam as told from the inside; interview. por U S News 59:76-81 O 18 '65
PYLE, Carter. See Schultz, J. jt. auth.
PYLE, Ernest Taylor. See Pyle, E.
PYLE, Ernie
By Ernie Pyle; anniversary of famed war correspondent's death. Newsweek 66:47 Ag 2 '65

PYLE, Gene
Experiment: take a dozen objects. il Pop Phot 56:68-9 Ap '65
Three photographers try the Swinger. il por Pop Phot 57:68-9+ S '65
PYLE, Howard
Seat belts save lives. por Parents Mag 40:32 Jl '65
PYLE, Howard S.
When it's 6 a.m. in Tokyo. Pop Electr 23:90-1 Ag '65
PYNCHON, Thomas
World, this one, the flesh, Mrs Oedipa Maas, and the testament of Pierce Inverarity; story. Esquire 64:170-3 D '65
PYRAMIDS
Tomb of the scientist-god; Imhotep. il Sci Digest 57:21 Mr '65
PYRAMIDS, Mexican. See Indians of Mexico—Antiquities
PYRITES
Fossil bacteria in pyrite. E. G. Ehlers and others. il Science 148:1719-21 Je 25 '65
PYROXENES
    See also
Ureyite
PYRRHO, pseud.
LBJ: political gamester. Nat R 18:67-9 Ja 25 '66
Vietnam: in and out of focus. Nat R 17:1161-3 D 14 '65
What exit for Asia? Nat R 17:638-41 Jl 27 '65
PYRUVATE kinase. See Pyruvates
PYRUVATES
Insulin: inducer of pyruvate kinase. G. Weber and others. bibliog il Science 149:65-7 Jl 2 '65

Q

QANTAS empire airways. See Airlines—Australia
QUACKENBUSH, Robert
Illustrations of Robert Quackenbush. J. H. Michel. il por Am Artist 29:28-33+ Ap '65
QUACKS and quackery
Our daughter was a victim of the world's cruelest hoax. L. David. Good H 161:81+ N '65
Quackery: Senate investigators concerned with billion-dollar business preying on elderly. E. Langer. Science 147:1119-20 Mr 5 '65
Vitamin healers; career of C. Fredericks. R. L. Smith. il Reporter 33:18-25 D 16 '65; Discussion. 34:6+ Ja 13 '66
QUADE, Quentin, L.
Vietnam background. America 113:17-19 Jl 3 '65
QUAIL shooting
Cajun quail. G. Gresham. il Field & S 70:43-5+ N '65
Covey birds. T. Trueblood. il Field & S 70:28+ O '65
Speed and the quail hunter; ed. by W. Page. il Field & S 70:138-43 My '65
Three kinds of quail. L. Watson. il Outdoor Life 137:36-7+ Ja '66
QUAISON-SACKEY, Alex
United Nations commemoration address, June 25, 1965. UN Mo Chron 2:79-84 Jl '65
    about
Alex Quaison-Sackey: UN's first black president. il pors Ebony 20:198-200+ My '65
QUAKER relief work. See American friends service committee
QUALIFICATIONS of teachers. See Teachers—Qualifications
QUALITY control
Navy propellent monitoring technique employs gauges embedded in grains. J. F. Judge. il Miss & Roc 16:22-3 Ap 19 '65
Revivalist zeal in the drive for perfect parts: Zero defects gaining converts in aerospace and defense industries. il Bsns W p 158+ My 8 '65
QUALITY of products
Basic principles of reliability. J. H. Wujek, jr. il Electr World 73:44-5 F '65
Buying guide issue (cont) Consumer Rep 30:1-448 D '65
JCII is quality control: Japan camera inspection institute. U S Camera 28:59 Je '65
Reliability is components lab mission: ERC's Component technology division. Miss & Roc 16:71 My 31 '65

QUALITY of products—*Continued*
Reliability of electronic components. J. H. Wujek, jr. il Electr World 73:40-1+ My '65
Search for quality; eastern Europe. Time 86: 115-16 N 19 '65
Speaker for the house. C. Montgomery. See issues of Good housekeeping
Standards to protect the buying public; proposed creation of a national standards institute. J. Ridgeway. New Repub 152:9-10 My 1 '65
Strict liability suits pile up for auto makers. Bsns W p30+ Ag 28 '65
U.S. standards needed? Bsns W p 178 Mr 20 '65
What's new at the Institute? lots of things. il Good H 161:124-7 S '65
Why the old products last. V. A. Adams. Duns R 85:46-7+ Ap '65
See also
Testing
QUALITY stabilization bill. See Price maintenance by industry
QUAM, Victor W.
Instant money for small-order purchases. Am City 80:118-19 My '65
QUANBECK, Warren A.
Compassionate pontiff. Christian Cent 83: 16-17 Ja 5 '66
QUANTITY cookery. See Church suppers, breakfasts, etc; Cookery, Quantity
QUANTUM electronics
Production of coherent radiation by atoms and molecules; address, December 11, 1964. C. H. Townes. bibliog il Science 149:831-41 Ag 20 '65
Quantum electronics; address, December 11, 1964. A. M. Prokhorov. bibliog Science 149: 828-30 Ag 20 '65
QUANTUM theory
Books; Schrödinger equation. J. Bernstein. New Yorker 41:180-2+ My 1 '65
Einstein, specific heats, and the early quantum theory; address, December 29, 1964. M. J. Klein. bibliog Science 148:173-80 Ap 9 '65
Fluorescence quantum yield measurements: vitamin B₆ compounds. R. F. Chen. bibliog il Science 150:1593-5 D 17 '65
Quantum theory and elementary particles; address, April 23, 1965. V. F. Weisskopf. il Science 149:1181-9 S 10 '65
QUANTUM yield. See Quantum theory
QUARANTINE, Plant. See Plant quarantine
QUARLES, Benjamin
Profile; The associated publishers. por Negro Hist Bul 28:81 Ja '65
QUARRELS
Can quarrels help a marriage? questions and answers. J. Brothers. Good H 162:34+ Ja '66
Marital quarrels involve psychological survival. Sci N L 87:169 Mr 13 '65
Why couples quarrel. S. Blum. il Redbook 125:46-7+ Je '65
QUARRIES and quarrying
McGrath quarry; state of Washington. H. D. Brown. il Hobbies 70:116-17 Ja '66
QUARTERBACKS. See Football players
QUARTERMAIN, David, and others
Brief temporal gradient of retrograde amnesia independent of situational change. bibliog Science 149:1116-18 S 3 '65
QUARTZ
Devil's digs; white crystal found near Cristalina, Brazil. il Time 85:37 Ap 9 '65
Phase relations in the system Na₂Si₂O₅SiO₂. J. Williamson and F. P. Glasser. bibliog il Science 148:1589-91 Je 18 '65
Temperature-resistant quartz produced; astroquartz. J. F. Judge. il Miss & Roc 16: 55-6 My 17 '65
QUASARS. See Radio astronomy
QUASI-stellar radio sources. See Radio astronomy
QUAT, Phan-huy-. See Phan-huy-Quat
QUEBEC (province)
Canada's quiet revolution; a degree of autonomy for Quebec. A. Deming. il Newsweek 65:58-60 Mr 15 '65
French-Canadian dilemma. C. Ryan. For Affairs 43:462-74 Ap '65
See also
French Canadians
Geology—Quebec (province)
Westmount

Economic conditions
Revolt of French Canada. P. Siekman. il Fortune 71:156-63+ F '65; Same abr. with title French Canada: a people in revolt. Read Digest 86:203-4+ My '65

Politics and government
Crisis in French Canada. W. E. Greening. Yale R 54:375-82 Mr '65
How far can the French opt out? concerning report of royal commission. Time 85:35 Mr 5 '65
Revolt of French Canada. P. Siekman. il Fortune 71:156-63+ F '65; Same abr. with title French Canada: a people in revolt. Read Digest 86:203-4+ My '65
We're nothing, but we want to be something; attitudes of students at University of Montreal, and McGill. R. Hoffmann. il Mlle 62:155-7+ N '65
QUEEN and the rebels; drama. See Betti, U.
QUEEN MAUD RANGE
Geology of the central portion of the Queen Maud Range, Transantarctic Mountains. F. A. Wade and others. bibliog Science 150:1808-9 D 31 '65
QUEEN of spades; opera. See Tchaikovsky, P. I.
QUEENS, N.Y.
Need for suburban planning; changes in Forest Hills. M. Polner. America 112:188-90 F 6 '65
QUEENS borough public library
Queens borough public library at work with the schools. H. W. Tucker and M. L. Hennessy. il ALA Bul 59:649-52 Jl '65
QUEEN'S Christmas cake; drama. See Watts, F. B.
QUEENSWARE. See Wedgwood ware
QUELLET, Maurice
Why and what. Commonweal 82:483-4 Jl 9 '65
QUESNELL, Quentin
On science and revelation. Sat R 49:27 Ja 1 '66
QUEST for the heart; story. See Young, M.
QUESTAR telescope. See Telescope—Photographic telescope
QUESTIONING
Delicate art of asking questions. J. K. Lagemann. Read Digest 86:87-91 Je '65
QUETICO-SUPERIOR wilderness region. See Wilderness areas
QUICHE. See Pastry
QUICK breads. See Bread
QUIDOR, John
Critics changed their minds; exhibition circulated throughout New York state. K. Kuh. Sat R 48:44-5 D 25 '65
Instinct for misanthropy. H. Cohen. Reporter 33:51-2 D 16 '65
Quidor. il Antiques 88:770+ D '65
QUIETUDE. See Silence
QUIGG, Philip W.
Japan in neutral. For Affairs 44:253-63 Ja '66
QUIHUIS, Lelia Lavine
Corn husk bags of the Nez Perce. Hobbies 70:114-16+ Mr '65
QUILL, Michael Joseph
Crush baptizes the new mayor. il Life 60: 32-3 Ja 14 '66
Inauguration: J. V. Lindsay as Mayor of New York city. New Yorker 41:20-3 Ja 8 '66
Intolerable strike. Life 60:5 Ja 14 '66
Never a kind word. il por Newsweek 66:27-8 D 20 '65
New York: a long week's walk into chaos. il por Newsweek 67:28-31 Ja 17 '66
What a union can do when it uses its power. il por U S News 60:84-6 Ja 17 '66
Will Quill win gamble? por Bsns W p32-3 Ja 8 '66
QUILTING
Island quilting is different; Hawaiian quilting. il Sunset 134:123-4+ Je '65
Stitch in another time. il Time 86:60-1 Ag 6 '65
QUILTS
Full enjoyment from quilts and comforters. Good H 161:255 O '65
Quilts and coverlets; homespuns of the Northwest Territory. il Antiques 87:327-9 Mr '65
QUIMBY, Harriet B.
Before the act. Library J 90:3694-5 S 15 '65
QUINCY, Mass.

Historic houses, etc.
Gardens at the Adams national historic site. R. C. Hands. il Horticulture 43:40-1+ My '65
QUININE
Quinine-resistant plasmodium berghei in mice. P. E. Thompson and others. bibliog il Science 148:1240-1 My 28 '65
Quinine shortage results as malaria drugs change. Sci N L 87:100 F 13 '65

QUINN, James Brian
National planning of science and technology in France; adaptation of address, October 1964. bibliog Science 150:993-1003 N 19 '65
QUINN, John Robert
Aging song. Christian Cent 83:40 Ja 12 '66
Christmas story; poem. Christian Cent 82: 1569 D 22 '65
QUINN, Joseph L.
Crash program for the Newman apostolate. Cath World 202:166-70 D '65
QUINN and Boden company, incorporated
Publishers learn about Linofilm in Quinn & Boden plant tours. il Pub W 187:102+ Mr 1 '65
QUINT, Beverly
Mysteries of art; poem. New Yorker 41:48 Ap 24 '65
QUINTUPLETS
Fischer quints at two. P. Wright. il pors Ladies Home J 83:53-7+ Ja '66
Fischer quints: summer on the farm. J. Bird. il Sat Eve Post 238:28-35 Jl 31 '65
Hormone that produces quints; Lawson quints. il Sci Digest 58:26-7 O '65
Merry Christmas for the quints; Fischers holiday. J. Bird. il Sat Eve Post 238:21-5 D 18 '65
Multiple-birth hormone; Lawson and Ohlsen quintuplets. il Time 86:64 Ag 6 '65
Narrowing the odds; Lawson and Olsen quintuplets. il Newsweek 66:78 Ag 9 '65
QUIRK, John
Rookie; story. Sat Eve Post 238:64-5 N 20; 56-60 D 4 '65
QUIZZES. See Information tests
QUMRAN scrolls. See Dead Sea scrolls
QUOIREZ, Françoise. See Sagan, F. pseud.
QUOTA controls. See Agricultural administration—United States
QUOTAS, Immigration. See Immigration and emigration—United States
QUOTAS, Import. See Import quotas
QUOTATIONS
Department of amplification: setting of lines in index of Bartlett's familiar quotations to resemble poetry. N. Hartman. New Yorker 40:88+ Ja 30 '65
Final say; last words of famous men; comp. by E. F. Murphy. N Y Times Mag p80 Mr 21 '65
Literary sampler; excerpts from new books. Sat R 48:37+ Ap 17 '65

R

RAF. See Great Britain—Royal air force
RCA. See Radio corporation of America
RCIA. See Retail clerks international association
REA. See United States—Rural electrification administration
RFE. See Radio free Europe
Rh factors
Expectant mother; what the Rh factor is. A. W. Liley. Redbook 126:38+ N '65
How the Rh factor in blood affects babies. Good H 161:169 S '65
Rh factor overcome. F. Marley. Sci N L 88: 115 Ag 21 '65
Vaccinating against Rh. Time 86:92-3 O 8 '65
R. H. Macy and company. See Macy, R. H. and company
RNA. See Ribonucleic acid
RPI. See Rensselaer polytechnic institute, Troy, N.Y.
RTCM. See Radio technical commission for marine services
RWDSU. See Retail, wholesale, and department store union
R one mended heart; story. See Shyer, M. F.
RAABE, Evelyn M.
CAP is born. America 112:608-10 Ap 24 '65
RABASSA, Gregory
(tr) See Amblard, M. Twenty-three years in Franco's jails
RABB, Herbert
Building reader confidence. Sr Schol 86: sup 13 Mr 25 '65
RABB, Miriam
Rhododendron trail ride. Am For 71:50-1+ S '65
RABBI; story. See Gordon, N.

RABBIS
Major Din Torah; dispute brought to rabbi for arbitration. I. B. Singer. Commentary 40:77-80 S '65
Rabbis or executives; views of A. Hertzberg. Newsweek 67:63 Ja 17 '66
Rabbis without God; Reform Judaism. Newsweek 65:66 My 24 '65
RABBIT fever. See Tularmia
RABBIT fleas. See Fleas
RABBIT hunting
Chair-lift rabbits; mountaintop rabbit hunt. H. Carroll. il Field & S 70:27-9+ D '65
Cottontail jungle. C. Vinson. il Outdoor Life 136:66-7+ N '65
Following the trail of the cottontail. H. Bradshaw and V. Bradshaw. il Todays Health 44:22-4+ Ja '66
Just rabbits. C. E. Gillham. il Field & S. 70: 76-8+ O '65
Rabbits: some with antlers. D. J. Anderson. il Field & S 70:48-50+ N '65
Sunshine cottontails. G. X. Sand. il Field & S 70:50-1+ S '65
To kill a cottontail. M. Ellis. il Field & S 70:44-6+ Ja '66
RABBITS and hares
Rabbit: frequency of suckling in the pup. M. X. Zarrow and others. bibliog il Science 150:1835-6 D 31 '65
See also
Cookery—Game

Hybrids
Sex-linkage of erythrocyte glucose-6-phosphate dehydrogenase in two species of wild hares. S. Ohno and others. bibliog il Science 150:1737-8 D 24 '65
RABE, Olive. See Fisher, A. jt. auth.
RABELAIS, François
Gargantua and Pantagruel. K. Rexroth. Sat R 48:20 Ag 28 '65
RABER, R. W.
Moveable feast; poem. Christian Cent 82:491 Ap 21 '65
RABIES
Rabid bats increase. Sci N L 87:75 Ja 30 '65
RABIN, Robert, and others
Glyoxylate in fatty-acid metabolism. bibliog Science 150:1548-58 D 17 '65
RABINOVE, Samuel
Corkscrew swamp sanctuary. Nat Parks Mag 39:8-9 O '65
RABINOVITZ, Marco. See Honig, G. R. jt. auth.
RABINOWITCH, Eugene
About Pugwash. Bul Atomic Sci 21:9-15 Ap '65
New perspective. Bul Atomic Sci 21:2-3 N '65
Open season on scientists. New Repub 154: 20-2 Ja 1 '66
Scientists in China. Bul Atomic Sci 21:29 N '65
Vietnam: facts and fictions. Bul Atomic Sci 21:45-8 Je '65
—and Govindjee
Role of chlorophyll in photosynthesis; with biographical sketches. Sci Am 213:16-17, 74-83 Jl '65
RABINOWITCH, Victor
Biology in Euratom. Bul Atomic Sci 21:46-7 Mr '65
—and Hasler, A. D.
International biological program. Bul Atomic Sci 21:32-4 O '65
RABINOWITZ, Jacob G.
Writing with light. Electr World 74:31 N '65
RABINOWITZ, Louis M, foundation. See Louis M. Rabinowitz foundation, incorporated
RABORN, William Francis, 1905-
Leaky ship. por Newsweek 66:25-6 D 27 '65
PERT man for the CIA. il por Time 85:27-8 Ap 23 '65
Public eye no. one. por Newsweek 65:27 Ap 26 '65
Shake-up ahead for supersecret agency? por U S News 58:29 Ap 26 '65
RABOTTI, Giancarlo F. and others
Brain tumors, gliomas induced in hamsters by Bryan's strain of Rous sarcoma virus. bibliog Science 147:504-6 Ja 29 '65
RACCOON hunting
Pilot was a pioneer. C. W. Bishop. il Outdoor Life 136:52-5+ D '65
RACE
Four-letter word that hurts. M. H. Fried. Sat R 48:21-3+ O 2 '65

Bibliography
UNESCO publications on race: articles on race published by the UNESCO courier. UNESCO Courier 18:28 Ap '65

RACE attitudes. See Attitudes

RACE cooperation. See Interracial cooperation

RACE differences. See Racial differences

RACE discrimination
Africans in darkest New York; United Nations delegates. J. K. Rosen. il N Y Times Mag p30-1+ F 28 '65
Biased broadcaster put on probation: United church of Christ petition to F.C.C. Christian Cent 82:732-3 Je 9 '65
Black man's burden; excerpts. J. O. Killens. il Ebony 20:173-5 Ag '65
High cost of discrimination. W. M. Young, jr. il Ebony 20:51-4 Ag '65
Race and shared belief as factors in social choice. M. Rokeach and L. Mezei. bibliog il Science 151:167-72 Ja 14 '66
Troubles of astronaut Edward Dwight. C. L. Sanders. il Ebony 20:29-32+ Je '65
White problem in America. L. Bennett, jr. il Ebony 20:29-30+ Ag '65
See also
Discrimination in employment
Negroes in the United States—Segregation
Race prejudice

RACE equality. See Equality

RACE horses
Add this pair to your Derby list; Isle of Greece and Tom Rolfe. W. Tower. Sports Illus 22:69 Mr 22 '65
And then there were only two; Tom Rolfe and Hail to All. W. Tower. il Sports Illus 23:53 Ag 30 '65
Bay and the gray were a perfect parlay; Native Charger and Lucky Debonair for Kentucky Derby. W. Tower. il Sports Illus 22:60+ Mr 15 '65
Blue-chip Bret; Bret Hanover. il Newsweek 65:98-9 My 24 '65
Bold is the badge of champions; Bold Ruler racing's foremost sire. W. Tower. il Sports Illus 22:22-4+ F 22 '65
Bond named Bret. il Time 85:81 Je 11 '65
Faith and form at Saratoga; Bishop McKinstry's devotion to Kelso. W. Tower. il Sports Illus 23:14-15 Ag 16 '65
Good one left is Jacinto; soundest potential Kentucky Derby favorite. W. Tower. il Sports Illus 22:55-6+ F 15 '65
Grass may not be greener; Roman Brother, best U.S. handicap horse at Laurel. W. Tower. Sports Illus 23:71 N 8 '65
He may run all the way to Churchill Downs; Buckpasser. W. Tower. il Sports Illus 23:54 S 6 '65
If at first you succeed, try, try again; Moccasin's victories. il Time 86:83 N 5 '65
Like father, like sons; Ribot's sons, Dapper Dan and Tom Rolfe in Preakness. W. Tower. il Sports Illus 22:30-1 My 24 '65
Little old ladies of Pasadena missed a good bet; G. Pope's Hill Rise to go off at 12-to-1 odds in the Santa Anita handicap. W. Tower. il Sports Illus 22:60-1 Mr 8 '65
Long trip in a short race; Bold Lad favorite of Kentucky Derby. W. Tower. il Sports Illus 22:30-1+ Ap 12 '65
Mink-lined millionaire; horse named Kelso. il Time 86:53 Jl 16 '65
Munificent obsession; pickings for Kentucky Derby. il Time 85:55 Ap 2 '65
Pickles, hosses and my man from Princeton; Greentree stable. J. Olsen. il Sports Illus 22:70-4+ Mr 15 '65
Race horses are a cash crop. S. Cady. il N Y Times Mag p26-7+ Je 13 '65
Race track. A. Minor. See issues of New Yorker
Ribot and a Tom Fool lead all the rest. W. Tower. il Sports Illus 23:112-13 S 20 '65
Rise of a new star named Pia; New York's Aqueduct racetrack. W. Tower. il Sports Illus 23:16-17 Ag 2 '65
Sentimental Derby; Bold Lad, trainer Winfrey and jockey Hartack. W. Tower. il Sports Illus 22:20-5 My 3 '65
Speedy son carries on the Adios tradition; Meadow Lenco at Laurel raceway. il Sports Illus 23:18-23 Jl 5 '65
Syndication is the new big game at the racetrack; trading thoroughbred stallions. J. McDonald. il Fortune 73:159-63+ Ja '66
This Native never left home; California's Native Diver. W. Tower. il Sports Illus 23:43 Jl 26 '65
'Twas a not-so-famous victory; early test for Derby horses at Hialeah. W. Tower. Sports Illus 22:49 Mr 1 '65

RACE of hairy men! drama. See Hunter. E.

RACE prejudice
Catch a bigot by the toe; Prince Georges County white citizens council. T. Kelly. Nation 200:169-70 F 15 '65
Fourth-grade course in color; experience of a white teacher in Harlem. B. Kremen. Holiday 37:24+ Mr '65
Intelligence or prejudice? questions and answers. E. Van Den Haag; discussion. Nat R 17:101-2 F 9 '65
Military ordeal of Sammy Davis jr; excerpt from Yes I can. S. Davis. il Ebony 21:151-4+ D '65
Public evil and private problems: segregation and psychiatry. R. Coles. Yale R 54:513-31 Je '65
Question of original sin; Britain and color discrimination. il Time 86:27 Ag 13 '65
Race hatred fear-based. Sci N L 87:307 My 15 '65
Racism and the Christian understanding of man, by G. D. Kelsey. Review
Christian Cent 83:50 Ja 12 '66. D Kitagawa
Snatch at Sydney. Time 86:28 Ag 13 '65
Structure of hate. G. Wills. Nat R 17:814-16 S 21 '65; Reply. Pyrrho. 17:898+ O 19 '65
Trials of an interracial couple. il Ebony 20:66-8+ O '65
What happens when Sigma chi pledges a Negro. il Look 29:36-40 Jl 27 '65
White man's guilt. J. Baldwin. il Ebony 20:47-8 Ag '65
White problem in America. L. Bennett, jr. il Ebony 20:29-30+ Ag '65
See also
Anti-Semitism
Negroes in the United States—Segregation
Race problems

Anecdotes, facetiae, satire, etc.

Humor in black and white. il Ebony 20:102-3 Ag '65
Negro, Jewish, and Italian hair; bristly reply to the American barber's most barbarous complaint. M. Mayer. Harper 231:44-6 Jl '65

RACE problems
Freedom to read and racial problems; address, January 1965. C. Morgan, jr. ALA Bul 59:484-90 Je '65
World races. Sr Schol 87:17+ S 30 '65: Discussion. 87:26 O 21 '65
See also
Church and race problems
Intermarriage of races
Interracial cooperation
Minorities
Race discrimination
Race prejudice
Race relations
also subhead Race problems under names of continents, countries, etc. e.g. South Africa—Race problems

RACE relations
Delusions of the white liberal; excerpt from Dark ghetto. K. B. Clark. il N Y Times Mag p27+ Ap 4 '65
Law and morality in race relations; civil rights laws restrict man's freedom to deny freedom to others. A. T. Davies. Christian Cent 82:1256-8 O 13 '65
Long, cold winter. il Ebony 20:102-3 O '65
Negro now; excerpts from Who speaks for the Negro? with quotations by four Negro leaders. R. P. Warren. il Look 29:23-31 Mr 23 '65
Southern girl's diary of discovery; North Carolina statewide interracial war on poverty. S. Sterling. il Look 29:107-13 Jl 13 '65
Tax funds for a hate the whites project; federal money for Black arts repertory theater-school in Harlem. U S News 59:16-17 D 13 '65
Trip to Leverton. C. Hunter. New Yorker 41:95-6+ Ap 24 '65
We can learn to be color-blind; Jamaica's racial mixture. P. Abrahams. il N Y Times Mag p38+ Ap 11 '65

RACE tracks
Out of the money? owner plans to sell Aintree course. Newsweek 65:56 Ap 5 '65
'Twas a not-so-famous victory; early test for Derby horses at Hialeah. W. Tower. Sports Illus 22:49 Mr 1 '65

RACIAL differences
Biology looks at race. G. F. Debetz. il UNESCO Courier 18:4-7 Ap '65
Document of paramount importance; biological aspects of the race; signed by participants at Unesco meeting, August 1964. UNESCO Courier 18:8-11 Ap '65
Flight from history, the heritage of the Negro. C. V. Woodward. Nation 201:142-6 S 20 '65

RACIAL discrimination. See Race discrimination

RACIAL equality. See Equality

RACING. See Automobile racing; Horse racing; Pigeon racing; Running

RACING. See Horse racing

RACING car engines. See Automobile engines

RACING car tires. See Tires, Automobile

RACING cars. See Automobiles, Racing

RACING fans. See Sports fans

RACISM
In defense of Uncle Toms. G. Wills. Commonweal 83:178-80 N 12 '65
White hate groups. J. N. Woodford. il Ebony 20:38-40+ Ag '65
Wonder is there have been so few riots. K. B. Clark. il N Y Times Mag p 10-11+ S 5 '65
See also
Race prejudice

RACKETEERING
New ways gangsters muscle into business; interview. F. M. Vinson, jr. il Nations Bsns 53:62-5 Ag '65
See also
Mafia

RACKETS, Tennis. See Tennis rackets

RACKETTY-packetty house; drama. See Kimball. R. F.

RACKS. See Shelves

RACKS, Bicycle. See Bicycle racks

RACKS, Gun. See Gun racks

RACKS, Spice. See Spice racks

RADANT, Else
Strange demise of W. A. Mozart. Hi Fi 15: 62-6 Mr '65

RADAR
Radar. ECM gains seen with Sperry delay line. M. Getler. Miss & Roc 16:34-6 Ap 26 '65

Antenna and scanning mechanisms
External radar on F-101B track missiles. il Aviation W 82:57-8 Je 7 '65
New look in radar; electronically steerable array radars. J. F. Bachmann. il Electr World 73:32-5+ F '65
Optical imaging unit shown feasible. C. D. La-Fond. il Miss & Roc 16:32-3+ Je 7 '65
Radar offers terrain following, mapping. B. Miller. il Aviation W 83:76-7+ N 8 '65
Valley of wire; Arecibo, Puerto Rico. il Sci Digest 57:inside back cover My '65

Mapping applications
Radar imagery; used for mapping purposes by reconnaissance aircraft. J. L. Nelson. il Electr World 74:42-3+ Ag '65

Meteorological applications
See Radar meteorology

Military applications
Air force optimistic about AWACS; airborne warning and control systems. M. Getler. Miss & Roc 18:16 Ja 10 '66
AWAC future hinges on feasibility tests; proposed airborne warning and control aircraft program. P. J. Klass. Aviation W 82:80-1+ F 22 '65
Navy improves accuracy, detection range of space surveillance chain. P. J. Klass. il Aviation W 83:56-7+ Ag 16 '65
New look in radar; electronically steerable array radars. J. F. Bachmann. il Electr World 73:32-5+ F '65

RADAR altimeters. See Altimeters

RADAR beacons. See Radar in aviation

RADAR defense network
See also
Guided missiles—Defenses

RADAR in astronomy
Mars: radar observations. R. M. Goldstein. il Science 150:1715-17 D 24 '65
New Arecibo findings about the planets. Sky & Tel 29:339+ Je '65
New radar studies of Venus. il Sky & Tel 29:356-7 Je '65
Tenuous surface layer on the moon: evidence derived from radar observations. T. Hagfors and others. bibliog il Science 150:1153-6 N 26 '65

RADAR in aviation
AWG-10 radar for F-4J detects, isolates malfunctions. P. J. Klass. il Aviation W 83: 72-3+ Ag 30 '65
Present radar systems insufficient for SST. Sci N L 88:100 Ag 14 '65

Radar beacon display system cuts costs. P. J. Klass. il Aviation W 82:60-1+ My 3 '65
Radar offers terrain following, mapping. B. Miller. il Aviation W 83:76-7+ N 8 '65
Stationkeeping system effective in tests. B. Miller. il Aviation W 82:36-7+ Mr 22 '65
USAF tests air-transportable surveillance and approach radar. il Aviation W 83:79-80 O 18 '65
See also
Airports—Traffic control
Radar meteorology
Transponders

RADAR in meteorology. See Radar meteorology

RADAR in navigation
New sounds underwater. E. Robberson. il Yachting 118:50-3+ Ag '65
Radar plotting. D. Shawn. il Motor B 115: 52-5 My '65
See also
Loran

RADAR in space flight
GT-5 will test rendezvous system. C. D. La-Fond. il Miss & Roc 16:22-3 Je 28 '65
LEM radar value shown by Gemini flight. W. J. Normyle. il Aviation W 84:91+ Ja 10 '66

RADAR interference
Technique predicts rocket interference. M. L. Yaffee. il Aviation W 82:58-9+ F 15 '65

RADAR meteorology
Doppler radar in weather research. il Electr World 73:45 My '65
What's that in the cloud, ahead? weather radar and how to use it. A. Trammell. il Flying 77:69-71 O '65

RADAR stations, Military. See Radar—Military applications

RADAR telescope. See Radar—Antenna and scanning mechanisms

RADATZ, Dick
Look! it's the monster. J. Jares. por Sports Illus 22:101-5 Ap 19 '65

RADCLIFFE, Woodward
Little touches that count. Flower Grower 52:30-1 Mr '65
Pot plants with a modern touch. Pop Gard 16:45 My '65
Serigraphy. Sch Arts 65:16-20 O '65
Succulents for color low maintenance and texture. Pop Gard 17:8+ Ja '66
Wax painting. Sch Arts 64:25-6 F '65

RADFORD, Va.
Brighter by night; more attractive by day. G. W. Hagy. il Am City 80:119-20 D '65

RADFORD ordnance works. See Munitions works

RADIAL saws. See Saws

RADIANT heating
Radiant heating: from wallboard! il Farm J 89:64G F '65

RADIATION
See also
Cosmic rays
Gamma rays
Light
Quantum theory

Accidents and injuries
Death by radiation. Sci Am 212:58+ Je '65

Agricultural applications
Life that's made to order; experiments at Atomic energy commission's research laboratory, University of Tennessee. A. Whitman. il Pop Mech 124:138-42 N '65

Measurement
Iron-55 in humans and their foods. H. E. Palmer and T. M. Beasley. bibliog il Science 149:431-2 Jl 23 '65

Physiological effects
Claimants of Hiroshima. R. A. Falk. il Nation 200:157-61 F 15 '65
Effect of gamma radiation on dietary and hormonal induction of enzymes in rat liver. H. C. Pitot and others. bibliog il Science 150:901-3 N 12 '65
Electron spin resonance of irradiated DNA. P. S. Pershan and others. bibliog il Science 148:378-80 Ap 16 '65
Hepatomas in mice: incidence increased after gamma irradiation at low dose rates. P. C. Nowell and L. J. Cole. bibliog il Science 148:96-7 Ap 2 '65
Ionizing radiation: effect of irradiated medium on synthetic processes. E. C. Pollard. bibliog il Science 147:1045-7 F 26 '65
Monkeys unfazed by radiation exposure. H. M. David. Miss & Roc 17:38 S 27 '65
Neutron affects heredity more than predicted. Sci N L 88:217 O 2 '65

RADIATION—Physiological effects—*Continued*
New lab will speed radiation studies. H. M. David. il Miss & Roc 17:34-5 N 15 '65
Protein synthesis in enucleated eggs of rana pipiens. L. D. Smith and R. E. Ecker. bibliog il Science 150:777-9 N 5 '65
Radiation and terrestrial ecosystems; report on symposium. F. P. Hungate. Science 150:1751-2 D 24 '65
Radiation carcinogenesis: the sequence of events. L. J. Cole and P. C. Nowell. bibliog il Science 150:1782-6 D 31 '65
Radiation-induced increases in fitness in the flour beetle tribolium confusum. J. W. Crenshaw. bibliog Science 149:426-7 Jl 23 '65
Radiation resistance in lipovirus-altered human cells. J. B. Little and R. S. Chang. bibliog il Science 148:1746-7 Je 25 '65
Selective mitochondrial damage by a ruby laser microbeam: an electron microscopic study. R. L. Amy and R. Storb. bibliog il Science 150:756-8 N 5 '65
Thymine photoproducts but not thymine dimers found in ultraviolet-irradiated bacterial spores. J. E. Donnellan, jr. and R. B. Setlow. bibliog il Science 149:308-10 Jl 16 '65
   See also
Plants, Effect of radiation on
Radiation—Agricultural applications
X rays—Physiological effects

Safety devices and measures
Compounds protect mice from radiation effects. Sci N L 87:149 Mr 6 '65

RADIATION, incorporated
Message units built for army in thirty days. G. Alexander. il Aviation W 83:90-1 S 27 '65

RADIATION, Planetary. See Planets—Temperature and radiation

RADIATION, Solar. See Solar radiation

RADIATION belts
   See also
Van Allen radiation belts

RADIATION burns. See Burns and scalds

RADIATION chemistry. See Radiochemistry

RADIATION ecology. See Ecology

RADIATION medicine. See Radiology, Medical

RADIATION sickness

Therapy
Four deadly minutes; accident at the Boris Kidrič institute of nuclear sciences, Yugoslavia. J. Kobler. il Sat Eve Post 238:42-4 N 6 '65

RADIATOR caps. See Automobiles—Equipment

RADIATORS
Workable ways to hide a radiator. il Bet Hom & Gard 43:154+ Ap '65

RADICAL left (politics) See Right and left (political science)

RADICAL right (politics) See Right and left (political science)

RADICALS and radicalism
Ability to face whatever comes; finding a basis for radical work. T. Hayden. New Repub 154:16-18 Ja 15 '66
New radicalism in America, 1889-1963, by C. Lasch. Review
   Commentary 40:85-6+ O '65. W. Phillips
   Commonweal 82:623-7 S 3 '65. M. Harrington
   Nation 200:564-6 My 24 '65. E. T. Chase
   Reporter 32:40+ Je 17 '65. P. Filene
   Sat R 48:42 Je 12 '65. A. Heckscher.
Rebel voices, ed. by J. L. Kornbluh. Review Nation 200:371-3 Ap 5 '65. H. Zinn
What's left of the left? H. Swados. Nation 201:108-14 S 20 '65
   See also
Free universities
Right and left (political science)

RADINOVSKY, Syd
Books in review. Natur Hist 74:8+ Ag '65

RADIO
History
De Forest and the triode detector. R. A. Chipman. il Sci Am 212:92-100 bibliog(p 140) Mr '65; Reply with rejoinder. L. Espenschied. 212:8+ My '65

RADIO, Single sideband. See Radio transmission—Single sideband system

RADIO, stereophonograph and tape recorder combination. See Television receiving apparatus—Radio, stereophonograph and tape recorder combination

RADIO aids to aviation. See Radio in aviation

RADIO altimeters. See Altimeters

RADIO amateurs. See Radio operators, Amateur

RADIO antennas
Build a 144-MC. Swiss quad antenna; directional antenna. H. S. Brier. il Pop Electr 23:52-3+ Jl '65
CB antennas then, now, and tomorrow. T. R. Merrick. il Pop Electr 22:62-7 My '65
EOS unveils unique passive reflector. il Miss & Roc 17:38+ O 18 '65
FM roof antennas. il Consumer Rep 30:86-8 F '65
Giant dish antennas for Caltech's observatory. Sky & Tel 29:199 Ap '65
Indispensable antenna; outdoor antenna a must for FM stereo. L. Cantor. il Hi Fi 15:64-7+ O '65
Largest mobile antennas to be built next year; Owens Valley radio observatory, Calif. Sci N L 87:131 F 27 '65
Marine radiotelephone antenna. E. Robberson. il Electr World 73:32-3 Ap '65
New generation of antennas. R. Cornell. il Pop Electr 22:46-51 My '65
Stereo FM antennas. H. Fantel. Opera N 30:33 Ja 22 '66

RADIO apparatus
Multiplex adapter for FM stereo. D. A. Williams. il Electr World 74:74-6 O '65

RADIO apparatus on aircraft
Single sideband radios urged on airlines. P. J. Klass. Aviation W 83:30 Jl 5 '65
   See also
Radio in aviation
Radio telephone on aircraft

RADIO apparatus on ships, boats, etc.
Marine band wavemeter. E. H. Marriner. il Pop Electr 22:44-5 My '65
SSB comes to marine radio. L. G. Sands. il Electr World 73:30-1 My '65
   See also
Radio telephone on ships, boats, etc.

RADIO apparatus on space vehicles
Receiver requirements for monitoring Gemini. J. C. Wright and W. L. Blair. il Electr World 73:33-5+ Je '65

RADIO astronomy
Andromeda galaxy: extension of the 610.5-megacyle-per-second map. J. R. Dickel and others. bibliog il Science 150:883-4 N 12 '65
Annihilation of matter seen source of quasars. Sci N L 87:310 My 15 '65
Big bang theory upheld; quasi-stellar blue galaxies. Sci N L 87:403 Je 26 '65
Celestial maser? Sci Am 214:48-9 Ja '66
Closer to the big bang. il Sci Am 213:44-6 Jl '65
Did the universe ever begin? D. Cohen. il Sci Digest 58:40-4 Ag '65
Enter the BSO's; blue stellar objects. il Newsweek 65:62 Je 21 '65
Exploding universe of quasars. L. Lessing. il Fortune 72:160-5+ D '65
Galactic X-ray astronomy. C. S. Bowyer. il Sky & Tel 30:264-6 N '65
Great quasar hunt. Sci Am 212:54-6 Mr '65
Ground-based astronomy: a ten-year program; summary of report; discussion. Science 147:1087-8, 1242 Mr 5-12 '65
Hydrogen aids star study. Sci N L 88:179 S 18 '65
Hydrogen emission line $n_{110} \rightarrow n_{109}$: detection at 5009 megahertz in galactic H II regions. B. Höglund and P. G. Mezger. bibliog il Science 150:339-40+ O 15 '65
Hydroxyl radicals in space. B. J. Robinson. il Sci Am 213:26-33 bibliog(p 124) Jl '65
Infrared astronomy. B. C. Murray and J. A. Westphal. il Sci Am 213:20-9 bibliog(p 118) Ag '65
Infrared glows around stars. G. S. Mumford. 3d. il Sky & Tel 29:158 Mr '65
Large radio telescope in use in West Virginia. il(p257) Sci N L 88:264 O 23 '65
Magnetic field of the galaxy. G. L. Berge and G. A. Seielstad. il Sci Am 212:46-54 bibliog(p 146) Je '65
Mathematical games; communication with intelligent organisms on other worlds. M. Gardner. il Sci Am 213:96-100 bibliog(p 120) Ag '65
More quasars found. W. Cloud. il Pop Sci 186:21-2+ Ap '65
Most remote objects ever identified; five quasi-stellar radio sources. il Sky & Tel 30:16 Jl '65
New antenna seen most precise radio telescope; Green Bank, W.Va. Miss & Roc 17:48+ O 18 '65
New class of radio star found in distant galaxy. Sci N L 87:105 F 13 '65
New evidence of intelligent life on other worlds. il Sci Digest 57:8-10 F '65
Oldest object found; 3C-9, most distant quasar. il Sci N L 87:338 My 29 '65

RADIO astronomy—*Continued*

Polarized radio waves from distant source. il(p353) Sci N L 88:356 D 4 '65

Quasars may be illusion. Sci N L 88:117 Ag 21 '65

Quasi-quasars. Time 85:64+ Je 18 '65

Quasi-stellar sources: variation in the radio emission of 3C 273. W. A. Dent. bibliog il Science 148:1458-60 Je 11 '65; Reply. G. B. Field. 150:78-9 O 1 '65

Radio Jupiter, right on time. il Sci Digest 57:27 Mr '65

Radio source spectra at centimeter wavelengths; cosmic radio observations at 11.4-meter wavelength. il Sky & Tel 29:221-2 Ap '65

Radio studies of Venus. G. S. Mumford. Sky & Tel 29:345 Je '65

Radio telescope for amateurs. J. K. Alexander and L. W. Brown. bibliog il Sky & Tel 29:212-14 Ap '65

Radio waves from sky object, 3C-273, variable; signals from three quasars. Sci N L 87:403 Je 26 '65

Relativistic astrophysics. L. C. Green. il Sky & Tel 29:145-9, 226-9 Mr-Ap '65

Relativistic astrophysics; report on symposium sponsored by the University of Texas and the Southwest center for advanced studies, Dallas. B. M. Biram. Science 148: 112-14 Ap 2 '65

Search for intergalactic hydrogen in the Virgo cluster. S. J. Goldstein, jr. bibliog il Science 151:71-3 Ja 7 '66

Search is on for quasars. il Sci N L 88:94 Ag 7 '65

Seek origin of universe. Sci N L 88:5 Jl 3 '65

Sizzling enigmas at the edge of space; quasars. J. F. Pearson. il Pop Mech 124: 94-7+ S '65

Space science stresses optics, antennas. K. Johnsen. Aviation W 82:34 Ap 5 '65

TV beacons in space; UHF transmissions and radio signals from space. Time 87:54 Ja 14 '66

They're solving the world's greatest mystery. C. P. Gilmore. il Pop Sci 187:102-5+ N '65

Those wild Russian stories. D. Cohen. il Sci Digest 58:66-8 Jl '65

Toward the edge of the universe; discovery of five new quasars. il Time 85:72 My 21 '65

U.S. awaits evidence on Russian space claim. Sci N L 87:264 Ap 24 '65

Variable radio emission from quasars. Sky & Tel 30:277-8 N '65

Youngest sky object yet found by radio waves; Cassiopea-A. Sci N L 87:261 Ap 24 '65

See also
National radio astronomy observatory, Green Bank, W.Va.
Radio telescope

RADIO astronomy explorer (satellite) See Artificial satellites—Astronomical applications

RADIO astronomy observatory. See Artificial satellites—Astronomical applications

RADIO-autography. See Autoradiography

RADIO broadcasting

Book programs

Children's books on the air; adaptation from discussion of Children's book council in New York. C. B. Grannis. Pub W 188:186 Jl 12 '65

No sale; libraries and Gateway to ideas program. R. L. Shayon. Sat R 48:34 Mr 20 '65

Comedy

See Radio broadcasting—Humor

Conversation programs

Airwaves' new era of refreshing blather. M. Mannes. Life 58:12 F 5 '65

Good evening; B. Gray on WMCA. New Yorker 41:18-21 Jl 3 '65

Hot hot-line. il Time 85:92+ Je 18 '65

Points of view; telephone conversation programs. R. L. Shayon. Sat R 48:122 Mr 13 '65

Documentary programs

Twenty-three seconds in Tuscaloosa; WBAI-FM programs, You must go home again. R. L. Shayon. Sat R 48:42 Mr 27 '65

Drama

See also
Radio plays

Frequency allocation

See Radio frequency allocation

Frequency modulation

See Radio frequency modulation

History

Program coming in fine; please play Japanese sandman. R. Saudek. il Am Heritage 16: 24-7 Ag '65

Humor

Nostalgic stroll up Allen's alley; return of F. Allen. S. Moore. Life 59:22 N 12 '65

Wayward reader. G. Frazier. Holiday 37:18+ My '65

International aspects

Broadcasting of world politics; address, November 3, 1965. H. Cleveland. Dept State Bul 53:896-901 D 6 '65

Multiplex system

Transistor FM multiplexer. O. D. Carlson. il Pop Electr 22:45-9+ F '65

See also
Radio broadcasting—Stereophonic transmission

Music

Air-borne jester; Canadian broadcasting corporation's Rigoletto. R. Ubriaco. il Opera N 29:32 Ap 3 '65

And still champ; interview on Texaco's opera quiz. ed. by Q. Eaton. S. Spaeth. il Opera N 29:6-7 Ap 10 '65

Magic note. R. N. Roth. Opera N 29:16 F 20 '65

Metropolitan opera is on the air; sponsored by Texaco. Opera N 30:3 O 23 '65

Recordings; Texaco-Metropolitan opera radio network. M. Mayer. Esquire 63:38+ F '65

Silver bells are ringing; then Telephone hour on radio; now Bell telephone hour on television. P. Dilts. il Sr Schol 86:31 Ap 29 '65

Texaco-Metropolitan opera radio network. Opera N 30:inside cover N 20 '65

News

All news, all the time; WINS; New York. Newsweek 65:91 My 3 '65

All the news all the time. R. L. Shayon. Sat R 48:30 Jl 31 '65

Sound of news; station WINS. New Yorker 41:18-19 Je 26 '65

Whose dissent do you hear? J. G. Dunne. New Repub 153:32+ N 6 '65

Opera

See Radio broadcasting—Music

Political applications

See Radio in politics

Programs

Jean Shepherd; radio's noble savage. E. Grossman. Harper 232:88-9 Ja '66

Look and listen. P. Dilts. See issues of Senior scholastic

Looking and listening. P. Dilts. |See issues of Senior scholastic

Value of speaking up; successful move to prevent dropping adult-level cultural programs by KHFM. Albuquerque, N.Mex. R. L. Shayon. Sat R 48:49 S 11 '65

Propaganda

See also
Radio free Europe

Religious programs

Airwave First amendment. America 112:213 F 13 '65

Churches and the airwaves; with editorial comment. D. Smith. Christian Cent 82:355-6, 364-7 Mr 24 '65; Discussion. 82:496-7, 681-2 Ap 21, My 26 '65

Religion and the FCC. M. Cohn; discussion. Reporter 32:6 F 11 '65

Some relevant religion; Night call changes format and widens audience. R. L. Shayon. Sat R 48:41 Ag 21 '65

Sports

Gamesmanship. il Newsweek 66:88B+ S 13 '65

Prince of Pittsburgh; Pirates brash broadcaster. M. Cope. il Sports Illus 23:84+ S 13 '65

Sweet sound of success; broadcaster. J. Garagiola. H. Horn. il Sports Illus 22:30-2+ Mr 15 '65

Stereophonic transmission

Booster for FM stereo. L. Cantor. il Electr World 73:83-4 My '65

Transoceanic stereo. Electr World 73:56 Je '65

Subscription programs

Plight of subscription radio. R. L. Shayon; reply. T. M. Ferguson. Sat R 48:21 Mr 6 '65

RADIO stations, Short wave—*Continued*
Short-wave listening (cont of) Monthly short-wave report. H. Bennett. See issues of Popular electronics

RADIO technical commission for marine services
How the RTCM helps boatmen. G. R. McLeod. il Motor B 115:52-3 Ap '65

RADIO telegraph
Codes
See Cipher and telegraph codes

RADIO telephone
Build the Paragon 144; 2-meter phone. H. B. Smith. il Pop Electr 22:55-9+ Ap '65
Equipment report; EICO 777 CB transceiver kit. il Pop Electr 22:60 Ap '65
More Canadian two-way channels. L. G. Sands. il Electr World 73:78 Je '65

RADIO telephone, Portable
Call alert for two-way radio. G. Childs. il Electr World 74:83 Jl '65

RADIO telephone on aircraft
HF transceiver for USAF F-111A has built-in malfunction isolation. il Aviation W 83:71 D 20 '65
I'll be home in time for dinner. il Flying 77:66-7 Jl '65

RADIO telephone on automobiles
Drivie-talkie. Newsweek 66:62-3 Jl 12 '65
Transistor CB-AM converter. C. J. Heron. il Electr World 73:76:7 Je '65

RADIO telephone on ships, boats, etc.
Get the most from your radio. H. C. Lawrence. il Motor B 115:26-9+ F '65
How the RTCM helps boatmen. G. R. McLeod. il Motor B 115:52-3 Ap '65
Marine radiotelephone antenna. E. Robberson. il Electr World 73:32-3 Ap '65
VHF; an answer to marine-phone congestion? R. Humphrey. il Motor B 115:48-9+ Mr '65

RADIO telescope
Deep-dish prober of far space; Green Bank radiotelescope. il Bsns W p 128+ O 23 '65
First observations at short wavelengths with the 140-foot radio telescope. J. W. M. Baars and P. G. Mezger. il Sky & Tel 31:7-10 Ja '66
He keeps score for the space race; B. Lovell and his radiotelescope at Britain's Jodrell bank. il Bsns W p96-8+ O 30 '65
Large radio telescope in use in West Virginia; National radio astronomy observatory, Green Bank. il(p257) Sci N L 88:264 O 23 '65
Looking up from down under. il Sci Digest 58:inside back cover Ag '65
NASA intensifies radiation studies. D. A. Anderton. il Miss & Roc 16:26+ Je 21 '65
New antenna seen most precise radio telescope; Green Bank, W.Va. Miss & Roc 17:48+ O 18 '65
New 140-foot radio telescope; Green Bank, W.Va. M. M. Small. il Sky & Tel 30:267-74 N '65
Radio telescope for amateurs. J. K. Alexander and L. W. Brown. bibliog il Sky & Tel 29:212-14 Ap '65
Valley of wire; Arecibo, Puerto Rico il Sci Digest 57:inside back cover My '65

RADIO time signals. See Time signals, Radio

RADIO transmission
Hats off to VHF. C. Sheridan. il Pop Electr 23:41-4 Ag '65

Single sideband system
SSB comes to marine radio. L. G. Sands. il Electr World 73:30-1 My '65

RADIO transmission, Short wave
Russians are winning the decibel war. S. Leinwoll. il Pop Electr 22:42-3+ Ap '65

RADIO transmitters
FM wireless microphone. D. Meyer. il Pop Electr 22:35-8 My '65
Sound-power space transmitter studied. il Aviation W 83:83 O 4 '65
Watchdog mobile monitor. H. Burgess. il Pop Electr 23:67-8+ O '65

Transistor transmitters
Camper's special. H. B. Smith. il Pop Electr 23:48-52 Ag '65
Wireless mike in your shirt pocket. J. P. Shields. il Pop Mech 125:194-5+ Ja '66

RADIO transmitters, Portable
Meanwhile, back at the lab. .; use in tracking animals. D. Mech. il Outdoor Life 136:16-17+ N '65
Night flight with a thrush. R. R. Graber. il Audubon Mag 67:368-74 N '65
Wireless mike in your shirt pocket. J. P. Shields. il Pop Mech 125:194-5+ Ja '66

RADIO transmitters, Short wave
R/C transmitter. D. Meyer. il Pop Electr 22:67-70 Je '65
VHF-FM: transmit and be heard. R. Humphrey. il Motor B 116:26-7+ N '65

RADIO waves
Cold tin sandwich found to send out radio waves. Sci N L 88:184 S 18 '65
Digital modulation tested; coding radio signals. A. Ewing. Sci N L 87:101 F 13 '65
Please explain. I. Asimov. Sci Digest 58:97-8 S '65
Radio waves that work under water. K. Warner. il Pop Sci 186:66-8 My '65
See also
Microwaves
Radio astronomy

RADIOACTIVATION analysis
Analytical chemistry in nuclear technology; report on eighth Conference on analytical chemistry in nuclear technology. C. D. Susano and others. Science 147:523 Ja 29 '65
Atomic-age Sherlock Holmes. W. McCann. il Sci N L 87:314-15 My 15 '65
Atomic fingerprints: our newest weapon in the war on crime. W. S. Griswold. il Pop Sci 187:54-6+ Ag '65
Hair may replace fingerprints for sleuths; experiments with activation analysis. Sci N L 88:232 O 9 '65
Taking nuclear fingerprints; activation analysis. il Bsns W p58+ My 1 '65

RADIOACTIVE dating
Ancient rocks hold key to supercontinent theory; dating South American and east African rocks, using radioactive potassium-argon and rubidium-strontium. Sci N L 88:297 N 6 '65
Fission-track dating of bed I, Odluvai Gorge. R. L. Fleischer and others. bibliog il Science 148:72-4 Ap 2 '65
Helium-uranium ratios for pleistocene and tertiary fossil aragonites. F. P. Fanale and O. A. Schaeffer. bibliog il Science 149:312-17 Jl 16 '65
Lead isotopes and the age of the earth. G. R. Tilton and R. H. Steiger. bibliog il Science 150:1805-8 D 31 '65
Potassium-argon age from a granite at Mount Wilbur, Queen Maud Range, Antarctica. V. H. Minshew. bibliog il Science 150:471-3 N 5 '65
Radiation dates meteorite; detecting tracks of plutonium 244. Sci N L 87:278 My 1 '65
Strontium-rubidium age of an iron meteorite. G. J. Wasserburg and others. bibliog il Science 150:1814-18 D 31 '65
Uranium-series ages of Pacific atoll coral. D. L. Thurber and others. bibliog Science 149:55-8 Jl 2 '65
Uranium-series dating of corals and oolites from Bahaman and Florida Key limestones. W. S. Broecker and D. L. Thurber. bibliog il Science 149:58-60 Jl 2 '65
See also
Radiocarbon dating

RADIOACTIVE fallout
Electronic system will send radioactivity data. Sci N L 88:328 N 20 '65
Nuclear power of China. R. E. Lapp. il Life 58:86-90+ My 28 '65; Same abr. with title Does red China understand the bomb? Read Digest 87:49-53 S '65
Radioactive fallout from nuclear weapons tests; report on second AEC conference. E. W. Bierly and A. W. Klement, jr. Science 147:1057-60 F 26 '65
Spring brings tornadoes; radioactive debris from the stratosphere to the earth's surface. B. Tufty. il(p257) Sci N L 87:263 Ap 24 '65
Wildlife will be safe from nuclear explosion. Sci N L 87:360 Je 5 '65

Measurement
Fallout from the nuclear explosion of 16 October 1964. P. K. Kuroda and others. bibliog il Science 147:1284-6 Mr 12 '65

Physiological effects
Fallout effect feared. Sci N L 88:310 N 13 '65

Alaska
Radioactive meat eaten; cesium 137 found among Eskimos at Anaktuvuk Pass. Sci N L 87:142 F 27 '65

California
Radioactive sewage gain. Sci N L 88:143 Ag 28 '65

Great Plains Region
Stratospheric tapping by intense convective storms; implication for public health in the United States. A. N. Dingle. bibliog Science 148:227-9 Ap 9 '65

RADIOACTIVE isotopes. See Radioisotopes
RADIOACTIVE particles. See Particles (nuclear physics)
RADIOACTIVE substances
Radioactivity of the Columbia River effluent. M. G. Gross and others. bibliog il Science 149:1088-90 S 3 '65
   See also
Radioisotopes
RADIOACTIVITY
   See also
Autoradiography
Gamma rays
Plutonium
Radiochemistry

Aeronautic applications
Varied uses developing for radioisotopes. B. Miller. il Aviation W 83:42-3+ Jl 19 '65

Measurement
Chromium-51 as a radioactive tracer of Columbia River water at sea. C. Osterberg and others. bibliog il Science 150:1585-7 D 17 '65
Meteorological evaluation of the sources of iodine-131 in pasteurized milk. R. J. List and others; reply. E. A. Martell. bibliog Science 148:1756-7 Je 25 '65
Polonium-210 analyses of vegetables, cured and uncured tobacco, and associated soils. K. C. Berger and others. bibliog il Science 150:1738-9 D 24 '65
Radioactivity: detection of gamma-ray emission in sediments in situ. D. Jennings and others. bibliog il Science 148:948-50 My 14 '65
Radioactivity: distribution from cratering in basalt. N. A. Bonner and J. A. Miskel. bibliog il Science 150:489-93 O 22 '65
Radioactivity measured in Alaskan natives, 1962-1964. H. E. Harvey and others. bibliog il Science 147:620 F 5 '65; Discussion. 147:1598; 148:1115 Mr 26, My 21 '65
Radioactivity of the Columbia River effluent. M. G. Gross and others. bibliog il Science 149:1088-90 S 3 '65
Strontium isotopes: global circulation after the Chinese nuclear explosion of 14 May 1965. P. K. Kuroda and others. bibliog il Science 150:1289-90 D 3 '65

Physiological effects
Bikini fallout victims show slight effects now. Sci N L 87:344 My 29 '65
Carbon traces changes. Sci N L 87:116 F 20 '65
Radioactive strontium: estimation of the amount accidentally ingested. J. Samachson and H. Spencer. bibliog il Science 148: 955-7 My 14 '65
Thyroid cancer removed in Marshall Islands. Sci N L 88:344 N 27 '65
Tritium: distribution in busycon canaliculatum (L.) injected with labeled reserpine. M. Mirolli. bibliog il Science 149:1503-4 S 24 '65
   See also
Radiation sickness

War use
See Radiological warfare
RADIOACTIVITY in milk. See Milk contamination
RADIOAUTOGRAPHY. See Radiography
RADIOBIOLOGY
Radiolysis of thymine in aqueous solutions: change in site of attack with change in pH. L. S. Myers, jr. and others. bibliog il Science 148:1234-5 My 28 '65
RADIOCARBON dating
Ancient U.S.-Mexico cultural bridge dated; dating of ceramic fragments. Sci N L 88: 233 O 9 '65
Carbon-14 and tritium dating: sixth international meeting. E. A. Olson and R. M. Chatters. Science 150:1488-92 D 10 '65
Half-life of radiocarbon; letter. F. Johnson. Science 149:1326 S 17 '65
Holocene submergence of the eastern shore of Virginia. W. S. Newman and G. A. Rusnak. bibliog il Science 148:1464-6 Je 11 '65
Mazama and Glacier Peak volcanic ash layers: relative ages. R. Fryxell. bibliog il Science 147:1288-90 Mr 12 '65
Radiocarbon age of a Nevada mummy. P. C. Orr and R. Berger. bibliog il Science 148: 1466-7 Je 11 '65
Radiocarbon date from the Lake St John area, Quebec. P. Lasalle. bibliog il Science 149:860-2 Ag 20 '65

Radiocarbon dates from a tomb in Mexico. P. T. Furst. bibliog il Science 147:612-13 F 5 '65
Radiocarbon determinations for estimating groundwater flow velocities in central Florida. B. B. Hanshaw and others. bibliog il Science 148:494-5 Ap 23 '65
Split twig figurines from northern Arizona: new radiocarbon dates. R. C. Euler and A. P. Olson. bibliog il Science 148:368-9 Ap 16 '65
RADIOCHEMISTRY
Chemistry at high velocities. R. Wolfgang. il Sci Am 214:82-90 Ja '66
Chemistry of isotopes; adaptation of address, October 16, 1963. J. Bigeleisen. bibliog il Science 147:463-71 Ja 29 '65
Mobility of the hydrated electron. K. H. Schmidt and W. L. Buck. bibliog il Science 151:70-1 Ja 7 '66
Radiolysis of thymine in aqueous solutions: change in site of attack with change in pH. L. S. Myers, jr. and others. bibliog il Science 148:1234-5 My 28 '65
Thymine addition to ethanol: induction by gamma irradiation. P. E. Brown and others. il Science 151:68-70 Ja 7 '66
RADIOGRAPHY
Growth rate of giant clam tridacna gigas at Bikini atoll as revealed by radioautography. K. Bonham. bibliog il Science 149:300-2 Jl 16 '65
Neutron radiographs. il Sci Digest 57:34-5 Je '65
   See also
Autoradiography
RADIOISOTOPE gages. See Gages
RADIOISOTOPES
AEC doubles space radioisotope efforts. M. L. Yaffee. il Aviation W 84:75+ Ja 10 '66
Cosmogenic radionuclides in the bondoc meteorite. P. J. Cressy, jr. and J. P. Shedlovsky bibliog il Science 148:1716-17 Je 25 '65
Nuclear medicine's two explosive decades. J. Breeling. il Todays Health 43:54-9+ Jl '65
Trinitite: cobalt-60, cesium-137, and europium-152. L. P. Salter and J. H. Harley. bibliog il Science 148:954-5 My 14 '65
   See also
Radiology, Medical

Aeronautic applications
See Radioactivity—Aeronautic applications
RADIOLOGICAL warfare
Forthright CBR policy urged. W. S. Beller. il Miss & Roc 16:27-8+ Ap 19 '65
RADIOLOGY, Medical
Nuclear energy as a medical tool. G. W. Tressel. il Todays Health 43:50-5 My '65
Nuclear medicine's two explosive decades. J. Breeling. il Todays Health 43:54-9+ Jl '65
RADIOLYSIS. See Radiochemistry
RADIOMETERS
Geophysical observations from Nimbus I. W. Nordberg. bibliog il Science 150:559-72 O 29 '65
Luminescence dosimetry; report on international conference. C. J. Karzmark and others. Science 150:391-2+ O 15 '65
RADIONUCLIDES. See Radioisotopes
RADIOSCOPIC diagnosis. See Diagnosis, Radioscopic
RADIOTELESCOPE. See Radio telescope
RADIOTHERAPY
Now, A-blasts for cancer. A. J. Snider. il Sci Digest 58:16-17 D '65
Nuclear medicine; report on symposium on clinical applications of nuclear medicine. D. B. Sodee. Science 147:761 F 12 '65
Radiation outside the body. il Time 85:54 Ap 9 '65
   See also
Radiology, Medical
X rays—Therapeutic applications
RADIUM
   See also
Polonium
RADOSH, Ronald
Open door of Henry Wallace. Nation 202:39-42 Ja 10 '66
RAFFAELLO (ship) See Ocean liners
RAFFEL, Burton
On translating Beowulf. Yale R 54:532-46 Je '65
RAFFERTY, Elizabeth
Snow bunny's 874-mile weekend. il pors Look 29:92 D 14 '65

RAFFERTY, Max Lewis
Cure for campus riots; interview. por U S News 58:70-2 My 17 '65
Education for patriotism in our schools. Sr Schol 86:10T+ F 4 '65

about

Little bit of censoring. R. L. Crowell. il Wilson Lib Bul 39:652-7 Ap '65

RAFTS
Jangada; a seaworthy Brazilian raft. E. C. Uruburu. il Américas 17:34-6 My '65

RAGO, Henry
T. S. Eliot: a memoir and a tribute. Poetry 105:392-5 Mr '65

RAGOTZIKE, Robert A. and Friedman, Irving
Low deuterium content of Lake Vanda, Antarctica. bibliog Science 148:1226-7 My 28 '65

RAHMAN, Abdul, tunku
Malaysia: key area in Southeast Asia. For Affairs 43:659-70 Jl '65

about

People of the week. por U S News 59:14 Ag 23 '65

RAHNER, Karl
Karl Rahner in New York; interview, ed. by E. C. Bianchi. America 112:860-3 Je 12 '65

RAHTZ, Robert
Paperbacks as textbooks. Sr Schol 87:sup 18 N 18 '65

RAHV, Philip
Myth and the powerhouse, by P. Rahv. Review
Sat R 48:55 O 2 '65. E. Capouya

RAICHLE, Elaine
Connoisseurs in the making. NEA J 54:29-30 N '65

RAIDS
More mosquito bites. Time 86:40+ N 26 '65
Storm troopers; terrorist group of Palestinian Arabs. Time 85:31A-31B Je 18 '65

RAIL mergers. See Railroads—Consolidations and mergers

RAILINGS. See Hand railings

RAILROAD accidents. See Railroads—Accidents

RAILROAD consolidation. See Railroads—Consolidations and mergers

RAILROAD employees. See Railroads—Employees

RAILROAD law
See also
United States—Interstate commerce commission

RAILROAD management. See Railroads—Management

RAILROAD models
Backyard & birdbath R.R. W. C. Lammey. il Pop Mech 124:118-28+ Ag '65
Bill Kromer's miniature railroad. S. A. Parvin. il Hobbies 70:122-3 Mr '65
Iron colts in the back yard. J. B. Kemmerer. il Pop Mech 124:80-4 Ag '65

Electric equipment
Super-X pulse power pack for HO railroading. W. Pope. il Pop Electr 23:41-6+ D '65

RAILROAD museums
How the English used to go; keepsakes of British transportation. il Sunset 134:38+ F '65

RAILROAD passengers. See Railroad travel; Railroads—Passenger traffic

RAILROAD strikes. See Strikes—United States—Railroads

RAILROAD travel
After finishing his morning coffee, this man hopped a freight. J. H. Doolittle. il Esquire 63:80-3+ My '65
Germans put a twist on travel by train; excursion for teen-agers. il Bsns W p84-5 Je 26 '65
Going nowhere and losing things on the Super Chief. R. Bailey. il House & Gard 127:29-30+ F '65
On rails in Wales. il Travel 123:43-5 Ap '65
Rail cruise encore. L. Martin. il Travel 123:10 Ap '65
To Grand Canyon Village by rail. il Sunset 134:33 Je '65
Wooing the passengers. il Time 86:55 D 24 '65

RAILROAD work rules. See Railroads—Work rules

RAILROADS
For travelers east, here are three rides behind steam. il Sunset 135:20-1 Ag '65
See also
Locomotive firemen
Locomotives

Accidents
Wreck of the 5:28; South Africa. Time 86:46 O 15 '65

Cars
See also
Railroads—Freight cars

Computer installations
Doubling the freight car's workday; electronic railroading. il Bsns W p 122-4+ D 18 '65

Consolidations and mergers
Bumpy line to merger; need for three strong eastern rail systems. il Bsns W p72+ Ap 3 '65
Getting mergers off the sidetrack; proposal for stepping up railroad mergers. Bsns W p98+ D 4 '65
High court clears a rail merger; judiciary upholds ICC approval of Seaboard and Atlantic Coast union. Bsns W p40 N 27 '65
Latest plan: biggest railroad; Chesapeake & Ohio and Norfolk & Western. il U S News 59:110 S 13 '65
Long courtship; Penn-Central merger. il Time 86:92 O 29 '65
Merger that takes a slow track; C&O-B&O. il Bsns W p66-8+ F 13 '65
New railroad giant on the way; merger of Pennsylvania and the New York central. il U S News 58:94 Ap 12 '65
Next-door sweethearts; Chicago and North Western railway and the Chicago, Milwaukee, St Paul & Pacific railroad. Newsweek 65:72-3 Mr 29 '65
On the right track; proposed Chicago, Milwaukee & North western transportation co. il Time 85:76 Mr 26 '65
One down, one to go; Pennsylvania-New York central merger. Newsweek 67:56 Ja 10 '66
Operation thunderbolt; C.&O. and Norfolk & Western railway. il Time 86:81-2 S 10 '65
Penn-Central: biggest merger yet? il Newsweek 65:81 Ap 12 '65
Pennsy and Central pass first ICC test; to create the Nation's largest rail system. il Bsns W p70+ Ap 3 '65
Railroads: how to think really big. il Newsweek 66:67 S 13 '65
Seven railroads to make one. il Bsns W p32-3 S 4 '65
Strength through union; Penn-Central merger announcement. il Time 85:89-90+ Ap 9 '65
Will two rich rails be allowed to wed? Atlantic Coast line and Seaboard. il Bsns W p90+ D 4 '65
World's biggest merger; Pennsylvania and New York central. G Burck. il Fortune 71:176-9+ Je; 72:128-31+ Jl '65

Employees
Firemen ask 25 per cent pay hike; demand could trigger strike and hasten job elimination. Bsns W p82 Ja 8 '66
Rail bargaining back on the tracks; carriers reach accord with five unions on job security. Bsns W p43 F 6 '65
Railroad employment protective agreement; excerpts. Mo Labor R 88:416-18 Ap '65
Railroads chip away at unnecessary jobs. Bsns W p85 Ap 3 '65
Timetable that missed; job reductions through attrition. Bsns W p54 F 27 '65
Trains without firemen: the record. U S News 60:86 Ja 17 '66
See also
Locomotive firemen
Station masters
Strikes—United States—Railroads

Federal aid
Bailing out the New Haven. Bsns W p27 Mr 13 '65

Finance
See also
Railroads—Federal aid

Freight cars
Comeback for a depressed industry. il U S News 58:90 Mr 1 '65
Doubling the freight car's workday; electronic railroading. il Bsns W p 122-4+ D 18 '65
Freight cars that pack a competitive wallop. il Fortune 72:132-7 Jl '65

Renting

Guided growth of leasing. il Duns R 85:pt2 132-3+ Je '65

Freight service
Rails: whistling a new tune. il Newsweek 65:72-5+ Ap 5 '65

RAILROADS—*Continued*

Government regulation
See Railroads and state—United States

Management
Chicago's miracle; unique railroad man making money out of commuters. A. Schiller. Harper 232:65-8+ Ja '66
One way to run a railroad: go to it! Brosnan's way. il Newsweek 66:89-90+ O 18 '65

Models
See Railroad models

Passenger service
Carrying people again; Florida East Coast ry. running passenger trains. il Bsns W p81 Ag 7 '65
Commuter railroads can be saved. H. B. Meyers. il Fortune 71:100-5+ My '65
Commuting at 1,000 m.p.h; Northeast corridor between Boston and Washington. L. Galton. il N Y Times Mag p76-7+ O 24 '65
Japan's crack train will get a longer run; Tokaido line to Okayama and Fukuoka. Bsns W p200 O 9 '65
Passenger trains that carry your auto, too. il U S News 59:10 Jl 26 '65
Reprieve for the New Haven; solution: New York central RR will operate New Haven's New York commuter service. Bsns W p34 Ap 24 '65

Passenger traffic
Chicago's miracle; unique railroad man making money out of commuters. A. Schiller. Harper 232:65-8+ Ja '66
Grant to measure rail commuter service; Southeastern Pennsylvania transportation compact. Am City 80:64 O '65
In Chicago, the rider is king; fast, sure rail service. il Bsns W p82+ Mr 20 '65
See also
Commuters
Railroad travel

Stations
See also
New York (city)—Stations
Station masters

Train speed
Commuting at 1,000 m.p.h; Northeast corridor between Boston and Washington. L. Galton. il N Y Times Mag p76-7+ O 24 '65
Due this year: trains that can go 150 m.p.h; electric cars between New York and Washington. A. P. Armagnac. il Pop Sci 188:88-93 Ja '66
400-mph passenger train. L. Lessing. il Fortune 71:124-9+ Ap '65
High speed tube transportation. L. K. Edwards. il Sci Am 213:30-40 bibliog(p 118) Ag '65; Discussion. 213:10+ S; 6 O '65
Jet-age approach to train travel; eventual high-speed service from Boston to Washington, D.C. il U S News 59:18 D 13 '65
Ninety minutes to Boston; rapid rail system needed. America 113:176 Ag 21 '65
Rails put on a high-speed drive; ultrafast trains in Northeast corridor. il Bsns W 80-3 Jl 17 '65
Take the air train? high-speed transportation methods. il Newsweek 65:56 F 15 '65
Train of the future in sight for 1966; segments between Washington and Boston, via New York. il U S News 59:110-11 O 4 '65
Trains at 300 mph, what travel of future will be like; interview. W. W. Seifert; R. J. Hansen. il U S News 59:96-9 Jl 26 '65

Trains
For travelers east, here are three rides behind steam. il Sunset 135:20-1 Ag '65
Japan's two-mile-a-minute train; Hikari. B. Hosokawa. il Read Digest 86:153-6+ Ap '65
Turbine train design uses aerospace technology heavily. W. H. Gregory. il Aviation W 83:84-5+ D 13 '65

Work rules
Railroads chip away at unnecessary jobs. Bsns W p85 Ap 3 '65
Trainmen yank brakes on featherbed label; AAR demands reforms in union work rules. il Bsns W p 102+ N 27 '65

Alaska
See also
White Pass and Yukon railroad

Bolivia
Watch out, here it comes! once-a-week express from Santa Cruz to Corumbá. T. Armbrister. il Sat Eve Post 238:74-7 F 27 '65

Brazil
Watch out, here it comes! once-a-week express from Santa Cruz to Corumbá. T. Armbrister. il Sat Eve Post 238:74-7 F 27 '65

Canada
See also
White Pass and Yukon railroad

Europe
New track for Wagons-Lits: diversification. il Time 86:107 O 8 '65

Germany (Federal Republic)
Germans put a twist on travel by train; excursion for teen-agers. il Bsns W p84-5 Je 26 '65

Japan
Japan's crack train will get a longer run; Tokaido line to Okayama and Fukuoka. Bsns W p200 O 9 '65
Japan's two-mile-a-minute train; Hikari. B. Hosokawa. il Read Digest 86:153-6+ Ap '65
Way of life; Tokaido express. il Newsweek 66:102 N 15 '65

Panama
Rails that linked the oceans. W. A. Naughton. il Américas 17:11-17 F '65

United States
Clear track for the rails; recovery of the railroads. il Duns R 85:pt2 98-101+ Je '65
Future of American railroads; what rail-industry leaders see ahead; symposium. il U S News 59:42-6 Ag 16 '65
Great railroads for the Great society; address, April 1, 1965. D. P. Loomis. Vital Speeches 31:424-7 My 1 '65
Notes and comment; five tips for reviving the rails. New Yorker 41:35 Mr 20 '65
Rail bargaining back on the tracks; carriers reach accord with five unions on job security. Bsns W p43 F 6 '65
Railroads are fighting back! J. N. Miller. Read Digest 87:153-6+ O '65
Railroads fight back. il(p97) Sci N L 87:103 F 13 '65
Railroads switch to other tracks. Bsns W p45-6 Ag 7 '65
Rails: whistling a new tune. il Newsweek 65:72-5+ Ap 5 '65
Total transportation. J. H. Wright. Duns R 86:76C-76D+ O '65
Train of the future in sight for 1966; segments between Washington and Boston, via New York. il U S News 59:110-11 O 4 '65
Train-watching in Arizona; Southwest's last standard-gauge steam-powered railroad. il Sunset 135:19 N '65
Twilight or dawn of a new era for railroads? il Sr Schol 86:12-14+ F 11 '65
Up the line: two executives moved on to new and bigger jobs. Time 86:101 S 24 '65
Wooing the passengers. il Time 86:55 D 24 '65
See also
Association of American railroads
Railroads—Consolidations and mergers
Railroads, Short line
Railroads and state—United States
also names of railroads, e.g. Florida East Coast railway

RAILROADS, Electric. See Electric railroads

RAILROADS, Narrow gage
Over Cumbres Pass on the narrow-gauge. il Sunset 134:46+ Je '65

RAILROADS, Private
See also
Railroads, Small size

RAILROADS, Short line
For travelers east, here are three rides behind steam. il Sunset 135:20-1 Ag '65
What a way to run a railroad! Manistee & Northeastern railroad. H. Titus. il Field & S 70:61-4 Jl '65

RAILROADS, Single rail
Here's the original monorail; Wuppertal; Germany (Federal Republic) il Sunset 134:72+ Ap '65

RAILROADS, Small size
Tiny trams; owned by Don Sorensen, Wilton, Conn. C. S. Wren. il Look 29:91-3 F 23 '65

RAILROADS, Toy
See also
Railroad models

RAILROADS and state

United States

400-Mph passenger train. L. Lessing. il Fortune 71:124-9+ Ap '65

If government does take over the railroads. il U S News 58:73-4 F 1 '65

Nationalization: when governments go into business. Sr Schol 86:21 Mr 18 '65

Subsidized commuting. Time 85:90+ Mr 5 '65
See also
Railroads—United States

RAILWAY regulation. See Railroads and state —United States

RAIN and rainfall

Collision characteristics of freely falling water drops. R. Gunn. bibliog il Science 150:695-701 N 5 '65; Reply. P. B. Scott. 150:1749 D 24 '65

Harvested rain: collecting rainfall in semiarid and desert regions. Sci Am 213:53 N '65

Water harvesting. Am City 81:47 Ja '66
See also
Droughts
Floods

RAIN forests
See also
Olympic National Park

RAIN making

Looking a hurricane in the eye; effect of cloud seeding. Bsns W p54 Ag 7 '65

No increase in rain found from seeding. Sci N L 88:296 N 6 '65

Rain decrease follows seeding sometimes. Sci N L 89:5 Ja 1 '66

Water: can cloud-seeding help? letter. F. W. Reichelderfer. Science 150:1103 N 26 '65

RAINBOW trout fishing. See Trout fishing

RAINCOATS

Light and shiny wet look; foul-weather apparel. il Sports Illus 22:52-8 Mr 15 '65

Quilted look. il Newsweek 65:108-9 Ap 12 '65

Raincoats, points to check before you buy. il Changing T 19:11-12 Ap '65

RAINE, Kathleen

Scala coeli; poem. New Yorker 41:56 D 4 '65

Three poems: Path; Lachesis; Last things. New Yorker 41:50-1 D 18 '65

RAINER, Yvonne

Brief biography. S. Goodman. pors Dance Mag 39:110-11 D '65

Yvonne Rainer and Robert Morris, Judson memorial church. J. Maskey. Dance Mag 39:64 My '65

RAINES, Max W.

Crossing the college threshold. por Am Ed 1:30-2 Jl '65

RAINEY, Lawrence

Two faces of Sheriff Rainey. R. Cleghorn. il por N Y Times Mag p 10-11+ F 21 '65

RAINEY, Sarita

New avenues of expression. Sch Arts 64:7-9 Je '65

RAINIER, MOUNT

Memorable Mount Rainier. J. Lange. il Travel 124:48-9 Ag '65

RAINS, D. W. and Epstein, Emanuel

Transport of sodium in plant tissue. bibliog Science 148:1611 Je 18 '65

RAINY LAKE

Sunny Rainy Lake. B. Cary. il Travel 124:40-4 Jl '65

RAINY RIVER

IJC recommendations approved for Rainy River pollution control. Dept State Bul 54:36 Ja 3 '66

RAISZ, Lawrence G. See Friedman, J. jt. auth.

RAJAN, M. S.

Future of nonalignment. Ann Am Acad 362:121-8 N '65

RAJAN, Sundar

India's linguistic dilemma. Reporter 32:31-2 My 6 '65

Kashmir: Shastri's time for decision. Reporter 33:41-3 S 23 '65

RALEIGH, C. B.

Glide mechanisms in experimentally deformed minerals. bibliog Science 150:739-41 N 5 '65

RALSTON, Dennis

Rain in Spain was cushions. F. Deford. il Sports Illus 23:20+ Ag 30 '65

RALSTON, S. Scott

House by the Brandywine. Read Digest 87:126-7 Jl '65

RAM Jet propulsion. See Jet propulsion

RAMA, S. N. I. and Hart, S. R.

Neon isotope fractionation during transient permeation. bibliog Science 147:737-8 F 12 '65

RAMA RAU, Santha

Christmas in the midday sun. House & Gard 128:162-3 D '65

Families are different in India. Read Digest 87:167-8+ Ag '65

Pearl on the toe of India. Horizon 7:50-63 Autumn '65

That much-abused word, friendship. McCalls 93:54+ N '65

Two descriptions of the elephant. Reporter 33:40+ S 9 '65

What's wrong with your judgement. Redbook 125:43+ Je '65

RAMACHANDRAN, G. N. and Parthasarathy, S.

Anomalous dispersion method: its power for protein structure analysis. bibliog Science 150:212-14 O 8 '65

RAMAKRISHNA

Ramakrishna and his disciples, by C. Isherwood. Review
America 113:82 Jl 17 '65
Commonweal 82:702-4 S 24 '65. G. Woodcock

RAMAKRISHNAN, Alladi

Mathematical sciences. Science 149:209-10 Jl 9 '65

RAMERREZ (operatic character) See Characters in opera

RAMINGTON, John

Of despair: poem. America 112:547 Ap 17 '65

RAMIREZ, Roberto

Death sails west on the Seven Seas. il por Life 59:68-71 Ag 20 '65

Nightmare afloat. Newsweek 66:23-4 Ag 23 '65

Slaughter on the Seven Seas. il por Time 86:35 Ag 20 '65

RAMO, Simon

Management of government programs. Harvard Bsns R 43:6-8+ Jl '65

RAMOND, Charles K.

Must advertising communicate to sell? bibliog f Harvard Bsns R 43:148-56+ S '65

RAMPAL, Jean Pierre

Ubiquitous flutist. R. McMullen. il pors Hi Fi 15:34-7+ My '65

RAMPART CANYON DAM (proposed) See Dams—Alaska

RAMPARTS (periodical)

Of many things; what has happened to Catholicism and editorial censorship. T. N. Davis. America 113:173 Ag 21 '65

RAMPERSAD, Oliver R. and Wool, I. G.

Protein synthesis by ribosomes from heart muscle: effect of insulin and diabetes. bibliog Science 149:1102-3 S 3 '65

RAMSAY, Theodore

Shades of Tom Sawyer. Sch Arts 65:16-19 S '65

RAMSDELL, H. J.

Ride to remember. J. C. Hunt. il Am Heritage 16:80-3 Ap '65

RAMSEY, Arthur Michael, abp

Rhodesia and the archbishop. J. M. Cameron. Commonweal 83:230-1 N 26 '65

RAMSEY, Diane

Information and control processes in living systems. Science 149:459 Jl 23 '65

RAMSEY, Jarold W.

Students, or grown-ups posing as students? NEA J 55:16-18 Ja '66

RAMSEY, Robert W. See Street, S. F. jt. auth.

RAMWELL, P. W. and others

Prostaglandin: release from the rat phrenic nerve-diaphragm preparation. bibliog Science 149:1390-1 S 17 '65

RANCH life

Ranchwoman's treasury of sounds and smells. B. L. Beck. il Farm J 89:76-7 O '65
See also
Gauchos

RANCHES

At the Gibson Ranch park, your children are welcome to meet the animals. il Sunset 135:64-5 Jl '65

Bradford Brinton memorial ranch; Wyo. Hobbies 70:123 O '65

Last of the divorce ranches; Donner Trail ranch. Nev. R. Wernick. il Sat Eve Post 238:30-2+ Jl 17 '65

Take them back to the farm: California's Gibson ranch county park. S. Parenteau. il Nat Parks Mag 39:12-13 N '65

This month's cover story; A. Rusk, rancher, Barber County, Kan. D. Malena. il Suc Farm 63:32 Je '65

RAND, Ayn

Ayn Rand: a voice in the wilderness. B. Cook. por Cath World 201:119-24 My '65

RAND, Christopher

Too much crusading. por Time 86:34 Ag 27 '65

Tourist in academe. E. R. Graubard. Nation 200:148 F 8 '65

RAND corporation

How to beat the traffic mess. S. V. Jones. il Sci Digest 57:77-9 My '65

RAND daily mall. See Newspapers—South
Africa
RAND McNally and company
Publisher wins map copyright suit; Pentron
corporation to pay and destroy the plates
used. Pub W 189:69 Ja 10 '66
RANDAL, Judith
Witch doctors and psychiatry. Harper 231:
56-61 D '65
RANDALL, Alex
Death of a newspaper. New Repub 153:29 O
30 '65
RANDALL, Betty, and Zabarsky, Nathan
Tools of selective focus. U S Camera 29:44-5+
Ja '66
RANDALL, Charles C. and others
Lability of host-cell NDA in growing cell cul-
tures due to mycoplasma. bibliog Science
149:1098-9 S 3 '65
RANDALL, Charles Edgar
George Perkins Marsh; conservation's for-
gotten man. Am For 71:20-3 Ap '65
So you want to be forester? Am For 71:18-34
S '65
Spain plants the plain. Am For 71:24-7+ Je
'65
RANDALL, Clarence B.
Whatever became of the village blacksmith?
por Pop Mech 124:106-7+ N '65
RANDALL, Florence Engel
No one kicks cans any more; story. Redbook
124:74-5 Ap '65
So near to me; story. Good H 160:64-5 Ja
'65
Watchers; story. Harper 230:96-8 Mr '65;
Excerpt. U S News 59:66 Ag 9 '65
RANDALL, Lyman K.
Organizational paradox. Harvard Bsns R 43:
86-7+ Jl '65
RANDALL, Martha
One for the old folks. Time 86:68 Ag 27 '65
RANDALL, Stanley J.
U.S. and Canada trade relations; address,
December 15, 1964. Vital Speeches 31:251-4
F 1 '65
RANDALL, Tony
Good-bye to a second banana. R. Lemon. il
pors Sat Eve Post 238:94-5+ N 6 '65
RANDOL, George
Financing the lay apostolate. America 113:233
S 4 '65
RANDOLPH, Chet
How to get two lamb crops a year. Suc Farm
63:102 S '65
RANDOLPH, Kay
Pet news. Ladies Home J 82:40 Ag; 34 O '65
RANDOM house, incorporated
RCA and Random house agree to merger
terms. Pub W 189:100 Ja 17 '66
Step-up books: Random's new children's
line. il Pub W 187:135-6 F 22 '65
RANGE finding
Varied tactical uses developing for laser.
B. Miller. il Aviation W 82:39+ My 31 '65
RANGE grasses. See Grasses
RANGE of aircraft. See Airplanes, Military—
Range
RANGEFINDER camera. See Cameras
RANGER project. See Lunar probes
RANGERS, Texas. See Texas—Police
RANGES, Electric. See Electric stoves
RANGES, Kitchen. See Gas stoves
RANGES, Missile. See Proving grounds
RANKIN, Allen
Augusto Ruschi's Garden of Eden. Read Di-
gest 86:216-18+ Je '65
RANKIN, R. F.
Press in developing countries. Sat R 48:124-5
S 18 '65
RANKIN, Virginia
Drama in the barn. Recreation 58:279+ Je
'65
RANN of Cutch. See Cutch, Rann of
RANSOHOFF, Martin
Hollywood's heedless horseman. J. G. Dunne.
il por Holiday 38:111-12+ D '65
RANSOM, Harry Howe
Containing Central intelligence. New Repub
153:12-15 D 11 '65
RANSOM, James
Beach-blanket babies. Esquire 64:90-5+ Jl '65
How to win at wine tasting, beer drinker's
guide. Esquire 63:30+ Mr '65
RANSOM, Jay Ellis
Travel far and near; the Kinishba Pueblo
ruins. Natur Hist 74:58-60+ My '65
RANSOM, Richard
Why Hickory farms goes to the fair. il por
Bsns W p70-2 S 4 '65
RANSTEAD, Donald D.
Breakthrough in Chile. Commonweal 82:82-3
Ap 9 '65

Dominican crisis. New Repub 152:8-9 My 29
'65
Latin America: continent on a teeterboard.
Nation 201:292-4 N 1 '65
Latin America reacts. Commonweal 82:613-15
S 3 '65
RANUNCULUS. See Buttercups
RAO, M. R. Ramachandra. See Novak, A. F.
jt. auth.
RAO, Potu N. and Engelberg, Joseph
HeLa cells: effects of temperature on the life
cycle. bibliog Science 148:1092-4 My 21 '65
RAPE
Death penalty for rape. Nation 200:156-7 F
15 '65
Mississippi justice; white man's life impris-
onment. Newsweek 66:42 N 22 '65
Reasonable rape; statutory rape. Time 87:49
Ja 21 '66
See also
Trials (rape)
RAPER, John R. See Mullins, J. T. jt. auth.
RAPF, Maurice
Life movie review. Life 59:10 S 3; 15 N 12 '65
RAPHAEL, Chaim
Department of amplification. New Yorker
41:150+ Mr 27 '65
RAPID cameras. See Cameras
RAPID films. See Photography—Films
RAPID transit
Many choices begin to form up. il Life 59:
158-9 D 24 '65
Mass transit. il Am City 80:66 Je; 52 Jl;
48 Ag; 47 S; 64 O; 28 N; 24 D '65
Moderate cost transit for smaller cities.
Sci N L 88:88 Ag 7 '65
Transportation in cities. J. W. Dyckman. il
Sci Am 213:162-74 bibliog(p278) S '65
See also
Transportation, High speed
also subhead Rapid transit under names
of cities, e.g. San Francisco—Rapid transit
RAPOPORT, Anatol
Sources of anguish. Bul Atomic Sci 21:31-6
D '65
RAPP, Fred, and others
Tumor and virus antigens of simian virus
40: differential inhibition of synthesis by
cytosine arabinoside. bibliog Science 147:
625-7 F 5 '65
RAPP, Herbert J. See Borsos, T. jt. auth.
RAPPLEYE, Willard C.
Where hospitals are weak, and what to do
about it; interview. por U S News 58:53-6
Mr 15 '65
RAPPORT, Victor A.
Some ways toward campus peace. Sch & Soc
93:296-7 Sum '65
RARE books section. See Association of
college and research libraries—Rare books
section
RARE gases. See Gases, Rare
RARE metals. See Metals
RARITAN RIVER
New Jersey revives a river. E. Kendall. Holi-
day 39:112+ Ja '66
River dies, and is born again. F. J. Cook.
il N Y Times Mag p22-3+ Ap 18 '65
RAS, Norberto
Books. Américas 17:38 Ag '65
RASCO, José Ignacio. See Ignacio Rasco, J.
RASKIN, A. H.
Automation has made strikes senseless. N Y
Times Mag p45+ O 31 '65
Berkeley affair: Mr Kerr vs. Mr Savio &
co. N Y Times Mag p24-5+ F 14 '65
Conciliator goes to the U.N. N Y Times
Mag p 10+ Ag 8 '65
Fat cats of labor. Nation 201:103-7 S 20 '65
Great Manhattan newspaper duel. Sat R 48:
58-60+ My 8 '65
What makes Teddy Kheel run. N Y Times
Mag p52-3+ D 5 '65
Who needs newspapers? Reporter 33:33-5 O
21 '65
about
It didn't fit to print. Newsweek 65:94 My 17
'65
RASKIN, Judith
American bel canto. Opera N 30:6 Ja 15 '66
about
Four Americans. M. Mayer. Esquire 63:36+
Ap '65
Music to my ears; first Town hall recital.
I. Kolodin. Sat R 48:26+ D 18 '65
RASMUSEN, B. A.
Isoantigens of gamma globulin in pigs. bib-
liog Science 148:1742-3 Je 25 '65

RASPBERRIES
Fresh raspberries. C. W. Norris. il Pop Gard 16:21+ Ap '65
Rosy future for raspberries. Farm J 89:46A S '65

RASPUTIN, Grigorii Efimovich
Killing the mad monk. il por Newsweek 66: 38 N 1 '65
Prince & the monk. il por Time 86:49-50 O 29 '65

RAT ISLAND earthquake. See Earthquakes—Aleutian Islands

RAT virus. See Viruses

RATCLIFF, John Drury
How man began. Read Digest 87:129-33 O '65
Italy's amazing amateur space watchers. Read Digest 86:110-14 Ap '65
Let's end these unnecessary deaths. Read Digest 87:124-8 S '65
Sleep: how much do you need? Read Digest 87:89-92 Ag '65
There's only one cure for hernia. Todays Health 43:60-1 N '65; Same abr. with title Quick repair for hernia. Read Digest 87: 120-2 N '65
Wonder of the winds. Read Digest 87:271-2+ '65
(ed) See Chain, E. B. We tamed penicillin

RATES. See Telephone—Rates; Water rates

RATHBONE, M. J.
Deciding the tough ones; interview. pors Nations Bsns 53:34-5+ Je '65
What kind of managers for tomorrow's world? January 19, 1965. Vital Speeches 31:372-5 Ap 1 '65

RATING of teachers. See College professors and instructors—Rating by students

RATING of television programs. See Television broadcasting—Program rating

RATIONING, Industrial. See Priorities and allocations, Industrial

RATNOFF, Oscar D. See Donaldson, V. H. jt. auth.

RATS
Rats attack when hurt. Sci N L 89:6 Ja 1 '66

RATS, Experiments on. See Animal experimentation

RATTE, John
Books. Commonweal 82:570-1; 83:247-9 Ag 6, N 26 '65
Specter of modernism. Commonweal 82:530-3 Jl 23 '65

RATTLESNAKES
How to get a rattle(r) out of your car. B. Fowler. Farm J 89:54 Ag '65
Rattlesnake, fact and fancy. C. Fletcher. il Read Digest 86:196-8+ Je '65
Snake hunt at Old Hollow. R. Starnes. Field & S 70:28+ N '65

RAU, Santha Rama. See Rama Rau, S.

RAUP, David M. and Michelson, Arnold
Theoretical morphology of the coiled shell. bibliog Science 147:1294-5 Mr 12 '65

RAUP, Henry A.
Pictured Rocks National Lakeshore. Nat Parks Mag 39:14-18 F '65

RAUSCHENBERG, Robert
Big show in Venice. C. Tomkins. il Harper 230:98-104 Ap '65
Modern inferno. il Life 59:44-9 D 17 '65
New old masters. L. Lerman. il pors Mlle 60:120-3 F '65
Unexpected assemblage! D. McDonagh. il por Dance Mag 39:42-5+ Je '65
World is a painting: Rauschenberg. L. Alloway. il por Vogue 146:100-3+ O 15 '65

RAUSCHER virus. See Leukemia viruses

RAUSCHKOLB, Elizabeth W.
Housewife and her hands. Todays Health 44:58-60 Ja '66

RAVEL, Maurice
Unraveling Ravel: the great leap sideways. F. V. Grunfeld. Reporter 32:35-8 My 6 '65

RAVEN awards. See Mystery writers of America

RAVENS
Curious gift. T. Capote. il Redbook 125:52-3+ Je '65

RAW materials
U.S. pledged to cooperate in solving commodity problems; statement, July 22, 1965. S. Nehmer. Dept State Bul 53:530-2 S 27 '65
See also
Stockpiling
Strategic materials

RAWLEY, Harold, and others
Square dancers do-si-do in their own building. Recreation 58:432-4 N '65

RAWLINGS, Marjorie Kinnan
Mother in Mannville; story. Parents Mag 40: 59-63 Ap '65

RAWLINS, Winifred
Sometimes my nights and days are spent; poem. Christian Cent 82:263 Mr 3 '65
Therefore choose life; poem. Christian Cent 82:778 Je 16 '65
Ultimate terror; poem. Christian Cent 82:1258 O 13 '65

RAY, Bill
Chinese patrol pops into view on rim of India; photographs. Life 59:36-43 O 8 '65
Long guns flash in the South China Sea; photographs. Life 59:16-23 Ag 6 '65

about
Each salvo bounced Bill inches in the air. G. P. Hunt. il por Life 59:3 Ag 6 '65
Two Life tourists in no man's land. G. P. Hunt. il por Life 59:7 O 8 '65

RAY, Carleton
Stalking seals under Antarctic ice. il por Nat Geog Mag 129:54-65 Ja '66

RAY, Sammy M. and Aldrich, D. V.
Gymnodinium breve: induction of shellfish poisoning in chicks. bibliog Science 148: 1748-9 Je 25 '65

RAYACK, Elton
AMA: the restrictive power. Nation 200:470-9 My 3 '65

RAYBURN, Sam
Clincher; making of the vice president 1960. Newsweek 66:32 S 13 '65

RAYBURN House office building. See Washington, D.C.—Public buildings

RAY-JONES, Tony
Ruffle of colors, flourish of brass; photographs. Sat Eve Post 238:30-5 Jl 3 '65

RAYMOND, George M.
Urban renewal. Commentary 40:72-6 Jl; 19 N '65

RAYMOND, H. S.
Soil sealant plugs a leak. Am City 80:106-7 Ag '65

RAYMOND, Jack
Brilliant administrator or human I.B.M. machine? N Y Times Mag p30-1+ Ap 11 '65
Draft is unfair. N Y Times Mag p5+ Ja 2 '66
Pilots of Danang aren't flyboys. N Y Times Mag p 16-17+ Ag 15 '65
When G.I. Joe meets ol' Charlie. N Y Times Mag p4-5+ Jl 25 '65

RAYMOND, Lilo
Is your sight asleep? H. D. Wieck. il U S Camera 29:62-5 Ja '66

RAYNAUD's disease
Case of the white hands; condition of K. Venturi. il Newsweek 65:64 My 3 '65

RAYNER, Gordon Z.
Soil fumigants control roots in sewers. por Am City 80:135-6 Je '65

RAYTHEON company
Raytheon continues acquisition program. M. Getler. Miss & Roc 16:35-7 My 10 '65
Raytheon to acquire D. C. Heath and company. Pub W 189:42-3 Ja 3 '66

RAZOR blades
Goliath has the upper sword; Wilkinson sword ltd. Time 87:87 Ja 7 '66
It was just a rumor; quality reduced to increase sales. Consumer Rep 30:472 O '65
See also
Gillette company

RAZORS
Electric shaver owners take note; Shaver Clean can be harmful. Consumer Rep 30:52 F '65
Pretty good shaver; very good guarantee; Shavex. il Consumer Rep 30:164 Ap '65

REA, D. G. and others
Mars: the origin of the 3.58-and 3.69-micron minima in the infrared spectra. bibliog Science 147:1286-8 Mr 12 '65

REA, John J.
Plywood sculptor. Design 67:20-3 N '65

REACTION rate theory. See Chemical reactions

REACTION time
How fast can you react? R. S. Tripp. il Sci Digest 57:50-4 My '65

REACTIONS, Chemical. See Chemical reactions

REACTORS, Nuclear. See Nuclear reactors

READ, James H.
Excerpt from testimony, March 16, 1965. Cong Digest 44:156+ My '65

READABILITY. See Printing—Legibility

READER guidance. See Libraries—Readers advisory service

READERS and libraries. See Libraries and readers

READER'S digest association, Incorporated
Reader's digest buys Funk & Wagnalls. Pub W 188:68 D 27 '65
Reader's digest talking merger with Funk & Wagnalls. Pub W 188:33 N 29 '65

READER'S digest gardens. See Gardens—New York (state)

READERS of newspapers. See Newspapers—Readers

READINESS for school
Folly of overplacement. J. H. Pollack. il NEA J 54:10-13 F '65
Is your child ready for kindergarten? W. Abraham. il Todays Health 43:40-1+ Mr '65
Kindergarten: off to a happy start. Todays Health 43:80 Mr '65
Much ado about school readiness. J. P. Elwart. Parents Mag 40:43+ Ag '65
Readily to school; with study-discussion program. R. Strang and M. Frobisher. bibliog il PTA Mag 59:10-13, 35 My '65

READING, Pa.
Pocketful of golumpkis. J. Kobrin. il Sat Eve Post 239:22 N 20 '65

READING
Reading and the disadvantaged; need for reading guidance of Negro youth. E. J. Josey. Negro Hist Bul 28:156-7+ Ap '65
See also
Books and reading
International reading association

Remedial teaching
Adults
New series with low vocabulary, mature content published; Mid-America publishing, inc. Library J 90:2346 My 15 '65

Study and teaching
American reading problem. S. Fraiberg. bibliog f Commentary 39:56-65 Je '65; Discussion. 40:30 S; 16+ O '65
Building reader confidence. H. Rabb. Sr Schol 86:sup 13 Mr 25 '65
Current approaches to teaching reading. bibliog il NEA J 54:18-20+ D '65
Dancing words; correlation of music and reading at P.S. 77, New York. il Time 86:64 O 22 '65
How to help babies learn without teaching them. J. Holt. il Redbook 126:54-5+ N '65
I/t/a: a reading revolution? initial teaching alphabet. il Library J 90:5058 N 15 '65
IRA focus: reading instruction in transition; statements. E. Malmquist. il Sr Schol 86: sup 1-2 My 20 '65
Learning to read; adaptation of address, October 31, 1963. E. J. Gibson. bibliog il Science 148:1066-72 My 21 '65; Reply with rejoinder. D. Elkind. 149:1325-6 S 17 '65
Learning to read with i/t/a; initial teaching alphabet. W. D. Boutwell. il Sr Schol 86: sup8-9 Mr 4 '65
Many roads to reading: Homestead school, Garden City, N.Y. A. Eisenberg and H. Eisenberg. il Look 29:M7-11 My 4 '65
Materials for the illiterate; symposium. bibliog il Wilson Lib Bul 40:51-64 S '65
New phonetic alphabets. N. Larrick. il Parents Mag 40:49-53+ O '65
Personalized reading. W. B. Barbe. il Library J 90:1978-80 Ap 15 '65; Reply. E. C. Saltus. 90:3644 S 15 '65; Rejoinder. 90:5442 D 15 '65
Poverty of condition and poverty of mind. R. Kirk. Nat R 17:467 Je 1 '65
Race and income keep Johnny from reading. Sci N L 88:67 Jl 31 '65
Reading and normality: phonics vs looksay, topic of Reading reform foundation conference. R. Kirk. Nat R 17:830 S 21 '65
Reading research and improvement: a time for change; federal support. W. G. Cutts. Sr Schol 86:sup6+ Ap 29 '65
SRA issues anti-poverty basic reading program; Reading in high gear. Pub W 187: 41 Mr 8 '65
Two exercises in educational policy making; excerpt from Cheerful prospect: a statement on the future of American education. C. S. Benson. il Sch & Soc 93:305-8 Sum '65
USOE studies focus on reading. Sr Schol 87: sup 16 D 9 '65
World i.t.a. thrust forecast at conference. il Sr Schol 87:sup4 S 23 '65
See also
Reading, Psychology of
Reading readiness

READING, Psychology of
Reading troubles seen. il Sci N L 88:147 S 4 '65

READING aloud. See Books and reading—Reading aloud

READING by children. See Childrens reading

READING lists
How to help students plan reading lists; Alexander Hamilton high school, Los Angeles. S. Cochell. Sr Schol 87:sup 10 D 2 '65

Past the middle range; booklist for college bound by Family circle. E. Geller. Library J 90:5016 N 15 '65
Summer reading lists for secondary schools; with Yale co-op's list of paperbacks. G. R. Smith. Pub W 188:108-14 S 27 '65

READING machines
Faster sort of mail; optical scanner. Time 87:44 Ja 7 '66
Optical readers turn a fresh page; optoscanning and disc scanning machines. il Bsns W p 185-6+ O 9 '65

READING railroad
Hardest look yet at rail commuters; in Philadelphia. il Bsns W p 164+ My 8 '65

READING readiness
Getting ready to read. P. L. Levin. il N Y Times Mag p93-4 Ap 11 '65

READING research
This reading thing. H. Levin and N. S. Meltzer. il Am Ed 1:30-2 Ap '65

READING rooms (in libraries) See Libraries—Reading rooms

READING to children. See Books and reading—Reading aloud

READY-mixed concrete. See Concrete

READY-to-cook food. See Food—Ready-to-cook food

REAGAN, Michael D.
Tax reform, four basic ideas. N Y Times Mag p32+ Mr 21 '65

REAGAN, Ronald
Down with plinkers. pors Am For 71:4-5 Ag '65
Moment of truth; address, June 8, 1965. Vital Speeches 31:681-6 S 1 '65
about
Brown vs Reagan. New Repub 154:7-8 Ja 22 '66
Enter Ronald Reagan. il por Newsweek 67: 31-2 Ja 17 '66
Good guy. S. Alsop. por Sat Eve Post 238:18 N 20 '65
How is Ronald Reagan doing? W. F. Buckley, jr. Nat R 18:17 Ja 11 '66
New role for Reagan. il por Time 87:28 Ja 14 '66
Reagan rides East. il por Newsweek 66:42 O 11 '65
Real Ronald Reagan stands up. R. Oulahan and W. Lambert. il pors Life 60:70-2+ Ja 21 '66
Ronald Reagan for governor? S. Alexander. Life 59:22 Ag 13 '65
Ronald Reagan story; or, Tom Sawyer enters politics. L. E. Litwak. il pors N Y Times Mag p46-7+ N 14 '65
Stage to Sacramento? il por Time 86:13-14 Jl 30 '65
Where's the rest of me? by R. Reagan and R. G. Hubler. Review
New Repub 152:23-4 My 8 '65. A. Kopkind
Will he size up? il por Newsweek 65:18-19 Je 7 '65

REAL estate. See Real property

REAL estate advertising. See Real property—Advertising

REAL estate business
Americans discover the West again; Mountain West. il U S News 58:80-2 Je 21 '65
Bubble in the sun; Florida real estate boom. G. B. Tindall. il Am Heritage 16:76-83+ Ag '65
Bust and boom of Florida homesites. il Fortune 72:172+ Jl '65
His bets are still on real estate; T. Crow. il Bsns W p 140+ S 18 '65
How to make a quick million in real estate. D. M. Friedenberg. il Esquire 63:122-3+ Je '65
Is real estate a smart investment? il Changing T 19:7-12 My '65
Now Uncle Sam's a real estate speculator. il Nations Bsns 53:46-8 N '65
Quiet giants; DiLorenzo and Goldman. Time 85:86 Mr 12 '65
Toughest woman in real estate: C. Benattar; with excerpts from interview with D. Lurie. il Life 59:49-50+ O 1 '65
Two realty partners tackle a big one alone; Wien and Helmsley plan to buy Schine enterprises, inc. il Bsns W p 105-6+ Ag 21 '65
See also
Corporations—Real estate operations
Webb, Del E. corporation
Webb and Knapp, incorporated

REAL presence. See Transubstantiation

REAL property
Does it pay to make a small investment in real estate? Bet Hom & Gard 43:8 O '65
Lure of the land; corporations moving into real estate. il Time 85:101A-101B F 5 '65

REAL property—*Continued*
Monuments to stubbornness; holdout property owners. il Time 86:61 Jl 9 '65
Rights of property, by B. Schwartz. Review
  Nat R 17:694 Ag 10 '65. G. M. Caplan
  See also
Land speculation
Land values
Real estate business

Advertising
Giving the picture to home buyers; gallery of homes, Rochester, N. Y. il Bsns W p87-8 My 29 '65

Valuation
Real-estate boom in sewage-works land. Am City 80:13 Ag '65

Caribbean Region
Executive land boom in the Caribbean. T. J. Murray. il Duns R 86:32-3+ Ag '65

France
Roof over your head with *viager*. J. Lewis. il Atlan 215:120+ F '65

Italy
Italian land bargains. P. Dallas. il Atlan 215:124+ Je '65

REAL property and taxation
Great urban tax tangle. Fortune 71:106-7+ Mr '65
Taxes and the death of cities. P. Prentice. Arch Forum 123:56-7 N '65; Reply. Christian Cent 82:1595-6 D 29 '65

REALISM (philosophy)
What is realism doing to American history? adaptation of address. A. MacLeish. il Sat R 48:10-12 Jl 3 '65; Discussion. 48:13-14+ Jl 3; 16-18 Jl 10; 38 Jl 24 '65

REALISM in art
Dickinson: reality of reflection; retrospective at the Whitney. D. Waldman. il Art N 64:28-31+ N '65
Ivan Albright: mystic-realist. M. W. Dulac. il Am Artist 30:32-7+ Ja '66
Waldmueller, master realist. A. Werner. il Am Artist 29:30-5+ D '65
  See also
Trompe-l'oeil

REALISM in literature
Off the cuff. L. Conger. Writer 78:8-10 S '65
Once upon a time. E. E. Philpott. ALA Bul 59:810-14 O '65
Uncorrupted consciousness: the stories of Katherine Anne Porter. R. P. Warren. Yale R 55:280-90 D '65

REALITY
Art, science, and reality. G. R. Walker; reply, B. Stewart. Bul Atomic Sci 21:34-5 F '65
I believe; ed. by C. Lydon. P. D. Brenner. Seventeen 24:220-1 Mr '65
  See also
Objectivity

REALS, Lucile Farnsworth
Four jade carvings of the Ch'ien Lung period. Hobbies 70:32 Ja '66

REALTY equities corporation of New York
Schine's surprise. Newsweek 66:74 S 13 '65

REANEY, James
Sun; poem. Atlan 215:80 F '65

REAPPORTIONMENT. See Apportionment (election law)

REARDEN, Jim
New: a big lift for salmon. Outdoor Life 136:26-8+ Jl '65
(ed) See Johnson, F. C. Hell on an island

REASON
Freedom of reason, by K. Kolenda. Review
  Christian Cent 82:1513-14 D 8 '65. W. E. Garrison

REASON for gladness; story. See Wallace, M.

REASONING
  See also
Hypothesis
Problem solving
Thought and thinking

REAVEY, Edward P. Jr.
Carving path to a top market spot. il pors Bsns W p78+ Ja 15 '66

REBEKAH Harkness foundation dance festival. See Dance festivals

REBHAN, John R.
Green garden. il Flower Grower 52:28-31+ Jl '65

REBUILT automobiles. See Automobiles, Remodeled

RECAPPING of tires. See Tires, Automobile—Retreading and recapping

RECAPTURE POCKET. See Utah—Description and travel

RECEPTIONS
Home wedding reception; menu with recipes. il Redbook 125:72-4+ Je '65

RECEPTORS, Sensory. See Nervous system, Sympathetic

RECESSION, Business. See Business depression

RECHY, John
I was always mad at the world. Nation 200:254-6 Mr 8 '65

RECIPE for rain; drama. See Huff, B. T.

RECIPES. See Cookery

RECIPES in literature. See Cookery in literature

RECIPROCITY
Antitrust aspects of reciprocity; address, February 18, 1965. J. R. Reilly. Vital Speeches 31:414-16 Ap 15 '65

RECK, Michael
Reading the Cantos. Commonweal 83:93-5 O 22 '65

RECLAMATION of land
Strip mining heals its own scars. il Bsns W p 140+ N 13 '65
  See also
Irrigation

California
Water; playing into the hands of large landholders; Westlands water district. D. Sanford. New Repub 153:14-15 S 4 '65
Wrested from the bay; site of Foster City, Calif. L. Ham. il Am City 80:102-3 Ag '65

Netherlands
War without end; projects progress. S. Hagerty. il Newsweek 66:58+ N 15 '65

RECONSTRUCTION (Civil war)
Black power. L. Bennett, jr. il Ebony 21:28-9+ N; 51-2+ D '65; 116-22 Ja '66 (to be cont)
1865: the great transition. A. S. Eisenstadt. il Nation 201:54-61 S 20 '65
Era of reconstruction: 1865-1877, by K. M. Stampp. Review
  Commonweal 82:388-91 Je 11 '65. H. N. Meyer
  Reporter 32:48 Ap 22 '65. K. S. Lynn
Grant or Greeley? the abolitionist dilemma in the election of 1872. J. M. McPherson. bibliog f Am Hist R 71:43-61 O '65
Is history repeating itself? excerpts from article in Atlantic monthly, January 1901, ed. by D. Lawrence. W. Wilson. U S News 58:112+ Je 7 '65
Sergeant Bates' march. M. Lomask. il Am Heritage 16:12-17 O '65
  See also

RECONSTRUCTION (World war, 1939-1945)
  See also
Germany—Reconstruction

RECONVERSION of war industries. See Factories—Reconversion

RECORD, Jane Cassels, and Record, Wilson
Ideological forces and the Negro protest. Ann Am Acad 357:89-96 Ja '65

RECORD, Wilson. See Record, J. C. jt. auth.

RECORD changers. See Phonograph—Record changers

RECORD club of America. See Phonograph record clubs

RECORD players. See Phonograph

RECORDER (musical instrument)
Fipple in the mouth; recorder popular in Seattle. D. Brink. il Recreation 58:399 O '65
Recordings. M. Mayer. Esquire 64:62+ D '65

RECORDING for the blind, incorporated
They help the blind to see; textbooks recorded on request. B. Clark. Read Digest 86:197-200 Mr '65

RECORDS
Opening government records; letter. E. M. Larrabee. Science 148:1172 My 28 '65; Reply. C. E. Dewing. 149:815-16 Ag 20 '65

RECORDS, Business. See Business records

RECORDS, Phonograph. See Phonograph records

RECORDS, School. See School reports and records

RECORDS, World. See World records

RECREATION
California playground. F. Dufresne. il Field & S 69:42-5 Mr '65
Family recreation scoresheet; promoting better family relationships through recreation. Recreation 58:447 N '65
Getting the most out of your leisure time; excerpt from Today's health guide. Todays Health 43:37-9 Jl '65
Wilderness and the Land and water conservation fund act; outdoor enjoyment. F. Gregg. il Liv Wild 29:25-8 Sum '65
  See also
Hobbies
Leisure

RECREATION—*Continued*

Activities

Barnyard serenade; park and recreation district operates popular small animal farm, Norwalk, Calif. B. Avenatti. il Recreation 58:425-6 N '65

College serves the community; cooperation in recreation programs, Cerritos college district, Calif. J. Larez. Recreation 58:485 D '65

Delinquency and recreation: fact and fiction! youth programs. R. G. Kraus. bibliog il Recreation 58:382-5 O '65

Developing an amateur radio project; summary of article in Jewish community center program aids. A. Dobrof and J. N. Jablin. Recreation 58:453-4 N '65

Recreation opens new doors. il Recreation 58:62-3 F '65

Retirement to leisure; adaptation of address, September 1964. V. Musselman. Recreation 58:239-40+ My '65

Summer in the park. R. Yeskey; M. Poston; V. Rankin. il Recreation 58:277-9+ Je '65

Sunday painting for beginners. H. Gasser. il Recreation 58:68-9 F '65

V.I.T.'s; programs for teenagers. il Recreation 58:242-4, 288-90+, 394-6+ My-Je, O '65

See also
Music as recreation
Recreation for the handicapped
Trade unions—Activities

Administration

Commercial recreation: an ally. J. L. Wilson. il Recreation 58:76+ F '65

Creative approach to parks and recreation. W. P. Mott, jr. il Recreation 58:340-1 S '65

Department-only vs community recreation. R. J. Andrews. Recreation 58:422 N '65

Highlights of public recreation, 1964; field reports. A. Todd. il Recreation 58:283-4 Je '65

Lively art of retirement; Sun City, Calif. G. D. Hunsaker. il Recreation 58:386-8+ O '65

Notes for the administrator. Recreation 58: 128+, 238, 451 Mr, My, N '65

Reduce your money needs; White Plains, N.Y. J. E. Curtis. il Am For 80:32 My '65

Sharing recreation services; community nursing homes, Middlesex County, N. J. A. Smutny. Recreation 58:348-9 S '65

Trojan horse tactics; cosponsorship to broaden recreation services. S. C. Newcombe. il Recreation 58:234-5+ My '65

Uncommon professional. B. Van Der Smissen. il Recreation 58:334-6+ S '65

What's in a budget? J. E. Curtis. il Recreation 58:82-3 F '65

Your playground manual. V. Musselman. Recreation 58:185 Ap '65

Aims and objectives

Delinquency and recreation: fact and fiction! youth programs. R. G. Kraus. bibliog il Recreation 58:382-5 O '65

Planning is basic to recreation philosophy; reprint. R. Andrews. Recreation 58:59 F '65

Social trends and recreation planning; address, 1964. G. W. Carter. il Recreation 58: 378-80 O '65

Bibliography

New publications; Books and pamphlets received; Magazine articles. See issues of Recreation to December 1965

Federal aid
See Recreation and state

Fees

$7 for all outdoors; outdoor recreation sticker. il Am For 71:62-3 My '65

Finance

What's in a budget? J. E. Curtis. il Recreation 58:82-3 F '65

Study and teaching

Colleges now teach recreatiton; excerpt from column Life begins at forty. R. Peterson. Recreation 58:450 N '65

Creative problem solving for executives; Tenth national institute for recreation and park administrators. W. C. Sutherland. Recreation 58:254 My '65

Japan

Carp on the Ginza; angling parlors Time 86: 31-2 Ag 20 '65

Malaysia

Nation building in Malaya; youth clubs and community centers. S. S. Winans. il Recreation 58:227-8 My '65

United States

Conflict in outdoor recreation; natural beauty versus economic interests. R. K. Davis and J. L. Knetsch. il Am For 71: 26-9+ N '65

Double life pays off; second home. il Bsns W p23-6 Jl 10 '65

Let's halt the federal land grab; no crisis in outdoor recreation. R. M. Hyatt. il Nat R 17:984-5 N 2 '65

State and local developments. E. Delany. See issues of Recreation to December 1965

Today's Arkansas traveler is a boatman. J. Houston. il Motor B 116:28-31 Jl '65

See also
National recreation month
Recreation, Rural
United States—Navy—Recreation
also subhead Recreation under names of cities, e.g. Minneapolis—Recreation

RECREATION (periodical)
Widening of horizons. S. Lee. Recreation 58:473-4 D '65

RECREATION, Rural
Farming for fun. H. Titus. il Field & S 69:53-5+ Ap '65

Meeting recreation area standards: the county. L. Lynch. il Recreation 58:80-1 F '65

Try some out-of-the-groove fun this summer; symposium. il Farm J 89:61 Jl '65

Finance

For profit from recreation. D. Hanson. Suc Farm 63:22 Jl '65

Recreation business: should you be in on it? R. K. Seim and R. C. Davids. il Farm J 89:28-9+ Jl '65

RECREATION activities. See Recreation—Activities

RECREATION and schools
Changing functions of parks; adaptation of St Cloud, Minn. park and recreation departments annual report. il Recreation 58: 225-6 My '65

New community idea; East Orange plans an education plaza. G. L. Lynch; G. M. Skea. Recreation 58:236-7 My '65

RECREATION and state
Recreation; buildings and facilities. il Arch Rec 138:151-70 Jl '65

RECREATION areas
Coming: more open spaces for Americans. Changing T 19:6 F '65

Disney's wider world; year-round resort at Mineral King, California's Sequoia national forest. il Bsns W p21 D 25 '65

Meeting recreation area standards (title varies) (cont) G. L. Lynch. Recreation 58: 80-1, 126-7 F-Mr '65

New recreation sticker bargain for tourists. Field & S 70:46 My '65

RECREATION buildings
Creative construction. il Recreation 58:427-30 N '65

Recreation; buildings and facilities. il Arch Rec 138:151-70 Jl '65

Square dancers do-si-do in their own building; Western dance center, Spokane, Wash. H. Rawley and others. il Recreation 58:432-4 N '65

RECREATION centers
Creative construction. il Recreation 58:427-30 N '65

New community idea; East Orange plans an education plaza. G. L. Lynch; G. M. Skea. Recreation 58:236-7 My '65

Recreation; buildings and facilities. il Arch Rec 138:151-70 Jl '65

Recreation center; with song of praise by third-grade students. E. A. Scholer. il Recreation 58:436 N '65

Remodeled and pre-engineered centers. il Recreation 58:488-90 D '65

Teen city; first teen-age country club, Denver. Newsweek 66:120+ N 15 '65

What a photography center should be. J. Deschin. il Pop Phot 57:32+ D '65

RECREATION departments
Future in retrospect! fiftieth birthday of Recreation department, Lynchburg, Va. M. F. Patterson. Recreation 58:486-7 D '65

RECREATION education. See Recreation—Study and teaching

RECREATION for the aged
Lively art of retirement; Sun City, Calif. G. D. Hunsaker. il Recreation 58:386-8+ O '65

Sharing recreation services; community nursing homes, Middlesex County, N. J. A. Smutny. Recreation 58:348-9 S '65

RECREATION for the aged—*Continued*
Tomorrow started yesterday; symposium. il Recreation 58:220-3+ My '65
United they built; Senior citizen center, Cedar Rapids, Ia. N. G. Zook. il Recreation 58:427-8 N '65

RECREATION for the handicapped
National survey of community recreation services to the mentally retarded and physically handicapped; summary. M. Thompson. bibliog Recreation 58:191-2 Ap '65
New hope for the homebound; Chicago homebound project. M. Thompson. il Recreation 58:435 N '65
R for the ill & handicapped. M. Thompson. See issues of Recreation to December 1965
Ward-activity programs. C. W. Williams. Recreation 58:55 F '65
See also
Recreational therapy

RECREATION rooms
For family fun. il House & Gard 128:110-11 Jl '65
How to build a sing-around music bar. H. Walton. il Pop Sci 186:164-7 Ap '65

RECREATION workers
Creative problem solving. W. C. Sutherland. Recreation 58:86 F '65
People in the news. See issues of Recreation to December 1965
Profile of a swimming pool manager. W. G. Riordan. Recreation 58:297 Je '65
Recreation en route; travel program for recreation professionals. Westchester County recreation and park society. B. J. Guagnini. il Recreation 58:403-4 O '65
Uncommon professional. B. Van Der Smissen. il Recreation 58:334-6+ S '65

Recruitment
Attracting and training junior leaders. W. F. Richardson. Recreation 58:197 Ap '65

Training
Professional preparation: the intern program. R. F. Toalson. Recreation 58:346-7 S '65
Two-year training courses. J. M. Caverly; L. Minshall. il Recreation 58:342-4 S '65
Youth officials association; training high school boys to officiate elementary athletic events. S. Peters. il Recreation 58:381 O '65

RECREATIONAL therapy
Enable the disabled. E. M. Avedon. Recreation 58:70-2 F '65

RECRUITING agencies. See Employment agencies

RECRUITING for business and industry. See Employment systems

RECRUITING for librarianship. See Librarians—Recruiting

RECRUITING of athletes. See Athletes—Recruiting

RECRUITMENT, Office for. See American library association—Library administration division

RECTUM, Cancer of the. See Cancer

RED alga. See Algae

RED BLUFF, Calif.
Biggest two-day rodeo comes April 17 and 18; Red Bluff round-up. il Sunset 134:52+ Ap '65

RED cross
Red cross calls for application of convention to war prisoners; statement, October 7, 1965, with text of U.E.-sponsored resolution. R. F. Woodward. Dept State Bul 53:725-6 N 1 '65
Strictly humanitarian; twentieth International conference, Vienna. Newsweek 66:63 O 18 '65

RED deer hunting. See Deer hunting

RED hot poker plants. See Torch lilies

RED sweater; story. See Jessop, E. J.

RED tape. See Bureaucracy

REDBOOK magazine
Fiction for Redbook. N. G. Stuart. Writer 78:24-5 N '65

REDD, John G. See Cordasco, F. M. jt. auth.

REDDICK, Glenn
Television. Christian Cent 82:1196-8 S 29 '65
To eccentricity and beyond; address, September 10, 1964. bibliog Vital Speeches 31:310-16 Mr 1 '65

REDDY, John
Fastest man on wheels. Read Digest 86:94-8 Mr '65
Few true friends. Read Digest 88:128-32 Ja '66

Shakespeare explosion. Read Digest 87:197-8+ Ag '65
Something belong friendship. Read Digest 86:224-8+ My '65
—See Kent, G. jt. auth.

REDECORATING. See House decoration

REDEFER, Frederick L.
Modest proposal. New Repub 154:37+ Ja 8 '66

REDEKER, Clark W.
Oxychloride floors; use and application. Arch Rec 137:235-6 Ap '65

REDEMPTION centers; story. See Meyers, J.

REDEVELOPMENT, Urban. See City planning

REDEVELOPMENT programs. See Economic assistance. Domestic

REDFIELD, Alfred C.
Terrestrial heat flow through salt-marsh peat. bibliog Science 148:1219-20 My 28 '65

REDFIELD, James
Archilochus not quite revived. Poetry 105:329-31 F '65

REDFORD, Mary
Spuria iris. Horticulture 43:48 Ap '65

REDFORD, Polly
Counting our eagles; excerpt from Raccoons and eagles. Atlan 216:64-8 Jl '65
Cows on the quay. Atlan 215:178+ Mr '65

REDING, Marcel
Marxism without atheism? Commonweal 82:216-18 My 7 '65

REDLANDS, Calif.
Upgrading downtown. il Arch Rec 137:188 Je '65

REDLICH, Don
Don Redlich dance concert, Henry street playhouse. J. Maskey. Dance Mag 39:34 Ap '65

REDONDO BEACH, Calif.
Civic center leads downtown renewal. il Arch Rec 137:172-3 My '65

REDSKINS (football club) See Football clubs

REDUCING. See Corpulence

REDUCING diet. See Diet

REDUCING exercises. See Exercise

REDUCING preparations. See Weight reducing preparations

REDUCTION of armaments. See Disarmament

REDWOOD
AFA's redwood recommendations adopted February 26, 1965; to convert Humboldt Redwoods State Park to national park status. il Am For 71:36 My '65
Fern Canyon, gold bluffs redwoods acquired for California park system. Am For 71:18 Je '65
Giant wave of wood; redwood structure. Hydraulic laboratory. E. J. Long. il Am For 71:31+ Ag '65
Must the redwoods fall? C. W. Buchheister. Audubon Mag 67:284 S '65
Protection of the redwoods. A. W. Smith. Nat Parks Mag 39:2 F '65
Redwood crisis. il Recreation 58:216 My '65
Redwood National Park, but where, and how much? R. D. Butcher. il Liv Wildn 29:11-15 Spr '65
Redwoods and parks. S. T. Dana and K. B. Pomeroy. bibliog f il Am For 71:1-32 My '65
Redwoods face a race against time. R. D. Butcher. il Audubon Mag 67:234-9 Jl '65
Redwoods for the Nation. C. W. Buchheister. Audubon Mag 67:181 My '65
Seeds for agreement; AFA for Humboldt. K. B. Pomeroy. il Am For 71:16-18+ Je '65
Vanishing redwoods; an album. il Audubon Mag 67:358-63 N '65
Very special redwoods. G. Collins. il Liv Wildn 87:22-6 Wint '64

REDWOOD CITY, Calif.

City planning
New waterfront for a bay city; San Francisco Bay area. il Fortune 72:183-4 Ag '65

REDWOOD highway. See Roads—California

REDWOODS NATIONAL PARK (proposed) See National parks and reserves—United States

REEB, James J.
James J. Reeb; recollections. Reporter 32:12 Mr 25 '65
To be a man. R. A. Reed. Christian Cent 82:466+ Ap 14 '65

REECE, F. N. See Knake, E. jt. auth.

REED, Charles F. See Witt, P. N. jt. auth.

REED, Christopher Dunham
Rugs of Turkestan. Antiques 89:94-8 Ja '66

REED, Clarence H.
Outboard motor speeds treatment of algae. Am City 80:38 N '65

REED, David
Rhino! Read Digest 87:222-4+ Jl '65
Stanleyville massacre; excerpt from 111 days in Stanleyville. Read Digest 87:233-8+ S '65
—See Hubbell, J. G. jt. auth.
REED, Donald J.
Tryptamine oxidation by extracts of pea seedlings: effect of growth retardant β-hydroxyethylhydrazine. bibliog Science 148:1097-9 My 21 '65
—and others
Plant growth retardant B-995; a possible mode of action. bibliog Science 148:1469-71 Je 11 '65
REED, Dorothy
I learned lighting in nursery school! Pop Phot 56:61 Je '65
REED, Harold
Build the master control SCR switching center. Pop Electr 22:53-5 Mr '65
REED, Ione
Petroglyphs. il Nat Parks Mag 39:9-10 S '65
REED, James, P.
Improved switching of inductive loads. Electr World 74:35+ S '65
REED, Louis S.
Consumer expenditures for health purposes. Mo Labor R 88:168-70 F '65
REED, Mary M.
Pilot program on occupational trends and career planning. ALA Bul 59:1006-9 D '65
REED, Mathilda Newman
Mysterious horseshoe tracks on Wolf Mountain. Am For 71:32-4 N '65
REED, N. D. and Juttia, J. W.
Wasting disease induced with cortisol acetate: studies in germ-free mice. bibliog Science 150:356-7 O 15 '65
REED, Robert A.
To be a man. Christian Cent 82:466+ Ap 14 '65
REED, Roy
Deacons, too, ride by night. N Y Times Mag p 10-11+ Ag 15 '65
REED, Samuel Pryor, family
Reed team. il pors Vogue 147:114-17+ Ja 15 '66
REED, Susan, A.
Mechanized monsters! Liv Wildn 29:17-19 Spr '65
REED, Wayne O.
Data link. Am Ed 1:31-2 Je '65
REED college, Portland, Ore.
Reed: the Mavericks and the Mandarinate. T. R. Bransten. il Mlle 60:188-90+ Ap '65
REEDER, Norm, and Bay, Ovid
Easier ways to keep records on dairy cows. Farm J 89:25 Je '65
REEDER, R. and Bell, E.
Short- and long-lived messenger RNA in embryonic chick lens. bibliog Science 150: 71-2 O 1 '65
REEDY, George E.
Change & chatter. il Time 86:15-16 Jl 16 '65
Change of tone; replacement of Presidential press secretary. il por Newsweek 66:19 Jl 19 '65
LBJ press job upgraded? U S News 59:19 Jl 19 '65
REEFS
New reefs for better fishing. O. Godbout. Yachting 117:153-4 Je '65
REEFS, Artificial
Regulating the reefs. T. N. Sandifer. il Motor B 115:118+ Mr '65
RE-ENTRY problem. See Guided missiles—Recovery
RE-ENTRY problems (space flight) See Space vehicles—Atmospheric entry
REES, Virginia
Reader's choice. Travel 124:44 S '65
REESE, Elmer J. See Smith, B. A. jt. auth.
REESE, Frederick D.
Law and the faithful. Reporter 33:18+ S 23 '65
Mistakes of the head? Newsweek 66:26 Jl 19 '65
Various forms of embezzlement. il por Time 86:20 Jl 16 '65
REESE, Terence
Four-finger exercise. por Sports Illus 22: 60+ Je 7 '65
about
Cheating scandal rocks the bridge world. M. Smith. il pors Life 58:32-3 Je 4 '65
Five-finger exercise. il por Time 85:42 Je 4 '65
Why do people cheat? C. H. Goren. il McCalls 92:30+ S '65
REEVE, F. D.
Alcoholic; poem. New Yorker 41:191 N 13 '65
Bells at Denton; poem. New Yorker 41:46 Ap 17 '65

REFEREEING (sports) See Sports officiating
REFERENCE books
State of reference book publishing; summary of address by Maurice B. Mitchell. Pub W 188:79+ N 8 '65
See also
Booksellers and bookselling—Reference books
Encyclopedias
Quotations

Bibliography
Current reference books. F. N. Cheney. See issues of Wilson library bulletin
Reference books: a personal choice. B. K. Scherman. Writer 79:15-18 Ja '66
Reference books of 1964; recommendations of a committee of the Reference services division of the American library association. J. Bartling. il Library J 90:1809-17 Ap 15 '65
Valuable library service to know about. il Good H 160:179 My '65
Well, what do we know? D. M. Glixon. il Sat R 48:30-1+ Mr 20 '65
REFERENCE work. See Libraries—Reference work
REFERENCES, Bibliographic. See Bibliographies
REFINISHING furniture. See Furniture—Finishing
REFLECTION (optics)
See also
Mirages
REFLECTIVE thinking. See Thought and thinking
REFLECTORS
Reflectors for small-object photography. C. W. Kennedy. il Pop Phot 56:76 Mr '65
See also
Prisms
REFLEXES
See also
Stimulus and response
REFORM Judaism. See Judaism
REFORM schools. See Reformatories
REFORMATION
Celebrating the reformation. Christian Cent 82:1275-6 O 20 '65
England's earliest Protestants 1520-1535, by W. A. Clebsch. Review
Christian Cent 82:1159 S 22 '65. C. S. Meyer
History of the reformation, by J. P. Dolan. Review
Commonweal 83:65-7 O 15 '65. R. H. Bainton
U.S. Protestantism: time for a second reformation. il Newsweek 67:33-7 Ja 3 '66
See also
Trent, Council of, 1545-1563
REFORMATION Sunday
Reforming Reformation Sunday. R. M. Brown. Commonweal 83:58-60 O 15 '65; Reply. R. E. McNally. 83:198-9 N 12 '65
REFORMATORIES
Last resort; approach to education. il Time 87:60-1 Ja 7 '66
Prison culture, from the inside; Federal correctional institutions. M. Arc. il N Y Times Mag p52-3+ F 28 '65
Reporter at large; Massachusetts correctional institution, Framingham. J. Colebrook. il New Yorker 41:47-8+ Je 12 '65
REFORMED church in America
Presbyterians, U.S: search for unity. J. A. Womeldorf. Christian Cent 82:660-2 My 19 '65
Way open to union. M. A. Vance. Christian Cent 82:842+ Je 30 '65
REFRIGERATION, Reversed. See Heat pumps
REFRIGERATION and refrigerating machinery
Danish industry grows amidst the farmlands; Danfoss. il Bsns W p60-2 Je 26 '65
Stirling refrigeration cycle. J. W. L. Köhler. il Sci Am 212:119-25+ bibliog(p 160) Ap '65
See also
Refrigerators, Electric
REFRIGERATOR desserts. See Desserts
REFRIGERATORS, Electric
Cold comfort; refrigerators. A. F. Rush. il McCalls 92:66+ My '65
Far-out refrigerators; pop art used to dress up new models. il Life 58:55-6 F 26 '65
Fresh foods, well preserved. il McCalls 92: 104-5+ Ag '65
Good use tips for refrigerators and freezers. Good H 160:135 Ja '65
How to choose and use a refrigerator. il Redbook 125:42+ Ag '65
No-frost refrigerator-freezer combinations. il Consumer Bul 48:6-12 Je; 18-24 Jl '65

REFRIGERATORS, Electric—*Continued*
Refrigeration. Consumer Rep 30:10-14 D '65
Refrigerator repairs. il Consumer Rep 31:25-7 Ja '66
Refrigerators: the news is outside. M. Davidson. il Ladies Home J 82:34 My '65

Care
Controlling food odors in refrigerators. Consumer Bul 48:38 Ap '65

REFUGEES
Refuge provisions of administration's proposals to revise immigration law; statement, March 3, 1965. A. P. Schwartz. il Dept State Bul 52:471-5 Mr 29 '65
World's refugees: living with heartache and hope. il Sr Schol 87:12-15 D 9 '65
See also
United Nations—High commissioner for refugees
United Nations relief and works agency for Palestine refugees in the Near East
Vietnamese war, 1957- —Refugees

REFUGEES, African
U.S. objectives and refugee relief programs in Africa; statements, January 21, 1965. G. M. Williams; A. P. Schwartz. Dept State Bul 52:219-28 F 15 '65

REFUGEES, Arab
Arab refugees; a Zionist view. M. Syrkin. Commentary 41:23-30 Ja '66
Arab refugees after eighteen years. E. Ben-Horin. Christian Cent 83:28-30 Ja 5 '66
Abraham's children. K. Haselden. Christian Cent 82:455-7 Ap 14 '65
Man to anger Nasser. Time 85:42+ My 7 '65
United States announces pledge for Palestine refugees; statement, February 17, 1965. F. T. P. Plimpton. Dept State Bul 52:390-1 Mr 15 '65

REFUGEES, Chinese
Sport with purpose: Peking's swimming campaign. Time 86:21B S 10 '65

REFUGEES, Cuban
And now by air. il Time 86:56 N 5 '65
Another Dunkirk? Newsweek 66:48+ O 18 '65
Another exodus. Christian Cent 82:1310 O 27 '65
Carnage off Key West; escaping refugees killed by Castro's patrols. H. J. Taylor. Read Digest 86:131-2 Ap '65
Compound at Camarioca. il Newsweek 66:33 O 25 '65
Cuban exodus resumes. America 114:3 Ja 1 '66
Cubans in Miami. C. K. Yearley. Commonweal 83:210-11 N 19 '65
Cuba's bestseller: A gusano returns. J. Yglesias. Nation 201:251-2 O 18 '65
Exodus. M. Frady. il Newsweek 66:54 N 1 '65
Exodus by air. il Time 86:46 D 10 '65
Farewell, dear hearts; free exit for anyone. il Time 86:51 O 15 '65
Fidel's challenge. Newsweek 66:70 N 15 '65
Fidel's pizzeria diplomacy paves the way for an exodus; Swiss ambassador acts as United States mediator. il Life 59:38-9 N 5 '65
Fly now; air shuttle agreement. Newsweek 66:33 N 8 '65
Free to leave. il Sr Schol 87:20 N 4 '65
Freedom flight plan: 200,000 to flee Cuba? U S News 59:16-17 N 22 '65
Full seats & a cruel promise. Time 86:24 D 31 '65
Gusanos' paradise; waiting for formal U.S.-Cuban agreement. il Time 86:48+ O 22 '65
How many more Cubans coming to U.S.? U S News 59:15 O 11 '65
Miami fears impact of another Cuban wave. il Bsns W p30-1 O 16 '65
More refugees, more blackmail. il Time 86: 38+ O 29 '65
New flight from Castro; new headache for U.S. il U S News 59:55-9 O 25 '65
New life for Cuban exiles. A. A. Micocci. il Am Ed 1:29-32 Mr '65
No place like it; Miami's little Havana. il Time 86:36-7 N 12 '65
OAS informed of U.S. move to help Cuban refugees; statement, October 6, 1965. W. P. Allen. Dept State Bul 53:663-4 O 25 '65
President signs immigration bill; offers asylum to Cubans; remarks, October 3, 1965. L. B. Johnson. Dept State Bul 53:661-3 O 25 '65
Procedures established for movement of Cuban refugees to United States; statement, November 6, 1965; with exchanges of notes. L. B. Johnson. Dept State Bul 53: 850-3 N 29 '65
Tony Oliva: Twins' lonely star. T. Cohane. il Look 29:83+ Je 1 '65

Why Castro allows Cubans to flee; the dictator's worries. il U S News 59:49-51 N 8 '65
Why Castro exports Cubans. G. Samuels. il N Y Times Mag p30-1+ N 7 '65

REFUGEES, European
See also
Intergovernmental committee for European migration

REFUGEES, German
Catacomb instinct; rescuing people from East Berlin. B. van Voorst. il Newsweek 66:36 Ag 23 '65
Defector's odyssey: personal look at Soviet-bloc science provided by high-ranking German physicist. D. S. Greenberg. Science 149:40-2 Jl 2 '65
O Tannenbaum; attempts to escape through Berlin wall. Time 87:30 Ja 7 '66
Under the Berlin wall. G. Bailey. il Reporter 33:18-23 N 4 '65

REFUGEES, Jewish
Contraband life. C. Ozick. Commentary 39:89-90+ Mr '65
M. Zuckerberg's heart. R. Berczeller. New Yorker 41:98+ S 4 '65

REFUGEES, Political
See also
Defectors, Political

REFUGEES, Portuguese
Hard way to France. Time 85:32 Ap 2 '65

REFUGEES, Religious
Ben-Gurion woos the Diaspora. Christian Cent 82:765 Je 16 '65

REFUGEES, Vietnamese
Problem to rival the war. il Time 86:28-9 S 3 '65
Refugees: Agency for international development sets up special relief division. il Newsweek 66:54-5 O 18 '65
Vietnamese refugee problem. P. Geyelin. il Reporter 33:43-5 S 23 '65

REFUGES, Wildlife. See Wildlife sanctuaries
REFUNDS, Tax. See Tax refunds
REFUSE, Utilization of
Compositing gets a tryout; San Fernando, Calif. il Am City 80:99-102 Ap '65
Solving the garbage explosion; salvage-compost operation. Sci Digest 57:24 My '65

REFUSE and refuse disposal
After the builder left. B. C. Kilvert, jr. il Flower Grower 52:34-6 Ap '65
Dump that trash, fill that hole; Los Angeles disposal gardens. Time 86:51 D 3 '65
Elmira to try composting; use in refuse disposal. C. F. Sanford. il Am City 80:93-4 Jl '65
For a more beautiful U.S; the President asks this; with interview with C. A. T. Johnson. il U S News 58:71-6+ F 22 '65
Good advice on getting rid of garbage. il Good H 160:177 Mr '65
Keep refuse collectors on the route; Montgomery, Ala. L. B. Green. il Am City 80: 110-11 Je '65
One-man refuse collection. J. P. McDonald. il Am City 80:93 S '65
Refuse collection and disposal. See issues of American city
Refuse-reduction plant saves landfill space. il Am City 80:92-3 N '65
Solid-waste disposal. R. R. Fleming. il Am City 81:101-4 Ja '66 (to be cont)
Trailers help to solve park refuse problem; Salisbury park, East Meadow, Long Island. il Am City 80:158 Ag '65
Vote for good service; Albuquerque, N.Mex. J. Gill. il Am City 80:96-7 My '65
West Virginia's big cleanup. D. Wharton. Read Digest 86:19-20+ Je '65
See also
Carcass disposal
Refuse, Utilization of
Refuse grinders
Trade waste

REFUSE collection trucks
Sanitary fill supermechanized; North Tonawonda, N.Y. il Am City 80:20 D '65

REFUSE grinders
Food waste disposers. il Consumer Bul 48: 6-11 O '65
Food waste disposers and incinerators. Bet Hom & Gard 43:137 Ap '65
Hurrah for garbage disposers! il Good H 161:164 O '65

REFUSE incinerators
Complete combustion with minimum excess air; Broward County, Fla. J. D. Easterlin. il Am City 80:99-101 F '65
Food waste disposers and incinerators. Bet Hom & Gard 43:137 Ap '65
How to dispose of dead birds. il Suc Farm 63:38B My '65

REFUSE incinerators—*Continued*
Less than $3,000 per ton; 250-ton-per-day incinerator in Ewing Township, N.J. A. Gruenwald and J. A. Reynolds. il Am City 80:100-1 O '65
Tepee refuse burner has extension dome; Lexington, Ky. W. M. Moore. il Am City 80:165 Ag '65

REFUSE receptacles
Refuse sacks are in; Mt Wolf, Pa. il Am City 80:96-7 D '65

REGAN, J. D. and Smith, J. B.
Triploidy in a human cell line. bibliog Science 149:1516-17 S 24 '65

REGAN, John J.
Religious tax exemptions and the First amendment. por Cath World 201:108-12 My '65
Supreme court and obscenity; address, May 2, 1965. Vital Speeches 31:592-5 Jl 15 '65

REGATTAS
Big week at Cowes; photographs by G. Cranham; with account by C. Mitchell. Sports Illus 23:30-6 Jl 12 '65
Block Island week; fog, frustration and fun. B. Robinson. il Yachting 118:50-2+ S '65
Championships minus the champ; Navy vs. Cornell, IRA annual championship on Onondaga Lake. il Sports Illus 22:34-5 Je 28 '65
Far flung circuit. B. Robinson. il Yachting 117:50-2+ My '65
Fog week at Block Island. F. Rohr. il Motor B 116:48-9+ S '65
High winds and muddy feet in a foggy, foggy do; Block Island race week. L. Smith. il Sports Illus 23:40-2 Jl 26 '65
Month in yachting. See issues of Yachting
Race in king-size dinghies; Harvard wins the first John F. Kennedy memorial regatta. H. Whall. il Sports Illus 22:68-9 My 3 '65
Regatta circuit; reports from Yachting's editors and correspondents. il Yachting 118:50-4+ O '65
Regatta results. Yachting 118:191-2 N; 167-8 D '65
Row fiercely, Harvard; 100th Harvard-Yale regatta. il Newsweek 65:52 Je 28 '65
Rubber race at Ratzeburg; Ratzeburg rowing club vs Vesper boat club of Philadelphia. H. Whall. il Sports Illus 23:18-19 Jl 19 '65
Sinking feeling on the Thames; Ratzeburg rowing club defeats Harvard and Vesper at Henley royal regatta. J. Lovesey. il Sports Illus 23:18-19 Jl 12 '65
Stichting stamboek ronde-en platbodemjachten zomer-reunie te Veere; yachting à la Hans Brinker on Holland's historic waters. E. F. Haylock. il Motor B 116:34-6+ D '65
Top strokes; Ratzeburg rowing club; in Henley Royal regatta. il Time 86:48+ Jl 16 '65
See also
Rowing

REGENCY electronics, Incorporated
Regency who. A. Trammell. Flying 77:45-6 Jl '65

REGENERATION (biology)
Hydra: induction of supernumerary heads by isolated neurosecretory granules. T. L. Lentz. bibliog il Science 150:633-5 O 29 '65
Lens fiber differentiation and gamma crystallins: immunofluorescent study of Wolffian regeneration. C. Takata and others. bibliog il Science 147:1299-301 Mr 12 '65
Neurons of insects: RNA changes during injury and regeneration. M. Cohen and J. W. Jacklet. bibliog il Science 148:1237-9 My 28 '65
Spermidine in regenerating liver: relation to rapid synthesis of ribonucleic acid. W. G. Dykstra, jr. and E. J. Herbst. bibliog il Science 149:428 Jl 23 '65

REGINA award
Regina medal presentation; to R. Sawyer, April 20, 1965. Mother Mary Cecile. il Horn Bk 41:477-8 O '65

REGIONAL ballet companies. See Ballet companies

REGIONAL organizations. See International organization, Regional

REGIONAL planning
Deeds, not words. H. J. Grossman. il Am For 71:18-21+ Mr '65
Half-finished society. E. K. Faltermayer. il Fortune 71:96-7+ Mr '65
New regional plan to arrest megalopolis; New York state's development program. L. Mumford. il Arch Rec 137:147-54 Mr '65
Priming the pump of area growth; combining public works with regional planning. il Bsns W p96-8+ O 9 '65

Small borough's comprehensive plan; Borough of Royersford, Pa. H. J. Grossman. il Am City 80:118-19 Je '65
Solving land-use determinations electronically; Norristown, Pa. D. B. Witwer. il Am City 80:90-1 F '65
See also
Cities and towns
City planning
Landscape improvement
Landscape protection
Metropolitan areas
New York (city)—Metropolitan district

United States
See Regional planning

Venezuela
Ciudad Guayana: a new city. L. Rodwin. il Sci Am 213:122-30+ S '65

REGISTRATION, Library. See Libraries—Registration

REGISTRATION of voters. See Voters, Registration of

REGNERY, Henry
Bias in book reviewing and book selection. por ALA Bul 60:57-62 Ja '66

REGULATION of prices. See Price regulation by government

REGULATORS, Voltage. See Voltage regulators

REGULATORY commissions. See Independent regulatory commissions

REGULY, Robert J.
Arctic maneuvers; the gimmicks of war. Nation 200:333-6 Mr 29 '65

REHABILITATION
Brighter future for disabled children. H. A. Rusk. il Parents Mag 40:66-7+ N '65
Face to face: with a girl who couldn't cry. S. Amoroso. Seventeen 24:202 My '65
Hard fight by a spunky cripple. M. Murphy. il Life 58:87-8+ F 5 '65
That accident did me good! M. L. Polk. Farm J 89:104 F '65

REHABILITATION, Rural. See Sociology, Rural

REHABILITATION centers
House of hands; rehabilitation center at Chapel Hill, N.C. il Life 58:113-14 Mr 19 '65
Three-level rehabilitation center; Ben R. Meyer rehabilitation center, Los Angeles. il Arch Rec 137:176-7 F '65

REHABILITATION of prisoners. See Prisoners—Rehabilitation

REHEARSALS, Theatrical. See Theatrical production

REHFIELD, John C.
Caging a river to build a skyscraper dam. Pop Sci 186:126-9 F '65

REHMUS, Charles M.
Multiemployer bargaining. Cur Hist 49:91-6+ Ag '65

REICH, Charles A.
Making free speech audible. Nation 200:138-41 F 8 '65

REICH, Wilhelm
World of Wilhelm Reich. P. Rieff; discussion. Commentary 39:18+ F '65

REID, Alastair
Letter from Spain. New Yorker 41:56+ Jl 10 '65
Reporter at large (cont) New Yorker 41:38-42+ Jl 31 '65

REID, Arch M. See Fredriksson, K. jt. auth.

REID, Charles
Patti at Craig-y-Nos. Hi Fi 15:43-7+ Jl '65

REID, Charles E.
Planning team. Library J 90:3214-15 Ag '65
Trustee's thoughts on censorship. ALA Bul 59:527-8 Je '65

REID, D. A.
Resistance soldering. Electr World 74:68-9 Jl '65

REID, Donald
Sub that sails in the sky. R. K. Massie. il pors Sat Eve Post 239:52-4 Ja 1 '66

REID, Frank A.
Refinishing a Firefly. Yachting 117:209-10 Ap '65

REID, Gene C.
Automatic watering pays its own way. Am City 80:106-7 Mr '65

REID, Oliver A.
Iris in July? yes! with the fabulous, fantastic Japanese iris. Flower Grower 52:37 Jl '65

REID, Susan
Learning of rules; poem. Seventeen 24:72 My '65

REIELS, James O.
Twin billing at Nicolet high. Library J 90:5472-5 D 15 '65

REIF, Rita
Home (cont) N Y Times Mag p80-1 Je 6; 24-5 Jl 4; 54-5 Ag 8; 54-5 Ag 22; 64-5 Ag 29; 114-15 S 19; 134-5+ O 24 '65; 36-7 Ja 2 '66

REIFF, Brenda
Civil righter's prayer; poem. Negro Hist Bul 28:144 Mr '65
REILLY, John F.
Ordeal of Otto Otepka. C. Stevenson and W. J. Gill. Read Digest 87:55-9 Ag '65
REILLY, John R.
Antitrust aspects of reciprocity; address, February 18, 1965. Vital Speeches 31:414-16 Ap 15 '65
REIMAN, Roy
New use for old horse barn. Suc Farm 63:50 O '65
Small-lot selling brings top beef prices. Suc Farm 63:116 Mr '65
REINDEER
Some Alaskan reindeer unfit for Santa's sleigh. il(p401) Sci N L 88:404 D 25 '65
REINER, Ernst, and Taylor, Alice
Afghanistan. bibliog Focus 15:1-6 Ja '65
REINHARDT, Adolph
Reinhardt paints a picture. il por Art N 64:39-41+ Mr '65

about

Black monk. il por Newsweek 65:90 Mr 15 '65
REINHART, Carole Dawn
Beauty on the trumpet. J. Shepherd. il pors Look 29:M8-11 Mr 23 '65
REINHART, Kenneth G. and Lull, H. W.
Manipulating forests for water. Am For 71:35-7+ N '65
REINHOLD, H. A.
No time to stop. Commonweal 82:583-5 Ag 20 '65
REINSURANCE. See Insurance—Reinsurance
REIS, Donald J. and Gunne, L.-M.
Brain catecholamines: relation to the defense reaction evoked by amygdaloid stimulation in cat. bibliog Science 149:450-1 Jl 23 '65
REIS, Ronald E.
Amateur's world. il U S Camera 28:80-3 My '65
REISCHAUER, Edwin Oldfather
Japan, the two Reischauers. A. Axelbank. New Repub 153:11-12 N 13 '65
REISCHE, Diana
(ed) Congress at work, 1965. por Sr Schol 86:6-29+ F 18 '65
REISMAN, Bonnie
Two woodcut artists. il Am Artist 29:64-8 O '65
REISS, Alvin H.
Contemporary look. Dance Mag 39:95-8+ D '65
(ed) See Hering, D. Dance and decentralization
REITER, Russel J. See Hoffman, R. A. jt. auth.
REITER, Thomas
Neighbor child; poem. Commonweal 82:409 Je 18 '65
REJ, Mikołaj
Life of Joseph. Criticism Vogue 146:169 O 1 '65
REJECTED manuscripts. See Editors and editing
RELATIVISM, Ethical. See Ethical relativism
RELATIVITY (philosophy and logic)
See also
Ethical relativism
RELATIVITY (physics)
Fountain of youth: Gemini 7's time slowdown. Time 87:44 Ja 7 '66
How to test relativity; reprint. W. Sullivan. il Sci Digest 57:69-72 My '65
New test of general relativity; Einstein's theory. G. S. Mumford, 3d. Sky & Tel 29:156-7 Mr '65
Relativity and solar evolution. Sky & Tel 30:275-6 N '65
See also
Space and time
RELAXATION
Great relaxing bonanza. W. I. Fischman. il Pop Mech 125:122-5+ Ja '66
Why I like the back forty. R. Gogerty. il Farm J 89:28 Ag '65
RELAY stations, Radio. See Radio relay systems
RELAYS
See also
Electronic relays
Radio relay systems
RELIABILITY of products. See Quality of products
RELICS and reliquaries
Magic presences; reliquaries on exhibit at Musée des arts décoratifs, Paris. P. M. Grand. il Art N 64:24-7+ My '65
Where is St Peter buried? E. M. Jung. il Cath World 202:107-13 N '65

RELIEF. See Unemployment—Relief measures
RELIEF work
Cooperation for disaster emergency relief. S. R. Tripp. Dept State Bul 53:419-23 S 6 '65
See also
Food relief
Medical relief work
Vietnamese war, 1957- —Relief work
RELIGION
Battle of the Bible; new Reformation. T. G. Harris. il Look 29:17-20 Jl 27 '65
Conservatism, liberalism, and religion. W. Herberg. il Nat R 17:1087-8 N 30 '65
Opinion on religion. J. Carmichael. Mlle 61:124+ S '65
Religion: a mystery. V. P. McCorry. il America 114:160 Ja 22 '66
See also
Atheism
Christian life
Christianity
Church
Creeds
Ethics
Faith
God
Modernism
Natural theology
Prayer
Religions
Religious education
Revelation
Secularism
Theology
Women and religion
Youth—Religion

Bibliography

Religious books: some fall highspots, September-December. il Pub W 188:51-76 S 27 '65
Religious books: some spring highspots January through May. il Pub W 187:58-83 F 8 '65
Religious books to come; ed. by J. Putnam and J. Lindheim. Library J 91:134-48 Ja 1 '66
Religious books to come; ed. by J. Putnam and R. Grossman. Library J 90:3482-97 S 1 '65

Study and teaching

Youth today. L. M. Grande. Cath World 202:41-4 O '65
RELIGION, Primitive
Temple and the house, by Lord Raglan. Review
Harper 230:150+ Mr '65. P. Pickrel
RELIGION, Psychology of
Faith: healthy v. neurotic. Time 85:78+ Ap 2 '65
Religious psychology, by V. V. Herr. Review
America 112:866-7 Je 12 '65. F. J. Ayd, jr
RELIGION and art. See Art and religion
RELIGION and communism. See Communism and religion
RELIGION and education. See Church and education
RELIGION and literature
Toward a Christian poetic. D. Rogers. Cath World 201:194-7 Je '65
RELIGION and politics. See Church and politics
RELIGION and psychiatry. See Psychiatry and religion
RELIGION and psychology. See Religion, Psychology of
RELIGION and science
Horizons in science. P. Hefner. Christian Cent 82:368-9 Mr 24 '65
On Teilhard de Chardin. S. Toulmin. Commentary 39:50-5 Mr '65; Discussion. 40:6+ Ag '65
Phenomenon of Teilhard. J. Collignon. Christian Cent 82:426-8 Ap 7 '65
Science and the scriptural view of the universe. J. V. Schall. Cath World 202:233-7 Ja '66
Teilhard de Chardin: the attack on man. F. S. Meyer. Nat R 17:596 Jl 13 '65
See also
Tennessee evolution controversy
RELIGION and sex. See Sex and religion
RELIGION and sociology
See also
Sociology, Christian
RELIGION and state. See Church and state
RELIGION and war. See War and religion
RELIGION in the public schools. See Public schools and religion
RELIGIONS
Eccentricity under the sun. R. Carson. il Holiday 38:112+ O '65

RELIGIONS—*Continued*
World religions. il Sr Schol 87:15-16 S 30 '65
  See also
Bahaism
Christian Science
Hinduism
New Thought
RELIGIOUS architecture. See Church architecture
RELIGIOUS art. See Christian art and symbolism
RELIGIOUS books. See Religious literature
RELIGIOUS conferences
Catholic, Orthodox, Protestant. E. T. Culver. Christian Cent 82:412-14 Mr 31 '65
Church and world in Louisiana; conference. F. H. Willhoite, jr. Christian Cent 82:402 Mr 31 '65
Consultative assembly; Latin American Lutheran conference. G. F. Hall. Christian Cent 82:1077-8 S 1 '65
Evanston after eleven years. C. Northcott. Christian Cent 32:1005-6 Ag 18 '65
Harvard conference on the new morality. J. L. Hofford. Christian Cent 82:408-10 Mr 31 '65
Highlights from denominational meetings. Christian Cent 82:996-8 Ag 11 '65
Kirchentag 1965: call for reform; summary of conference, Cologne, Germany. R. M. Herhold. Christian Cent 82:1064-5 S 1 '65; Discussion. 82:1168-70, 1296 S 22, O 20 '65
Lord's Supper: summary of discussion of Faith and order conference. L. Webb. Christian Cent 82:1063-4 S 1 '65
Meeting away from home; three-day conference in Rome on theme. How do we implement the council? R. Dodds. Christian Cent 83:92-4 Ja 19 '66
Ministry and union; fourth Consultation on church union. America 112:627 My 1 '65
Natural law probed; American society for Christian ethics. D. E. Smucker. Christian Cent 82:252-4 F 24 '65
Pacific Northwest conference on faith and order. W. Erickson. Christian Cent 82:1492-4 D 1 '65
Protestants, Catholics view religious liberty. B. Thompson. Christian Cent 82:788-90 Je 16 '65
Resolutionary Christianity? concerning World conference on church and society. J. R. Nelson. Christian Cent 82:639-40 My 19 '65
Scandal of particularity; Protestant-Roman Catholic conference on Judaism and the Christian seminary curriculum. A. P. Klausler. Christian Cent 82:563-6 Ap 28 '65
Toledo conference on clergy and race. G. E. Phibbs. Christian Cent 82:1522-4 D 8 '65
Toward Protestant union; Consultation on church union. Newsweek 65:67 Ap 19 '65
RELIGIOUS cooperation
Another job for all faiths; the war on poverty calls for ecumenical action. H. Smith. America 112:542-3 Ap 17 '65
Breakthroughs: Dubuque's experiment in ecumenism; cooperative graduate programs and open classes for undergraduates. W. E. Hulme. Christian Cent 82:1187-90 S 29 '65
Creed and witness; meeting of Catholic bishops and Lutherans in Baltimore. America 112:445 Ap 3 '65
RELIGIOUS discussion. See Discussion
RELIGIOUS drama
Man and God in dialogue; Sodom and Gomorrah, prologue, tr. by A. J. Skalafuris. N. Kazantzakis. Sat R 48:16-17+ Ag 28 '65
RELIGIOUS education
Teaching in the spirit. C. M. Bowman. Christian Cent 82:1229-30 O 6 '65
Teaching religion in Catholic high schools. D. J. Burke. Cath World 201:113-18 My '65
  See also
Catechetics
Catholic church—Education
Religion—Study and teaching
Sunday schools
RELIGIOUS emphasis week. See Colleges and universities—Religious life
RELIGIOUS faith. See Faith
RELIGIOUS freedom. See Religious liberty
RELIGIOUS history. See Church history
RELIGIOUS institutions and affairs
News of the Christian world. See issues of Christian century to December 29, 1965
World around us (cont of) News of the Christian world. Christian Cent 83:23-30, 53-4 Ja 5-12 '66
RELIGIOUS intermarriages. See Marriages, Mixed
RELIGIOUS liberty
Bishops approve liberty draft; Declaration on religious liberty. Christian Cent 82:1214 O 6 '65

Blow for liberty; Catholic bishops approve in principle declaration on religious liberty. Time 86:85-85A O 1 '65
Catholic vote for religious liberty. U S News 59:16 O 4 '65
Christian and religious liberty 1965; symposium; papers delivered at conference on First amendment freedoms, May 8, 1965. il Cath World 201:355-87 S '65
Church and religious liberty; council fathers favor of the declaration. America 113:393-4 O 9 '65
Conservative bishops win again; Declaration on religious liberty. Christian Cent 82:1405 N 17 '65
Declaration for freedom; views of Conference on the First amendment. America 112: 741 My 22 '65
Declaration on religious liberty. F. Canavan. America 113:635-6 N 20 '65
Freedom and public order. S. E. Mead. Christian Cent 82:1193-4 S 29 '65
Law of church and state; freedom of the mind; address, October 13, 1965. P. W. Bruton. Vital Speeches 32:149-54 D 15 '65
Letter from the council. R. E. Tracy. il America 113:364 O 2 '65
Letter from the council; steps toward Declaration on religious liberty. R. E. Tracy. America 113:397-9 O 9 '65
Peter and Caesar, by E. A. Goerner. Review America 113:345-7 S 25 '65. P. J. Henriot
Pope Paul VI on religious liberty. Paul VI. Cath World 201:400 S '65
Protestants, Catholics view religious liberty. B. Thompson. Christian Cent 82:788-90 Je 16 '65
Religion and American constitutions. by W. G. Katz. Review
  Christian Cent 82:144 F 3 '65. T. G. Sanders
Religious freedom: intrinsic or fortuitous? A. F. Carrillo de Albornoz. bibliog f Christian Cent 82:1122-6 S 15 '65
Religious liberty and the Vatican. E. Forcella. New Repub 153:15-16 O 9 '65
Religious liberty declaration. America 113: 358 O 2 '65
Religious liberty moves forward. J. B. Sheerin. Cath World 202:70-3 N '65; Reply with rejoinder. Marcellus. 202:194 Ja '66
Religious liberty: study in doctrinal development. B. S. Crittenden. Cath World 200:354-5+ Mr '65
Rights for Spanish Protestants? Franco pledged broadening of religious liberty. S. F. Wexler. Christian Cent 82:867-9 Jl 7 '65
Two interventions on behalf of religious liberty. J. C. Heenan; J. Beran. Cath World 202:176-7 D '65
Uses of ambiguity; schema on revelation and the Declaration on religious liberty. il Time 86:78 N 5 '65
Vote for liberty. Newsweek 66:86 O 4 '65
What about the concordats? Vatican council II's Declaration on religious liberty. Christian Cent 82:1244 O 13 '65
RELIGIOUS life. See Christian life
RELIGIOUS literature
Adclub examines handling of religious books. Pub W 188:70-2 D 27 '65
Religious books: some fall highspots, September-December. il Pub W 188:51-76 S 27 '65
  See also
Booksellers and bookselling—Religious literature
Catholic literature
Protestant church-owned publishers association
Publishers and publishing—Religious literature
RELIGIOUS news. See Newspapers—Religious news
RELIGIOUS newspapers and periodicals
Baptists' conscience; Texas Baptist standard's influence. Newsweek 66:65 O 25 '65
  See also
Christian century (periodical)
Christian herald
Christian tribune (periodical)
RELIGIOUS orders
Academic revolution at St John's. F. Canavan. America 113:136-40 Ag 7 '65
Family planning at St John's; insurrection against the Vincentian community. J. Leo. Commonweal 82:184-8 Ap 30 '65; Reply. T. F. Mader. 82:274 My 21 '65
More co-operation: new Committee for religious. America 112:183-4 F 6 '65
  See also
Capuchins
Jesuits
Secular institutes
RELIGIOUS plays. See Religious drama

RELIGIOUS psychology. See Religion, Psychology of
RELIGIOUS publishers group. See American book publishers council
RELIGIOUS radio programs. See Radio broadcasting—Religious programs
RELIGIOUS refugees. See Refugees, Religious
RELIGIOUS schools. See Sunday schools
RELIGIOUS statistics
Poll points to a paradox. Christian Cent 82:1118 S 15 '65
RELIGIOUS toleration. See Toleration
RELIGIOUS vacation schools. See Vacation schools, Religious
RELIQUARIES. See Relics and reliquaries
RELISHES. See Pickles and relishes
REMBRANDT Hermanszoon van Rijn
Fogg's find. il Time 85:94 Ap 16 '65
REMEDIAL teaching
Deprived student in the two-year college: new breed with a new need; summary of speeches at Conference on the teaching of remedial English and math. il Pub W 189:26-31 Ja 3 '66
Physical activity aids the three R's. D. E. Misner. bibliog Sr Schol 86:sup6 My 6 '65
REMINGTON, Frank L.
Every family needs a lawyer. Parents Mag 40:48-9+ Jl '65
REMINISCENCE
Medley of grievous things; bittersweet memories of childhood. R. Harris. Mlle 60:171+ Ap '65
REMODELED automobiles. See Automobiles, Remodeled
REMODELED buildings. See Buildings, Remodeled
REMODELED houses. See Houses, Remodeled
REMODELING (architecture)
Church is expanded, remodeled to needs of liturgical reform; St Thomas Aquinas center, West Lafayette, Ind. il Arch Rec 137:98+ Mr '65
They live in a loft over the family room. il Sunset 134:126+ My '65
See also
Apartments, Remodeled
Buildings, Remodeled
Houses, Remodeled
REMOTE control. See Electric control
REMOTE-control devices. See Magnetic recorders and recording—Control; Television receiving apparatus—Control
REMSBERG, Bonnie. See Remsberg, C. jt. auth.
REMSBERG, Charles, and Remsberg, Bonnie
Come alive, America. Esquire 63:102-5+ F '65
Heister increase their haul. N Y Times Mag p61+ Ja 16 '66
Teenagers who saved a town. Good H 161:82-3+ S '65
RENAISSANCE
Albany symposium on the renaissance. R. F. Creegan. Sch & Soc 93:302-3 Sum '65
RENAISSANCE art. See Art, Renaissance
RENAL cortex. See Kidneys
RENARD, Jules
Books. N. Bliven. New Yorker 41:153-5 Je 12 '65
RENAY, Liz
Mirage of beautiful air. L. H. Lapham. il pors Sat Eve Post 238:34-6+ Mr 27 '65
RENEGOTIATION board. See United States—Renegotiation board
RENIN
Renin production by organ cultures of renal cortex. A. L. Robertson and others. bibliog il Science 149:650-1 Ag 6 '65
RENNER, Richard R.
Student unrest in U.S. and Latin-American universities. Sch & Soc 93:294-5 Sum '65
RENO, Nev.
Rites of Reno. il Holiday 37:62-7 Je '65
RENSON, A. T.
Vacation notes; letter. Nat R 17:803 S 21 '65
RENSSELAER polytechnic institute, Troy, N.Y.
Old R.P.I. and new. il Sci Digest 59:64-9 Ja '66
RENSTROM, Richard
Festival flyer. Hot Rod 18:84-5 Je '65
RENT
Summer at On the rocks. S. Wright. il N Y Times Mag p20+ Ag 8 '65
RENTAL services
Leased landscapes put bloom on business. il Bsns W p 158 F 27 '65
You can rent almost anything! G. Daniels. il Pop Sci 186:132-4+ Je '65
See also subhead Renting under various subjects, e.g. Boats—Renting

RENTROP, Charles
Confusion at city hall. Time 86:31-2+ Ag 27 '65
REORGANIZATION (business) See Business management and organization
REPAIR men. See Repairmen
REPAIRING
Can you save any money on home repair services? Bet Hom & Gard 43:6+ O '65
Clinic for homeowners. See issues of Popular mechanics
Home section. il Pop Mech 124:125-67 S '65
Improve your home. il Pop Sci 187:107-54+ S '65
Linking up a chain, while you wait; Phillips-Ryan service empire. il Bsns W p 148+ O 9 '65
Seven home repairs you're most likely to face; questions and answers. R. C. Whitman. il Pop Sci 187:150-2+ O '65
See also
Houses—Maintenance and repair
Mending
also subhead Repairing under various subjects, e.g. Agricultural machinery—Repairing
REPAIRMEN
American repairman: a vanishing breed? il U S News 59:88-90 S 13 '65
How to escape the serviceman syndrome. E. S. Oshin. House & Gard 127:140-1+ Je '65
Let the right man fix it. Suc Farm 64:80 Ja '66
My love affair with the washing-machine man. J. K. Lubold. il Read Digest 87:60-2 Ag '65
REPARATION
Aiding the victims. Commonweal 83:139-40 N 5 '65
Britain pays the victim of the crime; state compensation for victims of criminal violence. C. Hussey. il N Y Times Mag p 19-20+ F 21 '65
Compensating the victim; first two state compensation laws in California. Newsweek 67:16 Ja 3 '66
Lead from California. Nat R 17:967 N 2 '65
Recompense for violence; compensation to victims of crimes of violence in California. J. Cross. il Nation 201:304-5 N 1 '65
Should the government compensate crime victims? pro and con discussion. Sr Schol 86:10-11 Ap 8 '65
REPARTEE. See Conversation
REPELLENTS, Animal. See Animal repellents
REPERTORY companies. See Theater—United States
REPERTORY theater. See Theater
REPERTORY theater of Lincoln Center for the performing arts. See Lincoln Center repertory theater company
REPORTERS and reporting
Alabama story; newspaper editors tour by invitation of Governor Wallace. W. J. Cook. il Newsweek 65:65 Je 21 '65
City room sagas. J. K. Hutchens. Sat R 48:27 Mr 20 '65
Correspondent in Saigon. G. Eagle. New Repub 152:25-7 My 15 '65
Dateline U.S. 80; covering Selma to Montgomery. il Newsweek 65:82 Ap 5 '65
Etiquette lessons; case of political reporter. W. Kovach vs. Tennessee state Senate. Newsweek 65:62 Mr 8 '65
Every man should have his say; free discussion; address, June 17, 1965. C. May. Vital Speeches 31:622-4 Ag 1 '65
Everybody sure glad; Indian correspondent for Yukon's newspaper, the Whitehorse star. D. J. Hamblin. il Life 58:69-70+ My 21 '65
Facts of life in Viet Nam. Time 85:62 My 7 '65
How do you cover hell? race riot in Los Angeles. il Newsweek 66:50+ Ag 30 '65
Image-polishing in Alabama; out-of-state editors and reporters on tour at invitation of Governor Wallace. il Time 85:38 Je 18 '65
In a novel way; Capote's report of a killing. Time 86:74+ O 8 '65
Lid in Vietnam; restrictions on newsmen. Newsweek 65:58-9 Mr 29 '65
Life magazine? of America? very sorry, goodby; G. De Carvalho's attempt to interview Chou En-lai. G. P. Hunt. Life 59:3 Jl 9 '65
Luci-Lynda beat; concerning H. Thomas and White House coverage. il Newsweek 66:89 D 6 '65

REPORTERS and reporting—*Continued*
Manner of speaking; concerning J. Pekkanen's report of an obscenity trial in Connecticut. J. Ciardi. Sat R 49:22 Ja 1 '66
Muffled in Moscow. il Time 86:83 D 10 '65
No limit? V. P. McCorry. America 112:195 F 6 '65
Pole ax; Warsaw correspondent expelled. Newsweek 67:42 Ja 10 '66
Prize for hungry horse; Pulitzer winners. il Newsweek 65:94+ My 17 '65
Reporting session four. P. E. O'Keefe. America 113:19 Jl 3 '65
Rigid restriction in Britain; conflict between a free press's right to report criminal proceedings and a defendant's right to an unprejudiced trial. Time 85:71 F 12 '65
School for Southerners. Newsweek 66:63 Jl 19 '65
Skirting the ban; reporter L. Hobbs in China. il Newsweek 65:50-1 Je 28 '65
Sociologist on the society beat. il Time 85:51 F 19 '65
T.R.B. from Washington; NY times series on red China from Canadian paper. New Repub 152:4 Je 19 '65
Taking sides in Santo Domingo. il Time 85:64 My 28 '65
Tale of wire and the rose garden; President Johnson and the press. J. N. Eller. America 112:385 Mr 20 '65
This world we live in; experiences as reporter on the old New York world. S. McKelway. New Yorker 41:155-6+ S 11 '65
To war in a taxi; covering Dominican revolt; Case of conscience; doubts about direction of American policy. il Newsweek 65:94-6 My 24 '65
Too much crusading; foreign correspondents. Time 86:34 Ag 27 '65
Two most eminent and strikingly different columnists. J. K. Jessup. il Life 58:40-1 My 7 '65
Up front once more: B. Mauldin in South Viet Nam. il Time 85:50-1 F 19 '65
Use & abuse of anonymity; concerning "highly reliable" news sources. Time 85:51 Je 11 '65
Whole truth. S. J. Adamo. il America 113:480-1 O 23 '65
With Senior's editor in Viet Nam; questions and answers. R. Hemming. il Sr Schol 86:13 Mr 4 '65
See also
Journalists
Newspaper court reporting
Press conferences
Radio broadcasting—Sports
War correspondents
Women as journalists
Women as reporters

REPORTS
Dear stockholders: everything looks rosy. W. H. Dinsmore. Harper 230:133-6+ Mr '65
New news. il Fortune 71:66 Mr '65

REPORTS. School. See School reports and records

REPOTTING of plants. See Plants, Potted

REPRESENTATIVE government and representation
Back to bossism. R. Moley. Newsweek 65:124 Je 14 '65
See also
Apportionment (election law)

REPRESENTATIVES, Congressional. See Congressmen

REPRINTS. See Books—Reprints

REPRODUCTION
Genetic transfer in bacterial mating. J. D. Gross and L. Caro. bibliog il Science 150:1679-84 D 24 '65
Lizard reproduction: refractory period and response to warmth in Uta stansburiana females. D. W. Tinkle and L. N. Irwin. bibliog il Science 148:1613-14 Je 18 '65
Right horn implantation in the common duiker. G. Child and A. S. Mossman. Science 149:1265-6 S 10 '65
Scenedesmus obliquus sexuality. F. R. Trainor and C. A. Burg. bibliog il Science 148:1094 My 21 '65
See also
Artificial insemination, Human
Plants—Reproduction

REPRODUCTION of works of art
Original or reproduction? N. Kent. Am Artist 29:3+ O '65

REPTILES
See also
Alligators

REPTILES, Fossil
See also
Dinosaurs

REPUBLIC aviation corporation
Republic adds modification facility. Aviation W 82:72 F 15 '65

REPUBLIC of the Philippines. See Philippines

REPUBLIC OF TOGO. See Togo

REPUBLICAN clubs. See Political clubs and associations

REPUBLICAN national committee. See Republican party

REPUBLICAN party
After hitting bottom. Commonweal 81:653 F 19 '65
After the fall. A. Hacker. Commentary 40:104+ S '65
Agony of the G.O.P. 1964, by R. D. Novak. Review
New Repub 152:28 F 20 '65. G. W. Johnson
Reporter 32:43-4+ Ap 22 '65. J. S. Saloma, 3d
And in this corner. . . Nat R 17:137-8 F 23 '65
And now there are two; no longer the one-party South. Time 86:13 D 24 '65
As Republicans hit the comeback trail. U S News 59:52 Jl 19 '65
Back to the drawing board; the Republicans and '68. W. D. Burnham. Commonweal 81:780-2 Mr 19 '65
Bliss rides the elephant; Republican national chairman. D. S. Broder. il N Y Times Mag p49-50+ Mr 21 '65
Business and the G.O.P. J. Berry. il Duns R 86:34-6+ D '65
Chuck's challenge; C. H. Percy's Senate bid. Newsweek 66:26 D 27 '65
Comeback for Republicans in '66? how big? il U S News 60:46-7 Ja 10 '66
Conviction or convenience; the trap of the Great society. R. F. Hamilton. il Nation 201:384-7 N 22 '65
Dance of the GOP. E. J. Hughes. Newsweek 66:19 N 1 '65
Election aftermath: how Republicans see the future; interview. R. C. Bliss. U S News 59:34-6 N 15 '65
Elections. Nat R 17:1012-13 N 16 '65
Enthusiasm gone sour. Time 86:17-18 Jl 2 '65
Every man should have his say; free discussion; address, June 17, 1965. C. May. Vital Speeches 31:622-4 Ag 1 '65
Final refrain; Burch analysis of Republican debacle. Newsweek 65:27 Mr 15 '65
Ghouls, ghosts and the GOP. Nation 201:513 D 27 '65
Goldwater rallies the troops. W. D. Burnham. Commonweal 82:552-5 Ag 6 '65
GOP attacks the John Birch society. F. Knebel. il Look 29:74-6 D 28 '65
Grand old party; celebration of Dwight Eisenhower's 75th birthday. il Newsweek 66:31-2 O 25 '65
GOP horoscope. Commonweal 83:425 Ja 14 '66
GOP today: schism within a dilemma. M. Viorst. Nation 201:375-8 N 22 '65
How many votes does Goldwater own? L. H. Bean and R. Drummond. il Look 29:75-6 Mr 23 '65
How Republicans hope to rebuild. il U S News 58:18 Ap 12 '65
How wide a tent? Newsweek 66:24-5 Ag 23 '65
In-fighting among the outs. W. V. Shannon. Commonweal 83:330-1 D 17 '65
Is silence loyalty? J. O'Gara. Commonweal 82:432 Je 25 '65
It won't go away. W. A. Rusher. Nat R 17:199-200 Mr 9 '65
Kelly caper. il Newsweek 66:20-1 Jl 5 '65
Key Republicans in the limelight. il U S News 60:22 Ja 17 '66
Liberals and John Lindsay. A. M. Bickel. New Repub 153:16-18 Jl 3 '65
Lindsay miracle. C. McWilliams. Nation 201:348-50 N 15 '65
Litany of defeat. il Newsweek 65:32 Ap 12 '65
Livy's ghost; Republican party and John Birch society. Newsweek 66:26-7 D 27 '65
Look ahead by the Republicans; interview. E. M. Dirksen. U S News 60:70-4 Ja 17 '66
Lyndon B. who? il Newsweek 65:22-3 Mr 22 '65
Mr Bliss' dilemma. W. F. Buckley, jr. Nat R 17:630 Jl 27 '65
Moment of truth; our rendezvous with destiny; address, June 8, 1965. R. Reagan. Vital Speeches 31:681-6 S 1 '65
More and more problems for Bliss. U S News 59:16 Jl 5 '65
Negro leader's advice to Republicans: interview. E. W. Brooke. U S News 58:66-70 F 1 '65
New era of Bliss. W. F. Buckley, jr. Nat R 17:318 Ap 20 '65

REPUBLICAN party—*Continued*

New GOP chairman. G. F. Jenks. New Repub 152:8-9 F 6 '65

New York and the GOP. Nat R 17:1014 N 16 '65

Next chief of the GOP. E. J. Hughes. Newsweek 66:19 N 29 '65

No comfort for Birchers. il Time 86:12 D 24 '65

Not very new GOP. E. J. Hughes. Newsweek 65:15 Mr 22 '65

Palmetto Republicans; South Carolina Republicans. J. C. Evans. Christian Cent 82: 1030 Ag 25 '65

Political economy of the Great society. O. Gass. bibliog f Commentary 40:31-6 O '65

Politics and federalism: party or anti-party? W. Buchanan. bibliog f il Ann Am Acad 359:107-15 My '65

Representative Lindsay steps to the fore. M. McGrory. America 112:820 Je 5 '65

Republican blueprint for Vietnam war. il U S News 59:10 D 27 '65

Republican future; interview. E. M. Dirksen. il U S News 58:60-4 My 3 '65

Republican parties. D. Danzig. Christian Cent 82:326 Mr 17 '65

Republicans after the debacle. P. Duke; S. Meisler; J. R. L. Sterne. Reporter 32:26-30 F 11 '65

Republicans at sea. A. Kopkind. New Repub 153:12-14 S 25 '65; Reply with rejoinder. C. E. Goddell. 153:37 O 9 '65

Republicans' comeback trail; where it begins. il U S News 58:70-1 F 8 '65

Republicans do think; alarming acceleration of federal debt; address, April 6, 1965. G. Allott. Vital Speeches 31:477-80 My 15 '65

Republicans in search of an issue. il U S News 58:34 Mr 22 '65

Ripon report: on Republican presidential campaign. il Time 85:24-5 F 19 '65

Same young fogies; Young Republican national federation convention. J. Duscha. New Repub 153:8 Jl 3 '65

Southern Republicans. New Repub 152:6-7 Je 26 '65

Splinters. Time 85:32-3 Je 25 '65

Splinters under the hide. il Newsweek 66:32 S 13 '65

T.R.B. from Washington; GOP's problem. New Repub 153:4 N 6 '65

Tips from the top; leadership training conference. Time 85:24 F 26 '65

Topic A; meeting of Republican coordinating committee. il Newsweek 65:43 Je 14 '65

Trials of being a Republican. M. McGrory. America 113:72 Jl 17 '65

Two-team league; Mississippi municipal elections. Time 85:27 Je 18 '65

Union now? il Time 85:31 Je 11 '65

What's new for the grand old party; Time essay. Time 86:26-7 O 22 '65

What's wrong with us? L. Hall. Time 85:24-5 Ap 2 '65

When Goldwater launched a new group. il U S News 58:15 Je 28 '65

Year of decision for the GOP. Nation 200:210 Mr 1 '65

See also
National conventions, Republican

REQUIEMS
La Scala requiem, by W. Josephs. B. Jacobson. Sat R 48:59 D 25 '65
See also
Phonograph records—Requiems

RESCH, George T.
How to get greater value from stock photographers. Pub W 188:82+ Ag 9 '65

RESCUE work
Daring lifesavers of the surf; Surf life saving association of Australia. il UNESCO Courier 18:30-1 Jl '65

How they rescued me 200 feet underground; National capital grotto rescue team. J. R. Berry. il Pop Sci 187:89-91+ O '65

Seventy-two hours of terror; on Teewinot Mountain in Grand Teton National Park. J. Lipscomb. il Sports Illus 22:86-90+ Je 14 '65

Under the Allalin; Switzerland's worst avalanche in eighty-four years. il Newsweek 66:40+ S 13 '65

Young lives, brave actions. B. Clark. il Read Digest 87:187-8+ N '65
See also
Animals—Protection
First aid in illness and injury
Helicopters in rescue work
Space rescue work
United States—Air force—Air rescue service
United States—Coast guard

RESEARCH
Changing environment of science; adaptation of address, December 28, 1964. A. T. Waterman; discussion. Science 147:1523-4 Mr 26 '65

Let's have more research on research; address, September 23, 1965. A. C. Daugherty. Vital Speeches 32:89-93 N 15 '65

Manner of speaking; future of scientific research. J. Ciardi. Sat R 49:26+ Ja 8 '66

Method of multiple working hypotheses; reprint from Science, 1890. T. C. Chamberlin. Science 148:754-9 My 7 '65; Reply. N. H. Eisen. 149:246+ Jl 16 '65

Priority. I. H. Page. Science 151:33 Ja 7 '66

Productive environment for innovation. D. Wolfle. Science 149:501 Jl 30 '65

Pure research, cultism, and the undergraduate. R. Wolfgang. Science 150:1563-5 D 17 '65

Science advances in 1965. W. Davis. il Sci N L 88:387-8 D 18 '65

Strong inference and weak interactions. E. M. Hafner and S. Presswood. bibliog il Science 149:503-10 Jl 30 '65

Teachers given research opportunities; science teachers. Sr Schol 87:sup3 D 2 '65

Thoughts on research. C. Stern. Science 148: 772-3 My 7 '65
See also Genetic research, and similar headings

Anecdotes, facetiae, satire, etc.

Breakthrough. D. S. Greenberg. Sat R 48: 54-5 F 6 '65

Cost

Indirect costs: House legislation embodies new cost-sharing formula for federal research grants. J. Walsh. Science 149:525-6 Jl 30 '65

Industry keeps pace as R&D outlays soar. il Bsns W p72 Jl 17 '65

West German research spending; plans for 1966 to 1968. V. K. McElheny. Science 148: 59-60 Ap 2 '65

Economic aspects

Foreign research: Reuss criticizes projects supported by the United States. D. S. Greenberg. Science 151:180-1 Ja 14 '66

Judging research and development payoff. L. R. Hafstad. Aviation W 82:21 Ap 19 '65

Paying for basic research; some economic issues. H. G. Johnson. Bul Atomic Sci 21: 12-16 D '65

Rib cage of a mighty giant; economy's non-economic support. il Sr Schol 86:10-11 Ap 15 '65

Federal aid

Adequate rate of growth. D. Wolfle. Science 14:13799 Mr 19 '65

Are the tame cats in charge? omens of Orwell. P. Abelson. Sat R 49:100-3 Ja 1 '66

Battle over funds opens. Sci N L 87:372 Je 12 '65

Big money and high politics of science. D. R. Fleming. Atlan 216:41-5 Ag '65; Reply. M. W. Keith. 216:56+ N '65

Billions for science: is it worth the price? interview. W. Weaver. il U S News 59:76-9 D 6 '65

Brawl for science dollars. B. H. Frisch. il Sci Digest 58:28-34 O '65

Budget: total funds for R&D rise modestly to 15.4 billion; research gets most of increase. J. Walsh. il Science 147:485-6 Ja 29 '65

Career awards; no more new ones will be made under NIH program. J. Walsh; discussion. Science 147:1395; 148:1040+; 149:7, 813-14 Mr 19, My 21, Jl 2, Ag 20 '65

Chaos in science; what space and defense are doing. A. Etzioni. Commonweal 82:494-7 Jl 9 '65

Chemistry: a little science would like a little more money; with editorial comment. D. S. Greenberg. il Science 150:1247, 1267-70 D 3 '65

Congress and science: tensions appear to be minimal as annual review begins on budget requests, with editorial comment. D. S. Greenberg. il Science 147:561, 582-4 F 5 '65; Reply. R. H. Alden. 147:1523 Mr 26 '65

DOD asked to reassess research policy. G. C. Wilson. il Aviation W 82:75-6 Je 28 '65

$15-billion question brings complex reply; National academy of sciences' answer to Congress concerning allocation of research funds. Bsns W p 122+ My 8 '65

Foreign research: Reuss criticizes projects supported by the United States. D. S. Greenberg. Science 151:180-1 Ja 14 '66

400-mph passenger train. L. Lessing. il Fortune 71:124-9+ Ap '65

RESEARCH—Federal aid—*Continued*
Fruits of research; patents ownership controversy. America 113:107 Jl 31 '65
Indirect costs: House legislation embodies new cost-sharing formula for federal research grants. J. Walsh. Science 149:525-6 Jl 30 '65
Industry keeps pace as R&D outlays soar. il Bsns W p72 Jl 17 '65
Institutional grants of the National science foundation. E. J. Merton. il Science 148:1693-6 Je 25 '65
Kept science ruinous. Sci N L 87:219 Ap 3 '65
LBJ directive: he says spread the research money. D. S. Greenberg. Science 149:1483-5 S 24 '65; Reply. P. H. Abelson. 150:11 O 1 '65
Military research; Congress generally goes along with RDT&E requests, but adds qualifications. J. Walsh. Science 149:403-5 Jl 23 '65
Money for research: Congress and scientists have different ideas on how the system should operate. D. S. Greenberg. Science 149:278-80 Jl 16 '65
Money for science: budget faces pressure from Vietnam conflict. D. S. Greenberg. Science 150:1790 D 31 '65
NSF budget: cuts by House group leave little leeway for growth in support of research proects. D. S. Greenberg. Science 148:928-30 My 14 '65
NSF: 14th annual report reveals efforts to devise new techniques in science-government relations. D. S. Greenberg. Science 147:1014-16 F 26 '65
Partnership in research. D. F. Shaughnessy. il Am Ed 1:1-4 F '65
Patents and copyrights: Congress moves toward comprehensive policy on federally financed research. J. Walsh. Science 148:54-6 Ap 2 '65
Pentagon's new R&D want list. il Bsns W p 120+ Mr 20 '65
Propose powerful role for NSF. C. A. Betts. Sci N L 87:275 My 1 '65
Public domain. W. E. Mylecraine. Am Ed 1:7-8 N '65
R&D boom: House report sees harm to higher education. D. S. Greenberg. Science 150:464-6 O 22 '65; Discussion. 150:1766-8+ D 31 '65
R&D can be useful. Nation 200:125-6 F 8 '65
Research grants hurt engineering education. Sci N L 88:88 Ag 7 '65
Research; the midas touch. H. S. Reuss. il Nation 202:69-71 Ja 17 '66
Reuss committee: new probe planned into priorities for R&D. D. S. Greenberg. Science 150:1565-6 D 17 '65
Some current problems of government science policy; address, April 26, 1965. H. Orlans. bibliog Science 149:37-40 Jl 2 '65
Spreading the research billions. il U S News 59:105 O 18 '65
Summer: the climate is changed for university scientists and the federal government did it. J. Walsh. Science 148:776-8 My 7 '65
Support of science in the U.S. D. Wolfle. il Sci Am 213:19-25 Jl '65
Technical services act: industry to benefit from new state programs paralleling farm extension service. L. J. Carter. Science 149:1485-6+ S 24 '65
U.S. patent policy and government research. R. L. Wright; discussion. Bul Atomic Sci 20:32-4 O '64; 21:34 F '65
Universities and federal science policies; address, October 11, 1965. D. F. Hornig. Science 150:847-51 N 12 '65
Way of the dinosaur? il Newsweek 65:104+ My 24 '65
What are we doing to engineering? J. R. Pierce. il Science 149:397-9 Jl 23 '65

International aspects
See Science—International aspects

Study and teaching
Research papers in high school English; pro and con discussion. T. E. Taylor; Sister M. Christina. NEA J 54:42-4 N '65
Your encyclopedia: tool for teaching research skills. W. D. Halsey. Sr Schol 86:sup9 My 6 '65

China (People's Republic)
How red China is taking science to its peasants; ed. by J. Lear. C. H. G. Oldham. il Sat R 48:45-6 Mr 6 '65

Germany (Federal Republic)
West German research spending: plans for 1966 to 1968. V. K. McElheny. Science 148:59-60 Ap 2 '65

India
Scientific research in India. J. Singh. Bul Atomic Sci 21:41-3 F '65

Israel
Fundamental biology at the Weizmann institute. V. K. McElheny. il Science 148:614-18 Ap 30 '65
Israel worries about its applied research. V. K. McElheny. il Science 147:1123-4+ Mr 5 '65

Italy
Public review Italian style; question of misappropriating government funds. Sci Am 213:82+ S '65
Research climate in Italy, I. V. K. McElheny; discussion. Science 145:1387; 147:556-7 S 25 '64, F 5 '65
Research climate in Italy, II. V. K. McElheny. il Science 148:205-7 Ap 9 '65
Support for Italian science; letter to Lyndon B. Johnson from eighty-two Italian scientists. A. Leonardi and others. Science 148:1037 My 21 '65

Latin America
Journal of Latin American research to be published by major universities; Latin American research review. Library J 90:4314 O 15 '65

Russia
Bunglers of the world, unite. Reporter 32:12+ Ap 8 '65
Soviet research and development: its organization, personnel, and funds, by A. Korol. Review
Science 148:785-6 My 7 '65. A. Vucinich
Trends in some areas of Soviet biomedical research. E. Simonson and J. Brožek. bibliog Science 150:1687-9 D 24 '65

United States
Impact of science on technology; ed. by A. W. Warner. Review
Science 148:1707-9 Je 25 '65. S. Dedijer
Judging research and development payoff. L. R. Hafstad. Aviation W 82:21 Ap 19 '65
Kansas City: new medical complex, university should complement Midwest research institute. J. Walsh. Science 148:1202-4 My 28 '65
Scholars and foreign policy: varieties of research experience; address, October 21, 1965. T. L. Hughes. Dept State Bul 53:747-58 N 8 '65; Excerpt. Science 150:1430 D 10 '65
Science in action: students in the museum. B. M. Hecht. Natur Hist 75:66-7 Ja '66
Support of science in the U.S. D. Wolfle. il Sci Am 213:19-25 Jl '65
Wanted: one million inventors. L. Velie. Read Digest 86:70-5 Ap '65
See also
Colleges and universities—Research
Government investigations—Government funded research
United States—National science foundation

Venezuela
Research on research in Venezuela. C. V. Kidd. bibliog il Science 149:727-9 Ag 13 '65

RESEARCH and engineering council of the graphic arts industry. See Graphic arts research council

RESEARCH centers. See Research laboratories

RESEARCH in colleges. See Colleges and universities—Research

RESEARCH laboratories
Clean industry every county covets. il Fortune 71:148+ My '65
Employment of women chemists in industrial laboratories. J. B. Parrish. bibliog il Science 148:657-8 Ap 30 '65
Mature research institutions and the older scientist. L. G. Cook and G. W. Hazzard. bibliog il Science 150:716-19 N 5 '65
R&D building, a new high. G. A. Christie. il Arch Rec 138:44 N '65
Research triangle seeks high-technology industry; center at Durham, N.C. L. J. Carter. il Science 150:867-71 N 12 '65
See also
United States—National aeronautics and space administration—Electronics research center

RESEARCH libraries

Circulation, loans, etc.

Lending research library; UCLA. J. R. Cox. il Library J 90:2219-25 My 15 '65

RESEARCH triangle institute, Durham, N.C. See Research laboratories

RESEGREGATION of schools. See Public schools—Desegregation

RESEMBLANCE, Protective. See Mimicry (biology)

RESENTMENT. See Anger

RESERPINE

Circadian rhythm in pineal serotonin: effect of monoamine oxidase inhibition and reserpine. S. H. Snyder and J. Axelrod. bibliog il Science 149:542-4 Jl 30 '65

RESERVATIONS, Indian. See Indians of North America—Reservations

RESERVE forces (United States) See United States—Armed forces—Reserves

RESERVE systems, Library. See College libraries—Reserve systems

RESERVOIRS

First we built the reservoir; triple benefits from dam in Brady, Tex. J. C. Feazelle. il Am City 80:135-6 N '65

Myths of the western dam. W. Stegner. il Sat R 48:29-31 O 23 '65

Evaporation control

Evaporation of water: its retardation by monolayers. V. K. LaMer and T. W. Healy. bibliog il Science 148:36-42 Ap 2 '65

Evaporation retardants: application by means of a water-soluble matrix. L. E. Myers. il Science 148:70-1 Ap 2 '65

RESHETAR, John S. Jr

Soviet Union and the neutralist world. bibliog f Ann Am Acad 362:102-12 N '65

RESHOVSKY, Zora L.

Fountain of youth. U S Camera 28:22-3+ F '65

RESIDENCE halls. See Dormitories

RESIDENCES, Official. See Official residences

RESIDENTIAL zoning. See Zoning

RESINOUS products

Inventor of the month; a tough new family; engineering plastics, polyimides. S. V. Jones. il Sci Digest 58:22 Jl '65

See also
Thermoplastics

RESISTANCE, Electric. See Electric resistance

RESISTANCE to disease. See Immunity

RESISTANCE to drugs. See Drugs, Resistance to

RESISTANCE to government. See Government; Resistance to; Passive resistance to government

RESISTANCE welding. See Electric welding

RESNIK, Muriel

How the flop flipped. por Newsweek 66:101-2 S 27 '65

RESOLUTIONS

What good are good resolutions? J. Brothers. Good H 160:30+ Ja '65

RESONANCE, Magnetic. See Magnetic resonance

RESORT houses. See Summer homes

RESORTS. See Summer resorts; Health resorts, watering places, etc; Winter resorts

RESOURCES, Conservation of. See Conservation of resources

RESOURCES, Natural. See Natural resources

RESPIRATION

Dogs breathe water. il Sci N L 87:229 Ap 10 '65

Fish that walks, breathes, changes sex. Sci Digest 57:12-13 Ap '65

Mammals that breathe under water; experimenting with liquid-filled chamber. il Sci Digest 58:18-19 Ag '65

Respiratory water exchange in two species of porpoise. H. N. Coulombe and others. bibliog il Science 149:86-8 Jl 2 '65

Take a deep breath. H. Durham. Read Digest 86:24J Mr '65

See also
Anoxemia
Emphysema

RESPIRATION, Artificial

Respiration study needed. Sci N L 88:69 Jl 31 '65

Tragedy of needless drowning deaths. G. Upton. il Todays Health 43:46-8+ Jl '65

See also
Respiratory apparatus

RESPIRATORY apparatus

Air compressor and breathing apparatus team up to save lives; equipment used by Syracuse, N.Y. Department of fire. il Am City 81:54 Ja '66

Mobile air supply cuts casualties; Baltimore, Md. il Am City 80:42 O '65

Smog box; oxygen-fortified air for persons with lung disorders. il Sci Digest 59:9 Ja '66

RESPIRATORY organs

Pinning down the suspects; industrial smog and cigarette smoke. Newsweek 66:96 N 8 '65

Diseases

Fastest growing killer is respiratory disease. Sci N L 87:297 My 8 '65

Three new miracle treatments to keep babies alive. B. Merson. Good H 161:68-9+ Jl '65

See also
Asthma
Cold (disease)
Hyaline membrane disease

RESPONSIBILITY

Are new laws needed for good samaritans? U S News 58:18 Ap 26 '65

Charter of accountability for executives P. N. Scheid. bibliog f Harvard Bsns R 43:88-98 Jl '65

How much responsibility can a youngster take? with discussion group program by M. R. Sherwin. H. F. Travers. il Parents Mag 41:12+, 40-1+ Ja '66

I don't want to get involved! pro and con discussion. Sr Schol 86:12-13 F 25; 17-18 My 13 '65

I'm glad I tried to help! ed. by L. David. V. A. McNeil. il Good H 160:92-3+ Ap '65

In the human interest; conflict with national interest. N. Cousins. Sat R 48:28 N 27 '65

Murder in Alabama; American wives think Viola Liuzzo should have stayed home. L. Tornabene. il Ladies Home J 82:42+ Jl '65

Self-reliance or self-destruction; address, April 27, 1965. G. Dudley, jr. Vital Speeches 31:632-4 Ag 1 '65

Should equal rights mean equal responsibility? excerpts from address, August 23, 1965. R. C. Byrd. U S News 59:14-15 S 6 '65

Some aspects of censorship; excerpts from address, October 13, 1964. M. L. Ernst. il Wilson Lib Bul 39:668-9 Ap '65

Story of a man who tried to help; Senn case. il U S News 58:64 Mr 29 '65

Transformation of a chronic nag. I. O. Tebbetts. il Redbook 125:6+ Ag '65

What is realism doing to American history? Adaptation of address. A. MacLeish. il Sat R 48:10-12 Jl 3 '65; Discussion. 48:13-14+ Jl 3; 16-18 Jl 10; 38 Jl 24 '65

RESPONSIBILITY (law) See Liability (law)

RESS, Paul Evan

Yankee dandies on the Danube. Sports Illus 23:20-1+ S 6 '65

REST

See also
Relaxation

REST homes. See Nursing homes

RESTAURANT associates, incorporated

Goulash in the making; Restaurant associates to merge with Waldorf system, inc. il Time 85:94+ My 21 '65

RESTAURANT management

Study and teaching

Changing the recipe for innkeepers; New York university's course in hotel, restaurant management. il Bsns W p66-8+ F 27 '65

RESTAURANTS

Splendors and miseries of the literary cafe. H. R. Lottman. il Sat R 48:34-5+ Mr 13 '65

Europe, Western

Europe's finest restaurants; 1966. il Holiday 39:72-4+ Ja '66

France

Chabert of Tain l'hermitage. C. Cate. il Atlan 216:168+ N '65

Real savoy; inn of Père Bise. A. J. McClane. il Esquire 63:92-4+ F '65

Success story; L'auberge Paul Bocuse. Newsweek 65:46-7 Je 21 '65

Hong Kong

Dining in the Far East. S. Spitzer. Holiday 38:98+ D '65

Notes from the East to paste in your hat. H. Sutton. il Sat R 48:74+ N 13 '65 (to be cont)

RESTAURANTS—*Continued*

Japan

Dining in the Far East. S. Spitzer. Holiday 38:98+ D '65

Mexico

Mexico's drug store changes prescription; Sanborns, restaurants, chain, and retail stores under Walgreen co. il Bsns W p72-3+ My 15 '65

United States

Country dining around Philadelphia. L. Dowst. il Holiday 37:80-1+ Je '65

Dining in/out with Esquire. Esquire 63:40A+ Je '65

Fast food and footloose Americans; conference on the problems of the Food service industries held in Fontana, Wis. R. Lynes. Harper 232:26+ Ja '66

Holiday's choice of American restaurants. S. Spitzer and H. Spitzer. il Holiday 38:66-71 Jl '65

Hot shoppes adds to its menu; Marriott-Hot shoppes, inc. il Bsns W p 160+ F 13 '65

Personal business: relaxed country dining. Bsns W p 115-16 Jl 24 '65

RESTITUTION claims

Claimants of Hiroshima. R. A. Falk. il Nation 200:157-61 F 15 '65

Closing the books: case of K. Koda family. il Newsweek 66:50-1 O 18 '65

RESTON, James Barrett

We may win the war but lose the people. N Y Times Mag p42-3+ S 12 '65

about

Pundit and the prole; J. B. Reston and J. E. Breslin in Saigon. il por Newsweek 66:49-50 S 6 '65

Two most eminent and strikingly different columnists. J. K. Jessup. por Life 58:40-1 My 7 '65

Two views of Lyndon Johnson; excerpts. U S News 58:34 F 1 '65

RESTON, Scotty. See Reston, J. B.

RESTON, Va.

Eighteen miles from the capital. il Time 85:77 My 21 '65

New way to live; self-contained town. J. Peter. il Look 29:52-7 N 30 '65

Progress in planning: a new town brings urban living patterns to the countryside. J. M. Dixon. il Arch Forum 123:84-9 Jl '65

Reston. R. Phillips. Am Home 68:34 Mr '65

Reston: first of the new satellite cities. il Life 59:144-5 D 24 '65

RESTORATION of books. See Books—Conservation and restoration

RESTORATION of buildings. See Architecture —Conservation and restoration

RESTORATION of works of art. See Art objects—Conservation and restoration

RESTORED airplanes. See Airplanes, Restored

RESTORED automobiles. See Automobiles, Remodeled

RESTORED houses. See Houses, Restored

RESTORED villages. See Villages, Restored

RESTRAINT of trade
See also
Boycott
Monopolies

RESTRICTIONS on travel. See Travel regulations

RESURFACING of pavements. See Pavements —Surface treatment

RESURRECTION
See also
Jesus Christ—Resurrection and ascension

RESUSCITATION

Can deep freeze conquer death? cryogenic interment. R. C. Ettinger. il Ebony 21:60-1+ Ja '66

Freeze on death? Newsweek 65:55 My 31 '65

Frozen Christian: cryogenic interment. R. C. W. Ettinger. Christian Cent 82:1313-15 O 27 '65; Reply. L. J. Putnam. 82:1550+ D 15 '65

How to delay death. V. Negovsky and V. Soboleva. il Sci Digest 57:60-5 Ap '65

Lasting indefinitely. R. C. W. Ettinger. il Esquire 63:63-5+ My '65

RETAIL clerks international association

Organizing with an adman's touch; southern California locals of RCIA applying Madison avenue techniques to recruit department store employees. il Bsns W p72+ O 16 '65

RETAIL stores

Employees

Unions will sell harder in stores. Bsns W p44+ F 6 '65

RETAIL trade

Another banner sales year coming up. il Bsns W p 13-14 Ja 1 '66

Early Christmas bells. Time 86:95 O 8 '65

Great discount delusion, by W. H. Nelson. Review
Nation 201:255-6 O 18 '65. V. Lebow

More for more. il Time 87:81-2 Ja 7 '66

Piling up more than lumber: Wickes lumberyards. il Bsns W p57-8 Ja 30 '65

Ratios of retailing; with table (cont) Duns R 86:48-9 S '65

Retailers jump gun on tax cut; pledge refunds. il Bsns W p28-30 My 29 '65

Retailers stake out snappy Easter. il Bsns W p28-9 Ap 10 '65

Trade: record boom goes on. il U S News 60:100 Ja 17 '66
See also
Chain stores
Christmas business
Dealer relations
Discount houses (retail trade)
Furniture industry and trade
Gift shops
Grocery trade
Merchandising clubs
Price marks
Sears, Roebuck and company

Hours of business

See Store hours

RETAIL, wholesale and department store union

New bargaining units for department stores. Mo Labor R 88:III-IV Mr '65

Unions will sell harder in stores. Bsns W p44+ F 6 '65

RETAIL workers
See also
Department stores—Employees

RETARDED children. See Slow learning children

RETARDED children, National association for. See National association for retarded children

RETICULOCYTES. See Erythrocytes

RETINA

Codominance of visual pigments in hybrid fishes. W. N. McFarland and F. W. Munz. bibliog il Science 150:1055-7 N 19 '65

Frog retina: detection of movement. D. Finkelstein and O. J. Grüsser. bibliog il Science 150:1050-1 N 19 '65

Geniculate unit responses to sine-wave photic stimulation during wakefulness and sleep. L. Maffei and others. bibliog il Science 149:563-4 Jl 30 '65

Mammalian retina: associational nerve cells in ganglion cell layer. A. Gallego and J. Cruz. bibliog il Science 150:1313-14 D 3 '65

Neural stage of adaptation between the receptors and inner nuclear layer of monkey retina. K. T. Brown and K. Watanabe. bibliog il Science 148:1111-13 My 21 '65

Primate retina: duplex function of dark-adapted ganglion cells. P. Gouras. bibliog il Science 147:1593-4 Mr 26 '65

Retina: pathology of neodymium and ruby laser burns. M. L. Wolbarsht and others. bibliog il Science 150:1453-4 D 10 '65

Synaptic connections of the centrifugal fibers in the pigeon retina. H. R. Maturana and S. Frenk. bibliog il Science 150:359-61 O 15 '65

RETINA, Detached. See Eye—Diseases and defects

RETINOBLASTOMA. See Cancer

RETINOL. See Vitamins—Vitamin A

RETIRED military officers

Retired at forty-five, and hunting for a job. il Changing T 19:25-8 F '65

RETIRED public officers. See Public officers

RETIRED service men. See Service men, Retired

RETIREMENT, Places of

Retire to the Caribbean? how practical, really? il Changing T 20:35-8 Ja '66

RETIREMENT from business, etc.

Beats working; experiment at three Southwest leisure villages. Newsweek 66:106 S 27 '65

Dilemma of retirement. T. R. Brooks. Duns R 86:81+ O '65

Drift to early retirement. E. K. Faltermayer. il Fortune 71:112-15+ My '65

Early retirement gets a big push. Bsns W p 170 S 11 '65

Early retirement: now White House takes a dim view. U S News 59:99-100 N 8 '65

Early retirement plan scores big; Big three-UAW pension innovations. il Bsns W p 166+ My 22 '65

RETIREMENT from business, etc.—*Continued*
For better, for worse, but not for lunch. P. McGinley. Ladies Home J 82:34+ F '65
Let's help farmers retire early. E. L. Butz. Farm J 89:20+ Mr '65
Retirement to leisure; adaptation of address, September 1964. V. Musselman. Recreation 58:239-40+ My '65
What they work at after they quit working. il Time 86:90+ N 26 '65
When should you retire? il Changing T 19:31-3 My '65
Where life begins at sixty-five; Rossmoor leisure world. P. Friggens. Read Digest 88: 157-8+ Ja '66
See also
Old age pensions
Pensions, Industrial
Retirement, Places of

RETIREMENT housing. See Aged—Housing

RETIREMENT income
How can you fight inflationary pressures when you retire? Bet Hom & Gard 44:8+ Ja '66
How workers like early retirement. il U S News 59:96-8+ O 18 '65

RETIREMENT systems. See Pensions, Industrial

RETOUCHING. See Photography—Retouching

RETRAINING programs. See Employees—Training

RETREADING of tires. See Tires, Automobile—Retreading and recapping

RETREAT from the sea; story. See Morris, T.

RETREATS, Spiritual
Christian ashrams in India; disciplined rule of worship, meditation. R. P. Beaver. Christian Cent 82:887-9 Jl 14 '65; Reply. E. S. Jones. 82:1160-2+ S 22 '65; Rejoinder. 82:1357-8 N 3 '65
United Christian ashrams. W. W. Richardson. Christian Cent 82:1020 Ag 18 '65

RETRIEVER trials. See Field trials (dogs)

RETRIEVERS
Trial or hunting retriever? D. M. Duffey. il Outdoor Life 136:110-13 D '65
See also
Labrador dogs

Training
See Dogs—Training

RETTALIATA, John T.
College teacher and the student. Sch & Soc 93:349-50 O 2 '65
University of science and technology. Sch & Soc 93:225 Ap 3 '65

RETURNS policy of booksellers. See Booksellers and bookselling—Returns policy

REUNIFICATION question, German. See Germany—Union (proposed)

REUSS, Henry S.
Let the U.N. handle it. Commonweal 82:523-6 Jl 23 '65
Research: the midas touch. Nation 202:69-71 Ja 17 '66
We need an American ombudsman. Christian Cent 82:269-71 Mr 3 '65

about
Reuss committee: new probe planned into priorities for R&D. D. S. Greenberg. Science 150:1565-6 D 17 '65

REUTHER, Walter Philip
How tough is Walter Reuther? J. R. Moskin. il pors Look 29:83-4+ Ag 10 '65
Labor's hardening arteries. T. R. Brooks. Duns R 86:45-7 Ag '65
Next IUD target: the working poor. por Bsns W p62+ N 13 '65
Push for full employment. T. R. Brooks. Duns R 85:33+ My '65
Reuther pours old zip into new campaigns. il por Bsns W p92+ N 20 '65
Reuther pushes toward an old goal. Bsns W p 128 F 20 '65
Reuther's offer to IUE: one stronger union. por Bsns W p28 F 13 '65
Walter Reuther looks ahead. U S News 59:88 N 29 '65

REVEL, Jean François
French revolution has been lost. N Y Times Mag p28-9+ N 7 '65

REVELATION
Uses of ambiguity; schema on revelation and the Declaration on religious liberty. il Time 86:78 N 5 '65

REVENUE bonds. See Bonds, Revenue

REVERBERATION. See Acoustics, Architectural

REVERSAL of time. See Time reversal

REVIEWS of books. See Book reviews

REVISED standard version of the Holy Bible. See Bible—Versions

REVLON, incorporated
Beauty with all the answers; Revlon research center. il Vogue 146:110-13 Ag 1 '65
New beauty university; Revlon research center opened. Vogue 146:36 Ag 1 '65
Vitamins for Revlon; wants to acquire U.S. vitamin & pharmaceutical corp. Time 86:75 Ag 27 '65

REVOLUTIONARY war (United States) See United States—History—Revolution

REVOLUTIONS
Bankruptcy of the liberals; address, November 27, 1965; with reply by P. Steinfels. C. Oglesby. Commonweal 83:396-401 Ja 7 '66
Counterinsurgency; political action required; address, July 9, 1965. R. F. Kennedy. Vital Speeches 31:649-52 Ag 15 '65
Iraq: seven years of revolution. G. Lenczowski. bibliog f Cur Hist 48:281-9+ My '65
Latin America and revolution. J. A. Mackay. Christian Cent 82:1409-12 N 17 '65
See also
Government, Resistance to

REVOLVERS
Colt model 1849 pocket revolver. W. R. Orbelo. il Hobbies 69:127 F '65
Colt's old model belt pistol. C. G. Worman. il Hobbies 70:122-3 Jl '65
Formidable Le Mat. C. G. Worman. il Hobbies 70:112+ Je '65
Schofield model Smith and Wesson. C Worman. il Hobbies 70:122-3 O '65

REVOLVING apartment houses. See Apartment houses

REVOLVING charge accounts. See Charge accounts (retail trade)

REW, Robert
Compatible. New Yorker 41:29-30 Je 12 '65

REWARDS, prizes, etc.
ALA invites 1966 awards nominations. Library J 90:5488-9 D 15 '65
Anna Freud receives White House award; Dolley Madison award for outstanding service to children. Sci N L 88:265 O 23 '65
Award-winning children's books. D. E. Leland. il Parents Mag 40:153 N '65
Awards. See issues of Wilson library bulletin
Fifteen books honored in Children's spring festival .Pub W 187:41-2 My 10 '65
Foundations: a welfare state for writers? D. Dempsey. Harper 231:165-71 O '65
Four projects vie for engineering award. Am City 80:177+ Mr '65
France presents its 1965 literary prizes. H. R. Lottman. il Pub W 188:32-7 D 27 '65
Governor Carl Sanders and Miss Emma; Golden key award. J. Shepherd. il Look 29:46+ F 23 '65
Grants, fellowships, and awards. See occasional issues of Science
Honoring the consensus. Nation 200:518 My 17 '65
Lifetime contribution, first newspaperman to win Evinrude award. B. Robinson. Yachting 117:60+ Mr '65
Literary prizes and awards, 1965. Pub W 189: 94-9 Ja 17 '66
Nominations sought for 1966 ALA awards. Library J 90:5230-4 D 1 '65
Prize offers and awards. See issues of Writer
Prizes and awards. See issues of Publishers' weekly
Publishers and printers win awards. il Pub W 188:84+ O 4 '65
Teachers' writing contest. NEA J 54:12-14 O '65
Under the rhubarb plant; France. il Time 86:43 D 10 '65
Unforeseen development on Mount Parnassus; awards of poetry prizes. D. Dempsey. Sat R 48:29 Mr 13 '65. Reply. M. Cowley. 48:21 Ap 3 '65
Year for teen-agers; 25th Peabody awards. Time 85:61 My 7 '65
Young scientists cited; winners of Arthur S. Flemming awards. Sci N L 87:116 F 20 '65
See also
Mademoiselle (periodical)
Poetry (periodical)
also names of organizations, societies, etc. granting awards, e.g. Mystery writers of America; *also* names of awards, e.g. Newbery medal

Anecdotes, facetiae, satire, etc.
For unsung heroes; Lj awards. J. Berry. Library J 90:5354 D 15 '65

REXALL drug and chemical company
Rexall Darts ahead. Newsweek 66:75 Jl 19 '65

REXROTH, Kenneth
Affluence; poem. Nation 201:481 D 13 '65
Chinese poems. Nation 201:425 N 29 '65
Classics revisited. Sat R 48:19 Mr 20; 17
  Mr 27; 18 Ap 3; 27 Ap 10; 27 My 1; 19 My
  15; 17 My 29; 15 Je 5; 29 Je 12; 19 Je 26;
  19 Jl 10; 21 Ag 14; 20 Ag 28; 31+ S 11;
  29 S 18; 25 O 2; 40 N 13; 27 N 27; 27 D 11
  '65; 49:19 Ja 1 '66
New American poets. Harper 230:65-7+ Je
  '65
Thar's culture in them thar hills. N Y Times
  Mag p28-9+ F 7 '65
William Golding. Atlan 215:96-8 My '65
REY, Madeleine Schlag-. See Schlag-Rey, M.
REYES, Gustavo de los
Imprisoned by Castro. Read Digest 86:114-18
  My '65
REYES, POINT, Calif.
Revolt in the provinces; BLM vs Oregon.
  J. C. Hunt. il Am For 71:40-1+ Je '65
REYNOLDS, Barbara
In witness to man's oneness. Christian Cent
  83:81 Ja 19 '66
REYNOLDS, Charles
Books for your summer reading. Pot Phot 57:
  108-9+ Jl '65
Films '65. Pop Phot 56:126+ F; 123 Ap; 57:
  129 O '65
Show the world's greatest movies. Pop Phot
  56:108-14 F '65
Three photographers try the Swinger. il Pop
  Phot 57:69 S '65
REYNOLDS, Don B.
Former White House aide's testimony: tie
  between LBJ's insurance and TV ads. por
  U S News 58:10 Mr 8 '65
Senator's insurance. Time 85:20 Mr 5 '65
REYNOLDS, Fred
Sweet and swinging. See issues of American
  record guide
REYNOLDS, Graham
Total immersion in landscape. Art N 64:42-
  5+ O '65
REYNOLDS, Harry W. Jr
(ed) Intergovernmental relations in the
  United States. bibliog f Ann Am Acad 359:
  1-156 My '65
Merit controls, the Hatch acts, and personnel
  standards in intergovernmental relations.
  bibliog f Ann Am Acad 359:81-93 My '65
REYNOLDS, John A. See Gruenwald, A. jt.
  auth.
REYNOLDS, Pat
Carpet composition. Sch Arts 65:36 O '65
REYNOLDS, Paul R.
Author, the publisher and the fifty-fifty split.
  Pub W 189:62-4 Ja 10 '66
I want to know: what does an author earn
  from a book? excerpt from The writing and
  selling of fiction. Writer 78:20-1 D '65
REYNOLDS, Quentin
Jennie; excerpts from Jennie went to the
  country, the Grossinger dream that came
  true. Look 29:86-8+ Jl 13 '65

about
Obituary
  Pub W 187:31-2 Mr 29 '65
REYNOLDS, Richard
Buffalo sculpture for a California high school.
  il por Am Artist 30:54-7+ Ja '66
REYNOLDS, Tim
Belle; poem. Atlan 216:128 Jl '65
Untitled; poem. Harper 230:69 Je '65
REYNOLDS, William H.
More sense about market segmentation. bib-
  liog f Harvard Bsns R 43:107-14 S '65
REYRE, Jean
Paris-Bas gets around. il Fortune 72:102+
  N '65
REZNIKOFF, Charles
Harmonies. M. Hindus. Commentary 41:76-8+
  Ja '66
RHEE, Syngman
Exile's last return. il por Time 86:25 Jl 30 '65
Tiger goes home. il por Newsweek 66:38 Ag
  2 '65
RHEINFRANK, W. J.
Snow-fighting by careful design. Am City 80:
  98-101 Ag '65
RHESUS factor. See Rh factors
RHESUS monkeys. See Monkeys
RHEUMATIC fever
Rheumatic fever. E. H. Freimer and M.
  McCarty. il Sci Am 213:66-70+ bib-
  liog(p 126+) D '65
Socioeconomic status, rheumatic fever linked.
  Sci N L 88:296 N 6 '65
RHEUMATOID arthritis. See Arthritis
RHINE, Joseph Banks
Science gets serious about E.S.P. D. Cohen.
  il por Sci Digest 58:62-72 N '65

RHINOCEROS
Rhino! D. Reed. il Read Digest 87:222-4+ Jl
  '65
RHINOCEROS; drama. See Ionesco, E.
RHOADS, Cornelius Packard
Unforgettable character of Dusty Rhoads.
  M. W. Lasker. por Read Digest 86:163-4+
  Ap '65
RHODE ISLAND
  See also
Fishing—Rhode Island
Narragansett Bay

Religious institutions and affairs
News of the Christian world (cont) Chris-
  tian Cent 82:503-4, 1456+ Ap 21, N 24 '65
RHODE ISLAND furniture. See Furniture,
  American
RHODE ISLAND school of design, Providence,
  R.I.
R.I.S.D. hypotheses. D. Manzella. il Sch Arts
  65:31-3 S '65
RHODES, Daniel
Japanese pottery; a report. Craft Horiz 25:
  38-40+ Mr '65
Twenty-third ceramic national. Craft Horiz
  25:18-23 Ja '65
RHODES, Lynwood Mark
LBJ country. Travel 123:29-32+ Mr '65
Year of terror. Todays Health 43:46-8+ D '65
RHODES (island)
Rhodes, Julius Caesar cut classes. G. Brad-
  shaw. Vogue 146:73 Ag 15 '65
RHODES scholars and scholarships
Fair Harvard's share. Newsweek 67:48 Ja 3
  66
RHODESIA
Canceling out Rhodesia's threat; neighbor-
  ing nations mapping alternative routes to
  isolate the rebels. il Bsns W p58 D 11 '65
Other, and first, Rhodesians. L. Fellows. il
  N Y Times Mag p36-7+ N 21 '65
Proposed solution to the Rhodesian crisis.
  W. B. George. Christian Cent 83:13-14 Ja
  5 '66
Southern Rhodesia today; address, June 15,
  1965. G. M. Williams. Dept State Bul 53:
  71-6 Jl 12 '65
Tightening the screws on rebellious Rho-
  desia; economic sanctions by Great Britain.
  il Bsns W p40-1 N 20 '65
Tightening the vise on Rhodesia. America
  113:699 D 4 '65
Zambia and Rhodesia: a study in contrast.
  R. Brown. il Cur Hist 48:201-6+ Ap '65
  See also
Elections—Rhodesia
Europeans in Rhodesia
Kariba Lake
United Nations—Rhodesia
United States—Foreign relations—Rhodesia

Economic conditions
And now for oil; economic sanctions. Time
  86:22+ D 24 '65
As U.S. and Britain begin oil squeeze. il U S
  News 60:6 Ja 10 '66
End of the road for whites in Rhodesia? ef-
  fects of economic sanctions. il U S News
  60:52-4 Ja 17 '66
Money & the flag; Britain's attack on the
  Rhodesian pound. Time 86:97 N 26 '65
Of oil & scotch. Time 86:23 D 31 '65
Other side of the Rhodesia story; interview,
  ed. by A. J. Meyers. I. D. Smith. il U S
  News 59:68-72 N 8 '65
Rhodesia creaks along. Newsweek 67:39-40 Ja
  17 '66
Squeeze on Rhodesia: who will really be hurt.
  il U S News 59:42-3 N 29 '65
White Rhodesia: can it survive? il U S News
  59:44-6 N 22 '65
Whites on wheels; Britain's oil embargo. il
  Time 87:33 Ja 7 '66

Foreign relations
Crying wolf: Wilson's brinkmanship. Newsweek 66:62+ N 15 '65
Rhodesia: hope of compromise. il Newsweek
  66:47 N 8 '65

Native races
Eleventh hour in Rhodesia. N. M. Shamuyarira. Nation 201:319-22 N 8 '65

Politics and government
Adding fuel; Organization of African unity
  ultimatum to Britain. il Newsweek 66:34+
  D 27 '65
Africa on the verge. Nation 201:261 O 25
  '65

RHODESIA—Politics and government—*Cont.*

Africa's new Verwoerd; the tightening white grip on Rhodesia; meaning of unilateral declaration of independence. A. Segal. New Repub 153:13-14 S 18 '65

Argument for patience. America 114:32 Ja 8 '66

Atlantic report. Atlan 216:26+ S '65

Bluster, threat, pressure. il Newsweek 66:37+ N 29 '65

Britain gropes for ways to dissolve an empire. il Bsns W p27-8 O 30 '65

Britain is right on Rhodesia. Life 59:4 N 26 '65

Bust or black? il Time 85:40 My 14 '65

Can Britain stop Rhodesia? question of economic sanctions. A. Lejeune. Nat R 18:22-3 Ja 11 '66

Cowboys; men who want independence at any price. P. R. Webb. il Newsweek 66:43 N 1 '65

Crisis in Rhodesia. B. V. Mtshali. America 113:712-13 D 4 '65

Crisis in Rhodesia: what the whites fear. A. J. Meyers. U S News 59:12 N 1 '65

Crying wolf; Wilson's brinkmanship. Newsweek 66:62+ N 15 '65

Decent opinion. Commonweal 83:172 N 12 '65

Defiance of Sir Humphrey. il Time 86:37 N 26 '65

Desperate mission; Rhodesia's threatened independence. il Time 86:31 O 29 '65

Eleventh hour in Rhodesia. N. M. Shamuyarira. Nation 201:319-22 N 8 '65

Fire burn, cauldron bubble. Nat R 17:1062-3 N 30 '65

Future of Rhodesia; extremes of political opinion in Britain. H. Brandon. Sat R 48:9 D 25 '65

Heart of the trouble in Rhodesia. America 113:518 N 6 '65

In Rhodesia, a crisis spills over into Zambia, where the fur hats plot. il Life 59:46-46B D 10 '65

Independence at 5 o'clock? il Time 85:26 Mr 12 '65

Independence day? Prime Minister H. Wilson's efforts to deter Rhodesia. il Newsweek 66:50+ N 22 '65

Lawn bowls and police dogs. J. Hicks. il Life 59:51-2 N 12 '65

Letter from London. M. Panter-Downes. New Yorker 41:198+ N 27; 225 D 11 '65

Letter from Washington. R. H. Rovere. New Yorker 41:201-2 N 20 '65

Many voices; Wilson bedeviled by crisis. Newsweek 66:45 D 20 '65

Mr Smith draws the line in Africa; unilateral declaration of independence. J. Lelyveld. il N Y Times Mag p22+ Ag 22 '65

No, we are not going to let that happen here; situation of white and black man. P. R. Webb. il Newsweek 66:51 N 22 '65

Not since 1776. il Newsweek 66:66 O 18 '65

One kind word; sanctions against Rhodesia making impact. Newsweek 67:29 Ja 10 '66

Opening & closing the door. Time 86:39 N 12 '65

Other side of the Rhodesia story; interview, ed. by A. J. Meyers. I. D. Smith. il U S News 59:68-72 N 8 '65

Outspoken Prince Philip in hot water again. il U S News 59:20 Jl 19 '65

Playing chicken; emergency airlift of oil supplies under way. il Newsweek 67:24 Ja 3 '66

Powder keg in Rhodesia. R. E. Hughes. Christian Cent 82:208-10+, 240+ F 17-24 '65

Rebellion brews in Rhodesia. R. W. Howe. il Reporter 32:26+ Je 3 '65; Reply with rejoinder. D. T. M. Williams. 33:6+ S 9 '65

Rhodesia. Commonweal 83:79-80 O 22 '65

Rhodesia and the archbishop. J. M. Cameron. Commonweal 83:230-1 N 26 '65

Rhodesia at the crossroads. T. Molnar. Nat R 17:971-2 N 2 '65

Rhodesia: eleventh-hour showdown: British prime minister's final effort to stop rebellion. il Newsweek 66:42 N 1 '65

Rhodesia: hope of compromise. il Newsweek 66:47 N 8 '65

Rhodesia makes its move. America 113:617 N 20 '65

Rhodesia: the loneliest country in all the world. il Life 59:38-38B N 26 '65

Rhodesia: the rebel fever rises. il Newsweek 66:43-4 O 25 '65

Rhodesia: unilateral independence; address, October 12, 1965. H. Wilson. Vital Speeches 32:39-41 N 1 '65

Rhodesian breakaway? il Sr Schol 87:16 O 28 '65

Rhodesian rebellion. G. I. Smith; R. W. Howe. il Reporter 33:27-32 D 2 '65

Rhodesian tea party. New Repub 153:7-8 N 27 '65

Rhodesia's next government. R. W. Howe. New Repub 154:15-16 Ja 15 '66

Right around the corner: independence. Time 86:38+ O 15 '65

1776 and all that vs. the data of history. America 113:488 O 30 '65

Sham in Rhodesia; Dissension in Africa. America 113:767-8 D 18 '65

Shortened fuse. il Time 86:34 D 3 '65

Smith's bet. New Repub 153:7 O 23 '65

Some planes arrive; K. Kaunda's demand for British troops. il Time 86:39-40 D 10 '65

Some questions for a friend; leaders of nineteen of the British Commonwealth's nations meet in Lagos. il Time 87:25 Ja 21 '66

Squeeze on Rhodesia: who will really be hurt. il U S News 59:42-3 N 29 '65

Sweat; approaching Washington visits of Harold Wilson and Ayub Khan. New Repub 153:8 D 11 '65

Sword, police dogs and tear gas; first session of Parliament since independence. il Newsweek 66:44 D 6 '65

UDI for Rhodesia. Sr Schol 87:18-19 D 9 '65

U.S. outlines interests in Southern Rhodesia; address, December 16, 1965. G. M. Williams. Dept State Bul 54:13-15 Ja 3 '66

Use of force in world affairs. America 113:662 N 27 '65

Voice of conscience; views of Judy Todd. Newsweek 66:44+ D 6 '65

We want our country. il Time 86:40-2+ N 5 '65

Where whites want to hold on in Africa. A. J. Meyers. il U S News 59:46-8 O 25 '65

White hot; independence wanted. il Time 86:40 O 22 '65

White rebels; sovereign independence. il Time 86:44-5 N 19 '65

White Rhodesia: can it survive? il U S News 59:44-6 N 22 '65

Wilson's razor's edge. R. W. Howe. New Repub 153:17-18 N 20 '65

Win some, lose some; Lagos conference on Rhodesian crisis. il Newsweek 67:39 Ja 24 '66

Race problems

No, we are not going to let that happen here; situation of white and black man. P. R. Webb. il Newsweek 66:51 N 22 '65

Teaching missionaries expelled from Rhodesia. Christian Cent 82:1003 Ag 18 '65

Religious institutions and affairs

Rhodesia's bishops go on record. America 113:740 D 11 '65

Speak-out in Rhodesia. Commonweal 83:297 D 10 '65

RHODODENDRONS

Don't eat the rhododendrons. T. Sterne. il Am For 71:40-1+ Mr '65

Dwarf rhododendrons. V. S. Jefferis. il Horticulture 43:18-19+ Ap '65

Why do rhododendron leaves curl? J. R. Havis. Horticulture 43:17 D '65

RHUBARB

See also

Cookery—Rhubarb

RHYTHM

See also

Eurythmics

RHYTHM bands, Childrens. See Bands, Childrens

RHYTHMIC phenomena. See Periodicity

RIBICOFF, Abraham

Dangerous ones; help for children with twisted minds. Harper 230:88-90 F '65

Gold for the Galloping Goose. Sat R 48:46 Je 12 '65

Harmony on the highways. Atlan 216:80-3 Jl '65

Senator Ribicoff challenges U.S. educational policy; summary of address, May 9, 1965. por Pub W 187:55-6 Je 14 '65

about

At stake: 48,000 lives. Bsns W p29 Mr 27 '65

RIBONUCLEIC acid

Actinomycin D and hydrocortisone: intracellular binding in rat liver. C. W. Dingman and M. B. Sporn. bibliog il Science 149:1251-4 S 10 '65

Active RNA from a test tube. Sci Am 213:50 N '65

Autocatalytic synthesis of a viral RNA in vitro. I. Haruna and S. Spiegelman. bibliog il Science 150:884-6 N 12 '65

Comparison of messenger RNA in photoperiodically induced and noninduced xanthium buds. J. H. Cherry and R. B. Van Huystee. bibliog il Science 150:1450-3 D 10 '65

RIBONUCLEIC acid—_Continued_

Conditional-lethal mutants of an animal virus: identification of two cistrons. B. W. Burge and E. R. Pfefferkorn. bibliog il Science 148:959-60 My 14 '65

Cracking the code. il Newsweek 65:57 Mr 29 '65

Defective RNA synthesis in lymphocytes from patients with primary agammaglobulinemia. M. J. Cline and H. H. Fudenberg. bibliog il Science 150:1311-12 D 3 '65

DNA-dependent synthesis of RNA is not implicated in growth response of chick comb to androgens. G. P. Talwar and others. bibliog il Science 150:1315-16 D 3 '65

DNA, RNA synthesized in lab the easy way. Sci N L 88:53 Jl 24 '65

Differential-approach tendencies produced by injection of RNA from trained rats. A. L. Jacobson and others. il Science 150:636-7 O 29 '65

Enrichment of serine-acceptor soluble RNA by nucleic acid gels. P. P. Hung. bibliog il Science 149:639-40 Ag 6 '65

Gene specificity aided; new kind of RNA discovered. Sci N L 88:227 O 9 '65

Glucose-6-phosphatase: reexamination of the RNA-induced activity in mouse ascites tumor cells. M. C. Niu. bibliog il Science 148:513-16 Ap 23 '65

Hormone-induced stabilization of soluble RNA in pea-stem tissue. F. E. Bendaña and A. W. Galston. bibliog il Science 150: 69-70 O 1 '65

Inactivation by nitrogen mustard of single- and double-stranded DNA and RNA bacteriophages. N. Yamamoto and T. Naito. bibliog il Science 150:1603-4 D 17 '65

Induction in vitro of antibodies to phage T2: antigens in the RNA extract employed. H. P. Friedman and others. bibliog il Science 149:1106-7 S 3 '65

Join links in life chain. Sci N L 88:195 S 25 '65

Key to life closer. F. Marley. Sci N L 87:195 Mr 27 '65

Memory transferred? Sci N L 89:39 Ja 15 '66

Messenger RNA in early sea-urchin embryos: cytoplasmic particles. A. S. Spirin and M. Nemer. bibliog il Science 150:214-17 O 8 '65

Messenger RNA in early sea-urchin embryos: size classes. M. Nemer and A. A. Infante. bibliog il Science 150:217-21 O 8 '65

Nearer the secret of life. il Sci Digest 57: 15-16 Je '65

Neurons of insects: RNA changes during injury and regeneration. M. Cohen and J. W. Jacklet. bibliog il Science 148:1237-9 My 28 '65

Polysomes from yeast: distribution of messenger RNA and capacity to support protein synthesis in vitro. L. Marcus and others. bibliog il Science 147:615-17 F 5 '65

Pseudouridine formation: evidence for RNA as an intermediate. S. B. Weiss and J. Legault-Demare. bibliog il Science 149:429-31 Jl 23 '65

Puromycin: effect on messenger RNA synthesis and β-galactosidase formation in escherichia coli 15T. B. H. Sells. bibliog il Science 148:371-3 Ap 16 '65

RNA codewords and protein synthesis. M. R. Bernfield and M. W. Nirenberg. bibliog il Science 147:479-84 Ja 29 '65

Ribosomes from escherichia coli: lack of specificity for viral RNA. J. E. Dahlberg and R. Haselkorn. bibliog il Science 149:78-80 Jl 2 '65

Secret of life; today's most fascinating mystery story. M. Gunther. il Sat Eve Post 238:25-9 Jl 3 '65

Short- and long-lived messenger RNA in embryonic chick lens. R. Reeder and E. Bell. bibliog il Science 150:71-2 O 1 '65

Spermidine in regenerating liver: relation to rapid synthesis of ribonucleic acid. W. G. Dykstra, jr. and E. J. Herbst. bibliog il Science 149:428 Jl 23 '65

Structure of a genetic molecule. Sci Am 212: 48-50 My '65

Structure of a ribonucleic acid. R. W. Holley and others. bibliog il Science 147:1462-5 Mr 19 '65; Discussion. 148:1410; 150:918-21 Je 11, N 12 '65

Sulfur: incorporation into the transfer fraction of soluble ribonucleic acid. T. Schleich and J. Goldstein. bibliog il Science 150: 1168-70 N 26 '65

Suppression in vitro: identification of a serine-sRNA as a nonsense suppressor. M. R. Capecchi and G. N. Gussin. bibliog il Science 149:417-22 Jl 23 '65

Template activity of RNA from antibody-producing tissues. B. Mach and P. Vassalli. bibliog il Science 150:622-6 O 29 '65

Transfer of a response to naive rats by injection of ribonucleic acid extracted from trained rats. F. R. Babich and others. bibliog il Science 149:656-7 Ag 6 '65; Discussion. 150:228, 1749 O 8, D 24 '65

Turnover of ribosomal RNA in rat liver J. N. Loeb and others. bibliog il Science 149:1093-5 S 3 '65

Vaccinia virus directed RNA: its fate in the presence of actinomycin. A. J. Shatkin and others. bibliog il Science 148:87-90 Ap 2 '65

Where the memory is. il Newsweek 66:70 Ag 23 '65

Will man create life? F. Marley. Sci N L 88:227 O 9 '65

RIBOSOMES. See Nucleoproteins

RICCA, Paul
Oh, to be in England. Newsweek 66:38 N 8 '65

RICCI, Corrado
Letter from an Italian: the final judgment. bibliog Esquire 63:46-7+ Je '65

RICCI, Ruggiero
Gifted child (handle with care) ed. by S. Frank. por McCalls 92:88+ F '65

RICE, Charles E.
Is a prayer amendment coming? Nat R 17: 597-9 Jl 13 '65

—and Feinstein, S. H.
Sonar system of the blind: size discrimination. bibliog Science 148:1107-8 My 21 '65

RICE, Elmer
Author! author! por Am Heritage 16:46-9+ Ap '65
On trial. Criticism
Am Heritage il por 16:46-9+ Ap '65

RICE, Grantland
My most unforgettable character. J. N. Wheeler. por Read Digest 87:99-103 D '65

RICE, Norman S.
Living with antiques. Antiques 88:806-11 D '65

RICE, Patrick J.
Book reviews. America 113:340+ S 25 '65

RICE, Robert
Reporter at large (cont) New Yorker 41: 50-2+ Mr 27 '65

RICE
See also
Cookery—Rice
International rice research institute

RICE, Wild. See Wild rice

RICH, Adrienne
Like this together: poem. Poetry 106:109-11 Ap '65
Reflections on Lawrence. Poetry 106:218-25 Je '65

RICH, Alan
Carmina Burana (but not by Orff) Hi Fi 15:88 Mr '65
Criticism disarmed, or the art of Maggie Teyte. Hi Fi 15:57-8 My '65
Disc for history, knowledge enhanced, esteem confirmed. Hi Fi 15:60 Je '65
From Furtwängler; the true Brucknerian affinity. Hi Fi 15:78-9 S '65
Golden horseshoe. Opera N 30:6 O 23 '65
Great Glagolitic mass, pagan, Christian, intensely personal. Hi Fi 15:66-7 Ag '65
Kurt Weill's Mahagonny. Hi Fi 15:158-9 S '65
Monoliths, flourishing and busy. Hi Fi 15:115 Jl '65
Schubert's symphonies, the scores corrected and a finish for the Unfinished. Hi Fi 16: 73-4 Ja '66
Singing actress. Opera N 29:26-7 Mr 6 '65

RICH, Leslie
Music for non-listening. Hi Fi 15:34+ N '65
Tempest in a milk carton. Duns R 86:pt2 101-6+ D '65

RICH, Marvin
Congress of racial equality and its strategy. Ann Am Acad 357:113-18 Ja '65

RICH, Richard C.
Planning a downtown parking deck. Arch Rec 137:177-82 My '65

RICH, The
Some reflections on the rich. L. Bart. Mlle 62:130+ D '65
See also
Millionaires

RICH HOLE country wilderness area (proposed) See Wilderness areas

RICHARD, Adrienne
One Christmas in Montana; story. Harper 231:102-6 D '65

RICHARD, Melvin
Elliott for mayor too. il Time 85:22 Mr 5 '65

RICHARD III; drama. See Shakespeare, W.— Plays

RICHARDS, Ben
D.C.-operated fluorescent light. Pop Electr 23:40-2 Jl '65

RICHARDS, Mary Caroline
Centering: toward a new humanism. E.
Navaretta. Craft Horiz 25:37+ Mr '65
World and self: instances. G. Sorrentino.
Poetry 106:308-9 Jl '65
RICHARDSON, Carol T.
Glittering novelties, easy to do. Design 67:
35 N '65
RICHARDSON, E. C. See Meggitt, W. jt. auth.
RICHARDSON, Eugene S. Jr
Wormlike fossil from the Pennsylvanian of
Illinois. Science 151:75-6 Ja 7 '66
RICHARDSON, Hugh F. See Ausland, J. C. jt.
auth.
RICHARDSON, Jack
Lincoln Center: act II. Commentary 41:55-6+
Ja '66
Poker. Esquire 64:144+ D '65
Xmas in Las Vegas. Criticism
Commonweal 83:243 N 26 '65
New Yorker 41:154+ N 13 '65
RICHARDSON, John, Jr
Colonization of the Lanikai Hills; poem.
Horn Bk 41:206 Ap '65
RICHARDSON, Robert S.
Discovery of Icarus; with biographical sketch
Sci Am 212:20, 106-15 bibliog(p 158+) Ap
'65
RICHARDSON, S. Dennis
Forestry in red China: modern-day Marco
Polo visits China. Am For 71:6-15+ F '65
RICHARDSON, Walter F.
Attracting and training junior leaders. por
Recreation 58:197 Ap '65
RICHARDSON, William J.
Book review. America 113:604 N 13 '65
RICHARDSON BAY wildlife sanctuary, Calif.
See Bird sanctuaries
RICHELIEU, Armand Jean du Plessis, car-
dinal, duc
For the glory of France. C. V. Wedgwood.
il por Horizon 7:20-9 Sum '65
RICHEY, Cliff
Highest ranking family in tennis. F. Deford.
il por Sports Illus 23:47-51 Jl 5 '65
RICHEY, George, family
All in the family; Richeys of Dallas. il por
Newsweek 66:62 Ag 2 '65
RICHEY, Nancy
Highest ranking family in tennis. F. Deford.
il por Sports Illus 23:47-51 Jl 5 '65
RICHIER, Xavier
French menus and master thieves. H. Frankel.
Sat R 49:79 Ja 8 '66
RICHLAND, Wash.
Town that wouldn't stay down; Richland,
Wash. and its sister cities. il U S News
59:96-7 Jl 19 '65
RICHLER, Mordecai
Catskills: land of milk and money. Holiday
38:56-63+ Jl '65
Pop goes the island. Commentary 39:67-70 My
'65
RICHMOND, Samuel S.
His first patient; drama. Plays 24:29-34 Ap
'65
RICHMOND, Va.

Education

What's new in business education? John
Marshall high school. il NEA J 54:12-13
Ap '65

Galleries and museums
See also
Virginia museum of fine arts

Newspapers

Spoofing the despots; Richmond news leader's
Beadle bumble fund. Time 87:47 Ja 21 '66
RICHTER, Conrad
Light in the forest; story. Read Digest 87:
207-10 Ag '65
RICHTER, Karl
Great recording by that other Richter. R.
Kammerer. Am Rec G 31:998 Je '65
RICHTER, Sviatoslav Teofilovich. See Rikhter,
S. T.
RICHWOOD, W.Va.
Cranberry Glades; scenic area. J. C. Beh-
rens. il Am For 71:12-13+ D '65
RICKARD, George Lewis
That was New York. A. Logan. New Yorker
41:80+ F 27 '65
RICKENBACKER, William F.
And still our enemy. por Nat R 17:1082-3
N 30 '65
Open question. por Nat R 17:877 O 5 '65
Reform or tinkering? Nat R 18:78-9 Ja 25 '66
RICKEY, Branch
Innovator. por Newsweek 66:58 D 20 '65
Mahatma. il por Time 86:76 D 17 '65

RICKING, Myrl
Recruitment (cont) ALA Bul 59:750-2, 835
S-O '65
—and Blasingame, Ralph, Jr
Recruitment. por Library J 90:2750-1 Je 15 '65
RICKMAN, Eric
Rooster tales. See issues of Hot rod
RIDDLE, Mrs C. A.
Royal fantasies. S. Bowen. il por Design 66:
32-5 Mr '65
RIDE a cock horse; drama. See Mercer, D.
RIDE your hobby; drama. See Fontaine, R.
RIDEAU CANAL
Cruising the Rideau. F. M. Paulson. il Field
& S 70:40-3 Ja '66
RIDENOUR, Margaret Murray
Spatter prints. Flower Grower 52:20-2 Ag '65
RIDGES, Ocean. See Ocean bottom
RIDGEWAY, James F.
Air, etc, we breathe. New Repub 152:36 Ap
17 '65
Atlanta fights poverty. New Repub 152:12-14
My 29 '65
Attack on Detroit. New Repub 152:13-14 Mr
6 '65
Feeling dizzy? New Repub 153:15-16 S 25 '65
How to cut down on pesticides. New Repub
152:11-12 Mr 27 '65
Johnson's model city. New Repub 152:15-18
F 13 '65
Lost Indians. New Repub 153:17-20 D 4 '65
More lost Indians. New Repub 153:19-22 D
11 '65
Not so educational TV. New Repub 153:16-18
Ag 21 '65
On the Mekong. New Repub 152:13-14 Ap 24
'65
Poor Chicago. New Repub 152:17-20 My 15;
27-9 Je 12 '65
Regulating natural gas in Texas. New Repub
152:11-12 F 20 '65
Snooping through the mails. New Repub 152:
11-13 Mr 20 '65
Standards to protect the buying public. New
Repub 152:9-10 My 1 '65
10,000,000 bottles. New Repub 153:12-14 N 6
'65
Way is hard for union insurgents. New Re-
pub 152:9-10 F 27 '65
Who's fit to serve? New Repub 152:9-11 Mr
13 '65
RIDGWAY, Matthew B.
1956 warning on land war in Asia; excerpts
from Soldier, ed. by H. H. Martin. por U S
News 60:32-3 Ja 3 '66
RIDING. See Horseback trips; Horsemanship
RIECKHOFF, Klaus E. and Peticolas, W. L.
Optical second-harmonic generation in crys-
talline amino acids. bibliog Science 147:610-
11 F 5 '65
RIENOW, Leona Train. See Rienow, R. jt.
auth.
RIENOW, Robert, and Rienow, L. T.
Last chance for the Nations waterways. Sat
R 48:35-6+ My 22 '65
Notes of a highwayman. Sat R 48:53-4+ Ap
10 '65
RIESEL, Victor
Boss nobody knows. Sat R 48:65-6 N 13 '65
RIESELBACH, Leroy N. See Deutsch, K. W.
jt. auth.
RIESSMAN, Frank
Lessons of poverty. por Am Ed 1:21-3 F '65
Mobilizing the poor. Commonweal 82:285-9 My
21 '65
RIETH, Marian
Lake-lover; story. Seventeen 24:138-9 S '65
Pitch, pass and dribble; story. Seventeen
24:154-5 Mr '65
RIFLE ranges. See Shooting ranges
RIFLES
Are you ready? W. Page. il Field & S 70:102-8
Jl '65
Billion dollar rifle; M-14 outmoded for army.
J. Morschauser. il Look 29:80+ F 23 '65
Changing sights on infantry rifles; Pentagon
trying to decide on new basic infantry
weapon. il Bsns W p80+ O 16 '65
Know your big-game rifle. J. O'Connor. il
Outdoor Life 136:70+ N '65
Now you can buy a hot combat rifle for
sport. P. Wahl. il Pop Sci 186:171 F '65
.35 caliber family. W. Page. il Field & S
69:126-31 Ap '65
.25's, dead or alive W. Page. il Field & S
70:66-70 Ag '65
U.S. model 1855 small arms. C. G. Worman.
il Hobbies 70:122-3 Ag '65
Year of the $300 sporter. W. Page. il Field &
S 70:110-14 Je '65
See also
Scabbards

RIFT valleys
Huge undersea valley found in Indian Ocean.
 Sci N L 87:296 My 8 '65
See also
Great Rift Valley
RIGGING. See Masts and rigging
RIGGS, Austen
Hemoglobin polymerization in mice. bibliog
 Science 147:621-3 F 5 '65
RIGHT and left (political science)
Beatnik unrest baffles LBJ. P. Lisagor. il
 Nations Bsns 53:23-4 Je '65
Bias in book reviewing and book selection.
 H. Regnery. ALA Bul 60:57-62 Ja '66
Danger of extremism. J. Moorhead. NEA J
 54:17 S '65
Explosive revival of the far left. R. Arm-
 strong. il Sat Eve Post 238:27-32+ My 8
 '65
Extremism in American politics. A. M.
 Schlesinger. il Sat R 48:21-5 N 27 '65
Freedom to read and the political problem;
 activities of right wing or radical right in
 American politics; address, January 1965.
 W. McCune. ALA Bul 59:500-8 Je '65
Honor bright and all that jazz. D. Trumbo.
 Nation 201:183-90 S 20 '65
In the hearts of the right, Goldwater lives!
 B. H. Bagdikian. il N Y Times Mag p6-7+
 Jl 18 '65
New look on the left: solidarity forever?
 il Newsweek 65:29-32 My 24 '65
New radicals in Dixie; those subversive civil
 rights workers. A. Kopkind. New Repub
 152:13-16 Ap 10 '65: Discussion. 152:30-1+
 My 1 '65
Paranoid style in American politics and other
 essays, by R. Hofstadter. Review
 Sat R 48:37-8 D 25 '65. J. M. Burns
Radicals on the march; but where to, and
 by what route? A. Kopkind. New Repub
 153:15-19 D 11 '65
To the right of reason: the patrioteers con-
 vene. R. R. Coffey. il Nation 200:520-1 My
 17 '65
White hate groups. J. N. Woodford. il Ebony
 20:38-40+ Ag '65
Why I quit the extreme left. P. A. Luce.
 Sat Eve Post 238:32-3 My 8 '65
See also
Conservatism
Free university of New York
Liberalism
RIGHT and wrong. See Ethics
RIGHT ascension and declination (astronomy)
 See Astronomy, Spherical and practical
RIGHT honourable gentleman; drama. See
 Dyne, M.
RIGHT of asylum. See Asylum, Right of
RIGHT of privacy. See Privacy
RIGHT to counsel
Confusion on confessions; ruling of U.S. Court
 of appeals in Philadelphia. Time 85:52 Je 4
 '65
Of families & fools. Time 85:57 Mr 19 '65
RIGHT to labor
See also
Discrimination in employment
RIGHT to travel. See Travel regulations
RIGHT to work laws. See Labor laws and leg-
 islation—United States
RIGHT wing (politics) See Right and left (po-
 litical science)
RIGHTS, Bill of (United States) See United
 States—Constitution—Bill of rights
RIGHTS, Civil. See Civil rights
RIGHTS, Personal. See Civil rights
RIGHTS, Property. See Real property
RIGHTS of women. See Woman—Equal rights
RIHA, Jeanne
Peace in an age of revolution. Bul Atomic
 Sci 21:39-40 O '65
RIJVEN, A. H. G. C. See Kefford. N. P. jt.
 auth.
RIKER, Audrey Palm. See Burns, J. T. jt.
 auth.
RIKHOFF, J. C.
Full house on leopards. por Outdoor Life 136:
 56-9+ O '65
RIKHTER, Sviatoslav Teofilovich
Richter on Scriabin; interview, ed. by F.
 Bowers. por Sat R 48:58-9 Je 12 '65
 about
Music to my ears; Richter's return. I. Kolo-
 din. Sat R 48:32 My 1 '65
Sviatoslav Richter returns. A. Chasins. por
 Hi Fi 15:100-1 Jl '65
RILEY, Bridget
Perception is the medium. por Art N 64:32-
 3+ O '65

RILEY, David
Who is Jimmie Lee Jackson? New Repub
 152:8 Ap 3 '65
RILEY, Nord
Cooking your own goose. Outdoor Life 136:
 42-3+ D '65
RILEY virus. See Viruses
RILLING, Mark, and McDiarmid, Colin
Signal detection in fixed-ratio schedules. bib-
 liog Science 148:526-7 Ap 23 '65
RIMSKII-KORSAKOV, Nikolai Andreevich
Scheherazade by Stokowski. J. Lyons. il Am
 Rec G 31:622-3 Mr '65
Stokowski's Scheherazade. R. D. Darrell. il
 Hi Fi 15:8-87 Mr '65
RINEHART, John S.
Earth tremors generated by Old Faithful
 geyser. bibliog Science 150:494-6 O 22 '65
RING-billed gulls. See Gulls
RING of the Nibelung; opera. See Wagner, R.
RING; story. See Smith, A.
RINGER, Alexander L.
Lives of Kodály. Sat R 48:33-4 Jl 31 '65
RINGER, Barbara A.
No place for poetic license; the copyright
 office at LC. por Library J 90:2958-63 Jl
 '65
RINGER, Vivian
Simple no; story. Redbook 125:52-3 My '65
RINGGENBERG, Harold
Quilting party. Design 67:38-9 N '65
Vanishing color. Design 66:27-9 My '65
RINGLING brothers
Florida's three-ring city; Ringling memora-
 bilia remains in Sarasota. H. Sutton. il
 Sat R 48:64+ O 16 '65
RINGLING brothers, Barnum and Bailey circus.
 See Circus
RINGLING brothers circus. See Circus
RINGOLD, Evelyn S.
Parent and child (cont) N Y Times Mag
 p59-60 Je 13; 109-10 S 19 '65
RINGS
Gold in those fingers; class rings. il News-
 week 65:74-5 Je 7 '65
Silver band rings. B. Proese. il Sch Arts
 64:18-19 Mr '65
RINGS of trees. See Tree rings
RINGWORM
Now, new treatment for athlete's foot. Good
 H 161:164 S '65
To wipe out athlete's foot. Time 86:102 N 19
 '65
RINKS, Skating. See Skating rinks
RIO DE JANEIRO
Birthday thoughts; 400th anniversary. il
 Newsweek 65:46 Mr 8 '65
Oozing death; torrential rains. Time 87:39
 Ja 21 '66
 See also
Stock exchange—Rio de Janeiro

        Description
Marvelous city: Rio's 400th anniversary. J.
 Guimarães. il Américas 17:1-10 Mr '65
On the railroad named delight. E. Bishop.
 il N Y Times Mag p30-1+ Mr 7 '65

        History
Marvelous city: Rio's 400th anniversary. J.
 Guimarães. il Américas 17:1-10 Mr '65

     Social life and customs
Rio de Janeiro: carnival and beach. J. Sims.
 il Sat R 49:86-8 Ja 1 '66
RIO DE JANEIRO flood. See Floods—Brazil
RIO GRANDE VALLEY
Visit to the living Pueblos. il Sunset 135:64-71
 S '65
RIORDAN, William F.
Swinging Salisbury. Newsweek 65:65 F 22 '65
RIORDAN, William G.
Profile of a swimming pool manager. por Rec-
 reation 58:297 Je '65
RIOTS
Bikies' fun; Weirs Beach, N.H. il Newsweek
 66:21 Jl 5 '65
Come to the riot. See Weirs Beach burn. M.
 Mok. il Life 59:88-9 Jl 2 '65
Embassies undergo attacks. il Sr Schol 86:
 18-19 Mr 18 '65
Long hot summer; concerning racial con-
 flict. New Repub 153:7-8 Jl 3 '65
Nobody wants to hear that nonsense in Har-
 lem; excerpts from television discussion.
 C. Brown; N. Podhoretz. New Repub 153:
 20 O 16 '65

RIOTS—*Continued*
U.S. embassies are under siege; the record of outrages and the protocol of protection; with editorial comment. il Life 58:4, 38-38B Mr 19 '65
Worldwide plague of city riots: a British view; reprint. Harper 231:44+ N '65
See also subhead Riots under names of countries, cities, etc. e.g. United States—Riots

RIPENING of fruit. See Fruit—Ripening

RIPLEY, S. Dillon
Saving the nene, world's rarest goose. por Nat Geog Mag 128:744-54 N '65

about

Powerhouse in the attic. D. Martin. il por Life 59:98+ N 19 '65
Smithsonian: under new secretary it is seeking to regain place as center for scientific research. D. S. Greenberg. il por Science 147:1266-9 Mr 12 '65
There's a windmill in the attic. D. S. Greenberg. por Sat R 48:48-50 Je 5 '65; Reply. C. G. Abbot. 48:58 S 4 '65

RIPON society. See Political clubs and associations

RISE and fall of the city of Mahagonny; opera. See Weill, K.

RISING Hill secondary school, England. See Schools—England

RISNER, James Robinson
Down in Thanh Hoa. por Time 86:28 S 24 '65
Fighting American. il por Time 85:22-3 Ap 23 '65

RITCHIE, Daniel L.
How to win star billing for an S&L. il por Bsns W p90-2 My 1 '65

RITES and ceremonies
See also
Hazing
Mourning customs

Brazil

Afro-Brazilian rites. J. Elbein. il Américas 17:16-19 Je '65

Congo (capital Leopoldville)

Death and the law in Bena Kanyoka. D. A. McLean. Reporter 33:44-5 D 2 '65

RITES of spring; ballet. See Ballets—Criticisms

RITNER, Peter
Problem of sanctions. Commonweal 82:315-19 My 28 '65

RITSCHL, Dietrich
Ecumenical confusion. Christian Cent 82:304-5 Mr 10 '65

RITTER, Colin
Walkin' and hollerin'. Am For 71:6-7+ Je '65

RITTER, Enrichetta
Pomodoro: the jewelry of Arnaldo and Giò. Craft Horiz 25:8-11 Jl '65

RITTER, Hope, Jr
Blood of a cockroach: unusual cellular behavior. bibliog Science 147:518-19 Ja 29 '65

RITTER, Lewis A.
Scum yields to a screw conveyor. Am City 80:108-9 Je '65

RITTS, R. E. Jr
Research with the brakes off. Todays Health 43:41-2 N '65

RITUAL. See Catholic church—Liturgy and ritual; Litanies; Liturgies

RITZ, Charles C.
Ritz has a cast system. J. Olsen. il pors Sports Illus 23:122-4+ S 20 '65

RIVER cement company. See Cement industry and trade

RIVER herring. See Alewives (fishes)

RIVER traffic
See also
St Lawrence Seaway

RIVER trips
Across Florida by outboard. E. White. il Yachting 117:62-3+ F '65
Barges on the Seine. C. Frankel. il Harper 230:60-5 My '65
Get a boat! let her float! C. G. Simonds. il Sr Schol 86:sup21 Ap 15 '65
Outboard cruising is in; adventure on the TVA's waterways. L. W. Bennett. il Motor B 115:35-7+ Ap '65
Pooling the pleasures of cruising; Mississippi River cruise. il Motor B 115:80+ Je '65
Yankee cruises the storied Nile. I. Johnson and E. Johnson. il Nat Geog Mag 127:583-633 My '65
See also
Canoe trips

RIVERA, Diego
Diego Rivera in San Francisco. il Sunset 136:37+ Ja '66

RIVERA, José Eustasio
Two novels of the Amazon. E. S. Urbanski. il Américas 17:33-8 Mr '65

RIVERHOUSE publishing company
New publishing company opens in Providence. Pub W 187:49 Mr 1 '65

RIVERS, Helen W.
Child's world opens wide. Horn Bk 41:81-5 F '65

RIVERS, Joan
For Joan, the woe must go on. C. L. Mee, jr. il pors N Y Times Mag p 137+ O 31 '65
Funny girl. por Newsweek 65:96+ Mr 22 '65

RIVERS, Larry
Jam session. il por Newsweek 65:86 Ap 26 '65
Larry Rivers' history of the Russian revolution; retrospective at the Jewish museum, New York. T. B. Hess. il Art N 64:36-7+ O '65
Quipster. il por Time 85:94-5 Ap 16 '65
Rivers' commedia dell' arte. H. Rosenberg. il Art N 64:35-7+ Ap '65

RIVERS, Lucius Mendel
He's gone, Mr Secretary. por Time 85:25A-25B Je 18 '65
New House foe fires on McNamara. por Bsns W p24-5 Jl 3 '65
Rivers delivers. D. Oberdorfer. il pors N Y Times Mag p30-1+ Ag 29 '65

RIVERS
Billions to clean up the rivers; industries and cities will have to split a huge tab. il Bsns W p50-2+ Ap 24 '65
Float trips U.S.A. A. J. McClane. il Field & S 70:102-7+ O; 86-93 N '65
On saving some wild rivers. C. W. Buchheister. Audubon Mag 67:181 My '65
Shall our wild rivers be eternally dammed? dam builders vs conservationists. R. Starnes. Field & S 69:14+ Mr '65
Washington newsletter; bill introduced to establish National wild rivers system. P. M. Tilden. Natur Hist 74:62 Ag '65
Wild rivers. Nat Parks Mag 39:20 Je '65
Wild rivers bill needs help. C. H. Callison. Audubon Mag 67:184 My '65
See also
Floods
Water pollution

Photographs

See also
Photography of rivers

Regulation

Missouri barges, dams ready for record thaw. Bsns W p67 Mr 13 '65

RIVERSIDE, Calif.
One-stop center for buying cars; Riverside auto center. il Bsns W p92-4 O 16 '65

RIVERSIDE, Calif, public library
Riverside in yellow brick. E. L. Farwell. il Library J 90:5161-3 D 1 '65

RIVETS and riveting
Now it's a cinch to clinch rivets and wall anchors. il Pop Sci 186:145 My '65

RIVIERA
Private seacoast in Italy; explorer in the Cinque Terre. J. Egan. il Sat R 48:42-3+ Mr 13 '65
Riviera treat: St Paul de Vence. il Sunset 135:8 N '65
You walk from village to village; Italy's Riviera. di Levante. il Sunset 134:50+ Mr '65

RIVIÈRE, André
Santo Domingo's activist adventurers. M. Clos. il Reporter 32:29-31 Je 17 '65

RIVKIN, Arnold
Lost goals in Africa. For Affairs 44:111-26 O '65
Organization of African unity; excerpts from Nation-building in Africa. bibliog f Cur Hist 48:193-200+ Ap '65

RIVKIN, Malcolm D.
Urban renewal. Commentary 40:76-7 Jl '65

RIVLIN, Harry N.
Where the talent goes. Sat R 48:89-90 F 20 '65

RIZKI, Rose M. and Rizki, T. M.
Morphogenetic effects of 6-azauracil and 6-azauridine. bibliog Science 150:222-3 O 8 '65

RIZKI, T. M. See Rizki, R. M. jt. auth.

RIZZOLI, Angelo
Molto, molto, molto. New Yorker 41:37-9 My 1 '65

RIZZOLI editore. See Publishers and publishing—Italy

ROACHE, James
California rancher. il pors Ebony 21:77-8+ Ja '66

ROAD accidents. See Traffic accidents

ROAD dividers. See Roads—Safety guards

ROAD guards. See Roads—Safety guards

ROAD law. See Highway law

ROAD signs
Fire signs go unnoticed. Sci N L 88:68 Jl 31 '65
Stupid highway signs can kill. L. D. Adams. il Pop Sci 186:104-8+ My '65

ROAD traffic
Exercise in slow motion. C. W. Morton. il Atlan 216:148+ O '65
See also
Radio broadcasting—Traffic reports

Radar control
Slow down, radar ahead! D. Wharton. il Read Digest 88:138-40+ Ja '66

England
Atlantic report. Atlan 216:43-4+ O '65
Our far-flung correspondents; road and the meadow in Oxford. A. Bailey. il New Yorker 41:129-30+ My 8 '65

ROAD transport. See Transportation, Automotive

ROADS
Roads in animal refuges. P. M. Tilden. Nat Parks Mag 39:2 My '65
See also
Tunnels and tunneling

Federal aid
Milestone; U.S. interstate road program. il Newsweek 66:56 Ag 2 '65

Finance
See also
Toll roads

Law
See Highway law

Lighting
Double-duty lights service new freeway link; Detroit, Mich. H. F. Wall. il Am City 80:115 F '65

Safety devices and measures
Hidden persuaders. W. M. Hall. il Am For 71:54-7 My '65
How to reduce road deaths with little spending. il U S News 58:58 Mr 1 '65
Life & death on U.S. 66. Changing T 19:10-12 Je '65
Rumble strips jar dreamy drivers; Contra Costa County, Calif. M. Kermit. il Am City 80:94-5 N '65
Tiny trees help keep expressways safe. Sci N L 87:72 Ja 30 '65

Safety guards
Ceramic granules protect guard rail. il Am City 81:39 Ja '66
Flexible guard posts; Cuyahoga Falls, Ohio. il Am City 80:117 My '65
New road barriers for safety; steel guard rails. W. McCann. il Sci N L 88:38+ Jl 17 '65

Superhighways
See Express highways

Arizona
Time saver on the Arizona border; north of Grand Canyon. il Sunset 135:27-8 O '65

Asia
Great Asian highway. M. S. Ahmad. il UNESCO Courier 18:12-17 Je '65

Brazil
On the road to dreams; effects of Belém to Brasília highway. il Time 87:34 Ja 7 '66

California
Four-lane menace to California's redwoods. L. P. Hudson. il Reporter 33:34-8 Ag 12 '65

Canada
Going to Quebec? here's a new route. J. T. Starr. il Am For 71:30-1+ Jl '65
Quebec prefabs a highway link; seven-section tunnel to link Quebec to 5,000-mile Trans-Canada highway. il Bsns W p 156 F 20 '65

Central America
See also
Pan American highway

Connecticut
Linseed oil cuts spalling damage; Connecticut state highway department. R. L. Booth. il Am City 80:96-7 S '65

England
Our far-flung correspondents; road and the meadow in Oxford. A. Bailey. il New Yorker 41:129-30+ My 8 '65

Germany (Federal Republic)
Eine kleine autobahn keeps traffic moving; West Germany's aging expressway system. il Bsns W p84+ My 15 '65

Great Britain
Our far-flung correspondents; driving route of Edinburgh royal mail up Old North road to Grantham. H. W. Wind. il New Yorker 41:138-46+ My 22 '65

Anecdotes, facetiae, satire, etc.
When the cows came home. D. Morgan. Reporter 32:41-2 My 20 '65

Hawaii
Hawaii's new jungle and volcano loop. il Sunset 136:24-6 Ja '66

New Jersey
Remote-controlled signs cut turnpike accidents; New Jersey turnpike. P. M. Weckesser. il Am City 80:118 F '65

New Mexico
New Mexico's crater country. J. V. Young. il Travel 124:30-4 S '65

New York (state)
New York's Adirondack trail. W. L. Wessels. il Travel 124:38-9 S '65

Oregon
Oregon's Coast highway. W. F. Heald. il Travel 124:24-9 S '65

Quebec
See Roads—Canada

South Dakota
On your way to the Black Hills. . . . E. Waltner. il Travel 124:35-7 S '65

United States
Bad bargain in the Smokies; destructive highways. A. W. Smith. il Nat Parks Mag 39:2 D '65
Future city; suggestions for tunneled freeways and parking beneath cities. G. A. Hoffman. il Sat R 48:42-4 Ag 7 '65
Going to Quebec? here's a new route. J. T. Starr. il Am For 71:30-1+ Jl '65
Hitting the road; fight-the-highway movement. il Time 85:48 Ap 9 '65
Ode to the road; Time essay. Time 86:32-3 S 10 '65
Transformation by road; American life and business. il Time 86:93-4 O 15 '65
Ubiquitous auto: man's servant or master? il Sr Schol 86:6-9 F 4 '65
See also
Express highways
Toll roads

ROADSIDE advertising. See Advertising, Outdoor

ROADSIDE improvement
Assault on the uglifiers; White House conference on natural beauty. New Repub 152:7 Je 12 '65
Beauty, beauty everywhere; White House conference on natural beauty. il Time 85:16 Je 4 '65
Beauty spot. New Repub 152:7 F 27 '65
Congress provides tools for a clean-up; prettier landscape and purer water. Bsns W p30 S 25 '65
Facelift for America; President's White House conference on natural beauty. Bsns W p33 My 29 '65
Flight from folly. il Time 86:62-72 S 17 '65
For a more beautiful U.S; the President asks this; with interview with C. A. T. Johnson. il U S News 58:71-6+ F 22 '65
Herbs for roadside plantings; ideas for beautifying America from our readers. Flower Grower 52:12 Ag '65
Hidden persuaders. W. M. Hall. il Am For 71:54-7 My '65
Lady Bird's beauty bill. E. B. Drew. il Atlan 216:68-72 D '65
LBJ's plan for roads: beauty; or no money. il U S News 58:62-3 Je 7 '65
On the way: less clutter along highways. il U S News 59:13 O 18 '65
President's conference on natural beauty. R. G. Miner. il Flower Grower 52:6-7 Ag '65

ROADSIDE improvement—*Continued*
Quality of environment; excerpts from remarks, May 21, 1965. L. S. Rockefeller. Am For 71:11 Je '65
Remaking the scene; White House conference on natural beauty. il Newsweek 65:56-7 Je 7 '65
Signs along the road. New Repub 153:6-7 O 2 '65
Signs of the times; proposed legislation to beautify US highways. il Newsweek 65: 89-89A+ Mr 8 '65
Some enchanted evening! House approved highway-beautification bill. Time 86:30-1 O 15 '65
Townscapes and turnpikes. F. Gutheim. Nation 200:622 Je 7 '65
Ugliness and the law. I. Silver. Commonweal 83:144-6 N 5 '65
White House conference on natural beauty. C. H. Callison. Audubon Mag 67:250-1 Jl '65
White House conference on natural beauty. J. B. Craig and I. M. Moore. il Am For 71:12-15 Je '65
Women to the rescue; women's clubs. America 113:313 S 25 '65
See also
Billboards

ROADSIDE planting. See Roadside improvement

ROAR of the greasepaint—The smell of the crowd; musical comedy. See Musical comedies, revues, etc.—Criticisms, plots, etc.

ROARK, Eugene
Our Wisconsin camp has winning ways. il Audubon Mag 67:103-7 Mr '65

ROASTING. See Cookery—Meat

ROBARGE, Margaret
Don't be a wreckreator. Recreation 58:274-6 Je '65

ROBB, Inez
In Tucson, Arizona, the frontier lives on. Vogue 146:43+ O 15 '65

RÖBBELEN, G.
Arabidopsis research. Science 150:1192 N 26 '65

ROBBERIES and assaults
Anatomy of bank robbery. M. Ottenberg. il Look 29:124+ O 19 '65
Bank robber sees his picture and gives up; United California bank. il Life 58:39 Mr 12 '65
Calling up the artillery; Syracuse vault theft. Newsweek 66:36 N 8 '65
College football hero's postgraduate course in horror; D. Pope's Big Springs bank killings. il Life 58:30-30A Je 25 '65
East side Earp. Time 86:21 Ag 20 '65
Heist from the play pen; robbery of vault at branch of the Royal bank of Canada, Montreal. il Newsweek 65:55 Ap 26 '65
Heisters increase their haul. C. Remsberg and B. Remsberg. il N Y Times Mag p61+ Ja 16 '66
Riddle of the nice killer; D. Pope. B. Lindeman. il Sat Eve Post 238:98+ O 23 '65
Split-second record of a bank robbery; Western-Manchester branch of the United California bank, Los Angeles. il Life 58:34-5 F 26 '65
Stranger in Big Springs; Nebraska bank robbery. il Newsweek 65:29-30 Je 21 '65
Topkapi revisited; biggest armed robbery in Turkish history. il Newsweek 66:52 S 27 '65

ROBBERSON, Elbert
A.C. afloat. Yachting 117:64-6+ Je '65
Electrical and electronic maintenance. il Yachting 117:74-5+ Ap '65
Marine radiotelephone antenna. Electr World 73:32-3 Ap '65
New sounds underwater. Yachting 118:50-3+ Ag '65
(ed) Yachting asks about wooden-kit boatbuilding. Yachting 117:61-4+ Mr '65

ROBBERSON, Winifred
Boating business. See issues of Yachting beginning March 1965

ROBBINS, Gerald
Recruiting and arming of Negroes in the South Carolina Sea Island, 1862-1865. bibliog Negro Hist Bul 28:150-1+ Ap '65

ROBBINS, Jhan
Happiest New Year of Greta Miller. Good H 160:34 Ja '65
Svetlana's Eastern bonnet. Read Digest 86: 137-40 Ap '65
We're flying the flag! Read Digest 86:128-30 Je '65
Woman who stayed. McCalls 92:96-7+ S '65
—and Robbins, June
Growing need for sex education in our schools. Good H 161:94-5+ N '65
Those new fertility drugs. Good H 160:88-9+ Mr '65
Young mother revisited. Redbook 125:8+ S '65

ROBBINS, June. See Robbins, Jhan, jt. auth.

ROBBINS, Richard
Books. Commonweal 82:540 Jl 23 '65

ROBBINS, W. E. and others
Feeding stimulants for the female house fly, musca domestica linneaus. bibliog Science 147:628-30 F 5 '65

ROBERT I, king of Scotland
Robert Bruce, by G. W. S. Barrow. Review Time por 85:106+ Ap 16 '65

ROBERT, earl of Gloucester
William of Malmesbury's Robert of Gloucester: a re-evaluation of the Historia novella. R. B. Patterson. bibliog f il Am Hist R 70:983-97 Jl '65

ROBERT the Bruce. See Robert I, king of Scotland

ROBERT Joffrey ballet (organization) See Ballet companies

ROBERT Morris junior college, Pittsburgh, Pa.
Pinwheel cluster of classrooms. il Arch Rec 138:156-7 O '65

ROBERTS, Derrell
Robert Toombs: an unreconstructed rebel on freedmen. bibliog Negro Hist Bul 28: 191-2 My '65

ROBERTS, Henry L.
(comp) Recent books on international relations. See issues of Foreign affairs

ROBERTS, Lillian
Woman fills man-size union job. il pors Ebony 20:91-2+ Ap '65

ROBERTS, Mary Carter
Snowtime surprise: Maryland. Travel 124:33-5 N '65

ROBERTS, Rachel
Rich, restless life of Rex Harrison. J. Hamilton. il pors Look 29:62-6 N 2 '65

ROBERTS, Richard W. and St Pierre, L. E.
Ultrahigh vacuum. bibliog Science 147:1529-42 Mr 26 '65

ROBERTS, Roy Allison
End of one-man rule. il por Time 86:68 O 1 '65

ROBERTS, Shepherd K.
Photoreception and entrainment of cockroach activity rhythms. bibliog Science 148:958-9 My 14 '65

ROBERTS, Steven V.
(ed) ...And this is what they have to say. Esquire 64:90-3+ N '65

ROBERTS, Walter Orr
Atmospheric research: a powerful concept emerges. Science 147:1093-8 Mr 5 '65

ROBERTS, Wyndham J.
How to make plants less thirsty. S. V. Jones. por Sci Digest 58:35 D '65

ROBERTSON, A. D. J. See Evans, C. R. jt. auth.

ROBERTSON, A. Willis
Excerpt from address, January 15, 1965. Cong Digest 44:143+ My '65

ROBERTSON, Abel L. and others
Renin production by organ cultures of renal cortex. bibliog Science 149:650-1 Ag 6 '65

ROBERTSON, Ann
Right or wrong, she's my roommate. Seventeen 25:18+ Ja '66

ROBERTSON, J. M.
Pros and cons of pre-bid conferences. Am City 81:96 Ja '66

ROBERTSON, Josephine
Homestead National Monument. Travel 124: 48-9 S '65

ROBERTSON, Lynn, and Zeman, L. E.
Five factors to consider when buying fertilizer. Suc Farm 63:30-1 D '65

ROBERTSON, Mary Ann
Found! summer jobs for teen-agers. Bet Hom & Gard 43:31 My '65

ROBERTSON, Nan
First lady's Lady Boswell. N Y Times Mag p 130-1+ Ap 11 '65
Second lady. Sat Eve Post 238:74-5+ Jl 3 '65
Why the President's daughter turned to the Catholic church. Ladies Home J 82:76+ Ag '65

ROBERTSON, Phyllis L. See Cavill, G. W. K. jt. auth.

ROBERTSON, William B. Jr
Inside the Everglades; excerpt from Bird watcher's America, ed. by O. S. Pettingill, jr. por Audubon Mag 67:274+ S '65

ROBEY, Donald
Origin of comets. Sat R 48:37-41 Ag 7 '65

ROBIDEAU, Merna
(comp) Detroit restaurants. ALA Bul 59:397-401 My '65

ROBIN, Ralph
Farewell to a chief of section; poem. Christian Cent 82:936 Jl 28 '65
I went to see a dying man; poem. Christian Cent 82:1509 D 8 '65
Just man; poem. New Repub 153:24 S 4 '65

ROBINS, Don W.
　250 feet of sewer obstruction. Am City 80:
　136+ F '65
ROBINS
　Birds in your garden. J. K. Terres. il Pop
　Gard 16:6 Ag '65
　Does the robin hear or see the worm? H.
　Saltford. Audubon Mag 67:255-6 Jl '65
ROBINSON, Arthur, and Puck, T. T.
　Sex chromatin in newborns: presumptive evi-
　dence for external factors in human non-
　disjunction. bibliog Science 148:83-5 Ap 2 '65
ROBINSON, Arthur B. and others
　Anesthesia of artemia larvae: method for
　quantitative study. bibliog Science 149:1255-
　8 S 10 '65
ROBINSON, Barbara
　Bed; story. McCalls 93:134-5 O '65
　For everything a season; story. McCalls 92:
　104-5 S '65
　Surprise package; story. McCalls 93:112-13
　D '65
　That day when I was lost; story. Good H
　161:84-5 O '65
　Thousand miles across the street; story.
　Good H 160:82-3 Je '65
ROBINSON, Beryl
　To Ruth Sawyer. Horn Bk 41:478-80 O '65
ROBINSON, Bill
　Stock talk. See issues of Motor trend
　With the racing classes. See issues of Yacht-
　ing
ROBINSON, Brian J.
　Hydroxyl radicals in space; with biographical
　sketch. Sci Am 213:16, 26-33 bibliog(p 124)
　Jl '65
ROBINSON, Bryan W. and others
　Brain telestimulator with solar cell power
　supply. Science 148:1111-13 My 21 '65
ROBINSON, Charles W.
　Area branches for Baltimore. Library J 90:
　5183-5 D 1 '65
　Book catalog: diving in. por Wilson Lib Bul
　40:262-8 N '65
ROBINSON, Donald W.
　Chaos in the social studies? por Sat R 48:79
　N 20 '65
ROBINSON, Edwin Arlington
　E.A.R.: a remembrance. L. Untermeyer. por
　Sat R 48:33-4 Ap 10 '65
　Poet of the recent past. G. Hicks. Sat R 48:
　31-2 Ap 10 '65
ROBINSON, Elizabeth
　Vacation in Las Vegas. il pors Ebony 20:180-
　2 Je '65
ROBINSON, Geroid Tanquary
　Bold proposal for Vietnam. Look 29:93-4 O
　19 '65
ROBINSON, Gladys Reed
　Favorite indoor plants. Horticulture 43:53
　Je '65
　Tamed zebra. Pop Gard 17:53 Ja '66
ROBINSON, Herbert
　Tino's day of reckoning. Reporter 33:54-7 D
　2 '65
ROBINSON, J. C. and others
　Leukocyte alkaline phosphatase: electro-
　phoretic variants associated with chronic
　myelogenous leukemia. bibliog Science 150:
　58-60 O 1 '65
ROBINSON, J. W. L.
　Chocós of the Taparal. Natur Hist 74:46-51
　Je '65
ROBINSON, John Arthur Thomas, bp
　Controversial bishop. America 112:598-9 Ap 24
　'65
　Profiles; concerning his Honest to God. V.
　Mehta. il New Yorker 41:63-4+ N 13; 60-2+
　N 20 '65
ROBINSON, Leif J. See McClure, A. jt. auth.
ROBINSON, Leonard Wallace
　Hearing color, smelling music, touching a
　scent. N Y Times Mag p 14-15+ Ag 22 '65
ROBINSON, Louie
　How two janitors bought white bank in
　Texas. Ebony 20:119-22+ Je '65
　Johnny Mathis: millionaire with problems.
　Ebony 20:99:102+ Mr '65
　Life and death of Nat King Cole. Ebony 20:
　123-34 Ap '65
　Rock 'n' roll becomes respectable. Ebony 21:
　48-50+ N '65
　This would never have happened. Ebony 20:
　114-24 O '65
　Tragic death of Sam Cooke. Ebony 20:92-6
　F '65
ROBINSON, Marion
　Holt series. Wilson Lib Bul 40:56-8 S '65
ROBINSON, Selma
　While you're in New York. McCalls 92:56+
　Ag '65
ROBINSON, Sugar Ray
　Bitter end for Sugar Ray. M. Kane. il por
　Sports Illus 23:89-90 N 22 '65
　Sugar: down but not quite out. L. L. King.
　il pors Sports Illus 23:58-66 S 6 '65

ROBINSON, Ted
　Roper's steamer; America's first car. Pop
　Mech 124:110-11+ O '65
ROBINSON, William M.
　Paper capacitors. Electr World 74:45-8 Jl '65
ROBLES, Richard
　Guilty as charged. il por Newsweek 66:32-3
　D 13 '65
ROBLES murder trial. See Trials (murder)
ROBOTS. See Automatons
ROCHE, James Michael
　Needed: better roads, drivers and vehicle
　maintenance; excerpts from testimony, July
　1965. por U S News 59:102-3 Ag 9 '65
　　　　　　　　　　about
　Businessmen in the news. R. Sheehan. il por
　Fortune 72:43-4 Jl '65
　GM's new driver. il por Newsweek 65:88 Je
　14 '65
　GM's new president; man with a world view.
　il por Bsns W p 114+ Je 5 '65
　Managing to succeed. il por Time 85:84 Je 11
　'65
　Up from the ranks; GM's new president. por
　U S News 58:14 Je 14 '65
ROCHE, John P.
　Chronicle of Camelot. Harper 231:117-18
　D '65
　Dissent, consensus, and McCarthyism. Re-
　porter 33:10 D 16 '65
　Professor votes for Mr Johnson. N Y Times
　Mag p45+ O 24; 16+ N 21 '65
ROCHE, Mary
　Desert traditions, decorative riches. House &
　Gard 128:254-9+ N '65
ROCHELLE, Pierre Drieu La. See Drieu La
　Rochelle, P.
ROCHESTER, Minn.
　Our own dredge proved best. W. M. Van
　Hook. il Am City 80:155+ O '65
ROCHESTER, N.Y.

　　　　　　　City planning
　Upgrading downtown. il Arch Rec 137:178-9
　Je '65

　　　　　　　Education
　Election and negotiation in Rochester. A.
　Cantor. il NEA J 54:22-3 S '65

　　　　　　　History
　City historian. B. McKelvey. il Am City 80:
　40d My '65

　　　　　　Social conditions
　Return to Rochester one year after. R. A.
　Schroth. America 113:163-4 Ag 14 '65
　Rochester braces for another July. J. Wit-
　cover. il Reporter 33:33-5 Jl 15 '65
　Saul Alinsky in smugtown. J. Ridgeway.
　New Repub 152:15-17 Je 26 '65
ROCHESTER, N.Y. public library
　One public library. M. E. Cashman. ALA Bul
　59:147-50 F '65
ROCHESTER, N.Y. University
　Fraternities at the University of Rochester.
　Sch & Soc 93:77+ F 6 '65
ROCHESTER Institute of technology, Rochester,
　N.Y.
　Campus designed by co-operation. il Arch
　Rec 137:162-6 Je '65
ROCK, Irvin, and others
　Perception of stroboscopic movement: evi-
　dence for its innate basis. bibliog Science
　147:1050-2 F 26 '65
ROCK carvings. See Petroglyphs
ROCK cotoneasters. See Cotoneasters
ROCK gardens. See Gardens, Rock
ROCK 'n' roll music
　Amps in the pants; amateur rock-'n'-roll
　combos. il Newsweek 66:67A+ S 6 '65
　California sound; rock 'n' roll music. P. Bart.
　il Atlan 215:140+ My '65
　Message time; rock 'n' roll. il Time 86:102+
　S 17 '65
　New sounds; rock-and-roll music. B. J.
　Friedman. il Holiday 38:44-5+ Jl '65
　One near-square who doesn't knock the rock;
　rock 'n' roll world championship. Lambert-
　ville, N.J. J. A. Michener. il N Y Times
　Mag p56-7+ O 31 '65
　Rock 'n' roll becomes respectable. L. Robin-
　son. il Ebony 21:48-50+ N '65
ROCK ISLAND, Ill.
　Teenagers who saved a town. C. Remsberg
　and B. Remsberg. il Good H 161:82-3+
　S '65
ROCK paintings. See Cave drawings and paint-
　ings
ROCK salt
　Softening rock salt's bite. il Bsns W p 160
　Mr 13 '65

ROCKEFELLER, John Davison, 1874-1960
Recollections of a trip with Mr John D. Rockefeller, jr, in California's Humboldt Redwoods State Park, July 1926. N. B. Drury. il por Nat Parks Mag 39:8-9 My '65

ROCKEFELLER, John Davison, 1906-
Hidden crisis. por Look 29:75-6+ F 9 '65

ROCKEFELLER, Laurance S.
Laurance Rockefeller awarded Audubon medal. por Audubon Mag 67:112-13 Mr '65
Quality of environment; excerpts from remarks, May 21, 1965. Am For 71:11 Je '65

about

Man from room 5600. il por Newsweek 66:44-5 Ag 2 '65
Mauna Kea caper. H. Sutton. Sat R 48:34+ Ag 21 '65
New organization now a reality. il por Recreation 58:315-17 S '65
Pioneers in every sense. G. S. Brown. il por Sports Illus 22:72-6+ Je 28 '65
Virgin Islands National Park. T. Gill. il Am For 71:38-41+ My '65

ROCKEFELLER, Nelson Aldrich, 1908-
Declaration & an elbow. Time 86:25 Ag 6 '65
How G.O.P. rivals destroyed themselves; excerpts from Making of the President—1964. T. H. White. il pors Life 58:82-4+ Je 25 '65
No room at the top. por Newsweek 65:39 My 17 '65
Rockefeller and Shriver clash, why. por U S News 59:20 Jl 12 '65
Rockefeller has to win. W. Weaver, jr. il pors N Y Times Mag p28-9+ My 9 '65
Rockefeller's re-entry. Nation 200:265 Mr 15 '65

ROCKEFELLER, Nelson Aldrich, 1964-
Meet Master Rockefeller; son of Happy and Rocky. il pors Life 59:66-8+ Ag 27 '65

ROCKEFELLER, Winthrop
On top of old Winrock. Newsweek 65:111 My 24 '65

ROCKEFELLER brothers fund
Performing arts; excerpts concerning opera from Performing arts: problems and prospects. il Opera N 29:6-10 Mr 20 '65

ROCKEFELLER center. See New York (city)—Rockefeller center

ROCKEFELLER foundation
Music to my ears; this, too, is New Orleans; Rockefeller foundation finances performance of contemporary music by a number of orchestras across the country. I. Kolodin. Sat R 48:30 Ap 17 '65
New music, big money; grants to university music departments. B. Boretz. Nation 201:47-8 Jl 19 '65

ROCKEFELLER institute. See Rockefeller university

ROCKEFELLER institute for medical research. See Rockefeller university

ROCKEFELLER university
Rockefeller institute's new mission: graduate education in natural sciences. il Bsns W p76-8+ F 20 '65
Rockefeller university: science in a different key. J. Walsh. il Science 150:1692-5 D 24 '65
See also
Institute for research in animal behavior

ROCKET engines
Cap pistol engines coming of age. D. A. Anderton. il Miss & Roc 17:25+ Ag 9 '65
DC motors stage comeback in space. W. S. Beller. il Miss & Roc 16:22-3 F 1 '65
Flygmotor develops small hybrid rocket. W. C. Wetmore. il Aviation W 83:55-6+ Jl 19 '65
ICBM studies focus on 156-in. motors. I. Stone. il Aviation W 82:141-3+ Mr 15 '65
Ion beam generation by laser studied at Cornell aeronautical. il Aviation W 82:65 F 1 '65
Rockets studied as laser power sources; magnetohydrodynamic generators. M. L. Yaffee. il Aviation W 82:85+ Je 28 '65
Subscale rockets used to study exhaust plume characteristics. Aviation W 83:123 S 13 '65
U.S. rocket motors; specifications (cont) Aviation W 82:210-13 Mr 15 '65
See also
Solid propellant rockets
Space vehicles—Propulsion systems

Exhaust

Launch pad poison. Sci N L 87:155 Mr 6 '65
Technique predicts rocket interference. M. L. Yaffee. il Aviation W 82:58-9+ F 15 '65

Ignition

Pyrofuze finds ordnance application. J. F. Judge. il Miss & Roc 16:32-4 My 24 '65

Manufacture

Firm creates new motor case process. J. F. Judge. il Miss & Roc 16:22-3 Mr 15 '65
Firm develops means for electroforming rocket engine chambers and nozzles. J. F. Judge. il Miss & Roc 17:24-5 Ag 2 '65

Materials

Acoustic liner damps rocket combustion instability. G. Alexander. il Aviation W 83:72-3+ Ag 9 '65
Firm creates new motor case process. J. F. Judge. il Miss & Roc 16:22-3 Mr 15 '65
Insulation liner for 260-in. motor. il Miss & Roc 16:27 Mr 1 '65
New filament winder can make 260-in. cases. Miss & Roc 16:35 Je 21 '65
Roll extrusion method chosen for UTC 120-in. motor case. J. F. Judge. il Miss & Roc 17:24-5 D 20 '65

Testing

Acoustic liner damps rocket combustion instability. G. Alexander. il Aviation W 83:72-3+ Ag 9 '65
Aerojet tests toroidal motor. il Miss & Roc 17:40 Ag 16 '65
New submerged-nozzle vector method tested. Aviation W 82:94 Je 21 '65
Titan 3A performs maneuvers in space. Aviation W 82:33 My 10 '65

Thrust control

Thiokol tests two thrust vector systems. M. L. Yaffee. il Aviation W 82:91+ Je 21 '65

ROCKET models
Making a bang with mini-missiles; rockets by mail to teen-agers. il Bsns W p79-80 Ap 24 '65

ROCKET propulsion
Did politics kill a major space project? Project Orion, involving nuclear explosions, abandoned. U S News 59:8 Jl 19 '65
Electric systems urged for 1970-75 missions. R. Pay. Miss & Roc 17:40+ N 8 '65
Ion beam generation by laser studied at Cornell aeronautical. il Aviation W 82:65 F 1 '65
New propulsion vistas; excerpts from remarks at symposium on advanced propulsion concepts. B. A. Schriever. Aviation W 82:21 My 10 '65
See also
Solid propellant rockets

ROCKET research corporation
Rocket research corp. expands market drive. J. F. Judge. il Miss & Roc 17:48+ S 13 '65

ROCKET sleds
Rocket sled to test nuclear effects. il Miss & Roc 17:17 D 13 '65

ROCKETS
Million-pound-thrust Hybrid proposed. J. F. Judge. Miss & Roc 16:26+ My 3 '65
Missiles and rockets world missile/space encyclopedia 1965. il Miss & Roc 17:37-44+ Jl 26 '65
Moscow parade features solid, liquid-fuel ICBMs and new battlefield-class missiles; with photographs and editorial comment. H. J. Coleman. Aviation W 82:21, 26-31 My 17 '65
See also
Guided missiles
Solid propellant rockets

Amateur experiments

5...4...3...2...1...0. il UNESCO Courier 18:42-3 Jl '65
Stop amateur rocketry says space group. Sci N L 87:89 F 6 '65
Things of science features Gemini model. Sci N L 87:361 Je 5 '65

Design

Navy meeting need for 2.75-in. rocket. J. F. Judge. il Miss & Roc 17:22-3 N 22 '65

Fuel

Gemini fuel filtration solved. L. A. Mavros. il Miss & Roc 17:26-8 Ag 2 '65
NASA to study liquid hydrogen behavior aboard orbiting S-4B. G. Alexander. Aviation W 82:29 F 22 '65
New rocket to use fluorocarbon. Aviation W 82:79 Mr 22 '65
Slush hydrogen seen as rocket engine fuel. Sci N L 89:11 Ja 1 '66

History

This high man. W. J. Coughlin. Miss & Roc 16:46 Mr 22 '65

ROCKETS—*Continued*

Launching

Pad built up for Titan III-C shot. Miss & Roc 16:18 Je 21 '65

Titan and Atlas-Centaur trials. R. N. Watts, jr. il Sky & Tel 29:95 F '65

Manufacture

Navy meeting need for 2.75-in. rocket. J. F. Judge. il Miss & Roc 17:22-3 N 22 '65

Materials

How Lukens turned out Titan plates. il Miss & Roc 17:35 Ag 30 '65

Recovery

Rocket recovery system nears flight; Germany's paraglider-ground control system. il Miss & Roc 17:35+ Jl 12 '65

Testing

More trouble for man's trip to moon; explosion during test firing. il Bsns W p34 Mr 6 '65

Pad built up for Titan III-C shot. Miss & Roc 16:18 Je 21 '65

S-1C-T test-fired at full power. Aviation W 82:33 Ap 26 '65

Transportation

Crawler problems won't delay Apollo. Miss & Roc 17:15 O 4 '65

Larger Guppy aimed at S-4B transport. H. D. Watkins. il Aviation W 82:43+ Ap 19 '65

Leveling trouble plagues crawler. S. Butler. il Miss & Roc 16:17 My 10 '65

S-4B flight article is shipped to Florida. Aviation W 83:51 S 13 '65

Super Guppy to make first flight Aug. 25. H. D. Watkins. il Aviation W 83:42-3 Ag 23 '65

Use in research

Fireflies to light the way in NASA effort to chart earth's biosphere. W. S. Beller. Miss & Roc 16:31 Mr 8 '65

Leading international research rockets; specifications. Aviation W 82:213-14 Mr 15 '65

Man-made comets. M. Morey. il Pop Mech 124:118 D '65

Rocket recovery system nears flight. il Miss & Roc 17:35+ Jl 12 '65

Rockets are flytrapping tiny micrometeorites. Sci N L 88:117 Ag 21 '65

U.S. research rockets; specifications. Aviation W 82:215 Mr 15 '65

ROCKETS, Atomic powered

Nuclear power; space system control tightened. il Miss & Roc 17:144-6+ N 29 '65

Rover commitment needed soon for early post-Apollo mission use. K. Johnsen. Aviation W 83:57 D 6 '65

Testing

Nerva engine handling facility completed. R. G. O'Lone. il Aviation W 83:52-3+ D 6 '65

ROCKETS, Sounding

Aerobee 350 heralded as scientific workhorse. W. S. Beller. il Miss & Roc 17:26-7+ S 27 '65

Interest grows in stabilized Skylark. M. Getler. Miss & Roc 17:28+ Jl 12 '65

Nitehawk provides reliability at low cost. R. Pay. il Miss & Roc 16:27+ Je 7 '65

Radar sounder will test Echo validity. R. Pay. Miss & Roc 16:33-5 My 3 '65

ROCKFORD, Ill.

Why the council bought eight more truck plows. C. E. Anderson. il Am City 80:27 D '65

Industries

Is a new plant in town always a blessing? il Bsns W p 124+ N 13 '65

Lighting

Brightest downtown in the world. il Am City 80:108-9 Jl '65

ROCKNE, Knute

Rockne, Parseghian and the Fighting Irish. T. Cohane. il por Look 29:88-9+ N 2 '65

ROCKPORT, Mass.

Conscience of an art colony. F. Potter. il Nation 201:410-14 N 29 '65

ROCKS

Finding rare beauty in common rocks. L. G. Collins. il Nat Geog Mag 129:120-9 Ja '66

Quiz; how we use rocks and minerals. J. Daugherty and M. Daugherty. il Sci Digest 57:89-91 Ap '65

Rock degradation by alkali metals: a possible lunar erosion mechanism. J. J. Naughton and others. bibliog il Science 149:630-2 Ag 6 '65

See also

Peridotite

Age

Rock ages measured. Sci N L 87:180 Mr 20 '65

Analysis

Structures in carbonate rocks made visible by luminescence petrography. R. F. Sippel and E. D. Glover. bibliog il Science 150: 1283-7 D 3 '65

Collectors and collecting

Rock lovers; collecting *suiseki* one of Japan's oldest and fastest-growing hobbies. il Newsweek 66:38-40 Ag 16 '65

Southeastern Oregon; Highland rock shop. H. D. Brown. il Hobbies 70:116-17 D '65

ROCKS, Igneous

Igneous rocks of the Indian Ocean floor. C. G. Engel and others. bibliog il Science 150:605-10 O 29 '65

Rock samples match lunar properties; upwelling or expanding magma in high order vacuums. J. F. Judge. il Miss & Roc 16:31 My 10 '65

ROCKS, Sedimentary

Carbonaceous rocks of the Soudan iron formation early Precambrain. E. P. Cloud, jr. and others. bibliog il Science 148:1713-16 Je 25 '65

Sedimentary origins of rock layering. P. E. Potter. il Natur Hist 74:50-5 bibliog(p66) D '65

ROCKVILLE CENTRE, N.Y.

Trial project spurs citywide lighting project. J. S. Fink. il Am City 81:122 Ja '66

ROCKWELL, F. A.

Translating reality into fiction; excerpt from Modern fiction techniques. Writer 78:16-18+ Jl '65

ROCKWELL, Frederick F. and Grayson, E. C.

Our small terrace pool; excerpt from Rockwells' complete guide to successful gardening. il Flower Grower 52:39 Mr '65

ROCKWELL, Norman

Longest step; space suits; with painting. B. Kocivar. il por Look 29:109-12 Ap 20 '65

Rockwell and rollers. il Look 30:34-5 Ja 11 '66

ROCKY MOUNTAIN goat hunting

Colorado's first goat hunt. J. J. Branney. il Outdoor Life 136:33-5+ O '65

ROCKY MOUNTAIN goats

Nature note; mountain goat. Sci N L 87:107 F 13 '65

ROCKY MOUNTAIN NATIONAL PARK

Colorado queen. W. F. Heald. il Travel 124: 36-8 Ag '65

Family approach to regional planning. D. S. Moore. Nat Parks Mag 39:19 S '65

ROCKY MOUNTAIN review

Shout & the whisper. il Time 85:74 Ap 2 '65

ROCOCO art. See Art, Rococo

ROCOCO furniture. See Furniture, Rococo

ROD, Ronald F.

Captain's legacy. por Time 86:10 D 24 '65

RODDEN, Robert J.

Early neolithic village in Greece; with biographical sketch. Sci Am 212:18, 82-8+ Ap '65

RODDIS, Louis H.

Columbus' doctors. Américas 17:35-7 Je '65

RODDY, Joseph

International university choral festival. Hi Fi 15:174-5 D '65

Presence of cellos; concerts. Hi Fi 15:86J-86K Mr '65

Sing unto the Lord; concerts. Hi Fi 15:117 My '65

RODENTS

See also names of rodents. e.g. Prairie dogs

RODEOS

Biggest two-day rodeo comes April 17 and 18; Red Bluff round-up. il Sunset 134:52+ Ap '65

Breakneck spectacle; with report by J. R. McDermott. il Life 59:50-60+ Ag 20 '65

King of the rope. il Time 86:74+ D 17 '65

Yankee caballeros, after hours; Charreadas, rodeo-like contest. il Bsns W p 154-5 F 27 '65

RODGERS, Guy

Name of the game is Cooty's turnabout. F. Deford. il pors Sports Illus 23:26-8+ D 13 '65

RODGERS, Mary Augusta

Rules of the game. Writer 78:11-14+ S '65

RODGERS, Richard
New word man for Rodgers; music in Do I hear a waltz? T. Prideaux. Life 58:20 Mr 19 '65
Number one melody man. G. Millstein. il pors Sat Eve Post 238:95-9 Mr 13 '65
RODIA, Simon
Reporter at large; Watts towers, Los Angeles. C. Trillin. il New Yorker 41:72+ My 29 '65
Watts: the forgotten slum. C. McWilliams. Nation 201:90 Ag 30 '65
Wonderful towers of Sabatino Rodia. il Sunset 134:108-9 My '65
RODILLA, Simon. See Rodia, S.
RODIN, Auguste
Great Rodin, his flagrant faker; with report by D. Seiberling. il por Life 58:64-71 Je 4 '65
RODINAL. See Photography—Developing and developers
RODITI, Edouard
Poor little Chagall from Vitebsk. N Y Times Mag p50-1+ D 5 '65
RODMAN, Selden
Close view of Santo Domingo. Reporter 33:20-7 Jl 15 '65
Maia Wojciechowska. Horn Bk 41:353-7 Ag '65
RODÓ, Laureano López. See López, Rodó, L.
RODRIGUEZ, Carlos Rafael
Down with the old guard. Time 85:42 F 26 '65
RODRIGUEZ, Carlos Sosa-. See Sosa-Rodriguez, C.
RODRIGUEZ, Eduardo Barreiros. See Barreiros Rodríguez, E.
RODRIGUEZ, Juan
For Chi Chi Rodriguez: which way is up? G. Zimmermann. il pors Look 29:M8-10 Je 29 '65
RODRIGUEZ-KABANA, Rodrigo, and others
Nematodes: biological control in rice fields: role of hydrogen sulfide. bibliog Science 148:524-6 Ap 23 '65
RODRIGUEZ-MONEGAL, Emir
In praise of Guimaraes Rosa. Commentary 41:65-7 Ja '66
RODWELL, Victor W. See Fimognari, G. M. jt. auth.
RODWIN, Lloyd
Ciudad Guayana: a new city; with biographical sketch. Sci Am 213:28+, 122-30+ S '65
ROE, Anne
Changes in scientific activities with age. bibliog Science 150:313-18 O 15 '65
ROE, Jim
Chicago: yachting at the office door. Yachting 117:44-5+ My '65
ROE, Kenn Sherwood
California loses another beach. il Audubon Mag 67:110-11 Mr '65
ROE, Lois Smethurst
In the manner of Matisse. Design 67:40-1 S '65
Secret of creative mask design. Design 67:28-30 S '65
ROE, Richard D.
Sweet and sour aristocrat. Am For 71:34-5+ Jl '65
Tradescantias. Horticulture 44:47-8 Ja '66
ROEBLING, John Augustus
Brooklyn bridge, by A. Trachtenberg. Review Reporter 33:36-7 Jl 1 '65. H. Cohen
ROEBLING, Mary G.
Power and influence of women; address, May 27, 1965. Vital Speeches 31:689-91 S 1 '65
ROEBLING, Washington Augustus
Brooklyn bridge, by A. Trachtenberg. Review Reporter 33:36-7 Jl 1 '65. H. Cohen
ROEDER, Kenneth D.
Moths and ultrasound; with biographical sketch. Sci Am 212:18+, 94-102 Ap '65
ROETHKE, Theodore
Light poem. New Yorker 41:21 Jl 10 '65

about

Couch and poetic insight. M. L. Rosenthal. Reporter 32:52-3 Mr 25 '65
Meeting the genuine mystery. G. Hicks. Sat R 48:15-16 Jl 31 '65
Trade winds. J. G. Fuller. Sat R 48:10-11 Mr 27 '65
ROETHLISBERGER, Fritz Jules
Foreman: master and victim of double talk: reprint from an issue of 1945. bibliog f por Harvard Bsns R 43:22-6+ S '65
ROEWADE, Svend A. K.
Unmelancholy Dane. Opera N 29:6-7 My 1 '65

ROGATCHEWSKY, Joseph
Historical records. A. Favia-Artsay. por Hobbies 70:35 Ja '66
ROGERS, Agnes
Lines to nobody in particular; poem. McCalls 92:191 Mr '65
Petulant thoughts toward the end of August; poem. Harper 231:75 Ag '65
ROGERS, David
Adam, fallen; poem. Cath World 200:363 Mr '65
Toward a Christian poetic. por Cath World 201:194-7 Je '65
ROGERS, Deborah Lee
Gift of Debbie. K. Baskette. il por Good H 160:92-3+ Mr '65
ROGERS, Donald H.
Remote control system. Electr World 74:92-3 O '65
ROGERS, Helen Priest
Films for notation. por Dance Mag 39:55-7 S '65
ROGERS, Mary
Christmas at Pine Mountain. Horn Bk 41:587-92 D '65
ROGERS, Roy, family
Gift of Debbie. K. Baskette. il Good H 160:92-3+ Mr '65
ROGERS, Rutherford David
Administering a giant: an intimate view. por Library J 90:4303-10 O 15 '65
Library position on copyright law revision; excerpts from statement, June 3, 1965. Library J 90:3403-5 S 1 '65

about

New ALA officer. L. Q. Mumford. por ALA Bul 59:655-8 Jl '65
ROGERS, Warren
(ed) See Donlon, R. H. C. Battle for Nam Dong
ROGGER, Hans
East Germany: stable or immobile? bibliog f Cur Hist 48:135-41 Mr '65
ROGIN, Gilbert
Lesser married; story. New Yorker 41:32-40 F 27 '65
Short novel; story. New Yorker 41:28-34 Ja 1 '66
ROGOFF, Gordon
At the Met: the unadventurous, repeated. Hi Fi 15:170-1 D '65
How absurd to be absurd. Nation 200:649-50 Je 14 '65
Met: some outstanding performances. Hi Fi 16:132-3 Ja '66
Moscow art theatre: surprises after Stanislavski. Reporter 32:49-50 Mr 25 '65
That true phoenix: Lorenzo da Ponte. Hi Fi 15:58-61+ N '65
Total theatre, part-time: operas. Hi Fi 15:133-4 Ap '65
ROGUES, Fidelio Despradel. See Despradel Rogues, F.
ROHDE, Barbara
Frog called Mystery; story. Redbook 124:64-5 F '65
Katrin's crusade; story. Redbook 126:64-5 N '65
ROHOLT, O. A. and others
Polypeptide chains of antibody: effective binding sites require specificity in combination. bibliog Science 147:613-15 F 5 '65
ROHRBACH, Heinrich
Fruiting pachysandra. Horticulture 43:15 D '65
ROHWEDER, Dwayne A. and Zeman, L. E.
How to get really top-quality hay. Suc Farm 63:46-7+ My '65
ROJAS, Carolina
On the gypsy circuit. W. Como. por Dance Mag 39:140-1 D '65
ROKEACH, Milton, and Mezel, Louis
Race and shared belief as factors in social choice. bibliog Science 151:167-72 Ja 14 '66
ROLAND Magruder, freelance writer; story. See Trillin, C.
ROLLAND, Romain
Telemann: the man and his music. por Sat R 48:80+ O 30 '65
ROLLAND, William W. See Burke, E. W. jr, jt. auth.
ROLLERS, Hair. See Hair curlers
ROLLIN, Betty
Pregnancy: then, now: excerpt from Mothers are funnier than children. Redbook 124:43 Ap '65
ROLLIN, Stephan H. and others
Thick-film resistors. Electr World 73:57-9 Ap '65
ROLLING (metal work)
Potentialities of roll-formed metal shapes. R. A. Biggs. il Arch Rec 137:225-6+ My '65

ROLLING MEADOWS, Ill.
Integrate your patching components. J. Mc-Feggan. il Am City 80:93-5 My '65

ROLLING mills
Rolling mill in miniature with a jeweler's touch; Hamilton watch co.'s Precision metals div, Lancaster. il Bsns W p 128-30 D 18 '65

ROLLING Stones. See Singers

ROLLINS, Alfred B. Jr
Whatever he did was notably done. Harper 231:126-8 N '65

ROLLINS, Howard A. Jr
New for your yard, an apple fence. Farm J 89:47 Mr '65

ROLLINS, Sonny
Rollins and Davis renewed. M. Williams. Sat R 48:91 O 30 '65

ROLLINS, Theodore Walter. See Rollins, S.

ROLLS. See Bread

ROLLS-Royce, limited
Rolls goes mad; Silver Shadow. il Time 86: 100+ O 15 '65
Rolls-Royce comes back flying high. il Bsns W p90-2+ My 29 '65

ROLOFF, Michael
Günter Grass. Atlan 215:94-7 Je '65

ROMAN, Nancy G.
Good look at NGC 4565. por Am Ed 1:5-8 O '65

ROMAN Catholic church. See Catholic church

ROMAN Catholics. See Catholics

ROMAN coins. See Coins

ROMAN curia. See Catholic church—Roman curia

ROMAN empire. See Rome

ROMAN Index. See Index librorum prohibitorum

ROMANCE
Epic love of Elmi Bonderi. M. Laurence. Holiday 38:35+ N '65

ROMANIDES, John S.
Condescending polemic. Christian Cent 82: 334 Mr 17 '65

ROMANINO, Girolamo
In his own dialect. il por Time 86:72-3+ Jl 9 '65

ROMANO, Tom
Dream department. Newsweek 65:27-8 Ap 26 '65

ROMANTIC love. See Love

ROME
Later Roman empire, by A. H. M. Jones. Review
New Yorker 41:114+ Ag 28 '65. J. Alsop

Antiquities
Birth of functional architecture: town planning and housing in ancient Rome. M. W. Frederiksen. il UNESCO Courier 18:30-2 My '65

Civilization
Research in America; Dr Gilfillan's theory of Rome's decay due to lead poisoning. J. Lear. Sat R 48:36 Ag 7 '65

History
Two views of Rome. A. Menen. il Holiday 37:68-73+ My '65

ROME (city)
Real citizens of Rome. A. Menen. Holiday 38:50-1+ S '65

Art
Rome: new and old, lost and found. M. Gendel. il Art N 64:36-7+ Sum '65

Description
Angel's roost: background of Puccini's Tosca. F. Stevenson. il Opera N 29:14-16 Ap 17 '65
Guided tour of tourists in Rome. I. Shenker. il N Y Times Mag p24-5+ Jl 11 '65
Rome, American style. H. Sutton. il Sat R 48:42-4 Ag 14 '65
Two views of Rome. A. Menen. il Holiday 37:68-73+ My '65

History
Real citizens of Rome. A. Menen. Holiday 38:50-1+ S '65

Music
Excitement below the surface. W. Weaver. il Hi Fi 15:130-1 My '65
Notes from our correspondents (cont) W. Weaver. Hi Fi 15:14+ Jl; 12+ O '65
Rome summary. F. Nuzzo. il Opera N 29:32 My 1 '65

Social life and customs
American in Rome. W. M. Kelley. Mlle 60: 202+ Mr '65

Making the *bella figura;* a letter from Rome. R. Espinosa. il Mlle 61:181-2 O '65

Street traffic
Moment for pedestrians; a pedestrian island. il Time 87:29 Ja 7 '66
Roman traffic holiday ends in all-out snarl; pedestrian island experiment backfired. il Bsns W p34-5 Ja 8 '66
When a traffic jam became traffic chaos. il U S News 60:12 Ja 10 '66

Streets
Flight from The Beach; Via Veneto. il Newsweek 66:36 Ag 16 '65

Theater
Deputy in Rome. il Newsweek 65:55 Mr 1 '65

ROMEO, Margaret M.
Eyes of the beholders. NEA J 54:41 Ap '65

ROMEO and Juliet; ballet. See Ballets—Criticisms

ROMEO and Juliet; drama. See Shakespeare, W.—Plays

ROMER, Alfred Sherwood
Alfred Sherwood Romer, president-elect. B. Patterson. por Science 147:891-2 F 19 '65

ROMERSTEIN, Herbert
American friends of the Vietcong. Nat R 17: 278-9 Ap 6 '65

ROMNEY, George, 1907-
Consumerism; address, April 19, 1965. Vital Speeches 31:489-93 Je 1 '65
From the bottom to the top; address, February 4, 1965. Vital Speeches 31:290-2 Mr 1 '65
Our unique economic principles; address, November 23, 1965. Vital Speeches 32:190-2 Ja 1 '66

about
Is Romney eying '66? or '68? por U S News 58:16 Mr 8 '65
Next chief of the GOP. E. J. Hughes. Newsweek 66:19 N 29 '65
On the track with George & Jack? por Time 85:24 Ap 2 '65
Run, run, run. il por Newsweek 65:46-7 My 10 '65
This Republican for 1968? D. R. Jones. il pors N Y Times Mag p28-9+ F 28 '65
Three up. Time 86:12 D 24 '65
Way with words. il por Time 85:34 Ap 30 '65

ROMOSER, George K.
Preview of a German controversy. Nation 201:172-4 S 27 '65
—and Foster, C. R.
Safety first: the West German election. Bul Atomic Sci 21:37-9 D '65

ROMULO, Carlos P.
Up-dating the pre-atomic United Nations; address, June 20, 1965. Vital Speeches 31: 658-61 Ag 15 '65; Excerpts. Sat R 48:34-5+ Jl 24 '65

RÓNAI, Paulo
Undoing Babel. Américas 17:26-30 Je '65

RONAN, Charles E.
Book review. America 113:542 N 6 '65

RONAN, Margaret
Following the films. Sr Schol 87:30-1 S 16; 32 S 23; 52 S 30; 22 O 7; 34 O 14; 24 O 21; 24 O 28; 28 N 4; 44 N 11; 32 N 18; 28 D 2; 33 D 9 '65
New movies. Sr Schol 87:sup 18 O 14; sup 10 N 18 '65

RONSON corporation
Bit much for a lighter company. il Time 86: 104 O 1 '65

RONY, Vera
Labor drives to close the South's open shop. Reporter 33:31-4 N 18 '65

ROOF drainage. See Drainage, House

ROOF heliports. See Heliports

ROOF trusses. See Trusses

ROOFING
New roofing: better than ever. J. Ingersoll. il Pop Sci 187:126-9 S '65

ROOFS
Bold roof expression for architect's own house. il Arch Rec 137:54-7 mid-My '65
Light pyramids add drama to flexible spaces. il Arch Rec 137:98-101 mid-My '65
Powerful roofs dominate design; family house. il Arch Rec 137:171-4 Je '65
Renewing a plastic roof. il Sunset 134:125-6+ F '65
Why not build a roof house? A. C. Borg. il Am Home 68:44 Ap '65
See also
Gutters (roof)
Roofing
Shells (structural engineering)
Vaults (architecture)

ROOFS—*Continued*

Leakage

Solving leakage problems of parapets. H. Edwards. il Arch Rec 137:222+ Ap '65
Who takes the blame when the roof leaks? E. Goble. Arch Rec 138:9 Jl '65

ROOKIE; story. See Quirk, J.

ROOM air conditioners. See Air conditioning equipment

ROOM dividers. See Partitions

ROOM; drama. See Pinter, H.

ROOM furnishings. See Household furnishings

ROOM painting. See Painting, Industrial and practical

ROOMMATES

Right or wrong, she's my roommate. A. Robertson. Seventeen 25:18+ Ja '66

ROOMS

Bright-on-a-budget: flower starred roomlets. il House & Gard 127:172-3 Ap '65
Convert the garage, add a car shelter. il Sunset 134:96+ F '65
Corner strategy. il House & Gard 127:142-7 Ap '65
Five ways to solve the long-room problem. il House & Gard 127:134-9 My '65
Living with fling in small quarters; rooms William Baldwin decorates. il Vogue 145: 142-7 Mr 15 '65
See also
Bedrooms
Childrens rooms
House decoration
Kitchens
Laundries
Living rooms
Music rooms and equipment
Nurseries
Studies (rooms)

ROOMS, Miniature

Miniature rooms of Helena Rubinstein. S. A. Parvin. il Hobbies 70:122-3 My; 120+ Jl '65

ROOMS, Remodeled. See Houses, Remodeled

ROONEY, Mickey

Many wives of Mickey Rooney; excerpts from I.E., an autobiography. pors Look 29:132-4+ O 19 '65

ROONEY, Paul M. See Rounds, J. B. jt. auth.

ROOSA, Robert Vincent

Federal debt management. por Duns R 85: 33+ Je '65
Inside story of the dollar and its future; interview. pors U S News 58:48-53+ F 8 '65

ROOSEVELT, Eleanor (Roosevelt)

Churchill at the White House. Atlan 215:77-80 Mr '65

about

Eleanor Roosevelt; excerpt from script of film. A. MacLeish. il pors McCalls 92:98-101+ My '65
Eleanor Roosevelt on film. T. Prideaux. Life 59:10 D 3 '65
Let us now praise famous men; concerning biographical film. A. Knight. Sat R 48: 74 D 4 '65

ROOSEVELT, Elliott

Elliott for mayor too. il por Times 85:22 Mr 5 '65
Like father. il por Newsweek 65:38+ Je 14 '65
May of the Beach. il por Time 85:32 Je 11 '65

ROOSEVELT, Franklin Delano, 1882-1945

FDR as we remember him; reminiscences by his daughter and four sons. il pors Sat Eve Post 238:38-40+ Ap 10 '65
From the Morgenthau diaries: years of urgency, 1938-1941, by J. M. Blum. Review
Harper 230:118+ F '65. J. M. Burns
Man for this age, too. R. H. Rovere. il por N Y Times Mag p23+ Ap 11 '65
Thirty-second President 1933-1945. F. Freidel. il pors Nat Geog Mag 129:70-9 Ja '66
Without portfolio. C. B. Luce. il McCalls 92:20 Ap '65

ROOSEVELT, Franklin Delano, 1914-

Frank's future. por Time 85:30 My 21 '65
Putting teeth in the hiring rules. por Bsns W p32-3 My 29 '65

ROOSEVELT, Franklin Delano, family

FDR's sons: all four active in politics. pors U S News 58:22 Mr 15 '65

ROOSEVELT, James

Excerpt from remarks, July 27, 1965. Cong Digest 44:204+ Ag '65
General assembly establishes U.N. development program; statement, November 22, 1965. Dept State Bul 53:958-9 D 13 '65

Toward a better life in larger freedom; statement, October 15, 1965. Dept State Bul 53: 798-805 N 15 '65
U.S. pledges $60 million to U.N. aid programs; statement, November 2, 1965. Dept State Bul 53:957-8 D 13 '65

about

Jimmy for mayor. il por Time 85:22 Mr 5 '65

ROOSEVELT, Jeanette

Interview about trimming, toning. Mlle 60: 137 F '65

ROOSEVELT, Julian K.

Accident prevention aboard an ocean racer. Yachting 117:225 Ap '65

ROOSEVELT, Theodore

Twenty-sixth President 1901-1909. F. Freidel. il pors Nat Geog Mag 128:540-7 O '65

Statues, portraits, etc.

Question of good taste; Theodore Roosevelt memorial island in the Potomac River. Nat Parks Mag 39:20 F '65

ROOSEVELT family

Roosevelts: American aristocrats, by A. Churchill. Review
Newsweek il 65:118-19 Je 14 '65
Sat R il 48:37 Jl 10 '65

ROOSEVELT hotel. See New York (city)—Hotels, restaurants, etc.

ROOSEVELT memorial. See Washington, D.C.—Monuments, statues, etc.

ROOT parasites. See Parasitic plants

ROOTES motors, incorporated

Chrysler's rescue mission; partnership with Rootes motors of Britain. il Fortune 72:63-4 Jl '65

ROOTS

Roots as organs of assimilation of sulfate. J. S. Pate. bibliog il Science 149:547-8 Jl 30 '65
Soil fumigants control roots in sewers; Milwaukee, Wis. G. Z. Rayner. il Am City 80: 135-6 Je '65
Transhydrogenation in root tissue: mediation by carbon dioxide. I. P. Ting and W. M. Dugger, jr. bibliog il Science 150: 1727-8 D 24 '65
Tree roots, do not disturb. Sunset 134:199 F '65

ROOTWORMS, Corn. See Corn rootworms

ROPE

Don't be a square; use two bowlines for joining nylon line. G. S. Smith. il Motor B 116:27 D '65
Practically seized. G. S. Smith. il Motor B 116:122 N '65
Whipping synthetic rope. G. S. Smith. il Motor B 116:68 N '65

ROPE tricks

King of the rope. il Time 86:74+ D 17 '65

ROPER, Elmo

Advertising in the 1970s. Sat R 48:74-5 F 13 '65

ROPER, Hugh Redwald Trevor-. See Trevor-Roper, H. R.

ROPER, James E. See Stevenson, C. jt. auth.

ROPER, Maurice K.

Ground-level transformers improve city skyline. Am City 80:100 N '65

RORABACK, Kenneth

Only anguish. il por Newsweek 66:48 O 11 '65

ROREM, Ned

Frozen interplay. por Time 86:83-4 N 12 '65
Miss Julie. Criticism
Hi Fi 16:126-7+ Ja '66
Newsweek il por 66:108 N 15 '65
Opera N il 30:29 D 18 '65
Opera N por 30:20-1 N 6 '65
Sat R 48:64+ N 20 '65
Time por 86:83-4 N 12 '65

RORIMER, James J.

Muses' marble acres. il por Time 85:80-5 Mr 19 '65

ROSATI, James

David Smith, 1906-1965. Art N 64:28-9+ S '65

ROSE, Arnold M.

American Negro problem in the context of social change; excerpts from Negro in America. Ann Am Acad 357:1-17 Ja '65
Minnesota professor wins libel suit. W. L. Thorkelson. Christian Cent 83:89-90 Ja 19 '66
(ed) Negro protest. bibliog f Ann Am Acad 357:1-133 Ja '65

ROSE, Billy

Rose garden; Billy Rose gives sculpture collection to Israel. il por Time 85:73 Mr 26 '65

ROSE, C. R. See Ewers, W. H. jt. auth.

ROSE, Dixie E.
Fall in the mountains. Horticulture 43:16 O
'65
For elegance, foxgloves. Flower Grower 52:
26-7 My '65
ROSE, Francis L. and others
Hepatic glycogen depletion in amphiuma dur-
ing induced anoxia. bibliog Science 147:
1467-8 Mr 19 '65
ROSE, Guenter H. and Lindsley, D. B.
Visually evoked electrocortical responses in
kittens: development of specific and non-
specific systems. bibliog Science 148:1244-6
My 28 '65
ROSE, Jerry A.
Communiqué from Hill 327 at Danang. N Y
Times Mag p 10-11+ Ap 25 '65
How strong is China's army? Reporter 32:
23-5 Mr 11 '65

about

Letters: death in South Vietnam. M. W.
Browne. por Sat Eve Post 238:6 N 6 '65
ROSE, Lloyd
In my opinion. por Seventeen 24:222 S '65
ROSE, Margaret
One camp, three nations, many friends.
UNESCO Courier 18:52-3+ Jl '65
ROSE, Pete
Joe Hustle may bring the flag to the Reds.
J. Mann. il por Sports Illus 23:114-15 S 20
'65
ROSE, Robert H.
Upheaval Dome. Nat Parks Mag 39:11-15 S
'65
ROSE potpourri. See Potpourri
ROSEBORO, John
Bat day. il por Newsweek 66:44 S 6 '65
Battle of San Francisco. J. Mann. il por
Sports Illus 23:12-15 Ag 30 '65
Time for tension. il por Time 86:64 S 3 '65
ROSELIEP, Raymond
Beholder; poem. America 112:772 My 22 '65
Good night, Mr Eliot; poem. Cath World
201:259 Jl '65
Michael Fox and applecheek day; poem.
Christian Cent 82:1378 N 10 '65
My father's trunk; Riverman; Kodachrome:
Katherine Anne Porter; Four haiku; poems.
Poetry 106:199-203 Je '65
Poems: My day as he goes; To his dark lady;
English sonnet; Ars poetica for Jeanne
Louise McHale making poems in her
eleventh year. Nation 200:538 My 17 '65
ROSELLE, Robert E.
Here's how to identify and control beef
cattle insects. Suc Farm 63:48-9+ My '65
ROSEMAN, Alvin
Thailand, Laos and Cambodia: a decade of
aid. Cur Hist 49:271-7+ N '65
ROSEMARY
Rosemary likes it in the sun. Sunset 135:156
Jl '65
ROSEN, Fred S. and others
Hereditary angioneurotic edema: two genetic
variants. bibliog Science 148:957-8 My 14
'65
ROSEN, Harold
Abortion: questions and answers: excerpt
from Encyclopedia of mental health. por
Todays Health 43:24-5+ Ap '65
ROSEN, Jane Krieger
Africans in darkest New York. N Y Times
Mag p30-1+ F 28 '65
ROSEN, Norma
Sheltering a life; story. Redbook 125:88-9
O '65
ROSENBERG, Harold
Art and work; adaptation of address, 1964.
Craft Horiz 25:26+ My '65
Books. Vogue 146:148-50 D '65
Books (cont) New Yorker 40:131-6 F 6;
41:129-36 F 27; 98-100+ Je 26 '65
Calendar of creation. Vogue 146:228-9 S 1 '65
Hans Hofmann. Vogue 145:192-5+ My '65
Psychoanalysis Americanized. Commentary
39:72-4 Ap '65
Rivers' commedia dell' arte. Art N 64:35-7+
Ap '65

about

Rosenberg and his Tower of Babel. E.
Stevens. New Repub 152:26-7 F 20 '65
ROSENBERG, Jakob
Expert's expert. il por Time 85:72-7 F 19 '65
ROSENBERG, Jessie
Return; poem. Atlan 216:95 S '65
ROSENBERG, Julius and Ethel, case
Invitation to an inquest, by W. Schneir and
M. Schneir. Review
Commentary 41:69-70+ Ja '66. A. M.
Bickel
Nation 201:361-3+ N 15 '65. F. J. Cook
Newsweek il 66:82 Ag 23 '65

ROSENBERG, P. E. See French, B. M. jt.
auth.
ROSENBERG, Shirley Sirota
Good health for every school child. Parents
Mag 40:50-1+ S '65
ROSENBLOOM, Carroll
Pleasure of dying on Sunday. R. H. Boyle.
il pors Sports Illus 23:84-6+ D 13 '65
ROSENBLUTH, Jack
Smooth muscle: an ultrastructural basis for
the dynamics of its contraction. bibliog Sci-
ence 148:1337-9 Je 4 '65
ROSENFELD, Albert
As Proteus he changed his shape. Life 58:57-8
Ap 23 '65
How will man suit up for space? Life 58:
56+ Ap 16 '65
New man; what will he be like? Life 59:
94-6+ O 1 '65; Same abr. with title Will
man direct his own evolution? Read Digest
88:37-42 Ja '66
Pushed out into a hostile world. Life 58:
70+ Ap 30 '65
ROSENFELD, David
Behind the scenes in a Gold cup race, 1964:
photographs. Yachting 118:24-5 S '65

about

White sails in the darkroom. il Pop Phot
56:60-1 F '65
ROSENFELD, Stephen
Muffled in Moscow. il por Time 86:83 D 10 '65
ROSENFIELD, Loyd
It figures! poem. Atlan 215:122 Je '65
Level best; poem Redbook 125:134 Ag '65
ROSENTHAL, Abraham Michael
Forgive them not, for they knew what they
did. N Y Times Mag p50-1+ O 24 '65
Taste of life in Hiroshima now. N Y Times
Mag p4-5+ Ag 1 '65
ROSENTHAL, Benjamin S.
Excerpt from debate, September 20, 1965. Cong
Digest 44:283+ N '65
ROSENTHAL, M. L.
Angst across the sea. Reporter 32:41-2 Mr 11
'65
Couch and poetic insight. Reporter 32:52-4
Mr 25 '65
New works on Pound. Poetry 106:361-5 Ag '65
To the rulers; poem. Nation 202:19 Ja 3 '66

about

Poetry chronicle. C. Urdang. Poetry 105:
340-1 F '65
ROSENWALD, Lessing Julius
Old Noel; wood and metal cuts on view at
Washington's National gallery of art. il
Newsweek 66:68 D 27 '65
ROSES
All-America recipes and All-America roses.
M. Johnston and H. Mason. il Bet Hom &
Gard 43:68-77+ F '65
Golden rose; rosa hugonis, or Father Hugo's
rose. il Flower Grower 52:24 F '65
How to train a climbing rose. M. M. Graff. il
Pop Gard 16:54+ S '65
Many faces of the rose. il House & Gard 127:
154-6 F '65
Never such roses. R. A. Browne. il Flower
Grower 52:40+ F '65
New roses for 1965. il Flower Grower 52:26-7
F '65
Old roses. R. Thomson. il Horticulture 43:
20-1+ Ag '65
Start the new year with the newest roses.
il Flower Grower 53:36-7, 41-2 Ja '66
Using roses as ground covers. il Sunset 134:
178+ F '65
Warm weather hardiness and roses. J. B.
Brimer. il Horticulture 43:22-3 N '65
Where to plant roses. il Bet Hom & Gard
43:24+ Ap '65
See also
Plants—All America selections

Diseases and pests

How, when and what of spraying roses. P.
P. Pirone. il Horticulture 43:36-7 Ap '65
ROSES, Symbolism of. See Symbolism
Le ROSEY (school) See Schools—Switzerland
ROSIN, A.
(tr) See Martinez, R. E. Europe's What is
man? exhibit
ROSKO, Milt
Wintertime codfishing. Travel 124:42-4 D '65
ROSS, Bertram
Bertram Ross dance concert, 92nd street
Y. D. Hering. Dance Mag 39:24 My '65
ROSS, D. M.
Preferential settling of the sea anemone
stomphia coccinea on the mussel modiolus
modiolus. bibliog Science 148:527-8 Ap 23 '65

ROSS, David
On apples; poem. New Yorker 41:48 O 2 '65
ROSS, Edward S.
Asian insects in disguise. il por Nat Geog
Mag 128:432-9 S '65
Birds that see in the dark with their ears.
il por Nat Geog Mag 127:282-90 F '65
ROSS, Elaine
Hot breads cook book. House & Gard 127:
163+ Mr '65
ROSS, Emory
Schweitzer in America. Sat R 48:25-6 S 25
'65
ROSS, Glynn
Pacific Sound. F. J. Warnke. il pors Opera N
29:30-1 F 6 '65
ROSS, Irwin
Britain's next prime minister? Read Digest
87:97-101 N '65
Case of the Swedish spy. Read Digest 86:
117-25 Ap '65
European slogan, go North, young man. N Y
Times Mag p34-6+ My 9 '65; Same abr. with
title Europe's workers on the move. Read
Digest 87:49-50+ N '65
Fraud fires flare up. Read Digest 86:33-5+
My '65
Pines and needles, and progress. Read Digest
86:37-8+ Mr '65
They fight to free the world's prisoners of
conscience. Read Digest 86:131-5 F '65
Trial by newspaper. Atlan 216:63-8 S '65
What nature teaches man. Sci Digest 59:
89-91 Ja '66
ROSS, James W. See Moore, E. W. jt. auth.
ROSS, Lillian
Our far-flung correspondents. New Yorker
41:185-6+ S 25 '65
Profiles. New Yorker 41:63-6+ O 30 '65
ROSS, Malcolm, and others
Mica polytypes: systematic description and
identification. bibliog Science 151:191-3 Ja
14 '66
ROSS, Marise
Child seller; with account by R. Stolley. il
por Life 59:109-10+ O 8 '65
ROSS, Nancy Wilson
Family circle: word and picture story. Opera
N 29:11-13 Mr 13 '65
Sir Tashi and the yeti. Horizon 7:104-11 Spr
'65
ROSS, Philip
National labor relations board. Cur Hist 49:
77-84+ Ag '65
ROSS, Walter Sanford
Best beast in your tank. Esquire 63:86-9+
Mr '65; Same abr. with title That beast in
your tank. Read Digest 86:139-41 Je '65
Let's stop these needless cancer deaths! ex-
cerpt from Climate is hope. McCalls 92:
82+ Ap '65
Peggy was dying. Ladies Home J 82:50-1+
Jl '65
Smoking is contagious. Parents Mag 40:68-9+
N '65
Something for everyone. Sat R 48:18-20 D
25 '65
ROSSELLAT, Robert
Feeling in your bones; ed. by J. Dougherty.
por Dance Mag 39:54-7 Ap '65
ROSSI, Alice
Case against full-time motherhood. Redbook
124:51+ Mr '65
Women in science: why so few? adaptation
of address, October 1964. bibliog Science
148:1196-202 My 28 '65
ROSSI, Irving
Hard rider with a feel for timing. il pors
Bsns W p 188-90+ My 15 '65
ROSSIDES, Zenon
United Nations commemoration address,
June 25, 1965. UN Mo Chron 2:108-11 Jl '65
ROSSINI, Gioacchino
Barber of Seville (Il barbiere di Siviglia)
Criticism
Opera N 30:26 N 20 '65
Cinderella. Criticism
New Yorker 41:237-8 N 13 '65
Opera N 30:22 O 23 '65
Sat R 48:64 N 20 '65
On records; La Cenerentola. Opera N 30:44
O 23 '65
Teresa Berganza as Rosina: London's Il bar-
biere di Siviglia. P. L. Miller. Am Rec G
32:122-4 O '65
Trump and no-trump. R. D. Daniels. Opera N
29:33 Mr 20 '65
Year for Rossini. W. Weaver. Hi Fi 15:119
Jl '65
ROSSIO, Joann D.
Our kids collect butterflies. Parents Mag
40:62-3+ Ag '65

ROSSKAM, Edwin
Style of the thirties. N. Fruchter. Nation
200:370-1 Ap 5 '65
ROSSMOOR leisure world. See Aged—Housing
ROSSO, Antonio da Monte. See Monte Rosso,
A. da
ROSTAND, Jean
Johann Gregor Mendel. UNESCO Courier 18:
16-19 Ap '65
ROSTEN, Leo
Broads were very skinny, or, Pop art, shmop
art, leave me alone. Harper 231:90-1 O '65;
Same abr. with title Pop art, shmop art,
leave me alone. Read Digest 87:75-7 D '65
Myths by which we live; address, March 7,
1965. Vital Speeches 31:410-14 Ap 15 '65
They made our world (cont) Look 29:80-1
Je 1; 78-9 O 5; 78-9 D 28 '65
World of Leo Rosten. Look 29:18 S 21; 79
O 5; 18 O 19; 16 N 16; 26 D 14 '65; 30:8
Ja 11 '66
ROSTOW, Eugene V.
Hard realities of power demand that we
must fight on. Life 59:40B-40C Jl 2 '65
Life book review. Life 59:10 Jl 9 '65
ROSTOW, Walt Whitman
Chapter that Keynes never wrote; address,
February 24, 1965. Dept State Bul 52:454-9
Mr 29 '65
Concept of a national market; address,
September 1, 1965. Vital Speeches 31:717-20
S 15 '65; Same. Dept State Bul 53:518-24 S
27 '65
Deeper roots for the Alliance. Américas 17:
37-41 Ap '65
Economic development in Asia; address, April
23, 1965. Dept State Bul 52:845-53 My 31 '65
Peace: the central task of foreign policy;
address, June 8, 1965. Dept State Bul 53:
21-7 Jl 5 '65
Regional organization: a planner's perspec-
tive. Dept State Bul 52:994-1000 Je 21 '65
Role of emerging nations in world politics;
address, March 15, 1965. Dept State Bul
52:492-7 Ap 5 '65
Three-part strategy. New Repub 152:17 My
29 '65
United States policy toward Europe; address,
March 19, 1965. Dept State Bul 52:576-82
Ap 19 '65
ROSTROPOVICH, Mstislav
Midsummer marathon. il por Time 86:54 Ag
13 '65
Music to my ears; Carnegie Hall recital and
accompanist for wife's recital in Philhar-
monic Hall. I. Kolodin. Sat R 49:76 Ja 8 '66
Musical events; performance of Dvořák's Cello
concerto with Moscow philharmonic or-
chestra. W. Sargeant. New Yorker 41:137-8
O 30 '65
Thirty-one by Rostropovich. E. Greenfield.
Hi Fi 15:166 O '65
ROSWAENGE, Helge
Helge Roswaenge. A. Favia-Artsay. il pors
Hobbies 70:32-3+ My '65
Helge Roswaenge, apparent eternal youth.
J. Maclain. por Am Rec G 31:624-5 Mr '65
ROSZAK, Theodore
British peace movement: looking for the
marchers. Nation 201:273-7 O 25 '65
Secret of moral action. Nation 200:426-8 Ap
19 '65
ROTARY International
Paul VI to the Rotarians. America 112:445
Ap 3 '65
ROTATORS, Antenna. See Television antennas
ROTH, Alice
Big top in the hangar. Recreation 58:444-5
N '65
ROTH, Barbara F. and Harvey, J. A.
Altered effect of potassium ions on cerebral
respiration in vitro following subcortical
lesions. bibliog Science 148:1356-7 Je 4 '65
ROTH, Jack
Beachboy caper. Esquire 64:118-19+ S '65
ROTH, Robert J.
Slogans and the Great society. America 112:
184 F 6 '65
William James and alcoholics anonymous.
America 113:48-50 Jl 10 '65
ROTH, Robert N.
Magic note. Opera N 29:16 F 20 '65
ROTH, Roberto
Alliance for what? Nat R 17:189-90+ Mr 9
'65
ROTH, William M.
Trade windows to the world. Dept State Bul
53:401-5 S 6 '65
ROTHENSTEIN, E. M.
Mica capacitors. Electr World 74:49-51 Jl
'65

ROTHFELS, Hans
  Preview of a German controversy. G. K. Romoser. Nation 201:172-4 S 27 '65
ROTHMAN, Stuart
  Let's stop Labor board's unfair practices. por Nations Bsns 53:34-5+ My '65
ROTHROCK, George A.
  Science in action; steps to new astronomy. Natur Hist 74:64-8 My '65
ROTHSCHILD, Miriam
  Fleas; with biographical sketch. Sci Am 213: 10, 44-53 D '65
ROTHSCHILD, Norman
  Rothschild reports. See issues of Popular photography

about

  How Norman Rothschild made the cover pictures. il Pop Phot 56:82 Mr '65
ROTHSCHILD, Pauline de, baronne
  Museum of wine in art. V. Lawford. il pors Vogue 145:172-83+ Mr 1 '65
ROTHSCHILD, Philippe de, baron
  Museum of wine in art. V. Lawford. il por Vogue 145:172-83+ Mr 1 '65
ROTHSTEIN, Arthur
  Creative color. See issues of U.S. camera & travel
ROTHSTEIN, Samuel
  Nobody's baby. por Library J 90:2226-7 My 15 '65
ROTHWELL, Frank N.
  Honolulu race nemesis. Yachting 117:64+ My '65
ROTOGRAVURE. See Photogravure
ROTOR aircraft
  Design for hot-cycle rotor/wing studied. il Aviation W 82:74 Je 21 '65
ROTORS (helicopters)
  Bell studies folding-rotor VTOL vehicles. il Aviation W 82:81+ Mr 22 '65
  Boelkow advances work on unconventional rotor systems. il Aviation W 82:314-16 Je 14 '65
  Lift fans gain favor for VTOL aircraft. M. L. Yaffee. il Aviation W 83:52-5+ Ag 9 '65
ROTZO, Italy
  Women of Rotzo; mayor and town council. il Newsweek 65:52+ Ap 12 '65
ROUAULT, Georges
  Georges Rouault. B. Kaufman. Commonweal 82:92-3 Ap 9 '65
ROUECHÉ, Berton
  Annals of medicine (cont) New Yorker 41: 51-2+ Ap 24; 180+ My 15; 205-10+ N 27 '65
  Phone call; story. New Yorker 41:38-9 Ag 28 '65
  Reporter at large (cont) New Yorker 41: 105-6+ O 23 '65
ROUKES, Nicholas
  Plastic paints. Sch Arts 64:20-4 F '65
ROULLIER, Jean
  Breakthrough in the facilitation of international maritime traffic. UN Mo Chron 2: 58-62 F '65
ROUNDS, George
  Electronic boating in your future. Motor B 116:22-5 N '65
ROUNDS, Joseph B. and Rooney, P. M.
  Buffalo bridges its site. Library J 90:5173-5 D 1 '65
ROUNDUPS
  See also
  Rodeos
ROUNDWORMS
  Nature note. Sci N L 88:285 O 30 '65
ROUNICK, Jack
  Great jumping swordfish. il por Yachting 117: 115-17 Je '65
ROUQUETTE, Robert
  Schism in French Catholicism? Cath World 202:34-9 O '65
ROUS sarcoma. See Sarcoma
ROUSSEAS, Stephen W.
  Great society: an old New deal. Nation 200: 499-501 My 10 '65
ROUSSEL, Hubert
  Lively accomplishments in the lively arts. Hi Fi 15:110 Jl '65
ROVELLO, Michael L.
  Don't make it look like a garage. Am City 80:114-15 Mr '65
ROVERE, Richard H.
  Books (cont) New Yorker 41:238+ D 11 '65
  Conservative mindlessness. Commentary 39: 38-42 Mr '65
  Letter from Washington. See issues of New Yorker
  Man for this age, too. N Y Times Mag p23+ Ap 11 '65
  Patriotic dissenters. NEA J 54:31 F '65

ROW houses
  Hospital staff housing opens to park; Highland view hospital family housing, Cuyahoga County, Ohio. il Arch Rec 137: 210-11 Ap '65
ROW spacing of plants. See Plants, Space arrangement of
ROWAN, Carl Thomas
  No whitewash for U.S. abroad. pors Ebony 20:56-8 Ag '65

about

  More than color. por Time 86:60 Ag 13 '65
  Now U.S. has one propaganda voice in Vietnam. por U S News 58:22 Ap 19 '65
ROWAN, Roy
  So far, yet it's so near. Life 59:98A-98B D 10 '65
ROWE, A. J. See Gibbons, I. R. jt. auth.
ROWE, David Nelson
  Korea 1965. Nat R 17:184 Mr 9 '65
ROWE, Leo S.
  OAS council. Américas 17:44-5 Je '65
ROWE, Leo S, scholarship loan fund. See Scholarships and fellowships
ROWELL, John
  New books for young adults. Sr Schol 86: sup2-3 Ap 15 '65
ROWELL, Robert L. and Stein, R. S.
  Electromagnetic scattering. Science 149:1399 S 17 '65
ROWEN, Herbert H.
  (comp) Articles and other books received; Low Countries. See issues of American historical review
ROWING
  Never before, at Harvard or in history; style of rowing patterned on Germany's Ratzeburg crew. H. Whall. il Sports Illus 22:36-8+ Je 28 '65
  Other times, other customs; Oxford-Cambridge boat race. Sports Illus 22:17 Ap 12 '65
  Think, feel, win; Harvard's crew. il Time 85: 68 Je 18 '65
  Up a muddy river in a beat-up shell; Fighting Irish of Notre Dame vs Harvard's oarsmen. H. Whall. il Sports Illus 22:60+ My 24 '65
  See also
  Regattas
ROWLAND, Stanley J, Jr
  Atypical giantitis. Christian Cent 82:1131-2 S 15 '65
  Matter of mind-set. Christian Cent 82:1226+ O 6 '65
ROWLAND, Wilmina
  How it is in Mississippi. Christian Cent 82: 340+ Mr 17 '65
ROWLEY, James J.
  Overhaul. il Newsweek 66:39 N 22 '65
ROWLEY, Peter
  Church and the couch. Nation 200:203-4 F 22 '65
ROWLINGSON, Donald T.
  Place of Jesus in theological reconstruction. Christian Cent 82:1034-6 Ag 25 '65
ROWSE, A. L.
  Sir Winston Churchill; excerpts from a tribute. Vogue 145:120-1 Mr 1 '65
ROWSOME, Frank, Jr
  Verse by the side of the road; excerpts. Am Heritage 17:102-5 D '65
ROWSON, K. E. K. See Mahy, B. W. J. jt. auth.
ROY, Gregor
  Morning song in a monastery valley; poem. Cath World 201:49 Ap '65
  Opinion: on the theatre. por Mlle 62:74+ N '65
  Plato, the penthouse, and the girl who hesitates. Mlle 60:199+ Mr '65
  Play of the month. Cath World 202:255-6 Ja '66
ROY, Jessie Hailstock
  Colored judges. por Negro Hist Bul 28:135-7, 158+ Mr-Ap '65
  Negro judges in the United States. por Negro Hist Bul 28:108-11 F '65
  Some personal recollections of Dr Woodson. por Negro Hist Bul 28:185-6+ My '65
ROY, Jules
  Jilted lover. il por Newsweek 66:58+ O 18 '65
ROYAL academy of dancing
  Royal academy. New Yorker 41:34-5 Je 5 '65
ROYAL air force. See Great Britain—Royal air force
ROYAL ballet, Great Britain
  Fourteen stars-in-ascendant of the greatest ballet company in the world, Britain's Royal. L. Lerman. il Mlle 60:218-19 Mr '65
  Letter from London; performance of Romeo and Juliet. M. Panter-Downes. New Yorker 41:118+ F 20 '65

ROYAL ballet, Great Britain—*Continued*
Man of the hour; Britain's Royal ballet in
Manhattan. il Time 85:52 Ap 30 '65
Music to my ears; new Swan lake. I.
Kolodin. il Sat R 48:54 My 22 '65
Music to my ears; the Royal ballet's Romeo.
I. Kolodin. Sat R 48:48 My 8 '65
Musical events; performance of Romeo and
Juliet. W. Sargeant. New Yorker 41:178-9
My 1 '65
New order at the Royal ballet. C. Barnes.
il Dance Mag 39:44-7+ Ap '65
Royal ballet; at Metropolitan opera house.
R. Krokover il Hi Fi 15:99+ Jl '65
Royal ballet's eighth New York season, Metro-
politan opera house. D. Hering Dance Mag
39:29-30+ Jl '65
Secret of the Nureyev spell. C. Barnes. il
N Y Times Mag p30-1+ Ap 18 '65
ROYAL Canadian mounted police. See Canada
—Royal Canadian mounted police
ROYAL Danish ballet
Bournonville preserved. T. G. Veale. il Dance
Mag 39:52-3+ Ag '65
High & the mighty; return to Manhattan.
il Time 86:62 D 10 '65
Introducing Flemming Flindt. J. Anderson.
il Dance Mag 39:26-9 N '65
Melancholy Dane; third American tour. il
Newsweek 66:92-3 D 13 '65
Music to my ears; Ashton's Romeo by the
Danes in New York state theater. Lincoln
Center. I. Kolodin. Sat R 48:56 D 11 '65
Musical events; first week of current season
at New York state theatre. W. Sargeant.
New Yorker 41:201-2 D 4 '65
Musical events; performance of Coppelia. W.
Sargeant. New Yorker 41:234 D 11 '65
Musical events; performance of La sylphide.
W. Sargeant. New Yorker 41:158 D 18 '65
What's different about the Danes? L. Moore.
il Dance Mag 39:44-9 O '65
ROYAL Dutch-Shell group
Rare kind of import; first American to be-
come a managing director. il Time 85:104
Ap 30 '65
ROYAL family of Monaco. See Monaco—Royal
family
ROYAL festival hall, London. See Concert
halls
ROYAL hunt of the sun; drama. See Shaffer,
P.
ROYAL institution of Great Britain
Schools lectures at the Royal institution; sci-
entific experiments to be shown to young
people. L. Bragg. il Science 150:1420-3 D
10 '65
ROYAL Marines tattoo.   See Great Britain—
Royal Marines
ROYAL OAK, Mich.
Dignity in detail for a corner bank. il Arch
Rec 137:196 Je '65
ROYAL society of London
Blackett chosen president of Royal society.
V. K. McElheny. Science 150:1437-9 D 10 '65
ROYAL Vancouver yacht club. See Yacht clubs
ROYAL Winnipeg ballet
Royal Winnipeg ballet, Hunter college play-
house. D. Hering. Dance Mag 39:159-60
D '65
ROYALTIES
Author, the publisher and the fifty-fifty split.
P. R. Reynolds. Pub W 189:62-4 Ja 10 '66
I want to know: what does an author earn
from a book? excerpt from The writing and
selling of fiction. P. R. Reynolds. Writer
78:20-1 D '65
Norton raises authors' cut on paperback re-
prints. Pub W 188:72 N 15 '65
Royalties: current patterns and practices.
Pub W 187:54-5 F 15 '65
Royalties: current practices affecting scientific
and technical books. Pub W 187:65-6 Ap 19
'65
Royalties: religious and children's book pub-
lishers. Pub W 187:39-42 Mr 1 '65
Some welcome fresh air in the subsidiary
rights field; 50-50 royalty split. R. H.
Smith. Pub W 188:45 N 29 '65
ROYCE, James E.
Book reviews. America 113:247-8 S 4 '65
ROYERSFORD, Pa.
Small borough's comprehensive plan. H. J.
Grossman. il Am City 80:118-19 Je '65
ROYSTER, Vermont Connecticut
Folksiness on Wall Street. il pors Time 85:
73 Ap 30 '65
ROZIN, Paul
Temperature independence of an arbitrary
temporal discrimination in the goldfish.
bibliog Science 149:561-3 Jl 30 '65

RÓZSA, Anna
Search for Anna Rózsa. G. Fitzgerald. por
Opera N 30:16-17 Ja 15 '66
RUARK, Robert Chester
Something of value. il por Newsweek 66:54-
5 Jl 12 '65
RUBBER
Undersea rubber under scrutiny. J. F. Judge.
il Miss & Roc 17:32 S 27 '65
RUBBER, Artificial
Goodrich, Gulf ready to end tie; joint syn-
thetic rubber venture. Bsns W p33 O 9 '65
RUBBER, Silicone
New silicone rubber foams detailed. J. F.
Judge. il Miss & Roc 16:81-2 My 31 '65
RUBBER balls. See Balls
RUBBER boats. See Boats, Rubber
RUBBER hearts. See Heart, Artificial
RUBBER industry and trade
Rumanian deal settled amid fuss over an-
other; Universal oil products case. Bsns
W p71 Jl 31 '65
    See also
Tire industry and trade
        Wages and hours
Snappy action in rubber; settlement reached
after contracts expired with big three tire
companies. Bsns W p 144 Ap 24 '65
RUBBER torsion suspension. See Motor trucks
—Springs and suspension
RUBBER tubes. See Tubes, Rubber
RUBBINGS
Rubbings of Maya monuments. D. Nichols.
il Am Artist 29:54-7 Ap '65
RUBBISH disposal.   See Refuse and refuse
disposal
RUBELLA
Agony of mothers about their unborn; with
editors' note. il Life 58:3, 24-31 Je 4 '65
Attack on the unborn; dangers of German
measles during pregnancy. S. M. Spencer.
il Sat Eve Post 238:82-4 Mr 13 '65
Catholic abortions; Life's admission of false-
hood. America 113:273 S 18 '65
Cytopathic effect of rubella virus in a rabbit-
cornea cell line. J. Leerhøy. bibliog il Science 149:633-4 Ag 6 '65
Dangerous babies. Time 85:77 F 26 '65
Hemadsorption-negative plaque test: new
assay for rubella virus revealing a unique
interference. P. I. Marcus and D. H.
Carver. bibliog il Science 149:983-6 Ag 27
'65
Major tragedy feared; defective births are
on the rise; epidemic of German measles.
il U S News 58:11 My 3 '65
Rubella complement fixation test. J. L. Sever
and others. bibliog il Science 148:385-7 Ap
16 '65
Rubella test quick. Sci N L 87:259 Ap 24 '65
Rubella vaccine urgent. Sci N L 88:293 N
6 '65
Three on hospital staff get rubella from
babies. Sci N L 88:169 S 11 '65
Tragic pregnancy; case of German measles.
il Good H 162:12+ Ja '66
RUBENS, Sir Peter Paul
Century of Rubens. il Newsweek 66:93 D 6 '65
Rare Rubens by Rubens; Daniel in the lions'
den. il Time 87:75 Ja 21 '66
RUBIDIUM
Portable atomic frequency standard. il Electr
World 73:45+ Je '65
Terrestrial ratio of potassium to rubidium
and the composition of earth's mantle.
P. W. Gast. bibliog il Science 147:858-60
F 19 '65
RUBIDIUM clocks. See Atomic clocks
RUBIDIUM magnetometers. See Magnetometers
RUBIDIUM-strontium dating. See Radioactive
dating
RUBIN, Dan
Photography's new breed. D. Becker. il U S
Camera 28:64-7+ F '65
RUBIN, Larry
Lookout point; poem. Commonweal 82:698
S 24 '65
To a girl who's been abroad too long; poem.
Sat R 48:34 O 9 '65
Warning; poem. Harper 232:100 Ja '66
RUBIN, Len S.
Reader's choice. Travel 123:7 My '65
RUBIN, Louis D. Jr
Notes on the literary scene: their own lan-
guage. Harper 230:173-5 Ap '65
RUBIN, Schulem
Rabbi as candidate. Newsweek 66:63 S 13 '65
RUBIN, Sol
Cops, guns and homicides. Nation 201:527-9 D
27 '65

RUBIN, Theodore Isaac
Thin book by a formerly fat psychiatrist. McCalls 93:54-5+ Ja '66

RUBINOFF, Ira
Science in action: mixing oceans and species. Natur Hist 74:69-72 Ag '65

RUBINSTEIN, Alvin Z.
Yugoslavia's opening society. Cur Hist 48:149-53+ Mr '65

RUBINSTEIN, Anton Grigor'evich
From ultraphone, Anton Rubinstein's The demon. R. Jones. por Am Rec G 31:649 Mr '65

RUBINSTEIN, Artur
Rubinstein, adventurer and elder statesman. A. Chasins. il por Hi Fi 15:113+ My '65

RUBINSTEIN, Helena
Beauty merchant. il por Time 85:98 Ap 9 '65
Madame. por Newsweek 65:87 Ap 12 '65
Miniature rooms of Helena Rubinstein. S. A. Parvin. il Hobbies 70:122-3 My; 120+ Jl '65

RUBIROSA, Porfirio
Great playboy. il por Newsweek 66:42 Jl 19 '65
Toujours Prêt. il pors Time 86:34 Jl 16 '65

RUBY, Jack
Clearing the air. S. T. Possony. Nat R 17:113-14+ F 9 '65
Critique of the Warren report. D. Macdonald. Esquire 63:59-63+ Mr '65
Jack Ruby case. Nation 200:323 Mr 29 '65

RUBY trial. See Trials (murder)

RUCK sack. See Packs

RUDD, Hughes
Short stories by a pair of young masters. C. Knickerbocker. Life 60:8+ Ja 14 '66

RUDENESS. See Courtesy

RUDJORD, Torstein. See Pansen, J. K. S. jt. auth.

RUDLOE, Jack J.
Amateur scientist. por Sci Am 212:119-20+ Mr '65

RUDNICK, A. and Chan, Y. C.
Dengue type 2 virus in naturally infected aedes albopictus mosquitoes in Singapore. bibliog Science 149:638-9 Ag 6 '65

RUDO, R. M.
Old irreplaceable me; story. Redbook 125:46-7 Ag '65

RUDOFF, Harvey
Should teachers join a union? yes. por Parents Mag 40:60+ O '65

RUDOFSKY, Bernard
Do you like kimono? excerpt from The kimono mind. Horizon 7:48-53 Spr '65

RUDOLF, Max
Public vs. modern music. Opera N 30:8-11 Ja 22 '66

RUDOLPH, Paul Marvin
Home in classic style. il Life 58:94-7+ F 26 '65
In pursuit of diversity. il Time 86:56-7 Jl 2 '65

RUDOLPH, Walter
Eight acres and independence. Am For 71:30-3 Mr '65

RUDY, Willis
Evaluations of American education by foreigners; excerpt from Schools in an age of mass culture. bibliog f Sch & Soc 93:93-104 F 6 '65

RUE, Leonard Lee, 3d
Publishing from the cider mill. A. L. Crosby. il por Pub W 188:41-3 Jl 5 '65; Reply. R. M. Huber. 188:11-12 Ag 16 '65

RUEFF, Jacques
Why de Gaulle said what he did; excerpt from interview. por U S News 58:44-5 F 15 '65

about
Missionary for gold wins few U.S. fans. pors Bsns W p31-2 Ap 24 '65

RUETHER, Rosemary
Is Roman Catholicism reformable? Christian Cent 82:1152-4 S 22 '65

RUFFED grouse shooting. See Grouse shooting

RUFFIN, Albert
Grizzly; story of five hikers. Life 59:73-4+ Ag 27 '65

RUFFIN, George Lewis
Colored judges. J. H. Roy. Negro Hist Bul 28:135-7 Mr '65

RUG making. See Rugs and carpets

RUGBY football
Have you ever watched a scrum? Monterey rugby tournament. il Sunset 134:56+ Mr '65
Playing and the partying were loovly; Notre Dame rugby club wins the Irish challenge cup. R. Lardner. il Sports Illus 22:65-6+ My 10 '65

RUGGIERO, Vincent Ryan
Rediscovering the obvious. America 112:613-15 Ap 24 '65

RUGS and carpets
Basic ways to make your own rugs. il Good H 160:136 Ja '65
Carpet for house and yard; Ozite outdoor-indoor carpet. Consumer Rep 30:274-5 Je '65
How to buy and care for carpeting. Am Home 68:104 Mr '65
How to make rya rugs. il House & Gard 127:170-1 My '65
Is carpet practical? carpets for libraries. M. Van Buren. il Library J 90:5152-6 D 1 '65; Reply with rejoinder. D. Schaffer. 90:5320+ D 15 '65
Keys to carpet buying. il Bet Hom & Gard 43:118+ O '65
Making a rug mural; interview. C. R. Perrin. il Am Artist 30:38-41+ Ja '66
Most effective decorating starts with the floor. A. C. Borg. il Am Home 68:48-53 Ap '65
New world at your feet. il McCalls 92:108-15 Mr '65
Questions and answers on buying carpets. il House & Gard 127:194-5 My '65
Ten don'ts for buyers of carpets and rugs. Good H 161:230+ N '65
Works of art to walk on, felt rugs. M. Garrity. il Bet Hom & Gard 43:60-1 F '65

RUGS and carpets, Oriental
Rugs of Turkestan; with editorial comment. C. D. Reed. il Antiques 89:77, 94-8 Ja '66
Timeless oriental rug. J. G. Staley. il Bet Hom & Gard 43:38+ N '65

RUHR RIVER
How Germany keeps the Ruhr River clean. il U S News 59:61 D 13 '65

RUHR VALLEY
West Germany's Ruhr: coal, steel, and trouble. il U S News 58:80-1 Mr 8 '65

RUIZ, Brunilda
Brief biography. S. Goodman. pors Dance Mag 39:46-7 Ag '65

RUKEYSER, Muriel
Backside of the academy; poem. Nation 200:146 F 8 '65
Little; story. Ladies Home J 82:82-5 F '65
Outer banks; poem. Poetry 106:381-7 S '65

RULE of law
Adlai Stevenson's last article; outline for a new American policy. A. E. Stevenson. il Look 29:71-2+ Ag 24 '65
Building a decent world order; address, June 5, 1965. D. Rusk. Dept State Bul 53:27-30 Jl 5 '65
Control of force in international relations; address, April 23, 1965. D. Rusk. Dept State Bul 52:694-701 My 10 '65
Prospects of law in a world of conflict; address, April 29, 1965. L. C. Meeker. Dept State Bul 52:900-5 Je 7 '65
Second Dublin declaration; text, with editorial note. Sat R 48:28-9 D 11 '65
Some fundamentals of American policy; address, March 4, 1965. D. Rusk. Dept State Bul 52:398-403 Mr 22 '65
World peace through law; addresses, September 16 and September 17, 1965. L. B. Johnson; A. J. Goldberg. Dept State Bul 53:542-8 O 4 '65
See also
World conference on world peace through the rule of law

RUM
Rum in the sun. il Esquire 64:90-1 Ag '65

RUMANIA
See also
Communism—Rumania
Communist party (Rumania)
Jews in Rumania
Music—Rumania
Sighet
United States—Commerce—Rumania
United States—Economic relations—Rumania

Description and travel
Sentimental journey to Dracula's home town; Borgo Pass. G. Smith. il Sat Eve Post 238:76-9 Mr 27 '65

Economic conditions
Romania's new national communism. P. Ben. Reporter 33:32-3 S 9 '65

Economic policy
Whither Rumania? W. S. Vucinich. bibliog f Cur Hist 48:161-7 Mr '65

Industries
Independent Rumanians industrialize. il Bsns W p 182 N 20 '65
See also
Rubber industry and trade

RUMANIA—*Continued*

Politics and government

Docile guests: Rumanian Communist party congress. il Time 86:23 Jl 30 '65
Holding the spotlight. F. Y. Blumenfeld. Newsweek 66:35-6 Ag 2 '65
Romania's new national communism. P. Ben. Reporter 33:32-3 S 9 '65
Whither Rumania? W. S. Vucinich. bibliog f Cur Hist 48:161-7 Mr '65

RUMANIA and Russia
Atlantic report. Atlan 215:32+ Je '65
Whither Rumania? W. S. Vucinich. bibliog f Cur Hist 48:161-7 Mr '65

RUMMELL, Frances V.
Maryland U.'s global classrooms. Read Digest 86:245-8+ Ap '65
Teaching kids to teach themselves. PTA Mag 60:16-29 O '65; Same abr. with title He teaches kids to teach themselves. Read Digest 87:246-7+ O '65

RUMMY (game)
There's no gambling like show gambling; playing gin rummy on stage. E. J. Kahn, jr. Vogue 147:12b+ Ja 1 '66

RUNAWAY bookmobile: drama. See Boiko, C.

RUNAWAY boys and girls
On running away. J. Keats. il Holiday 37:8+ Je '65

RUNGE, David
Lutheran church-Missouri synod in triennial session. Christian Cent 82:922-4 Jl 21 '65

RUNGE, Ted, and Forbes, Will
Darkroom aids and short cuts. Pop Phot 56:126-7 Je '65

RUNKLE, Mary
Walk carefully, your children are following. Suc Farm 63:61+ Ag '65

RUNNING
Ah, so; Boston marathon. il Newsweek 65:60 My 3 '65
Big three are miles apart. J. Underwood. il Sports Illus 22:26-7+ Je 21 '65
Fast teen-agers in grown-up time; J. Ryun beats P. Snell in mile run. G. S. Brown. il Sports Illus 23:14-15+ Jl 5 '65
Final blaze of non-success; once invincible P. Snell goes home. J. Underwood. il Sports Illus 23:14-15 Ag 2 '65
Flat out to thrash the bloke; P. Snell beats B. Crothers in indoor race. H. Horn. il Sports Illus 22:18-21+ F 22 '65
For the heart & soul. il Time 85:55 Je 4 '65
Jazy records. il Newsweek 66:52 Jl 5 '65
Jug of wine, and pow! M. Jazy. il Time 85:69 Je 18 '65
Land rush down under to overtake a record, New Zealand and Australian track circuit. G. S. Brown. il Sports Illus 24:44-5 Ja 3 '65
Near miss; American girl's wish to be a long distance runner. il Newsweek 66:52 Ag 16 '65
Number two lion in the land of Sheba; A. Bikila, Olympic champion marathon runner. J. Underwood. il Sports Illus 22:86-92+ Ap 12 '65
One Canadian takes charge of three meets; middle-distance runner B. Crothers. G. S. Brown. Sports Illus 22:48-9 F 8 '65
Ron runs the world ragged; Australia's R. Clarke has set four world records. G. S. Brown. il Sports Illus 23:24-5 Jl 26 '65
Some fanatics whose fun is playing old records: track nuts. G. Holland. il Sports Illus 3:46-7 Ag 2 '65
Sophisticate & the natural. il Time 86:37 D 24 '65
Two stirring triumphs over men and the clock: New Zealand's P. Snell, Australia's R. Clarke. G. S. Brown. il Sports Illus 22:79-81 Je 14 '65
Vas-y, Ja-zy! and he went; France's finest middle-distance runner. M. Jazy. E. Shrake. il Sports Illus 23:32-4+ Ag 30 '65

RUNNING of the deer: story. See Boles, P. D.

RUNWAYS, Airport. See Airports—Runways

RUPPENTHAL, Karl M.
Air safety. Nation 201:525-7 D 27 '65
Airplanes abroad: crashes and consequences. Nation 201:408-10 N 29 '65

RUPTURE. See Hernia

RURAL education. See Rural schools

RURAL electrification association. See United States—Rural electrification administration

RURAL library service
Books on the mountain; North Carolina. B. Davenport. il Am Ed 1:12-15 Mr '65

RURAL life. See Farm life

RURAL planning
Old agency up to new tricks. il Nations Bsns 53:48-50+ F '65

RURAL poverty. See Poverty

RURAL recreation. See Recreation, Rural

RURAL rehabilitation. See Sociology, Rural

RURAL schools
Our rural schools aren't half good enough! G. McConnell. Farm J 89:70D Ap '65

One-teacher schools

Survival of the one-room. il Time 85:45 Ap 9 '65

United States

Big ideas for small schools; Western states small schools project. O. F. Parody. il Am Ed 1:1-3 Jl '65

RURAL sociology. See Sociology, Rural

RURAL-urban conflict. See City and country

RURAL youth
What next for your teen-agers? symposium. Farm J 89:57-9 Je '65

RUSCHI, Augusto
Augusto Ruschi's Garden of Eden. A. Rankin. il por Read Digest 86:216-18+ Je '65

RUSH, Hazel S.
Christmas ornaments from fruit dividers. il Design 67:12-13 N '65
Frames and tempera. Sch Arts 64:38 My '65
Roman ladies. Design 67:27 S '65

RUSHER, William A.
It won't go away. Nat R 17:199-200 Mr 9 '65
What did happen in 1964? Nat R 17:690-2 Ag 10 '65

RUSHTON, John Henry
Personality of the month. L. Galton. il por Sci Digest 57:38-40 My '65

RUSK, Alice. See Wiese, M. B. jt. auth.

RUSK, Dean
ABC'S of U.S. aims in Vietnam; interview. por U S News 58:79-80 Ap 19 '65
Alliance for progress: a partnership of mutual help; address, June 10, 1965. Dept State Bul 53:2-5 Jl 5 '65
Anatomy of foreign policy decisions; address, September 7, 1965. Dept State Bul 53:502-9 S 27 '65; Same. Vital Speeches 31:744-7 O 1 '65
Building a decent world order; address, June 5, 1965. Dept State Bul 53:27-30 Jl 5 '65
Central treaty organization marks 10th anniversary; remarks. Dept State Bul 52:390 Mr 15 '65
Central treaty organization meets at Tehran; statement, April 7, 1965. Dept State Bul 52:685-8 My 3 '65
Common quest for freedom and prosperity in the American republics; address, November 22, 1965. bibliog f Dept State Bul 53:996-8 D 20 '65; Same with title Inter-American systems. Vital Speeches 32:130-5 D 15 '65
Consular convention with the Soviet Union; statement, July 30, 1965. Dept State Bul 53:375-8 Ag 30 '65
Control of force in international relations; address, April 23, 1965. Dept State Bul 52:694-701 My 10 '65
Eleventh anniversary of SEATO: statement, September 4, 1965. Dept State Bul 53:536-7 S 27 '65
Excerpt from statement, March 25, 1965. Cong Digest 44:175+ Je '65
Excerpt from testimony, February 24, 1965. Cong Digest 44:142+ My '65
Excerpt from testimony, July 30, 1965. Cong Digest 44:300+ D '65
Foreign assistance program for 1966; statement, March 9, 1965. Dept State Bul 52:482-8 Ap 5 '65
Foreign policy aspects of proposals to revise immigration law; statement, February 24, 1965. Dept State Bul 52:384-7 Mr 15 '65
From Dean Rusk: answers to key questions on Vietnam; excerpts from address, April 23, 1965. U S News 58:74-7 My 10 '65
Guidelines of U.S. foreign policy; address, June 6, 1965. Dept State Bul 52:1030-4 Je 28 '65
How reds block Vietnam peace, report from Rusk; summary. U S News 58:15 Je 28 '65
International visitors and the American society; address, March 19, 1965. Dept State Bul 52:588-92 Ap 19 '65
Letter to Foreign minister Fanfani, December 4, 1965. Dept State Bul 54:11-12 Ja 3 '66
Memorial to President Kennedy at Runnymede; remarks, May 14, 1965. Dept State Bul 52:897-8 Je 7 '65
OAS to help restore democratic order in Dominican Republic; statement, June 2, 1965. Dept State Bul 53:1017-18 Je 21 '65
Our Atlantic policy; address, March 6, 1965. Dept State Bul 52:427-31 Mr 22 '65

RUSK, Dean—*Continued*
Peace prospects, as Rusk sees them; excerpts from address, October 5, 1965. por U S News 59:20 O 18 '65
Political and military aspects of U.S. policy in Viet-Nam; interview, August 9, 1965. Dept State Bul 53:342-56 Ag 30 '65; Excerpts. por U S News 59:13 Ag 23 '65
Reform of our basic immigration law; address, April 19, 1965. Dept State Bul 52:806-9 My 24 '65
Rusk to Hanoi: no Vietnam backdown; excerpts from interview. U S News 59:10 D 20 '65
Secretary answers his critics; interview. por Newsweek 65:29 My 17 '65
Secretary discusses situation in Dominican Republic; interview, ed. by J. Hightower. Dept State Bul 52:842-4 My 31 '65
Secretary discusses Viet-Nam on USIA television; transcript of interview by members of the international press, June 24, 1965. Dept State Bul 53:105-10 Jl 19 '65
Secretary Rusk interviewed:
  Belgian television program, September 7, 1965. Dept State Bul 53:512-14 S 27 '65
  British broadcasting corporation, April 2, 1965. Dept State Bul 52:569-71 Ap 19 '65
  Columbia broadcasting system, August 23, 1965. Dept State Bul 53:431-44 S 13 '65
  Face the Nation program, March 7, 1965. Dept State Bul 52:442-8 Mr 29 '65
  Issues and answers program, July 11, 1965. Dept State Bul 53:183-90 Ag 2 '65
  NBC, January 3, 1965. bibliog f Dept State Bul 52:62-74 Ja 18 '65
  NBC, May 28, 1965. Dept State Bul 52:947-9 Je 14 '65
  NBC's American white paper, September 7, 1965. Dept State Bul 53:509-12 S 27 '65
Secretary Rusk reviews efforts to reach peaceful settlement in southeast Asia; remarks, June 18, 1965, with questions and answers. bibliog f Dept State Bul 53:6-12 Jl 5 '65
Secretary Rusk's news conference:
  February 25, 1965. Dept State Bul 52:362-71 Mr 15 '65
  March 24, 1965. Dept State Bul 52:528-32 Ap 12 '65
  May 26, 1965. Dept State Bul 52:938-47 Je 14 '65
  August 2, 1965. Dept State Bul 53:302-10 Ag 23 '65
  August 27, 1965. Dept State Bul 53:481-6 S 20 '65
  November 5, 1965. Dept State Bul 53:854-62 N 29 '65
  November 26, 1965. Dept State Bul 53:930-9 D 13 '65
  December 9, 1965. Dept State Bul 53:1006-13 D 27 '65
Secretary urges ratification of U.N. charter amendments; statement, April 28, 1965. Dept State Bul 52:827-30 My 24 '65
Some fundamentals of American policy; address, March 4, 1965. Dept State Bul 52:398-403 Mr 22 '65
Southeast Asia aid program; statement, June 3, 1965. Dept State Bul 52:1056-60 Je 28 '65
Tenth anniversary of signing of Austrian state treaty; remarks, May 15, 1965. Dept State Bul 52:898-9 Je 7 '65
United Nations holds memorial ceremony for Ambassador Stevenson; remarks, July 19, 1965. Dept State Bul 53:233-5 Ag 9 '65
U.S. continues to abide by Geneva conventions of 1949 in Viet-Nam; letter, August 10, 1965. Dept State Bul 53:447 S 13 '65
U.S.-Japan cabinet committee on trade and economic affairs holds fourth meeting at Washington; remarks, July 12, 1965; with joint communique. Dept State Bul 53:242-3, 247-9 Ag 9 '65
United States navy, watchdog of peace; address, January 23, 1965. Dept State Bul 52:165-7 F 8 '65
U.S. unwilling to maintain consular relations with Cambodia; letter, May 6, 1965. Dept State Bul 52:853-4 My 31 '65
U.S. willing to participate in conference on Cambodia; statement, April 25, 1965. Dept State Bul 52:711-12 My 10 '65
Unseen search for peace; address, October 16, 1965. Dept State Bul 53:690-9 N 1 '65; Same. Vital Speeches 32:66-71 N 15 '65
Viet-Nam: four steps to peace; address, June 23, 1965. Dept State Bul 53:50-5 Jl 12 '65
White House conference on international cooperation; remarks, December 1, 1965; with questions and answers. Dept State Bul 53:976-84 D 20 '65

World in our living room; statement. Time 86:18 D 17 '65
about
Bitter pen of Arthur M. Nat R 17:680 Ag 10 '65
Byzantium on the Potomac. M. Greenfield. Reporter 33:10+ Ag 12 '65
Change & chatter. il Time 86:16 Jl 16 '65
Credibility of commitment. il Time 86:9 D 24 '65
Dull old Dean. K. Crawford. Newsweek 66:28 Ag 16 '65
Empty chair. Newsweek 65:21 F 22 '65
Enigma of Dean Rusk. J. Kraft. Harper 231:100-3 Jl '65
How the State department baffled him; excerpts from A thousand days. A. M. Schlesinger, jr. il pors Life 59:18-27 Jl 30 '65
How two officials fared in South America. il por U S News 59:19 N 29 '65
Letter from Washington. R. H. Rovere. New Yorker 41:143-50 Je 12 '65
Of many things; concerning A. Schlesinger's recollections. T. N. Davis. America 113:124 Ag 7 '65
President's just-a-minute man. M. Frankel. il pors N Y Times Mag p48-9+ S 12 '65
Rusk rebuts policy critics. il Sr Schol 86:17 My 6 '65
Rusk's reply; reaction to A. Schlesinger, jr.'s attack. por Time 86:16 Ag 13 '65
What liberty means. il por Newsweek 66:26 N 29 '65

RUSK, Howard A.
Brighter future for disabled children. Parents Mag 40:66-7+ N '65
about
Green mansions. B. Black. il por Pop Gard 16:38-41 My '65

RUSK, R. Roy
Volunteership. por Recreation 58:212-13 My '65

RUSKAUFF, Bob
Sail paces power in the West. See issues of Motor boating
Un-natural wonder. Motor B 115:46-9 My '65
Westward ho! See issues of Motor boating

RUSNAK, Gene A. See Newman, W. S. jt. auth.

RUSS, Lavinia
For creatures great and small. Pub W 188:28-9 O 11 '65
I'm dreaming of a white tornado. Pub W 188:28 D 6 '65
Sheep in wolves' clothing; or Never judge a children's book by its cover. Pub W 187:57-8 My 10 '65

RUSSELL, Andy
Hunting knife. Field & S 70:54-7+ Je '65

RUSSELL, Bill
Psych. and my other tricks. por Sports Illus 23:32-4+ O 25 '65
about
Ol' Massa Russell? Nation 200:211 Mr 1 '65

RUSSELL, Cazzie
Nothing but the best. H. L. Masin. por Sr Schol 87:36-7 D 9 '65

RUSSELL, Charles Ellsworth
Resurgence of Pee Wee Russell. M. Williams. por Sat R 48:59 F 27 '65

RUSSELL, Charles Marion
Northern Montana loop. K. N. Anderson. il Todays Health 43:41-5+ S '65

RUSSELL, Charles W.
Fleet thinking. Recreation 58:132-3 Mr '65

RUSSELL, Dan M. Jr
How judges are made. New Repub 153:5-6 O 23 '65
Lowering the bench. New Repub 153:6 O 9 '65

RUSSELL, Donald B.
South Carolina's new senator. il por Time 85:33-4 Ap 30 '65

RUSSELL, Elizabeth S. See Margolis, F. L. jt. auth.

RUSSELL, Francis
Harding papers; and some were saved. Am Heritage 16:24-31+ F '65
Hundred years of Harding. Nat R 17:336-8 Ap 20 '65
Invitation to the dance. Nat R 17:202+ Mr 9 '65
Men and manners (cont) Nat R 17:1166-7 D 14 '65
Men of Vimy. Nat R 17:474-6 Je 1 '65
Movies (cont) Nat R 17:738, 886+ Ag 24, O 5 '65
Passing scene (cont) Nat R 17:1108-11 N 30 '65
Some non-encounters with Mr Eliot. Horizon 7:36-41 Autumn '65

RUSSELL, Franklin
Are animals more human than people? Life 58:12+ Mr 26 '65
Cold dawn run from Witless Bay to Erewhon. Sports Illus 22:64-6+ Ap 26 '65
How much for an eagle? Life 59:23 S 10 '65
Life and death on the Funks. Horizon 7:32-8 Sum '65

RUSSELL, Glen A. and Talaty, E. R.
Electron spin resonance spectroscopy: application to proof of structure of organic ketones. bibliog Science 148:1217-18 My 28 '65

RUSSELL, James E.
Response in elementary education; excerpt from Change and challenge in American education. Sch & Soc 93:120-4 F 20 '65

RUSSELL, John, 1919-
Adventure of making Private view. Vogue 146:97+ N 15 '65
Art news from London. See issues of Art news
London: from imperium to maniac. Art N 64: 48-9+ N '65
Man who invented modern art dealing. Vogue 146:146-9+ S 15 '65
Mark Tobey. Vogue 146:200-3+ N 1 '65
Previewing the Spencer-Churchill sale. Art N 63:40-3+ F '65

RUSSELL, Nicole (Schneider) Milinaire, duchess of Bedford. See Bedford, N. S. M. R.

RUSSELL, Peter
Decay of poetry. Nat R 17:428-30 My 18 '65

about

Ends and means. S. F. Morse. Poetry 105: 407-9 Mr '65

RUSSELL, Richard Brevard
What it will take to win in Vietnam; interview. por U S News 59:56-60 S 6 '65

about

Filibuster's best friend. D. Oberdorfer. il pors Sat Eve Post 238:90+ Mr 13 '65

RUSSELL, Rosalind
Dear, dear teen-agers. por Seventeen 24: 156+ N '65

about

Indestructible Roz. il pors Life 59:109-10+ S 10 '65

RUSSIA
Two miracles, Russian style. G. Feifer. Harper 230:106+ Je '65
U.S.S.R: the new regime; symposium. bibliog f il Cur Hist 49:193-234+ O '65
See also
Advertising—Russia
Agricultural administration—Russia
Airlines—Russia
Airplane industry and trade—Russia
Airplanes, Military—Russia
Art—Russia
Automobile industry and trade—Russia
Banks and banking—Russia
Budget—Russia
Camping—Russia
Chemical industries—Russia
Clothing industry—Russia
Coal mines and mining—Russia
Colleges and universities—Russia
Communism—Russia
Concentration camps—Russia
Crime and criminals—Russia
Education—Russia
Foreign students in Russia
Hotels, taverns, etc.—Russia
Hunting—Russia
Kazakhstan
Labor laws and legislation—Russia
Leningrad. Siege of, 1941-1944
Liquor problem—Russia
Marriage—Russia
Medicine—Russia
Merchant marine—Russia
Money—Russia
Moving picture industry—Russia
Moving pictures—Russia
Music—Russia
Newspapers—Russia
Phonograph record industry—Russia
Research—Russia
Science—Russia
Space research—Russia
Suzdal
Tashkent
Television broadcasting—Russia
Textbooks—Russia
Tourist trade—Russia
Trials—Russia
Unemployment—Russia
United Nations—Russia
Wages—Russia
Waterways—Russia
Women—Russia
World war, 1939-1945—Russia
Youth—Russia

Armed forces

Military policy: a Soviet dilemma. T. W. Wolfe. bibliog f Cur Hist 49:201-7+ O '65
See also
Russia—Navy

Officers

Men who run Russia's armed forces. S. Bialer. il N Y Times Mag p 14-15+ F 21 '65

Bibliography

Got anything new on Russia? E. Hall. Library J 90:5041-2+ N 15 '65

Boundaries

On the line; Sino-Soviet border. R. J. Korengold. il Newsweek 66:45 S 13 '65
Tourist trap, Soviet style; N. Mott's visa violation. Life 59:4 D 10 '65

Commerce

Closer trade ties; non-Communist world. Time 86:69 D 31 '65
Soviet trade and aid. M. Kovner. bibliog f il Cur Hist 49:227-34 O '65
Ugly Russian, by V. Lasky. Review Nat R il 17:731-2 Ag 24 '65. M. S. Evans
We should do more business with the Communists. J. H. Cerf. il N Y Times Mag p70-1+ D 5 '65
Why U.S. was left out of Russian wheat deal; with editorial comment. Bsns W p30-1, 144 Ag 21 '65

United States

Reappraising trade with Russia. T. F. Willers. Duns R 85:21+ Mr '65

Commercial treaties and agreements

Ally's reward; E. Apel suicide; protest against Russian-East German trade pact. Newsweek 66:39-40 D 20 '65
How Russia plunders its allies. il U S News 59:47 D 27 '65
United States and U.S.S.R. sign king crab fishing agreement; Department announcement, February 6, 1965, with text of agreement. Dept State Bul 52:320-1 Mr 1 '65

Cultural relations

Moscow—New York shuttle; Soviet-American musical relations. Hi Fi 15:49 O '65

Defenses

Is Russia slowing down in arms race? interview. R. S. McNamara. il U S News 58: 52-6+ Ap 12 '65
Military policy: a Soviet dilemma. T. W. Wolfe. bibliog f Cur Hist 49:201-7+ O '65
Moscow parade features solid, liquid-fuel ICBMs and new battlefield-class missiles; with photographs and editorial comment. H. J. Coleman. Aviation W 82:21, 26-31 My 17 '65
New rockets unveiled in Moscow; with editorial comment. il Miss & Roc 16:16-17, 74 My 17 '65
Pardon our nukes. Time 86:33 Jl 16 '65
Russia revamps its missile might; weapons reequipped with latest in rocketry and electronics. il Bsns W p 138+ N 20 '65
Russian SAM shows how it can kill. il Life 59:26B-26C Ag 6 '65
Soviet claim could spur space track. M. Getler. il Miss & Roc 17:14-15 N 15 '65
Soviets brandish medium, long range missiles; with photographs. Aviation W 82:20-3 My 24 '65
Soviets parade medium, long range missiles; photographs. Aviation W 83:64-5 D 6 '65
See also
Aeronautics, Military—Russia
Russia—Armed forces
Russia—Navy

Diplomatic and consular service

Consular convention with the Soviet Union; statement, July 30, 1965. D. Rusk. Dept State Bul 53:375-8 Ag 30 '65
Le plus parisien; change of ambassador in Paris. Newsweek 65:39+ Ap 5 '65
This month's feature: proposed U.S.-Soviet consular agreemnt. Cong Digest 44:289-310 D '65

Economic conditions

Borrowing from the capitalists; economic change in Communist-bloc. il Time 85:23-6+ F 12 '65; Same abr. with title Russia tests the profit system. Read Digest 86: 107-11 My '65
Bricklayers. il Time 85:39B Ap 30 '65
Depression in Russia? il U S News 59:42-5 S 13 '65

RUSSIA—Economic conditions—*Continued*
Economic policies after Khrushchev. M. T. Florinsky. Cur Hist 49:221-6+ O '65
How Russia has changed and what it means to us. J. P. Davies. il Look 29:81-3 My 18 '65
Revolt coming in Russia? with interview with M. Garder, ed. by F. C. Painton. il U S News 58:44-8 Je 21 '65
Revolution coming in Russia? a Yugoslav says this; summary of report. M. Mihajlov. il U S News 59:72-3 Jl 19 '65
Russia has lost its race with U.S; a French size-up; reprint. R. d'Abernat. U S News 59:84 N 8 '65
U.S.S.R. falters in economic growth race with the United States; memorandum, September 1965. il Dept State Bul 53:701-8 N 1 '65
Where Russia is losing; Moscow's reasons for taking a soft line. il U S News 58:53-Mr 22 '65
See also
Labor and laboring classes—Russia
Russia—Industries
Wages—Russia

Economic policy
Borrowing from the capitalists; economic change in Communist-bloc. il Time 85:23-6+ F 12 '65; Same abr. with title Russia tests the profit system. Read Digest 86:107-11 My '65
Can Soviet planners produce a speedup? il Bsns W p50+ S 4 '65
Capitalism in Russia: just how far will it go? il U S News 59:104-5 Ag 9 '65
Change: possibly for the better. N. Cousins. Sat R 48:22+ F 6 '65
Economic policies after Khrushchev. M. T. Florinsky. Cur Hist 49:221-6+ O '65
Horse-sense revolution; change in the Soviet economy. il Time 86:26 Jl 9 '65
Industrial revolution. il Newsweek 66:58+ O 11 '65
Management, distribution, planning: new Russian revolution. M. Miller. il Nation 201:437-9+ D 6 '65
Modernizing the Soviet economy. V. Zorza. New Repub 153:17-18 O 16 '65
Moscow restoration: dragon of bureaucracy. I. Deutscher. il Nation 201:264-6 O 25 '65
Nose of the camel? Liberman plan. il Newsweek 65:92-4 Ap 12 '65
On toward the goulash; Kosygin's economic shakeup. Time 86:48 O 8 '65
Russia discovers the customer is always right; Libermanism. D. Crankshaw. il N Y Times Mag p26-7+ Mr 28 '65
Russia puts a new spur to output; quotas dropped, and plant managers given more freedom of action. Bsns W p32 O 2 '65
Russians change but not much. Bsns W p202 O 9 '65
Russia's new economy. S. Lens. Christian Cent 82:236 F 24 '65
Russia's new five year plan; address, September 28, 1965. A. N. Kosygin. Vital Speeches 32:115-28 D 1 '65
Soviet economy since Stalin, by H. Schwartz. Review
Sat R 48:38 Ag 14 '65. L. Smolinski
Soviets set a style for profit; Moscow clothing plant aims to please consumer taste. il Bsns W p 104+ Mr 20 '65
Still trying to make socialism work. il U S News 59:45 O 11 '65
To catch a planner; excerpts from address. A. Kosygin. il Newsweek 65:43+ My 3 '65
What worries the men in the Kremlin. W. Benton. il Look 29:67-8+ Ap 20 '65

Economic relations
Moscow to sign patent agreement. Bsns W p42 Mr 20 '65

Foreign relations
Chance for Soviet-American diplomacy. H. Brandon. Sat R 48:18+ O 23 '65
Kremlin diplomacy: first year for the new team. I. Deutscher. Nation 202:32-3 Ja 10 '66
Kremlin's difficult choice; ideology vs. national interests. R. Lowenthal. Atlan 215:76-83 Ap '65
Legacies of Khrushchev. A. Werth. Nation 200:354-7 Ap 5 '65
Revolt coming in Russia? with interview with M. Garder, ed. by F. C. Painton. il U S News 58:44-8 Je 21 '65
Soviet foreign policy: a broad view. D. T. Cattell. bibliog f Cur Hist 49:208-13 O '65
Soviet leaders on the move. il Newsweek 67:36+ Ja 24 '66
Soviet Union and the neutralist world. J. S. Reshetar, jr. bibliog f Ann Am Acad 362:102-12 N '65

Soviets change their foreign policy. R. Lowenthal. il N Y Times Mag p30-1+ Ap 4 '65
Vacuum diplomacy. G. Lichtheim. Commentary 41:49-53 Ja '66
What worries the men in the Kremlin. W. Benton. il Look 29:67-8+ Ap 20 '65
See also
Communist strategy
Russia—Boundaries

Asia
Shelepin in Hanoi and Brezhnev in Ulan Bator. America 114:114 Ja 22 '66
U.S.S.R. policy in Asia. C. B. McLane. Cur Hist 49:214-20+ O '65

Asia, Southeastern
Russia's stake in Vietnam. R. Morris. New Repub 152:13-15 F 13 '65

China (People's Republic)
Communist division. Commonweal 81:684 F 26 '65
Deepening split. Newsweek 65:30+ Mr 22 '65
Dialectic of the split. J. Burnham. Nat R 17:274 Ap 6 '65
Enemies fall out; Russian-Chinese split. J. O'Gara. Commonweal 82:70 Ap 9 '65
High price of horse meat. Time 85:31 Ap 2 '65
Mao vs. Moscow. S. Slessinger. Commonweal 81:759-61 Mr 12 '65
Military aspects of the Sino-Soviet dispute. M. Mackintosh. Bul Atomic Sci 21:14-17 O '65
Russia vs. China; clash over Vietnam. I. Deutscher. Nation 201:3-4 Jl 5 '65
Strictly temporary. Time 85:34 Mr 19 '65
Where danger grows on a 4,500-mile border. R. P. Martin. il U S News 59:44-7 D 6 '65
With a tight smile; red Chinese inhospitality to Kosygin. il Time 85:20 F 12 '65

France
De Gaulle rings Kremlin bells. Bsns W p45 Ap 3 '65
Paris-Moscow flirtation. M. Gordey. New Repub 152:10-11 My 15 '65

Germany
Russia and Germany, by W. Laqueur. Review Nation 202:48-50 Ja 10 '66. J. Gimbel
Sat R 48:48+ N 13 '65. H. C. Wolfe

Germany (Federal Republic)
Autobahn stop-go; Communist harassment to protest West German parliament meeting in West Berlin. Sr Schol 86:27 Ap 29 '65
Island and the sea; Soviet harassment during Bundestag meeting in West Berlin. il Newsweek 65:38+ Ap 19 '65
Simple signpost; Bundestag session in West Berlin in defiance of Soviet wishes. il Time 85:32 Ap 16 '65
Smiles change to snarls in Berlin: the meaning; Communist harassment around Berlin to protest the meeting of the West German Parliament in West Berlin. il U S News 58:52 Ap 19 '65

India
Neutral attitude. il Time 85:38 My 28 '65
Soviet bid for India; hate America campaign. E. Taylor. il Reporter 33:18-23 N 18 '65

Rumania
Come to the funeral! Newsweek 65:43 Ap 5 '65

United States
Can we make common cause with Russia? R. Lowenthal. il N Y Times Mag p34-5+ N 21 '65
Mr Goldberg comments on speech by Soviet foreign minister; statement, September 24, 1965. A. J. Goldberg. Dept State Bul 53:683 O 25 '65
My visits with Kosygin and Tito. W. A. Harriman. il Life 59:89-90 Ag 27 '65
Russia, the US and Vietnam. H. J. Morgenthau. New Repub 152:12-13 My 1 '65; Discussion. 152:34-5 My 15 '65
Strategy of interdependence, by V. P. Rock. Review
Bul Atomic Sci 21:40 F '65. J. O. Coppock
U.S. protests harassment of ships by Soviets; rejects Soviet charges; Department announcements and notes, April 2 and April 5, 1965. Dept State Bul 52:655-8 My 3 '65
U.S.-Soviet Kula. M. Orans. Bul Atomic Sci 21:44-5 Mr '65
U.S. vs Russia: next round in arms race. il U S News 59:66-7 N 29 '65

RUSSIA—Foreign relations—United States—
Continued
Vietnam and the Russians; effect on U.S.
relations. H. Brandon. Sat R 48:22+ O 16
'65
Where Russia is losing; Moscow's reasons
for taking a soft line. il U S News 58:53-
6 Mr 22 '65
See also
Americans in Russia
United States—Treaties—Russia

Vietnam (Democratic Republic)
Deeper and deeper in Vietnam; now Russia
makes a move. U S News 59:,38-9 Jl 19 '65
Escalation & counter-escalation; question of
Russian position. Nation 201:50 Ag 2 '65
Kremlin dilemma over Vietnam. M. Kalb.
Reporter 33:22-3 Jl 1 '65
U.S.S.R. policy in Asia. C. B. McLane. Cur
Hist 49:214-20+ O '65
Vietnam: Mr Kosygin goes calling. il News-
week 65:36+ F 15 '65
View of the woods; importance of the
Soviet decision. K. Crawford. Newsweek
67:33 Ja 17 '66

Vietnam (Republic)
Addendum to Why Vietnam? a basis for
negotiation exists. J. Gittings. Nation 201:
111-15 S 6 '65
On the other side. il Newsweek 65:20 Mr 1
'65
Russia and Vietnam; Soviet prestige in eastern Europe. P. Ben. New Repub 153:15-16
Jl 10 '65
Vietnam, another Dienbienphu? with editorial
comment. I. Deutscher. Nation 200:209, 212-
14 Mr 1 '65
Vietnam: will Moscow move? il Newsweek
65:33 Je 7 '65

History
Polishing the escutcheons. Time 85:31A Je 18
'65
Was Lenin necessary? L. Schapiro; discussion. Commentary 39:16+ My '65

Bibliography
Articles and other books received; comp. by
R. V. Allen. See issues of American histor-
ical review

European war, 1914-1918
See European war, 1914-1918—Russia

Industries
Industrial revolution. il Newsweek 66:58+ O
11 '65
Management, distribution, planning: new
Russian revolution. M. Miller. il Nation
201:437-9+ D 6 '65
Russia puts a new spur to output; quotas
dropped, and plant managers given more
freedom of action. Bsns W p32 O 2 '65
Russia's new five year plan; address, Sep-
tember 28, 1965. A. N. Kosygin. Vital
Speeches 32:115-28 D 1 '65
Still trying to make socialism work. il U S
News 59:45 O 11 '65
See also
Chemical industries—Russia
Petroleum industry and trade—Russia

Intellectual life
Forever amber? A. Sinyavsky and Y. Daniel
arrested. Newsweek 66:48 N 1 '65
Inconvenient citizens; intellectual critics.
Time 85:36 My 21 '65
Legacies of Khrushchev. A. Werth. Nation
200:354-7 Ap 5 '65
Moscow summer, by M. Mihajlov. Review
Sat R 48:41-2 D 11 '65. P. Viereck
Muffled voice of Russian liberalism: Novy
mir, Russia's distinguished literary maga-
zine. D. Brown. il N Y Times Mag p 10-
11+ D 19 '65
Reporter at large. R. Blum. New Yorker 41:
40-2+ Ag 28; 32-6+ S 4; 168+ S 11 '65
Underground view of the U.S.S.R; concerning
articles by A. Tertz. il N Y Times Mag
p52-3+ O 31 '65

Maps
Map of Russia (cont) Sr Schol 87:27 S 30 '65

Moral conditions
Innocents at home; visit by Gorky and Mme
Andreyeva. J. Swan. il Am Heritage 16:
58-61+ F '65

Navy
Soviet sea power: how it's growing. il U S
News 59:9 D 27 '65

Submarine service
Russia outnumbers U.S. in submarine
strength. Sci N L 88:89 Ag 7 '65

Politics and government
Cults, coups and collective leaderships. H. R.
Swearer. bibliog f il Cur Hist 49:193-200+
O '65
Government and politics of the Soviet Union,
by L. Schapiro. Review
America 113:416-17 O 9 '65. S. L. Levitsky
Is a new revolution brewing in the U.S.S.R?
E. Lyons. Read Digest 87:213-14+ O '65
Kicks, upstairs & down; changes in Russian
hierarchy. il Time 86:27-8 D 17 '65
Kremlin mood: strain and anxiety. il News-
week 65:31 Mr 29 '65
Men who run Russia's armed forces. S.
Bialer. il N Y Times Mag p 14-15+ F 21
'65
Moscow: the quiet men. I. Deutscher; A.
Werth. Nation 200:252-7 Ap 5 '65
New Soviet oligarchy. C. W. Thayer. Harper
230:64-8+ Ap '65
One year, two views: on Soviet leaders. R. J.
Korengold; L. Volkov. il Newsweek 66:56-7
O 18 '65
Political succession in the USSR, by M. Rush.
Review
Sat R 48:40 F 13 '65. H. Schwartz
Problems of dictatorship; the Russian ex-
perience. J. R. Strayer. For Affairs 44:264-
74 Ja '66
Quiet men. Time 85:34-5 My 14 '65
Russia after Khrushchev, by R. Conquest.
Review
Sat R 48:35-6 My 8 '65. M. Kalb
Soviet Union today: Khrushchevism without
Khrushchev?-il Sr Schol 86:12-16 F 4 '65
Who's on third? Mikoyan's retirement;
Podgorny's promotion leaves vacuum. il
Newsweek 66:38-9 D 20 '65
See also
Communism—Russia
Communist party (Russia)

Social conditions
Covering the U.S.S.R. R. J. Korengold. il
Newsweek 66:90+ S 20 '65
Faces of Russia today; photo report: land of
change. R. P. Martin. U S News 59:80-5 O
25 '65
How Russia has changed and what it means
to us. J. P. Davies. il Look 29:81-3 My 18
'65
Moscow celebrates. A. Werth. il Nation 200:
603-6 Je 7 '65
Revolution coming in Russia? a Yugoslav
says this; summary of report. M. Mihajlov.
il U S News 59:72-3 Jl 19 '65
Russia, by H. E. Salisbury. Review
Sat R 49:34 Ja 15 '66. S. Heitman
See also
Labor and laboring classes—Russia
Women—Russia
Youth—Russia

Social life and customs
Brotherly cruise on the Black Sea. G. Feifer.
il Harper 230:78-84 Mr '65

Travel regulations
See Travel regulations

RUSSIA and Rumania. See **Rumania and
Russia**

RUSSIA and the United States
Hardest rendezvous of all, on the ground. J.
Hicks. il Life 59:113-14+ O 1 '65
Moscow celebrates. A. Werth. il Nation 200:
603-6 Je 7 '65
Two men from Moscow pay a call; Russian
journalists A. N. Druzhinin and S. Kon-
drashov. R. Dugger. il N Y Times Mag
p34-5+ F 14 '65
See also
Americans in Russia
United States—Foreign opinion—Russian

RUSSIA and the West. See World politics,
1945-
RUSSIAN artificial satellites. See Artificial
satellites, Russian
RUSSIAN authors. See Authors, Russian
RUSSIAN culture. See Russia—Intellectual
life
RUSSIAN economic assistance. See Economic
assistance, Russian
RUSSIAN liberalism. See Liberalism
RUSSIAN literature
Literature in the Soviet Union. R. Koste-
lanetz. Commonweal 81:740+ Mr 5 '65
See also
Authors, Russian
Literature, Comparative—English and Russian

RUSSIAN military assistance. See Military assistance, Russian
RUSSIAN opera. See Opera, Russian
RUSSIAN philosophy. See Philosophy, Russian
RUSSIAN poetry
Nabokov's Eugene Onegin. R. Conquest. Poetry 106:236-8 Je '65
RUSSIAN space probes. See Space probes, Russian
RUSSIAN spies. See Spies
RUSSIAN travel restrictions. See Travel regulations
RUSSIAN visitors in the United States. See Foreign visitors in the United States
RUSSIAN youth. See Youth—Russia
RUSSIANS
Brotherly cruise on the Black Sea. G. Feifer. il Harper 230:78-84 Mr '65
Faces of Russia today; photo report: land of change. R. P. Martin. U S News 59:80-5 O 25 '65
RUSSIANS in foreign countries
Ugly Russian, by V. Lasky. Review
Sat R 48:38-9+ Ag 14 '65. J. Allison
RUSSO, Bob
Famous transcontinentalists. Motor T 17:74-9 Mr '65
RUST, Robert, and Malena, Dave
Beef carcass checks, new help for feeders. Suc Farm 64:34-5+ Ja '66
RUST. See Corrosion and anticorrosives
RUST preventive paint. See Paint, Protective
RUSTIN, Bayard
From protest to politics: the future of the civil rights movement. Commentary 39:25-31 F '65
—and Kahn, Tom
Civil rights. Commentary 39:43-6 Je '65
RUSTS (botany)
Nucleic acid and protein changes in wheat leaf nuclei during rust infection. P. K. Bhattacharya and others. bibliog il Science 105:1605-7 D 17 '65
RUTENBER, Culbert G.
No access to God's diaries. bibliog f Christian Cent 82:1570-3 D 22 '65
RUTGERS university, New Brunswick, N.J.
Study in academic freedom: Genovese case. A. Beichman. il N Y Times Mag p 14-15+ D 19 '65

Graduate school of library service
This old gal went back to college. M. Bartley. il Library J 90:5351-3 D 15 '65
RUTH, Babe
Faces from the past. R. M. Ketchum. por Am Heritage 16:96-7 Ag '65
RUTH, George Herman. See Ruth, B.
RUTHERFOORD, Jim
Fewer fish to fry. Field & S 69:10-12+ Ap '65
RUTHERFORD, Ernest
Books. M. J. Klein. Sci Am 212:129-32+ Mr '65
RUTHERFORD, Margaret Taylor
Margaret Rutherford goes after England's ghosts; photographs. Travel 123:45-7 F '65
RUTHVEN, Courtney. See Mason, R. L. jt. auth.
RUTLEDGE, Archibald
Buck at the secret crossing. Outdoor Life 135:46-7+ Mr '65
RUTLEDGE, L. T.
Facilitation: electrical response enhanced by conditional excitation of cerebral cortex. bibliog Science 148:1246-8 My 28 '65
RUTTENBERG, Stanley H.
Manpower boss faces hornet's nest. por Bsns W p 102 Ja 30 '65
RUUD, Johan T.
Ice fish; with biographical sketch. Sci Am 213:17, 108-14 bibliog(p 144) N '65
RYAN, Claude
French-Canadian dilemma. For Affairs 43:462-74 Ap '65
RYAN, D. Hillsdon
Linking up a chain, while you wait. il por Bsns W p 148+ O 9 '65
RYAN, Eugene E.
Books. Commonweal 82:508 Jl 9 '65
RYAN, Frank
C≡(Frank Ryan)+2. R. Kahn. il pors Sat Eve Post 238:92+ N 20 '65
Doctor Ryan of the Browns: how smart is too smart? J. Olsen. il pors Sports Illus 23:64-70+ S 27 '65
RYAN, Jerry W.
Journey to Jordan's Petra. Travel 123:48-51 Ap '65
RYAN, John J.
Post-tribal worship. Commonweal 82:586-9; 83:4 Ag 20, O 8 '65
Post-Waugh insight. J. M. Cameron. Commonweal 83:114-15 O 29 '65

RYAN, Mary Perkins
One year later. Commonweal 82:139-41 Ap 23 '65
RYAN, Patricia
America's prize stays French. Sports Illus 22:20-1 F 8 '65
Hambo in the gloaming. Sports Illus 23:38-9 S 13 '65
Harness racing (cont) Sports Illus 23:60-1 Jl 19; 72+ O 4; 74 N 29 '65
Horse racing. Sports Illus 23:86+ O 18 '65
Rock and roll in the Rockies. Sports Illus 23:16-19 Ag 30 '65
RYAN, Patrick
Yorkshire. Holiday 37:84-91+ My '65
RYAN, Stephen P.
Book review. America 113:444 O 16 '65
RYAN, William
Savage discovery; the Moynihan report. Nation 201:380-4 N 22; inside cover, 526 D 27 '65
RYAN, William Fitts
Excerpt from remarks, February 24, 1965. Cong Digest 44:125+ Ap '65

about
Hearing. New Yorker 41:23-6 Ag 28 '65
Ryan and Lindsay. R. Lekachman. New Repub 153:8-9 Jl 24 '65
RYAN aeronautical company
Ryan sets up new electronics branch. R. Pay. il Miss & Roc 17:34+ D 6 '65
RYAS. See Rugs and carpets
RYBOVICH, John, and sons boat works. See Boatbuilding
RYCHLEWSKI, T. V. See Miller, R. C. jt. auth.
RYDER cup matches. See Golf—Tournaments
RYNNE, Xavier, pseud.
Letter from Vatican City (cont) New Yorker 41:135-6+ S 11; 34-6+ D 25 '65

about
Real Rynne revealed. Christian Cent 82:823 Je 23 '65
RYSANEK, Leonie
Singing actress. A. Rich. por Opera N 29:26-7 Mr 6 '65
RYSER, Hugues J.-P. and Hancock, Ronald
Histones and basic polyamino acids stimulate the uptake of albumin by tumor cells in culture. bibliog Science 150:501-3 O 22 '65
RYUKYU ISLANDS
Ryukyu Islands. S. McCune. bibliog il Focus 15:1-6 Mr '65
U.S. and Japan broaden functions of Ryukyus consultative committee; exchange of notes, April 2, 1965. E. O. Reischauer; E. Shiina. Dept State Bul 52:601-2 Ap 19 '65
RYUN, Jim
Fast teen-agers in grown-up time. G. S. Brown. il por Sports Illus 23:14-15+ Jl 5

S

SAG. See Screen actors guild
SAT. See College entrance examination board—Scholastic aptitude test
SBA. See United States—Small business administration
SCLC. See Southern Christian leadership conference
SCM. See Student Christian movement
SCM corporation
Turnaround; new copier unveiled. Newsweek 66:76+ S 27 '65
Typewriter maker shifts key. il Bsns W p 172+ Mr 27 '65
SCS. See United States—Soil conservation service
SCTA. See Southern California timing association
SDS. See Scientific data systems, incorporated; Students for a democratic society (organization)
SEATO. See Southeast Asia treaty organization
SEC. See United States—Securities and exchange commission
SEG. See Screen extras guild
SIDS (stellar inertial Doppler system) See Inertial guidance systems
SIGS (simplified inertial guidance system) See Inertial guidance systems
SIU. See Seafarers' international union of North America
SLA. See Special libraries association

SLANT (Self-leadership for all nationalities today) See Civil rights organizations

SLR cameras. See Single-lens reflex cameras

SNAP (secondary nuclear auxiliary power) See Space vehicles—Atomic power plants

SNCC. See Student non-violent coordinating committee

SOS. See Signals and signaling

SPAR (seagoing platform for acoustics research) See Ships, Research

SPD (Social democratic party) See Political parties—Germany (Federal Republic)

START (spacecraft technology and advance re-entry tests) See Space vehicles—Atmospheric entry

STOL airplanes. See Airplanes, Short take-off and landing

SUB. See Supplemental unemployment benefits

SUNY (State university of New York) See New York state university

SV40 (simian virus) See Cancer viruses

SAAB. See Airplane industry and trade—Sweden

SAAL, Hubert
He lives to dance. Read Digest 87:139-42 Jl '65

about
Top of the week. il por Newsweek 65:17 Ap 19 '65

SAAL, Rollene W.
Pick of the paperbacks. See issues of Saturday review

SAARI, J. M. See Shorthill, R. W. jt. auth.

SAARINEN, Aline B.
Legwomen. il por Newsweek 65:58 Je 21 '65

SAARINEN, Eero
Spirit of St Louis: a new arch of triumph. il Bsns W p34 Ap 3 '65
Tall tales. H. Sutton. il Sat R 48:44+ D 18 '65

SABAH. See North Borneo

SABAH al-Salim al-Sabah
Where people are getting richer fast. il por U S News 59:19 D 6 '65

SABBATH
See also
Sunday
Sunday legislation

SABENA Belgian world airlines. See Airlines—Belgium

SABER saws. See Saws

SABESIN, Seymour M.
Lymphocytes of small mammals: spontaneous transformation in culture of blastoids. bibliog Science 149:1385-7 S 17 '65
—and Isselbacher, K. J.
Protein synthesis inhibition: mechanism for the production of impaired fat absorption. bibliog Science 147:1149-51 Mr 5 '65

SABIN, Albert Bruce
Recognition for Sabin. Newsweek 66:93 N 22 '65

SABIN, Robert
Cherevichki. Am Rec G 31:1006 Je '65
DGG's extraordinary Daphne. Am Rec G 31:776-9 My '65
Marschallin looks back. Am Rec G 31:904-6 My '65
Rake's progress. Am Rec G 31:496-8 F '65

SABLE, Martin H.
Readings on Latin America. Cur Hist 49:363-6 D '65

SABLE hunting. See Antelope hunting

SABLE ISLAND
Safe landing on Sable: isle of 500 shipwrecks. M. B. Grosvenor. il Nat Geog Mag 128:398-431 S '65

SABOL, Stephen Douglas
Fearless tot from Possum Trot. T. C. Brody. il pors Sports Illus 23:64+ N 22 '65

SABRE saws. See Saws

SACCADIC eye movements. See Eye—Movements

SACCHARIN
Dulcin and saccharin taste in squirrel monkeys, rats, and men. G. L. Fisher and others. bibliog il Science 150:506-7 O 22 '65

SACCHAROMYCES. See Yeasts

SACHAR, Abram L.
Malady of love. Sat R 48:34 Je 19 '65

SACHS, Paul Joseph
In memoriam. A. Frankfurter. il por Art N 64:23+ Ap '65

SACK, Harold
Restorations in American furniture, what is acceptable? Antiques 89:116-21 Ja '66

SACKETT, William M. and others
Temperature dependence of carbon isotope composition in marine plankton and sediments. bibliog Science 148:235-7 Ap 9 '65

SACKEY, Alex Quaison-. See Quaison-Sackey, A.

SACRAMENTO, Calif.
Notes from a native daughter. J. Didion. il Holiday 38:76-7+ O '65

Le SACRE du printemps; ballet. See Ballets—Criticisms

SACRED college of cardinals. See Cardinals

SACRED cows. See Cows in religion, folklore, etc.

SACRED Heart, Devotion to
Word. V. P. McCorry. America 112:906+ Je 26 '65

SACRED music. See Church music

SACRED places. See Holy places

SADE, Donatien Alphonse François, comte de
Books. E. Wilson. New Yorker 41:175-86+ S 18 '65
Manner of speaking. J. Ciardi. Sat R 48:18 S 18; 36 O 2 '65
Sade: chronicles of a misanthrope. C. D. B. Bryan. New Repub 153:20-3 O 30 '65
Talent for evil. R. J. Clements. Sat R 48:45-6 S 11 '65

SADIRONS. See Flatirons

SADLER, Christine
Coming of age of Joan Kennedy. McCalls 92:126-7+ F '65

SADLER, William A. Jr
Canadian collegians and The comfortable pew. Christian Cent 82:1353-6 N 3 '65

SADLER'S Wells theatre. See London—Theater

SADRUDDIN Khan, prince
High commissioner. New Yorker 41:51-2 D 11 '65

SAENZ, Manuela
Bolivar's villa. L. Zalamea. il por Américas 17:22-7 D '65

SAFARI. See Hunting—Africa; Hunting—Tanganyika

SAFE deposit boxes
What to keep in a safe-deposit box. Good H 160:174 Je '65

SAFE little house; story. See Alexander. R. W.

SAFER, Morley
Invitation to return to Cam Ne. N. Cousins. Sat R 48:16+ S 4 '65
TV's first war. W. Tuohy. il por Newsweek 66:32 Ag 30 '65

SAFETY at sea
See also
Collisions at sea

SAFETY belts
Safety, front & back; safety belts as standard equipment in automobiles. Time 85:92 F 19 '65
Seat belts save lives. H. Pyle. Parents Mag 40:32 Jl '65

SAFETY campaigns
Off-the-job accidents; management responsibility in safety program training. T. R. Brooks. Duns R 85:62-4 F '65

SAFETY devices and measures
Hazard in a safety product; make bathtub or shower floor less slippery. Consumer Rep 30:424-5 S '65
How to make a home safer. il Bet Hom & Gard 43:30+ Jl '65
Today's health guide: safety in the home; excerpts. il Todays Health 43:35-42 Je '65
See also
Accidents—Prevention
Road signs
also subhead Safety devices and measures under various subjects, e.g. Automobiles—Safety devices and measures

SAFETY education
Beaches, boats and back-yard pools. B. Spock. Redbook 125:20+ Ag '65
Before it happens: bulb-snatchers turn outdoor Christmas lights into death trap. il Recreation 58:496 D '65
His first trip to school? make it a safe one. H. E. Dark. il Todays Health 43:50-1+ S '65
Traffic safety is no accident. il NEA J 54:44-5 My '65
See also
Accidents—Prevention
Automobile driving—Study and teaching

SAFETY glass. See Glass, Safety

SAFETY guards. See Roads—Safety guards

SAFETY movement
See also
Safety campaigns

SAFETY stud tires. See Tires, Automobile

SAFFIR, Leonard
Southwarr venture: first U.S. daily devoted exclusively to news from south of the border. Time 86:45 Jl 16 '65

SAFIRE, William L.
Silvertoe; financial adventure of James Debenture. Harvard Bsns R 43:110-18 My '65

SAFRAN printing company
Color in print; AIGA-Safran seminar on color language and reproduction. il Pub W 187:106-11 Mr 1 '65

SAG HARBOR, N.Y.
Whale of a time; Sag Harbor's Old whalers' festival. il Motor B 116:54+ Ag '65

SAGAN, Françoise, pseud.
France for Edward Albee. Esquire 63:60-2 F '65

about
Letter from Paris. Genêt. New Yorker 41: 200+ O 2 '65

SAGAS
Njal's saga. K. Rexroth. Sat R 48:27 My 1 '65

SAGE, Russell
Russell Sage: the money king, by P. Sarnoff. Review
  Time il por 86:98+ Jl 16 '65

SAGE, Tom
Giraffe in Piazza del popolo. Nat R 17:105-6 F 9 '65

SAGER, Donald J.
Interning in Kingston. Wilson Lib Bul 40: 252-4 N '65

SAGITTA setosa. See Arrowworms

SAGITTARIUS, Heinrich. See Schütz, H.

SAGUARO. See Cactus

SAGUARO NATIONAL MONUMENT
Saguaro problem and grazing in southwestern national monuments. W. A. Niering and R. H. Whittaker. bibliog il Nat Parks Mag 39:4-9 Je '65

SAHARA DESERT
Cruel desert is Algeria's wealth. P. Braestrup. ily N Y Times Mag p76-7+ Jl 7 '65
Guelta of the bleak Sahara; source of water is mystery in the Tchad. W. G. Dyer. il Natur Hist 74:36-9 N '65
I joined a Sahara salt caravan. V. Engelbert. il Nat Geog Mag 128:694-711 N '65
Landscape with mirages. T. Sterling. il Horizon 7:80-91 Autumn '65
Sahara holiday; excerpt from Children of Allah. A. N. Keith. il Atlan 216:92-4+ D '65
  See also
Timbuktu

SAHLINS, Marshall
Best torture; once you've broken him down. Nation 201:266-9 O 25 '65

SAIGON
Dreaming of a red Christmas; promise of terrorism against Americans in downtown Saigon. Time 86:19 D 24 '65
Letter from Saigon. R. Shaplen. New Yorker 41:192+ N 13 '65
Saigon; eye of the storm. P. T. White. il Nat Geog Mag 127:834-72 Je '65
Saigon tries to live in a hurry. J. Langguth. il N Y Times Mag p 12-13+ Ag 8 '65

Newspapers
Antic English in Saigon. Time 86:78+ D 17 '65

SAILBOARDING. See Aquatic sports

SAILBOAT masts. See Masts and rigging

SAILBOAT models. See Ship and boat models

SAILBOAT racing
Jib man winneth; Southern Ocean racing conference. il Newsweek 65:87 Mr 22 '65
Lake Erie's annual fiasco. M. Walley. il Motor B 116:80 O '65
Robbie Doyle: twice North America junior champion. B. D. Barker. 3d. Yachting 118: 30-1+ N '65
Sail for all seasons; photographs. Fortune 73:141-3 Ja '66
U.S. keeps the 5.5 Gold cup. T. R. Vickery. il Motor B 116:50-1+ D '65
Windward starts. J. Sutphen and A. Kostanecki. il Yachting 117:77-9+ Ap '65
With the racing classes. B. Robinson. See issues of Yachting
  See also
Regattas

SAILBOATS
Guide for sailboat watchers. il Sunset 134:68-70 Je '65
Teacup; a basic-basic sailboat. M. M. Matthews. il Pop Mech 125:146-51+ Ja '66
To Banzai with love. E. S. Mulligan. il Motor B 115:36-7+ F '65

What is a cutter? R. M. Clancy. Motor B 115:182-3+ My '65
  See also
Catboats
Masts and rigging
Trimarans

Care
Refinishing a Firefly. F. A. Reid. il Yachting 117:209-10 Ap '65

Design
Bill Lapworth on design. B. Lapworth. Yachting 117:204+ Je '65
Designs. W. H. deFontaine. See issues of Yachting
Great American sailboats; Fram: a North Sea type for American waters. B. Koelbel. il Motor B 115:43+ My '65
Great American sailboats; New York thirty-two. il Motor B 116:46-7 N '65
IYRU design competition winners. O. J. Stephens, 2d. il Yachting 117:54-5+ Mr '65
Look out for Tempest; two-man keel boat. R. N. Bavier, jr. il Yachting 118:46-7+ Jl '65
Poor man's yachts; Sailfish or Sunfish. il Newsweek 66:75 Ag 30 '65

Equipment
Case for roller reefing. R. W. Carrick. il Yachting 118:44-5+ Jl '65
Gear and gadgets for the one-design. N. D. Freeman. il Yachting 117:58-60+ F '65

SAILFISH fishing
Great tailwalker. J. Brooks. il Outdoor Life 136:58-60+ D '65
Mastery in billfishing; third Invitational masters angling tournament. M. Coan. il Motor B 115:43-4+ Ap '65

SAILING
Aboard the 35' ketch Wyntie with Walter Cronkite. G. Sloane. il Motor B 116:42-3 Ag '65
All the fun is getting there; sailing to Tahiti aboard the ketch Thane. H. Downs. il Sci Digest 58:92-4 Jl '65
Bob Allen on weather strategy. R. M. Allen, jr. il Yachting 117:40+ Je '65
Daysailing in Maine. F. L. Barton. il Motor B 116:101+ Jl '65
Handling the multihull; excerpt from Basic sailing; ed. by A. River. M. B. George. il Motor B 116:38-9 S '65
Monterey to San Francisco; what we wanted was wind. B. Cooke. il Motor B 115:138-9+ My '65
On the art of reefing. R. C. Taylor. Yachting 117:220-1 Ap '65
September hurricane. W. Brown. il Yachting 118:38-40+ S '65
To Banzai with love. E. S. Mulligan. il Motor B 115:36-7+ F '65
  See also
Cruising

Anecdotes, facetiae, satire, etc.
Captain of his ship. R. L. Day. il Yachting 117:59+ My '65

Study and teaching
A+ in spinnaker is easy at Ardell; California's Ardell sailing school. H. Whall. il Sports Illus 23:54-6+ N 1 '65
Community junior training; Norwalk, Conn. L. Miner. il Yachting 118:41-3+ Jl '65
Learning to sail: how and where. N. Atkins. bibliog il Motor B 115:41+ Je '65

SAILING vessels
Surgeons and ships in gold rush days; excerpt from Doctors on the American frontier. R. Dunlop. il Todays Health 43:50-1+ Mr '65
  See also
Sailboats
Schooners

Design
Great American sailboats; Barrie Anne; character in a 26-foot ketch. B. Koelbel. il Motor B 115:144-6 Mr '65

SAILORS. See Seamen

SAILORS knots. See Knots and splices

SAILPLANES. See Gliders (aeronautics)

SAILS
Case for roller reefing. R. W. Carrick. il Yachting 118:44-5+ Jl '65
Gene Trepte on spinnakers. G. Trepte. Yachting 117:209 Je '65
Roller wings. W. Britton. il Yachting 118: 54-6+ Ag '65

SAILS—*Continued*
Surplus parachute into balloon spinnaker. J. Siegel. il Motor B 115:57+ F '65
Tune up! a new look at an old problem. W. Britton. il Motor B 115:42+ My '65
SAIN, Johnny
In-Sain view of the Twins; interviews, ed. by H. L. Masin. Sr Schol 87:50 S 30 '65

about

Twins' miracle coach. M. Smith. il pors Life 59:83-4+ S 10 '65
SAINSBURY, Wilfred J.
Large groups and figures in the soft-paste biscuit of Vincennes-Sèvres. Antiques 87: 430-3 Ap '65
Small figures and groups in the soft-paste biscuit of Vincennes-Sèvres. Antiques 88: 824-8 D '65
ST ALBANS, Francis Bacon, viscount. See Bacon, F
ST ALBANS school, Washington, D.C. See Private schools
ST AUGUSTINE, Fla.
Nation's oldest city. il Sr Schol 86:8 My 20 '65
Of many things: 400th anniversary of founding. T. N. Davis. America 112:621 My 1 '65
Sort of Spanish town; 400th anniversary. H. Sutton. Sat R 48:43-5 N 6 '65
ST AUGUSTINE'S pigeon; story. See Connell, E. S. jr
ST BERNARD college, St Bernard, Ala.
Alabama oddity: Holyland U.S.A. il Travel 123:41-3 My '65
SAINT EXUPÉRY, Antoine de
Passion that poisons our daily bread. L. Fischer. por Sat R 48:27 Je 5 '65
Poet of the machine. il por Newsweek 65:87 My 31 '65
Saint-Exupéry's posthumous testament. W. Mathes. New Repub 152:22-3 Je 12 '65
ST GEORGE, Tim
War of the Never Sweats. Nat Parks Mag 39:16-17 S '65
ST GERMAIN, Robert
I was an innocent in the classroom. por NEA J 54:21 O '65
ST HONORÉ cake. See Pastry
ST JOHN ISLAND
Virgin Islands National Park. T. Gill il Am For 71:38-41+ My '65
ST JOHN the Divine, Cathedral of. See New York (city)—St John the Divine, Cathedral of
ST JOHN'S college, Annapolis, Md.
Grades, eyeball-to-eyeball; don rag. il Time 85:59 F 12 '65

Santa Fe campus

St John's; profile. M. Franklin. il Mlle 61: 149+ O '65
ST JOHNS university, Collegeville, Minn.
Subiaco, Italy, monastic manuscripts first to be microfilmed by St John's. Library J 90:1281 Mr 15 '65
ST JOHN'S university, Jamaica, N.Y.
Academic revolution at St John's. F. Canavan. America 113:136-40 Ag 7 '65
Family planning at St John's; insurrection against the Vincentian community. J. Leo. Commonweal 82:184-8 Ap 30 '65; Reply. T. F. Mader. 82:274 My 21 '65
In the vulgate. Nat R 18:58+ Ja 25 '66
Issue at St John's. R. Wines. America 114: 103 Ja 22 '66
Morally suffocating? teacher dismissals. Newsweek 66:65 D 27 '65
News and views. J. Leo. Commonweal 83: 110,390 O 29 '65, Ja 7 '66
Priest vs. priest as a strike disrupts a university; academic freedom issue. R. Vaughan. il Life 60:30B-30C Ja 21 '66
St John's university; the issues. F. Canavan. America 114:122-4 Ja 22 '66
Strife at St John's. il Time 86:34+ D 31 '65
ST JOHNSBURY athenaeum
Victoriana in Vermont. il Time 86:50-1 Ag 20 '65
ST LAURENT, H.
Build a smoke alarm for your home. Pop Electr 23:49-52 S '65
ST LAURENT, Yves Mathieu
For Yves St Laurent, it's a love story; ready-to-wear. por Bsns W p82 D 18 '65
Paris in the fall. il Newsweek 66:49 Ag 16 '65
ST LAWRENCE SEAWAY
Successful seaway season. Newsweek 66:76 D 20 '65
ST LOUIS

Art

Leaping time & space. il Time 86:94-5 N 19 '65

City planning

Blithe spirit of St Louis; LaClede town, moderate-income housing. il Fortune 73: 175 Ja '66
New St Louis. il Newsweek 66:123-123A+ N 15 '65
New spirit soars in mid-America's proud old city. R. P. Jordan. il Nat Geog Mag 128:605-41 N '65
St Louis snaps out of a long, costly lull. il Bsns W p 192-4+ S 18 '65

Description

New spirit soars in mid-America's proud old city. R. P. Jordan. il Nat Geog Mag 128: 605-41 N '65
St Louis snaps out of a long, costly lull. il Bsns W p 192-4+ S 18 '65

Education

School where children teach themselves; Valley Winds school. H. Black. il Sat Eve Post 238:80-1+ Je 19 '65

Elections

Fun, but futile; mayoral election. Time 85:27 Ap 16 '65
Ward heelers' revenge; Tucker defeated by A. J. Cervantes. Time 85:29-30 Mr 19 '65

History

So long, St Louis, we're heading West. W. C. Everhart. il Nat Geog Mag 128:642-69 N '65

Housing

Arcaded high-rise on a raised plaza. il Arch Rec 137:202-3 Ap '65
Case history of a failure; Pruitt-Igoe housing project. J. Bailey. il Arch Forum 123:22-5 D '65

Monuments, statues, etc.

Leaping time & space; St Louis arch. il Time 86:94-5 N 19 '65
St Louis memorial arch. il Am City 81:141-2 Ja '66
Spirit of St Louis: a new arch of triumph; Gateway arch. il Bsns W p34 Ap 3 '65
Tall tales Gateway arch, nearing completion. H. Sutton. il Sat R 48:44+ D 18 '65

Music

Sound maneuvers; Strategy for two orchestras and two conductors performance/battle by St Louis symphony. Newsweek 65:92 Mr 15 '65
See also
St Louis symphony orchestra

Police

Criminal identification in three seconds; new system at St Louis metropolitan police department. H. S. Priest. il Am City 80:46 Mr '65

Stores

Soft-sell salute boosts St Louis and a store; Stix, Baer & Fuller. il Bsns W p96-7 O 16 '65

Water supply

St Louis: one city's contribution. I. Dilliard. Sat R 48:77-8 O 23 '65
ST LOUIS Cardinals (baseball) See Baseball clubs
ST LOUIS Cardinals (football club) See Football clubs
ST LOUIS post-dispatch
Misinformed source; how Post-dispatch correspondent got his exclusive. il Newsweek 67:53-4 Ja 3 '66
Right not to know; irresponsible publication of North Vietnam peace feeler. K. Crawford. Newsweek 67:18 Ja 3 '66
ST LOUIS symphony orchestra
City to emulate. P. Yates. Hi Fi 15:122-13 Jl '65
ST LOUIS university, St Louis, Mo.
Local boys make very good; national soccer championships. J. Jares. il Sports Illus 23:22-5 D 13 '65
ST MARK'S school, Southborough, Mass. See Private schools
ST MARTIN (island)
Traveler's choice. F. R. Smith. Travel 124: 68 O '65
ST MARY, Ernest
Wild flower's fleeting moment of perfection. il por Pop Gard 16:30-1 N '65
ST MICHAEL'S college, Winooski, Vt.
Dialogue in Vermont. L. B. Bozell. Nat R 17: 1153-6 D 14 '65
SAINT MICHEL, MONT, France. See Mont Saint Michel, France

ST MORITZ, Switzerland
Palace in St Moritz. F. Morton. Holiday 38:
76-7+ N '65
Rooms at the top; Palace hotel. il Newsweek
67:46-7 Ja 10 '66

SAINT of Bleecker street; opera. See Menotti.
G. C.

ST PATRICK'S day

Drama
Leprechaun's pot of gold. F. B. Watts. Plays
24:43-50 Mr '65

ST PAUL

Libraries
Minneapolis-St Paul opinion survey reveals
high public library use. Library J 90:2790+
Je 15 '65

ST PETER and St Paul, Cathedral of. See
Washington, D.C.—Churches

ST PETERSBURG, Fla.
Moonlighting for Sunny Pete. Am City 80:
145-6 O '65

ST PIERRE, Leon E. See Roberts, R. W. jt.
auth.

ST PIERRE, Ronald L. and Ackerman, G. A.
Bursa of Fabricius in chickens: possible humoral factor. bibliog Science 147:1307-8 Mr
12 '65

SAINT PIERRE and Miquelon (islands)
Gone flying to St Pierre. R. C. Mock. il Flying 77:52-6 Jl '65

SAINT-SAËNS, Camille
Samson and Delilah. Criticism
Sat R 48:43+ D 25 '65
Thanks to Decca, the Cincinnati returns to
records. A. Cohn. il Am Rec G 31:698-9
Ap '65

ST THOMAS ISLAND
Alley shopping on St Thomas. il Sunset 135:
73-4 N '65
Where women's work has a golden touch;
gift shops. il Bsns W p 100-2 Mr 27 '65

SAINTE-MARIE, Buffy
Buffy's many voices. il pors Life 59:53-4+
D 10 '65
Solitary Indian. por Time 86:62 D 10 '65

SAINTS
Saints and sanctity, by W. J. Burghardt.
Review
America 113:760 D 11 '65. M. T. Miller
Saints: their place in the church, by P.
Molinari. Review
America 113:725-6 D 4 '65. P. Dent

SAITO, Fred. See Bennett, E. jt. auth.

SAITO, Kuniji
Japanese plans for May's eclipse. Sky &
Tel 29:149 Mr '65

SAKAMOTO, Yoshikazu
Japanese and Vietnam. New Repub 153:16-17
S 4 '65

SAKEY, Joseph
Birchers attack N.H. librarian with telephone
hate message. Library J 90:3231-2 Ag '65;
Correction. 90:4650 N 1 '65

SALAD dressings. See Salads

SALADS
Add something new to your tossed salads.
B. L. Henry. il Farm J 89:79 Je '65
All-season salad. il McCalls 92:144-6 F '65
Bountiful salads of summer; with recipes.
il Good H 160:114-33 Je '65
Cold salad soup; with recipes. il Seventeen
24:108-9+ Je '65
Cool for summer; gelatin salads. il Sunset 134:
220+ Je '65
Cranberry salads, relish. il Bet Hom & Gard
43:101-2 N '65
From Denmark, a six-salad buffet. il Sunset
135:152+ S '65
From Turkey, a relish salad. il Sunset 135:
137 Jl '65
Frosted gelatin-fruit molds for salad or des-
sert. B. Pierson. il Farm J 89:76-7 N '65
Great staples to help you turn out master-
pieces. V. T. Habeeb. il Am Home 68:60-
1+ Ap '65
Hollywood bowls. M. Eckley. il McCalls 92:
130-1+ My '65
Hot salads for cold days. il Bet Hom & Gard
43:82 F '65
How do you mold a main dish? salads with
recipes. il Bet Hom & Gard 43:74 Ag '65
Italians have a way with salads in summer;
with recipes. M. Kaytor. il Look 29:50-1
Je 29 '65
It's the super-tomato's season. il Sunset 135:
158+ S '65
Main-course salads add sparkle to meals. G.
Maddox. il Todays Health 43:60-5 Jl '65
Mediterranean classic salad has some Cali-
fornia cousins. il Sunset 135:58-9 Jl '65

Molded salads to make ahead. il Bet Hom &
Gard 43:83-4 Mr '65
Our favorite cookout salads. il Bet Hom &
Gard 43:80 Je '65
Salad days and ways; with recipes. C. Clai-
borne. il N Y Times Mag p50 Ag 8 '65
Salads that skip a step. il Bet Hom & Gard
43:102 S '65
Successful recipes; molded salads. il Suc
Farm 63:99-100 My '65
Summer salads. il Bet Hom & Gard 43:99-100
Jl '65
These salads use blue cheese. Sunset 134:195
My '65
See also
Aspic

SALAM, Abdus
New center for physics. Bul Atomic Sci 21:
43-5 D '65

SALAMA, Hannu
Finnish author, publisher prosecuted for
blasphemy. Pub W 187:100 F 8 '65

SALAMANDERS
Great hellbender. R. Beck. il Field & S 69:
64-6+ Ap '65
Hepatic glycogen depletion in amphiuma
during induced anoxia. F. L. Rose and
others. bibliog il Science 147:1467-8 Mr 19
'65
Orientation of ambystoma maculatum: movements to and from breeding ponds. C. R.
Shoop. bibliog il Science 149:558-9 Jl 30 '65

SALANDINI, Victor
Union organizing in the fields. America 113:
400-1 O 9 '65

SALARIES
Fifty best paying jobs today. Changing T
19:12 O '65
Washington report; lifetime earnings of college, high school and elementary graduates
and dropouts in relation to Higher education act. J. Lloyd. Sr Schol 86:sup4 My
6 '65
See also subhead Salaries under various
subjects. e.g. Clergy—Salaries

SALAS, Mariano Picón-. See Picón-Salas, M.

SALAZAR, António de Oliveira
Against the situation. por Time 86:39 N 12
'65
Dead end in Portugal; tr. by J. Drury. J.
Nabuco. Commonweal 83:240-2 N 26 '65
Portugal awakened. America 113:618 N 20 '65

SALAZAR, Jorge Mejia
Big stir in coffee. Read Digest 87:31-2+ D
'65

SALAZAR BONDY, Sebastián
Obituary
Américas por 17:39 O '65. O. B. Powell

SALE, J. Kirk
Loneliness of Kwame Nkrumah. N Y Times
Mag p20-1+ Je 27 '65

SALEM, Mass.
See also
Essex institute

Historic houses, etc.
Crowninshield-Bentley House in Salem, a
documentary restoration. D. A. Fales, jr.
il Antiques 88:486-93 O '65

SALEM, North Carolina. See Winston-Salem,
N.C.

SALEM, Ore.

Parks and playgrounds
Small park for a big tree; Big tree of Waldo
park. G. W. Taplin. il Nat Parks Mag 39:
21 My '65

SALEMINK, C. A. and others
Phytotoxin isolated from liquid cultures of
ceratocystis ulmi. bibliog Science 149:202
Jl 9 '65

SALES, Soupy
New York scene; ed. by E. Miller. pors
Seventeen 24:30+ S '65

about
Man who is also The mouse; with report by
S. Schmidt. il pors Life 58:49-50+ My 14 '65
Simple Simon pieman. il por Time 85:52 Ap
23 '65
Soupy and The mouse. W. J. Smith. Com-
monweal 82:446-8 Je 25 '65

SALES, Art. See Art sales

SALES conventions
All the world's a stage for business meetings.
il Bsns W p74-5 F 6 '65
Soft sell in sales meetings. L. A. Blumenthal.
il Duns R 86:48-9+ N '65

SALES forecasting. See Business forecasting

SALES managers
Forgotten field sales manager. V. Adams. il
Duns R 85:45-6+ Mr '65

SALES managers—*Continued*
New man in selling; national account manager. T. J. Murray. il Duns R 85:38-40+ F '65

SALES policies
How to sell now; symposium. il Nations Bsns 53:36-9+ My '65
Marketing strategy brings higher sales. il Nations Bsns 53:94-6+ N '65
Why the old products last. V. A. Adams. Duns R 85:46-7+ Ap '65

SALES promotion
Are sales incentives a waste? L. A. Blumenthal. il Duns R 86:66-8+ O '65
Come alive, America; family to keep all the groceries it can snatch from a supermarket in thirty minutes. C. Remsberg and B. Remsberg. il Esquire 63:102-5+ F '65
In the time it takes you to read these lines the American teen-ager will have spent $2,378.22. G. Hechinger and F. M. Hechinger. Esquire 64:65+ Jl '65
Indirect sell; hidden promotion efforts of automen. Time 86:90+ O 29 '65
Leverage in the product life cycle. D. K. Clifford, jr. il Duns R 85:62-4+ My '65
One way to sell anything; industrial shows. D. Seligman. il Fortune 71:162-5 Je '65
Selling by the book; use of books in sales campaigns. Time 85:82+ Je 18 '65
Strategy of price deals. C. L. Hinkle. Harvard Bsns R 43:75-85 Jl '65
Tupperware brings home party to Japan; marketing polyethylene containers. il Bsns W p 162-4 N 20 '65
See also
Competitions
Trading stamps

Anecdotes, facetiae, satire, etc.
Meet sugar bear. J. Ciardi. Sat R 48:26 My 22 '65

SALES techniques. See Salesmen and salesmanship

SALESMEN and salesmanship
Hollow ring; Oregon legislature passes bill to curb fast-talking salesmen. Newsweek 65:74 Mr 29 '65
How I sold $1,000,000 worth of insurance in a single month. C. A. McSween. il Ebony 20:208-9 My '65
How to sell now; symposium. il Nations Bsns 53:36-9+ My '65
New look in selling; intensive training requirements. L. Velie. Read Digest 86:251-2+ My '65
See also
Advertising
Booksellers and bookselling
Dealer relations
Saleswomen

SALESWOMEN
Oracle to high society girls; super-saleswoman at De Pinna. il Life 58:76-8+ My 7 '65

SALGADO, Antonio
Inca Garcilaso. Américas 17:22-8 Jl '65

SALINE water conversion. See Sea water—Desalting

SALINGER, J. D.
Hapworth 16, 1924; story. New Yorker 41:32-40 Je 19 '65

SALINITY of soils. See Soils, Salts in

SALISBURY, Harrison E.
Memories of the man of steel. Sat R 48:40-1 D 11 '65
Million miles of quiet land. Sat R 48:31 F 20 '65
Pearl of the Antilles. New Repub 153:23-5 Jl 3 '65
What the world owes Khrushchev. N Y Times Mag p 16-17+ Ap 25 '65

SALISBURY, Robert Arthur Talbot Gascoyne-Cecil, 3d marquis of
Patricians; excerpts from Proud tower. B. W. Tuchman. por Vogue 146:156-7+ N 1 '65

SALISBURY, Md.
Swinging Salisbury; Salisbury international tennis tournament. Newsweek 65:65 F 22 '65

SALISBURY cathedral. See Cathedrals—England

SALIVARY glands
Collagenase: effect on the morphogenesis of embryonic salivary epithelium in vitro. C. Grobstein and J. Cohen. bibliog il Science 150:626-8 O 29 '65
Lysosomal and free acid phosphatase in salivary glands of chironomus tentans. K. S. Schin and U. Clever. bibliog il Science 150:1053-5 N 19 '65
Submaxillary gland of mouse: effects of a fraction on tissues of mesodermal origin in vitro. D. G. Attardi and others. bibliog il Science 150:1307-9 D 3 '65

SALIX. See Willow

SALK, Jonas Edward
Doctor Salk to continue immunization studies. Sci N L 88:248 O 16 '65
Salk says man is challenge. il por Sci N L 87:258-9 Ap 24 '65

SALK institute for biological studies, San Diego, Calif.
No more triumphs? il Time 85:68 Ap 23 '65

SALK vaccine. See Poliomyelitis—Vaccines

SALKIN, Jeri
Sliver of hope. D. Hering. il Dance Mag 39:46-8 S '65

SALM, Walter G.
Home video tape recording, when? Pop Electr 23:63-7 D '65

SALMON
Fishing treaties and salmon of the North Pacific; address, October 21, 1965. W. F. Thompson. il Science 150:1786-9 D 31 '65
New: a big lift for salmon. J. Rearden. il Outdoor Life 136:26-8+ Jl '65
Sockeye that swims too far. il Time 85:86 Je 11 '65
Swimming energetics of salmon. J. R. Brett. il Sci Am 213:80-5 Ag '65
What's happening to Atlantic salmon? L. Wulff. il Yachting 117:100-1+ Je '65

Migration
See Fishes—Migration

SALMON fishing
Bulls of St Mary's; river in Nova Scotia. R. Tuttle. il Outdoor Life 136:46-7+ Jl '65
Death rode the surf. O. C. Johnson. il Outdoor Life 136:52-5+ Jl '65
Great steelhead hang-up. C. Conley. il Field & S 69:44-7+ Ap '65
Klamath slot. C. R. Hull. il Outdoor Life 136:40-3+ Jl '65
Landlock break-out. H. F. Blaisdell. il Outdoor Life 135:58-60+ My '65
Notes for a gazetteer; Golden north salmon derby, Juneau, Alaska. P. Hamburger. New Yorker 41:170+ Mr 13 '64
Peripatetic reviewer. E. Weeks. Atlan 216:142+ S '65
Salmon spree. C. Elliott. il Outdoor Life 135:52-5+ Je '65
Sebago starts back. Sports Illus 23:8+ N 1 '65
Son of the salmon. B. Geagan. il Field & S 69:42-3+ Ap '65
Spring salmon ring the bell. R. E. Landsburg. il Outdoor Life 135:40-3+ Ap '65
Steelheads on a rough river; Oregon's Rogue River. V. Kraft. Sports Illus 23:92+ N 15 '65
What's happening to Atlantic salmon? L. Wulff. il Yachting 117:100-1+ Je '65

SALMONELLA. See Bacteria, Pathogenic

SALOMA, John S. 3d
Trail to the Cow Palace. Reporter 32:43-4+ Ap 22 '65

SALOME: opera. See Strauss, R.

SALON internationale des techniques, papetieres et graphiques, TPG-65. See International exhibition of paper, printing and graphic arts industries, Paris, 1965

SALOONS. See Bars and barrooms

SALSAMENDI, A.
Opinion: on youth's conscience. por Mlle 62:56-7 D '65

SALSBURY, Edith Colgate
Expergation of Huckleberry Finn; excerpt from Susy and Mark Twain. Am Heritage 16:112 O '65

SALSIFY
For food, for arrangements, dual role for salsify. L. Burgess. il Flower Grower 52:63 Ap '65

SALT
Cationic glass electrode response in aqueous solutions of sodium chloride and potassium chloride. E. W. Moore and J. W. Ross. bibliog il Science 148:71-2 Ap 2 '65
Synthesis of block oligonucleotides. R. E. Thach and P. Doty. bibliog il Science 147:1310-11 Mr 12 '65
You are inside a mountain of salt; Salt cathedral. il Sunset 135:32 O '65
See also
Morton salt company

SALT and pepper shakers
Famous salt-shaker case. A. G. Peterson. il Hobbies 70:72 My '65

SALT glaze ware
Study of a group of English salt-glaze ware. K. Boney. il Antiques 88:834-7 D '65

SALT LAKE. See Great Salt Lake

SALT LAKE CITY

Description
Mormon city. il Sunset 134:76-87 Ap '65
Reader's choice. V. Rees. Travel 124:44 S '65

Historic houses, etc.
Brigham's home; the Beehive House. il Sunset 135:36+ S '65

Newspapers
See also
Rocky Mountain review

SALT marshes
Ebbtide of our salt marshes. W. Hanley; G. C. Matthiessen; S. L. Udall. il Recreation 58:271+ Je '65
Our coastal marshes: are they to become a vanishing resource? R. H. Goodwin. il Recreation 58:305-7 Je '65
Trembling prairie; great salt marshes of Louisiana. L. Dietz. il Field & S 69:57-9+ F '65

SALT RIVER
Keeping cool in Arizona; a float trip. il Sunset 134:80+ My '65

SALT water aquariums. See Aquariums

SALT water fishing
Anyway you look at cobia. K. Osborne. il Outdoor Life 135:50-2+ Mr '65
Beach boats. J. A. Emmett. il Outdoor Life 136:90-2 Ag '65
Billfish West, billfish East. C. West; B. Wisner. il Motor B 116:36-7+ S '65
Blue blitzes; Montauk trolling spree. G. Heinold. il Outdoor Life 136:42-3+ Ag '65
Fisherman's horn of plenty. G. X. Sand. il Outdoor Life 135:52-5+ My '65
Fishing for peace. B. Wisner. il Motor B 115:50-1+ My '65
Flies worth their salt. J. Brooks. il Outdoor Life 135:60-3+ Je '65
Great tailwalker: sailfish of Florida Keys. J. Brooks. il Outdoor Life 136:58-60+ D '65
Nothing like it on the Oregon coast; Cape Kiwanda. B. Behme. il Field & S 70:10-11+ S '65
Piñas Bay: jungle, Indians and the fightingest fish. Motor B 116:51-3 Jl '65
Salt water. G. Heinold. See issues of Outdoor life
Seasoned with salt; fly fishing. A. J. McClane. il Field & S 70:102-7 S '65
Special section on sportfishing; symposium. il Yachting 117:77+ Je '65
Sportfishing. N. Benedict. See issues of Yachting
Where sportfishermen meet. D. W. Thornton. il Motor B 115:144-7 F '65
See also
Bonefish fishing
Cod fishing
Harpooning
Mackerel fishing
Marlin fishing
Salmon fishing
Snook fishing
Swordfish fishing
Tarpon fishing

SALTER, Leonard P. and Harley, J. H.
Trinitite: cobalt-60, cesium-137, and europium-152. bibliog Science 148:954-5 My 14 '65

SALTFORD, Herb
Does the robin hear or see the worm? Audubon Mag 67:255-6 Jl '65

SALTON SEA
Un-natural wonder. B. Ruskauff. il Motor B 115:46-9 My '65

SALTONSTALL, Leverett
Free for all. il por Newsweek 67:20-1 Ja 10 '66
Last Brahmin. por Time 87:22 Ja 7 '66
Running Brooke. Reporter 34:12+ Ja 13 '66

SALTONSTALL, Richard, jr
Wawona, historic three-master. il Yachting 117:204-5 Mr '65

SALVADOR, Brazil
In search of Afro-Brazil. J. A. Page. il Reporter 33:44-7 N 4 '65

SALVAGE (ships)
Plastic bubbles help refloat capsized ship. il Pop Sci 186:118-19 Ap '65
Salvage. T. M. Prudden. Yachting 118:157-9 D '65
Trying to salvage Betsy's discards; Avondale shipyards. il Bsns W p 180+ O 23 '65

SALVAGE (torpedoes)
Navy hunts test debris; cable-controlled underwater research vehicle. Sci N L 88:309 N 13 '65

SALVATION
See also
Justification

SALVATION army
Booth led boldly with his big bass drum; Salvation army's 100th anniversary. Christian Cent 82:885-6 Jl 14 '65
General next to God; condensation. R. Collier. il Read Digest 86:265-8+ F '65
Hundred years' war. il Newsweek 66:55 Jl 5 '65
Salvation army beats a bigger, better drum; calling on industrial and community leaders for advice and help. il Bsns W p 114-16+ Je 19 '65

SALWAK, Stanley F.
Academic cooperation: Big ten style. Sch & Soc 93:397-8+ O 30 '65

SALZANO, John V. See Kilburn, K. H. jt. auth.

SALZBURG festival
Festival 1965. W. Legge. il Hi Fi 15:204-7+ N '65
Sound of Salzburg. J. Hamilton. il Look 29:44-9 Je 29 '65

SALZBURG seminar in American studies
Americana at Salzburg. il Time 86:49 Ag 13 '65

SAM Griffith memorial powerboat race. See Motor boat racing

SAMACHSON, Joseph, and Spencer, Herta
Radioactive strontium: estimation of the amount accidentally ingested. bibliog Science 148:955-7 My 14 '65

SAMARITANI, Aldo
Who's who in foreign business. por Fortune 71:92 Je '65

SAMOA, AMERICAN. See American Samoa

SAMOA, WESTERN
Press in developing countries. R. F. Rankin. il Sat R 48:124-5 S 18 '65

SAMOANS
Samoa: America's showplace of the South Seas. C. W. Hall. il Read Digest 87:157-64+ N '65

SAMPAIO, Nelson de Sousa
Latin America and neutralism. Ann Am Acad 362:62-70 N '65

SAMPLERS
See also
Needlework

SAMPLES, Kert
Seasoned skier shows them how. il pors Ebony 20:148-52+ Ap '65

SAMPLING
See also subhead Analysis under specific substances, e.g. Sea water—Analysis

SAMPSON, E. Lois. See O'Brien, J. S. jt. auth.

SAMPSON, Edith S.
Choose one of five: it's your life; address, May 30, 1965. Vital Speeches 31:661-3 Ag 15 '65

SAMPSON, M. and others
DNA synthesis in aluminum-treated roots of barley. bibliog Science 148:1476-7 Je 11 '65

SAMPSON, Paula D.
Patience Wright and her new style of picturing. Antiques 87:586-9 My '65

SAMSITES. See Guided missile bases

SAMSON and Delilah; opera. See Saint-Saëns, C.

SAMSON et Dalila; opera. See Saint-Saëns, C.

SAMSONITE corporation. See Shwayder brothers, incorporated

SAMSTAG, Nicholas
Because you have always told half-truths; excerpt from Bamboozled; or, How business is bamboozled by the ad-boys. Sat R 49:112-15 Ja 8 '66

SAMUELS, Gertrude
They no longer bop, they jap. N Y Times Mag p40+ Mr 7 '65
To Juárez on the divorce run. N Y Times Mag p78+ S 12 '65
Wanted: 1,000 Nazis still at large. N Y Times Mag p26-7+ F 28 '65
Where junkies learn to hang tough. N Y Times Mag p30-1+ My 9 '65
Why Castro exports Cubans. il N Y Times Mag p30-1+ N 7 '65
Working their way through jail. N Y Times Mag p 160+ N 14 '65

SAMUELS, Howard J.
Desperate need for more public debt. por Duns R 85:52+ F '65

SAMUELSON, Paul
Three experts on the outlook. por Newsweek 67:52-3 Ja 10 '66

SAN ANDREAS fault. See Faults (geology)

SAN ANTONIO, Tex.

Description
San Antonio, I love you! M. Cousins. il McCalls 93:72+ N '65

SAN ANTONIO, Tex.—*Continued*

Hotels, restaurants, etc.

Notes for a gazetteer; dining and cruising aboard Casa Rio barges. P. Hamburger. New Yorker 41:122+ F 20 '65

Music

See also

San Antonio symphony orchestra

Street traffic

Standardize traffic-control equipment. S. Fischer. il Am City 80:117 F '65

SAN ANTONIO grand opera festival. See Music festivals—Texas

SAN ANTONIO RIVER

Notes for a gazetteer; dining and cruising aboard Casa Rio barges. P. Hamburger. New Yorker 41:122+ F 20 '65

SAN ANTONIO symphony orchestra

Texas. A. Holmes. il Opera N 30:30 D 11 '65

SANAZARO, Paul J.

Research in patient care. Science 148:1489-90 Je 11 '65

SAN BERNARDINO, Calif.

Upgrading downtown. il Arch Rec 137:189 Je '65

SAN BERNARDINO MOUNTAINS

See also

San Gorgonio, Mount

SANBORN, Ia.

When the lights come on again; new downtown lighting system. J. Cravens. il Am City 80:130 O '65

SANBORNS. See Restaurants—Mexico

SANCHEZ MADERO, Luis Eduardo

Cuba's brazen blueprint for subversion. K. O. Gilmore. Read Digest 87:70-5 Ag '65

SANCHEZ VILELLA, Roberto

New man in La Fortaleza. A. W. Maldonado. il por Reporter 33:32-3 N 4 '65

SANCTIONS (international law)

Can Britain stop Rhodesia? question of economic sanctions. A. Lejeune. Nat R 18:22-3 Ja 11 '66

End of the road for whites in Rhodesia? effects of economic sanctions. il U S News 60:52-4 Ja 17 '66

How tight is the squeeze? R. W. Howe. il Reporter 33:29-32 D 2 '65

Many voices; Wilson bedeveled by Rhodesian crisis. Newsweek 66:45 D 20 '65

One kind word; sanctions against Rhodesia making impact. Newsweek 67:29 Ja 10 '66

Problem of sanctions; development of economic pressures against South Africa. P. Ritner. Commonweal 82:315-19 My 28 '65

Tightening the screws on rebellious Rhodesia; economic sanctions by Great Britain. il Bsns W p40-1 N 20 '65

Tightening the vise on Rhodesia. America 113:699 D 4 '65

SANCTIONS, Professional

Oklahoma's education war; NEA sanctions. S. Kalkstein. il Look 30:80+ Ja 25 '66

Sanctions are effective. R. B. Kennan. NEA J 54:31-2+ N '65

Teacher-opinion poll; professional sanctions. il NEA J 54:68 N '65

Teachers give Oklahoma a lesson; NEA sanctions against state. B. Carter. Reporter 33:34-7 S 9 '65

SANCTITY. See Holiness

SANCTUARIES, Bird. See Bird sanctuaries

SANCTUARIES, Wildlife. See Wildlife sanctuaries

SANCTUARY of the Dead Sea scrolls. See Dead Sea scrolls

SAND, George X.

Fisherman's horn of plenty. Outdoor Life 135:52-5+ My '65

Opening day on doves. Outdoor Life 136:54-7+ S '65

Sunshine cottontails. Field & S 70:50-1+ S '65

Tricky tilapia. Field & S 70:70-1+ Ja '66

SAND

Sands of the Mid-Atlantic Ridge. P. J. Fox and B. C. Heezen. bibliog il Science 149: 1367-70 S 17 '65

SAND and gravel pits

What to do with a highway borrow pit. R. L. Hall. il Farm J 89:60B-60C My '65

SAND buggies. See Motor vehicles

SAND casting. See Casting (sculpture)

SAND dunes

Dune-protection ordinance. A. J. Walnut and S. Sussna. il Am City 80:105-6 O '65

Early morning's the best time to read the face of a sand dune. il Sunset 135:26+ N '65

Living sand; Cape Henlopen, Del. W. H. Amos. il Nat Geog Mag 127:820-33 Je '65

SAND plovers. See Plovers

SAND sailboats. See Land sailboats

SAND storms. See Dust storms

SAND wedge (golf club) See Golf clubs (sticks)

SANDBACH, Walker

New executive director for CU. il por Consumer Rep 30:323 Jl '65

SANDBEACH isopod. See Isopoda

SANDBURG, Carl

Lincoln, man of steel and velvet; excerpts from address, February 12, 1959. Read Digest 86:61-4 F '65

SANDEEN, Ernest

Day in June; poem. Poetry 106:112-15 Ap '65

More comic spirit. Poetry 106:231-3 Je '65

SANDER, Ludwig R.

Sander at the mixolydian edge; exhibition at Kootz gallery, N.Y. J. Schuyler. il por Art N 64:26-7+ D '65

SANDERS, Aaron P. and others

Succinate; protective agent against hyperbaric oxygen toxicity. bibliog Science 150: 1830-1 D 31 '65

SANDERS, Bill

When extremists attack the press. J. F. Fixx. Sat R 48:72-3 F 13 '65

SANDERS, Carl E.

Governor Carl Sanders and Miss Emma. J. Shepherd. il pors Look 29:46+ F 23 '65

SANDERS, Charles L.

Ambassador is a lady. Ebony 21:23-6+ Ja '66

Race problem in Great Britain. il Ebony 21: 146-8+ N '65

Tortuous road to Oslo. Ebony 20:36+ Mr '65

Troubles of astronaut Edward Dwight. Ebony 20:29-32+ Je '65

SANDERS, Marion K.

New American female; demi-feminism takes over. Harper 231:37-43 Jl '65

Politics as a spectator sport. Harper 230: 152-4 Mr '65

(ed) See Alinsky, S. Professional radical

SANDERS, Ronald

Legacy of A. D. Gordon. Commentary 39:74-6 Ap '65

Reformers in the ghetto. Commentary 40:78-80+ N '65

Settling in Israel? Commentary 40:37-44 Ag: 28 N '65

SANDERS, Stanley

Riot as a weapon; the language of Watts. Nation 201:490-3 D 20 '65

about

My friend in Watts. S. Alexander. Life 59: 18 Ag 27 '65

SANDERS, Steve

Audition; boys for principal role in musical version of The yearling. New Yorker 41:23 S 4 '65

SANDERS, Thomas G.

Is neutrality the answer? Christian Cent 82: 144 F 3 '65

SANDERS, William

Creation and consolidation of the American community. Américas 17:4-9 Ap '65

SANDERS. See Sanding machines

SAN DIEGO, Calif.

Electronic equipment speeds survey work. F. G. Peters. il Am City 80:122-4 Mr '65

Galleries and museums

Biggest little museum; Putnam art collection. Timken art gallery. il Art N 64:26-7+ O '65

In San Diego, the history of flight; Aerospace museum, Balboa park. il Sunset 135:62+ N '65

Visit to Oaxaca in Balboa Park; Museum of man. il Sunset 134:50 My '65

Industries

At the end of the yo-yo, the federal city. W. Marx. Bul Atomic Sci 21:48-50 Mr '65

Music

San Diego dawn. S. A. Desick. il Opera N 30:28 S 25 '65

Parks and playgrounds

Whale tale and other stories; Mission Bay Park. H. Sutton. il Sat R 48:55-7 F 13 '65

Sanitary affairs

All-underwater pipe crew. il Am City 80:111 Ag '65

SAN DIEGO Chargers (football club) See Football clubs

SAN DIEGO yacht clubs. See Yacht clubs

SANDIFER, T. N.

Regulating the reefs. Motor B 115:118+ Mr '65

SANDING machines
Fastest orbital sander. C. E. Rhine. il Pop Sci 188:147 Ja '66
Finishing sanders. il Consumer Rep 30:112-17 Mr '65

Stands
See Machinery—Stands

SANDINO, Augusto César
In quest of Sandino, imperialism still rides. C. Beals. Nation 201:83-7 S 20 '65

SANDLER, Irving H.
Baziotes: modern mythologist. Art N 63:28-31+ F '65
Expressionism with corners. Art N 64:38-40+ Ap '65

SANDLER, Woodrow J.
Another worry for employers. por U S News 58:86-9 Mr 15 '65

SANDMAN, Charles W. Jr.
Chance for a change in the Garden state. J. J. Farmer. Reporter 33:27-9 Ag 12 '65

SANDS, Diana
Diana Sands: notes on a Broadway pussycat. S. Castan. il pors Look 29:38-9+ F 9 '65
Owl and the pussycat. il pors Ebony 20:98-103 F '65

SANDS, H. J. Jr
Technology for tomorrow's missile power; address, June 10, 1965. Vital Speeches 31:554-7 Jl 1 '65

SANDS, Leo G.
Additional channels for business radio. Electr World 74:62 S '65
More Canadian two-way channels. Electr World 73:78 Je '65
New industrial radio band. Electr World 73:29 Ap '65
SSB comes to marine radio. Electr World 73:30-1 My '65

SANDWICH construction
Beach house made of aluminum sandwiches; polystyrene foam between two sheets of aluminum. il Sports Illus 23:42-5 Ag 9 '65
Honeycomb used extensively in F-111A/B. E. J. Bulban. il Aviation W 83:73+ O 4 '65

SANDWICH spreads
Your blender makes spreads. Sunset 135:150 S '65

SANDWICHES
Fancy summer sandwiches. il Sunset 135:162+ S '65
Hearty sandwiches. R. Hanna. il Suc Farm 63:118-19 S '65
It's a sandwich! with recipes. il Seventeen 24:262-3+ Ag '65
Patio sandwich party. il Pop Gard 16:58+ My '65
Sandwich cookbook. il Good H 161:96-113 S '65
Sandwich makes the meal. il Parents Mag 40:94 S '65
Sunday-night supper; Danish modern. il Ladies Home J 82:82 Jl '65
What she's serving are seafood sandwiches Danish style. il Sunset 134:200-1 Ap '65
Wide-open sandwiches. il McCalls 92:90-1+ Jl '65
World's fastest meal-size sandwiches! il Bet Hom & Gard 43:76-7 Jl '65
See also
Sandwich spreads

SANE (organization) See National committee for a sane nuclear policy

SANFELICI, Arthur H.
Pilot report; Volaire 10A. Flying 77:47-9 Jl '65

SAN FERNANDO, Calif.
Composting gets a tryout. il Am City 80:99-102 Ap '65

SAN FERNANDO VALLEY, Calif.
High-fashion store with split-level massing; Bullock's Fashion square. il Arch Rec 137:194-9 My '65

SANFORD, Carl F.
Elmira to try composting. Am City 80:93-4 Jl '65

SANFORD, David
AMA and that disease. New Repub 153:10 S 18 '65

SANFORD, Nevitt
Morals on the campus. NEA J 54:20-3 Ap '65
—See Katz, J. jt. auth.

SANFORD, Terry
New era ahead for your state. pors Nations Bsns 53:56-8+ Jl '65

SAN FRANCISCO

Architecture
Rooms with a view in San Francisco. il Fortune 73:173 Ja '66

Banks
Crash on the Coast; San Francisco national bank closed by federal agents. il Newsweek 65:72-3 F 8 '65
Saxon on the stand; concerning testimony on failure of San Francisco national bank. il Newsweek 65:72 Mr 22 '65

Bridges
Seal and surface successfully in cool weather; San Francisco-Oakland Bay bridge. il Am City 80:112-13 Je '65

Chinatown
Now San Francisco has motorshaws. il Sunset 135:24 Ag '65

Churches
Grass-roots social justice; employment in building St Mary's cathedral. America 113:392 O 9 '65

City planning
In San Francisco, a renewal effort based on civic pride falls short of expectation. C. W. Moore. Arch Forum 123:58-63 Jl '65
San Francisco report: no easy road to the more handsome city. E. K. Thompson. il Arch Rec 138:151-66 S '65
San Francisco skyline: hard to spoil, but they're working on it. C. W. Moore. il Arch Forum 123:40-7 N '65

Description
Charm of San Francisco. H. Sutton. il McCalls 92:24+ Je '65
Our San Francisco, by H. Gilliam and others. Review
Pop Phot il 57:122 O '65. A. Young

Gardens
H&G's gardener's month: San Francisco's Strybing arboretum. il House & Gard 127:182-4 Mr '65

Housing
Nob Hill elegance by Warnecke. il Arch Rec 137:198-201 Ap '65

Intellectual life
Thar's culture in them thar hills. K. Rexroth. il N Y Times Mag p28-9+ F 7 '65

Lighting
Mercury vapors move in. S. M. Tatarian. Am City 80:136+ Ag '65

Music
Bay City success. A. Boucher. Opera N 30:28-9 S 25 '65
Lulu: West Coast premiere; San Francisco report. R. Commanday. il Hi Fi 15:176-7 D '65
San Francisco quake; major cultural scandal. N. Melnick. il Opera N 30:8-12 D 25 '65
See also
San Francisco opera company
Spring opera of San Francisco (organization)

Newspapers
Merger in San Francisco; Chronicle and Examiner. il Newsweek 66:61 S 20 '65
Out West, two more papers bite the dust. il Bsns W p30 S 18 '65
San Francisco merger leaves supplements' fate undecided. Pub W 188:47 S 20 '65
Survival, not sentiment; consolidation of Chronicle and Examiner. il Time 86:79 S 17 '65

Parks and playgrounds
Community action: once a neighborhood eyesore, now a place in the sun; San Francisco's Richmond district. il Sunset 136:88-9 Ja '66
New idea-gardens you can visit in San Francisco's Golden Gate park. il Sunset 135:74-7 S '65
Panhandle: it's a museum of living trees. il Sunset 135:70-1 Jl '65

Police
More on police brutality; L. Thompson vs. A. Gerrans and H. Clark. U S News 59:10 S 13 '65
Special unit revives police-community relations. T. J. Cahill. il Am City 80:166+ Je '65

Politics and government
San Francisco quake; major cultural scandal. N. Melnick. il Opera N 30:8-12 D 25 '65

SAN FRANCISCO—*Continued*

Rapid transit

BART: San Francisco's grand design; Bay area rapid transit. il Newsweek 66:69-71 Jl 19 '65

Super solution to the traffic tangle; BARTD or Bay area rapid transit district. M. Simons. il Look 29:62-3 S 21 '65

Transportation in cities; Bay area rapid transit district. J. W. Dyckman. il Sci Am 213:168-74 bibliog(p278) S '65

Traveling in high style; new transit system. B. R. Stokes. il Sat R 49:90-1 Ja 8 '66

Social life and customs

Intersection; point of meeting; enterprise in San Francisco. R. J. Hawthorne. Christian Cent 82:1599-602 D 29 '65

Stores

End of a landmark; White house closed. Newsweek 65:78 F 15 '65

Old S.F. department store goes out of business; closing of White house. Pub W 187:72-4 Mr 1 '65

Theater

Enter the gadflies; directors of San Francisco's Actors workship appointed to direct Lincoln Center repertory theater. Newsweek 65:82-3 F 8 '65

On stage in San Francisco. M. Harris. Holiday 38:180+ O '65

Transportation

Floating on air; Hovercraft shuttle between Oakland and San Francisco airports. il Time 86:59 Ag 20 '65

Toting commuters by computers; computer-controlled transportation complex. il Bsns W p 122-4+ Ap 10 '65

SAN FRANCISCO and Oakland helicopter airlines

Helicopter carrier petitions CAB for GEM trials at San Francisco. Aviation W 82:32 Mr 1 '65

SAN FRANCISCO ballet

Dash & control. il Time 85:67 Mr 5 '65

East meets West! Newsweek 65:88 Ap 26 '65

Musical events; week's run at the New York state theatre. W. Sargeant. New Yorker 41:88+ Ap 24 '65

San Francisco ballet; New York state theater. D. Hering. Dance Mag 39:30+ Je '65

San Francisco's pop art ballet. H. Caen. il Dance Mag 39:48-9 Ap '65

SAN FRANCISCO BAY REGION

San Francisco; getting together. S. C. Beise. il Sat R 49:50+ Ja 8 '66

San Francisco; telling the Bay area story; how the area council works. S. McCaffrey. il Sat R 49:52+ Ja 8 '66

Traveling in high style; new transit system. B. R. Stokes. il Sat R 49:90-1 Ja 8 '66

SAN FRANCISCO conference, 1945. See United Nations conference on international organization, San Francisco, 1945

SAN FRANCISCO national bank. See San Francisco—Banks

SAN FRANCISCO opera company

San Francisco (cont) A. Boucher. il Opera N 30:22 N 6; 24 N 20; 30 D 18 '65

Winning the West. P. J. Smith. il Opera N 30:6-7 D 18 '65

SAN FRANCISCO theological seminary, San Anselmo, Calif.

Balaam's ass in the seminary. R. Kirk. Nat R 17:934 O 19 '65

Doctoral studies for pastors; in-service doctoral program. H. B. Adams. Christian Cent 82:560+ Ap 28 '65

SAN FRANCISCO. University

Theology comes alive; summer school at University of San Francisco. America 113:198 Ag 28 '65

SAN GORGONIO, MOUNT

Battle for a mountain; sportsmen vs conservationists. C. Phinizy. il Sports Illus 22:18-21 F 1 '65

San Gorgonio; Southern California's rooftop. W. F. Heald. il Liv Wildn 29:12-16 Sum '65

SAN GORGONIO wilderness area. See Wilderness areas

SANGREN, Ward

Computing methods applied to reactor problems. Science 149:1268+ S 10 '65

SANITARY affairs. See subhead Sanitary affairs under names of countries, states, cities, e.g. Atlanta—Sanitary affairs

SANITARY bureau, Pan American. See Pan American sanitary bureau

SANITARY engineering

See also

Water supply

SANITARY fills. See Filling (earthwork)

SANITARY goods

Modern feminine products. M. B. Keiser. il Parents Mag 40:28+ Jl '65

SANITATION, Household

See also

Plumbing

SAN JOSE, Calif.

Campus plan for an office complex; California water service company offices. il Arch Rec 137:167-70 Je '65

SAN JUAN, Puerto Rico

Description

Caribbean Vegas. il Time 85:41 F 19 '65

Hotels, restaurants, etc.

Everything's up to date in Puerto Rico. H. Sutton. il Sat R 48:40+ Ap 17 '65

Water supply

Six years ahead of schedule. R. M. Guzman. il Am City 80:132-3 F '65

SAN JUAN ISLANDS, Wash.

Northwest's islands of discovery. F. C. Clark, jr. Yachting 117:66-8 Mr '65

Over the bounding wabes; San Juan Islands off Washington and British Columbia. J. Olsen. il Sports Illus 23:50-8 Ag 2 '65

Pig war was a one-shot war. il Sunset 135:40+ S '65

SAN JUAN wilderness areas, Colo. See Wilderness areas

SAN LEANDRO, Calif.

On-the-spot tests check gutter capacity. G. H. Hamlin and J. Bautista. il Am City 80:94-6 Ap '65

SAN MARTÍN, José de

Liberators of the South. E. Correas. il por Américas 17:14-21 S '65

SAN RAFAEL primitive area (proposed) See Wilderness areas

SAN REMO festival. See Music festivals—Italy

SANTA BARBARA, Calif.

Richard H. Dana was a visitor; De la Guerra adobe. il Sunset 134:36 F '65

SANTA BARBARA, Calif, public library

Santa Barbara public library again without chief librarian. Library J 90:606 F 1 '65

SANTA BARBARA botanic garden

Santa Barbara botanic garden; Santa Barbara, Calif. J. Broughton. il Horticulture 43:28-32 N '65

SANTA BARBARA historical society

For a Santa Barbara stopover; historical museum. il Sunset 135:19 O '65

SANTA BARBARA ISLANDS, Calif.

Channel Island skunk; spotted skunk. R. G. Van Gelder. il Natur Hist 74:30-5 Ag '65

SANTA CATALINA ISLAND

Long Island west? il Newsweek 66:50 Jl 5 '65

SANTA CLARA, Calif.

Slurry seal drops costs, boosts quality. S. Cristofano. il Am City 80:96-8 F '65

SANTA CLARA COUNTY, Calif.

Water supply

Small consultants join to provide engineering service. il Am City 80:160 My '65

SANTA CLARA COUNTY prison. See Prisons—California

SANTA CLARA VALLEY, Calif.

Santa Clara; the bulldozer crop. J. P. Degnan. il Nation 200:242-5 Mr 8 '65

SANTA CLAUS

Poetry

Night before Christmas. C. C. Moore. il Redbook 126:49-61 D '65

SANTA CRUZ, Calif.

Plastic sewers serve a wharf. C. R. Bergston. il Am City 80:94-5 S '65

SANTA FE, N. Mex.

Architecture

New look in Santa Fe; opera theater underwent a face-lifting. E. C. Munro. il Opera N 30:14-16 S 25 '65

Music

Fabulous Santa Fe. R. C. Marsh; R. Bright. il Opera N 30:23 S 25 '65

SANTA FE opera association

To serve the cause of opera. P. J. Smith. il Hi Fi 15:198+ N '65

SANTANA, Manuel
  Kangaroo rampant. il por Newsweek 67:44
    Ja 10 '66
  ¡Olé! Manolo, a little bit too late. E. Shirley.
    il Sports Illus 24:48-9 Ja 10 '66
SANTANDER, Francisco de Paula
  History, stuff of dreams. P. G. Valderrama.
    il por Américas 17:28-33 D '65
SANTA ROSA, Calif.
  New hope for old streets. il Am City 80:90-1
    N '65
SANTIAGO, Spain
  Here and there; pilgrimage. Holiday 37:170
    Ap '65
  Miracles of Santiago. J. A. Michener. il Read
    Digest 87:228-34 Jl '65
  Search for the Spanish soul; series of courses
    on the interpretation of Spanish music.
    C. Irizarry. il Hi Fi 15:186-7 D '65
SANTIAGO de Compostela, Spain. See Santiago,
  Spain
SANTIAM RIVER
  Down the river in or on kayaks, inner
    tubes, rafts, surfboards; North Santiam
    River run challenge. il Sunset 134:41 My '65
SANTO DOMINGO, Dominican Republic
  Nightmare of civil war; life in Dominican
    capital. U S News 58:27 My 31 '65
  Routine kill; death of student demonstrator.
    il Newsweek 66:64 O 11 '65
  Santo Domingo: a taunting boy killed. il Life
    59:46-46A O 8 '65
  U.S. troops in Santo Domingo: grim price of
    power. S. Castan. il Look 29:38-43 Je 15 '65
SANTO Tomé de Guayana. See Guayana,
  Venezuela
SÃO PAULO (city), Brazil

Galleries and museums
  Brazilian bouillabaisse; eighth São Paulo
    bienal. E. C. Baker. il Art N 64:30-1+
    D '65
SÃO PAULO biennial. See Art—Exhibitions
SAP
  Sap pressure in vascular plants. P. F.
    Scholander and others. bibliog il Science
    148:339-46, 1488 Ap 16, Je 11 '65; Reply
    with rejoinder. W. R. Gardner and S. L.
    Rawlins. 149:920+ Ag 27 '65
SAPPHO
  Sappho, poet and legend. K. Rexroth. Sat R
    48:27 N 27 '65
SARASOHN, Wendy
  Curl up and read. Seventeen 24:38 Je '65
SARASOTA, Fla.
  Florida's three-ring city: Ringling memora-
    bilia remains in Sarasota. H. Sutton. il
    Sat R 48:64+ O 16 '65
SARAYIOTES, James
  Are you ready for UHF? Pop Electr 22:58
    My '65
SARAZEN, Gene
  How businessmen can play smarter golf. por
    Nations Bsns 53:92-4+ O '65
SARBIN, Penny
  Yearbook photo journalism. Pop Phot 56:100
    F '65
SARCOLEMMA. See Muscle
SARCOMA
  Brain tumors, gliomas induced in hamsters
    by Bryan's strain of Rous sarcoma virus.
    G. F. Rabotti and others. bibliog il Science
    147:504-6 Ja 29 '65
  Mosquito transmission of a reticulum cell
    sarcoma of hamsters. W. G. Banfield and
    others. bibliog il Science 148:1239-40 My 28
    '65
  Reversion in hamster cells transformed by
    Rous sarcoma virus. I. Macpherson. il Sci-
    ence 148:1731-3 Je 25 '65
  Transformation by Rous sarcoma virus: a re-
    quirement for DNA synthesis. J. P. Bader.
    bibliog il Science 149:757-8 Ag 13 '65
SARCOPLASMIC reticulum. See Muscle
SARDINES
    See also
  Cookery—Fish
SARDINIA
  In search of Sardinia. S. O'Faolain. Holiday
    39:52-3+ Ja '66
SARDIS
  Sardis excavated further. il Sci N L 88:309
    N 13 '65
SARFF, Douglas P.
  Good-by to all that. Newsweek 65:68 Ap 19
    '65
SARGEANT, Winthrop
  Books (cont) New Yorker 41:189-94 Ap 17
    '65
  Musical events. See issues of New Yorker
  Profiles (cont) New Yorker 41:40-2+ Ja 15 '66

SARGENT, F. 2d, and Itoh, S.
  Bioclimatology. Science 147:761-2+ F 12 '65
SARGENT, Jo Ann
  Eyelash: fur or hair? Atlan 215:120-2 Je '65
SARK
  Other Eden. il Time 86:33 Ag 20 '65
SARMA, Padman S. and others
  Induction of tumors in hamsters with an
    avian adenovirus (CELO) bibliog Science
    149:1108 S 3 '65
SARMI, Ferdinando, count
  Bugles, bangles & all woman. il por Time
    85:62 Je 25 '65
SARMIENTO, Domingo Faustino
  From the editor. Am Ed 1:inside cover Ap
    '65
SARNOFF, David
  Switchboards in space: a look into the future;
    interview. por U S News 59:50-4 Jl 5 '65
  Where Soviets may challenge U.S. next; ex-
    cerpts from address May 26, 1965. por U S
    News 58:20 Je 7 '65

    about
  One world. Nation 201:207 O 11 '65
  One-world concept of mass communication.
    R. L. Tobin. Sat R 49:101-2 Ja 8 '66
  Sarnoff and son. por Newsweek 66:68 S 13 '65
SARNOFF, Robert W.
  Businessmen in the news. por Fortune 72:
    47 O '65
  Sarnoff and son. por Newsweek 66:68 S 13 '65
SAROYAN, William
  Ah-ha, the cat saw the mouse. Sat Eve Post
    238:70-2 F 27 '65
  Biggest watermelon anybody ever saw; story.
    Sat Eve Post 238:56-9 S 11 '65
  Pointy shoes; story. Sat Eve Post 238:44-6
    My 22 '65
SARRATT, Reed
  South: educational resources; address, April
    1965. por Wilson Lib Bul 39:860-6 Je '65
SARTRE, Jean Paul
  Sartre talks of Beauvoir; interview, ed. by
    M. Gobeil, tr. by B. Frechtman. por Vogue
    146:72-3 Jl '65
  Up all night; cable received by the teach-in
    group at Boston university, May 5, 1965.
    Nation 200:574 My 31 '65
  Why I will not go to the United States; tr.
    by L. Abel. por Nation 200:407-11 Ap 19
    '65
  (tr) See Euripides. Trojan women

    about
  Books. H. Rosenberg. New Yorker 40:131-6
    F 6 '65
  Force of circumstances, by S. de Beauvoir.
    Review
      Nat R 17:692-4 Ag 10 '65. W. S. Schlamm
      New Yorker 41:104+ Ja 8 '66. N. Bliven
  Free self in a captive society. E. Capouya.
    Sat R 48:40-1 Je 12 '65
  Little bourgeois. K. Nott. Commentary 39:
    82-6 F '65
  Marxism of Jean-Paul Sartre, by W. Desan.
    Review
      Commonweal 82:194-6 Ap 30 '65. A. May-
      hew
  Sartre and the cancelation. T. Molnar. Nat R
    17:270 Ap 6 '65
  Sartre as performer and literary illusionist.
    W. E. Arnold. Commonweal 82:566-7 Ag 6
    '65
  Sartre cancels U.S. visit in protest. Christian
    Cent 82:388 Mr 31 '65
  Les séquestrés d'Altona. Criticism
    New Yorker 41:206+ O 2 '65
SARVIS, Shirley
  Try a main-dish custard pie. Farm J 89:84-5
    O '65
SASANO, Takaaki
  Mosaics with eggshells. Design 66:13-15 Ja '65
SASKATCHEWAN
  Prairie winter. M. Creal. il Ladies Home J
    82:60-1+ D '65
    See also
  Education—Saskatchewan

Description and travel
  We explore Saskatchewan. C. B. Colby. il
    Outdoor Life 136:22-4+ D '65; 137:112-13+
    Ja '66

Economic policy
  Where socialism failed close to home. T.
    Drury. il Nations Bsns 53:66-8+ O '65
SASKATCHEWAN doctors strike. See Strikes
  —Canada
SASS, Daniel B. and others
  Shell structure of recent articulate brachio-
    poda. Science 149:181-2 Jl 9 '65

SASSOON, Vidal
Sassoon and his scissors. il pors Life 59:67-8
Jl 9 '65

SATELLITES
Atmosphere on Io? G. S. Mumford, 3d. il Sky
& Tel 29:157 Mr '65
Io-related radio emission from Jupiter. G.
A. Dulk. bibliog il Science 148:1585-9 Je
18 '65
Jupiter's decametric emission correlated with
the longitudes of the first three galilean
satellites. G. R. Lebo and others. bibliog
il Science 148:1724-5 Je 25 '65
Satellites of Saturn. il Sky & Tel 30:185 S '65
Saturn's ring and the satellites of Jupiter;
interpretations of infrared spectra. T.
Owen. bibliog Science 149:974-5 Ag 27 '65
See also
Artificial satellites

SATIN, Lowell Robert
Behind the scenes. J. F. Fixx. por Sat R 48:
32 Je 12 '65

SATINOFF, Evelyn
Impaired recovery from hypothermia after
anterior hypothalamic lesions in hibernators. bibliog Science 148:399-400 Ap 16 '65

SATIRE
Literature of the absurd. G. P. Nemes. il
Américas 17:6-10 F '65

SATISFACTION in work. See Job satisfaction

SATO, Akira
Compelling images of Akira Sato. il Pop
Phot 56:70-3 My '63

SATO, Eisaku
President Johnson and Prime Minister Sato
of Japan exchange views on matters of
mutual interest; greeting, January 12, 1965.
Dept State Bul 52:134 F 1 '65
about
Criticism at the polls. il por Time 86:33 Jl
16 '65
Positive but humble. Newsweek 66:32 Jl 19
'65

SATO, Gordon H. and others
Phenotypic alterations in adrenal tumor cultures. bibliog Science 148:1733-4 Je 25 '65

SATTLEY, Helen R.
Basic book courses for prospective teachers.
Wilson Lib Bul 39:797 My '65

SATURDAY evening post
Tradition of Ben Franklin. il Sat Eve Post
239:60 Ja 1 '66

SATURDAY review
Education in America. P. Woodring. Sat R
48:61 S 11 '65
Life begins at twenty-five; editor's twenty-
fifth anniversary on SR. N. Cousins. Sat
R 48:26-8 Ap 24 '65; Correction. 48:49 My
22 '65
Where have all the young writers gone? re-
port on the 1965 student magazine contest.
S. B. Chickering. il Sat R 48:26-7 O 9 '65
See also
Anisfield-Wolf awards

SATURDAY review of literature. See Saturday review

SATURN (planet)
Edgewise presentation of Saturn's rings.
J. W. Goodman. il Sky & Tel 30:128-31 S '65
Satellites
See Satellites
Spectra
Saturn's ring and the satellites of Jupiter;
interpretations of infrared spectra. T.
Owen. bibliog Science 149:974-5 Ag 27 '65

SATURN booster. See Space vehicles—Propulsion systems

SATURNIIDAE. See Imperial moths

SAUCERS, Flying. See Flying saucers

SAUCES
Enchantment in the Louisiana marshes;
manufacturers of tabasco sauce. K. Hamill.
il Fortune 72:158-64 O '65
Gourmet barbecue sauce. il Pop Gard 16:62
My '65
How the Swedes use mushrooms. il Sunset
134:150 F '65
Ice cream and sauces. R. Hanna. il Suc
Farm 63:74-5 Je '65
New toppings for angel food; with recipes.
B. Pierson. il Farm J 89:92-3 F '65
Saucery; subtle and spicy. il Redbook 125:
74-5+ My '65
Saucy suggestions! il Bet Hom & Gard 43:
106-7 Mr '65
Sweet. and hot; history of tabasco sauce
H. Sutton. il Sat R 49:46-7 Ja 15 '66

SAUDEK, Robert
Program coming in fine; please play Japanese
sandman. por Am Heritage 16:24-7 Ag '65

SAUDI ARABIA
Five kinds of time; problems of reform. J. A.
Morris, jr. il Newsweek 65:42-4 Mr 8 '65
Saudi Arabia; beyond the sands of Mecca.
T. J. Abercrombie. il Nat Geog Mag 129:
1-53 Ja '66
See also
Water supply—Saudi Arabia

Foreign relations
Death of a dream; Nasser and Faisal sign
Yemeni peace pact. il Newsweek 66:29 S 6
'65

Politics and government
King Faisal's first year. V. Sheean. For Affairs 44:304-13 Ja '66
Two to watch; new crown prince. il Time
85:29 Ap 9 '65

Social conditions
King Faisal's first year. V. Sheean. For
Affairs 44:304-13 Ja '66

SAUER, Louis W.
Your child's health. See issues of PTA magazine

SAUERBRATEN. See Cookery—Meat

SAUERKRAUT
Sausage sampler on top of sauerkraut. il Sunset 135:184-5 O '65

SAUGER fishing
Now is the time for sauger fishing. H. Bradshaw. il Suc Farm 63:88 Ap '65

SAUGERTIES, N.Y.

Historic houses, etc.
Living with antiques; Mynderse farmhouse.
E. Gaines. il Antiques 88:352-5 S '65

SAULNIER, Raymond J.
Three experts on the outlook. por Newsweek
67:52-3 Ja 10 '66

SAUNA. See Baths, Vapor

SAUNDERS, Robert J.
Books. Sch Arts 65:50 O '65

SAUNDERS, Stuart Thomas
Rail bargaining back on the tracks. por Bsns
W p43 F 6 '65

SAUSAGE
Sausage sampler on top of sauerkraut. il Sunset 135:184-5 O '65

SAUSALITO, Calif, public library
Confessions of a fellow traveler. R. Dillon.
Library J 90:5484-5 D 15 '65

SAVAGE, Charles H. Jr
Episode in intercultural misunderstanding.
America 113:778-9 D 18 '65

SAVAGE RIVER State forest, Maryland. See
Forests, State

SAVANNAH, Ga.

Churches
Secession in Savannah; St John's Episcopal
church refuses integration. il Time 85:70
My 7 '65

SAVANNAH RIVER AEC project. See Nuclear
reactors

SAVED; drama. See Bond, E.

SAVIDGE, George Paul
Twins become rival football captains. il pors
Life 59:119+ O 8 '65

SAVIDGE, George Peter
Twins become rival football captains. il pors
Life 59:119+ O 8 '65

SAVILE, D. B. O.
Spore discharge in basidiomycetes: a unified
theory. bibliog Science 147:165-6; 148:533
Ja 8, Ap 23 '65

SAVING and savings
Banks' scramble for your savings. U S News
60:97 Ja 17 '66
Glossary for savers. il U S News 60:97 Ja 24
'66
How much do you want to save up? il Chang-
ing T 19:45 N '65
Make your savings earn more. il Changing T
19:7-10 S '65
Savings incentives offered to West German
workers. K. Braun. Mo Labor R 88:971-3
Ag '65
What you can earn on your savings. il U S
News 59:91-4 O 11 '65
Why pension plans boost savings; concerning
G. Katona's book Private pensions and in-
dividual savings. Bsns W p98+ D 11 '65
See also
Banks and banking—Savings departments
Finance, Personal
Hoarding
Investments
Postal savings banks
Savings banks

SAVINGS and loan associations
Battle of interest. il Time 87:81 Ja 7 '66
Bigger dividends on savings? U S News 59: 110 D 13 '65
Critical look at banking; investigations starting in Washington. il U S News 58:39-41 Mr 15 '65
Lid put on California S&L rates; federal agency bars rise to 5 per cent. Bsns W p38 Ap 10 '65
Savers come out ahead in big drive for their money. il U S News 60:67-9 Ja 3 '66
Scramble for savings: meaning to borrowers, banks, builders. il U S News 60:96-7 Ja 24 '66
Squeeze on the S.&L.'s. il Fortune 71:63 My '65
Where insured savings earn the most. il Changing T 19:15-17 Mr '65
    See also
Columbia savings and loan association

SAVINGS banks
Battle of interest. il Time 87:81 Ja 7 '66
Scramble for savings: meaning to borrowers, banks, builders. il U S News 60:96-7 Ja 24 '66
    See also
Postal savings banks
Savings deposits

SAVINGS bonds. See Bonds, Government

SAVINGS certificates. See Savings deposits

SAVINGS deposits
Rate rise sharpens savings battle; Fed's boost of interest ceiling on time deposits. il Bsns W p56-8 D 18 '65
Want extra interest? let your savings sit; savings certificates. il Changing T 19:26 Je '65
    See also
Banks and banking—Savings departments

SAVIO, Mario
University has become a factory; interview, ed. by J. Fincher. por Life 58:100-1 F 26 '65
    about
Berkeley affair: Mr Kerr vs. Mr Savio & co. A. H. Raskin. il por N Y Times Mag p24-5+ F 14 '65
Bonaparte's retreat. Time 85:54 My 7 '65
Savio goes to jail. Time 85:48 Mr 12 '65

SAVORY, Theodore
Courtship behavior of arachnids. Natur Hist 74:52-6 My '65

SAW-whet owls. See Owls

SAWING
Offbeat tricks with your radial-arm saw. R. J. De Cristoforo. il Pop Mech 124:188-92 N '65

SAWMILL workers. See Lumber workers

SAWS
Five tricks with bandsaw. il Pop Sci 187: 136-7 Ag '65
New from Wen; circular saws. il Pop Mech 125:46 Ja '66
Nibbler attachment for your sabre saw. H. W. Teter. Pop Mech 125:190-1+ Ja '66
Offbeat tricks with your radial-arm saw. R. J. De Cristoforo. il Pop Mech 124:188-92 N '65
Pine-pole sawing partner; prop to use with crosscut saw. il Sunset 134:116 Ap '65
Quickie saw guide for cutting big panels. V. Kondra. il Pop Sci 187:144-5 O '65
Safety saw. C. Conley. il Field & S 70:102 Ag '65
Speed reducer for metal cutting. H. P. Strand. il Pop Mech 124:152-4 D '65
Your radial saw can sharpen itself. M. Banister. il Pop Mech 124:192-4 O '65
Your table saw will cut circles. R. J. De Cristoforo. il Pop Sci 188:136-9 Ja '66

SAWSILAK, Arnold B. See Duke, P. jt. auth.

SAWYER, Charles H. See Kawamura, H. jt. auth.

SAWYER, Kenneth
Arts in architecture. Craft Horiz 25:7-8 Ja '65
Fabric collage. Craft Horiz 25:16-21+ Mr '65

SAWYER, Ruth
Christmas that was nearly lost; story. Parents Mag 40:49-51 D '65
Laura Ingalls Wilder award; acceptance address, July 6, 1965. Horn Bk 41:474-6 O '65
    about
From deep springs. R. H. Viguers. Horn Bk 41:463 O '65
Our fair lady! M. D. McCloskey. il Horn Bk 41:481-6 O '65

Regina medal presentation; April 20, 1965. Mother Mary Cecile. por Horn Bk 41:477-8 O '65
To Ruth Sawyer. B. Robinson. Horn Bk 41:478-80 O '65

SAXÉN, Lauri
Tetracycline: effect on osteogenesis in vitro. bibliog Science 149:870-2 Ag 20 '65

SAXIFRAGES
How to succeed with saxifrages. D. Klaber. il Horticulture 43:16-17 Ag '65

SAXON, James J.
Central figure in inquries on banks. por U S News 58:15 Mr 1 '65
Comptroller Saxon: his critics speak out. por U S News 58:16 Mr 29 '65
Saxon charm draws Chase bank. il por Bsns W p 121+ Jl 24 '65
Saxon on the stand. il por Newsweek 65:72 Mr 22 '65
Trouble among the regulators. il por Time 85:79 Mr 26 '65
Who's on first? il por Newsweek 65:68 F 15 '65

SAY good night to owl; story. See Schulberg, B.

SAY nothing; drama. See Hanley, J.

SAYER, William R.
Washington report. Yachting 118:82+ Jl '65

SAYERS, Frances Clarke
If the trumpet be not sounded; address, November, 1964. por Wilson Lib Bul 39:658-62+ Ap '65
Lose not the nightingale; excerpts. Horn Bk 41:299-301 Je '65
Too long at the sugar bowls: Frances C. Sayers raps Disney; statements. Library J 90:4538 O 15 '65
Walt Disney accused; interview. Horn Bk 41:602-11 D '65
    about
Confessions of a fellow traveler. R. Dillon. Library J 90:5484-5 D 15 '65
Summoned by books. R. H. Viguers. Horn Bk 41:244-5 Je '65

SAYERS, Gale
Extravagant outing for a rare rookie. T. Maule. il Sports Illus 23:97-9 D 6 '65
Gale Sayers: pro football's rambling rookie. il pors Ebony 21:70-1+ Ja '66
In search of excitement. il por Time 86:90 D 10 '65

SAYINGS. See Aphorisms and apothegms; Quotations

SAYLOR, John P.
What the Wilderness act does; adaptation of statement, July 30, 1964. Liv Wildn 86: 9+ Spr '64

SAYLOR, Margaret D.
Study trip to Washington. NEA J 54:54-5 Mr '65

SAYRE, Francis B. Jr
Pastor's satirical poke at pastors. Life 58:20 Je 18 '65
    about
Free-swinging cleric in a high place; with quotations from conversations with R. Stolley. il pors Life 58:125-6+ Ap 2 '65

SAYRE, Joel
Life book review. Life 59:6 S 24 '65

SAYRE, Nora
Exquisite insultress. Harper 231:114-15 Ag '65

SCABBARDS
Rifle on the horse. J. O'Connor. il Outdoor Life 136:68+ Ag '65

SCALE models. See Models

SCALES (weighing instruments)
Bathroom scales. il Consumer Rep 31:14-16 Ja '66
Inexpensive household scales are not accurate. il Consumer Bul 48:37-9 Jl '65

SCALLI, Frank J.
Skin and scuba training games. Recreation 58:136-7 Mr '65

SCALLOPS
    See also
Cookery—Fish

SCALPELS. See Surgical instruments

SCAMMON, Richard M. See Wattenberg, B. J. jt. auth.

SCANDAL
That was New York; scandal column of Town topics, weekly magazine. A. Logan. il New Yorker 41:37-8+ Ag 14; 41-2+ Ag 21 '65

SCANDINAVIA
    See also
Opera—Scandinavia
Tourist trade—Scandinavia

SCANDINAVIANS
Nothing rotten in the states of Denmark, Norway, Sweden and Finland, especially the girls. R. Joseph. il Esquire 63:84-7 My '65

See also
Icelanders

SCARLATTI, Domenico
Horowitz's Scarlatti: a really new experience. C. J. Luten. por Am Rec G 31:621 Mr '65
Scarlatti by Landowska. C. J. Luten. il por Am Rec G 31:510 F '65

SCARLET ibises. See Ibises

SCARPELLI, Emile M. and others
Lung surfactants, counterions, and hysteresis. bibliog Science 148:1607-9 Je 18 '65

SCATTERGUNS. See Shotguns

SCATTERING (physics)
Electromagnetic scattering: report on second Interdisciplinary conference on electromagnetic scattering. R. L. Rowell and R. S. Stein. Science 149:1399 S 17 '65

SCENEDESMUS obliquus. See Algae

SCENERY. See Landscape

SCENERY, Stage. See Theater—Stage scenery

SCENIC areas. See Preservation of landmarks, scenery, etc.—United States

SCENT. See Perfumery

SCHAEFER, George Louis
Organization man. il por Time 86:60 N 26 '65

SCHAEFER, Jack
New Southwest. Holiday 37:50-65+ My '65

SCHAEFFER, Bobb, and Mangus, Marlyn
Fossil lakes from the eocene. Natur Hist 74:10-21 Ap '65

SCHAEFFER, O. A. See Fanale, F. P. jt. auth.

SCHAELING, Marianne
Last jack-o'-lantern; story. Seventeen 24:138-9 O '65
We have something in common; story. Seventeen 24:82-3 Je '65

SCHAETZEL, J. Robert
Impact of change in eastern Europe on the Atlantic partnership; address, April 3, 1965. Dept State Bul 53:161-71 Jl 26 '65

SCHAFER, Milton
Promenade concerts at Lincoln Center. Hi Fi 15:144+ S '65

SCHAFF, Adam
Heart. Schaff and Marx. por Newsweek 67:30 Ja 10 '66

SCHALK, Adolph
Return to Auschwitz. Commonweal 82:498-501 Jl 9 '65

SCHALL, James V.
Science and the scriptural view of the universe. Cath World 202:233-7 Ja '66

SCHALLER, George B.
My year with the tigers. por Life 58:60+ Je 25 '65

about
Tense assignment: stalking the tiger. G. P. Hunt. il Life 58:3 Je 25 '65

SCHALLER, Lyle E.
Housing for the Nation's poor. Christian Cent 83:10-13, 44-7 Ja 5-12 '66

SCHALOCK, Henry Delbert
I love you; and I like you! ed. by M. Longwell. Farm J 89:75+ O '65

SCHAPIRO, Boris
Cheating scandal rocks the bridge world. M. Smith. il pors Life 58:32-3 Je 4 '65
Five-finger exercise. il por Time 85:42 Je 4 '65
Why do people cheat? C. H. Goren. il McCalls 92:30+ S '65

SCHAPIRO, J. Salwyn
New continental community. Sat R 48:39 F 13 '65

SCHAPIRO, Leonard
Was Lenin necessary? Commentary 38:57-60 D '64; 39:18 My '65

SCHAPPER, Beatrice
What we now know about sex molesters. Todays Health 44:18-21+ Ja '66

SCHARDT, Arlie
Tension, not split, in the Negro ranks. Christian Cent 82:614-16 My 12 '65

SCHARFF, Matthew D. and Uhr, J. W.
Functional ribosomal unit of gamma-globulin synthesis. bibliog Science 148:646-8 Ap 30 '65

SCHARLEMANN, Robert P.
After Tillich, what? address, October 22, 1965. Christian Cent 82:1478-80 D 1 '65

SCHAUFFLER, Goodrich C.
Pregnancy & heart disease. McCalls 92:42+ Je '65

SCHAULIS, William
Veterinarian tells: how to treat fresh feedlot cattle. por Suc Farm 63:46+ S '65

SCHAWLOW, A. L.
Lasers; adaptation of address, December 28, 1963. bibliog Science 149:13-22 Jl 2 '65

SCHECHNER, Richard
Free theater for Mississippi. Harper 231:31-2+ O '65

SCHECTER, Bayla. See Melzack, R. jt. auth.

SCHECTER, Jerrold
Jewel Essence Goddess in blue brocade: Mrs Sukarno. Life 60:30-30A Ja 21 '66
Political price of Japan's China trade. Reporter 33:28-30 S 23 '65

SCHEDULES, Household. See Home economics

SCHEDULES, School
Brookhurst plan: an experiment in flexible scheduling. Brookhurst junior high school, Anaheim, Calif. E. B. Hofmann. il NEA J 54:50-2 S '65

SCHEER, Milton D. See Jackson, W. M. jt. auth.

SCHEER, Robert
Rim of hell. Nation 201:110 S 6 '65

SCHEFFLER, Harold W.
Big men and disks of shell. Natur Hist 74:20-5 D '65

SCHEID, Phil N.
Charter of accountability for executives. bibliog f Harvard Bsns R 43:88-98 Jl '65

SCHEINUK, Paula
For crunchy marmalade: make use of big zucchinis. Flower Grower 52:6 Jl '65

SCHELLSBURG, Pa.
Town with too many churches. N. M. Lobsenz. il Redbook 126:70-1+ N '65

SCHEMAN, L. Ronald
Books. Américas 17:39-40 Mr '65

SCHENECTADY, N.Y.

Streets
Just a shimmy, no bang-bang; pile driver in Schenectady, N.Y. il Am City 80:24 S '65

SCHENFELD, Abraham E.
Selecting a UHF antenna. Pop Electr 22:55-7 My '65

SCHENK, Gretchen Knief
(ed) Extending library service. See issues of Wilson library bulletin

SCHENK, Paul E.
Precambrian glaciated surface beneath the Gowganda formation, Lake Timagami, Ontario. bibliog Science 149:176-7 Jl 9 '65

SCHENKER, Donald
Picture of Mathew Brady; poem. Poetry 107:95-7 N '65

SCHERER, George
Reducing rectifier interference. Electr World 73:65 Mr '65

SCHERER, James A.
Lutheran introspection. Christian Cent 82:622+ My 12 '65

SCHERMAN, Bernardine Kielty
Reference books: a personal choice. Writer 79:15-18 Ja '66

SCHERMAN, David E.
His world of worms, eels and a mad dwarf Life 58:56 Je 4 '65

SCHERY, Robert W.
Landscape for casual living. Pop Gard 16:10-11+ Jl '65
Latest news about lawns. Horticulture 44:34-5+ Ja '66
Migration of a plant. Natur Hist 74:40-5 D '65

SCHEUER, Joseph F. See Wakin, E. jt. auth.

SCHEVILL, James
Cycle; poem. Nation 201:253 O 18 '65

about
Vision, celebration, and testimony. M. Van Duyn. Poetry 105:268 Ja '65

SCHICK, George
Preparing a performance; ed. by A. M. Lingg. pors Opera N 29:8-12 Mr 27 '65

SCHICKEL, Richard
Life book review. Life 57:13+ D 17 '65
Life movie review (cont) Life 58:19 Mr 12; 18 Ap 16; 16 My 7; 15 Je 18; 15 Je 25; 59:16 Jl 9; 11 Ag 6; 10 Ag 27; 8 S 17; 19 O 15; 22 N 5; 15 N 19; 20 D 3; 20 D 10 '65; 60:8+ Ja 7; 10 Ja 14 '66
Life TV review. Life 58:19 My 21; 59:27 N 12 '65
Marshall McLuhan: Canada's intellectual comet. Harper 231:62-8 N '65
Work of serious, genuine art. Life 60:62A Ja 21 '66

SCHICKELE, Peter
Properly neglected. il Time 87:62 Ja 7 '66

SCHIELE, Egon
Women of Klimt and Schiele. A. Werner. il Reporter 32:44+ F 25 '65

SCHIFF, Dorothy
Concession to Dolly. il por Time 86:59 Jl 2
'65
SCHIFF, Sydney. See Hudson, S. pseud.
SCHILD, Rudolph. See Hiltner, W. A. jt. auth.
SCHILLER, Andrew
Chicago's miracle. Harper 232:65-8+ Ja '66
Chicago's Oxford on the rocks. Harper 230:
87-90+ My '65
SCHILLER, Friedrich von. See Schiller, J. C.
F. von
SCHILLER, Helmut
Gourmet botanist. New Yorker 41:43 N 6 '65
SCHILLER, Johann Christoph Friedrich von
Problem child for both Schiller and Verdi:
Don Carlo. L. C. McGinn. por Opera N
30:24-5 D 11 '65
SCHILLER, Karl
Germany's economic requirements. For Af-
fairs 43:671-81 Jl '65
SCHIN, Ki Ssu, and Clever, Ulrich
Lysosomal and free acid phosphatase in sali-
vary glands of chironomus tentans. bibliog
Science 150:1053-5 N 19 '65
SCHINE, G. David
Days of shame, by C. E. Potter. Review
Sat R 48:49 O 16 '65. N. S. Finney
SCHINE, J. Myer
Dark horse wins out on Schine deal. Bsns W
p96 S 4 '65
Schine's surprise. Newsweek 66:74 S 13 '65
SCHINE enterprises, incorporated
Two realty partners tackle a big one alone:
Wien and Helmsley plan to buy Schine
enterprises, inc. il Bsns W p 105-6+ Ag 21
'65
SCHIPA, Tito
Obituary
Opera N por 30:33 Ja 22 '66. F. Robinson
SCHIPPERS, Thomas
People are talking about... il por Vogue
147:66-7 Ja 15 '66
Wedding of Miss Elaine Phipps and Mr
Thomas Schippers. il pors Vogue 145:138-9
Je '65
SCHIPPERS, Wim
Breathtaking show; from pop art to proboscis
art. il Newsweek 66:94B+ S 20 '65
SCHIRACH, Baldur von
Living symbols. Newsweek 66:53 N 8 '65
SCHIRRA, Walter Marty, 1923-
Astronauts' own reports from Gemini 6 and 7.
il por Life 60:66-7 Ja 14 '66
about
Shot that failed. L. Wainwright and H.
Suydam. il por Life 59:111-13 N 5 '65
Two for rendezvous. il por Newsweek 66:56
N 1 '65
See also
Space flight—Manned flights—Schirra-Staf-
ford flight, 1965
SCHISGAL, Murray
Luv. Criticism
America 112:232-3 F 13 '65
Cath World 200:383 Mr '65
SCHISGALL, Oscar
Village where people cared. Read Digest 86:
55-60 F '65
What you can do with an hour a day. Read
Digest 86:83-5 Ap '65
SCHISTOSOMIASIS
Drug for snail fever. Time 87:65-6 Ja 7 '66
Schistosomiasis attacked. Sci N L 88:130 Ag
28 '65
Worm that kills. Newsweek 67:57 Ja 10 '66
SCHIZOPHRENIA
Children in a shadow world. R. M. Harrison.
il Parents Mag 40:52-3+ My '65
Long hospitalization hit. Sci N L 89:14 Ja 1
'66
Many faces of schizophrenia. F. R. Schreiber
and M. Herman. Sci Digest 57:44-5 F '65
Pink spots spot schizoids. Sci N L 88:323 N
20 '65
Schizophrenics helped to return to own
homes. Sci N L 89:39 Ja 15 '66
When love is not enough; case of adopted
child suffering from schizophrenia. il Good
H 160:12+ Ap '65
World for Amy. N. E. Husting. il Redbook
125:70-1+ Ag '65
SCHLAEGER, Gerald J.
Follow me through. Flying 77:116 O '65
SCHLAGER, Gunther, and Dickie, M. M.
Spontaneous mutation rates at five coat-color
loci in mice. bibliog Science 151:205-6 Ja 14
'66
SCHLAG-REY, Madeleine. See Suppes, P. jt.
auth.
SCHLAMM, William S.
Der Alte returns. Nat R 17:811-12 S 21 '65
Death of Gaullism. Nat R 18:63-5 Ja 25 '66

Elections in wonderland. Nat R 17:651-2 Jl
27 '65
Letter from Rome. Nat R 18:23-4 Ja 11 '66
Second sex and second thoughts. Nat R 17:
692-4 Ag 10 '65
Willie Sutton and Abdel Nasser. Nat R 17:
238 Mr 23 '65
SCHLEICH, Thomas, and Goldstein, Jack
Sulfur: incorporation into the transfer frac-
tion of soluble ribonucleic acid. bibliog Sci-
ence 150:1168-70 N 26 '65
SCHLEIERMACHER, Friedrich Ernst Daniel
Schleiermacher on Christ and religion, by
R. R. Niebuhr. Review
Christian Cent 82:439-41 Ap 7 '65. W. A.
Johnson
Commonweal 82:56-7 Ap 2 '65. M. Novak
SCHLEISNER, Doris G. See Gottscho, S. H.
jt. auth.
SCHLESINGER, Arthur, 1888-1965
Extremism in American politics. por Sat R
48:21-5 N 27 '65
about
Father remembered. A. Schlesinger, jr. por
Sat R 48:21 N 27 '65
Obituary
Pub W 188:38 N 8 '65
SCHLESINGER, Arthur, 1917-
Annual rites at Cannes. Harper 230:79-84
F '65
Croly and The promise of American life.
New Repub 152:17-22 My 8 '65
Father remembered. Sat R 48:21 N 27 '65
Thousand days; excerpts. Life 59:28-37+,
68-9 Jl 16; 62-70+ Jl 23; 18-27 Jl 30; 84-6+
N 5; 110-12+ N 12; 124-6+ N 19 '65
about
Bay of Pigs revisited: lessons from a failure.
Time 86:16-17 Jl 30 '65
Bitter pen of Arthur M. Nat R 17:680 Ag 10
'65
Brief, not a history. R. Moley. Newsweek
66:108 D 20 '65
Byzantium on the Potomac. M. Greenfield.
Reporter 33:10+ Ag 12 '65
Combative chronicler. il pors Time 86:54-6+
D 17 '65
Controversial historian of the age of Ken-
nedy. W. V. Shannon. il pors N Y Times
Mag p30-1+ N 21 '65
Crawfie Schlesinger. W. F. Buckley, jr. Nat R
17:719 Ag 24 '65
From the Professor's notebook; concerning
A. M. Schlesinger's account. il por Time
86:22 Jl 23 '65
Gardner Jackson 1897-1965. New Repub 152:
17 My 1 '65
Instant and judicial history. Life 59:4 Ag 13
'65
Kennedy administration; shimmering essence.
il por Newsweek 66:34+ D 6 '65
Of many things. T. N. Davis. America 113:124
Ag 7 '65
Peephole journalism; Thousand days; exploita-
tion of position. Commonweal 82:613 S 3 '65
Schlesinger and John F. Kennedy. G. P.
Hunt. il por Life 59:5 Jl 16 '65
Taste of memory. Nation 201:49-50 Ag 2 '65
Trials of an instant author. Time 86:31 Ag 27
'65
SCHLESINGER, Ina
Soviet education in 1964. bibliog f Sch & Soc
93:270-1 My 1 '65
SCHLESINGER, James R.
Of pieties and policy. Reporter 33:47-50 Ag 12
'65
SCHLIEREN apparatus
Schlieren technique for studying water flow
in marine animals. J. A. Westphal. il Sci-
ence 149:1515-16 S 24 '65
Sedimentation velocity experiments; position
and motion of schlieren peaks. J. A.
Faucher and J. V. Koleske. il Science 147:
1152-3 Mr 5 '65
SCHLUETER, Paul
Eight lives. Christian Cent 82:1158-9 S 22
'65
SCHLUMBERGER, Jean
Second fame; good food. N. Lyon. il por
Vogue 146:140-2 Ag 15 '65
SCHMAIS, Claire
Learning is fun when you dance it. Dance
Mag 40:33-5 Ja '66
SCHMALZ, R. F.
Brucite in carbonate secreted by the red alga
goniolithon sp. bibliog Science 149:993-6 Ag
27 '65
SCHMANDT, Raymond H.
Vatican archives. Commonweal 82:190-1 Ap
30 '65

SCHMECK, Harold M. Jr
  Coming: a cancer breakthrough; reprint. Sci
    Digest 58:57-62 Ag '65
  Science marches on. N Y Times Mag p 129
    Ap 11 '65
SCHMELTZ, Irwin, and others
  Myristicin in cigarette smoke. bibliog Science
    151:96-7 Ja 7 '66
SCHMEMANN, Alexander
  World as sacrament. Cath World 201:132-7
    My '65
SCHMERTZ, Mildred F.
  Harvard holds ninth urban design conference.
    Arch Rec 137:23+ Je '65
  Philadelphia report: a long wait for the
    renaissance. Arch Rec 138:119-32 Jl '65
SCHMID, Carlo
  Unification of Germany; address, February
    18, 1965. Vital Speeches 31:403-5 Ap 15 '65
SCHMID, Charles Howard, Jr
  Secrets in the sand. por Time 86:27 N 26 '65
SCHMID, Peter
  Letter from Havana. Commentary 40:56-63
    S '65
SCHMID, William D.
  Energy intake of the mourning dove zenai-
    dura macroura marginella. bibliog Science
    150:1171-2 N 26 '65
SCHMIDT, Albert C.
  Above the clouds. Reporter 32:38+ Ap 22 '65
SCHMIDT, Edward
  Magnetic recording tape. Electr World 73:
    23-6 Mr '65
SCHMIDT, Franz
  Book with seven seals. P. L. Miller. il por
    Am Rec G 31:524-5 F '65
SCHMIDT, Klaus H. and Buck, W. L.
  Mobility of the hydrated electron. bibliog
    Science 151:70-1 Ja 7 '66
SCHMIDT, Richard A.
  Extraterrestrial dust as a source of atmos-
    pheric argon. bibliog Science 151:223 Ja 14
    '66
SCHMIDT, Sandra
  Prize always went to someone who sang
    Aïda. Life 58:56 My 14 '65
SCHMIDT, William J.
  Solar perplexus; poem. Christian Cent 82:367
    Mr 24 '65
SCHMIDTCHEN, Paul W.
  Books. See issues of Hobbies
SCHMIEG, A. L.
  Everybody uses this communications console.
    Am City 80:110-11 Ap '65
SCHMITT, Francis O.
  Physical basis of life and learning; adaptation
    of address, April 23, 1965. bibliog Science
    149:931-6 Ag 27 '65
SCHMITT, Rita Therese
  Other twenty-nine. por NEA J 54:12-14 O '65
SCHNEEMANN, Carolee
  Unexpected assemblage! D. McDonagh. il
    Dance Mag 39:42-5+ Je '65
SCHNEIDER, John A.
  Only you, Jim Aubrey. il por Newsweek 65:
    62-3 Mr 15 '65
SCHNEIDER, Phillip.   See Wallace, J. jt.
    auth.
SCHNEIDER, Pierre E.
  Charlemagne's dream. Art N 64:22-6+ N '65
  His men look like survivors of a shipwreck.
    N Y Times Mag p34-5+ Je 6 '65
SCHNEIDER, Ronald M.
  Interim regime in Brazil. bibliog f Cur Hist
    49:349-55+ D '65
SCHNEIDER, Rose G. and Jones, R. T.
  Hemoglobin F_{Texas}; gamma-chain variant.
    bibliog Science 148:240-2 Ap 9 '65
SCHNEIDER, William
  Follow these four cardinal rules. Am City
    80:104-6 D '65
SCHNEIDER-SIEMSSEN, Gunther
  Light touch; interview, ed. by H. Johnson.
    por Opera N 29:6 Mr 6 '65
SCHNEIDERMAN, Dan
  Man behind our mission to Mars. B. Kocivar.
    il pors Look 29:36-8+ Jl 13 '65
  Perils and triumphs of Mariner 4. il por
    Bsns W p 102-4 Jl 24 '65
SCHNEIDERMAN, Marvin A. and Myers, M. H.
  Assessment of drugs. Science 149:1398 S 17
    '65
SCHNEIRLA, T. C.
  Dorylines: raiding and in bivouac. Natur
    Hist 74:44-51 O; 40-7 N '65
SCHNÖS, Maria. See Caro, L. G. jt. auth.
SCHOEFFLER, Oscar E.
  Fashions. Esquire 63:62 My '65
SCHOEN, Barbara
  'Tis better to have loved; story. Seventeen
    24:150-1 My '65
SCHOENBAUM, David
  Nazi murders & German politics. Commen-
    tary 39:72-7 Je '65

Time runs out on Germany's war-crimes
    trials. Reporter 32:30-2 Mr 11 '65
  What German boys say about Hitler. N Y
    Times Mag p30-1+ Ja 9 '66
SCHOENBERG, Arnold. See Schönberg, A.
SCHOENBERNER, Franz
  Triumph of wit. E. Capouya. Sat R 48:19 F
    20 '65
SCHOENFELD, Madalynne
  Children's theater in Yonkers. por Wilson
    Lib Bul 40:352-5 D '65
SCHOENFELD, William N. and Baron, S. H.
  Ethology and experimental psychology. Sci-
    ence 147:634-5 F 5 '65
SCHOENMAECKERS, Ernest
  Birdcages in Dutch churches. America 113:
    408 O 9 '65
SCHOENMAN, Theodore
  Education vs. culture. ALA Bul 60:27-30 Ja
    '66
SCHOENSTEIN, Ralph
  Save the English language! excerpt from
    Time lurches on. Read Digest 87:45-6 Jl
    '65
  Swing low, sweet Siegfried. Sat R 48:91
    Ap 10 '65
SCHOLANDER, P. F.
  Tension gradients accompanying accelerated
    oxygen transport in a membrane. bibliog
    Science 149:876-7 Ag 20 '65
—and others
  Sap pressure in vascular plants. bibliog Sci-
    ence 148:339-46, 1488, 149:920+ Ap 16, Je 11,
    Ag 27 '65
SCHOLAR of Bourbon street; story. See Amen,
    G.
SCHOLARS
  Scholars, Catholic, who's got the? H. C.
    Gardiner. America 113:442-3 O 16 '65
SCHOLARS, Russian. See Russia—Intellectual
    life
SCHOLARSHIP. See Learning and scholarship
SCHOLARSHIPS and fellowships
  ALA invites 1966 awards nominations. Li-
    brary J 90:5488-9 D 15 '65
  Common noun spelled f-u-l-b-r-i-g-h-t. D.
    Oberdorfer. il N Y Times Mag p79-80+
    Ap 4 '65
  Description of union scholarship programs.
    J. F. Mead. il Mo Labor R 88:508-10 My
    '65
  Financing your college education. J. Beck.
    il Todays Health 43:32-5+ F '65
  Foundation of our educational system;
    teachers of high quality. J. Brademas.
    NEA J 54:17 D '65
  Girls and machine team up to spot style
    trends, or I was a teen-age computer;
    Bobbie Brooks company award scheme. il
    Life 59:81-3+ Ag 6 '65
  NDEA fellowships: expansion doubles and
    redoubles number. J. Walsh. Science 150:
    1270-2 D 3 '65
  Need money for graduate study? how &
    where to find it. il Changing T 19:43-4 O '65
  Nominations sought for 1966 ALA awards.
    Library J 90:5230-4 D 1 '65
  OAS council; tribute to founder of Leo S.
    Rowe fund. il Américas 17:44-5 Je '65
  Partial list of available scholarships. Ebony
    20:42+ Ap '65
  U.S. pledges funds to U.N. program for
    training of South Africans; note, June 25,
    1965. A. E. Stevenson. Dept State Bul 53:
    220-1 Ag 2 '65
  When foreign-student scholarships are
    misused. C. Haussamen. il Sat R 48:50+
    Ag 21 '65
    See also
  African scholarship program of American
    universities
  College students—Aid
  National achievement scholarship program
  National merit scholarship corporation
  Student loans
  United States—State, Department of—Foreign
    scholarships, Board of
SCHOLASTIC aptitude test. See College en-
    trance examination board—Scholastic apti-
    tude test
SCHOLASTIC aptitude tests. See Aptitude
    tests
SCHOLASTIC Institute of student opinion. See
    Scholastic research center
SCHOLASTIC magazines, Incorporated
  At our corner; new book fair kit. W. K.
    Richards. il Sr Schol 86:sup 16 Ap 29 '65
  At our corner; new services. il Sr Schol 87:
    sup 10 S 16 '65
  Presenting the 1965 Scholastic awards. il Sr
    Schol 86:17-22+ My 20 '65
  Scholastic family. Sr Schol 87:5 O 21 '65

SCHOLASTIC Magazines, incorporated—*Cont.*
Scholastic teacher travel awards (cont) il
Sr Schol 86:sup 13-14 Mr 18; sup21-7 Ap
15 '65
Vacation travel plans: yours and ours;
Scholastic teacher's new and enlarged travel and vacation department. A. H. Hepburn. Sr Schol 86:sup9 My 13 '65

SCHOLASTIC research center
As high school students see it! how fair is
the draft? Institute of student opinion. il
Sr Schol 87:16 D 2 '65
As high school students see the war in
Viet Nam; Institute of student opinion.
il Sr Schol 87:8 N 18 '65

SCHOLASTIC teacher. See Senior scholastic
(periodical)

SCHOLASTICISM
See also
Thomism

SCHOLEM, Gershom
Golem of Prague and the Golem of Rehovoth; excerpt from address, June 17, 1965.
Commentary 41:62-5 Ja '66

SCHOLER, E. A.
Playground in Kiwiland. por Recreation 58:
392-3 O '65
Recreation center. Recreation 58:436 N '65

SCHOLLANDER, Don
Face to face with the best swimmer in the
world. por Seventeen 24:107 Je '65
Olympic bulldog for old Eli. il pors Life
58:64+ Ap 16 '65

SCHOMBURG, Arthur
Role for librarians in the relevant war against
poverty; address, May 15, 1965. K. B. Clark.
il Wilson Lib Bul 40:45-7 S '65

SCHOMBURG collection. See New York public
library—135th Street branch

SCHOMER, Howard
Abstentionists and morticians. Christian
Cent 82:419 Ap 7 '65
Runaway war or deadlocked peace. Christian
Cent 82:957-9 Ag 4 '65

SCHÖNBERG, Arnold
Arnold Schönberg: an unknown correspondence. R. Steiner and E. Steiner. por Sat R
48:47-9+ Mr 27 '65
At last in stereo. Schoenberg's Gurre lieder.
J. Diether. il Am Rec G 32:208-12 N '65
BSO Schönberg; violin concerto played by
Boston symphony. M. Bernheimer. Sat R
48:30 Ap 17 '65
Moses and Aaron. Criticism
New Yorker 41:65-6 Jl 31 '65
Newsweek il 66:84 Jl 12 '65
Opera N il 30:21 S 30 '65
Sat R 48:43 Jl 31 '65
Time il 87:62 Ja 14 '66
Music of Arnold Schoenberg. A. Cohn. por
Am Rec G 32:12-13 S '65
New life for Gurre-lieder. R. Ericson. Sat
R 48:85 O 30 '65
Schoenberg's Gurrelieder, an event for a
generation. R. Lawrence. il Hi Fi 15:
79-80 O '65
Schoenberg's letters. I. Stravinsky. Hi Fi 15:
136-8 My '65
Schoenberg's odyssey. H. W. Heinsheimer.
il pors Opera N 29:6-10 Mr 13 '65

SCHONBERG, Harold C.
First comes the singing. N Y Times Mag
p54-5+ O 24 '65
Mystery man; reprint. Am Rec G 31:1132-4
Ag '65
Sound of sounds that is New York. N Y
Times Mag p38+ My 23 '65

SCHOOL activities. See Student activities

SCHOOL administration. See School management and organization

SCHOOL administrators. See School superintendents and principals

SCHOOL age
See also
Readiness for school

SCHOOL and social and economic problems
ACEI conference: a child and his potential.
Sr Schol 86:sup 1+ My 13 '65
Big-city school: problems and prospects. J. I.
Goodlad and M. C. Hunter. il PTA Mag
59:8-10 Ap '65
Education and our present social problems;
reprint of a 1933 article. J. Dewey. Sch &
Soc 93:39-43 Ja 23 '65
Everybody gets into the act; Wilmington
schools and other agencies. M. Crosby. il
NEA J 54:22-4 N '65
From rich homes or poor. H. R. Nieberl.
NEA J 54:45-6 O '65
Rafferty asks bonuses for slum teachers. Sr
Schol 87:sup2 O 7 '65
School and the Negro child. C. Stewart.
Negro Hist Bul 29:9-10 O '65

Schools and slums. J. O'Gara. Commonweal
82:551 Ag 6 '65
Schools in the cities; address, January 27,
1965. S. M. Brownell. Vital Speeches 31:380-4
Ap 1 '65
Teacher corps proposed by LBJ; summary of
address, July 1965. L. B. Johnson. il Sr Schol
86:sup 1 S 16 '65
Teachers in slum areas. W. W. Wayson. il Sr
Schol 86:4T+ F 11 '65
Washington report. J. Lloyd. Sr Schol 86:
sup3 Ap 8 '65
Wilmington finds an answer; city salvages
underprivileged pupils. il Ebony 20:57-60+
Jl '65
See also
Children of migrant laborers—Education
Socially handicapped children—Education

SCHOOL and society (periodical)
Half-century of School and society. W. W.
Brickman. Sch & Soc 93:34+ Ja 23 '65
School and society: the vision and the vitality. S. Lehrer. il Sch & Soc 93:33-4 Ja 23
'65
Status of School and society, 1964-65. W. W.
Brickman. Sch & Soc 93:335 O 2 '65

SCHOOL and the community
Allies for human renewal. R. Sorenson and
C. L. Marburger. NEA J 54:21 N '65
Aquila Romana; Pennsylvania station eagle
at Hicksville, N.Y. railroad station. S. A.
Goldberg. il NEA J 54:29 D '65
Bridging the gap between public administration and school administration. R. G.
Weintraub and L. D. Greisman. bibliog f
Sch & Soc 93:433-7 N 13 '65
Classroom incident; parental visits. NEA J
54:27-8 D '65
Coming of age in America, by E. Z. Friedenberg. Review
Nation 201:254-5 O 18 '65. M. V. Miller
Community leadership and education in a
crisis. T. L. Patrick. Sch & Soc 93:403-4
O 30 '65
Do tell; effective communications and public
relations. B. M. Gudridge. NEA J 54:32-3
My '65
Everybody gets into the act; Wilmington
schools and other agencies. M. Crosby. il
NEA J 54:22-4 N '65
Good schools attract industry. R. A. Will.
NEA J 54:28 Mr '65
Keeping the schools human. S. M. Brownell.
il PTA Mag 59:6-8 F '65
PTA and critical issues in education. J.
Moorhead. PTA Mag 59:2-3 Je '65
Public relations; questions and answers. J. H.
Starie. NEA J 54:28-9 S '65
School art festival; interview, ed. by I.
Arms. O. Gatti. il Sch Arts 64:31-3 My '65

SCHOOL and the home
Parent-teacher relationship issue; symposium. il Sr Schol 87:sup6+ O 21 '65
Parents' gripes; with reply by W. G. Hollister
and study-discussion program, by D. Harris
and E. Harris. bibliog il PTA Mag 59:16-19,
36 Ap '65
Preparing for a teacher-parent conference;
with study-discussion program, by E. Harris and D. Harris. E. D. Landau. bibliog
il PTA Mag 60:13-15, 34 N '65
See also
Parents and teachers associations

SCHOOL annuals. See High school annuals

SCHOOL architecture. See School buildings

SCHOOL arts (periodical)
Special issue of children's art in 1965. il
Sch Arts 64:20-8 Mr '65

SCHOOL athletics
Compulsory games may cause harmful stress.
Sci N L 88:313 N 13 '65
Public school that jumps; Millfield school,
Somerset, England. il Sports Illus 23:16-21
Ag 16 '65
See also
College athletics
Football

SCHOOL attendance
Dual enrollment; shared time. il Am Ed 1:24-
5 Mr '65

SCHOOL auditoriums. See Auditoriums

SCHOOL bells. See Bells

SCHOOL boards
Best weapon in the fight for better education. B. Asbell. il Redbook 125:58-9+ My
'65
Do school boards take education seriously?
J. Wallace and P. Schneider. il Sat R 48:
89-90+ O 16 '65
How to pick a school board. P. Binzen. il
Sat R 48:72-3+ Ap 17 '65

SCHOOL boards—*Continued*
I fought against hatred among my neighbors;
    ed. by J. N. Bell. A. Hollenbeck. il Good H
    161:71+ S '65
Parish school board. O. J. Murdick. Amer-
    ica 114:132-6 Ja 22 '66
School boards of the future. O. C. D'Amour.
    America 113:316-17 S 25 '65
School personnel and educational policy. J.
    E. Allen, jr. il PTA Mag 59:12-14 Je '65
Who speaks for teachers? M. Lieberman.
    il Sat R 48:64-6+ Je 19 '65
SCHOOL book fairs. See Book fairs
SCHOOL books. See Textbooks
SCHOOL buildings
Better schools built in 1965. G. A. Christie.
    il Arch Rec 138:44 O '65
Building types study (cont) il Arch Rec 137:
    167-86 Mr '65
Schoolhouses for big cities. W. W. Chase.
    il Am Ed 1:12-19 F '65
Unknown shaper; consultant for school
    construction. Time 86:90+ N 12 '65
Vote of confidence for educational construc-
    tion. G. A. Christie. il Arch Rec 137:18
    Mr '65

Air conditioning

Built-in flexibility for air conditioning;
    Pekin, Ill. community high school. il Arch
    Rec 137:228-30 Ap '65

Cost

We beat the educationists; extravagances of
    school board in South Burlington, Vt. A.
    Cismaru. Nat R 17:413-14 My 18 '65

Fires and fire protection

Parishioners v. church; damage suits of
    Chicago's Our Lady of the Angels' fire.
    il Time 86:48-9 S 24 '65
SCHOOL buildings, Remodeled
Unit additions convert an elementary school
    into a junior high. il Arch Rec 137:169-71
    Mr '65
SCHOOL bus transportation. See School chil-
    dren—Transportation
SCHOOL children
From the end spring new beginnings; end-
    ings children wrote for the NEA journal's
    Unfinished stories. D. Waleski. il NEA J
    54:14-18 Ap '65
I am a lone boy; excerpts from papers writ-
    ten by fifth-graders, ed. by E. F. Murphy.
    N Y Times Mag p86+ D 5 '65
School report; excerpts from published recol-
    lections of outstanding people, comp. by
    U. Mahoney. N Y Times Mag p57+ S 12
    '65
Schools are emasculating our boys. P. C.
    Sexton. Sat R 48:57 Je 19 '65; discussion. 48:
    53 Jl 17 '65
Teacher-opinion poll; pressure on pupils. il
    NEA J 55:51 Ja '66
Vietnamese tragedy. D. E. Luellen. NEA J
    54:18 Ap '65
    See also
High school students
Students
Teachers and students

Accident insurance

See Insurance, Accident

Adjustment

Big-city school; problems and prospects. J. I.
    Goodlad and M. C. Hunter. il PTA Mag 59:
    8-10 Ap '65
Classroom incident; symposium. NEA J 54:
    47-8 Ap '65

Health

See Children—Care and hygiene

Medical inspection

Good health for every school child. S. S.
    Rosenberg. il Parents Mag 40:50-1+ S '65

Migration

See Children of migrant laborers

Reading

See Childrens reading

Transportation

How to move 15,400,000 children. G. A.
    Crenson. il Am Ed 1:10-12 Jl '65
Pennsylvania school bus fight; public aid
    for parochial schools. C. W. Zunkel. Chris-
    tian Cent 82:1036-7 Ag 25 '65; Discussion.
    82:1322 O 27 '65
SCHOOL children, Free food for. See School
lunches

SCHOOL childrens boners. See Blunders
SCHOOL clothes. See Clothing and dress—Chil-
dren
SCHOOL committees. See School boards
SCHOOL construction. See School buildings
SCHOOL counselors
College guidance: good, bad or indifferent? D.
    Klein. Seventeen 24:20+ Jl '65
What does a school counselor do? R. Carson.
    il Parents Mag 40:66-8+ S '65
    See also
Personnel service (education)
SCHOOL discipline
Classroom incident; symposium. NEA J 54:
    40-1 F '65
Discipline is. . . Sister Marian Frances. il
    NEA J 54:26-8 S '65
Essay of school rules; governing student
    conduct in an eighteenth century common
    school in Pennsylvania. il Sat R 48:81 O
    16 '65
Hair styles and harebrains. J. Ciardi. Sat R
    48:18 My 1 '65
Long and short of it; aspects of student dress
    and grooming. il Newsweek 66:64-6 S 27
    '65
Splitting hairs over moptops; or, How
    lunatic is the fringe? il Sr Schol 87:20 O
    14 '65
Unkindest cut for student moptops. Life 59:
    4 S 24 '65
    See also
Corporal punishment
SCHOOL enrollment. See School attendance
SCHOOL excursions
Serendipity; camping trip with thirty teen-
    agers. P. L. Jones. il Sr Schol 86:sup24-5
    Ap 15 '65
Study trip to Washington. M. D. Saylor. il
    NEA J 54:54-5 Mr '65
SCHOOL finance
Costs students face in free schools. il Good H
    161:166-7 S '65
Editor's notebook. M. S. Fenner. NEA J 54:
    72 D '65
Education and the bond market. E. C.
    Deering and J. Du Von. il Am Ed 1:28 S;
    23 O; 28 N '65
Education and the bond market. E. C. Deer-
    ing and J. Trevor Thomas. il Am Ed 1:28
    Ap; 22 My; 30 Je; 29 Jl '65
Education and the bond market. E. C. Deer-
    ing and P. K. Nance. il Am Ed 1:22 D '64;
    20 F; 28 Mr '65
How Evanston passed its bond issue. J. F.
    Hall. il NEA J 54:42-4 D '65
Score on school finance. J. K. Norton. il
    PTA Mag 59:4-6 My '65
SCHOOL furniture, equipment, etc.
Children be seated. W. E. Martin. il Am Ed 1:
    4-6 Je '65
SCHOOL gardens
School gardens in Cleveland. H. G. Meyer. il
    Horticulture 43:24-5+ Ap '65
SCHOOL grounds
Park-school facilities do double duty; Mes-
    quite, Tex. G. Schrader and R. Poteet. il
    Am City 80:110-11 D '65
SCHOOL health education. See Health educa-
tion
SCHOOL journalism. See College and school
journalism
SCHOOL lands
Land-rich or land-poor schools; Open space
    land program, part of Housing act of 1961.
    D. E. Gardner. il Am Ed 1:12-14 N '65
SCHOOL laws and legislation

Arkansas

Evolution law and some archaic voices. Life
    59:8 O 8 '65
    See also
Evolution—Laws and legislation

United States

Congress: a higher education bill is con-
    sidered a likely prospect, but hard bargain-
    ing lies ahead. J. Walsh. Science 149:162-
    4 Jl 9 '65
Congress: higher education act including
    scholarship for needy passed in final days
    of session. J. Walsh. Science 150:591-2+
    O 29 '65
Hands-off policy continues; expanded NDEA
    and pending legislation without federal
    edict. E. Geller. Library J 90:916+ F 15
    '65
Junior college presidents' views on legisla-
    tion. Sch & Soc 93:362-3 O 16 '65
Legislation and the schools; new legislation
    of NDEA, ALA midwinter report. E. Gel-
    ler. il Library J 90:1481-2 Mr 15 '65

SCHOOL laws and legislation—United States
—*Continued*
Main features: higher education act of 1965.
Science 150:593 O 29 '65
NDEA funds in action. Sr Schol 87:sup 16-17
O 14 '65
NDEA institutes for school librarians. Library J 90:1495-6 Mr 15 '65
NDEA summer institute listings. Sr Schol 86:sup4+ Mr 4; sup2+ Mr 11 '65
President Kennedy and education: excerpt from John F. Kennedy on education. W. T. O'Hara. bibliog f Sch & Soc 93:444-50+ N 27 '65
Q and A: how to acquire books under NDEA, etc. J. H. Lloyd. Sr Schol 86:sup 29+ Mr 4 '65
Title III allotments under revised NDEA. Library J 90:948 F 15 '65
Washington report. J. Lloyd. Sr Schol 86: 14T F 4; 87:sup4 O 28 '65
We've got it started; Elementary and secondary education act of 1965. il NEA J 54:33-9 S '65
World we have to know; NDEA language and area centers programs. M. Flapan. il Am Ed 1:30-2 O '65
See also
Evolution—Laws and legislation
Federal aid to education
SCHOOL leaving. See Dropouts
SCHOOL librarians
Getting and keeping a school librarian. C. W. Tanner. il NEA J 54:48-50 O '65
Librarian talks to teachers. E. Kebabian. il Sr Schol 87:sup 12-13 S 30 '65
Why not listen to the librarian? E. R. Christine. ALA Bul 59:1010-11 D '65

Qualifications
Daddy Warbucks and the school librarians; excessive prosperity and selectivity. J. Shera. Wilson Lib Bul 39:573+ Mr '65
SCHOOL libraries
Books for the mountain children; providing libraries in the schools of Appalachia. J. Moorhead. il PTA Mag 59:2-3 Mr '65
Elementary school library collection, ed. by M. V. Gaver. Review
Library J 90:5492-4 D 15 '65. D. M. Broderick
From the editor. Am Ed 1:inside cover My '65
Good libraries are not enough. D. G. Emery; L. H. Freiser. il Sat R 48:74-6+ Ap 17 '65
Individualized instruction; symposium, ed. by M. P. Archer. bibliog il Library J 90:1977-90 Ap 15 '65
Librarian talks to teachers. E. Kebabian. il Sr Schol 87:sup 12-13 S 30 '65
Library school at Liberty bell; teachers' workshop on using children's literature in the elementary school, Coopersburg, Pa. A. Crosby. il Library J 90:2334-5 My 15 '65
Many roads to reading; Homestead school, Garden City, N.Y. A. Eisenberg and H. Eisenberg. il Look 29:M7-11 My 4 '65
Pattern of school library design; symposium. il Library J 90:5453-83 D 15 '65
Reading and the disadvantaged; need for reading guidance of Negro youth. E. J. Josey. Negro Hist Bul 28:156-7+ Ap '65
School libraries. See every other issue of Wilson library bulletin
School library development: a job for all bookmen. C. B. Grannis. Pub W 187:43 Mr 8 '65
Service to students; joint responsibility of school and public libraries; ed. by V. McJenkin. bibliog il ALA Bul 59:540-2, 649-52, 733-44; 60:63-72 Je-S '65, Ja '66
Theory of maximum use: flexible scheduling; Hueneme school district, Port Hueneme, Calif. P. M. Sturm. Library J 90:2341 My 15 '65
See also
Knapp school libraries project
School librarians

Acquisitions
Goals for service; survey of book ordering. N. Paige. il Library J 90:937-41 F 15 '65

Book selection
See Book selection

Censorship
Censorship and the public schools; address, January 1965. L. A. Burress, jr. bibliog ALA Bul 59:491-9 Je '65
Censorship and the school library. C. Crosthwait. bibliog il Wilson Lib Bul 39:670-2 Ap '65
Clear and present danger: the books, or the censors? reprint. H. Bach. bibliog il Library J 90:3681-5 S 15 '65

Wisconsin U. holds workshop on intellectual freedom for schools. Library J 90:3704 S 15 '65

Finance
Allisonville shapes up; Knapp project school works toward ALA standards. D. L. Barnes. il Library J 90:942-4 F 15 '65

Instruction in use
See Libraries—Instruction in use

Music collections
100 to grow on; core music collection. B. R. Purrington. bibliog Library J 90:4523-5 O 15 '65

Paperback books
Education paperbacks issue; symposium. Sr Schol 87:sup6+ O 28 '65
Paperback conference; Role of paperback books in education. N. Kirin. Wilson Lib Bul 40:232 N '65
Paperback conference: success at Columbia; Role of paperback books in education. il Sr Schol 87:sup 1-2 O 28 '65
Paperback in education: report on the Teachers college conference; with statements from popular poll. E. Geller. il Library J 90:5051-3 N 15 '65
Paperbacks for the elementary school. P. Johnson, jr. Library J 90:5054-5 N 15 '65

Publicity
That Knapp film catches on; elementary school libraries in And something more. R. Lindenmeyer. il Library J 90:1470-1 Mr 15 '65

Reference work
Study in self-reliance; Shaker Heights learning experiment. M. L. Krohn. il Library J 90:4520-2 O 15 '65

Standards
Books and the new media. E. Geller. Library J 90:2306 My 15 '65
Equal treatment for the blind. E. Geller. Library J 90:1485 Mr 15 '65
Something drastic must be done about school libraries, you can help! E. Castagna. Parents Mag 40:42+ Ap '65
What every library needs. D. G. Emery. il Sat R 48:74-5 Ap 17 '65

Work with blind
Equal treatment for the blind. E. Geller. Library J 90:1485 Mr 15 '65
SCHOOL libraries and research. See Libraries and research
SCHOOL libraries and social and economic problems. See Libraries and social and economic problems
SCHOOL libraries and state. See Libraries and state
SCHOOL library architecture. See Library architecture
SCHOOL library conferences. See Library conferences
SCHOOL lunches
Pilot school lunch program begins at Bogota. Dept State Bul 53:65-6 Jl 12 '65
SCHOOL magazines. See College and school journalism
SCHOOL management and organization
Bridging the gap between public administration and school administration. R. G. Weintraub and L. D. Greisman. bibliog f Sch & Soc 93:433-7 N 13 '65
Conditions of work for quality teaching. il NEA J 54:33-40 Mr '65
One campus for all schools: is this your city's solution? educational parks or school villages. il U S News 58:53-6 Je 14 '65
Teacher-administrator relationships. H. W. Schooling. il NEA J 54:32-4 F '65
Where a school of the future is holding classes today; complete education on one campus. South Florida education center, Broward County. il U S News 59:36-9 Jl 5 '65
Who runs our big city schools? F. M. Hechinger; P. Binzen. il Sat R 48:70-3+ Ap 17 '65; Discussion. 48:67 My 15 '65
See also
Colleges and universities—Administration
Corporal punishment
Schedules, School
School boards
School discipline
School superintendents and principals
Teachers—Contracts
Teachers—Selection and appointment

SCHOOL management and organization—*Cont.*

Teacher participation
Effective cooperative decision-making in education. M. Y. Nunnery. Sch & Soc 93:151-2 Mr 6 '65
Election and negotiation in Rochester. A. Cantor. il NEA J 54:22-3 S '65
Improvement of instruction. M. Stevenson and E. Q. Forman. il NEA J 54:28-9 My '65
NEA time to teach project. M. M. Provus. il NEA J 54:8-10 Ap '65
Please, Mr Superintendent. E. M. Blue. il NEA J 54:49-50 My '65
Professional negotiation. R. O. Daly. NEA J 54:30-1 My '65
School personnel and educational policy. J. E. Allen, jr. il PTA Mag 59:12-14 Je '65
Teacher-opinion poll; formal group action. il NEA J 54:23-4 S '65
Today's militant teachers. R. D. Batchelder. il NEA J 54:18-19 S '65

SCHOOL music
   See also
   Music—Instruction and study
SCHOOL news. See Newspapers—Educational news
SCHOOL of aerospace medicine. See United States—Air force—Systems command
SCHOOL of performing arts. See New York (city)—Education
SCHOOL officials. See School superintendents and principals
SCHOOL organization. See School management and organization
SCHOOL papers. See College and school journalism
SCHOOL prayer. See Public schools and religion
SCHOOL prayer decision. See United States—Supreme court—Decisions
SCHOOL reports and records
Automation in schools. F. C. Weed. il Sr Schol 87:sup40-1 S 23 '65
Confidentiality of student records; opinions differ; pro and con discussion. E. T. Burianek; R. O. Fitzsimmons. il NEA J 55:28-30 Ja '66
How to get into college; Hillhouse high school's unusual marking system. il Time 86:56 Ag 27 '65
   See also
   Personnel records in education

SCHOOL schedules. See Schedules, School
SCHOOL statistics. See Education—Statistics
SCHOOL subjects. See Courses of study
SCHOOL superintendents and principals
Breaking up the big systems; plans to decentralize authority. P. Woodring. Sat R 48:51-2 Jl 17 '65
New York's take-charge man. Time 85:57 Ap 16 '65
Nice guy's exit; Superintendent C. Gross asked to resign. Time 85:48 Mr 12 '65
Public school superintendent and his knowledge. W. W. Brickman. Sch & Soc 93:263 My 1 '65
Room for whom at the top? F. M. Hechinger. il Sat R 48:70-1+ Ap 17 '65
   See also
   National education association—Department of elementary school principals

SCHOOL surveys. See Educational surveys
SCHOOL teachers. See Teachers
SCHOOL teaching. See Teaching
SCHOOL transportation. See School children—Transportation
SCHOOL trustees. See School boards
SCHOOL year
School attendance of Swiss and American children. R. P. Whitfield and E. Egger. il Sch & Soc 93:254-6 Ap 17 '65
SCHOOLHOUSES. See School buildings
SCHOOLING, H. W.
Teacher-administrator relationships. NEA J 54:32-4 F '65
SCHOOLS
New views of schools. S. Leggett. Sat R 48:93-4 O 16 '65
   See also
   Military schools
   Parochial schools, Catholic
   Private schools
   Public schools
   School buildings

Names
Time for a halt; Marlboro high school reconsiders name change. Newsweek 67:22 Ja 10 '66

Statistics
See Education—Statistics

Denmark
Danish folkehojskole. R. Pedersen. il Sr Schol 86:sup 12 My 20 '65

Ecuador
John F. Kennedy school no. 1; El Esfuerzo jungle community. J. P. Blank. il Read Digest 86:54-8 Mr '65

England
Educating slum children in London; Rising Hill secondary school. R. N. Kirk. Sch & Soc 93:180-2 Mr 20 '65

Scotland
Catholic schools in Scotland. E. W. Schott. America 113:45 Jl 10 '65

Switzerland
School attendance of Swiss and American children. R. P. Whitfield and E. Egger. il Sch & Soc 93:254-6 Ap 17 '65
School for the rich and the royal: with interview with L. Jhannot. il Life 58:53-4+ My 7 '65

United States
See also
Education—United States

SCHOOLS, Elementary. See Education, Elementary
SCHOOLS, Experimental
Freeing the children; Lewis-Wadhams school, uses Summerhill concept of education. B. Brower. il Holiday 38:60-7+ S '65
   See also
   Reed college, Portland, Ore.
SCHOOLS, Traveling
   See also
   Colleges and universities, Traveling
SCHOOLS, Underground. See Underground structures
SCHOOLS and libraries. See Libraries and schools
SCHOOLS and politics. See Politics and education
SCHOOLS and recreation. See Recreation and schools
SCHOOLS and social and economic problems. See School and social and economic problems
SCHOOLS for dogs. See Dogs—Training
SCHOOLS for the blind. See Blind—Education
SCHOOLS of business. See Business education
SCHOONERS
Coastwise in a museum ship; from Puget Sound to San Francisco in the C.A. Thayer. G. P. Jones. il Yachting 117:45-7+ Mr '65
Wawona, historic three-master. R. Saltonstall, jr. il Yachting 117:204-5 Mr '65
SCHOOP, Trudi
Sliver of hope. D. Hering. il Dance Mag 39:46-8 S '65
SCHOPF, J. William, and others
Electron microscopy of fossil bacteria two billion years old. bibliog Science 149:1365-7 S 17 '65
—See Barghoorn, E. S. jt. auth.
SCHOR, Seth L.
Serotonin and adenosine triphosphate: synergistic effect on the beat frequency of cilia of mussel gills. bibliog Science 148:500-1 Ap 23 '65
SCHORR, Daniel
Sins of the fathers. Sat R 48:47-8 N 13 '65
SCHOTT, Edward W.
Catholic schools in Scotland. America 113:45 Jl 10 '65
SCHOTT, Webster
Flannery O'Connor: faith's stepchild. Nation 201:142-4+ S 13 '65
Teach-in: new forum for reason. Nation 200:575-9 My 31 '65
SCHRADER, George, and Poteet, Ralph
Park-school facilities do double duty. pors Am City 80:110-11 D '65
SCHRAG, Peter
Schools of Appalachia. Sat R 48:70-1+ My 15 '65
SCHRAGE, Chuck
With the power squadrons. See issues of Yachting
SCHRAGE, Harry
R&D entrepreneur: profile of success. bibliog f Harvard Bsns R 43:56-69 N '65
SCHRAM, Irene
Myth; mantle; poem. Nation 201:536 D 27 '65

SCHRAMM, Wilbur
What TV is doing to our children; summary of Effects of television on children and adolescents. UNESCO Courier 18:22-6 F '65
SCHRAMM, incorporated
Company that runs family style. il Bsns W p60+ Jl 24 '65
SCHREIBER, Flora Rheta
How to interpret your baby's cries. Todays Health 43:41-5 Ag '65
LBJ's feel for science. Sci Digest 57:9-11 Ap '65
—and Herman, Melvin
Marriage, neurotic and otherwise. Sci Digest 57:26-30 Je '65
SCHREIBER, Morris
New tool for English teachers. Sr Schol 87:sup5 O 7 '65
SCHREIDER, Frank. See Schreider, H. jt. auth.
SCHREIDER, Helen, and Schreider, Frank
Journey into the Great Rift. il pors Nat Geog Mag 128:254-90 Ag '65
SCHRIEVER, Bernard A.
New propulsion vistas; excerpts from remarks at symposium on advanced propulsion concepts. Aviation W 82:21 My 10 '65
SCHRIFTGIESSER, Karl
Keeping watch on the economy. Sat R 49:65-6+ Ja 8 '66
SCHRÖDER, Gerhard
Germany looks at eastern Europe. For Affairs 44:15-25 O '65

about

At the epicenter. por Newsweek 66:57-8 O 11 '65
SCHRÖDINGER, Erwin
Books. J. Bernstein. New Yorker 41:180-2+ My 1 '65
SCHROEDER, Alfred
Mechanical services for a large courthouse. Arch Rec 138:205-8 O '65
SCHROEDER, Eva M.
How to enjoy a longer season of sweet corn. Flower Grower 52:61 Ap '65
Miniature glads. Pop Gard 16:26+ Jl '65
SCHROEDER, R. J.
Etc. Commonweal 83:62-3 O 15 '65
Theatre. Nation 200:625-8, 681 Je 7, 21 '65
SCHROETER, James
Willa Cather and The professor's house. Yale R 54:494-512 Je '65
SCHROTH, Raymond A.
Between the lines. America 113:527; 114:41 N 6 '65, Ja 8 '66
Book reviews. America 113:413-14, 472-3, 782-3 O 9, 23, D 18 '65
In the promised land. America 113:213 Ag 28 '65
Return to Rochester one year after. America 113:163-4 Ag 14 '65
Tight pants and full wallets. America 113:80 Jl 17 '65
SCHUBERT, Franz Peter
Curzon's orchestrated Schubert. C. J. Luten. Am Rec G 31:871 My '65
From the Musical heritage society, a gem. E. Belov. Am Rec G 32:67 S '65
On records: Die schöne müllerin. Opera N 29:34 Mr 6 '65
On records: Die winterreise. Opera N 29:34 F 6 '65
Schubert symphonies. J. W. Barker. il Am Rec G 32:342-3+ D '65
Schubert symphonies; a revisionist view. D. Vaughan. il Hi Fi 15:60-3 O '65
Schubert's symphonies, the scores corrected and a finish for the Unfinished. A. Rich. Hi Fi 16:73-4 Ja '66
They shall have music. H. Kupferberg. il Atlan 217:112-13 Ja '66
SCHUCHMAN, Robert M.
Robert M. Hurt, RIP. Nat R 17:316 Ap 20 '65
SCHUCKMAN, Harold, and Orbach, J.
Detection thresholds as a function of interval separation between two successive targets. bibliog Science 150:1623-5 D 17 '65
SCHULBERG, Budd
Say good night to owl; story. Redbook 125:62-3 Ag '65
SCHULER, Stanley
AP; bright new tone in education. PTA Mag 59:4-7 Je '65; Same abr. with title Bright new horizons for the gifted student. Read Digest 87:33-4+ S '65
After dark garden. Flower Grower 52:37+ My '65
How to keep from going out of style. Nations Bsns 53:66+ F '65
They speed up slow minds. Todays Health 44:40-1+ Ja '66; Same. Read Digest 88:177-80 Ja '66

SCHULKE, Flip
Routine assignment? il por Mod Phot 29:18+ S '65
SCHULMAN, S. J.
How to zone for multi-family dwellings. Am City 80:92-4 D '65
SCHULMAN, Sam
Latin-American shantytown. N Y Times Mag p30-1+ Ja 16 '66
SCHULTE, Fritz Karl
Egg man. Time 86:76+ Ag 27 '65
SCHULTZ, Carl E.
Union tactics stall justice thirteen years. il por Nations Bsns 53:31-3 N '65
SCHULTZ, Gwen M.
More children; more hunger. Todays Health 43:18-23+ O '65
SCHULTZ, Harald
Waurá: Brazilian Indians of the hidden Xingu. il Nat Geog Mag 129:130-52 Ja '66
SCHULTZ, Jack, and Pyle, Carter
Cat bites whale. Yachting 118:48-50+ D '65
SCHULTZ, Morton J.
After tuneup, what? Pop Mech 124:182-5 N '65
Checking out your circuits. Pop Mech 124:177-81+ S; 180-4 O '65
Give your brakes a break. Pop Mech 124:154-7 Ag '65
Shocks shot? service 'em yourself! Pop Mech 124:166-70 D '65
Winter tune-up for your cycle. Pop Mech 125:152-5+ Ja '66
You can get more miles per gallon. Pop Mech 125:184-8 Ja '66
SCHULTZE, Charles Louis
Budget wins a new role. il pors Bsns W p128-30+ Ag 21 '65
How LBJ wins at the budget game; with editorial comment. il por Bsns W p30-1 Je 26 '65
New budgeteer. por Newsweek 65:76 My 3 '65
Shuffle at Budget. Time 85:31 Ap 30 '65
SCHULZ, Charles M.
Love is walking hand in hand; excerpt. il Ladies Home J 82:70-1 Jl '65

about

Good grief. il por Time 85:80-4 Ap 9 '65
Gospel according to Peanuts, by R. L. Short. Review
  Christian Cent 82:276 Mr 3 '65. R. P. Nelson
SCHULZE, Raymond A.
Editor's page. por Pop Mech 124:83 N '65
SCHUMANN, Robert Alexander
Vox boxful of Brahms and Schumann quartets. A. Cohn. Am Rec G 32:233-4 N '65
SCHUMANN, T. E. W.
Moon trip doomed to disaster? por U S News 59:55-8 N 1 '65
SCHUMANN-HEINK, Ernestine
From the depths. D. Warren. por Opera N 30:6-7 D 4 '65
SCHURMEIER, H. M. and others
Ranger missions to the moon; with biographical sketches. Sci Am 214:14, 52-67 bibliog(p 134-5) Ja '66
SCHUSTERMAN, Ronald J. and Feinstein, S. H.
Shaping and discriminative control of underwater click vocalizations in a California sea lion. bibliog Science 150:1743-4 D 24 '65
—and others
Underwater visual discrimination by the California sea lion. bibliog Science 147:1594-6 Mr 26 '65
SCHUTZ, George
Recordings. M. Mayer. Esquire 63:52+ Mr '65
SCHÜTZ, Heinrich
Miraculous inventions of Heinrich Schütz; with list of recordings. E. Helm. il por Hi Fi 15:51-5+ Ag '65
Schuetz, indispensable and otherwise. J. W. Barker. il Am Rec G 31:1084-7 Jl '65
SCHUYLER, James
Sander at the mixolydian edge. Art N 64:26-7+ D '65
White city; poem. Poetry 105:371 Mr '65
SCHWAB, Bernard
Madison cuts a corner. Library J 90:5170-2 D 1 '65
SCHWAB, H.
Unfinished diary; story. Read Digest 87:119-20 D '65
SCHWALBERG, Carol
Overture to a future. Mlle 60:194-5+ Ap '65
SCHWAN, Herman P. See Sher, L. D. jt. auth.
SCHWANN, William
Boswell of LP. J. M. Conly. por Opera N 30:22 N 20 '65

SCHWANN long playing record catalog. See
  Phonograph records—Catalogs
SCHWARCZ, June
  June Schwarcz: electroforming and enamel.
    A. Ventura. il Craft Horiz 25:36-7+ N '65
SCHWARTZ, Abba P.
  Problems of immigraton; letter. New Repub
    152:36-8 Mr 6 '65
  Refugee provisions of administration's pro-
    posals to revise immigration law; state-
    ment, March 3, 1965. Dept State Bul 52:
    471-5 Mr 29 '65
  U.S. objectives and refugee relief programs
    in Africa; statement, January 21, 1965. Dept
    State Bul 52:224-8 F 15 '65
  U.S. participates in meeting of migration
    committee; statement, December 1, 1965.
    Dept State Bul 54:39-41 Ja 3 '66
SCHWARTZ, Alexander
  (tr) See Wiesel, E. Last return
SCHWARTZ, Alvin
  Mud is more than just dirt to kids. Parents
    Mag 40:48-9+ Ap '65
  Why children are afraid of the dark. Parents
    Mag 40:44-5+ Je '65
SCHWARTZ, Bert
  Alumni find a new role. Sat R 48:68-9+ D 18
    '65
SCHWARTZ, Fred
  Books. Craft Horiz 25:60 My '65
  National art education association confer-
    ence. Craft Horiz 25:8-9 My '65
  Undergraduate training of an art teacher.
    bibliog por Sch Arts 64:36-8 F '65
SCHWARTZ, Harry
  Man who lost Russia. Sat R 48:38 N 20 '65
  Soviet power shift. Sat R 48:40 F 13 '65
  Why write a book? Sat R 48:22-3 Ag 14 '65
SCHWARTZ, Jerome
  Christmas window displays; interview. Pub
    W 188:86-8 Ag 23 '65
SCHWARTZ, Joan
  Sonnet 2; At eight the county came to
    slaughter trees. Commonweal 82:347-8 Je
    4 '65
SCHWARTZ, Louis B.
  Excerpt from statement, April 27, 1965. Cong
    Digest 44:253+ O '65
SCHWARTZ, Marvin. See Shagass, C. jt. auth.
SCHWARTZ, Murray L.
  Hard lesson for the law. Sat R 48:35-7+
    N 13 '65
SCHWARTZ, Robert S. and Beldotti, Lorraine
  Malignant lymphomas following allogenic
    disease: transition from an immunological
    to a neoplastic disorder. bibliog Science 149:
    1511-14 S 24 '65
SCHWARTZ, Stanley A. and Braun, Werner
  Bacteria as an indicator of formation of anti-
    bodies by single spleen cells in agar. bib-
    liog Science 149:200 Jl 9 '65
SCHWARTZ, Tony
  Tony Schwartz on sound. See issues of
    Popular photography
SCHWARTZLOSE, Richard A. See Isaacs. J.
  D. jt. auth.
SCHWARTZMAN, Daniel
  Check list for department store programing.
    Arch Rec 137:188-90 My '65
SCHWARZ, Boris
  Italian Baroque. Sat R 48:63+ Ap 24 '65
  Shaporin and Shebalin. Sat R 48:54-5 F 27
    '65
SCHWEID, Bernard
  Publishers should put more effort on their
    staple stock. Pub W 187:45 My 31 '65
SCHWEITZER, Albert
  Man belongs to man; excerpt from Teach-
    ing of reverence for life. por Read Digest
    87:77-8 Jl '65
  Schweitzer letter presented by librarian; ex-
    cerpts from letter to R. Bultmann. Wilson
    Lib Bul 40:217+ N '65

about

Albert Schweitzer, 1875-1965. Christian Cent
  82:1116-17 S 15 '65
Albert Schweitzer: his life, his work, his
  thought; symposium. il pors Sat R 48:18-
  32+ S 25 '65
Albert Schweitzer, RIP. Nat R 17:807-8 S 21
  '65
Goodby at Lambarene. R. Chelminski. il por
  Life 59:90-2+ S 17 '65
Last days of Albert Schweitzer. F. Pope.
  il por McCalls 93:76+ D '65
Living with a verity. il Time 86:108 S 17 '65
Obituary
  Pub W 188:93-4 S 27 '65
Schweitzer method hit. Sci N L 88:180 S 18
  '65
Schweitzer: reverence for life. por Newsweek
  66:62 S 13 '65

Verdict on Schweitzer, by G. McKnight. Review
  New Yorker 41:190+ Ap 24 '65. N. Bliven
What matters about Schweitzer. N. Cousins.
  pors Sat R 48:30-2 S 25 '65
White wizard's 90th. H. Moffett. il pors Life
  58:82-92+ F 19 '65

Statues, portraits, etc.

Schweitzer and Lambaréné. E. Anderson.
  Sat R 48:28-9 S 25 '65
SCHWEITZER, Pierre Paul
  Does the world need a new kind of money?
    interview. por U S News 59:78-81 O 4 '65
SCHWEPPES, limited
  Can Commander Whitehead save Britain? J.
    Weingarten. il Duns R 86:42-3+ Jl '65
SCHWIEBERT, Ernest
  Homage to Patagonia: a fisherman's tale.
    Esquire 63:90-2+ Mr '65
  Last great empty slopes. Esquire 65:88-9+
    Ja '66
  Strangest trout stream on earth. Field & S
    70:44-7+ Jl '65
  10,000 miles from Thuringia. pors Field & S
    70:67-9+ Ja '66
SCHWINGER, Julian
  Julian Schwinger on the future of funda-
    mental physics. por Science 147:1554 Mr 26
    '65

about

Nobel prize winners. por Sci N L 88:279 O
  30 '65
Tomonaga, Schwinger, and Feynman awarded
  Nobel prize for physics. F. J. Dyson. por
  Science 150:588-9 O 29 '65
SCHWITTERS, Kurt
  Revolution from refuse; retrospective of
    works in Manhattan's Marlborough-Gerson
    gallery. il Time 85:64 Je 4 '65
SCIENCE
  California's science monopoly. H. Pryor. il
    Sci Digest 57:22-5 F '65
  Can we buy quality in science? S. MacLane.
    Bul Atomic Sci 21:6-11 N '65
  Corruption of innocent neutrons. W. H.
    Auden. il N Y Times Mag p 18-20+ Ag 1
    '65; Same abr. with title Of man and the
    atom. Read Digest 87:219-20+ N '65
  Even science cannot make wishes come true.
    Sci N L 89:40 Ja 15 '66
  Evolution of science; adaptation from Re-
    port of the president. C. P. Haskins. Sci-
    ence 148:737 My 7 '65
  Kept science ruinous. Sci N L 87:219 Ap 3
    '65
  Limits to science. P. Auger. Bul Atomic Sci
    21:21-2 N '65
  Main competition lies ahead; address, March
    1, 1965. D. F. Hornig. Sci N L 87:165+
    Mr 13 '65
  1965 science review. Sci N L 88:395 D 18 '65
  Physical science. il Science 150:1058-62 N 19
    '65
  Please explain; questions and answers. See
    issues of Science digest
  Profits and risks of simplification. H. Eyring.
    Science 150:439 O 22 '65
  Science ABC's. See issues of Science digest
    to July 1965
  Science and scientists; excerpts from address,
    September 1, 1965. C. Hinshelwood. Sci N L
    88:182 S 18 '65
  Science forecast for 1966. W. Davis. Sci N L
    88:403 D 25 '65
  Warn against confusing science and tech-
    nology. Sci N L 89:9 Ja 1 '66
  World in 1984, ed. by N. Calder. Review
    New Repub 153:28-9 Jl 10 '65. E. T. Chase
    See also
  Geography
  Inventions
  Research
  Scientific method

Anecdotes, facetiae, satire, etc.

Funny side of science. D. Cohen. Sci Digest
  57:88 My '65

Bibliography

Book reviews. See issues of Science
Science crosses specialty lines. L. Engel.
  Harper 230:117-18 F '65
Science, technology: some outstanding titles.
  il Pub W 187:38-61 Ag 19: 188:42-67 N 15 '65
Scientific, technical, and medical books to
  come; ed. by J Putnam and R. Grossman.
  Library J 90:1160-201, 3038-119 Mr 1, '65
Scientific, technical, and medical books to
  come; ed. by J. Putnam and J. Lindheim.
  Library J 90:4820-65 N 1 '65

SCIENCE—*Continued*

Charts, graphs, etc.

Three dimensions in fine structure. H. C. Mitchell and J. C. Thaemert. bibliog il Science 148:1480-2 Je 11 '65

Exhibitions

Art in science; exhibit at 1965 annual meeting of the AAAS. D. G. Barry. il Science 150:1486-7 D 10 '65

Science display intrigues St Paul students. il Todays Health 43:88 Ap '65

Experiments

Making hospital rounds with the science lady. J. H. Pollack. il Todays Health 43: 37-41 My '65

Schools lectures at the Royal institution; scientific experiments to be shown to young people. L. Bragg. il Science 150:1420-3 D 10 '65

Federal aid
See Research—Federal aid

Fiction
See Science fiction

History

Our heritage from Galileo Galilei; address, May 21, 1964. R. E. Gibson; discussion. Science 146:997-8; 147:8, 459 N 20 '64, Ja 1, 29 '65

Information services

How can I find out? il Sci Digest 57:36-7 My '65

International aspects

Doctor Hornig studies establishment of science institute in Korea. Dept State Bul 53: 172 Jl 26 '65

Dollar wise, pound foolish. Nation 200:629-30 Je 14 '65

Free source materials. Sci N L 87:340 My 29 '65

Institute for technical economics. W. Leontief. Bul Atomic Sci 21:46 S '65

International biological program. V. Rabinowitch and A. D. Hasler. Bul Atomic Sci 21:32-4 O '65

International prospects of science; excerpts from address, 1964. N. M. Sisakian. il UNESCO Courier 18:4-8+ Mr '65

Is good science good politics? D. E. Kash. Bul Atomic Sci 21:34-6 Mr '65; Discussion. 21:25-7 S '65

New center for physics. A. Salam. Bul Atomic Sci 21:43-5 D '65

Paleomagnetism; report on second conference of a group of American and Japanese scientists. J. Verhoogen. Science 147:1060-1 F 26 '65

President authorizes medical science program with Japan. Dept State Bul 53:671-2 O 25 '65

President gratified by report on U.S.-Japan health program; statement, April 29, 1965. L. B. Johnson. Dept State Bul 52:761 My 17 '65

Science, a new social force; atmosphere of co-operation needed. M. Millionshchikov. il UNESCO Courier 18:24-6 O '65

Science and international cooperation; remarks, November 30, 1965. D. F. Hornig. Dept State Bul 54:20-2 Ja 3 '66

Science in the State department: a practical imperative; adaptation of address. J. R. Killian, jr. il Bul Atomic Sci 21:12-17 My '65

Science must serve the cause of peace; address. M. D. Millionshchikov. UN Mc Chron 2:53-65 Ap '65

Science of science. D. J. de S. Price. Bul Atomic Sci 21:2-8 O '65

Scientific research: the case for international support. A. A. Buzzati-Traverso. bibliog Science 148:1440-4 Je 11 '65

Slicing the pie: Russian argues astronomy in U.S.S.R. is neglected while nuclear physics prospers. D. S. Greenberg. Science 148:479 Ap 23 '65

State department seminar. L. F. Audrieth and H. I. Chinn. Bul Atomic Sci 21:43-4 My '65

Support for Italian science; letter to Lyndon B. Johnson from eighty-two Italian scientists. A. Leonardi and others. Science 148:1037 My 21 '65

Tsunami runup: United States-Japan cooperative science program; report on symposium. W. G. Van Dorn. Science 149:566 Jl 30 '65

U.S. and Argentina to launch meteorological sounding rockets. Dept State Bul 52:966-7 Je 14 '65

U.S. and Japan begin program of cooperation in medical science; statement, April 8, 1965, with text of U.S. advisory group. L. B. Johnson. Dept State Bul 52:667-8 My 3 '65

See also
European atomic energy community
International geophysical year
International Indian Ocean expedition
Project Camelot
United States—State, Department of—International scientific and technological affairs, Office of

Juvenile literature
See Scientific literature for children

Materials

Materials science in dentistry, medicine, and pharmacy; synthetic materials. il Science 150:784 N 5 '65

Methodology

See also
Hypothesis

Philosophy

Limitations of science. V. Bush. Time 85: 81 My 7 '65

See also
Nature, Laws of

Popularization
See Science news

Religious aspects
See Religion and science

Scholarships and fellowships

Grants, fellowships, and awards. See occasional issues of Science

Social aspects

But is the teacher also a citizen? adaptation of address, April 14, 1965. A. M. Weinberg. bibliog Science 149:601-6 Ag 6 '65; Discussion. 150:141-2+, 965 O 8, N 19 '65

Ethical basis of science; excerpt from Science and ethical values. B. Glass. bibliog Science 150:1254-61 D 3 '65

Science and the shabby curate of poetry; essays about the two cultures, by M. Green. Review
   Bul Atomic Sci 21:31-2 S '65. M. M. Simpson

Soviets take a new look at science. S. Dedijer. Bul Atomic Sci 21:40-1 Mr '65

Study and teaching

Academic organization in physical science. H. G. Booker; reply. H. J. Gray. Science 147:557-8 F 5 '65

Curriculum reform. J. Walsh; reply. L. Lisonbee. Science 148:733-4 My 7 '65

Elementary science: a new scheme of instruction. R. M. Gagné. bibliog il Science 151:49-53 Ja 7 '66

Philippine science school. Sci N L 87:132 F 27 '65

Role of the paperback in science teaching; summaries of addresses at Teachers college, Columbia university, conference. Pub W 188:68-71 N 15 '65

School laboratory supplies. D. Wolfle. Science 147:827 F 19 '65

Science in the small school; Green River, Wyoming. J. V. Bernard. Atlan 215:95-8 Ap '65; Discussion. 216:56+ S '65

Teacher's right arm: cooperation in teaching science. H. D. Moore. il Library J 90:1984-6 Ap 15 '65

Teaching kids to teach themselves. F. V. Rummell. il PTA Mag 60:16-19 O '65; Same abr. with title He teaches kids to teach themselves. Read Digest 87:246-7+ O '65

What's wrong with high school science. J. F. Etten. il Sci Digest 57:64-8 My '65
See also
Chemistry—Study and teaching
Natural history—Study and teaching
Science teachers
Scientific education

Projects

Beginning a science project. F. L. Snakenberg. il Sci N L 88:218-19 O 2 '65

How to cope with the project. E. Gibbs. Am Home 68:80 Ap '65

SCIENCE—*Continued*

Terminology

But, please George, write it in English! excerpt from Pomona today. M. Beadle. Sat R 48:53-4 Ap 3 '65

Textbooks

Schools, science & society. Nation 200:341-3 Mr 29 '65

China (People's Republic)

Science in mainland China: a tourist's impressions. C. H. G. Oldham. bibliog il Science 147:706-14 F 12 '65; Reply. P. A. Chenoweth. 148:1172 My 28 '65

Scientific revolution brews in red China. Sci N L 87:133 F 27 '65

France

France considers significance of Nobel awards. V. K. McElheny. il Science 150:1013-15 N 19 '65

Is French scientific policy chauvinist? V. K. McElheny. il Science 149:1216-18 S 10 '65

National planning of science and technology in France; adaptation of address, October 1964. J. B. Quinn. bibliog il Science 150:993-1003 N 19 '65

Germany (Federal Republic)

West Germany debates a cultural crisis. V. K. McElheny. il Science 147:589-91 F 5 '65

Great Britain

Blackett chosen president of Royal society. V. K. McElheny. Science 150:1437-9 D 10 '65

Britain wields a modernizing ax. V. K. McElheny. Science 147:1429-31 Mr 19 '65

Scientific policy in Britain; adaptation of address, December 14, 1964. A. R. Todd. Science 149:156-62 Jl 9 '65

Italy

E. B. Chain accused of contempt of Italian judiciary. V. K. McElheny. Science 150:1573-5 D 17 '65

Research climate in Italy. V. K. McElheny; discussion. Science 145:1387; 147:556-7 S 25 '64, F 5 '65

Japan

Insect biochemistry; report on pioneering insect biochemistry seminar, Chiba, Japan. L. Levenbook. Science 150:643-4 O 29 '65

Korea (Republic)

Advisory group reports on study of science institute in Korea; White House announcement; with remarks, August 5, 1965. L. B. Johnson. Dept State Bul 53:322-3 Ag 23 '65

Doctor Hornig studies establishment of science institute in Korea. Dept State Bul 53:172 Jl 26 '65

Poland

As I see it. L. Infeld. il Bul Atomic Sci 21:7-14 F '65

Russia

New science city in Siberia; Akademgorodok. H. Koprowski and others. il Science 149:947-9 Ag 27 '65

Rise and fall of Lysenko. E. W. Caspari and R. E. Marshak. Science 149:275-8 Jl 16 '65; Discussion. 149:1443-4+ S 24 '65

Slicing the pie: Russian argues astronomy in U.S.S.R. is neglected while nuclear physics prospers. D. S. Greenberg. Science 148:479 Ap 23 '65

Soviets take a new look at science. S. Dedijer. Bul Atomic Sci 21:40-1 Mr '65

See also

Research—Russia

United States

See Science; Science and state

SCIENCE (periodical)

Paid circulation of Science outside continental United States; June 30, 1965. Science 149:617 Ag 6 '65

SCIENCE advisory committee. See United States—President's science advisory committee

SCIENCE and civilization

Council on the future. V. Potter. il Nation 200:133-6 F 8 '65

Escape to the endless frontier; excerpt from Scientific estate. D. K. Price. bibliog Science 148:743-9 My 7 '65

Impact of science on technology; ed. by A. W. Warner. Review

Science 148:1707-9 Je 25 '65. S. Dedijer

Learning to live with science. E. G. Mesthene. Sat R 48:14-17 Jl 17 '65

Materials and the development of civilization and science; adaptation of seminar, September 1963. C. S. Smith. bibliog il Science 148:908-17 My 14 '65; Reply. L. F. Trueb. 149:246 Jl 16 '65

Open season on scientists. E. Rabinowitch. New Repub 154:20-2 Ja 1 '66; Reply. L. Dembart. 154:28 Ja 22 '66

Panic in modern man; excerpt from Identity of man. J. Bronowski. Sci Digest 58:82-5 D '65

Profiles; R. B. Fuller. C. Tomkins. New Yorker 41:35-6+ Ja 8 '66

Science and antiscience; address, December 27, 1964. W. R. Brain. bibliog Science 148:192-8 Ap 9 '65; Reply. D. J. Pletsch. 149:926 Ag 27 '65

Science and the common man. R. Calder. UNESCO Courier 18:4-8+ F; 17+ Mr '65

Science pauses. V. Bush. Fortune 71:116-19+ My '65

Society and science; adaptation of address. V. R. Potter; reply. F. E. Hahn. Science 147:823-4 F 19 '65

Sociobiology and man. A. M. Guhl. Bul Atomic Sci 21:22-4 O '65

Step to man; excerpt. J. R. Platt. Science 149:607-13 Ag 6 '65; Same. UNESCO Courier 18:4-9+ D '65

Teaching and the expanding knowledge. A. Szent-Györgyi; reply. W. F. Battig. Science 147:558 F 5 '65

Vision of the year 2000, scientific and technological revolution. C. B. Luce. McCalls 93:44+ Ja '66

Where is science taking us? excerpts from Nature of human conflict. C. A. McClelland. Sat R 48:45-6 Je 5 '65

SCIENCE and industry. See Industrial research

SCIENCE and literature. See Literature and science

SCIENCE and religion. See Religion and science

SCIENCE and state

Air conservation report reflects national concern. J. P. Dixon and J. P. Lodge. Science 148:1060-6 My 21 '65

Basic research and national goals. P. H. Abelson. Science 148:897 My 14 '65

Big money and high politics of science. D. R. Fleming. Atlan 216:41-5 Ag '65; Reply. M. W. Keith. 216:56+ N '65

Congress and scientific advice. G. E. Lowe. Bul Atomic Sci 21:39-42 D '65

E. B. Chain accused of contempt of Italian judiciary. V. K. McElheny. Science 150:1573-5 D 17 '65

Escape to the endless frontier; excerpt from Scientific estate. D. K. Price. bibliog Science 148:743-9 My 7 '65

Megaloscience; adaptation of address, November 5 ,1964. J. B. Adams. Science 148:1560-4 Je 18 '65

More power, less security. S. Chase. Sat R 48:32-3 Jl 17 '65

National planning for medical research; adaptation of address, March 1, 1965. P. Handler. bibliog Science 148:1688-92 Je 25 '65; Reply. J. D. Cooper. 149:1173 S 10 '65

Need science commission. C. A. Betts. Sci N L 88:20 Jl 10 '65

New level of understanding. D. Wolfle. Science 150:693 N 5 '65

New priesthood, by R. E. Lapp. Review

New Repub 152:19-20 Je 12 '65. A. Toffler

Open season on scientists. E. Rabinowitch. New Repub 154:20-2 Ja 1 '66; Reply. L. Dembart. 154:28 Ja 22 '66

Proposal for a yearly presidential report on science. W. D. Carey. Sat R 48:57-8 N 6 '65

Science and government: new currents flowing. D. S. Greenberg. Science 149:1209-11 S 10 '65

Scientific pork barrel. D. S. Greenberg. Harper 232:90-2 Ja '66

Scientist in the federal service. J. W. Macy, jr. Science 148:51-4 Ap 2 '65

Scientists and congressmen; address, August 17, 1965. C. A. Mosher. Vital Speeches 31:709-13 S 15 '65

Trends in some areas of Soviet biomedical research. E. Simonson and J. Brožek. bibliog Science 150:1687-9 D 24 '65

Where science and politics meet, by J. B. Wiesner. Review

Reporter 33:47-50 Ag 12 '65. J. R. Schlesinger

Why politics needs scientists. H. Pryor. Sci Digest 58:34-6 S '65

See also

Research—Federal aid

SCIENCE and the humanities

Congress: subcommittee surveys effects of federally supported research on higher education. J. Walsh. Science 149:42-4 Jl 2 '65; Reply. D. T. Denhardt. 149:918+ Ag 27 '65

Fields of scholarship. D. Wolfle. Science 147:1091 Mr 5 '65

Not by truth alone. F. Tilden. Science 148:1415 Je 11 '65

Opinion, please, from New York. S. Sontag. Mlle 60:58+ Ap '65

Science and the shabby curate of poetry, by M. Green. Review
  Commonweal 82:478-9 Jl 2 '65. G. Greene

SCIENCE aptitude tests. See Aptitude tests

SCIENCE as a profession

Building for a science career. F. L. Snakenberg. il Sci N L 88:234 O 9 '65

Changes in scientific activities with age. A. Roe. bibliog il Science 150:313-18 O 15 '65

Order from chaos; address, March 19, 1965. J. H. Hildebrand. bibliog il Science 150:441-50 O 22 '65

SCIENCE books for children. See Scientific literature for children

SCIENCE camps. See Camps

SCIENCE city. See Akademgorodok, Siberia

SCIENCE clubs

Science: thrills of exploration; excitement of discovery. F. Wattier. il UNESCO Courier 18:40-1+ Jl '65

SCIENCE clubs of America

See also
Science talent search

SCIENCE education. See Scientific education

SCIENCE fairs

Fairs: international, national, local. il Sci N L 88:174 S 11 '65

International science fair new name adopted; replacing National science fair-international. Sci N L 87:324 My 22 '65

One million youths enter local science fairs. Sci N L 87:233 Ap 10 '65

Science fair winners; Special award winners; Health awards winners; 16th National science fair-international. il Sci N L 87:323-9+ My 22 '65

Thousands attend first Guatemalan science fair; Costa Rica prepares National Science fair. Sci N L 88:219 O 2 '65

SCIENCE fiction

Imagination of disaster; excerpt from Against interpretation. S. Sontag. Commentary 40:42-8 O '65

Long John Nebel and the woodlouse; science-fiction writer looks at information science. address, December 8, 1964. F. Pohl. Library J 90:4704-8 N 1 '65

Men and morals in space; comment on C. S. Lewis' trilogy. J. M. Phelan. America 113:405-7 O 9 '65

Russian science fiction, ed. by R. Magidoff. Review
  Commonweal 82:27-8 Mr 26 '65. M. Green

Science fiction: a practical nightmare. K. Amis. il Holiday 37:8+ F '65

See also
Moving pictures—Science fiction

Single works

Harrison Bergeron. K. Vonnegut, jr. il Nat R 17:1020-1 N 16 '65

SCIENCE in art

Art galleries; exhibition: Art-in-science at Institute of history and art, Albany, N.Y. R. M. Coates. New Yorker 41:205-8+ O 16 '65

SCIENCE in criminal investigation. See Criminal investigation

SCIENCE in fiction. See Science fiction; Science in literature

SCIENCE in literature

Astronaut, the novelist, and Cadwalder Glotz; science in fiction. H. Searls. Writer 78:24-5+ S '65

See also
Science fiction

SCIENCE kits. See Scientific apparatus and instruments

SCIENCE librarians. See Librarians

SCIENCE news

Are we really telling the people about science? adaptation of address, December 28, 1964. V. Cohn. Science 148:750-3 My 7 '65

But, please George, write it in English! excerpt from Pomona today. M. Beadle. Sat R 48:53-4 Ap 3 '65

Information race; letters. W. Loveland; A. Mather. Science 148:314 Ap 16 '65

Late science news. See issues of Science digest

Public understanding of science. E. G. Sherburne, jr. Science 149:381 Jl 23 '65; Discussion. 150:7, 289, 1103-4 O 1, 15, N 26 '65

Science marches on. H. M. Schmeck, jr. il N Y Times Mag p 129 Ap 11 '65

Science newsfront. W. Cloud. See issues of Popular science monthly

Those wild Russian stories. D. Cohen. il Sci Digest 58:66-8 Jl '65

SCIENCE projects. See Science—Study and teaching—Projects

SCIENCE research associates, incorporated

Reading in high gear. L. Willey. il Wilson Lib Bul 40:61 S '65

SRA issues anti-poverty basic reading program; Reading in high gear. Pub W 187:41 Mr 8 '65

SCIENCE service, incorporated

See also
Science talent search

SCIENCE students

Building for a science career. F. L. Snakenber. il Sci N L 88:234 O 9 '65

Science scholarship winners. il Sci N L 87:166-7 Mr 13 '65

STS honors announced. Sci N L 87:70 Ja 30 '65

Science talent search winners. Sci N L 87:86+ F 6 '65

Teen-age space experts report science projects. Sci N L 88:25 Jl 10 '65

Trips, cruises to honor science fair winners. Sci N L 87:265 Ap 24 '65

See also
Science talent search

SCIENCE talent search

Remarks on talent search. D. C. Burnham; L. Carmichael. Sci N L 87:164+ Mr 13 '65

Science talent search. il Sci N L 88:175 S 11 '65

STS 25th anniversary. Sci N L 88:198 S 25 '65

1965 (24th)

Main competition lies ahead; address, March 1, 1965. D. F. Hornig. Sci N L 87:165+ Mr 13 '65

President meets winners; remarks, March 1, 1965. L. B. Johnson. il Sci N L 87:163+ Mr 13 '65

Science scholarship winners. il Sci N L 87:166-7 Mr 13 '65

STS honors announced. Sci N L 87:70 Ja 30 '65

Science talent search winners. Sci N L 87:86+ F 6 '65

SCIENCE teachers

Teachers given research opportunities. Sr Schol 87:sup3 D 2 '65

SCIENCE teaching. See Science—Study and teaching

SCIENCE youth month. See National science youth month

SCIENTIFIC apparatus and instruments

Christmas science selection. F. L. Snakenberg. il Sci N L 88:314-15 N 13 '65

Instrument issue; symposium (cont) bibliog il Science 150:149-99+ O 8 '65

New products. See issues of Science

School laboratory supplies. D. Wolfle. Science 147:827 F 19 '65

See also
Oceanographic instruments

Exhibitions

Instruments at the FASEB show. D. J. Prager. Science 148:1366+ Je 4 '65

SCIENTIFIC attachés (United States) See United States—Diplomatic and consular service

SCIENTIFIC conferences

Conference literature. E. H. Ahrens, jr. Science 148:313 Ap 16 '65

Meetings. See issues of Science

Obese degeneration of scientific congresses. G. E. W. Wolstenholme; discussion. Science 146:1001; 147:679-80 N 20 '64, F 12 '65

When and where. See issues of Missiles and rockets

SCIENTIFIC data systems, incorporated

New computer prodigy? J. F. Olesky. Duns R 86:71-2 N '65

Only no. 7, so it tries harder. il Bsns W p 172+ Mr 20 '65

SCIENTIFIC education

Big money and high politics of science. D. R. Fleming. Atlan 216:41-5 Ag '65; Reply. M. W. Keith. 216:56+ N '65

Education of professional physicists; report on international conference. R. Geballe. Science 150:1752+ D 24 '65

SCIENTIFIC education—*Continued*
Fiscal dilemma of academic science. W. V. Consolazio. il Bul Atomic Sci 21:15-18 F '65
Japan points a way. B. Glass. Science 150: 1107 N 26 '65
President meets winners; remarks, March 1, 1965. L. B. Johnson. il Sci N L 87:163+ Mr 13 '65
Pure research, cultism, and the undergraduate. R. Wolfgang. Science 150:1563-5 D 17 '65
Schools lectures at the Royal institution; scientific experiments to be shown to young people. L. Bragg. il Science 150:1420-3 D 10 '65
Science news in the classroom. A. H. Drummond, jr. Sat R 48:57 Jl 17 '65
See also
Engineering education
Science—Study and teaching

SCIENTIFIC libraries
See also
National lending library for science and technology, Boston Spa, Yorkshire

SCIENTIFIC literature
De Gaulle: president of France calls for a harder line in behalf of French in international science. J. Walsh. Science 148:350-1 Ap 16 '65
Distribution of U.S. scientific literature. P. H. Abelson. Science 149:589 Ag 6 '65
Networks of scientific papers; adaptation of address, March 17, 1964. D. J. de Price. bibliog il Science 149:510-15 Jl 30 '65
Reprints: a proposal; letter. A. F. Hofmann and others; discussion. Science 147:677+: 148:313, 1173, 1542 F 12, Ap 16, My 28, Je 18 '65
Rules for referees. B. K. Forscher. Science 150:319-21 O 15 '65; Discussion. 150:1407-8 D 10 '65
300 years of storing words: scientific communication; excerpt from address. J. R. Porter; reply. J. H. Wood. Sat R 48:56 Ap 3 '65
See also
Booksellers and bookselling—Scientific literature
Libraries—Science collections
Publishers and publishing—Scientific literature
Science—Bibliography

Translating
See Translations and translating

SCIENTIFIC literature for children
On writing science books for children. I. Adler. il Horn Bk 41:524-9 O '65

Bibliography
Annual survey of books about science addressed to young readers. J. R. Newman. Sci Am 213:114-17+ D '65
Natural history's 1965 survey of science books for young people. Natur Hist 74:4-6+ N '65
Selection criteria: science books for children. F. W. Doughty. Horn Bk 41:195-200 Ap '65
Teacher's right arm: cooperation in teaching science. H. D. Moore. il Library J 90:1984-6 Ap 15 '65
Views on science books. I. Asimov. See issues of Horn book magazine

SCIENTIFIC method
Strong inference and weak interactions. E. M. Hafner and S. Presswood. bibliog il Science 149:503-10 Jl 30 '65

SCIENTIFIC personnel, Government. See Government employees

SCIENTIFIC photography. See Photography—Scientific applications

SCIENTIFIC research. See Research

SCIENTIFIC terms. See Science—Terminology

SCIENTIFIC theories. See Science

SCIENTIFIC toys. See Toys

SCIENTIFIC workers. See Scientists

SCIENTISTS
Corruption of innocent neutrons. W. H. Auden. il N Y Times Mag p 18-20+ Ag 1 '65; Same abr. with title Of man and the atom. Read Digest 87:219-20+ N '65
Electronics industry: products, people, and prospects; special report. il Electr World 73:25-8+ Ap '65
Greatest discovery; excerpt from Inquiry into enoughness. D. Lang. Sat R 48:28 Ap 17 '65
Intuition in science: why cover it up? address. R. Jastrow. Sat R 48:55 My 1 '65
Kick the scientist; concerning articles in October issue of the Bulletin. H. Malamud. Bul Atomic Sci 21:34-5 My '65
Knowledge for what? W. Hirsch. Bul Atomic Sci 21:28-31 My '65

Poets and scientists. M. K. McCorquodale. Bul Atomic Sci 21:18-20 N '65
Science and scientists; excerpts from address, September 1, 1965. C. Hinshelwood. Sci N L 88:182 S 18 '65
Science fuels its own chain reaction; AAAS meeting in Berkeley. il Bsns W p 18-19 Ja 1 '66
Scientists drift from teaching. il Bsns W p52-3 Ja 8 '66
See also
Negro scientists
Physicists
Women as scientists

Political activities
Is good science good politics? D. E. Kash. Bul Atomic Sci 21:34-6 Mr '65; Discussion. 21:25-7 S '65
Peril and a hope, by A. K. Smith. Review Nation 201:124-7 S 6 '65. E. Langer
Scientists on tap or on top? we are missing the real issues. L. F. Audrieth. Bul Atomic Sci 21:24-5 S '65

Supply and demand
Chaos in science; what space and defense are doing. A. Etzioni. Commonweal 82:494-7 Jl 9 '65
Doctoral feedback into higher education. R. H. Bolt and others. bibliog il Science 148:918-28 My 14 '65
Scientist in the federal service. J. W. Macy, jr. Science 148:51-4 Ap 2 '65
West Germany debates a cultural crisis. V. K. McElheny. il Science 147:589-91 F 5 '65

SCIENTISTS, Amateur
Science: thrills of exploration; excitement of discovery. F. Wattier. il UNESCO Courier 18:40-1+ Jl '65

SCIENTISTS, American
Changes in scientific activities with age. A. Roe. bibliog il Science 150:313-18 O 15 '65
Mature research institutions and the older scientist. L. G. Cook and G. W. Hazzard. bibliog il Science 150:716-19 N 5 '65
Peril and a hope, by A. K. Smith. Review Nation 201:124-7 S 6 '65. E. Langer Sci Am 213:257-8+ S '65. P. Morrison
Summer: the climate is changed for university scientists and the federal government did it. J. Walsh. Science 148:776-8 My 7 '65

SCIENTISTS, Chinese
Soviet scientists in red China, by M. A. Klochko. Review Bul Atomic Sci 21:29 N '65. E. Rabinowitch

SCIENTISTS, Japanese
Japanese zoologists abroad; letter. A. Gorbman and T. Fujii. il Science 147:1395-6 Mr 19 '65

SCIENTISTS, Negro. See Negro scientists

SCINTILLATION of stars. See Stars—Scintillation

SCIURIDAE. See Squirrels

SCLAR, C. B. and others
Indium telluride (II'): transitory intermediate phase in the transformation InTe(II) to InTe(I) bibliog Science 147:1569-71 Mr 26 '65

SCLERA, Transplantation of. See Transplantation of organs, tissues, etc.

SCLEROSIS, Multiple
Clue to multiple sclerosis. il Time 85:65 Je 11 '65
Multiple sclerosis. il Todays Health 43:36-7 Ag '65
Multiple sclerosis linked to chicken pox virus. Sci N L 87:216 Ap 3 '65

SCOFIELD, John
Israel: land of promise. Nat Geog Mag 127: 394-434 Mr '65

SCOGGIN, Margaret C.
(comp) Outlook tower. See issues of Horn book magazine

SCOOTERS, Motor. See Motor scooters

SCOPES. See Oscillographs; Telescopic sights

SCOPES trial. See Tennessee evolution controversy

SCOREBOARDS
Big screen is watching: Houston's astrodome. J. Jares. il Sports Illus 22:30-1 My 31 '65

SCOTCH tape. See Adhesive tape

SCOTLAND
See also
Arran (island)
Edinburgh
Hebrides
Hotels, taverns, etc.—Scotland
Hunting—Scotland
Pittenweem
Schools—Scotland
Skye, Isle of

SCOTLAND—*Continued*

Description and travel
Bring rod, clubs and gun. F. R. Smith. il Sports Illus 22:55-6+ My 17 '65
Following a Scot on his holidays. Sunset 135:46-7 Jl '65
Inns of the Highlands. R. Postage. il Holiday 37:82-3+ Mr '65

Religious institutions and affairs
News of the Christian world (cont) Christian Cent 82:186+, 688, 1168, 1429-30 F 10, My 26, S 22, N 17 '65
See also
Church of Scotland

SCOTLAND, Church of. See Church of Scotland

SCOTT, Beverley
Please squeeze the caviar. Seventeen 25:26 Ja '66

SCOTT, David H.
Scott's corner. por Flying 77:70 Jl; 22 Ag '65

SCOTT, Foresman and company
Scott, Foresman consolidates warehousing at Pinola, Indiana. il Pub W 188:25-8 D 13 '65

SCOTT, George C.
Sorry about that. pors Esquire 64:208-11+ D '65

SCOTT, Jack Denton
His magnificence, the moose. Read Digest 87:118-22 O '65

SCOTT, Jim
Music in the redwoods. Am For 71:19+ Je '65

SCOTT, Joan
How to know when a child is happy. Bet Hom & Gard 43:40+ F '65

SCOTT, John Paul
Anatomy of violence. Nation 200:662-6 Je 21 '65
—and Fuller, J. L.
What dogs tell us about man's future. Sat R 48:47-51 Mr 6; 64 My 1 '65

SCOTT, Lin
Bangkok and beyond. Travel 123:33-5 Mr '65

SCOTT, Marion
Marion Scott and dance company, 92nd street Y. M. Marks. Dance Mag 39:64-5 My '65

SCOTT, Meredith A.
Atlas and the world of ships. il Motor B 116:54-5+ Jl '65
Florida, by sea. Travel 124:36-7 O '65

SCOTT, Vernon
Black and white: two worlds of Robert Matlock. Ladies Home J 82:92-3+ N '65
Why Barbara Stanwyck grinned all the way to the bank. McCalls 92:82 Mr '65

SCOTT, Winfield Townley
Music, image, and emotion. Sat R 48:57-9 O 9 '65
about
Three poets. H. Carruth. Poetry 106:309-10 Jl '65

SCOTTO, Renata
Bel canto Butterfly; interview, ed. by G. Fitzgerald. por Opera N 30:26 Ja 1 '66

SCOUR in swine. See Swine—Diseases and pests

SCOUTING, Basketball. See Basketball scouting

SCOUTING, Football. See Football scouting

SCOUTS and scouting
See also
Boy scouts

SCOUTTEN, E. F.
Retreat from excellence; address, June 25, 1965. Vital Speeches 31:761-5 O 1 '65

SCOVEL, Carl
Joy to the whole wide world; story. McCalls 93:108-9 D '65

SCOVEL, Myra
Poems: Two blades of grass; All beauty has its price; Trail, blazed. Am For 71:52 S '65

SCOVILL manufacturing company

Hamilton beach division
Carving path to a top market spot; electric knife as sales leader. il Bsns W p78+ Ja 15 '66

SCRAMJET propulsion. See Jet propulsion

SCRANTON, William Warren
Building a base. il por Time 87:28 Ja 14 '66
Firm foreign policy; address, May 28, 1965. Vital Speeches 31:652-4 Ag 15 '65

SCRANTON, Pa, public library
Librarian and bookdealer convicted in Scranton (Pa) book theft trial. Library J 90: 2774 Je 15 '65

SCRAP metal
Orders to clean up those junkyards. E. T. Folliard. America 112:215 F 13 '65
Process may put scrap back in steel mills. Sci N L 88:105 Ag 14 '65

SCRAPIE disease. See Sheep—Diseases and pests

SCREEN actors guild
SEG or SAG? what union for Hollywood dancers? V. H. Swisher. Dance Mag 39:108-9 D '65

SCREEN extras guild
SEG or SAG? what union for Hollywood dancers? V. H. Swisher. Dance Mag 39:108-9 D '65

SCREEN printing. See Silk screen printing

SCREEN producers guild
Uses of anonymity; how networks dominate the sources of program production. R. L. Shayon. Sat R 48:35 Mr 6 '65

SCREEN writing. See Moving picture authorship

SCREENS (doors, windows, etc)
Screening can do the job. il Pop Gard 16:30-1 Jl '65

SCREENS (fences) See Fences

SCREENS (furniture)
Create your own fancies for a folding screen. il House & Gard 127:54+ My '65
Screen inside your entry. il Sunset 135:137 O '65
Screen stars. il McCalls 92:96-9+ Ag '65

SCREENS (sun)
Canvas. P. Corey. il Pop Gard 16:28-31 Mr '65
Here are working defenses against the summer sun. il Sunset 135:72-4 Jl '65
Over the sun deck, a fabric sun shade. il Sunset 134:145 Je '65
Sun control on the west side of a house. il Sunset 135:156 O '65
This sun shelter is simple to build. il Bet Hom & Gard 43:120 F '65

SCREENS, Projector. See Projection apparatus

SCREVANE, Paul Rogers
Man who saved MFY. Nation 201:58 Ag 2 '65
Me & Screvane. il por Time 85:32 Je 25 '65

SCREW drivers
Choosing, using a screwdriver. il Sunset 134:130+ Mr '65

SCREW propellers. See Propellers

SCREWS
Inventor of the month; better way to hold things together; three-cornered screws. S. V. Jones. il Sci Digest 58:44 O '65
Make your own hand-screws. E. P. Kushner, sr. il Pop Mech 124:194-5 N '65

SCRIABIN, Alexander Nicholaevich. See Skriabin, A. N.

SCRIBNER, Dan
Fipple in the mouth. D. Brink. il por Recreation 58:399 O '65

SCRIPPS-Howard newspapers
Shade of difference; death of Indianapolis times. il Newsweek 66:96 O 25 '65

SCRIPPS institution of oceanography. See California. University—Scripps institution of oceanography

SCRIPTO, incorporated
Blacker ink at Scripto inc. Time 86:109 N 19

SCRIPTS, Moving picture. See Moving picture authorship

SCRIPTURES. See Bible

SCROLLS from the Dead Sea. See Dead Sea scrolls

SCUDDER, Thayer
Kariba case: manmade lakes and resource development in Africa. Bul Atomic Sci 21:6-11 D '65

SCUFFLE hoes. See Hoes

SCULL, Robert C.
Odd ball in. Newsweek 66:104 O 25 '65

SCULLING. See Rowing

SCULLY, James
Crew practice on Lake Bled, in Jugoslavia; poem. New Yorker 41:48 My 8 '65
Oracle of subocracy. Nation 200:144 F 8 '65

SCULLY, Vincent
His ideas are woven into the ages. Life 59:123-4 S 24 '65

SCULPTORS
Reviews and previews: new names this month. See issues of Art news

SCULPTURE
Abstract sculpture; work of high school art classes. J. Hadley. il Sch Arts 64:12-14 Mr '65
Bonanza or bust? bust, believed sculpted by da Vinci or del Verrocchio. il Newsweek 66:104+ N 8 '65

SCULPTURE—*Continued*
Sculptor's secret tool. R. McNesky. il Design 66:14-17 My '65
See also
Figurines
Metal sculpture
Portrait sculpture
Wire sculpture
Wood carving
    also subhead Monuments, statues, etc. under names of cities, e.g. Washington, D.C.—Monuments, statues, etc.

Conservation and restoration
Stones also die. R. Sneyers. il UNESCO Courier 18:26-7+ Ja '65

Exhibitions
Chez Rodin; largest exhibition of American sculpture ever shown in Europe at Rodin museum, Paris. il Time 86:56 Jl 2 '65
Figures in the sun; Athens' international sculpture show. il Time 86:84 O 8 '65
Life force; masterpieces of Indian sculpture at New York's Metropolitan museum of art. il Newsweek 65:68D-69 F 22 '65
Plastic people; F. Gallo exhibitions at New York's Graham and Chicago's Gilman galleries. il Newsweek 66:90 N 29 '65
See also
Museum of modern art, New York

Prices
See Art—Prices

Study and teaching
Materials
Coffee cup conversions; material for fourth graders. F. Irving. il Design 66:10-11 Mr '65
Instant sculpture. E. Welch. il Design 66:12-14 Mr '65

Technique
See also
Lost wax process

SCULPTURE, African
Africa. M. Leiris. il UNESCO Courier 18:10-16 D '65
See also
Sculpture, Bini

SCULPTURE, American
Chez Rodin; largest exhibition of American sculpture ever shown in Europe at Rodin museum, Paris. il Time 86:56 Jl 2 '65
New medium for sculpture. D. Mortillito. il Am Artist 29:44-9+ D '65
See also
Calder, A.
Gallo, F.
Laurent, R.
Lipton, S.
Nakian, R.
Nivola, C.
Smith, D.
Voulkos, P.
Wright, P. L.

SCULPTURE, Animal. See Animal sculpture
SCULPTURE, Architectural. See Decoration and ornament, Architectural
SCULPTURE, Bini
Bronzes of Benin. il Time 86:60 Ag 6 '65
SCULPTURE, British
Five British sculptors work and talk, by W. Forma. Review
    Sat R il 48:39-41 Mr 27 '65. M. R. Weiss
Intellectuals without trauma; new sculptors. il Time 85:66-70 Mr 12 '65
See also
Moore, H. S.
SCULPTURE, Buddhist
Well traveled camera. H. Keppler. Mod Phot 29:52 Mr '65
SCULPTURE, Egyptian
Split chief minister; bust of Sema-tawy-tefnakht rejoined with missing lower half. il Time 85:66-7 Ap 23 '65
SCULPTURE, Eskimo. See Eskimos—Art
SCULPTURE, French
Explosive forms of Piotr Kowalski; interview, ed. by B. P. Spring. P. Kowalski. il Arch Forum 123:30-5 D '65
See also
Gaudier-Brzeska, H.
Lipchitz, J.
SCULPTURE, German
See also
Lehmbruck, W.
SCULPTURE, Greek
Fundamental Venus; exhibition of Cycladic sculpture at Manhattan's Andre Emmerich gallery. il Time 85:70 Je 18 '65
SCULPTURE, Indian (East Indian)
Forty centuries of consistency; sculpture from India at the Metropolitan, New York. M. Neff. il Art N 63:46-9+ F '65

Life force; masterpieces of Indian sculpture at New York's Metropolitan museum of art. il Newsweek 65:68D-69 F 22 '65
SCULPTURE, Italian
See also
Manzù, G.
Michelangelo, Buonarroti
Pomodoro, A.
SCULPTURE, Norwegian
See also
Vigeland, G.
SCULPTURE, Polynesian
Oceania: sculpture. F. Girard. il UNESCO Courier 18:17-26 D '65
SCULPTURE, Primitive
Ancient ills in clay; collection of Dr Abner I. Weisman. il Life 59:99-100 Jl 16 '65
Case histories in clay; Dr Weisman's collection of pre-Columbian figures. il Time 86:75-6 Jl 9 '65
Latitudes of beauty; exhibition of the masterpieces of the Museum of man; excerpts from catalogue. M. Leiris; H. Lehmann; F. Girard. il UNESCO Courier 18:10-30 D '65
Medical sculpture; Weisman collection of pre-Columbian medical sculpture. New Yorker 41:15-16 Jl 10 '65
SCULPTURE, Swiss
See also
Giacometti, A.
SCURVY
How gold-rush-day doctors battled scurvy. il Todays Health 43:52-3+ O '65
SCUTELLARIA. See Skullcaps (flowers)
SCYTHIANS
Frozen tombs of the Scythians. M. I. Artamonov. il Sci Am 212:100-9 bibliog(p 151) My '65
SEA anemones
Nature note; sea flower. Sci N L 88:235 O 9 '65
Preferential settling of the sea anemone stomphia coccinea on the mussel modiolus modiolus. D. M. Moss. bibliog il Science 148:527-8 Ap 23 '65
SEA Christmas; story. See Enright, E.
SEA CLIFF yacht club. See Yacht clubs
SEA food
Inkfish and shark kabob; the sun and seafood of the Aegean; with recipes. F. Du Plessix. Vogue 146:288-90+ S 1 '65
What she's serving are seafood sandwiches Danish style. il Sunset 134:200-1 Ap '65
See also
Cookery—Fish
Fish as food
Shellfish
SEA gulls. See Gulls
SEA hares
Molecular memory of dawn; experiments on sea hares. Sci Am 213:41-2 O '65
SEA lampreys. See Lampreys
SEA law. See Maritime law
SEA-level canal. See Canals—Central America
SEA level changes
Sea-level changes during the last 2000 years at Point Barrow, Alaska. J. D. Hume. bibliog il Science 150:1165-6 N 26 '65
SEA life park, Hawaii. See Aquariums
SEA lilies. See Crinoids
SEA lions. See Seals (animals)
SEA nettles. See Jellyfish
SEA otters
Atomic blast vs otter? S. McCutcheon. il Audubon Mag 67:376-81 N '65
How to see the sea otters. Sunset 135:51-2+ O '65
Uproar over otters; Amchitka Island nuclear test dispute. il Life 59:151-2 O 15 '65
SEA shells. See Shells (conchology)
SEA snakes
Cobras of the sea. A. J. McClane. il Field & S 69:74+ F '65
SEA sounds. See Ocean sounds
SEA stars. See Starfishes
SEA stations. See Oceanographic buoys
SEA trout fishing. See Weakfish fishing
SEA urchins
Messenger RNA in early sea-urchin embryos: cytoplasmic particles. A. S. Spirin and M. Nemer. bibliog il Science 150:214-17 O 8 '65
Messenger RNA in early sea-urchin embryos: size classes. M. Nemer and A. A. Infante. bibliog il Science 150:217-21 O 8 '65
Nature note; hedgehogs of the sea. Sci N L 88:350 N 27 '65

SEA water
Mineralogy of particulate matter suspended in sea water. M. B. Jacobs and M. Ewing. bibliog il Science 149:179-80 Jl 9 '65
Silica: role in the buffering of natural waters. R. M. Garrels. bibliog Science 148:69 Ap 2 '65
Silicates: reactivity with sea water. F. T. Mackenzie and R. M. Garrels. bibliog il Science 150:57-8 O 1 '65
Suspended matter in deep ocean water. M. Ewing and E. M. Thorndike. bibliog il Science 147:1291-4 Mr 12 '65

Analysis
Sampling by helicopter; pollution-monitoring program in San Francisco and Daly City ocean area. R. V. Bernicchi. il Am City 80:80-2 N '65

Desalting
Atomic desalting costly. Sci N L 88:294 N 6 '65
Atoms for thirst. Time 86:63A-63B Jl 30 '65
Desalination: emphasis is on dual-purpose nuclear power and desalting plants. J. Walsh. il Science 147:1117-19 Mr 5 '65
Desalination of water. P. H. Abelson; reply. S. Loeb. Science 147:1241-2 Mr 12 '65
Desalinization progress. Am City 80:19 Ag '65
Desalted water builds up steam; with list of saline water conversion plants. il Bsns W p 120+ O 16 '65
Desalting, today and tomorrow. il Am City 81:87-9 Ja '66
Fifty-four nations to attend October meeting on water desalting; White House announcement. June 20, 1965, with statement. L. B. Johnson. Dept State Bul 53:86-7 Jl 12 '65
Fresh water from the sea, it's here! R. C. Davids. il Farm J 89:40+ D '65
Fresh water from the sea; next big industry for U.S? Race with Britain. il U S News 59:72-4 S 6 '65
Memorandum signed on study of desalting plant for Israel; announcement, April 9, 1965. Dept State Bul 52:635-6 Ap 26 '65
Pilot conversion plant. Nat Parks Mag 39: 18-19 Ap '65
Question of birthright; man's current concern over water. il Time 86:70-79B O 1 '65
Reverse osmosis purifies; Desalination advances. B. Tufty. il Sci N L 88:247 O 16 '65
Rivers of fresh water from the sea. A. P. Armagnac. il Pop Sci 187:82-5 N '65
They're turning salt water into sweet. H. Manchester. Read Digest 86:15-16+ Ap '65
U.S, Mexico, IAEA agree on joint saline water feasibility study; remarks, October 7, 1965. L. B. Johnson. Dept State Bul 53: 720-2 N 1 '65
Water and power. Nat Parks Mag 39:22 N '65
Water desalination seminar; first United Nations inter-regional seminar on the economic application of water desalination. UN Mo Chron 2:49 N '65
Worldwide cooperative effort in water desalination; address, October 4, 1965; with message from President Johnson. S. L. Udall. Dept State Bul 53:716-20 N 1 '65

Pollution
Radioactivity of the Columbia River effluent. M. G. Gross and others. bibliog il Science 149:1088-90 S 3 '65
Sampling by helicopter; pollution-monitoring program in San Francisco and Daly City ocean area. R. V. Bernicchi. il Am City 80:80-2 N '65
Wastes junked in ocean menace sea life, man. Sci N L 89:9 Ja 1 '66

SEA world, San Diego. See Aquariums

SEABOARD air line railway-Atlantic Coast line merger. See Railroads—Consolidations and mergers

SEABORG, Glenn T.
Atom in your future. por Seventeen 24:162+ Mr '65
Importance of scientific exchanges with U.S.S.R. and eastern Europe; report to Cabinet, June 18, 1965. Dept State Bul 53: 128-31 Jl 19 '65
International cooperation on the peaceful uses of atomic energy; statement, September 22, 1965. Dept State Bul 53:677-82 O 25 '65
Plowshare program, developing peaceful uses of nuclear explosives; statement, January 5, 1965. Dept State Bul 52:116-18 Ja 25 '65

U.S. to make further cutback in enriched uranium production; letter to President Johnson, February 2, 1965. Dept State Bul 52:339 Mr 8 '65
Worldwide race for A-bombs, can it be stopped? interview. por U S News 59:60-5 Jl 19 '65

about
Inventor of the month. S. V. Jones. por Sci Digest 57:15 F '65

SEABROOK, John Martin
Squires at large. il por Esquire 64:70 Ag '65

SEABURY, Paul
Antic politics of California. Harper 230:82-4+ Je '65

SEAFARERS' international union of North America
Collision in cab vote; SIU battle with teamsters for Chicago's taxi drivers. il Bsns W p 128 My 15 '65

SEAFARING life
See also
Seamen

SEAFOOD. See Sea food

SEAGER, Allan
No more roses; story. Sat Eve Post 238: 52-8 Mr 27 '65

SEAGER, Ralph W.
Wallpaper valentine; poem. McCalls 92:183 F '65

SEAGLE, Mary
Community action. Wilson Lib Bul 40:256 N '65

SEAGRAM, Joseph E, and sons
Bronfman's private stock. il Time 85:92 Mr 5 '65
Seagram's recipe: a dash of advice. il Bsns W p 126+ Ja 30 '65

SEAGRAVE, Gordon Stifler
Burma surgeon's last battle. S. Seagrave. il pors Sat Eve Post 238:38-40+ Jl 3 '65
Man with a mission. il por Newsweek 65:46+ Ap 12 '65
Obituary
Christian Cent 82:421 Ap 7 '65

SEAGRAVE, Sterling
Burma surgeon's last battle. pors Sat Eve Post 238:38-40+ Jl 3 '65
—and Jones, R. A.
From China, with love. Esquire 65:42-7+ Ja '66

SEAGULLS. See Gulls

SEAL BEACH, Calif.
Council votes electronically. J. T. Williams. il Am City 80:150 My '65

SEAL hunting
Hell on an island; interview, ed. by J. Rearden. F. C. Johnson. il Outdoor Life 136:50-3+ S '65

SEALAB II. See Underwater laboratories

SEALING compositions
For weeping seams a silicone sealant. W. A. Evanko. il Motor B 115:29 Mr '65

SEALS (animals)
Sammy, the sociable seal; condensation of Seal summer. N. W. Hooke. il Read Digest 86:233-9+ Mr '65
Shaping and discriminative control of underwater click vocalizations in a California sea lion. R. J. Schusterman and S. H. Feinstein. bibliog il Science 150:1743-4 D 24 '65
Stalking seals under Antarctic ice; Weddell seal. C. Ray. il Nat Geog Mag 129:54-65 Ja '66
Underwater visual discrimination by the California sea lion. R. J. Schusterman and others. bibliog il Science 147:1594-6 Mr 26 '65
What seals talk about. Sci Digest 57:83 Mr '65

SEAMAN, Barbara
Why did birth control fail for me? Ladies Home J 82:166-7 N '65

SEAMANS, Robert C. Jr
Space and society; excerpts from remarks. Aviation W 83:17 N 22 '65

SEAMANSHIP. See Navigation

SEAMEN
Admiralty's happy wards. il Time 85:63-4 Ap 2 '65
AMA hits free care for merchant seamen. Sci N L 88:41 Jl 17 '65
Great mutiny, by J. Dugan. Review
New Repub 153:23-5 N 6 '65. J. Featherstone
Time il 86:104+ O 29 '65

SEANCES. See Spiritualism

SEAPLANES
CL-215 water bomber design modified; utility transport flying boat for use in fighting Canadian forest fires. D. A. Brown. il Aviation W 83:96-9+ Ag 16 '65
See also
Airplanes, Amphibious

SEAPORTS. See Ports
SEARCH warrants. See Warrants (law)
SEARLS, Hank
Astronaut, the novelist, and Cadwalder Glotz. Writer 78:24-5+ S '65
SEARS, Paul B.
Man or motor? Atlan 216:74-8 Jl '65
SEARS, Roebuck and company
Assertive Sears in a concrete cage; Sears retail store, Baton Rouge, La. il Arch Rec 137:209 My '65
Sears sweeps a path with no-cord vacuum; Kenmore cordless vac. il Bsns W p41 Je 12 '65
$12 billion boom: the aftermarket; auto-repair center in Hicksville, N.Y. il Newsweek 66:55-6 D 27 '65
SEASCAPES. See Marine painting; Photography—Marines
SEASHORE
    See also
Beaches
Shore protection
SEASHORE houses. See Beach architecture
SEASIDE gardens. See Gardens, Seaside
SEASIDE regional center, Conn. See State institutions
SEASIDE resorts
Following the lure of the sun; resorts boom. il Bsns W p30-1 Mr 6 '65
SEASONAL labor
Found! summer jobs for teen-agers; Youth-power, inc. M. A. Robertson. Bet Hom & Gard 43:31 My '65
Summer jobs that pay off. B. M. Silverman. il Parents Mag 40:54-5+ My '65
    See also
Migrant labor
SEASONING of lumber. See Lumber—Drying
SEASONINGS
    See also
Herbs
Parsley
Spices
SEASONS
Four seasons. E. Weeks. Atlan 216:134+ D '65
    See also
Autumn
Spring
Winter
SEAT belts. See Safety belts
SEATTLE
Whale's progress; Namu nearing Seattle. Sports Illus 23:7 Ag 2 '65
Yoo-hoo to Namu the whale. D. Connelly. il Sports Illus 23:18-23+ Jl 26 '65

Architecture
Bearing wall expressed in a skyscraper; IBM building, Seattle; with account by J. S. Hornbeck. il Arch Rec 137:123-8 F '65

Description
Love lyrics to a lake. E. Crimmin. il Motor B 116:40-1+ S '65
People of Seattle. K. Lamott. il Holiday 38:44-51+ Ag '65

Education
America's most wanted students; Seattle's public schools' program of business education. G. B. Leonard. il Look 29:46-51 Jl 27 '65
Case for the junior high school: the Nathan Eckstein school in Seattle. J. R. Warren. Atlan 215:120-3 Mr '65

History
Revolution in Seattle: a memoir, by H. O'Connor. Review
    Nation 200:228-9 Mr 1 '65. C. Adcock

Hospitals
Pain clinic; University of Washington hospital and school of medicine. E. Crimmin. il Sci Digest 57:66-70 F '65

Music
Monoliths, flourishing and busy. A. Rich. Hi Fi 15:115 Jl '65
Northwestern progress. F. J. Warnke. Opera N 29:36 My 1 '65
Question of musical maturity; Seattle report. R. Stromberg. Hi Fi 16:143 Ja '66
    See also
Seattle opera association
Seattle opera company

Pacific science center
Doctor Warren Weaver wins Arches of science award. Sci N L 88:232 O 9 '65

For outstanding contributions; first Arches of science award. Sci Am 213:48-9 N '65

Recreation
Ready, set, ski! pre-ski conditioning program. D. Brink. il Recreation 58:443 N '65

Religious institutions and affairs
Sephardim; Spanish-speaking Jew. J. Dash. il Américas 17:8-14 O '65

Water supply
Seattle: nature was a good provider. R. L. Cunningham. Sat R 48:76-7 O 23 '65
SEATTLE earthquake. See Earthquakes—United States
SEATTLE opera association
Pacific Sound; Seattle's new operatic concord. F. J. Warnke. il Opera N 29:28-31 F 6 '65
SEATTLE opera company
Seattle. F. J. Warnke. Opera N 30:30 D 18 '65
SEAWEED
    See also
Carrageen
Kelp
SEBACEOUS glands
Hereditary absence of sebaceous glands in the mouse. A. H. Gates and M. Karasek. bibliog il Science 148:1471-3 Je 11 '65
SEBASTIAN, Sister
Birthday card; poem. Commonweal 81:691 F 26 '65
SEBASTIAN, Ferd
To catch a model! U S Camera 28:54-5 Mr '65
SEBEOK, Thomas A.
Animal communication. bibliog Science 147:1006-14 F 26 '65
SECOND-best girl; story. See Buechler, J.
SECOND committee of the General assembly. See United Nations—Economic and financial committee
SECOND hand cameras. See Cameras, Used
SECOND impressions; story. See Shyer, M. F.
SECOND nature; story. See Knowlton, R. A.
SECONDARY recovery of oil. See Petroleum engineering
SECONDARY school teachers. See Teachers
SECONDARY schools. See High schools
SECOR (satellite) See Artificial satellites—Mapping applications
SECRET agents. See Spies
SECRET diplomacy. See Diplomacy
SECRET infidelity of Arthur Nydes; story. See Bayer. A.
SECRET of the box; story. See Böll, H.
SECRET police; story. See Household, G.
SECRET service
    See also
European war, 1914-1918—Secret service
Spies

China (People's Republic)
From China, with love. S. Seagrave and R. A. Jones. il Esquire 65:42-7+ Ja '66

United States
How secret service is being modernized. il U S News 59:12 N 22 '65
Overhaul; new table of organization. il Newsweek 66:39 N 22 '65
    See also
Presidents—United States—Protection
United States—Central intelligence agency

Venezuela
Downfall of the man with the dog; arrest of Communist agents in Caracas. M. Acoca. il Life 58:72C-72D Ap 30 '65
SECRET societies
Extremism in American politics. A. M. Schlesinger. il Sat R 48:21-5 N 27 '65
    See also
Ku Klux klan
SECRET; story. See Brodeur, P.
SECRETARIES (furniture) See Desks
SECRETARIES of the army (United States)
Advocate for the army. il Time 85:26 My 28 '65
SECRETIONS
Ant venoms, attractants, and repellents. G. K. K. Cavill and P. L. Robertson. bibliog il Science 149:1337-45 S 17 '65
Defensive secretion of a caterpillar, Papilio. T. Eisner and Y. C. Mainwald. bibliog il Science 150:1733-5 D 24 '65

SECRETIONS—*Continued*
Odorous secretion of normal and mutant tribolium confusum. M. Engelhardt and others. bibliog il Science 150:632-3 O 29 '65
  See also
Pheromones

SECRETS, Book of. See Manuscripts, Hebrew

SECRETS, Trade. See Trade secrets

SECTS
My thirty years with Father Devine. R. Boaz. il Ebony 20:88-90+ My '65
  See also
Lumpa sect (Zambia)
Mennonites
Mormons and Mormonism
New Thought

SECTS, Jewish. See Jewish sects

SECULAR institutes
Aggiornamento in vocations. V. Leary. America 112:548-51 Ap 17 '65

SECULARISM
Secular city, by H. Cox. Review
  Christian Cent 82:1038-9 Ag 25 '65. G. B. Hall
  Commonweal 82:658-62 S 17 '65. D. Callahan; Discussion. 83:4-5+, 137+ O 8, N 5 '65
  Time il 85:78 Ap 2 '65
Secular city; symposium. Commonweal 83:181-90 N 12 '65; Reply. P. A. Lockrey. 83:327+ D 17 '65
Today's city; threat or promise? concerning H. Cox's Secular city. M. L. Stackhouse. Christian Cent 82:1537-41 D 15 '65
  See also
Agnosticism
Irreligion

SECURITIES
New setback in Tokyo: Yamaichi securities co. $214-million in debt. Bsns W p 122 My 29 '65
Why Tokyo stocks skid. il Bsns W p70+ Jl 3 '65
  See also
Bonds
Investments
Stock exchange
Stocks
  also subhead Securities under various subjects, e.g. Airlines—Securities

Advertising
Should companies promote their own stocks? SEC investigates Genesco. C. J. Loomis. il Fortune 72:184-6+ D '65

Marketing
New-issue angles. Fortune 73:220 Ja '66
Security analyst and the corporation. il Duns R 85:41-2+ Mr '65
Specialist wheels the biggest stock deal; $17.3-million transaction in Union carbide. il Bsns W p 156+ My 22 '65

Regulation
Telling their secrets; unlisted companies comply with SEC disclosure requirements. Bsns W p 170+ O 16 '65

SECURITIES and exchange commission. See United States—Securities and exchange commission

SECURITY. See International security

SECURITY, Internal. See Internal security

SECURITY analysts. See Investments—Advisers

SECURITY and insecurity (psychology)
Anxiety; hidden threat to children's health. M. B. Hoover. il Parents Mag 40:74-6+ N '65
Can we increase intelligence? with study-discussion program, by R. Strang. L. W. Sontag. bibliog il PTA Mag 60:20-2, 33 N '65
Teenagers in search of themselves. G. B. Blaine, jr. il Parents Mag 40:46-8+ D '65

SECURITY classification (government documents)
Eyes only? photograph in New York times magazine reveals special intelligence designation. Nat R 17:313 Ap 20 '65
  See also
Defense information, Classified

SECURITY council of the United Nations. See United Nations—Security council

SECURITY insurance group
Iconoclast of insurance. il Duns R 86:62-4 O '65

SEDER. See Passover

SEDGWICK, Edie
Edie & Andy. il por Time 86:65+ Ag 27 '65

SEDIMENTATION and deposition
Isoprenoid hydrocarbons in recent sediments: presence of pristane and probable absence of phytane. M. Blumer and W. D. Snyder. bibliog il Science 150:1588-9 D 17 '65
Quaternary correlations across Bering Strait. D. M. Hopkins and others. bibliog il Science 147:1107-14 Mr 5 '65
Radioactivity: detection of gamma-ray emission in sediments in situ. D. Jennings and others. bibliog il Science 148:948-50 My 14 '65
Systematic relationships between carbon and oxygen isotopes in carbonates deposited by modern corals and algae. M. L. Keith and J. N. Weber. bibliog il Science 150:498-501 O 22 '65
Vertical density currents. W. H. Bradley. bibliog il Science 150:1423-8 D 10 '65
  See also
Deep sea deposits
Rocks, Sedimentary

SEDUMS
Try something different. D. E. Stebbins. il Pop Gard 16:14-15+ N '65

SEDWITZ, Walter J.
Common goal; economic and social progress. Américas 17:10-15 Ap '65

SEED, Randolph W. and Goldberg, I. H.
Iodination in relation to thyroglobulin maturation and subunit aggregation. bibliog Science 149:1380-2 S 17 '65

SEED catalogs. See Catalogs, Seed and plant

SEED drills. See Seeding machinery

SEED trade
Blooming big business! J. N. Miller. il Read Digest 86:17-18+ Mr '65

SEEDING
Corn soybeans sorghum; how thick should you plant? W. L. Colville and L. E. Zeman. il Suc Farm 64:36-7+ Ja '66
Plants ninety acres a day. B. Hardy. il Farm J 89:52D My '65
Will we go to permanent rows? C. E. Ball. il Farm J 89:32-3+ D '65
  See also
Corn—Seeding
Seeding machinery

SEEDING machinery
Grain drill that plants row crops. il Farm J 89:66 Ap '65

SEEDLINGS
They grew inside a plastic bag. il Sunset 134:238 Mr '65

SEEDS
Patience with peas; dormant seed. Time 87:54 Ja 14 '66
Seed packets: 1966. il House & Gard 129:144-5+ Ja '66
  See also
Cottonseed
Seed trade

Dispersal
Angiosperm parasite and host: coordinated dispersal. P. R. Atsatt. bibliog il Science 149:1389-90 S 17 '65
Seed dispersal velocity in four dwarfmistletoes. T. E. Hinds and F. G. Hawksworth. bibliog il Science 148:517-19 Ap 23 '65
Spread of a parasite: dwarfmistletoe. F. C. Hawksworth and T. E. Hinds. il Natur Hist 74:52-7 Mr '65

SEEGER, Pete
Ballad of Pete Seeger. P. Lyon. por Holiday 38:83-4+ Jl '65
Needed: a Lutheran profile of courage. Christian Cent 82:356 Mr 24 '65

SEEGERS, Winnifred, and others
Double beta-lipoprotein: a new genetic variant in man. bibliog Science 149:303-4 Jl 16 '65

SEEMAN, Elizabeth
Tumblin' Creek's cabin library. S. C. Gross. il pors Sr Schol 87:sup 17-19 S 30 '65

SEEMAN, Ernest
Tumblin' Creek's cabin library. S. C. Gross. il pors Sr Schol 87:sup 17-19 S 30 '65

SEESE, Ronald
Simple self-resetting tamper-alarm. Pop Electr 23:61-2 Jl '65

SEGAL, Aaron
Africa's new Verwoerd. New Repub 153:13-14 S 18 '65

SEGAL, George, 1924-
Silent people; exhibition at New York's Sidney Janis gallery. il por Newsweek 66:104+ O 25 '65

SEGAL, George, 1934?-
Happy to be a king. A. Guerin. il pors Life 59:141-2 N 19 '65

SEGAL, Lore
Memories of a brownshirt girlhood. New Repub 153:23-8 Ag 21 '65

about

Contraband life. C. Ozick. Commentary 39: 89-90+ Mr '65

SEGREGATION, Social
See also
Discrimination in housing

SEGREGATION in education
Another first for Massachusetts; ban de facto school segregation. il Time 86:56 Ag 27 '65
Balancing imbalances; Massachusetts outlaws de facto segregation. Newsweek 66:74 Ag 30 '65
Black and white schools; separate and unequal schools in South. New Repub 153:5-6 O 9 '65
Boston's busing battle; Louise Day Hicks fight to keep Negroes from busing their children out of black districts into white neighborhood schools. il Time 86:70 S 24 '65
Boston's race dilemma; threat to cut off U.S. school funds. U S News 59:37 Ag 23 '65
Even Stephens; protests in Crawfordville, Ga. il Time 86:31 O 15 '65
Segregation in the North. il Newsweek 66: 56+ S 20 '65

SEGREGATION of Negroes. See Negroes in the United States—Segregation

SEHON, Alec
Stereospecificity. Science 148:401-4+ Ap 16 '65

SEIB, Charles B.
Every problem is an opportunity; interview. Nations Bsns 53:40-1+ My '65
How Congress may bust the budget. Nations Bsns 53:38-9+ Mr '65
Who the President listens to. Nations Bsns 53:32-3+ Ap '65

—and Otten, A. L.
Abe, help! LBJ. Esquire 63:86-8+ Je '65

SEIBEL, Kathryn
Make your own flowers. Farm J 89:76 S '65

SEIBERLING, Dorothy
Mastering the maze. Life 58:60A Ap 9 '65
Pursuing fame and the famous. Durig fell back on fraud. Life 58:68-71 Je 4 '65
Trying to be a genius. Life 59:75-6+ N 12 '65

SEIDEL, Frederick
Berryman's dream songs. Poetry 105:257-9 Ja '65

SEIDL, Anthony E.
Those expensive lay teachers. Commonweal 82:147-50+, 391 Ap 23, Je 11 '65

SEIDMAN, Arthur H.
Evolving transistor. Electr World 73:30-3+ Mr '65
Testers for semiconductor devices. Electr World 74:42-4+ S '65

SEIDMAN, Joel
Labor movement today; a diagnosis. Mo Labor R 88:149 F '65

SEIELSTAD, George A. See Berge, G. L. jt. auth.

SEIF, Morton
Béjart at the Paris festival. Sat R 49:49+ Ja 15 '66

SEIFERT, William W.
Trains at 300 mph, what travel of future will be like; interview. por U S News 59:96-9 Jl 26 '65

SEINE RIVER
Barges on the Seine. C. Frankel. il Harper 230:60-5 My '65

SEISMIC sea waves
Tsunami runup; United States-Japan cooperative science program; report on symposium. W. G. Van Dorn. Science 149: 566 Jl 30 '65

SEISMOGRAPHS
Earthquake detector. B. W. Powell. il Pop Sci 187:135-8+ D '65
Resonant vibrations of the earth. F. Press. il Sci Am 213:28-37 bibliog(p 142) N '65

SEISMOLOGICAL stations
Predicting the shock; seismograph network to predict earth tremors. Bsns W p 135 O 16 '65

SEISMOLOGY
Earth tremors generated by Old Faithful geyser. J. S. Rinehart. bibliog il Science 150:494-6 O 22 '65
Nuclear listening post; Montana system. Large aperture seismic array. il Time 86: 52-3 Ag 13 '65
Progress in seismic recording and analysis; report on meeting of the Royal society. V. K. McElheny. il Science 147:1271-3 Mr 12 '65

SEITZ, Frederick
Academy reelects Seitz. Sci N L 87:132 F 27 '65
National academy; Seitz elected to full-time, six year presidency amidst signs of greater activity. D. S. Greenberg. por Science 147: 715-16 F 12 '65

SEITZ, William
New perceptual art. Vogue 145:78-80+ F 15 '65

SELBY, Anne. See Selby, E. jt. auth.

SELBY, Earl, and Selby, Anne
California's jackpot for the jobless. Read Digest 86:67-70 Je '65
Three girls who were born again. Read Digest 87:133-6 S '65
Why the dole doesn't work. Read Digest 86:79-83 Mr '65

SELBY, Hope
Vietnamese students talk about the war. N Y Times Mag p 104-5+ O 31 '65

SELDEN, Armistead I.
Excerpt from debate, September 20, 1965. Cong Digest 44:280+ N '65

SELDEN, David
Personal opinion; needed: more teacher strikes. por Sat R 48:75 My 15 '65

SELDEN, William K.
Governance of higher education; adaptation of annual report. Science 149:711 Ag 13 '65

SELDON, Niles Avery
City cars; poem. Horn Bk 41:418 Ag '65

SELECT magazines, incorporated
Large magazine distributors charged by justice dept. Pub W 187:76 Je 21 '65

SELECTION of students. See Student selection

SELECTIONS, Literary. See Literature—Collections

SELECTIVE service, Military. See Military service, Compulsory

SELENOGRAPHY. See Moon—Surface

SELF
Images in the lonely crowd; awareness of self; address, April 3, 1965. J. A. Dyal. Vital Speeches 31:729-35 S 15 '65

SELF assurance. See Self reliance

SELF confidence. See Self reliance

SELF culture
Strategies for self-education. W. R. Dill and others. bibliog f Harvard Bsns R 43:119-30 N '65
What you can do with an hour a day. O. Schisgall. Read Digest 86:83-5 Ap '65

SELF defense
See also
Judo

SELF defense for women
Hatpin or tear gas for a lady's defense? concerning a booklet by G. Accas and J. H. Eckstein. Consumer Bul 48:17-18 S '65

SELF-denial
Self-denial. D. J. Lehman and J. E. Corrigan. il America 112:391-3 Mr 20 '65
Word. V. P. McCorry. America 112:233-4 F 13 '65

SELF disclosure. See Human relations

SELF education. See Self culture

SELF employed
New rules for self-pensioning? U S News 58:122 Je 21 '65

SELF evaluation
High school students' self-rating. Sch & Soc 93:291-2 Sum '65
Voice of the self. A. T. Jersild. NEA J 54: 23-5 O '65
What you can learn about yourself. M. R. Feinberg. il Nations Bsns 53:40-1+ F '65
Where do you stand with the boss? R. Dreyfack. il Nations Bsns 53:74-5+ N '65

SELF feeders, Cattle. See Cattle self feeders

SELF government. See Democracy

SELF improvement. See Self culture

SELF knowledge. See Self evaluation

SELF-leadership for all nationalities today (organization) See Civil rights organizations

SELF love
See also
Autism

SELF-medication. See Medicine

SELF murder. See Suicide

SELF portraits. See Portraits

SELF ratings. See Self evaluation

SELF reliance
Importance of self confidence; address, February 26, 1965. L. F. McCollum. Vital Speeches 31:441-4 My 1 '65
Self-reliance or self-destruction; address, April 27, 1965. G. Dudley, jr. Vital Speeches 31:632-4 Ag 1 '65

SELF respect
How to succeed as a teen-ager. P. L. Levin. il N Y Times Mag p94+ Ap 18 '65
SELIG, Richard
Poetry chronicle. C. Urdang. Poetry 105: 341-2 F '65
SELIGMAN, Ben B.
Capitalism today. Commentary 39:88-90 Ap '65
SELIGMAN, Daniel
One way to sell anything. Fortune 71:162-5 Je '65
SELIGMAN, Henry
Henry Seligman's Sisters of mercy. S. White. il por Sat R 48:68-71 O 2 '65
SELLARS, Dorothy Rainer
Small town teacher. J. Anderson. il por Dance Mag 39:52-5 Jl '65
SELLER, Arthur
Arthur Seller: pictures by design, not accident. il Pop Phot 57:150-1+ N '65
SELLERS, Johnny
Yow! make way for the new Sellers! il pors Sports Illus 23:22-4+ S 6 '65
SELLING. See Marketing
SELLING by telephone. See Telephone selling
SELLS, Bruce H.
Puromycin: effect on messenger RNA synthesis and β-galactosidase formation in escherichia coli 15T-. bibliog Science 148: 371-3 Ap 16 '65
SELMA, Ala.
American tragedy; state troopers charge marching Negroes. il Newsweek 65:18-21 Mr 22 '65
Behind the Selma march. M. L. King, jr. il Sat R 48:16-17+ Ap 3 '65
Beyond the bridge; race relations. P. Good. il Reporter 32:23-6 Ap 8 '65
Black eye; Sheriff Jim Clark vs. Mrs Cooper. il Newsweek 65:24 F 8 '65
Boomerang in Neverland. il Sr Schol 86:17-19 Mr 25 '65
Central point; Negro struggle to achieve the right to vote. il Time 85:23-8 Mr 19 '65
Charge to the jury; concerning J. A. Hare's address to the Selma grand jury investigating murder of J. J. Reeb. Time 85:28 Ap 23 '65
Ethics of Selma. M. L. Stackhouse. Commonweal 82:75-7 Ap 9 '65
Forced march; Negro voter-registration campaign. il Newsweek 65:24+ F 22 '65
From Selma: the stench of freedom. R. Featherstone. Negro Hist Bul 28:130 Mr '65
How the army got set to move into Selma; What really happened on Alabama march? excerpts from statement to Congress, April 27, 1965. W. L. Dickinson. il U S News 58:16-17 My 10 '65
It looks like a hot summer; with Selma the beginning. il U S News 58:32-3 Mr 22 '65
Letter from Selma. R. Adler. New Yorker 41:121-2+ Ap 10 '65
Letters from Washington. R. H. Rovere. New Yorker 41:177-8+ Mr 20 '65
Nuns at Selma. Sister Thomas Marguerite. America 112:454-6 Ap 3 '65
Perchance a good man will die for a friend; Negro or white, dies in the struggle for racial justice. Christian Cent 82:388-9 Mr 31 '65
Power to protect; use of federal forces. New Repub 152:5-6 Mr 20 '65
Registering Negro voters in the South; necessity for federal voting referees. A. M. Bickel. New Repub 152:9-10 F 20 '65
Remarks to the New York police department Holy name society, April 4, 1965. W. F. Buckley, jr. Nat R 17:324-6 Ap 20 '65
Salvaging Selma; efforts of the Edmundite fathers and brothers. America 112:238 F 20 '65
Selma. Commonweal 82:3-4 Mr 26 '65
Selma. A. Kopkind. New Repub 152:7-9 Mr 20 '65
Selma and Sharpeville. D. Berrigan. Commonweal 82:71-5 Ap 9 '65; Discussion. 82: 230 My '65
Selma; beatings start the savage season. il Life 58:30-7 Mr 19 '65
Selma campaign. Nat R 17:227 Mr 23 '65
Selma campaign; justification of non-violence. Commonweal 81:684-5 F 26 '65
Selma, civil rights, and the church militant. il Newsweek 65:75-6+ Mr 29 '65
Selma, contd; woman beaten by sheriff during registration drive. Time 85:24 F 5 '65
Selma: sustaining the momentum. D. Peerman and M. E. Marty. Christian Cent 82: 358-60 Mr 24 '65
Selma's shame. America 112:386 Mr 20 '65
Siege of Selma. Nation 200:154+ F 15 '65

So much Christian unity in Selma; congregation at the memorial service for the Rev. James Reeb. M. McGrory. America 112:448 Ap 3 '65
Stalemate in Selma. E. A. Smith. Christian Cent 82:1031-3 Ag 25 '65
Struggle in Selma. il Sr Schol 86:17-18 F 11 '65
Three strangers in Selma; day of the memorial service for the slain minister, Rev. James Reeb. S. Alexander. Life 58:28 Mr 26 '65
Victory in jail. il Time 85:16-17 F 12 '65
Walk in Alabama. A. Kopkind. New Repub 152:7-8 Ap 3 '65
Where's the spirit of Selma now? G. Talese. il N Y Times Mag p8-9+ My 30 '65
Why the Negro children march. P. Watters. il N Y Times Mag p28-9+ Mr 21 '65
SELTZER, Louis Benson
Cleveland: saving Lake Erie. Sat R 48:36+ O 23 '65

about

Mr Cleveland bows out. por Time 87:58 Ja 14 '66
Something missing here. Newsweek 67:83-4 Ja 17 '66
SELWAY, Neville Carr
Our far-flung correspondents. H. W. Wind. il New Yorker 41:138-46+ My 22 '65
SELWAY-BITTERROOT wilderness area. See Wilderness areas
SELYE, Hans
Induced hypersensitivity to cold. Science 149:201 Jl 9 '65
SELZNICK, David Oliver
Epic man. il por Newsweek 66:82 Jl 5 '65
Producer prince. il pors Time 86:62 Jl 2 '65
SEMANTICS
Words under a mask. S. Fersh. bibliog f il UNESCO Courier 18:9-12+ F '65; Reply. V. Zvegintsev. 18:33 S '65
SEMEN
Polymorphic spermatozoa in the hymenopterous wasp dahlbominus. P. E. Lee and A. Wilkes. bibliog il Science 147:1445-6 Mr 19 '65
Sperm capacitation by uterine fluid or beta-amylase in vitro. K. T. Kirton and H. D. Hafs. bibliog il Science 150:618-19 O 29 '65
SEMICONDUCTOR lasers. See Lasers
SEMICONDUCTOR transducers. See Transducers
SEMICONDUCTORS
European semiconductor code. P. Halliday. Electr World 74:62 Ag '65
IBM buys its own sales pitch: System 360 computers in six plants. il Bsns W p 140-2+ O 30 '65
See also
Electric current rectifiers
Transistors

Testing

Testers for semiconductor devices. A. H. Seidman. il Electr World 74:42-4+ S '65
Testing semiconductors with V.O.M. or V.T.V.M. C. D. Todd. il Electr World 74: 31-4+ S '65
SEMINARIANS. See Theological students
SEMINARIES. See Theological schools
SEMINOLE Indians
Seminoles' long road to victory; right to compensation for loss of lands in Florida. W. Hartley and E. Hartley. Read Digest 86:199-200+ F '65
SEMITIC civilization. See Civilization, Semitic
SEMONIN, Paul F.
No man's land. Nation 201:535-7 D 27 '65
SEMPERVIVA. See Houseleeks
SEMPLE, Robert B. Jr
White House on the Pedernales. N Y Times Mag p54-5+ O 31 '65
SEN, Dipak K.
Disarmament proposal. Bul Atomic Sci 21:35-6 F '65
SENANAYAKE, Dudley
Change in direction? por Sr Schol 86:25 Ap 15 '65
Madame's exit. por Time 85:29-30 Ap 2 '65
Pledge to battle. Time 85:28 Ap 9 '65
Shift to the center. Newsweek 65:44 Ap 5 '65
SENATE (United States) See United States—Congress—Senate
SENATE restaurant. See Washington, D.C.—Hotels, restaurants, etc.
SENATORS
Congress: a crop of bright young men. il Newsweek 66:35 N 8 '65
Requiem for a racist bloc. Life 58:4 My 21 '65

SENATORS—*Continued*
Southern bloc, how it's changing. il U S
News 58:17-18 My 3 '65
Time has come; H. F. Byrd's resignation.
il Newsweek 66:40 N 22 '65
Two senators named Kennedy. il Newsweek
67:17-20+ Ja 17 '66
See also
United States—Congress—Senate
SENATORS (baseball) See Baseball clubs
SENCOURT, Robert
Winston Churchill; letter. Commonweal 81:
750-1 Mr 12 '65
SENDAK, Maurice
Aliveness of Peter rabbit; address, June
1965. Wilson Lib Bul 40:345-8 D '65
SENECA, Lucius Annaeus
Seneca as educational thinker. W. W. Brick-
man. Sch & Soc 93:362 O 16 '65
SENECA Indians
Senecas lose again. Nat Parks Mag 39:21
F '65
SENEGAL
See also
United Nations—Senegal
SENESCENCE in plants. See Age (plants)
SENEY, Noel
What are you doing with the cars at your
house? Bet Hom & Gard 43:50-3 Ag '65
SENGHOR, Léopold Sédar
Teilhard de Chardin and the Afro-Asian
world. T. P. Melady and M. B. Melady.
Cath World 202:102-6 N '65
SENIOR citizen clubs. See Recreation for the
aged
SENIOR scholastic (periodical)
Introducing Scholastic teacher's contribut-
ing editors. il Sr Schol 87:sup 14 N 11 '65
Scholastic's 45th birthday. J. K. Lippert. il
Sr Schol 87:4-5 O 21 '65
SENN, Edouard
From a French friend; letter. Bul Atomic
Sci 21:49-51 Je '65
SENN, George R.
Story of a man who tried to help. il U S
News 58:64 Mr 29 '65
SENN, Milton J. E.
New light on an old mystery: the common
cold. McCalls 93:136-7 N '65
Pedodontics: children's own dentistry. Mc-
Calls 93:38+ Ja '66
What parents ask. See issues of McCall's
to October 1965
SENOFSKY, Berl
Musical truth; performance of Prokofiev's
Second violin concerto in Carnegie Hall.
il por Newsweek 67:80-1 Ja 24 '66
SENSE organs
See also
Nose
SENSENICH corporation
It all began with a bedstead. J. Gilbert. il
Flying 77:50-3 S '65
SENSES and sensation
Four sensations. A. Lebrón-Pumarol. il
Américas 17:31-4 Je '65
See also
Perception
Reaction time
Taste
SENSORY aid for the blind. See Blind, Ap-
paratus for the
SENSORY receptors. See Nervous system,
Sympathetic
SENTENCE, Imposing of. See Justice, Admin-
istration of
SENTENCES (grammar) See English language
—Grammar
SENTER, Raymond D. pseud.
McNamara-Kennedy doctrine. New Repub
152:21-2 F 13 '65
Military moves into space. New Repub 153:
11-13 S 11 '65
Nuclear weapons in orbit. New Repub 153:11-
12 N 27 '65; 154:36 Ja 1 '66
Up comes the navy. New Repub 152:12-13
F 27 '65
SENTRONIC system. See Library protection
systems
SEPARATIONS, Marital. See Domestic rela-
tions
SEPHARDIM
Sephardim. J. Dash. il Américas 17:8-14 O
'65
SEPTEMBER
In September; few of the dates, memorable
and not so, coming up next month (title
varies) (cont) il N Y Times Mag p36+ Ag
29 '65
Les SÉQUESTRÉS d'Altona; drama. See Sartre,
J. P.
SEQUOIA
See also
Redwood

SEQUOIA park, Salem, Ore. See Salem, Ore.
—Parks and playgrounds
SERF, Barbara
Fiery fatalist. por Newsweek 66:99 O 11 '65
SERGEANT, Elizabeth Shepley
Obituary
Pub W 187:102 F 8 '65
SERGEANT fish fishing
Anyway you look at cobia. K. Osborne. il
Outdoor Life 135:50-2+ Mr '65
SERGI, Arturo
Boomerang; interview, ed. by F. Stevenson.
por Opera N 29:30 Mr 27 '65
SERIAL publications
Cost indexes for 1965: U.S. periodicals and
serial services. H. M. Welch; N. B.
Brown and W. H. Huff. il Library J 90:
2964-7 Jl '65
SERIGRAPHY. See Silk screen printing
SERINE
Enrichment of serine-acceptor soluble RNA
by nucleic acid gels. P. P. Hung. bibliog
il Science 149:639-40 Ag 6 '65
SERKIN, Peter
Family affair. por Newsweek 65:81 Mr 1 '65
Music to my ears; playing of Mozart's F
major concerto with Philadelphia orchestra.
I. Kolodin. Sat R 48:30 Mr 6 '65
SERLING, Rod
Person who changed my life. por Seventeen
24:157 Ap '65
Will the real Dutch uncle please stand up?
por Seventeen 24:110+ Jl '65
SERLY, Tibor
Shadow of genius. R. Ellsworth. il pors Am
Rec G 32:26-33 S '65
SERMONS
Sermon seminar in a parish church; lay-
men participation. M. M. Eakin. Chris-
tian Cent 83:75-7 Ja 19 '66
See also
Preaching
SEROTONIN
5-Hydroxytryptamine in single neoplastic
mast cells: a microscopic spectrofluoro-
metric study. L. S. Van Orden and others.
bibliog il Science 148:642-4 Ap 30 '65
5-Hydroxytryptophan decarboxylase in rat
brain: effect of hypothalamic lesions. A.
Heller and others. bibliog il Science 147:
887-8 F 19 '65
Serotonin and adenosine triphosphate: synergistic effect of the beat frequency of
cilia of mussel gills. S. L. Schor. bibliog
il Science 148:500-1 Ap 23 '65
Serotonin: synthesis and release from the
myenteric plexus of the mouse intestine.
M. D. Gershon and others. bibliog il Science 149:197-9 Jl 9 '65
SERRA international
Forward stride of Serra; convention, Miami
Beach. America 113:70-1 Jl 17 '65; Discus-
sion. 113:146, 270, 423 Ag 14, S 18, O 16 '65
SERUM
Allograft survival: effect of antiserums to
thymus glands and lymphocytes. H. Nagaya
and H. O. Sieker. bibliog il Science 150:
1181-2 N 26 '65
Serum protein electrophoresis in acrylamide
gel: patterns from normal human subjects.
A. C. Peacock and others. bibliog il Science
147:1451-3 Mr 19 '65
See also
Blood—Plasma
Complements (immunity)
SERUM globulins
Genetic factors and polypeptide chain subclasses of human immunoglobulin G
detected in chimpanzee serums. F. P.
Alepa and W. D. Terry. bibliog il Science
150:1293-4 D 3 '65
Immunoglobulin A production in ataxia
telangiectasia. D. E. McFarlin and others.
bibliog il Science 150:1175-7 N 26 '65
Immunoglobulin structure: amino- and car-
boxyl-terminal peptides of type I Bence
Jones proteins. K. Titani and F. W. Put-
nam. bibliog Science 147:1304-5 Mr 12 '65
Immunoglobulin structure: partial amino acid
sequence of a Bence Jones protein. K.
Titani and others. bibliog il Science 149:
1090-2 S '65; Reply with rejoinder. D. W.
Talmage 150:1484-5 D 10 '65
SERVANTS. See Household employees
SERVICE
Big-hearted Buttercup. il Ebony 20:47-8+
F '65
Can I help? E. Hill. Read Digest 87:25+
N '65
SERVICE (in industry)
American repairman: a vanishing breed? il
U S News 59:88-90 S 13 '65
How to escape the serviceman syndrome.
E. S. Oshin. House & Gard 127:140-1+
Je '65

SERVICE, Community. See Community service

SERVICE, Volunteer. See Volunteer service

SERVICE hatches. See Pass-throughs

SERVICE industries
    See also
Public service industries
Repairing

SERVICE men

Pay, allowances, etc.
    See United States—Armed forces—Pay, allowances, etc.

Recreation
    See subhead Recreation under divisions of the armed forces, e.g. United States—Air force—Recreation

SERVICE men, Discharged
    See also
Discharge, Military

Benefits
Veteran against veteran; dollars wasted. J. E. Booth. il Atlan 216:88-91 O '65; Discussion. 216:38+ D '65

Education
Coming: new GI bill of rights? U S News 59:42 Ag 30 '65
Education begets education; GI bill twenty years later. J. R. Emens. il Am Ed 1:11-13 S '65
G.I. bill for all cold war veterans? pro and con discussion. il Sr Schol 86:18-20 Mr 4 '65
On the way: new bill of rights for GI's. il U S News 60:8 Ja 24 '66

United States
    See Service men, Discharged

SERVICE men, Retired
Retired at forty-five, and hunting for a job. il Changing T 19:25-8 F '65
SERVICE mens benefits. See Service men, Discharged—Benefits
SERVICE mens families
Christmas: at home and in Vietnam. il Newsweek 66:13-17 D 27 '65
U.S. dependents overseas: how many; and where they are. il U S News 58:6 F 22 '65
Vietnam as one family faces it; Boyt family; with reports by B. Wise, M. Silva and R. Morse. il Life 59:74-87+ D 10 '65
Vietnam crisis: what happens when war separates a young family; Captain D. Moore's family. W. C. Heinz. il Ladies Home J 82:74-5+ S '65
SERVICE mens graves
Still quiet on the western front. G. Smith. il Am Heritage 16:20-5+ O '65; Excerpt. Sat Eve Post 238:78-85 N 6 '65
SERVICE mens letters. See Letters from service men
SERVICE mens pensions. See Pensions, Military
SERVICE mens readjustment act of 1944. See Service men, Discharged—Education
SERVICE mens widows. See Widows
SERVICE stations. See Airplane service stations; Automobile service stations
SERVING trays. See Trays
SESPE wildlife area. See Wildlife sanctuaries
SESSA, Frank B.
Filling the gap in Miami. Wilson Lib Bul 40:255-6 N '65
SESTAK, Tom
King of crash, haul and hit. E. Shrake. il Sports Illus 23:71-4 O 25 '65
SETLOW, R. B. See Donnellan, J. E. jr. jt. auth.
SETON, Cynthia
Little girls lost: how parents fail their daughters. Redbook 125:45+ My '65
Reward the years bring. Redbook 125:67+ O '65
SETON Hall university, South Orange, N.J.
Newark; Francesca da Rimini. J. W. Freeman. il Opera N 30:32 Ja 15 '66
SEUSS, Dr, pseud. See Geisel, T. S.
SEVAREID, Eric
Final troubled hours of Adlai Stevenson. Look 29:81-4+ N 30 '65
SEVEN Sisters (constellation) See Pleiades
SEVENTEEN-nation disarmament conference, Geneva, 1962-. See Conference of the Eighteen-nation committee on disarmament, Geneva, 1962-
SEVER, John L. and others
Rubella complement fixation test. bibliog Science 148:385-7 Ap 16 '65

SEVERANCE pay. See Wages—Dismissal wage

SEVERIN, Kurt
Figurines of the Carajá: photographs. Natur Hist 74:54-5 Ap '65
SEVERO, Richard
Automation, printers and publishers. New Repub 152:16 Mr 13 '65
SEVILLE, Spain
Holy week in Seville. A. Mayor. il Holiday 37:80-5 Ap '65
SEWAGE
New way to clean water and reuse it; Hyperion treatment plant, Playa del Rey, Calif. P. Comen and R. Jacobson. il Sci Digest 57:89-91 My '65
SEWAGE disposal
New sewage-treatment process uses coal. il Am City 81:105+ Ja '66
Plastic sewers serve a wharf; Santa Cruz, Calif. C. R. Bengston. il Am City 80:94-5 S '65
Sewerage and sewage purification. See Issues of American city
    See also
Sewage lagoons
Sewage pumping
Water pollution

Activated sludge method
How biological oxidation works in theory and practice. H. Edde. il Am City 80:92-5 F '65

Filtration
Salt water in the sewers; North Miami, Fla. F. J. Miller. il Am City 80:112+ D '65
Scum yields to a screw conveyor at a sewage-purification plant, Harrisburg, Pa. L. A. Ritter. il Am City 80:108-9 Je '65
Trickling filter overcomes shock loads; Ortonville, Minn. R. L. Smith and T. N. Rodeberg. il Am City 80:29 O '65
Vacuum flotation replaces primary settling; Fresno, Calif. M. J. Carozza and R. J. Theroux. il Am City 80:79-81 F '65
We chose three-stage sewage purification; Mound, Minn. L. L. Kopp. il Am City 80:89-91 D '65

Grease and oil removal
Keeping grease traps free of accumulations. Consumer Bul 48:34 S '65
SEWAGE disposal plants
Duquesne, Pa, breaks precedent; new sewage treatment plant. W. T. McPhee. il Am City 80:93-6 O '65
Extras pay dividends; Missoula's water-pollution-control plant. R. A. Haverfield. il Am City 80:101-3 N '65
New idea in sludge dewatering; Caldwell, N.J. plant. G. A. Valente. il Am City 80:95-7 Jl '65
New way to clean water and reuse it; Hyperion treatment plant, Playa del Rey, Calif. P. Comen and R. Jacobson. il Sci Digest 57:89-91 My '65
People wanted this plant; first major sewage-treatment plant built on Oahu since 1927. Y. Kunimoto. il Am City 80:89-90 My '65
Scum yields to a screw conveyor at a sewage-purification plant, Harrisburg, Pa. L. A. Ritter. il Am City 80:108-9 Je '65
Sewerage and sewage purification. See Issues of American city
This plant can do tricks; Portland, Ore. il Am City 80:110-12 O '65
Vacuum flotation replaces primary settling; Fresno, Calif. M. J. Carozza and R. J. Theroux. il Am City 80:79-91 F '65

Electric equipment
Follow these four cardinal rules: ways to get maximum performance from electrical equipment in water and sewage plants. W. Schneider. il Am City 80:104-6 D '65
SEWAGE flow
Holding basin cuts bypasses; Ann Arbor, Mich. J. C. Seeley. Am City 80:22 D '65
SEWAGE lagoons
How biological oxidation works in theory and practice. H. Edde. il Am City 80:92-5 F '65
SEWAGE pumping
Progressive design ideas cancel corrosion; sewer lift stations, Alburquerque, N.M. K. Lawson. il Am City 81:90-1 Ja '66
SEWAGE treatment plants. See Sewage disposal plants
SEWALL family
Sewall coat-of-arms. H. K. Eilers. il Hobbies 70:126-7 Ja '66
SEWANEE college. See University of the South, Sewanee, Tenn.

SEWER cleaning
250 feet of sewer obstruction; Compton, Calif. D. W. Robins. il Am City 80:136+ F '65

SEWER inspection
Inspecting 11½ miles of sewers from the inside; Anchorage, Alaska. H. D. Shanks. il Am City 80:118+ S '65

SEWER pipes
All-underwater pipe crew; places San Diego's new outfall sewer. il Am City 80:111 Ag '65
Plastic sewers serve a wharf; Santa Cruz, Calif. C. R. Bengston. il Am City 80:94-5 S '65
Plea for short sewers. R. L. Smith; reply. J. D. Parkhurst. il Am City 80:120+ My '65
Zinc cable provides cathodic protection; Washington, D.C. il Am City 80:30 Mr '65
See also
Sewer cleaning

Leakage
Soil fumigants control roots in sewers; Milwaukee, Wis. G. Z. Rayner. il Am City 80: 135-6 Je '65

Repairing
New strength for an old sewer; Atlanta. R. A. Nixon. il Am City 80:33 Ap '65
Photographing sewers doesn't cost a cent; Westfield, N.J. B. F. Murphy. il Am City 80:112-13 Mr '65
TV plus grout; bargain repairs for leaking sewer systems; Indianapolis. il Am City 80: 112-13 Ap '65

SEWERAGE
Controlling pollution from combined sewers; studies in Chicago area. Am City 81:13 Ja '66

SEWING
How to sew a fine seam. C. Houck. il Parents Mag 40:105 Je '65
Redbook's guide to home sewing. il Redbook 126:85-92 N '65
Sewing is a mother's art for gifts galore. il Bet Hom & Gard 43:40-1+ D '65
Stay-stitch in time. C. Houck. il Parents Mag 40:78 Ap '65
What's new in home sewing; work saving innovations. M. Garrity. il Bet Hom & Gard 43:114+ My '65
See also
Needlework
Thread

Study and teaching
Best way to sew on buttons. C. Houck. il Parents Mag 41:104 Ja '66
See also
Clothing and dress—Study and teaching

Terminology
Simple glossary of sewing. Bet Hom & Gard 43:118+ Ap '65

SEWING boxes
Swing-out sewing caddy. S. Ellingson. il Pop Mech 124:166-7 N '65

SEWING cabinets. See Cabinets (furniture)

SEWING equipment
Fold-away cutting table. R. Martens. il Farm J 89:80 O '65
Hang on to your needle and thread; instant button-on. il Consumer Rep 30:474-5 O '65
Sewing center on wheels. R. Martens. il Farm J 89:81 O '65

SEWING machine cabinets. See Cabinets (furniture)

SEWING machines
Sewing machines. Consumer Bul 48:18 Mr '65

SEWING rooms
It's easy to create your own sewing center. B. G. Wadsworth. il Parents Mag 40:58+ Jl '65
Sewing-utility room. il Sunset 135:140+ N '65
Trim your sewing corner. C. Houck. il Parents Mag 40:116 S '65

SEX
Down with sex! M. Muggeridge. Esquire 63: 72-4 F '65
Pop sex; some sex symbols of the sixties. R. R. Lingeman. il Mlle 62:184-5+ N '65
Secrets of sex; climate for research. il Newsweek 65:58+ Ap 26 '65
Sex under socialism. E. Pawel. Commentary 40:90+ S '65; Reply with rejoinder. J. Weber. 41:14+ Ja '66

SEX (biology)
Heterothallism in biflagellate aquatic fungi; preliminary genetic analysis. J. T. Mullins and J. R. Raper. bibliog Science 150:1174-5 N 26 '65
Lovely lady with a very fishy reputation; E. Clark of Cape Haze marine laboratory, Sarasota, Fla. C. Phinizy. il Sports Illus 23: 46-50 O 4 '65

Sex-linkage of erythrocyte glucose-6-phosphate dehydrogenase in two species of wild hares. S. Ohno and others. bibliog il Science 150:1737-8 D 24 '65
See also
Gynandromorphism
Hermaphroditism

SEX and law
See also
Prostitution

SEX and religion
Christ's sexuality. il Time 85:59 Ap 9 '65
Love in place of law? gathering at Harvard divinity school to ponder the new morality and its significance for the church. Time 85:42+ Mr 5 '65
Sex and youth; pastoral directives of the German episcopate. Cath World 201:264-8 Jl '65

SEX attractants (insects) See Insect sex attractants

SEX behavior
Cerebral temperature changes accompanying sexual activity in the male rat. C. D. Hull and others. bibliog il Science 149:89-90 Jl 2 '65
Deviance and deviates. H. S. Becker. Nation 201:115-19 S 20 '65
Dialogue with mothers; young children's sex behavior. B. Bettelheim. Ladies Home J 82:62+ O '65
Don Marquis to the young; letter, ed. by C. O'Neill. D. Marquis. Esquire 63:77+ My '65
I'm sorry, dear; excerpt from Ways of the will. L. H. Farber; discussion. Commentary 39:14+ Ap; 8+ My '65
Mirror display in the squirrel monkey, saimiri sciureus. P. D. MacLean; reply with rejoinder. P. Hershkovitz. Science 147:1156-7 Mr 5 '65
Monkey business; experiment suggesting psychosexual behavior determined chemically in the fetus. il Newsweek 66:84 N 15 '65
Nature of sexual response; primary sex research at Washington university in St Louis. il Time 87:65 Ja 7 '66
Sex: the silent bell; excerpt from Wild heritage. S. Carrighar. il Atlan 215:102-9 Mr '65
See also
Courtship of animals
Courtship of insects

SEX chromatin. See Chromatin

SEX chromosomes. See Chromosomes

SEX crimes
1965 Kinsey report; concerning our sex laws. P. Gebhard. Ladies Home J 82:66-7+ My; 42+ Je '65
Sex crimes in the spotlight. R. Niebuhr. Harper 231:137-8 S '65
Sex offenders, by P. Gebhard and others. Review
New Repub 153:25-7 O 16 '65. R. Coles
Newsweek il 66:42 Ag 2 '65
Sci N L 88:68 Jl 31 '65
Social problem of sexual assault. A. M. Kross. Sat R 48:23-5+ Ag 7 '65
What we now know about sex molesters. B. Schapper. il Todays Health 44:18-21+ Ja '66
Where women fear to tread; assaults in District of Columbia. Time 86:17A Ag 13 '65
See also
Indecent exposure
Rape

SEX determination and control
Dimorphic development of transplanted juvenile gonads of mosquitoes. J. F. Anderson and W. R. Horsfall. bibliog il Science 147: 624-5 F 5 '65
Interspecific transfer of the sex-ratio agent of drosophila willistoni in drosophila bifasciata and drosophila melanogaster. H. Ikeda. bibliog il Science 147:1147-8 Mr 5 '65
Marmosets (hapiladae): breeding seasons, twinning, and sex of offspring. J. K. Hampton, jr. and S. H. Hampton. bibliog il Science 150:915-17 N 12 '65
Sex conversion induced by hydrostatic pressure in the marine copepod tigriopus californicus. V. D. Vacquier and W. L. Belser. bibliog il Science 150:1619-21 D 17 '65

SEX differences
How young men influence the girls who love them; adaptation of address. M. S. Calderone. il Redbook 125:45+ Jl '65

SEX education. See Sex instruction

SEX hormone creams. See Cosmetics

SEX hormones. See Hormones, Sex

SEX in literature
Memoirs of a female pornographer. M. Meeske. il Esquire 63:112-15 Ap '65
New immoralists. W. Phillips. Commentary 39:66-9 Ap '65; Discussion. 40:10+ Ag '65

SEX in literature—*Continued*
Sex as the writer's new myth. R. C. Erickson. Christian Cent 82:641-3 My 19 '65
Writers should be heard but not obscene. P. Gallico. Writer 78:15-16 O '65
SEX in moving pictures. See Moving pictures—Moral aspects
SEX instruction
Common sense about children and sex. J. Brothers. Good H 160:12+ My '65
Fourth R. il Time 86:35 D 31 '65
Growing need for sex education in our schools. J. Robbins and J. Robbins. Good H 161:94-5+ N '65
Preparation for puberty; with study-discussion program, by E. Harris and D. Harris. J. W. Kessler. bibliog il PTA Mag 59:25-7, 35-6 My '65
Sex and youth; pastoral directives of the German episcopate. Cath World 201:264-8 Jl '65
Subtle dangers in mother-daughter talks about sex. R. Wilkenson. il McCalls 93: 58-9+ Ja '66
Teacher-opinion poll. il NEA J 54:52 F '65
Teenagers and sex; with study-discussion program, by C. Smallenburg and H. Smallenburg. M. S. Calderone. bibliog il PTA Mag 60:4-7, 36-7 O '65
What is sex education? P. Woodring. Sat R 48:55-6 D 18 '65; Discussion. 49:58 Ja 15 '66

Anecdotes, facetiae, satire, etc.
Sex without popcorn. R. Fontaine. il Atlan 215:128+ My '65
SEX perversion
Sex offenders, by P. Gebhard and others. Review
  New Repub 153:25-7 O 16 '65. R. Coles
  Newsweek il 66:42 Ag 2 '65
  Sci N L 88:68 Jl 31 '65
  See also
  Homosexuality
SEX ratio
Cytological basis of sex ratio in drosophila pseudoobscura. E. Novitski and others. bibliog il Science 148:516-17 Ap 23 '65
Polymorphic spermatozoa in the hymenopterous wasp dahlbominus. P. E. Lee and A. Wilkes. bibliog il Science 147:1445-6 Mr 19 '65
SEX relations
I'm sorry, dear; excerpt from Ways of the will. L. H. Farber; discussion. Commentary 39:14+ Ap; 8+ My '65
Nature of sexual response; primary sex research at Washington university in St Louis. il Time 87:65 Ja 7 '66
Sex and pregnancy. J. P. Greenhill. Redbook 124:28+ Ap '65
SEXTANTS
Sextant studies scheduled for Gemini-4. il Aviation W 82:63-4 My 31 '65
SEXTON, Anne
For the year of the insane; prayer. Harper 230:68 Je '65
Little girl, my stringbean, my lovely woman; poem. New Yorker 41:30 Ag 7 '65
Two poems: Wedding night; KE 6-8018. Poetry 106:116-19 Ap '65
SEXTON, Patricia Cayo
Schools are emasculating our boys. por Sat R 48:57 Je 19 '65
SEXUAL behavior. See Sex behavior
SEXUAL diseases. See Venereal diseases
SEXUAL ethics
Big question for teens: morality; panel discussion, ed. by J. Beck. il Todays Health 43:24+ My '65
Down with sex! M. Muggeridge. Esquire 63: 72-4 F '65
Is sex morality out of date? with discussion group program, by E. G. Neisser. R. Thomas. Parents Mag 40:31-2+, 39+ My '65
Let's face it; prostitute-heroines. M. Mannes. McCalls 92:18+ Je '65
Little girls lost: how parents fail their daughters; values of virginity. C. Seton. il Redbook 125:45+ My '65
Love and sex. D. Sugarman and R. Hochstein. Seventeen 24:94-5+ Jl '65
Love is the only measure; with reply by H. McCabe. J. Fletcher. Commonweal 83: 427-32, 439-40 Ja 14 '66
Man, morals and maturity; excerpt from Sin, sex and self-control. N. V. Peale. Read Digest 87:253-6+ O '65
Morals on the campus; a professor and a minister disagree on the present state of student morality. N. Sanford; A. Kinsolving. NEA J 54:20-4 Ap '65
New rationalism; teenage moral crisis. America 112:846 Je 12 '65
Pill and morality. A. Hacker. il N Y Times Mag p32-3+ N 21 '65

Reflections on the revolution in sex. F. Canavan. America 112:312-15 Mr 6 '65; Discussion. 112:456-8, 509-11 Ap 3, 17 '65
Sex as the writer's new myth. R. C. Erickson. Christian Cent 82:641-3 My 19 '65
Sexual behavior of college girls. il Sch & Soc 93:208 Ap 3 '65
Should I tell everything? questions and answers. A. Wood. il Seventeen 24:242-3+ Ag '65
Sister considers chastity. M. R. Jones. America 112:488-90 Ap 10 '65; Reply. M. Chabanel. 112:651 My 8 '65
Toward a new sexual morality? R. A. McCormick. Cath World 202:10-16 O '65
Unmarried love, by E. Chesser. Review
  America 113:417+ O 9 '65. F. Canavan
Waiting till marriage. P. L. Levin. il N Y Times Mag p65-6 My 9 '65
When the sap begins to flow. G. Naismith. il Todays Health 43:44-6+ F '65
  See also
  Prostitution
  Sex and religion
SEXUAL sterilization. See Sterilization, Sexual
SEYCHELLES (islands)
Down with coconuts; independence demand. il Time 86:26 S 10 '65
For people with plenty of time. il Sunset 134:74+ Mr '65
Seychelles; really away from it all. J. P. Nugent. il Atlan 216:154+ O '65
SEYDOUX, Roger
United Nations commemoration address, June 26, 1965. UN Mo Chron 2:145-7 Jl '65
SEYMOUR, Paul
Lost Bullets in disasterville. M. Kram. il por Sports Illus 23:26-7 N 8 '65
SEYMOUR House. See Middlebury, Vt.—Historic houses, etc.
SEYNES, Philippe de
International action and the strategy of development. UN Mo Chron 2:55-8 F '65
SHABECOFF, Philip
Action atonement. N Y Times Mag p 149-51+ N 7 '65
SHACK, Eddie
Maple Leafs' Punchinello packs a real punch. T. C. Brody. il por Sports Illus 23:68+ D 13 '65
SHACKFORD, Charles
Musical events; method of measuring the precise pitches of notes. W. Sargeant. New Yorker 41:173 Ap 17 '65
SHAD
Rebirth of the shad. J. S. Martin. il Atlan 215:90-3 Je '65
SHAD fishing
100-a-day at Enfield. A. Davenport. il Field & S 70:43-5+ Je '65
SHADE, Christine
Dear babe that almost was. Redbook 125:48-9+ Jl '65
SHADE
  See also
  Screens (sun)
SHADE plants. See Plants, Shade
SHADES. See Window shades
SHADES and shadows
Shadow designs. W. Bock. il Sch Arts 65: 18-20 N '65
SHADOAN, George
Behind the crime scare. Nation 200:495-7 My 10 '65
SHADOW of kindness; story. See Brennan, M.
SHADOW pantomimes and plays
Shadow puppets. E. Weinberg. il Sch Arts 65:12-13 O '65
SHADOWS. See Shades and shadows
SHAFER, Burr
Muddled, mirthful world of Burr Shafer. J. F. Fixx. il por Sat R 48:54-5 Jl 10 '65
SHAFER, Floyd Doud
Pastoral counseling. Christian Cent 82:1420+ N 17 '65
SHAFER, Nathaniel
Venereal disease: plague of our atomic age. Todays Health 43:92 S '65
SHAFER, Susanne M.
Political conscience for West German youth. Sr Schol 86:sup 13 My 20 '65
SHAFFER, Peter
Royal hunt of the sun. Criticism
  America 113:648-9 N 20 '65
  Commonweal 83:215 N 19 '65
  Dance Mag il 39:138-9 D '65
  Life il 59:134-5+ D 10 '65
  Nat R 18:37 Ja 11 '66
  Nation 201:397 N 22 '65
  New Repub 153:45-6 N 27 '65
  New Yorker 41:115 N 6 '65
  Newsweek il 66:96 N 8 '65
  Sat R 48:31 My 29 '65
  Sat R 48:71 N 13 '65
  Time 86:77 N 5 '65

SHAGASS, Charles, and Schwartz, Marvin
Age, personality, and somatosensory cerebral evoked responses. bibliog Science 148:1359-61 Je 4 '65
SHAHEEN, John M.
Building an empire in oil, with leverage. il por Bsns W p 119-20+ Mr 6 '65
SHAHN, Ben
Glass houses and green rooms. H. Frankel. Sat R 48:30 My 15 '65
Personal backgrounds. il por House & Gard 128:178-9 D '65
SHAIN, Charles E.
That big word: integrity. Seventeen 24:94-5+ D '65
SHAKER cookery. See Cookery, American
SHAKER HEIGHTS, Ohio
Lomond learning center. M. L. Krohn. il Library J 90:5463-4 D 15 '65
Study in self-reliance; Shaker Heights learning experiment. M. L. Krohn. il Library J 90:4520-2 O 15 '65
SHAKESPEARE, William
Julius Caesar; drama, ed. by L. Olfson. Plays 24:81-90 F '65
Macbeth; drama, ed. by L. Olfson. Plays 25: 79-90 Ja '66

about

Great Shakespeare forgery, by B. Grebanier. Review
Sat R 48:61+ O 23 '65. H. T. Moore
Tragedie of Othello, the Moore of Venice. J. Diether. Am Rec G 31:739+ Ap '65

Authorship

Shakespeare and The two noble kinsmen, by P. Bertram. Review
Sat R 48:39 N 27 '65. B. Grebanier

Criticism and interpretation

Bottom: on Shakespeare, by L. Zukofsky and C. Zukofsky. Review
Nation 200:232-4 Mr 1 '65. D. Hayman

Plays

Shakespeare and The two noble kinsmen, by P. Bertram. Review
Sat R 48:39 N 27 '65. B. Grebanier

Coriolanus

Live blossoms in dead soil; Berliner ensemble. R. Brustein. New Repub 153:35-6 Ag 7 '65
Mugging the Bard in Central park. J. Simon. Commonweal 82:635-6 S 3 '65
Stratford II. J. Novick. Nation 201:65-6 Ag 2 '65

Henry IV

Master fibber; Stratford, Ontario. H. Hewes. Sat R 48:27 Ag 28 '65

Henry V

Thoughts from home and abroad. R. Brustein. New Repub 152:29-30 Je 26 '65

King Lear

Finding Shakespeare. J. Novick. Nation 201: 45-7 Jl 19 '65
Gags & good intentions can't tame a shrew; American Shakespeare festival theatre production. E. Coleman. Life 59:13 Jl 23 '65
Stratford: a theatre in search of itself. R. Hapgood. il Reporter 33:37-9 S 9 '65

Love's labour's lost

Broadway postscript; New York Shakespeare festival's production. H. Hewes. Sat R 48:22 Jl 3 '65

Midsummer night's dream

Letter from Paris; at Comédie-Française. Genêt. New Yorker 41:174+ N 13 '65

Much ado about nothing

Much ado, with garlic; production of Britain's National theater. il Time 85:47 Ap 2 '65

Richard III

Guthrie's production of Groucho the III. H. Popkin. Life 58:8+ Je 4 '65

Romeo and Juliet

Finding Shakespeare. J. Novick. Nation 201: 45-7 Jl 19 '65

Taming of the shrew

Gags & good intentions can't tame a shrew; American Shakespeare festival theatre production. E. Coleman. Life 59:13 Jl 23 '65
Stratford II. J. Novick. Nation 201:65 Ag 2 '65

Staging and acting of plays

Shakespeare for the people. J. Novick. Nation 201:146-8 S 13 '65
See also
Shakespeare, W.—Plays

Study and teaching

Play's the thing; National Shakespeare company. il Sr Schol 86:4T F 25 '65
SHAKESPEARE company
Fiberglas fairway. Newsweek 66:76 Jl 12 '65
SHAKESPEARE festival, Stratford, Ontario
Kurt Weill's Mahagonny. A. Rich. il Hi Fi 15:158-9 S '65
Master fibber. H. Hewes. Sat R 48:27 Ag 28 '65
Play's the thing . . . il Bsns W p32-3 Je 26 '65
Two Cherry orchards; Guthrie theatre, Minneapolis, and Shakespearean festival theatre, Stratford, Ont. productions. J. Novick. Nation 201:87-8 Ag 16 '65
SHAKESPEARE festivals
Repertory's rising requirements. H. Hewes. Sat R 48:22 Jl 3 '65
Shakespeare explosion; summer events. J. Reddy. il Read Digest 87:197-8+ Ag '65
See also
American Shakespeare festival theatre and academy, Stratford, Conn.
New York Shakespeare festival
SHAKESPEARE on phonograph records. See Phonograph records—Spoken records
SHALIT, Gene
New children's books. McCalls 92:64+ Je '65
SHALLOTS
Three unusual vegetables. R. Gannon. il Flower Grower 52:54-5 My '65
SHAMAN, Harvey
They taught me 35-mm underwater and then I soloed with a shark. il Pop Phot 57: 54-7+ Ag '65
SHAMUYARIRA, N. M.
Eleventh hour in Rhodesia. Nation 201:319-22 N 8 '65
SHANE, Harold G.
How do they rate you, professor? NEA J 54: 18-20 N '65
SHANE, Ted
Roamer's ramblings. See issues of Travel
SHANKS, Henry D.
Inspecting 11½ miles of sewers from the inside. Am City 80:118+ S '65
SHANNON, William V.
Controversial historian of the age of Kennedy. N Y Times Mag p30-1+ N 21 '65
Crisis of the cities. Commonweal 83:264-5 D 3 '65
Emergence of Senator Kennedy (D, Mass) N Y Times Mag p 16-17+ Ag 22 '65
Hamlet without the prince. Harper 231:110-12 Ag '65
Home rule almost. Commonweal 83:82-3 O 22 '65
How Ted Kennedy survived his ordeal. Good H 160:88-9+ Ap '65
In-fighting among the outs. Commonweal 83: 330-1 D 17 '65
Last days of Congress. Commonweal 83: 140-2 N 5 '65
Lindsay, Kennedy, and the power struggle in New York. Harper 232:37-45 Ja '66
Point of no return. Commonweal 82:580-1 Ag 20 '65
Political almanac for '66. Commonweal 83: 393-5 Ja 7 '66
Stevenson the politician. Commonweal 82: 549-50 Ag 6 '65
Supersonic question mark. Commonweal 82: 518-19 Jl 23 '65
SHAPE of the earth. See Earth—Figure
SHAPER, Richard S.
School aid: a threat to the parish. Christian Cent 82:394-6 Mr 31 '65
SHAPIRO, Charles
Hope and sorrow in the South. Sat R 48: 31-3 Ag 14 '65
SHAPIRO, David
Privacy; poem. Harper 232:62 Ja '66
SHAPIRO, Fred C.
Reporter at large. New Yorker 41:161-4+ Ap 10 '65
SHAPIRO, Frieda S.
Your liability for student accidents. NEA J 54:46-7 Mr '65
SHAPIRO, Karl
Decolonization of American literature; address, April 1965. por Wilson Lib Bul 39: 842-53 Je '65
Karl Shapiro's anti-poem. R. Howard. Poetry 106:225-8 Je '65
SHAPIRO, Samuel
Santo Domingo: can we withdraw? Nation 200:556-9 My 24 '65
Scoring the revolution. Nation 201:62-4 Ag 2 '65

SHAPLEN, Robert
Letter from Algeria. New Yorker 41:147-8+
() 30 '65
Letter from Algiers. New Yorker 41:38-40+
Jl 17 '65
Letter from Manila (cont) New Yorker 41:
84+ Ja 15 '66
Letter from Saigon (cont) New Yorker 41:
86+ Mr 20; 192+ N 13 '65
Letter from South Vietnam. New Yorker 41:
166+ Ap 24 '65
SHAPLEY, Harlow
Changing view of universe. A. Ewing. il por
Sci N L 88:10-11 Jl 3 '65
Harlow Shapley is eighty. Sky & Tel 30:
263 N '65
SHAPORIN, IUrii
Shaporin and Shebalin. B. Schwarz. Sat R
48:54-5 F 27 '65
SHARECROPPERS. See Farm tenancy
SHARED time (public and parochial schools)
See Educational cooperation
SHAREHOLDERS. See Stockholders
SHARK fishing
Shark-eating men. il Time 85:68+ Je 25 '65
SHARKS
Attacked by a killer shark! R. Fox. il Read
Digest 87:49-54 Ag '65
SHARMA, Madan, and Berkovitz, Robert
200-watt solid-state stereo amplifier. Electr
World 73:44-7 Mr '65
SHARON SPRINGS, Kan.
They wouldn't let their small town die! il
Suc Farm 63:74+ F '65
SHARP, Alan
Author. H. Frankel. il por Sat R 48:28 My 8
'65
SHARP, Evelyn
Progress report on the mathematics revolu-
tion. Sat R 48:62-3+ Mr 20 '65
SHARP, Gene
Political equivalent of war, civilian defense.
bibliog f Int Concil 555:5-67 N '65
SHARP, Ulysses Simpson Grant, 1906-
Thinking man's admiral. il pors Life 58:47-8+
Ap 23 '65
SHARPE, Donald M.
Threshold to the profession. NEA J 54:33-5
Ap '65
SHARPENING
Art of knife sharpening. il Sunset 134:149-
50+ Ap '65
Your radial saw can sharpen itself. M.
Banister. il Pop Mech 124:192-4 O '65
See also
Grinding machines
SHARPLESS (operatic character) See Char-
acters in opera
SHASTA daisies
Shastas all summer long. il Sunset 134:276
Je '65
SHASTRI, Lal Bahadur
Atlantic report. Atlan 215:14+ My '65
Bantam visitor. Newsweek 65:49 Je 28 '65
Ending the suspense. il por Time 86:44-8 S
17 '65
Fee and sympathy; visit to Russia. News-
week 65:40 My 31 '65
Gentle warrior. il Newsweek 67:37-8 Ja 24
'66
I am in fact a very ordinary human. L.
Kraar. il por Life 58:37 Je 11 '65
India: downhill toward disaster. S. Karnow.
il por Sat Eve Post 238:78-83 Je 5 '65
India looks for a new leader. Bsns W p27 Ja
15 '66
India without a leader. America 114:113 Ja
22 '66
Kashmir: Shastri's time for decision. S.
Rajan. Reporter 33:41-3 S 23 '65
Last journey of India's gentle leader; with
report by B. Farrell. il pors Life 60:20-9
Ja 21 '66
Nehru's munshi comes out of Nehru's shad-
ow. J. A. Lukas. il pors N Y Times Mag
p54-5+ N 28 '65
Playing the honest broker. il por News-
week 67:36+ Ja 17 '66
Pride & reality. il por Time 86:18-26B Ag
13 '65
Process of change. il por Time 87:22-5 Ja 21
'66
Shade of the banyan. por Newsweek 65:55
My 17 '65
Shastri: hard to follow, too. Life 60:4 Ja 21
'66
Shastri-Pearson talks. Nation 200:686 Je 28
'65
SHATKIN, A. J. and others
Vaccinia virus directed RNA: its fate in
the presence of actinomycin. bibliog Science
148:87-90 Ap 2 '65
SHATOUNI, Vahan
Shatouni the Magnificent. R. Mamoulian. il
por Read Digest 87:170-2+ Jl '65

SHATTER-proof glass. See Glass, Safety
SHAUGHNESSY, D. F.
Partnership in research. por Am Ed 1:1-4
F '65
SHAW, Arnold
Behind the folk-song frenzy. Read Digest
86:191+ Ap '65
SHAW, Artie
Statement to the friends of National review.
W. F. Buckley, jr. Nat R 17:448 Je 1 '65
SHAW, Bernard. See Shaw, G. B.
SHAW, Betty M.
Should homework be abolished? NEA J 54:23-
4 F '65
SHAW, Charles R.
Electrophoretic variation in enzymes. bib-
liog Science 149:936-43 Ag 27 '65
—and Barto, Elizabeth
Autosomally determined polymorphism of
glucose-6-phosphate dehydrogenase in pero-
myscus. bibliog Science 148:1099-100 My 21
'65
SHAW, Darla
Stop those Halloween hollows! Recreation 58:
397-8 O '65
SHAW, Elmer W.
Skylines of Alaska; poem. Am For 71:40-1
Ap '65
SHAW, George Bernard
Becoming Bernard Shaw. S. Kauffmann. New
Repub 153:21-4 N 27 '65
Bernard Shaw: collected letters (1874-1897)
ed. by D. H. Laurence. Review
Time por 87:83+ Ja 21 '66
Flawed giant. G. Wills. por Nat R 17:1197-8+
D 28 '65
Our far-flung correspondents. J. Bainbridge.
New Yorker 41:137-8+ N 6 '65
Shaw and Christianity, by A. S. Abbott.
Review
Christian Cent 82:1579 D 22 '65. J. A.
Davidson
Sublime monster. il por Newsweek 66:126+
N 15 '65
Those angry authors, why their protests
fail. I. Brown. Sat R 48:18-19+ Ag 28 '65
Unrepentant pilgrim, by J. P. Smith. Re-
view
Sat R 49:80-1 Ja 8 '66. A. Marshall
Whole world was his stage. S. Weintraub. il
Sat R 48:45+ N 13 '65
SHAW, Leonard
System theory; symposium at the Polytechnic
institute of Brooklyn, New York. Science
149:1005 Ag 27 '65
SHAW, Maud
My life with Caroline and John-John; ex-
cerpts. il por Ladies Home J 82:82-5+ D
'65; 83:68-71+ Ja '66 (to be cont)
SHAW, Ralph R.
Form and the substance; address, 1964. por
Library J 90:567-71, 1580+ F 1, Ap 1 '65
Integrated bibliography; address. Library J
90:819-22 F 15 '65
Let's all tell the truth. ALA Bul 59:594-6
Jl '65
SHAW, Spencer
Children's world, Library/USA. Library J
90:1996-7 Ap 15 '65
SHAWANGUNK MOUNTAINS
Of men and mountains. Nat Parks Mag 39:
20 S '65
SHAWCROSS, Hartley William Shawcross,
baron
Crime does pay because we do not back up
the police. N Y Times Mag p44-5+ Je 13
'65
Criminal is living in a golden age; excerpts
from address, October 11, 1965. por U S
News 59:80-2 N 1 '65
SHAWN, Donald
Radar plotting. Motor B 115:52-5 My '65
SHAWN, William
New Yorker at forty. il por Newsweek 65:
62-4 Mr 1 '65
Whisperer. por Time 85:60 Ap 16 '65
William and the Wolfe. il por Newsweek
65:62+ Ap 19 '65
SHAYON, Robert Lewis
Audio/video (cont) Sat R 48:80+ Ap 10 '65
TV and radio. See issues of Saturday review
Uphill fight of pay-TV. Sat R 48:55-7 Ap 24
'65
SHCHUKIN, Sergei Ivanovich
Adventurous taste of Sergei Shchukin. il
por(p44) Life 58:49-58 Ap 99 '65
SHEARER, John C.
Exporting U.S. standards to underdeveloped
countries. Mo Labor R 88:145-7 F '65
SHEARER, Thomas B.
Shallow cabinet for a hallway. Pop Sci 186:
172-3 F '65

SHEBA, Queen of
Africa's golden past. W. L. Hansberry and E. H. Johnson. il por Ebony 20:136-7+ Ap '65
SHEBALIN, Vissarion
Shaporin and Shebalin. B. Schwarz. Sat R 48:54-5 F 27 '65
SHEBESTA, Mary C.
Readings on labor-management. Cur Hist 49: 46-9+, 108-11+ Jl-Ag '65
SHECTER, Leonard
Take me out to the old yakyu. Sat Eve Post 238:82+ F 13 '65
SHEDD, Charlie W.
Letters to Karen; excerpt. Read Digest 88: 211-16+ Ja '66
SHEDESKY, Pat
Delphinium. Pop Gard 16:26-9 Jl '65
For summer color phlox. Pop Gard 16:12 Jl '65
My biggest garden helper. Flower Grower 52:44-5 Je '65
SHEDLOVSKY, Julian P. See Cressy, P. J. jr, jt. auth.
SHEDS
See also
Garden houses, shelters, etc.
SHEEAN, Vincent
King Faisal's first year. For Affairs 44:304-13 Ja '66
SHEED, Wilfrid
Growing up Catholic; excerpt from Generation of the third eye. Commonweal 81:692-5 F 26 '65
Revival of a salesman. Commonweal 81:670 F 19 '65
Stage. See issues of Commonweal
SHEEHAN, Arthur T.
Austrian apocalypse. America 112:81, 340 Ja 16, Mr 13 '65
SHEEHAN, Edward R. F.
Drama and anguish in Africa. Harper 231:128-33 D '65
Massachusetts: rogues and reformers in a state on trial. Sat Eve Post 238:25-32+ Je 5 '65
Trinity of nation-builders. Harper 230:142-4 My '65
SHEEHAN, Ethna
Best books of the season for children. America 113:637-40+ N 20 '65
Vacation reading for children. America 112: 899-902 Je 26 '65
SHEEHAN, George A. Jr
For the heart & soul. il por Time 85:55 Je 4 '65
SHEEHAN, Neil
Simple man in pursuit of power. N Y Times Mag p9+ Ag 15 '65
SHEEHAN, Robert
A.T.&T: a study in federalism. Fortune 71: 142-7+ F '65
Kodak picture, sunshine and shadow. Fortune 71:126-9+ My '65
Price of success at Chrysler. Fortune 72:138-43+ N '65
Red umbrella in a high wind. Fortune 72: 138-41+ Ag '65
Those fund-raising businessmen. Fortune 73: 148-50+ Ja '66
SHEEN, Fulton John, bp
Few true friends. J. Reddy. Read Digest 88: 128-32 Ja '66
SHEEP
What's new. See issues of Successful farming

Culling
How I cull my ewe flock. Mrs J. Stricklin. il Suc Farm 63:106C Mr '65

Diseases and pests
USDA announces change in scrapie program. Farm J 89:52F My '65

Feeding
See also
Lambs—Feeding
SHEEP breeding
Three lamb crops in two years. il Suc Farm 63:104 Ap '65
SHEEP dogs
Raggedy go at the Garden; Westminster dog show. L. Smith. il Sports Illus 22:22-5 Mr 1 '65
SHEERIN, John B.
Editorials. See issues of Catholic world
Nature of religious liberty. por Cath World 201:356-61 S '65
SHEET-fed gravure. See Photogravure
SHEET steel
Improving sheet steel; Inland steel co. Bsns W p 158 F 20 '65
SHEHAN, Lawrence Joseph, cardinal
Another U.S. cardinal. por U S News 58:16 F 8 '65

Baltimore cardinal. America 112:181 F 6 '65
Chiefly from the heart. A. Tehan and J. Tehan. Christian Cent 82:1548-50 D 15 '65
New red hats. il por Newsweek 65:80 F 8 '65
SHELBURNE, Mary Willis
Interpretation; poem. America 113:207 Ag 28 '65
SHELBY, Carroll Hall
Snakes, butter beans and Mister Cobra. C. Phinizy. il pors Sports Illus 22:36-8+ My 17 '65
SHELBY American, incorporated
Building fast cars on a shoestring; C. Shelby, ex-racing driver. il Bsns W p66-8+ Ag 14 '65
SHELEPIN, Aleksandr Nikolaevich
Who's on third? Newsweek 66:38-9 D 20 '65
SHELL aviation corporation
Shell way. J. Gilbert. il Flying 77:54-8 O '65
SHELL craft. See Shellwork
SHELL flowers
This annual likes a cool temperature. F. W. Patch. il Flower Grower 52:58 Ap '65
SHELL work. See Shellwork
SHELLCRACKER fishing. See Sunfish fishing
SHELLEY, Howard
World's rarest trophy? por Outdoor Life 136: 36-9+ Jl '65
SHELLFISH
Up from the sea: shellfish; with recipes. il Ladies Home J 82:86-7+ Je '65
See also
Cookery—Fish
Lobsters
Mussels
Oysters
SHELLFISH fisheries
Shrimp need fresh water, too; address, June 1965. C. P. Idyll. Nat Parks Mag 39:14-15 O '65
Shrimp nursery; science explores new ways to farm the sea. C. P. Idyll. il Nat Geog Mag 127:636-59 My '65
SHELLS (conchology)
Calcite deposition during shell repair by the aragonitic gastropod murex fulvescens. E. O. Muzii and H. C. W. Skinner. bibliog il Science 151:201-3 Ja 14 '66
Odd behavior of the slipper shells. A. G. Melvin. il Hobbies 70:130 Ja '66
Rare shells are expensive. A. G. Melvin. il Hobbies 69:130+ F '65
Snails lay eggs; moon shells and their sand collars. A. G. Melvin. il Hobbies 70:130 N '65
Spirals in shells. A. G. Melvin. il Hobbies 70:130 Ag '65
Theoretical morphology of the coiled shell. D. M. Raup and A. Michelson. bibliog il Science 147:1294-5 Mr 12 '65
Wonderful world of shells. R. T. Abbott. il Sci Digest 58:66-73 D '65
See also
Cowries

Collectors and collecting
Collect shells at Halibut Point. A. G. Melvin. il Hobbies 70:130 Jl '65
Jewels from the ocean deep. M. Hoyt. il Read Digest 86:146-51 My '65
Odd places to find shells. A. G. Melvin. il Hobbies 70:130 O '65
Shell boats of Acapulco. A. G. Melvin. il Hobbies 70:130+ D '65
Shells available to collectors (cont) A. G. Melvin. il Hobbies 70:130+ Mr '65
Wonder shell. A. G. Melvin. il Hobbies 70: 130+ S '65
SHELLS (projectiles) See Cartridges; Projectiles
SHELLS (structural engineering)
Curved roof elements make use of metal lath. il Arch Rec 138:179-80 Ag '65
Natural, appropriate use of concrete shells; Carleton college men's gymnasium. il Arch Rec 137:129-32 F '65
Welded pipe trussed frame roofs open air tabernacle. il Arch Rec 137:224-5 Ap '65
SHELLS, Orchestra. See Orchestra shells
SHELLWORK
Jewelry on the half shell. il Look 29:77 My 4 '65
SHELTERING a life; story. See Rosen, N.
SHELTERS
Butterfly carport. il Sunset 134:121 Mr '65
SHELTERS, Animal. See Animal shelters
SHELTERS, Atomic bomb. See Atomic bomb shelters
SHELTON, Arthur Edwin
Clerical error. Newsweek 65:32-3 Ap 12 '65
SHELTON, Isabelle
Lyndon Johnson's mother. Sat Eve Post 238: 94+ My 8 '65

SHINER, Larry
  Goodbye, death-of-God! Christian Cent 82:
  1418-19 N 17 '65
SHIP and boat models
  Sailing downwind in a nice, cozy yacht club.
  R. S. Hewlett. il Sports Illus 23:66-7 D 13
  '65
SHIP building. See Shipbuilding
SHIP canals. See Canals
SHIP photography. See Photography of ships
SHIP signals. See Signals and signaling
SHIP stability. See Ships—Stability and stabi-
  lizers
SHIP subsidies
  Container ships race for a route; U.S. and
  foreign operators competing. il Bsns W
  p 198+ N 13 '65
SHIP yard employees. See Shipworkers
SHIPBUILDING
  Looking out for no. 1; Japan's Mitsubishi. il
  Bsns W p59-62+ My 15 '65
  Queen's shipbuilder. il Time 85:92+ Mr 12
  '65
  Super shipbuilders; Japan's boom. il News-
  week 65:74-5 F 15 '65
  Weak spot in our defenses. J. D. Hayes.
  America 113:93-5 Jl 24 '65
    See also
  Shipworkers
  Sloops
  Sun shipbuilding and dry dock company
SHIPLEY, T.
  Visual contours in homogeneous space. bib-
  liog Science 150:348-50 O 15 '65
—and others
  Evoked visual potentials and human color
  vision. bibliog Science 150:1162-4 N 26 '65
SHIPMENT of goods
  One big package for the shippers. Bsns W
  p74+ S 4 '65
    See also
  Packing for shipment
SHIPMENT of works of art. See Transporta-
  tion of works of art
SHIPPEE, Robert
  Air taxi. Flying 77:60-1 D '65
SHIPPING
    See also
  Panama Canal
  Ports

Automation

  Automation goes to sea. J. H. Winchester.
  il Read Digest 86:119-22 My '65
  Merchant marine in deadly peril. America
  113:175-6 Ag 21 '65

Federal aid

  How to begin the end for maritime subsidies.
  Fortune 72:126 N '65

International aspects

  Agreed minute provides for exchange of ship-
  ping information. Dept State Bul 52:188-90
  F 8 '65
  Breakthrough in the facilitation of interna-
  tional maritime traffic. J. Roullier. UN Mo
  Chron 2:58-62 F '65
  U.S. and eleven OECD nations discuss in-
  ternational shipping problems. Dept State
  Bul 52:549 Ap 12 '65

Rates

  Agreed minute provides for exchange of
  shipping information. Dept State Bul 52:
  188-90 F 8 '65

United States

  Can union demands kill the U.S. shipping
  industry? role of Maritime administration.
  il U S News 59:61-2 Ag 2 '65
  Shipping all at sea: government silence on
  policy blamed. Bsns W p 142 Je 12 '65
  Troubled waters in shipping; obsolete equip-
  ment and high costs. il Duns R 85:pt2 120-
  3+ Je '65
  U.S. shipping; warnings of still rougher
  water. U S News 59:10 Jl 12 '65
    See also
  Merchant marine—United States
SHIPPING containers. See Containers for
  shipping
SHIPPING fever. See Cattle—Diseases and
  pests
SHIPPING subsidies. See Ship subsidies
SHIPS
    See also
  Armored vessels
  Constellation (frigate)
  Freight vessels

Merchant ships
Ocean liners
Salvage (ships)
Viking ships
Warships—United States

Crews

  See Seamen

Fires and fire protection

  Electronic lifeline on the high seas; Lakonia
  fire. T. Irwin. il Pop Sci 187:86-8+ S '65
  Fiery throes of a dying cruise ship; Yarmouth
  Castle; with report by D. Nevin. il Life 59:
  28-35 N 26 '65
  $59 to tragedy; Yarmouth castle disaster. il
  Time 86:28-9 N 26 '65
  Fun ship to Nassau; S.S. Yarmouth Castle
  disaster. il Newsweek 66:34+ N 22 '65
  Mystery at 400 fathoms; Yarmouth Castle
  fire. Time 86:43B N 19 '65
  Truth about safety at sea: lesson of one
  disaster; Yarmouth Castle. il U S News
  59:44-5 N 29 '65
  What went wrong? blazing example: Yar-
  mouth Castle fire. Newsweek 66:26 N 29 '65

Food service

    See also
  Freight vessels—Food service

Repairing

  Ship to aid Vietnam aircraft maintenance;
  USS Corpus Christi Bay, former USS Al-
  bermarle. R. D. Hibben. il Aviation W 83:
  63+ Ag 30 '65

Safety devices and measures

  Voyage to nowhere; need for foreign-flag
  cruise ships to upgrade safety standards.
  Nation 201:403 N 29 '65

Signals and signaling

  See Signals and signaling

Stability and stabilizers

  Excursion to death; overturning of Eastland.
  J. Griggs. il Am Heritage 16:32-5+ F '65
SHIPS, Atomic powered
  Protection of U.S. naval nuclear propulsion
  plant information; Department statement,
  February 9, 1965. Dept State Bul 52:300 Mr
  1 '65
SHIPS, Bureau of. See United States—Navy
  department—Ships, Bureau of
SHIPS, Model. See Ship and boat models
SHIPS, Research
  Oceanography: House subcommittee encour-
  ages use of merchant ships to gather data
  on the high seas. J. Walsh. Science 148:
  349-50 Ap 16 '65
  Practical astronomy from shipboard. W. S.
  Von Arx. bibliog il Sky & Tel 29:340-5
  Je '65
  Satellites to aid in sea studies; nine oceano-
  graphic ships planned. H. Taylor. il Miss &
  Roc 17:41-2+ S 6 '65
  Seagoing computer; aboard research vessel,
  Atlantis II. il Sci Digest 57:24-5 My '65
  Ship that stands on end; SPAR. il Sci Di-
  gest 57:inside cover Mr '65
SHIPS in art
    See also
  Photography of ships
SHIPWORKERS

Wages and hours

  Wage chronology: Bethlehem Atlantic ship-
  yards; supplement no. 4, 1962-65. W. Fridie.
  il Mo Labor R 88:421-4 Ap '65
SHIPWRECKS
  Excursion to death; overturning of Eastland.
  J. Griggs. il Am Heritage 16:32-5+ F '65
  Two famous cruise ships lost; Yankee;
  Wanderer. il Yachting 117:202-5 Ap '65
    See also
  Salvage (ships)
  Survival (after airplane accidents, shipwrecks,
  etc)
SHIPYARDS
  Trying to salvage Betsy's discards. il Bsns W
  p 180+ O 23 '65
SHIRLEY, Ernest
  Tennis. Sports Illus 24:48-9 Ja 10 '66
SHIRLEY, George
  Leading man at the Met. il pors Ebony
  21:84-6+ Ja '66
  Tenor in whiteface. il por Time 86:54 Ag
  13 '65
SHIRLEY Holmes and the FBI; drama. See
  Miller. H. L.

SHORE protection
Plastic seaweed helps build up beach sand.
Sci N L 88:123 Ag 21 '65
SHORT, Edward Watson
Tory ambush. por Newsweek 66:36 Jl 19 '65
SHORT, John Fulton
John Fulton, artist & matador. I. Murdoch.
il por Am Artist 29:22-7+ Ap '65
SHORT cake. See Shortcake
SHORT novel; story. See Rogin, G.
SHORT stories
Beckoning hand. M. E. Nutt. Writer 78:9-11+
Mr '65
Hurry with your snowball. G. H. Freitag.
Writer 78:28-9 My '65
Leaving out the snow on Park avenue. C.
Hubbell. Writer 78:22-3+ N '65
Short stories; how to begin and how to end.
D. Bates. Writer 79:19-20+ Ja '66
Short stories, preface to an episode in life.
B. Plagemann. Writer 78:14-15+ Je '65
What makes a salable confession? sin, suffer,
and repent formula. J. Jackson. Writer
78:17-22 Mr '65

Bibliography
Exploring the province of the short story.
G. P. Elliott. Harper 230:111-16 Ap '65
SHORT take-off and landing airplanes. See
Airplanes. Short take-off and landing
SHORT wave radio. See Radio receiving ap-
paratus, Short wave; Radio transmission,
Short wave
SHORT wave radio transmitters. See Radio
transmitters, Short wave
SHORTCAKE
Battle plan for the feast: strawberry short-
cake. E. Graves. Life 58:102-3+ My 28 '65
Strawberries and rhubarb. R. Hanna. il Suc
Farm 63:94-5+ My '65
Strawberry shortcake, three ways! il Bet
Hom & Gard 43:104 Je '65
SHORTHILL, R. W. and Saari, J. M.
Nonuniform cooling of the eclipsed moon:
a listing of thirty prominent anomalies.
bibliog Science 150:210-12 O 8 '65
SHORTLINE railroads. See Railroads. Short
line
SHORTNESS of breath. See Emphysema
SHOSTAKOVICH, Dmitrii Dmitrievich
Katerina Ismailova. Criticism
New Yorker 41:187-9 Mr 13 '65
Opera N 29:32 Ap 3 '65
Sat R 48:47+ Mr 20 '65
SHOT putting
Busting the seventy-foot barrier. il Life 58:
80A-80B My 21 '65
Champ from Pampa; R. Matson. il Time
85:65 Ap 30 '65
Record-slinging in the rain; Texas A&M's
R. Matson. E. Shrake. il Sports Illus 22:
26-7 My 3 '65
SHOTGUNS
Double-barreled shotguns. il Consumer Rep
30:506-9 O '65
Pattern your shotgun. W. C. Lammey. il Pop
Mech 124:172-5+ N '65
Shotgun barrel. J. O'Connor. il Outdoor Life
135:148+ Ap '65
Shotgun pointers. J. Madson. il Suc Farm 63:
56+ O '65
Shotgun tracer. W. Page. Field & S 70:114
Je '65
Shotguns in the field. V. Kraft. il Sports
Illus 23:64-6+ O 18 '65
20 gauge moves up. J. O'Connor. il Outdoor
Life 136:68+ S '65
Wheel-lock guns. C. G. Worman. il Hob-
bies 70:122-3 D '65
SHOTWELL, James Thomson
Historical necessity of peace. S. Chase. por
Sat R 48:129 Mr 13 '65
James Thomson Shotwell; a tribute. C. M.
Eichelberger. Sat R 48:16 Ag 7 '65
Obituary
Pub W 188:35-6 Ag 9 '65
SHOTWELL, Louisa R.
Roosevelt Grady and the children of Asia.
Horn Bk 41:252-4 Je '65
Thailand diary. NEA J 54:44 O '65
SHOW, Ralph E.
Using a transistor curve tracer. Electr World
74:49-52+ S '65
SHOW (periodical)
Show stopper. Newsweek 65:99 My 10 '65
SHOW cases. See Exhibition cases
SHOW windows
Christmas window displays; interview. J.
Schwartz. il Pub W 188:86-8 Ag 23 '65
Window display roundup; bookstores. il
Pub W 188:60-1 O 4 '65
Window displays in small and medium-sized
stores. Pub W 187:50-1 Mr 15 '65

SHOWER baths
Put a shower near the pool. il Sunset 135:
88+ Jl '65
SHOWER gifts. See Wedding gifts
SHOWERS (parties) See Entertaining
SHRAKE, Edwin
Boxing. Sports Illus 22:59-60+ Mr 22 '65
Once forbidding land. Sports Illus 22:76-80+
My 10 '65
Pro football (cont) Sports Illus 23:76+ O 4:
71-4 O 25; 86-8+ N 15 '65
SHREVE, James S.
Tachometer & engine idle speed calibrator.
Pop Electr 22:54-5+ F '65
SHREVEPORT, La.
Traffic control on a limited budget. T. Herline.
il Am City 80:183-4 Mr '65
SHRIMP fisheries. See Shellfish fisheries
SHRIMP fishing
Queen of shrimpers. il Ebony 21:131-4+ N '65
SHRIMPS
Shrimp nursery; science explores new ways
to farm the sea. C. P. Idyll. il Nat Geog
Mag 127:636-59 My '65
See also
Cookery—Fish
SHRIMPTON, Jean Rosemary
Truth about modeling; excerpt. por Ladies
Home J 82:66-7+ Ag '65
about
Encounter with Jean Shrimpton. P. Devlin.
il pors Vogue 146:28+ O 15 '65
Girl, the face, the Shrimp. il pors Newsweek
65:67-70 My 10 '65
Imposing proportions of Jean Shrimpton.
B. J. Friedman. il pors Esquire 63:70-5+
Ap '65
SHRINE of the book for biblical manuscripts
in Israel. See Israel museum, Jerusalem
SHRINER, Fleming
Admiral leads on: drama. Plays 25:79-82, 86
O '65
SHRINES
See also
Holy places
SHRIVER, Eunice Kennedy
Answer to the attacks on motherhood. Mc-
Calls 92:88-9+ Je '65
SHRIVER, Robert Sargent, 1915-
Dispute over blame for the Los Angeles
riots; statement. por U S News 59:16 Ag
30 '65
How goes the war on poverty? Look 29:30-
1+ Jl 27 '65
about
Just one job for Shriver? how LBJ plans to
end furor. por U S News 58:22 Je 21 '65
Mr Shriver and the savage politics of pov-
erty. W. F. Haddad. il Harper 231:43-50
D '65
Progress, protest & politics. il por Time 86:
19-20 Jl 16 '65
Rockefeller and Shriver clash, why. por U S
News 59:20 Jl 12 '65
Shriver and the war on poverty. il por
Newsweek 66:22-6+ S 13 '65
SHROVE Tuesday. See Carnival
SHRUBS
Bring a song to your garden. J. K. Terres.
il Pop Gard 16:24-5 S '65
Flowering shrubs are for every garden. I.
Zucker. il Flower Grower 53:30-3 Ja '66
Outstanding shrubs. E. S. Henderson. Horti-
culture 43:48-9 O '65
Shrubs for summer flowers. R. C. Hands. il
Horticulture 43:20-1 Jl '65
See also
Brooms (shrubs)
Crape myrtle
Holly
Myrtle
Silk tassel bushes
Planting
Placing and spacing trees, shrubs, and
vines. il Bet Hom & Gard 43:126 Ap '65
Spring planting, shrub send-off. il Flower
Grower 52:51 Ap '65
SHUEY, Bruce S. See Stout, R. C. jt. auth.
SHULDINER, Herbert
Educating yourself. Pop Sci 186:84-6+ My '65
Model dream cars build dream careers. Pop
Sci 187:170-2+ O '65
SHULL, Kenneth E.
Try a multi-bed filter. Am City 80:77-9 N '65
SHULL, Thelma
Bartered bride as seen on glassware. Hobbies
70:82 Ap '65

SHULMAN, Max
Humor is no laughing matter. por Seventeen 24:110+ Je '65
SHUMAN, Charles Baker
Food for freedom. il por Time 86:11 D 24 '65
How to shoot Santa Claus. il pors Time 86: 22-6 S 3 '65
SHUMAN, James B. See Daniel, J. jt. auth.
SHUMWAY, F. Ritter
Forecasting Great Lakes weather. por Motor B 115:53-6+ Je '65
SHUMWAY, Mary
Suddenly falling earth. J. Crawford, jr. Poetry 105:410 Mr '65
SHUNK, William R.
Successful foreign aid in education. Sch & Soc 93:437-8 N 13 '65
SHURTLEFF, Mal, and Feight, J. J.
How to identify and control corn diseases. il Suc Farm 63:44-5+ Ap '65
Latest report on maize dwarf mosaic. Suc Farm 63:56-7+ F '65
SHUSTER, George N.
Catholic education once more. Cath World 201:50-4 Ap '65
SHUTTLESWORTH, Fred
Benevolent dictator: all-Negro Revelation Baptist church. por Time 86:71 S 3 '65
Champion. por Time 86:73-4 N 26 '65
Shuttlesworth defies ouster demand. Christian Cent 82:1397 N 10 '65
SHUTTLEWORTH, Jack
John Held, jr, and his world. Am Heritage 16:28-32 Ag '65
SHWAYDER brothers, Incorporated
In the bag. il Time 85:88+ Je 25 '65
Samsonite: on land, in the air, on the sea. il Bsns W p98+ F 27 '65
SHYER, Marlene Fanta
Decision by firelight; story. Good H 161:74-5 Jl '65
Favorite; story. Good H 161:90-1 O '65
Gray house, black trim; story. Redbook 125: 66-7 Ag '65
Just the man for you; story. McCalls 93: 112-13 N '65
Life and love upstairs; story. Good H 160: 112-13 My '65
Pantry kiss; story. Redbook 126:46-7 Ja '66
R one mended heart; story. Good H 161:92-3 N '65
Second impressions; story. Redbook 124:50-1 F '65
Slick pattern. Writer 78:12-14 Ag '65
SIAMESE twins
Rare change from us to me; Foglia twins separated. il Life 58:41-2 Je 25 '65
SIBBISON, James B.
Rise & fall of Wm. C. Durant. Motor T 17:58-61 Ap '65
SIBELIUS, Jean Julius Christian
Centennial of the birth of Jean Sibelius; messages, January 1, 1965. L. B. Johnson; U. Kekkonen. Dept State Bul 52:111 Ja 25 '65
Sibelius and the tide of taste; with discography. W. R. Trotter. il pors Hi Fi 15: 48-53+ D '65
SIBERIA
See also
Akademgorodok

Antiquities
Frozen tombs of the Scythians. M. I. Artamonov. il Sci Am 212:100-9 bibliog(p 151) My '65

Description and travel
Giving Siberia a good name. R. J. Korengold. il Newsweek 66:38-9 Ag 30 '65
SIBLEY, Charles Kenneth
What is not in New York. F. Getlein. New Repub 153:34+ O 2 '65
SIBLEY, Hi
Folding dollhouse. Pop Mech 124:144-5 D '65
Lathe fun from Alpine novelties. Pop Mech 125:164-7 Ja '66
Tree well serves a double purpose. il Flower Grower 52:19 O '65
SIBLINGS
Dialogue with mothers: we got the baby for you. B. Bettelheim. Ladies Home J 82:55-6 N '65
Firstborns more anxious. Sci N L 88:311 N 13 '65
It's hard to be the middle child; with group-discussion program. by E. G. Neisser. A. Whitmer. bibliog il Parents Mag 40:34+, 64-5+ O '65
It's smart to play favorites. M. B. Hoover. il Parents Mag 40:48-9+ My '65
Life with the new baby. B. L. Goldsmith. il Parents Mag 40:52-4+ S '65

Mistakes many mothers make: will your children ever be friends? R. W. Bacmeister. il Parents Mag 40:54-5+ Ap '65
My parents play favorites: questions and answers. A. Wood. il Seventeen 24:144-5+ S '65
Should I tell everything? questions and answers. A. Wood. Seventeen 24:295-6 Ag '65
See also
Children, First-born
SICILY

Description and travel
Sicily by summer. E. Perényi. Vogue 146:46-7 Ag 1 '65
SICK, The
Heart patients need sleep. Sci N L 88:116 Ag 21 '65
How to prepare for a hospital stay. Good H 160:175 My '65
Living with illness in the family; questions and answers. A. Wood. il Seventeen 24:142-3+ Mr '65
Love: the essential medicine when your child is ailing; excerpt from Caring for your disabled child. B. Spock and M. O. Lerrigo. Ladies Home J 82:53+ My '65
See also
Incurables
Physicians and patients
Sickness

Recreation
See Recreation for the handicapped
SICK benefit programs. See Insurance, Health
SICKEL, Werner
Respiratory and electrical responses to light stimulation in the retina of the frog. bibliog Science 148:648-51 Ap 30 '65
SICKLE cell anemia. See Anemia
SICKNESS
Why get sick when you don't have to? E. Day. il Ladies Home J 83:46+ Ja '66
SICKNESS insurance. See Insurance, Health
SICOTTE, Sid
Church in Mississippi. Commonweal 82:487-8 Jl 9 '65
SICRE, José Gómez-. See Gómez-Sicre, J.
SIDE, Ronald K
Oliver Twist: dramatization of novel by C. Dickens. Plays 24:87-98 My '65
SIDENBLADH, Göran
Stockholm: a planned city; with biographical sketch. Sci Am 213:28, 106-10+ S '65
SIDERITE. See Iron ores
SIDERS, Harvey
Kenton at the Pavilion. Sat R 48:62-3 F 13 '65
SIDEWALKS, Elevated
Campus City, Chicago; the walks. il Arch Forum 123:30-3 S '65
Walk on the high side; plans for Morristown, Tenn, and London's Piccadilly circus. il Newsweek 66:62 Jl 12 '65
SIDEWALKS, Moving. See Moving platforms
SIDEWINDER (guided missile) See Guided missiles—Launching from airplanes
SIDEWINDERS. See Motor vehicles, Amphibious
SIDEY, Hugh
Measure of the man. Life 59:53+ D 3 '65
SIDING (building)
How to be sure about siding! Bet Hom & Gard 43:91-3 Jl '65
Those amazing new sidings with built-in paint. R. Treves. il Pop Sci 187:130-3+ S '65
SIDLEY, N. A. and others
Photopic spectral sensitivity in the monkey: methods for determining, and initial results. bibliog Science 150:1837-9 D 31 '65
SIDMAN, R. L. and others
Neurological mutants of the mouse. Science 150:513-14+ O 22 '65
SIDNEY, Margaret
Five little Peppers midway. See Kimball, R. P. Where is Phronsie Pepper?
SIEBEL, Julia
At seventy-five; poem. Poetry 107:93 N '65
SIEGEL, Benjamin
Free man; story. Redbook 124:155-78 Mr '65
SIEGEL, Dorothy
What young wives have learned about husbands. Redbook 126:58-9+ N '65
When to interfere with children's friendships. Parents Mag 40:56-8+ My '65
SIEGEL, Eli
What's there? Mod Phot 29:91+ O '65
SIEGEL, J.
Surplus parachute into balloon spinnaker. Motor B 115:57+ F '65

SIEGEL, Jerome, and Gordon, T. P.
Paradoxical sleep: deprivation in the cat.
bibliog Science 148:978-80 My 14 '65
SIEGEL, Sanford
What we'll see on Mars. B. H. Frisch. il
por Sci Digest 58:44-53 Jl '65
SIEGEL, Seymour
Christian Mishna. Commentary 40:73-5 Ag '65
SIEGFRIED, John B. and others
Evoked brain potential correlates of psycho-
physical responses: heterochromatic flicker
photometry. bibliog Science 149:321-3 Jl 16
'65
SIEKER, Herbert O. See Nagaya, H. jt. auth.
SIEKMAN, Philip
Revolt of French Canada. Fortune 71:156-63+
F '65; Same abr. with title French Canada:
a people in revolt. Read Digest 86:203-4+
My '65
South America's shattered showcase. Fortune
72:164-9+ N '65
SIEMSSEN, Gunther Schneider-. See Schnei-
der-Siemssen, G.
SIEPI, Cesare
Mephisto's musings. por Hi Fi 16:124 Ja '66
SIERRA club
Carey-Thomas awards are presented. il Pub W
187:32-4 My 3 '65
How the Sierra club does it; remarkable
color reproduction. il Pub W 187:94-5+
Mr 1 '65
Wilderness trips for the whole family. il
Sunset 134:30 Ap '65
SIERRA national forest. See National forests
SIERRA NEVADA, Calif.
Sierra Nevada has varied climate, plants. Sci
N L 87:290 My 8 '65
SIEVENPIPER, Don
Dragwinder. il Hot Rod 18:34-7 Mr '65
SIEVENPIPER, Jim
Dragwinder. il Hot Rod 18:34-7 Mr '65
SIGEL, Roberta
Assumptions about the learning of political
values. bibliog f Ann Am Acad 361:1-9 S
'65
In retrospect. Ann Am Acad 361:128-9 S '65
(ed) Political socialization: its role in the
political process. bibliog f Ann Am Acad
361:1-140 S '65
SIGHET, Rumania
Last return; tr. by A. Schwartz. E. Wiesel.
Commentary 39:43-9 Mr '65
SIGHT
Adaptation to prismatically rotated visual
fields. R. B. Morant and H. K. Beller. bib-
liog il Science 148:530-1 Ap 23 '65
Adrenaline and noradrenaline: relation to
performance in a visual vigilance task.
J. F. O'Hanlon. jr. bibliog il Science 150:
507-9 O 22 '65
Astronauts' vision acute. Sci N L 88:343 N 27
'65
Dermooptical perception: a cautionary re-
port; letter. J. Zubin. Science 147:985 F 26
'65
Detection thresholds as a function of interval
separation between two successive targets.
H. Schuckman and J. Orbach. bibliog il
Science 150:1623-5 D 17 '65
Eye doctor's advice for putters. il Sci Digest
58:34-6 N '65
New roles seen for human eyes in space.
R. G. O'Lone. Aviation W 83:51+ Ag 30
'65
Patricia couldn't see the board. J. Hunter. il
Parents Mag 40:68-9+ Mr '65
Preference for shapes of intermediate varia-
bility in the newborn human. M. Hershen-
son and others. bibliog il Science 147:630-1
F 5 '65
Visual accommodation in human infants. H.
Haynes and others. bibliog il Science 148:
528-30 Ap 23 '65
Visual excitation and blood clotting. G. Wald.
bibliog il Science 150:1028-30 N 19 '65
Visual resolution and the diffraction limit.
H. B. Barlow. bibliog il Science 149:553-5
Jl 30 '65
Your eyes, your auto and your life; with eye
tests. P. W. Kearney. il Read Digest 87:
115-18 D '65
See also
After images
Blindness
SIGHT (animals)
Perception of stroboscopic movement; evi-
dence for its innate basis. I. Rock and
others. bibliog Science 147:1050-2 F 26 '65
Uncrossed visual pathways of hooded and
albino rats. R. D. Lund. bibliog il Science
149:1506 S 24 '65
Underwater visual discrimination by the
California sea lion. R. J. Schusterman and
others. bibliog il Science 147:1594-6 Mr
26 '65

SIGHT (birds)
Pupillary response of the screech owl. otus
asio. L. G. Bishop and L. Stark. il Science
148:1750-2 Je 25 '65
SIGHT (insects)
Diffraction and visual acuity of insects. J.
Palka. bibliog il Science 149:551-3 Jl 30 '65
Visual resolution and the diffraction limit.
H. B. Barlow. bibliog il Science 149:553-5
Jl 30 '65
SIGHT testing
Preserving two good eyes. P. L. Levin. il
N Y Times Mag p 65-6 F 28 '65
SIGHTS for firearms. See Firearms—Sights
SIGLER, Howard T.
How to take your own picture. Field & S
69:100 Mr '65
SIGMAN, Carl T.
Eight landscape tricks for plastic pools. Pop
Sci 187:132-5 Jl '65
How two can live happily in the same room.
Pop Sci 187:120-3 D '65
Nine new plans for outdoor storage. Pop Sci
186:130-8 My '65
Seven ways to find space for a guest bed.
Pop Sci 186:140-4 Mr '65
SIGMUND, Paul E.
Books. Commonweal 82:360-1 Je 4 '65
New Tshombe. Commonweal 82:559-63 Ag 6
'65
SIGN in Sidney Brustein's window; drama. See
Hansberry, L.
SIGN language
High price of silent insults; illegal gestures
in Italy. il Time 85:67-8 Ap 9 '65
SIGNALITE, incorporated
Writing with light. J. G. Rabinowitz. il
Electr World 74:31 N '65
SIGNALS and signaling
Emergency flasher; auto warning signals.
D. Yeh. il Pop Electr 23:60 Jl '65
From CQ to Mayday. H. M. Anthony.
Motor B 115:140+ My '65
Sign talk. B. Lemon. il Motor B 116:84 D '65
SIGNATURES (writing)
See also
Autographs
SIGNER, Peter. See Pepin, R. O. jt. auth.
SIGNETICS corporation
Economical microcircuit package sought. B.
Miller. il Aviation W 82:44-5 Mr 1 '65
SIGNORELLI, Luca
Mother church, Orvieto. R. M. Coates. il
Horizon 7:85-9 Spr '65
SIGNS and signboards
Carving signs with router templates. R.
Shoberg. il Pop Mech 125:176-80+ Ja '66
Hobo signs: designs by students at the Her-
ron school of art. il Design 66:36-9 Mr '65
Signs; King displays, signmakers for Broad-
way theatres. New Yorker 41:42-5 O 2 '65
Signs of the times. R. Almquist. il Design
66:28-9 Ja '65
See also
Billboards
SIH, Paul K. T.
New books. Cath World 201:141-3 My '65
SIHANOUK, Norodom. See Norodom Sihanouk
SIK, A. E.
Weather while you wait. Motor B 116:42-
5+ O '65
SIKHS
They are staring at me; excerpt from Area of
darkness. V. S. Naipaul. il Sat Eve Post
238:82-4 Ap 10 '65
SIKKIM
Hope-la in Gangtok; coronation of Sikkim's
queen. il Time 85:39 Ap 16 '65
Land of Hope and yaks. J. Lieber. il Sat R
48:60+ S 18 '65
See also
Sino-Indian border dispute. 1957-
SILAGE
Cattle like cold-cut silage. D. Seim. il Farm J
89:56D F '65
Cold cut silage gets another boost. Farm J
89:46 O '65
Hybrid grass haylage. G. W. Wormley. il
Farm J 89:54F S '65
Latest on corn in silos for dairy cows. D.
Hillman. il Suc Farm 63:36-8+ Ag '65
New ideas on silage feeding for beef; corn
silage mixtures. D. Malena. il Suc Farm
63:36-8+ Ag '65
New silage-feeding ideas. J. R. Borcherding
and J. Albino. il Suc Farm 63:36-7 N '65
They fill silo all year around. J. Pates and
D. Malena. il Suc Farm 63:44-5 Je '65
Which way; hay or grass silage? Farm J
89:34 Jl '65
See also
Silos

SILAGE handling
Haylage gains fast in the East. B. Hardy. il Farm J 89:36-7+ O '65
SILBERMAN, Arlene
When Noël came home. Good H 161:80-1+ Ag '65
SILBERMAN, Charles E.
Beware the day they change their minds! Fortune 72:150-3+ N '65
Mixed-up war on poverty. Fortune 72:156-61+ Ag '65
Real news about automation. Fortune 71:124-6+ Ja; 78+ Mr '65
Technology and the labor market. Fortune 71:153-5+ F; 130-3+ Ap '65
SILENCE
On silence. F. Stark. il Holiday 38:12+ D '65
Word. V. P. McCorry. America 112:205-6 F 6 '65
SILHOUETTES
Blue and white paper silhouettes. J. Markos. il Design 67:17 S '65
How to make handsome duck silhouettes. D. Lewis. il Pop Sci 188:134-5 Ja '66
Vagabond camera. W. Lane. il Travel 124:64-5 D '65
SILICA
Clathrate crystalline form of silica. B. Kamb. bibliog il Science 148:232-4 Ap 9 '65
Silica: role in the buffering of natural waters. R. M. Garrels. bibliog Science 148:69 Ap 2 '65
See also
Chert
SILICA gel
Extend the abundance of summer. R. C. Hands. il Horticulture 43:24-5 N '65
SILICATES
Rock-forming silicates; conference on the crystal structures and crystal chemistry of rock-forming silicates at Lake Vermilion, Minn. T. Zoltai. Science 150:926-8 N 12 '65
Silicates: reactivity with sea water. F. T. Mackenzie and R. M. Garrels. bibliog il Science 150:57-8 O 1 '65
See also
Merrihueite
SILICON
Germanium and silicon disulfides: structure and synthesis. C. T. Prewitt and H. S. Young. bibliog il Science 149:535-7 Jl 30 '65
SILICON carbide
Inorganic fiber production readied. J. F. Judge. il Miss & Roc 17:32+ D 13 '65
Whiskers in quantity; silicon carbide. Sci Am 212:56 Mr '65
SILICON compounds
Clathrate structure of silicon Na₈Si₄₆ and Na₈Si₁₃₆. J. S. Kasper and others. bibliog il Science 150:1713-14 D 24 '65
SILICON controlled rectifiers. See Electric current rectifiers
SILICON diodes. See Diodes
SILICONE rubber. See Rubber, Silicone
SILICONES
Chemical background of silicones. J. F. Hyde. bibliog il Science 147:829-36 F 19 '65
SILK, George
Think big, that's Life. il Mod Phot 29:19+ My '65
SILK manufacture and trade
Millions from the mulberry bush; Thailand's soft, nubby silk cloth. il Time 86:91 Jl 16 '65
SILK screen printing
Serigraphy. W. Radcliffe. il Sch Arts 65:16-20 O '65
Silk screen. O. Locke. il Sch Arts 64:17-19 F '65
SILK tassel bushes
Coast silktassel puts on quite a winter show. il Sunset 135:241 N '65
SILK trees
They are splendid in summer. il Sunset 135:164 Ag '65
SILL, William
Living-room workbench licks the dust. Pop Sci 188:124-6 Ja '66
SILLIPHANT, Stirling
Take back your Kafka. J. G. Dunne. New Repub 153:32-4 S 4 '65
SILONE, Ignazio, pseud.
European literary scene. R. J. Clements. por Sat R 48:43 N 13 '65
SILOS
They fill silo all year around. J. Pates and D. Malena. il Suc Farm 63:44-5 Je '65
Two new silage ideas: roadbed silo, apron feeder. il Farm J 90:52F Ja '66
SILOS, Missile. See Guided missiles—Launching pads
SILVA, Artur da Costa e
Other barrel. por Time 86:46 N 12 '65

SILVA, Ruth C.
Reapportionment and redistricting; with biographical sketch. Sci Am 213:14, 20-7 bibliog(p 142) N '65
SILVER, Adele Zeidman
Parent and child. N Y Times Mag p 132+ N 14 '65
SILVER, George A.
Education: the forgotten patient. Nation 200:467-70 My 3 '65
SILVER, Isidore
McCarthy and the establishment. New Repub 153:28-31 N 20 '65
Ugliness and the law. Commonweal 83:144-6 N 5 '65
SILVER, James Wesley
Of many things. T. N. Davis. America 113:145 Ag 14 '65
SILVER, Sidney L.
Electronic timers for automatic control. Electr World 73:39-41+ Mr '65
SILVER
Is silver necessary? use in photographic industry. N. Rothschild. il Pop Phot 57:76-9+ O '65
New methods could aid search for silver. Sci N L 87:232 Ap 10 '65
Two new methods found to increase silver supply. il Sci N L 88:23 Jl 10 '65
See also
Silverware
SILVER All-America awards. See Sports illustrated silver anniversary All-America
SILVER as money
Base metal for our coins? C. French. Hobbies 70:102 Mr '65
Big change; possible silver substitutes for US coinage. Newsweek 65:79 My 17 '65
Change in change. Newsweek 65:88+ Je 14 '65
Change in coins. Time 85:84 Je 11 '65
Coins: no silver lining? W. F. Rickenbacker. Nat R 17:237 Mr 23 '65
Crisis in silver. U S Camera 28:41+ Ag '65
Gold, silver come into the news. il U S News 58:47 F 8 '65
In answer to your questions about silver. il U S News 58:118-19 Je 21 '65
Inside story of our new silver-saving coins. A. P. Armagnac. il Pop Sci 187:64-6 S '65; Same abr. with title Those new sandwich coins. Read Digest 87:21-2+ D '65
Our silver dolors. E. Lichtenstein. il Fortune 71:126-9+ Mr '65
Remember Gresham's law. A. M. Sullivan. Duns R 86:84 Ag '65
Silver cloud; shortage of U.S. coins; rising demand in industry. il Time 85:85 F 26 '65
Silver coin plan: a bit for everyone; plan to eliminate silver from dimes and quarters, leave some in half-dollars. il Bsns W p57-8+ Je 12 '65
Silver crisis; what it can mean to photographers. A. Wolfman. Mod Phot 29:16+ S '65
Silver shortage. America 112:816 Je 5 '65
Silverless coins lighter. W. McCann. Sci N L 88:23 Jl 10 '65
SILVER Burdett company
Building language skills. E. Griffin. Wilson Lib Bul 40:62-3 S '65
SILVER jewelry. See Jewelry
SILVER lance exercise. See United States—Marine corps—Maneuvers
SILVER mines and mining

Mexico
On trail of new riches in centuries-old mines. il Bsns W p 112-14 Mr 13 '65
SILVER nitrate
New burn treatment. Sci Digest 57:21 Je '65
SILVER polishes. See Polishing materials
SILVER question. See Silver as money
SILVER selenide
Pressure dependence of the alpha-beta transition temperature in silver selenide. M. D. Banus. bibliog Science 147:732-3 F 12 '65
SILVERBERG, Robert
Science in action; hoaxes and half-truths. Natur Hist 74:62-5 Mr '65
SILVERMAN, Eve
Senior-made primers. NEA J 54:32-3 O '65
SILVERS, Willys K.
Agouti locus: homology of its method of operation in rats and mice. bibliog Science 149:651-2 Ag 6 '65
SILVERSMITHS
Hester Bateman. G. Kaler. Hobbies 70:46 S '65
Powell? Potts? Pitts! the T P epergnes. E. Gaines. il Antiques 87:462-5 Ap '65
Sword hilts by early American silversmiths. J. K. Lattimer. il Antiques 87:196-9 F '65

SILVERT, K. H.
Parties and the masses. bibliog f Ann Am Acad 358:101-8 Mr '65

SILVERTHORNE, Don C.
Banky panky. Newsweek 65:68 Mr 29 '65
Failing banks & sporty bankers. M. Harris. il Nation 200:442-5 Ap 26 '65; Reply with rejoinder. W. R. Grubb. 200:inside cover My 31 '65
Hard twelve. il por Newsweek 65:78 Ap 5 '65

SILVERWARE
Chinese imagery on restoration silver. C. C. Dauterman. il Antiques 88:511-15 O '65
Constant craftsmen; Lunt's Lace Point. il Mlle 61:196-7 My '65
Fakes, forgeries, and duty dodgers in English silver; excerpts from Old English silver. J. Banister. Antiques 88:330-2 S '65
For someone special; special gifts in sterling. il Seventeen 24:138-9 Ap '65
Recent museum accessions in silver. R. Davidson. il Antiques 87:726+ Je '65
Silver made just for you. il Seventeen 24:142-3 N '65
Silver, pewter, and other metals: old Northwest Territory. il Antiques 87:322-3 Mr '65
What goes with what? choosing china and silver patterns. il Seventeen 24:114-15 S '65
What to call a spade: silver. il Vogue 145:148-9 Je '65
See also
Epergnes
Spoons

Care
Care and safekeeping of silver. il House & Gard 127:32+ Ap '65

Exhibitions
Silver for the dinner table; exhibiton at the Sterling and Francine Clark art institute, Williamstown, Mass. R. Davidson. il Antiques 88:158+ Ag '65

SIMANDLE, Sidney
Certification across state lines. NEA J 54:56-8 D '65

SIMBAS
Arrows to heaven. Time 85:40 Je 11 '65
Certain gain; clean up of Congolese rebels. il Time 85:32 Ap 23 '65
How to win wars & elections. il Time 85:30-1 Ap 2 '65
Red arsenals arm the Simbas; with eyewitness reports from Life correspondents. il Life 58:26-33 F 12 '65
Renouncing the rebels; Simbas shipped out of Egypt. Time 86:41 S 24 '65
Stanleyville massacre; excerpt from 111 days in Stanleyville. D. Reed. il Read Digest 87:233-8+ S '65

SIMENON, Georges
Practiced hand. por Time 86:120+ D 10 '65

SIMIAN adenoviruses. See Tumor viruses

SIMIAN malaria. See Malaria

SIMIC, Charles
My hand; My legs: Boss hires; poems. Nation 201:314 N 1 '65

SIMISON, Frank M.
Indiana's state parks. Travel 123:48-9 My '65

SIMISTER, R. Wayne
Capacitance touch-plate lighting switch. Electr World 74:44+ Ag '65

SIMKIN, William E.
Role of the federal mediator. T. R. Brooks. por Duns R 85:59-60+ Je '65

SIMMON Xenomega. See Photography—Enlarging

SIMMONS, Charles
Born to suffer and to serve. Sat R 49:40 Ja 22 '66

SIMMONS, Ernest
Law student overcomes handicap to win point. il pors Ebony 20:119-20+ My '65

SIMMONS, F. Blair, and others
Auditory nerve: electrical stimulation in man. bibliog Science 148:104-6 Ap 2 '65

SIMMONS, Jean
Jean Simmons: the mouse becomes a cat. C. R. Jennings. pors Sat Eve Post 238:77-8 Ag 28 '65

SIMMONS, John S.
Content specialist in English. Sch & Soc 93:153-4 Mr 6 '65

SIMMONS machine tool corporation
Gambling on the Czechs; exclusive sales agents in the western hemisphere for the heavy machine tools of the Skoda works. il Fortune 72:103-4 D '65

SIMMS, Jeptha Root
Man whose praise we sing; summary of his Trappers of New York. F. B. Leach. il Am Heritage 16:62-3+ Ap '65

SIMMS, Mildred E. See Larson, R. H. jt. auth.

SIMNEL cake. See Cake

SIMON, Andrew, and Simon, Richard
Automating the Model 11. il Pop Phot 56:48-9+ Mr '65

SIMON, E.
Recombination in bacteriophage T4: a mechanism. bibliog Science 150:760-3 N 5 '65

SIMON, John
Mugging the Bard in Central park. Commonweal 82:635-6 S 3 '65
Spotlight on the nonwoman. Holiday 38:153-4+ N '65

SIMON, Mina Lewiton
Crickets, raccoons, and writers. Library J 90:2336-7 My 15 '65

SIMON, Neil
Doc Simon's R for comedy. A. Levy. il pors N Y Times Mag p42-3+ Mr 7 '65
He loves to kill them. T. Prideaux. il por Life 58:39+ Ap 9 '65
Odd couple. Criticism
America 112:810-11 My 29 '65
Cath World 201:343-4 Ag '65
Commonweal 82:51-2 Ap 2 '65
Life il 58:35-6 Ap 9 '65
Nation 200:373-4 Ap 5 '65
New Yorker 41:83 Mr 20 '65
Newsweek il 65:90-1 Mr 22 '65
Sat R 48:44 Mr 27 '65
Time 85:66 Mr 19 '65
Vogue 145:142 My '65

SIMON, Noel
Of whales and whaling. Science 149:943-6 Ag 27 '65

SIMON, Norton
Collecting is its own reward. il Fortune 71:152-9 Je '65
Corporate Cézanne. il pors Time 85:74-6+ Je 4 '65
New St George. il por Time 87:69A Ja 21 '66
New show at ABC. por Time 86:64 Jl 30 '65
Norton Simon says thumbs down. R. J. Whalen. il pors Fortune 71:146-51+ Je '65
Simon says. il por Newsweek 65:80 Mr 29 '65
Who, me? por Newsweek 66:55-6 Ag 2 '65

SIMON, Paul
Cleaning up the Illinois legislature: a follow-up report. Harper 231:125 S '65

SIMON, Richard. See Simon, A. jt. auth.

SIMON, Richard A. See Frederick, W. H. jr. jt. auth.

SIMON, Sidney
From England's green and pleasant bowers. Art N 64:28-31+ Ap '65

SIMON, Stephen
Music to my ears; Schola cantorum concert in Philharmonic Hall. I. Kolodin. Sat R 48:30 Mr 6 '65

SIMON and Schuster, Incorporated
Simon & Schuster to issue Interpublic books line. il Pub W 188:35-6 D 6 '65

SIMON Fraser university, Burnaby, British Columbia
In Canada, the continent's first single-structure campus. D. Lyndon. il Arch Forum 123:13-21 D '65

SIMONDS, C. H.
Children's books. Nat R 17:1165 D 14 '65
Popcult orgy. Nat R 17:989-90 N 2 '65

SIMONDS, Charles G.
Get a boat! let her float! por Sr Schol 86:sup21 Ap 15 '65

SIMONDS, Edith
We like the suburbs but. Parents Mag 40:54-5+ D '65

SIMONS, George F.
Liturgy. Commonweal 82:678 S 24 '65

SIMONSON, Ernst, and Brožek, Josef
Trends in some areas of Soviet biomedical research. bibliog Science 150:1687-9 D 24 '65

SIMONSON, Solomon
New curriculum in English, speech, and communications. Sch & Soc 93:394-5 O 30 '65

SIMONSON, William N.
(comp) Articles and other books received; Latin America. See issues of American historical review

SIMONT, Marc
Afternoon in Spain; excerpts. il Horizon 7:118-20 Autumn '65
¡Olé! for the brave Club Taurino! paintings. Sports Illus 23:32-9 Ag 23 '65

SIMPKINS, John J.
Easy-to-make greenhouse. il Flower Grower 52:15-16 Mr '65
Root plants quickly under constant mist. il Flower Grower 52:20-1 Jl '65
Springtime photographs outdoors & indoors. il Flower Grower 52:33 Mr '65

SIMPLE no; story. See Ringer, V.

SIMPLEX time recorder company
Invading Britain in the old Yankee way;
opening of plant in Halifax, England. il
Bsns W p96-7 Ag 14 '65

SIMPLIFIED inertial guidance system. See
Inertial guidance systems

SIMPSON, Dale R.
Carbonate in hydroxylapatite. bibliog Science
147:501-2 Ja 29 '65

SIMPSON, Dwight J.
Israel: the state of siege. Cur Hist 48:263-8
My '65

SIMPSON, J. A. See O'Gallagher, J. J. jt. auth.

SIMPSON, Louis
Baudelaire in three injections. Harper 230:
48-50 Je '65
Confessions of an American poet. pors N Y
Times Mag p30-1+ My 2 '65
Dvonya; poem. Harper 231:56 N '65
One of their kings; poem. New Yorker 41:46
My 1 '65
Outward; poem. New Yorker 40:36 F 13 '65
Sacred objects; poem. Harper 231:102 O '65
Things; poem. New Yorker 41:56 My 15 '65
What's in it for me? Harper 231:173 O '65

SIMPSON, Mary M.
Two cultures revisited. Bul Atomic Sci 21:
31-2 S '65

SIMPSON, S. A.
Sailing through the Marquesas. Travel 125:
48-54 Ja '66

SIMPSON'S. See London—Hotels, restaurants,
etc.

SIMS, Charles
Visit Bogalusa and you will look for me. S.
Alexander. Life 59:28 Jl 2 '65

SIMS, Joseph
Rio de Janeiro; carnival and beach. Sat R
49:86-8 Ja 1 '66

SIMULATORS
Amateur scientist; apparatus for simulat-
ing high altitudes. il Sci Am 213:239-40+
S '65
Better cratering extrapolation seen; simula-
tion of moon's surface. il Miss & Roc 16:
23-4 Mr 1 '65
Celestial simulator is major advance. il Miss
& Roc 16:28+ Mr 15 '65
Douglas studying oil bath weightlessness. Miss
& Roc 17:36 O 4 '65
Lunar rover cabin space examined. il Miss
& Roc 17:30+ O 4 '65
Navy to build huge blast tube; Naval weap-
ons test laboratory, Dahlgren, Va, to simu-
late high-altitude blasts. il Miss & Roc
16:17 Ap 26 '65
Simulated accidents to help halt real ones;
automobile driving simulator system. Sci
N L 87:72 Ja 30 '65
See also
Space flight simulators
Space station simulators

SIMULATORS, Flight. See Flight simulators

SIN
Announcing mortal sins. C. Davis. America
112:193 F 6 '65; Discussion. 112:340-1 Mr 13
'65
Sin, liberty and law. by L. Monden. Review
Cath World 201:401 S '65. J. D. Conway
Speaking out; down with sin! T. Wolfe. Sat
Eve Post 238:12+ Je 19 '65

SINAI, I. Robert
Is foreign aid worth the price? interview
por U S News 59:64-7 Ag 30 '65

SINATRA, Frank
Me and my music. pors Life 58:86-96+ Ap
23 '65
about
At sea with Sinatra. il Newsweek 66:71 Ag
23 '65
Chairman of the board. Time 86:62 Jl 16 '65
Idol remembered. M. Evelyn. por Esquire 64:
84-5 Jl '65
No news is good news. Newsweek 66:88 N 29
'65
Private world and thoughts of Frank Sinatra.
il pors Life 58:84-96+ Ap 23 '65
Seagoing soap opera of captain Sinatra. T.
Thompson. il pors Life 59:34B Ag 20 '65
Sinatra at fifty. J. Bryson. il pors Look 29:
61-6+ D 14 '65
Sinatra: where the action is. il pors News-
week 66:39-42 S 6 '65
Voyage of the Southern Breeze. il por Time
86:64 Ag 20 '65

SINCLAIR, Harry
Tempest over Teapot. B. Bliven. il por Am
Heritage 16:22-3+ Ag '65

SINCLAIR, Thomas
Champion Red Archer; story. Yale R 55:227-
49 D '65

SINCLAIR, Warren K.
Hydroxyurea: differential lethal effects on
cultured mammalian cells during the cell
cycle. bibliog Science 150:1729-31 D 24 '65

SINDBIS virus. See Viruses

SINDLER, Allen P.
Protest against the political status of the
Negro. Ann Am Acad 357:48-54 Ja '65

SING me a song of left tackle; story. See
Weeks, M. L.

SING to me through open windows; drama.
See Kopit, A.

SINGAPORE
Art of dispelling anxiety. Time 86:20 Ag 27
'65
Atlantic report. Atlan 216:48+ N '65
Malaysia—Singapore=trouble. S. Huck. Nat
R 17:771+ S 7 '65
More bad news for U.S. from Asia. il U S
News 59:21-3 Ag 23 '65
Showcase city of the Orient. il Newsweek
66:34 Ag 23 '65
Singapore. A. Menen. il Vogue 145:200-3+ My
'65
Singapore splits. il Sr Schol 87:17 O 7 '65
Still good friends. Newsweek 66:37 Ag 30 '65
See also
United Nations—Singapore

Economic conditions
Boom that went bust. il Time 87:86 Ja 7 '66

Foreign relations
United States
Blasting off. il Time 86:21B S 10 '65
United States—Foreign relations—Singapore

Industries
Latest success story in Asia. il U S News 58:
76 My 3 '65

Politics and government
Anti-red bulwark weakens. il Bsns W p26
Ag 14 '65
As Jakarta and Peiping rejoice; Singapore's
eviction from Malaysia. America 113:200
Ag 28 '65
Bad day in a rear area of Asia; Singapore
leaves federation. Life 59:4 Ag 20 '65
Brand-new baby for the U.N; secession of
Singapore from Malaysia federation. R.
Morse. Life 59:65+ Ag 20 '65
Brilliant, but a bit of a thug; report and
interview by R. Morse. il Life 59:43-4+ Jl
16 '65
Expulsion of Singapore. C. P. FitzGerald. il
Nation 201:208-12 O 11 '65
Federal idea; Singapore to secede from the
Federation of Malaysia. Christian Cent 82:
1023-9 Ag 25 '65
Lee Kuan Yew is Singapore. S. Topping. il
N Y Times Mag p66-7+ O 31 '65
Malaysia: my dream is shattered. il News-
week 66:33-4 Ag 23 '65
Modest proposal. Time 86:35 S 24 '65
One of our islands is missing. il Time 86:26+
Ag 20 '65
Second fall of Singapore. D. Warner. il Re-
porter 33:27-9 S 9 '65
Singapore's restless Chinese. S. S. King. il
Reporter 33:20-2 Ag 12 '65

SINGER, Isaac Bashevis
Major din Torah. Commentary 40:77-80 S '65
Secret; excerpt from In my father's court.
Commentary 40:72+ O '65
Two corpses go dancing; story. Commentary
40:45-9 Ag '65
What's in it for me? Harper 231:172-3 O '65
about
Antic arts: Spinoza of Canal street. R. M.
Elman. por Holiday 38:83-7 Ag '65
Problem of Isaac Bashevis Singer. D. Jacob-
son. Commentary 39:48-52 F '65

SINGER, Paul, collection. See Art—Private
collections

SINGER, S. Fred
Case for man in space. Reporter 32:25-8 Je
17 '65

SINGERS
Air pollution? tasteless themes of the Rolling
Stones. il Newsweek 66:76 Ag 16 '65
Behind the folk-song frenzy. A. Shaw. il
Read Digest 86:191+ Ap '65
Cast for Metropolitan opera national com-
pany tour. il Opera N 30:29-31 O 23 '65
Children of Bobby Dylan: boom in protest
songs with a rock beat. il Life 59:43-4+ N 5
'65
Culp sings Schumann. A. Favia-Artsay. pors
Hobbies 70:32-3+ Ap '65
Dave Clark five make a movie! Having a
wild weekend; ed. by E. Miller. J. Boor-
man; D. Clark; M. Smith. il Seventeen 24:
90-1+ Jl '65

SINGERS—*Continued*

Debuts and reappearances; New York concerts. Hi Fi 15:173 D '65

Economics of singing. J. McCracken. il Opera N 30:8-11 N 20 '65

Folk and the rock. il Newsweek 66:88+ S 20 '65

Golden voices on LP. A. Favia-Artsay. il Hobbies 70:30-1+ Mr '65

Great vibration theory; or, Are singers really stupid? particularly tenors? Time 86:66+ Ag 6 '65

Hear that big sound; with report by T. Thompson. il Life 58:82-94+ My 21 '65

Kathy's wild weekend; I won a contest, and a date with the Dave Clark five! K. Sheron. il Seventeen 24:136-7 N '65

Ladies on the loose; itinerant prima donnas. Q. Eaton. il Opera N 30:32-4 O 23 '65

Last debuts; pre-Lincoln Center season. il Newsweek 66:96 N 22 '65

London scene: pop music. F. Gannon. Nat R 17:838-40 S 21 '65

Lonely as a lark; counter-tenor. A. Deller. il Time 86:54 N 26 '65

Message from Sparks; Back porch majority concerned with the American image. il Newsweek 66:77 Ag 30 '65

Music to my ears; Russian singers and American. I. Kolodin. Sat R 48:47 N 6 '65

Musical whirl; photographs. See issues of High fidelity incorporating Musical America

My name is, Tom Jones? Welsh singer. A. Carthew. il N Y Times Mag p67+ N 14 '65

New folklorist. C. M. Curtis. il Atlan 215: 139-40 My '65

Pappy, listen to Petula; bittersweet voice of Petula Clark. C. Harman. Life 59:23 D 10 '65

Pop rock. G. Shalit. il Look 29:77-82+ Je 15 '65

Pop's bad boys: the Rolling Stones. il Newsweek 66:92 N 29 '65

Public writer no. 1? B. Dylan. T. Meehan. il N Y Times Mag p44-5+ D 12 '65; Discussion. p4+ D 26 '65

Rock 'n' roll becomes respectable. L. Robinson. il Ebony 21:48-50+ N '65

Singing or acting? age-old dilemma for opera singers. B. Thebom. il Opera N 29:8-11 Ap 3 '65

Singing the way; New York's first folk festival at Carnegie Hall. pors Newsweek 65: 84 Je 28 '65

Song-&-glance man; today's crooners. il Time 86:69-70 Jl 9 '65

Stout-hearted men; well-rounded opera singers. A. M. Lingg. il Opera N 29:12-13 F 6 '65

Swingle sound; Swingle singers. il Newsweek 66:90 D 6 '65

Waive the rules, Britannia! il Nat R 17: 407 My 18 '65

Where's it at? pop groups and the new sound. L. Lerman. il Mlle 61:74-7 Je '65

See also

Beatles

Choral groups and societies

Singing

also names of singers, e.g. M. Freni

SINGH, Jagjit

Scientific research in India. Bul Atomic Sci 21:41-3 F '65

SINGH, K. Natwar-. See Natwar-Singh, K.

SINGH, Khushwant

Why Hindu and Moslem speak hate. N Y Times Mag p27-9+ S 19 '65

SINGH, Patwant

Visitor's appraisal; Toronto city hall. Arch Forum 123:22-3 N '65

SINGING

Peter, Paul and Mary: triple play! interview; ed. by E. Miller. P. Yarrow; P. Stookey; M. A. Travers. il Seventeen 24:128-9+ Ap '65

Senior scholastic interview: folk singing ambassadors; ed. by R. Hemming. S. Addiss; B. Crofut. il Sr Schol 86:20 Mr 11 '65

Sing and tell; with study-discussion program. by R. Strang, K. Osborn and P. P. W. Knapp. bibliog il PTA Mag 59:7-9, 34 Mr '65

Singing or acting? age-old dilemma for opera singers. B. Thebom. il Opera N 29:8-11 Ap 3 '65

See also

Singers

Competitions

Auditions 1965; and Metropolitan forecast. A. M. Lingg. il Opera N 29:16-17 My 1 '65

Show on the road; Cantagiro, or Singing tour. il Newsweek 66:63 Jl 26 '65

Diction

American bel canto. J. Raskin. Opera N 30:6 Ja 15 '66

SINGING contests. See Singing—Competitions

SINGLE-lens reflex cameras

Asahi Pentax Spotmatic. H. Bristol. il U S Camera 28:57-9+ Mr '65

Boom in BTL meters. M. Edelson. il U S Camera 28:50-1+ D '65

Directory of all single-lens-reflex cameras and test reports of leading ones. il U S Camera 28:61-83 D '65

Expanding world of the 120 SLR. N. Rothschild. il Pop Phot 57:150-3 D '65

Four new reflexes. il Pop Phot 56:80-1 Ap '65

Good buys in used SLR's. il Mod Phot 29:70-1+ S '65

How? with SLR! P. Caulfield. il Mod Phot 29:60-7 Mr '65

Keppler on the SLR. H. Keppler. See issues of Modern photography

Keppler's handy guide to an easier SLR technique. H. Keppler. il Mod Phot 29:72-3+ S '65

Leicaflex. C. W. Kennedy. il Pop Phot 56: 49-51+ Ap '65

Leicaflex. P. Leonian. il U S Camera 28: 46-9+ Ap '65

Leicaflex 35mm SLR: here at long last. il Mod Phot 29:96-8 Ap '65

Modern photography's complete annual comparison guide to all 35mm & 2¼ single lens reflex cameras; comp. by D. L. Miller. il Mod Phot 29:91+ Ag '65

New Spotmatic; a tryout at the Tokyo Olympics. F. Springer-Miller. il Pop Phot 56: 70-1+ Ap '65

SLR systems compared. D. L. Miller. il Mod Phot 29:82-7 S '65

SLR with no moving mirror! Canon Pellix reflex cameras. H. Keppler and E. Meyers. il Mod Phot 29:86+ Je '65

Speed Magny combines Polaroid film with 35mm versatility. J. Wolbarst. Mod Phot 29:46 O '65

Topcon auto 100: SLR with a meter behind the lens. E. H. Ortner. il Pop Sci 188:84-5+ Ja '66

Unhappy with your groundglass? C. W. Kennedy. il Pop Phot 57:50-3 Ag '65

What means what in SLR? Mod Phot 29:105 Ag '65

What's more versatile than an SLR? selection of photographs. P. Caulfield. il Mod Phot 29:74-81 S '65

Why are some SLRs brighter? B. Sherman. il Mod Phot 29:68-9+ Mr '65

SINGLE men. See Bachelors

SINGLE sideband receivers. See Radio receiving apparatus—Single sideband receivers

SINGLE sideband system. See Radio transmission—Single sideband system

SINGLE women

Cities and the single girl; C. Abrams view. il Newsweek 66:120 N 15 '65

How come a nice girl like you isn't married? L. Bergquist. il Look 30:54-5 Ja 11 '66

Needed: a new status for the single woman. V. Lindbeck. Cath World 202:151-7 D '65

When a girl doesn't marry. F. R. Schreiber and M. Herman. Sci Digest 58:41-3 Jl '65

SINGLETON, Zutty

Jazz. W. Balliett. New Yorker 41:132-4 N 6 '65

SINIAVSKII, Andrei D. See Tertz, A.

SINKERS. See Fishing tackle

SINO-INDIAN border dispute, 1957

Bluff, bombast, or a danse macabre? il Newsweek 66:25 S 27 '65

Cease-fire and backdown. il Newsweek 66: 42+ O 4 '65

China threatens war. il Sr Schol 87:10-11 S 30 '65

Chinese patrol pops into view on rim of India. il Life 59:36-43 O 8 '65

Himalayan rumbles. Nat R 17:856-8 O 5 '65

If China attacks us—. il Newsweek 66:42 S 27 '65

Looking into Chinese guns from twenty-five feet; eyewitness story. il U S News 59:76-7 N 1 '65

New threat of big war: red China goes to the brink. il U S News 59:38-9 S 27 '65

Not war, not peace. New Repub 153:5-6 O 2 '65

View at Natu Pass. il Time 86:37 O 1 '65

Voice from the mountains. il Time 86:32 S 24 '65

SINROD, Harold S.

Periodontal disease in developing nations. bibliog Science 149:400-2 Jl 23 '65

SINTON, William M. See Boyce, P. B. jt. auth.

SINUS disease
How sinusitis is best treated. il Good H 162:137 Ja '66

SINUSITIS. See Sinus disease

SIOUX Indians. See Dakota Indians

SIPPEL, Robert F. and Glover, E. D.
Structures in carbonate rocks made visible by luminescence petrography. bibliog Science 150:1283-7 D 3 '65

SIRENS. See Whistles

SIRI, Román Fresnedo. See Fresnedo Siri, R.

SIRIKIT Kitiyakara, consort of Bhumibol Adulyadej, king of Thailand
Golden court of Thailand. il pors Vogue 145: 82-91 F 15 '65

SIRIUS
Double star Sirius. S. L. Lippincott and M. D. Worth. il Sky & Tel 31:4-6 Ja '66

SISAKĬAN, Noraĭr Martirosovich
International prospects of science; excerpts from address, 1964. UNESCO Courier 18:4-8+ Mr '65

SISCO, Joseph J.
Days ahead for the United Nations; address, September 19, 1965. Dept State Bul 53: 636-40 O 18 '65
Hard choices at the U.N; address, February 27, 1965. Dept State Bul 52:460-5 Mr 29 '65; Same. Vital Speeches 31:357-60 Ap 1 '65

SISK, John P.
Citadel of prose. Commonweal 83:18-19+ O 8 '65
Late demon rum. Commonweal 82:113-16 Ap 16 '65
Specter of the poor. Commonweal 82:437-40 Je 25 '65

SISKIND, Aaron
Siskind's one-man show. il Pop Phot 57: 74-5+ Ag '65

about

Siskind canonization. B. Downes. Pop Phot 57:36 Ag '65

SISSMAN, L. E.
Envoy: poem. New Yorker 41:26 S 4 '65
Sweeney to Mrs Porter in the spring; poem. New Yorker 41:44 Ap 24 '65
Tree warden; poem. Atlan 215:88-9 Je '65

SISSON, Don. See Galloway, H. jt. auth.

SISSON, Edwin D.
Amateur scientist. Sci Am 213:106-10 Jl '65

SISTERHOODS
American nun; poor, chaste, and restive. E. Wakin and J. F. Scheuer. Harper 231:35-40 Ag '65; Discussion. 231:8+ O '65
Clergy heeds a new call; civil-rights movement. J. Cogley. il N Y Times Mag p42-3+ My 2 '65
Council and sisters' renewal. il Cath World 201:41-3+ Ap '65
Emerging nun. J. O'Gara. Commonweal 82: 104 Ap 16 '65
Ferris wheel, anyone? Sister Mary Stephanie. Commonweal 82:14-16 Mr 26 '65
GI's and the girls from Dubuque; condensation of address. M. Xavier. il Read Digest 86:164-7+ Je '65
Mother Cecilia's revolt. il Life 58:45-6 Je 4 '65
Nun as hero. Commonweal 82:37 Ap 2 '65; Reply with rejoinder. R. Ruether. 82:178 Ap 30 '65
Nuns at Selma. Sister Thomas Marguerite. America 112:454-6 Ap 3 '65
Putting sisters in their place. S. Kelly. il America 114:10-11 Ja 1 '66
Sister considers chastity. M. R. Jones. America 112:488-90 Ap 10 '65
Sisters pool ideas; religious orders in the St Louis area form Sisters' sharing group. America 112:213 F 13 '65

SIT-in demonstrations. See Negroes in the United States—Segregation, Resistance to

SITE planning. See Housing projects—Site planning

SITES, Historic. See United States—Historic houses, etc.

SITES, Industrial. See Location in business and industry

SITKA, Alaska
Reader's choice. P. Crittenden. Travel 124:5 Ag '65

SITTING rooms. See Living rooms

SITTLER, Joseph
Christmas, the Messiah and the small town. Christian Cent 82:1576-7 D 22 '65

SITTOW, Michel
Sittow Assumption C. T. Eisler. il Art N 64:34-7+ S '65

SITTS, Elizabeth, and Sitts, Marvin
All the children sculpture with wire. Sch Arts 64:9-13 F '65

SITTS, Marvin. See Sitts, E. jt. auth.

SITWELL, Dame Edith
Cast of characters: a Bloomsbury memoir; excerpt from Taken care of. Reporter 32: 43-5 Ap 8 '65
Edith Sitwell, poet. por Harper 230:56-8 Ap '65
Of what use is poetry? Read Digest 86:119-22 Je '65
When I was young and uneasy; excerpt from Taken care of. pors Atlan 215:159-65 Mr '65

about

Book of the month. A. T. Leone. Cath World 201:202-3 Je '65
Dame Edith Sitwell's sad, witty farewell. J. Purdy. Life 58:8+ Ap 30 '65
Edith Sitwell. A. Pryce-Jones. Commonweal 82:241-3 My 14 '65
Edith Sitwell: prophetess to an age. R. J. Mills, jr. Christian Cent 82:652+ My 19 '65
Exquisite insultress. N. Sayre. Harper 231: 114-15 Ag '65
Monster with melopoeia. D. Levertov. Nation 200:618-19 Je 7 '65
Peripatetic reviewer. E. Weeks. Atlan 215: 135-6 F '65
Rage against the night. L. Edel. por Sat R 48:34 My 29 '65
Three little Sitwells and how they grew. S. Spender. New Repub 152:19-20 Ap 24 '65

SIXTH amendment to the Constitution. See United States—Constitution—Bill of rights

SIZER, I. W. See Goodwin, B. C. jt. auth.

SIZER, Theodore R.
Reform movement or panacea? Sat R 48:52-4+ Je 19 '65

SJOBERG, Gideon
Origin and evolution of cities. Sci Am 213: 54-63 S '65

SKAGIT RIVER
Winter fishing the Skagit. il Sunset 136:28+ Ja '66

SKALAFURIS, Angelo James
(tr) See Kazantzakis, N. Man and God in dialogue

SKATEBOARDING
New sport, or a new menace? Consumer Rep 30:273-4 Je '65
Sidewalk surfing. il Newsweek 65:71 Ap 5 '65
Skateboard mania. il Life 58:126C-128+ My 14 '65
Skateboard skiddoo. Newsweek 65:40+ My 10 '65
Skateboarding: hazardous new fad for kids. il Good H 161:137 Ag '65
Skateboards, fun but dangerous. Consumer Bul 48:13-14 Ag '65
Taking the plunge. il Newsweek 65:110+ My 24 '65

SKATING
There is a doctor on the ice; former figure-skating champion, T. Albright. B. La Fontaine. il Sports Illus 22:28-30+ F 8 '65
See also
Ice shows

SKATING rinks
Cooperation constructs an ice rink; Anderson, Ind. R. Welch. il Am City 80:28 Mr '65
Snow removal from skating areas. R. Lachance. Recreation 58:452 N '65

SKEA, Graham M.
East Orange viewpoint. Recreation 58:237 My '65

SKEET (game)
See also
Trap shooting

SKELETON
Human skeletons of Tehuacán. J. E. Anderson. bibliog il Science 148:496-7 Ap 23 '65; Reply. E. A. Sweeney. 149:1118 S 3 '65

SKELETON clocks. See Clocks

SKELTON, R. A.
Mapping of Vinland; excerpt from Vinland map and the Tartar relation. Am Heritage 16:9-10+ O '65
—and Painter, G. D.
Was there a lasting colony? excerpt from Vinland map and the Tartar relation. Am Heritage 16:100-3 O '65

SKELTON, Red
Red Skelton: television's clown prince. N. F. Busch. il por Read Digest 86:145-8 Mr '65

SKELTON, Robin
Life at work. Poetry 106:234-6 Je '65

SKETCHING clubs. See Art clubs

SKI cabins. See Cabins

SKI clothing. See Clothing and dress—Sports clothes

SKI Jackets. See Clothing and dress—Sports clothes

SKI lodges. See Lodges (architecture)

SKI resorts. See Winter resorts

SKIING. See Skis and skiing

SKIING, Water. See Water skis and skiing

SKILLED workers. See Labor and laboring classes

SKILLET cookery. See Cookery

SKILLETS
Electric skillet's unusual talents. Good H 160:219 Je '65
Fry pan with a new kind of finish; Tufram. il Consumer Rep 31:4 Ja '66

SKIN
Skin. W. Montagna. il Sci Am 212:56-66 bibliog(p 134-5) F '65
Synthetic skin tests lift hopes in burn cases. il Bsns W p52 D 4 '65
Treated human skin stored for two years. Sci N L 88:296 N 6 '65
Why Americans have sallow skins. Sci Digest 57:25 Mr '65
See also
Birthmarks
Keratin

Care and hygiene
Beauty life: a compendium of skin care-fors. il Mlle 60:98-9 F '65
Choose your daily skin care plan! Good H 161:99 N '65
Face facts. Seventeen 24:140-1+ Ap '65
Forecast: cold and drying. il Redbook 126:54-5+ Ja '66
Four clean stories; reports from four Mlle editors. il Mlle 61:134-5+ O '65
Liquid detergent for skin care. M. B. Keiser. il Parents Mag 40:20+ F '65
Men and their looks; tape-talk straight from a famous doctor; questions and answers. Vogue 146:118-21 N 15 '65
Project: you. il Ladies Home J 82:20 Ap '65
Protect your skin from wind and weather. L. D. Kirk. il Parents Mag 40:106 F '65
Skin: a thirst for beauty. S. Harney. il Ladies Home J 82:74-5+ Ap '65

Diseases
Housewife and her hands. E. W. Rauschkolb. il Todays Health 44:58-60 Ja '66
How to turn green. Sci Digest 57:34 My '65
See also
Acne

SKIN, Artificial
Synthetic skin aids burns. Sci N L 88:243 O 16 '65

SKIN, Color of. See Color of man

SKIN anthrax. See Anthrax

SKIN banks. See Skin

SKIN diving. See Diving, Submarine

SKIN grafting. See Transplantation of organs, tissues, etc.

SKIN stimulus. See Stimulus and response

SKIN-surface lipids. See Lipides

SKINNER, B. F.
Why teachers fail; address. Sat R 48:80-1+ O 16 '65

SKINNER, H. Catherine W. See Muzii, E. O. jt. auth.

SKINNER, W. A. and others
Repellency of skin-surface lipids of humans to mosquitoes. Science 149:305 Jl 16 '65

SKIPWORTH, James T.
Many will say the President was not a cowboy. Esquire 63:84-5 Mr '65

SKIR, Leo
Other Chanukahs; story. Commentary 39:56-61 Mr '65

SKIRA, Albert
Skira art books on exhibit in Moscow. il por Pub W 187:78 Je 21 '65

SKIS and skiing
Aspen's awful problem: surfers on skis; with report by R. Bradford. il Life 58:42-4+ Mr 12 '65
Bullet in the Rockies; B. Kidd. D. Jenkins. il Sports Illus 22:26-31 Mr 8 '65
Comma & the fullback; M. and C. Goitschel. il Time 85:40+ F 12 '65
Killy & the Kidd; W. W. Kidd. il Time 87:68 Ja 21 '66
Let's travel: N.America ski-lands. J. Jay. il Mlle 62:204-10+ N '65
Low boom in the land of horizontal skiing; American Midwest. B. Ottum. il Sports Illus 22:48-50 F 15 '65
New ski boom in France. E. Bowen. il Mlle 62:202-3+ N '65

On their own snow; American international ski meet at Vail, Colo. il Time 85:45 Mr 26 '65
Perils of deep powder; photographs by J. G. Zimmerman; with account by E. Morris and P. Stewart. Sports Illus 23:52-65 N 15 '65
Racy herren and fast femmes; American international ski races in Colorado won by Austrian and French teams. D. Jenkins. il Sports Illus 22:24-7 Mr 22 '65
Ready, set, ski! pre-ski conditioning program. D. Brink. il Recreation 58:443 N '65
Rope-tow hill to Mascara Mountain. B. Hersh. il Holiday 37:161+ Mr '65
Schussboomers' blues; worst skiing conditions in three decades. il Newsweek 65:78 F 8 '65
Seasoned skier shows them how. il Ebony 20:148-52+ Ja '65
Ski-jumpers paradise; Duluth, Minn. J. Nowak. il Recreation 58:65+ F '65
Ski life at Aspen. il Mlle 62:106-7+ D '65
Ski touring. R. Mattesich. il Travel 125:42-4 Ja '66
Ski-touring the national parks and forests. C. M. Ouellette. il Nat Parks Mag 40:8-11 Ja '66
Skiing, family style; teaching your children to ski. C. W. Casewit. il Parents Mag 41:46-7+ Ja '66
Skiing in Norway. il Holiday 38:64-7 D '65
Skiing '66; symposium. il Look 29:79-83+ D 14 '65
Snowtime surprise; Maryland. M. C. Roberts. il Travel 124:33-5 N '65
Teen travel talk; Canada. il Seventeen 24:86 N '65
Top U.S. ski spots. C. W. Casewit. il Travel 124:25-9+ D '65
Travail at Vail; first American international team races. il Newsweek 65:60-1 Mr 29 '65
Traveling with Mlle; Sun Valley ski scene. il Mlle 62:189-90 N '65
Two Canadians raid Aspen; N. Greene and P. Duncan in Aspen's Roch cup meet. B. Ottum. Sports Illus 22:50-1 F 8 '65
Winter is vacation time, too! il Changing T 19:33-4 N '65
See also
National ski patrol system

Accidents and injuries
Busy, busy ski doctor; he sets 350 fractures a winter. il Life 58:111-12 F 19 '65
Never look back in sorrow; Jill Kinmont. il Good H 160:66-7+ Ja '65

Anecdotes, facetiae, satire, etc.
Last year at Sugarbush. I. Kampen. il McCalls 93:74+ O '65

Equipment
Snowless skiing on tank treads. S. James. il Pop Mech 124:140-1 O '65
Sport in which it pays to have the shorts; shorter skis. P. Stewart. il Sports Illus 23:60+ D 13 '65

SKLANSKY, Morris A. and Neisser, E. G.
Helping teenagers control their impulses. Parents Mag 40:40-1+ Jl '65

SKLAR, Robert
Aristocrat of the twenties. Reporter 32:51-2 F 11 '65

SKLARE, Marshall
Assimilation & the sociologists. Commentary 39:63-7 My '65

SKODA Lenin works. See Czechoslovakia—Industries

SKOKIE, Ill.
Skokie Swift, the answer to a commuter's prayer. B. L. Marsh. il Am City 80:122-3 Je '65

SKORNIA, Harry J.
They don't all see the same thing. PTA Mag 60:7-8 bibliog(p35) Ja '66

SKOURAS, Spyros P.
Bailing out the fleet. il por Time 86:84+ Jl 16 '65

SKOW, John
Confessions of a pun addict. Sat Eve Post 238:20 Je 19 '65
Dirty-clam caper. Sat Eve Post 238:44+ F 27 '65
Grits, magnolia and skiing. Sat Eve Post 238:86-9 Mr 13 '65
Importance of being poached. Sat Eve Post 238:88-91 My 8 '65
Out to launch. Sat Eve Post 238:20 Ag 28 '65
Sound of progress. Sat Eve Post 238:25-6 F 13 '65
Stop the train, I want to get off. Sat Eve Post 239:10 Ja 1 '66

SKRIABIN, Aleksandr Nikolaevich
Richter on Scriabin; interview. ed. by F Bowers. S. Richter. Sat R 48:58-9 Je 12 '65

SKUAS. See Gulls

SKULL
Unusual format and production in Hafner's Atlas of human skull. il Pub W 188:113-14+ N 8 '65

SKULLCAPS (flowers)
Favorite indoor plants. G. R. Robinson. il Horticulture 43:53 Je '65

SKUNKS
Channel Island skunk; spotted skunk. R. G. Van Gelder. il Natur Hist 74:30-5 Ag '65
Loner (cont) J. Stuart. il Am For 71:58-9+ My '65

SKURNIK, Walter A. E.
New motifs in West Africa. Cur Hist 48:207-12+ Ap '65

SKY
Search for cosmic light. Sky & Tel 30:211 O '65

SKY diving. See Parachuting

SKY roamers air travel, incorporated
Teaming up to roam the airways; Sky roamers of Los Angeles, cooperative flying group. il Bsns W p28-9 Ap 24 '65

SKYE, Erik. See Pearson. L. jt. auth.

SKYE, ISLE OF
Conquest of Skye; tourists on the Sabbath. il Newsweek 65:50 Je 21 '65

SKYLIGHTS
Cruciform window onto heaven; Kenzo Tange creates cathedral in Tokyo. R. Boyd. il Arch Forum 123:50-5 S '65
Five on one side, the cook on the other. il Sunset 134:126 Ap '65
Here are the skylights available and here are their costs. il Sunset 134:122-4 Mr '65
High light from the sky is marvelous indoors. il Sunset 134:110-16 Mr '65

SKYSCRAPER; musical comedy. See Musical comedies, revues, etc.—Criticisms, plots, etc.

SKYSCRAPERS
Above the hurly-burly; plans of John Hancock insurance co. for a 100-story building in Chicago. il Time 85:42 Ap 2 '65
Bearing wall expressed in a skyscraper; IBM building, Seattle; with account by J. S. Hornbeck. il Arch Rec 137:123-8 F '65
Cities higher than mountains. N. Mailer. il N Y Times Mag p 16-17+ Ja 31 '65
Letter from Paris; plans for Tour Montparnasse hotel. Genêt. New Yorker 41:126+ O 30 '65
Saarinen's skyscraper; Columbia broadcasting system's office tower, New York city. il Arch Rec 138:111-18 Jl '65
Tall buildings in prestressed concrete. T. Y. Lin. il Arch Rec 138:165-70 D '65
Tower in a new kind of urban space; Equitable's new headquarters. il Arch Rec 138:161-8 O '65
Triangular plot shapes triple tower. S. F. Blum. il Arch Rec 138:140-3 D '65

SLABS, Concrete. See Concrete slabs

SLACKS, Mens. See Clothing and dress—Men

SLACKS, Womens. See Clothing and dress

SLAFF, George
Five seats in Congress; Mississippi challenge. Nation 200:526-9 My 17 '65

SLANDER. See Libel and slander

SLANE, Willis H. Jr
Obituary
Motor B por 116:116 O '65

SLANG
Cool that low talk and that high talk. T. M. Bernstein. il N Y Times Mag p 12-13 Jl 4 '65
In the boonies, its's numbah ten thou; G.I. glossary, updated. Time 86:34 D 10 '65
Little bit of censoring; Dictionary of American slang. R. L. Crowell. il Wilson Lib Bul 39:652-7 Ap '65
What are they saying? teen-age slang. J. Wylie. Esquire 64:44-5 Jl '65
Whiz mob; a correlation of the technical argot of pickpockets with their behavior pattern. by D. W. Maurer. Review
Nation 200:261-2 Mr 8 '65. R. I. McDavid

SLAPSTICK moving pictures. See Moving pictures—Comedy

SLATE, George L.
Maintenance is easy with the right tools. Pop Gard 16:24-5 Mr '65
Quick way to stop the tarnished plant bug. Flower Grower 52:50 My '65

SLATE, John H.
Lay lobotomy, go slow. Atlan 216:166-7 N '65
Note on man-animal, animal-man, and animal perception. Atlan 215:84-7 Ap '65

SLATER, Jerome
Democracy versus stability; the recent Latin American policy of the United States. Yale R 55:169-81 D '65

SLATER, Joseph
On coming home to poetry. Sat R 48:30 F 6 '65
Pattern of days and ideas. Sat R 48:18-19 Jl 31 '65

SLATER, Peggy
Peggy Slater on boat preparation. Yachting 117:39-40 Je '65

SLATON, Bill, and Slaton, N. B.
Wanted, drugs to fight the new viruses. Sci Digest 57:81-4 F '65

SLATON, Nellie Becker. See Slaton, B. jt. auth.

SLATTED barn floors. See Barns and stables—Floors

SLATTERY, Margaret E.
Don't send for Hector; drama. Plays 25:1-13 Ja '66

SLAUGHTER, Frank G.
Confessions of a storyteller; address, July 1965. por ALA Bul 59:1003-5 D '65

SLAUGHTER, L. W.
On time. See issues of Hobbies

SLAVE; drama. See Jones, L.

SLAVE trade
Documents illustrative of the history of the slave trade to America, ed. by E. Donnan. Review
Am Heritage 16:46-8 Je '65. B. Catton
Newsweek il 65:106-7 Mr 15 '65
Journey in misery. D. L. Dumond. Sat R 48:30 Mr 13 '65

SLAVERY
See also
Abolitionists
Slave trade

United States
Insurrection in South Carolina; the turbulent world of Denmark Vesey, by J. Lofton. Review
Negro Hist Bul 28:202+ My '65. E. M. Lewis
Political economy of slavery, by E. D. Genovese. Review
Nation 201:390-2 N 22 '65. A. S. Kraditor
Sat R 49:33 Ja 1 '66. D. M. Potter
Slavery in the cities; the South 1820-1860, by R. C. Wade. Review
Negro Hist Bul 28:138 Mr '65. B. H. Nelson
This quiet dust. W. Styron. il Harper 230:134-46 Ap '65
Unfinished business of the Civil war; true freedom for the Negro; excerpt from the Centennial history of the Civil war. B. Catton. il N Y Times Mag p28-9+ Ap 4 '65
See also
Dred Scott case
Emancipation proclamation
Negroes—Colonization

SLAVITT, David R.
Carnivore; Speculations about the death of Eskimos; poems. Yale R 54:392-4 Mr '65

SLAYMAKER, S. R. 2d
Dutch country ringneck shoot. Outdoor Life 136:56-7+ N '65

SLAYTON, William
Total program in the fight against blight; address, January 15, 1965. Vital Speeches 31:267-71 F 15 '65

SLED; story. See Adams. T. E.

SLEDDING. See Coasting

SLEDDING, Dog. See Dog sleds and sledding

SLEDGE, G. Allen
Winsome, lose some; story. Seventeen 24:96 Ag '65

SLEDS
Not so smooth getaway; General motors bobsled. Newsweek 65:81 F 8 '65
Rule Britannia for now; new G.M. sleds. il Time 85:88 F 5 '65
See also
Ice boats and ice boating

SLEDS, Motor. See Motor sleds

SLEDS, Rocket. See Rocket sleds

SLEEP
Carotid sinus and aortic reflexes in the regulation of circulation during sleep. M. Guazzi and others. bibliog il Science 148:397-9 Ap 16 '65
Causes of arousal from sleep studied. Sci N L 88:130 Ag 28 '65
Discrimination and conditioning during sleep as indicated by the electroencephalogram. H. B. Beh and P. E. H. Barratt. bibliog il Science 147:1470-1 Mr 19 '65

SLEEP—*Continued*

Elevation in brain temperature during paradoxical sleep. H. Kawamura and C. H. Sawyer. bibliog il Science 150:912 N 12 '65

Geniculate unit responses to sine-wave photic stimulation during wakefulness and sleep. L. Maffei and others. bibliog il Science 149:563-4 Jl 30 '65

Great relaxing bonanza. W. I. Fischman. il Pop Mech 125:122-5+ Ja '66

Heart patients need sleep. Sci N L 88:116 Ag 21 '65

Nicotine: effect on the sleep cycle of the cat. E. F. Domino and K. Yamamoto. bibliog il Science 150:637-8 O 29 '65

Oxygen consumption rate and electroencephalographic stage of sleep. D. R. Brebbia and K. Z. Altshuler. bibliog il Science 150:1621-3 D 17 '65

Periodic respiratory pattern occurring in conjunction with eye movements during sleep. E. Aserinsky. bibliog il Science 150:763-6 N 5 '65

Reporter at large; Rapid eye movement sleep. C. Trillin. il New Yorker 41:58-60+ S 18 '65

Rhythmic enzyme changes in neurons and glia during sleep. H. Hydén and P. W. Lange. bibliog il Science 149:654-6 Ag 6 '65

Scientists use new techniques to study the complex activity called sleep. M. Markham. Parents Mag 40:60-1+ Ag '65

Sleep: changes in threshold to electroconvulsive shock in rats after deprivation of paradoxical phase. H. B. Cohen and W. C. Dement. bibliog il Science 150:1318-19 D 3 '65

Sleep: effects of a restricted regime. W. B. Webb and H. W. Agnew, jr. bibliog il Science 150:1745-7 D 24 '65

Sleep: how much do you need? J. D. Ratcliff. Read Digest 87:89-92 Ag '65

See also
Dreams
Insomnia

SLEEP habits of animals. See Animals—Habits and behavior

SLEEPING bags
Camper's report: sleeping bags. il Consumer Bul 49:2+ Ja '66
It's in the bag. C. Conley. il Field & S 69:64-7+ F '65

SLEEPING beauty; ballet. See Ballets—Criticisms

SLEEPING sickness
How a city faced an epidemic; Houston, Tex. B. Merson. il Good H 160:80-1+ Je '65

SLEEPLESSNESS. See Insomnia

SLEEPWALKING. See Somnambulism

SLEPIAN, Edward L.
Solving current problems by VTV. Motor B 115:48-51 Je '65

SLESSINGER, Seymour
Mao vs. Moscow. Commonweal 81:759-61 Mr 12 '65
600 million Chinese + communism + the bomb = ? Commonweal 82:506 Jl 9 '65

SLEVIN, Joseph R.
Washington desk. See issues of Dun's review and modern industry

SLIDE illuminators. See Transparencies—Viewers

SLIDE projectors. See Projection apparatus

SLIDE rule
Arithmetic on a stick. il Changing T 19:34 My '65

SLIDE viewers. See Transparencies—Viewers

SLIFE, Fred W. and Zeman, L. E.
1965 weed and insect control guide. Suc Farm 63:69-74+ Mr '65

SLIGH, Charles R. Jr
Fair practices and fair profits; address, February 20, 1965. bibliog Vital Speeches 31:430-4 My 1 '65

SLIGHT ache; drama. See Pinter, H.

SLIME molds. See Myxomycetes

SLIPPED disc. See Spine—Abnormalities and deformities

SLIPYI, Josyf, cardinal
Four men: four stories. America 112:449-50 Ap 3 '65

SLOAN, Irving J.
Negro in history. Sat R 48:90-2 F 20 '65

SLOAN, John
Artist's angle of vision. B. H. Hayes, jr. il Sat R 48:48 N 27 '65

SLOAN, Robert E. and Van Valen, Leigh
Cretaceous mammals from Montana. bibliog Science 148:220-7 Ap 9 '65
—See Van Valen, L. jt. auth.

SLOAN-Kettering institute for cancer research
Unforgettable character of Dusty Rhoads. M. W. Lasker. Read Digest 86:163-4+ Ap '65

SLOANE, Eric
What a painting reflects. il por Am Artist 29:56-61+ Mr '65

SLOANE, Gloria
Aboard the 35' ketch Wyntie with Walter Cronkite. Motor B 116:42-3 Ag '65
Aboard the 36' cruiser Queen Mary with Peter Lind Hayes and Mary Healy. Motor B 115:60-1+ Je '65
Captain Herlihy emcee of the 42' Big Jeanne. Motor B 116:56-7+ O '65
Hugh Downs; Today's star is South Sea bound. Motor B 116:76-8 Jl '65

SLOGANS
Tiger goes abroad; Esso's tiger with the high-octane tail. il Time 85:100-1 My 28 '65

SLOMAN, Joel
Insecta anonymous; Ate; Astronaut of waste; poems. Poetry 106:331-4 Ag '65

SLONIMSKY, Nicolas
A. C, his book. Am Rec G 32:4-5+ S '65

SLOOPS
Greatest little boat; Bahama sloop built in 1952. D. N. Brady. il Yachting 118:48-50+ Jl '65
Sloops of Friendship. R. F. Duncan. il Yachting 117:184-6 F '65
What a perfect Friendship; old lobster sloops built in Friendship, Me. G. Weller. il Sports Illus 22:42-6 Je 21 '65

SLOT-car racing. See Automobile models—Racing

SLOTE, Alfred
Falling leaves; story. Sat Eve Post 238:48-50 N 6 '65

SLOTTED angles. See Angles (metal work)

SLOTTED floors (swine houses) See Swine houses—Floors

SLOVAK, Mira
Duel at Rockford. il por Flying 77:49-51 Ag '65

SLOW dance on the killing ground; drama. See Hanley, W.

SLOW learning children
Catching failures in time; costly public boarding school in Winston-Salem for underachievers. il Time 85:49-50 Mr 19 '65
Our daughter was a victim of the world's cruelest hoax. L. David. Good H 161:81+ N '65
Retarded child: what to do? R. Kramer. il N Y Times Mag p 129-30 O 24 '65
Slow learner, surrounded and alone; hints for parents. W. Abraham. il Todays Health 43:58-61+ S '65
See also
National association for retarded children

Education

Discovering materials for the retarded; Lincoln school, Plainfield, N.J. M. Harayda. il Sr Schol 86:sup 10-11 My 6 '65
Motivating the slow learner; interests of teenagers; excerpt from an address, April 1965. W. D. Boutwell. Wilson Lib Bul 40:75-7+ S '65
Retarded children: out of the attic. F. R. Schreiber and M. Herman. il Sci Digest 58:18-23 O '65
Teacher of the unteachables; Springboards reading program. J. Tebbel. Sat R 48:72+ My 15 '65
Time for a special lesson; special education classes, Valley Oaks elementary, Houston, Tex. E. Norton. bibliog Library J 90:1987-8 Ap 15 '65

SLUDGE, Sewage. See Sewage

SLUM clearance. See Urban renewal

SLUMBER parties. See Entertaining

SLUMS
Dark ghetto, by K. B. Clark. Review
Reporter 33:59-62 O 21 '65. R. Coles
Dilemmas of urban America, by R. C. Weaver. Review
Sat R 49:85 Ja 8 '66. C. W. Griffin, jr
Failure of urban renewal; a critique and some proposals. H. J. Gans. Commentary 39:29-37 Ap '65; Discussion. 40:72-80 Jl; 14+ N '65
Housing the poor. W. Klein. Commonweal 82:377-9 Je 11 '65; Reply. T. E. Kristopeit. 82:515+ Jl 23 '65
Latin-American shantytown: Bogota's Barrio of 65. S. Schulman. il N Y Times Mag p30-1+ Ja 16 '66
Slum dwellings do not make a slum. N. Glazer. il N Y Times Mag p54-5+ N 21 '65

SLURRY seal. See Pavements—Surface treatment

SMALL, Arnold
From Monterey to the Sierras; excerpt from Bird watcher's America,, ed. by O. S. Pettingill, jr. por Audubon Mag 67:208-11 Jl '65

SMALL, Maxwell M.
New 140-foot radio telescope. Sky & Tel 30: 267-74 N '65

SMALL arms. See Firearms

SMALL business
Future for small business; report on study by Robert R. Nathan associates, inc. il Bsns W p35-6+ Jl 31 '65
Management assistance for small business. L. T. White. Harvard Bsns R 43:67-74 Jl '65
Small business: its prospects and problems. E. B. Shils. bibliog f il Cur Hist 49:36-44+ Jl '65
Think small. A. Uris. il Nations Bsns 53: 94-6+ My '65
What is a small businessman? address, September 13, 1965. W. C. Marquis. Vital Speeches 32:21-4 O 15 '65
Where small business goes wrong. L. A. Allen. il Duns R 85:60-1+ My '65
See also
Exclusive agencies
Self employed

Finance
Bad debts: threat to small business. W. A. Duvel. il Duns R 85:60-1 Ap '65

SMALL business administration. See United States—Small business administration

SMALL crimson parasol; drama. See Boiko, C.

SMALL favor; story. See Stanton, W.

SMALL miracle; story. See Gallico, P.

SMALLENBURG, Carol, and Smallenburg, Harry
Our hard-pressed teenagers. PTA Mag 59:34-6 bibliog(p44) F '65

SMALLENBURG, Harry. See Smallenburg, C. jt. auth.

SMALLPOX
Geneva: world headquarters in the fight against smallpox. il UNESCO Courier 18: 24-7 Mr '65
Smallpox: its threat persists. Good H 161: 141 Ag '65
U.S. to cooperate in smallpox eradication program in Africa. Dept State Bul 53:959 D 13 '65
World health organization observes 17th birthday; smallpox vaccination program in India. il Todays Health 43:50 Jl '65

SMART, Mollie
Five steps in the growth of a parent. Parents Mag 40:56-7+ bibliog(p22) D '65
How does a conscience grow? Parents Mag 40:58-9+ Ag '65

SMELL
Do you smell something? questions and answers. J. Daugherty and M. Daugherty. il Sci Digest 58:89-91 Jl '65
They're selling you with subtle smells. T. Irwin. il Pop Sci 186:60-1+ Je '65
Your mysterious nose. C. B. Hicks. Todays Health 43:35-7+ O '65
See also
Odors

SMETANA, Bedřich
Unknown Smetana. W. Weaver. il por Hi Fi 15:44-7 My '65

SMITH, Abigail (Adams)
Miss Adams in love. L. Mayo. il por Am Heritage 16:36-49+ F '65

SMITH, Adam
They made our world. L. Rosten. il Look 29:78-9 O 5 '65

SMITH, Alan
Can we improve on nature too much? Sci Digest 58:88-91 O '65
Were dinosaurs a failure? Sci Digest 58:86-9 S '65
Why not meters and kilos? Sci Digest 58: 90-3 N '65

SMITH, Alfred, and others
Absence of taste-bud papillae in familial dysautonomia. bibliog Science 147:1040-1 F 26 '65

SMITH, Andrew
Ring; story. Atlan 215:125-7 Ap '65

SMITH, Mrs Anson Howe
What we can learn from English church arrangements. Horticulture 43:20-3 Mr '65

SMITH, Anthony Wayne
Water for Arizona and Bridge and Marble Canyon Dams; statements, August 1965. Nat Parks Mag 39:I-IV D '65

SMITH, Bardwell L.
Meanwhile, in Mississippi. Commonweal 82: 39-42 Ap 2 '65

SMITH, Betty Cole
Reporter at large. J. Colebrook. il New Yorker 41:47-8+ Je 12 '65

SMITH, Beverly Bush
Are home haircuts for your family? Parents Mag 40:122-3 O '65
Do-ahead meals. Parents Mag 41:61+ Ja '66
Happiness is a yummy dessert. Parents Mag 40:69-72+ Je '65

SMITH, Bob
Bookmaker to a river. Field & S 70:52-5 Ag '65

SMITH, Bradford A. and Reese, E. J.
Jovian atmospheric feature of special interest. Sky & Tel 29:118-19 F '65

SMITH, Bruce C.
Performance ratings for induction units. Arch Rec 137:223-4+ Je '65

SMITH, C. Jay, jr
Great Britain and the 1914-1915 Straits agreement with Russia: the British promise of November 1914. bibliog f Am Hist R 70: 1015-34 Jl '65

SMITH, C. Lavett
Science in action; survey of the Bahamas. Natur Hist 74:62-5 D '65

SMITH, Charles William
Charles W. Smith of the Old Dominion. N. Kent. il por Am Artist 29:60-5+ Je '65

SMITH, Chloethiel Woodard
Leading lady in urban renewal. J. Peter. il pors Look 29:75-6+ S 21 '65

SMITH, Cyril Stanley
Materials and the development of civilization and science. bibliog Science 148:908-17 My 14 '65

SMITH, Datus C. Jr
Franklin book programs: global publishing aid is varied and expanded. il Pub W 187: 28-32 Mr 15 '65

SMITH, David
David Smith, 1906-1965. J. Rosati. il por Art N 64:28-9+ S '65
Farewell to the Vulcan of American art. il pors Life 58:129-30 Je 11 '65
Iron works closed. il por Newsweek 65:78 Je 7 '65

SMITH, David Loeffler
Great artists as art teachers. Am Artist 29: 58-63 S '65

SMITH, David S.
Flight muscles of insects; with biographical sketch. Sci Am 212:20, 76-82+ Je '65

SMITH, Desmond
AT&T; folksy octopus. Nation 202:16-18 Ja 3 '66
Churches and the airwaves. Christian Cent 82:364-7 Mr 24 '65
International exchange: a standard better than gold. Nation 200:437-9 Ap 26 '65
New look in war. Nation 200:200-2 F 22 '65
Overplaying it. Nation 200:566-7 My 24 '65

SMITH, Dido
Heesen's glass: risk and discipline. Craft Horiz 25:34-7+ Ja '65

SMITH, Don
Demand to delist. il por Time 86:67 Ag 13 '65

SMITH, E. Brooks
School-college cooperation. NEA J 54:36 Ap '65

SMITH, Edgar H. Jr
Approaching end of Edgar H. Smith, jr. W. F. Buckley, jr. por Esquire 64:116-20+ N '65

SMITH. Edmund Ware
Fly choice by the Omen method. Field & S 69: 62-4+ Mr '65
Mister Maine and the mountain. Field & S 70:10-11+ D '65
Strange places I have slept. Field & S 70:58-61+ My '65

SMITH, Edward J. and others
Magnetic field measurements near Mars. bibliog Science 149:1241-2 S 10 '65

SMITH, Eleanor T.
Return of the reader's adviser. Library J 90: 3215-16 Ag '65

SMITH, Elinor Goulding
Desk is a desk is a desk. Redbook 124:97 Ap '65
Those crazy Americans. Atlan 216:111-13 Ag '65

SMITH, Elwyn A.
Anti-Americanism, French style. Christian Cent 82:300-3 Mr 10 '65
Further proposal for federal aid to Catholic schools. por Cath World 201:162-9 Je '65
Is God changing our society? Cath World 202:74-9 N '65
Stalemate in Selma. Christian Cent 82:1031-3 Ag 25 '65

SMITH, Emily Nash
How to pursue a hobby. Suc Farm 63:119-23
F '65
SMITH, F. Robert
Reader's choice. Travel 123:9 Je '65
Traveler's choice. Travel 124:7 D '65; 125:58
Ja '66
SMITH, Frank Kingston
Weekend pilot. See issues of Flying
SMITH, Fred G.
Warden's view of bears. Outdoor Life 135:56-
7+ Je '65
SMITH, G. Roysce
Summer reading lists for secondary schools.
Pub W 188:108-14 S 27 '65
SMITH, Gale M.
Telephones for the deaf; reprint. Sci Digest
57:55-9 My '65
SMITH, Gene
Horseplayer's wild ride through Europe. Sat
Eve Post 238:80-2 Jl 3 '65
Sentimental journey to Dracula's home town.
Sat Eve Post 238:76-9 Mr 27 '65
Still quiet on the western front. il Am Herit-
age 16:20-5+ O '65; Excerpt. Sat Eve Post
238:78-85 N 6 '65
SMITH, George Cline
What's happened to the building boom? in-
terview. por U S News 59:90-5 N 29 '65
SMITH, George E.
Cardinal rule. por Newsweek 67:25 Ja 10 '66
On parole. por Newsweek 66:37-8 D 13 '65
SMITH, George Ivan
Chips are down. Reporter 33:27-9 D 2 '65
SMITH, Gerald
Have a field day. Recreation 58:445-6 N '65
SMITH, Gerard C.
Tomorrow's Atlantic alliance. America 113:
132-5 Ag 7 '65
SMITH, Godfrey
England's stingingest gadfly. N Y Times Mag
p26-7+ Ja 9 '66
SMITH, Gordon S.
Back splice; you don't stop at the bitter
end. Motor B 115:57 Je '65
Don't be a square. il Motor B 116:27 D '65
Practically seized. Motor B 116:122 N '65
Whipping synthetic rope. Motor B 116:68
N '65
SMITH, Grace Hunter
Effective orientation program calls for early
planning. NEA J 54:47-8 My '65
SMITH, H. A. P. See Lang, T. G. jt. auth.
SMITH, H. Allen
Coat hangers of the world, arise! Read Digest
86:24E-24F+ Mr '65
I hate winter postcards. Travel 125:55-7 Ja
'66
SMITH, H. T. U.
Anomalous erosional topography in Victoria
Land, Antarctica. bibliog Science 148:941-2
My 14 '65
SMITH, Harold H.
Genetic control of differentiation. Science
150:1847-9 D 31 '65
SMITH, Harrison
In the great tradition. Sat R 49:25 Ja 15 '66
SMITH, Hartland B.
Build steam powered ham rig. Pop Electr 23:
55-7+ Jl '65
Build the Paragon 144. Pop Electr 22:55-9+
Ap '65
Camper's special. Pop Electr 23:48-52 Ag '65
SMITH, Hazel Brannon
Appreciation day. Newsweek 66:70 D 13 '65
Eleven year siege of Mississippi's lady editor.
T. G. Harris. il por Look 29:121-2+ N 16 '65
SMITH, Hendrick
They call him El Rayis, the boss. N Y
Times Mag p32-3+ My 16 '65
SMITH, Herbert D.
Fight for inner space; address. April 7,
1965. Vital Speeches 31:493-5 Je 1 '65
SMITH, Hervey Garrett
Incredible saga of Twinkle-Twinkle. Yacht-
ing 117:217-18 My '65
SMITH, Hilary
Another job for all faiths. America 112:542-3
Ap 17 '65
SMITH, Howard K.
Television in the Nation's service; address,
October 13, 1965. Vital Speeches 32:79-81
N 15 '65
SMITH, Howard Worth
How a conservative upset the liberals. por
U S News 59:24 O 11 '65
SMITH, Huston
10,000 red-gilt envelopes. Nation 200:191-3 F
22 '65
SMITH, Ian Douglas
Other side of the Rhodesia story; interview,
ed. by A. J. Meyers. por U S News 59:68-72
N 8 '65

about

Africa's new Verwoerd. A. Segal. New Re-
pub 153:13-14 S 18 '65
Can Britain stop Rhodesia? A. Lejeune.
Nat R 18:22-3 Ja 11 '66
Independence day? il por Newsweek 66:50+
N 22 '65
Letter from London. M. Panter-Downes. New
Yorker 41:198+ N 27 '65
Mr Smith draws the line in Africa. J. Lely-
veld. il pors N Y Times Mag p22+ Ag 22
'65
People of the week. por U S News 59:18 O 18
'65
Powder keg in Rhodesia. R. E. Hughes.
Christian Cent 82:208-10+, 240+ F 17-24 '65
Rhodesia at the crossroads. T. Molnar. Nat
R 17:971-2 N 2 '65
Rhodesia: hope of compromise. il Newsweek
66:47 N 8 '65
Rhodesia: not since 1776. il Newsweek 66:66
O 18 '65
Rhodesia: the rebel fever rises. il por News-
week 66:43-4 O 25 '65
Smith vs. Wilson: two views on Rhodesia's
independence. il por U S News 59:22 N 22
'65
Victory for fear. por Newsweek 65:54-5 My 17
'65
We want our country. il por Time 86:40-2+
N 5 '65
White Rhodesia: can it survive? il pors U S
News 59:44-6 N 22 '65
SMITH, J. B. See Regan, J. D. jt. auth.
SMITH, J. Robert
Surinam animal rescue. Natur Hist 75:24-9
Ja '66
SMITH, Janell
This is the way the girls go. J. Underwood. il
por Sports Illus 22:34-6+ My 10 '65
SMITH, Jerry
Antique toys. il Hobbies 70:52-3 D '65
SMITH, Joan Merriam
Loser. J. Gilbert. il pors Flying 77:80-4 Ag '65
SMITH, Justin C. See Munster, J. H. jr, jt.
auth.
SMITH, Kendall O.
Cyclic structure of adenovirus DNA. bibliog
Science 148:100-2 Ap 2 '65
SMITH, Kirk
Outdoor dining oriental style. Pop Gard 16:48-
9 Mr '65
SMITH, L. Dennis, and Ecker, R. E.
Protein synthesis in enucleated eggs of rana
pipiens. bibliog Science 150:777-9 N 5 '65
SMITH, L. H.
Changes in the tail feathers of the adolescent
lyrebird. Science 147:510-13 Ja 29 '65; Cor-
rection. 149:565 Jl 30 '65
SMITH, Larry
Business can save America's cities. Nations
Bsns 53:38-9+ N '65
SMITH, Lawrence L.
Shibui & hade. U S Camera 28:60-3+ Je '65
When the moon is high. U S Camera 28:64-
5+ Mr '65
SMITH, Leon W. and others
Thin-layer chromatography of plant pigments
on mannitol or sucrose. Science 148:508-9
Ap 23 '65
SMITH, LeRoi
Disc brakes for early Fords. il Hot Rod 18:
56-8+ D '65
SCTA opener. El Mirage. il Hot Rod 18:48-51
S '65
SMITH, Lillian
Poets among the demagogues. Sat R 48:24+
O 2 '65
SMITH, Liz
Boating. Sports Illus 23:40-2 Jl 26 '65
SMITH, M. J.
Cataract; poem. New Yorker 41:164 My 8 '65
SMITH, M. J. Ashwood-. See Ashwood-Smith,
M. J.
SMITH, M. Mead
Labor and the Savannah River AEC project;
reprint from June 1952 issue. Mo Labor R
88:799-800 Jl '65
SMITH, McGregor, jr
Day-after-Christmas dialogue for Santa;
poem. Christian Cent 82:1598 D 29 '65
SMITH, Malcolm
Absence of gray. il Pop Phot 56:58-9 F '65
SMITH, Margaret D.
Beauty of imperfection. Am For 71:32-5+ Ag
'65
SMITH, Margoret
Waiting for George; poem. Atlan 216:55 Jl
'65
SMITH, Marshall
Bad boy of the pros. Life 59:85-6+ O 22 '65
Cheating scandal rocks the bridge world.
Life 58:32-3 Je 4 '65

SMITH, Marshall—*Continued*
If your back is out, you're in. Life 58:70-2+
Ap 9 '65; Same abr. Read Digest 87:157-8+
S '65
Twins' miracle coach. Life 59:83-4+ S 10 '65
SMITH, Mary Jo
And she cooks! por Seventeen 25:102-3+ Ja
'66
SMITH, Michael
Improbable cause. Time 87:55 Ja 14 '66
SMITH, Mike
Dave Clark five make a movie! ed. by
E. Miller. pors Seventeen 24:138-9 Jl '65
SMITH, Mortimer
Faddishness in education. por Sat R 48:53 Ag
21 '65
SMITH, Ned
We learned about elk. por Outdoor Life 136:
44-7+ D '65
Who needs a grouse dog? Outdoor Life 136:
44-7+ O '65
SMITH, Nellene
Santa Barbara public library again without
chief librarian. Library J 90:606 F 1 '65
SMITH, Oliver
Man for all scenes. il por Time 85:86+ Mr
19 '65
SMITH, Patrick J.
Churchill records. Hi Fi 15:71-2 Ap '65
Donizetti's Lucrezia Borgia. Hi Fi 15:98 Jl
'65
From France: classic and romantic. Hi Fi
15:115 Je '65
Metropolitan opera club. Opera N 29:6-7 Ap
3 '65
Of Spades and Turks; operas. Hi Fi 15:116
My '65
One who's right. Opera N 30:24-5 D 18 '65
Question of function. Hi Fi 15:67-9+ Mr '65
Tales for our time. Opera N 29:24-5 F 27 '65
To serve the cause of opera. Hi Fi 15:198+
N '65
Winning the West. Opera N 30:6-7 D 18 '65
(ed) See Barrault, J. L. Touch of magic
(ed) See Caballé, M. Spanish treasure
(ed) See Heinrich, R. Man engaged
SMITH, Paul J.
Baked: exhibition of traditional breads and
modern dough sculpture at Museum of
contemporary crafts, New York. New
Yorker 41:19-20 Ja 8 '66
SMITH, Perry Edward
Capricious flight, capture and a bloodcurd-
ling confession. il por Life 60:66-7 Ja 7 '66

about
Annals of crime; In cold blood. T. Capote.
New Yorker 41:66+ O 2; 58-62+ O 9; 62-
4+ O 16 '65
In cold blood: an American tragedy. il por
Newsweek 67:59-62 Ja 24 '66
Two killers, last faces the Clutters saw. por
Life 60:64-5 Ja 7 '65
SMITH, Philip R. Jr
Visit with the Dirksens. il Flower Grower
52:36-7 N '65
SMITH, R. Fremont-. See Fremont-Smith, R.
SMITH, Ralph A.
Forms of rationality. bibliog Sch Arts 64:19-
23 My '65
SMITH, Ralph Lee
Bunk about health foods. Todays Health 43:
24+ O '65
Chiropractic: science or swindle? excerpt
from Health hucksters. Todays Health 43:
56-61 My '65
Cops as robbers. Nation 200:102-7 F 1 '65
Vitamin healers. Reporter 33:18-25 D 16 '65
SMITH, Richard Austin
At Saint-Gobain, the first 300 years were the
easiest. Fortune 72:148-50+ O '65
Los Angeles, prototype of supercity. Fortune
71:98-101+ Mr '65
Nationalism threatens U.S. investment. For-
tune 72:126-31+ Ag '65
They play rough in the gas business. Fortune
73:132-5+ Ja '66
SMITH, Robert C.
Vista Alegre. Antiques 87:444-7 Ap '65
SMITH, Robert E. See Kleinsorge, P. L. jt.
auth.
SMITH, Robert Houston
Church of the Holy Sepulcher: toward an
ecumenical symbol. Yale R 55:34-56 O '65
SMITH, Ruth B.
(comp) Calendar of coming events. See is-
sues of Motor boating
SMITH, Sherwin D.
Boondoggle that helped 38 million people.
N Y Times Mag p37+ My 2 '65
Day for the rights of man. N Y Times Mag
p29-30+ Je 13 '65
Great Monkey trial. N Y Times Mag p8-9+
Jl 4 '65

SMITH, Stanley E.
Key to physical fitness. Parents Mag 40:46-
7+ Jl '65
SMITH, Stanley G.
Chilocorus similis Rossi: disinterment and
case history. bibliog Science 148:1614-16 Je
18 '65
SMITH, Stevie
To carry the child; poem. New Yorker 41:48
Ap 10 '65

about
Ends and means. S. F. Morse. Poetry 105:
406-7 Mr '65
SMITH, T. G. and others
Electrical connections between visual cells
in the ommatidium of limulus. bibliog Sci-
ence 147:1446-8 Mr 19 '65
SMITH, Terry
Bobby's image. Esquire 63:62-3+ Ap '65
SMITH, Tex
Carburetor overhaul. Motor T 17:57-9 Jl '65
SMITH, W. Eugene
Picture memo to the editor on the new
Leicaflex. Pop Phot 56:52-3 Ap '65

about
Shooting without stopping. H. M. Keppler.
il Pop Phot 57:46-9 Ag '65
W. Eugene Smith. H. M. Kinzer. il Pop Phot
56:74-9 F '65
SMITH, Warren Sylvester
Drama. Christian Cent 82:1066-7, 1096-7, 1578-
9 S 1-8, D 22 '65
SMITH, Wendell A.
Shareowner Smith, U.S.A. il por Newsweek
66:68 Jl 5 '65
SMITH, Wilbur S.
Ways to make the Nation's highways safer;
interview. por U S News 58:59-61 Mr 1 '65
SMITH, Willard H.
Maggie modernizes Mishawaka's methods.
Am City 80:124-5 Je '65
SMITH, William James
Angus Wilson's England. Commonweal 82:
18-21 Mr 26 '65
Books. Commonweal 82:507 Jl 9 '65
Soupy and The mouse. Commonweal 82:446-8
Je 25 '65
SMITH, William Jay
Bluestockings of New England. New Repub
152:22-4+ Mr 27 '65
New books of poems: from last August to
this. Harper 231:106+ Ag '65
Slave bracelets; poem. New Repub 152:18-19
Ap 17 '65
SMITH, William Stephens
Miss Adams in love. L. Mayo. il por Am
Heritage 16:36-49+ F '65
SMITH act. See Communism—United States—
Anti-Communist measures
SMITH and Wesson revolvers. See Revolvers
SMITHCRAFT corporation
Man who got the owner's job. il Bsns W p86+
Je 26 '65
SMITHERMAN, Joe T.
$107 misunderstanding. por Newsweek 65:27
Ap 19 '65
SMITHIES, Oliver
Antibody induction and tolerance: excerpts
from address, February 25, 1965. bibliog
Science 149:151-6 Jl 9 '65
Disulfide-bond cleavage and formation in pro-
teins. bibliog Science 150:1595-8 D 17 '65
SMITHSON, James
International gathering to mark Smithsonian
bicentennial, September 16-18, 1965. Science
149:954 Ag 27 '65
Smithsonian celebrates founder's 200th birth-
day. Sci N L 88:198 S 25 '65
Wellspring of a nation's pride; with report by
D. Martin. il por Life 59:86-98+ N 19 '65
SMITHSONIAN institution
Diffusing knowledge among men. H. Morales.
il Am Ed 1:1-5 S '65
International gathering to mark Smithsonian
bicentennial, September 16-18, 1965. Science
149:954 Ag 27 '65
Legacy of James Smithson: address, September 16, 1965. L. B. Johnson. Dept State Bul
53:550-2 O 4 '65; Same with title Smithsonian honored: remarks, September 16,
1965. Sci N L 89:199 S 25 '65; Same with
title President Johnson on international
education. Sch & Soc 93:481+ D 11 '65
National museum act could increase status.
Sci N L 87:219 Ap 3 '65
New York jeweler gives diamond to Smithsonian. Hobbies 70:113 My '65
Smithsonian institution. il NEA J 54:30-2 S
'65

SMITHSONIAN institution—*Continued*
Smithsonian: under new secretary it is seeking to regain place as center for scientific research. D. S. Greenberg. il Science 147: 1266-9 Mr 12 '65; Discussion. 148:580; 149:7-8 Ap 30, Jl 2 '65
There's a windmill in the attic. D. S. Greenberg. Sat R 48:48-50 Je 5 '65; Reply. C. G. Abbot. 48:58 S 4 '65
Underwater thesaurus: Smithsonian institution program of underwater exploration of historic sites. M. Peterson. il Antiques 88: 319-24 S '65
Van Alstyne American folk art collection. P. C. Welsh. il Antiques 88:208-11 Ag '65
Wellspring of a nation's pride; anniversary for the Smithsonian; with report by D. Martin. il Life 59:86-98+ N 19 '65

Museum of history and technology

Eighteenth-century porcelain at the Smithsonian; the Hans Syz collection. P. V. Gardner. il Antiques 88:336-40 S '65
Larsen and McCauley collections at the Smithsonian institution. J. J. Miller, 2d. il Antiques 88:522-5 O '65
Wellspring of a nation's pride; anniversary for the Smithsonian; with report by D. Martin. il Life 59:86-98+ N 19 '65

National air and space museum

$40-million museum will trace evolution of air, space flight; National air and space museum. il Aviation W 82:58 My 3 '65
Museum for the space age. il Arch Rec 137: 140-2 Mr '65

National collection of fine arts

Stuart Davis in memoriam. F. Getlein. New Repub 153:36-7 Jl 24 '65

National portrait gallery

Our national portrait gallery. il Antiques 87:416+ Ap '65

SMOG
Dilute smog by planting greenbelts by freeways. Sci N L 88:313 N 13 '65
How smog hurts your eyes. il Sci Digest 58:18 S '65
Smog today & smog tomorrow; main offender: motor vehicles. M. Neiburger. il Nation 201:432-5 D 6 '65
  See also
Los Angeles—Air pollution

SMOKE detectors
Build a smoke alarm for your home. H. St Laurent. il Pop Electr 23:49-52 S '65

SMOKE houses. See Smokehouses

SMOKE prevention
Smoke watch; Consolidated Edison company of New York. New Yorker 41:23-5 Jl 17 '65

SMOKEHOUSES
Smoke boxes you can make. il Sunset 135:86+ Ag '65

SMOKING
Confirm smoking theory; UCLA report. Sci N L 88:214 O 2 '65
Habit; classes sponsored by Smoking unit of the New York city department of health. New Yorker 41:31-3 Je 5 '65
Hartford's antismoking campaign; high schools. C. L. Towne. il Sr Schol 87:sup39+ S 23 '65
Herba nicotiana in history. P. W. Schmidtchen. Hobbies 70:107-8+ S '65
How to quit smoking. Sci Digest 59:35-6 Ja '66
If everybody stopped smoking—. il U S News 59:99 D 20 '65
Men quit smoking easier. Sci N L 87:251 Ap 17 '65
New smoking report; recommendations for continued research into the psychology of smoking. Sci N L 88:85 Ag 7 '65
No no smoking; Samsonite corp. ban lifted. Newsweek 66:81 D 13 '65
Quit smoking early. Sci N L 87:308 My 15 '65
Smokers seek masculinity. C. A. Betts. Sci N L 87:373 Je 12 '65
Smoking is contagious. W. S. Ross. il Parents Mag 40:68-9+ N '65
Smoking studies conflict. Sci N L 87:388 Je 19 '65
Washington report. J. Lloyd. Sr Schol 87:sup5 N 4 '65
Wethersfield plan; antismoking program in elementary schools. C. L. Towne. il Sr Schol 87:sup8-9 O 14 '65
  See also
Cigarettes
Tobacco—Physiological effects

SMOKING of food. See Food—Smoking

SMOLINSKI, Leon
Farm and factory in the USSR. Sat R 48:38 Ag 14 '65

SMOLLER, Carolyn G.
Neurosecretory processes extending into third ventricle: secretory or sensory? bibliog Science 147:882-4 F 19 '65

SMOLUCHOWSKI, R.
Is there vegetation on Mars? bibliog Science 148:946-7 My 14 '65
Radiation sintering of lunar dust. bibliog Science 150:1025-6 N 19 '65

SMOOTH muscle. See Muscle

SMOTHERS brothers
Tom, Dick, and money. Newsweek 65:80 Mr 1 '65

SMUCKER, David E.
Amateur scientist. il Sci Am 213:239-40+ S '65

SMUCKER, J. M. company
Smucker spreads out beyond jam and jelly. il Bsns W p 194+ N 13 '65

SMUGGLING
Dirty campaign on the corruption issue; Philippine smugglers. G. De Carvalho. il Life 59:78B-80+ N 26 '65
Dope-smuggling diplomats; ed. by J. C. G. Conniff. H. L. Giordano. il Pop Sci 186: 100-3+ Je '65
Smugglers I have known; experiences in Majorca. F. V. Grunfeld. il Opera N 30:8-12 N 6 '65
Travel for profit; smuggling goods and money between Hungary, Poland, Czechoslovakia, Rumania, Bulgaria and Austria. Newsweek 66:80-1 S 20 '65
Up front where it counts; cigarette smuggling across Swiss-Italian border. il Newsweek 66:84 O 25 '65
Where they still walk a mile for a Camel; cigarettes smuggled from Switzerland to Italy. Time 86:46 O 15 '65

SMUTNY, Anne
Sharing recreation services. Recreation 58: 348-9 S '65

SMYLIE, James H.
Conflict of concerns. Christian Cent 82:1602-6 D 29 '65
Freedom in action. Christian Cent 82:1067-8 S 1 '65

SMYLIE, Robert E.
Livy's ghost. Newsweek 66:26-7 D 27 '65

SMYTH, Henry D.
Nuclear power and proliferation; address, November 17, 1965. Dept State Bul 54:28-36 Ja 3 '66

SMYTH, Peter R.
To sleep: ay, there's the rub. Motor B 115: 30-2+ Mr '65

SMYTHE, John W. See Smythe, R. jt. auth.

SMYTHE, Rosena, and Smythe, J. W.
Outboard yachting in the Bahamas. il pors Yachting 118:58-9+ N '65

SNACKS. See Meals

SNAIL fever. See Schistosomiasis

SNAILS
Giant snail is used for muscle studies: research in the physiology of strophocheilidae. C. P. Jaeger. il Natur Hist 74:26-7 N '65
Great snail war; Swiss ban on snail hunters annoys the French. Newsweek 65:54 My 24 '65
Liguus, the Florida tree snail. G. K. Zimmer. il Nat Parks Mag 39:13 Ap '65
Tree snails, gems of the Everglades. T. Davidson. il Nat Geog Mag 127:372-87 Mr '65
Trematode parasitism and polymorphism in a marine snail. W. H. Ewers and C. R. Rose. il Science 148:1747-8 Je 25 '65

SNAKE bite. See Venom

SNAKE RIVER
Increase water supply, don't allocate shortages. S. B. Nelson. il Am City 80:96-8 Mr '65

SNAKE venom. See Venom

SNAKES
King snake dines on a sparrow egg; with photographs by R. H. Wright. Natur Hist 74:50-1 Mr '65
New facts on deadly snakes. B. East. il Outdoor Life 136:17-19+ Ag '65
Snakes, the legless ones. il Sci Digest 57: 92-4 F '65
Venomous babies; Australian tiger snakes. il Sci Digest 58:45 Ag '65
  See also
Rattlesnakes
Sea snakes

SNAP. See Space vehicles—Atomic power plants

SNAPPING turtles. See Turtles

SNAPSHOTS. See Photography

SNYDER, John Avery
Opinion, please from Philadelphia. Mlle 61:
144+ Ag '65
SNYDER, LeMoyne
Lee Oswald's guilt; how science nailed Kennedy's killer. por Pop Sci 186:68-73 Ap '65
SNYDER, Louis L.
America's role in world conflict. Sat R 48:
26 Jl 3 '65
Doubt came too late for Germany. Sat R 48:
25+ Ap 3 '65
SNYDER, Martin P.
Views of Philadelphia 1750-1770. Antiques
88:674-80 N '65
SNYDER, Russell L.
Air-sea interface. Science 149:766 Ag 13 '65
SNYDER, Samuel S.
Automation at LC: philosophy, plans, progress. por Library J 90:4709-14 N 1 '65
SNYDER, Solomon H. and Axelrod, Julius
Circadian rhythm in pineal serotonin: effect
of monoamine oxidase inhibition and reserpine. bibliog Science 149:542-4 Jl 30 '65
—See Fischer, J. E. jt. auth.
SNYDER, W. Dale. See Blumer, M. jt. auth.
SO dear to my heart; story. See Alexander,
R. W.
SO near to me; story. See Randall, F. E.
SOAP
Soap and water beauty; a guide to the right
soaps for you. il Redbook 125:66-7+ Je
'65
Soap making goes modern. M. B. Keiser. il
Parents Mag 40:18+ N '65

History

Art of cleanliness. J. G. Harmount. il Todays Health 43:49-51+ D '65
SOAP operas. See Television broadcasting—
Dramas
SOARES, Janet M.
Janet M. Soares, Judith Willis and companies,
92nd street Y. J. Maskey. Dance Mag 39:32
Jl '65
SOBEL, Ross
Teacher. il por Time 86:64-5 S 3 '65
SOBILOFF, Hy
To Millicent Smith, whom I didn't know;
Outside my autumn morning; To my doctor;
Three ladies with their hats on having
lunch; My windblown poem; Tom Jones my
tom cat; As the conversation goes; My wild
flowers anonymous; Waiting; poems. Poetry
105:318-23 F '65
SOBOLEVA, Valentina. See Negovsky, V. jt.
auth.
SOBY, James Thrall
Through Snowdon's lens. Sat R 48:34 D 11
'65
SOCCER
Chipping away at U.S. apathy; two foreign
teams draw SRO crowd in New York. M.
Kram. il Sports Illus 22:60-1 Je 21 '65
Local boys make very good; national soccer
championships. J. Jares. il Sports Illus 23:
22-5 D 13 '65
Soccer; the rabble game. D. Cort. il Nation
201:100-1 Ag 30 '65
Twenty minutes of horror; disaster at National stadium in Lima, Peru. J. P. Blank,
Read Digest 86:141-4 Ap '65
SOCCER players
Instep with the times; field-goals. H. L. Masin. il Sr Schol 87:26 N 18 '65
SOCHOR, Eugene
Unesco general conference of 1964. Sch & Soc
93:226-8 Ap 3 '65
SOCHUREK, Howard
Sweep of creative power; photographs. Life
59:70-1+ D 24 '65
SOCIAL adjustment. See Adjustment, Social
SOCIAL agencies, Voluntary
Royal Oak aids its problem youth. J. A.
Morris. il Read Digest 87:163-7 O '65
War on poverty; are the poor left out? R.
A. Cloward. il Nation 201:55-60 Ag 2 '65
**SOCIAL and economic council of the United
Nations.** See United Nations—Economic
and social council
SOCIAL and economic security
Welfare programs in evolution. E. M. Burns.
Mo Labor R 88:294-5 Mr '65
What big daddy, alias Uncle Sam, will do
for you; Time essay. Time 86:62-3 N 5 '65
See also
Insurance, Health
Insurance, Social

Great Britain

Creeping crisis for Britain's welfare state. il
U S News 59:59-61 N 22 '65
Welfarism vs. the masses. Nat R 17:1184
D 28 '65

Uruguay

If you want to know how far welfare can
go—. J. N. Wallace. il U S News 59:73-4+
S 27 '65
SOCIAL attitudes. See Attitudes; Moral attitudes
SOCIAL behavior. See Manners and customs
SOCIAL behavior of animals. See Animals—
Habits and behavior
SOCIAL change
Accidental century, by M. Harrington. Review
New Repub 153:25-6 Jl 24 '65. D. W.
Brogan
American idealism, 1965; role of youth. H.
Taylor. il Sat R 48:14-16 Je 26 '65
American Negro problem in the context of
social change; excerpts from Negro in
America. A. M. Rose. Ann Am Acad 357:
1-17 Ja '65
Automation and imagination. J. Hawkes.
Harper 231:92-4+ O '65
Can we cope with tomorrow? A. Toffler. il
Redbook 126:38-9+ Ja '66
Future as a way of life. A. Toffler. il Horizon
7:108-15 Sum '65
Hard problems of a turbulent world; address,
September 16, 1965. G. W. Ball. Dept State
Bul 53:588-92 O 11 '65
Help wanted; maybe Mary Poppins, inc;
Time essay. Time 86:42-3 Jl 9 '65
In only eight years, how U.S. is to change.
il U S News 58:56-60 My 17 '65
Is God changing our society? E. A. Smith.
Cath World 202:74-9 N '65
Nature of modernization; the Middle East and
north Africa. W. R. Polk. For Affairs
44:100-10 O '65
Patterns, structures, of modernization and
political development. M. J. Levy, jr. Ann
Am Acad 358:29-40 Mr '65
Post-industrial generation: roots of student
discontent. M. B. Freedman. il Nation 200:
639-43 Je 14 '65
Rate and costs of political development. M.
Halpern. bibliog f Ann Am Acad 358:20-8
Mr '65
Responsibility for social change; business or
government? R. W. Austin. Harvard Bsns
R 43:45-52 Jl '65
Time of juveniles. E. Hoffer. Harper 230:
16+ Je '65
Toward a concept of political development.
K. Von Vorys. Ann Am Acad 358:14-19 Mr
'65
Transformation of peasant societies; report
on symposium on Vicos, Peru, project. A.
R. Holmberg and H. F. Dobyns. Science
147:1062+ F 26 '65
Your kids when they grow up; interview.
D. N. Michael. il Changing T 19:7-13 Mr
'65
See also
Institute on social change in a democratic
society
Social progress
SOCIAL clubs. See Clubs
SOCIAL commission of the United Nations. See
United Nations—Social commission
SOCIAL conditions
Great, and good, society. W. Lippmann.
Newsweek 66:25 N 22 '65
Strengthening the international development
institutions; statement, July 9, 1965. A. E.
Stevenson. Dept State Bul 53:142-51 Jl 26
'65; Same with title International development. Vital Speeches 31:610-15 Ag 1 '65
See also
Civilization
Poverty
SOCIAL conflict
Worldwide plague of city riots: a British
view; reprint. Harper 231:44+ N '65
SOCIAL control
See also
Pressure groups
SOCIAL cooperation, International. See International cooperation
SOCIAL development. See Social progress
SOCIAL diseases. See Venereal diseases
SOCIAL education
Los Angeles riots: handling the topic in
class; symposium. il Sr Schol 87:sup8-10+
O 7; sup5 O 14; sup5 O 21 '65; Excerpts. 87:
9-12+ O 28 '65
See also
Social sciences—Study and teaching
SOCIAL equality. See Equality

SOCIAL ethics
Kind word for conformity; American life in the 1960s. M. W. Fishwick. il Sat R 48:22-4 D 11 '65
  See also
Christian ethics
Church and race problems
Sexual ethics
SOCIAL evolution. See Social change; Social progress
SOCIAL facilitation. See Social psychology
SOCIAL groups. See Groups (sociology)
SOCIAL history
  See also
United States—Social history
Urbanization
SOCIAL, humanitarian and cultural committee of the United Nations. See United Nations—Social, humanitarian and cultural committee
SOCIAL insurance. See Insurance, Social
SOCIAL interaction
Political socialization: its role in the political process; symposium, ed. by R. Sigel. bibliog f il Ann Am Acad 361:1-140 S '65
SOCIAL isolation. See Isolation, Social
SOCIAL legislation
  See also
Pensions—Laws and regulations

United States
Johnson oversell. W. V. Shannon. Commonweal 81:777-8 Mr 19 '65; Reply. Time 85:76 Ap 2 '65
What Congress did to change U.S; legislation to get the Great society under way. il U S News 59:29-32 N 1 '65
  See also
Family allowances—United States
Old age pensions—United States
SOCIAL life and customs. See Manners and customs
SOCIAL news. See Newspapers—Society page
SOCIAL planning, Rural. See Sociology, Rural
SOCIAL policy
  See also subhead Social policy under names of countries, e.g. United States—Social policy
SOCIAL problems
Wretched of the earth, by F. Fanon. Review New Repub 153:20+ S 18 '65. R. Coles
  See also
Church and social problems
Homosexuality
Illegitimacy
Juvenile delinquency
Libraries and social and economic problems
Prostitution
Race discrimination
Race problems
School and social and economic problems
Slums
Sociology, Christian
Suicide
Unemployables
SOCIAL progress
Conquering the ancient enemies of mankind; remarks, July 22, 1965. L. B. Johnson. Dept State Bul 53:236-8 Ag 9 '65
Idea of progress: a critical reassessment; adaptation of paper, September 1964. G. G. Iggers. bibliog f Am Hist R 71:1-17 O '65
Kind word for conformity; American life in the 1960s. M. W. Fishwick. il Sat R 48:22-4 D 11 '65
Teilhard de Chardin and the Afro-Asian world. T. P. Melady and M. B. Melady. Cath World 202:102-6 N '65
SOCIAL psychiatry
Poverty and social change. A. H. Leighton. il Sci Am 212:21-7 bibliog(p 150) My '65
SOCIAL psychology
Group structure and role behavior. J. Jackson and C. McGehee. bibliog f Ann Am Acad 361:130-40 S '65
Moral indignation and middle class psychology, by S. Ranulf. Review Nation 200:428-30 Ap 19 '65. C. McWilliams
Social facilitation. R. B. Zajonc. bibliog il Science 149:269-74 Jl 16 '65
  See also
Adjustment, Social
Attitudes
Human relations
Morale, National
Social psychiatry
SOCIAL responsibility. See Responsibility
SOCIAL satire. See Satire

SOCIAL science research
Foreign affairs research: review process rises on ruins of Camelot. J. Walsh. Science 150:1429-31 D 10 '65
In retrospect. R. Sigel. Ann Am Acad 361:128-9 S '65
Procedures for review of contract research on foreign affairs; Department statement, November 23, 1965. Dept State Bul 53:960-1 D 13 '65
SOCIAL sciences
What's happening in social studies; summaries of periodical articles and reports, ed. by H. L. Hurwitz (cont) Sr Schol 86:7T F 11; sup 19 Ap 29; 87:sup27 S 23 '65
  See also
Geography
Sociology

Bibliography
Curious whether and how: creative reading in the social sciences. R. K. Carlson. Library J 90:1981-3 Ap 15 '65
New paperbacks for high school teachers; new social studies books. H. L. Hurwitz. il Sr Schol 87:sup24-5+ O 28 '65

Courses of study
Curriculum revision projects: English and the social studies. W. K. Richards. il Sr Schol 86:13T-14T F 18 '65

Periodicals
  See also
Trans-action (periodical)

Study and teaching
Chaos in the social studies? D. W. Robinson. Sat R 48:79 N 20 '65
Curriculum revision projects: English and the social studies. W. K. Richards. il Sr Schol 86:13T-14T+ F 18 '65
Improving social science education. Sch & Soc 93:238 Ap 17 '65
New records for English and social studies; with discography. J. Muri. il Sr Schol 87:sup 13-14 O 7 '65
New social studies. Sch & Soc 93:174 Mr 20 '65
Political conscience for West German youth. S. M. Shafer. il Sr Schol 86:sup 13 My 20 '65
Reforming social studies in schools; Educational research council of Greater Cleveland. R. Kirk. Nat R 17:775 S 7 '65
Social studies in British schools. R. E. Gross. il Sr Schol 87:sup36-8 S 23 '65
  See also
Current events—Study and teaching
National council for the social studies
Social education

Textbooks
How to use a multiple textbook approach in junior high social studies classes; Madison junior high school, Madison, N.J. R. T. Hall. Sr Schol 87:sup 19 N 18 '65
World affairs workshop, ed. by New York times and Encyclopaedia Britannica. Review Sat R 49:74 Ja 15 '66. B. B. Stretch
SOCIAL sciences and humanities index
Committee on Wilson indexes; decision on International index. Wilson Lib Bul 39:802-3 My '65
SOCIAL security. See Insurance, Social; Social and economic security
SOCIAL security act
  See also
Old age, survivors' and disability insurance trust fund
SOCIAL security act amendments
Biggest change since the New deal; Mills medicare bill. il Newsweek 65:88-90 Ap 12 '65
How medicare will affect medicine. il Bsns W p 144+ Jl 10 '65
Medicare. H. C. Wallich. Newsweek 65:72 My 31 '65
Medicare program takes shape. Bsns W p 180 Ap 10 '65
Medicare vs. the AMA's latest substitute. Consumer Rep 30:148-9 Mr '65
One tax that will go up and up. il U S News 59:104 Jl 12 '65
Other changes coming in social security. Suc Farm 63:94 O '65
Pensions, benefits, taxes; how they go up under the new social security law. il U S News 59:48-9 Ag 2 '65
Reducing take-home pay. D. Lawrence. U S News 59:-108 Jl 19 '65
Social security: a growing giant; Congress to boost benefits and taxes. il Bsns W p76-7+ F 6 '65

SOCIAL security act amendments—*Continued*
Stepping up too fast. Bsns W p 164 Ap 3 '65
This month's feature: controversy in Congress over medicare. Cong Digest 44:67-77+ Mr '65
What the new social security means to you. il Changing T 19:19-23 D '65
Wrapping up medicare; biggest social security measure in history. Bsns W p25 Jl 3 '65
Wrapping up the medicare bill; House ways & means committee reports. Bsns W p32 Mr 27 '65

SOCIAL security administration. See United States—Social security administration

SOCIAL security benefits. See Insurance, Social —United States

SOCIAL status
High school extracurricular activities and political socialization. D. Ziblatt. bibliog f il Ann Am Acad 361:20-31 S '65
See also
Middle classes
Students—Social and economic status

SOCIAL status of teachers. See Teachers—Social status

SOCIAL studies. See Social sciences

SOCIAL usage. See Etiquette

SOCIAL welfare
Business role in tthe Great society. J. Terhorst; W. Welch. il Reporter 33:26-32 O 21 '65
See also
Sociology, Rural

SOCIALISM
Can we talk to Marxian atheists. P. Ehlen; D. I. MacLean. America 113:112-17 Jl 31 '65
Politics of socialism, by R. H. S. Crossman. Review
New Repub 153:25-7 D 25 '65. N. S. Care
Socialism and capitalism; an international misunderstanding. R. K. White. il For Affairs 44:216-28 Ja '66
Socialist humanism: an international symposium, ed. by E. Fromm. Review
Sat R 48:107-8 S 18 '65. H. Cox

Algeria
Algeria: zigzag path to socialism. S. Corvell. il Nation 200:277-9 Mr 15 '65

Burma
Sharing the shame; Burmese road to socialism. Time 86:20 D 24 '65

Canada
Where socialism failed close to home; test in Saskatchewan. T. Drury. il Nations Bsns 53:66-8+ O '65

Great Britain
See also
Labor party (Great Britain)

United States
Inheritors of the faith. M. Cantor. Nation 200:366-8 Ap 5 '65
See also
Socialist scholars conference, New York

SOCIALISM and communism. See Communism and socialism

SOCIALIST scholars conference, New York
What is a Socialist? J. O'Connor. Nation 201:195-6 O 4 '65

SOCIALIZED medicine. See Medical service, State

SOCIALLY handicapped children
Children Santa forgot; cases of seventeen children. il Ladies Home J 82:48+ D '65
Four days in May. J. Moorhead. PTA Mag 59:2-3 My '65
Mountain of books for mountain children; PTA project, Books for Appalachia. E. May. il PTA Mag 60:8-10 S '65
Special hell for children in Washington. J. W. Anderson. Harper 231:51-6 N '65; Discussion. 232:6+ Ja '66
Where kids are kings; Boys brotherhood republic, New York city. J. Olsen. il Sr Schol 86:sup 10-11 Mr 4 '65

Education
As a psychologist sees pressures on disadvantaged teen-agers. A. Pearl. il NEA J 54:18-19+ F '65
Compensatory education for cultural deprivation, by B. S. Bloom and others. Review
Sat R 48:81-2 My 15 '65. A. H. Passow
Disadvantaged defined; more oral English for the disadvantaged; NCTE meeting. Sr Schol 87:sup 13 D 9 '65

Educating slum children in London. R. N. Kirk. Sch & Soc 93:180-2 Mr 20 '65
Expose, don't impose; introducing middle-class values to disadvantaged children. J. D. Lohman. NEA J 55:24-6 Ja '66
I can be 'most anything! W. Hartley and E. Hartley. Good H 161:262 N '65
Learning is fun when you dance it; program in Washington, D.C. to prepare slum children for reading. C. Schmais. il Dance Mag 40:33-5 Ja '66
Lessons of poverty. F. Riessman. il Am Ed 1:21-3 F '65
Poverty of condition and poverty of mind. R. Kirk. Nat R 17:467 Je 1 '65
School library or bookatheque? education of youth and war on poverty. C. K. Brooks. Library J 90:1989-90 Ap 15 '65
Schools of Appalachia. P. Schrag. il Sat R 48:70-1+ My 15 '65
Summer study-skills program for minority group pupils; project of Educational counseling service. W. D. Martinson and others. Sch & Soc 93:300-2 Sum '65
Teaching the disadvantaged. B. Bettelheim. il NEA J 54:8-12 S '65
Tiger in Stephen's jungle. R. A. Hochstein. il Am Ed 1:5-7 Ap '65
Way it spozed to be. J. Herndon. il Harper 231:79-87 S '65
See also
Children of migrant laborers—Education
Project head start

SOCIÉTÉ générale de Belgique. See Belgium—Industries

SOCIETY. See subhead Social life and customs under names of countries, states, cities, e.g. Washington, D.C.—Social life and customs

SOCIETY, Primitive
See also
Eskimos—Culture
Indians of North America—Culture

SOCIETY and art. See Art and society

SOCIETY and the individual. See Individual and society

SOCIETY for research on meteorites. See Meteoritical society

SOCIETY Hill, Philadelphia. See Philadelphia—City planning

SOCIETY news reporting. See Reporters and reporting

SOCIETY of automotive engineers
Attack on Detroit. J. Ridgeway. New Repub 152:13-14 Mr 6 '65

SOCIETY of fellows. See Harvard university —Society of fellows

SOCIETY of illustrators
Artists and books surveyed at panel discussion and exhibition; summary of panel discussion, with list of award winners. il Pub W 188:86-8+ N 8 '65

SOCIETY of Jesus. See Jesuits

SOCIETY of photographer and artist representatives
Art, photographer agents form trade organization. Pub W 187:77 Ap 26 '65

SOCIETY of photo-optic instrumentation engineers
New roles seen for human eyes in space. R. G. O'Lone. Aviation W 83:51+ Ag 30 '65

SOCIETY page. See Newspapers—Society page

SOCIO-ECONOMIC status of students. See Students—Social and economic status

SOCIOLOGY
Global sociology urged. Sci N L 88:165 S 11 '65
Protestantism in American sociology. R. L. Means; reply. R. T. Wolcott. Christian Cent 82:146-7 F 3 '65; Rejoinder. 82:470-1+ Ap 14 '65
Report from a Chinese village, by J. Myrdal. Review
New Repub 152:22-3 Je 26 '65. E. Snow
See also
Attitudes

Periodicals
See also
American behavioral scientist

Study and teaching
Sociology in bloom. Time 86:64+ O 29 '65

SOCIOLOGY, Animal. See Animals—Habits and behavior

SOCIOLOGY, Christian
Helping and healing ministries. D. C. Taggart. Christian Cent 82:1510-11 D 8 '65
Karl Rahner in New York; interview, ed. by E. C. Bianchi. K. Rahner. America 112:860-3 Je 12 '65

SOCIOLOGY, Christian—*Continued*
Poor: French vs. American viewpoint. D. O'Grady. Cath World 201:177-82 Je '65
See also
Church and social problems
SOCIOLOGY, Industrial
Priests without cassocks. H. C. Bunke. Harvard Bsns R 43:103-9 My '65
SOCIOLOGY, Rural
Poverty and social change. A. H. Leighton. il Sci Am 212:21-7 bibliog(p 150) My '65
See also
Urbanization
SOCIOLOGY, Urban
Chicago's Archdiocesan office of urban affairs. J. H. Fichter. America 113:462-5 O 23 '65
Today's city: threat or promise? concerning H. Cox's Secular city. M. L. Stackhouse. Christian Cent 82:1537-41 D 15 '65
See also
Urban renewal
Urbanization
SOCIOLOGY and economics. See Economics—Social and ethical aspects
SOCKEYE salmon. See Salmon
SOCONY Mobil oil company, incorporated
Centralized control key to Socony Mobil's air operations. D. A. Brown. il Aviation W 82:60-1+ Je 21 '65
SOCRATES
Kierkegaard and Socrates. M. W. Hess. Christian Cent 82:736-8 Je 9 '65
Trial and death of Socrates; concerning four dialogues of Plato. K. Rexroth. por Sat R 48:31+ S 11 '65
SODAS, Ice cream. See Beverages
SODEE, D. Bruce
Nuclear medicine. Science 147:761 F 12 '65
SÖDERBLOM, Nathan
Söderblom: ecumenical churchman and theologian. C. J. Curtis. Christian Cent 83:47-8 Ja 12 '66
SODIUM
Viscosities of liquid sodium and potassium, from their melting points to their critical points. A. V. Grosse. bibliog il Science 147:1438-41 Mr 19 '65
Isotopes
Anomalous abundance of upper atmosphere sodium, 1964. C. R. Burnett. bibliog Science 147:736-7 F 12 '65
SODIUM chloride. See Salt
SODIUM compounds
Clathrate structure of silicon Na₈Si₄₆ and Na₂Si₁₃₆. J. S. Kasper and others. bibliog il Science 150:1713-14 D 24 '65
SODIUM in the body
Active uptake of sodium by softshell turtles, trionyx spinifer. W. A. Dunson and R. D. Weymouth. bibliog il Science 149:67-9 Jl 2 '65
Electron microscopy: sodium localization in normal and ouabain-treated transporting cells. G. I. Kaye and others. bibliog il Science 150:1167-8 N 26 '65
Sodium pump: its electrical effects in skeletal muscle. A. S. Frumento. bibliog il Science 147:1442-3 Mr 19 '65
Transepidermal potential difference: development in anuran larvae. R. E. Taylor, jr. and S. B. Barker. bibliog il Science 148:1612-13 Je 18 '65
SODIUM vapor lamps. See Electric lamps, Sodium vapor
SOFIA Christian peace conference. See Peace conferences
SOFT drinks. See Beverages
SOFTBALL
And then a good cry; U.S. loses series of ladies softball. Time 85:52+ Mr 5 '65
Play ball; Broadway show league. il Newsweek 65:54+ Je 28 '65
SOFTENING of water. See Water softening
SOFTSHELL turtles. See Turtles
SOGNNAES, Reidar F.
Fluoride protection of bones and teeth. bibliog Science 150:989-93 N 19 '65
SOHM ABYSSAL PLAIN. See Atlantic Ocean
SOHN, David A.
Programed instruction. PTA Mag 60:17-19 S '65
SÖHNGEN, Werner
Who's who in foreign business. por Fortune 72:66 S '65
SOHO. See London
SOIL acidity
See also
Lime

SOIL analysis. See Soils—Analysis
SOIL bacteriology
See also
Soil microbiology
SOIL bank. See Agricultural administration—United States
SOIL conservation service. See United States—Soil conservation service
SOIL disinfection
Faster fumigation with plastic. il Farm J 89:50E Mr '65
SOIL fertility
See also
Fertilizers and manures
SOIL fumigation. See Soil disinfection
SOIL microbiology
Amateur scientist; how to isolate from samples of topsoil microorganisms that secrete antibiotics. B. Hulett. il Sci Am 213:124-6+ N '65
Enzyme from soil bacterium hydrolyzes phenylcarbamate herbicides. P. C. Kearney and D. D. Kaufman. Science 147:740 F 12 '65
SOIL moisture
Testing
Tells when and how much to irrigate. il Farm J 89:47 Ap '65
SOIL pollution
Histoplasma capsulatum: occurrence in soil from the Emilia-Romagna region of Italy. G. Sotgiu and others. bibliog Science 147:624 F 5 '65
SOIL salinity. See Soils, Salts in
SOILLESS culture of plants. See Plants—Soilless culture
SOILS
What's new. See issues of Successful farming
Analysis
Test your soil. F. R. Laughton. il Pop Gard 16:6+ Mr '65
Why a complete soil analysis is important; foundation design. E. C. Nordquist. Arch Rec 137:215-16 Je '65
Nitrogen content
Will nitrates put you out of farming? B. Brantley. Suc Farm 63:49+ Mr '65
SOILS, Liming of. See Lime
SOILS, Salts in
They used an artificial soil. il Sunset 135:270 O '65
SOKA Gakkai (sect)
Soka Gakkai brings absolute happiness. I. Morris. il N Y Times Mag p8-9+ Jl 18 '65
SOKOLOW, Anna
I hate academies; modern dance is an individual quest; excerpt from Choreographers on choreography, ed. by S. J. Cohen. Dance Mag 39:38-9 Jl '65
about
Dance theatre workshop, inc. works by Valerie Bettis, Anna Sokolow, Deborah Jowitt; East 74th street theatre. J. Maskey. Dance Mag 39:160-1 D '65
SOLAR, Lucio Garcia del. See Garcia del Solar, L.
SOLAR batteries
Brain telestimulator with solar cell power supply. B. W. Robinson and others. il Science 148:1111-13 My 21 '65
How we're harnessing the sun. T. E. Weissmann. il Sci Digest 57:52-6 Je '65
Improved solar cells planned for IMP-D. R. D. Hibben. il Aviation W 83:53+ Jl 26 '65
Let the sun power your portable. H. L. Davidson. il Pop Electr 23:85-6 N '65
Thin-film solar cells boost output ratio. P. J. Klass. il Aviation W 83:67-70 N 29 '65
SOLAR boats. See Boats, Solar powered
SOLAR cells. See Solar batteries
SOLAR constant. See Solar radiation
SOLAR distillation. See Solar stills
SOLAR eclipses. See Eclipses, Solar
SOLAR-electric propulsion. See Rocket propulsion
SOLAR energy
How we're harnessing the sun. T. E. Weissmann. il Sci Digest 57:52-6 Je '65
Solar energy; report on Solar energy society. P. E. Glaser. Science 148:1127-9+ My 21 '65
See also
Solar batteries

SOLAR engines
Amazing no-fuel space engine you can build; operating on solar energy. H. Walton. il Pop Sci 187:106-10+ Jl '65
New engine for space does down-to-earth jobs. H. Walton. il Pop Sci 187:100-5+ Jl '65

SOLAR flares
How electricity in the air affects you. J. R. Free. il Sci Digest 58:50-4 N '65
Solar flare symposium: Goddard space flight center. G. S. Mumford. il Sky & Tel 29: 89 F '65
Sun affects Mars cap? Sci N L 87:180 Mr 20 '65
Sun-watchers keep alert. Sci N L 88:133 Ag 28 '65

SOLAR magnetic field. See Magnetic field (cosmic physics)

SOLAR motion. See Solar system—Motion in space

SOLAR photography. See Astronomical photography

SOLAR power. See Solar energy

SOLAR probes. See Space probes

SOLAR radiation
Atmospheric noble gases: solar-wind bombardment of extraterrestrial dust as a possible source mechanism. D. Tilles. bibliog Science 148:1085-8 My 21 '65
Decreased solar radiation. C. S. Mumford. Sky & Tel 30:140 S '65
Effect of solar wind seen. Sci N L 87:310 My 15 '65
NASA intensifies radiation studies. D. A. Anderton. il Miss & Roc 16:26+ Je 21 '65
Our life-giving star, the sun. H. Friedman. il Nat Geog Mag 128:712-43 N '65
Solar constant studies needed for spacemen. G. S. Mumford. Sky & Tel 30:219 O '65
Solar radiation: an anomalous decrease of direct solar radiation; atmospheric dust from the eruption of Mt Agung. E. C. Flowers and H. J. Viebrock. bibliog il Science 148:493-4 Ap 23 '65
See also
Plants, Effect of solar radiation on
Solar energy
Solar flares
Sunspots

Measurement
In-flight results from Mariner 4. R. N. Watts, jr. il Sky & Tel 29:359 Je '65
Sunlight measuring box calculates rain needs; integrating solarimeter. Sci N L 87: 390 Je 19 '65

SOLAR spectrum. See Spectrum, Solar

SOLAR stills
New simple solar still operating in Australia. il Sci N L 88:277 O 30 '65
New survival technique: get water anywhere. D. S. Halacy, jr. il Outdoor Life 136:14-15+ Ag '65
Portable solar still. Sci Digest 58:25 N '65
Simple solar still yields survival water in desert. Sci N L 88:215 O 2 '65
Solar distillation of water from soil and plant materials: a simple desert survival technique. R. D. Jackson and C. H. M. Van Bavel. il Science 149:1377-9 S 17 '65

SOLAR system
Great space debate. D. Cohen. il Sci Digest 58:28-32 D '65
Solar system exploration study planned. I. Stone. Aviation W 83:87-9+ Jl 12 '65
Solar system, the sun's family. il Sci Digest 57:84-7 Mr '65

Motion in space
Relativity and solar evolution. Sky & Tel 30: 275-6 N '65

SOLARIMETERS. See Solar radiation—Measurement

SOLDER and soldering
Fourth rule for soft soldering. J. Burroughs. il Pop Sci 186:130-3+ Mr '65
New soldering tools and techniques. W. H. Buchsbaum. il Electr World 73:46-8+ F '65
Resistance soldering. D. A. Reid. il Electr World 74:68-9 Jl '65
See also
Brazing

SOLDERING apparatus
New soldering tools and techniques. W. H. Buchsbaum. il Electr World 73:46-8+ F '65

SOLDIERS
Duty, honor, country; potential draftees in Las Vegas. il Newsweek 66:18 S 6 '65

SOLDIERS, American. See United States—Army

SOLDIERS, Unknown. See Unknown soldiers

SOLDIERS graves. See Service mens graves

SOLDIERS letters. See Letters from service men

SOLDIERS pensions. See Pensions, Military

SOLDIERS slang. See Slang

SOLDNER, Paul
California design nine. Craft Horiz 25:18-23 My '65
Workshop: a kiln is built. Craft Horiz 25: 38-9 Ja '65

SOLE (fish)
See also
Cookery—Fish

SOLENOID engines, Toy. See Engines, Toy

SOLI, Giorgio. See Hoyt, J. W. Jt. auth.

SOLICITOR General. See United States—Justice, Department of

SOLID-phase peptide synthesis. See Synthesis

SOLID propellant rockets
Adaptability designed into FW-4S motor. R. G. O'Lone. Aviation W 83:69 D 13 '65
AF discloses new upper stage. Miss & Roc 17:17 S 20 '65
Big-solid insurance needed. W. J. Coughlin. Miss & Roc 17:50 O 25 '65
Big solids cancellation resisted. J. F. Judge. Miss & Roc 17:21 O 11 '65
Congress may restore solids funds. H. M. David. Miss & Roc 16:12 F 8 '65
Congress seen as hope for 260-in. solids. W. J. Normyle. Aviation W 82:24 F 8 '65
Insulation liner for 260-in. motor. il Miss & Roc 16:27 Mr 1 '65
ICBM studies focus on 156-in. motors. I. Stone. il Aviation W 82:141-3+ Mr 15 '65
LPC big solids R&D leads to interest in volume-limited motor production. J. F. Judge. il Miss & Roc 16:28+ Mr 1 '65
New rocket to use fluorocarbon. Aviation W 82:79 Mr 22 '65
New rockets unveiled in Moscow; with editorial comment. il Miss & Roc 16:16-17, 74 My 17 '65
Solid core booster rockets to success; SL-1, solid rocket engine. il Bsns W p47-8 O 2 '65
Subliming solid thrustor set for test. W. S. Beller. il Miss & Roc 17:26-7 Ag 23 '65
UTC solves Scout stage spin problem. R. Lindsey. il Miss & Roc 17:28+ Ag 30 '65

Launching
Launch of large solids from silos studied. I. Stone. il Aviation W 83:69-70 S 6 '65

Manufacture
Solid groundwork for solid rockets; portfolio. Fortune 71:114-21 Mr '65

Materials
Hydrostatic test bursts 260-in. case. Aviation W 82:29 Ap 19 '65
260 case rupture traced. Miss & Roc 17:25-6+ Jl 26 '65

Testing
Aerojet demonstrates solid pulse motors. Aviation W 82:30 Ap 19 '65
Aftermath of Atlas-Centaur failure. il Miss & Roc 16:18 Mr 15 '65
Biggest booster yet. il Time 85:55 Mr 12 '65
Dilemma of a solid success. il Life 58:73+ Ap 23 '65
Facility refines motor testing. il Miss & Roc 16:32-3 My 10 '65
Final Titan 3A readied for test; first 3C vehicle is assembled. il Aviation W 82:32-3 Ap 12 '65
Hydrostatic test bursts 260-in. case. Aviation W 82:29 Ap 19 '65
Navy propellant monitoring technique employs gauges embedded in grains. J. F. Judge. il Miss & Roc 16:22-3 Ap 19 '65
156-in. firing scores major success. J. F. Judge. il Miss & Roc 16:16-17 Mr 8 '65
156-in. semi-prototype test successful. H. D. Watkins. il Aviation W 83:61+ D 27 '65
Roaring success, but will it fly? Thiokol's 156-in.-diameter solid rocket. il Bsns W p82+ Mr 6 '65
Solids support mounts in Congress. J. F. Judge. il Miss & Roc 17:18+ O 4 '65
Success marks Thiokol 156-in. solid firing. W. Hansen. il Aviation W 82:22 Mr 8 '65
Thiokol tests two thrust vector systems. M. L. Yaffee. il Aviation W 82:91+ Je 21 '65
260-in. motor success spurs new support. W. Hansen. il Aviation W 83:26-7 O 4 '65

SOLIDS
Hard-sphere fluid. H. L. Frisch. bibliog il Science 150:1249-54 D 3 '65
Tracks of charged particles in solids. R. L. Fleischer and others. bibliog il Science 149:383-93 Jl 23 '65

SOLITUDE
Loneliness can be a treasure. C. C. Park. Ladies Home J 82:58+ Mr '65
Rain and the rhinoceros. T. Merton. il Holiday 37:8+ My '65

SOLMSSEN, Lily
How David Attie creates montages in his darkroom. Mod Phot 29:80-5 Mr '65
Variations on two negatives. Mod Phot 29:66-9 F '65

SOLO projection system. See Projection apparatus

SOLOMON, Alan R.
Big show in Venice. C. Tomkins. il Harper 230:98-104 Ap '65

SOLOMON, Anthony M.
Challenges facing United States trade policy; address, October 21, 1965. Dept State Bul 53:787-93 N 15 '65
East-West trade; address, October 21, 1965. Dept State Bul 53:739-46 N 8 '65
U.S. trade policy in Latin America; statement, September 10, 1965. Dept State Bul 53:567-72 O 4 '65

SOLOMON, Eric
Free speech at Ohio state. Atlan 216:119-23 N '65

SOLOMON, Leonard A.
Cruising through history on Long Island Sound. il por Motor B 115:22-9+ Ap '65

SOLOMON ISLANDS
Big men and disks of shell; exchange of kesa in transactions. H. W. Scheffler. il Natur Hist 74:20-5 D '65

SOLOMON R. Guggenheim museum, New York
Cry of anguish; Munch exhibition. A. Werner. il Reporter 33:51-3 O 21 '65
Redressing a spiral showcase; Thannhauser collection bequeathed to Manhattan's Guggenheim museum. il Time 85:86 My 7 '65

SOLOVIOFF, Nicholas
Rig for sea, and showtime; paintings. Sports Illus 24:20-5 Ja 3 '66

SOLOW, Anatole A. See Powelson, J. P. jt. auth.

SOLTI, Georg
Other side; thwarted attempt to present Schönberg's Moses and Aaron at the Royal opera house. T. Heinitz. Sat R 48:43 Jl 31 '65

SOLUBILITY
Carbonates: association with organic matter in surface seawater. K. E. Chave. bibliog il Science 148:1723 Je 25 '65

SOLUTION (chemistry)
Sedimentation velocity experiments: position and motion of schlieren peaks. J. A. Faucher. and J. V. Koleske. il Science 147:1152-3 Mr 5 '65

SOLUTIONS
Nucleation of crystals from solution. A. G. Walton. bibliog il Science 148:601-7 Ap 30 '65
Radiolysis of thymine in aqueous solutions: change in site of attack with change in pH. L. S. Myers, jr. and others. bibliog il Science 148:1234-5 My 28 '65

SOLVENTS
Lewis acidity of polar organic solvents from thermodynamic measurements. R. V. Orye and others. bibliog il Science 148:74-5 Ap 2 '65
Sedimentation velocity experiments: position and motion of schlieren peaks. J. A. Faucher. and J. V. Koleske. il Science 147:1152-3 Mr 5 '65

SOMALIA
Somalia walks the tightrope. J. Contini. il N Y Times Mag p 14-15+ Ag 8 '65
See also
Food relief—Somalia

SOMALIS
Epic love of Elmi Bonderi. M. Laurence. Holiday 38:35+ N '65
Somalia walks the tightrope. J. Contini. il N Y Times Mag p 14-15+ Ag 8 '65

SOMATIC polysaccharides. See Polysaccharides

SOME of the time, all of the time; story. See Dorman, S.

SOMEONE to care; story. See Knowlton, R. A.

SOMEROSKI, James M. and Myers, Richard
Wood assemblage: a children's art project. Sch Arts 65:14-17 N '65
—See Mancini, M. R. jt. auth.

SOMERS, Florence
From Route 66 to the Mexican border. Redbook 125:38+ O '65
New movies. See issues of Redbook

SOMERSET, Henry Robert
H. R. (Bobby) Somerset; appreciation. E. F. Haylock. por Motor B 115:188 My '65

SOMERSON, Norman L. and others
Hemolysin of mycoplasma pneumoniae: tentative identification as a peroxide. bibliog Science 150:226-8 O 8 '65

SOMETHING nice; story. See Lyons, R.

SOMME, Battles of the. See European war, 1914-1918—Campaigns and battles

SOMMER, John W.
Ethiopia. bibliog Focus 15:1-6 Ap '65

SOMMERS, Joseph
Silencing the children of Sanchez. Nation 201:530-3 D 27 '65

SOMNAMBULISM
Dreamless sleepwalking. Sci Am 213:49 Jl '65
Somnambulism: all-night electroencephalographic studies. A. Jacobson and others. bibliog il Science 148:975-7 My 14 '65

SON et lumière. See Sound and light

SON-in-law; story. See Gordimer, N.

SONAR
How the blind use sonar. il Sci Digest 58:33 S '65
Modern sea search uses sonar, television; search for the Eastern air lines plane. il Sci N L 87:135 F 27 '65
No place to hide; Project Caesar, computer-coordinated deep-sea listening net. Newsweek 66:28 S 27 '65
Sonar system of the blind: size discrimination. C. E. Rice and S. H. Feinstein. bibliog il Science 148:1107-8 My 21 '65

SONATAS
See also
Phonograph records—Sonatas

SONDERICKER, Herbert
Review of books. Sr Schol 87:sup 10 S 30 '65

SONDERN, Frederic, jr
Many faces of the FBI. Read Digest 87:177-8+ D '65
Meet the men who guard your mail. Read Digest 87:186-8+ O '65
Other side of apathy. Read Digest 86:113-16 F '65

SONDHEIM, Stephen
New word man for Rodgers; music in Do I hear a waltz? T. Prideaux. Life 58:20 Mr 19 '65

SONG books. See Songbooks

SONG leading. See Conducting, Choral

SONGBOOKS
Reading and singing. C. H. Bishop. il Commonweal 83:153-4 N 5 '65

SONGS
See also
Folk songs
Phonograph records—Songs

SONGS, American
Flag or rag, it's still grand; Cohan and the grand old flag. P. O'Neil. Life 58:19 My 7 '65
Songs of freedom; with photographs by A. Kane. C. S. Wren. Look 29:83-9 N 16 '65
See also
Folk songs, American
Negro songs

Anecdotes, facetiae, satire, etc.
America the what? E. Zern. il Field & S 70:132 Ja '66

SONGS, English
Looking backward; Purcell's songs. P. L. Miller. il Sat R 48:68 N 27 '65
Old English music hall songs are new. C. MacInnes. il N Y Times Mag p62-3+ N 28 '65

SONGS, Negro. See Negro songs

SONGS, Popular. See Music, Popular (songs, etc)

SONGS of birds. See Birds—Song

SONIA; story. See Jacobson, D.

SONIC boom. See Shock waves

SONIC sounding. See Sounding and soundings

SONICS. See Sound waves

SONORAN DESERT
Organ Pipe Cactus National Monument. W. F. Heald. il Nat Parks Mag 39:9-12 Ap '65

SONS
See also
Fathers

SONS and fathers. See Parent-child relationship

SONS and mothers. See Parent-child relationship

SONTAG, L. W.
Can we increase intelligence? PTA Mag 60:20-2 bibliog(p33) N '65

SONTAG, Susan
Imagination of disaster; excerpt from Against interpretation. Commentary 40:42-8 O '65
Opinion, please, from New York. Mlle 60:58+ Ap '65
Theatre. Vogue 146:51-2 Ag 15 '65

about
Not good taste, not bad taste, it's camp. T. Meehan. il N Y Times Mag p30-1+ Mr 21 '65
Self-education of a brilliant highbrow. R. Phelps. Life 60:8+ Ja 21 '66

SOPHIA the seamstress; drama. See Dias, E. J.

SOPHOCLES
Sophocles: the Theban plays. K. Rexroth. Sat R 48:40 N 13 '65

SOPRANOS. See Singers

SORBITOL
Sorbitol pathway: presence in nerve and cord with substrate accumulation in diabetes. K. H. Gabbay and others. bibliog il Science 151:209-10 Ja 14 '66

SORBONNE. See Colleges and universities— France

SORELL, Walter
Edgar Degas: the sentimental cynic. Dance Mag 39:62-5 Je '65
Tatjana Gsovsky: a prayer to the deity. Dance Mag 39:14-15 Ag '65

SORENSEN, Theodore Chaikin
Kennedy; excerpts. pors Look 29:40-50 Ag 10; 37-51 Ag 24; 42-6+ S 7; 48-52+ S 21; 50-3 O 19 '65

about
Bay of Pigs revisited: lessons from a failure. Time 86:16-17 Jl 30 '65
Sorensen on Kennedy, a footnote; concerning articles by S. Alsop in Saturday evening post. S. Alsop. por Sat Eve Post 238:14 O 9 '65
Sorensen's Kennedy. M. Kempton. il por Atlan 216:71-4 O '65
Sorensen's Kennedy. R. Moley. Newsweek 66:120 N 8 '65

SORENSON, Roy, and **Marburger, C. L.**
Allies for human renewal. NEA J 54:21 N '65

SORGENFREY, Sven
Something new in Denmark. Dance Mag 39: 26-7 Ag '65

SORGHUM
How to control weeds in grain sorghum. Suc Farm 63:82 Ap '65
What we learned about growing sorghum. F. C. Stickler. Suc Farm 63:82 My '65
See also
Milo

SORIA, Dorle J.
Artist life. See issues of High fidelity incorporating Musical America
Under the stars. Opera N 29:8-12 My 1 '65

SORREL tree. See Sourwood

SORRENTINO, Gilbert
World and self: instances. Poetry 106:306-9 Jl '65
about
Gestures of deliberation. T. Clark. Poetry 107:121-2 N '65
Two against chaos. R. Howard. Nation 200: 289-90 Mr 15 '65

SOSA-RODRIGUEZ, Carlos
United Nations commemoration address, June 26, 1965. UN Mo Chron 2:169-71 Jl '65
United Nations holds memorial ceremony for Ambassador Stevenson; remarks, July 19, 1965. Dept State Bul 53:230-1 Ag 9 '65

SOSS, Wilma
Into orbit & out of order. il por Time 85:94 My 21 '65

SOTET, James G.
Poem; If my love did not mean as much. Seventeen 24:72 My '65

SOTGIU, Giulio, and others
Histoplasma capsulatum: occurrence in soil from the Emilia-Romagna region of Italy. bibliog Science 147:624 F 5 '65

SOTHEBY and company
Auction by Early bird. R. Lynes. il Harper 231:28+ Ag '65
Manuscripts at Sotheby's. K. V. Hostick. Hobbies 70:110-11 D '65
Sotheby builds up a bid for old-car collectors. il Bsns W p42-4 N 20 '65

SOUDAN formation. See Paleontology—Minnesota

SOUFFLES
Puffed with goodness. C. Claiborne. il N Y Times Mag p75 Mr 7 '65

Successful soufflé. il Am Home 68:64+ Ap '65
What she's serving is a vegetable soufflé; with recipes. il Sunset 135:172+ S '65

SOULE, Carl
Other side has a case. Christian Cent 82: 803-5 Je 23 '65

SOULE, Gardner
How Jon Lindbergh works on the ocean floor. Pop Sci 187:50-3 S '65

SOUND
See also
Music—Acoustics and physics
Noise
Ultrasonics
Voice

Apparatus
Artificial voice helps speechless to speak. Sci N L 89:40 Ja 15 '66
Cartridge sound projector. il U S Camera 28:64-5 My '65
Device sends more sound; speech analyzer. Sci N L 87:292 My 8 '65
Home entertainment. il Consumer Rep 30: 203-61 D '65
Local color: dead or alive. T. Schwartz. il Pop Phot 56:38+ Ap '65
Loudness under control. I. B. Berger. Sat R 48:59+ Mr 27 '65
Sound advice; tape deck or complete tape recorder? R. Flanzraich. Mod Phot 29:21+ S '65
Sound; cable data and other joint technical matters. J. Wesson. U S Camera 28:30 Mr '65
See also
Earphones
Hydrophones
Loud speaking apparatus
Microphones
Moving picture cameras—Sound equipment
Phonograph
Sonar
Spectrograph, Sonic
Tuning forks

Measurement
See Sound measurement

Recording and reproducing
Sound. J. Wesson. See issues of U.S. camera & travel
Sound advice. See issues of Modern photography
Sound test report (cont) il Pop Phot 56:125 Ap; 114-15 Jl '65
Tony Schwartz on sound. T. Schwartz. See issues of Popular photography
See also
Magnetic recorders and recording
Phonograph records—Recording

Stereophonic recording and reproducing
Audio. H. Fantel. See issues of Opera news
How much stereo is enough? Bet Hom & Gard 43:110-11 F '65
Inquiry into spatial stereo; with editorial comment. L. Feldman. il Hi Fi 15:33, 38-40+ My '65
See also
Stereophonic sound systems

SOUND and light
Vivid ghost; son et lumière on U.S.S. North Carolina. il Time 85:77-8 My 21 '65

SOUND conditioning. See Soundproofing

SOUND measurement
How loud is loud? I. B. Berger. Sat R 48: 61+ F 27 '65

SOUND of silence; drama. See Willis, H.

SOUND production by animals
Bullfrogs sing along with jets. S. W. Kress. il Audubon Mag 67:93-6 Mr '65
Communication between dolphins in separate tanks by way of an electronic acoustic link. T. G. Lang and H. A. P. Smith. bibliog il Science 150:1839-44 D 31 '65
Dolphins can mimic human voice duration. Sci N L 87:73 Ja 30 '65
Froggie went a-courtin; excerpt from Sex life of the animals. H. Wendt. il Sat R 48: 50 S 4 '65
Intelligent life on this world; bottle-nosed dolphins. H. Downs. il Sci Digest 57:88-91 Mr '65
Shaping and discriminative control of underwater click vocalizations in a California sea lion. R. J. Schusterman and S. H. Feinstein. bibliog il Science 150:1743-4 D 24 '65
What science knows about dolphin talk. A. Hamilton. il Sci Digest 57:9-13 My '65

SOUND production by animals—*Continued*
What seals talk about. Sci Digest 57:83 Mr
'65
See also
Insect sounds

SOUND production by fishes
Sound production by cichlid fishes. A. A.
Myrberg, jr. and others. bibliog il Science
149:555-8 Jl 30 '65

SOUND production by insects. See Insect
sounds

SOUND suppressors
High-Q detector and noise-limiter system;
communications receiver. R. L. Ives. il
Electr World 73:74-5 Mr '65

SOUND waves
Infrasound tests human tolerance. **H. M.**
David. Miss & Roc 17:31+ O 11 '65
Sound: waves that travel in the air. il Sci
Digest 57:84-5 Ap '65
When the earth rang like a bell. E. Ubell.
Read Digest 87:179-80+ Ag '65
See also
Ultrasonic waves

Medical applications
Detect disease by sound; echocardiography.
Sci N L 87:386 Je 19 '65
Sound detects bone disease in early stages.
Sci N L 88:201 S 25 '65

SOUNDING and soundings
Installing a depth sounder inside and out.
H. C. Lawrence. il Motor B 115:124-6 Mr
'65
New sounds underwater. E. Robberson. il
Yachting 118:50-3+ Ag '65

SOUNDING rockets. See Rockets, Sounding

SOUNDPROOFING
All quiet on the homefront; model homes
in San Antonio. Time 85:42-3 Je 4 '65
Building or buying? here's what to look for.
Todays Health 43:59 F '65
It's not the noise, it's the annoyance. il
House & Gard 127:148-55+ Ap '65
Let's take the din out of living. W. R.
Vath. il Todays Health 43:6-7+ F '65
Wherewithal of sound control; special prod-
ucts to help you. House & Gard 127:202-3
Ap '65
Wrap yourself in quiet. il Pop Mech 124:152-
8 S '65

SOUNDS of the sea. See Ocean sounds

SOUPS
Best-loved soups in the world. il McCalls 92:
124-5+ Ap '65
Cold day calls for hearty soup. B. S. Brown.
il Good H 160:136 F '65
Cold salad soup; with recipes. il Seventeen
24:108-9+ Je '65
First course by the fireplace; with recipes.
il McCalls 93:140-1+ N '65
Garden row soup. H. Groves. il Farm J 89:
90 S '65
Green pea soup. M. Kaytor. il Look 29:88-9
N 30 '65
Hot soup! with recipes. R. Hanna. il Suc
Farm 64:110-11 Ja '66
Let onion soup start a party française!
C. Brock. Good H 162:126 Ja '66
Put some wine in your soup? il Sunset 134:
216+ My '65
Two winter soups using lentils. Sunset 134:
136 F '65
See also
Chowder

SOUPY Sales program. See Television broadcasting—Childrens programs

SOUR cream. See Cream, Sour

SOURDOUGH. See Dough

SOURWOOD
Sweet and sour aristocrat. R. D. Roe. il Am
For 71:34-5+ Jl '65

SOUSA, John Philips
Sousa at Columbia: performance of El cap-
tian. A. M. Lingg. Opera N 29:33 F 20 '65

SOUSA SAMPAIO, Nelson de. See Sampaio,
N. de S.

SOUSTER, Raymond
Hunting of the deer; My nighthawk; Church
Street pawnshop; poems. Poetry 105:238-9
Ja '65

SOUTH
Century after Appomattox; symposium. bibliog il Wilson Lib Bul 39:840-68+ Je '65
Fast-changing South; symposium. il Look 29:
33-44+ N 16 '65
South today; symposium, ed. by W. Morris.
il Harper 230:126-84+ Ap '65; Discussion.
230:4+ Je '65
Which South? K. Haselden. Christian Cent
82:1055-6 S 1 '65

Who speaks for the South? by J. M. Dabbs.
Review
Reporter 32:46+ Mr 11 '65. C. Degler
See also
Agriculture—Southern states
Appalachian Region
Camping—Southern states
Colleges and universities—Southern states
Education—Southern states
Gulf states
Justice, Administration of—Southern states
Negroes in the United States—South
Tourist trade—Southern states

Civilization
W. J. Cash after a quarter century; excerpt
from South today: 100 years after Appomattox. E. M. Yoder. Harper 231:14+ S '65;
Reply. H. Golden. 231:6 N '65

Description and travel
Golfing along the Gulf. V. J. Flanagan. il
Travel 123:42-4 F '65
Plantation country. P. Deutsch and R.
Deutsch. il Holiday 37:30 My '65

Economic conditions
Ever-ever land. J. Daniels. il Harper 230:183-
4+ Ap '65
South: socioeconomic and cultural aspects;
address, April 1965. L. L. Durisch. il Wilson Lib Bul 39:854-9 Je '65

History
Era of reconstruction, 1865-1877, by K. M.
Stampp. Review
Nation 200:450-3 Ap 26 '65. B. A. Weis-
berger
Furl that banner. H. Carter. il N Y Times
Mag p8-9+ Jl 25 '65
South as it is: 1865-1866, by J. R. Dennett.
Review
Nation 201:197-8 O 4 '65. W. R. Brock
This quiet dust. W. Styron. il Harper 230:
134-46 Ap '65
See also
Ku Klux klan
Reconstruction (Civil war)
United States—History—Civil war

Industries
Air-conditioned sweatshop; criticism of public-financing programs. B. Kovach. il Reporter 33:29-31 O 7 '65
New trend for factories; go West! go South!
il U S News 59:94-5 N 1 '65
Pressure is on the diehards; behind the
scenes in Mississippi and Alabama. il
Bsns W p27-8 Ap 3 '65

Politics
And now there are two; no longer the one-
party South. Time 86:13 D 24 '65
Changing face of southern politics. F.
Knebel. il Look 29:50+ N 16 '65
Cracks widen in once solid South. il U S
News 58:11 Je 28 '65
From the first reconstruction to the second.
C. V. Woodward. il Harper 230:127-33 Ap
'65
Million more Negro voters; what happens on
Election day? il U S News 59:63-4 S 20 '65
Negro's strange bedfellows. Nation 201:346
N 15 '65
New politics in the South. V. F. Callahan,
jr; H. Wolman. Commonweal 83:312-14 D
10 '65
Rising Negro vote; what it will mean to the
South. il U S News 59:46-7 N 29 '65
Southern bloc, how it's changing. il U S
News 58:17-18 My 3 '65
South's new Negro voters; can they swing
an election? with chart. il U S News 59:
38-40 Ag 23 '65
W. J. Cash after a quarter century; excerpt
from South today: 100 years after Appomat-
tox. E. M. Yoder. Harper 231:14+ S '65;
Reply. H. Golden. 231:6 N '65
What the Negro vote will do to South; what
southern editors say about the Negro vote.
il U S News 58:30-8 Mr 29 '65

Popular culture
Southern mythology. C. V. Woodward. Commentary 39:60-3 My '65

Race problems
See also
Negroes in the United States—South

Social conditions
Deep South's other venerable tradition. E.
Caldwell. il N Y Times Mag p 10-11+ Jl
11 '65

SOUTH—Social conditions—*Continued*
Impending crisis of the deep South. D. W.
  Brogan. Harper 230:147-51 Ap '65
South: into a new century. il Newsweek 65:
  26 My 3 '65
South: socioeconomic and cultural aspects;
  address, April 1965. L. L. Durisch. il Wilson Lib Bul 39:854-9 Je '65
Unexpected dividend for the South. P. M.
  Stern. Harper 230:66-72 My '65
Voices from the South. R. Coles. Harper
  230:165 Ap '65
Why I returned. A. Bontemps. il Harper
  230:176-82 Ap '65

Social history

See also
Slavery—United States

Social life and customs

Last American hero is Junior Johnson, yes!
  T. Wolfe. il Esquire 63:68-75+ Mr '65
Southern mythology. C. V. Woodward. Commentary 39:60-3 My '65

SOUTH, University of the. See University of
  the South, Sewanee, Tenn.

SOUTH AFRICA

International court of justice; concerning
  public hearings. UN Mo Chron 2:50-2 Ap '65
Problem of sanctions: development of economic pressures against South Africa. P.
  Ritner. Commonweal 82:315-19 My 28 '65
Republic of South Africa. C. R. Lovell. il
  Cur Hist 48:226-31 Ap '65
South Africa; address, March 5, 1965. H. L.
  T. Taswell. Vital Speeches 31:495-7 Je 1 '65
See also
Investments, Foreign (in South Africa)
Prisons—South Africa
Public opinion—South Africa
Suffrage—South Africa
United Nations—South Africa

Commerce

Our stake in apartheid. S. Meisler. il Nation
  201:71-3 Ag 16 '65

Economic conditions

South Africa: rich, arrogant, self-righteous.
  il Newsweek 66:44+ O 25 '65

Foreign relations

South Africa bars American Negroes. New
  Repub 153:8-9 Jl 10 '65

History

See also
Zulu war, 1879

Industries

Where the cash grows in Africa. il Bsns W
  p 134+ Je 19 '65

Native races

Higher learning for the Bantu; separate institutions under the policy of apartheid.
  R. Kirk. Nat R 17:150 F 23 '65
See also
South Africa—Race problems

Politics and government

Beloved country 1965. A. Paton. Commonweal
  82:311-15 My 28 '65
Happiness in South Africa. America 113:
  466-8 O 23 '65
Solitary voice; H. Suzman's M.P.'s protest
  against white supremacist policies. Newsweek 65:44+ Je 21 '65
South Africa: rich, arrogant, self-righteous.
  il Newsweek 66:44+ O 25 '65

Race problems

Action for South Africa; report of British
  council of churches study. C. Northcott.
  Christian Cent 82:231 F 24 '65
All part of the game; South African P.G.A.
  tournament at Germiston. Time 87:40 Ja
  14 '66
Angry young bishop; food-raising for the
  Bantus. il Time 87:52 Ja 14 '66
Apartheid in South Africa. UN Mo Chron 2:
  51-5 Je; 42-7 Jl; 25-6 Ag '65
Apartheid in South Africa. il UNESCO Courier
  18:20-8 Ap '65
Happiness in South Africa. America 113:
  466-8 O 23 '65
Higher learning for the Bantu; separate
  institutions under the policy of apartheid.
  R. Kirk. Nat R 17:150 F 23 '65
Humanity in South Africa. Sat Eve Post 238:
  84 Ag 28 '65
It is still not too late; proposals for new
  course against apartheid. il UNESCO
  Courier 18:29-33 Ap '65

117 days, by R. First. Review
  America 113:188 Ag 21 '65. P. E. Khabele
One man, one vote in South Africa. R. Kirk.
  Nat R 17:198 Mr 9 '65
Onlookers and others. J. Squire. Christian
  Cent 82:1524-5 D 8 '65
Our stake in apartheid. S. Meisler. il Nation
  201:71-3 Ag 16 '65
Preventing a massacre. Christian Cent 83:
  36 Ja 12 '66
Prisons of apartheid. H. Kuper. Nation 202:
  76-8 Ja 17 '66
Selma and Sharpeville. D. Berrigan. Commonweal 82:71-5 Ap 9 '65; Discussion. 82:
  230 My 7 '65
South Africa bars American Negroes. New
  Repub 153:8-9 Jl 10 '65
South Africa takes still tougher line. Christian Cent 82:908 Jl 21 '65
There is no such thing as regulations here;
  South African jails. H. Strachan. il N Y
  Times Mag p 10-11+ Jl 25 '65
Vehicle for concern. V. E. Lowder. Christian
  Cent 82:508-10 Ap 21 '65
Verwoerd tightens the screws. A. Delius.
  il Reporter 33:29-31 Jl 1 '65
See also
United Nations—Expert committee on South
  Africa
United Nations—South Africa

Religious institutions and affairs

Beloved country 1965. A. Paton. Commonweal
  82:313-15 My 28 '65
Happiness in South Africa. America 113:
  466-8 O 23 '65
News of the Christian world (cont) Christian
  Cent 82:408, 750, 1202-5, 1524-5 Mr 31, Je 9,
  S 29, D 8 '65

SOUTH AFRICAN authors. See Authors, South
  African

SOUTH AMBOY, N.J.

Another city has 100 per cent-code-level
  lighting. M. F. Nagle. il Am City 80:131-2
  Ag '65

SOUTH AMERICA

See also
Amazon Valley
Latin America

Commerce

See Latin America—Commerce

Defenses

See Latin America—Defenses

Description and travel

See Latin America—Description and
  travel

Economic conditions

See Latin America—Economic conditions

Education

See Education—Latin America

Politics

See Latin America—Politics

SOUTH AMERICA and the United States. See
  Latin America and the United States
SOUTH AMERICAN literature. See Latin
  American literature

SOUTH BURLINGTON, Vt.

We beat the educationists; extravagances of
  school board. A. Cismaru. Nat R 17:413-14
  My 18 '65

SOUTH CAROLINA

See also
Housing—South Carolina
Hunting—South Carolina
Libraries—South Carolina

History

South Carolina: post bellum paradise for
  Negroes. L. Bennett, jr. il Ebony 21:116-
  22 Ja '66

Politics and government

Palmetto Republicans; South Carolina Republicans. J. C. Evans. Christian Cent 82:
  1030 Ag 25 '65
Same South Carolina. New Repub 153:11-12
  S 4 '65
South Carolina: post bellum paradise for
  Negroes. L. Bennett, jr. il Ebony 21:116-
  22 Ja '66
South Carolina's new senator. il Time 85:
  33-4 Ap 30 '65

SOUTH DAKOTA

Good fun in the Badlands. B. Ballantine. il
  Holiday 37:20+ Je '65
See also
Birds—South Dakota

SOUTH DAKOTA—*Continued*

Description and travel

On your way to the Black Hills... E. Waltner. il Travel 124:35-7 S '65

Religious institutions and affairs

News of the Christian world. Christian Cent 82:500+ Ap 21 '65

SOUTH END school. See Boston—Education

SOUTH Pacific; musical comedy. See Musical comedies, revues, etc. Criticisms, plots, etc.

SOUTH SEA ISLANDS

Far lands grow nearer; Asia and the Pacific; symposium. il Sat R 48:35-40+ S 18 '65

Mama Tala; visit to Puka-Puka, Cook Islands. J. Frisbie. il Atlan 215:69-74 F '65

See also
Easter Island
Marquesas Islands
Nauru (island)
Polynesia
Tahiti

SOUTHAM, Anna L.

What's new in family planning. Parents Mag 40:82-4+ N '65

SOUTHAMPTON, N.Y.

Summer living in Southampton. il House & Gard 128:100-15 Ag '65

SOUTHEAST ASIA. See Asia, Southeastern

SOUTHEAST ASIA treaty organization

Eleventh anniversary of SEATO; statement, September 4, 1965. D. Rusk. Dept State Bul 53:536-7 S 27 '65

Plan for peace in Vietnam; the U.N. and SEATO offer an alternative to war in southeast Asia. D. R. Larson and A. Larson. Sat R 48:21-4 Ap 24 '65

SEATO council ministers hold 10th meeting at London; statement, May 3, 1965, with text of communique, May 5, 1965. G. W. Ball. Dept State Bul 52:920-6 Je 7 '65

SOUTHEASTERN regional ballet festival. See Dance festivals

SOUTHERN, Terry

At the movies: Southern way of death. M. Barrett. Reporter 33:40-2 N 18 '65

Loved house of the Dennis Hoppers. Vogue 146:138-43+ Ag 1 '65

SOUTHERN Baptist convention. See Baptists in the United States

SOUTHERN Baptists. See Baptists in the United States

SOUTHERN CALIFORNIA timing association

SCTA opener, El Mirage. L. Smith. il Hot Rod 18:48-51 S '65

SOUTHERN CALIFORNIA university, Los Angeles

Married students housing. il Arch Rec 138:128-9 Ag '65

SOUTHERN Christian leadership conference

Helping hands; domestic Freedom corps. il Newsweek 65:24 Je 28 '65

Law and the faithful; Rev Reese, charged with embezzlement. Reporter 33:18+ S 23 '65

Men behind Martin Luther King. il Ebony 20:164-6+ Je '65

Summer delay; SCOPE students return to campuses. Nation 201:71 Ag 16 '65

Summer strategy. Newsweek 65:28-9 Ap 12 '65

Tension, not split, in the Negro ranks. A. Schardt. Christian Cent 82:614-16 My 12 '65

SOUTHERN cookery. See Cookery, American

SOUTHERN courier (newspaper) See Atlanta—Newspapers

SOUTHERN Methodist university, Dallas, Tex.

Contemporary revival; Religious emphasis week's Willson lectures. J. C. Evans. Christian Cent 82:392-3 Mr 31 '65

SOUTHERN mountaineers. See Mountaineers (southern states)

SOUTHERN OCEAN racing conference. See Sailboat racing

SOUTHERN railway company

One way to run a railroad: go to it! Brosnan's way. il Newsweek 66:89-90+ O 18 '65

SOUTHERN regional council

Federal courts practice racial exclusion. Christian Cent 82:605 My 12 '65

Southern regional council. L. W. Dunbar. Ann Am Acad 357:108-12 Ja '65

SOUTHERN RHODESIA. See Rhodesia

SOUTHERN state college, Magnolia, Ark.

Men's dormitories. il Arch Rec 138:122-3 Ag '65

SOUTHERN states. See South

SOUTHERNERS

Camden, Alabama; last summers of a dreamlike world; with excerpts from Ordways, by W. Humphrey. J. Poppy. il Look 29:64-8+ N 16 '65

My problem and how I solved it; a southern family's trials due to friendship with Negroes. il Good H 160:62+ Je '65

Southern girl's diary of discovery; North Carolina statewide interracial war on poverty. S. Sterling. il Look 29:107-13 Jl 13 '65

This was Montgomery; racial attitudes in the Deep South. G. H. Dunne. il America 112:660-1+ My 8 '65; Discussion. 113:78-9 Jl 17 '65

Weep no more, Columbia. il Newsweek 65:27-8+ My 3 '65

SOUTHWARK, Arthur Mervyn Stockwood, bp of. See Stockwood, A. M.

SOUTHWEST

See also
Botany—Southwestern states
Education—Southwestern states

Description and travel

New Southwest. J. Schaefer. il Holiday 37:50-65+ My '65

Economic conditions

Southwest poverty; archbishop stresses absence of unionism. America 112:183 F 6 '65

SOUTHWEST AFRICA

International court of justice; concerning public hearings. UN Mo Chron 2:50-2 Ap '65

Price of prosperity. P. Webb. il Newsweek 66:45 Ag 16 '65

SOUTHWEST water plan. See Colorado River

SOUTHWESTERN regional ballet festival. See Dance festivals

SOUTHWICK, Albert B.

James Baldwin's jeremiad. Christian Cent 82:362-4 Mr 24 '65

SOVEREIGN immunity. See Privileges and immunities

SOVIET CENTRAL ASIA. See Asia, Central

SOVIET education. See Education—Russia

SOVIET government. See Russia—Politics and government

SOVIET waterways. See Waterways—Russia

SOVIET women. See Women—Russia

SOVIET writers. See Authors, Russian

SOVIET youth. See Youth—Russia

SOWING. See Seeding

SOWS. See Swine

SOYBEANS

Fertilizers and soybeans. J. Russell. Farm J 89:60J My '65

Now, a dozen weed killers for soybeans. C. E. Ball. il Farm J 89:65-6 My '65

Report on hybrid soybeans. W. D. Pardee. il Suc Farm 63:46 Ag '65

Report on new soybean varieties. B. Pardee. il Suc Farm 63:52 Ap '65

73.5-bu soybeans, a record! D. Seim. il Farm J 89:44 Mr '65

Diseases and pests

Report on preemergence weed killers for corn and soybeans. Suc Farm 63:88-9 Mr '65

SOYER, Moses

Informal portraits of Moses Soyer; interview, ed. by R. Gill. il por Am Artist 29:50-5+ S '65

SOZANSKI, Edward J.

Life of a theoretical scientist. Sci Digest 57:28-31 F '65

SPACE (architecture)

Opinion, please from New York. R. Marker. il Mlle 61:38+ Je '65

Private space and public pleasure. il Esquire 64:217-19 D '65

SPACE, Outer

Anecdotes, facetiae, satire, etc.

Dumbbell's guide to the space age. il Esquire 63:122-5 My '65

Bibliography

Mandate of heaven. P. Morrison. il Nation 200:339-41 Mr 29 '65

Law

See Space law

Study and teaching

How far is space? inquiry-centered space science program. A. F. Eiss and C. Mulford. il NEA J 54:14-16 N '65

SPACE and information systems division. See North American aviation, incorporated—Space and information systems division

SPACE and time
Gravitational collapse and the death of a star. K. S. Thorne. bibliog il Science 150:1671-9 D 24 '65
See also
Relativity (physics)

SPACE arrangement of plants. See Plants, Space arrangement of

SPACE detection and tracking systems. See Radar—Military applications

SPACE environment chamber. See Testing laboratories

SPACE flight
Because it's there; evaluating the space program. Christian Cent 82:1597 D 29 '65
Chronology of fiscal 1965. Miss & Roc 17:150+ Jl 26 '65
Faster pace in the space race. Life 58:4 Ap 9 '65
Monkeys for the moon; with pictures. Sci Digest 58:66-9 O '65
See also
Computers—Space flight applications
Navigation (space flight)

Anecdotes, facetiae, satire, etc.
Let's go into orbit. J. G. Hubbell. il Read Digest 86:71-5 Je '65

Communication problems
Apollo communications system modified. P. J. Klass. il Aviation W 83:53+ O 11 '65
Apollo Comsats built for mutiple access. B. Miller. il Aviation W 84:78-80 Ja 17 '66
ATS expanding to study large antennas. D. E. Fink. Aviation W 83:91-2 N 8 '65
C-135 being refitted for communications. Aviation W 83:73+ N 15 '65
Electromagnetic research effort aimed at deep-space communications; ERC's Electromagnetic research division. il Miss & Roc 16:51-2+ My 31 '65
Microwave radiation laboratory to cost $5.9 million by FY '68; ERC's Electromagnetic research division. Miss & Roc 16:68 My 31 '65
Receiver requirements for monitoring Gemini. J. C. Wright and W. L. Blair. il Electr World 73:33-5+ Je '65
S-band shakedown slated at Guam. C. D. LaFond. il Miss & Roc 17:34-5 S 20 '65

Cost
AES costs estimated at $3 billion annually. Aviation W 83:29 Ag 30 '65
Cost key to military man-in-space. Miss & Roc 16:12 Mr 8 '65

Food problems
Keeping house in orbit. il Newsweek 66:64 S 20 '65
Menus in orbit; Gemini IV. il Fortune 72:198 Jl '65

International aspects
Arms race shifts to space, and reds have a head start. il U S News 58:40-4 Je 21 '65
As U.S. speeds up the space race. il U S News 58:31-2+ Je 14 '65
Outer space and the advancement of human understanding; remarks, September 15, 1965. G. W. Ball. Dept State Bul 53:552 O 4 '65
Politics of outer space; address, May 27, 1965. H. Cleveland. Dept State Bul 52:1007-13 Je 21 '65
President calls Gemini-5 flight a journey of peace; statement, August 29, 1965. L. B. Johnson. Dept State Bul 53:475 S 20 '65
Space race: who's ahead? Pop Sci 186:70-1 Je '65
See also
United Nations—Committee on the peaceful uses of outer space

Laws and legislation
See Space law

Manned flights
Accelerating Gemini pace clouds future of extra-vehicular plans. W. J. Normyle. Aviation W 83:18 O 18 '65
Acrobats in space. G. Bylinsky. New Repub 152:14-15 Ap 3 '65
Advanced manned research; Mars, Venus trips feasible by 1980. il Miss & Roc 17:75-6+ N 29 '65
Agena failure may deal moon program a blow. il Bsns W p29-30 O 30 '65
Apollo acceleration hinted by NASA. H. Taylor. il Miss & Roc 17:15 N 1 '65

Apollo applications system; FY '67 to bring hardware starts; with editorial comment. il Miss & Roc 17:48-50+. 170 N 29 '65
AES experiments may cost $700 million. Miss & Roc 17:14 Ag 9 '65
AES urged as transition space effort. H. M. David. Miss & Roc 17:18+ Ag 30 '65
Building the technical image. R. Hotz. Aviation W 83:21 S 20 '65
Celestial tag; rendezvous exercise of Gemini 5 flight. il Newsweek 66:20+ Ag 23 '65
Decision on Gemini mission profile for manned flight due this week. G. Alexander. Aviation W 82:25 F 15 '65
Docking last big goal as Gemini reaches halfway point. W. J. Normyle. il Aviation W 83:22-6 D 27 '65
Double Gemini. America 113:562 N 13 '65
Dual Gemini flight may start Dec. 8. J. Mercer. Miss & Roc 17:14-15 N 8 '65
Duration, reliability are keys to Gemini-4; with editorial comment. Aviation W 82:11, 16 My 31 '65
Eight years hindsight. R. Hotz. Aviation W 83:11 N 1 '65
Entire Gemini flight schedule slips; loss of Agena. il Miss & Roc 17:12-13 N 1 '65
Extravehicular exercise due in GT-4. H. Taylor. il Miss & Roc 16:14 My 24 '65
Extra-vehicular plans are revised by NASA. Aviation W 83:73 Ag 23 '65
First manned MOL mission slips to 1968. D. E. Fink. Aviation W 82:26-7 Ap 5 '65
Further AES experiments outlined; Apollo extension systems. H. Taylor. il Miss & Roc 17:14-15 Ag 16 '65
Gemini-4 mission plans near completion. W. J. Normyle. Aviation W 82:28 Ap 19 '65
Gemini 8 may still go in February. H. Taylor and J. Mercer. il Miss & Roc 17:12-14 D 13 '65
Gemini-5 set for busiest U.S. mission. G. Alexander. Aviation W 83:22-3 Jl 26 '65
Gemini 5 set for launch. J. Eberhart. Sci N L 88:102 Ag 14 '65
Gemini-4 to carry two defense experiments. W. J. Normyle. Aviation W 82:6 My 3 '65
Gemini 9 to test re-start of docked Agena. W. J. Normlye. Aviation W 83:32-3 N 15 '65
Gemini photos advance AES experiments; with photographs. D. E. Fink. Aviation W 83:61-2+ Ag 9 '65
Gemini planning, schedules being revised. W. J. Normyle. Aviation W 83:26-7 N 8 '65
Gemini profile allows friction re-entry. W. J. Normyle. Aviation W 82:30 F 22 '65
Gemini rendezvous hinges on countdown. G. Alexander. Aviation W 83:74+ O 18 '65
Gemini set to enter manned flight phase. G. Alexander. Aviation W 82:22+ Mr 22 '65
Gemini 6 flight could last five days. J. Mercer. il Miss & Roc 17:16-17 O 4 '65
Gemini 6 mission plans include four docking contacts with Agena. Aviation W 83:36 S 20 '65
Gemini-6 mission will include rendezvous, docking with Agena. Aviation W 82:30 Ap 12 '65
Gemini spectacular; its meaning to the moon race; setting man-in-space records. il U S News 59:11 D 13 '65
GT-4 crucial to manned flight plans. H. M. David. Miss & Roc 16:28+ My 24 '65
GT-7 crew wants shirtsleeve flight. Miss & Roc 17:17 Jl 19 '65
GT-3 to renew U.S. manned program; Project Gemini. H. Taylor. Miss & Roc 16:16-17 Mr 15 '65
Geminis to fly in tandem. Bsns W p58 N 6 '65
Here comes Gemini. il Time 85:25 F 19 65
House unit urges separate USAF MOL. G. C. Wilson. Aviation W 82:16 Je 7 '65
Inside while outside; astronaut maneuvering unity. il Time 86:46 N 26 '65
Little more poise. Nation 200:351 Ap 5 '65
Manned AES funding may hold to levels of Gemini-Apollo. W. J. Normyle. il Aviation W 83:62-3+ S 6 '65
Manned flight future keyed to program. W. J. Normyle. il Aviation W 83:64-5+ O 11 '65
MOL experiments may require Apollos. D. L. Zylstra. Miss & Roc 16:13 Ap 26 '65
Manned planetary flights studied in detail. D. E. Fink. Aviation W 83:67 S 6 '65
Manned planetary swing-bys proposed. D. E. Fink. Aviation W 83:30 Ag 30 '65
Manned space flight's new phase. R. Hotz. Aviation W 82:21 Ap 12 '65
Manned Venus flyby possible in '75. W. S. Beller. Miss & Roc 17:34 Ag 30 '65
Marshall to do AES integration. H. Taylor. Miss & Roc 17:14-15 S 20 '65

SPACE flight—Manned flights—*Continued*

Mathews outlines GT-5 flight plan. Miss & Roc 17:14 Jl 5 '65

Military space platform may get blastoff signal; manned orbiting laboratory. il Bsns W p66-8+ Jl 17 '65

Multi-manned fifteen-day space flight predicted as next Soviet mission. W. J. Normyle. Aviation W 83:18 N 1 '65

NASA alerts Congress to plans for major post-Apollo missions. Aviation W 82:23 F 22 '65

NASA cranking up for Gemini 6 & 7. J. Mercer. il Miss & Roc 17:14-15 S 6 '65

NASA rejects untethered Gemini excursions. Aviation W 83:36 S 27 '65

NASA seeks proposals for pallet to house experiments on Apollo. E. J. Bulban. Aviation W 83:27-8 S 27 '65

New steps put U.S. far ahead in space; with editorial comment. il Bsns W p30-1, 122 S 4 '65

No EVA in next three Gemini flights. Miss & Roc 17:14 Jl 12 '65

Plans told for manned observatories. W. S. Beller. il Miss & Roc 16:28-30+ My 17 '65

Post-Apollo projects detailed for Congress. W. J. Normyle. il Aviation W 82:54-7+ Mr 22 '65

Power surge, telemetry problem force delay of Gemini-5 launch. Aviation W 83:36 Ag 23 '65

Project Gemini. R. N. Watts, jr. Sky & Tel 29:211 Ap '65

Push on for extravehicular ability. H. Taylor. il Miss & Roc 16:14-15 Ap 5 '65

Race to moon: can U.S. still catch Russia? il U S News 58:46-8 Mr 29 '65

Real story of the space race: U.S. vs. Russia. il U S News 58:33-6 Ap 5 '65; Same abr. with title Are we running the right space race? Read Digest 86:109-10 Je '65

Rendezvous, EVA conditions may extend Gemini flights. J. Mercer. Miss & Roc 18: 16 Ja 17 '66

Shot that failed; Agena explosion halts Gemini 6 mission. L. Wainwright and H. Suydam. il Life 59:111-13 N 5 '65

Slippage possible in GT-5 launching. Miss & Roc 17:18 Ag 9 '65

Space race pace quickens. J. Eberhart. il Sci N L 87:387+ Je 19 '65

Television coverage of the Gemini program. E. G. Sherburne, jr. Science 149:1329 S 17 '65

Three steps to the moon; two U.S. and one Russian achievement in space. il Bsns W p 144-6+ Mr 27 '65

Twenty-year plan; manned missions to Mars and Venus. W. J. Coughlin. Miss & Roc 17: 50 Ag 16 '65

U.S. bids to seize space leadership. il Miss & Roc 17:15-16 Ag 23 '65

Untethered extra-vehicular tests slated. W. J. Normyle. Aviation W 83:29 Ag 9 '65

Walk around the world; plans for future flights. Newsweek 66:90 O 4 '65

Weight of space is on his shoulders; C. Kraft, jr. il Bsns W p64+ Je 12 '65

What happened with Gemini 6. Time 86:92 N 19 '65

When the countdown is one, his pulse is 135; C. Kraft masterminds Gemini 5 mission. G. Bylinsky. il N Y Times Mag p 14-15+ Ag 15 '65

White House push seen in excursion decision. G. Alexander. Aviation W 82:17 My 31 '65

See also

Orbital rendezvous (space flight)

Anecdotes, facetiae, satire, etc.

Funny thing happened. N. Benchley. New Yorker 41:78+ Ja 15 '66

Belíaev-Leonov flight, 1965

Adventure into emptiness; first human satellite. il Time 85:85-6 Mr 26 '65

Effects of Voskhod flights revealed. Miss & Roc 16:31 My 24 '65

In Moscow, a welcome to the space walker. il Life 58:42B Ap 2 '65

Leonov space activity called strenuous. W. C. Wetmore. Aviation W 82:25 Je 21 '65

Man in space. R. N. Watts, jr. il Sky & Tel 29:279-80 My '65

My first steps in space. A. Leonov. il UNESCO Courier 18:4-11 Je '65

Our walk in space; with report by P. Belíaev and A. Leonov. il Life 58:41-4+ My 14 '65

Problems with Voskhod 2 flight cancel rendezovus. il Aviation W 82:22-4 Mr 20 '65

Sequences record Leonov space excursion; with photographs. Aviation W 82:30-1 My 24 '65

Soviet moon statements give Congress pause on proposed NASA budget cuts. H. M. David. il Miss & Roc 16:22+ Mr 29 '65

Soviet somersault. il Sr Schol 86:10 Ap 1 '65

Space-walkers needed. J. Eberhart. Sci N L 87:196 Mr 27 '65

Take a giant step into space. il Newsweek 65:52-4+ Mr 29 '65

Voskhod 2 expands Soviet space lead; with editorial comments. D. Winston; E. H. Kolcum. Aviation W 82:11, 23 Mr 22 '65

Voskhod 2 forced into extra orbit by failures in orientation, control. D. Winston. Aviation W 82:30 Ap 5 '65

Borman-Lovell flight, 1965

Far-out date. il Time 86:29 D 10 '65

Gemini 8 may come in first quarter; special report on GT-7 and 6. H. Taylor and others. il Miss & Roc 18:16-18+ Ja 3 '66

Gemini 8 may still go in February. H. Taylor and J. Mercer. il Miss & Roc 17:12-14 D 13 '65

Gemini 7 crew finds zero-G no problem. E. J. Bulban. il Aviation W 83:53-5+ D 27 '65

Gemini triumphs; what's next? U S News 59:19-21 D 27 '65

Longest journey; flight of Gemini 7. il Newsweek 66:60 D 13 '65

Memorable Gemini triumphs. il Life 60:22-33 Ja 7 '66

Orbit above, scrub below. il Newsweek 66:57 D 20 '65

Perfection aloft, a scrub at the Cape. il Time 86:62 D 17 '65

Shirtsleeve garb eases tasks in Gemini 7. E. J. Bulban. il Aviation W 83:30-1 D 13 '65

Six new experiments on Gemini 7 schedule. E. J. Bulban. il Aviation W 83:33 D 6 '65

We felt content, cozy and safe and never got bored. F. Borman; J. Lovell. il Life 60:68-72 Ja 14 '66

What a quiet week in space really proved; Gemini VII. U S News 59:8 D 20 '65

See also

Orbital rendezvous (space flight)

Cooper-Conrad flight, 1965

Astronauts' personal stories about their Gemini 5 flight. P. Conrad; G. Cooper. il Life 59:84C-84D+ S 24 '65

Caught short. il Newsweek 66:56-7 S 13 '65

Crew of Gemini 5 vehicle provided detailed storm data. E. J. Bulban. il Aviation W 83:68-9+ S 20 '65

Element of chance. il Newsweek 66:72-3 Ag 30 '65

Flight to the finish. il Time 86:49-51 S 3 '65

Fuel-cell flight. il Time 86:46-8 Ag 27 '65

Gemini 5 experiments verify Apollo plans. E. J. Bulban. il Aviation W 83:26-7 S 6 '65

Gemini 5 flight improves outlook for space rendezvous, docking. G. Alexander. Aviation W 83:28-9 S 6 '65

Gemini 5: man's toughest test. il Newsweek 66:46-8 S 6 '65

Gemini-5 scores big as it goes for all eight. il Bsns W p26-7 Ag 28 '65

Gemini 5 sustains accelerated U.S. pace. il Aviation W 83:24-9 Ag 30 '65

Gemini program sets space records. R. N. Watts, jr. il Sky & Tel 30:214-15 O '65

GT-5 proves U.S. rendezvous ability. H. Taylor. il Miss & Roc 17:16-17 Ag 30 '65

Man can adapt to space. il Sci Digest 58: 15-17 N '65

Man is moon-rated. il Time 86:64-6 S 10 '65

NASA cranking up for Gemini 6 & 7. J. Mercer. il Miss & Roc 17:14-15 S 6 '65

Oversight cited in Gemini landing error. Aviation W 83:34 S 27 '65

Splashdown, all the records smashed. il Life 59:30-7 S 10 '65

Twin triumphs in space: Gemini 4 and 5. il Sr Schol 87:26-7 S 23 '65

U.S. and Russia in space; the pace quickens. il U S News 59:25-6 Ag 30 '65

World's experienced observers make report. Sci N L 88:197 S 25 '65

Grissom-Young flight, 1965

American manned spaceflights resume. R. N. Watts, jr. il Sky & Tel 29:279 My '65

Exceptional systems performance cited. il Aviation W 82:74-7+ Ap 5 '65

Flight of the Molly Brown. il Time 85:48-50 Ap 2 '65

Four manned Geminis now seen for 1965; with editorial comment. H. Taylor. il Miss & Roc 16:13-14+, 172 Mr 29 '65

SPACE flight—Physiological aspects—*Cont.*
GT-4 crucial to manned flight plans. H. M. David. Miss & Roc 16:28+ My 24 '65
GT-7 will emphasize calcium study. H. M. David. Miss & Roc 17:32-3 S 20 '65
Getting around by voice control; ways to control an astronaut maneuvering unit. il Time 85:80 Ap 23 '65
How much can you take? weightless maneuvers around scale-model space capsule. R. Vaughan. il Sat Eve Post 238:32-4+ My 22 '65
It's double or nothing in space; McDivitt and White Gemini flight. il Bsns W p 105-6 Je 19 '65
Leonov space activity called strenuous. W. C. Wetmore. Aviation W 82:25 Je 21 '65
Longest journey; Gemini 7/6 mission. il Newsweek 66:60 D 13 '65
Man is moon-rated. il Time 86:64-6 S 10 '65
NASA gets biolab recommendations; AES, MORL and Apollo-X. H. M. David. Miss & Roc 17:36-8 Ag 23 '65
NASA's firefly project. il Life 59:35-6 Jl 9 '65
No EVA in next three Gemini flights. Miss & Roc 17:14 Jl 12 '65
1-A for man in space; medical reports on space flight of Gemini-7. il Bsns W p54+ Ja 8 '66
Orbit above, scrub below; Gemini 7 mission. il Newsweek 66:57 D 20 '65
Outer space and the inner ear. il Bsns W p45-6+ Ja 30 '65
Remote biosensors sought for astronauts. Aviation W 82:36 Ap 19 '65
Space movement studied. il Sci N L 87:262 Ap 24 '65
Spinning for space; Coriolis acceleration platform. il Time 85:78 Mr 12 '65
Thermal manikin to aid MSC. M. Getler. il Miss & Roc 16:49+ My 17 '65
Well-suited for orbit; Gemini 7/6 astronauts. il Newsweek 67:45 Ja 10 '66
See also
Life support systems
Space medicine
Weightlessness

Psychological aspects
Mental effects of long space flights tolerable. Sci N L 88:168 S 11 '65

Social aspects
University and the exploration of space; address, October 11, 1965. H. L. Dryden. Science 150:1129-33 N 26 '65

SPACE flight simulators
AF conducting further space cabin atmosphere studies in sixty-eight day test. H. M. David. il Miss & Roc 17:29-30 O 18 '65
AF pilots to simulate Apollo flight. H. M. David. Miss & Roc 16:84-5 My 31 '65
Douglas tests helium as atmosphere. H. M. David. Miss & Roc 16:38-41 Je 28 '65
How much can you take? weightless maneuvers around scale-model space capsule. R. Vaughan. il Sat Eve Post 238:32-4+ My 22 '65
Huge space simulator designed C. D. LaFond. il Miss & Rec 17:45-6 S 13 '65
MSC plans first manned chamber tests soon. il Miss & Roc 17:14 N 22 '65
Outer space on earth. J. Eberhart. il Sci N L 87:154-5 Mr 6 '65
Pad turnaround completed day early. G. Alexander. il Aviation W 83:32-3 D 13 '65
Padding saves egg after eleven-story drop; protective padding used in zero-gravity tests. Sci N L 88:345 N 27 '65
Re-entry simulator will employ MHD. D. L. Zylstra. il Miss & Roc 16:24+ Ap 5 '65
TV camera to monitor biodynamics. M. Getler. il Miss & Roc 16:32-3 My 3 '65
Test rig simulates LEM landings. il Miss & Roc 16:43 My 17 '65
Vacuum chambers to check Apollo 011. S. Butler. Miss & Roc 17:27 D 6 '65
Zero and lunar gravity simulated by device. il(p 193) Sci N L 87:200 Mr 27 '65
Zero-G slows astronaut performance. H. M. David. il Miss & Roc 17:34+ N 8 '65
See also
Space station simulators

SPACE flight to Jupiter
See also
Space probes

SPACE flight to Mars
Advanced manned research; Mars, Venus trips feasible by 1980. il Miss & Roc 17:75-6+ N 29 '65
Early start on Mars systems urged. H. M. David. Miss & Roc 17:22 Jl 12 '65
Experts at odds over Mars goals. R. Pay. Miss & Roc 16:39+ F 22 '65

Soviets see Mars as manned space goal. W. J. Normyle. Aviation W 82:37 My 10 '65
To Mars or bust. I. Wolfert. il Read Digest 87:63-8 Jl '65
When will we land on Mars? W. Von Braun. il Pop Sci 186:86-8+ Mr '65
See also
Space probes

SPACE flight to Mercury
See also
Space probes

SPACE flight to the moon
Apollo blueprint 1970. J. Eberhart. il Sci N L 87:378-9+ Je 12 '65
AES management plan nears completion; Apollo extension system. D. E. Fink. Aviation W 83:16-17 Jl 19 '65
AES program definition to begin. Miss & Roc 16:17 Je 7 '65
Business on the moon; profits to be made from lunar exploration. il Time 86:89-90 O 29 '65
Conservative approach dictating lunar scientific research plan. W. J. Normyle. Aviation W 82:17 Je 7 '65
Funding boost might cut Apollo cost. Miss & Roc 17:18 O 25 '65
Funding to start for Apollo lunar science. W. J. Normyle. Aviation W 82:18-19 My 31 '65
How U.S. plans to conquer the moon; interview. G. E. Mueller. il U S News 59:33-7 D 27 '65
Kepler's dream; by J. Lear. Review Sat R il 48:41 Ap 3 '65. W. D. Stahlman
Lunar mission retains top U.S. priority. W. J. Normyle. il Aviation W 82:105-8+ Mr 15 '65
Moon landing possible in 1968? what U.S. proved with four days in space. il U S News 58:40-1 Je 21 '65
NASA alerts Congress to plans for major post-Apollo missions. Aviation W 82:23 F 22 '65
New post-1970 missions investigated. W. E. Wilks. il Miss & Roc 17:22-3 N 1 '65
Space race pace quickens. J. Eberhart. il Sci N L 87:387+ Je 19 '65
Special report, Apollo at mid-term; symposium. il Aviation W 83:55-7+ N 15 '65
Special report on Apollo applications. il Aviation W 83:64-5+ O 11 '65
Three giant steps to the moon. il Pop Mech 124:90-4+ O; 116-20+ N; 104-8+ D '65
Two spacemaps to the moon. G. Bylinsky. il N Y Times Mag p6-7+ My 30 '65
See also
Lunar probes
Space flight—Manned flights

Cost
Lunar landing; the big goal. il U S News 59:54 N 1 '65
Moon struck. W. J. Coughlin. Miss & Roc 16:46 Ap 12 '65
NASA's target; keep date with moon. il Bsns W p28-9 F 6 '65

International aspects
Moon race: is it worth while? statements from National youth conference on the atom. il Sr Schol 86:20-1 F 4 '65
Race to moon: can U.S. still catch Russia? il U S News 58:46-8 Mr 29 '65
U.S. and Russia in space; the pace quickens. il U S News 59:25-6 Ag 30 '65

SPACE flight to Venus
Advanced manned research; Mars, Venus trips feasible by 1980. il Miss & Roc 17:75-6+ N 29 '65
Manned Venus flyby possible in '75. W. S. Beller. Miss & Roc 17:34 Ag 30 '65
See also
Space probes

SPACE heaters. See Electric heaters
SPACE industry. See Aerospace industries
SPACE law
International regulation of outer space activities. E. Galloway. il Bul Atomic Sci 21:36-9 F '65
Laws for space debated. Sci N L 88:197 S 25 '65

SPACE medicine
Adaptation of medicine to space conditions seen. Sci N L 88:153 S 4 '65
AA experiment proposals studied. il Miss & Roc 17:23 D 6 '65
Birds aid space study. Sci N L 88:34 Jl 17 '65
Drugs studied to aid astronauts. il Miss & Roc 16:33 Mr 15 '65
Gazenko discusses Soviet space medicine. O. G. Gazenko. il Aviation W 82:40-1+ Je 7 '65

SPACE medicine—*Continued*
Tests show tooth needs. Sci N L 88:86 Ag 7 '65

See also
Space flight—Physiological aspects
Weightlessness

SPACE navigation. See Navigation (space flight)

SPACE perception
Stimulus variables determining space perception in infants. T. G. R. Bower. bibliog il Science 149:88-9 Jl 2 '65

SPACE photography
Apollo crater landing seen possible; Ranger IX photos. W. E. Wilks. Miss & Roc 16:26+ Mr 29 '65
Can you see the moon in 3-D? L. Mallan. il Pop Phot 57:52-5 S '65
Close tracking of Mariner continues. il Miss & Roc 17:14-15 Jl 19 '65
Complex system produced Mars photos. il Aviation W 83:67-8 Jl 26 '65
Crew of Gemini 5 vehicle provided detailed storm data. E. J. Bulban. il Aviation W 83:68-9+ S 20 '65
Drama from the moon; flight of Ranger IX. il Time 85:48 Ap 2 '65
First orbiter to picture moon's far side. Aviation W 83:30 O 4 '65
Gemini V experiments on zodiacal light and gegenschein. E. P. Ney and W. F. Huch. bibliog il Science 150:53-6, 1629 O 1, D 17 '65
Gemini photos advance AES experiments; with photographs. D. E. Fink. Aviation W 83:61-2+ Ag 9 '65
Gemini 7 may take photographs of Gemini 6 re-entry sequence. W. J. Normyle. Aviation W 83:23 N 29 '65
Gemini 6 crewmen to photograph Bahamas in storm damage study. W. J. Normyle. Aviation W 83:37 S 20 '65
GT-3 astronaut photographs Africa, Mexico. il Aviation W 82:68-9 Ap 12 '65
How they shot the space walk. il U S Camera 28:68-9+ S '65
John o' Groats to Timbuctoo; photographs taken by the Nimbus weather satellite. Sci Digest 57:inside back cover Mr '65
Looking sharp; Questar telescope for space photography. il Newsweek 66:88 S 27 '65
Lunar results from Rangers 7 to 9. G. P. Kuiper. bibliog il Sky & Tel 29:293-308 My '65
Mapping the moon; Ranger VIII. il Time 85:58-9 F 26 '65
Mariner 4 completes Mars mission. R. N. Watts, jr. il Sky & Tel 30:136-8 S '65
Mariner 4 photographs of Mars. il Sky & Tel 30:155-61 S '65
Mariner IV photography of Mars: initial results. R. B. Leighton and others. il Science 149:627-30 Ag 6 '65
Mariner 4 photos, data reducing unknowns about Mars. H. D. Watkins. il Aviation W 83:16-20 Jl 26 '65
Mariner observes Mars. il Sci N L 88:51 Jl 24 '65
Mariner photographic field determined. Aviation W 82:25 F 15 '65
Mars never seen. il Newsweek 66:54-6+ Jl 26 '65
NASA studies feasibility of color television from lunar surface. il Aviation W 84:71+ Ja 17 '66
Photos point to Mars landing difficulty. R. Pay. il Miss & Roc 17:13-14+ Jl 26 '65
Pictures of success; Gemini 7. il Time 86:55 D 31 '65
Portrait of a planet; flight of Mariner IV. il Time 86:36-8+ Jl 23 '65
Ranger 8 lunar photos appear to confirm Ranger 7 data. il Aviation W 82:20-3 Mr 1 '65
Ranger 8 lunar reconnaissance. il Sky & Tel 29:205-9 Ap '65
Ranger missions to the moon. H. M. Schurmeier and others. il Sci Am 214:52-67 bibliog(p 134-5) Ja '66
Ranger 9 data promises basic insights on lunar surface. H. D. Watkins. il Aviation W 82:84-9 Ap 5 '65
Ranger IX may shoot Surveyor site; with editorial comment. W. E. Wilks. il Miss & Roc 16:18+, 46 Mr 1 '65
Ranger program exceeds expectations. W. E. Wilks. il Miss & Roc 16:28+ Ap 5 '65
Rangers confirm moon landing areas. W. E. Wilks. Miss & Roc 16:22-3 Ap 12 '65
Ranger's-eye view. il Sci N L 87:149 Mr 6 '65
Research in America; Ranger 8 findings. J. Lear. il Sat R 48:47-8 Ap 3 '65
So vast, so beautiful, so overpowering; photographs of earth taken from Gemini 5. Life 59:30-9 S 24 '65

Surveyor unit permits live TV broadcast from Ranger 9. H. D. Watkins. il Aviation W 82:26-7 Mr 29 '65
Techniques tomorrow; cameras being used in space. B. Sherman. il Mod Phot 29:40+ D '65
Terrain of neighbor Mars; pictures taken 135 million miles away. il Life 59:62A-62C Ag 6 '65
Via Ranger, rills and dimples; Ranger 8. il Newsweek 65:64-5 Mr 1 '65
VAD group processed Mariner photos. R. Pay. il Miss & Roc 17:28+ Ag 9 '65
View from Gemini 7: the lonely moon and the homing-in of Gemini 6. il Life 60:24-31 Ja 7 '66
World's experienced observers make report. Sci N L 88:197 S 25 '65
Zond designed to transmit photos repeatedly from extreme ranges. il Aviation W 83:32 Ag 23 '65

SPACE power systems. See Space vehicles—Power supply

SPACE probes
Acrobats in space. G. Bylinsky. New Repub 152:14-15 Ap 3 '65
Advanced unmanned planetary missions; effort embraces entire solar system. il Miss & Roc 17:103+ N 29 '65
Appointment in Amazonis; Mars-bound Mariner 4. Newsweek 65:54 F 22 '65
Asteroid belt probe. J. Eberhart. Sci N L 87:115 F 20 '65
Atmosphere data to alter Voyager design. I. Stone. il Aviation W 83:66-7+ N 22 '65
Automated lab will search for Mars life. H. D. Watkins. il Aviation W 83:61+ Ag 2 '65
Close tracking of Mariner continues. il Miss & Roc 17:14-15 Jl 19 '65
Comet flyby studied for Mariner backup. W. C. Wetmore. il Aviation W 83:45-6+ N 29 '65
Distant space probe foreseen in ten years. Sci N L 87:338 My 29 '65
Earth to Mars in 229 days; Mariner 4. J. Eberhart. il Sci N L 88:19 Jl 10 '65
First close-up look at Mars. W. S. Griswold. il Pop Sci 187:82-6 Jl '65
Flight of Mariner II changes theories about planet Venus. T. D. Nicholson. il Natur Hist 75:52-4 Ja '66
Giant step. Sci Am 213:42 Ag '65
Gun-launched probes yield varied data. il Aviation W 83:54 O 4 '65
He keeps the space shots zooming; W. H. Pickering, director of JPL. il Bsns W p 118-20 Ag 14 '65
In-flight results from Mariner 4. R. N. Watts, jr. il Sky & Tel 29:359 Je '65
Interest rises in comets, asteroid belt. H. D. Watkins. il Aviation W 82:89-90+ F 22 '65
Is anybody out there? Mars-bound Mariner IV. S. M. Spencer. il Sat Eve Post 238:44-6 Je 19 '65
Is there life on Mars? J. Eberhart. il Sci N L 88:74-5 Jl 31 '65
JPL debating alternate methods for contacting Mariner 4 in 1967. H. D. Watkins. il Aviation W 83:32 Ag 2 '65
JPL to manage Voyager lander. H. Taylor. Miss & Roc 16:14 My 3 '65
Journey to Mars. il Newsweek 66:52 Jl 19 '65
Landing on a comet proposed by scientist. Sci N L 87:136 F 27 '65
Man behind our mission to Mars; Mariner IV. B. Kocivar. il Look 29:36-8+ Jl 13 '65
Mariner data may limit Voyager payload. I. Stone. Aviation W 83:55+ Ag 2 '65
Mariner flight continues. R. N. Watts, jr. Sky & Tel 29:95-6 F '65
Mariner 4 completes Mars mission. R. N. Watts, jr. il Sky & Tel 30:136-8 S '65
Mariner 4 contact ends. R. N. Watts, jr. Sky & Tel 30:285 N '65
Mariner IV may provide us with new knowledge about Mars. T. D. Nicholson. il Natur Hist 74:30-2 My '65
Mariner IV measurements near Mars: initial results; symposium; with editorial comment. bibliog il Science 149:1179, 1226-48 S 10 '65
Mariner 4 nearing final mission hurdles. H. D. Watkins. il Aviation W 83:50+ Jl 5 '65
Mariner 4 nears Mars. Sci N L 88:15 Jl 3 '65
Mariner 4 photos, data reducing unknowns about Mars. H. D. Watkins. il Aviation W 83:16-20 Jl 26 '65
Mariner 4 radio link to be tried in 1967. Aviation W 82:66-7 My 3 '65
Mariner IV's expense account; increase due to extreme tenuity of Martian atmosphere. J. Lear. Sat R 48:35 Ag 7 '65
Mariner nears moment of truth. Miss & Roc 17:11 Jl 12 '65

SPACE probes—*Continued*
Mars atmosphere probe proposed. R. Lindsey. Miss & Roc 16:13 F 8 '65
Mars in focus; Mariner IV probe. il Sr Schol 87:19-20 S 16 '65
Mars never seen. il Newsweek 66:54-6+ Jl 26 '65
Mars observations wanted; Mariner-4 probe. R. N. Watts, jr. il Sky & Tel 29:150 Mr '65
Mars, tantalizing question mark in the sky. W. Sullivan. il N Y Times Mag p 12-13+ Jl 11 '65
Mars vehicle becomes major scientific program. D. E. Fink. il Aviation W 82:116-18+ Mr 15 '65
Martian atmosphere experiment urged for 1969 Voyager vehicle. M. Yaffee. Aviation W 82:61+ F 8 '65
Masterminds of Mars. R. S. Lewis. Bul Atomic Sci 21:39-41 Ap '65
Mercury flyby proposed. J. Eberhart. Sci N L 87:83 F 6 '65
Meteors bombard Mariner. Sci N L 87:278 My 1 '65
Moonfaced Mars. il Newsweek 66:58 Ag 9 '65
Moon-faced Mars; concerning pictures taken by spaceship Mariner IV. il Time 86:58 Ag 6 '65
NASA promises versatile Voyager. H. M. David. Miss & Roc 16:10 Mr 1 '65
NASA rests Mariner, readies other probes. Bsns W p48 O 2 '65
NASA revamping Voyager development. D. E. Fink. Aviation W 83:20 N 1 '65
NASA still considering Mars capsule for 1969. Miss & Roc 16:36 Mr 22 '65
NASA's Mercury history irks air force. E. H. Kolcum. Aviation W 83:16-17 O 18 '65
Needle-nosed Mars probe suggested. W. S. Beller. il Miss & Roc 17:24-5 Jl 12 '65
Notes and comment: news from Mariner 4. New Yorker 41:17 Ag 7 '65
On the Mars! Mariner IV voyage. L. Lessing. il Fortune 72:106-11+ Jl '65
Our encounter with Mars; successful combination of men and machines. L. Wainwright. Life 59:14 Ag 6 '65
Perils and triumphs of Mariner 4. il Bsns W p 102-4 Jl 24 '65
Photos point to Mars landing difficulty. R. Pay. il Miss & Roc 17:13-14+ Jl 26 '65
Pioneer explores space. il Sci N L 89:23 Ja 8 '66
Planetary exploration hopes buoyed by Mariner flight. W. J. Normyle. il Aviation W 83:86-7+ Ag 9 '65
Portrait of a planet: flight of Mariner IV. il Time 86:36-8+ Jl 23 '65
Project Voyager; FY '67 request seen as $150 million. il Miss & Roc 17:61-2+ N 29 '65
Real meaning of the Mars flight. il U S News 59:41 Jl 26 '65
Scientists detail Mars priority argument; Voyager program. W. J. Normyle. Aviation W 82:69+ My 10 '65
Seamans crystallizes Voyager plans. H. Taylor. Miss & Roc 17:17 O 25 '65
Severe Voyager sterilization criteria set. H. D. Watkins. Aviation W 83:58+ D 6 '65
Solar system exploration study planned. I. Stone. Aviation W 83:87-9+ Jl 12 '65
Space life detection seen enhanced. H. M. David. Miss & Roc 17:41-2+ O 4 '65
Space life detector simulates firefly light. Sci N L 87:201 Mr 27 '65
They try harder; with Russian-U.S. deepspace box score. il Newsweek 66:62 N 29 '65
This is Mars; first close-up view. il Life 59:30-1 Jl 23 '65
To Mars or bust. I. Wolfert. il Read Digest 87:63-8 Jl '65
U.S. starts catching up in space. Bsns W p 164 Ap 3 '65
Unmanned launch studied. Sci N L 88:82 Ag 7 '65
Voyager capsule RFP's due in summer. H. Taylor. Miss & Roc 16:15 Mr 22 '65
Voyager experiment decisions due in July. D. E. Fink. Aviation W 83:71 N 22 '65
Voyager procurement plans uncertain. H. Taylor. Miss & Roc 17:13 Jl 5 '65
Voyager program facing reorganization. H. Taylor. Miss & Roc 17:14 O 4 '65
Voyager to avoid Surveyor errors. H. M. David. Miss & Roc 16:15 Mr 15 '65
Webb says Mariner winning Mars race; Zond a month behind. H. Taylor. Miss & Roc 16: 15 F 15 '65
What we'll see on Mars. B. H. Frisch. il Sci Digest 58:44-53 Jl '65
See also
Lunar probes

SPACE probes, Russian
Russians may skip Mars probe in 1966. D. Winston. Aviation W 83:31-2 Ag 30 '65
Russians report Mars probe failure; Zond II. H. Taylor. il Miss & Roc 16:12-13 My 10 '65
Soviet space problems. R. N. Watts, jr. il Sky & Tel 30:19 Jl '65
They try harder; with Russian-U.S. deepspace box score. il Newsweek 66:62 N 29 '65
Webb says Mariner winning Mars race; Zond a month behind. H. Taylor. Miss & Roc 16:15 F 15 '65
See also
Lunar probes, Russian

SPACE rescue work
Need seen for global space rescue code. W. J. Normyle. il Aviation W 83:69-71 O 18 '65

SPACE research
Chronology of fiscal 1965. Miss & Roc 17: 150+ Jl 26 '65
Eight years hindsight. R. Hotz. Aviation W 83:11 N 1 '65
Exploration explosion. il Sci Digest 58:9-12 Ag '65
1965 science review. il Sci N L 88:397-8 D 18 '65
Orbiting potato. J. Lear. il Sat R 48:47-50 S 4 '65; Discussion. 48:92 D 4 '65
Space notes. R. N. Watts, jr. Sky & Tel 30: 285 N '65
See also
International council of scientific unions—Committee on space research

International aspects
Across the sea. W. J. Coughlin. Miss & Roc 18:46 Ja 3 '66
After spending 30 billions; how U.S. stands in space. il U S News 59:41-3 S 6 '65
France in space: collaboration with both U.S. and U.S.S.R? V. K. McElheny. il Science 150:1700-1 D 24 '65
Gains, pitfalls seen in cooperation. Aviation W 82:17 My 3 '65
Greater joint space effort endorsed; report to White House conference on international cooperation; with editorial comment. W. S. Beller. Miss & Roc 17:15, 46 D 6 '65
Ike on the missile gap: there wasn't any; excerpts from White House years: waging peace, 1956-61. D. D. Eisenhower. il U S News 59:20 O 4 '65
International space surge; excerpts from congressional testimony. H. L. Dryden. Aviation W 82:17 F 22 '65
Japan's rockets: a future nuclear threat? il U S News 59:12 S 6 '65
Non-U.S. experiments are invited for Gemini, Apollo, later flights. E. J. Bulban. Aviation W 82:25 My 3 '65
One big race U.S. is winning: new products. il U S News 59:84-7 S 27 '65
So little in it. Commonweal 82:101 Ap 16 '65
Space and the International cooperation year: a national challenge. A. W. Frutkin. Dept State Bul 53:384-92 S 6 '65
See also
United Nations—Committee on the peaceful uses of outer space

Argentina
Argentina paces Latin space growth. W. S. Beller. il Miss & Roc 16:35+ Je 14 '65

Europe, Western
ELDO, ESRO programs meet slippages. W. Wetmore. il Aviation W 82:127+ Mr 15 '65
European space proposal. W. J. Coughlin. Miss & Roc 17:46 Jl 12 '65
Europeans frustrated in space hopes. W. S. Beller. il Miss & Roc 18:34-5 Ja 3 '66
Europeans reviewing space goals through early 1970s. Aviation W 82:198-201 Je 14 '65
Eurospace clings to transporter idea. Miss & Roc 16:18 My 17 '65
Eurospace debates its future; with editorial comment. il Miss & Roc 16:12-13, 46 My 3 '65
Eurospace proposes expanded program; with editorial comment. E. H. Kolcum. Aviation W 82:11, 16-17 My 3 '65
Eurospace views space program needs. E. Loewe; E. P. Wheaton. il Aviation W 82: 74-5+ My 10 '65

France
Astronauts recoup space prestige: Paris show. M. Getler. il Miss & Roc 16:16-17 Je 28 '65

SPACE probes—France—*Continued*

France in space: collaboration with both U.S. and U.S.S.R? V. K. McElheny. il Science 150:1700-1 D 24 '65

French retain ambitions in space despite tight budget. il Aviation W 82:206-9 Je 14 '65

How not to sell abroad. W. J. Coughlin. Miss & Roc 16:50 Je 28 '65

NASA may aid in French program. W. S. Beller. il Miss & Roc 17:22-3 Jl 5 '65

Germany (Federal Republic)

$460-million German space push urged. W. C. Wetmore. il Aviation W 83:50-1+ S 6 '65

German industry hungry for funding. M. Getler. il Miss & Roc 17:29-30+ Jl 19 '65

Increase sought in German space effort. il Aviation W 82:211-12+ Je 14 '65

Great Britain

U.K. industry awaits review findings; with editorial comment. Miss & Roc 17:15, 46 Jl 5 '65

India

India's nascent space program. V. K. McElheny. il Science 149:1487-9 S 24 '65

Japan

Japan moves toward launch of home-built satellite in '68. il Miss & Roc 17:29-30 D 20 '65

Russia

Assessment. W. J. Coughlin. Miss & Roc 17:168 Jl 26 '65

Hardly a time for complacency. W. J. Coughlin. Miss & Roc 17:62 O 18 '65

Men, pictures told space story. J. Eberhart. Sci N L 88:357 D 4 '65

Recent Russian activities. R. N. Watts, jr. Sky & Tel 30:285 N '65

Russia increases military space tempo. E. H. Kolcum. Aviation W 82:113+ Mr 15 '65

Russians report Mars probe failure. H. Taylor. il Miss & Roc 16:12-13 My 10 '65

Soviet sour grapes. R. Hotz. Aviation W 83: 21 S 13 '65

Soviets may attempt to eclipse Gemini-5. W. J. Normyle. Aviation W 83:24 Jl 26 '65

Soviets seen exploiting huge new vehicle. W. J. Normyle. Aviation W 83:32 O 11 '65

Withhold information on USSR space progress. Sci N L 88:72 Jl 31 '65

United States

After the moon landing: Senate hearings open way for debate. D. S. Greenberg. Science 150:1003-5 N 19 '65

After the moon, what? Sci N L 88:18 Jl 10 '65

AES management plan nears completion; Apollo extension system. D. E. Fink. Aviation W 83:16-17 Jl 19 '65

AES program definition to begin. Miss & Roc 16:17 Je 7 '65

Are the tame cats in charge? omens of Orwell. P. Abelson. Sat R 49:100-3 Ja 1 '66

Assessment. W. J. Coughlin. Miss & Roc 17: 168 Jl 26 '65

Avionics in space; excerpts from address, 1965. E. C. Welsh. Aviation W 83:21 N 8 '65

Case for man in space. S. F. Singer. il Reporter 32:25-8 Je 17 '65

Dandridge Cole: G.E.'s way-out man. B. H. Frisch. il Sci Digest 58:9-15 Jl '65

Death of a project; Project Orion. F. J. Dyson. Science 149:141-4 Jl 9 '65; Discussion. 149:912+ Ag 27 '65

Europeans get eyeful of U.S. space work; delegates to Eurospace conference amazed by U.S. plants. il Bsns W p 134+ My 15 '65

Experiments in space. J. H. Wujek, jr. il Electr World 74:30-1+ Jl '65

Fifth annual NASA issue; ed. by H. Taylor. il Miss & Roc 17:35+ N 29 '65

Guidance, control studies under way; ERC's Guidance and control div. il Miss & Roc 16: 32-5 My 31 '65

Hardly a time for complacency. W. J. Coughlin. Miss & Roc 17:62 O 18 '65

Humphrey vows dynamic space support; excerpts from address, March 19, 1965. H. H. Humphrey. Aviation W 82:25 Mr 29 '65

Immensity of space. J. Eberhart. il Sci N L 88:119+ Ag 21 '65

Letter from the editor. W. J. Coughlin. Miss & Roc 17:48 D 20 '65

Magic trees; effect of space research on American economy. W. J. Coughlin Miss & Roc 17:46 O 11 '65

Men, pictures told space story. J. Eberhart. Sci N L 88:357 D 4 '65

Mission-oriented R&D is called threat to U.S. civilian economy. R. G. O'Lone. Aviation W 83:99+ S 6 '65

NASA ponders AES integration team. H. Taylor. Miss & Roc 16:14 Je 21 '65

NASA promises versatile Voyager. H. M. David. Miss & Roc 16:10 Mr 1 '65

NASA to decide key AES issues in June; Apollo extension systems. W. J. Normyle. Aviation W 82:16-17 My 24 '65

Report from Cape Kennedy. J. Harabin. il Seventeen 25:88-9+ Ja '66

Row over rockets. Sci Digest 57:44-5 Ap '65

Soviet article raps DOD space role; summary of report. M. Golyshev. Miss & Roc 17:17 N 22 '65

Soviet sour grapes. R. Hotz. Aviation W 83: 21 S 13 '65

Soviet space activities. R. N. Watts, jr. Sky & Tel 31:27 Ja '66

Space (cont) il Life 59:35-6 Jl 9 '65

Space: a White House endorsement and a NASA view on the attitudes of scientists toward the program. D. S. Greenberg. Science 147:1269-70 Mr 12 '65

Space and society; excerpts from remarks. R. C. Seamans, jr. Aviation W 83:17 N 22 '65

Space goals for next twenty years should be set. Sci N L 89:25 Ja 8 '66

Space plans gain Congress' confidence. G. C. Wilson. Aviation W 82:28-9 Ap 5 '65

Successful summer in space. R. Hotz. Aviation W 83:21 Ag 16 '65

Sustain space exploration effort but keep guard up, U.S. urged R. G. O'Lone. Aviation W 83:33-4 Ag 9 '65

This month's feature: Congress considers the U.S. space program. Cong Digest 44:35-64 F '65

Three steps forward for U.S. spacemen. il U S News 58:6 Mr 1 '65

Top-level space support. W. J. Coughlin. Miss & Roc 16:46 Mr 8 '65

Triple space launch. R. Hotz. Aviation W 82: 13 Mr 29 '65

Twenty-year plan. W. J. Coughlin. Miss & Roc 17:50 Ag 16 '65

U.S. space teamwork comes of age. J. E. Webb. Miss & Roc 17:37 N 29 '65

University and the exploration of space; address, October 11, 1965. H. L. Dryden. Science 150:1129-33 N 26 '65

Vigor of space; excerpts from address. E. C. Welsh. Aviation W 83:21 O 11 '65

Where the space race is paying off for the U.S; chart. il U S News 58:46-7 Mr 29 '65; Same. Read Digest 86:108 Je '65

See also

United States—National aeronautics and space administration

SPACE sextants. See Sextants

SPACE-simulation chambers. See Testing laboratories

SPACE station simulators

Analog, digital computer combination will aid in MOL mission simulation. Miss & Roc 16: 34-5 Mr 15 '65

Helium looks feasible for use in MOL cabin. il Miss & Roc 17:38-9 D 20 '65

Zero-G slows astronaut performance. H. M. David. il Miss & Roc 17:34+ N 8 '65

SPACE stations

Across the sea; questions regarding a lunar international laboratory. W. J. Coughlin. Miss & Roc 18:46 Ja 3 '66

Aerospace corp. given MOL task. H. Taylor. Miss & Roc 17:15-16 O 18 '65

Aerospace to get key MOL task despite congressional criticism. K. Johnsen. Aviation W 83:33 Ag 30 '65

Air force given manned space role; MOL program. W. J. Normyle. Aviation W 83: 23 Ag 30 '65

Air force moves quickly to exploit MOL; with editorial comment. D. E. Fink. Aviation W 83:17, 22-3 S 6 '65

AF nears test in inflatable station. il Miss & Roc 16:16 Ap 5 '65

Assembly-in-orbit plan promising. W. E. Wilks. il Miss & Roc 16:38-40 Je 21 '65

Base where MOL will be born; air force's Vandenberg. il Bsns W p70-2+ N 13 '65

Behind the budget; military development of the manned orbiting laboratory. W. J. Coughlin. Miss & Roc 16:46 F 1 '65

Bioastronautics for survival; manned orbiting laboratory. il Time 86:58-9 Ag 6 '65

Case for man in space. S. F. Singer. il Reporter 32:25-8 Je 17 '65

CIA control bid slowed decision on MOL. D. E. Fink. il Aviation W 83:26-7 S 20 '65

Changes raise MORL concept reliability. W. J. Normyle. il Aviation W 84:65+ Ja 17 '66

SPACE stations—*Continued*
Committee asks LBJ for MOL ruling. L. J. Curran. Miss & Roc 16:16 Ap 12 '65
Decision made to launch manned laboratory; MOL. Sci N L 88:151 S 4 '65
Defense dept. expands capability of MOL. D. E. Fink. Aviation W 82:16-17 F 15 '65
Detection of ICBMs key in MOL approval. Aviation W 83:26-7 S 27 '65
Douglas gets a jump with MOL; manned space laboratory. il Bsns W p50-2 D 25 '65
Douglas reopens MOL subcontracting. Miss & Roc 17:18 S 27 '65
Douglas wins epochal MOL contract. D. L. Zylstra. il Miss & Roc 17:14-15 Ag 30 '65
Finally. W. J. Coughlin. Miss & Roc 17:46 Ag 30 '65
First manned MOL mission slips to 1968. D. E. Fink. Aviation W 82:26-7 Ap 5 '65
For $1.5 billion, a new air force eye in the sky; MOL. il Newsweek 66:46-7 S 6 '65
From Washington: the air force in space and peacekeeping assessments. H. Margolis. Bul Atomic Sci 21:34-7 O '65
House unit urges separate USAF MOL. G. C. Wilson. Aviation W 82:16 Je 7 '65
Long-delayed MOL. W. J. Coughlin. Miss & Roc 17:62 Jl 19 '65
McNamara says MOL awards are near. D. L. Zylstra. Miss & Roc 16:13-15 Mr 1 '65
Major MOL subsystem contracts near. Miss & Roc 17:16 N 22 '65
Manned AES funding may hold to levels of Gemini-Apollo. W. J. Normyle. il Aviation W 83:62-3+ S 6 '65
Manned orbiting lab gets push from LBJ. il Bsns W p27 Ag 28 '65
MOL, AES definition contractors named. D. E. Fink. Aviation W 82:24-5 Mr 8 '65
Manned orbiting laboratory: center of U.S. space controversy. il U S News 58:43 Je 21 '65
MOL experiments may require Apollos. D. L. Zylstra. Miss & Roc 16:13 Ap 26 '65
MOL proposals include new concepts. Miss & Roc 16:15 My 3 '65
Manned space stations; Administration funding nod awaited. il Miss & Roc 17: 68-70+ N 29 '65
Military moves into space; manned orbital laboratories. R. D. Senter. New Repub 153: 11-13 S 11 '65
Military space platform may get blastoff signal; manned orbiting laboratory. il Bsns W p66-8+ Jl 17 '65
NASA gets biolab recommendations; AES, MORL and Apollo-X. H. M. David. Miss & Roc 17:36-8 Ag 23 '65
NASA initiates study of orbital station. D. E. Fink. il Aviation W 82:52-3 F 1 '65
Orbiting lab; air force MOL. il Time 86:51 S 3 '65
Orbiting labs may be Soviet lunar key. W. C. Wetmore. Aviation W 83:33-4 S 27 '65
Report on Washington; MOL project. Atlan 216:13 D '65
Schriever given direction of MOL. Miss & Roc 17:16 S 6 '65
Senate committee bolsters MOL. Miss & Roc 17:17 Ag 23 '65
Space: MOL to give military first chance at manned flight; Soviet reaction unpredictable. L. J. Carter. Science 149:1357-9 S 17 '65
Space station gets go-ahead; air force MOL. W. Cloud. il Pop Sci 186:21+ Mr '65
Spaceport for the military; close-up of a mammoth base; Vandenberg air force base manned orbiting laboratory program. il U S News 59:42-4+ D 13 '65
Titan 3 test schedule emphasizes MOL. H. D. Watkins. Aviation W 82:53-5 Mr 1 '65
Top-level MOL policy committee formed. il Aviation W 83:25 O 4 '65
Truth and the MOL. W. J. Coughlin. Miss & Roc 17:46 N 22 '65
USAF continues MOL definition effort. il Aviation W 82:85+ Mr 15 '65
USAF imposes rigid MOL data ban. Aviation W 82:33 Ap 12 '65
USAF to launch two used NASA Geminis; orbital flights to qualify MOL systems. E. H. Kolcum. Aviation W 82:26 Ap 19 '65
USAF unit meets on MOL bids; recommendations due this week. D. E. Fink. Aviation W 82:24-5 F 22 '65
Vandenberg begins expanding for MOL. R. Lindsey. il Miss & Roc 18:35-6 Ja 10 '66
What ever happened to the manned space stations? W. Von Braun. il Pop Sci 186: 88-9+ F '65
What goes on in the sky? manned orbiting laboratory. N. Cousins. Sat R 48:32 S 11 '65

Why the space race is a defense problem; decision to build manned orbiting laboratories. il U S News 59:36-8 S 13 '65
SPACE suits. See Astronauts—Clothing
SPACE technology
Breakthrough foreseen in early 70s. Miss & Roc 16:32 F 15 '65
Building the technical image. R. Hotz. Aviation W 83:21 S 20 '65
Gains, pitfalls seen in cooperation. Aviation W 82:17 My 3 '65
Magic trees; effect of space research on American economy. W. J. Coughlin. Miss & Roc 17:46 O 11 '65
Space arms control. A. Frye. Bul Atomic Sci 21:30-3 Ap '65
Space science stresses optics, antennas. K. Johnsen. Aviation W 82:34 Ap 5 '65
SPACE telemetry
Adaptive telemetry gains reported. Miss & Roc 17:18 S 6 '65
ETR antenna gets wide-range ability. R. Pay. il Miss & Roc 16:26-7 My 24 '65
Ground-station automation imminent. il Miss & Roc 17:32-3 Ag 30 '65
1,500-mile-long data corridor nearly ready. C. D. LaFond. il Miss & Roc 17:34-6 N 1 '65
PCM system to get Apollo test; pulse code modulation telemetry system. C. D. La-Fond. il Miss & Roc 17:32-3 D 6 '65
Telemetry: our eyes and ears in space. J. W. Billups. il Pop Electr 23:53-7+ O '65
SPACE tools. See Space vehicles—Maintenance and repair
SPACE vehicle batteries. See Storage batteries
SPACE vehicle models
Space astronomy at the World's fair. P. A. Leavens. il Sky & Tel 30:68-70 Ag '65
SPACE vehicles
Apollo weight problems discounted. Miss & Roc 16:14 Mr 8 '65
Coming, ferries to space. W. Von Braun. il Pop Sci 187:68-9+ S '65
Fund bite halts Voyager bus work; lander capsule design to continue. D. E. Fink. Aviation W 84:24 Ja 3 '66
Gemini 5 set for launch. J. Eberhart. Sci N L 88:102 Ag 14 '65
Gemini set to enter manned flight phase. G. Alexander. Aviation W 82:22+ Mr 22 '65
Guidance, control studies under way; ERC's Guidance and control div. il Miss & Roc 16:32-5 My 31 '65
Mars vehicle becomes major scientific program. D. E. Fink. il Aviation W 82:116-18+ Mr 15 '65
Men, pictures told space story; with 1965 space calendar. J. Eberhart. Sci N L 88: 357-8 D 4 '65
Missiles and rockets astrolog; current status of U.S. missile and space programs. See occasional issues of Missiles and rockets
Missiles and rockets world missile/space encyclopedia 1965. il Miss & Roc 17:37-44+ Jl 26 '65
Planners alter lunar orbiter trajectory. D. E. Fink. il Aviation W 83:49+ O 4 '65
Pre-launch photos show Voskhod 2 spacecraft configuration. il Aviation W 82:32-3 Ap 19 '65
Russia displays Vostok with spherical cabin. il Aviation W 82:28-9 My 10 '65
Shifting orbits; Titan III A and Mariner IV. il Time 85:70 F 19 '65
Soviets seen exploiting huge new vehicle. W. J. Normyle. Aviation W 83:32 O 11 '65
Space vehicle log (cont) Aviation W 82:125 Mr 15 '65
U.S. spacecraft: International spacecraft; specifications (cont) Aviation W 82:189-90 Mr 15 '65
Voyager capsule RFP's due in summer. H. Taylor. Miss & Roc 16:15 Mr 22 '65
Voyager RFP's due this month. Miss & Roc 17:16 S 20 '65
See also
Lunar vehicles
Navigation (space flight)

Atmospheric entry

Air force, NASA finishing plans for joint manned lifting body test. W. J. Normyle. Aviation W 82:19 Je 28 '65
AF wants new lifting-body program; funding sought for PILOT project. Miss & Roc 17:21 Ag 16 '65
Athena impact accuracies point to possibility of longer unguided flights. R. Pay. il Miss & Roc 17:26-7 Jl 12 '65
Ejection times for heat shield adjusted for last Fire flight. Aviation W 82:24 My 3 '65
Gemini may use new re-entry mode. Miss & Roc 16:11 F 8 '65

SPACE vehicles—Atmospheric entry—*Cont.*
Gemini profile allows friction re-entry. W. J. Normyle. Aviation W 82:30 F 22 '65
Lifting-body studies seek problem areas. I. Stone. il Aviation W 82:65-7 My 31 '65
Lost ASSET bore important data. Miss & Roc 16:12 Mr 1 '65
On-board velocity meter tested. il Miss & Roc 16:76 My 31 '65
Re-entry considerations prompt Apollo changes. W. E. Wilks. Miss & Roc 17:38-9 O 11 '65
Second Project Fire launch set. il Miss & Roc 16:15 Ap 26 '65
Space transporter designed by Junkers; based on a manned delta wing booster. il Aviation W 82:219+ Je 14 '65
Spinning space net designed for reentry; Rotornet. Sci N L 88:51 Jl 24 '65
Start program manned flights eliminated. W. J. Normyle. il Aviation W 82:20-1 Ap 5 '65
USAF wants larger lifting body than M2/F2 for manned START; spacecraft technology and advanced re-entry tests. I. Stone. il Aviation W 83:34+ Ag 16 '65

Atomic power plants

AEC doubles space radioisotope efforts. M. L. Yaffee. il Aviation W 84:75+ Ja 10 '66
Atoms and ions in orbit; nuclear generator and ion engine in space. il Bsns W p 105-6 Ap 10 '65
EOS advances ion engine art; primary test involves operation of the SNAP 10A. J. F. Judge. il Miss & Roc 16:22-3 Ap 5 '65
Finger cites thermionic power gains. W. S. Beller. Miss & Roc 17:12 N 22 '65
Ion engine interferes with Snap 10A data. Aviation W 82:30 Ap 12 '65
Ninety-day orbital test of Snap 10A planned. I. Stone. il Aviation W 82:90-3 Ap 5 '65
Nuclear power; space system control tightened. il Miss & Roc 17:144-6+ N 29 '65
Orbiting reactor works; SNAP-10A. Sci N L 87:246 Ap 17 '65
Reactor in orbit; SNAP-10A. il Time 85:64-5 Ap 16 '65
Snap 8 gains support for more funding. K. Johnsen. Aviation W 82:20-1 F 15 '65
SNAP 8 support gathers momentum. H. M. David. il Miss & Roc 16:17 F 15 '65
Snap 50 cutback to close Canel. AEC moves project to California. W. J. Normyle. Aviation W 83:17 Jl 5 '65
SNAP systems get new emphasis. H. Taylor. Miss & Roc 16:16-17 Ap 19 '65
SNAP 10A test exceeds expectations. il Miss & Roc 16:13 Ap 12 '65
Thermionic space power considered. W. S. Beller. il Miss & Roc 17:24-5 O 18 '65

Auxiliary power

See Space vehicles—Power supply

Control systems

Abort backup for LEM near production. B. Miller. il Aviation W 84:106-7+ Ja 10 '66
Attitude control testing advanced by sophisticated magnetic facility. W. S. Beller. il Miss & Roc 17:22-3 S 13 '65
Control, information systems lab to cost $3.5 million, employ 180; section of ERC's Guidance and control division. Miss & Roc 16:74-5 My 31 '65
Exceptional systems performance cited; Gemini-3 spacecraft. il Aviation W 82:74-7+ Ap 5 '65
Gemini 5 utilized new attitude system. Aviation W 83:73 S 20 '65
GT-3 proves extended flights feasible. G. Alexander. il Aviation W 82:68-73 Ap 5 '65
Greater sensor utilization sought on Surveyor lander test vehicles. D. E. Fink. Aviation W 84:69-71 Ja 17 '66
Isotope microthruster proposed by Philco; spacecraft attitude control unit. il Aviation W 83:35-6 Jl 12 '65
Maneuvering unit may incorporate RMU; remote maneuvering unit. Aviation W 82:24 My 3 '65
Mid-course change puts Ranger on target. Aviation W 82:34 F 22 '65
NAA system would avoid booster bending. R. Pay. Miss & Roc 16:38-9 Ap 5 '65
New roles seen for human eyes in space. R. G. O'Lone. Aviation W 83:51+ Ag 30 '65
Oversight cited in Gemini landing error. Aviation W 83:34 S 27 '65
Space guidance work to be isolated; ERC space guidance laboratory. Miss & Roc 16:57 My 31 '65

Spacecraft could fly itself. Sci N L 87:83 F 6 '65
Star-sighting difficulties could alter Apollo guidance system. J. Mercer. Miss & Roc 18:17-18 Ja 10 '66
Vital Agena unit replaced for GTA-6. R. Pay. il Miss & Roc 17:24+ O 25 '65
See also
Inertial guidance systems

Cooling

See also
Space vehicles—Thermal control

Crews

See Astronauts

Design

Atmosphere data to alter Voyager design. I. Stone. il Aviation W 83:66-7+ N 22 '65
Design efforts for ELDO B accelerated. Aviation W 82:227 Je 14 '65
First Apollo flight-type vehicle readied for shipment. il Aviation W 83:30-1 Ag 23 '65
Gemini 8 cockpit near final form; White's proposals cause changes. Aviation W 83:95 N 8 '65
Inside our first two-man spacecraft; Gemini. W. S. Griswold. il Pop Sci 186:142-5+ F '56
Lunar orbiter nears final configuration. H. D. Watkins. il Aviation W 82:42-3+ F 1 '65
NASA emphasizes Apollo simplification. E. H. Kolcum. Aviation W 83:55-6 N 15 '65
Photos of Vostok display reveal new details of spacecraft. il Aviation W 82:76-8 My 24 '65
Spacecraft description and encounter sequence. H. R. Anderson. il Science 149:1226-8 S 10 '65
Voyager experiment decisions due in July. D. E. Fink. Aviation W 83:71 N 22 '65
Voyager hardware to get gradual buildup. D. E. Fink. Aviation W 82:45+ F 15 '65

Electric propulsion systems

See Space vehicles—Propulsion systems

Electronic equipment

Anatomy of the Gemini spacecraft. il Life 59:60-7 S 3 '65
Apollo data link may use microcircuits. B. Miller. il Aviation W 82:95-7 My 10 '65
Avionics in space; excerpts from address, 1965. E. C. Welsh. Aviation W 83:21 N 8 '65
Component technology has Core role; ERC's Component technology div. il Miss & Roc 16:37-9 My 31 '65
New navigation system developed for Apollo. Sci N L 88:18 Jl 10 '65
REA to utilize 750-1,000-ft. antennas; radio astronomy explorer satellite. D. E. Fink. il Aviation W 83:106-7+ S 27 '65
Relative radiation vulnerability analyzed in study of components. Aviation W 83:89 N 22 '65
Von Braun urges reusable transport. C. D. LaFond. Miss & Roc 17:16 N 8 '65
See also
Radar in space flight

Equipment

Assembly-in-orbit plan promising. W. E. Wilks. il Miss & Roc 16:38-40 Je 21 '65
Instrumentation and data processing; Instrumentation and data processing division of ERC. il Miss & Roc 16:45-7 My 31 '65
Instruments for the new celestial navigation. S. Moskowitz. il Sky & Tel 30:348-51 D '65
NASA emphasizes Apollo simplification. E. H. Kolcum. Aviation W 83:55-6 N 15 '65
NASA seeks proposals for pallet to house experiments on Apollo. E. J. Bulban. Aviation W 83:27-8 S 27 '65
Prototype telescope for OAO-C tested. R. D. Hibben. il Aviation W 82:71+ Mr 22 '65
Radiation, inc. equipping Nimbus-B satellite; Interrogation-recording-location system. M. Getler. Miss & Roc 16:35 Mr 8 '65
Rocket-riding cameras show how boosters behave. W. Von Braun. il Pop Sci 187:106-7+ D '65
Rocket troubleshooters spot trouble in advance. Sci N L 87:137 F 27 '65
VAD group processed Mariner photos. R. Pay. il Miss & Roc 17:28+ Ag 9 '65
See also
Life support systems
Television apparatus on space vehicles

Heat control

See Space vehicles—Thermal control

SPACE vehicles—*Continued*

Instrument boards
Exceptional systems performance cited; Gemini-3 spacecraft. il Aviation W 82:74-7+ Ap 5 '65
Instrumentation and data processing; Instrumentation and data processing division of ERC. il Miss & Roc 16:45-7 My 31 '65

Landing systems
Soft landing on hard ground. il Time 86:52 Ag 13 '65

Mars
Langley group assesses three Mars landers; Project Voyager Mars lander. Aviation W 83:28-9 S 20 '65
Martian atmosphere experiment urged for 1969 Voyager vehicle. M. Yaffee. Aviation W 82:61+ F 8 '65

Moon
Abort backup for LEM near production. B. Miller. il Aviation W 84:106-7+ Ja 10 '66
Apollo blueprint 1970. J. Eberhart. il Sci N L 87:378-9+ Je 12 '65
Apollo's scout runs into snags; unmanned Surveyor. il Bsns W p49-50+ D 18 '65
Astronauts could land LEM by earthshine. Miss & Roc 17:31 N 22 '65
Batteries will sub for LEM fuel cells. Miss & Roc 16:14 Mr 8 '65
Conservative approach dictating lunar scientific research plan. W. J. Normyle. Aviation W 82:17 Je 7 '65
Finding out how to land on the moon. il Pop Sci 187:100-1 N '65
First spacecraft LEM adapter delivered. il Aviation W 83:66-8 N 15 '65
Funding boost might cut Apollo cost. Miss & Roc 17:18 O 25 '65
Greater sensor utilization sought on Surveyor lander test vehicles. D. E. Fink. Aviation W 84:69-71 Ja 17 '66
How U.S. plans to conquer the moon; use of LEM, interview. G. E. Mueller. il U S News 59:33-7 D 27 '65
Lunar blindness; porous layer of moon's crust. Time 86:91 N 19 '65
Lunar debate still rages despite Ranger; designs of LEM and Surveyor landing gear may be redesigned. Aviation W 82:34 Ap 26 '65
LEM radar value shown by Gemini flight. W. J. Normyle. il Aviation W 84:91+ Ja 10 '66
LEM system readied for checkout. H. M. David. il Miss & Roc 16:22-3 My 3 '65
Lunar exploration systems advance. H. Taylor. Miss & Roc 17:10 Jl 12 '65
Lunar surface structure probes studied. I. Stone. il Aviation W 82:46-8 F 8 '65
Manned AES funding may hold to levels of Gemini-Apollo. W. J. Normyle. il Aviation W 83:62-3+ S 6 '65
Moon trip doomed to disaster? scientist's size-up. T. E. W. Schumann. il U S News 59:55-8 N 1 '65
NASA gets biolab recommendations; AES, MORL and Apollo-X. H. M. David. Miss & Roc 17:36-8 Ag 23 '65
Primary Apollo applications goals chosen. il Aviation W 83:73+ O 11 '65
Ranger's answer. il Newsweek 65:56-7 Mr 8 '65
Soft landing on the moon. W. S. Griswold. il Pop Sci 187:102-5+ O '65
Surface of the moon; research of Grumman scientists. il Fortune 72:191-2 Jl '65
Test rig simulates LEM landings. il Miss & Roc 16:43 My 17 '65
Tests set to define landing hazard. W. E. Wilks. il Miss & Roc 17:36-7 D 20 '65
Three giant steps to the moon. il Pop Mech 124:90-4+ O; 116-20+ N; 104-8+ D '65
To the moon, softly. W. J. Coughlin. Miss & Roc 17:46 N 1 '65

Launching
Fast analysis overruled Gemini 6 ejection. G. Alexander. Aviation W 83:19-20 D 20 '65
Immediate Gemini pad turnaround set. G. Alexander. Aviation W 83:22 N 29 '65
NASA orbits solar observatory. Aviation W 82:25 F 8 '65
Pilot rocket control seen. Sci N L 87:355 Je 5 '65
Story of a photograph; R. Morse's feat; Gemini 6-7 shoots eleven days apart. G. P. Hunt. il Life 60:3, 22-33 Ja 7 '66
Third Titan 3A vehicle carries experimental Comsat into orbit. il Aviation W 82:26 F 15 '65

Triple space launch. R. Hotz. Aviation W 82:13 Mr 29 '65
USAF official cites high cost of space launch operations. Aviation W 83:90 Ag 16 '65
See also
Artificial satellites—Launching

Launching pads
Coating withstands searing exhaust heat; Martyte FS. il Miss & Roc 17:25-6 Jl 5 '65
Facilities for Titan 3 keyed to short-notice launchings. G. Alexander. il Aviation W 83:36-7+ Jl 5 '65
Pad turnaround completed day early. G. Alexander. il Aviation W 83:32-3 D 13 '65

Launching sites
Amazing new Cape Kennedy. H. Pryor. il Sci Digest 57:47-51 Je '65
Argentina paces Latin space growth. W. S. Beller. il Miss & Roc 16:35+ Je 14 '65
As U.S. moonport takes shape; John F. Kennedy space center, Merritt Island launch area. il U S News 59:27-30 Ag 30 '65
MILA construction delays cramping space agency's launch schedulers; Merritt Island launch area. M. Getler. il Miss & Roc 16:26-7 Mr 15 '65

Maintenance and repair
Cold welding helpful? Sci N L 88:181 S 18 '65
Handy wrench for space. il Time 86:39 Jl 30 '65
Inflight spacecraft repair demonstrated. Aviation W 83:25 Ag 30 '65
Next EVA mission will test power tool. il Miss & Roc 17:39 Jl 19 '65
Space welding technique occurs only in vacuum. Sci N L 87:136 F 27 '65
USAF studying space tool development. R. D. Hibben. il Aviation W 83:58-9+ S 13 '65

Manufacture
Cosmic room to stagger the mind; Apollo project's Vehicle assembly building. J. Atwater. il Sat Eve Post 238:30-1 Ap 24 '65
S-1C for first moon flight to be accepted in June, 1968. W. J. Normyle. il Aviation W 83:60-1+ N 15 '65

Materials
Air force seeking data on toxicity of materials for use in space cabins. H. M. David. Miss & Roc 16:28+ Ap 12 '65
Beryllium material offers more ductility. il Aviation W 82:97+ F 22 '65
Lunar misson heat shield production to use established techniques. M. L. Yaffee. il Aviation W 83:56-7+ N 15 '65
NASA increasing use of brazed fittings. il Aviation W 83:63+ Jl 26 '65
Tape-wrapping technique refined. J. F. Judge. Miss & Roc 16:22-3 Ap 26 '65
See also
Shielding (heat)

Power supply
Amazing no-fuel space engine you can build; operating on solar energy. H. Walton. il Pop Sci 187:106-10+ Jl '65
Anatomy of the Gemini spacecraft. il Life 59:60-7 S 3 '65
Electric power in space. W. Von Braun. il Pop Sci 187:58-9+ Ag '65
Finger cites thermionic power gains. W. S. Beller. Miss & Roc 17:12 N 22 '65
Gemini fuel cell studied. Sci N L 88:151 S 4 '65
Improved solar cells planned for IMP-D. R. D. Hibben. il Aviation W 83:53+ Jl 26 '65
New engine for space does down-to-earth jobs. H. Walton. il Pop Sci 187:100-5+ Jl '65
Power conditioning and distribution lab will seek better electrical systems; section of ERC's systems division. Miss & Roc 16:67 My 31 '65
Systems division concerned with electronics analysis and integration; ERC's systems laboratory and the power conditioning and distribution laboratory. Miss & Roc 16:41-3 My 31 '65
Thermionic space power considered. W. S. Beller. il Miss & Roc 17:24-5 O 18 '65
Thin-film solar cells boost output ratio. P. J. Klass. il Aviation W 83:67-70 N 29 '65
See also
Space vehicles—Atomic power plants

Propulsion systems
Agena failure laid to new start sequence. Aviation W 83:33 N 15 '65

SPACE vehicles—Propulsion systems—*Cont.*

Agena failure may deal moon program a blow. il Bsns W p29-30 O 30 '65

Agena re-use in orbit considered. J. Mercer. Miss & Roc 17:18 S 13 '65

Air force in orbit. il Newsweek 65:56 Je 28 '65

AF seeks tests to requalify agena. H. Taylor. il Miss & Roc 17:13-14 N 22 '65

Atlas-Centaur shot bolsters Surveyor. Miss & Roc 17:16 Ag 16 '65

Atlas launch vehicle to be uprated. H. Taylor. Miss & Roc 16:14 My 17 '65

Big-solid insurance needed. W. J. Coughlin. Miss & Roc 17:50 O 25 '65

Breakthrough foreseen in early 70s. Miss & Roc 16:32 F 15 '65

Captive flight to check mating of modified M2-F2 with B-52. Aviation W 83:26 O 18 '65

Centaur propellant control succeeds. J. F. Judge. il Miss & Roc 17:28+ O 25 '65

Centaur ready for critical launching. H. Taylor. Miss & Roc 16:11 Mr 1 '65

Coming, ferries to space. W. Von Braun. il Pop Sci 187:68-9+ S '65

Congress may force NASA Titan 3 study. W. J. Normyle. Aviation W 83:30 Jl 12 '65

Death of a project; Project Orion. F. J. Dyson. Science 149:141-4 Jl 9 '65; Discussion. 149:912+ Ag 27 '65

Decision imminent on standard Atlas. H. Taylor. Miss & Roc 16:16 F 22 '65

DC motors stage comeback in space. W. S. Beller. il Miss & Roc 16:22-3 F 1 '65

Douglas studies re-usable launch vehicles. I. Stone. Aviation W 83:74-5 S 20 '65

Dual-fueled booster Titan. 3C. R. N. Watts, jr. il Sky & Tel 30:86-7 Ag '65

Electric systems urged for 1970-75 missions. R. Pay. Miss & Roc 17:40+ N 8 '65

Entire Gemini flight schedule slips; loss of Agena. il Miss & Roc 17:12-13 N 1 '65

Facilities for Titan 3 keyed to short-notice launchings. G. Alexander. il Aviation W 83:36-7+ Jl 5 '65

Final Titan 3A readied for test; first 3C vehicle is assembled. il Aviation W 82:32-3 Ap 12 '65

Flame-out; Atlas-Centaur failure. il Newsweek 65:69 Mr 15 '65

Flexible manned craft/booster urged. W. E. Wilks. il Miss & Roc 17:26 D 13 '65

Flight of the Hangar Queen; Centaur rocket. Time 86:62 Ag 20 '65

Gemini fuel filtration solved. L. A. Mavros. il Miss & Roc 17:26-8 Ag 2 '65

Gemini 9 to test re-start of docked Agena. W. J. Normyle. Aviation W 83:32-3 N 15 '65

Glitch & the Gemini; failure of Agena rocket. il Time 86:94 N 5 '65

Go for the moon; Saturn V booster. il Newsweek 66:57 Ag 16 '65

H_2O_2 oxidizer challenges other high-energy propulsion compounds. J. F. Judge. il Miss & Roc 17:23-4 Ag 9 '65

Improved Scout to loft piggyback. Aviation W 83:32 Ag 9 '65

Japan moves toward launch of home-built satellite in '68. il Miss & Roc 17:29-30 D 20 '65

Launch success ends Saturn 1 test series. Aviation W 83:30 Ag 9 '65

Limited work may be continued on Orion; system uses nuclear explosions. M. L. Yaffee. Aviation W 82:64-5+ My 10 '65

Little Joe II uprating proposed. W. E. Wilks. il Miss & Roc 16:44+ My 17 '65

Manned lifting body RFP issued. Aviation W 82:52+ F 15 '65

MSFC gets Saturn IB/Centaur job. Miss & Roc 16:14 Ap 19 '65

Million-pound-thrust Hybrid proposed. J. F. Judge. Miss & Roc 16:26+ My 3 '65

More powerful Delta introduced. S. Butler. Miss & Roc 16:21 Je 7 '65

Move up in space, win points; Martin co. steering Titan III program toward a profit. il Bsns W p92-4+ S 25 '65

NASA excludes Titan 3 vehicle in long-range mission forecast. E. H. Kolcum. Aviation W 82:27 My 10 '65

NASA orders four improved SLV-2 launch vehicle versions. Aviation W 83:29 Ag 2 '65

NASA's giant boosters. R. N. Watts, jr. Sky & Tel 31:27 Ja '66

New Delta may prove most economical. W. S. Beller. il Miss & Roc 17:24+ Ag 16 '65

New propulsion vistas; excerpts from remarks at symposium on advanced propulsion concepts. B. A. Schriever. Aviation W 82:21 My 10 '65

New third stage considered for Delta. Miss & Roc 17:18 N 15 '65

OAR to use own vehicles for OV shots. R. Pay. il Miss & Roc 18:32-4+ Ja 17 '66

Orion research may be resumed. W. E. Wilks. Miss & Roc 16:16 My 3 '65

Pace of advanced booster study drops. G. Alexander. il Aviation W 82:65+ Ap 19 '65

Recoverable booster studies aired. Miss & Roc 17:17 N 8 '65

Rocket-riding cameras show how boosters behave. W. Von Braun. il Pop Sci 187:106-7+ D '65

S-1 readied for Pegasus 2 launch. Aviation W 82:25 My 24 '65

S-1C for first moon flight to be accepted in June, 1968. W. J. Normyle. il Aviation W 83:60-1+ N 15 '65

Saturn 1B/Centaur likely victim as funding squeeze hits Voyager. D. E. Fink. Aviation W 83:30 O 11 '65

Schedule, performance problems threaten ELDO A booster program. D. E. Fink. il Aviation W 82:188-90+ Je 14 '65

Shot that failed; Agena explosion halts Gemini 6 mission. L. Wainwright and H. Suydam. il Life 59:111-13 N 5 '65

Solid core booster rockets to success; SL-1, solid rocket engine. il Bsns W p47-8 O 2 '65

Soviets seen using kick stages to separate Cosmos satellites. Aviation W 83:101 N 8 '65

Space boosters; fluorine upper stage now in prospect. il Miss & Roc 17:83-4+ N 29 '65

Space transporter designed by Junkers; based on a manned delta wing booster. il Aviation W 82:219+ Je 14 '65

Spacecraft design lags. Sci N L 88:103 Ag 14 '65

Surveyor's carrier makes the grade; performance of Atlas-Centaur 6. il Bsns W p 116 Ag 14 '65

TV system faces severe Saturn V test. R. Pay. Miss & Roc 18:38-9 Ja 3 '66

Third Titan 3A vehicle carries experimental Comsat into orbit. il Aviation W 82:26 F 15 '65

Titan and Atlas-Centaur trials. R. N. Watts, jr. il Sky & Tel 29:95 F '65

Titan III-A hits near-perfect orbit. D. L. Zylstra. il Miss & Roc 16:21 F 22 '65

Titan III-C is powerful space launch vehicle. Sci N L 88:9 Jl 3 '65

Titan IIIC tumbles on brink of triumph. il Bsns W p 123-4 O 23 '65

Titan III family may fill Atlas silos. D. L. Zylstra. Miss & Roc 17:12-13 Jl 12 '65

Titan 3 program involves five major incentive fee contracts. W. H. Gregory. il Aviation W 83:42-3+ Jl 5 '65

Titan III shot to set stage for defense Comsat project. M. Getler. il Miss & Roc 17:18 D 20 '65

Titan 3 test schedule emphasizes MOL. H. D. Watkins. Aviation W 82:53-5 Mr 1 '65

Titan III-X to fly in summer of 1966. Miss & Roc 16:18 F 15 '65

Two Centaurs are modified for restart. il Aviation W 83:77-9 Ag 23 '65

U.S. launch vehicles; International launch vehicles; specifications (cont) Aviation W 82:191-2 Mr 15 '65

UTC solves Scout stage spin problem. R. Lindsey. il Miss & Roc 17:28+ Ag 30 '65

Uprated Atlas confidence vote likely. H. Taylor. Miss & Roc 16:14 Ap 12 '65

Use of Centaur as Saturn 1B upper stage to give NASA significant payload increase. G. Alexander. il Aviation W 82:68-9+ My 17 '65

Vital Agena unit replaced for GTA-6. R. Pay. il Miss & Roc 17:24+ O 25 '65

Vital space plan killed; Project Orion. Sci N L 88:70 Jl 31 '65

Von Braun urges reusable transport. C. D. LaFond. Miss & Roc 17:16 N 8 '65; Reply. W. von Braun. 17:6 N 22 '65

What happens to rocket booster. W. Von Braun. il Pop Sci 188:68-70 Ja '66

See also

Ion engines

Rocket engines

Solid propellant rockets

Testing

Agena tests key to April Gemini shot. J. Mercer. il Miss & Roc 17:16-17 D 6 '65

Air force wins its space gamble; Titan IIIC. il Bsns W p 106-8+ Je 26 '65

Almost flawless Centaur flight viewed as development milestone. Aviation W 83:29 Ag 16 '65

Control system caused Titan failure. il Miss & Roc 18:14-15 Ja 3 '66

Eight Saturn IB,V launches set. Miss & Roc 17:17 O 11 '65

SPACE vehicles—Propulsion systems—Testing
—*Continued*
First industry-built Saturn 1 puts Pegasus-2 in precise orbit. Aviation W 82:21 My 31 '65
Giant stride by U.S. in space weaponry; Titan III-C. il U S News 58:8 Je 28 '65
Industry's Saturn I scores hit; booster built by Chrysler. il Bsns W p52+ My 29 '65
Next: Titan III; greatest U.S. rocket yet, military booster. il U S News 58:42 Je 21 '65
Pad built up for Titan III-C shot. Miss & Roc 16:18 Je 21 '65
Solid success; Titan III-C. il Time 85:64 Je 25 '65
Subliming solid thrustor set for test. W. S. Beller. il Miss & Roc 17:26-7 Ag 23 '65
Success revives USAF hopes for Titan 3C as national launch vehicle. G. Alexander. il Aviation W 82:16-19 Je 28 '65
Successful firings sustain Saturn pace. G. Alexander. il Aviation W 83:69+ Ag 23 '65
Titan III-C also managerial success. il Miss & Roc 16:14-15 Je 28 '65
Titan 3C transtage malfunctions, fails to achieve circular orbit. G. Alexander. Aviation W 83:27 D 27 '65

Protection
Relative radiation vulnerability analyzed in study of components. Aviation W 83:89 N 22 '65

Recovery
Air force, Nasa finishing plans for joint manned lifting body test. W. J. Normyle. Aviation W 82:19 Je 28 '65
Little bit of Russia: game of satellite catch between Russia and US. H. Simmons. Newsweek 65:57 Ap 19 '65
Martin developing SV-5 lifting body. il Miss & Roc 16:15 Mr 8 '65
Parafoil shows potential for spacecraft recovery. R. Pay. il Miss & Roc 16:38-9 My 10 '65
Start to a photo finish. il Newsweek 65:84 Mr 22 '65

Refueling
Orbiting fuel tanks to service spacecraft. Sci N L 88:82 Ag 7 '65

Shielding from heat
See Shielding (heat)

Stability and stabilizers
Magnets hold satellite; Atmosphere explorer satellite. Sci N L 88:70 Jl 31 '65

Sterilization
Canned Voyager; to rid Voyager of its terrestrial bugs. Time 86:82+ D 3 '65
Contaminant removal equipment is readied. il Miss & Roc 17:26+ S 13 '65
Earth could infect Mars. Sci N L 88:50 Jl 24 '65
GE proposes sterilization facility. H. M. David. il Miss & Roc 17:24-5 D 13 '65
GE sterilization techniques promising for planet probes. Miss & Roc 18:39-40 Ja 3 '66
Severe Voyager sterilization criteria set. H. D. Watkins. Aviation W 83:58+ D 6 '65
Voyager effort focuses on sterilization. H. D. Watkins. il Aviation W 84:58-9+ Ja 3 '66
Voyager sterilization sets precedent. H. M. David. Miss & Roc 17:32-3 Ag 9 '65

Testing
Agena target effort pushed for Gemini 8. R. G. O'Lone. il Aviation W 83:59-60 D 27 '65
AF seeks tests to requalify agena. H. Taylor. il Miss & Roc 17:13-14 N 22 '65
Checkout requirements push Apollo flight into February. il Miss & Roc 18:17 Ja 17 '66
DOD approved pre-MOL flights. D. L. Zylstra. il Miss & Roc 16:12-13 Ap 19 '65
Gemini hatch opening tests successful. W. J. Normyle. Aviation W 82:27-8 Ap 5 '65
Greater sensor utilization sought on Surveyor lander test vehicles. D. E. Fink. Aviation W 84:69-71 Ja 17 '66
Lab to simulate radiation environment; to test spacecraft. W. S. Beller. il Miss & Roc 16:24+ Mr 22 '65
Little lift, late bird; Gemini test. il Newsweek 65:83 My 3 '65
Mercury data aids Apollo checkout gear. G. Alexander. il Aviation W 82:48-9+ Mr 29 '65
Qualifications & standards lab will codify environmental testing methods; Core laboratory of the ERC. Miss & Roc 16:72+ My 31 '65

USAF to launch two used NASA Geminis; orbital flights to qualify MOL systems. E. H. Kolcum. Aviation W 82:26 Ap 19 '65

Thermal control
AIAA meeting focuses on thermal degradation. R. Pay. Miss & Roc 17:41+ S 27 '65
Which side is up? il Sci Digest 58:47 D '65

Tracking
Close tracking of Mariner continues. il Miss & Roc 17:14-15 Jl 19 '65
How we track our spacecraft. W. Von Braun. il Pop Sci 187:108-9+ N '65
Italy's amazing amateur space watchers. J. D. Ratcliff. il Read Digest 86:110-14 Ap '65
New U.S. spacecraft tracking station opens in Australia; message to Prime Minister Robert Menzies. L. B. Johnson. Dept State Bul 52:550 Ap 12 '65
S-band shakedown slated at Guam. C. D. LaFond. il Miss & Roc 17:34-5 S 20 '65
Telemetry: our eyes and ears in space. J. W. Billups. il Pop Electr 23:53-7+ O '65
Tracking on an island and around the world. il Life 58:78-9 Je 18 '65

Transportation
Apollo crawler bearing design changed. il Aviation W 83:100 N 8 '65
Larger Guppy aimed at S-4B transport. H. D. Watkins. il Aviation W 82:43+ Ap 19 '65
Leveling trouble plagues crawler. S. Butler. il Miss & Roc 16:17 My 10 '65
Super Guppy to make first flight Aug. 25. H. D. Watkins. il Aviation W 83:42-3 Ag 23 '65

SPACE vehicles, Atomic powered
Libby calls for nuclear space ship development. R. Pay. Miss & Roc 17:35-7 O 11 '65
Limited work may be continued on Orion; system uses nuclear explosions. M. L. Yaffee. Aviation W 82:64-5+ My 10 '65
Orion research may be resumed. W. E. Wilks. Miss & Roc 16:16 My 3 '65

SPACE vehicles, Russian
Biggest boost; Proton 1. Newsweek 66:59 Ag 2 '65
Full-scale Vostok exhibited by USSR; display at the Paris air show. il Aviation W 83:68-9 Jl 19 '65
Men, pictures told space story; with 1965 space calendar. J. Eberhart. Sci N L 88:357-8 D 4 '65
Photos show details of Vostok cabin, suit. il Aviation W 82:58-60 My 31 '65

SPACEMEN. See Astronauts

SPACESHIP Santa Maria; drama. See Boiko, C.

SPACKS, Barry
How to learn a secret name. por Am Ed 1:7-12 Je '65

SPADATS (space detection and tracking system) See Radar—Military applications

SPADEA spectaculars. See Comics (books, strips, etc)

SPAETH, Sigmund
And still champ; interview on Texaco's opera quiz, ed. by Q. Eaton. por Opera N 29:6-7 Ap 10 '65
Winning friends for opera. por Opera N 30:8-11 D 11 '65

SPAGHETTI. See Macaroni

SPAGHT, Monroe Edward
Rare kind of import. il por Time 85:104 Ap 30 '65

SPAHN, Warren Edward
Left out. il por Time 86:74 Jl 23 '65
Pitcher at forty-four. por Newsweek 65:72 My 10 '65

SPAIN
Spain; symposium. il Holiday 37:10+ Ap '65
See also
Andalusia
Arts and crafts—Spain
Automobile industry and trade—Spain
Banks and banking—Spain
Booksellers and bookselling—Spain
Catalonia
Censorship—Spain
Colleges and universities—Spain
Festivals—Spain
Forests and forestry—Spain
Investments, Foreign (in Spain)
Jews in Spain
Labor laws and legislation—Spain
Málaga
Moving pictures—Spain
Oviedo
Paleontology—Spain
Prisoners—Spain
Publishers and publishing—Spain
Santiago
Seville
Youth—Spain

SPAIN—*Continued*

Church history

All-pervasive church. H. Thomas. Holiday 37:86-7+ Ap '65
See also
Inquisition

Civilization

Soul of Spain. V. S. Pritchett. il Holiday 37:52-67+ Ap '65

Colonies

Spain's discreet decolonization. R. Pélissier. il For Affairs 43:519-27 Ap '65
Spain's new role in Africa. T. P. Melady. America 114:17-19 Ja 1 '66
See also
Latin America—History
Majorca

Description and travel

Before Ava Gardner arrived, Tartessians, Iberians, Phoenicians, Romans, Visigoths, Moors and Spaniards all lived here. R. Joseph. il Esquire 63:98-103+ Ap '65
Changing face of Old Spain. B. McDowell. il Nat Geog Mag 127:291-339 Mr '65
Love letter to Spain. F. P. Keyes. il Ladies Home J 82:68-9+ F '65
Road to Santiago; Spain's ancient road refurbished for modern pilgrims. F. V. Grunfeld. il Reporter 34:40+ Ja 13 '66
Travel in Spain. D. Dodge. il Holiday 37:153-60 Ap '65
Travel notes. R. Joseph. Esquire 63:48+ Ap '65
Travel's picture portfolio. Travel 123:50-5 Mr '65
We travel in Spain. E. Cary. il Mlle 61:233-4 Ag '65
Young girl, an old horse, and astonishing journey; experiences in southern Spain and France. L. Moffat. Vogue 146:16+ N 1 '65

Economic conditions

Awakening land. il Time 87:26-34D+ Ja 21 '66
Boom in Spain. G. Lazarus. Sat R 48:69+ O 9 '65
Letter from Spain. J. G. B. Nation 200:230-2 Mr 1 '65
Letter from Spain. A. Reid. il New Yorker 41:56+ Jl 10 '65

Economic policy

Spain and the E.E.C. L. López Rodó. For Affairs 44:127-33 O '65

Foreign relations

Great Britain

Reporter at large; Gibraltar question. A. Reid. New Yorker 41:38-42+ Jl 31 '65

Latin America

Return of the bullion billion. il Time 86:44 D 10 '65

History

Before Ava Gardner arrived, Tartessians, Iberians, Phoenicians, Romans, Visigoths, Moors and Spaniards all lived here. R. Joseph. il Esquire 63:98-103+ Ap '65
Violent past. J. Morris. Holiday 37:68-9+ Ap '65

Bibliography

Articles and other books received; comp. by C. J. Bishko. See issues of American historical review

Republic, 1931-1939

Spanish Republic and the Civil war: 1931-1939, by G. Jackson. Review
Nation 201:418-20 N 29 '65. J. Yglesias
Spanish tragedy. A. Guttmann. Commentary 40:73-80 Ag '65; Reply with rejoinder. H. M. Pachter. 41:20-1 Ja '66

Civil war, 1936-1939

Spanish Republic and the Civil war: 1931-1939, by G. Jackson. Review
Nation 201:418-20 N 29 '65. J. Yglesias
Wounded generation. A. M. Matute. Nation 201:420-4 N 29 '65

Civil war, 1936-1939—Volunteers

International brigades, by V. Brome. Review
Nat R 18:31-2 Ja 11 '66. J. Hart

Industries

Boom in Spain. G. Lazarus. Sat R 48:69+ O 9 '65

Maps

Lands of the bold captains mapped anew. il Nat Geog Mag 127:340-1, sup(folded map) Mr '65

Politics and government

Awakening land. il Time 87:26-34D+ Ja 21 '66
Franco's foes stop hoping. C. Sterling. il Reporter 32:33-6 F 25 '65
Hint from the Caudillo. il Time 87:30 Ja 7 '66
Letter from Spain. A. Reid. il New Yorker 41:56+ Jl 10 '65
More liberal Spain. E. M. von Kuehnelt-Leddihn. Nat R 17:323 Ap 20 '65
Spain, by B. Welles. Review
Sat R 49:36-7 Ja 15 '66. J. Kaplow
Spain's new role in Africa. T. P. Melady. America 114:17-19 Ja 1 '66
Steps forward. il Time 85:38-9 Ap 23 '65
Twenty-three years in Franco's jails; tr. by G. Rabassa. M. Amblard. il Nation 200:305-7 Mr 22 '65

Religious institutions and affairs

See also
Catholic church in Spain
Protestants in Spain

Social conditions

Letter from Spain. J. G. B. Nation 200:230-2 Mr 1 '65

Social life and customs

Connecticut Yankee finds her destiny in Spain. M. Daly. il Ladies Home J 82:60-1+ F '65

SPALDING, Alice B.
Eating low on the hog. Harper 230:139-40+ Mr '65

SPANIARDS
Leader and some notable Spanish faces. il Holiday 37:70-7 Ap '65
Letter from Spain. A. Reid. il New Yorker 41:56+ Jl 10 '65
Soul of Spain. V. S. Pritchett. il Holiday 37:52-67+ Ap '65

SPANIELS
Basic training for spaniels. D. M. Duffey. il Outdoor Life 136:160-4 O '65
National springer stake. D. M. Duffey. il Outdoor Life 135:138-40+ Mr '65

SPANISH. See Spaniards

SPANISH AMERICA. See Latin America

SPANISH AMERICAN literature. See Latin American literature

SPANISH AMERICANS in the United States. See Latin Americans in the United States

SPANISH cookery. See Cookery, Spanish

SPANISH fiction
Don Quixote. K. Rexroth. Sat R 48:19 My 15 '65

SPANISH HARLEM. See New York (city)—Harlem

SPANISH inquisition. See Inquisition

SPANISH Jews. See Sephardim

SPANISH literature
Passionate authors. G. Thomas. il Holiday 37:10+ Ap '65
See also
Authors, Spanish
Spanish fiction

SPANISH missions in California. See California—Missions

SPANISH music. See Music, Spanish

SPANISH PEAKS wilderness area (proposed) See Wilderness areas

SPANISH peanuts. See Peanuts

SPANISH REPUBLIC. See Spain—History—Republic, 1931-1939

SPANISH students
Franco and the students. America 112:346 Mr 13 '65

SPARE time. See Leisure

SPARERIBS. See Cookery—Meat

SPARGO, Larry, and others
Probing Viet Cong strongholds; excerpts from report. Aviation W 83:21 Jl 12 '65

SPARGUR, Ronn
Annunciation; poem. Christian Cent 82:1545 D 15 '65

SPARK, Muriel
Ladies and gentlemen; story. Harper 231:60-4 Jl '65
Liturgy of time past; poem. Atlan 216:91 Ag '65
Mandelbaum gate; story. New Yorker 41:54-9 My 15; 25-32 Jl 10; 26-34 Jl 24; 28-34 Ag 7 '65
Note by the wayside; poem. Atlan 216:102 N '65

SPARK, Muriel—*Continued*
about
Novel as Jerusalem. F. Kermode. por Atlan 216:92-4+ O '65

SPARK plugs
Inside story: outboard spark plugs. J. Roe. il Pop Sci 187:66-9 D '65
Spark plug care. R. E. Jennings. il Motor T 17:42-4 Je '65

SPARKMAN, John
Poor John. por Time 85:24-5 My 28 '65
Portrait of a southern liberal in trouble. R. Sherrill. il pors N Y Times Mag p46-7+ N 7 '65

SPARKS, Fred
As it happens (cont) Sat R 48:23 F 27; 21 Mr 20 '65
Writer at sea in Asia. Sat R 48:50+ S 18 '65

SPARKS, Morgan. See Hittinger, W. C. jt. auth.

SPARKS, Randy
Message from Sparks. il por Newsweek 66:77 Ag 30 '65

SPARKS, Will
Terror in the streets? Commonweal 82:345-8 Je 4 '65

SPARLING, Joseph J.
Lapidary experiments for elementary children. Sch Arts 64:41-3 Je '65

SPARROW, Arnold H. See Sparrow, R. C. jt. auth.

SPARROW, Rhoda C. and Sparrow, A. H.
Relative radiosensitivities of woody and herbaceous spermatophytes. bibliog Science 147:1449-51 Mr 19 '65

SPARROWS
English sparrows with American accents. D. Halyard. il Audubon Mag 67:178-9 My '65

SPAS. See Health resorts, watering places, etc.

SPASMS, Habit. See Tic

SPASTIC paralysis. See Paralysis

SPATTER prints. See Prints—Technique

SPEAKEASIES. See Liquor traffic—United States

SPEAKING. See Public speaking; Voice

SPEARMAN, Walter
Town's reputation and reality. Sat R 48:38 My 1 '65

SPEAS, Jan Cox
Happy anniversary darling; story. Good H 160:92-3 Je '65

SPECIAL classes and special schools
Saving the trouble-prone. N. E. Hall, jr. il NEA J 54:26-8 Ap '65
Something for the special child; with editorial comment. M. A. Wirtz. il Am Ed 1:inside cover, 14-21 S '65
Special education reaches nearly 2 million children. R. P. Mackie. Sch Life 47:8-9 D '64
Time for a special lesson: special education classes, Valley Oaks elementary, Houston, Tex. E. Norton. bibliog Library J 90:1987-8 Ap 15 '65
See also
Slow learning children—Education

SPECIAL collections in libraries. See Libraries—Special collections

SPECIAL committee of twenty-four on colonialism. See United Nations—Special committee on the situation with regard to implementation of declaration on granting of independence to colonial countries and peoples

SPECIAL days, weeks, and months
Goal of the week: the year's safety; National safe boating week. N. C. Barnard. Motor B 115:126-7 Je '65
National teachers' day endorsed by Senate. Sr Schol 87:sup3 28 '65
1965 National electronics week set for N.Y. Electr World 73:80 Ap '65
Of the greatest importance; World law day. Time 86:18 Jl 16 '65
World law day; remarks, July 8, 1965, with proclamation. L. B. Johnson. Dept State Bul 53:216-17 Ag 2 '65

SPECIAL education. See Special classes and special schools

SPECIAL forces of the United States army. See United States—Army—Special forces

SPECIAL fund. See United Nations—Special fund

SPECIAL librarians. See Librarians

SPECIAL libraries association
Evaluations on an IBM card; annual conference. il Library J 90:2974-8 Jl '65
SLA awards. Library J 90:2996 Jl '65
SLA convention to be held in Philadelphia. Wilson Lib Bul 39:723 My '65
SLA translation center gets renewed backing Pub W 189:106 Ja 17 '66

SPECIALISTS
Specialists try a wider track; management development problem. il Bsns W p56-7 Jl 31 '65

SPECIALIZATION in medicine
Guide to specialists and what they do. G. G. Greer. Bet Hom & Gard 43:38-9 Mr '65

SPECIALIZED agencies of the United Nations. See United Nations—Specialized agencies

SPECIES
Trend curves of the rate of species description in zoology. G. C. Steyskal. bibliog il Science 149:880-2 Ag 20 '65

SPECIFIC gravity
Density gradients. G. Oster. il Sci Am 213:70-6 Ag '65
Specifics of specific gravity; proving Archimedes' principle. H. P. Strand. il Pop Mech 125:168-9 Ja '66
Stability of lakes near the temperature of maximum density. H. Eklund. il Science 149:632-3 Ag 6 '65

SPECIFICATIONS
See also subhead Specifications under various subjects, e.g. Automobiles—Specifications

SPECIMENS, Botanical. See Plants—Collection and preservation

SPECTACLES. See Eyeglasses

SPECTER, Arlen
Parallel pattern. il por Newsweek 66:36 N 15 '65
People of the week. por U S News 59:21-2 N 15 '65

SPECTINOMYCIN. See Antibiotics

SPECTOR, Phil
Giant stands 5 ft. 7 in. por Time 85:44 F 19 '65

SPECTOR, Robert Donald
Poet's voice in the crowd. Sat R 48:29 Ag 7 '65
Way to say what a man can see. Sat R 48:46-8 F 13 '65

SPECTROGRAPH, Sonic
Bird song: the anatomy of a miracle. D. J. Borror. il Audubon Mag 67:159-63 My '65

SPECTROPHOTOFLUOROMETERS. See Spectrophotometers

SPECTROPHOTOMETERS
Fluorescence polarization: measurement with ultraviolet-polarizing filters in a spectrophotofluorometer. R. F. Chen and R. L. Bowman. bibliog il Science 147:729-32 F 12 '65
Spectrophotometer: new instrument for ultrarapid cell analysis. L. A. Kamentsky and others. bibliog il Science 150:630-1 O 29 '65

SPECTROSCOPY. See Spectrum analysis

SPECTRUM
Spectrum: all colors of the rainbow. il Sci Digest 57:85-7 Ap '65
Spectrum analyzers. J. Kyle. il Electr World 73:51-4+ My '65
See also
Comets—Spectra
Stars—Spectra

SPECTRUM, Infrared
Infrared spectra as a means of determining botanical sources of amber. J. H. Langenheim and C. W. Beck. bibliog il Science 149:52-5 Jl 2 '65

SPECTRUM, Solar
Solar energy spectrum. H. H. Malitson. il Sky & Tel 29:162-5 Mr '65

SPECTRUM analysis
Electron spin resonance spectroscopy: application to proof of structure of organic ketones. G. A. Russell and E. R. Talaty. bibliog il Science 148:1217-18 My 28 '65
Frequency or wavelength? letter. G. Wald. Science 150:1239 D 3 '65
Infrared spectroscopy with an interferometer. P. B. Boyce and W. M. Sinton. il Sky & Tel 29:78-80 F '65
New method for studying the atom. S. Bashkin. bibliog il Science 148:1047-53 My 21 '65
Spectrum analyzers. J. Kyle. il Electr World 73:51-4+ My '65
Spectrum of the intensity variations in 3C 273B. P. Maltby and A. T. Moffett. bibliog il Science 150:63-4 O 1 '65

SPECULATION
See also
Investments
Investments, Foreign
Land speculation
Stock exchange

SPEECH
Compressed speech helps. P. McBroom. Sci N L 88:214 O 2 '65

SPEECH—*Continued*
I teach famous men to talk; ed. by H. Markel. M. Von Hesse. il McCalls 92:98+ F '65
See also
Children—Language
English language
Voice
Study and teaching
See Speech education
SPEECH, Disorders of. See Speech defects
SPEECH, Freedom of. See Free speech
SPEECH, Liberty of
See also
Free speech
SPEECH analyzer. See Sound—Apparatus
SPEECH correction. See Speech therapy
SPEECH defects
Gift of speech. M. Marge. il Am Ed 1:23-5 N '65
See also
Institute of logopedics, Wichita, Kan.
SPEECH education
Denatured man; address, November 24, 1964. R. T. Eubanks. bibliog Vital Speeches 31:241-3 F 1 '65
Helping children to speak effectively. J. W. Bridges. il NEA J 54:20-1 Mr '65
Role of human values in communication; address, April 2, 1965. V. L. Baker. bibliog Vital Speeches 31:434-7 My 1 '65
See also
Children—Language
SPEECH of animals. See Animal communication
SPEECH research
Acoustic methods in psychiatry. P. F. Ostwald. il Sci Am 212:82-9+ bibliog (p 139) Mr '65
How's that again? American institutes for research study of speeded speech. Newsweek 66:84 S 13 '65
Speech research progress aided by computer. Sci N L 88:265 O 23 '65
SPEECH therapy
Artificial voice helps speechless to speak. Sci N L 89:40 Ja 15 '66
I teach famous men to talk; ed. by H. Markel. M. Von Hesse. il McCalls 92:98+ F '65
Speech therapy in the secondary school. S. H. Haimoff and M. P. De La Fuente. NEA J 54:52-3 N '65
SPEECH writing. See Authorship—Collaboration
SPEECHES, addresses, etc.
Who's writing LBJ's speeches. il U S News 58:57 Je 28 '65
See also
Public speaking
SPEED
See also
Automobiles—Speed
SPEED boat racing. See Motor boat racing
SPEED indicators
See also
Tachometers
SPEED limit signs. See Traffic signs
SPEED of trains. See Railroads—Train speed
SPEED traps, Radar. See Road traffic—Radar control
SPEEDLIGHT. See Photography—Apparatus and supplies
SPEEDOMETERS
Keep tab on your speedometer. G. S. Bondor. il Pop Sci 187:28 Jl '65
Marine speedometers. il Consumer Rep 30: 552-5 N '65
SPEEDWAYS
Leader of the pack: Daytona 500. il Newsweek 65:56 Mr 1 '65
SPEER, R. D.
Crematory for animal disposal. Am City 80: 121-2 Ag '65
SPEER, R. E. Jr
City girds for the Dutch-elm-disease battle. Am City 80:132-3 Je '65
SPEIRS, Jack
We're being swamped with boating laws. Pop Mech 124:106-9+ Ag '65
SPELEOLOGY. See Caves
SPELL of the rainbow; story. See Brown, G.
SPELLMAN, A. B.
Jazz at the Judson. Nation 200:149-51 F 8 '65
SPELMAN, Franz
I took the wrong baby home from the hospital. McCalls 92:62+ Ap '65

SPENCER, Elizabeth
Adult holiday; story. New Yorker 41:35-6 Je 12 '65
Knights and dragons; story. Redbook 125: 127 Jl '65
SPENCER, Herta. See Samachson, J. jt. auth.
SPENCER, Marion D.
Reading center for adults in the public library. por Wilson Lib Bul 40:78-9 S '65
SPENCER, Steven M.
Attack on the unborn. Sat Eve Post 238: 82-4 Mr 13 '65
Birth control revolution. Sat Eve Post 239: 21-5+ Ja 15 '66
Is anybody out there? Sat Eve Post 238: 44-6 Je 19 '65
Killer that stalks the newborn. Sat Eve Post 238:32-5 Ag 28 '65
SPENCER-CHURCHILL, Edward George
Letter from London. M. Panter-Downes. New Yorker 41:88-9 Je 26 '65
SPENCER-CHURCHILL collection. See Art— Private collections
SPENDER, Stephen
Three little Sitwells and how they grew. New Repub 152:19-20 Ap 24 '65
about
British poet is chosen for Library of Congress post. Pub W 187:76 Je 21 '65
Losses, engagements, privacies. W. Stafford. Poetry 106:295 Jl '65
SPENDING. See Consumption (economics)
SPERBER, Ann
Wozzeck. Am Rec G 32:338-41 D '65
You cannot lose, DGG's Die zauberflöte. Am Rec G 32:14-17 S '65
SPERM. See Semen
SPERMATOZOA. See Semen
SPERMIDINE
Spermidine in regenerating liver: relation to rapid synthesis of ribonucleic acid. W. G. Dykstra, jr. and E. J. Herbst. bibliog il Science 149:428 Jl 23 '65
SPERO, Robert
Father watches the birth of his son. Redbook 125:54-5+ My '65
SPERRY Rand corporation
Radar, ECM gains seen with Sperry delay line. M. Getler. Miss & Roc 16:34-6 Ap 26 '65
Univac isn't a business to jump in and out of. S. H. Brown. Fortune 71:120-3+ Ap '65
SPHERICAL astronomy. See Astronomy, Spherical and practical
SPHINX moths. See Moths
SPICE orchids. See Orchids
SPICE racks
Two easy-to-make spice racks. R. Gilmore. il Pop Sci 187:154-5 N '65
SPICES
Spices and herbs have an intriguing history. il Todays Health 43:31 O '65
Spices rate a place of their own. J. Gillies. il Farm J 89:81 Je '65
See also
Curry
SPIDER webs
Spider-web building. P. N. Witt and C. F. Reed. bibliog il Science 149:1190-7 S 10 '65
Wizardry of webs. J. George. il Read Digest 87:115-19 Ag '65
SPIDERS
Spider quiz. J. Daugherty and M. Daugherty. il Sci Digest 58:90-2 S '65
SPIDERWORTS
Tradescantias. R. D. Roe. Horticulture 44:47-8 Ja '66
SPIEGEL, Clara G.
Day on safari. Reporter 33:38+ Jl 1 '65
SPIEGEL, Der. See Periodicals—Germany (Federal Republic)
SPIEGELMAN, Judith M.
Are we preparing our children for world citizenship? Parents Mag 40:42 S '65
SPIEGELMAN, S. See Haruna, I. jt. auth.
SPIES, Tom Douglas
Battler against hidden starvation. por Todays Health 43:18 F '65
SPIES
As Penkovsky saw it; concerning his papers. J. Burnham. Nat R 17:1150 D 14 '65
British agent supports Penkovsky papers. Pub W 188:39-40 N 22 '65
Case of the Swedish spy: Col S. Wennerström. I. Ross. Read Digest 86:117-25 Ap '65
Cloak and dollar; E. Helbig and F. C. Bossard. Newsweek 65:40 Ap 19 '65

SPIES—*Continued*

Domestic scandal; E. Helbig on trial in West Germany. il Newsweek 65:56+ Ap 12 '65

Downfall of the man with the dog; arrest of Communist agents in Caracas. M. Acoca. il Life 58:72C-72D Ap 30 '65

Honest-to-badness; two spy memoirs. il Time 86:44-5 N 12 '65

I spied for the Russians; ed. by H. H. Martin. R. G. Thompson. il Sat Eve Post 238:23-9 My 22; 38-40+ Je 5 '65

I stole America's secrets; Lonsdale memoirs in London newspaper. il Newsweek 65:33 Ap 12 '65

Lenin, mon amour; R. G. Thompson. il Newsweek 65:23-4 Mr 22 '65

Lo, the poor spy; financial aspirations of French spies. Newsweek 66:50 S 27 '65

Man from S.K.U.N.K; case of Syrian-born Farhan Attassi. Time 85:35 F 26 '65

New meaning of treason, by R. West. Review Nat R il 17:156+ F 23 '65. G. Wills

Of hate & espionage; Attassi & Elie Cohn cases. il Time 85:31 Mr 5 '65

Soviet spymasters; Soviet espionage apparatus in the U.S. S. Alsop. Sat Eve Post 238:16 My 22 '65

Spies. Nat R 17:316 Ap 20 '65

Spy of God. L. Poliakov. Commentary 40:67-70 Ag '65

Spy season; wave of espionage in Syria. il Newsweek 65:44 My 8 '65

Spy who broke & told; case of James Mintkenbaugh and Robert Lee Johnson. Time 85:25 Ap 16 '65

Stupid spy; R. G. Thompson. il Time 85:31 Mr 19 '65

Under the table; British security procedures. Time 85:38 My 21 '65

Well-informed spy. D. Cort. il Nation 200:136-8 F 8 '65

See also

Espionage

European war, 1914-1918—Secret service

Rosenberg, Julius and Ethel, case

SPIES, Industrial

Corporate spies. il Time 85:76 Mr 26 '65

Crestfallen spy; Eugene Mayfield offers Crest marketing plans to Colgate-Palmolive. Time 85:97 Ap 9 '65

From Cincinnati, with love; attempted sale of Crest marketing plan. Newsweek 65:90 Ap 12 '65

From Du Pont, with love; industrial spying and corporate paranoia. E. Engberg. Commonweal 82:465-8 Jl 2 '65

I spy becomes big business. L. Stessin. il N Y Times Mag p 105-6+ N 28 '65

Operation air bubble; East German engineer convicted by French court. il Newsweek 65:79 Ap 19 '65

SPIES in literature

Agent 008, where are you? boredom with Bond. S. Alexander. Life 59:27 Jl 19 '65

Bond phenomenon. il Newsweek 65:95-6 Ap 19 '65

Bondanza; 007 products boom. il Newsweek 65:92+ My 10 '65

Cold war fiction; spy stories as literature. B. Cook. Commonweal 83:342-5 D 17 '65

Does James Bond really hate women? excerpt from James Bond dossier. K. Amis. il Ladies Home J 82:47+ Jl '65

007 knows what to do. il pors Life 60:79-81 Ja 7 '66

007-the spy with the golden touch; creation of James Bond. F. Stewart-Gordon. Read Digest 87:113-17 O '65

Incredible James Bond; merchandising program. J. F. Olesky. il Duns R 86:75-6 O '65

James Bond: modern-day dragonslayer. A. S. Boyd. Christian Cent 82:644-7 My 19 '65

Organization spies; Moscow's KGB, Washington's CIA and London's MI-6 spy-thrillers to challenge Fleming's James Bond stories. S. Alsop. il Sat Eve Post 238-14 D 18 '65

Spies who come in from next door; spy novel syndrome. C. Knickerbocker. Life 58:13 Ap 30 '65

SPIEZIO, Edward Wayne

Please, please, Ed Spiezio, won't you please pop up? T. C. Brody. il por Sports Illus 22:80-1 Ap 12 '65

SPIKE, Robert W.

Our churches' sin against the Negro; excerpts from Freedom revolution and the churches. Look 29:29-31 My 18 '65

SPINACH

See also

Cookery—Vegetables

SPINAL cord

Surgery

New way to relieve pain within minutes; cordotomy; reprint. L. Getz. Sci Digest 58:80-3 O '65

SPINE

Abnormities and deformities

What is a slipped disc? Good H 161:148-9 Jl '65

SPINELLO, Matt P.

On the citizens band. See issues of Popular electronics

SPINGARN, Lawrence P.

Episode at Vigo; poem. Sat R 48:17 F 13 '65

Foreclosure; poem. Sat R 48:30 My 8 '65

Healthy Henry; poem. Sat R 48:86 S 11 '65

SPINNAKERS. See Sails

SPINRAD, Bernard I.

Ramifications of nuclear energy. Bul Atomic Sci 21:21-4 My '65

SPINSTERS. See Single women

SPIRIN, Alexander S. and Nemer, Martin

Messenger RNA in early sea-urchin embryos: cytoplasmic particles. bibliog Science 150:214-17 O 8 '65

SPIRIT communication. See Spiritualism

SPIRITS. See Ghosts

SPIRITUAL direction. See Spiritual life

SPIRITUAL exercises

Spiritual exercises, by K. Rahner. Review America 113:347-8 S 25 '65. T. A. Burke

SPIRITUAL life

Education for responsible citizenship; adaptation of address. S. K. Bailey. NEA J 54:16-18 My '65

Faith and the facts of life. W. Hamilton. Nation 200:424-6 Ap 19 '65

Is there a tragic sense of life? L. Abel; discussion. Commentary 39:18+ My '65

Matter and spirit. R. O. Johann. America 113:52 Jl 10 '65

SPIRITUAL retreats. See Retreats, Spiritual

SPIRITUAL values. See Worth

SPIRITUALISM

Through the years with Ethel and Albert. H. Frankel. Sat R 48:28-30 Ag 14 '65

SPITZER, Alan B. See Lasch, C. jt. auth.

SPITZER, Silas

Dining in the Far East. Holiday 38:98+ D '65

Spanish food: a new excitement. Holiday 37:94-6+ Ap '65

SPIVACK, Kathleen

Eating; poem. Harper 231:48 N '65

March 1st; poem. New Yorker 41:40 Mr 6 '65

Metamorphosis; poem. Atlan 215:105 Ap '65

Straining; poem. Atlan 216:109 O '65

SPIVAK, Jonathan

Education's muddled bureaucracy. Reporter 32:33-6 Ap 8 '65

SPLEEN

Spleen as a production site for erythropoietin. P. de Franciscis and others. bibliog il Science 150:1831-3 D 31 '65

SPLEEN cells. See Cells

SPLICES. See Knots and splices

SPLICING of moving pictures. See Moving pictures—Editing

SPLIT-level houses. See Architecture, Domestic

SPOCK, Benjamin

How can we protect our children from obscenity? por Redbook 124:18+ Ap '65

How well nourished should our children be? por Redbook 125:44+ S '65

[Monthly column] See issues of Redbook

—and Lerrigo, M. O.

Love: the essential medicine when your child is ailing; excerpt from Caring for your disabled child. Ladies Home J 82:53+ My '65

about

Bah and humbug to Dr Spock. Life 59:4 D 10 '65

Doctor Spock loses first round in Pocket books suit. Pub W 188:67 D 27 '65

Doctor Spock sues pocket books for ruling to end inserts. Pub W 188:52 O 25 '65

Scholastic teacher interview; ed. by H. J. Langer, por Sr Schol 86:sup9-11 Ap 1; sup7-8 Ap 8 '65

What to do about fussy eating habits. por Redbook 125:28+ Jl '65

SPOILER; story. See Brodeur, P.

SPOILING of children. See Children—Management and training

SPOILS system. See Patronage, Political

SPOKANE, Wash.

Education

City friends for farmers; farm tour for fourth graders. il Farm J 89:51 N '65

Recreation

Square dancers do-si-do in their own building; Western dance center. H. Rawley and others. il Recreation 58:432-4 N '65

SPOKEN phonograph records. See Phonograph records—Spoken records

SPOLETO festival. See Music festivals—Italy

SPONG, Paul, and others

Selective attentiveness and cortical evoked responses to visual and auditory stimuli. bibliog Science 148:395-7 Ap 16 '65

SPONGE fishing

What is the lady looking at? with lithograph. il Am Heritage 16:17-19 O '65

SPONGES

Nature note; Venus flower basket. Sci N L 88:189 S 18 '65

Proteins and disulfide groups in the aggregation of dissociated cells of sea sponges. G. J. Gasic and N. L. Galanti. bibliog il Science 151:203-5 Ja 14 '66

SPONSORS, Advertising. See Television advertising

SPOON shelves. See Shelves

SPOONS

Some trade spoons. M. Alves. il Hobbies 70:46 S '65

Tea caddy spoons. M. M. Bridwell. il Antiques 88:528-31 O '65

SPORANGIUM

Bacterial stimulation of sporangium production in phytophthora cinnamomi. G. A. Zentmyer. bibliog Science 150:1178-9 N 26 '65

SPORES (botany)

Conidia of botrytis cinerea: labeling by fluorescent vital staining. H. M. Wilson. bibliog il Science 151:212 Ja 14 '66

Spore discharge in basidiomycetes: a unified theory. D. B. O. Savile; reply with rejoinder. L. S. Olive. Science 148:533 Ap 23 '65

See also
Sporangium

SPORN, Michael B. See Dingman, C. W. jt. auth.

SPORT fishing boats. See Fishing boats

SPORT parachuting. See Parachuting

SPORT trophies. See Trophies, Sport

SPORTCASTER company

Long-distance jumper on the ski wear trail; ski jackets. il Bsns W p 140-1 F 27 '65

SPORTING goods

Only the game remains the same; synthetics replace traditional materials of sport; with account by L. Smith. il Sports Illus 23:32-9 S 27 '65

This stuff is to keep him from getting hurt, it doesn't always work. il Esquire 64:74-5 O '65

Trade! trade! who'll hoss trade? swapfest of sports equipment; Jefferson County, Ky. J. McLain. il Recreation 58:187-8 Ap '65

What's new. See issues of Outdoor Life

SPORTS

Adapt sports for special needs. il Recreation 58:497-8 D '65

SR/1966 world travel calendar. R. Meyer, jr. Sat R 49:55-6+ Ja 1 '66

See also
Radio broadcasting—Sports
School athletics
Sportsmanship
Television broadcasting—Sports
Track athletics
also names of sports, e.g. Shot putting

Accidents and injuries

How your own strength can hurt you. K. N. Anderson. il Todays Health 43:18-23+ Ap '65

See also subhead Accidents and injuries under various subjects, e.g. Baseball—Accidents and injuries

Anecdotes, facetiae, satire, etc.

Short monograph on the uses of frailty in physical competition. S. Potter. il Nation 200:506-8 My 10 '65

Anecdotes, facetiae, satire, etc.

Moment-of-truth menace. B. Gilbert. Esquire 64:98+ D '65

Fiction

Second letter to sports writers. D. M. Broderick; reply. J. P. Colby. Library J 90:1368 Mr 15 '65

International aspects

Yankee dandies on the Danube; World university games. P. E. Ress. il Sports Illus 23:20-1+ S 6 '65

Periodicals

See also
Sports illustrated (periodical)

Photographs

Perils of picture making. M. Ornitz. il U S Camera 29:42-3+ Ja '66

Records

See Sports records

England

See also
Cricket (game)

Ethiopia

Number two lion in the land of Sheba; A. Bikila, Olympic champion marathon runner. J. Underwood. il Sports Illus 22:86-92+ Ap 12 '65

France

New vigor in French sports. C. R. Agnew, jr. il Recreation 58:66-7+ F '65

Latin America

Latins storm *las grandes ligas.* R. H. Boyle. il Sports Illus 23:24-6+ Ag 9 '65

Scotland

Misty haven for sportsmen; photographs by P. Beard; with account by F. R. Smith. Sports Illus 22:50-6+ My 17 '65

Spain

See also
Bullfights

United States

For the record. See issues of Sports illustrated

O.K. everybody: beat America! D. Jenkins. il Sports Illus 23:12-17 Jl 26 '65

Sports. H. L. Masin. See issues of Senior scholastic

Sports. See issues of Newsweek

Then my arm glassed up. J. Steinbeck. Sports Illus 23:94-6+ D 20 '65

See also
Amateur athletic union of the United States

SPORTS arenas. See Stadiums

SPORTS car club of America. See Automobile clubs

SPORTS car racing. See Automobile racing

SPORTS cars

Cars; photographs. See issues of Hot rod

Chevy showcase: Mako Shark II. il Motor T 17:66-7 Jl '65

Mako Shark super 'Vette. E. Dahlquist. il Hot Rod 18:48-51+ D '65

Mustang with fangs, GT-350. E. Rickman. il Hot Rod 18:50-3 Ag '65

Runaway success; Ford Mustang. il Newsweek 65:76 Ap 26 '65

Snakes, butter beans and Mister Cobra; American sports car. C. Phinizy. il Sports Illus 22:36-8+ My 17 '65

Wisconsin warrior; sports car racing at Elkhart Lake, Wis; photographs. J. Cooke. Sports Illus 22:28-33 Je 21 '65

See also
Automobiles, Racing

Testing

Corvette Sting Ray road test. B. McVay. il Motor T 17:46-51 Je '65

MT road test:
Ford makes a tiger of the Sunbeam. B. McVay. il Motor T 17:80-3 F '65

2+2 for excitement. B. McVay. il Motor T 17:36-9+ F '65

SPORTS clothes. See Clothing and dress—Sports clothes

SPORTS clubs

Public joins Winchester in a shotgun revolution; Thunder Mountain public shooting center, Ringwood, N.J. V. Kraft. il Sports Illus 24:46-8 Ja 17 '66

School for anglers; Miami Beach rod and reel club. J. Brooks. il Field & S 70:32-3 Jl '65

See also
Fishing clubs

SPORTS columns. See Newspapers—Sections, columns, etc.

SPORTS equipment. See Sporting goods

SPORTS exhibits. See Exhibits

SPORTS fans
Celestial hell of the superfan; pro football. G. Plimpton. il Sports Illus 23:104-6+ S 13 '65
49ers lose their cool and get hot; won their second straight at Kezar stadium. T. Maule. il Sports Illus 23:34-6+ O 11 '65
Grand prix was a gasser; Los Angeles times Grand prix, Riverside, Calif. L. Smith. il Sports Illus 23:42-4+ N 15 '65
Their business is peanuts; feeding spectators at sports events. J. Jares. il Sports Illus 24:52-8 Ja 17 '66
To be seen seeing the Redskins; Washington Redskins. E. Shrake. il Sports Illus 23:52-4+ O 4 '65

SPORTS films. See Moving pictures—Sports films

SPORTS for the deaf. See International games for the deaf

SPORTS illustrated (periodical)
Sportsman of the year; interview, ed. by J. Olsen. S. Koufax. il Sports Illus 23:34-8+ D 20 '65

SPORTS illustrated silver anniversary All-America
1965 silver anniversary awards. il Sports Illus 23:77-83 D 20 '65

SPORTS journalism
Esquire is a paid-up member in the fellowship of American sport. A. Gingrich. Esquire 64:6 O '65

SPORTS network, incorporated
Maitre d' of sports TV; Dick Bailey of SNI. G. S. Brown. il Sports Illus 23:52-4 N 8 '65

SPORTS officiating
Little pal on the dead run; college basketball official, L. Wirtz. B. Gilbert. il Sports Illus 22:38-43 Mr 1 '65
See also
Baseball—Organization and administration

SPORTS promoting. See Promoters and promoting

SPORTS records
Here is the odd paradise of the record maniac. Guinness book of records. J. A. M. Graham. il Sports Illus 22:54-8+ F 8 '65; Same abr. with title Book to end arguments. Read Digest 86:152-4+ My '65
Mouse who builds the mountains; Dodger's M. Wills, holder of stolen-base record. W. Leggett. il Sports Illus 23:38-42 Jl 12 '65
Ron runs the world ragged; Australia's R. Clarke has set four world records. G. S. Brown. il Sports Illus 23:24-5 Jl 26 '65
Sandy makes a pitch for posterity; compares with Feller and Diz. J. Jares. il Sports Illus 23:10-13 Ag 2 '65
Some fanatics whose fun is playing old records; track nuts. G. Holland. il Sports Illus 23:46-7 Ag 2 '65

SPORTSMANSHIP
On being good sports in sports; address. G. Turbeville. Vital Speeches 31:542-4 Je 15 '65
One winner, two victories; first International fair play trophy. il UNESCO Courier 18:22-5 Jl '65
Pour le sport. Nation 200:633 Je 14 '65
Shooting is the least important part of basketball; UCLA team. J. Wooden. il Look 30:66+ Ja 25 '66
We rejoice in our sufferings; letter. C. Cushman. il Sr Schol 86:30 Mr 4 '65

SPORTSMEN
Are sportsmen becoming extinct? R. T. Allen. il Read Digest 87:43+ N '65

SPOTMATIC cameras. See Single-lens reflex cameras

SPOTS, Removal of. See Cleaning

SPOTTED skunk. See Skunks

SPOTTED spurges. See Spurges

SPRAGG, Bruce C.
Regional dog-control program. Am City 80:104-5 N '65

SPRAGUE, Lucian M.
Fish immunogenetics research. Science 148:1252+ My 28 '65

SPRAYING and dusting
How, when and what of spraying roses. P. P. Pirone. il Horticulture 43:36-7 Ap '65
Is spraying necessary? C. Westcott. il Horticulture 43:20-1+ N '65
Pest control on plants indoors. P. P. Pirone. il Horticulture 43:26-8 S '65

Spray schedule for the flower garden. P. P. Pirone. il Horticulture 43:34-5 My '65
Spray schedule for vegetables. P. P. Pirone. il Horticulture 43:32-4 Je '65
Spraying evergreens; schedule for narrow-leaved evergreens. P. P. Pirone. il Horticulture 43:34-7 F '65
Spraying small fruits. P. P. Pirone. il Horticulture 43:38-9 Mr '65
See also
Airplanes in agriculture
Fungicides
Helicopters in insect control

Safety devices and measures
Safe use of chemicals. J. Antoine. Recreation 58:93 F '65

SPRAYING and dusting apparatus
Faster spraying, fewer weeds. il Farm J 89:32-3 Je '65
Insect control calendar. P. P. Pirone. il Pop Gard 17:20-1 Ja '66
PTO sprayer bucks the breeze. B. Hardy. il Farm J 89:81 Ap '65
See also
Aerosols

SPREADERS, Fertilizer. See Fertilizer spreaders

SPREADS, Sandwich. See Sandwich spreads

SPREIREGEN, Paul D.
City as a work of art; excerpts from Urban design: the architecture of towns and cities. Sat R 49:38-41 Ja 8 '66

SPREMULLI, Estelle
Sub-environments and the individual. Sch & Soc 93:104-5 F 6 '65

SPRING, Bernard P.
(ed) See Kowalski, P. Explosive forms of Piotr Kowalski

SPRING
Springtime at Trail Wood. E. W. Teale; S. H. Gottscho. il Audubon Mag 67:164-9 My '65
Unfolding of spring. B. Tufty. il Sci N L 87:186-7 Mr 20 '65

SPRING cleaning. See House cleaning

SPRING fever; drama. See Hark, M. and McQueen, N.

SPRING opera of San Francisco (organization)
Quality in several forms; Spring opera. R. C. Marsh. il Hi Fi 15:156 S '65

SPRING tonic; drama. See McQueen, M. H.

SPRINGER, Barbara
Stitchery for wall hanging. Sch Arts 64:22 Je '65

SPRINGER, Ethel M.
Canal-boat children; reprint from February 1923 issue. Mo Labor R 88:798 Jl '65

SPRINGER, Lois E.
Bells. See issues of Hobbies

SPRINGER-MILLER, Fred
New Spotmatic; a tryout at the Tokyo Olympics. il Pop Phot 56:70-1+ Ap '65

SPRINGFIELD, Ill.
Stump removal wins public favor. W. F. Cellini. il Am City 80:82-3 F '65

Historic houses, etc.
Lincolns' Globe tavern; reprint. J. T. Hickey. Hobbies 70:110-13 Ap '65

SPRINGFIELD, Mass.

Hospitals
New kind of doctor; emergency room of Wesson memorial hospital. R. H. Berg. il Look 29:22-6 Je 29 '65

Negroes
Trigger of hate. il Time 86:19 Ag 20 '65
When Negroes tried to shock a friendly city. il U S News 59:46-8 S 13 '65

SPRINGFIELD, Ohio
Changing times; R. Henry sworn in as mayor. Newsweek 67:27 Ja 17 '66

SPRINGS
Spring. R. Starnes. Field & S 70:12+ Ja '66

SPRINKLERS
Automatic watering pays its own way; Tucson, Ariz. G. C. Reid. il Am City 80:106-7 Mr '65
Lawn sprinklers. il Consumer Bul 48:25-7 Ag '65

SPRUCE KNOB MOUNTAIN. See Allegheny Mountains

SPRUCH, Grace Marmor
One man's adventures with a shiny suit. Sat R 48:88-90 D 4 '65

SPURGES
Is it the decade's worst weed? spotted spurge. il Sunset 135:152 Ag '65

SPURIA irises. See Irises

SPY stories. See Spies in literature

SPYING. See Spies

SQUARE dancing
Square dancers do-si-do in their own building; Western dance center, Spokane, Wash. H. Rawley and others. il Recreation 58: 432-4 N '65

SQUARE in the eye; drama. See Gelber, J.

SQUARE knotting. See Macramé

SQUASHES
Can you judge a squash by its cover? with cooking instructions. il Bet Hom & Gard 43:82 O '65
Save room for eat-all squash. B. C. Kilvert, jr. il Flower Grower 52:32 Mr '65
See also
Cookery—Vegetables

SQUAW VALLEY, Calif.
Summer camp; High camp. il Time 86:62 Ag 13 '65

SQUIDS
Electrophysiological studies of Chilean squid axons under internal perfusion with sodium-rich media. I. Tasaki and others. bibliog il Science 150:899-901 N 12 '65

SQUIRE, James R. and Hogan, R. F.
Where is the danger? PTA Mag 59:12 bibliog(p36) Mr '65

SQUIRE Puntila and his servant Matti; drama. See Brecht, B.

SQUIRES, Donald F.
Neoplasia in a coral? bibliog Science 148: 503-5; 150:78 Ap 23, O 1 '65

SQUIRES, Raymond
Morals of a teen. PTA Mag 59:4-7 bibliog (p37) Ap '65

SQUIRREL hunting
Spooky grays of Tate's hell. R. F. Burgess. il Outdoor Life 136:48-51+ Jl '65

SQUIRRELS
Color vision in the antelope ground squirrel. F. Crescitelli and J. D. Pollack. bibliog il Science 150:1316-18 D 3 '65
Control of tree squirrels. E. M. Mills. il Consumer Bul 48:43+ S '65
Day length and food caches; photoperiods cue the flying squirrel. I. Muul. il Natur Hist 74:22-7 Mr '65
Desert ground squirrel needs blue for life; antelope ground squirrel. Sci N L 88:184 S 18 '65
Hemoglobin and oxygen: affinities in seven species of sciuridae. F. G. Hall. bibliog il Science 148:1350-1 Je 4 '65
See also
Chipmunks

SQUIRRU, Rafael
Antonio Berni; reprint. Américas 17:20-9 O '65
Books. Américas 17:39-40 My '65
Culture we share. Américas 17:42-9 Ap '65
Edward Hopper. Américas 17:11-17 My '65

SREBRO, Richard. See Krauskopf, J. jt. auth.

SRIHONGSE, Sunthorn, and Johnson, C. M.
Wyeomyia subgroup of arbovirus: isolation from man. bibliog Science 149:863-4 Ag 20 '65

SRINIVAS, M. N. and Béteille, André
Untouchables of India; with biographical sketches. Sci Am 213:10, 13-17 D '65

STAAR, Richard
Retrogression in Poland. bibliog f Cur Hist 48:154-60+ Mr '65

STABA, E. John. See Kaul, B. jt. auth.

STABILE, Toni
New approach to Mexico. Redbook 125:28+ Ag '65

STABILITY of ships. See Ships—Stability and stabilizers

STABILIZATION of employment. See Employment stabilization

STACEY, Nicolas
Profiles; concerning Honest to God, by J. Robinson. V. Mehta. il New Yorker 41: 105-6+ N 20 '65

STACKHOUSE, Max L.
Ethics of Selma. Commonweal 82:75-7 Ap 9 '65
Today's city: threat or promise? Christian Cent 82:1537-41 D 15 '65

STACKHOUSE, Sally
Brief biography. S. Goodman. pors Dance Mag 39:54-5 My '65

STACKPOLE, Peter
35mm techniques. See issues of U.S. camera & travel

STADE, George
Variation on a theme by Robert Graves; poem. Nation 202:56 Ja 10 '66

STADELHOFER, Emil Anton
Fidel's pizzeria diplomacy paves the way for an exodus. il Life 59:38-9 N 5 '65

STADIUMS
Ballplayers under glass; Houston's new astrodome. H. Sutton. il Sat R 48:36-8 Mr 6 '65
Big screen is watching; Houston's astrodome. J. Jares. il Sports Illus 22:30-1 My 31 '65
Business of baseball; Houston astrodome. il Newsweek 65:66-70 Ap 26 '65
Daymares in the dome; Houston's new astrodome. il Time 85:97 Ap 16 '65
Domed stadium: spark to city's economy; Houston's astrodome. il U S News 59:10 O 11 '65
Giltfinger's golden dome; Houston astrodome. L. Smith. il Sports Illus 22:44-6+ Ap 12 '65
Great wall of Boston; Fenway park's left-field fence. J. Mann. il Sports Illus 22: 42-8+ Je 28 '65
Incredible Houston dome. F. X. Tolbert. il Look 29:96-8 Ap 20 '65
Lost in the stars; Houston astrodome stadium opens. il Newsweek 65:64 Ap 19 '65
Outdoor sports with indoor comfort: Houston's new astrodome stadium. il U S News 58:16 F 22 '65
Rain or shine, play ball! Houston's astrodome. il Life 58:86-8 Ap 9 '65
Small flaw in Houston's diamond; astrodome. il Bsns W p30-2 Ap 17 '65
What a wonder! what a blunder! Houston's new enclosed baseball stadium; with report by J. R. McDermott. il Life 58:76A-78 Ap 23 '65

STADTMUELLER, Frederick
Investiture controversy. America 113:88 Jl 24 '65

STAEL, Nicolas de
Sunburst; exhibition of paintings touring the U.S. il por Newsweek 66:112 O 18 '65
Thousand vibrations. il Time 86:88-9 O 22 '65

STAEMPFI, George W.
Op; exhibition at Staempfi gallery of K. Gerstner's works. New Yorker 41:29-30 F 20 '65

STAFFORD, Jean
Books. See issues of Vogue
(ed) See Oswald, M. Strange world of Marguerite Oswald

STAFFORD, Thomas P.
Astronauts' own reports from Gemini 6 and 7. il por Life 60:66-7 Ja 14 '66
about
Shot that failed. L. Wainwright and H. Suydam. il por Life 59:111-13 N 5 '65
See also
Space flight—Manned flights—Schirra-Stafford flight, 1965

STAFFORD, William
Following the Markings of Dag Hammarskjöld: a gathering in the spirit of his life and writings; poems. Poetry 106:319-27 Ag '65
Indirections of reason. Poetry 105:262-4 Ja '65
Inner legislation. Poetry 106:356-8 Ag '65
Losses, engagements, privacies. Poetry 106: 294-5 Jl '65
Monday; poem. New Yorker 41:184 D 11 '65
Out West; poem. Sat R 48:56 Ap 10 '65
Uncle George; poem. Sat R 48:15 Mr 13 '65
Weighed and found wanted. Poetry 106:429-32 S '65
When I was young; poem. Sat R 48:20 My 1 '65

STAFFORDSHIRE ware
Identification of Staffordshire ladles. N. F. Little. il Antiques 88:212-15 Ag '65
Larsen and McCauley collections at the Smithsonian institution. J. J. Miller, 2d. il Antiques 88:522-5 O '65

STAG hunting. See Deer hunting

STAG king; opera. See Henze, H. W.

STAGE. See Acting; Theater

STAGE coaches. See Coaches and coaching

STAGE photography. See Photography, Theatrical

STAGE scenery. See Theater—Stage scenery

STAGECOACHES. See Coaches and coaching

STAGG, Amos Alonzo
Coach. il por Time 85:45 Mr 26 '65

STAGGERS, Harley Orrin
Key chairmanship for an LBJ liberal. por U S News 60:10 Ja 10 '66

STAGGS, Reba
Modern meat primer. por Parents Mag 40: 77+ O '65

STAHL, Walter R.
Organ weights in primates and other mammals. bibliog Science 150:1039-41 N 19 '65
STAHLMAN, William D.
Project moon shot: 1609. Sat R 48:41 Ap 3 '65
STAHNKE, Herbert L.
Stress and the toxicity of venoms. bibliog Science 150:1456-7 D 10 '65
STAIB, Bjørn O.
North toward the Pole on skis. pors Nat Geog Mag 127:254-81 F '65
STAINED glass. See Glass painting and staining
STAINLESS steel. See Steel, Stainless
STAINLESS steel blades. See Razor blades
STAINPROOF textiles. See Textile fabrics—Protection
STAINS, Removal of. See Cleaning
STAINS and staining (microscopy)
Conidia of botrytis cinerea: labeling by fluorescent vital staining. H. M. Wilson. bibliog il Science 151:212 Ja 14 '66
STAIRWAYS
Secret of successful stairs. R. J. DeCristoforo. il Pop Mech 124:158-62 D '65
STALEY, Jane Goss
Timeless oriental rug. Bet Hom & Gard 43: 38+ N '65
STALEY, Thomas F.
Carlo Coccioli. Commonweal 83:95-8 O 22 '65
STALIN, Iosif
Memories of the man of steel. H. E. Salisbury. il por Sat R 48:40-1 D 11 '65
Rise and fall of Stalin, by R. Payne. Review
New Repub 154:27-9 Ja 1 '66. A. Field
Selective objectivity; partial rehabilitation. il por Newsweek 65:54-5 My 24 '65
STALLS, Airplane. See Airplanes—Stalling
STALVEY, Lois Mark
Who won, mom? Parents Mag 40:87 O '65
STAMFORD, Conn.

City planning
Upgrading downtown. il Arch Rec 137:184-5 Je '65
STAMLER, Jeremiah
Stamler vs. HUAC: heart specialist, called by committee, responds by challenging HUAC's legality. E. Langer. Science 149: 405-7 Jl 23 '65
STAMOS, Theodoros
Personal backgrounds. il por House & Gard 128:181 D '65
STAMP, James
How to get the most grain in 35-mm. il Pop Phot 57:66-7+ Ag '65
STAMP collecting. See Postage stamps—Collectors and collecting
STAMPS, Postage. See Postage stamps
STANBURY, C. M. 2d
One QSL too many. Pop Electr 22:65+ Ap '65
STANDARD and Poors corporation
McGraw-Hill delays merger with Standard & Poor's. Pub W 188:67 D 27 '65
McGraw-Hill set to acquire Standard & Poor's. Pub W 188:55 O 25 '65
Putting facts together; Standard & Poors to merge with McGraw-Hill. Time 86:92 O 29 '65
STANDARD of living
Behind the mask of success; excerpt from Our depleted society. S. Melman. Sat R 48:8-10+ Jl 31 '65
Employed poor: their characteristics and occupations. L. D. Cummings. il Mo Labor R 88:828-35 Jl '65
Heritage of going without. R. Hunter. Read Digest 87:120-2 Ag '65
See also
Budget, Household
Poverty
STANDARD oil company (New Jersey)
Change at Jersey. Time 85:86 F 26 '65
Oil and power mix; Esso Standard eastern. Fortune 71:70+ F '65
Oil is no longer enough; Jersey Standard moves into chemicals, power, realty. il Bsns W p48-50+ Jl 3 '65
STANDARDIZATION
See also
Quality of products
STANDARDS
See subhead Standards under various subjects, e.g. Hospitals—Standards
STANDARDS (ethics) See Ethics
STANDARDS association, American. See American standards association
STANDARDS of measurement. See Weights and measures

STANDARDS of production. See Production standards
STANDING congressional committees. See United States—Congress—Committees
STANDISH, Burt L.
Sort of postscript. J. K. Hutchens. Sat R 48:23 Ag 21 '65
STANDS, Machine. See Machinery—Stands
STANFORD, John, Jr
Supreme court quashes Texas book seizure. Pub W 187:57 F 1 '65
STANFORD research institute
Home furnishings head toward a new design; All-industry home furnishings conference. il Bsns W p45-6+ Ag 14 '65
STANFORD university, Stanford, Calif.
Palo Alto in Europe; Stanford's permanent campuses in Europe. il Time 87:43 Ja 14 '66
Sex at Stanford; Dean of women L. Allen resigns. Newsweek 65:53-4 Mr 1 '65
STANFORD university summer festival. See Music festivals—California
STANISLAUS RIVER
Sometimes it's peaceful and then again, sometimes it's not. il Sunset 134:30-2 My '65
STANISLAVSKI system. See Acting
STANISLAVSKII, Konstantin Sergeevich
MATmen. il Newsweek 65:84 F 15 '65
Stanislavsky and opera. K. Adler. por Opera N 29:6-7 F 6 '65
STANLEY, John
Books. Commonweal 83:67-9 O 15 '65
STANLEY, Marian
But I'm glad I'm my farmer's wife; ed. by M. Longwell. Farm J 89:107 Ap '65
STANLEY, Arnold and associates
Factory for million-dollar ideas. il Bsns W p64+ O 30 '65
STANLEY steamer. See Automobiles, Steam
STANLEYVILLE, Congo (capital Leopoldville)
Grim siesta of Stanleyville. J. Lelyveld. il N Y Times Mag p28-9+ My 16 '65
STANLEYVILLE massacre. See Congo massacre. 1964
STANS, Maurice H.
Other side of the new economics. por U S News 59:82+ D 13 '65
STANTON, Edward S.
Books to be noted; religion (cont) America 112:679-81 My 8 '65
Religion. America 113:684-6 N 27 '65
STANTON, Edwin McMasters
Assassination! excerpt from Twenty days. D. M. Kunhardt and P. B. Kunhardt, jr. il pors Am Heritage 16:9-35 Ap '65; Discussion. 16:7 Ap; 93 O '65
STANTON, Frank
Science and democratic progress; address, June 11, 1965. Vital Speeches 31:605-8 Jl 15 '65

about
CBS: the money machine. il por Newsweek 65:60-2 F 22 '65
STANTON, Will
Few words of advice; story. Redbook 124:60-1 Ap '65
Latest thing. McCalls 93:86+ O '65
People at parties. McCalls 92:55 My '65
Small favor; story. McCalls 93:122-3 N '65
There's a fire truck in the hall. Redbook 126: 44-5+ Ja '66
STAPHYLOCOCCI
Fighting staph with staph. il Time 86:46 S 10 '65
Hemolysin production in the development of staphylococcal lesions. E. A. Foster. bibliog il Science 149:1395-6 S 17 '65
Lysis of pleuropneumonia-like organisms by staphylococcal and streptococcal toxins. A. W. Bernheimer and M. Davidson. bibliog il Science 148:1229-31 My 28 '65
Staph resists antibiotics. Sci N L 87:69 Ja 30 '65
Staphylolytic substance from a species of pseudomonas. J. W. Zyskind and others. bibliog il Science 147:1458-9 Mr 19 '65
Temperature-sensitive repression of staphylococcal penicillinase. S. Cohen and others. bibliog il Science 149:877-9 Ag 20 '65
STAPLES, James T.
First rain; poem. Nat Parks Mag 39:15 S '65
STAPLES, Richard C. and others
Heat stabilities of acid phosphatases from pinto bean leaves. bibliog Science 149:1248-9 S 10 '65
STAPLES, Roebuck, family
First family of gospel; Staple singers. il Ebony 20:79-81+ S '65
STAPLES and stapling machines
Staple guns. il Consumer Rep 30:448-52 S '65
STAR, Kansas City. See Kansas City star

STATE and individual. See Individual and state
STATE and industry. See Industry and state
STATE and libraries. See Libraries and state
STATE and local relations
State and local government participation in the design and administration of intergovernmental programs. C. R. Adrian. bibliog f Ann Am Acad 359:35-43 My '65
STATE and municipal relations
Conflict and co-operation among local governments in the metropolis. W. W. Crouch. bibliog f Ann Am Acad 359:60-70 My '65
Etiquette lessons; case of political reporter, W. Kovach vs. Tennessee state Senate. Newsweek 65:62 Mr 8 '65
National-state-local systems of government and intergovernmental aid. A. K. Campbell. bibliog f il Ann Am Acad 359:94-106 My '65
STATE and music. See Music and state
STATE and science. See Science and state
STATE and the church. See Church and state
STATE and theater. See Theater and state
STATE banks. See Banks and banking—United States
STATE bonds
As states woo new industries. U S News 58:108 Ap 26 '65
Voters O.K. 70 per cent of bond issues. Bsns W p 160 N 6 '65
STATE colleges. See Colleges and universities, State
STATE control of education. See Education and state
STATE department (United States) See United States—State, Department of
STATE departments of education. See Education, State departments of
STATE election laws. See Election laws—United States
STATE elections. See Elections—United States
STATE employees
Merit controls, the Hatch acts, and personnel standards in intergovernmental relations. H. W. Reynolds, jr. bibliog f Ann Am Acad 359:81-93 My '65
STATE encouragement of science, literature and art
Federal foundations for arts & humanities; condensation of testimony before Senate subcommittee. D. Lacy. Pub W 187:14-18 Mr 29 '65
Ferment for public support of the arts and humanities. R. H. Smith. Pub W 187:42 Mr 15 '65
LBJ pushes photography in his first 365 days; symposium. il Pop Phot 57:58-60+ N '65
Now being human is an art. F. Morley. il Nations Bsns 53:27-8 S '65
Recreation, government, and the arts. J. Prendergast. il Recreation 58:377 O '65
Stuart Davis in memoriam. F. Getlein. New Repub 153:36-7 Jl 24 '65
This culture boom: how real is it? il Changing T 19:37-40 O '65
See also
White House festival of the arts, 1965

Ethiopia
Ethiopian artist extols his land; government support pays off. il Ebony 20:90-2+ Je '65

STATE fairs. See Agricultural exhibitions
STATE farms. See Collective farms
STATE finance
No-strings federal aid finds backers at forum; Heller plan, supported at ABA symposium. il Bsns W p28-9 Ap 3 '65
State-local finances. R. Moley. Newsweek 65:100 My 3 '65
See also
Taxation, State
STATE flowers
Your state flower: forget-me-not, Alaska. L. Krelove. Flower Grower 52:45 Ag '65
Your state flower: Indian paint-brush Wyoming. L. Krelove. Flower Grower 52:38 Jl '65
Your state flower: sagebrush, Nevada. L. Krelove. il Flower Grower 52:39 Je '65
STATE forests. See Forests, State
STATE governments
Interstate relations, some emergent trends. P. Monypenny. bibliog f Ann Am Acad 359:53-9 My '65
New era ahead for your state. T. Sanford. il Nations Bsns 53:56-8+ Jl '65
STATE historical society libraries. See Historical libraries

STATE institutions
They speed up slow minds; Connecticut's Seaside regional center for mentally retarded. S. Schuler. Todays Health 44:40-1+ Ja 66; Same. Read Digest 88:177-80 Ja '66
Where toys are locked away; Senator R. F. Kennedy's indictment of New York state's institutions for mentally retarded children. Christian Cent 82:1179 S 29 '65
See also
Mentally ill—Care and treatment
STATE laws, Uniform. See Uniform state laws
STATE legislatures
I spent a winter in politics; confessions of farmer. S. Bledsoe. il Farm J 90:38+ Ja '66
One-man, one-vote rule. W. Lippmann. Newsweek 65:33 My 10 '65
Our horse-and-buggy state legislatures. J. N. Miller. Read Digest 86:49-54 My '65
Sick state of the state legislatures. il Newsweek 65:29-32 Ap 19 '65
See also subhead Legislature under names of states, e.g. Maine—Legislature
STATE medicine. See Medical service, State
STATE ownership. See Government ownership
STATE parks and reserves
See also subhead Parks and reserves under names of states, e.g. Indiana—Parks and reserves
STATE police. See Police, State
STATE regulation of industry. See Industry and state
STATE rights
See also
Federal and state relations
STATE senators. See Senators
STATE taxation. See Taxation, State
STATE technical services, Office of. See United States—Commerce, Department of
STATE trees
Trees for the states. R. M. Pierce. il Am For 71:4-5+ Ap '65
STATE tuition grants. See College students—Aid
STATE universities. See Colleges and universities, State
STATE university of New York. See New York state university
STATEN ISLAND
Split-level compact for economy; Doctors hospital. il Arch Rec 137:180 F '65
Staten Island I love you. D. Powell. il Esquire 64:120-5 O '65
STATES (United States)
Chart of the fifty states (cont) Sr Schol 87:23-4 S 30 '65
STATES, New
New nations: the problem of political development; symposium, ed. by K. Von Vorys. bibliog f il Ann Am Acad 358:1-179 Mr '65
See also
Underdeveloped areas
STATESMEN
Arab unity: the cast of characters. pors Sr Schol 86:15-16 My 6 '65
Forgotten founding fathers. A. Mongin. il Antiques 88:516-21 O '65
Men involved in peace-talk proposals? il U S News 58:14 Mr 8 '65
See also
Heads of state
STATION masters
Faces from the past. R. M. Ketchum. il Am Heritage 16:60-1 Ap '65
STATION wagons
Four-wheel drives; they're great in the boondocks; Ford's new Bronco and Wagoneer. A. Markovich. il Pop Mech 124:104-5+ O '65
1966 station wagons. il Changing T 19:12 D '65
Spotlight on Dodge's new fastback; four-seater Dodge Charger. J. Dunne. il Pop Mech 125:42+ Ja '66
Station wagons; review of 1965's offerings. il Consumer Rep 30:302-9 Je '65

Testing
Test-driving the big three station wagons; Plymouth; Chevrolet; Ford. J. P. Norbye. il Pop Sci 186:88-92+ My '65
STATIONERY
Monogramming R for writing paper. il House & Gard 127:150-1 My '65
Vivid riposite. il Vogue 146:250-3 O 1 '65
Writing a letter? il Seventeen 24:166 S '65
STATIONMASTERS. See Station masters
STATIONS in space. See Space stations
STATISM
1965: age of the shrug; or, age of decision; address, November 9, 1965. R. M. Besse. Vital Speeches 32:154-8 D 15 '65

STATISTICAL commission of the United Nations. See United Nations—Statistical commission

STATISTICS
How do you figure? questions and answers. J. Daugherty and M. Daugherty. il Sci Digest 57:95-7 F '65
Not so vital statistics; comp. by H. Helfer (cont) il N Y Times Mag p38 Ap 18; 74 My 16 '65
  See also subhead Statistics under various subjects, and names of countries, e.g. Baseball—Statistics; United States—Statistics

Study and teaching
Writing unit on statistics. S. Cochell. Sr Schol 86:8T F 11 '65

STATUES
  See also
  Portrait sculpture
STATUES taken down; story. See Gallant, M.

STATUETTES. See Figurines

STATURE
How to grow tall. il Sci Digest 57:17-19 Je '65

STATUS (periodical)
Brave new entries. Newsweek 66:72 O 11 '65
Status cymbal. M. Mannes. New Repub 153:12 D 18 '65

STATUS of women, Commission on the. See United Nations—Commission on the status of women

STATUTE of limitations. See Limitation of actions

STAUFFER, Karl W. See Teichert, C. jt. auth.

STAUFFER chemical company
Stauffer board meeting moves south of border; to Mexico City. il Bsns W p112-14 F 6 '65

STEAD, Christina
Huntress; story. Sat Eve Post 238:76-8 O 23 '65
Man who loved children; excerpt from introduction to C. Stead's Man who loved children. R. Jarrell. Atlan 215:166-71 Mr '65
Marx as muse. J. Yglesias. Nation 200:368-70 Ap 5 '65

STEAKLEY, Melvin
Shot in the dark. il Time 85:50 My 14 '65

STEALING
Beware the outboard thief! B. Whittier. il Yachting 118:53 S '65
Cartnappers; theft of supermarket shopping carts. Newsweek 65:109-10 Ap 12 '65
Controlling pilferage in the college store. Pub W 187:67-8 Je 14 '65
Gold of Naples. il Time 85:25B-26 Mr 12 '65
Robbing Peter; theft of Vatican treasures. il Newsweek 66:59 D 6 '65
  See also
  Animal stealing
  Art thefts
  Book thefts
  Burglary and burglars
  Embezzlement
  Shoplifting

STEAM, Natural
Now we're drilling for steam; discovery of geothermal energy in the Salton Sea. J. L. Parker. il Sci Digest 57:78-80 F '65

STEAM automobiles. See Automobiles, Steam

STEAM baths. See Baths, Vapor

STEAM boilers. See Boilers

STEAM carriages
  See also
  Automobiles, Steam

STEAM engines
  See also
  Locomotives

STEAM locomotives. See Locomotives

STEAM turbines
Make a model Tesla turbine. W. E. Burton. il Pop Mech 124:188-93 S '65

STEAMER routes. See Ocean travel

STEAMSHIP lines
Italian beauty's maiden voyage: Michelangelo. F. Kappler. il Life 58:109-10 Je 18 '65
South American cruise; Moore-McCormack luxury cruise. T. B. Lesure. il Travel 124:28-32+ N '65
  See also
  Cunard steamship company
  Ocean liners

STEAMSHIPS and steamboats
  See also
  Ocean liners
  Ocean travel

STEARNS, Charles M.
It's the crew that kills you! Yachting 117:52+ F '65

STEBBINS, Doris E.
Blue grows the iris. Pop Gard 16:28-9 My '65
Try something different. Pop Gard 16:14-15+ N '65

STEBBINS, Robert L.
How to save uprooted trees. il Farm J 89:67 Mr '65

STECHOW, Wolfgang
Terbrugghen in America. Art N 64:46-51+ O '65

STECK-Vaughn company
Learning core. H. F. Teague. Wilson Lib Bul 40:60 S '65

STEDMAN, Jane W.
Fiddling devil. Opera N 29:14-16 F 27 '65
Ramerrez rides again. Opera N 30:6-7 Ja 8 '66

STEEGMULLER, Francis
System. New Yorker 41:181-4 Mr 13 '65

STEEL, Ronald
Bonn, the morning after. Commonweal 83:55-7 O 15 '65
Book reviews: politics; at home and abroad. Sr Schol 86:sup 13 Ap 1 '65
Books. Commonweal 83:104-6 O 22 '65
Can Germany be united? Commonweal 82:433-6 Je 25 '65
Cloaking the dagger. Commentary 39:87-9 Mr '65

STEEL
Marketing
How steel widens its targets; promotes offbeat uses. il Bsns W p 119-20+ Mr 27 '65

Prices
After the steel settlement. B. L. Masse. America 114:137-9 Ja 22 '66
Big steel ups prices but avoids a row. il Bsns W p28-9 Ja 8 '66
Bitter fruit. Newsweek 66:56 Ag 2 '65
LBJ vs. steel: negotiated peace. il Newsweek 67:69-70 Ja 17 '66
New yardstick for export prices; National bureau of economic research report: International price competitiveness. il Bsns W p74+ Jl 10 '65
Price fight. il Time 87:77-8 Ja 14 '66
Price-fixing verdict. Time 86:63A Jl 30 '65
Price rise. Time 87:81 Ja 7 '66
Steel-price dispute: a lesson for business. U S News 60:88-9 Ja 17 '66
Why they buy abroad; Fordham's price study. il Bsns W p34 My 22 '65

Strength
What you need to know about special steels. Suc Farm 64:88 Ja '66

STEEL, Stainless
Oil from the medicine cabinet; oil for titanium and steel. Time 86:84 D 3 '65
Stainless steel surprises. E. Kopecki. il Motor B 115:56-9 My '65

STEEL bands. See Bands (music)

STEEL bridges. See Bridges, Iron and steel

STEEL castings
Hard rider with a feel for timing; I. Rossi, promoter of continuous steel casting. il Bsns W p 188-90+ My 15 '65
  See also
  Armco steel corporation
  Steel ingots

STEEL construction
Welded apartment framing cuts costs. H. Allison. il Arch Rec 138:223-6 S '65
  See also
  Bridges, Iron and steel

STEEL doors. See Doors

STEEL framing. See Framing (building)

STEEL industry and trade
Race to the seacoasts; revolution in economics and geography. il Time 85:88+ Je 18 '65
  See also
  Rolling mills

Finance
Steel: no longer the bellwether? R. Lekachman. il Duns R 85:56-7+ Ap '65

International aspects
New yardstick for export prices; National bureau of economic research report: International price competitiveness. il Bsns W p74+ Jl 10 '65
Steel feels weight of global surplus. il Bsns W p31-2 N 27 '65

Wages and hours
Earnings in fabricated structural steel, 1964. C. M. O'Connor. il Mo Labor R 88:1219-22 O '65
Growing attack on steel report; Council of economic advisers. U S News 58:87 My 24 '65

STEEL industry and trade—*Continued*
Is White House backing union in dispute over steel wages? summary of report by Council of economic advisers. U S News 58:92 My 17 '65
Raises vs. jobs: an industry view. U S News 59:92 D 13 '65
Steel company answers the White House on wages; Republic steel corporation; excerpts from report. J. Backman. U S News 59:77 Ag 16 '65
Steel ready for action; contract talks to move to money issues. Bsns W p46 Jl 24 '65
Steel tightens belt, chafes at cost pinch. Bsns W p38 O 16 '65
Wage chronology: United States steel corp; 1960-64. J. Griest. il Mo Labor R 88:178-89 F '65
See also
Collective bargaining—Steel industry

Europe, Western
Hard times for steel. il Time 86:98 D 3 '65
See also
European coal and steel community

Germany (Federal Republic)
West Germany's Ruhr: coal, steel, and trouble. il U S News 58:80-1 Mr 8 '65

Great Britain
As Britain moves to take over steel. il U S News 58:95 My 17 '65
Can Wilson win fight on steel? nationalization of steel. Bsns W p36 My 8 '65
Gamble in steel; vote on proposals for renationalization. Newsweek 65:52+ My 17 '65
Labor's bid for steel. Newsweek 65:92 My 10 '65
Letter from London; steel debate in the House of commons. M. Panter-Downes. New Yorker 41:123-5 My 22 '65
Listener: proposed nationalization of the steel industry. il Time 85:36 My 14 '65
Nationalizing steel. America 112:703-4 My 15 '65
Steel gauntlet. Time 85:39-40 My 7 '65
Steel nationalization is not around the corner. B. Wenham. New Repub 152:9-10 My 22 '65
Steel no more. Time 86:46 N 19 '65

United States
After the steel settlement. B. L. Masse. America 114:137-9 Ja 22 '66
Booming steel has little left for hedge. il Bsns W p45-6 F 20 '65
Chances now for a steel strike. U S News 58:91-3 Ap 5 '65
Chaotic antitrust. H. Hazlitt. Newsweek 66:73 Ag 16 '65
Closer to a strike? Newsweek 65:73 My 3 '65
CEA report on steel prices; excerpt. Mo Labor R 88:673-4 Je '65
Cyclical steels. il Duns R 86:71-3 Jl '65
Effect of the mere threat of a strike in steel. il U S News 58:91-3 Mr 22 '65
Four-month truce in steel; what it will mean. il U S News 58:89-90 My 10 '65
How steel widens its targets; promotes offbeat uses. il Bsns W p 119-20+ Mr 27 '65
Latest big wrinkle in steel; portfolio. Fortune 72:159-63 S '65
LBJ vs. steel: negotiated peace. il Newsweek 67:69-70 Ja 17 '66
Man steel is watching; I. W. Abel. Bsns W p48+ Mr 27 '65
New guide for bargaining in steel; study by Council of economic advisers. Bsns W p202 My 15 '65
Next threat is in steel. il Bsns W p23 F 20 '65
Pacesetter's pace; falling orders, shrinking inventories, rising prices? il Time 86:113-14 S 17 '65
Pressure on prices; concerning President's council for economic advisers report. Newsweek 65:74 My 17 '65
Questions to debate; report on findings of a four-month study. il Time 85:91 My 14 '65
Real price of steel peace; here's industry's view. il U S News 59:92-4 S 20 '65
Relieved of a burden; steel settlement. Time 85:91 My 7 '65
Resurgence in Bunyan country; taconite boom. il Time 86:105 O 22 '65
Should steel build a new yardstick? controversy over ingot capacity. Bsns W p 124+ F 6 '65
Steel as scapegoat. H. Hazlitt. Newsweek 65:92 My 24 '65
Steel gets a report without frosting; CEA urges price stability. il Bsns W p26-7 My 8 '65

Steel makes peace with Justice. Bsns W p 18-19 Jl 31 '65
Steel negotiators get down to brass tacks. Bsns W p55-6 Je 19 '65
Steel-pact effects: in second month. U S News 59:93 N 1 '65
Steel pins its hopes on contract extension. Bsns Wp25 Ap 17 '65
Steel reprieve bolsters the boom. il Newsweek 65:83-4 My 10 '65
Steel sees little lag in tempo during '66. il Bsns W p27-8 D 18 '65
Steel settlement: now the protests; excerpts from statements. L. B. Worthington; A. S. Glossbrenner. U S News 59:113 O 11 '65
Steel takes stock, stays on cheerful side; AISI meeting. il Bsns W p30-1 Je 5 '65
Steel tightens belt, chafes at cost pinch. Bsns W p38 O 16 '65
Steel turns to the Midwest, back of big expansion. il U S News 59:101-3 Jl 19 '65
Steel's pace set to taper off. Bsns W p22-3 My 1 '65
Streamlining. Newsweek 66:64 Ag 30 '65
Toward the steel deadline. il Time 85:95 Ap 30 '65
USW closes ranks against the industry; bargaining impossible because of McDonald-Abel split. Bsns W p 30 Ap 24 '65
Whatever happened to Lukens steel? small company thriving among the giants. il Duns R 86:39+ Jl '65
Why they buy abroad; Fordham's price study. il Bsns W p34 My 22 '65
See also
Collective bargaining—Steel industry
Strikes—United States—Steel industry and trade
United steelworkers of America
STEEL ingots
Should steel build a new yardstick? controversy over ingot capacity. Bsns W p 124+ F 6 '65
STEEL scrap. See Scrap metal
STEEL strikes. See Strikes—United States—Steel industry and trade
STEEL workers
See also
Steel industry and trade—Wages and hours
United steelworkers of America
STEEL works
See also
Jones and Laughlin steel corporation
Rolling mills
STEELE, Arthur J.
Selecting the proper fuse. Electr World 74:28-30+ Ag '65
STEELE, Emmett
Champagne case. por Time 85:103 Ap 30 '65
Get it in writing. Newsweek 65:78-9 My 3 '65
STEELE, John
Coming up seventy-five, all roses for Ike. Life 59:49-50+ S 24 '65
STEELE, Max
From the French quarter; story. Esquire 64:109-10 N '65
STEELE, Tommy
Boy of Bermondsey. New Yorker 41:32-4 Je 12 '65
Cockney star bounces in; from rock'n'roll to Broadway. il pors Life 59:45-6+ Jl 2 '65
STEELE, William O.
Reader as eye-witness of the past. Writer 78:15-16+ Mr '65
STEELMAN, Julien R.
Koehring co. digs out its share. il pors Bsns W p 148-50 D 4 '65
STEELWORKERS union. See United steelworkers of America
STEEN, Virginia C. and Fryxell, Roald
Mazama and Glacier Peak pummice glass: uniformity of refractive index after weathering. bibliog Science 150:878-80 N 12 '65
STEER, Margery W.
(ed) See Blake, J. L. Parson Blake and the farmer's wife
STEER wrestling. See Rodeos
STEERE, William C.
Climate and plants. Horticulture 43:26-7+ F '65
about
Antarcticana. New Yorker 41:33-4 Je 5 '65
STEERING gear, Automobile. See Automobiles—Steering gear
STEEVENS, George Washington
When Churchill was twenty-three. Atlan 215:63-4 Mr '65
STEGNER, Wallace
Good-bye to all t—t! Atlan 215:119 Mr '65
Myths of the western dam. Sat R 48:29-31 O 23 '65
What ever happened to the great outdoors? Sat R 48:37-8+ My 22 '65

STEHLI, F. G.
Paleontologic technique for defining ancient ocean currents. bibliog Science 148:943-6 My 14 '65

STEIF, William
Why the copyright law needs revision. Sat R 48:126-8 S 18 '65

STEIGER, R. H. See Tilton, G. R. jt. auth.

STEIGER, Rod
Beauty and the beast; ed. by A. Guerin. il pors Life 59:45-6+ O 29 '65

STEIN, Emanuel
Unions and their members. Cur Hist 49:23-8+ Jl '65

STEIN, Gerald
Milk is good for skinny kids; story. Redbook 126:62-3 D '65

STEIN, Gertrude
About Four saints. V. Thomson. Am Rec G 31:520-1 F '65

STEIN, Richard S. See Rowell, R. L. jt. auth.

STEIN, Ruth
Books for developing countries. Sr Schol 86:sup 14 My 20 '65

STEINBACH, T. B. See Grey, S. jt. auth.

STEINBECK, John
Then my arm glassed up. por Sports Illus 23:94-6+ D 20 '65

about

Letters from Steinbeck. Newsweek 66:68 N 22 '65

STEINBERG, Alfred
How to build a better body. Read Digest 86:102-5 Mr '65

STEINBERG, Leo
BB as collector. Harper 230:154-6 Mr '65

STEINBERG, Michael
Special repertoire in a special way. Hi Fi 15:125 Ag '65

STEINBERG, Rafael
Hiroshima: in a flash it was gone. Sat Eve Post 238:28-35 Ag 14 '65

STEINBERG, Saul
Straight from the hand and mouth of Steinberg; excerpts from New world; with interview. ed. by J. Vanden Heuvel. il Life 59:59-60+ D 10 '65

about

Steinberg and the others. R. Lynes. il Harper 231:30+ D '65

STEINBERG, Sheldon S.
Formula for beating cancer. Todays Health 43:36-7+ Ap '65

STEINBERG, William
Early days with Klemperer. por Sat R 48:47-8+ My 29 '65
High-voltage conductor; interview. ed. by Q. Eaton. por Opera N 29:11 Mr 20 '65

STEINBICKER, Earl
Lighting on the run. il Pop Phot 57:156-7+ N '65
Stamp out the enemies of 35-mm. Pop Phot 57:76-7+ Ag '65

STEINBICKER, William
Flash is easier on, but take it off! Mod Phot 29:107 Je '65

STEINBRECHER, Herbert
Operation air bubble. il por Newsweek 65:79 Ap 19 '65

STEINDLER, E. M.
Nature's built-in clocks. Todays Health 43:48-53+ N '65

STEINEM, Gloria
Gernreich's progress; or, Eve unbound. N Y Times Mag p 18-22+ Ja 31 '65
Ins and outs of pop culture. Life 59:72-3+ Ag 20 '65
Julie Andrews. Vogue 145:124-5+ Mr 15 '65
She will not vegetate in Gracie mansion. N Y Times Mag p22-3+ Ja 9 '66
What's in it for me. Harper 231:169-70 N '65

about

News girl. il por Newsweek 65:98-9 My 10 '65

STEINER, Ena. See Steiner, R. jt. auth.

STEINER, George
Dying is an art. Reporter 33:51-4 O 7 '65
Kind of survivor. Commentary 39:32-8 F '65

STEINER, Rudolf, and Steiner, Ena
Arnold Schönberg: an unknown correspondence. Sat R 48:47-9+ Mr 27 '65

STEINFELS, Peter
Peace and reality. Commonweal 81:785-6 Mr 19 '65

STEINHART, J. S. See Hart, S. R. jt. auth.

STEINMAN, Gary, and others
Dicyandiamide possible role in peptide synthesis during chemical evolution. bibliog Science 147:1574 Mr 26 '65

STEINMANN, Marion
Future jobs for the beam. Life 59:73 Jl 9 '65
Wormholes in the map fill a big gap in Norse history. Life 59:65 O 22 '65

STEINMETZ, Charles Proteus
Thunderer's legacy; with report by A. Rosenfeld. il pors Life 58:53-4+ Ap 23 '65

STELLAR atmospheres. See Stars—Atmospheres

STELLAR eclipses. See Eclipses, Stellar

STELLAR inertial Doppler system. See Inertial guidance systems

STELLAR-inertial guidance systems. See Inertial guidance systems

STELLAR spectroscopy. See Spectrum analysis

STELOFF, Frances
Wise men fish here: the story of Frances Steloff and the Gotham book mart. by W. G. Rogers. Review
Sat R 48:31 F '65. W. Bower

STEM rust. See Rusts (botany)

STEMKE, G. W. and Fischer, R. J.
Rabbit 19S antibodies with allotypic specificities of the a-locus group. bibliog Science 150:1298+ D 3 '65

STENCHES. See Odors

STENCIL work
See also
Silk screen printing

STENDHAL, pseud. See Beyle, M. H.

STENGEL, Casey
Exit the genius-clown. il pors Time 86:91 S 10 '65
Last angry old man. E. Linn. il pors Sat Eve Post 238:75-8 Jl 31 '65
Lively one; celebrating 75th birthday in Roosevelt hospital. il por Newsweek 66:71-2 Ag 9 '65
You could look it up. il pors Newsweek 66:58 S 13 '65

STENGEL, Charles Dillon. See Stengel, C.

STENNIS, John Cornelius
Stripped & shortchanged. il por Time 86:16 Ag 13 '65

STENT, Gunther S.
1965 Nobel laureates in medicine or physiology. Science 150:462-4 O 22 '65

STÉNUIT, Robert
Deepest days. pors Nat Geog Mag 127:534-47 Ap '65

STEP stools. See Stools

STEPANCHEV, Stephen
Philosopher; poem. Nation 200:508 My 10 '65

STEPHANIE Marie Elisabeth, princess of Monaco
New princess in Monaco. il pors Look 29:43-8 Je 1 '65

STEPHANIE, Sister Mary. See Mary Stephanie, Sister

STEPHANOPOULOS, Stephanos
Government at last. il por Time 86:43 O 1 '65

STEPHEN, king of England
William of Malmesbury's Robert of Gloucester: a re-evaluation of the Historia novella. R. B. Patterson. bibliog f il Am Hist R 70:983-97 Jl '65

STEPHEN of Blois. See Stephen, king of England

STEPHEN, Edith
Edith Stephen dance company, 41st street theater. J. Maskey. Dance Mag 39:61+ Je '65

STEPHEN, John
Minneapolis mods. I. Bauer. il por Look 29:M7-11 N 30 '65
Will U.S. males turn into mods? il por Bsns W p74-6 Ag 28 '65

STEPHENS, Donald
More cracks in Malaysia. D. Warner. il Reporter 33:40-2 O 7 '65

STEPHENS, Olin J. 2d
IYRU design competition winners. Yachting 117:54-5+ Mr '65

about

Designer for all seasons. Sports Illus 23:8 Ag 9 '65

STEPHENS, Roderick, Jr
Tuning a twelve-meter. Yachting 117:48-50+ Mr; 80-1+ Ap '65

STEPHENS, William M.
Art of fish watching; adaptation of paper. Yachting 117:156+ Je '65

STEPHENSON, D. A. See Perrotta, A. J. jt. auth.

STEPPARENTS
Can a man learn to love a stepson? il Good H 161:14+ Ag '65
Six on a honeymoon. A. Lee. il Parents Mag 41:42-3+ Ja '66

STEPPING stones. See Garden walks

STEREO amplifiers. See Amplifiers

STEREO broadcasting. See Radio broadcasting

STEREO cartridges. See Phonograph—Stereophonic pickup

STEREO loud speakers. See Loud speaking apparatus

STEREOPHONIC pickup. See Phonograph—Stereophonic pickup

STEREOPHONIC recorders. See Magnetic recorders and recording—Stereophonic recorders

STEREOPHONIC sound systems
British audio establishment. N. Eisenberg. il Hi Fi 15:56–60+ Ap '65
Extension speakers. L. Buckwalter. il Hi Fi 15:70–3 Mr '65
Portfolio of stereo décor, 1965. il Hi Fi 15:54–61 Mr '65
Stereo or hi-fi? E. Villchur. il Am Rec G 31:596–8 Mr '65
   See also
Sound—Stereophonic recording and reproducing

STEREOPHOTOGRAPHY
Can you see the moon in 3-D? L. Mallan. il Pop Phot 57:52–5 S '65
Meanwhile, back on earth, where's 3-D today? C. Burger. il Pop Phot 57:56–9+ S '65
New 3-D photo allows looking behind objects. Sci N L 87:153 Mr 6 '65
3-D updated. P. Farber. il U S Camera 29:46–7+ Ja '66
True 3-D image from laser photography. E. N. Leith and J. Upatnieks. il Electr World 74:34–5+ O '65

STEREOSCOPIC cameras. See Cameras

STEREOSCOPY
Visual contours in homogeneous space. T. Shipley. bibliog il Science 150:348–50 O 15 '65

STEREOTYPE characters. See Characterization

STERILITY
High IQ and the small bosom: do they really go together? L. R. Chevalier. McCalls 92:87+ Mr '65
Those new fertility drugs. J. Robbins and J. Robbins. il Good H 160:88–9+ Mr '65

STERILITY, Induced. See Sterilization, Sexual

STERILITY in animals
Chromosome complement: differences between equus caballus and equus przewalskii. Poliakoff. K. Benirschke and others. bibliog il Science 148:382–3 Ap 16 '65
How to avoid sterility in your dairy cattle. Suc Farm 63:64D Je '65

STERILIZATION
   See also
Space vehicles—Sterilization

STERILIZATION, Sexual
Abortion and sterilization: the search for answers. W. Goodman. Redbook 125:70–1+ O '65
Response of the rabbit oviduct to a tissue adhesive. P. A. Corfman and others. bibliog il Science 148:1348–50 Je 4 '65

STERLING, Albert
Basics for the tape recordist. Hi Fi 15:43–50 Ag '65

STERLING, Claire
Africa's latest Caesar. Reporter 32:10–13 Je 3 '65
Franco's foes stop hoping. Reporter 32:33–6 F 25 '65
Italy's Catholic-Communist dialogue. Reporter 32:18–22 Ap 22 '65
Morocco's troubled young king. Reporter 32:21–5 Je 17 '65
Old man and the young Sabras. Reporter 33:35–8 N 4 '65
Serpentine politics in latter-day Eden. Reporter 33:30–2 D 30 '65

STERLING, Rupert
Soul of Antigua. F. E. Vasta. il por Negro Hist Bul 28:131+ Mr '65

STERLING, Suzy
Southern girl's diary of discovery. pors Look 29:107–13 Jl 13 '65

STERLING, Thomas
African encounter. Holiday 38:52–3+ Ag '65
Indian looks at Africa. Reporter 32:55+ Mr 25 '65
Landscape with mirages. Horizon 7:80–91 Autumn '65

STERLING airways. See Airlines—Denmark

STERLING and Francine Clark art institute, Williamstown, Mass.
Art library; Duveen library purchased from the Norton Simon foundation. il Am Artist 29:4+ D '65

Mr Anonymous. il Newsweek 66:78 Ag 16 '65
Silver for the dinner table. R. Davidson. il Antiques 88:158+ Ag '65

STERLING FOREST, N.Y.
Community for scientists. Am City 80:98–9 S '65

STERLING FOREST corporation
Community for scientists; Sterling Forest, N.Y. il Am City 80:98–9 S '65

STERLING silver. See Silverware

STERN, Albert
North Dakota runs down. Nation 201:41 Jl 19 '65

STERN, Bert
Marilyn Monroe. Pop Phot 58:139–40 Ja '66

STERN, Curt
Thoughts on research. Science 148:772–3 My 7 '65

STERN, Isaac
David and Isaac. Newsweek 65:102 My 10 '65
Music to my ears; performance of Beethoven's violin concerto with the Boston symphony. I. Kolodin. Sat R 48:24 F 6 '65
Profiles. J. Wechsberg. por(p49) New Yorker 41:58+ Je 5 '65

STERN, Joseph
Israeli illustrators, teacher discusses bookmaking; interview. il por Pub W 188:104–5 S 6 '65

STERN, Laurence
John J. Williams, watchdog of the Senate. Reporter 32:37–9 F 11 '65
Princefish comes into his own. Reporter 32:34–6 Mr 25 '65

STERN, Louis W. and Heskett, J. L.
Grass roots market research. bibliog f Harvard Bsns R 43:83–96 Mr '65

STERN, Philip M.
Open letter to the Ford foundation. Harper 232:83–7 Ja '66
Unexpected dividend for the South. Harper 230:66–72 My '65

STERN, Richard Martin
Turning point; story. Redbook 125:131–53 Je '65

STERN, Robbie
Turning the tables. M. Adler. il por U S Camera 28:50–1 Ag '65

STERN, T. Noel
Progress at Vermont state colleges. bibliog f Sch & Soc 93:267–9 My 1 '65

STERN drives. See Marine engines

STERNE, Joseph R. L.
Old guard returns. Reporter 32:28–30 F 11 '65

STERNE, Richard Clark
Nation and its century. bibliog Nation 201:42–53+ S 20 '65

STERNE, Thomas
Don't eat the rhododendrons. Am For 71:40–1+ Mr '65

STEROID hormones. See Hormones, Sex

STEROIDS
   See also
Testosterone
Triamcinolone

STEROLS
Sterols and temperature tolerance in the fungus pythium R., H. Haskins. bibliog Science 150:1615–16 D 17 '65
Unique sterol in the ecology and nutrition of drosophila pachea. W. B. Heed and H. W. Kircher. bibliog il Science 149:758–61 Ag 13 '65
   See also
Cholesterol

STESSIN, Lawrence
I spy becomes big business. N Y Times Mag p 105–6+ N 28 '65
They're not trying to succeed in business. N Y Times Mag p76+ Mr 28 '65

STETLER, David A. and Laetsch, W. M.
Kinetin-induced chloroplast maturatiton in cultures of tobacco tissue. bibliog Science 149:1387–8 S 17 '65

STETSON, Joe
(ed) Gun dogs. See issues of Field & stream

STEUBEN, Friedrich Wilhelm von
U.S. reaffirms interest in German unity in Von Steuben day message; text of President Johnson's message, September 25, 1965. L. B. Johnson. Dept State Bul 53:592 O 11 '65

STEVEN, William Pickford
Modern editor gets the boot. New Repub 153:8 S 25 '65
Successful, but sacked; editor of the Houston chronicle. por Time 86:79–80 S 17 '65

STEVENS, Clyde LoveJoy
On the eve of tomorrow; poem. Commonweal 81:763 Mr 12 '65

STEVENS, David
Magic lantern. Opera N 29:12-13 F 27 '65
STEVENS, Denis
Five-part harmony at Philharmonic Hall. Hi
Fi 16:136 Ja '66
Musical Yuletide in New York; concerts. Hi Fi
15:86H-86I Mr '65
STEVENS, Edwin D.
Do-it-yourself in Granby. Sat R 48:62-3 Jl
17 '65
STEVENS, Elisabeth
Rosenberg and his Tower of Babel. New
Repub 152:26-7 F 20 '65
STEVENS, Isaac Ingalls
Most satisfactory council; excerpts from Nez
Perce Indians and the opening of the
Northwest. A. M. Josephy, jr. il Am
Heritage 16:26-31+ O '65
STEVENS, J. P, and company
Labor drives to close the South's open shop;
illegal reprisals by Stevens company for
union activities. V. Rony. il Reporter 33:
31-4 N 18 '65
Union bid meets rebuff in South; North
Carolina vs AFL-CIO campaign. Bsns W
p 116 Mr 20 '65
STEVENS, James
Greenkeepers. por Am For 71:20-1+ D '65
STEVENS, Risë
At least 130 people in love; interview, ed. by
L. Lerman. por Mlle 61:146-7+ O '65
STEVENS, Roger L.
John F. Kennedy center for the performing
arts. Opera N 30:11-12 O 23 '65

about

Real conflict. Nation 201:234 O 18 '65
Roger and the rabbits. F. Getlein. New
Repub 152:25+ Ap 3 '65
STEVENS, Sylvester Kirby
Instant and judicial history. Life 59:4 Ag
13 '65
STEVENS, Thaddeus
Architects of Negro liberation. L. Bennett,
jr. il pors Ebony 20:123-6+ F '65
STEVENSON, Adlai Ewing
Adlai Stevenson's last article; outline for a
new American policy. pors Look 29:71-2+
Ag 24 '65
Congo question: position of the United States;
address, December 14, 1964. Vital Speeches
31:231-6 F 1 '65
Disarmament conference: United States posi-
tion; address. Vital Speeches 31:482-8 Je 1
'65
Fundamental meaning of the United Nations;
address, June 23, 1965. Vital Speeches 31:
615-17 Ag 1 '65
Grandmother Stevenson, elder stateswoman
of the PTA. PTA Mag 60:20-1 S '65
Hard kind of patriotism; reprint. Harper 231:
102 S '65
In quiet people there is vision and purpose;
sampling from speeches and writing. pors
Life 59:26-7 Jl 23 '65
Interdependence of nations; address, June 1,
1965. Vital Speeches 31:548-51 Jl 1 '65
Partnership in world affairs; address, June
17, 1965. Dept State Bul 53:123-8 Jl 19 '65
Principles of U.N.-OAS relationship in
Dominican Republic; statements, May 22
and May 24, 1965. Dept State Bul 52:975-80
Je 14 '65
Security council authorizes U.N. representa-
tive in Dominican Republic; statements,
May 3-5, 1965. bibliog f Dept State Bul 52:
869-85 My 31 '65
Security council renews mandate of Cyprus
peacekeeping force; statement, March 18,
1965. Dept State Bul 52:551-3 Ap 12 '65
Stevenson's last thoughts on world affairs;
ed. by J. Fromm. por U S News 59:46-7
Jl 26 '65
Strengthening the international development
institutions; statement, July 9, 1965. Dept
State Bul 53:142-51 Jl 26 '65; Same
with title International development. Vital
Speeches 31:610-15 Ag 1 '65
Twentieth anniversary of the United Nations;
address, June 26, 1965. Dept State Bul 53:
101-5 Jl 19 '65
U.N. asks all states to refrain from inter-
vention in Congo; address, December
30, 1964. Dept State Bul 52:118-20 Ja 25 '65
United Nations commemoration address,
June 26, 1965. UN Mo Chron 2:171-5 Jl '65
U.N. General assembly recesses; statements,
February 18, 1965. Dept State Bul 52:354-5
Mr 8 '65
U.N. Security council considers situation in
Dominican Republic; statements, May 19-
21, 1965. Dept State Bul 52:913-19 Je 7
'65

U.S. denounces Soviet circulation of note on
use of gas in Viet-Nam; letter, April 2,
1965. Dept State Bul 52:688 My 3 '65
U.S. expresses views on convening of U.N.
disarmament committee; statement. Dept
State Bul 52:601 Ap 19 '65
U.S. expresses views on Southern Rhodesian
independence in U.N. committee of 24 and
Security council; statement, May 5, 1965.
Dept State Bul 52:1063-6 Je 28 '65
U.S. letter to president of U.N. Security
council, February 7, 1965. Dept State Bul
52:240-1 F 22 '65
U.S. pledges funds to U.N. program for
training of South Africans; note, June 25,
1965. Dept State Bul 53:220-1 Ag 2 '65
U.S. reports to United Nations on ICY ac-
tivities; letter, May 20, 1965. Dept State
Bul 52:1067-9 Je 28 '65
United States reviews the U.N. constitutional
crisis; statement, January 26, 1965. Dept
State Bul 52:198-206 F 15 '65
U.S. submits report on Viet-Nam to U.N.
Security council; letter, February 27, 1965.
Dept State Bul 52:419 Mr 22 '65
U.S. submits to U.N. Security council OAS
documents on Dominican Republic; state-
ment, June 18, 1965. Dept State Bul 53:
132-5 Jl 19 '65
United States summarizes position on dis-
armament and arms control; statement,
April 26, 1965. bibliog f Dept State Bul 52:
762-74 My 17 '65
Why hold the line in Vietnam? Adlai Steven-
son's answer. por Newsweek 66:20 D 27 '65

about

Adlai, Adlai, what was the fifth word? E.
De Lanux. New Yorker 41:176+ S 25 '65
Adlai E. Stevenson, 1900-1965. E. Rabino-
witch. Bul Atomic Sci 21:2 S '65
Adlai E. Stevenson: voice for humanity. J.
Posada. por Américas 17:1-2 Ag '65
Adlai Stevenson. New Repub 153:5 Jl 24 '65
Adlai Stevenson. J. C. Cort. Commonweal
82:556-8 Ag 6 '65
Adlai Stevenson. R. H. Smith. Pub W 188:
35 Jl 26 '65
Adlai Stevenson of Illinois, 1900-1965. il pors
Newsweek 66:24-6+ Jl 26 '65
Adlai Stevenson: politician. D. O'Brien.
Christian Cent 82:1009-11 Ag 18 '65
Adlai Stevenson, RIP. Nat R 17:629-30 Jl 27
'65
Adlai Stevenson: successful also-ran. J. B.
Sheerin. Cath World 201:351-4 S '65
Atlantic report. Atlan 216:12 S '65
Bureau chief's memory of Stevenson; John
Steele recollections. G. P. Hunt. Life 59:3
Jl 23 '65
Eloquence stilled. por Sr Schol 87:20+ S 16
'65
Final troubled hours of Adlai Stevenson.
E. Sevareid. por Look 29:81-4+ N 30 '65
First gentleman of the world. Life 59:4 Jl
23 '65
Footnote on Adlai E. Stevenson. J. Fischer.
Harper 231:18+ N '65
Governor at work at the U.N. M. Mayer.
il pors N Y Times Mag p22-3+ F 7 '65
Graceful loser il pors Time 86:20-2 Jl 23 '65
He dignified our political dialogue. K. Nat-
war-Singh. il por Sat R 49:35 Ja 1 '66
Letter from London. M. Panter-Downes. New
Yorker 41:59 Jl 31 '65
Letter from Paris. Genêt. New Yorker 41:82
Ag 7 '65
Lonesome place against the sky. E. T.
Folliard. America 113:111 Jl 31 '65
Memories of A.E.S. N. Cousins. por Sat R
48:12-13+ Jl 31 '65
Notes and comment; review of career. New
Yorker 41:17-23 Jl 24 '65; Reply. S. Lippin-
cott. 41:101-3 Ag 21 '65
President Johnson and Secretary Rusk pay
tribute to Ambassador Stevenson; state-
ments, July 14, 1965. L. B. Johnson;
D. Rusk. Dept State Bul 53:229 Ag 9 '65
Rebuttal from the grave. Time 86:10 D 24 '65
Stevenson and ourselves. E. W. Thacker.
Christian Cent 82:993 Ag 11 '65
Stevenson: beachhead on world opinion.
Christian Cent 82:934 Jl 28 '65
Stevenson of Illinois. il pors Life 59:22-5+
Jl 23 '65
Stevenson, public servant. America 113:87 Jl
24 '65
Stevenson the politician. W. V. Shannon.
Commonweal 82:549-50 Ag 6 '65
Stevenson, tragedy and greatness. H. J. Mor-
genthau. New Repub 153:17-19 Ag 7 '65;
Reply. G. W. Johnson. 153:36+ Ag 21 '65
Tributes in the United Nations. il por UN
Mo Chron 2:54-8 Ag '65

STEVENSON, Adlai Ewing—about—*Continued*
United Nations holds memorial ceremony for
Ambassador Stevenson; remarks, July 19,
1965. Thant. Dept State Bul 53:226-30 Ag
9 '65
World remembers Adlai Stevenson; press trib-
utes. Sat R 48:43 Ag 21 '65
STEVENSON, Charles, and Gill, W. J.
Ordeal of Otto Otepka. Read Digest 87:55-9
Ag '65
—and Roper, J. E.
When the income-tax man looks over your
shoulder. Read Digest 86:49-50+ Ap '65
STEVENSON, Florence
Angel's roost. Opera N 29:14-16 Ap 17 '65
STEVENSON, Gordon
(ed) Music in libraries; symposium. bibliog
por Library J 90:1243-70 Mr 15 '65
Music in medium-sized libraries. por Li-
brary J 90:1255-8 Mr 15 '65
STEVENSON, Grace T.
Another tribute. C. W. Stone. ALA Bul 59:
238 Ap '65
Memo to members. D. H. Clift. ALA Bul
59:248-9 Ap '65
STEVENSON, James
Opening night. il Opera N 30:16-18 N 6 '65
STEVENSON, Letitia Green
Grandmother Stevenson, elder stateswoman
of the PTA. por PTA Mag 60:20-1 S '65
STEVENSON, Margaret, and Forman, E. Q.
Improvement of instruction. NEA J 54:28-9
My '65
STEVENSON, Robert P.
Shop talk. Pop Sci 186:137 Je; 187:131 Jl; 115
Ag; 141 O; 141 N; 119 D '65; 188:151 Ja '66
STEVENSON, W. B.
Hornsey goes long and low. Library J 90:
5215-17 D 1 '65
STEW
Magnificent half-hour stews; with recipes.
P. Cannon. il Ladies Home J 83:80-1 Ja
'66
Mystery of cioppino. il Sunset 134:100-1 Mr
'65
STEWARD, Hal D.
Right to know; letter. Sat R 48:29 Ap 17
'65
Route to magazine article sales. Writer 78:
19-21+ N '65
STEWARDESSES, Air. See Airlines—Host-
esses
STEWART, Bruce
Think big: open letter to the Secretary of the
Interior. Harper 231:62-3 Ag '65
STEWART, Charles E.
Count down to horror. Negro Hist Bul 29:17
O '65
STEWART, Cornelius
School and the Negro child. por Negro Hist
Bul 29:9-10 O '65
STEWART, Craig
Chicago street; poem. Christian Cent 82:1252
O 13 '65
STEWART, David C.
Celluloid syllabus. por Am Ed 1:29-32 S '65
Movies on the campus. Sat R 48:82-3 F 20 '65
Movies students make new wave on campus.
Harper 231:66-72 O '65
STEWART, David Marshall
Nashville respects tradition. Library J 90:
5167-9 D 1 '65
STEWART, Desmond
Turk who turned West. Nation 200:512 My 10
'65
STEWART, Donald
Ferry to Vermont; story. New Yorker 40:
26-7 Ja 30 '65
Forty; poem. New Yorker 41:160 Ap 10 '65
STEWART, Edward
Never let a cat go hungry; story. Ladies
Home J 82:58-9 S '65
STEWART, Ethelbert
Productivity of labor and industry; reprint
from March 1929 issue. Mo Labor R 88:793-4
Jl '65
STEWART, Evelyn Seeley
Do teenagers make good parents? Parents
Mag 40:46-9+ F '65
STEWART, J. George
Monster builder. il por Newsweek 66:41 O 11
'65
On guard, architect! Life 59:40D Jl 2 '65
STEWART, J. I. M.
Edinburgh boyhood. Holiday 38:60-71+ Ag '65
STEWART, Kenneth D. See Gifford, E. M. jr.
jt. auth.
STEWART, Mary
Airs above the ground; story. Good H 161:
59-63 Ag; 76-7 S '65
STEWART, Michael
Ironworker on high. il pors Ebony 20:64-6+
Mr '65

STEWART, Michael, 1906-
European political cooperation; address, Feb-
ruary 11, 1965. Vital Speeches 31:329-31 Mr
15 '65
STEWART, Natacha
Bottles; story. New Yorker 41:33-7 Jl 17 '65
Mack Sennett comedy. New Yorker 41:46-8
O 2 '65
STEWART, Paul
Gymnastics. Sports Illus 23:52-3 Jl 12 '65
Sport in which it pays to have the shorts.
Sports Illus 23:60+ D 13 '65
—See Morris, E. jt. auth.
STEWART, R. S.
Dr Zhivago: the making of a movie. Atlan
216:58-64 Ag '65
(ed) See Lerner, A. J. Sixth sense of Alan
Jay Lerner
STEWART, Robert
Forevers; poem. Commonweal 81:667 F 19 '65
STEWART, Robert H. See Whitmore, F. C.
jr, jt. auth.
STEWART, Sarah E. and others
Herpes-like virus isolated from neonatal and
fetal dogs. bibliog Science 148:1341-3 Je 4
'65
STEWART, Shan
Place to pot and putter. Pop Gard 17:12-13
Ja '66
STEWART, William Huffman
New Surgeon General. por Science 150:38 O
1 '65
New Surgeon General seeks high quality
staff. Sci N L 88:242 O 16 '65
STEWART-GORDON, James
Case of the durable detective. Read Digest
86:207-10 F '65
007-the spy with the golden touch. Read
Digest 87:113-17 O '65
Monte, test of toughness and technique.
Read Digest 87:137-41 D '65
Moss bros. suits the British. Read Digest
86:188-90+ Je '65
Tough old man in the saddle. Read Digest
87:19-20+ Jl '65
STEWS. See Stew
STEYSKAL, George C.
Trend curves of the rate of species de-
scription in zoology. bibliog Science 149:
880-2 Ag 20 '65
STICKLER, F. C.
What we learned about growing sorghum.
Suc Farm 63:82 My '65
STICKY my fingers, fleet my feet; story. See
Williams, G.
STIEVE, Helen
Can we keep on being neighborly? Farm J
89:C2 S '65
STILES, Martha Bennett
Sylvia's mother; story. Seventeen 24:142-3
O '65
STILL, C. C. and others
Inhibitory oxidation products of indole-3-
acetic acid: enzymic formation and detoxi-
fication by pea seedlings. bibliog Science
149:1249-51 S 10 '65
STILL life painting
Bottle; third grade project. M. Takach. il
Sch Arts 65:17-18 D '65
Object: still life; interview. C. Oldenburg. il
Craft Horiz 25:31-2+ S '65
See also
Trompe-l'oeil
STILL life photography. See Photography—
Still life
STILLINGER, Elizabeth
History in houses. Antiques 88:190-4 Ag '65
STILLWELL, Glen F.
Quick cures for sick recorders. Pop Electr
23:57-8+ D '65
STILLWELL, Rosalie H. See Lilly, D. M. jt.
auth.
STILWELL, Hart
Wings over the jungle. Field & S 70:116-18+
Jl '65
STIMPFLING, J. H. See Cudkowicz, G. jt.
auth.
STIMULUS and response
Adrenal response to fighting in mice: separa-
tion of physical and psychological causes.
F. H. Bronson and B. E. Eleftheriou. bib-
liog il Science 147:627-8 F 5 '65
Age, personality, and somatosensory cerebral
evoked responses. C. Shagass and M.
Schwartz. bibliog il Science 148:1359-61 Je
4 '65
Attenuation of aversive properties of peri-
pheral shock by hypothalamic stimulation.
V. C. Cox and E. S. Valenstein. bibliog il
Science 149:323-5 Jl 16 '65
Attitude and pupil size. E. H. Hess. il Sci
Am 212:46-54 Ap '65
Background and evoked activity in the audi-
tory pathway: effects of noise-shock pair-
ing. D. Galin. bibliog il Science 149:761-3
Ag 13 '65

STIMULUS and response—*Continued*
Brain catecholamines: relation to the defense reaction evoked by amygdaloid stimulation in cat. D. J. Reis and L.-M. Gunne. bibliog il Science 149:450-1 Jl 23 '65
Color adaptation of edge-detectors in the human visual system. C. McCollough. bibliog il Science 149:1115-16 S 3 '65
Evoked-potential correlates of stimulus uncertainty. S. Sutton and others. bibliog il Science 150:1187-8 N 26 '65
Evoked visual potentials and human color vision. T. Shipley and others. bibliog il Science 150:1162-4 N 26 '65
Galvanic skin reflex in newborn humans. D. H. Crowell and others. bibliog il Science 148:1108-11 My 21 '65
Geniculate unit responses to sine-wave photic stimulation during wakefulness and sleep. L. Maffei and others. bibliog il Science 149:563-4 Jl 30 '65
Increased activities of glycogenolytic enzymes in liver after splanchnic-nerve stimulation. T. Shimazu and A. Fukuda. bibliog il Science 150:1607-8 D 17 '65
Intracranial reinforcement compared with sugar-water reinforcement. W. E. Gibson and others. bibliog il Science 148:1357-9 Je 4 '65
Judgments of sameness and difference: experiments on decision time. D. Bindra and others. bibliog il Science 150:1625-7 D 17 '65
Lateral hypothalamic stimulation in satiated rats: T-Maze learning for food. J. Mendelson and S. L. Chorover. bibliog il Science 149:559-61 Jl 30 '65
Parkinsonism: electromyographic studies of monosynaptic reflex. M. Ioku and others. bibliog il Science 150:1472-5 D 10 '65
Perception of stroboscopic movement: evidence for its innate basis. I. Rock and others. bibliog Science 147:1050-2 F 26 '65
Photopic spectral sensitivity in the monkey: methods for determining, and initial results. N. A. Sidley and others. bibliog il Science 150:1837-9 D 31 '65
Prenatal auditory sensitivity in chickens and ducks. G. Gottlieb. bibliog il Science 147:1597-8 Mr 26 '65
Prolonged excitation in the visual cortex of the cat. C. R. Evans and A. D. J. Robertson. bibliog il Science 150:913-15 N 12 '65
Pupillary response of the screech owl, otus asio. L. G. Bishop and L. Stark. il Science 148:1750-2 Je 25 '65
Response of the pupil to steady-state retinal illumination: contribution by cones. J. ten Doesschate and M. Alpern. bibliog il Science 149:989-91 Ag 27 '65
Selective attentiveness and cortical evoked responses to visual and auditory stimuli. P. Spong and others. bibliog il Science 148:395-7 Ap 16 '65
Sequential behavior induced repeatedly by stimulation of the red nucleus in free monkeys. J. M. R. Delgado. bibliog il Science 148:1361-3 Je 4 '65
Visually evoked electrocortical responses in kittens: development of specific and nonspecific systems. G. H. Rose and D. B. Lindsley. bibliog il Science 148:1244-6 My 28 '65
STINCHCOMB, Bruce L. and others
Precambrian graphitic compressions of possible biologic origin from Canada. Science 148:75-6 Ap 2 '65
STINGLESS bees. See Bees
STINGS, Insect. See Insect bites and stings
STINNETT, Caskie
Speaking of travel. Holiday 39:16+ Ja '66
Under cover (cont) Ladies Home J 82:20+ F '65
STINNETT, Loni
First love, first heartbreak. McCalls 93:26+ O '65
STINNETT, T. M.
Helping teachers stand tall. NEA J 55:19 Ja '66
Million dollar fund for teacher rights. NEA J 54:38-9 O '65
STIRLING, Robert
Stirling refrigeration cycle. J. W. L. Köhler. il Sci Am 212:119-25+ bibliog(p 160) Ap '65
STITCHERY. See Embroidery
STIVENS, Dal
Going places, finding things in Australia. House & Gard 128:62-4+ O '65
Return of the mighty bison. Sci Digest 58:59-61 N '65
STIX, Baer and Fuller (store) See St Louis—Stores
STOCK, Dennis
Dennis Stock. P. Caulfield. il Mod Phot 29:66-9 S '65

STOCK, Jurgen
Site survey for the inter-American observatory in Chile. Science 148:1054-9 My 21 '65
STOCK averages. See Stocks—Price indexes and averages
STOCK brokers. See Brokers
STOCK-car racing. See Automobile racing
STOCK control (bookstores) See Booksellers and bookselling—Stock
STOCK dividends. See Dividends
STOCK exchange
Pros see clouds over the '66 market; opinions of investment analysts. il Bsns W p 14-15 Ja 1 '66
Those other exchanges; regional exchanges' growth. il Time 86:78+ S 3 '65
See also
Brokers
United States—Securities and exchange commission

Crisis, October 1929

Good-bye to everything! T. J. Fleming. il Am Heritage 16:88-95+ Ag '65
Yesteryear's grim lesson. Sr Schol 86:8 Ap 15 '65

Regulation

Big board sees antitrust shadow. Bsns W p 138+ Ap 3 '65
Big changes inside the stock market, and what they mean to you. il Changing T 19:15-20 Jl '65
Eleventh commandment? SEC still pushing reform. Newsweek 66:79+ D 13 '65
Fed holds the key on action; brokers look for trouble if Fed should tighten money. il Bsns W p 141-2 D 11 '65
SEC draws a bead on top men. Bsns W p 151 N 20 '65
Spotlight on margin trading; selective credit controls against speculators. Bsns W p98 D 18 '65
Toronto exchange cleans house; Sassoon swindle. Bsns W p 156+ Je 19 '65

Chicago

LaSalle Street runs to catch up. il Bsns W p 110-12+ Ap 3 '65

Los Angeles

Stock exchange action in L.A. il Sunset 134:71 Ap '65

New York (city)

Aiming higher. il Time 86:102 O 1 '65
Back to the blue chips. Time 85:87 Ap 23 '65
Big board sees antitrust shadow. Bsns W p 138+ Ap 3 '65
Bulls make a stand. il Bsns W p 15-16 Jl 3 '65
Buyers balk, waiting for a clear sign. il Bsns W p35 Je 12 '65
Compatible; automation of stock-quotation service. New Yorker 41:29-30 Je 12 '65
Crisis under control; reaction to events in Vietnam. Newsweek 65:84+ F 22 '65
Demand to delist. il Time 86:67 Ag 13 '65
Educating the investor. L. L. L. Golden. Sat R 48:74 O 9 '65
For market bears, every day is Halloween. il Bsns W p 154+ N 6 '65
Haze over brokers' fees. il Fortune 72:89-90 S '65
Here come the bears. Fortune 72:93 Ag '65
Instant quotes. il Time 85:88 Mr 12 '65
It's easier to win than to lose; U of Chicago study of stocks in 1926-60 period. il Bsns W p 118+ My 29 '65
Jolt to the stock market; how the experts see it. il U S News 58:120-1 Je 21 '65
Ladies' day; J. M. Walsh and P. S. Peterson approved by the Amex admissions committee. il Newsweek 66:88 N 22 '65
Market rides a roller coaster; result of W. M. Martin's disquieting remarks. il Bsns W p25-7 Je 19 '65
Market spooks itself; experts give views. il Life 58:35 Je 25 '65
Market, where the fireworks are. il Newsweek 66:15-16 Jl 12 '65
Martin market? Johnson market? il Newsweek 65:69 Je 21 '65
New kind of bull; new high plateau for trading activity. il Time 86:89 O 29 '65
Now for an encore; through the 900 mark. il Time 85:101 F 5 '65
One for the bulls; good week for Wall Street. il Time 86:87 Jl 9 '65
Out of the Garage; expansion plans. Newsweek 65:87 Ap 12 '65
Scent in the air; second big advance in as many weeks. Time 86:113 S 17 '65
Signs still point up, with a few go-slows. il Bsns W p92+ S 4 '65
Two-sided market. Time 86:100 D 10 '65

STOCK exchange—New York (city)—*Continued*
Wall Street: bears who walk like bulls; short sellers. il Newsweek 66:69 N 1 '65
Wall Street: booming prices, wary optimism. il Newsweek 66:78-9 O 11 '65
Wall Street heads for the West. il Bsns W p90+ Ag 28 '65
Wall Street: how to gauge the market? New York exchange considering own index. il Newsweek 67:75 Ja 24 '66
Wall Street: how to save on '65 losses. il Newsweek 66:85 N 22 '65
Wall Street puts its chips on a big year. il Bsns W p25-6 S 25 '65
Wall Street: sky's the limit, or is it? il Newsweek 66:83 N 8 '65
Wall St talks. See issues of Business week
Wall Street: the spell of splitting. il Newsweek 66:97 N 15 '65
Wall Street turns a little edgy. il Bsns W p25 Ap 3 '65
Wall St where capital changes hands. Sr Schol 86:18+ Ap 15 '65
Watching & waiting; market's uncertainty. Time 86:73 Jl 2 '65
Wavering bull. il Newsweek 65:76 Je 7 '65
What the stock market is saying; views of experts. il U S News 59:119-20+ O 25 '65
What went wrong in the market. U S News 58:86-7 Je 7 '65
What's ahead in stock market now; as experts see it; symposium. il U S News 58:44-50 Je 28 '65
Where are the bears of yesterday? il Newsweek 66:75 S 27 '65
Worries of Wall Street. il Newsweek 65:63+ Je 28 '65

Pacific coast
Wall Street heads for the West. il Bsns W p90+ Ag 28 '65

Rio de Janeiro
Out of chaos, order. Time 86:72 Ag 20 '65

Tokyo
Tokyo upsurge buoys Japan fund; closed-end investment company. il Bsns W p93-4+ D 18 '65
Why Tokyo stocks skid. il Bsns W p70+ Jl 3 '65

Toronto
Sasoon caper. Newsweek 65:70+ Je 28 '65
Toronto exchange cleans house; Sassoon swindle. Bsns W p 156+ Je 19 '65
STOCK exchange, American. See American stock exchange
STOCK margin requirements. See Stock exchange—Regulation
STOCK market. See Stock exchange
STOCK market charts. See Stocks—Price indexes and averages
STOCK tenders. See Stocks—Tender offers
STOCKDALE, Harold, and Gunderson, Harold
1965 dairy fly control guide. Suc Farm 63: 46-7 Je '65
STOCKHAUSEN, Karlheinz
Letter from Paris; performance of his Gruppen für drei orchester. Genêt. New Yorker 41:111-12 Je 12 '65
STOCKHOLDERS
Big blocks make more of a splash; growth of the institutional investor. il Bsns W p 110-12 Ja 15 '66
Educating the investor. L. L. L. Golden. Sat R 48:74 O 9 '65
Power of institutional investors. il Fortune 72:233+ D '65
20 million stockholders; who they are. il U S News 59:84 Jl 5 '65
Where is the big money? institutional investors. il Time 86:73-4 Jl 2 '65
Who's buying stocks now. il U S News 59: 101-2 N 29 '65
See also
Executives as stockholders
STOCKHOLDERS meetings
Clowns. il Time 85:98 Ap 30 '65
Into orbit & out of order; heckler expelled from Comsat's annual meeting. il Time 85:94 My 21 '65
Shushing the annual heckler. il Bsns W p 118+ My 22 '65
Where was I? il Newsweek 65:70+ My 3 '65
Will the annual meeting please come to order! S. Mahoney. il Fortune 71:140-2+ My '65
STOCKHOLM

City planning
Mathematical games; superellipse; answer to city-planning problem. M. Gardner. il Sci Am 213:222+ S '65
Stockholm: a planned city. G. Sidenbladh. il Sci Am 213:106-10+ S '65

Music
Nilsson's own Elektra. M. Mayer. Hi Fi 15: 134 Ag '65
Notes from our correspondents (cont) F. Hedman. Hi Fi 15:20+ Ag '65

Parks and playgrounds
Swedish modern. E. L. Weisman. il Recreation 58:163 Ap '65

Subways
Grandma Siri; art to decorate trains and stations. Newsweek 66:107-8 O 25 '65
STOCKHOLM festival. See Music festivals—Sweden
STOCKINGS. See Hosiery
STOCKLIN, William A.
For the record. See issues of Electronics world
STOCKMAN, Harry E.
Amateur scientist. Sci Am 213:112 O '65
STOCKMANN'S store. See Helsinki—Stores
STOCKPILING
Chinese hoard; London gold purchases. Newsweek 66:65 Ag 9 '65
What lies ahead for stockpiles? il Bsns W p 132+ D 4 '65
Why the lid will stay on prices for metals; stockpile sales. il Bsns W p32-3 N 27 '65
STOCKS
Buying strategy; promising stocks. il Duns R 86:77-9 Ag '65
Common stocks make the big difference. il Bsns W p 132+ Je 26 '65
Cyclical steels. il Duns R 86:71-3 Jl '65
How your stocks are really doing; with chart. Changing T 19:24-5 Ap '65
It's easier to win than to lose; U of Chicago study of stocks in 1926-60 period. il Bsns W p 118+ My 29 '65
New offerings perk up. il Bsns W p 134 Ap 3 '65
Should companies promote their own stocks? SEC investigates Genesco. C. J. Loomis. il Fortune 72:184-6+ D '65
Stocks the investment funds are buying now. il U S News 59:77-9 Ag 23 '65
Wall Street: which stocks to buy in '66? il Newsweek 67:54 Ja 10 '66
Wary now, bullish for later; corporate pension funds. il Bsns W p 160+ N 13 '65
Way officials size up stocks of their companies. il U S News 59:107-8 O 18 '65
What the new year holds for investors and savers. il U S News 60:78-80 Ja 10 '66
What's ahead in stock market now; as experts see it; symposium. il U S News 58:44-50 Je 28 '65
Without really trying; computer study made of movements of stock prices. Newsweek 65:66-7 My 31 '65
See also
Banks and banking—Securities
Bonds
Saving and savings
Stock exchange

Insider trading
Analysts run into a security blackout. il Bsns W p 142+ My 8 '65
New moves by government to protect investors. il U S News 58:96+ My 10 '65
SEC vs. Texas Gulf raises sticky questions; bonanza trouble; charges and issues at stake. C. Welles. il Life 59:29-30+ Ag 6 '65; Reply. C. O. Stephens. 59:19 Ag 13 '65

Marketing
Big blocks make more of a splash; growth of the institutional investor. il Bsns W p 110-12 Ja 15 '66
Over-the-counter revival. il Time 85:101 F 5 '65
Prohibiting stop orders. Fortune 72:236+ D '65

Price indexes and averages
As stocks pass 900; advice experts are giving to investors. il U S News 58:40-2 F 15 '65
Bear run? Newsweek 66:68 Jl 5 '65
Bumps along the way; higher margin rumor scotched. il Bsns W p27 O 2 '65
Buyers balk, waiting for a clear sign. il Bsns W p35 Je 12 '65
Can the average be improved? il Bsns W p 104+ Je 5 '65
Closer look at stock prices; with chart. il U S News 59:106-8 O 4 '65
Dow Jones: barometer of profits and confidence. il Sr Schol 86:22 Ap 8 '65
Dow Jones industrials, RIP. Nat R 17-580-1 Jl 13 '65
Eight stocks, their ups and downs. il Duns R 85:105-7 F '65

STOCKS—Price indexes and averages—*Cont.*
Executive investor; change in concept. il
Duns R 86:111-13 S '65
Fatter profits and slimmer margins. il News-
week 66:68 N 1 '65
Growth stocks again set pace. il Bsns W
p 169-70 S 18 '65
How much recovery for stocks? il Bsns W
p 114+ Jl 17 '65
How to buy stocks by the calendar. il Fortune
71:62 Mr '65
In stocks: still a bull market. il U S News
58:122-3 Ap 26 '65
Investors again see glow in growth stocks.
il Bsns W p 136+ Ap 3 '65
Investors overseas stay on the wary side.
il Bsns W p 114+ My 1 '65
Market crosses 900. Bsns W p 128 F 6 '65
Market rides a roller coaster; result of W. M.
Martin's disquieting remarks. il Bsns W
p25-7 Je 19 '65
Market, where the fireworks are. il Newsweek
66:15-16 Jl 12 '65
Not much gain in the picture; with table.
Bsns W p 108 N 27 '65
On toward 1000; Dow-Jones industrial average
breaks its own alltime records. Time 87:78
Ja 14 '66
Outlook for stocks: as market experts see
it. il U S News 58:91-4 My 31 '65
Pros see clouds over the '66 market; opinions
of investment analysts. il Bsns W p 14-15
Ja 1 '66
Reading the future in the past; technique
of the chartist. il Bsns W p 107-8+ Ag 14
'65
Setting records already; with charts. Bsns
W p23-5 F 6 '65
Solid gain to high ground. il Bsns W p27
O 16 '65
Stocks and inflation. C. J. Loomis. il For-
tune 72:85-6 O '65
Those misleading averages. Time 86:68 Ag 20
'65
Ups and downs of stock market; the meaning.
il U S News 59:42-4 Jl 12 '65
Wall Street: a rosy trend for blue chips. il
Newsweek 67:71 Ja 17 '66
Wall Street: booming prices, wary optimism.
il Newsweek 66:78-9 O 11 '65
Wall Street goes into a mood of caution;
results of W. M. Martin's comments. il
Bsns W p28-9 Je 5 '65
Wall Street: how to gauge the market? New
York exchange considering own index. il
Newsweek 67:75 Ja 24 '66
Wall Street puts its chips on a big year. il
Bsns W p25-6 S 25 '65
Wall Street: the fine art of the charts. il
Newsweek 66:88 O 18 '65
Wall Street: the history book indicates high-
er prices. il Newsweek 66:82-3 O 25 '65
When is a bull not a bull? symposium. il
Newsweek 65:64 Je 28 '65
When stocks recovered; who made the gains,
with chart. U S News 59:84 Ag 30 '65
Where are the bears of yesterday? il News-
week 66:75 S 27 '65
Which are the hot issues? il Bsns W p 166
Ap 17 '65
Worries of Wall Street. il Newsweek 65:63+
Je 28 '65

Taxation
See Taxation of bonds, securities, etc.

Tender offers
Glen Alden settles for less. Bsns W p74 Jl
31 '65

Valuation
See also
Corporations—Valuation
STOCKTON, Ann
Ann Stockton's porcelain. J. Pugliese. il por
Craft Horiz 25:34-6 Mr '65
STOCKTON, Robert Field
Beauty and chivalry of the United States
assembled. D. B. Webster, jr. il por Am
Heritage 17:50-3+ D '65
STOCKTON, Calif.
Put new life in old streets. F. Fargo. il Am
City 80:93-5 Mr '65
STOCKWOOD, Arthur Mervyn, bp
Profiles; concerning Honest to God, by
J. Robinson. V. Mehta. il New Yorker 41:
61 N 20 '65
STODDARD, Charles H.
Revolt in the provinces. J. C. Hunt. il por
Am For 71:40-1+ Je '65
STODDARD, George D.
New design for the college of liberal arts and
sciences. Sch & Soc 93:265-7 My 1 '65
STODELLE, Ernestine
College or career for dancers? UCLA's an-
swer. Dance Mag 39:48-53 My; 40-1+ Je '65
Repertory dance theater. Nat R 17:205-6 Mr
9 '65

STOENNER, R. W. and others
Half-lives of argon-37, argon-39, and argon-
42. bibliog Science 148:1325-8 Je 4 '65
STOKES, B. R.
Traveling in high style. Sat R 49:90-1 Ja 8
'66
STOKES, Carl
Black and white issue. il por Newsweek 66:
36+ N 15 '65
STOKES, Roy
New deal on an old frontier. por Library J
90:1608-11 Ap 1 '65
STOKES, Walter R.
Off limits. PTA Mag 60:6 S '65
STOKES, William S.
Honduras: problems and prospects. Cur Hist
50:22-6+ Ja '66
What hope for Latin America? Nat R 17:591-
4 Jl 13 '65
STOKLEY, James
Astronomy. See issues of Science news letter
STOKOWSKI, Leopold Anton Stanislaw
Musical events: concerts performed by Ameri-
can symphony orchestra in Carnegie Hall
(cont) W. Sargeant. New Yorker 41:170
Ap 17 '65
STOKVIS, Irene Ellen
(ed) First novelists, summer-fall 1965. Li-
brary J 90:2589-97+, 4119-25+ Je 1, O 1 '65
—and Putnam, Judith
(eds) Books to come (cont) Library J 90:
686-772+ F 1 '65
STOLEN automobiles. See Automobiles, Theft
of
STOLLER, Ezra
Architect's weekend home. il Holiday 38:52-7
S '65
STOLLEY, Richard
Dear President: I'm a sculptor and need help.
Life 59:76 N 26 '65
I couldn't put wigs on Harriman and Gold-
berg. Life 60:24-7 Ja 14 '66
Inside the White House: pressures build up to
the momentous speech. Life 58:34-5 Mr 26
'65
Life movie review: Synanon. Life 58:19 My
14 '65
Marise pushes a brainy brood. Life 59:110+
O 8 '65
Presidents are awful with the press; Johnson
is worse. Life 58:36 My 7 '65
Re-entry crisis. Life 58:100+ Mr 19 '65
Vietnam step-up: the secret councils. Life
59:26D Ag 6 '65
(ed) Washington report. See issues of Life
STOLZ, Mary
I love you truly; story. Good H 162:68-9 Ja '66
Ici, on parle what? story. Seventeen 24:148-9
Ap '65

STOMACH

Diseases
How upset stomach is best treated. Good H
160:129-30 Ja '65

Secretions
See also
Gastric juice
STOMACH cameras. See Medical instruments
and apparatus
STOMACH ulcers. See Peptic ulcers
STOMATA
Transpiration and the stomata of leaves.
P. E. Waggoner and I. Zelitch. bibliog il
Science 150:1413-20 D 10 '65
STONAKER, H. H. and Rohlf, J. A.
Are A.I. rules strangling purebreds? Farm J
89:31+ D '65
STONE, C. Walter
Another tribute. ALA Bul 59:238 Ap '65
STONE, Donald C.
Hard way south. Yachting 118:60-1+ N '65
STONE, Edward C.
Preserving vegetation in parks and wilder-
ness. bibliog Science 150:1261-7 D 3 '65
STONE, Edward Durell
America's unconventional master builder. B.
Clark. il por Read Digest 86:192-6 F '65
STONE, Emily Whitehurst
How a writer finds his material. Harper 231:
157-61 N '65
STONE, Gillian
Golden fan; poem. New Yorker 41:42 Ap 3
'65
STONE, I. F.
Official turns state's evidence. New Repub
152:24-6 My 29 '65
STONE, Jeremy J.
Containing the arms race. Bul Atomic Sci
21:18-21 S '65
On proliferation: where's the danger? Bul
Atomic Sci 21:15-18 N '65
—See Kaysen, C. jt. auth.
STONE, Michael
Author: G. Grass. Sat R 48:26 My 29 '65
STONE, Millard E.
Shifting winds of collective bargaining. Mo
Labor R 88:401 Ap '65

STONE, Robert B.
It was hi-fi to grandma. Hobbies 70:31-3 Ag '65

STONE, Ruth
Poet's workshop. Writer 78:23-6+ Mr; 22-5 My; 21-4+ Jl; 23-7 O; 27-30 D '65

STONE, W. H. and others
Skin grafts: delayed rejection between pairs of cattle twins showing erythrocyte chimerism. bibliog Science 148:1335-6 Je 4 '65

STONE, William T.
New boating laws and regulations. Yachting 117:68-71+ Ap '65
Washington report. See issues of Yachting

STONE
    See also
Rocks

STONE age
Early neolithic village in Greece; excavations at Nea Nikomedeia. R. J. Rodden. il Sci Am 212:82-8+ Ap '65
Later pleistocene cultures of Africa. J. D. Clark. bibliog il Science 150:833-47 N 12 '65
Paleolithic funeral. Sci Am 212:53-4 F '65
Sahara dried, divided African nations, people. Sci N L 88:361 D 4 '65
Search for Greece of the stone age. E. S. Higgs. il Natur Hist 74:18-25 N '65

STONE implements and weapons
America's oldest hunting weapon; stonepointed lance. F. C. Hibben. il Field & S 70:48-50+ Jl '65
Artifact from deposits of mid-Wisconsin age in Illinois. P. J. Munson and J. C. Frye. bibliog il Science 150:1722-3 D 24 '65
Artifact of ice age discovered in Illinois. Sci N L 89:41 Ja 15 '66
Later pleistocene cultures of Africa. J. D. Clark. bibliog il Science 150:833-47 N 12 '65
Lunar calendar from the Hungarian upper paleolithic. L. Vértes. bibliog il Science 149:855-6 Ag 20 '65
Recognizing the emergence of man; Tolchaco stone tool industry. R. Ascher and M. Ascher; discussion. Science 148:167-8 Ap 9 '65
    See also
Stone age

STONE MOUNTAIN
Georgia jinx. J. Dabney. il Travel 123:47-51 Je '65

STONE MOUNTAIN memorial
Georgia jinx. J. Dabney. il Travel 123:47-51 Je '65
They're burning a memorial into a mountain; southern memorial on Georgia's Stone Mountain. B. Wilson and J. Wilson. il Pop Mech 124:134-7+ N '65

STONE-pointed lance. See Stone implements and weapons

STONE tools. See Stone implements and weapons

STONE walks. See Walks (paths)

STONEBERG, Everett. See Harl, N. E. jt. auth.

STONEHAM, Horace
For he's a jolly good fellow; excerpt from Hustler's handbook. W. L. Veeck and E. Linn. il pors Sports Illus 22:50-2+ My 31 '65

STONEHENGE, England
Eighth wonder; ancient observatory. il Time 86:98 N 12 '65

STONER, J. Thomas. See Lytle, F. W. jt. auth.

STONER, Nicholas
Man whose praise we sing; summary of Trappers of New York, by J. R. Simms. F. B. Leach. il Am Heritage 16:62-3+ Ap '65

STONES
    See also
Rocks

STONEWARE crocks. See Flower pots

STONG, C. L.
(ed) Amateur scientist. See issues of Scientific American

STONY BROOK campus, New York state university. See New York state university—Long Island center, Stony Brook

STOOKEY, Paul
Peter, Paul and Mary: triple play! interview; ed. by E. Miller. pors Seventeen 24:128-9+ Ap '65

STOOLS
Helmsman's step-toolbox. H. Clark. il Pop Mech 124:183 S '65
Pine fireside stool. A. A. Altomare. il Pop Sci 187:154-5 N '65

STOOP, Bert
Unfinished war? Christian Cent 82:166 F 10 '65

STOPPERS, Bottle. See Bottle caps and seals

STOPPING of automobiles. See Automobiles—Stopping

STORAGE
Nine new plans for outdoor storage. C. Sigman. il Pop Sci 186:130-8 My '65
    See also
Cupboards
Kitchen cabinets
    also subhead Storage under various subjects, e.g. Gasoline—Storage

STORAGE, Underground
Double duty from hidden assets; rich vein of limestone in Kansas City, Kan. il Fortune 73:175-6 Ja '66

STORAGE batteries
Alkaline batteries. H. J. Strauss. il Electr World 74:49-52 O '65
Battery, heat riser & radiator check-out. R. E. Jennings. il Motor T 17:84-7+ F '65
Battery renaissance. W. A. Stocklin. Electr World 74:6 S '65
Carbon-zinc batteries. F. B. Pipal. il Electr World 74:42-5 O '65
Douglas improves battery materials; Astropower batteries. Miss & Roc 16:36 Ap 26 '65
Mercury batteries. G. E. Kaye. il Electr World 74:46-8 O '65
More life from your car battery. H. T. Gurley. il Pop Sci 188:120-3+ Ja '66
Nickel-cadmium batteries. L. Hofstatter. il Electr World 74:37-41 O '65

STORAGE battery chargers
Charging nickel cadmium cells. Electr World 73:77 F '65
New life for old dry cells. W. Temcor. il Pop Electr 22:69-70 F '65

STORAGE cabinets. See Cabinets (furniture)

STORAGE in boats. See Boats—Equipment

STORAGE in the home
Big problem with portables. il Sunset 135:86-9 N '65
Built-in storage wall. il Pop Mech 124:162-5 O '65
Built-out storage. E. Sverbeyeff. il N Y Times Mag p48-9 F 21 '65
Cleanup carousel. il Bet Hom & Gard 43:112 S '65
Designs for storage. il House & Gard 128:130 Jl '65
How to find a place for everything you own. il House & Gard 128:63-113 Jl '65
How to store your special interests. il Bet Hom & Gard 44:25 Ja '66
Making room; problem in converting a dilapidated West side rooming house into a duplex. B. Plumb. il N Y Times Mag p120-1+ N 28 '65
Six ways to put crawl space to work. il Pop Mech 124:160-3 S '65
Storage for work and play. il Bet Hom & Gard 43:110-11 O '65
Three kitchens with character. il Good H 162:110+ Ja '66
    See also
Pantries

STORAGE tubes
Direct-view storage tubes. J. B. Pegram. il Electr World 73:25-8 F '65

STORAGE walls
Clever cover-alls for storage walls. il Bet Hom & Gard 43:106 F '65
Clutter-free house. il House & Gard 128:82-9 Jl '65
Demountable storage wall. il House & Gard 128:76-7 Jl 7 '65
Different storage wall. il Bet Hom & Gard 43:68 Ap '65
Hard-working storage wall. il Bet Hom & Gard 43:22 Ap '65
Mr Storage Wall at home; G. Nelson's home. R. Reif. il N Y Times Mag p36-7 Ja 2 '66
More storage, more personality for your home. il Am Home 68:56-9 Ap '65
Open the wall and there's what you need. il Sunset 134:114-15+ Je '65
Storage walls; how can any house get along without one? il Bet Hom & Gard 43:32+ S '65
Why settle for a bad house? il Bet Hom & Gard 43:56-7 N '65

STORB, R. See Amy, R. L. jt. auth.

STORE decorations. See Christmas decorations

STORE hours
Snaring sales while others sleep; convenience stores. il Bsns W p 128+ N 6 '65

STORE signs. See Signs and signboards

STORE windows. See Show windows

STORER, George Butler
Northeast's next pilot? il por Bsns W p39-40 Je 12 '65

STORER broadcasting company
Northeast may have a buyer. Bsns W p31 Je 5 '65

STORES
Boutiquiana; New York, London, Paris. il Newsweek 66:92+ N 29 '65
Building types study (cont) il Arch Rec 137: 187-210 My '65
See also
Antiques shops
Chain stores
Retail trade
Sears, Roebuck and company
also subhead Stores under names of cities, e.g. New York (city)—Stores

Equipment
Computers begin to solve the marketing puzzle. il Bsns W p 114-15+ Ap 17 '65
STORIES. See Short stories
STORK club, New York. See Nightclubs
STORK showers. See Entertaining
STORKS
See also
Wood storks
STORM KING hydroelectric project. See Hydroelectric plants
STORMPROOF construction. See Building, Stormproof
STORMS
For whom do storm signals fly? T. Cofield. il Motor B 116:46-7+ O '65
Hard way south; voyage to St Thomas. D. C. Stone. il Yachting 118:60-1+ N '65
Los Angeles: the rains came. Newsweek 66: 38 D 6 '65
Stratospheric tapping by intense convective storms: implication for public health in the United States. A. N. Dingle. bibliog Science 148:227-9 Ap 9 '65
See also
Aviation—Storm hazards
Hurricanes
Magnetic storms
STORROW, James J. Jr
Statements to our readers. Nation 202:4 Ja 3 '66
about
Fiduciary of this trust. por Newsweek 67:42 Ja 10 '66
STORY dancers of India. See Dancing, Indian (East Indian)
STORY hour. See Story telling
STORY telling
Ethos of the teller of tales; address. 1965. A. T. Allen. bibliog Wilson Lib Bul 40:356-8 D '65
Once upon a bedtime. A. P. Eliasberg. il N Y Times Mag p 129+ O 31 '65
To Ruth Sawyer. B. Robinson. Horn Bk 41: 478-80 O '65
When grandma was a girl. M. C. Moore. il Parents Mag 40:54+ Jl '65
See also
Television broadcasting—Childrens programs
STORYBOOK revolt; drama. See Watts, F. B.
STORYTELLING. See Story telling
STOTT, Robert Leslie
Specialist wheels the biggest stock deal. il por Bsns W p 156+ My 22 '65
STOUGH, Donald B.
Natural lands: the big country. Am For 71: 64-5+ My '65
STOUT, Ellis
Handy feeder for corn silage. il Suc Farm 63:44 D '65
Step up to better pictures. U S Camera 28: 16-17+ O '65
STOUT, Juanita (Kidd)
Why must the taxpayer subsidize immorality? Read Digest 86:66-9 Ap '65
about
Her honor bops the hoodlums. D. J. Hamblin. il pors Life 59:74+ Jl 9 '65
Unfrightened crusader. por Time 85:47 Ap 16 '65
STOUT, P. R. See Burau, R. jt. auth.
STOUT, Rex
Author. H. Frankel. Sat R 48:55 O 9 '65
Author Rex Stout vs. the FBI; observations; ed. by S. Schmidt. il pors Life 59:127-8+ D 10 '65
Perils of omnipotence; concerning novel, Doorbell rang. Nation 201:291 N 1 '65
STOUT, Robert C. and Shuey, B. S.
Designed for split treatment. Am City 80:108-11 My '65
STOUTENBURGH, John L. Jr
Museum world. See issues of Hobbies
STOVER, Francis W.
Excerpt from testimony, August 10, 1964. Cong Digest 44:149+ My '65

STOVES
How to keep your range clean. Redbook 125:81 Jl '65
See also
Electric stoves
Gas stoves
STOWE, Leland
Eugenie Anderson shows the flag. Read Digest 86:173+ Mr '65
STOWELL, Earl
Interflex. Pop Mech 124:194-8 S '65
STOWELL, Joseph R.
Hex wrecks 'em in Peoria. J. Jares. il Sports Illus 24:14-15 Ja 17 '66
STRACHAN, Harold
There is no such thing as regulations here. N Y Times Mag p 10-11+ Jl 25 '65
STRACHAN, Ruth, and Comstock, Helen
Renewed study of Salem secretaries. Antiques 88:502-5 O '65
STRACHEY, Giles Lytton
Education of Lytton Strachey. J. Wain. New Repub 152:20-2 Ap 17 '65
STRACHEY, Lytton. See Strachey, G. L.
STRAIGHT, Michael
Days with Henry Wallace. New Repub 153: 9-11 D 4 '65
Something for the arts. New Repub 152:11-15 Mr 13 '65
Water picture in Everglades National Park. Nat Parks Mag 39:4-9 Ag '65
STRAILE, William E. See Mann, S. J. jt. auth.
STRAIN, Roy Q.
Credit union reverie. NEA J 54:29-30 Mr '65
STRAINS and stresses
Stress equation devised; ratio of elastic energy. Sci N L 87:198 Mr 27 '65
See also
Bending
STRAITS, Turkish. See Dardanelles
STRAND, Harold P.
Specifics of specific gravity. Pop Mech 125: 168-9 Ja '66
Speed reducer for metal cutting. Pop Mech 124:152-4 D '65
STRAND, Mark
Kite; poem. New Yorker 41:50 Mr 20 '65
Moontan; poem. New Yorker 41:152 S 11 '65
STRAND, Mette. See Valentine, R. C. jt. auth.
STRANG, Charles D.
Long happy life of the phenomenal outboard motor. Motor B 115:31-4+ Je: 116:43-5+ Jl; 44-7+ Ag '65
STRANG, Ruth
How the child's identity grows. PTA Mag 60:28-30 bibliog(p35) O '65
—and Frobisher, Mary
Readily to school. PTA Mag 59:10-13 bibliog(p35) My '65
STRANG Clinic, New York
Ounce of prevention. Time 86:31 Jl 30 '65
STRANSKY, Thomas F.
Ecumenical ennui? por Cath World 201:22-6 Ap '65
Wonderful communion of the faithful; excerpt from commentary on the Decree on ecumenism. Cath World 202:48-51 O '65
STRASBERG, Lee
How to succeed in the theatre without really being successful. E. Dundy. il Esquire 63: 88-9+ My '65
STRASFOGEL, Ignace
Matter of style. Opera N 29:8-11 Mr 6 '65
STRASSMANN, Erwin O.
High IQ and the small bosom: do they really go together? L. R. Chevalier. McCalls 92: 87+ Mr '65
STRATAS, Teresa
Bright star; interview, ed. by E. R. Rizzo. por Opera N 30:24-5 D 25 '65
about
Music to my ears; role of Perichole. I. Kolodin. Sat R 49:76 Ja 8 '66
Small body, big voice. por Time 85:73-4 Ap 9 '65
Tiny diva's big triumph. T. Thompson. il pors Life 59:129-30+ N 12 '65
STRATEGIC materials
Battle act report, 1964; seventeenth report to Congress, January 13, 1965. Dept State Bul 52:148-54 F 1 '65
How Washington controls critical defense materials. Bsns W p24 Ag 7 '65
Materials development is crucial to all areas of military weaponry. il Miss & Roc 16:54-8 Mr 29 '65
STRATEGIC space plans. See Space flight—Military applications
STRATEGY
Bigger wars ahead? interview. H. Kahn. il U S News 58:42-9 Je 7 '65

STRATEGY—*Continued*

Dialectic of force. W. R. Kinter. il Sat R 48:29-30 Je 26 '65

Escalation as a strategy: excerpts from On escalation: metaphors and scenarios, with editorial comment. H. Kahn. Fortune 71:105. 100-12+ Ap '65

Great debate: theories of nuclear strategy. by R. Aron; tr. by E. Pawel. Review
  Nation 200:198-200 F 22 '65. S. Hoffmann
  New Repub 152:21-2 F 13 '65. R. D. Senter
  Sat R 48:28 F 6 '65. K. W. Thompson

Heart of deterrence. R. K. Coffey. il Bul Atomic Sci 21:27-9 Ap '65

Herman's ladder. Nation 200:405 Ap 19 '65

Military appraisal: shift in U.S. strategy: its meaning. M. S. Johnson. il US News 58:53-4 My 17 '65

NATO strategy: what is past is prologue. H. Owen. For Affairs 43:682-90 Jl '65

On escalation, by H. Kahn. Review
  Nat R il 17:601-3 Jl 13 '65. S. T. Possony
  New Repub 152:19-21 Je 5 '65. A. Buchan

U.S. secret army: fighting reds by red methods. il U S News 58:49-50 Ap 12 '65

Why U.S. strategy is out of date. M. S. Johnson. il U S News 58:29 My 31 '65
  See also
  Vietnamese war, 1957- —Strategy

STRATEGY, Communist. See Communist strategy

STRATFORD, Conn. Shakespeare festival. See American Shakespeare festival theatre and academy, Stratford, Conn.

STRATFORD, Ontario, music festival. See Music festivals—Canada

STRATFORD, Ontario, Shakespeare festival. See Shakespeare festival, Stratford, Ontario

STRATOSPHERE. See Atmosphere, Upper

STRATTON, Burton L.
Authors' alterations: are they really necessary? Pub W 187:21-2 Ap 5 '65

STRATTON, James H.
Sea-level canal: how and where. For Affairs 43:513-18 Ap '65

STRATTON, Julius A.
Advice to a new academy; address, April 27, 1965. Science 149:1206-8 S 10 '65

STRATTON, William G.
High cost of politics. il por Time 85:30-1 Mr 19 '65

Political gifts and taxes; ex-governor acquitted. il por U S News 58:16 Mr 22 '65

STRAUS, Jack Isidor
Wanted: concern for the customer; address, September 29, 1965. Vital Speeches 32:109-12 D 1 '65
  about
Macy's puts its stamp on every store it owns. il por Bsns W p64+ O 2 '65

STRAUSS, Frances
On learning Shona. Horizon 7:112-15 Spr '65

STRAUSS, Franz Josef
Again Franz-Josef. por Newsweek 66:38 S 20 '65

March of oblivion. por Newsweek 66:40+ N 29 '65

Other Franz Josef. il por Time 85:34 Ap 23 '65

STRAUSS, Howard J.
Alkaline batteries. Electr World 74:49-52 O '65

STRAUSS, Lewis L.
Business, Washington, and conflict of interest; interview. ed. by J. Berry. por Duns R 86:48-50+ O '65

Inches, pounds, pints: the case for changing them all. por U S News 58:96-7 Je 28 '65

STRAUSS, Richard
Arabella. Criticism
  New Yorker 41:118 F 20 '65
  New Yorker 41:230-1 O 9 '65
  Opera N il 30:17-20 D 18 '65

Capriccio. Criticism
  New Yorker 41:127-8+ N 6 '65
  Opera N il 30:28 D 4 '65
  Sat R 48:72 N 13 '65

DGG's extraordinary Daphne. R. Sabin. il Am Rec G 31:776-9 My '65

Five operas and Richard Strauss, by L. Lehmann. Review
  Am Rec G 31:904-6 My '65. R. Sabin

Genius of Richard Strauss. E. Leinsdorf. por Atlan 216:79-83 Ag '65

More Strauss: again the Festival prelude. J. Diether. Am Rec G 31:779 My '65

On records; Daphne, Der Rosenkavalier, Arabella. Opera N 30:34 D 18 '65

On records; Salome; Die frau ohne schatten; Daphne. Opera N 29:34 Mr 13 '65

On records; Songs. Opera N 29:34 Ap 17 '65

Salome. Criticism
  New Yorker 40:152-3 F 13 '65
  Newsweek il 65:86 F 15 '65
  Opera N 29:24-5 Mr 13 '65
  Opera N il 29:17-20 Mr 13 '65
  Opera N il 29:29 My 1 '65
  Opera N 30:32 Ja 1 '66
  Sat R 48:45 F 20 '65
  Sat R 48:39 F 27 '65
  Time il 85:57 F 12 '65

STRAUSS, Theodore
Place for Jimmy; story. Good H 160:54-5 Ja '65

STRAUSS, William S.
Laboratory for the world's laws. por Library J 90:2504-8 Je 1 '65

STRAUSZ-HUPE, Robert
Between the ideal and the ideology. Sat R 48:38-9 Je 12 '65
  about
Two ways to one world. J. M. Allison. por Sat R 48:39-40 S 25 '65

Unprogressive pilgrim. por Time 86:62 D 24 '65

STRAVINSKY, Igor Fedorovich
Memories of T. S. Eliot; excerpt from Table talk. Esquire 64:92-3 Ag '65

Sacre de Diaghilev. Vogue 145:124-5+ Ap 15 '65

Schoenberg's letters. Hi Fi 15:136-8 My '65
  about
From Philips, the best complete recording of L'histoire du soldat. J. Diether. il Am Rec G 31:610-11+ Mr '65

On records; Rake's progress. Opera N 29:34 Ap 3 '65

Orpheus and Apollo as never before. C. J. Luten. Am Rec G 32:69 S '65

Rake's progress. R. Sabin. il por Am Rec G 31:496-8 F '65

STRAW, Ronnie J.
Electric power: runaway rates. Nation 200:364-5 Ap 5 '65

STRAWBERRIES
Amazing climbing strawberries prove to be earthbound! il Consumer Bul 48:34 Mr '65

How to grow mouthwatering strawberries. E. Gantner. il Pop Gard 16:32 Mr '65
  See also
  Cookery—Fruit

Diseases and pests
  See also
  Tarnished plant bugs

STRAWBERRY jars. See Flower boxes, planters, etc.

STRAWBERRY marks. See Birthmarks

STRAWBERRY shortcake. See Shortcake

STRAWN, Bernice
Solutions to your laundry quandary. Bet Hom & Gard 43:112-13 Mr '65

STRAY dogs. See Dogs

STRAYER, Joseph R.
Problems of dictatorship. For Affairs 44:264-74 Ja '66

STREAM pollution. See Water pollution

STREET, Donald, Jr
World's wackiest wayfarers. Yachting 118:50-1+ N '65

STREET, Sibyl F. and Ramsey, R. W.
Sarcolemma: transmitter of active tension in frog skeletal muscle. bibliog Science 149:1379-80; 150:1846 S 17, D 31 '65

STREET cars
Rapid transit pays own fare; Cleveland's little Shaker Heights line. il Bsns W p80+ S 11 '65

STREET cleaning
Flush before sweeping for cleaner streets; Minneapolis. L. C. Pratt. il Am City 80:118-20 Mr '65

Rate and upgrade your street cleaning. R. E. Denison. il Am City 80:120-2 Ap '65

Street cleaning. See issues of American city

Street cleaning involves more than sweeping; Hempstead, N.Y. H. Haff. il Am City 80:100-1 Jl '65
  See also
  Refuse and refuse disposal

Competitions
Cincinnati wins clean-up contest; expanded National cleanest town contest. il Am City 80:105-7 Ap '65

STREET cleaning apparatus
Flush before sweeping for cleaner streets; Minneapolis. L. C. Pratt. il Am City 80:118-20 Mr '65

STREET cleaning apparatus—*Continued*
Maggie modernizes Mishawaka's methods. W. H. Smith. il Am City 80:124-5 Je '65
Street cleaning. See issues of American city
We vacuum and flush our streets; Montgomery, Ala. L. B. Green. il Am City 80:104-5 My '65

STREET lighting
Lighting of cities. W. M. C. Lam. Arch Rec 137:210-14 Je '65
Modern lighting brings the shopper back downtown. il Am City 80:130-1 Je '65
Outdoor lighting. See issues of American city
Outdoor lighting scene in review. bibliog il Am City 80:73-5 F; 109-11 Mr; 114-16 Ap; 112-15 My '65
Tenfold more light with fluorescents; Virginia, Minn. E. F. B. Johnson. il Am City 80:111 F '65
See also subhead Lighting under names of cities, e.g. New York (city)—Lighting

STREET lighting fixtures
Outdoor lighting scene in review. bibliog il Am City 80:73-5 F; 109-11 Mr; 114-16 Ap; 112-15 My '65
Private lighting goes public; Duncannon, Pa. M. Cooper. il Am City 80:113 F '65

STREET markings. See Traffic markings

STREET parades. See Parades

STREET paving. See Pavements

STREET signs
Inventor of the month; signs you can see at night. S. V. Jones. Sci Digest 57:32 Mr '65
New street signs spell out good community relations; Berwyn, Ill. il Am City 80:129 My '65
Now you can read the signs; Columbia, Mo. T. I. Maupin. il Am City 80:114-15 Ag '65

STREET sweepers. See Street cleaning apparatus

STREET traffic
Britain: the unpolice state; traffic jams. C. W. Morton. il Atlan 215:172+ Mr '65
Other cities get on board. il Look 29:65 S 21 '65
Our car-strangled cities. W. Langewiesche. il Read Digest 87:71-6 Jl '65
See also
Automobile parking
Radio broadcasting—Traffic reports
also subhead Street traffic under names of cities, e.g. New York (city)—Street traffic

Automatic control
World's largest traffic-control system; New York city. il Am City 80:129 N '65

STREET trees. See Trees in cities

STREET vacuum sweepers. See Street cleaning apparatus

STREETER, Edward
Keep moving, please; story. McCalls 93:56-7 Ja '66

STREETS
See also
Gutters

Lighting
See Street lighting

Maintenance and repair
Integrate your patching components; Rolling Meadows, Ill. J. McFeggan. il Am City 80:93-5 My '65
Put new life in old streets; Stockton, Calif. F. Fargo. il Am City 80:93-5 Mr '65
See also
Pavements—Surface treatment

Safety devices and measures
Galvanizing guards a people barrier; fencing in Cincinnati. F. V. Cornelius. il Am City 80:22 N '65

STREHLOW, Loretta
Anyone can buy an Easter lily; story. Redbook 125:64-5 Je '65

STREIBIG, Don
Ideas & scripts. See issues of Popular photography

STREISAND, Barbra
Goodbye Jackie, hello Amanda! pecking order among the world's best-dressed women. il Time 87:56 Ja 21 '66
Miss Streisand's New York for Marcello Mastroianni. Esquire 63:56+ My '65
Person who changed my life. por Seventeen 24:156-7 Ap '65
We talk to..; interview. por Mlle 61:228-9 Ag '65

about
Redbook dialogue: Barbra Streisand and Marcello Mastroianni. pors Redbook 125:50-1+ Jl '65
She is tough, she is earthy, she is kicky. M. W. Lear. il pors N Y Times Mag p 10-11+ Jl 4 '65
Streisand at twenty-three. por Time 85:68 Ap 30 '65

STRENGE, F. A.
Wood research in a hymn to Hippocrates. Am For 71:42-5+ My '65

STRENGTH of materials
Fiber-reinforced metals. A. Kelly. il Sci Am 212:28-37 F '65
See also
Steel—Strength

STREPP, Hans G.
Wankel engine. il Motor B 116:28-31 D '65

STREPTOCOCCI
Lysis of pleuropneumonia-like organisms by staphylococcal and streptococcal toxins. A. W. Bernheimer and M. Davidson. bibliog il Science 148:1229-31 My 28 '65
Rheumatic fever. E. H. Freimer and M. McCarty. il Sci Am 213:66-70+ bibliog(p 126+) D '65

STREPTOCOCCUS sore throat. See Throat—Diseases

STREPTOMYCIN
Amino acid changes provoked by streptomycin in a polypeptide synthesized in vitro. D. Old and L. Gorini. bibliog il Science 150:1290-2 D 3 '65
Drug risky in pregnancy. Sci N L 88:98 Ag 14 '65

STRESS (physiology)
Dog response like man's. Sci N L 87:242 Ap 17 '65
Genotype and prenatal and premating stress interact to affect adult behavior in rats. J. M. Joffe. bibliog il Science 150:1844-5 D 31 '65
Keeping mentally fit; excerpts from Today's health guide. Parents Mag 40:38+ N '65
Moral equivalents. W. G. Hollister. PTA Mag 60:7 S '65
Our hard-pressed teenagers; with study-discussion program. C. Smallenburg and H. Smallenburg. bibliog il PTA Mag 59:34-6, 44 F '65
Stress and the toxicity of venoms. H. L. Stahnke. bibliog il Science 150:1456-7 D 10 '65
Twelve ways to handle the stress of modern living. D. Valentry. il Sci Digest 58:44-8 N '65
What stress can do to you and for you; discussion group program, by M. Smart. B. Burke. il Parents Mag 40:37-8+, 45+ Ap '65
What to do about that all-in, dragged-out feeling. J. Brothers. Good H 161:48+ N '65
Who's pressuring Johnny, home or school? with study-discussion program, by E. Harris and D. Harris. bibliog il PTA Mag 60:22-4, 36 S '65

STRESSES. See Strains and stresses

STRETCH, Bonnie Barrett
Classroom learning is not enough. Sat R 48:62-3+ Je 19 '65
Times as teacher. Sat R 49:74 Ja 15 '66

STRETCH fabrics. See Textile fabrics. Synthetic

STRICKER, Verne
Kirtland's warbler: feathers and flame. il Nat Parks Mag 39:16-19 O '65

STRICKHAUSEN, Harry
Seven poets. Poetry 107:183-91 D '65

STRICKLIN, Mrs John
How I cull my ewe flock. por Suc Farm 63:106C Mr '65

STRIDULATION. See Insect sounds

STRIKES

Economic aspects
Business struggles on as strike cuts deep; New York's crippling transit strike. il Bsns W p30 Ja 15 '66
Cost of a seven-week strike: the story told by a computer; Piper aircraft corporation, Lock Haven, Pa. U S News 59:64 D 27 '65
How a strike looks to a computer; Piper aircraft corporation, Lock Haven, Pa. il U S News 59:98-100 N 15 '65
How losses soar when transit stops; New York transit strike. il Bsns W p28-9 Ja 15 '66
How the strike cost New York $800 million. il Newsweek 67:70-1+ Ja 24 '66

STRIKES—Economic aspects—*Continued*
New York transit tieup jams business gears; department store losses. il Bsns W p30-1 Ja 8 '66
Strike shock waves; New York city's twelve-day transit strike. Time 87:69-70 Ja 21 '66

Law
See Labor laws and legislation—United States

Argentina
Holiday odors; municipal workers strike. il Newsweek 67:39 Ja 10 '66

Australia
Plenty of jobs, more strikes. U S News 58:89 F 15 '65

Canada
Two and a half years later: Canada's doctor strike; surprise ending to Saskatchewan's bitter battle over socialized medicine. J. Star. il Look 29:101+ Mr 23 '65

Europe, Western
Where strikes are few and far between. il U S News 59:90-2 N 1 '65

France
Taunting the teacher; civil workers' strike. Newsweek 65:69-70 F 8 '65

Great Britain
Letter from London; bakers' strike. M. Panter-Downes. New Yorker 41:226-7 D 11 '65
Letter from London; workers from British aircraft corporation. M. Panter-Downes. New Yorker 40:106+ Ja 30 '65
Not all right, Jack. Time 96:52-3 S 17 '65
Taming the wildcat in British industry; labor government looks hard at unauthorized strikes. il Bsns W p 152+ S 18 '65

Hungary
Wild kittens; Hungarian fashion models strike. Newsweek 65:40+ F 22 '65

Italy
Hot iron. Time 85:33 Ap 23 '65
Italy's thick minestrone of strikes. il Life 58:36 Ap 30 '65

Japan
Hot water; strike of public bathhouse attendants. il Time 85:47 My 7 '65
When Japanese go on strike; nationwide strike of seamen. U S News 59:75 D 20 '65

United States
Back of the growing unrest among workers. U S News 58:80-1 F 8 '65
Can the U.S. still afford big strikes? U S News 58:87-90 My 3 '65
Coordination. D. Lawrence. U S News 59:124 S 27 '65
End of a long, bitter dispute: will Kohler have labor peace? il U S News 60:70-1 Ja 3 '66
Golden handshake; longest major labor dispute in U.S. history, Kohler strike. Time 86:14-15 D 24 '65
How unions are adding to Johnson's worries. U S News 58:76+ Je 14 '65
In the strike season: where showdowns will come. il U S News 58:81-3 Mr 15 '65
Perils of prosperity. il Time 85:89 Ap 9 '65
Review of work stoppages during 1964. E. D. Onanian. il Mo Labor R 88:661-8 Je '65
Saboteurs at work; reprint from Wall street journal, September 20, 1965. J. E. Evans. U S News 59:120 O 4 '65
Why the recent wave of strikes. U S News 59:84 Jl 19 '65
Work stoppages; tables. See issues of Monthly labor review

Aerospace industries
U.S. keeps wary eye on strike at Boeing; dispute centers on job security and employee rating. il Bsns W p 166+ S 25 '65

Agricultural workers
See Strikes—United States—Farm labor

Airlines
Duty hours major issue in Pan Am strike. Aviation W 82:45 Ap 5 '65
Pilotless Pan Am. Newsweek 65:82 Ap 12 '65

Automobile industry and trade
General motors sit-down strike, 1937: a re-examination. S. Fine. bibliog f Am Hist R 70:691-713 Ap '65
How to bury a job; U.A.W.'s Kenosha strike. il Time 86:77-8 S 3 '65

Coal mines and mining
Wildcats in coal start pulling in their claws; UMW walkouts after firing of six men. Bsns W p 168 S 25 '65

Cotton workers
New alliance shapes up in Dixie; AFL-CIO's interest in strike on cotton plantation. il Bsns W p 124+ Jl 10 '65

Farm labor
Grape strike. M. Novak. Commonweal 83: 366-9 D 24 '65
Grapes of wrath; Delano district strike. il Newsweek 66:57-8 D 27 '65
Grapes of wrath in California. America 114: 33 Ja 8 '66
Nothin' to lose; sharecropper strike in Mississippi. Newsweek 65:33+ Je 21 '65
Revolution in the vineyards. A. Ogle. America 113:747-8 D 11 '65

Government employees
See also
Strikes—United States—Municipal employees

Government intervention
Federal pressure in ship strike. U S News 59:74+ Jl 26 '65
Strike talk fades to a whisper; Vietnam war and tougher White House position. Bsns W p 112 Ag 21 '65
Who needs newspapers? Goldberg's strike aversion plan. A. H. Raskin. Reporter 33: 33-5 O 21 '65

History
Right to strike. P. Taft. Cur Hist 49:17-22 Jl '65
What happens to bargaining now? il Newsweek 66:72+ S 20 '65

Maritime workers
As the Nation adds up the toll of the dock strike. il U S News 58:79-80 Mr 1 '65
Back to work. Newsweek 65:78 F 22 '65
Dock peace leaves some question marks. il Bsns W p90+ Mr 13 '65
Dock strike hurts, but there's no crisis yet. il Bsns W p29 F 13 '65
Dock strike; loss of $1.7 billion. T. R. Brooks. Commonweal 81:728-30 Mr 5 '65
High cost of the dock strike. U S News 58: 90 F 22 '65
High, dry & disastrous. il Time 86:67 Ag 13 '65
How LBJ ended a shipping strike. U S News 59:99 S 13 '65
How to damage the economy. il Time 85:90 F 19 '65
Is our merchant fleet really afloat? il Bsns W p 128+ S 25 '65
Long voyage nowhere. il Newsweek 66:64 Ag 9 '65
Maritime milestone. il Newsweek 66:63-4 Ag 30 '65
Merchant marine in deadly peril. America 113:175-6 Ag 21 '65
Real issue in the ship strikes. U S News 58:71 Je 28 '65
Sink or swim for U.S. ships; Marine engineers strike. Life 59:4 Jl 30 '65
Tieup eases, for liners only. Bsns W p84 Ag 28 '65
Where the next big strike can come: crisis in shipping. U S News 58:76-7 Je 7 '65

Motor bus drivers
See Strikes—United States—Transportation workers

Municipal employees
Cure for strikes against the public? il Newsweek 67:30 Ja 24 '66
Growing trend: strikes against government. U S News 60:84-5 Ja 24 '66

Newspapers
Another blackout in New York; Times-Guild dispute. il Time 86:53 S 24 '65
Another news blackout; why; American newspaper guild vs. New York times. U S News 59:92 S 27 '65
Back to print in Baltimore. Time 85:85 Je 4 '65
Baltimore blackout. Time 85:73 Ap 30 '65
Crack appears in press deadlock; Herald tribune resumes publication. il Bsns W p 116+ O 2 '65
Dismal situation; New York newspaper strike. Time 86:68-9 O 1 '65
Eclipse of the Sun. New Repub 152:9 My 15 '65
End without an end; New York city newspapers' precarious peace. Time 86:85 O 22 '65

STRIKES—United States—Newspapers—*Cont.*

Honorably ended; strike against Baltimore sunpapers. Newsweek 65:98 Je 14 '65

Inviting strikes; automation and union shop are issues in New York newspaper strike. H. Hazlitt. Newsweek 66:90 O 11 '65

Light-years apart; strike against Baltimore sunpapers. Newsweek 65:57 My 31 '65

N.Y. newspaper strike ends as Kheel solution is accepted. Pub W 188:26 O 18 '65

No more doves; Newspaper guild of New York vs New York times. il Newsweek 66:69 S 27 '65

No news or, what killed the dog; destruction of big city newspapers due to Newspaper guild's strike against the New York times. Nat R 17:858 O 5 '65

Other side of the Sun; strike against Sunpapers, Baltimore. il Newsweek 65:82 My 3 '65

Reporter at large; 1962-63 strike, N.Y. F. C. Shapiro. New Yorker 41:161-4+ Ap 10 '65

Right & wrong; New York newspaper strike ended. il Time 86:110 O 15 '65

Solidarity forever; Baltimore sunpapers strike ends. Newsweek 65:22 Je 7 '65

Story of a five year strike: cost to company and unions; Oregonian, and Oregon journal, Portland. il U S News 58:90+ Ap 19 '65

Strike ends; Newspaper guild vs New York times. il Newsweek 66:74+ O 18 '65

Stubbornness in Baltimore. Time 85:55 My 21 '65

Who needs newspapers? Goldberg's strike aversion plan. A. H. Raskin. Reporter 33:33-5 O 21 '65

Why printers broke strike; Sunpapers, Baltimore. U S News 58:77 Je 7 '65

Printers

NLRB dismisses unfair labor charges against Kingsport. Pub W 188:32-3 Ag 9 '65

PIA's annual meeting looks at labor; summaries of speeches at convention. il Pub W 188:76-8+ O 4 '65

Three unions certified in Kingsport strike. Pub W 187:48 Mr 1 '65

Wrong approach; two year strike at Kingsport press. C. B. Grannis. Pub W 187:54 Mr 22 '65

Railroads

Carrying people again; Florida East Coast ry. running passenger trains. il Bsns W p81 Ag 7 '65

Rail firemen fuel fight. Bsns W p52+ O 23 '65

Strike of the railroad shopmen; reprint from December 1922 issue. M. Gadsby. Mo Labor R 88:796 Jl '65

Steel industry and trade

Battle at Homestead; excerpt from Lockout. L. Wolff. il Am Heritage 16:64-79 Ap '65

Steel strike threat loses impact. Bsns W p79-80 Ag 7 '65

See also
Homestead strike, 1892

Taxicab drivers

Taxi turmoil. il Newsweek 66:77 Jl 12 '65

Teachers

Personal opinion; needed; more teacher strikes. D. Selden. Sat R 48:75 My 15 '65

Teachers on the march; the militant mice. M. Lieberman. il Nation 200:107-10 F 1 '65

Transportation workers

Back to normal; New York city transit strike. Time 87:19D-20 Ja 21 '66

Collective bargaining? New York transit strike. Nation 202:58 Ja 17 '66

Does New York city have a future? il U S News 60:44-7 Ja 24 '66

How losses soar when transit stops; New York transit strike. il Bsns W p28-9 Ja 15 '66

How the strike cost New York $800 million. il Newsweek 67:70-1+ Ja 24 '66

Inauguration; J. V. Lindsay as Mayor of New York city. New Yorker 41:20-3 Ja 8 '66

Intolerable strike; New York city transit system. Life 60:4 Ja 14 '66

Lucky Lindsay; New York city finds its avenger. M. Kempton. New Repub 154:10-11 Ja 15 '66

Mike's strike; New York transit strike. il Time 87:22-7 Ja 14 '66

New York; a long week's walk into chaos. il Newsweek 67:28-31 Ja 17 '66

New York transit tieup jams business gears; department store losses. il Bsns W p30-1 Ja 8 '66

No dice; New York transit strike. Nat R 18:54-6 Ja 25 '66

Organized contempt. D. Lawrence. U S News 60:104 Ja 24 '66

Picture of a mayor in deep trouble; New York transit strike. il U S News 60:46-7 Ja 17 '66

Signs and portents: paralysis of New York. J. Burnham. Nat R 18:70 Ja 25 '66

Spectacle New Yorkers hope never to see again. il Life 60:62D-67 Ja 21 '66

Strike shock waves; New York city's twelve-day transit strike. Time 87:69-70 Ja 21 '66

Transit mess; New York on foot. T. Grubisich. Commonweal 83:456-7 Ja 21 '66

Transit tie-up hurts labor's fight on 14(b); New York city subway-bus tie-up. Bsns W p31 Ja 15 '66

Transit union gets a half nelson on New York. il Life 60:28-34B Ja 14 '66

Victory for honest John. Newsweek 67:29-31 Ja 24 '66

Walking; Mayor's sixty block walks to city hall. New Yorker 41:26-7 Ja 15 '66

What a union can do when it uses its power. il U S News 60:84-6 Ja 17 '66

Truck drivers

Philadelphia truckers defy courts and Hoffa. il Bsns W p124 Je 26 '65

STRING quartets

Juilliard string quartet; Bartók string Quartets nos. 1-6. C. J. Luten. il Am Rec G 31:772-4 My '65

STRINGED instruments

See also
Baritone (musical instrument)

STRINGFELLOW, William

Liturgy as political event. Christian Cent 82:1573-5 D 22 '65

Sin, morality and poverty. Christian Cent 82:703-6 Je 2 '65

about

Of many things; what has happened to Catholicism and editorial censorship. T. N. Davis. America 113:173 Ag 21 '65

STRINGFIELD, Lonnie

Shoeshine. New Yorker 41:40-1 My 22 '65

STRIP mine dumps, Reclamation of. See Reclamation of land

STRIP mining. See Coal mines and mining—Stripping operations

STROBOSCOPE

Simple 60-cycle stroboscope. L. E. Greenlee. il Pop Electr 22:71 Je '65

STROETZEL, Donald S.

Fishing for meal. Américas 17:18-22 My '65

Go South, young man! Read Digest 88:189-94 Ja '66

STROHMEIER, William

Gone flying to Bermuda. Flying 77:44-9+ S '65

STROHMEYER, John

What passes for American news in Africa. Harper 231:98+ N '65; 232:8+ Ja '66

STROKES, Apoplectic. See Cerebral hemorrhage

STROKES, Cardiovascular. See Heart—Diseases

STROM, Anita

As we live and breathe! letter. M. Hoffman. Nat R 17:682 Ag 10 '65

STROMA cells. See Cells

STROMBERG, Rolf

Question of musical maturity. Hi Fi 16:143 Ja '66

STRONG, E. W.

What's ahead for the university? address, September 10, 1965. Vital Speeches 32:24-8 O 15 '65

STRONG, Lydia

Parent and child (cont) N Y Times Mag p53-4 Ja 16 '66

Worlds to share. Am Home 68:18 Mr '65

STRONG, Ray

Art of the diorama. Am Artist 29:34-9+ O '65

STRONTIUM

Strontium and magnesium in water and in crassostrea calcite. A. Lerman. bibliog il Science 150:745-6+ N 5 '65

Isotopes

Radioactive strontium: estimation of the amount accidentally ingested. J. Samachson and H. Spencer. bibliog il Science 148:955-7 My 14 '65

Strontium isotopes; global circulation after the Chinese nuclear explosion of 14 May 1965. P. K. Kuroda and others. bibliog il Science 150:1289-90 D 3 '65

STRONTIUM in the body

Strontium in fossil bones and the reconstruction of food chains. H. Toots and M. R. Voorhies. bibliog il Science 149:854-5 Ag 20 '65

STROPHOCHEILIDAE. See Snails

STROSS, Cynthia
Moss amid the oaks. Library J 90:5206-7 D 1 '65

STROSS, Raymond G. and Hill, J. C.
Diapause induction in daphnia requires two stimuli. bibliog Science 150:1462-4 D 10 '65

STROTHER, Robert S.
Cadet who refused to quit. Read Digest 87: 71-5 S '65
How Castro spreads the revolution. Read Digest 87:205-6+ N '65
Self-help: an answer to urban renewal. Read Digest 86:223-6 F '65

STROUT, Donald E. and Strout, R. B.
Sixty-one forty-five in nineteen sixty-four. Library J 90:2741-9 Je 15 '65

STROUT, Richard L.
Eternal manager. New Repub 153:31 D 11 '65
Space, and all that. New Repub 152:11-12 My 8 '65; Correction. 152:38 My 29 '65

STROUT, Ruth B. See Strout, D. E. jt. auth.

STRUCTURAL aluminum. See Aluminum, Structural

STRUCTURAL engineering
High-rise apartment structures of masonry. R. M. Gensert. il Arch Rec 137:182-7 F '65
Some radical proposals. il Esquire 64:222-3 D '65
See also
Shells (structural engineering)

STRUCTURES, Underground. See Underground structures

STRUCTURES, Underwater. See Underwater structures

STRULO, Rodney
Wreck of the Guinevere. Read Digest 87:110-15 Jl '65

STRUVE, Walter
Hans Zehrer as a neoconservative elite theorist. bibliog f Am Hist R 70:1035-57 Jl '65

STRYBING arboretum and botanical garden. See San Francisco—Gardens

STRYK, Lucien
At Virgil's tomb; poem. Sat R 48:99 F 20 '65
Oeuvre; poem. Sat R 48:47 F 20 '65

STRYKER, Perrin
Can you analyze this problem? Harvard Bsns R 43:73-8 My '65
How to analyze that problem. Harvard Bsns R 43:99-110 Jl '65

STUART, Dabney
Birthday poem. New Yorker 41:48 My 22 '65
I love you; For the birds; Dry leaves; Building a snow man; poems. Poetry 105: 232-6 Ja '65
Rescue; poem. New Yorker 41:96 S 4 '65
River; poem. New Yorker 41:50 O 9 '65
Separate parties; poem. New Yorker 41:30 Je 26 '65

STUART, Jesse
Airport guest. Am For 71:4+ Jl '65
Grassy. NEA J 54:53-4 D '65
How like the great Greek God Apollo is our king; poem. Esquire 64:242 D '65
Loner (cont) Am For 71:58-9+ My '65
My fourteen originals. por Sr Schol 86:sup5-6 My 20 '65
Shinglemill symphony; poem. Am For 71: 28-9 D '65

STUART, Jessica Jane
Winds of March; poem. Am For 71:55 Mr '65

STUART, Neal G.
Fiction for Redbook. Writer 78:24-5 N '65

STUART, Robert Lee
Writer-in-waiting. Christian Cent 82:647-9 My 19 '65

STUART, Walker
Just plain Jim, commercial Cassidy. Reporter 32:46-8 Je 17 '65

STUBBS, Peter
Enigma of the moon, how did it get there? N Y Times Mag p30-1+ Mr 28 '65

STUCKER, Gilbert F.
Whither the wide Missouri? il Nat Parks Mag 39:10-15 Ag '65

STUDENT achievements
Do junior college transfers make the grade? survey findings. J. H. Nelson. il NEA J 54:55-7 O '65
Editor's notebook. M. S. Fenner. NEA J 54: 72 N '65
Health, physical education, and academic achievement. C. A. Bucher. il NEA J 54: 38-40 My '65
Patterns of academic achievement. G. T. Kowitz and C. M. Armstrong. Sch & Soc 93: 91-2 F 6 '65
Solving the dilemma of the underachiever. W. Abraham. il Todays Health 43:34-7+ D '65
When bright children fail. E. W. Johnson. il Parents Mag 40:48-9+ S '65

Who's pressuring Johnny, home or school? with study-discussion program, by E. Harris and D. Harris. bibliog il PTA Mag 60:22-4, 36 S '65

STUDENT activities
Beautification from sea to shining sea. il NEA J 54:34-7 N '65
High school extracurricular activities and political socialization. D. Ziblatt. bibliog f il Ann Am Acad 361:20-31 S '65
In my opinion; high school extracurriculars are overrated and overdone. M. Bernson. Seventeen 24:246 N '65
New voices on campus; symposium of student-activists. il Mlle 61:303-5+ Ag '65
Q. are teens overworked? pro and con discussion. il Seventeen 24:132-3+ Ap '65
Truth about college weekends; excerpt from Boys and other beasts. B. Lang. McCalls 92:32-3 Ap '65
See also
College and school journalism
College students—Political activities
Debating societies
Science clubs

Caricatures and cartoons
Cal kid. D. Newman and R. Benton. Esquire 64:81-4 S '65

STUDENT aid
See also
College students—Aid

STUDENT Christian movement
Forward, march! SCM in England. C. Northcott. Christian Cent 82:1328-9 O 27 '65
See also
National student Christian federation

STUDENT conferences
See also
United States national student association

STUDENT demonstrations
Antiwar marches and how they happen; with report by S. Angeloff from Berkeley campus. il Life 59:108-10+ D 10 '65
Bashful revolutionary; a Japanese student's war against war. il Look 20:34-5+ Ag 10 '65
Behind the campus revolt: California uprising. J. Poppy; L. Gross. il Look 29:30-8+ F 23 '65
Behind the protests at Berkeley. J. F. Boler. Commonweal 81:602-5 F 5 '65
Behind the student rebellions. Christian Cent 82:421-2 Ap 7 '65
Behind those campus demonstrations. E. H. Methvin. Read Digest 88:43-8 Ja '66
Berkeley affair: Mr Kerr vs. Mr Savio & co. A. H. Raskin. il N Y Times Mag p24-5+ F 14 '65
Berkeley effect; various protests. il Time 85:48-9 Mr 19 '65
Berkeley student revolt, ed. by S. M. Lipset and S. S. Wolin. Review Sat R 48:77 S 11 '65. P. Woodring
Berkeley's civil war. New Repub 152:6-7 Mr 27 '65
Bonaparte's retreat; Savio quits as leader of the Free speech movement. Time 85:54 My 7 '65
Campus revolts: why students act that way; interview. B. G. Gallagher. il U S News 58:66-7 Mr 29 '65
Causes of the student revolution. J. Katz and N. Sanford. il Sat R 48:64-6+ D 18 '65
Choices at Berkeley; convicted students sentenced. il Newsweek 66:74-5 Ag 9 '65
Columbia buckles under; demonstration against and postponement of Naval reserve officer training corps awards ceremony. E. J. Bell. il Nat R 17:506-7 Je 15 '65; Reply with rejoinder. J. S. Reed, jr. 17:575 Jl 13 '65
Crisis at Berkeley. E. Langer. bibliog f Science 148:198-202, 346-9 Ap 9-16 '65; Discussion. 148:1273-8 Je 4 '65
Cure for campus riots; interview. M. Rafferty. il U S News 58:70-2 My 17 '65
Dissent on dissent. il Newsweek 65:86 Je 21 '65
Down with the Cossacks! Moscow students protest against the U.S. air raids on North Viet Nam. il Time 85:24-5 Mr 12 '65
Escalation in California. N. Cousins; reply. C. Kerr. Sat R 48:21+ Mr 6 '65
Extremism in the defense of. . . R. E. Fitch; discussion. Christian Cent 82:147-50 F 3 '65
Focus on Berkeley. P. G. Altbach. Christian Cent 82:1356-7 N 3 '65
From J. Edgar Hoover: a report on campus reds; excerpts from testimony. March 4, 1965. J. E. Hoover. il U S News 58:84 My 31 '65

STUDENT demonstrations—*Continued*
How campus discord forced a university president to resign. il U S News 58:22 Mr 22 '65
Lesson of Berkeley. S. M. Lipset and P. Seabury; discussion. Reporter 32:6+ F 25 '65
Letter from Berkeley. C. Trillin. New Yorker 41:52-4+ Mr 13 '65
Man for tomorrow; Yesterday's rebels; Berkeley students. il Time 86:49 Ag 6 '65
More campus unrest: are reds to blame? Howard university; statements. J. M. Nabrit, jr. il U S News 58:14 My 10 '65
New tool; Moscow students protest U.S. air attacks on North Vietnam. il Newsweek 65:46+ Mr 15 '65
New twist to anti-U.S. riots: reds vs. reds. il U S News 58:11 Mr 15 '65
Nonstudent left; significance of the Mulford law. H. S. Thompson. il Nation 201:154-8 S 27 '65
Now, a backlash to anti-Vietnam protests. il U S News 59:11-12 N 8 '65
On the campus: a troubled reflection of the U.S. M. Ways. il Fortune 72:130-5+ S; 140-7+ O '65
Rebels with cause. New Repub 152:5-6 My 1 '65
Revolt without dogma: the student left. J. Newfield. il Nation 200:491-5 My 10 '65
Self-criticism at Cal; reports on student disorders at the University of California. Time 85:58 My 21 '65
Sowing future trouble; Berkeley judge passes sentence on students involved in the demonstrations. Nation 201:70 Ag 16 '65
Storm at home: anti-draft and anti-Viet demonstrations; with press comments. il Sr Schol 87:18-20 N 4 '65
Student violence and rebellion, how big a problem? D. Iwamoto. il NEA J 54:10-13 D '65
Students in a ferment chew out the nation; with reports by four student leaders and by W. S. Coffin, jr. il Life 58:24-33 Ap 30 '65
Students move for peace. Sci N L 88:302 N 6 '65
Students speak for action. R. F. Wagner, jr; R. Gatlin. il Sat R 48:82-3+ O 16 '65
Students, teachers, bureaucrats; protests of university students. Nat R 17:228+ Mr 23 '65
Teach-ins and walk-outs. Nation 200:378 Ap 12 '65
To the big game and to the barricades; University of California at Berkeley a symbol of campus unrest. A. Wright. il Sports Illus 24:48-54 Ja 3 '66
University has become a factory; interview, ed. by J. Fincher. M. Savio. Life 58:100-1 F 26 '65
Uprising at Yale; students protest denial of tenure to R. J. Bernstein. il Newsweek 65:89 Mr 15 '65
Vietnam: growing war and campus protests threaten student deferments. E. Langer. Science 150:1567-70 D 17 '65
What happened at Berkeley. J. Cass; discussion. Sat R 48:62+ F 20; 56 Mr 20 '65
What happened at Berkeley. N. Glazer. Commentary 39:39-47 F '65; Reply with rejoinder. P. Selznick. 39:80-5 Mr '65
What the students want. J. L. Walsh. Commonweal 83:206-9 N 19 '65
When the drumbeats are not always heard; Students for a democratic society pickets the White House. J. N. Eller. America 112:628 My 1 '65
Why campus crisis flares again; University of California at Berkeley. il Bsns W p38-9 Mr 20 '65
Why the students revolt. B. Ward; reply. K. Auletta. Nation 200:inside cover F 22 '65
See also
Vietnamese war, 1957- —Protests, demonstrations, etc. against

Anecdotes, facetiae, satire, etc.
Anatomy of a revolt; reprint. A. Buchwald. Sch & Soc 93:371-2 O 16 '65

Caricatures and cartoons
Cal kid. D. Newman and R. Benton. Esquire 64:81-4 S '65

History
Student protest and commitment; address, June 15, 1965. N. M. Pusey. Sch & Soc 93:471-4 D 11 '65

STUDENT drinking. See Liquor problem—United States
STUDENT employment
Employment of school age youth, October 1964. T. E. Swanstrom. il Mo Labor R 88:851-6 Jl '65
In the grown-up world of teen-agers. il UNESCO Courier 18:26-9 Jl '65
Teen travel talk; jobs for American students in West Germany. il Seventeen 24:180 S '65
Ten best ways to land a summer job. Seventeen 24:158-9+ My '65
See also
College students—Employment
STUDENT enrollment. See School attendance
STUDENT ethics
Little sex without love. Time 85:46 Ap 9 '65
STUDENT fees. See Colleges and universities—Finance
STUDENT forums. See Forums (discussion and debate)
STUDENT interracial ministry (organization)
Doing is the difference; reply. R. C. Assenheimer. America 112:560-1 Ap 17 '65
STUDENT life
Man talk; bull session. D. Newman and R. Benton. Mlle 61:10+ Ag '65
Something to talk about on campus. J. Adams and H. Dubrow. il Mlle 61:312-15 Ag '65
Tigers on the prowl; Princeton booklet. il Newsweek 66:58 N 1 '65
See also
College students
Hazing
Student activities
STUDENT loans
Battling for student loan market. il Bsns W p 47:50 Jl 17 '65
Financing your college education. J. Beck. il Todays Health 43:32-5+ F '65
How to beat the high cost of college; excerpts. C. Cox. il Seventeen 24:134-5+ F '65
STUDENT newspapers. See College and school journalism
STUDENT non-violent coordinating committee
Inside Snick. il Time 85:73-4 Ap 30 '65
New fraternity; student and crypto-student organizations. F. Powledge. il Esquire 64:88-9+ S '65
New radicals in Dixie; those subversive civil rights workers. A. Kopkind. New Repub 152:13-16 Ap 10 '65; Discussion. 152:30-1+ My 1 '65
Of, by and for the poor; new generation of student organizers. A. Kopkind. New Repub 152:15-19 Je 19 '65
Question of SNCC. J. Newfield. il Nation 201:38-40 Jl 19 '65
Revolt without dogma: the student left. J. Newfield. il Nation 200:491-5 My 10 '65
Selma. A. Kopkind. New Repub 152:7-9 Mr 20 '65
SNCC photographers find cameras make good crash helmets. M. A. Matzkin. il Mod Phot 29:22+ Jl '65
SNCC: rebels with a cause: southern freedom movement. L. Bennett, jr. il Ebony 20:146-53 Jl '65
SNCC: the new abolitionists, by H. Zinn. Review
    Commonweal 81:616-17 F 5 '65. M. O'Brien
Tension, not split, in the Negro ranks. A. Schardt. Christian Cent 82:614-16 My 12 '65
Waving the red flag; fear of Communist infiltration. il Newsweek 65:30-1 Ap 12 '65
Will Snick overcome? R. Armstrong. il Sat Eve Post 238:79-83 Ag 28 '65
STUDENT opinion
Black-banders; government team for explaining the U.S. presence in Viet Nam to college students and professors. il Time 85:26-7 My 14 '65
Ideal man: they remember JFK; Kennedy image among college students. il Newsweek 65:47 Mr 22 '65
Now campus liberals denounce LBJ. U S News 58:36 My 24 '65
Vietnamese students talk about the war. H. Selby. il N Y Times Mag p 104-5+ O 31 '65
STUDENT peace movement. See Pacifism
STUDENT publications. See College and school journalism
STUDENT rating of teachers. See College professors and instructors—Rating by students
STUDENT residences. See Dormitories
STUDENT riots. See Riots
STUDENT selection
Alumni find a new role. B. Schwartz. il Sat R 48:68-9+ D 18 '65

STUDENT selection—*Continued*
Freshman class. D. Wolfe. Science 149:1453 S 24 '65; Discussion. 150:965-6 N 19 '65
Talent grows in small towns, too. M. Beadle. il Sat R 48:64-5 Jl 17 '65
Those thin letters; rejections. il Time 85:53 My 7 '65
When federal aid can backfire. Nations Bsns 53:27-8 Je '65
See also
College entrance examination board

STUDENT self-support. See College students—Employment

STUDENT teachers
Lesson of Jackie Brant; Student education corps. il Newsweek 65:62 F 22 '65
Student teacher. D. Corrigan. NEA J 54:40 Ap '65
Threshold to the profession. D. M. Sharpe. NEA J 54:33-5 Ap '65

STUDENT teaching
Special feature on student teaching; symposium. NEA J 54:32-40 Ap '65
They lead two lives in Central Michigan university's five-year teacher intern program. C. E. Nash and others. il NEA J 54:12-14 My '65

STUDENT tours. See Travel study courses

STUDENT travel. See Travel

STUDENT tutors. See Tutors and tutoring

STUDENT volunteer movement
John R. Mott remembered. J. R. Nelson. Christian Cent 8:671 My 26 '65

STUDENT volunteer service. See Volunteer service

STUDENT withdrawals. See Dropouts

STUDENT Woodlawn area project. See Chicago—Education

STUDENTS
School report; excerpts from published recollections of outstanding people, comp. by U. Mahoney. N Y Times Mag p57+ S 12 '65
Where the girls are; Easter vacation. Newsweek 65:25 My 3 '65
See also
African students
Catholic students
College students
Engineering students
High school students
Negro students

Employment
See Student employment

Grading and promotion
See Grading and marking (students)

Rating
See also
High school students—Rating

Social and economic status
Financial status of National merit finalists. R. C. Nichols. bibliog il Science 149:1071-4 S 3 '65; Reply. A. Thorne. 150:827 N 12 '65

STUDENTS, Interchange of
See also
Foreign students in the United States

STUDENTS, Married
See also
College students, Married
High school students, Married

STUDENTS, Women. See College students, Women

STUDENTS and teachers. See Teachers and students

STUDENTS for a democratic society (organization)
Apparatchik; action projects to correct abuses of the underprivileged. New Repub 153:7 Jl 24 '65
Demonstrators: why? how many? anti-Vietnam movement. il Newsweek 66:25-6+ N 1 '65
New fraternity; student and crypto-student organizations. F. Powledge. il Esquire 64:88-9+ S '65
Of, by and for the poor; new generation of student organizers. A. Kopkind. New Repub 152:15-19 Je 19 '65
Perennial marchers. Reporter 32:8+ My 6 '65
Revolt without dogma: the student left. J. Newfield. il Nation 200:491-5 My 10 '65
Student left; idealism and action; background history and aims of organization. J. Newfield. il Nation 201:330-3 N 8 '65
Vietnam protest. W. C. McWilliams and D. Hale. Commonweal 83:333-6 D 17 '65
Voice of the new campus underclass. T. R. Brooks. il N Y Times Mag p25-7+ N 7 '65; Discussion. p66+ N 28 '65

STUDENTS letters. See Letter writing

STUDENTS of theology. See Theological students

STUDENTS socio-economic status. See Students—Social and economic status

STUDIER, Martin H. and others
Organic compounds in carbonaceous chondrites. bibliog Science 149:1455-9 S 24 '65

STUDIES (rooms)
How to get that homework done; study centers. R. Martens. il Farm J 89:74-5 S '65

STUDIOS
Truman Capote and the country studio he designed for work. il Vogue 146:208-11 N 1 '65
See also
Artists studios
Moving picture studios

STUDY
Use & abuse of the cept. il Time 85:46+ Mr 26 '65
See also
Home study

STUDY tours. See Travel study courses

STUDY-work plan. See Education, Cooperative

STUECK, Hans Jurgen
How Hitler's war ended, for a German boy. por N Y Times Mag p8-9+ Je 27 '65

STUFFING. See Cookery—Poultry

STUIVER, Minze
Carbon-14 content of 18th- and 19th-century wood: variations correlated with sunspot activity. bibliog Science 149:533-5 Jl 30 '65

STUMP removal
Stump removal wins public favor; Springfield, Ill. W. F. Cellini. il Am City 80:82-3 F '65

STUNKARD, Albert J.
Night eating; excerpts from Overweight society. P. Wyden. Ladies Home J 82:39-40+ Ap '65

STUNT flying. See Aviation—Stunt flying

STUNT men
They die on cue for cash. D. Zeitlin. il Life 58:78B-82+ Mr 26 '65

STURDEVANT, Mary
More girl than sweater. il por Life 58:59-60 My 14 '65

STURGEON, Theodore
Avalanche. Nat R 17:634-7 Jl 27 '65

STURGEON, William
Additional notes on SCR auto ignition system. Electr World 73:70-1 My '65

STURGEONS
See also
Caviar

STURGES, Walter Knight
American romantic landscapes. Antiques 88:689-93 N '65

STURKEY, Don
Hometown faces. il U S Camera 28:68-71 Ag '65

STURM, Paul M.
Theory of maximum use. Library J 90:2341 My 15 '65

STURRUP, Ron
New life for Ron Sturrup. H. Bims. il pors Ebony 21:115-20+ D '65

STUTTS, Patricia, and Fridovich, Irwin
Square root variations of reciprocal graphing of enzyme kinetic data. Science 149:447 Jl 23 '65

STYCOS, J. Malone
Opinions of Latin-American intellectuals on population problems and birth control; with questions and answers. bibliog f Ann Am Acad 360:11-26 Jl '65

STYER, J. Franklin
Hardy orange. Horticulture 43:21 Je '65

STYLE, Literary
Coming revolution in literature. H. Swados. Sat R 48:14-17 Ag 21 '65
Writer-in-waiting. R. L. Stuart. Christian Cent 82:647-9 My 19 '65
See also
Words

Anecdotes, facetiae, satire, etc.
Snap snap. D. Barthelme. New Yorker 41:108+ Ag 28 '65
Word made Flesch; summary of his ABC of style, by D. Hucklesmudge, transcribed and paragraphed by H. Kenner. Nat R 17:558-60 Je 29 '65

STYLE, Musical
Matter of style. I. Strasfogel. il Opera N 29:8-11 Mr 6 '65

STYLE in dress. See Fashion

STYLE shows. See Fashion shows

STYLES in furniture. See Furniture

STYLING, Automobile. See Automobiles—Design

STYRON, Rose
Roxbury; Katama; Home; poems. Yale R 55: 86-7 O '65
STYRON, William
John Fitzgerald Kennedy . . . as we remember him. Hi Fi 16:38+ Ja '66
This quiet dust. Harper 230:134-46 Ap '65
SUBANDRIO, 1914-
Smoldering struggle. il Newsweek 66:56 N 8 '65
SUBCONTRACTING
   See also
Contracts, Government—Subcontracting
SUBJECT departments in libraries. See College libraries—Departmental and divisional libraries
SUBJECT was marigolds; drama. See Zindel, P.
SUBJECTS, School. See Courses of study
SUBMARINE archeology. See Archeology, Submarine
SUBMARINE boats
Alvin dives a mile; deep-diving submarine. il Sci Digest 58:inside cover O '65
New science submarine. il Yachting 117:82 Je '65
Searchers beneath the seas. il Newsweek 66: 84-5 S 27 '65
   See also
Periscopes
Submarine warfare

Airplane combination
Flying submarine designed. il Sci N L 87:221 Ap 3 '65
Flying submersible found practical; Convair study of Sub-plane. R. Pay. Miss & Roc 16:12-13 Mr 15 '65
Sub that sails in the sky. R. K. Massie. il Sat Eve Post 239:52-4 Ja 1 '66

Detection
Navy relies on variety of ASW sensors, platforms. Aviation W 82:83 Ap 12 '65
Systems integration boosts ASW effort. P. J. Klass. il Aviation W 82:36-7+ Mr 1 '65

Equipment
Navy relies on variety of ASW sensors, platforms. Aviation W 82:83 Ap 12 '65

Safety devices and measures
Navy plans rescue craft; Deep submergence systems project. Sci N L 89:13 Ja 1 '66
SUBMARINE boats, Atomic powered
Atomic sub no. 1 Nautilus. E. E. Kintner. il N Y Times Mag p30+ F 21 '65
Lockheed gets go-sign for improved Polaris. il Bsns W p86+ F 20 '65
Silent sea engine for nuclear subs. J. G. Busse. il Pop Sci 188:112-14+ Ja '66
U.K. Polaris program on schedule. R. Lindsey. Miss & Roc 16:22 Je 14 '65
SUBMARINE boats, Research. See Ships, Research
SUBMARINE detection and ranging devices. See Sonar
SUBMARINE diving. See Diving, Submarine
SUBMARINE drilling. See Underwater drilling
SUBMARINE geology
Colston symposium: marine geology and geophysics; report on 17th conference sponsored by the Colston research society. R. S. Dietz. Science 149:94-5 Jl 2 '65
Deep-sea stratigraphy; report on conference supported by the National science foundation. R. F. Flint. Science 149:660-1 Ag 6 '65
East Pacific rise: the magnetic pattern and the fracture zones. M. Talwani and others. bibliog il Science 150:1109-15 N 26 '65
Ocean drilling on the continental margin; Joint oceanographic institutions' deep earth sampling program. bibliog il Science 150: 709-16 N 5 '65
Phosphate may lie under continental shelf. Sci N L 88:345 N 27 '65
Potassium, rubidium, strontium, thorium, uranium, and the ratio of strontium-87 to strontium-86 in oceanic tholeiitic basalt. M. Tatsumoto and others. bibliog il Science 150:886-8 N 12 '65
Uranium-series dating of corals and oolites from Bahaman and Florida Key limestones. W. S. Broecker and D. L. Thurber. bibliog il Science 149:58-60 Jl 2 '65
SUBMARINE oil well drilling. See Oil well drilling, Submarine
SUBMARINE research. See Oceanographic research
SUBMARINE sounds. See Ocean sounds
SUBMARINE structures. See Underwater structures

SUBMARINE warfare
Flying submersible found practical; Convair study of Sub-plane. R. Pay. Miss & Roc 16:12-13 Mr 15 '65
Full speed ahead; ASW. Time 86:19-20 S 10 '65
Navy plans center around ASW. tactical aircraft. il Aviation W 82:76-7+ Mr 15 '65
Navy seeking improved ASW integration. M. L. Yaffee. Aviation W 82:81+ Ap 12 '65
RCA high-speed film processor to aid ASW. M. Getler. il Miss & Roc 16:34-6 Mr 1 '65
Systems integration boosts ASW effort. P. J. Klass. il Aviation W 82:36-7+ Mr 1 '65
   See also
Guided missiles—Launching from submarine boats

Study and teaching
Battle simulator aids navy planning; Naval submarine school, New London, Conn. il Miss & Roc 16:41-2+ Je 7 '65
SUBMERSION
From seal to man; diving reflex in relation to heart disturbances. il Newsweek 65:68 My 17 '65
   See also
Underwater physiology
SUB-PLANES. See Submarine boats—Airplane combination
SUBROC missile. See Guided missiles—Launching from submarine boats
SUBSCRIPTION television, incorporated
Reprieve for pay TV. Time 85:86 My 28 '65
SUBSCRIPTION television programs. See Television broadcasting—Subscription programs
SUBSIDIES
Can subsidies solve America's problems? symposium. il Nations Bsns 53:29-37+ Ag '65
Good and bad subsidies; privately-owned Public service company of Colorado. New Repub 153:7 D 25 '65
Integrate or get nothing; how big is the crackdown? il U S News 58:41-4 My 3 '65
King cotton; completely subsidized. Time 85: 21-2 Mr 5 '65
Myth of American conservatism. R. Lechtreck. America 114:44-6 Ja 8 '66
   See also
Agricultural administration—United States
Family allowances—United States
Ship subsidies
also subhead Federal aid under various subjects, e.g. Railroads—Federal aid
SUBSIDIES, Music. See Music and state
SUBSTITUTE teachers
Save our substitutes. S. S. Allen. il Sr Schol 87:sup20-1 S 23 '65
SUBSURFACE structures. See Underground structures
SUBTERRANEAN houses. See Architecture, Domestic
SUBURBAN life
Maryland's Montgomery County: the changing suburban dream. T. Coffin. Holiday 38: 54-5+ Jl '65
Typical white suburbanite; Gordon Chittenden family of Glendora, Calif. il Ebony 20: 123-6+ Ag '65
SUBURBS
Crime in the suburbs. P. Pierce. il Ebony 20:167-72 Ag '65
Genial suburb. il Esquire 64:220-1 D '65
Suburban renewal; subsidy on the rise. il Nations Bsns 53:42-3+ F '65
SUBVERSIVE activities
FBI's secret war against the Ku Klux klan. J. Barron. il Read Digest 88:87-92 Ja '66
How Castro spreads the revolution; FALN goals. R. S. Strother. Read Digest 87:205-6+ N '65
   See also
Communism—United States
SUBWAY cave. See Caves
SUBWAY strike. See Strikes—United States —Transportation workers
SUBWAYS

Anecdotes, facetiae, satire, etc.
Subways are for dancing. P. T. Hayes. il Atlan 216:132-3 S '65
SUCARYL. See Sugar substitutes
SUCCESS
Deciding the tough ones; interview. M. J. Rathbone. Nations Bsns 53:34-5+ Je '65
For success: work twenty-five hours a day. C. A. Cerami. il Nations Bsns 53:78-80 Ag '65
High cost of success. J. Brothers. Good H 161: 40+ Ag '65
How to become a millionaire. il Time 86: 87-8+ Jl 9 '65

SUCCESS—*Continued*
When a top rung breaks on the success ladder; two books for the executive. il Bsns W p 106+ N 6 '65
See also
Self reliance
SUCCESSION, Presidential. See Presidents—United States—Succession
SUCCINIC acid
See also
Growth inhibiting substances (plants)
SUCCULENT plants
Cacti and succulents in the garden. L. Cutak. il Horticulture 43:18-21+ O '65
Succulents for color low maintenance and texture. W. Radcliffe. il Pop Gard 17:8+ Ja '66
SUCKOW, Ruth
Prairie woods and wild flowers. Am Heritage 16:36-43 Ap '65
SUCROSE. See Sugars
SUDAN
Bad medicine. il Time 86:24 Jl 30 '65
Balloting in blood. Newsweek 65:48 My 3 '65
Odor is of genocide. America 113:149-50 Ag 14 '65
Post for a poet. Time 85:42+ Je 25 '65
Scorpions at work; rebels of the southern Sudan. P. Webb. il Newsweek 66:46+ S 13 '65
Terror down south. Time 86:43 D 10 '65
Too late for peace? Time 86:27 Ag 13 '65
Toward democracy. Time 85:40 My 28 '65

Religious institutions and affairs
They must be kidding; government appeals to Pope Paul VI to aid peace. America 113:232-3 S 4 '65
SUDDEN silence; story. See Alexander, R. W.
SUDERBURG, Ted
New refinements in meter maintenance. por Am City 80:114-16 Je '65
SUEPPEL, William F.
Can driver's license laws really save lives? interview. ed. by D. Gregg. Bet Hom & Gard 43:23-4+ Jl '65
SUERTH, John Charles
How to feed profits as well as babies. il por Bsns W p64-6+ Ja 8 '66
SUEZ CANAL
Decision at Sinai. J. C. Campbell. Sat R 48:55-6 Ap 17 '65
SUEZ crisis. See Egypt—History—Invasion, 1956
SUFFERING
See also
Pain
SUFFOCATION. See Asphyxia
SUFFRAGE
Who votes in other countries. Sr Schol 86:9 Ap 8 '65
See also
Voters, Registration of
Voting

South Africa
One man, one vote in South Africa. R. Kirk. Nat R 17:198 Mr 9 '65

United States
Clean sweep? voting rights bill. Commonweal 82:36 Ap 2 '65
Enforcing the Fifteenth. il Time 85:22-3 Mr 26 '65
Even if they can't read, they should have the vote. A. Hacker. il N Y Times Mag p26-7+ Ap 18 '65
See also
Negroes in the United States—Politics and suffrage
SUGAR
Harm in irradiated sugar? Sci N L 89:43 Ja 15 '66
Sweet talk; hearings on sugar legislation. Reporter 33:10 S 9 '65
See also
International sugar agreement

Physiological effects
Common sugar cures skin, tissue ulcers. Sci N L 89:9 Ja 1 '66

Prices
Sugar stick-up. Nation 201:206 O 11 '65
SUGAR beets
New way to control weeds in sugar beets. W. Meggitt and E. C. Richardson. Suc Farm 63:82 Ap '65
SUGAR cane

Cultivation
Raising cane in a reclaimed swamp; Florida Everglades; portfolio. Fortune 71:169-75 Je '65

SUGAR industry and trade
Cotton candy from Congress. A. Hamilton. New Repub 153:9-10 O 9 '65; Reply with rejoinder. J. A. Schnittker. 153:35+ N 20 '65
Lobbyists: cloud of doubt; Findley plan to amend Sugar act. Newsweek 66:34 O 25 '65
Playing sugar daddy to sugar. Life 59:4 O 29 '65
Salt in the sugar. il Time 85:35 Je 18 '65
Sweet success. il Time 85:105 F 5 '65
Sweeteners; extension of Sugar act. New Repub 153:7 O 9 '65
See also
International sugar conference

Regulation
Sugar quotas go through grinder. il Bsns W p84+ O 30 '65
SUGAR lobby. See Lobbying
SUGAR maple. See Maple
SUGAR substitutes
Animals fed Sucaryl grow more slowly. Sci N L 88:281 O 30 '65
SUGARBUSH VALLEY, Vt.
September is sweet in Sugarbush. il Sports Illus 23:80-3 S 13 '65
SUGARMAN, Daniel, and Hochstein, Rollie
How well do you handle your worries and fears? Seventeen 24:120-1+ F '65
Love and sex. Seventeen 24:94-5+ Jl '65
Why your parents don't understand you. Seventeen 24:134-5+ O '65
You and the dragon jealousy! Seventeen 24:146-7+ N '65
—See Hochstein, R. jt. auth.
SUGARMAN, Tracy
Second invasion. il por Am Artist 29:48-53+ N '65
SUGARS
Paired comparison method for measurement of sugar preference in squirrel monkeys. M. W. Wagner and others. bibliog il Science 148:1473-4 Je 11 '65
Thin-layer chromatography of plant pigments on mannitol or sucrose. L. W. Smith and others. il Science 148:508-9 Ap 23 '65
See also
Glucose
SUGGESTION systems
See also
Ideas in business
SUICIDE
Avert imminent suicide; emergency centers. Sci N L 88:362 D 4 '65
Collegians threaten suicide most often. Sci N L 88:278 O 30 '65
Do they really want to die? K. B. Murphy. il Todays Health 43:48-9+ Ap '65
Freedom to choose one's death. J. A. M. Meerloo. Nation 200:344-5 Mr 29 '65
Giving and taking one's life; case of N. R. Morrison. Christian Cent 82:1404 N 17 '65; Discussion. 83:84 Ja 19 '66
Human voice means more; means of protest. Time 86:118 N 19 '65
Immolations and consensus: the justification of innocence. A. Towne. Christian Cent 83:72-5 Ja 19 '66
In witness to man's oneness; concerning self-immolations of N. Morrison and R. LaPorte. B. Reynolds. Christian Cent 83:81 Ja 19 '66
Incompleat suicide; concerning Symposium on suicide held in Washington, D.C. M. Huxley. il Nation 201:414-17 N 29 '65
Meaningful death. J. C. Evans. Christian Cent 82:1598 D 29 '65
Mortal statistics. K. Nott; reply with rejoinder. M. L. Farber. Commentary 39:6+ Ap '65
Student suicides. America 112:344-5 Mr 13 '65; Reply. D. Brock. 112:470 Ap 10 '65
Suicide that lives in all of us; report of a symposium held in Washington. L. Wainwright. Life 59:26 O 29 '65
Ultimate Goldberg; death of Russell Aubrey Pennington. Newsweek 66:30-1 Jl 12 '65
Welfare, suicide linked? Sci N L 88:111 Ag 14 '65
Why Negro suicides are increasing. J. N. Woodford. il Ebony 20:89-90+ Jl '65
SUITES
See also
Phonograph records—Suites
SUITS, Mens. See Clothing and dress—Men
SUKARNO, 1901-
For Sukarno so loves the world; interview. ed. by C. Adams. por Esquire 64:128-9+ O '65
Sukarno sampler; quotations. por Newsweek 65:42 F 15 '65

about
After an evening with Morning Star. il por Time 86:41-2 O 8 '65

SUKARNO—about—*Continued*
Another Asian country in a weird war with reds. R. P. Martin. il por U S News 58:74-6 My 3 '65
Another big country about to go to the reds. S. W. Sanders. il por U S News 58:80-2 My 17 '65
Blowup in Indonesia: what it means to U.S. and reds. il por U S News 59:43-4 O 11 '65
Down with the Beatles! il por Time 86:19 Ag 27 '65
End of the road for U.S. in Indonesia. por U S News 58:49 Mr 15 '65
Fading dictator flails away, with clipped wings. il pors Life 59:41 N 26 '65
Fumbling juggler. il por Newsweek 66:41 D 27 '65
He wants to keep his people steeped in struggle. T. B. Morgan. il por Life 58:63-4+ F 12 '65
Indonesia: generals who got away. D. Warner. Reporter 33:39-40 O 21 '65
Indonesia: pride & politics. D. Hindley. il Nation 200:636-8 Je 14 '65
Indonesia talks big about nuclear club. Bsns W p32 F 6 '65
Indonesia: the confused coup. il por Newsweek 66:51-4 O 11 '65
Indonesia: the reds are on the run, but... S. W. Sanders. il por U S News 59:63-4 N 1 '65
Indonesia: to brink of civil war. S. W. Sanders. U S News 59:39 O 25 '65
Indonesian army sets back Communists. por Bsns W p31-2 O 16 '65
Indonesia's Communists: down but not out. D. Warner. il Reporter 33:23-6 N 18 '65
No substitute. Newsweek 66:69 N 15 '65
On the southern flank. J. Burnham. Nat R 17:146 F 23 '65
One place Communists met a setback. il por U S News 59:46+ O 18 '65
Peking-Djakarta axis. D. Warner. il Reporter 33:25-7 S 23 '65
Preference for privacy. il por Time 87:25B Ja 21 '66
Question of unanimity. Newsweek 66:54+ N 22 '65
Red paper tiger: failure in Indonesia; interview. S. W. Sanders. il por U S News 59:82+ N 22 '65
Revolt rocks Indonesia. Sr Schol 87:18 O 14 '65
Still swinging. F. Sully. il por Newsweek 66:53-4 D 13 '65
Struggle for power. il Sr Schol 87:17 O 21 '65
Sukarno: headman to a nation. il Newsweek 65:40-4 F 15 '65; Same abr. with title Sukarno: the other Asian problem. por Read Digest 86:97-102 My '65
Sukarno plods on. America 113:617-18 N 20 '65
Sukarno struts as Chen Yi snoozes. il Life 59:36-36A S 3 '65
Sukarno, the would-be emperor. D. Warner. il Reporter 32:24-7 My 20 '65
Sukarno's Indonesia. il por N Y Times Mag p36-9 Mr 21 '65
Sukarno's scheme: all-out break with U.S? il por U S News 58:18 My 3 '65
Sukarno's war against Malaysia. J. Jacquet-Francillon. New Repub 152:16-18 Ap 10 '65
U.S. survivors await Sukarno's ax. il Bsns W p52+ Je 26 '65
Way to the man is the heart. J. M. Allison. il Sat R 48:37-8 N 20 '65
What is Sukarno up to in southeast Asia? por Sr Schol 86:8-11 F 25 '65

SUKARNO, Mme
Jewel Essence Goddess in blue brocade: Mrs Sukarno. J. Schecter. por Life 60:30-30A Ja 21 '66

SULFATES
Ribosomes: analysis by cesium sulfate gradient centrifugation. F. M. DeFilippes. bibliog il Science 150:610-12 O 29 '65

SULFHYDRYL group. See Mercapto group

SULFIDES
Disulfide-bond cleavage and formation in proteins. O. Smithies. bibliog il Science 150:1595-8 D 17 '65
Germanium and silicon disulfides: structure and synthesis. C. T. Prewitt and H. S. Young. bibliog il Science 149:535-7 Jl 30 '65

SULFOXIDES
See also
Methyl sulfoxide

SULFUR
Process cleans sulfur economically and simply. Sci N L 87:232 Ap 10 '65
Sulfur: a new high-pressure form. T. Bååk. bibliog il Science 148:1220-1 My 28 '65
Sulfur: incorporation into the transfer fraction of soluble ribonucleic acid. T. Schleich and J. Goldstein. bibliog il Science 150:1168-70 N 26 '65

Sulfur: role in genesis of petroleum. A. G. Douglas and B. J. Mair. bibliog il Science 147:499-501 Ja 29 '65
SULFUR in plants. See Plants—Sulfur content
SULFUR mines and mining

Canada
See also
Texas gulf sulphur company

Mexico
Heat's on sulfur in Mexico. Bsns W p30 My 1 '65

United States
See also
Texas gulf sulphur company
SULFUR mustard. See Mustard gas
SULLEY, Anita
One man's land of romance. Am For 71:12-15+ Jl '65
SULLIVAN, Aloysius Michael
Reviewing stand. See issues of Dun's review and modern industry
Sanctification of the ordinary. Sat R 48:34-5 D 25 '65
SULLIVAN, Sister Bede
Movie making in high school. Sr Schol 87:sup 13-14 N 4 '65
What every high school English teacher should know about using films in the classroom. Sr Schol 87:sup43-4 S 23 '65
SULLIVAN, Clayton
Speaking out. por Sat Eve Post 238:10+ Ap 10 '65
SULLIVAN, Frances
Laura Ingalls Wilder award; presentation. Horn Bk 41:474 O '65
SULLIVAN, Frank
Greetings, friends! poem. New Yorker 41:25 D 25 '65
SULLIVAN, Fred R.
To reorganize, turn bottom up. por Bsns W p81-2+ Ap 10 '65
SULLIVAN, James
Diffidence; poem. Commonweal 82:154 Ap 23 '65
SULLIVAN, John L.
That was New York. A. Logan. New Yorker 41:44+ F 27 '65
SULLIVAN, Kevin
Last playboy of the western world. Nation 200:283-7 Mr 15 '65
SULLIVAN, Nancy
After the summer; poem. Sat R 48:46 N 13 '65
Fear and disaster; poem. Sat R 48:10 Je 5 '65
Money; poem. Sat R 48:138 Mr 13 '65
SULLIVAN, Peggy
In full swing. por Library J 90:2328-30 My 15 '65
SULLIVAN, Philip R.
Mental health act. America 112:773-5 My 22 '65
SULLIVAN, Walter
How to test relativity; reprint. Sci Digest 57:69-72 My '65
Mars, tantalizing question mark in the sky. N Y Times Mag p 12-13+ Jl 11 '65
SULLIVAN, Wilson
It's Tuesday on Sundays. Sat R 48:90-1 N 13 '65
SULZBERGER, Cyrus L.
King is on trial in Greece. N Y Times Mag p 12-13+ Ag 15 '65
SUMMER
Spacious days of summer; excerpt from Sundial of the seasons. H. Borland. il Read Digest 87:187-8+ Ag '65
Summer delights. il House & Gard 127:104-13 Je '65
SUMMER, Indian. See Indian summer
SUMMER camping. See Camping
SUMMER camps. See Camps
SUMMER community organization and political education. See Southern Christian leadership conference
SUMMER cookery. See Cookery
SUMMER drinks. See Beverages
SUMMER furniture. See Furniture, Outdoor
SUMMER homes
Colorado cliff-hanger. G. O'Brien. il N Y Times Mag p42-3 Ja 31 '65
Fortress by the sea; home of Lawrence Buttenwieser family. il Life 59:82-5+ Ag 13 '65
High-up house; T. Rantoul's home at Martha's Vineyard with plans. il Life 59:78-81+ S 3 '65
How to live like a European in Europe; spend the summer in a rented home. R. Joseph. Esquire 64:121+ S '65
Second home for vacations. il Pop Sci 186:141-5 Je '65

SUMMER homes—*Continued*
Summer at On the rocks. S. Wright. il N Y Times Mag p20+ Ag 8 '65
Summer living in Southampton. il House & Gard 128:100-15 Ag '65
Two-house idea keeps gaining favor; Honolulu house of Mr and Mrs David Barry, jr. il Sunset 135:86-7 S '65
Two houses for busmen's holidays. il House & Gard 127:118-25+ Je '65
Ways to finance a vacation home. il Sunset 134:146-8+ Je '65
SUMMER houses. See Garden houses, shelters, etc.
SUMMER institutes. See Teachers institutes
SUMMER jobs. See Seasonal labor
SUMMER jobs for students. See Student employment
SUMMER meals. See Meals
SUMMER menus. See Menus
SUMMER music camps. See Music camps
SUMMER photography. See Photography
SUMMER reading. See Books and reading
SUMMER reading projects. See Libraries, Childrens—Projects
SUMMER resorts
Don't call it the borscht belt. D. Boroff. il N Y Times Mag p48+ My 9 '65
Splendors at home. il Time 86:38-50 Jl 2 '65
Summer resort pays off a profit for all seasons; Sandusky's Cedar Point, Ohio. il Bsns W p60-2+ S 18 '65
    See also
Fishers Island
Sugarbush Valley, Vt.
SUMMER schools
Art on a fence; summer art class, Beverly Hills, Calif. P. Vandervoort, 3d. il Sch Arts 64:12-14 My '65
Bright-D-minus kids; Upward bound. il Time 86:55 Ag 20 '65
Foreign language summer camps for children. T. O. Brandt. Sch & Soc 93:372-3 O 16 '65
Holiday handbook of summer escape. M. Frome. il Holiday 37:105-10 F '65
June and beyond. N. Kent. Am Artist 29:3+ Je '65
1965 world guide to summer study. il Sr Schol 86:sup5-10+ Mr 18 '65
Summer art workshop for high school students; State university college at Buffalo. S. Kassman. il Sch Arts 64:18-22 Ap '65
Summer seminars; International seminars program sponsored by the St Albans school, Washington, D.C. il Newsweek 66:86+ Jl 26 '65
Summer study-skills program for minority group pupils; project of Educational counseling service. W. D. Martinson and others. Sch & Soc 93:300-2 Sum '65
Travel & study: survey of study opportunities, with directory. il Craft Horiz 25:27-41 My '65
    See also
University extension
SUMMER theater. See Theater—United States
SUMMER vacations. See Vacations
SUMMERS, Bill
Four in a row gotta go! E. Rickman. il por Hot Rod 18:44-7 Mr '65
SUMMERS, Bob
Four in a row gotta go! E. Rickman. il por Hot Rod 18:44-7 Mr '65
SUMMERS, Clyde W.
Labor relations in the Common market. Harvard Bsns R 43:148-50+ Mr '65
SUMMERS, Hollis
Hickory dickory; poem. Sat R 48:35 Ap 24 '65
SUMMIT conferences. See International conferences
SUMNER, Charles
Architects of Negro liberation. L. Bennett. jr. il por Ebony 20:123-6+ F '65
SUMNER, Michael
Varoom at the top: the Madison avenue motorcycle club. Esquire 64:141 N '65
SUN
Controlling the effects of sun's heat on steel doors. J. I. Yellott. il Arch Rec 138:177-8 D '65
Our life-giving star, the sun. H. Friedman. il Nat Geog Mag 128:712-43 N '65
Sun, moon, and planets this month. See issues of Sky and telescope
Which is older, the earth or the sun? quiz. J. Daugherty and M. Daugherty. il Sci Digest 59:92-4 Ja '66
    See also
Eclipses, Solar
International years of the quiet sun
Solar radiation
Sunspots

Atmosphere
Sun as a radar target. Sci Am 212:54 F '65
Spectrum
    See Spectrum, Solar
SUN (newspaper)
Heart trouble at the Sun. Time 85:74+ Ap 2 '65
SUN. Photography of. See Astronomical photography
SUN burn. See Sunburn
SUN CITY, Calif.
Lively art of retirement. G. D. Hunsaker. il Recreation 58:386-8+ O '65
SUN gas. See Helium
SUN glasses
Buying guide to sunglasses. il Good H 160:178 My '65
Instant sunglasses. Sci Digest 58:40 S '65
Instant sunglasses; Bestlite photochromic glass. il Sci Digest 59:28 Ja '66
Something new between the sun and you; Astro-Matic glasses. il Consumer Bul 48:40 Je '65
Something novel in sunglasses; Astro-Matic and Renauld sunglasses. il Consumer Rep 30:272 Je '65
Wraparound Polaroids. C. Conley. il Field & S 70:117 Je '65
SUN screens. See Screens (sun)
SUN shipbuilding and dry dock company
Sun ship rides new building crest. il Bsns W p58-60+ N 27 '65
SUN spots. See Sunspots
SUN tan. See Tan
SUN tan preparations. See Cosmetics
SUN VALLEY, Idaho
How now, Shangri-La? sale by Union Pacific railroad to the Janss corporation. M. W. Lear. il N Y Times Mag p26-7+ Ja 31 '65
Traveling with Mlle: Sun Valley ski scene. il Mlle 62:189-90 N '65
SUNBURN
Case of the sunburned mannequins; with Safety tips for sun worshippers. T. F. Walsh. il Todays Health 43:24-8 Ag '65
Travel well. E. N. Dye. Travel 124:45-6 Jl '65
SUNBURY, Pa.
Versatile new dam that comes and goes away. il Pop Sci 187:52-3 D '65
SUNDAES. See Ice cream, ices, etc.
SUNDARALINGAM, M. and Jensen, L. H.
Crystal and molecular structure of a phospholipid component: L-α-glycerophosphorylcholine cadmium chloride trihydrate. Science 150:1035-6 N 19 '65
SUNDAY
On the seventh day; custom of Sunday observance. Time 87:52 Ja 14 '66
SUNDAY legislation
Never on Sunday. D. Sanford. New Repub 153:7 D 4 '65
SUNDAY lunch; story. See Hale, N.
SUNDAY schools
Sunday school in a pagan culture. E. S. Ringold. il N Y Times Mag p 109-10 S 19 '65
SUNDAY supplements. See Newspapers—Sunday editions
SUNDEW
Caterpillar feeding on a sundew plant. T. Eisner and J. Shepherd. bibliog il Science 150:1608-9 D 17 '65
SUNDIALS
Liénard de Beaujeu's compass-sundial. C. H. Lewis. il Antiques 87:336-7 Mr '65
Sundial monument. H. Egger. il Sky & Tel 30:220 O '65
SUNFISH fishing
Chinks are bedded! G. Gresham. il Outdoor Life 135:34-5+ Mr '65
Living end for bluegills. B. W. Dalrymple. il Outdoor Life 136:64-5+ Jl '65
Shellcracker fever. C. Vinson. il Outdoor Life 135:58-9+ Je '65
SUNFLOWERS
Sunflower. C. B. Lees. il Horticulture 43:24-5 Ag '65
SUNGLASSES. See Sun glasses
SUNKEN gardens. See Gardens, Sunken
SUNKEN treasure. See Treasure trove
SUNSET (periodical)
Golden glow of Sunset. T. Peterson. il Sat R 48:146-7 Mr 13 '65
Ways to store and use old Sunsets. il Sunset 134:139-40+ Mr '65
SUNSET garden. See Gardens—California
SUNSHINE (periodical) See Periodicals—India
SUNSPOTS
Carbon-14 content of 18th- and 19th-century wood: variations correlated with sunspot activity. M. Stuiver. bibliog il Science 149:533-5 Jl 30 '65

SUNSPOTS—*Continued*
Mixed-up sun seen. A. Ewing. il Sci N L 87:293 My 8 '65
Trees, carbon-14, and the sunspot cycle. G. S. Mumford. Sky & Tel 30:279 N '65
SUNTORY, limited. See Japan—Industries
SUPER 8 film. See Moving picture films
SUPER markets. See Supermarkets
SUPER valu stores, Incorporated
Uncle to 1,700 grocers. S. Freedgood. il Fortune 71:130-3 Mr '65
SUPERCHARGERS. See Automobile engines—Superchargers
SUPERCONDUCTIVITY
Coherent matter waves. Sci Am 212:61 Je '65
Cryogenics in electronics. W. Nelson. il Electr World 74:28-9+ D '65
Quantum effects in superconductors. R. D. Parks. il Sci Am 213:57-62+ bibliog(p 127) O '65
Superconducting gallium antimonide. D. B. McWhan and others. bibliog il Science 147: 1441-2 Mr 19 '65
Superconductivity at room temperature. W. A. Little. il Sci Am 212:21-7 bibliog(p 134) F '65
SUPERELLIPSE. See Ellipses
SUPERFLUIDITY. See Fluid dynamics
SUPERHIGHWAYS. See Express highways
SUPERINTENDENTS, School. See School superintendents and principals
SUPERIOR, LAKE
Journey to Gitchee Gumee. M. L. Daly. il Travel 124:40-2 S '65
See also
Isle Royale National Park
SUPERIOR men. See Great men
SUPERIOR national forest, Minn. See National forests
SUPERMARKETS
Cartnappers; theft of supermarket shopping carts. Newsweek 65:109-10 Ap 12 '65
Inside tips on the supermarket; questions and answers. R. Hillery. il Changing T 19: 7-11 F '65
Why you spend so much on groceries. il Changing T 19:25-8 S '65
Yankee marketeers; Italy's largest supermarket. il Time 85:97 Ap 23 '65
SUPERNATURAL
See also
Ghosts
SUPERSONIC air travel. See Air travel
SUPERSONIC airplanes. See Airplanes, Supersonic
SUPERSONIC combustion ramjet. See Jet propulsion
SUPERSTITION
Trading old superstitions for new. M. Mead. Redbook 126:16+ Ja '66
See also
Charms
Demonology
Evil eye
Magic
SUPERVISION in industry. See Industrial management and organization
SUPERVISORY workers
See also
Foremen
SUPPERS
Fondue suppers. il Bet Hom & Gard 43:75+ N '65
Hearty suppers for cold nights; with recipes and menus. il McCalls 93:84-5+ Ja '66
New Year's revel in black and white; with menu. il House & Gard 128:161+ D '65
Speedy supper off the shelf. B. Pierson. il Farm J 89:94 My '65
Sunday-night supper; Danish modern. il Ladies Home J 82:82 Jl '65
Supper for sixteen dancers; with menu. il House & Gard 128:160+ D '65
See also
Buffet meals
SUPPES, Patrick
Adding up the new math. PTA Mag 60:8-10 bibliog(p36) O '65
—and Schlag-Rey, Madeleine
Observable changes of hypotheses under positive reinforcement. bibliog Science 148:661-2 Ap 30 '65
SUPPLEMENTAL airlines. See Local service airlines
SUPPLEMENTAL unemployment benefits
Supplemental unemployment benefit plans in major agreements. D. R. Kittner. il Mo Labor R 88:19-26 Ja '65
Worker to split a jackpot at GM. Bsns W p 104 N 27 '65
SUPPLEMENTARY employment
Medics who moonlight. R. H. Berg. il Look 29:28-32+ F 9 '65

Multiple jobholders in May 1964. H. R. Hamel and F. A. Bogan. il Mo Labor R 88:266-74 Mr '65
SUPPLY and demand
Leverage in the product life cycle. D. K. Clifford, jr. il Duns R 85:62-4+ My '65
Phasing out weak products. P. Kotler. bibliog f il Harvard Bsns R 43:107-18 Mr '65
SUPPLY and demand of college professors. See College professors and instructors—Supply and demand
SUPREME court of the United States. See United States—Supreme court
SUPREME headquarters, Allied powers, Europe
Admiral Moorer appointed Supreme allied commander, Atlantic. Dept State Bul 52: 299 Mr 1 '65
SUPREMES (singers) See Negro singers
SURF fishing. See Salt water fishing
SURF riding
Cool on a hot curl. J. P. Deagan. il N Y Times Mag p72-3 Ag 22 '65
Explorers in the surf; Coronado, Calif. G. D. Hunsacker. il Recreation 58:286-7+ Je '65
Go east, golden boy. il Time 85:62-3 Je 25 '65
Knee & the board; surfer's knobs. il Time 85:75 My 7 '65
Odd sport, and an unusual champion; J. Hoffmann. G. Rogin. il Sports Illus 23:94-8+ O 18 '65
Surfing. il Ebony 20:109-13 Ap '65
SURFACE chemistry
Surface phenomena; report on third annual symposium. L. J. Bonis. Science 150:1630-1 D 17 '65
SURFACE drainage. See Drainage
SURFACE platforms. See Oceanographic buoys
SURFACE to air missiles. See Guided missiles
SURFACE treatment of pavements. See Pavements—Surface treatment
SURFACES
Structure of crystal surfaces. L. H. Germer. il Sci Am 212:32-41 Mr '65
SURFBOARDS
Lifesaving surfboard designed by surgeon. Sci N L 89:8 Ja 1 '66
SURFING. See Surf riding
SURGERY
Bypassing the small bowel; super-surgery for the super-obese. il Time 86:77 O 29 '65
Intern. by Dr X. Review
Newsweek il 66:54 Jl 19 '65
Pig liver; new spare for humans. il Ebony 20:57-8+ S '65
Plastic parts for the human body. Read Digest 86:135-7 My '65
See also
Anesthesia
Children—Surgery
Cryogenic surgery
Foreign bodies (surgery)
Surgery, Military
Veterinary surgery
also subhead Surgery under names of organs and regions of the body, e.g. Heart —Surgery

Anecdotes, facetiae, satire, etc.
Lay lobotomy, go slow. J. H. Slate. il Atlan 216:166-7 N '65
SURGERY, Cosmetic. See Surgery, Plastic
SURGERY, Military
Disarming Mr Chin; removal of grenade. il Time 86:62 N 12 '65
This may hurt; grenade removed from chest of Nguyen Van Chinh. il Newsweek 66:50+ N 15 '65
SURGERY, Plastic
Face maker; cleft-lip and cleft-palate repairs by D. W. MacCollum of Children's hospital, Boston. il Newsweek 67:52 Ja 24 '66
Illusion of a future. J. Medelman. Esquire 64:137+ N '65
Now you can have your hair restored ($1 a hair) your eyelids tightened ($500) D. D. Harris. il Esquire 64:134-6+ N '65
They rebuild broken faces; Institute of reconstructive plastic surgery, N.Y. G. D. Kittler. Read Digest 87:195-6+ S '65
SURGICAL instruments
Clip that artery. il Sci Digest 58:16 Ag '65
Hot blade seals tissue; plasma arc scalpel. F. Marley. Sci N L 87:99 F 13 '65
Neurosurgeons save time with cutting tool; Neurairtome. il Sci N L 87:285 My 1 '65
Promise of bloodless surgery; testing plasma arc scalpel; reprint. il Sci Digest 58:66-9 S '65
SURGICAL operations. See Surgery
SURINAM
Where free enterprise is building a new frontier. M. C. Faught and A. Fairweather. il Nations Bsns 53:40-1+ Je '65

SURO, Darío
New pictorial language. Américas 17:9-13 S
'65
Torres-García of Uruguay, universal con-
structionist. Américas 17:24-9 Mr '65
SURPLUS products, Agricultural
Dwindling farm surplus. S. De Paul. America
114:37 Ja 8 '66
Fading farm surpluses. il U S News 59:116-17
D 6 '65
Farm bureau plan: end food surpluses. Farm
J 90:62 Ja '66
Time for a food reserve. il Farm J 90:118
Ja '66
SURPRISE package; story. See Robinson, B.
SURREALISM
History of surrealism, by M. Nadeau. Re-
view
Sat R il 48:59 O 30 '65. A. Darack
SURREALISM (art)
Avida dollars; Dali show at Huntington
Hartford's Gallery of modern art. A. Wer-
ner. il Reporter 34:45-7 Ja 13 '66
Comedian & the straight man; two shows in
Manhattan. il Time 86:74 D 31 '65
Giacometti and surrealism. F. Getlein. New
Repub 153:31-2 S 4 '65
Square surrealist; Magritte exhibition at
Museum of modern art. il Newsweek 67:57
Ja 3 '66
See also
Dali, S.
SURRENDER. See Capitulations, Military
SURREY, Stanley S.
Great society and taxes; address, October 5,
1965. Vital Speeches 32:145-9 D 15 '65
SURTEES, John
Five against the gods. R. Daley. por Esquire
64:99+ N '65
SURTSEY (island) See Volcanoes
SURVEILLANCE drone. See Airplanes, Drone
SURVEYING
Mosquitoes, mules, and men: Pacific North-
west; with sketches by A. Downing. B.
Le Roy. Am Heritage 16:102-7 Ap '65
See also
Electronics in surveying
United States—Coast and geodetic survey
SURVEYING, Aerial
See also
Helicopters in surveying
SURVEYOR probe. See Lunar probes
SURVEYS. See Library surveys; Educational
surveys; and similar headings
SURVIVAL (after airplane accidents, ship-
wrecks, etc)
Art of survival, by C. C. Troebst. Review
Time il 86:96+ S 10 '65
Fiery throes of a dying cruise ship: Yar-
mouth Castle; with report by D. Nevin. il
Life 59:28-35 N 26 '65
I made my death bed; ed. by B. East, R.
Fisher. il Outdoor Life 135:60-1+ Ap '65
New survival technique: get water anywhere.
D. S. Halacy, jr. il Outdoor Life 136:14-15+
Ag '65
Outdoors. T. Williams. Esquire 64:62+ O '65
Sight few have seen and lived to tell about:
engine fire of Pan American jet after take-
off from San Francisco; with comments by
passengers. il Life 59:20-7 Jl 9 '65
Solar distillation of water from soil and plant
materials; a simple desert survival techni-
que. R. D. Jackson and C. H. M. Van
Bavel. il Science 149:1377-9 S 17 '65
Taste for security; J. W. English's thirty-
three mile swim to Sicily. Newsweek 66:41
S 20 '65
Wreck of the Guinevere. R. Strulo. il Read
Digest 87:110-15 Jl '65
SURVIVAL after death. See Immortality
SURVIVAL of man. See Man—Survival
SURVIVAL tests. See Military training
SURVIVORS; story. See Weesner, T.
SURVIVORS; story. See Williams, T.
SUSANNAH; opera. See Floyd, C.
SUSANO, C. D. and others
Analytical chemistry in nuclear technology.
Science 147:523 Ja 29 '65
SUSPENSION of atomic bomb testing. See
Atomic bombs—Testing, Suspension of
SUSS, Irving D.
Dylan Thomas legend. Commonweal 83:350 D
17 '65
SUSSEX COUNTY, N. J.
Regional dog-control program. B. C. Spragg.
il Am City 80:104-5 N '65
SUSSMAN, Leonard R.
Dilemmas of American Jewry; address,
February 9, 1965. Vital Speeches 31:340-5
Mr 15 '65

SUSSNA, Stephen. See Walnut, A. J. jt. auth.
SUTHERLAND, Elizabeth
Mississippi; summer of discontent. Nation
201:212-15 O 11 '65
SUTHERLAND, Joan
Singing in a tree. por Seventeen 24:164+ S
'65
about
Diva & the orangutans. il por Time 86:61-2
S 10 '65
Mephisto's musings. il Hi Fi 15:161 D '65
Orchids from the Outback; return to Aus-
tralia. por Time 86:51 Jl 23 '65
Sutherland back home. T. Durdin. il por
Opera N 30:36+ O 23 '65
Sutherland comes home. R. Covell. il por Hi
Fi 15:162-3 O '65
SUTHERLAND, W. C.
Creative problem solving. Recreation 58:36
F '65
Creative problem solving for executives. por
Recreation 58:254 My '65
SUTHERS, Hannah Bonsey
Religion and the feminine mystique. Chris-
tian Cent 82:911-14 Jl 21 '65
SUTIN, Helen Gorn
New dimension (calorie-counter's dept.)
poem. McCalls 92:103 Jl '65
SUTOR, Jack A.
Florida boatbuilding. Yachting 117:172 F '65
SUTPHEN, Jack
Distance racing starts. Yachting 117:56-8+
My '65
—and Kostanecki, Andrew
Windward starts. Yachting 117:77-9+ Ap '65
SUTTON, H. Eldon
Biochemical genetics and man: accomplish-
ments and problems. bibliog Science 150:
858-62 N 12 '65
—See Wang, A. C. jt. auth.
SUTTON, Horace
Booked for travel. See issues of Saturday
review
Charm of San Francisco. McCalls 92:24+ Je
'65
Hong Kong high life. Sat R 48:42+ S 18 '65
I remember winter. Sat R 49:42-3+ Ja 1 '66
Primeval wilderness, the Everglades. Mc-
Calls 93:18+ Ja '66
Stop & go with Horace Sutton. See issues
of McCall's to July 1965
Those golden Greek isles. Holiday 39:62-71
Ja '66
SUTTON, Max
In the first place; poem. Christian Cent 82:
1470 D 1 '65
SUTTON, Samuel, and others
Evoked-potential correlates of stimulus un-
certainty. bibliog Science 150:1187-8 N 26
'65
SUYDAM, Henry. See Wainwright, L. jt.
auth.
SUYIN, Han
Chinese side of the story. D. Dodge. por
Sat R 48:60 O 23 '65
SUZANNE Kelly, Sister. See Kelly, S.
SUZDAL, Russia
Saturday in Suzdal. R. Morris. Reporter 33:
42+ Jl 15 '65
SUZMAN, Helen G.
Solitary voice. por Newsweek 65:44+ Je 21
'65
SUZUKA circuit amusement park. See Amuse-
ment parks
SVERBEYEFF, Elizabeth
Home (cont) N Y Times Mag p48-9 F 21;
94-5+ Ap 4; 98-9 Ap 11; 90-1 Ap 18; 84-5
Ap 25; 98-9 My 2; 70-1 My 23; 34-5 My
30; 38-9 Je 20; 36-7 Je 27 '65
SVERDLIK, Jean
Wrap-up senior lesson. Library J 90:4516-
19+ O 15 '65
SWADOS, Harvey
Coming revolution in literature. Sat R 48:14-
17 Ag 21 '65
Tree of life; story. McCalls 92:84-5 Je '65
What's left of the left? Nation 201:108-14 S
20 '65
about
Writer as subject. E. Capouya. Sat R 48:35
Ag 14 '65
SWAGEL, William
Time; poem. Horn Bk 41:531 O '65
SWAIN, Dwight V.
Conflict and how to build it. Writer 78:22-6
D '65; 79:21-8+ Ja '66
Words you write; excerpt from Tricks and
techniques of the selling writer. Writer 78:
18-23 S '65
SWALLOWED objects. See Foreign bodies
(surgery)
SWALLOWTAILS. See Butterflies
SWAMP rabbits hunting. See Rabbit hunting

SWAN, Jon
  Innocents at home. Am Heritage 16:58-61+
    F '65
  Kingdom; poem. New Yorker 41:197 D 4 '65
  Spring changes; poem. New Yorker 41:42
    My 1 '65
SWAN, Joyce Ferris
  When a woman has a whim. . . Farm J
    89:77+ My '65
SWAN, Lester A.
  Pest destroyers; excerpt from Beneficial in-
    sects (cont) bibliog il Audubon Mag 67:
    172-7 My '65
SWAN family
  Swan coat-of-arms. H. K. Eilers. Hobbies
    70:126-7 Je '65
SWAN Lake; ballet. See Ballets—Criticisms
SWANBERG, W. A.
  Dreiser among the slicks; excerpt from
    Dreiser. Horizon 7:5461 Spr '65
  On the fringe; ed. by H. Frankel. Sat R 48:
    40+ Jl 24 '65
  Two novelists: outsider and insider. P.
    Pickrel. Harper 230:116-18 Je '65
SWANDER, Homer D.
  Shakespeare and the Harlem clowns: illusion
    and comic form in Genet's The blacks.
    Yale R 55:209-26 D '65
SWANS
  Endangered species report; whooping crane
    and trumpeter swan. Nat Parks Mag 40:21
    Ja '66
  Mute swans of England; photographs by Lord
    Snowdon. Vogue 146:212-17 D '65
  Painting swans for science. P. Innis. il
    Audubon Mag 67:292-5 S '65

    Anecdotes, facetiae, satire, etc.
  Quiet day with the chavender. J. A. M.
    Graham. Harper 230:32+ Je '65
SWANSTON, Hamish
  Books. Commonweal 83:196-8 N 12 '65
SWANSTROM, Edward Ernest, bp
  World poverty secretariat. America 113:455
    O 23 '65
SWAP funds. See Investment trusts
SWAPPING. See Barter
SWARD, Robert
  Granite for John Torres; poem. Nation 200:
    230 Mr 1 '65
  Italian films; Historical society; Old postal
    cards; Arrival; Pavane; There's no way
    out; poems. Poetry 105:310-12 F '65
  Movies, left to right; poem. New Yorker 41:
    44 Je 5 '65
SWARMING of insects. See Insects—Habits
  and behavior
SWARTHMORE college, Swarthmore, Pa.
  Revising the gothic revival; dining hall at
    Swarthmore. il Arch Rec 137: 137:154-5 Je
    '65
SWARTHOUT, Glendon
  Going to see George; story. Esquire 64:72
    Jl '65
SWARTWOUT, Dave
  Add action to your Christmas displays. Pop
    Mech 124:128-33 D '65
  Animal pinup plaques. Pop Mech 124:156-9
    O '65
  Old door into new door. Pop Mech 124:136-7
    Ag '65
  Your home in replica. Pop Mech 124:146-7
    D '65
SWARTZ, Harold M. and Molenda, R. P.
  Electron spin resonance characteristics of
    some normal tissues: effect of microwave
    power. bibliog Science 148:94-5 Ap 2 '65
SWAYDUCK, Edward
  Gospel according to Swayduck. il por For-
    tune 73:118 Ja '66
SWEARER, Howard R.
  Cults, coups and collective leaderships. bib-
    liog f Cur Hist 49:193-200+ O '65
SWEARING (law) See Oaths
SWEARINGEN, John E.
  Advertising as a communicating force; ad-
    dress, February 9, 1965. Vital Speeches 31:
    304-7 Mr 1 '65
SWEARINGEN company
  Swearingen of San Antone; manufacturer of
    Merlin II. A. Trammell. il Flying 77:70-3
    N '65
SWEATERS
  Sweater care: easy does it! L. Chapman. il
    Good H 161:158 O '65
SWEATING. See Perspiration
SWEDEN
    See also
  Aeronautics. Military—Sweden
  Aerospace industries—Sweden
  Airplane industry and trade—Sweden
  Airplanes, Military—Sweden
  Astronomical observatories—Sweden
  Automobile industry and trade—Sweden

  Ballet—Sweden
  Book industries and trade—Sweden
  Dance schools—Sweden
  Electronic apparatus industry and trade—
    Sweden
  Göta Canal
  Insurance, Health—Sweden
  Music festivals—Sweden
  Oland (island)
  Taxation—Sweden

    Description and travel
  Sweden's pagan beauty. P. Coffin. il Look
    29:49-57 F 9 '65

    Industries
  Keeping mistakes from computers; Addo. il
    Bsns W p 166+ Je 12 '65

    Intellectual life
  Sweden. K. Bernadotte. il Look 29:60-2 F 9
    '65
SWEDEN freezer manufacturing company
  Freezer manufacturer builds a life saver. il
    Bsns W p88+ Mr 6 '65
SWEDES
  Sweden's pagan beauty. P. Coffin. il Look
    29:49-57 F 9 '65
SWEDISH cookery. See Cookery, Swedish
SWEDISH spies. See Spies
SWEENEY, Ben
  Arsenal in miniature. Hobbies 70:122 Je '65
SWEENEY, James W.
  Sweeney's miracle. il pors Look 29:117-18 N
    16 '65
SWEENEY, John L.
  Appalachia, a new greenery this spring. por
    Bsns W p32+ Ap 24 '65
SWEENEY, Pat
  Weekend; poem. America 113:20 Jl 3 '65
SWEEPERS, Lawn. See Lawn sweepers
SWEEPERS, Street. See Street cleaning ap-
  paratus
SWEET, Bruce
  Third day promised; poem. Commonweal 82:
    141 Ap 23 '65
SWEET, Marian
  Yachting interviews: a lady yacht broker.
    M. Wiley. por Yachting 117:61+ F '65
SWEET corn. See Corn, Sweet
SWEET enemy; drama. See Oates, J. C.
SWEETBREADS
    See also
  Cookery—Meat
SWEETENING agents. See Sugar substitutes
SWEETS. See Confectionery
SWEGLE, Wayne
  How to dock and depart with dignity. Pop
    Sci 186:118-21 F '65
  How to equip your boat. Suc Farm 63:52
    Je '65
SWENSON, Carl A.
  America's oldest worker; age: 100. J. Star.
    il pors Look 29:M8+ D 14 '65
SWENSON, G. R.
  Is Dali disgusting? Art N 64:50-1+ D '65
SWENSON, Harvey F.
  Freezer manufacturer builds a life saver.
    il por Bsns W p88+ Mr 6 '65
SWENSON, May
  Colors without objects; poem. New Yorker
    40:30 F 13 '65
  Dear Elizabeth; poem. New Yorker 41:56 O
    9 '65
  Drawing the cat; poem. Sat R 48:13 Jl 17 '65
  11th floor, West 4th street; poem. Sat R
    48:60 Jl 10 '65
  Flying home from Utah; poem. New Yorker
    41:50 My 15 '65
  Four-word lines; poem. Atlan 215:73 Je '65
  Gods. children; poem. Poetry 105:227-31 Ja
    '65
  In a museum cabinet; poem. New Yorker
    41:36 F 20 '65
  Sightseeing in Provincetown; poem. Nation
    202:20 Ja 3 '66
  Wave and the dune; poem. New Yorker 41:79
    Ag 7 '65
SWETS, John A. and Feurzeig, Wallace
  Computer-aided instruction. bibliog Science
    150:572-6 O 29 '65
SWIDLER, Leonard
  Books. Commonweal 82:702 S 24 '65
  Catholic colleges; a modest proposal. Com-
    monweal 81:559-62; 82:174 Ja 29, Ap 23 '65
SWIFT, Joan
  Sestina for Bart; poem. Atlan 217:62 Ja '66
SWIM; story. See Cullinan, E.
SWIMMING
  Last one in is a zero figure! keeping in shape.
    F. Chadwick. il Mlle 61:148-9 My '65
  One for the old folks; A.A.U. championship
    in Maumee, Ohio. Time 86:68 Ag 27 '65

SWIMMING—*Continued*
Strikes and strokes. il Newsweek 66:68-9 Ag 23 '65
See also
Diving

Safety devices and measures
Five water skills every child should know. E. H. Matthew. il Parents Mag 40:53-5+ Ag '65
How to cope with water emergencies. il Good H 160:168 Je '65

Study and teaching
How to prepare children for swimming lessons. il Good H 161:148-9 Jl '65
SWIMMING platforms. See Boats—Equipment
SWIMMING pool heaters. See Water heaters
SWIMMING pool managers. See Recreation workers
SWIMMING pools
Eight landscape tricks for plastic pools. C. Sigman. il Pop Sci 187:132-5 Jl '65
Get ready to get in the swim. Pop Gard 16:50 Ap '65
House divided by a glimmering pool. il House & Gard 128:190-5 S '65
How to test your swimming pool. Sunset 134:153 Je '65
Personal business. Bsns W p 157-8 Ap 10 '65
Plastic pool gets a beauty treatment. R. Hoppough. il Pop Sci 187:136-7 Jl '65
Pool house folly. il House & Gard 129:90-1 Ja '66
Sometimes the color changes. Sunset 135:77 Jl '65
Their remodel plan pulled things together. il Sunset 134:112+ F '65
This pool house is also a greenhouse. il Sunset 135:132+ O '65
Ups and downs of pool alkalinity. Sunset 134:155-6+ Ap '65
You can remove this pool fence. il Sunset 135:104 Jl '65

Cleaning
Special care that portable swim pools need. Good H 160:169 Je '65

Equipment
Things that go with a pool. il Sunset 134:138 Je '65

Heating
Cold figures promote warm water; Waterloo, Ia. R. Forsberg and G. Dietz. il Am City 80:120-1 Je '65
SWIMMING suits. See Bathing suits
SWINDLERS and swindling. See Fraud
SWINE
Eighty litters per year, the low-cost way. C. F. Marley. il Suc Farm 63:34A Jl '65
Hog news. See issues of Farm journal
How to make more money raising hogs. Suc Farm 63:70D Ap '65
Thirty-five top-notch hogmen tell how to farrow on slats. J. Russell. il Farm J 90:30-1+ Ja '66
What's new. See issues of Successful farming
See also
Woods hogs

Diseases and pests
New TGE vaccine gets USDA approval. Farm J 89:45 O '65
Tips on stopping scours. J. B. Herrick. il Suc Farm 63:60-1 Mr '65

Feeding
Blueprint for feeding sows. M. Whiteker. il Suc Farm 63:110 Mr '65
Easier ways to feed a lot of hogs. P. B. Jones and R. L. Maddex. il Suc Farm 63:50-1 F '65
Engineers report on nozzle feeding. J. Russell. il Farm J 89:31 Ag '65
How to cut sow feed costs in half; ed. by D. Wolf. il Farm J 89:D10-11 Mr '65
How to manage feeder pigs for a profit. J. Harvey. il Suc Farm 63:34-5 O '65
New way to manage sows. J. Harvey. il Suc Farm 63:112 F '65
Should you feed hogs a new way? T. W. Perry. il Suc Farm 63:52-3 My '65
Wean every pig farrowed? G. Lorang. il Farm J 89:68 D '65

Grading and standardization
How to save the best gilts. J. Harvey. il Suc Farm 63:34 Jl '65

Judging
Look what's happening to hog shows. R. C. Black. il Farm J 89:32-3+ S '65

Marketing
Feeder pigs, big new business. J. Bickers. il Farm J 89:21+ N '65
New way to sell hogs, auction by phone. D. Hagen. Farm J 89:54A Mr '65
Sell hogs now, or feed them longer? il Suc Farm 63:34B Jl '65

Performance records and registration
Here's how to buy a better boar. J. Harvey. il Suc Farm 63:32-3+ Ag '65

Prices
After $24 hogs, what's next? R. C. Black. Farm J 89:32 Jl '65
Coming soon: futures trading on live hogs. R. C. Black. Farm J 89:37 S '65
Hog outlook: better all the time. R. C. Black. Farm J 89:46 Ap '65
New way to bargain on livestock prices. Farm J 89:64J F '65
Sell hogs now, or feed them longer? il Suc Farm 63:34B Jl '65
What will hog farmers do now? J. Harvey. il Suc Farm 63:54-5+ S '65
Why corn-belt farmers are happy. il U S News 59:69 D 27 '65
SWINE, Cooling of. See Livestock, Cooling of
SWINE, Wild. See Woods hogs
SWINE breeding
How to get big litters. Suc Farm 63:58F O '65
See also
Swine—Performance records and registration
SWINE dysentery. See Swine—Diseases and pests
SWINE farms
Easier ways to feed a lot of hogs. P. B. Jones and R. L. Maddex. il Suc Farm 63:50-1 F '65
How I breed and feed for no. 1 hogs. C. Frederick. il Suc Farm 63:26-7 Jl '65
New way to manage sows. J. Harvey. il Suc Farm 63:112 F '65
SWINE farrowing crates and pens
How to avoid winter farrowing problems. J. Harvey. il Suc Farm 63:54-5+ F '65
Keep 'em cool, save an extra pig per litter. J. Harvey. il Suc Farm 63:48-9 Je '65
New ways to farrow pigs. J. Harvey. il Suc Farm 64:38-9+ Ja '66
Not one pig crushed in 100,000 farrowed! B. Hardy. il Farm J 89:22-3 Ag '65
SWINE house floors. See Swine houses—Floors
SWINE houses
Three buildings, 1,200 hogs, all under roof. J. Harvey. il Suc Farm 63:54-5 Ap '65
See also
Swine farrowing crates and pens

Equipment
Handy ideas for hog raisers. J. Harvey. il Suc Farm 63:53 Ap '65
Scientists zero in on hog confinement; of growing-finishing hogs. R. C. Black. il Farm J 89:44 My '65

Floors
How to convert barns to slats. D. Seim and D. Hagen. il Farm J 89:66B-66C+ Mr '65
Now, cast slats in place; for on-farm slotted floor. A. Gehlbach. il Suc Farm 63:76 S '65
Thirty-five top-notch hogmen tell how to farrow on slats. J. Russell. il Farm J 90:30-1+ Ja '66

Heating and ventilation
Keep 'em cool, save an extra pig per litter. J. Harvey. il Suc Farm 63:48-9 Je '65
SWINE shows. See Livestock shows
SWINE testing. See Swine—Performance records and registration
SWINEHART, Bob
Big ones of Africa hit back. pors Outdoor Life 135:28-31+ My '65
SWING (golf)
Cure for a stiff arm. J. Nicklaus. il Sports Illus 23:55 D 13 '65
One place that you must put the squeeze on. J. Nicklaus. il Sports Illus 24:49 Ja 17 '66
Seeing through some dirty lies. A. Palmer. il Sports Illus 23:32-8 Ag 9 '65
Use a helping hand to steady the head. J. Nicklaus. il Sports Illus 23:60 Ag 23 '65
SWING now, madam! story. See O'Brien, T.
SWINGER cameras. See Polaroid Land cameras
SWINGLE singers. See Singers
SWINTON, Philip Cunliffe-Lister, 1st earl of
In Parliament and Cabinet. Atlan 215:54-8 Mr '65
SWINTZ, Martha
Posies for the potentate; drama. Plays 25:45-53 Ja '66

SWISS opera. See Opera—Switzerland
SWISSAIR. See Airlines—Switzerland
SWITCHES. See Wigs
SWITCHES, Electric. See Electric switches
SWITZERLAND
    See also
  Airlines—Switzerland
  Airplanes, Military—Switzerland
  Alps
  Banks and banking—Switzerland
  Crime and criminals—Switzerland
  Festivals—Switzerland
  Finance—Switzerland
  Libraries—Switzerland
  Merchant marine—Switzerland
  Music—Switzerland
  Opera—Switzerland
  St Moritz
  Schools—Switzerland
  Valais
  Zermatt

    Economic conditions
Good times get out of hand; troubles of a model nation. il U S News 58:71-2 Mr 15 '65

    Economic policy
U.S. companies recross the Alps; ban on hiring Swiss personnel. il Bsns W p90-2+ My 8 '65

    Economic relations
Good times get out of hand; troubles of a model nation. il U S News 58:71-2 Mr 15 '65

    History
     Bibliography
Articles and other books received comp. by A. H. Price. See issues of American historical review

    Industries
Bring money! restrictions on foreign workers. il Newsweek 66:27-8 S 6 '65

    Literary landmarks
  See Literary landmarks

    Religious institutions and affairs
News of the Christian world (cont) Christian Cent 82:1017, 1520-2 Ag 18, D 8 '65
Note on Swiss democracy; anti-Jesuit laws. America 112:346 Mr 13 '65
    See also
  Church and state in Switzerland
SWOBODA, Ron
Sultan of swat from Sparrows Point. W. Leggett. il por Sports Illus 22:70+ Je 14 '65
SWOMLEY, John M. Jr
Limited objectors. Christian Cent 82:1541-2 D 15 '65
SWOPE, Herbert Bayard
Legend emeritus. por Newsweek 66:120+ O 25 '65
World of Swope, by E. J. Kahn, jr. Review
  New Repub 153:31 D 11 '65. R. L. Strout
  Time il por 86:133+ N 19 '65
  Vogue 146:167 O 1 '65. T. Wicker
SWORDFISH
Toughest trophy in the sea. D. Barnes. Sports Illus 23:35 Jl 19 '65
SWORDFISH fishing
Billfish East. B. Wisner. il Motor B 116:37+ S '65
Great jumping swordfish. il Yachting 117:115-17 Je '65
Search for the big swords; paintings, with account by D. Barnes. D. Passalacqua. Sports Illus 23:30-5 Jl 19 '65
SWORDS
Sword hilts by early American silversmiths. J. K. Lattimer. il Antiques 87:196-9 F '65
SYDNEY, Australia
    Architecture
Fifth façade; Sydney's opera house. il Time 86:86 D 10 '65
SYER, Warren B.
Lohengrin complete. Hi Fi 15:203+ N '65
Opera in Connecticut. Hi Fi 15:126-7 Je '65
SYKES, Christopher
Useful victorian. Nation 200:708-10 Je 28 '65
SYKES, Gail
Rock and roll in the Rockies. P. Ryan. il por Sports Illus 23:16-19 Ag 30 '65
La SYLPHIDE; ballet. See Ballets—Criticisms
SYLVANIA electric products, Incorporated
Sylvania steps up IC market drive. Miss & Roc 17:35 Ag 23 '65
SYLVESTER, Robert
Strictly for laughs. il por Newsweek 66:50 S 6 '65
SYLVIA, Avis L. See Humm, D. G. jt. auth.

SYLVIA'S mother; story. See Stiles, M. B.
SYMBOLISM
One red rose, symbol of a bond. E. M. Shisler. il Pop Gard 16:58 S '65
SYMBOLISM (psychology)
In my opinion; mania for finding hidden meanings in everything is a menace! L. Rose. Seventeen 24:222 S '65
SYMBOLISM in architecture. See Architecture—Philosophy
SYMBOLISM of numbers
Mathematical games; Dr Matrix in the guise of a neo-Freudian psychonumeranalyst. M. Gardner. il Sci Am 214:112-15 Ja '66
SYMINGTON, Stuart
Excerpt from debate, June 22 and June 24, 1964. Cong Digest 44:54+ F '65
SYMMETRY
Violations of symmetry in physics. E. P. Wigner. il Sci Am 213:28-36 bibliog(p 126) D '65
SYMONS, Vivian
Faith that moved a church. G. Kent. Read Digest 86:61-5 Ap '65
SYMPHONIES
Postscript of Ives's Fourth. R. Franceschini. Am Rec G 32:223 N '65
    See also
  Phonograph records—Symphonies
SYMPHONY orchestras. See Orchestras
SYNANON foundation, incorporated
Tunnel back, by L. Yablonsky. Review
  Nation 200:256-61 Mr 8 '65. E. Friedenberg
Where junkies learn to hang tough. G. Samuels. il N Y Times Mag p30-1+ My 9 '65
SYNCHRODROPPERS. See Meteorological instruments
SYNCHROMISM
Art galleries; exhibition of some sixty works by members of the group that is currently on view at the Knoedler. R. M. Coates. New Yorker 41:218 O 30 '65
Synchromism, the first American movement; exhibition at Knoedler, New York. W. C. Agee. il Art N 64:28-31+ O '65
SYNDICATE, Chicago. See Chicago—Crime
SYNECTICS, incorporated
Ideas to order. il Sci Digest 59:61-3 Ja '66
Synectics: inventing by the madness method. Fortune 72:165+ Ag '65
SYNER, Frank N. and Goodman, Morris
Polymorphism of lactate dehydrogenase in gelada baboons. bibliog Science 151:206-8 Ja 14 '66
SYNERGISM
Evidence of synergism absent on GT-3. H. M. David. il Miss & Roc 17:22 Ag 2 '65
SYNOPTIC gospels. See Bible—New Testament—Gospels
SYNOVIAL membranes. See Membranes (biology)
SYNTEX corporation
Master of the pill. il Time 87:85 Ja 7 '66
SYNTHESIS
Automated synthesis of peptides. R. B. Merrifield. bibliog il Science 150:178-85 O 8 '65
Periodic compounds: syntheses at high pressures and temperatures. H. T. Hall. bibliog il Science 148:1331-3 Je 4 '65
RNA codewords and protein synthesis. M. R. Bernfield and M. W. Nirenberg. bibliog il Science 147:479-84 Ja 29 '65
    See also
  Biosynthesis
SYNTHETIC food. See Food substitutes
SYNTHETIC intelligence machines. See Automatons
SYNTHETIC metals. See Metals, Synthetic
SYNTHETIC products
    See also
  Silicones
SYNTHETIC quinine. See Quinine
SYNTHETIC rope. See Rope
SYNTHETIC textile fabrics. See Textile fabrics, Synthetic
SYNTHETIC vitamins. See Vitamins
SYPHILIS
Syphilis & the young. Time 86:57 Ag 13 '65
    Diagnosis
False positive syphilis may be danger signal. Sci N L 88:168 S 11 '65
SYRACUSE, N.Y.
    Anti-poverty program
Politics and the poor: Shriver's second thought. J. Witcover and E. Knoll. Reporter 33:23-5 D 30 '65

    Music
Syracuse directions. Q. Eaton. Opera N 29:29-30 My 1 '65

SYRACUSE, N.Y.—*Continued*

Social work

Fighting poverty and city hall. E. Knoll and J. Witcover. il Reporter 32:19-22 Je 3 '65

SYRACUSE university

Poverty-war project under fire; training school for agitators? Community action training center. il U S News 59:52 Ag 23 '65

SYRIA

Right with the crowd. Time 87:33 Ja 7 '66
See also
Government ownership—Syria
Jordan River
United Nations—Syria

SYRKIN, Marie

Arab refugees. Commentary 41:23-30 Ja '66

SYSTEM analysis

System theory; symposium at the Polytechnic institute of Brooklyn, New York. L. Shaw. Science 149:1005 Ag 27 '65

SYSTEM simulation
See also
Computers—Simulation programs

SYSTEM theory. See System analysis

SYSTEMIC insecticides. See Insecticides

SYSTEMS engineering

Information explosion in the factory. H. E. Klein. Duns R 85:pt2 112-13+ Mr '65
Social engineering. Nation 201:486-7 D 20 '65
Systems division concerned with electronics analysis and integration; ERC's systems laboratory and the power conditioning and distribution laboratory. Miss & Roc 16:41-3 My 31 '65
See also
Weapons systems

SYSTEMS management

Firm matches computers with jobs; systems and computers evaluation and review technique. J. F. Judge. il Miss & Roc 16:24-5 Je 7 '65
How to organize information systems. J. Dearden. bibliog f il Harvard Bsns R 43:65-73 Mr '65
McNamara's management revolution; with case study of the impact of systems analysis on airlift and sea-lift capabilities. D. Seligman. il Fortune 72:116-21+ Jl '65
Systems facility has broad duties; ERC systems laboratory. Miss & Roc 16:58 My 31 '65

SYZ, Hans, collection. See Smithsonian institution—Museum of history and technology

SZASZ, Suzanne

Betsy's wonderful blanket. il Parents Mag 40:64-5 Ap '65
—See Gallico, P. W. jt. auth.

SZASZ, Thomas S.

Portrait of a secular moralist. New Repub 153:32-3 N 27 '65
Toward the therapeutic state. New Repub 153:26-9 D 11 '65

about

Psychoanalysis and morality. L. H. Farber. Commentary 40:69-74 N '65

SZELL, George

Profiles. J. Wechsberg. por New Yorker 41:59-62+ N 6 '65
They shall have music. H. Kupferberg. il Atlan 217:112-13 Ja '66

SZENT-GYÖRGYI, Albert

Cell division and cancer; address, May 13, 1965. bibliog Science 149:34-7 Jl 2 '65

SZERYNG, Henryk

Cultural ambassador. il por Time 86:58 S 3 '65

SZILARD, Leo

Sting of the bee in saturation parity. Bul Atomic Sci 21:8-13 Mr '65

SZULC, Tad

Communists, Socialists, and Christian democrats; with questions and answers. Ann Am Acad 360:19-109 Jl '65
When the marines stormed ashore in Santo Domingo; excerpt from 30 days in May. Sat Eve Post 238:36-8+ Jl 31 '65

T

T Flex converter. See Photography—Exposure

T men. See United States—Internal revenue service

TFX. See Airplanes, Military—United States

TGE virus. See Swine—Diseases and pests

TIROS (television infrared observation satellite) See Artificial satellites—Meteorological applications

TRG, incorporated

Synchronization technique used by TRG; Synchrotac adaptation to tactical air navigation. il Aviation W 82:45-6 Mr 22 '65

TRW systems. See Thompson Ramo Wooldridge, incorporated

TV tape recorders. See Video tape recorders and recording

TVA. See Tennessee Valley authority

TWA. See Trans World airlines

TWU. See Transport workers union

TAAFFE, Gerald

Fiction, humor and cartoons for the Montrealer. Writer 78:26-7 My '65

TAAL, MOUNT. See Volcanoes

TABASCO sauce. See Sauces

TABELLINI, Mariella

Training for adult education and rural development in southern Italy. Sch & Soc 93:395-6 O 30 '65

TABLE, The. See Table setting

TABLE decoration

All-America recipes and All-America roses. M. Johnston and H. Mason. il Bet Hom & Gard 43:68-77+ F '65
Bright tables for the bride. E. D. Craster. il Bet Hom & Gard 43:112 Je '65
Centerpieces grow big these days! E. D. Craster. il Bet Hom & Gard 43:56-7 S '65
Fresh uses for silver; centerpieces. Bet Hom & Gard 43:154+ O '65
Glass: dancing lights for party tables. il House & Gard 127:112-15 F '65
Parties with paper. E. D. Craster. il Bet Hom & Gard 43:25-6 Mr '65
Please do eat the centerpieces! with recipes. E. D. Craster. il Bet Hom & Gard 43:132 My '65
Set a fine table in the style that suits you. il Good H 161:120-40 N '65
Six ways to make your party fun. il Seventeen 24:122-5 F '65
Tables that invite you out. E. D. Craster. il Bet Hom & Gard 43:60-1 Je '65
Tips on wedding tables. Bet Hom & Gard 43:114 O '65

TABLE linen

Care tips for table linens. B. G. Wadsworth. il Parents Mag 40:146 O '65
For prettier tables; easy-to-clean cloths. B. G. Wadsworth. il Parents Mag 40:74+ O '65
More merry makings, tassel-tossed tablecloth! il Good H 161:119+ D '65
Two new ways to store your table linens. il House & Gard 128:236-7 S '65

TABLE manners. See Etiquette

TABLE saws. See Saws

TABLE setting

New ways to seat your guests. il House & Gard 129:108-11 Ja '66
Three table setting wardrobes for three personal tastes. il House & Gard 127:144-9 My '65
What a lovely way to dine; outdoor meals. il McCalls 92:94-9 Je '65

TABLE silver. See Silverware

TABLE tennis

Game of war; world table-tennis championships. il Time 85:82-3 My 7 '65

Anecdotes, facetiae, satire, etc.

Spongers seldom chisel. D. Miles. il Sports Illus 23:102-4+ N 15 '65

TABLER, William Benjamin

New big-city hotel. il Arch Rec 138:143-50 Jl '65
With a view of the dollar. il por Time 86:78 Ag 6 '65

TABLES

All-important matter of elbow room. il Consumer Bul 48:43 Ap '65
Drop-leaf table with a new twist. J. F. Bogash. il Pop Sci 186:154 My '65
Folding portable tables. il Consumer Bul 48:33-4 Ap '65
Hang a table on the wall! il Bet Hom & Gard 43:28 Mr '65
Sliding-top cocktail table. S. Ellingson. il Pop Mech 124:175-6 S '65
See also
Billiard tables

TABLEWARE

Silver for Bacchus; elegant ways of offering wine. il House & Gard 128:326-7 N '65

TABORSKY, Edward

Change in Czechoslovakia. bibliog f Cur Hist 48:168-74+ Mr '65

TACHOMETERS

Build your own wireless tach; portable automotive tachometer. R. M. Benrey. il Pop Sci 186:110-12 My '65
Electric eye that measures r.p.m. R. M. Benrey. il Pop Sci 188:98-100 Ja '66

TACHOMETERS—*Continued*
Tachometer & engine idle speed calibrator.
J. S. Shreve. il Pop Electr 22:54-5+ F '65
TACITUS, Cornelius
Tacitus. K. Rexroth. Sat R 48:19 Je 26 '65
TACOMA, Wash.

Water supply
Small-water-works automation earnings. R.
W. McCann and C. G. Kempe. il Am City
80:91-2 My '65
TACONITE
Pellet gives iron ore industry shot in the
arm. il Bsns W p 106-8+ D 4 '65
Resurgence in Bunyan country; taconite
boom. il Time 86:105 O 22 '65
TACTILE receptors. See Nervous system,
Sympathetic
TACTILES. See Touch
TACTUAL perception. See Touch
TADPOLES
Transepidermal potential difference: develop-
ment in anuran larvae. R. E. Taylor, jr. and
S. B. Barker. bibliog il Science 148:1612-13
Je 18 '65
TAEUBER, Conrad
Population growth. Science 151:226-7 Ja 14
'66
TAEUBER, Karl E.
Residential segregation; with biographical
sketch. Sci Am 213:11, 12-19 Ag '65
TAFAWA BALEWA, Sir Abubakar. See
Balewa, A. T.
TAFFEL, Alexander
Challenging the gifted. Atlan 215:99-102+
My '65
TAFT, Pauline Dakin
Green leaves of summer; excerpts from
Happy valley. Am Heritage 16:56-63 O '65
TAFT, Philip
Right to strike. Cur Hist 49:17-22 Jl '65
TAFT, William Howard, 1857-1930
Supreme court justice steps down. D. J.
Danelski. Yale R 54:411-25 Mr '65
Twenty-seventh president 1909-1913. F.
Freidel. il pors Nat Geog Mag 128:548-53 O
'65
TAFT, William Howard, 1915-
United States scientific attaché program.
Dept State Bul 52:113-15 Ja 25 '65
TAFT-Hartley law. See Labor laws and legisla-
tion—United States—Taft-Hartley law
TAGGART, D. Coyd
Helping and healing ministries. Christian
Cent 82:1510-11 D 8 '65
TAGIURI, Renato
—See Guth, W. D. jt. auth.

about
Pattern for success. W. Wingo. il por Na-
tions Bsns 53:48-52+ O '65
TAGUS RIVER
U.S. builders tie Portugal together; span
across Tagus River at Lisbon. il Bsns W
p28-9 Ag 14 '65
TAHITI
Tahiti. D. Messinesi. Vogue 145:255+ My
'65
Tahiti learns about the bomb. H. B. Jacobs.
il N Y Times Mag p45-7+ D 5 '65
See also
Tourist trade—Tahiti
TAHOE, LAKE
Tahoe notebook. J. Brown. il Holiday 38:
76-86+ D '65
TAILORING
Disguising the man. L. Wainwright. Life 58:
33 Ap 2 '65
TAIT, Charles W.
Whatever happened to the State department?
Nation 201:137-41 S 13 '65
TAIWAN
On their own. il Time 86:24 Jl 2 '65

Description and travel
China for Americans. J. P. Gabriel. il Travel
123:58-61 Ap '65

Religious institutions and affairs
See also
Protestant churches—Taiwan
TAIZÉ monastery. See Monasteries
TAKAHASHI, Taro, and Bassett, W. A.
Composition of the earth's interior; with bio-
graphical sketches Sci Am 212:22, 100-6+ Je
'65
TAKASAKI, Takeshi
Nature and function of missionaries. Chris-
tian Cent 83:19-20+ Ja 5 '66
TAKATA, Chinami, and others
Lens fiber differentiation and gamma crys-
tallins: immunofluorescent study of Wolf-
fian regeneration. bibliog Science 147:1299-
301 Mr 12 '65

TAKE my advice; drama. See Murray, J.
TAKE my hand; story. See Norman, G.
TAKEO, Yuji, and Himwich, H. E.
Mescaline,3,4-dimethoxyphenylethylamine, and
adrenaline: sites of electroencephalographic
arousal. bibliog Science 150:1309-10 D 3 '65
TALATY, Erach R. See Russell, G. A. jt. auth.
TALBERT, Bill
How to serve and win. Sports Illus 23:41-4
Jl 5 '65
TALBOT, Norman
Beetpullers; poem. Nation 200:654 Je 14 '65
TALENSKY, N.
Antimissile systems and disarmament; re-
print. Bul Atomic Sci 21:26-9 F '65
TALENT agents. See Theatrical agencies
TALENTED children. See Children, Gifted
TALES of Hoffmann; opera. See Offenbach, J.
TALESE, Gay
Where's the spirit of Selma now? N Y Times
Mag p8-9+ My 30 '65
TALIAFERRO, Mike
Battle of the QBs. por Time 86:96 S 17 '65
TALK. See Children—Language; Conversation
TALK to me; story. See Kassan, R.
TALKING books
Blind can now hear Farm journal. C. P.
Streeter. il Farm J 89:5 Ag '65
See also
Recording for the blind, incorporated
TALKING typewriters. See Teaching machines
TALL men. See Stature
TALLCHIEF, Maria
I cannot wait. il por Newsweek 66:100 O
25 '65
TALLMAN, Frank
Lockheed Vega; a pilot report. Flying 77:74-9
S '65
TALMADGE, Herman E.
Negroes' future in the South; interview. por
U S News 59:66-8+ O 11 '65
TALMUD
Talmud in paperback. il Time 86:68+ N 12 '65
TALOS (guided missile) See Guided missiles—
Launching from ships
TALOUMIS, George
Good ideas from home gardens in Greece. il
Flower Grower 52:28-9 F '65
Plants grow everywhere. Horticulture 43:44-7
Mr '65
Weatherproof plants for the seashore. House
& Gard 128:128-30+ Ag '65
Yuletide geography; New England. Pop Gard
16:27 N '65
TALWANI, Manik, and others
East Pacific rise: the magnetic pattern and
the fracture zones. bibliog Science 150:1109-
15 N 26 '65
TALWAR, G. P. and others
DNA-dependent synthesis of RNA is not im-
plicated in growth response of chick comb
to androgens. bibliog Science 150:1315-16 D
3 '65
TAMAMUSHI, B.
Education in chemistry: United States and
Japan. Science 147:1163 Mr 5 '65
TAMBLYN, Eldon W.
They play it safe. por Library J 90:2495-8 Je
1 '65
TAMES, George
More a kaleidoscope than a still picture. J.
Durniak. il Pop Phot 57:154-5 N '65
TAMING of the shrew; drama. See Shakespeare,
W.—Plays
TAMIRIS, Helen
First and second thoughts about a dance
career; interview, ed. by J. Anderson. pors
Dance Mag 39:30+ My '65
TAMM, Igor. See Eggers, H. J. jt. auth.
TAMPA, Fla.
Apartment tower with two-story base. il
Arch Rec 137:204-5 Ap '65
Raised plaza lends prestige; provides a view;
IBM building. il Arch Rec 138:156-7 D '65
Street lights and traffic signals share one
pole. S. Heller. il Am City 80:124 N '65
Tempest in Tampa; railroads to move out of
town. il Newsweek 66:86+ N 22 '65

Parks and playgrounds
Playground surfing. D. M. Barksdale. il Re-
creation 58:183-4 Ap '65
TAMPA BAY, Fla.
World of Tampa Bay. R. Marston. il Yacht-
ing 118:47-9+ N '65
TAN
Be careful of that blazing sun. L. D. Kirk. il
Parents Mag 40:82 Je '65
New natural look in sun and water. il Look
30:62-3 Ja 11 '66
Tender is the skin. Mlle 61:142+ My '65

TAN—*Continued*

Anecdotes, facetiae, satire, etc.

Letter from Stan Delaplane. S. Delaplane. Todays Health 43:72 Ag '65

TANAGERS
Tanager and a bluebird jousting. J. Vosbergh. il Audubon Mag 67:374-5 N '65

TANCRETO, Anthony Edward
Chief. New Yorker 41:24-6 Ag 21 '65

TANEY, Roger Brooke
Without fear or favor, by W. Lewis. Review Time por 86:122+ D 10 '65

TANGANYIKA
See also
Geology—Tanganyika
Huting—Tanganyika
Political parties—Tanganyika

Politics and government

Nation that tried to help itself. F. L. Howley. Read Digest 86:142-4+ Je '65

TANGERINES
Tangerine boom. il Sunset 134:76-9 F '65

TANGLEWOOD music festival. See Berkshire symphonic festival

TANGO; drama. See Mrozek, S.

TANK ships
Foiling oil down under; first Australian ship to carry Australian oil. il Time 85:106+ F 5 '65

TANKERS. See Tank ships

TANKS, Airplane. See Airplanes—Fuel tanks

TANKS, Military
Army tanks come down the line; portfolio. Fortune 71:120-5 My '65
Common market idea wins a role in defense; U.S. West Germany pool talent and money to develop tank for 1970s. Bsns W p21 Jl 3 '65

TANNER, Clarabel Weir
Getting and keeping a school librarian. NEA J 54:48-50 O '65

TANTRUMS. See Temper tantrums

TANZANIA
From one, many; visit of Chou En-lai. il Newsweek 65:44 Je 21 '65
Tanzania: myth and reality. L. Cliffe. Cur Hist 48:219-23+ Ap '65
Why we guard against subversion. il Time 85:40 Je 11 '65
See also
Elections—Tanzania

TAPE, Adhesive. See Adhesive tape

TAPE, Magnetic. See Magnetic tape

TAPE recorders and recording. See Magnetic recorders and recording

TAPE recordings
Anyone can call predators. R. Tinsley. il Field & S 70:10-12+ N '65
Don't waste a good performance, record it! adapted from Music journal. J. M. Woram. Recreation 58:87-8 F '65
Operas on tape, a bumper harvest. R. D. Darrell. Hi Fi 15:176 N '65
Sound advice; choosing tapes. R. Angus. il Mod Phot 29:36+ Mr '65
Sound, preserved & pirated; sound stealers. il Time 86:98+ N 19 '65
Tape deck. R. D. Darrell. See issues of High fidelity incorporating Musical America
Tape in transition; question and answer. N. Eisenberg. il Hi Fi 15:36-9+ Ag '65
World of sound at the fair. T. Schwartz. il Pop Phot 56:58-9+ My '65

Editing

Sound tape editing made easy. L. Zide. il Mod Phot 29:97+ F '65

Stereophonic recordings

Stereotape reviews. J. W. Barker and others. See issues of American record guide
Tapes: vogue or revolution? Discus. Harper 231:117-18 Ag '65

Storage

Sound advice. L. Zide. il Mod Phot 29:94+ N '65

TAPER, Bernard
Letter from Caracas. New Yorker 41:101-2+ Mr 6 '65
Letter from Port Of Spain. New Yorker 41:203-4+ O 23 '65
Reporter at large. New Yorker 41:58+ Jl 24 '65

TAPESTRY
Outweaving the French; International tapestry biennial. il Newsweek 66:78 Ag 23 '65

TAPLIN, Glen W.
Small park for a big tree. il Nat Parks Mag 39:21 My '65

TAPP, Jesse W.
Staying on top of change; interview. por Nations Bsns 53:46-8+ Ag '65

TAPPLY, H. G.
Sportsman's notebook. See issues of Field & stream

TARABANOV, Milko
United Nations commemoration address, June 25. 1965. UN Mo Chron 2:96-9 Jl '65

TARANTO, Italy
Bridge that splits the city it unites. il Newsweek 65:78 Mr 22 '65

TARDIGRADES. See Arthropods

TARDINESS
Latest thing; being late. W. Stanton. il McCalls 93:86+ O '65

TARGET locators
Cubic proposes sharpening targeting; high accuracy targeting sub-system. R. Pay. Miss & Roc 16:36+ My 17 '65

TARGET practice. See Shooting

TARIFF
Commercial policy at the crossroads; address, September 16, 1965. W. M. Blumenthal. Dept State Bul 53:665-71 O 25 '65
Kennedy round: a progress report; address, May 20, 1965. C. A. Herter. Dept State Bul 53:31-5 Jl 5 '65
Kennedy round; address, March 8, 1965. W. M. Blumenthal. Dept State Bul 52:628-35 Ap 26 '65
See also
General agreement on tariffs and trade

Canada

Ottawa restricts U.S. ads. Bsns W p36 S 4 '65

Germany (Federal Republic)

If you're living abroad and you want an American car: license and customs regulations in Munich; letter from an American citizen. il U S News 58:75 Ap 19 '65

United States

Tabling of agricultural offers in Kennedy round announced; statement, August 19, 1965. C. A. Herter. Dept State Bul 53:452-3 S 13 '65
See also
Duty free importation

TARIFF, Exemption from. See Duty free importation

TARIFF on watches
Watch movement, to West Indies; loopholes in tariff permits duty-free entry into U.S. il Bsns W p 132+ Je 5 '65

TARKENTON, Francis Asbury
Football's blue-chip scrambler. il pors Life 59:57-8+ N 19 '65
Scrambler; quarterback of the Minnesota Vikings. il Newsweek 66:61 S 13 '65

TARNISH preventives. See Polishing materials

TARNISHED plant bugs
Quick way to stop the tarnished plant bug. G. L. Slate. il Flower Grower 52:50 My '65

TARPON fishing
Guide to violence. A. J. McClane. il Field & S 70:74-8+ My '65
Tarpon fever. R. Tinsley. il Travel 123:46-7+ Ap '65
Tarpon of the jungle; paintings. T. Allen. Sports Illus 22:44-9 Mr 8 '65

TARRYTOWN, N.Y.
Police and fire reporting on a single circuit. il Am City 80:103 Mr '65

TARSIS, Valerii
Inconvenient citizens. por Time 85:36 My 21 '65
Man abused. Time 86:78-9 Ag 20 '65
Underground letters. S. K. Oberbeck. Reporter 33:58 O 21 '65

TARTAR (guided missile) See Guided missiles—Launching from ships

TARTAS, Joseph
Receiver noise from antenna to detector. Electr World 74:45-8+ Ag '65

TARTS
They have honest open faces; open-faced fruit and nut tarts; with recipes. il Sunset 135:185 N '65
To serve with tea; with recipes. il McCalls 92:134-5+ My '65

TARTUFFE; drama. See Molière, J. B. P.

TASAKI, Ichiji, and others
Electrophysiological studies of Chilean squid axons under internal perfusion with sodium-rich media. bibliog Science 150:899-901 N 12 '65

TASHI Namgyal, maharaja of Sikkim
Sir Tashi and the yeti. N. W. Ross. il por Horizon 7:104-11 Spr '65

TASHKENT, Russia
Sprucing up. il Newsweek 67:39 Ja 17 '66
Talk in Tashkent; Ayub and Shastri. Time 87:26-7 Ja 7 '66

TASMANIA
See also
Port Arthur

TASTE
Absence of taste-bud papillae in familial dysautonomia. A. Smith and others. bibliog il Science 147:1040-1 F 26 '65
Duplexity theory of taste. G. Von Békésy; reply. R. P. Erickson. Science 147:890 F 19 '65
Matter of taste; taste buds control your appetite. R. Dunlop. il Todays Health 43: 32-4 O '65

TASTE (aesthetics) See Aesthetics

TASWELL, H. L. T.
South Africa; address, March 5, 1965. Vital Speeches 31:495-7 Je 1 '65

TATARIAN, S. M.
Mercury vapors move in. Am City 80:136+ Ag '65

TATE, Allen
Courage of irony; poetry of Allen Tate. K. G. Chapin. New Repub 153:22-4 Jl 24 '65

TATE, Buddy
Jazz concerts; performance in last of this season's Museum of modern art series. W. Balliett. New Yorker 41:112-13 Ag 28 '65

TATE, Peggy Mapes
Grandad. Read Digest 87:66-9 O '65

TATSU, Eisaku
Two nudes. L. Solmssen. il Mod Phot 29:84-5 Je '65

TATSUMOTO, M. and others
Potassium, rubidium, strontium, thorium, uranium, and the ratio of strontium-87 to strontium-86 in oceanic tholeiitic basalt. bibliog Science 150:886-8 N 12 '65

TATTERSFIELD, Shirley, associates, incorporated
There's good money in art by the acre. il Bsns W p 150-2+ Ap 3 '65

TAUBE, Myron
Explosion; story. Seventeen 24:130-1 Mr '65

TAUBINGER, Laszlo M. and Musulin, Stella
Two Communist fronts at work. Nat R 17:328 Ap 20 '65
Youth festival that wasn't. Nat R 17:688+ Ag 10 '65

TAURINE
Gallstones produced experimentally by lithocholic acid in rats. R. H. Palmer. bibliog il Science 148:1339-40 Je 4 '65

TAUSSIG, Helen Brooke
Lady's hand guides fight on heart disease. il pors Bsns W p 130-2+ N 20 '65

TAUTOG fishing
Tip for topflight sport. G. Heinold. il Outdoor Life 136:10+ S '65

TAVARD, George H.
Books. Commonweal 82:572-3 Ag 6 '65
On the snares of mariology. Commonweal 81: 792-4; 82:98 Mr 19, Ap 16 '65

TAVES, Isabella
Hawaiian culture and prestige. Look 29:65-6+ F 23 '65
Revolution on Third avenue. Look 29:34-9 Ap 20 '65
—See Damon, V. G. jt. auth.

TAX collection
See also
Tax returns
United States—Internal revenue service
Withholding tax

TAX deductions. See Income tax—Deductions

TAX evasion
Dog's life; J. De Lyra uses dog as tax gimmick. Newsweek 66:27 D 20 '65
High cost of politics; W. G. Stratton acquitted of income tax evasion charges. il Time 85:30-1 Mr 19 '65
Kind of charity. Nation 201:30 Jl 19 '65
McCrackin reprise. F. Stauffer. Christian Cent 82:186 F 10 '65

TAX exemption. See Taxation, Exemption from

TAX forms
Changes coming in income tax forms. il U S News 59:18 N 1 '65
Do you need these special tax forms? Changing T 20:20 Ja '66
Form 1040. H. C. Wallich. Newsweek 65:84 Ap 19 '65

TAX planning
Can year-end planning save you tax dollars? N. Kuehnl and G. Bush. Bet Hom & Gard 43:11 D '65
Personal business; yearend tax selling. Bsns W p 117-18 N 27 '65
Tax rules you should know before you sell property. F. Bailey, jr. Suc Farm 63:34+ F '65
Tax-saving techniques; investment considerations. il Duns R 86:77-8 D '65

Year-end tips to lower income taxes. N. E. Harl and E. Stoneberg. il Suc Farm 63:34-5+ D '65
Your investments and taxes; what to do before year-end. il U S News 59:111-14 N 15 '65

TAX reduction. See Taxation—United States

TAX refunds
How to get your full gas tax refund. Suc Farm 63:98 S '65
Oil and water; Marvin Shurbet test case brings tax refund. Newsweek 66:82 D 6 '65

TAX returns
Dependents you can deduct on tax returns. il Good H 160:184 Mr '65
Gospel truth; incredible church contributions. Newsweek 65:39 My 17 '65
Here are ways to save on your 1964 taxes. il U S News 58:112-14 F 22 '65
Many unhappy returns; taxpayers moan, but no stampede to moneylenders. Bsns W p32 Ap 10 '65
Personal business; audits will be tougher this year. Bsns W p 183-4 My 15 '65
Tax windfall; computers produce ethical result? America 112:816 Je 5 '65
What computers are doing to your tax return. il Changing T 19:31-2 N '65
When the income-tax man looks over your shoulder. C. Stevenson and J. E. Roper. Read Digest 86:49-50+ Ap '65
When the machines get your tax return. il U S News 58:110-11 Ap 26 '65
Your income tax; five things to do now. il Changing T 20:17-20 Ja '66
Your 1965 tax; with chart. U S News 58:95 Mr 1 '65

TAX sales
Overhead projector aids property sales; Township of Ocean, Monmouth County, N.J. M. H. Worth. Am City 80:155 Ag '65

TAX selling. See Tax planning

TAX write-off program. See Amortization deductions

TAXATION
What other countries are doing about taxes. il U S News 58:82-4 Mr 8 '65
See also
Poll tax
also subhead Taxation under various subjects, e.g. Church property—Taxation

Brazil
Brazil's rich feel the tax man's bite. il Bsns W p60-2+ Mr 27 '65

Canada
Tax cut fever hits Canada. Bsns W p34 Ja 30 '65
See also
Income tax—Canada

Europe, Western
Expense-account living in trouble abroad, too; western Europe. il U S News 58:106-7 Ap 26 '65

Great Britain
Britain props the pound; tightens domestic spending and overseas investment. il Bsns W p27-8 Ap 10 '65

India
Slow death by taxes. Time 85:88 F 12 '65

Sweden
If you wonder where welfare is heading; United States v. Sweden. il U S News 59: 86-7 Jl 19 '65

United States
Ahead; a tax overhauling that will affect everybody. il U S News 58:92+ My 24 '65
Allocation of responsibilities and resources among the three levels of government. J. C. Charlesworth. il Ann Am Acad 359:71-80 My '65
Big issues; debt and taxes; report on study by forty-eight economists; with editorial comment. Bsns W p66+, 156 Mr 6 '65
Broadening the base of tax cuts. il Bsns W p28-9 Jl 10 '65
Budget boost; taxes without tears; concerning President's State of the Union address. il Newsweek 67:67-8 Ja 24 '66
Carriers dig in for tax fight. Bsns W p72 F 6 '65
First a round of tax cuts, and now . . . concerning State-of-the-Union message. U S News 60:89-90 Ja 24 '66
Fiscal policy for the year ahead. Bsns W p 128 Jl 24 '65
Great society and taxes; address, October 5, 1965. S. S. Surrey. Vital Speeches 32:145-9 D 15 '65

TAXATION—United States—*Continued*
Higher taxes? H. C. Wallich. Newsweek 67:
56 Ja 10 '66
If you wonder where welfare is heading;
United States v Sweden. il U S News 59:
86-7 Jl 19 '65
Marilyn Monroe versus Uncle Sam. Sat Eve
Post 238:88 Jl 31 '65
Pay as you use; specialized federal services.
Time 85:101B-2 F 5 '65
Plan for perpetual prosperity: more spend-
ing and tax cuts. il U S News 59:106-8
S 20 '65
Planning to tax less, spend more. Bsns W
p21 Jl 24 '65
Soak the poor is the new trend in taxation.
H. Aaron. New Repub 153:12 S 4 '65
Sweet & sour. Time 87:80 Ja 14 '66
Tax-cut habit. R. A. Musgrave. il Nation
200:643-5 Je 14 '65
Tax man cometh! il Ebony 20:156-7 Mr '65
Tax reform, four basic ideas. M. D. Reagan.
il N Y Times Mag p32+ Mr 21 '65
Tax reform gets lost. New Repub 152:6 My
29 '65
Tax relief denied creator of an idea. H. F.
Pilpel. Pub W 187:73 Ap 26 '65
Tax theory that has proved out in practice.
il U S News 59:85 Jl 26 '65
Thinking ahead in federal tax policy; U.S.
balance of payment; address, November 9,
1965. J. F. Oates, jr. Vital Speeches 32:
105-9 D 1 '65
U.S. counts its gain from tax cut. U S News
58:100+ My 17 '65
War's demands: must taxes rise? il U S
News 60:19-20 Ja 3 '66
What's wrong with our tax system? inter-
view; ed. by G. R. Rosen. M. M. Caplin.
Duns R 85:36-7+ F '65
When next big tax cut will come. Nations
Bsns 53:29-31+ My '65
With all the talk about a tax cut; what
you can expect in 1966. il U S News 59:78
Jl 19 '65
You are paying too many taxes. il Nations
Bsns 53:36-7+ Je '65
See also
Excise tax
Income tax—United States
Local taxation
Property tax
Real property and taxation
Taxation, Exemption from
Taxation, State
Taxation of bonds, securities, etc.
United States—Internal revenue service
also subhead Taxation under various sub-
jects, e.g. Gasoline—Taxation; *also* sub-
head Taxation under names of cities, e.g.
New York (city)—Taxation

TAXATION, Double
How to be rich without paying taxes. A.
Gore. il N Y Times Mag p28-9+ Ap 11 '65
Income tax protocol signed with Federal Re-
public of Germany. Dept State Bul 53:573
O 4 '65
Income tax protocol with Japan enters into
force. Dept State Bul 52:815 My 24 '65
Private initiative for the public good. J. W.
Gardner. Read Digest 87:98-102 O '65
Protocol amending double-taxation conven-
tion with Germany: message, September 29,
1965. L. B. Johnson. Dept State Bul 53:
722-3 N 1 '65
Religious tax exemptions and the First
amendment. J. J. Regan. Cath World 201:
108-12 My '65
Repairing cracks in foundations; Treasury
report on private tax-exempt groups. Bsns
W p34 F 13 '65
Tax crackdown; right-wing organizations.
Nat R 17:315-16 Ap 20 '65
United States and Belgium sign income tax
protocol. Dept State Bul 52:1020-1 Je 21 '65
United States and Israel sign income tax
convention. Dept State Bul 53:122-3 Jl
19 '65
United States and Thailand sign income tax
convention. Dept State Bul 52:437 Mr 22 '65
You are paying too many taxes. il Nations
Bsns 53:36-7+ Je '65

TAXATION, Exemption from
Challenge to tax exemption. D. Wolfe; reply.
L. P. McCarthy. Science 147:986-; 148:734
F 26, My 7 '65
Full tax exemption granted to AAUP. Pub W
188:44 Ag 2 '65

TAXATION, Municipal. See Local taxation

TAXATION, State
Curbing the states' tax reach; taxes on out-
of-state companies and on interstate sales.
Bsns W p85-6+ S 11 '65

In one pocket, out the other; excises cut,
state taxes up. il U S News 59:72-4 Jl 5 '65

Just ahead: a record rise in state taxes.
U S News 58:93-5 Mr 1 '65
Monumental muddle in state taxes. J. F.
Olesky. il Duns R 86:61+ N '65
New U.S. agency urged to run some state
taxes; sales and use levies on out-of-
state companies. Bsns W p58-9 Jl 3 '65
State taxes: problem of soaring demands,
shrinking sources. il Sr Schol 86:12-15 Ap
1 '65
States dig for new revenues. il Bsns W p 108-
10+ My 1 '65
Tax proposal to help states. U S News 59:
117-18 N 1 '65
Tax rises that are snowballing. U S News 59:
121 O 11 '65
Where taxes keep going up and up. il U S
News 59:100+ O 25 '65

TAXATION of bonds, securities, etc.
Deal for du Pont; tax problem over holdings
of GM stock. Newsweek 65:75-6 F 15 '65
In Du Pont-GM divorce: how everybody
fared. il U S News 58:98 Mr 1 '65
Tax-saving techniques; investment considerations. il Duns R 86:77-8 D '65

TAXICAB drivers
Collision in cab vote; SIU battle with
teamsters for Chicago's taxi drivers. il
Bsns W p 128 My 15 '65
Hell on wheels. G. Ace. Sat R 48:12 F 27
'65; Reply. M. M. Reid. 48:29 Ap 17 '65
Our far-flung correspondents; knowledge-of-
London test. J. Bainbridge. New Yorker
41:62+ Jl 3 '65
See also
Strikes—United States—Taxicab drivers

TAXICABS, Aerial. See Air taxi service

TAXIDERMY
Trophy to remember; the skinning of a deer.
C. Elliott. il Outdoor Life 136:40-5+ S '65

TAXONOMY. See Geology—Classification

TAYLOR, Alice. See Reiner, E.; Vouras, P. P.
jt. auths.

TAYLOR, Anne
I don't know where to look for me. por
Redbook 126:8+ Ja '66

TAYLOR, B. J.
This baby will be my last. por Redbook
125:6+ Jl '65

TAYLOR, Bill
How to buy a good used car. Pop Sci 186:
96-9 Ap '65

TAYLOR, Carl E.
Health and population. For Affairs 43:475-
86 Ap '65

TAYLOR, Cecil
Jazz concerts; performance of the new thing
at Town Hall. W. Balliett. New Yorker
41:175-6 Mr 20 '65

TAYLOR, Charles
Image and reality; China from within. Nation
201:180-4 O 4 '65

TAYLOR, Duncan Norton-. See Norton-Taylor,
D.

TAYLOR, Edmond
Algeria: a rude awakening for the left. Re-
porter 33:31-2 Jl 15 '65
Battle in the Delta. Reporter 34:21-5 Ja 13
'66
Battle over Tan Hiep. Reporter 33:26-9 D 16
'65
De Gaulle, Europe, and the dollar. Reporter
32:20-3 F 25 '65
De Gaulle looks left. Reporter 32:13-14 Je 3 '65
First report from India. Reporter 33:14+ O
7 '65
French Africa. Reporter 32:29-31 Mr 25 '65
French politics at the municipal level. Re-
porter 32:31-2 Ap 8 '65
French press warms up to LBJ. Reporter 32:
29-30 Ap 22 '65
Making Gromyko smile. Reporter 32:28-9 My
20 '65
New Communist propaganda strategy. Re-
porter 33:27-9 Jl 1 '65
Permissive planning and the French econ-
omy. Reporter 32:25-8 My 6 '65
Smoke and the fire. Reporter 33:24-7 N 4 '65
Soviet bid for India. Reporter 33:18-23 N 18
'65
Unrequited friendship; economic-warfare. Re-
porter 32:12 Ap 8 '65
Up front in Kashmir. Reporter 33:36-9 O
21 '65

TAYLOR, Edwin W.
Cellular dynamics; the cell cycle. Science 148:
1364 Je 4 '65

TAYLOR, Elizabeth, 1912-
Setting a scene. Writer 78:9-11 Jl '65

TAYLOR, Elizabeth, 1932-
Elizabeth Taylor; excerpts. pors Ladies
Home J 82:79-83+ N '65
Let him...be the first to throw a stone..;
quotations from Elizabeth Taylor. Christian
Cent 82:1463 N 24 '65

TAYLOR, Elizabeth, 1932—*Continued*

about

Burton writes of Taylor. R. Burton. pors Vogue 145:128-33 Mr 1 '65

King and queen. J. Hamilton. il pors Look 29:26-8+ Mr 9 '65

Liz and I. A. Buchwald. Ladies Home J 83:26 Ja '66

TAYLOR, Emily

Keeping house with Emily Taylor. See issues of Good housekeeping

TAYLOR, Fannie

Questions and answers about college bookings; interview. ed. by I. Fisher. por Dance Mag 40:52-3+ Ja '66

TAYLOR, Frank J.

Can your wife afford to be a widow? Read Digest 86:149-52 Ap '65

"Consider the (new-style) lilies..." Read Digest 87:154-9 Ag '65

TAYLOR, George C. Jr

Water, history, and the Indus Plain. Natur Hist 74:40-9 bibliog(p70) My '65

TAYLOR, Harold

American idealism, 1965. Sat R 48:14-16 Je 26 '65

Arts in America. por Dance Mag 39:35-9+ N '65

Need for radical reform. Sat R 48:75-6+ N 20 '65

TAYLOR, Henry J.

Boy borrowed for Christmas; reprint. Good H 161:107+ D '65

Carnage off Key West. Read Digest 86:131-2 Ap '65

TAYLOR, James L. and Christian, Johnie

Home economics facilities. Sch Life 47:13-16 D '64

TAYLOR, Jeff H.

Build a TV picture tube tester and rejuvenator. Pop Electr 23:42-5+ O '65

TAYLOR, John F. A.

Is the corporation above the law? bibliog f Harvard Bsns R 43:119-30 Mr '65

TAYLOR, John Renwick

Apples and new Eve; poem. Christian Cent 82:1008 Ag 18 '65

TAYLOR, Kathryn S.

Hardy orchids. Horticulture 43:20-3 Ap '65

TAYLOR, Kenneth I.

Function before form. por Library J 90:5481-3 D 15 '65

TAYLOR, L. B. Jr

Making the Yuletide count. Audubon Mag 67:350-5 N '65; Same abr. with title Great day for bird lovers. Read Digest 87:83-7 D '65

TAYLOR, Lee

World's fastest man on water. pors Pop Sci 187:96-9+ Ag '65

TAYLOR, Marjorie F.

Book fair exhibit for international understanding. Sr Schol 86:sup 18 Ap 29 '65

TAYLOR, Mark M.

Mahonias. Horticulture 43:20 F '65

Seashore gardens on the Pacific coast. Pop Gard 16:22-3+ Jl '65

Wonderful mahonias. Pop Gard 16:12-13 Mr '65

TAYLOR, Maxwell Davenport

Behind Lodge's reappointment. R. Stolley. Life 59:32B Jl 23 '65

To have a part in it. Time 86:15 Jl 16 '65

Vietnam: new blows, same strategy. il por Newsweek 65:27-8 Ap 12 '65

Vietnam: where do we go from here? S. Karnow. il por Sat Eve Post 238:28-30+ Mr 27 '65

War by any other name. Nat R 17:625-7 Jl 27 '65

Worse before it gets better; H. C. Lodge returns to Saigon. il por Newsweek 66:17-18 Jl 19 '65

TAYLOR, Nathan

Nightmare gobbler. por Outdoor Life 137:46-7+ Ja '66

TAYLOR, Paul

Paul Taylor dance company, Hunter college playhouse. M. Marks. Dance Mag 39:61-3 My '65

TAYLOR, Prince Albert, Jr, bp

Negro heads bishops' council. Christian Cent 82:606 My 12 '65

TAYLOR, R. E. Jr, and Barker, S. B.

Transepidermal potential difference: development in anuran larvae. bibliog Science 148:1612-13 Je 18 '65

TAYLOR, Raymond L.

Fourth Berkeley meeting. il Science 148:1116-25; 149:454-8 My 21, Jl 23 '65

TAYLOR, Richard N.

What good is paving anyway? Am City 80:102-3 O '65

TAYLOR, Roger C.

On the art of reefing. Yachting 117:220-1 Ap '65

TAYLOR, Samuel W.

Improbable successes of Ettie Lee. Read Digest 87:187-8+ D '65

TAYLOR, Theodore, and Atwater, James

I'll put on one hell of a show. Sat Eve Post 238:74-7 O 9 '65

TAYLOR, Thomas E.

Research papers in high school English. NEA J 54:42+ N '65

TAYLOR, Thomas Jefferson

LBJ as a determined suitor; excerpts from letter. U S News 58:51 F 15 '65

TAYLOR, Walter P.

North American ecology. Liv Wildn 87:27 Wint '64

TAYLOR, Zack

Wild horses couldn't hold us back. il Motor B 115:30-3+ Ap '65

TAYLORVILLE, Ill.

Come alive, America; family to keep all the groceries it can snatch from a supermarket in thirty minutes. C. Remsberg and B. Remsberg. il Esquire 63:102-5+ F '65

TAZI, Tamy

Two worlds of Mme Tamy Tazi. il pors Vogue 145:116-23 Ap 15 '65

TAZIEFF, Haroun

Confronting the irascible Irazu. UNESCO Courier 18:18-23+ N '65

TCHAD. See Chad

TCHAIKOVSKY, Peter Ilyitch

Cherevichki. R. Sabin. Am Rec G 31:1006 Je '65

Dorati's early Tchaikovsky on Mercury. C. J. Luten. il Am Rec G 32:381 D '65

Iolanthe (Yolanta) Criticism

Opera N 30:33 D 25 '65

Kogan's Tchaikovsky: violin Concerto in D. E. Belov. Am Rec G 31:1088 Jl '65

Musical events; concert performance of Pique dame by Concert opera association. W. Sargeant. New Yorker 41:119-21 F 27 '65

On records; Queen of spades. Opera N 30:38 Ja 15 '66

Queen of spades (Pique dame) Criticism

New Yorker 41:229 O 9 '65

Opera N 30:27 Ja 15 '66

Opera N il 30:19-22 Ja 15 '66

Sat R 48:39 O 16 '65

Richnesses of Russian opera. C. L. Osborne. por Hi Fi 16:74-6 Ja '66

Trump and no-trump. F. Merkling. Opera N 29:33 Mr 20 '65

TEA

Tea and the teapot story. T. H. Marsh. il Hobbies 70:82-3+ Ag '65

Tea: from medicine to beverage. J. F. Montague. il Todays Health 43:30-5 Ap '65

Tea-totalers? British home sales campaign. il Newsweek 66:86 O 18 '65

Time out for tea, piping hot or icy cold. Good H 161:145-6 D '65

TEA caddy spoons. See Spoons

TEA parties. See Entertaining

TEA pots. See Teapots

TEACH ins. See Teach-ins

TEACHER participation in school administration. See School management and organization—Teacher participation

TEACHER pupil relations. See Teachers and students

TEACHERS

Aid for teachers, what LBJ proposes. U S News 59:8 Jl 12 '65

Editor's notebook. M. S. Fenner. See issues of NEA journal

Governor Carl Sanders and Miss Emma. J. Shepherd. il Look 29:46+ F 23 '65

Modest proposal; misspellings in letters from Texas teachers. Newsweek 65:61 Mr 8 '65

New careers in America's classrooms. L. Velie. Read Digest 86:78-82 F '65

New intermediate school; return to four-year system. P. Woodring. Sat R 48:77-8 O 16 '65

Richard Klinck: teacher of the year. J. Poppy. il Look 29:47-50+ Ap 20 '65

Teachers in slum areas. W. W. Wayson. il Sr Schol 86:4T+ F 11 '65

Teachers: partners in progress; Teaching career month. A. D. Olson. il NEA J 55:62 Ja '66

Teaching the disadvantaged. B. Bettelheim. il NEA J 54:8-12 S '65

Those expensive lay teachers. A. E. Seidl. Commonweal 82:147-50+ Ap 23 '65

Washington report; project to resolve teacher displacement problems. J. Lloyd. Sr Schol 87:sup4 S 30 '65

What's bugging teachers. A. M. West. Sat R 48:88 O 16 '65

TEACHERS—*Continued*

Why teachers fail; address. B. F. Skinner. il Sat R 48:80-1+ O 16 '65; Discussion. 48: 71 N 20 '65

See also
Academic freedom
American teachers in foreign countries
Art teachers
College professors and instructors
Dance teachers
National education association
Negro teachers
Sanctions, Professional
School management and organization—Teacher participation
Science teachers
Substitute teachers

Adjustment

Beginning teacher; symposium. il NEA J 54: 16-31 O '65
Classroom incident. NEA J 54:40-1 O '65
Effective orientation program calls for early planning. G. H. Smith. NEA J 54:47-8 My '65

Anecdotes, facetiae, satire, etc.

Light touch. See issues of NEA journal

Certification

Certification across state lines. S. Simandle. NEA J 54:56-8 D '65
Teacher-opinion poll; nationwide certification. il NEA J 54:50 Mr '65

Contracts

New York averts teacher walkout. Sr Schol 86:sup2 S 30 '65
Professional negotiation. R. O. Daly. NEA J 54:30-1 My '65
Who speaks for teachers? M. Lieberman. il Sat R 48:64-6+ Je 19 '65
See also
College professors and instructors—Tenure

Duties

Crux of the matter. A. Mitchell. Sat R 49: 66 Ja 15 '66

Education

Basic book courses for prospective teachers: young adult literature, bibliography, reference. H. R. Sattley. Wilson Lib Bul 39:797 My '65
Conant's fight for better teaching. M. Borrowman. Atlan 215:113-17 Ap '65
Education courses. L. A. Lemons. il NEA J 54:26-8 O '65
Education of teachers of the disadvantaged; excerpt from American education and the search for equal opportunity. NEA J 54: 12-13 S '65
Foundation of our educational system; teachers of high quality. J. Brademas. NEA J 54:17 D '65
Improvement of teacher education. Sch & Soc 93:442 N 27 '65
India trains teachers for a new age. E. S. Obourn. il Am Ed 1:16-22 Mr '65
Japan points a way. B. Glass. Science 150: 1107 N 26 '65
Need for radical reform; teacher education. H. Taylor. il Sat R 48:75-6+ N 20 '65
Northwestern's new teacher education plan. Sch & Soc 93:76 F 6 '65
Preparation of teachers for school and college. W. W. Anderson. Sch & Soc 93:274 My 1 '65
Preparation of teachers in a liberal arts college. T. M. Carter. Sch & Soc 93:242-4 Ap 17 '65
Standards in teacher education and the new image makers. B. Mehl. Sch & Soc 93:81-2 F 6 '65
Successful executives: now successful teachers; fellowship program at Columbia university. Sat R 48:74 S 11 '65
Teacher education and school libraries. M. V. Gaver. il bibliog f ALA Bul 60:63-72 Ja '66
Teaching the school teachers; Wharton focuses on secondary schools; with editorial comment. il Bsns W p63-4, 144 Ag 14 '65
Threshold to the profession. D. M. Sharpe. NEA J 54:33-5 Ap '65
See also
Art teachers—Education
Educational workshops
Student teaching

Education in service

Albuquerque's climate for in-service education. il NEA J 54:26-7 Mr '65
Fifth year makes the difference; University of Pittsburgh's intern program. C. P. Williams. il Am Ed 1:6-8 My '65
Microteaching; program at Stanford university. D. W. Allen and R. E. Gross. NEA J 54:25-6 D '65

Operation brainstorm; projects of Denver classroom teachers association. J. E. Larson. NEA J 54:41 N '65
POINT points the way; Project for the orientation and induction of new teachers, Washington (state) V. B. Archer and others. NEA J 54:29-30 O '65
Sharing good teaching practices; Michigan Diffusion project. R. O. Lippitt and M. P. Flanders. il NEA J 54:30-2 D '65
Suggestions for the supervising teacher. S. W. Webster. NEA J 54:38 Ap '65

Ethics

See Teachers ethics

Oaths of allegiance, etc.

See Loyalty, Oaths of

Political activities

Fit to teach, fit to vote. W. G. Carr. NEA J 54:11 Ap '65
Local associations ask about teacher's political activities. J. H. Starie and L. Ellison. NEA J 54:50 N '65
Teacher-opinion poll; teachers and politics. il NEA J 54:64 O '65
Teachers, a political force; Washington. C. J. Hannan. NEA J 54:49 N '65
See also
College professors and instructors—Political activities

Qualifications

Achieving quality. G. R. Myers. NEA J 54: 37 Ap '65
Scholar in an age of conflicts; reprint of a 1936 article. C. A. Beard. Sch & Soc 93:43-4+ Ja 23 '65
Teacher-opinion poll; teacher qualifications. NEA J 54:10 Ap '65
Teacher today; amateurs not tolerated in Catholic education; adaptation of address at National Catholic educational association convention, April 21, 1965. A. Thomas. Cath World 202:40+ O '65
Teachers to police their own ranks. Sch & Soc 93:336 O 2 '65

Rating

Evaluating teacher effectiveness. G. Brain. NEA J 54:35-6 F '65
Great teachers. D. Wolfle; discussion. Science 147:556 F 5 '65
What teachers say about evaluation of teachers. H. Davis. il NEA J 54:37-9 F '65

Rating by students

See also
College professors and instructors—Rating by students

Recruiting

Recruiting teachers. New Repub 152:8 F 27 '65

Salaries

Behind a controversy over pay teachers; Oklahoma. U S News 58:16 My 24 '65
City public school teachers' salaries, 1961-63. R. A. Comer. il Mo Labor R 88:396-400 Ap '65
Election and negotiation in Rochester. A. Cantor. il NEA J 54:22-3 S '65
Raising salaries. J. H. Starie. NEA J 54:60 O '65
Teacher salary trends. il NEA J 54:20-1 S '65
Those expensive lay teachers. A. E. Seidl. Commonweal 82:147-50+ Ap 23 '65; Reply with rejoinder. Sister Mary Adele Francis. 82:370-1+ Je 11 '65
Who speaks for teachers? M. Lieberman. il Sat R 48:64-6+ Je 19 '65

Selection and appointment

Misassigning teachers called serious problem; excerpts from Assignment and misassignment of American teachers. Sr Schol 87:sup28 S 23 '65

Social status

Better status for teachers. Sch & Soc 93:478 D 11 '65

Supplementary employment

Dairying and a town job. J. Russell. Farm J 89:64 N '65
Moonlighting in Kanawha County. B. J. Lambert. NEA J 54:21 D '65

Supply and demand

Teacher-opinion poll; staffing slum schools. NEA J 54:64 My '65

TEACHERS—*Continued*

Tenure

All for one, one for all; Overseas education association pledge to million dollar fund for teacher rights. C. Driver. il NEA J 54: 45 N '65

Displacement of experienced teachers without due process. J. R. Picott. NEA J 54: 41 D '65

Million dollar fund for teacher rights. T. M. Stinnett. NEA J 54:38-9 O '65

Publish or perish. Commonweal 81:776-7 Mr 19 '65

Training

See Teachers—Education

TEACHERS, Interchange of

Seis meses en Akron. A. E. Fitzpatrick. il Am Ed 1:6-7 S '65

TEACHERS, New. See Teachers—Adjustment

TEACHERS aides

Volunteer services for schools; National school volunteer program, on NSVP. A. B. Tunick. il Sr Schol 87:sup 10 O 21 '65

TEACHERS and students

Can I so teach? il Sr Schol 87:sup7 S 16 '65

Classroom incident; symposium. NEA J 54: 52-3 Mr '65

College teacher and the student. J. T. Rettaliata. Sch & Soc 93:349-50 O 2 '65

Editor's notebook. M. S. Fenner. NEA J 54:72 S; 72 N '65

Education: worth of the individual; address, February 24, 1965. A. R. Broadhurst. Vital Speeches 31:360-2 Ap 1 '65

Eyes of the beholders. M. M. Romeo. il NEA J 54:41 Ap '65

Fourth-grade course in color; experience of a white teacher in Harlem. B. Kremen. Holiday 37:24+ Mr '65

Jet-age professors; University of California at Berkeley. L. Cross. il Look 29:36-8 F 23 '65

Manner of speaking; university faculty withdrawal from undergraduate teaching. J. Ciardi. Sat R 48:13 Mr 27 '65

Other twenty-nine; prize winning story. R. T. Schmitt. NEA J 54:12-14 O '65

Real world of the beginning teacher; adaptation of address. B. Kaufman. il NEA J 54: 16-19 O '65

Ricardo. V. H. Ormsby. NEA J 54:24-5 Ap '65

Student violence and rebellion, how big a problem D. Iwamoto. il NEA J 54:10-13 D '65

Students, teachers, bureaucrats; protests of university students. Nat R 17:228+ Mr 23 '65

Students to grade college teachers; plans of Oregon and at Yale. Sr Schol 87:sup4 N 4 '65

Teachers who make children hate school. S. Grafton. il McCalls 93:68-9+ Ja '66

Teaching kids to teach themselves. F. V. Rummell. il PTA Mag 60:16-19 O '65; Same abr. with title He teaches kids to teach themselves. Read Digest 87:246-7+ O '65

Way it spozed to be. J. Herndon. il Harper 231:79-87 S '65

Way teaching is; excerpts from address. P. W. Jackson. il NEA J 54:10-13+ N '65

What can the schools do? D. M. Lee. il NEA J 54:25-7 F '65

TEACHERS children. See Children of teachers

TEACHERS contracts. See Teachers—Contracts

TEACHERS education. See Teachers—Education

TEACHERS ethics

Classroom incident. NEA J 54:40-1 O '65

Coercing subordinates to join. NEA J 54:62 Mr '65

Teachers to police their own ranks. Sch & Soc 93:336 O 2 '65

TEACHERS institutes

NDEA institutes for school librarians. Library J 90:1495-6 Mr 15 '65

NDEA summer institute listings. Sr Schol 86:sup4+ Mr 4; sup2+ Mr 11 '65

TEACHERS liability. See Liability (law)

TEACHERS loyalty oath law. See Loyalty, Oaths of

TEACHERS salaries. See Teachers—Salaries

TEACHERS unions

Case for independent professional teachers' associations. S. Dorros; reply. J. M. Glasgow. Mo Labor R 88:535 My '65

Public interest in how teachers organize; Educational policies commission report; reply. L. Fleischer and H. T. Woodworth. Sr Schol 86:sup 10-11 Mr 25 '65

Teachers' unions: rift without differences. S. Elam. il Nation 201:247-9 O 18 '65

See also

American federation of teachers

TEACHERS workshops. See Educational workshops

TEACHING

Constitution: team teaching approach with A-V aids. M. Benefield. Sr Schol 86:sup7-8 Mr 11 '65

Human dimension in college teaching. E. R. Hilgard. il NEA J 54:43-5 S '65

Pressures on students and teachers; questions and answers. G. Hechinger and F. M. Hechinger. McCalls 92:180-1 Ap '65

Reform movement or panacea? curriculum development. T. R. Sizer. il Sat R 48:52-4+ Je 19 '65

Self-direction for teachers; Time to teach project; summary of report. M. M. Provus; A. De Lauter. NEA J 55:49-51 Ja '66

Teaching is better than ever. J. R. Killian, jr. il Atlan 216:53-6 D '65

Teaching kids to teach themselves. F. V. Rummell. il PTA Mag 60:16-19 O '65; Same abr. with title He teaches kids to teach themselves. Read Digest 87:246-7+ O '65

Teaching through stagesetting. G. E. Carrothers. Sch & Soc 93:220-2 Ap 3 '65

Team teaching; Wisconsin improvement program. D. W. Darling. il NEA J 54:24-5 My '65

Way teaching is; excerpts from address. P. W. Jackson. il NEA J 54:10-13+ N '65

Why teachers fail; address. B. F. Skinner. il Sat R 48:80-1+ O 16 '65; Discussion. 48:71 N 20 '65

See also

Academic freedom

Audio-visual instruction

Colleges and universities—Teaching

Education

Individual instruction

Montessori method of education

Psychology, Educational

Remedial teaching

Teachers

Teachers—Education

also subhead Study and teaching under various subjects, e.g. Reading—Study and teaching

Aids and devices

All that glitters is not electronic; exhibit at American management association's conference on The impact of educational technology. R. H. Smith. Pub W 188:37 Ag 9 '65

Change in thinking needed about texts, clinic is told; non-book materials. Pub W 189: 102 Ja 3 '66

Discovering materials for the retarded; Lincoln school, Plainfield, N.J. M. Harayda. il Sr Schol 86:sup 10-11 My 6 '65

Education by electronics; address, December 3, 1965. R. Brent. Vital Speeches 32:175-8 Ja 1 '66

Instructional materials issue; symposium. il Sr Schol 87:6-7 N 4 '65

Mathematics laboratory. H. L. Phillips. il Am Ed 1:1-3 Mr '65

Motivating the slow learner; interests of teen-agers; excerpt from an address, April 1965. W. D. Boutwell. Wilson Lib Bul 40: 75-7+ S '65

New firm will finance educational technology. Pub W 188:30-1 Jl 26 '65

New products. Sr Schol 87:sup31 S 23 '65

Please, Mr Superintendent. E. M. Blue. il NEA J 54:49-50 My '65

Simulators in driver education. R. B. Hayes. NEA J 54:58 Ap '65

Trump plan applied to modern language teaching. J. L. Trump. il NEA J 54:50-4 Ap '65

See also

Audio-visual aids

Phonograph in education

Teaching machines

Television in education

TEACHING, Freedom of. See Academic freedom

TEACHING as a profession

Breakthrough for professional autonomy; status of teaching profession in Oregon. E. S. Crowley. NEA J 54:46-7 N '65

TEACHING assistants. See College professors and instructors

TEACHING fellows. See College professors and instructors

TEACHING-learning laboratory. See Chicago. University

TEACHING load

Conditions of work for quality teaching. il NEA J 54:33-40 Mr '65

NEA time to teach project. M. M. Provus. il NEA J 54:8-10 Ap '65

See also

Class size

TEACHING machines
Alpha-ccm. E. Bukstein il Pop Electr 23: 81-2 N '65
How they make a typewriter talk. W. S. Bacon. il Pop Sci 187:110-12+ D '65
Invasion of classroom by gadgets foreseen. Sci N L 88:67 Jl 31 '65
Machine in the classroom. Newsweek 66:86 Jl 26 '65
New world of teaching machines or Brave new teaching machines? T. Morello. il UNESCO Courier 18:10-16 Mr '65
Omar Khayyam and his talking typewriter; machine teaches two-year-olds to read, spell, punctuate and touch-type. C. P. Gilmore. il Sat Eve Post 238:40-1 N 20 '65
Survey of programmed materials. P. P. Coleman. Sr Schol 86:20T-21T F 18 '65
What the talking typewriter says; Edison responsive environment. M. Pines. il N Y Times Mag p23+ My 9 '65
See also
Programmed teaching

TEACH-ins
Advice to young academic propagandists. D. Acheson. Reporter 33:30 Ag 12 '65
After the Washington teach-in; debate on government's policies and aims in Vietnam. M. Greenfield. il Reporter 32:16-19 Je 3 '65
Egghead soufflé; Washington teach-in. K. Crawford. Newsweek 65:30 My 31 '65
Highbrow to highbrow; Washington teach-ins on United States policy in Vietnam. il Newsweek 65:28 My 24 '65
Intellectuals and Vietnam. S. Alsop. il Sat Eve Post 238:18 Je 5 '65; Same abr. Read Digest 87:136-8 Ag '65
Long lectures for LBJ; protest in colleges over policies in Vietnam and Dominican Republic. il Bsns W p27 My 22 '65
National teach-in: professors, debating Viet Nam, question role of scholarship in policy-making. E. Langer. Science 148:1075-7 My 21 '65; Discussion. 148:1541; 149:498-9 Je 18, Jl 30 '65
New curriculum for teach-ins. C. Lasch. il Nation 201:239-41 O 18 '65
Notes on the Toronto teach-in: the irrelevance of morality. R. H. Welker. il Nation 201:301-4 N 1 '65
President Johnson vs. the intellectuals. Life 58:4 Je 25 '65
Professors and the teach-ins. W. Herberg. Nat R 17:590 Jl 13 '65
Reflections on protest; movement against escalation of war in Vietnam. K. E. Boulding. Bul Atomic Sci 21:18-20 O '65
Revolt of the professors; teach-ins. E. Knoll. il Sat R 48:60-1+ Je 19 '65
Some social implications of the teach-ins. R. Flacks. Bul Atomic Sci 21:21 O '65
Teach-in: new forum for reason; with editorial comment. W. Schott. il Nation 200: 573, 575-9 My 31 '65
Teach-ins. New Repub 152:9 Ap 17 '65
Teach-ins: new force for the times. A. S. Kaufman. il Nation 200:666-70 Je 21 '65
Up all night; called received by the teach-in group at Boston university, May 5, 1965. J. P. Sartre. Nation 200:574 My 31 '65

TEAGUE, Dorwin
High speed in the Caribbean. por Yachting 117:58-9+ Je '65

TEAGUE, H. F.
Learning core. Wilson Lib Bul 40:60 S '65

TEAGUE, Olin E.
Excerpt from debate, March 25, 1964. Cong Digest 44:58+ F '65

TEAGUE, Richard
Designing the Marlin. Motor T 17:28-9 Mr '65

TEALE, Edwin Way
Day with Samuel Gottscho. Audubon Mag 67:164+ My '65
In the valley of ice age wildlife; excerpt from Wandering through winter. Audubon Mag 67:286-91 S '65
Sleeping one of the Hopis; excerpts from Wandering through winter. Natur Hist 74: 26-9 D '65
Wondrous birds and a wondrous lady. il Audubon Mag 67:222-8 Jl '65

about
Four seasons. E. Weeks. Atlan 216:134+ D '65
Visit with Edwin Way Teale. S. H. Gottscho. il Audubon Mag 67:164-9 My '65
TEAM management (business) See Executives
TEAM teaching. See Teaching
TEAMS, Baseball. See Baseball clubs
TEAMSTERS union. See International brotherhood of teamsters, chauffeurs, warehousemen and helpers of America

TEAPOT DOME case
Tempest over Teapot. B. Bliven. il Am Heritage 16:20-3+ Ag '65
TEAPOT trouble; drama. See Nicholson, J.

TEAPOTS
Tea and the teapot story. T. H. Marsh. il Hobbies 70:82-3+ Ag '65

TEAS, Howard J. and others
Cycasin: radiomimetic effect. bibliog Science 149:541-2 Jl 30 '65
TEATRO Amazonas, Manaus. See Opera houses

TEBBEL, John
Amazing communications world of Roy Thomson. Sat R 48:66-8+ O 9 '65
Are authors obsolete? Sat R 48:68-9 D 11 '65
Electronic composing room: how near is it? Sat R 48:75-6 Je 12 '65
Journalism education: myth and reality. Sat R 48:92+ N 13 '65
Keeping up with knowledge. Sat R 48:52-3 Jl 10 '65
Little giant of Nassau County. Sat R 48:68-70 F 13 '65
New life for the Cheshire cat. Sat R 48:64-5 My 8 '65
Newsletters; the ubiquitous medium. Sat R 48:57-8 Ag 14 '65
Strong and steady light. Sat R 48:145+ Mr 13 '65
Teacher of the unteachables. Sat R 48:72+ My 15 '65
What's happening to Sunday newspapers? Sat R 49:110-11 Ja 8 '66

TEBBETTS, Ilse Opton
Transformation of a chronic nag. por Redbook 125:6+ Ag '65

TECHNICAL assistance
See also
Underdeveloped areas
United Nations—Technical assistance program
Volunteers for international technical assistance

TECHNICAL assistance, American
They can't eat our know-how; excerpt from Hungry nations. W. Paddock and P. Paddock. Read Digest 86:83-6 Je '65
See also
United States—Peace corps
TECHNICAL assistance in Afghanistan
Afghanistan: a land 90 per cent unexploited. il UNESCO Courier 18:16-17 O '65
TECHNICAL assistance in Chile
Chile-California experiment. E. P. Dvorin. Bul Atomic Sci 21:35-8 N '65
TECHNICAL assistance in Colombia
Colombia's fabulous valley of the Cauca. il UNESCO Courier 18:6-7 O '65
TECHNICAL assistance in Korea
Advisory group reports on study of science institute in Korea; White House announcement; with remarks, August 5, 1965. L. B. Johnson. Dept State Bul 53:322-3 Ag 23 '65
TECHNICAL assistance in Latin America
Technical assistance, report by the OAS program of direct technical assistance; summary. Américas 17:42-3 D '65
TECHNICAL assistance in the Cameroon Republic
Praise the Lord and pass the lug wrench. K. Engh. il Pop Mech 124:82-5+ D '65
TECHNICAL assistance in the Philippines
Life returns to Death Valley; development of the Tabuk plateau. il UNESCO Courier 18:15 O '65
TECHNICAL assistance in Vietnam
True test; E. Lansdale helps organize rural construction program. il Newsweek 67:34-5 Ja 17 '66
TECHNICAL assistance program. See United Nations—Technical assistance program
TECHNICAL book company
Technical book co. nears 50th anniversary. il Pub W 188:90-2 N 15 '65
TECHNICAL book sales associates. See Professional and scientific sales group
TECHNICAL education
Continuing education. P. H. Abelson. Science 150:831 N 12 '65; Discussion. 151:27 Ja 7 '66
Impact educational technology; excerpts from address, July 1965. F. Keppel. Sr Schol 87: sup 4 O 7 '65
Project choose: Resident schools. K. Gilmore. il Pop Electr 23:41-8 S '65
University of science and technology. J. T. Rettaliata. Sch & Soc 93:225 Ap 3 '65
See also
Delgado trades and technical institute, New Orleans
Massachusetts institute of technology, Cambridge
Trade schools
Vocational education

TECHNICAL high schools. See Trade schools

TECHNICAL information
How do you keep informed? symposium. il Duns R 85:50-1+ My '65

TECHNICAL libraries
See also
Linda Hall library, Kansas City, Mo.

TECHNICAL literature
See also
Booksellers and bookselling—Technical literature
Publishers and publishing—Technical literature

TECHNICAL processes in libraries. See Libraries—Technical processes

TECHNICAL progress. See Progress

TECHNICAL schools. See Technical education

TECHNICAL universities. See Technical education

TECHNICAL workers. See Technicians in industry

TECHNICIANS, Electronic. See Electric workers

TECHNICIANS, Missionary. See Missionaries

TECHNICIANS in industry
Training of optical technicians; Citrus college precision optical school, Azusa, Calif. R. E. Cox. il Sky & Tel 30:41-2 Jl '65
See also
Electric workers

Supply and demand
Your career barometer (title varies) C. Peet. il Pop Mech 124:32+ O; 44+ N '65

TECHNIQUES, papetieres et graphiques exposition. See International exhibition of paper, printing and graphic arts industries, Paris, 1965

TECHNOLOGICAL change
Collective bargaining solutions to technological change; excerpt from address, December 1964. A. Weber. Mo Labor R 88:17-18 Ja '65
Engineering of change in the U.S. Consititution; excerpt from Technology, social change, and the Constitution. A. S. Miller. il Sat R 48:52-5 F 6 '65
Epochal change. Duns R 85:37 Ap '65
Firm of the future. H. I. Ansoff. il Harvard Bsns R 43:162-3+ S '65
From Du Pont, with love; industrial spying and corporate paranoia. E. Engberg. Commonweal 82:465-8 Jl 2 '65
Lockheed scrambles for the battle of the primes. C. J. V. Murphy. il Fortune 71:148-52+ F '65
New look at how machines make jobs. il Nations Bsns 53:58-60+ S '65
Technological dilemma. Nation 200:435 Ap 26 '65
See also
Automatons

TECHNOLOGICAL research. See Industrial research

TECHNOLOGICAL unemployment. See Unemployment, Technological

TECHNOLOGY
Inventor gap; excerpts from address. E. Teller. Newsweek 65:65 Ap 26 '65
Science and scientists; excerpts from address, September 1, 1965. C. Hinshelwood. Sci N L 88:182 S 18 '65
Warn against confusing science and technology. Sci N L 89:9 Ja 1 '66
See also
Engineering
Fluids
Inventions
Space technology

Bibliography
Science, technology; some outstanding titles. il Pub W 187:38-61 Ap 19; 188:42-67 N 15 '65
Scientific, technical, and medical books to come; ed. by J. Putnam and J. Lindheim. Library J 90:4820-65 N 1 '65
Scientific, technical, and medical books to come; ed. by J. Putnam and R. Grossman. Library J 90:1160-201, 3083-119 Mr 1, Jl '65
Technical books of 1964; one hundred outstanding titles for a general collection; comp. by G. S. Bonn. il Library J 90:1041-7 Mr 1 '65

TECHNOLOGY and civilization
Is it a dream or a nightmare? excerpt from Technological society. J. Ellul. Sat R 48:58-9 F 6 '65
National planning of science and technology in France; adaptation of address, October 1964. J. B. Quinn. bibliog il Science 150:993-1003 N 19 '65
Profiles; R. B. Fuller. C. Tomkins. New Yorker 41:35-6+ Ja 8 '66

Technological society, by J. Ellul. Review
Nation 199:249-52 O 19 '64. R. Theobald; Reply with rejoinder. J. Ellul. 200:567-9 My 24 '65
Sci Am 212:125-6+ F '65. A. R. Hall
Vision of the year 2000; scientific and technological revolution. C. B. Luce. McCalls 93:44+ Ja '66

TECTONICS. See Geology, Structural

TEEN-age audiences. See Audiences

TEEN-age automobile drivers. See Automobile drivers

TEEN-age buying. See Youth market

TEEN-age centers. See Recreation centers

TEEN-age clothes. See Clothing and dress

TEEN-age drinking. See Liquor problem—United States

TEEN-age drivers. See Automobile drivers

TEEN-age drug addicts. See Narcotic addicts

TEEN-age employment. See Youth—Employment

TEEN-age entertaining. See Entertaining

TEEN-age fads. See Fads

TEEN-age gambling. See Gambling

TEEN-age marriage. See High school students, Married

TEEN-age parties. See Entertaining

TEEN-age reading. See Books and reading

TEEN-age reading lists. See Reading lists

TEEN-age slang. See Slang

TEEN-age smoking. See Smoking

TEEN-age spending. See Budget, Personal

TEEN-agers. See Adolescence; Youth

TEEN-agers amusements. See Amusements

TEEN-agers food preferences. See Food preferences

TEEN city, Denver. See Recreation centers

TEEPLE, John B.
Recent arms control research in Europe. Bul Atomic Sci 21:37-9 O '65

TEES
For a direct hit, tee the target high. J. Nicklaus. il Sports Illus 22:47 F 8 '65
Use your head and use a tee. J. Nicklaus. il Sports Illus 22:42 F 1 '65

TEETH
Little fluorine is good. il Time 86:44 S 3 '65
More malocclusion than once believed. Sci N L 88:114 Ag 21 '65
See also
Dentists
Orthodontics

Care and hygiene
Cavities can be prevented. F. H. Allen and J. E. Allen. il Parents Mag 40:52-3+ Jl '65
Fluoride protection of bones and teeth. R. F. Sognnaes. bibliog il Science 150:989-93 N 19 '65
Home care program brings dentists to patients; Cleveland's Dental home care program. il Todays Health 43:74 S '65
Pedodontics: children's own dentistry. M. J. E. Senn. il McCalls 93:38+ Ja '66
Your children's teeth. A. N. Cranin and N. M. Lobsenz. il Redbook 125:55-62 O '65

Diseases
Double mating: its use to study heritable factors in dental caries. R. H. Larson and M. E. Simms. bibliog Science 149:982-3 Ag 27 '65
Mouth cells possible factor in tooth decay. Sci N L 87:73 Ja 30 '65
No nibbling, says dentist. il Sci Digest 58:35 Jl '65
To end leaky fillings. Sci N L 89:22 Ja 8 '66
Tooth decay and loss prevalent in adults. Sci N L 88:120 Ag 21 '65

TEETH, Artificial
Do-it-yourself denture repairs prove costly. Sci N L 88:185 S 18 '65
New materials & new techniques for dentures. il Changing T 19:43-4 Ap '65
Replacing teeth with plastic. il Time 86:57 Ag 13 '65

TEETH, Transplantation of. See Transplantation of organs, tissues, etc.

TEFFT, Elden
Workshop: the primitive foundry. Craft Horiz 25:26-31 Mr '65

TEFLON
Fantastic Fabroid. E. Rickman. il Hot Rod 18:68-9 O '65

TEFLON-coated cookware. See Kitchen utensils

TEFLON-coated electric skillets. See Electric apparatus and appliances, Domestic

TEHACHAPI MOUNTAINS
Another way across the Tehachapi; Oak Creek Pass. il Sunset 136:19 Ja '66

TEHAN, Arline, and Tehan, John
Chiefly from the heart. Christian Cent 82:1548-50 D 15 '65

TEHAN, John. See Than, A. jt. auth.

TEHO, Fortunato
Yuletide geography; Hawaii. Pop Gard 16:26 N '65

TEICHER, Louis
Theme team. por Time 85:72 F 5 '65

TEICHERT, Curt, and Stauffer, K. W.
Paleozoic reef in Pakistan. bibliog Science 150:1287-8 D 3 '65

TEIID lizards. See Lizards

TEILHARD DE CHARDIN, Pierre
Books. H. Swanston. Commonweal 83:196-8 N 12 '65
On Teilhard de Chardin. S. Toulmin. Commentary 39:50-5 Mr '65; Discussion. 40:6+ Ag '65
Phenomenon of Teilhard. D. R. Campion. America 112:480-1 Ap 10 '65; Reply with rejoinder. T. Molnar. 112:696-7 My 15 '65
Phenomenon of Teilhard. J. Collignon. Christian Cent 82:426-8 Ap 7 '65
Teilhard de Chardin and the Afro-Asian world. T. P. Melady and M. B. Melady. Cath World 202:102-6 N '65
Teilhard de Chardin: the attack on man. F. S. Meyer. Nat R 17:596 Jl 13 '65
Teilhard de Chardin: the man and his meaning, by H. de Lubac. Review
  America 113:754 D 11 '65. D. A. Drennen
Vision of Father Pierre. H. Downs. por Sci Digest 57:85-91 F '65

TEKLE, Afewerk
Ethiopian artist extols his land. il pors Ebony 20:90-2+ Je '65

TEKTITES
Coesite discovered in tektites; Muong Nong type tektites from Thailand. L. S. Walter. bibliog il Science 147:1029-32 F 26 '65; Reply. S. R. Taylor. 149:658-9 Ag 6 '65
Glass from outer space has ripples like water. Sci N L 87:121 F 20 '65

TELECOMMUNICATION
See also
International telecommunication union
Telephone

TELEGRAMS
Things you can send by wire. il Good H 160:134 Ja '65

TELEGRAPH
Telegraph: long-distance writing; reprint. il Sci Digest 57:80-1 My '65

History
Real inventor of wireless. T. Appleby. il Pop Electr 23:64-6+ O '65

TELEGRAPH, Wireless
Real inventor of wireless. T. Appleby. il Pop Electr 23:64-6+ O '65

TELEGRAPH codes. See Cipher and telegraph codes

TELEGRAPH company, Western union. See Western union telegraph company

TELEMANN, Georg Philipp
Feast at Telemann's table; reports by R. Rolland and R. Freed with introductory note by I. Kolodin. por Sat R 48:79-81+ O 30 '65
Passion according to Saint Mark; more Telemann, and especially Musique de table. J. W. Barker. Am Rec G 31:792-6 My '65

TELEMETER
Advanced TM/MDI proposed for three-T's: Terrier, Tartar and Talos. C. D. LaFond. il Miss & Roc 16:22-3 My 24 '65
Telemetering ties cut operating costs; centralizing the operation of five small water districts with a large distribution area. S. Friedman. il Am City 80:96-7 N '65
See also
Range finding
Space telemetry

TELEPATHY
Pseudo experience in parapsychology; letter. L. W. Alvarez. Science 148:1541 Je 18 '65; Discussion. 149:910; 150:436 Ag 27, O 22 '65
See also
Extrasensory perception

TELEPHONE
Day the phone rang false; vicious attack on the PTA. PTA Mag 60:31-2 N '65
Dial-a-diatribe; attack on the PTA over recording service. New Repub 153:7 O 16 '65
From telephone to telly-phone. il UNESCO Courier 18:10-13 My '65
Hate line is still busy; concerning anonymous dial-a-hate messages. Christian Cent 82:1276 O 20 '65
Hello, is anyone there? answering machines. Time 86:66 S 3 '65

Nine far-out ways to talk and see. il Sci Digest 57:48-52 Mr '65
Telephone: long-distance talking; reprint. il Sci Digest 57:81-2 My '65
Telephones for the deaf; reprint. G. M. Smith. il Sci Digest 57:55-9 My '65
They're still inventing the telephone. H. Fantel. il Pop Sci 187:94-6+ D '65
See also
Radio telephone on ships, boats, etc.
Telephone selling

Anecdotes, facetiae, satire, etc.
Irish phone call. D. S. Matthews. il America 112:395-6 Mr 20 '65

History
Voice heard round the world; excerpt from Conquest of silence. L. Barnett. il Am Heritage 16:50-9+ Ap '65

Intercommunicating systems
See Intercommunicating systems

Rates
See also
Government investigations—American telephone and telegraph company

Television combination
Business gets eye-to-eye by phone; Picturephone. il Bsns W p30-1 Ag 14 '65
Dial F for future. il Sci N L 88:134+ Ag 28 '65
Nine far-out ways to talk and see. il Sci Digest 57:48-52 Mr '65
Picturephone as a photo tool. F. Wilson. il Pop Phot 57:36 O '65

Wire tapping
See Wire tapping

Europe, Western
Up the down escalator. Newsweek 66:58 Ag 23 '65

TELEPHONE, Dial
Dial F for future. il Sci N L 88:134+ Ag 28 '65

TELEPHONE calls
Basic rules of telephone etiquette. Good H 160:180 My '65
How to cope with crank telephone calls. D. J. Giese. Read Digest 86:138-40 My '65
Telephone terrorism; hate calls. P. Watters. Atlan 215:118-21 Ap '65
What to do about crank calls and mail. il Good H 160:174 My '65

TELEPHONE companies
See also
American telephone and telegraph company
Bell telephone system
General telephone and electronics corporation
Universal telephone, incorporated

Consolidations and mergers
Continental dials M for merger. il Bsns W p86+ N 6 '65

TELEPHONE exchanges
High-speed switch; use in automated telephone systems. il Electr World 74:85 N '65

TELEPHONE hour (radio program) See Radio broadcasting—Music

TELEPHONE in business
Next in banking: pay bills by phone; Bank of Delaware Touch-tone card dial system. il Bsns W p82+ N 13 '65
See also
Telephone selling

TELEPHONE in education
Spreading the word on the new math; use of telephone lines and the Electrowriter. il Bsns W p 110-12 Ap 10 '65

TELEPHONE numbers
When a telephone number is unlisted. il Good H 161:173 O '65

TELEPHONE poles. See Electric lines—Poles

TELEPHONE selling
Your time is their time; telephone solicitors. il Consumer Rep 30:331-3 Jl '65

TELEPHONE soliciting. See Telephone selling

TELEPHONE switches. See Electric switches

TELEPHOTO lenses. See Lenses, Photographic

TELEPHOTOGRAPHY
Low-cost ways to telephoto pictures. P. Wahl. il Pop Sci 186:120-3 Ap '65

TELESCOPE
Europe's second largest Schmidt telescope; Uppsala observatory, Sweden. A. Wallenquist. il Sky & Tel 29:136-40 Mr '65
Five telescopes in orbit to study stars in 1967; for one of the orbiting astronomical observatories. Sci N L 87:248 Ap 17 '65

TELESCOPE—Continued
Gleanings for ATM's; ed. by R. E. Cox. See issues of Sky and telescope
Kitt Peak 150-inch telescope. D. L. Crawford. il Sky & Tel 29:268-73 My '65
Large new telescopes for the southern hemisphere. V. K. McElheny; reply with rejoinder. J. Stock. Science 148:1039 My 21 '65
Novel dual-field 8-inch telescope. W. N. Lindsay. il Sky & Tel 29:112-17 F '65
OAO-B telescope will scan stars mapped by first OAO; orbiting astronomical observatory. R. D. Hibben. il Aviation W 83:74-6+ Jl 19 '65
Problems of constructing large telescopes. D. L. Crawford. il Sky & Tel 29:354-5 Je '65
Prototype telescope for OAO-C tested. R. D. Hibben. il Aviation W 82:71+ Mr 22 '65
Rotatable telescope for polarization studies. W. A. Hiltner and R. Schild. il Sky & Tel 30:144-7 S '65
See also
Mirrors for telescopes
Periscopes

Photographic telescope

Looking sharp; Questar telescope for space photography. il Newsweek 66:88 S 27 '65
TELESCOPE mirrors. See Mirrors for telescopes
TELESCOPIC sights
New Bushnells. W. Page. Field & S 70:89 S '65
TELESTIMULATOR. See Physiological apparatus
TELETYPE
Message units built for army in thirty days. G. Alexander. il Aviation W 83:90-1 S 27 '65
TELEVISION
Television: long-distance seeing. il Sci Digest 57:82-4 My '65

Color
See Television, Color

Photographic aspects
TV for proofs without printing. W. F. Wilson. il Pop Phot 57:44-5 Ag '65
See also
Video tape recorders and recording

Police applications
See Television in criminal investigation

Social aspects
See Television broadcasting—Social aspects

TELEVISION, Closed circuit
Astrovision; an in-flight entertainment system. L. C. Keene and T. E. Pierson. il Electr World 73:42-3+ Mr '65
Hidden TV monitors animal breeding cage. Sci N L 88:120 Ag 21 '65
Remote-control hypnosis. il Time 86:37 Jl 2 '65
TELEVISION, Color
Admen catch the color TV fever. il Bsns W p62-3 O 2 '65
Boom in color TV. il Duns R 85:81-2 Je '65
Color derby. il Newsweek 65:69-70 Je 28 '65
Color TV's astonishing boom. il Newsweek 65:70-2 Mr 29 '65
Colorimetry in color television. J. F. Holahan. il Electr World 74:21-3+ D '65
Coming of color. il Time 85:95-6 Mr 5 '65
Crystal valve feasible for color TV. R. Pay. il Miss & Roc 16:35-6 Mr 22 '65
Great color TV war. J. F. Olesky. il Duns R 86:38-40+ Ag '65
Paris-Moscow axis; political aspects of decision on color-TV system in Europe. J. Burnham. Nat R 17:362 My 4 '65
Pretty picture; color-TV sales to climb. Time 85:75 Mr 26 '65
Prime-time rainbow. Time 85:88 Mr 19 '65
Ripples of color; profits to satellite industries. Time 86:89-90 N 26 '65
Some black thoughts about color TV. R. L. Shayon. Sat R 48:80+ Ap 10 '65
Worldwide standards for color television. P. F. Geren. Dept State Bul 53:597-601 O 11 '65
TELEVISION actors and actresses. See Television broadcasting—Performers
TELEVISION advertising
Admen catch the color TV fever. il Bsns W p62-3 O 2 '65
And now, a message about commercials. S. Blum. il N Y Times Mag p26-7+ Ap 11 '65
And now, a $30,000 message from our sponsor. il Fortune 72:173-8 N '65
Artful pitchman; avant-garde commercials. il Newsweek 65:93-4 Ap 26 '65

Britain's TV ban; blackout on TV commercials for cigarettes. Newsweek 65:88 F 22 '65
British ban TV cigarette ads. Bsns W p 100 F 13 '65
Calories do count. Nation 200:351-2 Ap 5 '65
Color derby. il Newsweek 65:69-70 Je 28 '65
Fairfax Cone, the FCC, and TV advertising. R. L. Tobin. Sat R 48:49-50 Ag 14 '65
Frustrations of a satisfied viewer. J. F. Fixx. Sat R 48:73 O 9 '65
Long, hard night of the TV commercial; nationwide poll on television programing and commercials. R. L. Tobin. Sat R 48: 65-6 Ap 10 '65; Discussion. 48:55-7 My 8; 66-7 Je 12 '65
Now watch what happens; the people who deliver the commercials. C. W. Morton. il Atlan 216:109 Ag '65
Old movies are newer than ever; merging of the message and the movie. G. Ace. Sat R 48:8 D 25 '65
Pulling the props out; Supreme court decision on accurate representation of claims. il Newsweek 65:81 Ap 19 '65
Smokeless screen; British government bans cigarette advertising. Time 85:94+ F 19 '65
Sponsor who cares. Newsweek 66:64 N 1 '65
They're doing something right; tasteful new commercials. Time 86:95 N 12 '65
Thriving on the tube; TV advertising outside the U.S. il Time 86:82 S 3 '65
What's bad for TV is worse for advertising. F. M. Cone. Fortune 72:102+ Jl '65
Where there's smoke; TV commercial hooks actor. R. L. Shayon. Sat R 48:51 S 25 '65
Why Barbara Stanwyck grinned all the way to the bank. V. Scott. il McCalls 92:82 Mr '65

Anecdotes, facetiae, satire, etc.
Vacuum hat. C. W. Morton. il Atlan 215: 116 Je '65
TELEVISION and children. See Television broadcasting and children
TELEVISION and libraries. See Libraries and television
TELEVISION antennas
Antenna rotators pinpoint signals. G. Wayne. il Pop Electr 22:59-61 My '65
Antennas: which, why, when, and how much? R. Freas. Am Home 68:27-8 Ap '65
Are you ready for UHF? J. Sarayiotes. il Pop Electr 22:58 My '65
Community antennas enter the big TV picture. il Fortune 72:146-7+ Ag '65
CATV gets new viewer. Bsns W p30 My 1 '65
Golden antenna of CATV. T. J. Murray. il Duns R 85:44-6+ My '65
How to improve color TV antenna installations. L. Cantor. il Pop Electr 22:52-3+ My '65
How to stack TV antennas to increase signal strength and to reduce ghosts. L. Cantor. il Pop Electr 23:63-5+ N '65
Improved all-channel TV antenna. Consumer Rep 30:323 Jl '65
Line-of-sight nomogram; required antenna heights for various reception ranges. D. L. Pippen. il Electr World 73:27 Mr '65
Modern broadband CATV system. J. Frye. il Electr World 73:37-40+ F '65
Multiset couplers; operation and problems. il Electr World 73:36+ F '65
New generation of antennas. R. Cornell. il Pop Electr 22:46-51 My '65
Selecting a UHF antenna. A. E. Schenfeld. il Pop Electr 22:55-7 My '65
TELEVISION apparatus
Are you ready for UHF? J. Sarayiotes. il Pop Electr 22:58 My '65
TELEVISION apparatus industry and trade
Coming battle for the color-TV market. E. K. Faltermayer. il Fortune 73:144-7+ Ja '66
TELEVISION apparatus on space missions
TV system faces severe Saturn V test. R. Pay. Miss & Roc 18:38-9 Ja 3 '66
TELEVISION audiences
Habit; hard-core television watchers among college students. il Time 85:52+ Mr 26 '65
Rating the audience. Newsweek 65:70 Ap 12 '65
TELEVISION awards. See McCall's (periodical)
TELEVISION broadcasting
Television. G. E. Reddick. Christian Cent 82:1196-8 S 29 '65

Advertising
See Television advertising

Animal programs
See Animals on television programs

Baseball
See Television broadcasting—Sports

TELEVISION broadcasting—*Continued*

Book programs

Children's books on the air; adaptation from discussion of Children's book council in New York. C. B. Grannis. Pub W 188:186 Jl 12 '65

Censorship

Discriminating TV in Jackson, Mississippi; question of renewing WLBT's license. W. Pincus. New Repub 152:7-8 Je 5 '65

Heat on TV. Nation 202:1-2 Ja 3 '66

Time of the bloop; TV's self-censorious attitude. il Newsweek 67:54 Ja 24 '66

Children, Effect on

See Television broadcasting and children

Childrens programs

Literary adventure in educational television; series Let's read together. E. D. Landau. il Horn Bk 41:28-33 F '65

Soupy and the mouse; Soupy Sales success. W. J. Smith. Commonweal 82:446-8 Je 25 '65

Time out for television. See issues of PTA magazine

Comedy

See Television broadcasting—Humor

Conversation programs

Clash via Early bird; CBS's Town meeting of the world. il Newsweek 66:71 N 8 '65

Cut short. Time 86:38 Ag 27 '65

Debate by satellite; CBS reports Town meeting of the world. R. L. Shayon. Sat R 48:49 D 11 '65

Insomniacs-ville; late-night TV. il Newsweek 66:78 Jl 19 '65

Johnny Carson, the prince of chitchat, is a loner; Tonight show. B. Rollin. il Look 30:98-102 Ja 25 '66

Lowering the Crane; ABC drops Les Crane show. Newsweek 65:83 Mr 8 '65

TV talk shows, great conversation killers. W. Kerr. il McCalls 92:74-5+ Jl '65

Twenty-four hours in the life of Johnny Carson; Tonight show. E. Havemann. McCalls 92:58+ Mr '65

What's in a handshake? lessening of racial antagonisms the subject of Open end program. R. L. Shayon. Sat R 48:35 My 15 '65

Court proceedings

See Television broadcasting—Trials

Crime programs

Great TV spy scramble; competitors open fire on U.N.C.L.E.'s domain. il Life 59:118-20 O 1 '65

Criticism

See Television criticism

Dancing

Dancing in the dark; filming of dance sequence at the Museum of modern art. il Dance Mag 39:103-7 D '65

Danny Daniels says, grumble, J. Anderson. il Dance Mag 39:122-3+ D '65

Educational TV loves dance. J. Venza il Dance Mag 39:43-5+ S '65

Looking at television. A. Barzel. See issues of Dance magazine

Documentary programs

Affairs of state. il Newsweek 66:76 Ag 23 '65

Along the Volga with C.B.S; skillful piece of propaganda. Christian Cent 83:70 Ja 19 '66

Big show; American white paper; United States foreign policy on NBC. Newsweek 66:90 S 20 '65

Campaign document; Making of the President 1964. Newsweek 66:108 O 18 '65

Consensus television; review of summer schedule. N. Compton. Commentary 40:67-8+ O '65

Covering the U.S.S.R. R. J. Korengold. il Newsweek 66:90+ S 20 '65

Examination time; CBS National driver's test sponsored by Shell. Newsweek 66:76 Ag 23 '65

Frank talk; Vietnam: December, 1965. Newsweek 67:52 Ja 3 '66

Getting away from it all; National educational radio coverage of German national elections. R. L. Shayon. Sat R 48:53 O 23 '65

How Alfred Knopf saw his authors; A. A. Knopf's documentary film. Dialogue. M. R. Weiss. il Sat R 48:26-8 Je 12 '65

How do you cover hell? race riot in Los Angeles. il Newsweek 66:50+ Ag 30 '65

Incomplete Casals; television portrait. R. L. Shayon. Sat R 48:47 F 6 '65

Instant citizenship; United States and Communist China. R. L. Shayon. Sat R 48:56 Je 12 '65

Lady Bird's Washington; making of Visit to Washington with Mrs Lyndon B. Johnson. il Newsweek 66:92-3 N 22 '65

Lesson of history; Profiles in courage series on NBC. il Newsweek 65:58 F 15 '65

National citizenship test. P. Dilts. il Sr Schol 87:29 N 4 '65

Networks on Vietnam. J. G. Dunne. New Repub 154:36-7 Ja 8 '66

No news is good news; CBS's Sinatra. Newsweek 66:88 N 29 '65

Question of emphasis; CBS special report, Abortion and the law. America 112:513 Ap 17 '65

Seeing red; Soviets reaction to CBS's Volga narration. Newsweek 67:80 Ja 17 '66

Sense of the past; NBC's Of men and freedom series. il Newsweek 65:70 My 24 '65

Televising the real world. R. E. Kintner. Harper 230:94-6+ Je '65

TV's first war. W. Tuohy. il Newsweek 66:32 Ag 30 '65

Testing what? National drivers' test. R. L. Shayon. Sat R 48:48 Je 19 '65

Truman and the voice of history. M. Kempton. Life 58:16 Mr 5 '65

Wild, wild East; first in This proud land series. Newsweek 65:58 Je 21 '65

Drama

Boost for rep boom; Esso repertory theatre. T. Prideaux. Life 58:19 Ap 2 '65

Every woman's life is a soap opera; ed. by H. Markel. I. Phillips. il McCalls 92:116-17+ Mr '65

Extraordinary girl; working on Peyton Place; ed. by E. Miller. M. Farrow. il Seventeen 24:136-7+ O '65

Killing the mad monk; charge against CBS dramatization. il Newsweek 66:38 N 1 '65

Take back your Kafka. J. G. Dunne. New Repub 153:32-4 S 4 '65

TV's longest chase; Fugitive. S. Gordon. il Look 29:M10+ My 18 '65

TV's Peyton Place; sweet virtue's county seat; with account by Ira Mothner. il Look 29:78-81+ O 19 '65

Triple jeopardy; Peyton Place. il Time 86:65 Ag 20 '65

Visit to a town of the mind; Peyton Place. L. E. Litwak. il N Y Times Mag p46-7+ Ap 4 '65

Where oomph has gone; daytime dramas attract stars. il Newsweek 66:88 N 29 '65

Where theater lives; opening of Esso repertory theatre. il Newsweek 65:80 Mr 1 '65

Educational applications

See Television in education

Football

See Television broadcasting—Sports

Government programs

Not Bonanza, not Peyton Place, but the U.S. Senate! K. B. Keating. il N Y Times Mag p66-7+ Ap 25 '65

Humor

Deception as a TV comedy tool. G. E. Reddick. Christian Cent 82:1196-8 S 29 '65

Dim future; ineptitude trend. Newsweek 66:94+ D 20 '65

Fun with the Nazis; Hogan's heroes. il Newsweek 66:64 N 1 '65

Gomer Pyle; country boy next door. S. Gordon. il Look 29:99-102 Je 1 '65

Great TV spy scramble; competitors open fire on U.N.C.L.E.'s domain; and a spook sweepstakes. il Life 59:118-20 O 1 '65

Smart money; Get Smart! insane, absurd comedy. il Time 86:109 O 15 '65

TV's favorite comedy team breaks up. R. Hochstein. il Good H 161:30+ O '65

International aspects

Birds on the wing; cost of using Early bird for transatlantic broadcasts. Newsweek 65:70 My 24 '65

Broadcasting of world politics; address, November 3, 1965. H. Cleveland. Dept State Bul 53:896-901 D 6 '65

Feeding the Bird; first telecasts via Early bird. il Newsweek 65:86 My 17 '65

Worldwide standards for color television. P. F. Geren. Dept State Bul 53:597-601 O 11 '65

Merchandising tie-in

Tie-in sales bubbling with old black magic; TV's Bewitched to license marketing of merchandise based on popular program characters. il Bsns W p 132+ N 6 '65

TELEVISION broadcasting—*Continued*

Moral aspects

See also
Television broadcasting and children

Moving pictures

I spy. il Ebony 20:65-6+ S '65
Reel attraction. il Newsweek 66:116+ N 15 '65

Music

Music in two dimensions in a twenty-one
inch box. F. Bowers. House & Gard 128:
246-7+ O '65
Silver bells are ringing: then Telephone hour
on radio; now Bell telephone hour on television. P. Dilts. il Sr Schol 86:31 Ap 29 '65

Musical comedies, revues, etc.

Bouncy hour really tuned to teens; Hullabaloo,
musical. R. Schickel. Life 58:19 My 21 '65

News

Broadcasting and the news. R. E. Kintner.
Harper 230:49-55 Ap '65 (to be cont)
Consensus television: review of summer
schedule. N. Compton. Commentary 40:67-
8+ O '65
Covering the Pope. il Newsweek 66:106 O 18
'65
Editing for viewers. il Time 85:52 F 26 '65
Electronic hodgepodge; ABC vice president
James Hagerty's charges. Time 85:63 Mr
12 '65
Letter from the publisher; new March of
time. B. M. Auer. Time 85:17 Mr 12 '65
Presidential catarrh; TV reports of President
Johnson's cold. Nat R 17:93-4 F 9 '65
Press and television. America 112:657-8 My 8
'65
Rather rattled; CBS White House correspond-
ent. il Time 85:94+ F 5 '65
Teen-age TV reporter. S. Gordon il Look
29:44+ O 5 '65
Televising the real world. R. E. Kintner.
Harper 230:94-6+ Je '65
Television in the Nation's service; address,
October 13, 1965. H. K. Smith. Vital
Speeches 32:79-81 N 15 '65
TV's cold war; networks' special coverage
of the President's cold. Newsweek 65:76
F 8 '65
TV's female brain trust. C. Berman. il Good
H 161:42 Jl '65
TV's riot squad; bias in news coverage. J. G.
Dunne. New Repub 153:27-9 S 11 '65
Whose dissent do you hear? J. G. Dunne.
New Repub 153:32+ N 6 '65
See also
Television broadcasting—War news

Performers

Big push for Danny's charmer. il Life 58:
57-8+ Mr 19 '65
I spy; role of B. Cosby. il Ebony 20:65-6+
S '65
Man from U.N.C.L.E: R. Vaughn. D. Free-
man. il Sat Eve Post 238:76+ Je 19 '65
2,000-year-old man; Mel Brooks. il Newsweek
66:88-9 O 4 '65
Visit to a town of the mind; Peyton Place.
L. E. Litwak. il N Y Times Mag p46-7+
Ap 4 '65
Where oomph has gone; daytime dramas at-
tract stars. il Newsweek 66:88 N 29 '65
See also names of television performers,
e.g. M. T. Moore

Political programs

See Television in politics

Program production

Crazy gadgets of The man from U.N.C.L.E.
W. S. Bacon. il Pop Sci 187:46-7+ D '65
Exodus; departure of top directors. il News-
week 65:86-87A Mr 29 '65
Four-shot zoomed into a closeup; production
of one-hour television special. New York,
New York. New Yorker 41:47-9 O 23 '65
Organization man; director G. Shaefer. il
Time 86:60 N 26 '65
Punk who made good: S. Leonard. Time 86:
75 N 19 '65
What a TV producer produces. J. Barthel.
il N Y Times Mag p38-9+ N 21 '65

Program rating

First down: NBC ahead. Time 86:78 O 22 '65
Let them eat crow; Nielsen top ten. Time 86:
71 D 3 '65
Not my cup of TV; Nielsen system. G. Ace.
Sat R 48:6 Jl 31 '65
Rest in peace. G. Ace. Sat R 48:40 F 20 '65;
Reply. D. Levy. 48:25 Mr 13 '65; Rejoinder.
48:18 Ap 10 '65

TV and the ultimate public service. R. L.
Tobin. Sat R 48:65-6 Je 12 '65; Discussion.
48:46-7 Jl 10 '65
TV looks at TV ratings; CBS reports. Bsns
W p62 Jl 17 '65
Television vagaries. G. Ace. Sat R 48:14 N
27 '65
TV's power elite. il Newsweek 66:53 Jl 26 '65
Those that will not see; failings of audience
research. G. Ace. Sat R 48:20 S 18 '65
Trials of O'Brien. il Newsweek 66:94 D 6 '65
Upheaval in the networks; NBC and CBS
in close race, ABC losing heavily. il Bsns
W p46+ N 13 '65
Who killed your favorite TV show? B. David-
son. il Sat Eve Post 238:84-7 F 27 '65
Winner & now champion; NBC. Time 85:68
Ap 30 '65
Winner take nothing. Newsweek 66:88 O 4 '65

Programming

. . .And protests from sports fans; canceled
football games for Gemini 5. America 113:
231 S 4 '65
FCC (fat chance commission) G. Ace. Sat R
48:14 My 8 '65
Lollipop trap. R. L. Shayon. Sat R 49:37+
Ja 1 '66
Minority TV should cultivate. Life 59:8 O 1 '65
TV and the ultimate public service. R. L.
Tobin. Sat R 48:65-6 Je 12 '65; Discussion.
48:46-7 Jl 10 '65
TV programing; the fight for prime time.
H. Junker. il Nation 200:279-81 Mr 15 '65
Three men theme; networks versus advertis-
ing agency control of TV programs. Time
85:81A Mr 12 '65

Programs

Back to work; exposition of American foreign
policy since the end of World war II. R. L.
Shayon. Sat R 48:40 S 4 '65
Bill Cosby: variety is the life of spies; costar
of I spy. S. Karnow. il Sat Eve Post 238:
86+ S 25 '65
Blam! pow! . . fizzle; new programs. News-
week 67:55 Ja 24 '66
But is it science? il Sci Digest 58:93-5 S '65
Camping in the wasteland. N. Compton.
Commentary 41:58-60+ Ja '66
Candles of culture; independent and educa-
tional channels. il Time 85:88 Mr 19 '65
Choose your jungle. R. L. Shayon. il Sat R
49:44 Ja 15 '66
Consensus television; review of summer
schedule. N. Compton. Commentary 40:67-
8+ O '65
Country slicker; P. Henning's hillbilly pro-
grams. il Newsweek 66:97 D 6 '65
Crazy gadgets of The man from U.N.C.L.E.
W. S. Bacon. il Pop Sci 187:46-7+ D '65
Eight days that made one weak; first week
of new season. G. Ace. Sat R 48:18 O 9
'65
Everything's coming up loners. R. Schickel.
Life 59:27 N 12 '65
Ghostess with the mostest; Margaret Ruth-
erford in Stately ghosts of England. R. L.
Shayon. Sat R 48:54 F 13 '65
How's everything on the Ponderosa? current
shows. P. Dilts. Sr Schol 87:sup 18-19 N
4 '65
Inside UNCLE. il Newsweek 66:54 Jl 5 '65
Let it be forgot; the Burtons on Sammy
Davis jr show. il Time 87:46 Ja 14 '66
Let's face it; bedtime stories for the millions;
serials. M. Mannes. McCalls 93:34+ N '65
Letter from the publisher; new March of
time. B. M. Auer. Time 85:17 Mr 12 '65
Life TV review (cont) Life 58:17 F 19; 16
Mr 5; 19 Ap 2; 19 My 21; 22 Je 11 '65
Look and listen. P. Dilts. See issues of Senior
scholastic
Looking and listening. P. Dilts. See issues
of Senior scholastic
Man called I-l-l-y-a. B. Wolfe. il N Y Times
Mag p56-7+ O 24 '65
More class; two new daytime television
shows. il Time 86:36 D 31 '65
MD is for moving day; time switch of sick
shows. G. Ace. Sat R 48:14 N 6 '65
NBC gets smart; Get smart success. il News-
week 67:52 Ja 3 '66
Networks turn to teen-agers. J. Roddy. il
Look 29:34+ O 5 '65
New TV season, more of the same. Chang-
ing T 19:6 Ag '65
One man's Miami; Jackie Gleason's show.
H. Sutton. il Sat R 48:36+ O 9 '65
Or would you rather be a fish? shape of
forthcoming season. G. Ace. Sat R 48:15
Ag 28 '65
Out of the bag; shows for next season. il
Newsweek 65:58 F 15 '65
**Overstuffed tube; new shows. il Time 86:56+
S 24 '65**

TELEVISION broadcasting—Programs—*Cont.*
Queen of the little Kings. H. Ehrlich. il Look 29:80-4 Je 29 '65
Quoth the ratings: ever more; new shows and holdovers scheduled for the new fall season. il Time 86:76-7 Jl 23 '65
Return of Batman; ABC acquire TV rights to Kane's characters. il Newsweek 66:97 D 20 '65
Rock 'n' roll call; It's what's happening, baby. il Newsweek 66:85 Jl 12 '65
Rocking Congress; it's what's happening, baby. Sr Schol 87:22 S 16 '65
Samantha gets her way; bewitching L. Montgomery in Bewitched. J. Hyams. Sat Eve Post 238:32-3 Mr 13 '65
Same old new season; 1965-66 programs. il Newsweek 66:70 Ag 9 '65
Sampling the new season. B. Prelutsky. Holiday 38:176+ O '65
Security is a good show; Charlie Brown Christmas. il Time 86:89 D 10 '65
Sight & sound. L. Benjamin. See issues of McCall's
Slattery's saga; Slattery's people on CBS. il Newsweek 65:82+ My 31 '65
Spotlight! E. Miller. See issues of Seventeen, beginning April, 1965
Spreading wasteland; export of U.S. shows. il Time 86:78+ O 22 '65
Spy who'd rather not be known: costar of Man from U.N.C.L.E; ed. by E. Miller. D. McCallum. Seventeen 24:116-17 S '65
TV-radio. See issues of Newsweek
TV segment. R. Lynes. il Harper 231:36+ D '65
TV sweepstakes; new shows and returning hits. S. Peck. il N Y Times Mag p28-9 S 5 '65
TV; the 21" bore. R. A. Aurthur. Nation 201: 227-31 S 20 '65
Television vagaries. G. Ace. Sat R 48:14 N 27 '65
Television's tailfin age. J. G. Dunne. New Repub 153:27-9 D 25 '65
TV's topmost, this is America? A. Hano. il N Y Times Mag p 10-11+ D 26 '65
Time listings. See issues of Time
Time out for television. See issues of PTA magazine
Week that was; opening of new shows. Newsweek 66:90 S 27 '65
What's coming on TV. il Good H 161:78-9+ S '65
Xerox proves a point; effect of U.N. film drama experiment. R. L. Tobin. Sat R 48:87-8 N 13 '65
See also
National association for better radio and television
Television broadcasting—Dancing
Television broadcasting—Drama
Television criticism

Anecdotes, facetiae, satire, etc.
This is television, 1966. G. Ace. Sat R 49: 15+ Ja 1 '66

Psychological aspects
Rage in the lab; Feshbach experiment. R. G. G. Price. il Atlan 216:116-18 D '65

Public service programs
Message messes up a fine idea; Xerox United Nations series. D. Martin. Life 58:17 F 19 '65

Quiz programs
Dubious achievements of a TV contestant. A. Gingrich. Esquire 63:6 My '65

Religious programs
Airwave First amendment. America 112:213 F 13 '65
Churches and the airwaves; with editorial comment. D. Smith. Christian Cent 82:355-6, 364-7 Mr 24 '65; Discussion. 82:496-7, 681-2 Ap 21, My 26 '65
Religion and the FCC. M. Cohn; discussion. Reporter 32:6 F 11 '65

Scientific programs
Television coverage of the Gemini program. E. G. Sherburne, jr. Science 149:1329 S 17 '65

Social aspects
Disease that Dr Kildare couldn't cure: NBC cancels TV film on syphilis. J. Mitford. McCalls 92:102-3+ S '65

What happened, baby? Murray the K show for dropouts and unemployed youth. il Time 86:69 Jl 9 '65
See also
Television broadcasting—Psychological aspects
Television broadcasting and children

Sports
. . .And protests from sports fans: canceled football games for Gemini 5. America 113: 231 S 4 '65
Bigger than all of us; agreement between CBS and the N.F.L. il Time 87:68 Ja 7 '66
Gamesmanship. il Newsweek 66:88B+ S 13 '65
NFL-CBS pact nails prime time, top cash. il Bsns W p 17 Ja 1 '66
New tradition; U.S. Open and U.S. Amateur championship format changed to enhance televising. Sports Illus 22:6 F 8 '65
Prince of Pittsburgh; Pirates brash broadcaster. M. Cope. il Sports Illus 23:34+ S 13 '65
Sporting proposition; CBS plans to 1969. Newsweek 66:94+ D 6 '65
Sweet sound of success: broadcaster, J. Garagiola. H. Horn. il Sports Illus 22:30-2+ Mr 15 '65
TV kidnaps sports. J. R. Griffin. il Nation 200:336-8 Mr 29 '65
Unbreakable sports records. Sports Illus 23:11 Ag 9 '65
Word for TV golf is fore! J. R. McDermott. Life 58:18 Mr 26 '65
See also
Sports network, incorporated

Student programs
Debate by satellite; CBS reports Town meeting of the world. R. L. Shayon. Sat R 48:49 D 11 '65

Subscription programs
Reprieve for pay TV. Time 85:86 l(y 28 '65
Subscription TV test results. Electr World 73:80 My '65
Uphill fight of pay-TV. R. L. Shayon. il Sat R 48:55-7 Ap 24 '65
Who pays to watch the video show? report on study by Oxtoby-Smith, inc. il Bsns W p32 Ja 30 '65

Travel films
Ménage à trois. R. G. G. Price. il Atlan 215: 123 F '65

Travel programs
National geographic's newest adventure: a color television series. M. B. Grosvenor. il Nat Geog Mag 128:448-52 S '65

Trials
Billie Sol Estes's civil rights. R. L. Shayon. Sat R 48:50 My 1 '65
Crack in Canon 35; television in the courtroom. H. Brucker. Sat R 48:48-9 Jl 10 '65; Discussion. 48:50-1 Ag 14 '65
Should TV be allowed in the courtroom? il U S News 58:16 Je 21 '65
Television & fair trial. il Time 85:44 Je 18 '65
Television in the courtroom? pro and con discussion. J. McLaughlin; R. F. Drinan; discussion. America 112:208-9, 273 F 13, 27 '65

War news
Worthy try at covering a big story; Vietnam on TV. B. Brower. Life 60:15 Ja 21 '66

Westerns
Bonanza. R. W. Lewis. il Sat Eve Post 238: 84-9 D 4 '65
TV fakeroo. C. E. Gillham. il Field & S 70: 10-12+ Jl '65
Trigger-happy; who needs Jesse James? R. L. Shayon. Sat R 48:31 O 2 '65

Great Britain
Auntie's indiscretions; AWOL program canceled. il Newsweek 65:70 Ap 12 '65
Doctor's orders; American TV shows. Time 86:22 Ag 27 '65
Startled look at British television; realism to nudist film. J. F. Fixx. il Sat R 48:98+ N 13 '65; Reply. D. C. Mason. 48:67 D 11 '65
Word; four-letter words on television. Time 86:39 N 26 '65

Netherlands
Because of a tube; government crisis over commercial TV. il Newsweek 65:50 Mr 15 '65
Dutch tune out cabinet; clash over radio-TV programming and commercials. Bsns W p27 Mr 6 '65

TELEVISION broadcasting—*Continued*

Russia

Opiate of the masses. Newsweek 65:83 Mr 8 '65

United States

Case of the missing testimony; concerning D. Levy's The chameIons. R. L. Shayon. Sat R 48:42 F 27 '65

Finest hours; continuous and comprehensive coverage of the funeral rites of Sir Winston Churchill. il Newsweek 65:76 F 8 '65

Live from space; coverage of GT-4. il Newsweek 65:72 Je 14 '65

Monopoly over minds? why officials worry about TV; concentration of ownership of very-high frequency stations. il U S News 58:50-1 F 1 '65

Negro on TV; case of Jackson, Miss, station, WLBT. Nation 201:374 N 22 '65

Television. J. G. Dunne. See issues of New republic

TV: the 21" bore. R. A. Aurthur. Nation 201: 227-31 S 20 '65

Top of my head. G. Ace. See issues of Saturday review

See also

National broadcasting company
United States—Federal communications commission

TELEVISION broadcasting and children

Deception as a TV comedy tool. G. E. Reddick. Christian Cent 82:1196-8 S 29 '65

Lollipop trap. R. L. Shayon. Sat R 49:37+ Ja 1 '66

Ostriches, parents and television. S. Lindstrom. Parents Mag 40:20+ O '65

Tune out the bad, tune in the good on TV. F. Orme. il Parents Mag 40:56-7+ F '65

We're teaching our children that violence is fun. E. Merriam. Read Digest 86:39+ F '65

What TV is doing to our children; summary of Effects of television on children and adolescents. W. Schramm. il UNESCO Courier 18:22-6 F '65

What's TV doing to children? with study-discussion program by R. Strang. H. J. Skornia; G. D. Ewing. bibliog il PTA Mag 60:7-9, 35 Ja '66

See also

Television broadcasting—Childrens programs

TELEVISION broadcasting in court rooms. See Television broadcasting—Trials

TELEVISION broadcasting stations. See Television stations

TELEVISION cables

Coax vs twinlead. L. Cantor. il Electr World 74:34-6 Jl '65

New shielded twin-lead for color TV & U.H.F. R. Miracle. il Electr World 74: 29+ O '65

TELEVISION cameras

Choosing a closed-circuit TV camera. L. A. Wortman. il Electr World 73:50-2+ Mr '65

Dark is light enough; Perkin-Elmer corporation's laser camera for TV. Newsweek 66:98 D 20 '65

NASA studies feasibility of color television from lunar surface. il Aviation W 84:71+ Ja 17 '66

Operation of a high-quality CCTV camera. G. L. Hansen. il Electr World 74:44-7+ D '65

Real TV camera you build from a kit. R. M. Benrey. il Pop Sci 187:132-3 O '65

TV for proofs without printing. W. F. Wilson. il Pop Phot 57:44-5 Ag '65

Television in space. L. Solomon. il Electr World 74:21-4 Ag '65

TELEVISION censorship. See Television broadcasting—Censorship

TELEVISION channels. See Television stations

TELEVISION circuits

Semiconductor sweeps for large-screen TV. F. Gross. il Electr World 73:30-2+ Je '65

TELEVISION commentators. See Television broadcasting—News

TELEVISION commercials. See Television advertising

TELEVISION converters. See Television apparatus

TELEVISION criticism

Not so educational TV. J. Ridgeway. New Repub 153:16-18 Ag 21 '65

Watch out for children; inclusive critique of all prime-time TV, judged on its potential value, or harm, to children. Time 85:96 F 5 '65

What's bad for TV is worse for advertising. F. M. Cone. Fortune 72:102+ Jl '65

See also

Television broadcasting—Program rating

TELEVISION drama. See Television broadcasting—Drama

TELEVISION in criminal investigation

Television eyes catch criminals in the act. D. Scott. il Pop Sci 187:102-3 D '65

TELEVISION in education

Broadcasting of world politics; address, November 3, 1965. H. Cleveland. Dept State Bul 53:896-901 D 6 '65

Carnegie corp. plans education TV study. Sr Schol 87:sup3-4 D 2 '65

Do raise your voice! H. Humphrey. NEA J 54:57 My '65

Educational television is still just a promise; with editorial comment. E. W. Henry. il Am Ed 1:inside cover. 26-8 F '65

Educational TV: the timid crusaders. R. M. Elman. il Nation 200:217-21 Mr 1 '65; Reply with rejoinder. W. Kobin. 200:inside cover, 421 Ap 19 '65

Operation alphabet; Philadelphia public schools with WFIL. R. A. Luke. il Wilson Lib Bul 40:54-6 S '65

Relating to ETV; attempts by McGraw-Hill book company to relate to educational television. C. G. Benjamin. Pub W 187: 15-17 Ap 5 '65

Student teaching via closed circuit television. J. E. Van Haren. il Sch Arts 65:29-31 O '65

Talofa, Norma! N. Anderson. il Ebony 21:54-6+ Ja '66

While school keeps; ETV to receive scrutiny. J. Cass. Sat R 48:71 D 18 '65

See also

National educational television and radio center

Television stations, Educational

TELEVISION in medicine

TV camera to monitor biodynamics. M. Getler. il Miss & Roc 16:32-3 My 3 '65

TV monitors operations. il Sci N L 88:341 N 27 '65

TELEVISION in politics

Bobby's image. T. Smith. Esquire 63:62-3+ Ap '65

Broadcasting and the news. R. E. Kintner. Harper 230:49-55 Ap '65 (to be cont)

Every man should have his say; free discussion; address, June 17, 1965. C. May. Vital Speeches 31:622-4 Ag 1 '65

Is TV changing U.S. politics for better or worse? pro and con discussion. Sr Schol 87:10-11 O 7 '65

Looking at the Birchers. R. L. Shayon. Sat R 48:41 Ag 14 '65

Putting presidents in the picture. il Sr Schol 86:5 Ap 29 '65

Television and the world of politics. R. E. Kintner. Harper 230:121-3+ My '65; Reply with rejoinder R. Manning. 231:6+ Jl '65

Television in the Nation's service; address, October 13, 1965. H. K. Smith. Vital Speeches 32:79-81 N 15 '65

Where the money is; Reagan show created for West Coast GOP. Newsweek 65:39 My 17 '65

Anecdotes, facetiae, satire, etc.

How Barry Sosostris will save TV. R. Baker. il Sat Eve Post 238:24 N 6 '65

TELEVISION industry

United States

Equal time. by N. N. Minow; ed. by L. Laurent. Review

Commentary 39:80+ F '65. W. Goodman

FCC stirs new TV program clash; proposes tougher programming rule. Bsns W p27-8 Mr 27 '65

Great color TV war. J. F. Olesky. il Duns R 86:38-40+ Ag '65

On with the show. il Newsweek 66:96 O 11 '65

Prime-time target; FCC proposals. Newsweek 65:58 Ap 5 '65

Ripples of color; profits to satellite industries. Time 86:89+ N 26 '65

TV programing; the fight for prime time. H. Junker. il Nation 200:279-81 Mr 15 '65

Uses of anonymity; how networks dominate the sources of program production. R. L. Shayon. Sat R 48:35 Mr 6 '65

Who killed your favorite TV show? B. Davidson. il Sat Eve Post 238:84-7 F 27 '65

TELEVISION interference

Color-TV ghosts. W. H. Buchsbaum. il Electr World 74:33-5 D '65

How to stack TV antennas to increase signal strength and to reduce ghosts. L. Cantor. il Pop Electr 23:63-5+ N '65

Reducing rectifier interference. G. Scherer. il Electr World 73:65 Mr '65

U.H.F.-TV half-wave shorting-stub nomogram. M. H. Applebaum. il Electr World 73:29 Je '65

TELEVISION laws and regulations
See also
United States—Federal communications commission
TELEVISION lines. See Television cables
TELEVISION performers. See Television broadcasting—Performers
TELEVISION plays
History game; war stories turn tragedy into farce. R. L. Shayon. Sat R 48:76 O 30 '65
TELEVISION prizes. See Rewards, prizes, etc.
TELEVISION production. See Television broadcasting—Program production
TELEVISION program rating. See Television broadcasting—Program rating
TELEVISION programming. See Television broadcasting—Programming
TELEVISION programs. See Television broadcasting—Programs
TELEVISION projection
Crystal valve feasible for color TV. R. Pay. il Miss & Roc 16:35-6 Mr 22 '65
TELEVISION receiving apparatus
Semiconductor sweeps for large-screen TV. F. Gross. il Electr World 73:30-2+ Je '65
Zenith aims at the top in color TV. il Bsns W p 128+ S 11 '65

Anecdotes, facetiae, satire, etc.
Manner of speaking; no more TV in this house. J. Ciardi. il Sat R 48:22+ D 4 '65

Color receivers
Big-screen color TV comes in a small package. R. Benrey. il Pop Sci 187:100 Ag '65
Color TV. il Consumer Rep 31:8-13 Ja '66
Color-TV for Europe. Electr World 73:65 My '65
Color TV; how to live with it and love it. il Pop Sci 187:75-86 D '65
Color TV is in. L. Steckler. il Pop Mech 124:76-8+ Ag '65
Color TV makers dial a sharp profit picture. il Bsns W p80-2 D 25 '65
Color TV rides high, selling all it can make. Bsns W p24-5 O 30 '65
Color-TV set-up problems & adjustments. V. Bell. il Electr World 74:24-5+ D '65
Color-TV shortage. W. A. Stocklin. Electr World 74:6 D '65
Color TV, the picture is improving; Sylvania. il Consumer Rep 30:284-5 Je '65
Color TV's bottleneck; shortage of picture tubes. il Bsns W p29-30 My 15 '65
Coming battle for the color-TV market. E. K. Faltermayer. il Fortune 73:144-7+ Ja '66
How to buy a color TV set. R. M. Benrey. il Pop Sci 187:70-4+ D '65
How to improve color TV antenna installations. L. Cantor. il Pop Electr 22:52-3+ My '65
New color television receivers and five black-and-white sets. il Consumer Bul 49:6-11 Ja '66
New shielded twin-lead for color TV & U.H.F. R. Miracle. il Electr World 74:29+ O '65
1966 color-TV set chassis directory. Electr World 74:38-41 D '65
Personal business; buying a color TV set. Bsns W p 181-2 O 9 '65
RCA in Russia selling color TV. Bsns W p94 F 6 '65
Small-screen color; GE portable color set. Newsweek 65:64+ My 31 '65

Control
Refinement for TV silencers. Consumer Rep 30:475 O '65
TV silencers; remote-control devices. il Consumer Rep 30:398 Ag '65

Interference
See Television interference

Picture tubes
How to get more life out of your TV picture tube. R. Cornell. il Pop Electr 23:39-41+ O '65
Manufacture of color picture tubes. J. F. Holahan. il Electr World 74:30-2+ D '65
Rare-earth phosphors for color-TV tubes. R. C. Miller and T. V. Rychlewski. il Electr World 74:48 D '65

Testing
Build a TV picture tube tester and rejuvenator. J. H. Taylor. il Pop Electr 23:42-5+ O '65

Radio, stereophonograph and tape recorder combination
Ghost of Christmas yet to come? RCA's Dimensia IV. Consumer Rep 30:520-1 N '65

Repairing
Picture-shooting your television troubles. L. Steckler. il Pop Mech 124:170-3 Ag '65

Transistor receivers
Line-operated transistor TV sets; RCA. W. H. Buchsbaum. il Electr World 74:32-3 N '65
Tiny TV sets are in; transistor TV. R. M. Benrey. il Pop Sci 186:84-7 F '65
TELEVISION receiving apparatus, Portable
New ways to make a vacation happier. Bet Hom & Gard 43:142+ My '65
See also
Television receiving apparatus—Transistor receivers
TELEVISION reception
Color-TV set-up problems & adjustments. V. Bell. il Electr World 74:24-5+ D '65
Dialing in on UHF. il Newsweek 67:42-3 Ja 10 '66
Ten sure ways to improve your TV picture. R. M. Benrey. il Pop Sci 187:122-6 N '65
TELEVISION stations
Dialing in on UHF. il Newsweek 67:42-3 Ja 10 '66
Discriminating TV in Jackson, Mississippi; question of renewing WLBT's license. W. Pincus. New Repub 152:7-8 Je 5 '65
Hawaiian heresy; ABC affiliate KHVH-TV. R. L. Shayon. Sat R 48:49 My 8 '65
Johnsons' financial empire: up a million, branching out; Competition facing Johnson station. il U S News 58:44-5 My 31 '65
Monopoly over minds? why officials worry about TV; concentration of ownership of very-high frequency stations. il U S News 58:50-1 F 1 '65
Negro on TV; case of Jackson, Miss. station, WLBT. Nation 201:374 N 22 '65
Planning another TV network; Prime network for Sunday evenings. Bsns W p98 O 16 '65
Public may be heard; FCC investigation of station WLBT, Jackson, Miss. R. L. Shayon. Sat R 48:44 Je 26 '65
UHF: as profitable as CATV? Duns R 85:46 My '65
See also
Columbia broadcasting system
TELEVISION stations, Educational
Classroom TV comes to Samoa. T. Kaser. il Sat R 48:58-9+ Je 19 '65
Educational television is still just a promise; with editorial comment. E. W. Henry. il Am Ed 1:inside cover, 26-8 F '65
Relating to ETV; attempts by McGraw-Hill book company to relate to educational television. C. G. Benjamin. Pub W 187:15-17 Ap 5 '65
TV without commercials. il Changing T 19:19-23 S '65
TELEVISION towers
Scott's corner; lighting of television towers. D. H. Scott. il Flying 77:70 Jl '65
TELEVISION transmission
Facts about UHF-TV. Good H 160:136 Ja '65
Laser carries seven TV channels. Electr World 74:84 S '65
Single laser beam relays seven channels. Sci N L 87:131 F 27 '65
TV beacons in space; UHF transmissions and radio signals from space. Time 87:54 Ja 14 '66
Up-to-the-minute picture; Videx. il Time 86:64+ S 10 '65
See also
Television, Color
TELEVISION tubes. See Television receiving apparatus—Picture tubes
TELL es-Sa'idiyeh. See Jordan—Antiquities
TELLEFSEN, Robert N.
Economy-line transistors. Electr World 74:36+ Ag '65
—and Gabrielson, H. C.
Oscar III; ham radio's new 2-meter space station. Pop Electr 22:39-42+ Mr '65
TELLER, Edward
Inventor gap; excerpts from address. Newsweek 65:65 Ap 26 '65
TELLER, Walter
Sojourn in Haifa. Atlan 215:132+ My '65
TELLICO DAM (proposed) See Dams
TELLURIDES
See also
Indium telluride
TEMCO aircraft corporation. See Ling-Temco-Vought, incorporated
TEMCOR, Walter
New life for old dry cells. Pop Electr 22:69-70 F '65
TEMPER
How to cope with your child's temper tantrums. D. B. Thompson. Am Home 68:36+ Ap '65
See also
Anger

TEMPERANCE
Life and times of the late demon rum, by J. C. Furnas. Review
America 112:225 F 13 '65. V. P. McCorry
Commonweal 82:113-16 Ap 16 '65. J. P. Sisk
Whatever happened to the temperance movement? R. Burgess. Christian Cent 82:984-7 Ag 11 '65; Discussion 82:1166 S 22 '65
See also
Alcoholics anonymous

TEMPERATURE
Temperature dependence of carbon isotope composition in marine plankton and sediments. W. M. Sackett and others. bibliog il Science 148:235-7 Ap 9 '65
See also
Lakes—Temperature
Stars—Temperature
Thermistors

Physiological effects
HeLa cells: effects of temperature on the life cycle. P. N. Rao and J. Engelberg. bibliog Science 148:1092-4 My 21 '65
Life at 60 below; Arctic aeromedical laboratory for cold-weather testing of men, machines and materials. J. H. Winchester. il Sci Digest 57:63-7 Mr '65
Temperature effects on the peripheral auditory apparatus. A. C. Coats. bibliog il Science 150:1481-3 D 10 '65
Temperature-sensitive repression of staphylococcal penicillinase. S. Cohen and others. bibliog il Science 149:877-9 Ag 20 '65
See also
Cold—Physiological effects
Heat—Physiological effects

Regulation
Controlling the effects of sun's heat on steel doors. J. I. Yellott. il Arch Rec 138:177-8 D '65

TEMPERATURE, Animal and human
Cerebral temperature changes accompanying sexual activity in the male rat. C. D. Hull and others. bibliog il Science 149:89-90 Jl 2 '65
Cold rats work hard. Sci N L 88:132 Ag 28 '65
Impaired recovery from hypothermia after anterior hypothalamic lesions in hibernators. E. Satinoff. bibliog il Science 148:399-400 Ap 16 '65
Reptilian thermoregulation: evaluation of field studies. J. E. Heath; discussion. Science il 148:1250-1 My 28 '65
Sweating: direct influence of skin temperature. W. Van Beaumont and R. W. Bullard. bibliog il Science 147:1465-7 Mr 19 '65

TEMPERATURE, Planetary. See Planets—Temperature and radiation

TEMPERATURE of the earth. See Earth temperature

TEMPERATURES, Low. See Low temperatures

TEMPLATES. See Templets

TEMPLE, Shirley
Shirley Temple: her eyes are still dancing. C. R. Jennings. il pors Sat Eve Post 238:93-7 Je 5 '65
Shirley's big daughter. il pors Life 59:65-6+ Jl 30 '65

TEMPLE, W. C.
New Lincoln letter: Lincoln aids John McConnell. Hobbies 69:110-11 F '65

TEMPLE, Willard H.
Local girl makes good; story. Good H 160:88-9 Je '65

TEMPLES

Egypt
See also
Abu Simbel, Temples of

TEMPLETS
Carving signs with router templates. R. Shoberg. il Pop Mech 125:176-80+ Ja '66

TEMPO. See General electric company

TEMPTATION
Word. V. P. McCorry. America 112:337-8 Mr 6 '65

TENEMENT houses
See also
Slums

TENEN, S. S.
Retrograde amnesia from electroconvulsive shock in one-trial appetitive learning task. bibliog Science 148:1248-50; 149:1521 My 28, S 24 '65

TENNESSEE
See also
Airports—Tennessee
Booksellers and bookselling—Tennessee
Fishing—Tennessee
Hunting—Tennessee

Historic houses, etc.
Capital surroundings; historic homes circle Nashville. B. G. Loveless. il Travel 124:42-4 Ag '65

Industries
Air-conditioned sweatshop; criticism of public-financing programs. B. Kovach. il Reporter 33:29-31 O 7 '65

Race problems
News of the Christian world. W. A. Geier. Christian Cent 82:1109-10 S 8 '65
No plumbing for Negroes; Ames plantation. S. Barraclough. il Atlan 216:105-9 S '65

Religious institutions and affairs
News of the Christian world (cont) Christian Cent 82:820, 1584 Je 23, D 22 '65

Social conditions
Air-conditioned sweatshop; criticism of public-financing programs. B. Kovach. il Reporter 33:29-31 O 7 '65

TENNESSEE evolution controversy
After Scopes. T. A. Cowan. Science 150:435 O 22 '65
Great Monkey trial. S. D. Smith. il N Y Times Mag p8-9+ Jl 4 '65

TENNESSEE gas transmission company
Burning issue for gas pipelines; southern California natural gas market. il Bsns W p 138+ Ag 14 '65
They play rough in the gas business; T.G.T. vs. El Paso fight for southern California market. R. A. Smith. il Fortune 73:132-5+ Ja '66

TENNESSEE mountaineers. See Mountaineers (southern states)

TENNESSEE RIVER
Outboard cruising is in. L. W. Bennett. il Motor B 115:35-7+ Ap '65

TENNESSEE, University, Knoxville
From horseplay to homicide; three men killed during snowball fight. Time 85:59 F 12 '65
Life that's made to order; experiments at Atomic energy commission's research laboratory. A. Whitman. il Pop Mech 124:138-42 N '65
Red on white; student snowball fight results in three deaths. Newsweek 65:28+ F 15 '65

TENNESSEE VALLEY authority
Journals, by D. E. Lilienthal. Review
Bul Atomic Sci 21:42-3 Mr '65. C. P. Anderson
Land between the Lakes. G. Laycock. il Field & S 69:130-3+ Mr '65
Look toward the future in the TVA-Smokies region; with editorial comment. il Nat Parks Mag 39:2, 8-15 Mr '65
Now Uncle Sam's a real estate speculator. il Nations Bsns 53:46-8 N '65
Strip mining; TVA in middle in reclamation controversy. J. Walsh. il Science 150:194-8 O 8 '65

TENNIS
All in the family; Richeys of Dallas. il Newsweek 66:62 Ag 2 '65
Anyone care to play some VASSS? Van Alen simplified scoring system. F. Deford. il Sports Illus 23:20-2+ Jl 19 '65
Arthur was king for a day; U.S. national singles championships, Forest Hills. J. Jares. il Sports Illus 23:36-7+ S 20 '65
As long as there's a place to go, let it snow. H. Horn. il Sports Illus 22:58-9 Mr 8 '65
Charlito at twenty-one; walloped Australian Davis cup team. Sports Illus 23:9 Ag 2 '65
Kangaroo rampant; Spanish team in Australia. il Newsweek 67:44 Ja 10 '66
New rules enrage Pancho but excite fans; Van Alen simplified scoring system. il Life 59:52+ Ag 13 '65
¡Ole! Manolo, a little bit too late; Davis cup matches. E. Shirley. il Sports Illus 24:48-9 Ja 10 '66
Pain in Spain; Davis cup. il Time 86:68 Ag 27 '65
Pioneer in short white pants; A. Ashe, first male Negro to invade the highest levels of lawn tennis. H. Gordon. il N Y Times Mag p6-7+ Ja 2 '66
Rain in Spain was cushions; U.S. team lost to Spanish Davis cup team in Barcelona. F. Deford. il Sports Illus 23:20+ Ag 30 '65
Sporting scene: 1965 United States lawn tennis championships at Forest Hills, Newport casino invitation tournament. H. W. Wind. New Yorker 41:192+ O 9 '65
Swinging Salisbury; Salisbury international tennis tournament. Newsweek 65:65 F 22 '65

TENNIS—*Continued*
Tennis on the grass; photographs by J. G. Zimmerman; with accounts by B. Talbert and F. Deford. Sports Illus 23:32:44+ Jl 5 '65
Twentieth for Australia; Davis cup match. il Time 87:76 Ja 7 '66
Understudy takes charge; A. Ashe, first Negro to win Davis cup. F. Deford. il Sports Illus 23:18-19 Ag 9 '65
Winter madmen on the courts; Long Islanders play outdoor tennis in winter. R. Lardner. il N Y Times Mag p44-5+ N 21 '65
TENNIS, Table. See Table tennis
TENNIS balls
Tennis balls. il Consumer Rep 30:239-41 My '65
TENNIS courts
Tennis on top of the tank; water reservoir, Ada, Okla. P. S. Karr. il Am City 80:108-9 O '65
TENNIS courts, Indoor
Ad in. il Time 85:88+ F 5 '65
As long as there's a place to go, let it snow. H. Horn. il Sports Illus 22:58-9 Mr 8 '65
Indoor tennis scores with fancy service. il Bsns W p30-1 Mr 27 '65
TENNIS players
Ace; Davis cup zone finals. il Time 86:50 Ag 13 '65
Best and best-paid amateur; Australian R. Emerson. H. Gordon. il N Y Times Mag p36-7+ My 16 '65
Enter Arthur Ashe; first Negro to play on a U.S. Davis cup team; with report by R. Bradford. il Life 59:61-2+ O 15 '65
Highest ranking family in tennis; Richeys of Dallas. F. Deford. il Sports Illus 23:47-51 Jl 5 '65
How to serve and win. B. Talbert. il Sports Illus 23:40-4 Jl 5 '65
Net gains on the coconut beat; forty players on the Caribbean tennis tour. F. Deford. il Sports Illus 22:54-6+ My 10 '65
Pain in Spain; Davis cup. il Time 86:68 Ag 27 '65
Pioneer in short white pants; A. Ashe, first male Negro to invade the highest levels of lawn tennis. H. Gordon. il N Y Times Mag p6-7+ Ja 2 '66
Reign in Spain; M. Santana and L. Arilla winning the doubles. il Newsweek 66:54 Ag 30 '65
Sporting scene; 1965 United States lawn tennis championships at Forest Hills, Newport casino invitation tournament. H. W. Wind. New Yorker 41:192+ O 9 '65
Understudy takes charge; A. Ashe, first Negro to win Davis cup. F. Deford. il Sports Illus 23:18-19 Ag 9 '65
Winter madmen on the courts; Long Islanders play outdoor tennis in winter. R. Lardner. il N Y Times Mag p44-5+ N 21 '65
See also names of tennis players, e.g. A. Ashe
TENNIS rackets
Lacoste tries for an ace with a steel racket. il Bsns W p70+ O 30 '65
TENORS. See Singers
TENSION (psychology) See Stress (physiology)
TENTS
Pros and cons of tents. C. B. Colby. il Outdoor Life 136:28+ O '65
What ever happened to the ridgepole tent? P. Knight. il Sports Illus 22:68-9 Je 14 '65
TENURE, Academic. See College professors and instructors—Tenure
TEOTIHUACAN, Mexico
New marvel; Mexico's pyramids. H. M. Kovar. il Sci Digest 57:62-8 Je '65
TEPLITZ, Raymond L.
Sex chromatin of cone cells of human retina. bibliog Science 150:1828-9 D 31 '65
TEPLITZ, Zelda
Psychiatry and anti-psychiatry. New Repub 153:31-3 Ag 7 '65
TER BORCH, Gerard. See Borch, G. ter
TERBRUGGHEN, Hendrick
Master rediscovered; Dayton art institute exhibition. il Newsweek 66:108+ N 8 '65
Merry mimes. il Time 86:76-7 N 26 '65
Terbrugghen in America. W. Stechow. il Art N 64:46-51+ O '65
TER HORST, Jerald
Computers tackle social problems. Reporter 33:26-30 O 21 '65
No more pork barrel; the Appalachia approach. Reporter 32:27-9 Mr 11 '65
TERHUNE, William B.
Rising tide of alcoholism. Read Digest 86:123-6 Je '65
TERMINAL buildings, Airport. See Airport buildings

TERMINALS
See also
New York (city)—Stations
TERMINOLOGY. See subhead Terminology under various subjects, e.g. Politics—Terminology
TERMITES
Nature note. Sci N L 88:27 Jl 10 '65
Temperature extremes exterminate termites. Sci N L 88:104 Ag 14 '65
TERNBERG, Jessie L. and Butcher, H. R. Jr
Blood-flow relation between hepatic artery and portal vein. bibliog Science 150:1030-1 N 19 '65
TER-OVANESYAN, Igor
With a quarter inch between. il por Time 85:80 F 26 '65
TERPENES
Cyclopentanoid terpene biosynthesis in a phasmid insect and in catmint. J. Meinwald and others. bibliog il Science 151:79-80 Ja 7 '66
TERPIN. See Terpinol
TERPINOL
Vanillin, cis-terpin hydrate, and cis-terpin as ice nucleators. B. A. Power and R. F. Power. bibliog Science 148:1088 My 21 '65
TERPINOL hydrate
Vanillin, cis-terpin hydrate, and cis-terpin as ice nucleators. B. A. Power and R. F. Power. bibliog Science 148:1088 My 21 '65
TERRACES (outdoor living rooms) See Outdoor rooms
TERREBONNE, Quebec
One control operates eight filters. Am City 80:90-2 S '65
TERRELL, Ernie
Mouth and the mitt. T. Maule. il por Sports Illus 22:30-2+ Mr 1 '65
No place to wear his crown. T. Maule. il pors Sports Illus 22:28-9 Mr 15 '65
This laughing image. Time 86:75 N 12 '65
TERRELL, Robert Heberton
Colored judges J. H. Roy. por Negro Hist Bul 28:158+ Ap '65
TERRES, John K.
American goldfinches. Pop Gard 16:14 Jl '65
Birds in your garden (cont) Pop Gard 16:10-11 Mr; 6 Ap; 6 My '65
Bring a song to your garden. Pop Gard 16:24-5 S '65
Friendly ones. Flower Grower 52:36+ My '65
Know the birds by name. Flower Grower 52:23+ Ag '65
TERRESTRIAL heat. See Earth temperature
TERRESTRIAL magnetism. See Magnetism, Terrestrial
TERRIER (guided missile) See Guided missiles —Launching from ships
TERRILL, Ross
China, birth control and Bibles. New Repub 152:13-14 F 6 '65
Church in the storm of our time. Christian Cent 82:1280-3 O 20 '65
TERRITORIAL expansion
See also
Colonies
TERRITORIAL waters
Herring war; Ireland vs Northern Ireland. Newsweek 67:40 Ja 17 '66
See also
Fishery laws and legislation
TERRITORIALISM (animals) See Animals—Habits and behavior
TERRORISM
Dreaming of a red Christmas; promise of terrorism against Americans in downtown Saigon. Time 86:19 D 24 '65
Embassy bombed; Saigon. il Sr Schol 86:25-6 Ap 1 '65
Eyewitness report; a single, heavy blast, bodies everywhere; U.S. embassy, Saigon. R. P. Martin. il U S News 58:36-7 Ap 12 '65
Letter from Caracas; tactics of F.A.L.N. B. Taper. il New Yorker 41:111-12+ Mr 6 '65
Moments after Saigon bomb, a torn flag flies. il Life 58:28-9 Ap 9 '65
Outrages like this; attack on U.S. embassy in Saigon. il Time 85:21-2 Ap 9 '65
Saigon savagery; bombing of U.S. embassy. il Newsweek 65:39-40 Ap 12 '65
Will Viet war step up? bombing of U.S. embassy in Saigon. il Bsns W p29 Ap 3 '65
TERRORISM, Telephone. See Telephone calls
TERRY, Emilio
Squires at large. il por Esquire 63:78 My '65
TERRY, Fernando Belaúnde. See Belaúnde Terry, F.
TERRY, William D. See Alepa, F. P. jt. auth.
TERRY-THOMAS
Which is the real Hoar-Stevens? por Time 85:61 Je 25 '65

TERTZ, Abram, pseud.
Makepeace experiment; story; excerpt from novel, tr. from Russian by M. Harari. Harper 230:51-8 Je '65

about

Elusive Abram Tertz. J. Renshaw. N Y Times Mag p52 O 31 '65
Forever amber? Newsweek 66:48 N 1 '65
World power through witchcraft. P. Viereck. Sat R 48:45-6 Jl 24 '65
TERZIEV, Marc G.
We blazed wild new trails. pors Outdoor Life 135:32-5+ My '65
TESHIGAHARA, Hiroshi
Documentary fantasist. New Yorker 41:35-6 Ap 10 '65
TESSMAN, Irwin, and others
Mutagenic effects of hydroxylamine in vivo. bibliog Science 148:507-8 Ap 23 '65
TEST ban treaty. See Nuclear test ban treaty, 1963
TESTING
Corrosion hampers AF development; comprehensive materials symposium. J. F. Judge. il Miss & Roc 16:26-7+ Je 14 '65
Nondestructive testing fundamental to advanced materials development. J. F. Judge. il Miss & Roc 16:27+ F 22 '65
See also subhead Testing under various subjects, e.g. Airplanes—Testing
TESTING, Educational. See Educational tests and measurements
TESTING, Psychological. See Psychological examinations
TESTING instruments
Auto-engine analyzer you build from a kit. R. M. Benrey. il Pop Sci 186:136-7 Ap '65
Directory of test equipment for solid-state devices. Electr World 74:30 S '65
Don't let electrical problems stop your car; alternator, battery, generator and regulator tester. B. Ward. il Pop Mech 124:198-201 N '65
Guide to picture tube testers and rejuvenators. G. Wayne. il Pop Electr 23:46-8 O '65
Make a continuity tester for your appliance test bench. J. Braunstein. il Pop Mech 125:189 Ja '66
Test equipment product report. See issues of Electronics world
Testers for semiconductor devices. A. H. Seidman. il Electr World 74:42-4+ S '65
Using a transistor curve tracer. R. E. Show. il Electr World 74:49-52+ S '65
See also
Calibrators
TESTING laboratories
Lab to simulate radiation environment; to test spacecraft. W. S. Beller. il Miss & Roc 16:24+ Mr 22 '65
Outer space on earth. J. Eberhart. il Sci N L 87:154-5 Mr 6 '65
Some earth life seen adaptable to Mars; simulated environment tests. R. D. Hibben. il Aviation W 82:71+ Ap 12 '65
Space simulation: man-rated testing and vacuum generation; report on second national Space simulation testing conference. A. C. Bond. Science 147:523-7 Ja 29 '65
Spinning for space; Coriolis acceleration platform. il Time 85:78 Mr 12 '65
See also
Good housekeeping institute
Underwriters' laboratories, incorporated
TESTOSTERONE
Hormone cream restores lost hair. il Sci Digest 57:22-3 Mr '65
Hormone hazard; use of steroids by athletes. il Newsweek 66:66 S 27 '65
Male hormone produces hair on bald heads. Sci N L 87:184 Mr 20 '65
Significance of a dark spot; possible correlation between Barr spots and the effects of testosterone. Time 85:78 Mr 19 '65
TESTS, Information. See Information tests
TESTS, Laboratory. See Diagnosis
TETER, Howard W.
Nibbler attachment for your sabre saw. Pop Mech 125:190-1+ Ja '66
TETLEY, Glen
Rembrandt's The anatomy lesson. J. Anderson. il Dance Mag 39:46-8 Je '65
TETON national forest. See National forests
TETON studs, incorporated
Timber in the Tetons: the dangerous Mr D: dendroctonus monticolae. mountain pine beetle. il Am For 71:54-5+ S '65
TETRACHLOROANTHRACENE. See Anthracene
TETRACYCLINES
Tetracycline: effect on osteogenesis in vitro. L. Saxén. bibliog il Science 149:870-2 Ag 20 '65

TETRAHYMENA pyriformis. See Protozoa
TETRALOGY of Fallot
Total surgery effective for some blue babies. Sci N L 87:150 Mr 6 '65
TETRANUCLEOTIDES. See Nucleotides
TETRAULT, Barbara
Peace corps in art: a report. F. Friedman. il por Am Artist 29:80+ Je '65
TETRODOTOXIN. See Toxins and antitoxins
TEXANS
Once forbidding land; central Texas. E. Shrake. il Sports Illus 22:76-80+ My 10 '65
Texanization of Washington. I. Mothner. il Look 29:30-4 Ap 6 '65
TEXAS
See also
Birds—Texas
Housing—Texas
Houston
Hunting—Texas
Labor and laboring classes—Texas
Music festivals—Texas
Water supply—Texas

Description and travel

From Route 66 to the Mexican border; west Texas. F. Somers. il Redbook 125:38+ O '65
LBJ country. L. M. Rhodes. Travel 123:29-32+ Mr '65
Once forbidding land; central Texas. E. Shrake. il Sports Illus 22:76-80+ My 10 '65
Texas: good times gone, or here again? L. McMurtry. Holiday 38:58-9+ S '65
White House on the Pedernales; LBJ ranch near Johnson City. R. B. Semple, jr. il N Y Times Mag p54-5+ O 31 '65

Economic conditions

What people think in the land of LBJ. il Nations Bsns 53:34-7+ Ap '65

History

Sam Houston's last fight. A. Castel. il Am Heritage 17:80-7 D '65

Parks and reserves

What's new on plans for Johnson Park. U S News 60:10 Ja 10 '66

Police

Texas Rangers, by W. P. Webb. Review Time 87:88+ Ja 7 '66

Politics and government

Connally's Texas. A. Kopkind. New Repub 153:9-12 N 20 '65
Will LBJ take a hand in Texas political fight? U S News 59:12 O 4 '65

Religious institutions and affairs

Ecumenism and teetotalism. J. C. Evans. Christian Cent 82:798-9 Je 23 '65; Discussion. 82:1040-1 Ag 25 '65
News of the Christian world (cont) Christian Cent 82:498+, 1557-8 Ap 21, D 15 '65

Social conditions

What people think in the land of LBJ. il Nations Bsns 53:34-7+ Ap '65
TEXAS Gulf sulphur company
Analysts run into a security blackout. il Bsns W p 142+ My 8 '65
From Texas Gulf: a reply to SEC. U S News 59:87-8 Jl 19 '65
Inside the insider issue. il Fortune 72:69-70+ Jl '65
Insider stock buying; and what came next: suit by Securities and exchange commission. U S News 58:8+ My 3 '65
New moves by government to protect investors. il U S News 58:96+ My 10 '65
On the inside track; SEC charges Texas Gulf with violation of Securities exchange act. il Time 85:96+ Ap 30 '65
Phosphate bonanza ready to be tapped; Beaufort County, N.C. il Bsns W p88+ Mr 27 '65
SEC vs. Texas Gulf raises sticky questions; bonanza trouble; charges and issues at stake. C. Welles. il Life 59:29-30+ Ag 6 '65; Reply. C. O. Stephens. 59:19 Ag 13 '65
Texas Gulf suit opens new door for SEC. il Bsns W p24-5 Ap 24 '65
Texas Gulf's rebuttal to SEC complaint. Newsweek 66:68 Jl 19 '65
Wall Street: a sulphurous scandal; SEC investigation. il Newsweek 65:69-70 My 3 '65
When private news is public. Time 86:86 Jl 16 '65
TEXAS manufacturers association
For Texas employers, word from other side; union and government speakers at labor-management conference. il Bsns W p 122-4 N 6 '65

TEXAS Rangers. See Texas—Police

TEXAS. University, Austin
English with tears; Ford grant to establish a national translation center. D. Dempsey. Sat R 48:38+ F 13 '65
Ford foundation grants $750,000 to establish translation center. Library J 90:600 F 1 '65

TEXTBOOK publishers institute, American. See American textbook publishers institute

TEXTBOOKS
Aid for all. America 112:796 My 29 '65
Grammar in the cold war; propaganda in foreign language texts. A. Tillett and L. Tillett. New Repub 153:17-20 S 11 '65
Integrated texts on the rise; opposition met in South. il Library J 90:2344-5 My 15 '65
New York textbook bill. America 112:512 Ap 17 '65
Non-woven cover materials approved for textbook use; joint committee on textbook specifications. Pub W 188:96-8 S 6 '65
Rhode Island textbooks; Issue discussed. America 112:381 Mr 20 '65
Scholastic's fall book lineup. il Sr Schol 87: sup26 S 30 '65
Special textbook issue; symposium. Sr Schol 87:sup7+ N 18 '65
Trouble with textbooks. R. J. Margolis. il Redbook 124:64-5+ Mr '65
See also
Chemistry—Textbooks
Publishers and publishing—Textbooks
Social sciences—Textbooks
United States—History—Textbooks

Bibliography
Special textbook issue; symposium. Sr Schol 87:sup7+ N 18 '65

Russia
Grammar in the cold war; propaganda in foreign language texts. A. Tillett and L. Tillett. New Repub 153:17-20 S 11 '65

United States
See Textbooks

TEXTILE design
How Tzaims Luksus became a Vermont industrialist. Life 60:54A Ja 14 '66
See also
Batik

TEXTILE fabrics
Documentary fabrics and papers. R. Davidson. il Antiques 87:524+ My '65
Fabric moods: yours for the setting. il Good H 161:116-23+ S '65
Great expectations; 1966 viewpoints. il House & Gard 129:106-7 Ja '66
See also
Plastic fabrics
Textile finishing
Woolen and worsted fabrics

Coating
Light and shiny wet look; foul-weather apparel. il Sports Illus 22:52-8 Mr 15 '65

Creasing
See Creasing of textiles

Protection
Stain-resistant fabrics, are they really? il Changing T 19:27-8 Je '65

TEXTILE fabrics, Bonded web
Garment makers bolt to bonded materials. il Bsns W p40-1 D 25 '65
Stuck on each other; bonded fabric. Time 86: 86 N 19 '65

TEXTILE fabrics, Laminated. See Textile fabrics, Bonded web

TEXTILE fabrics, Metallized
Girl with a golden bra; metallic dresses and pants. il Newsweek 66:69 D 13 '65

TEXTILE fabrics, Synthetic
All those fibers, fabrics and finishes; how to tell them apart. Good H 161:228 O '65
British textiles spin revival with synthetics. il Bsns W p50-2+ Ja 15 '66
Catching up with synthetics; European textile makers. il Time 86:100-1 N 5 '65
Fancy pants maker stretches into new lines; Jack Winter, inc. Milwaukee. il Bsns W p60-2 Mr 20 '65
Let's get up-to-date on wash-and-wear. il Good H 160:234+ Ap '65
New sewing venture: stretch fabrics for active people. C. D. Legg. il Farm J 89:84-5 F '65
Remodeling with fabric: Celanese contemporary fibers. il House & Gard 28:276-83 N '65
Revolution in fit and comfort; stretch fabrics and expandable fashions. il Good H 160: 102-3+ My '65

What's all this about stretch? McCalls 92:107 Ap '65

TEXTILE fabrics, Waterproof
Stain-resistant fabrics, are they really? il Changing T 19:27-8 Je '65

TEXTILE finishing
All those fibers, fabrics and finishes: how to tell them apart. Good H 161:228 O '65
Clothes that never need ironing; wash-and-wears with permanent press. Changing T 19:11-12 N '65
Farewell to wrinkles; permanent press fabrics. il Bsns W p34+ S 18 '65
Permanent press. il Newsweek 65:82+ Ap 12 '65
Permanent press clothing. il Consumer Bul 48:6-10 N '65
Permanent-press shirts. il Consumer Rep 30: 534-5 N '65
Wash-and-wear innovation; permanent press. il Good H 160:6 Ap '65

TEXTILE industry
See also
Textile finishing

Europe, Western
Catching up with synthetics. il Time 86:100-1 N 5 '65

Great Britain
British textiles spin revival with synthetics. il Bsns W p50-2+ Ja 15 '66

United States
How one ailing industry has recovered. il U S News 58:96-8 Ap 19 '65
Textiles spin into a swifter pattern. il Bsns W p82-4+ O 2 '65
See also
Burlington industries, incorporated
Deering, Milliken and company
Stevens, J. P. and company

TEXTILE workers union of America
Labor drives to close the South's open shop; illegal reprisals by Stevens company for union activities. V. Rony. il Reporter 33: 31-4 N 18 '65
Rebellion in steel. R. W. Gibbons; reply with rejoinder. H. Peck. Commonweal 81:682 F 26 '65

TEXTILES. See Textile fabrics

TEXTRON, incorporated
Perilous quest for acquisitions. J. B. Weiner. il Duns R 86:32-5+ Jl '65
Taking the right tack. il Time 85:86+ Ap 16 '65

TEXTURE
Texture and visual perception. B. Julesz. il Sci Am 212:38-48 bibliog (p 134) F '65
Textures you can touch; with photographs by Ted Kessler. il U S Camera 28:27 S '65

TEYTE, Maggie
Criticism disarmed, or the art of Maggie Teyte. A. Rich. por Hi Fi 15:57-8 My '65

THACH, R. E. and Doty, Paul
Enzymatic synthesis of tri- and tetranucleotides of defined sequence. bibliog Science 148:632-4 Ap 30 '65
Synthesis of block oligonucleotides. bibliog Science 147:1310-11 Mr 12 '65

THACKER, Ernest W.
Stevenson and ourselves. Christian Cent 82: 993 Ag 11 '65

THACKRAY, John
Atlantic refining steps out. Duns R 86:40-2+ S '65
Bright lights of American electric. Duns R 86:37-8+ D '65
Bubbling retort at Allied chemical. Duns R 85:51-4 Je '65
Dominican military. New Repub 153:12 Ag 7 '65

THACKREY, Ted O.
Pittsburgh: how one city did it. Sat R 48:46-7 My 22 '65

THAEMERT, J. C. See Mitchell, H. C. jt. auth.

THAILAND
Golden court of Thailand. il Vogue 145:82-91 F 15 '65
Palace in the sun. M. Cable. il Horizon 7:65-75 Spr '65
Rural revolution; development in the Northeast. il Time 85:37-8 My 28 '65
Thailand, next Asian domino? P. S. McGhee. New Repub 153:11-12 Jl 10 '65
Thailand's fight to the finish. C. J. V. Murphy. il Fortune 72:122-7+ O '65
See also
Banks and banking—Thailand
Communism—Thailand
Economic assistance in Thailand
Education—Thailand
Investments, Foreign (in Thailand)
United States—Foreign relations—Thailand
Women—Thailand

THAILAND—*Continued*

Description and travel
Bangkok and beyond. L. Scott. il Travel 123: 33-5 Mr '65
Travel's picture portfolio. Travel 124:50-5 Ag '65

Foreign relations
Cheers from a cheerleader. il Time 85:26 My 21 '65

Industries
Silk of Thailand; Thai silk company. M. Cable. il Atlan 217:107-11 Ja '66

Politics and government
See also
Communism—Thailand

Royal family
Golden court of Thailand. il Vogue 145:82-91 F 15 '65

Social conditions
Model village rises in critical Northeast; Fa Huan. R. P. Martin. il U S News 58: 72-3 Mr 22 '65

THALASSEMIA. See Anemia

THALES, Robert
Voyage to the Marquesas. Motor B 115:22-5+ F '65

THALIDOMIDE
More about thalidomide. J. Ridgeway. New Repub 154:12-15 Ja 8 '66
New use for thalidomide? Time 86:59 Jl 23 '65
Thalidomide aids graft. Sci N L 88:211 O 2 '65

THALIDOMIDE babies. See Deformities

THANAT Khoman
To U.S. from an ally: stand firm; interview, ed. by R. P. Martin. por U S News 58:36 Mr 15 '65
about
Cheers from a cheerleader. il por Time 85:26 My 21 '65

THANE, Adele
Dummling and the golden goose; dramatization of Grimms' fairy tale. Plays 25:35-44 Ja '66
Elves and the shoemaker; dramatization of Grimms' fairy tale. Plays 25:33-40, 62 D '65
Hansel and Gretel; dramatization of Grimms' fairy tale. Plays 24:41-50 F '65

THANET, Octave, pseud. See French, A.

THANKSGIVING day
Every day is Thanksgiving day. D. Lawrence. U S News 59:124 D 6 '65

Drama
Meet the Pilgrims! C. Boiko. Plays 25:74-8 N '65
Our famous ancestors. M. Hark- and N. McQueen. Plays 25:26-36 N '65
Over the river. A. C. Martens. Plays 25: 1-14, 26 N '65

Fiction
This day for thanks. S. Weyer. il Good H 161:82-3 N '65

THANKSGIVING day parades. See Parades
THANKSGIVING dinners
How to celebrate Thanksgiving in ten languages; recipes. G. Maddox. il Todays Health 43:70-5 N '65
How to manage a big family dinner. Good H 161:234 N '65
Set a fine table in the style that suits you; with menus. il Good H 161:120-40 N '65
Shortcuts to wonderful holiday eating. Mrs W. Zigeler. il Farm J 89:78-9+ N '65
Small birds for the big feast; with recipes and menus. il McCalls 93:138-9+ N '65
Thanksgiving in easy stages. il Sunset 135: 160-2+ N '65
Travel well. E. N. Dye. Travel 124:45-6 N '65
Twentieth anniversary dinner. il Ebony 21: 188+ N '65
Work time: one hour new-fashioned Thanksgiving feast; recipes. P. Cannon. il Ladies Home J 82:110-11+ N '65

THANNHAUSER, Justin K, collection. See Art—Private collections

THANT, 1909-
Address to non-governmental organizations; May 27, 1965. UN Mo Chron 2:68-70 Je '65
Charter day 1965; message. UN Mo Chron 2:i-ii Jl '65
Development decade; excerpts from report. UN Mo Chron 2:39-41 Ag '65
Disarmament committee reconvenes; summary of message. UN Mo Chron 2:26-7 Ag '65

General assembly; nineteenth session reconvenes; summary of statement, January 18, 1965. UN Mo Chron 2:3-4 F '65
Harmonizing functions of the United Nations; address read at the convocation of Queen's university, Kingston, Ontario, May 22, 1965. UN Mo Chron 2:102-4 Je '65
Human rights day 1965; message. UN Mo Chron 2:iii-iv D '65
International co-operation year; statement. UN Mo Chron 2:1 F '65
Introduction to the annual report of the Secretary-General on the work of the organization. UN Mo Chron 2:92-117 O '65
New ideas for a new world; address. Sat R 48:24-5 Jl 24 '65
Press conference, February 24, 1965; summary of answers to questions. UN Mo Chron 2:31-3 Mr '65
Problems of peace-making; address, September 9, 1965. UN Mo Chron 2:118-22 O '65
Secretary-General to President Johnson; letter, July 29, 1965. Dept State Bul 53:275 Ag 16 '65
Situation in Kashmir; statement, August 24, 1965. UN Mo Chron 2:17 Ag '65
Situation in Viet-Nam; statement, February 12, 1965. UN Mo Chron 2:21-2 Mr '65
Statement by Secretary-General. UN Mo Chron 2:88 D '65
Turning point; excerpts from United Nations development decade at midpoint. UNESCO Courier 18:4-5+ O '65
United Nations commemoration address, June 26, 1965. UN Mo Chron 2:141-5 Jl '65
United Nations development programme; statement. UN Mo Chron 2:121-3 D '65
United Nations holds memorial ceremony for Ambassador Stevenson; remarks, July 19, 1965. Dept State Bul 53:226-30 Ag 9 '65
United Nations in a changing world; address, February 1965. UN Mo Chron 2:41-6 Mr '65

about
U Thant's credibility; use of gas in South Vietnam. Nation 200:349 Ap 5 '65
Visit with U Thant. New Repub 154:10-12 Ja 8 '66

THAO, Pham-ngoc-. See Pham-ngoc-Thao
THAR she blows; drama. See Dias, E. J.
THARP, Twyla
Cede blue lake, Hunter college. M. Marks. Dance Mag 40:58 Ja '66

THAT cat; story. See Hochstein, R.
THAT day when I was lost; story. See Robinson, B.
THAT thing at the Cherry lane; revue. See Musical comedies, revues, etc.—Criticisms, plots, etc.

THATCH, Lawn. See Lawn thatch
THATCHER, Norm
One hairy sedan! D. Francisco. il Hot Rod 18:40-1 F '65

THATCHER, Wilbert Ross
Where socialism failed close to home. T. Drury. il por Nations Bsns 53:66-8+ O '65

THAWING
Particle sorting by repeated freezing and thawing. A. E. Corte; reply with rejoinder. D. R. Inglis. il Science 148:1616-17 Je 18 '65

THAYER, Charles W.
New Soviet oligarchy. Harper 230:64-8+ Ap '65

THAYER, Harold Eugene
Chemical maker finds the formula. il por Bsns W p93-4+ N 13 '65

THAYER, V. T.
Relation of the school to the social order; excerpt from Formative ideas in American education. biblio f Sch & Soc 93:183-96 Mr 20 '65

THEATER
John Gielgud and Edward Albee talk about the theater; ed. by R. S. Stewart. E. Albee; J. Gielgud. Atlan 215:61-8 Ap '65
See also
Acting
Ballet
Drama
Dramatic criticism
Mime

Advertising
Pitching for Holmes; production of new musical Baker street. New Yorker 41:31-3 F 20 '65

Bibliography
New dimensions in theaters. Recreation 58: 258 My '65

Community and little theater movement
See also
American playwrights theater (organization)

THEATER—*Continued*

International aspects

America on the Paris stage. N. Biel. Nation 200:652-3+ Je 14 '65
U.S. showtime abroad. J. Dalrymple. il Travel 122:44-6 Je '65

Moral and religious aspects

Contemporary theatre and the Christian faith, by K. M. Baxter. Review
 Christian Cent 82:1226+ O 6 '65. S. J. Rowland, jr
Where the people are; Rev Boyd's idea of the church as a theater. il Newsweek 65:91 My 3 '65

Political aspects

Plays and politics. H. Clurman. il Nation 201:270-3 O 25 '65

Stage scenery

Designing for the theatre, by J. Mielziner. Review
 Sat R il 48:30+ N 27 '65. H. Hewes
Man for all scenes. il Time 85:86+ Mr 19 '65
 See also
Opera—Stage scenery

Czechoslovakia

Magic lantern; Offenbach's Tales of Hoffmann, combination of stage and film. D. Stevens. il Opera N 29:12-13 F 27 '65
 See also
Prague—Theater

Europe

Critic's holiday: a theatre fling in Europe. H. Popkin. Vogue 145:42+ Mr 15 '65

Europe, Eastern

Ring up that iron curtain: drama explosion in east Europe. H. Popkin. Life 59:19 S 17 '65

Germany (Democratic Republic)

 See also
Berlin—Theater

Germany (Federal Republic)

Letter from Paris: contributions to the international-theatre season. Genêt. New Yorker 41:120 Je 12 '65

Great Britain

Letter from London: opening of Yvonne Arnaud theatre, Guildford, with performance of Turgenev's Month in the country. M. Panter-Downes. New Yorker 41:82 Je 26 '65
 See also
London—Theater

Italy

 See also
Rome (city)—Theater

Japan

 See also
Japanese drama
Tokyo—Theater

Poland

 See also
Warsaw—Theater

Russia

 See also
Moscow art theatre

United States

America on the Paris stage. N. Biel. Nation 200:652-3+ Je 14 '65
Augmented theater; performances at Dallas, University of Oklahoma and Minneapolis. H. Hewes. Sat R 48:62 N 20 '65
Opinion: on the theatre; American repertory groups. G. Roy. Mlle 62:74+ N '65
Reader's choice; play-by-play vacation, thru New England. L. S. Rubin. Travel 123:7 My '65
Theatre. T. Lewis. See issues of America
Thespian marathon; country-wide, repertory-theater movement. Newsweek 65:98-9 Ap 12 '65
 See also
Amateur theatricals
American drama
American playwrights theatre (organization)
Biographical encyclopaedia and who's who of the American theatre
College and school drama
Theater, Negro

History

Theatre: the laggard art. H. Clurman. Nation 201:221-6 S 20 '65

THEATER, Amateur. See Amateur theatricals
THEATER, Childrens
Children's theater in Yonkers; Sprain Brook library theatre. M. Schoenfeld. il Wilson Lib Bul 40:352-5 D '65
Merry-go-rounders, 92nd street Y. J. Maskey. Dance Mag 39:72-4 Ap '65
Ostrich feathers, Martinique theatre. M. Marks. il Dance Mag 39:25 N '65
Paper bag players, Henry street playhouse. M. Marks. Dance Mag 39:156 D '65
THEATER, Negro
Free theater for Mississippi. R. Schechner. Harper 231:31-2+ O '65
THEATER, Traveling
Free theater for Mississppi. R. Schechner. Harper 231:31-2+ O '65
THEATER and state
Next on the subsidy list: plays, opera, orchestras. il U S News 58:64-5 Mr 15 '65
THEATER buildings
Modern theater concepts and community drama; theater design. S. H. Frieswyk. il Recreation 58:229-33 My '65
Theatres too big for dance? O. Maynard. Dance Mag 39:19+ Mr '65
Up their alley; proposed Alley theater. il Newsweek 66:74 Ag 16 '65
THEATER festivals. See Drama festivals
THEATER 1965. See New York (city)—Theater
THEATER 1966. See New York (city)—Theater
THEATRE of the living arts. See Philadelphia —Theater
THEATER photography. See Photography, Theatrical
THEATER signs. See Signs and signboards
THEATER tickets
Plight of the out-of-town theatergoer, ticket problems; with round-up of opinion by critics, and report by H. Hewes. J. F. Wharton. il Sat R 49:29-31+ Ja 22 '66
Stage; concerning the price of theater seats on Broadway. W. Sheed. Commonweal 81:703-4 F 26 '65
THEATRICAL agencies
Trade winds; image of the talent agent. J. G Fuller. il Sat R 48:16+ O 16 '65
THEATRICAL photography. See Photography, Theatrical
THEATRICAL production
Abe Burrows: what he does to earn $2,000 a day. E. J. Kahn, jr. il McCalls 92:116-17+ F '65
Audition: boys for principal role in musical version of The yearling. New Yorker 41:20-3 S 4 '65
Author! author! writing and production of On trial. E. Rice. il Am Heritage 16:46-9+ Ap '65
Experience: rehearsal of Anya. New Yorker 41:49-50 N 27 '65
Has anybody here seen Kelly? L. H. Lapham. il Sat Eve Post 238:32-4+ Ap 24 '65
How to succeed in the theatre without really being successful. E. Dundy. il Esquire 63:88-9+ My '65
Pitching for Holmes; production of new musical Baker street. New Yorker 41:31-3 F 20 '65
 See also
American playwrights theatre (organization)
Greek drama—Production. Modern
Shakespeare, W.—Staging and acting of plays
Television broadcasting—Program production
THEBOM, Blanche
Singing or acting? por Opera N 29:8-11 Ap 3 '65
THEFT. See Burglary and burglars; Embezzlement; Shoplifting; Stealing
THEISM
Christian natural theology and Christian existence. J. B. Cobb, jr. Christian Cent 82:265-7 Mr 3 '65; Discussion. 82:496 Ap 21 '65
THELEN, Al
Miracle on Main Street. Am City 80:75-6 N '65
THEME writing. See English language—Composition
THEOBALD, Robert
House that homo sapiens built. Nation 199:249-52; 200:568-9 O 19 '64, My 24 '65
THEODORE, Lee
Busy Lee Theodore. il pors Dance Mag 39:45 Jl '65
THEODORE ROOSEVELT NATIONAL MEMORIAL PARK
Theodore Roosevelt Memorial Park. R. W. Meyer. il Nat Parks Mag 39:17-20 My '65
THEOLOGIANS
Beyond Bonhoeffer? future of religionless Christianity. H. Cox. Commonweal 82:653-7 S 17 '65
Why this non-God-talk? death-of-God theologians. Christian Cent 82:1467-8 D 1 '65; Discussion. 83:85-6 Ja 19 '66

THEOLOGICAL education
American academy of parish clergy: why not?
G. E. Westberg. Christian Cent 82:557-8 Ap
28 '65
Diocesan priest and the intellectual life; excerpt from Seminary in crisis. S. Poole.
Commonweal 82:78-81 Ap 9 '65
Missing dimension. J. J. Kavanaugh. America 112:604-5+ Ap 24 '65
See also
Clergy—Education
Theological schools

THEOLOGICAL schools
American seminary education. S. Poole.
America 113:288-9 S 18 '65
Blueprint for seminaries. H. Ottensmeyer.
America 113:780-1 D 18 '65
Breakthrough: Dubuque's experiment in ecumenism; cooperative graduate programs and open classes for undergraduates. W. E. Hulme. Christian Cent 82:1187-90 S 29 '65
Do seminaries teach religion? W. H. Clark.
Christian Cent 82:520-2+ Ap 28 '65
Neither male nor female. D. Hunter and H. Hunter. Christian Cent 82:527-8+ Ap 28 '65; Discussion. 82:814 Je 23 '65
New trends for seminaries. America 113:660 N 27 '65
Put seminary eggs in fewer baskets; policy regarding Baptist seminaries. Christian Cent 82:1341 N 3 '65
Spirit of Sixth avenue; proposals for seminary reform. il Newsweek 65:85 My 3 '65
Unwarranted search; Christian institute of southern Africa and police. D. M. Norman. Christian Cent 82:820-1 Je 23 '65
See also
Holy Cross college, Washington, D.C.
San Francisco theological seminary, San Anselmo, Calif.

Curriculum

Agenda for a seminary board meeting; challenge to trustees, deans and faculties. W. D. Wagoner. Christian Cent 82:525-6 Ap 28 '65
Ecumenism and the Catholic seminary. K. Conley. Christian Cent 82:523-5 Ap 28 '65

Directories

Directory: seminary offerings (cont) il Christian Cent 82:529-56 Ap 28 '65

THEOLOGICAL students
Adman in the pulpit; future dual-vocation Episcopal priest. J. Shepherd. il Look 29: M14+ D 14 '65
Answering the call after thirty. il Time 85:88 Ap 30 '65
Neither male nor female. D. Hunter and H. Hunter. Christian Cent 82:527-8+ Ap 28 '65; Discussion. 82:814 Je 23 '65
New breed seminarians. R. L. Richard. America 112:194 F 6 '65; Discussion. 112:529-32+ Ap 17 '65
Post-seminary thoughts. M. Novak. Commonweal 83:9-12 O 8 '65; Discussion. 83: 111+, 166-7 O 29-N 5 '65
Understanding the ex-seminarian. America 113:129-30 Ag 7 '65

THEOLOGOS, Jim
On-the-spot picture sources. il Pub W 188: 104-5 N 8 '65

THEOLOGY
Changing world's challenge to theology. J. W. Goetz. Cath World 201:97-101 My '65
Christian atheism: God is dead movement. il Time 86:61-2 O 22 '65
Contra the new theologies. P. L. Holmer. Christian Cent 82:329-32 Mr 17 '65; Discussion. 82:742-3 Je 9 '65
Creative negation in theology. T. J. J. Altizer. Christian Cent 82:864-7 Jl 7 '65; Discussion. 82:1015-16, 1195, 1351-2 Ag 18, S 29, N 3 '65
Defenders of the faith; Evangelical theological society. Time 87:70 Ja 7 '66
Dissolution and reconstruction in theology. L. Gilkey. Christian Cent 82:135-9 F 3 '65; Discussion. 82:433-5 Ap 7 '65
Faith and truth. S. M. Ogden. Christian Cent 82:1057-60 S 1 '65; Reply. H. E. Jensen. 82:1321 O 27 '65
God is changing. il Time 85:68+ My 7 '65
God without God. G. Vahanian. Christian Cent 82:745-6 Je 9 '65
If all else fails. Christian Cent 83:3 Ja 5 '66
Is God changing our society? E. A. Smith. Cath World 202:74-9 N '65
Is God dead? comment on radical theology. D. Callahan. Commonweal 83:149-51 N 5 '65; Reply with rejoinder. R. Ruether. 83: 260-1 D 3 '65
Logic of religion. D. Callahan. Commonweal 83:346-8 D 17 '65

Modernity of fundamentalism. J. Opie, jr. Christian Cent 82:608-11 My 12 '65; Reply. J. Goodwin. 82:872-3 Jl 7 '65
Nature and function of faith. V. A. Harvey. Christian Cent 82:962-6 Ag 4 '65
New reality; God is dead; proclamation by T. J. J. Altizer. Newsweek 66:71-2 N 22 '65
Place and purpose of theology. H. Cox. Christian Cent 83:7-9 Ja 5 '66
Power and a goodness. R. R. Niebuhr. Christian Cent 82:1472-5 D 1 '65
Protestant & Catholic: the disparity beyond dogma. il Time 87:51-2 Ja 14 '66
Putting the new liturgy to work; understanding the meaning of the changes. O. V. Foxhoven. America 113:204-6 Ag 28 '65
Rebirth of Christ; essay on C. S. Lewis. J. Hart. il Nat R 17:1192-6 D 28 '65
Shape of a radical theology. W Hamilton. Christian Cent 82:1219-22 O 6 '65; Discussion. 82:1412-19; 83:18, 86 N 17 '65, Ja 5 19 '66
Swallowed up by godlessness. G. Vahanian. Christian Cent 82:1505-7 D 8 '65
Systematic theology of Paul Tillich, by A. J. McKelway. Review
Christian Cent 82:1481 D 1 '65. T. C. Oden
Theological asides (cont) C. Davis. America 112:193, 394, 667; 113:97; 284 F 6, Mr 20, My 8, Jl 24, S 18 '65
Theology as risk. C. Welch. Christian Cent 82:707-10 Je 2 '65
Theology in the context of culture. P. M. Van Buren. Christian Cent 82:428-30 Ap 7 '65
Third session, by X. Rynne. Review
Cath World 202:249-50 Ja '66. C. L. Palms
What on earth is happening to Protestantism. D. Norton-Taylor. il Fortune 72:170-3+ D '65
Where is theology going? M. Novak. Christian Cent 82:1342-3 N 3 '65
See also
Baptism
Belief and doubt
Christianity
Church
Creeds
Death
Ethics
God
Jesus Christ
Justification
Natural theology
Religion and science
Revelation
Secularism
Time (theology)

Bibliography

What the theologians are saying. W. Birmingham. Commonweal 81:705-8 F 26 '65

Study and teaching

Agenda for a seminary board meeting; challenge to trustees, deans and faculties. W. D. Wagoner. Christian Cent 82:525-6 Ap 28 '65
Do seminaries teach religion? W. H. Clark. Christian Cent 82:520-2+ Ap 28 '65
Theology comes alive; summer school at University of San Francisco. America 113: 198 Ag 28 '65
See also
Theological schools

THEOLOGY, Liberal. See Modernism
THEOLOGY, Natural. See Natural theology
THEORY of games. See Games, Theory of
THERAPEUTIC abortion. See Abortion
THERAPEUTICS
300-year weekend: marathon practice total honesty. S. Alexander. Life 59:28 S 24 '65
Toxicity, the therapeutic index, and the ranking of drugs. M. A. Schneiderman and others; discussion. il Science 149:1396-8 S 17 '65
See also
Cellular therapy
Occupational therapy
also subhead Therapy under names of diseases, e.g. Cancer—Therapy

THERE were pigeons in the square; story. See Greenbaum, E.
THERE'S some milk in the icebox; drama. See Henderson, B. J.
THÉRÈSE, Sister Mary. See Mary Thérèse, Sister
THERMAL analysis
Thermal analysis; report on first International conference on thermal analysis. C. B. Murphy. Science 151:111 Ja 7 '66
Thermal analysis; report on international symposium. B. R. Currell. Science 149:765-6 Ag 13 '65

THERMAL blankets. See Blankets
THERMAL ionization of gases. See Ionization of gases
THERMAL recovery of petroleum. See Petroleum engineering
THERMISTORS
Thermistor bridge design made easy. il Electr World 74:66 Jl '65
THERMODYNAMIC temperature scale. See Low temperature research
THERMODYNAMICS
Nonequilibrium thermodynamics, variational techniques, and stability; report on symposium. R. J. Donnelly. Science 149:1119-20 S 3 '65
Organic compounds in carbonaceous chondrites. M. H. Studier and others. bibliog il Science 149:1455-9 S 24 '65
THERMOGRAPHY, Medical. See Photography, Medical
THERMOLUMINESCENCE. See Luminescence
THERMOMETERS, Cooking
Oven thermometers. il Consumer Rep 30: 486-7 O '65
THERMOMETERS, Photographic. See Photography—Apparatus and supplies
THERMOMETERS and thermometry
Acoustical thermometer; ultrasonic interferometer. H. H. Plumb and G. Cataland. bibliog il Science 150:155-61 O 8 '65
Candy & deep-frying thermometers. il Consumer Rep 30:453-5 S '65
Rocket troubleshooters spot trouble in advance. Sci N L 87:137 F 27 '65
THERMOPLASTICS
Plyfoam: incredible new workshop wonder; with project ideas. A. Mikesell. il Pop Mech 124:146-55+ N '65
THEROUX, R. J. See Carozza, M. J. jt. auth.
THIBODEAU, Jean
Out of the ordinary small bulbs. Horticulture 43:28-9 Mr '65
THIELEN, Benedict
Florida nobody knows. Holiday 37:21-3+ F '65
Princeton: the enlightened exurbia. Holiday 38:58-65+ N '65
Woods Hole. Holiday 38:64-5+ Jl '65
THIEVES
I was always mad at the world. J. Rechy. Nation 200:254-6 Mr 8 '65
Whiz mob: a correlation of the technical argot of pickpockets with their behavior pattern, by D. W. Maurer. Review
Nation 200:261-2 Mr 8 '65. R. I. McDavid
THINK of them; story. See Polikoff, B.
THINKING. See Thought and thinking
THIOKOL chemical corporation
Biggest booster yet. il Time 85:55 Mr 12 '65
Hercules, Thiokol win Poseidon work. Miss & Roc 17:16 O 25 '65
Roaring success, but will it fly? Thiokol's 156-in.-diameter solid rocket. il Bsns W p82+ Mr 6 '65
Thiokol tests two thrust vector systems. M. L. Yaffee. il Aviation W 82:91+ Je 21 '65
THIRD avenue. See New York (city)—Streets
THIRST; story. See Andric, I.
THIRTIETH birthday of Clara Hawkins; story. See Banks, L. R.
35mm cameras. See Cameras
THIRTY-nine; story. See Weiss, M.
THIS day for thanks; story. See Weyer, S.
THIS small stranger; story. See Alexander, R. W.
THOMAS Aquinas, Saint
Aquinas' search for wisdom, by V. J. Bourke. Review
America 112:572+ Ap 17 '65. J. A. Mann
See also
Thomism
THOMAS More, Saint. See More, T. Saint
THOMAS Aquinas, Brother
Teacher today; adaptation of address at National Catholic educational association convention, April 21, 1965. por Cath World 202: 40+ O '65
THOMAS, Alexander. See Chess, S. jt. auth.
THOMAS, Audrey C.
If one green bottle; story. Atlan 215:83-7 Je '65
THOMAS, Bertram D.
Fast-growing lab regroups on the run. il por Bsns W p67-70 F 6 '65
THOMAS, Bruce
Scholarship on a budget. bibliog por Library J 90:2209-14 My 15 '65
THOMAS, Carole
Impressions. il U S Camera 28:54-5 Jl '65

THOMAS, Charles Walker
February issue: a dedication to Charles Wesley. Negro Hist Bul 28:99 F '65
Historical notes. Negro Hist Bul 28:149+ Ap '65
Make Negro history week an open-end activity in '65. Negro Hist Bul 28:75 Ja '65
THOMAS, David W. See Blumer, M. jt. auth.
THOMAS, Dylan
Solace from Swansea; letter. por Esquire 64: 151+ D '65
about
Bard reborn. il por Newsweek 66:96 N 1 '65
Life of Dylan Thomas, by C. FitzGibbon. Review
Commonweal 83:350 D 17 '65. I. D. Suss
Sat R il por 48:44 O 30 '65. W. Bittner
Time il por 86:102+ O 29 '65
Weighed and found wanted. W. Stafford. Poetry 106:432 S '65
Young Dylan Thomas; excerpts from The life of Dylan Thomas. C. Fitzgibbon. por Atlan 216:63-70 O; 66-72 N '65
THOMAS, Elizabeth Marshall
Reporter at large. New Yorker 41:51-2+ My 1; 50-2+ My 8; 61-2+ My 15; 54-6+ My 22 '65
THOMAS, Elsie M.
Magic pumpkin patch; drama. Plays 25:73-8 O '65
THOMAS, Gerald
Something new every day. Recreation 58: 129 Mr '65
THOMAS, Gertrude Z.
Picture worth a thousand words. Antiques 88:686-8 N '65
THOMAS, Gilbert
Behind New Guinea's masks. Sat R 48:68+ S 18 '65
THOMAS, Gwyn
Passionate authors. Holiday 37:10+ Ap '65
THOMAS, Harold E.
Reality of drought is always with us. Natur Hist 74:50-7 N '65
THOMAS, Helen
Luci-Lynda beat. il por Newsweek 66:89 D 6 '65
THOMAS, Hugh
All-pervasive church. Holiday 37:86-7+ Ap '65
THOMAS, J. Trevor. See Trevor Thomas, J.
THOMAS, Jess
For humanity. il por Time 87:58 Ja 21 '66
Four Americans. M. Mayer. Esquire 63:36+ Ap '65
THOMAS, John
Brumel drives a Rambler and gets his apartment free. por Life 58:72A Je 18 '65
THOMAS, Lowell, Jr
Scientists ride ice islands on Arctic odysseys. por Nat Geog Mag 128:670-91 N '65
THOMAS, Sister Marguerite. See Marguerite Thomas, Sister
THOMAS, Norman
Dean of protest; with report by S. Wright. il pors Life 60:56-65 Ja 14 '66
They are saying on the circuit. . . W. F. Buckley, jr. Nat R 17:1186 D 28 '65
THOMAS, Rachele
Is sex morality out of date? Parents Mag 40:39+ My '65
Mistakes many mothers make; dawdling is a necessary nuisance. Parents Mag 40:70-1+ Mr '65
THOMAS, Richard D.
Records protection system with a plus. por Am City 80:109 S '65
THOMAS, Robert
Piege pour un homme seul; adaptation. See Weinstock, J. Catch me if you can
THOMAS, W. Lamar
City gets the green light. Am City 80:123-4 S '65
THOMASSON, R. R.
Hawthorns. Horticulture 43:45 Je '65
THOMISM
Objections to Thomism. G. F. Pollard. America 112:842 Je 12 '65; Discussion. 113: 66 Jl 17 '65
Post-seminary thoughts. J. Gaffney. Commonweal 83:111+ O 29 '65
Thomism in an age of renewal. R. M. McInerny. America 113:258-60 S 11 '65
THOMPSON, Benjamin
Good design makes good giving. il por Look 29:M10+ D 28 '65
THOMPSON, Betty
Coordinated for mission. Christian Cent 82: 370+ Mr 24 '65
Protestants, Catholics view religious liberty. Christian Cent 82:788-90 Je 16 '65
THOMPSON, Bruce
Gesneriads. Horticulture 43:14-17+ S '65
Gloxinias. Horticulture 43:28-9+ F '65
THOMPSON, C. J. See Crawhall, J. C. jt. auth.

THOMPSON, Clive
Brief biography. S. Goodman. pors Dance
Mag 40:50-1 Ja '66
THOMPSON, Daniel C.
Rise of the Negro protest. bibliog f Ann Am
Acad 357:18-29 Ja '65
THOMPSON, Donald E.
Education for building. por Library J 90:
5157-60 D 1 '65
THOMPSON, Dorothy Barclay
How to cope with your child's temper tan-
trums. Am Home 68:36+ Ap '65
THOMPSON, Dorothy Brown
Answer to Emerson; poem. McCalls 92:161
Mr '65
THOMPSON, Elisabeth Kendall
San Francisco report: no easy road to the
more handsome city. Arch Rec 138:151-66
S '65
THOMPSON, Era Bell
Does amalgamation work in Brazil? Ebony
20:27-30+ Jl; 33-42 S '65
How Israel solves its cultural lag. Ebony
21:121-6+ N '65
Instant hair. Ebony 21:139-40+ N '65
Some of my best friends are white. Ebony
20:154+ Ag '65
THOMPSON, Evelyn
Our daughter Ivan the Terrible. Redbook
125:8+ O '65
THOMPSON, Frank, Jr
Excerpt from debate, July 26, 1965. Cong
Digest 44:202+ Ag '65
THOMPSON, Hunter S.
Motorcycle gangs: losers and outsiders. Na-
tion 200:522-6 My 17 '65
Nonstudent left. Nation 201:154-8 S 27 '65
THOMPSON, J. E. Jr
Boyce Thompson southwestern arboretum.
Horticulture 43:44-5+ F '65
THOMPSON, James H. W.
Silk of Thailand. M. Cable. il Atlan 217:
107-11 Ja '66
THOMPSON, John Beauchamp
For Martin Buber; poem. Christian Cent
82:863 Jl 7 '65
Good news of nothing; poem. Christian Cent
82:916 Jl 21 '65
Midnight; poem. Christian Cent 83:14 Ja 5 '66
North beach; poem. Commonweal 82:83 Ap 9
'65
THOMPSON, John G.
Math for the few; reprint. il por Sci Digest
57:38-41 Mr '65
THOMPSON, Kenneth W.
De Gaulle's doctrine of deterrence. Sat R 48:
28 F 6 '65
Fire of a thousand suns. Sat R 48:112-13
S 18 '65
Peace by evolutionary progress. Sat R 48:36
D 18 '65
Staying alive to solve the problems. Sat R
48:22-3 Ap 3 '65
THOMPSON, Lawrence S.
Thirty-four books chosen for Ninth annual
midwestern show. Pub W 188:125+ Jl 19 '65
THOMPSON, Milt
I'll fly anything! ed. by W. S. Griswold. por
Pop Sci 186:62-4+ Mr '65
THOMPSON, Morton
National survey of community recreation
services to the mentally retarded and physi-
cally handicapped; summary. bibliog Re-
creation 58:191-2 Ap '65
New hope for the homebound. Recreation
58:435 N '65
R for the ill & handicapped. See issues of
Recreation
THOMPSON, N. C.
Financing: the not-so-tender trap; excerpt
from How to get the best car deal, every
time. Motor T 17:36-8 Je '65
THOMPSON, Paul E. and others
Quinine-resistant plasmodium berghei in mice.
bibliog Science 148:1240-1 My 28 '65
THOMPSON, Robert Farris
Mid-month recordings. Sat R 48:58-9 F 13 '65
THOMPSON, Robert Glenn
I spied for the Russians; ed. by H. H. Mar-
tin. pors Sat Eve Post 238:23-9 My 22; 38-
40+ Je 5 '65

about

Lenin, mon amour. il por Newsweek 65:
23-4 Mr 22 '65
Stupid spy. il por Time 85:31 Mr 19 '65
THOMPSON, Sir Robert Grainger Ker
Doing the right things; interview, ed. by
F. Melville. por Newsweek 66:33 Jl 5 '65
This is guerrilla warfare; Vietnam extracts
from conversation with F. Melville. Read
Digest 87:90-1 S '65
THOMPSON, Sally Anne
Siesta time, or royalty out on a limb. Natur
Hist 74:34-7 O '65

THOMPSON, Thomas
King of song dies, and a friend remembers
him. Life 58:36 F 26 '65
Life movie review (cont) Life 59:16 Jl 23 '65
Life theater review (cont) Life 58:16 My 14
'65
Seagoing soap opera of captain Sinatra. Life
59:34B Ag 20 '65
Sound flowed out of old music streams. Life
58:92-4+ My 21 '65
Tiny diva's big triumph. Life 59:129-30+
N 12 '65
Tuning U.S. musicals to overseas box office.
Life 58:55+ Mr 12 '65
THOMPSON, W. B.
Where is science taking us? excerpt from
Trieste symposium published under title,
Plasma physics. Sat R 48:72 O 2 '65
THOMPSON, W. F.
Fishing treaties and salmon of the North
Pacific; address, October 21, 1965. Science
150:1786-9 D 31 '65
THOMPSON, Wade
Custodians of the language convene. Nation
200:145-8 F 8 '65
THOMPSON Ramo Wooldridge, incorporated
TRW systems wins Comsat nod. il Miss &
Roc 17:19 D 20 '65
THOMS, Wayne
Global trailer travel. Travel 123:26-31+ My
'65
THOMSON, J. Richard
Electronic detectives of medicine. Todays
Health 43:22-5+ Mr '65
THOMSON, Jean C.
(comp) Children's paperbacks. Library J 90:
2355-70+, 3725-6+ My 15, S 15 '65
(comp) New fall children's books. Library J
90:4560-600 O 15 '65
(comp) New spring children's books. Li-
brary J 90:1508-40 Mr 15 '65
—See Davis, E. L. jt. ed.
THOMSON, Margaret
Children in their masks; story. Redbook
125:72-3 O '65
THOMSON, Peter
Aussie menace. il por Time 86:48 Jl 16 '65
Man from down under laughs it up. J.
Lovesey. il por Sports Illus 23:16-17+ Jl
19 '65
Short, shy and sure. il por Newsweek 66:48
Jl 19 '65
THOMSON, Richard
Old roses. Horticulture 43:20-1+ Ag '65
THOMSON, Roy Herbert, 1st baron Thomson
of Fleet. See Thomson of Fleet, R. H. T.
THOMSON, Virgil
About Four saints. por Am Rec G 31:520-1
F '65

about

Four saints in three acts. Criticism
Am Rec G 31:521-2 F '65
Four saints in three acts. J. Lyons. il Am
Rec G 31:518-19 F '65
On records; Four saints in three acts. Opera
N 29:34 Ap 3 '65
THOMSON of Fleet, Roy Herbert Thomson, 1st
baron
(ed) See Kosygin, A. Sort of dialogue

about

Amazing communications world of Roy
Thomson. J. Tebbel. il por Sat R 48:66-8+
O 9 '65
Collector. il pors Time 86:53 N 26 '65
Roy Thomson of Fleet Street. by R. Braddon.
Review
Newsweek il por 66:90+ N 1 '65
THOMSON organization, limited
Thomson organization buys Hamish Hamil-
ton, ltd. Pub W 188:33 N 29 '65
THORARINSSON, Sigurdur
Surtsey: island born of fire. por Nat Geog
Mag 127:712-26 My '65
THORAZINE. See Chlorpromazine
THORBECKE, William J.
Coexistence or cooperation? Sat R 49:39 Ja
22 '66

about

Peace by evolutionary progress. K. W.
Thompson. Sat R 48:36 D 18 '65
THORNDIKE, Edward M. See Ewing, M. jt.
auth.
THOREAU, Henry David
Frog's-eye view at Walden Pond. S. North.
Sat R 49:39 Ja 15 '66
Harvard's Algonquin. G. Byron. por Liv
Wildn 29:17-19 Sum '65
Thoreau's social criticism as poetry. L.
Bowling. Yale R 55:255-64 D '65
Too tame for the Chippeway. R. Fleck. Liv
Wildn 29:20-1 Sum '65
THORNE, Kip S.
Gravitational collapse and the death of a
star. bibliog Science 150:1671-9 D 24 '65

THORNE, Samuel
Northern route to discovery. Sat R 48:33 D 18 '65
Record of a visit from the Vikings. Sat R 48:46-8 O 16 '65
THORNTON, Dade W.
Where sportfishermen meet. Motor B 115: 144-7 F '65
THORNTON, Michael V. See Bundy, M. L. jt. auth.
THORNTOWN, Ind.
Meter readers, throw away your pencils. il Am City 80:19 Ag '65
THORP, Edward O.
How many beans in the jar? Pop Mech 124: 96-7+ N '65
THORPE, Azalea
Institute of American Indian arts, Santa Fe. Craft Horiz 25:12-13+ Jl '65
THORPE, W. H. and North, M. E. W.
Lonely tunesmiths of nature, men and the birds. Sat R 48:85-7 D 4 '65
THOUGHT and thinking
Critical comments on some inconsistencies in modern thought. L. P. Williams. Sch & Soc 93:177-9 Mr 20 '65
Give your mind a chance. P. Dudley. Read Digest 87:94-6 N '65
Power of the mind; dedication to a contributing life; address, June 14, 1965. R. A. Charpie. Vital Speeches 31:668-70 Ag 15 '65
Primary thinking. F. R. Schreiber and M. Herman. Sci Digest 59:23 Ja '66
Publisher's foreword. J. J. Starrow, jr. Nation 201:15-17 S 20 '65
Stimulating productive thinking in students. Sch & Soc 93:443+ N 27 '65
What makes a company creative? symposium. Nations Bsns 53:76-9 Je '65
Working mind. A. M. Sullivan. Duns R 86: 76 Jl '65
See also
Attention
Problem solving
Reason
THOUGHT control. See Intellectual liberty
THOUGHT transference. See Telepathy
THOUSAND miles across the street; story. See Robinson, B.
THREAD
Sewing thread. il Consumer Rep 30:356-9 Jl '65
THREE-cornered screws. See Screws
THREE dimensional photography. See Stereo-photography
THREE-mile limit. See Territorial waters
THREE shapes of love; story. See O'Faolain, S.
THREE sisters; drama. See Chekhov, A. P.
THREEPENNY opera; opera. See Weill, K.
THREONINE
Thermal stability of threonine in the presence of a marine polyphenolic material. J. R. Vallentyne. bibliog il Science 151:214-15 Ja 14 '66
THRESHING
Threshing sledge. J. Bordaz. il Natur Hist 74:26-9 Ap '65
THRESHOLD, Visual. See Sight
THRIFT, Walter
What is not in New York. F. Getlein. New Repub 153:34+ O 2 '65
THRIFT
See also
Domestic finance
THRIFT shops and rummage sales
Purple thread shop; Clarksburg, Calif. R. Martens. il Farm J 89:87 Ap '65
THROAT

Diseases
No easy cure for a sore throat. il Consumer Bul 48:21-2 O '65
Strep throats among school children. L. W. Sauer. PTA Mag 60:25 D '65

Surgery
Tonsillectomy, in or out? il Newsweek 66: 94+ N 8 '65
THROCKMORTON, Helen J.
Eden revisited; poem. Christian Cent 82:778 Je 16 '65
THROMBIN
Peptides attached to thrombin: their influence on proteolysis. R. H. Landaburu and others. bibliog il Science 148:380-1 Ap 16 '65
THROMBOSIS
Lethal abscess. il Time 87:68+ Ja 14 '66
THROWERS, Snow. See Snow blowers, throwers, etc.
THRUPP, Sylvia L.
Writing of west European history: a bird's-eye view of trends between 1960 and 1964. bibliog f Ann Am Acad 359:157-64 My '65

THRUSHES
Night flight with a thrush. R. R. Graber. il Audubon Mag 67:368-74 N '65
THUCYDIDES
Thucydides: the historian as prophet. W. H. Chamberlin. il Sat R 48:22-3+ My 8 '65
THUNDER
See also
Lightning
THUNDER Mountain (shooting club) See Sports clubs
THUNDERSTORMS
Man-made storms boom over Old Faithful. Sci N L 88:57 Jl 24 '65
See also
Aviation—Storm hazards
Lightning
THURBER, David L. and others
Uranium-series ages of Pacific atoll coral. bibliog Science 149:55-8 Jl 2 '65
—See Broecker, W. S. jt. auth.
THURBER, James
Secret life of James Thurber; reply to a letter by Guy F. Smith. por Esquire 64: 152+ D '65
about
James Thurber and the art of fantasy. C. S. Holmes. Yale R 55:17-33 O '65
James Thurber, doodler extraordinary. B. Klaw. il por Am Heritage 16:56-7 F '65
THURMOND, Strom
Choice for Americans; address, January 9, 1965. Vital Speeches 31:259-62 F 15 '65
Cult of relativism; address, September 25, 1965. Vital Speeches 32:46-8 N 1 '65
about
Southern Republicans. New Repub 152:6-7 Je 26 '65
THURSDAY literature and luncheon society. See New York (city)—Clubs
THURSTONE, F. L. and others
Ultrasonic scanning of biologic tissue by a new technique. Science 149:302-3 Jl 16 '65
THWAITE, Anthony
Pond; poem. New Yorker 41:34 Ag 14 '65
THYBON DE COURTRY, Sylvaine, baroness
Dream and reality. Newsweek 66:49-50 S 27 '65
THYMINE
Thymine addition to ethanol: induction by gamma irradiation. P. E. Brown and others. il Science 151:68-70 Ja 7 '66
Thymine photoproducts but not thymine dimers found in ultraviolet-irradiated bacterial spores. J. E. Donnellan, jr. and R. B. Setlow. bibliog il Science 149:308-10 Jl 16 '65
THYMUS gland
Adult thymectomy: effect on recovery from immunologic depression in mice. A. P. Monaco and others. bibliog il Science 149: 432-5 Jl 23 '65
Allograft survival: effect of antiserums to thymus glands and lymphocytes. H. Nagaya and H. O. Sieker. bibliog il Science 150: 1181-2 N 26 '65
Immunity and the thymus. Sci Am 213:40+ D '65
Inhibition of L1210 tumor growth by thymus DNA. J. L. Glick and A. R. Goldberg. bibliog il Science 149:997-8 Ag 27 '65
Involvement of thymus in immune response of rabbits to somatic polysaccharides of gram-negative bacteria. M. Landy and others. bibliog il Science 147:1591-2 Mr 26 '65
Zeroing in on a cancer cure. Bsns W p142+ Ap 17 '65
THYMUS gland, Transplantation of. See Transplantation of organs, tissues, etc.
THYROCALCITONIN. See Thyroid extracts
THYROID extracts
Thyrocalcitonin: inhibitor of bone resorption in tissue culture. J. Friedman and L. G. Raisz. bibliog il Science 150:1465-7 D 10 '65
THYROID gland
Iodination in relation to thyroglobulin maturation and subunit aggregation. R. W. Seed and I. H. Goldberg. bibliog il Science 149:1380-2 S 17 '65
Partial thyroid removal helps hyperthyroidism. Sci N L 87:99 F 13 '65
Thyroid and parathyroid roles in hypercalcemia: evidence for a thyrocalcitonin-releasing factor. R. F. Gittes and G. L. Irvin. bibliog il Science 148:1737-9 Je 25 '65
THYROXINE
Metabolism of iodine-131-labeled thyroxine-binding prealbumin in man. J. H. Oppenheimer and others. bibliog il Science 149: 748-51 Ag 13 '65

TI plant
After five years, bloom! il Sunset 136:128-9 Ja '66
Our ti plant is a tree. S. Villers. il Flower Grower 53:45 Ja '66

TIBET
Mountain revolt. R. Ramanujam. il Newsweek 66:37-8 Ag 2 '65
See also
Guerrillas

Boundaries
Himalayas; disputed border between India and Tibet. Life 58:68 My 28 '65

TIC
Tics. M. J. E. Senn. McCalls 92:34 Jl '65
TIC douloureux. See Neuralgia, Trigeminal

TICHENOR, Tom
King Merrily's Merry Christmas; story. Good H 161:72-81 D '65
TICK bites. See Insect bites and stings
TICKET speculators. See Theater tickets

TICKETS
See also
Baseball—Tickets
Theater tickets

TICKNOR, R. L.
Weed control. Horticulture 43:29-31 Ap '65
TIDAL currents. See Ocean currents
TIDAL marshes. See Salt marshes
TIDAL power. See Tide power
TIDAL waves. See Seismic sea waves

TIDE power
Tides to drive mammoth power plant; Rance River plant, France. D. Scott. il Pop Sci 186:90-3+ Je '65

TIDES
Survey of sea tides set. Sci N L 89:13 Ja 1 '66
Tides: the moon's pull on the sea; reprint. il Sci Digest 57:84-5 Je '65
See also
Earth tides

TIDWELL, Roy, and Wiseblood, Edward
Oregon plan. Library J 90:3686-9 S 15 '65
TIE-in merchandise. See Merchandising
TIE racks. See Necktie racks

TIEL, Vicki
Two American girls show Paris. il pors Life 58:94-6+ F 5 '64
El TIEMPO (newspaper)
Batista in Bay Shore. Newsweek 65:82 Ap 5 '65

TIERNAN, Robert J.
Ten ways to sell them. Nations Bsns 53:84-6+ Je '65
TIFFIN boxes. See Lunch boxes

TIGER, Dick
Angry Tiger jumps on Joey. W. Leggett. il por Sports Illus 23:20-1 N 1 '65
Sad case of a neglected Tiger. M. Kram. il por Sports Illus 22:28-9 My 31 '65

TIGER hunting
First day tiger; thirty-day India hunt. J. O'Connor. il Outdoor Life 136:33-5+ N '65
In the land of the tiger. V. Kraft. il Sports Illus 23:44-67 D 20 '65
Tiger's kill; with report by G. Schaller. il Life 58:52-60+ Je 25 '65
Tigress of Elephantville; Eleanor O'Connor. J. O'Connor. il Outdoor Life 137:32-5+ Ja '66

TIGER snakes. See Snakes

TIGERFLOWERS
Tigridias. A. D. Hawkes. Horticulture 43:61 Mr '65

TIGERS
See also
Tiger hunting
TIGRIDIAS. See Tigerflowers

TIJERINA, Reies Lopez
Crusade against gringos. il por Newsweek 67:17-18 Ja 3 '66

TIJUANA, Mexico
Amigo Americans; college students aid Juarez-Lincoln social center. il Time 85:49 Ap 30 '65
Driving south and east of Tijuana. il Sunset 136:20 Ja '66
Surprises of Tijuana. il Sunset 136:45-57 Ja '66

TIKAL. See Mayas
TILAPIAS. See Mouthbreeders

TILDEN, Freeman
Not by truth alone. Science 148:1415 Je 11 '65

TILDEN, Paul Mason
Washington newsletter (cont) Natur Hist 74:62+ Ag '65; 75:12-13 Ja '66

TILE setting
Three steps to installing ceramic tile anywhere. J. Hand. il Pop Sci 187:144-7+ S '65

TILES
How to remove stains from ceramic tile. il Sunset 134:152+ Mr '65
Make your own tiles and trivets. il Design 66:26-7 Mr '65
Three steps to installing ceramic tile anywhere. J. Hand. il Pop Sci 187:144-7+ S '65
Tile: brilliant ceramic tiles grace four dramatic rooms. il McCalls 93:106-11 O '65
TILES, Floor
Inlaid vinyl floor coverings. il Consumer Rep 30:388-91 Ag '65

TILLAGE
Biggest year yet for minimum tillage. il Farm J 89:36-7 My '65
Minimum tillage for the southern corn belt. W. J. Fletcher. il Suc Farm 63:94 F '65

TILLES, David
Atmospheric noble gases: solar-wind bombardment of extraterrestrial dust as a possible source mechanism. bibliog Science 148:1085-8 My 21 '65

TILLETT, Anne, and Tillett, Lowell
Grammar in the cold war. New Repub 153:17-20 S 11 '65

TILLETT, Gladys A.
Expanding the participation of women in national life; eighteenth session. Tehran, Iran, March 1-20, 1965. Dept State Bul 53:39-44 Jl 5 '65
Family law and the women of Africa. Dept State Bul 52:229-33 F 15 '65
Journey to Mongolia. Dept State Bul 53:918-23 D 6 '65

TILLETT, Lowell. See Tillett, A. jt. auth.

TILLICH, Paul
Limit of hope: summary of address on Pacem in terris. por Time 85:38 F 26 '65

about
After Tillich, what? address, October 22, 1965. R. P. Scharlemann. Christian Cent 82:1478-80 D 1 '65
Courage to be. Christian Cent 82:1340 N 3 '65
Great radical theologian was apostle to the skeptics. por Life 59:40D N 5 '65
Man of ultimate concern. il por Time 86:80+ O 29 '65
Obituary
Pub W 188:39 N 1 '65
Passionate Protestant. por Newsweek 66:60 N 1 '65
Paul Tillich. R. M. Brown. Commonweal 83:471-3 Ja 21 '66
Paul Tillich and Christian realism. America 113:514-15 N 6 '65
Paul Tillich in Catholic thought. ed. by T. A. O'Meara and C. D. Weisser. Review
Cath World 201:72+ Ap '65. H. D. Noyes
Profiles; concerning Honest to God, by J. Robinson. V. Mehta. New Yorker 41:64+ N 13 '65
Systematic theology of Paul Tillich. by A. J. McKelway. Review
Christian Cent 82:1481 D 1 '65. T. C. Oden
Ultimate concern: Tillich in dialogue. ed. by D. M. Brown. Review
Christian Cent 82:1012 Ag 18 '65. C. W. Kegley

TILLIM, Sidney
Katz cocktail: grand and cozy. Art N 64:46-9+ D '65

TILLINGHAST, Charles Carpenter, 1911-
T.W.A: prosperity but no peace. J. McDonald. il Fortune 72:122-5+ Jl '65

TILLINGHAST, Richard
Praise for a household; poem. Yale R 55:254 D '65

TILTON, G. R. and Steiger, R. H.
Lead isotopes and the age of the earth. bibliog Science 150:1805-8 D 31 '65

TIMBUCTOO. See Timbuktu

TIMBUKTU
From here to Timbuktu. T. L. Christie. il Sat R 48:41-2+ S 4 '65

TIME
Discovery of time, by S. Toulmin and J. Goodfield. Review
New Yorker 41:231-8+ N 6 '65. J. Bernstein
Time halted for forty-five hours; Project time out, North Conway, N.H. Sci N L 88:78 Jl 31 '65
See also
Calendar
Geological time

TIME (periodical)
Letter from the publisher; magazines circulation. B. M. Auer. il Time 86:11 D 31 '65
Letter from the publisher; printing Time. B. M. Auer. il Time 85:11 F 12 '65
Letter from the publisher; Time covers. B. M. Auer. Time 85:25 Ap 30 '65
Letter from the publisher; Time's news tour of Asia. B. M. Auer. il Time 85:14-15 F 19 '65

TIME (periodical)—*Continued*
Time magazine on the Holy Eucharist.
America 113:90 Jl 24 '65
TIME (theology)
It is now the hour. . . J. Knoedel. America
113:666-9 N 27 '65
TIME, Daylight saving. See Daylight saving
TIME, incorporated
Federal court considers where is a corporation: Louisiana case against Time, inc.
H. F. Pilpel. Pub W 187:74 Ap 26 '65
Letter from the publisher; joint enterprise
to create and market educational materials, systems and services. B. M. Auer.
Time 86:19 N 26 '65
Time, inc. and G.E. plan educational materials unit. Pub W 188:32-3 N 29 '65
TIME, Reaction. See Reaction time
TIME and space. See Space and time
TIME capsules. See Civilization—Preservation
of records
TIME-delay switches. See Electric switches
TIME-lapse photography. See Photography,
Time-lapse
TIME-Life International
Time-Life uses effective 3-D models. il Pub
W 188:110-13 N 8 '65
TIME measurements
When it's 6 a.m. in Tokyo; world time indicator. H. S. Pyle. il Pop Electr 23:90-1
Ag '65
    See also
Astronomical clocks
TIME out of yesterday; story. See Crossman, P.
TIME payment sales. See Instalment plan
TIME perception
Don't ring, I'm already awake. H. Downs.
Sci Digest 57:91-4 Je '65
TIME reversal
European tests show backwardness of time.
Sci N L 87:169 Mr 13 '65
Lost force; fifth force in addition to four
known forces: nuclear, electromagnetic,
weak and gravitational. Sci Am 212:56-8 Ap
'65
New headache for physicists; fifth force and
CPT. B. H. Frisch. il Sci Digest 58:28-32
Jl '65
TIME sharing computers. See Computers—Cooperative use
TIME signals, Radio
New v.l.f. transmissions: Fort Collins, Colo.
low-frequency station WWVB. Electr World
74:78 D '65
TIME switches. See Electric switches
TIMERS. See Timing devices
TIMES, Los Angeles
Censoring sex; screening board. il Time 85:71
F 12 '65
New look at the Times. P. Bart. Sat R 48:68+
Je 12 '65
TIMES, New York. See New York times
TIMES-Mirror company
Times Mirror to acquire year book medical.
Pub W 188:35 N 8 '65
TIMES square, New York city. See New York
(city)—Times square
TIMES Tower building. See New York (city)—
Architecture
TIMING devices
Audible exposure timer. H. Hilton. il Pop
Mech 124:150-1+ D '65
By the clock; cycle dial to show a woman's
period of probable fertility. il Time 86:61
Jl 9 '65
Electronic timers for automatic control.
S. L. Silver. il Electr World 73:39-41+
Mr '65
Practical nanosecond timer developed. il Miss
& Roc 16:34-5 My 24 '65
Timers quiet satellites. Sci N L 87:262 Ap 24
'65
Tonal darkroom timer or metronome. F. W.
Chesson. il Pop Electr 23:95-6 N '65
TIMKEN art gallery. See San Diego, Calif.—
Galleries and museums
TIN cans
    See also
Beer containers
TIN industry and trade
    See also
International council
United Nations tin conference
TIN mines and mining
    Bolivia
More trouble from the mines. Time 86:46 O
1 '65
TINDALL, George B.
Bubble in the sun. Am Heritage 16:76-83+
Ag '65

TING, Irwin P. and Dugger, W. M. Jr
Transhydrogenation in root tissue; mediation
by carbon dioxide. bibliog Science 150:1727-8
D 24 '65
TINKER, Frank
They help stamp out firebugs. Pop Mech 124:
98-102+ S '65
TINKERS. See Gipsies in Ireland
TINKLE, Donald W. and Irwin, L. N.
Lizard reproduction: refractory period and
response to warmth in Uta stansburiana
females. bibliog Science 148:1613-14 Je 18
'65
TINNITUS
Tinnitus: that puzzling buzzing in your ears.
D. S. Hatton. Todays Health 43:14+ N '65
TINSLEY, Russell
Anyone can call predators. Field & S 70:10-
12+ N '65
Tarpon fever. Travel 123:46-7+ Ap '65
TINY Alice; drama. See Albee, E.
TIPPETT, Michael
Going like sixty. il por Time 85:57 F 12 '65
Tippett in the Rockies; Aspen report. A.
Young. il por Hi Fi 15:152 O '65
TIPPING
How to tip just enough; interview. J. Berger;
J. Nassikas. il Changing T 19:33-6 S '65
Tips on tipping; tipping the minister. Christian Cent 82:727 Je 2 '65
TIRE industry and trade
Michelin stretches its rubber empire; first in
tire sales in France. il Bsns W p 136-8+
Jl 17 '65
Wider track for tire sales. il Bsns W p55-
6+ Mr 20 '65
    See also
Goodyear tire and rubber company
TIREDNESS. See Fatigue
TIRES, Automobile
Are the tires on 1966 cars safe? il Consumer
Bul 49:21-2 Ja '66
Automobile tires. il Consumer Rep 30:428-33 S
'65
Goodyear gets back on the race track; Indianapolis 500. il Bsns W p 144-6+ My 22
'65
Have you checked your tires lately? P. W.
Kearney. Read Digest 87:103-5 Jl '65
How to buy tires. K. D. Gage. il Motor T
17:48-50+ My '65
How to make a giant tire. Sci Digest 58:40
O '65
Mars and motor cars; legislation to establish minimum safety and performance
standards for tires. Nation 201:51 Ag 2 '65
New rubber for new tires; radial-ply tires.
J. Eberhart. Sci N L 87:179 Mr 20 '65
New tires promise fastest 500 in history.
J. P. Norbye. il Pop Sci 186:78-80+ My '65
Numbers game in tires; maximum load standard set. New Repub 153:9 S 18 '65
Snow tires, recaps, chains, studded tires;
which to buy? Bet Hom & Gard 44:14 Ja
'66
Super tires for sportsmen. V. L. Oertle. il
Field & S 69:145+ Ap '65
Why the sudden furor over automobile tires.
il U S News 58:99-100 Ap 12 '65
Wider track for tire sales. il Bsns W p55-6+
Mr 20 '65

    Retreading and recapping
Legal cheaters; slick ways to retire your
competition. J. McFarland. il Hot Rod 18:
78-80 D '65
TIRES, Motor truck
Fat truck tires for farm hauling. L. Oertle.
il Suc Farm 63:65 Je '65
Tire failure no longer a problem; Batavia,
N.Y. G. A. Kandra. il Am City 80:104-5
Mr '65
TIRES, Rubber
New rubber for new tires; radial-ply tires.
J. Eberhart. Sci N L 87:179 Mr 20 '65
TIROS (artificial satellites) See Artificial
satellites—Meteorological applications
'TIS better to have loved; story. See Schoen, B.
TISDALE, D. E. W.
Reader's choice. Travel 123:13 Mr '65
TISSUE culture. See Tissues—Culture
TISSUE metabolism
Extracellular matrices; report on conference
at Arden House. K. Meyer and others. Science 147:760-1 F 12 '65
Lactate dehydrogenase isozymes: substrate
inhibition in various human tissues. E. S.
Vesell. bibliog il Science 150:1590-3 D 17 '65
TISSUES
Electron spin resonance characteristics of
some normal tissues: effect of microwave
power. H. M. Swartz and R. P. Molenda.
bibliog il Science 148:94-5 Ap 2 '65

TISSUES—*Continued*

Three dimensions in fine structure. H. C. Mitchell and J. C. Thaemert. bibliog il Science 148:1480-2 Je 11 '65

Ultrasonic scanning of biologic tissue by a new technique. F. L. Thurstone and others. il Science 149:302-3 Jl 16 '65

See also
Bone
Cells
Membranes (biology)

Culture

Functional studies of cultured brain tissues as related to demyelinative disorders. M. B. Bornstein and S. M. Crain. bibliog il Science 148:1242-4 My 28 '65

Growth and tissue formation from single, isolated tobacco cells in microculture. V. Vasil and A. C. Hildebrandt. bibliog il Science 147:1454-5 Mr 19 '65

Growth of mouse mammary glands in vivo after monolayer culture. C. W. Daniel and K. B. DeOme. bibliog il Science 149:634-6 Ag 6 '65

HeLa cells: effects of temperature on the life cycle P. N. Rao and J. Engelberg. bibliog Science 148:1092-4 My 21 '65

Hurler's syndrome: demonstration of an inherited disorder of connective tissue in cell culture. B. S. Daners and A. G. Bearn. bibliog il Science 149:987-9 Ag 27 '65

Hydroxyurea; differential lethal effects on cultured mammalian cells during the cell cycle. W. K. Sinclair. bibliog il Science 150:1729-31 D 24 '65

Immunization against Rauscher mouse leukemia with tissue culture material. G. Barski and K. Y. Jung. bibliog il Science 149:751-2 Ag 13 '65

Ionizing radiation: effect of irradiated medium on synthetic processes. E. C. Pollard. bibliog il Science 147:1045-7 F 26 '65

Lability of host-cell DNA in growing cell cultures due to mycoplasma. C. C. Randall and others. bibliog il Science 149:1098-9 S 3 '65

Lung surfactants, counterions, and hysteresis. E. M. Scarpelli and others. bibliog il Science 148:1607-9 Je 18 '65

Lymphocytes of small mammals: spontaneous transformation in culture of blastoids. S. M. Sabesin. bibliog il Science 149:1385-7 S 17 '65

Metabolic controls in cultured mammalian cells; adaptation of address, June 2, 1964. H. Eagle. bibliog il Science 148:42-51 Ap 2 '65

Neoplasia in a coral? D. F. Squires. bibliog il Science 148:503-5 Ap 23 '65

Nucleoside incorporation into strain L cells: inhibition by pleuropneumonia-like organisms. R. M. Nardone and others. bibliog il Science 149:1100-1 S 3 '65

Polyribosomes from escherichia coli: enzymatic method for isolation. M. Dresden and M. B. Hoagland. bibliog il Science 149:647-9 Ag 6 '65

Preservation of mammalian cells in a chemically defined medium and dimethylsulfoxide. B. L. Brown and S. C. Nagle, jr. bibliog il Science 149:1266-7 S 10 '65

Primary immune reactions in organ cultures. A. Globerson and R. Auerbach. bibliog il Science 149:991-3 Ag 27 '65

Renin production by organ cultures of renal cortex. A. L. Robertson and others. bibliog il Science 149:650-1 Ag 6 '65

Respiratory and electrical responses to light stimulation in the retina of the frog. W. Sickel. bibliog il Science 148:648-51 Ap 30 '65

Reversion in hamster cells transformed by Rous sarcoma virus. I. Macpherson. il Science 148:1731-3 Je 25 '65

Spare parts surgery: what lies ahead? excerpt from The rebuilt man. F. Warshofsky. il Todays Health 43:44-6+ Je '65

Steroid stimulation of beating of cultured rat-heart cells. R. L. McCarl and others. bibliog il Science 150:1611-13 D 17 '65

Tetracycline: effect on osteogenesis in vitro. L. Saxén. bibliog il Science 149:870-2 Ag 20 '65

See also
Plant cells and tissues—Culture

TISSUES analysis, Clinical. See Diagnosis

TITAN silo explosion. See Explosions

TITAN III-C test. See Space vehicles—Propulsion systems—Testing

TITANI, Koiti, and Putnam, F. W.
Immunoglobulin structure: amino- and carboxyl-terminal peptides of type I Bence Jones proteins. bibliog Science 147: 1304-5 Mr 12 '65

—and others
Immunoglobulin structure: partial amino acid sequence of a Bence Jones protein. bibliog Science 149:1090-2; 150:1485 S 3, D 10 '65

TITANIUM
Expert sees future of titanium as promising but demanding. J. F. Judge. il Miss & Roc 17:36+ S 20 '65

Oil from the medicine cabinet; oil for titanium and steel. Time 86:84 D 3 '65

Titanium's amazing comeback. G. Berkwitt. il Duns R 86:50-1+ N '65

TITANIUM borides
Room temperature slip in titanium diboride produced by high pressure. F. W. Vahldiek and others. bibliog il Science 149:747-8 Ag 13 '65

TITANIUM diboride. See Titanium borides

TITHONIA
Bright flower from Mexico. M. L. Donahue and R. Donahue. il Flower Grower 52:18 Mr '65

TITIAN
Titian: master painter of Venice. G. Kent. il por Read Digest 87:198-202 D '65

TITLES of books, stories, etc.
Titles that tantalize. K. M. Wilson. Writer 78:25 Jl '65

Anecdotes, facetiae, satire, etc.

Shortest-book game. Christian Cent **82:759** Je 9 '65

TITLES of honor and nobility
Chest-high handshake; use of titles in the church. America 112:213 F 13 '65

His Excellency Dmitri Kessel. G. P. Hunt. Life 59:3 D 3 '65

TITMUSS, Richard M.
Poverty vs. inequality: diagnosis. Nation 200: 130-3 F 8 '65

TITO
My visits with Kosygin and Tito. W. A. Harriman. il por Life 59:89-90 Ag 27 '65

Paunchy revolution. M. Mestrovic. Commonweal 83:336-9 D 17 '65

TITTLE, Y. A.
My life in pro football; ed. by T. Maule. por Sports Illus 23:27-32 Ag 16; 40-2+ Ag 23; 42-4+ Ag 30 '65

TITUS, Harold
Big fishing hole. Field & S 70:64-6 N '65
(ed) Conservation. See issues of Field & stream
Farming for fun. Field & S 69:53-5+ Ap '65
Fight to save Lake Erie. Field & S 69:10-12+ Mr '65
Goose pays the way. Field & S 70:100-1 Je '65
What a way to run a railroad! Field & S 70:61-4 Jl '65

TIXIER-VIGNANCOUR, Jean Louis
Circus star. il por Newsweek 66:35-6 Ag 16 '65
One candidate against de Gaulle. H. de Turenne. il pors N Y Times Mag p40-1+ Ag 29 '65

TO be a hero; story. See Yates, R.

TO ride an elephant; story. See Deal, B. H.

TO trust in Andy; story. See Cave, H.

TOALSON, Robert F.
Professional preparation: the intern program. por Recreation 58:346-7 S '65

TOBACCO
Amount of polonium 210 in tobacco differs. Sci N L 88:249 O 16 '65

Differentiation of tobacco plants from single, isolated cells in microcultures. V. Vasil and A. C. Hildebrandt. bibliog il Science 150: 889-92 N 12 '65

Growth and tissue formation from single, isolated tobacco cells in microculture. V. Vasil and A. C. Hildebrandt. bibliog il Science 147:1454-5 Mr 19 '65

Kinetin-induced chloroplast maturation in cultures of tobacco tissue. D. A. Stetler and W. M. Laetsch. bibliog il Science 149: 1387-8 S 17 '65

Polonium-210 in leaf tobacco from four countries. L. P. Gregory. bibliog il Science 150:74-6 O 1 '65

Tobacco seedlings: damage by excessive nitrogen lessened by added phosphorus. N. L. Pal and R. J. Ojha. Science 151: 106 Ja 7 '66

See also
Nicotine
Smoking

Physiological effects

Carboxyhemoglobin: hemodynamic and respiratory responses to small concentrations. S. M. Ayres and others. bibliog il Science 149:193-4 Jl 9 '65

TOBACCO—Physiological effects—*Continued*
How AMA research into smoking will help you. R. M. McKeown. Todays Health 43:12-13 Ag '65
Smoker must be studied to explain disease cause. Sci N L 88:152 S 4 '65
Smoking & the bladder. Time 85:37 Mr 26 '65
Tobacco and health; research report. K. N. Anderson. il Todays Health 43:26-34 Jl: 34-40+ S; 18-21 N '65
Tobacco: Congress moves closer to requiring warning of danger included on cigarette packages. D. S. Greenberg. Science 148:478-9 Ap 23 '65
Tobacco material itself causes tumors in mice. Sci N L 88:329 N 20 '65
See also
Smoking

TOBACCO habit. See Smoking
TOBACCO industry and trade
If everybody stopped smoking—. il U S News 59:99 D 20 '65
Tobacco industry thrives on danger. America 114:62-3 Ja 15 '66
Tobacco's taxing dielmma. il Time 85:98-9 My 7 '65
U.S. position on importation of Yugoslav tobacco; letter to cigarette manufacturers, October 11, 1965, with statement of manufacturers. D. Rusk and others. Dept State Bul 53:700-1 N 1 '65
See also
Cigarettes

Advertising
Caution: cigarette smoking may be hazardous to your health; warning to be on every cigarette pack and carton. Consumer Rep 30:488-91 O '65

Anecdotes, facetiae, satire, etc.
Tobacco farmer speaks out. G. Walker. il Atlan 215:122 F '65

TOBEY, Mark
Mark Tobey: master painter. il por Vogue 146:200-3+ N 1 '65
TOBIAS, Philip V.
Early man in East Africa. bibliog Science 149:22-33 Jl 2 '65
TOBIN, James
What is the lesson of 1929? New Repub 152:11-12 Je 19; 153:38 Jl 24 '65
TOBIN, Richard L.
Blood of change. Sat R 48:36-7 S 4 '65
(ed) Communications. See issues of Saturday review
Europe of the great war. Sat R 48:28 Jl 3 '65
TOBIN, Robert L. B.
Man on the move; interview, ed. by A. M. Lingg. por Opera N 30:13 N 6 '65
TODARO, George J. and Green, Howard
Successive transformations of an established cell line by polyoma virus and SV40. bibliog Science 147:513-14 Ja 29 '65
TODAY is tonight; novel. See Harlow, J.
TODD, Alexander Roberts
Scientific policy in Britain; adaptation of address, December 14, 1964. Science 149:156-62 Jl 9 '65
TODD, Arthur
Dance. bibliog NEA J 54:16-19 Mr '65
Highlights of public recreation, 1964. por Recreation 58:283-4 Je '65
TODD, Carl David
Integrated circuit techniques. Electr World 74:25-8+ N '65
Testing semiconductors with V.O.M. or V.T.V.M. Electr World 74:31-4+ S '65
TODD, Dan
Race cars of the world. Pop Sci 186:130-1 F '65
TODD, Hollis N. and Zakia, R. D.
Is it true? (cont) Pop Phot 56:26 My; 54 Je; 57:103 Jl '65
TODD, Judith
Voice of conscience. por Newsweek 66:44+ D 6 '65
TOFFLER, Alvin
Can we cope with tomorrow? Redbook 126:38-9+ Ja '66
Future as a way of life. Horizon 7:108-15 Sum '65
Solons and specialists. New Repub 152:19-20 Je 12 '65
Why the high cost of braces for teeth? Good H 160:87+ My '65
TOGO
Death does not scare easily; trucks ram crowd. Time 86:30+ D 17 '65
TOGOLAND, FRENCH. See Togo

TOILET
Fashions: grooming aids. O. E. Schoeffler. Esquire 63:62 My '65
See also
Beauty, Personal
Perfumery
TOILET; drama. See Jones, L.
TOILET preparations
See also
Cosmetics
Deodorants
TOILET soap. See Soap
TOILET training. See Infants—Care and hygiene
TOKAIDO line. See Railroads—Japan
TOKYO
See also
Stock exchange—Tokyo

Architecture
Emperor's new palace. il Time 86:72 Jl 9 '65

Description
Always on Sunday. H. Sutton. il Sat R 48:31-3 Je 5 '65
Travel notes. R. Joseph. Esquire 64:12+ Ag '65

Hotels, restaurants, etc.
In the dark in Tokyo. H. Sutton. il Sat R 48:44-6 Je 19 '65

Social life and customs
See also
Night clubs

Stores
Always on Sunday. H. Sutton. il Sat R 48:31-3 Je 5 '65
Rocks and rotten eggs. il Newsweek 65:69 Je 28 '65

Theater
Made in Japan. il Newsweek 66:78-9 Ag 23 '65
Notes from afar: report on traditional and western theater in Tokyo. H. Clurman. Nation 201:84-6 Ag 16 '65
Soap opera, Japanese style. J. Nathan. il N Y Times Mag p 12-13+ D 19 '65
West side story in Japan. J. Paull. il Dance Mag 39:35-8 Ap '65
TOKYO cathedral. See Cathedrals—Japan
TOKYO international trade fair. See Exhibitions
TOLAND, John
Last 100 days; excerpts. Look 29:34-40+ My 4; 38-40+ My 18; 70-2+ Je 1 '65
TOLBERT, Frank X.
Incredible Houston dome. Look 29:96-8 Ap 20 '65
TOLEDO, Ohio, museum of art
Gift of glass; Duckworth collection. R. Davidson. il Antiques 89:20 Ja '66
TOLEDO conference on clergy and race. See Religious conferences
TOLER, Burl
Burl Toler blows a whistle. il pors Ebony 21:142-7 D '65
TOLERATION
Principles for the dialogue: more friendliness to non-Catholics urged. America 113:311 S 25 '65
Uses of tolerance; a consideration of the encyclical Pacem in terris. H. J. Muller. il Sat R 48:23-5 F 13 '65
Word. V. P. McCorry. America 112:692 My 8 '65
See also
Prejudice
TOLKIEN, John Ronald Reuel
Elvish art of enchantment; reprint. L. Eiseley. Horn Bk 41:364-7 Ag '65
Elvish mode. New Yorker 41:24 Ja 15 '66
TOLL roads
Chicago's toll skyway hits a fiscal pothole. il Bsns W p68+ D 4 '65
New life for toll roads: why more are planned. il U S News 59:106-7 Ag 9 '65
TOLLYMORE estate. See Country estates—Ireland
TOLLYMORE FOREST PARK. See Parks—Ireland
TOLSON, Melvin Beaunorus
Poet's voice in the crowd. R. D. Spector. Sat R 48:29 Ag 7 '65
TOLSTOI, Lev Nikolaevich, graf
War and peace; dramatization. See Neumann, A. and others
about
Tolstoy, by H. Troyat. Review
New Yorker 41:182 Ap 17 '65. Genêt
TOLSTOY, Leo. See Tolstoi, L. N.
TOMATO relish. See Pickles and relishes

TOMATOES
Nature note. Sci N L 88:95 Ag 7 '65
New lamp ripens green tomatoes. Farm J 89:
42B Ag '65
Pick tomatoes indoors in May. M. Helleiner.
Flower Grower 52:16 F '65
TOMBSTONE, Ariz.
Help wanted in Tombstone. L. Barry. il Pop
Phot 56:28+ My '65
Old Tombstone. il Sunset 135:80-5 N '65
TOMIC, Radomiro
United Nations commemoration address, June
25, 1965. UN Mo Chron 2:102-5 Jl '65
TOMKINS, Calvin
Big show in Venice. Harper 230:98-104 Ap
'65
Profiles (cont) New Yorker 40:37-40+ F 6
'65; 41:35-6+ Ja 8 '66
TOMLINSON, Charles
Eight poems: Arizona desert; Death in the
desert; On the mountain; Arroyo seco;
Las trampas U.S.A; Old man at Valdez;
Weeper in Jalisco; News from nowhere.
Poetry 106:123-35 Ap '65
In winter woods; Door; Bone; Hill; Fox:
poems. Poetry 107:159-67 D '65
TOMLINSON, Edward
Boomland south of the border. Read Digest
86:201-2+ Mr '65
TOMONAGA, Shin'ichiro
Nobel prize winners. por Sci N L 88:279 O
30 '65
Tomonaga, Schwinger, and Feynmam
awarded Nobel prize for physics. F. J.
Dyson. por Science 150:588-9 O 29 '65
TOMPKINS, Jerry
Anti-evolution law tested. Sci N L 89:7+ Ja
1 '66
TONE
Musical events; tonality in symphonic music.
W. Sargeant. New Yorker 41:200-1 D 4 '65
TONE arm, Phonograph. See Phonograph
—Tone arm
TONE-separation process. See Photography—
Printing processes
TONG, James L. and others
Kidney homografts: uptake of fluorochrome-
labeled tissue extracts by lymph node cells.
bibliog Science 149:753 Ag 13 '65
TONGASS National Forest, Alaska. See Na-
tional forests
TONING (photography)   See Photography—
Printing processes
TONSILLECTOMY. See Throat—Surgery
TONSOR, Stephen J.
Who's afraid of Edmund Burke? Nat R 17:
112-13 F 9 '65
TOOHEY, Barbara. See Biermann, J. jt. auth.
TOOL boxes, racks, etc.
For Christmas, a real tool box. il Sunset 135:
84+ D '65
This toolbox helps do the work. C. E. Rhine.
il Pop Sci 187:142-4 D '65
TOOL houses. See Garden houses, shelters, etc.
TOOL rooms
Build a tool-shed fort. D. D. Lonie, jr. il
Pop Gard 17:14-15 Ja '66
TOOLS
Decorative appeal of hand tools. P. C. Welsh.
il Antiques 87:204-7 F '65
Shop talk. S. M. Gallager. See issues of Pop-
ular science monthly
Shopping for tools. R. B. Berger. See issues
of Popular mechanics
Tools for the distaff side. il Consumer Bul
48:16-17+ Jl '65
Tools for the electronic hobbyist. D. Lan-
caster. il Pop Electr 22:65-70+ Mr '65
See also
Electric tools, Portable
Garden tools, equipment and supplies
Jigs
TOOMBS, Robert
Robert Toombs: an unreconstructed rebel on
freedmen. D. Roberts. bibliog Negro Hist
Bul 28:191-2 My '65
TOOTH decay. See Teeth—Diseases
TOOTH transplantation. See Transplantation
of organs, tissues, etc.
TOOTS, Heinrich, and Voorhies, M. R.
Strontium in fossil bones and the reconstruc-
tion of food chains. bibliog Science 149:854-5
Ag 20 '65
TOPEL, Bernard J, bp
Catholic press, beware. Commonweal 81:753
Mr 12 '65
TOPLESS bathing suits. See Bathing suits
TOPOGRAPHY
Anomalous erosional topography in Victoria
Land, Antarctica; Wright Dry Valley. H.
T. U. Smith. bibliog il Science 148:941-2
My 14 '65

TOPOLOGY
Fixed-point theorems. M. Shinbrot. il Sci Am
214:105-10 Ja '66
TOPOLSKI, Feliks
Artist's record. il N Y Times Mag p 146-7
Ap 4 '65
Man in motion. New Yorker 41:35-6 Ap 24
'65
Topolski: contemporary Chronicler; first
American showing of Topolski's Chronicle.
M. R. Weiss. il por Sat R 48:20-1 My 15 '65
TOPPER, Harvey
Art & the city. Sch Arts 65:12-13 N '65
TOPPIN, Edgar A.
Book review. Negro Hist Bul 28:202 My '65
Half-century of struggle for equal rights;
1915-1965. bibliog por Negro Hist Bul 28:
176-7+ My '65
TOPPING, Seymour
Lee Kuan Yew is Singapore. N Y Times Mag
p66-7+ O 31 '65
Southeast Asia isn't scared of the Chinese
dragon. N Y Times Mag p 12-13+ Ja 16
'66
What goes in Hong Kong? everything. N Y
Times Mag p40-1+ Ap 11 '65
TOPPINGS, Whipped. See Icings
TOPS, Bottle. See Bottle caps and seals
TOPSY (thermally operated plasma system)
See Ionization of gases
TORCH lilies
Flaming rockets. A. L. Warren. Horticulture
44:46 Ja '66
TORGESEN, John L. and Jackson, R. W.
Growth layers on ammonium dihydrogen
phosphate. bibliog Science 148:952-4 My 14
'65
TORII, Tetsuya, and Ossaka, Joyo
Antarcticite: a new mineral, calcium chloride
hexahydrate, discovered in Antarctica. bib-
liog Science 149:975-7 Ag 27 '65
TORNABENE, Lyn
Murder in Alabama. Ladies Home J 82:42+
Jl '65
Tomorrow's stars. Good H 160:20+ Mr '65
Way-out minister of Washington square.
N Y Times Mag p 116-17+ Je 6 '65
TORNABENE, T. See Oró, J. jt. auth.
TORNADOES
Along tornado alley; meteorologists' knowl-
edge of tornadoes. Newsweek 65:65 Ap 26
'65
Eighty miles of faith; Farm journal follows
the trail of a tornado. J. Carlson. il Farm
J 89:40-1+ O '65
First the wind, then the waters; six Midwest
states suffer disaster. il Newsweek 65:25-6
Ap 26 '65
Man vs. nature: still a losing fight. il U S
News 58:50-2 Ap 26 '65
On the rampage. il Sr Schol 86:28 Ap 29 '65
Spring brings tornadoes; radioactive debris
from the stratosphere to the earth's sur-
face. B. Tufty. il(p257) Sci N L 87:263
Ap 24 '65
Tornadoes: Weather bureau office in Kansas
City is nerve center for severe storm warn-
ing network. J. Walsh. il Science 148:1306-8
Je 4 '65; Reply. W. S. Barney. 149:924 Ag
27 '65
Up the alley; Midwest twisters. il Time 85:
29 Ap 23 '65
Were warnings on time in tornado alley?
il Bsns W p27 Ap 17 '65

TORONTO

Architecture
Symbol for a city; new city hall. il Time
86:98 S 17 '65

Education
Castle Frank high school; new concept in
secondary education. W. A. McLauchlin.
il Sr Schol 86:sup 10 My 20 '65

Education, Board of
Education centre library
Toronto's Education centre library.   L. H.
Freiser. il Sat R 48:76+ Ap 17 '65

Hospitals
Gray heads for white caps; Quo Vadis
nursing school. il Life 59:41-2+ Jl 30 '65

Libraries
Public libraries in metro Toronto automate
reordering of paperbacks. Library J 90:
2232 My 15 '65
See also
Toronto—Education, Board of—Education centre library

Music
CBC, camera-wise. H. Von Hochmeister.
Hi Fi 15:86P-86Q Mr '65

TORONTO—*Continued*

Newspapers

See also

Globe and mail (Toronto)

Public buildings

Singular symbol for Toronto. il Arch Forum 123:15-21 N '65

Stores

Mix discounts and art and make sales jump; Honest Ed's. il Bsns W p50-2 F 20 '65

TORONTO stock exchange. See Stock exchange —Toronto

TORPEDOES

See also

Salvage (torpedoes)

TORQUE

How to tackle torque. J. Martenhoff. il Pop Sci 187:78+ Jl '65

TORRANCE, Calif.

Each park enjoys a distinctive personality. H. B. Van Bellehem. il Am City 80:30 Ap '65

TORRES, Camilo

Rebel priest in Colombia. V. Andrade. America 113:287, 512-13 S 18, N 6 '65

TORRES, José

American dream. Newsweek 65:102 Ap 12 '65

Documentary fantasist; film about preparations for championship fight. New Yorker 41:35-6 Ap 10 '65

Liver trouble and high living. E. Shrake. il Sports Illus 22:28-9+ Ap 12 '65

Svengali returns. R. H. Boyle. il por Sports Illus 22:24-7 Ap 12 '65

TORRES-GARCIA, Joaquin

Torres-Garcia of Uruguay, universal constructionist. D. Suro. il Américas 17:24-9 Mr '65

TORREY, Gordon H.

Nasser's Egypt. il Cur Hist 48:290-5+ My '65

TORREY pine. See Pine

TORREY PINES STATE PARK. See California—Parks and reserves

TORT liability. See Liability (law)

TORTE. See Cake; Meringue

TORTOISES, Fossil

Huge ancient tortoise unearthed in south China. Sci N L 87:376 Je 12 '65

TORY party (Great Britain) See Conservative party (Great Britain)

TOSCA; opera. See Puccini, G.

TOSCANINI, Arturo

Toscanini archives. J. W. Freeman. il Opera N 30:30-1 Ja 15 '66

TOTALITARIANISM

It's halfway to 1984; concerning G. Orwell's novel. J. Lukacs. il N Y Times Mag p8-9+ Ja 2 '66

See also

Authoritarianism

TOTE bags. See Bags

TOTH, William J.

Your car needs a spring cleaning too. Am Home 68:24-5 Ap '65

TOTMAN, Jeannette

Tanager and a bluebird jousting. J. Vosbergh. il por Audubon Mag 67:374-5 N '65

TOTTEN, Stanley M. See White, G. W. jt. auth.

TOUCH

Eyeless vision unmasked. Sci Am 212:57 Mr '65

Tactiles; touch art. P. Barron. il Design 67:24-6 S '65

TOUCH-me-nots

Impatiens for the shady garden. J. Lindeman. Horticulture 43:19 F '65

TOULMIN, Stephen

On Teilhard de Chardin. Commentary 39:50-5 Mr '65

TOULOUSE geese. See Geese

TOURÉ, Sékou

Reason to worry. il por Time 87:27-8 Ja 7 '66

TOUREL, Jennie

Music to my ears; production of Tchaikovsky's Pique dame, by Concert opera association. I. Kolodin. Sat R 48:30 Mr 6 '65

TOURING. See Automobile touring

TOURIST guides. See Guides

TOURIST trade

Autumn collectors' items. il Mlle 61:207-8 S '65

Big leak in dollars as Americans rush abroad. il U S News 59:40-1 Jl 12 '65

Boom in foreign travel, and in the U.S. too. U S News 58:10 Je 28 '65

Despite LBJ plea : boom in travel abroad? il U S News 58:8 Mr 29 '65

If you're planning a trip abroad; some useful news. il U S News 58:70-6 Ap 12 '65

Lo! the poor tourist; proposed restrictions on travel abroad by Americans. R. Moley. Newsweek 65:108 Mr 15 '65

Money for tourists; J. W. Fulbright's suggestion for curbing dollar drain by tourists. R. Moley. Newsweek 65:100 Mr 22 '65

Phantom funds; U.S.-owned foreign currency abroad. R. Moley. Newsweek 65:92 Mr 29 '65

Practical planner, Honolulu, Norway and Lake Tahoe. Holiday 38:126+ D '65

Practical planner, Sardinia, Greek islands. Holiday 39:88+ Ja '66

Bahama Islands

Let's travel: Nassau. il Mlle 61:214-15 My '65

Prize ports of call. il Motor B 116:30-5 O '65

Travel notes. R. Joseph. Esquire 64:39-40+ D '65

Bermuda

35mm techniques. P. Stackpole. U S Camera 28:30+ Je '65

California, Lower

Prize ports of call. il Motor B 116:40-1 O '65

Canada

More for your travel dollar! il Bet Hom & Gard 43:128+ Ap '65

Caribbean Region

Prize ports of call. il Motor B 116:36-9 O '65

Your own special island. R. Joseph. il Esquire 64:240-1 D '65

Columbia

Travel notes. R. Joseph. Esquire 63:19-20+ Mr '65

England

England for Sol Hurok; with notes by R. Joseph, K. Tynan. il Esquire 63:64-7 F '65

Europe

Traveling with Mlle: Europe; fifteen correspondents view the high spots. il Mlle 60:115-22 Mr '65

Europe, Eastern

Bikinis on the Black Sea. il Newsweek 65:42 My 3 '65

Europe, Western

Could these three Americans find happiness in Europe? with notes by R. Joseph. F. Sagan; K. Tynan; M. Mastroianni. il Esquire 63:58-71+ F '65

Get ready, Europe, here we come! il Bsns W p 102+ My 29 '65

More for your travel dollar! il Bet Hom & Gard 43:21-2+ F; 40+ Je '65

Florida

Prize ports of call. il Motor B 116:24-9 O '65

France

France for Edward Albee; with notes by R. Joseph. F. Sagan. il Esquire 63:60-3 F '65

French smile; at Americans! campaign of welcome and amiability. T. Foote. il N Y Times Mag p24-6+ Je 20 '65

Garçon! souriez! campaign of welcome and amiability. Time 85:37 Ap 23 '65

One for the money, one for the show. H. Sutton. Sat R 48:40+ My 8 '65

Hawaii

Hawaiian culture and prestige. I. Taves. il Look 29:65-6+ F 23 '65

Hong Kong

Travel notes. R. Joseph. Esquire 64:44+ O '65

Italy

Italy for Barbra Streisand; with notes by R. Joseph. M. Mastroianni. il Esquire 63:68-71+ F '65

Letter from Italy; love and the tourist trade. E. Forcella. New Repub 153:34-6 S 4 '65

Russia

Red carpet for tourism. il Bsns W p 133-4 My 22 '65

Scandinavia

Travel notes. R. Joseph. Esquire 63:32+ My '65

Southern states

Great vacations in the South. il Bet Hom & Gard 43:123-8 F '65

Tahiti

35mm techniques. P. Stackpole. U S Camera 28:30+ Je '65

TOURIST trade—*Continued*

United States

Let's travel: summer vacations. il Mlle 61: 208-13 My '65
Practical planner: California. Holiday 38:136+ O '65
Travel in the U.S. and spend your dollars at home! Consumer Bul 48:23-4 Je '65
U.S. travel push. C. S. Murphy. Aviation W 83:11 N 29 '65

West Indies

Travel notes. R. Joseph. Esquire 64:39-40+ D '65

Yugoslavia

By the Socialist sea; German girls go after Yugoslav men. E. Y. Blumenfeld. il Newsweek 66:50 O 4 '65
Practical planner; Yugoslavia and Munich. Holiday 38:120+ N '65

TOURISTS. See Tourist trade; Travelers

TOURNACHON, Félix. See Nadar

TOURNAMENTS, Bridge. See Bridge tournaments

TOURS, Garden. See Garden tours

TOURS, Package. See Travel

TOURTELLOT, Arthur Bernon
Kashmir: dilemma of a people adrift. Sat R 48:16-19 Mr 6; 44 My 29 '65

TOWBOATS. See Tugboats

TOWER, Whitney
Horse racing. See issues of Sports illustrated

TOWERS
Campus City, Chicago; the tower. il Arch Forum 123:38-9 S '65
Reporter at large; Watts towers, Los Angeles. C. Trillin. il New Yorker 41:72+ My 29 '65
Towers in the West. il Life 59:86-7 D 24 '65
See also
Television towers

TOWHEES
Rufous-sided towhee. J. K. Terres. il Pop Gard 16:6 S '65

TOWL, Andrew R.
Outside directors under attack. Harvard Bsns R 43:135-47 S '65

TOWN life. See City and town life

TOWN planning. See City planning

TOWNE, Anthony
Immolations and consensus: the justification of innocence. Christian Cent 83:72-5 Ja 19 '66
None is worthy, not even one: poem. Christian Cent 82:268 Mr 3 '65

TOWNE, Charles L.
Hartford's antismoking campaign. Sr Schol 87:sup39+ S 23 '65
Wethersfield plan. Sr Schol 87:sup8-9 O 14 '65

TOWNER, Emilie
When grandchildren come to visit. Suc Farm 63:51+ Jl '65

TOWNES, Charles H.
Production of coherent radiation by atoms and molecules; address, December 11, 1964. bibliog Science 149:831-41 Ag 20 '65

TOWNS. See Cities and towns

TOWNSEND, Lynn Alfred
Communicator; employer, employee relations; address, June 24, 1965. Vital Speeches 31: 670-2 Ag 15 '65
Multi-national corporation; address, January 13, 1965. Vital Speeches 31:444-8 My 1 '65; Excerpts. US News 58:94-5 F 1 '65
Price of success at Chrysler. R. Sheehan. il por Fortune 72:138-43+ N '65

TOWNSEND, Peter
You're all right, Pete. A. Wright. il pors Sports Illus 23:32-5 S 13 '65

TOXEMIA. See Pregnancy, Complications of

TOXINS and antitoxins
Botulinum toxin, type A: effects on central nervous system. E. H. Polley and others. bibliog il Science 147:1036-7 F 26 '65
Phytotoxin isolated from liquid cultures of ceratocystis ulmi. C. A. Salemink and others. bibliog Science 149:202 Jl 9 '65
Tetrodotoxin and manganese ion: effects on action potential of the frog heart. S. Hagiwara and S. Nakajima. bibliog il Science 149:1254-5 S 10 '65

TOY airplanes. See Airplanes, Toy

TOY automobiles. See Automobiles, Toy

TOY chests. See Chests

TOY engines. See Engines, Toy

TOY garages. See Garages, Toy

TOY houses. See Doll houses

TOY Industry
See also
Fisher-Price toys, incorporated

TOYNBEE, Arnold Joseph
Speaking out. por Sat Eve Post 238:10+ Jl 17 '65
War is not the normal condition of man. N Y Times Mag 122+ N 7 '65

about

Toynbee the sightseer. A. Campbell. New Repub 153:28 S 4 '65

TOYS
Batty boxers. W. Waltner and E. Waltner. il Pop Mech 124:134-5 D '65
Can you invent a million-dollar fad? W. S. Griswold. il Pop Sci 188:78-81+ Ja '66
Chemistry sets. il Consumer Rep 30:548-51 N '65
Choice toys for Christmas. D. Harris and E. Harris. PTA Mag 60:27-9 D '65
Christmas toys with a purpose. L. Steckler. il Pop Mech 124:124-7 D '65
Full cycle. il Design 66:38-41 My '65
Jeffrey giraffe. S. Ellingson. il Pop Mech 124:139 D '65
Merry bang-bang (and happy New Year) war toys. W. H. Honan. New Repub 153: 11-12 D 25 '65
Newest in Christmas toys. il Parents Mag 40:64-5 D '65
On and off the avenue (cont) New Yorker 41:151-2+ D 11 '65
Toys, holidays are fun time. il Consumer Bul 48:6-9 D '65
Trade winds; influence of military toys on children. J. G. Fuller. Sat R 48:7 D 25 '65
What do they need to play with? with study-discussion program by D. Harris and E. Harris. R. H. Ojemann. bibliog il PTA Mag 59:37-9, 43-4 F '65
What is a good toy? Good H 161:214 N '65
Who bombed Santa's workshop? should war toys be banned? panel discussion at Edgewood elementary school, Scarsdale. E. W. Buzbee. il N Y Times Mag p87+ D 12 '65
See also
Christmas gifts for children
Creative playthings, incorporated
Kites

Collectors and collecting

Antique toys; J. Smith's collection. il Hobbies 70:52-3 D '65

History

Teddy's bear; how the teddy bear got its name. il Newsweek 66:85 D 20 '65; Reply. B. F. Michtom. 67:2+ Ja 17 '66

Safety devices and measures

How to be sure a toy is safe. il Good H 161: 177 N '65

Storage

Here's where the toys go: bins serve as additional sitting space. il Sunset 134:131 F '65

TRACER shot shells. See Projectiles

TRACHOMA
End of world scourge. O. Mendels. Sci Digest 57:36 F '65
Less trachoma results from home treatment. Sci N L 88:216 O 2 '65

TRACHTENBERG, Alan
America, the sublime. Nation 201:446-8 D 6 '65
American view of life. Nation 201:42-5 Jl 19 '65

TRACK athletics
Bunch of the boys were whooping it up; Golden West invitational track and field meet, Sacramento. J. Jares. il Sports Illus 22:56+ Je 28 '65
Enchantment in the land of the Lobos. G. S. Brown. il Sports Illus 22:66-7 My 31 '65
Measuring up; National AAU meet, New York. il Newsweek 65:65 F 22 '65
Off to Russia, without love; AAU women's track and field team at Kiev. J. Jares. il Sports Illus 23:20-1+ Jl 12 '65
Quick young ladies of quality; U.S. women's track team invade Europe. J. Lovesey. Sports Illus 22:108+ Ap 19 '65
Startling invasion of women; AAU indoor track meet. il Sports Illus 22:18-19 Mr 1 '65
What the men can do for an encore; Russia's Brumel and U.S.'s Mills at the National AAU indoor championship. G. S. Brown. il Sports Illus 22:45-7 Mr 1 '65
Why they lost; U.S. men's teams defeated by the Russians in Kiev. Time 86:50-1 Ag 13 '65
With a quarter inch between; winter's big indoor track meets. il Time 85:80 F 26 '65
See also
Running
Shot putting

TRACKING and trailing
Meanwhile, back at the lab . . ; use of a radio transmitter attached to animal's collar. D. Mech. il Outdoor Life 136:16-17+ N '65

TRACTOR engines
Install a vacuum gauge for top tractor efficiency. G. E. Melvin. il Suc Farm 63:68 S '65

Repairing
Your tractor acting up? Suc Farm 64:76A Ja '66

TRACTORS
Backyard tractors. il Time 85:88 Je 11 '65
Gasoline, diesel, or LP tractor? Suc Farm 64:72 Ja '66
Shopping for a suburban tractor. J. Hand. il Pop Sci 186:154-7+ Mr '65
    See also
Crawler tractors

Care
Get ready for fall plowing. F. Buckingham and W. J. Fletcher. il Suc Farm 63:40-1 O '65

TRACY, Robert
Literature and obscenity. Christian Cent 82: 769-72 Je 16 '65

TRACY, Robert Emmet, bp
Early report from Rome and the council. America 113:330+ S 25 '65
Failure of session three. America 112:284-6 F 27 '65
Letter from the council. America 113:364, 397-9, 432-3, 494-5, 566-7, 706 O 2-16, 30, N 13, D 4, 18 '65
Postscript on the council. America 114:40 Ja 8 '66
Vatican City. America 113:461 O 23 '65

TRACY, Mrs Spencer
Talk, talk, talk to deaf children. pors Am Ed 1:4-7 D '64

TRADE. See Commerce

TRADE agreements
Collective bargaining agreements in the federal service. H. P. Cohany and H. J. Neary. il Mo Labor R 88:944-50 Ag '65
Developments in industrial relations. See issues of Monthly labor review
Developments under major bargaining agreements, 1964. G. Ruben. il Mo Labor R 88: 1189-95 O '65
Heat is back on for pay raises; job security and job expansion, labor's primary demands. il Bsns W p33-4 Jl 3 '65
Labor contract; key to industrial harmony. il Sr Schol 86:22 F 4 '65
New steel pact; its meaning. il U S News 59:96+ S 13 '65
Outlook for '66; few strikes, but big gains for unions. il U S News 60:68-71 Ja 10 '66
Railroad employment protective agreement; excerpts. Mo Labor R 88:416-18 Ap '65
Real price of steel peace; here's industry's view. il U S News 59:92-4 S 20 '65
Severance pay and layoff benefit plans. L. E. Lunden and E. M. Moore. bibliog f il Mo Labor R 88:27-34 Ja '65
Supplemental unemployment benefit plans in major agreements. D. R. Kittner. il Mo Labor R 88:19-26 Ja '65
Wage developments in manufacturing. R. W. Benny. il Mo Labor R 88:1182-8 O '65

TRADE associations
Business ethics, your trade association, and the invisible hand; address, May 10, 1965. D. Fromson. Vital Speeches 32:28-32 O 15 '65
What's a trade association worth? T. O'Hanlon. il Duns R 85:32-3+ Mr '65

TRADE balance. See Balance of payments

TRADE book clinic. See American institute of graphic arts—Trade book clinic

TRADE discount. See Discount, Trade

TRADE fairs. See Exhibitions

TRADE journals
Six rules for selling to the trade journals. F. Hamlin. Writer 78:26-7 N '65

TRADE marks
Story behind . . See issues of Changing times
Why the old products last. V. A. Adams. Duns R 85:46-7+ Ap '65
Will the real Zeiss please stand up? trademark controversy between Zeiss East and Zeiss West. il Bsns W p54-6+ O 30 '65

TRADE names
Fight for inner space; address, April 7, 1965. H. D. Smith. Vital Speeches 31:493-5 Je 1 '65
Incredible James Bond; merchandising program. J. F. Olesky. il Duns R 86:75-6 O '65
Name of the game; the name. il Newsweek 66:89-90+ O 25 '65
Story behind . . . See issues of Changing times

We've got to call it something; picking a name for new gadget, or company. M. Gunther. il Sat Eve Post 238:60-1 S 11 '65

TRADE practices
Customer is a company's best friend; reciprocity practices. E. McCreary, jr. and W. Guzzardi, jr. il Fortune 71:180-2+ Je '65
    See also
Trade secrets

TRADE schools
Area technical high school. S. Danovitz. NEA J 54:41-3 My '65
Best place for vocational education; the vocational and technical high school. B. D. Coe. NEA J 54:50-1 D '65

TRADE secrets
Care and feeding of intellectual property. J. H. Munster, jr. and J. C. Smith. bibliog Science 148:739-43 My 7 '65
From Du Pont, with love; industrial spying and corporate paranoia. E. Engberg. Commonweal 82:465-8 Jl 2 '65
How much of your job belongs to you? H. Shuldiner. il Pop Sci 187:98-100 D '65
Legal protection of computer programs. M. R. Wessel. Harvard Bsns R 43:97-106 Mr '65

TRADE shows. See Exhibitions

TRADE union leaders. See Trade unions—Officials

TRADE union scholarship programs. See Scholarships and fellowships

TRADE unions
Fate of 14(b); aid for the unions. S. Lens. Commonweal 82:662-5 S 17 '65
    See also
Industrial relations
Open and closed shop

Activities
How unions spend their off-hours; odd mix of activities. il Bsns W p 156+ S 18 '65

Benefit funds
Business of health insurance. T. R. Brooks. Duns R 86:47-8 Ag '65
Unions see windfall from medicare. Bsns W p 116+ Ag 21 '65

Communist activities
Reds and unions; a new ruling. U S News 58:106 Je 21 '65
Unions briefed on red goals; ex-Communist J. Lovestone says that Russia's aim is still world domination. Bsns W p 127 My 15 '65

Dues, fees, etc.
When workers defy their union; fines. U S News 59:102 O 4 '65

Elections
Carey's comeuppance; fraudulent election. Time 85:26 Ap 16 '65
Carey's fall causes union quake; Labor dept. report of misconduct in IUE's election. il Bsns W p 140+ Ap 10 '65
Counted out. M. Kempton. New Repub 152: 16-18 Ap 24 '65
Great vote steal; president resigns after vote-counting irregularities. il Newsweek 65:82-3 Ap 19 '65
Interim report on the IUE election. W. W. Wirtz. Mo Labor R 88:562-5 My '65
Policing the vote count; Labor dept. involved in disputed union elections. Bsns W p 114 Mr 20 '65
Union election challenges under the LMRDA. M. F. Riche. il Mo Labor R 88:1-7 Ja '65
Union votes spotlight gaps in election rules. il Bsns W p51-2+ F 27 '65
USW may escape family fight. il Bsns W p49-50 My 1 '65

Finance
Tighter rules for union funds? U S News 59:63 Ag 2 '65

History
Influence of the New deal. J. S. Auerbach. bibliog f Cur Hist 48:334-9+ Je '65
Labor and the federal government; 1850-1933. A. A. Blum. bibliog f il Cur Hist 48:328-33+ Je '65
Lessons of the Detroit experience; early injustices. R. Niebuhr. Christian Cent 82: 487-90 Ap 21 '65
Unions and their members. E. Stein. Cur Hist 49:23-8+ Jl '65

International aspects
American labor abroad; Lovestone diplomacy; with editorial comment. S. Lens. il Nation 201:2, 10-16+ Jl 5 '65
U.S. labor on the move. il Sr Schol 86:11+ Mr 11 '65
    See also
International labor organization

TRADE unions—*Continued*

Jurisdictional disputes

Collision in cab vote: SIU battle with teamsters for Chicago's taxi drivers. il Bsns W p 128 My 15 '65

Is Hoffa getting set to raid? brewery workers challenge to Toledo teamsters. Bsns W p55 Mr 27 '65

Print unions cast mold for merger. il Bsns W p84+ S 4 '65

Law

See Labor laws and legislation—United States

Management

Fat cats of labor. A. H. Raskin. Nation 201: 103-7 S 20 '65

Print unions cast mold for merger. il Bsns W p84+ S 4 '65

Steelworkers vote: prelude to the strike. B. J. Widick. il Nation 200:214-16 Mr 1 '65

Trade union as an organization. F. C. Munson. Mo Labor R 88:497-501 My '65

What guides the steelworkers? S. H. Brown. il Fortune 72:156-8+ S '65

Membership

Another worry for employers: union pledge cards. W. J. Sandler. U S News 58:86-9 Mr 15 '65

Bolstering the rolls: unions campaign for members. il Bsns W p60+ Je 19 '65

Labor drives to close the South's open shop: illegal reprisals by Stevens company for union activities. V. Rony. il Reporter 33: 31-4 N 18 '65

Law professor spells out: dangers in more forced unionism; interview. S. Petro. il Nations Bsns 53:31-3+ Mr '65

Next IUD target: the working poor; low-paid service industries. il Bsns W p62+ N 13 '65

Union representation election. J. E. Drotning. bibliog f il Mo Labor R 88:938-43 Ag '65

Unions gain members, but the going's slow. il Bsns W p 114+ N 6 '65

Will organizing be made easier? NLRB reviewing rules governing drives for representation. Bsns W p 111 My 29 '65

Workers vs. unions. il Nations Bsns 53:60-2+ Ap '65

Negro membership

Negroes in South push to sign up. il Bsns W p59-60 N 13 '65

Organized labor's ten years together. New Repub 153:7-8 D 11 '65

Officials

AFL-CIO council girds for a shake-up; shift to younger leaders. il Bsns W p 162+ S 25 '65

Another union changes the guard; J. Knight of Oil, chemical & atomic workers retires. il Bsns W p 124+ Jl 17 '65

Fat cats of labor. A. H. Raskin. Nation 201: 103-7 S 20 '65

Hidden power of labor's professionals. T. O' Hanlon. il Duns R 85:58-9+ Ap '65

Labor: the rank-and-file revolt. T. R. Brooks. il Duns R 85:34-5+ Mr '65

Labor's captains begin to change. Bsns W p28-9 My 22 '65

Labor's hardening arteries. T. R. Brooks. Duns R 86:45-7 Ag '65

New temper in the steelworkers: new leaders seek more influence, show more militancy. Bsns W p43-4 Je 5 '65

Nudging out the old guard; AFL-CIO putting younger leaders on its executive council. il Bsns W p 124+ F 20 '65

Old-age club: question of age of members of AFL-CIO council. il Newsweek 65:77 Mr 8 '65

Revolt of the left-outs; union malaise. S. Lens. Commonweal 82:441-4 Je 25 '65; Reply with rejoinder. D. J. McDonald. 82:514 Jl 23 '65

Tired old guard. il Time 85:87-8 Mr 5 '65

Union scale for union leaders: up to $102,000 a year; with chart. U S News 58:88+ My 17 '65

Woman fills man-size union job. il Ebony 20:91-2+ Ap '65

Political activities

American labor abroad; Lovestone diplomacy; with editorial comment. S. Lens. il Nation 201:2, 10-16+ Jl 5 '65

Architecture of union political action. J. Barbash. Mo Labor R 88:653-5 Je '65

How the unions would change the country. U S News 59:62-3 D 27 '65

How unions are adding to Johnson's worries. U S News 58:76+ Je 14 '65

In England, it's unions vs. a Labor government. J. Fromm. il U S News 59:116 S 20 '65

Is the Supreme court increasing power of unions? H. L. Browne. il U S News 58:104-6 Je 7 '65

Labor's comeback in Congress; after eighteen years. U S News 59:80-1 Ag 9 '65

Looking for issues to excite them; shifted emphasis toward social and political goals. il Bsns W p 104-6 D 18 '65

LBJ and the unions; an uneasy honeymoon. il U S News 58:69-71 Mr 8 '65

Steel's warning on union power; excerpts from address, October 14, 1965. R. C. Cooper. U S News 59:98 O 25 '65

Unions' big goals for '66. il U S News 59: 73-4 D 20 '65

What unions asked of LBJ: and what they got. U S News 58:67-9 My 31 '65

See also

American federation of labor and Congress of industrial organizations—Committee on political education

Trade unions—Communist activities

Publications

Off the barricades; U.S. unions' 1,000 publications. il Time 85:48+ My 14 '65

Australia

UAW faces GM abroad; sends negotiator to help Australian unions. Bsns W p 126+ D 4 '65

See also

Strikes—Australia

Colombia

New force in Colombia; Unión de trabajadores de Colombia. V. Andrade. America 112:828-9 Je 5 '65

Great Britain

In England, it's unions vs. a Labor government. J. Fromm. il U S News 59:116 S 20 '65

Unions and a lid on wages; government lays down law to labor. B. Wenham. New Repub 153:17 S 25 '65

Latin America

American institute for free labor development. M. F. Riche. bibliog f il Mo Labor R 88:1049-55 S '65

Labor organizations in Latin America and the Caribbean. M. F. Riche. Mo Labor R 88:298-300 Mr '65

Latin labor's alarming Christians. G. Delmas. il Reporter 32:27-30 F 25 '65; Reply. G. Packard. 32:6+ Mr 25 '65

United States

Bargaining weather: fair and mild; few contracts open; with chart. Bsns W p37-9 Ja 1 '66

Chronicle of trade union positions on government ownership. P. Henle. bibliog f Mo Labor R 88:805-16 Jl '65

Developments in industrial relations. See issues of Monthly labor review

Entertainment unions: a progress report. Mo Labor R 88:III-IV N '65

Everyone else is organized; farmers should be, too. D. Paarlberg. Suc Farm 63:31+ O '65

Fair practices and fair profits: union monopolies; address, February 20, 1965. C. R. Sligh, jr. bibliog Vital Speeches 31:430-4 My 1 '65

General motors sit-down strike, 1937: a re-examination. S. Fine. bibliog f Am Hist R 70:691-713 Ap '65

How tough is Walter Reuther? J. R. Moskin. il Look 29:83-4+ Ag 10 '65

How workers feel about early retirement. il U S News 58:78+ Mr 29 '65

Is our merchant fleet really afloat? il Bsns W p 128+ S 25 '65

Labor and the federal government: 1850-1933. A. A. Blum. bibliog f il Cur Hist 48:328-33+ Je '65

Labor month in review. See issues of Monthly labor review

Labor movement today: a diagnosis. J. Seidman. Mo Labor R 88:149 F '65

Labor's captains begin to change. Bsns W p28-9 My 22 '65

Now it's internal trouble for the unions. il U S News 58:81-2 Mr 1 '65

Outlook for '66: few strikes, but big gains for unions. il U S News 60:68-71 Ja 10 '66

Perils of prosperity. il Time 85:89 Ap 9 '65

Revolt of the left-outs; union malaise. S. Lens. Commonweal 82:441-4 Je 25 '65; Reply with rejoinder. D. J. McDonald. 82:514 Jl 23 '65

TRADE unions—United States—*Continued*
State of the unionists: griping, but living well. il Bsns W p24-6 F 20 '65
Support from labor; for Metropolitan opera's Lewisohn stadium concerts. il Opera N 29: 18 My 1 '65
Union labor: less militant, more affluent; Time essay. Time 86:42-3 S 17 '65
Unions and their members. E. Stein. Cur Hist 49:23-8+ Jl '65
Unions vs. management: the public battleground; transportation unions' use of public relations techniques. T. R. Brooks. il Duns R 85:pt2 138-9+ Je '65
    See also
American federation of labor and Congress of industrial organizations
Arbitration, Industrial—United States
Housing projects, Trade union
Strikes—United States
Teachers unions
Trade unions—Officials
    also names of unions, e.g; International typographical union

TRADE waste
Industry combats pollution. G. Hill. Bul Atomic Sci 21:42-3 D '65
Pollution fight picks up force; boom for makers of waste treatment equipment. il Bsns W p 108-10+ N 13 '65

TRADESCANTIA. See Spiderworts

TRADING. See Barter

TRADING stamps
Are trading stamps losing their punch? il Bsns W p66+ S 4 '65
Biggest gimmick. Nation 201:130-1 S 13 '65
Looking into the Green stamp business. D. Sanford. New Repub 153:9 O 16 '65
New licks in the stamp battle. il Time 86: 114 S 17 '65
Not as good as gold; court case dealing with exchange and purchase of stamps. New Repub 153:7 N 20 '65
Trading-stamp outlook. il U S News 59:67 N 15 '65
Trading stamps and the CPI. E. D. Hoover and M. L. Drake. bibliog f il Mo Labor R 88:429-33 Ap '65

Anecdotes, facetiae, satire, etc.
Cost reduction. W. J. Coughlin. Miss & Roc 16:54 F 15 '65

TRADITIONALIST movement. See Catholic church

TRAFFIC. See Road traffic

TRAFFIC, Tunnel. See Tunnel traffic

TRAFFIC accidents
Auto safety: new study criticizes manufacturers and universities. E. Langer. Science 150:1136-9 N 26 '65
Auto safety: who will take the lead? il Newsweek 66:67-8 Jl 26 '65
Automobile first aid supplies. C. J. Potthoff. Todays Health 43:76 Ap '65
Automotive safety. R. Moley. Newsweek 67:92 Ja 24 '66
Cars, roads, drivers and safety. Life 59:4 Jl 23 '65
Defensive driving. Motor T 17:61-2 Jl '65
Driving tests should be tougher. C. Leedham. il N Y Times Mag p40+ F 14 '65
Face to face: with a girl who couldn't cry. S. Amoroso. Seventeen 24:202 My '65
Highway casualties soar; what to do about it? with interview with W. S. Smith. il U S News 58:56-61 Mr 1 '65
How can we stop the slaughter on our nation's highways? forum discussion. il Sr Schol 87:14-15 O 14 '65
How good a driver are you? J. E. Gibson. il Todays Health 43:34-6 My '65
Murder on the highways: things are being done about it. Changing T 19:7-16 Je '65
On highways, still no holiday for death; record during Fourth of July week-end. U S News 59:14 Jl 19 '65
Passing the buck; manufacturers blame drivers. Nation 201:150-1 S 27 '65
Physicians as activists. Nation 200:463 My 3 '65
What to do if you're in an auto accident. il Good H 160:137 Ja '65
    See also
Automobile driving
Automobiles—Safety devices and measures
Insurance, Automobile
Safety belts

TRAFFIC congestion. See Street traffic

TRAFFIC control, Airport. See Airports—Traffic control

TRAFFIC control, Airway. See Air traffic control

TRAFFIC engineering
Computer-produced traffic-flow maps. il Am City 80:126 Ap '65
Future city; suggestions for tunneled freeways and parking beneath cities. G. A. Hoffman. il Sat R 48:42-4 Ag 7 '65
How to beat the traffic mess. S. V. Jones. il Sci Digest 57:77-9 My '65
Master modemixer; devised by Cornell lab team il Life 59:160-1 D 24 '65
New device forerunner of all-electric highway. Sci N L 87:153 Mr 6 '65
Notes for fretless traffic. il Esquire 64:216-17 D '65
Our car-strangled cities. W. Langewiesche. il Read Digest 87:71-6 Jl '65

Study and teaching
Yale offers traffic-engineering fellowships. Am City 81:28 Ja '66

TRAFFIC in arms. See Export controls

TRAFFIC markings
Arrows mark the way; Colorado Springs. D. L. Smith. il Am City 80:124+ D '65
Parade-tested traffic markings; District of Columbia. il Am City 80:128 Ag '65
Wet-proof safety lines; Florida state road department. il Am City 80:125 Jl '65

TRAFFIC regulations
Harmony on the highways. A. Ribicoff. Atlan 216:80-3 Jl '65
Passenger-car radios get traffic directions. Am City 80:152 Mr '65
Traffic control. See issues of American city
Traffic control on a limited budget; Shreveport, La. T. Herline. il Am City 80:183-4 Mr '65
    See also
Automobile parking
Computers—Traffic control applications
Moving pictures in traffic control

TRAFFIC signals

Control
Controller that meters traffic electronically; Binghamton, N.Y. il Am City 80:120+ Jl '65
Two master controllers, one smooth-flowing traffic network; Champaign, Ill. F. B. Noonan. il Am City 80:150 Je '65

TRAFFIC signs
Remote-controlled signs cut turnpike accidents; New Jersey turnpike. P. M. Weckesser. il Am City 80:118 F '65

TRAFFIC violations
Computer & Mrs Placente; New York city's Computer oriented retrieval of auto larcenists. il Time 86:72 S 3 '65

TRAGEDY
Is there a tragic sense of life? L. Abel; discussion. Commentary 39:18+ My '65

TRAGER, Frank N.
U.S. and Indonesia, a tragedy in diplomacy. N Y Times Mag p26-7+ Ag 29 '65

TRAIL riders of the Canadian Rockies
Horse by day, tepee at night. il Sunset 134: 58+ My '65

TRAIL riders of the wilderness
Lure of the wilderness. D. Dixon. il Am For 71:42-4+ Mr '65

TRAIL scooters. See Motor scooters

TRAILER camps. See Automobile trailer camps

TRAILERS
    See also
Automobile trailers

Transportation
Container ship lines get a play; Seatrain lines, inc, and Sea-land service, inc. il Bsns W p45-6+ Jl 10 '65

TRAILS
Jackson, Mississippi's nature trail. B. Horne. Horticulture 43:44 O '65
Motor scooter pressure. Liv Wildn 87:29 Wint '64
    See also
Appalachian trail
National parks and reserves—Trails

Canada
Hitting the trail in Canada. M. Woelflé. il Recreation 58:390-1 O '65

TRAIN ferries
Container ship lines get a play; Seatrain lines, inc, and Sea-land service, inc. il Bsns W p45-6+ Jl 10 '65

TRAIN speed. See Railroads—Train speed

TRAIN travel. See Railroad travel

TRAINING, Transfer of. See Transfer of training

TRAINING camps. See Military training camps

TRAINING of children. See Children—Management and training

TRAINING of plants. See Plants, Training of

TRAINING schools for delinquents. See Reformatories

TRAINOR, Francis R. and Burg, C. A.
Scenedesmus obliquus sexuality. bibliog Science 148:1094 My 21 '65

TRAINS. See Railroads—Trains

TRAINS, Model. See Railroad models

TRAMMELL, Archie
Al's place. Flying 77:45-7 D '65
Horse of a different color. Flying 77:57-60 Ag '65
O₂ fly in the troposphere. Flying 77:36-40 S '65
Regency who? Flying 77:45-6 Jl '65
Swearingen of San Antone. Flying 77:70-3 N '65
Thinking man's autopilot. Flying 77:45-8 N '65
What's that in the cloud, ahead? Flying 77:69-71 O '65

TRAMPOLINES
New bounce on the trampoline. P. Stewart. il Sports Illus 23:52-3 Jl 12 '65

TRAMPS
See also
Vagabonds

TRANQUILIZING drugs
Letdown for Miltown; dropped from the U.S. pharmacopeia. Time 85:85 Ap 30 '65
Tranquilizing drugs act on damaged brain areas. Sci N L 87:87 F 6 '65
See also
Chlorpromazine
Reserpine

TRANQUILLI, Secondo. See Silone, I. pseud.

TRANS-action (periodical)
Sociology without tears; new bimonthly magazine called Trans-action. Newsweek 65:82 F 15 '65

TRANSAMERICA corporation
Merchandising money. il Time 86:54 D 24 '65

TRANS ANDEAN railroad. See Railroads—Bolivia

TRANSATLANTIC travel. See Travel

TRANSATLANTIC voyages. See Voyages

TRANSCEIVERS. See Radio telephone

TRANSDUCERS
New semiconductor phono transducer. J. F. Wood. il Electr World 73:50-1+ F '65
Ultrasonic scanning of biologic tissue by a new technique. F. L. Thurstone and others. il Science 149:302-3 Jl 16 '65

TRANSFER of employees. See Employees, Transfer of

TRANSFER of learning. See Transfer of training

TRANSFER of training
Learning transfer hit. Sci N L 88:386 D 18 '65

TRANSFER students. See College students

TRANSFERRIN
Hemoglobin and transferrin electrophoresis and relationships of island populations of anolis lizards. G. C. Gorman and H. C. Dessauer. bibliog il Science 150:1454-5 D 10 '65
Human transferrins C and D₁: chemical difference in a peptide. A. C. Wang and H. E. Sutton. bibliog il Science 149:435-7 Jl 23 '65
Species and geographic differences in the transferrin polymorphism of macaques. M. Goodman and others. bibliog il Science 147:884-6 F 19 '65; Reply with rejoinder. J. Fooden. 148:255 Ap 9 '65

TRANSFERS, Job. See Job transfers

TRANSFIGURATION of Christ. See Jesus Christ—Transfiguration

TRANSFUSION of blood. See Blood—Transfusion

TRANSISTOR circuits
Designing a transistor power supply. T. J. Barmore. il Electr World 73:46-7 My '65

TRANSISTOR clocks. See Clocks, Electronic

TRANSISTOR radios. See Radio receiving apparatus—Transistor receivers

TRANSISTOR television receiving apparatus. See Television receiving apparatus—Transistor receivers

TRANSISTOR vibrators. See Multivibrators

TRANSISTORS
Economy-line transistors. R. Tellefsen. il Electr World 74:36+ Ag '65
Evolving transistor. A. H. Seidman. il Electr World 73:30-3+ Mr '65
Field-effect transistor. G. L. Jackson. il Electr World 74:81-4 N '65
Field-effect transistors for FM front-ends. D. R. Von Recklinghausen. il Electr World 74:36-7+ D '65
Hi-Fi stereo for '66, in solid. H. Fantel. il Pop Electr 23:47-51+ N '65
New line-cord-operated transistors. il Electr World 73:34-6 Ap '65

Solid state (cont of) Transistor topics. L. Garner. See issues of Popular electronics
Understanding the transistor data sheet. il Electr World 74:40-1+ S '65
See also
Radio receiving apparatus—Transistor receivers
Radio transmitters—Transistor transmitters
Television receiving apparatus—Transistor receivers
Transistor circuits

Testing

Transistor and diode curve tracer. A. A. Mangieri. il Electr World 73:65-8 Je '65
Transistor testing with an ohmmeter. Electr World 73:73 Mr '65
Using a transistor curve tracer. R. E. Show. il Electr World 74:49-52+ S '65

TRANSIT strike, New York. See Strikes—United States—Transportation workers

TRANSIT systems. See Rapid transit

TRANSITIONAL metals. See Metals

TRANSLATING machines
Mechanical translation: U.S.-Japan joint conference. F. L. Alt. Science 147:1599-600 Mr 26 '65

TRANSLATION, Opera. See Opera—Language

TRANSLATIONS and translating
Better off in Latin? translating Roman Catholic mass into vernacular languages. il Time 86:53 Jl 30 '65
English with tears; literary translators. D. Dempsey. Sat R 48:38+ F 13 '65
Gift of tongues; simultaneous interpreters. Newsweek 65:52 Mr 15 '65
On translating Mao's poetry. D. Davie. Nation 200:704-5 Je 28 '65
Polite lie. R. Graves. Atlan 215:74-80 Je '65
Translation of scientific literature. P. H. Abelson. Science 149:929 Ag 27 '65
Translator and publisher: the popular technical book. T. E. Burton. Pub W 187:62-4 Ap 19 '65
See also
Childrens literature—Translating
Poetry—Translating

TRANSMISSION, Automobile. See Automobiles—Transmission

TRANSPAC race. See Yacht racing

TRANS-PACIFIC yacht race. See Yacht racing

TRANSPARENCIES
Color a la carte; a prize picture by Robert Routh. il Pop Phot 58:114-15 Ja '66
Color clinic; salvaging transparencies. D. B. Eisendrath, jr. Pop Phot 56:10+ Ap; 20+ My '65
Color slides. R. Miller. See issues of U.S. camera & travel
How to put on a slide show without boring your friends. Bet Hom & Gard 43:56 Ap '65
Slide transparencies. E. Welch. il Design 66:37-9 Ja '65

Copying

Poor man's slide copier; Kingdon slide copier. N. Rothschild. il Pop Phot 56:62-3+ Mr '65
Slide duplicating made easy. D. L. Miller and E. Meyers. il Mod Phot 29:84-6+ Ap '65

Editing

Sight and sound. R. Miller. U S Camera 28:32+ Ag '65

Projection

Caulfield on color. P. Caulfield. Mod Phot 29:48 F '65
Caulfield on color; projecting 2¼x2¼ color. P. Caulfield. Mod Phot 29:34+ N '65
Color slides. R. Miller. U S Camera 28:18 Mr '65
Edit the dullness out of slide shows. D. B. Eisendrath, jr. Pop Phot 56:8+ F '65
Take the toughest test for slide shows. R. Miller. U S Camera 28:28+ Ag '65

Sound accompaniment

Sight and sound. R. Miller. il U S Camera 28:70-1+ Jl; 32+ Ag '65

Storage

Caulfield on color. P. Caulfield. Mod Phot 29:24+ O '65

Titles

How to make perfect slide captions. R. Miller. il U S Camera 28:24-5 Ap '65

Viewers

Caulfield on color. P. Caulfield. il Mod Phot 29:46 Mr '65

TRANSPARENT plastics. See Plastics, Transparent

TRANSPIRATION of plants.   See Plants—
    Transpiration
TRANSPLANTATION of organs, tissues, etc.
    Abrogation of allogeneic inhibition by
        cortisone. K. E. Hellström and others. bib-
        liog il Science 149:82-4 Jl 2 '65
    Adult thymectomy: effect on recovery from
        immunologic depression in mice. A. P.
        Monaco and others. bibliog il Science 149:
        432-5 Jl 23 '65
    Agouti locus: homology of its method of
        operation in rats and mice. W. K. Silvers.
        bibliog il Science 149:651-2 Ag 6 '65
    Artificial heart inside the body. W. J. Kolff.
        il Sci Am 213:38-46 bibliog(p 142) N '65
    Bone: formation by autoinduction. M. R.
        Urist. bibliog il Science 150:893-9 N 12 '65
    Brain transplantation: prolonged survival of
        brain after carotid-jugular interposition.
        R. J. White and others. bibliog il Science
        150:779-81 N 5 '65
    Cadaver transplants seen. Sci N L 87:195
        Mr 27 '65
    Calf bones to mend people. il Life 58:41+
        F 26 '65
    Clues from the placenta. il Time 85:58-9 Ap
        16 '65
    Control of life. il Life 59:66-83+ S 24 '65
    Dimorphic development of transplanted juve-
        nile gonads of mosquitoes. J. F. Anderson
        and W. R. Horsfall. bibliog il Science 147:
        624-5 F 5 '65
    Dog brain transplanted. F. Marley. il Sci
        N L 88:307 N 13 '65
    Ethics in new medicine: tissue transplants.
        F. D. Moore. Nation 200:358-62 Ap 5 '65
    Filigree of skin; new grafting technique for
        severe burns. il Life 59:51+ O 29 '65
    Gift of life from the dead; Wolf Sturmer
        transplant. il Life 59:78-88 S 17 '65
    Helped by a clean cut; severed hand replaced
        at North Carolina Baptist hospital, Winston-
        Salem. il Time 86:59 Jl 23 '65
    Homograft rabbit skin protection by pheno-
        thiazine derivatives. Z. Eyal and others.
        bibliog il Science 148:1468-9 Je 11 '65
    Hybrid resistance to parental marrow grafts:
        association with the K region of H-2. G.
        Cudkowicz and J. H. Stimpfling. bibliog il
        Science 144:1339-40 Je 12 '64; Correction.
        147:1056 F 26 '65
    Immunologic tolerance in thymectomized, ir-
        radiated rats grafted with thymus from
        tolerant donors. K. Isaković and others.
        bibliog il Science 148:1333-5 Je 4 '65
    Kidney & the cancer. il Time 85:83 My 21 '65
    Kidney homografts: uptake of fluorochrome-
        labeled tissue extracts by lymph node cells.
        J. L. Tong and others. bibliog il Science
        149:753 Ag 13 '65
    Mission of mercy; fight for young African's
        life. H. J. Massaquoi. il Ebony 20:149-52+
        My '65
    New eye transplants. il Sci Digest 59:35 Ja
        '66
    Now they're transplanting teeth! L. Joseph.
        il Todays Health 43:70-1+ My '65
    Rejoined at the ankle. il Time 86:102 N 19 '65
    Replanting teeth. Sci Digest 58:34 Jl '65
    Sclera graft aids sight. F. Marley. Sci N L
        88:275 O 30 '65
    Skin grafts: delayed rejection between pairs
        of cattle twins showing erythrocyte chimer-
        ism. W. H. Stone and others. bibliog il Sci-
        ence 148:1335-6 Je 4 '65
    Spare parts surgery: what lies ahead. ex-
        cerpt from The rebuilt man. F. Warshofsky.
        il Todays Health 43:44-6+ Je '65
    Surgery in the womb; study of immune
        reaction in lamb. il Newsweek 66:42-3 Ag
        2 '65
    Texas tornado. il Time 85:54-5 My 28 '65
    Thalidomide aids graft. Sci N L 88:211 O 2 '65
    Transfer of a response to naive rats by in-
        jection of ribonucleic acid extracted from
        trained rats. F. R. Babich and others. bib-
        liog il Science 149:656-7 Ag 6 '65; Dis-
        cussion. 150:228, 1749 O 8, D 24 '65
    Transplantation immunity of gestational ori-
        gin in infant rats. R. E. Billingham and
        others. bibliog il Science 147:514-16 Ja 29
        '65
    Treated human skin stored for two years.
        Sci N L 88:296 N 6 '65
    When missing teeth are replaced with real
        teeth. Good H 160:148 F '65
TRANSPLANTING
    Here's a tool for transplanting. il Sunset
        134:253 Mr '65
TRANSPLANTING of trees. See Tree planting
TRANSPONDERS
    New radar cuts hazard of mid-air collisions.
        P. Geraci. il Pop Sci 186:74-7+ Ap '65
    Regency who? miniscule navcom systems. A.
        Trammell. Flying 77:45-6 Jl '65

TRANSPORT planes, Military. See Airplanes,
    Military transport
TRANSPORT workers. See Transportation
    workers
TRANSPORT workers union
    Mike's strike; New York transit strike. il
        Time 87:22-7 Ja 14 '66
    New York transit settlement: what union
        demanded, what it got. U S News 60:34 Ja
        24 '66
    Transit mess; New York on foot. T.
        Grubisich. Commonweal 83:456-7 Ja 21 '66
    Unions vs. management: the public battle-
        ground; transportation unions' use of public
        relations techniques. T. R. Brooks. il Duns
        R 85:pt2 138-9+ Je '65
    Will Quill win gamble? TWU vs TA. Bsns W
        p32-3 Ja 8 '66
TRANSPORTATION
    Master modemixer; devised by Cornell lab
        team. il Life 59:160-1 D 24 '65
    Redesigning the twentieth century; with
        editorial comment. il Esquire 64:8, 214-23
        D '65
    Transportation on earth; address, October
        20, 1964. W. Owen. il Vital Speeches 31:
        292-7 Mr 1 '65
            See also
    Barges
            also subhead Transportation under vari-
            ous subjects, e.g. Boats—Transportation

        Federal aid
    Commuter rail cost set; service between
        Boston or New York and Washington.
        Sci N L 88:39 Jl 17 '65
    Federal official redefines mass-transit act.
        Am City 81:53 Ja '66
    Future of mass transportation; address. R.
        A. Nelson. Duns R 85:pt2 158A-158C+ Je
        '65
    Ground conveyance under scrutiny; intercity
        transportation. M. Getler. Miss & Roc 16:
        24-5 My 24 '65
    $6,000,000 in mass-transit grants approved.
        Am City 80:132+ My '65

        Finance
    Transport profits ride up. il Bsns W p66+
        Mr 20 '65

        International aspects
    International cooperation year, a challenge
        to transportation. L. K. Bridwell. Dept
        State Bul 53:835-9 N 22 '65

        Laws and regulations
    Renascent role of the regulatory agencies.
        J. F. Olesky. il Duns R 85:pt2 96-7+ Je '65
    Repeal of restrictive trade clause in trans-
        portation act urged; statement, March 30,
        1965. T. C. Mann. Dept State Bul 52:636-7
        Ap 26 '65

        Private operations
    Private transportation: cost is the criterion.
        il Duns R 85:pt2 130-1+ Je '65

        Research
    Big payoff in R&D. il Duns R 85:pt2 94-5+ Je
        '65

        Speed
        See also
    Transportation, High-speed

        Taxation
    Overseas travel tax idea dropped. Aviation W
        82:31 F 15 '65

        Japan
        See also
    Railroads—Japan

        United States
    Can he set an industry course? A. S. Boyd
        tackles problems of transportation. Bsns W
        p49-50+ S 18 '65
    Crisis in transportation. il Sr Schol 86:6-9
        F 4; 12-14+ F 11 '65
    400-Mph passenger train. L. Lessing. il
        Fortune 71:124-9+ Ap '65
    Getting there and back. A. H. Hepburn. il
        Sr Schol 87:sup 16-17 O 28 '65
    Getting to work and back. R. Brecher and
        E. Brecher. il Consumer Rep 30:56-65, 128-
        33, 206-9 F-Ap '65; Discussion. 30:299-301
        Je '65
    Ground conveyance under scrutiny; intercity
        transportation. M. Getler. Miss & Roc 16:
        24-5 My 24 '65
    Many choices begin to form up. il Life 59:
        158-9 D 24 '65
    Planes, trains, ships, roads: an official look
        ahead; interview. A. S. Boyd. U S News
        60:48-51 Ja 24 '66

TRANSPORTATION—United States—*Cont.*
R&D needs outlined; NAA transportation study to go on. Miss & Roc 18:23 Ja 17 '66
Special report on transportation; symposium. il Duns R 85:pt2 91-105+ Je '65
Transport for the corridor. Sci Am 212:56 Ap '65

See also
Air travel—United States
Ferries
Railroads—United States

History
How we got here. E. Zern. il Field & S 70:52-5 Jl '65

TRANSPORTATION, Automotive
See also
Trucking

Taxation
Carriers dig in for tax fight. Bsns W p72 F 6 '65

TRANSPORTATION, High-speed
Amazing plans for speeding travel. U S News 58:54-6 Ap 5 '65
Barriers to innovation. D. Wolfle. Science 150:295 O 15 '65
Breaking the travel bottleneck; MIT study report on high-speed travel. Bsns W p32-3 D 25 '65
British hovercar planned for high speed transit; land version of air-cushioned vehicle. Sci N L 88:104 Ag 14 '65
Commuting at 1,000 m.p.h. L. Galton. il N Y Times Mag p76-7+ O 24 '65
From subways to urbmobiles. il Sr Schol 87:5 O 28 '65
Magnetic highway seen for high-speed transit. Sci N L 87:393 Je 19 '65
Magnificent men in their whooshing machines. il Time 86:88 Jl 16 '65
New deal for the harried commuter. A. Williams. il Pop Mech 124:100-4+ N '65
Rapid transit plans grow; Glideway, Boston to Washington project. Sci N L 88:39 Jl 17 '65
350-mph train. il Sci Digest 58:49 N '65
See also
Railroads—Train speed

TRANSPORTATION, Military
Wrapping mobility in a total package; C-5A cargo plane and the fast deployment logistics ship. Bsns W p34 N 27 '65
See also
Landing craft
United States—Military airlift command
United States—Military sea transportation service
Vietnamese war, 1957- —Transportation

TRANSPORTATION of works of art
Message for the millions from the Pietà. il(cover) America 113:428 O 16 '65
Mona Lisa; V.I.P. protection par excellence. il UNESCO Courier 18:11-13 N '65
Pietà safe. Am Artist 30:6 Ja '66

TRANSPORTATION to airports. See Airports —Transportation problems

TRANSPORTATION workers
Unions vs. management: the public battleground; transportation unions' of public relations techniques. T. R. Brooks. il Duns R 85:pt2 138-9+ Je '65
See also
Strikes—United States—Transportation workers

TRANSUBSTANTIATION
Beyond transubstantiation: new theory of the real presence. il Time 86:68+ Jl 2 '65
See also
Catholic church—Eucharist

TRANS WORLD airlines
Boyd warns of possible major international dispute on movies. J. W. Carter. Aviation W 82:30 My 3 '65
Inflight movies rebound from TWA blow. J. W. Carter. Aviation W 82:28 Mr 22 '65
Matrices illustrate TWA's authority. il Aviation W 83:48 Ag 30 '65
TWA buys Lockheed recorders for DC-9s. Aviation W 83:46 Ag 23 '65
TWA move may be death blow for films. J. W. Carter. Aviation W 82:26-7 Mr 8 '65
TWA proposes experimental cut in domestic family coach fares. Aviation W 82:42 Ap 26 '65
T.W.A: prosperity but no peace. J. McDonald il Fortune 72:122-5+ Jl '65
TWA reliability program quickens lengthening of jet engine TBOs. Aviation W 82:41 F 22 '65
T.W.A: the struggle for the corporate cockpit. J. McDonald. il Fortune 71:106-11+ My '65
TWA to renew movie contract; entertainment future uncertain. J. W. Carter. Aviation W 82:39 Ap 19 '65

TRAP shooting
Safe trapshooting with a .22. M. Lindberg. il Pop Sci 187:134-5 Ag '65
Some bright, icy birds challenge clay pigeons; colorful ice targets replace clay pigeons of trap and skeet shooting. D. Barnes. il Sports Illus 22:58-9 My 3 '65

TRAPPERS
Old fur trader. D. J. Anderson. il Field & S 70:50-2+ O '65

TRAPPING
Rock-a-bye turkey; tranquilizers in catching wild turkeys. W. Lovett. il Field & S 70:8-9 D '65
See also
Fur trade

TRASCHEN, Isadore
Robert Frost: some divisions in a whole man. Yale R 55:57-70 O '65

TRAUMATIC neuroses. See Neuroses

TRAVEL
Booked for travel. H. Sutton. See issues of Saturday review
Esquire the younger. J. Berendt. Esquire 63: 158-61 Ap '65
Executive suites go on the road; company presidents spend over third of their working year traveling. il Bsns W p92+ O 2 '65
From America with love; teen-age travel. R. Joseph. Esquire 64:62 Jl '65
Got to be away for a while? things to attend to before departure. il Changing T 19:31-2 O '65
Half the fun of travel is reading Richard Joseph. A. Gingrich. Esquire 64:6 Ag '65
Here and there. See issues of Holiday
Holiday travel; with questions and answers. A. H. Hepburn. il Sr Schol 87:sup 12-13 S 23: sup 16-17 O 28: sup 12-13 N 11 '65
I remember. M. B. Tucker. il NEA J 54:46-8+ F '65
Is there a best way to take money on a foreign trip? Bet Hom & Gard 43:15 S '65
Just take off, brother! E. M. White. il Farm J 89:52L My '65
Keeping faith with the traveler; expanding international travel. W. D. Patterson. Sat R 48:30 S 18 '65
Let's travel: student specials. il Mlle 61:335-8 Ag '65
Life travel (cont) Life 58:64-73 Mr 19 '65
Life travel review. Life 58:17+ Je 18 '65: 60:46-53 Ja 7 '66
[Month] travel in and beyond the West. See issues of Sunset
More for your travel dollar! il Bet Hom & Gard 43:110 Mr: 128+ Ap '65
Recreation en route; travel program for recreation professionals, Westchester County recreation and park society. B. J. Guagnini. il Recreation 58:403-4 O '65
Roamer's ramblings. T. Shane. See issues of Travel
Roamin' the globe with travel. See issues of Travel
Sampling of student programs. il Sat R 48: 79-81 F 20 '65
Sayonara, Agamemnon; initiation into the world of genuine tourism. M. Laurence. Holiday 39:21-4+ Ja '66
Shoot it from your car. E. Scully. il U S Camera 28:72-5+ Mr '65
Should Americans travel? N. Cousins. Sat R 48:24 Mr 13 '65
Speaking of travel. C. Stinnett. Holiday 39: 16+ Ja '66
Stop & go with Horace Sutton. H. Sutton. See issues of McCall's to July 1965
Travel (cont) Vogue 145:82 Mr 1; 58 Mr 15; 98 Ap 1; 149 Ap 15; 138-40, 255+ My; 66 Je; 146:46-7 Ag 1; 178 S 1; 164-5 O 1; 118+ N 1 '65
Travel. L. Barry. Pop Phot 57:44+ S; 28+ O; 10+ D '65; 58:24+ Ja '66
Travel & camera. See issues of U.S. camera & travel
Travel digest. See issues of Travel
Travel notes. R. Joseph. See issues of Esquire
Travel the NEA way; with list of summer tours. il NEA J 55:60-1 Ja '66
Travel well: tonic for spring fever. E. N. Dye. Travel 123:61-2 My '65
Traveler's choice conducted tours. C. W. Morton. Atlan 216:162+ N '65
Travesties of educational travel. W. W. Brickman. Sch & Soc 93:170+ Mr 20 '65
Vacationing with purpose; special interest trips. Time 85:60+ Ap 23 '65
Well-traveled camera? the well-spoken camera! with set of phrases, in four languages. R. Burgess. Mod Phot 29:14+ Je '65
Why should so many people be afraid to travel? group tour best for first-timer. Bet Hom & Gard 43:128 O '65

TRAVEL—*Continued*
World travel issue 1966; world in winter; symposium. il Sat R 49:41-4+ Ja 1 '66
Your wife may be right. J. Faber. il U S Camera 28:52-3+ O '65
See also
Air travel
Automobile touring
Guidebooks
Ocean travel
Packing of luggage
Railroad travel
Tourist trade
Vacations
Youth hostels
 also subhead Description and travel under names of countries, states, etc. e.g. Spain—Description and travel

Anecdotes, facetiae, satire, etc.
Booked for travel; ruminations of a roamer. E. Bedell. Sat R 48:40+ Mr 20 '65

Bibliography
Helpful free booklets. A. H. Hepburn. il Sr Schol 87:sup 16-17 O 28 '65

Economic aspects
How to travel when you can't afford to. D. Huff. Redbook 126:118-19 D '65
Let's travel to Europe; sixty-one money-saving tricks. il Mlle 60:124+ Mr '65
See also
Tourist trade

Health aspects
Staying healthy while traveling aboard. G. G. Greer. Bet Hom & Gard 43:167-9 Ap '65
Turista; bane of travelers abroad and at home. Consumer Bul 48:16-17 Mr '65

Taxation
Travel notes; question of a travel tax. R. Joseph. Esquire 64:18+ Jl '65
TRAVEL (periodical)
See also
Mr Travel award
TRAVEL agencies
Airlines vs. travel agents; proposed new commissions add fuel to smoldering fire. Bsns W p200 My 15 '65
Commission rate change proposals stir row among agents, carriers. J. R. Ashlock. Aviation W 82:45 My 17 '65
TRAVEL agents
What a travel agent can do for you at no extra cost. Bet Hom & Gard 43:126-7 O '65
TRAVEL guides. See Guidebooks
TRAVEL literature
See also
Guidebooks
TRAVEL regulations
Bit chillier; N. Mott sentenced for illegal entry. il Newsweek 66:48+ D 6 '65
Get ready, Europe, here we come! il Bsns W p 102+ My 29 '65
Keeping faith with the traveler; expanding international travel. W. D. Patterson. Sat R 48:30 S 18 '65
Limits on travel. il Time 85:56 My 14 '65
Lo! the poor tourist; proposed restrictions on travel abroad by Americans. R. Moley. Newsweek 65:108 Mr 15 '65
Patriotic duty to stay at home? E. T. Folliard. America 112:519 Ap 17 '65
Restricting travel. Commonweal 83:425 Ja 14 '66
Right to travel; question of passport restrictions. Reporter 32:12+ My 20 '65
U.S. tourists abroad: footloose and almost fancy free. il Sr Schol 86:18-19+ Mr 11 '65
Use of Mexican border-crossing cards extended; White House statement, August 10, 1965. Dept State Bul 53:368-9 Ag 30 '65
Well traveled camera; India. H. Keppler. il Mod Phot 29:38+ Ag '65
TRAVEL study courses
Breather year; precollege travel and European studies program at American school in Switzerland. il Time 85:77-8 My 28 '65
Should you let a teen-ager travel alone? programs and addresses. Bet Hom & Gard 43:14 Ag '65
Summer school across the Atlantic; American institute for foreign study. E. Kolowrat. il Sr Schol 87:18 O 7 '65
See also
Colleges and universities, Traveling
TRAVEL tax. See Travel—Taxation
TRAVEL trailers. See Automobile trailers
TRAVEL with children
Children aboard. N. A. Kline. il Yachting 118:148-9 S '65

It's easy to travel with a baby. P. Bassett. il Parents Mag 40:56-7+ Ag '65
Let's take a family camping vacation! R. Charles. Parents Mag 40:68+ Ap '65
Shall we take the kids? G. West. il Motor B 115:82+ Ap '65
What youngsters learn from foreign lands. B. Miles. il Parents Mag 40:52-3+ Ap '65
TRAVEL with pets
How to take your pet to Europe. B. Edgar. il House & Gard 128:88+ S '65
Traveling with a pet? what to do. il Good H 161:153 Jl '65
You can take them with you; dogs go everywhere. il Time 86:54 O 1 '65
TRAVELERS
Doubtful bargain for tourists. Consumer Rep 30:272-3 Je '65
How beauty travels and what it takes. il Vogue 145:158-61+ Ap 1 '65
Song of the open road map; excerpt from Bird thou never wert. B. Vaughan. Read Digest 87:190B-190C Ag '65
Talking it over with Gay Head; travel manners. Gay Head. Sr Schol 86:42 My 13 '65
U.S. tourists abroad: footloose and almost fancy free. il Sr Schol 86:18-19+ Mr 11 '65
U.S. tourist's legal sampler; foreign laws. il Time 85:84-5 My 7 '65
See also
Women as travelers

Anecdotes, facetiae, satire, etc.
Europe with some reservations; excerpts from Europe without George. I. Kampen. il McCalls 92:124-5+ My '65
Happy hardware salesman. J. Glashan. il Holiday 38:54-9 Ag '65
TRAVELERS checks
Is there a best way to take money on a foreign trip? Bet Hom & Gard 43:15 S '65
TRAVELERS insurance companies
Red umbrella in a high wind. R. Sheehan. il Fortune 72:138-41+ Ag '65
TRAVELING exhibitions. See Exhibitions, Traveling
TRAVELING hospitals. See Hospitals, Traveling
TRAVELING theater. See Theater, Traveling
TRAVELING wave tubes
MEC turning out TWT's with increased power. Miss & Roc 17:42+ O 18 '65
TRAVELS
See also
Cruising
Horseback trips
Travel
TRAVERS, Helen F.
How much responsibility can a youngster take? Parents Mag 41:40-1+ Ja '66
TRAVERS, Mary Allin
Peter, Paul and Mary; triple play! interview; ed. by E. Miller. pors Seventeen 24:128-9+ Ap '65
TRAVERSO, Adriano A. Buzzati-. See Buzzati-Traverso, A. A.
TRAWLS and trawling
Tricks of trolling. G. Heinold. Outdoor Life 136:8+ Ag '65
TRAYNOR, Roger John
Pioneering California. il por Time 87:48-9 Ja 21 '66
TRAYS
Pictures to make and feel. L. Lindeman. il Design 66:25-7 Ja '65
Serving trays; new vintage. il House & Gard 128:306-7 N '65
Three trays you can make. R. Day; W. E. Burton. il Pop Sci 187:148-51 N '65
Tray storage. il House & Gard 128:106-9 Jl '65
TREADWAY, Lauris Goldsmith
Colonial innkeepers. il por Time 85:85 Je 18 '65
TREADWAY inns. See Hotels, taverns, etc.
TREASON trials. See Trials (treason)
TREASURE hunts
Why Mr Jarvis deserves torture; nightmarish trek through darkest Illinois, unscrambling riddles and scrambling for treasure. L. H. Lapham. il Sat Eve Post 238:80+ D 18 '65
TREASURE trove
Big find; richest treasure to date; silver coins from ancient Spanish ship found off Grand Bahama Island. W. I. Fischman. il Look 29:102+ Mr 9 '65
Florida's lucky treasure hunt. R. G. Sherrill. il Nation 200:221-3 Mr 1 '65
Florida's numismatist convention and treasure ships. C. French. il Hobbies 70:102 My '65

TREASURE trove—*Continued*
Ghost in the blue hole; Banner Reef, southwest of Jamaica in the open Caribbean. C. Phinizy. il Sports Illus 22:68-70+ Mr 8 '65
Lost treasures. C. French. Hobbies 70:102 Ap '65
They dive into history. G. Gaskill. il Read Digest 86:131-6 Je '65
Underwater thesaurus; Smithsonian institution program of underwater exploration of historic sites. M. Peterson. il Antiques 88: 319-24 S '65

TREASURY department (United States) See United States—Treasury department

TREATIES
Great Britain and the 1914-1915 Straits agreement with Russia: the British promise of November 1914. C. J. Smith, jr. bibliog f Am Hist R 70:1015-34 Jl '65
See also
Geneva conventions
North Atlantic treaty organization
also subhead Treaties under names of countries. e.g. United States—Treaties

TREATMENTS, Medical. See Medical service

TREDWAY, Thomas
Newman: patristics, liberalism and ecumenism. Christian Cent 82:987-9 Ag 11 '65

TREE, Marietta P.
It's a good time to be a woman. Mlle 61: 124+ O '65
U.S. expresses views on Southern Rhodesian independence in U.N. committee of 24 and Security council; statement, April 14, 1965. Dept State Bul 52:1061-3 Je 28 '65

TREE ants. See Ants

TREE frogs and tree toads
Neurosecretory processes extending into third ventricle: secretory or sensory? C. G. Smoller. bibliog il Science 147:882-4 F 19 '65

TREE full of stars; story. See Grubb, D.

TREE of life; story. See Swados, H.

TREE peonies. See Peonies

TREE planting
Bulbs & trees, ideal companions. R. M. Peters. il Pop Gard 16:44-5 S '65
Freedom project; Easton area high school. C. H. Peterson. il NEA J 54:40 N '65
Handy guide to planting trees. il Good H 160:175 Mr '65
How to plant a tree right. il Flower Grower 52:17-18 O '65
New way to move big young trees. il Sunset 135:142-3 Ag '65
Placing and spacing trees, shrubs, and vines. il Bet Hom & Gard 43:126 Ap '65
Trees and vines. il Bet Hom & Gard 43:22 Mr '65
See also
Arbor day

TREE protection. See Trees, Care of

TREE rings
Carbon-14 content of 18th- and 19th-century wood: variations correlated with sunspot activity. M. Stuiver. bibliog il Science 149: 533-5 Jl 30 '65

TREE roots. See Roots

TREE snails. See Snails

TREE surgery. See Trees, Care of

TREE wells. See Trees, Care of

TREES
Check list of 1,027 trees. Liv Wildn 29:39 Spr '65
Choose the right tree for your terrace. W. Flemer, 3d. il Pop Gard 16:26-7+ S '65
Panhandle: it's a museum of living trees. il Sunset 135:70-1 Jl '65
Tree is forever. B. Black. il Pop Gard 16: 18-20 Mr '65
Trees and vines for every setting. H. Mason and others. il Bet Hom & Gard 43:56-61 Mr '65
See also
Christmas trees
Flowering trees
Fruit trees
Nut trees
Tree planting
Tree rings
Woodlots
also names of trees, e.g. Myrtle

Diseases and pests
See also
Fruit trees—Diseases and pests

Planting
See Tree planting

Roots
See Roots

TREES, Care of
Build a well to save a tree. il Pop Gard 16: 8-9 N '65
How to save uprooted trees. R. L. Stebbins. il Farm J 89:67 Mr '65
Now's the time to save your split trees. J. M. Haller. il Pop Sci 187:148-9 O '65
Tree supporting in Japan. il Sunset 135:268-9 O '65
Tree well serves a double purpose. H. Sibley. il Flower Grower 52:19 O '65

TREES, Dwarf
Learn to create bonsai. G. S. Avery. il Horticulture 43:26-8 D '65
Small trees for big effect. H. Mason. il Bet Hom & Gard 43:56-9 Je '65
See also
Fruit trees, Dwarf

TREES, Fossil
Fossil beds of Florissant. E. E. Gamer. il Nat Parks Mag 39:16-19 Jl '65
Stone flowers for posterity. S. Pearl. il Am For 71:40-2 F '65
See also
Petrified Forest National Park

TREES, Historic
Liberty tree. V. L. Hebert. il Horticulture 43:38-9+ Ap '65

TREES, Moving of. See Tree planting

TREES, State. See State trees

TREES, Training of
Training plants. J. B. Brimer. il Flower Grower 52:35-6 Jl '65

TREES in cities
Ann Arbor's trees; Miss Dean's bequest to city for planting, care, replacement and maintenance of its trees. A. H. Wing. Horticulture 43:16 D '65
City girds for the Dutch-elm-disease battle; Ames, Ia. R. E. Speer, jr. il Am City 80: 132-3 Je '65
It's easy to plant trees downtown; Englewood, N.J. C. C. Guerrina. il Am City 80: 108-9 Ap '65
Tree: sapling from G. Washington's estate planted for opening of City parks week. New Yorker 41:44-6 My 15 '65
Trees for New York. Nat Parks Mag 39:22 Ag '65

Stump removal
See Stump removal

TREGER, Charles
Mephisto's musings. Hi Fi 15:142 O '65

TRELLISES
One-piece trellis. H. Jackson. il Pop Mech 124:220L O '65
Yuan trellis. J. Burroughs. il Pop Mech 124: 161 O '65

TREMATODES
Trematode parasitism and polymorphism in a marine snail. W. H. Ewers and C. R. Rose. Science 148:1747-8 Je 25 '65

TREMBLAY, Paul
United Nations commemoration address, June 25, 1965. UN Mo Chron 2:88-91 Jl '65

TRENT, Council of, 1545-1563
Applied collegiality. Commonweal 83:171-2 N 12 '65

TRENTON, N.J.

Social conditions
Mayor picks deprived area. il Ebony 20:132-4+ Ag '65

TREPTE, Gene
Gene Trepte on spinnakers. Yachting 117:209 Je '65

TRESS, Madeline
Curl up and read. Seventeen 25:31 Ja '66

TRESSEL, George W.
Nuclear energy as a medical tool. Todays Health 43:50-5 My '65

TRESSLER, Marcile F.
Toothpick structures. Sch Arts 64:12-14 Ap '65

TREVES, Ralph
Those amazing new sidings with built-in paint. Pop Sci 187:130-3+ S '65

TREVOR-ROPER, Hugh Redwald
Why Hitler did not invade England. N Y Times Mag p28-9+ Je 6 '65

TREVOR THOMAS, J. See Deering, E. C. jt. auth.

TREYZ, Joseph H. See Voigt, M. J. jt. auth.

TRIAL by jury. See Jury

TRIALS
Another confession problem: unjoining the joint trial. il Time 86:31 D 24 '65
Embattled nurse of Jackrabbit Flats; P. Gardelius on trial for practicing medicine without a license. J. G. Dunne. il Sat Eve Post 238:42-4+ N 20 '65

TRILLIUMS
DNA content of a chromosome of trillium erectum: effect of cold treatment. J. Woodard and others. bibliog il Science 151:215-16 Ja 14 '66
Trilliums. E. F. Steffek. il Horticulture 43: 30-1+ F '65
TRIMARANS
Handling the multihull; excerpt from Basic sailing; ed. by A. Piver. M. B. George. il Motor B 116:38-9 S '65
What about trimarans? M. Badham; D. Teague. il Yachting 117:56-9+ Je '65
TRIMETHYLENE dipyridyl
Reduction of trimethylene dipyridyl with illuminated chloroplasts. C. C. Black. bibliog il Science 149:62-3 Jl 2 '65
TRINER, L. and Nahas, G. G.
Acidosis: effect on lipolytic activity of norepinephrine in isolated fat cells. bibliog Science 150:1725-7 D 24 '65
TRINH, Nguyen-duy-. See Nguyen-duy-Trinh
TRINIDAD (island)
Trinidad and bad research. A. M. Greenhall. il Natur Hist 74:14-21 Je '65
See also
Port-Of-Spain
TRINITY RIVER, Tex.
Dallas and Fort Worth: new seaports? il U S News 59:10 O 4 '65
TRINUCLEOTIDES. See Nucleotides
TRIODES. See Vacuum tubes
TRIONYX spinifer. See Turtles
TRIOSEPHOSPHATE dehydrogenase. See Dehydrogenases
TRIOSEPHOSPHATE isomerase
Researchers report new blood disorder; enzyme deficiency. Sci N L 87:184 Mr 20 '65
TRIPARTITE conference, Potsdam, 1945. See Berlin conference, 1945
TRIPLETAIL fishing
Tips for tripletails. G. Heinold. il Outdoor Life 136:24+ O '65
TRIPLETS
Day the triplets came. F. Ziner. il Good H 160:114-15+ Ap '65
Triplets take a bow. B. Leavitt. il Look 29: M9-13 O 19 '65
TRIPP, Edward
On library panic; excerpt from address, February 1965. Library J 90:4514-16 O 15 '65
TRIPP, R. S.
How fast can you react? Sci Digest 57:50-4 My '65
TRIPP, Stephen R.
Cooperation for disaster emergency relief. Dept State Bul 53:419-23 S 6 '65
TRITIUM
Enrichment of tritium by thermal diffusion and measurement of dated Antarctic snow samples. H. von Buttlar and B. Wiik. bibliog il Science 149:1371-3 S 17 '65
Half-life of radiocarbon; letter. F. Johnson. Science 149:1326 S 17 '65
Tritium and phosphorus-32 in high-resolution autoradiography. L. G. Caro and M. Schnös. bibliog il Science 149:60-2 Jl 2 '65
Tritium: distribution in busycon canaliculatum (L.) injected with labeled reserpine. M. Mirolli. bibliog il Science 149:1503-4 S 24 '65
TRITIUM dating. See Radiocarbon dating
TRITOMAS. See Torch lilies
TRIVETS
Make your own titles and trivets. il Design 66:26-7 Mr '65
TROJAN women; drama. See Euripides
TROLLING. See Trawls and trawling
TROMBLEY, William
Fresh look at the University of California. New Repub 153:14-15 Jl 3 '65
TROMPE-l'oeil
Meta-trompe-l'oeil. S. Gablik. il Art N 64: 46-9 Mr '65
TROPHIES, Sport
Guessing the giants. W. Page. il Field & S 70:79-81+ O '65
One winner, two victories; first International fair play trophy. il UNESCO Courier 18:22-5 Jl '65
Trophy to remember; the skinning of a deer. C. Elliott. il Outdoor Life 136:40-5+ S '65
TROPICAL diseases. See Tropics—Diseases and hygiene
TROPICAL fishes. See Fishes
TROPICAL medicine. See Tropics—Diseases and hygiene
TROPICAL plants
See also
Gesneriaceae
TROPICS
See also
Jungle

Diseases and hygiene
Specialist finds many tropical diseases on Brooklyn waterfront. il Todays Health 43:71 Ag '65
See also
Malaria
TROPOSPHERE. See Atmosphere
TROPOSPHERIC radio wave propagation
Tropo system complements satellite links. Aviation W 83:87 O 25 '65
TROPOSPHERIC scatter communications. See Tropospheric radio wave propagation
TROTSKY, Leon
Trotsky in the Bronx. B. K. Hoffer. Esquire 63:156-7 Ap '65
TROTT, Susan
Francis: the city, the saint, the statue, the boy; story. Mlle 62:104-5 D '65
TROTTER, William R.
Sibelius and the tide of taste. Hi Fi 15:48-52 D '65
TROTTERS. See Race horses
TROTTIER, Alfred
One control operates eight filters. Am City 80:90-2 S '65
TROTTING races. See Harness racing
TROUBLED waters; drama. See Betti, U.
TROUSERS
Inventor of the month; he gave cotton a reprieve; pre-formed cuffs. S. V. Jones. il Sci Digest 57:27 My '65
TROUT
Lactate dehydrogenases in trout: evidence for a third subunit. E. Goldberg. bibliog il Science 148:391-2 Ap 16 '65
New hope for the Gila. R. B. Whitaker. il Field & S 70:48-9+ Ag '65
Saving drought-stricken trout streams. E. Gilligan. il Yachting 117:105+ Je '65
TROUT fishing
Angling in Austria. A. J. McClane. il Field & S 69:39-41+ Ap '65
Backwoods browns. H. L. Lawrence. il Field & S 69:12-14+ F '65
Best trout in the West. F. Dufresne. Field & S 69:84-5 Mr '65
Best trout stream in the East; West Branch of the Ausable River. A. Glowka. il Field & S 70:54-7+ My '65
Big fishing hole; Lake Superior. H. Titus. il Field & S 70:64-6 N '65
Big trout! C. Chatfield. il Outdoor Life 135: 48-9+ Mr '65
Bog-trot for trout. N. Bryant. il Outdoor Life 135:46-7+ Ap '65
Browns and rainbows in a deep, steep box; forbidding canyon on the Rio Grande. E. White. il Sports Illus 22:49-50+ Je 21 '65
Case for the flea rod. A. J. McClane. il Field & S 69:86-90 F '65
Deadliest dries. W. Davis. il Outdoor Life 135:70+ Je '65
Don't change that fly! H. T. Walden, 2d. il Outdoor Life 135:50-1+ My '65
Five tips for opening day. W. Davis. il Outdoor Life 135:33-5+ Ap '65
Flight to never-never land. C. Chatfield. il Outdoor Life 135:52-3+ Ap '65
Fly choice by the Omen method. E. W. Smith. il Field & S 69:62-4+ Mr '65
Fly leaders for wary trout. W. Davis. il Outdoor Life 135:56+ Mr '65
Fly of last resort. B. Elliot. il Outdoor Life 136:62-4+ O '65
How to catch springtime lakers. W. Davis. il Outdoor Life 135:62+ My '65
I got the message. G. B. Gordon. il Outdoor Life 136:66-8+ Jl '65
If weather holds, the fishing's fine; June Lakes loop. il Sunset 135:63 O '65
Land of record breakers. B. Warner. il Field & S 69:152-4+ Ap '65
Neglected cutthroats. P. Alport and F. Dufresne, jr. il Field & S 69:48-9 Ap '65
Pan-sized rainbows are waiting; Cave Falls on the Falls River. il Sunset 134:53 Je '65
Rainbows in a strange land; Brazil. D. C. Proper. il Outdoor Life 136:40-3+ O '65
Saving drought-stricken trout streams. E. Gilligan. il Yachting 117:105+ Je '65
Squaretail country. W. Davis. il Outdoor Life 135:48-9+ Je '65
Strangest trout stream on earth; Firehole River in Yellowstone National Park. E. Schwiebert. il Field & S 70:44-7+ Jl '65
Tenacious tiger. M. Ellis. il Field & S 70: 80-4+ My '65
Tricks for big trout. W. Davis. il Outdoor Life 135:82+ Ap '65
Trophy of gold. M. Hayden. il Outdoor Life 135:44-7+ My '65
Trouting with heart and mind. C. K. Fox. il Esquire 63:112-14 Je '65

TROUT fishing—*Continued*
Turnabout for trout. J. T. Fowler. il Outdoor Life 136:58-9+ S '65
Waters of the big fish. C. Elliott. il Outdoor Life 135:40-3+ Mr '65
We blazed wild new trails. M. G. Terziev. il Outdoor Life 135:32-5+ My '65
We gambled on Poison. M. Hayden. il Outdoor Life 136:36-9+ S '65
Wyoming roundup. A. J. McClane. il Field & S 70:48-52+ Je '65
See also
Grayling fishing
Il TROVATORE; opera. See Verdi. G.
TROWBRIDGE, Alexander B.
Business and industry in International cooperation year. Dept State Bul 53:406-11 S 6 '65
TRUAX, Hawley
Tolling of the bells at Winchester cathedral; poem. New Yorker 41:30 Je 19 '65
TRUCIAL states
Two down for Nasser. il Time 86:28+ Jl 9 '65
TRUCK campers. See Campers and coaches, Truck
TRUCK farming
Can Mexico take your vegetable market? B. Fowler. il Farm J 89:28-9+ Je '65
TRUCK lines. See Motor truck lines
TRUCK suspension systems. See Motor trucks— Springs and suspension
TRUCK tires. See Tires, Motor truck
TRUCKING
Truckers shift gears for a changing load; surge of less-than-truckload freight. il Bsns W p 166+ N 6 '65
Trucking: an industry in transition. il Duns R 85:pt2 102-5+ Je '65
Yellow transit, trucker in a hurry. il Bsns W p61-2+ Ag 28 '65
See also
Motor truck lines
Yale express system, incorporated

Finance

Trucking paradox: revenues up; profits down. Sr Schol 86:9 F 4 '65

Statistics

Transport changes the index. il Bsns W p 176 Ap 17 '65
TRUCKS
See also
Motor trucks
TRUDEAU, Edward Livingston
Physician who healed himself. il por Todays Health 43:5+ Ap '65
TRUE believer; story. See Duncan, L.
TRUEBLOOD, Ted, pseud.
[Monthly article on outdoor life] See issues of Field & stream
TRUED, Merlyn
Development of international cooperation in financial and monetary affairs. Dept State Bul 53:843-7 N 22 '65
TRUESCHLER, Josephine
Mammoth hunger; poem. Commonweal 82: 212 My 7 '65
TRUEX, Phillip
City gardens. il Horticulture 43:26-7+ My '65
TRUFFLES
Mere truffle; truffle snufflers at Battista Monchiero school, Alba, Italy. il Newsweek 66:51-2 D 13 '65
Trifle about truffles. R. Dunlop. il Todays Health 43:34-6 O '65
TRUJILLO, Flor de Oro
My life as Trujillo's prisoner; ed. by L. Bergquist. pors Look 29:52-3+ Je 29 '65
My tormented life as Trujillo's daughter; ed. by L. Bergquist. pors Look 29:44-6+ Je 15 '65
TRUJILLO, Jose M. and others
Sex-linkage of glucose-6-phosphate dehydrogenase in the horse and donkey. bibliog il Science 148:1603-4 Je 18 '65
TRUJILLO MOLINA, Rafael Leonidas
Communism and democracy in the Dominican Republic. J. Bosch. Sat R 48:13-15+ Ag 7 '65
My life as Trujillo's prisoner; ed. by L. Bergquist. F. de O. Trujillo. il por Look 29: 52-3+ Je 29 '65
My tormented life as Trujillo's daughter; ed. by L. Bergquist. F. de O. Trujillo. il pors Look 29:44-6+ Je 15 '65
TRUJILLO MOLINA family
My life as Trujillo's prisoner; ed. by L. Bergquist. F. de O. Trujillo. il Look 29: 52-3+ Je 29 '65
My tormented life as Trujillo's daughter; ed. by L. Bergquist. F. de O. Trujillo. il Look 29:44-6+ Je 15 '65

TRUMAN, Harry S.
Chip off the Chippendale. il por Newsweek 65:28-9 Ap 26 '65
Press conference; on the avenue. il Time 85:73 Ap 23 '65
Thirty-third President 1945-1953. F. Freidel. il pors Nat Geog Mag 129:80-9 Ja '66
U.S. leadership: at peak under Truman? excerpts from address, April 13, 1965. D. Acheson. il por U S News 58:30 Ap 26 '65
TRUMBO, Dalton
Honor bright and all that jazz. Nation 201: 183-90 S 20 '65
TRUMBORE, C. N. See Cohen, E. D. jt. auth.
TRUMBULL, Robert
Huks bring terror to the Philippines. N Y Times Mag p28-9+ Mr 14 '65
To Baguio and beyond. Sat R 48:52+ S 18 '65
TRUMPET music
Jazz: R. Eldridge's music. W. Balliett. New Yorker 41:156-8 Ap 3 '65
TRUMPETER swans. See Swans
TRUNG, Vo Cong. See Vo Cong Trung
TRUNKS
Old trunks; how to turn them into treasures. A. Coberg. il House & Gard 128:78+ S '65
TRUSSELL, Ray E.
Changes medicare will bring to patients, doctors, hospitals; interview. por U S News 59:36-7 Jl 26 '65
TRUSSES
New ways to make roof trusses. W. J. Fletcher. il Suc Farm 63:108 Mr '65
TRUST funds. See Trusts and trustees
TRUST TERRITORY OF THE PACIFIC ISLANDS
Trust Territory of the Pacific Islands; statements, May 28 and June 2, 1965. D. Dickinson; M. W. Goding; B. Olter. Dept State Bul 53:280-97 Ag 16 '65
TRUSTEES. See Trusts and trustees
TRUSTEES, Library. See Libraries—Trustees, boards, committees, etc.
TRUSTEES, School. See School boards
TRUSTEESHIP council. See United Nations— Trusteeship council
TRUSTS, Industrial
See also
Business consolidations and mergers

Law

Ace books and distributors told to stop discriminating; violation of Clayton and Sherman anti-trust acts. Pub W 188:31-2 Jl 26 '65
Anti-trust. Commonweal 82:4-5 Mr 26 '65
Antitrust, patents lead Court list. Bsns W p30-1 O 2 '65
Antitrust policy gets a long, hard look; Katzenbach sees trouble ahead. il Bsns W p45-6+ My 8 '65
Antitrust tops docket. Bsns W p36 O 16 '65
Chaotic antitrust. H. Hazlitt. Newsweek 66: 73 Ag 16 '65
FTC scores one, tries for another. Bsns W p22 Ja 1 '66
FTC spells out a merger guide; Beatrice foods case. Bsns W p32 My 22 '65
First word from new trustbuster; excerpts from address, August 10, 1965. D. F. Turner. U S News 59:56 Ag 23 '65
Is insurance the next big antitrust target? Bsns W p52 Je 19 '65
Is the franchise system legal? General motors vs Supreme court. Bsns W p66+ Ap 3 '65
Labor and antitrust: new worry for unions. il U S News 58:101+ Je 21 '65
Merger tide is swelling; antitrusters' hostility. il Bsns W p27-8 My 29 '65
Nolo contendere given a fresh treatment; Judge Juergens' decision of 3M's no contest plea. Bsns W p88 Ja 15 '66
Pushing for tougher rules on directors; extending Clayton act. Bsns W p26 Mr 27 '65
Rash of mergers: new crackdown? il U S News 58:72 Mr 29 '65
Recent U.S. Supreme court decision on antitrust law and labor unions; opinion and dissent. B. R. White; A. J. Goldberg; W. O. Douglas. Cong Digest 44:216-23 Ag '65
Report on Washington; debate on how to bring antitrust laws up to date. Atlan 216: 8+ Ag '65
Why auto dealers don't like cash buyers; Supreme court vs General motors franchise system. il Consumer Rep 30:258-61 My '65

United States

CBS, Yankees score in capital. Bsns W p42 F 27 '65
See also
United States—Justice, Department of— Antitrust division

TRUSTS, Investment. See Investment trusts

TRUSTS, Pension. See Pension trusts

TRUSTS and trustees
Personal business: potential pitfalls in trusts. Bsns W p 117 Ja 30 '65
Trust funds, yes, they can help average folks. il Changing T 19:17-20 N '65
Why the next portfolio gains may come harder; trust investing. Bsns W p 152+ N 20 '65
See also
Executors and administrators

TRUTH
Brutal truth. M. M. Shideler. Christian Cent 82:1375-8 N 10 '65
Nothing but the truth? H. Cecil. il Holiday 37:14+ Mr '65
Speaking out; hypocrisy is no sin. D. W. Brogan. Sat Eve Post 238:10+ Ag 14 '65
See also
Honesty

TRYPTAMINE
Tryptamine oxidation by extracts of pea seedlings: effect of growth retardant β-hydroxyethylhydrazine. D. J. Reed. bibliog Science 148:1097-9 My 21 '65

TRYPTOPHAN
Adaptive enzyme synthesis: its inhibition as a possible analogue of immunological tolerance. D. W. van Bekkum and H. T. M. Nieuwerkerk. bibliog il Science 149:548-50 Jl 30 '65

TSAI, Gerald, jr
Fresh face in money management. por Bsns W p54+ F 20 '65

TSETSE flies
Ill-advised program: tsetse-fly control through elimination of big-game animal populations in Southern Rhodesia. Nat Parks Mag 39: 19 Ap '65

TSHOMBE, Moise
Improbable elections. il por Newsweek 65:44 Ap 5 '65
Katanga's comeback: bright spot in Africa. A. J. Meyers. il U S News 58:70-1 My 24 '65
Kind of progress. por Newsweek 66:48 O 25 '65
Moise's black magic. il por Time 85:34 F 19 '65
Nervous at the top. Time 85:40+ My 14 '65
New Tshombe. P. E. Sigmund. Commonweal 82:559-63 Ag 6 '65
Premier Tshombe. R. W. Howe. New Repub 152:8-9 Ap 24 '65
Tshombe may seek anti-white role. R. W. Howe. New Repub 153:14-15 S 18 '65
Tshombe's election campaign. Time 85:41 Mr 19 '65
Visit with Tshombe. E. Dunbar. il pors Look 29:83-6+ Mr 9 '65

TSIANG, Tingfu F.
Tsingfu F. Tsiang, RIP. Nat R 17:968 N 2 '65

TSIRIMOKOS, Elias
Continuing crisis. por Time 86:21 Ag 27 '65

TSUNAMI. See Seismic sea waves

TSUNAMI; story. See Briskin, J.

TUAREGS
Landscape with mirages. T. Sterling. il Horizon 7:80-91 Autumn '65

TUBE testers. See Testing instruments

TUBERCULOSIS
Physician who healed himself. il Todays Health 43:5+ Ap '65
Tuberculosis and today's children. L. W. Sauer. PTA Mag 60:33-4 S '65

Prevention and control
TB: no longer so fearsome, but still a problem. il Todays Health 43:37-40 Ag '65
Two new experimental TB drugs effective: capreomycin and ethambutol. Sci N L 88: 221 O 2 '65

Vaccines
Case for and case against tuberculosis vaccine. D. S. Greenberg. il Todays Health 43:38-9+ D '65; Same abr. with title Let's use BCG to fight TB. Read Digest 87:58-62 D '65

TUBEROUS begonias. See Begonias

TUBES, Rubber
Low-cost relief for droughts? dam of rubberized fabric, answer to water shortage. il Bsns W p54+ Ag 7 '65
Versatile new dam that comes and goes away; Fabridam, inflatable dam for Sunbury, Pa. il Pop Sci 187:52-3 D '65

TUBING. See Aquatic sports

TUCCI, Niccolo
Worst; story. Esquire 64:79-80 Ag '65

TUCHMAN, Barbara W.
First anti-imperialists; excerpt from Proud tower; a portrait of the world before the war, 1890-1914. Nation 20..:77-82 S 20 '65
History by the ounce; adaptation of address. Harper 231:65-8+ Jl '65
Patricians; excerpts from Proud tower. Vogue 146:156-7+ N 1 '65

TUCKER, Gerald J.
Swede compass. Outdoor life 137:108-9 Ja '66

TUCKER, Harold W. and Hennessy, M. L.
Queens borough public library at work with the schools. pors ALA Bul 59:649-52 Jl '65

TUCKER, Martin
Books. Commonweal 82:387-8 Je 11 '65

TUCKER, Raymond Roche
Ward heelers' revenge. Time 85:29-30 Mr 19 '65

TUCKERMAN, Anne Weill-. See Weill-Tuckerman, A.

TUCKNER, Howard
Making of a heavyweight. N Y Times Mag p32+ F 7 '65

TUCSON, Ariz.
Description
In Tucson, Arizona, the frontier lives on. I. Robb. Vogue 146:43+ O 15 '65

Sanitary affairs
How to solve the holiday collection problem. H. L. Danforth. il Am City 80:20 Mr '65

Water supply
Automatic watering pays its own way. G. C. Reid. il Am City 80:106-7 Mr '65

TUCSON, Ariz, public library
Desert dove in Tucson: Wilmot branch. J. F. Anderson. il Library J 90:5180-2 D 1 '65

TUFTS university, Medford, Mass.
Minority view: tradition of free student expression upheld. Commonweal 82:276 My 21 '65
Student publications and the Tufts plan (or alma mater, yours in pride) J. Ciardi. Sat R 48:20-2 S 11 '65
Tufts library terraces with site. il Arch Rec 138:150-3 O '65
Tufts steps down a slope: new Nils Yngve Wessell library. J. S. Komidar. il Library J 90:5189-91 D 1 '65

TUGBOATS
Atlas and the world of ships. M. A. Scott. il Motor B 116:54-5+ Jl '65

TUGGLE, Robert A.
Reaching for the young. Opera N 29:27 F 13 '65

TUITION fees. See Colleges and universities
—Finance

TUKEY, John W.
Data analysis and the frontiers of geophysics; adaptation of address, February 26, 1964. bibliog Science 148:1283-9 Je 4 '65

TULAREMIA
Could you get rabbit fever? H. G. Tapply. il Field & S 70:56 D '65

TULE elk. See Elk

TULIPS
Good mixers: tulips & perennials. R. M. Peters. il Pop Gard 16:42-4 S '65
Three months of tulips. B. Miles. il Flower Grower 52:30+ O '65

TULLIMONSTRUM gregarium. See Invertebrates. Fossil

TULLIUS, F. P.
Heart of darkness. New Yorker 41:125-6 F 27 '65
Making a pastime: 1971. New Yorker 41:212-14 O 16 '65

TULLOCK, Gordon
Curbing bureaucracy. Nat R 17:1200-1 D 28 '65

TULLY monster. See Invertebrates, Fossil

TULSA, Okla, city-county library system
Tulsa in orbit. A. B. Martin and C. W. Ward. il Library J 90:5164-7 D 1 '65

TULSA opera, incorporated
Tulsa; Donizetti's Elisir d' amore. M. De Vinna. Opera N 30:33 Ja 15 '66

TUMOR transplants. See Transplantation of organs, tissues, etc.

TUMOR viruses
Circulating DNA as a possible factor in oncogenesis. A. Bendich and others. bibliog il Science 148:374-6 Ap 16 '65
Lymphocytic-choriomeningitis virus in hamster tumor: spread to hamsters and humans. A. M. Lewis, jr. and others. bibliog Science 150:363-4 O 15 '65
Mammary tumor virus in mice; report on informal working conference. D. H. Moore. Science 147:1158-60 Mr 5 '65
Successive transformations of an established cell line by polyoma virus and SV 40. G. J. Todaro and H. Green. bibliog il Science 147:513-14 Ja 29 '65

TUMORS
Brain tumors, gliomas induced in hamsters by Bryan's strain of Rous sarcoma virus. G. F. Rabotti and others. bibliog il Science 147:504-6 Ja 29 '65

Glucose-6-phosphatase: reexamination of the RNA-induced activity in mouse ascites tumor cells. M. C. Niu. bibliog il Science 148:513-16 Ap 23 '65

Glucose-6-phosphate dehydrogenase mosaicism: utilization as a cell marker in the study of leiomyomas. D. Linder and S. M. Gartler. bibliog il Science 150:67-9 O 1 '65

Granulocytosis-promoting extract of mouse tumor tissue: partial purification. L. Delmonte and R. A. Liebelt. bibliog il Science 148:521-3 Ap 23 '65

Hepatomas in mice: incidence increased after gamma irradiation at low dose rates. P. C. Nowell and L. J. Cole. bibliog il Science 148:96-7 Ap 2 '65

Histones and basic polyamino acids stimulate the uptake of albumin by tumor cells in culture. H. J.-P. Ryser and R. Hancock. bibliog il Science 150:501-3 O 22 '65

5-Hydroxytryptamine in single neoplastic mast cells: a microscopic spectrofluorometric study. L. S. Van Orden and others. bibliog il Science 148:642-4 Ap 30 '65

Induction of tumors in hamsters with an avian adenovirus (CELO) P. S. Sarma and others. bibliog il Science 149:1108 S 3 '65

Lymphoma growth in vivo: electronic discrimination between tumor and stroma cells. G. Haughton and others. il Science 150:769-71 N 5 '65

Macroglobulin-producing plasma-cell tumor in mice: identification of a new light chain. K. R. McIntire and others. bibliog il Science 150:361-3 O 15 '65

Malignant lymphomas following allogenic disease: transition from an immunological to a neoplastic disorder. R. S. Schwartz and L. Beldotti. bibliog il Science 149:1511-14 S 24 '65

Neoplasia in a coral? D. F. Squires. bibliog il Science 148:503-5 Ap 23 '65; Discussion. 150:77-8 O 1 '65

Phenotypic alterations in adrenal tumor culture. G. H. Sato and others. bibliog il Science 148:1733-4 Je 25 '65

Reversal of tumor growth. A. C. Braun. il Sci Am 213:75-81+ bibliog(p 143) N '65

Tenderness may indicate breast tumors in women. Sci N L 87:312 My 15 '65

See also
Melanoma
Sarcoma

TUMORS, Malignant. See Cancer

TUMORS, Plant
See also
Crown gall

TUNA fishing
Big one! Bimini, 1965. N. Benedict. il Yachting 118:32-3+ Ag '65

TUNGSTEN
Wound Tungsten offers new shapes. J. F. Judge. il Miss & Roc 16:27 Ap 12 '65

TUNGSTEN borides
Tungsten diboride: preparation and structure. H. P. Woods and others. il Science 151:75 Ja 7 '66

TUNGSTEN films. See Photography—Films

TUNGSTEN tip pens. See Pens

TUNGUS meteorite. See Meteorites

TUNGUSKA catastrophe. See Explosions

TUNGUSKA meteor. See Meteorites

TUNICK, Adele B.
Volunteer services for schools. Sr Schol 87:sup 10 O 21 '65

TUNING, Radio. See Radio receiving apparatus—Tuning

TUNING forks
Tuning fork as an electronic component. J. Verruso. il Electr World 73:37-9 My '65

TUNISIA
Foreign relations
Atlantic report. Atlan 216:24+ N '65

Bourguiba: portrait of a nonconformist. J. Lacouture. il N Y Times Mag p26-7+ Je 6 '65

Politics and government
Atlantic report. Atlan 216:24+ N '65

TUNLEY, Roul
(ed) See Wahle, A. Ordeal by fire

TUNNEL diodes
Crystal diode gains as microwave source. P. J. Klass. il Aviation W 83:68+ N 8 '65

NOL develops nerve-like diode. W. S. Beller. il Miss & Roc 16:14-15 F 8 '65

Tunnel diode sweep trigger. D. P. Adams. il Electr World 74:94-6 N '65

Tunnel diodes improve modified radar. B. Miller. il Aviation W 82:56-7+ Mr 8 '65

TUNNEL traffic
Future city; suggestions for tunneled freeways and parking beneath cities. G. A. Hoffman. Sat R 48:42-4 Ag 7 '65

TUNNELS and tunneling
Atomic defense tunnels. Sci N L 89:3 Ja 1 '66

Future city; suggestions for tunneled freeways and parking beneath cities. G. A. Hoffman. il Sat R 48:42-4 Ag 7 '65

Link for a continent; Mont Blanc tunnel. il Time 86:29 Jl 23 '65

Open, world's longest tunnel for autos; Mont Blanc tunnel. il U S News 59:14 Jl 26 '65

View from Mont Blanc. il Newsweek 66:74 Jl 19 '65

TUNNELS and tunneling, Underwater
Quebec prefabs a highway link; seven-section tunnel to link Quebec to 5,000-mile Trans-Canada highway. il Bsns W p 156 F 20 '65

See also
English Channel tunnel (proposed)

TUOHY, Frank
Floral tribute; story. New Yorker 41:40-4 Ap 10 '65

TUOHY, William
Big dirty little war. N Y Times Mag p43+ N 28 '65

TUPPERWARE home parties, Incorporated
Live it up, ladies; Tupperware convention. il Newsweek 66:70 Ag 30 '65

Tupperware brings home party to Japan; marketing polyethylene containers. il Bsns W p 162-4 N 20 '65

TURBEVILLE, Gus
On being good sports in sports; address. Vital Speeches 31:542-4 Je 15 '65

TURBINES, Steam. See Steam turbines

TURBOFAN engines. See Gas turbines, Aircraft

TURBOJETS. See Gas Turbines, Aircraft

TURCO, Lewis
Inventing to discover. Poetry 106:369-70 Ag '65

Some pinfeather blues; poem. Commonweal 83:468 Ja 21 '66

This town of strangers; poem. Atlan 216:124 O '65

Villagers; poem. Poetry 106:409 S '65

TURCOTTE, Ron
Education of a jockey. il Time 85:70 My 21 '65

TURECK, Rosalyn
Albert Schweitzer: in music, a new approach. Sat R 48:23-4 S 25 '65

TURENNE, Henri de
Grand subject. N Y Times Mag p 114 S 12 '65

One candidate against de Gaulle. N Y Times Mag p40-1+ Ag 29 '65

TURKEY
See also
Agriculture—Turkey
Americans in Turkey
Crime and criminals—Turkey
Dardanelles
Elections—Turkey
Investments, Foreign (in Turkey)

Air force
Turks want F-4 to meet MiG-21 threat. G. C. Wilson. Aviation W 83:22-3 O 4 '65

Antiquities
See also
Sardis

Description and travel
Travel's picture portfolio. Travel 123:52-7 Je '65

Turkish delights; Turkish Riviera. il Time 86:58 Ag 20 '65

Foreign relations
Greece and Turkey: the second round. G. Bailey; C. Sterling. il Reporter 33:14-22 S 9 '65

Russia
Hug of the bear. Time 86:32 Ag 20 '65

Politics and government
Ankara: Inönü looks left. C. Sterling. il Reporter 33:18-22 S 9 '65; Reply. S. J. Markiewicz. 33:8 O 7 '65

Changes in Turkey. H. N. Howard. bibliog f il Cur Hist 48:296-300 My '65

Discovery of politics. C. Poulos. il Nation 201:378-80 N 22 '65

Ghost on the go. Time 85:33 F 19 '65

TURKEY—Politics and government—*Continued*
Who is indispensable? after the fall of Ismet.
il Time 85:35 F 26 '65
Who profits? Newsweek 65:42 Mr 1 '65
See also
Elections—Turkey

Religious institutions and affairs
Turks persecute religion; persecution against
Patriarch Athenagoras. America 113:454 O
23 '65
See also
Orthodox Eastern church in Turkey

Social conditions
Yankee please stay; overseas exploits of
ex G.I.'s. K. Baldwin and H. F. Downey.
H. Bowser. Sat R 48:18 Ag 21 '65

TURKEY and the United States
Wavering ally. Newsweek 66:64 O 18 '65

TURKEY as food. See Cookery—Poultry

TURKEY hunting
Bow and arrow turkey. G. Hornbeck. il Field
& S 70:70-1+ Jl '65
New techniques for old toms. B. W. Dalrymple.
il Field & S 70:51-3+ N '65
Nightmare gobbler. N. Taylor. il Outdoor
Life 137:46-7+ Ja '66

TURKEYS
Thanks for the turkey. B. Tufty. il Sci N L
88:330 N 20 '65

Marketing
Case of the golden turkey eggs; B. Matthews of Norfolk, England, owner of
world's largest turkey farm. G. Kent. il
Read Digest 87:148-51 N '65

TURKEYS, Wild
Rock-a-bye turkey; tranquilizers in catching
wild turkeys. W. Lovett. il Field & S 70:
8-9 D '65
Thanks for the turkey. B. Tufty. il Sci N L
88:330 N 20 '65
See also
Turkey hunting

TURKISH cookery. See Cookery, Turkish

TURKISH dancing. See Dancing, Turkish

TURKISH STRAITS. See Dardanelles

TURNBULL, Agnes Sligh
Merry Little Christmas; excerpt from Little
Christmas. Read Digest 88:65-70 Ja '66

TURNBULL, Gael
Twenty words: twenty days: a sketchbook &
a morula; poem. Poetry 106:136-59 Ap '65

TURNELL, Martin
Malraux's fate. Commonweal 82:410-13 Je 18
'65

TURNER, C.
Lady in blue; story. Good H 161:80-1 S '65

TURNER, Donald Frank
First word from new trustbuster; excerpts
from address, August 10, 1965. por U S
News 59:56 Ag 23 '65

about
Antitrust gets a new gospel. por Bsns W
p27 Ag 14 '65
Professor Turner's turn at antitrust. H. B.
Meyers. por Fortune 72:168-71+ S '65

TURNER, Ewald
Mutual funds, a modern way to invest.
NEA J 54:24-5 S '65

TURNER, F. R. and Whaley, W. G.
Intercisternal elements of the Golgi apparatus. Science 147:1303-4 Mr 12 '65

TURNER, Geneva C.
Colored presidents and rulers (title varies)
(cont) bibliog por Negro Hist Bul 28:89-90,
107-8, 134-5, 201; 29:13-14 Ja-Mr, My-O '65
Look at the association. por Negro Hist Bul
28:184-5 My '65

TURNER, Joseph Mallord William
He made beauty his business. G. Kent. il
por Read Digest 87:260-5 N '65

TURNER, Nat
This quiet dust. W. Styron. il Harper 230:
134-46 Ap '65

TURNER, Pete
Shocking approach to tranquillity; photographs. Sports Illus 22:68-71 Je 28 '65
Sport on the far shores of Eden; photographs. Sports Illus 22:38-48 Mr 29 '65

TURNER, Reginald
Reggie, by S. Weintraub. Review
Sat R por 48:100-1 S 18 '65. A. Darack

TURNER, William W.
Crime is too big for the FBI. Nation 201:
322-8 N 8 '65

TURNING point; story. See Stern, R. M.

TURNOVERS, Meat. See Cookery—Meat

TURNTABLES
Use of turntables in buildings. D. B. John-
ston. il Arch Rec 138:235-6 S '65
See also
Phonograph—Turntables

TURPIN, Dick
Brains, newts, legs, eggs, and sea shells.
por Am Ed 1:1-4 Ap '65

TURTLE; story. See Brodeur, P.

TURTLES
Active uptake of sodium by softshell turtles,
trionyx spinifer. W. A. Dunson and R. D.
Weymouth. bibliog il Science 149:67-9 Jl 2
'65
Food imprinting in the snapping turtle,
chelydra serpentina. G. M. Burghardt and
E. H. Hess. bibliog il Science 151:108-9
Ja 7 '66
Probability-learning by the turtle. K. L.
Kirk and M. E. Bitterman. bibliog il Sci-
ence 148:1484-5 Je 11 '65

TURTLES, Green
Navigation of the green turtle. A. Carr. il
Sci Am 212:78-86 bibliog(p 151) My '65

TUSHINGHAM, Rita
People are talking about... por Vogue 146:
152-3 N 1 '65

TUSIANI, Joseph
Ornithology: footnote number one; poem.
Cath World 202:25 O '65

TUSKEGEE, Ala.
End of the facade; Sammy Younge shot to
death. Time 87:29 Ja 14 '66
Model community; S. Younge murder. Newsweek 67:25-6 Ja 17 '66
Reporter at large; attempts of Negroes to
register. B. Taper. New Yorker 41:58+ Jl
24 '65
Tuskegee's Negro majority. P. Good. il Reporter 33:18-21 Jl 1 '65

TUTORS, Volunteer. See Volunteer service

TUTORS and tutoring
When college students teach neighborhood
kids; tutoring programs. S. G. Welton. il
Parents Mag 40:64-6+ Je '65

TUTTLE, Anthony
Out-of-towner; story. Redbook 124:64-5 Ap
'65

TUTTLE, Irving P.
Visit with the glass artist, Emil Larsen.
Hobbies 70:66-7 S '65

TUTTLE, Ralph
Bulls of St Mary's. por Outdoor Life 136:
46-7+ Jl '65

TWAIN, Mark, pseud. See Clemens, S. L.

TWEED, William Marcy
Boss Tweed's New York, by S. J. Mandel-
baum. Review
Newsweek il por 65:122 Je 14 '65
House that Tweed built. A. B. Callow, jr. il
Am Heritage 16:64-9 O '65

TWEEDSMUIR, John Buchan, 1st baron. See
Buchan, J.

12 international photographers. See Photography—Exhibitions

TWENTIETH century
Accidental century, by M. Harrington. Re-
view
Nat R 17:878+ O 5 '65. M. S. Evans
Sat R 48:39 S 11 '65 G. W. Linden
Relics from the 20th century; excerpt from
My war with the 20th century. P. Berton.
il Read Digest 88:105-6 Ja '66
20th century began in 1945. I. Kristol. il N Y
Times Mag p25+ My 2 '65
See also
Nineteen hundred and thirties

TWENTIETH century-Fox film corporation
Bring on the dancing girls; injunction prohibiting showing of John Goldfarb, please
come home, reversed. America 112:276-7 F
27 '65

TWIN-engine boats. See Motor boats

TWIN-lens cameras
That rugged, reliable twin-lens reflex. N.
Rothschild. il Pop Phot 56:42-7+ Mr '65

TWINS
Extrasensory electroencephalographic induc-
tion between identical twins. T. D. Duane
and T. Behrendt. il Science 150:367 O 15
'65; Discussion. 150:1240+; 151:28+ D 3 '65,
Ja 7 '66
Is it true what they say about twins? P.
Pierce. il Ebony 20:148-50+ S '65
Marmosets (hapiladae): breeding seasons,
twinning, and sex of offspring. J. K. Hamp-
ton, jr. and S. H. Hampton. bibliog il
Science 150:915-17 N 12 '65
Study shows that twins are slower than
others. Sci N L 88:370 D 11 '65
Twins, alike as two peas? P. Williams. il
Parents Mag 40:44-5+ My '65
Will it be twins? A. F. Guttmacher. Redbook
124:20+ F '65

TWINS (baseball) See Baseball clubs

TWIST drills. See Drilling and boring machinery

TWO corpses go dancing; story. See Singer, I. B.

TWO for the money; drama. See Murray, J.

TWO-way radio. See Radio telephone, Portable

TWO-year colleges. See Junior colleges

TYKOCINSKI, Wladislaw
Exit the Gypsy Baron. por Newsweek 65:48 My 31 '65

TYLER, Anne
Everything but roses; story. Reporter 33: 47-8 S 23 '65
I'm not going to ask you again; story. Harper 231:88-98 S '65

TYLER, Nancy Carole
Silent secretary. il por Newsweek 65:32+ My 24 '65

TYLER, Stanley A. See Barghoorn, E. S. jt. auth.

TYLER, William R.
U.S. and Rumania sign cultural exchange agreement for 1965-66; text of U.S. note; December 23, 1964. Dept State Bul 52:88-90 Ja 18 '65

TYLOTRICH follicles. See Follicles

TYNAN, Kenneth
England for Sol Hurok. Esquire 63:64-5 F '65
Life movie review. Life 59:23 O 8 '65
Soho synthesis. Holiday 37:54-9 F '65

about

England's stingingest gadfly. G. Smith. il pors N Y Times Mag p26-7+ Ja 9 '66
Kenneth Tynan in the news. W. F. Buckley, jr. Nat R 18:62 Ja 25 '66

TYPE and typefounding
Monotype introduces new machinery, photo faces. il Pub W 189:97 Ja 3 '66
Shorewood's New York uses fourteen antique faces for heads. il Pub W 188:96-8+ D 6 '65

TYPESETTING
Behind the glamor of computer composition. A. E. Gardner. Pub W 188:90+ O 4 '65
PIA convention, publisher as printer; electronics house to become typesetting house; summaries of speeches. il Pub W 188:97-8+ N 8 '65
See also
Photocomposing machines
Printing—Legibility

TYPESETTING machines
Are authors obsolete? proof correction cost dispute. J. Tebbel. Sat R 48:68-9 D 11 '65
Monotype introduces new machinery, photo faces. il Pub W 189:97 Ja 3 '66
Next big jump is near in printing. il Bsns W p92 Ap 24 '65

TYPEWRITERS
New portable typewriters. il House & Gard 128:46-7 N '65
Typewriter rental; coin-operated electric ones for the use of patrons. il Library J 91:85 Ja 1 '66
Up-to-date advice on buying a portable typewriter. il Consumer Bul 48:11-17 My '65
See also
SCM corporation

TYPEWRITERS, Talking. See Teaching machines

TYPEWRITING

Study and teaching
How to teach typewriting with tape recorders; Hammond, Ind. high school. J. H. Nichols. Sr Schol 87:sup7 N 4 '65

TYPHOID fever

Preventive inoculation
Typhoid vaccination has limited use in children. Sci N L 88:147 S 4 '65

TYPOGRAPHIC errors. See Errors, Typographic

TYPOGRAPHICAL union, International. See International typographical union

TYPOGRAPHICAL workers. See Printers

TYPOGRAPHY. See Printing

TYRANNY. See Dictatorship

TYROSINE
Degeneration of the eyes of tyrosine-deficient chick embryos. C. R. Grau and others. bibliog il Science 148:1743-5 Je 25 '65
Exchange of carbon-bound hydrogen atoms ortho to the hydroxyl group in tyrosine. R. B. Martin and V. J. Morlino. bibliog Science 150:493 O 22 '65

Immunogenicity and role of size: response of guinea pigs to oligotyrosine and tyrosine derivatives. F. Borek and others. bibliog il Science 150:1177-8 N 26 '65

TYSON, Charles B.
On-site meter testing. Am City 80:113 S '65

TYSON, Robert C.
Freedom and enterprise; address, April 26, 1965. Vital Speeches 31:497-500 Je 1 '65
Profits make for growth; excerpts from address. Read Digest 86:99-101 Mr '65

U

UAW. See United automobile, aerospace and agricultural implement workers of America

UCLA. See California. University—Los Angeles campus

UCLA Neuropsychiatric institute. See Los Angeles—Hospitals

UHF television stations. See Television stations

UJA. See United Jewish appeal

UL. See Underwriters' laboratories

ULC (Université libre du Congo) See Colleges and universities—Congo (capital Leopoldville)

UMW. See United mine workers of America

UN. See United Nations

UNCTAD. See United Nations conference on trade and development

UNESCO. See United Nations educational, scientific and cultural organization

UNHCR. See United Nations—High commissioner for refugees

UNICEF. See United Nations children's fund

UNLA (National union for the struggle against illiteracy) See Education—Italy

UNRWA. See United Nations relief and works agency for Palestine refugees in the Near East

UPU. See Universal postal union

URAI. See Universities research association, incorporated

URS (Universal reference system) See Information storage and retrieval systems

URW. See United rubber, cork, linoleum and plastic workers of America

USGS. See United States—Geological survey

USIA. See United States—Information agency

USIA libraries. See American libraries abroad

USLTA. See United States lawn tennis association

USNSA. See United States national student association

USO. See United service organizations

USOE. See United States—Education, Office of

USS Glacier. See Ice breaking vessels

USWA. See United steelworkers of America

UWF. See United world federalists

UBELL, Earl
When the earth rang like a bell. Read Digest 87:179-80+ Ag '65

UCHIDA, Yoshiko
Jewelry by Margaret DePatta. Craft Horiz 25:22-5 Mr '65

UDALL, Lee
Ladies launch a gallery. I. Moore. Am For 71:22-5 Mr '65

UDALL, Stewart Lee
Duty to the future. Sat R 48:48+ My 22 '65
Ecology of man and the land ethic. Natur Hist 74:32-41 Je '65
Ending the water crisis. Sat R 48:46 O 23 '65
Interview on hunting; ed. by D. Hanson. por Suc Farm 63:6+ N '65
Now look here, voyager. Life 58:17+ Je 18 '65
Swamps can save cities. Recreation 58:308 Je '65
Worldwide cooperative effort in water desalination; address, October 4, 1965. Dept State Bul 53:716-20 N 1 '65

about

LBJ gives Udall wider role. il por Bsns W p98-100+ Ap 3 '65
Think big: open letter to the Secretary of the Interior. B. Stewart. il Harper 231:62-3 Ag '65

UEBERWASSER, Walter
Fire and water: obscurities in the late Paul Klee. Art N 64:40-1+ Sum '65

UELSMANN, Jerry
I like to present a problematical situation, and let the viewer come to grips with it; interview, ed. by H. M. Kinzer. il Pop Phot 57:140-3+ N '65
Jerry Uelsmann; involved with the celebration of life; photographs. Pop Phot 57:136-9 N '65

UGANDA
Colored rulers. G. C. Turner. Negro Hist Bul 28:201 My '65
Double intrusion; charges made that Congolese planes bombed two Ugandan villages. P. Webb. Newsweek 65:44 Mr 8 '65
See also
Hunting—Uganda
United Nations—Uganda

Description and travel
Sketches of Uganda. J. Nagenda. il Reporter 33:46-9 O 7 '65

Native races
Reporter at large: Dodoth tribe. E. M. Thomas. il New Yorker 41:51-2+ My 1; 50-2+ My 8; 61-2+ My 15; 54-6+ My 22 '65

UHDE, Hermann
Obituary
Opera N por 30:28 N 20 '65. E. Davidson

UHLENHAUT, Rudolph
Herr Uhlenhaut: the great lap forward. D. Bartley. il Esquire 63:96-9+ F '65

UHR, Jonathan W. See Scharff, M. D. jt. auth.

UKIAH, Calif.
Ground-level transformers improve city skyline. M. K. Roper. il Am City 80:100 N '65

ULANOV, Barry
Play of the month (cont) Cath World 200: 383; 201:343-4 Mr, Ag '65

ULBRICHT, Walter
Culture commissars. il por Newsweek 67: 47 Ja 17 '66

ULCERS. See Peptic ulcers

ULLMAN, Barbara
Ready when you are, H.Z! U S Camera 29: 48-51+ Ja '66

ULTRA-HIGH frequency television reception. See Television reception

ULTRA-HIGH frequency television stations. See Television stations

ULTRA-HIGH frequency television transmission. See Television transmission

ULTRAHIGH pressure. See Pressure

ULTRAHIGH vacuum. See Vacuum

ULTRASONIC interferometers. See Interferometers, Sonic

ULTRASONIC scanning. See Ultrasonic waves—Scientific applications

ULTRASONIC soldering. See Solder and soldering

ULTRASONIC transducers. See Transducers

ULTRASONIC waves
Ultrasound chemical effects on pure organic liquids. A. Weissler and others. bibliog Science 150:1288-9 D 3 '65

Medical applications
Sound technique. Newsweek 66:67 O 4 '65
Sound waves that see through people. H. Fantel. il Pop Mech 124:124-8+ O '65
Ultrasound sees tumors. A. Ewing. il Sci N L 87:389 Je 19 '65
See also
Sound waves—Medical applications

Scientific applications
Ultrasonic scanning of biologic tissue by a new technique. F. L. Thurstone and others. il Science 149:302-3 Jl 16 '65

ULTRASONICS
Moths and ultrasound. K. D. Roeder. il Sci Am 212:94-102 Ap '65

ULTRAVIOLET rays

Physiological effects
Blepharisma intermedium: ultraviolet resistance of pigmented and albino clones. A. C. Giese. bibliog il Science 149:540-1 Jl 30 '65
Case of the sunburned mannequins; with safety tips for sun worshippers. T. F. Walsh. il Todays Health 43:24-8 Ag '65
Ultraviolet damage to bacteria and bacteriophage at low temperatures. M. J. Ashwood-Smith and others. bibliog il Science 149:1103-5 S 3 '65

ULTRAVIOLET telescope. See Telescope

UMBELLIFERAE
Visnagin: biosynthesis and isolation from ammi visnagi suspension cultures. B. Kaul and E. J. Staba. bibliog il Science 150:1731-2 D 24 '65

UMBILICAL cord
Specificity of macroglobulin antibody synthesized by the normal human fetus. W. V. Epstein. bibliog il Science 148:1591-2 Je 18 '65

UMBRELLAS
Esthetics for a rainy day; the *bangasa*. il Time 87:42 Ja 7 '66

UMPIRES (sports)
Umpire's revenge. Sports Illus 22:18 My 24 '65

UMSTED, Truxtun
Fate of the America. Yachting 117:232+ Ap '65

UN-AMERICAN activities committee. See United States—Congress—House of representatives—Un-American activities committee

UNAUTHORIZED reprints. See Copyright—Unauthorized reprints

UNBORN children (law)
Unborn plaintiff. il Time 85:58+ Ap 30 '65

UNCLE Sam (nickname)
Many faces of a legend. il Sr Schol 86:5 Mr 11 '65

UNCLE Tom (term)
In defense of Uncle Toms. G. Wills. Commonweal 83:178-80 N 12 '65

UNDECLARED war. See War

UNDERACHIEVEMENT, Student. See Student achievements

UNDERDEVELOPED areas
Challenge of the developing countries; address, May 23, 1965. D. E. Bell. Dept State Bul 53:173-7 Jl 26 '65
Concept of a national market and its economic growth implications; address, September 1, 1965. W. W. Rostow. Dept State Bul 53:518-24 S 27 '65; Same. Vital Speeches 31:717-20 S 15 '65
Development decade in the balance. G. D. Woods. For Affairs 44:206-15 Ja '66
Disparities in progress among nations. T. C. Mann. Ann Am Acad 360:63-7 Jl '65
Exporting U.S. standards to underdeveloped countries. J. C. Shearer. Mo Labor R 88: 145-7 F '65
Global poverty. America 112:848 Je 12 '65
IPA education section: ways sought for international publishing aid; meeting in Frankfurt. il Pub W 188:32-8 N 22 '65
Last revolution, by L. J. Lebret. Review Commonweal 83:250-2 N 26 '65. V. C. Ferkiss
More projects than money. H. C. Wallich. Newsweek 66:96 O 18 '65
Neighbors to all the world; World neighbors, inc. achievements. C. W. Hall. il Read Digest 87:127-32 Ag '65
New era in world development. C. H. Malik. America 113:496-8 O 30 '65
Press in developing countries R. F. Rankin. il Sat R 48:124-5 S 18 '65
Role of emerging nations in world politics; address, March 15, 1965. W. W. Rostow. Dept State Bul 52:492-7 Ap 5 '65
Touch of tyranny; views of W. P. Bundy. R. F. Hamilton. Nation 201:75-8 Ag 16 '65
Toward international aid for educational publishing. R. H. Smith. Pub W 188:46 N 22 '65
Turning point; symposium. il UNESCO Courier 18:4-34 O '65
UNESCO and the world of books; program for book development. J. Behrstock. UNESCO Courier 18:21-2 S '65
Unfinished revolution: America and the third world, by C. L. Sulzberger. Review Sat R 48:42-3 Jl 24 '65. A. A. Castagno
World apartheid. T. Balasuriya. il Commonweal 83:363-6 D 24 '65
See also
Agricultural administration—Underdeveloped areas
Agriculture—Underdeveloped areas
Colleges and universities—Underdeveloped areas
Education—Underdeveloped areas
Food supply—Underdeveloped areas
Forests and forestry—Underdeveloped areas
Housing—Underdeveloped areas
Investments, Foreign (in underdeveloped areas)
Public health—Underdeveloped areas
United Nations—Technical assistance program
United States—Commerce—Underdeveloped areas
Youth—Underdeveloped areas

UNDEREMPLOYMENT. See Employment

UNDERGRADUATES. See College students

UNDERGROUND atomic testing. See Atomic bombs—Testing, Underground

UNDERGROUND drainage. See Drainage

UNDERGROUND houses. See Architecture, Domestic

UNDERGROUND living
Room at the bottom; underground homes. il Newsweek 65:87 My 3 '65

UNDERGROUND storage. See Storage, Underground

UNDERGROUND structures
Come visit the village inside a mountain. D. Francis. il Pop Phot 187:96-9+ N '65
Down with art? underground art gallery, Conn. G. O'Brien. il N Y Times Mag p 70-1 F 28 '65
Finally: an attack-proof center for U.S. defense; NORAD's Combat operations center at Cheyenne Mountain, Colo. il U S News 60:54-7 Ja 24 '66
Invisible architecture in the Paris underground; UNESCO three-story underground building. il Fortune 73:176 Ja '66
New digs; Lake Worth junior high school. Time 85:62 F 5 '65

UNDERGROUND water. See Water, Underground

UNDERHILL, A. Heaton
Land and water conservation fund; summary of address. Liv Wildn 86:47 Spr '64

UNDERPRIVILEGED children. See Socially handicapped children

UNDERTAKERS and undertaking
Another visit to the undertaker. D. Cort. il Nation 200:420-1 Ap 19 '65
Have the undertakers reformed? J. Mitford. Atlan 215:69-73 Je '65
Mortician groups fight critics, and each other; National funeral directors assn. and National selected morticians. Bsns W p34 Ag 21 '65
See also
National funeral directors association

UNDERWATER archeology. See Archeology, Submarine

UNDERWATER drilling
Ocean drilling on the continental margin; Joint oceanographic institutions' deep earth sampling program. bibliog il Science 150:709-16 N 5 '65
Phosphate may lie under continental shelf; Joint oceanographic institutions' deep earth sampling. Sci N L 88:345 N 27 '65

UNDERWATER laboratories
Deep submergence project is upgraded. H. M. David. Miss & Roc 18:18 Ja 17 '66
Exploring depths of sea and men; navy undersea project. L. Wainwright. Life 59:21 Ag 20 '65
Journey to inner space; Sealab II. il Time 86:90+ S 17 '65
Life under pressure; Sealab II. il Newsweek 66:56 S 13 '65
Man can dwell undersea. B. Tuffy. Sci N L 87:405 Je 26 '65
Man in the sea. A. F. Spilhaus; discussion. Science 146:471, 1113; 147:1396 O 23, N 27 '64, Mr 19 '65
Man tests his limits in the ocean's depths; navy's Sealab II. il Bsns W p66-8+ S 11 '65
Sealab, Gemini similar. Sci N L 88:163 S 11 '65
Sealab III target date is October. H. M. David. Miss & Roc 17:28 N 22 '65
Up from success; Sealab II and Con Shelf III. il Time 86:72 O 22 '65
What's going on down there? J. Dugan. il Holiday 37:70-9+ Je '65

UNDERWATER oil well drilling. See Oil well drilling, Submarine

UNDERWATER physiology
Can man live undersea? Sci N L 88:54 Jl 24 '65
Deep submergence project is upgraded. H. M. David. Miss & Roc 18:18 Ja 17 '66
Exploring depths of sea and men; navy undersea project. L. Wainwright. Life 59:21 Ag 20 '65
Life under pressure; Sealab II. il Newsweek 66:56 S 13 '65
Mammals that breathe under water; experimenting with liquid-filled chamber. il Sci Digest 58:18-19 Ag '65
Thirty days in Sealab. S. Carpenter. il Life 59:100A-100B+ O 15 '65
Up from success; Sealab II and Con Shelf III. il Time 86:72 O 22 '65

UNDERWATER sound system. See Hydrophones

UNDERWATER sounds. See Ocean sounds

UNDERWATER structures
See also
Underwater laboratories

UNDERWEAR
Zip, and also pop. il Time 86:67 Ag 27 '65
See also
Brassieres

UNDERWOOD, John
College basketball. Sports Illus 22:70-1 Mr 22 '65
Flying. Sports Illus 23:68-70 O 4 '65
Pro football. Sports Illus 23:46-9 Ag 9 '65

UNDERWORLD. See Crime and criminals

UNDERWRITERS' laboratories, incorporated
Public gives UL its seal of approval. il Bsns W p92+ S 18 '65

UNEMPLOYABLES
I picked apples with the unemployed; with editorial comment. G. Logsdon. il Farm J 89:36-7+, 118 N '65

UNEMPLOYMENT

Relief measures
Business pumps millions into depressed areas; job-creating investments. il Nations Bsns 53:36-7+ Mr '65
California's jackpot for the jobless. E. Selby and A. Selby. Read Digest 86:67-70 Je '65
Can subsidies solve America's problems? a city's answer, Oakland, Calif. il Nations Bsns 53:32-3+ Ag '65
See also
United States—Job corps
United States—Work projects administration

Statistics
International unemployment rates, 1960-64. A. F. Neef. bibliog f il Mo Labor R 88:256-9 Mr '65
Labor force and employment in 1964. S. S. Holland and J. R. Wetzel. il Mo Labor R 88:384-95 Ap '65

California
Affluent poor. J. Burgess. il Esquire 63:82-7+ Ap '65

Russia
Are the jobless unemployed? il Time 86:72 Ag 20 '65

United States
Almost full; dwindling steadily and less acute than some statistics show. il Time 86:103 N 12 '65
Business widens its hiring range; stockpiling of employees. il Bsns W p 125-6 D 4 '65
Double pay for overtime: robbing Peter won't give Paul a job. C. D. Long. il Nations Bsns 53:84-6 Jl '65
Employment experience of discharged defense workers. R. Brandwein. il Mo Labor R 88:1213-14 O '65
Great risk of the Great society. F. Morley. Nations Bsns 53:27-8 Mr '65
Help wanted almost everywhere; shortage of skilled workers. il Bsns W p28-9 O 16 '65
How much unemployment? il Fortune 71:34+ F '65
How they figure; statistics. Time 86:65-6 Ag 13 '65
I'm out of a job. I'm all through. B. H. Bagdikian. il Sat Eve Post 238:32-6+ D 18 '65
Long-term unemployment in the 1960's. S. S. Holland. bibliog f il Mo Labor R 88:1069-76 S '65
Myth of big-scale unemployment. il U S News 58:80-2 My 10 '65
Push for full employment. T. R. Brooks. Duns R 85:83+ My '65
Unemployed: why they started looking for work. C. L. Smith, jr. il Mo Labor R 88:1196-203 O '65
Wages and prices by formula? address. A. F. Burns. Harvard Bsns R 43:55-64 Mr '65
Wanted: 9-million new jobs. Bsns W p34 Mr 13 '65
Washington desk. J. R. Slevin. Duns R 85:5-6 Mr '65
What's happened to the will to work? il Nations Bsns 53:56-8+ My '65
When the war is over, mass job program and negative income tax. New Repub 154:7 Ja 1 '66
Where the jobs are & are not. il Time 85:85 Ap 16 '65
Who's working, who's not; hard facts on unemployment. U S News 58:87-9 F 15 '65
See also
Labor supply—United States

UNEMPLOYMENT, Technological
Automation: a job creator not a job destroyer; excerpts from address. Y. Brozen. il U S News 58:94-8 Mr 8 '65
Automation and jobs. R. Cissell and H. Cissell. il America 112:459-61 Ap 3 '65
Automation and jobs. il Sr Schol 87:12-14 N 11 '65
Automation is here to liberate us. E. Hoffer. il N Y Times Mag p48-9+ O 24 '65

UNEMPLOYMENT, Technological—*Continued*
Automation panel splits on report. Bsns W p66 D 25 '65
How steel jobs are dwindling; computer-controlled mills. il Bsns W p75-6+ Ag 14 '65
I'm out of a job, I'm all through. B. H. Bagdikian. il Sat Eve Post 238:32-6+ D 18 '65
Jeremiahs and pacifiers. Nation 200:127 F 8 '65
Manpower implications of technological change. Mo Labor R 88:III-IV F '65
Productivity of labor and industry; reprint from March 1929 issue. E. Stewart. Mo Labor R 88:793-4 Jl '65
Take charge of your career. R. Dunlop. Pop Mech 124:20+ Ag '65
Technology and the labor market. il Fortune 71:153-5+ F; 130-3+ Ap; 112-15+ My; 72:156-61+ Ag '65
Ten corporations and automation; report on questions sent to presidents of twenty California corporations. A. Juvinall. Christian Cent 82:271-3 Mr 3 '65
Time to kill, automation, leisure and jobs. E. Larrabee. Nation 201:198-202 S 20 '65
Town that wouldn't stay down; Richland, Wash, and its sister cities. il U S News 59:96-7 Jl 19 '65
Worker reaction to job displacement; adaptation of address. H. L. Sheppard. Mo Labor R 88:170-2 F '65
UNEMPLOYMENT benefits, Supplemental. See Supplemental unemployment benefits
UNEMPLOYMENT insurance. See Insurance, Unemployment
UNFINISHED diary; story. See Schwab. H.
UNFINISHED furniture. See Furniture
UNGER, Leonard
Thinking about her poems again; poem. Nation 200:483 My 3 '65
UNGER, Leonard, 1917-
Present objectives and future possibilities in southeast Asia; address, April 19, 1965. Dept State Bul 52:712-19 My 10 '65
UNGRADED classes
Meeting children where they are; nongraded classes at University elementary school. University of California, Los Angeles. J. I. Goodlad. il Sat R 48:57-9+ Mr 20 '65
Nongraded school. S. E. Dean. bibliog f il Sch Life 47:19-23 D '64
School for the future; Garden Springs elementary school, Lexington, Ky. C. Brossard. il Look 29:55-6+ Mr 9 '65
UNHAPPINESS. See Happiness
UNICORN plants
Unicorn still lives! R. Gatzke. Flower Grower 52:42 D '65
UNIDENTIFIED flying objects. See Flying saucers
UNIFON alphabet. See Alphabet
UNIFORM state laws
Interstate relations, some emergent trends. P. Monypenny. bibliog f Ann Am Acad 359:53-9 My '65
UNIFORMS, Police
Smartness in police uniform; Covina, Calif. il Am City 80:22 Jl '65
UNION activities. See Trade unions—Activities
UNION bank of Switzerland. See Banks and banking—Switzerland
UNION carbide and carbon corporation
Business gets eye-to-eye by phone; Picturephone. il Bsns W p30-1 Ag 14 '65
Specialist wheels the biggest stock deal; $17.3-million transaction in Union carbide. il Bsns W p 156+ My 22 '65
There is life at Union carbide. il Time 85:86 Je 18 '65
Union carbide breaks out of an earnings rut. il Bsns W p 174 O 9 '65
Union carbide's patient schemers; with portfolio. G. Burck. Fortune 72:146-53+ D '65
UNION catalog of Library of Congress. See United States—Library of Congress—Union catalog
UNIÓN de trabajadores de Colombia. See Trade unions—Colombia
UNION for research and experimentation in higher education
Union of experimental colleges. Sch & Soc 93:239 Ap 17 '65
UNION international motorboating. See Motor boat racing
UNION oil company of California
Curious pursuit of Pure oil. T. A. Wise. il Fortune 72:112-15+ Jl '65
Pure's stockholders ask for more. il Bsns W p58-60 Ap 17 '65
UNION publications. See Trade unions—Publications
UNION scholarship programs. See Scholarships and fellowships

UNION shops. See Open and closed shop
UNION wide collective bargaining. See Collective bargaining, Industry wide
UNITARIAN Universalist association
Unitarian religiocentricity. Christian Cent 82:387 Mr 31 '65; Discussion. 82:715-17 Je 2 '65
UNITAS, Johnny
Big man in Baltimore. T. Cohane. il pors Look 29:90+ S 21 '65
UNITED air lines
Record jet sale: what it means to air travel. il U S News 58:16 Ap 19 '65
Seat pallet van is developed for 727QC. R. G. O'Lone. il Aviation W 83:66-7 N 1 '65
United begins equipment program; all-jet carrier by 1970. J. W. Carter. il Aviation W 82:38+ Ap 12 '65
United bets a bundle; contracting for $750-million worth of new jet planes by 1970. Bsns W p36 Ap 10 '65
United charts a new flight plan; G. E. Keck replaces W. A. Patterson next April. il Bsns W p 128-30+ Ag 14 '65
United expands use of leasing. Aviation W 82:39 My 17 '65
United for Boeing; choice of a short-range jet. il Newsweek 65:80 Ap 19 '65
United order stresses spending requirements. W. H. Gregory. Aviation W 82:39 Ap 12 '65
United uses underground service system; renovations at San Francisco international airport. il Aviation W 82:49+ My 10 '65
Univac flies with United. Bsns W p33 D 25 '65
UNITED aircraft corporation
Roll extrusion method chosen for UTC 120-in. Motor case. J. F. Judge. il Miss & Roc 17:24-5 D 20 '65

Pratt and Whitney aircraft division
P&W seen continuing JTF-14E effort. il Aviation W 83:67+ D 6 '65
UNITED ARAB REPUBLIC
See also
Economic assistance in the United Arab Republic
UNITED automobile, aerospace and agricultural implement workers of America
End of a long, bitter dispute: will Kohler have labor peace? il U S News 60:70-1 Ja 3 '66
Helping the have nots; members ready for on-scene trouble shooting in foreign auto production centers. Newsweek 66:88 N 22 '65
How workers like early retirement. il U S News 59:96-8+ O 18 '65
Is auto union asking a veto? il U S News 59:77-8 S 6 '65
Reuther pushes toward an old goal; merger of UAW and IUE. Bsns W p 128 F 20 '65
Reuther's offer to IUE: one stronger union; UAW-IUE merger proposal. Bsns W p28 F 13 '65
Sour notes mar auto pact harmony; disputes over GM's cancellation of strikers' Christmas bonus, and Ford plant's white-collar organizers. Bsns W p 108 D 18 '65
Union tactics stall justice thirteen years. il Nations Bsns 53:31-3 N '65
UAW expected to stress job security. W. H. Gregory. Aviation W 82:55+ Mr 29 '65
UAW faces GM abroad; sends negotiator to help Australian unions. Bsns W p 126+ D 4 '65
UAW mounts campaign against monopsony; vs Detroit's Big three. Bsns W p43-4 Jl 24 '65
UNITED cement, lime and gypsum workers international union
Cement workers win thirty-five cents gain. Bsns W p 140 Je 12 '65
UNITED church of Christ
Agony and the wild cry; worship service, Chicago's First congregational church. Christian Cent 82:910 Jl 21 '65; Discussion. 82:1070-2, 1211-12, 1516 S 1, O 6, D 8 '65
Biased broadcaster put on probation; United church of Christ petition to F.C.C. Christian Cent 82:732-3 Je 9 '65
It pays to advertise. Time 86:106+ S 17 '65
Justice and beyond justice; United church's Council for Christian social action. Christian Cent 82:227-8 F 24 '65; Reply with rejoinder. R. M. Davidson. 82:436 Ap 7 '65
United church of Christ general synod: ministries approved. M. Frakes. Christian Cent 82:919-20+ Jl 21 '65
UNITED church of Christ in Japan
Missionary exodus from Japan? R. H. Drummond. Christian Cent 82:672-4 My 26 '65; Discussion. 82:892; 83:19-20+ Jl 14 '65, Ja 5 '66

UNITED daughters of the confederacy
Georgia jinx. J. Dabney. il Travel 123:47-51
Je '65

UNITED federation of teachers
Case for teachers' unions; excerpt from address. G. Brooks; discussion. Mo Labor R
87:543; 88:535-6 My '64, My '65

UNITED hatters, cap and millinery workers
international union
Millinery workers put heads together. il
Bsns W p60 Je 19 '65

UNITED Jewish appeal
Miracle of Jewish giving. Fortune 73:149 Ja
'66

UNITED mine workers of America
Way is hard for union insurgents. J. Ridge-
way. New Repub 152:9-10 F 27 '65
Wildcats in coal start pulling in their claws;
UMW walkouts after firing of six men.
Bsns W p 168 S 25 '65

UNITED mine workers of America welfare and
retirement fund
Brighter picture for miners' fund. U S News
59:72 Ag 23 '65

UNITED NATIONS
Addendum on the U.N. Christian Cent 82:637
My 19 '65
Advancing the goals of the U.N. charter;
address, October 26, 1965. A. J. Goldberg.
Dept State Bul 53:868-71 N 29 '65
Ambassador Goldberg holds news conference
at New York; transcript of conference,
July 28, 1965; with questions and answers.
A. J. Goldberg. Dept State Bul 53:272-4+
Ag 16 '65
Can the U.N. be saved? N. Cousins. Sat R
48:32 F 13 '65
China's presence at the UN; decay of old
alliances, birth of new alignments. P. Ben.
New Repub 153:9-10 O 2 '65
Commemoration; addresses delivered at the
meetings held in San Francisco on June 25
and June 26 to commemorate the twentieth
anniversary of the signing of the United
Nations charter. il UN Mo Chron 2:73-175
Jl '65
Crisis in the United Nations; address, De-
cember 10, 1964. C. B. Luce. Vital Speeches
31:236-41 F 1 '65
Days ahead for the United Nations; address,
September 19, 1965. J. J. Sisco. Dept State
Bul 53:636-40 O 18 '65
Do we really need the UN? A. Eban. il Look
29:75-6 Je 29 '65
Fall and rise of the U.N. D. Lawrence.
U S News 59:88 Jl 5 '65
From LBJ: a call for U.N. help; excerpts
from address, June 25, 1965. L. B. John-
son. U S News 59:8 Jl 5 '65
Fundamental meaning of the United Nations;
world of law and justice; address, June 23,
1965. A. E. Stevenson. Vital Speeches 31:
615-17 Ag 1 '65
Future of peacekeeping. A. Larson. il Sat R
48:22-3+ Jl 24 '65
Future of the United Nations; problems of
Asia & Rhodesia; address, December 16,
1965. H. Wilson. Vital Speeches 32:162-7
Ja 1 '66
Goal of the United Nations; a Great society
for all men; statement, September 23, 1965.
A. J. Goldberg. Dept State Bul 53:578-87
O 11 '65
Governor at work at the U.N; role of A. E.
Stevenson. M. Mayer. il N Y Times Mag
p22-3+ F 7 '65
Hard choices at the U.N; address, February
27, 1965. J. J. Sisco. Dept State Bul 52:460-
5 Mr 29 '65; Same. Vital Speeches 31:357-60
Ap 1 '65
Harmonizing functions of the United Na-
tions; address read at the convocation of
Queen's university, Kingston, Ontario, May
22, 1965. Thant. UN Mo Chron 2:102-4 Je
'65
Here's Pope Paul's historic message to the
United Nations; tr. of address, October 4,
1965. Paul VI. il U S News 59:84-8 O 18
'65; Same with title Message for humanity.
Vital Speeches 32:2-4 O 15 '65; Same with
title Address of Pope Paul VI to the
United Nations. UN Mo Chron 2:65-70 N
'65
How to stop the war yet assure peace. D.
Lawrence. il U S News 59:112 Ag 9 '65
In twenty years: rise and decline of the U.N.
il U S News 58:40-2 Je 28 '65
Indestructibility of the U.N. W. Lippmann.
Newsweek 66:27 O 25 '65
International co-operation: twenty years
after the San Francisco conference; ad-
dress. A. Lleras Camargo. UN Mo Chron
2:63-73 F '65
Introduction to the annual report of the
Secretary-General on the work of the orga-
nization. Thant. UN Mo Chron 2:92-117 O
'65

Is the U.N. dying? constitutional crisis. H.
E. Fey. Christian Cent 82:263-4 Mr 3 '65
Limits of the U.N. P. Ben. Reporter 34:
32-3 Ja 13 '66
Man who wasn't there; text of a radio programme first produced in 1955; hopes and
ideals surrounding the creation of the
United Nations. UN Mo Chron 2:93-101 Je
'65
Meanwhile back at the UN; apathy of the
press. Nation 200:181-2 F 22 '65
Meeting U.N. crises: let us seek basic solutions. J. W. Pomerance. Bul Atomic Sci
21:31-2 My '65
Meetings for [month] See issues of UN
monthly chronicle
Moment of reflection; Pope Paul's visit to
the United Nations; with text of papal
brief presented to the Secretary-General
and text of address. il UN Mo Chron 2:
57-70 N '65
Mounting trouble for U.N; is it facing collapse? il U S News 58:52-4 F 22 '65
No. 1 crisis: UN peace-keeping role in
jeopardy. N. Cousins. Sat R 48:26+ Je 19
'65
Notes of the month. See issues of UN monthly chronicle
Of ghosts and the UN. America 112:417 Mr
27 '65
Ominous laughs in Dag's cracked mirror.
Life 58:4 F 26 '65
Ordeal of the U.N. E. J. Hughes. Newsweek
65:19 Mr 8 '65
Peace and pathos; study of Pope John's
encyclical Pacem in terris. N. O'Gorman.
Commonweal 81:783-5 Mr 19 '65
Peace comes in parcels; address, March 31,
1965. H. Cleveland. Dept State Bul 52:613-
18 Ap 26 '65
Peace on earth; address, February 17, 1965.
H. H. Humphrey. Vital Speeches 31:322-5
Mr 15 '65; Same. Dept State Bul 52:326-32
Mr 8 '65
Problems of peace-making; address, Septem-
ber 9, 1965. Thant. UN Mo Chron 2:118-22
O '65
Prospects of law in a world of conflict; ad-
dress, April 29, 1965. L. C. Meeker. Dept
State Bul 52:900-5 Je 7 '65
Rediscovery of the UN. Nation 200:433 Ap 26
'65
Second Dublin declaration; text, with edi-
torial note. Sat R 48:28-9 D 11 '65
Secretary urges ratification of U.N. charter
amendments; statement, April 28, 1965. D.
Rusk. Dept State Bul 52:827-30 My 24 '65
Society for all men; address, September 23,
1965. A. J. Goldberg. Vital Speeches 32:34-9
N 1 '65
State of affairs; crisis of the world organiza-
tion and U Thant's warnings. H. Brandon.
Sat R 48:10+ Jl 24 '65
Third force and the United Nations. K. I.
Babaa. bibliog f il Ann Am Acad 362:81-91
N '65
Toward a better life in larger freedom;
statement, October 15, 1965. J. Roosevelt.
Dept State Bul 53:798-805 N 15 '65
Turning point; symposium. il UNESCO
Courier 18:4-34 O '65
Twentieth anniversary of the United Nations;
address, June 25, 1965. L. B. Johnson. Dept
State Bul 53:98-101 Jl 19 '65; Excerpts.
U S News 59:8 Jl 5 '65
Unhappy birthday; 20th anniversary celebra-
tion in San Francisco. Time 86:15 Jl 2
'65
U.N. after Kashmir. Commonweal 83:45 O 15
'65
U.N. an effective arm of U.S. foreign policy;
address, November 3, 1965. P. H. B. Fre-
linghuysen. Dept State Bul 53:1021-8 D 27
'65
UN at twenty; with editorial comment. A.
Weill-Tuckerman; A. Gabriel. il Nation 200:
685, 690-6 Je 28 '65
U.N: battered, broke, alive. il Newsweek 66:
17-18 Jl 5 '65
United Nations' future: a Christian concern.
A. G. Mower, jr. Christian Cent 82:800-2 Je
23 '65
United Nations in a changing world; ad-
dress, February 1965. Thant. UN Mo Chron
2:41-6 Mr '65
U.N. of Dag Hammarskjöld is dead. H. J.
Morgenthau. il N Y Times Mag p32-3+
Mr 14 '65
U.N. out of its teens. I. D. Talmadge. il Sr
Schol 87:16-17+ S 16 '65
UN peacekeeping. Commonweal 81:753 Mr 12
'65
UN power shifts: decline of the unaligned.
A. Weill-Tuckerman. Nation 201:488-90 D
20 '65

UNITED NATIONS—*Continued*

U.N: prospects beyond paralysis; Time essay. Time 85:26-7 Ap 2 '65

U.N. revision? Commonweal 81:683-4 F 26 '65

U.N: the next twenty years; symposium. il Sat R 48:21-35+ Jl 24 '65

U.N. tries hard, but—; letter to a friend in London. D. Middleton. il N Y Times Mag p28-9+ Ja 9 '66

U.N.'s unhappy birthday. Sr Schol 87:38-9 S 30 '65

United States reviews the U.N. constitutional crisis; statement, January 26, 1965. A. E. Stevenson. Dept State Bul 52:198-206 F 15 '65

Using the United Nations; the endless task of reconciliation; adaptation of address. B. V. Cohen. New Repub 152:13-16 My 8 '65

View from the world bridge: big power competition; address, December 3, 1964. P. Frederick. Vital Speeches 31:265-7 F 15 '65

Whatever became of the United Nations? America 113:235 S 4 '65

What's wrong with the U.N. Christian Cent 82:603-5 My 12 '65

What's wrong with the U.N. il Sat Eve Post 238:94 F 13 '65

Why the U.N. survives. S. Harrington. Commonweal 82:527-9 Jl 23 '65

World federalists view the U.N. H. Y. Williams. Christian Cent 82:992-3 Ag 11 '65

See also

World health organization

Advisory committee on the application of science and technology to development

Concerted attack proposed. UN Mo Chron 2:59-60 My '65

Science and technology; session in Paris. UN Mo Chron 2:47-8 Ap '65

Armed forces

Books; from Suez to the Congo. L. S. Finkelstein. Bul Atomic Sci 21:36-7 My '65

Hard choices at the U.N; address, February 27, 1965. J. J. Sisco. Dept State Bul 52:460-5 Mr 29 '65

Peacekeeping operations; address, November 24, 1965. A. J. Goldberg. Vital Speeches 32:167-70 Ja 1 '66

Peace-keeping operations; Special political committee hears statements by Ireland, Liberia and Ceylon. UN Mo Chron 2:29-32 N '65

Preserving the peacekeeping powers of the General assembly; statement, June 15, 1965. F. T. P. Plimpton. Dept State Bul 53:218-20 Ag 2 '65

U.N: hope for the future; remarks, February 19, 1965. H. Cleveland. Dept State Bul 52:380-1 Mr 15 '65

U.S. finds U.N. majority unwilling to enforce article 19; statement, August 16, 1965. A. J. Goldberg. Dept State Bul 53:454-7 S 13 '65

Weaponry of quiet diplomacy. A. W. Cordier. il Sat R 48:28-9+ Jl 24 '65

Forces in Cyprus

Cyprus; Security council extends UNFICYP. UN Mo Chron 2:11-17 Jl '65

Security council extends UNFICYP; with text of resolution. UN Mo Chron 2:3-17 Ap '65

Security council renews mandate of Cyprus peacekeeping force; statement, March 19, 1965; with text of resolution. A. E. Stevenson. Dept State Bul 52:551-4 Ap 12 '65

U.N. extension of Cyprus peace force; text of approved resolution. Cur Hist 48:301 My '65

Budget

See United Nations—Finance

Charter

Amending U.N. charter to enlarge Security council and ECOSOC; message, April 6, 1965. L. B. Johnson. Dept State 52:678-81 My 3 '65

Birth of the U.N. A. Eden. il N Y Times Mag p 12-13+ Je 20 '65

Charter day 1965; message. Thant. UN Mo Chron 2:i-ii Jl '65

Charter review conference; committee's recommendations. UN Mo Chron 2:31 O '65

Crisis in the United Nations; over solvency and Article nineteen. C. B. Luce. il McCalls 92:28+ S '65

De Gaulle proposes U.N. revision. Christian Cent 82:198 F 17 '65

New era in world development. C. H. Malik. America 113:496-8 O 30 '65

New ideas for a new world; address. Thant. il Sat R 48:24-5 Jl 24 '65

Peace-keeping: a new chapter? J. A. Joyce. Christian Cent 82:306-8 Mr 10 '65

Secretary urges ratification of U.N. charter amendments; statement, April 28, 1965. D. Rusk. Dept State Bul 52:827-30 My 24 '65

United Nations charter; amendments go into effect. UN Mo Chron 2:24-5 Ag '65

United Nations charter; twentieth anniversary commemorated. UN Mo Chron 2:3 Jl '65

United Nations in a changing world; address, February 1965. Thant. UN Mo Chron 2:41-6 Mr '65

U.S. states views on procedures to amend U.N. charter; statement, September 16, 1965. S. M. Finger. Dept State Bul 53:642-3 O 18 '65

Up-dating the pre-atomic United Nations; address, June 20, 1965. C. P. Romulo. Vital Speeches 31:658-61 Ag 15 '65; Excerpts. Sat R 48:34-5+ Jl 24 '65

Commission on human rights

Commission on human rights; twenty-first session. UN Mo Chron 2:39 Ap '65; 62-4 My '65

See also

United Nations—Sub-commission on prevention of discrimination and protection of minorities

Commission on the status of women

Commission on the status of women; eighteenth session. UN Mo Chron 2:42-5 Ap '65

Expanding the participation of women in national life; eighteenth session, Tehran, Iran, March 1-20, 1965. G. A. Tillett. Dept State Bul 53:39-44 Jl 5 '65

Family law and the women of Africa; U.N. seminar on the status of women in family law, Lomé, Togo. G. A. Tillett. Dept State Bul 52:229-33 F 15 '65

Journey to Mongolia; Seminar on participation of women in public life. G. A. Tillett. Dept State Bul 53:918-23 D 6 '65

Committee for industrial development

Fifth session. UN Mo Chron 2:76-7 Je '65

Committee of twenty-four

See United Nations—Special committee on the situation with regard to implementation of declaration on granting of independence to colonial countries and peoples

Committee on housing, building and planning

Housing committee holds third session. UN Mo Chron 2:37-8 O '65

Committee on the peaceful uses of outer space

Committee holds seventh session. UN Mo Chron 2:34-5 N '65

International regulation of outer space activities. E. Galloway. il Bul Atomic Sci 21:36-9 F '65

Committee on the question of defining aggression

Committee on the question of defining aggression. UN Mo Chron 2:26-32 My '65

Development programme

Development programme created; combining the Expanded programme of technical assistance and the Special fund. UN Mo Chron 2:88-91 D '65

General assembly establishes U.N. development program; statement, November 22, 1965. J. Roosevelt. Dept State Bul 53:958-9 D 13 '65

1965 pledging conference. UN Mo Chron 2:91-2 D '65

$200 million target sought. UN Mo Chron 2:92-3 D '65

United Nations development programme; statement. Thant. UN Mo Chron 2:121-3 D '65

Disarmament commission

Commission adopts resolutions. UN Mo Chron 2:17-31 Jl '65

Disarmament at the U.N. H. A. Jack. Christian Cent 82:991-2 Ag 11 '65

Disarmament commission concludes general debate. UN Mo Chron 2:27-45 Je '65

Disarmament commission convenes. UN Mo Chron 2:3-10 My '65

Disarmament conference; United States position; address. A. E. Stevenson. Vital Speeches 31:482-8 Je 1 '65

UNDC: for a world disarmament conference. H. A. Jack. Bul Atomic Sci 21:39-40 S '65

UNITED NATIONS—Disarmament commission
—*Continued*
U.S. agrees to discuss holding of world disarmament conference; statements, November 18, and November 23, 1965; with text of resolution. W. C. Foster; A. J. Goldberg. Dept State Bul 53:1029-34 D 27 '65

Economic and financial committee
Campaign for world literacy. UN Mo Chron 2:96-7 D '65
International perspective on the world economy; statement, October 5, 1965. P. De Seynes. UN Mo Chron 2:146-58 N '65
Record of the month. UN Mo Chron 2:92-6 D '65
World economic problems; discussion. UN Mo Chron 2:37-40 N '65

Economic and social council
Amending U.S. charter to enlarge Security council and ECOSOC; message, April 6, 1965. L. B. Johnson. Dept State Bul 52:678-81 My 3 '65
Vision of a world economy. A. Gabriel. il Nation 200:694-6 Je 28 '65

Meetings, 1965
Economic and social council; resumption of thirty-seventh session. UN Mo Chron 2:35-8 Ap '65
Economic and social council; summer sessions. UN Mo Chron 2:36-9 Ag '65
ECOSOC, thirty-ninth session in Geneva. UN Mo Chron 2:59 Jl '65
International concern for social justice and human rights; statement, July 25, 1965. F. H. Williams. Dept State Bul 53:532-6 S 27 '65
39th session resumed. UN Mo Chron 2:103-4 D '65

Economic commission for Africa
African economic community; East African economic community suggested. UN Mo Chron 2:124 D '65
Seventh session. UN Mo Chron 2:34-6 Mr '65

Economic commission for Asia and the Far East
Asian development bank. UN Mo Chron 2: 48-9 Ag '65
ECAFE; twenty-first session. UN Mo Chron 2:46-7 Ap '65
Mekong work in Cambodia. UN Mo Chron 2:106 D '65
Sharing the wealth. Newsweek 66:57-8 N 8 '65
Vietnam: the fourth course; international cooperation in science. G. F. White; reply. H. Newcombe. Bul Atomic Sci 21:29-30 S '65

Economic commission for Europe
Adoption of report to economic and social council; conclusion of twentieth session. UN Mo Chron 2:70-2 Je '65

Economic commission for Latin America
Eleventh session held in Mexico City. UN Mo Chron 2:72-3 Je '65
Latin America: myths and realities; address, May 13, 1965. G. A. Costanzo. Vital Speeches 31:551-4 Jl 1 '65

Expanded program of technical assistance
See United Nations—Technical assistance program

Expert committee on South Africa
Apartheid in South Africa; concerning report of expert committee. UN Mo Chron 2:23-30 Ap '65

Finance
Back in business. Time 86:21 Ag 27 '65
Backdown; end of dues dispute. Newsweek 66:45 Ag 30 '65
Budget estimates for 1966. il UN Mo Chron 2:49-52 Ag; 106-17 D '65
Clearing the slate at the U.N; with editorial comment. il Bsns W p32-3, 144 Ag 21 '65
Collection of contributions; summaries of letters to Secretary-General by member states. UN Mo Chron 2:11-15 F '65
Crisis in the United Nations; over solvency and Article nineteen. C. B. Luce. il McCalls 92:28+ S '65
Goldberg at the UN; diplomacy as the art of the possible. N. McKitterick. New Repub 153:13-15 S 11 '65 Reply. H. M. Pachter. 153:38 S 25 '65
Let the U.N. handle it; peace-keeping in Vietnam; with editorial comment. H. S. Reuss. Commonweal 82:515-16, 523-6 Jl 23 '65

Lost session at the U.N; dues dispute. M. Greenfield. il Reporter 32:14-20 My 6 '65
Other side has a case; Soviet position on United Nations assessments. C. Soule. Christian Cent 82:803-5 Je 23 '65
Peace-keeping costs; address, August 16, 1965. A. J. Goldberg. Vital Speeches 31:674-6 S 1 '65
Supplementary estimates for 1964. UN Mo Chron 2:49-53 N '65
Thunderous silence; back assessments of Russia and France. Time 86:31 D 3 '65
UN abused. New Repub 152:5-7 F 13 '65; Reply with rejoinder. H. Cleveland. 152: 25-9 Ap 24 '65
U.N: hope for the future; remarks, February 19, 1965. H. Cleveland. Dept State Bul 52: 380-1 Mr 15 '65
U.S. finds U.N. majority unwilling to enforce article 19; statement, August 16, 1965. A. J. Goldberg. Dept State Bul 53:454-7 S 13 '65
United States reviews the U.N. constitutional crisis; statement, January 26, 1965. A. E. Stevenson. Dept State Bul 52:198-206 F 15 '65
Weaponry of quiet diplomacy. A. W. Cordier. il Sat R 48:28-9+ Jl 24 '65
What is left of the United Nations now. il U S News 59:34-5 Ag 30 '65

General assembly
U.N. calls for renewed efforts on non-proliferation treaty; statements, October 18, 27 and November 8, 1965; with text of resolution. W. C. Foster. Dept State Bul 53:873-84 N 29 '65
U.N.'s gobbledygook. D. Lawrence. U S News 60:82 Ja 3 '66

Sessions (19th)
Alex Quaison-Sackey: UN's first black president. il Ebony 20:198-200+ My '65
Back into limbo; procedural vote allowed. il Time 85:31 F 26 '65
Backdown by the U.S. at the U.N; procedural vote. U S News 58:9 Mr 1 '65
Decisions taken in February. UN Mo Chron 2:3-33 Mr '65
Embarrassed & embittered. Time 85:27 F 19 '65
General debate; summaries of representatives' statements, with replies (cont) UN Mo Chron 2:23-46 F '65
Lost session at the U.N; dues dispute. M. Greenfield. il Reporter 32:14-20 My 6 '65
Nineteenth session reconvenes. UN Mo Chron 2:3-6 F '65
U.N: a concession to recess. il Newsweek 65:41 Mr 1 '65
U.N. General assembly recesses; statements, February 18, 1965. A. E. Stevenson. Dept State Bul 52:354-5 Mr 8 '65

Sessions (20th)
Back in business. il Time 86:36 O 1 '65
Cautious optimism. Sr Schol 87:14-15 O 7 '65
Convened: opening day. New Yorker 41:41-2 O 2 '65
Farewell to no. 20. Time 86:22 D 31 '65
General assembly adopts resolution; co-operation with OAU. UN Mo Chron 2:17 N '65
General assembly; conclusion of nineteenth session; opening of twentieth session. UN Mo Chron 2:23-9 O '65
General assembly twentieth regular session; notes on the provisional agenda. UN Mo Chron 2:71-96 Ag '65
General debate; summaries of representatives statements. UN Mo Chron 2:39-91 O; 71-145 N '65
Issues before the 20th General assembly. bibliog f il Int Concil 554:5-191 S '65
Provisional agenda of twentieth session of U.N. General assembly. Dept State Bul 53: 457-60 S 13 '65
Record of the month. UN Mo Chron 2:46-66 D '65
Supplementary list of items proposed for U.N. agenda. Dept State Bul 53:529 S 27 '65

High commissioner for refugees
Contributions to refugee programmes. il UN Mo Chron 2:36-8 Mr '65
High commissioner. New Yorker 41:51-2 D 11 '65
U.S. objectives and refugee relief programs in Africa; statements, January 21, 1965. G. M. Williams; A. P. Schwartz. Dept State Bul 52:219-28 F 15 '65

International law commission
International law commission; seventeenth session. UN Mo Chron 2:53-4 Ag '65
Sixth committee recommendations; Law commission reports. UN Mo Chron 2:53-4 N '65

UNITED NATIONS—*Continued*

Legal affairs, Office of

Conventions and agreements; list. UN Mo Chron 2:87 F '65

Legal committee

League of Nations treaties; Assembly adopts resolution. UN Mo Chron 2:117-18 D '65
League of Nations treaties; recommendations of Sixth committee. UN Mo Chron 2:54-5 N '65
Sixth committee recommendations; Law commission reports. UN Mo Chron 2:53-4 N '65
Special committee on wider appreciation of international law. UN Mo Chron 2:15 F '65
Technical assistance to promote study of international law. UN Mo Chron 2:118-19 D '65

Membership

Alternative to anarchy. C. M. Eichelberger. il Sat R 48:35+ Jl 24 '65
Malaise of sovereignty. A. Weill-Tuckerman. il Nation 200:690-4 Je 28 '65
Other side has a case; Soviet position on United Nations assessments. C. Soule. Christian Cent 82:803-5 Je 23 '65
United Nations procedures and power realities: the international apportionment problem; address, April 23, 1965. R. N. Gardner. Dept State Bul 52:701-11 My 10 '65

Non-governmental organizations

Role of non-governmental organizations in the United Nations. UN Mo Chron 2:79-82 My '65

Political and security committee

Committee considers draft resolutions; non-proliferation of nuclear weapons. UN Mo Chron 2:18-23 N '65
First committee adopts resolution; nuclear tests suspension. UN Mo Chron 2:66-70 D '65
First committee considers twenty-seven power draft resolution; denuclearization of Africa. UN Mo Chron 2:70-2 D '65

Population commission

Population commission; thirteenth session. UN Mo Chron 2:45-6 Ap '65; 57-9 My '65

Publications

1963 World trade annual. UN Mo Chron 2: 9-10 F '65

Bibliography

Current U.N. documents: a selected bibliography. See issues of Department of state bulletin
Documents; selected list. See issues of UN monthly chronicle
Recent publications; descriptive list. See issues of UN monthly chronicle

Security council

Amending U.N. charter to enlarge Security council and ECOSOC: message, April 6, 1965. L. B. Johnson. Dept State Bul 52:678-81 My 3 '65
Dominican situation; jurisdiction of the regional organization. F. V. García Amador. il Américas 17:1-3 Jl '65
Same mandate, a different world. R. C. Hottelet. il Sat R 48:26-7+ Jl 24 '65
Security council authorizes U.N. representative in Dominican Republic: statements, May 3-5, 1965; with text of resolution adopted May 14, 1965. A. E. Stevenson. bibliog f Dept State Bul 52:869-85 My 31 '65
Security council urged to respond to challenge in southeast Asia; letter, July 30, 1965. A. J. Goldberg. Dept State Bul 53:278-80 Ag 16 '65
U.N. Security council demands cease-fire between armed forces of India and Pakistan; statements, September 17, 18, 20 and 22, 1965; with text of resolution. A. J. Goldberg. Dept State Bul 53:602-8 O 11 '65
United States supports call for India-Pakistan cease-fire; statements, September 4 and September 6, 1965, with texts of resolutions. A. J. Goldberg. Dept State Bul 53:526-9 S 27 '65

Meetings, 1964

Resolutions on the Congo; excerpts from the O.A.U. resolution, September 10 and text of the Security council resolution, December 30, 1964. Cur Hist 48:237-8 Ap '65

Meetings, 1965

Council considers situation; conditions in the Dominican Republic. UN Mo Chron 2:10-16 Ag '65

India-Pakistan question. il UN Mo Chron 2:2-23 O '65
New hope, new purpose; emergency meeting on the India-Pakistan war. il Newsweek 66:25-7 O 4 '65
Record of the month:
  Cyprus. UN Mo Chron 2:31-8 D '65
  India-Pakistan question. UN Mo Chron 2:26-31 D '65
  Portuguese territories. UN Mo Chron 2: 38-46 D '65
  Southern Rhodesia. UN Mo Chron 2:3-4 26 D '65
Record of the month. UN Mo Chron 2:3-35 Ap '65
Security council adopts resolution; question of Cyprus. UN Mo Chron 2:3-10 Ag '65
Security council calls for prevention of unilateral declaration of independence; situation in Southern Rhodesia. UN Mo Chron 2: 13-21 Je '65
Security council considers situation; conditions in the Dominican Republic. il UN Mo Chron 2:3-12 Je '65
Security council considers situation; problem of Southern Rhodesia. UN Mo Chron 2:37-9 My '65
Security council renews mandate of Cyprus peacekeeping force; statement, March 19, 1965; with text of resolution. A. E. Stevenson. Dept State Bul 52:551-4 Ap 12 '65
Security council resumes consideration; India-Pakistan question. UN Mo Chron 2:3-12 N '65
Senegal's complaint against Portugal. UN Mo Chron 2:21-7 Je '65

Sixth committee

See United Nations—Legal committee

Social commission

Adoption of report to Economic and social council. UN Mo Chron 2:74-6 Je '65

Social, humanitarian and cultural committee

Discussions in Third committee. UN Mo Chron 2:40-6 N '65
Record of the month. UN Mo Chron 2:97-103 D '65

Special committee on peace-keeping operations

Committee adopts report to Assembly. UN Mo Chron 2:17-24 Ag '65
Committee hears statements; peace-keeping operations. UN Mo Chron 2:72-6 D '65
Meeting of Special committee. UN Mo Chron 2:45-51 Je '65
Peace-keeping operations. UN Mo Chron 2: 10-21 My '65
Peace-keeping operations; organization of work of special committee. UN Mo Chron 2:17-22 Ap '65
Special committee adopts report to General assembly. UN Mo Chron 2:31-42 Jl '65

Special committee on the situation with regard to implementation of declaration on granting of independence to colonial countries and peoples

Declaration on granting of independence to colonial countries and peoples; consideration of Special committee's report; by Trusteeship committee of the General assembly. UN Mo Chron 2:82-8 D '65
Report to General assembly. UN Mo Chron 2:35-7 N '65
Special committee of twenty-four (cont) UN Mo Chron 2:39-53 My; 55-68 Je; 47-55 Jl; 27-36 Ag; 32-6 O '65

Special fund

Buttressing the foundations. P. G. Hoffman. il Sat R 48:30-1+ Jl 24 '65
Locust fighters. J. Gunther. il Look 29:40-2 Ap 20 '65
New aid programme under Special fund approved. UN Mo Chron 2:55-8 Jl '65
New special fund programme authorized. UN Mo Chron 2:7-9 F '65
Report on special fund. UN Mo Chron 2:81-2 Je '65
U.S. commends development activities of U.N. special fund; statement, January 12, 1965. F. H. Williams. Dept State Bul 52: 155-7 F 1 '65
United States pledges funds to U.N. development program for 1965; note to correspondents, March 2, 1965; with text of letter from Ambassador Stevenson. Dept State Bul 52:475-6 Mr 29 '65
U.S. pledges $60 million to U.N. aid programs; statement, November 2, 1965. J. Roosevelt. Dept State Bul 53:957-8 D 13 '65
See also
United Nations—Development programme

UNITED NATIONS—*Continued*

Special political committee

Apartheid in South Africa. UN Mo Chron 2: 79-81 D '65

Committee hears statements; peace-keeping operations. UN Mo Chron 2:72-6 D '65

Meetings of Special political committee; Palestine refugees. UN Mo Chron 2:76-9 D '65

Specialized agencies

United Nations commemoration address, June 25, 1965. A. Quaison-Sackey. UN Mo Chron 2:79-84 Jl '65

United Nations commemoration address, June 25, 1965. M. G. Candau. UN Mo Chron 2: 138-40 Jl '65

Statistical commission

Statistical commission; considerations during thirteenth session. UN Mo Chron 2:78-80 Je '65

Sub-commission on prevention of discrimination and protection of minorities

Draft convention against religious intolerance. UN Mo Chron 2:10-11 F '65

Study of discrimination in respect of the right of everyone to leave any country, including his own, and to return to his country, by J. D. Ingles. Review
Negro Hist Bul 28:95 Ja '65. E. B. Jackson

Technical assistance program

Buttressing the foundations. P. G. Hoffman. il Sat R 48:30-1+ Jl 24 '65

Development decade; excerpts from report. Thant. UN Mo Chron 2:39-41 Ag '65

EPTA, assistance reaches record level. UN Mo Chron 2:58-9 Jl '65

Fifteen years and 150,000 skills; Expanded programme. D. Owen. UN Mo Chron 2:105-9 Je '65

Technical co-operation in a world of change; with editorial comment. D. Owen. il UNESCO Courier 18:12-14+ O '65

Technical co-operation in the Congo. UN Mo Chron 2:60-2 My '65

United States pledges funds to U.N. development program for 1965; note to correspondents, March 2, 1965; with text of letter from Ambassador Stevenson. Dept State Bul 52:475-6 Mr 29 '65

U.S. pledges $60 million to U.N. aid programs; statement, November 2, 1965. J. Roosevelt. Dept State Bul 53:957-8 D 13 '65
See also
United Nations—Development programme

Trusteeship committee

Declaration on granting of independence to colonial countries and peoples. UN Mo Chron 2:82-8 D '65

Trusteeship council

Thirty-second session. UN Mo Chron 2:82-4 Je '65

Trust Territory of the Pacific Islands; statements, May 28 and June 2, 1965. D. Dickinson; M. W. Goding; B. Olter. Dept State Bul 53:280-97 Ag 16 '65

Trusteeship council; thirty-second session. UN Mo Chron 2:62-71 Jl '65

United Nations commemoration address, June 25, 1965. F. H. Corner. UN Mo Chron 2: 129-32 Jl '65

Visiting mission to New Guinea and Nauru. UN Mo Chron 2:48-50 Ap '65

Voting

United Nations procedures and power realities: the international apportionment problem; address, April 23, 1965. R. N. Gardner. Dept State Bul 52:701-11 My 10 '65

Aden

Discussions in Fourth committee. UN Mo Chron 2:32-3 N '65

General assembly adopts resolution; with text of resolution. UN Mo Chron 2:57-62 D '65

Special committee of 24; with text of resolution. UN Mo Chron 2:55-63 Je '65

Asia, Southeastern

Security council urged to respond to challenge in southeast Asia; letter, July 30, 1965. A. J. Goldberg. Dept State Bul 53: 278-80 Ag 16 '65

Cambodia

United Nations resolution on Cambodia; text. June 4, 1964. Cur Hist 48:109 F '65

China (People's Republic)

Assembly decision; representation of China. UN Mo Chron 2:52-7 D '65

Catalytic China; U.S. and U.S.S.R. peace depends on peril. Christian Cent 82:1307-8 O 27 '65

China the peacemaker; behind India and Pakistan's cease-fire. Nation 201:177 O 4 '65

Comes the millennium. America 113:703 D 4 '65

Instant citizenship; TV symposium. R. L. Shayon. Sat R 48:56 Je 12 '65

Losing ground; question of a seat for red China? il Newsweek 66:56 N 22 '65

None of the UN's business. America 113: 308 S 25 '65

Not war, not peace. New Repub 153:5-6 O 2 '65

Peiping's admission to the U.N; address, November 8, 1965. A. J. Goldberg. Vital Speeches 32:98-102 D 1 '65

Recalcitrant candidate. Time 86:48 N 19 '65

Sniping from the Sedan chair. Time 86:34+ N 26 '65

U.N. defeat for red China, but—. il U S News 59:8 N 29 '65

U.N. General assembly again rejects move to change representation of China; statements, November 8, 16 and 17, 1965; with texts of resolutions. A. J. Goldberg; C. W. Yost. Dept State Bul 53:940-52 D 13 '65

U.S. and China; policy or obsession? il Newsweek 66:44-6 N 29 '65

U.S. sponsor red China? Commonweal 83:139 N 5 '65

Vote. Newsweek 41:52-3 N 27 '65

What about mainland China? D. M. Stowe; discussion. Christian Cent 82:405-7 Mr 31 '65

Whither Goldberg? Nation 201:205 O 11 '65

Congo (capital Leopoldville)

Congo question; position of the United States; address, December 14, 1964. A. E. Stevenson. Vital Speeches 31:231-6 F 1 '65

Congo realities and United States policy; address, April 25, 1965. G. M. Williams. Dept State Bul 52:793-805 My 24 '65

Crisis in the Congo, by E. W. Lefever. Review
America 112:863-4 Je 12 '65. V. S. Kearney

Resolutions on the Congo; excerpts from the O.A.U. resolution, September 10 and text of the Security council resolution, December 30, 1964. Cur Hist 48:237-8 Ap '65

Technical co-operation in the Congo. UN Mo Chron 2:60-2 My '65

U.N. asks all states to refrain from intervention in Congo; statements, December 30, 1964; with resolution adopted by the Security council. A. E. Stevenson. Dept State Bul 52:118-20 Ja 25 '65

Cook Islands

Special committee of twenty-four; with text of resolution. UN Mo Chron 2:27-36 Ag '65

Cyprus

Record of the month. UN Mo Chron 2:24-6 My '65

Security council adopts resolution. UN Mo Chron 2:3-10 Ag '65

Security council considers situation. UN Mo Chron 2:31-8 D '65

Dominican Republic

Communications on situation. UN Mo Chron 2:36 My '65

Council considers situation. UN Mo Chron 2:10-16 Ag '65

Dominican Republic; Council considers situation. UN Mo Chron 2:3-11 Jl '65

Dominican situation; jurisdiction of the regional organization. F. V. García Amador. il Américas 17:1-3 Jl '65

Principles of U.N.-OAS relationship in Dominican Republic; statements, May 22 and May 24, 1965. A. E. Stevenson. Dept State Bul 52:975-80 Je 14 '65

Security council authorizes U.N. representative in Dominican Republic; statements, May 3-5, 1965; with text of resolution adopted May 14, 1965. A. E. Stevenson. biblíog f Dept State Bul 52:869-85 My 31 '65

Security council considers situation; conditions in the Dominican Republic il UN Mo Chron 2:3-12 Je '65

U.N. Security council considers situation in Dominican Republic; statements, May 19-21, 1965. A. E. Stevenson. Dept State Bul 52:913-19 Je 7 '65

UNITED NATIONS—*Continued*

Taiwan

U.N. General assembly again rejects move to change representation of China; statements, November 8, 16 and 17, 1965; with texts of resolutions. A. J. Goldberg; C. W. Yost. Dept State Bul 53:940-52 D 13 '65

Turkey

See also
United Nations—Cyprus

Uganda

U.S. replies to Uganda charges at Nairobi conference. Dept State Bul 52:337-8 Mr 8 '65

United States

Absent powers. Reporter 32:12-13 Je 17 '65
Alternative to anarchy. C. M. Eichelberger. il Sat R 48:35+ Jl 24 '65
Congress passes concurrent resolution on 20th anniversary of United Nations; text of resolution. Dept State Bul 53:103 Jl 19 '65
Crisis in the United Nations; address, December 10, 1964. C. B. Luce. Vital Speeches 31:236-41 F 1 '65
Double jeopardy: U.N. and Vietnam. N. Cousins. Sat R 48:20 Mr 27 '65
Duty overrules Justice Goldberg. J. Neary. il Life 59:30B Jl 30 '65
Effectiveness of U.S. delegation to U.N. enhanced by new law; statement, September 28, 1965. L. B. Johnson. Dept State Bul 53:641 O 18 '65
Goal of the United Nations; a Great society for all men; statement, September 23, 1965. A. J. Goldberg. Dept State Bul 53:578-87 O 11 '65
Goldberg and world rule by law. Life 59:4 Jl 30 '65
Goldberg at the U.N: an ambassador who loves a fight. U S News 59:12-13 Ag 2 '65
Goldberg at the UN; diplomacy as the art of the possible. N. McKitterick. New Repub 153:13-15 S 11 '65
Goldberg's new guard. Time 86:20 S 3 '65
Johnson at San Francisco. UN anniversary. Nation 200:685-6 Je 28 '65
Justice Goldberg sworn in as representative to U.N; remarks, July 26, 1965. L. B. Johnson; A. J. Goldberg. Dept State Bul 53:265-7 Ag 16 '65
Lost session at the U.N; dues dispute. M. Greenfield. il Reporter 32:14-20 My 6 '65
Meanwhile back at the UN; apathy of the press. Nation 200:181-2 F 22 '65
Peace-keeping costs; address, August 16, 1965. A. J. Goldberg. Vital Speeches 31:674-6 S 1 '65
President names Justice Goldberg as U.S. Ambassador to U.N; remarks, July 20, 1965. A. J. Goldberg; L. B. Johnson. Dept State Bul 53:240-1 Ag 9 '65
Proconsuls and ambassadors: appointment of Justice Goldberg as United States representative to the United Nations. Nation 201:49 Ag 2 '65
Society for all men; address, September 23, 1965. A. J. Goldberg. Vital Speeches 32:34-9 N 1 '65
U.N, an effective arm of U.S. foreign policy; address, November 3, 1965. P. H. B. Frelingfihuysen. Dept State Bul 53:1021-8 D 27 '65
U.N. General assembly again rejects move to change representation of China; statements, November 8, 16 and 17, 1965; with texts of resolutions. A. J. Goldberg; C. W. Yost. Dept State Bul 53:940-52 D 13 '65
U.N. General assembly recesses; statements, February 18, 1965. A. E. Stevenson. Dept State Bul 52:354-5 Mr 8 '65
UN on the rack. A. Weill-Tuckerman. Nation 200:128-9 F 8 '65
U.S. denies plaque violates U.N. headquarters agreement; exchanges of notes between the U.S. and U.S.S.R. missions, January 15, February 24, April 24, and May 28, 1965. Dept State Bul 53:84-6 Jl 12 '65
U.S. expresses views on Southern Rhodesian independence in U.N. committee of 24 and Security council; statements, April 14 and May 5, 1965. M. P. Tree; A. E. Stevenson. Dept State Bul 52:1061-6 Je 28 '65
U.S. finds U.N. majority unwilling to enforce article 19; statement, August 16, 1965. A. J. Goldberg. Dept State Bul 53:454-7 S 13 '65
United States pledges funds to U.N. development program for 1965; note to correspondents, March 2, 1965; with text of letter from Ambassador Stevenson. Dept State Bul 52:475-6 Mr 29 '65

U.S. pledges $60 million to U.N. aid programs; statement, November 2, 1965. J. Roosevelt. Dept State Bul 53:957-8 D 13 '65
U.S. replies to Uganda charges at Nairobi conference. Dept State Bul 52:337-8 Mr 8 '65
U.S. reports to United Nations on ICY activities; letter, May 20, 1965, with U.S. note to Secretary-General, May 17, 1965. A. E. Stvenson. Dept State Bul 52:1067-9 Je 28 '65
United States reviews the U.N. constitutional crisis; statement, January 26, 1965. A. E. Stevenson. Dept State Bul 52:198-206 F 15 '65
U.S. states views on procedures to amend U.N. charter; statement, September 16, 1965. S. M. Finger. Dept State Bul 53:642-3 O 18 '65
Why LBJ wants men ten feet tall. P. Lisagor. il Nations Bsns 53:23-4 O '65
Why the U.N. survives. S. Harrington Commonweal 82:527-9 Jl 23 '65

Anecdotes facetiae, satire, etc.

UN aid to the USA, 1980 R. E. Asher. New Repub 153:13-15 Jl 10 '65

Vietnam (Republic)

Ambassador Goldberg holds news conference at New York; transcript of conference, July 28, 1965; with questions and answers. A. J. Goldberg. Dept State Bul 53:272-4+ Ag 16 '65
Communications received on developments in Viet-Nam. UN Mo Chron 2:30-3 Ap '65
Future of the peacekeeping. A. Larson. il Sat R 48:22-3+ Jl 24 '65
Let the U.N. handle it; peace-keeping in Vietnam; with editorial comment. H. S. Reuss. Commonweal 82:515-16, 523-6 Jl 23 '65
Plan for peace in Vietnam; the U.N. and SEATO offer an alternative to war in southeast Asia. D. R. Larson and A. Larson. Sat R 48:21-4 Ap 24 '65; Reply. D. Keys. 48:49 My 22 '65
Situation in Viet-Nam. UN Mo Chron 2:21-5 Mr '65
Statement by Secretary-General. Thant. UN Mo Chron 2:88 D '65
UN blackout on Vietnam. A. Weill-Tuckerman. Nation 200:324-6 Mr 29 '65
U.N. peacekeeping committee meets; U.S. refutes charges on Viet-Nam; statement, March 26, 1965. F. T. P. Plimpton. Dept State Bul 52:598-600 Ap 19 '65
Vietnam at the UN; President Johnson appeals to UN. Nation 201:69 Ag 16 '65
Viet-Nam; summary of statements by Secretary-General on recent developments. UN Mo Chron 2:21-4 My '65

UNITED NATIONS children's fund

Are we preparing our children for world citizenship? J. M. Spiegelman. il Parents Mag 40:42 S '65
For helping children, a Nobel peace prize. U S News 59:21 N 8 '65
Nobel peace prize for the love of children. il Life 59:30-7 N 5 '65
Peace prize. New Yorker 41:44-7 N 6 '65
Peace prize to UNICEF. Sr Schol 87:10 N 11 '65
They scare up pennies; UNICEF trick or treat program celebrates fifteenth anniversary. Recreation 58:398 O '65
UNICEF executive director. UN Mo Chron 2:81 Ap '65
UNICEF fights on for the world's children. M. Pate. Parents Mag 40:50+ Mr '65

UNITED NATIONS conference on international organization, San Francisco, 1945

San Francisco, 1945; picture section. UN Mo Chron 2:85-92 Je '65

UNITED NATIONS conference on trade and development

Trade and development board; recommendation of Geneva as the UNCTAD headquarters. UN Mo Chron 2:46-7 N '65
Trade board meeting in Geneva; second session. UN Mo Chron 2:42-3 Ag '65
U.S. pledged to cooperate in solving commodity problems; statement, July 22, 1965. S. Nehmer. Dept State Bul 53:530-2 S 27 '65

UNITED NATIONS conference on transit trade of land-locked countries

Aid for land-locked countries. UN Mo Chron 2:43-4 Ag '65

UNITED NATIONS conference on world population. See World population conference

UNITED NATIONS congress on the prevention of crime and the treatment of offenders

Congress on prevention of crime and treatment of offenders; third meeting. UN Mo Chron 2:46-7 Ag '65

UNITED NATIONS day
  Religion and the UN. America 113:37 Jl 10
    '65
  United Nations day, 1965. UN Mo Chron
    2:i–iii O '65
  United Nations day, 1965; proclamation, April
    9, 1965. L. B. Johnson. Dept State Bul 52:
    731-2 My 10 '65
UNITED NATIONS educational, scientific and
    cultural organization
  Asia and Africa programs to develop pub-
    lishing. Pub W 187:78 Je 14 '65
  Document of paramount importance; biologi-
    cal aspects of race; signed by partici-
    pants at Unesco meeting, August, 1964.
    UNESCO Courier 18:8-11 Ap '65
  Educational progress around the world; re-
    port of general conference. il UNESCO
    Courier 18:8-9 Mr '65
  International prospects of science; excerpts
    from address, 1964. N. M. Sisakian. il
    UNESCO Courier 18:4-8+ Mr '65
  IPA education section: ways sought for
    international publishing aid; meeting in
    Frankfurt. il Pub W 188:32-8 N 22 '65
  Map of UNESCO conservation missions. il
    UNESCO Courier 18:24-5 Ja '65
  Menace of the bulldozers; excerpts from
    study. J. O. Brew. il UNESCO Courier 18:
    33-6 Ja '65
  Toward international aid for educational
    publishing. R. H. Smith. Pub W 188:46 N 22
    '65
  Uncomprehending 40 per cent; new UNESCO
    project. il Time 86:67-8 N 19 '65
  UNESCO and the world of books. J. Behr-
    stock. UNESCO Courier 18:21-2 S '65
  UNESCO and youth. UNESCO Courier 18:66-7
    Jl '65
  Unesco general conference of 1964. E. Sochor.
    Sch & Soc 93:226-8 Ap 3 '65
  UNESCO is your organization. R. Maheu.
    NEA J 54:30 Mr '65
    See also
  International theatre institute

      Division of libraries, documen-
          tation and archives
  New Unesco department for libraries recom-
    mended by Advisory committee. M. J.
    Voigt. Library J 90:2515-16 Je 1 '65

      International advisory committee
        on bibliography, documentation
            and terminology
  New Unesco department for libraries recom-
    mended by Advisory committee. M. J. Voigt.
    Library J 90:2515-16 Je 1 '65
UNITED NATIONS general assembly. See
    United Nations—General assembly
UNITED NATIONS institute for training and
    research
  Institute for training and research. UN Mo
    Chron 2:81-2 Ap '65
UNITED NATIONS international atomic energy
    agency. See International atomic energy
    agency
UNITED NATIONS International children's
    emergency fund. See United Nations chil-
    dren's fund
UNITED NATIONS relief and works agency
    for Palestine refugees in the Near East
  Contributions to refugee programmes. il UN
    Mo Chron 2:36-8 Mr '65
  Meetings of Special political committee;
    Palestine refugees. UN Mo Chron 2:23-9
    N; 76-9 D '65
UNITED NATIONS scientific and cultural
    organization
  Metamorphosis in Unesco. il UNESCO Courier
    18:27-9 O '65
UNITED NATIONS tin conference
  International tin agreement. UN Mo Chron
    2:64-6 My '65
  Third tin conference. UN Mo Chron 2:41-2 Ap
    '65
UNITED NATIONS trade and development
    board
  First session of board. UN Mo Chron 2:53-6
    My '65
UNITED Presbyterian church in the United
    States of America
  Calvin reformed. Newsweek 65:54-5 Mr 1 '65
  Changing the confession. Time 85:68 F 26 '65
  Changing the confession. il Newsweek 65:42
    Je 7 '65
  New direction, a new birth; 177th general
    assembly. il Time 85:61-2 Je 4 '65
  Presbyterians on unity. America 112:846 Je
    12 '65
  Script-writers take over. M. E. Marty. Chris-
    tian Cent 82:733-5 Je 9 '65

  Summer study-skills program for minority
    group pupils; project of Educational coun-
    seling service. W. D Martinson and others.
    Sch & Soc 93:300-2 Sum '65
UNITED Presbyterian general assembly. See
    United Presbyterian church in the United
    States of America
UNITED rubber, cork, linoleum and plastic
    workers of America
  Snappy action in rubber; settlement reached
    after contracts expired with big three tire
    companies. Bsns W p 144 Ap 24 '65
UNITED service organizations
  Hello, Saigon! international company of Hello,
    Dolly. Time 86:109 O 15 '65
UNITED STATES
  America the middle-aged. L. Heren. Harper
    231:100+ Ag '65
  Churchill on America: a legacy in words;
    quotations. W. L. S. Churchill. il U S News
    58:38-9 F 8 '65; Same abr. with title Church-
    ill legacy in words. Read Digest 86:214B-
    214C My '65
  Four simple words: the right to choose. W.
    McMillen. Read Digest 86:24B F '65
  In only eight years, how U.S. is to change.
    il U S News 58:56-60 My 17 '65
  Moment of truth: our rendezvous with
    destiny; address, June 8, 1965. R. Reagan.
    Vital Speeches 31:681-6 S 1 '65
  Morality of nations; address, June 6, 1965.
    L. B. Johnson. Dept State Bul 52:1026-9
    Je 28 '65
  1966: year of decision. il U S News 60:23-8+
    Ja 10 '66
  Our growing responsibilities in a changing
    world; address, December 8, 1964. G. Cham-
    pion. Vital Speeches 31:282-5 F 15 '65
  Paradise deferred; President Johnson's great
    society. Christian Cent 82:931-2 Jl 28 '65
  Peace of mankind; address, June 3, 1965.
    L. B. Johnson. Dept State Bul 52.986-9
    Je 21 '65; Excerpts. U S News 58:4 Je 14
    '65
  Promise of America, by J. Morton. Review
    Sat R 49:37 Ja 15 '66. M. R. Konvitz
  Transcendent issues in today's world; ad-
    dress, February 22, 1965. L. B. Johnson.
    Dept State Bul 52:372-4 Mr 15 '65
  Trends: the state of the Nation. F. Morley.
    See issues of Nation's business
  Why fear the future? complacency in a land
    of plenty; address, June 28, 1965. W. C.
    Mainwaring Vital Speeches 31:691-6 S 1
    See also
  Americans
  South
  States (United States)
    also subhead United States under various
    subjects, e.g. Education—United States

      Advanced research projects agency
    See United States—Defense, Department of
      —Advanced research projects agency

      Advisory committee on monetary
              arrangements
  Advisory committee on monetary arrange-
    ments has first meeting; announcement of
    meeting, July 16, 1965, with statements.
    Henry H. Fowler; Douglas Dillon; L. B.
    Johnson. Dept State Bul 53:238-9 Ag 9 '65

      Agency for international development
  A.I.D. a symbol of help. il Todays Health 43:
    14 D '65
  Business enlists in South Vietnam. il Bsns W
    p 114 Je 12 '65
  Can the U.S. teach whole world to read?
    school aid for backward lands. Bsns W
    p34 O 23 '65
  Cooperation, international development, and
    the problem of hunger. H. J. Waters. Dept
    State Bul 53:816-19 N 22 '65
  Escalated welfare. K. Crawford. Newsweek
    65:28 Je 28 '65
  Foreign aid and the liberal dissent. I. Frank;
    reply. L. E. Gordon. New Repub 152:29-30
    Mr 20 '65
  Foreign aid is for help, not for cheers. Life
    58:4 F 12 '65
  Refugees; special relief division set up for
    Vietnam. il Newsweek 66:54-5 O 18 '65

      Aging, Administration on
  Administration on aging: new HEW unit will
    offer grants to states, universities for
    studies of aging. E. Langer. Science 149:
    617-19 Ag 6 '65; Reply. R. R. Kohn. 150:
    685 N 5 '65

      Agriculture, Department of
  Department of agriculture. Farm J 89:126
    D '65
  Old agency up to new tricks. il Nations
    Bsns 53:48-50+ F '65

UNITED STATES—Agriculture, Department of
—*Continued*
On the outside looking out. E. Peter, jr.
New Repub 152:18 Je 26 '65
USDA's role as the consumer's adviser. Consumer Bul 48:39-40 N '65
See also
United States—National seed storage laboratory
United States—Soil conservation service

Forest service
See United States—Forest service

Air force
AF discloses new upper stage. Miss & Roc 17:17 S 20 '65
Air force expands range dominance. D. L. Zylstra. il Miss & Roc 16:33-5 Mr 8 '65
Air force given manned space role; MOL program. W. J. Normyle. Aviation W 83:23 Ag 30 '65
Air force moves quickly to exploit MOL; with editorial comment. D. E. Fink. Aviation W 83:17, 22-3 S 6 '65
Air force plans F-111A briefing. il Aviation W 83:29 D 13 '65
CIA control bid slowed decision on MOL. D. E. Fink. il Aviation W 83:26-7 S 20 '65
Military moves to space; manned orbital laboratories. R. D. Senter. New Repub 153: 11-13 S 11 '65
Of planes and men; U.S. air force wages cold war and hot. K. F. Weaver. il Nat Geog Mag 128:298-349 S '65
Personality of the month; scientist takes over the air force. Sci Digest 58:17 O '65
Tactical weaponry pushed by air force. il Aviation W 82:72-5 Mr 15 '65
USAF continues MOL definition effort. il Aviation W 82:85+ Mr 15 '65
U.S. air force: power for peace. C. E. LeMay. il Nat Geog Mag 128:291-7 S '65
USAF seeks funds to speed its scramjet, hypersonic flight program. M. L. Yaffee. il Aviation W 83:52-3+ Jl 12 '65

Aerospace medical division
See United States—Air force—Systems command

Aerospace research, Office of
OAR to use own vehicles for OV shots. R. Pay. il Miss & Roc 18:32-4+ Ja 17 '66
See also
United States—Air force—Cambridge research laboratories

Air defense command
Fifteen year alert. Time 86:22 Jl 9 '65

Air national guard
See United States—Air national guard

Air proving grounds
See Proving grounds

Air rescue service
They jump to save lives. G. E. Maxwell. il Todays Health 43:42-5+ Mr '65

Appropriations and expenditures
Bomber slash follows B-111 fund rebuff. Aviation W 83:26-7 D 13 '65
McNamara killed YF-12A request. Aviation W 82:31 Ap 12 '65
SRAM funding slashed by House. Miss & Roc 16:18 Je 28 '65

Cambridge research laboratories
USAF plans attempt to transmit radio signals between satellites. M. L. Yaffee. il Aviation W 83:80-1+ Ag 16 '65

Communication systems
1,500-mile-long data corridor nearly ready. C. D. LaFond. il Miss & Roc 17:34-6 N 1 '65

Education
See also
Air pilots—Training
United States air force academy, Colorado Springs

Forces in France
French town, an American base, a frontier; Châteauroux air base. A. Menen. il N Y Times Mag p 14-15+ Ja 31 '65

Forces in Japan
Two happy GI's in Japan; F. W. LeSueur, jr. and W. A. McFarland. il Look 29:30-2 Ag 10 '65

Forces in Laos
Bombings disclosed. Sr Schol 86:19 F 4 '65

Forces in Vietnam (Republic)
Aboard a carrier off Vietnam. L. Wainwright. Life 58:28 My 14 '65
Aircraft availability averages over 80 per cent. C. Brownlow. il Aviation W 82:65-6+ Je 7 '65
Mac the Fac's last mission. Time 85:31 Ap 30 '65
Pilots of Danang aren't flyboys. J. Raymond. il N Y Times Mag p 16-17+ Ag 15 '65

Logistics command
Air lift enhancing Vietnam maintenance. Aviation W 82:91 Ap 19 '65

Military airlift command
See United States—Military airlift command

Negroes
Cadet who refused to quit: B. O. Davis, a Negro lieutenant general. R. S. Strother. Read Digest 87:71-5 S '65

Officers
Cadet who refused to quit: B. O. Davis, a Negro lieutenant general. R. S. Strother. Read Digest 87:71-5 S '65

Procurement
Air force tightens rein on required data. H. D. Watkins. Aviation W 83:39+ O 18 '65
Air force to charge interference by GAO as lingering feud erupts. Aviation W 82:17 My 24 '65
Impact of Vietnam procurement nearing. Aviation W 83:26-7 Ag 16 '65
McNamara says MOL awards are near. D. L. Zylstra. Miss & Roc 16:13-15 Mr 1 '65
Major MOL subsystem contracts near. Miss & Roc 17:16 N 22 '65
Titan 3 program involves five major incentive fee contracts. W. H. Gregory. il Aviation W 83:42-3+ Jl 5 '65
USAF contracts. See issues of Aviation week & space technology

Recreation
Have a field day; Lowry air force base, Colo. G. Smith. il Recreation 58:445-6 N '65

Strategic air command
35,000 hours through the looking glass; Strategic air command's airborne emergency headquarters. il Time 85:19 F 12 '65

Systems command
Major command and control communications systems managed by USAF's electronic systems division. Aviation W 82:240-1 Mr 15 '65
New lab will speed radiation studies; Air force systems command's school of aerospace medicine. H. M. David. il Miss & Roc 17:34-5 N 15 '65

Training
See Military training

Air force, Army
Air mobility boosts army effectiveness. il Aviation W 82:70-1+ Je 7 '65
DOD approves army air assault concept. G. C. Wilson. Aviation W 82:32 Ap 26 '65
Detailed analysis to affect selection of army aircraft. G. Wilson. il Aviation W 82:80-1+ Mr 15 '65

Air force, Navy
Navy plans center around ASW, tactical aircraft. il Aviation W 82:76-7+ Mr 15 '65
Navy tests light water airborne fire-fighting system. il Aviation W 83:90-1 Ag 23 '65

Air national guard
Smoother deployment of air guard is urged. Aviation W 82:77 Je 7 '65

Anti-Communist measures
See Communism—United States—Anti-Communist measures; United States—Foreign relations—Anti-Communist measures

Antiquities
Federal law to guard ancient relics urged. Sci N L 88:24 Jl 10 '65

Appalachian regional commission
New way to beat poverty; the plan for Appalchia. il U S News 59:68-70 S 27 '65

Appropriations and expenditures
Computer and the pork barrel; President may try economy measures. H. Brandon. Sat R 48:14-15 Ag 28 '65

UNITED STATES—Appropriations and expenditures—*Continued*

Engineering misdirected; misuse of national resources by cold war. Nation 201:111 S 6 '65

Forestry appropriations; fiscal year ending June 30, 1966 compared with 1965. Am For 71:62 Ag '65

Forestry in the federal budget, fiscal year ending June 30, 1966. il Am For 71:8 Mr '65

Government: biggest growth industry? il U S News 59:62-5 N 22 '65

Great society: new kind of balance sheet is needed. L. H. Keyserling. New Repub 152: 11-14 Je 12 '65

Great society's cost. H. Hazlitt. Newsweek 66:90 N 22 '65

How federal spending will soar in '66, war or no war. il U S News 60:75-7 Ja 10 '66

Our depleted society, by S. Melman. Review Commentary 41:80-2 Ja '66. R. Lekachman

Republicans do think: alarming acceleration of federal debt; address, April 6, 1965. G. Allott. Vital Speeches 31:477-80 My 15 '65

Seductive odor of pork; congressmen's pet projects. Life 59:4 S 17 '65

Sweet and sour pork. il Newsweek 66:29-30 O 4 '65

Time for federal housecleaning. Life 60:4 Ja 21 '66

See also
Budget—United States
Government spending policy
United States—Armed forces—Appropriations and expenditures
United States—Economic policy

Area redevelopment administration

Depressed areas built to order. B. B. VanDusen. Read Digest 86:79-82 My '65

Federal aid to depressed areas, by S. A Levitan. Review
Christian Cent 82:1097-8 S 8 '65. C. M. Cook

Hope for depressed areas. B. L. Masse. America 112:479 Ap 10 '65

Priming the pump of area growth; combining public works with regional planning. il Bsns W p96-8+ O 9 '65

Proliferating Appalachias. D. Oberdorfer. il Reporter 33:22-3+ S 9 '65; Discussion. 33:8+ O 7 '65

Armed forces

How many left? plenty. il Time 85:26 My 14 '65

Power for peace; address, May 13, 1965. S. Ailes. Vital Speeches 31:534-7 Je 15 '65

State of our defenses; message to Congress, January 18, 1965. L. B. Johnson. Dept State Bul 52:211-18 F 15 '65

See also
Military training
United States—Air force
United States—Army
United States—Defense, Department of
United States—Joint chiefs of staff
United States—Marine corps
United States—Navy

Appropriations and expenditures

At home: growing pressure to get ready for big war. U S News 59:45 Jl 26 '65

Bad news, good news; costs of war eat into national budget. il Newsweek 66:25 D 20 '65

Biggest bill. R. Hotz. Aviation W 84:21 Ja 10 '66

Conference unit restores funds for E-2A; AMSA gets $22 million. Aviation W 82:19 My 31 '65

Congress, DOD renewing bomber clash. G. C. Wilson. Aviation W 82:18-19 Mr 1 '65

Defense is no longer a big growth business. Bsns W p29 S 11 '65

DOD asked to reassess research policy. G. C. Wilson. il Aviation W 82:75-6 Je 28 '65

DOD briefing emphasizes tactical needs. H. D. Watkins. Aviation W 82:16-17 Mr 8 '65

DOD spending decline is about over. M. Getler. Miss & Roc 16:17-18 Mr 22 '65

FY '67 Defense budget may remain $60 billion. Miss & Roc 18:14 Ja 10 '66

FY '66 budget programs at a glance. il Miss & Roc 16:12-13 F 1 '65

From Washington: McNamara's new budget. H. Margolis. Bul Atomic Sci 21:54-6 Mr '65

Higher DOD spending hinges on Nike X. C. Brownlow. il Aviation W 82:18-23 F 1 '65

Industry may receive $23.7 billion. il Miss & Roc 16:10-11+ F 1 '65

Johnson allots $180 million for aircraft. G. C. Wilson. Aviation W 82:26-7 My 10 '65

Johnson maps strong aerospace efforts; with editorial comment. G. C. Wilson. il Aviation W 82:11, 16-18 F 1 '65

LBJ's third veto. Reporter 33:10+ S 9 '65

McNamara delays aircraft buy decision. G. C. Wilson. Aviation W 82:24 My 24 '65

McNamara: no diversion from R&D. Miss & Roc 17:17 Ag 16 '65

Men and money. Newsweek 66:12 Ag 16 '65

Military research: Congress generally goes along with RDT&E requests, but adds qualifications. J. Walsh. Science 149:403-5 Jl 23 '65

Military spending: on the way up again. U S News 58:11 My 17 '65

Mr McNamara reports on use of supplemental appropriations; White House announcement, May 18, 1965; with memorandum for the President. il Dept State Bul 52:896-7 Je 7 '65

Mobilization outlook; with interview with B. Ellington. il U S News 59:19-29 Ag 2 '65

National defense message; excerpts. L. B. Johnson. Sci N L 87:67 Ja 30 '65

New look at defense; why Congress worries. il U S News 58:37-41 Mr 1 '65

Onward and upward. W. J. Coughlin. Miss & Roc 16:54 F 8 '65

Our depleted society, by S. Melman. Review Commentary 41:80-2 Ja '66. R. Lekachman

Pentagon's new R&D want list. il Bsns W p 120+ Mr 20 '65

Pivotal $5 billion. il Fortune 72:27-8 S '65

Planning to tax less, spend more. Bsns W p21 Jl 24 '65

Pressure growing for DOD budget boast. G. C. Wilson. Aviation W 83:16 Jl 5 '65

Problems for the Hill. W. J. Coughlin. Miss & Roc 16:54 F 22 '65

Report released on economic impact of defense and disarmament; letter, September 4, 1965; with White House announcement. L. B. Johnson. Dept State Bul 53: 515-18 S 27 '65

R&D funding continues to increase. il Miss & Roc 16:125-6+ Mr 29 '65

Rising cost of overkill. A. E. Burns. Sat R 48:26 Ag 7 '65

Senate fears DOD fund reprogramming. Miss & Roc 17:15 Ag 9 '65

Senate okays $15.28 billion for DOD. Miss & Roc 16:15 Ap 12 '65

Standardization gains momentum in DOD. C. Brownlow. il Aviation W 82:69-72 Mr 15 '65

Status of FY 1966 budgets; Dept. of defense appropriations. Miss & Roc 17:160-6 Jl 26 '65

Tactical capabilities stressed in budget. Aviation W 82:64-5 Mr 8 '65

Vietnam spurs DOD boost, reprogramming. il Aviation W 83:26-8 Ag 2 '65

Who's afraid of peace? massive defense spending not essential to nation's prosperity. Time 86:38-9 S 17 '65

Civilian employees

Pentagon plan that will cut draft calls. U S News 59:8 S 27 '65

Education

Careers in the armed forces; with charts. Sr Schol 87:21-2 N 11 '65

Cheating and symbols; report of a special committee called by the secretary of the air force to consider cases of cheating. Commonweal 82:277 My 21 '65

How the armed forces create careers for specialists. S. L. Englebardt. il Pop Sci 186:136-8+ F '65

Equipment and supplies

Stripped & shortchanged; Senate's preparedness subcommittee report. il Time 86:16 Ag 13 '65

See also
Vietnamese war, 1957—Equipment and supplies

Forces in Ethiopia

Yankee please stay; overseas exploits of ex-G.I.'s. K. Baldwin and H. F. Downey. H. Bowser. Sat R 48:18 Ag 21 '65

Forces in Europe

51st state; regions in West Germany inhabited by U.S. servicemen and their dependents. il Newsweek 67:42+ Ja 17 '66

Will arms build-up in Asia cut U.S. role in Europe? interview. A. E. Heusinger. il U S News 59:64-7 Ag 23 '65

Forces in foreign countries

Guns, butter, and then-some economy. G. Burck. il Fortune 72:118-21+ O '65

UNITED STATES—Armed forces—Forces in foreign countries—*Continued*
How many Dominican Republics and Vietnams can we take on? F. Church. il N Y Times Mag p44-5+ N 28 '65
Military members of the country team. S. Horwitz. Dept State Bul 53:268-71 Ag 16 '65
Sentinels of freedom. il Sr Schol 86:14-15 Mr 11 '65
To keep the peace, GI's on duty around the world. il U S News 60:22-3 Ja 3 '66
We are too deep in Asia and Africa. F. Church. il N Y Times Mag p30-1+ F 14 '65

Forces in Latin America

See also
United States—Marine corps—Forces in Latin America

Forces in Southeast Asia

Why we are fighting in Asia. F. V. Drake. il Read Digest 87:61-5 O '65

Forces in Taiwan

Status-of-forces agreement signed with China. Dept State Bul 53:480 S 20 '65

Forces in the Dominican Republic

After the battle in the Caribbean. H. Handleman. il U S News 58:33-7 My 17 '65
Assessment of the situation in the Dominican Republic; statement, June 17, 1965. L. B. Johnson. Dept State Bul 53:19-21 Jl 5 '65
Congress approves supplemental appropriation for Viet-Nam, remarks, May 4, 1965, with message to Congress. L. B. Johnson. Dept State Bul 52:816-26 My 24 '65
Coup that became a war. il Time 85:28-32 My 7 '65
Death and jasmine. il Newsweek 65:46+ My 17 '65
From firefighting to revolution in three days; Dominican Republic. M. S. Lowden. il Am For 71:16-19+ Ag '65
How Latin America sees it; with editorial comment. L. E. Odell and others. Christian Cent 82:797, 805-6 Je 23 '65
Iron sights and a family reunion; Cesar Encarnacion of Brooklyn. il Life 58:44-44A My 21 '65
Lessons of Santo Domingo. il Sat Eve Post 238:92 Jl 3 '65
Moving in was easy, but. . . U S News 58:75 Je 21 '65
On a sun-drenched isle, smoke of a sudden war. il Life 58:30-38A My 14 '65
OAS foreign ministers provide for establishment of inter-American force in Dominican Republic; statements, May 1-14, 1965, with texts of resolutions and Act of Santo Domingo. E. Bunker. Dept State Bul 52:854-69 My 31 '65
OAS Secretary General to represent meeting of consultation of Dominican Republic; Brazilian to command inter-American force; statements and notes, May 15, 1965, with resolutions adopted by the meeting. E. Bunker. Dept State Bul 52:908-13 Je 7 '65
Our one-package landing force. G. F. Eliot. il Pop Sci 187:40-3+ Jl '65
Record airlift: what it means to U.S. strategy. U S News 58:10 My 24 '65
Report from Santo Domingo. J. F. Fixx. il Sat R 48:30-2+ Je 12 '65
Santo Domingo: what next? Nation 200:545 My 24 '65
Secretary discusses Dominican situation on NBC-TV; interview. ed. by J. Chancellor. D. Rusk. Dept State Bul 52:947-9 Je 14 '65
Secretary discusses situation in Dominican Republic; interview. ed. by J. Hightower. D. Rusk. Dept State Bul 52:842-4 My 31 '65
Two governments, face to face. il Time 85:31-2 My 14 '65
U.N. Security council considers situation in Dominican Republic; statements, May 19-21, 1965. A. E. Stevenson. Dept State Bul 52:913-19 Je 7 '65
U.S. acts to meet threat in Dominican Republic; statements and letter, April 28-May 2, 1965, with texts of three resolutions. L. B. Johnson; A. E. Stevenson; E. Bunker. bibliog f Dept State Bul 52:738-48 My 17 '65
U.S. troops in Santo Domingo: grim price of power. S. Castan. il Look 29:38-43 Je 15 '65
Whiff of buckshot; U.S. sergeant kills rioter. il Newsweek 67:49 Ja 24 '66
See also
United States—Marine corps—Forces in the Dominican Republic

Forces in the Far East

Test for tigers. il Time 85:25-9 F 26 '65

Forces in Turkey

Yankee please stay; overseas exploits of ex-G.I.'s, K. Baldwin and H. F. Downey. H. Bowser. Sat R 48:18 Ag 21 '65

Forces in Vietnam

Adding up, up, up; number of U.S. servicemen in South Viet Nam. Time 86:51 S 17 '65
American policy in South Viet-Nam and southeast Asia; address, January 23, 1965. W. P. Bundy. Dept State Bul 52:168-75 F 8 '65
Big dirty little war. W. Tuohy. il N Y Times Mag p43+ N 28 '65
Bigger war. Nation 201:233 O 18 '65
Broadway show in a theater of war; Hello Dolly! troupe. S. Alexander. Life 59:30 O 22 '65
Christmas: at home and in Vietnam. il Newsweek 66:13-17 D 27 '65
Christmas letters from Vietnam; excerpts from servicemen's letters. Look 29:29 D 28 '65
Communiqué from Hill 327 at Danang. J. Rose. il N Y Times Mag p 10-11+ Ap 25 '65
Draft prospect as war speeds up; Department of defense answers questions. il U S News 59:40-1 Jl 19 '65
Fighting American. il Time 85:22-6 Ap 23 '65
Hello, Dolly, and hellish ambush. il Life 59:32-3 O 22 '65
How the U.S. would expand its forces. il Newsweek 66:20 Jl 26 '65
In search of a Vietnam hero; H. D. Meyerkord's death. L. Wainwright. Life 58:23-4 My 28 '65
Ingenious Americans; Thanksgiving dinners. Newsweek 66:42 D 6 '65
Johnson means business in Vietnam. Life 59:4 Ag 6 '65
Little parcel of commitment; U S forces morale. L. Wainwright. Life 58:28 Je 11 '65
Lonely stand on a peak in Danang. G. P. Hunt. il Life 58:3 Ap 9 '65
Long guns flash on the South China Sea; Seventh fleet in action; with report by B. Wise. il Life 59:16-23 Ag 6 '65
Making of a quagmire, by D. Halberstam. Review
  Nation 200:536-7 My 17 '65. C. Mohr
Man for the job in Vietnam: General Westmoreland. J. G. Hubbell and D. Reed. Read Digest 88:55-60 Ja '66
Mission of U.S. troops in Viet-Nam defined; White House statement, June 9, 1965. Dept State Bul 52:1041 Je 28 '65
More & faster. il Time 86:25A O 22 '65
Negroes in Vietnam: we, too, are Americans. S. Booker. il Ebony 21:89-90+ N '65
New guns & old problems. Time 85:29 Je 4 '65
Only five minutes to darkness in Vietnam; bitter dilemmas and a new U.S. strategy; with interview with General Nguyen Cao Ky. il Life 59:54-61 Jl 23 '65
Only one color: Negroes in Vietnam. il Newsweek 66:42-3 D 6 '65
Our new commitment in Vietnam; with report by B. Mauldin. il Life 58:30-5 F 19 '65
Pleiku and Qui Nhon: decision points. il Newsweek 65:32-5 F 22 '65
Protests on principle and some practical options. il Life 59:30-1 Ag 20 '65
Road past North C pier. il Newsweek 65:19-20 Je 28 '65
Saigon's Santa; gifts to U.S. soldiers in Viet Nam. il Time 86:22-3 D 17 '65
Secretary McNamara discusses buildup of forces in Viet-Nam; news conference, June 16, 1965. R. S. McNamara. Dept State Bul 53:12-19 Jl 5 '65
Status & strategy. il Time 86:28-30 Ag 6 '65
Terror in the streets; Viet Cong attacks in Saigon. il Newsweek 67:30+ Ja 3 '66
Those CBS reports; distorted report of marine assault on Camne. America 113:175 Ag 21 '65
United States in Vietnam. G. M. Kahin and J. W. Lewis. bibliog f il Bul Atomic Sci 21:28-40 Je '65
Vietnam: a bid to parley. il Newsweek 65:40-8 My 24 '65
Vietnam as one family faces it; Boyt family; with reports by B. Wise, M. Silva and R. Morse. il Life 59:74-87+ D 10 '65
Vietnam crisis: what happens when war separates a young family; Captain D. Moore's family. W. C. Heinz. il Ladies Home J 82:74-5+ S '65
Vietnam: new policy in the making. H. W. Baldwin. il Reporter 33:16-20 Ag 12 '65

UNITED STATES—Armed forces—Forces in Vietnam—*Continued*
Vietnam step-up: the secret councils; President Johnson's seven days of deliberation before decision. R. B. Stolley. il Life 59:26D Ag 6 '65
Vietnam: where do we go from here? S. Karnow. il Sat Eve Post 238:28-30+ Mr 27 '65
War no one wants, or can end. il Newsweek 66:17-19 Ag 9 '65
We can't let them down. S. Alsop. il Sat Eve Post 238:18 Mr 27 '65; Same abr. Read Digest 86:116-18 Je '65
We must choose: (1) bug out; (2) negotiate; (3) fight. H. W. Baldwin. il N Y Times Mag p8-9+ F 21 '65; Reply. Christian Cent 82:291-2 Mr 10 '65
With Senior's editor in Viet Nam; questions and answers. R. Hemming. il Sr Schol 86: 15-16 F 11: 17+ F 25 '65 (to be cont)
See also
United States—Air force—Forces in Vietnam
United States—Marine corps—Forces in Vietnam
Vietnamese war, 1957—American participation

Medical and sanitary affairs
Surgeon on a hot seat; colonel battles killer disease as senior medic of sixth army. il Ebony 20:87-90 F '65

Mobilization
LBJ's decision: meaning to U.S. il U S News 59:34-5 Ag 9 '65

Negroes
Only one color: Negroes in Vietnam. il Newsweek 66:42-3 D 6 '65
See also
United States—Air force—Negroes

Officers
McNamara's plan, less seniority, more talent. U S News 59:19 Jl 19 '65
What military offers college men now. U S News 59:48-9 D 6 '65

Pay, allowances, etc.
Boost for the boys. Time 86:23 Ag 20 '65
How big a pay boost for men in service? U S News 59:9 Ag 2 '65
How to end the draft. R. Wilhelm. il Nation 201:350-2 N 15 '65
In the works: another big boost in military pay. il U S News 58:14 Mr 15 '65
Military pay boost: who'll get how much; some examples. il U S News 59:8 Ag 23 '65
Paupers in uniform. F. Drake and K. Drake. Read Digest 86:49-53 Mr '65
Upgrading Uncle Sam's payroll. Bsns W p 100+ Je 19 '65

Post exchanges
Myths and misconceptions; corporation marketing techniques. T. O'Hanlon. Duns R 85:85-6 F '65
Worldwide PX: $2 billion in bargains. il Newsweek 67:72-3+ Ja 17 '66

Procurement
Guns, butter, and then-some economy. G. Burck. il Fortune 72:118-21+ O '65
Higher DOD spending hinges on Nike X. C. Brownlow. il Aviation W 82:18-23 F 1 '65
Lockheed tops DOD contractor list. il Miss & Roc 16:21 Mr 22 '65
Military procurement bill nears passage in Congress; table. Aviation W 82:89 My 17 '65
Ordeal of the plane makers: the C-5. J. Mecklin. il Fortune 72:158-9+ D '65
Peacetime guides to govern Viet buildup. C. Brownlow. il Aviation W 83:28-9 Ag 23 '65
Services draft source selection guides. G. C. Wilson. Aviation W 82:88-9 My 17 '65
Slow-down in the Pentagon. H. W. Baldwin; reply. J. Burnham. Nat R 17:104 F 9 '65
Standardization gains momentum in DOD; prime contract awards by state. C. Brownlow. il Aviation W 82:69-72 Mr 15 '65

Recreation
Big top in the hangar; open-house fundraising carnival, Fort Wainwright. A. Roth. il Recreation 58:444-5 N '65
Broadway show in a theater of war; Hello, Dolly! troupe. S. Alexander. Life 59:30 O 22 '65
GI's and the girls from Dubuque; condensation of address. M. Xavier. il Read Digest 86:164-7+ Je '65
Hello, David! trouble over Dolly troupe in South Vietnam. il Newsweek 66:36+ O 25 '65

Recreation
Hello, Dolly, and hellish ambush. il Life 59: 32-3 O 22 '65
See also
United service organizations

Recruiting and enlistment
See also
Military service, Compulsory—United States

Relations with civilians
Doc Lucier, who fights his war with a tin washbasin. M. Mok. il Life 59:64-9+ N 26 '65
Saigon tries to live in a hurry. J. Langguth. il N Y Times Mag p 12-13+ Ag 8 '65

Reserves
Outlook now for draft, reserves, armed force build-up; interview. N. S. Paul. il U S News 59:36-40 Ag 16 '65
See also
United States—Army—Reserves
United States—National guard

Training
See Military training

Transportation
See also
United States—Military sea transportation service

Arms control and disarmament agency
ACDA: LBJ supports agency plea for bigger budget, longer life; but old problems still remain. E. Langer. Science 147:584-6 F 5 '65
Arms control and disarmament: some sober truths; remarks, May 27, 1965. L. B. Johnson. Dept State Bul 52:973-4 Je 14 '65
Arms control, foundation stone in the ramparts we watch; address, March 31, 1965. W. C. Foster. Dept State Bul 52:659-64 My 3 '65
Disarmament inches ahead: new lease of life for ACDA. N. K. Herzfeld. Commonweal 82:631-5 S 3 '65
Government sponsored research for disarmament. B. G. Lall. Bul Atomic Sci 21:44-6 F '65
President Johnson asks four-year extension of ACDA authorization; letters, January 13 and January 15, 1965; with text of proposed legislation. L. B. Johnson; W. C. Foster. Dept State Bul 52:144-6 F 1 '65
United States arms control and disarmament agency; excerpts from report to Congress, January 1, 1964–December 31, 1964. W. C. Foster. bibliog f Dept State Bul 52:308-19 Mr 1 '65

Army
Airmobile division. Time 85:31 Je 25 '65
Army presses for better field systems; tactical power supplies. il Miss & Roc 16:77-8+ Mr 29 '65
Renaissance in the ranks. il Time 86:30-4 D 10 '65
TOW, Shillelagh face showdown; year of decision for army's tactical missile development program. D. L. Zylstra. Miss & Roc 16:14-15 My 10 '65
See also
Military training camps

Administration
What's wrong with our army? S. Alsop. Sat Eve Post 238:18 F 13 '65

Appropriations and expenditures
Army spells out its $253.7-million missile request. il Miss & Roc 16:13 Mr 15 '65
Senate probe may bolster army funding. G. C. Wilson. il Aviation W 83:28-9 S 13 '65
20-billion-dollar build-up for army. il U S News 59:94 N 8 '65

Corps of engineers
Case of the vanishing beaches; California. W. Marx. il Am For 71:10-13+ N '65
Ditched again; Washington's pork-barrel engineers. Nation 201:290 N 1 '65

Defense language institute
Lingo tech; importance of knowing the Vietnamese language in battlefields of Vietnam. il Time 86:54+ Jl 16 '65
Military foreign language factory. il Ebony 20:126-8+ O '65

Education
See also
United States military academy, West Point

UNITED STATES—Armed forces—*Continued*

Equipment and supplies

Economizing blamed for army shortages. Aviation W 83:27-8 S 20 '65

How big a shortage in army weapons? U S News 59:22 S 20 '65

Forces in Vietnam (Republic)

Fighting gets tougher; so does American GI; report from Vietnam, with letter by K. W. Bagby. il U S News 59:39-41 D 13 '65

Team players; U.S. Special forces. il Newsweek 66:29 Ag 23 '65

They are not jolly in the foxholes. J. Langguth. il N Y Times Mag p26-7+ My 9 '65

Whirling dervishes; First cavalry division (airmobile) in central Vietnam highlands and Ia Drang Valley. Newsweek 66:28 D 13 '65

Hospitals

See Hospitals, Military

Maneuvers

See Military maneuvers

Materiel command

Army weighs new air-defense system. M. Getler. Miss & Roc 17:14 N 1 '65

Medical and sanitary affairs

See also
Hospitals, Military

Missile command

See United States—Army—Materiel command

Negroes

Freedom fighters. J. W. Blassingame. bibliog Negro Hist Bul 28:105-6 F '65

Post exchanges

See United States—Armed forces—Post exchanges

Procurement

McNamara, Senate group gird for procurement policy battle. G. C. Wilson. Aviation W 83:27-9 Ag 16 '65

Recreation

See also
United service organizations

Reserves

McNamara at the bar; proposed abolition of the Reserve. W. F. Buckley, jr. Nat R 17:361 My 4 '65

New Pentagon plan· short-term soldiers. il U S News 59:6 O 4 '65

Tough new role for reserves. U S News 59:63 O 11 '65

Special forces

Green berets, by R. Moore. Review
Nation 201:64-5 Ag 2 '65. D. Ford

Team players; action in Vietnam. il Newsweek 66:29 Ag 23 '65

Training

See Military training

Army hospitals

See Hospitals, Military

Army research office

Inventors' utopia; Limited war laboratory. · D. Francis. il Pop Sci 187:54-7+ S '65

Atomic energy commission

AEC doubles space radioisotope efforts. M. L. Yaffee. il Aviation W 84:75+ Ja 10 '66

AEC unlocks some files for business; Y-12 facilities near Oak Ridge. il Bsns W p50+ O 2 '65

Atoms for peace: the dream, the reality. C. P. Anderson. il N Y Times Mag p 10-11+ Ag 1 '65

Competing with AT&T; Los Alamos telephone system. New Repub 152:7 F 6 '65

Deep nuclear blasts tap lodes of data; AEC's underground test program. il Bsns W p 134+ O 9 '65

Experiment in womanhood. A. P. Cooper. Sat R 48:52-3 Mr 6 '65

High-energy politics; forces now jockeying for position as plans proceed for giant new accelerator. D. S. Greenberg. il Science 147:1423-6 Mr 19 '65

Life that's made to order; experiments at Atomic energy commission's research laboratory, University of Tennessee. A. Whitman. il Pop Mech 124:138-42 N '65

NASA sees rising need for isotopes. H. Taylor. Miss & Roc 16:12 Ap 26 '65

Nuclear reactors; the between generation. il Fortune 71:219 Je '65

Town that wouldn't stay down; Richland, Wash, and its sister cities. il U S News 59:96-7 Jl 19 '65

U.S. to make further cutback in enriched uranium production; Atomic energy commission announcement of February 15, 1965, with letter to President Johnson from AEC chairman. Dept State Bul 52:339 Mr 8 '65

Appropriations and expenditures

AEC funding reduced on space, defense. K. Johnsen. Aviation W 82:38-9 F 8 '65

Funding for nuclear test detection reaches $250-million annual level. Aviation W 83:68 Jl 5 '65

SNAP 8 support gathers momentum. H. M. David. il Miss & Roc 16:17 F 15 '65

Attorney General

See United States—Justice, Department of

Budget, Bureau of the

Budget wins a new role. il Bsns W p 128-30+ Ag 21 '65

New budgeteer; appointment of C. L. Schultze. Newsweek 65:76 My 3 '65

Remarkable Mr Gordon and his quiet power center. J. Kraft. Harper 230:40+ My '65

Shuffle at Budget; C. L. Schultze appointed director. Time 85:31 Ap 30 '65

$20 million footnote. M. S. Monk, jr. il Am For 71:24-7 Ap '65; Discussion. 71:11 Ap; 2 Jl '65

Bureau of Indian affairs

See United States—Indian affairs, Bureau of

Cabinet

Cabinet charade. Time 85:21-2 Ap 16 '65

Gardner appointment. J. Lear. Sat R 48:46 Ag 21 '65

Head for HUD; first Negro Cabinet officer in Nation's history. Newsweek 67:26 Ja 24 '66

How Johnson uses his cabinet. il Bsns W p 180+ My 22 '65

Surrogate for the cities. Time 86:22-3 Ag 20 '65

Their master's voice; reversing policies. New Repub 152:8-9 Ap 17 '65

When newsmen interviewed the Cabinet en masse. il U S News 58:6 Ap 5 '65

Capital

See also
Washington, D.C.

Capitol

Get our Capitol a real architect! Life 59:4 Jl 9 '65

House of Stewart; west wall extension. il Time 86:26 D 3 '65

New concern over safety of the Capitol. il U S News 58:12 Je 7 '65

No vacancy; problem of office space for Vice-President and his staff. Reporter 32:16+ Mr 25 '65

Reflecting pool for the Capitol, too. il U S News 59:14 N 15 '65

To keep the Capitol from falling down. il U S News 59:12 O 25 '65

Census

This U.S.A. by B. J. Wattenberg and R. M. Scammon. Review
Newsweek 66:109C+ D 6 '65
Sr Schol il 87:8-11+ D 9 '65

Central intelligence agency

Containing Central intelligence. H. H. Ransom. New Repub 153:12-15 D 11 '65

Invisible government, by D. Wise and T. B. Ross. Review
Commentary 39:87-9 Mr '65. R. Steel

Leaky ship. Newsweek 66:25-6 D 27 '65

Marines have had it; attractions of CIA. Nation 201:207-8 O 11 '65

New tools for the CIA. H. Brandon. Sat R 48:16+ My 22 '65

Oh, oh, 007; adventures of the CIA. New Repub 153:8 S 18 '65

PERT man for the CIA. il Time 85:27-8 Ap 23 '65

Public eye no. one. Newsweek 65:27 Ap 26 '65

Search for someone to fill the cloak. Time 85:26 Ap 9 '65

Shake-up ahead for supersecret agency? U S News 58:29 Ap 26 '65

Shaky domino; CIA agent plotting subversion in Singapore. il Newsweek 66:44-5 S 13 '65

UNITED STATES—Central intelligence agency
—*Continued*
Soviet spymasters; Soviet espionage apparatus in the U.S. S. Alsop. Sat Eve Post 238:16 My 22 '65
When the spy business gets in the news. il U S News 59:70-1 N 15 '65

Chamber of commerce
See Chamber of commerce of the United States

Civil aeronautics board
Air fares flying on collision course. Bsns W p75 Ja 1 '66
Board delays Hawaii route award. Aviation W 83:41 S 13 '65
Board refuses to back inflight movie ban. J. R. Ashlock. Aviation W 82:28 Je 7 '65
CAB asks participants' assistance in reopening Pacific routes case. Aviation W 83:43 Ag 9 '65
CAB awards Florida-Texas route to Eastern, affirming 1961 ruling. R. G. O'Lone. Aviation W 82:29 Je 7 '65
CAB calls meeting with airlines to analyze jet fare policy impact. Aviation W 83:33 O 4 '65
CAB chairman pledges firm fare limits. J. R. Ashlock. Aviation W 83:37 S 13 '65
CAB cool to airline aid for NY airways. Aviation W 83:28 Jl 5 '65
CAB seeks surcharge dilemma solution. J. R. Ashlock. il Aviation W 84:28-9 Ja 3 '66
CAB seen delaying inflight movie ruling. J. R. Ashlock. Aviation W 82:30 My 24 '65
CAB weighs appeal on blocked-space. R. G. O'Lone. Aviation W 82:41 Ap 26 '65
CAB will weigh new cargo aids if courts rule out blocked space. J. W. Carter. Aviation W 82:34 Mr 29 '65
Flak from the boss; rejection of airlines proposal to raise fares. Time 86:76+ Ag 6 '65
Pending CAB decisions could alter U.S. international route pattern. W. Wright. Aviation W 83:28-9 Jl 26 '65
Two basic charter decisions facing CAB. R. G. O'Lone. Aviation W 82:36-7 F 22 '65
United jet fare rejection shakes industry. J. R. Ashlock. Aviation W 83:34-5 S 6 '65
Will CAB get tough now? Bsns W p34 Ag 7 '65

Civil air patrol
CAP goes aloft. il Flying 77:86 Ag '65

Civil defense, Office of
Hospitals in storage. Nation 201:514 D 27 '65

Civil rights commission
See United States—Commission on civil rights

Civil service commission
Charge of immorality; concerning Civil service commission hiring procedures. New Repub 153:6-7 Jl 3 '65
Exodus of federal employees. America 114:62 Ja 15 '66
Test bans; government tightening regulations over use of psychological tests. New Repub 152:8 Je 19 '65

Civilization
Culture we share; American hemisphere as single cultural entity. R. Squirru. il Américas 17:42-9 Ap '65
Great society: an old New deal. S. W. Rousseas. Nation 200:499-501 My 10 '65
House of law. R. Moley. Newsweek 66:96 S 13 '65
Inaugural address; January 20, 1965. L. B. Johnson. Dept State Bul 52:162-4 F 8 '65
Is America ready for a Great society? interview. R. E. Fitch. il U S News 58:50-4 Mr 8 '65; Same abr. with title America's potential for greatness. Read Digest 86:62-6 Je '65
LBJ keynote: a prosperous, great and mighty nation; inaugural address, January 20, 1965. L. B. Johnson. il U S News 58:102-3 F 1 '65; Same. Vital Speeches 31:258-9 F 15 '65
Man in the American mask. J. Barzun. For Affairs 43:426-35 Ap '65
On seeing and believing. A. Heckscher. Sat R 48:125-6 Mr 13 '65
Priests without cassocks. H. C. Bunke. Harvard Bsns R 43:103-9 My '65
State of the Union; address to the Congress. January 4, 1965. L. B. Johnson. Dept State Bul 52:94-100 Ja 25 '65; Excerpts. Cur Hist 48:176-8+ Mr '65
See also
United States—Intellectual life
United States—Social conditions

History
Americans: the national experience, by D. J. Boorstin. Review
Time il 86:118+ O 1 '65
Life of the mind in America: from the Revolution to the Civil war, by P. Miller. Review
Nation 201:446-8 D 6 '65. A. Trachtenberg
Nation and its century. R. C. Sterne. bibliog il Nation 201:42-53+ S 20 '65
Theories of the American experience; between Revolutionary and Civil wars. L. Grauman, jr. New Repub 153:23-6 O 2 '65

Coast and geodetic survey
Current situation; Long Island Sound. M. L. Hersey. il Motor B 115:102+ Ap '65
See also
United States—Environmental science services administration

Coast guard
Death rode the surf. O. C. Johnson. il Outdoor Life 136:52-5+ Jl '65
Electronic lifeline on the high seas; AMVER to the rescue. T. Irwin il Pop Sci 187:86-8+ S '65
Emergency radio calls. R. Fremont-Smith. Yachting 117:190+ Ap '65
Rescue at tin can grounds; Long Island Sound. J. Ridgeway. New Repub 153:14-16 Jl 24 '65
See also
United States coast guard academy, New London, Conn.

History
Coast guard's 175th. J. C. Goldthorpe. il Motor B 116:39+ Ag '65

Coast guard auxiliary
Coast guard auxiliary offers free boating courses. il Motor B 116:123-4 Ag '65
Coast guard's extra arm. S. Castan. il Look 29:M8-11 Jl 13 '65
Under the blue ensign. B. Woodward. See issues of Motor boating
U.S. Coast guard auxiliary. R. Birnn. See issues of Yachting

Commerce
Charting a new course; U.S. shipping. il Bsns W p 166+ Ap 24 '65
DOD overhauls procedures for export. C. Brownlow. Aviation W 84:26-7 Ja 17 '66
Department opposes bill to amend export control act of 1949; statement, May 24, 1965. G. W. Ball. Dept State Bul 53:35-7 Jl 5 '65
Exporters pin hopes on second-half sales. il Bsns W p28 Jl 17 '65
How New York pushes its wares overseas. il Bsns W p32 S 11 '65
How U.S. makes markets abroad; exports displayed in trade shows. il U S News 59:70 Ag 30 '65
Look at U.S. export prospects. il Fortune 72:58 Jl '65
Making a strong pitch to build U.S. exports; government and businessmen unite. il Bsns W p80+ My 8 '65
Piggyback sales gain momentum; piggyback exporting. Bsns W p70+ D 18 '65
President reports to Congress on trade agreements program; text of message, October 13, 1965. L. B. Johnson. Dept State Bul 53:761 N 8 '65
Shrinking surplus; imports soar. il Time 86:97 N 5 '65
Trade and the balance of payments; statement, March 16, 1965. G. G. Johnson. Dept State Bul 52:502-7 Ap 5 '65
U.S. exports fight to hold '64 level. il Bsns W p 138+ O 16 '65
Why U.S. is pushing the sale of weapons. il U S News 59:122 O 11 '65
See also
Import quotas
Merchant marine—United States
Railroads—United States
Shipping—United States

Australia
Arms U.S. is selling to two key allies. il U S News 58:8 F 22 '65

Canada
Common market for U.S. and Canada? interview. H. G. Johnson. il U S News 58:98-101 F 8 '65
Department supports bill to carry out auto agreement with Canada; statement, April 27, 1965. T. C. Mann. Dept State Bul 52:830-3 My 24 '65

UNITED STATES—Commerce—Canada—*Cont.*
U.S. and Canada trade relations; address,
December 15, 1964. S. J. Randall. Vital
Speeches 31:251-4 F 1 '65

China (People's Republic)
10,000 red-gilt envelopes. H. Smith. il Nation
200:191-3 F 22 '65

Communist countries
East-West trade; address, October 21, 1965.
A. M. Solomon. Dept State Bul 53:739-46
N 8 '65
Pressure rises for trade with reds; business
groups urge easing of U.S. policy, right-
wing groups continue fighting for hard line.
Bsns W p96+ My 8 '65
Selling wheat to Communist countries: gain
or loss for the free world? pro and con
discussion. il Sr Schol 87:12-13 D 2 '65
Trade with the reds. Nat R 17:408+ My 18
'65

Europe, Eastern
Group to study trade relations with eastern
Europe and U.S.S.R. Dept State Bul 52:
724 My 10 '65
President acknowledges report on east Europe
and Soviet trade; letter, May 20, 1965. L. B.
Johnson. Dept State Bul 52:954 Je 14 '65

Europe, Western
Feeding western Europe; U.S. farm exports.
il Time 86:78 Ag 27 '65
Hard-sell arms race, U.S. style. il Newsweek
65:59 Je 14 '65
Kennedy round; address, March 8, 1965. W.
M. Blumenthal. Dept State Bul 52:628-35
Ap 26 '65

France
Behind the nickel curtain; order bans U.S.
imports of any products containing Le
nickel's metal. il Time 86:107 N 12 '65

Great Britain
Arms U.S. is selling to two key allies. il U S
News 58:8 F 22 '65
Buying overseas for U.S. arsenal; policy of
reciprocity. il Bsns W p 142+ O 9 '65
Now that Britain decides to buy U.S. planes.
U S News 58:16 F 15 '65

Greece
U.S. renews agricultural aid to Greece; De-
partment statement, December 10, 1965.
Dept State Bul 53:1020 D 27 '65

Latin America
U.S. trade policy in Latin America; state-
ment, September 10, 1965. A. M. Solomon.
Dept State Bul 53:567-72 O 4 '65

Mexico
U.S.-Mexican trade committee holds first
meeting; Department announcement, October 12; joint communique, October 16,
1965. Dept State Bul 53:738 N 8 '65

Poland
U.S. trade mission visits Poland and Rumania. Dept State Bul 53:553 O 4 '65

Rumania
Rumanian deal settled amid fuss over another; Universal oil products case. Bsns W
p71 Jl 31 '65
U.S. trade mission visits Poland and Rumania. Dept State Bul 53:553 O 4 '65

Russia
East-West trade; address, October 21, 1965.
A. M. Solomon. Dept State Bul 53:739-46
N 8 '65
Group to study trade relations with eastern
Europe and U.S.S.R. Dept State Bul 52:
724 My 10 '65
Making Soviet trade a U.S. political asset.
il Bsns W p94+ F 27 '65
President acknowledges report on east Europe
and Soviet trade; letter, May 20, 1965. L. B.
Johnson. Dept State Bul 52:954 Je 14 '65
President Johnson receives report on increas-
ing trade with U.S.S.R; remarks, January 7,
1965. W. Blackie; L. B. Johnson. Dept State
Bul 52:101-3 Ja 25 '65
Reappraising trade with Russia. T. F.
Willers. Duns R 85:21+ Mr '65
We should do more business with the Communists. J. H. Cerf. il N Y Times Mag
p70-1+ D 5 '65
Why U.S. was left out of Russian wheat
deal; with editorial comment. Bsns W
p30-1, 144 Ag 21 '65

Underdeveloped areas
Challenges facing United States trade policy;
address, October 21, 1965. A. M. Solomon.
Dept State Bul 53:787-93 N 15 '65

Commerce, Department of
Boyd views new Commerce post as focus of
transportation policy. Aviation W 82:26 My
31 '65
Connor: how he works for business; seeking
bigger voice for business in government.
il Nations Bsns 53:36-7+ N '65
Technical services act: industry to benefit
from new state programs paralleling farm
extension service. L. J. Carter. Science 149:
1485-6+ S 24 '65
Voice for business in U.S. policy. il Bsns W
p96-8+ Mr 13 '65
Why can't we make cars safer? R. F. Kennedy. il Pop Sci 187:63-7+ N '65
See also
United States—International commerce, Bureau of

Institute of oceanography
Commerce bids for sea research role. W. S.
Beller. il Miss & Roc 18:28+ Ja 17 '66

Commercial treaties and agreements
President asks authority to remove duties on
Canadian auto products; letter, March 31,
1965. L. B. Johnson. Dept State Bul 52:
638-9 Ap 26 '65
U.S. and Canada sign agreement on trade
in automotive products; exchange of remarks, with text of agreement, January 16,
1965. L. B. Johnson; L. B. Pearson. Dept
State Bul 52:191-4 F 8 '65
U.S. and Colombia conclude cotton textile
agreement; Department announcement,
June 9, 1965, with agreement and related
letters. il Dept State Bul 53:89-92 Jl 12 '65
U.S. and Japan amend bilateral cotton textile
arrangement; joint announcement, May 19,
1965, with U.S. note. Dept State Bul 52:980-1
Je 14 '65
U.S. and Pakistan conclude cotton textile
agreement; Department announcement,
with text of U.S. note, February 26, 1965.
G. G. Johnson. il Dept State Bul 52:391-4
Mr 15 '65
United States and U.S.S.R. sign king crab
fishing agreement; Department announcement, February 6, 1965, with text of agreement. Dept State Bul 52:320-1 Mr 1 '65
United States expresses views on Laurel-
Langley agreement; statement, March 8,
1965. W. P. Bundy. Dept State Bul 52:
664 My 3 '65

Canada
Automotive products agreement with Canada
becomes effective; statements, October 2,
1965, with texts of the proclamation and
the order. L. B. Johnson. Dept State Bul
53:793-5 N 15 '65

Korea (Republic)
U.S. and Korea conclude cotton textile agreement; Department announcement, January
26, 1965, with agreement and related letters.
il Dept State Bul 52:274-8 F 22 '65

Mexico
U.S. and Mexico agree on measures to solve
Lower Colorado River salinity problem;
statement, March 22, 1965; with joint State-
Interior department announcement. L. B.
Johnson. Dept State Bul 52:555-7 Ap 12 '65

Commission on civil rights
Coming: new laws to help rights workers?
Commission recommendations. U S News
59:8 N 22 '65
Interpretation, anyone? public hearings concerning tests for voter registration in Mississippi. il Time 85:23-4 F 26 '65

Commission on national goals
See United States—President's commission on national goals

Committee for economic development
See Committee for economic development

Community relations service
Long hot summer; concerning racial conflict.
New Repub 153:7-8 Jl 3 '65

Conciliation service
See United States—Federal mediation and
conciliation service

Congress
Congress at work, 1965; symposium, ed. by
D. Reische. il Sr Schol 86:6-29+ F 18 '65

UNITED STATES—Congress—*Continued*
Engineering of change in the U.S. Constitution; excerpt from Technology, social change, and the Constitution. A. S. Miller. il Sat R 48:52-5 F 6 '65
Leading from strength: LBJ in action. D. Brinkley. Atlan 215:49-54 F '65
Profiles without courage. D. Lawrence. U S News 58:128 Ap 26 '65
Undeclared wars; no congressional debates. Commonweal 82:276-7 My 21 '65
  See also
Congressional record
Congressmen
Legislation—United States
Lobbying
Presidents—United States—Relations with Congress

  Caricatures and cartoons
Comment around the Nation. Sr Schol 86:20-1 F 18 '65

  Committees
Committee system: Congress' key to getting things done. il Sr Schol 86:12-14+ F 18 '65
Congress has its own closed shop; closed hearings on controversial subjects. J. Ridgeway. New Repub 152:9 Je 19 '65
How to out-fox the majority. J. Deakin. New Repub 152:13-14 F 27 '65

  Pages
Couple of whizzes go to Washington; first Negroes to serve as congressional pages. il Ebony 20:75-8 Je '65

  Powers and duties
Congress: legislative oversight problem acquires new dimensions as Great society bills are passed. J. Walsh. Science 148:479-82 Ap 23 '65
Congressional foreign policy. New Repub 152:6-7 F 6 '65
Where's Congress? Nation 200:657 Je 21 '65

  Professional staff members
Congress: legislative oversight problem acquires new dimensions as Great society bills are passed. J. Walsh. Science 148:479-82 Ap 23 '65

  Rules and practice
Congress: more action than reform. M. Viorst. Nation 200:581-4 My 31 '65
Effort toward efficiency. Time 85:28 My 21 '65
House out of order, by R. Bolling. Review Nation 200:600 My 31 '65. J. V. Morris
Push for reforms; forum topic of the week. Sr Schol 86:20-2 F 18 '65

  Terminology
Congressional glossary. Sr Schol 86:38 F 18 '65

  89th Congress
Congress and business: Senators Mansfield and Dirksen debate outlook; ed. by J. W. Bunting. M. Mansfield and E. M. Dirksen. il Nations Bsns 53:76-80+ Mr '65
Congressional scorecard; bills and acts of interest to recreation. Recreation 58:264-5 Je '65
89th: LBJ's do-plenty Congress. il Newsweek 65:21-2 F 15 '65
Revolutionizing the U.S, the changes Congress is making. il U S News 59:29-32 Jl 26 '65

  89th Congress—1st session
And there's more on the way; President calls for passing of more bills. il Bsns W p28-9 Ag 7 '65
As Congress rushes to go home—. il U S News 59:35-6 O 25 '65
Atlantic report; 1965 review. Atlan 217:6 Ja '66
Best crop of legislation in years. il Bsns W p 17-18 Jl 3 '65
Bills already enacted; bills not yet enacted, and their outlook. U S News 58:33 Je 28 '65
Breaking down the old order; Johnson Congress. Bsns W p25-6 S 18 '65
Cheer for Congress. Sat Eve Post 238:80 S 11 '65
Congress. See issues of Newsweek
Congress. See issues of Time
Congress: in session of heavy legislative output legislators paid new attention to environment. J. Walsh. Science 150:724-5 N 5 '65
Congress is nobody's lapdog. Life 59:4 N 5 '65

Congress: more action than reform. M. Viorst. Nation 200:581-4 My 31 '65
Domestic record. Commonweal 83:111-12 O 29 '65
89th Congress: acting on the visionary. Time 86:22 O 29 '65
89th Congress in perspective; what LBJ wants, LBJ gets; address, November 15, 1965. R. P. Griffin. Vital Speeches 32:140-3 D 15 '65
89th's massive record. il Sr Schol 87:15-16 O 28 '65
GOP salutes President for 89th's record. J. N. Eller. America 113:520 N 6 '65
Grand old problem; Republican opposition policy. Reporter 32:11-12 Je 17 '65
Holiday for builders; first session adjourns. il Time 86:21+ O 29 '65
In Congress, major bills move ahead. U S News 59:6 Ag 2 '65
In home stretch, Congress speeds up. il U S News 59:8 Ag 30 '65
Johnson message; first seven messages to Congress. New Repub 152:1+ F 6 '65
Key men in the 89th. Sr Schol 86:15 F 18 '65
Last days of Congress. W. V. Shannon. Commonweal 83:140-2 N 5 '65
Legislative oversight; critical review. New Repub 152:5-6 Je 26 '65
Legislative scorecard. Time 86:21 Ag 6 '65
Let us praise tired men at the harvest. J. N. Eller. America 113:257 S 11 '65
LBJ and Congress; after a fast start, harder tests ahead. il U S News 58:52-3 Mr 1 '65
LBJ and the fabulous 89th go home; achievements and future implications. S. Shaffer. il Newsweek 66:21-3 N 1 '65
LBJ is asking for all this. il U S News 58:35-6 F 1 '65
LBJ's new experiment in government. il U S News 58:64-8+ Ap 5 '65
LBJ's 100 days: a record piling up; Way LBJ runs Congress. il U S News 58:41-4 Ap 26 '65
Members of the 89th Congress. Sr Schol 86:24-5 F 18 '65
Month in Congress. Cong Digest 44:33-4+, 65-6+, 97-8, 129-30, 161-2+ F-Je '65
Mood of Congress. W. V. Shannon. Commonweal 82:462-3 Jl 2 '65
New look at defense: why Congress worries. il U S News 58:37-41 Mr 1 '65
Putting Congress through hoops. Bsns W p32 Ap 3 '65
Scant rest in sight for weary Congress; with editorial comment. Bsns W p27-8, 196 O 23 '65
School aid bill: attention to controversial issues overshadows discussion of educational R&D. J. Walsh. Science 147:717-19 F 12 '65
There's never been anything like the 89th. H. Hamilton. America 113:181 Ag 21 '65
This week in Congress. Sr Schol 86:15 F 25 '65 24 Mr 4; 23 Mr 11; 20 Mr 18; 19 Mr 25; 27 Ap 15; 27 Ap 29 '65
Time for a breather. Bsns W p96 Jl 31 '65
Washington wire; cold eye on Johnson. R. G. Sherrill. Nation 202:4-7 Ja 3 '66
What Congress did to change U.S; legislation to get the Great society under way. il U S News 59:29-32 N 1 '65
Why labor didn't get all it wanted from Congress. U S News 59:93-4+ O 25 '65
Work for the fabulous 89th; ineffectiveness in foreign affairs. Nation 201:317 N 8 '65

  89th Congress—2d session
Active & concerned. Time 87:19B-19C Ja 21 '66
Bubbles and blanks; reactions to L. B. Johnson's State of the Union message. Newsweek 67:22 Ja 24 '66
Congress. il Time 87:21A Ja 14 '66
For Congress, tax rise may be the big issue. Bsns W p20+ Ja 1 '66
Fretful Congress confronts Vietnam. il Newsweek 67:16-17 Ja 17 '66
Midterm '66 hopes and fears. E. T. Folliard. America 114:9 Ja 1 '66
Outlook for LBJ's legislative plans. il U S News 60:4 Ja 24 '66
Return of the 89th. America 114:65-6 Ja 15 '66
State of the Congress. A. Kopkind. New Repub 154:13-16 Ja 22 '66
What LBJ can expect from Congress now. il U S News 60:50-1 Ja 10 '66

  House of representatives
Changes in the House. Commonweal 81:629 F 12 '65
Disorderly house; attitude of House of representatives to Supreme court. K. Crawford. Newsweek 65:34 Ap 5 '65

UNITED STATES—Congress—House of representatives—*Continued*
Group that runs the House; Democratic study group. P. Duke and A. B. Sawsilak. il Reporter 32:29-31 My 20 '65
Home place, by W. S. White. Review
 Harper 230:152-4 Mr '65. M. K. Sanders
 Nat R 17:286-7 Ap 6 '65. R. E. Bauman
House out of order, by R. Bolling. Review
 Nation 200:600 My 31 '65. J. V. Morris
 New Repub 152:23-4+ F 13 '65. W. A. Korns
Legislation with representation. M. L. Coit. Sat R 48:62-3 Ap 10 '65
Representing the House. N. W. Polsby. il Reporter 32:40+ My 6 '65
When Congress got its back up; defeat of Johnson-backed home rule bill. il U S News 59:41-2 O 11 '65
When violence struck at the Capitol; congressman in House shot by members of Nationalist party, Puerto Rico, March 1, 1954. il Sr Schol 86:4 F 25 '65

House of representatives—Armed services committee
He's gone, Mr Secretary. Time 85:25A-25B Je 18 '65
House committee to investigate air power. G. C. Wilson. Aviation W 83:26 Ag 23 '65
Rivers delivers; powerful armed forces chairman. D. Oberdorfer. il N Y Times Mag p30-1+ Ag 29 '65

House of representatives—Banking and currency committee
Hanky-panky in the House. J. Ridgeway. New Repub 153:8 O 30 '65
Patman vs. Martin: new clash on money; hearing of the House banking and currency committee, July 6. U S News 59:20 Jl 19 '65

House of representatives—Committee on science and astronautics
Academy and Congress: NAS panel completes its first assignment in new relationship with Congress. D. S. Greenberg. Science 148: 608-9 Ap 30 '65

House of representatives—Committees
Oceanography: House subcommittee encourages use of merchant ships to gather data on the high seas. J. Walsh. Science 148:349-50 Ap 16 '65

House of representatives—Un-American activities committee
Abolish it. New Repub 152:5 Mr 6 '65
Committee on contempt; disgraceful behavior in Chicago. New Repub 152:8 Je 19 '65
Dark days in weird week; public hearings before House un-American activities committee. Time 86:29 O 29 '65
Focus on HUAC. Nation 200:238-9 Mr 8 '65
Gambling on HUAC. Commonweal 82:101 Ap 16 '65
Honor bright and all that jazz. D. Trumbo. Nation 201:183-90 S 20 '65
HUAC in Chicago: this is not a court. R. R. Coffey. Nation 200:633-6 Je 14 '65
HUAC; indictment of two members of the Women strike for peace movement. Commonweal 81:596 F 5 '65
H.U.A.C. meets the K.K.K. W. Goodman. il N Y Times Mag p48-9+ D 5 '65
HUAC versus the Klan. Reporter 32:9-10 Ap 22 '65
HUAC's feint. Nation 200:183 F 22 '65
Investigating the klans. New Repub 152:5-6 Ap 10 '65
Klan clams up. M. Kempton. New Repub 153:11-13 O 30 '65
Klan discovers HUAC; R. M. Shelton Ku Klux klan contributions. W. Goodman. il Nation 201:328-30 N 8 '65; Reply with rejoinder. S. E. Crane. 201:inside cover, 428 N 29 '65
Klan on the pan. Sr Schol 86:27 Ap 15 '65
Same old HUAC. Nation 201:290-1 N 1 '65
Sending a goose to catch a fox; HUAC to investigate K.K.K. Christian Cent 82:453 Ap 14 '65; Reply. 82:1432 N 24 '65
Shooting at the Klan but wounding the Negro; clergymen denounce H.U.A.C.'s impending investigation of KKK. Christian Cent 82: 1149 S 22 '65
Sleep softly, myth; L. Currie case. Nat R 17:494+ Je 15 '65
Stamler vs. HUAC: heart specialist, called by committee, responds by challenging HUAC's legality. E. Langer. Science 149:405-7 Jl 23 '65

Un-American; two women from Women strike for peace indicted at behest of HUAC; reply. F. J. Donner. New Repub 152:28 F 6 '65
Unsheeting the Klan. il Newsweek 65:29-30 Ap 12 '65

Senate
Free for all; contenders for Saltonstall's seat. il Newsweek 67:20-1 Ja 10 '66
Ted Kennedy on his own: coming up strong in the Senate. J. Roddy. il Look 29:29-35 Jl 13 '65
Uhuru comes to the Senate; deterioration of the Senate club. M. Greenfield. il Reporter 33:32-7 S 23 '65
Winds of change in the Senate. T. Wicker. il N Y Times Mag p52-3+ S 12 '65
 See also
Senators

Senate—Banking and currency committee
How to out-fox the majority. J. Deakin. New Repub 152:13-14 F 27 '65

Senate—Committees
Anatomy of copyright revision; subcommittee of the House committee on the judiciary. R. H. Smith. Pub W 187:81 Je 14 '65
99th senator; R. Kennedy answers charges made at hearings of subcommittee on government snooping. il Newsweek 65:29-30 Mr 15 '65
Robbing the aged; findings of subcommittee of Senate special committee on aging. America 112:244 F 20 '65
Uhuru comes to the Senate; deterioration of the Senate club. M. Greenfield. il Reporter 33:32-7 S 23 '65

Senate—History
Of snuff, sin and the Senate, by R. Rienow and L. T. Rienow. Review
 Sat R 48:24-5 Jl 31 '65. M. L. Coit

Senate—Rules and practice
Filibuster's best friend; R. Russell, dean of southern senators. D. Oberdorfer. il Sat Eve Post 238:90+ Mr 13 '65
World's most exclusive delaying tactic: filibuster. il Sr Schol 86:5 F 11 '65

Senate—Rules committee
FBI report: publication of Don B. Reynolds testimony with document rebutting his charges. Time 85:23A Mr 12 '65

Conservation, Department of (proposed)
Public land review. M. Clawson. il Am For 71:26-9+ Jl '65

Constitution
Bowing to the new extremists. D. Lawrence. U S News 58:112 Mr 29 '65
Constitutional framework: place for Congress. Sr Schol 86:6-7 F 18 '65
Engineering of change in the U.S. Constitution; excerpt from Technology, social change, and the Constitution. A. S. Miller. il Sat R 48:52-5 F 6 '65
Founders confounded. K. Crawford. Newsweek 65:35 Ap 19 '65
Magna charta: forerunner of the U.S. Constitution. H. G. Earl. il Todays Health 43: 54-7 Je '65
Must we repeal the Constitution to give the Negro the vote? with editorial comment. J. J. Kilpatrick. il Nat R 17:312, 319-22, 350+ Ap 20-My 4 '65

Amendments
Art of amending; giving full power to vice-president during a president's disability. il Time 85:49 F 26 '65
Baseball, pure and undefiled; anti-reapportionment amendment. A. Kopkind. New Repub 153:9-10 Ag 7 '65
Constitutional view: right to vote. Sr Schol 86:7 Ap 8 '65
Enforcing the Fifteenth. il Time 85:22-3 Mr 26 '65
Immoral law; excerpts from editorials in Wall Street journal, March 22 and March 24, 1965. U S News 58:116+ Ap 5 '65
Lynching the states; proposed Voting rights act of 1965. D. Lawrence. U S News 58: 124 Ap 12 '65
Profiles without courage. D. Lawrence. U S News 58:128 Ap 26 '65
Remarkably unamended document. Sr Schol 87:13 O 14 '65
Senator Dirksen vs. the Court; proposed amendment to nullify one man, one vote reapportionment ruling. R. M. Christenson. Nation 201:60-1 Ag Ag 2 '65

UNITED STATES—Constitution—Amendments
—*Continued*
Trend: legislating by constitutional amendment. J. N. Eller. America 112:278 F 27 '65
25th amendment, we hope; replacing a disabled president. Life 59:6 Jl 16 '65
Urge to amend; proposed amendment of one-man, one-vote ruling as applied to state legislatures. Time 86:24-5 Ag 6 '65
Voting bill and the Constitution. il U S News 58:40-1 Ap 5 '65
See also
Presidents—United States—Succession

Bill of rights

Bill of rights, by I. Brant. Review
    Sat R 49:28 Ja 1 '66. R. Baldwin
Citizen as activist. Nation 200:603 Je 7 '65
Conflict without calumny; interpretation of First amendment. Christian Cent 82:933 Jl 28 '65
Criminal law and the Bill of rights. J. S. Wright. il Reporter 32:23-5 Je 3 '65
Forgotten amendment; Griswold v. Connecticut, right to marital privacy and rediscovery of Ninth amendment. J. D. Carroll. Nation 201:121-2 S 6 '65
Life, liberty and privacy; added to 5 amendments. Life 59:4 Jl 2 '65
New life for a forgotten amendment: Ninth, involving right to privacy. il U S News 59:14 Jl 5 '65
Now comes the Sixth amendment; the confrontation clause. Time 85:46 Ap 16 '65

Study and teaching

Constitution: team teaching approach with A-V aids. M. Benefield. Sr Schol 86:sup7-8 Mr 11 '65

Copyright office

No place for poetic license; the copyright office at LC. B. A. Ringer. il Library J 90:2958-63 Jl '65

Council of economic advisers

Forecaster for the forecasters; D. W. Lusher. il Bsns W p 158+ Ap 3 '65
Growing attack on steel report. U S News 58:87 My 24 '65
How the style shifts at CEA; chairman G. Ackley. il Bsns W p73-4+ Ja 30 '65
Is White House backing union in dispute over steel wages? U S News 58:92 My 17 '65
Keeping a delicate balance; concerning report of the Council. il Time 85:93 My 21 '65
No miracles; concerning President's annual Economic report to Congress and report by the Council of economic advisers. Commonweal 81:628-9 F 12 '65
Planning for economic stability in 1966. Bsns W p 148 O 30 '65
Road ahead looks smooth to a point. il Bsns W p27-9 Ja 30 '65
Steel company answers the White House on wages: Republic steel corporation; excerpts from report. J. Backman. U S News 59:77 Ag 16 '65
Steel gets a report without frosting; CEA urges price stability. il Bsns W p26-7 My 8 '65
To & from Harvard in the middle of the road. Time 87:82 Ja 7 '66
Vigorous growth in the year ahead; annual Economic report. il Newsweek 65:63-4 F 8 '65

Council on the arts

See United States—National council on the arts

Court of customs and patent appeals

Who invented the laser? C. H. Townes' and A. L. Schawlow's patent rights challenged. il Bsns W p 132-7 N 27 '65

Crime commission

See United States—National crime commission

Cultural relations

Arts committee reports progress on cultural presentations; letter, with Committee's recommendations. R. E. Larsen. Dept State Bul 52:108-11 Ja 25 '65
Finding out about red China; need for exchange of information. L. H. Evans. il Sat R 48:17-18 Je 26 '65
Moscow-New York shuttle; Soviet-American musical relations. Hi Fi 15:49 O '65
President sends Congress reports on cultural and exhibits programs; letters, October 6, 1965. L. B. Johnson. Dept State Bul 53: 673-4 O 25 '65

Scribblers and international relations. C. Frankel. For Affairs 44:1-14 O '65
Seven cups of tea. W. Starr. il Am Ed 1:10-11 My '65
Soft sound in the U.S.S.R: New York pro musica in the Soviet Union. N. Greenberg. il Hi Fi 15:41-3+ My '65
Theater study group given permanent advisory status. Dept State Bul 52:253 F 22 '65
Toward world literacy; address, April 1965. L. Carnovsky. bibliog il Wilson Lib Bul 39: 887-95 Je '65
West side story in Japan. P. Paull. il Dance Mag 39:35-8 Ap '65
See also
American libraries abroad
People-to-people-program

Culture, Popular

See United States—Popular culture

Customs

See United States—Social life and customs

Customs, Bureau of

See Customs service—United States

Declaration of independence

It wasn't easy; getting the Declaration written. G. Ace. Sat R 48:7 Jl 3 '65

Defense, Department of

Computerized diplomacy. W. Pfaff. Commonweal 82:520-1 Jl 23 '65
Defense dept. lists 100 top contractors. Aviation W 83:75+ D 20 '65
Defense: McNamara's comptroller, Charles J. Hitch, leaves after four pioneering years at DOD. J. Walsh. Science 149:1074-6 S 3 '65
Defense without competition. Nation 202:59 Ja 17 '66
DOD broadening plans of action for faster weapon production. C. Brownlow. Aviation W 83:25-6 Jl 26 '65
DOD, GAO reach truce on pricing policy. K. Johnsen. Aviation W 83:68-70 D 27 '65
Department of defense lists top 100 prime contractors for fiscal 1964. il Aviation W 82:88-91 Ap 12 '65
Lockheed tops DOD contractor list. il Miss & Roc 16:21 Mr 22 '65
McNamara methods arousing fresh criticism in Congress; with editorial comment. M. Getler. Miss & Roc 18:15, 46 Ja 17 '66
McNamara shuffles Pentagon managers. Bsns W p31 S 18 '65
McNamara team extending sphere into top operation service posts. G. C. Wilson. Aviation W 83:24 Jl 19 '65
McNamara's management revolution; with case study of the impact of systems analysis on airlift and sea-lift capabilities. D. Seligman. il Fortune 72:116-21+ Jl '65
New House foe fires on McNamara. Bsns W p24-5 Jl 3 '65
Power in the Pentagon; duties of R. McNamara. il Newsweek 66:30-4 D 6 '65
Senate fears DOD fund reprogramming. Miss & Roc 17:15 Ag 9 '65
Slow-down in the Pentagon. H. W. Baldwin; reply. J. Burnham. Nat R 17:104 F 9 '65
Standardization gains momentum in DOD. C. Brownlow. il Aviation W 82:69-72 Mr 15 '65
Support service fight has $8 billion stake. C. Brownlow. Aviation W 82:16-18 Mr 22 '65
Tactical warfare and technology. il Miss & Roc 16:39-43+ Mr 29 '65
Two on the aisle. W. J. Coughlin. Miss & Roc 16:46 Mr 15 '65
U.S. agencies get order; join McNamara's band; cost system imposed by Defense secretary on the Pentagon. Bsns W p 182+ N 13 '65
What a whiz kid did; C. J. Hitch's accounting revolution at Pentagon. il Newsweek 66:21 Jl 19 '65
Whatever happened to the State department? C. W. Tait. il Nation 201:137-41 S 13 '65
See also
United States—Defense research and engineering. Director of

Advanced research projects agency

H-bomb blast gives U.S. seismic test earful. il Bsns W p56 N 6 '65
Linking two sides of research; ARPA's experimental program. Bsns W p 140 N 20 '65
On-line computing dominance forseen. R. Pay. Miss & Roc 16:32-4 Mr 1 '65

Appropriations and expenditures

More bucks for the bang. Newsweek 66:100+ N 15 '65

UNITED STATES—Defense, Department of—
Continued

Procurement

New profits for the primes. C. J. Loomis. il
Fortune 71:75-6+ Ap '65

Defense research and engineering, Director of

DOD to overhaul internal R&D policies;
laboratory improvement program. K. Johnsen. Aviation W 83:28-9 S 27 '65
DDR&E changes dilute space role. H. M.
David. il Miss & Roc 17:14 S 13 '65
DDR&E reorganization nears finish. Miss &
Roc 17:15 O 11 '65
Project hindsight to isolate gains of DOD's
fundamental research. K. Johnsen. Aviation W 83:47-8+ O 18 '65
Reorganized DDR&E to put more emphasis on
systems engineering. Aviation W 83:33 S
20 '65

Defenses

American merchant marine; foruth arm of our
defense; address, September 29, 1965. L. E.
James. Vital Speeches 32:51-3 N 1 '65
Anti-missile defense: should Nike X be deployed? L. J. Carter. il Science 150:1696-9
D 24 '65
Bombers vs. missiles: showdown ahead. il
U S News 59:30-2 D 27 '65
Defense budget. Nation 200:97 F 1 '65
DOD briefing emphasizes tactical needs. H.
D. Watkins. Aviation W 82:16-17 Mr 8 '65
Design for survival, by T. S. Power. Review
Time il 85:23A Mr 26 '65
From Washington: notes on defense matters.
H. Margolis. Bul Atomic Sci 21:36-8 S '65
Greater joint space effort endorsed; report
to White House conference on international
cooperation; with editorial comment. W.
S. Beller. Miss & Roc 17:15, 46 D 6 '65
Is Russia slowing down in arms race? interview. R. S. McNamara. il U S News 58:52-
6+ Ap 12 '65
LeMay's warning; excerpts from address.
C. E. LeMay. Aviation W 82:21 Ap 5 '65
Message on megadeaths; McNamara presents
annual report on strategy and defense to
Congress. il Newsweek 65:23-4 Mr 1 '65
NASA budget to be squeezed by boost in
DOD spending. H. M. David. Miss & Roc
18:15 Ja 3 '66
National defense message; excerpts. L. B.
Johnson. Sci N L 87:67 Ja 30 '65
National security and the nuclear-test ban.
J. B. Wiesner and H. F. York; discussion.
Sci Am 211:8+ D '64; 212:8+ F; 6+ Ap '65
New cutback in big bombers: effect on U.S.
defense; with statements by members of
armed-services committees and former
SAC chiefs. il U S News 59:56-7 D 20 '65
President's committee optimistic on impact
of defense fund shifts. K. Johnsen. Aviation W 83:105+ O 11 '65
Should U.S. reshape its strategic might? il
Bsns W p33-4 Jl 17 '65
State of our defenses; message to Congress,
January 18, 1965. L. B. Johnson. Dept State
Bul 52:211-18 F 15 '65
Strategic problems detailed by McNamara;
testimony before the House armed services
committee. R. S. McNamara. Aviation W
82:62-6 Mr 1 '65
Strategic realignment; McNamara's controversial canons. il Time 86:22 D 17 '65
Strategy for the Pacific. C. J. V. Murphy.
il Fortune 73:167-8+ Ja '66
Strongest peace force in the world. R. S.
McNamara. Read Digest 86:83-7 F '65
Tactical capabilities stressed in budget. Aviation W 82:64-5 Mr 8 '65
Tactical warfare and technology. il Miss &
Roc 16:39-43+ Mr 29 '65
35,000 hours through the looking glass;
Strategic air command's airborne emergency headquarters. il Time 85:19 F 12 '65
Truth about our missile defense. H. O.
Johansen. il Pop Sci 187:84-7+ O '65
U.S. defense: the changes Johnson wants;
summary of special message. L. B. Johnson. il U S News 58:14 F 1 '65
See also
Aeronautics, Military—United States
Atomic warfare—Defenses
Civil defense
North American air defense command
United States—Defense, Department of
United States—Navy

Description and travel

Adventure without a passport. M. Frome. il
NEA J 55:54-6 Ja '66
America in summer; with editorial comment.
B. H. Pearse. il Am Ed 1:inside cover,
16-23 Je '65

Autumn foliage: few of this fall's opportunities. il Changing T 19:24 S '65
Do U.S. sights surpass those of Europe? il
U S News 58:12 Mr 8 '65
Fall travel has a special charm. A. H. Hepburn. il Sr Schol 87:sup 12 S 23 '65
Family-planned travel program by the editors
of Better homes & gardens; best vacations
in mid-America. il Bet Hom & Gard 43:
113-18 Jl '65
Family-planned travel program by the editors
of Better homes & gardens highlights of
the historic East. il Bet Hom & Gard 43:
133-8 Je '65
Going nowhere and losing things on the
Super Chief. R. Bailey. il House & Gard
127:29-30+ F '65
Grand tour, family style: a Redbook guide
to travel vacations. M. Cohen. il Redbook
124:49-56 Ap '65
I see America first: diary of the President's
daughter. L. B. Johnson. il Nat Geog Mag
128:874-904 D '65
Now look here, voyager; case for seeing
America first. S. L. Udall. Life 58:17+ Je
18 '65
See America first. A. Chamberlin. il Sat Eve
Post 238:25-31+ Ag 28 '65
Splendors at home. il Time 86:38-50 Jl 2 '65
Teen travel talk; calendar of events. il Seventeen 24:333-4+ Ag '65

Anecdotes, facetiae, satire, etc.

Lighthearted tour of America. R. Bissell.
il Holiday 38:30-43+ Jl '65
Long way to go. P. S. Beagle. il Holiday 37:
62-7+ F '65 (to be cont)

Diplomatic and consular service

Consular convention with the Soviet Union;
statement. July 30, 1965. D. Rusk. Dept
State Bul 53:375-8 Ag 30 '65
Consulate at Vigo, Spain, closed; Embassy
Madrid to handle duties; Department statement, December 1, 1965. Dept State Bul
53:984 D 20 '65
Josy and the king; Burundi demands recall
of Donald A. Dumont. il Newsweek 67:41 Ja
24 '66
No club for cookie-pushers. M. Higgins. NEA
J 54:15 Mr '65
President notes anniversary of American
specialist program; letter, April 15, 1965.
L. B. Johnson. Dept State Bul 52:725 My
10 '65
Science in the State department. D. Wolfle.
Science 148:1181 Je 4 '65
This month's feature: proposed U.S.-Soviet
consular agreement. Cong Digest 44:289-310
D '65
Three consulates in United Kingdom to close
on October 31; Department statement.
September 30, 1965. Dept State Bul 53:645
O 18 '65
U.S. embassies are under siege; the record
of outrages and the protocol of protection;
with editorial comment. il Life 58:4, 38-
38B Mr 19 '65
United States scientific attaché program.
W. H. Taft. Dept State Bul 52:113-15 Ja 25
'65
Wawa moves East; ouster of R. Gordon and
F. Carlucci. Time 85:40 F 5 '65
See also
Negro ambassadors
United States—State, Department of
Women as ambassadors

Discovery and exploration
See United States—History—Discovery
and exploration

Economic conditions

Ackley's answer to Martin: no pitfalls ahead.
Bsns W p27 Je 19 '65
Amazing boom: can it last? il Newsweek 65:
77-8+ Je 14 '65; Same abr. Read Digest
87:76-80 S '65
American economy; symposium. ed. by G.
Nikolaieff. il Sr Schol 86:5-22+ Ap 15 '65
America's great success story. H. H. Humphrey. Read Digest 87:71-4 D '65
Balance of economy cools fear of inflation.
il Bsns W p 104+ S 25 '65
Big gun on poverty. E. L. Dale, jr. New
Repub 153:13-15 Ag 7 '65; Reply. R. M.
Paige. 153:29-30 S 11 '65
Bittersweet smell of success. il Newsweek
66:63 Ag 30 '65
Boom without bust? President's economic
report to Congress. il Time 85:19-20 F 5 '65
Booming economy with only small ifs. Life
59:4 O 22 '65
Challenge to affluence, by G. Myrdal. Review
Sr Schol 86:sup 12 Ap 15 '65. H. L.
Hurwitz

UNITED STATES—Economic conditions—*Cont.*
Consumerism; address, April 19, 1965. G.
Romney. Vital Speeches 31:489-93 Je 1 '65
Could we ever have another depression? il
Changing T 20:7-12 Ja '66
Economics in the news (cont) il Sr Schol
86:22 F 4; 16 F 25; 25 Mr 4; 21 Mr 18; 22
Ap 8; 87:14-15 S 16; 12-13+ O 7; 16+ O 14;
12-13 O 21; 13-14 O 28; 21-2 N 4; 17-18 D
2; 21 D 9 '65
Economy: full of life and vigor. il Newsweek
65:67 Mr 29 '65
Excellent, buoyant & ebullient. il Time 85:21
Ap 23 '65
Fifty-three months of prosperity, how it
looks. il Changing T 19:6 Jl '65
Fight inside the Fed. il Newsweek 66:78 N 8
'65
Five more boom years ahead; interview. A.
F. Brimmer. il Nations Bsns 53:60-2+ Je
'65
Going into the sixth year: future of the
boom. il U S News 60:24-6 Ja 10 '66
Great society: new kind of balance sheet is
needed. L. H. Keyserling. New Repub 152:
11-14 Je 12 '65
Happy face. Newsweek 65:76 Mr 8 '65
Is credit quality getting too low? private
debt outpaced economic growth. il Bsns W
p75-6+ O 2 '65
It never looked better: consumer confidence.
il Bsns W p23-5 Mr 27 '65
Johnson gives the cheerful earful; sees no
slackening of boom. Bsns W p26-7 Je 26
'65
Keeping a delicate balance; concerning report of the Council of economic advisers.
il Time 85:93 My 21 '65
Labor month in review. See issues of Monthly
labor review
Low-pressure economy. H. C. Wallich. Newsweek 66:82 N 1 '65
Monetary cassandra; W. M. Martin, jr. B. L.
Masse. America 112:873 Je 19 '65
1966: booming but look out. Life 60:4 Ja 7
'66
No letup in sight; business boom. il News-
week 65:75 My 24 '65
No miracles; concerning President's annual
Economic report to Congress and report by
the Council of economic advisers. Common-
weal 81:628-9 F 12 '65
Now 1966: problems of prosperity. il News-
week 67:49-52 Ja 10 '66
On your marks, get set, spend. il Newsweek
66:55 S 6 '65
Open-mouth campaign. Time 85:87 Je 25 '65
Optimism reinforced. Time 85:87 Mr 5 '65
President Johnson on the economy; address,
January 28, 1965. L. B. Johnson. Cur Hist
48:362-3+ Je '65
Problem: to keep a lid on; with editorial
comment. il Bsns W p 11-13, 84 Ja 1 '66
Problems of abundance. il Time 86:53 D 24
'65
Problems of success. Time 86:25 D 3 '65
Ready for escalation. il Time 86:63-4 Jl 30 '65
Road ahead looks smooth to a point; high-
lights of report of the Council of economic
advisers. il Bsns W p27-9 Ja 30 '65
Steel reprieve bolsters the boom. il News-
week 65:83-4 My 10 '65
Structure of the U.S. economy. W. W. Leon-
tief. il Sci Am 212:25-35 Ap '65
Talk with Gardner Ackley; interview, ed.
by G. R. Rosen. G. Ackley. Duns R 86:36-8
Jl '65
Three anxieties; excerpt from Our depleted
society. S. Melman. Sat R 48:14-15 Ap 3
'65
Time of trouble; Lyndon Johnson's admin-
istration. S. Alsop. Sat Eve Post 238:16 Jl
17 '65
Touch of economicare; effect of President
Johnson's welfare programs on American
society. il Time 86:67 Ag 20 '65
Two approaches to welfare. O. A. Ornati. bib-
liog f Mo Labor R 88:296-7 Mr '65
United States economy; overview. B. J.
Widick. bibliog f il Cur Hist 49:1-8+ Jl '65
Vigorous growth in the year ahead; annual
Economic report. il Newsweek 65:63-4 F 8
'65
Warning to cool the boom, not kill it. Life
58:4 Je 18 '65
We are depression (but not recession) proof.
E. L. Dale, jr. il N Y Times Mag p36-7+
Ap 4 '65
What is the lesson of 1929? J. Tobin. New
Repub 152:11-12 Je 19 '65; Reply with re-
joinder. C. C. Killingsworth. 153:37-8 Jl 24
'65
Where the mood means so much. il Time
85:81-2 Je 18 '65
Whiz-bang! 1965's first quarter. il Newsweek
65:75-6 Ap 26 '65

Who's afraid of peace? massive defense
spending not essential to nation's prosperity.
Time 86:38-9 S 17 '65
Why recessions are obsolete. R. Newcomb.
Nations Bsns 53:62-4 My '65
See also
Business conditions
Cost of living—United States
Debts, Public—United States
Finance—United States
Immigration and emigration—United States
Labor and laboring classes—United States
Minimum wage—United States
Negroes in the United States—Economic
conditions
Prices—United States
Prosperity
Taxation—United States
Unemployment—United States
United States—Industries
Wages—United States

Economic history

If Lincoln lived today; profile in poverty.
il U S News 58:74-6 F 15 '65
Industry and the federal government: 1850-
1933. G. D. Nash. Cur Hist 48:321-7+ Je '65
See also
Money—United States—History

Economic opportunity, Office of

Bright-D-minus kids; Upward bound. il Time
86:55 Ag 20 '65
Bureaucracy's long arm; too heady a start
in Mississippi? A. Kopkind. New Repub
153:19-22 Ag 21 '65
Can the Job corps do the job? B. Carter.
il Reporter 32:21-6 Mr 25 '65
Fighting poverty and city hall. E. Knoll and
J. Witcover. il Reporter 32:19-22 Je 3 '65
Mr Powell and OEO. America 112:658 My 8
'65
Office of economic opportunity. J. G. Patton.
New Repub 153:38 D 11 '65
Politics and the poor: Shriver's second
thoughts. Reporter 33:23-5 D 30 '65
Poverty war: birth pains. il Newsweek 65:
23-4 Mr 29 '65
What poverty war is about. Life 59:6 Jl
16 '65
Why the poverty war seems a muddle. J.
Ridgeway. New Repub 153:7-8 O 9 '65; Dis-
cussion. 153:36-8 O 23; 39 N 6 '65
See also
Anti-poverty program, 1964-
United States—Job corps

Economic policy

Abundant peace, by R. C. Garretson. Re-
view
Sat R 48:30-1 F 20 '65. L. J. Walinsky;
Reply. R. C. Garretson. 48:21 Ap 3
'65
As events close in on Johnson—. il U S
News 59:27-8 D 20 '65
Bad guys, good guys; economic expansion
v. balanced budget. H. C. Wallich. News-
week 65:85 My 17 '65
Battle over money. America 113:740-1 D 11 '65
Big business & the Democrats; excerpts from
What is power? D. T. Bazelon. Commen-
tary 39:39-46 My '65
Big changes in major policies: decisions LBJ
faces. il U S News 59:29-31 D 13 '65
Big issues: debt and taxes; report on study
by forty-eight economists; with editorial
comment. Bsns W p66+, 156 Mr 6 '65
Booming economy tests self-control. America
113:561-2 N 13 '65
Budget boost: taxes without tears; concern-
ing President's State of the Union address.
il Newsweek 67:67-8 Ja 24 '66
Consumerism; address, April 19, 1965. G.
Romney. Vital Speeches 31:489-93 Je 1 '65
Diehard on the left: L. H. Keyserling.
Duns R 85:41 Je '65
Does monetary history repeat itself? present
& the past; address, June 1, 1965. W. M.
Martin, jr. Vital Speeches 31:580-3 Jl 15 '65;
Excerpts. U S News 58:84-6 Je 14 '65; Sum-
mary. Newsweek 65:79 Je 14 '65
Economic report. H. C. Wallich. Newsweek
65:90 F 22 '65
Economy under new management; with edi-
torial comment. L. Banks. il Fortune 71:
90-1, 96-9+ My '65
Embattled guidelines; Council of economic
advisors' guidelines. Time 86:81 S 10 '65
Expensive economics. Reporter 33:11 Jl 1 '65
Government and the economy; how much
federal control? is still a burning issue.
il Sr Schol 86:20-1+ Ap 15 '65
Great society. R. Lekachman. Commentary
39:37-42 Je '65
How to make guidelines work; among business, labor, and government. Bsns W p200
N 20 '65

UNITED STATES—Economic policy—*Cont.*
Is America ready for a Great society? interview. R. E. Fitch. il U S News 58:50-4 Mr 8 '65; Same abr. with title America's potential for greatness. Read Digest 86:62-6 Je '65
Is there a new economy? G. R. Rosen. il Duns R 85:38-41+ Je '65
Johnson charts his economics; with editorial comment. il Bsns W p25-6, 136 Ja 30 '65
Keeping watch on the economy; meaning of 1946 Employment act. K. Schriftgiesser. Sat R 49:65-6+ Ja 8 '66
Kept society. R. Moley. Newsweek 65:92 F 8 '65
Lid coming off U.S. spending; promises of the Great society. il U S News 58:44-6 Ap 12 '65
LBJ's decision: guns and butter; concerning State-of-the Union message. il U S News 60:27-8 Ja 24 '66
LBJ's Great society, what will it be? Read Digest 86:136-9 F '65
LBJ's outside man; D. C. Cook. Bsns W p27 F 13 '65
LBJ's revolution: the big changes; New deal, Great society. il U S News 59:46-9 O 11 '65
Mr Goodwin's Great society. W. F. Buckley, jr. Nat R 17:760 S 7 '65
Money managers air their differences; highlights of speeches, by four Federal reserve governors. il Bsns W p 113-14+ O 30 '65
Money men punt on first down. J. N. Eller. America 113:773 D 18 '65
Money policy; the case for restraint. Bsns W p 140 N 27 '65
New complacency. D. Lawrence. U S News 58:124 F 22 '65
Next step; aerospace programs to apply space-age know-how to the Nation's social and economic problems. W. J. Coughlin. Miss & Roc 17:46 N 15 '65
No more recessions? what the planners say. il U S News 58:36-9 F 15 '65
Other side of the new economics. M. H. Stans. U S News 59:82+ D 13 '65
Our unique economic principles; market place should determine price; address, November 23, 1965. G. Romney. Vital Speeches 32:190-2 Ja 1 '66
Pity the poor dirigiste. Nat R 17:1185 D 28 '65
Political economy of the Great society. O. Gass. bibliog f Commentary 40:31-6 O '65
President Johnson on the economy; address, January 28, 1965. L. B. Johnson. Cur Hist 48:362-3+ Je '65
Signal callers on the economic front. U S News 59:21 D 13 '65
State of LBJ; concerning State of the Union address. K. Crawford. Newsweek 67:35 Ja 24 '66
State of the Union; address to the Congress, January 4, 1965. L. B. Johnson. Dept State Bul 52:94-100 Ja 25 '65; Excerpts. Cur Hist 48:176-8+ Mr '65
Taking the rise in stride; stepped-up spending plans by corporations and government. il Bsns W p25-7 D 11 '65
To build, to help, and to fight; concerning President's State of the Union message. il Newsweek 67:21-3 Ja 24 '66
Top economist's formula for keeping the boom alive; excerpts from address, November 9, 1965. A. F. Burns. U S News 59:94+ N 22 '65
Wages and prices by formula? address. A. F. Burns. Harvard Bsns R 43:55-64 Mr '65
War, taxes, labor, rights; LBJ's plans for 1966; State of the Union message, January 12, 1966. L. B. Johnson. U S News 60:62-6+ Ja 24 '66
We are all Keynesians now. il Time 86:64-67B D 31 '65
What Congress did to change U.S; legislation to get the Great society under way. il U S News 59:29-32 N 1 '65
What the Great society is going to cost. il U S News 59:50-2 O 18 '65
Where do we go from here? S. Alsop. il Sat Eve Post 238:14 S 25 '65
Why the Federal reserve raised interest rates; excerpts from address, December 8, 1965. W. M. Martin, jr. U S News 59:92-4 D 20 '65
Will business tempo start to slow in '66? impact of Johnson's programs. il Bsns W p60+ F 13 '65
See also
Agricultural administration—United States
Budget—United States
Economic assistance, Domestic
Finance—United States
Government spending policy
Income tax—United States

Price regulation by government—United States
Taxation—United States
United States—Appropriations and expenditures
United States—Council of economic advisers
United States—National recovery administration

Economic relations

Economic responsibilities of the United States; address, February 4, 1965. W. A. Harriman. Dept State Bul 52:245-50 F 22 '65
International economic policies; excerpt from economic report of the President and annual report of the Council of economic advisers. Dept State Bul 52:254-60 F 22 '65
Monetary talks get go-ahead. Bsns W p26-7 Jl 17 '65
Reason U.S. bears world burden. il U S News 58:42-3 My 10 '65
Rise of nationalism; criticism by France and Japan of US economic policies. Time 86:65 Jl 30 '65
Scare over money; what's back of it. il U S News 59:37-9 Jl 12 '65
This month's feature: Congress & the U.S. foreign aid program. Cong Digest 44:163-91 Je '65
See also
Economic assistance, American
United States—Commerce

Africa
United States policy in Africa; address, March 18, 1965. G. M. Williams. Dept State Bul 52:539-48 Ap 12 '65

Brazil
What is so rare? il Newsweek 66:45-6 Ag 23 '65

Canada
Canada and the United States, principles for partnership; report, June 28, 1965. L. T. Merchant and A. D. P. Heeney. Dept State Bul 53:193-208 Ag 2 '65

Communist countries
Battle act report, 1964; seventeenth report to Congress, January 13, 1965. Dept State Bul 52:148-54 F 1 '65
Fresh East-West winds. Newsweek 65:79 My 17 '65
We should do more business with the Communists. J. H. Cerf. il N Y Times Mag p70-1+ D 5 '65

Europe, Eastern
U.S. policy in east Europe. A. Korbonski. bibliog f Cur Hist 48:129-34+ Mr '65

Europe, Western
Battle the U.S. is winning; recovery for the dollar. il U S News 58:46-8 Ap 19 '65
Europe's distaste for dollars. Bsns W p 192 My 22 '65
President of EEC commission meets with President Johnson; joint communique, March 18, 1965. L. B. Johnson and W. Hallstein. Dept State Bul 52:491-2 Ap 5 '65
Prestige abroad can be no stronger than dollar. F. Morley. Nations Bsns 53:25-6 My '65
Washington desk; voluntary credit control program. J. R. Slevin. Duns R 85:5-6 My '65
Where U.S. patience is wearing thin; Europe gets rich, finds fault, but still wants help. il U S News 58:50-3 Ap 5 '65

Japan
See also
Joint United States-Japan committee on trade and economic affairs

Latin America
Real enemy. J. O'Gara. Commonweal 82:400 Je 18 '65
U.S. trade policy in Latin America; statements, September 10, 1965. J. H. Vaughn; A. M. Solomon. Dept State Bul 53:559-72 O 4 '65

Mexico
Mexico and the United States; address, February 1, 1965. B. Pagliai. Vital Speeches 31:472-5 My 15 '65

Rumania
Firestone case; cancellation of contract to build plant in Rumania. il Newsweek 66:64 Ag 9 '65

Russia
Commerce with Communists; appointment of panel to study the possibility of expanded commercial relations with the Soviet empire. B. L. Masse. America 112:639-41 My 1 '65

UNITED STATES—*Continued*

Education, Office of

Doc Howe. New Repub 154:8 Ja 1 '66

Education: new commissioner champions change and reform. L. J. Carter. Science 150:1794-6 D 31 '65

Grant programs for fiscal 1966; with list of programs. G. O. Dane. Am Ed 1:5-9 Jl '65

Howe to do it. Newsweek 67:48 Ja 3 '66

New commissioner. Time 86:34 D 31 '65

OE's open doors. R. A. Hochstein. il Am Ed 1:10-11 O '65

Organizing for continuing change. F. A. J. Ianni and B. D. McNeill. il Sat R 48:55-6+ Je 19 '65

Public domain. W. E. Mylecraine. Am Ed 1:7-8 N '65

United States Office of education, by H. Kursh. Review
Sat R 48:82-3 Ap 17 '65. C. Hanson; Reply. H. Kursh. 48:51 Je 19 '65

USOE contract to put school programs on microfiche. Pub W 189:42 Ja 3 '66

USOE reports on academic libraries. Library J 90:1277 Mr 15 '65

USOE studies focus on reading. Sr Schol 87: sup 16 D 9 '65

Washington report: project to resolve teacher displacement problems. J. Lloyd. Sr Schol 87:sup4 S 30 '65

Arts and humanities branch

Arts & humanities in the U.S. Office of education. H. E. Hoffa. Sch Arts 64:52 My '65

Library services branch

Washington report: from the Library services branch. P. P. Price and H. A. Carl. See issues of ALA bulletin

Emergency planning, Office of

Man at the controls: the need is unlikely; B. Ellington runs OEP. Bsns W p32-3 Jl 17 '65

Engineer corps

See United States—Army—Corps of engineers

Engraving and printing, Bureau of

Nonprofit money-makers. W. McCann. il Sci N L 87:138-9 F 27 '65

Environmental science services administration

Earthquake prediction: ESSA and USGS vie for leadership. L. J. Carter. il Science 151:181-3 Ja 14 '66

Environmental agency; merger of U.S. weather bureau and U.S. coast and geodetic survey. Sci N L 87:340 My 29 '65

Environmental sciences: Johnson proposes new agency merging U.S. research and service programs. E. Langer. Science 148:1446-7 Je 11 '65

Executive departments

Antarctica: congressional urge for tidy research administration manifests itself in new proposal. D. S. Greenberg. Science 148:1304-5 Je 4 '65

Briefing the brass: Business council meets with Cabinet members. il Bsns W p30-1 My 8 '65

Crisis management: Berlin, Cyprus, Laos. J. C. Ausland and H. F. Richardson. For Affairs 44:291-303 Ja '66

Economy under new management; with editorial comment. L. Banks. il Fortune 71:90-1, 96-9+ My '65

Education's muddled bureaucracy. J. Spivak. il Reporter 32:33-6 Ap 8 '65; Reply. R. L. Thackrey. 32:6 My 6 '65

Johnson's talent hunt. J. Kraft. Harper 230:40+ Mr '65

President calls for full use of resources in overseas programs; statement, March 25, 1965. L. B. Johnson. Dept State Bul 52:538 Ap 12 '65

Role of the federal government in the design and administration of intergovernmental programs. W. G. Colman. Ann Am Acad 359:23-34 My '65

Time for federal housecleaning. Life 60:4 Ja 21 '66

U.S. agencies get order: join McNamara's band; cost system imposed by Defense secretary on the Pentagon. Bsns W p 182+ N 13 '65

See also
Independent regulatory commissions
Presidents—United States

Executive office of the president

Bill Moyers: Johnson's good angel. T. Wicker. il Harper 231:41-9 O '65; Same abr. with title Remarkable rise of Bill D. Moyers. Read Digest 88:72-7 Ja '66

Johnson's talent hunt. J. Kraft. Harper 230:40+ Mr '65

King's men: a British view of the White House. L. Heren. Harper 230:108+ F '65

Lyndon's lobbyists: how they get what he wants. il Nations Bsns 53:38-9+ Ap '65

West wing story. J. Kraft. Harper 230:106-10 Ap '65

Expenditures

See United States—Appropriations and expenditures

Exploration

See United States—History—Discovery and exploration

Federal aviation agency

Anti-skid coating aids wet runway stops; new requirements for jet landing. R. G. O'Lone. il Aviation W 83:39+ D 20 '65

Departure of Bain spurs concern over future FAA direction of SST. Aviation W 83:36 Ag 30 '65

FAA census records new gains in aircraft, pilots, airports facilities. il Aviation W 83:34 S 20 '65

FAA considers standby radars after major traffic jam at O'Hare. Aviation W 83:43 S 20 '65

FAA plans to consolidate R&D functions. Aviation W 83:95 Ag 16 '65

FAA tightens wet runway rules. Aviation W 83:40 Jl 12 '65

General aviation category 2 rules follow pattern set for airlines. H. D. Watkins. Aviation W 83:20 O 18 '65

Learning to love the boom; tests to evaluate effect of sonic booms. Time 85:64+ My 7 '65

McKee confirmation follows quiet hearing. Aviation W 83:25 Jl 5 '65

Report criticizes airport planning by FAA. R. G. O'Lone. Aviation W 82:28-9 My 24 '65

Sound of progress; sonic boom over Oklahoma City. J. Skow. il Sat Eve Post 238:25-6 F 13 '65

Things to come. R. B. Parke. il Flying 77:26 Jl '65

Appropriations and expenditures

FAA allocates $84.5 million for airports. il Aviation W 83:40 S 13 '65

Research funds sought to cut accidents. R. G. O'Lone. Aviation W 82:41-2 My 10 '65

Federal bureau of investigation

Crime is too big for the FBI. W. W. Turner. il Nation 201:322-8 N 8 '65; Discussion. 201:inside cover D 20 '65

FBI's secret war against the Ku Klux klan. J. Barron. il Read Digest 88:87-92 Ja '66

His master's voice; C. D. DeLoach boost in FBI hierarchy. Newsweek 66:25 D 27 '65

Hoover of the FBI. J. Phelan. il Sat Eve Post 238:23-8+ S 25 '65

In defense of J. Edgar Hoover. Time 85:41 Mr 5 '65

Informer; Gary Thomas Rowe, jr, informer against the K.K.K. Time 85:32 Ap 30 '65

J. Edgar Hoover, the compleat bureaucrat. J. Kraft. Commentary 39:59-62 F '65

Many faces of the FBI. F. Sondern, jr. il Read Digest 87:177-8+ D '65

National police force? no, says FBI chief Hoover; excerpts from statements. J. E. Hoover. U S News 58:20 Ap 12 '65

Routine checkup; concerning the sending of agents to additional Latin-American posts. New Repub 153:8 N 6 '65

Safest large city. Am City 80:160+ Ag '65

What's ahead for the FBI. M. Ottenberg. Look 29:27-9 F 23 '65

When Hoover corrected the record. U S News 59:13 Ag 2 '65

Federal communications commission

Airwave First amendment. America 112:213 F 13 '65

Big changes ahead for TV's prime hours? il U S News 58:16 Mr 15 '65

Choosing sides; FCC decision in St Louis. R. L. Shayon. Sat R 48:32 My 29 '65

CATV gets new viewer. Bsns W p30 My 1 '65

Community antennas enter the big TV picture. il Fortune 72:146-7+ Ag '65

Discriminating TV in Jackson, Mississippi; question of renewing WLBT's license. W. Pincus. New Repub 152:7-8 Je 5 '65

UNITED STATES—Federal communications commission—*Continued*

Equal time, by N. N. Minow; ed. by L. Laurent. Review
Commentary 39:80+ F '65. W. Goodman

Fairfax Cone, the FCC, and TV advertising. R. L. Tobin. Sat R 48:49-50 Ag 14 '65

FCC stirs new TV program clash; proposes tougher programming rule. Bsns W p27-8 Mr 27 '65

Hate line is still busy; protests and warnings by National council of churches. Christian Cent 82:1276 O 20 '65

Heat on TV. Nation 202:1-2 Ja 3 '66

How the FCC proposes to change TV programs. U S News 58:14 Ap 5 '65

Monopoly over minds? why officials worry about TV; concentration of ownership of very-high frequency stations. il U S News 58:50-1 F 1 '65

New CB rules: HELP. W. A. Stocklin. Electr World 73:8 My '65

Prime-time target; FCC proposals. Newsweek 65:58 Ap 5 '65

Public may be heard; FCC investigation of station WLBT, Jackson, Miss. R. L. Shayon. Sat R 48:44 Je 26 '65

Religion and the FCC. M. Cohn; discussion. Reporter 32:6 F 11 '65

TV programing; the fight for prime time. H. Junker. il Nation 200:279-81 Mr 15 '65

Three men theme; networks versus advertising agency control of TV programs. Time 85:81A Mr 12 '65

Western union hums with data; computer data transmission. il Bsns W p 150-2+ F 20 '65

Federal council for science and technology

National information program impends. W. S. Beller. Miss & Roc 17:17-18 N 1 '65

Federal deposit insurance corporation

See Federal deposit insurance corporation

Federal home loan bank board

Lid put on California S&L rates; federal agency bars rise to 5 per cent. Bsns W p38 Ap 10 '65

Why some savings may earn less. U S News 58:123 Je 21 '65

Federal housing administration

From Washington, homes for sale; FHA and VA. il U S News 58:105 Ap 26 '65

How home loans are guaranteed. il Changing T 19:26 D '65

Making cities fit for people. H. H. Humphrey. Sat R 48:16-17 Jl 3 '65

Federal library committee

Formation of Federal library committee announced by Library of Congress. Library J 90:1846 Ap 15 '65

Federal maritime commission

Agreed minute provides for exchange of shipping information. Dept State Bul 52:188-90 F 8 '65

Federal mediation and conciliation service

Joint consultation devices in collective bargaining. Mo Labor R 88:173 F '65

Role of the federal mediator. T. R. Brooks. Duns R 85:59-60+ Je '65

Federal power commission

Burning issue for gas pipelines; southern California natural gas market. il Bsns W p 138+ Ag 14 '65

FPC tightens the cap on natural gas prices. il Bsns W p31-2 Ag 14 '65

Gas pricing: wellhead warriors. M. Wax. il Nation 200:417-19 Ap 19 '65

Rebuke to the FPC; failure to investigate Storm King Mountain project. New Repub 154:7 Ja 15 '66

Should U.S. use power on power companies? debate on whether electric utilities should be tied into national grid. Bsns W p45-6 N 13 '65

Stink of dead stripers; Con Ed under attack over killing of fish at Hudson's bass spawning grounds. R. H. Boyle. il Sports Illus 22:81-2+ Ap 26 '65

Federal reserve board

Behind the tug of war on money; administration, lenders clash on need for higher rates; with editorial comment. il Bsns W p51-2+, 198 O 16 '65

Credit joins the payments battle. il Bsns W p34-5 F 27 '65

Economics of the long war. Nation 201:485 D 20 '65

Fait accompli. Time 86:18-19 D 17 '65

Fed holds the key on action; brokers look for trouble if Fed should tighten money. il Bsns W p 141-2 D 11 '65

Fed lineup veers to the liberal side. il Bsns W p 146+ S 11 '65

Fed puts quiet hand on interest rates; U.S. monetary policy; with editorial comment. il Bsns W p 104+, 180 Mr 27 '65

FRB Chairman Martin: a clash developing with the President? il U S News 58:14 Je 14 '65

Federal reserve's Martin: no to LBJ. il U S News 59:15 D 20 '65

Fed's surprise: tighter money; raise in discount rate. il Newsweek 66:75-6+ D 13 '65

Fixing interest rates. H. Hazlitt. Newsweek 66:86 D 20 '65

Gold warriors. il Time 85:88+ Ap 23 '65

Growing fight over money. il U S News 58:91 Je 21 '65

Haves vs. have-nots; disagreements between Johnson and Martin over discount rate. K. Crawford. Newsweek 66:30 D 20 '65

Is credit quality getting too low? private debt outpaced economic growth. il Bsns W p75-6+ O 2 '65

LBJ vs. Reserve board: who gets last word on money. U S News 59:47 D 20 '65

Manipulating money. H. Hazlitt. Newsweek 67:47 Ja 3 '66

Money managers air their differences; highlights of speeches, by four Federal reserve governors. il Bsns W p 113-14+ O 30 '65

New limit on bank interest? U S News 59:89 Ag 16 '65

Patman on the warpath. il Newsweek 66:51 D 27 '65

Planning the economy. Commonweal 83:361-2 D 24 '65

Pressure goes on Fed not to tighten credit. Bsns W p40 N 13 '65

Pressures & passions. il Time 86:53-4 D 24 '65

Rate & its ripples; effects of the Federal reserve's move. il Time 86:85 D 17 '65

Rate rise sharpens savings battle; Fed's boost of interest ceiling on time deposits. il Bsns W p56-8 D 18 '65

Raising the cost of money. New Repub 153:8-9 D 18 '65

Restrain the boom? how the money managers see it. il U S News 59:30-1 D 13 '65

T.R.B. from Washington; the market and FRB chairman Martin. New Repub 153:4 D 18 '65; Reply. H. M. Goldstein. 154:28 Ja 22 '66

Up go the rates and the roof; protests. il Newsweek 66:75-6 D 20 '65

Up with the discount rate. il Time 86:99 D 10 '65

Warrior from Patman's switch. H. Kay. il Fortune 71:154-6+ Ap '65

Why the Federal reserve raised interest rates; excerpts from address, December 8, 1965. W. M. Martin, jr. U S News 59:92-4 D 20 '65

Federal trade commission

Can you merge? now even government isn't sure. il U S News 58:102-3 My 24 '65

Company in a quandary; competing too aggressively. Time 86:54-5 D 24 '65

Court catches up with Holland furnace co. Consumer Bul 48:25-6 Ap '65

End of a thirty years' war on consumers; FTC vs Holland furnace. Consumer Rep 30:238 My '65

FTC hearing forecasts federal book banning; opinions in advertising. S. Wagner. Pub W 188:30-1 O 11 '65

FTC offers a plan for voluntary compliance; determination to eliminate anticompetitive discriminatory promotional programs. C. B. Grannis. Pub W 188:33 O 18 '65

FTC scores one, tries for another. Bsns W p22 Ja 1 '66

Halting department store mergers. Bsns W p36 Ag 21 '65

Merger tide is swelling; antitrusters' hostility. il Bsns W p27-8 My 29 '65

New look in mergers frowned on by FTC. Bsns W p 136 Mr 13 '65

Old lady's new look. il Time 85:86 Ap 16 '65

Only when CU consents, says FTC. Consumer Rep 30:425 S '65

Quiet victory of the cigarette lobby. E. B. Drew. Atlan 216:76-80 S '65

Fish and wildlife service

Close look at predator control. T. Trueblood. il Field & S 69:28+ Ap '65

Fish and wildlife service urges delay. C. W. Buchheister. Audubon Mag 67:285 S '65

UNITED STATES—Fish and wildlife service
—*Continued*
New look in predator control. C. H. Callison.
Audubon Mag 67:321 S '65

Food and drug administration

Drug abuse: tighter controls placed on amphetamines and barbiturates: law to cover other drugs later. J. Walsh. Science 149:951-3 Ag 27 '65
Drug lab caught in crossfire; FDA's handling of label mixups. Bsns W p30 O 30 '65
Drugs that work around the clock. Bsns W p58+ S 4 '65
Feeling dizzy? drug labels. J. Ridgeway. New Repub 153:15-16 S 25 '65
FDA: scientific, medical groups support agency in dispute with Fountain over access to drug data. E. Langer. Science 149: 731-4 Ag 13 '65; Reply. W. L. Nyhan. 150: 1533 D 17 '65
Mess in FDA. il Time 87:62 Ja 21 '66
More about thalidomide. J. Ridgeway. New Repub 154:12-15 Ja 8 '66
10,000,000 bottles; inspection of intravenous solutions manufacturing department; at Abbott jaboratories. J. Ridgeway. New Repub 153:12-14 N 6 '65
What's in food standards for you? Consumer Bul 48:31-3 Mr '65

Foreign opinion

American image will take care of itself; anti-American world opinion. D. Acheson. il N Y Times Mag p24-5+ F 28 '65
As others see us; ed. by J. F. Fixx. See issues of Saturday review
Back home; foreign opinion of American role in Vietnam. M. Ascoli. Reporter 32: 20 Mr 25 '65
Burdens of power. C. Marcy. Sat R 48:11-13 S 4 '65
Great debate on Viet Nam. Sr Schol 87:6-9 S 23 '65
Hitting the target; use of gas in Vietnam. il Newsweek 65:37 Ap 5 '65
How the world views the U.S. il Newsweek 65:39-40 Je 21 '65
I couldn't put wigs on Harriman and Goldberg. R. B. Stolley. il Life 60:24-7 Ja 14 '66
Messianic pose; post-cold-war delusions. H. S. Hughes. il Nation 202:7-10 Ja 3 '66
No whitewash for U.S. abroad. C. T. Rowan. il Ebony 20:56-8 Ag '65
Rest of the world. W. Lippmann. Newsweek 65:21 Je 21 '65
Socialism and capitalism; an international misunderstanding. R. K White.. il For Affairs 44:216-28 Ja '66
Trigger-happy charge and the U.S. answer. il U S News 58:34-5 Je 28 '65
What is realism doing to American history? adaptation of address. A. MacLeish. il Sat R 48:10-12 Jl 3 '65; Discussion. 48:13-14+ Jl 3; 16-18 Jl 10; 38 Jl 24 '65
World's size-up of LBJ now. il U S News 59:26-9 D 27 '65

African

As others see us. Newsweek 66:35 Ag 23 '65
Letter from Africa; reactions to our foreign policy. America 112:554+ Ap 17 '65
What passes for American news in Africa. J. Strohmeyer. Harper 231:98+ N '65; Reply with rejoinder. G. Long. 232:8+ Ja '66

British

British press postscript. J. Fletcher. il Nat R 18:25-6 Ja 11 '66
From Britain: U.S. is abdicating. U S News 58:53 Ap 5 '65
In Britain, anti-U.S. feeling over Vietnam. il U S News 59:8 Jl 12 '65

Cuban

What Cubans think of the U.S. il Sr Schol 87:22-3 N 18 '65

European

How Europe sees outlook for U.S. boom. il U S News 59:32-5 Jl 5 '65
LBJ: a view from Europe. il U S News 60: 41 Ja 17 '66
Mounting tide of anti-Americanism. E. M. von Kuehnelt-Leddihn. Nat R 17:503 Je 15 '65
Notes of a bad American. A. Karlen. il Holiday 38:8+ Jl '65
Open letter to the American people. B. Hutchison. Read Digest 87:96-100 Ag '65
Vietnam, LBJ, good times: what Europeans are saying. il U S News 59:72-4 Ag 9 '65
See also
Europe and the United States

French

Anti-Americanism, French style; culture against barbarism. E. A. Smith. Christian Cent 82:300-3 Mr 10 '65; Reply. G. H. Pigueron, 3d. 82:747 Je 9 '65
French press warms up to LBJ. E. Taylor Reporter 32:29-30 Ap 22 '65
New Communist propaganda strategy; French anti-Americanism. E. Taylor. il Reporter 33:27-9 Jl 1 '65

Japanese

American policy and Japanese opinion. Nation 200:632 Je 14 '65
Japan: a sense of independence. il Newsweek 66:46+ D 20 '65
Japan, the two Reischauers. A. Axelbank. New Repub 153:11-12 N 13 '65
Japanese and Vietnam; war is popularizing anti-Americanism. Y. Sakamoto. New Repub 153:16-17 S 4 '65

Latin American

Latin America: continent on a teeterboard. D. D. Ranstead. Nation 201:292-4 N 1 '65

Russian

Sort of dialogue; excerpts from interview, ed. by Lord Thomson. A. Kosygin. Newsweek 66:40 S 20 '65

Vietnamese

Who wants us out? Nat R 17:966-7 N 2 '65

Foreign population

See also
Immigrants in the United States
Immigration and emigration—United States
also Hungarians in the United States, and similar headings

Foreign relations

Adlai Stevenson's last article; outline for a new American policy. A. E. Stevenson. il Look 29:71-2+ Ag 24 '65
All-purpose myth; policy based on threat of Communist take-over. W. Lippmann. Newsweek 65:23 My 24 '65
Alliance immobilized. W. V. Shannon. Commonweal 82:102-3 Ap 16 '65
Amateur. K. Crawford. Newsweek 66:25 Ag 23 '65
American empire. Fortune 72:119-20 Ag '65
American image will take care of itself. D. Acheson. il N Y Times Mag p24-5+ F 28 '65
Americans around the world; symposium, ed. by G. Nikolaiess. il Sr Schol 86:6-20+ Mr 11 '65
America's place in the world. D. D. Eisenhower. Read Digest 87:75-81 O '65
Anatomy of foreign policy decisions; address, September 7, 1965. D. Rusk. Dept State Bul 53:502-9 S 27 '65
As LBJ starts his third year, new problems, bigger plans. il U S News 59:58-60 D 6 '65
As the world struggles against war and famine. il U S News 60:30-2 Ja 10 '66
As winds of change sweep the world. il U S News 59:23-4 Jl 5 '65
Atlantic report (cont) Atlan 215:8+ My; 216: 4+ Jl '65
Big show: American white paper; United States foreign policy on NBC. Newsweek 66:90 S 20 '65
Burden of leadership. A. Eden. For Affairs 44:229-38 Ja '66
Can Pax Americana succeed? D. F. Fleming. Ann Am Acad 360:127-38 Jl '65
Can the question of war be debated? W. Lippmann. Newsweek 65:23 Mr 15 '65
Cheer for American imperialism. H. Fairlie. il N Y Times Mag p7+ Jl 11 '65
Chimeras in Viet Nam; concerning article in the current New leader. Time 85:63 Mr 12 '65
Choice for Americans: address, January 9, 1965. S. Thurmond. Vital Speeches 31:259-62 F 15 '65
Cold war idealism. Commonweal 83:361 D 24 '65
Congressional foreign policy. New Repub 152:6-7 F 6 '65
Contagion of hope. E. J. Hughes. Newsweek 66:23 O 4 '65
Crackdown; US policy dissenters. Nation 201: 205-6 O 11 '65
Credibility of commitment. il Time 86:9 D 24 '65
Crisis management: Berlin, Cyprus, Laos. J. C. Ausland and H. F. Richardson. For Affairs 44:291-303 Ja '66
Dangers of nostalgia; address, March 16, 1965. G. W. Ball. Dept State Bul 52:532-7 Ap 12 '65

UNITED STATES—Foreign relations—*Cont.*

Dangers of the consensus. H. Brandon. Sat R 48:14+ F 27 '65

Department officers address foreign policy conference at Dallas; address, February 27, 1965. J. J. Sisco; E. Bunker. Dept State Bul 52:460-71 Mr 29 '65

Détente: cold war strategies in transition, ed. by E. L. Dulles and R. D. Crane. Review Sat R 48:54-5 Ap 17 '65. F. Altschul

Diplomacy a la Johnson. Nation 200:461 My 3 '65

Diplomacy of drift. E. J. Hughes. Newsweek 67:17 Ja 24 '66

Ethics in international relations today; address, December 9, 1964. D. Acheson. Vital Speeches 31:226-8 F 1 '65; Same abr. with title We need a hardheaded foreign policy. Read Digest 86:66-8 Mr '65

Facts, fallacies and foreign policy; address, May 4, 1965. H. M. Jackson. Vital Speeches 31:515-18 Je 15 '65

Firm foreign policy; unity with Europe; address, May 28, 1965. W. W. Scranton. Vital Speeches 31:652-4 Ag 15 '65

Foreign-policy changes? Fulbright has some in mind; statements. R. Long. U S News 58:20 F 1 '65

Foreign policy decisions; address, September 7, 1965. D. Rusk. Vital Speeches 31:744-7 O 1 '65

Foreign policy: drift or design? il Newsweek 65:27-34 My 17 '65

Foreign policy fever. Commonweal 82:307-8 My 28 '65

Foreign policy: the stuck whistle. J. K. Galbraith. Atlan 215:64-8 F '65

Former librarian of Congress questions US foreign policy. Library J 90:2984 Jl '65

Free world colossus, by D. Horowitz. Review New Repub 154:26-8 Ja 15 '66. R. G. Hazo

Growing ordeal of LBJ. il U S News 58:29-30 Mr 15 '65

Guidelines of U.S. foreign policy; address, June 6, 1965. D. Rusk. Dept State Bul 52:1030-4 Je 28 '65

Handcuffs on foreign policy. Nation 201:109-10 S 6 '65

How Europe sees the President. H. Brandon. Sat R 48:22-3 Ap 10 '65

How helpful are U.S. allies? what the record shows. il U S News 59:50-2+ S 13 '65

How the State department baffled him; excerpts from Thousand days. A. M. Schlesinger, jr. il Life 59:18-27 Jl 30 '65

How to lose the world. N. Cousins. Sat R 48:28 Ap 10 '65; Discussion. 48:23 My 15 '65

How U.S. is doing in Europe and Asia, a French size-up; interview. P. M. Gallois. il U S News 59:58-60 D 20 '65

If we fail to meet it here and now; excerpts from testimony to the House armed services committee. R. McNamara. Time 85:20 F 26 '65

Inside word: the world as seen by Washington. il U S News 58:31-3 My 3 '65

IPA congress hits U.S. on copyright and foreign policies. Pub W 187:141-3 Je 7 '65

Isolating America? D. Lawrence. U S News 58:108 Mr 8 '65

Isolationism again, with a difference. H. F. Graff. il N Y Times Mag p26-7+ My 16 '65

It's world-travel season for Congress; with a record in sight. il U S News 59:72-3 D 6 '65

Johnson abroad. New Repub 152:5-6 Je 12 '65

Johnson corollary; legality and morality of U.S. intervention in foreign states. il Time 85:24-5 My 14 '65

Lexicon of force. N. Cousins. Sat R 48:16+ Je 5 '65

Long lectures for LBJ; protest in colleges over policies in Vietnam and Dominican Republic. il Bsns W p27 My 22 '65

LBJ and his critics. R. Moley. Newsweek 65:88 Je 7 '65

L.B.J's foreign policy: manner and matter. S. Alsop. Sat Eve Post 238:18 Je 19 '65

LBJ's troubles begin to mount. il U S News 58:8 Je 21 '65

LBJ's visitors; country's responsibilities East-West and worldwide. New Repub 153:5-6 D 25 '65

Messianic pose post-cold-war delusions. H. S. Hughes. il Nation 202:7-10 Ja 3 '66

Mr Rusk, Mr McNamara discuss Rhodesia, Rio meeting, Viet-Nam; news conference, November 11, 1965. D. Rusk; R. S. McNamara. Dept State Bul 53:894-6 D 6 '65

Mobs and embassies; policy concerning unfriendly demonstrations in front of our embassies. America 112:387 Mr 20 '66

More heat and light; concern about the President's handling of foreign policy. H. Brandon. Sat R 48:10 Je 5 '65

Needed: better war and peace aims. Fortune 73:113+ Ja '66

New complacency. D. Lawrence. U S News 58:124 F 22 '65

New word; neo-isolationism. Nation 200:98 F 1 '65

Newspapers: support from most. Time 85:55 My 21 '65

Notes on the Toronto teach-in: the irrelevance of morality. R. H. Welker. il Nation 201:301-4 N 1 '65

Nothing personal, by R. Avedon and J. Baldwin. Review Nat R 17:98 F 9 '65. W. F. Buckley, jr

No. 1 crisis; UN peace-keeping role in jeopardy. N. Cousins. Sat R 48:26+ Je 19 '65

One year of L.B.J. T. Wicker. il New Repub 153:13-22 N 13 '65

Our no-nonsense President. M. Ascoli. Reporter 32:18 My 20 '65

Palmerstonian America. G. Lichtheim. Commentary 40:58-62 Jl '65

Paranoid style; American foreign policy in post-World-war II period. Nation 201:401-2 N 29 '65

Partnership in world affairs; address, June 17, 1965. A. E. Stevenson. Dept State Bul 53:123-8 Jl 19 '65

Peace: the central task of foreign policy; address, June 8, 1965. W. W. Rostow. Dept State Bul 53:21-7 Jl 5 '65

Perplexing, and potentially tragic. il Newsweek 66:23-4 S 20 '65

Plain talk on foreign policy. D. Lawrence. U S News 58:112 F 15 '65

President comments on several foreign policy developments; statement, August 29, 1965. L. B. Johnson. Dept State Bul 53:476 S 20 '65

President Johnson discusses Viet-Nam, Dominican Republic, disarmament; statements, July 13, 1965. L. B. Johnson. Dept State Bul 53:182-3 Ag 2 '65

President's constituency; relation of cold war operations to the working of democracy. C. C. O'Brien. New Repub 153:28-31 Ag 21 '65

Public opinion and the war in Vietnam; Great debate. L. Markel. il N Y Times Mag p9+ Ag 8 '65

Reason U.S. bears world burden. il U S News 58:42-3 My 10 '65

Red Sea to Singapore: new burden for U.S? il U S News 59:72-3 N 15 '65

Regional organization: a planner's perspective. W. W. Rostow. Dept State Bul 52:994-1000 Je 21 '65

Rest of the world. W. Lippmann. Newsweek 65:21 Je 21 '65

Return to isolation? W. Pfaff. Commonweal 82:6-7 Mr 26 '65

Scholars and foreign policy: varieties of research experience; address, October 21, 1965. T. L. Hughes. Dept State Bul 53:747-58 N 8 '65

Secretary Rusk interviewed:
NBC, January 3, 1965. bibliog f Dept State Bul 52:62-74 Ja 18 '65
NBC's American white paper, September 7, 1965. Dept State Bul 53:509-12 S 27 '65

Secretary Rusk's news conference:
February 25, 1965. Dept State Bul 52:362-71 Mr 15 '65
May 26, 1965. Dept State Bul 52:938-47 Je 14 '65
August 2, 1965. Dept State Bul 53:302-10 Ag 23 '65
August 27, 1965. Dept State Bul 53:481-6 S 20 '65
November 5, 1965. Dept State Bul 53:854-62 N 29 '65
November 26 1965. Dept State Bul 53:930-9 D 13 '65
December 9, 1965. Dept State Bul 53:1006-13 D 27 '65

Senator Fulbright dissents. Nation 201:177-8 O 4 '65

Separate worlds: isolationism is back with us. M. Ascoli. Reporter 33:12 Jl 1 '65

Shift of focus, LBJ looks abroad. il Newsweek 66:23-4 D 20 '65

Some payoffs for patience. Life 59:4 N 12 '65

Spoiled spring; leadership and methods of LBJ. E. J. Hughes. Newsweek 65:17 My 31 '65

Squeeze: President Johnson's thinking of foreign-policy in terms of domestic politics. Nation 201:1 Jl 5 '65

UNITED STATES—Foreign relations—*Cont.*
State of the Union; address to the Congress, January 4, 1965. L. B. Johnson. Dept State Bul 52:94-100 Ja 25 '65; Excerpts. Cur Hist 48:176-8+ Mr '65
Stepping into fights. New Repub 152:5-6 My 29 '65
Time of trouble; Lyndon Johnson's administration. S. Alsop. Sat Eve Post 238:16 Jl 17 '65
Two views of America's task abroad; Evolutionary concept; Three-part strategy. S. Hoffmann; W. W. Rostow. New Repub 152:17 My 29 '65
Undeclared wars; no congressional debates. Commonweal 82:276-7 My 21 '65
Uneasy alliance; President Johnson and liberal intellectuals. H. Brandon. Sat R 48:8 Jl 3 '65
U.N, an effective arm of U.S. foreign policy; address, November 3, 1965. P. H. B. Frelinghuysen. Dept State Bul 53:1021-8 D 27 '65
United States and the neutralists: a decade in perspective. C. V. Crabb, jr. bibliog f Ann Am Acad 362:92-101 N '65
U.S. & world opinion; Time essay. Time 85:30-1 My 28 '65; Same abr. with title United States and world opinion. Read Digest 87:59-62 S '65
U.S. at the crossroads; Growing debate on world policy. il U S News 58:25-7 Mr 8 '65
U.S. foreign policy: who makes it? il Sr Schol 87:9-11+ D 2 '65
U.S. leadership: at peak under Truman? excerpts from address, April 13, 1965. D. Acheson. il U S News 58:30 Ap 26 '65
Unseen search for peace; involvement in world affairs; address, October 16, 1965. D. Rusk. Vital Speeches 32:66-71 N 15 '65
Uses of flexibility; adaptation of address. J. W. Fulbright. Sat R 48:19-21+ My 8 '65; Discussion. 48:21 My 29 '65
Vacuum diplomacy. G. Lichtheim. Commentary 41:49-53 Ja '66
Veteran diplomat looks at U.S. in today's world; interview. W. A. Harriman. il U S News 59:70-2 Jl 12 '65
View from up there; address, July 2, 1965. H. Cleveland. Dept State Bul 53:151-6 Jl 26 '65
Wartime leader. il Time 85:23-4 My 14 '65
Wave of the past. New Repub 152:1+ My 15 '65
We are in too deep in Asia and Africa. F. Church. il N Y Times Mag p30-1+ F 14 '65
What is realism doing to American history? adaptation of address. A. MacLeish. il Sat R 48:10-12 Jl 3 '65; Discussion. 48:13-14+ Jl 3; 16-18 Jl 10; 38 Jl 24 '65
What's going on here? Nat R 17:226 Mr 23 '65
White House conference on international cooperation; remarks, December 1, 1965; with questions and answers. D. Rusk. Dept State Bul 53:976-84 D 20 '65
Why allies don't help U.S. in Vietnam. U S News 59:60 S 6 '65
Why de Gaulle thinks U.S. is through as world leader. il U S News 58:47-8 Mr 1 '65
Why White House troubles mount. U S News 58:31-3 Je 28 '65
Will to stay the course; address, November 23, 1965. H. M. Jackson. Vital Speeches 32:138-40 D 15 '65
With what little wisdom the world is ruled. G. Myrdal. il N Y Times Mag p20-1+ Jl 18 '65
World in a mess. il U S News 59:38-42 D 6 '65
World politics of responsibility. O. Gass. Commentary 40:85-90 D '65
World troubles closing in on U.S. with excerpts from television broadcast by A. Krock. il U S News 58:27-9 Mr 1 '65
World's size-up of LBJ now. il U S News 59:26-9 D 27 '65
See also
Economic assistance, American
Military assistance, American
Monroe doctrine
United Nations—United States
United States—State, Department of
United States—Treaties

Anecdotes, facetiae, satire, etc.
Are we losing East Frambesia to the Communists? T. Meehan. New Yorker 41:50-1 O 2 '65

Anti-Communist measures
Bigger wars ahead? interview. H. Kahn. il U S News 58:42-9 Je 7 '65
Castro's turn next? il U S News 58:44-7 My 17 '65

Containing communism East and West. W. E. Griffith. Atlan 215:71-5 My '65
Crucial conflict. E. J. Hughes. Newsweek 65:21 Ap 5 '65
Dominican crisis: correcting some misconceptions; address, October 12, 1965. T. C. Mann. Dept State Bul 53:730-8 N 8 '65
Fighting in Kashmir; Washington obsessed by communism. New Repub 153:7-8 S 11 '65
From Ike, some strong backing for Johnson; policy in Vietnam, Dominican Republic and Hungary, excerpts from news conference. D. D. Eisenhower. U S News 58:8 My 24 '65
Globalism; Johnson's moral crusade. H. J. Morgenthau. New Repub 153:19-22 Jl 3 '65
How many Dominican Republics and Vietnams can we take on? F. Church. il N Y Times Mag p44-5+ N 28 '65
Letter from Washington. R. H. Rovere. New Yorker 41:160+ Ap 17; 143-50 Je 12 '65
Must we fight alone? D. Lawrence. U S News 59:124 D 13 '65
New forward thrust of freedom; how Vietnam victory can lead way toward global containment of communism. R. Drummond. Read Digest 87:133-5 Ag '65
New warning to the Latins. Time 86:28 O 1 '65
Roll call in the House; resolution concerning communism in western hemisphere. New Repub 153:7 O 16 '65
Stepping into fights. New Repub 152:5-6 My 29 '65
This month's feature: the U.S. and western hemisphere security. Cong Digest 44:257-88 N '65
Trying times. M. Ascoli. Reporter 32:14 Je 17 '65
Two views from the top. L. B. Johnson; D. Rusk. Time 85:15 Je 4 '65
United States summarizes position on disarmament and arms control; statement, April 26, 1965. A. E. Stevenson. bibliog f Dept State Bul 52:762-5 My 17 '65
Uproar over resolution aimed at communism. U S News 59:14 O 4 '65
Wave of the past. New Repub 152:1+ My 15 '65
When to intervene; nonintervention, keystone of structure of inter-American system. Time 86:53 O 22 '65

Bibliography
Congressional documents relating to foreign policy. See issues of Department of state bulletin

History
First anti-imperialists; excerpt from Proud tower; a portrait of the world before the war, 1890-1914. B. W. Tuchman. Nation 201:77-82 S 20 '65
Oldest new nation. C. Bowles. Yale R 54:321-30 Mr '65
Some timely advice from President Washington. J. J. Wadsworth. Sat R 48:18+ F 20 '65

Africa
Albatross; African leaders outraged by US support of Tshombe. il Newsweek 65:43-4 Mr 1 '65
Lost goals in Africa. A. Rivkin. For Affairs 44:111-26 O '65
Red China's year in Africa. E. Huxley. il Nat R 17:95-6+ F 9 '65
United States policy in Africa; address, March 18, 1965. G. M. Williams. Dept State Bul 52:539-48 Ap 12 '65

Africa, North
North Africa: active crossroads. D. D. Newsom. il Dept State Bul 53:315-22 Ag 23 '65

Asia
As U.S.-Soviet tensions grew: North Vietnam, North Korea and red China threats. il U S News 58:4 F 22 '65
Asia out of control? interview. R. P. Martin. il U S News 59:38-42 O 4 '65
Encirclement in Asia. il Time 86:35-6 S 17 '65
Is peace still possible? the United States, China and Vietnam. E. Snow. New Repub 152:15-20 My 22 '65
President's decision. P. Horton. Reporter 32:12 F 25 '65
Twenty years after; why GI's are still fighting in Asia; with interview with K. S. Chiang. il U S News 59:41-9 Ag 9 '65

Asia, Southeastern
American policy in South Viet-Nam and southeast Asia; address, January 23, 1965. W. P. Bundy. Dept State Bul 52:168-75 F 8 '65

UNITED STATES—Foreign relations—France
—*Continued*
On dealing with de Gaulle. J. M. Gavin.
Atlan 215:49-54 Je '65
This electoral season; French-US antagonism.
M. Ascoli. Reporter 33:10 N 18 '65
What shall we do about de Gaulle? P. H.
Douglas. New Repub 152:7-10 Je 12 '65;
Discussion. 152:35-7 Je 26 '65
See also
United States—Commerce—France

Germany
Twenty years after; German people and mis-
deeds of Nazi faction; excerpts from the
editorial, May 1945. D. Lawrence. U S
News 58:124 My 17 '65

Germany (Federal Republic)
Der Alte returns. W. S. Schlamm. Nat R
17:811-12 S 21 '65
Anniversary of sovereignty of German Federal
Republic; message, May 5, 1965. L. B.
Johnson. Dept State Bul 52:814 My 24 '65
Atlantic report. Atlan 216:48-51 S '65
Chancellor Erhard of Germany talks with
President Johnson; joint statement, June
4, 1965. L. B. Johnson and L. Erhard. Dept
State Bul 52:1051-3 Je 28 '65
Frank look at some current issues in German-
American relations; address, October 22,
1965. G. C. McGhee. Dept State Bul 53:902-
7 D 6 '65
New deal for Bonn? America 112:876 Je 19
'65
West Germany's aim: closer ties with the
U.S.; interview. L. Erhard. U S News 59:
36-7 D 20 '65

Great Britain
Pig war was a one-shot war. il Sunset 135:
40+ S '65
Why Humphrey didn't go; controversy over
representation at Churchill funeral. il U S
News 58:53-4 F 15 '65

India
Beaut; postponement of scheduled visits by
Ayub Khan and Shastri. Newsweek 65:48+
My 3 '65
What about a nuclear guarantee for India?
R. D. Masters. New Repub 153:9-10 D 25
'65; Reply. C. Kaysen and J. J. Stone. 154:
13-14 Ja 15 '66

Indonesia
Ambassador Bunker concludes meetings with
Indonesian leaders; joint communique, April
15, 1965. Dept State Bul 52:654-5 My 3 '65
Another big country about to go to the
reds. S. W. Sanders. il U S News 58:80-2
My 17 '65
Bitter champagne; U.S. to maintain open
diplomatic line to Djakarta and Sukarno.
Newsweek 66:48 Ag 9 '65
Bunker and Bung. Reporter 32:8 My 6 '65
Coping with the Bung. il Time 86:30 Ag 6 '65
End of the line? il Time 85:28 Ap 2 '65
End of the road for U.S. in Indonesia. U S
News 58:49 Mr 15 '65
Failure in Indonesia. New Repub 152:7 My
1 '65
South seas under. Nat R 17:271-2 Ap 6 '65
U.S. and Indonesia, a tragedy in diplomacy.
F .N. Trager. il N Y Times Mag p26-7+
Ag 29 '65

Italy
United States and Italy reaffirm close ties
of friendship; exchange of greetings, with
text of joint communique, April 21, 1965.
L. B. Johnson; A. Moro. Dept State Bul
52:809-12 My 24 '65

Japan
Direct hit; using Okinawa as a launching
pad for Vietnam-bound bombers. il News-
week 66:40+ Ag 16 '65
Japan and the United States: the essentials
of partnership; address, October 25, 1965.
W. P. Bundy. Dept State Bul 53:777-80
N 15 '65
President Johnson and Prime Minister Sato
of Japan exchange views on matters of
mutual interest; exchange of greetings, with
joint communique, January 13, 1965. L. B.
Johnson; E. Sato. Dept State Bul 52:133-6
F 1 '65
U.S.-Japanese trends and prospects; address,
October 30, 1965. W. P. Bundy. Dept State
Bul 53:770-7 N 15 '65

Korea (Peoples Democratic Republic)
USAF plane attacked by MIG's off North
Korean coast; Department statement, April
30, 1965. Dept State Bul 52:812-13 My 24 '65

Korea (Republic)
Korean foreign minister holds talks with
Secretary Rusk; joint statement, March 17,
1965. T. W. Lee and D. Rusk. Dept State
Bul 52:491 Ap 5 '65
Something of value; U.S. visit of South
Korea's President Chung Hee Park. il Time
85:22-3 My 28 '65
United States and Korea reaffirm strong
bonds of friendship; exchange of greetings,
with joint communique, May 18, 1965. L. B.
Johnson; C. H. Park. Dept State Bul 52:
950-4 Je 14 '65

Laos
Little war in Laos. V. S. Kearney. America
112:250-1 F 20 '65
Neutralization experiment in Laos. A. J.
Dommen. Cur Hist 48:89-94+ F '65
Our secret war in Laos. D. Warner. il Re-
porter 32:23-6 Ap 22 '65

Latin America
Another view from Latin America. G. Driver
and G. Fritz. Christian Cent 82:1292+ O
20 '65
Campaign tour; R. Kennedy's Latin-American
tour. il Newsweek 66:39-40 N 22 '65
Charity begins abroad; Senators Fulbright and
Mansfield pronouncements. M. Ascoli. Re-
porter 33:24 O 7 '65
Cooperating for progress in Latin America;
address, February 27,1965. E. Bunker. Dept
State Bul 52:465-71 Mr 29 '65
Democracy versus stability: the recent Latin
American policy of the United States. J.
Slater. Yale R 55:169-81 D '65
Dominican crisis; case study in American
policy. T. Draper. Commentary 40:33-68 D
'65
Dominican crisis; issue is nonintervention.
D. D. Ranstead. New Repub 152:8-9 My
29 '65
Dominican Republic: the necessary risk; Time
essay. Time 85:33 Je 11 '65
Field trip. il Time 86:41 S 3 '65
Hispaniola. M. Ascoli. Reporter 33:14 Jl 15 '65
Johnson so far: foreign policy. M. J. Gold-
bloom. Commentary 39:47-55 Je '65; Discus-
sion. 40:6+ N '65
Latin America: continent on a teeterboard.
D. D. Ranstead. Nation 201:292-4 N 1 '65
Man behind our Latin-American actions. L.
Gross. il Look 29:35-7 Je 15 '65
Mann to watch. A. Campbell. New Repub
152:13-15 Je 5 '65
Mann's divided mind. New Repub 153:6-7
O 23 '65
Marines have landed; intellectual poverty of
administration's policy. W. V. Shannon.
Commonweal 82:278-9 My 21 '65
New warning to the Latins. Time 86:28 O
1 '65
Report from the Dominican Republic. R. Dud-
man. New Repub 152:15-16 Je 5 '65
Roberto south of the border. Nat R 17:1144-6
D 14 '65
Roll call in the House; resolution concerning
communism in western hemisphere. New
Repub 153:7 O 16 '65
Situation in the Dominican Republic; com-
pliance with the law; address, September
15, 1965. J. W. Fulbright. Vital Speeches
31:753-5 O 1 '65
Spiritless alliance. R. B. Goldmann. New
Repub 153:13-15 O 30 '65; Reply. D. B.
Atkinson. 153:34-5 N 13 '65
This month's feature: the U.S. and western
hemisphere security. Cong Digest 44:257-
88 N '65
U.S. establishes a new doctrine; unilateral
intervention to forestall Castro-type Com-
munist government in this hemisphere.
Bsns W p 170 My 8 '65
Vietnam and Latin America; danger of a
hemispheric Vietnam; address, August 25,
1965. T. J. Dodd. Vital Speeches 31:706-9
S 15 '65
When reds move in; how U.S. responds;
excerpts from address, October 12, 1965.
T. C. Mann. U S News 59:19 O 25 '65
When to intervene; nonintervention, key-
stone of structure of inter-American sys-
tem. Time 86:53 O 22 '65
Yankee go home? stay home? intervene? J.
P. Davies, jr. il N Y Times Mag p28-9+
My 23 '65
Yankees vs. Latins. W. Pfaff. Commonweal
82:309-10 My 28 '65
See also
Latin America and the United States
Monroe doctrine

UNITED STATES—Foreign relations—*Cont.*

Malaysia

U.S. regrets Malaysia unable to accept military credit proposal; Department statement, December 29, 1964; with text of joint communique, November 23, 1964. Dept State Bul 52:75 Ja 18 '65

Mali (Republic)

Mission from Mali concludes visit to United States; joint statement, July 14, 1965. Dept State Bul 53:192 Ag 2 '65

Mexico

Good neighbor who opposes U.S. now; action in the Dominican Republic. il U S News 58:10 My 24 '65

Middle East

Good samaritan; arms race. Newsweek 65:45-6 Ap 26 '65
Middle East; address, April 21, 1965. P. H. Nitze. Vital Speeches 31:504-9 Je 1 '65
Middle East: temperature rising. R. D. Heinl, jr. New Repub 152:9-11 Mr 20 '65; Reply. R. L. Cleveland. 152:28 My 8 '65
United States and the Middle East; address, November 4, 1965. E. Berger. Vital Speeches 32:184-90 Ja 1 '66
U.S. in the Middle East: policy in transition. H. L. Hoskins. Cur Hist 48:257-62 My '65

Nicaragua

In quest of Sandino, imperialism still rides. C. Beals. Nation 201:83-7 S 20 '65

Pakistan

Beaut; postponement of scheduled visits by Ayub Khan and Shastri. Newsweek 65:48+ My 3 '65
Hard talk about hardware. Time 86:20 D 17 '65
Pakistan's Ayub: once an ally; now? il U S News 59:24 S 20 '65
Plugged in; President Ayub Khan's U.S. visit. il Newsweek 66:20+ D 27 '65
Sweat; approaching Washington visits of Harold Wilson and Ayub Khan. New Repub 153:8 D 11 '65
U.S. and Pakistan agree on need for peaceful settlement of Asian conflicts; exchange of greetings and exchange of toasts, December 14, 1965; with joint communique. M. Ayub Khan; L. B. Johnson. Dept State Bul 54:2-7 Ja 3 '66

Panama

President: revisionist; treaty revised. Newsweek 66:27-8 O 4 '65

Philippines

Now: an old friend turning away from U.S? with interview with D. Macapagal. il U S News 58:68-71 Je 14 '65

Rhodesia

Letter from Washington. R. H. Rovere. New Yorker 41:201-2 N 20 '65
U.N. condemns Rhodesia's attempt to perpetuate minority rule; statement, October 12, 1965, with text of resolution. A. J. Goldberg. Dept State Bul 53:762-3 N 8 '65

Russia

Atomic diplomacy: Hiroshima and Potsdam, by G. Alperovitz. Review
  Nation 201:123-4 S 6 '65. C. Lasch
Beyond the cold war, by M. D. Shulman. Review
  Sat R 49:39 Ja 22 '66. W. J. Thorbecke
Can we make common cause with Russia? R. Lowenthal. il N Y Times Mag p34-5+ N 21 '65
Chance for Soviet-American diplomacy. H. Brandon. Sat R 48:18+ O 23 '65
Cold wind from Moscow: detente illusions die hard; Radio Moscow commentary on ceasefire. A. Brumberg. il Reporter 33:40-2 O 21; 10 D 2 '65
Heil Hoover; ratification of consular convention postponed. New Repub 153:9 S 4 '65
Mr Ball discusses U.S. relations with Europe on BBC; interview, ed. by A. Burnet. October 2, 1965. G. W. Ball. Dept State Bul 53:653-60 O 25 '65
Mr Goldberg comments on speech by Soviet foreign minister; statement, September 24, 1965. A. J. Goldberg. Dept State Bul 53:683 O 25 '65
On dealing with Russia. Sat Eve Post 238:98 S 25 '65

Open door of Henry Wallace. R. Radosh. Nation 202:39-42 Ja 10 '66
President sends New Year's message to Soviet leaders; letter, December 30, 1964. L. B. Johnson. Dept State Bul 52:74 Ja 18 '65
Russia, the US and Vietnam. H. J. Morgenthau. New Repub 152:12-13 My 1 '65; Discussion. 152:34-5 My 15 '65
[Soviet cold war strategy] reprint, March 14, 1956. J. Burnham. Nat R 17:1068 N 30 '65
Strategy of interdependence, by V. P. Rock. Review
  Bul Atomic Sci 21:40 F '65. J. O. Coppock
U.S. calls police protection of Moscow embassy inadequate; White House statement, February 10, 1965. Dept State Bul 52:289 Mr 1 '65
U.S. protests harassment of ships by Soviets; rejects Soviet charges; Department announcement and notes, April 2 and April 5, 1965. Dept State Bul 52:655-8 My 3 '65
U.S.-Soviet Kula. M. Orans. Bul Atomic Sci 21:44-5 Mr '65
U.S. vs. Russia: next round in arms race. il U S News 59:66-7 N 29 '65
Unity, the legacy of American democracy; address, February 3, 1965. L. B. Johnson. Dept State Bul 52:242-4 F 22 '65
What's a little war between friends? Nat R 17:756-8 S 7 '65
  See also
United States—Treaties—Russia

Singapore

U.S. recognizes Singapore as sovereign, independent state; Department statement, with message from Secretary Rusk August 11, 1965. Dept State Bul 53:357 Ag 30 '65

South Africa

American policy toward South Africa; address, March 22, 1965. D. M. Fraser. Vital Speeches 31:398-400 Ap 15 '65
Our stake in apartheid. S. Meisler. il Nation 201:71-3 Ag 16 '65

Tanganyika

Nation that tried to help itself. F. L. Howley. Read Digest 86:142-4+ Je '65

Tanzania

U.S. asks departure of Tanzanian counselor of embassy; Department statement, February 14, 1965. Dept State Bul 52:432 Mr 22 '65
U.S. recalls Ambassador from Tanzania; Department statement, January 30, 1965. Dept State Bul 52:244 F 22 '65

Thailand

And now Thailand. Nation 202:29 Ja 10 '66
Reciprocating a kindness; American-Thai buildup. il Time 86:20-2 D 24 '65

Turkey

Ankara: Inönü looks left. C. Sterling. il Reporter 33:18-22 S 9 '65; Reply. S. J. Markiewicz. 33:8 O 7 '65

Uganda

U.S. replies to Uganda charges at Nairobi conference. Dept State Bul 52:337-8 Mr 8 '65

Underdeveloped areas

Secretary Rusk appears on NBC's American white paper; interview, September 7, 1965. D. Rusk. Dept State Bul 53:509-10 S 27 '65

Upper Volta

President Yameogo of Upper Volta visits the United States; exchange of greetings, with joint communique, March 30, 1965. L. B. Johnson; M. Yameogo. Dept State Bul 52:618-21 Ap 26 '65

Vietnam

Vietnam: a diplomatic tragedy, by V. Bator. Review
  New Repub 153:23-4 Jl 10 '65. B. B. Fall

Vietnam (Democratic Republic)

Congress reluctant to declare war. J. N. Eller. America 114:67 Ja 15 '66
Speak up, Mr. Johnson. Commonweal 83:262 D 3 '65
U.S. case against Hanoi. U S News 58:27 Mr 8 '65

Vietnam (Republic)

Acid test. W. Lippmann. Newsweek 66:15 Jl 5 '65
After the Washington teach-in; debate on government's policies and aims in Vietnam. M. Greenfield. il Reporter 32:16-19 Je 3 '65

UNITED STATES—Foreign relations—Vietnam
(Republic)—*Continued*
Test in Vietnam. W. Lippmann. Newsweek
65:23 Ap 26 '65
They march, doubting they will overcome;
Vietnam day committee marchers. New
Repub 153:9 O 30 '65
Third bird; President's position in debate
over policy. K. Crawford. Newsweek 65:32
Mr 8 '65
This month's feature: U.S. and the situa-
tion in Vietnam. il Cong Digest 44:99-128
Ap '65
Three Afro-Asian fronts; Vietnam. D.
Warner. il Reporter 32:27-9 Mr 25 '65
To have a part in it; Lodge succeeds Taylor
as ambassador. il Time 86:15 Jl 16 '65
To my pacifist friends. J. O'Gara. Common-
weal 82:208 My 7 '65
Treason of the experts. E. Bentley. Nation
201:466-70 D 13 '65
Truth in Vietnam. America 112:350-1 Mr 13
'65
U.S. and Viet Nam; symposium, ed. by R.
Hemming. il Sr Schol 87:5-19+ S 23 '65
U.S. embassy at Saigon damaged; funds for
new building requested; statement, March
30, and letter, April 1, 1965, with bill. L.
B. Johnson. Dept State Bul 52:571-2 Ap
19 '65
U.S. objective in Viet-Nam; remarks, Feb-
ruary 17, 1965. L. B. Johnson. Dept State
Bul 52:332 Mr 8 '65
U.S. tries armed force and persuasive power;
in Dominican Republic and Vietnam.
Bsns W p26 My 22 '65
Unmistakable message; purpose and policy
in Vietnam. M. Greenfield. Reporter 33:10
Ag 12 '65
Vietnam. N. Cousins. Sat R 48:38+ N 13 '65
Vietnam and beyond: hard decisions. News-
week 65:19-20 Mr 1 '65
Vietnam and Cuba. Commonweal 82:5-6 Mr
26 '65
Vietnam and reality. W. Pfaff. Commonweal
81:685-6 F 26 '65; Reply with rejoinder.
D. R. Weidman. 82:2 Mr 26 '65
Vietnam and the American conscience. N.
Cousins. Sat R 48:22-3 F 27 '65
Vietnam and U.S. policy continuity. N.
Cousins. Sat R 48:32 N 20 '65
Vietnam background. Q. L. Quade. il America
113:17-19 Jl 3 '65
Vietnam choice: hysteria or stamina. E. T.
Folliard. America 112:306 Mr 6 '65
Vietnam: in and out of focus. Pyrrho. Nat R
17:1161-3 D 14 '65
Vietnam: Mr Kosygin goes calling; Second
traveler; Bundy's trip. il Newsweek 65:36+
F 15 '65
Vietnam: new blows, same strategy. il News-
week 65:27-8 Ap 12 '65
Vietnam policy; letter. H. W. Edgerton. New
Repub 152:28-30 My 22 '65
Vietnam: problems and progress; address,
January 14, 1965. H. K. Johnson. Vital
Speeches 31:262-5 F 15 '65
Viet Nam: the right war at the right time;
Time essay. Time 85:30 My 14 '65
Vietnam: way to victory? excerpts. T. K.
Young. il Newsweek 65:42-3 Mr 29 '65
Vietniks: self-defeating dissent; Time essay.
Time 86:44-5 O 29 '65
View from the brink. E. J. Hughes. News-
week 67:15 Ja 10 '66
Vox Vietnik fires a volley of protest; with
report by J. K. Jessup. il Life 59:40B-40D O
29 '65
War by any other name. Nat R 17:625-7 Jl
27 '65
We can win in southeast Asia. A. Harrigan.
Nat R 17:187-8+ Mr 9 '65
We will be far better off facing the issue.
il Time 85:19-21 F 26 '65
What are we doing in Vietnam? J. Burnham.
Nat R 17:232 Mr 23 '65
What next in Vietnam? Commonweal 81:775-6
Mr 19 '65
Where's Congress? Nation 200:657 Je 21 '65
While the bullets whiz. il Time 85:21-21A
Mr 12 '65
White paper. New Repub 152:5-7 Mr 13 '65
Why hold the line in Vietnam? Adlai Steven-
son's answer. A. E. Stevenson. il Newsweek
66:20 D 27 '65
Why the protests? demonstrations. New
Repub 153:5-7 O 30 '65
Will Johnson do it? and can he take it?
Nat R 17:355-6 My 4 '65
With Senior's editor in Viet Nam; questions
and answers R. Hemming. il Sr Schol 86:
12-13 Mr 4 '65
Word to my critics. W. V. Shannon. Com-
monweal 82:206-7 My 7 '65; Reply. P.
Batten. 82:338 Je 4 '65

Worse before it gets better. il Newsweek 66:
17-18 Jl 19 '65
See also
Vietnamese war, 1957- —American participation

Vietnam (Republic)—Bibliography
War in Asia: more questions than answers.
R. Dudman. Sat R 48:34-5 N 27 '65

Yugoslavia
My visits with Kosygin and Tito. W. A.
Harriman. il Life 59:89-90 Ag 27 '65

Foreign service
Aim, FAIM, fire! civilians to assist ambas-
sadors. New Repub 153:7-8 O 23 '65
Begrudged diplomats: the stepsons of foggy
bottom. H. S. Villard. il Nation 202:36-9
Ja 10 '66
Face to face with a working diplomat, for-
eign service officer's son. C. Adams. Seven-
teen 24:145 O '65
Federal civilian employment in foreign coun-
tries reduced. il Dept State Bul 52:1015-16
Je 21 '65
Military members of the country team. S.
Horwitz. Dept State Bul 53:268-71 Ag 16 '65
President asks strengthening of foreign af-
fairs agencies; letters, May 6, 1965; with
executive order. L. B. Johnson. Dept State
Bul 52:930-3 Je 7 '65
President submits promotion list, asks FSO
appointments for USIA; letter, April 13,
1965. L. B. Johnson. Dept State Bul 52:733
My 10 '65
Public members added to teams of foreign
service inspectors. Dept State Bul 53:256-
7 Ag 9 '65
State of the Department of state; Time
essay. Time 86:34-5 O 15 '65

Forest products laboratory
Forestry's scientific U.N. R. H. Lysager. il
Am For 71:28-30+ Ag '65
Preserving the natural beauty of wood ex-
posed to weather. il Consumer Bul 48:2 Mr
'65
They work wonders with wood. K. Detzer.
Read Digest 86:233-4+ My '65

Forest service
But can they crack a nut? Emerson's views
on commodity values vs. beauty. J. B.
Craig. Am For 71:7 Jl '65
From firefighting to revolution in three days;
Dominican Republic. M. S. Lowden. il Am
For 71:16-19+ Ag '65
Life as a fire lookout in Crater Lake National
Park. L. Neuberger and R. Neuberger. il
Nat Parks Mag 39:16-19 Ag '65
They help stamp out firebugs. F. Tinker.
il Pop Mech 124:98-102+ S '65
They work wonders with wood. K. Detzer.
Read Digest 86:233-4+ My '65
Wildlife and multiple use. V. Metcalfe. il
Am For 71:30-1+ N '65

General accounting office
DOD, GAO reach truce on pricing policy.
K. Johnsen. Aviation W 83:68-70 D 27 '65
GAO contracts policy is criticized. Miss &
Roc 16:18 My 31 '65
GAO policies hit; with editorial comment.
Miss & Roc 16:10, 54 Je 7 '65
GAO willing to help protect contractors. K.
Johnsen. Aviation W 83:87 Jl 19 '65
House group will recommend changes in GAO
defense contract audit practices. H. M.
David. Miss & Roc 17:23 Jl 19 '65
Industry voices concern over GAO power. K.
Johnsen. Aviation W 82:20 Je 7 '65
More responsive GAO attitude seen. Miss &
Roc 17:15 D 13 '65
Watchdog agency tugs on leash; GAO checks
U.S. expenditures. Bsns W p76+ Je 12 '65

General services administration
Auto safety inquiry. New Repub 153:6 Jl 24
'65
Crashproof car? il Newsweek 65:69 F 8 '65
Lawson B. Knott, jr. named administrator
of General services. Arch Rec 138:365+ S
'65

Geological survey
Earthquake prediction: ESSA and USGS vie
for leadership. L. J. Carter. il Science 151:
181-3 Ja 14 '66

Government
See United States—Politics and government

Government printing office
Decision on new GPO building postponed at
least one year. Pub W 188:114 O 4 '65

UNITED STATES—Government printing office
—*Continued*
Implementing the depository law; proposal for
the distribution of non-GPO publications
to depository libraries, 1962 statute. C.
Brock. bibliog il Library J 90:1825-33 Ap 15
'65
Government publications
See Government publications
**Health, education and welfare.
Department of**
Congress: House subcommittee to concentrate
on PHS, NIH, FDA in study of parent de-
partment. J. Walsh. Science 148:609-10 Ap
30 '65
Educator takes on problem pupil. HEW;
Secretary J. W. Gardner. Bsns W p32+
Ag 14 '65
Excellence for HEW. Newsweek 66:27 Ag
9 '65
Explorer for excellence; new Secretary. Time
86:23 Ag 6 '65
Gardner appointment. J. Lear. Sat R 48:46
Ag 21 '65
Health, education, and welfare; excerpts
from address, November 18, 1965. J. W.
Gardner. Science 150:1684-6 D 24 '65
HEW: as Secretary of Department of health,
education and welfare Gardner faces for-
midable tasks. J. Walsh. Science 149:613-16
Ag 6 '65
HEW: running the Great society. E. Langer.
il Science 150:1272-4 D 3 '65
Hospital discrimination: HEW criticized by
civil rights groups. E. Langer. Science
149:1355-7 S 17 '65
How welfare provisions of the civil-rights
act will be enforced; questions and answers.
U S News 58:43 My 3 '65
Leadership for education; new appointments.
J. Cass. Sat R 49:57-8 Ja 15 '66
What the pending federal bill would do. Bul
Atomic Sci 21:18-22 Ap '65
See also
United States—Aging, Administration on

Historic houses, etc.
In pursuit of Honest Abe; Lincoln heritage
trail. T. J. Fleming. il Good H 160:138+ F
'65
Monumental shame. J. H. Winchester. il
Travel 123:58-60 My '65
Preserving America's past. M. Frome. il
Holiday 37:151-6 Mr '65
Special case: presidents' houses. il Sr Schol
86:16 Mr 18 '65
Target: historic houses. A. H. Hepburn. il
Sr Schol 87:sup 13 S 23 '65
See also
Monticello (historic house)
Mount Vernon (historic house)
Williamsburg, Va.
also subhead Historic houses, etc. under
names of states, cities, etc. e.g. New York
(state)—Historic houses, etc.

History
Americans: the national experience, by D.
J. Boorstin. Review
America 113:412-13 O 9 '65. W. L. Lucey
Sat R 48:64-5 O 23 '65. R. D. Heffner
Bold men, bold dreams. C. D. Bowen. Read
Digest 87:49-53 Jl '65
Oxford history of the American people, by S.
E. Morison. Review
Newsweek 65:100+ Ap 26 '65
Search for a usable past. H. S. Commager.
il Am Heritage 16:4-9+ F '65
See also
Cities and towns—United States—History
Frontier and pioneer life—United States
United States—Social history
also subhead History under names of
regions, states, etc. e.g. West—History

Bibliography
Articles and other books received; comp. by
W. Gray. See issues of American historical
review
New books for your history shelf. H. L.
Hurwitz. il Sr Schol 87:sup22-4 S 30 '65
New books in American history. H. L. Hur-
witz. Sr Schol 87:sup 17 N 18 '65

Discovery and exploration
How lost was Zebulon Pike? Louisiana pur-
chase. D. Jackson. il Am Heritage 16:10-15+
F '65
See also
America—Discovery and exploration

Textbooks
History is a dangerous subject; findings of
Anglo-United States team survey of sec-
ondary school textbooks. R. A. Billington.
il Sat R 49:59-61+ Ja 15 '66
Colonial period
Americans loyal to the crown. R. B. Morris.
il Sat R 48:30-1 D 18 '65
Catholics in colonial America, by J. T. Ellis.
Review
America 113:100 Jl 24 '65. C. E. O'Neill
See also
Puritans

Colonial period—Sources
Colonial court records and the study of early
American history: a bibliographical review.
M. G. Kammen. bibliog f Am Hist R 70:
732-9 Ap '65

French and Indian war, 1755-1763
Guns at the forks, by W. O'Meara. Review
Sat R 48:30+ Ag 14 '65. E. Wright
Most extraordinary adventures of Major
Robert Stobo, by R. C. Alberts. Review
Sat R 48:66 O 23 '65. W. C. Kiessel

Revolution
Meaning of the American revolution, by
D. Lacy. Review
Sr Schol 86:sup21 Mr 18 '65. H. L. Hur-
witz
Peacemakers, by R. B. Morris. Review
Sat R il 48:56-7 O 2 '65. S. F. Bemis
Revolutionary character of the American rev-
olution. W. H. Nelson. bibliog f Am Hist
R 70:998-1014 Jl '65
Truth and illusion: meaning of the American
revolution today; address, February 22, 1965.
T. J. Fleming. Vital Speeches 31:345-9 Mr 15
'65

Revolution—Campaigns and battles
Sons of liberty; excerpt from the Oxford
history of the American people. S. E.
Morison. il Read Digest 87:281-6+ N '65

Revolution—Causes
Sons of liberty; excerpt from The Oxford history of the American people. S. E. Morison.
il Read Digest 87:281-6+ N '65

Revolution—Drama
Star for Old Glory. A. Fisher and O. Rabe.
Plays 24:57-61 Ap '65
Yankee Doodle dandy. A. Fisher. Plays 25:
61-2 Ja '66

Revolution—Personal narratives
Documents of freedom; with facsimiles of letters, ed. by H. H. Peckham. il Am Heritage
16:65-73 Je '65
Revolution—Personal narratives—British
We was amazingly fortunate; excerpts from
journal of British naval officer, ed. by T. J.
Fleming. B. James. il Am Heritage 16:32-
5+ O '65

1783-1812
See also
Louisiana purchase

1849-1877
Pig war was a one-shot war. il Sunset 135:
40+ S '65

Civil war
Cabin boy's diary of action aboard the Cairo.
G. Yost. Life 58:44 F 12 '65
Lincolniana in 1964. B. E. Wheeler. il Hobbies
69:28-9+ F; 70:28-9+ Mr '65
Never call retreat, by B. Catton. Review
Sat R 48:58 O 2 '65
Unfinished business of the Civil war; true
freedom for the Negro; excerpt from the
Centennial history of the Civil war. B.
Catton. il N Y Times Mag p28-9+ Ap 4
'65
War within a war, by C. Beals. Review
America 113:120-1 Jl 31 '65. W. D. Hoyt,
jr

Civil war—Campaigns and battles
See also
Appomattox campaign, 1865
Bull Run, First battle of, 1861
Confederate States of America—Army
Reconstruction (Civil war)

Civil war—Centennial, 1961-1965
Centennial notes: report on a New Jersey
observance. G. M. Fishman. Negro Hist
Bul 28:82-3 Ja '65

UNITED STATES—History—Civil war—Centennial, 1961-1965—*Continued*
Lost: one centennial. W. K. Zinsser. il Sat Eve Post 238:22 My 8 '65
This hallowed ground; centennial commemoration at the Appomattox court house. il Time 85:27 Ap 16 '65

Civil war—Negro troops

Worth fighting for: a history of the Negro in the United States during the Civil war and reconstruction, by A. McCarthy and L. Reddick. Review
Negro Hist Bul 28:202 My '65. E. A. Toppin

Civil war—Negroes

Centennial notes: report on a New Jersey observance. G. M. Fishman. Negro Hist Bul 28:82-3 Ja '65
Recruiting and arming of Negroes in the South Carolina Sea Islands, 1862-1865. G. Robbins. bibliog Negro Hist Bul 28:150-1+ Ap '65

Civil war—Personal narratives

So eager were we all; condensation, with an introd. by B. Catton. L. H. Metcalf. il Am Heritage 16:32-41 Je '65

1865-

Age of excess: the United States from 1877 to 1914, by R. Ginger. Review
Sat R 48:41 Ap 10 '65. M. Cantor
Of snuff, sin and the Senate, by R. Rienow and L. T. Rienow. Review
Sat R 48:24-5 Jl 31 '65. M. L. Coit

1865-1898

Era of reconstruction, 1865-1877, by K. M. Stampp. Review
Nation 200:450-3 Ap 26 '65. B. A. Weisberger
Old vision of a new South. H. Hansen. il Sat R 48:42-3 Ap 10 '65
See also
Reconstruction (Civil war)

Spanish American war, 1898-1899

First anti-imperialists; excerpt from Proud tower; a portrait of the world before the war, 1890-1914. B. W. Tuchman. Nation 201:77-82 S 20 '65

20th century

America enters the modern era. F. Freidel. il Nat Geog Mag 128:536-77 O '65

1933-1945

Atomic age: its problems and promises. F. Freidel. il Nat Geog Mag 129:66-9 Ja '66

1945-

Atomic age: its problems and promises. F. Freidel. il Nat Geog Mag 129:66-9 Ja '66

History, Pictorial

Look of the twenties. Am Heritage 16:41-55 Ag '65

House of representatives

See United States—Congress—House of representatives

Housing and home finance agency

Washington dateline. Am City 80:7 F '65

Housing and urban development, Department of

Department of headaches. W. Von Eckardt. New Repub 153:19-22 N 6 '65
Department of urban affairs. R. H. Leach. il America 112:388-91 Mr 20 '65
First for the new Cabinet post. il U S News 60:14 Ja 24 '66
Head for HUD; first Negro Cabinet officer in Nation's history. Newsweek 67:26 Ja 24 '66
Manhunt; R. Weaver's chances of becoming first Negro Cabinet officer. Newsweek 66:42 N 22 '65
Soon, a Cabinet secretary for cities. U S News 59:10 Ag 23 '65
Surrogate for the cities. Time 86:22-3 Ag 20 '65
What new urban department will do; questions and answers. il U S News 59:63 Ag 30 '65

Indian affairs, Bureau of

American Indian: citizen in captivity; plight of Navajo Indians and a land sale case. B. W. Young. il Sat R 48:25-6 D 11 '65; Discussion. 49:21 Ja 1; 34 Ja 22 '66

Indian claims commission

Seminoles' long road to victory; right to compensation for loss of lands in Florida. W. Hartley and E. Hartley. Read Digest 86:199-200+ F '65

Industries

As boom goes into its fifth year; with charts. U S News 58:102-3 My 3 '65
Behind the mask of success; excerpt from Our depleted society. S. Melman. Sat R 48:8-10+ Jl 31 '65
Dollars in figures; effect on industries. T. R. Brooks. il Duns R 85:62-4+ Ap '65
Interindustry employment requirements; with input-output tables. J. Alterman. Mo Labor R 88:841-50 Jl '65
U.S. industry 1965, another record shattering year. il Sr Schol 86:16-17 Ap 15 '65
See also
Building industry
Industrial mobilization
Shipbuilding
Tobacco industry and trade
United States—Commerce
also subhead Industries under names of sections, states, cities, etc. e.g. New York (city)—Industries; *also* subhead United States under names of industries, e.g. Steel industry and trade—United States

Information agency

Crucial battle for the minds of men; USIA libraries. H. W. Axford. bibliog Library J 90:2499-503 Je 1 '65
IMG sets country allocation for fiscal 1966. Pub W 188:72 N 15 '65
President submits promotion list, asks FSO appointments for USIA; letter, April 13, 1965. L. B. Johnson. Dept State Bul 52:733 My 10 '65
Split personality of USIA. A. Bermel. il Harper 231:116-18+ S '65
U.S. closes libraries and reading rooms in Indonesia. Dept State Bul 52:448 Mr 29 '65
USIA sees donated books building export markets. Pub W 188:31 D 13 '65
USIA tells U.S. story with pictures. il Pop Phot 57:58+ N; 134+ D '65
War of words; America's un-used weapon; address, June 21, 1965. A. E. Meyerhoff. Vital Speeches 31:600-3 Jl 15 '65

Information service

How to riot tactfully; Indonesian mobs storm USIS offices; USIS libraries in Indonesia to be closed. Time 85:24 Mr 12 '65
Who closed the library? Grosvenor square closed by USIS. Newsweek 67:21-2 Ja 10 '66

Intellectual life

Angst across the sea; concerning British broadcasting corporation program. Under pressure: U.S.A. M. L. Rosenthal. Reporter 32:41-2 Mr 11 '65
Culture fizzle; Rockefeller brothers fund report. Newsweek 65:82 Mr 8 '65
Flourishing intellectuals; Time essay. Time 85:32-3 My 21 '65
Intellectualism in American life. J. Epstein. New Repub 152:21-4 Je 5 '65
Machine in the garden, by L. Marx. Review Nation 201:42-5 Jl 19 '65. A. Trachtenberg
Room for culture too, in the President's plans. il U S News 58:41-2 F 1 '65
This culture boom: how real is it? il Changing T 19:37-40 O '65
Who are the Americans? V. Miller. Nat R 17:1035-7 N 16 '65
See also
American literature
Books and reading
Colleges and universities—United States
National education association
United States—Popular culture

Interagency committee on oceanography (proposed)

Industry within. W. J. Coughlin. Miss & Roc 17:70 S 6 '65

Interior, Department of

Think big: open letter to the Secretary of the Interior to build two dams on Colorado River. B. Stewart. il Harper 231:62-3 Ag '65
See also
United States—Land management, Bureau of

Internal revenue service

Globe-trotting t-men follow the taxpayers; help Americans abroad with tax returns. il Bsns W p 112+ Mr 27 '65

UNITED STATES—Internal revenue service
—*Continued*

IRS: please note! tax-exempt POAU. Nat R 17:681-2 Ag 10 '65

Men from Uncle Sam; techniques used by the tax man. il Newsweek 66:27-8 Ag 2 '65

New drive on tax crooks; collectors, accountants, taxpayers. U S News 58:95-6 My 24 '65

New tax collector tells his goals. S. S. Cohen. Nations Bsns 53:31+ Ap '65

Now: social clubs face new taxes. U S News 58:99-101 Mr 22 '65

Payoff for informers. Time 85:68 Ap 9 '65

Personal business; audits will be tougher this year. Bsns W p 183-4 My 15 '65

Profiles. J. Brooks. il New Yorker 41:66+ Ap 3; 51-2+ Ap 10 '65

Speaking out; we must stop tax snooping. E. V. Long. Sat Eve Post 238:10+ N 20 '65

T-men's tactics are disallowed; subcommittee investigating IRS agents invasion of privacy. il Bsns W p24 Jl 31 '65

Tax crackdown; right-wing organizations. Nat R 17:315-16 Ap 20 '65

Uncle Sam's wonderful tax machine. D. Oberdorfer. il Sat Eve Post 238:28-9 Ap 10 '65

When machines check on taxes. U S News 58:103-4 Ap 19 '65

When tax agent asks for more: many fight, and win; IRS appeals division. il U S News 58:99-100 Mr 15 '65

When the income-tax man looks over your shoulder. C. Stevenson and J. E. Roper. Read Digest 86:49-50+ Ap '65

When the machines get your tax return. il U S News 58:110-11 Ap 26 '65

Your friendly tax collector; use of instruments of snoopery to get evidence against tax dodgers. il Time 86:14-15 Jl 30 '65

International commerce, Bureau of

They lead small business to bigger markets. R. S. Knowles. Read Digest 87:107-10 O '65

Interoceanic canal commission

President asks for funds for canal commission. Dept State Bul 53:70 Jl 12 '65

Interstate commerce commission

Getting mergers off the sidetrack; proposal for stepping up railroad mergers. Bsns W p98+ D 4 '65

Old ways at the ICC nearing end of line. Bsns W p74 Ja 1 '66

Thanks for nothing; J. Jones of Atlanta, hopes crushed by Interstate commerce commission's Trucking authority board. il Newsweek 66:82 D 6 '65

Trucking rolls into an age of giants. il Bsns W p 174-6+ Je 12 '65

Job corps

Be somebody; Catoctin job corps conservation center, Md. L. E. Mathis. il Am Ed 1:28-32 My '65

Business role in the Great society. J. Terhorst; W. Welch. il Reporter 33:26-32 O 21 '65

Can the Job corps do the job? B. Carter. il Reporter 32:21-6 Mr 25 '65

Changing liabilities to assets; Job corps program to train school dropouts. il Bsns W p 156+ Mr 20 '65

Expectations, great & small; Women's job corps center in Cleveland. il Time 85:27-8 My 21 '65

For Youth corps: $1.25 an hour. U S News 58:74 F 1 '65

It's what's happening, baby; Camp Atterbury job corps center near Columbus, Ind. D. E. Cope. il Nat R 17:930-2 O 19 '65

Job corps=human+natural conservation; Catoctin job corps conservation center, Md. D. B. Huyck. il Am For 71:22-5 Jl '65

Job corps in Oregon. il Newsweek 66:25 S 13 '65

Job corps: what boys will it take? P. Anderson. New Repub 152:15-16 F 20 '65; Discussion. 152:34-5 Mr 6 '65

Jobbing the job corps? deficiencies in Kilmer program. il Newsweek 66:65 N 29 '65

My neighbor needs me. il Time 85:21 Mr 5 '65

Neighborhood youth corps. P. P. Price and H. A. Carl. ALA Bul 59:185-6 Mr '65

One poverty cure already in trouble. il U S News 58:93 F 22 '65

Planning for education's forgotten men. V. R. Alden. il Sat R 48:68-9+ My 15 '65

Poor don't want to be middle-class. R. Coles. il N Y Times Mag p7+ D 19 '65; Discussion. p 10+ Ja 9 '66

Providing jobs and skills for young people. Mo Labor R 88:III-IV Je '65

Shape-up starts for Job corps grads; drive for placement service. il Bsns W p32-3 N 6 '65

Troubles in the Job corps, report from a showplace: Camp Kilmer, N.J; with interview with F. Purcell. il U S News 59:51-5 D 27 '65

Welfare market; contracts to open and operate Job corps training center awarded to private industry. Newsweek 65:75-6 My 24 '65

What's going on in the Job corps. il U S News 59:57-60 Jl 26 '65

Where wage-fixing keeps kids idle. il Nations Bsns 53:34-5+ Jl '65

Libraries

Books for the Job corps. Library J 90:1472-7+ Mr 15 '65

Books for the Job corps; with excerpts from guidelines by J. M. Carroll. J. Manthorne. il Library J 90:932-4 F 15 '65

Joint chiefs of staff

JCS questionnaire. T. D. White. Newsweek 65:22 F 15 '65

Management team. il Time 85:22-23A F 5 '65

Justice, Department of

Advocate for U.S; T. Marshall; with report by S. McBee. il Life 59:57-8+ N 12 '65

Attorney General of the United States, talks; statements ed. by J. R. Moskin, N deB. Katzenbach. il Look 29:27-33 Je 1 '65

Battler from Baltimore; T. Marshall, first Negro Solicitor General. Newsweek 66:22 Jl 26 '65

Daily dilemmas of the Attorney General. D. Oberdorfer. il N Y Times Mag p28-9+ Mr 7 '65

From robe to swallowtail; T. Marshall, first Negro Solicitor General. il Time 86:18 Jl 23 '65

Justice dept. keeps heat on Hoffa. Bsns W p48 F 13 '65

Katzenbach's commission. A. Kopkind. New Repub 154:7-8 Ja 15 '66

Solicitor General. P. Pierce. il Ebony 21:67-9+ N '65

Tenth member: Solicitor General. il Time 86:94 O 22 '65

Thurgood Marshall takes a new tush-tush job; Solicitor General. S. E. Zion. N Y Times Mag p 11+ Ag 22 '65

Up from slavery; Thurgood Marshall begins as Solicitor General. por Newsweek 66:41 O 18 '65

See also

United States—Federal bureau of investigation

Antitrust division

Antitrust gets a new gospel. Bsns W p27 Ag 14 '65

Antitrust policy gets a long, hard look; Katzenbach sees trouble ahead. il Bsns W p45-6+ My 8 '65

First word from new trustbuster; excerpts from address, August 10, 1965. D. F. Turner. U S News 59:56 Ag 23 '65

In a few hands, by E. Kefauver. Review Nation 200:680 Je 21 '65. C. D. Edwards

One more try to show price-fixing in oil. Bsns W p26 Ap 17 '65

Professor Turner's turn at antitrust. H. B. Meyers. Fortune 72:168-71+ S '65

T.R.B. from Washington; evidence about mergers gathered by the Judiciary subcommittee on antitrust and monopoly. New Repub 152:4 Ap 24 '65

Office of criminal justice

Justice at justice. New Repub 152:7 My 1 '65

Labor, Department of

Manpower boss faces hornet's nest; S. H. Ruttenberg. Bsns W p 102 Ja 30 '65

Policing the vote count. Bsns W p 114 Mr 20 '65

Youth corps

See United States—Job corps

Labor policy

14(b) pending. Commonweal 82:712 O 1 '65

Labor-management under the Johnson administration. J. R. Wason. Cur Hist 49:65-70+ Ag '65

President's message to Congress on labor; address, May 18, 1965. L. B. Johnson. Cur Hist 48:106-7+ Ag '65

Toward an integrated manpower policy. G. L. Mangum. Mo Labor R 88:547-9 My '65

UNITED States—Labor policy—*Continued*

What happens to bargaining now? il Newsweek 66:71-2+ S 20 '65

See also

Labor laws and legislation—United States

United States—National labor relations board

Labor statistics, Bureau of

Analyst and economic policy; excerpt from remarks, October 21, 1965. A. M. Ross. Mo Labor R 88:II N '65

Land management, Bureau of

Preservation and the public lands. il Nat Parks Mag 39:20-1 N '65

Revolt in the provinces; BLM vs Oregon over Point Reyes, Calif. J. C. Hunt. il Am For 71:40-1+ Je '65

Who's boss? concerning T. Hallock's criticism of BLM director. J. B. Craig. Am For 71:53 Jl '65

Library of Congress

Another Capitol-hill building, and another controversy. il U S News 58:10 Je 21 '65

British poet is chosen for Library of Congress post. Pub W 187:76 Je 21 '65

Brush of a comet. F. Frankfurter; D. C. Mearns. Atlan 215:90-2 My '65

Death of a President; excerpt from the introd. to Annual report of the librarian of Congress for the fiscal year ending June 30, 1964. il Library J 90:3173-6 Ag '65

Formation of Federal library committee announced by Library of Congress. Library J 90:1846 Ap 15 '65

How can I find out? il Sci Digest 57:36-7 My '65

LC, CRL division of duties suggested by ARL committee. Library J 90:3410 S 1 '65

Library of Congress glows as reading room opens; culmination of renovation and restoration. Pub W 188:58+ Ag 23 '65

Library of Congress series (cont) il Library J 90:572-7, 1053-7, 1600-7, 1834-40, 2094-103, 2504-8, 2958-63, 3179-83, 3397-402, 4005-12, 4303-10, 4709-14, 5333-40 F 1, Mr 1, Ap 1-My 1, Je 1, Jl-S 1, O 1-N 1, D 15 '65

L.C. to house National register of microfilms. Pub W 187:137 F 22 '65

LC's main reading room opens after year-long restoration. Library J 90:3574 S 15 '65

LC's 1964 annual report notes year of records. Library J 90:2989 Jl '65

Monumental amends; James Madison memorial building. il Time 86:32 O 8 '65

New center at LC to coordinate copying of foreign manuscripts. Library J 90:3413 S 1 '65

Poetry and power; Consultant in poetry. Newsweek 65:94-94B F 15 '65

Profile: Luther H. Evans; reprint, with editorial comment. V. W. Clapp. il Library J 90:3386-91 S 1 '65

Third building for the Library of Congress. A. McCormick. ALA Bul 59:779 O '65

Washington report: from the Library of Congress. E. Hamer and A. McCormick. See issues of ALA bulletin

Administration

Administering a giant: an intimate view. R. D. Rogers. il Library J 90:4303-10 O 15 '65

Appropriations and expenditures

LC appropriations. ALA Bul 59:613 Jl '65

Automation

Automation at LC: philosophy, plans, progress. S. S. Snyder. il Library J 90:4709-14 N 1 '65

Law library

Laboratory for the world's laws. W. S. Strauss. il Library J 90:2504-8 Je 1 '65

Legislative reference service

Librarians to the Congress. C. A. Goodrum. il Library J 90:572-7 F 1 '65

Weather: new report sketches anatomy of national program and of coordination problem. J. Walsh. Science 148:610-11 Ap 30 '65

Manuscript division

African game preserve: a scholar's view of LC. L. H. Butterfield. il Library J 90:5333-40 D 15 '65

Quarterly notes. K. V. Hostick. Hobbies 70:111+ O '65

Quarterly notes concerning the Library of Congress; acquisitions. Hobbies 70:111-12 My; 111+ Je '65

Quarterly notes from the Manuscript division, Library of Congress. Hobbies 70:110 Mr '65

Music division

Quiet ferment; LC's role as a patron of the arts. H.-A. Hilker. il Library J 90:2094-103 My 1 '65

Processing department

Windows on the world: LC's processing department. S. L. Wallace. il Library J 90:4005-12 O 1 '65

Reference department

Service to an infinite public. M. W. McFarland. il Library J 90:1053-7 Mr 1 '65

Science policy research division

See United States—Library of Congress—Legislative reference service

Special collections

African game preserve: a scholar's view of LC. L. H. Butterfield. il Library J 90:5333-40 D 15 '65

Answers: fog-laden panorama of LC's collections. D. C. Mearns. il Library J 90:1600-7, 1834-40 Ap 1-15 '65

Continuing quest: care of LC's collections. P. E. Edlund. il Library J 90:3397-402 S 1 '65

Quiet ferment; LC's role as a patron of the arts. H.-A. Hilker. il Library J 90:2094-103 My 1 '65

Union catalog

National register of microform masters to be issued; role of National union catalog. E. Hamer and A. McCormick. ALA Bul 59:791-2 O '65

Publication of the National union catalog of pre-1956 imprints; report. ALA Bul 59:403 My '65; Library J 90:2230 My 15 '65

Literature

See American literature

Manners and customs

See United States—Social life and customs

Maps

Map of the United States (cont) Sr Schol 87:28 S 30 '65

Marine corps

Going back to boot camp, Parris Island, S.C. R. A. Aurthur. il Esquire 64:127-30+ S '65

More boot camp than campus; Marine military academy, Harlingen, Tex. il Life 59:51-2+ O 22 '65

War steps up; where it's headed; with report by H. Handleman. il U S News 58:31-5 My 10 '65

Forces in Latin America

U.S. intervention in Latin America, 1900-1965. il Sr Schol 87:8-9+ S 16 '65

Forces in the Dominican Republic

Marines into the Dominican crossfire. il Life 58:85-6+ My 7 '65

Two governments, face to face. il Time 85:31-2 My 14 '65

U.S. steps into another hornet's nest; sending troops to Santo Domingo. il Bsns W p28-9 My 8 '65

When the marines stormed ashore in Santo Domingo; excerpt from 30 days in May. T. Szulc. il Sat Eve Post 238:36-8+ Jl 31 '65

Forces in Vietnam

As the marines scored in Vietnam. il U S News 59:6 Ag 30 '65

Marine victory and optimism; battle of Van Tuong. W. Tuohy. il Newsweek 66:28-9 Ag 30 '65

Marines and a message; guarding of Da Nang air base. il Newsweek 65:37-8 Mr 22 '65

Marines get flowers for a tough mission. J. Flynn. il Life 58:44-5 Mr 19 '65

Mission is to kill; marine brigade at Da Nang air base. il Newsweek 65:49-50 My 10 '65

Nineteen-year-old marine in Vietnam. C. S. Wren. il Look 29:19-23 Ag 24 '65

One ride with Yankee Papa 13; U.S. Marines' helicopter squadron 163 in Vietnam. L. Burrows. il Life 58:24-34C Ap 16 '65

Prospect of action; U.S. marines the first combat troops to arrive in South Viet Nam. il Time 85:32-3 Mr 19 '65

Maneuvers

Games, but grim; Silver lance exercise by the marines. il Time 85:21A-21B Mr 12 '65

UNITED States—Marine corps—*Continued*

Training

See Military training

Maritime administration

Bailing out the fleet. il Time 86:84+ Jl 16 '65

Can union demands kill the U.S. shipping industry? il U S News 59:61-2 Ag 2 '65

Mexico air agreement

See Aviation—International aspects

Military airlift command

All-jet airlift begins to shape up. il Bsns W p28-9 My 1 '65

USAF channels 75 per cent of airlift to Vietnam. C. Brownlow. Aviation W 84:35-6 Ja 10 '66

Viet war boosts contract airlift demands; MATS Pacific airlift contracts. W. Wright. Aviation W 83:37 S 27 '65

Military cooperation

See Military assistance, American

Military sea transportation service

Lifeline to the war; shippers object to operate. il Newsweek 66:79 D 6 '65

Withered arm. R. Moley. Newsweek 66:84 Ag 23; 84 Ag 30 '65

Moral conditions

Morals of a teen; poll of PTA presidents; with study-discussion program. by C. Smallenberg and H. Smallenberg. R. Squires. bibliog il PTA Mag 59:4-7, 36-7 Ap '65

Speaking out; down with sin! T. Wolfe. Sat Eve Post 238:12+ Je 19 '65

What worries Ike: the breakdown in American morals; statements. D. D. Eisenhower. U S News 59:19 O 25 '65

Who is deprived? address. D. Berrigan. Commonweal 82:53-5 Ap 2 '65

Why slap a helping hand? Life 58:4 Ap 30 '65

See also

Crime and criminals—United States

Narcotics, Bureau of

Dope-smuggling diplomats; ed. by J. C. G. Conniff. H. L. Giordano. il Pop Sci 186:100-3+ Je '65

National academy of medicine (proposed)

Where's the doctor? excerpt from Modern medicine. I. H. Page. Sat R 48:59-60 F 6 '65

National aeronautics and space administration

AES management plan nears completion; Apollo extension system. D. E. Fink. Aviation W 83:16-17 Jl 19 '65

AES program definition to begin. Miss & Roc 16:17 Je 7 '65

Arms race shifts to space, and reds have a head start. il U S News 58:40-4 Je 21 '65

As U.S. moonport takes shape; John F. Kennedy space center, Merritt Island launch area. il U S News 59:27-30 Ag 30 '65

Fifth annual NASA issue; ed. by H. Taylor. il Miss & Roc 17:35+ N 29 '65

Management structure; charts. Miss & Roc 17:125-8+ N 29 '65

MILA construction delays cramping space agency's launch schedulers; Merritt Island launch area. M. Getler. il Miss & Roc 16:26-7 Mr 15 '65

NASA emphasizes Apollo simplification. E. H. Kolcum. Aviation W 83:55-6 N 15 '65

NASA may aid in French program. W. S. Beller. il Miss & Roc 17:22-3 Jl 5 '65

NASA sees rising need for isotopes. H. Taylor. Miss & Roc 16:12 Ap 26 '65

NASA to decide key AES issues in June; Apollo extension systems. W. J. Normyle. Aviation W 82:16-17 My 24 '65

NASA weather satellite plans. il Aviation W 84:40-2+ Ja 3 '66

NASA's Mercury history irks air force. E. H. Kolcum. Aviation W 83:16-17 O 18 '65

Space agency to have new office; Apollo/Saturn applications office. H. Taylor. Miss & Roc 17:16 Ag 2 '65

Special report on NASA's advanced mission plans. il Aviation W 82:54-7+ Mr 22 '65

This month's feature: Congress considers the U.S. space program. Cong Digest 44:35-64 F '65

Ugly American; proposed interview between American astronauts and Soviet cosmonauts in Athens not held due to poor NASA press relations. W. J. Coughlin. Miss & Roc 17:54 O 4 '65

Uprated Atlas confidence vote likely. H. Taylor. Miss & Roc 16:14 Ap 12 '65

Advanced research and technology, Office of

OART projects; hypersonic, planetary flight pace effort. il Miss & Roc 17:116-18+ N 29 '65

Appropriations and expenditures

Agency pressed to hold spending level. il Miss & Roc 17:40-2 N 29 '65

Apollo applications planners see need for $250 million next year. W. J. Normyle. Aviation W 83:23-4 N 22 '65

Apollo applications RFP due this week. H. Taylor. Miss & Roc 18:14 Ja 17 '66

Apollo exploitation key to space awards. W. J. Normyle. il Aviation W 82:24-7 F 1 '65

Ceiling limited; new budget. Newsweek 65:58 F 8 '65

Committee may restore NASA funds. H. M. David. Miss & Roc 16:13 Ap 5 '65

First Apollo flight hardware funded. il Miss & Roc 16:16 F 15 '65

FY '66 budget programs at a glance. il Miss & Roc 16:12-13 F 1 '65

Fund bite halts Voyager bus work; lander capsule design to continue. D. E. Fink. Aviation W 84:24 Ja 3 '66

Funding to start for Apollo lunar science. W. J. Normyle. Aviation W 82:18-19 My 31 '65

House group sets stage to restore key NASA development projects. D. E. Fink. Aviation W 82:24 Mr 1 '65

House space group approves NASA cuts. Aviation W 82:37 Ap 19 '65

House subcommittees would cut $63.3 million from NASA budget. Aviation W 82:29 Ap 12 '65

House unit chips Apollo research $30 million; deeper cut rejected. Aviation W 82:29 Ap 5 '65

House unit cuts space fund $100 million. Aviation W 82:28-9 My 10 '65

Industry may receive $23.7 billion. il Miss & Roc 16:10-11+ F 1 '65

Lunar mission retains top U.S. priority. W. J. Normyle. il Aviation W 82:105-8+ Mr 15 '65

NASA applications program funds to rise. Aviation W 82:45 F 8 '65

NASA asks fund shift to end programs. D. E. Fink. Aviation W 82:288-9 Mr 15 '65

NASA asks to reshuffle '65 funds. Miss & Roc 16:14 Mr 15 '65

NASA budget ceiling will delay new launch vehicle until 1970s. D. E. Fink. Aviation W 83:17 O 18 '65

NASA budget set for conference. Aviation W 83:25 Jl 19 '65

NASA budget to be squeezed by boost in DOD spending. H. M. David. Miss & Roc 18:15 Ja 3 '66

NASA funding bill advances in House. H. M. David. Miss & Roc 16:16 Mr 22 '65

NASA prepares post-Apollo groundwork. il Aviation W 82:103-4 Mr 15 '65

NASA reorients lunar, planet missions. D. E. Fink. Aviation W 83:20-1 D 27 '65

NASA request pegged at $5.1-5.2 billion. Miss & Roc 18:14 Ja 10 '66

NASA science projects boosted; Voyager design funds included. D. E. Fink. il Aviation W 82:27-9 F 1 '65

NASA space science & applications FY'66 R&D request. Miss & Roc 16:17 F 22 '65

NASA to begin budget defense; prospects good for full request. W. J. Normyle. Aviation W 82:17 F 15 '65

NASA's target: keep date with moon. il Bsns W p28-9 F 6 '65

New push for extra Apollo funding. Miss & Roc 16:21 Je 14 '65

$90-million NASA request cut seen. H. M. David. Miss & Roc 16:15 My 17 '65

Priority funding for Apollo, Mariner. H. Taylor. Miss & Roc 18:13 Ja 3 '66

Senate reduces AES funding by $24 million. Aviation W 82:19 Je 7 '65

Space agency facilities past budget peaks. il Aviation W 82:41+ F 8 '65

Space budget goes to conference. Aviation W 82:37 My 17 '65

Space, Vietnam spur record expenditures; NASA to fight Budget bureau cuts. G. C. Wilson. Aviation W 83:26-7 D 6 '65

UNITED STATES—National aeronautics and space administration—Appropriations and expenditures—*Continued*

Start of funding peaks for Apollo mission lifts NASA procurement 42 per cent in fiscal 1964. W. J. Normyle. il Aviation W 82:70-2 Mr 1 '65

Wider NASA fund distribution urged. H. M. David. il Miss & Roc 16:15 Ap 19 '65

Electronics research center

ERC will issue first major RFP's soon. M. Getler. Miss & Roc 17:21 Ag 23 '65

ERC's future; symposium; with editorial comment. il Miss & Roc 16:24-6+, 94 My 31 '65

Ready to launch a lab. il Bsns W p72+ S 11 '65

Goddard space flight center

Lab to simulate radiation environment; to test spacecraft. W. S. Beller. il Miss & Roc 16:24+ Mr 22 '65

Research in America; Ranger 8 findings. J. Lear. il Sat R 48:46-8 Ap 3 '65

Jet propulsion laboratory

See Jet propulsion laboratory

Manned spacecraft center

Air force details 128 officers to NASA's center in Houston. W. J. Normyle. Aviation W 83:27 Ag 23 '65

And now over to Houston. il Newsweek 65:34-6 Je 14 '65

Conductor in a command post. il Time 86:48-54 Ag 27 '65

Man at the switch with no time to argue. M. Durham. il Life 58:74-6 Je 18 '65

Manned spacecraft center officials praise incentive contribution to Gemini progress. Miss & Roc 18:31 Ja 3 '66

MSC plans first manned chamber tests soon. il Miss & Roc 17:14 N 22 '65

Memo from moonville. H. Sutton. Sat R 48:45 Mr 27 '65

Mercury data aids Apollo checkout gear. G. Alexander. il Aviation W 82:48-9+ Mr 29 '65

Personal business; Houston: new magnet for business. Bsns W p 125-6 O 2 '65

Weight of space is on his shoulders; C. Kraft, jr. il Bsns W p64+ Je 12 '65

What Houston won when NASA came to town. il Bsns W p90-1+ S 11 '65

Where space race is bringing a twenty-five year boom; Houston, Tex. il U S News 59:44-7 S 6 '65

Manned space flight, Office of

MSFC gets Saturn IB/Centaur job. Miss & Roc 16:14 Ap 19 '65

Special report on Apollo applications. il Aviation W 83:64-5+ O 11 '65

Marshall space flight center

Marshall to do AES integration. H. Taylor. Miss & Roc 17:14-15 S 20 '65

Pace of advanced booster study drops. G. Alexander. il Aviation W 82:65+ Ap 19 '65

Rocket age comes to tiny Triana. H. Bims. il Ebony 20:106-8+ Mr '65

Space age comes to Mississippi. il U S News 58:78-80 F 15 '65

Procurement

California aerospace firms again lead nation in space agency dollars. il Miss & Roc 16:21 Je 21 '65

Great Boston power play. W. Hines. Read Digest 88:99-104 Ja '66

Major applications contracting to start. D. E. Fink. Aviation W 83:29 N 8 '65

MSC FY '65 awards total $1.48 billion. Aviation W 83:95 D 6 '65

NASA awards. Aviation W 82:101+ My 17; 72 Je 28 '65

NASA list of FY 1965 top 100 prime contractors. il Miss & Roc 17:20 D 20 '65

NASA list of FY 1964 top 100 prime contractors. il Miss & Roc 16:21 F 15 '65; Same. Aviation W 82:70-1 Mr 1 '65

NASA ponders AES integration team. H. Taylor. Miss & Roc 16:14 Je 21 '65

NASA procurement up 51 per cent in first half of fiscal 1965; North American top contractor; with tables. Aviation W 83:82-3 Jl 12 '65

NASA promises versatile Voyager. H. M. David. Miss & Roc 16:10 Mr 1 '65

NASA will pick two contractors for preliminary OTS design work; optical technology satellite. Aviation W 83:22 Jl 5 '65

New NASA contract policies; excerpts from statement. G. Friedl, jr. Aviation W 82:11 Mr 1 '65

North American continues to lead NASA contractors in fiscal 1965. Aviation W 83:34 D 13 '65

Research mission prompts new thinking on procurement methods. il Miss & Roc 16:29-30 My '65

Top 100 fiscal 1965 NASA contractors listed. il Aviation W 83:66-8 D 27 '65

Total buying jumped 13 per cent in FY '65. Miss & Roc 17:43-4 N 29 '65

Wider NASA fund distribution urged. H. M. David. il Miss & Roc 16:15 Ap 19 '65

National archives

Presidential libraries. A. R. Pastore, jr. il Travel 124:50-1+ O '65

National commission on technology, automation and economic progress

Automation panel splits on report. Bsns W p66 D 25 '65

New formula for meeting automation. U S News 60:8 Ja 3 '66

National council on the arts

Disbursement of funds. F. Getlein. New Republic 154:36+ Ja 15 '66

President Johnson names members of National council on the arts. Library J 90:1276 Mr 15 '65

President outlines housing and arts subsidy programs, names National council on arts. Arch Rec 137:20+ Ap '65

Problem of how to spend $3 million; with account by R. B. Stolley. il Life 59:75-6 N 26 '65

Real conflict. Nation 201:234 O 18 '65

National crime commission

Target; establishment of National crime commission. Newsweek 66:26 S 20 '65

We ask the wrong questions about crime. W. M. McCord. il N Y Times Mag p27+ N 21 '65

National foundation for the arts and humanities

Arts and humanities: new national foundation. Science 150:41 O 1 '65

Can culture explode? notes on subsidizing the arts. S. Kauffmann. Commentary 40:19-28 Ag '65

Congress: birth of NSF recalled as new foundation is established to strengthen arts, humanities. L. J. Carter. Science 150:40-2+ O 1 '65

Historic occasion; address, September 29, 1965. L. B. Johnson. Dance Mag 39:34 N '65

H.R. 334; text of bill. W. S. Moorhead. Sch & Soc 93:214-18 Ap 3 '65

Humanities foundation; proposal for a National humanities foundation. America 112:414 Mr 27 '65

Legislation to create a national foundation for the arts and humanities; new bill H.R. 6051, supersedes H.R. 334. W. S. Moorhead. Sch & Soc 93:256-7 Ap 17 '65

Now being human is an art. F. Morley. il Nations Bsns 53:27-8 S '65

President seeks national foundation on arts. Sr Schol 86:sup 1 Ap 1 '65

President submits $10 million plan for arts and humanities foundation. Library J 90:1682 Ap 1 '65

Proposal for a national foundation for the humanities; adaptation of address, August 31, 1964. B. C. Keeney. Sch & Soc 93:211-14 Ap 3 '65

Thanks, without enthusiasm; intellectual world's regard for Johnson. il Time 86:30 O 8 '65

Washington report. J. Lloyd. Sr Schol 86:sup4 Ap 1 '65

Why we need a national humanities foundation. B. C. Keeney. il Sat R 48:68-70 Mr 20 '65

National guard

Reserves; short of men, weapons, equipment; 33rd infantry of Illinois. il U S News 59:27-9 Ag 2 '65

Tough new role for reserves. U S News 59:63 O 11 '65

See also

United States—Air national guard

National institutes of health

Biomedical science and its administration. P. H. Abelson. Science 148:171 Ap 9 '65

Career awards; no more new ones will be made under NIH program. J. Walsh; discussion. Science 147:1395; 148:1040+; 149:7, 813-14 Mr 19, My 21, Jl 2, Ag 20 '65

UNITED STATES—National institutes of health
—*Continued*

Findings and recommendations of the Wooldridge study. Science 147:1556-7 Mr 26 '65

Health program evaluated. Sci N L 87:299 My 8 '65

Healthy NIH; committee report on use of funds. Newsweek 65:57 Mr 29 '65

Latest word on heart disease, arthritis, leukemia, viruses. il U S News 58:68-9 My 10 '65

NIH study: Wooldridge committee praises past efforts, but urges major organizational revisions. D. S. Greenberg. il Science 147:1556-9 Mr 26 '65; Discussion. 149:6, 133+, 1047-8 Jl 2-9. S 3 '65

Onward the management of science: The Wooldridge report. J. D. Cooper. Science 148:1433-9 Je 11 '65; Discussion. 149:705-7 Ag 13 '65

Woolridge report: study of NIH producing conflicting reactions among congressional figures. D. S. Greenberg. Science 148:351-2 Ap 16 '65

National labor relations board

Call for full investigation of the Labor relations board; excerpts from testimony, September 16, 1965 E. A. Keeney. il U S News 59:106-7 O 11 '65

Collective bargaining; address, April 14, 1965. V. B. Day. Vital Speeches 31:437-41 My 1 '65

Influence of the New deal. J. S. Auerbach. bibliog f Cur Hist 48:334-9+ Je '65

Let's stop Labor board's unfair practices. S. Rothman. il Nations Bsns 53:34-5+ My '65

Liberal NLRB faces tougher road; Supreme court upsets three rulings. Bsns W p78+ Ap 3 '65

Limits on labor & management. il Time 85:66-7 Ap 9 '65

National labor relations board. P. Ross. Cur Hist 49:77-84+ Ag '65

National labor relations board in fiscal year 1964; excerpt from annual report. il Mo Labor R 88:960-4 Ag '65

New policy for the NLRB? T. R. Brooks. Duns R 86:49-50+ Jl '65

New rules for employers from the Supreme court; Deering, Milliken and company and other cases. il U S News 58:101-4 Ap 12 '65

Significant decisions in labor cases. See issues of Monthly labor review

Union representation election. J. E. Drotning. bibliog f il Mo Labor R 88:938-43 Ag '65

Who runs the Labor board: complaints of employers. il Nations Bsns 53:31-3+ S '65

Why court ruled against NLRB. U S News 58:81 Mr 29 '65

Will organizing be made easier? NLRB reviewing rules governing drives for representation. Bsns W p 111 My 29 '65

National library of medicine

Computerized bibliographic services for biomedicine. L. Karel and others. bibliog il Science 148:766-72 My 7 '65

NLM publications to be buried in World's fair time capsule. Library J 90:1270 Mr 15 '65

Nursing index, Dental abstract journal; NLM cooperates on new publications. Library J 90:3416 S 1 '65

National park service

Basic guide for national park visits. il Good H 161:147 Jl '65

Job corps=human+natural conservation; Catoctin job corps conservation center, Md. D. B. Huyck. il Am For 71:22-5 Jl '65

Life as a fire lookout in Crater Lake National Park. L. Neuberger and R. Neuberger. il Nat Parks Mag 39:16-19 Ag '65

Summary of the preliminary report of the National park service on its special study of the California Coast redwoods. il Nat Parks Mag 39:10-11 F '65

National parks and reserves

See National parks and reserves—United States

National recovery administration

Influence of the New deal. J. S. Auerbach. bibliog f Cur Hist 48:334-9+ Je '65

National science foundation

Adequate rate of growth. D. Wolfle. Science 147:1399 Mr 19 '65

Annual report of National science foundation sent to Congress; message, February 15, 1965. L. B. Johnson. Dept State Bul 52:434-6 Mr 22 '65

Curriculum reform: success hasn't spoiled NSF program, but biology study's status reflects problems; Biological sciences curriculum study. J. Walsh. Science 149:280-2 Jl 16 '65

Daddario study says NSF should be in forefront of policymaking. D. S. Greenberg. Science 151:177-9 Ja 14 '66

Institutional grants of the National science foundation. E. J. Merton. il Science 148:1693-6 Je 25 '65

Life at Antarctic U. T. O. Jones. il Am Ed 1:29-32 N '65

Mohole: drilling site in Pacific favored as time nears to award construction contract for vessel. D. S. Greenberg. Science 147:487 Ja 29 '65

Money for research: Congress and scientists have different ideas on how the system should operate. D. S. Greenberg. Science 149:278-80 Jl 16 '65

NSF budget: cuts by House group leave little leeway for growth in support of research projects. D. S. Greenberg. Science 148:928-30 My 14 '65

NSF: 14th annual report reveals efforts to devise new techniques in science-government relations. D. S. Greenberg. Science 147:1014-16 F 26 '65

NSF: friendly reorganization plan and hearings impending in House indicate how the agency has grown. J. Walsh. il Science 148:1444-6 Je 11 '65

New directions for the National science foundation. D. Wolfle. Science 148:1673 Je 25 '65

Propose powerful role for NSF. C. A. Betts. Sci N L 87:275 My 1 '65

Public understanding of science. E. G. Sherburne, jr. Science 149:381 Jl 23 '65; Discussion. 150:7, 289, 1103-4 O 1, 15, N 26 '65

See also
Ernest Orlando Lawrence memorial awards

National security agency

Eavesdropper. Newsweek 65:21 My 31 '65

National security council

Big three: executive committee of the National security council. il Time 85:29-30 Ap 30 '65

National seed storage laboratory

National seed storage laboratory, Fort Collins, Colorado. R. C. Hands. il Horticulture 43:34-5 D '65

National service corps

See Volunteers in service to America

Nationalism

Search for a usable past. H. S. Commager. il Am Heritage 16:4-9+ F '65

Naval observatory

Observatory is the U.S. navy's oldest official scientific agency. T. D. Nicholson. il Natur Hist 74:42-5 Je '65

Naval ordnance laboratory

See United States—Navy department—Weapons, Bureau of

Naval propellant plant

Navy propellant monitoring technique employs gauges embedded in grains. J. F. Judge. il Miss & Roc 16:22-3 Ap 19 '65

Navy

Four-ocean navy in the nuclear age. T. W. McKnew. il Nat Geog Mag 127:145-87 F '65

Long guns flash on the South China Sea; Seventh fleet in action; with report by B. Wise. il Life 59:16-23 Ag 6 '65

Navy improves accuracy, detection range of space surveillance chain. P. J. Klass. il Aviation W 83:56-7+ Ag 16 '65

Navy plans center around ASW, tactical aircraft. il Aviation W 82:76-7+ Mr 15 '65

Soviet sea power: how it's growing. il U S News 59:9 D 27 '65

United States navy, watchdog of peace; address, January 23, 1965. D. Rusk. Dept State Bul 52:165-7 F 8 '65

Up comes the navy. R. D. Senter. New Repub 152:12-13 F 27 '65
See also
Landing craft
Navy yards and naval stations
Warships—United States

Boats

Knox on the rocks; U.S.S. Frank Knox aground on reef in China Sea. il Newsweek 66:36 N 8 '65

UNITED STATES—Navy—*Continued*

Education

Battle simulator aids navy planning; Naval submarine school, New London, Conn. il Miss & Roc 16:41-2+ Je 7 '65
    See also
United States naval academy, Annapolis

Officers

Admiral goes home. Newsweek 66:36 N 8 '65

Procurement

Navy/LTV A-7A vendors listed. Aviation W 83:87 N 15 '65

Recreation

Recreation afloat; USS Kitty Hawk. R. C. Hallberg. il Recreation 58:439-42 N '65

Navy department
Ships, Bureau of

Navy seeking improved ASW integration. M. L. Yaffee. Aviation W 82:81+ Ap 12 '65

Weapons, Bureau of

ASW missile test site readied. M. Getler. il Miss & Roc 17:18 N 8 '65
NOL develops nerve-like diode. W. S. Beller. il Miss & Roc 16:14-15 F 8 '65
NOL tunnel advances arc heater art. W. S. Beller. il Miss & Roc 17:27 O 4 '65
New power supplies show high reliability. il Aviation W 83:119+ N 15 '65

Neighborhood youth corps
    See United States—Job corps

Office of education
    See United States—Education. Office of

Officials and employees
    See Government employees

Patent office

Patent law comes under fire. il Bsns W p 132+ S 18 '65

Peace corps

Are they asking too much? Peace corps veterans. F. G. Jennings. Sat R 48:65-6 My 15 '65
Are we turning away from talent? excerpt from address. F. Keppel. Sat R 48:66 My 15 '65
Behind the scenes; Bob Satin in the Dominican Republic. J. F. Fixx. Sat R 48:32 Je 12 '65; Reply. B. Satin. 48:18 Jl 3 '65
Culture shock; adjusting to life back home. il Newsweek 65:30+ Mr 15 '65
John F. Kennedy school no. 1; El Esfuerzo jungle community. J. P. Blank. il Read Digest 86:54-8 Mr '65
Letter from Washington; conference to celebrate four years of survival. R. H. Rovere. New Yorker 41:184-6 Mr 20 '65
Notes of a peace corps reject. J. McDonough. il Esquire 65:90+ Ja '66
Other America. Nation 200:546 My 24 '65
Peace corps forestry: there's a forest in your future! F. Friedman. il Am For 71:20-1+ F '65
Peace corps in art: a report. F. Friedman. il Am Artist 29:80+ Je '65
Peace corps in perspective. N. Barron; discussion. Library J 90:200-1, 988 Ja 15, Mr 1 '65
Peace corps test hit. E. Lederer. Sci N L 87:404 Je 26 '65
Peace corps volunteers fool psychiatrists. Sci N L 88:183 S 18 '65
Peace corps volunteers return; what are they doing now? R. Hartley. il Seventeen 24:20+ My '65
Peace corpsman returns to darkest America. J. Horwitz. il N Y Times Mag p74+ O 24 '65
Pilgrims of peace. il Sr Schol 86:16-17 Mr 11 '65
President Johnson establishes new personnel system for Peace corps; White House announcement, October 11, 1965, with text of executive order. L. B. Johnson. Dept State Bul 53:765 N 8 '65
President Johnson recommends expansion of Peace corps; letter, February 25, 1965. L. B. Johnson. Dept State Bul 52:433-4 Mr 22 '65
Promises of home; experiences of Peace corps teachers. W. W. Wiggins. il Am Ed 1:21-5 Ap '65
Rattling good history; three-day conference of Peace corps returnees. H. Bowser. Sat R 48:26 Ap 3 '65

Recruiting the activists. il Newsweek 66:66 N 8 '65
Re-entry crisis; return of Peace corps volunteers to U.S. R. B. Stolley. il Life 58:98-100+ Mr 19 '65
Speaking out; the Peace corps isn't doing its job. A. Zeitlin and M. Zeitlin. Sat Eve Post 239:7-8 Ja 1 '66
Statement on returning Peace corps teachers. Vice President Humphrey to head Peace corps advisory council; letter, January 26, 1965. L. B. Johnson. Dept State Bul 52:250 Sch & Soc 93:304 Sum '65 F 22 '65
Wanted: skilled hands for the Peace corps. H. Shuldiner. il Pop Sci 186:72-5+ Je '65
Why I'm staying in teaching. L. Bergthold. NEA J 54:20+ O '65
Young publisher with problems; Brooklyn Peace corps volunteer puts out Spanish newspaper in slum of Lima, Peru. il Ebony 21:101-2+ N '65

Pictorial history
    See United States—History, Pictorial

Politics and government

Affairs of state. S. Alsop. See issues of Saturday evening post
America, 1965: hidden meaning of consensus. H. Fairlie. New Repub 154:15-20 Ja 1 '66
America will be different because of you; address, May 6, 1965. A. N. Booth. Vital Speeches 31:537-9 Je 15 '65
American directions: a forecast. P. F. Drucker. Harper 230:39-45 F '65; Reply. E. A. Menuez. 230:6 My '65
Are Americans more comfortable with Lyndon Johnson? Q. de Manila. Nat R 17:552-4+ Je 29 '65
As LBJ starts his third year, new problems, bigger plans. il U S News 59:58-60 D 6 '65
At the center of our concerns: State of the Union message. L. B. Johnson. Bsns W p25-6 Ja 15 '66
Atlantic report. See issues of Atlantic
Change in the scenery; looking forward to the President's State of the Union address. Time 87:21 Ja 14 '66
Choice for Americans; address, January 9, 1965. S. Thurmond. Vital Speeches 31:259-62 F 15 '65
Conviction or convenience; the trap of the Great society. R. F. Hamilton. il Nation 201:384-7 N 22 '65
Crrrack! criticism of Johnson administration by ADA. Nat R 17:1061-2 N 30 '65
Cult of relativism; harder right or the easier wrong; address, September 25, 1965. S. Thurmond. Vital Speeches 32:46-8 N 1 '65
Federalism's twilight. R. Moley. Newsweek 65:104 Ap 26 '65
Focus on Washington. Cato. Nat R 17:91, 139, 179, 225, 267, 311, 357, 405, 449, 493, 535, 580, 625 F 9-Jl 27 '65
Forecast: change; summaries of inaugural address and message to Congress. L. B. Johnson. il Sr Schol 86:18-19 F 4 '65
Group that runs the House; Democratic study group. P. Duke and A. B. Sawsilak. il Reporter 32:29-31 My 20 '65
Growing ordeal of LBJ. il U S News 58:29-30 Mr 15 '65
Handcuffs on foreign policy. Nation 201:109-10 S 6 '65
Hard limits of government by consensus. L. W. Koenig. il N Y Times Mag p26-7+ Mr 7 '65
Harvest time: reforms planted by minority groups. K. Crawford. Newsweek 65:33 F 15 '65
Historic picture of the New frontier, and this is what they have to say; symposium, ed. by S. V. Roberts. il Esquire 64:88-95+ N '65
Inaugural address; January 20, 1965. L. B. Johnson. Dept State Bul 52:162-4 F 8 '65
Johnson era starts: What's ahead now under LBJ? il U S News 58:29-34 F 1 '65
Johnson so far; symposium. Commentary 39: 37-55 Je '65
Leading from strength: LBJ in action. D. Brinkley. Atlan 215:49-54 F '65
Letter from Washington. R. H. Rovere. See issues of New Yorker
Lindsay miracle. C. McWilliams. Nation 201: 348-50 N 15 '65
LBJ keynote: a prosperous, great and mighty nation: inaugural address, January 20, 1965. L. B. Johnson. il U S News 58:102-3 F 1 '65; Same. Vital Speeches 31:258-9 F 15 '65
LBJ phenomenon: a whirlwind pace. il Bsns W p26-8 Je 5 '65
LBJ: political gamester. Nat R 18:67-9 Ja 25 '66

UNITED STATES—Politics and government
—*Continued*

LBJ's troubles begin to mount. il U S News 58:8 Je 21 '65

Lyndon Johnson vs the ghost of Jack Kennedy. T. Wicker. Esquire 64:87+ N '65

Machiavelli of the New deal. J. Featherstone. New Repub 153:22-6 Ag 7 '65; Reply. J. F. Bowen. 153:36 S 4 '65

National affairs. See issues of Newsweek

Need for politics. Commonweal 83:327-8 D 17 '65

New political non-job. D. Oberdorfer. il Harper 231:108+ O '65

1965: age of the shrug; or, age of decision; address, November 9, 1965. R. M. Besse. Vital Speeches 32:154-8 D 15 '65

Open letter from a military intellectual to a sophisticated liberal leader. R. A. Levine; discussion. Bul Atomic Sci 21:31 Ja; 31-3 Mr; 28-9 O '65

Paranoid style in American politics, by R. Hofstadter. Review
New Repub 153:43-5 N 27 '65. L. Grauman, jr

Presidential system; summary of television interview. L. F. O'Brien. Nat R 17:627-8 Jl 27 '65

Shadow presidency. J. M. Burns. il Nation 201:115-18 S 6 '65; Reply. B. M. Goldwater. 201:inside cover O 4 '65

Shaping of intergovernmental relations in the twentieth century. D. J. Elazer. bibliog f il Ann Am Acad 359:10-22 My '65

State of affairs (cont) H. Brandon. Sat R 48:14+ F 27; 16 Mr 13; 16-17 My 8; 16+ My 22 '65

State of the Union, and the war; President prepares message. il Newsweek 67:15-16 Ja 17 '66

T.R.B. from Washington. See issues of New republic

Trends: Washington mood. P. Lisagor. See issues of Nation's business

Union & the war; concerning State of the Union address. il Time 87:19-19B Ja 21 '66

Washington front. See issues of America

Washington outlook. See issues of Business week

Washington wire; cold eye on Johnson. R. G. Sherrill. Nation 202:4-7 Ja 3 '66

What's new in Washington. See issues of Successful farming

Why White House troubles mount. U S News 58:31-3 Je 28 '65

See also
Conservatism
Democratic party
Elections—United States
Federal and state relations
Legislation—United States
Lobbying
Local government—United States
Political campaigns
Political parties—United States
Presidents—United States
Republican party
Socialism—United States
Trade unions—Political activities
United States—Constitution
United States—Executive departments
United States—National recovery administration

Vice-presidents—United States
also subheads Politics; Politics and government under names of sections, states, cities, e.g. South—Politics

Bibliography

Book reviews: politics: at home and abroad. R. Steel. Sr Schol 86:sup 13 Ap 1 '65

Books in the field: political science. N. W. Polsby. il Wilson Lib Bul 40:432-9 Ja '66

Popular culture

Assimilation & the sociologists. M. Sklare. Commentary 39:63-7 My '65

Comic prison. A. Goldman. Nation 200:142-4 F 8 '65

Crisis in American culture: addresses. D. Macdonald; W. M. Young; M. Kempton. il Wilson Lib Bul 39:739-47 My '65

Cultural explosion and musical myths. J. H. Mueller. bibliog il Library J 90:1243-7 Mr 15 '65

Fear of positive thinking. L. A. Coser. Nation 201:166-70 S 20 '65

Ins and outs of pop culture: how to play the game. G. Steinem. il Life 59:72-3+ Ag 20 '65

Kandy-kolored tangerine-flake streamline baby, by T. Wolfe. Review
Nat R 17:989-90 N 2 '65. C. H. Simonds

Lingering tastemasters. H. Kenner. Nat R 17:1098+ N 30 '65

Machine in the garden: technology and the pastoral ideal in America, by L. Marx. Review
Commentary 39:73-4+ My '65. N. Compton

Staggered culture. L. Kronenberger. Nation 201:67-71 S 20 '65

Two worlds of American art: the private and the popular, by B. Ulanov. Review
America 113:545 N 6 '65. C. J. McNaspy
Sat R il 48:37-8 S 11 '65. A. Darack

Anecdotes, facetiae, satire, etc.

NCMSB report; culture explosion. R. Angell. il New Yorker 41:47-8+ F 20 '65

Population

Another baby boom? il Sci Digest 58:38 O '65

Intelligent woman's guide to the population explosion. G. Cant. McCalls 92:32+ F '65; Same abr. with title What the population explosion really means. Read Digest 86:103-6 My '65

Is quality of U.S. population declining? interview. W. Shockley. il U S News 59:68-71 N 22 '65

Meaning of the changes in U.S. population. il U S News 60:48-9 Ja 10 '66

Our population: the statistics explosion. B. J. Wattenberg and R. M. Scammon. il Reporter 32:40-1 Mr 25 '65; Discussion. 32:4-5 Ap 22 '65

Population only slightly affected by longevity. Sci N L 88:280 O 30 '65

Saturation: a problem evaded in planning land use; environmental consequences of sustained population growth. G. Macinko. bibliog il Science 149:516-21 Jl 30 '65

300,000,000 Americans would be wrong. D. E. Lilienthal. il N Y Times Mag p24-5+ Ja 9 '66

Will markets develop as hoped? population explosion taking new twists. il Bsns W p32-4 My 15 '65

See also
Birth rate—United States
Cities and towns—United States
Migration, Internal
United States—Census

Post office department

Can he really put zip in the mails? Postmaster General Gronouski. il Bsns W p83-4+ Je 19 '65

Farley mold. Newsweek 66:21 S 13 '65

Mail snooping. New Repub 153:6-7 Ag 21 '65

Now O'Brien delivers the mail; Postmaster General of the United States. P. Anderson. il N Y Times Mag p54-5+ N 14 '65

What's the matter with the mails? M. Greenfield. il Reporter 32:21-5 F 11 '65; Discussion. 32:6+ Mr 11 '65

See also
Mail handling
Postal censorship
Postal employees
Postal service—United States

President's commission on heart disease, cancer and stroke

Aim to conquer killers; network of regional medical complexes for heart disease, cancer and stroke. Sci N L 87:151 Mr 6 '65

Doctor's first job: preventing sickness. J. Mayer. il N Y Times Mag p48-9+ N 28 '65

Heart, cancer, and stroke: bill based on presidential commission calls for regional medical centers. E. Langer. Science 148:930-3 My 14 '65; Reply. C. B. Chapman. 149:246 Jl 16 '65

President's commission on law enforcement and administration of justice

War on evil. Reporter 33:18 S 23 '65

President's commission on national goals

Taking the national pulse. H. M. Wriston. Sat R 48:25-9 S 11 '65

President's commission to investigate the assassination of President Kennedy

Critique of the Warren report. D. Macdonald. Esquire 63:59-63+ Mr '65

Death of a president: the established facts. Devlin. Atlan 215:112-18 Mr '65

Lee Oswald's guilt, how science nailed Kennedy's killer; Warren commission. L. Snyder. il Pop Sci 186:68-73 Ap '65

Unanswered questions about President Kennedy's assassination, by S. Fox. Review
Nat R 18:34-7 Ja 11 '66. M. S. Evans

UNITED STATES—*Continued*

President's committee on equal employment opportunity
See United States—President's equal employment opportunity commission

President's equal employment opportunity commission
Coming soon: new rules for hiring, firing, promoting; Equal employment opportunity commission. U S News 58:84+ My 24 '65

Job-rights unit asks new power. U S News 59:63 Ag 2 '65

New paper work for employers; women's job rights. U S News 59:93 D 6 '65

Now: new rights for workers, new rules for employers; questions and answers. il U S News 58:69-70 Je 28 '65

Official word on job rights for women. U S News 59:90-1 N 22 '65

Placing a want ad? there are federal rules to follow now. U S News 59:100-1 O 4 '65

Putting teeth in the hiring rules. Bsns W p32-3 My 29 '65

Two months of job-rights law: who complains about what. U S News 59:75-6 S 6 '65

Unfinished business of Negro jobs; Title VII of Civil rights act. il Bsns W p82-4+ Je 12 '65

Where civil rights law is going wrong. Nations Bsns 53:60-2+ N '65

Why the delay? New Repub 152:7 Ap 24 '65

President's science advisory committee
Advisory set: newappointments reduce Harvard-MIT presence on President's science committee. D. S. Greenberg. Science 148:352 Ap 16 '65

Pollution: PSAC panel takes a panoramic view. J. Walsh. Science 150:1006-8 N 19 '65

Science in the State department: a practical imperative; adaptation of address. J. R. Killian, jr. il Bul Atomic Sci 21:12-17 My '65

Public buildings
See Public buildings

Public buildings service
New federal architecture. il Arch Rec 137:135-46 Mr '65

Public health service
Test case on pollution: big clean-up begins; Lake Erie. il Bsns W p25-6 Ag 14 '65

They stopped a tropical epidemic. J. Winchester. il Todays Health 43:32-3+ D '65

Washington dateline. Am City 80:7 F '65
See also
United States—National institutes of health

Public land law review commission (proposed)
Goddard named by President Johnson. Am For 71:16 F '65

Off to a good start! Am For 71:11 Ag '65

Public land review. M. Clawson. il Am For 71:10-13+ Mr; 34-9+ Ap; 50-3+ My; 12-15+ Ag '65; Discussion. 71:9 Mr; 2-3 Je '65

Public roads, Bureau of
More for the roads; cost allocation report on interstate highway system. il Bsns W p81+ Mr 27 '65

Race problems
Negroes & Jews; the new challenge to pluralism. N. Glazer; discussion. Commentary 39:8 My; 6+ Je '65

Peoples of America. N. Glazer. il Nation 201:137-41 S 20 '65
See also
Church and race problems
Japanese Americans
Negroes in the United States

Relations (diplomatic)
Catholic church
See Catholic church—Relations (diplomatic)—United States

Religious institutions and affairs
Battle of the Bible: new Reformation. T. G. Harris. il Look 29:17-20 Jl 27 '65

Beyond Bonhoeffer? future of religionless Christianity. H. Cox. Commonweal 82:653-7 S 17 '65

Highlights from denominational meetings. Christian Cent 82:996-8 Ag 11 '65
See also
Baptists in the United States
Catholic church in the United States
Catholics in the United States
Methodist church in the United States
Presbyterian church in the United States
Presbyterian church in the United States (South)
Protestant churches—United States
Protestant Episcopal church
Protestants in the United States

Renegotiation board
Excess profit claims settled by four firms. Aviation W 83:20 Jl 5 '65

Reserve forces
See United States—Armed forces—Reserves

Revenue
See also
Taxation—United States

Riots
Beyond the Los Angeles riots. M. L. King; M. L. Schwartz. Sat R 48:33-7+ N 13 '65

Holiday riots: tougher penalties the answer? il U S News 59:10 Jl 19 '65

New racial violence in North and South. U S News 58:12 Mr 1 '65

Northern race violence: the season opens. il U S News 58:6 Mr 29 '65

Police neutral in riots. Sci N L 88:135 Ag 28 '65

Police under pressure. D. Clark. Cath World 202:228-32 Ja '66

Shift in the wind in Washington; violent defiance of law and order gone too far. il U S News 59:27-8 S 6 '65

That riotous feeling. Time 86:78-9 Jl 16 '65

Why Negroes riot; excerpt from The making of the President, 1964. T. H. White. Read Digest 87:67-73 N '65

Rural electrification administration
Profits from subsidies. R. Moley. Newsweek 66:112 S 27 '65

School laws and legislation
See School laws and legislation—United States

Science and technology, Office of
Congress and scientific advice. G. E. Lowe. Bul Atomic Sci 21:39-42 D '65

Secretaries of the army
See Secretaries of the army (United States)

Securities and exchange commission
Analysts run into a security blackout. il Bsns W p 142+ My 8 '65

Better reports for investors? U S News 59:84 D 20 '65

Inside the insider issue; Texas Gulf sulphur case. il Fortune 72:69-70+ Jl '65

New moves by government to protect investors. il U S News 58:96+ My 10 '65

On the inside track; SEC charges Texas Gulf with violation of Securities exchange act. il Time 85:96+ Ap 30 '65

SEC draws a bead on top men. Bsns W p 151 N 20 '65

SEC prods accountants; ruling how installment sales shall be carried on balance sheets. Bsns W p 102 Ja 15 '66

SEC vs. Texas Gulf raises sticky questions; bonanza trouble; charges and issues at stake. C. Welles. il Life 59:29-30+ Ag 6 '65; Reply. C. O. Stephens. 59:19 Ag 13 '65

Should companies promote their own stocks? SEC investigates Genesco. C. J. Loomis. il Fortune 72:184-6+ D '65

Telling their secrets; unlisted companies comply with SEC disclosure requirements. Bsns W p 170+ O 16 '65

Texas Gulf suit opens new door for SEC. il Bsns W p24-5 Ap 24 '65

Wall Street: a sulphurous scandal; SEC investigation of Texas Gulf sulphur company. il Newsweek 65:69-70 My 3 '65

Senate
See United States—Congress—Senate

Small business administration
Future for small business; report on study by Robert R. Nathan associates, inc. il Bsns W p35-6+ Jl 31 '65

Small business in search of loans. D. Sanford. New Repub 154:13-14 Ja 1 '66

UNITED STATES—Small business administration—*Continued*

Thanks for nothing; J. Jones of Atlanta, hopes crushed by Interstate commerce commission's Trucking authority board. il Newsweek 66:82 D 6 '65

Social conditions

Civil rights. B. Rustin and T. Kahn. Commentary 39:43-6 Je '65

Crisis in American culture; address. M. Kempton. Wilson Lib Bul 39:746-7 My '65

People or personnel, by P. Goodman. Review Atlan 216:88-91 Ag '65. M. Harrington New Yorker 41:124-7 Ag 21 '65. N. Bliven

Postscript: a moderately Great society. K. E. Boulding. New Repub 153:15-16 D 18 '65

Proud tower, by B. Tuchman. Review Newsweek il 67:86+ Ja 17 '66

Reformers in the ghetto. R. Sanders. Commentary 40:78-80+ N '65

Sin, morality and poverty; social upheavals afflicting American society. W. Stringfellow. Christian Cent 82:703-6 Je 2 '65

Social trends and recreation planning; address, 1964. G. W. Carter. il Recreation 58:378-80 O '65

This U.S.A. by B. J. Wattenberg and R. M. Scammon. Review
 Sr Schol il 87:8-11+ D 9 '65

Thoughts of the young radicals; series of personal statements. New Repub 153:13-15 D 18; 19-21 D 25 '65; 154:20-2 Ja 8; 16-18 Ja 15; 9-10 Ja 22 '66

What motivates American whites? K. B. Clark. il Ebony 20:69-74 Ag '65

See also
Child labor—United States
Child welfare—United States
Cities and towns—United States
Cost of living—United States
Crime and criminals—United States
Divorce—United States
Housing—United States
Immigration and emigration—United States
Labor and laboring classes—United States
Poor—United States
United States—Population
Women—United States
Youth—United States
 also subhead Social conditions under names of sections, states, cities, e.g. New York (city)—Social conditions

Bibliography

Home scene. D. R. Campion. America 112:684-7+ My 8 '65

Home scene. W. L. Lucey. America 113:680-2 N 27 '65

Social history

Hometown USA; excerpt from The situation in Flushing. E. G. Love. il Sat Eve Post 238:32-6+ S 11 '65

If Lincoln lived today; profile in poverty. il U S News 58:74-6 F 15 '64

Proud tower, by B. W. Tuchman. Review Sat R il 49:33 Ja 15 '66. J. H. Plumb

See also
Slavery—United States

Social life and customs

Bringing up children; the American vs. the British way. E. Wintour; discussion. Harper 229:11-12 O '64; 230:13-14 My '65

Green leaves of summer; excerpts from Happy valley. P. D. Taft. il Am Heritage 16:56-63 O '65

Next dance will be what is Meyer Davis doing while Oedipus and the mothers drop trousers? G. Frazier. Esquire 65:60-1+ Ja '66

Piano in the parlor; excerpts from Polite Americans. G. Carson. il Am Heritage 17:54-9+ D '65

Twenties; symposium. il Am Heritage 16:2-112 Ag '65

Social policy

America's commitment to social justice and progress for all; excerpt from address, June 1, 1965. L. B. Johnson. Dept State Bul 52:1005-6 Je 21 '65

Creative federalism and the Great society; more to L.B.J.'s domestic policies than meets the eye. M. Ways. il Fortune 73:120-3+ Ja '66

Family policy for the Nations; with editorial comment. D. P. Moynihan. il America 113:277, 280-3 S 18 '65

Great society. S. Booker. il Ebony 20:148-50+ Ag '65

Great society. R. Lekachman. Commentary 39:37-42 Je '65

Is America ready for a Great society? interview. R. E. Fitch. il U S News 58:50-4 Mr 8 '65; Same abr. with title America's potential for greatness. Read Digest 86:62-6 Je '65

Kept society. R. Moley. Newsweek 65:92 F 8 '65

Legacy of James Smithson; address, September 16, 1965. L. B. Johnson. Dept State Bul 53:550-2 O 4 '65; Same with title President Johnson on international education. Sch & Soc 93:481+ D 11 '65

LBJ's decision: guns and butter; concerning State-of-the Union message. il U S News 60:27-8 Ja 24 '66

LBJ's Great society, what will it be? Read Digest 86:136-9 F '65

LBJ's revolution: the big changes; New deal, Great society. il U S News 59:46-9 O 11 '65

Mr Goodwin's Great society. W. F. Buckley, jr. Nat R 17:760 S 7 '65

Pause would be refreshing; planners, eager for new proposals. P. Lisagor. Nations Bsns 53:23-4 S '65

Revolutionizing the U.S, the changes Congress is making. il U S News 59:29-32 Jl 26 '65

Slogans and the Great society. R. J. Roth. America 112:184 F 6 '65

State of LBJ; concerning State of the Union address. K. Crawford. Newsweek 67:35 Ja 24 '66

State of the Union; address to the Congress, January 4, 1965. L. B. Johnson. Dept State Bul 52:94-100 Ja 25 '65; Excerpts. Cur Hist 48:176-8+ Mr '65

Surviving the age of the city. R. Lazarus. Sat R 49:44 Ja 8 '66

To build, to help, and to fight; concerning President's State of the Union message. il Newsweek 67:21-3 Ja 24 '66

Unity, the legacy of American democracy; address, February 3, 1965. L. B. Johnson. Dept State Bul 52:242-4 F 22 '65

War, taxes, labor, rights; LBJ's plans for 1966; State of the Union message, January 12, 1966. L. B. Johnson. U S News 60:62-6+ Ja 24 '66

What the Great society is going to cost. il U S News 59:50-2 O 18 '65

Where consensus breaks down; Great society. H. J. Morgenthau. New Repub 154:16-18 Ja 22 '66

Where do we go from here? S. Alsop. il Sat Eve Post 238:14 S 25 '65

Social security administration

Social security: a growing giant; Congress to boost benefits and taxes. il Bsns W p76-7+ F 6 '65

Soil conservation service

$20 million footnote. M. S. Monk, jr. il Am For 71:24-7 Ap '65; Discussion. 71:11 Ap; 2 Jl '65

Solicitor General

See United States—Justice, Department of

State, Department of

Aggression from the North; the record of North Viet-Nam's campaign to conquer South Viet-Nam; report, February 27, 1965. il Dept State Bul 52:404-27 Mr 22 '65

Decision in Viet Nam; how Johnson makes foreign policy. H. F. Graff. il N Y Times Mag p4-7+ Jl 4 '65

Decline of State: Firm denial. Nation 201:129-30 S 13 '65

Department to hold conference for editors and broadcasters. Dept State Bul 52:550 Ap 12 '65

Diplomatic logjam; esprit without a corps. N. McKitterick. New Repub 152:8-11 Mr 27 '65

Education and world affairs: a search for new techniques. J. E. Horner. Dept State Bul 53:1017-20 D 27 '65

Foreign policy conference to be held at Dallas. Dept State Bul 52:253 F 22 '65

Foreign policy conference to be held at Flint, Michigan. Dept State Bul 53:453 S 13 '65

Foreign policy conference to be held at Pittsburgh. Dept State Bul 52:905 Je 7 '65

Foreign policy conference to be held at Portland. Dept State Bul 52:757 My 17 '65

How the State department baffled him; excerpts from Thousand days. A. M. Schlesinger, jr. il Life 59:18-27 Jl 30 '65

National review board appointed for East-West center. Dept State Bul 52:383-4 Mr 15 '65

Not so ugly Americans. E. J. Hughes. Newsweek 66:15 Ag 9 '65

UNITED STATES—Supreme court—Decisions
—*Continued*
Mobs vs. the law: what High court says;
Cox case. U S News 58:16 F 1 '65
Multiemployer bargaining and the balancing
of power. Mo Labor R 88:III-IV Ap '65
Negro in the Supreme court, 1940. R. L. Gill.
Negro Hist Bul 28:194+ My '65
Negro in the Supreme court, 1954-64; address,
1964 (cont) R. L. Gill. bibliog Negro Hist
Bul 28:86-8, 117-19 Ja-F '65
New rules for employers from the Supreme
court; Deering, Milliken and company and
other cases. il U S News 58:101-4 Ap 12
'65
Now comes the Sixth amendment; case of
Pointer v. Texas. Time 85:46 Ap 16 '65
Now, legal family planning; Connecticut birth
control law unconstitutional. H. G. Lewis.
Christian Cent 82:970+ Ag 4 '65
Population control takes a forward step;
ruling against Connecticut's anti-birth
control statutes. Bsns W p 108+ Je 19 '65
Profiles without couarge. D. Lawrence. U S
News 58:128 Ap 26 '65
Reapportionment: shall the Court or the
people decide? H. Harvey and K. O. Gil-
more. Read Digest 86:111-16 Mr '65
Recent U.S. Supreme court decision on anti-
trust law and labor unions; opinion and
dissent. B. R. White; A. J. Goldberg; W. O.
Douglas. Cong Digest 44:216-23 Ag '65
Reds' registration overruled. Sr Schol 87:14
D 2 '65
Retroactivity riddle. Time 85:44+ Je 18 '65
Revolution in criminal justice; Time essay.
Time 86:22-3 Jl 16 '65
Senator Dirksen vs. the Court; proposed
amendment to nullify one man, one vote
reapportionment ruling. R. M. Christenson.
Nation 201:60-1 Ag 2 '65
Significant decisions in labor cases. See is-
sues of Monthly labor review
Still waiting on confessions. il Time 85:61 Je
11 '65
Strike vs. lockout. Newsweek 65:82 Ap 12
'65
Supreme court: guardian or dictator of the
Nation's laws? with key arguments from
key decisions. il Sr Schol 86:6-11 Mr 4 '65
Supreme court quashes Texas book seizure.
Pub W 187:57 F 1 '65
Supreme court reverses birth control law;
Connecticut birth control laws banned.
Christian Cent 82:796 Je 23 '65
Supreme court: which way now. il U S News
59:56 Ag 2 '65
Television & fair trial. il Time 85:44 Je 18 '65
Test for believers; rights of conscientious
objectors. il Newsweek 65:64 Mr 22 '65
Under review by Supreme court: just what
rights do suspects have? il U S News 59:
10 D 6 '65
Up from the underground; court prohibits
government from compelling individual
party members to register. il Time 86:26
N 26 '65
Verdict; pilot study of Supreme court
decisions. E. W. Lichtenberger. il NEA J
54:48-50 Mr '65
Voluntary prayer? Time 86:31 D 24 '65
Warren court by the Warren court; quota-
tions. P. C. Bartholomew. il Nat R 17:143-5
F 23 '65
When judges disagree; case of S. Sheppard.
Time 85:56 My 14 '65
Winner take nothing. il Time 85:46 Ap 23
'65
See also
Dred Scott case

History
Supreme court: guardian or dictator of the
Nation's laws? with key arguments from
key decisions. il Sr Schol 86:6-11 Mr 4 '65

Technical assistance program
See Technical assistance, American

Territorial expansion
See also
Louisiana purchase

Territories and possessions
See also
Guam

Trade policy
See United States—Commerce

Travel regulations
See Travel regulations

Treasury department
Balance-of-payments program and the Con-
gress; Cabinet report, May 13, 1965. H. H.
Fowler. Dept State Bul 52:963-4 Je 14 '65

Gold warriors. il Time 85:88+ Ap 23 '65
Silverless lining; new coinage revenues Time
86:39 S 17 '65
Turndown; D. C. Cook refuses secretary-
ship. Time 85:29 Mr 19 '65

Treaties
Department releases 1965 edition of Treaties
in force. Dept State Bul 52:233 F 16 '65
Treaty information. See issues of Depart-
ment of state bulletin
Where U.S. is pledged to defend more than
forty other nations around the world. il
U S News 58:36-7 My 10 '65

Mexico
Triumph of goodwill; problem of salt water
solved. il Newsweek 65:54 Ap 5 '65

Panama
New canal treaty. il Sr Schol 87:19 O 14 '65

Russia
Under fire: treaty that may aid Soviet spies.
U S News 59:10-11 S 6 '65

Urban renewal administration
Great Boston power play. W. Hines. Read
Digest 88:99-104 Ja '66
Land-rich or land-poor schools; Open space
land program, part of Housing act of 1961.
D. E. Gardner. il Am Ed 1:12-14 N '65

Veterans administration
From Washington, homes for sale; FHA and
VA. il U S News 58:105 Ap 26 '65
Those homes you can buy from the VA
Good H 160:151 F '65

Veterans administration hospitals
Veterans medicine: imbroglio over closing of
VA facilities is partly clash of old and new.
J. Walsh. Science 147:1426-8 Mr 19 '65;
Discussion. 148:1411; 149:708 Je 11, Ag 13
'65

Libraries
Three-dimensional program: Veterans administration library service. H. J. Gartland. il Library J 90:4296-9 O 15 '65

Vital statistics
Births and deaths. Newsweek 66:54 Jl 19 '65
See also
Birth rate—United States

Water pollution control administration
Water pollution: federal role is strengthened
by law authorizing new agency and quality
standards. E. Langer. Science 150:198-9+
O 8 '65

Weather bureau
Tornadoes: Weather bureau office in Kansas
City is nerve center for severe storm
warning network. J. Walsh. il Science 148:
1306-8 Je 4 '65
Weather while you wait. A. E. Sik. il Motor
B 116:42-5+ O '65
See also
United States—Environmental science serv-
ices administration

Work projects administration
Boondoggle that helped 38 million people.
S. D. Smith. il N Y Times Mag p37+ My
2 '65

Youth corps
See also
United States—Job corps

UNITED STATES (ship) See Ocean liners
UNITED STATES air force academy, Colorado
Springs
Cadet involved sizes up the scandal; honor
code violation. il Life 58:68-73 F 12 '65
Cheating and symbols; report of a special
committee called by the secretary of the
air force to consider cases of cheating.
Commonweal 82:277 My 21 '65
Cheating by air cadets; the brass is blamed.
U S News 58:16 My 17 '65
Clipping AF wings; report of committee on
cheating scandal. Newsweek 65:67 My 17
'65
Honor bound to what? Air force academy
code of honor. New Repub 152:9-10 F 13
'65; Discussion. 152:26-7 Mr 13; 28-9 Ap 3
'65
Lengthening list; buying and selling of stolen
exams by cadets. Newsweek 65:83-4 F 8 '65
Rules of the game; revision of administration of honor code. Newsweek 66:65 N
29 '65

UNITED STATES air force academy, Colorado Springs—Continued
Scandal at Colorado Springs; sale of exam papers. il Time 85:62 F 5 '65
Smudge on the cadet code; cheating ring at Air force academy. J. Bride, jr. il Life 58:82+ F 5 '65
Tarnished buttons; cheating scandal. S. Alexander. Life 58:25 F 12 '65
Topkapi in Colorado; cheating scandal. il Newsweek 65:82 F 15 '65

UNITED STATES and Australia; United States and Japan; etc. See Australia and the United States; Japan and the United States; etc.

UNITED STATES book publishers association. See American book publishers council

UNITED STATES-Canada permanent joint board on defense. See Permanent joint board on defense, United States and Canada

UNITED STATES chamber of commerce. See Chamber of commerce of the United States

UNITED STATES coast guard academy, New London, Conn.
Cadet life at the Academy. B. Woodward. il Motor B 115:60+ My '65

UNITED STATES embassy, Saigon. See Embassies (buildings)

UNITED STATES freight company
One big package for the shippers. Bsns W p74+ S 4 '65

UNITED STATES girls' junior championship. See Golf—Tournaments

UNITED STATES golf association
Jolly Bob finds his game; winner of U.S. Amateur championship. A. Wright. il Sports Illus 23:22-3 S 27 '65
Man who makes the grass grow. A. Wright. il Sports Illus 22:40-4+ Je 14 '65

UNITED STATES in art
See also
Mississippi in art
West in art

UNITED STATES information agency. See United States—Information agency

UNITED STATES information libraries. See American libraries abroad

UNITED STATES-Japan cooperative science program. See Science—International aspects

UNITED STATES junior chamber of commerce
America's ten outstanding young men of 1965. il Look 30:35+ Ja 25 '66

UNITED STATES lawn tennis association
Rally in tennis. Sports Illus 22:16 My 17 '65
Sporting scene (cont) H. W. Wind. New Yorker 41:192+ O 9 '65

UNITED STATES libraries of information. See American libraries abroad

UNITED STATES military academy, West Point
Army makes a new Point; modifying its curriculum and discipline. il Bsns W p 130-2+ Mr 27 '65

UNITED STATES national student association
Polite encounter between the generations; conference on Student stress in the college experience. E. Z. Friedenberg. il N Y Times Mag p 10-11+ Ja 16 '66
Resolved, more action. il Newsweek 66:82 S 13 '65
Summer and scope; directory offers details on summer programs. Newsweek 65:102+ Je 14 '65
Two conventions; one: NSA. Wm. F. Buckley, jr. Nat R 17:810 S 21 '65
Where have all the young writers gone? report on the 1965 student magazine contest. S. B. Chickering. il Sat R 48:26-7 O 9 '65

UNITED STATES naval academy, Annapolis
Formal facades for Annapolis; Naval academy laboratories by John Carl Warnecke. il Arch Rec 137:156-7 Je '65
Naval academy; lockstep program is abandoned. L. J. Carter. il Science 150:1008-12 N 19 '65
New tack at Annapolis. il Newsweek 66:66 N 8 '65

UNITED STATES news and world report (periodical)
U.S. news & world report given human relations award. il U S News 58:8 Ap 12 '65

UNITED STATES office of education. See United States—Education, Office of

UNITED STATES plywood corporation
New growth rings for U.S. plywood. il Bsns W p72-5 Jl 24 '65

UNITED STATES power squadrons, incorporated
Under way with the USPS. See issues of Motor boating
With the power squadrons. C. Schrage. See issues of Yachting

UNITED STATES savings bonds. See Bonds, Government

UNITED STATES service academies. See United States—Armed forces—Education

UNITED STATES steel corporation
Big steel ups prices but avoids a row. il Bsns W p28-9 Ja 8 '66
Capital ideas. Time 86:74 Ag 27 '65
Design a bridge and win a prize. il Am City 80:30 D '65
Early frost hits Steel and USW; U.S. steel's Cooper vs union chief Abel. il Bsns W p43-4+ O 30 '65
Wage chronology: United States steel corp; 1960-64. J. Griest. il Mo Labor R 88:178-89 F '65

UNITED STATES steel International, New York, incorporated
U.S. builders tie Portugal together; span across Tagus River at Lisbon. il Bsns W p28-9 Ag 14 '65

UNITED STATES trust company of New York. See New York (city)—Banks

UNITED steelworkers of America
Abel holds edge in USW tally; election results. Bsns W p31 Mr 6 '65
After steel election, the strike outlook now. il U S News 58:87-8 F 22 '65
Aluminum comes next; bargaining spotlight shifts. Bsns W p 136 My 8 '65
Campaign '65; men of steel. il Newsweek 65:64+ F 8 '65
Chances of avoiding a steel strike. U S News 58:93-4 Ap 26 '65
Decision time again: is a steel strike coming? il U S News 59:70-1 Ag 23 '65
Early frost hits Steel and USW; U.S. steel's Cooper vs union chief Abel. il Bsns W p43-4+ O 30 '65
Eye to eye; negotiations between the United steelworkers union and the steel industry. il Newsweek 66:56 S 6 '65
From steel union, surprise demands. U S News 58:104 Ap 12 '65
Glower & glow in Pittsburgh. il Time 86:76 Ag 6 '65
How steel jobs are dwindling; computer-controlled mills. il Bsns W p75-6+ Ag 14 '65
In steel, a deal close to guidelines; with editorial comment. il Bsns W p28-30, 122 S 4 '65
Man steel is watching; I. W. Abel. Bsns W p48+ Mr 27 '65
New dispute over steel pattern. U S News 59:102 N 8 '65
New leader for a big union; here's a look at his ideas. U S News 58:70 My 31 '65
New temper in the steelworkers; new leaders seek more influence, show more militancy. Bsns W p43-4 Je 5 '65
Next threat is in steel. il Bsns W p23 F 20 '65
Passing the gavel; inauguration of I. W. Abel. il Newsweek 65:90 Je 14 '65
Photo finish in USW? McDonald-Abel contest for presidency. il Bsns W p98-100 Ja 30 '65
Pressure on steel union to extend May 1 deadline for strike. il U S News 58:72 Mr 8 '65
Rebellion in steel. R. W. Gibbons; reply with rejoinder. H. Peck. Commonweal 81:682 F 26 '65
Revolt of the left-outs; union malaise. S. Lens. Commonweal 82:441-4 Je 25 '65; Reply with rejoinder. D. J. McDonald. 82:514 Jl 23 '65
Say a prayer; United steelworkers president refrains from contesting election. il Time 85:24 My 28 '65
Snarl in steel; dead lock in election of president. Newsweek 65:75-6 Mr 15 '65
Steel pins its hopes on contract extension. Bsns W p25 Ap 17 '65
Steelworkers' hard-nosed boss; I. W. Abel, tough man at the contract table. il Life 58:45-6+ Je 25 '65
Steelworkers vote: prelude to the strike. B. J. Widick. il Nation 200:214-16 Mr 1 '65
That's an election? protests of voting violations. il Time 85:23B Mr 12 '65
To the brink in steel; Pittsburgh. il Time 86:19-20 S 3 '65
Toward the steel deadline. il Time 85:95 Ap 30 '65
Trouble ahead; steelworkers' presidential election. il Time 85:22 F 19 '65
Truce in USW may get steel talks going again. Bsns W p42 F 27 '65
Union votes spotlight gaps in election rules. il Bsns W p51-2+ F 27 '65
U.S. sweats out the steel vote. il Newsweek 65:77-8 F 22 '65
USW closes ranks against the industry; bargaining impossible because of McDonald-Abel split. il Bsns W p30 Ap 24 '65

UNITED steelworkers of America—*Continued*
USW hears rumble on local issues; dissatisfaction over bargaining techniques. Bsns W p69 O 16 '65
USW may escape family fight. il Bsns W p49-50 My 1 '65
USW nears hour of decision: voting for McDonald vs Abel. Bsns W p28 F 6 '65
Wage barrier looms in steel bargaining. il Bsns W p 144+ Ap 10 '65
What guides the steelworkers? S. H. Brown. il Fortune 72:156-8+ S '65
Where do unions go after steel? Bsns W p 150 S 18 '65

UNITED technology center. See United aircraft corporation

UNITED world federalists
World federalists view the U.N. H. Y. Williams. Christian Cent 82:992-3 Ag 11 '65

UNIVERSAL CITY, Calif.
Hollywood changes script on sightseers; Universal City tours. il Bsns W p30-1 Jl 10 '65

UNIVERSAL declaration of human rights
Human rights day 1965: messages. A. Fanfani; Thant. UN Mo Chron 2:i-iv D '65

UNIVERSAL history. See World history

UNIVERSAL language. See Language, Universal

UNIVERSAL postal union
Universal postal union. M. A. K. Menon. bibliog f il Int Concil 552:3-64 Mr '65

UNIVERSAL reference system. See Information storage and retrieval systems

UNIVERSAL telephone, incorporated
Competing with AT&T; Los Alamos telephone system. New Repub 152:7 F 6 '65

UNIVERSAL time. See Time measurements

UNIVERSALISM (politics) See Internationalism

UNIVERSE
Big bang theory upheld; quasi-stellar blue galaxies. Sci N L 87:403 Je 26 '65
Celestial coexistence. Time 86:91 N 19 '65
Changing view of universe. A. Ewing. il Sci N L 88:10-11 Jl 3 '65
Closer to the big bang. il Sci Am 213:44-6 Jl '65
Did the universe ever begin? D. Cohen. il Sci Digest 58:40-4 Ag '65
Is there a second universe? B. H. Frisch. il Sci Digest 58:10-12 S '65
New look at the universe. Sci Digest 59:24-5 Ja '66
Seek origin of universe. Sci N L 88:5 Jl 3 '65
Space, and all that. R. L. Strout. New Repub 152:11-12 My 8 '65; Correction. 152:38 My 29 '65
They're solving the world's greatest mystery. C. P. Gilmore. il Pop Sci 187:102-5+ N '65
See also
Cosmogony
Life on other planets
Solar system

UNIVERSITIES of science and technology. See Technical education

UNIVERSITIES research association, incorporated
200-bev machine: university compact offers its services. D. S. Greenberg. Science 150:1566-7 D 17 '65

UNIVERSITY administration. See Colleges and universities—Administration

UNIVERSITY bookstores. See College bookstores

UNIVERSITY choral festival. See Music festivals

UNIVERSITY degrees. See Degrees, Academic

UNIVERSITY dining halls. See Colleges and universities—Dining halls

UNIVERSITY extension
Holiday U; Vacation college, an eight-day session for adults. il Newsweek 66:74 Ag 30 '65
Paid learning for all employees. Sch & Soc 93:204+ Ap 3 '65

UNIVERSITY microfilms, Ann Arbor, Mich.
Alice ms. facsimile starts Xerox subsidiary's program. il Pub W 188:41-2 Ag 2 '65
Boast of Englishmen: project to microfilm British periodicals from the Restoration to the death of Queen Victoria. D. Fader. bibliog il Library J 90:1841-3 Ap 15 '65
University microfilm head requests inquiry; charges of conflict of interests between roles as officer of the publishing house and regent of University of Michigan. Pub W 188:34-5 N 29 '65

UNIVERSITY of St Thomas, Houston, Tex.
Processional elements in Houston; chapel for St Thomas university. il Arch Rec 137:159 Je '65

UNIVERSITY of the Seven Seas. See Colleges and universities. Traveling

UNIVERSITY of the South, Sewanee, Tenn.
In appreciation of excellence. Time 86:45 S 10 '65

UNIVERSITY of California; University of Texas; etc. See California. University; Texas. University; etc

UNIVERSITY of Washington arboretum. See Arboretums

UNIVERSITY presses
From the university presses; selection of books. il Library J 90:2766-71 Je 15 '65
Paradox of university publishing. J. J. Foley. America 114:84+ Ja 15 '66
SR's check list of University press books; comp. by R. Brown. Sat R 48:91-2 My 22 '65
University presses review domestic and world concerns; AAUP convention. il Pub W 188:36-57+ Jl 19 '65
See also
Association of American university presses
Kentucky university press
Louisiana state university press

UNIVERSITY professors. See College professors and instructors

UNIVERSITY professors, American association of. See American association of university professors

UNIVERSITY professors conference. See Economic conferences

UNIVERSITY research. See Colleges and universities—Research

UNIVERSITY students. See College students

UNIVIS, incorporated
Univis' marketing feat. T. J. Murray. Duns R 85:83-4 Ap '65

UNKNOWN rooms; story. See Henderson, R.

UNKNOWN soldiers
Honoring three, and half a million. il Sr Schol 87:7 N 11 '65

UNLOVED; story. See Hitchens, D.

UNMARRIED men. See Bachelors

UNMARRIED mothers. See Mothers, Unmarried

UNMARRIED women. See Single women

UNRUH, Jesse
Big Daddy vs. Pat. por Newsweek 65:30+ Ap 5 '65
Great row in California. S. Alsop. por Sat Eve Post 238:18 My 8 '65

UNTERECKER, John
Ampurias, Spain; poem. Yale R 55:253 D '65

UNTERMEYER, Louis
E.A.R: a remembrance. Sat R 48:33-4 Ap 10 '65
Sporting occupation. Sat R 48:37 N 27 '65
Vagabond muse. Sat R 48:51+ O 16 '65
about
On the fringe. H. Frankel. Sat R 48:46+ O 2 '65
Patriarch of poetry. por Newsweek 66:104A-104B O 4 '65

UNTOUCHABLES
Untouchables of India. M. N. Srinivas and A. Béteille. il Sci Am 213:13-17 D '65

UPATNIEKS, Juris. See Leith, E. N. jt. auth.

UPDIKE, John
Alligators; story. Parents Mag 40:62-3 S '65
Avec la bébé-sitter; story. New Yorker 41:24-7 Ja 1 '66
Books (cont) New Yorker 41:216+ O 2; 223-4+ O 30 '65
Bulgarian poetess; story. New Yorker 41:44-51 Mr 13 '65
Deus dixit; story. Esquire 64:100-2 S '65
Family meadow; story. New Yorker 41:24-5 Jl 24 '65
Four sides of one story; story. New Yorker 41:48-52 O 9 '65
Hermit; story. New Yorker 41:38-46 F 20 '65
Home movies; poem. New Repub 154:23 Ja 8 '66
My lover has dirty fingernails; story. New Yorker 41:28-31 Jl 17 '65
Poem for a far land. New Repub 152:17 Mr 13 '65
Postcards from Soviet cities: Moscow; Kiev; Leningrad; Yerevan; poems. New Yorker 41:34 My 29 '65
Roman portrait busts; poem. New Repub 152:21 F 6 '65
Stare; story. New Yorker 41:41-3 Ap 3 '65
Sunshine on sandstone; poem. New Repub 152:26 Ap 17 '65
about
They also serve who write well. G. Hicks. Sat R 48:25-6 My 15 '65
Updike's ups and downs. D. J. Enright. Holiday 38:162+ N '65

UPHOLSTERY
Shampooing upholstery. E. Taylor. il Good H 161:219 S '65

UPPER classes
Beautiful people in Mexico. il Vogue 145:172-7 Ap 1 '65

UPPER Mantle project. See Earth—Internal structure

UPPER RIO GRANDE wilderness areas. See Wilderness areas

UPPER VOLTA
Fast shuffle; government coup. il Newsweek 67:40 Ja 17 '66
President Yameogo of Upper Volta visits the United States; exchange of greetings, with joint communique, March 30, 1965. L. B. Johnson; M. Yameogo. Dept State Bul 52:618-21 Ap 26 '65
Soldiers on the march. Time 87:39 Ja 14 '66

UPPSALA observatory. See Astronomical observatories—Sweden

UPTON, George
Tragedy of needless drowning deaths. Todays Health 43:46-8+ Jl '65

UPTON, T. Graydon
Inter-American development bank; address, February 3, 1965. Vital Speeches 31:375-80 Ap 1 '65

URACIL
Hydrogen-bonded dimers of adenine and uracil derivatives. R. M. Hamlin, jr. and others. bibliog il Science 148:1734-7 Je 25 '65
Uracil mustard: a potent inducer in lung tumors in mice. C. W. Abell and others. bibliog il Science 147:1443-5 Mr 19 '65

URANIUM
Why it's time for atom police. S. Eklund. il Sat R 48:66-7 O 2 '65

Isotopes
Fossil particle tracks and uranium distributions in minerals of the Vaca Muerta meteorite. R. L. Fleischer and others. bibliog il Science 148:629-32 Ap 30 '65

URANIUM-helium dating. See Radioactive dating

URANIUM mines and mining

United States
U.S. to make further cutback in enriched uranium production; Atomic energy commission announcement of February 15, 1965, with letter to President Johnson from AEC chairman. Dept State Bul 52:339 Mr 8 '65

URBAN, Joseph
Opera urbanized. Q. Eaton. il por Opera N 29:26-30 F 27 '65

URBAN education. See Education, Urban

URBAN freeways. See Express highways

URBAN growth. See Cities and towns—Growth

URBAN league, National. See National urban league

URBAN renewal
American city: crisis or renaissance? il Sr Schol 86:6-9 Ap 29 '65
Birds, beaches, bistros, urban renewal goes astray. il Nations Bsns 53:98-9+ Mr '65
Can subsidies solve America's problems? a university's answer, Detroit's Wayne state university survey. il Nations Bsns 53:34-5+ Ag '65
Church and urban renewal, by G. D. Younger. Review
  Commonweal 82:540 Jl 23 '65. R. Robbins.
City is the frontier, by C. Abrams. Review
  Atlan 216:151 D '65
Comeback of downtown: big plans in big cities. il U S News 59:64-9 Jl 26 '65
Exploding the myths of urban renewal; excerpts from Federal bulldozer. M. Anderson. Read Digest 86:86-90 Ap '65
Factory sites in rural areas. B. L. Masse. America 113:440 O 16 '65
Failure of urban renewal; a critique and some proposals. H. J. Gans. Commentary 39:29-37 Ap '65; Discussion. 40:72-80 Jl; 14+ N '65
Federal bulldozer: a critical analysis of urban renewal, 1949-1962, by M. Anderson. Review
  Reporter 32:49-50+ F 25 '65. W. W. Nash, jr. and C. W. Hartman
  Sat R 48:30-1 F 27 '65. C. W. Griffin, jr
Housing design: quality returns to the city; symposium. Arch Forum 123:40-69 Jl '65
Housing progress: four steps forward; how many back? il Arch Forum 123:70-89 Jl '65
Instant slum clearance: R. B. Fuller's plan for Harlem. J. Meyer. il Esquire 63:108-11 Ap '65

Latest plan for perpetual prosperity: city building; LBJ's proposals to Congress. il U S News 58:42-4 Mr 15 '65
Lighting of cities; proposed urban redesign of New Haven, Conn. W. M. C. Lam. il Arch Rec 138:173-80 Jl '65
Making cities fit for people. H. H. Humphrey. Sat R 48:16-17 Jl 3 '65
New directions for urban renewal; excerpts from address, March 30, 1965. R. C. Weaver. Arch Rec 138:137-42 Ag '65
New focus on the city. il Sr Schol 87:10-11 O 21 '65
New spirit soars in mid-America's proud old city. R. P. Jordan. il Nat Geog Mag 128:605-41 N '65
New town in Washington. W. Von Eckardt. il Américas 17:6-12 Je '65
Our sick cities; symposium. il Look 29:27-38+ S 21 '65
Philadelphia report: a long wait for the renaissance. M. F. Schmertz. il Arch Rec 138:119-32 Jl '65
Pope Paul VI on urbanization. America 113:107 Jl 31 '65
Renewal of cities. N. Glazer. il Sci Am 213:194-202+ bibliog(p278+) S '65
Reporter at large; effects of urban renewal on old people in South End of Boston. J. Colebrook. New Yorker 41:35-6+ Ja 1 '66
Row over urban renewal. J. Epstein. Harper 230:55-61 F '65; Discussion. 230:16+ Ap '65
San Francisco report: no easy road to the more handsome city. E. K. Thompson. il Arch Rec 138:151-66 S '65
Saving the cities. America 112:217 F 13 '65
Schemes for the cities; President's proposals. Bsns W p32+ Mr 6 '65
Slum dwellings do not make a slum. N. Glazer. il N Y Times Mag p54-5+ N 21 '65
Small borough's comprehensive plan; borough of Royersford, Pa. H. J. Grossman. il Am City 80:118-19 Je '65
Speaking out; slum clearance is a hoax. D. M. Friedenberg. Sat Eve Post 238:12+ Ag 28 '65
State of the cities. C. W. Griffin, jr. il Reporter 33:52-4 D 16 '65
Suburban renewal: subsidy on the rise. il Nations Bsns 53:42-3+ F '65
Total program in the fight against blight; address, January 15, 1965. W. L. Slayton. Vital Speeches 31:267-71 F 15 '65
Urban renewal: a case study in emerging goals in an intergovernmental setting. C. C. Ham. bibliog f Ann Am Acad 359:44-52 My '65
Urban renewal wastelands. il Nations Bsns 53:86-7 Ap '65
We'd rather do it ourselves; communities rebuilding without federal doles. il Nations Bsns 53:36-7+ S '65
We're wasting billions on our cities. Nations Bsns 53:43+ F '65
What hope of good urban planning? R. Kirk. Nat R 17:1160 D 14 '65
Why a city turned down federal dollars; case of Orlando, Fla. il Nations Bsns 53:38-9+ O '65
You shove out the poor to make houses for the rich: urban renewal means Negro removal. W. L. Miller and L. T. Appleby. il N Y Times Mag p36+ Ap 11 '65
  See also
Business districts
City planning
United States—Urban renewal administration

URBAN renewal administration. See United States—Urban renewal administration

URBAN-rural conflict. See City and country

URBAN sociology. See Sociology, Urban

URBAN training center for Christian mission
Plunge. il Newsweek 65:83 F 15 '65
School for a new creation. il Time 86:124+ N 19 '65

URBAN universities. See Colleges and universities, Municipal

URBANA, Ill.
Upgrading downtown. il Arch Rec 137:186-7 Je '65

URBANISM. See Cities and towns

URBANIZATION
Secular city, by H. Cox. Review
  Christian Cent 82:1038-9 Ag 25 '65. G. B. Hall
Urbanization of the human population. K. Davis. il Sci Am 213:40-53 S '65
Waiting for reality, birth of the megalopolis. S. Greer. Nation 201:98-102 S 20 '65

Latin America
Urban and rural development in Latin America; with questions and answers. J. P. Powelson and A. A. Solow. bibliog f Ann Am Acad 360:48-62 Jl '65

URBANIZED areas. See Metropolitan areas

URBANSKI, Edmund S.
Two novels of the Amazon. Américas 17:33-8 Mr '65

URBMOBILES. See Automobiles, Electric

URCHINS, Sea. See Sea urchins

URDANG, Constance
Poetry chronicle. Poetry 105:336-42 F '65
These also wait for death; Exhortation: Songs for stones; poems. Poetry 106:347-9 Ag '65

UREA
Hydroxyurea: differential lethal effects on cultured mammalian cells during the cell cycle. W. K. Sinclair. bibliog il Science 150:1729-31 D 24 '65
New high-urea rations, when and how to use them. D. Malena. il Suc Farm 63:88 F '65

UREN, Laurel S.
Audubon stamp bird moves to the U.S. Audubon Mag 67:101-2 Mr '65

UREY, Harold C.
Biological material in meteorites: a review. bibliog Science 151:157-66 Ja 14 '66
Meteorites and the moon. bibliog Science 147:1262-5 Mr 12 '65

UREYITE
Ureyite, NaCrSi₂O₆: a new meteoritic pyroxene. C. Frondel and C. Klein, jr. bibliog il Science 149:742-4 Ag 13 '65

URI, Pierre
Persistent friend of Atlantic unity. il por Bsns W p68+ My 8 '65

URIBURU, Ernesto C.
Jangada; a seaworthy Brazilian raft. por Américas 17:34-6 My '65
World in miniature. Américas 17:34-6 O '65

URICEMIA. See Urinary organs—Diseases

URICH, Ted, and Mauck, Joe
Best place for vocational education. NEA J 54:51-2 D '65

URIDINE
Pseudouridine formation: evidence for RNA as an intermediate. S. B. Weiss and J. Legault-Demare. bibliog il Science 149:429-31 Jl 23 '65

URINARY calculi. See Calculi, Urinary

URINARY organs
Bradykinin: effect on ureteral peristalsis. P. Catacutan-Labay and S. Boyarsky. bibliog il Science 151:78-9 Ja 7 '66

Diseases
Lactic acid metabolism in hypertensive patients. F. E. Demartini and others. bibliog il Science 148:1482-4 Je 11 '65
Pacemaker corrects backflow of urine. Sci N L 88:233 O 9 '65
Urinary infections may lead to kidney trouble. Sci N L 87:151 Mr 6 '65

URINARY proteins. See Proteins

URINE
Endoplasmic reticulum in rat renal interstitial cells: molecular rearrangement after water deprivation. R. E. Bulger and others bibliog il Science 151:83-6 Ja 7 '66

Incontinence
If a child is a bed wetter. il Good H 161:175 O '65

URIS, Auren
Put new life in your career. Nations Bsns 53:78+ S '65
Think small. Nations Bsns 53:94-6+ My '65

URIST, Marshall R.
Bone: formation by autoinduction. bibliog Science 150:893-9 N 12 '65

UROKINASE. See Enzymes

URQUHART, Clara
Albert Schweitzer: behind the legend. Sat R 48:26-7 S 25 '65

URQUHART, D. J.
Model of simplicity: Britain's National lending library for science & technology. bibliog por Library J 90:4926-8 N 15 '65

URUGUAY

Economic conditions
Rot in the barrel. M. J. Kubic. Newsweek 66:46-7 Ag 30 '65
Toward the brink. Time 86:30 Ag 13 '65
Woe in welfareland. Time 86:59 N 19 '65

Economic policy
Land of funny money. il Fortune 72:65-6+ S '65

Politics and government
Proposal for leadership. Time 85:31 Mr 26 '65

Religious institutions and affairs
News of the Christian world (cont) Christian Cent 82:1202 S 29 '65

Social conditions
See also
Social and economic security—Uruguay

USED automobiles. See Automobiles, Used

USTINOV, Peter
Art of asking questions; adaptation of address. Sat R 48:22 D 25 '65
Frontiers of the sea; story. Atlan 217:43-51 Ja '66

UTAH
See also
Architecture, Domestic—Utah
Brian Head
Camping—Utah
Great Salt Lake
Hunting—Utah
Kings Peak
Mormons and Mormonism
Paleontology—Utah

Description and travel
Among the books: Standing up country. M. T. Musselman. il Liv Wildn 29:29-31 Sum '65
Before you leave Salt Lake Valley, here are side trips too good to miss. il Sunset 134:90-1 Ap '65
He's standing in Recapture Pocket. il Sunset 135:54+ S '65

Parks and reserves
See also
Canyonlands National Park

Religious institutions and affairs
See also
Mormons and Mormonism

UTE Indians
Utes invite you in; reservation in northeastern Utah. il Sunset 134:66 Ap '65

UTERINE cancer. See Cancer

UTERUS
Surgery
Hysterectomy: when it's needed, what it does. Good H 160:139 Ja '65

UTILITY poles. See Electric lines—Poles

UTILIZATION of land. See Land utilization

UTZON, Jørn
Fifth façade. il Time 86:86 D 10 '65

UYS, Stanley
Letter from South Africa. New Repub 153:36-7 S 25 '65

UZIELLI, Anne (Ford) See Ford, A.

UZIELLI, Giancarlo
Watching Fords go by; party at New York's Delmonico hotel before wedding. il por Newsweek 67:46 Ja 10 '66

UZZLE, Burk
Right under the eyes of the Vietcong. G. P. Hunt. por Life 58:3 Mr 12 '65

V

VA. See United States—Veterans administration

V-belts. See Belting

VD. See Venereal diseases

V-E day
Fiery skies salute V-E day; 20th anniversary. Life 58:40-3 My 21 '65
Flags of freedom fly; twentieth anniversary. il Newsweek 65:50-1 My 17 '65
Germany '45: the day the Americans came. H. H. Kirst. il N Y Times Mag p26-7+ My 2 '65

VFW. See Veterans of foreign wars

VGH recorders. See Aeronautic instruments

VHF (very high frequency) radio transmission. See Radio transmission

VHF television stations. See Television stations

VIM conveyor. See Mail handling

VISTA. See Volunteers in service to America

VITA. See Volunteers for international technical assistance

VOA. See Voice of America (radio program)

VOM. See Voltohmmeters

VOR (visual omnirange) See Radio in aviation

V/STOL (vertical or short take-off and landing) See Airplanes, Vertical take-off and landing

VTOL. See Airplanes, Vertical take-off and landing

VTVM (vacuum tube voltmeters) See Voltmeters

VACATION
How to budget now for next year's vacation. Bet Hom & Gard 43:151 O '65

VACATION cabins. See Cabins

VACATION houses
Vacation house that can travel. A. Mikesell. il Pop Mech 125:93 Ja '66
See also
Cottages
Summer homes

VACATION reading. See Books and reading

VACATION schools. See Summer schools

VACATION schools, Religious
Mustard-seed Bible schools; organization and operation of a summer Bible school. M. A. Carey. America 112:361-4 Mr 13 '65

VACATION spending. See Vacations

VACATION villages
Bikinis in the desert. J. Lieber. il Sat R 48:68+ Mr 13 '65

VACATIONS
And what are your vacation plans? Changing T 19:6 Je '65
Double life pays off; second home. il Bsns W p23-6 Jl 10 '65
Let's travel; spring vacations. il Mlle 60:150-3 F '65
More for your travel dollar! (cont) il Bet Hom & Gard 43:21-2+ F: 110 Mr: 128+ Ap '65
Novel vacations. D. B. Warnick. il Travel 123:37-9 Je '65
One-day vacations. E. Pearson. Farm J 89:58 N '65
Stay-at-home vacation. R. Holter. il Parents Mag 40:50-1+ Jl '65
Sunny Rainy Lake. B. Cary. il Travel 124:40-4 Jl '65
Surf, snow, sex & protest; spring-vacationing students. il Time 85:61 Ap 2 '65
There's no place like someone else's home; home swapping. Time 86:63 Ag 13 '65
Time to loaf. E. J. LeShan. il N Y Times Mag p73-4 Je 6 '65
Vacation high spots in Canada. il Bet Hom & Gard 43:151-6 My '65
We had a wild time. A. W. Prince. il Outdoor Life 136:33-5+ Jl '65
Where to go fishing, vacationing, hunting. See issues of Outdoor life
Why some people always vacation off-season. Bet Hom & Gard 43:30+ S '65
Winter is vacation time, too! il Changing T 19:33-4 N '65
See also
Outdoor life

Anecdotes, facetiae, satire, etc.
I hate winter postcards. H. A. Smith. il Travel 125:55-7 Ja '66

VACATIONS, Employee
Plant and paid leave hours in manufacturing, 1959 and 1962. A. Strasser. il Mo Labor R 88:413-15 Ap '65

VACCARO, Louis C.
Three ways out for small Catholic colleges. America 113:580-2 N 13 '65

VACCINATION
Edward Jenner, the father of vaccination. il UNESCO Courier 18:28-31 Mr '65
See also
Immunity
Typhoid fever—Preventive inoculation

VACCINES
Cat fever tamed by vaccine; oral vaccine for catarrh. Bsns W p60 Ap 24 '65
Cow to the rescue; vaccines against various diseases. il Sr Schol 86:7 My 13 '65
Roundabout vaccination; live-virus vaccines. Time 85:86 Ap 30 '65
See also subhead Vaccines under names of diseases, e.g. Poliomyelitis—Vaccines

VACCINIA virus
Vaccinia virus directed RNA: its fate in the presence of actinomycin. A. J. Shatkin and others. bibliog il Science 148:87-90 Ap 2 '65

VACQUIER, Victor D. and Belser, W. L.
Sex conversion induced by hydrostatic pressure in the marine copepod tigriopus californicus. bibliog Science 150:1619-21 D 17 '65

VACUUM
Ultrahigh vacuum. R. W. Roberts and L. E. St Pierre. bibliog il Science 147:1529-42 Mr 26 '65

VACUUM cleaners
Central vacuum system for your home? E. F. Lindsley. il Pop Sci 186:160-2 Ap '65
Portable vacuum cleaners. il House & Gard 128:82 O '65

Sears sweeps a path with no-cord vacuum; Kenmore cordless vac. il Bsns W p41 Je 12 '65
Vacuum cleaners, now they're built in. il Changing T 19:37-8 Ap '65

VACUUM filtration. See Sewage disposal—Filtration

VACUUM presses. See Presses

VACUUM sweepers, Street. See Street cleaning apparatus

VACUUM tubes
See also
Diodes
Storage tubes
Traveling wave tubes

History
De Forest and the triode detector. R. A. Chipman. il Sci Am 212:92-100 bibliog (p 140) Mr '65; Reply with rejoinder. L. Espenschied. 212:8+ My '65

VADON, Jim
Family affair. Outdoor Life 136:54-5+ O '65

VAGABONDS
Hobo signs; designs by students at the Herron school of art. il Design 66:36-9 Mr '65

VAHANIAN, Gabriel
God without God. Christian Cent 82:745-6 Je 9 '65
Swallowed up by godlessness. Christian Cent 82:1505-7 D 8 '65

VAHL, Rod
Circus magic; drama. Plays 25:63-6 Ja '66
Indian boy without a name; drama. Plays 25:55-60, 86 O '65

VAHLDIEK, F. W. and others
Room temperature slip in titanium diboride produced by high pressure. bibliog Science 149:747-8 Ag 13 '65

VAIL, Thomas Van Husen
Tigerish. il por Newsweek 66:78-9 Jl 5 '65

VAIONT DAM, Italy. See Dams—Italy

VALACHI, Joseph
Penthouse Proust. por Time 87:23 Ja 7 '66

VALAIS, Switzerland
Valais variety. R. Deardorff. il Travel 123:58-61 Je '65

VALAITIS, Vytas
Two's a crowd. il Parents Mag 40:42-3 Jl '65

VALBRACHT, Louis H.
Christmas is for joy. por Suc Farm 63:55+ D '65

VALDERRAMA, Pedro A. Gómez. See Gómez Valderrama, P. A.

VALDIVIA, Enrique, and others
Fatty change of the granular pneumocyte. bibliog Science 151:213-14 Ja 14 '66

VALDIVIA pottery. See Pottery, Ecuadorian

VALDOSTA, Ga.
Georgia boy goes home. L. E. Lomax. il Harper 230:152-9 Ap '65

VALENCIA, León
Another Latin-American country that can blow up. J. N. Wallace. il por U S News 58:70-2 Je 21 '65

VALENSTEIN, Elliot S. See Cox, V. C. jt. auth.

VALENTE, G. A.
New idea in sludge dewatering. Am City 80:95-7 Jl '65

VALENTE, Richard
Enduring Saint Brendan. Américas 17:22-7 N '65

VALENTI, Jack
Loyal lieutenant views LBJ; excerpts from address. por Newsweek 66:16-17 Jl 12 '65
Of extra glands, giant agony and the grey stone mountain; excerpts from address. Time 86:19-20 Jl 9 '65
Top aide's close-up of a President who never says I'm tired; summary of address, June 28, 1965. por U S News 59:22 Jl 12 '65

about
Valenti's valentine. Reporter 33:18 Jl 15 '65

VALENTINE, Helen
Young wife's world. See issues of Good housekeeping

VALENTINE, Jean
Solomon; poem. Commonweal 82:657 S 17 '65

about
Bell, book, and candle. por Newsweek 65:89 Mr 1 '65

VALENTINE, Luis
Dawn; poem. Am For 71:48 Ap '65

VALENTINE, Raymond C. and Strand, Mette
Complexes of F-pili and RNA bacteriophage. bibliog Science 148:511-13 Ap 23 '65

VALENTINE for Kate; drama. See Miller, H. L.

VALENTINES day
Who was St Valentine? Good H 160:152 F '65

Drama
Valentine for Kate. H. L. Miller. Plays 24:29-40 F '65

Poetry
I'm no saint, but I have my doubts about Valentine, too. O. Nash. il Ladies Home J 82:79 F '65

VALENTINO, Rudolph
Overloved one. M. M. Marberry. il por Am Heritage 16:84-7+ Ag '65

VALENTRY, Duane
Twelve ways to handle the stress of modern living. Sci Digest 58:44-8 N '65

VALÉRY, Paul
Technology and insight. G. S. Fraser. Poetry 106:367-8 Ag '65

VALLE, José Cecilio del
José Cecilio del Valle, Pan Americanist. P. F. Lavin. il pors Américas 17:7-9 Ag '65

VALLENTYNE, J. R.
Thermal stability of threonine in the presence of a marine polyphenolic material. bibliog Science 151:214-15 Ja 14 '66

VALLEY Winds school, St Louis. See St Louis —Education

VALUABLE papers. See Family records

VALUATION (psychology) See Value (psychology)

VALUE (philosophy) See Worth

VALUE (psychology)
Why I am not going to the moon. J. W. Krutch. Sat R 48:29-31 N 20 '65

VALUE, Moral. See Worth

VALUE analysis
How valuable is value analysis? il Bsns W p78+ My 15 '65
Live better, spend less; cost-cutting formula. il Changing T 19:21-3 Je '65
Value analysis in purchasing; Virginia. G. L. Nunnally. Am City 80:162+ Je '65

VALUE of college education. See College education. Value of

VALUE of education. See Education, Value of

VALVES
Get more hours between valve jobs; farm engine. G. E. Melvin. Suc Farm 64:76D Ja '66
See also
Automobile engines—Valves

VAMPIRES
Sentimental journey to Dracula's home town; Borgo Pass. G. Smith. il Sat Eve Post 238:76-9 Mr 27 '65

VAN, George E.
Detroit: Cadillac liked it. Yachting 117:42-3+ My '65
Gypsy sweeps Bayview Mackinac for second straight year. Yachting 118:47+ S '65

VAN ALEN, Jimmy
New rules enrage Pancho but excite fans. il por Life 59:52+ Ag 13 '65

VAN ALLEN, J. A. and others
Absence of Martian radiation belts and implications thereof. bibliog Science 149:1228-33 S 10 '65

VAN ALLEN radiation belts
OV2-1 will seek to determine extent of Van Allen belt threat; orbital vehicle. il Aviation W 83:113+ S 27 '65

VAN ALSTYNE, William W.
Right to vote: small fruit of a bold promise. Nation 200:411-13 Ap 19 '65

VAN ALSTYNE folk art collection. See Smithsonian institution

VAN ANDEL, Tjeerd H. and others
Morphology and sediments of a portion of the Mid-Atlantic ridge. bibliog Science 148:1214-16 My 28 '65

VAN ARK, Dorothy
I can say no to my teenagers. Parents Mag 40:58-9+ S '65

VAN BAALEN, Chase
Mutation of the blue-green alga, anacystis nidulans. bibliog Science 149:70 Jl 2 '65

VAN BAVEL, C. H. M. See Jackson, R. D. jt. auth.

VAN BEAUMONT, W. and Bullard, R. W.
Sweating: direct influence of skin temperature. bibliog Science 147:1465-7 Mr 19 '65

VAN BROCKLIN, Norman Mack
Dutchman is half an inch away. T. Maule and M. H. Sharnik. il por Sports Illus 23:46-51 S 13 '65

VAN BUREN, Abigail, pseud.
Very Dear Abby. por Newsweek 66:62 N 8 '65

VAN BUREN, Martin
Is carpet practical? por Library J 90:5152-6, 5322 D 1-15 '65
What to look for when buying shelving. por Library J 90:1614-17 Ap 1 '65

VAN BUREN, Martin, 1782-1862
Speech that toppled a president; excerpts from address, April 14, 1840, ed. with introd. by G. Carson. C. Ogle; reply, G. I. Bushfield. Am Heritage 16:87 Ap '65

VAN BUREN, Paul M.
Intelligent subjectivity. Christian Cent 83:49 Ja 12 '66
Theology in the context of culture. Christian Cent 82:428-30 Ap 7 '65

about
Profiles; concerning Honest to God, by J. Robinson. V. Mehta. New Yorker 41:137-8+ N 13 '65

VAN BUSKIRK, Alden
Carol; Hate poem; poems. Poetry 105:250-1 Ja '65

VANCE, Ben F.
Answers to vegetable and garden questions. Suc Farm 63:114+ F '65

VANCE, Monk
Branding makes cattle record keeping easy. il Suc Farm 63:108 Ap '65
He uses records+common sense in beef herd improvement. Suc Farm 63:26B Ag '65

VANCE, Velma J. and others
Brightness discrimination in the collared lizard. bibliog Science 147:758-9 F 12 '65

VANCE, Vivian
TV's favorite comedy team breaks up. R. Hochstein. il por Good H 161:30+ O '65

VAN COEVERING, Jack
Dead loon mystery. Audubon Mag 67:229-30 Jl '65

VANCOUVER, British Columbia
Vancouver; yachting center of Canada's photogenic Pacific waterways. H. Glynn-Ward. il Motor B 115:40-1 My '65

VANCOUVER music festival. See Music festivals—Canada

VANCOUVER opera association
Vancouver's high priest; interview, ed. by F. Stevenson. I. Guttman. il Opera N 29:29-31 F 20 '65

VANDALISM
City's shame; Bamberg, Germany. il Newsweek 66:40 Jl 5 '65
Destruction of California, by R. F. Dasmann. Review
Nation 201:252-4 O 18 '65. K. Lamott
Don't be a wreckreator. M. Robarge. il Recreation 58:274-6 Je '65
Havoc wrought by vandals. il UNESCO Courier 18:16-17 N '65
Monumental shame. J. H. Winchester. il Travel 123:58-60 My '65
Vandalism. N. Kent. Am Artist 29:3+ Ap '65
Vandalism past and present; library burning as censorship. E. J. Gaines. ALA Bul 60:26-7 Ja '66
Vandals. il Sat Eve Post 238:102 My 8 '65

VANDENBERG air force base. See Air bases

VAN DEN BOSCH, Robert
Integrated pest control in California. Bul Atomic Sci 21:22-6 Mr '65

VAN DEN HAAG, Ernest
Analysis, not prescription. Nat R 17:1031-2 N 16 '65
Intelligence or prejudice? questions and answers. Nat R 16:1059-63; 17:102 D 1 '64. F 9 '65
More immigration? Nat R 17:821-2+, 956+ S 21, N 2 '65

VANDEN HEUVEL, Jean
(ed) See Longworth, A. R. Sharpest wit in Washington
(ed) See Steinberg, S. Straight from the hand and mouth of Steinberg

VANDERBEEK, Stan
VanDerBeek: master of animation. R. Christgau. il pors Pop Phot 57:106-11 S '65

VANDERBILT, Amy
Children's manners. por Ladies Home J 82:52 Je '65
Etiquette; questions and answers. See issues of Ladies' home journal

VANDERBILT, Kermit
Last words of E.H. Nation 201:284-5 O 25 '65
Norton and Godkin: launching The nation. Nation 200:165-9 F 15 '65

VANDERBILT family
Marble cottages; the Breakers and Marble House. M. Cable. il Horizon 7:18-27 Autumn '65

VAN DER SMISSEN, Betty
Uncommon professional. por Recreation 58:334-6+ S '65

VANDERVOORT, Paul, 3d
Art on a fence. Sch Arts 64:12-14 My '65
VANDERVOORT, Peter O.
Age of the Orion nebula: with biographical
sketch. Sci Am 212:17, 90-6+ bibliog(p 135)
F '65
VANDER WAL, Mary Claire
India is centuries away. Sat R 48:51-2+ Ag
21 '65
VANDERWICKEN, Peter
Big noise. Esquire 64:38-9+ Jl '65
Liability revolution. Esquire 64:88+ Ag '65
New Stanley hotel. Esquire 63:106 My '65
VAN DEUSEN, Hobart M.
Books in review. Natur Hist 75:6 Ja '66
VANDIVER, Frank
Man in the marble image. Sat R 49:34 Ja 1
'66
VAN DOREN, Mark
Personal note. por Nation 201:35-6 S 20 '65
VAN DOREN, Tandy
Mlle's inside report on summer 1965; young
Caribbean. Mlle 60:211+ Ap '65
VAN DORN, William G.
Tsunami runup: United States-Japan coop-
erative science program. Science 149:566 Jl
30 '65
VANDUSEN, Bruce B.
Depressed areas built to order. Read Digest
86:79-82 My '65
VAN DUSEN, Henry P.
Indonesia today. Christian Cent 82:584-8, 616-
17 My 5-12 '65
VAN DUYN, Mona
Good man; What I want to say; Wish to be
believed; Challenger; poems. Poetry 107:
100-6 N '65
Vision, celebration, and testimony. Poetry
105:264-9 Ja '65
about
Poetry chronicle. R. Howard. Poetry 106:301-3
Jl '65
VAN DYKE, Frank
Medicare: the major defects. Nation 200:697-
700 Je 28 '65
VAN DYKE, Willard
Focus on Willard Van Dyke. pors Pop Phot
56:118-19+ Ap '65
VANES. See Weather vanes
VANESSA; opera. See Barber, S.
VAN GELDER, Richard G.
Books in review. Natur Hist 74:4+ Ap '65
Channel Island skunk. Natur Hist 74:30-5 Ag
'65
VAN HANDEL, Emile, and Lea, A. O.
Medial neurosecretory cells as regulators of
glycogen and triglyceride synthesis. bibliog
Science 149:298-300 Jl 16 '65
VAN HAREN, John E.
Student teaching via closed circuit television.
Sch Arts 65:29-31 O '65
VAN HECKE, Charles O. See Bieck, O. H.
jt. auth.
VAN HOOK, W. M.
Our own dredge proved best. Am City 80:
155+ O '65
VAN HUYSTEE, Robert B. See Cherry, J. H.
jt. auth.
VANILLIN
Vanillin, cis-terpin hydrate, and cis-terpin
as ice nucleators. B. A. Power and R. F.
Power. bibliog Science 148:1088 My 21 '65
VANITY fair (periodical)
Epitaphs for an era; reprints. il Am Heritage
16:112 Ag '65
VAN LAWICK, Jane (Goodall) baroness
New discoveries among Africa's chimpanzees.
pors Nat Geog Mag 128:802-31 D '65
VANN, John Paul
This is all bad news country. il por News-
week 66:40-1 Jl 26 '65
VANN, Sarah K.
Dewey abroad. bibliog pors Wilson Lib Bul
39:550-4 Mr '65
VAN ORDEN, Lucas S. and others
5-Hydroxytryptamine in single neoplastic
mast cells: a microscopic spectrofluoro-
metric study. bibliog Science 148:642-4 Ap
30 '65
VAN OVERBEEK, J. See Crane, J. C. jt. auth.
VAN PATTEN, James J.
Dichotomies in American education. Sch &
Soc 93:474-5 D 11 '65
VANSITTART, Sir Robert Gilbert
None so blind, by I. Colvin. Review
New Repub 153:25-6 O 30 '65. A. Camp-
bell
VAN SLYCK, Philip
Toward a larger western alliance. Sat R
48:37 D 18 '65

VAN STOCKUM, Hilda
How much is too much discipline? Parents
Mag 40:56-7+ Je '65
VAN TIL, William
Five bold ways to attack the dropout prob-
lem. Parents Mag 40:58-9+ Mr '65
VAN VALEN, Leigh, and Sloan, R. E.
Earliest primates. bibliog Science 150:743-5
N 5 '65
—See Sloan, R. E. jt. auth.
VAN VECHTEN, Carl
On words and music. Am Rec G 31:521-2
F '65
about
Carl Van Vechten: memorial album of opera
singers photographs. Opera N 29:14-16 F 13
'65
VAN VLISSINGEN, Henry Louis Fentener
Exile. il por Newsweek 66:56 O 25 '65
VARÈSE, Edgard
Sound of infinity. por Newsweek 66:94+ N
22 '65
Varèse. B. Boretz. Nation 201:426-7 N 29 '65
VARGAS, Enrique
Jet-age malady. Sat R 48:18-19 My 29 '65
VARGAS, Jesús V.
Sukarno makes trouble in the Philippines. O.
S. Villadolid. Reporter 33:22-4 Ag 12 '65
VARGAS, Manuela
Back to the singing cafés il por Time 85:73
Je 18 '65
Brief biography. S. Goodman. pors Dance
Mag 39:50-1 S '65
VARIATION (biology) See Mutation (biology)
VARIEGATION
Genetic mosaicism in adult mice of quad-
riparental lineage. B. Mintz. bibliog il Sci-
ence 148:1232-3 My 28 '65
VARIG airlines. See Airlines—Brazil
VARNER, Velma V.
Beni Montresor. Horn Bk 41:374-9 Ag '65
VARNEY, Joyce E.
Get those people out of my cellar! Read
Digest 86:244-6+ F '65
VARNISH and varnishing
See also
Furniture—Finishing
VASES
Tin can vases. K. Seibel. il Farm J 89:66 Je
'65
VASIL, Vimla, and Hildebrandt, A. C.
Differentiation of tobacco plants from single,
isolated cells in microcultures. bibliog Sci-
ence 150:889-92 N 12 '65
Growth and tissue formation from single,
isolated tobacco cells in microculture. bib-
liog Science 147:1454-5 Mr 19 '65
VASSALLI, Pierre. See Mach, B. jt. auth.
VASSEUR, Jacques
Maman's boy. il por Time 86:46-7 N 19 '65
VASTA, Florence Evan
Soul of Antigua. Negro Hist Bul 28:131+ Mr
'65
VATICAN
Story of the Vatican and its wealth. il U S
News 58:70-2 Ap 26 '65
Vatican wealth. America 112:416-17 Mr 27
'65
Vatican's wealth. il Time 85:68+ F 26 '65
See also
Catholic church
Catholic church—Relations (diplomatic)
Archives
Vatican archives. R. H. Schmandt. Common-
weal 82:190-1 Ap 30 '65
Library
Robbing Peter; theft of Vatican treasures.
il Newsweek 66:59 D 6 '65
VATICAN council, 1869-1870
Council and reform. E. Engberg. Common-
weal 83:171+ N 12 '65
VATICAN council, 2d
And after the council? H. Kung. Common-
weal 82:619-23 S 3 '65; Reply. A. Poulin,
jr. 83:76-7 O 22 '65
Another view of Vatican II: short sighted
view of C. Stanley Lowell, P.O.A.U.
director. Christian Cent 82:1596 D 29 '65
Catholic aggiornamento. O. Hastings. il Re-
porter 33:19-22 D 30 '65
Christian in the world; drafting of a final
conciliar text on the church in the modern
world. America 112:350 Mr 13 '65
Church tomorrow, by G. M. Tavard. Review
Cath World 201:269-70 Jl '65. D. R. Campion
Conciliar Rome. J. J. Wright; J. Cogley;
G. E. Carter. America 112:418-25 Mr 27 '65

VATICAN council, 2d—Continued

Conciliar Rome; laymen at the council. J. Cogley. America 112:420-2 Mr 27 '65; Reply. J. J. Norris. 112:594 Ap 24 '65

Council and the bomb. J. Douglass. Commonweal 81:725-8 Mr 5 '65

Council condemnation of communism? America 113:561 N 13 '65

Council: end or beginning? tr. by H. R. Bronk, H. Kung. Commonweal 81:631-7 F 12 '65; Reply. America 112:279-80 F 27 '65

Council ends. G. Baum. Commonweal 83: 402-5 Ja 7 '66

Council ends its epochal task; with report by J. K. Jessup. il Life 59:22-9+ D 17 '65

Council of new beginnings. America 113:771-2 D 18 '65

Council, the church and the human person; end of session observations. J. B. Sheerin. Cath World 202:199-203 Ja '66

Declaration on religious liberty. F. Canavan. America 113:635-6 N 20 '65

Dialogue on the way, ed. by G. A. Lindbeck. Review
  Cath World 202:116-17 N '65. J. B. Sheerin

Ecumenical escalation; concerning the schema De oecumenismo. R. M. Brown. Commonweal 81:787-90 Mr 19 '65

Ecumenical publication of Vatican council documents. il Pub W 189:68 Ja 10 '66

Ecumenicity of Vatican II. America 114:8 Ja 1 '66

An end to the shame? Christian and anti-Semitism. Commonweal 82:237-8 My 14 '65

Five decrees. G. Baum. Commonweal 83:237-40 N 26 '65

How the Jews changed Catholic thinking. J. Roddy. il Look 30:18-23 Ja 25 '66

How Vatican II turned the church toward the world; Time essay. Time 86:24-5 D 17 '65

Imperious ecumenism. Christian Cent 82: 1499-500 D 8 '65

Impressions of the council. M. G. McGrath. America 113:182-3 Ag 21 '65

Irrelevance of Vatican II. L. Baldwin. Cath World 201:260-3 Jl '65

Letter from the council. R. E. Tracy. America 113:494-5 O 30 '65

New Constitution on the church: a new approach. F. X. Murphy. Cath World 200: 346-53 Mr '65

On changes in the church. America 113:150 Ag 14 '65

Our 100th anniversary and the new era of the Holy Spirit; analysis of the Vatican council's Constitution on the church. J. B. Sheerin. Cath World 201:11-14 Ap '65

Outsider in the Vatican, by F. Franck. Review
  America 113:502+ O 30 '65. J. A. Hardon
  Commonweal 83:318 D 10 '65. D. R. Campion

Papacy, the episcopacy, and collegiality, by W. Bertrams. Review
  Commonweal 82:360-1 Je 4 '65. P. E. Sigmund

Pope is clearly worried; warns of danger threatening Catholic orthodoxy. America 113:177 Ag 21 '65

Postscript on the council. R. E. Tracy. America 114:40 Ja 8 '66

Price of freedom. America 112:513+ Ap 17 '65

Protestant surveys schema thirteen; The church in the modern world. C. Nelson. Cath World 201:394-9 S '65

Punctures balloon words; Lukas Vischer, observer at the Vatican council. C. Northcott. Christian Cent 82:134 F 3 '65

Reflections on Vatican II: Christianity in a secularized world. A. Lunn. il Nat R 18:19-21 Ja 11 '66

Religious liberty: study in doctrinal development. B. S. Crittenden. Cath World 200: 354-5+ Mr '65

Reporting session four; personal details of reporters. P. E. O'Keefe. America 113:19 Jl 3 '65

Revolution for Christmas. E. J. Hughes. Newsweek 66:11 D 27 '65

Second Vatican council and the new Catholicism, by G. C. Berkouwer. Review
  Commonweal 8:572-3 Ag 6 '65. G. H. Tavard

Some of the Pope's problems. A. L. Moats. Nat R 17:367 My 4 '65

Two interventions on behalf of religious liberty. J. C. Heenan; J. Beran. Cath World 202:176-7 D '65

Uses of ambiguity; schema on revelation and the Declaration on religious liberty. il Time 86:78 N 5 '65

Vatican council ends: reform on borrowed time. F. E. Cartus. Harper 231:100-3+ S '65; Reply. T. N. Davis. America 113:inside cover S 11 '65

Vatican II and responsible parenthood. R. Fagley. Christian Cent 82:332-3 Mr 17 '65

Vatican II & the Jews. F. E. Cartus; discussion. Commentary 39:31-2+ Je '65

Vatican II and U.S. peace aims. America 113: 701 D 4 '65

Vatican II's test. Newsweek 66:55-6 S 20 '65

Vatican's dilemma. Christian Cent 82:859-60 Jl 7 '65

What has the council done? tr. by J. Dwyer and H. Bronk. H. Kung. il Commonweal 83:461-8 Ja 21 '66

What the council did. il Newsweek 66:60+ D 20 '65

While the cable editor slept; false story about council and Jews. America 113:67 Jl 17 '65

3d session

Catholic revolution; authority of bishops and supremacy of the pope. J. Roddy. il Look 29:21-7 F 9 '65; Reply. America 112:213 F 13 '65

Declaration on the Jews. America 113:5-6 Jl 3 '65

Failure of session three. R. E. Tracy. America 112:284-6 F 27 '65

Less ecumenism, please. Time 85:74 Mr 12 '65

Lonely pope or first of the brethren? H. A. Oberman. Christian Cent 82:835-7 Je 30 '65

Third session, by X. Rynne. Review
  America 113:166-8 Ag 14 '65. D. R. Campion
  Cath World 202:249-50 Ja '66. C. L. Palms

4th session

American princes of the church. G. Zimmermann. il Look 29:24-8+ Ag 24 '65

Balancing act. D. Peerman. Christian Cent 82:1534-5 D 15 '65

Belgium's apostle of working youth; concerning Cardinal Cardijns speech. America 113:455 O 23 '65

Council calls for change; On the adaptation and renovation of the religious life. America 113:559 N 13 '65

Council: fourth session; symposium. il Commonweal 82:685-96 S 24 '65

Council, the popes and peace. R. A. Graham. America 113:365-7 O 2 '65

Debate on schema thirteen. America 113:390 O 9 '65

Decree on religious life. L. M. Örsy. America 114:12-13+ Ja 1 '66

Dialogue in the church clarified. America 113:662-3 N 27 '65

Early report from Rome and the council. R. E. Tracy. America 113:330+ S 25 '65

Ecumenical council; address, September 15, 1965. Paul VI. Vital Speeches 31:738-41 O 1 '65

Final days of the second Vatican council. America 113:255 S 11 '65

Final session: off to a good start. G. Baum. Commonweal 83:52-5 O 15 '65

Fourth session. Time 86:74 S 10 '65

Freud and man in Rome. C. G. Pepper. il Newsweek 66:95 O 11 '65

From atheism to analysis; Father Pedro Arrupe's speech. Time 86:70 O 8 '65

How life will be different for Catholics. il U S News 59:52-3 D 20 '65

Innovation at Vatican II; fourth and probably final session. il Newsweek 66:62 S 27 '65

Jesuit general's speech at the Vatican council. America 113:429-30 O 16 '65

Jews absolved; and other decisions. Newsweek 66:65 O 25 '65

Letter from the council. R. E. Tracy. il America 113:364, 397-9, 432-3, 566-7, 706, 774-5 O 2-16, N 13, D 4, 18 '65

Letter from Vatican City. X. Rynne. New Yorker 41:135-6+ S 11; 34-6+ D 25 '65

Mood for the council. America 113:278 S 18 '65

More major changes in Catholic beliefs. U S News 59:12 N 8 '65

On the modern world; council discussion of schema 13 and of the Jews. G. Baum. il Commonweal 83:117-20 O 29 '65

Options at the fourth session. Christian Cent 82:1147-8 S 22 '65

Peace, priests and the missions. G. Baum. Commonweal 83:175-8 N 12 '65

Placet! Christian Cent 82:1563-4 D 22 '65

Pope Paul: liberal, conservative, or compromiser? U S News 59:19 S 27 '65

Pope's keynote; synod of bishops. America 113:358 O 2 '65

Protestant hopes for the fourth session. J. B. Sheerin. Cath World 202:5-9 O '65

VATICAN council, 2d—4th session—*Continued*
Religious liberty moves forward. J. B. Sheerin. Cath World 202:70-3 N '65; Reply with rejoinder. Marcellus. 202:194 Ja '66
Reluctant revolutionary. il Time 86:62-4+ S 24 '65
Statement on the Jews: an inadequate document. D. Polish. Christian Cent 82:1475-7 D 1 '65; Reply. A. B. Williams. 83:84-5 Ja 19 '66
Those latest council decrees. America 113: 518-19 N 6 '65
Vatican City; progress report. R. E. Tracy. America 113:461 O 23 '65
Vatican II: the final stretch. America 113: 486 O 30 '65
Vote against prejudice; declaration accepted by Vatican council. il Time 86:61 O 22 '65
See also
Religious liberty

VAUDABLE, Louis
I'm going to Maxim's; interview, ed. by P. Dragadze. il pors Life 60:39-42 Ja 7 '66

VAUDEVILLE
Broads and baggy pants; This was burlesque on Broadway. il Newsweek 65:82 Mr 29 '65
Comic; This was burlesque. New Yorker 41: 37-9 Ap 17 '65
Life theater review; This was burlesque. T. Prideaux. Life 58:18 Ap 23 '65
Vaudeville ritual. J. K. Hutchens. Sat R 48:33 N 27 '65

VAUGHAN, Bill
Song of the open road map; excerpt from Bird thou never wert. Read Digest 87:190B-190C Ag '65

VAUGHAN, Denis
Schubert symphonies. Hi Fi 15:60-3 O '65
They shall have music. H. Kupferberg. il Atlan 217:112-13 Ja '66

VAUGHAN, Richard P.
Psychotherapeutic abortion. America 113:436-8 O 16 '65

VAUGHAN, Roger
How much can you take? Sat Eve Post 238: 32-4+ My 22 '65
Priest vs. priest as a strike disrupts a university. Life 60:30B-30C Ja 21 '66

VAUGHN, Jack Hood
Housing and urban development in Latin America; address, June 14, 1965. Dept State Bul 53:66-70 Jl 12 '65
Review of U.S. policy in Latin America; report, September 10, 1965. Dept State Bul 53:548-9 O 4 '65
U.S. trade policy in Latin America; statement, September 10, 1965. Dept State Bul 53:559-67 O 4 '65

about
Field trip. il por Time 86:41 S 3 '65
New man in Rio. il por Newsweek 66:48-9 N 29 '65
Peace corps approach. por Time 85:41 F 26 '65

VAUGHN, Robert Francis
Man from U.N.C.L.E. D. Freeman. pors Sat Eve Post 238:76+ Je 19 '65

VAULTING (sport)
Heights school; Earl Warren senior high school, Downey, Calif. il Newsweek 65:98 My 24 '65

VAULTS (architecture)
Ingenuity in building an elliptical roof. Arch Rec 138:177-8 Ag '65

VAVREK, Bernard
Book catalog: one step backward? por Wilson Lib Bul 40:269-70 N '65

VAWTER, Bruce
New New Testament. por Cath World 201: 290-5 Ag '65

VAZZANO, Stephen
Stomping on the Savoy. por Newsweek 67: 46 Ja 3 '66

VEAL
See also
Cookery—Meat

VEALE, Tom G.
Bournonville preserved. Dance Mag 39:52-3+ Ag '65

VECELLIO, Tiziano. See Titian

VEECK, Bill, and Linn, Edward
Hustler's handbook; excerpts. por (cover) Sports Illus 22:87-9+ My 17; 40-2+ My 24; 50-2+ My 31; 32-4+ Je 7; 48-50+ Je 14 '65

VEGA, Garcilaso de la, el Inca. See Garcilaso de la Vega

VEGETABLE arrangements. See Fruits, vegetables, etc. in decoration

VEGETABLE gardening
Answers to vegetable and garden questions. B. F. Vance. Suc Farm 63:114+ F '65
Bigger profits with plastic tunnels. B. Hardy. il Farm J 90:52H Ja '66

Fall garden notes; some things to do before winter. B. Brinhart. il Pop Gard 16:8+ S '65
Gardening inside a cage; protection from birds and animals. il Sunset 134:287 My '65
Kitchen gardener. See issues of Flower grower, the home garden magazine
Paul's garden. P. Mawicke. il Flower Grower 52:34-5 Je '65
Plant now; Cook later; with recipes. M. Kaytor and J. Peter. il Look 29:51-3 My 4 '65
September's the time to plant cole crops. il Sunset 135:184-5 S '65
When a cook grows her own; baby carrots and petit peas. il Sunset 134:266-7 Mr '65
See also
Greenhouses
Truck farming

VEGETABLE oyster. See Salsify

VEGETABLES
For 1966. il Horticulture 44:18-21+ Ja '66
New fruits and vegetables for '66. G. Logsdon. il Farm J 90:60 Ja '66
New kinds of vegetables for your garden. P. F. Frese. Pop Gard 16:55 Mr '65
Newer vegetables to grow and freeze. S. Munson. il Farm J 89:101-2+ Ap '65
See also
Cookery—Vegetables
Vegetable gardening
also names of vegetables, e.g. Tomatoes

Harvesting
Time to pick vegetables. E. F. Steffek. il Horticulture 43:30-1+ Je '65

VEGETABLES, Canned
See also
Green giant company

VEGETABLES, Frozen
Boil-in-the-bag vegetables, with butter sauce. il Consumer Rep 30:334-5 Jl '65

VEGETATION
Preserving vegetation in parks and wilderness. E. C. Stone. bibliog il Science 150: 1261-7 D 3 '65

VEINS
Blood-flow relation between hepatic artery and portal vein. J. L. Ternberg and H. R. Butcher, jr. bibliog il Science 150:1030-1 N 19 '65

VELA hotel nuclear detection satellite. See Atomic bombs—Testing, Detection of

VELACUMANTUS australiss. See Snails

VELARDE, Pablita
Pablita Velarde: Pubelo painter. W. T. Le Viness. il por Am Artist 29:40-5+ Ap '65

VELASCO, Marcos, and Lindsley, D. B.
Role of orbital cortex in regulation of thalamocortical electrical activity. bibliog Science 149:1375-7 S 17 '65

VELAZQUEZ, Carlos Maria
Some legal aspects of the colonial problem in Latin America; address, April 10, 1965; with questions and answers. bibliog f Ann Am Acad 360:110-19 Jl '65

VELDE, Paul
Books; themes in Shadow and act. Commonweal 81:674-6 F 19 '65
China on film. Commonweal 82:535-6 Jl 23 '65
Master builder; poem. Commonweal 83:217 N 19 '65

VELIA, Italy
Arch that was Grecian for the road that was Roman; Greek arches found in Elea. il Time 86:47 Jl 9 '65

VELIE, Lester
Come back to the work force, mother! Read Digest 87:01-2+ S '65
Health careers unlimited. Read Digest 87: 108-12 Ag '65
How to choose your job, and land it: questions and answers. Read Digest 87:140-3 N '65
Should you see a career doctor? Read Digest 88:112-17 Ja '66
Where the jobs are. Read Digest 86:78-82 F; 70-5 Ap; 251-2+ My; 151-2+ Je '65

VELLECOUR, Josy
Josy and the king. il Newsweek 67:41 Ja 24 '66

VELLOSO, Wilson
Alliance comes of age. Américas 17:1-5 F '65

VENDING machines
From bubble gum to vitamin pills. il Consumer Rep 31:7 Ja '66

VENEERS and veneering
Wood: what the new flooring, paneling and furniture can do for a room! D. Popplestone and D. Jordan. il Bet Hom & Gard 43:50-63 My '65

VENEREAL diseases
AMA and that disease; campaign to eradicate VD. D. Sanford. New Repub 153:10 S 18 '65
Disease that Dr Kildare couldn't cure. J. Mitford. McCalls 92:102-3+ S '65
Do you know the facts about VD? Todays Health 43:29 D '65
Faith and morals. America 112:699 My 15 '65
Price of prudery. Nation 200:406 Ap 19 '65
VD epidemic. Newsweek 66:80 S 13 '65
Venereal disease international problem. Sci N L 87:217 Ap 3 '65
Venereal disease: plague of our atomic age. N. Shafer. Todays Health 43:92 S '65
Venereal disease: why and where it flourishes; with chart. U S News 59:12 S 20 '65
Venereal epidemic: now urgent city problem. U S News 59:12 S 13 '65
Why the rise in teen-age venereal disease? G. E. Maxwell. il Todays Health 43:18-23+ S '65
See also
Gonorrhea
Syphilis

VENETIAN blinds. See Blinds
VENEZIA, Mike
Bugged. Sports Illus 22:16 My 31 '65
VENEZUELA
Political experiment in Venezuela. R. J. Alexander. Cur Hist 49:336-41+ D '65
View from Caracas. R. Leoni. For Affairs 43:639-46 Jl '65
See also
Angel Falls
Ciudad Guayana
Guayana
Guerrillas—Venezuela
Political parties—Venezuela
Regional planning—Venezuela
Research—Venezuela
Trials—Venezuela

Description and travel
Fastest way to the other side of time. R. Joseph. il Esquire 65:98+ Ja '66
Travel notes. R. Joseph. Esquire 65:32+ Ja '66

Politics and government
Cuba's brazen blueprint for subversion. K. O. Gilmore. Read Digest 87:67-75 Ag '65
Democratic revolution in Venezuela. R. J. Alexander. Ann Am Acad 358:150-8 Mr '65
Letter from Caracas. B. Taper. il New Yorker 41:101-2+ Mr 6 '65
Questionable coup. Newsweek 65:55 Ap 26 '65
With a velvet glove. il Time 85:42+ Mr 19 '65

VENICE
Architecture
Open hand in Venice; Le Corbusier's design for municipal hospital to replace the old hospital of Sts John and Paul. il Time 85:82 Ap 30 '65
Venice, a sinking city. P. Gazzola. il UNESCO Courier 18:11-13 Ja '65

City planning
Venice, a sinking city. P. Gazzola. il UNESCO Courier 18:11-13 Ja '65

Description
Opera-lover's guide to Venice. M. J. Matz. il Opera N 30:14-17 D 11 '65
Venice: no one asks, gondola? H. R. Lottman. il Sat R 49:47+ Ja 1 '66

Music
Opera-lover's guide to Venice. M. J. Matz. il Opera N 30:14-17 D 11 '65
VENICE biennale. See Art—Exhibitions; Music festivals—Italy
VENNEWITZ, Leila
(tr) See Böll, H. Like a bad dream
VENOM
Ice aids snakebite cure. Sci N L 88:99 Ag 14 '65
Stress and the toxicity of venoms. H. L. Stahnke. bibliog il Science 150:1456-7 D 10 '65
VENTANA wild area. See Wilderness areas
VENTILATION
See also subhead Heating and ventilation under various subjects, e.g. Barns and stables—Heating and ventilation
VENTILATORS
There's more than one way to cool a kitchen. il McCalls 92:44+ Jl '65

Window fans. il Consumer Rep 30:325-30 Jl '65

VENTOSA JIMÉNEZ, Josefa
Downfall of the man with the dog. M. Acoca. il Life 58:72C-72D Ap 30 '65
VENTRICLE. See Heart
VENTURA, Anita
June Schwarcz: electroforming and enamel. Craft Horiz 25:36-7+ N '65
VENTURA, Frank L.
Data-processing system you can bank on. por Am City 81:114+ Ja '66
VENTURI, Ken
Case of the white hands. il Newsweek 65:64 My 3 '65
Renewed hope for a special pair of hands. G. Crozier. il por Sports Illus 23:48-50 Jl 12 '65
Warm hopes for a man with a cold touch. G. S. Brown. por Sports Illus 22:64-7 Mr 15 '65
VENUS (planet)
Flight of Mariner II changes theories about planet Venus. T. D. Nicholson. il Natur Hist 75:52-4 Ja '66
Mountains of Venus. Sci Am 213:40 D '65
New radar studies of Venus. il Sky & Tel 29:356-7 Je '65
Parting the veil of Venus. Time 86:53 Ag 13 '65
See also
Space flight to Venus

Atmosphere
Molecular oxygen in the atmosphere of Venus. G. S. Mumford. il Sky & Tel 30:278 N '65
Surface conditions on Venus. G. S. Mumford. 3d. il Sky & Tel 29:156 Mr '65
VENUS flower basket. See Sponges
VENUS probe. See Space probes
VENZA, Jac
Educational TV loves dance. por Dance Mag 39:43-5+ S '65
VERA foundation, incorporated
Freeing people & police. Time 86:47 Ag 20 '65
VERANDAS. See Porches
VERDI, Giuseppe
Aïda. Criticism
Opera N il por 29:17-20 Mr 20 '65
Opera N il 29:24-5 Mr 20 '65
Sat R 49:30 Ja 15 '66
Almost terrifying dynamic contrasts: Verdi from DGG. J. Diether. Am Rec G 32:74-5 S '65
Angel's Il Trovatore. J. Maclain. il Am Rec G 31:1048-50 Jl '65
Anna Moffo: RCA Victor's Luisa Miller. P. L. Miller. Am Rec G 32:118-19+ O '65
Birgit Nilsson as London's Lady Macbeth. P. L. Miller. Am Rec G 31:780-1+ My '65
Don Carlo. Criticism
New Yorker 41:200 O 16 '65
Opera N 30:18-21 D 11 '65
Opera N 30:35 Ja 15 '66
Sat R 48:54 O 23 '65
Sat R 48:69 D 4 '65
Ernani. Criticism
Opera N 29:24-5 Ap 10 '65
Opera N il 29:8-11 Ap 10 '65
Opera N il 29:17-20 Ap 10 '65
La forza del destino. Criticism
Opera N 29:24-5 F 6 '65
Opera N il 29:17-20 F 6 '65
La forza del destino. P. L. Miller. Am Rec G 31:798-9+ My '65
Kindling word; Verdi as a man of the theater. E. Downes. il Opera N 29:24-5 Mr 20 '65
Luisa Miller in new stereo dress. C. L. Osborne. il Hi Fi 15:84-5 N '65
On records: Aïda; Rigoletto. Opera N 29:34 Mr 20 '65
On records: Don Carlo. Opera N 30:34 D 11 '65
On records: Ernani; Macbeth. Opera N 29:34 Ap 10 '65
On records: La forza del destino. Opera N 29:34 F 6 '65
On records: La forza del destino. Opera N 30:30 N 20 '65
On records: Luisa Miller; Il Trovatore; Four sacred pieces. Opera N 30:34 D 4 '65
On records: Il Trovatore. Opera N 30:44 O 23 '65
Outlaw as hero. H. Peyre. il Opera N 29:8-11 Ap 10 '65
Problem child for both Schiller and Verdi. Don Carlo. L. C. McGinn. Opera N 30:24-5 D 11 '65
Il Trovatore. Criticism
Opera N il 30:18-20 D 4 '65
Opera N il 30:24-5 D 4 '65
Two new recordings of Rigoletto. P. L. Miller. Am Rec G 31:561-3 F '65

VERDI, Giuseppe—*Continued*
Verdi's gardener; interview, ed. by M. J. Matz. L. Grandini. Opera N 29:28 Mr 20 '65
VERDIER, Philippe
Brothers Huaud and their enameled Swiss watches. Antiques 88:829-33 D '65
VERDON, René
Adieu to pease porridge. Time 86:13 D 24 '65
Rhubarb in the kitchen. il por Newsweek 66:24 D 27 '65
VERGA, Bob
Lonely and lively hours of a star; photographs. J. Drake. Sports Illus 23:68-75 D 6 '65
VERHOOGEN, John
Paleomagnetism. Science 147:1060-1 F 26 '65
VERHULST, Henry L.
What do you know about accidental poisoning? PTA Mag 59:29-31 Mr '65
VERITY, Calvin William, 1917-
Businessmen in the news. por Fortune 72:79 N '65
VERMONT
See also
Booksellers and bookselling—Vermont
Fishing—Vermont
Hunting—Vermont
Music festivals—Vermont

Capitol
Vermont statehouse and its furniture. W. Ames. il Antiques 88:200-4 Ag '65

Economic conditions
Waiting for realty, death of a small town. D. Wakefield. Nation 201:92-7 S 20 '65

Historic houses, etc.
Vermont statehouse and its furniture. W. Ames. il Antiques 88:200-4 Ag '65
See also
Middlebury, Vt.—Historic houses, etc.

Politics and government
Themselves again? Time 86:26 D 3 '65
Vermont: first straws for '66. U S News 59: 74 D 13 '65
Vermont House gets remodeled; new House of representatives. V. Maerki. il Reporter 33:38-9 O 7 '65
VERNON, Jackie
Dying pan. por Time 86:54+ S 10 '65
VERONICA; drama. See White, J.
VERRETT-CARTER, Shirley
Four Americans. M. Mayer. Esquire 63:36+ Ap '65
VERRUSO, Joseph
Tuning fork as an electronic component. Electr World 73:37-9 My '65
VERSACE, Humbert Roque
Only anguish. il por Newsweek 66:48 O 11 '65
VERSAILLES, Palace of
Letter from Paris; opening of rooms authentically restored to the times and styles of Louis XIV, XV, and XVI. Genêt. New Yorker 41:88+ S 4 '65
VERSE. See Poetry
VERSIFICATION
See also
Poetics
VÉRTES, László
Lunar calendar from the Hungarian upper paleolithic. bibliog Science 149:855-6 Ag 20 '65
VERTICAL density currents. See Hydrodynamics
VERTICAL improved mail. See Mail handling
VERTICAL take-off and landing airplanes. See Airplanes, Vertical take-off and landing
VERTOL division. See Boeing company—Vertol division
VERWOERD, Hendrik Frensch
South Africa bars American Negroes. New Repub 153:8-9 Jl 10 '65
Verwoerd tightens the screws. A. Delius. il Reporter 33:29-31 Jl 1 '65
VERY high frequency radio transmission. See Radio transmission
VERY high frequency radiophone. See Radio telephone on ships, boats, etc.
VERY high frequency television stations. See Television stations
VERY rich woman; drama. See Gordon, R.
VESALIUS, Andreas
Vesalius commemoration at Brussels; report on international celebration of his fourth centennial. W. F. H. M. Mommaerts and C. D. O'Malley. Science 147:1603-5 Mr 26 '65

VESELL, Elliot S.
Lactate dehydrogenase isozyme patterns of human platelets and bovine lens fibers. bibliog Science 150:1735-7 D 24 '65
Lactate dehydrogenase isozymes: substrate inhibition in various human tissues. bibliog Science 150:1590-3 D 17 '65
Polymorphism of human lactate dehydrogenase isozymes. bibliog Science 148:1103-5 My 21 '65
VESEY, Denmark
Insurrection in South Carolina: the turbulent world of Denmark Vesey, by J. Lofton. Review
Negro Hist Bul 28:202+ My '65. E. M. Lewis
VESSELS, Armored. See Armored vessels
VEST, Eugene B.
Chicago's newest showcase: U. of Illinois bookstore. Pub W 189:32-5 Ja 3 '66
VESTAL, David
Decomposition. Pop Phot 56:82-3+ Je '65
Look without prejudging; interview, ed. by J. Deschin. por Pop Phot 57:34+ N '65
VESTAL, N.Y.
Inherit the wind production barred in upstate New York; high school. Library J 90:5486 D 15 '65
VESTMENTS. See Church vestments
VETERINARIANS
Jobs for kids who love animals. il Changing T 20:39-41 Ja '66
VETERINARY medicine
See also
Veterinarians
VETERANS. See Service men, Discharged
VETERANS administration. See United States—Veterans administration
VETERANS administration hospitals. See United States—Veterans administration hospitals
VETERANS of foreign wars
Mr Ottinger sees it through. Nation 200:518 My 17 '65
VETERANS pensions. See Pensions, Military
VETERINARY first aid
First aid a pet may need. il Good H 161: 175 O '65
VETERINARY medicine
Veterinarian tells: how to treat fresh feedlot cattle. W. Schaulis. il Suc Farm 63: 46+ S '65
Veterinary helps. J. W. Bailey. See issues of Successful farming
When your pet needs a vet in a hurry; emergency medical services for pets. il Good H 160:181 Mr '65
See also
Domestic animal—Vaccination
Veterinary first aid
VETERINARY surgery
Sex and the single bull; operation performed on prize bull, Lindertis Evulse. il Newsweek 66:53 Ag 2 '65
VETO
See also
Presidents—United States—Powers and duties
VEXLER, Erica
(ed) See Johnson, L. B. Luci Baines Johnson
VIA VENETO. See Rome (city)—Streets
VIAGER. See Real property—France
VIAN, Boris
Le goûter des généraux. Criticism
New Yorker 41:222-3 O 16 '65
VIARDOT-GARCIA, Pauline
Price of genius, by A. Fitzlyon. Review
Am Rec G por 32:314-16 D '65. R. Ellsworth
Opera N 30:31 D 25 '65, D. Warren
VIBRATION
Itch and vibration. R. Melzack and B. Schecter. bibliog il Science 147:1047-8 F 26 '65
VIBRATION absorbers
Inertial platform performance improved by internal isolator. il Aviation W 83:87 O 4 '65
VIBRATORS
See also
Multivibrators
VIBRIOSIS. See Abortion, Vibrionic
VICAS, George
Sense of the past. il por Newsweek 65:70 My 24 '65
VICE
See also
Prostitution

VICE-PRESIDENTS
United States
American roulette: the history and dilemma of the vice presidency, by D. Young. Review
New Repub 153:26-7 Jl 3 '65. G. W. Johnson
Author's view on how Johnson was chosen; excerpt from A thousand days. A. M. Schlesinger, jr. il Life 59:68-9 Jl 16 '65
Backup man winds up Congress and has a few tense hours. R. B. Stolley. il Life 59:38-42A O 22 '65
Bob dropped, Hubert kept dangling; excerpts from Making of the President-1964. T. H. White. il Life 59:70-2+ Jl 2 '65
Can you name three former VP's? E. T. Folliard. America 113:363 O 2 '65
Go-between's memo on the wild day L.B.J. was named Vice President. Life 58:90 Je 18 '65
Happy understudy. H. Brandon. Sat R 48:16-17 My 8 '65
Home for Hubert; official residence for the veep. il Time 86:30-1 O 1 '65
Humphrey: a strong no. 2. il Bsns W p 175-6+ N 13 '65
I enjoy it; Humphrey's first seven weeks in office. il Newsweek 65:28-9 Mr 15 '65
Making of the veep; controversy over how L. B. Johnson was chosen. il Newsweek 66:23 Jl 26 '65
Plan for a stand-in president. U S News 59:10 Jl 19 '65
25th amendment, we hope: replacing a disabled president. Life 59:6 Jl 16 '65
View from Capitol hill. L. W. Koenig. il Sat R 48:32 Jl 10 '65
What's new about the new Hubert Humphrey. W. Bowen. il Fortune 72:142-5+ Ag '65

VICENTE, Esteban
Importance of being casual. N. Edgar. il Art N 64:44-5 D '65

VICKERS, Harry Franklin
Univac isn't a business to jump in and out of. S. H. Brown. por Fortune 71:120-3+ Ap '65

VICKERS, James
Safari for science. G. E. Maxwell. il pors Todays Health 43:22-31 N '65

VICKERS, Jon
Thinking man's tenor. R. Jacobson. por Opera N 30:12-13 D 11 '65

VICKERY, Thomas R.
U.S. keeps the 5.5 Gold cup. Motor B 116:50-1+ D '65

VICKSBURG, Miss.
Lighting
Vicksburg's 100 per cent relighting program. J. D. Holland. il Am City 80:127 S '65

VICKSBURG, Miss. hydraulics testing station. See Hydraulic laboratories

VICOS Indians. See Indians of South America—Peru

VICTOR Gruen associates. See Gruen, Victor, associates

VICTORIA, queen of Great Britain
Books. N. Bliven. New Yorker 41:80-4 Jl 10 '65
Dearest child: letters between Queen Victoria and the Princess Royal, ed. by R. Fulford. Review
Sat R il por 48:24 Ap 3 '65. H. Laski
Queen Victoria, by E. Longford. Review
Nat R por 17:109-10+ F 9 '65. S. Leslie
New Repub 152:19-20 Mr 13 '65. J. Epstein
Reporter 32:50+ Ap 8 '65. A. West
Vogue 145:96 Mr 1 '65. J. Stafford
Traitor and a queen. H. M. Hyde. Harper 230:156-8 Mr '65

VICTORIA, British Columbia
Victoria, city of charm; 1966 garden tours. M. Perry. il Flower Grower 52:44 D '65

VICTORIA and Albert museum, South Kensington
First for Fleet Street's cameras; acquisition of contemporary press photos. M. R. Weiss. il Sat R 48:122-3 S 18 '65
Galleries of nineteenth-century art in the Victoria and Albert museum. J. F. Hayward. il Antiques 87:690-5 Je '65

VICTORIAN furniture. See Furniture, Victorian

VIDAL, Gore
Byzantine mosaic. Reporter 33:54-7 O 7 '65
Vidal to Vidal: on misusing the past. Harper 231:162-4 O '65

VIDAURRE, Antonio Alvarez. See Alvarez Vidaurre, A.
VIDEO records
Grooves of this record contain 400 pictures and sound; Phonovid. W. F. Wilson. il Pop Phot 58:116-17+ Ja '66
VIDEO tape recorders and recording
Astrovision; an in-flight entertainment system. L. C. Keene and T. E. Pierson. il Electr World 73:42-3+ Mr '65
At last! a home TV tape recorder kit! H. F. Kutschbach. il Pop Electr 22:44+ Ap '65
At last: home videotape. Dance Mag 39:19 S '65
Home video tape recorders. W. A. Stocklin. Electr World 74:6 N '65
Home video tape recording, when? W. G. Salm. il Pop Electr 23:63-7 D '65
Home videocorder works like a real TV studio. R. Benrey. il Pop Sci 187:68-9 N '65
PS builds a TV tape recorder. R. M. Benrey. il Pop Sci 187:102-6 Ag '65
Tape home movies for your TV screen. L. Steckler. il Pop Mech 124:92-5 N '65
Tape-it-yourself TV. il Life 59:57-8+ S 17 '65
Taping untapped markets. Time 85:90+ F 19 '65
Three days with Sony's home videotape recorder. W. F. Wilson. il Pop Phot 57:82-3+ O '65
Town that saw itself on a home videotape recorder. W. F. Wilson. il Pop Phot 57:146-7 N '65
Video tape: tomorrow's 35-mm? B. Pierce. il Pop Phot 57:40-3+ Ag '65

VIDICON. See Television cameras

VIEBROCK, Herbert J. See Flowers, E. C. jt. auth.

VIEHMEYER, Glenn
Evergreens for the Plains. Horticulture 43:18+ Ag '65

VIENNA
Airports
Vienna airport plans expansion program. il Aviation W 82:38-9 F 1 '65

History
Siege of Vienna, by J. Stoye. Review
Sat R 48:41 S 11 '65. H. C. Wolfe

Music
Vienna. J. Wechsberg. il Opera N 30:32 D 11 '65

VIENNA festival weeks. See Music festivals—Austria

VIENNESE cookery. See Cookery, Austrian
VIENNESE humor. See Humor, Austrian
VIERECK, Peter
Intellectual travelogue. Sat R 48:41-2 D 11 '65
World power through witchcraft. Sat R 48:45-6 Jl 24 '65

VIERTEL, Peter
Redbook dialogue: Deborah Kerr, Peter Viertel and Miguel Domingufn. por Redbook 125:50-1+ My '65

VIET-Report (periodical)
Two views of Viet Nam; new magazines. Time 86:52-3 N 26 '65

VIETNAM
History
That Geneva agreement: how the French got out of Vietnam. B. B. Fall. il N Y Times Mag p28-9+ My 2 '65
Vietnam. F. Hung. bibliog il Focus 16:1-6 D '65
Vietnam year by year; September 1940 to November 1965. Sat R 48:18-19 D 18 '65

VIETNAM (Democratic Republic)
Enemy: 20,000 missions later. C. Koch. il Newsweek 66:44-8 O 11 '65
Inside Hanoi; impressions of J. Cameron and F. Greene after visit and Ho interviews. il Newsweek 66:69 D 20 '65
Uncovered country. il Time 85:30-2 Ap 16 '65
Vietnam background. V. S. Kearney. il America 113:8-11 Jl 3 '65
See also
Communism—Vietnam (Democratic Republic)
Foreign visitors in Vietnam (Democratic Republic)
Guerrillas—Vietnam (Democratic Republic)
Hanoi
Public health—Vietnam (Democratic Republic)
Army
Advance party? PAVN infiltration. il Newsweek 66:23-4 N 29 '65
Back from a Vietcong hellhole in the jungle. A. Okamura. il Life 59:56D-63 Jl 2 '65
Cautionary report on Laos; developments along the Ho Chi Minh trail. D. Warner. il Reporter 33:35-8 D 2 '65

VIETNAM (Democratic Republic)—Army—
Continued

Getting to know the enemy. D. Warner. il Reporter 33:14-17 D 30 '65

If Ho Chi Minh's army moves south in force—. B. B. Fall. il N Y Times Mag p7+ S 5 '65

Price of victory; Vietcong manpower and materials infiltration methods. D. Warner. il Reporter 33:29-32 D 16 '65

Why reds scorn peace in Vietnam. il U S News 58:55 My 31 '65

Economic conditions

Hard times in North Vietnam: hunger, failures, dissension; excerpts from address, May 13, 1965. P. J. Honey. il U S News 58:56-7 My 31 '65

Here's how North Vietnam is doing in the war; interview, ed. by J. Fromm. P. J. Honey. il U S News 58:40-2 Ap 12 '65

Why war in Vietnam goes on and on. il U S News 59:24-5 Ag 23 '65

Foreign relations

Here's how North Vietnam is doing in the war; interview, ed. by J. Fromm. P. J. Honey. il U S News 58:40-2 Ap 12 '65

Point of no return. W. V. Shannon. Commonweal 8:580-1 Ag 20 '65

Uncle Ho defies Uncle Sam. J. Lacouture. il N Y Times Mag p25+ Mr 28 '65

Why don't they negotiate? Chinese influence. N. Cousins. Sat R 48:24+ D 25 '65

Industries

Vietnam. F. Hung. bibliog il Focus 16:1-6 D '65

Politics and government

Hard times in North Vietnam: hunger failures, dissension; excerpts from address, May 13, 1965. P. J. Honey. il U S News 58:56-7 My 31 '65

Jungle Marxist. il Time 86:24-8 Jl 16 '65

They propagandize peasants, patrol the jungle; French journalist's show how Vietcong operate. il Life 59:64-7 Jl 2 '65

Viet Cong: who are they, what do they want? J. Lacouture. New Repub 152:21-4 Mr 6 '65

Vietnam: a debate. S. Gottlieb; L. Cherne; H. S. Commager. il Sat R 48:16-23+ D 18 '65; Discussion. 49:29 Ja 15 '66

VIETNAM (Republic)

Busy week for Ky and troops. Newsweek 66: 44+ S 20 '65

Defense of freedom in Viet-Nam; address, January 14, 1965. H. K. Johnson. Dept State Bul 52:176-80 F 8 '65

Luong Hoa: village besieged. F. Sully. il Newsweek 66:20-2 Ag 9 '65

This is all bad news country. il Newsweek 66:40-1 Jl 26 '65

Vietnam background. V. S. Kearney. il America 113:8-11 Jl 3 '65

Vietnam: facts and fictions. E. Rabinowitch. Bul Atomic Sci 21:45-8 Je '65; Discussion. 21:23 N '65

Vietnam: problems and progress; address, January 14, 1965. H. K. Johnson. Vital Speeches 31:262-5 F 15 '65

See also
Americans in Vietnam
Camranh Bay
Communism—Vietnam (Republic)
Economic assistance in Vietnam (Republic)
Education—Vietnam (Republic)
Elections—Vietnam (Republic)
Food supply—Vietnam (Republic)
Guerrillas—Vietnam (Republic)
Investments, Foreign (in Vietnam [Republic])
Land tenure—Vietnam (Republic)
Medical relief work—Vietnam (Republic)
Police—Vietnam (Republic)
Saigon
United Nations—Vietnam (Republic)
United States—Armed forces—Forces in Vietnam (Republic)
Women—Vietnam (Republic)
Youth—Vietnam (Republic)

Air force

VNAF effectiveness keyed to leadership. C. Brownlow. il Aviation W 82:30-2 My 10 '65

VNAF seeks means to train own pilots. C. Brownlow. il Aviation W 82:62-3 Je 7 '65

Armed forces

Evaluating the Arvins. il Newsweek 66:34-5 D 20 '65

Our friends, the Buddhists; impending purge of Catholic generals from the South Vietnamese armed forces. America 112:597 Ap 24 '65

See also
Military service, Compulsory—Vietnam (Republic)

Army

How good is Vietnamese army? il U S News 59:55 S 6 '65

Defenses

Defense of freedom in Viet-Nam; address, January 14, 1965. H. K. Johnson. Dept State Bul 52:176-80 F 8 '65

Vietnam: the agonizing reappraisal. B. B. Fall. bibliog f il Cur Hist 48:95-102+ F '65

Weapons: what U.S. is using in Asia. il U S News 58:4+ F 22 '65

Description and travel

Sorry about that. G. C. Scott. il Esquire 64:209-11+ D '65

Economic conditions

Other war in Vietnam; fight against inflation. il U S News 59:32-3 Ag 30 '65

Surfeit of money. il Newsweek 66:30 Ag 23 '65

U.S. winning a battle on Vietnam economy. il Bsns W p30-1 D 4 '65

Vietnam revisited: the big changes. G. Troelstrup. il U S News 59:41 N 15 '65

Viet-Nam: the third face of the war: address, May 13, 1965. L. B. Johnson. Dept State Bul 52:838-41 My 31 '65

Foreign relations

Getting to know them. il Time 86:19 Ag 27 '65

History

Atlantic report. Atlan 215:28+ Mr '65

Historical profile: peace-loving people. il Sr Schol 87:10-13 S 23 '65

Two views of Vietnam; report on books by M. West and B. Fall. P. O'Connor. America 113:240-3 S 4 '65; Reply with rejoinder. B. B. Fall. 113:735 D 11 '65

Industries

Vietnam. F. Hung. bibliog il Focus 16:1-6 D '65

Navy

Death on the river; River assult groups mission in Kien Hoa Province. il Newsweek 66:41 N 1 '65

Politics and government

Addendum to Why Vietnam? a basis for negotiation exists. J. Gittings. Nation 201: 111-15 S 6 '65

American aid to Vietnam. W. R. Fishel. il Cur Hist 49:294-9 N '65

Atlantic report (cont) Atlan 215:28+ Mr '65

Bourgeois gentlemen of Saigon. C. Oglesby. il Nation 201:352-5 N 15 '65

Buddhists weigh in. Newsweek 66:31 Jl 19 '65

Coup, counter-coup. Sr Schol 86:18+ F 11 '65

Coup is dead, long live the coup! D. Warner. Reporter 32:25-6 Mr 11 '65

Coup that failed. il Newsweek 65:21+ Mr 1 '65

Department officers discuss Viet-Nam situation; broadcast over WNEW-TV, New York, on February 7, 1965. W. P. Bundy; J. A. Mendenhall. Dept State Bul 52:291-4 Mr 1 '65

From crisis to crisis in Saigon. il U S News 58:28-9 Mr 8 '65

General is back. Time 85:33B-34 F 5 '65

Go on fighting in Vietnam? interview. H. C. Lodge. il U S News 58:62-7 F 15 '65; Excerpts. 59:66-7 Jl 19 '65

Historical profile: peace-loving people. il Sr Schol 87:10-13 S 23 '65

How democracy returned to Vietnam. B. B. Fall. Nation 200:362-4 Ap 5 '65

If you wonder how the U.S. got into the war in Vietnam. P. Martin. il U S News 59:56-62 S 13 '65

Invisible enemy. il Time 86:25 Jl 9 '65

Key senators tell what to do about Vietnam. U S News 58:68-72 F 15 '65

Khanh's farewell. il Newsweek 65:36 Mr 8 '65

Ky: who rules Vietnam? M. D. Perry. il Newsweek 66:32+ S 27 '65

Last days for South Vietnam? close look at latest crisis. R. P. Martin. il U S News 58: 36-7 F 8 '65

Letter from a dead man; excerpts. Phamngoc-Thao. Newsweek 66:40 Jl 26 '65

VIETNAM (Republic)—Politics and government—*Continued*
Letter from Saigon. R. Shaplen. New Yorker 41:86+ Mr 20; 192+ N 13 '65
Mission in torment, by J. Mecklin. Review Time 85:95 Je 11 '65
Negotiating out of Vietnam. J. Kraft. il Harper 231:38+ S '65
New leaders in South Vietman. U S News 58:16 Je 28 '65
Our man in Saigon. Commonweal 82:484 Jl 9 '65
Perspective on U.S. policy in Viet-Nam; address, November 5, 1965. W. P. Bundy. Dept State Bul 53:890-4 D 6 '65
Physician among warriors. il Time 85:33 My 7 '65
Playboy to premier. il Newsweek 66:34+ Jl 12 '65
Present objectives and future possibilities in southeast Asia; address, April 19, 1965. L. Unger. Dept State Bul 52:712-19 My 10 '65
Real revolution in South Viet Nam. G. A. Carver, jr. For Affairs 43:387-408 Ap '65
Reality and myth concerning South Viet-Nam; address, May 13, 1965. W. P. Bundy. Dept State Bul 52:890-6 Je 7 '65
Return of the generals. Time 85:28 Je 18 '65
Saigon merry-go-round. America 112:890 Je 26 '65
Shattered filigree; another coup nipped in the bud. il Time 85:38 My 28 '65
Situation in southeast Asia. K. T. Young, jr. Sat R 48:35-6 My 29 '65
Something big. Newsweek 65:33-4 Je 7 '65
Swinging door; South Vietnam's rulers. il Newsweek 66:41 S 27 '65
Ten days of action. il Time 86:24 Jl 2 '65
Toward a sterner life. il Time 85:37-8 Je 25 '65
Tragedy of Diem and the paradox of Asia; interview, ed. by D. L. Flaherty. M. L. West. America 112:352-6 Mr 13 '65
Trial for patience. il Time 85:30 F 26 '65
True test; E. Lansdale helps organize rural construction program. il Newsweek 67:34-5 Ja 17 '66
United States in Vietnam. G. M. Kahin and J. W. Lewis. bibliog f il Bul Atomic Sci 21:28-40 Je '65
Viet Cong presence in a pacified area. New Repub 152:7-8 Je 26 '65
Vietcong terror in a village: Loc Dien; with report by D. Moser. il Life 59:28-33+ S 3 '65
Viet Cong; who are they, what do they want? J. Lacouture. New Repub 152:21-4 Mr 6 '65
Vietnam: a debate. S. Gottlieb; L. Cherne; H. S. Commager. il Sat R 48:16-23+ D 18 '65; Discussion. 49:29 Ja 15 '66
Vietnam: a monk and two generals. il Newsweek 65:36 F 8 '65
Vietnam background. P. O'Connor. il America 113:11-13+ Jl 3 '65
Vietnam: in and out of focus. Pyrrho. Nat R 17:1161-3 D 14 '65
Vietnam: new policy in the making. H. W. Baldwin. il Reporter 33:16-20 Ag 12 '65
Vietnam: the agonizing reappraisal. B. B. Fall. bibliog f il Cur Hist 48:95-102+ F '65
Vietnam: the politics of peace. D. Warner. il Reporter 32:40-2 Ap 8 '65
Viet-Nam today; address, September 16, 1965. U. A. Johnson. Dept State Bul 53: 626-35 O 18 '65
Vietnam youth in revolt. M. Hope. il Mlle 61:96-7+ Je '65
Vietnam's young generals face the old problems. T. Oka. il Reporter 33:36-8 Jl 15 '65
What we must do to win in Asia. H. W. Baldwin. il Read Digest 87:111-16 N '65
See also
Elections—Vietnam (Republic)

Relief work
Vietnamese refugee problem. P. Geyelin. il Reporter 33:43-5 S 23 '65

Religious Institutions and affairs
Another Eden; An Giang province, bastion of the Hoa Hao religious sect. F. Sully. Newsweek 66:30+ Ag 30 '65
New guns & old problems. Time 85:29 Je 4 '65
Saigon merry-go-round. America 112:890 Je 26 '65
Two views of Vietnam; report on books by M. West and B. Fall. P. O'Connor. America 113:240-3 S 4 '65; Reply with rejoinder. B. B. Fall. 113:735 D 11 '65
Vietnam youth in revolt. M. Hope. il Mlle 61:96-7+ Je '65

Social conditions
Geographic aspects of the struggle in Viet-Nam. G. E. Pearcy. il Dept State Bul 53: 487-96 S 20 '65

VIETNAM (Republic) and the United States
Campus letter from Saigon; excerpts. il U S News 59:46 N 8 '65
Gifts of comfort and compassion; America's Christmas train and trucks, for villagers of South Vietnam. Life 59:4 D 17 '65
See also
United States—Foreign opinion—Vietnamese

VIETNAMESE
Bourgeois gentlemen of Saigon. C. Oglesby. il Nation 201:352-5 N 15 '65
Human profile; to bend, without breaking. il Sr Schol 87:16-18 S 23 '65
Luong Hoa; village besieged. F. Sully. il Newsweek 66:20-2 Ag 9 '65
People beneath the war. R. R. Coffey. Nation 202:61-3 Ja 17 '66
Vietnamese tragedy. D. E. Luellen. NEA 54:18 Ap '65
See also
Montagnards

VIETNAMESE language
Lingo tech; importance of knowing the Vietnamese language in battlefields of Vietnam. il Time 86:54+ Jl 16 '65

VIETNAMESE refugees. See Refugees. Vietnamese; Vietnamese war, 1957- —Refugees

VIETNAMESE soldiers. See Vietnam (Republic)—Army

VIETNAMESE students
Campus letter from Saigon; excerpts. il U S News 59:46 N 8 '65
Vietnamese students talk about the war. H. Selby. il N Y Times Mag p 104-5+ O 31 '65

VIETNAMESE war, 1957-
ABC's of U.S. aims in Vietnam; interview. D. Rusk. il U S News 58:79-80 Ap 19 '65
According to informed sources; unanswered questions about Vietnam. New Repub 152: 6-7 F 20 '65
Aggression detailed. il Sr Schol 86:21-2 Mr 11 '65
Aggression from the North; the record of North Viet-Nam's campaign to conquer South Viet-Nam; report, February 27, 1965. il Dept State Bul 52:404-27 Mr 22 '65
Air raids hit reds' bases. il Sr Schol 86:30 F 18 '65
Ambush! success of Vietcong. J. Langguth. il N Y Times Mag p4-5+ Je 27 '65
American crisis. Nation 200:517 My 17 '65
Anxious days. il Newsweek 65:40+ Je 21 '65
As a British observer reports the war; weapons in daily use. A. Carthew. New Repub 152:7 Ap 17 '65
As real as an invading army; concerning U.S. white paper, aggression from the North. il Time 85:27-8 Mr 5 '65
As Vietnam war gets bigger; what to look for next. U S News 58:34-5 My 3 '65
Back from a Vietcong hellhole in the jungle. A. Okamura. il Life 59:56D-63 Jl 2 '65
Bad news from Vietnam. Christian Cent 82: 419-20 Ap 7 '65
Big dirty little war. W. Tuohy. il N Y Times Mag p43+ N 28 '65
Case of optimism. il Newsweek 65:55-6 My 17 '65
Cautionary report on Laos; developments along the Ho Chi Minh trail. D. Warner. il Reporter 33:35-8 D 2 '65
Closer than ever to Hanoi. il Time 85:27-8 Mr 26 '65
Come , let us reason together. Nation 200: 489 My 10 '65
Control of force in international relations; address, April 23, 1965. D. Rusk. Dept State Bul 52:694-701 My 10 '65
Counterblows heighten crisis. il Sr Schol 86: 14-15 F 25 '65
Dead end of nonalignment. P. Ben. il Reporter 32:19-22 My 20 '65
Decision time near in Vietnam? U S News 58:35-8 Ap 12 '65
Deep-breathing season; lull in the fighting and diplomatic activity. Time 86:15A Ag 13 '65
Deeper and deeper in Vietnam; now Russia makes a move. U S News 59:38-9 Jl 19 '65
De Gaulle on Vietnam; way out of the jungle; with editorial comment. A. Werth. Nation 200:237, 239-42 Mr 8 '65
Department officers discuss Viet-Nam situation; broadcast over WNEW-TV, New York, on February 7, 1965. W. P. Bundy; J. A. Mendenhall. Dept State Bul 52:291-4 Mr 1 '65
Diagnosis: battle fatigue R: transfusion. Time 85:43 Ap 30 '65

VIETNAMESE war, 1957- —*Continued*

Diplomatic feelers; pressure on U.S. to negotiate settlement. Newsweek 65:22 Mr 8 '65

Edgy truce; Christmas cease-fire. il Time 86:13 D 31 '65

Ending a pause, raising the ante. il Newsweek 65:39 My 31 '65

Escalation & counter-escalation; question of Russian position. Nation 201:50 Ag 2 '65

Extremism by default. Christian Cent 82:452 Ap 14 '65

Facing the facts in Vietnam; address, January 26, 1965. R. M. Nixon. Vital Speeches 31:337-40 Mr 15 '65

Floating island; capture of Russian and Chinese arms from sunken ship. il Newsweek 65:36+ Mr 8 '65

Forecast: showers & a showdown. il Time 85:34 My 21 '65

From Washington; notes on Vietnam; with editorial comment. H. Margolis. Bul Atomic Sci 21:2-3+ Ap '65

Fury after the lull. Newsweek 66:36+ Jl 26 '65

Go on fighting in Vietnam? interview. H. C. Lodge. il U S News 58:62-7 F 15 '65; Excerpts. 59:66-7 Jl 19 '65

Good copters, but bum tactics; U.S. helicopter tactics in South Vietnam. J. Dille. Life 58:34D Ap 16 '65

Hawks and the President. Nation 200:377 Ap 12 '65

Help for the junkmen. Time 85:33+ My 7 '65

Here's how North Vietnam is doing in the war; interview, ed. by J. Fromm. P. J. Honey. il U S News 58:40-2 Ap 12 '65

High cost of fantasy; retreat unthinkable. E. J. Hughes. Newsweek 66:25 D 13 '65

If red China does jump into Vietnam war—. il U S News 58:68-9 Mr 29 '65

In Vietnam; signs of red buildup for a showdown with U.S. il U S News 58:38-9 Ap 19 '65

Inside Hanoi; impressions of J. Cameron and F. Greene after visit and Ho interviews. il Newsweek 66:69 D 20 '65

Intelligence, where everything starts. il Newsweek 65:38-9 Ap 26 '65

Is Vietnam a junkyard for U.S. arms? il U S News 58:10 Mr 22 '65

Is Vietnam to become a civil rights issue? Dr M. L. King urges negotiations with Viet Cong. U S News 59:12 Jl 19 '65

Johnson's goal in Vietnam; similarity between Vietnam and Korea. E. T. Folliard. America 113:39 Jl 10 '65

Kidding the kids; concerning professorial comment on Vietnam. K. Crawford. Newsweek 65:47 My 10 '65; Same abr. with title Let's not kid the kids about Vietnam. Read Digest 87:56-7 Jl '65

Largest raids. Sr Schol 86:19 Mr 18 '65

Last year's illusions. Commonweal 83:391-2 Ja 7 '66

Letter from Saigon. R. Shaplen. New Yorker 41:86+ Mr 20; 192+ N 13 '65

Letter from South Vietnam. R. Shaplen. New Yorker 41:166+ Ap 24 '65

Letter from Washington. R. H. Rovere. New Yorker 41:131-6 F 20; 177-8+ Mr 20 '65

Limit on war; policy of minimizing civilian casualties. il Time 86:38 O 1 '65

Listen to the marine. Nation 200:433 Ap 26 '65

Look down that long road. il Time 85:16-21 F 19 '65

McGovern versus Nixon. Nation 200:126-7 F 8 '65

McNamara predicts long Vietnam fight; excerpts from statement, April 26, 1965. R. S. McNamara. Aviation W 82:20 My 3 '65

Making of a quagmire, by D. Halberstam. Review
Nation 200:536-7 My 17 '65. C. Mohr
New Repub 152:25-7 My 15 '65. G. Eagle

Matter of time? il Time 85:25-6 Mr 12 '65

Mess; three views. B. B. Fall. Nation 200: 534-6 My 17 '65

Military situation in Vietnam; excerpt. J. Lacouture. New Repub 152:20 My 22 '65

Moving up; new escalation. il Newsweek 65: 45 Mr 15 '65

Murder at the Metropole. il Newsweek 66:37 D 13 '65

National teach-in; professors debating Viet Nam, question role of scholarship in policymaking. E. Langer. Science 148:1075-7 My 21 '65

Nearing the brink in Vietnam. W. Lippmann. Newsweek 65:25 Ap 12 '65

Neglected sea power; US navy patrolling coast of South Vietnam. R. Moley. Newsweek 65: 112 My 17 '65

Networks on Vietnam; hopes that a documentary can serve as comment. J. G. Dunne. New Repub 154:36-7 Ja 8 '66; Reply. E. S. Herman. 154:28 Ja 22 '66

New decisiveness. il Newsweek 65:36-7 Ap 5 '65

New forward thrust of freedom. R. Drummond. Read Digest 87:133-5 Ag '65

New weapons, new experience. New Repub 152:7-8 Ap 17 '65

Not for attribution; State department briefing on aggression from the North. A. Campbell. New Repub 152:7-8 Mr 13 '65

Odds of March. il Time 85:30 Ap 16 '65

On the edge of town; battle for Saigon's edge. Time 86:21A-21B S 10 '65

On the use of gas. W. J. Couglin. Miss & Roc 16:46 Ap 19 '65

Only five minutes to darkness in Vietnam; bitter dilemmas and a new U.S. strategy; with interview with General Nguyen Cao Ky. il Life 59:54-61 Jl 23 '65

Opinion in Paris; China won't fight. P. Ben. New Repub 153:18 S 25 '65

Password is green; U.S. fuel supply trucks in Viet Cong territory. W. Tuohy. il Newsweek 65:42+ Mr 29 '65

Peace opposition. Nation 200:462 My 3 '65

Peking statement on North Vietnam; excerpts from resolution of National people's congress, April 20, 1965. Cur Hist 49:177-8 S '65

Pleiku and Qui Nhon; decision points. il Newsweek 65:32-5 F 22 '65

President Johnson and Secretary McNamara review situation in Viet-Nam. L. B. Johnson; R. S. McNamara. Dept State Bul 52: 748-57 My 17 '65

President reaffirms U.S. goal of peace in southeast Asia; statement, March 20, 1965. L. B. Johnson. Dept State Bul 52:488-9 Ap 5 '65

Problem of communication. Nat R 17:136-7 F 23 '65

Profile of the Viet Cong. il Newsweek 65: 40-1+ Ap 12 '65

Propaganda stage; Passive resistance? Nation 200:293 Mr 22 '65

Prospect for southeast Asia; symposium. il Sat R 48:25-37+ O 30 '65

Prospects in Vietnam; with editorial comment. F. Kuh. Nation 200:209, 213 Mr 1 '65

Raids on the North. Commonweal 81:651-2 F 19 '65

Real story of Vietnam as told from the inside; interview. L. W. Pye. il U S News 59:76-81 O 18 '65

Reality and myth concerning South Vietnam; address, May 13, 1965. W. P. Bundy. Dept State Bul 52:890-6 Je 7 '65

Reductio ad Vietnam. R. J. Leng. il Nation 200:445-7 Ap 26 '65

Retaliation; the war in Vietnam moves north. Newsweek 65:19-20 F 22 '65

Revolutionary warfare; how to tell when the rebels have won. E. Ahmad. il Nation 201:95-100 Ag 30 '65

Revolving door leadership; with comment on the world's news fronts. Sr Schol 86: 22-3 Mr 4 '65

Rules they use in Vietnam. R. Dudman. New Repub 152:20-1 Je 12 '65

Russia vs. China; clash over Vietnam. I. Deutscher. Nation 201:3-4 Jl 5 '65

Sartre cancels U.S. visit in protest. Christian Cent 82:388 Mr 31 '65

Secretary Rusk discusses use of tear gas in Viet-Nam; statement, March 24, 1965. D. Rusk. Dept State Bul 52:528-32 Ap 12 '65

Secretary Rusk discusses Viet-Nam situation on BBC; broadcast, April 2, 1965. D. Rusk. Dept State Bul 52:569-71 Ap 19 '65

Secretary Rusk discusses Viet-Nam situation on Face the Nation program. D. Rusk. Dept State Bul 52:442-8 Mr 29 '65

Secretary Rusk's news conference, August 2, 1965. D. Rusk. Dept State Bul 53:203-10 Ag 23 '65

Secretary Rusk's news conference of February 25, 1965. D. Rusk. Dept State Bul 52: 362-71 Mr 15 '65

Secretary talks about Viet-Nam on Issues and answers; interview, July 11, 1965. D. Rusk. Dept State Bul 53:183-90 Ag 2 '65

Silent night; Christmas truce. il Newsweek 67:30 Ja 3 '66

Situation in southeast Asia. K. T. Young, jr. Sat R 48:35-6 My 29 '65

Six HH-43Fs handle bulk of air rescue. C. Brownlow. il Aviation W 82:71+ My 3 '65

Stepped-up war. E. Taylor; D. Warner. il Reporter 33:26-32 D 16 '65

VIETNAMESE war, 1957- —*Continued*
Summer of discontent. H. Brandon. Sat R
48:19 Je 19 '65
Taking the initiative. il Time 85:27 Ap 9 '65
Teach-ins and walk-outs. Nation 200:378 Ap
12 '65
They are not jolly in the foxholes. J. Lang-
guth. il N Y Times Mag p26-7+ My
9 '65
This month's feature: U.S. and the situation
in Vietnam. il Cong Digest 44:99-128 Ap '65
Three Afro-Asian fronts; Vietnam. D. Warn-
er. il Reporter 32:27-9 Mr 25 '65
Tragedy, disappointment, and progress in
southeast Asia; statement, April 17, 1965.
L. B. Johnson. Dept State Bul 52:650-2
My 3 '65
Turning point near in Vietnam war? il U S
News 58:11 My 17 '65
250 lbs. of plastique; Metropole bombing in
Saigon. il Time 86:38 D 10 '65
Two views of Vietnam; report on books by
M. West and B. Fall. P. O'Connor. Amer-
ica 113:240-3 S 4 '65; Reply with rejoinder.
B. B. Fall. 113:735 D 11 '65
U Thant's credibility; use of gas in South
Vietnam. Nation 200:349 Ap 5 '65
UN blackout on Vietnam. A. Weill-Tucker-
man. Nation 200:324-6 Mr 29 '65
U.N. peacekeeping committee meets; U.S
refutes charges on Viet-Nam; statement,
March 26, 1965. F. T. P. Plimpton. Dept
State Bul 52:598-600 Ap 19 '65
U.S. and South Viet-Nam hit North Viet-
namese targets again; White House state-
ment, February 11, 1965, with joint U.S.-
South Viet-Nam statement. Dept State
Bul 52:290-1 Mr 1 '65
U.S. at the crossroads; with report by S.
Sanders. il U S News 58:25-31 Mr 8 '65
U.S. calls for deeds, not words, in U.N. com-
mittee on defining aggression; statements,
April 5 and April 8, 1965. F. T. P. Plimp-
ton. Dept State Bul 52:775-85 My 17 '65
U.S. replies to seventeen-nation appeal on
Viet-Nam; U.S. reply and the seventeen-
nation appeal. Dept State Bul 52:610-12 Ap
26 '65
U.S. submits report on Viet-Nam to U.N.
Security council; letter, February 27, 1965.
A. E. Stevenson. Dept State Bul 52:419
Mr 22 '65
Unlearned lesson of Korea. Nation 200:322
Mr 29 '65
Use of gas in Vietnam draws a rising pro-
test; non-lethal type used. Bsns W p34
Mr 27 '65
Victory at Kannack. il Time 85:33-4 Mr 19
'65
Victory in Vietnam? K. Crawford. News-
week 66:35 O 25 '65
Viet Cong diplomat sizes up the war; inter-
viewed by E. Behr. Vo Cong Trung. News-
week 65:42 Ap 12 '65
Vietnam: a bid to parley. il Newsweek 65:40-8
My 24 '65
Vietnam: a debate. S. Gottlieb; L. Cherne;
H. S. Commager. il Sat R 48:16-23+ D 18
'65; Discussion. 49:29 Ja 15 '66
Vietnam: a matter of interpretation. il Newsweek 65:37-8 Ap 26 '65
Viet-Nam action called collective defense
against armed aggression; Department
statement, March 4, 1965. Dept State Bul
52:403 Mr 22 '65
Vietnam and China. G. Lichtheim. Commen-
tary 39:56-9 My '65
Viet Nam & Korea: a comparison. Time 86:
16 Jl 23 '65
Vietnam and the Russians; effect on U.S.
relations. H. Brandon. Sat R 48:22+ O 16
'65
Vietnam, another Dienbienphu? with edi-
torial comment. I. Deutscher. Nation 200:
209, 212-14 Mr 1 '65
Vietnam convoy. D. Ford. New Repub 152:
11-12 F 6 '65
Vietnam: no contact. il Newsweek 66:34 Jl
12 '65
Vietnam: problems and progress; address,
January 14, 1965. H. K. Johnson. Vital
Speeches 31:262-5 F 15 '65
Vietnam question: pull out or all-out? with
editorial comment. il Bsns W p39-40, 160
F 27 '65
Vietnam: the agonizing reappraisal. B. B.
Fall. bibliog f il Cur Hist 48:95-102+ F '65
Viet-Nam today; address, September 16,
1965. U. A. Johnson. Dept State Bul 53:
626-35 O 18 '65
Vietnam war steps up; a crisis nears. il
U S News 58:4 Je 14 '65

Vietnam war; with editorial comment. C.
Brownlow. il Aviation W 82:21, 26-31 Ap 26
'65 (to be cont)
Vietnam: where do we go from here? S.
Karnow. il Sat Eve Post 238:28-30+ Mr 27
'65
View from the brink. E. J. Hughes. News-
week 67:15 Ja 10 '66
View of the woods; importance of the Soviet
decision. K. Crawford. Newsweek 67:33
Ja 17 '66
War crisis: how dangerous now? with report
by M. S. Johnson. il U S News 58:45-9 Ap
26 '65
War in Vietnam can be won but—. J. Lang-
guth. il N Y Times Mag p30-1+ S 19 '65
War in Vietnam; with editorial comment. C.
Brownlow. il Aviation W 82:21, 26-31 Ap
26; 18-21 My 3; 30-2 My 10; 32-4 My 17;
48-50+ My 24; 29-30+ My 31, 62-3+ Je 7
'65
War of words & deeds. il Time 85:19 Ap 2
'65
War: on the escalator. il U S News 58:29-
31 Mr 22 '65
We can win in southeast Asia. A. Harrigan.
Nat R 17:187-8+ Mr 9 '65
We can't let them down. S. Alsop. il Sat Eve
Post 238:18 Mr 27 '65; Same abr. Read Digest
86:116-18 Je '65
We must choose: (1) bug out; (2) negotiate;
(3) fight. H. W. Baldwin. il N Y Times
Mag p8-9+ F 21 '65; Reply. Christian Cent
82:291-2 Mr 10 '65
What it would take to turn the tide in Viet-
nam. R. P. Martin. il U S News 59:46-8 Jl
12 '65
What we must do to win in Asia. H. W.
Baldwin. il Read Digest 87:111-16 N '65
While the bullets whiz. il Time 85:21-21A
Mr 12 '65
While the sun shines. il Newsweek 65:36 Ap
19 '65
White paper. New Repub 152:5-7 Mr 13 '65
Why I will not go to the United States; tr.
by L. Abel; with reply by the editors of
Nation. J. P. Sartre. Nation 200:407-11 Ap
19 '65
Why reds scorn peace in Vietnam. il U S
News 58:55 My 31 '65
Why Vietnam's reds scorn peace talks; inter-
view. S. W. Sanders. il U S News 59:50-5 N
29 '65
Why war in Vietnam goes on and on. il U S
News 59:24-5 Ag 23 '65
Will Vietnam lead to world war III? R. L.
Gilpatric. il N Y Times Mag p 10-11+ My
30 '65
See also
Vietnam (Democratic Republic)—Army

Aerial operations

A-6A fills interdiction mission in Vietnam.
D. A. Brown. il Aviation W 83:18-20 D 27
'65
Air war in Vietnam; army employs Sikorsky
CH-37 to save downed aircraft. C. Brown-
low. il Aviation W 82:108-9+ My 10 '65
Attack: Pleiku, South Vietnam. B. Mauldin.
New Repub 152:8-9 F 20 '65
B-52s: raids effect on war course. il News-
week 66:41 O 25 '65
Battle over Tan Hiep; with Lieutenant G.
Walters. E. Taylor. il Reporter 33:26-9 D
16 '65
Big bombers: how useful in Vietnam? il U S
News 58:8 Je 28 '65
Bombing, North and South. Commonweal 83:
77-8 O 22 '65
Bombing reds' lifeline in Laos; eyewitness
report. Ho Chi Minh trail. Laos. S. W.
Sanders. il U S News 60:37-9 Ja 24 '66
Bombs away. il Time 86:32 O 29 '65
Bombsight & handsight at the O.K. Corral;
use of the B-52 Stratofortress. Time 85:37
Je 25 '65
Burgeoning U.S. use of air power aimed at
forestalling ground war with Chinese. C.
Brownlow. il Aviation W 82:26-31 Ap 26 '65
Buzz saw & a bunker; action by 101st air-
borne division. il Time 86:38 O 1 '65
Communiqué from Hill 327 at Danang. J.
Rose. il N Y Times Mag p 10-11+ Ap 25
'65
Da Nang security boosted against Viet Cong
raids. il Aviation W 82:60-1 Mr 1 '65
Dogfighting with MiGs; interview. E. A.
Greathouse; C. B. Johnson. Aviation W 83:
11 Jl 26 '65
Enemy: 20,000 missions later. C. Koch. il
Newsweek 66:44-8 O 11 '65
First mission; Capt. M. W. Burr's crash and
survival. W. J. Cook. il Newsweek 66:44 N
8 '65

VIETNAMESE war, 1957- —Aerial operations
—Continued
First team: U.S. 1st cavalry (airmobile)
division. il Time 86:33-4 S 24 '65
Ho's blasted bridges. il Time 85:34-5 My 7
'65
How it happened; two U.S. Thunderchiefs
shot down by North Vietnamese MIGs. il
Time 85:24 Ap 16 '65
Hunting skunks. F. Sully. il Newsweek 66:
25 S 6 '65
Into a new blue yonder; objective: red
sanctuary. il Life 58:28-33 F 26 '65
Jet-seat view of an air strike; battle of Plei
Me. G. C. Troelstrup. il U S News 59:51-2
N 22 '65
Jungle Marxist. il Time 86:24-8 Jl 16 '65
Lesson of Vietnam; air power; address, De-
cember 6, 1965. J. P. McConnell. Vital
Speeches 32:182-4 Ja 1 '66; Excerpts. Avia-
tion W 83:21 D 13 '65; U S News 60:36
Ja 17 '66
Look down that long road. il Time 85:16-21
F 19 '65
Message; strikes against North Vietnam. Na-
tion 200:181 F 22 '65
Military size-up of the truce effort. U S
News 60:35-6 Ja 17 '66
Monsoon may alter war. Sci N L 87:287 My
1 '65
Navy war in Vietnam; assault from U.S.S.
Coral Sea. S. Castan. il Look 29:28-31 N 30
'65
New ball game? il Newsweek 65:53-4 My 3 '65
New war. R. Hotz. Aviation W 82:11 Mr 8 '65
Next: bomb Vietnam where it hurts? il U S
News 59:35-7 D 6 '65
Opening the envelope. Time 86:19 D 24 '65
Operation rescue; Fifth air rescue detach-
ment in South Viet Nam. il Time 85:21A
Mr 12 '65
Our new commitment in Vietnam; with re-
port by B. Mauldin. il Life 58:30-5 F 19 '65
Pandora's box. il Newsweek 65:32-3 Je 28 '65
Peace through bombing. Nation 200:265 Mr
15 '65
Pilots of Danang aren't flyboys. J. Raymond.
il N Y Times Mag p 16-17+ Ja 16 '66
Prayer, a take-off and the B-52 strike is on.
il Life 59:36-41 N 12 '65
Probing Viet Cong strongholds; excerpts from
report. L. Spargo and others. Aviation W
83:21 Jl 12 '65
Proving ground. Nation 200:489-90 My 10 '65
Report from Vietnam. J. J. Murphy. il
Seventeen 25:91+ Ja '66
Role of airpower in Viet-Nam; address,
September 16, 1965. J. P. McConnell. Vital
Speeches 32:12-15 O 15 '65
SAM the sham; antiaircraft weapons. il Time
86:29 D 17 '65
Shot down in North Vietnam, pilot tells his
story of pursuit and rescue; ed. by B.
Wise. P. Ilg. il Life 59:24-5 Ag 6 '65
Tactical raids by B-52s stun Viet Cong. C. M.
Plattner. il Aviation W 83:16-21 N 29 '65
Tale of two airports. il Time 85:26-7 Mr 5 '65
Target: SAM. il Time 86:28 S 3 '65
Telephone poles; bombing of Soviet SAM
missile sites. il Newsweek 66:22 Ag 9 '65
Tide turning in Vietnam war? il U S News
59:35-7 S 27 '65
Time for decision. Nation 200:601-2 Je 7 '65
Truce, or bigger war; showdown ahead in
Vietnam. il U S News 60:27-8 Ja 10 '66
USAF wins right to use jets in Vietnam.
C. Brownlow. Aviation W 82:18 Mr 8 '65
United States and South Vietnamese forces
launch retaliatory attacks against North
Viet-Nam; White House statement, Feb-
ruary 7, 1965, with statements and letter
to U.N. Security council. L. B. Johnson;
R. S. McNamara; A. E. Stevenson. Dept
State Bul 52:238-41 F 22 '65
U.S. and Viet-Nam initiate combined air-
strikes. Dept State Bul 52:371-2 Mr 15 '65
U.S. to double strength in South Vietnam;
with editorial comment. C. Brownlow. il
Aviation W 82:11, 18-20 F 15 '65
Unthinkable target; why the bombing has to
stop. C. Lasch and A. B. Spitzer. Nation
201:74-5+ Ag 16 '65
Vietnam; reality of war, talk of peace. il
U S News 60:6 Ja 3 '66
Vietnam: the war turns North. Life 58:4 F
19 '65
Vietnam; view from the cockpit. il Life 58:
42B-42D My 7 65
War in Vietnam. C. Brownlow. il Aviation
W 82:18-21 My 3; 30-2 My 10; 32-4 My 17;
48-50+ My24; 29-30+ My 31; 62-3+ Je 7
'65
War in Vietnam; O-1F observers perform
major role in aerial recon. C. Brownlow.
il Aviation W 82:52-3+ My 17 '65

War in Vietnam; with editorial comment. C.
M. Plattner. il Aviation W 84:11, 16-21 Ja
3; 26-32 Ja 10; 28-32 Ja 17 '66
We are not hot-shot Charlies; U.S. pilots.
il Newsweek 65:36-7 Ap 19 '65
What congressmen found in Vietnam; per-
sonal reports; symposium. il U S News 60:
24-31 Ja 3 '66
Who's signaling what? United States air
raids on North Vietnam. New Repub 152:
5-6 F 20 '65
Wings of destruction. Time 86:33-4 N 26 '65
See also
Helicopters—Military applications

American participation
ABC's of the war in Vietnam; questions and
answers. il U S News 58:36-9 Je 28 '65
After Vietnam lull; bigger war ahead? U S
News 58:8 My 31 '65
America and Belgium; a community of in-
terests; address, June 16, 1965. D. Mac-
Arthur, 2d. Dept State Bul 53:118-22 Jl 19
'65
American folly; British view. J. M. Cameron.
Commonweal 82:343-4 Je 4 '65
American policy and Japanese opinion. Na-
tion 200:632 Je 14 '65
Another county is heard from; Freedom
House backs government. America 113:232
S 4 '65
As the marines scored in Vietnam. il U S
News 59:6 Ag 30 '65
Australian looks at Vietnam; weighing prob-
able future moves. A. Walker. Christian
Cent 82:960-2 Ag 4 '65
Awaiting negotiations; concerning President
Johnson's speech. Commonweal 82:133-4 Ap
23 '65
Bell for the next round. J. Burnham. Nat R
17:583 Jl 13 '65
Build-up in Vietnam. Commonweal 82:428-9
Je 25 '65
Buildup of U.S. forces in Viet-Nam; state-
ment, August 4, 1965. R. S. McNamara.
Dept State Bul 53:369-74 Ag 30 '65
Burden of leadership. A. Eden. For Affairs
44:229-38 Ja '66
Changed war in Vietnam. Life 59:4 Jl 9 '65
Close to his vest; concerning press confer-
ence of July 28, 1965. Nat R 17:680 Ag 10
'65
Commitment; more battalions sent to South
Viet Nam. il Time 85:25 Je 25 '65
Congress approves supplemental appropriation
for Viet-Nam, remarks, May 4, 1965, with
message to Congress. L. B. Johnson. Dept
State Bul 52:816-26 My 24 '65
Debate; M. Bundy and supporters vs. critics
of the administration's firm Viet Nam poli-
cies. il Time 86:14-15 Jl 2 '65
Decision in Viet Nam; how Johnson makes
foreign policy. H. F. Graff. il N Y Times
Mag p4-7+ Jl 4 '65
Decisions in Vietnam. W. Lippmann. News-
week 66:13 Ag 2 '65
Deepening war. Nation 200:461 My 3 '65
Deeper and deeper in Vietnam; now Russia
makes a move. U S News 59:38-9 Jl 19 '65
Deeper & wider. Time 86:35 N 19 '65
Deeper into the trap; Christmas message on
Vietnam. E. Snow. New Repub 153:15-18
D 25 '65
Defense of South Viet-Nam; proclamation,
November 6, 1965. L. B. Johnson. Dept
State Bul 53:894 D 6 '65
Delusions of power. New Repub 153:5-6 O 16
'65
Doing the right things; interview, ed. by
F. Melville. R. G. K. Thompson. Newsweek
66:33 Jl 5 '65
Doves' chance in Vietnam; concerning Pres-
ident Johnson's address at Johns Hopkins
university. Christian Cent 82:484 Ap 21 '65
Duty of Congress; representatives organize
public discussions in own districts. Nation
201:457-8 D 13 '65
E pluribus unum; Vietnam policy under at-
tack. il Newsweek 66:21 Ag 30 '65
Editor's easy chair. J. Fischer. Harper 231:
21-2+ Ag '65; Discussion. 231:6+ O; 13-14+
N '65
Escalating at a high pace; new push in Vietnam buildup. il Bsns W p25-7 D 4 '65
Escalation & counter-escalation; question of
Russian position. Nation 201:50 Ag 2 '65
Face of victory; Van Tuong. il Time 86:
18-19 Ag 27 '65
Fiery pangs of conscience; why N. Morrison
committed suicide. L. Wainwright. Life 59:
34 N 12 '65
Find 'em & fight 'em. Time 86:45 N 12 '65
Finland and the United States, an enduring
friendship; address, September 5, 1965; with
message from President Johnson. W. A.
Harriman. Dept State Bul 53:555-8 O 4 '65

VIETNAMESE war, 1957- —American partici-
pation—*Continued*
Ft. Riley shipping them out; for the war in
Vietnam. il Newsweek 65:20-1 Je 28 '65
Forum; focus on Vietnam; symposium. bib-
liog f il Bul Atomic Sci 21:26-49 Je '65;
Reply. J. Barden. 21:31 S '65
Frank talk; Vietnam: December, 1965. News-
week 67:52 Ja 3 '66
From Dean Rusk; answers to key questions on
Vietnam; excerpts from address, April 23,
1965. D. Rusk. il U S News 58:74-7 My 10
'65
From U.S. leaders: a briefing on war and
policy. il U S News 58:39-41 My 10 '65
From Washington; some problems in Vietnam.
H. Margolis. Bul Atomic Sci 21:40-3 My '65
Goliath's peril. Nation 201:29 Jl 19 '65
Guardians at the gate. il Time 87:15-21 Ja 7
'66
Hard lesson; Laird-Ford formula for victory.
W. Lippmann, Newsweek 66:15 Jl 19 '65
Hard realities of power demand that we must
fight on. E. V. Rostow. il Life 59:40B-40C
Jl 2 '65
Hearing: called locally and unofficially by W.
F. Ryan in his district. New Yorker 41:23-
6 Ag 28 '65
Heart of the matter; American stake in
Viet Nam. il Time 86:13-14 Jl 2 '65
Hotter war? Sr Schol 86:15-16 My 20 '65
How Johnson changed the war in Vietnam.
S. Castan. il Look 29:32-4+ N 30 '65
How we bungled our way in. W. C. Mc-
Williams. Commonweal 82:537-8 Jl 23 '65
If you wonder how the U.S. got into the war
in Vietnam. P. Martin. il U S News 59:56-
62 S 13 '65
Improved outlook in Vietnam. Life 59:4 S 10
'65
In they go to the reality of this war;
Seventh marine regiment's mission at Cape
Batangan. M. Mok. il Life 59:50-69+ N 26
'65
In Vietnam: new grimness, new moves to-
ward total war. U S News 59:8 Jl 5 '65
International law, morality and American
interventions. W. V. O'Brien. Cath World
201:388-93 S '65
Is the Vietcong such a sure winner after all?
excerpt. G. Chaffard. il Life 58:87+ Ap
30 '65
Johnson facing critical Vietnam decisions.
C. Brownlow. Aviation W 83:18 Jl 19 '65
Johnson means business in Vietnam. Life 59:4
Ag 6 '65
Johnson's dilemma: coping with a half-war.
il Bsns W p27-8 D 4 '65
Keeping the consensus. Commonweal 83:7-8
O 8 '65
Key senator warns: appeasers are hurting
U.S. excerpts from statement, June 10,
1965. T. J. Dodd. U S News 58:21 Je 21
'65
Key senators tell what to do about Vietnam.
U S News 58:68-72 F 15 '65
Key to victory in Vietnam. M. McGrory.
America 113:201 Ag 28 '65
Knots of our own tying. J. Burnham. Nat R
17:762 S 7 '65
Letter from Washington. R. H. Rovere. New
Yorker 41:160+ Ap 17; 99-102+ Jl 17; 108-9
Ag 14; 202-5 N 20; 191-4+ D 18 '65
Liberated village; misunderstanding between
Americans and Vietnamese. New Repub
153:10-11 S 11 '65
Long guns flash on the South China Sea;
Seventh fleet in action; with report by B.
Wise. il Life 59:16-23 Ag 6 '65
Lull that lapsed. Time 85:21-2 My 28 '65
LBJ and Congress; secrets of a briefing. il
U S News 59:30-1 Ag 23 '65
LBJ's Vietnam policy; what the polls show.
U S News 58:11 My 10 '65
McNamara and Vietnam: sharp questions;
statements. R. S. McNamara. il U S News
59:32 D 27 '65
Military size-up of the truce effort; with
excerpts from address, by J. P. McConnell.
il U S News 60:35-6 Ja 17 '66
Mission is to kill; Marine brigade at Da
Nang air base. il Newsweek 65:49-50 My 10
'65
Mr Ball discusses Viet-Nam on Issues and
answers; interview, August 1, 1965; ed. by
W. R. Downs, jr. and J. Scali. G. W. Ball.
Dept State Bul 53:310-14 Ag 23 '65
Mr McNamara reports on use of supplemental
appropriation; White House announcement,
May 18, 1965; with memorandum for the
President. il Dept State Bul 52:896-7 Je
7 '65
Mobilization outlook; with interview with
B. Ellington. il U S News 59:19-29 Ag 2 '65

Morality, moralism and Vietnam. W. H. Har-
ris. Christian Cent 82:1155-7 S 22 '65; Dis-
cussion. 82:1452+ N 24 '65
More escalation. Nation 201:457 D 13 '65
More shooters. Time 86:36-7 O 15 '65
Most agonizing build-up. il Sr Schol 87:19
S 16 '65
Naive idealists and wanton realists. Christian
Cent 82:1403-4 N 17 '65
Nation underwrites L.B.J. E. T. Folliard.
America 113:565 N 13 '65
New and serious decisions. il Newsweek 66:
19-21 Jl 26 '65
New war in Vietnam; address, July 23, 1965.
H. K. Johnson. Vital Speeches 31:676-9 S
1 '65
No victory in Vietnam. W. Pfaff. Common-
weal 82:135-7 Ap 23 '65
Now the Vietnik; demonstrations against U.S.
policy in Viet Nam. il Time 86:25A O 22
'65
On two fronts; find Viet Cong. il Time 85:
23-4 My 7 '65
One more shift in the Vietnam war. il U S
News 58:40 Je 7 '65
One-two punch. il Time 86:17-18 S 3 '65
Our course in Vietnam. J. O'Gara. Common-
weal 82:464 Jl 2 '65
Our war in Vietnam. Commonweal 82:547-8
Ag 6 '65
Our way of life. Nation 201:69-70 Ag 16 '65
Parochial American. W. Pfaff. Commonweal
82:581-2 Ag 20 '65
Peace and Protestantism. Nation 201:513-14
D 27 '65
Peace or war: the Johnson plan; address,
April 7, 1965. L. B. Johnson. il U S News
58:76-8 Ap 19 '65; Same. Vital Speeches 31:
386-8 Ap 15 '65; Dept State Bul 52:606-10 Ap
26 '65
Peace through war. New Repub 152:7 Ap 24
'65
Pentagon's dilemma; Goliath and the guer-
rilla. E. Hobsbawn. il Nation 201:33-8 Jl 19
'65; Discussion. 201:inside cover S 6 '65
Perspective on U.S. policy in Viet Nam; ad-
dress, May 27, 1965. W. P. Bundy. Dept
State Bul 52:1001-5 Je 21 '65
Point of no return. W. V. Shannon. Com-
monweal 82:580-1 Ag 20 '65
Political and military aspects of U.S. policy
in Viet-Nam; interview, August 9, 1965
D. Rusk; R. S. McNamara. Dept State
Bul 53:342-56 Ag 30 '65
Political skirmishing in Vietnam war. U S
News 59:13 S 6 '65
President reiterates U.S. policy on Viet-Nam;
statement, March 25, 1965. L. B. Johnson.
Dept State Bul 52:527-8 Ap 12 '65
Presidential war. Nation 201:401 N 29 '65
President's days of crisis and decision: in
LBJ's own words; excerpts from statements,
May 4, 1965. L. B. Johnson. il U S News
58:43 My 17 '65
President's perplexity. Nation 200:658 Je 21
'65
Probing Viet Cong strongholds; excerpts
from report. L. Spargo and others. Aviation
W 83:21 Jl 12 '65
Problem in Vietnam. C. Brownlow. Aviation
W 82:11 Je 7 '65
Psywar. il Newsweek 66:40 O 4 '65
Public opinion and the war in Vietnam;
Great debate. L. Markel. il N Y Times
Mag p9+ Ag 8 '65
Public opinion and Vietnam. Nat R 17:678-9
Ag 10 '65
Questions unanswered. Nation 201:486 D 20
'65
Real negotiations on South Vietnam. F. C.
Ikle. Reporter 32:15-16 Je 3 '65
Real war. R. Hotz. Aviation W 83:21 Ag 2
'65
Republican blueprint for Vietnam war. il U S
News 59:10 D 27 '65
Republicans and Vietnam. J. O'Gara. Com-
monweal 82:489 Jl 9 '65
Rim of hell: How the United States got
involved. Nation 201:110 S 6 '65
Runaway war or deadlocked peace. H. Scho-
mer. Christian Cent 82:957-9 Ag 4 '65
Rusk rebuts policy critics. il Sr Schol 86:
17 My 6 '65
SR's readers and Cam Ne. N. Cousins. Sat R
48:30 O 9 '65
Secretary discusses U.S. policy in Viet-Nam
on Belgian TV; interview, September 7,
1965. D. Rusk. Dept State Bul 53:512-14
S 27 '65
Secretary discusses Viet-Nam on USIA television; transcript of interview by members of the international press, June 24,
1965. D. Rusk. Dept State Bul 53:105-10
Jl 19 '65

VIETNAMESE war, 1957- —American participation—*Continued*
Secretary McNamara discusses U.S. operations in Viet-Nam; questions and answers,
July 14, 1965. R. S. McNamara. Dept
State Bul 53:190-1 Ag 2 '65
Secretary of defense McNamara explains how
things are going in Vietnam. Nat R 17:
1182-3 D 28 '65
Secretary Rusk's news conference of Novem-
ber 26, 1965. D. Rusk. Dept State Bul 53:
930-9 D 13 '65
Secretary Rusk's news conference of Decem-
ber 9, 1965. D. Rusk. Dept State Bul 53:
1006-13 D 27 '65
Senate on Viet Nam; statements of senators.
il Time 86:15A-15B Ag 13 '65
Shift in U.S. policy? concerning President's
address at John Hopkins university. il Sr
Schol 86:26-7 Ap 29 '65
Snipers, fever, confusion; this is the Vietnamese war. il U S News 59:26-9 Ag 23
'65
Some tears & some blood. il Time 86:15-16
Jl 23 '65
Sooner, the better. New Repub 152:5-6 Je 19
'65
Stepping up pressure for a Viet cease-fire;
U.S. sends its first organized combat
unit. il Bsns W p 19-20 Jl 3 '65
Summer of discontent. H. Brandon. Sat R
48:19 Je 19 '65
Suspense. M. Ascoli. Reporter 34:20 Ja 13
'66
There is no one else; turning point in U.S.
policy toward the war in Viet Nam; Press
conference. il Time 86:17-18 Ag 6 '65
This is really war; White House press con-
ference, July 28, 1965. il Bsns W p 15-16
Jl 31 '65
Tough ground war multiplies the costs. il
Bsns W p22-3 Jl 24 '65
Tougher & then some. il Time 85:30-1 Ap 30
'65
Toward a winning commitment. il Time 85:
19 Je 18 '65
Traveler to the Pacific wars; letter on the
larger war in Vietnam. C. J. V. Murphy.
il Fortune 72:132-4+ Ag '65
Truth about war in Vietnam. R. P. Martin
and S. W. Sanders il U S News 59:42-5 Jl
26 '65
Two front row seats to a bitter tragedy. M.
West. Life 58:12 My 7 '65
Two-pronged attack on Vietcong. Life 58:4
Ap 30 '65
Union & the war; concerning State of the
Union address. il Time 87:19-19B Ja 21 '66
U.S. and Viet Nam; symposium, ed. by R.
Hemming. il Sr Schol 87:5-19+ S 23 '65
U.S. goals in Vietnam as set by the Presi-
dent; excerpts from news conference, July
29, 1965. L. B. Johnson. il U S News 59:
50-1 Ag 9 '65
U.S. has the initiative. il Time 86:42 O 8 '65
U.S. sets record straight on position in Viet-
Nam; statement, October 7, 1965. A. J.
Goldberg. Dept State Bul 53:724-5 N 1 '65
Unthinkable target; why the bombing has to
stop. C. Lasch and A. B. Spitzer. Nation
201:74-5+ Ag 16 '65
Untold story of Vietnam war. il U S News
60:29-32 Ja 24 '66
Vietnam blitz; report on the impersonal war.
B. B. Fall. New Repub 153:17-21 O 9 '65;
Discussion. 153:32-4 N 13 '65
Vietnam: European viewpoints. B. B. Fall.
New Repub 153:13-15 Ag 21 '65
Vietnam: holding action; address, June 15,
1965. J. W. Fulbright. Vital Speeches 31:
546-8 Jl 1 '65
Vietnam: new policy in the making. H. W.
Baldwin. il Reporter 33:16-20 Ag 12 '65
Vietnam: sharp words and hints of parley;
with views of leading columnists and com-
mentators. il Newsweek 65:23-5 My 3 '65
Vietnam spurs DOD boost, reprogramming. il
Aviation W 83:26-8 Ag 2 '65
Vietnam step-up: the secret councils; Presi-
dent Johnson's seven days of deliberation
before decision. R. B. Stolley. il Life 59:
26D Ag 6 '65
Vietnam: still on the escalator; recasting
and hardening of U.S. aims and long-term
planning. il Newsweek 66:27-8 D 13 '65
Vietnam: the new war. il Newsweek 66:30-2+
Jl 5 '65
Vietnam: the problem of candor; concerning
President's State of the Union message. il
Newsweek 67:24-6 Ja 24 '66
Vietnam: the ritual of decision. il Newsweek
66:15-17 Ag 2 '65
Vietnam: to be another Korea? il U S News
58:37-9 Je 21 '65
Vietnam war: a harvest of votes for Re-
publicans? il U S News 58:32 Je 28 '65

Viet-Nam: winning the peace; television in-
terview, August 23, 1965. D. Rusk; A. J.
Goldberg; M. Bundy. Dept State Bul 53:
431-44 S 13 '65
Viet war boosts contract airlift demands;
MATS Pacific airlift contracts. W. Wright.
Aviation W 83:37 S 27 '65
Vietnamese war today. W. Lippmann. News-
week 66:17 S 13 '65
War council; sessions after return of R. Mc-
Namara from a five-day inspection trip to
South Viet Nam. il Time 86:9-10 Jl 30 '65
War in Asia, why? New Repub 153:5-6 Ag 7
'65
War in Vietnam; with editorial comment.
C. M. Plattner. il Aviation W 84:11, 16-21
Ja 3; 26-32 Ja 10; 28-32 Ja 17 '66
War steps up; where it's headed. il U S
News 58:31-3 My 10 '65
War, taxes, labor, rights: LBJ's plans for
1966; State of the Union message, January
12, 1966. L. B. Johnson. U S News 60:62-
6+ Ja 24 '66
War's awful logic. S. Alsop. il Sat Eve Post
238:14 S 11 '65
We are deluding ourselves in Vietnam. H. J.
Morgenthau. il N Y Times Mag p24-5+
Ap 18 '65
We can solve the Vietnam dilemma; excerpt
from address, July 27, 1965. G. McGovern.
Sat R 48:37-8 O 16 '65
We have to finish the job. il Newsweek 66:27
S 20 '65
We may win the war but lose the people. J
Reston. il N Y Times Mag p42-3+ S 12 '65
We will stand in Viet-Nam; statement, July
28, 1965. L. B. Johnson. Dept State Bul
53:262-5 Ag 16 '65
Weakest front. J. Burnham. Nat R 17:499 Je
15 '65
What aim in Vietnam? Sat R 17:536 Je 29
'65
What are we doing in Vietnam? J. Burnham.
Nat R 17:232 Mr 23 '65
What congressmen found in Vietnam; per-
sonal reports; symposium. il U S News
60:24-31 Ja 3 '66
What it will take to win in Vietnam; inter-
view. R. B. Russell. U S News 59:56-60
S 6 '65
What next in Vietnam? with report by S. W.
Sanders. il U S News 59:33-40 Ag 9 '65
What senators' mail says about Vietnam.
U S News 59:9 Ag 23 '65
What the people really think. S. Alsop. il
Sat Eve Post 238:18, 27-31 O 23 '65
What the President says now about U.S.
role in Vietnam; news conference, April
27, 1965. L. B. Johnson. il U S News 58:
73 My 10 '65
What Vietnam war means to U.S; with re-
port by R. P. Martin. il U S News 58:35-9
F 22 '65
What we must do to win in Asia. H. W.
Baldwin. il Read Digest 87:111-16 N '65
Wheeler and the dealer. W. J. Coughlin. Miss
& Roc 17:74 S 13 '65
When G.I. Joe meets ol' Charlie. J. Ray-
mond. il N Y Times Mag p4-5+ Jl 25 '65
White House teach-in. il Time 86:21 Ag 20
'65
Who pledged what in Vietnam? excerpts
from news conference, August 17, 1965.
D. D. Eisenhower. U S News 59:15 Ag 30
'65
Who said irrational? reductio ad absurdum
of war. Nation 201:149 S 27 '65
Why are we fighting a war in Vietnam?
Christian Cent 82:230 F 24 '65
Why is U.S. in a war? here are answers to
questions being asked about Vietnam. R. P.
Martin and S. W. Sanders. il U S News
58:42-4 Ap 5 '65
Why the U.S. took chance on bigger war.
il Bsns W p30-1 F 13 '65
Why U.S. risks big war in Asia; with inter-
view with Thanat Khoman; ed. by R. P.
Martin. il U S News 58:31-4+ Mr 15 '65
Why war is undeclared in Vietnam. il U S
News 59:33 D 20 '65
Why we are fighting in Asia. F. V. Drake. il
Read Digest 87:61-5 O '65
Why we are in Viet-Nam; excerpts from re-
marks, December 9, 1965. L. B. Johnson.
Dept State Bul 53:1014 D 27 '65
Will arms build-up in Asia cut U.S. role in
Europe? interview. A. E. Heusinger. il U S
News 59:64-7 Ag 23 '65
Winning instead of wishing. il Time 86:31-
31A N 5 '65
World in our living room; statement. D.
Rusk. Time 86:18 D 17 '65
Worse before it gets better. il Newsweek 66:
17-18 Jl 19 '65

VIETNAMESE war, 1957- —American partici-
pation—*Continued*
Wrong-way Johnson. Nation 201:91 Ag 30 '65
  See also
United States—Armed forces—Forces in Viet-
nam

Anecdotes, facetiae, satire, etc.

Notes and comment; nomenclature suitable
for use by country not at war. New Yorker
41:49 D 11 '65

Atrocities

Degree of moderation; last hours of recon-
naissance patrol. il Newsweek 67:24 Ja
10 '66
Green berets, by R. Moore. Review
  Commonweal 82:568 Ag 6 '65. E. Capouya
Only anguish; reprisal against two Ameri-
cans. il Newsweek 66:48 O 11 '65
Vietcong terror in a village; Loc Dien; with
report by D. Moser. il Life 59:28-33+ S 3
'65
War within. il Time 85:22 My 28 '65
Where terror is practiced; Hoa Long. E.
Taylor. il Reporter 33:17-18 D 30 '65

Bibliography

War in Asia: more questions than answers.
R. Dudman. Sat R 48:34-5 N 27 '65

Campaigns and battles

American soldier in action; 173rd airborne
brigade in Zone D. il Newsweek 66:61-2 N
22 '65
Battle for Nam Dong; excerpt from Outpost
of freedom; ed. by W. Rogers. R. H. C.
Donlon. il Sat Eve Post 238:38-42+ O 23 '65
Battle for the hills. il Time 86:18 Jl 30 '65
Battle in the Chu Phong massif. il Life 59:
42D D 3 '65
Battle in the Delta; Co Cong victory. E.
Taylor. il Reporter 34:21-5 Ja 13 '66
Battle of Chu Lai, the instant a marine is
shot. il Life 59:22-7 S 3 '65
Bigger & uglier; Viet Cong raid against
Danang and other operations. il Time 86:
20-1 Jl 9 '65
Bloody hills; Viet Cong summer offensive. il
Time 85:34-5 Je 11 '65
Conflict heats up. il Sr Schol 87:18 D 9 '65
Degree of moderation; post-truce actions. il
Newsweek 67:24 Ja 10 '66
Face of victory; Van Tuong. il Time 86:18-19
Ag 27 '65
Fighting gets tougher; so does American GI;
report from Vietnam, with letter by K. W.
Bagby. il U S News 59:39-41 D 13 '65
First major U.S.-North Viet battle. il Avia-
tion W 84:30-1 Ja 10 '66
Forgotten war; Mekong delta. il Newsweek
67:24-5 Ja 10 '66
Fury at Ia Drang: now the regulars; US
First air cavalry activities. il Newsweek
66:21-3 N 29 '65
GI's pour in and the war looks up. il News-
week 66:38+ O 4 '65
How Plei Me survived. W. J. Cook. il News-
week 66:43 N 8 '65
In they go to the reality of this war; Seventh
marine regiment's mission at Cape Batan-
gan. M. Mok. il Life 59:50-69+ N 26 '65
In Vietnam: suddenly it's a stepped-up war;
battle of Plei Me, with report by G. C.
Troelstrup. il U S News 59:50-2 N 22 '65
Marine victory and optimism; battle of Van
Tuong. W. Tuohy. il Newsweek 66:28-9
Ag 30 '65
Name of the game is zap, zap, zap; operation
near Ben Cat. il Time 86:34 S 24 '65
New fury in Viet Nam; Dong Xoai battle.
il Life 59:30-40A Jl 2 '65
Most of the dying. il Time 86:30-1 D 3 '65
No give: Death on the river. il Newsweek
66:41 N 1 '65
No victory, no defeat. il Newsweek 66:36
O 25 '65
Now it's a major war in Vietnam. il U S
News 59:37-8 N 29 '65
On the trial; ambush by First cavalry divi-
sion. Newsweek 66:52 N 15 '65
One kind of routine; Ap Nha Mat area and
operation Harvest moon at Tam Ky. il
Newsweek 66:34 D 20 '65
Relief of Duc Co. W. Tuohy. il Newsweek
66:28-9 Ag 23 '65
Same war, with a big difference; siege of
Plei Me. il Newsweek 66:31-2 N 8 '65
Seven days of zap; siege of Plei Me. il
Time 86:31A-35 N 5 '65
Stepped-up war; battle over Tan Hiep. E.
Taylor. il Reporter 33:26-9 D 16 '65
Those who must die; battle at Dongxoai. il
Time 85:28-30 Je 18 '65

Trap of the harvest moon. Time 86:28 D 17
'65
Valleys of death; Chu Pong foothills. il Time
86:32-3 N 26 '65
Vietcong terror in a village; Loc Dien; with
report by D. Moser. il Life 59:28-33+ S 3
'65
Vietnam: a black week's omen; battle of
Quang Ngai. M. Perry. il Newsweek 65:
53-4 Je 14 '65
Whirling dervishes; First cavalry division
(airmobile) in central Vietnam highlands
and Ia Drang Valley. Newsweek 66:28 D
13 '65

Casualties

As U.S. casualties mount in Vietnam. U S
News 59:6 N 22 '65
B-52s and live ducks il Newsweek 66:54 O
18 '65
Blood all over. il Time 86:24 Jl 16 '65
Busy life came to a close; death and home-
coming of Sgt. L. C. Blake. K. Fleming.
il Newsweek 66:18-19 D 27 '65
Down in Thanh Hoa; jet ace, J. R. Risner.
Time 86:28 S 24 '65
Folks, by all rights I should be dead; letter.
K. W. Bagby. U S News 59:41 D 13 '65
Fury at Ia Drang: now the regulars; US
First air cavalry activities. il Newsweek
66:21-3 N 29 '65
Hero comes home. K. O. Gilmore. Read
Digest 87:61-6 N '65
Humor, horror & heroism. il Time 86:30 D 3
'65
I loved that man so much; how wives re-
ceived death messages in Columbus, Ga,
and details of four survivors. il Newsweek
66:27-8 D 6 '65
In search of a Vietnam hero; H. D. Meyer-
kord's death. L. Wainwright. Life 58:23-4
My 28 '65
Into the iron triangle and ominous stillness.
il Life 59:34-7 O 22 '65
Killed in action in Vietnam; 1961 to Nov.
27, 1965. Sat R 48:20 D 18 '65
Letters; death of J. A. Rose. M. W. Browne.
Sat Eve Post 238:6 N 6 '65
Little parcel of commitment; death of J.
LaHaye. L. Wainwright. Life 58:28 Je 11
'65
Lone American; U.S. civilians killed in the
Viet Nam war. Time 85:27 Ap 23 '65
Meaning of the dead. S. Alsop. il Sat Eve
Post 238:16 Ap 24 '65; Same abr. Read
Digest 87:54-6 Jl '65
Moderation in all; characterizing losses as
light, moderate or heavy. Newsweek 66:
42 D 6 '65
Moment of rescue in biggest U.S. victory;
battle in the Ia Drang Valley. il Life 59:
42B-42D D 3 '65
New ball game? il Newsweek 65:53-4 My 3
'65
Notes and comment. New Yorker 41:49 D 4
'65
Time of blood. Time 86:48+ N 19 '65
Toll; U.S. casualties in action since January
1, 1961. il Time 85:25 Ap 23 '65
Valleys of death; Chu Pong foothills. il Time
86:32-3 N 26 '65
Vietnam widow; S. Isaacs. J. Star. il Look
30:24-8+ Ja 25 '66

Censorship

Right to know; letter. H. D. Steward. Sat
R 48:29 Ap 17 '65

Economic aspects

America at war; war profits. Commonweal
82:650 S 17 '65
As events close in on Johnson—. il U S News
59:27-8 D 20 '65
Budget escalates; $12-billion added for Viet-
namese war, with editorial comment. Bsns
W p27-8, 114 Ja 8 '66
Butter plus guns; new boom ahead? il U S
News 59:70-2 Ag 16 '65
Decisions under the gun; with editorial com-
ment. il Bsns W p 11-13, 84 D 25 '65
Expanding without strain. Bsns W p23-4 Ag
7 '65
If truce comes, or, if no truce; what to ex-
pect. il U S News 60:28-31 Ja 17 '66
If war ends soon; what happens to business.
il U S News 59:115-16 O 4 '65
Impact of Vietnam begins to register; increase
in defense spending. Bsns W p27-8 My 15
'65
Peacetime guides to govern Viet buildup. C.
Brownlow. il Aviation W 83:28-9 Ag 23 '65
Real reason LBJ was irked. il U S News
59:41 Ag 16 '65
Shift of signals on government spending. il
U S News 59:32 D 13 '65

VIETNAMESE war, 1957- —Economic aspects
—*Continued*
'66 budget; war takes precedence over the Great society. G. L. Perry. New Repub 153:12-15 D 25 '65
U.S. winning a battle on Vietnam economy. il Bsns W p30-1 D 4 '65
Vietnam puts squeeze on the Great society; with editorial comment. il Bsns W p31, 132 D 18 '65
Waiting for the next big move. Bsns W p25 Ag 7 '65
War costs set pace for jump in spending. il Bsns W p28-30 D 4 '65
War pinch. il Time 87:79 Ja 14 '66
War's demands: must taxes rise? il U S News 60:19-20 Ja 3 '66
War's widening ripples; U.S. commitment in Vietnam. il Newsweek 66:51-3 Ag 2 '65
See also
Industrial mobilization

Equipment and supplies
Big bottleneck in Vietnam war. il U S News 59:38-40 D 27 '65
Blockade saves lives. R. Moley. Newsweek 67:60 Ja 3 '66
Freedom of the seas; goods of war to North Vietnam. R. Moley. Newsweek 66:74 D 27 '65
Giant bottleneck. il Time 86:19-20 D 24 '65
Jungle proving ground; use of new weapons and novel equipment in Vietnam. il Time 86:47 Jl 9 '65
Lifeline to the war; shippers object to operate for Military sea transport service. il Newsweek 66:79 D 6 '65
Mecca on the bay; supply base at Cam Ranh Bay. F. Sully. Newsweek 66:34+ S 13 '65
Port of entry for U.S. power; Cam Ranh Bay. K. M. Chrysler. il U S News 59:50-2 O 11 '65
Price of victory; Vietcong manpower and materials infiltration methods. D. Warner. il Reporter 33:29-32 D 16 '65
Vietnam needs strain logistics pipeline; with editorial comment. C. Brownlow. Aviation W 83:21, 30-1 S 27 '65
Vietnam snafu: how shortages hamper combat troops. il U S News 59:32-4 Ag 16 '65
Vietnam war pace strains C-141 program Aviation W 83:30-1 S 13 '65
Wheeler and the dealer. W. J. Coughlin. Miss & Roc 17:74 S 13 '65

Foreign participation
More flags: allies in the field; Australia, New Zealand and South Korea. il Newsweek 66:50 N 15 '65
One painful lesson for U.S. in Vietnam. il U S News 60:32-4 Ja 17 '66
When U.S. asks allies for help. il U S News 59:24 D 27 '65

Guerrillas
Airmobile concept proves effectiveness in guerrilla fight. C. M. Plattner. il Aviation W 84:26-32 Ja 10 '66
Ambush! success of Vietcong. J. Langguth. il N Y Times Mag p4-5+ Je 27 '65
Bigger war ahead in Vietnam? il U S News 59:11 N 15 '65
Face of the enemy in Vietnam; excerpts from Making of a quagmire. D. Halberstam. Harper 230:62-4+ F '65
Forgotten war; Mekong delta. il Newsweek 67:24-5 Ja 10 '66
Guerrilla bosses in jungle war. U S News 58:26 My 17 '65
Guerrilla meat grinder; assault on Ba Gia, South Vietnam. il Newsweek 66:30 Jl 19 '65
How Viet Cong rules the roads. il U S News 59:47 Jl 12 '65
Infiltration from the North; the vital transfusion. il Time 85:34 F 5 '65
Life with the Viet Cong. Time 86:25-6 Jl 2 '65
Long, hot walk. M. Perry; F. Sully. il Newsweek 66:32-3 Ag 16 '65
Look down that long road. il Time 85:16-21 F 19 '65
Luong Hoa: village besieged. F. Sully. il Newsweek 66:20-2 Ag 9 '65
Military profile: Yankee, you die; guerrilla fighter of the Viet Cong. il Sr Schol 87: 14-15+ S 23 '65
Pentagon's dilemma; Goliath and the guerrilla. E. Hobsbawn. il Nation 201:33-8 Jl 19 '65; Discussion. 201:inside cover S 6 '65
Pond and the fish; condemnation by Pope Paul. Commonweal 82:339-40 Je 4 '65
Profile of the Viet Cong. il Newsweek 65:40-1+ Ap 12 '65
Revolutionary warfare; how to tell when the rebels have won. E. Ahmad. il Nation 201:95-100 Ag 30 '65

Runaway war or deadlocked peace. H. Schomer. Christian Cent 82:957-9 Ag 4 '65
Terror in the streets; Viet Cong attacks in Saigon. il Newsweek 67:30+ Ja 3 '66
This is guerrilla warfare; Vietcong's silent subversion. M. W. Browne. Read Digest 87:87-93 S '65
Where red guerrillas burrow like moles. il U S News 60:4+ Ja 24 '66

Legal aspects
Is a declaration of a state of war needed? D. Lawrence. U S News 59:108+ Jl 26 '65

Medical and sanitary affairs
Doc Lucier, who fights his war with a tin washbasin. M. Mok. il Life 59:64-9+ N 26 '65
Gamest bastards of all; medical evacuation team. il Time 86:25 Jl 2 '65
Leprosy: another, older enemy in Viet Nam. il Todays Health 43:76-8 N '65
Malaria in Viet Nam. Time 86:43 Ag 20 '65
Medics' new strides in Vietnam. il Newsweek 66:98+ D 13 '65
More action, more malaria. il Time 86:92 D 10 '65
Woman who stayed; to aid Project concern. J. Robbins. il McCalls 92:96-7+ S '65
Working against death. il Time 86:62-3 D 31 '65
See also
Surgery, Military

Moral and religious aspects
Australian looks at Vietnam: weighing probable future moves. A. Walker. Christian Cent 82:960-2 Ag 4 '65
Call to vigil on Vietnam; Interreligious committee on Vietnam. Christian Cent 82:605 My 12 '65
Churches speak on Vietnam. Christian Cent 82:325 Mr 17 '65
Invitation to return to Cam Ne; Saturday review project to rebuild destroyed houses. N. Cousins. Sat R 48:16+ S 4 '65; Discussion. 48:33-4+ S 25; 47-8+ O 23 '65
Morality, moralism and Vietnam. W. H. Harris. Christian Cent 82:1155-7 S 22 '65; Discussion. 82:1452+ N 24 '65
No place to hide; morality of U.S. policy. Nation 201:179-80 O 4 '65
SR's readers and Cam Ne. N. Cousins. Sat R 48:30 O 9 '65
Svenska Vietnamkommittén; Swedish Vietnam committee formed. B. Svahnström. Nation 201:inside cover S 27 '65
Urge cease-fire in South Vietnam; religious leaders polled in Washington, D.C.; discussion. Christian Cent 82:274, 495-6 Mr 3, Ap 21 '65
Vietnam: setting the moral equation. H. Zinn. il Nation 202:64-9 Ja 17 '66
Who is adequate, Monsignor? criticism of current Vietnamese policy. Christian Cent 82:668 My 26 '65

Naval operations
Navy war in Vietnam; assault from U.S.S. Coral Sea. S. Castan. il Look 29:28-31 N 30 '65

Peace and mediation
Addendum to Why Vietnam? a basis for negotiation exists. J. Gittings. Nation 201: 111-15 S 6 '65
Amateur hour; tragedy of errors performed by diplomatic amateurs. Newsweek 66:19 D 27 '65
And now what? U.S. peace offensive. il Newsweek 67:34 Ja 17 '66
Another no from Ho. il Time 86:24 D 3 '65
As others see us; Japanese Christian peace mission in US. Christian Cent 82:1181-2 S 29 '65
Awaiting negotiations; concerning President Johnson's speech Commonweal 82:133-4 Ap 23 '65
Back door to peace? proposed international conference on Cambodia. Commonweal 82: 205 My 7 '65
Basic U.S. position on Viet-Nam reaffirmed in note to U.K; text of U.S. note, August 8, 1965. Dept State Bul 53:444-7 S 13 '65
Behind the scenes in Vietnam. H. Brandon. Sat R 48:10+ Ag 14 '65
Cautious optimism about Vietnam. il U S News 59:14 S 6 '65
Cease-fire and after; North Vietnam. Nat R 18:10+ Ja 11 '66
Certain reversal. Time 85:32 Ap 32 '65
Chances for peace in Vietnam. il U S News 59:29-31 Ag 16 '65
Christian consensus on Vietnam. Christian Cent 82:1083-4 S 8 '65

VIETNAMESE war, 1957- —Peace and Mediation—*Continued*

Anecdotes, facetiae, satire, etc.

How to fail in negotiations without really trying. A. Fraleigh. New Repub 154:9 Ja 1 '66

Personal narratives

Ambush. J. Morris. il Esquire 64:76-7+ Ag '65

Battle for Nam Dong; excerpt from Outpost of freedom; ed. by W. Rogers. R. H. C. Donlon. il Sat Eve Post 238:38-42+ O 23 '65

Bombing reds' lifeline in Laos; eyewitness report, Ho Chi Minh trail. Laos. S. W. Sanders. il U S News 60:37-9 Ja 24 '66

Folks, by all rights I should be dead; letter. K. W. Bagby. U S News 59:41 D 13 '65

Growing plea from GI's in Vietnam; the least those at home can do is support us; excerpts from letters. il U S News 59:51-2 N 1 '65

I finally met the Vietcong and became their prisoner; with introduction. D. Dawson. il Life 59:121-2+ O 8 '65

Jet-seat view of an air strike; battle of Plei Me. G. C. Troelstrup. il U S News 59:51-2 N 22 '65

Letters from a soldier; ed. by R. G. Deindorfer. il Good H 161:68-9+ D '65

Lot of luck in one whack; rescue of N. Huggins. Time 86:45 N 12 '65

Nineteen-year-old marine in Vietnam. C. S. Wren. il Look 29:19-23 Ag 24 '65

Password to no man's land: friendship. G. P. Hunt. il Life 59:3 S 3 '65

Report from Vietnam. J. J. Murphy. il Seventeen 25:91+ Ja '66

Shot down in North Vietnam, pilot tells his story of pursuit and rescue; ed. by B. Wise. P. Ilg. il Life 59:24-5 Ag 6 '65

Sorry about that. G. C. Scott. il Esquire 64:208-11+ D '65

This is guerrilla warfare; Vietcong's silent subversion. M. W. Browne. Read Digest 87:87-93 S '65

Trying to put the fires out; excerpts from letter. Nat R 17:1144 D 14 '65

Viet vignettes. il Sr Schol 87:18-19+ S 23 '65

Vietnam as one family faces it; Boyt family; with reports by B. Wise. M. Silva and R. Morse. il Life 59:74-87+ D 10 '65

Vietnam diary; notes from the journal of a young American in Saigon. il Reporter 34:25-7 Ja 13 '66

Vietnam: Washington's biggest problem; with recollections from notebook lost in Vietnam. S. Castan. il Look 29:70-6+ Ap 6 '65

Photography

Where the action is; press photographer. H. Faas. il Time 85:66-7 Je 25 '65

Prisoners and prisons

Best torture; once you've broken him down. M. Sahlins. il Nation 201:266-9 O 25 '65

Cardinal rule; case of G. E. Smith and C. McClure. il Newsweek 67:25 Ja 10 '66

Code for soldiers; US military command to abide by the Geneva prisoner of war conventions of 1949. New Repub 153:8 D 11 '65

Getting to know the enemy. D. Warner. il Reporter 33:14-17 D 30 '65

I finally met the Vietcong and became their prisoner; with introduction. D. Dawson. il Life 59:121-2+ O 8 '65

Nasty war that is turning nastier. il U S News 59:8 O 11 '65

No quarter. il Newsweek 66:36 S 13 '65

On parole; cases of G. E. Smith and C. McClure. il Newsweek 66:37-8 D 13 '65

Two for the show; freed G.I.s denounced U.S. involvement in the war. il Time 86:39 D 10 '65

U.S. condemns Viet Cong execution of American military prisoners; Department statement, September 27, 1965. Dept State Bul 53:635 O 18 '65

Use of torture in Vietnam. America 113:148 Ag 14 '65

Propaganda

Air force U-10Bs play key role in psychological warfare tactics. C. Brownlow. Aviation W 82:69 Je 7 '65

Numbing the public. Commonweal 82:35-6 Ap 2 '65

Psywar. il Newsweek 66:40 O 4 '65

Sizing up Viet Nam; newspaper editorials. Time 85:50 F 19 '65

U.S. reaction: talk or fight? U.S. policy in Vietnam. Newsweek 65:20-1 F 22 '65

U.S. role in Vietnam: how Americans react. U S News 58:6 Mr 1 '65

Unrepresented; demonstrations by Assembly of unrepresented people in Washington. Nat R 17:716 Ag 24 '65

Vietnam comes to Oregon U; campus protest called the teach-in. M. Levitas. il N Y Times Mag p24-5+ My 9 '65

War on words; Washington phrase-mongers. B. Forer. Sat R 48:27 Ap 3 '65

What people write on Vietnam war. U S News 58:8 Mr 8 '65

Protests, demonstrations, etc, against

Advise & dissent. Time 86:15 D 31 '65

Again, Moscow stages anti-U.S. protests. il U S News 59:10 D 20 '65

And now the *nouvelle gauche;* self-anointed emissaries. il Time 87:23 Ja 7 '66

And now the Soulnik. Time 86:35 D 10 '65

Antiwar marches and how they happen; with report by S. Angeloff from Berkeley campus. il Life 59:108-10+ D 10 '65

Bankruptcy of the liberals; address, November 27, 1965; with reply by P. Steinfels. C. Oglesby. Commonweal 83:396-401 Ja 7 '66

Battle of conscience; Clergymen's concern over U.S. policies in southeast Asia. il Newsweek 66:78 N 15 '65

Battle of Vietnam day; protest against U.S. policy in Vietnam. il Newsweek 66:98 O 25 '65

Behind those campus demonstrations. E. H. Methvin. Read Digest 88:43-8 Ja '66

Burning draft cards. Commonweal 83:203-5 N 19 '65; Reply. C. Emmet. 83:385-6 D 24 '65

Catholic worker; R. A. LaPorte burns self to death. il Newsweek 66:71 N 22 '65

Children in the line of march. K. D. Fishman. il N Y Times Mag p92+ N 7 '65

Crime of David Miller. J. O'Gara. Commonweal 83:174 N 12 '65

Crisis of confidence. J. O'Gara. Commonweal 83:426 Ja 14 '66

Day the Vietcong attacked the United States; October 15 and October 16, demonstrations in cities across the country and in foreign capitals. T. J. Wheeler. Nat R 17:1157-9 D 14 '65

Defend right of dissent. Christian Cent 82:1373 N 10 '65

Demonstrators: why? how many? anti-Vietnam movement. il Newsweek 66:25-6+ N 1 '65

Draft resisters 1965. C. Brossard. il Look 29:13-17 D 28 '65

Draft riots on college campuses? Sch & Soc 93:420+ N 13 '65

Draftniks and Vietniks; evaluating the opposition. Nation 201:317-18 N 8 '65

Drop the baby! N. Morrison burns self. Newsweek 66:44+ N 15 '65

Epidemic of the heart. Nation 201:375 N 22 '65

Evolution of a peace creep. S. Alexander. Life 59:35 D 10 '65

Great draft-card hubbub. Nation 201:373-4 N 22 '65

Gulliver and the Vietniks. J. Burnham. Nat R 17:1188 D 28 '65

Immolations and consensus: the justification of innocence. A. Towne. Christian Cent 83:72-5 Ja 19 '66

March for peace; Washington march. Christian Cent 82:1501 D 8 '65

Messianic pose; post-cold-war delusions. H. S. Hughes. il Nation 202:7-10 Ja 3 '66

Patriotism of protest. R. G. Sherrill. il Nation 201:463-6 D 13 '65; Correction. 202: inside cover 45 Ja 10 '66

Peace demonstrations, rights and wrongs. America 113:490 O 30 '65; Discussion. 113:656 N 27 '65; Christian Cent 82:1372 N 10 '65

Present dilemma of dissent. America 113:619 N 20 '65

Principles and facts. Commonweal 83:137-8 N 5 '65

Problem of dissent. H. S. Commager. il Sat R 48:21-3+ D 18 '65

Protests against Vietnam policy; address, October 19, 1965. W. Morse. Vital Speeches 32:74-8 N 15 '65

Punishment by conscription; General Hershey's big stick. C. Cohen. il Nation 201:520-2 D 27 '65; Reply with rejoinder by editors. L. Hershey. 202:inside cover. 28 Ja 3 '66

Radicals on the march: but where to, and by what route? A. Kopkind. New Repub 153:15-19 D 11 '65

VIETNAMESE war, 1957- —Protests, demonstrations, etc. against—*Continued*

Reporter at large; student peace movement over Thanksgiving weekend in Washington, D.C. R. Adler. New Yorker 41:195-202 D 11 '65

Ruckus on campus; reaction to demonstrations against war in Vietnam. K. Crawford. Newsweek 66:38 N 1 '65

Spectrum on Viet Nam; campus activity in support of U.S. policy. il Time 86:67 N 19 '65

Squawk and flutter; Washington march. il Newsweek 66:28-9 D 6 '65

Straws in the wind. Nation 201:514 D 27 '65

Students' sturm und drang. Christian Cent 82:1339 N 3 '65; Discussion. 82:1581 D 22 '65

They are saying on the circuit. . ; concerning speech by N. Thomas. W. F. Buckley, jr. Nat R 17:1186 D 28 '65

They march, doubting they will overcome; Vietnam day committee marchers. New Repub 153:9 O 30 '65

To Hanoi, from Dr Spock; demonstrating in Washington. il Time 86:27 D 3 '65

Treason of the experts. E. Bentley. Nation 201:466-70 D 13 '65

Ungentlemanly conduct; H. W. Howe's court-martial. New Repub 154:7 Ja 15 '66

Unteachables. Nat R 17:1181-2 D 28 '65

Vietnam comes to Oregon U; campus protest called the teach-in. M. Levitas. il N Y Times Mag p24-5+ My 9 '65

Vietnam panic button; administration's desire for consensus on foreign policy. J. Whipple. New Repub 153:38 N 20 '65

Vietnam protest. W. C. McWilliams and D. Hale. Commonweal 83:333-6 D 17 '65

Vietniks and the F.B.I. Commonweal 83:392-3 Ja 7 '66

Voice of the new campus underclass. T. R. Brooks. il N Y Times Mag p25-7+ N 7 '65; Discussion. p66+ N 28 '65

Vox Vietnik fires a volley of protest; with report by J. K. Jessup. il Life 59:40B-40D O 29 '65

Weighty unanimity; by Protestant, Catholic and Jews. Christian Cent 82:1564-5 D 22 '65

Psychological aspects

Psywar; handling of propaganda by Joint United States public affairs office. Time 86:32+ O 29 '65

Public opinion

As high school students see the war in Viet Nam; Institute of student opinion. il Sr Schol 87:8 N 18 '65

Letter from Washington; findings of latest Louis Harris survey. R. H. Rovere. New Yorker 41:191-4+ D 18 '65

People beneath the war; the Vietnamese. R. R. Coffey. Nation 202:61-3 Ja 17 '66

Problem of dissent. H. S. Commager. il Sat R 48:21-3+ D 18 '65

Vietnam war: how Americans see it. il U S News 59:11 D 27 '65

Vietnamese students talk about the war. H. Selby. il N Y Times Mag p 104-5+ O 31 '65

Refugees

Captain's legacy. Time 86:10 D 24 '65

Relief work

If your enemy is hungry: two ways to aid the victims of the Vietnamese war. Christian Cent 82:1117 S 15 '65

Statistics

Korea and Vietnam: how two wars compare; table. il U S News 59:6 D 6 '65

Strategy

Big hole; Operation Piranha. il Time 86:51 S 17 '65

Chances for peace in Vietnam. il U S News 59:29-31 Ag 16 '65

Curious passivity; Operations crimp and matador. il Time 87:25A Ja 21 '66

Getting to know the enemy. D. Warner. il Reporter 33:14-17 D 30 '65

End to inertia. il Time 86:24-5 Ag 20 '65

Is the U.S. armed for the wrong war? interview. E. G. Fubini. il U S News 59:60-3 Ag 16 '65

New kind of war il Time 86:28-39B O 22 '65

No easy formula. il Time 86:23 D 3 '65

Now reds must fight, or run. il U S News 59:43 O 4 '65

Now that the choice is made; here's the new strategy. S. W. Sanders. il U S News 59:36-40 Ag 9 '65

Status & strategy. il Time 86:28-30 Ag 6 '65

Stepped-up war. D. Warner. Reporter 33:32 D 16 '65

Strictly military; strategy's by-products. il Newsweek 66:30+ Ag 16 '65

Tears or death? ill-informed public opinion. Time 86:51 S 17 '65

Tide turning in Vietnam war? il U S News 59:35-7 S 27 '65

Vietnam: new policy in the making. H. W. Baldwin. il Reporter 33:16-20 Ag 12 '65

Television reports

See Television broadcasting—War news

Transportation

Giant venture in Viet Nam; large and swift construction programs. il Time 86:86 D 17 '65

War correspondents

Battle in the Delta; Co Cong victory. E. Taylor. il Reporter 34:21-5 Ja 13 '66

Conduit in North Viet Nam; J. Cameron. il Time 86:78 D 17 '65

Dickey Chapelle killed. Sr Schol 87:7 N 18 '65

Git or git got; C. Black of Columbus, Ga, Enquirer. il Newsweek 66:88 D 6 '65

Our man Mok with the marines. G. F. Hunt. il Life 59:3 N 26 '65

Pundit and the prole; J. B. Reston and J. E. Breslin in Saigon. il Newsweek 66:49-50 S 6 '65

Reporter's death; D. Chapelle. Newsweek 66:52 N 15 '65

Woman at war; D. Chapelle killed in Vietnam. il Time 86:54 N 12 '65

Women and the war

Girls under fire; South Vietnamese women in the war. il Time 86:23 Jl 23 '65

Woman who stayed; to aid Project concern. J. Robbins. il McCalls 92:96-7+ S '65

VIEW cameras. See Cameras

VIEW finders

Are 8mm movie finder images bright enough? M. A. Matzkin. il Mod Phot 29:91-2 My '65

Keppler on the SLR; dirt in your finder. H. Keppler. il Mod Phot 29:42+ S '65

VIEW from the bridge; drama. See Miller, A.

VIEW of the sea; drama. See Nolan, P. T.

VIEWERS for transparencies. See Transparencies—Viewers

VIGELAND, Gustav

Astonishing sculptures in Oslo. il Sunset 134:63 My '65

VIGILANCE committees

Deacons; for defense and justice. Negro vigilantes. il Newsweek 66:28-9 Ag 2 '65

See also

Civil rights organizations

VIGLIERCHIO, David R. and Yu, P. K.

Plant parasitic nematode: a new mechanism for injury of hosts. bibliog Science 147:1301-3 Mr 12 '65

VIGNANCOUR, Jean Louis Tixier-. See Tixier-Vignancour, J. L.

VIGUERS, Ruth Hill

Arm of the starfish; review. Horn Bk 41:161 Ap '65

Bushbabies; review. Horn Bk 41:613-15 D '65

North to freedom; review. Horn Bk 41:380-1 Ag '65

On spies and applesauce and such. Horn Bk 41:74-6 F '65

—and others

Booklist (title varies) See issues of Horn book magazine

VIKING press, incorporated

Studio books' formula for quality includes faithful reproduction of good material. il Pub W 188:82+ D 6 '65

VIKING ships

Six viking ships; found in Roskildefjord. P. L. Adams. Atlan 215:88-92 Ap '65

VIKINGS

Columbus vs. Ericson, what science says. D. Cohen. il Sci Digest 59:10-15 Ja '66

Map of history; Vinland map. il Time 86:120+ O 15 '65

New light on discovery of the New World. il U S News 59:8-9 O 25 '65

New world mapped, 1440. il Sci N L 88:263 O 23 '65

Seeing America first; Viking map of 1440. il Newsweek 66:103-4 O 18 '65

Vinland map and the Tartar relation, by R. A. Skelton and others. Review America 114:87 Ja 15 '66. H. Musurillo

VIKINGS—*Continued*
Vinland map and the Tartar relation; excerpts, with introd. by O. Jensen. R. Skelton and G. D. Painter. il Am Heritage 16:4-10+ O '65
Westviking: the ancient Norse in Greenland and North America, by F. Mowat. Review
Sat R il 48:33 D 18 '65. S. Thorne
What did the Norsemen discover? il Sat R 48:49-52 N 6 '65; Discussion. 48:90-1 D 4 '65
Who was first? il Sr Schol 87:17 O 28 '65
Windblown Leif. il Time 86:25B O 22 '65
Yale press publishes map discovery of the century. il Pub W 188:31-4 O 11 '65
VIKINGS (football club) See Football clubs
VILA, George Raymond
Who pays the profit? por Duns R 86:50-2+ S '65

about

U.S. rubber's Vila: he makes the profit. il Duns R 86:51 S '65
VILAS, Charles H.
North Channel cruise. Yachting 117:46-8+ My; 60-2+ Je '65
VILELLA, Roberto Sánchez. See Sánchez Vilella, R.
VILLA, Francisco
Memoirs of Pancho Villa, by M. L. Guzmán. Review
Time il por 86:82+ Jl 2 '65
VILLADOLID, Oscar S.
Sukarno makes trouble in the Philippines. Reporter 33:22-4 Ag 12 '65
VILLAGE life
Continent of villages. R. G. Wesson. Nation 200:705-7 Je 28 '65
Small towns: a new role for old communities? M. Mead. Redbook 125:20+ S '65
VILLAGES
Congo is Kibweta, not Leopoldville. J. A. Lukas. il N Y Times Mag p24-5+ Mr 7 '65
VILLAGES, Historical. See Historical museums
VILLAGES, Restored
Women who bought Main Street; Winnebago, Ill. V. Cadden. il Redbook 124:60-1+ Mr '65
See also
Tombstone. Ariz.
VILLA-LOBOS, Heitor
Something new for Joan Baez, Villa-Lobos. J. Diether. il por Am Rec G 31:502-4 F '65
VILLANOVA university, Villanova, Pa.
University theater. R. A. Duprey. il Cath World 201:240-6 Jl '65
VILLARD, Henry S.
Begrudged diplomats: the stepsons of foggy bottom. Nation 202:36-9 Ja 10 '66
VILLARD, Oswald Garrison
Oswald Garrison Villard: pacifist at war, by M. Wreszin. Review
Christian Cent 82:968 Ag 4 '65. H. E. Fey
Pacifist rough rider. M. Wreszin. por Nation 200:671-3+ Je 21 '65
VILLCHUR, Edgar
Stereo or hi-fi? Am Rec G 31:596-8 Mr '65
VILLELLA, Edward
Dance magazine's 1964 awards. por Dance Mag 39:35+ Mr '65
VILLERS, Stevana
Our ti plant is a tree. il Flower Grower 53:45 Ja '66
Le VILLI; opera. See Puccini, G.
VILLIARD, Paul
Gift of understanding. Read Digest 86:58-61 Je '65
Nature and photography. Natur Hist 74:64-6 N '65
VILLIERS, Alan
Wales, land of bards. Nat Geog Mag 127:727-69 Je '65
VILMORIN, Louise de
Louise de Vilmorin; second fame: good food. N. Lyon. por Vogue 146:122-4 Jl '65
VIMY RIDGE, Battle of. See European war, 1914-1918—Campaigns and battles
VINACKE, Harold M.
Communist China and the uncommitted zone. bibliog f Ann Am Acad 362:113-20 N '65
VINCENNES-Sèvres figurines. See Figurines
VINCENT, G. Robert
Sound of history. por Library J 90:4282-90 O 15 '65
VINCENT, Harold S.
Education for industry. Sat R 49:58+ Ja 8 '66
VINDING, Kirsten
Binding with vat-made papers. A. Karlikow. il Craft Horiz 25:12-15+ Mr '65
VINE, F. J. and Wilson, J. T.
Magnetic anomalies over a young oceanic ridge off Vancouver Island. bibliog Science 150:485-9 O 22 '65

VINEBERG, Arthur M.
Second chance for a dying heart. il pors Look 29:66-71 D 28 '65
VINES. See Climbing plants
VINLAND map. See America—Discovery and exploration—Maps
VINOGRADOV, Sergei
Le plus parisien. por Newsweek 65:39+ Ap 5 '65
VINSON, Carlos
Cottontail jungle. Outdoor Life 136:66-7+ N '65
Shellcracker fever. Outdoor Life 135:58-9+ Je '65
VINSON, Fred M. Jr
New ways gangsters muscle into business; interview. pors Nations Bsns 53:62-5 Ag '65
VINSON, Kenneth
Prohibition's last stand. New Repub 153:10-11 O 16 '65
VINTON, Bobby
So who is this Bobby Vinton? A. Levy. il pors Life 58:76-8+ Mr 12 '65
VINYL
Wet look; expanded-vinyl cloth. il Time 85:54 My 14 '65
VINYL floor tiles. See Tiles, Floor
VIOLENCE
Anatomy of violence. J. P. Scott. il Nation 200:662-6 Je 21 '65
Attack on crime; And the Haters. America 112:412 Mr 27 '65
Home to roost; violence between white and black in America. Commonweal 81:752 Mr 12 '65
Is violence un-American? Nation 201:109 S 6 '65
Negro leaders on violence. Time 86:17 Ag 20 '65
Psychiatrists analyze the Los Angeles riots. F. R. Schreiber and M. Herman. il Sci Digest 58:18-22 N '65
Student violence and rebellion, how big a problem? D. Iwamoto. il NEA J 54:10-13 D '65
Substitutes for violence. J. Fischer. Harper 232:16+ Ja '66
Trade winds; influence of military toys on children. J. G. Fuller. Sat R 48:7 D 25 '65
Unwitting partners to youthful violence. M. Mead. Redbook 125:24+ My '65
What does violence say about man? J. W. Krutch. Sat R 48:18-19 Mr 27 '65
Wretched of the earth, by F. Fanon. Review
New Yorker 41:115-17 Ja 15 '66. N. Hentoff
Sat R 48:33-4 Ap 24 '65. E. Capouya
See also
Terrorism
VIOLETS
Nature note. Sci N L 87:174 Mr 13 '65
VIOLIN playing
Face to face: with an unsentimental violinist. C. Yorke, jr. il Seventeen 24:70 Ap '65
Profiles. J. Wechsberg. il New Yorker 41:49-50+ Je 5 '65
VIOLINCELLO music
See also
Phonograph records—Violincello music
VIOLINISTS
Profiles. J. Wechsberg. il New Yorker 41:49-50+ Je 5 '65
See also
Perlman, I.
Szeryng, H.
VIOLONCELLISTS
Midsummer marathon. Time 86:54 Ag 13 '65
VIORST, Milton
Congress: more action than reform. Nation 200:581-4 My 31 '65
GOP today: schism within a dilemma. Nation 201:375-8 N 22 '65
Nuclear club; why the outs want in. Nation 201:235-9 O 18 '65
VIRDEN, Helen
Faith of a farmer; poem. Farm J 89:113 Ap '65
VIRGIN Mary. See Mary, Virgin
VIRGIN ISLANDS
See also
Airlines—Virgin Islands
St John Island
Saint Thomas Island
Women—Virgin Islands

Industries

Watch movement, to West Indies: loophole in tariff permits duty-free entry into U.S. il Bsns W p 132+ Je 5 '65
VIRGIN ISLANDS NATIONAL PARK
Virgin Islands National Park. T. Gill. il Am For 71:38-41+ My '65

VIRGINIA
See also
Booksellers and bookselling—Virginia
Chincoteague Island
Colleges and universities—Virginia
Education—Virginia
Fairfax County
Fishing—Virginia
Prince Edward County
Shenandoah National Park

Description and travel
Gone flying to Virginia. K. Magner and J. Magner. il Flying 77:52-6 Ag '65
Rich delights of Tidewater, Virginia. E. S. Maloney. bibliog il Motor B 116:22-7+ S '65
We took the high road. W. Hartley. il Redbook 124:70-1+ Mr '65

Historic houses, etc.
Custis-Lee mansion. il Travel 124:37-9 Jl '65
Living with antiques; Virginia home of Mr and Mrs Walter Major. L. P. McGrath. il Antiques 87:208-11 F '65
Virginia in the spring. J. E. Dwyer. il Pop Gard 16:16 Mr '65
See also
Monticello (historic house)
Mount Vernon (historic house)
Williamsburg

History
Rich delights of Tidewater, Virginia. E. S. Maloney. bibliog il Motor B 116:22-7+ S '65

Politics and government
Flutter in Byrdland; governorship race. il Time 86:32 O 15 '65
Goldwater thing. il Time 86:34 N 12 '65
New Byrd men. New Repub 153:9 N 13 '65
New dominion; pre-election problems. Reporter 33:20+ O 21 '65
Sic transit Byrd. V. F. Callahan, jr. Commonweal 83:312-13 D 10 '65
Sit down, you're rocking the boat. E. J. Bell. Nat R 17:983+ N 2 '65
Yes, Virginia, there is a G.O.P. J. Kenneth Robinson victory. il Time 86:13 D 24 '65

Religious institutions and affairs
News of the Christian world (cont) Christian Cent 82:152, 842 F 3, Je 30 '65

VIRGINIA, Minn.
Tenfold more light with fluorescents. E. F. B. Johnson. il Am City 80:111 F '65

VIRGINIA coal and iron company
America's most profitable company? Duns R 85:43 Ap '65

VIRGINIA inside passage. See Waterways—United States

VIRGINIA Kirkus service, incorporated. See Kirkus, Virginia, service, incorporated

VIRGINIA museum of fine arts
Split chief minister; bust of Sematawytefnakht rejoined with missing lower half. il Time 85:66-7 Ap 23 '65

VIRGINITY
Sister considers chastity. M. R. Jones. America 112:488-90 Ap 10 '65

VIRUS
Ribosomes from escherichia coli; lack of specificity for viral RNA. J. E. Dahlberg and R. Haselkorn. bibliog il Science 149:78-80 Jl 2 '65

VIRUS diseases
See also
Cold (disease)
Foot-and-mouth disease
Virus research

Vaccines
New hope for drugs to fight viruses. Good H 160:143-5 F '65
Vaccine aids recruits. Sci N L 87:285 My 1 '65

VIRUS diseases in plants
See also
Viruses, Plant

VIRUS research
Viral diseases related; infectious mononucleosis and leukemia. Sci N L 87:260 Ap 24 '65

VIRUS X; story. See Gallant, M.

VIRUSES
Adenovirus multiplication; genetic relatedness of tumorigenic human adenovirus types 7, 12, and 18. S. Lacy and M. Green. bibliog il Science 150:1296-8 D 3 '65

Adenovirus-associated defective virus particles. R. W. Atchison and others. bibliog il Science 149:754-6 Ag 13 '65; Reply. R. Haselkorn. 150:921 N 12 '65
All about bugs. I. Asimov. il Sci Digest 58:34-5 N '65
Autocatalytic synthesis of a viral RNA in vitro. I. Haruna and S. Spiegelman. bibliog il Science 150:884-6 N 12 '65
Cerebellar disease in cats induced by inoculation rat virus. L. Kilham and G. Margolis. bibliog il Science 148:244-6 Ap 9 '65
Chronic infection of rodents by machupo virus. K. M. Johnson and others. bibliog il Science 150:1618-19 D 17 '65
Conditional-lethal mutants of an animal virus; identification of two cistrons. B. W. Burge and E. R. Pfefferkorn. bibliog il Science 148:959-60 My 14 '65
Cyclic structure of adenovirus DNA. K. O. Smith. bibliog il Science 148:100-2 Ap 2 '65
Herpes-like virus isolated from neonatal and fetal dogs. S. E. Stewart and others. bibliog il Science 148:1341-3 Je 4 '65
Induction of tumors in hamsters with an avian adenovirus (CELO) P. S. Sarma and others. bibliog il Science 149:1108 S 3 '65
Interferon-like virus-inhibitor induced in human leukocytes by phytohemagglutinin. E. F. Wheelock. bibliog il Science 149:310-11 Jl 16 '65
Isoenzymic specificity of impaired clearance in mice infected with Riley virus. B. W. J. Mahy and K. E. K. Rowson. bibliog il Science 149:756-7 Ag 13 '65
Oncogenicity of the simian adenoviruses. R. N. Hull and others. bibliog il Science 150:1044-6 N 19 '65
Particles resembling papova viruses in human cerebral demyelinating disease. G. M. Zu Rhein and S. Chou. bibliog il Science 148:1477-9 Je 11 '65
Radiation resistance in lipovirus-altered human cells. J. B. Little and R. S. Chang. bibliog il Science 148:1746-7 Je 25 '65
Revolution in the cell; Lwoff and others discover. Newsweek 66:77 O 25 '65
Rotation technique in electron microscopy of viruses. H. O. Agrawal and others. bibliog il Science 148:638-40 Ap 30 '65
Soviet search for viruses that cause chronic neurologic diseases in the U.S.S.R. J. A. Brody and others. bibliog Science 147:1114-16 Mr 5 '65
Viruses: smallest bits of living matter. il Sci Digest 57:86-7 Je '65
Wyeomyia subgroup of arbovirus; isolation from man. S. Srihongse and C. M. Johnson. bibliog il Science 149:863-4 Ag 20 '65
See also
Bacteriophage
Coxsackie viruses
Vaccinia virus
Virus research

Culture mediums
Phenotypic alterations in adrenal tumor culture G. H. Sato and others. bibliog il Science 148:1733-4 Je 25 '65

VIRUSES, Plant
Corn stunt disease; is it slowing down? maize dwarf mosaic. Farm J 89:42 S '65
Latest report on maize dwarf mosaic. M. C. Shurtleff and J. J. Feight. il Suc Farm 63:56-7+ F '65

VISHNEVSKAIA, Galina
Music to my ears; Carnegie Hall concert. I. Kolodin. Sat R 48:47 N 6 '65
Music to my ears; Philharmonic Hall recital. I. Kolodin. Sat R 49:76 Ja 8 '66

VISHNIAC, Roman
Art in science. P. Caulfield. il Mod Phot 29:56-7 O '65

VISION. See Sight

VISION (animals) See Sight (animals)

VISION tests. See Sight testing

VISIT home; story. See Bode, E.

VISITING housekeepers
Substitute mothers. C. W. Blackburn. il PTA Mag 59:28-30 Je '65

VISITING nurses. See Nurses and nursing, Public health

VISITOR; story. See Boughton, A. A.

VISITS of state
Are exchange visits of U.S. and Soviet leaders worthwhile? pro and con discussion. il Sr Schol 86:10-11 F 11 '65
As world leaders come to LBJ; what they ask, what they offer. il U S News 59:22-3 D 27 '65

VISITS of state—*Continued*
As world leaders prepare to meet. il U S News 59:22 D 13 '65
Ruffled feelings; postponement of visits by President Ayub Khan and Prime Minister Shastri of India; no postponement of visit by President Park. il Sr Schol 86:18 My 6 '65

Anecdotes, facetiae, satire, etc.
Visit that didn't come off. A. Buchwald. Read Digest 86:235-6 F '65
VISNAGIN. See Benzopyrano
VISSER 'T HOOFT, Willem Adolf
Enugu: second thoughts. G. Murray. Christian Cent 82:167-8 F 10 '65
VISTA. See Volunteers in service to America
VISTA ALEGRE. See Pottery, Portuguese
VISUAL adaptation. See Eye—Accommodation and refraction
VISUAL aids. See Audio-visual aids
VISUAL instruction. See Audio-visual instruction
VISUAL organs (animals) See Sight (animals)
VISUAL perception. See Perception
VISUAL pigments. See Retina
VISUAL stimulus. See Stimulus and response
VITAL statistics
See also
Marriage—Statistics
Population
also subhead Vital statistics under names of countries, e.g. United States—Vital statistics
VITAMIN A. See Vitamins—Vitamin A
VITAMIN deficiency. See Diet, Deficient
VITAMINS
Are vitamin pills necessary? il Consumer Bul 48:18-21 Ap '65
Common sense about vitamins. M. J. Babcock. il Ladies Home J 82:26+ F '65
Vitamin healers; career of C. Fredericks. R. L. Smith. il Reporter 33:18-25 D 16 '65; Discussion. 34:6+ Ja 13 '66
Vitamins restore old books at Vatican City laboratory. il Pub W 188:79+ Ag 9 '65

Vitamin A
Biosynthesis of vitamin A with rat intestinal enzymes. D. S. Goodman and H. S. Huang. bibliog il Science 149:879-80 Ag 20 '65
Retinoyl beta-glucuronic acid: a major metabolite of vitamin A in rat bile. P. E. Dunagin, jr. and others. bibliog il Science 148:86-7 Ap 2 '65
Vitamin A, how much is too much. D. Malena. il Suc Farm 63:124 Mr '65

Vitamin B₆
Fluorescence quantum yield measurements: vitamin B₆ compounds. R. F. Chen. bibliog il Science 150:1593-5 D 17 '65

Vitamin C
Fast reactions of ascorbic acid and hydrogen peroxide in ice, a presumptive early environment. N. H. Grant and H. E. Alburn. bibliog il Science 150:1589-90 D 17 '65

Vitamin D
Actinomycin D and the response to vitamin D. A. W. Norman. bibliog il Science 149:184-6 Jl 9 '65
Actinomycin D inhibition of vitamin D action. J. E. Zull and others. bibliog il Science 149:182-4 Jl 9 '65

Vitamin E
Vitamin E harmful? Sci N L 88:402 D 25 '65
VITTI, Monica
Platinum bonds. por Newsweek 66:98B S 20 '65
VIVALDI, Antonio
From Angelicum, a recording of great musical and pedagogical value. H. Glass. Am Rec G 31:534 F '65
Little Vivaldi festival. S. Fleming. Hi Fi 15:172 D '65
Manhattan Olympiad. Q. Eaton. Opera N 29:31 Mr 20 '65
VIVANTE, Arturo
Last rites; story. New Yorker 41:42-3 My 22 '65
Visit. New Yorker 41:29-31 Jl 3 '65
Waiting room; story. New Yorker 41:40-5 Mr 20 '65
VIVIAN, Weston E.
Congress: one new member brings an engineering PH.D background in research, business to the job. J. Walsh. il por Science **147:1016-18 F 26 '65**

VIVIAN Beaumont theater. See Lincoln Center for the performing arts, New York—Vivian Beaumont theater
VIVISECTION
Antivivisection bill hit. Sci N L 88:111 Ag 14 '65
VIZZARD, James L.
Book review. America 114:88-9 Ja 15 '66
Faces of poverty. America 112:552 Ap 17 '65
Water poachers. America 112:220-3 F 13 '65
VLAHOS, C. J.
This is zero force. Sci Digest 58:77-9 O '65
VLERICK, Richard H.
Research programs can solve purchasing problem, reduce costs. Am City 80:150+ Ap '65
VO Cong Trung
Viet Cong diplomat sizes up the war; interviewed by E. Behr. Newsweek 65:42 Ap 12 '65
VOBORIL, Virginia V.
Dessert of the month. See issues of Good housekeeping
VOCABULARY
Good-bye to all t—t! strong language in literature. W. Stegner. Atlan 215:119 Mr '65
When you speak; excerpt from Seventeen book of etiquette and entertaining. E. A. Haupt. Seventeen 24:175 Mr '65
See also
Words
VOCABULARY tests
It pays to increase your word power. W. Funk. See issues of Reader's digest
VOCAL pitch. See Voice
VOCALISTS. See Singers
VOCATIONAL education
All-age, all-job program. W. M. Arnold. il Am Ed 1:8-11 D '64
Best place for vocational education; opinions differ. J. B. Zack; B. D. Coe; T. Urich; J. Mauck. il NEA J 54:48-52 D '65
Castle Frank high school: new concept in secondary education; Toronto. W. A. McLauchlin. il Sr Schol 86:sup 10 My 20 '65
Conversation on industrial arts and vocational education; interviews. K. E. Dawson; L. A. Burkett. NEA J 54:25-8 N '65
Meeting changing manpower needs; NEA project in Quincy, Mass. and Wood County-Parkersburg, W.Va. il NEA J 55:20-2 Ja '66
Men and boys on Lost Creek road. G. Norman. il Am Ed 1:8-12 Ap '65
Pilot program on occupational trends and career planning. M. M. Reed. ALA Bul 59:1006-9 D '65
Road up hill. Sr Schol 87:19-20 N 11 '65
Schooling kids for today's jobs. il Changing T 19:41-5 S '65
Two exercises in educational policy making; excerpt from Cheerful prospect: a statement on the future of American education. C. S. Benson. il Sch & Soc 93:305-8 Sum '65
Ultimate weapon in war on poverty. il Nations Bsns 53:36-7+ F '65

United States
See Vocational education
VOCATIONAL guidance
College and career; questions and answers. H. Zuckerman. See issues of Senior scholastic
Focusing on careers with a purpose. il Sr Schol 87:11-22+ N 11 '65
Should you see a career doctor? L. Velie. Read Digest 88:112-17 Ja '66
See also
American personnel and guidance association
Occupations
Vocational education
VOCATIONAL literature
Career classified: guide to free job information. il Sr Schol 87:31-4+ N 11 '65
VOCATIONAL psychology
Human side of industry. F. R. Schreiber and M. Herman. il Sci Digest 57:41-3 F '65
VOGEL, Carol A.
Librarian-for-a-day 1964. Library J 90:1468-70 Mr 15 '65
Profession's bottleneck: library education. por Library J 91:65-6 Ja 1 '66
VOGELHUT, P. O. See Chai, S. Y. jt. auth.
VOGT, William
Books in review. Natur Hist 74:4+ D '65
We help build the population bomb. N Y Times Mag p32+ Ap 4 '65
VOICE
When you speak; excerpt from Seventeen book of etiquette and entertaining. E. A. Haupt Seventeen 24:175 Mr '65
Your voice is you. R. Match. Read Digest 87:135-7 N '65

VOICE of America (radio program)
His master's voice; White House censorship of news broadcasts. il Newsweek 65: 16-17 Je 7 '65
New voice at VOA. Time 86:52 Ag 6 '65
Speaking to the Russians in a new voice. J. Osborne. New Repub 153:9-10 N 6 '65
Voice of the Voice. Newsweek 66:27+ Ag 9 '65

VOICE training
Seven-year Cinderella. R. Peters. Seventeen 24:146+ F '65
See also
Speech

VOICEPRINTS
Voiceprints: poison for the telephone rat. J. R. Berry. il Pop Sci 187:80-3 S '65

VOIGT, Melvin J. and Treyz, J. H.
New campuses program. pors Library J 90: 2204-8 My 15 '65

VOLCANIC ash, tuff, etc.
Mazama and Glacier Peak pumice glass: uniformity of refractive index after weathering. V. C. Steen and R. Fryxell. bibliog il Science 150:878-80 N 12 '65
Photometry at Cerro Tololo, Shile: effects of Mount Agung eruption. H. Moreno and others. bibliog il Science 148:364-6 Ap 16 '65
Solar radiation: an anomalous decrease of direct solar radiation; atmospheric dust from the eruption of Mt Agung. E. C. Flowers and H. J. Viebrock. bibliog il Science 148:493-4 Ap 23 '65
Titanium dioxide in pyroclastic layers from volcanoes in the Cascade Range. G. K. Czamanske and S. C. Porter. bibliog il Science 150:1022-5 N 19 '65

VOLCANIC lightning. See Lightning

VOLCANIC rocks. See Rocks, Igneous

VOLCANOES
Beauty's toll; eruption of Mount Taal. il Newsweek 66:54 O 11 '65
Belch of a killer: Mt Taal, Philippines. il Time 86:47 O 8 '65
Confronting the irascible Irazu. H. Tazieff. il UNESCO Courier 18:18-23+ N '65
Electricity in volcanic clouds. R. Anderson and others. bibliog il Science 148:1179-89 My 28 '65
Fiery birth of a new island; Surtsey. H. Shuldiner. il Pop Sci 187:92-3 O '65
Light watches volcanoes. Sci N L 88:325 N 20 '65
Lovely island pearl suddenly erupts; Alas-as village, Volcano Island; with report by R. Morse. il Life 59:108-16+ O 15 '65
Most dangerous science. B. H. Frisch. il Sci Digest 58:9-11 D '65
No thundercloud needed; volcanic lightning. il Time 85:102 Je 11 '65
Photometry at Cerro Tololo, Chile: effects of Mount Agung eruption. H. Moreno and others. bibliog il Science 148:364-6 Ap 16 '65
Surtsey, child of an expanding earth? J. Lear. il Sat R 48:33-9 Jl 3 '65; Discussion. 48:45 Ag 7 '65
Surtsey: island born of fire. S. Thorarinsson. il Nat Geog Mag 127:712-26 My '65
Volcano hard to predict; Taal volcano studied. B. Tufty. il Sci N L 88:231+ O 9 '65
See also
Craters
Etna, Mount
Haleakala

VOLK, Harry J.
Expanding the unusual. il por(cover) Bsns W p68-70+ Ag 28 '65

VOLKOV, Leon
One year, two views. por Newsweek 66:57 O 18 '65

VOLKSWAGEN. See Automobiles, Foreign

VOLLEYBALL
Wising up to a down game. J. Jares. il Sports Illus 22:28-9 My 17 '65

VOLPI, Anna Haria Cicogna, contessa
Villa Volpi. R. Cameron. il por Vogue 145:126-33+ Ap 15 '65

VOLT ohmmeter. See Voltohmmeters

VOLTAGE
Voltage function quiz. R. P. Balin. il Pop Electr 22:73+ F '65

VOLTAGE calibrators. See Calibrators

VOLTAGE regulators
Low-voltage regulator. il Electr World 73:60 F '65

VOLTAIRE, François Marie Arouet de
Age of Voltaire, by W. Durant and A. Durant. Review
Sat R por 48:65-6 O 23 '65. L. Gershoy
Time por 86:118+ O 8 '65

VOLTMETERS
Put your best meter face forward. D. Lancaster. il Pop Electr 22:71-2+ F '65
Testing semiconductors with V.O.M. or V.T.V.M. C. D. Todd. il Electr World 74:31-4+ S '65
See also
Voltohmmeters

VOLTOHMMETERS
Testing semiconductors with V.O.M. or V.T.V.M. C. D. Todd. il Electr World 74: 31-4+ S '65

VOLUNTARY social agencies. See Social agencies, Voluntary

VOLUNTEER service
Amigo Americans; Project Amigos. il Time 85:49 Ap 30 '65
Case of the shocking-purple school. J. Fetterman. Good H 161:276 N '65
Classroom learning is not enough. B. B. Stretch. il Sat R 48:62-3+ Je 19 '65
Conference on Latin American volunteer problems; message to President Arturo U. Illia, September 9, 1965. L. B. Johnson. Dept State Bul 53:608 O 11 '65
Here come the tutors! A. Hamilton. il PTA Mag 60:7-9 D '65
In the grown-up world of teen-agers. il UNESCO Courier 18:26-9 Jl '65
Operation community service; volunteers in Peru's university community co-operation movement. E. Barclay. il UNESCO Courier 18:17-20 Jl '65
Social service projects in English schools. R. Kirk. Sch & Soc 93:476-7 D 11 '65
Teenagers who saved a town; Rock Island, Ill. C. Remsberg and B. Remsberg. il Good H 161:82-3+ S '65
Trojan horse tactics; cosponsorship to broaden recreation services. S. C. Newcombe. il Recreation 58:234-5+ My '65
20,000 volunteer workers for progress and friendship; in fifty developing nations. A. Gillette. il UNESCO Courier 18:57-9 Jl '65
Village where people cared; Humlikon, Switzerland. O. Schisgall. il Read Digest 86:55-60 F '65
Voluntarism in retirement; address, 1964. G. Meyer. Recreation 58:219+ My '65
Volunteership. R. R. Rusk. Recreation 58:212-13 My '65
See also
Teachers aides

VOLUNTEER service, International
Action atonement; German volunteers in nations that suffered under the Nazi invasion. P. Shabecoff. il N Y Times Mag p 149-51+ N 7 '65
I failed in Puno; Papal volunteer. R. F. Clark; discussion. America 112:152, 470 Ja 30, Ap 10 '65
See also
United States—Peace corps
Volunteers for international technical assistance

VOLUNTEER workers. See Volunteer service

VOLUNTEERS for international technical assistance
International technical assistance. D. Wolfle. Science 149:1053 S 3 '65
VITA has the answer. J. Daniel. Read Digest 87:123-6 O '65

VOLUNTEERS in service to America
Bright new spirit in Tonyville. B. Asbell. il Good H 162:60-1+ Ja '66
Domestic Peace corps formed. Christian Cent 82:165 F 10 '65
Domestic peace corps tackles poverty. J. Star. il Look 29:100-3 Ap 20 '65
My neighbor needs me. il Time 85:21 Mr 5 '65
Off the reservation; Red Cliff ousts VISTA workers. il Newsweek 66:27-8 D 27 '65
Report from Appalachia. N. Krell. il Seventeen 25:92-3+ Ja '66
VISTA: a new kind of public service. H. Lees. il Reporter 32:31-2 Ap 22 '65
VISTA brings aid to Indians. il Ebony 20: 88-90+ S '65
VISTA welcomed. E. C. Parker. Christian Cent 82:721-2 Je 2 '65

VON ARX, William S.
Practical astronomy from shipboard. bibliog Sky & Tel 29:340-5 Je '65

VON BRAUN, Wernher
Coming, ferries to space. por Pop Sci 187: 68-9+ S '65
Electric power in space. por Pop Sci 187:58-9+ Ag '65
How we track our spacecraft. Pop Sci 187: 108-9+ N '65
Rendezvous in space. il por Pop Sci 187: 58-9+ Jl '65

VON BRAUN, Wernher—*Continued*
Rocket-riding cameras show how boosters behave. por Pop Sci 187:106-7+ D '65
Ships and planes navigated by satellites. por Pop Sci 186:76-7+ My '65
Strange world of zero gravity. por Pop Sci 186:68-9+ Je '65
Tiny computers steer mightiest rockets. por Pop Sci 187:94-5+ O '65
What an astronaut will wear on the moon. por Pop Sci 186:87-8+ Ap '65
What ever happened to the manned space stations? por Pop Sci 186:88-9+ F '65
What happens to a rocket booster. por Pop Sci 188:68-70 Ja '66
When will we land on Mars? por Pop Sci 186:86-8+ Mr '65

about

Von Braun receives Hill space award. por Miss & Roc 17:58-9 Jl 19 '65
Von Braun urges reusable transport. C. D. LaFond. Miss & Roc 17:16 N 8 '65

VON DER BORCH, C. C. See Peterson, M. N. A. jt. auth.

VON DREELE, W. H.
Here we go a-wassailing with LBJ; poems. Nat R 17:1191 D 28 '65
Reporting the campaign. Nat R 17:980-1 N 2 '65

VON ECKARDT, Wolf
Case for building 350 new towns. Harper 231: 85-8+ D '65
Department of headaches. New Repub 153: 19-22 N 6 '65
New town in Washington. Américas 17:6-12 Je '65

VON GOETZ, Cecile
Introitus; poem. Cath World 201:118 My '65

VON HESSE, Maxeda
I teach famous men to talk; ed. by H. Markel. McCalls 92:98+ F '65

VON HOCHMEISTER, Herbert
CBC. camera-wise. Hi Fi 15:86P-86Q Mr '65
L'esprit de jeunesse, et de corps, et d'art. Hi Fi 15:188-90 D '65
Of time and time beaters. Hi Fi 15:136-7 Ag '65

VON LAUE, Theodore H.
Subversive West. Bul Atomic Sci 21:25-8 My '65

VONNEGUT, Kurt, Jr
Harrison Bergeron; story. Nat R 17:1020-1 N 16 '65
Life book review. Life 58:15+ Je 11 '65

about

Life book review. C. Knickerbocker. Life 58: 6+ Ap 9 '65

VON RECKLINGHAUSEN, Daniel R.
Field-effect transistors for FM front-ends. Electr World 74:36-7+ D '65
Silicon transistor i.f. amplifier for FM tuner. Electr World 74:32-3+ O '65

VON SYDOW, Max
In the role of Jesus. il pors Life 58:92+ Mr 19 '65

VON VORYS, Karl
(ed) New nations: the problem of political development. Ann Am Acad 358:1-179 Mr '65
Toward a concept of political development. Ann Am Acad 358:14-19 Mr '65

VOODOOISM
Haunted Haiti. H. Gold. il Holiday 37:64-9 Mr '65

VOORHEES, Stephen Francis
Stephen Francis Voorhees is dead at eighty-six. por Arch Rec 137:26 Mr '65

VOORHIES, M. R. See Toots, H. jt. auth.

VORKAPICH, Slavko
Reasons of the eye. New Yorker 40:25-7 F 13 '65

VORTEX motion
Australian bath drain has clockwise whirl. Sci N L 88:185 S 18 '65
Bathtub vortex. Sci Am 213:54 N '65
Bathtub vortex. il Time 86:74 S 24 '65

VOSPER, Robert G.
Libraries and the inquiring mind; address, July 9, 1965. ALA Bul 59:709-17 S '65
Memo to members; comments on conference, ed. by R. Warncke. ALA Bul 59:688-9 S '65

VOSS, Carl Hermann
Ways to a willing oneness. Sat R 48:40 F 6 '65

VOSS, Grace Ann
Mo-maids in the swim. Recreation 58:499-500 D '65

VOSS, Virginia
Monteith. Mlle 61:149+ O '65

VOSTOK (space vehicle) See Space vehicles, Russian

VOTERS, Registration of
Amending the voting rights bill. A. M. Bickel. New Repub 152:10-11 My 1 '65
As Alabama arrests neared 3,500; voter-registration drive by Negroes in Selma and Marion. il U S News 58:10 F 15 '65
Beyond the voting rights act. P. Good. il Reporter 33:25-9 O 7 '65
Boomerang in Neverland; Selma, Ala. il Sr Schol 86:17-19 Mr 25 '65
Bowing to the new extremists. D. Lawrence. U S News 58:112 Mr 29 '65
Case of the missing registrars; LBJ and the Negro vote. W. L. Higgs. il Nation 201: 460-2 D 13 '65
Central point; Negro struggle to achieve the right to vote. il Time 85:23-8 Mr 19 '65
Civil right no. 1: the right to vote. M. L. King, jr. il N Y Times Mag p26-7+ Mr 14 '65
Deluge; Negro registrations in the South. il Newsweek 66:17-18 Ag 23 '65
Difference of impact; nonviolent civil rights drives in Montgomery, Ala. and Selma, Ala. il Time 85:23 F 19 '65
Doubters with points; new voting-rights bill. Time 85:22-3 Ap 2 '65
Fact of life; Deep South. Time 86:21 S 3 '65
Forced march; Negro voter-registration campaign in Selma, Ala. il Newsweek 65:24+ F 22 '65
Freedom fever; civil rights violence in Marion. Time 85:23 F 26 '65
Government unlimited; voting rights bill. Nat R 17:712-13 Ag 24 '65
How the voting-rights bill would work. U S News 58:8 Je 7 '65
Interpretation, anyone? public hearings concerning tests for voter registration in Mississippi. il Time 85:23-4 F 26 '65
It looks like a hot summer; with Selma the beginning. il U S News 58:32-3 Mr 22 '65
Kiss of death; voting rights bill. Time 86:17-18 Jl 16 '65
Law & de lawd; slowdown in enrollment of Negro voters. Time 86:38 N 5 '65
Letter from Selma. R. Adler. New Yorker 41:121-2+ Ap 10 '65
Letters from Washington. R. H. Rovere. New Yorker 41:177-8+ Mr 20 '65
Million new Negro voters? il U S News 59:8 Ag 16 '65
Mississippi's new way to register voters. U S News 59:11 Ag 30 '65
More registrars head South. America 113: 560 N 13 '65
Negro registration. New Repub 153:7-8 N 13 '65
New voting law goes into action. il Life 59: 34-34A Ag 20 '65
No peace for winner of peace prize; drive for mass registration of Negro voters in the South. il U S News 58:19 F 1 '65
Opening a second front. Newsweek 66:34 N 8 '65
Other side of the voting-rights bill; excerpts from statement. H. F. Byrd. U S News 58:86-8 Ap 12 '65
President's voting bill. America 112:411 Mr 27 '65
Real stakes in Negro-vote drive. il U S News 58:37-8 Mr 8 '65
Registering Negro voters in the South; necessity for federal voting referees. A. M. Bickel. New Repub 152:9-10 F 20 '65
Report from Mississippi. E. Evans. il Seventeen 25:90+ Ja '66
Reporter at large; attempts of Negroes to register in Tuskegee, Ala. B. Taper. New Yorker 41:58+ Jl 24 '65
Selma, contd; woman beaten by sheriff during registration drive in Selma, Ala. Time 85: 24 F 5 '65
Selma; sustaining the momentum. D. Peerman and M. E. Marty. Christian Cent 82: 358-60 Mr 24 '65
Siege of Selma. Nation 200:154+ F 15 '65
Speedup ordered; Negro voter registration. Sr Schol 86:31+ F 18 '65
Squeezing the trigger; failures to comply with voting rights act. Time 86:12-13 Ag 27 '65
Struggle in Selma; voter registration drive in Alabama's black belt. il Sr Schol 86:17-18 F 11 '65
Summer delay; SCOPE students return to campuses. Nation 201:71 Ag 16 '65
Trigger of hope. il Time 86:19-20 Ag 20 '65
Two nuns in Georgia; gentle crusaders; Project SCOPE, Albany. il Look 29:M9+ N 2 '65

VOTERS, Registration of—*Continued*
Victory in jail. il Time 85:16-17 F 12 '65
Voting rights act of 1965; address, March 18, 1965. N. deB. Katzenbach. Vital Speeches 31:391-8 Ap 15 '65
Voting rights bill. Newsweek 65:21 Mr 22 '65
Voting rights bill, third edition. A. M. Bickel. New Repub 152:13-14 My 22 '65
Voting rights law; victory for freedom; address, August 6, 1965. L. B. Johnson. Vital Speeches 31:642-3 Ag 15 '65
What the Negro vote will do to South; what southern editors say about the Negro vote. il U S News 58:30-8 Mr 29 '65
Who should vote? il Sr Schol 86:6-9+ Ap 8 '65
Will Snick overcome? R. Armstrong. il Sat Eve Post 238:79-83 Ag 28 '65
Year of the vote: the how and whither. Life 58:4 Mr 26 '65
Your future depends on it; signing of voting rights bill and its effect. il Time 86:15 Ag 13 '65
See also
Election laws—United States

VOTING
Obstacles to voting. Nation 201:2-3 Jl 5 '65
Science and democratic progress; election reforms; address, June 11, 1965. F. Stanton. Vital Speeches 31:605-8 Jl 15 '65
Toward voting as a positive pleasure; Time essay. Time 86:37 D 10 '65
See also
Election day
Literacy tests (election law)
Voters, Registration of

Literacy tests
See Literacy tests (election law)
VOTING laws. See Election laws
VOTING machines
Council votes electronically; electronic vote indicator; Seal Beach, Calif. J. T. Williams. il Am City 80:150 My '65
Punched-card votes meet with instant success; use of the Votomatic in Atlanta, Ga. A. F. Kiepper and others. il Am City 80:110-12 S '65
Science and democratic progress; election reforms; address, June 11, 1965. F. Stanton. Vital Speeches 31:605-8 Jl 15 '65
Toward voting as a positive pleasure; Time essay. Time 86:37 D 10 '65

History
First voting machine a hit. il Am City 80:122 Ag '65
VOTOMATIC. See Voting machines
VOULKAS, Peter
Peter Voulkas. D. Cyril. pors Sch Arts 65:27-30 S '65
VOULKOS, Peter
Voulkos: redemption through ceramics. J. Coplans. il por Art N 64:38-9+ Sum '65
VOURAS, Paul P. and Taylor, Alice
Lebanon. bibliog Focus 15:1-6 Je '65
VOYAGE of the lollipop; story. See Dunovan, C.
VOYAGER probe. See Space probes
VOYAGES
Aboard Tinkerbelle on her run to glory R. Manry. il Life 59:30-9 S 17 '65
Alone against the sea; from Samoa to Australia on raft. W. Willis. il Sat Eve Post 238:38-42+ S 25 '65; Same abr. Read Digest 88:118-23 Ja '66
Brave self far at sea; R. Manry's Atlantic crossing. L. Wainwright. Life 59:18 S 3 '65
Coastwise in a museum ship; from Puget Sound to San Francisco in the C.A. Thayer. G. P. Jones. il Yachting 117:45-7+ Mr '65
Conquering copyreader; R. Manry's return after crossing the Atlantic in sloop. il Time 86:61 S 10 '65
Cruise of the Alsanal. S. A. Bell. il Motor B 116:22-5+ Ag; 44-6+ S; 74+ O '65
Hawaii, here we come. G. Mayer. il Motor B 116:48-50+ Jl '65
Hugh Downs: Today's star is South Seas bound. G. Sloane. il Motor B 116:76-8 Jl '65
Scoop at sea; rivalry between Cleveland plain dealer and Cleveland press in reporting R. Manry's voyage. il Time 86:48 Ag 20 '65
Seventy-eight days to fame. il Time 86:22 Ag 27 '65
Suburbanite's saga; R. Manry sailing from Falmouth, Mass. to Falmouth, England. M. Lydon. il Newsweek 66:37-8 Ag 30 '65
Swedish odyssey. il Motor B 116:82+ O '65

Transatlantic passage. M. Badham. il Yachting 117:56-7+ Je '65
World's wackiest wayfarers; boats that cross from Europe to the West Indies. D. Street. jr. il Yachting 118:50-1+ N '65
See also
Cruising
VREELAND, Diana
What is fashion? pors Look 30:58-9 Ja 11 '66
about
Vogue's Diana Vreeland: she sets the fashion. P. Coffin. il pors Look 30:56-9 Ja 11 '66
VUCINICH, Alexander
Science, the index of Soviet power: R&D in the U.S.S.R. Science 148:785-6 My 7 '65
VUCINICH, Wayne S.
Whither Rumania? bibliog f Cur Hist 48:161-7 Mr '65
VULGARITY
Let's face it; what is vulgar? who is vulgar? M. Mannes. McCalls 82:16+ Ag '65
VUREK, Gerald G. and Bowman, R. L.
Helium-glow photometer for picomole analysis of alkali metals. bibliog Science 149:448-50 Jl 23 '65

W

WBOX (radio station) See Radio station
WCOTP. See World confederation of organizations of the teaching profession
WERM (World's encyclopaedia of recorded music) See Phonograph records—Catalogs
WFTU. See World federation of trade unions
WHO. See World health organization
WINS (radio station) See Radio stations
WLBT, Jackson, Miss. See Television stations
WMNB-FM (radio station) See Radio stations, Frequency modulation
WNBA. See Women's national book association
WPA. See United States—Work projects administration
W. R. Grace and company. See Grace, W. R. and company
W. W. Norton and company, incorporated. See Norton, W. W. and company, incorporated
WWVB (radio station) See Radio stations
WACHOVIA bank and trust company
Southern money for southerners. Time 85:88 F 26 '65
WADE, F. A. and others
Geology of the central portion of the Queen Maud Range, Transantarctic Mountains. bibliog Science 150:1808-9 D 31 '65
WADE, John Stevens
Centuries of peasant blood in me; poem. Nation 200:174 F 15 '65
Jimmy's father; poem. Nation 200:143 F 8 '65
Ticktacktoe; poem. Nation 200:174 F 15 '65
WADLER, Joyce
In my opinion. por Seventeen 24:244 My '65
WADSWORTH, Betty G.
Ideas from Parents' magazine's better homemaking center. See issues of Parents' magazine and better homemaking
It's easy to create your own sewing center. Parents Mag 40:58+ Jl '65
WADSWORTH, James J.
Some timely advice from President Washington. Sat R 48:18+ F 20 '65
WADSWORTH atheneum, Hartford, Conn.
Hartford glimpses the pre-renaissance; exhibition of early Florentine and Sienese art. S. J. Wagstaff, jr. il Art N 64:32-4+ My '65
WAFFLES
How to make the waffles on our cover. il Bet Hom & Gard 44:27 Ja '66
Way of the waffle. il Ladies Home J 82:46+ Ap '65
WAGE agreements. See Trade agreements
WAGE differentials
Occupational wage differentials, 1907-47. H. Ober. Mo Labor R 88:787-9 Jl '65
WAGE-price policy. See Price regulation by government—United States
WAGENHEIM, Kal
Cracks in the showcase. New Repub 153:15-16 O 16 '65

WAGES
See also
Income
Non-wage payments
Overtime
Salaries

Dismissal wage
Severance pay and layoff benefit plans. L. E. Lunden and E. M. Moore. bibliog f il Mo Labor R 88:27-34 Ja '65

Economic aspects
Five-way push on wage cost coming. il Nations Bsns 53:31-3 F '65

Regulation
Wages and poverty. America 113:130 Ag 7 '65

Statistics
Developments under major bargaining agreements, 1964. G. Ruben. il Mo Labor R 88: 1189-95 O '65
Trends in average annual earnings and income. A. Sackley. Mo Labor R 88:1302-6 N '65
See also
Wage differentials

Great Britain
Britain's plan to control wages. U S News 58:96 Ap 26 '65

Japan
How Japan's top brass makes the job pay off; through liberal system of expense accounts and fringe benefits. il Bsns W p 100-2+ My 8 '65

Russia
Monthly survey of family budgets in the U.S.S.R. J. W. De Pauw. bibliog f il Mo Labor R 88:681-7 Je '65

United States
Earnings and hours; tables. See issues of Monthly labor review
Earnings and weekly hours of factory workers. J. Cocco. il Mo Labor R 88:1206-12 O '65
Employed poor: their characteristics and occupations. L. D. Cummings. il Mo Labor R 88:828-35 Jl '65
LBJ's views on big pay in industry, government; excerpts from news conference, August 25, 1965. L. B. Jonhson. U S News 59:75 S 6 '65
Metropolitan area pay differences, 1964. K. J. Hoffmann. il Mo Labor R 88:407-12 Ap '65
New report: raises speed up. U S News 59: 94 D 6 '65
People never had it so good: who does best? il U S News 59:110+ O 11 '65
Question of stability. il Time 86:77 S 3 '65
Ranking of U.S. occupations by earnings. M. A. Rutzick. bibliog f il Mo Labor R 88:249-55 Mr '65
Reducing take-home pay. D. Lawrence. U S News 59:108 Jl 19 '65
When $10.00 an hour will be going wage. il U S News 59:83-4 Jl 12 '65
Where raises are headed now. U S News 59: 81-2 Ag 9 '65
Why workers don't mind a little inflation. il U S News 59:99-100 O 4 '65
See also
Government employees—Salaries, allowances, etc.
Minimum wage—United States
Night work
Wages—Statistics
also subhead Wages and hours under names of industries, e.g. Steel industry and trade—Wages and hours

WAGGONER, Paul E. and Zelitch, Israel
Transpiration and the stomata of leaves. bibliog Science 150:1413-20 D 10 '65

WAGGONER, William G.
Band grinder smooths and sharpens; Pop Mech 124:172-4 D '65
Five accessories for your drill press. Pop Sci 186:168-70 Ap '65

WAGMAN, Frederick H.
New member and ALA; address, July 1965. ALA Bul 59:995-1002 D '65

WAGNER, Mahlon W. and others
Paired comparison method for measurement of sugar preference in squirrel monkeys. bibliog Science 148:1473-4 Je 11 '65

WAGNER, Richard, 1813-1883
Avant-garde. N. Dana. il Opera N 29:8-13 F 13 '65

Commemorating Wagner. C. McAlister. il por Opera N 29:17 F 13 '65
Flying Dutchman (Der fliegende Holländer)
Criticism
New Yorker 40:64 Ja 30 '65
Opera N il 29:18-20 F 13 '65
Opera N il 29:24-6 F 13 '65
Sat R 48:24 F 6 '65
From Bayreuth, via Philips, a live Tannhäuser. B. Igesz. il Am Rec G 32:108-11 O '65
From Bayreuth (and Philips), a stunning stereo, Parsifal. G. L. Mayer. il Am Rec G 31:684-7 Ap '65
Götterdämmerung. C. J. Luten. il Am Rec G 31:952-5 Je '65
Hi-fi hit for Wagner's masterwork. E. Coleman. Life 59:22 Jl 2 '65
Lohengrin. Criticism
Hi Fi il 15:203+ N '65
Opera N 30:30 S 25 '65
On records: Der fliegende Holländer; Wagner excerpts. Opera N 29:34 F 13 '65
On records; Die Walküre. Opera N 29:34 Mr 6 '65
On records; Götterdämmerung. Opera N 30:30 N 6 '65
On records; Parsifal. Opera N 29:34 Ap 10 '65
On records; Tannhäuser; Der fliegende Holländer. Opera N 30:34 Ja 22 '66
Perfect achievement. H. Bailey. Opera N 29: 24-5 Mr 6 '65
Richard und Ludwig. por Time 85:73 Je 18 '65
Ring of the Nibelung. Criticism
Opera N 29:24-5 Mr 6 '65
Opera N il 30:25-6 N 6 '65
Stereo Parsifal for the faithful and new converts. C. L. Osborne. il Hi Fi 15:85-6+ Mr '65
Stupendous stereo for the Gods in Twilight. C. L. Osborne. il Hi Fi 15:57-8 Jl '65
Swing low, sweet Siegfried. R. Schoenstein. Sat R 48:91 Ap 10 '65
Wagner and Tristan. A. M. Lingg. Opera N 29:29 Mr 20 '65
Wagner for young and old. J. Browning. Opera N 29:32 F 13 '65
Die Walküre. Criticism
New Yorker 41:89 Mr 6 '65
Opera N il 29:17-20 Mr 6 '65
Sat R 48:26 Mr 13 '65
Who's afraid of the Furtwängler Ring? M. Mayer. Hi Fi 15:32+ O '65
Wings of the storm. E. Downes. il Opera N 29:24-6 F 13 '65
See also
Bayreuth festival

WAGNER, Robert F. Jr
Dimension of commitment. Sat R 48:82-3 O 16 '65

WAGNER, Robert Ferdinand, 1910-
New Yorker goes to the fair. N Y Times Mag p52-3+ Ap 18 '65

about
Best-kept secret. il por Newsweek 65:27-8 Je 21 '65
Can Wagner stop Kennedy in New York? il por U S News 58:59-60 F 22 '65
Dropout? por Newsweek 65:18 Je 7 '65
GOP hope; Lindsay of N.Y. il pors Newsweek 65:23-4+ My 31 '65
Mayor Wagner. New Yorker 41:17-21 D 25 '65
Mischievous Robert Wagner. J. Desmond. il Nation 200:688-90 Je 28 '65
No inferences, please. il por Time 85:25 F 5 '65
There sits Mayor Wagner. J. Newfield. Nation 200:267-9 Mr 15 '65
What New York mayor's race can mean. U S News 58:20 My 24 '65
Who v. Lindsay? il por Time 85:27 Je 18 '65

WAGNER, Ruth H.
I remember Dobry. Horn Bk 41:342-8 Ag '65

WAGNER, Susan
FTC hearing forecasts federal book banning. Pub W 188:30-1 O 11 '65

WAGNER, Wieland
Freudian ring. il Time 86:66 Ag 6 '65
Vienna. J. Wechsberg. Opera N 30:32 Ja 1 '66
Wieland Wagner's Fidelio; Brussels report. R. McMullen. Hi Fi 16:148-9 Ja '66

WAGONER, David
Burying a weasel; poem. Sat R 48:29 My 1 '65
Escape artist; story. Harper 230:102-4 My '65
Osprey's nest; poem. Sat R 48:34 Mr 27 '65

WALL, Albert
Look what's happening to bicycles. Pop Sci 187:108-11+ Ag '65
WALL, E. H.
Power and the intellectuals. Nat R 17:780+ S 7 '65
WALL, James M.
Movies. Christian Cent 82:144-5 F 3 '65
Toward Christian film criteria. Christian Cent 82:775-8 Je 16 '65
WALL, Patrick D. See Melzack, R. jt. auth.
WALL coverings
Burlap's a good answer if you have a problem wall. il Sunset 135:145-6+ O '65
See also
Wallpaper
WALL hangings
Another way to decorate a wall; musical instruments on wall. il Sunset 136:86 Ja '66
Stitchery for wall hanging; junior high school. B. Springer. il Sch Arts 64:22 Je '65
WALL painting. See Mural painting and decoration
WALL paper. See Wallpaper
WALL plaques. See Plaques, plaquettes
WALL Street Journal
Folksiness on Wall Street. il Time 85:73 Ap 30 '65
Wall Street and religion. Christian Cent 82: 357 Mr 24 '65
WALL-to-wall carpeting. See Rugs and carpets
WALLACE, Cecelia
Pacem in terris, Ecclesiam Suam and communism. Cath World 200:231-8; 201:220 Ja, Jl '65
WALLACE, George Corley
Debut of a theologian; interview. Christian Cent 82:511 Ap 21 '65

about

Alabama story; newspaper editors tour by invitation of Governor Wallace. W. J. Cook. il por Newsweek 65:65 Je 21 '65
Alabama unbound. A. Kopkind. New Repub 153:12-16 N 27 '65
Filibustered. Newsweek 66:34-5 O 25 '65
Image-polishing in Alabama; out-of-state editors and reporters on tour at invitation of Governor. il por Time 85:38 Je 18 '65
Lurleen gambit. Time 86:35 N 12 '65
Wallace for president. Time 86:35 O 8 '65
Wallace hangs on. H. Wolman. Commonweal 83:313-14 D 10 '65
Wallace's pottage; expected to run for Senate. Time 86:25A-25B O 22 '65
WALLACE, Henry Agard
Days with Henry Wallace. M. Straight. New Repub 153:9-11 D 4 '65
Henry Wallace dies. por Sr Schol 87:14 D 2 '65
Henry Wallace, RIP. Nat R 17:1149 D 14 '65; Reply. F. C. Waldrop. 18:6+ Ja 11 '66
Henry Wallace; review of career. il por Newsweek 66:28+ N 29 '65
Henry Wallace's legacy. Fortune 73:116 Ja '66
Man who tried to stop the cold war. Nation 201:431 D 6 '65
Man with a hoe. il por Time 86:24-5 N 26 '65
Open door of Henry Wallace. R. Radosh. por Nation 202:39-42 Ja 10 '66
Wallace years. por U S News 59:10 N 29 '65
WALLACE, John, and Schneider, Phillip
Do school boards take education seriously? Sat R 48:89-90+ O 16 '65
WALLACE, Mary
Reason for gladness; story. McCalls 92:72-5 Ag '65
WALLACE, Robert
Fly in December; poem. New Yorker 41:190 D 18 '65
In a spring still not written of; poem. Harper 230:61 F '65
In the field forever; poem. New Yorker 41:43 My 22 '65
Last photograph, being divorced; Directions for keeping a muse; poems. Poetry 106:190-1 Je '65
Love poem. Reporter 33:42 D 30 '65
WALLACE, Sarah L.
Windows on the world: LC's processing department. por Library J 90:4005-12 O 1 '65
WALLACH, Donald F. Hoelzl. See Kamat, V. B. jt. auth.
WALLENQUIST, Ake
Europe's second largest Schmidt telescope. Sky & Tel 29:136-40 Mr '65
WALLEY, Martin
Lake Erie's annual fiasco. Motor B 116:80 O '65

WALLEYE fishing. See Perch fishing

WALLICH, Henry C.
[Column on economic questions] See issues of Newsweek
WALLIS, C. Lamar
Too much ado about too little? letter. ALA Bul 59:100 F '65
WALLIS, W. Allen
Plight of the small college. Atlan 216:124-6 N '65
WALLMANN, Margherita
Lady general. il por Time 85:50 Mr 12 '65
WALLPAPER
Documentary fabrics and papers. R. Davidson. il Antiques 87:524+ My '65
Excise marks on English and Irish wallpapers. A. L. Leask. il Antiques 88:216-19 Ag '65
What wallpaper can do for a room. il Bet Hom & Gard 43:82+ Ag '65
WALLS
Art on a fence; summer art class, Beverly Hills, Calif. P. Vandervoort, 3d. il Sch Arts 64:12-14 My '65
Bearing wall expressed in a skyscraper; IBM building, Seattle; with account by J. S. Hornbeck. il Arch Rec 137:123-8 F '65
Beauty treatment for blank walls. il Bet Hom & Gard 43:115 Mr '65
How to tell a bearing wall. il Pop Mech 124: 134-5 Ag '65
New ideas for dramatic wall treatments. il Bet Hom & Gard 43:80-1 Ap '65
Three precast bearing walls. il Arch Rec 137:218-20+ My '65
See also
Paneling
Plaster and plastering
Storage walls
WALLS, Brick
Build an open brick wall. J. B. Brimer. il Flower Grower 52:40-1 Je '65
WALLS, Concrete
Instant walls; bonding hollow concrete blocks with hot-sulphur-fibre coating. il Sci Digest 58:24-5 N '65
Motel walls angled to view serve also to resist wind; Howard Johnson motor hotel on Cleveland's lakefront. il Arch Rec 137: 226-7 Ap '65
WALLS, Glass
Brick columns and a broad roof shelter a glass-walled house. il Arch Rec 138:167-70 Ag '65
Treetop living pavilion of steel and glass. il Arch Rec 137:66-9 mid-My '65
WALNUT, A. J. and Sussna, Stephen
Dune-protection ordinance. Am City 80:105-6 O '65
WALSH, Ann
Pills to keep women young; excerpt from ERT: the pills to keep women young. McCalls 93:104-5+ O '65
WALSH, Chad
All the creatures of the earth. Sat R 48:52-3 Ap 24 '65
Good old man; poem. America 113:207 Ag 28 '65
O apple tree; poem. Reporter 33:45 O 7 '65
Ode on a plastic stapes. Sat R 49:33 Ja 22 '66
Uneconomic determinism; poem. Reporter 32: 42 Mr 11 '65

about

World dances between our eyes. K. Irby. Poetry 105:414-16 Mr '65
WALSH, F. J.
Energy plants and systems. Arch Rec 137: 212-17 My '65 (to be cont)
WALSH, Jim
Favorite pioneer recording artists. See issues of Hobbies
Three memorable days in and near Washington. pors Hobbies 69:32-4+ F; 70:32-5+ Mr '65
WALSH, Joseph L.
What the students want. Commonweal 83: 206-9 N 19 '65
WALSH, Moira
Films. See issues of America
WALSH, Thomas F.
Case of the sunburned mannequins. Todays Health 43:24-8 Ag '65
WALSH, Thomas James
Tempest over Teapot. B. Bliven. il por Am Heritage 16:20-3+ Ag '65
WALT, Lewis
In they go to the reality of this war. M. Mok. il por Life 59:50-69+ N 26 '65
WALT Disney productions. See Disney, Walt, productions
WALTER, Eugene
Federico Fellini; wizard of films. Atlan 216: 62-7 D '65

WALTER, Eugene—*Continued*
Isak Dinesen conquers Rome. Harper 230:
46-54 F '65
Private jokes of Federico Fellini. por Vogue
146:274-5+ S 1 '65

WALTER, L. S.
Coesite discovered in tektites. bibliog Science
147:1029-32 F 26 '65

WALTER Kidde and company. See Kidde,
Walter, and company

WALTERS, Everett
Immutable Ph.D. Sat R 49:62-3+ Ja 15 '66

WALTERS, Gary
Battle over Tan Hiep. E. Taylor. il Reporter
33:26-9 D 16 '65

WALTHAM, Clae
Not for every eye; story. Redbook 125:147-
59 Ag '65

WALTNER, Elma
On your way to the Black Hills... Travel
124:35-7 S '65
—See Waltner, W. jt. auth.

WALTNER, Willard, and Waltner, Elma
Band of angels. Pop Mech 124:136-7 D '65
Batty boxers. Pop Mech 124:134-5 D '65
Rainbow star. Pop Mech 124:140-1 D '65
Vintage gems from jalopy graveyards. Pop
Mech 124:106-9+ O '65

WALTON, Alan G.
Nucleation of crystals from solution. bibliog
Science 148:601-7 Ap 30 '65
Nucleation phenomena. Science 148:1490+ Je
11 '65

WALTON, Harry
Amazing no-fuel space engine you can build.
Pop Sci 187:106-10+ Jl '65
How good are GE's new power tools? Pop
Sci 187:170-2 N '65
How to build a sing-around music bar. Pop
Sci 186:164-7 Ap '65
How to get the best from twist drills. Pop
Sci 186:148-50+ F '65
Improving your home wiring. Pop Sci 187:156-
61 D '65
It pays to know the best bits for boring
wood. Pop Sci 186:146-9+ Ap '65
Motor mounts that solve shop problems. Pop
Sci 186:152-6 My '65
New engine for space does down-to-earth
jobs. Pop Sci 187:100-5+ Jl '65
Newspaper logs keep the home fires burning.
Pop Sci 187:140-1 D '65
Take your slide show with you. Pop Sci 187:
132-5 N '65
—See McEntee, H. G. jt. auth.

WALZ, Jay
Guy Trimble vs. Guy Tremblay. N Y Times
Mag p38-9+ S 19 '65

WANAMAKER, Temple
Bullets for a consul. il por Newsweek 65:
55 Je 21 '65

WANDERER; story. See Jordan, E. H.

WANDERONE, Rudolf
Famous hustler tells you how to win at
home. por Life 58:161-2 My 14 '65
Proper english. por Esquire 63:79-81 Ap '65

WANG, An-chuan, and Sutton, H. E.
Human transferrins C and D_1: chemical difference in a peptide. bibliog Science 149:
435-7 Jl 23 '65

WANG, Hao
Games, logic and computers; with biographical sketch. Sci Am 213:17, 98-104+ N '65

WANKEL engines. See Automobile engines

WANKEL engines, Marine. See Marine engines

WAPITI. See Elk

WAR
On escalation, by H. Kahn. Review
Commentary 40:101-2+ N '65. G. Kateb
On war as a permanent condition; Time
essay. Time 86:30-1 S 24 '65
People's wars. New Repub 153:7-8 S 18 '65
War is not the normal condition of man. A.
Toynbee. il N Y Times Mag p 122+ N 7
'65
Wars of liberation. H. E. Fey. Christian
Cent 82:1054 S 1 '65
See also
Armaments
Atomic warfare
Disarmament
European war, 1914-1918
Gases in warfare
Guerrilla warfare
Pacifism
Strategy
Vietnamese war, 1957-

Caricatures and cartoons
That was the war that was. Am Heritage
16:84-9 F '65

Economic aspects
Economics of the long war. Nation 201:485 D
20 '65
See also
Vietnamese war, 1957- —Economic aspects

Moral aspects
Loud little handful; wars that offended Abra-
ham Lincoln and Mark Twain. Nation 202:
2-3 Ja 3 '66
Pursuit of peace. E. Larrabee. Atlan 216:61-5
N '65
See also
Atomic warfare—Ethical aspects
War, Ethics of

Psychological aspects
Pursuit of peace. E. Larrabee. Atlan 216:61-5
N '65
See also
Psychological warfare
Vietnamese war, 1957- —Psychological as-
pects

Social aspects
See also
Atomic warfare—Social aspects

WAR, Declaration of
Is a declaration of a state of war needed?
D. Lawrence. U S News 59:108+ Jl 26 '65
Why war is undeclared in Vietnam. il U S
News 59:33 D 20 '65

WAR, Ethics of
Gas in Vietnam. Commonweal 82:67-8 Ap 9
'65
Strategy and conscience, by A. Rapoport. Re-
view
Bul Atomic Sci 21:25-30 D '65; D. G.
Brennan; with reply by A. Rapoport.
21:31-6 D '65

WAR, Prevention of
Alternative to war: peaceful co-existence, an
objective necessity; address. February 18,
1965. N. N. Inozemstev. Vital Speeches 31:
421-4 My 1 '65
Can science prevent war? A. Larson. Sat R
48:15-17+ F 20 '65; Reply. J. J. Agria.
48:25 Mr 13 '65; Rejoinder. 48:27 Ap 3 '65
Can we take chances on survival? D. Law-
rence. U S News 58:104 F 1 '65
Disarmament and international cooperation;
statements, May 12, 1965. H. Cleveland;
A. S. Fisher. Dept State Bul 52:967-73 Je
14 '65
Heart of deterrence. R. K. Coffey. il Bul
Atomic Sci 21:27-9 Ap '65
Peace and pathos; study of Pope John's en-
cyclical Pacem in terris. N. O'Gorman.
Commonweal 81:783-5 Mr 19 '65
Peace and reality; convocation on Pacem in
terris. P. Steinfels. Commonweal 81:785-6
Mr 19 '65
Peace that can be; most commonly ad-
vocated means of survival. S. T. Possony;
reply. C. A. Zebot. America 112:237 F 20
'65
Political equivalent of war, civilian defense.
G. Sharp. bibliog f il Int Concil 555:5-67 N
'65
Same mandate, a different world. R. C. Hot-
telet. il Sat R 48:26+ Jl 24 '65
United Nations commemoration address,
June 25, 1965. L. B. Johnson. UN Mo
Chron 2:84-8 Jl '65
War safety control. D. L. Flaherty. Amer-
ica 112:656 My 8 '65
White House conference on international co-
operation; remarks, December 1, 1965; with
questions and answers. D. Rusk. Dept
State Bul 53:976-84 D 20 '65
Works of peace; remarks, April 10, 1965.
L. B. Johnson. Dept State Bul 52:652-4
My 3 '65

WAR, Psychology of. See War—Psychological
aspects

WAR aims
See also
World war, 1939-1945—War aims

WAR and children
Girl of the paper cranes; Children's monu-
ment in the Peace park. B. J. Lifton. il
N Y Times Mag p35 Ag 1 '65
How Hitler's war ended, for a German boy.
H. J. Stueck. il N Y Times Mag p8-9+ Je
27 '65

WAR and Christianity. See War and religion

WAR and morals. See War—Moral aspects

WAR and peace; drama. See Neumann, A. and
others

WAR and religion
Antiwar sentiment; Japan. G. K. Chapman.
Christian Cent 82:1332-4 O 27 '65
Are we serious about social action? E. R.
Wilson. Christian Cent 82:169-71 F 10 '65

WAR and religion—*Continued*
As others see us; Japanese Christian peace mission in US. Christian Cent 82:1181-2 S 29 '65
Battle of conscience; clergymen's concern over U.S. policies in southeast Asia. il Newsweek 66:78 N 15 '65
Church and modern war. America 114:7-8 Ja 1 '66
Council and the bomb. J. Douglass. Commonweal 81:725-8 Mr 5 '65; Reply. T. Merton. 82:62-3 Ap 2 '65
Council, the popes and peace. R. A. Graham. America 113:365-7 O 2 '65
Japanese peace mission; meeting in New York. H. E. Fey. Christian Cent 82:982-3 Ag 11 '65
Men of peace. J. O'Gara. Commonweal 81:779 Mr 19 '65; Discussion. 82:99+, 175, 202 Ap 16-23, My 7 '65
Peace, priests and the missions. G. Baum. Commonweal 83:175-8 N 12 '65
   See also
Vietnamese war, 1957- —Moral and religious aspects
WAR casualties
   See also
Geneva conventions
WAR correspondents
   See also
Vietnamese war, 1957- —War correspondents
WAR crime trials. See World war, 1939-1945—War criminals
WAR criminals
   See also
World war, 1939-1945—War criminals
WAR debts. See Debts, Public
WAR dogs. See Dogs, War use of
WAR games
   See also
Military maneuvers
WAR graves. See Service mens graves
WAR heroes. See Heroes
WAR in literature
   See also
World war, 1939-1945—Fiction
WAR in poetry. See War poetry
WAR industries. See Munitions industries
WAR inventions. See Inventions
WAR materials
   See also
Munitions
Strategic materials
WAR memorial auditorium, Boston. See Auditoriums
WAR memorials
   See also
Stone Mountain memorial
WAR neuroses. See Neuroses
WAR news
   See also
Television broadcasting—War news
WAR novels. See World war, 1939-1945—Fiction
WAR objectors. See Conscientious objectors
WAR on poverty (program) See Anti-poverty program, 1964-
WAR/Peace report (periodical)
On war and peace. Nat R 17:90 F 9 '65
WAR pensions. See Pensions, Military
WAR poetry
Heroes' twilight, by B. Bergonzi. Review Sat R 49:31-2 Ja 15 '66. G. Hicks
WAR supplies
   See also
Vietnamese war, 1957- —Equipment and supplies
WAR surgery. See Surgery, Military
WAR toys. See Toys
WAR use of dogs. See Dogs, War use of
WAR veterans. See Service men, Discharged
WAR widows. See Widows
WARBLERS
Kirtland's warbler: feathers and flame. V. Stricker. il Nat Parks Mag 39:16-19 O '65
WARD, Aileen
Rescuing Jane Austen. Reporter 32:45-6+ My 20 '65
WARD, Barbara (Lady Jackson)
Lyndon's other bible: Rich nations and the poor nations. il Time 86:19 S 3 '65
WARD, Brice
Automotive electronics. Pop Electr 22:51-3 F '65
Don't let electrical problems stop your car. Pop Mech 124:198-201 N '65
Electronic go-go for your car. Pop Mech 124:196-9 O '65

WARD, Catherine E.
Epic of the gaucho. Américas 17:8-15 N '65
WARD, Charles W. See Martin, A. B. jt. auth.
WARD, Clint
Skiing team. Motor B 116:40-2+ Jl '65
WARD, D. C. and others
Base specificity in the interaction of polynucleotides with antibiotic drugs. bibliog Science 149:1259-63 S 10 '65
WARD, Darrell N.
Cancer research. Science 150:1063-4+ N 19 '65
WARD, Donald O.
Common problems in specifying resistors. Electr World 73:41 Ap '65
WARD, Donovan F.
How eldercare protects the elderly in need of medical care. Todays Health 43:67+ Mr '65
More doctors needed? America 112:850-2 Je 12 '65
Why the medical profession is opposed to medicare; adaptation of address. Todays Health 43:8+ F '65
   about
Doctor Ward's last words. Time 85:28-9 My 21 '65
WARD, Douglas Turner
Day of absence. Criticism
   New Yorker 41:50 D 25 '65
Happy ending. Criticism
   New Yorker 41:50 D 25 '65
WARD, H. Glynn-. See Glynn-Ward, H.
WARD, John William
Enlightenment's evangel. Reporter 33:52+ D 2 '65
WARD, Lewis B.
Ethnics of executive selection. bibliog f Harvard Bsns R 43:6-8+ Mr '65
WARD, Lynd
Illustrating a book in lithography; reprint. Am Artist 29:21+ N '65
WARD, Muriel
Family affair; drama. Plays 25:21-34, 44 Ja '66
WARD, Nancy
Sainte Therese and the dart of fire; poem. Commonweal 81:637 F 12 '65
WARD, Pete
Mecca lunch kid: White Sox third-baseman. M. Cope. il pors Sat Eve Post 238:70+ Ag 14 '65
WARD, Priscilla
Sunday sermon: pew; poem. Cath World 201:301 Ag '65
WARD, R. A. and others
Susceptibility of the gibbon hylobates lar to falciparum malaria. bibliog Science 150:1604-5 D 17 '65
WARD, Samuel
Sam Ward, king of the lobby, by L. Thomas. Review
   Time 85:121+ Ap 30 '65
WARD, William
Low and inside: views from the arena. Nation 200:508-10 My 10 '65
WARD, William B. and Borcherding, J. R.
Thinking of expanding? Suc Farm 63:46-7+ Ap '65
WARDLAW, Frank H.
They never left Texas. Sat R 48:25-8 S 18 '65
WARDWELL, Allen
English decorative arts at the Art institute of Chicago. Antiques 89:78-93 Ja '66
WAREHOUSES
All-rush service the goal at new Dell warehouse; Montvill warehouse, New Jersey. il Pub W 188:19-22 O 18 '65
Bags vs bulk: savings and storage; how communities store de-icing chemicals in bulk. il Am City 81:108-9 Ja '66
Book wholesaling and supply in California. F. H. Potter. Pub W 188:57-9 N 22 '65
Scott, Foresman consolidates warehousing at Pinola, Indiana. il Pub W 188:25-8 D 13 '65
University of Chicago press streamlines its warehouse. il Pub W 187:55-6 F 1 '65
WARFARE, Submarine. See Submarine warfare
WARFIELD, Rebecca
Who are you? and who are all those others? Vogue 146:84-5+ S 15 '65
WARHOL, Andrew
Andy Warhol, movie maker. H. Junker. Nation 200:206-8 F 22 '65
Edie & Andy. il por Time 86:65+ Ag 27 '65
Second fame. N. Lyon. il Vogue 145:184-6 Mr 1 '65

WARING, James
About dancing. Dance Mag 39:35 F '65

about

James Waring and dance company, Judson dance theater. D. Hering. Dance Mag 39: 64+ Mr '65
Works by Deborah Lee, Carol Marcy, and James Waring; Judson memorial church. J. Anderson. Dance Mag 39:158 D '65

WARMINSTER broom. See Brooms (shrubs)

WARNCKE, Ruth E.
Memo to members. D. H. Clift. por(p212) ALA Bul 59:170 Mr '65

WARNER, Bob
Land of record breakers. Field & S 69:152-4+ Ap '65

WARNER, David
People are talking about... por Vogue 145: 80-1 Ap 15 '65

WARNER, Denis
Australia girds for defense. Reporter 32:20-2 Mr 11 '65
Cautionary report on Laos. Reporter 33:35-8 D 2 '65
Coup is dead, long live the coup! Reporter 32:25-6 Mr 11 '65
Getting to know the enemy. Reporter 33:14-17 D 30 '65
Indonesia: generals who got away. Reporter 33:39-40 O 21 '65
Indonesia's Communists: down but not out. Reporter 33:23-6 N 18 '65
More cracks in Malaysia. Reporter 33:40-2 O 7 '65
Our secret war in Laos. Reporter 32:23-6 Ap 22 '65
Peking-Djakarta axis. Reporter 33:25-7 S 23 '65
Price of victory. Reporter 33:29-32 D 16 '65
Second fall of Singapore. Reporter 33:27-9 S 9 '65
Stepped-up war. Reporter 33:32 D 16 '65
Sukarno, the would-be emperor. Reporter 32:24-7 My 20 '65
Thailand: Peking's new front. Reporter 32:32-4 Je 17 '65
Three Afro-Asian fronts; Vietnam. Reporter 32:27-9 Mr 25 '65
Vietnam: the politics of peace. Reporter 32:40-2 Ap 8 '65

WARNER, Ed
Mephisto's musings. Hi Fi 16:125 Ja '66

WARNER, Jack L.
Last tycoon. por Newsweek 65:112+ My 24 '65

WARNER, John
Mobile status symbol. Sat R 49:83 Ja 8 '66

WARNER, Ken
Radio waves that work under water. Pop Sci 186:66-8 My '65

WARNER, Sylvia Townsend
Johnnie Brewer; story. New Yorker 41:45-50 Ap 10 '65

WARNER-Lambert pharmaceutical company
Governor's face lift; new products. il Time 86:63B-64 Jl 30 '65

WARNICK, Dorothy Brant
Fun under floodlights. Travel 123:39-42 Ap '65
Novel vacations. Travel 123:37-9 Je '65

WARNING lights. See Signals and signaling

WARNKE, Frank J.
Pacific Sound. Opera N 29:28-31 F 6 '65
Slender affirmations. New Repub 154:28+ Ja 15 '66

WARRANTS (law)
Importance of good police work; search without warrant. Time 85:56 F 19 '65
Supreme court quashes Texas book seizure. Pub W 187:57 F 1 '65

WARRANTY
Don't get hooked buying a camera. T. Karp. Mod Phot 29:67+ D '65
Warranty war. P. Hillary. il Motor T 17: 27-9 Je '65
See also
Guaranty of goods

WARREN, A. Louise
Flaming rockets. Horticulture 44:46 Ja '66

WARREN, Dale
Boston opera. Opera N 29:29 Ap 17 '65
Boston opera company, 1909-1914. Am Rec G 32:130-2, 382 O, D '65
From the depths. Opera N 30:6-7 D 4 '65
Herbs for summer bouquets. Horticulture 43: 29 Jl '65
Price of genius. Opera N 30:31 D 25 '65

WARREN, Harry V.
Medical geology and geography. Science 148: 534-7+ Ap 23 '65

WARREN, Herbert J.
Thought for the day; poem. Atlan 215:136 Ap '65

WARREN, James R.
Case for the junior high school. Atlan 215: 120-3 Mr '65

WARREN, Mary
Hefner chooses a special girl who finds it an honor. il pors Life 59:68D-69 O 29 '65

WARREN, Mary Phraner
Memory of a writers' conference. Writer 78: 23-4 Ap '65

WARREN, Philip, Jr
Here come the trailers! Am For 71:36-9+ Je '65

WARREN, Robert Penn
Fall comes in back-country Vermont; poem. New Yorker 41:56-7 O 23 '65
Negro now; excerpts from Who speaks for the Negro? Look 29:23-31 Mr 23 '65
Robert Penn Warren and Ralph Ellison: dialogue; excerpt from Who speaks for the Negro? Reporter 32:42-6+ Mr 25 '65
Uncorrupted consciousness: the stories of Katherine Anne Porter. Yale R 55:280-90 D '65
Unity of experience. Commentary 39:91-6 My '65
(ed) See Carmichael, S. Two for SNCC
(ed) See Moses, R. Two for SNCC

WARREN, Stanley, Jr
Palmares: a Negro state in colonial Brazil. Negro Hist Bul 28:79-80 Ja '65

WARSAW

Music

Renaissance in Warsaw; Grand theater of opera and ballet reopened. V. C. Gibbs and E. L. Howard. il Opera N 30:28-9 Ja 1 '66
Thorn grows in Warsaw. P. Heyworth. il Hi Fi 15:60-5 S '65

Theater

Theatre. H. Popkin. Vogue 146:169 O 1 '65

WARSAW book fair. See Book fairs

WARSAW convention
Dropping the pact; damages for death outdated. Newsweek 66:68+ N 1 '65
IATA members vote liability limit raise. J. R. Ashlock. Aviation W 83:24-5 N 1 '65
U.S. gives notice of denunciation of Warsaw convention; Department announcement, November 15, 1965, with text of notice. Dept State Bul 53:923-5 D 6 '65
Warsaw convention decision seen near. Aviation W 83:43 S 20 '65
Warsaw move seen threat to cooperation. J. R. Ashlock. Aviation W 83:35 D 6 '65
What is a life worth? U.S. proposes raise of liability limit. Time 86:98 O 29 '65

WARSAW ghetto. See Jews in Poland

WARSAW international festival of contemporary music. See Music festivals—Poland

WARSHIPS
Dreadnought: a history of the modern battleship, by R. Hough, with introd. by C. S. Forester. Review
Am Heritage il 16:110-11 Ap '65. B. Catton
See also
Armored vessels

Armaments

Beauty and chivalry of the United States assembled; explosion of Peacemaker, cannon on U.S. steam sloop Princeton, 1844. D. B. Webster, jr. il Am Heritage 17:50-3+ D '65

United States

Beauty and chivalry of the United States assembled; explosion of Peacemaker, cannon on U.S. steam sloop Princeton, 1844. D. B. Webster, jr. il Am Heritage 17:50-3+ D '65
Historic U.S. ships. J. H. Winchester. il Travel 124:31-3 Jl '65
Navy to brief industry on FDL ships; fast deployment logistics ships. M. Getler. Miss & Roc 17:15-16 N 22 '65
U.S. to sell or lend eleven warships to friendly foreign countries. Dept State Bul 53:871-2 N 29 '65
See also
Constellation (frigate)

WARSHOFSKY, Fred
Spare parts surgery: what lies ahead? excerpt from The rebuilt man. Todays Health 43:44-6+ Je '65

WASH and wear fabrics. See Textile fabrics, Synthetic

WASHBURN, Bradford
Canada's Mount Kennedy. il por Nat Geog Mag 128:1-3 Jl '65

WASHBURN, Paul
Is this renewal? Christian Cent 82:809-11 Je 23 '65

WASHBURN, S. L. and others
Field studies of Old World monkeys and apes. bibliog Science 150:1541-7 D 17 '65

WASHING machines
Automatic washing machines. il Consumer Bul 48:6-12 Ag '65
Just push a button. il McCalls 93:56+ O '65

WASHING of clothes. See Laundry

WASHING of eggs. See Eggs—Washing

WASHINGTON, George
George Washington, businessman; excerpt from George Washington: the forge of experience, with editorial comment. J. T. Flexner. il Am Heritage 16:94-8 O '65
George Washington, by J. T. Flexner. Review
    Sat R 49:38 Ja 15 '66. E. Wright
Nothing but the tooth; report from Washington post on teeth donated to Smithsonian institution. Reporter 33:14+ D 16 '65
Reflections on Washington's birthday. por Sat Eve Post 238:88 F 27 '65
Some timely advice from President Washington. J. J. Wadsworth. por Sat R 48:18+ F 20 '65
Visit to Mount Vernon; excerpts from Travels through America; tr. and ed. by M. J. E. Budka. J. U. Niemcewicz. il por Am Heritage 16:64-71 F '65
Washington at Monmouth; with painting. Am Heritage 16:14-17 Je '65

WASHINGTON, Martha
Visit to Mount Vernon; excerpts from Travels through America; tr. and ed. by M. J. E. Budka. J. U. Niemcewicz. il Am Heritage 16:64-71 F '65

WASHINGTON, D.C.
Big change in Washington; symposium. il Look 29:21-34+ Ap 6 '65
Five different Washingtons. B. H. Bagdikian. il N Y Times Mag p8-9+ D 26 '65
It's Middletown-on-the-Potomac. R. Baker. il N Y Times Mag p32-3+ F 14 '65
Washington code: zip; report on the generation now at peak energy. peak ideas. il Vogue 146:98-103 Ag 15 '65
    See also
Gardens—Washington, D.C.
Public welfare—Washington, D.C.
White House

Airports
Washington jet access closes major gap; opening of Washington national airport. J. R. Ashlock. Aviation W 84:43+ Ja 17 '66
Where's everybody? Dulles international airport. il Newsweek 65:89 My 10 '65

Anti-poverty program
Fighting poverty in the Nation's capital. U S News 59:56 N 22 '65

Architecture
In Washington, the power of persuasion helps overcome a maze of controls. J. Bailey. il Arch Forum 123:48-51 Jl '65
Monster builder; J. G. Stewart and his Capitol campus. il Newsweek 66:41 O 11 '65
New building houses health organizations; Pan American health organization and World health organization. il(p209) Sci N L 88:217 O 2 '65
On guard, architect! J. G. Stewart criticized. R. Stolley. Life 59:40D Jl 2 '65
    See also
Washington, D.C.—Public buildings

Art
Knaths and Morris in Washington. F. Getlein. New Repub 152:30-1 My 15 '65

Buildings
See Washington, D.C.—Architecture

Churches
    See also
Washington, D.C.—Washington cathedral

City planning
Anti-urban design for Washington. D. Canty. il Arch Forum 123:24-5 N '65
New town in Washington. W. Von Eckardt. il Américas 17:6-12 Je '65

Climate
White House located in Washington heat island. Sci N L 87:121 F 20 '65

Crime
Alarmed capital fights violent crime. il U S News 59:54-5 Ag 23 '65

Capitol crime; District of Columbia committee introduces bill to the House. Reporter 32:18+ Ap 8 '65
In the Nation's capital, crisis in crime; excerpts from article in Washington Sunday star. M. Ottenberg. il U S News 58:58-60 My 24 '65
Where women fear to tread. Time 86:17A Ag 13 '65

Description
Coming to Washington? J. Miller. il Suc Farm 63:111+ Ap '65
Offbeat guide to Washington. D. Chapman. il Look 29:46-55 Ap 6 '65
When you visit Washington... il Changing T 19:21-3 Ap '65

Education
Big-city answers; innovations of superintendent Hansen. il Time 86:56 Jl 9 '65
School that smiles; John Eaton school, District of Columbia. E. Ferber. il Am Ed 1:8-10 S '65

Galleries and museums
Ladies launch a gallery; sculpture and paintings by American Indians in the Department of the interior building. I. Moore. il Am For 71:22-5 Mr '65
Plastic history; capital's new National historical wax museum. il Time 85:71 Mr 12 '65
    See also
National gallery of art
Smithsonian institution
Smithsonian institution—National collection of fine arts

Gardens
In the great gardens of Dumbarton Oaks, nature joins art and artifice. il House & Gard 127:130-3 Mr '65
New White House garden dedicated. il Flower Grower 52:38-9 Ag '65

Hotels, restaurants, etc.
Senators' choice: soup of the inner sanctum, also other specialties; with recipes. M. Kaytor. il Look 29:38-9 Ap 6 '65

Housing
Foggy Bottom's dolce vita; executives cooperative overlooking the Potomac. F. Gutheim. Nation 201:395-7 N 22 '65
Johnson's model city; the poverty program in Washington. J. Ridgeway. New Repub 152:15-18 F 13 '65
Leading lady in urban renewal. J. Peter. il Look 29:75-6+ S 21 '65

Intellectual life
Changing Washington. H. Ehrlich. il Look 29:21-9 Ap 6 '65

Monuments, statues, etc.
Honoring the presidents: more memorials. il U S News 59:14 O 18 '65
Try again; proposed Franklin Delano Roosevelt memorial. il Newsweek 66:20 Jl 5 '65
What's being done about FDR and JFK memorials. il U S News 58:11 Ap 12 '65
    See also
Washington monument, Washington, D.C.

Music
Cio-Cio-San arrives. A. M. Lingg. il Opera N 30:24-5 Ja 1 '66
Inter-American festival: third; sponsored by the Pan American union. Américas 17:42 Mr '65
Inter-American music festival. G. Lafay. Hi Fi 15:124 Ag '65
Thirty world premieres; third Inter-American music festival. I. Lowens. il Américas 17:18-21 Jl '65
Twin capitals. F. C. Smith; J. Ardoin. il Opera N 29:31 Ap 3 '65
Variety in the capital. G. Lafay. il Hi Fi 15:114 Jl '65
    See also
Opera society of Washington

Negroes
If nation's capital rules itself. il U S News 59:50-2 S 20 '65
Race rule in Washington. A. Kopkind. New Repub 152:18-20 Mr 27 '65
Race trouble if D.C. doesn't get home rule? U S News 59:8 S 6 '65
Shoes for God's children; Brother Joe's project. M. McGrory. America 113:396 O 9 '65
Warning for Washington. Time 86:21 S 3 '65

WASHINGTON, D.C—Negroes—*Continued*
Washington's Negro elite. S. Hyman. il Look 29:60+ Ap 6 '65
Why whites flee the Nation's capital. il U S News 59:58-61 O 25 '65

Police
Unhappy lot of men in blue. America 113: 128 Ag 7 '65

Politics and government
Business not as usual on Monday; struggle for independence. J. N. Eller. America 113: 314 S 25 '65
Decolonizing Columbia. il Time 86:16 S 10 '65
DC home rule; letter. F. C. Waldrop. New Repub 152:45 Ap 17 '65
Home rule almost. W. V. Shannon. Commonweal 83:82-3 O 22 '65
Home rule for D.C? what Johnson proposes. U S News 58:10 F 15 '65
Home sweet home rule. Nat R 17:910 O 19 '65
How a conservative upset the liberals; defeat of home-rule bill. U S News 59:24 O 11 '65
If nation's capital rules itself. il U S News 59:50-2 S 20 '65
Last colony; killing of Johnson's bill by House. Time 86:31-2 O 8 '65
Never jam today; Home rule bill. New Repub 153:8 S 11 '65
Premature birth; selfgovernment to the District of Columbia stalled. Newsweek 66:33 O 11 '65
Race rule in Washington. A. Kopkind. New Repub 152:18-20 Mr 27 '65
Some other time, perhaps. New Repub 153:7 O 9 '65
Washington, D.C: a city in search of a government. il Sr Schol 86:28-9 F 18 '65
Washington, our worst-governed city. il Changing T 19:25-8 Ag '65
When Congress got its back up; defeat of Johnson-backed home rule bill. il U S News 59:41-2 O 11 '65

Public buildings
House that Sam built; Rayburn House office building. D. G. Lowe. il Am Heritage 16:67 O '65
House the House built; Rayburn House office building. il Newsweek 65:31 Ap 12 '65
Monument to power. H. B. Meyers. il Fortune 71:122-5+ Mr '65
New federal architecture. il Arch Rec 137: 135-46 Mr '65
See also
United States—Capitol

Rapid transit
House passes transit bill for the capital. Am City 80:47 S '65

Religious institutions and affairs
News of the Christian world (cont) Christian Cent 82:219 F 17 '65

Sanitary affairs
Trash-tapping; segregating the trash of special individuals into separate bundles. Reporter 32:7-8 Je 3 '65

Social conditions
Shoes for God's children; Brother Joe's project. M. McGrory. America 113:396 O 9 '65

Social life and customs
Changing Washington. H. Ehrlich. il Look 29:21-9 Ap 6 '65
Girl in Georgetown; Jo Ann Christiansen. C. S. Wren. il Look 29:93-6 Ap 6 '65
Offbeat guide to Washington. D. Chapman. il Look 29:46-55 Ap 6 '65
Race to succeed Nicole; the entries. M. Cheshire. il Life 59:93-4+ N 12 '65

Stores
Hecht's art gallery complements its book section. il Pub W 187:62-3 My 24 '65

Street traffic
Parade-tested traffic markings. il Am City 80:128 Ag '65

Streets
Washington's Pennsylvania avenue; Grand avenue for the Great society. J. Peter. il Look 29:40-1 Ap 6 '65

Theater
See also
John F. Kennedy Center for the performing arts. Washington, D.C.

Washington cathedral
Gargoyles for Washington; National cathedral. E. L. Horwitz. il Horizon 7:46-8 Sum '65
Rare book display marks Cathedral library opening. il Pub W 187:42-3 My 3 '65

Water supply
Zinc cable provides cathodic protection. il Am City 80:30 Mr '65

WASHINGTON (state)
See also
Architecture, Domestic—Washington (state)
Booksellers and bookselling — Washington (state)
Crab Creek
Education—Washington (state)
Fishing—Washington (state)
Glacier Peak
Hunting—Washington (state)
Labor and laboring classes—Washington (state)
Legislation—Washington (state)
Mines and mineral resources—Washington (state)
Public welfare—Washington (state)
San Juan Islands
Skagit River
Washington, Lake

Description and travel
Gone flying to Washington. K. Magner and J. Magner. il Flying 77:62-7 N '65
Salt-water highways of Puget Sound; how to use them on any visit to western Washington. il Sunset 135:42-51 Ag '65

Politics and government
Lumps in Olympia. il Newsweek 65:29 F 8 '65

Religious institutions and affairs
News of the Christian world (cont) Christian Cent 82:1328 O 27 '65

WASHINGTON (state) University, Seattle
Iron man at Washington. il Time 86:69 N 5 '65
Liberal arts seminars for high school pupils. C. B. Ovens. Sch & Soc 93:350-1 O 2 '65

School of fisheries
College-bred fish for man's delight. M. Morgan. il Harper 231:47-51 Jl '65; Same abr. Read Digest 87:193-5+ O '65

WASHINGTON, LAKE
Love lyrics to a lake. E. Crimmin. il Motor B 116:40-1+ S '65
WASHINGTON cathedral. See Washington, D.C.—Washington cathedral
WASHINGTON correspondents. See Reporters and reporting
WASHINGTON COUNTY free library, Hagerstown, Md.
Washington County free library. il Library J 90:5179 D 1 '65
WASHINGTON earthquake. See Earthquakes—United States
WASHINGTON library association
Another strong state program. M. Ricking. ALA Bul 59:835 O '65
WASHINGTON market, New York. See New York (city)—Markets
WASHINGTON monument, Washington, D.C.
Tall tales; building of the monument. H. Sutton. il Sat R 48:44+ D 18 '65
WASHINGTON national airport. See Washington, D.C.—Airports
WASHINGTON rallying the troops at Monmouth; painting. See Leutze, E.
WASHINGTON Redskins (football club) See Football clubs
WASHINGTON Senators (baseball) See Baseball clubs
WASHINGTON square, New York. See New York (city)—Washington square
WASHINGTON square; drama. See Olfson, L.
WASHINGTON state library
Cooperative program for institutions started by Washington state library. Library J 90:4317 O 15 '65
WASHINGTON university, St Louis
Getting out of the hometown class. il Bsns W p 154-6+ Je 26 '65
WASHINGTON university arboretum. See Arboretums
WASHINGTONIAN (periodical)
Brave new entries. Newsweek 66:72 O 11 '65
WASHINGTONIANS
We were eyeball to eyeball with victory; why Washington Senators were removed to Minnesota and renamed Minnesota Twins. R. Baker. Sports Illus 23:40-1 O 11 '65

WASHSTANDS
Treasure hunt; washstands. J. Mebane. il Bet Hom & Gard 43:82-3 Je '65

WASKOW, Arthur I.
Nonviolence and creative disorder. Christian Cent 82:1253-5 O 13 '65
Young America's newest vocation. Sat R 48:12-14+ Je 5 '65

WASON, James R.
Labor-management under the Johnson administration. Cur Hist 49:65-70+ Ag '65

WASPS
Polymorphic spermatozoa in the hymenopterous wasp dahlbominus. P. E. Lee and A. Wilkes. bibliog il Science 147:1445-6 Mr 19 '65
See also
Hornets

WASSEF, Rameses Wissa
Poetic world fashioned on the weaver's loom. UNESCO Courier 18:32-9 Jl '65

WASSERBURG, G. J. and others
Strontium-rubidium age of an iron meteorite. bibliog Science 150:1814-18 D 31 '65

WASSERMAN, Paul
New library school at Maryland starts classes under Wasserman. Library J 90:3570+ S 15 '65

WASTE disposers. See Refuse grinders

WASTE in government spending. See United States—Appropriations and expenditures

WASTING disease. See Animals—Diseases and pests

WATANABE, Kosuke. See Brown, K. T. jt. auth.

WATCH dogs. See Watchdogs

WATCH making. See Clock and watch making

WATCHDOGS
Criminal's worst friend; guard dogs. il Life 58:107-8 Ap 23 '65

WATCHERS; story. See Randall, E. E.

WATCHES
Capsule history of timepieces. R. Condon. Holiday 38:42-3 Ag '65
See also
Hamilton watch company
Time measurements

History
Brothers Huaud and their enameled Swiss watches. P. Verdier. il Antiques 88:829-33 D '65

WATER
Is your plumbing double-crossing you? danger of cross-connections. R. Day. il Pop Mech 124:160-3+ Ag '65
Question of birthright; man's current concern over water. il Time 86:70-79B O 1 '65
Stability of lakes near the temperature of maximum density. H. Eklund. il Science 149:632-3 Ag 6 '65
Strontium and magnesium in water and in crassostrea calcite. A. Lerman. bibliog il Science 150:745-6+ N 5 '65
Water myths; know the facts. il Good H 161:162 S '65
See also
Floods

Desalting
Making sea fit to drink. G. T. Seaborg. U S News 59:64 Jl 19 '65

Pollution
See Water pollution

Purification
See Water purification

WATER, Distilled
Desalted water builds up steam; with list of saline water conversion plants. il Bsns W p 120+ O 16 '65

WATER, Saline
Pilot conversion plant. Nat Parks Mag 39:18-19 Ap '65
Saline water program. Nat Parks Mag 39:20 Mr '65

WATER, Underground
Ancient water tapped; 40,000-year-old rainwater found in Saudi Arabia. Sci N L 88:277 O 30 '65
Guelta of the bleak Sahara; source of water is mystery in the Tchad. W. G. Dyer. il Natur Hist 74:36-9 N '65
Now we're drilling for steam; discovery of geothermal energy in the Salton Sea. J. L. Parker. il Sci Digest 57:78-80 F '65
Radiocarbon determinations for estimating groundwater flow velocities in central Florida. B. B. Hanshaw and others. bibliog il Science 148:494-5 Ap 23 '65
See also
Springs

WATER bear. See Arthropods

WATER billing. See Billing

WATER birds
Ducks and geese survive on U.S. private lands. Sci N L 87:264 Ap 24 '65
See also name of water birds, e.g. Pelicans

WATER coagulation. See Water purification

WATER color painting
Visions from the greenhouse; A. Christ-Janer. il Time 86:74-5 D 31 '65
Warren Baumgartner, 1894-1963. N. Kent. il Am Artist 29:46-7+ Ap '65
Water color page. See issues of American artist

WATER conservation
Ending the water crisis. S. L. Udall. Sat R 48:46 O 23 '65
Evaporation of water; its retardation by monolayers. V. K. LaMer and T. W. Healy. bibliog il Science 148:36-42 Ap 2 '65
Evaporation retardants; application by means of a water-soluble matrix. L. E. Myers. il Science 148:70-1 Ap 2 '65
Friend in need. R. C. Wilson. Recreation 58:268+ Je '65
Myths of the western dam. W. Stegner. il Sat R 48:29-31 O 23 '65
Precious water; handle with care. il McCalls 93:70-1+ Ja '66

WATER consumption
See also
Water meters

WATER departments
Water service beyond the meter. L. R. Burzell. Am City 80:122-3+ O '65

WATER desalting. See Sea water—Desalting; Water purification—Desalting

WATER distribution
Water service beyond the meter. L. R. Burzell. Am City 80:122-3+ O '65
Water shortage; a frame of mind. W. Bowen. il Fortune 71:144-6+ Ap '65

WATER flies. See Cladoceran

WATER heaters
Bargain electric water heater? Consumer Bul 49:36 Ja '66
Safer water heaters; incorrectly installed heater may explode. il Consumer Bul 48:2+ Ap '65

WATER hyacinths
Beautiful nuisance. Time 86:59 Jl 16 '65

WATER in the body
Nuclear magnetic resonance studies of living muscle. C. B. Bratton and others. bibliog Science 147:738-9 F 12 '65
Why man cannot live without water; Doctor Carrasquer research findings. Todays Health 43:76 Je '65

WATER meters
Closer eye on water. il Bsns W p44+ Jl 31 '65
Everybody gains with this meter; remote-reading system, Holidaysburg, Pa. il Am City 81:17 Ja '66
Meter readers, throw away your pencils; Thorntown, Ind. il Am City 70:19 Ag '65
Put a price on water. H. Hazlitt. Newsweek 66:71 Ag 30 '65
Use gallons, not cubic feet in your water-rate schedules. Am City 80:117+ Ap '65

Repairing
New refinements in meter maintenance; Portland, Ore. T. Suderburg. il Am City 80:114-16 Je '65

WATER pipes

Cleaning
Vaults combine with biennial conduit cleaning to transport water economically; Kingston, N.Y. C. A. Manganaro. il Am City 80:126-8 Je '65

Leakage
Leak; New York's methods of dealing with leakage. New Yorker 41:19-20 S 4 '65

WATER plants. See Aquatic plants

WATER pollution
Air and water; enforcement of legislation. New Repub 152:6-7 Ap 24 '65
Are we running out of water? G. Hill. Look 29:31-3 D 14 '65
Beauty spot. New Repub 152:7 F 27 '65
Billions to clean up the rivers; industries and cities will have to split a huge tab. il Bsns W p50-2+ Ap 24 '65
Brighter picture for the Great Lakes. H. Titus. Field & S 70:24+ S '65
Bullhead weakened by traces of detergents. Sci N L 80:40 Jl 17 '65
Cleaner water drive steps up. Bsns W p78 Mr 13 '65

WATER pollution—*Continued*

Congress provides tools for a clean-up; prettier landscape and purer water. Bsns W p30 S 25 '65

Crisis in water: its sources, pollution and depletion; symposium. il Sat R 48:23-8+ O 23 '65; Discussion. 48:29 N 27 '65

Day we run out of water; reprint. J. E. Bylin. il Sci Digest 58:74-9 Jl '65

Dead sea; Lake Erie. il Newsweek 65:33-4 Ap 12 '65

Dry season; drought-stricken Northeast. New Repub 153:5-6 Ag 21 '65

Excessive nitrate making water unsafe. Sci N L 88:41 Jl 1 7'65

Federal water-pollution control act uses both carrot and stick. Am City 80:17 D '65

Fight to save Lake Erie. H. Titus. il Field & S 69:10-12+ Mr '65

Filth in the Great Lakes: what can be done about it; interview. G. B. Langford. il U S News 59:58-61 D 13 '65

Fouling of the American environment; symposium. il Sat R 48:31-48+ My 22 '65; Discussion. 48:21 Je 26 '65

Guarding clean water; federal emphasis on keeping rivers and streams from becoming polluted. Bsns W p36 Ja 30 '65

Hideous Hudson River; Lake Erie is dirty, too. America 113:148 Ag 14 '65

Hudson. New Yorker 41:41-3 S 11 '65

Hudson, an open, running sewer. il Newsweek 66:50-1 Ag 23 '65

Man and his habitat: problems of pollution; symposium. Bul Atomic Sci 21:18-30 Mr '65

Man and his habitat: problems of water pollution. il Bul Atomic Sci 21:16-26 Ap '65

Metabolism of cities. A. Wolman. il Sci Am 213:178-88+ bibliog(p278) S '65

Model river aids stream-pollution study; University of Texas project. il Am City 80:30 Jl '65

Muskie starts pollution control drive. C. H. Callison. Audubon Mag 67:114 Mr '65

National disgrace. Nation 200:462 My 3 '65

New Jersey revives a river. E. Kendall. Holiday 39:112+ Ja '66

New York leads pollution attack. il Am For 71:38-9 Mr '65

North River, town of Norwell, Plymouth County, Mass. W. O. Douglas. Bul Atomic Sci 21:11 My '65

Our great scenic rivers. il Recreation 58:266-7 Je '65

Poison in the well. Sci Digest 59:37 Ja '66

Poisoned waters; endrin in lower Mississippi; reply. J. F. Flanagan. Commonweal 81:746 Mr 5 '65

Poisoning our own wells. Christian Cent 82:828 Je 30 '65

Politics of pollution. G. Hill. il Nation 201:220-3 O 11 '65

Pollution fight picks up force; boom for makers of waste treatment equipment. il Bsns W p 108-10+ N 13 '65

Pollution kills 7,800,000 fish. Am City 80:133 Mr '65

Pollution: PSAC panel takes a panoramic view. J. Walsh. Science 150:1006-8 N 19 '65

Presidential findings on air, water pollution. Am City 80:8 D '65

Progress report; Newburgh, N.Y. to build sewage plant. il Newsweek 66:37 N 8 '65

River dies, and is born again; Raritan River, N.J. F. J. Cook. il N Y Times Mag p22-3+ Ap 18 '65

Salmonella in the water; Riverside County, Calif. Newsweek 66:56 Jl 12 '65

Saving the rivers from resource raiders. New Repub 152:10-11 F 13 '65

Test case on pollution: big clean-up begins; Lake Erie. il Bsns W p25-6 Ag 14 '65

Time for transfusion. il Time 86:62 Ag 20 '65

U.S. offers timetable on cleaning up Hudson; conference on pollution of the Hudson River. Bsns W p31 O 2 '65

War on pollution; Water quality act. Nat Parks Mag 39:22 D '65

Water fresh, clear, clean-or polluted? House & Gard 127:103 Je '65

Water needs cleaning. B. Tufty. Sci N L 87:117 F 20 '65

Water pollution: bill endorsing strong federal war on polluters received favorably in Congress. E. Langer. Science 147:1018-20 F 26 '65

Water-pollution challenge. Am City 80:8 O '65

Water pollution: federal role is strengthened by law authorizing new agency and quality standards. E. Langer. Science 150:198-9+ O 8 '65

Water pollution, who's holding up progress? Am City 80:8 My '65

See also

Trade waste

Water purification

WATER pollution control administration. See United States—Water pollution control administration

WATER pressure. See Hydrostatic pressure

WATER purification

Approved coagulant aids. il Am City 80:28 S '65

Desalinization makes brackish water fresh. Sci N L 88:57 Jl 24 '65

Drums along Otter Creek; limestone neutralizes acid trout waters. J. Hayes. il Outdoor Life 137:40-3+ Ja '66

50-billion-dollar job: cleaning up the Nation's waters. il U S News 59:44-6 O 4 '65

Good-neighbor plant; Westchester County, N.Y. G. E. Griffin. il Am City 80:99-102 Mr '65

How Germany keeps the Ruhr River clean. il U S News 59:61 D 13 '65

How good is your water? House & Gard 128:37-8+ O '65

New mill no threat to Lake Michigan. il Am City 80:12 N '65

New way to clean water and reuse it; Hyperion treatment plant, Playa del Rey, Calif. P. Comen and R. Jacobson. il Sci Digest 57:89-91 My '65

One control operates eight filters; Terrebonne, Quebec. A. Trottier. il Am City 80:90-2 S '65

Outboard motor speeds treatment of algae; device used in Boston. C. H. Reed. il Am City 80:38 N '65

Pure water for America; editorial. A. W. Smith. Nat Parks Mag 39:2 N '65

Research built this water plant; Chicago's Central district filtration plant. il Am City 80:82-5 Jl '65

Safe water for drinking and cooking; gadgets attached to faucets ineffectual. il Consumer Bul 48:19-20 O '65

Try a multi-bed filter; Bryn Mawr, Pa. K. E. Shull. il Am City 80:77-9 N '65

We solved a filter-media problem; Erie, Pa. W. E. DeArment. il Am City 80:83-5 D '65

Why sewage effluents must be chlorinated; summary of Masters thesis. A. F. Lehmann. bibliog il Am City 80:79-81 Jl '65

See also

Swimming pools

Water softening

Water supply

Desalting

Atomic water vs. atomic power; difficulties of nuclear control compounded. Nation 201:263-4 O 25 '65

Desalinization progress. Am City 80:19 Ag '65

Salt free; municipally-owned water desalting plant in Texas. Recreation 58:451 N '65

Salt water in the sewers; North Miami, Fla. F. J. Miller. il Am City 80:112+ D '65

Sixty-three nations to attend symposium on water desalination. Dept State Bul 53:537 S 27 '65

Where is science taking us? excerpt from the 1964 report of the director of Oak Ridge national laboratory. A. M. Weinberg. il Sat R 48:56-7 F 6 '65

See also

Sea water—Desalting

WATER rates

Modern water rates. See issues of American city to October 1965

Oil and water; Marvin Shurbet test case brings tax refund. Newsweek 66:82 D 6 '65

Pilot plant points the way to a rate decrease; Minneapolis, Minn. T. B. Corlett, jr. and J. R. Hoffer. il Am City 80:113-15 O '65

WATER skis and skiing

Look, mom, no boat! il Time 85:64 My 7 '65

Skiing team: skiboat driving. C. Ward. il Motor B 116:40-2+ Jl '65

Water skiing is easier than it looks. W. Heyman. il Pop Sci 186:110-13 Je '65

Anecdotes, facetiae, satire, etc.

Down to the sea on skis. H. Bottel. il Motor B 116:38-9 Jl '65

WATER softening

Conditioning the water we use; with equipment that softens water. il Consumer Bul 48:33-8 N '65

Is soft water really important? R. Charles. il Parents Mag 40:80-1+ F '65

Precious water: handle with care. il McCalls 93:70-1+ Ja '66

WATSON, Aldren A.
Mural panels for a publisher's office. Am Artist 29:46-51+ O '65
WATSON, Debbie
I like people to like me. por Seventeen 25:37 Ja '66
about
Debbie Watson: she'll be dangerous at twenty. S. Gordon. il pors Look 30:73-5 Ja 25 '66
WATSON, Donald P. See Hylin, J. W. jt. auth.
WATSON, F. J. B.
Paris *marchands-merciers* and French eighteenth-century taste; adaptation of address, May 1964. Antiques 88:347-51 S '65
WATSON, Harold M.
French authors and Roman indexers. America 114:79-83 Ja 15 '66
WATSON, Ivan
How to put that zing in your screenings! Pop Phot 56:122+ Ap '65
WATSON, John
PEN congress in Bled forecasts '66 session in U.S. Pub W 188:14-15 Ag 16 '65
WATSON, John B.
Calipers on the human mind. J. W. Krutch. Sat R 48:22-5 Je 19 '65
WATSON, Lewis
Three kinds of quail. por Outdoor Life 137: 36-7+ Ja '66
WATSON, Paul G.
DeForest's early audions. Electr World 74: 82-3 S '65
WATSON, Robert
Woman's question; poem. Poetry 105:244 Ja '65
WATSON, Thomas Augustus
Voice heard round the world; excerpt from Conquest of silence. L. Barnett. il Am Heritage 16:50-9+ Ap '65
WATSON, Thomas J. Jr
Automation; address, October 8, 1965. Vital Speeches 32:48-51 N 1 '65
WATSON, W. Marvin
Games as usual. il por Newsweek 65:22 F 22 '65
WATSON-Wilson transportation system
Yellow transit, trucker in a hurry. il Bsns W p61-2+ Ag 28 '65
WATT, D. C.
European students strike for academic reforms. Reporter 33:42-4 D 16 '65
WATT, Douglas
Concert records (cont) New Yorker 41:134+ Je 12 '65
Popular records (cont) New Yorker 40:65+ Ja 30 '65
WATT, James
International cooperation for health: a modern imperative. Dept State Bul 53:412-18 S 6 '65
WATTENBERG, Ben J.
Not great, but good; excerpts from This U.S.A. Time 86:29-30 O 8 '65
—and Scammon, R. M.
Our population: the statistics explosion. Reporter 32:40-1 Mr 25 '65
WATTERS, Pat
Telephone terrorism. Atlan 215:118-21 Ap '65
Why the Negro children march. N Y Times Mag p28-9+ Mr 21 '65
WATTIE, Robert T.
Robert Wattie's road back. il por Newsweek 65:54-5 F 8 '65
WATTIER, Francis
Science: thrills of exploration; excitement of discovery. UNESCO Courier 18:40-1+ Jl '65
WATTMETERS
Audio power wattmeter. S. Davis. il Electr World 74:77 D '65
WATTS, Alan
Mystic more Freudian than Freud. New Repub 152:22-4 My 1 '65
WATTS, Frances B.
Leprechaun's pot of gold; drama. Plays 24: 43-50 Mr '65
Queen's Christmas cake; drama. Plays 25: 69-75 D '65
Storybook revolt; drama. Plays 25:67-73 N '65
Witch in the golden hat; drama. Plays 25: 68-72, 86 O '65
WATTS, Franklin
Getting a children's book published. Writer 78:21-2 O '65
WATTS, Mango
Fragrance hall of fame. Mlle 61:147 My '65
WATTS, Raymond N. Jr
Space notes. Sky & Tel 30:285 N '65
WATTS towers, Los Angeles. See Architecture, Fantastic
WATUSI. See Burundi—Native races

WATZEK, Peter F.
Watzek elected AFA president membership gains are shown. por Am For 71:5 Mr '65
WAUGH, Dorothy
Adrienne Adams. Am Artist 29:54-9+ N '65
WAUGH, Evelyn
Fizz, bubbly, pop. Vogue 146:156+ S 1 '65
about
Books. W. H. Auden. New Yorker 41:159-60+ Ap 3 '65
Post-Waugh insight. J. M. Cameron. Commonweal 83:114-15 O 29 '65
WAURÁ Indians. See Indians of South America—Brazil
WAUWATOSA, Wis.
Designed for the people who use it. F. D. Kuckuck. il Am City 80:108-10 Ag '65
WAVE functions
Is there a fifth force in the universe? conservation of parity. B. H. Frisch. il Sci Digest 57:37-40 F '65
WAVE mechanics
See also
Wave functions
WAVELL, Archibald Percival Wavell, 1st earl
Wavell: scholar and soldier, by J. Connell. Review
Reporter 33:43-5 S 9 '65. G. A. Craig
WAVES, Sound. See Sound waves
WAX, Mel
Gas pricing: wellhead warriors. Nation 200: 417-19 Ap 19 '65
WAX bullets. See Bullets
WAX dolls. See Dolls
WAX figures
Plastic history; capital's new National historical wax museum. il Time 85:71 Mr 12 '65
WAX modeling
Patience Wright and her new style of picturing. P. D. Sampson. il Antiques 87:586-9 My '65
WAX painting. See Encaustic painting
WAY of the world; drama. See Congreve, W.
WAYMAN, Cooper H.
Hard look at soft detergents. Bul Atomic Sci 21:22-6 Ap '65
WAYMAN, Stan
Tiger's kill; photographs. Life 58:52-9 Je 25 '65
about
Tense assignment: stalking the tiger. G. P. Hunt. il por Life 58:3 Je 25 '65
WAYNE, Gary
Antenna rotators pinpoint signals. Pop Electr 22:59-61 My '65
Guide to picture tube testers and rejuvenators. Pop Electr 23:46-8 O '65
WAYNE, John
Big John. por Newsweek 65:86+ Mr 1 '65
John Wayne. A. Hano. il por Good H 161: 82-3+ O '65
John Wayne: a love song. J. Didion. il pors Sat Eve Post 238:76-9 Ag 14 '65
John Wayne rides again. il pors Life 58:69-70+ My 7 '65
Man's man. W. Page. il pors Field & S 70: 31-3 Ja '66
WAYNE state university, Detroit
Can subsidies solve America's problems? a university's answer. il Nations Bsns 53: 34-5+ Ag '65
Cantilevered tiers for Hall of pharmacy. il Arch Rec 138:154-5 O '65
Women's dormitory. il Arch Rec 138:134-5 Ag '65
Monteith college
Monteith; profile. V. Voss. il Mlle 61:149+ O '65
WAYS, Max
Creative federalism and the Great society. Fortune 73:120-3+ Ja '66
On the campus: a troubled reflection of the U.S. Fortune 72:130-5+ S; 140-7+ O '65
WAYSON, William W.
Teachers in slum areas. Sr Schol 86:4T+ F 11 '65
WE have something in common; story. See Schaeling, M.
WEAKFISH fishing
Campout on Cape Sable. V. Dunaway. il Outdoor Life 135:62-4+ Ap '65
Spring tide plugging. A. J. McClane. il Field & S 69:100 Ap '65
WEALES, Gerald
Books. Commonweal 82:599-600 Ag 20 '65
How now, Herb Blau? Reporter 34:43-5 Ja 13 '66

WEALES, Gerald—*Continued*
Knack; and how to lose it. Reporter 33:64
S 23 '65
Newley pretentious. Reporter 32:45-6 Ap 8
'65
Virtue rewarded. Reporter 32:38-40 My 6 '65

WEALTH
See also
Millionaires
Poverty
Prosperity
Rich, The
Success

Anecdotes, facetiae, satire, etc.
Flatten your wallet; high style ahead. S. J.
Perelman. New Yorker 41:34-6 F 20 '65

WEALTH, Distribution of
Jeremiahs and pacifiers. Nation 200:127 F 8
'65

WEANING of pigs. See Swine—Feeding

WEAPONS
As a British observer reports the war; wea-
pons in daily use in the Vietnamese war.
A. Carthew. New Repub 152:7 Ap 17 '65
In Vietnam, a blank check to try out new
weapons. il U S News 58:38 Ap 12 '65
Inventors' utopia; Limited war laboratory.
D. Francis. il Pop Sci 187:54-7+ S '65
Is Vietnam a junkyard for U.S. arms? il
U S News 58:10 Mr 22 '65
Military situation in Vietnam; excerpt. J.
Lacouture. New Repub 152:20 My 22 '65
New weapons, new experience; war in Viet-
nam. New Repub 152:7-8 Ap 17 '65
Questions and answers; need for increased
attention for limited-warfare weapons. W.
J. Coughlin. Miss & Roc 17:54 N 8 '65
See also
Atomic weapons
Firearms
Munitions
Rockets
Stone implements and weapons

Control systems
Systems planners stress modularity. il Miss
& Roc 16:109-11+ Mr 29 '65

WEAPONS, Bureau of. See United States—
Navy department—Weapons, Bureau of

WEAPONS control. See Disarmament

WEAPONS systems
Air force analyzing Minuteman 2 for hind-
sight payoff evaluations. Aviation W 83:
104 D 13 '65
Low-level flight capabilities studied. I. Stone.
Aviation W 83:101-2 O 11 '65
McNamara seeks improved anti-aircraft. G.
C. Wilson. Aviation W 82:25-6 F 22 '65
McNamara stresses air defense system. Miss
& Roc 16:18 F 22 '65
Materials development is crucial to all areas
of military weaponry. il Miss & Roc 16:
54-8 Mr 29 '65
Military objectives spur work. il Miss &
Roc 16:83-4+ Mr 29 '65
Myriad R&D problems await solution. il
Miss & Roc 16:40-3+ Mr 29 '65
Systems approach sought for avionics. B.
Miller. il Aviation W 82:235-6+ Mr 15 '65
Systems planners stress modularity. il Miss
& Roc 16:109-11+ Mr 29 '65
TOW, Shillelagh face showdown; year of
decision for army's tactical missile de-
velopment program. D. L. Zylstra. Miss &
Roc 16:14-15 My 10 '65

WEARY, Marcia Dale
Ballet in the barn. il Dance Mag 39:64-5
F '65

WEATHER
Drought in East, floods in West, why the
strange weather; interview. J. Namias. il
U S News 59:48-50 D 27 '65
Those crazy Americans; extremes of Ameri-
can climate. E. G. Smith. il Atlan 216:
111-13 Ag '65
Weather for a gardener. T. M. Longstreth. il
Horticulture 43:26-8+ Ap '65
What's happening to the weather; with in-
terview with R. M. White. il U S News 59:
49-52 Ag 30 '65
See also
Droughts
Meteorology
Storms
Winds

WEATHER and business
Drought dries up business, too. il Bsns W
p29-30 Jl 17 '65

WEATHER and plants. See Plants, Effect of
climate on

WEATHER buoys. See Buoys

WEATHER bureau (United States) See United
States—Weather bureau

WEATHER control
Change of climate. Newsweek 66:90 O 4 '65
Notes and comment; battle between fruit
growers and truck farmers. New Yorker
40:23 F 13 '65
Weather modification; NAS panel report and
new program approved by Congress reveal
split on policy. J. Walsh; reply. G. P.
Miller. Science 148:22 Ap 2 '65
Weather; now we can do something about
it. A. P. Armagnac. il Pop Sci 186:80-4+
Mr '65
See also
Rain making

Laws and regulations
Weather, legal problem? Sci N L 88:405 D 25
'65

WEATHER forecasts
Chief; New York weather bureau area fore-
cast center. New Yorker 41:24-6 Ag 21 '65
Environmental agency. Sci N L 87:340 My 29
'65
Numerical weather prediction in daily use.
G. P. Cressman. bibliog il Science 148:319-
27 Ap 16 '65
Speed weather forecasts; development of the
world weather watch. A. Ewing. Sci N L
88:405 D 25 '65
Weather forecasts; good now, will get better.
Changing T 20:6 Ja '66
What's new. See issues of Successful farm-
ing
Your weather. See issues of Farm journal
See also
Radar meteorology
Radio broadcasting—Weather forecasts
United States—Weather bureau

WEATHER instruments. See Meteorological instruments

WEATHER lore
Weather signs in the back country; reprint
from Out of the woods. il Recreation 58:
144 Mr '65

WEATHER maps
Early bird speeds chart transmission; data
gathered by Tiros IX. il Miss & Roc 17:
35+ Jl 5 '65
Extraordinary photograph shows earth pole
to pole. il Nat Geog Mag 127:190-3 F '65

WEATHER modification. See Weather control

WEATHER predictions. See Weather forecasts

WEATHER radar. See Radar meteorology

WEATHER records
Weather; new report sketches anatomy of
national program and of coordination problem. J. Walsh. Science 148:610-11 Ap 30 '65

WEATHER research
Doppler radar in weather research. il Electr
World 73:45 My '65
Need weather research. Sci N L 87:402 Je
26 '65

WEATHER vanes
Treasure hunt; weathervanes. J. Mebane.
il Bet Hom & Gard 43:96 Ag '65
Turnings in the wind; exhibition at Manhattan's Museum of early American folk
arts. il Time 86:70 Jl 16 '65

WEATHERCOCKS. See Weather vanes

WEATHERFORD, John
On the grindstone. Library J 91:70 Ja 1 '66
Usual; visit to the United States university
average library. por Library J 90:5345-7
D 15 '65

WEATHERS, Winston
Lazarus as hero; the novels of Lagerkvist.
Commonweal 81:688-91 F 26 '65

WEATHERVANES. See Weather vanes

WEAVER, Charles E.
Potassium content of illite. bibliog Science
147:603-5 F 5 '65

WEAVER, George
Rebuke to Dr King? Negro official speaks
out; excerpts from address, August 19,
1965. por U S News 59:16 Ag 30 '65

WEAVER, John D.
California wines. Holiday 38:36+ O '65
Drawing blood; political cartoonists. Holiday
38:72-3+ Ag '65
Where does all the money go? McCalls 93:
26+ Ja '66

WEAVER, Kenneth F.
Of planes and men. por Nat Geog Mag 128:
298-349 S '65

WEAVER, Loyd
Where's that drain stoppage? Pop Sci 187:
126-7 D '65

WEAVER, Pat. See Weaver, S. L. 1908-

WEAVER, Robert Clifton
New directions for urban renewal; excerpts from address. March 30, 1965. Arch Rec 138:137-42 Ag '65
New look of campus living. por Am Ed 1:14-21 D '64

about

First for the new Cabinet post. il por U S News 60:14 Ja 24 '66
Head for HUD. por Newsweek 67:26 Ja 24 '66
Manhunt. Newsweek 66:42 N 22 '65
Weaver's long wait. il por Time 87:19C Ja 21 '66
Will we have a Negro in the Cabinet? Christian Cent 82:1533 D 15 '65

WEAVER, Sylvester L. 1908-
Planning another TV network. Bsns W p98 O 16 '65

WEAVER, Warren
Billions for science: is it worth the price? interview. por U S News 59:76-9 D 6 '65

about

Doctor Warren Weaver wins Arches of science award. Sci N L 88:232 O 9 '65
Personality of the month. por Sci Digest 58:21-2 D '65

WEAVER, Warren, Jr
Big gamble of John Vliet Lindsay. N Y Times Mag p30-1+ My 23 '65
Paradox of Jacob Javits. N Y Times Mag p34-5+ Ap 4 '65
Rockefeller has to win. N Y Times Mag p28-9+ My 9 '65
This Tuesday's winner, and loser. N Y Times Mag p46-7+ O 31 '65
Will the real Robert Kennedy stand up? N Y Times Mag p8-9+ Je 20 '65

WEAVER, William
Audience. Opera N 29:8-11 F 6 '65
Boxing match at La Scala. Hi Fi 15:86U Mr '65
Excitement below the surface. Hi Fi 15:130-1 My '65
In Italy, festivals old and new. Hi Fi 15:163 S '65
Intimate festivals. Hi Fi 15:178+ D '65
Notes from our correspondents (cont) Hi Fi 15:14+ Jl; 12+ O '65
Unknown Smetana. Hi Fi 15:44-7 My '65
Year for Rossini. Hi Fi 15:119 Jl '65

WEAVING
Dominic DiMare. H. Giambruni. il Craft Horiz 25:18-21+ N '65
New avenues of expression; the challenge of screen weaving. S. Rainey. il Sch Arts 64:7-9 Je '65
Poetic world fashioned on the weaver's loom. R. W. Wassef. il UNESCO Courier 18:32-9 Jl '65
Weaving; junior high school. K. Lakewold. il Sch Arts 64:33 Mr '65

History

Conversation with Anni Albers; interview, ed. by N. Welliver. A. Albers. il Craft Horiz 25:17-21+ Jl '65

Study and teaching

Weaving. P. Greenberg. il Sch Arts 64:15-18 Je '65

WEBB, Anne
Ann Webb, girl forester. W. B. Morse. il pors Am For 71:28-9+ Ap '65

WEBB, Del E. corporation
What Del Webb is up to in Nevada. T. Alexander. il Fortune 71:130-2+ My '65

WEBB, J. A.
Canadian plant physiology. Science 150:787+ N 5 '65

WEBB, James E.
U.S. space teamwork comes of age. por Miss & Roc 17:37 N 29 '65

WEBB, James W.
(ed) See Falkner, M. Day the balloon came to town

WEBB, Kenneth L. See Johannes, R. E. jt. auth.

WEBB, Lance
Lord's Supper: summary of conference. Christian Cent 82:1063-4 S 1 '65

WEBB, Walter Prescott
They never left Texas. F. H. Wardlaw. Sat R 48:25-8 S 18 '65

WEBB, William C.
Industrial park gives rare plants a showcase. il Bsns W p 122-4 Ja 15 '66

WEBB, Wilse B. and Agnew, H. W. Jr
Sleep: effects of a restricted regime. bibliog Science 150:1745-7 D 24 '65

WEBB and Knapp, incorporated
Big man on the thin edge. C. Welles. il Life 58:74-6+ F 12 '65
End of an empire. il Newsweek 65:84+ My 24 '65
New York bank blows whistle on Zeckendorf; action against Webb & Knapp in bankruptcy court. il Bsns W p30-1 My 15 '65
Operators. Newsweek 65:82+ My 17 '65
Sad saga of Big Bill. Time 85:96+ My 21 '65

WEBBER, Linda
Black clouds & pink rain. Sch Arts 65:13 D '65

WEBER, Arnold
Collective bargaining solutions to technological change; excerpt from address, December 1964. Mo Labor R 88:17-18 Ja '65

WEBER, David
Mexico city: roses on the Reforma. Sat R 49:52+ Ja 1 '66
—See Hamill, P. jt. auth.

WEBER, George, and others
Insulin: inducer of pyruvate kinase. bibliog Science 149:65-7 Jl 2 '65

WEBER, Jon N. and Kaufman, J. W.
Brucite in the calcareous alga goniolithon. bibliog Science 149:996-7 Ag 27 '65
—See Keith. M. L. jt. auth.

WEBER, L. E.
Better-water benefits start early. Am City 80:97-8 Ap '65

WEBER, Ursula M. See Mitchell, H. K. jt. auth.

WEBERN, Anton von
World of Webern. por Newsweek 66:77-8 Ag 16 '65

WEBRE, Alfred L. 3d
We wait: poem. America 113:671 N 27 '65

WEBSTER, David B. and Currier, H. H.
Callose: lateral movement of assimilates from phloem. bibliog Science 150:1610-11 D 17 '65

WEBSTER, Donald B. Jr
Beauty and chivalry of the United States assembled. Am Heritage 17:50-3+ D '65

WEBSTER, John
White devil. Criticism
Nation 202:54-5 Ja 10 '66
New Repub 154:35-6 Ja 1 '66
Time 86:40+ D 17 '65

WEBSTER, Noah
Americans nobody knows. C. W. Ferguson. por PTA Mag 59:20-2 My '65

WEBSTER, Staten W.
Suggestions for the supervising teacher. NEA J 54:38 Ap '65

WEBSTER, W. R. and others
Auditory habituation: a test of a centrifugal and a peripheral theory. bibliog Science 148:654-6 Ap 30 '65

WEBSTER college, Webster Groves, Mo.
One small college and research. J. Grennan. Am Ed 1:14-15 Je '65

WECHSBERG, Joseph
Freudian slip. N Y Times Mag p 105-8 Je 6 '65
Gastronomy. Esquire 64:45-6+ N; 126-8+ D '65
John le Carré: will his success spoil David Cornwell? Ladies Home J 82:122+ Ap '65
Profiles (cont) New Yorker 41:49-50+ Je 5; 59-62+ N 6 '65
Tall tales of the Vienna woods. Sat R 48:36+ Mr 13 '65

WECHSLER, G. A.
Computerize your purchases and save. Am City 80:86-7 N '65

WECHSLER, Margaret
Crusade for the arts in Britain. New Repub 154:23-4 Ja 1 '66

WECK, Egon
Birthday party. U S Camera 28:52-3 D '65

WED enterprises, incorporated
Disney's live-action profits. il Bsns W p78-82 Jl 24 '65

WEDDELL seals. See Seals (animals)

WEDDING gifts
Presents that are perfect for showers and weddings; excerpt from Seventeen book of etiquette and entertaining. E. A. Haupt. Seventeen 24:170 My '65

WEDDING meals
Wedding cook book. T. McKenna. il House & Gard 127:175+ My '65

WEDDING receptions. See Receptions

WEDDINGS
African scion takes a bride; son of Houphouët-Boigny wed in Paris. il Ebony 20:25-8+ O '65
It was a beautiful wedding, but... J. McGregor. il Good H 161:90-1+ N '65

WEDDINGS—*Continued*
On a Greek island, the bride looked like a Byzantine princess; marriage of Cornelia Embiricos to M. Barbet Schroeder. il Vogue 146:120-1 O 15 '65
Wedding of the Hon Lucinda Lambton and Henry Harrod in England's North country. il Vogue 145:140-1 Ap 1 '65
When the daughter of Madame Grès married. il Vogue 146:184-5 N 1 '65
See also
Wedding gifts
Wedding meals

Anecdotes, facetiae, satire, etc.
Magyar wedding, Irish funeral. J. Lukacs. Esquire 64:34+ Ag '65

WEDGWOOD, C. V.
For the glory of France. Horizon 7:20-9 Sum '65
When black death stalked in London. N Y Times Mag p92+ S 12 '65

WEDGWOOD, Josiah
Britain's royal potter. il por Time 85:66-7 My 21 '65
Josiah Wedgwood: Potter to the Queen. R. N. Gregg. il Hobbies 70:24-5+ Je '65

WEDGWOOD ware
Britain's royal potter. il Time 85:66-7 My 21 '65
Josiah Wedgwood: Potter to the Queen. R. N. Gregg. il Hobbies 70:24-5+ Je '65
Wedgwood from midwestern collections. R. N. Gregg and M. M. Delhom. il Antiques 87:705-8 Je '65

WEED, Florence Collins
Automation in schools. Sr Schol 87:sup40-1 S 23 '65

WEEDS
Weed is where you find it; photographs by E. Javorsky. Natur Hist 74:22-5 Ap '65
See also
Greens, Edible
Jimson weed

Chemical control
How to control common lawn weeds. il Good H 160:176-7 My '65
How to control weeds in grain sorghum. Suc Farm 63:82 Ap '65
How to control weeds in small grains. Suc Farm 63:76 My '65
New way to control weeds in sugar beets. W. Meggitt and E. C. Richardson. Suc Farm 63:82 Ap '65
New weed killers for corn, sugar beets. Farm J 89:48 F '65
1965 weed and insect control guide; symposium. il Suc Farm 63:69-74+ Mr '65
Now, a dozen weed killers for soybeans. C. E. Ball. il Farm J 89:65-6 My '65
Soil incorporation: hottest thing in weed killing. C. E. Ball. il Farm J 89:36-7+ F '65
To knock corn weeds, mix two chemicals. il Farm J 89:56 Mr '65
Weed control with modern herbicides. R. L. Ticknor. il Horticulture 43:29-31 Ap '65
See also
Herbicides

Control
January attack on weeds. Sunset 136:130-1 Ja '66
Whip Johnsongrass with chemicals, good management. J. Everly. il Suc Farm 63:102 Ap '65
See also
Weeds—Chemical control

Control by fire
Anti-tumbleweed heat treatment; use of weed burner in Albuquerque, N.M. il Am City 81:18 Ja '66
Report on flame cultivation; questions and answers. E. Knake and F. N. Reece. Suc Farm 63:95 Mr '65

WEEKEND cabins. See Cabins
WEEK-end houses. See Cottages
WEEKEND vacations. See Vacations
WEEKLY newspapers. See Newspapers
WEEKS, Edward Augustus
Peripatetic reviewer. See issues of Atlantic
WEEKS, Mary Lyle
Sing me a song of left tackle; story. Seventeen 24:130-1 O '65
WEEKS, Percy S.
Obituary
Motor B por 115:134 Ap '65
WEEKS, Robert Lewis
Appalachian front; poem. New Yorker 41:176 My 1 '65

WEEKS, Sara
Early bird. Atlan 215:135-6 Ap '65
WEEMS, David B.
Build the Cinderella. Pop Electr 23:49-52 O '65
Mr Thuras' magic box. Pop Electr 22:45-9 Ap '65
WEESNER, Theodore
Survivors; story. Sat Eve Post 238:62-4 Je 5 '65
WEETALL, H. H. and Weliky, N.
Immunoadsorbent for the isolation of purine-specific antibodies. bibliog Science 148:1235-7 My 28 '65
WEEVILS
See also
Alfalfa weevils
WEGENER woods. See Forests and forestry—Missouri
WEGNER, Robert E.
Woman with concave breasts; story. Esquire 63:83 F '65
WEIDHAAS, Arthur
Flower boy; interview, ed. by A. M. Lingg. Opera N 29:12-13 Ap 3 '65
WEIDMAN, Jerome
Absolute darlings; story. McCalls 92:62-3 Jl '65
Friends of Mary Fowler; story. Redbook 125:58-9 Jl '65
WEIERBACH, Idelle
Femme supreme; poem. McCalls 92:124 Jl '65
WEIGELAS
June rivals. E. S. Henderson. il Pop Gard 16:31+ My '65
WEIGHT (physiology)
Body composition and coat color correlation in different phenotypes of viable yellow mice. G. L. Wolff. bibliog il Science 147:1145-7 Mr 5 '65
How to keep your weight down: advice from specialists. il U S News 58:66-70 Je 7 '65
Organ weights in primates and other mammals. W. R. Stahl. bibliog Science 150:1039-41 N 19 '65
See also
Corpulence
WEIGHT lifting
How to build a better body. A. Steinberg. il Read Digest 86:102-5 Mr '65
WEIGHT reducing preparations
Dieting drugs: how good and how safe? Good H 162:131-2 Ja '66
WEIGHT throwing
See also
Shot putting
WEIGHTLESSNESS
Douglas studying oil bath weightlessness. Miss & Roc 17:36 O 4 '65
Gemini 7 crew finds zero-G no problem. E. J. Bulban. il Aviation W 83:53-5+ D 27 '65
Otolith function not markedly affected by weightlessness. Miss & Roc 18:39 Ja 17 '66
Outer space and the inner ear. il Bsns W p45-6+ Ja 30 '65
Strange world of zero gravity. W. Von Braun. il Pop Sci 186:68-9+ Je '65
Weightlessness unsolved. Sci N L 87:370 Je 12 '65
Zero-G slows astronaut performance. H. M. David. il Miss & Roc 17:34+ N 8 '65
WEIGHTMAN, J. G.
Mandarin left. Commentary 39:96-8 Mr '65
Reconsidering Gide. Commentary 40:102-4 S '65
WEIGHTMAN, John
Stories women tell. Harper 231:162-7 N '65
WEIGHTS and measures
In defense of drams and scruples. Sat Eve Post 238:84 Ag 28 '65
Latin Americans trained in standardized weights. Sci N L 88:217 O 2 '65
See also
Cookery—Measurements
Metric system
WEIL, Irwin
Prophet and a prisoner. Sat R 48:44-5 Jl 24 '65
WEIL, Simone
Simone Weil, by J. Cabaud. Review
Christian Cent 82:683 My 26 '65. N. Hardesty
Nation 200:422-4 Ap 19 '65. P. West
New Yorker 41:106-10 Ja 8 '66. N. Bliven.
Sat R por 48:26-7 F 20 '65. G. Bree
WEILER, Howard
Skip, skip, skip, and thwack! H. Whall. il Sport Illus 22:30-1 Ap 19 '65
WEILL, Kurt
Mahagonny. Criticism
Hi Fi il 15:158-9 S '65
Nation 201:107 Ag 30 '65
Newsweek il 66:82 Jl 19 '65
Opera N il 30:26 N 6 '65

WEILL, Kurt—*Continued*
Threepenny opera (Die dreigroschenoper)
Criticism
New Repub 153:35 Ag 7 '65
New Yorker 41:172-3 Mr 20 '65
Sat R 48:22 Mr 27 '65
WEILL-TUCKERMAN, Anne
Kashmir: the UN's perilous chance. Nation
201:151-3 S 27 '65
Malaise of sovereignty. Nation 200:690-4
Je 28 '65
UN blackout on Vietnam. Nation 200:324-6
Mr 29 '65
UN on the rack. Nation 200:128-9 F 8 '65
UN power shifts: decline of the unaligned.
Nation 201:488-90 D 20 '65
WEIMAR REPUBLIC. See Germany—History—
Weimar Republic, 1918-1933
WEIMARANERS. See Pointers (dogs)
WEIMER, Paul
Inventor of the month. S. V. Jones. il por
Sci Digest 58:22 S '65
WEINBERG, Alvin M.
But is the teacher also a citizen? adaptation
of address, April 14, 1965. bibliog Science
149:601-6; 150:142+ Ag 6, O 8 '65
Where is science taking us? excerpt from
the 1964 report of the director of Oak Ridge
national laboratory. por Sat R 48:56-7 F 6
'65
WEINBERG, Ephraim
Shadow puppets. Sch Arts 65:12-13 O '65
WEINER, Herbert
Wedding in B'nai Brak. Commentary 40:
39-46 Jl 14 N '65
WEINER, Jack
Whole secret is feeling. J. Lidstone. il Sch
Arts 64:24-8 Mr '65
WEINER, Lester Keith
Subversion in a sonnet. Christian Cent 82:
606 My 12 '65
Teaching missionaries expelled from Rho-
desia. Christian Cent 82:1003 Ag 18 '65
WEINER, Myron
Political integration and political development.
bibliog f Ann Am Acad 358:52-64 Mr '65
WEINLAND, James D.
Take labels off your men. Nations Bsns 53:
56+ N '65
WEINMAN, Barbara
Notes to Mrs Charterer. Yachting 117:173-4
F '65
WEINSTOCK, Herbert
Barber from London. Sat R 48:59 S 11 '65
Dawn of opera. Sat R 48:53 Mr 27 '65
Double Donizetti. Sat R 48:58 My 29 '65
Eternal Handel. Sat R 48:60 Ap 24 '65
Germ and the virus. Sat R 48:47-9 D 25 '65
Music to my ears. Sat R 48:49 My 8 '65
Serse and Samson. Sat R 48:53 D 18 '65
Woman of the week. Opera N 29:26-7 Mr 20
'65
WEINSTOCK, Jack
Catch me if you can; adaptation of Piege
pour un homme seul, by R. Thomas. Crit-
icism
America 112:690 My 8 '65
Commonweal 82:118-19 Ap 16 '65
Sat R 48:44 Mr 27 '65
WEINTRAUB, Ruth G. and Greisman, L. D.
Bridging the gap between public administra-
tion and school administration. bibliog f Sch
& Soc 93:433-7 N 13 '65
WEINTRAUB, Stanley
Alone with his wit. Sat R 48:46-7 Ap 17 '65
Whole world was his stage. Sat R 48:45+
N 13 '65
WEIR, Walter John
House her way; poem. McCalls 92:196 F '65
WEISBERG, David E.
Big eight computer spectrum. Duns R 86:pt2
152 S '65
WEISBERGER, Bernard A.
Carpetbagger's new clothes. Nation 200:450-
3 Ap 26 '65
WEISBROD, Christian
Threepenny tragedy. il Time 86:54 N 5 '65
WEISER, Russell S. See Granger, G. A. jt.
auth.
WEISKOPF, Herman
Baseball's week. See issues of Sports il-
lustrated
WEISMAN, Abner I.
Case histories in clay. il por Time 86:75-6
Jl 9 '65
Medical sculpture. New Yorker 41:15-16 Jl 10
'65
WEISMAN, Eli L.
Swedish modern. Recreation 58:163 Ap '65
WEISMILLER, Edward
Private services; poem. Atlan 215:95 My '65
WEISS, Bernard, and Laties, V. G.
Reinforcement schedule generated by an on-
line digital computer. bibliog Science 148:
658-61 Ap 30 '65

WEISS, Herbert F. See Markowitz, M. D. jt.
auth.
WEISS, Margaret R.
Drama in two dimensions. Sat R 48:96-7 N 13
'65
First for Fleet Street's cameras. Sat R 48:
122-3 S 18 '65
How Alfred Knopf saw his authors. Sat R 48:
26-8 Je 12 '65
Laurels for lensmen. Sat R 48:62-3 My 8 '65
Maestros of survival. Sat R 48:103-5 S 18 '65
Photo forecast, 1975. Sat R 48:50-1 Jl 10 '65
Questing camera. Sat R 48:33-9 Ag 28 '65
Sight, sound, and substance. Sat R 48:39-
41 Mr 27 '65
Through Snowdon's lens. Sat R 48:33-4 D 11
'65
Topolski: contemporary Chronicler. Sat R 48:
20-1 My 15 '65
WEISS, Miriam S.
Arrivals and departures; story. McCalls 92:
58-9 Jl '65
Thirty-nine; story. Ladies Home J 82:90-1 N
'65
WEISS, Nathan
General Benjamin Franklin Butler and the
Negro: the evolution of the racial views
of a practical politician. bibliog por Negro
Hist Bul 29:3-4+ O '65
WEISS, Neil
Word; poem. New Yorker 41:69 Jl 3 '65
WEISS, Peter
Marat/Sade. Criticism
Commonweal 83:476-7 Ja 21 '66
Nation 202:82-4 Ja 17 '66
New Repub 154:23-4+ Ja 22 '66
New Yorker 41:98+ Ja 8 '66
Newsweek il 67:63 Ja 10 '66
Sat R 49:45+ Ja 15 '66
Time il 87:51 Ja 7 '66
Vogue 147:102-5 Ja 1 '66
Peter Weiss and Wolf Biermann. E. Bentley.
Nation 202:31 Ja 10 '66
WEISS, Robert B.
Small community gets big-time data process-
ing. Am City 80:103-4 Ap '65
WEISS, Samuel B. and Legault-Demare, Jean
Pseudouridine formation: evidence for RNA
as an intermediate. bibliog Science 149:
429-31 Jl 23 '65
WEISS, Theodore
Eighth day; poem. Yale R 55:250 D '65
Into summer; poem. Nation 200:620 Je 7 '65
Robes of the gods; poem. Nation 202:80 Ja 17
'66
Through the strings; poem. Poetry 106:160-5
Ap '65
WEISSKOPF, Victor F.
Nature of matter: purposes of high energy
physics; defence. por Science 147:1552-4
Mr 26 '65
Quantum theory and elementary particles;
address, April 23, 1965. Science 149:1181-9
S 10 '65
Why pure science? with biographical sketch.
Bul Atomic Sci 21:4-8 Ap '65
WEISSLER, Alfred, and others
Ultrasound chemical effects on pure organic
liquids. bibliog Science 150:1288-9 D 3 '65
WEISSMANN, Tom E.
How we're harnessing the sun. Sci Digest
57:52-6 Je '65
Those amazing fuel cells. Sci Digest 58:79-
82 S '65
WEIZMANN institute of science
Fundamental biology at the Weizmann in-
stitute. V. K. McElheny. il Science 148:
614-18 Ap 30 '65
Golem of Prague and the Golem of Rehovoth;
reason for computer's name; excerpt from
address, June 17, 1965. G. Scholem. Com-
mentary 41:62-5 Ja '66
WELCH, Claude
Pope John and Luther. Christian Cent 82:
244+ F 24 '65
Theology as risk. Christian Cent 82:707-10 Je
2 '65
WELCH, Edna
Instant sculpture. Design 66:12-14 Mr '65
Shape, color, space, a la Mondrian. Design
67:20-1 S '65
Slide transparencies. Design 66:37-9 Ja '65
WELCH, Helen M.
Cost indexes for 1965: periodicals. Library J
90:2964-5 Jl '65
WELCH, Norman A.
Excerpt from statement, August 13, 1964.
Cong Digest 44:91+ Mr '65
WELCH, Paul
Grim conclusions; life in Gordon towers. Life
59:119-21 D 24 '65
WELCH, Raquel
Raquel Welch: the definitive chickie. B. J.
Friedman. pors Esquire 64:84-7+ O '65

WELCH, Robert Henry Winborne
Birchers have birthday party. America 113: 457 O 23 '65; Reply. R. F. Drinan. 113: 657 N 27 '65
Little old pink man who called Ike red; concerning address at Howard university. D. Sanford. New Repub 153:8 N 20 '65

WELCH, Wayne
Experiment at Camp Kilmer. Reporter 33:30-2 O 21 '65

WELCOME, parents; drama. See Cole, E.

WELCOME, strangers and others too; story. See Hughes, M. G.

WELDING
Cold welding helpful? Sci N L 88:181 S 18 '65
Explosive joining for hostile metals. il Fortune 72:197-8 Jl '65
Fiery point of fusion. Fortune 71:134-41 Ap '65
Space welding technique occurs only in vacuum. Sci N L 87:136 F 27 '65
See also
Brazing
Electric welding

WELDING machines, Electric. See Electric welding machines

WELFARE, Public. See Public welfare

WELFARE, Social. See Social welfare

WELFARE economics. See Economics—Social and ethical aspects

WELFARE state. See Social and economic security

WELFARE work. See Public welfare

WELIKY, N. See Weetall, H. H. jt. auth.

WELITSCH, Ljuba
Lady from Vienna. R. Ackart. il por Opera N 30:26-8 D 18 '65

WELKER, Robert H.
Notes on the Toronto teach-in: the irrelevance of morality. Nation 201:301-4 N 1 '65

WELLER, George
What a perfect Friendship. Sports Illus 22: 42-6 Je 21 '65

WELLER, Jack
Is there a future for yesteday's people? excerpt from Yesterday's people: life in contemporary Appalachia. Sat R 48:33-6 O 16 '65
Ministering to Appalachia. Christian Cent 82:935-6 Jl 28 '65

WELLES, Chris
Big bash that is running short of cash. Life 58:136-8+ My 14 '65
Big boom in men's beauty aids; not by soap alone. Life 59:39-40 Ag 13 '65
Big man on the thin edge. Life 58:74-6+ F 12 '65
Helen Gurley Brown turns editor. Life 59: 65-6+ N 19 '65
Man with two wives: amnesia or hoax? Life 58:41-2+ Mr 5 '65
SEC vs. Texas Gulf raises sticky questions; bonanza trouble. Life 59:29-30+ Ag 6 '65
Takes a heap of gadgets to make a car a home. Life 59:86+ N 12 '65

WELLES, Sara. See Blum, S. jt. auth.

WELLESLEY college, Wellesley, Mass.
Point in time at Wellesley; M. Clapp to resign. Time 86:55-6 Ag 20 '65
Stopping in midstream. Newsweek 66:72-3 Ag 23 '65

WELLIVER, Neil
(ed) See Albers, A. Conversation with Anni Albers

WELLNER, Daniel, and Meister, Alton
New symbols for the amino acid residues of peptides and proteins. Science 151:77-8 Ja 7 '66

WELLS, David I.
One man, one vote. New Repub 152:11-12 Je 26 '65

WELLS, Dickie
Jazz records. W. Balliett. New Yorker 41: 156+ N 20 '65

WELLS, George S.
Bark beetle: his own worst enemy. Am For 71:28-31+ Je '65
We rented a roving cabin. McCalls 93:60+ O '65
Yukon's golden railroad. Travel 123:32-6 My '65

WELLS, H. G.
Inexperienced ghost; dramatization. See Nolan, P. T.

WELLS, Henry
Turmoil in the Dominican Republic. Cur Hist 50:14-21 Ja '66

WELLS, Henry P.
Well governed angler. H. Clepper. il por Am For 71:4-5+ F '65

WELLS, Philip V.
Scrap woodlands, transported grassland soils, and concept of grassland climate in the Great Plains Region. bibliog Science 148:246-9 Ap 9 '65

WELLS, Robert W.
Country feast. Ladies Home J 82:23 Mr '65
Good-by, my son. Read Digest 86:130-2 Mr '65
Why I bought my children a woods. Ladies Home J 82:39-40 F '65

WELLS, W. D.
Two dawns (New Orleans); poem. America 113:20 Jl 3 '65

WELLS
For the garden handyman build a wishing well. R. A. Henry, jr. il Pop Gard 17:19 Ja '66
See also
Cisterns

WELLS, Pollution of. See Water pollution

WELLS CREEK crater. See Meteorite craters

WELS, Byron G.
Batteries: the inside story. U S Camera 28: 62-3+ F '65
Inside tips from the pros. Pop Electr 23: 51-3 D '65

WELSH, Edward C.
Avionics in space: excerpts from address, 1965. Aviation W 83:21 N 8 '65
Excerpt from address, November 5, 1964. Cong Digest 44:46+ F '65
Vigor of space; excerpts from address. Aviation W 83:21 O 11 '65

WELSH, Peter C.
Decorative appeal of hand tools. Antiques 87:204-7 F '65
Van Alstyne American folk art collection. Antiques 88:208-11 Ag '65

WELSHONS, W. J.
Analysis of a gene in drosophila. bibliog Science 150:1122-9 N 26 '65

WELTNER, Charles Longstreet
That changing climate. il por Time 85:17-18 F 12 '65

WELTON, Shirley G.
When college students teach neighborhood kids. Parents Mag 40:64-6+ Je '65

WELTY, Eudora
Eye of the story. Yale R 55:265-74 D '65
Must the novelist crusade? por Atlan 216: 104-8 O '65
Season of dreams, by A. Appel. Review Sat R 48:27-8 D 18 '65. G. Hicks

WENATCHEE youth circus. See Circus

WENDELL, William G.
History in houses; Macpheadris-Warner House. Antiques 87:712-15 Je '65

WENDT, Herbert
Froggie went a-courtin: excerpt from Sex life of the animals. Sat R 48:50 S 4 '65

WENGER, Otto Paul
Ambassadors of art and history. UNESCO Courier 18:27-31 F '65

WENHAM, Brian
Britain's angry doctors. New Repub 152:9-10 Ap 10 '65
Color in Britain. New Repub 152:14-15 Mr 6 '65
Commons debate on banning discrimination. New Repub 152:7-8 My 29 '65
Privileged education in Britain. New Repub 153:10-12 D 11 '65
Steel nationalization is not around the corner. New Repub 152:9-10 My 22 '65
Train-wreckers. New Repub 152:8-9 Je 26 '65
Unions and a lid on wages. New Repub 153: 17 S 25 '65
West is best. New Repub 153:18-19 N 20 '65
Wilson's unhappy hundred days. New Repub 152:9-10 F 6 '65

WENNERSTRÖM, Stig
Case of the Swedish spy. I. Ross. por Read Digest 86:117-25 Ap '65
Well-informed spy. D. Cort. il Nation 200: 136-8 F 8 '65

WENSBERG, Erik
Damned with loud praise. Reporter 32:50-1 F 11 '65
Redcoats on Broadway: whites of their eyes. Reporter 33:48+ N 18 '65
Wise man in Gotham. Reporter 32:48-50 My 20 '65

WENTWORTH, E. F. Jr
Foster Wheeler mends its house from within. il por Bsns W p 116-18+ D 18 '65

WENTZ, Richard E.
Pertinent pastor. Christian Cent 82:582-3 My 5 '65

WERBLIN, Sonny
Show-biz Sonny and his quest for stars. R. H. Boyle. il pors Sports Illus 23:66-72 Jl 19 '65

WERLEY, Bill
Phoenix: drought underground. Sat R 48:44+
O 23 '65
WERNER, Alfred
Avida dollars. Reporter 34:45-7 Ja 13 '66
Cry of anguish. Reporter 33:51-3 O 21 '65
Eternal Olympia. Am Artist 29:48-53+ Ap
'65
Tender monumentality of Wilhelm Lehm-
bruck. Am Artist 29:54-9+ Je '65
Waldmueller, master realist. Am Artist 29:
30-5+ D '65
Women of Klimt and Schiele. Reporter 32:
44+ F 25 '65
WERNER, Oskar
New star, his name is Oskar. il pors Life
59:32-4+ Jl 30 '65
People are talking about... por Vogue 146:
226-7 S 1 '65
WERNER, Pat
Prayer: Lord, let me be like the pine tree.
Am For 71:51 Ap '65
WERNICK, Robert
Down the wide Missouri with an old S.O.B.
Sat Eve Post 238:92-7 O 23 '65
I wrote The drinking man's diet. Sat Eve
Post 238:84+ My 22 '65
Last of the divorce ranches. Sat Eve Post
238:30-2+ Jl 17 '65
Speaking out. por Sat Eve Post 238:12+ N 6
'65
World's biggest gambler. Sat Eve Post 238:
27-32 F 13 '65
WERTH, Alexander
De Gaulle: America's elder statesman. Na-
tion 201:404-8 N 29 '65
De Gaulle on Vietnam; way out of the jungle.
Nation 200:239-42 Mr 8 '65
His pen was a welcome weapon. Sat R 48:32-
3 Je 19 '65
Legacies of Khrushchev. Nation 200:354-7 Ap
5 '65
Moscow celebrates. Nation 200:603-6 Je 7 '65
Thank God for Goering! Nation 202:50-1 Ja
10 '66
WERTMAN, C. D.
Emergency prop. Field & S 69:40 F '65
**WESCON electronics show. See Electronics—
Exhibitions**
WESCOTT, Jimmy
From a boy's point of view. See issues of
Seventeen
WESLEY, Charles H.
Great man theory of emancipation. Negro
Hist Bul 28:101-2+ F '65
Our fiftieth year. Negro Hist Bul 28:172-3+
My '65
about
February issue: a dedication to Charles Wes-
ley. il pors Negro Hist Bul 28:99-100+ F '65
WESLEYAN university press
Xerox pays $56 million for Wesleyan univer-
sity press. Pub W 187:32 My 31 '65
WESLING, Donald
Berkeley: free speech and free verse. Nation
201:338-40 N 8 '65
WESSEL, Milton R.
Legal protection of computer programs. Har-
vard Bsns R 43:97-106 Mr '65
WESSEL, Morris A.
Breast feeding made easy. Parents Mag 40:
70-1+ N '65
WESSELS, William L.
New York's Adirondack trail. Travel 124:
38-9 S '65
WESSIN Y WESSIN, Elias
Bitter salt of a stranger's bread; letter. Nat
R 17:911 O 19 '65
New terror planned by Dominican reds? ex-
cerpts from testimony. por U S News 59:16
N 29 '65
about
Exile of the general. por Time 86:54 S 17 '65
Farewell to arms. Newsweek 66:50 S 20 '65
Two key men in the Dominican flare-up.
U S News 58:20 My 10 '65
**WESSLING, Lucy Ellen. See Posey, C. W. jt.
auth.**
WESSON, Jerry
Sound. See issues of U.S. camera & travel
Tiny lights for closeups. U S Camera 28:
52-3 F '65
WESSON, Robert G.
Continent of villages. Nation 200:705-7 Je 28
'65
WEST, Allan M.
What's bugging teachers. por Sat R 48:88 O
16 '65
WEST, Anthony
Suspension of belief. Reporter 33:50 N 18 '65
Troubles of a golden age. Reporter 33:48-50+
D 2 '65
Watch for the birdie. Reporter 32:50+ Ap 8
'65

WEST, Anthony C.
Surviving Ireland. A. Karlen. Nation 200:
486-8 My 3 '65
WEST, Carolyn
Best by test. Motor B 115:32-4+ My '65
Billfish West. Motor B 116:36+ S '65
Mardi gras. por Motor B 115:38-9+ My '65
WEST, Chuck
Church in the Wildwood. Am For 71:8-9 Je
'65
WEST, Gordon
Shall we take the kids? por Motor B 115:82+
Ap '65
WEST, Jerry
Smashing hurrah for the Lakers. J. Under-
wood. il por Sports Illus 22:12-17 F 8 '65
WEST, Jessamyn
Good-bye, Bossy; story. Ladies Home J 82:
82-3 Je '65
Trouble with doctors is me. Ladies Home J
82:42+ Mr '65
WEST, John Foster
Time was, a long time coming. Writer 78:
15-18 Ag '65
WEST, Morris L.
Tragedy of Diem and the paradox of Asia;
interview, ed. by D. L. Flaherty. America
112:352-6 Mr 13 '65
Two front row seats to a bitter tragedy.
Life 58:12 My 7 '65
about
Novelist named West faces East. il Life
58:79-80+ Mr 19 '65
WEST, Paul
Divinity's iron maiden. Nation 200:422-4 Ap
19 '65
WEST
Country living in the West (cont) Sunset
134:116 Ap; 135:124 O '65
See also
Frontier and pioneer life—United States
Hunting—Western states
Irrigation—Western states
Pacific coast

Description and travel
Great vacations in the West. N. Kuehnl. il
Bet Hom & Gard 43:121-6 Mr '65
Long way to go. P. S. Beagle. il Holiday
37:78-81+ Mr '65
[Month] travel in and beyond the West. See
issues of Sunset
Personal business; explore the Pacific
Northwest. Bsns W p 141-2 Jl 10 '65
Wild, wise West; excerpts from The Oregon
desert, by R. A. Long and E. R. Jackman.
il Farm J 89:72+ Mr '65

Discovery and exploration
So long, St Louis, we're heading West. W. C.
Everhart. il Nat Geog Mag 128:642-69 N '65

History
How lost was Zebulon Pike? Louisiana pur-
chase. D. Jackson. il Am Heritage 16:10-
15+ F '65
Peddlers in Eldorado. L. Berg. Commentary
40:63-7 Jl '65
See also
Lewis and Clark expedition

Industries
New trend for factories: go West! go South!
il U S News 59:94-5 N 1 '65

Population
Americans discover the West again; Mountain
West. il U S News 58:80-2 Je 21 '65
WEST AFRICA. See Africa, West
WEST BERLINERS. See Berliners
WEST Coast flood. See Floods—United States
WEST in art
Range burial; a monumental canvas. F. Get-
lein. il Am Artist 29:60-4+ N '65
**WEST INDIAN cookery. See Cookery, West
Indian**
WEST INDIANS in Great Britain
Color in England. J. B. Gerald. Common-
weal 83:304-6 D 10 '65
Race relations in Britain. P. Mason. Chris-
tian Cent 82:738-41 Je 9 '65
WEST INDIES
Isle-hoppers, aisle-walkers; new hotel on
Young Island. H. Sutton. il Sat R 48:36-
7+ My 15 '65
See also
Caribbean Region
East Indians in the West Indies
Hotels, taverns, etc.—West Indies
St Martin (island)
Tourist trade—West Indies

WEST INDIES—*Continued*

Description and travel

Finisterre sails the Windward Islands. G. Mitchell. il Nat Geog Mag 128:755-801 D '65

WEST INDIES (Federation)

Central America today; symposium. bibliog f il Cur Hist 50:1-44 Ja '66

Letter from Port Of Spain. B. Taper. New Yorker 41:209-12+ O 23 '65

Economic conditions

Those troubled islands in America's front yard. il U S News 59:77-80 Jl 12 '65

West Indies after the federation. T. Mathews. bibliog f Cur Hist 50:27-31+ Ja '66

Politics

West Indies after the federation. T. Mathews. bibliog f Cur Hist 50:27-31+ Ja '66

WEST INDIES, BRITISH

See also
Nevis (island)
West Indies (Federation)

WEST INDIES, FRENCH

See also
Guadeloupe Island

WEST POINT military academy. See United States military academy, West Point

WEST side story; musical comedy. See Musical comedies, revues, etc.—Criticisms, plots, etc.

WEST VIRGINIA

West Virginia's big cleanup. D. Wharton. Read Digest 86:19-20+ Je '65

See also
Fishing—West Virginia

Economic conditions

Poverty state? look at West Virginia today. il U S News 59:100-3 Jl 12 '65

WESTBERG, Granger E.

American academy of parish clergy: why not? Christian Cent 82:557-8 Ap 28 '65

WESTBY, Barbara

Commercial cataloging services. por Wilson Lib Bul 39:560-1+ Mr '65

WESTCHESTER COUNTY, N.Y.

Good-neighbor plant. G. E. Griffin. il Am City 80:99-102 Mr '65

How to zone for multi-family dwellings. S. J. Schulman. il Am City 80:92-4 D '65

WESTCOTT, Cynthia

(comp) H&G's 1965 guide to plant protection. House & Gard 127:210-14 Ap '65

Is spraying necessary? Horticulture 43:20-1+ N '65

WESTER, R. E. and Edgerley, W. E.

Portable frame. Horticulture 43:24-5 Mr '65

WESTERN air lines, incorporated

Western's jets fly over profit ceiling. il Bsns W p54-5+ Mr 6 '65

WESTERN amateur astronomers (organization)

Convention highlights from Reno. A. McClure and L. J. Robinson. il Sky & Tel 30:206-10 O '65

WESTERN AUSTRALIA

World's newest frontier; western Australia, attracts U.S. companies. E. J. Drechsel. il U S News 58:68-72 Ap 19 '65

WESTERN bloc and Russia. See World politics, 1945-

WESTERN books exhibition. See Book exhibits

WESTERN catalpa. See Catalpa

WESTERN civilization. See Civilization

WESTERN EUROPE. See Europe, Western

WESTERN films. See Moving pictures—Westerns

WESTERN hemisphere

See also
America

WESTERN home awards

1965-1966 AIA Sunset Western home awards. il Sunset 135:74-93 O '65

WESTERN states small schools project. See Rural schools—United States

WESTERN stories

Poem of the West. F. Cleva. il Opera N 30: 24-5 Ja 8 '66

Ramerrez rides again; Dick Johnson alias Ramerrez, in Girl of the golden West. J. W. Stedman. il Opera N 30:6-7 Ja 8 '66

Wild western rides again. T. Curry. il Sat R 48:70+ D 11 '65

See also
Television broadcasting—Westerns

WESTERN test range. See Proving grounds

WESTERN union telegraph company

AT&T; folksy octopus; Western union-AT&T-Bell battle. D. Smith. il Nation 202:16-18 Ja 3 '66

Western union hums with data; computer data transmission. il Bsns W p 150-2+ F 20 '65

WESTERNERS

See also
Texans

WESTFIELD, N.J.

Photographing sewers doesn't cost a cent. B. F. Murphy. il Am City 80:112-13 Mr '65

WESTHAMPTON, N.Y.

Westhampton group weekends. B. Leavitt. il Look 29:78-81 S 7 '65

WESTIN, Alan F.

Anti-communism & the corporations. Commentary 36:479-87 D '63; 37:23-4 Ap; 38:6 N '64; 39:16+ F '65

WESTIN, Av

Bird. New Yorker 41:46-8 My 15 '65

WESTINGHOUSE electric corporation

Escape from the grapevine. L. L. L. Golden. Sat R 48:79 D 11 '65

Magnetic highway proposed. il Am City 80: 64 O '65

Westinghouse aims high with a bus; skybus for urban rapid transit. il Bsns W p57-8 S 18 '65

WESTINGHOUSE time capsule. See Civilization—Preservation of records

WESTLAKE, Robert E.

Physician's image. Sat R 48:84 D 4 '65

WESTLUND, Edward J.

Ham radio plan now for your license. Pop Electr 23:48-51+ Jl '65

WESTMEYER, Eleanor

Japanese iris. il Horticulture 43:14-15+ Jl '65

WESTMINSTER abbey. See London—Westminster abbey

WESTMINSTER kennel club show. See Dog shows

WESTMORELAND, William Childs

Guardians at the gate. il Time 87:15-21 Ja 7 '66

about

Man for the job in Vietnam. J. G. Hubbell and D. Reed. por Read Digest 88:55-60 Ja '66

WESTMOUNT, Quebec

Stationary snow melter overcomes dumping dilemma. J. R. Daye and A. deF. Heron. il Am City 80:86-9 F '65

WESTON, Christine

First frost; story. Redbook 126:66-7 D '65

WESTON, Edward

Way-out Weston. P. Caulfield. il Mod Phot 29:78-81 N '65

WESTON, Elizabeth

Food forum (cont) McCalls 92:38 Mr; 34 Ap; 44 My; 36 Je '65

WESTPHAL, James A.

Schlieren technique for studying water flow in marine animals. Science 149:1515-16 S 24 '65

—See Murray, B. C. jt. auth.

WESTWOOD, Andrew F.

Politics of distrust in Iran. Ann Am Acad 358:123-35 Mr '65

WET paint; revue. See Musical comedies, revues, etc.—Criticisms, plots, etc.

WETHERED, Joyce

Sporting scene. H. W. Wind. New Yorker 41:104+ Ag 21 '65

WETHERELL, Donald F. See Halperin, W. jt. auth.

WETHERSFIELD, Conn.

Wethersfield plan; antismoking program in elementary schools. C. L. Towne. il Sr Schol 87:sup8-9 O 14 '65

WEVER, Ernest Glen, and others

Electrical output of lizard ear: relation to hair-cell population. Science 150:1172-4 N 26 '65

WEXLER, Sidney F.

Rights for Spanish Protestants? Christian Cent 82:867-9 Jl 7 '65

WEYER, Susan

This day for thanks; story. Good H 161:82-3 N '65

WEYMOUTH, Robert D. See Dunson, W. A. jt. auth.

WHALEN, Edward

John F. Kennedy school no. 1. J. P. Blank. il Read Digest 86:54-8 Mr '65

WHALEN, Philip

Invocation and theophany; poem. Poetry 106: 166-8 Ap '65

WHALEN, Richard J.

Big skid at Yale express. Fortune 72:144-9+ N '65

I.M.C: the miner who shook the fertilizer market. Fortune 71:108-13+ Mr '65

Norton Simon says thumbs down. Fortune 71:146-51+ Je '65

WHALES

Conversation-starved killer in a salmon net. E. Whitehead. il Sports Illus 23:54+ Jl 12 '65

WHALES—*Continued*
Decline of the whale. Nat Parks Mag 39:20 Ap '65
Gentle killer; Namu, the killer whale. Sports Illus 23:24+ O 18 '65
Last whales. Sci Am 212:58 Je '65
Namu of the North; killer whale. il Newsweek 66:51 Jl 26 '65
Of whales and whaling. N. Simon. Science 149:943-6 Ag 27 '65
Saga of Moby Doll; captive killer whale in Vancouver, B.C. D. MacDonald. il Read Digest 86:95-9 Ap '65
Seattle's big blowout for a killer whale; Namu's voyage to aquarium. il Life 59:34-5 Ag 13 '65
South Atlantic: death of the whales. J. Hillaby. il Nation 200:245-7 Mr 8 '65
Unicorn in the pool. M. J. Kempner. il Harper 231:57-61 N '65
Whale suicide tales believed untrue. Sci N L 88:229 O 9 '65
Whale's progress; Namu nearing Seattle. Sports Illus 23:7 Ag 2 '65
Yoo-hoo to Namu the whale. D. Connelly. il Sports Illus 23:18-23+ Jl 26 '65
See also
International whaling commission

WHALEY, W. Gordon. See Turner, F. R. jt. auth.

WHALING
Cat bites whale. J. Schultz and C. Pyle. il Yachting 118:48-50+ D '65
Voyage to the Marquesas; cannibals, whalermen and A. Lincoln's timepiece. R. Thales. il Motor B 115:22-5+ F '65

WHALL, Hugh
Boating (cont) Sports Illus 22:72+ Mr 22; 68-9 My 3 '65
Motor sports. Sports Illus 22:93-6+ Ap 5 '65
Rowing (cont) Sports Illus 22:60+ My 24 '65

WHAM-O manufacturing company
Can you invent a million-dollar fad? W. S. Griswold. il Pop Sci 188:78-81+ Ja '66

WHARTON, Don
Slowdown, radar ahead! Read Digest 88:138-40+ Ja '66
West Virginia's big cleanup. Read Digest 86:19-20+ Je '65
Xerox: the invention that hit the jackpot. Read Digest 86:121-4 Mr '65

WHARTON, Edith Newbold (Jones)
Edith Wharton and Henry James: the story of their friendship, by M. Bell. Review.
  Commonweal 82:417-18 Je 18 '65. J. R. Mellow
  New Repub 152:21-4 My 29 '65. J. L. Featherstone
  Reporter 33:44+ Ag 12 '65. A. Kazin
Henry James, Edith Wharton, and the age of leisure. W. Andrews. Harper 230:137-40 My '65
Two lives of Edith Wharton, by G. Kellogg. Review.
  America 113:444-5 O 16 '65. J. J. McAleer

WHARTON, John F.
Plight of the out-of-town theatergoer. Sat R 49:29-31+ Ja 22 '66

WHEAT
How to understand and use this year's wheat-feed grain programs. B. Brantley and F. Bailey, jr. Suc Farm 63:52-3 Mr '65
Revolution on the pampas, by J. S. Scobie. Review
  Américas il 17:38 Ag '65. N. Ras
Who'll be first to grow 250-bu. wheat? G. Lorang. il Farm J 89:24-5+ Ag '65
Why U.S. was left out of Russian wheat deal; with editorial comment. Bsns W p30-1, 144 Ag 21 '65

Prices
And now, wheat. Newsweek 66:79 D 6 '65
Buttering the bread tax. Time 86:13 Ag 27 '65
Letter from Washington; to George S. Moore from Orville L. Freeman. Newsweek 66:78 Jl 26 '65
Now there's talk of a bread tax. il U S News 59:32 Jl 26 '65
Protecting the freshmen; no vote on farm bill. New Repub 153:10-11 S 4 '65

WHEAT-cotton act. See Agricultural laws and legislation

WHEAT trade
Moving wheat to Russia. il Time 86:34 Ag 20 '65
Selling wheat to Communist countries: gain or loss for the free world? pro and con discussion. Sr Schol 87:12-13 D 2 '65

WHEATON, Elmer P.
Wheaton outlines U.S. industry response. por Aviation W 82:82-4+ My 10 '65

WHEATON, III.
Warning strips protect underground spaghetti. S. J. Kennedy. il Am City 80:98 Mr '65

WHEATON, III, public library
Contemporary contrast for Wheaton. M. Lincoln. il Library J 90:5176-8 D 1 '65

WHEEL barrows. See Wheelbarrows

WHEELBARROWS
Big wheel. il House & Gard 128:44+ O '65
How to invent the wheelbarrow or the wheel. T. Irwin. il Pop Sci 187:162-3 D '65

WHEELER, Bradner D. Jr. See Chave, K. E. jt. auth.

WHEELER, Bruce E.
Lincolniana in 1964. Hobbies 69:28-9+ F; 70:28-9+ Mr '65

WHEELER, C. A.
America's most beautiful animal. Field & S 70:58+ S '65

WHEELER, Earle Gilmore
Management team. il por Time 85:22-23A F 5 '65
Wheeler and the dealer. W. J. Coughlin. Miss & Roc 17:74 S 13 '65

WHEELER, John N.
My most unforgettable character. Read Digest 87:99-103 D '65

WHEELER, Joseph L.
Providence pioneer: William E. Foster. Wilson Lib Bul 40:275-8 N '65

WHEELER, Keith
Billion-dollar baby, the birth of XB-70. Read Digest 87:128-33 Jl '65
Brotherly boom in burglaries. Life 59:71-2+ Ag 6 '65
Cursed gun, the track of C2766. Life 59:62-5 Ag 27 '65

WHEELER, Owen H. and Montalvo, Rafael
Radiolysis of estrone and estradiol. bibliog Science 150:493-4 O 22 '65

WHEELER, Richard
Facts behind the fiction. H. Frankel. Sat R 48:31 N 6 '65

WHEELER, Thomas C.
New York tries a new approach. Reporter 32:18-20 Je 17 '65

WHEELER, Timothy J.
Day the Vietcong attacked the United States. Nat R 17:1157-9 D 14 '65

WHEELER, Wilfred
Cheerful holly tree. J. P. Wood. il Read Digest 87:171-2+ D '65

WHEELER national wildlife refuge. See Wildlife sanctuaries

WHEELING steel corporation
Spring cleaning: new president. Newsweek 65:84+ My 10 '65

WHEELOCK, E. Frederick
Interferon-like virus-inhibitor induced in human leukocytes by phytohemagglutinin. bibliog Science 149:310-11 Jl 16 '65

WHEELOCK, John Hall
Bathing beach; poem. New Yorker 41:36 Jl 17 '65

WHEELS
Wheels for tykes and teens. M. B. Keiser. il Parents Mag 40:15-16 Je '65
See also
Automobiles—Wheels
Flywheels

WHEELS within wheels; drama. See Fisher, A. and Rabe, O.

WHELAN, Hilda
African mother; poem. Christian Cent 82: 1056 S 1 '65

WHELAN, Thomas J.
Slide-rule Caesar. por Time 86:15A D 31 '65

WHEN is a captain; story. See Ezell, M. K.

WHEN the heart remembers; story. See Dowty, L.

WHERE did all the flowers go? story. See Block, L.

WHERE is Phronsie Pepper? drama. See Kimball, R. P.

WHIPPETS (dogs)
Dog's big haul; Ch. Courtenay Fleetfoot's awards. il Life 58:49-50 F 5 '65

WHIPPING. See Corporal punishment

WHIPPLE, J.
Vietnam panic button. New Repub 153:38 N 20 '65

WHIPS (desserts) See Desserts

WHISKEY barrels. See Barrels

WHISTLER, James Abbott McNeill
Gallery for young people. C. B. Johnson. il Sch Arts 65:42-3 N '65

WHISTLERS (marmots) See Marmots

WHISTLES
Pocket policeman; alarm siren. W. S. Gohl. il Pop Mech 125:198 Ja '66

WHISTLING swans. See Swans

WHITAKER, Frederic
Day with Disney. Am Artist 29:44-8+ S '65
Illustrations of Raymond F. Houlihan. Am
Artist 29:47-53+ Mr '65
Robert Abbett, illustrator. Am Artist 29:48-
53+ Je '65

WHITAKER, Robert B.
New hope for the Gila. Field & S 70:48-9+
Ag '65

WHITBREAD, Thomas
Shiloh: the bloody pond; poem. Harper 231:75
Jl '65

WHITE, Alison
With birds in his beard. Sat R 49:26-7 Ja
15 '66

WHITE, Antonia
(tr) See Leduc, V. Balenciaga
(tr) See Leduc, V. Great craftsmen of Paris

WHITE, Bruce
Arc welding as a means of expression. il Sch
Arts 65:29-31 N '65

WHITE, Byron R.
Excerpts from the opinion of the Court, June
7, 1965. Cong Digest 44:216+ Ag '65

WHITE, Carroll T. See Bartlett, N. R. jt. auth.

WHITE, Charles C.
One-man war on poverty. il pors Ebony
20:77-8+ F '65

WHITE, E. B.
What do our hearts treasure? New Yorker
41:29-30 Ja 15 '66

WHITE, Edna M.
Just take off, brother! Farm J 89:52L My '65

WHITE, Edward Higgins, 2d
I felt red, white and blue all over. por Life
58:70A-70B Je 25 '65
I'm thankful to be first; historic voices from
space; conversation. U S News 58:35 Je
14 '65
about
Closing the gap. il por Time 85:24-8 Je 11 '65
How they shot the space walk. il por U S
Camera 28:68-9+ S '65
Men, the wives, the kids. il Newsweek 65:32
Je 14 '65
Tumult on earth; series of tumultuous recep-
tions. il por Time 85:33 Je 25 '65
See also
Space flight—Manned flights—McDivitt-White
flight, 1965

WHITE, Edward Higgins, family
Down on earth, their kids plotted for bubble
gum. J. Howard. il Life 58:40B Je 18 '65

WHITE, Elgin
Across Florida by outboard. Yachting 117:
62-3+ F '65

WHITE, Ellington
Fishing. Sports Illus 22:49-50+ Je 21 '65

WHITE, George W. and Totten, S. M.
Wisconsinan age of the Titusville till, formerly called inner Illinoian, northwestern Pennsylvania. bibliog Science 148:234-5 Ap 9 '65

WHITE, Gilbert F.
Rediscovering the earth. por Am Ed 1:8-11
F '65

WHITE, John
Bugs. Criticism
New Repub 153:29+ D 18 '65
Veronica. Criticism
Commonweal 83:410-11 Ja 7 '66
New Repub 153:29+ D 18 '65

WHITE, John F.
Not so educational TV. J. Ridgeway. New
Repub 153:16-18 Ag 21 '65

WHITE, Joseph M. and Holm, G. C.
Colony of hemophilic dogs. Science 150:1766
D 31 '65

WHITE, Josh
Josh White talks to teens. por Seventeen 24:
172+ Ap '65

WHITE, Katherine S.
Department of amplification. New Yorker
41:70 Jl 10 '65
Onward and upward in the garden. New
Yorker 41:164+ D 18 '65

WHITE, L. T.
Management assistance for small business.
Harvard Bsns R 43:67-74 Jl '65

WHITE, Paul Dudley. See Estes, J. W. jt.
auth.

WHITE, Peter T.
Saigon; eye of the storm. Nat Geog Mag 127:
834-72 Je '65

WHITE, Philip L.
Challenge to the American diet; interview.
Todays Health 44:12-13+ Ja '66
(ed) Let's talk about food. See issues of
Today's health

WHITE, Ralph K.
Socialism and capitalism. For Affairs 44:216-
28 Ja '66

WHITE, Robert J. and others
Brain transplantation: prolonged survival of
brain after carotid-jugular interposition.
bibliog Science 150:779-81 N 5 '65

WHITE, Robert M.
Weatherman talks about the weather; interview. por U S News 59:51-2 Ag 30 '65

WHITE, Sheffield
Underdeveloped British businessman. Atlan
217:75-8 Ja '66

WHITE, Sidney
Art as a way of life. Sch Arts 64:5-8 F '65

WHITE, Stanford
Stanford White and the wherewithal. W.
McQuade. il por Arch Forum 123:70 N '65
That was New York. A. Logan. New Yorker
41:56+ F 27 '65

WHITE, Stanley
Henry Seligman's Sisters of mercy. Sat R 48:
68-71 O 2 '65

WHITE, Theodore Harold
Big city faces its decisive moment. Life 59:
34-40A+ O 29 '65
Making of the President—1964; excerpts. Life
58:86-7+ Je 18; 82-4+ Je 25; 59:70-2+ Jl
2 '65
Unmaking of a vice president; excerpts from
Making of the President—1964. U S News
59:15 Jl 5 '65
What went wrong? something called 345 KV.
Life 59:46B+ N 19 '65
Why Negroes riot; excerpt from The making
of the President, 1964. Read Digest 87:
67-73 N '65
about
Indomitable spirit, compassion for people. G.
P. Hunt. por Life 58:3 Je 18 '65
Wordsmith at work. il pors Newsweek 66:21-
2+ Jl 12 '65

WHITE, Thomas Dresser
JCS questionnaire. por Newsweek 65:22 F 15
'65
Obituary
Newsweek por 67:7 Ja 3 '66

WHITE, Vera Randal
Night for celebration; story. Sat Eve Post
238:50-4 D 4 '65

WHITE, Wallace
Wood; story. Atlan 215:76-81 My '65

WHITE, William C.
Chinese lawyer. il por Time 86:14-15 Ag
27 '65
Return of a native. S. Liu. il por Newsweek
66:45 Ag 30 '65

WHITE, William S.
Home is where the heart is. R. E. Bauman.
Nat R 17:286-7 Ap 6 '65

WHITE citizens councils
Catch a bigot by the toe; Prince Georges
County white citizens council. T. Kelly.
Nation 200:169-70 F 15 '65
Ringers; Prince Georges County, Md, white
citizens' council. Newsweek 65:24+ F 8
'65

WHITE collar workers. See Office workers

WHITE devil; drama. See Webster, J.

WHITE dwarf stars. See Stars, Dwarf

WHITE House
Atlantic report; small talk in the yellow
room; the President and the ambassadors.
Atlan 217:10 Ja '66
Christmas at the White House. Sr Schol
87:29 D 9 '65
Life in the White House; excerpt from A
thousand days. A. M. Schlesinger, jr. il
Life 59:84-6+ N 5 '65
Moderns in the White House. F. Getlein.
New Repub 153:34-5 O 23 '65
New White House garden dedicated. il Flower
Grower 52:38-9 Ag '65
Not the sort of place to live in; White House
vs. LBJ ranch. E. T. Folliard. America
112:797 My 29 '65
Now, White House help for tourists. il US
News 59:14-15 Ag 16 '65
Paintings in the President's house. F. Getlein.
New Repub 153:34-6 O 16 '65
Presidents and their Christmas trees. W. K.
Williams. il Am For 71:16-19+ D '65
Radiant interlude in history; dinner and
dance for Princess Margaret and her hus-
band. il Life 59:32-41 D 3 '65
Rhubarb in the kitchen. il Newsweek 66:24
D 27 '65
White House cuisine: quenelles are out, chili
is in. il U S News 59:8 D 27 '65
White House flowers. il Good H 162:64-7
Ja '66
White House: no fit place to live? il U S
News 58:48-52 My 24 '65

WHITE House—*Continued*

History

Speech that toppled a president; excerpts from address, April 14, 1840, ed. with introd. by G. Carson. C. Ogle; reply. G. I. Bushfield. Am Heritage 16:87 Ap '65

WHITE House conference on civil rights, 1966 (proposed)

Moynihan report: Negro family, the case for national action. Christian Cent 82:1531-2 D 15 '65

WHITE House conference on education, 1965

Alice in Washington. il Newsweek 66:60 Ag 2 '65

Innovation called for at White House conference. Library J 90:3708 S 15 '65

Memo to members; comments on conference, ed. by R. Warncke. R. G. Vosper. ALA Bul 59:688-9 S '65

Need for radical reform; teacher education. H. Taylor. il Sat R 48:75-6+ N 20 '65

Prelude to a new push. il Time 86:40 Jl 30 '65

Teach and learn urged. A. Ewing. Sci N L 88:67 Jl 31 '65

Washington report. J. Lloyd. Sr Schol 87: sup4 S 16 '65

White House conference: harbinger of change. J. Cass. Sat R 48:45-6 Ag 21 '65

White House conference on education and the emergence of the new guard. F. Parker. Sch & Soc 93:425-8 N 13 '65

White House conference on education; with editorial comment. il Am Ed 1:inside cover, 13-27 Jl '65

White House conference revisited; quotations. Sr Schol 87:sup33 S 23 '65

WHITE House conference on International cooperation, 1965

Conference conference; recommendations. Reporter 33:12+ D 16 '65

Greater joint space effort endorsed; with editorial comment. W. S. Beller. Miss & Roc 17:15; 46 D 6 '65

ICY; report on the White House conference on International cooperation year. A. Balk. Sat R 49:24-8 Ja 22 '66

ICY; US program. N. Cousins. Sat R 48:24 D 18 '65

International cooperation: LBJ gets conference proposals. L. J. Carter. il Science 150:1431-2+ D 10 '65

State department's *nyet*. Nation 201:485 D 20 '65

White House conference on international cooperation; addresses, November 29-December 1, 1965. Dept State Bul 53:966-84 D 20 '65

World is a campus; recommendations by committees on aviation, transportation, and cultural exchange. W. D. Patterson. Sat R 49:20 Ja 1 '66

WHITE House conference on natural beauty

Beauty, beauty everywhere; White House conference on natural beauty. il Time 85:16 Je 4 '65

Facelift for America; President's White House conference on natural beauty. Bsns W p33 My 29 '65

Remaking the scene; White House conference on natural beauty. il Newsweek 65:56-7 Je 7 '65

White House conference on natural beauty. C. H. Callison. Audubon Mag 67:250-1 Jl '65

White House conference on natural beauty. J. B. Craig and I. M. Moore. il Am For 71:12-15 Je '65

White House conference on natural beauty, May 24 and May 25, 1965; excerpts from addresses. il Recreation 58:318-20 S '65

Word at the White House conference; on natural beauty. C. W. Buchheister. Audubon Mag 67:220 Jl '65

WHITE house department store. See San Francisco—Stores

WHITE House entertaining. See Government entertaining

WHITE House festival of the arts, 1965

Art, and politics, at the White House; Festival of the arts. il U S News 58:10-11 Je 28 '65

Art-in; White House festival of the arts. Reporter 33:10 Jl 1 '65

Artists in the Great society? T. B. Hess. Art N 64:21 S '65

Arts and the man, and the state; first White House festival of the arts. il Newsweek 65:22-4 Je 28 '65

Arts in America. H. Taylor. il Dance Mag 39:35-7 N '65

Festival of the arts. il Time 85:30-1 Je 25 '65

Mrs Johnson's cultural cookout. R. Lynes. il Harper 231:28+ S '65

My day at the White House; White House festival of the arts. F. Getlein. New Repub 152:33+ Je 26 '65

Polit art; White House festival of the arts. Nation 206:687-8 Je 28 '65

White House festival. S. Maloff. Commonweal 82:485-7 Jl 9 '65

White House festival of the arts. il Dance Mag 39:36-8 Ag '65

White House presents photography as art. C. Reynolds. il Pop Phot 57:59+ N '65

WHITE House press photographers association photo contest. See Photography—Competitions

WHITE House staff. See Public officers

WHITE ISLAND

White Island; owner's reminiscences. R. B. Fosdick. il Atlan 216:110-12+ O '65

WHITE men in Africa. See Africa—Race problems

WHITE motor company

White molds the parts; has acquired five competitors and three farm equipment companies. il Bsns W p 159-60+ O 16 '65

WHITE MOUNTAINS, Ariz.

Very unusual vacation; among the Pueblo ruins at Grasshopper, Ariz. L. B. Johnson. il McCalls 92:58+ S '65

WHITE MOUNTAINS, New Hampshire

Summer in the White Mountains; a historical account. D. H. Giffen. il Antiques 88:195-9 Ag '65

WHITE PASS and Yukon railroad

Yukon's golden railroad. G. S. Wells. il Travel 123:32-6 My '65

WHITE PLAINS, N.Y.

Putting jarrah wood to the test. A. Howard. il Recreation 58:299 Je '65

Reduce your money needs. J. E. Curtis. il Am City 80:32 My '65

This parking garage. W. H. Bruder. il Am City 80:98-100 D '65

WHITE salmon fishing. See Yellowtail fishing

WHITE SANDS missile range. See Proving grounds

WHITE Sox (baseball) See Baseball clubs

WHITEBARK pine. See Pine

WHITEHEAD, Alfred North

Christian natural theology, by J. B. Cobb, jr. Review

Christian Cent 82:712-13 Je 2 '65. F. Ferré

WHITEHEAD, Donald R.

Prehistoric maize in southeastern Virginia. bibliog Science 150:881-3 N 12 '65

WHITEHEAD, Edward

Can Commander Whitehead save Britain? J. Weingarttn. il Duns R 86:42-3+ Jl '65

WHITEHEAD, Eric

Nature. Sports Illus 23:54+ Jl 12 '65

WHITEHORN, Ethel. See McMahan, I. jt. auth.

WHITEHORSE star. See Newspapers—Canada

WHITEKER, McElwyn

Blueprint for feeding sows. Suc Farm 63:110 Mr '65

WHITEMAN, Philip M.

Wind of change in British library education. por Library J 90:4921-5 N 15 '65

WHITENACK, Carolyn I.

Educational media index; interview, ed. by D. DuBose. por Sr Schol 86:7T-8T F 25 '65

WHITFIELD, Raymond P. and Egger, Eugene

School attendance of Swiss and American children. Sch & Soc 93:254-6 Ap 17 '65

WHITING, Mrs J. D.

Charms and amulets. Hobbies 70:45+ O '65

WHITING, John

Devils; dramatization of Devils of Loudun. by A. Huxley. Criticism

Cath World 202:255-6 Ja '66
Commonweal 83:348-9 D 17 '65
Nat R 18:38-9 Ja 11 '66
Nation 201:483-4 D 13 '65
New Repub 153:28 D 18 '65
New Yorker 41:170+ N 27 '65
Newsweek il 66:91 N 29 '65
Reporter 33:46+ D 16 '65
Sat R 48:76 D 4 '65
Time il 86:67 N 26 '65
Vogue 147:72 Ja 1 '66

WHITMAN, Ainsley A.

Asheville-Biltmore in red, white and black. Library J 90:5204-5 D 1 '65

WHITMAN, Ardis

How the civil rights struggle challenges our churches. Redbook 125:55-7+ Ag '65

Our churches answer the challenge of civil rights. Redbook 125:64-5+ S '65

WHITMAN, Ardis—*Continued*
Overtaken by joy. Read Digest 86:105-9 Ap '65
Power of the open heart. Read Digest 86:
179-80+ My '65
Why good parents have problem children.
Read Digest 87:144-7 N '65
WHITMAN, Arthur
Life that's made to order. Pop Mech 124:
138-42 N '65
Toys to train army tankmen for battle. Pop
Mech 124:142-6 O '65
WHITMAN, Roger C.
Easy way to paint a room. Am Home 68:80+
Mr '65
Seven home repairs you're most likely to face:
questions and answers. Pop Sci 187:150-2+
O '65
With today's miracle adhesives, you can
mend anything. Am Home 68:98-9 Ap '65
WHITMAN, Ruth
Dead center; poem. New Yorker 41:43 My
8 '65
Spider on my poem; Three letters; poems.
Poetry 106:336-7 Ag '65
WHITMER, Anne
It's hard to be the middle child. Parents
Mag 40:64-5+ bibliog(p38) O '65
WHITMORE, Frank C. jr, and Stewart, R. H.
Miocene mammals and Central American
seaways. bibliog. Science 148:180-5 Ap 9 '65
WHITMORE, George, jr
Right guy. il por Newsweek 65:30-1 F 8
'65
Suspect confesses, but who believes him? S. E.
Zion. il por N Y Times Mag p30-1+ My
16 '65
WHITNEY, Edgar A.
Edgar A. Whitney describes some new ap-
proaches. il por Am Artist 30:58-9+ Ja '66
WHITNEY, Monroe
Transatlantic view of American education.
Sat R 48:66-7 Mr 20 '65
WHITNEY, Phyllis A.
Map is not a journey. Writer 78:7-12 N '65
Satisfying element. Writer 78:11-14+ F '65
WHITNEY, John Hay, foundation. See John
Hay Whitney foundation
**WHITNEY museum of American art, New
York**
Art galleries; annual exhibition of contem-
porary American painting (cont) R. M.
Coates. New Yorker 41:52+ Ja 1 '66
WHITTAKER, Charles E.
Dangers of mass disobedience. Read Digest
87:121-4 D '65
Lawlessness in U.S. warning from a top
jurist; address, June 17, 1965. por U S News
59:60-33 Jl 5 '65

about
Ex-justice severs Supreme court ties. U S
News 59:14 N 1 '65
WHITTAKER, Helene
Genie of the bottle; drama. Plays 25:79-84
N '65
WHITTAKER, James W.
Mount Kennedy: first ascent. pors Nat Geog
Mag 128:10-33 Jl '65
WHITTAKER, R. H. See Niering, W. A. jt.
auth.
WHITTALL, Gertrude Clarke
Mrs Matthew John Whittall dies; great pa-
tron of Library of Congress. Library J 90:
3241 Ag '65
WHITTEMORE, Reed
Clamming; poem. New Yorker 41:30 Ag 28
'65
Poetry and power. il por Newsweek 65:94-94B
F 15 '65
WHITTEN, Joseph N.
Maritime remodels. Library J 90:5201-3 D 1
'65
WHITTIER, Bob
Beware the outboard thief! Yachting 118:53
S '65
Build this flyweight boat trailer. Pop Sci
186:116-17 F '65
Outboard in fog. Yachting 117:66-7+ My '65
WHITWORTH, Bill
Ornette Coleman: innovator or incompetent?
Holiday 38:81-2+ S '65
WHITWORTH, Kathy
Heiress apparent. il por Newsweek 66:66 D
13 '65
New girl in town. por Time 86:63 Ag 6 '65
WHOLESALE price index. See Price indexes
WHOLESALE trade
Ratios of the wholesalers. il Duns R 86:70-1
O '65

Wages and hours
Wholesale trade: employee earnings and
hours, 1964. H. A. Donoian. bibliog f il
Mo Labor R 88:1307-12 N '65

WHOLESALERS, Book. See Book jobbers
WHOOPING cough

Vaccines
New whooping cough kills, resists vaccine;
pertussis vaccine. Sci N L 88:35 Jl 17 '65
WHOOPING cranes. See Cranes (birds)
WHO'S who in library service
Final call for Who's who; letter to the editor.
L. Ash. Library J 90:3830 O 1 '65
WHO'S who of the American theatre. See
Biographical encyclopaedia and who's who
of the American theatre
WHYMPER, Edward
Reporter at large. J. Bernstein. New Yorker
41:134+ Mr 13 '65
WIBBERLEY, Leonard
Portugal. Travel 123:30-5 Ap '65
Stories are about people. Writer 78:9-11+
Ag '65
WICHITA, Kan.

Water supply
Do-it-yourself pays in many ways. O. K.
Brandon. il Am City 80:97 O '65
WICK, G. C.
High energy physics and the rest of physical
science. por Science 147:1554-5 Mr 26 '65
WICKER, Tom
Bill Moyers: Johnson's good angel. Harper
231:41-9 O '65; Same abr with title Re-
markable rise of Bill D. Moyers. Read
Digest 88:72-7 Ja '66
Books. Vogue 146:167 O 1 '65
Johnson-Goldwater clash. New Repub 153:
17-21 Jl 10 '65
Lyndon Johnson is ten feet tall. N Y Times
Mag p23+ My 23 '65
Lyndon Johnson vs the ghost of Jack Ken-
nedy. Esquire 64:87+ N '65
One year of L.B.J. New Repub 153:13-22 N
13 '65
Son of the Kingfish. N Y Times Mag p76-
7+ Ap 4 '65
Winds of change in the Senate. N Y Times
Mag p52-3+ S 12 '65
WICKERSHAM, David Clifford
Somebody up there. Newsweek 66:62 Ag 2
'65
WICKES corporation
Building-supply supermarkets. J. F. Olesky.
il Duns R 85:85 F '65
Piling up more than lumber. il Bsns W p57-8
Ja 30 '65
WICKFORD, R.I.
Wickford tales. A. W. Hinckley. il Am Heri-
tage 16:80-90 Je '65
WICKWIRE, Franklin B.
King's friends, civil servants, or politicians.
bibliog f Am Hist R 71:18-42 O '65
WIDE-angle lenses. See Lenses, Photographic
WIDGERY, David
Travels among the Americans. Sat R 49:55-
6 Ja 15 '66
WIDICK, B. J.
AFL-CIO convention. Nation 201:516-18 D 27
'65
Steelworkers vote: prelude to the strike. Na-
tion 200:214-16 Mr 1 '65
United States economy: overview. bibliog f
Cur Hist 49:1-8+ Jl '65
WIDOM, B.
Molecular transitions and chemical reaction
rates. bibliog Science 148:1555-60 Je 18 '65
WIDOWS
Helping the widows; policemen's widows. il
Time 86:38+ S 10 '65
How Jackie Kennedy & other young widows
have rebuilt their lives. A. Levy. il Good H
160:96-9+ Mr '65
Vietnam widow; S. Isaacs. J. Star. il Look
30:24-8+ Ja 25 '66
Young widow speaks to young wives. Red-
book 125:6+ My '65
WIECK, Herman D.
Is your sight asleep? U S Camera 29:62-5
Ja '66
WIECK, Paul R.
Dirksen's double play. New Repub 152:13-14
Ap 17 '65
Unrepresented Negro farmers in the South.
New Repub 153:8-9 D 25 '65
WIEGAND, Dorothea
People like cul-de-sacs. Am City 80:108 Mr
'65
WIELAND, William
Ordeal of Otto Otepka. C. Stevenson and
W. J. Gill. Read Digest 87:56-9 Ag '65
WIEN, Lawrence Arthur
Two realty partners tackle a big one alone.
por Bsns W p 105-6+ Ag 21 '65

WIENERS, Charlie
Hawk is a mighty hunter. F. Deford. il
Sports Illus 24:20-3 Ja 10 '66
WIENERS, John
Taking away from God his sound. R. Duncan.
Nation 200:595-8 My 31 '65
To write is to listen. D. Levertov. Poetry
105:326-9 F '65
WIENS, A. Wayne, and Gilbert, L. I.
Regulation of cockroach fat-body metabolism
by the corpus cardiacum in vitro. bibliog
Science 150:614-16 O 29 '65
WIESBADEN festival. See Music festivals—
Germany (Federal Republic)
WIESE, M. Bernice, and Rusk, Alice
Mount Royal elementary. Library J 90:5457-9
D 15 '65
WIESEL, Elie
Last return; tr. by A. Schwartz. Commentary
39:43-9 Mr '65
WIFE beating
When did you stop beating your wife? F. R.
Schreiber and M. Herman. Sci Digest 57:20
Mr '65
WIGGAM, Lionel
Outer space; poem. Atlan 216:167 N '65
WIGGIN, Kate Douglas
Birds' Christmas carol; dramatization. See
Miller, H. L.
WIGGINS, Warren W.
Promises of home. por Am Ed 1:21-5 Ap '65
WIGNER, Eugene P.
Violations of symmetry in physics; with
biographical sketch. Sci Am 213:10, 28-36
bibliog(p 126) D '65
WIGS
Beauty life; the won't-wilt coifs. il Mlle 61:
100-1 Je '65
Bewitching switching. il Seventeen 24:138 Je
'65
Fake hair flattery. il Life 58:89-90 F 12
'65
Pin on a gay, new hairdo; switches and
braids. il Seventeen 24:118-19 N '65
Wiglets: pretty little pin-on pieces that go to
your head. il McCalls 92:120-1+ Mr '65

Anecdotes, facetiae, satire, etc.
Instant hair. E. B. Thompson. il Ebony 21:
139-40+ N '65
WIIK, B. See Buttlar, H. von jt. auth.
WIKGREN, J. Arthur
Fighting the flurries. Am City 80:98-9 O '65
WILBUR, Richard
On the marginal way; poem. New Yorker 41:
48 S 25 '65
(tr) See Molière, J. B. P. Tartuffe
WILCOX, John M. See Ness, N. F. jt. auth.
WILCOX, Wayne
Politicians, bureaucrats, and development in
India. bibliog f Ann Am Acad 358:114-22
Mr '65
WILCOX, William H.
Philadelphia: look at techniques. Sat R 49:
98-9 Ja 8 '66
WILD animal pets. See Pets
WILD bees. See Bees
WILD cats. See Lynxes
WILD dogs
Wild dogs keep order. Sci N L 87:142 F 27
'65
WILD ducks. See Ducks, Wild
WILD flowers
Conservation: New Jersey style. E. Finch.
il Pop Gard 16:34-5+ Ap '65
Fall in the mountains. D. E. Rose. Horticul-
ture 43:16 O '65
Growing wildflowers from seed; excerpt from
Wild flowers and how to grow them. E. F.
Steffek. il Horticulture 43:40-2 O '65
Joy of wildflowering. S. H. Gottscho and
D. G. Schleisner. il Audubon Mag 67:97-101
Mr '65
Prairie woods and wild flowers. R. Suckow.
il Am Heritage 16:36-43 Ap '65
Redding to Red Bluff in flowers; Cascade
foothills, Calif. il Sunset 134:44-5 Mr '65
Weed is where you find it; photographs by
E. Javorsky. Natur Hist 74:22-5 Ap '65
Wild flower rescue squad; Flower fanciers'
garden club, Hagerstown, Md. H. A.
Arnold. Flower Grower 53:13 Ja '66
Wildflowers at home or close to home. il
Sunset 135:252-3 O '65
Wildflowers in Alaska. E. Baldwin. il Horti-
culture 43:22-3 Ag '65
Wild flowers to grow. M. J. Dietz. il Flower
Grower 52:26+ Ap '65
WILD geese. See Geese, Wild
WILD honey; story. See Ballard, J.
WILD horses. See Horses

WILD rice
Luxury food item, with a wild price. il Bsns
W p32-3 S 18 '65
WILD swine. See Woods hogs
WILD turkeys. See Turkeys, Wild
WILD West shows. See Rodeos
WILDE, John
U.S. power squadrons free instruction in boat
operation starts next month. Motor B 116:
120-2 Ag '65
WILDE, Oscar
Birthday of the infanta; dramatization. See
Nolan, P. T.
WILDE, Patricia
Tchaikovsky Promenade-1, Philharmonic Hall.
M. Marks. Dance Mag 39:28 Ag '65
WILDER, Amos N.
Hard death; poem. Poetry 107:168-9 D '65
Nativity; poem. Christian Cent 82:1568 D 22
'65
Third day; poem. Christian Cent 82:458 Ap 14
'65
WILDER, Laura (Ingalls)
From deep springs. R. H. Viguers. Horn Bk
41:463 O '65
Frontier faith revisited. W. J. Jacobs. il
Horn Bk 41:464-73 O '65
WILDER, Norman J.
Amateur scientist. Sci Am 213:102-6 Ag '65
WILDER, Thornton Niven
Thornton Wilder wins first National medal
for literature. por Pub W 187:36 My 10 '65
Universe of Thornton Wilder. H. I. Popper.
Harper 230:72-8+ Je '65
WILDER award
Laura Ingalls Wilder award; presentation
and acceptance. F. Sullivan; R. Sawyer.
Horn Bk 41:474-6 O '65
WILDERNESS areas
After your nine-mile hike, a choice of thirty
fishing lakes; Oregon's Lake Basin. il Sun-
set 135:47-8 S '65
Allagash; Maine's counter proposal; with
text. il Am For 71:26-9 F '65
Battle at Mason Neck. il Nat Parks Mag
39:20-1 D '65
Boundary waters canoe area decision; Su-
perior national forest, Minn. il Liv Wildn
29:20-6 Spr '65
By horseback into the Marble Mountain
wilderness. il Sunset 135:22-4 Jl '65
Conflict in outdoor recreation; natural beauty
versus economic interests. R. K. Davis and
J. L. Knetsch. il Am For 71:26-9+ N '65
Handbook on the Wilderness act; with text
of act; symposium. il Liv Wildn 86:1-9+
Spr '64
Journey into wilderness. J. V. Lone. il Liv
Wildn 29:9-11 Sum '65
Land between the Lakes. C. Laycock. il
Field & S 69:130-3+ Mr '65
Lincoln back country wilderness proposed.
Liv Wildn 29:37 Spr '65
Living museums. C. Foley. il Am For 71:
14-17+ N '65
Mechanized monsters! S. A. Reed. il Liv
Wildn 29:17-19 Spr '65
Message from the President of the United
States, February 8, 1965; excerpt. L. B.
Johnson. Liv Wildn 87:2 Wint '64
Minnesota compromise; AFA's Minnesota
land ownership study. Am For 71:18-19
F '65
Nature center grows in the Land between the
Lakes. J. J. Shomon. il Audubon Mag 67:
212-14 Jl '65
P.R. in the forests; North Cascades struggle
for conservation. G. McConnell. il Nation
201:522-4 D 27 '65
Rich Hole country. R. H. Giles, jr. il Liv
Wildn 29:3-6 Sum '65
Roadless area, by P. Brooks. Review
Liv Wildn il 29:29-31 Spr '65. H. Broome
San Gorgonio; Southern California's rooftop.
W. F. Heald. il Liv Wildn 29:12-16 Sum '65
San Rafael wilderness the first. Liv Wildn
29:37 Sum '65
Save the Selway. Liv Wildn 87:29 Wint '64
Spanish Peaks wilderness proposal announc-
ed. Liv Wildn 29:38 Sum '65
Speaking out; let's spoil the wilderness. R.
Wernick. il Sat Eve Post 238:12+ N 6 '65
To big Bald Rock and plunging Feather Falls.
il Sunset 135:30+ Jl '65
Twenty dudes in the wilderness; reprint.
C. Harper. il Liv Wildn 87:13-15 Wint '64
Udall acts to preserve natural areas. C. H.
Callison. Audubon Mag 67:184-5 My '65
Westchester gorillas. D. Cort. il Nation 201:
249-50+ O 18 '65
Wilderness and the condor. Nat Parks Mag
40:19-20 Ja '66

WILDERNESS areas—*Continued*
Wilderness and the Land and water conservation fund act; outdoor enjoyment. F. Gregg. il Liv Wildn 29:25-8 Sum '65
Wilderness in the parks; need for new wilderness bill. A. W. Smith. Nat Parks Mag 39:2 O '65
Wilderness trail: autumn; Quetico-Superior. H. Hoover. il Liv Wildn 87:11-12 Wint '64
Wilderness trail: winter; Quetico-Superior country. H. Hoover. il Liv Wildn 29:8-10 Spr '65
Wilderness walk back of Big Sur; Ventana wild area. il Sunset 134:48-9 My '65

WILDERNESS society
Twenty dudes in the wilderness; reprint. C. Harper. il Liv Wildn 87:13-15 Wint '64
Wilderness council in Montana; August 7 to 14, 1964. il Liv Wildn 87:30-1 Wint '64

WILDEST ride; story. See Nicoloff, P.

WILDEY, Robert L.
Hot shadows of Jupiter. Science 147:1035-6 F 26 '65

WILDFLOWERS. See Wild flowers

WILDGEN, Jerome
Day in the life of a family doctor. T. Gallagher. il pors Good H 160:78-81+ F '65

WILDI, Ernst
Close-up on close-ups. Pop Phot 56:104-7+ Mr '65
Creating perspective. U S Camera 28:66-7+ N '65
Is Super-8 the filmsize of the future? por U S Camera 28:74+ Jl '65

WILDLIFE
New ban proposed on wildlife imports. Sci N L 87:296 My 8 '65

WILDLIFE conservation
Churchill's interest in animal life. L. H. Newman. il Audubon Mag 67:240-3 Jl '65
Down with plinkers. R. Reagan. il Am For 71:4-5 Ag '65
Survival or surrender? C. W. Buchheister. Audubon Mag 67:221 Jl '65
Westchester gorillas. D. Cort. il Nation 201: 249-50+ O 18 '65
Wildlife and multiple use. V. Metcalfe. il Am For 71:30-1+ N '65
        See also
Animals—Protection
Wildlife sanctuaries

WILDLIFE management. See Game preserves

WILDLIFE photography. See Photography of animals

WILDLIFE populations. See Animal populations

WILDLIFE sanctuaries
Atomic blast vs otter? S. McCutcheon. il Audubon Mag 67:376-81 N '65
Corkscrew swamp sanctuary; Fla. S. Rabinove. il Nat Parks Mag 39:8-9 O '65
Goose pays the way. H. Titus. il Field & S 70:100-1 Je '65
Grave threat to the condor; Sespe wildlife area. C. W. Buchheister. il Audubon Mag 67:82-3 Mr '65
Great Swamp refuge addition. Nat Parks Mag 39:25 My '65
Oregon's Hart Mountain antelope and sage hen refuge. A. Antrei. il Nat Parks Mag 39:16-19 Je '65
Plaque for Corkscrew sanctuary. il Audubon Mag 67:249 Jl '65
Ratchet and the wildlife refuges; caught in a recent economy squeeze. il Nat Parks Mag 39:9-12 D '65
Roads in animal refuges. P. M. Tilden. Nat Parks Mag 39:2 My '65
Sanctuaries astride frontiers. F. Bourlière. il UNESCO Courier 18:15-21 F '65
        See also
Bird sanctuaries

WILDSMITH, Brian
Antic disposition: a young British illustrator interviews himself. il por Library J 90: 5035-8 N 15 '65

WILEY, Bradford
Franklin book programs: global publishing aid is varied and expanded. il pors Pub W 187:28-32 Mr 15 '65

WILEY, Charles W.
Dickey Chapelle, RIP. Nat R 17:1066 N 30 '65
Who was Malcolm X? Nat R 17:239-40 Mr 23 '65

WILEY, David
Fire this time. Christian Cent 82:200-3 F 17 '65

WILEY, John, and sons, incorporated
Wiley holds receptions for its West Coast authors. il Pub W 187:39-40 Ap 12 '65

WILEY, Marcia
Cabin talk. See issues of Yachting
Waterfront news. See issues of Yachting
Yachting interviews: a lady yacht broker. Yachting 117:61+ F '65

WILHELM, Eugene J. jr
New Ozark scenic riverways. il Nat Parks Mag 39:12-15 Jl '65

WILHELM, Ross
How to end the draft. Nation 201:350-2 N 15 '65
Rash of student riots aimed at the draft? excerpts from statements. U S News 59:18 S 20 '65

WILHELMSEN, Frederick D.
Notes towards a grammar of the dialogue. Nat R 17:450 Je 1 '65
Who wants a third eye anyway? Nat R 17: 380+ My 4 '65

WILKENLOH, Mrs W. E.
Fresh flowers. il Horticulture 43:43 F '65

WILKENSON, Ruth
Subtle dangers in mother-daughter talks about sex. McCalls 93:58-9+ Ja '66

WILKES, A. See Lee, P. E. jt. auth.

WILKES, Ralph S.
How you can build an A-frame playhouse. Pop Sci 187:124-6 Jl '65
Job-proven ideas for better kitchen cabinets. Pop Sci 186:152-4 F '65

WILKIE, Jane
Deborah Kerr: the lady is a scamp. Good H 160:86-7+ F '65

WILKINS, Collie Leroy
Cooler for Collie. il por Time 86:15B D 31 '65
Hung jury. il por Newsweek 65:40-2 My 17 '65
Juries & justice in Alabama. por Time 86: 49 O 29 '65
Not guilty again. Sr Schol 87:8-9 N 11 '65
Pictorial summation of a tragicomic mistrial; with excerpts from defense counsel's speech and report by J. Frook. il por Life 58:32-9 My 21 '65
Trial. il por Time 85:27-9 My 14 '65
Trial by jury. Newsweek 66:36 N 1 '65
Trial of the Klansman. M. Kempton. New Repub 152:10-13 My 22 '65

WILKINS, Elsie
Stillwater; poem. Liv Wildn 29:10 Spr '65

WILKINS, Roy
Los Angeles riots; handling the topic in class. Sr Schol 87:sup 19 O 7 '65; Same with additions 87:11 O 28 '65
Spirit of '76 in the 1960's. por Seventeen 24:150+ O '65
        about
Confusing the cause; civil rights groups U.S. foreign policy. Time 86:20 Jl 16 '65
Moment of history. New Yorker 41:38-9 Mr 27 '65
Wilkins calls Little Rock integration top achievement. il pors Ebony 20:134+ My '65

WILKINSON, Alfred
British plan a cup caper. J. Lovesey. il por Sports Illus 23:28-9 D 20 '65

WILKINSON, Barbara Lynne
Come take my hand. Seventeen 24:98-9+ D '65

WILKINSON, Emma Lonsdale
Governor Carl Sanders and Miss Emma. J. Shepherd. il pors Look 29:46+ F 23 '65

WILKINSON, James
How lost was Zebulon Pike? D. Jackson. il por Am Heritage 16:10-15+ F '65

WILKINSON sword, limited
Goliath has the upper sword. Time 87:87 Ja 7 '66

WILKS, Robert C.
Whirlybird whiz of the coast guard. il pors Ebony 20:26-8+ My '65

WILL, Ed
How to operate a small-city airport. Am City 80:129 Je '65
Return of the wild beasts. Am For 71:6-7+ Ag '65

WILL, Frederic
Notes on Robert Duncan. Poetry 106:427-8 S '65
Six poems: Subaquatic; In time of tapping; After Keats; In memoriam; Né en Illinois; For a childhood. Poetry 107:85-90 N '65

WILL, James E.
Union without renewal? Christian Cent 82: 588+ My 5 '65

WILL, Robert A.
Good schools attract industry. por NEA J 54:28 Mr '65

WILLAMETTE RIVER, Ore.
Get a boat! let her float! C. G. Simonds. il Sr Schol 86:sup21 Ap 15 '65

WILLARD, Charlotte
Corporation as art collector. Look 29:67-72 Mr 23 '65

WILLE, Lois
  Confrontation in Chicago; Mayor Daley meets
    the movement. Nation 201:92-5 Ag 30 '65
  Good Samaritans; law and the golden rule.
    Nation 200:47-9 Ap 26 '65
  Payoff in Chicago. New Repub 153:11 O 23 '65
WILLETT, Henry I.
  Good citizenship must begin in childhood.
    por Parents Mag 40:40 Je '65
WILLETTS, Elwood H.
  Inventor of the month. S. V. Jones. il Sci
    Digest 57:31 Je '65
WILLEY, Lawrence
  Reading in high gear. Wilson Lib Bul 40:61
    S '65
WILLHOITE, Fred H. Jr
  Church and world in Louisiana. Christian
    Cent 82:402 Mr 31 '65
WILLIAM of Malmesbury
  William of Malmesbury's Robert of Glou-
    cester: a re-evaluation of the Historia
    novella. R. B. Patterson. bibliog f il Am
    Hist R 70:983-97 Jl '65
WILLIAMS, Alfred
  New deal for the harried commuter. Pop
    Mech 124:100-4+ N '65
WILLIAMS, Andy
  Person who changed my life. por Seventeen
    24:156 Ap '65
WILLIAMS, Barbara C.
  Manageable meals. Parents Mag 40:65+ My
    '65
WILLIAMS, Barbara Fischer-. See Fischer-
    Williams, B.
WILLIAMS, Daniel Hale
  Surgeon who dared; excerpt from Doctor
    Dan. H. Buckler. por Todays Health 43:
    46-7+ S '65
WILLIAMS, David A.
  Multiplex adapter for FM stereo. Electr World
    74:74-6 O '65
WILLIAMS, Donald E.
  Crystal packing of molecules. bibliog Sci-
    ence 147:605-6 F 5 '65
WILLIAMS, Eric Eustace
  Letter from Port of Spain. B. Taper. New
    Yorker 41:216-19+ O 23 '65
WILLIAMS, Franklin H.
  International concern for social justice and
    human rights; statement, July 26, 1965. Dept
    State Bul 53:532-6 S 27 '65
  U.S. commends development activities of
    U.N. special fund; statement, January 12,
    1965. Dept State Bul 52:155-7 F 1 '65
WILLIAMS, G. See Carey, J. B. jr, jt. auth.
WILLIAMS, Gene
  Deterrent; story. New Yorker 41:141-3 F 20
    '65
  Les enfants du Thalia; story. New Yorker
    40:28-9 F 6 '65
  Paper tiger, burning bright; story. New
    Yorker 41:52-4 O 30 '65
  Sticky my fingers, fleet my feet; story. New
    Yorker 41:46-8 S 11 '65
WILLIAMS, Gerhard Mennen
  Agricultural development in Africa; address,
    January 7, 1965. Dept State Bul 52:104-7
    Ja 25 '65
  Congo realities and United States policy;
    address, April 25, 1965. Dept State Bul 52:
    793-805 My 24 '65
  More on inside story of how JFK picked
    LBJ; statement. U S News 59:9 Ag 9 '65
  Southern Rhodesia today; address, June 15,
    1965. Dept State Bul 53:71-6 Jl 12 '65
  U.S. objectives and refugee relief programs
    in Africa; statement, January 21, 1965.
    Dept State Bul 52:219-24 F 15 '65
  U.S. outlines interests in Southern Rhodesia;
    address, December 16, 1965. Dept State Bul
    54:13-15 Ja 3 '66
  United States policy in Africa; address, March
    18, 1965. Dept State Bul 52:539-48 Ap 12 '65
  U.S. program of economic assistance to
    Africa; statement, February 10, 1965. Dept
    State Bul 52:349-54 Mr 8 '65

  about
  Assistant Secretary Williams visits six Afri-
    can areas. Dept State Bul 52:333 Mr 8 '65
WILLIAMS, Gordon
  Center for research libraries: its new organ-
    ization and programs. por Library J 90:
    2947-51 Jl '65
  Preservation of deteriorating books; excerpts
    from report. bibliog por Library J 91:51-6
    Ja 1 '66
  US support for book preservation proposed
    in ARL committee report; summary. Li-
    brary J 90:1272+ Mr 15 '65
WILLIAMS, Gweneira M.
  Kettle of brains; drama. Plays 24:77-80 Ap
    '65

WILLIAMS, Howard Y.
  World federalists view the U.N. Christian
    Cent 82:992-3 Ag 11 '65
WILLIAMS, J. Paul
  Church and state: is the wall of separation
    rising or falling? Sch & Soc 93:112-13 F
    20 '65
WILLIAMS, John J.
  Case of Bobby Baker and the courageous
    senator. J. Barron. Read Digest 87:112-18
    S '65
  Echoes of the Baker case: Williams tangles
    with critics. por U S News 58:16 My 31
    '65
  John J. Williams, watchdog of the Senate.
    L. Stern. il por Reporter 32:37-9 F 11 '65
  People's spoilsport. Fortune 72:114 O '65
  Watchdog beware! por Time 85:25 My 28 '65
WILLIAMS, Keith
  Down with Michelin! Atlan 216:130-3 Jl '65
WILLIAMS, Kenneth I. H. and others
  Oxidation of dimethyl sulfoxide to dimethyl
    sulfone in the rabbit. bibliog Science 149:
    203-4 Jl 9 '65
WILLIAMS, Lloyd P.
  Critical comments on some inconsistencies in
    modern thought. Sch & Soc 93:177-9 Mr
    20 '65
WILLIAMS, Martin
  Mostly modernists. See Recordings issues of
    Saturday review
  Resurgence of Pee Wee Russell. Sat R 48:59
    F 27 '65
WILLIAMS, Mary Elizabeth
  Quiet one; poem. America 112:320 Mr 6 '65
WILLIAMS, Mary Frances
  Our teenage cook. See issues of Good house-
    keeping
WILLIAMS, Miller
  Inventing to discover. L. Turco. Poetry 106:
    369 Ag '65
WILLIAMS, Neil
  Three new, cool, bright imagists. E. H.
    Johnson. il por Art N 64:42-4+ Sum '65
WILLIAMS, Norman, Jr
  Zoning and planning decisions. See issues
    of American city
WILLIAMS, Peter
  Twins, alike as two peas? Parents Mag 40:
    44-5+ My '65
WILLIAMS, Ralph Vaughan
  V.W. E. Jablonski. il por Am Rec G 31:
    882-4 My '65
WILLIAMS, Robert E.
  Man on the moon; address, March 11, 1965.
    Vital Speeches 31:624-9 Ag 1 '65
WILLIAMS, Simon
  Private investment in world agriculture.
    Harvard Bsns R 43:95-105 N '65
WILLIAMS, Tennessee
  Gnädiges fräulein; text. Esquire 64:102+
    Ag '65
  Mutilated; text. Esquire 64:96-101 Ag '65
  Slapstick tragedy; preface to production script
    of his two one-act plays. Esquire 64:95-
    102+ Ag '65

  about
  Glass menagerie. Criticism
    America 112:888 Je 19 '65
    Commonweal 82:356-7 Je 4 '65
    Life 58:16 My 28 '65
    New Yorker 41:158 My 15 '65
    Newsweek il 65:92 My 17 '65
    Time il 85:64 My 14 '65
WILLIAMS, Thomas
  All trades, their tackle and trim; story.
    Esquire 64:102-3 N '65
  Outdoors. Esquire 64:72+ S; 62+ O; 50+ D
    '65
  Survivors; story. New Yorker 41:32-40 Ag
    21 '65
WILLIAMS, W. K.
  Presidents and their Christmas trees. Am
    For 71:16-19+ D '65
WILLIAMS, William Carlos
  Gift; poem. Good H 161:70-1 D '65
WILLIAMS-ELLIS, Clough
  In praise of a folly. J. Morris. il por Horizon
    7:16-19 Sum '65
WILLIAMSBURG, Va.
  Business meetings add a dash of the past;
    Conference center. il Bsns W p 178-80+
    N 6 '65
  Colonial kaleidoscope. B. Laatsch. il Sr Schol
    86:sup22-3 Ap 15 '65
  Travel tips. P. P. Coleman. il Sr Schol 86:
    10T F 25 '65
WILLIAMSBURG student burgesses. See
  Forums (discussion and debate)
WILLIAMSON, Charles C.
  Obituary
    Library J 90:798 F 15 '65. P. A. Winckler

WILSON, Harold—about—*Continued*
Independence day? il por Newsweek 66:50+ N 22 '65
Letter from London (cont) M. Panter-Downes. New Yorker 41:136-7 Je 5; 198+ N 27; 225 D 11 '65
Man with a four-seat margin. il pors Time 85:35-39A Ap 30 '65; Same abr. with title Britain's benign socialist. Read Digest 87: 121-5 Jl '65
Many voices. Newsweek 66:45 D 20 '65
Mr Wilson is master of the House. A. Lewis. il pors N Y Times Mag p24-5+ Ap 11 '65
Most popular P. M. Newsweek 66:52 N 22 '65
Now Britain tries a planned recession. por U S News 59:96 S 6 '65
Perils of Harold. Newsweek 65:32+ Mr 22 '65
Plugged in. il por Newsweek 66:20+ D 27 '65
Rhodesia: eleventh-hour showdown. il por Newsweek 66:42 N 1 '65
Rhodesia: hope of compromise. il Newsweek 66:47 N 8 '65
Slightly warmer. Newsweek 65:54+ Ap 12 '65
Smith vs. Wilson: two views on Rhodesia's independence. il por U S News 59:22 N 22 '65
Sterling and steel sour Wilson's hopes. por Bsns W p38-9 Je 12 '65
Surrounded by trouble; Wilson postpones U.S. visit. por U S News 58:20 F 15 '65
Trouble for another Socialist experiment. il por U S News 58:42-3 Je 14 '65
Victory without advance. Time 86:27 Ag 13 '65
Vietnam peacemaker? now Wilson will make a try. por U S News 60:13 Ja 3 '66
We want our country. il por Time 86:48-9 N 5 '65
Wilson's razor's edge. R. W. Howe. New Repub 153:17-18 N 20 '65
Win some, lose some. il por Newsweek 67: 39 Ja 24 '66

WILSON, Helen Van Pelt
Miniature geraniums. Flower Grower 52:31-2 S '65

WILSON, J. Gilchrist
Appearance of board-formed concrete. bibliog Arch Rec 138:173-6 Ag '65

WILSON, J. Tuzo
Transform faults, oceanic ridges, and magnetic anomalies southwest of Vancouver Island. bibliog Science 150:482-5 O 22 '65
—See Vine, F. J. jt. auth.

WILSON, James L.
Commercial recreation: an ally. Recreation 58:76+ F '65

WILSON, James Q.
Flamboyant Mr Powell. Commentary 41:31-5 Ja '66

WILSON, John S.
Jazz. See issues of High fidelity incorporating Musical America

WILSON, José
Going places, finding things in the Pennsylvania Dutch country. House & Gard 128:8+ Jl '65

WILSON, Joseph Chamberlain
Can Xerox be copied? il por Bsns W p66-8+ O 9 '65
SR's businessman of the year. W. D. Patterson. por Sat R 49:72+ Ja 8 '66

WILSON, Juana. See Wilson, B. jt. auth.

WILSON, Julian K.
Brains, newts, legs, eggs, and sea shells. D. Turpin. il por Am Ed 1:1-4 Ap '65

WILSON, Kathryn M.
Titles that tantalize. Writer 78:25 Jl '65

WILSON, Kemmons
Southern business: the boomman. T. G. Harris. il pors Look 29:40-4 N 16 '65

WILSON, Kenneth A.
Biology of reproduction in ferns. Natur Hist 74:52-9 Je '65

WILSON, Lanford
Home free! Criticism Newsweek il por 65:93 F 22 '65

WILSON, Logan
Higher educaation and 1984; adaptation of address, November 2, 1964. Sch & Soc 93: 343-6 O 2 '65
Is the college student becoming a forgotten man? adaptation of address, October 22, 1964. Sch & Soc 93:78-81 F 6 '65

WILSON, M. Curtis
Report on cereal leaf beetle. Suc Farm 63:80 Mr '65

WILSON, Marion Ball
Yuletide feasting in Pennsylvania. por Parents Mag 40:71-4+ D '65

WILSON, Mary
Housewife at no. 10. S. King. il por N Y Times Mag p43+ F 7 '65

WILSON, Orlando Winfield
Excerpt from testimony, October 22, 1963. Cong Digest 44:250+ O '65

about

Chicago shows a way to police reform. J. Star. il por Look 29:43-9 O 19 '65
How Atlanta and Chicago reduced crime. por Fortune 72:259 D '65

WILSON, Peter
Auction by Early bird. R. Lynes. il Harper 231:28+ Ag '65

WILSON, Ralph C.
Friend in need. por Recreation 58:268+ Je '65

WILSON, Robert A.
Key to staying young; excerpts from Feminine forever. Look 30:66+ Ja 11 '66

WILSON, Robley, jr
On a Maine beach; poem. Commonweal 83: 408 Ja 7 '66

WILSON, Rosalind
Famous Rutland pearls; story. Ladies Home J 82:68-9 My '65

WILSON, Sloan
Should you offer teen-agers drinks in your home? Read Digest 86:100-2 Ap '65

WILSON, Thelma, and Niehans, Ken
Better health for every baby. Parents Mag 40:59-61+ N '65

WILSON, Thomas W. jr
Elaborate fantasy. New Repub 153:25-7 D 18 '65

WILSON, Tom
City hall should be a show place. por Am City 80:106-7 My '65

WILSON, W. Frederic
TV for proofs without printing. Pop Phot 57:44-5 Ag '65

WILSON, William E.
Long, hot summer in Indiana. Am Heritage 16:56-64 Ag '65

WILSON, Woodrow
Is history repeating itself? excerpts from article in Atlantic monthly, January 1901, ed. by D. Lawrence. U S News 58:112+ Je 7 '65

about

Twenty-eighth president 1913-1921, F. Freidel. il pors Nat Geog Mag 128:554-61 O '65
Wilson: campaigns for progressiveness and peace, 1916-1917, by A. S. Link. Review America 113:605-6 N 13 '65. F. J. Gallagher

WILSON and company
Wilson, lean, fit, ready for action. il Bsns W p80-3 N 27 '65

WILT, Fred H.
Erythropoiesis in the chick embryo: the role of endoderm. bibliog Science 147:1588-90 Mr 26 '65

WILT pruf
My biggest garden helper. P. Shedesky. il Flower Grower 52:44-5 Je '65

WIMBUSH, Roger
Notes from our correspondents. Hi Fi 16:22+ Ja '66

WIMSATT, William Kurtz
Portraits of Alexander Pope. Antiques 87: 188-92 F '65

WIN a few, lose a few; story. See Lacy, R.

WINANS, Sterling S.
Nation building in Malaya. por Recreation 58:227-8 My '65

WINCHES. See Windlasses

WINCHESTER, Alice
Some eighteenth-century classics from the collection of I. Austin Kelly III. Antiques 87:200-3 F '65

WINCHESTER, James H.
Automation goes to sea. Read Digest 86:119-22 My '65
Food poisoning, and how to avoid it. Read Digest 86:161-2+ My '65
Historic U.S. ships. Travel 124:31-3 Jl '65
Life at 60 below. Sci Digest 57:63-7 Mr '65
Monumental shame. Travel 123:58-60 My '65
Oklahoma powwows. Travel 123:32-6+ Je '65
They stopped a tropical epidemic. Todays Health 43:32-3+ D '65

WINCHESTER cathedral. See Cathedrals—England

WIND, Herbert Warren
Our far-flung correspondents. New Yorker 41:138-46+ My 22 '65
Sporting scene (cont) New Yorker 41:140+ My 1; 72+ Jl 17; 104+ Ag 21; 192+ O 9; 209-10+ N 13 '65

WIND. See Winds

WIND ensembles
See also
Phonograph records—Wind ensembles

WIND pressure
Air-sea interface; report on conference. R. L. Snyder. Science 149:766 Ag 13 '65
WIND tunnels
NOL tunnel advances arc heater art. W. S. Beller. il Miss & Roc 17:27 O 4 '65
WINDFALL oils and mines, limited
Windfall stock stirs demand for Toronto reform; Royal commission report. Bsns W p 172+ O 16 '65
WINDHORST, Dorothy B. and others
Chediak-Higashi syndrome: hereditary gigantism of cytoplasmic organelles. bibliog Science 151:81-3 Ja 7 '66
WINDISCHGRAETZ, Lajos, prince
Windischgraetz caper. G. Bailey. Reporter 32:30-4 F 11 '65
WINDJAMMER cruises. See Cruising
WINDLASSES
Winches have taken a turn for the better. R. W. Carrick. il Yachting 118:58-60+ D '65
WINDLE, William F.
Fertility experiment recalled. Science 149: 1444+ S 24 '65
WINDMILLS
Windmill Island; Holland, Mich; with editorial comment. H. Holt. il Am City 80:8, 98-9 Jl '65
WINDOW blinds. See Blinds
WINDOW boxes. See Flower boxes, planters, etc.
WINDOW curtains and draperies. See Curtains and draperies
WINDOW decoration. See Show windows
WINDOW displays. See Show windows
WINDOW gardening
Gardener's kitchen. L. Burgess. il Flower Grower 53:46-7 Ja '66
Greenhouse in my window. E. D. Ballard. il Horticulture 43:26-7 O '65
WINDOW shades
Making a fabric shade. il Sunset 134:158+ My '65
Timeless traditions for windows; Austrian shade. il House & Gard 127:196-7 My '65
Timeless traditions for windows; patterned window shade. il House & Gard 128:232-3 S '65
Timeless traditions for windows; Roman shade. il House & Gard 127:198-9 Ap '65
WINDOW ventilators. See Ventilators
WINDOWS
Choosing the right windows. G. K. Geerlings. il Pop Sci 186:156-9 Ap; 146-9 My '65
Give windows a fresh outlook. il Bet Hom & Gard 43:63 Ap '65
How to compose a new window look: sliding, floor-to-ceiling fabric panels. il House & Gard 128:255 O '65
Picture window. il Flower Grower 52:40-2 Mr '65
Portrait windows. il McCalls 92:128-33 F '65
Windows: the romantic view. M. White. il Ladies Home J 82:70-7 Je '65
See also
Glass painting and staining
Skylights
WINDS
Restless wind; photographs. C. Harbutt. Sat Eve Post 239:18-23 Ja 1 '66
Wind, the air in motion. il Sci Digest 58: 86-7 Jl '65
Winds of the world. J. Martenhoff. il Motor B 115:45-7+ Mr '65
Wonder of the winds. J. D. Ratcliff. il Read Digest 87:271-2+ N '65
See also
Hurricanes
Monsoons
Mountain waves
Tornadoes
Wind pressure
WINDS, Solar. See Solar radiation
WINDSHIELD wipers. See Automobiles—Windshield wipers
WINDSOR, Edward, duke of. See Edward VIII, king of Great Britain
WINDSOR, Wallis (Warfield) duchess of
Once upon a time. il Time 85:36+ Mr 19 '65
Queen finally meets her aunt. il por Life 58:41 Mr 26 '65
WINDSOR, Conn.
Small community gets big-time data processing. R. B. Weiss. il Am City 80:103-4 Ap '65
WINDSOR, Ontario
Introducing Windsor. R. Hedy. ALA Bul 59: 395-6 My '65
WINDWARD ISLANDS. See West Indies
WINE
California wines. J. D. Weaver. Holiday 38: 36+ O '65

Chabert of Tain l'hermitage. C. Cate. il Atlan 216:168+ N '65
Choosing wine for a casserole. H. Johnson. House & Gard 129:130+ Ja '66
Corkscrew: light, summery wines of Alsace. H. Johnson. House & Gard 128:116+ Ag '65
Happy marriages of wine and meat; chart. J. A. Beard. House & Gard 128:226+ O '65
Lighter side of Christmas drinking. J. A. Beard. House & Gard 128:186+ D '65
On drinking American. Life 58:4 Je 4 '65
Recent European vintages. R. Postgate. il Holiday 38:125-30 N '65
Subtle emanations of the noblest grape; Château Lafite-Rothschild. il Esquire 64: 104-9 S '65
'Tis the season to give wine. House & Gard 128:197 D '65
Toast from LBJ: drink American. il Newsweek 65:67-8+ Je 7 '65
Vintage review. S. Aaron. House & Gard 128: 292+ N '65
Wine and spaghetti; alcoholism more prevalent in France than in Italy. il Sci Digest 59:36-7 Ja '66
Wine list for patriots. G. J. Barry. il Esquire 64:238-9+ D '65
Wine lovers rack up savings in futures; paying in advance for 1964 vintage. il Bsns W p72-4 Jl 31 '65
Wine: the farsighted wedding gift. J. A. Beard. il House & Gard 127:172+ My '65
Wine, women and so on; American wines. P. Cannon. Ladies Home J 82:60 N '65
Wine, women, & so on; California wines. P. Cannon. Ladies Home J 82:36 Ag '65
Wine women & so on; sherries. P. Cannon. Ladies Home J 82:103 S '65
Wines of Italy. P. Dallas. il House & Gard 127:136+ F '65
See also
Champagne
Cookery—Wine

Anecdotes, facetiae, satire, etc.
How to win at wine tasting, beer drinker's guide. J. Ransome. Esquire 63:30+ Mr '65

Bibliography
Book gifts for a wine fancier. Sunset 135:138+ D '65
WINE trade
Of grapes and gripes; conditions in France. il Fortune 72:71-2 S '65
WINELAND, Lynn
Lion's share. il Hot Rod 18:84-7 Mr '65
WINES, Roger
Issue at St John's. America 114:103 Ja 22 '66
WING, Anne H.
Ann Arbor's trees. Horticulture 43:16 D '65
WING shooting. See Shooting
WINGERTER, R. G.
Tiny flame; address, October 26, 1965. Vital Speeches 32:158-60 D 15 '65
WINGLESS glider. See Gliders (aeronautics)
WINGO, Walter
Pattern for success. Nations Bsns 53:46-50+ S. 48-52+ O '65 (to be cont)
WINGS
See also
Insects—Wings
WINKS, Donald
How to know when you're being F.I.R.E.D. Esquire 64:104-5+ Ag '65
WINNEBAGO, Ill.
Women who bought Main Street. V. Cadden. il Redbook 124:60-1+ Mr '65
WINNETKA, Ill.

Religious institutions and affairs
What the consumer wants; Nielsen survey to plan program of church activities. Newsweek 67:53 Ja 24 '66
WINSOME, lose some; story. See Sledge, G. A.
WINSOR, Kathleen
11,623 hours. il por Newsweek 65:114 My 24 '65
WINSTON, Alexander
Yale's new treasure house. Harper 230:32+ Mr '65
WINSTON, Donald
Voskhod 2 expands Soviet space lead. Aviation W 82:23 Mr 22 '65
WINSTON, Harry
New York jeweler gives diamond to Smithsonian. Hobbies 70:113 My '65
WINSTON-SALEM, N.C.
World for the lonely piper; dance, theatre and music. D. Hering. il Dance Mag 39:38-41 Mr '65

WINSTON-SALEM, N.C.—*Continued*

Architecture

Architecture of Salem. W. J. Murtagh. il Antiques 88:69-80 Jl '65

History

Old Salem. R. P. Hanes. Antiques 88:99 Jl '65

Music

Musical life in Salem. D. M. McCorkle. il Antiques 88:65-8 Jl '65

Rapid transit

Dixie bus company at a crossroads; Safe bus, inc. il Ebony 21:70-4 D '65

Religious institutions and affairs

Moravians of Salem. C. Davis. il Antiques 88: 60-4 Jl '65

WINTER, Elmer L.
Milwaukee: a fair deal. Sat R 49:54+ Ja 8 '66

WINTER, Gibson
Theology of demonstration. Christian Cent 82: 1249-52 O 13 '65

WINTER, Harry
Protestant celibacy. America 113:470-1 O 23 '65

WINTER, Jack A.
Fancy pants maker stretches into new lines. il por Bsns W p60-2 Mr 20 '65

WINTER, Paul
Person of Jesus. Commentary 40:107-8+ S '65
Trial of Jesus. bibliog f Commentary 38:35-41 S '64; 39:20+ Mr '65

WINTER
I remember winter. H. Sutton. il Sat R 49: 42-3+ Ja 1 '66
Wandering through winter. by E. W. Teale. Review
    Atlan 216:134+ D '65. E. Weeks

WINTER branch; story. See Irving, J.

WINTER conditioning of automobiles. See Automobiles—Care

WINTER fishing. See Fishing, Winter

WINTER gardening
    See also
Window gardening

WINTER in Berlin; story. See Licht, F.

WINTER king hawthorn. See Hawthorns

WINTER nationals, Pomona, Calif. See Automobile racing

WINTER PARK, Fla.

Stores

Fully enclosed axis mall. il Arch Rec 137: 206-7 My '65

WINTER protection of plants. See Plants, Protection of

WINTER resorts
Grits, magnolia and skiing. J. Skow. il Sat Eve Post 238:86-9 Mr 13 '65
Last great empty slopes. E. Schwiebert. il Esquire 65:88-9+ Ja '66
Low boom in the land of horizontal skiing; American Midwest. B. Ottum. il Sports Illus 22:48-50 F 15 '65
On the slopes, where to ski when. D. Messinesi. Vogue 146:118+ N 1 '65
Powder line: Whitefish to Santa Fe. F. R. Smith. il Sports Illus 23:66-7 N 15 '65
Relaxing in Gagra; Black Sea resort town. L. Gottlieb. Mile 62:16+ N '65
Rope-tow hill to Mascara Mountain. B. Hersh. il Holiday 37:161+ Mr '65
Ski East by Northeast. G. E. Maxwell. il Todays Health 44:50-1+ Ja '66
Skiing; its dollars keep winter green. C. S. Wren. il Look 29:104+ D 14 '65
Top U.S. ski spots. C. W. Casewit. il Travel 124:25-9+ D '65
    See also
Aspen, Colo.
Bakuriani, Russia
St Moritz, Switzerland
Sugarbush Valley, Vt.
Sun Valley, Idaho

WINTER sleep. See Hibernation

WINTER sports
Winter sport for bowmen. G. H. Gillelan. il Outdoor Life 136:12+ D '65
    See also
Curling
Ice boats and ice boating
Skis and skiing

WINTER tennis, Outdoor. See Tennis

WINTER tires. See Tires, Automobile

WINTER travel. See Travel

WINTER vacation houses. See Cabins

WINTER vacations. See Vacations

WINTER wrens. See Wrens

WINTERICH, John Tracy
Brothers Harper. Pub W 188:38-40 Ag 2 '65
Criminal record. See last issue of each month of Saturday review
Time and telepathy. Sat R 48:44 S 11 '65
—and Glixon, D. M.
    (eds) Your literary I.Q. See issues of Saturday review

WINTERS, David
Don't say you're a dancer! J. Anderson. il pors Dance Mag 39:47-9 F '65

WINTERS, John E.
Youth crime: some suggested treatments; statement. por U S News 59:46-7 N 15 '65

WINTERS, Jonathan
Jonathan Winters: always on. T. Berger. por Holiday 38:101-3+ N '65
Jonathan Winters of our discontent. G. Ace. Sat R 48:14 Ap 24 '65
Winging it with Jonathan Winters. M. W. Lear. il pors N Y Times Mag p36-7+ Mr 28 '65

WINTERS, Walter F.
Beefy seal coats work best. Am City 81:92-3 Ja '66

WINTERS, Warrington
Transcendentalist in the basement. Sat R 48:39 Je 19 '65
We two, the world, and the whale. Sat R 48:27-8 My 15 '65

WINTERSTEEN, Bernice McIlhenny
Paintings and antiques. Antiques 88:644-9 N '65

WINTERTHUR, Switzerland

Music

Notes from our correspondents. K. Blaukopf. Hi Fi 15:18+ Ag '65

WINTHROP, Theodore
Theodore Winthrop, by E. Colby. Review
    America 113:224 Ag 28 '65. C. W. McCue

WINTHROP laboratories
Liquid detergent for skin care. M. B. Keiser. il Parents Mag 40:20+ F '65

WINTON, Kay Grogan
Turnabout recipes. Parents Mag 40:74+ F '65

WINTZ, George A.
Mad bull of Bristol Head. Outdoor Life 135: 56-7+ My '65

WIONCZEK, Miguel S.
Latin American free trade association. bibliog f Int Concil 551:3-62 Ja '65

WIRE sculpture
All the children sculpture with wire. E. Sitts and M. Sitts. il Sch Arts 64:9-13 F '65
Metal lathe cutting as art form. W. F. Dominick. il Sch Arts 64:36-7 My '65
Wire sculpture. C. Heiple. il Sch Arts 64:15-17 Ap '65

WIRE tapping
Improper practice; investigation of wiretapping by federal employees. Newsweek 66:23 Jl 26 '65
Ordeal of Otto Otepka. C. Stevenson and W. J. Gill. Read Digest 87:55-9 Ag '65
Speaking out; we must stop tax snooping. E. V. Long. Sat Eve Post 238:10+ N 20 '65
T-men's tactics are disallowed; subcommittee investigating IRS agents invasion of privacy. il Bsns W p24 Jl 31 '65

WIRE weaving. See Weaving

WIRELESS earphones. See Earphones

WIRELESS telegraph. See Telegraph, Wireless

WIREMAN, Billy O.
Education, democracy, and the human condition. Sch & Soc 93:366-8 O 16 '65

WIRETAPPING. See Wire tapping

WIRING electric. See Electric wire and wiring

WIRTZ, Lennie
Little pal on the dead run. B. Gilbert. il pors Sports Illus 22:38-43 Mr 1 '65

WIRTZ, Morvin A.
Something for the special child. por Am Ed 1:14-21 S '65

WIRTZ, William Willard
Civil equity; address, November 17, 1965
Vital Speeches 32:135-8 D 15 '65

about

Education of Willard Wirtz. Nation 200:379 Ap 12 '65
Secretary Wirtz on farming. Farm J 89:86 Ag '65

WISCONSIN
Fresh look at Wisconsin. E. Waldron. Holiday 37:52-3+ F '65
    See also
Apostle Islands
Colleges and universities—Wisconsin
Hunting—Wisconsin

WISCONSIN—*Continued*

Description and travel

Journey to Gitchee Gumee. M. L. Daly. il Travel 124:40-2 S '65

Religious institutions and affairs

News of the Christian world (cont) Christian Cent 82:345-6, 750+, 1104+, 1525-6 Mr 17, Je 9, S 20, D 8 '65

WISCONSIN library association
Wisconsin program a three-year plan. M. Ricking. ALA Bul 59:750-2 S '65

WISCONSIN stage. See Geology, Stratigraphic—Pleistocene

WISCONSIN. University, Madison
India is centuries away; Wisconsin undergraduate year in India; a student recalls. M. C. Vander Wal. il Sat R 48:51-2+ Ag 21 '65
Research and development center for learning and re-education. Sch & Soc 93:106 F 6 '65
Research and development center for learning and re-education. H. J. Klausmeier. Sch & Soc 93:182-3 Mr 20 '65

WISE, T. A.
Bank with the boardinghouse reach. Fortune 72:136-9+ S '65
Those uncertain actuaries. Fortune 72:154-7+ D '65; 73:164-6+ Ja '66

WISE, Wayne R.
Electronic draftsman. Electr World 74:70-1 Jl '65

WISEBLOOD, Edward. See Tidwell, R. jt. auth.

WISEMILLER, James
Young master with the old touch. C. Goren. il Sports Illus 22:72 My 10 '65

WISENTS. See Bison, European

WISER, William
Cannes caper. Reporter 33:43-4+ N 18 '65

WISHERD, Edwin L.
Two men behind the scene. por Pop Phot 57: 63+ Jl '65

WISHING wells. See Wells

WISNER, Bill
Billfish East. il Motor B 116:37+ S '65
Fishing for peace. Motor B 115:50-1+ My '65

WISTER, Gertrude S. See Wister, J. C. jt. auth.

WISTER, John C. and Wister, G. S.
Tree peonies. Horticulture 43:30-1+ My '65

WISTERIA
Plant wisteria this month for bloom year after year in March and April. il Sunset 136:58-9 Ja '66
Wisteria. C. E. Lewis. il Horticulture 43:18-20 Je '65

WITCH in the golden hat; drama. See Watts, F. B.

WITCHCRAFT
Witch, is she, or isn't she? P. W. Schmidtchen. il Hobbies 70:106-8 Ja '66
Witch's garden. D. Jacob. il Pop Gard 16:32-3+ N '65
See also
Demonology

WITCOVER, Jules
Poverty's neglected battlefront. Sat R 48: 29-30 S 11 '65
Rochester braces for another July. Reporter 33:33-5 Jl 15 '65
We Birchers are trained to look for patterns. New Repub 152:8-9 My 8 '65
Who's afraid of those new Negro voters? New Repub 153:10 O 30 '65
—and Knoll, Erwin
Politics and the poor: Shriver's second thoughts. Reporter 33:23-5 D 30 '65
—See Knoll, E. jt. auth.

WITH love and cold water soap; story. See Bentham, J.

WITHERING, William
William Withering and the purple foxglove. J. W. Estes and P. D. White. il por Sci Am 212:110-16+ Je '65

WITHHOLDING tax
New payroll plan: more taxes from weekly checks. il U S News 59:74-5 D 27 '65
New tax plan: graduated withholding. il U S News 58:98-9 Mr 22 '65
Unkindest tax cut. il Newsweek 65:73-4 Ap 19 '65
Who has a dime to spare? cut in withholding rate. Time 85:21-2 Ap 23 '65

WITLOOF chicory. See Chicory

WITNESSES
I'm glad I tried to help! ed. by L. David. V. A. McNeil. il Good H 160:92-3+ Ap '65
Story of a man who tried to help; Senn case. il U S News 58:64 Mr 29 '65

WITT, Harold
Certainty; poem. Sat R 48:71 Je 12 '65
To Eric, not to make too much of time; poem. Sat R 48:36 My 29 '65
Written on the wind; poem. Sat R 48:49 Jl 24 '65

WITT, J. A.
Seattle, Washington's University of Washington arboretum. Horticulture 43:30-1+ Jl '65

WITT, Peter N. and Reed, C. F.
Spider-web building. bibliog Science 149: 1190-7 S 10 '65

WITTEN, Victor H.
Hemangiomas: Mother Nature's vanishing act. Todays Health 43:48-9+ S '65

WITTENBERG, Ernest
How ya gonna keep 'em down in Upper Volta after they've met Lloyd Hand? Esquire 64: 24+ D '65
Thrifty spy on the Sixth avenue el. Am Heritage 17:60-4+ D '65

WITTING, Amy
Goodbye, Ady, goodbye, Joe; story New Yorker 41:51-8 N 6 '65

WITTING, J. and others
Mars: age of its craters. bibliog Science 149: 1496-8 S 24 '65

WITTMANN, Otto
How's that again? Mod Phot 29:108 S '65

WITTY, Helen S.
Season's fare. See issues of Flower grower, the home garden

WITWER, David B.
Solving land-use determinations electronically. Am City 80:90-1 F '65

WIVES
Bill of rights for wives and mothers. J. Brothers. Good H 160:48+ Ap '65
Few words with the wife of our travel editor. Esquire 63:130-1 F '65
I don't know where to look for me. A. Taylor. Redbook 126:8+ Ja '66
L.B.J.'s grass widows; wives of presidential assistants. P. Cavin. Ladies Home J 82: 64+ N '65
What young wives have learned about husbands. D. Siegel. il Redbook 126:58-9+ N '65
Young wife's world. H. Valentine. See issues of Good housekeeping
See also
Husbands
Marriage
Widows
Woman

WIVES; drama. See Abel, L.

WODEHOUSE, P. G.
Battle of Squashy Hollow; story. Sat Eve Post 238:50-1 Je 5 '65

WOELFLE, Melba
Hitting the trail in Canada. Recreation 58: 390-1 O '65

WOETZEL, Robert K.
Do our homosexuality laws make sense? Sat R 48:23-5 O 9 '65

WOGAMAN, Philip
California churches in the aftermath of defeat. Christian Cent 82:139-41 F 3 '65

WOHL, Paul
Gospel according to Bonn. Nation 200:453-6 Ap 26 '65

WOHLSTETTER, Roberta
Cuba and Pearl Harbor: hindsight and foresight. For Affairs 43:691-707 Jl '65

WOIWODE, L.
Deathless lovers; story. New Yorker 41:20-1 Jl 10 '65

WOJCIECHOWSKA, Maia
Shadow of a kid; Newbery award acceptance, July 6, 1965. Horn Bk 41:349-52 Ag '65
Their improbable treasure; excerpts from address, 1965. por Library J 90:4511-13 O 15 '65
about
Maia Wojciechowska. J. Karl. por Library J 90:1464-6 Mr 15 '65
Maia Wojciechowska. S. Rodman. il por Horn Bk 41:353-7 Ag '65
Newbery and Caldecott winners: Wojciechowska. Montresor. il por Pub W 187:26-7 Mr 8 '65
Newbery-Caldecott awards. por Wilson Library Bul 39:627 Ap '65
Say I'm eccentric. H. Frankel. por Sat R 48:25 Mr 27 '65

WOLBARSHT, M. L. and others
Retina: pathology of neodymium and ruby laser burns. bibliog Science 150:1453-4 D 10 '65

WOLBARST, John
Pictures in a moment. See issues of Modern photography
Take a negative view. Mod Phot 29:70-5 F '65
35mm. See issues of Modern photography

WOLCOTT, Derek
Choices and risks. M. Benedikt. Poetry 105: 332 F '65

WOLCOTT, Jean
Think Christmas! Recreation 58:455 N '65

WOLF, Henry
Photography for inept sophisticates. Esquire 65:62-4 Ja '66

WOLF, Hugo
Now on Vox: Brahms, Loewe, and Wolf lieder by Prey, magnificent. H. Glass. Am Rec G 31:526-7 F '65
On records; Italian song book. Opera N 30: 34 Ja 22 '66
Reissued by Angel: Gerhardt's Hugo Wolf, perhaps the greatest of all collectors' items. P. L. Miller. il por Am Rec G 32:126-9 O '65

WOLF, Leonard
Cleaning up the Merrimack. Bul Atomic Sci 21:16-18 Ap '65
Myself; poem. Yale R 54:549 Je '65

WOLF, Milton
Busy, busy ski doctor. il por Life 58:111-12 F 19 '65

WOLF, Susan
Come take my hand. Seventeen 24:159+ D '65

WOLFE, Bernard
Man called I-l-l-y-a. N Y Times Mag p56-7+ O 24 '65

WOLFE, Edwin, 2d
Rare books and bing bing boys. Library J 90:3210-11 Ag '65

WOLFE, Henry C.
Leopold mused as Moslems marched. Sat R 48:41 S 11 '65
Natural allies but national enemies. Sat R 48:48+ N 13 '65
Saving the City of light. Sat R 48:27 Jl 3 '65

WOLFE, Thomas K.
Last American hero is Junior Johnson, yes! Esquire 63:68-75+ Mr '65
Speaking out. por Sat Eve Post 238:12+ Je 19 '65
Wayward reader. Holiday 38:14+ Ag '65

about

Akond of swock. M. Barrett. Reporter 33: 50+ Ag 12 '65
Author. H. Frankel. por Sat R 48:23-4 Jl 31 '65
Department of amplification. Newsweek 65:82-3 My 3 '65
In chic's clothing. por Time 86:59-60 Jl 2 '65
Popcult orgy. C. H. Simonds. Nat R 17:989-90 N 2 '65
Rococo and roll. J. Epstein. New Repub 153: 27-9 Jl 24 '65
Talk of the town. Nat R 17:359-60 My 4 '65
Whisperer. por Time 85:60 Ap 16 '65
William and the Wolfe. il por Newsweek 65: 62+ Ap 19 '65

WOLFE, Tom. See Wolfe, T. K.

WOLFE, Thomas W.
Military policy: a Soviet dilemma. bibliog f Cur Hist 49:201-7+ O '65

WOLFENDEN, Jeremy
Western village in Moscow. N Y Times Mag p21+ F 7 '65

WOLFENSTEIN, Lincoln. See Orear, J. jt. auth.

WOLFERT, Ira
Antarctica: world's most fascinating ice-box. Read Digest 87:119-23 S '65
To Mars or bust. Read Digest 87:63-8 Jl '65

WOLFF, George L.
Body composition and coat color correlation in different phenotypes of viable yellow mice. bibliog Science 147:1145-7 Mr 5 '65

WOLFF, Leon
Battle at Homestead; excerpt from Lockout. Am Heritage 16:64-79 Ap '65

WOLFF, Lester L.
Biggest gimmick. Nation 201:130-1 S 13 '65
How to beat a good congressman. N. Freeman. por Nat R 17:547-50 Je 29 '65; Discussion. 17:672-3 Ag 10 '65

WOLFF, Maurice
Detailing a precast panel facade. Arch Rec 137:191-3 Mr '65

WOLFF, Robert P.
Race to college. Atlan 216:145-8 N '65

WOLFFIAN regeneration. See Regeneration (biology)

WÖLFFLIN, Heinrich
Two centenarians. A. Frankfurter. Art N 63: 23 F '65

WOLFGANG, Richard
Chemistry at high velocities; with biographical sketch. Sci Am 214:14, 82-90 Ja '66
Pure research, cultism, and the undergraduate. Science 150:1563-5 D 17 '65
—See MacKay, C. jt. auth.

WOLFLE, Dael
Support of science in the U.S; with biographical sketch. Sci Am 213:16, 19-25 Jl '65

WOLFMAN, Augustus
Silver crisis. Mod Phot 29:16+ S '65
Wolfman on printing. por Mod Phot 29:30+ N; 28+ D '65; 30:20+ Ja '66

WOLMAN, Abel
Metabolism of cities; with biographical sketch. Sci Am 213:30. 178-88+ bibliog (p278) S '65

WOLMAN, Harold
Wallace hangs on.   Commonweal 83:313-14 D 10 '65

WOLSELEY, Roland E.
Author's anguish. ALA Bul 59:1002 D '65

WOLTERS, Richard A.
New tools for training. Field & S 70:178-9+ My '65

WOLVES
Farewell, dear wolf: pet belonging to George and Ruth Wilson. il Life 59:81-2 O 8 '65
Last of the outlaw wolves. R. K. Massie. il Sat Eve Post 239:71-4 Ja 15 '66

WOMAN
Allure: continental woman; American woman. il Vogue 146:186-91+ O 1 '65
American women; symposium, ed. by P. Coffin. il Look 30:15-30+ Ja 11 '66
Descendants of Eve. E. Capouya. il Sat R 48:34-5 Jl 17 '65
Fun of being a woman. M. Furlong. il Read Digest 86:59-60 Mr '65
It's a good time to be a woman. M. Tree. Mlle 61:124+ O '65
Ladies, God bless 'em. Christian Cent 82:927 Jl 21 '65
On being a woman. J. Brothers. See issues of Good housekeeping
Without portfolio; status of women today. C. B. Luce. McCalls 92:26+ Mr '65
Women's prejudices against women. W. Goodman. il Redbook 124:46-7+ F '65
Word. V. P. McCorry. il America 113:612 N 13 '65

See also
Indians of North America—Women
Prostitution
Single women
Widows
Wives
Women and the church
World war, 1939-1945—Women and the war
Young women

Anecdotes, facetiae, satire, etc.

How to tell a man from a woman. J. Goodsell. il Good H 160:12+ Mr '65; Same abr. Read Digest 86:112-13 My '65
Man talk. D .Newman and R. Benton. Mlle 61:132 S '65
Twilight of the goddess? R. Gray. Ladies Home J 82:90-1 Mr '65

Crime

Reporter at large; Massachusetts correctional institution, Framingham. J. Colebrook. il New Yorker 41:47-8+ Je 12 '65
See also
Prostitution

Defense
See Self defense for women

Diseases

What a girl should know about her first gynecological checkup. Good H 160:183 Mr '65

Employment

Employment of women chemists in industrial laboratories. J. B. Parrish. bibliog il Science 148:657-8 Ap 30 '65
What a man looks for when he hires a girl; a candid view. N. Breckenridge. Mlle 60: 146+ F '65
Where the best job opportunities will be. il Good H 161:138 Ag '65
Why women start and stop working: a study in mobility. C. Rosenfeld and V. C. Perrella. il Mo Labor R 88:1077-82 S '65
See also
Household employees
Woman—Equal rights
Women as farmers

Equal rights

Are women executives people? survey of attitudes of 2,000 executives. G. W. Bowman and others. il Harvard Bsns R 43:14-16+ Jl '65
Family law and the women of Africa; U.N. seminar on the status of women in family law. Lomé, Togo. G. A. Tillett. Dept State Bul 52:229-33 F 15 '65

WOMAN—Equal rights—*Continued*

Journey to Mongolia; Seminar on participation of women in public life. G. A. Tillett. Dept State Bul 53:918-23 D 6 '65

Monstrous regiment, by D. Mitchell. Review New Repub 153:21-2 D 18 '65. E. Dienstag

Needed: a new status for the single woman. V. Lindbeck. Cath World 202:151-7 D '65

New paper work for employers; women's job rights; advice from Equal employment opportunity commission. U S News 59:93 D 6 '65

Official word on job rights for women; official guidance by Equal employment opportunity commission. U S News 59:90-1 N 22 '65

Placing a want ad? there are federal rules to follow now; Equal employment opportunity commission. U S News 59:100-1 O 4 '65

Problems on job rights of women. U S News 59:77 Ag 30 '65

Sex and the job. Newsweek 66:72 Jl 12 '65

Women are equal, but. M. Mannes. McCalls 92:18+ S '65
See also
United Nations—Commission on the status of women

Health and hygiene

Modern feminine products. M. B. Keiser. il Parents Mag 40:28+ Jl '65

Speaking of feminine hygiene. G. Naismith. il Todays Health 43:22-3+ D '65

Why women are aging more slowly. Sci Digest 57:17 Ap '65
See also
Beauty, Personal
Menopause

Intelligence
See Intelligence levels—Women

Legal status, laws, etc.
See also
Woman—Equal rights

Occupations

Academic women. M. Ellmann. Commentary 39:67-70 Mr '65

Overture to a future; jobs in the music world. C. Schwalberg. por Mlle 60:194-5+ Ap '65

Women are equal, but. M. Mannes. McCalls 92:18+ S '65
See also
Business and professional women
Models (persons)
Women as authors

Professions
See Woman—Occupations

Psychology

How women see themselves. V. Cadden. Redbook 125:46-7+ My '65

Identity of modern woman. H. S. Krech. il Nation 201:125-8 S 20 '65

Man and superwoman! D. Newman and R. Benton. il Mlle 60:88-9 F '65

Men, women and music. F. V. Grunfeld. il Read Digest 87:35-6 N '65

On being a woman. J. Brothers. See issues of Good housekeeping

What kind of girl are you, anyway? L. Wyse. il McCalls 92:68+ Je '65

Women cooperate less. P. McBroom. Sci N L 88:362 D 4 '65

Rights of women
See Woman—Equal rights

Social and moral questions

Plato, the penthouse, and the girl who hesitates. G. Roy. Mlle 60:199+ Mr '65

Religion and the feminine mystique; concerning Betty Friedan's book The feminine mystique. H. B. Suthers. Christian Cent 82:911-14 Jl 21 '65
See also
Alcoholism
Divorce
Girls
Prostitution
Woman—Crime

WOMAN at the seaside; story. See O'Brien, E.

WOMAN with concave breasts; story. See Wegner, R. E.

WOMELDORF, John A.
Presbyterians, U.S: search for unity. Christian Cent 82:660-2 My 19 '65

WOMEN

Africa

Family law and the women of Africa; U.N. seminar on the status of women in family law, Lomé, Togo. G. A. Tillett. Dept State Bul 52:229-33 F 15 '65

Algeria

Algerian woman. G. Estivals. Holiday 37:60-1+ Je '65

France

End to tears? sweeping changes in marriage laws proposed in France. Time 85:41 Mr 19 '65

Germany (Federal Republic)

By the Socialist sea; German girls go after Yugoslav men. F. Y. Blumenfeld. il Newsweek 66:50 O 4 '65

Down with dumplings. Newsweek 66:63 O 18 '65

Italy

Bravura year for Italian beauty. il Life 59:70-9 O 22 '65

Slim, jaunty, with deep, velvety eyes. L. Barzini. il Life 59:81-2 O 22 '65

Japan

Eight Japanese women. C. Bernstein. il Look 29:53-9 Ag 24 '65
See also
Geishas

Russia

Russian woman; her amazing success. O. Carlisle. il Sat Eve Post 238:28-38+ Je 19 '65

Thailand

Behind every successful woman. il Time 86:91-2 D 17 '65

United States

American women; symposium. ed. by P. Coffin. il Look 30:15-30+ Ja 11 '66

Are women people? A. Perkins. Christian Cent 82:917-18 Jl 21 '65

Feminine mistake; excerpt from This half of the apple is mine. J. K. Lubold. Read Digest 86:55-7 Je '65

New American female: demi-feminism takes over. M. K. Sanders. il Harper 231:37-43 Jl '65; Discussion. 231:6+ S '65

Power and influence of women: address, May 27, 1965. M. G. Roebling. Vital Speeches 31:689-91 S 1 '65

Religion and the feminine mystique; concerning Betty Friedan's book The feminine mystique. H. B. Suthers. Christian Cent 82:911-14 Jl 21 '65
See also
Divorce—United States
Education of women—United States
Woman—Equal rights

Vietnam (Republic)

Girls under fire; South Vietnamese women in the war. il Time 86:23 Jl 23 '65

Virgin Islands

Where women's work has a golden touch. il Bsns W p 100-2 Mr 27 '65

WOMEN, Famous

How Jackie Kennedy & other young widows have rebuilt their lives. A. Levy. il Good H 160:96-9+ Mr '65

100 best people in the world. il Esquire 64:64-5 Ag '65

Without portfolio; status of women today. C. B. Luce. McCalls 92:26+ Mr '65
See also names of famous women, e.g. S. J. B. Halle

WOMEN, Negro. See Negro women

WOMEN and men

Academic women. M. Ellmann. Commentary 39:67-70 Mr '65

Approach to Mr Everest; letter. E. C. Moore. il Am Heritage 16:112 Ap '65

Battle of the species: he vs. she. J. Collins. Mlle 62:93+ D '65

Flight from woman, by K. Stern. Review America 113:289-90 S 18 '65. F. J. Braceland

How do bachelors get away with it? five young men tell all to a tape recorder. Mlle 60:105-6+ F '65; Discussion. 61:183-5+ S '65

How women see themselves. V. Cadden. Redbook 125:46-7+ My '65

Legitimate pickup. A. Ellis and R. Nathan. il Mlle 61:198+ My '65

WOMEN and men—*Continued*
Man talk; sex appeal and the single girl. D. Newman and R. Benton. Mlle 60:26 Mr '65
Man talk; the disguise. D. Newman and R. Benton. il Mlle 61:52 My '65
Men really don't like women. J. Feiffer. Look 30:60 Ja 11 '66

Anecdotes, facetiae, satire, etc.
Sex and the single boy. S. J. Perelman. New Yorker 41:40-3 My 8 '65
Stop the train, I want to get off. J. Skow. il Sat Eve Post 239:10 Ja 1 '66

WOMEN and peace
HUAC; indictment of two members of the Women strike for peace movement. Commonweal 81:596 F 5 '65
Un-American; two women from Women strike for peace indicted at behest of HUAC; reply. F. J. Donner. New Repub 152:28 F 6 '65
See also
Women's international league for peace and freedom

WOMEN and politics
That Pellet woman! by B. Pellet and A. Klein. Review
Sat R 48:46 Je 12 '65. A. Ribicoff
Women of Rotzo; mayor and town council. il Newsweek 65:52+ Ap 12 '65

WOMEN and religion
Mature married woman. S. C. Callahan. Cath World 201:102-6 My '65
Prayers of women, ed. by L. Sergio. Review
Christian Cent 82:918 Jl 21 '65. M. H. Bro
Religion and the feminine mystique; concerning Betty Friedan's book The feminine mystique. H. B. Suthers. Christian Cent 82:911-14 Jl 21 '65

WOMEN and the church
Putting sisters in their place. S. Kelly. il America 114:10-11 Ja 1 '66

WOMEN and war
See also
Vietnamese war, 1957—Women and the war
World war, 1939-1945—Women and the war

WOMEN as air pilots
Invisible 99s. R. Bach. il Flying 77:38-41 Ag '65
Skirts flying. S. Buegeleisen. Flying 77:22 N; 20 D '65; 78:28 Ja '66
Women and aviation; symposium, with editorial comment. il Flying 77:28, 30-45+ Ag '65

WOMEN as ambassadors
Eugenie Anderson shows the flag; U.S. minister in Bulgaria. L. Stowe. Read Digest 86:173+ Mr '65

WOMEN as architects
Face to face; with an architect of the future. B. Karten. il Seventeen 24:339 Ag '65

WOMEN as artists
Art galleries; exhibition: Women artists of America, 1707-1964 at Newark museum. R. M. Coates. New Yorker 41:94+ Ap 10 '65

WOMEN as astronauts
Space may be a man's world. il Sci Digest 57:23-4 Mr '65

WOMEN as athletes
Amazons. B. Glanville. il Mlle 61:166-7+ My '65
Fitness should be fun. C. Mangel. il Look 29:88-90+ Ag 24 '65
Measuring up; National AAU meet. New York. il Newsweek 65:65 F 22 '65
Off to Russia, without love; AAU women's track and field team at Kiev. J. Jares. il Sports Illus 23:20-1+ Jl 12 '65
Quick young ladies of quality; U.S. women's track team invade Europe. J. Lovesey. Sports Illus 22:108+ Ap 19 '65
Startling invasion of women; AAU indoor track meet. il Sports Illus 22:18-19 Mr 1 '65
This is the way the girls go; distance runners. J. Smith and M. Mulder. J. Underwood. il Sports Illus 22:34-6+ My 10 '65

WOMEN as authors
Pioneers and caretakers, by L. Auchincloss. Review
Sat R 48:19-20 Je 5 '65. G. Hicks
Puritan promenade, by M. Bacon. Review
New Repub 152:22-4+ Mr 27 '65. W. J. Smith
Stories women tell. J. Weightman. Harper 231:162-7 N '65

Anecdotes, facetiae, satire, etc.
Off the cuff. L. Conger. Writer 79:7-8 Ja '66

WOMEN as brokers
Ladies' day; J. M. Walsh and P. S. Peterson approved by the Amex admissions committee. il Newsweek 66:88 N 22 '65

WOMEN as chemists
Employment of women chemists in industrial laboratories. J. B. Parrish. bibliog il Science 148:657-8 Ap 30 '65
Very favorable outlook for women in research. Sci N L 87:392 Je 19 '65

WOMEN as criminals. See Woman—Crime

WOMEN as doctors. See Women as physicians

WOMEN as editors
All in all, a most enlightening happening. G. Buckman. il Mlle 61:162-3+ O '65
Eleven year siege of Mississippi's lady editor. T. G. Harris. il Look 29:121-2+ N 16 '65

WOMEN as educators
See also
National council of administrative women in education

WOMEN as engineers
Women in science and engineering. D. Wolfle; discussion. Science 148:21, 893-4 Ap 2, My 14 '65

WOMEN as executives
Are women executives people? survey of attitudes of 2,000 executives. G. W. Bowman and others. il Harvard Bsns R 43:14-16+ Jl '65

WOMEN as farmers
So your daughter wants to take ag? C. Eckhardt. il Farm J 89:99 N '65

WOMEN as journalists
Early history of Negro women in journalism. A. E. Dunnigan. Negro Hist Bul 28:178-9+ My '65
See also
Women as editors
Women as reporters

WOMEN as judges
Her honor bops the hoodlums. D. J. Hamblin. il Life 59:74+ Jl 9 '65

WOMEN as lawyers
Case for girls in law. R. Connable. il Mlle 61: 188-90+ My '65

WOMEN as ministers
God, male or female? il Newsweek 66:60-2 Jl 12 '65
Neither male nor female. D. Hunter and H. Hunter. Christian Cent 82:527-8+ Ap 28 '65; Discussion. 82:814 Je 23 '65
See also
Women as priests

WOMEN as musicians
Beauty on the trumpet. J. Shepherd. il Look 29:M8-11 Mr 23 '65

WOMEN as novelists. See Women as authors

WOMEN as painters. See Women as artists

WOMEN as physicians
Elizabeth McSherry, M.D. il Good H 161: 54-5+ S '65

WOMEN as priests
Lady in waiting; Episcopal deaconess refused Holy orders. il Newsweek 65:62 Ap 26 '65
Priesthood and women; tr. by W. Kramer. G. Heinzelmann; discussion. Commonweal 81:626, 682, 746-7 F 12, 26-Mr 5 '65

WOMEN as public officers
Her honor, the mayor, in 112 cities. N. Flesch. Am City 80:110 Ag '65

WOMEN as real estate agents
See also
Real estate business

WOMEN as reporters
Legwomen. il Newsweek 65:58 Je 21 '65
Maggie. il Newsweek 67:83 Ja 17 '66
Teen-age TV reporter. S. Gordon. il Look 29:44+ O 5 '65

WOMEN as scientists
Why nobody wants women in science; reprint. R. B. Kundsin. il Sci Digest 58:60-5 O '65
Women in science and engineering. D. Wolfle; discussion. Science 148:21, 893-4 Ap 2, My 14 '65
Women in science; why so few? adaptation of address, October 1964. A. S. Rossi. bibliog il Science 148:1196-202 My 28 '65; Discussion. 149:707 Ag 13 '65
See also
Women as chemists

WOMEN as teachers
Academic women. M. Ellman. Commentary 29:67-70 Mr '65

WOMEN as travelers
Victorian lady travelers, by D. Middleton. Review
Newsweek il 66:108 S 27 '65

WOMEN college graduates. See College graduates, Women

WOMEN college students. See College students, Women

WOMEN criminals. See Woman—Crime

WOMEN; drama. See Luce, C. B.

WOMEN golf players. See Golfers

WOMEN in aeronautics. See Women as air pilots

WOMEN in boating
Cabin talk. M. Wiley. See issues of Yachting
Companionway. R. L. Williamson. See issues of Motor boating
Hawaii, here we come. G. Mayer. il Motor B 116:48-50+ Jl '65
Portrait of a racing lady. E. Crimmin. Motor B 116:115-16 Ag '65

WOMEN in literature
Pioneers and caretakers, by L. Auchincloss. Review
Harper 231:112 Ag '65

WOMEN in politics. See Women and politics

WOMEN in publishing. See Publishers and publishing

WOMEN shoppers. See Shoppers and shopping

WOMEN strike for peace movement. See Women and peace

WOMENS clothes. See Clothing and dress

WOMENS clubs and societies
Women to the rescue. America 113:313 S 25 '65

WOMEN'S international league for peace and freedom
Long war for peace. Nation 200:323-4 Mr 29 '65

WOMEN'S job corps. See United States—Job corps

WOMEN'S national book association
WNBA honors booksellers at meeting in New York. Pub W 187:105 Ap 26 '65

WOMENS organizations. See Womens clubs and societies

WOMENS periodicals. See Periodicals for women

WOMENS reformatories. See Reformatories

WOMEN'S wear daily
Man from WWD. il Newsweek 66:50 Ag 16 '65

WONDER drugs. See Drugs

WONDERFUL prize; story. See Cavanaugh, A.

WONG, Harry K.
Teaching kids to teach themselves. F. V. Rummell. il por PTA Mag 60:16-19 O '65; Same abr. with title He teaches kids to teach themselves. Read Digest 87:246-7+ O '65

WOOD, Abigail
Young living; questions and answers. See issues of Seventeen

WOOD, Bryce
(ed) See Cerda, L. E. Social science and development

WOOD, Charles W.
Plants out-of-the-ordinary.   See issues of Flower grower. the home garden magazine to October 1965
about

Obituary
Flower Grower por 52:27 My '65

WOOD, Edsal A. and Potter, C. H.
Groundcovers for the Northwest. Horticulture 43:36-7+ N '65

WOOD, Ginny Hill
Rampart, foolish dam. Liv Wildn 29:3-7 Spr '65

WOOD, James Playsted
Cheerful holly tree. Read Digest 87:171-2+ D '65

WOOD, John F.
New semiconductor phono transducer. Electr World 73:50-1+ F '65

WOOD, Kay. See Coats, B. jt. auth.

WOOD, Kerry
How to cook a bony fish. Field & S 69:56-9 Ap '65

WOOD, Lee
Most unforgettable character I've met. Read Digest 87:82-6 N '65

WOOD, Malcolm
Appraiser; story. Sat Eve Post 238:54-6 Ap 10 '65
Home fires burning; story. Sat Eve Post 238:52-3 Jl 3 '65

WOOD, Robert C.
From MIT to LBJ. por Newsweek 67:60 Ja 17 '66

WOOD, Robert E.
Profiting from foresight; interview. por Nations Bsns 53:40-1+ Jl '65

WOOD, Thomas A.
Computer company president. il pors Ebony 21:95-8+ Ja '66

WOOD
Wood goes atomic; wood-plastic composites. R. Yoshioka. il Sci N L 87:394-5 Je 19 '65
Wood-plastic composite to be tested, evaluated. Sci N L 88:294 N 6 '65
See also
Lignin

Research
See Wood research

Testing
Irradiated wood-plastic to be industry tested. Sci N L 88:73 Jl 31 '65
Putting jarrah wood to the test; White Plains, N.Y. A. Howard. il Recreation 58: 299 Je '65

WOOD, Fossil. See Trees, Fossil

WOOD alcohol. See Methanol

WOOD as fuel
Compleat firewooder. R. Bailey. Field & S 69:109-11 Mr '65
Wood keeps him warm. R. H. Lysager. il Am For 71:25+ F '65

WOOD carving
Emil Janel: lumberjack artist. il Design 67:26-9 N '65
Famous wooden statues or effigies and dolls. C. H. Fawcett. il Hobbies 70:40-2+ Ja '66
Found-wood trio. il Art N 64:27 N '65
Lumberjack artist; ed. by I. Moore. E. Janel. il Am For 71:20-3+ Ag '65
My wood sculpture. E. Bell. il Am Artist 29:34-9+ Mr '65
Plywood sculptor. J. J. Rea. il Design 67:20-3 N '65
Wood carvings; Northwest Territory. il Antiques 87:330-1 Mr '65

WOOD drying. See Lumber—Drying

WOOD ducks. See Ducks, Wild

WOOD engravings
Gauguin woodblocks rediscovered. H. Lass. il Am Artist 29:36-41+ My '65
Illustrations of Robert Quackenbush. J. H. Michel. il Am Artist 29:28-33+ Ap '65
Two woodcut artists. B. Reisman; G. Miret. il Am Artist 29:64-70+ O '65

WOOD finishing
Fantasy finishes at work. il House & Gard 127:142-5+ Mr '65
Preserving the natural beauty of wood exposed to weather. il Consumer Bul 48:2 Mr '65
See also
Furniture—Finishing

WOOD flooring. See Flooring

WOOD floors. See Floors, Wood

WOOD ibises. See Wood storks

WOOD lots. See Woodlots

WOOD mosaics. See Mosaics

WOOD paneling. See Paneling

WOOD-plastic composites. See Wood

WOOD pulp and paper mill waste. See Trade waste

WOOD pulp paper. See Paper

WOOD research
They work wonders with wood. K. Detzer. Read Digest 86:233-4+ My '65
Wood goes atomic; wood-plastic composites. R. Yoshioka. il Sci N L 87:394-5 Je 19 '65

WOOD roses
Ergoline alkaloids in tropical wood roses. J. W. Hylin and D. P. Watson. bibliog il Science 148:499-500 Ap 23 '65

WOOD seasoning. See Lumber—Drying

WOOD storks
Nesting of the wood stork. G. Heinzman and D. Heinzman. il Natur Hist 74:30-5 Ap '65

WOOD; story. See White, W.

WOODARD, John, and others
DNA content of a chromosome of trillium erectum: effect of cold treatment. bibliog Science 151:215-16 Ja 14 '66

WOODBRIDGE, N.J.
WAM builds a street in on day. C. Beagle. il Am City 80:86-8 D '65

WOODCARVING. See Wood carving

WOODCHUCK hunting
Bowhunting for chucks. G. H. Gillelan. il Outdoor Life 135:14+ My '65
We hunt the littlest big game. F. McKinley. il Outdoor Life 135:32-3+ Mr '65

WOODCOCK, George
Books. Commonweal 82:702-4 S 24 '65
India's civil war. Commonweal 82:352-5 Je 4 '65
Kutch and Kashmir, how the war started. Commonweal 82:724-6 O 1 '65

WOODCOCK shooting
Odd fellow of the alder runs. L. Dietz. il Field & S 70:56-7+ S '65
Where the woodcock are. T. Janes. il Outdoor Life 136:32-5+ S '65
WOODEN, John
Hot Brubabes. J. Jares. il Sports Illus 23:46-7 D 6 '65
Shooting is the least important part of basketball. pors Look 30:66+ Ja 25 '66
WOODEN bridges
See also
Covered bridges
WOODEN dolls. See Dolls
WOODEN posts. See Posts, Wooden
WOODEN propellers. See Airplane propellers
WOODFORD, John N.
White hate groups. Ebony 20:38-40+ Ag '65
Why Negro suicides are increasing. Ebony 20:89-90+ Jl '65
WOODLE, Allan
Let's go gunkholing. Motor B 115:30+ Je '65
WOODLOTS
Eight acres and independence. W. Rudolph. il Am For 71:30-3 Mr '65
WOODPECKERS
Nature note; ivory-billed woodpecker. Sci N L 87:351 My 29 '65
WOODRING, Paul
Editor's bookshelf. See issues of Saturday review
—and Cass, James
(eds) Education in America. See issues of Saturday review
WOODRING, W. P.
Endemism in middle Miocene Caribbean molluscan faunas. bibliog Science 148:961-3 My 14 '65
WOODS, E. J.
Theoretical physics conference. Science 148:107-8 Ap 2 '65
WOODS, George D.
Development decade in the balance. For Affairs 44:206-15 Ja '66
WOODS, H. P. and others
Tungsten diboride: preparation and structure. Science 151:75 Ja 7 '66
WOODS, John
Going to the field; poem. Poetry 106:411-12 S '65
WOODS
Outdoors: concerning two boys lost in the woods. T. Williams. Esquire 64:50+ D '65
Prairie woods and wild flowers. R. Suckow. il Am Heritage 16:36-43 Ap '65
Why I bought my children a woods. R. W. Wells. Ladies Home J 82:39-40 F '65
WOODS hogs
Five little pigs; excerpt from The elderberry tree. I. Petite. il Read Digest 87:225-6+ N '65
WOODS HOLE, Mass, marine biological laboratory
Committee for professional opportunity; letter. T. Hayashi. Science 148:1411 Je 11 '65
WOODS HOLE, Mass, oceanographic institution
Woods Hole. B. Thielen. il Holiday 38:64-5+ Jl '65
Yachtsmen and marine science. F. T. Moss. il Yachting 117:44-5+ F '65
WOODSMEN
Old Snakeroot; Abe Scholl, hex doctor, healer, teacher, and friend. D. J. Anderson. il Field & S 69:40-1+ Mr '65
WOODSON, C. W.
Tricks for milling on a lathe. Pop Sci 188:144-5 Ja '66
WOODSON, Carter Godwin
Doctor Woodson prepares for Negro history week, 1930; excerpts from diary. L. J. Greene. Negro Hist Bul 28:174-5+ My '65
Some personal recollections of Dr Woodson. J. H. Roy. Negro Hist Bul 28:185-6+ My '65
WOODSON, Weldon D.
ABC's of filming bees. Pop Phot 56:120-1+ Ap '65
WOODSTOCK, Joseph, family
This family is big on Christmas! il Bet Hom & Gard 43:35-65 D '65
WOODSTOCK, L. W. and Pollock, B. M.
Physiological predetermination: imbibition, respiration, and growth of lima bean seeds. Science 150:1031-2 N 19 '65
WOODWARD, Abishai
Thomas Harland's clock, whose case? A. R. Chase and H. Bulkeley. il Antiques 87:700-1 Je '65
WOODWARD, Bliss
Cadet life at the Academy. Motor B 115:60+ My '65
Under the blue ensign. See issues of Motor boating

WOODWARD, C. Vann
After Watts, where is the Negro revolution headed? N Y Times Mag p24-5+ Ag 29 '65
Flight from history, the heritage of the Negro. Nation 201:142-6 S 20 '65
From the first reconstruction to the second. Harper 230:127-33 Ap '65
Southern mythology. Commentary 39:60-3 My '65
Warren's challenge to race dogma. New Repub 152:21-3 My 22 '65
WOODWARD, Joanne
Second fame: good food. N. Lyon. il por Vogue 146:144-6 Ag 1 '65
WOODWARD, Kenneth L.
Nonecclesiastical Catholicism. Christian Cent 82:779-80 Je 16 '65
WOODWARD, Mary
In my opinion. por Seventeen 24:402 Ag '65
WOODWARD, Robert Burns
Nobel prize winners. por Science N L 88:279 O 30 '65
Robert Burns Woodward, Nobel prize in chemistry for 1965. P. D. Bartlett and others. il por Science 150:585-7 O 29 '65
WOODWARD, Robert F.
Red cross calls for application of convention to war prisoners; statement, October 7, 1965. Dept State Bul 53:725 N 1 '65
WOODWARD, Robert H.
Old Kentucky home. Hobbies 70:120 My '65
WOODWARD, Stanley
Rage on the sports page. por Time 86:83-4 D 10 '65
WOODWORKING
See also
Drilling and boring (woodwork)
Joints (carpentry)
Sawing
Projects
Animal pinup plaques. D. Swartwout. il Pop Mech 124:156-9 O '65
Lathe fun from Alpine novelties; smoking caliph and bottle stoppers. H. Sibley. il Pop Mech 125:164-7 Ja '66
PM ideas for Christmas. il Pop Mech 124:128-47 D '65
Three projects for a child's room; plywood rocker; trumpet lamp; drum toy box. il Pop Sci 187:124-5 D '65
Three woodworking projects for the weekend. il Pop Sci 187:142-3 O '65
Wordless workshop. R. Doty. See issues of Popular science monthly
See also
Doll houses
Furniture, Childrens
WOODYARD, David O.
For all times. Christian Cent 82:1230+ O 6 '65
WOOL, Ira G. See Rampersad, O. R. jt. auth.
WOOL fabrics. See Woolen and worsted fabrics
WOOLDRIDGE, Dean E.
Human body; master control, the brain; reprint. Sci Digest 57:77-81 Mr '65
WOOLEN and worsted fabrics
Wool research; report on third international wool textile research conference. J. Menkart. Science 150:1750 D 24 '65
WOOLF, Leonard
Books. W. H. Auden. New Yorker 41:159-60+ Ap 3 '65
WOOLFE, Ray, Jr
Faces at the races. M. Orovan. il U S Camera 28:68-9 O '65
WOOLLEY, D. W.
New insight into mental illness: philosophical implications. Atlan 216:46-50 Jl '65
WOOLNER, Frank
Thing called early blur. Outdoor Life 136:48-9+ N '65
WOOLSON, Robert
Backyard & birdbath R.R. W. C. Lammey. il Pop Mech 124:118-28+ Ag '65
WOOLWICH, John Arthur Thomas Robinson, bp of. See Robinson, J. A. T.
WOOLWORTH, F. W. company
Changing world of Woolworth: modernization and acquisition. T. J. Murray. il Duns R 86:46-7+ N '65
Originals; sale of paintings at Menlo Park branch. New Yorker 41:36-8 Ap 10 '65
WOOSTER, Harold
Post-mortems can be fun: the cost analysis of information systems. por Library J 90:2968-73 Jl '65
WORAM, John M.
Don't waste a good performance, record it! adapted from Music journal. Recreation 58:87-8 F '65

WORCESTER, Mass.

Education
School art festival; interview, ed. by I. Arms.
O. Gatti. il Sch Arts 64:31-3 My '65

WORD games
Trade winds. J. G. Fuller. Sat R 48:12+ Je
12 '65
See also
Crossword puzzles

WORDEN, Helen
I took the Niehans treatment. Vogue 147:
76-7+ Ja 15 '66

WORDS
Building word power. H. L. Herber. Sr
Schol 86:9T F 11 '65
Careful writer. by T. M. Bernstein. Review
Reporter il 33:60+ S 23 '65. R. C. Wald
Language of democracy. E. Capouya. Sat R
48:31-2 My 8 '65
Language on vacation, by D. Borgmann.
Review
Sat R 48:130 S 18 '65. J. F. Fixx
Time il 86:133 S 17 '65
Sneaky summer word-makers; creators of
magazine journalese. R. L. Dean. America
113:135 Ag 7 '65
Trials of a word-watcher. C. Ogburn, jr.
Harper 230:88-90+ Ap '65
See also
English language—Terms and phrases
Vocabulary

WORDS, New
Language of democracy. E. Capouya. Sat R
48:31-2 My 8 '65

WORK benches
Four-way workbench you can build. S. M.
Gallager. il Pop Sci 186:180-3 F '65
Living-room workbench licks the dust. W.
Sill. il Pop Sci 188:124-6 Ja '66
Lock-up workbench protects your tools. C.
E. Rhine. il Pop Sci 187:164-9+ N '65

WORK camps. See Labor camps

WORK experience. See Vocational education

WORK furlough programs. See Prisoners—Rehabilitation

WORK holders. See Holding devices (machine
work)

WORK measurement
Desk work gets faster countdown; work
measurement programs. Bsns W p91-2+ O
30 '65

WORK projects administration. See United
States—Work projects administration

WORK rules. See Railroads—Work rules

WORK satisfaction. See Job satisfaction

WORK simplification. See Home economics

WORK-study plan. See Education, Cooperative

WORKER priests
New life for priest workers. R. Bertrand.
America 113:669-70 N 27 '65
Not cassocks but coveralls. Time 86:80 N
5 '65
Priest-worker flare-up. America 112:240 F
20 '65
Priest-workers. Commonweal 83:393 Ja 7 '66
Priests for the factories. America 113:515 N
6 '65
They are priests and workers, both. J. Cog-
ley. il N Y Times Mag p6-7+ D 26 '65

WORKERS education. See Labor and laboring
classes—Education

WORKING classes. See Labor and laboring
classes

WORKING day. See Hours of labor

WORKING girls and women. See Business and
professional women

WORKING mothers. See Married women—Employment

WORKING week. See Hours of labor

WORKINGMENS clubs. See Clubs

WORKMAN, Wendy
Mountains of misery. M. Orovan. il U S
Camera 28:58-61+ My '65

WORKMENS compensation

United States
Workmen's compensation enactments in 1965.
L. W. Larson. il Mo Labor R 88:1322-4
N '65

WORKS progress administration. See United
States—Work projects administration

WORKSHOPS
Great hobby corners in waste space; instant
office; closet projection room; collectors'
corner; hunting and fishing hideaway. il
Pop Mech 124:144-51 S '65
He works inside three wine tanks. il Sunset 135:76+ Ag '65

Improving your home wiring; wiring your
home shop for power. J. Burroughs. il Pop
Sci 187:159-63+ N '65
These workrooms are closet-sized. il Sunset
136:79 Ja '66

Equipment
This farm shop has nearly everything! B.
Brantley. il Suc Farm 64:42-3 Ja '66
Two accessories for any workshop. il Pop
Sci 187:157 N '65

WORKSHOPS, Dance. See Dance institutes and
workshops

WORKSHOPS, Educational. See Educational
workshops

WORKSHOPS, Library. See Library institutes
and workshops

WORKSHOPS, Opera. See Opera—Instruction
and study

WORLD (New York) See New York world

WORLD bank. See International bank for
reconstruction and development

WORLD championship coonhound water races.
See Dog racing

WORLD citizenship, Education for. See International education

WORLD confederation of organizations of the
teaching profession
World's children; WCOTP conference. J.
Moorhead. il PTA Mag 60:18-19 N '65

WORLD conference on church and society. See
Religious conferences

WORLD conference on world peace through
the rule of law
From many lands. H. Y. Williams. Christian
Cent 82:1331-2 O 27 '65

WORLD congress of writers. See PEN club

WORLD cooperation. See International cooperation

WORLD council of churches
Enugu: second thoughts; Central committee's
attempt to choose successor to Visser't
Hooft. G. Murray. Christian Cent 82:167-8
F 10 '65
New Missions journal dress. G. Murray.
Christian Cent 82:723-4 Je 2 '65
New words; diakonia and lability. G. Murray.
Christian Cent 82:1297 O 20 '65
Power struggle at Enugu; Central commit-
tee meeting. Enugu, Nigeria. Christian
Cent 82:131 F 3 '65
Protestant Vatican. Newsweek 66:82-3 Jl 26
'65
Religious liberty or public order? Christian
Cent 82:1003-4 Ag 18 '65; Reply. S. E. Mead.
82:1193-4 S 29 '65
Resolutionary Christianity? concerning World
conference on church and society. J. R.
Nelson. Christian Cent 82:639-40 My 19 '65
Visser 't Hooft's successor. Christian Cent
82:1468 D 1 '65
We nominate Blake. Christian Cent 83:68-9
Ja 19 '66

WORLD crafts council
World crafts council. Craft Horiz 25:4 My
'65

WORLD economics. See Economic conditions

WORLD federation of trade unions
Two Communist fronts at work. L. M. Taubinger and S. Musulin. Nat R 17:328 Ap 20
'65

WORLD festival of youth and students for
peace and friendship
Youth festival that wasn't; Algiers-sched-
uled World youth festival. L. Taubinger
and E. Musulin. Nat R 17:688+ Ag 10 '65

WORLD flights. See Aviation—World flights

WORLD food program. See Food supply

WORLD food supply. See Food supply

WORLD fund. See International monetary fund

WORLD health organization
Geneva: world headquarters in the fight
against smallpox. il UNESCO Courier 18:
24-7 Mr '65
Sculpture in light and concrete. J. Villaverde.
il Américas 17:22-8 S '65
World health organization observes 17th
birthday; smallpox vaccination program in
India. il Todays Health 43:50 Jl '65
World health organization shelves research
center plan. V. K. McElheny. Science 148:
1576-8 Je 18 '65

WORLD history
Twenty years of challenge and change 1945-
65. Sr Schol 87:35 S 30 '65

Bibliography
New books for your history shelf. H. L.
Hurwitz. il Sr Schol 87:sup24 S 30 '65

WORLD language. See Language, Universal

WORLD law. See International law

WORLD law day. See Special days, weeks, and months

WORLD maps
Changing world sits for a new portrait. il Nat Geog Mag 127:188-90, sup(folded map) F '65
Map of the world (cont) Sr Schol 87:29-31 S 30 '65

WORLD Methodist council
Eyes to the past? B. Thompson. Christian Cent 82:947-8+ Jl 28 '65

WORLD mindedness. See Internationalism

WORLD neighbors, incorporated
Neighbors to all the world. C. W. Hall. il Read Digest 87:127-32 Ag '65

WORLD of Charles Aznavour: musical comedy. See Musical comedies, revues, etc.—Criticisms, plots, etc.

WORLD of Ray Bradbury; drama. See Bradbury, R.

WORLD opinion. See Public opinion

WORLD order study conference
Red China at St Louis. K. Haselden. Christian Cent 82:1343-4 N 3 '65

WORLD organization. See United Nations

WORLD organization for early childhood education
For young children in a changing world; education facilities in Scandinavia. L. L. Gore. il Sch Life 47:4-7 D '64

WORLD outside; story. See Holland, B.

WORLD politics, 1945-
Adlai Stevenson's last article; outline for a new American policy. A. E. Stevenson. il Look 29:71-2+ Ag 24 '65
Alternative to war: peaceful co-existence, an objective necessity; address, February 18, 1965. N. N. Inozemstev. Vital Speeches 31: 421-4 My 1 '65
Arguments for accommodation. F. Altschul. Sat R 48:40 Ag 14 '65
Atomic diplomacy: Hiroshima and Potsdam, by G. Alperovitz. Review
Nation 201:123-4 S 6 '65. C. Lasch
Broadcasting of world politics; address, November 3, 1965. H. Cleveland. Dept State Bul 53:896-901 D 6 '65
Burden of leadership. A. Eden. For Affairs 44:229-38 Ja '66
Can Pax Americana succeed? D. F. Fleming. Ann Am Acad 360:127-38 Jl '65
Challenges to freedom and peace; address, October 31, 1965. W. A. Harriman. Dept State Bul 53:863-7 N 29 '65
China's strategy: a critique. D. S. Zagoria. Commentary 40:61-6 N '65
Current documents. See issues of Current history
Dangers of nostaglia; address, March 16, 1965. G. W. Ball. Dept State Bul 52:532-7 Ap 12 '65
Existence through co-existence: cooperation, not conflict; address May 29, 1965. Vital Speeches 31:562-5 Jl 1 '65
France and Germany: divergent outlooks. A. Grosser. For Affairs 44:26-36 O '65
Great debate: theories of nuclear strategy, by R. Aron; tr. by E. Pawel. Review
New Repub 152:21-2 F 13 '65. R. D. Senter
Hard problems of a turbulent world; address, September 16, 1965. G. W. Ball. Dept State Bul 53:588-92 O 11 '65
Interdependence of nations: shades of gray; address, June 1, 1965. A. E. Stevenson. Vital Speeches 31:548-51 Jl 1 '65
New diplomacy; address, June 6, 1965. J. W. Ball. Dept State Bul 52:1042-8 Je 28 '65
New perspective. E. Rabinowitch. Bul Atomic Sci 21:2-3 N '65
Nonalignment in foreign affairs; symposium, ed. by C. V. Crabb, jr. bibliog f Ann Am Acad 362:1-138 N '65
Other end of the telescope; address, October 21, 1965. H. Cleveland. Dept State Bul 53: 781-7 N 15 '65
Peace: the central task of foreign policy; address, June 8, 1965. W. W. Rostow. Dept State Bul 53:21-7 Jl 5 '65
Roadblock to arms control and disarmament negotiations; address, June 4, 1965. W. C. Foster. Dept State Bul 53:77-84 Jl 12 '65
Role of emerging nations in world politics; address, March 15, 1965. W. W. Rostow. Dept State Bul 52:492-7 Ap 5 '65
Tasks of the free-world community; address, July 14, 1965. G. C. McGhee. Dept State Bul 53:324-30 Ag 23 '65
20th anniversary of V-E day; address, May 7, 1965. L. B. Johnson. Dept State Bul 52:790-3 My 24 '65

Unfinished revolution: America and the third world, by C. L. Sulzberger. Review
Sat R 48:42-3 Jl 24 '65. A. A. Castagno
United Nations commemoration address, June 26, 1965. Thant. UN Mo Chron 2:141-5 Jl '65
U.S. and world affairs annual, 1965-66; ed. by E. R. Floyd and others. il Sr Schol 87: 12-41+ S 30 '65
U.S. calls for deeds, not words, in U.N. committee on defining aggression; statements, April 5 and April 8, 1965. F. T. P. Plimpton. Dept State Bul 52:775-85 My 17 '65
United States summarizes position on disarmament and arms control; statement, April 26, 1965. A. E. Stevenson. bibliog f Dept State Bul 52:762-74 My 17 '65
What the world owes Khurshchev. H. E. Salisbury. il N Y Times Mag p 16-17+ Ap 25 '65
World politics of responsibility. O. Gass. Commentary 40:85-90 D '65
Worldgram: from the capitals of the world. See issues of U.S. news & World report
See also
Balance of power
Current events
International relations

Bibliography
Book reviews: politics: at home and abroad. R. Steel. Sr Schol 86:sup 13 Ap 1 '65
Since Hiroshima. A. Campbell. New Repub 153:27-8 Ag 7 '65
Unofficial volunteers for the great debate. R. Drummond. Harper 231:122+ N '65

WORLD population. See Population

WORLD population conference, Belgrade, 1965
Population conference. UN Mo Chron 2:77-8 Je: 44-6 Ag '65
Population growth; World conference on population, Belgrade, Yugoslavia, 30 August-10 September 1965. C. Taeuber. Science 151: 226-7 Ja 14 '66
Problems of world population; interview, ed. by F. Canavan. F. C. Madigan. America 113:524-6 N 6 '65
U.S. pledges support to World population conference; August 30, 1965. L. B. Johnson. Dept State Bul 53:480 S 20 '65
World population conference; meeting in Belgrade, Yugoslavia. UN Mo Chron 2:36-7 O '65

WORLD records
Trade winds; concerning The Guinness book of world records. J. G. Fuller. il Sat R 48: 8 N 27 '65

WORLD rule of law. See Rule of law

WORLD samplers club. See Aviation clubs

WORLD security. See International security

WORLD series (baseball)
Dodgers down and up. J. Mann. il Sports Illus 23:28-35 O 18 '65
Final strength was Sandy; best pitcher in baseball. W. Leggett. il Sports Illus 23: 28-9 O 25 '65
Home, sweet home? il Time 86:76 O 15 '65
How the Twins should do with the National league. il Sports Illus 23:28-9 O 4 '65
Mr Cool & the pros. il Time 86:93+ O 22 '65
Scratch, slide and steal. il Newsweek 66:80 O 18 '65
Sporting scene; world series. R. Angell. il New Yorker 41:192+ O 30 '65

WORLD series tickets. See Baseball—Tickets

WORLD student Christian federation
Students talk of their faith; Joint consultation of Pax Romana and the World student Christian federation at Taizé. J. J. Megivern. America 112:636-8 My 1 '65

WORLD theater season, London. See Drama festivals

WORLD, this one, the flesh, Mrs Oedipa Maas, and the testament of Pierce Inverarity; story. See Pynchon, T.

WORLD trade. See Commerce

WORLD trade corporation. See International business machine corporation

WORLD trade week
World trade week, 1965; proclamation, March 24, 1965. L. B. Johnson. Dept State Bul 52:549 Ap 12 '65

WORLD travel. See Travel

WORLD unity. See International organization; Internationalism

WORLD war, 1914-1918. See European war, 1914-1918

WORLD war, 1939-1945
Last 100 days; excerpts. J. Toland. il Look 29:34-40+ My 4; 38-40+ My 18; 70-2+ Je 1 '65
See also
Japan—History—Allied occupation, 1945-1952

WRECKING
Penn station: arriving on schedule. il Bsns W p32-3 O 30 '65
Wreckers rip into old downtown hotels. il Bsns W p63-4 Ag 21 '65

WRENS
Nature note; winter wren. Sci N L 87:75 Ja 30 '65

WRESTLING
Day the Cowboys got lassoed for a loss; Iowa state's winning of NCAA championship. M. Kram. Sports Illus 22:82-4 Ap 5 '65
Pittsburgh Hurricane roars into wrestling. il Ebony 20:100-2+ Je '65
See also
Judo

WRESZIN, Michael
Pacifist rough rider. Nation 200:671-3+ Je 21 '65
Taking man's measure. Nation 202:19-22 Ja 3 '66

WRETCHED mess news (periodical)
Wretched mess of type, mostly about fishing. R. Cantwell. il Sports Illus 23:71-4 D 20 '65

WRIGHT, Beatrice
Wrights. New Yorker 41:36 Mr 20 '65

WRIGHT, Bruce S.
South to Caicos. pors Field & S 70:49-51+ D '65

WRIGHT, Esmond
Making of a president, 1789. Sat R 49:38 Ja 15 '66
Roadway called war. Sat R 48:30+ Ag 14 '65

WRIGHT, Frank Lloyd
What nature teaches man. I. Ross. il Sci Digest 59:89-91 Ja '66

WRIGHT, Helen
Helen Wright; a way of responding. J. Deschin. por Pop Phot 57:36+ S '65

WRIGHT, Henry
Air-conditioning the whole house. Arch Rec 137:7+ mid-My '65

WRIGHT, J. Handly
Total transportation. Duns R 86:76C-76D+ O '65

WRIGHT, J. Skelly
Crime in the streets and the new McCarthyism. New Repub 153:10-11 O 9 '65
Criminal law and the Bill of rights. Reporter 32:23-5 Je 3 '65

WRIGHT, James
Before the cashier's window in a department store; poem. New Yorker 41:50 Mr 13 '65
For the marsh's birthday; poem. New Yorker 41:71 Jl 10 '65
Micromutations; poem. New Yorker 41:97 Je 26 '65
Poems to a brown cricket. New Yorker 41:31 Jl '65

WRIGHT, James Couper
Watercolors of James Couper Wright. J. Lovoos. il por Am Artist 29:52-7+ O '65

WRIGHT, Jess C. and Blair, W. L.
Receiver requirements for monitoring Gemini. Electr World 73:33-5+ Je '65

WRIGHT, John J. bp
Conciliar Rome. America 112:418-20 Mr 27 '65

WRIGHT, Martha R.
Bijah's Luce of Guilford, Vermont. Negro Hist Bul 28:152-3+ Ap '65

WRIGHT, Mary Kathryn
Mickey Wright: a retreat from a flawless image. pors Sports Illus 23:24+ Jl 12 '65
Sporting scene. H. W. Wind. New Yorker 41:104+ Ag 21 '65

WRIGHT, Patience Lovell
Patience Wright and her new style of picturing. P. D. Sampson. il por Antiques 87:586-9 My '65

WRIGHT, Paul
Wrights. New Yorker 41:36 Mr 20 '65

WRIGHT, Phyllis M.
Fischer quints at two. Ladies Home J 83:53-7+ Ja '66
Medicine today; ed. by V. Cohn. Ladies Home J 82:38+ Je; 38 Jl; 48 Ag; 24 S; 26 O; 44+ N; 24 D '65

WRIGHT, R. H.
Metarchons: insect control through recognition signals. Bul Atomic Sci 21:28-30 Mr '65

WRIGHT, Robert H.
King snake dines on a sparrow egg; photographs. Natur Hist 74:50-1 Mr '65

WRIGHT, Stanton MacDonald-. See MacDonald-Wright, S.

WRIGHT, Sylvia
He goads and chides the young and gains new followers. Life 60:60-5 Ja 14 '66
How to complicate a trip. Harper 230:84-7 Ap '65
Summer at On the rocks. N Y Times Mag p20+ Ag 8 '65

WRIGHT, Vincent, family
Trials of an interracial couple. il Ebony 20:66-8+ O '65

WRIGHT DRY VALLEY. See Antarctic Regions

WRIGLEY, Walter, and Hollister, W. M.
Gyroscope: theory and application. bibliog Science 149:713-21 Ag 13 '65

WRINKLING. See Creasing of textiles

WRISTON, Henry M.
Publish or perish. por Sat R 48:59 Jl 17 '65
Taking the national pulse. Sat R 48:25-9 S 11 '65

WRITERS. See Authors

WRITERS, World congress of. See PEN club

WRITERS conference. See Authors conferences

WRITERS vocabulary. See Vocabulary

WRITING
See also
Alphabet
Authorship
    History
Ancestors of the ball-point pen. L. Pareti. il UNESCO Courier 18:25-7 My '65

WRITING (authorship) See Authorship

WRITING (composition) See English language —Composition

WRITING, Minoan
Rediscovery of Crete. M. I. Finley. il Horizon 7:64-75 Sum '65

WRITING paper. See Stationery

WRONG, Dennis H.
Jews, gentiles & the New establishment. Commentary 39:83-6 Je '65

WROUGHT-iron furniture. See Furniture, Metal

WU, Yuan-li
Communist China's economy: critical questions. bibliog f Cur Hist 49:164-9 S '65

WUJEK, Joseph H. Jr
Basic principles of reliability. Electr World 73:44-5 F '65
Experiments in space. Electr World 74:30-1+ Jl '65
Micrometeoroid measurements. Electr World 74:42-3+ N '65
Reliability of electronic components. Electr World 73:40-1+ My '65

WULFF, Lee
What's happening to Atlantic salmon? il Yachting 117:100-1+ Je '65

WUPPERTAL, Germany (Federal Republic)
Here's the original monorail. il Sunset 134:72+ Ap '65

WURSTER, Charles F. Jr, and Wurster, D. H.
DDT spray and bird mortality. bibliog Science 149:326 Jl 16 '65
—and others
Bird mortality after spraying for Dutch elm disease with DDT. bibliog Science 148:90-1 Ap 2 '65

WURSTER, Doris H. See Wurster, C. F. Jr, jt. auth.

WURTMAN, Richard J. and Axelrod, Julius
Adrenaline synthesis: control by the pituitary gland and adrenal glucocorticoids. bibliog Science 150:1464-5 D 10 '65
Pineal gland; with biographical sketches. Sci Am 213:16, 50-60 bibliog(p 124) Jl '65

WYANDOTTE cave. See Caves

WYANT, Rowena
Business failures. See issues of Dun's review and modern industry

WYCHERLEY, William
Country wife. Criticism
    Nation 201:538-9 D 27 '65
    New Repub 154:35 Ja 1 '66
    Newsweek il 66:92-3 D 20 '65
    Reporter 34:44-5 Ja 13 '66
    Sat R 48:41+ D 25 '65
    Time il 86:40 D 17 '65

WYDEN, Peter
Night eating; excerpts from Overweight society. Ladies Home J 82:39-40+ Ap '65

WYEOMYIA viruses. See Viruses

WYER, Malcolm Glenn
Wyer at 88; letter to the editor. L. C. Powell. Library J 90:2182 My 15 '65

WYETH, Andrew
Andrew Wyeth; interview, ed. by R. Meryman. il pors Life 58:92-106+ My 14 '65
    about
Patriot talks about his portrait. R. Cline. il Life 58:122 My 14 '65

WYETH, Newell Convers
N. C. Wyeth. H. C. Pitz. il pors Am Heritage 16:36-55+ O '65

WYETH family
N. C. Wyeth. H. C. Pitz. il Am Heritage
16:36-55+ O '65
WYLER, William
Great Gallic welcome. J. F. Fixx. por p 14
Sat R 48:16 D 25 '65
Wyler's wiles. il por Time 85:92 Je 18 '65
WYLIE, Evan McLeod
Last year of little Sal. Good H 161:12+ N '65
Mrs John Glenn talks about the years
since. . . Good H 161:76-81+ Jl '65
WYLIE, Jim
What are they saying? Esquire 64:44-5 Jl '65
WYLIE, Philip
Making of a man. Read Digest 87:63-8 D '65
Speaking out. por Sat Eve Post 238:10+ S
11 '65
WYMAN, Donald
Make room for birch trees. Pop Gard 16:32-3+
My '65
WYMAN, Louis C.
Excerpts from remarks, May 21 and August
3, and from debate, August 13, 1964. Cong
Digest 44:57+ F '65
WYNNE, Greville Maynard
British agent supports Penkovskiy papers.
Pub W 188:39-40 N 22 '65
WYNNE, Jim
He drives a hairy race. B. Ottum. il pors
Sports Illus 23:30-5 Ag 2 '65
WYNNE-EDWARDS, V. C.
Self-regulating systems in populations of
animals; adaptation of address, December
26, 1964. bibliog Science 147:1543-8 Mr 26 '65
WYOMING
See also
Fishing—Wyoming
Jackson Hole Valley
Paleontology—Wyoming

Religious institutions and affairs
News of the Christian world. Christian Cent
82:1076-7 S 1 '65
WYSE, Lois
What kind of girl are you, anyway? McCalls
92:68+ Je '65
WYSZYŃSKI, Stefan, cardinal
Four men: four stories. America 112:450 Ap 3
'65
Who may come to Czestochowa? Time 87:
34 Ja 14 '66

X

X-15 (airplane) See Airplanes. Experimental—
Testing
X RAY analysis. See Crystallography—X ray
studies
X RAY densitometers. See Densitometers
X RAYS
Heart X-rays advised; X-ray risk kept small.
Sci N L 88:242 O 16 '65
X-rays, seeing inside solid substances. Sci
Digest 58:88 Jl '65
See also
Crystallography—X ray studies
Diagnosis, Radioscopic

Physiological effects
Irradiated cells repaired. F. Marley. Sci
N L 87:259 Ap 24 '65
X-ray exposure causes hereditary rat cat-
aracts. Sci N L 87:121 F 20 '65

Therapeutic applications
Normal tissue may be spared during X-ray.
Sci N L 88:221 O 2 '65
X 21 (airplane) See Airplanes, Experimental
XANTHIUM
Comparison of messenger RNA in photo-
periodically induced and noninduced xan-
thium buds. J. H. Cherry and R. B. Van
Huystee. bibliog il Science 150:1450-3 D 10
'65
XAVIER, Sister Mary
GI's and the girls from Dubuque; condensa-
tion of address. Read Digest 86:164-7+ Je
'65
XENAKIS, Yannis
Beat me in St Louis; U.S. première of Stra-
tégie for two orchestras and two conduc-
tors. il Time 85:50 Mr 12 '65
XENON
Vehicle for a noble gas. Sci Am 213:84+ S
'65

Xenon-photosensitized formation of meta-
stable nitrogen. W. M. Jackson and M. D.
Scheer. bibliog il Science 148:1718-19 Je
25 '65
XEROGRAPHY
Art of xerography. C. M. Celent. il Electr
World 74:25-8+ Jl '65
Can Xerox be copied? acquisitions point to
further growth. il Bsns W p66-8+ O 9 '65
Copy machine boom, and Xerox xoom; Man
who started it all. il Newsweek 66:84-6+
N 8 '65
Xerox: the invention that hit the jackpot.
D. Wharton. il Read Digest 86:121-4 Mr '65
XEROX corporation
Can Xerox be copied? acquisitions point to
further growth. il Bsns W p66-8+ O 9 '65
Copy machine boom, and Xerox xoom; Man
who started it all. il Newsweek 66:84-6+
N 8 '65
Message messes up a fine idea; Xerox United
Nations series. D. Martin. Life 58:17 F 19
'65
Research & development. W. A. Stocklin.
Electr World 73:6 F '65
Shushing the annual heckler; professional
stockholders. il Bsns Wp 118+ My 22 '65
SR's businessman of the year: J. C. Wilson.
W. D. Patterson. Sat R 49:72+ Ja 8 '66
Xerox pays $56 million for Wesleyan univer-
sity press. Pub W 187:32 My 31 '65
Xerox proves a point; effect of U.N. film
drama experiment. R. L. Tobin. Sat R 48:
87-8 N 13 '65
XMAS in Las Vegas; drama. See Richardson,
J.

Y

YAF. See Young Americans for freedom (or-
ganization)
YASD. See American library association—
Young adult services division
YMCA. See Young men's Christian association
YABLONSKY, Lewis
Watch out, whitey. New Repub 154:10-12 Ja 1
'66
YACHT building
Building a stock fiberglass cruiser (cont)
B. Cobb, jr. il Yachting 117:49-51+ F '65
Challenge; Dame Pattie, Australian challenge
for the America's cup. L. D'Alpuget. il
Yachting 118:42-4+ D '65
Sailing yacht research; use of computers in
tests at MIT. H. C. Herreshoff and J. E.
Kerwin. il Yachting 118:51-3+ Jl '65
See also
Chrysler corporation
YACHT clubs
Birth of a yacht club. P. Paine. Atlan 216:
110-11 Ag '65
Chicago: yachting at the office door. J. Roe.
il Yachting 117:44-5+ My '65
Sailing downwind in a nice, cozy yacht club;
Sea Cliff yacht club. R. S. Hewlett. il
Sports Illus 23:66-7 D 13 '65
They work together; San Diego's yacht clubs.
H. Monahan. il Yachting 117:48-9+ Je '65
Vancouver; Royal Vancouver yacht club. H.
Glynn-Ward. il Motor B 115:40-1 My '65
YACHT insurance. See Insurance, Marine
YACHT propellers. See Propellers
YACHT racing
Admiral's cup. A. F. Loomis. il Yachting
118:47-9+ Ag '65
Admiral's cup. E. F. Haylock. il Motor B
116:86-7+ O '65
Another Morgan sails the sea for treasure;
skipper, designer C. Morgan. H. Whall.
il Sports Illus 22:72+ Mr 22 '65
Certain elation; Ondine wins Buenos Aires-
Rio race. il Time 85:52 Mr 5 '65
Distance racing starts. J. Sutphen. il Yacht-
ing 117:56-8+ My '65
Figaro trims the SORC. F. Rohr. il Motor B
115:156-60+ My '65
Honolulu race nemesis; final test for Transpac
crews in Molokai Channel. F. N. Rothwell.
il Yachting 117:64+ My '65
Ice boating: watch it grow. E. Knudsen.
See issues of Motor boating
Largest and fastest Transpac. A. Lockabey.
il Yachting 118:41-3+ S '65
Mackinacs won by two old ladies of the
lakes. F. Heyes; G. E. Van. il Yachting
118:46-7+ S '65

YACHT racing—*Continued*
Match racing tactics (cont) R. N. Bavier, jr.
  il Yachting 117:46-8+ F '65
Midwest watch. See issues of Motor boating
  to May 1965
Month in yachting. See issues of Yachting
On the racing circuit. See issues of Motor
  boating
Psyche snares the Transpac. A. F. H. Goetz.
  il Motor B 116:106-8+ S '65
Race that broke the Bird; Eagle vs. Constel-
  lation in picking defender for America's
  cup. R. N. Bavier, jr. il Sports Illus 23:34-
  40 Ag 16 '65
Sail paces power in the West. B. Ruskauff.
  See issues of Motor boating
Soviets at bay; world championships, Bay of
  Naples. il Newsweek 65:96 Je 14 '65
Tuning a twelve-meter; Constellation. R.
  Stephens, jr. il Yachting 117:48-50+ Mr;
  80-1+ Ap '65
Very special race; symposium. il Yachting
  117:39-40+ Je '65
Victorious skipper to ship designer; letter.
  R. Johnson. il Esquire 64:151+ D '65
Vineyard race. E. B. Morris. il Yachting 118:
  173-5 O '65
Western sailing; what's coming; what was.
  A. F. H. Goetz. il Motor B 115:35-7 My '65
Westward ho! B. Ruskauff. See issues of
  Motor boating
What sort of power next? J. Martenhoff. See
  issues of Motor boating
With the racing classes. B. Robinson. See
  issues of Yachting

Administration
Gordon Curtis on race organization. G. Curtis.
  il Yachting 117:210+ Je '65

Rules
Changes in the racing rules. R. N. Bavier, jr.
  Yachting 117:51+ Mr '65
YACHTS

Berths
To sleep: there's the rub. P. R. Smyth. il
  Motor B 115:30-2+ Mr '65

Care
Tuning a twelve-meter; Constellation. R.
  Stephens, jr. il Yachting 117:48-50+ Mr;
  80-1+ Ap '65

Chartering
Handy Pied-à-Terre for a sailorman. C.
  Mitchell. il Sports Illus 22:79-80+ My 24 '65

Design
Another Morgan sails the sea for treasure;
  Maredea, the biggest fiber-glass boat. H.
  Whall. il Sports Illus 22:72+ Mr 22 '65
Blue Fox. il Yachting 117:56-7+ F '65
Boats we meet: Distant Star; medium size
  ocean-going power yachts. J. Emmett. il
  Yachting 118:57-9+ Jl '65
Boats we meet: Out Islander. J. Emmett. il
  Yachting 117:85-7+ Ap '65
Boats we meet: Rocking Chair. J. Emmett.
  il Yachting 117:41-3 F '65
Burr Bartram's Exact. B. Robinson. il
  Yachting 117:52-3+ Mr '65
Designer for all seasons; O. Stephens de-
  signed Finisterre. Sports Illus 23:8 Ag 9 '65
Designs. W. H. deFontaine. See issues of
  Yachting
Disco Volante, the saucer that flies; new
  James Bond epic Thunderball. J. Marten-
  hoff. il Motor B 116:32-3+ D '65
Great American sailboats. Dorade; Olin
  Stephens yawl design. il Motor B 115:42-3+
  Je '65
Great American sailboats; Stormy Weather.
  il Motor B 116:32-3+ Ag '65
N.A.'s art in action. il Motor B 115:38-51 F;
  51-60 Mr '65
Other man's boat; Effie Jean. il Yachting
  118:70-1+ Ag '65
Other man's boat; Evening Star V. il Yacht-
  ing 118:72-3+ O '65
Other man's boat; Integrity. W. Howland. il
  Yachting 118:62-3+ N '65
Other man's boat; Jack Tar. il Yachting 117:
  68-9+ My '65; Reply. G. Braidwood. 118:
  147 S '65
Other man's boat; Sunquest II. il Yachting
  117:70-1+ Mr '65

Materials
Building a stock fiberglass cruiser (cont)
  B. Cobb, jr. il Yachting 117:49-51+ F '65

YACHTS and yachting
Aboard the 36' cruiser Queen Mary with
  Peter Lind Hayes and Mary Healy. G.
  Sloane. il Motor B 115:60-1+ Je '65
Big stern-drive cruise handles like out-
  board. J. Roe. il Pop Sci 186:96-8 Mr '65
Boats we meet: Out Islander. J. Emmett. il
  Yachting 117:85-7+ Ap '65
Calendar of coming events; comp. by R. B.
  Smith. See issues of Motor boating
Captain Herlihy emcee of the 42' Big Jeanne.
  G. Sloane. il Motor B 116:56-7+ O '65
Charm of small boats. J. Pazereskis. Yacht-
  ing 117:174+ F '65
Great Lakes yachting; symposium. il Yacht-
  ing 117:40-53+ My '65
Hideaway for LBJ: a yacht on the Potomac.
  il U S News 58:12 Je 21 '65
News from yachting centers. See issues of
  Yachting
Over the bounding wabes: San Juan Islands
  off Washington and British Columbia. J.
  Olsen. il Sports Illus 23:50-8 Ag 2 '65
Plug-in boats. il Time 86:66 S 3 '65
Sailing with Uncle Charlie; C. F. Adams.
  G. C. Homans. il Atlan 216:39-45 Jl '65
Seasoned skipper. See issues of Motor boat-
  ing
Southern yachting; symposium. Yachting 118:
  38-59+ N '65
Under the lee of the longboat. See issues of
  Yachting
Vancouver; yachting center of Canada's
  photogenic Pacific waterways. H. Glynn-
  Ward. il Motor B 115:40-1 My '65
Whatta way to go! E. Crimmin. See issues
  of Motor boating
Yachting in the grand style. il Life 59:46-61
  Jl 9 '65
      See also
Cookery, Marine
Cruising
Decks
Sloops
Voyages
Women in boating

Accidents
Emergency radio calls. R. Fremont-Smith.
  Yachting 117:190+ Ap '65
Piloting blooper and the lesson it taught.
  H. H. Maxim. Yachting 117:193-4 Ap '65

Anecdotes, facetiae, satire, etc.
It's the crew that kills you! C. M. Stearns.
  il Yachting 117:52+ F '65

Bibliography
Book reviews. See issues of Yachting

History
Fate of the America. T. Umsted. il Yachting
  117:232+ Ap '65

Laws and regulations
See Boats and boating—Laws and regulations

Safety devices and measures
Accident prevention aboard an ocean racer.
  J. K. Roosevelt. il Yachting 117:225 Ap '65

France
Beat boatmen of the lazy shore; drawings by
  D. Gorsline; with account by C. Mitchell.
  Sports Illus 22:74-80+ My 24 '65

Ireland
Wee bit of Irish yachting. B. Davis. il Motor
  B 116:26-7+ Ag '65
YADDO (art colony) See Artists colonies
YAGI, Yasuo, and others
Antibodies against the component polypeptide
  chains of bovine insulin. bibliog Science
  147:617-19 F 5 '65
YALE express system, incorporated
Big skid at Yale express. R. J. Whalen. il
  Fortune 72:144-9+ N '65
Mystery at Yale. Newsweek 65:68 Ap 5 '65
YALE graduates. See College graduates
YALE university
Ivyless halls of Yale. il Holiday 37:76-81 My
  '65
Master Hersey; J. Hersey named new master
  at Pierson. il Newsweek 65:52 Je 7 '65
Master novelist; J. Hersey, master of Pierson
  college. il Time 85:50 Je 4 '65
Protest at Yale. Nation 200:266-7 Mr 15 '65
Students & tenure at Yale. Time 86:64 O 22
  '65

YALE university—*Continued*
Uprising at Yale; students protest denial of tenure to R. J. Bernstein. il Newsweek 65:89 Mr 15 '65
Yale's tenure trouble; case of R. J. Bernstein. N. S. Care. New Repub 152:13-14 Mr 27 '65; Reply. C. Mitchell. 152:29 Ap 10 '65
See also
Gesell institute of child development

Libraries
Yale's new treasure house. A. Winston. il Harper 230:32+ Mr '65

YALE university press
Yale press publishes map discovery of the century. il Pub W 188:31-4 O 11 '65

YALTA conference. See Crimea conference, Yalta, Russia, 1945

YAMAMOTO, Ken-ichi. See Domino, E. F. jt. auth.

YAMAMOTO, Nobuto, and Naito, Tatsuro
Inactivation by nitrogen mustard of single- and double-stranded DNA and RNA bacteriophages. bibliog Science 150:1603-4 D 17 '65

YAMASAKI, Minoru
Lofty portico, a termination and a transition. Arch Rec 138:146-9 D '65

YAMÉOGO, Maurice
Presdient Yameogo of Upper Volta visits the United States; greetings, March 29, 1965. Dept State Bul 52:619-20 Ap 26 '65

about
How ya gonna keep 'em down in Upper Volta after they've met Lloyd Hand? E. Wittenberg. Esquire 64:24+ D '65

YANKEE Doodle dandy; drama. See Fisher, A.

YANKEES (baseball) See Baseball clubs

YANNONI, N. F. and others
Structure of 9,9,10,10-tetrachloroanthracene. bibliog Science 148:231 Ap 9 '65

YARDS. See Home grounds

YARMOLINSKY, Adam
Always a bridemaid. Newsweek 66:32 N 8 '65
People of the week. il por U S News 59:24 N 8 '65
Yarmolinsky affair. R. Evans and R. Novak. il Esquire 63:80-2+ F '65

YARMOUTH Castle fire. See Ships—Fire and fire protection

YARROW, Peter
Peter, Paul and Mary: triple play! interview; ed. by E. Miller. pors Seventeen 24: 128-9+ Ap '65

YARY, Ron
Fast, huge and only a pup. por Sports Illus 23:70 S 20 '65

YATES, J. Michael
Ice rider; poem. Poetry 105:246 Ja '65
Scorpion; It hardly matters; poems. Poetry 106:403-4 S '65

YATES, Peter
City to emulate. Hi Fi 15:112-13 Jl '65
Contemporary arts at the University of Illinois. Hi Fi 15:128-9 Je '65
Dallas symphony at North Texas state. Hi Fi 15:127+ Ag '65

YATES, Richard
Good and gallant woman; story. Sat Eve Post 238:48-55 S 11 '65
To be a hero; story. Sat Eve Post 238:52-8 S 25 '65

YEAR book medical publishers, incorporated
Times Mirror to acquire year book medical. Pub W 188:35 N 8 '65

YEARBOOKS, High school. See High school annuals

YEARLEY, C. K.
Cubans in Miami. Commonweal 83:210-11 N 19 '65

YEASTS
Tricarboxylic acid cycle mutants in saccharomyces: comparison of independently derived mutants. M. Ogur and others. bibliog Science 147:1590 Mr 26 '65

YEATS, William Butler
On Yeats and others. H. Carruth. Poetry 107:192-4 D '65
Willie is so silly. F. O'Connor. Vogue 145: 122+ Mr 1 '65

Bibliography
Time pardons him for writing well; books to commemorate centennial. H. T. Moore. por Sat R 48:39+ D 11 '65

YELLOTT, John I.
Controlling the effects of sun's heat on steel doors. Arch Rec 138:177-8 D '65

YELLOW fever
Yellow fever, a new airborne threat. D. A. Dukelow and R. Alden. il Todays Health 43:30-1+ Mr '65

YELLOW-fever mosquitoes. See Mosquitoes

YELLOW SPRINGS school forest, Ohio. See Conservation of resources—Study and teaching

YELLOW transit freight lines, incorporated
Yellow transit, trucker in a hurry. il Bsns W p61-2+ Ag 28 '65

YELLOWSTONE NATIONAL PARK
Our first national park: Yellowstone or Yosemite? W. R. Jones. il Audubon Mag 67: 382-4 N '65
Winter animal show is now under way in snowy Yellowstone. il Sunset 135:31-2 D '65

YELLOWTAIL fishing
Tips for yellowtails. G. Heinold. il Outdoor Life 135:16+ Je '65

YEMEN
Appointment in Khamir; peace conference. il Time 85:42 My 14 '65
Death of a dream; Nasser and Faisal sign Yemeni peace pact. il Newsweek 66:29 S 6 '65
Dialogue of the deaf; truce talks to settle three-year civil war. il Time 86:30 D 17 '65
Diplomatic farce in Yemen. S. Guldesca. il Nat R 17:510-11 Je 15 '65
Fear knows no fast; civil war. Time 86:23 D 31 '65
Forgotten war in the desert: a first-hand report. J. Law. il U S News 58:67-9 My 24 '65
Man to end the war; Premier Noman. Time 85:42 My 7 '65
Preference for war. il Time 86:33 Jl 16 '65
Yemen's desert fox. G. De Carvalho. il Life 58:97-8+ F 19 '65

YEON, John
House of wood today. il House & Gard 128: 188-91 O '65

YERKES observatory. See Astronomical observatories

YESKEY, Ronald
Oompah in the park. Recreation 58:277-8 Je '65

YETI. See Animals, Mythical

YEVTUSHENKO, Yevgeny Aleksandrovich. See Evtushenko, E. A.

YGLESIAS, José
Cuba's bestseller: A gusano returns. Nation 201:251-2 O 18 '65
Doña Franco comes to town. Holiday 37:44+ Ap '65
Marx as muse. Nation 200:368-70 Ap 5 '65

YIDDISH language

Dictionaries
$1,275,000 Yiddish dictionary project. Pub W 187:70 F 15 '65

YILMAZ, Huseyin
Seeing is deceiving. il Newsweek 65:56-7 F 15 '65

YLVISAKER, Paul
Villains are greed, indifference, and you. Life 59:92-4+ D 24 '65

YODER, Edwin M. Jr
Flight into confederacy. Sat R 48:43 Ap 10 '65
They hated a myth, murdered a man. Sat R 48:32 D 25 '65
W. J. Cash after a quarter century; excerpt from South today: 100 years after Appomattox. Harper 231:14+ S '65

YOGURT
These coolers use yogurt. Sunset 135:110 Jl '65
See also
Cookery—Yogurt

YOHO NATIONAL PARK. See National parks and reserves—Canada

YOLANTA; opera. See Tchaikovsky, P. I.

YOLEN, Will
Go fly a fishing kite. Todays Health 43:58-61+ Mr '65

YOLLES, Stanley F.
Mental health and the poor; summary of address, March 15, 1965. America 112:449 Ap 3 '65

YONKERS, N.Y., public library
Children's theater in Yonkers; Sprain Brook library theatre. M. Schoenfeld. il Wilson Lib Bul 40:352-5 D '65

YORK, Pa.

Lighting
King-sized lighting for Continental square. il Am City 80:128 S '65

YORKE, Craig, Jr
Face to face. por Seventeen 24:70 Ap '65

YORKSHIRE, England
Yorkshire. P. Ryan. il Holiday 37:84-91+ My '65

YORTY, Samuel William
Dispute over blame for the Los Angeles riots; statement. por U S News 59:16 Ag 30 '65
Wins by ins. Newsweek 65:26-7 Ap 19 '65

about

Best weapons. Nation 201:515 D 27 '65
Democrats' minuet. il por Time 86:17B Ag 13 '65
Parks and politics in Los Angeles. F. M. Brodie. il Reporter 32:39-42 F 11 '65
Somebody out there hates the Mayor. A. Costy. New Repub 153:8-9 S 4 '65
Who's to blame? il por Time 86:10-11 Ag 27 '65

YOSEMITE NATIONAL PARK
Our first national park: Yellowstone or Yosemite? W. R. Jones. il Audubon Mag 67:382-4 N '65
Yosemite's hundredth birthday. W. R. Jones. il Nat Parks Mag 39:14-17 Ap '65

YOSEMITE VALLEY
View from Sentinel Dome. il Sunset 134:64+ My '65

YOSHIMURA, Junzo
Emperor's new palace. il por Time 86:72 Jl 9 '65

YOSHINA, Shizue
We are legion. por PTA Mag 59:22 F '65

YOST, Charles W.
Raising children to know their neighbors, near and far. por Parents Mag 40:46 O '65
Security council recommends the Gambia for U.N. membership; statement, March 15, 1965. Dept State Bul 52:511-12 Ap 5 '65
U.N. General assembly again rejects move to change representation of China; statements, November 16 and November 17, 1965. Dept State Bul 53:947-51 D 13 '65
U.S.S.R. vetoes U.S.-U.K. resolution on Syrian-Israeli complaint; statement, December 21, 1964. Dept State Bul 52:86 Ja 18 '65

YOST, George
Cabin boy's diary of action aboard the Cairo. Life 58:44 F 12 '65

YOU can't take it with you; drama. See Hart, M. and Kaufman, G. S.

YOU don't belong to me; drama. See McCoy, P. S.

YOULOU, Fulbert
Abbé in exile. Time 85:34+ Ap 16 '65

YOUMANS, Vincent
Popular records. D. Watt. New Yorker 40: 65+ Ja 30 '65

YOUNG, Allen
Critics at large. Pop Phot 57:122 O '65
Golschmann's quiet conquest. Hi Fi 15:86L-86M Mr '65
Tippet in the Rockies: Aspen report. Hi Fi 15:152 O '65

YOUNG, Anne
Elegy in E. Commonweal 82:346 Je 4 '65

YOUNG, Augusta Adams Cobb
She who shall be nameless. M. Cable. il por Am Heritage 16:50-5 F '65

YOUNG, Biloine W.
American Indian: citizen in captivity. Sat R 48:25-6 D 11 '65

YOUNG, Brigham
Brigham's home; the Beehive House. il Sunset 135:36+ S '65
She who shall be nameless. M. Cable. il por Am Heritage 16:50-5 F '65

YOUNG, Doris
Their business is going under. G. Rogin. il pors Sports Illus 22:80-4+ Je 7 '65

YOUNG, Ellsworth
Planning and making the move to a new store. Pub W 188:56-60 O 11 '65

YOUNG, Gardner
Their business is going under. G. Rogin. il por Sports Illus 22:80-4+ Je 7 '65

YOUNG, H. S. See Prewitt, C. T. jt. auth.

YOUNG, Hugo H.
Bus competitor GM helped build. il por Bsns W p 172+ D 11 '65

YOUNG, James Webb
Madison avenue. Sat R 48:67 Ap 10 '65

YOUNG, Jean M.
Individualized physical activity. NEA J 54: 22-3 D '65

YOUNG, John
—See Grissom, V. jt. auth.
See also
Space flight—Manned flights—Grissom-Young flight, 1965

YOUNG, John, family
He's on his way and it couldn't be prettier. M. Acoca. il Life 58:36-40 Ap 2 '65

YOUNG, John V.
New Mexico's crater country. Travel 124: 30-4 S '65

YOUNG, Kenneth T. Jr
Situation in southeast Asia. Sat R 48:35-6 My 29 '65

YOUNG, Leontine R.
High cost of conscience. McCalls 93:81-2+ O '65
Mysterious disappearances. McCalls 92:60+ My '65
Truth about children's lying; excerpt from life among the giants. McCalls 93:186+ N '65

YOUNG, M. Ada
Five secretaries and the Cogswells. Antiques 88:478-85 O '65

YOUNG, Marguerite
Inviting the muses. Mlle 61:194+ S '65
Quest for the heart; story; excerpt from Miss Macintosh, my darling. Mlle 61:195+ S '65

about

Adrift on a sea of dreams. G. Hicks. Sat R 48:35-6 S 11 '65
Something to talk about: on being young. L. Lerman. por Mlle 61:193 S '65

YOUNG, Marjabelle
Let's be little ladies; with excerpts from her book. il pors Life 59:83-4+ D 3 '65

YOUNG, Thailand Kenneth
Vietnam: way to victory? excerpts. por Newsweek 65:42-3 Mr 29 '65

YOUNG, Virginia Brady
Elegy for a P.F.C. Christian Cent 82:1447 N 24 '65

YOUNG, Warren R.
Mysterious air crashes: why they happen. Read Digest 86:106-10 Mr '65
What's to come. Life 59:143+ D 24 '65

YOUNG, Wayland
Prospects for arms control in Europe. Bul Atomic Sci 21:22-4 S '65

YOUNG, Whitney M. Jr
Crisis in American culture; address. por Wilson Lib Bul 39:744-6 My '65
High cost of discrimination. por Ebony 20: 51-4 Ag '65
Integration: opportunity and obligation. por Parents Mag 41:30 Ja '66
Positive side of the racial story; address, May 31, 1965. Vital Speeches 31:572-6 Jl 1 '65
Urban league and its strategy. Ann Am Acad 357:102-7 Ja '65
Vanishing era. Harper 230:172 Ap '65

about

New look for the Urban league. A. Morrison. il pors Ebony 21:164-6+ N '65

YOUNG American medal for bravery
Young lives, brave actions. B. Clark. il Read Digest 87:187-8+ N '65

YOUNG Americans for freedom (organization)
Resolved, more action. il Newsweek 66:82 S 13 '65
Should Fulbright be muzzled? summary of address. J. W. Fulbright. Nat R 17:718 Ag 24 '65
YAF convention: personal notes. Nat R 17: 806-7 S 21 '65

YOUNG automobile drivers. See Automobile drivers

YOUNG lord; opera. See Henze, H. W.

YOUNG men
America's ten outstanding young men of 1965. il Look 30:35+ Ja 25 '66
Big sprout-out of male mop-tops; revolt against the close-trimmed male haircut. il Life 59:56-9+ Jl 30 '65
People are talking about youthquakers. il Vogue 146:86-91 Ag 1 '65
Résumé of the young man as a non-generation. H. Junker. Esquire 64:169 D '65
Washington code: zip; report on the generation now at peak energy, peak ideas. il Vogue 146:98-103 Ag 15 '65

YOUNG men's Christian association
Y unbanned. America 112:304 Mr 6 '65
Y.M.C.A. worldwide, in Tokyo. G. K. Chapman. Christian Cent 82:1458-10 N 24 '65

YOUNG people. See Young men; Youth

YOUNG peoples consultation centre, London. See Youth—Great Britain

YOUNG Republicans. See Political clubs and associations

YOUNG women
Opinion, please: from New York. C. P. Lockridge. Mlle 60:44+ F '65

YOUNG women—*Continued*
People are talking about youthquakers. il Vogue 146:86-91 Ag 1 '65
Townies; quartet of off-campus cuties. il Esquire 64:92-5 S '65
Washington code: zip; report on the generation now at peak energy, peak ideas. il Vogue 146:98-103 Ag 15 '65
See also
College students. Women

YOUNGBLOOD, Arthur
Out of a clay pit. Recreation 58:429-30 N '65

YOUNGERMAN, Jack
Youngerman: liberty in limits. M. Benedikt. il Art N 64:43-5+ S '65

YOUR a grand old rag (song) See Songs, American

YOUSKEVITCH, Igor
Ballet romantique, High school of printing. M. Marks. il Dance Mag 39:66 Mr '65

YOUTH
Are student moral values slipping? round-table discussion from 1965 student burgesses at Williamsburg. il Sr Schol 86:14-16 Ap 29 '65
Calendar of creation. H. Rosenberg. Vogue 146:228-9 S 1 '65
Death of hip; the changing hipster. M. Magid. il Esquire 63:89-103+ Je '65
Locomotives; excerpt from Fashionable savages. J. Fairchild. il Ladies Home J 82:47+ S '65
Stimulus to dialogue; impact of mass culture. M. L. Goldberg. Sat R 48:87-9 N 20 '65
Teen-age aristocracy. F. Musgrove. il Nation 200:439-42 Ap 26 '65
Teen city; first teen-age country club, Denver. Newsweek 66:120+ N 15 '65
V.I.T.'s; seventeen-year-olds. il Recreation 58:242-4 My '65 (to be cont)
Youth is not an age. H. R. Miller. Vogue 145:84 Mr 1 '65
Youth; symposium. il UNESCO Courier 18:4-68 Jl '65
See also
Adolescence
Boys
High school students
Libraries—Work with young people
Negro youth
Students

Adjustment
See Adjustment, Social

Employment
Employment of high school graduates and dropouts. F. A. Bogan. il Mo Labor R 88:637-43 Je '65
Employment of school age youth, October 1964. T. E. Swanstrom. il Mo Labor R 88:851-6 Jl '65
How much unemployment? il Fortune 71:34+ F '65
It's a dead-end road for the dropout. J. N. Miller. il Read Digest 86:125-30 My '65
Kids and money; with case history of the Martin family of Barrington, Ill. G. Zimmermann. il Look 29:49-53+ N 2 '65
Labor force status of youth, 1964. H. R. Hamel. il Mo Labor R 88:932-7 Ag '65
Opportunities for farm boys. Farm J 89:146 Mr '65
Small, fine print; Athletics in temporary employment as agricultural manpower contract. New Repub 153:7 Jl 3 '65
Summer jobs that pay off. B. M. Silverman. il Parents Mag 40:54-5+ My '65
What hit the teenagers. C. E. Silberman. il Fortune 71:130-3+ Ap '65
Youth wants to work; City of New York seasonal helper trainee program. J. B. Kelley. America 112:428-30 Mr 27 '65
See also
College students—Employment
Labor camps
Student employment
United States—Job corps
Youthpower, incorporated

Health and hygiene
Chins up; US teen-agers more fit than in 1958. Newsweek 66:64 D 20 '65
Emerging specialty: adolescent medicine. D. W. Lewis. il Todays Health 43:38-41 F '65

Management and training
I can say no to my teenagers. D. Van Ark. il Parents Mag 40:58-9+ S '65

Nutrition
See Children—Nutrition

Political activities
American idealism, 1965. H. Taylor. il Sat R 48:14-16 Je 26 '65
Do it yourself; meeting of group protesting foreign policy, in Madison Square Garden. Nation 200:657 Je 21 '65
I've been working on the doorbells. D. C. Johnston. il Nat R 17:726-7 Ag 24 '65
Nature of dissent in a democracy; student action; address, August 23, 1965. H. H. Humphrey. Vital Speeches 31:741-3 O 1 '65
Spirit of '76 in the 1960's. R. Wilkins. Seventeen 24:150+ O '65
What you can do for human rights in your own home town. D. Klein. il Seventeen 24:130-1+ My '65

Reading
See Books and reading

Recreation
See Recreation

Religion
Youth today. L. M. Grande. Cath World 202:41-4 O '65

Australia
Daring lifesavers of the surf; Surf life saving association of Australia. il- UNESCO Courier 18:30-1 Jl '65

China (People's Republic)
Molding the future; anti-American campaign. Newsweek 67:25+ Ja 3 '66

Cuba
See also
Cuban students

England
See Youth—Great Britain

Germany (Federal Republic)
Action atonement; German volunteers in nations that suffered under the Nazi invasion. P. Shabecoff. il N Y Times Mag p149-51+ N 7 '65
New voters. Time 86:20+ Jl 30 '65
Rabbi asks: isn't it time we forgave the Germans? J. Asher. il Look 29:84-6+ Ap 20 '65

Great Britain
Britain's with-it society. S. Hagerty. il Newsweek 66:52-3 D 6 '65
Dave Clark five make a movie! Having a wild weekend; ed. by E. Miller. J. Boorman; D. Clark; M. Smith. il Seventeen 24:90-1+ Jl '65
Dear sir, or madam? mods and rockers. A. Carthew. il N Y Times Mag p59-60+ N 7 '65
Teenagers need someone to tell their troubles to; Young peoples consultation centre, London. J. Wakeman. il Parents Mag 40:56-8+ Ap '65
Train-wreckers. B. Wenham. New Repub 152:8-9 Je 26 '65
Young London. il Seventeen 24:108-9 Mr '65

Hungary
Impatient Hungarian youth. D. Snyder. New Repub 153:12 D 4 '65

Japan
They were born when the bomb dropped. G. R. Packard. il N Y Times Mag p28-9+ Ag 29 '65
See also
Japanese students

Poland
Letter from Poland. M. Kuncewicz. Nation 201:537-8 D 27 '65

Russia
Generation of builders. Y. Kotler. il UNESCO Courier 18:62-5 Jl '65
Where the action isn't restrictions on youth. Time 87:34 Ja 14 '66

Spain
Restive youth of Spain. S. Birmingham. il Holiday 37:88-93+ Ap '65

Underdeveloped areas
20,000 volunteer workers for progress and friendship: in fifty developing nations. A. Gillette. il UNESCO Courier 18:57-9 Jl '65

YOUTH—*Continued*

United States

American idealism. 1965. H. Taylor. il Sat R 48:14-16 Je 26 '65

American youth: a generation under the gun; with editorial comment. S. Birmingham. il Holiday 37:41, 42-61+ Mr '65

Beatnik unrest baffles LBJ. P. Lisagor. il Nations Bsns 53:23-4 Je '65

Behind the search for kicks; symposium; with study-discussion program, by C. Smallenburg and H. Smallenburg. bibliog il PTA Mag 60:4, 36-7 S '65

Big question for teens: morality; panel discussion, ed. by J. Beck. il Todays Health 43:24+ My '65

Code for teens, updated. A. P. Eliasberg. N Y Times Mag p 112+ N 21 '65

Coming of age in America, by E. Z. Friedenberg. Review
  New Repub 153:30-1 Ag 7 '65. R. Kluger
  Newsweek il 65:98+ Je 21 '65

Esquire: a special issue: teen-agers in America; symposium. il Esquire 64:30-9+ Jl '65

In my opinion; teens: timid, lazy, afraid to express deep emotion. M. Crist. Seventeen 24:179 Je '65

In the grown-up world of teen-agers. il UNESCO Courier 18:26-9 Jl '65

Morals of a teen; poll of PTA presidents; with study-discussion program, by C. Smallenberg and H. Smallenberg. R. Squires. bibliog il PTA Mag 59:4-7, 36-7 Ap '65

On not losing one's cool about the young; Time essay. Time 86:16-17 D 24 '65

Opinion: on youth's conscience. A. Salsamendi. Mlle 62:56-7 D '65

Our hard-pressed teenagers; with study-discussion program. C. Smallenburg and H. Smallenburg. bibliog il PTA Mag 59:34-6, 44 F '65

Profile of normality; reprint. R. E. Nixon. Sr Schol 87:sup8 N 18 '65

Speaking out; teen-agers are the greatest people. P. Wylie. Sat Eve Post 238:10+ S 11 '65

Teen-ager tames the city; Karen Koscuik of New York. D. R. Maxey. il Look 29:99-101+ S 21 '65

Teen-agers an American invention. B. M. Berger. il N Y Times Mag p12-13+ Je 13 '65

Teen scene. See issues of Seventeen

Temptation of the new breed. A. M. Greeley. America 112:750-2 My 22 '65; Discussion. 113:318-19+, 422 S 25, O 16 '65

That riotous feeling. Time 86:78-9 Jl 16 '65

Tight pants and full wallets; comment on Esquire's coverage of the American teenager. R. A. Schroth. America 113:80 Jl 17 '65

V.I.T.'S; programs for teenagers. il Recreation. 58:242-4, 288-90+, 394-6+ My-O '65

Youth explosion; address, May 3, 1965. W. I. Nichols. Vital Speeches 31:524-7 Je 15 '65
  See also
College students
Dating
United States—Job corps
Youth market

Vietnam (Republic)

Vietnam youth in revolt. M. Hope. il Mlle 61:96-7+ Je '65
  See also
Vietnamese students

YOUTH and race relations. See Interracial cooperation

YOUTH associations
  See also
Young Americans for freedom (organization)

YOUTH centers. See Recreation centers

YOUTH conference on the atom. See National youth conference on the atom

YOUTH conferences
Youth makes sound criticism; Ecumenical youth study conference. America 113:177 Ag 21 '65
  See also
World festival of youth and students for peace and friendship

YOUTH group achievement awards
P/M's eleventh annual youth awards. Parents Mag 40:70+ O '65

YOUTH hostels
Community recreation tries hosteling programs. F. D. Cosgrove. il Recreation 58:337 S '65

Global network of youth hostels. P. François. il UNESCO Courier 18:12-13 Jl '65

Go! go! go! what makes hosteling fun in Europe. K. Goff. il Seventeen 24:80-1+ Je '65

YOUTH jury
Teens in the jury box. il Changing T 19:36 O '65

Youth juries: help, or hindrance to justice? pro and con discussion. Sr Schol 87:16-17 D 9 '65

YOUTH market
Affluent teen. and it's all his. il Esquire 64:66-8 Jl '65

And a little child shall control TV. G. Ace. Sat R 48:14 Mr 13 '65

Grown-ups à go-go. il Esquire 64:41-3 Jl '65

In the time it takes you to read these lines the American teen-ager will have spent $2,378.22 G. Hechinger and F. M. Hechinger. Esquire 64:65+ Jl '65

Kids and money; with case history of the Martin family of Barrington, Ill. G. Zimmermann. il Look 29:49-53+ N 2 '65

Teen-age consumers: dynamic force in the U.S. economy. il Sr Schol 86:5-7 F 25 '65

Teen-ager tunes them out. Consumer Rep 30:164-5 Ap '65

Young, single spenders pour it on the market. il Bsns W p62-3 Ja 1 '66

YOUTH movement

Germany

Account rendered, by M. Maschmann. Review
  New Repub 153:23-8 Ag 21 '65. L. Segal

YOUTH movement, Communist. See World festival of youth and students for peace and friendship

YOUTH volunteer service. See Volunteer service

YOUTHPOWER, incorporated
Found! summer jobs for teen-agers. M. A. Robertson. Bet Hom & Gard 43:31 My '65

YU, Pyung K. See Viglierchio, D. R. jt. auth.

YUAN, Luke C. L.
Introduction to nature of matter. por Science 147:1548-51 Mr 26 '65

YUCATAN
  See also
Cozumel Island
Mayas

YUGOSLAV cookery. See Cookery, Yugoslav

YUGOSLAV visitors in the United States. See Foreign visitors in the United States

YUGOSLAVIA
Atlantic report. Atlan 216:13-14+ Jl '65

How Yugoslavs mix communism with capitalism. Bsns W p 196 N 20 '65
  See also
Belgrade
Censorship—Yugoslavia
Communism—Yugoslavia
Music festivals—Yugoslavia
Tourist trade—Yugoslavia
Trials—Yugoslavia

Description and travel

Yugoslavia. A. Karlen. il Holiday 38:42-55+ N '65

Yugoslavia's coast. F. Perea. il Travel 123: 62-4 Je '65

Economic conditions

Half Karl & half Groucho. il Time 85:97-8 My 7 '65

Where Titoism was tried. G. Bailey. il Reporter 33:13-18 Jl 1 '65
  See also
Communism—Yugoslavia

Politics and government

Constitutional socialism in Yugoslavia. I. Maksimović. bibliog f Ann Am Acad 358: 159-69 Mr '65

Where Titoism was tried. G. Bailey. il Reporter 33:13-18 Jl 1 '65

Yugoslavia's opening society. A. Z. Rubinstein. Cur Hist 48:149-53+ Mr '65
  See also
Communism—Yugoslavia

Social policy

Yugoslavia's opening society. A. Z. Rubinstein. Cur Hist 48:149-53+ Mr '65

YUGOSLAVS
By the Socialist sea; German girls go after Yugoslav men. E. Y. Blumenfeld. il Newsweek 66:50 O 4 '65

YUKON
Everybody sure glad; Indian correspondent for Yukon's newspaper, the Whitehorse star. D. J. Hamblin. il Life 58:69-70+ My 21 '65
See also
Kennedy, Mount
YUKON RIVER
Our land speaks. D. V. Baxter. il Liv Wildn 87:16-21 Wint '64
Plot to drown Alaska; Rampart Dam project. P. Brooks. il Atlan 215:53-9 My '65; Same abr. Read Digest 87:79-83 Ag '65; Discussion. Atlan 216:26+ Jl '65
Rampart Dam: white elephant of the Yukon Flats. T. T. Brady. il Nat Parks Mag 39:4-7 O '65
Rampart, foolish dam. G. H. Wood. il Liv Wildn 29:3-7 Spr '65
YULAN magnolia. See Magnolias
YUNCKER, Barbara
Keep up with medicine. See issues of Good housekeeping
YUNGMEYER, Elinor, and others
Cooperation in action. por ALA Bul 59:733-44 S '65
YUNICH, David L. See Bingham, W. H. jt. auth.
YUNICK, Henry. See Yunick, S.
YUNICK, Smokey
Inside Indy. por Pop Sci 186:81 F; 85 Mr; 67 Ap; 81 My '65
Say, Smokey; questions and answers. See issues of Popular science monthly
Secrets of a trouble-free automobile. Pop Sci 186:77-88 Je '65
396 wedge, Yunick style. pors Hot Rod 18:34-8+ D '65
Today's hero at the 500 is often tomorrow's bum. por Pop Sci 186:81 F '65
YURCHENCO, Henrietta
Folk music. See issues of American record guide
YURICK, Sol
Correspondent to the underworld. Nation 201:283-4 O 25 '65
YURIKO
Yuriko and dance company, 92nd street Y. D. Hering. Dance Mag 39:34+ Ap '65
YUSUPOV, Feliks Feliksovich, kni͡az'. See I͡Usupov, F. F.

Z

ZIP (Zoning improvement plan) See Postal service—United States
ZABARSKY, Nathan. See Randall, B. jt. auth.
ZABEL, William D.
Interracial marriage and the law. Atlan 216:75-9 O '65
ZACCHINI, Edmondo, family
Cannon fodder. New Yorker 41:25-7 Jl 17 '65
ZACHAI, Dorian
Fiber, clay, metal. Craft Horiz 25:10-17+ Ja '65
ZACK, Jacob B.
Best place for vocational education. NEA J 54:48-50 D '65
ZAGORIA, Donald S.
China's strategy; a critique. Commentary 40:61-6 N '65
Communism in Asia. Commentary 39:53-8 F; 12 Ap '65
ZAGREB biennale. See Music festivals—Yugoslavia
ZAHARIAS, Babe Didrikson
Sporting scene. H. W. Wind. New Yorker 41:104+ Ag 21 '65
ZAHIR, king of Afghanistan. See Mohammed Zahir
ZAHL, Paul A.
Bizarre world of the fungi. il Nat Geog Mag 128:502-27 O '65
ZAHNISER, Howard
People and wilderness; excerpt from Wilderness, April 18-19, 1964. Liv Wildn 86:39-42 Spr '64
ZAJONC, Robert B.
Social facilitation. bibliog Science 149:269-74 Jl 16 '65
ZAKIA, Richard D. See Todd, H. N. jt. auth.
ZAKIN, Alexander
Profiles: I. Stern. J. Wechsberg. New Yorker 41:78-9+ Je 5 '65

ZALAMEA, Luis
Bolívar's villa. Américas 17:20 D '65
ZALEZNIK, Abraham
Dynamics of subordinacy; excerpt. Harvard Bsns R 43:119-31 My '65
ZAMBEZI RIVER
See also
Kariba Lake
ZAMBIA
Another Suez? Kaunda's demand for British troops. Newsweek 66:52 D 13 '65
As U.S. and Britain begin oil squeeze. il U S News 60:6 Ja 10 '66
Canceling out Rhodesia's threat; neighboring nations mapping alternative routes to isolate the rebels. il Bsns W p58+ D 11 '65
Colored rulers; Kenneth David Kaunda. G. C. Turner. bibliog Negro Hist Bul 28:134-5 Mr '65
End of the road for whites in Rhodesia? il U S News 60:52-4 Ja 17 '66
Five colors. il Time 86:25 S 10 '65
How tight is the squeeze? possible soft spot in sanctions ring. R. W. Howe. il Reporter 33:29-32 D 2 '65
Imperiled president; call for British troops. il Newsweek 66:40+ D 20 '65
In Rhodesia, a crisis spills over into Zambia, where the fur hats plot. il Life 59:46-46B D 10 '65
Independence comes to Zambia. il Ebony 20:27-30+ F '65
Letter from Lusaka. V. P. McCorry. America 113:528-30 N 6 '65
Of oil & scotch; British economic sanctions felt. Time 86:23 D 31 '65
Playing chicken; emergency airlift of oil supplies under way. il Newsweek 67:24 Ja 3 '66
Report from Africa; from Lusaka, with love. V. P. McCorry. il America 112:881-2 Je 19 '65
Shortened fuse; under pressure to do something about Smith takeover. il Time 86:34 D 3 '65
Some planes arrive; K. Kaunda's demand for British troops. il Time 86:39-40 D 10 '65
Zambia and Rhodesia: a study in contrast. R. Brown. il Cur Hist 48:201-6+ Ap '65
See also
Kariba Lake
Lumpa sect (Zambia)
ZAMBON, Joseph
Shoes for God's children. M. McGrory. America 113:396 O 9 '65
ZANDONAI, Riccardo
In Dante's wake; Zandonai's Francesca da Rimini. J. W. Freeman. il por Opera N 30:6-7 D 11 '65
Newark. J. W. Freeman. il Opera N 30:32 Ja 15 '66
On records: Romeo and Juliet. P. Elvins. Opera N 30:31 N 6 '65
ZANESVILLE, Ohio
Zanesville and the mass-transit act. S. Grey and T. B. Steinbach. Am City 80:144+ S '65
ZARBOCK, Robert
First, and beautiful, recording of Rusalka. Am Rec G 32:348-9 D '65
ZARROW, M. X. and others
Rabbit: frequency of suckling in the pup. bibliog Science 150:1835-6 D 31 '65
ZARTMAN, I. William
Morocco. bibliog Focus 15:1-6 F '65
ZAVALA ORTIZ, Miguel Angel
Door is open; excerpts from address. Américas 17:inside cover F '65
ZEBOT, Cyril A.
Efficiency and equity in welfare economics. bibliog f Mo Labor R 88:528-34 My '65
Needed: a secularized Marxism. America 113:439 O 16 '65
ZECKENDORF, William
Big man on the thin edge. C. Welles. il pors Life 58:74-6+ F 12 '65
End of an empire. il por Newsweek 65:84+ My 24 '65
New York bank blows whistle on Zeckendorf; action against Webb & Knapp in bankruptcy court. il Bsns W p30-1 My 15 '65
Operators. por Newsweek 65:82+ My 17 '65
Sad saga of Big Bill. por Time 85:96+ My 21 '65
ZEFFIRELLI, Franco
Second fame: good food. N. Lyon. por Vogue 145:134-6 F 15 '65
ZEHRER, Hans
Hans Zehrer as a neoconservative elite theorist. W. Struve. bibliog f Am Hist R 70:1035-57 Jl '65

ZEIK, Michael D.
  Books. Commonweal 82:600-2 Ag 20 '65
  Pope and the Jews. Commonweal 82:181-2 Ap
    30 '65
ZEITLIN, Alexander
  High-pressure technology; with biographical
    sketch. Sci Am 212:18, 38-46 bibliog(p 150)
    My '65
ZEITLIN, Arnold, and Zeitlin, Marian
  Speaking out. pors Sat Eve Post 239:7-8 Ja
    1 '66
ZEITLIN, David
  Day we listened to Rocky's mother-in-law
    and other photographic stories. Pop Phot
    56:56-7+ F '65
  Good drizzle after a big sizzle. Life 58:45-6+
    F 26 '65
  Greatest pie fight ever creates a horrendous
    splaat! Life 59:84-5+ Jl 9 '65
  They die on cue for cash. Life 58:78B-82+
    Mr 26 '65
ZEITLIN, Denny
  Doctor digs jazz. N. Hentoff. il por Holiday
    37:109-10+ My '65
  Doctor jazz. il por Newsweek 66:94 S 27 '65
ZEITLIN, Jake
  Who shall silence all the airs and madrigals?
    address, November 1964. por Library J 90:
    2479-83 Je 1 '65
ZEITLIN, Marian. See Zeitlin, A. jt. auth.
ZELITCH, Israel. See Waggoner, P. E. jt. auth.
ZELKO, Harold P.
  How to be a better speaker. Nations Bsns
    53:88+ Ap '65
ZEN Buddhism
  Buddhism in the U.S: a yen for Zen? Sr
    Schol 86:12 Mr 25 '65
  Go West, young Zen; cultists at Chico, Calif.
    R. B. Young. il Newsweek 65:46+ Je 14 '65
ZÉNDEGUI, Guillermo de
  Idea whose time had come. Américas 17:
    16-23 Ap '65
ZENITH radio corporation
  Great color TV war. J. F. Olesky. il Duns R
    86:38-40+ Ag '65
  Zenith aims at the top in color TV. il Bsns W
    p 128+ S 11 '65
ZENTMYER, George A.
  Bacterial stimulation of sporangium produc-
    tion in phytophthora cinnamomi. bibliog
    Science 150:1178-9 N 26 '65
ZEPPELINS. See Airships
ZERMATT, Switzerland
  Zermatt. C. Cate. il Atlan 215:138+ Ap '65
ZERN, Ed
  Exit, laughing. See issues of Field & stream
  How we got here. Field & S 70:52-5 Jl '65
  Tutors for shooters. por Field & S 70:46-8+
    D '65
ZERO defects. See Quality control
ZERO gravity. See Weightlessness
ZERO on the compass; story. See Dorman, S.
ZETTERSTRÖM, Bengt E. M. See Dahlström,
  A. B. jt. auth.
ZEUS project. See Guided missiles—Defenses
ZHUKOV, Georgii Konstantinovich
  Polishing the escutcheons. por Time 85:31A
    Je 18 '65
ZIBLATT, David
  High school extracurricular activities and
    political socialization. bibliog f Ann Am
    Acad 361:20-31 S '65
ZIDE, Larry
  1965 audio show: notes and impressions.
    Am Rec G 32:206-7 N '65
  Sound advice (cont) Mod Phot 29:58+ Je;
    94+ N '65
  Sound ideas. See issues of American record
    guide
  Sound tape editing made easy. Mod Phot 29:
    97+ F '65
  —See Marcus, P. jt. auth.
ZIEFF, Howard
  Ready when you are, H.Z! B. Ullman. il U S
    Camera 29:48-51+ Ja '66
ZIETLOW, D. D.
  $25 got my goat. Outdoor Life 136:46-7+ S
    '65
ZIFF, Larzer
  Other lost generation. Sat R 48:15-18 Mr 20
    '65
ZIGELER, Mrs Wayne
  Shortcuts to wonderful holiday eating. il por
    Farm J 89:78-9+ N '65
ZILVERSMIT, D. B.
  Oxygen-hemoglobin system: a model for facil-
    itated membranous transport. bibliog Sci-
    ence 149:874-6 Ag 20 '65

ZIMBARDO, Philip G. and others
  Control of pain motivation by cognitive dis-
    sonance. bibliog Science 151:217-19 Ja 14
    '66
ZIMMER, Gale Koschmann
  Liguus, the Florida tree snail Nat Parks
    Mag 39:13 Ap '65
ZIMMERMAN, John G.
  Perils of deep powder: photographs. Sports
    Illus 23:52-60 N 15 '65
  Tennis on the grass: photographs. Sports
    Illus 23:32-40 Jl 5 '65
ZIMMERMAN, M.
  Library and librarian attacked in California
    censorship case. Library J 90:1683 Ap 1 '65
ZIMMERMAN, Peter J.
  Libraries behind the news. por Library J
    90:4291-5 O 15 '65
ZIMPEL, Lloyd
  When equality is not enough. Christian Cent
    82:1060-3 S 1 '65
ZINC
  Limits terminated on imports of unmanu-
    factured lead and zinc; statement, October
    22, 1965, with proclamation. L. B. Johnson.
    Dept State Bul 53:795-7 N 15 '65
ZINC in the body
  Unexpected properties of zinc. Time 86:102+
    N 19 '65
ZINDEL, Paul
  Subject was marigolds. Criticism
    Sat R 48:45 Je 26 '65
ZINER, Feenie
  Day the triplets came. Good H 160:114-15+
    Ap '65
ZINGG, David Drew
  Walk softly and carry a long lens. L. Barry.
    il Pop Phot 57:68-71+ Ag '65
ZINN, Howard
  New World: fragments of the Old. Nation
    200:562-4 My 24 '65
  South revisited. Nation 201:147-53 S 20 '65
  Vietnam: setting the moral equation. Na-
    tion 202:64-9 Ja 17 '66
  Wobbly spirit. Nation 200:371-3 Ap 5 '65
              about
  Southern mythology. C. V. Woodward. Com-
    mentary 39:60-3 My '65
ZINNIAS
  Envy; new zinnia. M. C. Ohlander. il Flower
    Grower 52:30 F '65
  Zinnias, rainbow colors all season bloom. B.
    Brinhart. il Flower Grower 52:36-7+ Mr '65
ZINSSER, William K.
  Big Bond bonanza. Sat Eve Post 238:76-81
    Jl 17 '65
  Ceiling zero. Sat Eve Post 238:22 Je 5 '65
  Does he or doesn't he? Sat Eve Post 238:16
    O 9 '65
  Good-by, Burma-Shave. Read Digest 86:103-6
    F '65
  Inside Xenobia. Horizon 7:112-13 Autumn '65
  Lost: one centennial. Sat Eve Post 238:22
    My 8 '65
  Past, present and yet to come. Life 59:82+
    D 17 '65
ZINZANIA acquatica. See Wild rice
ZION, Sidney E.
  Frank O'Connor takes the high road. N Y
    Times Mag p9+ Ja 16 '65
  Suspect confesses, but who believes him?
    N Y Times Mag p30-1+ My 16 '65
  Thurgood Marshall takes a new tush-tush
    job. N Y Times Mag p 11+ Ag 22 '65
ZIONISM
  Ancient hatred builds toward war. G. De
    Carvalho. il Life 58:44+ Je 18 '65
  Dissenters in Zion. E. Wakin. Sat R 48:35
    Je 19 '65
      See also
  Israel
ZIPAQUIRÁ, Colombia
  You are inside a mountain of salt; Salt
    cathedral. il Sunset 135:32 O '65
ZIPPERS
  Hip zip. il Time 85:87 F 5 '65
  Zipper that doesn't show. il Consumer Bul
    48:14-15 O '65
ZIRCONIUM
  Explosion of burning zirconium droplets
    caused by nitrogen. L. S. Nelson. bibliog il
    Science 148:1594-5 Je 18 '65
ZMOLEK, William
  Ways to cut costs on new cattle. Suc Farm
    63:64 O '65
ZNAMIEROWSKI, Nell
  Spencer Depas and knotting. Craft Horiz
    25:32-3+ Mr '65
ZODIACAL dust. See Matter, Interstellar

ZODIACAL light
Gemini V experiments on zodiacal light and gegenschein. E. P. Ney and W. F. Huch. bibliog il Science 150:53-6, 1629 O 1, D 17 '65
Photographing the zodiacal light. H. G. Solberg, jr. il Sky & Tel 29:323-5 My '65

ZOETTL, Joseph
Alabama oddity: Holyland U.S.A. il por Travel 123:41-3 My '65

ZOND probes. See Lunar probes, Russian

ZONDERVAN publishing house
Harper Bible department sold to Zondervan. Pub W 188:40+ N 22 '65

ZONING
Big zoning battle. L. Gross. il Look 29:93-8 O 5 '65
How to zone for multi-family dwellings; Westchester County, N.Y. S. J. Schulman. il Am City 80:92-4 D '65
Zoning and planning decisions. N. Williams, jr. See issues of American city

ZONING improvement plan. See Postal service —United States

ZONING law
Manure odors can land you in court! J. Russell. Farm J 89:19+ Ag '65

ZON-O-PHONE records. See Phonograph records

ZOO story; drama. See Albee, E.

ZOOK, Nancy Gibbons
United they built. Recreation 58:427-8 N '65

ZOOLOGICAL gardens
Monkey's marriage & other improbable tales; excerpt from Menagerie manor. G. Durrell. il McCalls 92:80+ M '65
New life for museums; proposed National museum act of 1965. B. Tufty. il Sci N L 88:122-3 Ag 21 '65
New Mexico's four-footed refugees; animals from Africa and the Near East. il Nat Parks Mag 39:14-16 N '65
Walk on the wild side; Knowland park zoo, Oakland, Calif. Am City 80:20 N '65
Zoo with tame animals; Deer ranch park and zoo. il Sunset 135:41 Ag '65
See also names of zoological gardens, e.g. Lincoln park zoo, Chicago

Buildings
Plastics and steel wire to modernize zoos. Sci N L 87:120 F 20 '65

ZOOLOGY

Classification
Trend curves of the rate of species description in zoology. G. C. Steyskal. bibliog il Science 149:880-2 Ag 20 '65

Ecology
Entrainment of a tidal rhythm. J. T. Enright. bibliog il Science 147:864-7 F 19 '65
See also
Animal populations

Geographical distribution
See Geographical distribution of animals and plants

Africa, East
Camera safari to East Africa. H. Nipson. il Ebony 20:148-50+ O '65
Safari for science. G. E. Maxwell. il Todays Health 43:22-31 N '65

Antarctic Regions
Ice fish. J. T. Ruud. il Sci Am 213:108-14 bibliog(p 144) N '65
Pink creature lives closest to South Pole. Sci N L 87:183 Mr 20 '65

Australia
Saved: Australia's delightful wildlife. il Sci Digest 58:58-65 S '65
See also
Kangaroos

Maine
Beaver returns to Maine. B. Geagan. il Nat Parks Mag 40:12-14 Ja '66

Mexico
Sabino grove ecology study. E. Leshan and others. il Natur Hist 74:14-23 My '65

Montana
April in Montana; excerpts from Blue hen's chick. A. B. Guthrie, jr. Holiday 37:70-1 Mr '65

ZOOM lenses
Are tele zooms practical? symposium. il Mod Phot 29:60-1 Ag '65
Right way to zoom. B. Campbell. il U S Camera 28:66-7+ Ap '65
Unusual zoom. il Mod Phot 29:74-5 Mr '65
Zoom lenses for 35-mm SLR's. Pop Phot 57:58-9 Ag '65

ZOOPLANKTON. See Plankton

ZOOS. See Zoological gardens

ZORIN, Valerian Aleksandrovich
De Gaulle rings Kremlin bells. por Bsns W p45 Ap 3 '65

ZORTHIAN, Barry
Psywar. il por Newsweek 66:40 O 4 '65

ZORZA, Victor
Modernizing the Soviet economy. New Repub 153:17-18 O 16 '65

ZOUNGRANA, Paul, cardinal
Government of the missions: African cardinal's view. America 113:660-1 N 27 '65

ZOYSIA grass. See Grasses

ZUBER, B. L. and Stark, L.
Microsaccades and the velocity-amplitude relationship for saccadic eye movements. bibliog Science 150:1459-60 D 10 '65

ZUCKER, A. and Bromley, D. A.
Nuclear physics: a status report. Science 149:1197-205 S 10 '65

ZUCKER, Isabel
Flowering shrubs are for every garden. Flower Grower 53:30-3 Ja '66

ZUCKERKANDL, Emile
Evolution of hemoglobin; with biographical sketch. Sci Am 212:18, 110-18 bibliog(p 152) My '65

ZUCKERMAN, Art
Electronic magic at the World's fair. Pop Electr 23:63-5+ Jl '65
Focus on Willard Van Dyke. Pop Phot 56:118-19+ Ap '65
Sound effects. Pop Phot 57:110-11+ Jl '65
Sound test report. Pop Phot 56:125 Ap; 114-15 Jl '65

ZUCKERMAN, Harold
College and career; questions and answers. See issues of Senior scholastic

ZUKMANN, Marion
I just paint. il por Am Artist 29:42-6 N '65

ZUKOFSKY, Louis
A-14 beginning An; poem. Poetry 107:1-51 O '65
Pronounced golgonoozà? Poetry 107:65-8 O '65

about
After Sedley, after Pound. D. Davie. Nation 201:311-13 N 1 '65
. . . Paradise/our/speech. . . R. Creeley. Poetry 107:52-5 O '65
Some thoughts on bottom and after I's. G. Malanga. Poetry 107:60-4 O '65
Zukofsky's all. T. Clark. Poetry 107:55-9 O '65

ZUKOSKY, Jerome
NYPL restrictions on Moses' papers queried in Herald tribune report; summary. Library J 90:1088+ M 1 '65

ZULL, J. Elwood, and others
Actinomycin D inhibition of vitamin D action. bibliog Science 149:182-4 Jl 9 '65

ZULU war, 1879
Washing of the spears, by D. R. Morris. Review
Nat R 17:882-3 O 5 '65. J. Hart
Sat R 48:27-8 S 4 '65. C. Miller

ZULU and the zayda; drama. See De Silva, H. and Leon, F.

ZULUS. See Africa—Native races

ZUNKEL, C. Wayne
Pennsylvania school bus fight. Christian Cent 82:1036-7 Ag 25 '65

ZU RHEIN, Gabriele M. and Chou, Shi-ming
Particles resembling papova viruses in human cerebral demyelinating disease. bibliog Science 148:1477-9 Je 11 '65

ZURICH, Switzerland

Music
Zurich upswing. E. V. Epstein. il Opera N 29:33-4 My 1 '65

ZWEIG, Paul
Bells; poems. Poetry 105:373 Mr '65
Invisible man. Nation 201:307-8+ N 1 '65

ZWINGLI, Ulrich
Zwingli, by J. Rilliet. Review
Christian Cent 82:1236-8 O 6 '65. G. Fackre

ZYSKIND, Judith Weaver, and others
Staphylolytic substance from a species of pseudomonas. bibliog Science 147:1458-9 Mr 19 '65